N ATIO RESULT

CW00766933

The Sporting Life

Published 1997 by The Sporting Life
One Canada Square, Canary Wharf, London E14 5AP

© 1997 The Sporting Life

ISBN 0 901091 93 6

Editorial and Production by Martin Pickering Bloodstock Services
Cover printed by Colour Splash, London E14
Preliminaries typeset by LBJ Enterprises Ltd, Chilcompton and Aldermaston
Text printed by The Bath Press, Bath and London

Cover picture
Tote Cheltenham Gold Cup winner, Mr Mulligan, Tony McCoy up.

(Photograph: Allsport)

Contents

National Hunt Average Times 1996–97

(Revised up to and including 1995–96 season)

SPORTING LIFE Adjusted Average Times represent the theoretical time a top class horse can be expected to clock under ideal conditions carrying 12 stone.

They embrace previous fast times over each individual course and distance, are adjusted to compensate for the state of the ground, weight carried, calibre of horse and revised to 12 stone. They provide an accurate and reliable benchmark for each individual trip and track with which we can compare the actual times recorded at a meeting.

AINTREE
Chases
National Course

2m 1f 110yds	4m 10s
2m about 6f	5m 26s
3m 3f	6m 45s
4m about 4f	8m 58s

Mildmay Course

About 2m	3m 47s
2m about 4f	4m 48s
3m about 1f	6m 5s

Hurdles

2m about 110yds	3m 48s
2m about 4f	4m 38s
3m about 110yds	5m 48s

ASCOT
Chases

About 2m	3m 48s
2m about 3f 110yds	4m 41s
3m about 110yds	6m 1s
3m about 5f	7m 18s

Hurdles

2m about 110 yds	3m 46s
2m about 4f	4m 41s
About 3m	5m 36s
3m about 1f 110yds	5m 59s

AYR
Chases

About 2m	3m 45s
2m about 4f	4m 47s
2m about 5f 110yds	5m 6s
3m about 1f	6m
3m about 3f 110yds	6m 42s
4m about 1f	8m 4s

Hurdles

About 2m	3m 36s
2m about 4f	4m 38s
2m about 6f	5m 7s
3m about 110yds	5m 41s
3m about 2f 110yds	6m 13s

BANGOR
Chases

2m about 1f 110yds	4m 2s
2m about 4f 110yds	4m 46s
3m about 110yds	5m 45s
3m about 6f	7m 10s
4m about 1f	8m

Hurdles

2m about 1f	3m 50s
2m about 4f	4m 30s
3m	5m 29s

CARLISLE
Chases

About 2m	3m 54s
2m about 4f 110yds	4m 55s
About 3m	5m 52s
3m about 2f	6m 28s

Hurdles

2m about 1f	4m 3s
2m about 4f 110yds	4m 42s
3m about 110yds	5m 51s

CARTMEL
Chases

2m about 1f 110yds	4m 11s
2m about 5f 110yds	5m 10s
3m about 2f	6m 17s

Hurdles

2m about 1f 110yds	4m
2m 6f	5m 7s
3m about 2f	5m 58s

CATTERICK
Chases

About 2m	3m 47s
2m 3f	4m 30s
3m about 1f 110yds	6m 15s
3m about 4f 110yds	7m 2s

Hurdles

About 2m	3m 40s
2m 3f	4m 20s
3m about 1f 110yds	6m 1s

CHELTENHAM (New Course)
Chases

2m about 110yds	3m 53s
2m about 5f	5m 4s
3m about 1f 110yds	6m 15s
3m about 2f 110yds	6m 32s
3m about 4f 110yds	7m 2s
4m about 1f	8m 17s

Hurdles

2m about 1f	3m 54s
2m 4f	4m 40s
2m about 5f 110yds	4m 58s
3m about 110yds	5m 39s

CHELTENHAM (Old Course)
Chases

About 2m	3m 52s
2m about 4f 110yds	4m 57s
3m about 1f	6m 8s
3m about 2f	6m 24s
3m about 3f 110yds	6m 50s
About 4m	8m 5s

Hurdles

2m about 110yds	3m 49s
2m about 5f	4m 56s
3m about 2f	6m 16s

CHELTENHAM (Park Course)
Chases

2m about 110 yds	3m 54s
2m 5f	5m 3s
3m 1f 110yds	6m 8s

Hurdles

2m 110yds	3m 52s
2m 5f 110yds	5m 1s
2m 7f 110yds	5m 26s

CHEPSTOW
Chases

2m about 110yds	3m 57s
2m about 3f 110yds	4m 43s
About 3m	5m 50s
3m about 2f 110yds	6m 35s
3m 5f about 110yds	7m 26s

Hurdles

2m about 110yds	3m 47s
2m about 4f 110yds	4m 38s
About 3m	5m 35s

DONCASTER
Chases

2m about 110yds	3m 54s
2m about 3f 110yds	4m 45s
About 3m	5m 54s
3m about 2f	6m 21s
3m 4f	6m 47s
About 4m	7m 59s

Hurdles

2m about 110yds	3m 50s
2m 4f	4m 35s
3m about 110yds	5m 42s

EXETER (Summer Course)
Chases

2m about 1f 110yds	4m 5s
2m about 3f	4m 28s
2m about 6f 110yds	5m 20s
3m about 1f	5m 56s

Hurdles

2m about 1f 110yds	3m 56s
2m about 3f	4m 16s
2m about 6f	4m 57s
3m about 1f 110yds	5m 49s

(Winter Course)
Chases

2m about 2f	4m 10s
2m about 3f 110yds	4m 33s
2m about 7f 110yds	5m 34s
3m about 1f 110yds	6m 3s

Hurdles

2m about 2f	3m 59s
2m about 3f 110yds	4m 21s
3m about 2f	5m 56s

FAIRYHOUSE
Chases

2m	3m 54s
2m 2f	4m 25s
2m 4f	4m 55s
2m 6f	5m 27s
2m 6f about 110 yds	5m 33s
3m	5m 59s
3m 1f	6m 15s
3m 2f	6m 30s
3m 4f	7m 4s
3m 5f	7m 20s
4m 1f	8m 23s

Hurdles

2m	3m 44s
2m 2f	4m 12s
2m 4f	4m 44s
2m 6f	5m 11s
3m	5m 40s

FAKENHAM
Chases

2m about 110yds	3m 57s
2m 5f about 110yds	5m 12s
3m about 110yds	5m 57s

Hurdles

2m	3m 44s
2m about 4f	4m 41s
2m about 7f 110yds	5m 27s

FOLKESTONE
Chases

About 2m	3m 51s
2m about 5f	5m 11s
3m about 2f	6m 15s
3m about 7f	7m 30s

Hurdles

2m about 1f 110yds	3m 57s
2m about 4f 110yds	4m 35s
2m about 6f 110yds	5m 10s
3m about 4f	6m 30s

FONTWELL
Chases

2m about 2f	4m 20s
2m about 3f	4m 35s
3m about 2f 110yds	6m 30s
3m about 7f	7m 35s

Hurdles

2m about 2f 110yds	4m 17s
2m about 6f 110yds	5m 14s
3m about 3f	6m 24s

HAYDOCK
Chases

About 2m	3m 56s
2m about 4f	4m 57s
About 3m	6m 5s
3m about 4f 110yds	7m 12s
4m about 110yds	8m 20s

Hurdles

About 2m	3m 38s
2m about 4f	4m 36s
2m about 6f	5m 7s
2m about 7f 110yds	5m 31s

AVERAGE TIMES FOR COURSES

HEREFORD
Chases

About 2m	3m 47s
2m about 3f	4m 25s
3m about 1f 110yds	6m 6s

Hurdles

2m about 1f	3m 45s
2m about 3f 110yds	4m 18s
3m about 2f	6m 2s

HEXHAM
Chases

2m about 110yds	3m 58s
2m about 4f 110yds	4m 58s
3m about 1f	6m 5s
4m	8m 3s

Hurdles

About 2m	3m 49s
2m about 4f 110yds	4m 51s
About 3m	5m 48s

HUNTINGDON
Chases

2m about 110 yds	3m 54s
2m about 4f 110yds	4m 47s
About 3m	5m 40s

Hurdles

2m about 110yds	3m 41s
2m about 4f 110yds	4m 35s
2m about 5f 110yds	4m 49s
3m about 2f	5m 52s

KELSO
Chases

2m about 1f	4m 5s
2m about 6f 110yds	5m 24s
3m about 1f	5m 57s
3m about 4f	6m 46s

Hurdles

2m about 110yds	3m 43s
2m about 2f	4m 7s
2m about 4f 110yds	4m 42s
2m about 6f 110yds	5m 9s
3m about 3f	6m 14s

KEMPTON
Chases

About 2m	3m 46s
2m about 4f 110yds	4m 53s
About 3m	5m 49s
3m about 4f 100yds	6m 56s

Hurdles

About 2m	3m 40s
2m about 5f	4m 46s
3m about 110yds	5m 45s

LEICESTER
Chases

2m about 1f	4m 8s
2m about 4f 110yds	5m 2s
About 3m	5m 45s

Hurdles

About 2m	3m 43s
2m about 4f 110yds	4m 48s
About 3m	5m 47s

LEOPARDSTOWN
Chases

2m 1f	4m 10s
2m 2f	4m 25s
2m 3f	4m 39s
2m 5f	5m 9s
2m 6f	5m 25s
2m 7f	5m 40s
3m	6m 7s

Hurdles

2m	3m 44s
2m 2f	4m 12s
2m 4f	4m 40s
2m 6f	5m 6s
3m	5m 37s

LINGFIELD
Chases

About 2m	3m 54s
2m about 4f 110yds	5m 1s
About 3m	5m 54s

Hurdles

2m about 110yds	3m 51s
2m about 3f 110yds	4m 33s
2m about 7f	5m 26s

LUDLOW
Chases

About 2m	3m 50s
2m about 4f	4m 49s
About 3m	5m 47s

Hurdles

About 2m	3m 32s
2m about 5f 110yds	4m 55s
3m about 2f 110yds	6m 5s

MARKET RASEN
Chases

2m about 1f 110yds	4m 14s
2m about 4f	4m 49s
2m 6f 110yds	5m 27s
3m about 1f	6m
3m about 4f 110yds	6m 59s
4m about 1f	8m 6s
4m about 3f 110yds	8m 46s

Hurdles

2m about 1f 110yds	4m 1s
2m about 3f 110yds	4m 30s
2m about 5f 110yds	5m 3s
About 3m	5m 39s

MUSSELBURGH
Chases

About 2m	3m 49s
2m about 4f	4m 47s
About 3m	5m 49s

Hurdles

About 2m	3m 37s
2m about 4f	4m 38s
About 3m	5m 37s

NEWBURY
Chases

2m about 1f	4m
2m about 4f	4m 48s
About 3m	5m 45s
3m 2f about 110yds	6m 28s

Hurdles

2m about 110yds	3m 49s
2m about 5f	4m 54s
3m about 110yds	5m 46s

NEWCASTLE
Chases

2m about 110yds	3m 59s
2m about 4f	4m 47s
About 3m	5m 46s
3m about 6f	7m 25s
4m about 1f	8m 11s

Hurdles

2m about 110yds	3m 40s
2m about 4f	4m 38s
About 3m	5m 31s

NEWTON ABBOT
Chases

2m about 110yds	3m 58s
2m about 5f 110yds	5m 2s
3m about 2f 110yds	6m 20s

Hurdles

2m about 1f	3m 49s
2m about 6f	5m 1s
3m about 3f	6m 16s

PERTH
Chases

About 2m	3m 51s
2m about 4f 110yds	4m 52s
About 3m	5m 55s

Hurdles

2m about 110yds	3m 41s
2m about 4f 110yds	4m 40s
3m about 110yds	5m 42s

PLUMPTON
Chases

About 2m	3m 52s
2m 2f	4m 21s
2m about 5f	5m 6s
3m about 1f 110yds	6m 14s

Hurdles

2m about 1f	3m 57s
2m about 4f	4m 37s

PUNCHESTOWN
Chases

2m	3m 59s
2m 2f	4m 28s
2m 4f	4m 57s
2m 5f	5m 12s
3m	6m
3m 1f	6m 15s
3m 2f	6m 31s
3m 2f 110yds	6m 38s
3m 4f	7m 3s
4m 1f	8m 24s

Hurdles

2m	3m 45s
2m 2f	4m 7s
2m 4f	4m 42s
3m	5m 45s

SANDOWN
Chases

About 2m	3m 49s
2m about 4f 110yds	5m
3m about 110yds	5m 59s
3m 5f about 110yds	7m 13s

Hurdles

2m about 110yds	3m 47s
2m about 6f	5m 3s

SEDGEFIELD
Chases

2m about 110yds	3m 52s
2m about 5f	4m 56s
3m about 3f	6m 33s
3m about 4f	6m 47s

Hurdles

2m about 1f	3m 46s
2m about 5f 110yds	4m 48s
3m 3f 110yds	6m 22s

SOUTHWELL
Chases

About 2m	3m 54s
2m about 4f 110yds	5m
2m about 6f	5m 20s
3m about 110yds	5m 54s

Hurdles

About 2m	3m 46s
2m 2f	4m 15s
2m about 4f 110yds	4m 46s
2m about 6f	5m 6s
3m about 110yds	5m 42s

STRATFORD
Chases

2m about 1f 110yds	4m 2s
2m about 4f	4m 40s
2m about 5f 110yds	5m
About 3m	5m 45s
3m about 4f	6m 45s

Hurdles

2m about 110yds	3m 46s
2m about 3f	4m 20s
2m about 6f 110yds	5m 12s
3m about 3f	6m 18s

TAUNTON
Chases

2m about 110yds	3m 52s
2m about 3f	4m 31s
About 3m	5m 43s
3m about 3f	6m 30s
3m about 6f	7m 12s
4m about 2f 110yds	8m 21s

Hurdles

2m about 1f	3m 43s
2m about 3f 110yds	4m 18s
3m about 110yds	5m 28s

TOWCESTER
Chases

2m about 110 yds	3m 57s
2m about 6f	5m 26s
3m about 1f	6m 12s

Hurdles

About 2m	3m 43s
2m about 5f	4m 59s
About 3m	5m 42s

UTTOXETER
Chases

2m	3m 47s
2m about 4f	4m 44s
2m about 5f	4m 58s
2m about 7f	5m 28s
3m about 2f	6m 12s
4m about 2f	8m 30s

Hurdles

About 2m	3m 37s
2m about 4f 110yds	4m 39s
2m about 6f 110yds	5m 7s
3m about 110yds	5m 37s

WARWICK
Chases

About 2m	3m 52s
2m about 4f 110yds	4m 55s
3m about 2f	6m 14s
3m about 5f	7m 9s
4m about 1f 110yds	8m 19s

Hurdles

About 2m	3m 39s
2m about 4f 110yds	4m 45s

WETHERBY
Chases

About 2m	3m 47s
2m about 4f 110yds	4m 53s
3m about 110yds	6m 1s
3m about 5f	7m 12s

Hurdles

About 2m	3m 41s
2m about 4f 110yds	4m 42s
2m about 7f 110yds	5m 25s
3m about 1f	5m 46s

WINCANTON
Chases

About 2m	3m 48s
2m about 5f	5m 4s
3m about 1f 110yds	6m 16s

Hurdles

About 2m	3m 34s
2m about 6f	5m 6s

WINDSOR
Chases

About 2m	3m 54s
2m about 5f	5m 9s
About 3m	5m 53s
3m about 4f 110yds	6m 59s

Hurdles

About 2m	3m 45s
2m about 4f	4m 40s
2m about 6f 110yds	5m 15s

WORCESTER
Chases

About 2m	3m 49s
2m about 4f 110yds	4m 57s
2m about 7f	5m 38s
3m about 4f 110yds	6m 54s

Hurdles

About 2m	3m 40s
2m about 2f	4m 7s
2m about 4f	4m 36s
2m about 5f 110yds	4m 54s
About 3m	5m 36s

The Sporting Life-Coral nap award winners 1947–97

Jumping

		W.	L.	N.R.	Longest seq. W.	Longest seq. L.	Profit £1 level Stakes £	s.	d.
1947–48	Daily Graphic Gimcrack	24	41	3	*	*	20	6	6
1948–49	Sporting Chronicle Stable Boy	10	38	10	*	*	32	6	9
1949–50	Sporting Chronicle Traveller	35	43	4	7	9	22	4	8
1950–51	News Chronicle Capt Heath	29	47	4	4	6	21	17	2
1951–52	Birmingham Post Veritas	27	40	14	7	6	18	3	0
1952–53	Daily Mirror Newsboy	24	51	11	3	11	10	10	6
1953–54	Sporting Life Man on the Spot	37	39	5	5	5	31	0	8
1954–55	Sporting Life Man on the Spot	28	37	7	5	8	23	1	0
1955–56	Daily Telegraph Hotspur	29	36	11	4	7	19	13	3
1956–57	Daily Mail Robin Goodfellow	25	51	14	2	6	32	19	0
1957–58	Sporting Life Solon	33	39	6	8	6	39	2	2
1958–59	Morning Advertiser Gainsborough	24	39	7	3	7	12	17	0
1959–60	Yorkshire Post The Duke	24	56	6	6	11	24	7	1
1960–61	Sheffield Telegraph Fortunatus	29	60	6	3	10	15	11	3
1961–62	Daily Express The Scout	29	48	5	4	7	15	8	2
1962–63	Western Mail Carlton	10	32	2	2	15	26	18	6
1963–64	Daily Sketch Gimcrack	31	48	4	3	6	36	16	8
1964–65	Irish Times Brown Jack	29	60	4	3	14	33	5	1
1965–66	Irish Press Merlin	23	50	6	4	15	16	8	3
1966–67	Irish Times Brown Jack	26	63	3	3	11	29	4	2
1967–68	Daily Mail Robin Goodfellow	28	44	1	4	4	34	9	1
1968–69	Sporting Life Solon	25	38	6	6	8	32	15	8
1969–70	Sun Templegate	33	62	5	3	8	16	8	8

		W.	L.	N.R.	Longest seq. W.	Longest seq. L.	Profit £1 level Stakes £	p	
1970–71	Western Mail Carlton	46	57	6	7	8	30.51		
1971–72	Daily Mirror Newsboy	44	66	2	5	8	25.53		
1972–73	Morning Star Cayton	22	82	4	2	12	25.92½		
1973–74	Morning Star Cayton	46	46	12	5	5	29.57½		
1974–75	Morning Advertiser Gainsborough	30	53	7	4	5	31.96½		
1975–76	Scottish Daily Express Scotia	39	64	4	6	9	16.22½		
1976–77	Liverpool Post Argus	20	63	6	3	16	20.96		
1977–78	Sporting Life Form	41	48	3	5	9	30.66		
1978–79	Western Mail Carlton	16	24	5	3	7	22.64		
1979–80	Daily Mail Robin Goodfellow	35	60	5	4	7	23.22		
1980–81	Morning Star Cayton	42	56	8	10	11	26.84		
1981–82	Northern Echo Capt Day	34	51	6	4	8	29.73		
1982–83	Daily Mail Robin Goodfellow	40	58	4	2	5	33.80		
1983–84	East Anglian Daily Times	47	47	11	7	4	27.92		
1984–85	Sporting Life, Stop Watch	32	47	5	4	5	29.07		
1985–86	Sunday Express, Tom Forrest	35	37	3	3	4	38.01		
1986–87	Daily Mirror, Newsboy	27	63	8	3	11	42.21		
1987–88	The Sporting Life, Nick Deacon	43	49	4	7	7	45.74		
1988–89	The Independent, John Karter	34	74	6	4	11	40.15		
1989–90	Daily Telegraph, Tony Stafford	41	56	9	4	10	42.20		
1990–91	Glasgow Herald, Martin Gale	37	55	10	4	12	42.45		
1991–92	Western Daily Press, Bob Watts	50	49	5	6	7	30.13		
1992–93	Sun, Templegate	33	70	8	6	9	27.88		
1993–94	Coventry Evening Telegraph, Jimmy Marshall	34	65	12	4	7	31.13		
1994–95	Sporting Life, Northern View (Jon Freeman)	25	73	14	2	8	36.63		
1995–96	Daily Telegraph, Tony Stafford	31	67	12	4	8	36.09		
1996–97	Sporting Life Form (Nigel Shields)	38	58	13	5	8	27.85		

* Figures not recorded in contemporary records

Licensed trainers 1996–97

The following received licences (valid until January 31, 1998) to train under Rule 50(i)

FLAT RACES AND FOR STEEPLE CHASES, HURDLE RACES AND NATIONAL HUNT FLAT RACES

Aconley, Mrs Vivien Ann
Akehurst, Jonathan
Akehurst, Reginald Peter John
Allan, Adam Richard
Allen, Conrad Norman
Alston, Eric James
Arbuthnot, David William Patrick
Armstrong, Robert Walter

Babbage, Norman Mark
Bailey, Alan
Bailey, Kim Charles
Baker, Rodney John
Balding, Gerald Barnard
Balding, Ian Anthony
Balding, John
Banks, John Edward
Barker, David William
Barnett, George William
Barr, Ronald Edward,
†Barraclough, Melvyn Frederick
Barratt, Lowther James
Barron, Thomas David
Barrow, Arthur Kendall
Barwell, Charles Robin
Bastiman, Robin
Baugh, Brian Philip John
Beaumont, Peter
Bennett, James Anthony
Benstead, Christopher John
Berry, Jack
Berry, John Claude de Pomeroy
Berry, Norman Edward
Bevan, Peter John
Bielby, Martin Peter
Bill, Tom Trivett
Birkett, John James
Bishop, Kevin Shaun
Blanshard, Michael Thomas William
Bolton, Michael John
Booth, Charles Benjamin Brodie
Bosley, Martin Read
Bottomley, John Frederick
Bowen, Peter
Bower, Miss Jane
Bowlby, Mrs Amanda
Bowring, Sidney Roy
Bradburne, Mrs Susan
Bradley, John Milton
Bradstock, Mark Fitzherbert
Bravery, Giles Colin
Brazington, Robert George

Brennan, Owen
Bridger, John James
Bridgwater, Kenneth Stanley
Brisbourne, William Mark
Brittain, Clive Edward
Brittain, Melvyn Anthony
Brooks, Charles Patrick Evelyn
Brotherton, Roy
Buckler, Robert Hamilton
Burchell, Walter David
Burke, Karl Richard
Butler, Patrick
Bycroft, Neville

Caldwell, Terence Harvey
Callaghan, Neville Anthony
Calver, Peter
Camacho, Maurice James Christopher
Cambidge, Burnup Roy
Campbell, Ian
Campion, Andrew Mark
†Campion, Stephen William
Candy, Henry Derrick Nicholas Bourne
Carr, John Michael
Carroll, Anthony William
Casey, William Terence
Cecil, Mrs Julia
Chamberlain, Adrian John
Chamberlain, Norman
Champion, Robert
Chance, Noel Thomas
Channon, Michael Roger
Chapman, Michael Christopher
Chappell, Major David Nigel
Chapple-Hyam, Peter William
Charles-Jones, Gareth Francis Hugh
Charlton, John Irving Alistair
Clarke, Peter Cedric
Clay, William
Clement, Terence Thomas
Cole, Paul Frederick Irvine
Collingridge, Hugh John
Cosgrove, David Joseph Simon
Cottrell, Leslie Gerald
Craggs, Raymond
Craze, Miss Julie Frances
Cullinan, John
Cundell, Peter David
Cunningham, William Scott
Cunningham-Brown Kenneth Owen

Curley, Barney Joseph
Curtis Roger
Cuthbert, Thomas Alexander Keir
Cyzer, Charles Alan

Dalton, Paul Thomas
DeHaan, Benjamin
Dickin, Robin
Dods, Michael Joseph Keil
Donnelly, Terence William
Dow, Simon Langley
Drewe, Christopher James
Dunlop, John Leeper
Dutfield, Mrs Pauline Nerys
Dwyer, Christopher Ambrose

Earle, Simon Alexander
Easterby, Michael William
Easterby, Timothy David
Eccles, Paul
Eckley, Malcolm Willis
Egerton, Charles Ralph
Ellison, Brian
Elsworth, David Raymond Cecil
Embiricos, Miss Alexandra Eugenie
Enright, Gerard Patrick
Etherington, Timothy James
Eustace, James Maurice Percy
Evans, Paul David
Eyre, John Leslie

Fahey, Richard Aiden
Fairhurst, Christopher William
Fanshawe, James Robert
Farrell, Patrick
Felgate, Paul Stanley
Ffitch-Heyes, John Ronald
Ffrench Davis, Dominic John Simon
Fierro, Giuseppe
FitzGerald, James Gerard
Flower, Richard Mark
Foster, Alexander George
Fox, James Christopher
Frost, Richard George

Gandolfo, David Rostron
Gaselee, Nicholas Auriol Digby Charles
George, Miss Karen Mary
George, Tom Richard
Gifford, Joshua Thomas

Glover, Jeremy Anton
Goldie, James Sloan
Gollings, Stephen
Goulding, John Lennox
Graham, Neil Anthony
Green, Miss Zoe Ann

Haggas, William John
Haigh, William Wilson
Haine, Diana Elizabeth Solna
Haldane, John Swanson
Hall, Leslie Montague
Hall, Miss Sarah Elizabeth
Ham, Gerald Antony
Hammond, Michael David
Hannon, Richard Michael
Harris, James Lawrence
Harris, John Arthur
Harris, Roger
Haslam, Patrick Charles
Haynes, Michael John
Hayward, Peter Alfred
Heaton-Ellis, Michael James Brabazon
Hedger, Peter Ronald
Henderson, Nicholas John
Hern, Major William Richard
Herries, Lady Anne Elizabeth
Hetherton, James
Hide, Anthony Gatehouse
Hills, Barrington William
Hills, John William
Hind, Terry
Hobbs, Philip John
Hodges, Ronald James
Hollinshead, Reginald
Holmes, Gordon
Horgan, Cornelius Augustus
Howe, Harry Stuart
Howling, Paul
Hubbard, Geoffrey Ambrose
Huntingdon, Lord William Edward Robin Hood
Hyde, Dermid Michael

Ingram, Roger
Ivory, Kenneth Thomas

Jackson, Colin Frederick Charles
James, Anthony Paul
James, Charles John
Jarvis, Alan Peter
Jarvis, Michael Andrew

LICENSED TRAINERS 1996–97

Jefferson, Joseph Malcolm
Jenkins, John Renfield
Jenks, William Percival
Jewell, Mrs Linda Christine
Johnsey, Miss Clair Jayne
Johnson Houghton, Gordon Fulke
Johnson Houghton, Richard Fulke
Johnston, Mark Steven
Jones, Anthony Paul
Jones, Derek Haydn
Jones, Mrs Merrita Anne
Jones, Robert Walter
Jones, Thomas Michael
Jones, Timothy Thomson
Jordan, Frank Thomas James
Jordan, Mrs Joan
Juckes, Roderick Thomas

Keddy, Thomas
Kelleway, Miss Gay Marie
Kelleway, Paul Anthony
Kelly, Gerald Patrick
Kemp, William Thomas
Kersey, Trevor
Kettlewell, Steven Edward
King, Mrs Anabel Louise Moss
King, Jeffrey Steven
Knight, Miss Henrietta Catherine
Knight, Steven George

Lamb, David Antony
Lampard, Nicholas Mark
Leadbetter, Stephen John
Lee, Richard Anthony
Leight, James Patrick
Littmoden, Nicholas Paul
Llewellyn, Bernard John
Lloyd-James, Lee Russell
Long, John Edward
Lungo, Leonard

Macauley, Mrs Norma Jacqueline
Mackie, William John Wilkinson
MacTaggart, Alexander Bruce
Madgwick, Michael John
Makin, Peter James
Mann, Charles James
Margarson, George Graham
Marks, Douglas
Marvin, Richard Frank
McAuliffe, Kevin William John
McCain, Donald
McConnochie, John Calvin
McCourt, Graham Matthew
McGovern, Thomas Patrick
McKellar, Robert McNaughton
McKeown, William Joseph
McMahon, Bryan Arthur
McMath, Brian James

Meade, Christopher Martyn
Meagher, Michael Gerard
Meehan, Brian Joseph
Mellor, Stanley Thomas Edward
Milligan, Miss Mary Kate
Millman, Brian Roderick
Mills, Terence George
Mitchell, Patrick Kenneth
Mitchell, Philip
Moffatt, Dudley
Monteith, Peter
Mooney, Peter
Moore, Gary Lee
Moore, George Mervin
Moore, James Stanley
Morgan, Barry Clive
Morgan, Kevin Alan
Morlock, Charles Philip Herbert
Morris, David
Morrison, Hugh
Muggeridge, Menin Patrick
Muir, William Robert
Mulholland, Anthony Bernard
Mullins, James William
Murphy, Ferdinand
Murphy, Patrick Gerard
Murray, Brendan William
Murray, Christopher
Murray Smith, David John George
Musson, William James

Naughton, Mrs Ann Muriel
Naughton, Thomas Joseph
Neville, James Joseph
Newcombe, Anthony Gilbert
Nicholls, David
Nicholls, Paul Frank
Nicholson, David
Nolan, Dolan Alphonsos
Norton, John

O'Brien, Daniel Christopher
O'Neill, John Joseph
O'Neill, Owen
O'Shea, John Gerard Martin
O'Sullivan, Roland Jeffrey
Old, James Andrew Bertram
Oldroyd, Geoffrey Reginald

Palling, Brynley
Parker, Colin
Parkes, John Edwin
Payne, John William
Peacock, John Harris
Peacock, Raymond Eric
Pearce, Brian Arthur
Pearce, Jeffrey
Perratt, Miss Linda Agnes

Perrett, Mrs Amanda Jill
Phillips, Richard Timothy
Pickering, John Alan
Pipe, Martin Charles
Pitman, Mrs Jennifer Susan
Polglase, Mark Julyan
Popham, Christopher Leslie
Poulton, James Raymond
Preece, William George
Prescott, Sir Mark
Price, Richard John
Pritchard, Peter Anthony

Quinn, John Joseph

Ramsden, Mrs Lynda Elaine
Retter, Mrs Jacqueline Gay
Reveley, Mrs Mary Christiana
Richards, Gordon Waugh
Richards, Mrs Lydia
Ringer, David John
Ritchens, Paul Cyril
Rothwell, Brian Samuel
Rowe, Richard
Rowland, Miss Mandy Elizabeth
Ryan, Michael John

Salaman, Marshalla Ali
Sanders, Miss Brooke Virginia Jane
Saunders, Malcolm Sydney
Scargill, Dr Jon David
Shaw, Derek
Sheehan, John Joseph
Sherwood, Oliver Martin Carwardine
Siddall, Miss Lynn Christina
Simpson, Rodney
Sly, Mrs Pamela Marigold
Smart, Bryan
Smith, Alfred
Smith, Charles
Smith, Craig Anthony
Smith, Denys
Smith, John Peter
Smith, Nigel Alan
Smith, Mrs Susan Jane
Smyth-Osbourne, Julian George
Soane, Victor St John
Sowersby, Michael Edward
Spearing, John Lionel
Spicer, Roger Charles
Stokell, Miss Ann
Storey, Wilfred Luke
Stoute, Michael Ronald
Streeter, Andrew Paul
Stronge, Robert Maynard
Stubbs, Mrs Linda
Swinbank, Mrs Ann

Tate, Frederick Martin
Tate, Thomas Patrick
Thom, David Trenchard
Thompson, Ronald
Thompson, Victor
Thomson, Mrs Dorothy
Thomson, Neil Barrett
Thorner, Graham Edward
Thornton, Christopher William
Tinkler, Nigel Delfosse
Todhunter, Duncan Martin
Toller, James Arthur Richard
Tompkins, Mark Harding
Turnell, Andrew
Turner, William George Michael
Twiston-Davies, Nigel Anthony

Upson, John Ralph
Usher, Mark Donald Ian

Wainwright, John Stanley
†Walker, Nicholas James Howard
Wall, Christian Frederick
Wall, Trevor Richard
Walwyn, Peter Tyndall
Wane, Martyn
Waring, Mrs Barbara
Watson, Frederick
Watson, Toby Richard
Weaver, Redvers John
Webber, Paul Richard
Weedon, Colin Victor
Weymes, Ernest
Wharton, John Raymond
Wheeler, Eric Archibald
Whitaker, Richard Mawson
White, John Raymond
Wilkinson, Mark John
Williams, David Lyndon
Williams, Ian Paul
Williams, Robert James Royston
Williams, Mrs Sarah Daphne
Wilson, Andrew James
Wilson, Captain James Hume
Wilton, Miss Susan Jayne
Wingrove, Kenneth George
Wintle, David John
Woodhouse, Robert Dickson Edgar
Woodman, Stephen
Woods, Sean Peter Charles

Yardley, Francis John
Yardley, George Henry

† Relinquished

RESTRICTED FOR FLAT RACES

Akbary, Hooman
Arnold, Jeremy Rupert

Bell, Michael Leopold
Wentworth
Bethell, James David
William
bin Suroor, Saeed
Boss, Ronald

Cecil, Henry Richard
Amherst

Chapman, David William
Charlton, Roger John
Cumani, Luca Matteo

Dunlop, Edward Alexander
Leeper

Fetherston-Godley, Martin
John

Gosden, John Harry Martin
Gubby, Brian

Guest, Rae

Hanbury, Benjamin
Harris, Peter Woodstock
Hill, Courtney John

Incisa, Don Enrico

Jarvis, William

Lee, Francis Henry
Lewis, Geoffrey
Loder, David Richard

Morley, Michael Frederick
David

O'Gorman, William Andrew

Powell, Thomas Edward

Stewart, Alexander Christie

Watts, John William
Williams, Stuart Charles
Wragg, Geoffrey

RESTRICTED FOR STEEPLE CHASES, HURDLE RACES AND NATIONAL HUNT FLAT RACES

Alexander, Hamish Harold
Ferguson
Alner, Robert Henry
Ayliffe, Nicholas George

Barclay, James
Barnes, Maurice Allen
Bell, Simon Bernard
Best, John Robert
Bower, Miss Lindsay Jane
Brookshaw, Steven
Anthony
Brown, Mrs Jeannie

Caroe, Miss Clarissa Janet
Elizabeth
Carr, Timothy Julian
Chamings, Patrick Richard
Cheesbrough, Peter Ralph
Cole, Sydney Newman

Dodds, John Peter
Dunn, Allan John Keith

Eckley, Richard Jones
Edwards, Miss Stephanie
Susan

Forster, Captain Timothy
Arthur

Geraghty, David Patrick
Goldie, Robert Howie
Grant, Christopher
Grassick, Liam Patrick
Grissell, Delagarde Michael

Harvey, Alexander Henry
Hawke, Nigel John
Hemsley, Colin John
Henderson, Mrs Rosemary
Gillian
Hewitt, Mrs Shirley Anne
Hobbs, Andrew Geoffrey

Johnson, John Howard
Jones, Christopher Harry

†Keddy, Thomas

McCune, David
McDonald, Robert
McKie, Mrs Victoria Jane
Mitchell, Norman Richard
Murtagh, Finbarr Patrick

Newton-Smith, Miss Anna
Marguerite

†Oliver, Henry Joseph
Oliver, James Kenneth
Murray

Poulton, Julian Charles

Reed, William George
Rodford, Patrick Reginald
Roe, Colin Graeme
Algernon Maitland
Russell, Miss Lucinda
Valerie

Sheppard, Matthew Ian
Smith, Julian Simon
Smith, Ralph John
Storey, Mrs Jane Margaret

Tate, Robin
Townsley, Mrs Prudence
Laxton
Tuck, John Colin
Turner, James Richard

Ward, Mrs Valerie Claire
Wells, Lawrence
Whillans, Alistair Charles
Whittle, Miss Pamela May
Williams, Miss Venetia
Mary
Williamson, Mrs Lisa
Victoria
Williamson, Miss Sally Lynn
Winkworth, Peter Leslie
†Wintle, David John

† Relinquished

Permit trainers: hurdles and chases

Permits to train for steeplechases, hurdle races and National Hunt Flat races for the season 1996-97 under Rule 50(ii) of the Rules of Racing

Adam, James Raleigh
Alder, Derek Stanley
Alford, Gordon Norman
Allen, John Scot
†Andrews, Jack
Armson, Richard John
Arthur, Hon Mrs Veronica
   Rosemary
Avison, Mrs Penelope Mary
   Ann
Aynsley, John William Faill

Banks, Michael Charles
Barclay, Mrs Althea
Barlow, George
Barlow, Sir John Kemp
Bartlett, Ronnie Alexander
Bassett, David Francis
Batchelor, Julian
   Christopher Alexander
Bethell, William
Bevan, Edward George
Bewley, Joseph Robert
Bickerton, Mrs Philippa
   Frances
Billinge, Jeremy Nicholas
   Russell
Bishop, Vivian Roger
Black, Mrs Charmian
   Jennifer
Blackmore, Alan Grenville
Bousfield, Bryan
Bowen, Simon Alexander
Bowlby, Lady Anne Lavinia
   Maud
Bowman, Mrs Carol
   Margaret
Brace, David
Bradley, Paul
Brewis, Robert
Broad, Mrs Beryl Kathleen
Brooks, Mrs Elizabeth Mary
Brown, David Henry
Brown, Ian Robertson
Brown, John Leslie
Brown, Reginald Leslie
Broyd, Miss Alison
   Elizabeth

Caine, Edward Malcolm
Cantillon, Donald Edward
Carey, Derek Norman
Caro, Denis John
Carson, Robert Martin
Carter, Oliver John
Castle, James Merry
Chadwick, Stephen George
Chesney, Dr David

Churches, Maxwell Robert
Clark, Stephen Bradly
Clutterbuck, Kenneth Frank
Cockburn, Robert George
Cole, Henry Toogood
Collins, Richard
Conway, Mrs Jillian
Coombe, Michael John
Cornwell, John Edward
Coton, Frank
Coward, Mrs Cherry Ann
Cresswell, John Kenneth
   Silvers
Curtis, John William Parker

Dalgetty, Thomas Norman
Dalton, James Neale
Davies, David Janway
Davies, Gerald Walter
   James
Day, Miss Joy Hilary
Dean, Richard
Dennis, Paul Jeffrey
Dennis, Walter William
Dixon, John Edward
Douch, Selwyn Alun
Downes, John Derek
Du Plessis, Miss
   Jacqueline Mary
Dun, John Michael
Dun, Thomas Dixon
   Connochie

Eckley, Brian John
Edwards, Gordon Francis
Elliott, Eric Alan
England, Miss Evelyn Mary
   Victoria
Evans, John Thomas
Evans, Richard Rhys
Ewer, Mrs Justina Ann

Findlay, Mrs Anthea June
Forbes, Anthony Leslie
Forster, Donald Michael
Frost, Kevin

Gee, Brian
Giddings, Gordon Wilfrid
Gledson, James Lewis
Goodfellow, Mrs Anne
   Cicely Dawn
Gray, Frederick
Greathead, Terence
   Richard
Greenway, Victor Gerald
Griffin, Michael Albert
Griffiths, Sirrell George

Hanson, John
Harker, Geoffrey Alan
Harriman, John
Harriss, Paul Richards
Hawkins, Mrs Joanne
   Elizabeth
Haynes, Hedley Edward
Haynes, Jonathan Charles
Heath, Mrs Elizabeth Helen
Hewitt, Philip Stanley
Hiatt, Peter William
Hill, Martin Edwin
Hodge, Hugh Baird
Hollingsworth, Alan
   Frederick
Hollis, Frederick George
Homewood, John Stanley
†Hope, John Wallace
†Hope, Mrs Nancy
Horler, Miss Carol Jane
Horner-Harker, Mrs Sarah
   Louise
Hubbuck, John Sidney

Jackson, Frank Samuel
Jessop, Alan Ernest
   Michael
Jestin, Fergus
Johnson, Patrick Roy
Johnson, Robert William
Johnson, Mrs Susan Mary
Jones, Gruffydd Elwyn
Jones, Ivor Reginald
Jones, Peter John
Joseph, Jack

Kavanagh, Henry Michael
Kendall, Mrs Margaret Ann
Kinsey, Thomas Richard
Kirby, Fred
Kirby, John

Lamb, Mrs Kathleen
   Margaret
Lamyman, Mrs Susan
Ledger, Roger Roy
Livermore, Richard Ewart
   Allison
Llewellyn, William Brinley
Lloyd, David Michael
Lloyd, Frank

Manners, Herbert John
Marshall, Mrs Leslie Ann
Mason, Norman Beresford
Mathew, Robert Knox
Mays-Smith, Lady Elizabeth
   Maria

McInnes Skinner, Mrs
   Caroline Ann Patricia
McKenzie-Coles, William
   George
†McKeown, William Joseph
McMillan, Malcolm
   Douglas
Millington, Charles
   Roderick
Minty, Desmond John
Mitchell, Colin Walter
Moore, James Alan
Morton, Thomas
Moscrop, Mrs Edna

Neaves, Albert Stanley
Needham, John Lees
Needham, Thomas
Nelson, Walter Maxwell
Nixon, George Rayson
   Steele
Nock, Mrs Susan

O'Neill, John Gerard
Odell, Mrs Shaena
   Margaret
Owen, Edward Hollister
Owen, Mrs Fiona Margaret

Panvert, John Francis
Parfitt, John
Park, Ian
Payne, James Ronald
   George
Phillips, Miss Cherry
   Elizabeth
Pilkington, Mrs Jane St
   Clare
Pittendrigh, Stewart Ian
Plater, Ms Linda Christine
Pocock, Robert Edward
Price, Andrew Ernest
Price, Mrs Ann
Price, George Michael
Pritchard, Dr Philip Leslie
   James
Prodromou, George
Pugh, Roger Charles

Ratcliffe, Christopher Ian
Raw, William
Rich, Paul Michael
*Richards, Graham
Richardson, Mrs Susan
   Leonhardt
Roberts, Michael John
Robertson, David

Robeson, Mrs Renee Louise Marie
Robinson, Simon John
†Rowland, Miss Mandy Elizabeth
Ryall, Bertram John Miller

Sawyer, Harry
Sayer, Mrs Heather Dianne
Scott, Mrs Elizabeth Beryl
Scriven, Bernard Anthony Victor
Scrivens, Mrs Janet
Shally, Miss Laura Angela
†Shaw, Bernard
Shiels, Raymond
Sidebottom, Mrs Janice
Sisterson, John
Slack, Mrs Doris Evelyn
Smith, Alan Dennis
Smith, Miss Diana Jean
Smith, Geofrey Richard

Smith, Malcolm John
Smith, William James Frederick
Snook, Laurence Arthur
Spottiswood, Philip
Stephens, Miss Victoria Alison
Stirk, Mrs Maxine Katrina
†Stone, Miss Frances Mary
Storey, Frederick Stalker
Supple, Kevin Roy
Swiers, Joseph Edward
Swindlehurst, Derek Gordon

Taylor, Frank
Taylor, Mrs Lavinia Clare
Temple, Bruce Michael
Thomas, Mrs Delyth
Thomson, Alexander Moffat
Thomson, Rennie Watt
Tinning, William Hodge

Todd, David Thomas
Tucker, Frederick George
Turner, Dennis Charles

Vincent, Kenneth

Wade, John
Wadham, Mrs Lucy Ann Mhari
Waggott, Norman
Waley-Cohen, Robert Bernard
Walshe, Thomas Patrick
Walton, Frank Teasdale
Walton, Mrs Helen Louise
†Ward, Mrs Valerie Claire
Waring, Louis Edwin
Warner, Keith Oswald
Waterman, Miss Susan Elizabeth
Watkins, Philip George

Webb, Henry John Montague
Weeden, Martin John
Wegmann, Peter
†Wells, Lawrence
Weston, Martin Henry
Whillans, Donald Wilson
White, Mrs Frances Elizabeth
White, George Francis
Whyte, John William
Williams, Lyndon James
Wood, Robert Stuart
Woodrow, Mrs Ann Mary
Wordingham, Leonard Walter

Young, Mrs Judith Anne Frances
Young, William Gilchrist

† Relinquished
* Revoked

Licensed jockeys: hurdles and chases

Licensed to ride in steeplechases and hurdle races for the season 1996–97 under Rule 60(ii) of the Rules of Racing

Anderson, Stephen George 9 7

Bellamy, Robert John 10 0
Bentley, David Branwell 10 0
Bentley, Nicholas Andrew 10 0
Bohane, Gerry, 10 0
†Bosley, Martin Read 10 3
Bradley, Graham John 10 3
Brennan, Martin Joseph 10 0
Bridgwater, David George 10 0
Burchell, David John 10 0
Burke, John Henry 10 0
Burrough, Simon Charles 10 2
Byrne, Derek Cyril 10 0
Byrne, Edmond Martin 10 0

Cahill, Gearoid Patrick 10 0
Callaghan, Jason Glen 10 0
Carberry, Paul Alice 10 0
Clarke, Michael Joseph 9 10
Clifford, Brian Martin 10 0
Crone, Gary Steven 10 0
Culloty, James Hugh 9 7
Curran, Sean 10 0
Cuthbert, Miss Carol 10 0

†Dalton, Bernard Patrick 10 0
=Davis, Richard John 10 0
Dicken, Anthony Robert 10 0
Dobbin, Anthony Gerald 10 0
Dunwoody, Thomas Richard 10 2
Dwan, William Joseph 10 0
Dwyer, Mark Peter 10 3

Eley, Timothy James 10 0
†Evans, Jamie Kenneth 10 0

Farrant, Rodney Alan 10 0
Fenton, Barry Dennis 10 0
Fitzgerald, Michael Anthony 10 4
Foster, Martin Robin 10 0
Fox, Sean 10 0
Frost, James Douglas 10 4
Fry, William Stanley 10 0

Gallagher, Dean Thomas 10 0
Garritty, Russell John 10 3
Gaule, Kieran Patrick 10 0
Greene, Roderick Joseph 10 0
Guest, Richard Charles 10 1

Harding, Brian Patrick 10 0
†Harker, Geoffrey Alan 10 4
Harvey, Lucien John 10 0
Hide, Philip Edward 10 0
Hodge, Robert James 10 0
Holley, Paul Stephen 10 0
Hughes, Richard David 8 9
†Humphreys, William George 10 0

Jenks, Tom Percival 10 0
Johnson, Kenneth 10 0
Johnson, Richard Evan 10 0
†Jones, Kevin 10 0
Jousset, Freddy Nicolas Alain 10 3

Kavanagh, John Robert 10 0
Kent, Terence John 10 0

Larnach, Andrew Alexander 10 0
Lawrence, Ian Russell 10 0
Leach, Neil Richard 10 0
Leahy, Denis 10 0
Leech, Jonathan Peter 10 0
Llewellyn, Carl 10 0
Lodder, Jonathan David 10 0
Long, Miss Leesa Georgina 10 0
Lyons, Gary 10 2

Maguire, Adrian 10 0
Mann, Nicholas James William 10 0
Marley, Roger John 10 0
Marston, Warren John 10 0
Maude, Christopher George 10 0
McCabe, Alan Joseph 10 0
McCain, Donald Richard 10 4
McCarthy, James Andrew 10 0
McCoy, Anthony Peter 10 0
McDougall, Stephen James 10 0
McFarland, William John 10 0
McLaughlin, John Fletcher Stephen 10 0
McLaughlin, Thomas Gary 10 0
McLoughlin, Patrick Joseph 10 0
McNeill, Simon Robert Onslow 10 0
Moffatt, Dudley James 10 0
Moloney, Michael John 10 0
Morris, Derrick 10 0
†Murphy, Eamon Robert 10 0
Murphy, Timothy James 9 7

Niven, Peter David 10 3

O'Dwyer, Conor 10 0
O'Hara, Liam Stuart 10 0
O'Sullivan, Darren Kenneth 10 1
O'Sullivan, Timothy Joseph 10 0
Oliver, Miss Jacqueline 10 0
Osborne, James Anthony 10 0

Parker, David 10 0
Pears, Oliver John 10 0
Perratt, William Fraser 10 0
Powell, Brendan Gerard 10 0
Procter, Anthony Richard 10 0

Railton, James Andrew 10 2
Ranger, Mark 10 0
Reed, William Timothy 10 5
Richards, Mark Robert 10 0
Roche, Alan John 9 10
Rourke, Robin Richard 10 0
Ryan, Diarmuid Anthony 10 0
Ryan, John Barry 10 0

Sharratt, Mark Raymond 10 0
Skyrme, David Vaughan 10 0
Slattery, John Vincent 10 0
Smith, Adrian Stewart 10 0
Smith, Charles Nicholas 10 0
Smith, Vince 10 0
Stokell, Miss Ann 10 0
Storey, Brian 10 0
Supple, John Anthony 10 0
Supple, Robert John 10 0

Thornton, Andrew Robert 10 0
Titley, Jason Francis 10 0
Tormey, Glenn Eugene 10 0

Upton, Guy 10 3

Verco, David Ian 10 2

†Waggott, Peter 10 2
Walsh, David John 10 0
Williamson, Norman 10 0
Worthington, William Martin 10 0
Wyer, Lorcan Andrew 10 0
Wynne, Stephen 9 10

† Relinquished
= Deceased

Conditional jockeys

Licensed to ride in steeplechases, hurdle races and National Hunt Flat races for the season 1996–97 under Rule 60(iv) of the Rules of Racing

Aizpuru, Xavier (Mr R Dickin) 9 7
Arnold, Richard Walker (Mr G B Balding) 9 7
Aspell, Leighton (Mr J T Gifford) 9 9
Attwater, Michael James (Mr G L Moore) 10 0

Bastiman, Harvey James (Mr R Bastiman) 9 9
Batchelor, Mathew Alexander (Mr G L Moore) 9 7
Bates, Aaron (Capt T A Forster) 9 9
Berry, Martin (Mr C P E Brooks) 10 0
Berry, Ross Keith (Mr M C Chapman) 9 7
Bogle, Fergus (Mr I Williams) 9 7
Bohan, David Joseph (Mr J R White) 9 7
Brace, Gary James (Mr C P E Brooks) 9 7
Brennan, Michael Anthony (Mr J G M O'Shea) 9 10
Brown, Kevin (Mr N A Twiston-Davies) 9 7
Brown, Mark (Mr K R Burke) 9 7
Burns, Robert Patrick (Mr G Richards) 9 7
Burrows, Owen James (Mr P Nicholls) 9 7

†Cahill, Gearoid Patrick (Mrs M Reveley) 9 11
Callaghan, Edward Gerald (Mr J M Jefferson) 10 0
†Carson, Derek Alexander (Mr J Sheehan) 9 7
†Clarke, Bradley James (Mr C Smith) 9 8
Clinton, Mark Andrew (Mr P R Hedger) 9 10
†Comerford, Thomas Joseph (Mrs M Reveley) 9 7
Cooke, Jason Lee (Mrs M A Jones) 9 7
Cooper, Liam Philip (Mr J J O'Neill) 9 7
Creech, David Phillip (Mr G Foster) 10 0
†Culloty, James Hugh (Miss H Knight) 9 7
Cummins, Liam Patrick (Mr P Nicholls) 9 7

Dascombe, Thomas Geoffrey (Mr R J Hodges) 9 11
Davidson, John Tristran (Mr C Parker) 9 7
Davies, Carl Anthony William (Mr A P Jarvis) 9 7
†Dempsey, Keith Anthony David (Mr Rod Simpson) 9 7
Dowling, Andrew Geraed (Mr H J Manners) 9 7
Dowling, William Joseph (Mr L Lungo) 9 7
Dunne, Martin Patrick (Mrs M A Jones) 9 7

Egan, Niall Thomas (Mr J R Jenkins) 9 7
Elkins, Richard John (Mr S Dow) 9 10
Elliott, Christopher James (Mr J L Eyre) 9 7

†Fenton, Barry Dennis (Mr G B Balding) 8 12
†Finnegan, David (Mr N J H Walker) 9 10
Fortt, Daniel Lloyd (Mr D R Gandolfo) 9 9
†Fowler, Simon Roy (Mr P Wegmann) 10 2

Gallagher, Gordon Robert Patrick (Mr B A Pearce) 9 7
Garrity, Andrew (Mr R Rowe) 9 7
†Gaule, Kieran Patrick (Mr G A Hubbard) 9 7
Graham, Shuan Richard (Mr G Roe) 9 7
Grattan, Brian Denis (Mr P Beaumont) 9 7
Greatrex, Warren James (Mr J T Gifford) 9 7

Greehy, Enda Patrick (Mr J A B Old) 9 7
Griffiths, Mark John (Mr A Turnell) 9 7

Hagger, Trevor (Mr N J Henderson) 9 7
Hambidge, Miss Katharine Rose (Mr M Bradstock) 9 7
Hannity, Niall (Mr G M Moore) 9 7
Harris, Jay Edward (Mr R J Hodges) 9 7
Haworth, Steven Michael (Mr N B Mason) 9 9
Hayes, William Michael (Mrs J Pitman) 9 7
Henley, Peter John (Mr R Alner) 9 11
Herrington, Michael (Mrs M Reveley) 10 0
Hibbert, Kevin Matthew (Miss P M Whittle) 9 7
Hobson, Richard Henry (Mr G McCourt) 9 7
Hogan, Gerard Patrick (Mr D Nicholson) 9 11
Horrocks, Nathan (Mr C W Thornton) 9 7
Husband, Eugene Llewellyn (Mr N Tinkler) 9 11
Hynes, Columban Brendan (Mr T R George) 9 5

Irvine, Andrew James (Mr J E Long) 9 7

Jardine, Iain James (Mr L Lungo) 9 7

Kavanagh, David James (Mr P J Hobbs) 9 9
Keenan, Joseph (Mr J S Moore) 9 7
Keighley, Martin Holmes (Mr N A Twiston-Davies) 9 10
Kiernan, David Noel Brendan (Mr C Mann) 9 7

Laird, Stephen Bernard (Mr J T Gifford) 9 9
Lane, Mark Anthony Phillip (Mrs M A Jones) 9 7
Leahy, Finbarr Timothy (Mr J FitzGerald) 9 7
Lee, Graham Martin (Mrs M Reveley) 9 11
Lewis, Guy Miles (Mr W Clay) 9 11
Lucas, Andrew Keith (Mr J Bennett) 9 11
Lycett, Shaun (Mr N A Twiston-Davies) 9 13

Magee, Jamie (Mr C Mann) 10 0
Maher, Patrick Joseph (Mr N J Henderson) 9 7
Massey, Robert Ian (Mr David Nicholson) 9 9
McCarthy, James Keith (Mr R M Flower) 9 7
McCarthy, Raymond (Mr T P Tate) 10 0
McCormack, Calvin John (Mr M Todhunter) 9 7
McGann, Barry Thomas (Mr S A Earle) 9 7
†McGirr, Fergus Joseph (Mr J A B Old) 9 7
McGrath, Laurence Richard (Mr W S Cunningham) 9 7
McGrath, Richard (Mr J J O'Neill) 9 7
Melrose, Stephen (Mr R Allan) 9 10
Middleton, David John (Mr D Marks) 9 7
Midgley, Paul Thomas (Mr M W Easterby) 10 5
Mitchell, Miss Sophie Jane (Mr D R Gandolfo) 8 10
Mogford, Jodie (Capt T A Forster) 9 0
Moore, Benjamin Hiram (Mr M C Pipe) 9 7
Moran, Mark Patrick (Mr P J Hobbs) 9 7

†Murphy, Richard Mathais (Mrs M Reveley) 9 10
Murphy, Thomas Cyril (Mr N J Henderson) 9 10
†Murphy, Timothy James (Mr K C Bailey) 9 7
Newton, Michael Joseph (Mr J M Jefferson) 9 7
Nolan, James Thomas (Mr J G M O'Shea) 9 7

†O'Connor, Donald Christopher (Mr M Wilkinson) 9 7
O'Connor, Thomas Anthony (Mr C L Popham) 9 7
O'Shaughnessy, Jason Patrick (Mr J Pearce) 9 7
O'Shea, Seamus Martin (Mr G B Balding) 9 7

Painter, Richard Bentley (Mr K R Burke) 9 9
Parker, David (Mr C Parker) 9 11
Parkhouse, Jason Stephen (Mr R Curtis) 9 7
Parkin, Gyles (Mr M W Easterby) 9 0
Porritt, Stephen (Mr O Brennan) 9 7
Power, John Gerard (Mr Bill Turner) 9 7
Prior, John Haydn (Mr D Burchell) 10 0

Quinlan, Frank (Mr P M Mooney) 9 12

Rae, Colin (Mr A Turnell) 9 7
Reynolds, Leslie Richard (Miss G Kelleway) 10 7
†Righton, Shashi Marvin (Mr J Spearing) 9 7
Roche, Alan John (Mr J J O'Neill) 9 10
Rossiter, Nathan Ian McColm (Mr A G Newcombe) 10 0
Ryan, Gerard Finbarr (Mrs S Smith) 9 0
Ryan, Shane (Mr R Akehurst) 9 10

Salter, Darren Geoffrey (Mr B R Millman) 9 9
†Scholes, Adrian Paul (Mr N Bycroft) 9 7
Scudder, Christopher (Mr K C Bailey) 9 7
Siddall, Tom James (Miss L C Siddall) 9 7
†Smith, Andrew Kenneth (Mr W T Kemp) 10 0
Smith, Glen Edvard (Mr D Nicholson) 9 7
Smith, Martin Philip Bruce (Mr Richard Phillips) 9 7
Studholme, Ross (Mr G McCourt) 9 7
Supple, Gerard David (Mr M C Pipe) 9 7
Supple, John Anthony (Mrs A Swinbank) 9 11
Suthern, Lee (Mr N A Twiston-Davies) 9 7

Taylor, Scott Duncan (Mr M Barnes) 9 9
Thomas, Darren (Mr O M C Sherwood) 9 7
Thorner, Miss Clare Victoria (Mr G Thorner) 10 0
†Todd, Alan William (Miss S Williamson) 9 0
†Tormey, Glenn Eugene (Mr P J Hobbs) 9 11
Turner, David Ian (Mr S Mullins) 9 7

†Walsh, David John (Mr N A Twiston-Davies) 9 11
Walsh, William John (Mr K C Bailey) 9 7

Watt, Andrew Robert (Mr K R Burke) 8 12
Webb, Christopher Lee (Mr S Mellor) 9 9
Webb, David Christopher (Mrs M Reveley) 9 7

Wilkinson, Richard David James (Mrs S Smith) 9 7
Willmington, Nathan Scott (Mr B Turner) 9 7

Yellowlees, Darren (Mr J R Jenkins) 9 7

† Relinquished

Restricted conditional jockeys

Restricted to Steeplechases and hurdle races for the season 1996–97.

†Bogle, Fergus (Mr F Murphy) 9 7
Branton, Grant John (Mr R Akehurst) 9 7
Brewer, John Charles (Mr C Egerton) 9 10

Carey, Declan Martin (Mr A P Jones) 9 10
Carnaby, Christopher (Miss H Knight) 9 7
†Cooper, Liam Philip (Mr J J O'Neill) 9 7
Currie, Alistair James (Mr B Rothwell) 9 7

Dove, Barry Robert (Mr R Ingram) 9 7
†Dowling, William Joseph (Mr L Lungo) 9 7

Ede, Alexander Charles (Mr M D Hammond) 9 7
Egan, Anthony Francis (Mr D McCain) 9 7

Froggitt, Miss Claudine Anne (Miss J Bower) 9 7

Garrard, Ross (Mrs J Pitman) 9 7

†Garrity, Andrew (Mr R Rowe) 9 7

Handley, Mark John (Mr C P H Morlock) 9 7
Hearn, Simon Paul (Mr S Mellor) 9 0
†Hobson, Richard Henry (Mr G McCourt) 9 7
Hodges, Robert James (Mr F Jordan) 9 0
Hogg, Timothy Tristram (Mr G M Moore) 9 7
†Hoggart, Craig Darren (Mr D McCain) 9 7

†Irvine, Andrew James (Mrs M E Long) 9 7

Jewett, Dale Jonathan (Mr J J O'Neill) 8 7

†Mortimer, Terry James (Mr S A Brookshaw) 9 7

Parker, Simon Brenan (Mr J R White) 9 7
†Parkhouse, Jason Stephen (Mr K A Morgan) 9 7

Pike, Ian William (Mr D Moffatt) 9 7

Rafter, Carl John (Mr C P E Brooks) 9 7
†Rossiter, Nathan Ian McColm (Mr G A Hubbard) 10 0
†Rudd, Stephen Thomas (Mr J J Quinn) 9 7
Ryan, Peter Edward (Mr N T Chance) 9 7

Sangster, Christopher (Mr A M Campion) 9 7
†Scales, Michael Noel (Mr B Smart) 9 0
Shilton, Shaune (Mr N A Gaselee) 9 6
Slattery, David Martin (Mr K O Cunningham-Brown) 9 13

†Turner, David Ian (Mr S Mullins) 9 7
Tynan, Fergal Cronan (Mr G B Balding) 8 7

†Wallwork, Colin David (Mr A P Jarvis) 9 7
Waugh, Shane (Mr R G Brazington) 9 10
Weaver, Charlie Redvers (Mr D Nicholson) 9 7

† Relinquished

Amateur riders 1996–97

Riders who have been granted permits to ride in Flat races, steeplechases and hurdle races. Valid from July 1, 1996 to June 30, 1997 under Rule 60(v).

CATEGORY "A"

Apiafi, Joshua 11 10
Armitage, Miss Annabelle Sophie Jane 8 4
Auvray, Jean-Rene Georges 10 4

†Babington, Edward Patrick 9 7
Baker, Ian 9 7
Barnes, Miss Fiona Alison 9 10
Barrett, Mrs Lucinda Marie 8 0
Bennison, Mark 9 9
Black, Richard Leslie, 10 12
Blane, Paul 10 0
Bradburne, Miss Lorna Charlotte 9 7
Brennan, Finbarr Joseph Edward 10 2
Brown, Anthony Gerrard 9 13
Brown, Miss Susan Eileen 9 7

Cassels, Miss Sharon 10 4
Cave, Miss Tabitha Christiane 9 7
Chapman, Nicholas Earl 10 0
Clarke, Peter Cedric 10 4
Clinton, Patrick Lawrence 10 7
Coogan, Vincent Lindley 10 2
Cooper, Paul Reuben 10 5
Copper, Miss Caroline Louise 8 12
†Corcoran, Liam Anthony 9 7
Cosgrave, Paul Joseph 9 7
Courier, Miss Lucy Anne 9 0
Cowley, Mark Robert John 10 9
Craggs, Miss Joanne Nicola 9 0
Crossland, David Kenneth 10 2
Crowley, James Vincent 9 0
Cuthbert, Miss Helen Elsie 9 0

Dare, Miss Tessa Sarah 7 10
Davis, Stephen James 9 10
Dixon, William George 10 6
Dudgeon, Miss Hazel Gilcrest 9 7
†Dudley, Miss Anne 9 0
Dunbar, Colin Morrison 10 5

Eastwood, Miss Jeanette 9 0
Elliott, Miss Caroline Jane 9 7
Emmanuel, Michael 10 7
Evans, Miss Charlotte Mary 9 7

Findlay, Stephen Robert 9 7

Gallagher, John 10 5
Gibson, Bruce Samual 9 7
†Goldstein, Jamie 9 7
Gowlett, William Gordon James 12 0
†Graham, Brian George 9 7
Grant, Brian Douglas 10 0
Gritton, Miss Samantha Ann 9 7

†Haigh, Miss Victoria 9 6
Hannaford, Miss Christine 9 0
Henderson, James Harold 11 0
Hetherton, James 10 6
Holder, Mark James 11 0
Howe, Simon Peter 10 0
Howson, Jamie 10 5

Jones, Timothy 10 10

Kerswell, Miss Sarah Louise 9 4
Kneafsey, Matthew Peter 8 12

Lake, Miss Catherine Jane 9 4
Lake, Geoffrey 9 0
Loads, Keith Frederick John 10 4

@Mackley, Matthew Robert 10 2
Mannish, Dr Michael 9 9
Markham, Gordon James 10 0
Marshall Miss Victoria Ruth 8 7
McAllister, Paul Mark 9 0
McEntee, Carl Joseph 9 3
McGregor, Mrs Jean Catherine 9 10
McIntosh, Miss Lois Samantha 8 7
†McLaughlin, William John 9 7
Michael, Alexander Harry Law 9 8
Mongan, Ian Bernard 8 0
Morrison, Stewart Guy Brander 11 7

Naughton, Miss Joanne Clare 8 12
Naylor, Dr Jeremy Richmond James 11 0

O'Sullivan, Miss Margaret 9 3
Oliver, Nicholas Henry 9 7
Osmond, Miss Claire Elizabeth 10 0
Owens, Patrick Philip 9 10

Patman, Miss Rebecca Jane 7 7
Pope, Miss Lara 9 0
Poulton, Mrs Camilla Dawn 9 0
Price, David Anthony 10 5

†Quinlan, Frank 9 10

Roberts, Miss Victoria Carly 9 7
Russell, Christopher Lee 9 7
Russell, Miss Diane Valerie 9 10
Ryan, James Joseph 10 5

Samworth, Miss Susannah Lorraine 8 11
Southcombe, Miss Wendy Louise 8 0
Spillane, Maurice James 10 4

Thatcher, John Gerald 10 7
†Thuillier, Ryan Joseph 10 3
†Townsley, Miss Charlotte Anne 9 0

Walters, Mark John Humphrey 10 0
Walton, Mrs Helen Louise 8 10
Weatherley, Guy 9 7
Wells, Matthew Richard 8 7
Wharfe, Mrs Patricia Jane 9 6
Wheate, Kenneth John 9 8
Whitaker, Thomas Edward 9 7
†Widger, Robert Peter 9 7
Wilkinson, Mrs Diane Shirley 7 7
Williams, Miss Emma Jane 9 2
Willoughby, Guy Nesbit John 10 4
Wilson, Miss Fiona Jane 9 7
Wrighton, Mrs Luisa 10 0

† Relinquished
@ Withdrawn

CATEGORY "B"

*Alers-Hankey, Dominic Guy 10 12
*Allan, Miss Victoria Louise 9 4
*Allison, Miss Jane Karen 9 2
*%Andrews, Simon Richard 11 7
*Appleby, Michael 10 0
*Armson, Richard John 10 7
*%Armytage, Marcus David 10 5
*Astaire, Steven 11 8

Babington, Edward Patrick 9 7
Baines, Graham 9 7
Baker, Louis Mark 9 0
Balding, Andrew Matthews 10 10
*Barfoot-Saunt, Geoffrey Charles 10 9
*Barlow, Charles James Bulkeley 10 12
*Barlow, Thomas David Bradwall 11 5
*Barraclough, Miss Susannah Mary 9 3
*Barrett, Raymond Ernest 9 4
Barrett, Richard John 9 11
Barry, Tristan James 10 5
*Batters, Malcolm John 11 7
*Beddoes, Miss Samantha Jane 9 7
†Beedles, Alistair Edwin 10 5
*Bevis, Richard Norman 10 0
*Blackford, Miss Linda Ann 10 9
*Blackwell, Stephen Christopher 10 5
*Bloom, Nigel Michael 11 2
%Bonner, Christopher Colin Malcolm 9 11
*Bosley, Mrs Sarah Jane 8 7
Boswell, Miss Louise 9 7
*Bowie, Miss Alison Campbell 9 7
Bradburne, Mark Sachevral Gordon 10 7
*%Bradley, Noel Andrew 9 7
*Brotherton, Miss Serena 9 7
*Brown, Adrian Conrad 9 9
*Brown, Hilary Stephen Leigh 11 0
*Bulgin, Toby Stuart Mark 10 7
*Bull, Peter Anthony 10 6
*Burnell, Wayne Martin 10 0
*Burrows, Mark William 9 12
Burton, Richard Peter Lingen 10 2
*%Bush, Stephen 11 0

*%Charles-Jones, Alexander Skeel 10 1
Clark, Miss Ruth Amanda 9 7
*Close, Peter Leslie 8 12
Coe, Alan Richard 10 7
*Coglan, Mark Victor 9 10
*Coombe, Miss Miranda Susan 9 0
Cornes, Jonathan Francis 11 2
*Cowdrey, Mrs Maxine 9 0
*Cowell, Simon Andrew 11 0
*%Craggs, Peter Foxton 10 4
Creighton, Joseph Patrick Declan 10 7
*Crow, Alastair Henry 10 11
†%Culloty, James Hugh 9 7
*Cumings, Miss Joanne Mary 10 0
Cunningham, Finbarr Patrick 10 7
*Curling, Miss Polly 10 7

*Dalton, Andrew Neale 11 0
*Dare, Miss Alison 10 0

Davies, John Joseph 10 0
*Davis, Mrs Angela Ella May 9 0
*Deniel, Miss Alyson Jodi 9 0
Dennis, Timothy Walter 10 5
Dixon, Ben 10 12
Docker, Joseph Michael 10 0
*Dowrick, Ian Stewart 10 7
@*Duckett, Miss Sally Jane 10 0
Dudley, Miss Anne 9 0
Dunlop, Harry James Leeper 10 10
Durack, Seamus Edmund 9 7
*%Durkan, John Patrick Peter 10 7
*Dyson, Miss Claire 9 7

*Ellis, Miss Katie Jane 8 0
*Ellwood, Major Oliver Charles Beauclerk 10 0
*Embiricos, Miss Alexandra Eugenie 10 2
*%Evatt, David Brook 11 9

%Farrant, Ashley James 11 0
Fitzgerald, Mrs Jane 9 12
Fitzgerald, Martin Paul 9 13
*Ford, Mrs Carol-Ann 9 0
*Ford, Richard 11 2
*Forster, Miss Sandra Eleanor 9 12
*%French, Miss Sarah 10 0
Frith, Matthew Giles 9 10

*Garton, Tim Alastair 11 7
*Gee, Michael Patrick 10 0
*Gingell, Matthew James 11 0
*Gladders, Miss Sarah Gillian 9 7
*Goble, Karl Rowan 9 3
*Godfrey, Mrs Sally Ann 10 0
Goldstein, Jamie 9 7
*Grassick, James Robert 9 7
*Greed, Tom Richard 10 10
*%Green, Kevin Andrew 10 0
Gundry, Miss Polly-Anna Beatrice 9 12

*Hacking, William Paul 11 7
*Haigh, Michael Philip 9 7
*Haigh, Miss Victoria 9 7
*%Hale, Richard Andrew 10 4
*Hand, Mrs Amanda Jane 10 7
*Hanly, Patrick Joseph 10 4
*%Hanmer, Gary Duncan 11 4
*Harding, Hon Miss Diana Mary 9 7
*Harris, Michael Charles Masson 11 0
*Harris, Neil John 10 0
*Haynes, Miss Fiona Alexandra 9 5
*Henderson, Mrs Rosemary Gillian 10 0
*Henderson, William John 10 7
†*%Henley, Peter John 9 9
Higgins, Miss Stefanie Alice 9 4
*Hill, Alan 11 11
*Hill, Miss Minette Bridget 9 7
*Hill, Miss Trelawney Jane 10 7
*Hills, Mrs Katherine Mary 9 7
*Hills, Thomas James 11 5
*Holdsworth, Anthony Sam Tarragon 9 5
*Howse, Philip Henry 11 4
Hutsby, Frederick Andrew 10 0

*Illsley, Thomas Charles 11 5
*Irving, Miss Heather Mary Oriane 9 12

*Jackson, Mark Joseph 10 2
*Jackson, Miss Sarah 10 0
*%Jackson, Mrs Valerie Susan 10 0
*James, Edward Daniel Luke John 10 0
James, Miss Emma Elizabeth Louise 9 7
*Jefford, Leslie David Battershill 9 12
*%Johnson, Peter 11 0
*Johnson Houghton, Miss Eve Annette 9 7
*Jones, David Samuel 10 10
Jones, Miss Emily Jane 9 0
*%Jones, Miss Isobel Diana Whitfield 9 2

*Jones, Miss Philippa Lindy 9 0
%Joynes, Scott 10 0
*Jukes, Jamie 9 7

*%Kendall, Mrs Margaret Ann 9 7
*Kent, John Nicholas 10 0
*Kettlewell, Mrs Deborah Jane 9 7
*Kinane, Anthony 9 7
*King, Neil Bernard 10 12

%Lamb, Miss Sarah Kathleen 9 7
*Lawther, John Rory 10 7
*%Lay, Anthony Lawrence 11 0
*Ledger, Mrs Cynthia (rides as Nicky) 9 7
*Lewis, Mark 10 7
*%Llewellyn, John Lewis 10 0
*Lloyd, Stephen David 11 2
*Luck, James Guy Alexander 10 0
*Lukaniuk, Victor Casimir 9 0

McCarthy, Timothy Daniel 10 0
McGrath, Murty Joseph 10 0
*McHale, Mrs Denise Alison 8 7
*McLaughlin, William John 9 10
McPhail, Oliver James 9 7
Meakins, Miss Amanda May 10 0
Metcalfe, Miss Claire 9 7
*Middleton, Philip William 10 0
*Miller, Michael Geoffrey 11 7
Mitchell, Andrew Francis 9 12
*Mitchell, Nicholas Richard 11 3
*%Mitchell, Timothy Llewelyn John 11 12
†Moore, John Daniel 9 8
*Morgan, William Giles Newberry 10 10
*Morris, Mrs Margaret Ann 9 0
*Morrison, Thomas 10 2
*%Morshead, Mrs Anthea Louise 8 7
*Mulcaire, Sean Patrick 10 0
*Mulhall, Clive Anthony 10 3
*Munrowd, Mark Ashley 10 7
%Murray, Patrick James 9 10

Naughton, Michael Henry 9 7
*%Needham, Mrs Fiona Emma 9 7
*Nichol, Miss Susan Ann 9 7
*Nuttall, Rupert Ellis Gurney 10 5

O'Keeffe, Patrick Augustin 10 4
*Ogden, Adam Craig 10 7

*Parker, Andrew 10 4
*Payne, Ryan James 10 0
*Perrett, Mrs Amanda Jill 9 0
*Phillips, Alan John 10 2
Phillips, Paul 9 7
Plunkett, Miss Alice 9 7
Pollock, Benjamin Nicholas 10 5
%Potts, Barry Joseph 10 12
*Price, Andrew Raymond 11 7
*Price, J J E 11 9
*Pritchard, John Ian 11 7
*Pritchard, Julian Michael 11 0
*%Pritchard, Dr Philip Leslie James 9 11
Pritchard-Gordon, Patrick 10 0
*Purdy, Miss Alison Jane 9 2

*Ramsay, Capt William Bertram 11 7
*Rebori, Anthony Dominic 11 0
*Rees, James 9 10
*%Rimell, Mark Guy 10 2
*Ritson, William Alexander 10 4
*%Robson, Andrew William 10 10
*%Robson, Miss Pauline 9 3
*Rowe, Miss Lisa Jeanette 10 0
*Rowsell, Hamish Giles Morley 11 0
†*Ryan, James Joseph 10 7

*Sansome, Andrew David 10 12

*Saunders, Mrs Julia Aline 8 5
*Scott, James Alexander 10 7
*Scott, Patrick Barry 9 10
*Scott, Thomas Walton 11 7
*Sharratt, Miss Susan 10 4
%Shenkin, Gordon Richman 9 9
*%Shiels, Raymond 11 4
*Shinton, Stephen Norman 11 0
*Smith, Mrs Deborah Anne 9 7
*Smith, Nigel Forster 11 0
*%Smith, Terry Ernest George 10 7
Spearing, Miss Caroline Mary-Anne 9 7
*Spearing, Miss Teressa Sally 9 0
*Speight, Mrs Jayne Elizabeth 8 10
Sporborg, Simon Richard 11 0
*Stephens, Miss Victoria Alison 9 7
*Stockton, Christopher John 11 7
*%Storey, Clive 10 4
*Sunderland, Mrs Katie Joanne 8 7
*%Swiers, Stephen James 10 5
*%Swindlehurst, David James 10 4

*Thomas, Miss Candy Jane 9 7
*%Thompson, Mark 11 0
%Thornton, Robert Alan 9 7
*Tingey, Mrs Melanie Alison 8 3
Tizzard, Joe Colin Leslie 10 0
Tolhurst, Edward James 9 10
Townsley, Miss Charlotte Anne 9 0
Townson, Jonathan George 10 7
*%Treloggen, Ronald Morley 10 10
*Trice-Rolph, Jonathan Campbell 11 0
*%Tutty, Nigel David 11 0

†*Verco, David Ian 10 2
*Vickery, Miss Shirley Anne 9 0
Vigors, Charles Stewart Cliffe 10 2

Wakley, Rupert James 9 9
*Wales, William Anthony 11 2
Walker, Simon Anthony 9 7
*Wallin, Miss Samantha Louise 9 7
*Walmsley, Robert William 11 0
*Walton, Ashley Edward 9 4
*Ward, Charles Edward 11 0
*Ward Thomas, Christian Rupert Francis 10 7
*Warr, Anthony James 11 0
*Watson, Christopher Phillip Edward 8 12
*Watson, Major Miles Ronald Marcus 11 0
*Webb-Bowen. Lt Col Robert Ince 11 5
*Welsh, Adam 10 7
*Weymes, John Robert 10 2
*Wheeler, Gerald Felix 10 10
*White, Miss Susan Elizabeth 9 8
Widger, Robert Peter 9 7
*Williams, Richard Evan Rhys 10 9
*Wilson, Christopher Ralph 10 10
*%Wilson, Noel 10 7
%Wintle, Adrian Allan 10 3
*Wood, Capt Angus William 10 10
Wormall, Miss Jill 9 0

*Yardley, Miss Alison Jayne 8 0
Young, James 10 0
*Young, Miss Susan Elizabeth Maria 10 7

† Relinquished
@ Withdrawn

* Indicates over 25 years of age at the time the Permit was granted — Rule 109(iii)(a)
% Indicates over 75 rides against professional jockeys under Rules of Racing at the time the Permit was granted

Winners of Big Races

(The figures in parentheses indicate the number of runners)

MURPHY'S (MACKESON) GOLD CUP (Cheltenham)

(2½ miles 110 yds)

1960 Fortria 8y 12st (19)
1961 Scottish Memories 7y 10st 12lb (17)
1962 Fortria 10y 12st (25)
1963 Richard of Bordeaux 8y 10st 5lb (20)
1964 Super Flash 9y 10st 5lb (9)
1965 Dunkirk 8y 12st 7lb (8)
1966 Panwbroker 8y 11st 9lb (5)
1967 Charlie Worcester 10y 10st 11lb (13)
1968 Jupiter Boy 7y 10st 3lb (13)
1969 Gay Trip 7y 11st 5lb (14)
1970 Chatham 6y 10st 3lb (17)
1971 Gay Trip 9y 11st 3lb (10)
1972 Red Candle 8y 10st (11)
1973 Skymas 8y 10st 5lb (15)
1974 Bruslee 8y 10st 7lb (11)
1975 Clear Cut 11y 10st 9lb (13)
1976*Cancello 7y 11st 1lb (13)
1977 Bachelor's Hall 7y 10st 6lb (16)
1978 Bawnogues 7y 10st 7lb (11)
1979 Man Alive 8y 10st 9lb (11)
1980 Bright Highway 6y 11st 11lb (15)
1981 Henry Kissinger 7y 10st 13lb (11)
1982 Fifty Dollars More 7y 11st (11)
1983 Pounentes 6y 10st 6lb (9)
1984 Half Free 8y 11st 10lb (10)
1985 Half Free 9y 11st 10lb (10)
1986 Very Promising 8y IIst 13lb (11)
1987 Beau Ranger 9y 10st 2lb (14)
1988 Pegwell Bay 7y 11st 2lb (13)
1989 Joint Sovereignty 9y 10st 4lb (15)
1990 Multum In Parvo 7y 10st 2lb (13)
1991 Another Coral 8y 10st 1lb (11)
1992 Tipping Tim 7y 10st 10lb (16)
1993 Bradbury Star 8y 11st 8lb (15)
1994 Bradbury Star 9y 11st 11lb (14)
1995 Dublin Flyer 8y 10st 8lb (12)
1996 Challenger du Luc (FR) 6y 10st 2lb (12)

*Run at Haydock

HENNESSY COGNAC GOLD CUP CHASE (Newbury)

(3¼ miles 110 yds)

1957*Mandarin 6y 11st (19)
1958*Taxidermist 6y 11st 1lb (13)
1959*Kerstin 9y 11st 10lb (26)
1960 Knucklecracker 7y 11st 1lb (20)
1961 Mandarin 10y 11st 5lb (22)
1962 Springbok 9y 10st 8lb (27)
1963 Mill House 6y 12st (10)
1964 Arkle 7y 12st 7lb (8)
1965 Arkle 8y 12st 7lb (8)
1966 Stalbridge Colonist 7y 10st (6)
1967 Rondetto 11y 10st 1lb (13)
1968 Man of the West 7y 10st (11)
1969 Spanish Steps 6y 11st 8lb (15)
1970 Border Mask 8y 11st 1lb (12)
1971 Bighorn 7y 10st 11lb (13)
1972 Charlie Potheen 7y 11st 4lb (13)

1973 Red Candle 9y 10st 4lb (11)
1974 Royal Marshal II 7y 10st (13)
1975 April Seventh 9y 11st 2lb (13)
1976 Zeta's Son 7y 10st 9lb (21)
1977 Bachelor's Hall 7y 10st 10lb (13)
1978 Approaching 7y 10st 6lb (8)
1979 Fighting Fit 7y 11st 7lb (15)
1980 Bright Highway 6y 11st 6lb (14)
1981 Diamond Edge 10y 11st 10lb (14)
1982 Bregawn 8y 11st 10lb (11)
1983 Brown Chamberlain 8y 11st 8lb (12)
1984 Burrough Hill Lad 8y 12st (13)
1985 Galway Blaze 9y 10st (13)
1986 Broadheath 9y 10st 5lb (15)
1987 Playschool 9y 10st 8lb (12)
1988 Strands of Gold 9y 10st (12)
1989 Ghofar 6y 10st 2lb (8)
1990 Arctic Call 7y 11st (13)
1991 Chatam (USA) 7y 10st 6lb (15)
1992 Sibton Abbey 7y 10st (13)
1993 Cogent 9y 10st 1lb (9)
1994 One Man 6y 10st (16)
1995 Couldnt Be Better 8y 10st 8lb (11)
1996 Coome Hill 7y 10st (11)

*Run at Cheltenham

TRIPLEPRINT GOLD CUP HANDICAP CHASE (Cheltenham)

(2 miles 5 fur)

1963 Limeking 7y 10st 12lb (14)
1964 Flying Wild 8y 10st 6lb (7)
1965 Flyingbolt 6y 12st 6lb (8)
1966 The Laird 5y 10st 9lb (8)
1967 No race
1968 Tassilo 10y 10st 1lb (14)
1969 Titus Oates 7y 11st 13lb (11)
1970 Simian 8y 11st 8lb (7)
1971 Leap Frog 7y 12st 1lb (12)
1972 Arctic Bow 7y 10st 12lb (11)
1973 Pendil 8y 12st 7lb (8)
1974 Garnishee 10y 10st 6lb (9)
1975 Easby Abbey 8y 11st 10lb (9)
1976 No race
1977 Even Melody 8y 11st 2lb (11)
1978 The Snipe 8y 10st (14)
1979 Father Delaney 7y 10st 10lb (12)
1980 Bueche Giorod 9y 10st (15)
1981 No race
1982 Observe 6y 10st 11lb (15)
1983 Fifty Dollars More 8y 11st 10lb (13)
1984 Beau Ranger 9st 10lb (10)
1985 Combs Ditch 9y 11st 9lb (7)
1986 Oregon Trail 6y 10st 7lb (6)
1987 Bishops Yarn 8y 10st 7lb (5)
1988 Pegwell Bay 7y 10st 13lb (10)
1989 Clever Folly 9y 10st 4lb (6)
1990 No race
1991 Kings Fountain 8y 11st 10lb (8)
1992 Another Coral 9y 11st 4lb (10)
1993 Fragrant Dawn 9y 10st 2lb (11)
1994 Dublin Flyer 8y 10st 2lb (11)
1995 No race
1996 Addington Boy 8y 11st 10lb (10)

PERTEMPS KING GEORGE VI CHASE (Kempton)

(3 miles)

1937 Southern Hero 12y 12st (4)
1938 Airgead Sios 8y 11st 10lb (4)
1939–46 No race
1947 Rowland Roy 8y 11st 13lb (10)
1948 Cottage Rake 9y 12st 6lb (9)
1949 Finnure 8y 11st 10lb (4)
1950 Manicou 5y 11st 8lb (7)
1951 Statecraft 9y 11st 11lb (6)
1952 Halloween 7y 11st 13lb (6)
1953 Galloway Braes 8y 12st 6lb (7)
1954 Halloween 9y 11st 10lb (8)
1955 Limber Hill 8y 11st 13lb (8)
1956 Rose Park 10y 11st 7lb (6)
1957 Mandarin 6y 12st (9)
1958 Lochroe 10y 11st 7lb (7)
1959 Mandarin 8y 11st 5lb (9)
1960 Saffron Tartan 9y 11st 7lb (10)
1961 and 1962 No race
1963 Mill House 6y 12st (3)
1964 Frenchman's Cove 9y 11st 7lb (2)
1965 Arkle 8y 12st (4)
1966 Dormant 9y 11st (7)
1967 and 1968 No race
1969 Titus Oates 7y 11st 10lb (5)
1970 No race
1971 The Dikler 8y 11st 7lb (10)
1972 Pendil 7y 12st (6)
1973 Pendil 8y 12st (4)
1974 Captain Christy 7y 12st (6)
1975 Captain Christy 8y 12st (7)
1976 Royal Marshal II 9y 11st 7lb (10)
1977 Bachelor's Hall 7y 11st 7lb (9)
1978 Gay Spartan 7y 11st 10lb (16)
1979 Silver Buck 7y 11st 10lb (9)
1980 Silver Buck 8y 11st 10lb (8)
1981 No race
1982 Wayward Lad 7y 11st 10lb (6)
1983 Wayward Lad 8y 11st 10lb (5)
1984 Burrough Hill Lad 8y 11st 10lb (3)
1985 Wayward Lad 10y 11st 10lb (5)
1986 Desert Orchid 7y 11st 10lb (9)
1987 Nupsala (FR) 8y 11st 10lb (9)
1988 Desert Orchid 9y 11st 10lb (5)
1989 Desert Orchid 10y 11st 10lb (6)
1990 Desert Orchid 11y 11st 10lb (6)
1991 The Fellow (FR) 6y 11st 10lb (8)
1992 The Fellow (FR) 7y 11st 10lb (8)
1993 Barton Bank 7y 11st 10lb (10)
1994 Algan (FR) 6y 11st 10lb (9)
1995*One Man 8y 11st 10lb (11)
1996 One Man 8y 11st 10lb (5)

*Run at Sandown 6/1/96
over 3 miles, 110yards

CORAL WELSH NATIONAL (Chepstow)

(3 miles 5 fur 110 yds)
(First run 1895)

1920 Mark Back 9y 11st 9lb (9)
1921 Mythical 7y 10st 6lb (10)
1922 Simonides 9y 10st 5lb (10)
1923 Clonree 9y 11st 6lb (12)

1924 Dwarf of the Forest 7y 10st 5lb (11)
1925 Vaulx 11y 12st 1lb (16)
1926 Miss Balscadden 7y 9st 9lb (12)
1927 Snipe's Bridge 13y 11st 2lb (12)
1928 Miss Balscadden 9y 9st 7lb (15)
1929 Monduco 7y 10st 2lb (21)
1930 Boomlet 10y 11st 6lb (11)
1931 Wise Don 9y 10st 5lb (15)
1932 Miss Gaynus 6y 11st (10)
1933 Pebble Ridge 8y 10st 11lb (9)
1934 Dream Ship 8y 11st 7lb (10)
1935 Lacatoi 7y 10st 8lb (12)
1936 Sorley Boy 10y 10st 12lb (11)
1937 Lacatoi 9y 10st 5lb (13)
1938 Timber Wolf 10y 11st 3lb (3)
1939 Lacatoi 11y 10st 11lb (11)
1940–47 No race
1948 Bora's Cottage 10y 10st 2lb (16)
1949 Fighting Line 10y 10st 9lb (15)
1950 Gallery 12y 10st 8lb (12)
1951 Skyreholme 8y 10st 13lb (16)
1952 Dinton Lass 10y 10st (16)
1953 Stalbridge Rock 10y 11st 3lb (15)
1954 Blow Horn 10y 10st 6lb (17)
1955 Monaleen 10y 9st 7lb (17)
1956 Crudwell 10y 11st 6lb (16)
1957 Creeola II 9y 10st 5lb (11)
1958 Oscar Wilde 8y 9st 13lb (14)
1959 Limonali 8y 10st 2lb (10)
1960 Clover Bud 10y 10st 10lb (14)
1961 Limonali 9y 11st 12lb (9)
1962 Forty Secrets 8y 10st 11lb (15)
1963 Motel 9y 10st 6lb (10)
1964 Rainbow Battle 8y 10st (11)
1965 Norther 8y 11st (11)
1966 Kilburn 8y 11st 2lb (11)
1967 Happy Spring 11y 10st 4lb (6)
1968 Glenn 7y 10st 4lb (8)
1969 No race
1970 French Excuse 8y 10st 9lb (11)
1971 Royal Toss 9y 10st 12lb (13)
1972 Charlie H 10y 11st 3lb (9)
1973 Deblin's Green 10y 9st 12lb (16)
1974 Pattered 8y 10st 2lb (24)
1975 No race
1976 Rag Trade 10y 11st 2lb (17)
1977 No race
1978 No race
1979 (Feb) No race
1979 (Dec) Peter Scot 8y 10st 2lb (15)
1980 Narvik 7y 10st 10lb (10)
1981 Peaty Sandy 7y 10st 3lb (23)
1982 Corbierre 7y 10st 10lb (10)
1983 Burrough Hill Lad 7y 10st 9lb (18)
1984 Righthand Man 7y 11 st 5lb (18)
1985 Run And Skip 7y 10st 8lb (18)
1986 Stearsby 7y 11st 5lb (17)
1987 Playschool 9y 10st 11lb (13)
1988 Bonanza Boy 7y 10st 1lb (12)
1989 Bonanza Boy 8y 11st 11lb (12)
1990 Cool Ground 8y 10st (14)
1991 Carvill's Hill 9y 11st 12lb (17)
1992 Run For Free 8y 10st 9lb (11)
1993 Riverside Boy 10y 10st (8)
1994*Master Oats 8y 11st 6lb (8)
1995 No race
1996 No race

Run over 2¹/₂ miles at Cardiff from 1895 to 1898, over 3 miles from 1899 to 1912, over 3 miles 100 yds in 1914, and over 3 ¹/₂ miles from 1920 to 1939. Run over 3 miles 4 fur 150 yds at Newport in 1948
  *Run at Newbury over 3³/₄ miles

THE LADBROKE HANDICAP HURDLE (Leopardstown)

(2 miles)
1969†Normandy 4y 11st 2lb (15)
1970†Persian War 7y 12st (11)
1971 Kelanne 7y 11st 6lb (6)
1972 Captain Christy 6y 11st 6lb (13)
1973 Comedy of Errors 6y 12st (9)
1974 Comedy of Errors 7y 12st (8)
1975 Night Nurse 4y 11st 5lb (9)
1976 Master Monday 6y 10st 2lb (19)
1977 Decent Fellow 4y 11st 4lb (18)
1978 Chinrullah 6y 10st 6lb (12)
1979 Irian (Fr) 5y 10st (20)
1980 Carrig Willy 5y 10st (26)
1981 No race
1982 For Auction 6y 10st 10lb (20)
1983 Fredcoteri 7y 10st (15)
1984 Fredcoteri 8y 10st 4lb (18)
1985 Hansel Rag 5y 10st (20)
1986 Bonalma 6y 10st 13lb (22)
1987 Barnbrook Again 6y 11st 8lb (22)
1988 Roark 6y 11st 1lb (15)
1989 Redundant Pal 6y 10st (7)
1990 Redundant Pal 7y 11st 5lb (27)
1991 The Illiad 10y 10st 13lb (17)
1992 How's The Boss 6y 10st 2lb (20)
1993 Glencloud 5y 10st 13lb (25)
1994 Atone 7y 10st 8lb (25)
1995 Anusha 5y 10st 2lb (17)
1996 Dance Beat 5y 9st 12lb (22)
1997 Master Tribe 7y 10st 4lb (23)

†Run at Fairyhouse

TOTE GOLD TROPHY H'CAP HURDLE (Newbury)

(2 miles 110 yds)
1963*Rosyth 5y 10st (41)
1964 Rosyth 6y 10st 2lb (24)
1965 Elan 6y 10st 7lb (21)
1966 Le Vermontois 5y 11st 3lb (28)
1967 Hill House 7y 10st 10lb (28)
1968 Persian War 5y 11st 13lb (33)
1969 No race
1970 No race
1971 Cala Mesquida 7y 10st 9lb (23)
1972 Good Review 5y 10st 9lb (26)
1973 Indianapolis 6y 10st 6lb (26)
1974 No race
1975 Tammuz (Fr) 7y 10st 13lb (28)
1976 Irish Fashion 5y 10st 4lb (29)
1977 True Lad 7y 10st 4lb (27)
1978 No race
1979 Within The Law 5y 11st 4lb (28)
1980 Bootlaces 6y 10st 9lb (21)
1981 No race
1982 Dongal Prince 6y 10st 8lb (27)
1983 No race
1984 Ra Nova 5y 10st 6lb (26)
1985 No race
1986 No race
1987 Neblin 8y 10st (21)
1988 Jamesmead 7y 10st (19)
1989 Grey Salute 6y 11st 5lb (10)
1990 Deep Sensation 5y 11st 3lb (17)
1991 No race
1992 Rodeo Star (USA) 6y 10st 10lb (15)
1993 King Credo 8y 10st (16)
1994 Large Action 6y 10st 8lb (11)
1995 Mysilv 5y 10st 8lb (8)

1996 Squire Silk 7y 10st 12lb (18)
1997 Make A Stand 6y 11st 7lb (18)

  ★Run at Liverpool over 2 miles 1 fur and a few yards

SCHLITZ VICTOR LUDORUM HURDLE (Haydock)

(2 miles)
(For four year olds)
1962 Pillock's Green 10st 13lb (9)
1963 No race
1964 Makaldar 11st 3lb (11)
1965 Anselmo 11st 3lb (15)
1966 Harwell 11st 3lb (9)
1967 Persian War 11st 3lb (9)
1968 Wing Master 11st 3lb (6)
1969 Coral Diver 11st (11)
1970 No race
1971 Nerak 11st (13)
1972 North Pole 11st (7)
1973 Mythical King (USA) 11st 4lb (12)
1974 Relevant 11st 4lb (15)
1975 Zip Fastener 11st 4lb (11)
1976 Sweet Joe (USA) 11st 9lb
1977 Rathconrath 11st 9lb (12)
1978 Mixed Melody 11st 4lb (13)
1979 Exalted 11st 4lb (13)
1980 Jubilee Saint 11st 4lb (8)
1981 No race
1982 Azaam 11st 4lb (11)
1983 Wollow Will 11st 9lb (8)
1984 Childown (USA) 11st 9lb (11)
1985 Wing And A Prayer 11st 10lb (8)
1986 No race
1987 Cashew King 4y 11st 4lb (6)
1988 Royal Illusion 11st 10lb (13)
1989 Liadett (USA) 11st 10lb (7)
1990 Ninja 11st 4lb (5)
1991 Reve de Valse (USA) 11st 4lb (8)
1992 Snowy Lane 11st 4lb (6)
1993 Bold Boss 11st 10lb (7)
1994 No race
1995 Muntafi 11st 5lb (8)
1996 Marchant Ming 11st 4lb (9)
1997 No More Hassle 10st 11lb (7)

SUNDERLANDS IMPERIAL CUP H'CAP HURDLE (Sandown)

(2 miles 110 yds)
(First run 1907)
1920 Trespasser 4y 12st (9)
1921 Trespasser 5y 12st 7lb (10)
1922 Trespasser 6y 12st 7lb (11)
1923 North Waltham 6y 12st 4lb (11)
1924 Noce d'Argent 4y 11st 2lb (11)
1925 Scotch Pearl 4y 10st 7lb (18)
1926 Peeping Tom 4y 10st 7lb (13)
1927 Zeno 4y 10st 12lb (12)
1928 Royal Falcon 5y 11st 6lb (16)
1929 Hercules 6y 11st 5lb (18)
1930 Rubicon II 4y 11st 3lb (15)
1931 Residue 7y 12st 3lb (14)
1932 Last of the Dandies 5y 11st 4lb (21)
1933 Flaming 6y 11st 4lb (18)
1934 Lion Courage 8y 10st 7lb (13)
1935 Negro 6y 11st 6lb (21)
1936 Negro 7y 11st 3lb (23)
1937 le Maestro 6y 11st (18)
1938 Bimco 5y 10st 12lb (11)
1939 Mange Tout 5y 11st 10lb (20)

1940–46 No race
1947 Tant Pis 5y 10st 9lb (33)
1948 Anglesey 6y 11st 8lb (12)
1949 Secret Service 6y 11st 11lb (17)
1950 Secret Service 7y 11st 10lb (13)
1951 Master Bidar 6y 10st 11lb (21)
1952 High Point 6y 10st 4lb (19)
1953 High Point 7y 10st 7lb (19)
1954 The Pills 6y 10st 5lb (26)
1955 Bon Mot II 6y 10st 11lb (32)
1956 Peggy Jones 6y 10st 10lb (22)
1957 Camugliano 7y 10st 10lb (29)
1958 Flaming East 9y 10st 5lb (23)
1959 Langton Heath 5y 10st 9lb (21)
1960 Farmer's Boy 7y 11st 7lb (20)
1961 Fidus Achates 6y 10st 4lb (23)
1962 Irish Imp 5y 10st 12lb (26)
1963 Antiar 5y 11st 2lb (21)
1964 Invader 6y 11st 4lb (15)

1965 Kildavin 7y 10st 7lb (19)
1966 Royal Sanction 7y 10st 1lb (18)
1967 Sir Thopas 6y 11st 8lb (20)
1968 Persian Empire 5y 11st 4lb (18)
1969 No race
1970 Solomon II 6y 11st 1lb (17)
1971 Churchwood 7y 11st 3lb (12)
1972 Spy Net (Fr) 5y 10st (18)
1973 Lanzarote 5y 12st 4lb (14)
1974 Flash Imp 5y 10st 9lb (17)
1975 No race
1976 Nougat (Fr) 6y 10st 6lb (11)
1977 Acquaint 6y 11st 12lb (20)
1978 Winter Melody 7y 11st 3lb (15)
1979 Flying Diplomat (USA) 8y 10st 6lb
　　(9)
1980 Prayukta 5y 11st (16)
1981 Ekbalco 5y 11st 3lb (14)
1982★Holemoor Star 5y 11st 7lb (7)

1983 Desert Hero 9y 9st 8lb (16)
1984 Dalbury 6y 9st 12lb (13)
1985 Floyd 5y 10st 3lb (16)
1986 Insular 6y 10st (19)
1987 Inlander 6y 10st 3lb (21)
1988 Sprowstown Boy 5y 10st 11lb (15)
1989 Travel Mystery 6y 10st (8)
1990 Moody Man 5y 10st 13lb (15)
1991 Precious Boy 5y 10st 6lb (13)
1992 King Credo 7y 10st 4lb (10)
1993 Olympian 6y 10st (15)
1994 Precious Boy 8y 11st 7lb (13)
1995 Collier Bay 5y 10st 2lb (10)
1996 Amancio (USA) 5y 10st 8lb (11)
1997 Carlito Brigante 5y 10st (18)

★Run at Kempton

SMURFIT CHAMPION HURDLE

(Cheltenham)　(2 miles 110 yds)　(First run 1927)

1927 Mrs H M Hollins's Blaris b g by Achtoi 6–12–0 . . . . G Duller		11–10
Mr A H Tennent's Boddam 8–12–0 . . . . W Speck		7–2
Col A E Jenkins's Harpist 6–12–0 . . . . F Rees		9–4
8l,1l. 4m 13³/₅s. 4 ran. W Payne		
1928 Maj H A Werner's Brown Jack br g by Jackdaw 4–11–0 . . . . L Rees		4–1
Maj D Dixon's Peace River 5–11–10 . . . . T Leader		5–1
Mrs H M Hollins's Blaris 7–12–0 . . . . G Duller		2–1
1¹/₂l, 6l. 4m 5s. 6 ran. Hon A Hastings		
1929 Miss Williams-Bulkeley's Royal Falcon ch h by White Eagle 6–12–0 . . . . . F Rees		11–2
Mr T R Rimell's Rolie 8–12–0 . . . . W Stott		4–1
Sir John Grey's Clear Cash 4–11–0 . . . . G Pellerin		7–4
4l, 5l. 4m 1¹/₅s. 6 ran. R Gore		
1930 Mrs J de Selincourt's Brown Tony br g by Jackdaw 4–11–0 . . . . T Cullinan		7–2
Sir John Grey's Clear Cash 5–11–10 . . . . G Pellerin		6–4
Mr S Wootton's Peertoi 5–11–10 . . . . S Ingham		7–2
Hd, sht. hd. 4m 20¹/₅s. 5 ran. J Anthony		
1931 No race		
1932 Miss D Paget's Insurance b g by Achtoi 5–11–10 . . . . T Leader		4–5
Sir H Nugent's Song of Essex 6–12–0 . . . . W Parvin		5–4
Lord Stalbridge's Jack Drummer 4–11–0 . . . . T Cullinan		33–1
12l, bad. 4 m 14¹/₄s. 3 ran. A Briscoe		
1933 Miss D Paget's Insurance b g by Achtoi 6–12–0 . . . . W Stott		10–11
Mr R Bownass's Windermere Laddie 9–12–0 . . . . S Ingham		4–1
H.H. Aga Khan's Indian Salmon 4–11–0 . . . . G Pellerin		100–8
³/₄l, 8l. 4m 373/5s. 5 ran. A Briscoe		
1934 Mr G H Bostwick's Chenago b g by Hapsburg 7–12–0 . . . . D Morgan		4–9
Mr R Smith's Pompelmoose 4–11–0 . . . . P Fitzgerald		9–2
Mr G M King's Black Duncan 4–11–0 . . . . T Cullinan		20–1
5l, 6l. 4m 17s. 5 ran. I Anthony		

1935 Mr R Fox-Carlyon's Lion Courage b or br g by Jackdaw 7–12–0 . . . . . . G Wilson		100–8
Mrs Crossman's Gay Light 9–12–0 . . . . S Ingham		9–4
Mr M Pilkington's Hill Song 6–12–0 . . . . G Pellerin		3–1
¹/₂l, ³/₄l. 4m 0¹/₅s. 11 ran. F Brown		
1936 Mrs M Stephen's Victor Norman gr g by King Sol 5–11–10 . . . . H Nicholson		4–1
Mr B Warner's Free Fare 8–12–0 . . . . G Pellerin		5–2
Mrs G S L Whitelaw's Cactus II 6–12–0 . . . . M Blair		20–1
3l, 1¹/₂l. 3m 58²/₅s. 8 ran. M Blair		
1937 Mr B Warner's Free Fare ch g by Werwolf 9–12–0 . . . . G Pellerin		2–1
Mr R Gubbins's Our Hope 8–12–0 . . . . Capt R Harding		100–8
Miss D Paget's Menton 5–11–10 . . . . S Ingham		11–2
2l, sht. hd. 4m 19²/₅s. 7 ran. E Gwilt		
1938 Mr R Gubbins's Our Hope gr g by Son and Heir 9–12–0 . . . . . . Cap R Harding		5–1
Vicomte de Chambure's Chuchoteur 6–12–0 . . . . M Plaine		9–2
Mr R Dick's Lobau 6–12–0 . . . . H Nicholson		100–6
1¹/₂l, 10l. 4m 4⁴/₅s. 5 ran. R Gubbins		
1939 Mr H J Brueton's African Sister ch m by Prester John 7–12–0 . . . . . . .K Piggott		10–1
Mr A F Jack's Vitement 6–12–0 . . . . E Vinall		20–1
Maj J M J Evans's Apple Peel 9–12–0 . . . . S Ingham		100–8
3l, ¹/₂l. 4m 13³/₅s. 13 ran. C Piggott		
1940 Miss D Paget's Solford 9 b g by Soldennis 9–12–0 . . . . S Magee		5–2
Mr H J Brueton's African Sister 4–11–0 . . . . K Piggott		8–1
Mrs J C Lewis's Carton 5–11–10 . . . . F Rickaby		3–1
11/2l, 4m 13³/₅s. 8 ran. O Anthony		
1941 Sir M McAlpine's Seneca ch c by Caligula 4–11–0 . . . . R Smyth		7–1
Miss D Paget's Anarchist 4–11–0 . . . . M Jones		33–1
Mr F Walwyn's Ephorus 5–11–0 . . . . H Nicholson		8–1
Hd, 2l. 4m 9s. 6 ran. V Smyth		
1942 Mr V Smyth's Forestation b g by Felicitation 4–11–0 . . . . R Smyth		10–1

Miss D Paget's Anarchist 5–11–10
.... T Isaac 100–8
Mr J Barker's Southport 6–12–0
.... F Rickaby 9–2
3l, 3l. 20 ran. V Smyth
1943 and 1944 No race
1945 Mr F Blakeway's Brains Trust ch g by
Rhodes Scholar-Easter Bonnet 5–11–
10 .... T F Rimell 9–2
Mr A E Saunder's Vidi 4–11–0
.... D Butchers 100–6
Lord Stalbridge's Red April 8–12–0
.... D L Jones 10–1
3/4l, 3/4l. 4m 9 2/5s. 16 ran. Gerald Wilson
1946 Miss D Paget's Distel b g by Rosewell 5–
11–10 .... R O'Ryan 4–5
Mr A Gibbes's Carnival Boy 5–11–0
.... T F Rimell 7–2
Mrs J Skinner's Robin O'Chantry 6–12–0
.... J Goodgame 100–6
4l,1/2l. 4m 5 1/5s. 8 ran. M Arnott, in Ireland
1947 Mr L A Abelson's National Spirit ch g by
Scottish Union 6–12–0 ..... D Morgan 7–1
Mme L Aurousseau's Le Paillon 5–11–10
.... A Head 2–1
Lord Bicester's Freddy Fox 8–12–0
.... R Smyth 8–1
1l, 2l. 4m 34/5s. 14 ran. V Smyth
1948 Mr L A Abelson's National Spirit ch g by
Scottish Union 7–12–0 ..... R Smyth 6–4
Lt-Col Philips's DUKW 5–11–10
.... J Maguire 5–1
Lady Latymer's Encoroll 5–11–10
.... M Connors 20–1
2l, 3/4l. 3m 55s. 12 ran. V Smyth
1949 Mrs M H Keogh's Hatton's Grace b g by
His Grace 9–12–0 .... A Brabazon 100–7
Mrs V M Pulham's Vatelys 9–12–0
.... R Bates 10–1
Mr F W Chandler's Captain Fox 4–11–0
.... K Mullins 100–9
6l, 1l. 4m 0 2/5s. 14 ran. M V O'Brien in Ireland
1950 Mrs M H Keogh's Hatton's Grace b g by
His Grace 10–12–0 ...... A Brabazon 5–2
Mrs E Williams's Harlech 5–11–12
.... M Moloney 9–2
Mrs Z E Lambert's Speciality 5–11–12
.... K Mullins 100–6
1 1/2l, 2l, 3m 59 1/5s. 12 ran. M V O'Brien in Ireland
1951 Mrs M H Keogh's Hatton's Grace b g by
His Grace 11–12–0 ......T Molony 4–1
M G Chastenet's Pyrrhus III 8–12–0
.... A Gill 11–2
M G Beauvois's Prince Hindou 5–11–12
.... M Larraun 9–2
5l, 1/2l. 4m 10 1/5s. 8 ran. M V O'Brien in Ireland
1952 Mr M Kingsley's Sir ken b g by Laeken 5–
11–12 .... T Molony 4–1
Mr S Wootton's Noholme 5–11–0
.... B Marshall 100–7
Mr L A Abelson's Approval 6–12–0
.... D Dillon 9–1
2l, 4l. 4m 2 2/5s. 16 ran. W Stephenson
1953 Mr M Kingsley's Sir Ken b g by Laeken
6–12–0 .... T Molony 2–5
Mr J H Griffin's Galatian 6–12–0
.... B Marshall 4–1
Mrs C Magnier's Teapot II 8–12–0
.... P Taaffe 100–9
2l, 1 1/2l. 3m 55 2/5s. 7 ran. W. Stephenson
1954 Mr M Kingsley's Sir Ken b g by Laeken
7–12–0 .... T Molony 4–9
Mr S W Everitt's Impney 5–11–12
.... M Pumfrey 9–1
Mr J H Griffin's Galatian 7–12–0
.... P Taaffe 10–1
1l, 3l. 4m 10 1/5s. 13 ran. W Stephenson
1955 Mr G C Judd's Clair Soleil br g by
Maravedis 6–12–0 .... F Winter 5–2
Mr B Hamilton's Stroller 7–12–0
.... T P Burns 7–2

Mrs A C leggatt's Cruachan 7–12–0
.... G Slack 50–1
Hd, 4l. 4m 11 3/5s. 21 ran. H R Price
1956 Mr C Nicholson's Doornocker ch g by
Cacador 8–12–0 ....H Sprague 100–9
Mrs L Brand's Quita Que 7–12–0
.... Mr J R Cox 33–1
Mr M Kingsley's Baby Don 6–12–0
.... T Molony 100–8
3/4l, 4l. 4m 2s. 14 ran. W A Hall
1957 Mrs D Jones's Merry Deal b g by Straight
Deal 7–12–0 ...... G Underwood 28–1
Mrs L Brand's Quita Que 8–12–0
.... Mr J R Cox 15–2
Comte de Monteynard's Tout ou Rien 5–
11–12 .... R Emery 100–8
5l, 5l. 4m 6 7/5s. 16 ran. A Jones
1958 Mrs D Wright's Bandalore b g by Tam-
bourin 7–12–0 .... G Slack 20–1
Mr D Deyong's Tokoroa 7–12–0
.... D V Dick 5–1
Mr Jos Bennett's Retour de Flamme 5–
11–12 .... J Lindley 11–2
2l, 3l. 3m 56s. 18 ran. J S Wright
1959 Mr G C Judd's Fare Time b g by Thor-
oughfare 6–12–0 .... F Winter 13–2
Mr J G Duggan's Ivy Green 9–12–0
.... P Taaffe 40–1
Mrs G R Westmacott's Prudent King 7–
12–0 .... T P Burns 13–2
4l, 11l. 4m 7 1/5s. 14 ran. H R Price
1960 Mr J J Byrne's Another Flash b g by Roi
d'Egypte 6–12–0 .... H Beasley 11–4
Mrs C Magnier's Albergo 6–12–0
.... D Page 11–2
Lady Cottenham's Saffron Tartan 9–12–0
.... T P Burns 3–1
2l, 3l, 3m 55s. 12 ran. P Sleator in Ireland
1961 Dr B N Pajgar's Eborneezer b h by
Ocean Swell 6–12–0 .... F Winter 4–1
Mrs T O'Brien's Moss Bank 5–11–12
.... J J Rafferty 7–4
Mr A H Birtwhistle's Farmer's Boy 8–12–0
.... D Nicholson 8–1
3l, 11/2l. 4m 10s. 17 ran. H R Price
1962 Sir T Ainsworth's Anzio ro h by Vic Day 5–
11–12 .... G W Robinson 11–2
Mrs I R Pitman's Quelle Chance 7–12–0
.... D V Dick 11–2
Mr J J Byrne's Another Flash 8–12–0
.... H Beasley 11–10
3l, 1 1/2l. 4m 0 1/5s. 14 ran. F Walwyn
1963 Mr G Spencer's Winning Fair bl or br g by
Fun Fair 8–12–0 ...... Mr A Lillingston 100–9
Mrs M E Donnelly's Farrney Fox 8–12–0
.... P Powell 10–1
Mrs I R Pitman's Quelle Chance 8–12–0
.... B Wilkinson 100–7
3l, nk. 4m 152/5s. 21 ran. G Spencer in Ireland
1964 Mr J McGhie's Magic Court br g by
Supreme Court 6–12–0 ... P McCarron 100–6
Mr J J Byrne's Another Flash 10–12–0
.... H Beasley 6–1
Mrs D Beddington's Kirriemuir 4–11–4
.... G W Robinson 100–6
4l, 3/4l. 4m 8s. 24 ran. T Robson
1965 Mrs D Beddington's Kirriemuir br g by
Tangle 5–11–12 .... G W Robinson 50–1
Mme P Logut's Spartan General 6–12–0
.... T W Biddlecombe 8–1
Queen Elizabeth's Worcran 7–12–0
.... D Nicholson 8–1
1l, 1 1/2l. 4m 6 1/5s. 19 ran. F Walwyn
1966 Mrs J Rogerson's Salmon Spray ch g by
Vulgan 8–12–0 .... J Haine 4–1
Lady Aitken's Sempervivum 8–12–0
.... J King 20–1
Mrs T G Williamson's Flyingbolt 7–12–0
.... P Taaffe 15–8
3l, 3/4l. 4m 10 1/5s. 17 ran. R Turnell
1967 Mr K F Alder's Saucy Kit b h by Hard
Sauce 6–12–0 .... R Edwards 100–6

Queen Elizabeth's Makaldar 7-12-0
.... D Mould   11-4
Mr M L Healey's Talgo Abbess 8-12-0
.... F Carroll   100-8
Aurelius finished second, beaten 4
lengths, but was disqualified. Makaldar
was 1 length further away.
4m. 11¹/₅s. 23 ran. M H Easterby

1968 Mr H S Alper's Persian War b g by
Persian Gulf 5-11-12 .... J Uttley   4-1
Lord James Crichton-Stuart's Chorus 7-
12-0 ....A Turnell   7-2
Mr R J Cohen's Black Justice 6-12-0
.... B Scott   100-6
4l, 5l. 4m 3³/₅s. 16 ran. C Davies

1969 Mr H S Alper's Persian War b g by
Persian Gulf 6-12-0 .... J Uttley   6-4
Mr I H Stuart Black's Drumikill 8-12-0
.... B Brogan   100-7
Maj G Glover's Privy Seal 5-11-12
.... J Cook   33-1
4l, 2¹/₂l. 4m 41¹/₅s. 17 ran. C Davies

1970 Mr H S Alper's Persian War b g by
Persian Gulf 7-12-0 .... J Uttley   5-4
Mr K E Wheldon's Major Rose 8-12-0
.... J Gifford   8-1
Queen Elizabeth's Escalus 5-11-12
.... D Mould   25-1
1¹/₂l, 1¹/₂l. 4m 13⁴/₅s. 14 ran. C Davies

1971 Capt E J Edwards-Heathcote's Bula b g
by Raincheck 6-12-0 ..... P Kelleway   15-8
Mr H S Alper's Persian War 8-12-0
.... J Uttley   9-2
Mr K E Wheldon's Major Rose 9-12-0
.... T W Biddlecombe   4-1
4l, 1l. 4m 22¹/₂s. 9 ran. F Winter

1972 Capt E J Edwards-Heathcote's Bula b g
by Raincheck 7-12-0 ..... P Kellaway   8-11
Lord Blakenham's Boxer 5-11-12
.... J Uttley   25-1
Mrs E Swainson's Lyford Cay 8-12-0
.... D Cartwright   66-1
8l, 3l. 4m 25¹/₅s. 12 ran. F Winter

1973 Mr E Wheatley's Comedy of Errors br h
by Goldhill 6-12-0 .... W Smith   8-1
Mrs W Blow's Easby Abbey 6-12-0
.... R Barry   20-1
Mrs J Samuel's Captain Christy 6-12-0
.... H Beasley   85-40
1¹/₂l, 2l. 4m 7⁴/₅s. 8 ran. T F Rimell

1974 Lord Howard de Walden's Lanzarote br g
by Milesian 6-12-0 .... R Pitman   7-4
Mr E Wheatley's Comedy of Errors 7-12-
0 .... W Smith   4-6
Mr D W Samuel's Yenisei (NZ) 7-12-0
.... H Beasley   100-1
3l, 8l. 4m 17·70s. 7 ran F Winter

1975 Mr E Wheatley's Comedy of Errors br h
by Goldhill 8-12-0 .... K White   11-8
Mrs O Negus-Fancey's Flash Imp 6-12-0
.... T Stack   12-1
Mrs C Williams's Tree Tangle 6-12-0
.... A Turnell   10-1
8l, hd. 4m 28·50s. 13 ran. T F Rimell

1976 Mr R Spencer's Night Nurse b g by
Falcon 5-12-0 .... P Broderick   2-1
Mr I Scott's Birds Nest 6-12-0
.... A Turnell   100-30
Mrs O Negus-Fancey's Flash Imp 7-12-0
.... R Mann   40-1
2¹/₂l, 8l. 4m 5·9s. 8 ran. M H Easterby

1977 Mr R Spencer's Night Nurse b g by
Falcon 6-12-0 .... P Broderick   15-2
Dr M Mangan's Monksfield 5-12-0
.... T Kinane   15-1
Mr L Thwaite's Dramatist 6-12-0
.... W Smith   6-1
2l, 2l. 4m 24s. 10 ran. M H Easterby

1978 Dr M Mangan's Monksfield b h by Gala
Performance 6-12-0 .... T Kinane   11-2
Mr P Muldoon's Sea Pigeon (USA) 8-12-
0 .... F Berry   5-1
Mr R Spencer's Night Nurse 7-12-0
.... C Tinkler   3-1
2l, 6l. 4m 12·70s. 13 ran. D McDonogh in Ireland

1979 Mr M Mangan's Monksfield b h by Gala
Performance 7-12-0 ..... D T Hughes   9-4
Mr P Muldoon's Sea Pigeon (USA) 9-12-
0 .... J J O'Neill   6-1
Mr H Joel's Beacon Light 8-12-0
.... J Francome   22-1
³/₄l, 15l. 4m 27s. 10 ran. D McDonogh in Ireland

1980 Mr P Muldoon's Sea Pigeon (USA) br g
by Sea-Bird II 10-12-0 .....J J O'Neill   13-2
Mr M Mangan's Monksfield 8-12-0
.... D T Hughes   6-5
Mr Scott's Birds Nest 10-12-0
.... A Turnell   11-1
7l, 1¹/₂l. 4m 6s. 9 ran. M H Easterby

1981 Mr P Muldoon's Sea Pigeon (USA) br g
by Sea-Bird II 11-12-0 ... J Francome   7-4
Mr R Formby's Pollardstown 6-12-0
.... P Blacker   9-1
Mrs H Doyle's Daring Run 6-12-0
.... Mr T Walsh   8-1
1¹/₂l, nk. 4m 111o40s. 14 ran. M H Easterby

1982 Mr P Heaslip's For Auction b g by Royal
Trip 6-12-0 .... Mr C Magnier   40-1
Lord Northampton's Broadsword 5-12-0
.... P Scudamore   100-30
Tawfuk Fakhouri's Ekbalco 6-12-0
.... D Goulding   7-2
7l, 1¹/₂l, 1¹/₂l. 4m 12·4s. 14 ran. M Cunningham

1983 Sheikh Ali Abu Khamsin's Gaye Brief b g
by Lucky Brief 6-12-0 .... R Linley   7-1
Mr W Lenehan's Boreen Prince 6-12-0
.... N Madden   50-1
Mr F Heaslip's For Auction 7-12-0
.... Mr C Magnier   3-1
3l; 7l. 3m 57·08s. 17 ran. Mrs M Rimell

1984 Mrs C D Hill's Dawn Run b m by Deep
Run, 6-11-9 .... J J O'Neill   4-5
Mr R A Padmore's Cima 6-12-0
.... P Scudamore   66-1
Mr R H Mann's Very Promising 6-12-0
.... S Moorshead   16-1
³/₄l, 4l. 3m 52·6s 14 ran. P Mullins in Ireland

1985 The Stype Wood Stud Ltd's See You
Then br g by Royal Palace, 5-12-0
.... S Smith Eccles   16-1
Mr A Hunt's Robin Wonder 7-12-0
.... J J O'Neill   66-1
Mrs M C Margan's Stans Pride 8-11-9
.... S Moorshead   100-1
7l; 31.3m 51·7s. 14 ran. N J Henderson

1986 The Stype Wood Stud Ltd's See You
Then br g by Royal Palace 6-12-0
.... S Smith Eccles   5-6
Sheikh Ali Abu Khamsin's Gaye Brief 9-
12-0 .... P Scudamore   14-1
Ulceby Farm Ltd's Nohalmdun 5-12-0
.... J J O'Neill   20-1
7l; 1¹/₂l. 3m 53·3s. 23 ran. N J Henderson

1987 The Stype Wood Stud Ltd's See You
Then br g by Royal Palace 7-12-0
.... S Smith Eccles   11-10
Mr W L Pape's Flatterer (USA) 8-12-0
.... J Fishback   10-1
Mr M Davies's Barnbrook Again, 6-12-0
.... S Sherwood   14-1
1¹/₂l; 1l. 3m 57·3s. 18 ran. N J Henderson

1988 Mr D Horton's Celtic Shot b g by Celtic
  Cone 6–12–0 . . . . P Scudamore   7–1
  Mr J O'Connell's Classical Charm 5–12–0
  . . . . K Morgan   33–1
  Mrs L Sewell's Celtic Chief 5–12–0
  . . . . R Dunwoody   5–2
  4l; 3l. 4m 14·4s. 21 ran. F Winter
1989 Mr A Geake's Beech Road ch g by
  Nearly A Hand 7–12–0 . . . . . . R Guest   50–1
  Mrs L Sewell's Celtic Chief 6–12–0
  . . . . G McCourt   6–1
  Mr D Horton's Celtic Shot 7–12–0
  . . . . P Scudamore   8–1
  2l; 1l. 4m 2·10s. 15 ran. G B Balding
1990 Sheikh Mohammed's Kribensis gr g by
  Henbit 6–12–0 . . . . R Dunwoody   95–40
  Mr R Sangster's Nomadic Way 5–12–0   P
  Scudamore   8–1
  Mr N Hetherton's Past Glories 7–12–0
  . . . . J Quinn   150–1
  3l ³/₄l. 3m 50.7s. 19 ran. M Stoute
1991 Michael Jackson Bloodstock Ltd's Morley
  Street ch g by Deep Run 7–12–0
  . . . . J Frost   4–1
  Mr. R Sangster's Nomadic Way 6–12–0
  . . . . R Dunwoody   9–1
  Mr G D Groarke's Ruling 5–12–0   P Niven   50–1
  1¹/₂l. head, 3m 54.6s. 24 ran. G B Balding
1992 Sheikh Mohammed's Royal Gait b g by
  Gunner B 9–12–0 . . . . G McCourt   6–1
  Oh So Risky Syndicate's Oh So Risky 5–
  12–0 . . . . P Holley   20–1
  I MacDonald/J Short's Ruling 6–12–0
  . . . . P Niven   20–1
  ¹/₂l, short head. 3m 57.2s. 16 ran. J R Fanshawe

1993 Mr E Scarth's Granville Again ch g by
  Deep Run 7–12–0 . . . . . P Scudamore   13–2
  Mr M Tabor's Royal Derbi 8–12–0
  . . . . M Perrett   50–1
  Mr A Christodoulou's Halkopous 7–12–0
  . . . . A Maguire   9–1
  1l, 2¹/₂l, 3m 51.6s. 18 ran. M C Pipe
1994 Mr J T Price's Flakey Dove b m by Oats
  8–11–9 . . . . M Dwyer   9–1
  The Oh So Risky Syndicate's Oh So Risky
  7–12–0 . . . . P Holley   9–4
  Mr B T Stewart-Brown's Large Action 6–
  12–0 . . . . J Osborne   8–1
  1¹/₄l, ³/₄l, 4m 2s. 15 ran. R J Price
1995 Mr E Pick's Alderbrook b h by Ardross
  6–12–0 . . . . N Williamson   11–2
  Mr B T Stewart-Brown's Large Action
  7–12–0 . . . . J Osborne   4–1 j-fav
  Mr D J O'Neill's Danoli 7–12–0 C F Swan   4–1 j-fav
  5l, 2l, 4m 3s. 14 ran. K C Bailey
1996 Mr W E Sturt's Collier Bay b g by Green
  Desert (USA) 6–12–0 . . . . . . G Bradley   9–1
  Mr E Pick's Alderbrook 7–12–0
  . . . . R Dunwoody   10–11 fav
  Messrs Jones, Berstock and Fleet Part-
  nership's Pridwell 6–12–0 . . . . C Maude   33–1
  2¹/₂l, 6l, 3m 59s. 16 ran. J A B Old
1997 Mr P A Deal's Make A Stand ch g by
  Master Willie 6–12–0 . . . . . . A P McCoy   7–1
  Mrs John Magnier's Theatreworld 5–12–0
  . . . . N Williamson   33–1
  Mrs E Queally's Space Trucker 6–12–0
  . . . . J Shortt   9–2
  5l, ³/₄l, 3m 48.4s (course record), 17 ran, M C Pipe

THE QUEEN MOTHER CHAMPION CHASE (Cheltenham)

(2 miles)

1959 Quita Que 10y 12st (9)
1960 Fortria 8y 12st (7)
1961 Fortria 9y 12st (5)
1962 Piperton 8y 12st (7)
1963 Sandy Abbot 8y 12st (5)
1964 Ben Stack 7y 12st (5)
1965 Dunkirk 8y 12st (6)
1966 Flyingbolt 7y 12st (6)
1967 Drinny's Double 9y 12st (8)
1968 Drinny's Double 10y 12st (5)
1969 Muir 10y 12st (11)
1970 Straight Fort 7y 12st (6)
1971 Crisp (Aus) 8y 12st (8)
1972 Royal Relief 9y 12st (6)
1973 Inkslinger (USA) 6y 12st (6)
1974 Royal Relief 10y 12st (6)
1975 Lough Inagh 8y 12st (8)
1976 Skymas 11y 12st (7)
1977 Skymas 12y 12st (9)
1978 Hilly Way 8y 12st (10)
1979 Hilly Way 9y 12st (9)
1980 Another Dolly 10y 12st (7)
  Chinrullah came in first but was
  later disqualified
1981 Drumgora 9y 12st (9)
1982 Rathgorman 10y 12st (9)
1983 Badsworth Boy 8y 12st (6)
1984 Badsworth Boy 9y 12st (10)
1985 Badsworth Boy 10y 12st (5)
1986 Buck House 8y 12st (11)
1987 Pearlyman 8y 12st (8)

1988 Pearlyman 9y 12st (8)
1989 Barnbrook Again 8y 12st (8)
1990 Barnbrook Again 9y 12st (9)
1991 Katabatic 8y 12st (7)
1992 Remittance Man 8y 12st (6)
1993 Deep Sensation 8y 12st (9)
1994 Viking Flagship 7y 12st (8)
1995 Viking Flagship 8y 12st (10)
1996 Klairon Davis (FR) 7y 12st (7)
1997 Martha's Son 10y 12st (6)

ROYAL SUNALLIANCE CHASE (Cheltenham)

(3 miles 1 fur)

1964 Buona notte 7y 12st 4lb (16)
1965 Arkloin 6y 11st 7lb (17)
1966 Different Class 6y 11st 12lb (17)
1967 Border Jet 7y 11st (19)
1968 Herring Gull 6y 11st 12lb (16)
1969 Spanish Steps 6y 11st 12lb (22)
1970 Proud Tarquin 7y 11st 12lb (17)
1971 Tantalum 7y 11st 7lb (16)
1972 Clever Scot 7y 11st 7lb (18)
1973 Killiney 7y 11st 3lb (9)
1974 Ten Up 7y 11st (12)
1975 Pengrail 7y 11st (11)
1976 Tied Cottage 8y 11st (15)
1977 Gay Spartan 6y 11st 4lb (15)
1978 Sweet Joe 6y 11st 4lb (17)
1979 Master Smudge 7y 11st 4lb (17)
1980 Lacson 8y 11st 4lb (17)
1981 Lesley Ann 7y 11st 4lb (17)

1982 Brown Chamberlin 7y 11st 4lb (15)
1983 Canny Danny 7y 11st 4lb (14)
1984 A Kinsman 8y 11st 4lb (18)
1985 Antarctica Bay 8y 11st 4lb (11)
1986 Cross Master 9y 11st 4lb (30)
1987 Kildimo 7y 11st 4lb (18)
1988 The West Awake 7y 11st 4lb (14)
1989 Enropak Token 8y 11st 4lb (13)
1990 Garrison Savannah 7y 11st 4lb (9)
1991 Rolling Ball (FR) 8y 11st 4lb (20)
1992 Miinnehoma 9y 11st 4lb (18)
1993 Young Hustler 6y 11st 4lb (8)
1994 Monsieur le Cure 8y 11st 4lb (18)
1995 Brief Gale 8y 10st 13lb (13)
1996 Nahthen Lad 7y 11st 4lb (12)
1997 Hanakham 8y 11st 4lb (14)

ELITE RACING CLUB TRIUMPH HURDLE (Cheltenham)

(2 miles 1 fur)
For four year olds

1939 Grey Talk 11st 7lb (15)
1940–49 No race
1950 Abrupto 11st 6lb (19)
1951 Blue Song II 10st 7lb (12)
1952 Hoggar 10st 10lb (15)
1953 Clair Soleil 11st 5lb (13)
1954 Prince Charlemagne 10st 10lb (12)
1955 Kwannin 10st 10lb (12)
1956 Square Dance 10st 12lb (11)
1957 Meritorious 10st 12lb (14)

1958 Pundit 11st 4lb (14)
1959 Amazons Choice 10st 10lb (13)
1960 Turpial 10st 10lb (13)
1961 Cantab 10st 10lb (15)
1962 Beaver II 10st 10lb (11)
1963–64 No race
1965 Blarney Beacon 11st 4lb (7)
1966 Black Ice 11st 4lb (11)
1967 Persian War 11st 8lb (13)
1968 England's Glory 10st 10lb (16)
1969 Coral Diver 11st 4lb (26)
1970 Varma 11st 4lb (31)
1971 Boxer 11st 3lb (18)
1972 Zarib 11st (16)
1973 Moonlight Bay 11st (18)

1974 Attivo 11st (21)
1975 Royal Epic 11st (28)
1976 Peterhof 11st (23)
1977 Meladon 11st (30)
1978 Connaught Ranger 11st (14)
1979 Pollardstown 11st (28)
1980 Heighlin 11st (26)
1981 Baron Blakeney 11st (29)
1982 Shiny Copper 11st (29)
1983 Saxon Farm 11st (30)
1984 Northern Game 11st (30)
1985 First Bout 11st (27)
1986 Solar Cloud 11st (28)
1987 Alone Success 11st (29)
1988 Kribensis 11st (26)

1989 Ikdam 11st (27)
1990 Rare Holiday 11st (30)
1991 Oh So Risky 11st (27)
1992 Duke of Monmouth (USA) 11st (30)
1993 Shawiya 10st 9lb (25)
1994 Mysilv 10st 9lb (28)
1995 Kissair 11st (26)
1996 Paddy's Return 11st b (29)
1997 Commanche Court 11st (28)

Run as Triumph Hurdle over 2 miles at Hurst Park from 1939 to 1962

TOTE CHELTENHAM GOLD CUP CHASE

(Cheltenham)   (3 miles 2f 110 yds)   (First run 1924)

1924 Maj H Wyndham's Red Splash ch g by Copper Ore 5–11–5 . . . . F Rees	5–1	
Maj C Dewhurst's Conjurer II 12–12–0 . . . . Mr H A Brown	7–1	
Maj F J Scott Murray's Gerald L 10–12–0 . . . . I Morgan	5–1	
Hd, nk. 9 ran. F E Withington		
1925 M J C Bentley's Ballinode ch m by Machakos 9–12–0 . . . . T Leader	3–1	
Mr W H McAlpine's Alcazar 9–12–0 . . . . F Rees	8–13	
Mr B lemon's Patsey V 11–12–0 . . . . Mr B Lemon	10–1	
5l, bad. 7m 29³/₅s. 4 ran. F Morgan in Ireland		
1926 Mr F Barbour's Koko b g by Santoi 8–12–0 . . . . J Hamey	10–1	
Mrs W H Dixon's Old Tay Bridge 12–12–0 . . . . J Hogan	3–1	
Mr W Filmer-Sankey's Ruddyglow 8–12–0 . . . . Mr W Filmer-Sankey	6–5	
4l, 5l. 7m 11s. 8 ran. A Bickley		
1927 Lord Stalbridge's Thrown In ch g by Beau Bill 11–12–0 . . . . Mr H R Grosvenor	10–1	
Mr T Ka Laidlaw's Grakle 5–11–5 . . . . J Moloney	5–1	
Mr W H Midwood's Silvo 11–12–0 . . . . F Rees	13–8	
2l, 1¹/₂l. 7m 28s. 8 ran. O Anthony		
1928 Mr F W Keen's Patron Saint br g by St Girons 5–11–5 . . . . F Rees	7–2	
Col J H Starkey's Vive 13–12–0 . . . . P Powell	4–5	
4l, 2l. 7m 29³/₅s. 7 ran. H Harrison		
1929 Mr J H Whitney's Easter Hero ch g by My Prince 9–12–0 . . . . F Rees	7–4	
Capt R F H Norman's Lloydie 7–12–0 . . . . R McCarthy	100–9	
Mr C R Taylor's Grakle 7–12–0 . . . . K Piggott	11–4	
20l, 2l. 6m 57s. 10 ran. J Anthony		
1930 Mr J H Whitney's Easter Hero ch g by My Prince 10–12–0 . . . . T Cullinan	8–11	
Mr C R Taylor's Grakle 8–12–0 . . . . K Piggott	10–1	
Only 2 finished		
20l. 7m 6s. 4 ran. J Anthony		
1931 No race		
1932 Miss D Paget's Golden Miller b g by Goldcourt 5–11–5 . . . . T Leader	13–2	
Lady Lindsay's Inverse 6–12–0 . . . . R Lyall	8–1	
Mr M D Blair's Aruntius 11–12–0 . . . . D McCann	20–1	
4l, bad. 7m 33³/₅s. 6 ran. A Briscoe		
1933 Miss D Paget's Golden Miller b g by Goldcourt 6–12–0 . . . . W Stott	4–7	
Mr J H Whitney's Thomond II 7–12–0 . . . . W Speck	11–4	
Mr J B Snow's Delaneige 8–12–0 . . . . J Moloney	20–1	
10l, 5l. 7m 33s. 7 ran. A Briscoe		
1934 Miss D Paget's Golden Miller b g by Goldcourt 7–12–0 6–5		
Mrs V Mundy's Avenger 5–11–5 . . . . R Lyall	6–1	
Mrs F Ambrose Clark's Kellsboro' Jack 8–12–0 . . . . D Morgan	10–1	
6l, 6l. 7m 4³/₅s. 7 ran. A Briscoe		
1935 Miss D Paget's Golden Miller b g by Goldcourt 8–12–0 . . . . G Wilson	1–2	
Mr J H Whitney's Thomond II 9–12–0 . . . . W Speck	5–2	
Mrs F Ambrose Clark's Kellsboro' Jack 9–12–0 . . . . D Morgan	100–7	
³/₄l, 5l. 6m 30s. 5 ran. A Briscoe		
1936 Miss D Paget's Golden Miller b g by Goldcourt 9–12–0 . . . . E Williams	21–20	
Mr H Lloyd Thomas's Royal Mail 7–12–0 . . . . Mr F Walwyn	5–1	
Mrs F Ambrose Clark's Kellsboro' Jack 10–12–0 . . . . D Morgan	10–1	
12l, 2l. 7m 5¹/₅s. 6 ran. O Anthony		
1937 No race		
1938 Lt-Col D C Part's Morse Code b or ch g by The Pilot 9–12–0 . . . . D Morgan	13–2	
Miss D Paget's Golden Miller 11–12–0 . . . . H Nicholson	7–4	
Mr H A Steel's Macaulay 7–12–0 . . . . D Butchers	3–1	
2l, 3l. 6m 35¹/₅s. 6 ran. I Anthony		
1939 Mrs A Smith-Bingham's Brendan's Cottage b h by Cottage 9–12–0 G Owen	8–1	
Capt J W Bridge's Morse Code 10–12–0 . . . . D Morgan	4–7	
Mr G S L Whitelaw's Embarrassed 6–12–0 . . . . Capt P Herbert	25–1	
5l, bad. 7m 34¹/₅s. 5 ran. G Beeby		

1940 Miss D Paget's Homan Hackle b g by
Yutoi 7–12–0 .... E Williams — Evens
Mrs C Jones's Black Hawk 9–12–0
.... T F Rimell — 20–1
Mrs C Evans's Royal Mail 11–12–0
.... D Morgan — 100–8
10l, 2l. 6m 46²/₅s. 7 ran. O Anthony

1941 Mr D Sherbooke's Poet Prince ch g by
Milton 91–12–0 .... R Burford — 7–2
Maj L Montagu's Savon 9–12–0
.... G Archibald — 100–30
Lady Sybil Phipp's Red Rower 7–12–0
.... D Morgan — 8–1
3l, sht. hd. 15³/₅s. 10 ran. I Anthony

1942 Lord Sefton's Medoc II b g by Van
8–12–0 .... H Nicholson — 9–2
Lady Sybil Phipp's Red Rower 8–12–0
.... D Morgan — 3–1
Lord Bicester's Asterabad 11–12–0
.... T F Carey — 20–1
8l, 4l. 6m 38s. 12 ran. R Hobbs

1943 and 1944 No race

1945 Lord Stalbridge's Red Rower b g by
Rameses the Second 11–12–0
.... D L Jones — 11–4
Mrs K Cameron's Schubert 11–12–0
.... C Beechener — 11–2
Mr R A Holbech's Paladin 11–12–0
.... P Conlon — 100–30
3l, 1¹/₂l. 6m 16¹/₅s. 16 ran. Lord Stalbridge

1946 Mr J V Rank's Prince Regent b g by My
Prince 11–12–0 .... T Hyde — 4–7
Mrs D Nelson's Poor Flame 8–12–0
.... G Kelly — 9–2
5l, 4l. 6m 47³/₅s. 6 ran. T Dreaper in Ireland

1947 Lord Grimthorpe's Fortina ch h by For-
mor 6–12–0 .... Mr R Black — 8–1
Miss D Paget's Happy Holme 8–12–0
.... D L Moore — 3–1
Lord Bicester's Prince Blackthorn 9–12–0
.... R Turnell — 8–1
10l, 6l. 6m 41¹/₅s. 12 ran. H Christie

1948 Mr F L Vickerman's Cottage Rake b or br
g by Cottage 9–12–0 .... A Brabazon — 10–1
Miss D Paget's Happy Home 9–12–0
.... M Molony — 6–1
Mr W F Highnam's Coloured School Boy
8–12–0 .... E Vinall — 10–1
1¹/₂l, 10l. 6m 56³/₅s. 12 ran. M V O'Brien in Ireland

1949 Mr F L Vickerman's Cottage Rake b or br
g by Cottage 10–12–0 .... A Brabazon — 4–6
Maj R Stirling-Stuart's Cool Customer
10–12–0 .... P J Murphy — 13–2
Mr W F Highnam's Coloured School Boy
9–12–0 .... E Vinall — 8–1
2l, 6l. 6m 36s. 6 ran. M V O'Brien in Ireland
† Run at April Meeting

1950 Mr F L Vickerman's Cottage Rake b or br
g by Cottage 11–12–0 .. A Brabazon — 5–6
Lord Bicester's Finnure 9–12–0
.... M Molony — 5–4
Marquis de Portago's Garde Toi 9–12–0
.... Marquis de Portago — 100–1
10l, 8l. 7m 0³/₅s. 6 ran. M V O'Brien in Ireland

1951 Lord Bicester's Silver Fame ch g by
Werwolf 12–12–0 ...... M Molony — 6–4
Mr J V Rank's Greenogue 9–12–0
.... G Kelly — 100–8
Mr L B Chugg's Mighty Fine 9–12–0
.... J A Bullock — 10–1
Sht. hd, 2l. 6m 23²/₅s. 6 ran. G Beeby

1952 Miss D Paget's Mont Tremblant ch g by
Gris Perle 6–12–0 ...... D V Dick — 8–1
Mr G Hemsleys Shaef 8–12–0 F Winter — 7–1
Lady Orde's Galloway Braes 8–12–0
.... R Morrow — 66–1
10l, 4l. 7m 2¹/₅s. 13 ran. F Walwyn

1953 Mrs M H Keogh's Knock Hard ch g by
Domaha 9–12–0 .... T Moloney — 11–2
Contessa di Sant Elia's Halloween
8–12–0 .... F Winter — 5–2
Lady Orde's Galloway Braes 8–12–0
.... R Morrow — 33–1
5l, 2l. 6m 28²/₅s. 12 ran. M V O'Brien in Ireland

1954 Mr A Strange's Four Ten b g by Blunder-
buss 8–12–0 .... T Cusack — 100–6
Lord Bicester's Mariner's Log 7–12–0
.... P Taaffe — 20–1
Contessa di Sant Elia's Halloween
9–12–0 .... G Slack — 100–6
4l, 4l. 7m 12¹/₅s. 9 ran. J F Roberts

1955 Mr P J Burt's Gay Donald b g by Gay
Light 9–12–0 .... A Grantham — 33–1
Contessa di Sant Elia's Halloween
10–12–0 .... F Winter — 7–2
Mr A Strange's Four Ten 9–12–0
.... T Cusack — 3–1
10l, 8l. 6m 59¹/₅s. 9 ran. J J Ford

1956 Mr J Davey's Limber Hill ch g by Bassam
9–12–0 .... J Power — 11–8
Mr A R B Owen's Vigor 9–12–0
.... R Emery — 50–1
Contessa di Sant Elia's Halloween
11–12–0 .... F Winter — 100–8
4l, 1¹/₂l. 6m 42s. 11 ran. W P Dutton

1957 Mr D Brown's Linwell b g by Rosewell
9–12–0 .... M Scudamore — 100–9
Mr G H Moore's Kerstin 7–12–0
.... G Milburn — 6–1
Mr G G Lawrence's Rose Park 11–12–0
.... G Nicholls — 100–8
1l, 1l. 6m 55¹/₅s. 13 ran. C Mallon

1958 Mr G H Moore's Kerstin br m by Honor's
Choice 8–12–0 .... S Hayhurst — 7–1
Mrs P Pleydell-Bouverie's Polar Flight
8–12–0 .... G Slack — 11–2
Mr P J Burt's Gay Donald 12–12–0
.... F Winter — 13–2
¹/₂l, bad. 6m 55³/₅s. 9 ran. C Bewicke

1959 Lord Fingall's Roddy Owen b g by
Owenstown 10–12–0 ...... H Beasley — 5–1
Mr D Brown's Linwell 11–12–0
.... F Winter — 11–2
Mrs J Mildmay-White's Lochroe 11–12–0
.... A Freeman — 100–9
3l, 10l. 7m 28²/₅s. 11 ran. D Morgan in Ireland

1960 Mr J Rogerson's Pas Seul b or br g by
Erin's Pride 7–12–0 ...... W Rees — 6–1
Mrs J Mildmay-White's Lochroe 12–12–0
.... D Mould — 25–1
Mrs G St John Nolan's Zonda 9–12–0
.... G W Robinson — 8–1
1l, 5l. 7m 0s. 12 ran. R Turnell

1961 Col G R Westmacott's Saffron Tartan b or
br g by Tartan 10–12–0 ..... F Winter — 2–1
Mr J Rogerson's Pas Seul 8–12–0
.... D V Dick — 100–30
Mme K Hennessy's Mandarin 10–12–0
.... P Madden — 100–7
1¹/₂l, 3l. 6m 49⁴/₅s. 11 ran. D Butchers

1962 Mme K Hennessy's Mandarin b g by
Deux pour Cent 11–12–0 .... F Winter — 7–2
Mr G Ansley's Fortria 10–12–0 P Taaffe — 3–1
Mr W Nodding's Cocky Consort 9–12–0
.... C Stobbs — 50–1
1l, 10l. 6m 39²/₅s. 9 ran. F Walwyn

1963 Mr W H Golling's Mill House b g by King
Hal 6–12–0 .... G W Robinson — 7–2
Mr G Ansley's Fortria 11–20–0 P Taaffe — 4–1
Mr J Tilling's Duke of York 8–12–0
.... F Winter — 7–1
12l, 4l. 7m 8²/₅s. 9 ran. F Walwyn

1964 Anne, Duchess of Westminster's Arkle b
g by Archive 7–12–0 ...... P Taaffe — 7–4
Mr W H Golling's Mill House 7–12–0
.... G W Robinson — 8–13

Mr J Rogerson's Pas Seul 11–12–0
.... D V Dick   50–1
5l, 25l. 6m 45³/₅s. 4 ran. T Dreaper in Ireland
1965 Anne, Duchess of Westminster's Arkle b
g by Archive 8–12–0 .... P Taaffe   30–100
Mr W H Golling's Mill House 8–12–0
.... G W Robinson   100–30
Mr W Roycroft's Stoney Crossing 7–12–0
.... Mr W Roycroft   100–1
10l, 30l. 6m 41¹/₅s. 4 ran. T Dreaper in Ireland
1966 Anne, Duchess of Westminster's Arkle b
g by Archive 9–12–0 .... P Taaffe   1–10
Mrs D M Wells-Kendrew's Dormant
9–12–0 .... M Scudamore   20–1
Lord Cadogan's Snaigow 7–12–0
.... D Nicholson   100–7
30l, 10l. 6m 54¹/₅s. 5 ran. T Dreaper in Ireland
1967 Mr H H Collins' Woodland Venture b g by
Eastern Venture 7–12–0
.... T W Biddlecombe   100–8
Mr R J R Blindell's Stalbridge Colonist
8–12–0 .... S Mellor   11–2
Lady Weir's What a Myth 10–12–0
.... P Kelleway   3–1
³/₄l, 2l. 6m 59¹/₅s. 8 ran. T F Rimell
1968 Col J Thomson's Fort Leney b g by
Fortina 10–12–0 .... P Taaffe   11–2
Mr H J Joel's The Laird 7–12–0 .. J King   3–1
Mr R J R Blindell's Stalbridge Colonist
9–12–0 .... T W Biddlecombe   7–2
Nk, 1l. 6m 51s. 5 ran. T Dreaper in Ireland
1969 Lady Weir's What a Myth ch g by Coup
de Myth 12–12–0 .... P Kelleway   8–1
Mr B P Jenks's Domacorn 7–12–0
.... T W Biddlecombe   7–2
Mr P Cussin's Playlord 8–12–0 .. R Barry   4–1
1¹/₂l, 20l. 7m 30¹/₅s. 11 ran. H R Price
1970 Mr R R Guest's L'Escargot ch g by
Escart III 7–12–0 .... T Carberry   33–1
Mr K Stewart's French Tan 8–12–0
.... P Taaffe   8–1
Mr E R Courage's Spanish Steps 7–12–0
.... J Cook   9–4
1¹/₂l, 10l. 6m 47⁷/₅s. 12 ran. D L Moore in Ireland
1971 Mr R R Guest's L'Escargot ch g by
Escart III 8–12–0 .... T Carberry   7–2
Mrs R K Mellon's Leap Frog 7–12–0
.... V O'Brien   7–2
Mrs D W August's The Dikler 8–12–0
.... B Brogan   15–2
10l, 15l. 8m 0³/₅s. 8 ran. D L Moore in Ireland
1972 Mr P Doyle's Glencaraig Lady ch m by
Fortina 8–12–0 .... F Berry   6–1
Mr H Handel's Royal Toss 10–12–0
.... N Wakley   22–1
Mrs D August's The Dikler 9–12–0
.... B Brogan   11–1
³/₄l, hd. 7m 17¹/₅s. 12 ran. F Flood in Ireland
1973 Mrs D August's The Dikler b g by Vulgan
10–12–0 .... R Barry   9–1
Mrs C Swallow's Pendil 8–12–0
.... R Pitman   4–6
Mrs B Heath's Charlie Potheen 8–12–0
.... T W Biddlecombe   9–2
Sht. hd., 6l. 6m 37¹/₅s. 8 ran. F Walwyn
1974 Mrs J M A Samuel's Captain Christy b g
by Mon Capitaine 7–12–0 .. H Beasley   7–1
Mrs D August's The Dikler 11–12–0
.... R Barry   5–1
Queen Elizabeth's Game Spirit 8–12–0
.... T Biddlecombe   20–1
5l, 20l. 7m 5·50s. 7 ran. P Taaffe in Ireland
1975 Anne, Duchess of Westminster's Ten Up
b g by Raise You Ten 8–12–0
.... T Carberry   2–1
Mrs M Scott's Soothsayer (USA) 8–12–0
.... R Pitman   28–1
Capt E Edwards-Heathcote's Bula
10–12–0 .... J Francombe   5–1

6l, ¹/₂l. 7m 51·40s. 8 ran. J Dreaper in Ireland
1976 Sir E Hanmer's Royal Frolic b g by Royal
Buck 7–12–0 .... J Burke   14–1
Mrs P Burrell's Brown Lad 10–12–0
.... T Carberry   13–8
Mrs P Burrell's Colebridge 12–12–0
.... F Berry   12–1
5l, 5l. 6m 40·1s. 11 ran. T F Rimell
1977 Mrs J McGowan's Davy Lad, b g by
David Jack 7–12–0 ...... D T Hughes   14–1
Mr A Robinson's Tied Cottage 9–12–0
.... T Carberry   20–1
Mr H J Joel's Summerville 11–12–0
.... J King   15–1
6l, 20l. 7m 13·80s. 13 ran. M O'Toole in Ireland
1978 Mrs O Jackson's Midnight Court b g by
Twilight Alley 7–12–0 .. J Francombe   5–2
Mrs P E Burrell's Brown Lad 12–12–0
.... T Carberry   8–1
Mr S P Marsh's Master H 9–12–0
.... R Crank   18–1
7l, 1l. 6m 57·30s. 10 ran. F Winter
1979 Snailwell Stud Company's Alverton ch g
by Midsummer Night II 9–12–0
.... J J O'Neill   5–1
Mr S Burgess's Royal Mail (NZ) 9–12–0
.... P Blacker   7–1
Mr S Embiricos's Aldaniti 9–12–0
.... R Champion   40–1
25l, 20l. 7m 1s. 14 ran. M H Easterby
1980 Mr A Barrow's Master Smudge ch g by
Master Stephen 8–12–0 ..... R Hoare   14–1
Miss P Neal's Mac Vidi 15–12–0
.... P Leach   66–1
Major D Wigan's Approaching 9–12–0
.... B R Davies   11–1
8l, 5l, 2¹/₂l. 7m 14·20s. 15 ran. A Barrow
Tied Cottage came in first, but, following
a dope test, was later disqualified.
1981 Mr R Wilson's Little Owl b g by Cantab
7–12–0 .... Mr A J Wilson   6–1
Mr R Spencer's Night Nurse 10–12–0
.... A Brown   6–1
Mrs C Feather's Silver Buck 9–12–0
.... T Carmody   7–2
1¹/₂l, 10l. 7m 9·90s. 15 ran. M H Easterby
1982 Mrs C Feather's Silver Buck br g by Silver
Cloud 10–12–0 .... R Earnshaw   8–1
Mr M Kennelly's Bregawn 8–12–0
.... G Bradley   18–1
Miss C Hawkey's Sunset Cristo 8–12–0
.... C Grant   100–1
2l, 12l. 7m 11·3s. 22 ran. M Dickinson
1983 Mr J Kennelly's Bregawn ch g by Saint
Denys 9–12–0 .... G Bradley   100–30
Mr F Emami's Captain John 9–12–0
.... D Goulding   11–1
Mrs S N Thewlis's Wayward Lad 8–12–0
.... J J O'Neill   6–1
5l; 1¹/₂l. 6m 57·60s. 11 ran. M Dickinson
1984 Mr R S Riley's Burrough Hill Lad b g by
Richboy 8–12–0 .... P Tuck   7–2
Mrs B Samuel's Brown Chamberlain
9–12–0 .... J Francombe   5–1
Mr Michael Cuddy's Drumlargan 10–12–0
.... Mr F Codd   16–1
3l, 8l. 6m 44·4s. 12 ran. Mrs J Pitman
1985 T Kilroe and Sons Ltd's Forgive 'N' For-
get ch g by Precipice Wood 8–12–0 ..
.... M Dwyer   7–1
Mrs M M Haggas's Righthand Man
8–12–0 .... G Bradley   15–2
Mr W Hamilton's Earls Brig 10–12–0
.... P Tuck   13–2
1¹/₂l, 2¹/₂l. 6m 48·3s. 15 ran. J FitzGerald
1986 Mrs C D Hill's Dawn Run b m by Deep
Run 8–11–9 .... J J O'Neill   15–8
Mrs S N Thewlis's Wayward Lad, 11–12–0
.... G Bradley   8–1

T Kilroe and Sons Ltd's Forgive 'N' Forget
9-12-0 .... M Dwyer 7-2
1l; 2½l. 6m 35.3s. 11 ran. P Mullins in Ireland
1987 T P M McDonagh Ltd's The Thinker ch g
by Cantab 9-12-0 .... R Lamb 13-2
Mr I Bray's Cybrandian 9-12-0
.... C Grant 25-1
Mr H J Joel's Door Latch 9-12-0
.... R Rowe 9-1
1½l; 2½l. 6m 56.1s. 12 ran. W A Stephenson
1988 Mrs C Smith's Charter Party br g by
Document 10-12-0 ..... R Dunwoody 10-1
Mrs J Ollivant's Cavvies Clown 8-12-0
.... S Sherwood 6-1
White Bros. (Taunton) Ltd's Beau Ranger
10-12-0 .... P Scudamore 33-1
6l; 10l. 6m 58.9s. 15 ran. D Nicholson
1989 Mr R Burridge's Desert Orchid gr g by
Grey Mirage 10-12-0 .... S Sherwood 5-2
Mr A Parker's Yahoo 8-12-0
.... T Morgan 25-1
Mr C Smith's Charter Party 11-12-0
.... R Dunwoody 14-1
1½l; 8l. 7m 17.60s. 13 ran. D Elsworth
1990 Mr S Griffiths's Norton's Coin ch g by
Mount Cassino 9-12-0 ....G McCourt 100-1
.... M Pitman 8-1
Mrs E Hitchins's Toby Tobias 8-12-0
.... R Dunwoody 10-11
Mr R Burridge's Desert Orchid 11-12-0
¾l, 4l. 6m 30.9s. 12 ran. S. Griffiths
1991 Autofour Engineering's Garrison Savan-
nah b g by Random Shot 8-12-0
.... M Pitman 16-1
Marquesa de Moratalla's The Fellow (FR)
6-12-0 .... A Kondrat 28-1
Mr R Burridge's Desert Orchid 12-12-0
.... R Dunwoody 4-1
Short head, 15l. 6m 49.8s. 14 ran. Mrs J Pitman
1992 Whitcombe Manor Racing Stables Ltd's
Cool Ground ch g Over the River
10-12-0 .... A Maguire 25-1

Marquesa de Moratalla's The Fellow (FR)
7-12-0 .... A Kondrat 7-2
R H Baines's Docklands Express
10-12-0 .... M Perrett 16-1
Short head, 1l. 6m 47.5s. 8 ran. G B Balding
1993 Mr J N Yeadon's Jodami b g by Crash
Course 8-12-0 ....M Dwyer 8-1
Hunt & Co (Bournemouth) Ltd's Rushing
Wild 8-12-0 ....R Dunwoody 11-1
Messrs G & L Johnson's Royal Athlete
10-12-0 ....B de Haan 66-1
2l, 7l. 6m 34.4s. 16 ran. P Beaumont
1994 Marquesa de Moratalla's The Fellow (FR)
b g by Italic (FR) 9-12-0 .. A Kondrat 7-1
Mr J N Yeadon's Jodami 9-12-0
.... M Dwyer 6-4
Mr G MacEchern's Young Hustler 7-12-0
.... C Llewellyn 20-1
1½l, 4l. 6m 40.6s. 15 ran. F Doumen in France
1995 Mr P A Matthews's Master Oats ch g by
Oats 9-12-0 ....N Williamson 100-30F
Mr H T Cole's Dubacilla 9-11-9
.... D Gallagher 20-1
Mr Freddie Starr's Miinnehoma 12-12-0
.... R Dunwoody 9-1
15l, 15l, 6m 56.1s. 15 ran. K C Bailey
1996 Lisselan Farms Ltd's Imperial Call br g by
Callernish 7-12-0 ....C O'Dwyer 9-2
Mr A T A Wates' Rough Quest 10-12-0
.... M A Fitzgerald 12-1
Mr R A B Whittle's Couldnt Be Better
9-12-0 .... G Bradley 11-1
4l, 19l, 6m 42.5s. 10 ran. F Sutherland in Ireland
1997 Mr Michael Worcester's Mr Mulligan ch g
by Torus 9-12-0 ....A P McCoy 20-1
Mrs J Mould's Barton Bank 11-12-0
.... D Walsh 33-1
Mr T J Doran's Dorans Pride 8-12-0
.... J P Broderick 10-1
9l, ½l, 6m 35.5s. 14 ran. N T Chance

JAMESON IRISH GRAND NATIONAL (Fairyhouse)

(3 miles 5 fur)

(First run 1870)

1900 Mavis of Meath 6y 12st 12lb (5)
1901 Tipperary Boy 7y 12st (9)
1902 Patlander 6y 11st (7)
1903 Kirko 6y 11st 7lb (9)
1904 Ascetic's Silver 7y 11st 7lb (12)
1905 Red Lad 5y 10st 7lb (13)
1906 Brown Bess 5y 10st 11lb (6)
1907 Sweet Cecil 6y 11st 4lb (5)
1908 Lord Rivers 6y 11st 12lb (6)
1909 Little Hack II 10st (9)
1910 Oniche 8y 10st 3lb (8)
1911 Repeater II 10st 6lb (13)
1912 Small Polly 7y 10st 10lb (17)
1913 Little Hack II 10st 10lb (15)
1914 Civil War 5y 10st 7lb (14)
1915 Punch 7y 11st 8lb (19)
1916 All Sorts 6y 11st (11)
1917 Pay Only 7y 12st (14)
1918 Ballyboggan 7y 11st 4lb (14)
1919 No race
1920 Halston 8y 10st 5lb (11)
1921 Bohernore 8y 10st 7lb (11)
1922 Halston 10y 12st 11lb (16)
1923 Be Careful 14y 10st 2lb (11)
1924 Kilbarry 9y 10st 1lb (16)
1925 Dog Fox 11y 10st 2lb (19)
1926 Amberwave 8y 10st (15)
1927 Jerpoint 7y 12st (15)

1928 Don Sancho 8y 12st 1lb (19)
1929 Alike 6y 10st 5lb (11)
1930 Fanmond 7y 9st 8lb (22)
1931 Impudent Barney 9y 10st 3lb (11)
1932 Copper Court 9y 10st 9lb (15)
1933 Red Park 7y 11st 5lb (16)
1934 Poolgowran 4y 9st 11lb (12)
1935 Rathfriland 7y 10st 10lb (9)
1936 Alice Maythorn 6y 10st 1lb (19)
1937 Pontet 7y 10st 2lb (14)
1938 Clare County 7y 11st 3lb (9)
1939 Shaun Peel 7y 9st 7lb (16)
1940 Jack Chaucer 9y 11st 11lb (14)
1941 No race
1942 Prince Regent 7y 12st 7lb (10)
1943 Golden Jack 8y 10st 3lb (8)
1944 Knight's Crest 7y 9st 7lb (13)
1945 Heirdom 13y 9st 7lb (12)
1946 Golden View II 11y 12st 7lb (11)
1947 Revelry 7y 11st 5lb (17)
1948 Hamstar 8y 9st 7lb (17)
1949 Shagreen 8y 10st 10lb (20)
1950 Dominick's Bar 6y 10st 6lb (12)
1951 Icy Calm 8y 10st 3lb (11)
1952 Alberoni 9y 10st 1lb (11)
1953 Overshadow 10y 10st 4lb (15)
1954 Royal Approach 6y 12st (11)
1955 Umm 8y 10st 5lb (16)
1956 Air Prince 12y 10st (19)
1957 Kilballyown 10y 9st 10lb (26)
1958 Gold Legend 8y 9st 7lb (21)
1959 Zonda 8y 10st 6lb (15)
1960 Olympia 6y 9st 11lb (16)
1961 Fortria 9y 12st (14)
1962 Kerforo 8y 10st 3lb (11)

1963 Last Link 7y 9st 7lb (10)
1964 Arkle 7y 12st (7)
1965 Splash 7y 10st 13lb (4)
1966 Flyingbolt 7y 12st 7lb (6)
1967 Vulpine 6y 11st 6lb (12)
1968 Herring Gull 6y 11st 13lb (12)
1969 Sweet Dreams 8y 9st 10lb (18)
1970 Garoupe 6y 9st 9lb (13)
1971 King's Sprite 9y 9st 13lb (12)
1972 Dim Wit 7y 10st 13lb (14)
1973 Tartan Ace 6y 9st 7lb (14)
1974 Colebridge 10y 11st 2lb (10)
1975 Brown Lad 9y 10st 5lb (8)
1976 Brown Lad 10y 12st 2lb (15)
1977 Billycan 7y 10st (20)
1978 Brown Lad 12y 12st 2lb (19)
1979 Tied Cottage 11y 10st 12lb (20)
1980 Daletta 7y 11st 4lb (25)
1981 Luska 7y 9st 9lb (20)
1982 King Spruce 8y 10st 2lb (25)
1983 Bit of a Skite 7y 9st 7lb (27)
1984 Bentom Boy 9y 9st 9lb (29)
1985 Rhyme 'N' Reason 6y 10st 6lb (23)
1986 Insure 8y 9st 11lb (15)
1987 Brittany Boy 8y 10st 10lb (26)
1988 Perris Valley 7y 10st (18)
1989 Maid of Money 8y 11st 6lb (22)
1990 Desert Orchid 11y 12st (14)
1991 Omerta 11y 10st 9lb (22)
1992 Vanton 8y 10st 11lb (23)
1993 Ebony Jane 8y 10st 7lb (21)
1994 Son of War 9y 10st (18)
1995 Flashing Steel 10y 12st (18)
1996 Feathered Gale 9y 10st (17)
1997 Mudahim 11y 10st 3lb (20)

MARTELL GRAND NATIONAL H'CAP CHASE

(Aintree) (About 4½ miles) (First run 1837)

1837*The Duke (6)
1838*Sir Henry (10)
1839 Lottery 12st (12)
1840 Jerry 12st (12)
1841 Charity 12st (11)
1842 Gaylad 12st (15)
1843 Vanguard 11st 10lb (16)
1844 Discount 6y 10st 12lb (15)
1845 Cure-All 11st 5lb (15)
1846 Pioneer 6y 11st 12lb (22)
1847 Matthew 10st 6lb (28)
1848 Chandler 11st 12lb (29)
1849 Peter Simple 11st (23)
1850 Abd el Kader 9st 12lb (32)
1851 Abd el Kader 10st 4lb (21)
1852 Miss Mowbray 10st 4lb (24)
1853 Peter Simple 10st 10lb (21)
1854 Bourton 11st 12lb (20)
1855 Wanderer 9st 8lb (20)
1856 The Free-trader 7y 9st 6lb (21)
1857 Emigrant 9st 10lb (28)
1858 Little Charley 12y 10st 7lb (16)
1859 Half-Caste 6y 9st 7lb (16)
1860 Anatis 10y 9st 10lb (19)
1861 Jealousy 7y 9st 12lb (24)
1862 Huntsman 9y 11st (13)
1863 Emblem 7y 10st 10lb (16)
1864 Emblematic 6y 10st 6lb (25)
1865 Alcibiade 5y 11st 4lb (23)
1866 Salamander 7y 10st 7lb (30)
1867 Cortolvin 8y 11st 13lb (23)
1868 The Lamb 6y 10st 7lb (21)
1869 The Colonel 6y 10st 7lb (22)
1870 The Colonel 7y 11st 12lb (23)
1871 The Lamb 9y 11st 5lb (25)
1872 Casse Tete 7y 10st (25)
1873 Disturbance 6y 11st 11lb (28)
1874 Reugny 6y 10st 12lb (22)
1875 Pathfinder 10st 11lb (19)
1876 Regal 5y 11st 3lb (19)
1877 Austerlitz 5y 10st 8lb (16)
1878 Shifnal 9y 10st 12lb (12)
1879 The Liberator 9y 11st 4lb (18)
1880 Empress 5y 10st 7lb (14)
1881 Woodbrook 7y 11st 3lb (13)
1882 Seaman 6y 11st 6lb (12)
1883 Zoedone 6y 11st (10)
1884 Voluptuary 6y 10st 5lb (15)
1885 Roquefort 6y 11st (19)
1886 Old Joe 8y 10st 9lb (23)
1887 Gamecock 8y 11st (16)
1888 Playfair 7y 10st 7lb (20)
1889 Frigate 10y 11st 5lb (20)
1890 Ilex 6y 10st 5lb (16)
1891 Come Away 7y 11st 12lb (21)
1892 Father O'Flynn 7y 10st 5lb (25)
1893 Cloister 9y 12st 7lb (15)
1894 Why Not 13y 11st 13lb (14)
1895 Wild Man From Borneo 7y 10st 11lb (19)
1896 The Soarer 7y 9st 13lb (28)
1897 Manifesto 9y 11st 3lb (28)
1898 Drogheda 6y 10st 12lb (24)
1899 Manifesto 11y 12st 7lb (9)

*Run at Maghull

1900 H.R.H. The Prince of Wales's Ambush II b g by Ben Battle 6–11–3 . . . . A Anthony 4–1
Mr C H Brown's Barsac 8–9–12 . . . . W Halsey 25–1
Mr J G Bulteel's Manifesto 12–12–13 . . . . G Williamson 6–1
4l, nk. 10m 1s. 16 ran. Trained A Anthony in Ireland

1901 Mr B Bletsoe's Gruden, br h by Old Back 11–10–0 . . . . A Nightingall 9–1
Mr O J Williams's Drumcree 7–10–0 . . . . Mr H Nugent 10–1
Mr J E Rogerson's Buffalo Bill 7–9–7 . . . . H Taylor 33–1
4l, 6l. 9m 47⅕s. 24 ran. Trained J Holland

1902 Mr A Gorham's Shannon Lass b or br m by Butterscotch 7–10–1 . . . . . . D Read 20–1
Mr John Widger's Matthew 6–9–12 . . . . W Morgan 50–1
Mr J G Bulteel's Manifesto 14–12–8 . . . . A E Piggott 100–6
3l, same. 10m 3s. 21 ran. Trained J F Hackett

1903 Mr J S Morrison's Drumcree b g by Ascetic 9–11–3 . . . . P Woodland 13–2fav
Mr White-Heather's Detail 7–19–13 . . . . A Nightingale 100–14
Mr J G Bulteel's Manifesto 15–12–3 . . . . G Williamson 25–1
3l, 20l. 10m 9⅖s. 23 ran. Trained Sir Charles Nugent

1904 Mr Spencer Gollan's Moifaa br g by Natator 8–10–7 . . . . A Birch 25–1
Mr F Bibby's Kirkland 8–10–10 . . . . F Mason 100–7
Mr John Widger's The Gunner 7–10–4 . . . . Mr John Widger 25–1
8l, nk. 9m 58⅗s. 26 ran. Trained O'Hickey

1905 Mr F Bibby's Kirkland ch g by Kirkham 9–11–5 . . . . F Mason 6–1
Capt McLaren's Napper Tandy 8–10–0 . . . . P Woodland 25–1
Mr P E Speakman's Buckaway II 7–9–11 . . . . A Newey 100–1
3l, 4l. 9m 48⅘s. 27 ran. Trained E Thomas

1906 Prince Hatzfeldt's Ascetic's Silver ch h by Ascetic 9–10–9 . . . . . . Hon A Hastings 20–1
Mr E M Lucas's Red Lad 6–10–2 . . . . C Kelly 33–1
Mr B W Parr's Aunt May 10–11–2 . . . . Mr H Persse 25–1
10l, 2l. 9m 34⅖s. 23 ran. Trained Hon A Hastings

1907 Mr S Howard's Eremon b g by Thurles 7–10–1 . . . . A Newey 8–1
Mr H Hardy's Tom West 8–9–12 . . . . H Murphy 100–6
Mr W Nelson's Patlander 11–10–7 . . . . J Lynn 50–1
6l, bad. 9m 47⅕s. 23 ran. Trained T Coulthwaite

1908 Maj F Doublas Pennant's Rubio ch g by Star Ruby 10–10–5 . . . . H Bletsoe 66–1
Mr W Cooper's Mattie Macgregor 6–10–6 . . . . W Bissill 25–1
Mr P Whitaker's The Lawyer III 11–10–13 . . . . Owner 100–7
10l, 6l. 10m 33⅕s. 24 ran. Trained W Costello

1909 Mr J Hennessy's Lutteur III ch h by St Damien 5–10–11 . . . . G Parfrement 100–9co–f
Mr B W Parr's Judas 8–10–10 . . . . R Chadwick 33–1
Mr F Bibby's Caubeen 8–11–7 . . . . F Mason 20–1
2l, bad. 9m 53⅘s. 32 ran. Trained H Escott

1910 Mr S Howard's Jenkinstown b g by Hackler 9–10–5 . . . . R Chadwick 100–8
Mr C Assheton Smith's Jerry M 7–12–7 . . . . E Driscoll 6–1fav
Mr R Hall's Odor 9–9–8 . . . . Owner 100–1
3l, same. 10m 44⅕s. 25 ran. Trained T Coulthwaite

1911 Mr F Bibby's Glenside b g by St Gris 9–10–3 . . . . Mr J R Anthony 20–1
Mr O H Jones's Rathnally 6–11–0 . . . . R Chadwick 8–1
Mr P Nelke's Shady Girl 10–10–5 . . . . G Clancy 33–1
20l, 3l (2nd and 3rd fell but were remounted). 10m 35s. 26 ran. Trained Capt Collis

1912 Sir C Assheton-Smith's Jerry M bg by Walmsgate 9–12–7 . . . . E Piggott 4–1co–f
Mr C Bower Ismay's Bloodstone 10–11–6 . . . . F Lyall 40–1
Ld Derby's Axle Pin 8–10–4 . . . I Anthony 20–1
6l, 4l. 10m 13⅖s. 24 ran. Trained R Gore

1913 Sir C Assheton-Smith's Covertcoat b g by Hackler 7–11–6 . . . . P Woodland 100–9
Mr Tyrwhitt Drake's Irish Mail 6–11–4 . . . . Mr O Anthony 25–1
Mr C H Wildenburg's Carsey 10–12–0 . . . . Mr H Drake 100–9
Distance, same (3rd fell but was remounted). 10m 19s. 22 ran. Trained R Gore

1914 Mr T Tyler's Sunloch b g by Sundorne 8–9–7 .... W J Smith 100–6
Mr H de Mumm's Trianon III 9–11–9 .... C Hawkins 100–8
Mr J Hennessy's Lutteur III 10–12–6 .... A Carter 10–1
8l, same. 9m 58$^{4}/_{5}$s. 20 ran. Trained Owner
1915 Lady Nelson's Ally Sloper br g by Travelling Lad 6–10–5 ...... Mr J R Anthony 100–8
Mr C Bower Ismay's Jacobus 8–11–0 .... A Newey 25–1
Lord Suffolk's Father Confessor 6–9–10 .... A Aylin 10–1
2l, 8l. 9m 47$^{4}/_{5}$s. 20 ran. Trained Hon A Hastings
†1916 Mr P F Heybourn's Vermouth b g by Barcadelle 6–11–10 .... J Reardon 100–8
Mr E Platt's Irish Mail 9–12–5 .... C Hawkins 20–1
Mr H C Davey's Schoolmoney 6–10–2 .... A Saxby 33–1
2l, 6l. 10m 22s. 21 ran. Trained J Bell
†1917 Sir G Bullough's Ballymacad b g by Laveno 10–9–12 .... E Driscoll 100–9
Mr H Trimmer's Chang 7–9–9 .... W Smith 11–2
Lady Nelson's Ally Sloper 8–11–10 .... I Anthony 20–1
8l, 4l. 10m 12$^{2}/_{5}$s. 19 ran. Trained Hon A Hastings
†1918 Mrs Hugh Peel's Poethlyn b g by Rydal Head 8–11–6 .... E Piggott 5–1co–f
Mr F R Hunt's Captain Drefuss 10–12–7 .... J Reardon 20–1
Sir G Bullough's Ballymacad 11–11–3 .... I Anthony 7–1
4l, bad. 9m 50$^{2}/_{5}$s. 17 ran. Trained H Escott
†Run at Gatwick
1919 Mrs Hugh Peel's Poethlyn b g by Rydal Head 9–12–7 .... E Piggott 11–4fav
Mr E W Hope Johnstone's Ballyboggan 8–11–10 .... W Head 9–1
Mr J L Dugdale's Pollen 10–11–4 .... H Escott 100–7
8l, 6l. 10m 8$^{2}/_{5}$s. 22 ran. Trained H Escott
1920 Maj T G C Gerrard's Troytown br g by Zria 7–11–9 .... Mr J R Anthony 6–1
Mr C L Willcox's The Turk II 10–9–7 .... R Burford 66–1
Mr H A Brown's The Bore 9–10–1 .... Owner 28–1
12l, 6l. 10m 20$^{2}/_{5}$s. 24 ran. Trained A Anthony in Ireland
1921 Mr T M McAlpine's Shaun Spadah b g by Easter Prize 10–11–7 ...... F B Rees 100–9
Mr H A Brown's The Bore 10–11–8 .... Owner 9–1fav
Ld Wavertree's All White 7–10–13 .... R Chadwick 33–1
Distance, same (2nd and 3rd fell but were remounted). 10m 26s. 35 ran. Trained G C Poole
1922 Mr Hugh Kershaw's Music Hall b g by Cliftonhall 9–11–8 .... L B Rees 100–9
Mr Jos. Widger's Drifter 8–10–0 .... W Watkinson 18–1
Mr J C Bulteel's Taffytus 9–11–10 .... T Leader jun 66–1
12l, 6l. 9m 55$^{4}/_{5}$s. 32 ran. Trained Owen Anthony
1923 Mr S Sanford's Sergeant Murphy ch g by General Symons 13–11–3 .... Capt G N Bennet 100–6
Sir M McAlpine's Shaun Spadah 12–12–7 .... F B Rees 20–1
Maj C Dewhurst's Conjuror II 11–11–0 .... Mr C P Dewhurst 100–6
3l, 6l. 9m 36s. 28 ran. Trained G Blackwell
1924 Ld Airlie's Master Robert ch g by Moorside II 11–10–5 .... R Trudgill 25–1
Mr T K Laidlaw's Fly Mask 10–10–12 .... J Moylan 100–7
Mr W H Midwood's Silvo 8–12–2 .... G Goswell 100–7
4l, 6l. 9m 40s. 30 ran. Trained Hon A Hastings
1925 Mr D Goold's Double Chance ch g by Roi Herode or Day Comet 9–10–9 .... Maj J P Wilson 100–9
Mrs W H Dixon's Old Tay Bridge 11–11–12 .... J R Anthony 9–1fav
Mr T K Laidlaw's Fly Mask 11–11–11 .... E C Doyle 10–1
4l, 6l. 9m 42$^{3}/_{5}$s. 33 ran. Trained F Archer
1926 Mr A C Schwartz's Jack Horner ch g by Cyllius 9–10–5 .... W Watkinson 25–1
Mrs W H Dixon's Old Tay Bridge 12–12–2 .... J R Anthony 8–1
Mr S Sanford's Bright Boy 7–11–8 .... E Doyle 25–1
3l, 1l. 9m 36s. 30 ran. Trained H Leader
1927 Mrs M Partridge's Sprig ch g by Marco 10–12–4 .... T E Leader 8–1fav
Mr G W Pennington's Bovril III 9–10–12 .... Owner 100–1
Mr S Sanford's Bright Boy 8–12–27 .... J R Anthony 100–7
1l, same. 10m 20$^{1}/_{5}$s. 37 ran. Trained T Leader
1928 Mr H S Kenyon's Tipperary Tim b g by Cipango 10–10–0 ..... Mr W P Dutton 100–1
Mr H Bruce's Billy Barton 10–10–11 .... T Cullinan 33–1
Distance; only two finished. 10m 23$^{3}/_{5}$s. 42 ran. Trained J J Dodd
1929 Mrs M A Gemmell's Gregalach ch g by My Prince 7–11–4 .... R Everett 100–1
Mr J H Whitney's Easter Hero 9–12–7 .... J Moloney 9–2fav
Mr R McAlpine's Richmond II 6–10–6 .... W Stott 40–1
6l, bad. 9m 47$^{3}/_{5}$s. 66 ran. Trained T R Leader
1930 Mr W H Midwood's Shaun Goilin ch g sire's ped unknown 10–11–7 .... T Cullinan 100–8
Mr W Wilson's Melleray's Belle 11–10–0 .... J Mason 20–1
Mr J H Whitney's Sir Lindsay 9–10–6 .... D Williams 100–7
Nk, 1$^{1}/_{2}$l. 9m 40$^{3}/_{5}$s. 41 ran. Trained F Hartigan
1931 Mr C R Taylor's Grakle b g by Jackdaw 9–11–7 .... R Lyall 100–6
Mrs M A Gemmell's Gregalach 9–12–0 .... J Moloney 25–1
Lady Glenapp's Annandale 9–10–7 .... T Morgan 100–1
1$^{1}/_{2}$l, 10l. 9m 32$^{4}/_{5}$s. 43 ran. Trained T Coulthwaite
1932 Mr W Parsonage's Forbra br g by Foresight 7–10–7 .... J Hamey 50–1
Mrs Ireland's Egremont 8–10–7 .... Mr E C Paget 33–1
Mr W H Midwood's Shaun Goilin 12–12–4 .... D Williams 40–1
3l, bad. 9m 44$^{3}/_{5}$s. 36 ran. Trained T R Rimell
1933 Mrs F Ambrose Clarke's Kellsboro' Jack b g by Jackdaw 7–11–9 ... D Williams 25–1
Maj Noel Furlong's Really True 9–10–12 .... Mr F Furlong 66–1
Mr G S L Whitelaw's Slater 8–10–7 .... Mr M Barry 50–1
3l, nk. 9m 28s. 34 ran. Trained I Anthony
1934 Miss D Paget's Golden Miller b g by Goldcourt 7–12–2 .... G Wilson 8–1
Mr J B Snow's Delaneige 9–11–6 .... J Moloney 100–7
Mr J H Whitney's Thomond II 8–12–4 .... W Speck 18–1
5l, same. 9m 20$^{2}/_{5}$s. 30 ran. Trained A Briscoe
1935 Maj N Furlong's Reynoldstown br or bl g by My Prince 8–11–4 .... Mr F Furlong 22–1
Lady Lindsay's Blue Prince 7–10–7 .... W Parvin 40–1
Mr J H Whitney's Thomond II 9–11–13 .... W Speck 9–2
3l, 8l. 9m 21s. 27 ran. Trained by Owner

1936 Maj N Furlong's Reynoldstown br or bl g
by My Prince 9-12-2
.....................Mr F Walwyn 10-1
Sir D Llewellyn's Ego 9-10-8
.....................Mr H Llewellyn 50-1
Mr James V Rank's Bachelor Prince
9-10-9 ....J Fawcus 66-1
12l, 6l. 9m 37s. 35 ran. Trained by Owner
1937 Mr H Lloyd Thomas's Royal Mail bl g by
My Prince 8-11-13 ....E Williams 100-6
Mr James V Rank's Cooleen 9-11-4
.....................J Fawcus 33-1
Mr E W W Bailey's Pucka Belle 11-10-7
.....................Owner 100-6
3l, 10l. 9m 59³/₅s. 33 ran. Trained I Anthony
1938 Mrs Marion Scott's Battleship ch h by
Man o'War 11-11-6 ....D L Moore 18-1
Mr H C McNally's Royal Danieli 7-11-3
.....................J Brogan 28-1
Sir A Maguire's Workman 8-10-2
Hd, bad. 9m 29⁴/₅s. 36 ran. Trained R Hobbs
1939 Sir A Maguire's Workman br g by Cot-
tage 9-10-6 ....T Hyde 100-8
Capt L Scott-Briggs's Mac Moffat 7-10-3
.....................I Alder 25-1
Miss D Paget's Kilstar 8-10-3
.....................G Archibald 8-1fav
3l, 15l. 9m 42¹/₅s. 37 ran. Trained J Ruttle in Ireland
1940 Ld Stalbridge's Bogskar br g by Werwolf
7-10-4 ....M A Jones 25-1
Capt L Scott-Briggs's Mac Moffat
8-10-10 ....I Alder 8-1
Mr J R Neill's Gold Arrow 8-10-3
.....................P Lay 50-1
4l, 6l. 9m 20³/₅s. 30 ran. Trained by Owner
1941–1945 No race
1946 Mr J Morant's Lovely Cottage br g by
Cottage 9-10-8 ....Capt R Petre 25-1
Mr L S Elwell's Jack Finlay 7-10-2
.....................W Kidney 100-1
Mr James V Rank's Prince Regent
11-12-5 ....T Hyde 3-1fav
4l, 3l. 9m 38¹/₅s. 34 ran. Trained T Rayson
1947 Mr J J McDowell's Caughoo br g by
Within-the-Law 8-10-0 ...E Dempsey 100-1
Mrs M Rowe's Lough Conn 11-10-1
.....................D McCann 33-1
Sir A Gordon-Smith's Kami 10-10-13
.....................Mr J Hislop 33-1
20l, 4l. 10m 3¹/₅s. 57 ran. Trained H McDowell, in Ireland
1948 Mr J Proctor's Sheila's Cottage b m by
Cottage 9-10-7 ....A P Thompson 50-1
Maj D J Vaughan's First of the Dandies
11-10-4 ....J Brogan 25-1
Ld Mildmay's Cromwell 7-10-11
.....................Owner 33-1
1l, 6l. 9m 25²/₅s. 43 ran. Trained N Crump
1949 Mr W F Williamson's Russian Hero b g by
Peter the Great 9-10-8
.....................L McMorrow 66-1
Ld Bicester's Roimond 8-11-12
.....................R Francis 22-1
Mrs M Harvey's Royal Mount 10-10-12
.....................Patrick Doyle 18-1
8l, 1l. 9m 24¹/₅s. 43 ran. Trained G Owen
1950 Mr L Brotherton's Freebooter b g by
Steel-point 9-11-11 ....J Power 10-1 co-f
Capt T D Wilson's Wot No Sun 8-11-8
.....................A P Thompson 100-7
Mrs J S Gorman's Acthon Major 10-11-2
.....................R O'Ryan 33-1
15l, 10l. 9m 24¹/₅s. 49 ran. Trained R Renton
1951 Mr J Royle's Nickel Coin b m by Pay Up
9-10-1 ....J A Bullock 40-1
Mrs M H Keogh's Royal Tan 7-10-13
.....................Mr A O'Brien 22-1
Mr P Digney's Derrinstown 11-10-0
.....................A Power 66-1

Won by 6l; Derrinstown fell, was remounted, and finished a bad third. 9m 48⁴/₅s. 36 ran. Trained J O'Donoghue
1952 Mr H Lane's Teal b g by Bimco 10-10-12
.....................A P Thompson 100-7
Miss D Paget's Legal Joy 9-10-4
.....................M Scudamore 100-6
Capt T D Wilson's Wot No Sun 10-11-7
.....................D V Dick 33-1
5l, bad 3rd. 9m 20²/₅s. 47 ran. Trained N Crump
1953 Mr J H Griffin's Early Mist ch g by Bru-
meux 8-11-12 ....B Marshall 20-1
Miss D Paget's Mont Tremblant 7-12-5
.....................D V Dick 18-1
Ld Sefton's Irish Lizard 10-10-6
.....................R Turnell 33-1
20l, 4l. 9m 22⁴/₅s. 31 ran. Trained M V O'Brien in Ireland
1954 Mr J H Griffin's Royal Tan ch g by Tarton
10-11-7 ....B Marshall 8-1
Mrs E Truelove's Tudor Line 9-10-17
.....................G Slack 10-1
Ld Sefton's Irish Lizard 11-10-5
.....................M Scudamore 15-2fav
Nk, 10l. 9m 32⁴/₅s. 29 ran. Trained M V O'Brien in Ireland
1955 Mrs W H E Welman's Quare Times b g
by Artist's Son 9-11-0 ....P Taaffe 100-9
Mrs E Truelove's Tudor Line 10-11-3
.....................G Slack 10-1
Mr D J Coughlan's Carey's Cottage
8-10-11 ....T Taaffe 20-1
12l, 4l. 10m 19¹/₅s. 30 ran. Trained M V O'Brien in Ireland
1956 Mrs L Carver's E.S.B. b or br g by Bidar
10-11-3 ....D V Dick 100-7
Mr J J Straker's Gentle Moya 10-10-2
.....................G Milburn 22-1
Prince Aly Khan's Royal Tan 12-12-1
.....................T Taaffe 28-1
10l, same. 9m 21²/₅s. 29 ran. Trained T F Rimell
1957 Mrs G Kohn's Sundew, ch g by Sun King
11-11-7 ....F Winter 20-1
Miss R M P Wilkinson's Wyndburgh
7-10-7 ....M Batchelor 25-1
Mr E R Courage's Tiberetta 9-10-0
.....................A Oughton 66-1
8l, 6l. 9m 42²/₅s. 35 ran. Trained F Hudson
1958 Mr D J Coughlan's Mr What b g by
Grand Inquisitor 8-10-6 ...A Freeman 18-1
Mr E R Courage's Tiberetta 10-10-6
.....................G Slack 28-1
Ld Cadogan's Green Drill 8-10-10
.....................G Milburn 28-1
30l, 15l. 9m 59⁴/₅s. 31 ran. Trained T J Taaffe in Ireland
1959 Mr J E Bigg's Oxo b g by Bobsleigh
8-10-13 ....M Scudamore 8-1
Mrs J K M Oliver's Wyndburgh 9-10-12
.....................T Brookshaw 10-1
Mr D J Coughlan's Mr What 9-11-9
.....................T Taaffe 6-1fav
1¹/₂l, 8l. 9m 37⁴/₅s. 34 ran. Trained W Stephenson
1960 Miss W H S Wallace's Merryman II b g by
Carnival Boy 9-10-12 ....G Scott 13-2fav
Ld Leverhulme's Badanloch 10-10-9
.....................S Mellor 100-7
Mr B Sunley's Clear Profit 10-10-1
.....................B Wilkinson 20-1
15l, 2l. 9m 27s. 26 ran. Trained N Crump
1961 Mr C Vaughan's Nicolaus Silver gr g by
Nicolaus 9-10-1 ....H Beasley 28-1
Miss W H S Wallace's Merryman II
10-11-12 ....D Ancil 8-1
Mrs S Elliott's O'Malley Point 10-11-4
.....................P Farrell 100-6
5l, nk. 9m 22¹/₅s. 35 ran. Trained T F Rimell
1962 Mr N Cohen's Kilmore b g by Zalophus
12-10-4 ....F Winter 28-1
Mrs J K M Oliver's Wyndburgh 12-10-9
.....................T Barnes 45-1

Mr G V Keeling's Mr What 12-10-9 .... J Lehane 22-1
10l, same. 9m 50s. 32 ran. Trained Ryan Price
1963 Mr P B Raymond's Ayala ch g by Super-
tello 9-10-0 .... P Buckley 66-1
Mr G Kindersley's Carrickbeg 7-10-3 .... Mr J Lawrence 20-1
Mr W Stephenson's Hawa's Song 10-10-0 .... P Broderick 28-1
¾l, 5l. 9m 35⅕s. 47 ran. K Piggott
1964 Mr J K Goodman's Team Spirit b g by Vulgan 12-10-3 .... G W Robinson 18-1
Mr T Beattie's Purple Silk 9-10-4 .... J Kenneally 100-6
Mrs F Williams's Peacetown 10-10-1 .... R Edwards 40-1
¹/₁l. 6l. 9m 47s. 33 ran. F Walwyn
1965 Mrs M Stephenson's Jay Trump b g by Tonga Prince 8-11-5 ..... Mr C Smith 100-6
Mr R R Tweedie's Freddie 8-11-10 .... P McCarron 7-2fav
Mr C D Collins's Mr Jones 10-11-5 .... Mr C Collins 50-1
¹/₁l, 20l. 9m 30¹/₁s. 47 ran. F T Winter
1966 Mr S Levy's Anglo ch g by Greek Star 8-10-0 .... T Norman 50-1
Mr R R Tweedie's Freddie 9-11-7 .... P McCarron 11-4fav
Mrs D Thompson's Forest Prince 8-10-8 .... G Scott 100-7
20l, 5l. 9m 52¹/₁s. 47 ran. F T Winter
1967 Mr C P T Watkins's Foinavon br g by Vulgan 9-10-0 .... J Buckingham 100-1
Mr C Pugh's Honey End 10-10-4 .... J Gifford 15-2fav
Mr J Manners's Red Alligator 8-10-0 .... B Fletcher 50-1
15l, 3l. 9m 49¹/₁s. 44 ran. J H Kempton
1968 Mr J Manners's Red Alligator ch g by Magic Red 9-10-0 ...... B Fletcher 100-7
Miss P Harrower's Moidore's Token 11-10-8 .... B Brogan 100-6
Mr Gregory Peck's Different Class 8-11-5 .... D Mould 17-2fav
20l, nk. 9m 28¹/₁s. 45 ran. Denys Smith
1969 Mr T H McKoy jun's Highland Wedding br g by Question 12-10-4 .. E P Harty 100-9
Mr J L Drabble's Steel Bridge 11-10-0 .... R Pitman 50-1
Mr A B Mitchell's Rondetto 13-10-6 .... J King 25-1
12l, 1l. 9m 29¹/₁s. 30 ran. G Balding
1970 Mr A Chambers's Gay Trip b g by Vulgan 8-11-5 .... P Taaffe 15-1
Gen R K Mellon's Vulture 9-10-0 .... S Barker 15-1
Mrs W Macaulay's Miss Hunter 9-10-0 .... F Shortt 33-1
20l, ¹/₁l. 9m 38s. 28 ran T F Rimell
1971 Mr F Pontin's Specify br g by Specific 9-10-13 .... J Cook 28-1
Mrs J Watney's Black Secret 7-11-5 .... Mr J Dreaper 20-1
Mr B Jenks's Astbury 8-10-0 .. J Bourke 33-1
Nk, 2l. 9m 34¹/₁s. 38 ran. J E Sutcliffe
1972 Capt T Forster's Well To Do ch g by Phebus 9-10-1 .... G Thorner 14-1
Mr A Chambers's Gay Trip 11-11-9 .... T Biddlecombe 12-1
Mrs J Watney's Black Secret 8-11-2 .... S Barker 14-1
and
Mrs E Newman's General Symons 9-10-0 .... P Kiely 40-1
dead-heated for third place
2l, 3l. 10m 8¹/₁s. 42 ran. Capt T Forster
1973 Mr N Le Mare's Red Rum b g by Quorum 8-10-5 .... B Fletcher 9-1co-f
Sir C Manifold's Crisp (Aus) 10-12-0 .... R Pitman 9-1co-f

Mr R Guest's L'Escargot 10-12-0 .... T Carberry 11-1
¾l, 25l. 9m 1·9s. 38 ran. D McCain
1974 Mr N Le Mare's Red Rum b g by Quorum 9-12-0 .... B Fletcher 11-1
Mr R Guest's L'Escargot 11-11-13 .... T Carberry 17-2
Lt-Col P Bengough's Charles Dickens 10-10-0 .... A Turnell 50-1
7l, sht. hd. 9m 20·50s. 42 ran. D McCain
1975 Mr R Guest's L'Escargot ch g by Escart III 12-11-3 .... T Carberry 13-2
Mr N Le Mare's Red Rum 10-12-0 .... B Fletcher 7-2fav
Mr E Courage's Spanish Steps 12-10-3 .... W Smith 20-1
15l, 8l. 9m 31·10s. 31 ran. D L Moore in Ireland
1976 Mr P B Raymond's Rag Trade ch g by Menelek 10-10-12 .... J Burke 14-1
Mr N Le Mare's Red Rum 11-11-10 .... T Stack 10-1
Mr J Bosley's Eyecatcher 10-10-7 .... B Fletcher 28-1
2l, 8l. 9m 20·90s. 32 ran. T F Rimell
1977 Mr N Le Mare's Red Rum b g by Quorum 12-11-8 .... T Stack 9-1
Mr B Arnold's Churchtown Boy 10-10-0 .... M Blackshaw 20-1
Mr J Bosley's Eyecatcher 11-10-1 .... C Read 18-1
25l, 5l. 9m 30·30s. 42 ran. D McCain
1978 Mrs D Whitaker's Lucius b g by Perhapsburg 9-10-9 .... B R Davies 14-1
Mr R Jeffrey's Sebastian V 10-10-1 .... R Lamb 25-1
Mrs G St John Nolan's Drumroan 10-10-0 .... G Newman 50-1
¼l, nk. 9m 33·90s. 37 ran. G W Richards
1979 Mr J Douglas's Rubstic br g by I Say 10-10-0 .... M Barnes 25-1
Mr D Montagu's Zongalero 9-10-5 .... B R Davies 20-1
Mr L Dormer's Rough and Tumble 9-10-7 .... J Francombe 14-1
1¹/₁l, 5l. 9m 53s. 34 ran. S J Leadbetter
1980 Mr R C Stewart's Ben Nevis ch g by Casmiri 12-10-12 .... Mr C Fenwick 40-1
Mr L Dormer's Rough and Tumble 10-10-11 .... J Francome 11-1
Mrs G Poole's The Pilgarlic 12-10-4 .... R Hyett 33-1
20l, 10l. 10m 17·40s. 30 ran. Capt T Forster
1981 Mr S Embiricos's Aldaniti ch g by Derek H 11-10-13 .... R Champion 10-1
Mr M J Thorne's Spartan Missile 9-11-5 .... Mr M J Thorne 8-1
Mr John Murray Begg's Royal Mail (NZ) 11-11-7 .... P Blacker 16-1
4l, 2l. 9m 47·20s. 39 ran. J Gifford
1982 Mr F Gilman's Grittar b g by Grisaille 9-11-5 .... Mr C Saunders 7-1fav
Lady Wates's Hard Outlook 11-10-1 .... A Webber 50-1
Mr A Nettley's Loving Words 10-10-11 .... R Hoare 16-1
15l, Distance. 9m 12.6s. 39 ran. Owner
1983 Mr B R H Burrough's Corbiere ch g by Harwell 8-11-4 .... B de Haan 13-1
Mrs N Todd's Greasepaint 8-10-7 .... Mr C Magnier 14-1
Mr N Keane's Yer Man 8-10-0 .... T V O'Neill 80-1
¾l, 20l. 9m 47·4s. 41 ran. Mrs J Pitman
1984 Mr Richard Shaw's Hallo Dandy b g by Menelek 10-10-2 .... N Doughty 13-1
Mr M W J Smurfit's Greasepaint 9-11-12 .... T Carmody 9-1
Mr B R H Burrough's Corbiere 9-12-0 .... B de Haan 16-1
4l, 1¹/₁l. 9m 21·4s. 40 ran. G W Richards

1985 Anne, Duchess of Westminster's Last
Suspect b or br g by Above Suspicion
11–10–5 .... H Davies — 50–1
Mr A Greenwood's Mr Snugfit 8–10–0
.... P Tuck — 12–1
Mr B R H Burrough's Corbiere 10–11–10
.... P Scudamore — 9–1
1¹/₄l; 3l. 9m 42·7s. 40 ran. Capt T Forster
1986 Mr P Luff's West Tip b g by Gala Perfor-
mance 9–10–11 .... R Dunwoody — 15–2
Mr J B Russell's Young Driver 9–10–0
.... C Grant — 66–1
Cheveley Park Stud's Classified 10–10–3
.... S Smith Eccles — 22–1
2l, 20l, 9m 33s. 40 ran. M Oliver
1987 Mr H J Joel's Maori Venture ch g by St
Columbus 11–10–13 ...... S C Knight — 28–1
Major I C Straker's The Tsarevich
11–10–5 .... J White — 20–1
Mrs W Tulloch's Lean Ar Aghaidh
10–10–0 .... G Landau — 14–1
5l, 4l, 9m 19·3s. 40 ran. A Turnell
1988 Miss J Reed's Rhyme 'N' Reason b g by
Kemal, 9–11–0 .... B Powell — 10–1
Mr R Oxley's Durham Edition 10–10–9
.... C Grant — 20–1
Mr J Meagher's Monanore 11–10–4
.... T Taaffe — 33–1
4l; 15l. 9m 53·5s. 40 ran. D Elsworth
1989 Mr E Harvey's Little Polveir b g by Cantab, 12–10–3 .... J Frost — 28–1
Mr P Luff's West Tip 12–10–11
.... R Dunwoody — 12–1
TPM McDonagh Ltd's The Thinker
11–11–10 .... S Sherwood — 10–1
7l; ¹/₄l. 10m 6·80s. 40 ran. G B Balding
1990 Mr H Duffey's Mr Frisk ch g by Bivouac
11–10–6 .... Mr M Armytage — 16–1
Mr R Oxley's Durham Edition 12–10–9
.... C Grant — 9–1
Mr A Proos's Rinus 9–10–4 .. N Doughty — 13–1
³/₄l, 20l. 8m 47·8s (record). 38 ran. K Bailey
1991 Sir Eric Parker's Seagram (NZ) ch g by
Balak 11–10–6 .... N Hawke — 12–1

Autofour Engineering's Garrison Savan-
nah 8–11–1 .... M Pitman — 7–1
Mrs R Wilson's Auntie Dot 10–10–4
.... M Dwyer — 50–1
5l, 8l, 9m 29.9s. 40 ran. D H Barons
1992 Mrs D Thompson's Party Politics br g by
Politico 8–10–7 .... C Llewellyn — 14–1
Mr L J Garrett's Romany King 8–10–3
.... R Guest — 16–1
Mr J P McManus's Laura's Beau 8–10–0
.... C O'Dwyer — 12–1
2¹/₄l, 15l. 9m 6·3s. 40 ran. N A Gaselee
1993 Race declared void after two false starts.
39 starters
1994 Mr Freddie Starr's Miinnehoma b or br g
by Kambalda 11–10–8 ..R Dunwoody — 16–1
Mr H T Cole's Just So 11–10–3
.... S Burrough — 20–1
Mr K G Manley's Moorcroft Boy 9–10–0
.... A Maguire — 5–1 fav
1¹/₄l, 20l, 10m 18·8s. 36 ran. M C Pipe
1995 Messrs G & L Johnson's Royal Athlete ch
g by Roselier 12–10–6 .... J Titley — 40–1
Mrs D Thompson's Party Politics 11–10–2
.... M Dwyer — 16–1
Mr G Tobitt's Over The Deel 9–10–0
.... Mr C Bonner — 100–1
7l, 6l, 9m 4s. 35 ran. Mrs J Pitman
1996 Mr A T A Wates's Rough Quest b g by
Crash Course 10–10–7 M A Fitzgerald — 7–1 fav
Mr V Nally's Encore un Peu (FR) 9–10–0
.... D Bridgwater — 14–1
Mr P McGrane's Superior Finish 10–10–3
.... R Dunwoody — 9–1
1¹/₄l, 16l, 9m 0·8s. 27 ran. T Casey
1997 Mr Stanley W Clarke's Lord Gyllene (NZ)
b g by Ring the Bell (NZ) 9–10–0
.... A Dobbin — 14–1
Uplands Bloodstock's Suny Bay 8–10–3
.... J Osborne — 8–1
Mr Michael Gates' Camelot Knight
11–10–0................. C Llewellyn — 100–1
25l, 2l, 9m 5.8s. 36 ran. S A Brookshaw

STAKIS CASINOS SCOTTISH GRAND NATIONAL (Ayr)

(4 miles 1 fur)
(First run 1867)
1920 Music Hall 7y 11st 11lb (9)
1921 No race
1922 Sergeant Murphy 12y 11st 7lb (15)
1923 Harrismith 8y 11st 11lb (13)
1924 Royal Chancellor 9y 11st (18)
1925 Gerald L 11y 12st 6lb (11)
1926 Estuna 8y 9st 11lb (18)
1927 Estuna 9y 11st 11lb (12)
1928 Ardeen 11y 11st 1lb (23)
1929 Donzelon 8y 11st 5lb (21)
1930 Drintyre 7y 11st 5lb (15)
1931 Annandale 9y 10st 5lb (10)
1932 Clydesdale 6y 11st 3lb (15)
1933 Libourg 7y 10st 10lb (21)
1934 Southern Hero 9y 11st 5lb (9)
1935 Kellsboro' Jack 9y 11st 10lb (6)
1936 Southern Hero 11y 11st 7lb (10)
1937 Rightun 7y 11st 10lb (14)
1938 Young Mischief 7y 9st 11lb (10)
1939 Southern Hero 14y 12st 3lb (11)
1940–46 No race
1947 Rowland Roy 8y 11st 2lb (15)
1948 Magnetic Fin 9y 10st 5lb (12)
1949 Wot No Sun 7y 11st 5lb (10)
1950 Sanvina 10y 12st 2lb (19)
1951 Court Painter 11y 9st 7lb (13)
1952 Flagrant Mac 8y 11st 12lb (17)
1953 Queen's Taste 7y 10st 2lb (21)
1954 Queen's Taste 8y 10st 9lb (15)
1955 Bar Point 8y 10st 2lb (18)
1956 Queen's Taste 10y 11st (14)
1957 Bremontier 10y 10st 12lb (13)
1958 Game Field 8y 11st 10lb (14)
1959 Merryman II 8y 10st 12lb (18)
1960 Fincham 8y 10st (8)
1961 Kinmont Wullie 7y 10st 7lb (18)

1962 Sham Fight 10y 10st (18)
1963 Pappageno's Cottage 8y 10st 9lb (18)
1964 Popham Down 7y 10st (14)
1965 Brasher 9y 10st 5lb (9)
1966 African Patrol 7y 10st 7lb (17)
1967 The Fossa 10y 9st 12lb (18)
1968 Arcturus 7y 10st 4lb (10)
1969 Playlord 8y 12st (17)
1970 The Spaniard 8y 10st (10)
1971 Young Ash Leaf 7y 10st 2lb (21)
1972 Quick Reply 7y 9st 9lb (17)
1973 Esban 9y 9st 11lb (21)
1974 Red Rum 9y 11st 13lb (17)
1975 Barona 9y 9st 10lb (17)
1976 Barona 10y 10st (23)
1977 Sebastian V 9y 10st 2lb (18)
1978 King Con 9y 9st 13lb (21)
1979 Fighting Fit 7y 10st 10lb (19)
1980 Salkeld 8y 10st (23)
1981 Astral Charmer 8y 9st 10lb (21)
1982 Cockle Strand 9y 9st 11lb (15)
1983 Canton 9y 10st 2lb (22)
1984 Androma 7y 10st (19)
1985 Androma 8y 10st (18)
1986 Hardy Lad 9y 10st (24)
1987 Little Polveir 10y 10st (11)
1988 Mighty Mark 9y 10st 4lb (17)
1989 Roll-A-Joint 11y 10st (11)
1990 Four Trix 9y 10st (28)
1991 Killone Abbey 8y 10st (18)
1992 Captain Dibble 7y 11st (21)
1993 Run For Free 9y 11st 10lb (21)
1994 Earth Summit 6y 10st (22)
1995 Willsford 12y 10st 12lb (22)
1996 Moorcroft Boy 11y 10st 2lb (20)
1997 Belmont King 9y 11st 10lb (17)

Run over 3 miles 7 fur at Bogside from 1867 to 1965

WHITBREAD GOLD CUP (Sandown)

(3 miles 5 fur 110 yds)
1957 Much Obliged 9y 10st 12lb (24)
1958 Taxidermist 6y 10st 8lb (31)
1959 Done Up 9y 10st 13lb (23)
1960 Plummers Plain 7y 10st (21)
1961 Pas Seul 8y 12st (23)
1962 Frenchman's Cove 7y 11st 3lb (22)
1963 Hoodwinked 8y 10st 9lb (32)
1964 Dormant 7y 9st 7lb (11)
1965 Arkle 8y 12st 7lb (7)
1966 What A Myth 9y 9st 8lb (8)
1967 Mill House 10y 11st 11lb (13)
1968 Larbawn 9y 10st 9lb (16)
1969 Larbawn 10y 11st 4lb (18)
1970 Royal Toss 8y 10st (17)
1971 Titus Oates 9y 11st 13lb (18)
1972 Grey Sombrero 8y 9st 10lb (28)
1973†Charlie Potheen 8y 12st (21)
1974 The Dikler 11y 11st 13lb (16)
1975 April Seventh 9y 9st 13lb (12)
1976 Otter Way 8y 10st 10lb (14)
1977 Andy Pandy 8y 10st 12lb (15)
1978 Strombolus 7y 10st (15)
1979 Diamond Edge 8y 11st 11lb (14)
1980 Royal Mail (NZ) 10y 11st 5lb (12)
1981 Diamond Edge 10y 11st 7lb (18)
1982 Shady Deal 9y 10st (9)
1983 Drumlargan 9y 10st 10lb (15)
1984 Special Cargo 11y 11st 2lb (13)
1985 By The Way 7y 10st (20)
1986 Plundering 9y 10st 6lb (16)
1987 Lean Ar Aghaidh 10y 9st 10lb (9)
1988 Desert Orchid 9y 11st 11lb (12)
1989 Brown Windsor 7y 10st (18)
1990 Mr Frisk 11y 10st 5lb (13)
1991 Docklands Express 9y 10st 3lb (10)
1992 Topsham Bay 9y 10st 1lb (11)
1993 Topsham Bay 10y 10st 1lb (13)
1994 Ushers Island 8y 10st (12)
1995 Cache Fleur (FR) 9y 10st 1lb (14)
1996 Life of A Lord 10y 11st 10lb (17)
1997 Harwell Lad 8y 10st (9)

†Run at Newcastle over 3m 6f

Season Leaders 1996–97

TOP 25 OWNERS
(Prize Money Order)

H = Horses R = Runners W = Winners 2 = 2nd 3 = 3rd
%W-R = Percentage of winners to runners £ Win = Win Money £ £ W/P = Win/Place Money £

	H	R	W	2	3	%W-R	£ Win	£ W/P
Ogden, Robert	28	142	42	24	17	29.6	201,500	283,986
Deal, P A	4	15	6	1	1	40.0	245,392	256,553
Clarke, Stanley W	7	37	8	5	5	21.6	224,760	246,901
Johnson, D A	11	52	18	8	7	34.6	158,983	225,379
Hubbard, G A	22	78	11	7	10	14.1	109,099	158,681
Worcester, Michael & Gerry	11	24	3	4	3	12.5	139,506	150,905
Uplands Bloodstock	17	51	6	5	7	11.8	64,321	138,642
Hales, J	3	14	5	6	1	35.7	105,083	136,694
Mould, Mrs J	11	45	5	7	5	11.1	54,287	135,243
Hartigan, P J	1	3	2	0	0	66.7	129,110	129,110
Stewart-Brown, B T	9	28	6	4	0	21.4	80,747	120,929
Green, Mr & Mrs Raymond Anderson	24	101	16	16	19	15.8	96,151	116,016
Vestey, Lord	5	16	6	3	5	37.5	87,098	112,300
Martin Pipe Racing Club	24	106	25	14	12	23.6	78,759	107,438
Harris , Lady	8	27	8	6	3	29.6	60,465	84,556
Murray, Mrs E A	2	7	4	0	1	57.1	83,995	84,366
Dennis, Mrs Jill	2	11	5	0	0	45.5	81,566	81,976
McManus, J P	12	24	2	3	2	8.3	58,142	80,539
Bowen, P	1	23	10	5	2	43.5	64,299	78,149
Queally, Mrs E	1	4	2	1	1	50.0	49,148	76,587
Blackshaw, James	2	5	4	0	0	80.0	68,689	68,689
Sturt, W E	7	25	9	5	1	36.0	43,286	68,644
Wellstead, H	3	11	3	1	2	27.3	66,428	68,556
Broadhurst, Miss Jean & Archer, Matt	4	24	6	4	2	25.0	51,940	67,456
Tory, R J	3	8	2	1	1	25.0	44,616	66,440

TOP 25 TRAINERS
(Prize Money Order)

H = Horses R = Runners W = Winners 2 = 2nd 3 = 3rd
%W-R = Percentage of winners to runners £ Win = Win Money £ £ W/P = Win/Place Money £

	H	R	W	2	3	%W-R	£ Win	£ W/P
Pipe, M C	161	820	212	121	104	25.9	1,048,373	1,362,652
Nicholson, D	103	391	100	75	61	25.6	596,701	1,020,092
Richards, G	65	292	74	39	35	25.3	429,581	592,699
Reveley, Mrs M	97	386	87	69	48	22.5	337,175	460,617
Bailey, K C	98	382	77	59	41	20.2	296,591	422,828
Twiston-Davies, N A	92	362	52	48	30	14.4	221,668	382,806
Nicholls, P F	66	279	56	53	35	20.1	262,722	359,402
Henderson, N J	93	303	58	45	32	19.1	225,332	349,935
Hobbs, P J	96	384	64	47	47	16.7	247,308	349,523
Forster, Capt T A	61	187	36	36	24	19.3	269,485	324,453
Sherwood, O	63	243	49	36	32	20.2	242,828	316,884
Brooks, C P E	57	208	27	28	28	13.0	164,456	303,904
Knight, Miss H C	87	306	47	44	36	15.4	218,780	300,018

Brookshaw, S A	23	76	15	11	9	19.7	242,318	270,361
Smith, Mrs S J	52	274	42	44	42	15.3	158,437	253,998
Alner, R H	55	208	24	36	28	11.5	173,906	252,102
Gifford, J T	67	254	41	41	25	16.1	173,678	249,894
Hammond, M D	88	364	47	56	46	12.9	151,115	243,334
Bowen, P	29	158	33	20	19	20.9	175,565	217,574
FitzGerald, J G	43	169	29	24	26	17.2	149,702	202,418
Gandolfo, D R	49	201	30	42	30	14.9	108,596	200,963
Webber, P R	42	151	27	13	21	17.9	122,872	177,453
Easterby, T D	32	153	32	22	18	20.9	132,570	176,816
Chance, Noel T	19	47	9	8	4	19.1	155,102	170,387
Johnson, J Howard	54	217	23	27	19	10.6	102,509	164,843

TOP 25 JOCKEYS
(Winners Order)

M = Mounts   W = Winners   2 = 2nd   3 = 3rd   F = Fell
%W-R = Percentage of winners to runners   £ Win = Win Money £   £ W/P = Win/Place Money £

	M	W	2	3	F	%W-R	£ Win	£ W/P
McCoy, A P	665	190	130	78	26	28.6	1,025,885	1,288,915
Osborne, J	530	131	82	63	13	24.7	847,025	1,150,431
Dunwoody, R	558	111	101	70	26	19.9	779,965	1,112,793
Johnson, R	564	102	78	91	22	18.1	414,173	648,012
Williamson, N	530	85	71	66	31	16.0	508,189	758,405
Niven, P	379	84	57	50	12	22.2	316,246	421,353
Fitzgerald, M A	445	82	61	53	17	18.4	315,866	481,608
Maguire, A	398	81	72	61	25	20.4	367,732	546,812
Dobbin, A	393	73	52	46	12	18.6	474,961	634,476
Bridgwater, D	389	69	47	49	12	17.7	255,010	338,201
Garritty, R	354	62	66	51	8	17.5	221,605	351,358
Carberry, P	249	61	40	29	8	24.5	240,296	337,688
Llewellyn, C	411	57	42	48	13	13.9	297,041	431,639
Maude, C	359	56	45	37	15	15.3	238,333	352,477
Guest, Richard	322	50	47	41	14	15.5	843,369	946,553
Supple, R	337	49	39	43	15	14.5	163,499	227,599
Storey, B	398	48	48	49	16	12.1	225,553	299,122
Thornton, A	454	38	66	55	30	8.4	117,260	243,984
Powell, B	451	36	43	49	12	8.0	160,261	242,097
*Fenton, B	404	35	55	44	15	8.7	113,677	196,887
*Walsh, D	272	35	26	26	12	12.9	132,272	237,022
Hide, P	141	35	23	16	8	24.8	130,976	172,257
Bradley, G	261	33	40	37	7	12.6	136,067	244,232
Culloty, J	240	32	22	24	10	13.3	108,051	158,248
†Thornton, Mr A	304	30	41	50	7	9.9	159,337	242,928

* Leading Conditionals   † Leading Amateur

Abandoned Meetings

1996

Fri	Aug	9	Plumpton	Abandoned after 5th race due to slippery nature of course
Mon	Sep	2	Hexham	Abandoned after 1st race due to slippery state of course
Tue	Nov	19	Wetherby	Heavy Snow
Thur	Nov	21	Sedgefield	Course Snowbound
Sat	Nov	23	Market Rasen	Frost
Mon	Nov	25	Catterick	Snow on the course
Thur	Nov	28	Carlisle	Frost
			Uttoxeter	Frost
Thur	Dec	5	Leicester	Fog
Sat	Dec	14	Haydock	Frost
Tue	Dec	17	Southwell	Fog
Mon	Dec	23	Kelso	Frost
Thur	Dec	26	Ayr	Frost
			Hereford	Frost
			Huntingdon	Frost
			Market Rasen	Frost
			Newton Abbot	Frost
			Sedgefield	Frost
			Wetherby	Frost
			Wincanton	Frost
			Wolverhampton	Frost
Fri	Dec	27	Chepstow	Frost
			Kempton	Frost
			Leicester	Frost
			Wetherby	Frost
Sat	Dec	28	Folkestone	Frost
			Huntingdon	Frost
			Newbury	Frost
			Newcastle	Frost
Sun	Dec	29	Limerick	Frost
Mon	Dec	30	Carlisle	Frost
			Newbury	Frost
			Plumpton	Frost
			Stratford	Frost
Tue	Dec	31	Catterick	Frost
			Fontwell	Frost and Snow
			Taunton	Frost
			Warwick	Frost
			Punchestown	Snow

1997

Wed	Jan	1	Catterick	Frost
			Cheltenham	Frost
			Exeter	Frost
			Leicester	Frost
			Uttoxeter	Frost
			Windsor	Frost
			Fairyhouse	Snow

			Tramore	Snow
Thur	Jan	2	Ayr	Frost
			Market Rasen	Snow
Fri	Jan	3	Lingfield	Frost and Snow
			Sedgefield	Frost and Snow
			Towcester	Frost and Snow
Sat	Jan	4	Haydock	Frost and Snow
			Musselburgh	Frost
			Sandown	Frost
			Warwick	Frost and Snow
			Naas	Snow
Mon	Jan	6	Folkestone	Frost and Snow
Tue	Jan	7	Leicester	Frost and Snow
			Punchestown	Snow
Wed	Jan	8	Kelso	Snow
			Plumpton	Frost
Thur	Jan	9	Wetherby	Snow
			Wincanton	Frost
Fri	Jan	10	Ascot	Frost
Sat	Jan	11	Ascot	Frost
			Newcastle	Frost
			Warwick	Frost
Mon	Jan	13	Fontwell	Frost
Wed	Jan	15	Huntingdon	Frost
			Windsor	Frost
Wed	Jan	22	Sedgefield	Frost
Thur	Jan	30	Sedgefield	Part of course unsafe to race
Tue	Feb	11	Sedgefield	Transferred to Ayr due to drainage problem
Tue	Feb	18	Carlisle	Waterlogged
Wed	Feb	19	Sedgefield	Transferred to Hexham due to drainage problem but subsequently abandoned there because of waterlogging
Mon	Feb	24	Plumpton	Waterlogged
Tue	Mar	4	Sedgefield	Transferred to Kelso due to continued drainage problems
Sun	Mar	30	Cork (Mallow)	Postponed due to problems with the ground
Mon	Mar	31	Cork (Mallow)	Postponed due to problems with the ground
Sat	Apr	5	Aintree	Abandoned after 3rd race due to security alert and evacuation of race course
Sat	May	3	Hexham	Abandoned after 4th race due to fog

Index to Meetings

National Hunt Results 1996-97

SLIGO (IRE) (yielding)
Sunday June 2nd

1   **Yeats Maiden Hurdle (4-y-o and up) £2,740 2m.........................(2:25)**

EARP (Ire) 4-11-6 P Carberry, ... (6 to 1)	1
ADARAMANN (Ire) 4-10-8 (7*) Mr R Walsh, ... (2 to 1 fav)	2
MIGHTY TRUST (Ire) 7-11-6 W T Slattery, ... (12 to 1)	3
CORMAC LADY (Ire) 5-11-0 J K Kinane, ...(20 to 1)	4
SHINDARAM (Ire) 5-11-5 H Rogers, ... (5 to 2)	5
EIRE (Ire) 7-12-0 A Powell, ... (12 to 1)	6
MANNIX (Ire) 7-10-13 (7*) S P McCann, ... (20 to 1)	7
EMYGUY (Ire) 4-11-1 P Leech, ... (12 to 1)	8
TOUREEN LODGE (Ire) 6-10-13 (7*) L J Fleming, .. (4 to 1)	9
GORT NA SHEOTG (Ire) 7-11-1 F Woods, ... (33 to 1)	10
DOCUMMINS (Ire) 6-11-6 K F O'Brien, ... (33 to 1)	11

Dist: 2l, 9l, 1½l, 4½l. 4m 4.10s. (11 Ran).

(John O'Meara), Noel Meade

2   **N.C.F. Meats Handicap Hurdle (0-109 4-y-o and up) £3,253 2m.........(2:55)**

HAIL TO HOME (Ire) [-] 6-9-11 T Horgan, ... (5 to 2)	1
SHARLENE (Ire) [-] 5-10-4 P Carberry, ...(8 to 1)	2
YOUR THE MAN [-] 10-11-7 F Woods, ... (9 to 1)	3
RUSHEEN BAY (Ire) [-] (bl) 7-9-2 (5*) G Cotter, ...(20 to 1)	4
PRINTOUT (Ire) [-] 6-11-10 H Rogers, ... (4 to 1)	5
AITEANN (Ire) [-] 6-10-1 P L Malone, ... (12 to 1)	6
BARNAGEERA BOY (Ire) [-] 7-11-13 K F O'Brien,	
.... (2 to 1 fav)	7
PRACTICIAN (Ire) [-] 6-10-3 (7*) J M Maguire, ... (10 to 1)	pu

Dist: 9l, ½l, nk, ¾l. 3m 54.90s. (8 Ran).

(M O Cullinane), M O Cullinane

3   **Larkhill Beginners Chase (5-y-o and up) £2,740 2½m.......................(4:55)**

REUTER 8-11-9 P L Malone, ...(16 to 1)	1
THE ODIN LINE 7-11-9 K F O'Brien, ... (6 to 1)	2
CUBAN QUESTION 9-11-9 (5*) G Cotter, ...(10 to 1)	3
ASK THE LEADER (Ire) 7-11-4 F Woods, ... (3 to 1)	4
JUMPING FOR JOY (Ire) 7-11-9 A Powell, ... (5 to 2 fav)	5
NOELS DANCER (Ire) 6-12-0 P Carberry, ... (6 to 1)	6
DROP THE ACT (Ire) 6-11-9 S H O'Donovan, ... (12 to 1)	7
CHENE ROSE 8-10-13 (5*) T Martin, ... (12 to 1)	8
LET THE RIVER RUN 10-10-11 (7*) R P Hogan, ... (25 to 1)	9
BOLD BOREEN (Ire) 7-11-9 W T Slattery, ... (12 to 1)	10
ARDFARNIA LAD 13-11-9 T Horgan, ... (12 to 1)	pu
BUCKANEER BAY 9-11-9 H Rogers, ... (20 to 1)	pu
CARRIGANS LAD (Ire) 8-11-9 J K Kinane, ... (14 to 1)	pu

Dist: 1l, 4l, 1½l, 2l. 5m 18.00s. (13 Ran).

(Mrs Monica Cogan), F Flood

4   **Sportsmans I.N.H. Flat Race (4 & 5-y-o) £2,740 2m.........................(5:25)**

SUPREME CHARM (Ire) 4-11-1 (5*) A J Slattery, ...(10 to 1)	1
GLADIATORIAL (Ire) 4-11-6 Mr P Fenton, ...(9 to 4)	2
THE HOLY PARSON (Ire) 4-10-13 (7*) M P Cooney, (8 to 1)	3
MC CLATCHEY (Ire) 5-11-13 Mr P F Graffin, ... (8 to 1)	4
NASOWAS (Ire) 5-11-1 (7*) D W O'Sullivan, ... (7 to 4 fav)	5
SHERMAYA (Fr) 4-10-10 (5*) J Butler, ... (3 to 1)	6

Dist: 3½l, 7l, 9l, 6l. 4m 2.30s. (6 Ran).

(D M O'Meara), Michael O'Meara

TRALEE (IRE) (yielding to soft)
Sunday June 2nd

5   **Ballybeggan Racegoers Club Maiden Hurdle (4-y-o and up) £3,425 2½m (2:35)**

FLY ROSEY (Ire) 6-11-9 C F Swan, ...(10 to 9 on)	1
MISS BERTAINE (Ire) 7-11-9 T J Murphy, ...(10 to 1)	2
VAIN PRINCESS (Ire) 7-11-9 M P Hourigan, ...(9 to 2)	3
BROTHER NICHOLAS (Ire) 5-11-13 T P Treacy, ... (12 to 1)	4
LOUGH N UISCE (Ire) 6-11-6 (3*) J R Barry, ...(10 to 1)	5
DOOK'S DELIGHT (Ire) 5-11-4 P L Cusack, ... (3 to 1)	6
ROSETOWN GIRL (Ire) 5-11-8 J F Titley, ...(33 to 1)	7
BURGESS HILL VI 11-11-7 (7*) A O'Shea, ... (20 to 1)	8
CANDY IS DANDY (Ire) 7-11-9 B Sheridan, ... (20 to 1)	9
CHAPEL CHAT (Ire) (bl) 6-11-9 (5*) Mr B M Cash, ..(14 to 1)	10
GLACIAL GIRL 4-10-10 (5*) J M Donnelly, ... (33 to 1)	11

FORCE THIRTEEN (Ire) 5-11-8 C O'Dwyer, ... (12 to 1)	f
HAUNTED FOR SURE (Ire) 5-11-8 J Shortt, ...(33 to 1)	pu

Dist: 20l, 15l, 9l, 3½l. 5m 14.90s. (13 Ran).

(Sean Spillane), A P O'Brien

6   **Stanley Racing Handicap Hurdle (0-137 4-y-o and up) £4,110 2m............(3:05)**

NOTCOMPLAININGBUT (Ire) [-] 5-11-12 T P Treacy,	
.... (6 to 4 fav)	1
POKONO TRAIL (Ire) [-] 7-10-8 F J Flood, ...(9 to 2)	2
MISTER CHIPPY (Ire) [-] 4-10-0 C F Swan, ...(7 to 2)	3
PERSIAN MYSTIC (Ire) [-] 4-9-10 T J O'Sullivan, ...(6 to 1)	4
BOB THE YANK (Ire) [-] 6-9-10 (3*) D J Casey, ...(5 to 1)	5

Dist: 1l, 3½l, ½l, sht-hd. 4m 8.00s. (5 Ran).

(Mrs C A Moore), P Mullins

7   **Kingdom Beginners Chase (5-y-o and up) £2,740 2m..........................(3:35)**

MOUSSAHIM (USA) 6-12-0 L P Cusack, ... (13 to 2)	1
WINTER BELLE (USA) (bl) 8-12-0 J Shortt, ... (5 to 4 fav)	2
DORANS WAY (Ire) 5-11-7 M P Hourigan, ... (12 to 1)	3
ICANTELYA (Ire) 7-12-0 T P Treacy, ...(9 to 1)	4
NORDIC THORN (Ire) 6-12-0 J F Titley, ...(10 to 1)	5
FERRYCARRIG HOTEL (Ire) 7-11-9 (5*) B Bowens, (10 to 1)	6
CELTIC BUCK 10-11-7 (7*) Mr Patrick O'Keeffe, ..(10 to 1)	7
DOONEGA (Ire) 8-12-0 T J O'Sullivan, ... (12 to 1)	8
GLOWING LINES 6-11-9 C F Swan, ... (6 to 1)	9
KILKEN CHOICE (Ire) 5-11-7 J P Broderick, ... (25 to 1)	10
ROYAL COMPANY 9-11-7 (7*) A O'Shea, ... (25 to 1)	11
BALLYBEGGAN BOY (Ire) 5-11-4 (3*) J R Barry, .. (40 to 1)	12
TRIPTODICKS (Ire) 6-11-9 P A Roche, ... (20 to 1)	13
VERUNA (Ire) 6-11-9 C O'Dwyer, ... (20 to 1)	f
SANDY FOREST LADY (Ire) (bl) 7-11-9 T J Murphy, (12 to 1)	ur
CAPITULAR (Ire) (bl) 6-12-0 F J Flood, ...(25 to 1)	pu

Dist: Sht-hd, 1l, 3½l, 3l. 4m 15.30s. (16 Ran).

(O B P Carroll), G A Cusack

8   **Ballybeggan Racegoers Club INH Flat Race (6-y-o and up) £3,425 2m 1f (5:05)**

FONTAINE LODGE (Ire) 6-11-9 Mr D Marnane, ...(12 to 1)	1
CLONGOUR (Ire) 6-11-9 (5*) Mr B M Cash, ...(9 to 4 fav)	2
MALICE 10-11-6 (3*) Mr E Norris, ...(20 to 1)	3
ROMANCEINTHEDARK (Ire) 6-11-9 Mr B A Murphy,	
..................................(12 to 1)	4
MYSTERY BREEZE (Ire) 6-11-7 (7*) Mr J Bright, ...(7 to 1)	5
HIGH MOAT (Ire) 6-11-7 (7*) Mr P J Coleman, ...(13 to 2)	6
BUGGSY BLADE 10-11-7 (7*) Mr G Elliott, ...(14 to 1)	7
GALATASOR JANE (Ire) 6-11-2 (7*) Mr B O'Keeffe, (16 to 1)	8
ART PRINCE (Ire) 6-11-7 (7*) Mr B N Doyle, ...(14 to 1)	9
FAT BARNEY (Ire) 6-11-7 (7*) Miss J Lee, ...(20 to 1)	10
BARRIGAN'S HILL (Ire) 6-11-7 (7*) Mr John P Moloney,	
..................................(25 to 1)	11
PRINCESS LENA (Ire) 6-11-4² (7*) Mr T J Nagle Jnr, (20 to 1)	12
STAND ALONE (Ire) 7-11-7 (7*) Mr B Hassett, ...(12 to 1)	13
PREMIER WALK 7-11-7 (7*) Mr S P Hennessy, ...(14 to 1)	14
MUSKERRY EXPRESS (Ire) 6-11-7 (7*) Mr M J Walsh,	
..................................(20 to 1)	15
CARNMORE CASTLE (Ire) (bl) 8-11-7 (7*) Mr K N McDonagh,	
..................................(20 to 1)	16
SHAREZA RIVER (Ire) 6-11-7 (7*) Mr J T McNamara, (5 to 1)	17
LAUGHING FONTAINE (Ire) 6-11-7 (7*) Mr H Murphy,	
..................................(10 to 1)	18
MAGICAL WAY (Ire) 6-12-0 Mr J A Nash, ...(16 to 1)	19
PERCY HANNON (Ire) 6-11-7 (7*) Mr D Russell, .. (20 to 1)	20

Dist: Nk, 10l, 7l, 5l. 4m 16.90s. (20 Ran).

(ABC Syndicate), Anthony Mullins

LEOPARDSTOWN (IRE) (good)
Monday June 3rd

9   **Clonskeagh INH Flat Race (4-y-o and up) £3,082 2m..........................(5:30)**

ERRAMICA 4-11-1 Miss F M Crowley, (100 to 30 fav)	1
MINELLA MILLER (Ire) 6-11-9 (5*) Mr B M Cash, ...(5 to 1)	2
PRINCE DANTE 4-11-6 Mr M McNulty, ...(7 to 2)	3
RED RADICAL (Ire) 6-11-7 (7*) Mr P E I Newell, ...(25 to 1)	4
ANOTHER KAV (Ire) 6-11-9 Mr J A Berry, ...(20 to 1)	5
BOBBIT BACK ON (Ire) 6-12-0 Mr J A Nash, ... (4 to 1)	6
TINERANA GLOW (Ire) 4-10-12 (3*) D T Evans, ...(25 to 1)	7
IVERK'S PRIDE (Ire) 5-11-8 (5*) J Butler, ...(4 to 1)	8
STRONG RAIDER (Ire) 6-12-0 Mr H F Cleary, ...(8 to 1)	9

1

Dist: 14l, 1½l, 2l, 5l. 3m 39.10s. (9 Ran).

(J J Byrne), A P O'Brien

TRALEE (IRE) (yielding to soft)
Monday June 3rd

10 **Kirbys Steakhouse Handicap Chase (0-116 4-y-o and up) £3,425 2½m (4:05)**

SPRINGFORT LADY [-] 7-10-2 P Carberry,	(5 to 1)	1
ANOTHER GROUSE [-] 9-12-0 T P Treacy,	(6 to 1)	2
THERE TIS FOR YA (Ire) [-] 8-10-5 C O'Dwyer,	(12 to 1)	3
STEVIE BE (Ire) [-] 8-11-6 K F O'Brien,	(7 to 1)	4
ROSSBEIGH CREEK [-] 9-11-3 F J Flood,	(6 to 1)	5
MICKS DELIGHT (Ire) [-] 6-11-10 C F Swan,	(2 to 1 fav)	6
NATIVE VENTURE (Ire) [-] 8-11-10 J F Titley,	(5 to 1)	7
ROSSMANAGHER (Ire) [-] 7-11-2 (5*) G Cotter,	(6 to 1)	8

Dist: 1l, 1l, 6l, 20l. 5m 30.30s. (8 Ran).

(Patrick Cagney), John J Walsh

11 **Kerry Maiden Hurdle (4-y-o and up) £2,740 2m 1f. (4:35)**

SPANKY (Ire) 4-11-1 L P Cusack,	(7 to 1)	1
TARAJAN (USA) (bl) 4-11-6 J Shortt,	(9 to 1)	2
REAL TAOISEACH (Ire) 6-11-7 (7*) Mr A K Wyse,	(7 to 4 fav)	3
THATS MY WIFE (Ire) 5-11-1 (3*) J R Barry,	(16 to 1)	4
OLD FONTAINE 8-10-8 (7*) S O'Donnell,	(12 to 1)	5
COOLING CHIMES (Ire) 6-11-6 Mr M Phillips,	(20 to 1)	6
CROHANE PRINCESS (Ire) 7-11-1 S H O'Donovan,	(14 to 1)	7
MIDNIGHT JAZZ (Ire) 6-12-0 J P Broderick,	(6 to 1)	8
BRIGHT SHARES (Ire) 6-11-1 K F O'Brien,	(14 to 1)	9
PHARRAMBLING (Ire) 5-11-0 M P Hourigan,	(20 to 1)	10
BRAVE COMMITMENT (Ire) 5-11-8 C F Swan,	(6 to 1)	11
DEREENGLOSS (Ire) 5-11-0 C O'Dwyer,	(10 to 1)	12
SNUGVILLE SALLY 4-10-3 (7*) S FitzGerald,	(16 to 1)	13
FORT DEELY (Ire) 5-11-5 J Jones,	(20 to 1)	14
MILLA'S DELIGHT (Ire) 5-11-5 P Carberry,	(14 to 1)	15
APHRIKE (Ire) 5-10-12 (7*) A O'Shea,	(16 to 1)	16
SHAKARAYA (Ire) 5-11-0 T P Treacy,	(20 to 1)	17
ARGIDEEN VALE 4-11-1 J F Titley,	(8 to 1)	pu
SCARLET RIVER (Ire) 6-11-8 B P Harding,	(25 to 1)	pu
LADY SHALOM (Ire) 5-11-0 F J Flood,	(14 to 1)	pu

Dist: 5½l, 10l, 3l, 10l. 4m 28.80s. (20 Ran).

(Mrs D J Coleman), Mrs D J Coleman

12 **Joseph J Grace Memorial Handicap Hurdle (0-109 4-y-o and up) £3,425 2½m (5:05)**

HELLO MONKEY [-] 9-11-7 T P Treacy,	(8 to 1)	1
OFFICIAL PORTRAIT (Ire) [-] 7-11-6 (6ex) C F Swan,	(11 to 10 fav)	2
CLASHWILLIAM GIRL (Ire) [-] 8-11-5 (7*) Mr R M Walsh,	(7 to 1)	3
MARIES POLLY [-] 6-10-7 D H O'Connor,	(8 to 1)	4
ANDROS DAWN [-] 6-10-7 C O'Dwyer,	(8 to 1)	5
SHOREWOOD (Ire) [-] 6-10-5 F Woods,	(14 to 1)	6
GOLDEN RAPPER [-] 11-9-9 J P Broderick,	(25 to 1)	7
FALCARRAGH (Ire) [-] 6-9-11 (7*) Mr G Elliott,	(9 to 2)	8
BITRAN [-] 6-10-7 A Powell,	(12 to 1)	9

Dist: 2½l, 3½l, 20l, 8l. 5m 23.50s. (9 Ran).

(Mrs Audrey Healy), P Mullins

13 **Ballybeggan Racegoers Club INH Flat Race (4 & 5-y-o) £3,425 2m. (5:35)**

SENTOSA STAR (Ire) 5-11-13 Mr P Fenton,	(10 to 9 on)	1
PERAMBIE (Ire) (bl) 4-10-8 (7*) Mr R M Walsh,	(9 to 2)	2
MALADANTE (Ire) 4-10-8 (7*) Mr J P Hayden,	(8 to 1)	3
MUST GO LADY (Ire) 4-11-1 Mr J P Dempsey,	(13 to 2)	4
MR MAGNETIC (Ire) 5-11-13 Mr T Doyle,	(5 to 1)	5
AMERICAN CONKER (Ire) 5-11-1 (7*) Mr J T McNamara,	(7 to 1)	6
THE THIN FELLOW (Ire) 5-11-6 (7*) Mr C Amerian,	(12 to 1)	7
ASTRID (Ire) 5-11-1 (7*) Mr A Jordan,	(10 to 1)	8
RUN OF FASHION (Ire) 5-11-8 Mr M Phillips,	(12 to 1)	9
PROPHETS FIST (Ire) 5-11-6 (7*) Mr D A Harney,	(16 to 1)	10
BALLYMAC HERO (Ire) 5-11-6 (7*) Mr P J Gilligan,	(8 to 1)	pu

Dist: 10l, 9l, 15l, 4l. 4m 9.10s. (11 Ran).

(C J Deasy), Michael Hourigan

BADEN-BADEN (GER) (good to soft)
Tuesday June 4th

14 **Badener Roulette-Preis (Hurdle) (4-y-o) £11,261 2m 110yds. (5:10)**

LAST CORNER 10-8 K Hviid,		1
MULTY (Ire) (bl) 10-12 R Dunwoody, improved hfwy, cl 3rd 2 out, kpt on one pace,		2
REVEILLON (Ger) 11-0 S Hickey,		3

Dist: 4½l, 4½l, 1½l, 3l. 3m 53.50s. (8 Ran).

(B Raber), C Von Der Recke

BADEN-BADEN (GER) (good)
Wednesday June 5th

15 **Bader-Preis-Hurdenrennen Hurdle (5-y-o and up) £15,766 2½m 165yds (3:25)**

REGISTANO (Ger) 9-10-6 D Fuhrmann,		1
WEISSENSTEIN (Ire) 5-10-8 D Byrne,		2
ACONCAGUE (Ger) 9-10-11 P Gehm,		3
DECIDE YOURSELF (Ire) 6-10-8 G Bradley, in tch till hfwy, beh whn btn at 2 out,		pu

Dist: 4l, 2½l, 13l, 1¾l, 14l, 10l, 2l. 4m 47.80s. (12 Ran).

(Gestut Sybille), U Stoltefuss

NAVAN (IRE) (good to yielding)
Wednesday June 5th

16 **Breeders Supporting Navan Handicap Hurdle (0-130 4-y-o and up) £4,110 2m (8:00)**

6² POKONO TRAIL (Ire) [-] 7-10-12 F J Flood,	(5 to 2 co-fav)	1
KATIYMANN (Ire) [-] 4-9-7¹ T Horgan,	(5 to 2 co-fav)	2
DASHING ROSE [-] 8-10-8 P Carberry,	(5 to 2 co-fav)	3
DEVIL'S HOLIDAY (USA) [-] 6-9-7 (7*) Miss S Kauntze,	(5 to 1)	4
OH SO GRUMPY [-] 8-11-7 J Shortt,	(9 to 1)	5

Dist: 4½l, hd, 15l, 4½l. 3m 53.10s. (5 Ran).

(Mrs Miriam Byrne), F Flood

17 **Meath Farm Machinery Hurdle (4-y-o and up) £3,596 2½m (8:30)**

923² BAMAPOUR (Ire) 6-11-7 P Carberry,	(Evens fav)	1
GAZALANI (Ire) 4-10-9 (3*) D Bromley,	(9 to 4)	2
MAKING THE POINT (Ire) 5-11-12 K F O'Brien,	(7 to 2)	3
CLEVER JACK (Ire) 6-11-7 J P Broderick,	(16 to 1)	4
KING'S MANDATE (Ire) 7-11-7 J K Kinane,	(33 to 1)	5
PINTPLEASE PAT (Ire) 5-11-1 L P Cusack,	(16 to 1)	6
HIDDEN SPRINGS (Ire) 5-11-6 J Shortt,	(25 to 1)	7
ROSSI (Ire) 7-11-7 B Sheridan,	(33 to 1)	pu

Dist: 1½l, 6l, ½l, 3l. 4m 56.90s. (8 Ran).

(Michael Hilary Burke), Michael Cunningham

18 **Green And Gold I.N.H. Flat Race (4-y-o and up) £2,740 2m (9:00)**

PHARDUBH (Ire) 5-11-13 Miss F M Crowley,	(3 to 1 fav)	1
ST CAROL (Ire) 5-11-8 Mr T Mullins,	(7 to 1)	2
LAGEN BRIDGE (Ire) 7-12-0 Mr M Phillips,	(4 to 1)	3
VARTRY BOY (Ire) 5-11-13 Mr D Marnane,	(5 to 1)	4
TRY ONCE MORE (Ire) 5-11-6 (7*) Mr A J Dempsey,	(14 to 1)	5
MONTANA KING (Ire) 5-11-6 (7*) Mr G Elliott,	(7 to 1)	6
ROLL OVER (Ire) 6-11-7 (7*) Mr A C Coyle,	(8 to 1)	7
KNOCKAULIN (Ire) 5-11-13 Mr H F Cleary,	(9 to 1)	8
GALACTUS (Ire) 5-11-6 (7*) Mr L P King,	(10 to 1)	9
FORGE AHEAD (Ire) 5-11-13 Mr J A Nash,	(14 to 1)	10
MAY BLOOM (Ire) 5-11-8 Mr A R Coonan,	(14 to 1)	11
MOLLY WHACK (Ire) 5-11-1 (7*) Mr R Walsh,	(14 to 1)	12
BANNOW ISLAND (Ire) 8-11-7 (7*) Mr E Gallagher,	(20 to 1)	13
COCO (Ire) 5-11-6 (7*) Mr D P Coakley,	(12 to 1)	14
AWAY IN A HACK (Ire) 6-11-7 (7*) Mr P M Cloke,	(20 to 1)	15
ROSEY BUCK (Ire) 4-10-8 (7*) Mr J P Kilfeather,	(25 to 1)	16

Dist: ¾l, 2l, 8l, 2l. 3m 38.10s. (16 Ran).

(T Conroy), A P O'Brien

AUTEUIL (FR) (good to soft)
Thursday June 6th

19 **Prix la Barka (Hurdle) (5-y-o and up) £39,526 2m 5f 110yds. (3:25)**

MONTPERLE (Fr) 7-10-2 Y Fouin,		1
MYSILV 6-10-0 J Osborne, prmnt, led 4th till mstk 7th, 5th and rdn 3 out, hdwy last, ran on r-in,		2
EARL GRANT (Fr) 7-10-4 J-Y Beaurain,		3

Dist: 1½l, ½l, nk, 1½l, 15l, 4l, 10l, 20l. 5m 22.00s. (10 Ran).

(Mme H Carion), H Bedran de Balanda

BALLINROBE (IRE) (good)
Thursday June 6th

20 **Harp Lager Handicap Chase (0-102 5-y-o and up) £3,425 2½m (7:25)**

IRISH FOUNTAIN (Ire) [-] 8-11-8 J P Broderick,	(8 to 1)	1
ARISTODEMUS [-] 7-11-4 F Woods,	(9 to 4 fav)	2
JUMPING FOR JOY (Ire) [-] 7-10-12 A Powell,	(8 to 1)	3
ANY PORT [-] 6-10-10 D H O'Connor,	(7 to 1)	4
BALLYBRIKEN CASTLE [-] 9-9-1 (7*) M D Murphy,	(9 to 1)	5
WHITBY [-] 8-9-6 (7*) A O'Shea,	(20 to 1)	6

AMME ENAEK (Ire) [-] (bl) 7-11-0 H Rogers, ...(8 to 1)   7
LISNAGREE BOY (Ire) [-] 8-10-11 P McWilliams, . . (16 to 1)   8
DEEP REFRAIN (Ire) [-] (bl) 6-9-11 (5*) G Cotter, ...(7 to 2)   ur
SONNY SULLIVAN [-] 9-9-5 (5*) T Martin, ...(33 to 1)   pu
Dist: 3l, 1½l, 5½l, 4½l. 5m 25.00s. (10 Ran).

(Michael J McDonagh), Michael J McDonagh

21   Lough Carra Maiden Hurdle (4-y-o and up) £2,226 2m. . . . . (7:55)

MARADYKE BRIDGE (Ire) 7-12-0 Mr G J Harford,
. . . . (7 to 4 fav)   1
WHEREWILITALL END (Ire) 5-11-2 (3*) U Smyth, . . (12 to 1)   2
KING SHOES (Ire) 5-10-9 (5*) D J Kavanagh, ...(9 to 1)   3
MARGUERITA SONG 6-11-1 L P Cusack, ...(2 to 1)   4
BRIGHT PROJECT (Ire) 4-10-8 (7*) A O'Shea, ... (14 to 1)   5
QAMOOS (Ire) 6-12-0 F Woods, ...(8 to 1)   6
MANTON GIRL (Ire) 5-11-0 J F Titley, ... (16 to 1)   7
THIRD AGENDA (Ire) 5-11-5 J P Byrne. . . . . (10 to 1)   8
GALE HAMSHIRE (Ire) 7-11-1 A Powell, ...(10 to 1)   9
LIOS NA MAOL (Ire) 5-10-7 (7*) M D Murphy, ...(20 to 1)   10
WARLOCKFOE (Ire) 5-10-9 (5*) G Cotter, ... (20 to 1)   11
Dist: 2l, 1l, 5l, 4½l. 4m 17.30s. (11 Ran).

(Mrs Monica Hackett), Noel Meade

22   Partry I.N.H. Flat Race (4-y-o and up) £2,226 2m. . . . .(8:25)

SHRAMORE LAD (Ire) 5-11-6 (7*) Mr R J Cooper, . . .(7 to 2)   1
NATIVE BABY (Ire) 6-11-2 (7*) Mr A C Coyle, . . (3 to 1 jt-fav)   2
PREMIER WALK 7-11-7 (7*) Mr S P Hennessy, ...(14 to 1)   3
MASK RIVER (Ire) 7-11-2 (7*) Mr A Daly. . . . . (20 to 1)   4
THE YELLOW BOG (Ire) 6-12-0 Mr G J Harford, ...(6 to 1)   5
ORCHARD SUNSET (Ire) 6-11-7 (7*) Mr D M Fogarty, (7 to 2)   6
BIDDY HUNT (Ire) 5-11-1 (7*) Mr P J Gilligan, ... (14 to 1)   7
GLEN RUADH (Ire) 5-11-6 (7*) Mr G Elliott, . . . (3 to 1 jt-fav)   8
MOSCOWSBANNER (Ire) 4-10-13 (7*) Mr R D Lee, . (14 to 1)   9
Dist: 1½l, 1½l, 6l, nk. 4m 11.30s. (9 Ran).

(P M Reilly), G T Lynch

PERTH (good to firm)
Thursday June 6th
Going Correction: MINUS 0.30 sec. per fur.

23   Jolly Miller Novices' Hurdle Class D (4-y-o and up) £2,788 2½m 110yds. . (7:00)

MUZRAK (Can) 5-11-1 R Garritty, trkd ldrs, led bef 2 out, sn
clr, very easily. (Evens fav op 5 to 4)   1
BIREQUEST 5-11-1 D J Moffatt, led till hdd bef 2 out, no ch
wth wnr. . . . .(20 to 1 op 14 to 1)   2
BALLYALLIA CASTLE (Ire) (bl) 7-11-1 P Niven, hld up, hdwy
aftr 6th, sn drvn alng, no imprsn on 1st 2.
. . . .(14 to 1 op 10 to 1)   3
EXCUSE ME (Ire) (bl) 7-11-1 P Carberry, in tch, hdwy bef 7th,
rdn aftr 3 out, sn wknd. . . . .(33 to 1 op 14 to 1)   4
KITZBERG (Ire) 5-10-10 A P McCoy, prmnt till wkned quickly
aftr 6th, tld off. . . . .(9 to 1 op 8 to 1 tchd 10 to 1)   5
JUST A GUESS (Ire) (bl) 5-10-12 (3*) A Roche, mstks, hld up,
lost tch frm hfwy, tld off whn pld up bef 3 out.
. . . .(50 to 1 op 25 to 1)   pu
GAWN INN (Ire) 6-11-7 Mr R J Patton, trkd ldrs till lost pl rpdly
aftr 5th, lost tch and pld up bef nxt. . . . . . .(9 to 4 op 6 to 4)   pu
Dist: 18l, 14l, 16l, dist. 4m 55.00s. a 15.00s (7 Ran).

(The Gemini Partnership), M D Hammond

24   Riverboat Casino Handicap Chase Class D (0-125 5-y-o and up) £4,052 3m (7:30)

HILLWALK [110] 10-11-4 D Morris, hld up in tch, hdwy bef
15th, rdn to ld fnl 100 yards.
. . . .(11 to 2 op 4 to 1 tchd 6 to 1)   1
THE YANK [97] (v) 10-10-2 (3*) Mr C Bonner, nvr far away, led
15th, rdn and hdd fnl 100 yards, no extr.
. . . . (25 to 1 op 16 to 1 tchd 33 to 1)   2
EAST HOUSTON [96] 7-10-4 A P McCoy, nvr far away, ch 2
out, kpt on same pace. . . . . .(9 to 2 op 4 to 1 tchd 5 to 1)   3
ROCKET RUN (Ire) [107] 8-11-1 A Thornton, led till hdd 15th,
disputing second and und pres whn blun 2 out, sn btn.
. . . .(9 to 4 fav tchd 5 to 2)   4
BALD JOKER [92] 11-10-0 P Carberry, prmnt till wknd aftr
15th, tld off. . . . .(14 to 1 op 16 to 1)   5
SWORD BEACH [112] 12-11-6 P Niven, sn beh, tld off.
. . . .(14 to 1 op 10 to 1 tchd 16 to 1)   6
POSITIVE ACTION [92] (bl) 10-10-0 A Dobbin, prmnt till wknd
bef 14th, tld off. . . . .(50 to 1 op 33 to 1)   7
CROSS CANNON [115] 10-11-9 B Storey, tracking ldrs whn f
11th (water). . . . .(9 to 1 op 7 to 1 tchd 10 to 1)   f
OFF THE BRU [97] 11-10-5¹⁰ (7*) Mr M Bradburne, mstks, al
beh, tld off whn pld up bef 13th.
. . . .(8 to 1 op 7 to 1 tchd 10 to 1)   pu
CEILIDH BOY [120] 10-11-11 (3*) G Cahill, mstks, beh, tld up
whn pld up bef 3 out. . . . . .(14 to 1 op 10 to 1 tchd 16 to 1)   pu
JIMS CHOICE [94] 9-10-2 R Davis, prmnt, drvn alng whn pld
up lme bef 15th. . . . .(12 to 1 op 10 to 1 tchd 16 to 1)   pu
Dist: 1¼l, 3l, 11l, 24l, 20l, 10l. 6m 0.40s. a 5.40s (11 Ran).

(M L Shone), R Curtis

25   Bruce Wilson Sports And Leisure Handicap Hurdle Class E (0-110 5-y-o and up) £2,723 2½m 110yds. . . . . (8:00)

TABU LADY (Ire) [90] (bl) 5-10-12 A P McCoy, made all, kckd
bef 2 out, styd on wl. . . . . . .(7 to 1 op 4 to 1 tchd 8 to 1)   1
LEVEL EDGE [86] 5-10-3 (5*) R McGrath, in tch, hdwy to
chase wnr bef 3 out, rdn before nxt, no imprsn.
. . . .(11 to 8 fav op 5 to 4 tchd 13 to 8)   2
MASTER OFTHE HOUSE [90] 10-10-12 R Garritty, hld up,
hdwy bef 3 out, sn drvn alng and btn.
. . . .(5 to 2 op 9 to 4 tchd 11 to 4)   3
DALUSMAN (Ire) [79] 8-10-1 L O'Hara, chsd wnr till wknd bef
3 out. . . . .(12 to 1 op 14 to 1 tchd 10 to 1)   4
CANDID LAD [82] 9-10-4 (7ex) B Storey, in tch, wkng whn
blun badly 3 out, tld off when pld up bef nxt.
. . . .(7 to 1 op 5 to 1 tchd 8 to 1)   pu
SYLVAN CELEBRATION [78] 5-9-11 (3*) G Cahill, beh, mstk
7th, losing tch whn hmpd 3 out, tld off when pld up bef nxt.
. . . .(25 to 1 op 12 to 1)   pu
Dist: 8l, 14l, 10l. 4m 54.10s. a 14.10s (6 Ran).

(P McWilliams), W Rock

26   Earl Grey Novices' Chase Class D (5-y-o and up) £3,761 2m. . . . . (8:30)

SECRETARY OF STATE 10-11-2 A P McCoy, led 4th, made
rst, clr frm 9th, easily. . . . .(9 to 2 op 5 to 1)   1
MOVAC (Ire) 7-11-9 A Thornton, in tch, chsd wnr frm 9th, no
imprsn. . . . .(11 to 8 on op 6 to 4 on tchd 5 to 4 on)   2
BORING (USA) 7-10-11 (5*) R McGrath, hld up, some hdwy
bef 9th, sn drvn alng and btn.
. . . .(10 to 1 op 8 to 1 tchd 12 to 1)   3
REVE DE VALSE (USA) 9-11-2 Mr P Johnson, led to 4th, chsd
wnr till wknd aftr 9th. . . . .(12 to 1 op 8 to 1)   4
MISTER BLACK (Ire) 8-11-2 P Carberry, mstks, lost tch frm
hfwy, tld off. . . . .(9 to 1 op 8 to 1 tchd 10 to 1)   5
EXCISE MAN 8-11-9 B Storey, in tch, wkng whn f 3 out.
. . . .(12 to 1 tchd 14 to 1)   f
BOETHIUS (Ire) 7-11-2 A Dobbin, reminders aftr 5th, lost
tch and pld up bef 9th. . . . .(25 to 1 op 33 to 1)   pu
LE DENSTAN 9-11-2 R Davis, reluctant to line up, jmpd badly,
sn tld off, pld up bef 9th. . . . .(100 to 1 op 50 to 1)   pu
POP IN THERE (Ire) 8-11-2 L O'Hara, not jump wl, sn tld off,
pld up bef 8th. . . . .(100 to 1 op 50 to 1)   pu
Dist: 11l, 25l, 3½l, dist. 3m 53.10s. a 2.10s (9 Ran).
SR: 19/15/-/-/-/-/

(W H Ponsonby), D W P Arbuthnot

27   Snuggles Break Novices' Handicap Hurdle Class E (0-100 4-y-o and up) £2,388 2m 110yds. . . . . (9:00)

BOURDONNER [70] 4-10-2 P Carberry, made all, clr aftr 3
out, ran on wl. . . . .(13 to 2 op 9 to 2 tchd 7 to 1)   1
TEEJAY'N'AITCH (Ire) [72] 4-10-1 (3*) G Cahill, in tch, chsd
wnr frm 3 out, no imprsn. . . . .(9 to 2 op 3 to 1)   2
CHARLISTIONA [68] 5-9-11 (3*) B Fenton, chsd ldrs, kpt on
same pace frm 3 out. . . (16 to 1 op 14 to 1 tchd 20 to 1)   3
TRIENNIUM (USA) [81] 7-10-6 (7*) S Melrose, hld up in tch,
effrt bef 3 out, no real hdwy. . . . . . .(9 to 4 fav tchd 5 to 2)   4
LAC DE GRAS (Ire) [68] 5-10-0 D Morris, towards rear, effrt
whn blun 2 out, kpt on, nvr dngrs. . . . . .(25 to 1 op 20 to 1)   5
MISTER CASUAL [72] 7-9-13 (5*) R McGrath, nvr better than
mid-div. . . . .(12 to 1 op 10 to 1)   6
PATS CROSS (Ire) [72] 7-11-10 A P McCoy, mstk second,
chsd ldrs till wknd aftr 3 out.
. . . .(9 to 2 op 4 to 1 tchd 5 to 1)   7
COQUET GOLD [68] 5-10-0 B Storey, beh most of way.
. . . .(10 to 1 op 8 to 1)   8
DAYTIME DAWN (Ire) [77] 5-10-9 D J Moffatt, sn beh.
. . . .(50 to 1 op 33 to 1)   9
MELODY DANCER [68] 5-10-0⁷ (7*) R Murphy, chsd wnr till
wknd quickly aftr 3 out.
. . . .(66 to 1 op 50 to 1 tchd 100 to 1)   10
GRINNELL [70] 6-10-2 R Davis, tld off frm hfwy.
. . . .(50 to 1 op 33 to 1)   11
ON THE MOVE [76] 5-10-8 W Fry, towards rear, lost tch and
pld up bef 2 out. . . . .(20 to 1 op 14 to 1)   pu
Dist: 7l, 11l, 8l, 8l, 1¾l, 7l, 4l, 14l, 1¾l, dist. 3m 48.40s. a 7.40s (12 Ran).

(Cornelius Lysaght), M D Hammond

28   Glasgow West End Conditional Jockeys' Handicap Hurdle Class E (0-110 4-y-o and up) £2,786 3m 110yds. . . . . . . (9:30)

TOUGH TEST (Ire) [93] 6-11-8 B Fenton, trkd ldrs, led 3 out,
mstk nxt, ran on wl. . . . .(3 to 1 op 9 to 4)   1
NICHOLAS PLANT [92] 7-11-7 G Cahill, made most till hdd 3
out, chsd wnr aftr, no imprsn. . . . .(4 to 1 op 3 to 1)   2
SCRABO VIEW (Ire) [99] 8-11-8 (6*) B Grattan, hld up, effrt bef
9th, sn drvn alng, kpt on same pace frm 3 out.
. . . .(10 to 1 op 7 to 1)   3
SLAUGHT SON (Ire) [91] 8-11-6 F Leahy, hld up, pushed alng
bef 9th, sn btn, tld off. . . . .(2 to 1 fav op 6 to 4)   4

CLASSIC STATEMENT [81] (bl) 10-10-7 (3*) S Taylor, *dsptd ld, hrd rdn aftr 8th, wknd aftr nxt, wl beh whn pld up bef 2 out.*
....(4 to 1 op 10 to 1) pu
Dist: 12l, 8l, dist. 5m 56.90s. a 14.90s (5 Ran).

(J D Goodfellow), Mrs J D Goodfellow

TIPPERARY (IRE) (firm)
Thursday June 6th

29 Brookville Handicap Hurdle (0-116 4-y-o and up) £2,740 2m.................(6:00)

GALLETINA (Ire) [-] 6-11-5 B Sheridan, ...(11 to 2)	1
WEST ON BRIDGE ST (Ire) [-] 6-10-2 (3*) D J Casey, (9 to 2)	2
BALMYRA (Ire) [-] (bl) 4-9-13 W T Slattery, ...(9 to 2)	3
NOBULL (Ire) [-] 6-10-6 J Shortt, ...(4 to 1 fav)	4
ANGAREB (Ire) [-] 7-10-8 T P Treacy, ...(10 to 1)	5
QUINTILIANI (Ire) [-] 5-10-6 C O'Dwyer, ...(8 to 1)	6
THE TOM'S ERROR (Ire) [-] 6-9-11 (3*) J R Barry, ..(20 to 1)	7
ILLBETHEREFORYOU (Ire) [-] 5-9-7 T Horgan, ...(5 to 1)	8
LITTLE(?)... (Ire) ...	pu
Dist: Sht-hd, 6l, 1l, 3½l. 3m 49.60s. (9 Ran).

(Trevor C Stewart), D Hanley

30 Bansha Maiden Hurdle (4-y-o) £2,397 2m ....(6:30)

KATES CHOICE (Ire) 11-1 T P Treacy, ...(10 to 1)	1
FRASER CAREY (Ire) 10-10 M P Hourigan, ...(5 to 4 fav)	2
I REMEMBER IT WELL (Ire) 10-10 M P Hourigan, ..(10 to 1)	3
ONE WORD (Ire) 11-1 J Shortt, ...(12 to 1)	4
ADARAMANN (Ire) 10-8 (7*) Mr R Walsh, ...(7 to 2)	5
VINTAGE PLAY (Ire) 10-7 (3*) D T Evans, ...(12 to 1)	6
DANCING POSER (Ire) 11-1 K F O'Brien, ...(12 to 1)	7
MEDIA MISS (Ire) 10-10 J K Kinane, ...(12 to 1)	8
TIFFANY VICTORIA (Ire) 10-10 C O'Dwyer, ...(12 to 1)	9
STONE COLD MAGIC (Ire) 10-3 (7*) R P Hogan, ..(25 to 1)	10
GLACIAL GIRL (Ire) 10-5 (5*) J M Donnelly, ...(20 to 1)	11
QUAH (Ire) 10-3 (7*) D McCullagh, ...(20 to 1)	12
JEWEL OF THE NIGHT (Ire) 10-12 (3*) J R Barry, ..(20 to 1)	13
LOSLOMOS (Ire) 10-8 (7*) Mr D Duggan, ...(20 to 1)	14
BIG STORM (Ire) 10-3 (7*) S FitzGerald, ...(20 to 1)	f
Dist: 11l, 1l, hd, 9l. 3m 48.00s. (15 Ran).

(Mrs Geraldine Treacy), S J Treacy

31 Knockaney I.N.H. Flat Race (4-y-o and up) £2,740 2m................(8:30)

NATIVE-DARRIG (Ire) 5-12-3 Mr J A Nash, ...(5 to 1)	1
LISS DE PAOR (Ire) 5-11-12 Miss F M Crowley, (10 to 9 on)	2
JAY MAN (Ire) 6-11-13 (5*) Mr E J Kearns Jnr, ..(12 to 1)	3
DUISKE ABBEY (Ire) 6-11-6 (7*) Mr J P McNamara, (3 to 1)	4
BALLYDUFF ROSE (Ire) 6-10-13 (7*) Mrs C Doyle, (14 to 1)	5
DEEP BIT (Ire) 5-11-10 Mr P Fenton, ...(14 to 1)	6
BARLEY COURT (Ire) 6-11-6 (5*) Mr P A Deegan, ..(14 to 1)	7
TRIPLE ACTION (Ire) 7-11-4 (7*) Mr D Duggan, ...(12 to 1)	8
PIXIE BLUE (Ire) 5-10-12 (7*) Mr John P Moloney, (20 to 1)	9
FORD CLASSIC (Ire) 4-10-5 (7*) Mr M Hickey, ...(20 to 1)	10
Dist: 15l, 6l, 1l, 3½l. 3m 40.20s. (10 Ran).

(W P Kerwin), W P Mullins

DUNDALK (IRE) (good (races 1,2), good to yielding (3))
Friday June 7th

32 Carrickarnon Handicap Hurdle (0-102 4-y-o and up) £2,226 2½m 153yds (5:30)

DIFFICULT TIMES (Ire) [-] 4-11-8 (3*) S C Lyons, ...(4 to 1)	1
YOUR THE MAN [-] 10-11-12 F Woods, ...(10 to 1)	2
KING BRIAN (Ire) [-] 6-10-3 (7*) L J Fleming, ...(8 to 1)	3
STRAIGHT ON (Ire) [-] 5-11-3 J Shortt, ...(6 to 1)	4
DANGEROUS REEF (Ire) [-] 8-11-3 (3*) D J Casey, ..(6 to 1)	5
MIDNIGHT HOUR (Ire) [-] 7-11-8 (5*) G Cotter, ..(3 to 1 fav)	6
CLAIRE ME (Ire) [-] 7-9-13 (5*) T Martin, ...(12 to 1)	7
HOLLOW SOUND (Ire) [-] 7-9-10 (7*) R Burke, ...(20 to 1)	8
COLOURED SPARROW (Ire) [-] 6-9-12 (7*) S M McGovern,	
....(6 to 1)	9
NATIVE BORN [-] 11-9-2 (5*) J Butler, ...(20 to 1)	10
THE BOURDA [-] 10-10-0 C O'Dwyer, ...(8 to 1)	11
RUNNING SLIPPER (Ire) [-] (bl) 6-11-1 L P Cusack, (33 to 1)	12
HENRY G'S (Ire) [-] 10-10-9 F J Flood, ...(7 to 1)	13
LESS HASSLE (Ire) [-] 6-10-10 K F O'Brien, ...(10 to 1)	14
Dist: 1l, ¾l, 3l, ½l. 4m 44.90s. (14 Ran).

(P M Dowling), G M Lyons

33 Fane Hurdle (4-y-o and up) £2,397 2m 135yds..........................(6:00)

FINCHPALM (Ire) 6-12-0 F J Flood, ...(Evens fav)	1
GHALAYAN 4-10-13 C O'Dwyer, ...(20 to 1)	2
BACK TO BLACK (Ire) (bl) 7-11-9 K F O'Brien, ...(4 to 1)	3
TALE GAIL (Ire) 6-11-7 W T Slattery, ...(7 to 2)	4
PETITE MEWS (Ire) 5-11-1 D H O'Connor, ...(16 to 1)	5

ASHLEY'S PRINCESS (Ire) 4-10-8 C N Bowens, .. (16 to 1)	6
LAKE MAJESTIC (Ire) 5-10-10 (5*) T Martin, ...(25 to 1)	7
TENDER LASS (Ire) 5-11-1 P L Malone, ...(12 to 1)	8
CNOC AN RIOG (Ire) 6-11-2 (5*) J Butler, ...(20 to 1)	9
BOLD TERM (Ire) 5-10-12 (3*) U Smyth, ...(25 to 1)	10
Dist: 8l, 1½l, 1½l, 2l. 3m 54.20s. (10 Ran).

(Finchpalm Limited), F Flood

34 Faughart I.N.H. Flat Race (4-y-o and up) £2,226 2m 135yds...............(8:30)

NATIVE COIN (Ire) 7-12-0 Mr R Walsh, ...(7 to 4 on)	1
MOTOQUA 4-10-8 (7*) Mr G Elliott, ...(8 to 1)	2
JOHNNY'S DREAM (Ire) 6-11-7 (7*) Mr A J Dempsey,	
....(4 to 1)	3
JUST A VODKA (Ire) 6-11-7 (7*) Mr A Fleming, ...(20 to 1)	4
PEACEFULL RIVER (Ire) 7-11-2 (7*) Mr D Delaney, ..(8 to 1)	5
BARLEY MEADOW (Ire) 4-11-5 (7*) Mr B M Cash, .(14 to 1)	6
ARCTIC COURT (Ire) 5-11-1 (7*) Mr N Hannity, ...(12 to 1)	7
FANORE (Ire) 5-11-6 (7*) Mr M O'Connor, ...(12 to 1)	8
JARSUN QUEEN (Ire) 4-11-1 Mr H F Cleary, ...(7 to 1)	9
YOUR WORSHIP (Ire) 6-11-7 (7*) Mr J Bright, ...(25 to 1)	10
Dist: 6l, 1½l, 2l, 10l. 3m 41.60s. (10 Ran).

(Mrs J E Rothwell), W P Mullins

PERTH (good to firm)
Friday June 7th
Going Correction: MINUS 0.25 sec. per fur.

35 Wetter Better People Novices' Hurdle Class E (4-y-o and up) £2,332 2m 110yds ....(2:30)

TUKANO (Can) 5-10-12 A P McCoy, *prmnt, lft in ld aftr 3rd, drvn alng bef 2 out, styd on.*	
..........................(11 to 10 fav op 6 to 4 tchd 7 to 4)	1
FORGOTTEN EMPRESS 4-10-2 P Carberry, *hld up, smooth hdwy to track wnr aftr 3 out, drvn alng bef nxt, no imprsn.*	
....(33 to 1 op 20 to 1)	2
MULLINS (Ire) 5-10-12 D J Moffatt, *in tch, hdwy to chase ldrs hfwy, wknd appr 2 out.* ....(6 to 1 op 4 to 1)	3
SARACEN PRINCE (USA) (v) 4-10-7 P Niven, *mid-div, hdwy to chase wnr hfwy, blun 3 out, sn wknd.*	
...........................(5 to 1 op 7 to 2 tchd 9 to 2)	4
MAC'S TAXI 4-10-7 M Foster, *in tch till wknd aftr 3 out, tld off.* ....(12 to 1 op 10 to 1)	5
27 GRINNELL 6-10-12 R Davis, *sn lost tch, wl tld off.*	
..........................(100 to 1 tchd 200 to 1)	6
PATTER MERCHANT 7-10-12 B Storey, *led till swrvd badly lft and ran out paddock bend aftr 3rd.* ....(50 to 1)	ro
GORODENKA BOY 6-10-12 D Morris, *sn lost tch, tld off whn pld up bef 3 out.* ....(100 to 1 tchd 150 to 1)	pu
BALMAHA 5-10-7 Mr A Phillips, *lost tch frm 4th, tld off whn pld up bef 3 out.*..........(9 to 1 op 10 to 1 tchd 8 to 1)	pu
DRAKEWRATH (Ire) 6-10-9 (3*) D Parker, *chsd ldrs till wknd aftr 5th, tld off whn pld up bef 2 out.*	
.........................(9 to 2 op 3 to 1 tchd 5 to 1)	pu
Dist: 2l, 16l, 1¼l, dist, dist. 3m 48.30s. a 7.30s (10 Ran).

(Mrs T McCoubrey), J R Jenkins

36 Water Options For Growth Novices' Chase Class E (5-y-o and up) £3,178 3m ....(3:00)

TEMPLE GARTH 7-12-1 R Supple, *sn chasing clr ldr, led aftr 13th, blun last, styd on wl.*	
..........................(6 to 4 op 11 to 8 tchd 5 to 4)	1
CABBERY ROSE (Ire) 8-10-10 P Carberry, *led to second, in tch, hdwy to dispute ld aftr 13th, one drvn alng, no imprsn on wnr.* ....(11 to 4 tchd 3 to 1 and 7 to 2)	2
WHITE DIAMOND (bl) 8-11-1 M Foster, *jmpd lft, led second till hdd aftr 13th, sn btn.* ..(9 to 4 op 2 to 1 tchd 5 to 2)	3
27° MISTER CASUAL 7-10-10 (5*) R McGrath, *beh, blun 8th, lost tch frm tenth.* ....(20 to 1 op 16 to 1)	4
BECCY BROWN 8-10-7 (3*) D Parker, *in tch till wknd aftr tenth, sn wl beh.* ....(50 to 1 tchd 66 to 1)	5
ESTABLISH (Ire) 8-10-10 A Thornton, *sn lost tch, tld off whn pld up bef 7th.* ....(20 to 1 op 14 to 1)	pu
Dist: 10l, 14l, 16l, 15l. 6m 1.40s. a 6.40s (6 Ran).

(Mrs Jos Wilson), P Beaumont

37 Irrigation By Design Handicap Chase Class E (0-115 5-y-o and up) £3,590 2½m 110yds....................(3:30)

UNOR (Fr) [101] 10-11-4 A Dobbin, *nvr far away, led 11th, drw clr frm 3 out, eased considerably r-in.*	
...................(5 to 2 fav op 9 to 4 tchd 11 to 4)	1
BITACRACK [83] 9-10-0 L O'Hara, *in tch, hdwy to chase ldrs hfwy, outpcd aftr tenth, styd on wl frm betw last 2, no ch with wnr.* ....(10 to 1 op 7 to 1)	2
BLAZING DAWN [83] 9-10-0 (6ex) B Storey, *led till hdd 11th, kpt on same pace.*......................(10 to 1 op 9 to 2)	3
24° BALD JOKER [84] 11-9-12 (3*) B Fenton, *in tch till wknd aftr tenth, tld off.*...................(25 to 1 op 20 to 1)	4

CHARMING GALE [92] 9-10-9 P Carberry, *chsd ldrs till wknd bef tenth, tld off*..........(10 to 1 op 6 to 1) 5
OLD MONEY [83] 10-10-0 (6ex) A P McCoy, *lost tch frm hfwy, tld off*..........(5 to 1 op 7 to 2 tchd 6 to 1) 6
WISE ADVICE (Ire) [104] (bl) 6-11-7 R Garritty, *chsd ldrs, drvn alng and wknd bef 9th, tld off.*..........(7 to 1 op 5 to 1 tchd 8 to 1) 7
FUNNY OLD GAME [83] 9-10-0 R Davis, *sn wl tld off, pld up aftr 7th*..........(20 to 1 op 14 to 1) pu
WILLCHRIS [107] 9-11-10 T P Rudd, *lost tch frm 5th, tld off whn pld up aftr 7th*..........(9 to 2 tchd 5 to 1) pu
Dist: 1¾l, 1¼l, dist, 12l, 17l, 4l. 4m 58.20s. a 6.20s (9 Ran).
(Miss H B Hamilton), P Monteith

38 Sprinkled Excellence Novices' Hurdle Class E (4-y-o and up) £2,332 3m 110yds .... (4:00)

BLOOMING SPRING (Ire) 7-10-9 L O'Hara, *nvr far away, led 9th, drw clr frm 2 out, easily*..........(7 to 2 tchd 4 to 1) 1
MICKSDILEMMA 9-11-0 Mr A Phillips, *in tch, led 7th, blun and hdd 9th, drvn alng to chase wnr aftr, no imprsn.*..........(4 to 1 op 3 to 1) 2
VILPRANO 5-11-7 D J Moffatt, *in tch, pushed alng bef 3 out, grad wknd*..........(7 to 4 on tchd 13 to 8 on) 3
23 JUST A GUESS (Ire) (bl) 5-11-0 A P McCoy, *mstks, led till hdd 7th, lost tch aftr nxt, tld off*..........(33 to 1 op 20 to 1) 4
SALLY SMITH 7-10-4 (5*) R McGrath, *lost tch aftr 5th, tld off whn pld up after 7th*..........(33 to 1 op 20 to 1) pu
Dist: 13l, 16l, dist. 5m 56.00s. a 14.00s (5 Ran).
(Capt Ben Coutts), Mrs D Thomson

39 Giving Nature A Hand Handicap Chase Class E (0-115 5-y-o and up) £3,403 2m .... (4:30)

GROUSE-N-HEATHER [89] 7-10-7 A Dobbin, *trkd ldrs, led bef 8th, styd on wl und pres frm 2 out*...(2 to 1 op 11 to 8) 1
GONE BY (Ire) [82] 8-10-0 A P McCoy, *hld up in tch, effrt bef 3 out, sn chasing wnr, styd on wl und pres frm nxt.*..........(5 to 4 fav op 7 to 4) 2
LOCHNAGRAIN (Ire) [110] 8-12-0 P Niven, *led to 4th, prmnt, outpcd appr 3 out, kpt on frm nxt*..........(5 to 2 op 6 to 4) 3
CARDENDEN (Ire) [82] 8-10-0 B Storey, *led 4th till hdd bef 8th, rdn and wknd aftr 3 out*..........(33 to 1 op 20 to 1) 4
Dist: ¾l, 4l, 14l. 3m 54.00s. a 3.00s (4 Ran).
SR: 9/1/25/-/ (D J Fairbairn), P Monteith

40 Drops Equal Good Crops Handicap Hurdle Class E (0-115 4-y-o and up) £2,762 2m 110yds.......... (5:00)

KEEP BATTLING [88] 6-10-11 (3*) G Cahill, *hld up, hdwy bef 2 out, led aftr last, ran on und pres.*..........(6 to 1 op 5 to 1 tchd 13 to 2) 1
SARMATIAN (USA) [91] 5-11-3 R Garritty, *hld up, hdwy bef 5th, led on bit appr last, sn rdn and hdd, no extr.*..........(11 to 8 fav op 5 to 4) 2
25* TABU LADY (Ire) [96] (bl) 5-11-8⁶ A P McCoy, *led, rdn bef 2 out, hdd appr last, no extr*..........(6 to 1 op 5 to 1) 3
FLINTLOCK (Ire) [87] 6-10-8 (5*) R McGrath, *chsd ldrs, ev ch 2 out, wkng whn mstk last*...(9 to 2 op 4 to 1 tchd 5 to 1) 4
WELL APPOINTED (Ire) [98] 7-11-10 B Storey, *lost tch frm 5th, tld off*..........(9 to 2 op 4 to 1) 5
LIABILITY ORDER [85] (bl) 7-10-11 M Moloney, *chsd ldr to 5th, wknd quickly, tld off*..........(100 to 1 op 50 to 1) 6
Dist: 3½l, hd, 12l, dist, 8l. 3m 43.60s. a 2.60s (6 Ran).
SR: 19/18/22/1/-/-/ (J S Goldie), J S Goldie

SOUTHWELL (good to firm) Saturday June 8th

Going Correction: PLUS 0.10 sec. per fur.

41 Summer Jumping Novices' Chase Class D (5-y-o and up) £4,253 2½m 110yds .... (6:50)

TUFFNUT GEORGE 9-11-7 Mr A Phillips, *trkd ldrs, led tenth, made rst, kpt on wl*..........(11 to 4 op 4 to 1) 1
CALL ME ALBI (Ire) 5-10-7 M Richards, *hdwy frm tenth, styd on from 3 out, no ch wth wnr.*..........(11 to 1 op 10 to 1 tchd 12 to 1) 2
TOP SPIN 7-11-0 J Osborne, *not go early pace, rdn and styd on frm 13th, nrst finish.*..........(6 to 4 fav tchd 7 to 4 and 15 to 8) 3
HIZAL 7-11-0 Mr A Charles-Jones, *hld up, styd on appr 3 out, not trble ldrs*..........(50 to 1 op 33 to 1) 4
MARINERS COVE 8-11-0 R Farrant, *hdwy frm 6th, kpt on one pace from 13th*..........(7 to 1 op 9 to 2) 5
GOLDEN SAVANNAH (bl) 6-11-0 A Thornton, *led, hdd tenth, sn wknd*..........(10 to 1 op 8 to 1) 6
BIT OF A DREAM (Ire) 6-11-0 Richard Guest, *mstk 1st, sn prmnt, chsd wnr frm 9th, rdn and lost pl appr 3 out.*..........(25 to 1 op 20 to 1) 7
DORMSTON BOYO 6-10-11 (3*) R Massey, *prmnt to 7th, sn lost pl, no ch frm 13th*..........(33 to 1 tchd 50 to 1) 8
WITHOUT A FLAG (USA) 6-11-0 W McFarland, *mstk second, rear grp most of way, tld off*..........(14 to 1) 9
RUSHHOME 9-10-9 S Burrough, *beh most of way, refused 3 out*..........(50 to 1 op 33 to 1) ref
PRINCE ROCKAWAY (Ire) 8-10-11 (3*) Guy Lewis, *wth ldrs to tenth, grad lost pl, tld off whn pld up bef 3 out.*..........(50 to 1 op 33 to 1) pu
Dist: 2½l, 6l, ½l, 14l, 6l, 7l, 13l, 22l, dist. 5m 23.50s. a 23.50s (11 Ran).
(P T Cartridge), Mrs P Grainger

42 J.T.F. Wholesale Distribution Handicap Chase Class F (0-100 5-y-o and up) £3,980 3m 110yds.......... (7:15)

ROYAL VACATION [95] 7-11-10 N Bentley, *hld up, hdwy frm 12th, chlgd and led 3 out, rdn out*..........(6 to 1 tchd 7 to 1) 1
SEA BREAKER (Ire) [92] 8-11-7 Richard Guest, *tucked in beh ldrs, str run appr last, no extr nr finish*..........(7 to 2 jt-fav op 11 to 4) 2
ALBERT BLAKE [92] 9-11-7 A P McCoy, *led, hdd 3 out, no extr flt*..........(13 to 2 op 5 to 1 tchd 7 to 1) 3
MISS ENRICO [89] 10-11-4 A Thornton, *styd on frm 16th, not trble ldrs*..........(14 to 1 tchd 16 to 1) 4
BRINDLEY HOUSE [82] 9-10-11 W McFarland, *prmnt to 16th, kpt on one pace*..........(14 to 1) 5
TENBIT (Ire) [73] 6-10-2 C Llewellyn, *chsd ldr to 13th, grad lost pl, beh frm 16th*..........(11 to 2 op 6 to 1 tchd 7 to 1) 6
TWO STEP RHYTHM [82] 12-10-11 M Sharratt, *chsd ldrs to 14th, sn rdn and btn*..........(33 to 1 op 20 to 1) 7
TRUSS [85] 9-11-0 R Supple, *al prmnt, in tch whn f 13th.*..........(7 to 1 op 5 to 1) f
ROYAL MILE [75] 11-10-4¹ Mr N Kent, *mid-div, wknd quickly and pld up bef 15th*..........(33 to 1 op 20 to 1) pu
HAWAIIAN GODDESS (USA) [77] 9-10-6 D Leahy, *mstks, sn tld off, pld up bef 3 out*..........(33 to 1 op 20 to 1) pu
LADY BLAKENEY [86] 10-11-1 J Osborne, *prmnt till pld up aftr 12th*..........(7 to 2 jt-fav op 3 to 1 tchd 4 to 1) pu
Dist: 2l, 3l, 16l, 3l, 1l, dist. 6m 24.80s. a 30.80s (11 Ran).
(G P Edwards), G M Moore

43 Maun Motors Handicap Chase Class E (0-115 5-y-o and up) £4,230 2m... (7:45)

SASKIA'S HERO [104] 9-11-10 D Byrne, *hld up, hdwy to ld 8th, made rst, hit 3 out, ran on wl.* (5 to 2 jt-fav op 9 to 4) 1
GESNERA [88] 8-10-1 (7*) Michael Brennan, *wth ldrs frm 6th, ev ch 9th, no extr from 2 out*..........(7 to 1 op 6 to 1) 2
DR ROCKET [86] (bl) 11-10-3 (3*) J Culloty, *wth wnr frm 6th, lost pl 3 out*..........(5 to 1 op 4 to 1) 3
EMERALD MOON [82] 9-10-2² S Burrough, *mid-div, kpt on one pace frm tenth*..........(25 to 1 op 20 to 1) 4
RAMSTAR [99] 8-11-5 A P McCoy, *quickly into strd, led to 8th, hit 9th, wknd*....(5 to 2 jt-fav op 3 to 1 tchd 100 to 30) 5
FULL O'PRAISE (NZ) [108] 9-12-0 Gary Lyons, *chsd ldr to 5th, lost tch 7th, beh frm tenth*..........(4 to 1 tchd 9 to 2) 6
MASTER SALESMAN [80] 13-9-11 (3*) D Parker, *mstks, sn beh, tld off whn pld up bef 3 out*..........(16 to 1) pu
Dist: 3l, 7l, 7l, 10l, 14l. 4m 23.00s. a 29.00s (7 Ran).
(Qualitair Holdings Limited), J F Bottomley

44 Nottingham Evening Post Handicap Hurdle Class D (0-125 4-y-o and up) £2,976 2½m 110yds.......... (8:15)

EID (USA) [118] 7-12-0 Richard Guest, *al prmnt, wth ldrs 2 out, slight ld last, ran on wl, fnshd feelingly.*..........(9 to 2 op 5 to 1 tchd 11 to 2) 1
RED VALERIAN [111] (v) 5-11-0 (7*) Michael Brennan, *chsd ldrs, rdn alng frm 3 out, slight ld aftr 2 out, hdd last, ridden out.*..........(7 to 2 op 3 to 1) 2
BLUE RAVEN [90] 5-10-0 A P McCoy, *chsd ldr, led aftr 3 out, mstk 2 out, unbl to quicken last.*..........(9 to 2 op 5 to 1 tchd 11 to 2) 3
DIBLOOM [90] 8-10-0 R Johnson, *led, hdd aftr 3 out, one pace frm 2 out*..........(16 to 1 op 12 to 1) 4
TOPFORMER [90] 9-10-0 R Supple, *al in rear, nvr able to chal*..........(25 to 1 op 16 to 1) 5
CIRCUS COLOURS [98] 6-10-8 J Osborne, *al in rear, rdn appr 7th, no hdwy, tld off*..........(6 to 1 op 4 to 1) 6
MR GENEAOLOGY (USA) [96] 6-10-6 A Thornton, *prmnt to 6th, sn lost pl, tld off*..........(7 to 1 op 6 to 1 tchd 8 to 1) 7
ALL ON [110] 5-11-6 R Marley, *bumped and uns rdr 1st.*..........(100 to 30 fav op 3 to 1) ur
Dist: Hd, 5l, 14l, 12l, dist, dist. 5m 4.10s. a 18.10s (8 Ran).
(N Wilby), Mrs S J Smith

45 Top Of The Ground Selling Handicap Hurdle Class G (0-90 4 - 7-y-o) £2,027 2m .... (8:45)

NOCATCHIM [85] 7-11-7 (3*) R Massey, *led to 3 out, wth ldr nxt, rdn to led ag'n, pushed out.*..........(11 to 2 op 5 to 1 tchd 6 to 1) 1

PARISH WALK (Ire) [85] 5-11-10 S Wynne, *al prmnt, jmpd rght 2 out, hld last, unbl to quicken.
.... (100 to 30 fav op 11 to 4 tchd 7 to 2) 2
AGAINST THE CLOCK [65] 4-10-4 R Greene, *hld up, styd on frm 2 out, not rch ldrs*............(11 to 1 op 7 to 1) 3
HIGH FLOWN (USA) [74] 4-10-13 A P McCoy, *chsd ldr to 3 out, rdn 2 out, one pace*....(7 to 1 op 6 to 1 tchd 8 to 1) 4
CLASSIC IMAGE (Ire) [72] 6-10-11 Mr A Charles-Jones, *trkd ldr, wknd appr 3 out*....(16 to 1 op 12 to 1 tchd 20 to 1) 5
SPEAKER'S HOUSE (USA) [89] 7-12-0 A Thornton, *mid-div, no hdwy frm 3 out*.....................(6 to 1 op 9 to 2) 6
LEGAL DRAMA (USA) [65] 4-9-12[1] (7*) C Rae, *hld up, hdwy frm 6th, sn rdn and btn*.............................(20 to 1) 7
WOODLANDS ENERGY [61] 5-10-9 R Davis, *prmnt, wknd appr 2 out*...................(9 to 1 op 16 to 1) 8
NIGHT BOAT [76] (v) 5-10-12 (3*) Guy Lewis, *rear div most of way*.............................(8 to 1 tchd 7 to 1) 9
SIESTA TIME (USA) [64] (bl) 6-10-3[3] D O'Sullivan, *beh, hdwy frm 4th, 5th, sn behind*..................(25 to 1) 10
SAKBAH (USA) [65] 7-10-1 (3*) T Dascombe, *no oth whn f 3 out*.........................(14 to 1 op 12 to 1) f
3 out, hdd aftr 2 out, second and btn whn f last.
.............................(12 to 1 op 14 to 1) pu
Dist: 6l, 3l, 11l, 2½l, 2l, hd, 11l, sht-hd, 6l. 3m 56.10s. a 10.10s (12 Ran).
SR: 11/5/-/-/-/-/

(R E Gray), K A Morgan

46 Fast Ground Maiden Hurdle Class E (4-y-o and up) £2,511 2m............ (9:15)

ZAHID (USA) 5-11-8 R Johnson, *hld up, gd hdwy appr 3 out, slight ld last, rdn out*........................(9 to 2 op 5 to 1) 1
ORDOG MOR (Ire) 7-11-5 A P McCoy, *led 5th, hdd last, hrd rdn, no extr last strds*...........(11 to 4 fav op 3 to 1) 2
SCAMALLACH (Ire) (bl) 6-11-0 J Osborne, *wth ldrs, ev ch appr 2 out, wknd last*........(3 to 1 op 7 to 2 tchd 4 to 1) 3
JUST BRUCE 7-11-5 A Thornton, *led to 5th, kpt on one pace appr 2 out*....................(9 to 2 op 3 to 1 tchd 5 to 1) 4
PEGASUS BAY 5-11-5 R Garritty, *prmnt, mstk 6th, no hdwy frm 3 out*........................(8 to 1 op 7 to 1) 5
DEEP FAIR 9-11-5 Richard Guest, *hld up, hdwy aftr 4th, rdn 3 out, unbl to quicken*...............(14 to 1 op 12 to 1) 6
PAPA'S BOY (Ire) 5-11-5 M Foster, *prmnt, wknd appr 2 out.*
.............................(11 to 2 op 9 to 2 tchd 6 to 1) 7
NEVER SAY SO 4-10-9 Mr N Kent, *beh, pld up bef 2 out.*
.............................(50 to 1 op 33 to 1) pu
Dist: ½l, 4l, 10l, 10l, 8l, 2l. 3m 55.70s. a 9.70s (8 Ran).
SR: 10/9/-/-/-/-/

(Keith W R Booth), K R Burke

WORCESTER (good)
Saturday June 8th
Going Correction: NIL

47 Bransford Novices' Handicap Hurdle Class F (0-95 5-y-o and up) £2,143 3m
.... (3:00)

VALISKY [75] 6-11-0 C Llewellyn, *wtd wth, hdwy appr 3 out, chlgd last, led r-in, drvn out*........(12 to 1 op 10 to 1) 1
HIGH POST [75] 7-10-11 (3*) R Massey, *hld up, hdwy 8th, led 3 out, hdd and unbl to quicken r-in .*
.............................(10 to 1 op 8 to 1 tchd 11 to 1) 2
WYNBERG [89] 5-11-9 (5*) L Aspell, *hld up beh ldrs, clr order 7th, led 3 out, hdd 3 out, no extr last.*
.............................(8 to 1 op 5 to 1 tchd 9 to 1) 3
PALACE PARADE (USA) [65] 6-10-4 S Burrough, *hld up, hdwy frm 4 out, effrt nxt, one pace 2 out*..............(33 to 1) 4
LIMOSA [81] 5-11-6 M Richards, *trkd ldrs, effrt appr 3 out, wknd nxt*........................(7 to 1 op 5 to 1) 5
MR POPPLETON [71] (bl) 7-10-7 (3*) Guy Lewis, *chsd ldrs, effrt aftr 4 out, btn 2 out*...............(14 to 1 op 12 to 1) 6
SPANISH BLAZE (Ire) [68] 8-10-7 D Byrne, *hld up, rdn alng aftr 8th, btn appr 3 out*.........(2 to 1 fav op 7 to 1) 7
LITTLE COURT [61] 5-10-0 R Johnson, *hld up beh ldrs, rdn and wknd appr 3 out*............................ 8
HIDDEN FLOWER [61] (v) 7-9-11 (3*) B Fenton, *led to 7th, sn wknd, tld off whn pld up bef 3 out.*
.............................(20 to 1 op 16 to 1) pu
STONECROP [79] 5-11-4 J R Kavanagh, *al beh, tld off whn pld up bef 2 out*..................(20 to 1 op 16 to 1) pu
VAN DER GRASS [63] 7-10-2[2] Gary Lyons, *hld up in mid-div, wknd 8th, tld off whn pld up bef 3 out.* (33 to 1 op 20 to 1) pu
UP THE TEMPO (Ire) [72] 7-10-11 R Greene, *hld up, rdn and lost to aftr 6th, tld off whn pld up bef 4 out, broke blood vessel*..................(12 to 1 op 10 to 1 tchd 14 to 1) pu
RED EIKON [72] (bl) 5-10-11 A P McCoy, *chsd ldr, led 7th to nxt, sn wknd, tld off whn pld up bef 3 out* (6 to 1 op 5 to 1) pu
AKIYMANN (USA) [87] 6-11-12 D Bridgwater, *al beh, tld off whn pld up bef 3 out*......(6 to 1 op 7 to 2 tchd 7 to 1) pu
WINTER ROSE [75] 5-11-0 B Powell, *al beh, tld off whn pld up bef 2 out*...........................(10 to 1 op 7 to 1) pu
Dist: 1¼l, 3½l, 7l, 6l, 17l, 3l, 3½l. 5m 49.40s. a 13.40s (15 Ran).

(Risk Another Partnership), R Lee

48 Redhill Handicap Chase Class D (0-120 5-y-o and up) £4,500 2½m 110yds (3:30)

SARTORIUS [100] (v) 10-10-9 B Powell, *led to second, rgned ld 7th, made rst, all out*............(10 to 1 op 8 to 1) 1
POLDEN PRIDE [112] 8-11-4 (3*) B Fenton, *hld up, rdn and styd on frm 4 out, chlgd r-in, ran on.*
.............................(7 to 2 op 3 to 1 tchd 4 to 1) 2
HENLEY REGATTA [94] 8-10-3[3] S Burrough, *hld up, mstks 5th and 11th, styd on frm nxt, ran on r-in.* (20 to 1 tchd 25 to 1) 3
MONKS JAY (Ire) [91] 7-10-0 I Lawrence, *hld up, rdn alng 8th, effrt 4 out, one pace appr 2 out*.............(11 to 2) 4
MUSKORA (Ire) [119] (bl) 7-12-0 R Dunwoody, *wth wnr, led second, jmpd slwly and hdd 7th, jumped slowly ag'n nxt, wknd appr 4 out*.....................(7 to 4 fav op 2 to 1) 5
BLACK CHURCH [100] 10-10-9 D O'Sullivan, *hld up, hdwy aftr 6th, lost pl 9th, no dngr after*....(12 to 1 op 10 to 1) 6
PONTYNYSWEN [111] (v) 8-11-6 D J Burchell, *hld up, hdwy 8th, 3rd and btn whn blun and uns rdr last.*
.............................(6 to 1 op 9 to 2) ur
CASTLE KING [119] 9-12-0 M Richards, *prmnt till wknd 4 out, tld off whn pld up bef 2 out*.......(10 to 1 tchd 12 to 1) pu
NADJATI (USA) [100] 7-10-9 G Upton, *hld up, lost tch aftr 9th, tld off whn pld up after last*......(10 to 1 op 8 to 1) pu
FATHER SHARP [91] 10-9-5[5] A Dowling, *prmnt till wknd 5th, hdwy 9th, wknd appr 2 out, tld off whn pld up bef last* mstk 1st, hdwy 9th, wknd appr 2 out
.............................(33 to 1 op 25 to 1) pu
Dist: ½l, ¾l, 12l, 1l, 9l. 5m 10.80s. a 13.80s (10 Ran).

(M Popham), T Thomson Jones

49 Boxfoldia Jubilee Handicap Hurdle Class F (0-105 4-y-o and up) £2,512 2m (4:00)

PHALAROPE (Ire) [84] 8-10-10 R Dunwoody, *hld up, hdwy aftr 5th, led 2 out, rdn out.* (9 to 4 fav op 3 to 1 tchd 7 to 2) 1
CALL THE GUV'NOR [90] 7-11-2 J R Kavanagh, *hld up, hdwy appr 3 out, mstk nxt, chalg whn hng lft aftr last, unbl to quicken last one hundred yards*....................(6 to 1) 2
BOLTROSE [92] 6-11-4 R Davis, *hld up, hdwy 3 out, kpt on frm nxt*..................(16 to 1 op 8 to 1) 3
LEGATEE [90] (v) 5-10-11 T Eley, *hld up beh ldrs, effrt 5th, one pace 2 out, rn on*............(11 to 1 op 10 to 1) 4
HOW'S IT GOIN (Ire) [98] 5-11-10 M Richards, *beh frm 4th, kpt on ag'n from 2 out*.............(10 to 1 tchd 11 to 1) 5
ELEANORA MUSE [74] 6-9-9 (5*) Chris Webb, *in tch to 3 out.*
.............................(8 to 1 tchd 9 to 1 and 10 to 1) 6
BUGLET [90] 6-11-2 D Bridgwater, *beh frm 3rd, tld off.*
.............................(6 to 1 op 4 to 1) 7
WHISTLING BUCK (Ire) [80] 8-10-6 D O'Sullivan, *prmnt to 5th.*
.............................(10 to 1 op 8 to 1 tchd 11 to 1) 8
FRONTIER FLIGHT (USA) [88] 6-10-11 (3*) E Husband, *hld up, hdwy frm 3 out, staying on 6th whn f nxt.*
.............................(10 to 1 op 14 to 1 tchd 8 to 1) f
JAVA SHRINE (USA) [76] (bl) 5-10-2 S McNeill, *prmnt, led 3rd, hdd 2 out, 4th and btn whn f last*.........(20 to 1 op 14 to 1) f
WILL JAMES [80] (bl) 10-10-3 (3*) J Culloty, *hld up, lost tch 5th, tld off whn pld up bef last.*
.............................(16 to 1 op 14 to 1 tchd 20 to 1) pu
HAVE A NIGHTCAP [102] (bl) 7-12-0 B Powell, *led to 3rd, wknd quickly, tld off whn pld up bef 3 out.*
.............................(20 to 1 op 14 to 1) pu
Dist: 2l, 7l, 4l, 5l, 1¼l, 28l, 8l. 3m 46.90s. a 6.90s (12 Ran).
SR: 13/17/12/1/9/-/

(Foreneish Racing), K A Morgan

50 Holt Novices' Hurdle Class E (4-y-o and up) £2,617 2m............... (4:30)

BRAVE PATRIARCH (Ire) 5-10-12 J R Kavanagh, *hld up beh ldrs, led 3 out, rdn out, ran on wl.*
.............................(Evens fav op 5 to 4 tchd 5 to 4 on) 1
BORN TO PLEASE (Ire) 4-10-7 A P McCoy, *ran green, led to 4th, rgned ld briefly appr 3 out, ran on frm last.*
.............................(4 to 1 op 3 to 1 tchd 9 to 2) 2
BRAMLEY MAY 6-10-12 B Powell, *hld up in rear, hdwy 5th, ev ch 2 out, unbl to quicken r-in.*
.............................(11 to 2 op 5 to 1 tchd 6 to 1) 3
GENERAL SHIRLEY (Ire) 5-10-12 (7*) M Clinton, *hld up, hdwy frm 5th, effrt from 3 out, one pace nxt.*
.............................(15 to 2 op 6 to 1 tchd 8 to 1) 4
OUT FOR A DUCK 5-10-12 R Davis, *hld up, lost tch frm 5th, no impsn aftr*..........(50 to 1 op 25 to 1 tchd 66 to 1) 5
MANABOUTHEHOUSE 9-10-12 L Harvey, *in tch, rdn appr 3 out, sn btn*.........................(25 to 1 op 16 to 1) 6
MAFUTA (Ire) (bl) 4-9-13 (3*) T Dascombe, *hld up beh ldrs, effrt whn not fluent 3 out, wknd nxt*....(25 to 1 op 16 to 1) 7
LASER LIGHT LADY 4-10-2 S Wynne, *prmnt, jmpd slwly 3rd, wknd 5th*.........................(150 to 1 op 50 to 1) 8
FRANKIE HARRY 4-10-7 T Eley, *hld up lost tch 5th, no dngr aftr*.........................(150 to 1 op 50 to 1) 9
KUTAN (Ire) (bl) 6-10-12 E Byrne, *hld up in tch, led 4th till appr 3 out, wkng whn f nxt*.........(33 to 1 op 20 to 1) f
Dist: 2½l, 1l, 6l, 14l, 5l, 8l, 3½l, 6l. 3m 50.60s. a 10.60s (10 Ran).

(Peter S Winfield), N J Henderson

51 P & O Handicap Chase Class E (0-100 5-y-o and up) £3,104 2m 7f....... (5:05)

FUNCHEON GALE [85] 9-10-3 D Morris, *hld up in tch, led 14th, drw clr frm 4 out*.................(5 to 2 jt-fav tchd 3 to 1 and 9 to 4) 1

HOWGILL [94] (bl) 10-10-12 S Wynne, *al prmnt, led 8th till 11th, outpcd frm 4 out*.................(8 to 1 op 5 to 1) 2
CHARGED [97] 7-11-1 A P McCoy, *chsd ldrs, second and hld whn blun 4 out*..........(5 to 2 jt-fav op 7 to 2) 3
BRAVO STAR (USA) [82] 11-9-9 (5*) Chris Webb, *prmnt, lost pl tenth, no imprsn aftr.*
........(16 to 1 op 14 to 1 tchd 20 to 1 and 25 to 1) 4
ARTFUL ARTHUR [82] 10-10-0 Mr J Grassick, *al beh.*
..................(50 to 1 op 33 to 1) 5
VICTORY ANTHEM [82] 10-9-11 (3*) B Fenton, *led to 8th, rgned ld 11th, hdd 14th, sn wknd, tld off*............(16 to 1) 6
THE BLUE BOY (Ire) [100] (bl) 8-11-4 R Johnson, *prmnt to 9th, grad wknd, tld off whn pld up aftr last*... (10 to 1 op 6 to 1) pu
VICAR OF BRAY [90] 9-10-8 J R Kavanagh, *al beh, tld off whn pld up bef 4 out*..........(9 to 1 op 6 to 1 tchd 10 to 1) pu
MERIVEL [110] 9-12-0 D O'Sullivan, *al beh, tld off whn pld up bef 4 out*..................(13 to 2 op 9 to 2) pu
Dist: 12l, 30l, 2½l, sht-hd, dist. 5m 54.50s. a 16.50p (9 Ran).

(Kings Of The Road Partnership), R Curtis

52 Grimley Standard Open National Hunt Flat Class H (Div I) (4,5,6-y-o) £1,280 2m
.... (5:40)

REGAL GEM (Ire) 5-11-0 (3*) B Fenton, *wtd wth, prog hfwy, led o'r 2 fs out, drvn out.*
..........(5 to 4 on op 6 to 4 on tchd 6 to 4 on) 1
OH DEAR ME 5-10-10 D O'Sullivan, *hld up beh ldrs, rdn o'r 2 fs out, ev ch ins last, kpt on*...........(25 to 1 op 14 to 1) 2
BOUNDTOHONOUR (Ire) 4-10-10 Jacqui Oliver, *hld up in tch, str chal und pres frm 3 fs out, no extr ins last*......(12 to 1) 3
SEVEN WELLS 4-10-10 R Greene, *trkd ldg grp, effrt 3 fs out, one pace*......................(33 to 1 op 20 to 1) 4
ROC AGE 5-10-10 R Davis, *prmnt, led 5 fs out, hdd o'r 2 furlongs out, one pace*..................(33 to 1) 5
FOOLS NOOK 5-10-12 (3*) T Dascombe, *hdwy hfwy, effrt 4 fs out, wknd o'r 2 out*........(4 to 1 op 3 to 1 tchd 9 to 2) 6
BLUE HAVANA 4-9-12 (7*) Shaun Graham, *hld up, hdwy hfwy, btn o'r 2 fs out*..................(33 to 1 op 50 to 1) 7
JACKAMUS (Ire) 5-10-8 (7*) Mr M Frith, *nvr able to chal.*
..................(33 to 1 op 16 to 1) 8
FUTURE HEALTH 6-11-1 V Smith, *trkd ldg grp, lost pl frm hfwy*..............(10 to 1 op 6 to 1 tchd 12 to 1) 9
TIGER BEE 5-10-5 (5*) Sophie Mitchell, *led to 5 fs out, wknd quickly*..........(25 to 1 op 16 to 1 tchd 33 to 1) 10
SONRISA (Ire) 4-10-10 J R Kavanagh, *al beh.*
..................(7 to 1 op 3 to 1 tchd 10 to 1) 11
ABER GLEN 6-10-10 Mr M Rodda, *keen hold, in tch till wknd 6 fs out*......................(33 to 1 op 20 to 1) 12
ANOTHER BULA (Ire) 5-11-1 B Powell, *beh frm hfwy.*
..................(20 to 1 op 16 to 1 tchd 25 to 1) 13
DERRING COURT 6-10-10 G Upton, *prmnt early, beh frm hfwy, tld off*..................(33 to 1 op 16 to 1) 14
Dist: ½l, 1½l, 11l, 2l, 9l, 1¼l, 12l, 8l, 2l, 16l. 3m 43.60s. (14 Ran).

(D W E Coombs), C R Barwell

53 Grimley Standard Open National Hunt Flat Class H (Div II) (4,5,6-y-o) £1,269 2m
.... (6:10)

KAILASH (USA) 5-11-8 D Bridgwater, *hld up beh ldrs, led o'r 4 fs out, all out*..................(5 to 2 op 3 to 1) 1
TANGLEFOOT TIPPLE 5-11-1 P Holley, *hld up, steady hdwy frm hfwy, ev ch whn hng lft ins last, ran on.*
..................(12 to 1 op 10 to 1) 2
POPSI'S CLOGGS 4-10-10 D Morris, *hld up, hdwy frm 6 fs out, kpt on one pace and hng lft fnl 3 furlongs, no imprsn on 1st 2*..................(33 to 1 op 16 to 1 tchd 50 to 1) 3
PROFIT AND LOSS 5-10-10 R Dunwoody, *hld up beh ldrs, effrt o'r 4 fs out, btn over 3 out*.....(7 to 4 fav tchd 2 to 1) 4
CARNIVAL CLOWN 4-10-10 R Greene, *nvr nr to chal.*
..................(50 to 1 op 6 to 1) 5
SARENACARE (Ire) 4-10-10 B Powell, *mid-div, effrt o'r 4 fs out, btn over 3 out*..................(16 to 1 op 7 to 1) 6
SUFFOLK GIRL 4-10-9 (3*) G Cahill, *hld up and beh, hdwy and effrt 5 fs out, sn wl o'r 3 out*
..................(11 to 4 op 6 to 4 tchd 3 to 1) 7
DERRYBELLE 5-10-7 (3*) T Dascombe, *chsd clr ldr, led 7 fs out, hdd o'r 4 out, sn btn*..........(16 to 1 op 12 to 1) 8
ARCTIC CHANTER 4-10-10 J R Kavanagh, *nvr on terms.*
..................(33 to 1 op 16 to 1) 9
ROSSLAYNE SERENADE 5-10-5 P McLoughlin, *trkd ldrs, wknd hfwy, tld off*..........(50 to 1 op 20 to 1) 10
WOTANITE 6-11-1 V Slattery, *led, sn clr, hdd 7 fs out, soon wknd, tld off*............(50 to 1 op 16 to 1) 11
BARTON BULLDOZER (Ire) 6-10-12 (3*) B Fenton, *chsd ldrs, wknd frm hfwy, tld off*..................(50 to 1) 12
MAGNUM FORCE (Ire) 5-11-1 T Eley, *hld up, pld up and dismounted o'r 7 fs out* (40 to 1 op 16 to 1 tchd 50 to 1) pu
Dist: Hd, 16l, 1½l, ¾l, 3l, 8l, 2l, 12l, dist, ¾l. 3m 42.10s. (13 Ran).

(Mick Fletcher), M C Pipe

STROMSHOLM (SWE) (good)
Sunday June 9th

54 Svenskt Grand National (Chase) (5-y-o and up) £9,718 2m 5f............ (2:45)

BLACK HERO (Fr) 7-10-10 J Twomey,................... 1
SERAFIN (Pol) 12-11-0 J McLaughlin,................... 2
HORRIBLE HATTA (Ire) 8-10-3 Mr A Gammell,.......... 3
RAGLAN ROAD 12-10-4 J Ryan,........................ 6
Dist: 2l, 5l, 6½l, 1l, ½l, dist. 5m 4.30s. (9 Ran).

(Stall Nor), Mrs R Nilsen

UTTOXETER (good to firm)
Sunday June 9th
Going Correction: MINUS 0.35 sec. per fur.

55 Janerite Services 'Military' Maiden Hurdle Class D (4-y-o and up) £3,048 2m
.... (2:15)

BIRTHDAY BOY (Ire) (v) 4-11-0 J Osborne, *al prmnt, chlgd 2 out, hrd rdn to ld last, all out*...........(7 to 2 jt-fav op 4 to 1 tchd 3 to 1) 1
IMLAK (Ire) 4-11-0 R Dunwoody, *al prmnt, led sn aftr 4 out, hrd rdn 2 out, kpt on, no extr*.........(4 to 1 op 3 to 1) 2
EFHARISTO (bl) 7-11-5 D Bridgwater, *hld up, gd hdwy appr 4 out, one pace frm 2 out*..................(7 to 2 jt-fav op 4 to 1 tchd 3 to 1) 3
DOUBLE PENDANT (Ire) 5-11-5 A P McCoy, *hld up, hdwy appr 5th, wknd 2 out, btn whn hit last.*
..................(9 to 1 op 8 to 1 tchd 10 to 1) 4
ILEWIN JANINE (Ire) 5-11-0 C Maude, *hld up, gd hdwy appr 4 out, ev ch nxt, wknd approaching last*..(10 to 1 op 7 to 1) 5
TOM'S GEMINI STAR 8-11-5 Richard Guest, *in rear, styd on frm 3 out, nvr dngrs*..................(50 to 1 op 33 to 1) 6
POT BLACKBIRD 7-11-0 R Johnson, *mid-div, lost tch 4 out, tld off*..............(10 to 1 op 12 to 1 tchd 16 to 1) 7
KAMA SIMBA 4-11-0 W McFarland, *mstk 1st, mid-div till wknd 4 out, tld off*..................(16 to 1 op 12 to 1) 8
DANCING AT LAHARN (Ire) (v) 6-10-12 (7*) N Willmington, *led second, hdd and wknd aftr 4 out, tld off*. (15 to 2 op 5 to 1) 9
HATTA RIVER (USA) 6-11-5 T Eley, *prmnt, rdn 4 out, sn wknd, tld off*..................(33 to 1 op 16 to 1) 10
TRINA'S COTTAGE (Ire) 7-11-5 R Supple, *slwly away, al beh, tld off*..................(50 to 1 op 33 to 1) 11
WATCH SOOTY 5-10-7 (7*) D Finnegan, *led to second, wknd 4 out, tld off*........(66 to 1 op 50 to 1 tchd 100 to 1) 12
AWS CONTRACTS 11-11-2 (3*) B Fenton, *mstk 4th, al beh, tld off whn virtually pld up r-in, lme*......(33 to 1 op 25 to 1) 13
WINTER GEM 7-11-0 P McLoughlin, *pld hrd, mstk second, tld off whn pulled up bef 4 out*........(100 to 1 op 50 to 1) pu
SISTER JIM 6 11 0 R Davis, *mstk second, sn tld off, pld up bef 3 out*..................(100 to 1 op 50 to 1) pu
FERN GROVE 4-11-0 A Thornton, *beh whn jmpd slwly 5th, pld up bef nxt*..................(50 to 1 op 33 to 1) pu
Dist: ½l, 6l, 7l, 1¾l, 18l, 9l, 4l, 1¾l, 1½l, 1¼l. 3m 40.90s. a 3.90s (16 Ran).

(T R Pearson), J R Jenkins

56 Senate Conditional Jockeys' Selling Handicap Hurdle Class G (4-y-o and up) £2,134 2½m 110yds............ (2:50)

CRAZY HORSE DANCER (USA) [77] 8-11-2 L Aspell, *trkd ldrs, led appr 3 out, clr nxt, rdn out.*
..................(8 to 1 op 10 to 1 tchd 7 to 1) 1
SOVEREIGN NICHE (Ire) [84] (v) 8-11-9 E Husband, *slwly away, sn trkd ldr, led 4 out, hdd appr nxt, rallied r-in.*
..................(4 to 1 fav op 9 to 2 tchd 5 to 1) 2
WHISTLING GIPSY [66] 11-10-5 Chris Webb, *hld up, hdwy appr 6th, ev ch 2 out, held whn mstk last.* (10 to 1 op 8 to 1) 3
SWEET NOBLE [85] 7-11-7 (3*) B Grattan, *led, hdd 4 out, styd in tch, rdn and wknd 2 out*..................(33 to 1) 4
ANTARTICTERN (USA) [78] 6-11-3 P Midgley, *hld up, hdwy 6th, rdn and wknd 2 out*... (7 to 1 op 6 to 1 tchd 15 to 2) 5
MISS PIMPERNEL [77] (bl) 6-11-2 Sophie Mitchell, *trkd ldrs, wknd appr 3 out*..................(12 to 1) 6
JOBBER'S FIDDLE [66] 4-10-5 T Dascombe, *trkd ldrs, wknd appr 3 out*..........(12 to 1 op 10 to 1) 7
TUDOR FLIGHT [63] 5-10-2 B Fenton, *in tch, wknd appr 3 out.*
..................(5 to 1 op 7 to 1) 8
STATION EXPRESS (Ire) [61] 8-10-0 F Leahy, *nvr on terms, tld off*..........(25 to 1 op 33 to 1) 9
THE SECRET SEVEN [65] 6-10-4 R Massey, *al toward rear, tld off*..................(20 to 1) 10
LADY LOIS [61] 5-9-11 (3*) D Finnegan, *mstk 4th, al beh, tld off*..................(7 to 1 op 8 to 1) 11
MINITURE MELODY (Ire) [61] 8-9-11² (5*) M Keighley, *mid-div, wknd 6th, tld off*..................(33 to 1) 12
LOVELARK [61] 7-10-0 S Ryan, *al beh, tld off 6th*...(20 to 1) 13
SKITTLE ALLEY [82] 10-11-7 Guy Lewis, *al beh, tld off.*
..................(16 to 1 op 14 to 1) 14
MASON DIXON [74] 7-10-10 (3*) C Rae, *beh, hdwy 5th, wknd quickly aftr 4 out, sn pld up*........(8 to 1 tchd 9 to 1) pu
ROSCOMMON LAD (Ire) [61] 4-10-0 D Parker, *al beh, tld off whn pld up bef 3 out*..................(25 to 1) pu
Dist: 1¼l, 5l, 3l, 1¼l, 9l, 2½l, ½l, 16l, 6l, 4l. 4m 47.80s. a 8.80s (16 Ran).

(Mrs A Roddis), F Jordan

57 Ladbroke Handicap Chase Class D (0-120 5-y-o and up) £4,221 2m 7f (3:25)

CERTAIN ANGLE [105] 7-10-13 A P McCoy, *wth ldr, led 7th, bumped 2 out and whn hdd last, rallied gmely to ld r-in.*
............................(9 to 4 op 3 to 1)   1
LEMON'S MILL (USA) [120] (bl) 7-12-0 D Bridgwater, *beh, hdwy to track ldrs 7th, chalg whn jmpd rght 2 out and ag'n when led last, hdd r-in.*
............................(6 to 5 on op Evens tchd 11 to 10)   2
COUNTERBALANCE [99] 9-10-7 S McNeill, *trkd ldrs, outpcd appr 4 out.*......................(10 to 1 op 9 to 1)   3
ABBOTSHAM [98] 11-10-6 A Thornton, *al beh, lost tch 11th, tld off.*...(16 to 1 op 14 to 1)   4
SHANNON GLEN [102] (bl) 10-10-10 R Supple, *trkd ldrs to hfwy, lost tch 9th, tld off.*(14 to 1 op 10 to 1 tchd 16 to 1)   5
MUTUAL TRUST [112] 12-11-6 R Johnson, *made most to 7th, wkng whn blun 11th, pld up bef nxt....*(20 to 1 op 16 to 1) pu
HURRYUP [96] 9-10-4 B Powell, *al beh, tld off 8th, pld up bef 5 pl.*......................(20 to 1 op 16 to 1) pu
Dist: Hd, 16l, dist, ½l. 5m 26.80s. b 1.20s (7 Ran).
SR: 17/32/-/-/

(The Plyform Syndicate), P J Hobbs

58 Senate Handicap Hurdle Class D (0-125 4-y-o and up) £3,204 3m 110yds.. (3:55)

MORNING BLUSH (Ire) [95] 6-10-0 D Bridgwater, *made all, styd on wl whn chlgd 2 out.*
............................(6 to 1 op 5 to 1 tchd 13 to 2)   1
SOUTH WESTERLY (Ire) [111] 8-11-2 P Niven, *hld up, hdwy 6th, rdn to go second 2 out, sn held, eased r-in.*
............................(5 to 1 op 4 to 1)   2
CATS RUN (Ire) [118] 8-11-9 R Supple, *chsd wnr to 2 out, styd on one pace.*......................(5 to 1 op 4 to 1)   3
TALLYWAGGER [118] 9-11-2 (7*) T Hogg, *hld up in rear, hdwy appr 3 out, not rch ldrs.*.........(9 to 4 fav op 3 to 1)   4
ABLE PLAYER (USA) [95] 9-10-0 M Sharratt, *chsd ldrs, wknd appr 3 out.*......................(14 to 1 op 12 to 1)   5
LA FONTAINBLEAU (Ire) [97] 8-10-2 A P McCoy, *chsd ldrs, wknd 4 out, tld off.*..................(9 to 1 op 8 to 1)   6
MACEDONAS [95] 8-10-0 B Powell, *hld up, hdwy 4th, wknd quickly appr four out, tld off.*...........(33 to 1)   7
FIRST CRACK [95] 11-10-0 R Greene, *al in rear, mstk 5th, tld off.*...............................(14 to 1 op 12 to 1)   8
FAR OUT [95] (v) 10-10-0 M Brennan, *hld up, hdwy 8th, 4th and btn whn pld up lme bef 3 out......*(9 to 1 op 10 to 1) pu
Dist: 8l, 1l, 12l, 1¾l, 25l, 18l, 18l. 5m 38.70s. a 1.70s (9 Ran).

(Bisgrove Partnership), M C Pipe

59 City Of Stoke On Trent Celebration Plate Novices' Chase Class C (5-y-o and up) £5,174 2m 5f................. (4:25)

FACTOR TEN (Ire) 8-12-0 J F Titley, *hld up in tch, cld on ldr 5 out, rdn to ld last, drvn out.*
(11 to 8 on op 5 to 4 on tchd 11 to 10 on and 6 to 4 on) 1
BALLYLINE (Ire) 5-10-7 R Supple, *led 3rd, jmpd wl, rdn and hdd last, no extr.*.................(14 to 1 tchd 16 to 1)   2
NESCAF (NZ) 6-11-0 R Dunwoody, *al prmnt, blun 4th, sn reco'red, wknd 3 out....*(100 to 30 op 7 to 2 tchd 9 to 1)   3
MUSIC SCORE 10-11-0 A Thornton, *led to 3rd, lost tch appr 4 out.*....................(20 to 1 op 12 to 1 tchd 25 to 1)   4
MANOR RHYME 9-11-0 S McNeill, *al towards rear, lost tch frm 11th....*...............................(12 to 1 op 10 to 1)   5
AND WHY NOT 8-11-0 Richard Guest, *al in rear, lost tch tenth....*...............................(33 to 1 op 20 to 1)   6
TRISTAN'S COMET 9-11-0 B Dalton, *al beh, lost tch 9th.*
............................(16 to 1 op 14 to 1)   7
WELSH'S GAMBLE 7-11-0 W McFarland, *hld up, hdwy 11th, hit nxt, sn btn....*.........(50 to 1 op 20 to 1)   8
MISTY GREY 7-10-8[1] (7*) S Lycett, *jmpd poorly in rear, lost tch frm hfwy.*......................(50 to 1)   9
PRECIS 8-10-9 R Davis, *sn tld off, pld up aftr 8th.*.. (50 to 1) pu
Dist: 4l, 11l, 4l, 9l, 1½l, 1½l, 2½l, 2l. 5m 5.50s. a 6.50s (10 Ran).

(Premier Crops Limited), Miss H C Knight

60 Bet With The Tote Novices' Hurdle Class C (4-y-o and up) £4,494 2½m 110yds................................ (4:55)

ROLFE (NZ) (bl) 6-11-12 R Johnson, *hld up in tch, led and mstk 2 out, drvn clr....*(2 to 1 fav op 6 to 4 tchd 9 to 4)   1
PEMBRIDGE PLACE 5-11-0 A Thornton, *led, hdd 2 out, rallied r-in.*......................(6 to 1 op 7 to 1)   2
AMERICIUS 8-10-8 R Dunwoody, *trkd ldr to 4 out, outpcd till rallied 2 out, kpt on....*(4 to 1 tchd 7 to 2)   3
SUPERMODEL 4-10-9 P Hide, *trkd ldrs, wknt second 4 out, ev ch till rdn and wknd appr last.*
............................(5 to 2 op 3 to 2 tchd 2 to 1)   4
MRS ROBINSON (Ire) 5-10-6 (3*) E Husband, *al in rear, tld off....*...............................(20 to 1)   5
LEAP IN THE DARK (Ire) 7-11-0 M Richards, *in tch, wknd appr 4 out, tld off....*..........................(20 to 1)   6
RAH WAN (USA) 10-11-0 B Powell, *hld up, hdwy 5th, wknd 4 out, tld off....*...........................(33 to 1)   7

CROWN IVORY (NZ) 8-11-0 S Fox, *beh frm 6th, tld off.*
............................(33 to 1 op 50 to 1)   8
SHERS DELIGHT (Ire) (v) 6-11-12 M Brennan, *al beh, lost tch hfwy, tld off....*...............................(12 to 1)   9
MATACHON 6-11-0 R Supple, *al beh, tld off 6th, pld up 3 out.*
............................(50 to 1) pu
TRUE RHYME 6-10-9 J Slattery, *mstk 1st, beh frm hfwy, tld off whn pld up bef 3 out....*..................(50 to 1) pu
Dist: 4l, nk, 1l, dist, 1½l, 1l, 18l, 10l. 4m 43.10s. a 4.10s (11 Ran).

(Stanley W Clarke), D Nicholson

61 Senate Electrical Handicap Hurdle Class E (0-115 4-y-o and up) £2,284 2m (5:25)

LADY CONFESS [87] 6-10-1 R Supple, *made all, rdn and mstk 2 out, drvn out....*(11 to 1 op 8 to 1)   1
KALZARI (USA) [86] 11-10-0 A P McCoy, *hld up, hdwy aftr 5th, wnt second 3 out, no rdn and no imprsn after nxt.*
............................(12 to 1 op 8 to 1 tchd 14 to 1)   2
TOUTE BAGAILLE (Fr) [93] 4-10-7 D Bridgwater, *prmnt, pll 5th, styd on frm 2 out, no chn wth 1st two.*
............................(11 to 4 fav op 3 to 1 tchd 5 to 2)   3
NAVTSATNT(Irc)[114](t)7-11-0A, *
wnr 4 out to nxt, one pace aftr, lost 3rd pl on line.*
............................(9 to 2 op 3 to 1)   4
COAST ALONG (Ire) [86] 4-10-0 W Worthington, *in tch, wknd quickly 3 out....*.........(6 to 1 op 7 to 1)   5
NORTHERN TRIAL [95] 8-10-9 R Dunwoody, *hld up, outpcd 5th, reminders and effrt 4 out, sn wknd.*
............................(9 to 2 op 5 to 1)   6
MARSH'S LAW [89] (v) 9-10-3 M Brennan, *al beh.*
............................(9 to 1 op 6 to 1)   7
WORDSMITH (Ire) [92] 10-10-6 B Dalton, *al beh, lost tch 5th.*
............................(9 to 1 op 8 to 1)   8
BUD'S BET (Ire) [86] 8-10-0 R Johnson, *trkd wnr till wknd 4 out....*...............................(14 to 1 op 10 to 1)   9
Dist: 2½l, 14l, hd, 1¼l, 5l, 1l, 2½l, 3l. 3m 37.00s. (9 Ran).
SR: 19/15/8/28/-/2/

(Mrs R E Tate), John R Upson

ROSCOMMON (IRE) (good)
Monday June 10th

62 Roscommon Town & District Vintners Maiden Hurdle (5-y-o and up) £2,740 2m (5:30)

DONTLEAVETHENEST (Ire) 6-11-6 P L Malone, ... (16 to 1)   1
HIGH MOAT (Ire) 6-11-1 (5*) Susan A Finn, ...(6 to 1)   2
DROMINAGH (Ire) 8-11-1 (5*) J M Donnelly, ...(12 to 1)   3
HIGH TONE (Ire) 7-11-6 H Rogers, ...(5 to 1)   4
THATS MY WIFE (Ire) 5-10-9 (5*) J Butler, ...(6 to 1)   5
GRANUALE (Ire) 5-11-6 J F Titley, ...(10 to 1)   6
ROSSI (Ire) 7-11-6 A Powell, ...(20 to 1)   7
MISS AGARBIE (Ire) 5-10-9 (3*) D T Evans, ...(14 to 1)   8
DEABHAILIN (Ire) 6-11-3 (3*) D J Casey, ...(16 to 1)   9
WOODY 5-11-13 P Carberry, ...(9 to 4 fav) 10
CHAMPAGNE HURLEY (Ire) 5-11-1 (7*) C Eyre, ...(9 to 2) 11
DOCUMMINS (Ire) 6-11-6 K F O'Brien, ...(33 to 1) 12
STAR OF FERMANAGH (Ire) 7-10-13 (7*) F McGirr, (33 to 1) 13
CARNMORE CASTLE (Ire) (bl) 8-11-6 W T Slattery, (25 to 1) 14
DOLLDYEDEE (Ire) 5-11-0 T Horgan, ...(20 to 1) 15
THE RURAL DEAN (Ire) 5-11-5 S H O'Donovan, ...(12 to 1) 16
APHRIKE (Ire) (bl) 5-11-5 J P Broderick, ...(14 to 1) 17
Dist: 1½l, ½l, 8l, 2½l. 3m 57.40s. (17 Ran).

(T Cox), Francis Berry

63 Roscommon Chase (5-y-o and up) £2,740 3m........................ (7:00)

HEARNS HILL (Ire) 7-11-4 J Shortt, ...(8 to 1)   1
MILE A MINUTE (Ire) 5-11-1 A Powell, ...(10 to 1)   2
PUNTERS BAR 9-11-4 T P Treacy, ...(5 to 2 fav)   3
FRIDAY THIRTEENTH (Ire) 7-11-4 J P Broderick, . (33 to 1)   4
YOUNG ENTRY 10-11-7 (7*) Mr C Andrews, ...(14 to 1)   5
MURPHY'S LADY (Ire) 6-10-13 P Carberry, ...(12 to 1)   6
MASTER MILLER 10-11-6 (5*) G Cotter, ...(12 to 1)   7
LUCKY SALUTE (Ire) 7-11-4 T Horgan, ...(14 to 1)   8
DROP THE ACT (Ire) 6-11-4 S H O'Donovan, ...(20 to 1)   9
DECENT LUKE (Ire) 8-11-4 J F Titley, ...(7 to 1) ur
Dist: 4½l, hd, hd, 20l. 6m 15.20s. (10 Ran).

(George J Kent), Mrs John Harrington

64 Roscommon Town & District Vintners Flat Race (6-y-o and up) £2,568 2m (8:30)

ARCTIC RED RIVER (Ire) 7-11-9 (5*) Mr J Connolly, (4 to 1)   1
US FOUR (Ire) 6-11-7 (7*) Mr C A Murphy, ...(33 to 1)   2
SYNIEYOURMISSED (Ire) 7-11-7 (7*) Mr B Hassett, (14 to 1)   3
A THOUSAND DREAMS (Ire) 6-11-9 (5*) Mr B M Cash,
............................(5 to 4 fav)   4
SIBERIAN TALE (Ire) 6-11-11 (3*) Mr P J Casey, ..(10 to 1)   5
BAY FALLOUGH (Ire) 7-11-7 (7*) Mr R F Coonan, ..(8 to 1)   6
RED RADICAL (Ire) 6-11-7 (7*) Mr P E I Newell, ...(16 to 1)   7
SHINOUMA 6-12-0 Mr D Marnane, ...(12 to 1)   8
BALLYWHAT (Ire) 7-11-2 (7*) Mr R Walsh, ...(20 to 1)   9
HOT SUP (Ire) 6-11-2 (7*) Mr J T McNamara, ...(25 to 1) 10

MALICE 10-11-6 (3*) Mr E Norris, ...(12 to 1) 11
TURBET LASS (Ire) 6-11-2 (7*) Mr J Jones, ...(33 to 1) 12
TREMBLES CHOICE (Ire) 6-11-2 (7*) Mr B N Doyle, .(33 to 1) 13
DREAMIN GEORGE (Ire) 6-12-0 Mr P F Graffin, . . .(14 to 1) 14
FRISKY THYNE (Ire) 7-11-7 (7*) Mr F M Hanley, . . .(33 to 1) 15
TURRAMURRA GIRL (Ire) 7-11-9 Mr H F Cleary, . . .(16 to 1) 16
MOY VALLEY (Ire) 6-11-2 (7*) Mr A Daly, ...(25 to 1) 17
HASTY HOURS (Ire) 6-11-2 (7*) Mr G Elliott, ... (8 to 1) 18
FINGERHILL (Ire) (bl) 7-11-7 (7*) Mr M O'Connor, . .(20 to 1) 19
COMMANCHE ROSE (Ire) 6-11-7 (7*) Mr R Kehoe, .(33 to 1) pu
Dist: 2l, 3½l, 2½l, 9l. 3m 50.30s. (20 Ran).

(Mrs Noeleen Roche), P Burke

CLONMEL (IRE) (good to firm)
Thursday June 13th

65 Dungarvan Beginners Chase (5-y-o and up) £2,226 2¼m . . . . (7:30)

NORDIC THORN (Ire) 6-12-0 K F O'Brien, ...(3 to 1 fav) 1
THE OUTBACK WAY (Ire) 6-12-0 D H O'Connor, ...(7 to 1) 2
COOLGREEN 8-12-0 S H O'Donovan, ...(7 to 1) 3
BARNAMIRE BAY (Ire) 7-11-7 (7*) M D Murphy, . . .(14 to 1) 4
ICANTELYA (Ire) 7-12-0 T P Treacy, ...(7 to 1) 5
CUBAN QUESTION 9-11-9 (5*) G Cotter, ...(10 to 1) 6
PAT THE HAT (Ire) 6-12-0 J P Broderick, ...(20 to 1) 7
IRENES TREASURE (Ire) 6-11-8[1] (7*) Mr S J Mahon,
. . . .(33 to 1) 8
KILLALIGAN KIM (Ire) 6-11-6 (3*) D T Evans, ...(33 to 1) 9
KING TYRANT (Ire) 7-12-0 P A Roche, ...(16 to 1) 10
NAGLE RICE (Ire) 7-11-2 (7*) A O'Shea, ...(33 to 1) 11
DOONEGA (Ire) 8-12-0 T Horgan, ...(10 to 1) 12
DORANS WAY (Ire) 5-11-7 A P McCoy, ...(4 to 1) f
CHUCK (Ire) 6-11-7 (7*) D McCullagh, ...(25 to 1) ur
SANDY FOREST LADY (Ire) (bl) 7-11-9 P Carberry, .(7 to 1) pu
Dist: 2l, 1l, sht-hd, sht-hd. 4m 32.10s. (15 Ran).

(Peter Malone), Martin Brassil

66 Lombard & Ulster Maiden Hurdle (4-y-o and up) £2,740 2m . . . . (8:00)

GALAVOTTI (Ire) 7-12-0 P Carberry, ...(10 to 1) 1
SCOUTS HONOUR (Ire) 5-11-8 F Woods, ...(3 to 1) 2
HONEY TRADER 4-11-1 J P Broderick, ...(14 to 1) 3
NORDIC QUEEN (Ire) 6-11-9 J F Titley, ...(10 to 1) 4
BRIGHT SHARES (Ire) 6-11-1 K F O'Brien, ...(20 to 1) 5
21[9] GALE HAMSHIRE (Ire) 7-11-1 J Shortt, ...(12 to 1) 6
I'LL FLY AWAY (Ire) 7-11-6 P A Roche, ...(20 to 1) 7
CROOM ABU (Ire) 5-10-12 (7*) Mr P P O'Brien, ...(33 to 1) 8
ARDMORE KELINKA (Ire) 6-11-1 H Rogers, ...(33 to 1) 9
THE SENATOR (Ire) 5-11-5 D H O'Connor, ...(6 to 1) 10
21 LIOS NA MAOL (Ire) 5-10-7 (7*) M D Murphy, ...(33 to 1) 11
31[9] PIXIE BLUE (Ire) 5-11-0 T P Treacy, ...(33 to 1) 12
CRUCIAL MOVE (Ire) 5-10-11 (3*) D J Casey, . .(6 to 4 fav) f
MILLA'S DELIGHT (Ire) 5-11-5 A P McCoy, ...(16 to 1) f
GUILLIG LADY (Ire) 6-10-8 (7*) A O'Shea, ...(20 to 1) ur
30 BIG STORM (Ire) 4-10-10 M P Hourigan, ...(20 to 1) ur
SPANISH CASTLE (Ire) 5-11-5 T Horgan, ...(12 to 1) bd
CHUCKAWALLA (Ire) 4-10-10 A Powell, ...(14 to 1) pu
Dist: Hd, sht-hd, 2l, 3l. 3m 59.00s. (18 Ran).

(C Caldwell), Noel Meade

67 Sportsmans Handicap Hurdle (0-109 4-y-o and up) £2,226 2m . . . . (8:30)

30* KATES CHOICE (Ire) [-] 4-10-3 P Carberry, ...(5 to 2 fav) 1
30[3] I REMEMBER IT WELL (Ire) [-] 4-9-0 (7*) S FitzGerald,
. . . .(10 to 1) 2
FRESH DEAL (Ire) [-] 4-11-10 B Sheridan, ...(10 to 1) 3
FATHER RECTOR (Ire) [-] 7-10-13 T Horgan, ...(10 to 1) 4
DANCING CLODAGH (Ire) [-] 4-10-8 S C Lyons, ...(7 to 1) 5
MR GREENFIELD [-] 12-10-4 F Woods, ...(14 to 1) 6
HELLO EXCUSE ME (USA) [-] 6-10-4 (7*) J M Sullivan,
. . . .(12 to 1) 7
INNOVATIVE (Ire) [-] 5-10-8 L P Cusack, ...(12 to 1) 8
OFFICIAL PORTRAIT (Ire) [-] 7-11-7 J F Titley, ...(4 to 1) 9
PHARLINDO (Ire) [-] (bl) 5-10-5 A P McCoy, ...(14 to 1) 10
FONTAINE LODGE (Ire) [-] 6-9-13 (7*) A O'Shea, . . .(10 to 1) 11
MOUNTHENRY STAR (Ire) [-] 8-10-13 J Shortt, . . .(12 to 1) 12
ANOTHER COURSE (Ire) [-] 8-11-2 (5*) G Cotter, . .(12 to 1) 13
CHIEF RANI (Ire) [-] 6-10-7 T P Treacy, ...(14 to 1) 14
Dist: 3l, 1½l, 2½l, 1l. 3m 46.60s. (14 Ran).

(Mrs Geraldine Treacy), S J Treacy

68 Park I.N.H. Flat Race (4-y-o and up) £2,226 2m . . . . (9:00)

NUTTY SOLERA 6-12-0 Mr J A Berry, ...(6 to 4 fav) 1
22[2] NATIVE BABY 6-11-2 (7*) Mr A C Coyle, ...(11 to 2) 2
MASTER CHUZZLEWIT (Ire) 5-11-6 (7*) Mr T N Cloke,
. . . .(20 to 1) 3
ONEOFTHECLAN (Ire) 6-11-2 (7*) Mr V P Devereux, .(20 to 1) 4
EASTERN CUSTOM (Ire) 5-11-1 (7*) Miss D O'Neill, .(12 to 1) 5
RADICAL ACTION (Ire) 6-11-7 (7*) Miss S McDonagh,
. . . .(12 to 1) 6
JOLLY TEAR (Ire) 5-11-6 (7*) Mr E Gallagher, ...(10 to 1) 7

CASTLE DOVE (Ire) (bl) 5-11-1 (7*) Mr E Sheehy, . . .(10 to 1) 8
POLLYROE (Ire) 5-11-1 (7*) Mr P M Cloke, ...(14 to 1) 9
BOSTON MELODY (Ire) 4-10-8 (7*) Mr M J Walsh, .(20 to 1) 10
ISLAND SHADOW (Ire) 6-11-2 (7*) Mr G Elliott, ...(14 to 1) 11
CALICO KATE (Ire) 4-10-8 (7*) Mr R Walsh, ...(10 to 1) 12
RUN OF FASHION (Ire) 5-11-8 Mr M Phillips, ...(20 to 1) 13
GLIDING AWAY (Ire) 6-11-2 (7*) Mr J T McNamara, .(20 to 1) 14
CRAFTY FROGGIE (Ire) 4-10-13 (7*) Mr Sean O O'Brien,
. . . .(9 to 2) ur
PIANO MELODY (Ire) 5-11-1 (7*) Mr J L Cullen, . . .(16 to 1) pu
SUPERSONIA (Ire) 5-11-9 Mr P Fenton, ...(12 to 1) pu
Dist: ½l, 2l, 1½l, 4½l. 3m 46.40s. (17 Ran).

(P M Berry), J A Berry

MARKET RASEN (good to firm)
Friday June 14th
Going Correction: MINUS 0.20 sec. per fur.

69 Promota 'Jockeys Title' Selling Hurdle Class G (4-y-o and up) £2,057 2m 1f 110yds . . . . (6:50)

SIAN WYN 6-11-1 R Dunwoody, nvr far away, improved to ld
aftr 2 out, rdn out frm last . . . . (5 to 2 fav tchd 11 to 4) 1
ELITE JUSTICE (bl) 4-11-1 A P McCoy, led, clr second, hdd
aftr 2 out, no extr r-in . . . . . (7 to 1 op 5 to 1 tchd 8 to 1) 2
SWISS MOUNTAIN 6-10-8 W Worthington, handily plcd, effrt
3 out, one pace appr last . . . . (4 to 1 tchd 9 to 2) 3
EASTERN CHARLY (Bel) 6-10-13 Richard Guest, hld up,
improved into midfield hfwy, effrt 2 out, no extr last . . .
. . . .(10 to 1 op 8 to 1) 4
NANDUPA 5-10-8 J Ryan, midfield, struggling aftr 4 out, btn
last 2 . . . . (9 to 1 op 14 to 1) 5
LAGO LAGO (Ire) 4-10-7 (3*) G Cahill, settled towards rear,
drvn aftr 4 out, nvr able to chal . . . .(11 to 4 op 5 to 2) 6
MENDIP SON (bl) 6-10-13 Mr A Phillips, hld up, shrtlvd effrt
4th, struggling last 3 . . . .(25 to 1 op 16 to 1) 7
SURGICAL SPIRIT (bl) 6-10-5 (3*) K Gaule, chsd ldrs, rdn 4th,
struggling aftr nxt . . . .(25 to 1 op 20 to 1) 8
NORMEAD LASS 8-10-8 M Ranger, beh, struggling fnl cir-
cuit, tld off . . . .(16 to 1 op 12 to 1) 9
NEEDWOOD CUBE 5-10-10 (3*) R Massey, beh, drvn alng
4th, nvr on terms . . . .(20 to 1 op 16 to 1) 10
FREE TYSON 5-10-13 M Brennan, beh, struggling fnl circuit,
tld off . . . .(25 to 1 op 20 to 1) 11
JUNGLE HIGHWAY (bl) 7-10-1 (7*) Mr R Thornton, chsd ldrs,
struggling bef 4th, tld off . . . .
. . . .(25 to 1 op 20 to 1 tchd 33 to 1) 12
Dist: 2½l, 2l, 1¼l, 10l, 2l, 14l, 22l, hd, 15l, 1½l. 4m 8.30s. 4 3.30s (12 Ran).

(D G & D J Robinson), K R Burke

70 Roseland Group Handicap Hurdle Class E (0-110 4-y-o and up) £2,990 2m 3f 110yds . . . . (7:20)

SUPERHOO [86] 5-11-3 (3*) B Fenton, in tch, chalg whn lft clr
2 out, easily . . . . (6 to 1 op 4 to 1) 1
PASJA (Ire) [88] (v) 5-11-8 J Osborne, led, hdd 3 out, one pace
nxt . . . .(3 to 1 jt-fav op 11 to 4 tchd 100 to 30) 2
JENNYELLEN (Ire) [90] 7-11-10 M Foster, hld up, effrt whn hit
3 out, outpcd bef nxt, no imprsn . . . . .(12 to 1 op 8 to 1) 3
49* PHALAROPE [90] 8-11-10 (6ex) R Dunwoody, cl up, drvn
alng 3 out, fdd nxt . . . .(3 to 1 jt-fav op 5 to 2) 4
EASY OVER (USA) [70] 10-10-4 S Fox, hld up, struggling 4
out, no imprsn fnl 2 . . . .(25 to 1 op 20 to 1) 5
CROMABOO CROWN [78] 5-10-12 W Worthington, hndy,
drvn alng 6th, struggling nxt . . . .(10 to 1 tchd 11 to 1) 6
CHRIS'S GLEN [84] (v) 7-11-4 A P McCoy, nvr far away, ev ch
3 out, sn rdn, btn nxt . . . .(7 to 1 tchd 13 to 2) 7
DARK SILHOUETTE (Ire) [75] 7-10-9 M Brennan, nvr far
away, led 3 out, f heavily nxt . . . .(5 to 1 op 6 to 1) f
Dist: 5l, 3½l, 3l, 3l, 20l, dist. 4m 41.50s. a 11.50s (8 Ran).

(Prince Bishop Racing), R Craggs

71 Tote Bookmakers Summer Festival Handicap Chase Class C (0-130 5-y-o and up) £8,689 2½m . . . . (7:50)

BOBBY SOCKS [110] 10-10-8 R Johnson, dsptd ld frm 6th,
led 5 out, blun badly 2 out, styd on wl . . . .(4 to 1 op 5 to 1) 1
WISE APPROACH [130] 9-12-0 S McNeill, led, hdd 5 out, one
pace fnl 2 . . . .(5 to 2 fav op 3 to 1) 2
24[6] SWORD BEACH [112] 12-10-10 P Niven, mid-div, drpd rear
9th, styd on last 2, nrst finish.
. . . .(16 to 1 op 12 to 1 tchd 20 to 1) 3
CHANNEL PASTIME [102] 12-9-11 (3*) Guy Lewis, cl up,
outpcd 4 out, no dngr aftr . . . .(16 to 1 op 12 to 1) 4
BALLY PARSON [116] 10-10-11 (3*) J Culloty, hld up, drvn
alng 8th, nvr on terms.
. . . .(9 to 1 op 10 to 1 tchd 8 to 1) 5
POSTAGE STAMP [126] 9-11-10 P Carberry, cl up, outpcd bef
4 out, sn btn . . . .(7 to 2 fav op 3 to 1 tchd 4 to 1) 6
24 CROSS CANNON [115] 10-10-13 R Dunwoody, hld up,
improved 8th, wknd quickly appr last . . . .(7 to 1 op 6 to 1) 7

SHAARID (USA) [112] 8-10-10 J Osborne, *hld up, struggling 5 out, pld up bef 3 out*...... (4 to 1 op 7 to 2 tchd 9 to 2)   pu
STRONG SOUND [103] 9-9-12 (3*) G Cahill, *cl up, sddl slpd bef 9th, pld up before nxt*.............(8 to 1 op 7 to 1)   pu
Dist: 6l, 2l, 1l, 1½l, ½l, hd. 4m 51.40s. a 1.90s (9 Ran).
SR: 21/35/15/4/16/25/13/-/-/   (Risk Factor Partnership), R Lee

72 Lincolnshire Echo Handicap Chase Class E (0-110 5-y-o and up) £4,703 3m 1f.............................. (8:20)

24[3] EAST HOUSTON [96] 7-11-5 A P McCoy, *settled midfield, improved 12th, led 3 out, ran on strly*.
..............................(3 to 1 op 4 to 1 tchd 9 to 2)   1
KNOCKUMSHIN [84] 13-10-7 R Supple, *mid-div, outpcd 4 out, styd on fnl 2, no ch wth wnr*......(10 to 1 tchd 12 to 1)   2
COSMIC FORCE (NZ) [83] (v) 12-10-6 Jacqui Oliver, *prmnt, lost by 9th, rallied to ld 5 out, hdd 3 out, no extr*.
..............................(25 to 1 tchd 33 to 1)   3
STORM WARRIOR [77] (bl) 11-9-11 (3*) R Massey, *pressed ldr, hit 6 out and 4 out, no imprsn frm nxt*......(25 to 1)   4
▓▓▓▓▓▓▓▓▓▓▓▓▓▓▓▓▓▓▓▓ out, tdd last 2*....................... (16 to 1 tchd 20 to 1)   5
ADRIEN (Fr) [103] (bl) 8-11-12 P Carberry, *beh, some hdwy bef 3 out, nvr able to chal*.
..............................(11 to 4 fav op 2 to 1 tchd 5 to 1)   6
K C'S DANCER [83] 11-10-3 (3*) J Culloty, *chsd ldrs, outpcd aftr 12th, struggling last 4*............(16 to 1 op 14 to 1)   7
GALE AHEAD (Ire) [104] 6-11-13 N Bentley, *beh, struggling fnl circuit, tld off*....................................(4 to 1 tchd 9 to 2)   8
REGARDLESS [77] 14-9-11 (3*) K Gaule, *in tch, drvn 6 out, blun badly nxt, sn btn*..........................(25 to 1)   9
ROMANY KING [102] 12-11-11 J Osborne, *in tch, lost pl 8th, pld up bef 4 out*....................(8 to 1 tchd 9 to 1)   pu
WINNIE LORRAINE [99] 11-11-3 (5*) Mr P Henley, *hld up, effrt 12th, struggling 4 out, pld up bef nxt*....(6 to 1 op 11 to 2)   pu
Dist: 8l, 1½l, 3l, 13l, 7l, 9l, dist, 14l. 6m 16.20s. a 16.20s (11 Ran).
(Highgreen Partnership), J J O'Neill

73 Rotary Club Novices' Hurdle Class D (4-y-o and up) £2,924 2m 3f 110yds.. (8:50)

RIVER ROOM 6-11-0 J Osborne, *led to 3 out, slightly outpcd nxt, ran on wl frm last to ld cl hme*..(10 to 1 tchd 11 to 1)   1
23[*] MUZRAK (Can) 5-11-6 R Garritty, *al wl plcd, led 3 out, hrd pressed r-in, jst ct*.
..............................(Evens to 1 op 11 to 10 on tchd 11 to 10)   2
35[*] TUKANO (Can) 5-11-6 A P McCoy, *nvr far away, ev ch 4 out, outpcd aftr nxt, effrt 2 out, one pace r-in*.
..............................(13 to 8 op 6 to 4 tchd 7 to 4)   3
SIMON SAYS 6-10-11 (3*) B Fenton, *chsd ldg grp, outpcd aftr 4 out, sn btn*..........(9 to 1 op 20 to 1 tchd 33 to 1)   4
IRBEE 4-10-1 (7*) Michael Brennan, *hndy on ins, outpcd 4 out, sn btn*..........................(33 to 1 op 25 to 1)   5
OAKBURY (Ire) 4-10-8 A Thornton, *chsd ldrs, outpcd 6th, btn last 4*..........................(16 to 1 op 12 to 1)   6
CLASHAWAN (Ire) 6-10-9 R Guest, *beh, struggling hfwy, pld up bef last*....................(25 to 1 op 14 to 1)   7
Dist: Hd, 2l, dist, 1¼l, 28l. 4m 43.20s. a 13.20s (7 Ran).
(Douglas Allum), K C Bailey

74 Promota Summer Festival Standard Open National Hunt Flat Class H (4,5,6-y-o) £1,273 1m 5f 110yds.......... (9:20)

PETIT FLORA 4-10-7 R Garritty, *hld up, gd hdwy on outer to ld one furlong out, hng rght, ran on strly* (5 to 2 tchd 11 to 4)   1
SUPREME COMFORT (Ire) 4-10-0 (7*) Mr R Thornton, *hld up, improved to ld 2 fs out, hdd one out, no extr*.
..............................(10 to 1 op 20 to 1)   2
ROCKET RON 4-10-12 R Guest, *mid-div, lost pl 5 fs out, styd on fnl 2 furlongs*......(7 to 1 op 5 to 1)   3
GENERAL MONTY 4-10-12 Miss A Embiricos, *made most till hdd 2 fs out, one pace fnl furlong*.......(10 to 1 op 14 to 1)   4
FLAME OF DANCE 5-11-3 T Eley, *hld up, improved 5 fs out, drvn o'r 3 out, kpt on same pace over one out*.
..............................(7 to 1 op 4 to 1 tchd 8 to 1)   5
SABOTEUSE 4-10-7 L O'Hara, *wnt rght strt, pld hrd, trkd ldrs, drvn o'r 2 fs out, not quicken over one out*........(20 to 1)   6
OUSEFLEET BOY 4-10-9 (3*) G Cahill, *in tch, improved 5 fs out, ev ch o'r 2 out, btn fnl furlong*.....(25 to 1 op 16 to 1)   7
TAMSIN'S GEM 5-10-9 (3*) T Dascombe, *in tch, pushed alng 5 fs out, no dngr aftr*..............(14 to 1 tchd 16 to 1)   8
CHIEF OF KHORASSAN (Fr) 4-10-7 (5*) S Taylor, *pld hrd, dsptd ld aftr 3 fs, drvn o'r three out, struggling 2 out*.
..............................(9 to 4 fav op 6 to 4)   9
LIFE OF BRIAN (Ire) 5-11-3 Mr A Phillips, *cl up, drvn and wknd o'r 2 fs out*............(20 to 1 op 14 to 1)   10
BUGSYSIEGEL 6-11-0 (3*) R Massey, *hld up, ran wide bend appr strt, sn lost tch*............(25 to 1 op 16 to 1)   11
Dist: 1½l, 1¾l, ½l, ¾l, 1l, 8l, 4l, nk, nk, 16l. 3m 20.90s. (11 Ran).
(G W Singleton), G Holmes

LES LANDES (JER) (good)
Friday June 14th

75 Rowlands Recruitment 21st Anniversary Hurdle (4-y-o and up) £720 2m.... (7:15)

BIRSTWITH (USA) 11-11-10 B Powell...........(2 to 1 on)   1
CLEAR COMEDY (Ire) 8-10-9 R Darke,............(2 to 1)   2
KINGSWOOD STAR (Ire) 5-11-0 A McCabe,......(4 to 1)   3
Dist: 5l, dist. 3m 58.00s. (3 Ran).
(A J Greenwood), Miss A A Vibert

GOWRAN PARK (IRE) (good to firm)
Saturday June 15th

76 Norevale Handicap Hurdle (0-135 4-y-o and up) £5,480 3m 1f............. (5:30)

LE GRANDE BARD (Ire) [-] (bl) 7-9-7 T P Treacy, ..(16 to 1)   1
SAMBARA (Ire) [-] 5-11-4 (3*) D J Casey,.........(6 to 1)   2
DROMKEEN (Ire) [-] 6-10-8 (5*) G Cotter, ...(4 to 1 jt-fav)   3
CULLENSTOWN LADY (Ire) [-] 5-10-12 A Powell, ..(13 to 2)   4
FINAL TUB [-] 13-9-9 T Horgan,................(20 to 1)   5
▓▓▓▓▓▓▓▓▓▓▓▓▓▓▓▓▓▓▓▓..............................(7 to 1)   6
MINISTER FOR FUN (Ire) [-] 8-10-10 R Dunwoody, ..(5 to 1)   7
32[2] YOUR THE MAN [-] 10-10-3 F Woods,..........(12 to 1)   pu
TOMMY PAUD [-] 7-10-12 M Duffy, ...(11 to 2)   pu
NORTHERN SLOPE (Ire) [-] 5-12-0 B Sheridan, ..(4 to 1 jt-fav)   pu
Dist: 13l, 7l, 3l, 10l. 5m 33.80s. (10 Ran).
(Mrs D J Tarrant), Mrs F M O'Brien

77 Barrowvale I.N.H. Flat Race (4-y-o) £2,226 2m.....................(6:00)

34[2] MOTOQUA 10-11 (7*) Mr G Elliott, ...(7 to 2)   1
FISHIN CABIN (Ire) 11-2 (7*) Mr P Moore, ...(16 to 1)   2
BOBSANNA (Ire) 11-1 (3*) Mr C Bonner, ...(5 to 2 fav)   3
SOPHIE VICTORIA (Ire) 11-4 Mr P Fenton, ...(9 to 1)   4
LUCKY TIME 11-2 (7*) Mr D Whelan, ...(14 to 1)   5
DANTE'S MOON (Ire) 11-4 Mr H F Cleary, ...(10 to 1)   6
PERAMBIE (Ire) (bl) 10-11 (7*) Mr R M Walsh, ...(3 to 1)   7
ARMY BARIGNS (Ire) 10-11 (7*) Mr J P McNamara, ..(9 to 2)   8
LITTLE DUCHESS (Ire) 10-11 (7*) Miss C Linnane, (12 to 1)   9
Dist: 10l, sht-hd, 1l, 2½l. 3m 43.30s. (9 Ran).
(Mrs Michael Cunningham), Michael Cunningham

MARKET RASEN (good to firm)
Saturday June 15th
Going Correction: MINUS 0.25 sec. per fur.

78 Tote Bookmakers Novices' Hurdle Class D (4-y-o and up) £2,974 3m....... (2:10)

SANTELLA BOY (USA) 4-10-9 A P McCoy, *nvr far away, improved to ld 2 out, rdn clr frm last*.
..............................(7 to 2 op 5 to 2 tchd 4 to 1)   1
TIPPING THE LINE 6-11-9 R Johnson, *nvr far away, led aftr 3 out to nxt, sn one pace*..........(9 to 2 tchd 4 to 1)   2
BIG TREAT (Ire) 4-10-6 (3*) E Husband, *settled midfield, improved 7th, drvn bef 2 out, no pace*.
..............................(14 to 1 op 12 to 1 tchd 16 to 1)   3
SUJUD (Ire) 4-10-4 M Dwyer, *hld up, improved hfwy, effrt bef 2 out, fdd before last*..........(3 to 1 fav op 5 to 2)   4
60[2] PEMBRIDGE PLACE 5-11-2 A Thornton, *wth ldr, led 5th till aftr 3 out, rallied and ch nxt, wknd quickly*.
..............................(4 to 1 op 5 to 1)   5
APACHE RAIDER 4-10-9 P Carberry, *hld up, steady hdwy 4 out, rdn bef 2 out, sn btn*............(20 to 1 op 14 to 1)   6
YOUNG KENNY 5-11-9 R Supple, *hld up, struggling aftr 4 out, nvr on terms*....................(8 to 1 op 7 to 1)   7
PATSCILLA 5-10-8 (3*) J Culloty, *towards rear, struggling fnl circuit, btn 3 out*................(50 to 1 op 33 to 1)   8
CLASSIC CREST (Ire) (v) 5-11-9 N Bentley, *cl up, struggling 8th, sn btn*..........................(14 to 1 op 10 to 1)   9
TREMBLE 7-11-2 J Osborne, *led to 5th, cl up, outpcd aftr 8th, tld off whn pld up bef 2 out*..........(5 to 1 op 6 to 1)   pu
POLITICAL SKIRMISH 7-10-11 L O'Hara, *towards rear, lost tch fnl circuit, pld up bef 2 out*.......(66 to 1 op 33 to 1)   pu
SWISS COMFORT (Ire) 5-10-4 (7*) Mr R Thornton, *beh, struggling whn pld up aftr 7th*........(50 to 1 op 33 to 1)   pu
TIMUR'S STAR 7-10-11 Richard Guest, *mid-div, struggling 7th, pld up bef 4 out*..........(50 to 1 op 33 to 1)   pu
Dist: 6l, 3l, 4l, 4l, 3½l, dist, 16l, 20l. 5m 57.50s. a 18.50s (13 Ran).
(The Link Leasing Partnership), C J Mann

79 Lincs FM Novices' Chase Class D (5-y-o and up) £4,323 2m 1f 110yds.. (2:40)

ROBERT'S TOY (Ire) (bl) 5-11-3 A P McCoy, *cl up, hit 4th, led 5 out, drw clr frm nxt, eased r-in*.
..............................(6 to 4 fav op 7 to 4 tchd 2 to 1)   1
MICHERADO (Fr) 6-11-9 P Carberry, *jmpd badly, led till hdd 5 out, struggling whn blun 2 out*........(6 to 1 op 5 to 1)   2
DEAR EMILY 8-10-11 R Johnson, *hld up, pushed alng 4 out, nvr on terms*....................(25 to 1 op 20 to 1)   3

LOWAWATHA 8-11-9 A Thornton, *chsd ldrs, struggling aftr 4 out, eased*..........................(3 to 1 op 5 to 2)   4
MISS DOTTY 6-10-11 R Farrant, *jmpd badly in rear, al wl beh*.....................................(14 to 1 op 12 to 1)   5
COLWAY PRINCE (Ire) 8-11-2 S McNeill, *beh, improved 5 out, 4th but no imprsn whn f nxt*...........(20 to 1 op 16 to 1)   f
SHERWOOD BOY 7-11-2 J Osborne, *chsd clr ldr, blun second, struggling 8th, pld up bef 3 out*......(4 to 1 op 7 to 2)   pu
Dist: 16l, 1¾l, 6l, 29l. 4m 26.00s. a 12.00s (7 Ran).

(Clive D Smith), M C Pipe

80   Summer Festival Handicap Hurdle Class C (0-130 4-y-o and up) £8,559 2m 1f 110yds..........................(3:10)

MISTER DRUM (Ire) [120] 7-11-4 M Dwyer, *al cl up, led 4 out, styd on gmely last 2.*
................(3 to 1 fav op 11 to 4 tchd 100 to 30)   1
SUIVEZ [123] 6-11-7 P Hide, *nvr far away, chlgd 2 out, hld towards finish.*............(4 to 1 op 7 to 2 tchd 9 to 2)   2
MAGSLAD [112] 6-10-10 A P McCoy, *chsd ldg grp, outpcd aftr 3 out, improved nxt, kpt on finish...* (7 to 1 op 6 to 1)   3
NON VINTAGE (Ire) [130] 5-11-7 (7*) G Supple, *al wl plcd, led bef 4th to nxt, cl up whn blun 2 out, rallied, no imprsn.*
..................................(11 to 2 op 4 to 1 tchd 6 to 1)   4
NO LIGHT [106] 9-10-4 L Harvey, *hld up, improved to chase ldrs aftr 3 out, one pace after....*(8 to 1 tchd 9 to 1)   5
GLENUGIE [104] (v) 5-10-2 N Bentley, *prmnt, lost pl 4th, styd on frm last, no imprsn.*...............(9 to 1 op 8 to 1)   6
SASSIVER (USA) [102] (bl) 6-10-0 P Carberry, *settled on outer, improved 4th, drvn aftr nxt, struggling last 2.*
.....................................(16 to 1 op 12 to 1)   7
SYLVAN SABRE (Ire) [112] 7-10-7 (3*) R Massey, *led to bef 4th, cl up, fdd fnl 2.*.....................(10 to 1 op 8 to 1)   8
WAMDHA (Ire) [107] 6-10-5² A Thornton, *hld up, drvn aftr 3 out, btn nxt.*.............................(8 to 1 op 6 to 1)   9
BURES (Ire) [122] (v) 5-11-3 (3*) K Gaule, *hld up, improved bef 4th, hrd drvn nxt, btn 2 out.*..........(9 to 1 op 7 to 1)   10
Dist: Nk, 2l, 2½l, nk, 2½l, 3l, 7l, 9l, 28l. 4m 5.70s. a 4.70s (10 Ran).

SR: -/3/-/5/-/-/   (Malcolm Batchelor), M J Wilkinson

81   Systematic Printing Handicap Chase Class D (0-125 5-y-o and up) £4,618 2m 1f 110yds........................(3:45)

RODEO STAR (USA) [100] (bl) 10-10-12 R Garritty, *hld up, improved aftr 4 out, led after last, ran on strly.*
.....................................(9 to 2 op 5 to 1)   1
43* SASKIA'S HERO [110] 9-11-8 D Byrne, *hld up, improved 7th, led appr 2 out till aftr last, no extr.*
........................(100 to 30 op 3 to 1 tchd 7 to 2)   2
RIJPPI FS [88] 9-10-0 W Worthington, *hld up, outpcd bef 3 out, no imprsn aftr.*.............(25 to 1 op 16 to 1)   3
SUPER SHARP (NZ) [89] 8-10-1 Jacqui Oliver, *chsd ldrs, mstks 8th and 9th, led nxt, hdd whn mistake 2 out, sn btn.*
...................(14 to 1 op 16 to 1 tchd 20 to 1)   4
SYDNEY BARRY (NZ) [93] 11-10-5 B Powell, *led, hdd 4 out, hmpd by faller nxt, eased.*...........(10 to 1 op 8 to 1)   5
OSCAIL AN DORAS (Ire) [110] 7-11-8 P Carberry, *strted slwly, beh, mstk 6th, struggling whn hit 4 out, eased.*
....................(11 to 4 fav op 3 to 1 tchd 5 to 2)   6
PERSIAN TACTICS [116] 7-12-0 J Osborne, *beh, struggling fnl circuit, tld off.*.................(6 to 1 op 7 to 2)   7
STRONG APPROACH [108] 11-11-6 A P McCoy, *cl up, outpcd 4 out, rallied and chalg whn f and broke leg nxt, dead.*
...................................(9 to 2 op 4 to 1)   f
Dist: 4l, 13l, ½l, 14l, 20l, 6l. 4m 16.10s. a 2.10s (8 Ran).

SR: 20/26/-/-/-/   (J C Bradbury), N Tinkler

82   Scunthorpe Slag Novices' Handicap Chase Class D (0-105 5-y-o and up) £4,107 2¾m 110yds..........(4:15)

DARINGLY [71] 7-10-3 D Morris, *hld up, gd hdwy fnl circuit, led bef 3 out, drw clr...* (14 to 1 op 12 to 1 tchd 16 to 1)   1
SOUTHERLY GALE [94] 9-11-7 (5*) Mr A Farrant, *prmnt, led tenth to bef 3 out, no ch wth wnr.*........(6 to 1 op 11 to 2)   2
39² GONE BY (Ire) [86] 8-11-4 A P McCoy, *mid-div, outpcd and drvn 4 out, no imprsn nxt.*.......(3 to 1 fav tchd 7 to 2)   3
GORBY'S MYTH [73] 6-10-2 (3*) K Gaule, *hld up, improved 8th, outpcd 5 out, hdwy bef 3 out, sn rdn and btn.*
..................................(5 to 1 op 7 to 1)   4
TOUR LEADER (NZ) [89] 7-11-7 B Powell, *hndy, effrt and rdn bef 3 out, struggling nxt.*............(8 to 1 op 6 to 1)   5
KILLY'S FILLY [68] 6-9-11 (3*) B Fenton, *hndy, effrt whn blun 4 out, struggling nxt.*................(25 to 1)   6
LITTLE THYNE [68] (bl) 11-10-0 Dr P Pritchard, *sn wl beh, nvr on terms.*.............................(33 to 1)   7
LO-FLYING MISSILE [68] 8-9-11 (3*) J Culloty, *al prmnt, struggling aftr 4 out, pld up bef nxt...*(6 to 1 tchd 11 to 2)   pu
ITS GRAND [69] 7-10-1 R Johnson, *chsd ldr, blun badly and lost pl second, blunded 5th, sn tld off, pld up bef 4 out.*
...............................(10 to 1 op 12 to 1)   pu
WILLIE MAKEIT (Ire) [72] 6-10-4 J Osborne, *led to tenth, struggling aftr 4 out, pld up nxt......*(10 to 1 tchd 8 to 1)   pu

DARLEYFORDBAY [78] 7-10-10 A Thornton, *cl up, already lost pl whn pld up aftr 8th, sddl slpd.*
.....................(11 to 1 op 10 to 1 tchd 12 to 1)   pu
Dist: 6l, 10l, 3l, 8l, 16l, dist. 5m 28.40s. a 1.40s (11 Ran).
SR: -/22/4/-/-/-/   (Michael Appleby), R Curtis

83   Peter Rhodes Novices' Handicap Hurdle Class E (0-100 4-y-o and up) £2,425 2m 1f 110yds.......................(4:50)

KARINSKA [90] 6-11-4 W Worthington, *hld up, improved to chase ldr whn blun 2 out, styd on to ld nr finish.*
......................................(3 to 1 tchd 9 to 1)   1
PICKENS (USA) [87] 4-10-12 (3*) E Husband, *hld up, improved 3 out, rdn to ld aftr last, hdd nr finish.*
..................(13 to 2 op 6 to 1 tchd 7 to 1)   2
PLINTH [74] 5-10-2 A P McCoy, *cl up, led 3 out, sn clr, hdd aftr last, no extr..........*(3 to 1 jt-fav op 7 to 2 tchd 11 to 4)   3
27* BOURDONNER [80] 4-10-8 R Garritty, *sn led, hdd 3 out, hit last, one pace....*(3 to 1 jt-fav op 2 to 1 tchd 7 to 2)   4
LITTLE TINCTURE (Ire) [72] 6-10-0 D Leahy, *beh, struggling hfwy, styd on wl frm 2 out........*(33 to 1 op 16 to 1)   5
REEFA'S MILL (Ire) [81] (v) 4-10-9 P Carberry, *hld up, improved 4 out, wknd aftr 2 out....*(10 to 1 op 8 to 1)   6
CAVIL [72] 4-9-11 (3*) Guy Lewis, *chsd ldrs, struggling 4 out, fdd..................*(5 to 1 op 12 to 1 tchd 6 to 1)   7
CONEYGREE [72] 4-10-0 B Dalton, *in tch, outpcd aftr 3 out, sn btn................*(16 to 1 op 12 to 1 tchd 25 to 1)   8
M'BEBE [72] 6-10-0 R Farrant, *beh, struggling fnl circuit, pld up bef 2 out................*(50 to 1 op 33 to 1)   pu
ASTROLABE [72] 4-10-0 R Johnson, *chsd ldrs, struggling hfwy, pld up bef 2 out.........*(20 to 1 op 12 to 1)   pu
LIMITED LIABILITY [100] 6-12-0 M Dwyer, *pld hrd in rear, struggling aftr 4 out, pulled up bef 2 out*
........................(9 to 1 op 6 to 1 tchd 10 to 1)   pu
RED LIGHT [83] (v) 4-10-11 J Osborne, *mid-div, struggling bef 3 out, pld up before nxt....*(12 to 1 op 10 to 1)   pu
CRAMBELLA (Ire) [76] 4-10-4⁴ R Guest, *not jump wl in rear, al struggling, tld off whn pld up bef 2 out.*
......................................(50 to 1 op 20 to 1)   pu
Dist: Hd, 2l, 1¼l, 4l, 2½l, 16l, 6l. 4m 7.10s. a 6.10s (13 Ran).
(Geoff Whiting), M C Chapman

AUTEUIL (FR) (soft)
Sunday June 16th

84   Grand Steeplechase de Paris (5-y-o and up) £158,103 3m 5f..............(4:35)

ARENICE (Fr) 8-10-1 P Sourzac, ...   1
AL CAPONE II (Fr) 8-10-1 J-Y Beaurain, ...   2
BANNIKIPOUR (Fr) 7 10 1 C Pieux, ...   3
Dist: 2½l, 3l, 2½l, 8l, 6l, 3l. 7m 7.00s. (7 Ran).
(Mrs F Montauban), G Macaire

GOWRAN PARK (IRE) (good to firm)
Sunday June 16th

85   RTE For Sport Handicap Chase (0-137 4-y-o and up) £3,425 2m 5f....... (3:30)

BOLD FLYER [-] 13-11-13 K F O'Brien, ...(11 to 2)   1
HEIST [-] 7-12-0 P Carberry, ...(7 to 2 fav)   2
ROSSBEIGH CREEK [-] 9-10-9 F J Flood, ...(4 to 1)   3
63³ PUNTERS BAR [-] 9-11-3 J Shortt, ...(7 to 1)   4
GLEN OG LANE [-] 13-9-7 F Woods, ...(14 to 1)   5
QUATTRO [-] 6-10-6 J P Broderick, ...(13 to 2)   6
ANOTHER GROUSE [-] 9-11-8 T P Treacy, ...(9 to 2)   7
Dist: Sht-hd, 1½l, 11l, 8l. 5m 7.40s. (7 Ran).
(S W N Collen), Miss Anne Collen

86   Royal Oak Maiden Hurdle (4-y-o and up) £2,740 2m........................(5:00)

WESPERADA (Ire) 4-11-7 P Carberry, ...(7 to 2)   1
MUSKERRY KING (Ire) 5-11-5 W T Slattery, ...(8 to 1)   2
33² GHALAYAN 4-10-10 (5*) G Cotter, ...(6 to 1)   3
DREAM ETERNAL (Ire) 5-11-7 T Horgan, ...(14 to 1)   4
62³ DROMINAGH (Ire) 8-11-1 (5*) J M Donnelly, ...(10 to 1)   5
HELORHIWATER (Ire) 5-11-5 (3*) D J Casey, ...(5 to 4 on)   6
MARCHEGIANI (Ire) 10-10-7 (7*) J A Robinson, ...(25 to 1)   7
PINGO HILL (Ire) 4-11-1 J Shortt, ...(14 to 1)   8
CROGHAN BRIDGE (Ire) 7-11-6 F Woods, ...(20 to 1)   9
DUSTY ROSE (Ire) (bl) 7-11-1 M Moran, ...(14 to 1)   10
WEST CLIFF (Ire) 8-11-1 B Sheridan, ...(20 to 1)   11
Dist: 3l, sht-hd, 2l, 4l. 3m 44.40s. (11 Ran).
(Mrs A McAleer), Noel Meade

87   Jack Duggan Coolmore Handicap Hurdle (0-140 4-y-o and up) £4,795 2m... (5:30)

POKONO TRAIL (Ire) [-] 7-11-5 F J Flood, ...(7 to 4 fav)   1
29⁵ ANGAREB (Ire) [-] (bl) 7-10-1 P Carberry, ...(8 to 1)   2
SLANEY GLOW (Ire) [-] 5-11-4 F Woods, ...(5 to 1)   3
HELLO MONKEY (Ire) [-] 9-10-13 T P Treacy, ...(3 to 1)   4

NORDIC RACE [-] 9-10-5 P A Roche, ... (12 to 1)   5
JUSTAWAY (Ire) [-] 6-10-11 K P Gaule, ... (12 to 1)   6
GLOWING LINES [-] [-] (bl) 6-11-9 (5*) J M Donnelly,
. . . . (8 to 1)   7
Dist: Hd, 2½l, 8l, dist. 3m 40.20s. (7 Ran).

(Mrs Miriam Byrne), F Flood

88   Thomastown Summer I.N.H. Flat Race (5-y-o and up) £2,740 2½m. . . . . . . (6:00)

CLONAGAM (Ire) 7-11-9 (5*) Mr B M Cash, ... (12 to 1)   1
YOUNG DUBLINER (Ire) 7-11-7 (7*) Mr M Walsh, . . (8 to 1)   2
ART PRINCE (Ire) 6-11-7 (7*) Mr B N Doyle, ... (14 to 1)   3
64⁴ A THOUSAND DREAMS (Ire) 6-11-7 (7*) Mr C A Murphy,
. . . . (3 to 1)   4
DO POP IN 5-11-6 (7*) Mr P M Cloke, ... (8 to 1)   5
CELIO LUCY (Ire) 6-11-2 (7*) Mr A C Coyle, ... (7 to 1)   6
LITTLE-K (Ire) 6-11-7 (7*) Mr P R Lenihan, ... (9 to 1)   7
ANOTHER KAV (Ire) 6-11-2 (7*) Mr T N Cloke, ... (16 to 1)   8
COCKPIT (Ire) 5-11-6 (7*) Mr D A Harney, ... (14 to 1)   9
ST CAROL (Ire) 5-11-8 Mr T Mullins, ... (7 to 4 fav) 10
MR PRECISION (Ire) 5-11-7 (7*) Mr G Elliott, ... (25 to 1) 11
MACKLETTE (Ire) 5-11-7 (7*) Mr O Sullivan, ... (25 to 1) 12
CHILLY LORD (Ire) 6-11-7 (7*) Mr R J Barnwell, . . . (33 to 1) 13
64 TREMBLES CHOICE (Ire) 6-11-9 Mr H F Cleary, . . (33 to 1) 14
WOLF ELLA (Ire) (bl) 7-11-7 (7*) Mr A J Dempsey, . (10 to 1) 15
MOLLY WHACK (Ire) 5-11-1 (7*) Mr D P Coakley, . . (25 to 1) 16
ONLY IF (Ire) 7-11-2 (7*) Mr J T McNamara, ... (12 to 1) pu
WHO'S PAYIN (Ire) 5-11-6 (7*) Mr R M Walsh, ... (14 to 1) pu
Dist: 5½l, nk, 7l, 3½l. 4m 37.30s. (18 Ran).

(R Galvin), A P O'Brien

KILBEGGAN (IRE) (good to firm)
Monday June 17th

89   William Glynn Memorial Handicap Hurdle (0-116 4-y-o and up) £2,226 2m 3f . . . . (6:00)

PARSKIN (Ire) [-] 6-11-3 T P Treacy, ... (100 to 30)   1
SANDRA LOUISE (Ire) [-] 6-9-1 (7*) L J Fleming, . . (4 to 1)   2
LIMAHEIGHTS (Ire) [-] 6-10-11 (3*) D T Evans, . . . (16 to 1)   3
29⁸ ILLBETHEREFORYOU (Ire) [-] 5-10-5 M P Hourigan, (9 to 1)   4
CHOICE COMPANY (Ire) [-] 7-9-10 F Woods, ... (33 to 1)   5
LET IT RIDE (Ire) [-] 7-11-9 (5*) T Martin, ... (7 to 4 fav) co
32⁴ STRAIGHT ON (Ire) [-] 5-11-0 J Shortt, ... (6 to 1) ro
Dist: ¾l, 7l, 3l, 25l. 4m 35.30s. (7 Ran).

(Mrs P Mullins), P Mullins

90   Bank Of Ireland Maiden Hurdle (4-y-o and up) £2,740 2m 3f . . . . (6:30)

MIGHTY TRUST (Ire) 7-11-6 W T Slattery, ... (8 to 1)   1
CLODAGHS FANCY (Ire) 5-11-8 J F Titley, ... (7 to 1)   2
ALPINE MIST (Ire) 4-11-1 T Horgan, ... (10 to 1)   3
NEPHIN FAR (Ire) 6-11-1 T P Treacy, ... (7 to 2)   4
BURGEES HILL VI 11-11-6 K F O'Brien, ... (14 to 1)   5
LEMOIRE 5-11-0 P Leech, ... (8 to 1)   6
21⁸ THIRD AGENDA (Ire) 5-11-5 J P Byrne, ... (10 to 1)   7
CREGMORE BOY (Ire) 6-10-13 (7*) M McCormack, . (20 to 1)   8
TIMELY AFFAIR (Ire) 7-11-7 F Woods, ... (9 to 4 fav)   9
62⁹ DEABHAILIN (Ire) 6-11-1 (5*) G Cotter, ... (20 to 1) 10
31⁸ TRIPLE ACTION (Ire) 7-11-3 (7*) Mr D Duggan, . . (16 to 1) 11
SNUGVILLE SALLY 4-10-10 J P Broderick, ... (25 to 1) 12
THE CONVINCER (Ire) 6-11-6 J Shortt, ... (20 to 1) 13
Dist: 2½l, nk, 2½l, 3l. 4m 33.10s. (13 Ran).

(G Kennedy), W P Browne

91   T & V Maiden Hurdle (5-y-o and up) £2,740 3m . . . . (7:00)

BOBSVILLE (Ire) 8-11-6 F Woods, ... (14 to 1)   1
KILCARAMORE (Ire) 5-11-5 Mr P J Healy, ... (14 to 1)   2
22⁵ THE YELLOW BOG (Ire) 6-11-6 (7*) T Martin, ... (9 to 1)   3
PUNGAYNOR (Ire) 6-11-1 (5*) J M Donnelly, ... (16 to 1)   4
DROMOD POINT (Ire) 7-11-6 D H O'Connor, ... (16 to 1)   5
DUCHESS OF PADUA (Ire) 6-11-1 W T Slattery, . . . (20 to 1)   6
SHIR ROSE (Ire) 6-11-9 T Horgan, ... (7 to 2)   7
BROTHER NICHOLAS (Ire) 5-11-5 T P Treacy, ... (8 to 1)   8
VAIN PRINCESS (Ire) 6-11-6 M P Hourigan, ... (5 to 2 fav)   9
VITAL APPROACH (Ire) 6-10-8 (7*) M D Murphy, . . (20 to 1) 10
LANGRETTA (Ire) 5-10-7 (7*) A O'Shea, ... (20 to 1) 11
88 WOLF ELLA (Ire) (bl) 7-11-1 (5*) G Cotter, ... (7 to 1) 12
COOLING CHIMES (Ire) 6-11-6 Mr M Phillips, ... (6 to 1) 13
Dist: 3½l, 5½l, 25l, 6½l. 5m 56.90s. (13 Ran).

(J B Reilly), A L T Moore

92   Summer Handicap Hurdle (0-102 4-y-o and up) £2,226 3m . . . . (7:30)

DUNDOCK WOOD [-] 8-10-5 K F O'Brien, ... (5 to 1)   1
ARCTIC KATE [-] 10-12-0 B Sheridan, ... (8 to 1)   2
32 NATIVE BORN [-] 11-9-2 (5*) J Butler, ... (25 to 1)   3
29⁷ THE TOM'S ERROR (Ire) [-] 6-10-10 (3*) R Barry, . (9 to 1)   4
VALAMIR (Ire) [-] 6-9-0 (7*) R P Hogan, ... (25 to 1)   5
WINDYHOUSE WAY (Ire) [-] 6-9-13 K P Gaule, ... (14 to 1)   6

BUCKANEER BAY [-] 9-9-9 F Woods, ... (33 to 1)   7
MARIE'S PRIDE [-] 5-9-7 J P Broderick, ... (8 to 1)   8
SUDDEN STORM (Ire) [-] 5-11-2 T P Treacy, ... (2 to 1 fav)   9
ANOTHER IDEA (Ire) [-] 8-10-2 (7*) Mr A Ross, . . . (20 to 1) 10
OVER THE GREEN (Ire) [-] 8-10-8 T Horgan, ... (20 to 1) f
PLOUGH THE LEA (Ire) [-] 6-9-10 (7*) J F Clarke, . . (8 to 1) f
LADY HA HA [-] 9-9-2 (7*) M D Murphy, ... (14 to 1) bd
THATS MY BOY [-] 8-10-6 (5*) B Bowens, ... (14 to 1) pu
Dist: 8l, 6l, 1½l, 15l. 5m 49.80s. (14 Ran).

(N Enright), L T Reilly

93   Bloomfield House Hotel Handicap Chase (0-102 4-y-o and up) £2,740 2m 5f (8:00)

FAYS FOLLY (Ire) [-] 7-9-8 (7*) R P Hogan, ... (8 to 1)   1
STEVIE BE (Ire) [-] 8-11-12 K F O'Brien, ... (7 to 4 fav)   2
FIXED ASSETS [-] 9-10-9 J F Titley, ... (7 to 1)   3
63⁶ MURPHY'S LADY (Ire) [-] 7-9-10 T P Treacy, ... (10 to 1)   4
20⁵ BALLYBRIKEN CASTLE [-] 9-9-1 (7*) M D Murphy, . (10 to 1)   5
BALLYVERANE (Ire) [-] 9-9-3 (7*) C Rae, ... (20 to 1)   6
ROTEK [-] 12-9-4 (3*) D Bromley, ... (25 to 1)   7
CHARLIES DELIGHT (Ire) [-] 8-11-0 K P Gaule, . . . (16 to 1)   8
COCKTAIL GOLD (Ire) [-] 7-10-7 T Horgan, ... (20 to 1) f
ORIENT ROVER [-] 12-9-7 P L Malone, ... (25 to 1) ro
Dist: ½l, 3½l, nk, 7l. 5m 19.70s. (10 Ran).

(T Cox), Francis Berry

94   Tullamore Beginners Chase (5-y-o and up) £2,226 2m 5f . . . . (8:30)

36² CABBERY ROSE 8-11-4 T P Treacy, ... (2 to 1)   1
PRECEPTOR (Ire) 7-11-9 C N Bowens, ... (12 to 1)   2
TREENS FOLLY (bl) 7-11-9 F Woods, ... (25 to 1)   3
SPORTING VISION (Ire) 5-10-13 H Rogers, ... (25 to 1)   4
SIMPLY PERKY (Ire) 5-10-13 J P Broderick, ... (9 to 1)   5
65 DORANS WAY (Ire) 5-11-7 M P Hourigan, ... (5 to 4 on) f
COZY CORNER (Ire) 6-11-4 P A Roche, ... (25 to 1) f
Dist: 15l. 5m 26.70s. (7 Ran).

(Mike Futter), P F Graffin

95   Coola Mills I.N.H. Flat Race (4-y-o and up) £2,226 2m 3f . . . . (9:00)

LAURA GALE (Ire) 7-11-9 Mr P Fenton, ... (11 to 10 fav)   1
FAIR SOCIETY (Ire) 5-11-1 (7*) Mr John P Moloney, (3 to 1)   2
22⁷ BIDDY HUNT (Ire) 5-11-1 (7*) Mr P J Gilligan, ... (10 to 1)   3
ZUZUS PETALS (Ire) 6-11-2 (7*) Mr G Elliott, ... (25 to 1)   4
WESTPARK EXPRESS (Ire) 6-11-7 (7*) Miss R Hickey,
. . . . (25 to 1)   5
68 CRAFTY FROGGIE (Ire) (bl) 4-10-13 (7*) Mr Sean O O'Brien,
. . . . (5 to 2) f
Dist: 20l, dist, dist, dist. 4m 21.10s. (6 Ran).

(J M Foley), S J Treacy

TRAMORE (IRE) (good)
Tuesday June 18th

96   Lismore Handicap Hurdle (0-109 4-y-o and up) £2,226 2m . . . . (5:30)

KEPHREN (USA) [-] 7-10-12 B Sheridan, ... (7 to 4 fav)   1
BOB THE YANK (Ire) [-] 6-11-3 J Shortt, ... (5 to 2)   2
PHARDY (Ire) [-] 5-11-0 G M O'Neill, ... (5 to 1)   3
TEXAS FRIDAY (Ire) [-] 6-11-1 K F O'Brien, ... (5 to 1)   4
INGMAR [-] 10-10-4 W T Slattery, ... (16 to 1)   5
67⁸ INNOVATIVE (Ire) [-] 5-10-8 L P Cusack, ... (10 to 1)   6
MAKE THAT CALL (Ire) [-] 5-9-8¹ F Woods, ... (10 to 1)   7
PRINCE JUAN [-] 9-9-13³ (7*) Mr P R Lenihan, . . . (12 to 1)   8
Dist: 6l, 7l, 7l, 2l. 3m 55.60s. (8 Ran).

(Paul Davis), V Kennedy

97   Brownstown Beginners Chase (5 & 6-y-o) £2,226 2m . . . . (6:00)

STROLL HOME (Ire) 6-11-11 (3*) Mr D P Costello, . (8 to 1)   1
RATES RELIEF (Ire) 6-12-0 J P Broderick, ... (9 to 4)   2
BOBSTAR DANCER (Ire) 5-11-7 J Shortt, ... (5 to 2)   3
65² THE OUTBACK WAY (Ire) (bl) 6-12-0 D H O'Connor,
. . . . (6 to 4 fav) f
Dist: 1l, dist. 3m 57.60s. (4 Ran).

(Mrs M Mangan), James Joseph Mangan

98   Portlaw Handicap Chase (0-102 4-y-o and up) £2,226 2½m. . . . . (6:30)

THERE TIS FOR YA (Ire) [-] 8-10-9 (7*) Mr K O'Sullivan,
. . . . (4 to 1)   1
TRIPTODICKS (Ire) [-] 6-9-11¹ T P Treacy, ... (8 to 1)   2
KYLE HOUSE VI (Ire) [-] 7-9-10¹ J P Broderick, . . . (7 to 1)   3
COOLADERRA LADY [-] 9-10-13 F Woods, ... (4 to 1)   4
WHAT THING [-] 9-10-12 (5*) G Cotter, ... (3 to 1)   5
KILKEN CHOICE (Ire) [-] 5-9-7 (7*) M D Murphy, . . (20 to 1)   6
LET THE RIVER RUN [-] 10-9-0 (7*) R P Hogan, . . . (20 to 1)   7
SILENTBROOK [-] 11-9-7 (3*) A O'Shea, ... (6 to 1)   8
EVEN CALL [-] 10-9-12 S H O'Donovan, ... (14 to 1)   9
WALKERS LADY (Ire) [-] 8-11-1 (3*) D T Evans, . . . (10 to 1) bd
Dist: 3l, ½l, 11l, 3½l. 4m 42.60s. (10 Ran).

(T Cronin), Gerard Cully

99 Tramore I.N.H. Flat Race (6-y-o and up) £2,226 2m......................(8:00)

ROLL OVER (Ire) 6-11-7 (7") Mr A C Coyle, ... (100 to 30)	1
MAJOR GALE (Ire) 7-11-7 (7") Mr M D Hennessy, . .(12 to 1)	2
21⁴ MARGUERITA SONG 6-11-2 (7") Mr J T McNamara,	
. . . . (6 to 4 fav)	3
CRAZY DREAMS (Ire) 8-12-0 Mr P J Healy, ...(8 to 1)	4
66 GUILLIG LADY 6-11-2 (7") Mr G Elliott, ...(12 to 1)	5
64² US FOUR (Ire) 6-11-7 (7") Mr C A Murphy, ... (5 to 1)	6
BALLY UPPER 8-12-0 Mr H F Cleary, ... (12 to 1)	7
DROP THE LOT (Ire) 6-11-7 (7") Mr P M Cloke, ... (8 to 1)	8
COMIC ACT (bl) 6-11-9 (5") Mr B M Cash, ... (10 to 1)	pu
GLENBEG GROVE (Ire) 6-11-2 (7") Mr B J Hallahan, (10 to 1)	pu

Dist: 3l, 4½l, 3l, 2l. 3m 52.40s. (10 Ran).

(Joseph P Ryan), P A Fahy

WORCESTER (good to firm)
Wednesday June 19th
Going Correction: MINUS 0.20 sec. per fur.

100 St Martins Selling Handicap Hurdle Class G (0-90 4-y-o and up) £2,185 2m ....(6:45)

HIGHLY REPUTABLE (Ire) [81] 6-11-8 R Dunwoody, al prmnt, led 3 out, rdn out. . . . . (6 to 1 op 5 to 1)	1
FLUIDITY (USA) [87] (bl) 8-12-0 D Bridgwater, al prmnt, led 5th to nxt, rdn 2 out, kpt on r-in.	
. . . . (5 to 1 fav op 8 to 1 tchd 9 to 1)	2
MILZIG (USA) [69] 7-10-10 C Llewellyn, hld up, hdwy 2 out, ran on und pres r-in. . . . (9 to 1 op 10 to 1 tchd 12 to 1)	3
MOST INTERESTING [64] 11-10-2 (3") B Fenton, hld up, hdwy 3 out, kpt on r-in. . . . . (20 to 1 op 14 to 1)	4
MYLORDMAYOR [59] 9-9-7 (7") Mr R Thornton, prmnt, ev ch whn mstk 3 out, rdn and blun last, no extr. . . . . . . (33 to 1)	5
THE EXECUTOR [76] 6-11-3 J Frost, hld up, hdwy 3 out, styd on same pace frm last. . . . . (20 to 1)	6
BECKY BOO [72] 6-10-13 D J Burchell, chsd ldrs, ev ch 3 out, ran on one pace frm nxt. . . . . (7 to 1 op 11 to 2)	7
STAY HAPPY (Fr) [65] 7-10-6³ A Thornton, mid-div, rdn 3 out, no imprsn frm nxt. . . . . . (11 to 1 op 10 to 1 tchd 12 to 1)	8
45³ AGAINST THE CLOCK [64] (v) 4-10-5 R Greene, hld up, hdwy appr 3 out, no extr approaching last. . . (11 to 1 op 8 to 1)	9
45⁸ CLASSIC IMAGE (Ire) [69] 6-10-10 Mr A Charles-Jones, hld up, hdwy 5th, one pace appr 2 out. . . . . . (25 to 1 op 20 to 1)	10
69³ SWISS MOUNTAIN [69] 6-10-10 W Worthington, prmnt, rdn 5th, wknd 3 out. . . . . (8 to 1 op 6 to 1)	11
50 KUTAN (Ire) [65] 6-10-6 J R Kavanagh, hld up, hdwy 5th, wknd 2 out. . . . . (12 to 1 op 10 to 1)	12
45² PARISH WALK (Ire) [85] 5-11-12 S Wynne, nvr trble ldrs. . . . . (10 to 1 op 6 to 1)	13
DOCTOR-J (Ire) [84] 6-11-11 R Supple, hld up, nvr better than mid-div. . . . . (14 to 1 op 10 to 1)	14
CELCIUS [74] 12-11-1 C Maude, nvr rch chalg pos.	
. . . . (16 to 1 op 12 to 1)	15
SIDE BAR [67] (bl) 6-10-3 (5") Mr P Henley, prmnt to 4th, sn rdn and pld up. . . . . (20 to 1 op 14 to 1)	16
HUGH DANIELS [76] 8-11-3 Gary Lyons, prmnt, jnd ldrs 4th, wknd 3 out. . . . . (20 to 1 op 16 to 1)	17
ORCHESTRAL DESIGNS (Ire) [59] 5-9-11 (3") R Massey, hld up, al rear. . . . . (40 to 1 op 33 to 1)	18
ARDEARNED [59] 9-10-0 R Davis, beh 5th.	
. . . . (50 to 1 op 33 to 1)	19
WAAZA (USA) [72] 7-10-13 J Osborne, prmnt to 4th, lost pl quickly. . . . . (14 to 1 op 10 to 1 tchd 16 to 1)	20
PAID ELATION [59] 11-9-9 (5") Sophie Mitchell, led to 5th, wknd quickly, tld off whn pld up bef 3 out.	
. . . . (33 to 1 op 33 to 1)	pu

Dist: 2l, 1l, nk, 2½l, hd, hd, ¾l, 1l, 1¾l, 5l. 3m 45.40s. a 5.40s (21 Ran).
SR: 8/12/-/-/-/-/

(Michael C Whatley), G C Bravery

101 Whitbourne Novices' Claiming Hurdle Class F (4-y-o and up) £2,129 2m (7:15)

NIGHT TIME 4-10-0 (5") L Aspell, hld up, hdwy 3 out, led r-in, ran on wl. . . . . (1 to 1 jt-fav op 7 to 4 tchd 9 to 4)	1
BETABETCORBETT 5-11-2 T Eley, led, rdn appr 2 out, hdd r-in, not quicken. . . . . (25 to 1)	2
MINNESOTA FATS (Ire) 4-10-5 Gary Lyons, al prmnt, ev ch 3 out, no extr r-in. . . . . (8 to 1 op 6 to 1)	3
PLEASANT SURPRISE (Fr) 4-11-11 D Bridgwater, hld up in tch, drvn alng 5th, ev ch whn blun last, not reco'r. (2 to 1 jt-fav op 7 to 4)	4
LANCER (USA) 4-11-3 R Dunwoody, hld up, hdwy 5th, rdn 3 out, styd on same pace. . . . . (4 to 1 op 3 to 1)	5
MIDNIGHT JESTOR (Ire) 8-10-7 M Sharratt, hld up, hdwy 4th, wknd 2 out. . . . . (33 to 1)	6
45⁸ WOODLANDS ENERGY 5-10-11 R Davis, hld up, hdwy 3 out, wknd appr last. . . . . (12 to 1 tchd 16 to 1)	7
50⁸ FRANKIE HARRY 4-10-5 D Morris, hld up, hdwy 3 out, wknd nxt. . . . . (33 to 1)	8
50⁸ LASER LIGHT LADY 4-10-0 B Powell, chsd ldrs, mstk 3rd, drvn alng 5th, wknd appr 2 out. . . . . . . (40 to 1 op 33 to 1)	9

REALLY NEAT 10-10-6 (5") Sophie Mitchell, chsd ldr, rdn 3 out, wknd quickly. . . . . (40 to 1 op 33 to 1)	10
PATS FOLLY 5-10-3 P McLoughlin, trkd ldrs till wknd quickly 3 out, tld off. . . . . (33 to 1 op 20 to 1)	11
BIDE OUR TIME (USA) 4-10-6 (7") Shaun Graham, in tch to 4th, wknd quickly, tld off whn I last. . . (40 to 1 op 33 to 1)	f

Dist: 3½l, 2l, ¾l, hd, 8l, 6l, 3l, 18l, 2½l, dist. 3m 46.90s. a 6.90s (12 Ran).

(D Bentley), A Streeter

102 Overbury Club Athletica Handicap Chase Class E (0-115 5-y-o and up) £3,327 2½m 110yds............(7:45)

COMEDY ROAD [90] 12-10-3 R Johnson, al prmnt, led 8th to nxt, led and mstk 2 out, drvn out. . . . . . . (8 to 1 op 7 to 1)	1
48³ HENLEY REGATTA [94] 8-10-7 S Burrough, hld up, hdwy 7th, led 11th, hit 3 out, hdd nxt, no extr r-in. . . (5 to 1 op 7 to 2)	2
37² BITACRACK [87] 9-10-0 L O'Hara, prmnt, lost pl 11th, rallied appr 4 out, wknd nxt. . . . . (9 to 2 op 5 to 1)	3
FINAL PRIDE [100] 10-10-6 (7") Mr R Thornton, hld up, hdwy to ld 9th, hit tenth, hdd nxt, wknd 4 out.	
. . . . (7 to 2 fav op 5 to 2)	4
HAMPER [87] (bl) 13-9-11 (3") K Gaule, hld up, hdwy to ld 7th, hdd nxt, rdn and wknd 4 out. . . . . . (16 to 1 op 10 to 1)	5
DRUMSTICK [100] 10-10-13 A Thornton, prmnt, rdn 11th, wknd 4 out. . . . . (6 to 1 op 4 to 1)	6
GOLDEN MADJAMBO [95] 10-10-8 R Greene, hld up to 3rd, led 5th to 7th, wknd 9th, tld off whn pld up bef 5 out.	
. . . . (5 to 1 op 7 to 2)	pu
SALCOMBE HARBOUR (NZ) [87] 12-10-0 Dr P Pritchard, beh 6th, tld off whn pld up bef 8th. . . . . . (33 to 1 op 20 to 1)	pu
48 CASTLE KING [115] 9-12-0 B Powell, hld up, hdwy 6th, wknd 9th, tld off whn pld up bef 4 out.	
. . . . (9 to 1 op 10 to 1 tchd 12 to 1)	pu
THE LORRYMAN (Ire) [97] 8-10-10 G Upton, led 3rd to 5th, wknd 9th, tld off whn pld up bef 5 out. (14 to 1 op 10 to 1)	pu

Dist: 6l, 6l, 9l, 1¾l, 1½l. 5m 4.00s. a 7.00s (10 Ran).

(Winsbury Livestock), R Lee

103 Hereford & Worcester Chamber Of Commerce Novices' Hurdle Class E (4-y-o and up) £2,547 2½m........ (8:15)

SIGMA WIRELESS (Ire) 7-11-2 S Wynne, hld up, hdwy to chase ldr 5th, edgd rght and led 2 out, drvn out.	
. . . . (5 to 1 op 9 to 2 tchd 6 to 1)	1
MILNGAVIE (Ire) 6-11-2 C Llewellyn, hld up, hdwy whn mstk 4 out, chasing wnr whn pckd last, no imprsn.	
. . . . (4 to 1 op 3 to 1)	2
DAMAS (Fr) (v) 5-11-2 D Bridgwater, prmnt, drvn alng 3 out, no extr r-in. . . . . (11 to 4 op 9 to 4)	3
DREAM HERE 8-11-2 S Fox, hld up, hdwy 5th, rdn and mstk 2 out, wknd r-in. . . . . (10 to 1 op 5 to 2)	4
BLENNERVILLE (Ire) 6-10-8 (3") T Dascombe, prmnt, led appr 5th, rdn and hdd 2 out, wknd last. . . . (10 to 1 op 50 to 1)	5
I DON'T THINK SO 5-10-11 P McLoughlin, mid-div, drvn alng 5th, sn beh, tld off. . . . . (50 to 1 tchd 66 to 1)	6
DICKIES GIRL 6-10-8 (3") B Fenton, beh 5th, tld off.	
. . . . (12 to 1 op 8 to 1 tchd 14 to 1)	7
SANDFORD THYNE (Ire) 6-10-4 (7") Mr R Thornton, pld hrd, led second till appr 5th, wknd 4 out, beh whn uns rdr 3 out.	
. . . . (50 to 1 op 33 to 1)	ur
MUTLEY 6-11-2 C Maude, beh 5th, tld off whn pld up r-in, dismounted. . . . . (25 to 1 op 16 to 1)	pu
MISS SPENT YOUTH 5-10-6 (5") Mr P Henley, mid-div, drvn alng 5th, wknd, pld up bef 3 out. . . . (50 to 1 tchd 66 to 1)	pu
RORY'M (Ire) 7-11-2 D Leahy, beh hfwy, tld off whn pld up bef 4 out. . . . . (50 to 1 op 33 to 1)	pu
CLASSIC JESTER (Ire) (bl) 5-11-2 B Powell, strted slwly, al beh, tld off whn pld up bef 3 out. . . . . . . (33 to 1)	pu
SAXON BLADE 8-11-2 W McFarland, led to second, wknd quickly appr 5th, pld up bef nxt. . . (33 to 1 op 20 to 1)	pu

Dist: 4l, 10l, nk, 1¼l, dist, 14l. 4m 44.60s. a 8.60s (13 Ran).

(Mrs Richard Strachan & Mrs David Lewis), Capt T A Forster

104 Green Street Novices' Chase Class E (5-y-o and up) £3,535 2m 7f..... (8:45)

FLY THE WIND 11-10-11 D Bridgwater, chsd ldr, led 4th, quickened clr aftr tenth, eased r-in. . . . . (7 to 2)	1
47 RED EIKON 5-10-8 Richard Guest, hld up, styd on appr last, nvr plcd to chal. . . . . (33 to 1 tchd 50 to 1)	2
59⁵ MANOR RHYME 9-11-2 S Wynne, prmnt, lost pl 3rd, tld off hfwy, ran on outpcd. . . . . (20 to 1 op 16 to 1)	3
DUSTYS TRAIL (Ire) 7-10-9 (7") Mr R Thornton, prmnt, chsd wnr tenth, sn outpcd. . . . . (10 to 1 op 6 to 1)	4
SPY DESSA 8-11-2 A Thornton, prmnt to hfwy.	
. . . . (33 to 1 op 25 to 1)	5
41⁴ HIZAL 7-11-2 Mr A Charles-Jones, tld off 9th, styd on frm 2 out. . . . . (16 to 1 op 12 to 1 tchd 20 to 1)	6
CRACKING IDEA (Ire) (bl) 8-11-9 R Dunwoody, chsd ldrs till wknd 11th. . . . . (9 to 1 op 7 to 1 tchd 10 to 1)	7
SEA SEARCH 9-11-2 R Johnson, prmnt, hit 9th, wknd 11th, beh whn blun 4 out. . . . . . (8 to 1 op 7 to 1 tchd 9 to 1)	8
59² BALLYLINE (Ire) 5-10-8 R Supple, led to 4th, wknd 11th.	
. . . . (3 to 1 fav tchd 4 to 1)	9

59^{8} WELSH'S GAMBLE 7-11-2 W McFarland, *hld up, al rear.* ....(33 to 1) 10
51^{5} ARTFUL ARTHUR 10-11-2 Mr J Grassick, *beh hfwy, tld off whn f 4 out*..........(50 to 1 op 33 to 1) f
PINK SUNSET (Ire) 8-11-2 C Maude, *f second.* ....(33 to 1 op 25 to 1) f
BENGAZEE (Ire) 8-11-2 V Slattery, *blun and uns rdr 1st.* ....(50 to 1) ur
BRORA ROSE (Ire) (bl) 8-10-11 S Burrough, *tld off hfwy, jmpd slwly 4 out, sn pld up*..........(33 to 1) pu
ARR EFF BEE (bl) 9-11-2 T Eley, *al beh, tld off hfwy, pld up bef 4 out*..........(50 to 1 op 33 to 1) pu
42^{5} BRINDLEY HOUSE 9-11-2 D Morris, *beh hfwy, tld off whn pld up bef 13th*..........(10 to 1 op 12 to 1 tchd 14 to 1) pu
41^{3} TOP SPIN 7-11-2 J Osborne, *not jump wl, sn well beh, tld off whn pld up bef 4 out*..........(100 to 30 op 2 to 1) pu

Dist: 9l, hd, 7l, 4l, ¾l, ¾l, 3l, 24l, 11l. 5m 54.50s. a 16.50s (17 Ran).
(Mrs Pam Pengelly), M C Pipe

105 High Green Handicap Hurdle Class D (0-120 4-y-o and up) £3,965 2½m (9:15)

NINE O THREE (Ire) [96] 7-10-9 A Thornton, *hld up, hdwy 7th, led 2 out, ran on strly*..........(9 to 2 op 4 to 1) 1
SHIKAREE (Ire) [111] 5-11-10 D Bridgwater, *hld up, hdwy 5th, evrey ch 2 out, ran on one pace appr last.* (7 to 1 op 9 to 2) 2
49^{2} CALL THE GUV'NOR [96] 7-10-9 J R Kavanagh, *hld up, hdwy 6th, led 3 out to nxt, wknd appr last.* ....(3 to 1 fav op 4 to 1 tchd 11 to 4) 3
FIRST CLASS [94] 6-10-7 R Greene, *hld up, hdwy 4 out, styd on same pace frm 2 out*..........(14 to 1 tchd 16 to 1) 4
RAY RIVER [87] 4-10-0 J Ryan, *hld up, hdwy 5th, ev ch 3 out, wknd appr last*..........(16 to 1 op 10 to 1) 5
STICKY MONEY [97] 8-10-10 C Maude, *led to second, hrd rdn appr 6th, wknd 3 out.* (9 to 1 op 6 to 1 tchd 10 to 1) 6
KIPPANOUR (USA) [109] (bl) 4-11-8 R Dunwoody, *prmnt, led 5th till appr 3 out, sn btn*..........(13 to 2 op 5 to 1) 7
ADMIRALTY WAY [95] 10-10-8 L Harvey, *hld up, nvr trble ldrs*..........(33 to 1) 8
HOLY JOE [105] 14-11-4 D J Burchell, *prmnt till wknd 6th.* ....(25 to 1 op 16 to 1) 9
56^{4} SWEET NOBLE (Ire) [87] 7-10-0 M Sharratt, *prmnt, led second to 5th, wknd 4 out*..........(20 to 1 op 12 to 1) 10
BEAM ME UP SCOTTY (Ire) [94] 7-10-7 C Llewellyn, *prmnt, rdn 4 out, wknd quickly*..........(25 to 1 op 20 to 1) 11
BATTY'S ISLAND [109] (v) 7-11-8 Gary Lyons, *chsd ldrs, rdn 5th, wknd nxt, tld off*..........(20 to 1 op 14 to 1) 12
TWICE THE GROOM (Ire) [90] 6-10-3 P McLoughlin, *slwly into strd, mid-div whn f 3rd.* ....(10 to 1 op 6 to 1 tchd 12 to 1) f
49^{5} HOW'S IT GOIN (Ire) [98] 5-10-11 M Richards, *slwly into strd, hld up, f 4th*..........(12 to 1) f

Dist: 6l, 6l, 2½l, 2l, 11l, 2l, 18l, ½l, 9l, 30l. 4m 40.00s. a 4.00s (14 Ran).
SR: 1/10/-/-/-/-/ (Bideford Tool Ltd), A G Newcombe

STRATFORD (good to firm)
Thursday June 20th
Going Correction: MINUS 0.05 sec. per fur.

106 Dudley Castle And Zoo 'As You Like It' Novices' Chase Class E (5-y-o and up) £3,324 2½m..........(6:45)

48 NADJATI (USA) (v) 7-11-0 R Dunwoody, *hld up in tch, led 3 out, hdd r-in, rallied to ld last strd*..........(4 to 1 op 7 to 4) 1
SIMPLY (Ire) 7-11-0 P Hide, *led 3rd, jmpd slwly and hdd tenth, led 11th, headed 3 out, led r-in, headed post*..........(11 to 4 jt-fav op 3 to 1 tchd 7 to 2 and 9 to 4) 2
LEGAL ARTIST (Ire) 6-11-0 L Harvey, *mid-div, effrt tenth, 4th and btn whn hit 2 out*..........(12 to 1 op 8 to 1) 3
BEAT THE RAP (v) 10-11-0 Richard Guest, *prmnt, mstk 8th, wknd appr 2 out*..........(50 to 1 op 25 to 1) 4
100^{2} FLUIDITY (USA) (bl) 8-11-0 D Bridgwater, *strted slwly, hld up, pld hrd, hdwy tenth, jnd ldrs and hit 11th, wknd appr 2 out.* ....(11 to 4 jt-fav op 7 to 2 tchd 5 to 1) 5
DUKE OF DREAMS 6-11-0 B Powell, *prmnt, led tenth, hdd nxt, ev ch 4 out, wknd appr 2 out*..........(12 to 1 op 10 to 1) 6
THE FOOLISH ONE 9-10-9 R Johnson, *hld up, mstk 4th, hdwy und pres tenth, wknd 3 out.* ....(9 to 1 op 7 to 1 tchd 10 to 1) 7
79^{5} MISS DOTTY 6-10-9 R Farrant, *prmnt, lost pl 5th, beh frm 5 out*..........(14 to 1 op 8 to 1) 8
41 PRINCE ROCKAWAY (Ire) 8-10-11 (3*) Guy Lewis, *led to 3rd, wknd 4 out*..........(20 to 1 tchd 25 to 1) 9
APRIL CRUISE 9-10-9 G Upton, *not jump wl, al beh, tld off whn pld up aftr 8th*..........(50 to 1 op 33 to 1) pu
MUSICAL VOCATION (Ire) (bl) 5-10-2 Gary Lyons, *al in rear, lost tch hfwy, tld off whn pld up bef 2 out.* ....(50 to 1 op 33 to 1) pu

Dist: Sht-hd, 13l, 3½l, 6l, 6l, 1½l, 10l, 13l. 4m 59.00s. a 19.00s (11 Ran).
(T J Whitley), D R Gandolfo

107 Baggeridge Bricks Sedgley 'Comedy Of Errors' Novices' Hurdle Class E (4-y-o and up) £2,416 2m 110yds..(7:15)

COUREUR 7-10-12 R Garritty, *hld up, hdwy 6th, led last, rdn out*..........(11 to 4 op 5 to 2) 1
50* BRAVE PATRIARCH (Ire) 5-11-5 J R Kavanagh, *al prmnt, led 2 out, hdd last, unbl to quicken*..........(2 to 1 fav op 6 to 4) 2
ZINE LANE 4-10-7 R Farrant, *led to 4th, led 6th till rdn and hdd 2 out, styd on same pace.* ....(11 to 2 op 9 to 2 tchd 6 to 1) 3
I'M A DREAMER (Ire) 6-11-5 Gary Lyons, *prmnt, ev ch 3 out, wknd nxt*..........(4 to 1 op 7 to 2 tchd 9 to 2) 4
IRISH WILDCARD (NZ) 8-10-12 V Slattery, *trkd ldr, led 4th to 6th, wknd 3 out*..........(6 to 1 op 10 to 1) 5
THE CAMPDONIAN (Ire) 5-10-12 R Dunwoody, *hld up, nvr trble ldrs*..........(14 to 1 op 10 to 1) 6
SEVEN BROOKS 6-10-12 S Fox, *hld up, nvr dngrs.* ....(25 to 1 op 14 to 1) 7
BEST OF BOLD 4-10-7 P Hide, *hld up, effrt 5th, sn beh.* ....(33 to 1 op 20 to 1) 8
WELL SUITED 6-10-12 D O'Sullivan, *al in rear, tld off frm 5th.* ....(50 to 1 op 33 to 1) 9
SAYITAGAIN 4-10-7 J Osborne, *prmnt to 5th, tld off whn pld* [illegible] pu
SPARTS FAULT (Ire) (bl) 6-10-12 Richard Guest, *mid-div, rdn 5th, sn beh, tld off whn pld up bef 3 out.* ....(33 to 1 op 20 to 1 tchd 50 to 1) pu
MERELY MORTAL 5-10-12 R Johnson, *mid-div, lost pl 5th, rallied appr nxt, wknd quickly, beh whn pld up bef 3 out.* ....(33 to 1 op 16 to 1) pu

Dist: 2l, 8l, 10l, 18l, 3l, 1½l, 22l, 7l. 3m 51.60s. a 5.60s (12 Ran).
SR: 19/24/4/6/-/-/ (Frank Hanson), M D Hammond

108 J. Round Machinery Wednesbury 'Midsummer Night's Dream' Handicap Chase Class D (0-125 5-y-o and up) £3,658 3m..........(7:45)

CHANGE THE REIGN [103] 9-10-12 J Ryan, *al prmnt, led 8th, drvn out*..........(11 to 4 tchd 3 to 1) 1
24* HILLWALK [115] 10-11-10 D Morris, *hld up, jmpd slwly 4th and 5th, hdwy 11th, rdn four out, ev ch last, not quicken.* ....(11 to 10 fav op 5 to 4 tchd 11 to 8) 2
DOONLOUGHAN [104] 11-10-10 (3*) B Fenton, *led to 3rd, lft in ld 7th, hdd nxt, ev ch frm 4 out, no extr last.* ....(5 to 1 op 7 to 2) 3
DONNA DEL LAGO [107] (bl) 10-10-9 (7*) R Hobson, *prmnt, hit 3rd, outpcd 3 out, styd on r-in.* ....(10 to 1 op 5 to 1 tchd 11 to 1) 4
PETTY BRIDGE [96] 12-10-5 B Powell, *led 3rd, blun and hdd 7th, sn lost pl, tld off whn pld up bef 4 out.* ....(11 to 1 op 7 to 1) pu

Dist: 1½l, 4l, nk. 5m 57.30s. a 12.30s (5 Ran).
(E D Nicolson), Miss A E Embiricos

109 John Davies Interiors West Bromwich Garrick Jubilee Challenge Cup Handicap Hurdle Class D (0-120 4-y-o and up) £3,116 2m 110yds..........(8:15)

FISIO SANDS [96] 7-10-6 P Hide, *led to second, led appr 3 out, ran on wl*..........(14 to 1 op 6 to 1 tchd 16 to 1) 1
COMMANCHE CREEK [90] 6-9-9 (5*) Sophie Mitchell, *hld up and beh, hdwy 6th, trkd wnr 3 out, no extr appr last.* ....(16 to 1 op 20 to 1 tchd 25 to 1) 2
61* LADY CONFESS [93] 6-10-3 R Supple, *prmnt, mstk 6th, one pace frm 2 out*..........(7 to 1 op 8 to 1) 3
CLASSIC EXHIBIT [96] 7-10-6 T Eley, *mid-div, hdwy 5th, wknd appr 2 out*..........(10 to 1 op 8 to 1) 4
HAM N'EGGS [110] 5-11-6 R Garritty, *beh till styd on appr last, nvr nrr*..........(100 to 30 fav op 3 to 1 tchd 7 to 2) 5
YUBRALEE (USA) [106] 4-11-2 D Bridgwater, *trkd ldr, led 5th, hdd appr 3 out, sn wknd*..........(6 to 1 op 5 to 1) 6
IVY EDITH [114] 6-11-10 D O'Sullivan, *hld up, hdwy and mstk 5th, sn lost pl*..........(11 to 1 op 8 to 1 tchd 12 to 1) 7
80^{5} NO LIGHT [106] 9-11-2 L Harvey, *hld up, effrt 4 out, btn nxt.* ....(11 to 2 op 6 to 1 tchd 7 to 1) 8
YACHT [90] (bl) 4-10-0 P McLoughlin, *prmnt, rdn appr 5th, sn beh*..........(16 to 1 tchd 20 to 1) 9
HACKETTS CROSS (Ire) [113] 8-11-9 Richard Guest, *al in rear*..........(16 to 1 op 12 to 1) 10
BUNGEE JUMPER [108] (bl) 6-11-4 R Dunwoody, *led second, hdd 5th, sn hrd rdn and wknd*..........(11 to 2 op 7 to 2) 11
ROYAL GLINT [90] 7-9-7 (7*) Miss E J Jones, *al in rear, tld off whn pld up bef 3 out*..........(33 to 1 op 20 to 1) pu

Dist: 6l, 3l, 16l, 1½l, nk, 22l, 1½l, 1¾l, 4l, 8l. 3m 51.20s. a 5.20s (12 Ran).
SR: 18/6/6/-/5/-/ (The Best Of Luck Partnership), T P McGovern

110 KPMG Birmingham 'Twelfth Night' Handicap Chase Class E (0-115 5-y-o and up) £3,031 2m 1f 110yds... (8:45)

NOBLELY (USA) [105] 9-11-12 R Farrant, *led aftr 1st, hdd 6th, led 5 out, hit nxt, jmpd slwly 3 out, hrd rdn r-in, all out.* ....(3 to 1 op 9 to 4 tchd 7 to 2) 1
FLYING ZIAD (Can) [82] 13-10-3^{3} Mr A Charles-Jones, *prmnt, effrt appr 2 out, styd on r-in*..........(25 to 1 op 16 to 1) 2

81[4] SUPER SHARP (NZ) [89] 8-10-10 Jacqui Oliver, *hld up, hdwy to ld 6th, hdd 5 out, ev ch appr 2 out, wknd last.* ....(7 to 2 tchd 3 to 1) 3
TANGO'S DELIGHT [79] 8-10-0 B Powell, *hld up, hit 5th, wknd 7th.*........................ (7 to 2 op 9 to 2) 4
FIERCE [92] (v) 8-10-13 J Osborne, *led, jmpd slwly 1st, sn hdd, wknd appr 5 out, tld off.* ....(15 to 8 fav op 2 to 1 tchd 9 to 4) 5
STRIDING EDGE [79] (bl) 11-10-0 P McLoughlin, *prmnt till wknd 7th, tld off*........................(16 to 1 op 12 to 1) 6
Dist: ½l, 16l, 5l, 19l, 4l. 4m 16.30s. a 14.30s (6 Ran).
(D H Cowgill), N J H Walker

111 A.H.P. Trailers Wombourne 'Troilus And Cressida' Novices' Handicap Hurdle Class F (0-95 4-y-o and up) £2,234 2¾m 110yds.................. (9:15)

47[8] LITTLE COURT [61] 5-10-0 R Johnson, *al prmnt, led and blun 3 out, sn hdd, rdn whn lft in ld 2 out, all out.* ....(33 to 1 op 20 to 1) 1
46[3] SCAMALLACH (Ire) [85] (bl) 6-11-10 J Osborne, *hld up, hdwy to ld 8th, hdd 3 out, styd on und pres r-in.* ....(8 to 1 op 5 to 1 tchd 9 to 1) 2
47[2] HIGH POST [81] 7-11-3 (3*) R Massey, *hld up in tch, slpd bend appr 4 out, sn rdn, one pace frm 3 out.* ....(2 to 1 fav op 9 to 4) 3
ONE MORE DIME (Ire) [75] 6-10-11 (3*) B Fenton, *led to 8th, wknd 3 out.*........................ (8 to 1 op 6 to 1 tchd 10 to 1) 4
47[7] SPANISH BLAZE (Ire) [67] 8-10-6 D Byrne, *prmnt till blun and uns rdr 6th.*........................(3 to 1 op 5 to 2 tchd 7 to 2) ur
55[9] DANCING AT LAHARN (Ire) [85] 6-11-3 (7*) N Willmington, *hld up, hdwy 5th, lost pl 8th, rallied and lft in ld aftr 3 out, blun and uns rdr 2 out*........................(10 to 1 op 6 to 1) ur
27[5] LAC DE GRAS (Ire) [63] 5-10-2 D Morris, *hld up, beh frm 7th, tld off whn pld up bef 2 out.*........................ (11 to 1 op 8 to 1) pu
NICK THE BISCUIT [83] (v) 5-11-8 R Dunwoody, *trkd ldr, led briefly appr 8th, lost pl and hmpd bend approaching 9th, tld off whn pld up bef 3 out.*......(9 to 2 op 3 to 1 tchd 5 to 2) pu
Dist: Hd, 7l, 18l. 5m 32.80s. a 20.80s (8 Ran).
(E G Bevan), E G Bevan

THURLES (IRE) (firm)
Thursday June 20th

112 Tipperary Maiden Hurdle (4-y-o and up) £2,226 2m.................. (5:45)

FORCE THIRTEEN (Ire) 5-11-0 J F Titley,........................ (3 to 1) 1
62 WOODY 5-11-13 J Shortt,........................ (2 to 1 fav) 2
HE'S NO ANGEL (Ire) 6-11-1 (5*) Mr B M Cash,... (10 to 1) 3
ELLE CARVOEIRO (Ire) 5-10-9 (5*) T Martin,...... (10 to 1) 4
QUEEN'S FLAGSHIP (Ire) 4-10-10 T Horgan,........(3 to 1) 5
NOBODYWANTSME (Ire) 5-10-13[1] (7*) Mr J Creighton, ...(20 to 1) 6
UNDERSTANDING (Ire) 7-10-8 (7*) Mr P J McGarry, (20 to 1) 7
EMYGUY (Ire) 4-11-1 P Leech,........................(14 to 1) f
Dist: 2l, 2½l, 25l, dist. 3m 55.80s. (8 Ran).
(Mrs P F N Fanning), M F Morris

113 Shannon Handicap Hurdle (0-116 4-y-o and up) £2,226 2m............ (6:15)

67* KATES CHOICE (Ire) [-] 4-10-13 T P Treacy,..(11 to 10 fav) 1
33[3] BACK TO BLACK (Ire) [-] (bl) 7-10-8 K F O'Brien,..(11 to 2) 2
RUSHEEN BAY (Ire) [-] (bl) 7-9-0 (7*) A O'Shea,....(20 to 1) 3
ANDROS DAWN (Ire) [-] 6-10-7 J F Titley,..........(7 to 1) 4
GREAT ADVENTURE (Ire) [-] 8-12-0 J P Broderick, (10 to 1) 5
TIBOULEN (Ire) [-] 6-11-6 P Leech,..............(6 to 1) 6
ASHPARK ROSE (Ire) [-] 6-9-10 (5*) G Cotter,..... (10 to 1) 7
DEVIL'S HOLIDAY (USA) [-] 6-10-11 (5*) T Martin,...(4 to 1) f
Dist: 3l, ¾l, 11l, 1½l. 3m 46.00s. (8 Ran).
(Mrs Geraldine Treacy), S J Treacy

114 Moycarkey Beginners Chase (5-y-o and up) £2,226 2¾m............(7:45)

LOFTUS LAD (Ire) 8-11-4 (5*) Mr W M O'Sullivan,...(6 to 1) 1
65[6] CUBAN QUESTION 9-11-9 (5*) G Cotter,..........(9 to 2) 2
BEET STATEMENT (Ire) 7-10-11 (7*) Mr B Valentine, (8 to 1) 3
RASCAL STREET LAD (Ire) 8-11-4 J P Broderick,...(8 to 1) 4
CELTIC BUCK 10-11-7 (7*) Mr Patrick O'Keeffe, (7 to 2 fav) 5
STEALING HOME (Ire) 6-10-11 (7*) M D Murphy,... (9 to 1) 6
65 KING TYRANT (Ire) 7-11-9 K F O'Brien,.......... (20 to 1) 7
NATURAL ABILITY 11-12-0 C N Bowens,............(5 to 1) 8
BALLINVUSKIG LADY (Ire) 6-11-4 S H O'Donovan, (12 to 1) 9
65[8] IRENES TREASURE (Ire) 6-11-3[1] (7*) Mr S J Mahon, ...(20 to 1) 10
OKDO 9-11-9 G M O'Neill,........................ (20 to 1) pu
65[9] KILLALIGAN KIM (Ire) 6-11-1 (3*) D T Evans,......(20 to 1) pu
MR PIPE MAN (Ire) 7-11-2 (7*) A O'Shea,......(12 to 1) pu
Dist: 1½l, ¾l, 7l, 20l. 5m 30.50s. (13 Ran).
(Mrs Fiona O'Sullivan), Eugene M O'Sullivan

115 Devil's Bit I.N.H. Flat Race (4-y-o and up) £2,226 2m.................. (8:15)

MISTER GIGI (Ire) 5-11-6 (7*) Mr J T McNamara,... (4 to 1) 1
64[9] BALLYWHAT (Ire) 7-11-2 (7*) Mr R Walsh,.... (7 to 2 jt-fav) 2
BERCLUB (Ire) 5-11-6 (7*) Mr M Walsh,.......... (14 to 1) 3
ANNFIELD HERITAGE (Ire) 5-11-5 (3*) Mr P English, ...(7 to 2 jt-fav) 4
FRESHFIELD GALE (Ire) 6-11-2 (7*) Mr A C Coyle, (13 to 2) 5
SPRINGWELL MAY (Ire) 4-11-1 Mr P Fenton,...... (8 to 1) 6
DERRYNAFLAN LAD (Ire) 4-11-1 (5*) Mr B M Cash, (8 to 1) 7
THE THIN FELLOW (Ire) 5-11-6 (7*) Mr C Amerian, (16 to 1) 8
FRANCOSKID (Ire) 4-10-13 (7*) Mr J P McNamara, (7 to 1) ro
Dist: 12l, 1½l, 2½l, 6l. 3m 40.50s. (9 Ran).
(Leo Glennon), Donal Hassett

116 Golden Vale Handicap Chase (0-116 4-y-o and up) £2,226 2m 110yds (8:45)

97[2] RATES RELIEF (Ire) [-] 6-10-9 (7*) Mr G Elliott, (9 to 4 jt-fav) 1
HANNIES GIRL (Ire) [-] 7-10-9 F J Flood,.......... (5 to 2) 2
LA MODE LADY [-] 11-10-10 K F O'Brien,....(9 to 4 jt-fav) 3
NO SIR ROM [-] 10-9-7 T Horgan,................ (9 to 2) 4
Dist: 15l, 7l, 13l. 3m 57.30s. (4 Ran).
(Nikral Racing Syndicate), L Young

WEXFORD (IRE) (good)
Friday June 21st

117 Kilmore Maiden Hurdle (4-y-o and up) £2,226 2½m...................(6:00)

SHOREWOOD (Ire) 5-11-13 F Woods,.......(3 to 1 jt-fav) 1
CLASSIC SILK (Ire) 4-11-1 L P Cusack,........... (5 to 1) 2
CHANOBLE (Ire) 4-11-1 (5*) G Cotter,............(14 to 1) 3
66 THE SENATOR (Ire) 5-11-13 D H O'Connor,........(7 to 1) 4
86 DUSTY ROSE (Ire) 7-11-9 M Moran,............ (20 to 1) 5
66[6] GALE HAMSHIRE (Ire) 7-11-9 J Shortt,............(8 to 1) 6
62[7] ROSSI (Ire) 7-12-0 A Powell,....................(25 to 1) 7
TIGERALI (Ire) 6-11-9 T Horgan,..................(12 to 1) 8
THE CUSHMAN (Ire) 5-11-13 P A Roche,.... (3 to 1 jt-fav) pu
Dist: 1l, 15l, ½l, ½l. 4m 57.30s. (9 Ran).
(Lloyd Thompson), E J O'Grady

118 Bree Handicap Hurdle (0-102 4-y-o and up) £2,226 2¼m...........(6:30)

FERRYCARRIG HOTEL (Ire) [-] 7-11-6 C N Bowens, (9 to 2) 1
67[4] FATHER RECTOR (Ire) [-] 7-11-5 J Shortt,......(4 to 1 fav) 2
THE SOUTH POLE INN (Ire) [-] 4-9-4 (5*) J Butler, (20 to 1) 3
BUGGSY BLADE [-] 10-10-12 L P Cusack,....... (14 to 1) 4
30[7] DANCING POSER (Ire) [-] (bl) 4-10-8 K F O'Brien, (10 to 1) 5
BITRAN [-] 6-10-12 A Powell,....................(20 to 1) 6
PRINCE SABI (Ire) [-] 6-10-6 P L Malone,........(20 to 1) 7
TISRARA LADY (Ire) [-] 6-11-13 T P Treacy,...... (8 to 1) 8
29[9] LORD BENTLEY [-] (bl) 6-10-8 (7*) M W Martin,.... (8 to 1) 9
THE WICKED CHICKEN (Ire) [-] 7-10-12 T Horgan, (12 to 1) 10
65 CHUCK (Ire) [-] 6-10-12 F Woods,............... (20 to 1) 11
THE BRIDGE TAVERN (Ire) [-] 7-11-1 (3*) D P Murphy, ...(14 to 1) f
RADIF (USA) [-] 5-10-1 J P Byrne,............... (10 to 1) bd
FORTUNES LUCK (Ire) [-] 8-11-1 D H O'Connor,... (7 to 1) pu
Dist: 10l, 1l, nk, 6l. 4m 12.20s. (14 Ran).
(Ferrycarrig Hotel Syndicate), Victor Bowens

119 Hilary Murphy Travel Novice Hurdle (4-y-o and up) £3,082 2¼m....... (7:00)

SPANKY (Ire) 4-11-0 L P Cusack,..................(4 to 1) 1
EARP (Ire) 4-11-0 J Shortt,........................(4 to 1) 2
FLY ROSEY (Ire) 6-11-3 T Horgan,............(11 to 8 on) 3
RUDDS HILL (Ire) 8-11-2 J H Burke,............. (12 to 1) 4
MATTS DILEMMA (Ire) 8-10-13 (3*) D P Murphy,...(20 to 1) 5
PHANTOMS GIRL (Ire) 5-10-10 D H O'Connor,.....(33 to 1) 6
BENALF (Ire) 6-10-13 (3*) D T Evans,..............(50 to 1) 7
30 QUAH (Ire) 4-10-3 F Woods,.....................(33 to 1) 8
Dist: 10l, 1l, 8l, dist. 4m 10.40s. (8 Ran).
(Mrs D J Coleman), Mrs D J Coleman

120 Wexford Mares I.N.H. Flat Race (4-y-o and up) £2,226 2½m............(8:30)

64 TURRAMURRA GIRL (Ire) 7-12-0 Mr H F Cleary,...(14 to 1) 1
GALATASORI JANE (Ire) 6-11-7 (7*) Mr Patrick O'Keeffe, ...(14 to 1) 2
CARNACREEVA GANE (Ire) 5-11-6 (7*) Mr E Sheehy, (8 to 1) 3
LOUGHLINS PRIDE 7-12-0 Mr M Phillips,......... (7 to 1) 4
LANTINA (Ire) 5-11-6 (7*) Mr R Walsh,............(10 to 1) 5
SEA BRETA (Ire) 6-11-7 (7*) Mr Sean O O'Brien,.... (8 to 1) 6
68[4] ONEOFTHECLAN (Ire) 6-11-7 (7*) Mr V P Devereux, (6 to 1) 7
ROMANCEINTHEDARK (Ire) 6-11-7 (7*) Mr B A Murphy, ...(6 to 1) 8
RAHANINE MELODY (Ire) 4-10-13 (7*) Mr P R Crowley, ...(16 to 1) 9
68[8] CASTLE DOVE (Ire) 5-11-8 (5*) Mr B M Cash,...... (8 to 1) 10
GENNY'S SERENADE (Ire) 5-11-6 (7*) Mr A J Dempsey, ... (7 to 2 fav) 11
HARDTOBEGOOD (Ire) 5-11-6 (7*) Mr T N Cloke,..(10 to 1) 12

GRACIES MARE (Ire) 5-11-10 (3*) Mr P English, ... (8 to 1) 13
TREMOLLINA (Ire) 5-11-6 (7*) Mr J P McNamara, . .(20 to 1) 14
68⁵ EASTERN CUSTOM (Ire) 5-11-6 (7*) Miss D O'Neill, (8 to 1) 15
Dist: 3l, 4½l, sht-hd, 2½l. 4m 57.60s. (15 Ran).

(Henry Cleary), Henry Cleary

121 Duncannon I.N.H. Flat Race (5-y-o) £2,226 2¼m. . . . . (9:00)

DRAMATIST (Ire) 11-8 (5*) Mr B Mash, ...(11 to 10 fav) 1
68³ MASTER CHUZZLEWIT (Ire) 11-6 (7*) Mr T N Cloke,
. . . .(100 to 30) 2
ATTACK AT DAWN (Ire) 11-8 Mr P Fenton, ...(9 to 1) 3
BUCK AND A HALF (Ire) 11-6 (7*) Mr R Walsh, ...(20 to 1) 4
VALLEY TINGO (Ire) 11-6 (7*) Mr S Durack, ...(14 to 1) 5
COLONIA SKY (Ire) 11-1 (7*) Mr P R Lenihan, ...(16 to 1) 6
GRANNY'S COTTAGE (Ire) 11-1 (7*) Mr M A Cahill, (20 to 1) 7
TRY ONCE MORE (Ire) 11-6 (7*) Mr A J Dempsey, . .(5 to 1) 8
Dist: 1½l, 9l, 4l, 1l. 4m 9.70s. (8 Ran).

(Joseph Crowley), A P O'Brien

NAAS (IRE) (good to firm)
Saturday June 22nd

122 Eadestown I.N.H. Flat Race (4-y-o and up) £2,740 2m. . . . . (5:30)

VARTRY BOY (Ire) 5-11-13 Mr D Marnane, . . . (3 to 1 jt-fav) 1
SIR GANDOUGE (Ire) 7-12-0 Mr M Halford, ...(3 to 1 fav) 2
34⁴ JUST A VODKA (Ire) 6-11-7 (7*) Mr R Walsh, ...(8 to 1) 3
DOTTIE'S DOUBLE (Ire) 5-11-1 (7*) Miss K Rudd, (16 to 1) 4
MC CLATCHEY (Ire) 5-11-13 Mr P F Graffin, ...(7 to 1) 5
HILL OF HOPE (Ire) 5-11-6 (7*) Mr M A Cahill, ...(14 to 1) 6
64 DREAMIN GEORGE (Ire) 6-12-0 Mr G J Harford, . .(12 to 1) 7
THE HOLY PARSON (Ire) 4-11-1 (5*) Mr B M Cash, (7 to 1) 8
115⁴ ANNFIELD HERITAGE (Ire) 5-11-5 (3*) Mr A C Coyle, (8 to 1) 9
ROCK ON BUD (Ire) 5-11-10 (3*) Mr D Valentine, . .(12 to 1) 10
68⁶ RADICAL ACTION (Ire) 6-11-7 (7*) Miss S McDonogh,
. . . .(8 to 1) 11
GALACTUS (Ire) 5-11-6 (7*) Mr L P King, ...(8 to 1) 12
SLIGO CHAMPION (Ire) 5-11-13 Mr H F Cleary, . . .(12 to 1) 13
Dist: Hd, 1l, 7l, 6l, 4l. 3m 44.70s. (13 Ran).

(Miss P M Kavanagh), J Fanning

SOUTHWELL (good to firm)
Saturday June 22nd
Going Correction: PLUS 0.25 sec. per fur.

123 Will Scarlet Novices' Chase Class D (5-y-o and up) £4,092 2m. . . . .(1:55)

43² GESNERA 8-10-2 (7*) Michael Brennan, al prmnt, chsd ldr
7th, lft in ld 4 out, clr nxt, fnshd lme. . . . . .(5 to 2 op 3 to 1) 1
MORCAT 7-10-11² Mr C Mulhall, chsd ldrs, hdwy 5 out, hmpd
nxt, chased wnr 3 out, kpt on. . . . .(50 to 1 op 25 to 1) 2
26* SECRETARY OF STATE 10-11-7 J Osborne, prmnt, led 3rd till
aftr 6th, rdn alng and blun 8th, wknd after 4 out.
. . . .(100 to 30 op 9 to 4) 3
43⁴ EMERALD MOON 9-11-0 S Burrough, in tch, blun 5th and 7th,
wknd nxt, beh 4 out. . . . . (33 to 1 op 20 to 1 tchd 40 to 1) 4
SPANISH MONEY 9-11-0 Mr N Kent, led to 3rd, prmnt whn f
. . . .(33 to 1 op 20 to 1) f
79* ROBERT'S TOY (Ire) (bl) 5-11-8 D Bridgwater, prmnt, jmpd
slwly 1st, hit 4th, led aftr 6th till f four out.
. . . . (Evens fav op 6 to 4 on) f
QUICK DECISION (Ire) 5-10-5 (3*) R Massey, not fluent, al
beh, tld off hfwy, pld up aftr 2 out. . . . .(50 to 1 op 25 to 1) pu
Dist: 3½l, 11l, 10l. 4m 9.20s. 4s 15.20s (7 Ran).

(Catch-42), J G M O'Shea

124 Robin Hood Handicap Chase Class F (0-100 5-y-o and up) £4,962 3m 110yds. . . . . (2:25)

82² SOUTHERLY GALE [97] 9-11-11 B Powell, led second, clr 4
out, hit 2 out, kpt on. . . . .(7 to 2 fav op 3 to 1 tchd 4 to 1) 1
42 TRUSS [85] 9-10-13 R Supple, in tch, hdwy 13th, chsd wnr 4
out, hld whn blun last. . . . .(5 to 1 op 7 to 2) 2
UPWELL [72] 12-9-11 (3*) G Cahill, beh, hdwy 4 out, styd on
frm nxt, nvr dngrs. . . . .(33 to 1 op 33 to 1) 3
72⁹ REGARDLESS [72] 14-9-11 (3*) K Gaule, in tch, hdwy to join
ldr 12th, hit nxt, rdn alng 5 out, one pace whn blun 3 out.
. . . .(33 to 1) 4
RUSTY BRIDGE [91] (bl) 9-11-5 R Johnson, beh, sn drvn
alng, styd on und pres frm 4 out, nvr a factor.
. . . .(15 to 2 op 7 to 1 tchd 9 to 1) 5
JIMMY O'DEA [95] (v) 9-11-9 J Osborne, prmnt, rdn alng
14th, wknd nxt. . . . .(7 to 1 tchd 8 to 1) 6
DRUMCULLEN (Ire) [88] 7-11-2 R Dunwoody, led to second,
chsd wnr till rdn appr 4 out, sn wknd.
. . . .(5 to 1 op 9 to 2 tchd 11 to 1 2) 7
72⁴ STORM WARRIOR [72] (bl) 11-9-11 (3*) R Massey, chsd ldrs,
hit 4th, hit tenth and nxt, wknd 12th, beh whn pld up bef last.
. . . .(9 to 1 op 7 to 1 tchd 8 to 1) pu

424 MISS ENRICO [89] 10-11-3 A Thornton, in tch, rdn alng hfwy,
wknd 5 out, pld up bef 3 out. . . . .(10 to 1 op 8 to 1) pu
VAZON EXPRESS [86] 10-10-11 (3*) D Parker, sn beh, rdn
alng and tld off whn pld up aftr 14th. . .(20 to 1 op 16 to 1) pu
MAGIC BLOOM [100] 10-12-0 M Dwyer, mid-div, lost pl 11th,
beh whn pld up bef 13th. . . .(8 to 1 op 6 to 1 tchd 9 to 1) pu
Dist: 5l, 12l, ¾l, 13l, 5l, 6l. 6m 30.20s. 4s 36.20s (11 Ran).

(405200 Racing), M C Pipe

125 Alexandra Motors Handicap Hurdle Class E (0-110 4-y-o and up) £3,054 3m 110yds. . . . . (2:55)

DERRING BRIDGE [85] 6-10-10 R Johnson, hld up, hdwy 8th,
led and hit 3 out, clr nxt, ran on. . . . .(9 to 1 tchd 10 to 1) 1
28⁴ SLAUGHT SON (Ire) [91] 8-11-2 M Dwyer, hld up mid-div,
hdwy 8th, effrt 3 out, kpt on. . . . .(7 to 1 tchd 8 to 1) 2
70⁵ EASY OVER (USA) [75] 10-10-0 S Fox, in tch, hdwy 4 out,
chsd wnr nxt, sn rdn, one pace frm 2 out.
. . . .(20 to 1 tchd 25 to 1) 3
56⁶ MISS PIMPERNEL [75] (bl) 6-10-0 L O'Hara, mid-div, hdwy
8th, led 4 out, rdn and hdd nxt, sn one pace. . . .(16 to 1) 4
58⁶ LA FONTAINBLEAU (Ire) [91] 8-11-2 W Fry, beh, hit 6th, hdwy
und pres appr 3 out, no imprsn nxt. . .(14 to 1 op 16 to 1) 5
58⁵ ABLE PLAYER (USA) [93] 9-11-4 M Sharratt, mid-div, hdwy
8th, ev ch 4 out, rdn nxt, wknd. . . . . .(20 to 1 tchd 25 to 1) 6
28³ SCRABO VIEW (Ire) [99] 8-11-10 R Supple, al rear.
. . . .(15 to 2 op 6 to 1 tchd 8 to 1) 7
COURT CIRCULAR [95] 7-11-3 (3*) Guy Lewis, chsd ldrs, rdn
alng 9th, wknd nxt. . . .(16 to 1 op 14 to 1 tchd 20 to 1) 8
59³ NESCAF (NZ) [92] 6-11-3 R Dunwoody, al rear, tld off 3 out.
. . . .(11 to 2 op 5 to 1 tchd 6 to 1) 9
STRONG JOHN (Ire) [90] 8-10-12 (3*) K Gaule, cl up, rdn 9th,
wknd nxt, sn beh. . . . .(14 to 1) 10
MOOBAKKR (USA) [100] 5-11-11 J Osborne, chsd ldrs, lost
pl and pld up aftr 8th. . . . .(7 to 1 tchd 8 to 1) pu
58* MORNING BLUSH (Ire) [103] 6-12-0 B Powell, made most till
aftr 9th, wknd quickly, pld up aftr 3 out.
. . . .(5 to 2 fav tchd 2 to 1) pu
Dist: 6l, 2½l, 8l, 12l, 3l, 1¼l, 19l, dist, dist. 6m 16.60s. 4s 34.60s (12 Ran).

(I K Johnson), Mrs S M Johnson

126 Derby Building Services Novices' Hurdle Class E (4-y-o and up) £2,322 2m . . . . (3:30)

46* ZAHID (USA) 5-11-7 R Johnson, hld up, hdwy 5th, led 2 out,
quickened clr frm last. . . . .(2 to 1 fav op 6 to 4) 1
CUBAN NIGHTS (USA) 4-10-9 B Powell, trkd ldrs, hdwy 5th,
ev ch 2 out, sn rdn, not quicken r-in. . . .(7 to 1 op 6 to 1) 2
SUAS LEAT (Ire) 6-11-0 M Dwyer, prmnt, led 6th, rdn and hdd
appr 2 out, sn one pace. . . . .(5 to 2 op 7 to 2) 3
PRINZAL 9-10-7 (7*) R Hobson, led tll aftr second, led 4th to
6th, cl up and ev ch whn hit 2 out, 3rd and btn when blun last.
. . . .(11 to 2 op 6 to 1 tchd 7 to 1) 4
HAMADRYAD (Ire) 8-11-7 R Davis, hld up beh, hit 5th, hdwy
aftr 3 out, hit nxt, sn btn. . . . .(7 to 1 op 6 to 1) 5
PIMSBOY 9-10-11 (3*) P Midgley, lost tch 5th, sn beh.
. . . .(33 to 1) 6
83 MB'EBE 6-11-0 T Kent, al prmnt, ev ch whn rdn alng 3 out,
wkng when pld up bef nxt.
. . . .(5 to 1 op 33 to 1 tchd 20 to 1) pu
BOLD LOOK 5-11-0 R Bellamy, in tch, rdn alng 7th, sn wknd,
beh whn pld up bef 2 out. . . . .(12 to 1 op 10 to 1) pu
46 NEVER SAY SO 4-10-1 (3*) G Cahill, cl up, led aftr second to
3rd, sn pld up quickly nxt, beh whn pld up 3 out. . . . .(33 to 1) pu
Dist: 6l, 16l, 1¾l, 3l, 9l. 4m 1.20s. 4s 15.20s (9 Ran).

(Keith W R Booth), K R Burke

127 Maid Marion Handicap Hurdle Class F (0-105 4-y-o and up) £2,211 2m (4:00)

ISLAND VISION (Ire) [85] (bl) 6-10-6 (7*) Michael Brennan, al
prmnt, effrt 3 out, led last, rdn and ran on wl, disqualified.
. . . .(9 to 2 fav op 8 to 1) 1D
45* NOCATCHIM [85] 7-10-10 (3*) R Massey, trkd ldrs, hdwy to ld
6th, rdn alng 2 out, hdd last, kpt on und pres, fnshd second,
awarded race. . . . .(13 to 2 op 6 to 1 tchd 7 to 1) 1
44⁴ DIBLOOM [80] 8-10-8 R Johnson, al prmnt, ev ch 3 out, sn
rdn, one pace frm 2 out, fnshd 3rd, plcd second. . . .(12 to 1) 2
PLAYFUL JULIET (Can) [75] 8-10-3³ T Kent, beh and rdn alng
hfwy, styd on frm 2 out, nvr a factor, fnshd 4th, plcd 3rd.
. . . .(15 to 2 op 7 to 1 tchd 8 to 1) 3
NORDIC VALLEY (Ire) [105] 5-12-0 B Powell, al rear, tld off 4
out, fnshd 5th, plcd fourth. . . . .(6 to 1 op 4 to 1) 4
STAY WITH ME (Fr) [90] 6-11-4 J Osborne, beh, effrt and
son hdwy 3 out, sn wknd, fnshd 6th, plcd 5th.
. . . . 5
MCGILLYCUDDY REEKS (Ire) [95] 5-11-4 R Dunwoody, cl up,
led 3rd to 6th, sn rdn, wknd aftr 3 out. . .(6 to 1 op 9 to 2) 7
NORTHERN NATION [84] 8-10-9 (3*) Guy Lewis, in tch to 4th,
beh 6th, pld up bef 2 out. . . . .(20 to 1 op 16 to 1) pu
ERINY (USA) [88] 7-11-2 M Dwyer, hld up, hdwy 5th, 3rd and
rdn alng whn pld up bef 2 out, lme. . . .(5 to 1 tchd 6 to 1) pu
SHELLHOUSE (Ire) [89] 8-11-3 A Thornton, led, hit second,
hdd nxt, wknd 6th, beh whn pld up bef 2 out.
. . . .(7 to 1 op 6 to 1) pu

Dist: ½l, 18l, 12l, 8l, 1¼l, 10l. 3m 57.50s. a 11.50s (10 Ran).
SR: 10/9/-/-/-/-/ (R E Gray), K A Morgan

128 Sheriff Of Nottingham Conditional Jockeys' Novices' Selling Handicap Hurdle Class G (0-90 4-y-o and up) £1,943 2½m 110yds............ (4:35)

```
       ROSIE (Ire) [56] 6-10-0 B Fenton, beh, hdwy 7th, chlgd 2 out,
         sn led, clr last, into nxt....................(16 to 1 op 20 to 1)   1
78     TREMBLE [63] 7-10-7 D Parker, hld up, hdwy 6th, cl up nxt,
         led 3 out to next, one pace und pres.
         ...................................(16 to 1 op 14 to 1 tchd 20 to 1)  2
69⁶    LAGO LAGO (Ire) [80] 4-11-4 G Cahill, hld up in tch, hdwy 7th,
         led 2 out, sn rdn and hdd, wknd appr last.
         ......................................(7 to 4 fav op 7 to 2)          3
       WORDY'S WIND [70] 7-10-11 (3ˣ) C Rae, in tch, hdwy 7th, rdn
         3 out, sn one pace.......................(16 to 1 op 14 to 1)         4
       KINGFISHER BLUES (Ire) [56] 8-9-13² (3ˣ) Michael Brennan,
         chsd ldrs, 6th 7th, wknd bef 3 out.... (33 to 1 op 25 to 1)          5
       DAN DE LYON [71] 8-11-1 J Magee, led till aftr 6th, wknd
         quickly, pld up after nxt. (10 to 1 op 7 to 1 tchd 12 to 1)         pu
       TUKUM [84] 8-11-11 (3ˣ) B Grattan, hld up, hdwy 7th, ev ch
         whn pld up bef 2 out, lme..................(10 to 1 op 7 to 1)       pu
       MARKETING MAN [60] 6-10-4 Guy Lewis, chsd ldr, rdn alng
         and lost pl 7th, beh whn pld up aftr 3 out.
         ...................................(10 to 1 op 12 to 1 tchd 14 to 1)  pu
       DENOMINATION (USA) [65] 4-11-9 E Husband, prmnt, led 7th
         till rdn and hdd 3 out, wknd appr nxt, pld up bef last.
         .......................................(9 to 4 op 5 to 4)            pu
Dist: 3½l, 7l, 8l, 5l. 5m 15.70s. a 29.70s (9 Ran).
```
(W E Dudley), C J Hemsley

129 King John Intermediate National Hunt Flat Class H (4,5,6-y-o) £1,269 2m
.... (5:05)

```
       ULTIMATE SMOOTHIE 4-10-11 (3ˣ) R Massey, trkd ldrs gng
         wl, hdwy 2 fs out, led o'r one out, sn clr.
         ...........................(5 to 1 op 4 to 1 tchd 11 to 1)          1
       ARRANGE 4-10-7 (7ˣ) N Horrocks, reared strt, sn prmnt, led 3
         fs out, rdn 2 out, hdd and one pace appr last.
         .......................................(15 to 2 op 4 to 1 tchd 8 to 1)  2
       NENAGH GUNNER 6-10-11 (3ˣ) B Fenton, hld up, hdwy 6 fs
         out, ev ch 2 out, sn rdn, kpt on same pace appr last.
         .............................................(14 to 1 op 10 to 1)    3
       MILLENNIUM MAN 5-11-5 Mr J Weymes, in tch, hdwy hfwy,
         chlgd and ev ch o'r 2 fs out, sn rdn, one pace appr last.
         .............................(12 to 1 op 10 to 1 tchd 14 to 1)       4
74*    PETIT FLORA 4-10-13 (3ˣ) G Cahill, hld up beh, hdwy 7 fs out,
         effrt and chsd ldrs o'r 2 out, sn rdn, one pace appr last.
         ........................................(5 to 2 fav op 9 to 4)       5
       OATS FOR NOTES 6-11-0 Mr M Rimell, led, rdn alng 5 fs out,
         hdd 3 out, wknd....................(20 to 1 op 16 to 1)             6
       CRUSTYGUN 6-11-2 (3ˣ) J Culloty, hld up, hdwy hfwy, rdn 4 fs
         out, wknd o'r 2 out..........(5 to 1 op 6 to 1 tchd 7 to 1)          7
       KNIGHTON 5-11-0 (5ˣ) S Ryan, prmnt, rdn alng 6 fs out, sn
         wknd...........................................(14 to 1 op 12 to 1)  8
       ROBERT SAMUEL 5-11-0 (5ˣ) Mr C Vigors, chsd ldrs, lost pl
         and beh 6 fs out................(9 to 2 op 3 to 1 tchd 5 to 1)       9
       ALICE SHEER THORN 6-10-7 (7ˣ) Miss E Tomlinson,
         hdwy to join ldrs aftr 5 fs, cl up till rdn and wknd five out.
         ...........................................(20 to 1 op 16 to 1)     10
       SWEET TALKER 4-11-0 Mr A Phillips, in tch, rdn alng
         hfwy, sn wknd.............................(20 to 1 op 16 to 1)      11
       STORMIN GIFT 5-11-2 (3ˣ) A Roche, al rear.
         ...................................(16 to 1 op 14 to 1)            12
       GREENS BRIDE 4-10-11 (3ˣ) E Husband, chsd ldrs, wknd aftr
         7 fs, tld off 5 out......... (14 to 1 op 12 to 1 tchd 16 to 1)      13
       LITTLE DERRING 5-10-7 (7ˣ) Mr R Thornton, tld off hfwy.
         ...........................................(25 to 1 op 14 to 1)    14
Dist: 5l, sht-hd, sht-hd, 3l, 11l, 4l, 4l, ¾l, 20l, 5l. 3m 59.10s. (14 Ran).
```
(Isca Bloodstock), M C Pipe

LIMERICK (IRE) (good)
Monday June 24th

130 BDO Simpson Xavier Handicap Hurdle (0-112 4-y-o and up) £3,425 2m 5f
.... (5:30)

```
76*    LE GRANDE BARD (Ire) [-] (bl) 7-10-0 T P Treacy, (6 to 4)            1
76⁴    CULLENSTOWN LADY (Ire) [-] 5-11-7 A Powell, .... (7 to 4)            2
67     MOUNTHENRY STAR (Ire) [-] 8-9-9 (7ˣ) C B Hynes,  (7 to 1)            3
93³    FIXED ASSETS (Ire) [-] 9-11-0 K F O'Brien,...........(6 to 1)       4
Dist: 5l, dist, 20l. 4m 46.00s. (4 Ran).
```
(Mrs D J Tarrant), Mrs F M O'Brien

131 Kevin McManus Bookmaker Handicap Hurdle (0-116 4-y-o and up) £3,425 2m
.... (6:00)

```
       PRACTICIAN (Ire) [-] 6-9-4 (7ˣ) J M Maguire, ...... (12 to 1)        1
29³    BALMYRA (Ire) [-] (bl) 4-10-0 W T Slattery,.......(100 to 30)        2
       NATALIES FANCY [-] 10-11-7 (7ˣ) Mr P Cashman,  (10 to 1)            3
```

```
       BALLINAGREEN (Ire) [-] 6-10-10 A Powell, ...... (12 to 1)            4
       TEMPLEROAN PRINCE [-] 9-11-4 M Duffy, ......... (9 to 2)            5
66⁸    CROOM ABU (Ire) [-] 5-9-7 T Horgan, ............. (9 to 1)          6
67²    I REMEMBER IT WELL (Ire) [-] (bl) 4-9-0 (7ˣ) S FitzGerald,
         .................................................(9 to 2)            ur
89     LET IT RIDE (Ire) [-] 7-11-1 T P Treacy, .........(9 to 4 fav)        pu
Dist: Hd, 1½l, dist, 1½l. 3m 37.30s. (8 Ran).
```
(P Beirne), P Beirne

132 Punch's Pub & Restaurant Maiden Hurdle (4-y-o and up) £3,425 2¼m.. (6:30)

```
86⁸    PINGO HILL (Ire) 4-11-1 J Shortt, ...............(12 to 1)           1
30⁵    ADARAMANN (Ire) 4-11-6 (7ˣ) Mr R Walsh, .........(3 to 1)           2
86⁵    DROMINAGH (Ire) 8-10-13 (7ˣ) A O'Shea, ..........(6 to 1)           3
       JONATHAN'S ROSE (Ire) 7-10-8 (7ˣ) Mr G Gallagher,
         ...................................................(25 to 1)        4
       BRAVE COMMITMENT (Ire) 5-11-8 T Horgan, ...... (4 to 1)             5
90     SNUGVILLE SALLY 4-10-10 M P Hourigan, ........(14 to 1)            6
66³    HONEY TRADER 4-11-1 J P Broderick, ....... (9 to 4 fav)            7
30     GLACIAL GIRL 4-10-5 (5ˣ) G Cotter, ......... (14 to 1)             8
66     PIXIE BLUE (Ire) 5-11-0 T P Treacy, .............(20 to 1)          9
       LOCH WEE (Ire) 5-11-0 J Jones, ...............(20 to 1)            10
Dist: 1½l, ½l, 3½l, 4½l. 4m 16.80s. (10 Ran).
```
(J E B Jobson), Mrs John Harrington

133 Aeorbord Ltd I.N.H. Flat Race (5-y-o and up) £3,425 2½m........... (8:00)

```
       SOUTHERN MARINER (Ire) 6-11-4 (5ˣ) Mr B M Cash, (8 to 1)            1
88³    ART PRINCE (Ire) 6-11-7 (7ˣ) Mr J T McNamara, (9 to 2 co-
         fav)                                                                2
       STRADBALLY JANE (Ire) 6-11-2 (7ˣ) Mr M Walsh, ..(16 to 1)            3
95³    BIDDY HUNT (Ire) 5-11-1 (7ˣ) Mr R Walsh, ........(20 to 1)          4
92⁸    MARE'S PRIDE (Ire) (bl) 5-11-1 (7ˣ) Mr J L Cullen,  (16 to 1)        5
       FATHER MICHAEL (Ire) 6-11-7 (7ˣ) Mr A C Coyle, (9 to 2 co-
         fav)                                                                6
86²    MUSKERRY KING (Ire) 5-11-13 Mr P Fenton, (9 to 2 co-fav)            7
       MUSKERRY EXPRESS (Ire) 6-11-7 (7ˣ) Mr M J Walsh,
         ...................................................(20 to 1)        8
       CANTELIER 7-11-11 (3ˣ) Mr E Norris, ...........(8 to 1)             9
       SARAH'S VISION (Ire) 5-11-8 Mr D Marnane, ...(12 to 1)            10
94     NEPHIN FAR (Ire) 6-11-2 (7ˣ) Mr John P Moloney,  (12 to 1)         11
       TULLAGHFIN (Ire) 6-11-7 (7ˣ) Mr G Elliott, .......(14 to 1)         12
       MEGS MOMENT (Ire) 5-11-1 (7ˣ) Mr J Keville, ...(20 to 1)           13
       WELSH LANE (Ire) 5-11-2 (7ˣ) Mr C A Murphy, .....(7 to 1)          14
       ATHY PRINCESS (Ire) 6-11-2 (7ˣ) Mr D P Daly, .....(8 to 1)         15
       MAC-DUAGH (Ire) 6-11-7 (7ˣ) Mr R D Lee, ......(16 to 1)            16
       CAMLA LAD (Ire) 5-11-6 (7ˣ) Mr P J Gilligan, ....(11 to 1)         17
Dist: 1½l, 2½l, 5½l, 3l. 4m 35.20s. (17 Ran).
```
(Philip O'Connor), A P O'Brien

SLIGO (IRE) (good to firm)
Tuesday June 25th

134 Garavogue Maiden Hurdle (4-y-o and up) £2,226 2m.................. (5:30)

```
21⁵    BRIGHT PROJECT (Ire) 4-10-8 (7ˣ) A O'Shea, ......(7 to 2)           1
21²    WHEREWILITALL END (Ire) 5-11-2 (3ˣ) U Smyth, (7 to 4 fav)           2
       CORMAC LADY (Ire) 5-11-0 J K Kinane, ............(9 to 2)           3
       SLIEVROE (Ire) 5-11-0 J Shortt, .................(5 to 1)           4
       ROYAL ARISTOCRAT (Ire) 7-11-1 P McWilliams, .. (7 to 1)            5
       OG'S DESIRE (Ire) 5-11-0 L P Cusack, ...........(12 to 1)          6
       ROCK COTTAGE 5-11-5 A Powell, ..................(16 to 1)          7
       AUGHNANURE (Ire) 5-11-5 K F O'Brien, ...........(16 to 1)          8
Dist: ¾l, 13l, 11l, 2l. 3m 51.00s. (8 Ran).
```
(Sean Geary), Donal Hassett

135 Oates Conlon Life & Pensions Handicap Hurdle (0-102 4-y-o and up) £2,740 2m.................... (6:00)

```
       MASCOT [-] 5-11-9 P L Malone, ..................(5 to 1)            1
95²    FAIR SOCIETY (Ire) [-] 5-9-12 J P Broderick, ...... (5 to 1)        2
113³   RUSHEEN BAY (Ire) [-] (bl) 7-9-1 (7ˣ) A O'Shea, ...(8 to 1)         3
       LAWYER'S BRIEF (Fr) [-] 9-10-1 T P Treacy, .... (14 to 1)          4
       MAJESTIC PADDY (Ire) [-] 6-11-10 F Woods, .. (2 to 1 fav)          5
32     THE BOURDA [-] 10-10-6 T P Rudd, ..............(12 to 1)           6
       LEGITMAN (Ire) [-] 6-9-11 T Horgan, ..............(7 to 1)          7
89⁵    CHOICE COMPANY (Ire) [-] 7-9-2 (5ˣ) T Martin, ...(33 to 1)         8
90     DEABHAILIN (Ire) [-] 6-9-13 (5ˣ) G Cotter, .......(25 to 1)        9
23⁴    EXCUSE ME (Ire) [-] 7-10-3 P McWilliams, .......(12 to 1)         10
Dist: ½l, 1l, 3l, 5l. 3m 49.50s. (10 Ran).
```
(Rudy Weiss), M J Grassick

136 M.Reilly Mitsubishi Connaught National Chase (4-y-o and up) £2,740 2½m........................... (7:30)

```
37⁴    BALD JOKER [-] 11-9-11 F Woods, ...............(20 to 1)           1
       PENNYBRIDGE (Ire) [-] 7-11-8 L P Cusack, .......(5 to 1)           2
       SPINDANTE (Ire) [-] 6-10-2 P McWilliams, ......(12 to 1)           3
       CASTALINO [-] 10-10-2 (5ˣ) G Cotter, ............(4 to 1)          4
       ANOTHER COQ HARDI (Ire) [-] 8-10-9 J Shortt, .... (4 to 1)         5
       MAN OF IRON [-] 9-9-11 T Horgan, ..............(14 to 1)           6
```

GREEK MAGIC [-] 9-10-2 A Powell, ...(10 to 1) 7
37 WILLCHRIS [-] 9-10-8 T P Rudd, ...(12 to 1) 8
TRASSEY BRIDGE [-] 9-11-6 C O'Dwyer, ...(11 to 4 fav) 9
Dist: Sht-hd, 2l, 2½l, 2l. 5m 1.00s. (9 Ran).

137 Grange I.N.H. Flat Race (4-y-o and up) £2,226 2m......................(8:00)

SINDABEZI (Ire) 4-10-12 (7") Mr A J Dempsey, ... (3 to 1) 1
PHARDUBH (Ire) 5-11-10 (7") Mr R M Walsh, ...(Evens fav) 2
22* SHRAMORE LAD (Ire) 5-11-10 (7") Mr R J Cooper, ..(5 to 1) 3
GRAPHIC LADY (Ire) 4-10-12 Mr J P Dempsey, .. (14 to 1) 4
HARRY HEANEY (Ire) 7-11-13 (5") Mr B M Cash, ... (8 to 1) 5
DUNMORE DOM (Ire) 4-11-3 Mr D Marnane, ... (33 to 1) 6
MAIASAURA (Ire) 7-11-11 Mr P F Graffin, ...(20 to 1) 7
MISS TOP (Ire) 6-10-13 (7") Mr G Elliott, ...(20 to 1) 8
SILKEN ASH (Ire) 6-11-4 (7") Mr D M Christie, ...(33 to 1) bd
64 MOY VALLEY (Ire) 6-10-13 (7") Mr A Daly, ...(33 to 1) su
Dist: 3l, 4l, 6l, 20l. 3m 51.60s. (10 Ran).

(Mrs J M Harley), J C Harley

GOWRAN PARK (IRE) (yielding) Wednesday June 26th

138 Evergreen Handicap Chase (0-116 5-y-o and up) £2,740 2¾m..........(7:30)

114* LOFTUS LAD (Ire) [-] 8-10-1 (4ex) T P Treacy, ...(5 to 1) 1
85³ ROSSBEIGH CREEK [-] 9-10-10 F J Flood, ...(7 to 2) 2
32⁶ MIDNIGHT HOUR (Ire) [-] 7-11-5 C O'Dwyer, ...(6 to 1) 3
MICKS DELIGHT (Ire) [-] 6-11-6 M P Dwyer, ...(7 to 2) 4
SPRINGFORT LADY (Ire) [-] 7-10-5 J P Broderick,
......................................(5 to 2 fav) 5
85⁵ GLEN OG LANE [-] 8-13-9-8¹ F Woods, ...(20 to 1) 6
Dist: 4l, ½l, 6l, 7l. 5m 28.30s. (6 Ran).

(Mrs Fiona O'Sullivan), Eugene M O'Sullivan

139 John M Foley Hurdle (4-y-o and up) £3,425 2m......................(8:00)

86* WESPERADA (Ire) 4-10-6 J Shortt, ...(3 to 1) 1
67³ FRESH DEAL (Ire) 4-10-6 L P Cusack, ...(13 to 8 fav) 2+
119³ FLY ROSEY (Ire) 6-10-9 T Horgan, ...(5 to 2) 2+
MY TRELAWNY (Ire) 6-11-4 C O'Dwyer, ...(5 to 1) 4
DREAMCATCHER (Ire) 6-11-0 T P Treacy, ...(8 to 1) 5
RONDELLI (Ire) 6-11-0 J K Kinane, ...(12 to 1) 6
33⁶ ASHLEY'S PRINCESS (Ire) 4-10-1 C N Bowens, .. (25 to 1) ro
Dist: Nk, dd-ht, dist, dist. 3m 45.50s. (7 Ran).

(Mrs A McAleer), Noel Meade

140 Midsummer Maiden Hurdle (5-y-o and up) £2,397 2½m...............(8:30)

91⁹ VAIN PRINCESS (Ire) 7-11-9 M P Hourigan, ...(10 to 1) 1
88² YOUNG DUBLINER (Ire) 7-11-6 J Shortt, ...(9 to 2) 2
MISS BERTAINE (Ire) 7-11-1 J P Broderick, ...(9 to 1) 3
CLEVER JACK (Ire) 6-11-6 K F O'Brien, ...(7 to 1) 4
SLANEY RASHER 9-11-3 (3") D P Murphy, ...(10 to 1) 5
99⁷ BALLY UPPER (Ire) 8-11-6 C O'Dwyer, ...(20 to 1) 6
SLAVE GALE (Ire) 5-11-8 T Horgan, ...(7 to 2) 7
BABY WHALE (Ire) 6-11-1 T J O'Sullivan, ...(20 to 1) 8
BISHOP'S HILL (Ire) 7-12-0 T P Treacy, ...(100 to 30 fav) 9
HAY DANCE 5-11-0 (5") Mr M W O'Sullivan, ...(20 to 1) 10
MOONVOOR (Ire) 5-11-5 M P Dwyer, ...(8 to 1) 11
RATHNAGEERA GIRL (Ire) 8-11-9 S H O'Donovan, (7 to 1) 12
JOSALADY (Ire) 7-10-8 (7") M P Dunne, ...(20 to 1) 13
Dist: ¾l, 10l, 2½l, 8l. 4m 58.10s. (13 Ran).

(D O'Leary), Michael Hourigan

LES LANDES (JER) (good) Thursday June 27th

141 Barings International Handicap Hurdle (4-y-o and up) £720 2m 1f.......(7:00)

WOLLBULL 6-12-0 V Smith, ...(5 to 4 on) 1
75* BIRSTWITH (USA) 11-9-9 B Powell, ...(5 to 4) 2
CLEAR HOME 10-11-2 A McCabe, ...(5 to 1) 3
FOOLS OF PRIDE (Ire) 4-10-8 P Henley, ...(4 to 1) 4
Dist: 15l, 8l, 6l. 4m 0.00s. (4 Ran).

(M J Weaver), J S O Arthur

TIPPERARY (IRE) (good to firm) Thursday June 27th

142 Limerick Junction Maiden Hurdle (4-y-o and up) £2,226 2m..........(7:00)

30² FRASER CAREY (Ire) (bl) 4-11-6 C O'Dwyer, ...(5 to 2) 1
SHANRUE (Ire) 6-12-0 T Horgan, ...(6 to 1) 2
62² HIGH MOAT (Ire) 6-11-1 (5") Susan A Finn, ...(8 to 1) 3
62⁶ GRANUALE (Ire) 5-10-7 (7") A O'Shea, ...(10 to 1) 4
LOUGH N UISCE (Ire) 6-11-6 (3") J R Barry, ...(10 to 1) 5

66² SCOUTS HONOUR (Ire) 5-11-8 F Woods, ...(9 to 4 fav) 6
111² WOODY (bl) 5-11-13 J Shortt, ...(8 to 1) 7
112³ HE'S NO ANGEL (Ire) 6-11-9 (5") Mr B M Cash, .. (12 to 1) 8
NEW WEST (Ire) 6-11-1 (5") J Butler, ...(20 to 1) 9
BELLE OF KILBRIDE (Ire) 6-10-8 (7") L A Hurley, .. (20 to 1) 10
62 DOLLDYEDEE (Ire) 5-11-0 T P Treacy, ...(25 to 1) 11
68 PIANO MELODY (Ire) (bl) 5-11-0 J P Broderick, ...(25 to 1) 12
99 GLENBEG GROVE (Ire) 6-11-1 K F O'Brien, ...(25 to 1) pu
Dist: 7l, 9l, 3½l, 4½l. 3m 49.10s. (13 Ran).

(Mrs M Burridge), Declan Gillespie

143 Primus Advertising Handicap Hurdle (0-130 4-y-o and up) £3,596 2m (7:30)

KATIYMANN (Ire) [-] 4-10-10 T Horgan, ...(11 to 8 fav) 1
96² BOB THE YANK (Ire) [-] 6-11-2 J Shortt, ...(9 to 2) 2
PERSIAN MYSTIC (Ire) [-] 4-11-0 G M O'Neill, ...(5 to 1) 3
MISTER CHIPPY (Ire) [-] 4-12-0 C O'Dwyer, ...(4 to 1) 4
65 SANDY FOREST LADY (Ire) [-] 7-10-9 T P Treacy, (12 to 1) 5
SUNDANCE MADERA (Ire) [-] 6-10-5 (3") D T Evans,
......................................(14 to 1) 6
REGIO DANGEREUX (Ire) [-] 6-10-10 ....(9 to 1) pu
Dist: 3h-hd, 2l, 8l, 2l. 3m 44.80s. (7 Ran).

(Frank Hardy), Thomas J Taaffe

144 Bansha I.N.H. Flat Race (4-y-o and up) £2,740 2m......................(9:00)

ERRAMORE (Ire) 4-11-0 (5") Mr B M Cash, ...(11 to 10 fav) 1
STANSWAY 8-11-4 (7") Mr Patrick O'Keeffe, .. (16 to 1) 2
99* ROLL OVER (Ire) 6-11-11 (7") Mr J T McNamara, .. (10 to 1) 3
REAL TAOISEACH (Ire) 6-11-11 (7") Mr A K Wyse, .. (16 to 1) 4
DEL PIERO (Ire) 5-11-10 (7") Mr A C Coyle, ...(100 to 30) 5
31⁷ BARLEY COURT (Ire) 6-11-6 (5") Mr P A Deegan, .. (25 to 1) 6
JOLLY SIGNAL (Ire) 5-10-12 (7") Mr J Cullen, ... (25 to 1) 7
SHADOW CHASER (Ire) 4-10-5 (7") Mr R Walsh, .. (14 to 1) 8
GILLYS HOPE (Ire) 5-11-3 (7") Mr A J Dempsey, .. (25 to 1) 9
TOBARELLA (Ire) 6-10-13 (7") Mr J G Sheehan, .. (25 to 1) 10
64 MALICE 10-11-3 (3") Mr E Norris, ...(16 to 1) 11
OSMUNDS PRIDE (Ire) 4-10-10 (7") Mr S P Hennessy,
......................................(20 to 1) 12
66 BIG STORM 4-10-5 (7") Mr John P Moloney, .. (16 to 1) 13
Dist: 1l, ½l, 2l, 1l. 3m 39.00s. (13 Ran).

(J J Byrne), A P O'Brien

UTTOXETER (good to firm) Thursday June 27th
Going Correction: MINUS 0.35 sec. per fur.

145 Uttoxeter Advertiser Ashbourne News Telegraph Maiden Hurdle Class E (4-y-o and up) £2,232 3m 110yds. . (6:45)

47³ WYNBERG 5-11-3 S Wynne, hndy, drvn to ld last, styd on und
pres...............(5 to 2 fav tchd 11 to 4 and 3 to 1) 1
46² ORDOG MOR (Ire) 7-11-3 D Byrne, led aftr 4th, rdn and hdd
last, no extr...................(13 to 2 op 11 to 2) 2
102² MILNGAVIE (Ire) 6-11-3 C Llewellyn, cl up, outpcd appr 3 out,
styd on stdly....................(7 to 2 op 3 to 1) 3
111 DANCING AT LAHARN (Ire) 6-11-3 R Dunwoody, hld up, chsd
ldrs 4 out, ev ch nxt, wknd betw last 2..(8 to 1 op 10 to 1) 4
47⁵ LIMOSA 5-10-12 M Richards, midfield, pushed alng hfwy,
outpcd appr 2 out....................(20 to 1) 5
47 HIDDEN FLOWER (v) 7-10-9 (3") R Massey, prmnt till rdn and
wknd appr 3 out...........(100 to 1 op 66 to 1) 6
SILVER BIRD (Ire) 4-10-2 (3") K Gaule, sn led, hdd aftr 4th,
reminders 5 out, wknd nxt........(33 to 1 op 25 to 1) 7
WYE OATS 7-10-12 R Johnson, blun 3rd, hit 4th, struggling
frm 5 out, tld off....................(50 to 1) 8
STORM DANCE 5-11-0 (3") J Culloty, hld up, struggling appr
4 out, btm whn mstk nxt..........(12 to 1 op 10 to 1) 9
103⁶ I DON'T THINK SO (bl) 5-10-12 P McLoughlin, reminders in
rear 5th, struggling 5 out, tld off frm nxt.
......................................(100 to 1 op 66 to 1) 10
BROOMHILL BOY 7-11-3 J Osborne, hld up, in tch whn f 5
out....................(9 to 2 op 4 to 1 tchd 11 to 2) f
47 STONECROP (bl) 5-10-0 (3") B Fenton, beh, pushed alng whn
mstk and rdr lost irons 5 out, tld off and pld up nxt. (50 to 1) pu
Dist: 3l, 10l, 1¼l, 16l, 3l, ¾l, 1½l, 8l, dist. 5m 43.70s. a 6.70s (12 Ran).

(Mrs D Pridden), Capt T A Forster

146 Springbank Industries Staffordshire Newsletter Selling Handicap Hurdle Class G (0-90 4-y-o and up) £2,036 2 ½m 110yds.....................(7:15)

100³ MILZIG (USA) [69] 7-10-9 C Llewellyn, midfield, steady hdwy
3 out, chlgd last, ran on und pres to ld cl hme.
......................................(100 to 30 fav op 9 to 2) 1
ERLEMO [76] 7-11-7 R Johnson, sn pushed alng, chsd ldrs
fnl circuit, hrd rdn to ld 2 out, hdd and no extr cl hme.
......................................(9 to 2 op 3 to 1 tchd 12 to 1) 2
56³ WHISTLING GIPSY [66] 11-10-6 Jacqui Oliver, beh, hdwy
appr 4 out, ev ch last, kpt on same pace.
......................................(9 to 1 op 7 to 1 tchd 10 to 1) 3
MISS SOUTER [70] (v) 7-10-10 R Dunwoody, chsd ldrs, drvn
alng 3 out, one pace frm nxt..........(9 to 1 op 8 to 1) 4

70[6] CROMABOO CROWN [82] 5-11-2 W Worthington, *cl up, led 3 out, hdd nxt, fdd stdly* . . . . (12 to 1 op 10 to 1) 5

RIVA'S BOOK (USA) [89] 5-11-9 D Byrne, *patiently rdn, shaken up and hdwy 2 out, nvr a factor.* (16 to 1 op 14 to 1) 6

51[4] BRAVO STAR (USA) [65] 11-10-0 (5*) Chris Webb, *made most, rdn and hdd 3 out, fdd aftr nxt.* . . . . (16 to 1) 7

MARYJO (Ire) [73] 7-10-13 S Wynne, *beh, niggled alng 4 out, nvr dngrs.* . . . . (33 to 1) 8

100[4] MOST INTERESTING [64] 11-10-4 R Greene, *hld up, outpcd 4 out, no dngr aftr.* . . . . (10 to 1 op 8 to 1) 9

THEY ALL FORGOT ME [70] 9-10-10 Miss G Dyson, *chsd ldrs, struggling 4 out, sn btn.* . . . . (33 to 1) 10

56[2] SOVEREIGN NICHE (Ire) [88] (v) 8-12-0 D Bridgwater, *chsd ldr, reminders 4 out, hng lft and outpcd 2 out, eased.*
. . . . (4 to 1 op 6 to 1) 11

OLIVER-J [75] 5-10-9 R Supple, *midfield, reminders 5th, no dngr frm 4 out.* . . . . (20 to 1) 12

CARDEA CASTLE (Ire) [61] 8-9-10 (5*) S Taylor, *midfield, lost tch appr 4 out, tld off.* . . . . (25 to 1) 13

INJUNCTION (Ire) [93] (bl) 5-11-6 (7*) C Rae, *al beh, tld off frm 3 out.* . . . .(9 to 1 op 8 to 1 tchd 10 to 1) 14

106[9] PRINCE ROCKAWAY (Ire) [60] (bl) 8-9-11 (3*) B Fenton, *hld up, struggling 5 out, tld off aftr nxt.* . . . . (50 to 1) 15

69[5] NANDURA [71] 5-10-5 N Mann, *midfield, lost tch 4 out, wl beh whn pld up and dismounted last.* . . . . (20 to 1) pu

ARROGANT BOY [60] 7-9-9² (7*) Miss R Clark, *jmpd poorly in rear, tld off whn pld up bef 4 out.* . . . . (50 to 1) pu

SOUPREME [71] (bl) 4-10-2 (3*) G Cahill, *struggling in rear, tld off whn pld up bef 4 out.* . . . . (10 to 1 op 9 to 1) pu

Dist: Hd, 5l, 3l, ¾l, 2½l, 4l, hd, 7l, 7l, 18l. 4m 48.00s. a 9.00s (18 Ran).

(Jack Joseph), J Joseph

147 Burton Mail Novices' Chase Class D (5-y-o and up) £3,517 2m 7f . . . .(7:45)

IMPERIAL VINTAGE (Ire) 6-11-2 R Dunwoody, *made most, jmpd boldly, clr whn blun 3 out, rdn and styd on strly frm nxt.*
. . . . (11 to 2 op 4 to 1) 1

104³ FLY THE WIND 11-11-3 D Bridgwater, *with ldr, blun 4th, rdn and outpcd 3 out, styd on betw last 2, no ch with nnr.*
. . . . (6 to 4 fav op 7 to 4) 2

MENATURE (Ire) 7-10-13 (3*) J Culloty, *midfield, hdwy to chase ldrs 5 out, outpcd 3 out, hld in 3rd whn hit last.*
. . . . (33 to 1 op 20 to 1) 3

104³ DUSTYS TRAIL (Ire) 7-10-9 (7*) Mr R Thornton, *jmpd slwly, reminders in rear 5th, struggling whn blun 5 out, no dngr aftr.*
. . . . (16 to 1 op 12 to 1) 4

26² MOVAC (Ire) 7-11-8 A Thornton, *pressed ldrs, rdn and lost tch 5 out, sn no dngr.* . . . .(11 to 4 op 3 to 1 tchd 5 to 2) 5

WAKT 6-10-8 (3*) B Fenton, *hld up, hdwy 6 out, disputing second but held whn f 2 out.* . . . .(10 to 1 op 8 to 1) f

59⁴ MUSIC SCORE 10-11-2 R Supple, *hld up, niggled alng hfwy, beh frm 4 out, pld up betw last 2* . . . . . .(25 to 1 op 20 to 1) pu

104⁶ HIZAL 7-11-2 Mr A Charles-Jones, *hld up, lost tch appr 4 out, tld off whn pld up 2 out.* . . . .(20 to 1 op 14 to 1) pu

41² CALL ME ALBI (Ire) 5-10-8 M Richards, *jmpd slwly in rear, tld off frm 9th, pld up bef 12th.* . . . . (8 to 1 op 6 to 1) pu

Dist: 9l, 7l, 10l, 1½l. 5m 30.70s. a 2.70s (9 Ran).

(May We Never Be Found Out), K C Bailey

148 Advertiser Guinness Galway Handicap Hurdle Trial Class C (0-130 4-y-o and up) £3,371 2m . . . . (8:15)

109⁷ IVY EDITH [114] 6-11-3 D Bridgwater, *pld hrd, sn clr, drvn alng 2 out, strly pressed r-in, jst hld on.* (10 to 1 op 8 to 1) 1

80² SUIVEZ [125] 6-12-0 R Dunwoody, *chsd clr ldr, blun 3 out, rallied betw last 2, styd on strly und pres.*
. . . . (13 to 8 fav op 7 to 4 tchd 15 to 8) 2

61² KALZARI (USA) [97] 11-9-7 (7*) B Moore, *hld up, hdwy to chase ldrs 4 out, rdn and one pace frm 2 out.*
. . . . (10 to 1 op 8 to 1) 3

AMAZON EXPRESS [111] 7-11-0 R Johnson, *pld hrd, in tch, rdn alng 4 out, outpcd frm nxt.* . . . .(33 to 1 op 20 to 1) 4

109⁴ CLASSIC EXHIBIT [97] 7-10-0 T Eley, *hld up, niggled alng whn hmpd 4 out, no dngr aftr.*
. . . .(4 to 1 op 9 to 2 tchd 7 to 2) 5

109 HACKETTS CROSS (Ire) [113] 8-11-2 Richard Guest, *sn beh, tld off 5th, no dngr aftr.* . . . .(25 to 1 op 20 to 1) 6

GREEN LANE (USA) [119] 8-11-8 C Llewellyn, *beh, tld off frm 5th.* . . . . (10 to 1 op 16 to 1) 7

80⁹ WAMDHA (Ire) [103] 6-10-6 A Thornton, *hld up, in tch and keeping on whn f 4 out.* . . . .(10 to 1 op 8 to 1) f

DJAIS (Fr) [119] 7-11-5 (3*) J Culloty, *hld up, rdn and outpcd appr 3 out, 4th and btn whn f last.*
. . . .(9 to 2 op 5 to 2 tchd 11 to 2) f

Dist: Nk, 5l, 8l, 6l, 10l, dist. 3m 38.10s. a 1.10s (9 Ran).

SR: 22/33/-/6/-/-/ (Glen Antill), T G Mills

149 Lichfield Cathedral Digital Galway Plate Trial Handicap Chase Class C (0-130 5-y-o and up) £4,331 2m 5f
. . . . (8:45)

81² SASKIA'S HERO [111] 9-11-5 D Byrne, *patiently rdn, led on bit aftr 3 out, jmpd lft nxt, cmftbly.*
. . . .(13 to 8 fav op 2 to 1 tchd 6 to 4) 1

71³ SWORD BEACH [112] 12-11-6 P Niven, *led, clr 7th, jnd 9th, mstk and hdd 3 out, unbl to quicken.*
. . . . (15 to 8 op 9 to 4 tchd 5 to 2) 2

110² FLYING ZIAD (Can) [96] 13-10-4⁴ Mr A Charles-Jones, *chsd ldr, drw level 9th, blun 5 out, sn outpcd, kpt on ag'n appr last.*
. . . .(10 to 1 op 12 to 1 tchd 14 to 1) 3

CROSULA [120] 8-12-0 D Bridgwater, *settled 3rd, gd hdwy whn jmpd slwly 5 out, cl second when f nxt, dead.*
. . . .(3 to 1 op 2 to 1) f

Dist: 3l, 1¼l. 5m 12.70s. a 14.70s (4 Ran).

(Qualitair Holdings Limited), J F Bottomley

150 Brindley Honda Staffordshire Life Novices' Hurdle Class D (4-y-o and up) £2,857 2m . . . .(9:15)

SHAHRANI 4-10-9 D Bridgwater, *pld hrd and led, jmpd rght early, pushed clr 3 out, cmftbly.* . . . .(8 to 1 op 10 to 1) 1

55* BIRTHDAY BOY (Ire) (v) 4-11-2 R Supple, *midfield, drvn alng 4 out, styd on stdly frm 2 out, no ch with nnr.*
. . . . (7 to 2 tchd 4 to 1) 2

PRUSSIA 5-11-0 R Johnson, *al hndy, hit 5th, outpcd appr 2 out, sn no extr.* . . . . (3 to 1 op 5 to 2) 3

GOVERNOR DANIEL 5-11-7 R Dunwoody, *chsd ldrs, reminders 4 out, outpcd appr 2 out.* (7 to 4 fav op 11 to 4) 4

46⁵ PEGASUS BAY 5-11-0 R Garritty, *beh, hdwy to track ldrs 3 out, fdd frm nxt.* . . . . (16 to 1 op 14 to 1) 5

LITTLE ROUSILLON 4-11-0 W Humphreys, *pld hrd, moderate hdwy appr 3 out, nvr a factor.* . . . .(33 to 1) 6

POSITIVO 5-11-0 I Lawrence, *midfield, struggling 4 out, no dngr frm nxt.* . . . .(14 to 1 op 10 to 1) 7

GUARDS BRIGADE 5-11-0 R Marley, *cl up, rdn and no imprsn whn btn 4 out, eased whn btn.* . . . .(25 to 1) 8

SPECIALIZE 4-10-9 A Larnach, *al beh.*
. . . .(16 to 1 op 14 to 1 tchd 20 to 1) 9

SLIGHTLY SPECIAL (Ire) 4-10-9 Mr A Phillips, *al beh.*
. . . .(25 to 1 op 20 to 1) 10

BOOST (bl) 4-10-9 S Wynne, *und pres in rear hfwy, sn tld off.* . . . . (50 to 1) 11

TROUBLE'S BREWING 5-10-9 C Llewellyn, *blun in rear second, tld off frm 4 out.* . . . . (33 to 1) 12

TOP BANK 8-11-0 Miss S Sharratt, *tld off frm hfwy.* (50 to 1) 13

COME ON WINN 4-10-4 T Eley, *refused to race.*
. . . . (33 to 1 tchd 50 to 1) ref

Dist: 6l, sht-hd, 4l, 13l, 4l, sht-hd, 9l, 20l, nk, ¾l. 3m 41.30s. a 4.30s (14 Ran).

(A S Helaissi And Mr S Helaissi), M C Pipe

AUTEUIL (FR) (soft)
Saturday June 29th

151 Grande Course de Haies d'Auteuil Hurdle (5-y-o and up) £105,402 3m 1f 110yds. . . . . (3:40)

19³ EARL GRANT (Fr) 7-10-5 J-Y Beaurain, *rcd in 3rd, chlgd 5 out, led 3 out, run on* 1

19² MYSILV 6-10-1 J Osborne, *jmpd wl, led till jnd 5 out, hdd 3 out, run on gmely und pres r-in.* 2

19* MONTPERLE (Fr) 7-10-5 D Bressou, ... 3

Dist: 2l, 15l, 20l, 2l, 1l, 4l. 6m 19.00s. (10 Ran).

(L Gautier), B Secly

WORCESTER (good to firm)
Saturday June 29th
Going Correction: MINUS 0.05 sec. per fur.

152 Hawford Conditional Jockeys' Handicap Hurdle Class E (0-110 4-y-o and up) £2,337 2m . . . . (2:35)

COURAGEOUS KNIGHT [82] 7-10-9 B Fenton, *hld up, drvn alng frm 5th, hdwy appr 2 out, led r-in, driven out.*
. . . . (100 to 30 fav op 3 to 1 tchd 7 to 2) 1

127 ISLAND VISION (Ire) [97] (bl) 6-11-7 (3*) Michael Brennan, *wtd wth, hdwy appr 3 out, led briefly r-in, kpt on.*
. . . . (11 to 2 op 3 to 1 tchd 6 to 1) 2

STATELY HOME (Ire) [100] 5-11-3 (5*) B Moore, *led second till r-in, unbl to quicken.* . . . . (12 to 1 op 8 to 1) 3

STAPLEFORD LADY [86] 8-10-13 J Magee, *hld up, rdn alng and effrt appr 3 out, styd on wl r-in.* . . . . .(20 to 1 op 16 to 1) 4

69* SIAN WYN [83] 6-10-10 G Lee, *chsd ldrs, effrt appr 3 out, kpt on same pace frm nxt.* . . . .(5 to 1 tchd 6 to 1) 5

109² COMMANCHE CREEK [84] 6-10-11 Sophie Mitchell, *led to second, chsd ldr aftr, ev ch frm 3 out, wknd r-in.*
. . . . (10 to 1 tchd 11 to 2) 6

109 ROYAL GLINT [73] 7-9-9 (5*) A Dowling, *hld up, effrt 3 out, btn nxt.* . . . .(20 to 1 op 16 to 1) 7

LAWNSWOOD JUNIOR [89] 9-11-2 D Walsh, *hld up, rdn appr 3 out, sn btn.* . . . .(11 to 1 op 12 to 1) 8

127 SHELLHOUSE (Ire) [91] 8-11-4 T J Murphy, *hld up in rear, rdn appr 3 out, wknd nxt.* . . . .(10 to 1 op 6 to 1) 9

COUNTRYWIDE LAD [73] 7-9-11 (3*) S Ryan, *hld up, rdn 3 out, fdd.* . . . .(50 to 1 op 33 to 1) 10

SECRET CASTLE [73] (bl) 8-10-0 Chris Webb, *bolted bef strt, tld off frm 3rd, pld up before 5th*......(66 to 1 op 33 to 1) pu
Dist: Nk, 1¾l, ½l, 3l, ½l, nk, 7l, ¾l, 26l. 3m 47.10s. a 7.10s (11 Ran).

SR: 2/17/13/3/-/-/ (L Kirkwood), P Hayward

153 Ferry Maiden Hurdle Class F (4-y-o and up) £2,339 2½m............... (3:05)

SEARCHLIGHT (Ire) 8-11-5 D Bridgwater, *hld up beh ldrs, led appr 7th, rdn bef nxt, clr frm 2 out*......(9 to 2 tchd 5 to 1) 1
GREYCOAT BOY 4-10-13 R Dunwoody, *in tch, ev ch on bit frm 7th till outpcd appr 2 out.*
........................(7 to 4 fav op 6 to 4 tchd 2 to 1) 2
MURBERRY (Ire) 6-11-0 L Harvey, *hld up beh ldrs, outpcd frm 7th, no dngr aftr*......................(7 to 1 op 6 to 1) 3
MIRAMARE 6-11-5 G Upton, *hld up, effrt 7th, wknd bef nxt.*
........................(50 to 1 op 33 to 1) 4
PHARRAGO (Ire) 7-11-5 D J Burchell, *beh, moderate hdwy frm 2 out, nvr a dngr...* (20 to 1 op 16 to 1 tchd 25 to 1) 5
CHEER'S BABY 6-11-5 Richard Guest, *hld up, effrt 7th, wknd bef nxt.*......................(33 to 1 op 33 to 1) 6
103 SANDFORD THYNE (Ire) 6-11-0 S Wynne, *ht in mid-div, some hdwy appr nxt, wknd 3 out* (66 to 1 op 33 to 1) 7
101⁹ LASER LIGHT LADY 4-10-8 B Powell, *hld up in mid-div, beh frm 7th.*......................(50 to 1) 8
PRIESTHILL (Ire) 7-11-2 (3*) K Gaule, *prmnt till mstk and wknd 5th.*......................(50 to 1) 9
COOLMOREEN (Ire) 8-11-0 (5*) Chris Webb, *nvr dngrs.*
........................(66 to 1 op 33 to 1) 10
DARING HEN (Ire) 6-11-0 A P McCoy, *led till appr 7th, wknd quickly.*......(11 to 4 op 3 to 1 tchd 5 to 2) 11
DOTTEREL (Ire) 8-11-5 W Humphreys, *al beh.*
........................(14 to 1 op 10 to 1) 12
LORD OF THE MILL (Ire) 5-11-5 W McFarland, *nvr on terms, tld off.*......................(50 to 1 op 33 to 1) 13
101 REALLY NEAT 10-10-9 (5*) Sophie Mitchell, *beh whn pld up bef 6th.*......................(66 to 1 op 33 to 1) pu
55⁶ TOM'S GEMINI STAR 8-11-5 Mr J Jukes, *al beh, tld off whn pld up bef 3 out.*......................(20 to 1 op 33 to 1) pu
BRENSHAM FOLLY 5-11-5 T Eley, *tld off whn blun 5th, pld up bef nxt.*......................(66 to 1 op 33 to 1) pu
100 ORCHESTRAL DESIGNS (Ire) (bl) 5-11-5 S Burrough, *prmnt, wknd quicky appr 5th, tld off whn pld up bef 7th.*
........................(50 to 1 op 33 to 1) pu
TROPWEN MARROY 7-11-0 Gary Lyons, *mstk 1st, al wl beh, tld off whn pld up bef 5th.*......(66 to 1 op 33 to 1) pu
PERTEMPS ZOLA 7-11-0 V Slattery, *mstk second, al beh, tld off whn pld up bef 7th.*......(50 to 1 op 33 to 1) pu
Dist: 9l, 14l, 8l, 13l, 7l, 9l, 6l, 4l, 1¼l, 2l. 4m 48.40s. a 12.40s (19 Ran).

(Mrs R T Watson), T R Watson

154 M Joan Swift Handicap Chase Class D (0-125 5-y-o and up) £4,500 2m 7f .... (3:35)

WATERFORD CASTLE [103] 9-10-3 (3*) T J Murphy, *beh, hdwy 9th, led 4 out, drvn out*........(9 to 2 tchd 11 to 2) 1
FATHER DOWLING [97] (v) 9-9-11 (3*) B Fenton, *hld up, hdwy frm tenth, rdn and ev ch 4 out, btn last.* (25 to 1 op 16 to 1) 2
ANDRELOT [115] (bl) 9-11-4 R Dunwoody, *chsd ldrs, ev ch 4 out, btn nxt.*......................(10 to 1 op 6 to 1) 3
57⁴ ABBOTSHAM [98] 11-10-2¹ Mr J Jukes, *chsd ldrs, led 8th, hdd 4 out, sn wknd.*......................(50 to 1 op 25 to 1) 4
104 ARTFUL ARTHUR [97] 10-10-0 Mr J Grassick, *nvr nr to chal.*......................(66 to 1 op 50 to 1) 5
57 HURRYUP [97] (bl) 9-9-11 (3*) J Culloty, *dsptd ld till blun tenth, wknd quickly, tld off....* (25 to 1 op 20 to 1) 6
51* FUNCHEON GALE [97] 9-10-0 D Morris, *blun and uns rdr second*......(9 to 4 op 3 to 1 tchd 7 to 2) ur
TAUREAN TYCOON [97] 12-10-0 T Eley, *blun second, al beh, tld off whn pld up bef 4 out....* (66 to 1 op 33 to 1) pu
108 PETTY BRIDGE [97] 12-10-0 B Powell, *al beh, tld off whn pld up bef 4 out....* (33 to 1 op 20 to 1) pu
72² KNOCKUMSHIN [97] 13-10-0 R Supple, *hld up, rdn 14th, wknd frm nxt, tld off whn pld up bef last.*
......................(12 to 1 op 12 to 1) pu
RYTON GUARD [97] 11-10-0 S Wynne, *prmnt early, beh frm 4th, tld off whn pld up bef four out....* (66 to 1 op 33 to 1) pu
SEAL KING [97] 11-10-0 V Slattery, *led to 8th, dsptd ld till wknd frm tenth, tld off whn pld up bef 4 out.*
......................(14 to 1 tchd 20 to 1) pu
57² LEMON'S MILL (USA) [125] (bl) 7-12-0 D Bridgwater, *hld up in tch, rdn aing tenth, jnd ldr nxt, ev ch 4 out, sn wknd, tld off whn pld up bef 2 out.*
......(85 to 40 fav op 6 to 4 tchd 9 to 4 and 5 to 2) pu
Dist: 8l, 4l, 22l, 1l, dist. 6m 4.70s. a 26.70s (13 Ran).

(Sybil Lady Joseph), K C Bailey

155 Malvern Blinds Handicap Hurdle Class D (0-120 4-y-o and up) £3,760 3m .... (4:10)

78² TIPPING THE LINE [100] 6-10-10 D Bridgwater, *chsd ldr, led 8th to nxt, outpcd appr 3 out, rallied approaching last, led r-in, drvn out*......(5 to 1 tchd 6 to 1 and 13 to 2) 1

58³ CATS RUN (Ire) [117] 8-11-13 R Supple, *chsd ldrs, led 3 out, hdd and unbl to quicken r-in.*
......................(11 to 1 op 5 to 1 tchd 12 to 1) 2
78* SANTELLA BOY (USA) [100] 4-10-3 R Dunwoody, *hld up, hdwy frm 8th, chsd ldr and effrt 3 out, one pace appr last.*
......................(15 to 8 fav op 3 to 1 tchd 7 to 2) 3
125⁴ MISS PIMPERNEL [90] 6-9-9 (5*) Sophie Mitchell, *beh frm 3rd, rallied from 3 out, styd on one pace.*
......................(50 to 1 op 33 to 1) 4
JOHNNY WILL [104] 11-11-0 J Ryan, *mid-div, hdwy 9th, effrt whn mstk 3 out, wknd nxt, fnshd lme...*(25 to 1 op 20 to 1) 5
44 ALL ON [117] 5-11-6 R Marley, *hld up, hdwy 7th, led frm 9th to 3 out, sn btn...*......................(9 to 1 op 5 to 1) 6
58² SOUTH WESTERLY (Ire) [111] 8-11-7 P Niven, *beh, hdwy 6th, wknd appr 3 out.*......................(5 to 1 op 13 to 2) 7
LAUGHING GAS (Ire) [100] 7-10-10 S Wynne, *led to 8th, wknd quickly.*......................(12 to 1 tchd 14 to 1) 8
72* EAST HOUSTON [101] 7-10-11 A P McCoy, *nvr on terms.*
......................(9 to 1 op 8 to 1 tchd 10 to 1) 9
125* DERRING BRIDGE [91] 6-9-12 (3*) B Fenton, *chsd ldrs, blun and uns rdr 5th...*......(9 to 1 op 10 to 1 tchd 11 to 1) ur
KHAZARI [91] 6-9-12 (3*) D Walsh, *hld up, effrt appr 3 out, sn wknd, fnshd lme....*......................(50 to 1) 11
THE FLYING FOOTMAN (Ire) [91] 6-10-1 W McFarland, *beh, tld off whn pld up r-in.*......................(50 to 1) pu
Dist: ½l, 3l, 13l, 5l, 3½l, sht-hd, 16l, 16l. 5m 51.70s. a 15.70s (13 Ran).

(Mrs L M Sewell), M C Pipe

156 Besford Novices' Handicap Chase Class E (0-100 5-y-o and up) £3,353 2m............................ (4:45)

CASPIAN BELUGA [93] 8-12-0 G Upton, *made all, sn clr, unchlgd, fnshd lme.*...........(5 to 1 jt-fav op 7 to 2) 1
82 WILLIE MAKEIT (Ire) [69] 6-10-1 (3*) J Culloty, *hld up, prog 8th, chsd wnr frm 3 out, ran on....*...(8 to 1 tchd 9 to 1) 2
QUINTA ROYALE [74] 9-10-9 Richard Guest, *hld up, styd on one pace frm 4 out, not rch ldrs...*(25 to 1 op 16 to 1) 3
106⁶ DUKE OF DREAMS [72] 6-10-7 B Powell, *in tch, lft in second 5th, wknd 3 out.*......................(8 to 1 op 6 to 1) 4
TELMAR SYSTEMS [65] 7-9-11 (3*) B Fenton, *nvr nr to chal.*
......................(16 to 1 op 20 to 1 tchd 25 to 1) 5
JAMESWICK [65] 6-9-12³ (5*) Mr P Henley, *nvr nr ldrs.*
......................(20 to 1 tchd 33 to 1) 6
41⁵ MARINERS COVE [81] 8-10-13 (3*) T J Murphy, *al beh.*
......................(15 to 2 op 6 to 1 tchd 8 to 1) 7
LOFTY DEED (USA) [65] 6-9-11 (3*) K Gaule, *nvr on terms.*
......................(16 to 1 op 12 to 1) 8
EXCLUSION [84] 7-11-5 R Marley, *trkd ldrs, wknd quickly 8th.*......................(12 to 1 op 10 to 1) 9
OUR NIKKI [70] 6-10-5⁵ S Burrough, *al rear, no ch whn blun last.*......................(50 to 1 op 33 to 1) 10
50⁶ MANABOUTTHEHOUSE [86] 9-11-7 L Harvey, *hld up beh ldrs, mstk 7th, sn wknd....*......................(33 to 1) 11
GIMME (Ire) [90] 6-11-11 A P McCoy, *chsd wnr till f 5th.*
......................(5 to 1 jt-fav op 11 to 2 tchd 13 to 2) f
GEORGE LANE [68] 8-10-3 R Greene, *chsd ldrs till blun and uns rdr 5th.*
........(12 to 1 op 10 to 1 tchd 14 to 1 and 16 to 1) ur
Dist: 4l, 10l, 8l, 3l, 1¼l, nk, 1¼l, 13l, ½l, ¾l. 4m 0.90s. a 11.90s (13 Ran).

(L J Hawkings), S G Knight

157 Luisley Standard Open National Hunt Flat Class H (4,5,6-y-o) £1,322 2m .... (5:15)

52* REGAL GEM (Ire) 5-11-7 (3*) B Fenton, *hld up towards rear, prog hfwy, led 2 ls out, easily.*.........(5 to 1 op 3 to 1) 1
52² OH DEAR ME 5-11-0 B Powell, *trkd ldrs, rdn aing 4 out, styd on fnl 2 ls....*......(7 to 2 op 11 to 4 tchd 4 to 1) 2
SMART REMARK 4-11-0 P McLoughlin, *hld up, improved hfwy, effrt 4 fs out, styd on one pace frm 2 out.*
......................(50 to 1 op 33 to 1) 3
DRAGON FLY (Ire) 5-11-5 B Clifford, *towards rear, styd on frm 4 fs out, nrst finish..............*(33 to 1 op 20 to 1) 4
IRISH DELIGHT 4-10-11 (3*) D Walsh, *trkd ldrs, lost pl hfwy, styd on ag'n frm o'r 2 fs out.......*(13 to 1 op 14 to 1) 5
53⁵ CARNIVAL CLOWN 4-11-0 R Greene, *nvr nrr.*
......................(20 to 1 op 16 to 1) 6
DOUBLE TROUBLE 5-11-2 (3*) D Fortt, *towards rear, styd on frm o'r 3 fs out, nvr nrr.............*(16 to 1 op 10 to 1) 7
DISCO'S WELL 5-11-5 O Pears, *chsd ldr, lft in ld 7 fs out, hdd 2 out, sn wknd.*......................(50 to 1 op 20 to 1) 8
74⁵ FLAME OF DANCE 5-11-5 T Eley, *hld up, hdwy 6 fs out, effrt 4 out, wknd fnl quarter m....*(10 to 1 op 8 to 1) 9
52⁴ SEVEN WELLS 4-11-0 R Bellamy, *nvr better than mid-div.*
......................(25 to 1 op 16 to 1 tchd 33 to 1) 10
THE BRATPACK (Ire) 6-11-0 G Upton, *nvr trbld ldrs.*
......................(33 to 1 op 25 to 1) 11
FINAL SCORE (Ire) 6-10-9 (5*) Chris Webb, *hld up beh ldrs, lost pl hfwy, tld off....*......................(33 to 1) 12
TIPSY QUEEN 5-10-11 (3*) J Culloty, *nvr on terms, tld off.*
......................(11 to 1 op 8 to 1 tchd 12 to 1) 13
MRS MOLOTOFF 5-11-0 V Slattery, *trkd ldrs, rdn appr hfwy, sn wknd, tld off.*......................(33 to 1 op 20 to 1) 14
52⁸ JACKAMUS (Ire) 5-10-12 (7*) Mr M Frith, *al beh, tld off.*
......................(33 to 1 op 25 to 1) 15
LYSANDER 4-10-11 (3*) G Cahill, *al beh, tld off.*
......................(33 to 1 op 25 to 1) 16

53³ POPSI'S CLOGGS 4-11-0 D Morris, *chsd ldrs, 3rd and rdn whn ran out and uns rdr appr fnl 3 fs.*
.... (9 to 1 op 7 to 1 tchd 10 to 1) ro
RARE SPREAD (Ire) 6-11-5 D Bridgwater, *led till ran out 7 fs out*.............. (2 to 1 fav tchd 7 to 4 and 5 to 2) ro
Dist: 2½l, 4l, 4l, ¾l, 4l, hd, ¾l, 1¼l, 10l, nk. 3m 45.60s. (18 Ran).

(D W E Coombs), C R Barwell

BELLEWSTOWN (IRE) (good to firm)
Tuesday July 2nd

158 **Agrifert Handicap Hurdle (0-116 4-y-o and up) £2,740 3m..............(6:30)**

92³ ARCTIC KATE [-] 10-11-5 C O'Dwyer,......... (9 to 2 fav) 1
MERRY PEOPLE (Ire) [-] 8-12-0 T Horgan,........(5 to 1) 2
MURPHY'S TROUBLE (Ire) [-] 8-9-4 (3*) D Bromley, (9 to 1) 3
114² CUBAN QUESTION [-] 9-9-12 (5*) G Cotter,.......(7 to 1) 4
40³ TABU LADY (Ire) [-] (bl) 5-9-8 T P Treacy,..........(6 to 1) 5
RISING BREEZE (Ire) [-] 7-10-4 (5*) J Butler,......(12 to 1) 6
92⁴ THE TOM'S ERROR (Ire) [-] (bl) 6-10-0 (3*) J R Barry,
.......................(10 to 1) 7
67⁷ HELLO EXCUSE ME (USA) [-] 6-10-0 (7*) J M Sullivan,
.......................(10 to 1) 8
136⁸ WILLCHRIS [-] 9-9-13 T P Rudd,...............(16 to 1) 9
32 HENRY G'S (Ire) [-] 6-9-4 (7*) L J Fleming,........(10 to 1) 10
92 OVER THE GREEN (Ire) [-] 8-9-13 F Woods,.......(7 to 1) pu
BARNISH DAWN (Ire) [-] 6-9-0 (7*) S P Kelly,......(33 to 1) pu
Dist: 2l, 1l, 25l, 6l. 5m 56.20s. (12 Ran).

(Mrs R D Richards), James O'Haire

159 **McLoughlins Oil I.N.H. Flat Race (5-y-o and up) £2,740 2m 1f...........(8:30)**

MOONLIGHT ESCAPADE (Ire) 5-11-13 Mr P Fenton,
.......................(11 to 4 jt-fav) 1
NO DIAMOND (Ire) 7-11-7 (7*) Mr D W Cullen,......(7 to 1) 2
122³ JUST A VODKA (Ire) 6-11-7 (7*) Mr R Walsh, (11 to 4 jt-fav) 3
117⁶ GALE HAMSHIRE (Ire) 7-11-9 Mr J A Nash,.......(10 to 1) 4
NEW LEGISLATION (Ire) (bl) 6-11-9 Mr J P Dempsey,
.......................(14 to 1) 5
TWENTYFIVEQUID (Ire) 5-11-13 Mr P F Graffin,......(9 to 1) 6
TROJAN OAK (Ire) 5-11-10 (3*) Mr B M Cash,......(12 to 1) 7
CLOVER MOR LASS (Ire) 7-11-2 (7*) Mr G A Kingston,
.......................(14 to 1) 8
115² BALLYWHAT (Ire) 7-11-2 (7*) Mr J T McNamara,.....(7 to 1) 9
MUTUAL DECISION (Ire) 5-11-1 (7*) Mr A K Wyse, (14 to 1) 10
PROUDSTOWN LADY (Ire) 5-11-3 (5*) Mr D McGoona,
.......................(25 to 1) 11
120⁸ ROMANCEINTHEDARK (Ire) 6-11-2 (7*) Mr Edgar Byrne,
.......................(14 to 1) 12
KILLINEY'S IMAGE (Ire) 6-11-2 (7*) Mr Ig Elliott,...(25 to 1) 13
SUPER SECRETARY (Ire) 5-11-1 (7*) Mr S J Mahon, (25 to 1) 14
LAERGY CRIPPERTY (Ire) 8-12-0 Mr H F Cleary,..(25 to 1) 15
Dist: 1½l, 2½l, 4½l, ½l. 3m 54.90s. (15 Ran).

(Paul Shanahan), Anthony Mullins

160 **Michael Moore Car Sales Hurdle (4-y-o and up) £2,911 2½m...........(9:00)**

64⁵ SIBERIAN TALE (Ire) 6-10-13 (3*) Mr P J Casey,....(3 to 1) 1
67⁵ DANCING CLODAGH (Ire) 4-10-9 J Shortt,.........(7 to 4) 2
85* BOLD FLYER 13-11-2 K F O'Brien,...........(11 to 10 fav) 3
VIENNA WALTZ (Ire) 6-10-11 H Rogers,..........(50 to 1) 4
122⁵ MC CLATCHEY (Ire) 5-11-1 A Powell,..........(12 to 1) 5
Dist: 6l, dist, 25l, dist. 5m 4.40s. (5 Ran).

(Mrs Peter Casey), Peter Casey

BELLEWSTOWN (IRE) (good to firm)
Wednesday July 3rd

161 **Potato Protection Novice Hurdle (4-y-o) £2,911 2m 1f..............(6:00)**

139* WESPERADA (Ire) 11-12 P Carberry,...............(5 to 4) 1
119* SPANKY (Ire) 11-12 L P Cusack,...........(11 to 10 fav) 2
30⁹ TIFFANY VICTORIA (Ire) 10-9 C O'Dwyer,..........(8 to 1) 3
SAWAALEFF (Ire) 11-0 H Rogers,.............(8 to 1) 4
FRENCH LADY (Ire) 10-9 K F O'Brien,..........(16 to 1) 5
30 JEWEL OF THE NIGHT (Ire) 10-11 (3*) J R Barry,... (33 to 1) 6
SERGEANT BILL (Ire) 10-7 (7*) D Fisher,..........(25 to 1) 7
Dist: ¾l, 3½l, 1½l, 8l. 4m 13.00s. (7 Ran).

(Mrs A McAleer), Noel Meade

162 **Tayto Growers Handicap Hurdle (0-123 4-y-o and up) £2,740 2m 1f.....(8:00)**

NEAR GALE (Ire) [-] 6-11-10 T P Treacy,......(11 to 4 fav) 1
NORTHERN FANCY [-] 5-10-7 F Woods,........(7 to 2) 2
OPEN MARKET (USA) [-] 7-11-11 (3*) D T Evans,....(8 to 1) 3
BETTER STYLE (Ire) [-] 5-10-8 C O'Dwyer,.......(16 to 1) 4
KENTUCKY BABY (Ire) [-] 6-10-9 (5*) G Cotter,....(7 to 1) 5
113⁶ TIBOULEN (Ire) [-] 6-10-6 (3*) J R Barry,.........(12 to 1) 6
66* GALAVOTTI (Ire) [-] 7-10-4 P Carberry,..........(4 to 1) f
87³ SLANEY GLOW (Ire) [-] 5-11-11 C F Swan,.........(7 to 2) f

---

Dist: 3l, 5l, 7l, 8l. 4m 14.20s. (8 Ran).

(Patrick F Kehoe), P Mullins

MARKET RASEN (good)
Wednesday July 3rd
Going Correction: PLUS 0.30 sec. per fur.

163 **'Summer Season' Conditional Jockeys' Selling Handicap Hurdle Class G (0-90 4-y-o and up) £1,993 2m 5f 110yds........................(2:10)**

RED JAM JAR [85] 11-11-12 G Cahill, *trkd ldr frm 3rd, led 3 out, sn wl clr*.......... (11 to 1 op 10 to 1 tchd 12 to 1) 1
NORTH BANNISTER [73] 9-11-0 T J Murphy, *wl plcd, squeezed for room on bend aftr 3rd, chsd wnr appr 2 out, no imprsn*.............(11 to 4 fav op 5 to 2 tchd 3 to 1) 2
128² TREMBLE [65] 7-10-6 D Parker, *wl in tch, rdn and outpcd frm 3 out*....................(9 to 1 op 7 to 1) 3
NORDIC CROWN (Ire) [83] (bl) 5-11-7 E Husband, *chsd ldr to 3rd, prmnt till rdn and wknd 4 out*.......(7 to 2 op 3 to 1) 4
146 SOVEREIGN NICHE (Ire) [86] (bl) 8-11-13 D Walsh, *led, hdd 3 out, sn wknd*.............(8 to 1 op 7 to 1 tchd 9 to 1) 5
145⁷ SILVER BIRD (Ire) [84] 4-10-5 K Gaule, *mid-div, outpcd frm 4 out*...... (14 to 1 op 12 to 1 tchd 16 to 1 and 20 to 1) 6
125³ EASY OVER (USA) [73] 10-11-0 D Fortt, *hld up in rear, nvr rch ldrs*..................(13 to 2 op 8 to 1 tchd 9 to 1) 7
100 CLASSIC IMAGE (Ire) [68] 6-10-4 (5*) A Dowling, *prog 5th, wknd frm 3 out*..........(7 to 1 op 6 to 1 tchd 8 to 1) 8
JOLI'S GREAT [69] (bl) 8-10-10 Guy Lewis, *hld up towards rear, rdn and btn 4 out*.............(9 to 1 op 6 to 1) 9
146 CARDEA CASTLE (Ire) [59] 8-10-0 S Taylor, *in tch, beh aftr 3rd*...........................(25 to 1) 10
Dist: 27l, 9l, 9l, 2l, 1¼l, 9l, 20l, 2½l, sht-hd. 5m 24.60s. a 21.60s (10 Ran).

(C H P Bell), S B Bell

164 **'Bar-B-Q' Novices' Handicap Chase Class E (0-100 5-y-o and up) £3,185 3m 1f..........................(2:40)**

104³ MANOR RHYME [74] 9-10-12 B Powell, *wl plcd, hit 6th, rdn 14th, hit last, styd on to ld r-in*..........(9 to 1 op 7 to 1) 1
82* DARINGLY [78] 7-11-2 D Morris, *chsd ldrs, led 14th, clr 4 out, wknd and hdd r-in*.... (2 to 1 fav op 7 to 4 tchd 9 to 4) 2
92⁷ BUCKANEER BAY [69] 9-10-4 (3*) G Cahill, *mstks, effrt 13th, rdn and outpcd frm 4 out*.
.......................(14 to 1 op 20 to 1 tchd 10 to 1) 3
79³ DEAR EMILY [77] 8-11-1 A P McCoy, *chsd ldrs, rdn and outpcd frm 4 out*............(11 to 2 op 5 to 1 tchd 6 to 1) 4
CUCHULLAINS GOLD (Ire) [86] 8-11-10 R Dunwoody, *hld up, rdn and outpcd frm 14th*...(7 to 2 op 3 to 1 tchd 4 to 1) 5
82⁷ LITTLE THYNE [63] (bl) 11-10-1 Dr P Pritchard, *wth ldrs, reminder 12th, rdn nxt, wknd and f 14th*..........(33 to 1) f
QUIXALL CROSSETT [67] 11-9-12 (7*) Mr M H Naughton, *not jump wl, sn well beh, tld off whn pld up bef 9th*.
.......................(33 to 1 tchd 40 to 1) pu
RUBER [74] 9-10-12 B Storey, *sn beh, tld off whn pld up bef 9th*.......................(25 to 1 op 20 to 1) pu
125 MORNING BLUSH (Ire) [86] 6-11-10 D Bridgwater, *made most, hdd 14th, sn wknd, pld up bef 3 out*. (5 to 1 tchd 6 to 1) pu
104² RED EIKON [75] 5-10-8 Richard Guest, *chsd ldrs, mstk 12th, rdn and outpcd aftr nxt, pld up bef 15th*..(8 to 1 op 6 to 1) pu
Dist: 3½l, 27l, 12l, 20l. 6m 23.90s. a 23.90s (10 Ran).

(Major H R M Porter), J C McConnochie

165 **Roseland Group Handicap Chase Class D (0-120 5-y-o and up) £3,822 2½m..........................(3:10)**

NORDIC SUN (Ire) [110] 8-11-12 M Dwyer, *ldg grp, jnd ldr 8th, led last, pushed clr*.............(11 to 2 op 5 to 1) 1
71⁴ CHANNEL PASTIME [94] 12-10-7 (3*) Guy Lewis, *made most, hdd last, outpcd r-in*. (7 to 2 fav tchd 3 to 1 and 4 to 1) 2
102³ BITACRACK [84] 9-10-0 L O'Hara, *wth ldrs, ch appr 3 out, outpcd nxt*...................(8 to 1 op 6 to 1) 3
149² SWORD BEACH [112] 12-12-0 P Niven, *hld up, cld on ldrs frm 8th, one pace appr 2 out*.
.......................(9 to 2 op 5 to 1 tchd 11 to 2) 4
71 STRONG SOUND [103] 9-11-2 (3*) G Cahill, *wl plcd, hit 7th, ch appr 3 out, hit nxt, sn btn*..........(9 to 2 op 11 to 2) 5
ITS UNBELIEVABLE [90] 6-10-6 P McLoughlin, *hld up towards rear, blundered 4th, wknd 11th, tld off 3 out*.
.......................(16 to 1) 6
102⁶ DRUMSTICK [96] 10-10-12 R Dunwoody, *hld up, reminders 8th, wknd aftr tenth, tld off*........(10 to 1) 7
103³ DAMAS (Fr) [110] (bl) 5-11-8 D Bridgwater, *al beh, tld off 9th, pld up bef 3 out*............(5 to 1 op 9 to 2) pu
Dist: 7l, ½l, 4l, 13l, 17l, 20l. 5m 3.00s. a 13.50s (8 Ran).
SR: 23/-/-/13/-/-/

(J B Slatcher), L R Lloyd-James

166 **Roseland Group Maiden Hurdle Class E (4-y-o and up) £2,477 2m 1f 110yds
...........................(3:40)**

55³ EFHARISTO (bl) 7-11-1 R Dunwoody, *hld up, steady prog 3 out, slight ld last, quickened cir. . .*(5 to 2 jt-fav op 2 to 1) 1
SEA GOD 5-11-1 W Worthington, *hld up, hdwy 4th, led 2 out, hdd last, kpt on same pace.*
. . . .(6 to 1 op 5 to 1 tchd 13 to 2) 2
ELLY FLEETFOOT (Ire) 4-10-7 J Ryan, *wl in tch, effrt 3 out, not quicken appr nxt, staying on whn mstk last.*
. . . .(20 to 1 op 14 to 1) 3
150⁷ POSITIVO 5-11-11 Lawrence, *in tch, cld on ldr 4th, led 3 out, hdd nxt, sn outpcd . . . .*(12 to 1 op 14 to 1) 4
83² PICKENS (USA) 4-10-12 J Osborne, *chsd ldrs, rdn and outpcd aftr 3 out . . . .*(5 to 2 jt-fav tchd 11 to 4) 5
35⁴ SARACEN PRINCE (USA) 4-10-12 P Niven, *mid-div, no imprsn on ldrs frm 3 out . . . .*(12 to 1 op 10 to 1) 6
KINDERGARTEN BOY (Ire) 5-10-12 (3*) T J Murphy, *led, jmpd lft second, hdd 3 out, sn wknd. . . . . . .*(20 to 1 op 16 to 1) 7
INSTANTANEOUS 4-10-7 R Garritty, *took keen hold, mid-div, not fluent 3 out, sn btn . . . .*(6 to 1 op 5 to 1) 8
103⁵ BLENNERVILLE (Ire) 6-10-10 M Foster, *wth ldrs, wknd aftr 5th . . . .*(14 to 1 op 10 to 1) 9
SMOCKING 6-10-10 P McLoughlin, *nvr nr to chal. (33 to 1)* 10
IRIE MON (Ire) 4-10-12 A P McCoy, *mid-div, effrt 5th, outpcd 3rd . . . .* 11
WOODBINE 6-11-1 D Byrne, *took keen hold, wth ldr whn bumped second, wknd 4th, tld off when f 3 out.*
126⁸ PIMSBOY 9-10-12 (3*) P Midgley, *nvr on terms, tld off whn pld up bef 2 out. . . . .*(25 to 1 op 33 to 1) f
ON THE LEDGE (USA) 6-10-8 (7*) A Dowling, *al beh, tld off whn pld up bef 2 out. . . . .*(33 to 1) pu
MALZOOM 4-10-12 B Storey, *al beh, tld off 4th, pld up bef 2 out . . . .*(50 to 1) pu
. . . .(25 to 1 op 20 to 1) pu
Dist: 1¾l, 6l, 4l, 14l, 6l, 1¼l, hd, 10l, 12l, 2½l. 4m 15.70s. a 14.70s (15 Ran).
(Adrian Fitzpatrick), J White

167 'Strawberries & Cream' Handicap Chase Class F (0-105 5-y-o and up) £2,861 2m 1f 110yds. . . . . (4:10)

RHOSSILI BAY [97] 8-11-6 P Niven, *ldg grp, ev ch whn slpd 3 out, slight ld nxt, drvn out frm last.*
. . . .(13 to 8 fav op 7 to 4 tchd 2 to 1) 1
THE TOASTER [97] 9-11-6 M Dwyer, *hld up in tch, outpcd 4 out, ran on 2 out, str brst frm last, jst fld. (9 to 2 op 4 to 1)* 2
110* NOBLEY (USA) [105] 9-12-0 R Farrant, *led till hdd and mstk 2 out, sn wknd . . . .*(5 to 1 op 3 to 1) 3
FORGETFUL [87] 7-10-10 D J Burchell, *wth ldrs, rdn and outpcd 4 out, rallied and mstk nxt, sn wknd.*
. . . .(9 to 2 tchd 5 to 1) 4
81³ RUPPLES [87] 9-10-10 W Worthington, *hld up in tch, rdn and outpcd 4 out . . . .*(12 to 1) 5
SHREWD JOHN [102] 10-11-11 D Byrne, *hld up rear, effrt and rdn 9th, wknd 4 out . . . .*(8 to 1 op 10 to 1) 6
OLD MORTALITY [78] 10-11-7 B Storey, *mstk second, rear 4th, tch 6th, tld off whn pld up bef four out.*
. . . .(33 to 1 op 20 to 1) pu
Dist: Hd, 10l, 12l, 3½l, 12l. 4m 28.20s. a 14.20s (7 Ran).
(Mrs M Williams), Mrs M Reveley

168 'Ice Cream' Novices' Hurdle Class D (4-y-o and up) £2,819 2m 3f 110yds . . . . (4:40)

73* RIVER ROOM 6-11-6 J Osborne, *wl plcd, led appr 2 out, clr last, cmftbly . . . .*(7 to 2 op 7 to 4) 1
CLEAN EDGE (USA) 4-10-8 (3*) E Husband, *hld up in rear, ran on appr 2 out, no imprsn on wnr frm last.*
. . . .(9 to 1 op 8 to 1) 2
POLITICAL PANTO (Ire) 5-11-6 D Bridgwater, *led, hdd appr 2 out, no extr last.*
. . . .(2 to 1 fav op 5 to 2 tchd 3 to 1 and 7 to 4) 3
604 SUPERMODEL 4-10-12 R Dunwoody, *trkd ldr, stumbled appr 6th, wknd approaching 2 out.*
. . . .(7 to 2 op 5 to 2 tchd 4 to 1) 4
60³ AMERCIUS (bl) 4-10-11 D Gallagher, *mid-div, in tch till rdn and wknd 3 out, tld off. . . . . . .*(6 to 1 tchd 13 to 2) 5
POPLIN 5-10-9 B Dalton, *in 3rd pl whn f 5th.*
. . . .(20 to 1 op 16 to 1) f
TEETER THE PEETH 6-11-0 P McLoughlin, *beh frm 5th, ran out on bend appr 6th . . . .*(33 to 1 tchd 40 to 1) ro
25² LEVEL EDGE 5-10-8 (7*) Mr R Thornton, *hld up in rear, hmpd 5th, no ch whn pld up bef 3 out . . . . .*(9 to 1 op 8 to 1) pu
123 SPANISH MONEY 9-11-0 A P McCoy, *sn rdn alng in rear, hmpd 5th, lost tch and pld up bef nxt. .*(16 to 1 op 12 to 1) pu
Dist: 5l, 9l, 3l, 20l. 4m 48.50s. a 18.50s (9 Ran).
(Douglas Allum), K C Bailey

BELLEWSTOWN (IRE) (good) Thursday July 4th

169 Sam Dennigan And Co Maiden Hurdle (4-y-o and up) £2,740 2m 1f. . . . . (6:30)

RED GLITTER (USA) 6-11-6 C F Swan, ...(5 to 1) 1
117² CLASSIC SILK (Ire) 4-11-2 L P Cusack, ...(5 to 2 fav) 2
BENNY THE BISHOP (Ire) 6-10-13 (7*) Mr A Ross, (25 to 1) 3

SHINDARAR (Ire) 5-11-5 H Rogers, ...(9 to 1) 4
327 CLAIRE ME (Ire) 7-10-10 (5*) T Martin, ...(10 to 1) 5
NORDIC AIR (Ire) 5-12-7 C O'Neill, ...(14 to 1) 6
1344 SLIEVROE (Ire) 5-11-0 C O'Dwyer, ...(14 to 1) 7
1595 NEW LEGISLATION (Ire) bl 6-11-1 Mr J P Dempsey,
. . . .(11 to 1) 8
RAHAN BRIDGE (Ire) 7-11-6 (3*) IJ Smyth, ...(4 to 1) 9
CHASE THE SUN (Ire) 5-11-5 T P Treacy, ...(20 to 1) 10
FREE AND EQUAL (Ire) 5-11-5 J P Broderick, ...(25 to 1) 11
1346 OG'S DESIRE (Ire) (bl) 5-11-0 P McWilliams, ...(25 to 1) 12
1358 CHOICE COMPANY (Ire) 7-11-6 T P Rudd, ...(33 to 1) 13
INCENSE DOLL (USA) 8-10-8 (7*) D W O'Sullivan, (33 to 1) 14
907 THIRD AGENDA (Ire) 5-11-2 (3*) Mr B M Cash, ...(9 to 2) f
112 EMYGUY (Ire) 4-10-13 (3*) D T Evans, ...(20 to 1) f
SAMMY HALL 6-11-6 A Powell, ...(25 to 1) pu
Dist: 6l, 8l, 3l, 1l. 4m 0.40s. (17 Ran).
(William Godfrey), John A Quinn

170 Tipperary Natural Mineral Water Maiden Hurdle (5-y-o and up) £2,911 3m. . . . . ([**] **)

91² KILCARAMORE (Ire) 5-11-13 Mr P J Healy, ...(5 to 2 fav) 1
118⁴ BUGGSY BLADE 10-12-0 L P Cusack, ...(8 to 1) 2
132⁴ JONATHAN'S ROSE (Ire) 7-11-2 (7*) Mr G Gallagher,
. . . .(10 to 1) 3
1377 MAIASAURA (Ire) 7-12-0 C O'Dwyer, ...(12 to 1) 4
915 DROMOD POINT (Ire) (bl) 7-12-0 T J Mitchell, ...(14 to 1) 5
88⁴ A THOUSAND DREAMS (Ire) 8-12-0 C F Swan, (100 to 30) 6
SHEER INDULGENCE (Ire) 8-12-0 J P Broderick, . .(8 to 1) 7
122⁴ DOTTIE'S DOUBLE (Ire) 5-11-8 T P Rudd, ...(5 to 1) 8
1347 ROCK COTTAGE (Ire) 5-11-13 F Woods, ...(33 to 1) 9
133 MEGS MOMENT (Ire) 5-11-1 (7*) R P Hogan, ...(33 to 1) 10
HANNAH'S PET (Ire) 6-11-9 P Carberry, ...(14 to 1) 11
114 IRENES TREASURE (Ire) 6-11-7 (7*) Mr S J Mahon, (25 to 1) 12
66⁹ ARDMORE KELINKA (Ire) 6-11-9 H Rogers, ...(25 to 1) 13
1345 ROYAL ARISTOCRAT (Ire) 7-11-13 Mr J McWilliams, . . (10 to 1) pu
62 THE RURAL DEAN (Ire) 5-11-13 S H O'Donovan, . .(20 to 1) pu
1126 NOBODYWANTSME (Ire) 5-11-6 (7*) Mr J Creighton,
. . . .(16 to 1) pu
Dist: 1l, 1l, 25l, ½l. 6m 0.90s. (16 Ran).
(P J Healy), P J Healy

171 Seamus Mulvaney Crockafotha Handicap Hurdle (0-102 4-y-o and up) £2,740 2½m. . . . . (8:00)

117* SHOREWOOD (Ire) [-] 5-10-13 F Woods, ...(7 to 2) 1
CONCLAVE (Ire) [-] 6-11-3 (5*) G Cotter, ...(11 to 1) 2
89² SANDRA LOUISE (Ire) [-] 6-9-2 (7*) L J Fleming, (11 to 4 fav) 3
1185 DANCING POSER (Ire) [-] (bl) 4-10-6 K F O'Brien, (14 to 1) 4
FONTAINE LODGE (Ire) [-] 6-10-12 P Carberry, ...(7 to 1) 5
1357 LEGITMAN (Ire) [-] 6-9-11² C F Swan, ...(7 to 1) 6
65⁸ ICANTELYA (Ire) [-] 7-11-7 T P Treacy, ...(6 to 1) 7
89 STRAIGHT ON (Ire) [-] (bl) 5-11-1 C O'Dwyer, ...(3 to 1) 8
1187 PRINCE SABI (Ire) [-] 6-10-4 P L Malone, ...(16 to 1) 9
HAWTHORN'S WAY (Ire) [-] 8-9-8² S H O'Donovan, (33 to 1) 10
EXTRA STOUT (Ire) [-] 4-9-7³ (3*) J R Barry, ...(20 to 1) 11
Dist: 1l, nk, 3l, 12l. 5m 2.90s. (11 Ran).
(Lloyd Thompson), E J O'Grady

172 Vincent Keating Oil Distributors INH Flat Race (4-y-o and up) £3,575 2m 1f. . . . . (9:00)

SUPREME CHARM (Ire) 4-11-11 Mr P Fenton, (2 to 1 jt-fav) 1
121* DRAMATIST (Ire) 5-12-0 (3*) Mr B M Cash, ...(9 to 4) 2
MONTE'S EVENING (Ire) 8-11-8 (3*) Mr P J Casey, (12 to 1) 3
122² SIR GANDOUGE (Ire) 7-11-4 (7*) Mr A K Wyse, (2 to 1 jt-fav) 4
346 BARLEY MEADOW (Ire) 4-10-11 (7*) Mr G Elliott, . .(12 to 1) 5
BOREEN BOY 6-11-4 (7*) Miss C O'Connell, ...(20 to 1) 6
CHARLIEADAMS (Ire) 6-11-4 (7*) Mr A G Cash, ...(33 to 1) 7
SISTER JUDE 5-10-12 (7*) Mr P J Burke, ...(20 to 1) 8
Dist: 6l, 2l, 8l, 1l. 4m 1.40s. (8 Ran).
(D M O'Meara), Michael O'Meara

WEXFORD (IRE) (yielding) Friday July 5th

173 Enniscorthy (Mares) Maiden Hurdle (5-y-o and up) £2,226 2¼m. . . . . . (5:45)

95* LAURA GALE (Ire) 7-12-0 T P Treacy, ...(2 to 1 fav) 1
1407 SLAVE GALE (Ire) 5-11-13 C F Swan, ...(6 to 1) 2
1175 DUSTY ROSE (Ire) 7-11-6 M Moran, ...(14 to 1) 3
665 BRIGHT SHARES (Ire) 6-11-6 K F O'Brien, ...(10 to 1) 4
1343 CORMAC LADY (Ire) 5-11-5 J K Kinane, ...(12 to 1) 5
64 HASTY HOURS (Ire) 6-11-6 F Woods, ...(11 to 2) 6
1703 JONATHAN'S ROSE (Ire) 7-10-13 (7*) Mr G Gallagher,
. . . .(25 to 1) 7
SOLAR CASTLE (Ire) (bl) 6-11-3⁴ (7*) Mr T J Nagle Jnr, ...(25 to 1) 8
RUN ROSE RUN (bl) 6-11-6 T Horgan, ...(20 to 1) 9
864 DREAM ETERNAL (Ire) 5-11-5 W T Slattery, ...(8 to 1) 10
1205 LANTINA (Ire) 5-11-5 D H O'Connor, ...(12 to 1) 11

112[7] UNDERSTANDING (Ire) 7-10-13 (7*) Mr P J McGarry,
....(33 to 1) 12
140[8] BABY WHALE (Ire) 6-11-6 T J O'Sullivan, ...(25 to 1) 13
FRAU DANTE (Ire) 6-12-0 C O'Dwyer, ...(11 to 2) pu
RIVERRUNSTHROUGHIT (Ire) 5-11-5 F J Flood, ..(40 to 1) pu
Dist: 3½l, 15l, 6l, 4½l. 4m 27.90s. (15 Ran).

(J M Foley), S J Treacy

174 Tusker House Hotel Handicap Hurdle (0-109 4-y-o and up) £2,568 2¼m
....(6:15)

118* FERRYCARRIG HOTEL (Ire) [-] 7-11-6 C N Bowens,
....(5 to 4 on) 1
118 CHUCK (Ire) [-] 6-9-11 (7*) D McCullagh, ...(20 to 1) 2
CARRAIG-AN-OIR (Ire) [-] 7-9-1 (7*) J D Pratt, ...(12 to 1) 3
118 THE WICKED CHICKEN (Ire) [-] 7-10-3 T Horgan, ..(10 to 1) 4
87[6] JUSTAWAY (Ire) [-] 6-11-9 K P Gaule, ...(7 to 2) 5
SHAYISTA (Ire) [-] 11-10-7 (7*) Miss C O'Neill, ...(10 to 1) 6
DONERAILE PARK [-] 9-11-0 (7*) Mr B Walsh, ...(8 to 1) 7
Dist: ¾l, 9l, 2l, 2l. 4m 31.10s. (7 Ran).

(Ferrycarrig Hotel Syndicate), Victor Bowens

175 Rosslare Maiden Hurdle (4-y-o and up) £2,226 2¼m
.....................................(6:45)

132[2] ADARAMANN (Ire) 4-11-8 (7*) Mr R Walsh, ...(9 to 4) 1
132[3] DROMINAGH (Ire) 8-11-6 C F Swan, ...(2 to 1 fav) 2
90 TRIPLE ACTION (Ire) 7-10-13 (7*) A O'Shea, ...(14 to 1) 3
THE ROAD TO MOSCOW (Ire) 5-11-2 (3*) J R Barry, (10 to 1) 4
CORKERS FLAME (Ire) 5-11-9 W T Slattery, ...(20 to 1) 5
30 LOSLOMOS (Ire) 4-10-8 (7*) Mr D Duggan, ...(16 to 1) 6
TELL THE COUNTRY (Ire) 4-10-10 T Horgan, ...(10 to 1) 7
TOUREEN LODGE (Ire) 6-11-6 F J Flood, ...(10 to 1) 8
MOON-FROG 9-11-6 F Woods, ...(16 to 1) 9
115[6] SPRINGWELL MAY (Ire) 4-10-3 (7*) M D Murphy, ..(14 to 1) 10
MOSHER (Ire) 4-10-8 (7*) Mrs C Harrison, ...(20 to 1) 11
118 FORTUNES LUCK (Ire) 8-12-0 D H O'Connor, ...(8 to 1) pu
Dist: 3l, 15l, 5½l, 1½l. 4m 36.10s. (12 Ran).

(Mrs Helen Walsh), T M Walsh

176 Cedars Hotel Rosslare Hurdle (4-y-o and up) £2,568 2½m
.........................(7:15)

132[2] PINGO HILL (Ire) 4-11-5 C O'Dwyer, ...(9 to 1) 1
139[2] FLY ROSEY (Ire) 6-11-9 C F Swan, ...(11 to 8 on) 2
32* DIFFICULT TIMES (Ire) 4-11-5 S C Lyons, ...(4 to 1) 3
92[9] SUDDEN STORM (Ire) 5-11-8 T P Treacy, ...(8 to 1) 4
140[9] BISHOP'S HILL (Ire) 7-11-7 K F O'Brien, ...(12 to 1) 5
118[2] FARTHER RECTOR (Ire) 7-12-0 T J Murphy, ...(6 to 1) 6
ANTICS (Ire) 4-10-0 (7*) Mrs C Harrison, ...(14 to 1) 7
66 CHUCKAWALLA (Ire) 4-10-2 A Powell, ...(16 to 1) 8
86[9] CROGHAN BRIDGE (Ire) 7-11-7 J H Burke, ...(33 to 1) pu
118 THE BRIDGE TAVERN (Ire) 7-11-11 (3*) D P Murphy,
....(20 to 1) pu
SWINGER (Ire) 7-12-0 P Carberry, ...(10 to 1) pu
Dist: 1½l, 11l, 5l, 15l. 5m 15.80s. (11 Ran).

(J E B Jobson), Mrs John Harrington

177 Duncannon I.N.H. Flat Race (6-y-o and up) £2,226 2¼m
.........................(8:45)

88[6] CELIO LUCY (Ire) 6-11-9 Mr J A Nash, ...(8 to 1) 1
144[2] STANSWAY (Ire) 8-12-0 Mr P Fenton, ...(7 to 4 fav) 2
DAWN INFIDEL (Ire) 6-11-2 (7*) Mr R Walsh, ...(8 to 1) 3D
OX EYE DAISY (Ire) 8-11-2 (7*) Mr E Sheehy, ...(10 to 1) 3
120[2] GALATASSIR JANE (Ire) 6-11-2 (7*) Mr Patrick O'Keeffe,
....(10 to 1) 4
BUZZ ABOUT (Ire) 6-11-2 (7*) Mr J P Murphy, ...(14 to 1) 5
99[5] GUILLIG LADY (Ire) 6-11-4 (3*) Mr B M Cash, ...(14 to 1) 6
PRINCESS LENA (Ire) 6-11-3[1] (7*) Mr T J Nagle Jnr, (20 to 1) 7
CROCHAUN (Ire) 6-11-2 (7*) Mr G Finlay, ...(20 to 1) 8
TULLIBARDS SWALLOW (Ire) 7-11-2 (7*) Mr G Elliott,
....(7 to 1) 9
20 DEEP REFRAIN (Ire) (bl) 6-11-7 (7*) Mr B Hassett, ..(6 to 1) 10
LISCAHILL BREEZE (Ire) 7-11-9 Mr H F Cleary, ...(14 to 1) 11
65[4] BARNAMIRE BAY (Ire) 7-12-0 Mr D Marnane, ...(12 to 1) 12
GERRY O MALLEY (Ire) 6-11-7 (7*) Mr D W Cullen, (16 to 1) 13
Dist: Sht-hd, 3l, 2½l. 4m 23.80s. (14 Ran).

(Mrs J E Rothwell), W P Mullins

DUNDALK (IRE) (firm)
Sunday July 7th

178 Annagassan Maiden Hurdle (4-y-o and up) £2,740 2m 135yds
.........(2:30)

134[2] WHEREWILITALL END (Ire) 5-11-2 (3*) U Smyth, ...(6 to 1) 1
MAGICAL FUN (Ire) 4-11-7 C F Swan, ...(6 to 4 on) 2
90[3] ALPINE MIST (Ire) 4-11-2 T Horgan, ...(6 to 1) 3
90[6] LEMOIRE (Ire) 5-10-11 (3*) D T Evans, ...(14 to 1) 4
SPECTACLE (Ire) 6-10-13 (7*) A O'Shea, ...(25 to 1) 5
GROVE VICTOR (Ire) (bl) 5-11-5 C O'Dwyer, ...(25 to 1) 6
FOREST LADY (Ire) 4-10-11 L P Cusack, ...(33 to 1) 7
BUBBLY PROSPECT (USA) 5-11-10 (3*) C Everard, ..(8 to 1) f
Dist: Sht-hd, 5½l, ½l, 14l. 4m 8.50s. (8 Ran).

(S P Mahon), Peter McCreery

179 Tallonstown Handicap Hurdle (0-109 4-y-o and up) £2,740 2½m 153yds
....(3:00)

158* ARCTIC KATE [-] 10-11-13 (6ex) C O'Dwyer, ...(100 to 30) 1
118[6] BITRAN [-] 6-10-3 F Woods, ...(16 to 1) 2+
MAKING THE POINT (Ire) 5-11-7 K F O'Brien, ...(5 to 1) 2+
130[2] CULLENSTOWN LADY (Ire) [-] 5-12-0 A Powell, (2 to 1 fav) 4
92 PLOUGH THE LEA (Ire) [-] 6-9-5 (5*) Mr J Connolly, (8 to 1) 5
169[4] SHINDARAR (Ire) [-] 5-10-9 H Rogers, ...(10 to 1) 6
136[6] MAN OF IRON [-] 9-9-8 (7*) A O'Shea, ...(33 to 1) 7
32 RUNNING SLIPPER (Ire) [-] (bl) 6-10-5 L P Cusack, (33 to 1) bd
171[9] PRINCE SABI (Ire) [-] (bl) 6-9-11 P L Malone, ...(33 to 1) bd
169[ ] RED GLITTER (USA) [-] 6-11-4 (6ex) C F Swan, (100 to 30) pu
Dist: Nk, dd-ht, 2l, dist. 4m 46.60s. (10 Ran).

(Mrs R D Richards), James O'Haire

180 Louth I.N.H. Flat Race (4-y-o and up) £2,740 2m 135yds.........(5:30)

34[3] JOHNNY'S DREAM (Ire) 6-11-7 (7*) Mr A J Dempsey,
....(6 to 1) 1
68[2] NATIVE BABY (Ire) 6-11-2 (7*) Mr R Walsh, ...(7 to 2) 2
FANE PATH (Ire) 4-11-0 (7*) Mr M Madden, ...(8 to 1) 3
SABANIYA (Ire) 4-10-9 (7*) Miss A Croke, ...(10 to 1) 4
BRISBUCK LADY (Ire) 6-11-9 Mr P Fenton, ...(20 to 1) 5
MIDNIGHT CYCLONE (Ire) 5-11-8 Mr J A Nash, (6 to 4 fav) 6
MY CLASSIC 6-11-2 (7*) Mr Joss Saville, ...(12 to 1) 7
APPOLLO VISION (Ire) 5-11-6 (7*) Mr P Barcoe, ...(12 to 1) 8
RAPID PLAYER (Ire) 6-11-2 (7*) Mr P Fahey, ...(14 to 1) 9
26[5] MISTER BLACK (Ire) 8-12-0 Mr P F Graffin, ...(20 to 1) 10
BEHY BRIDGE (Ire) 4-10-9 (7*) Mr D P Coakley, ...(14 to 1) 11
159[3] JUST A VODKA (Ire) 6-11-7 (7*) Mr A Fleming, ...(13 to 2) pu
Dist: ¾l, 2½l, 4½l, 10l. 4m 47.10s. (12 Ran).

(Mrs James Nicholson), D T Hughes

ROSCOMMON (IRE) (good to firm)
Monday July 8th

181 Red Mills Maiden Hurdle (4-y-o and up) £3,082 2m.........(6:00)

94[2] PRECEPTOR (Ire) 7-11-1 (5*) B Bowens, ...(16 to 1) 1
DON'T LOOSE FAITH (Ire) (bl) 4-10-11 S C Lyons, ..(9 to 2) 2
140[6] BALLY UPPER (Ire) 8-11-6 C O'Dwyer, ...(6 to 1) 3
62[4] HIGH TONE (Ire) 7-11-6 H Rogers, ...(4 to 1) 4
DIAMOND CLUSTER 6-11-6 W T Slattery, ...(25 to 1) 5
159[2] NO DIAMOND (Ire) 7-11-6 J P Broderick, ...(13 to 2) 6
CASTI F FLLEN BOY (Ire) 4-11-2 J F Titley, ...(12 to 1) 7
MANNIX (Ire) 7-10-13 (7*) S P McCann, ...(20 to 1) 8
144[4] REAL TAOISEACH (Ire) 6-11-7 (7*) Mr A K Wyse, (6 to 4 fav) 9
Dist: 2l, 10l, 10l, 12l. 3m 51.60s. (9 Ran).

(P A McMahon), Victor Bowens

182 Pat Hughes Handicap Hurdle (0-102 4-y-o and up) £2,911 2m.......(6:30)

29[2] WEST ON BRIDGE ST (Ire) [-] 6-11-7 C O'Dwyer,
....(13 to 8 fav) 1
171[6] LEGITMAN (Ire) [-] 6-9-10 P Carberry, ...(8 to 1) 2
174* FERRYCARRIG HOTEL (Ire) [-] 7-12-0 (5*,6ex) B Bowens,
....(7 to 1) 3
135[6] THE BOURDA [-] 10-10-2 F Woods, ...(10 to 1) 4
135[3] RUSHEEN BAY (Ire) [-] (bl) 7-9-2 (7*) A O'Shea, ...(7 to 1) 5
117[7] ROSSI (Ire) [-] 7-9-6 (5*) G Cotter, ...(20 to 1) 6
RUNABOUT (Ire) [-] 4-10-2 C F Swan, ...(12 to 1) 7
JUST AN ILLUSION (Ire) [-] 4-11-9 (3*) D T Evans, ..(8 to 1) 8
CANDY IS DANDY (Ire) [-] 7-10-6 L P Cusack, ...(25 to 1) 9
134[8] AUGHNANURE (Ire) [-] (bl) 5-9-8 P L Malone, ...(20 to 1) f
143 DEGO DANCER [-] 9-9-12 T P Treacy, ...(14 to 1) f
FLYING IN THE GALE (Ire) [-] 5-9-9 (3*) J R Barry, (20 to 1) ur
Dist: 10l, 2l, 1l, 4½l. 3m 43.30s. (12 Ran).

(Robert Hennelly), V T O'Brien

183 Keenans Bookmakers INH Flat Race (4-y-o and up) £2,740 2m.......(9:00)

STAR DEFECTOR (Ire) 5-11-8 (5*) G Cotter, ...(3 to 1) 1
MURPHY'S MALT (Ire) 4-11-4 (3*) Mr B M Cash, (100 to 30) 2
BELLE PERK (Ire) 5-11-3 (5*) Mr J Connolly, ...(7 to 4 fav) 3
JACKIE'S PERSIAN (Ire) 7-11-2 (7*) M P Dunne, ...(14 to 1) 4
144[9] GILLYS HOPE (Ire) 5-11-6 (7*) Mr A J Dempsey, ..(33 to 1) 5
122[7] DREAMIN GEORGE (Ire) 6-12-0 Mr P F Graffin, ...(20 to 1) 6
HOLLOW WOOD (Ire) 5-11-6 (7*) Mr D A Harney, (10 to 1) 7
62 DOCUMMINS (Ire) 6-11-7 (7*) Mr B P Galvin, ...(33 to 1) 8
99[6] US FOUR (Ire) 5-11-7 (7*) Mr C A Murphy, ...(9 to 1) 9
GOLD DEVON (Ire) 6-12-0 Mr T Doyle, ...(25 to 1) 10
NUAN (Ire) 6-11-2 (7*) Mr Joseph G McMahon, ...(14 to 1) 11
KIDSTUFF (Ire) 5-11-6 (7*) Mr P J Gilligan, ...(16 to 1) 12
GARLAND ROSE (Ire) 6-11-2 (7*) P Morris, ...(12 to 1) 13
137 MOY VALLEY (Ire) 6-11-2 (7*) Mr A Daly, ...(33 to 1) 14
KU KAMARI (Ire) 5-11-8 Mr J P Dempsey, ...(33 to 1) 15
133 CAMLA LAD (Ire) 5-11-6 (7*) Mr R Walsh, ...(20 to 1) 16
137[6] DUNMORE DOM (Ire) 4-11-0 (7*) Mr M P Brown, ..(33 to 1) 17

Dist: 8l, 7l, 4l, 2½l. 3m 35.60s. (17 Ran).

(Yoshiki Akazawa), John Muldoon

NAAS (IRE) (good to firm)
Wednesday July 10th

184 Furness Handicap Hurdle (0-123 4-y-o
and up) £3,425 2m.............(6:30)

139²	FRESH DEAL (Ire) [-] 4-11-10 L P Cusack,..... (6 to 1 4 fav)	1
131⁵	TEMPLERAN PRINCE [-] 9-11-8 M Duffy,......... (8 to 1)	2
96⁶	INNOVATIVE (Ire) [-] 5-10-3 C O'Dwyer,........ (10 to 1)	3
	LOUGH ATALIA [-] 9-10-2 A Powell,............. (12 to 1)	4
143*	KATIYMANN (Ire) [-] 4-11-0 T Horgan,........... (11 to 4)	5
162	GALAVOTTI (Ire) [-] 7-10-8 P Carberry,.......... (9 to 1)	6
143⁴	MISTER CHIPPY (Ire) [-] 4-12-0 C F Swan,........(5 to 1)	7

Dist: 2l, 7l, nk, 3l. 3m 46.40s. (7 Ran).

(F Dunne), F Dunne

185 Go Racing In Kildare INH Flat Race (4-8
.............................(8:30)

	REEVES (Ire) 4-11-0 (7*) Mr R Walsh,.............(2 to 1)	1
	CROSSCHILD (Ire) 5-11-8 Mr J A Berry,........... (8 to 1)	2
	WELL ARMED (Ire) 5-11-10 (3*) Mr B R Hamilton, (11 to 2)	3
	CASTLE COIN (Ire) 4-11-4 (3*) Mr B M Cash, ... (7 to 4 fav)	4
122⁶	HILL OF HOPE (Ire) 5-11-6 (7*) Mr M A Cahill, ...(12 to 1)	5
88⁹	COCKPIT (Ire) 5-11-13 Mr P Fenton,............. (12 to 1)	6
121³	ATTACK AT DAWN (Ire) 5-11-1 (7*) Mr J P McNamara,	
	...................................(9 to 1)	7
	PROPHETS FIST (Ire) 5-11-6 (7*) Mr D A Harney, ... (14 to 1)	8
	ROSEY BUCK (Ire) 4-10-9 (7*) Mr J P Kilfeather, ...(33 to 1)	9
	BASINGER (Ire) 5-11-3 (5*) Mr E J Kearns Jnr, ... (14 to 1)	10
	FLY BY WIRE (Ire) 4-11-0 (7*) Mr S T Nolan,......(8 to 1)	11

Dist: 4½l, ½l, 3½l, 8l. 4m 28.10s. (11 Ran).

(Alexander McCarthy), W P Mullins

WORCESTER (good to firm)
Wednesday July 10th
Going Correction: MINUS 0.45 sec. per fur.

186 Harpley Novices' Claiming Hurdle
Class F (4-y-o and up) £2,087 2½m
...................................(6:45)

107	SPARTS FAULT (Ire) 6-10-10 Richard Guest, hld up, hdwy to	
	ld appr last, drvn out..........(25 to 1 tchd 33 to 1)	1
103	MUTLEY 6-10-7 C Maude, early to post, beh, gd hdwy and	
	slight ld whn hmpd 2 out, sn hdd, no extr.	
	......................(14 to 1 tchd 16 to 1)	2
165⁵	PICKENS (USA) 4-11-5 J Osborne, nvr far away, not fluent	
	6th, ev ch whn hng lft 2 out, one pace whn jmpd rght last.	
	....................(3 to 1 tchd 4 to 1)	3
165³	ELLY FLEETFOOT (Ire) 4-10-9 J Ryan, chsd ldrs, jmpd slwly 5	
	out and nxt, led 3 out, hdd next, unbl to quicken	
	......................(5 to 2 fav op 7 to 4)	4
	EWAR IMPERIAL 4-10-11 D Gallagher, in tch, ev ch 3 out, btn	
	whn hit last...............(33 to 1 op 25 to 1)	5
	COOLEGALE 10-10-7 S McNeill, set steady pace, hdd appr 3	
	out, sn outpcd................(20 to 1 op 14 to 1)	6
101	PATS FOLLY 5-10-2 P McLoughlin, hld up, hdwy hfwy, hit 4	
	out, lost tch aftr nxt...........(50 to 1 op 33 to 1)	7
	ADMIRAL'S GUEST (Ire) 4-10-11 T Eley, midfield, improved to	
	chase ldrs 3 out, sn outpcd.	
	................(20 to 1 op 14 to 1 tchd 25 to 1)	8
	DON TOCINO 6-11-2 A P McCoy, cl up, drvn to ld briefly appr	
	3 out, wknd bef nxt...............(9 to 2 op 5 to 2)	9
	EMPERORS WOOD 5-10-10 B Fenton, unruly strt, al beh, tld	
	off.......................(33 to 1 op 25 to 1)	10
	SALTIS (Ire) 4-10-5 V Slattery, blun badly second, jmpd poorly	
	in rear, tld off whn pld up 3 out........(33 to 1 op 20 to 1)	11
111	NICK THE BISCUIT (v) 5-10-13 R Dunwoody, cl up,	
	reminders appr 3 out, sn wknd, tld off...(9 to 2 op 5 to 1)	12
100	ARDEARNED 9-10-4² Mr A Charles-Jones, jmpd slwly 1st,	
	beh frm 6th, tld off whn pld up bef last, lme.	
	......................(50 to 1 op 33 to 1)	pu
153	BRENSHAM FOLLY (bl) 5-10-7 L Harvey, tld off frm 5th, pld up	
	4 out........................(50 to 1 op 33 to 1)	pu

Dist: 6l, 2½l, 1½l, 14l, 2½l, 4l, 3l, 4l, 15l, ½l. 4m 53.40s. a 17.40s (14 Ran).

(Brian A Lewendon), P Eccles

187 Pershore Novices' Handicap Hurdle
Class E (0-100 4-y-o and up) £2,250
3m............................(7:15)

83⁵	LITTLE TINCTURE (Ire) [66] 6-10-2 (5*) Sophie Mitchell, made	
	most, str pressed appr last, hld on wl. (5 to 1 tchd 6 to 1)	1
47⁴	PALACE PARADE (USA) [65] 6-10-6 A Thornton, nvr far away,	
	reminders 4 out, chlgd 2 out, kpt on und pres.	
	................(5 to 2 op 3 to 1 tchd 100 to 30)	2
	MOUNTAIN LEADER [69] 6-10-10 B Powell, in tch, rdn and	
	outpcd appr 2 out, rallied und pres fll. (20 to 1 op 16 to 1)	3
111*	LITTLE COURT [66] 5-10-3 A P McCoy, led to 3rd, chsd ldrs	
	till wknd appr 3 out, tld off...........(9 to 2 op 4 to 1)	4

47*	VALISKY [85] 6-11-12 C Llewellyn, f second, dead.	
	....................(9 to 4 fav op 7 to 4)	f
	CREDIT CALL (Ire) [59] 8-10-0 W Humphreys, beh, lost tch 4	
	out, tld off whn pld up bef last.	
	...............(50 to 1 op 33 to 1 tchd 66 to 1)	pu
	RUMI [76] 5-10-13 J Osborne, hld up, hdwy jmpd slwly 4	
	out, wknd quickly and pld up bef nxt.	
	....................(9 to 2 op 7 to 2 tchd 5 to 1)	pu

Dist: 1¼l, ¾l, dist. 5m 54.80s. a 18.80s (7 Ran).

(Mrs T J McInnes Skinner), Mrs T J McInnes Skinner

188 Wadham Kenning Worcester Vauxhall
Handicap Chase Class F (0-105 5-y-o
and up) £3,099 2m 7f............(7:45)

	EVANGELICA (USA) [105] 6-12-0 D Bridgwater, in tch, gd	
	hdwy 4 out, led last, drvn out............. (9 to 2 op 5 to 1)	1
51	THE BLUE BOY (Ire) [100] (bl) 8-11-9 R Dunwoody, hndy,	
	chlgd betw last 2, ran on............(16 to 1 op 12 to 1)	2
147³	MENATURE (Ire) [77] 7-9-11 (3*) J Culloty, led 11th, mstk and	
	hng left............................(10 to 1)	3
124⁵	RUSTY BRIDGE [88] 9-10-4 (7*) Mr R Thornton, hld up, drvn	
	alng hfwy, blun tenth, styd on frm 2 out, nvr dngrs. (20 to 1)	4
	JIM VALENTINE [93] 10-11-2 W Marston, blun badly second,	
	jmpd slwly towards rear, nvr dngrs...........(14 to 1)	5
	MANAMOUR [82] 9-10-5² Richard Guest, hld up, hdwy gng	
	wl appr 4 out, shaken up and outpcd nxt.	
	....................(20 to 1 op 16 to 1)	6
	BOXING MATCH [89] 9-10-1 B Fenton, chsd ldrs till wknd 4	
	out..........................(20 to 1 tchd 25 to 1)	7
154	FUNCHEON GALE [94] 9-11-3 D Morris, beh, hdwy and in tch	
	twelfth, lost pl 4 out.........(11 to 4 fav op 4 to 1)	8
	TRUST DEED (USA) [77] (bl) 8-10-0 M Richards, mstk 1st,	
	hdwy and in tch tenth, hrd drvn twelfth, sn btn.	
	....................(12 to 1 op 10 to 1)	9
102⁵	HAMPER [83] (bl) 13-10-3 (3*) K Gaule, in tch, drvn and	
	outpcd twelfth, sn no dngr..........(25 to 1 op 16 to 1)	10
124²	TRUSS [87] 9-10-10 R Supple, led to 4th, in tch whn blun 5	
	wknd frm nxt.........(11 to 1 op 10 to 1 tchd 12 to 1)	11
102	THE LORRYMAN (Ire) [97] 8-11-6 G Upton, led 4th, hdd 11th,	
	wknd appr four out.................(33 to 1)	12
154²	FATHER DOWLING [82] 9-10-5 A P McCoy, al beh, tld off.	
	....................(11 to 2 op 5 to 1)	13
	GILSTON LASS [101] 9-11-10 A S Smith, hdwy to track ldrs	
	7th, struggling 5 out, sn beh.......(25 to 1 op 20 to 1)	14
154⁴	ABBOTSHAM [11-10-3 (7*) Miss E J Jones, f 5th.	
	....................(20 to 1 op 14 to 1)	f
124	STORM WARRIOR [77] (bl) 11-9-11 (3*) R Massey, hld up,	
	mstk 6th, struggling whn blun 3 out, pld up bef nxt. (33 to 1)	pu
	CANTANTIVY [77] 11-9-7 (7*) Mr O McPhail, cl up, lost tch 6	
	out, tld off whn pld up bef last............(50 to 1)	pu
106⁷	THE FOOLISH ONE [7] 9-10-0 D Gallagher, hmpd 5th, tld off	
	whn pld up tenth...................(33 to 1)	pu
124⁶	JIMMY O'DEA [95] (v) 9-11-4 J Osborne, hld up struggling fnl	
	circuit, tld off whn pld up 5 out..........(14 to 1)	pu
42⁶	TENBIT (Ire) [81] 6-10-4⁴ C Maude, midfield, beh whn pld up	
	5 out.......................(16 to 1)	pu

Dist: 1¼l, 8l, 12l, ½l, 2l, sht-hd, 11l, 2l, 9l, 1¼l. 5m 58.90s. a 20.90s (20 Ran).

(Martin Pipe Racing Club), M C Pipe

189 Radio Wyvern Handicap Hurdle Class
E (0-115 4-y-o and up) £2,512 2m
...................................(8:15)

	ROUTING [102] 8-11-5 C Maude, al gng wl, led and hit 2 out,	
	clr whn jmpd rght last, easily...... (16 to 1 tchd 20 to 1)	1
	EL GRANDO [83] 6-10-0 D Gallagher, hld up, some hdwy	
	hfwy, kpt on und pres betw last 2, no ch wth wnr.	
	....................(20 to 1 op 33 to 1)	2
	OUT RANKING (Fr) [100] 4-11-0 D Bridgwater, cl up, led appr	
	3 out, hdd and mstk nxt, no extr.......(13 to 2 op 5 to 1)	3
148³	KALZARI (USA) [90] 11-10-7 B Powell, hld up, unbl to quicken	
	3 out, some hdwy betw last 2, kpt on sdly.	
	....................(10 to 1 op 7 to 1)	4
109³	LADY CONFESS [93] 6-10-10 R Supple, made most, hdd	
	appr 3 out, wknd frm nxt...........(8 to 1 op 7 to 1)	5
	KING'S SHILLING (USA) [99] 9-11-2 R Davis, beh, some	
	hdwy appr 3 out, nvr dngrs.........(25 to 1 op 20 to 1)	6
152*	COURAGEOUS KNIGHT [85] 7-10-2 B Fenton, nvr gng wl,	
	lost tch appr 3 out...........(3 to 1 op 11 to 4)	7
148	WAMDHA (Ire) [103] 6-11-6 A S Smith, settled rear, lost tch	
	appr 3 out, nvr dngrs....(10 to 1 op 8 to 1 tchd 12 to 1)	8
	CAVO GRECO (USA) [83] 7-10-0 D Skyrme, pld hrd, chsd ldrs	
	till lost tch 4 out, tld off.................	9
	MOYMET [83] 10-10-0 J Osborne, chsd ldrs, struggling 4 out,	
	tld off.........................(33 to 1)	10
	SHIFTING MOON [98] 4-10-12 W Marston, midfield, hrd drvn	
	hfwy, sn beh, tld off............(14 to 1 op 12 to 1)	11
148⁴	AMAZON EXPRESS [106] 7-11-9 R Dunwoody, cl up, mstk 4	
	out, wkng whn f nxt.......................(10 to 1 op 8 to 1)	f
109*	FISIO SANDS [103] 7-11-6 A P McCoy, chsd ldrs, lost tch	
	hfwy, sn pld up.........(5 to 2 fav tchd 9 to 4)	pu

Dist: 6l, 1½l, 1l, 1½l, 8l, 6l, nk, 22l, 28l, 10l. 3m 40.10s. a 0.10s (13 Ran).
SR: 18/-/3/-/-/-/

(Derek Jones), N G Ayliffe

190 Promota Novices' Chase Class E (5-y-o
and up) £3,036 2m............(8:45)

153³ STATELY HOME (Ire) 5-10-8 A P McCoy, *led, jmpd wl, clr hfwy, jnd 4 out, rallied and drvn clear appr last.*
....(4 to 1 op 5 to 1) 1
PONTOON BRIDGE 9-11-4 R Dunwoody, *chsd ldr, mstk 7th, ev ch frm 4 out, one pace appr last.*
....(11 to 8 on 6 to 4 on tchd 5 to 4 on) 2
127⁴ NORDIC VALLEY (Ire) 6-10-8 D Bridgwater, *hld up, outpcd 4 out, no dngr aftr.*..........(7 to 2 op 11 to 4 tchd 4 to 1) 3
106³ LEGAL ARTIST (Ire) 6-10-11 L Harvey, *hld up, drvn alng frm 7th, no dngr from 4 out.*.....(8 to 1 op 7 to 1 tchd 9 to 1) 4
MASTER ART 6-10-6 (5*) Mr P Henley, *beh, tld off frm 8th.*
....(50 to 1 op 33 to 1) 5
100 PAID ELATION 11-10-1 (5*) Sophie Mitchell, *chsd ldrs, struggling appr 4 out, wknd quickly.......*(100 to 1 op 66 to 1) 6
BALLYRANEBOW (Ire) 8-10-11⁵ Mr G Barfoot-Saunt, *beh, tld off frm 5 out.*..............................(100 to 1 op 66 to 1) 7
Dist: 5l, 20l, 2½l, 6l, 2l, 28l. 3m 55.80s. a 6.80s (7 Ran).

(P Bowen), P Bowen

191 Worcester Standard Open National Hunt Flat Class H (4,5,6-y-o) £1,259 2m...........................(9:15)

53* KAILASH (USA) 5-12-0 D Bridgwater, *al gng best, led on bit 3 fs out, easily.*......................(5 to 2 op 2 to 1) 1
MARLOUSION 4-10-10 D Gallagher, *hld up, niggled alng hfwy, kpt on appr fnl furlong, no ch wth wnr.*
....(10 to 1 op 5 to 1) 2
POWERFUL SPIRIT 4-10-10 (5*) Michael Brennan, *keen hold, hld up, hdwy to ld 5 fs out, hdd 3 out, one pace.*
....(9 to 1 op 25 to 1 tchd 8 to 1) 3
157² OH DEAR ME 5-10-13 B Powell, *chsd ldrs, pushed alng and outpcd 4 fs out, styd on stdly ins last.....*(5 to 1 op 7 to 2) 4
SWYNFORD KING 4-11-1 D Byrne, *hld up, drvn to improve 5 fs out, wknd fnl 2 furlongs.*
....(7 to 4 fav op 9 to 4 tchd 5 to 2) 5
MORECEVA 6-11-4 R Greene, *nvr nr ldrs.*
....(33 to 1 op 25 to 1) 6
HEADING NORTH 5-10-11 (7*) Miss E J Jones, *heading midfield, drvn aing hfwy, lost tch fnl 4 fs........*(33 to 1) 7
129⁶ OATS FOR NOTES 6-10-13 Mr M Rimell, *hld up, some hdwy fhwy, outpcd entering strt.............*(20 to 1 op 16 to 1) 8
157⁹ FLAME OF DANCE 5-11-4 T Eley, *in tch, outpcd o'r 3 fs out, eased whn btn............*(25 to 1) 9
NO SACRIFICE 4-10-5 (5*) Sophie Mitchell, *nvr a factor.*
....(33 to 1) 10
HILDENS MEMORY 6-10-13 S McNeill, *keen hold, cl up, rdn alng o'r 3 fs out, sn wknd..........*(10 to 1 op 33 to 1) 11
MOLLIE SILVERS 4-10-7 (3*) R Massey, *led aftr 3 fs, hdd 5 out, wl btn whn run wide strt............*(33 to 1) 12
53 WOTANITE 6-11-4 V Slattery, *led 3 fs, cl up till lost tch 5 out, sn beh............*(33 to 1) 13
KATHARINE'S SONG 6-10-13 R Dunwoody, *cl up, lost pl quickly entering strt, tld off...*(16 to 1 op 12 to 1) 14
OVERSEAS INVADER (Ire) 4-11-1 W McFarland, *al beh, tld off entering strt.*...................(33 to 1) 15
Dist: 4l, 5l, nk, 6l, 12l, 2½l, 1¼l, 4l, 3l, ¾l. 3m 43.20s. (15 Ran).

(Mick Fletcher), M C Pipe

TIPPERARY (IRE) (good to firm)
Thursday July 11th

192 Powers Solicitors Maiden Hurdle (4-y-o and up) £2,911 2m...........(7:30)

171⁵ FONTAINE LODGE (Ire) 6-11-2 (7*) A O'Shea, ...(7 to 2) 1
140 HAY DANCE 5-11-2² (5*) Mr W M O'Sullivan, ...(12 to 1) 2
PHARDANTE GIRL 5-11-0 M P Hourigan, ...(5 to 1) 3
DEREENGLOSS (Ire) 5-11-0 C O'Dwyer, ...(6 to 4 fav) 4
175 SPRINGWELL MAY (Ire) (bl) 4-10-11 P Carberry, ...(16 to 1) 5
142⁹ NEW WEST (Ire) 6-11-1 (5*) J Butler, ...(12 to 1) 6
117⁸ TIGERALI (Ire) 6-11-1 C F Swan, ...(7 to 1) 7
33⁸ TENDER LASS (Ire) 5-11-0 P L Malone, ...(7 to 1) 8
175 MOSHER (Ire) 4-10-9 (7*) Mrs C Harrison, ...(25 to 1) 9
132 LOCH WEE (Ire) 5-11-0 J Jones, ...(33 to 1) 10
142 BELLE OF KILBRIDE (Ire) 6-11-1 J Shortt, ...(12 to 1) pu
Dist: 6l, 2½l, 4½l, ¾l. 4m 3.80s. (11 Ran).

(ABC Syndicate), Anthony Mullins

193 Pierse Motors I.N.H. Flat Race (4-y-o and up) £2,911 2m...........(9:00)

RATHGIBBON (Ire) 5-10-13 (7*) Mr J P McNamara, (6 to 1) 1
88* CLONAGAM (Ire) 7-11-11 (3*) Mr B M Cash, ...(7 to 4 fav) 2
173 FRAU DANTE (Ire) 6-11-6 (3*) Mr K Whelan, ...(5 to 1) 3
135² FAIR SOCIETY (Ire) (bl) 5-10-8 (7*) Mr John P Moloney,
....(10 to 1) 4
159* MOONLIGHT ESCAPADE (Ire) 5-11-13 Mr P Fenton, (2 to 1) 5
MONTETAN (Ire) 5-11-1 (7*) Miss A Reilly, ...(10 to 1) 6
DOON LOVE (Ire) 4-10-2 (7*) Mr G Elliott, ...(20 to 1) 7
DRUMELLA (Ire) 4-10-7 (7*) Mr J T McNamara, ...(14 to 1) 8
Dist: 5l, 2½l, 1½l, 1l. 3m 49.90s. (8 Ran).

(Mrs Margaret Marshall), S J Treacy

DUNDALK (IRE) (firm)

Friday July 12th

194 Dromiskin Novice Hurdle (4-y-o and up) £2,397 2m 135yds.........(6:00)

178* WHEREWILITALL END (Ire) 5-11-3 (3*) U Smyth, ...(5 to 1) 1
142* FRASER CAREY (Ire) (bl) 4-11-0 C O'Dwyer, ...(11 to 8 on) 2
176* PINGO HILL (Ire) 4-11-7 J Shortt, ...(9 to 4) 3
139⁶ RONDELLI (Ire) 6-11-0 J K Kinane, ...(14 to 1) 4
DEARMISTERSHATTER (Ire) 5-10-13 M Duffy, ...(100 to 1) 5
LADY PHARDANTE (Ire) (bl) 6-10-6 (3*) D Bromley, (33 to 1) 6
Dist: 1½l, 6l, 8l, 8l. 3m 52.70s. (6 Ran).

(S P Mahon), Peter McCreery

195 Forkhill Opportunity Handicap Hurdle (0-102 4-y-o and up) £2,568 2½m 153yds........................(6:30)

WILD COUNTRY (Ire) [-] 5-10-9 (4*) S M McGovern,
....(11 to 4 fav) 1
179⁵ PLOUGH THE LEA (Ire) [-] 6-10-9 U Smyth, ...(8 to 1) 2
179 PRINCE SABI (Ire) [-] (bl) 6-10-4 (4*) R Burke, ...(20 to 1) 3
158⁵ TABU LADY (Ire) [-] (bl) 5-10-5 (2*) G Cotter, ...(6 to 1) 4
178⁵ SPECTACLE (Ire) [-] (bl) 6-10-1 (4*) A O'Shea, ...(33 to 1) 5
142⁷ CHUCK (Ire) [-] 6-11-0 (4*) D McCullagh, ...(5 to 1) 6
179 RED GLITTER (USA) [-] 6-11-13 D Bromley, ...(3 to 1) 7
92⁵ VALAMIR (Ire) [-] 6-9-8 (2*) J Butler, ...(33 to 1) 8
93⁸ CHARLIES DELIGHT (Ire) [-] 8-11-6 (4*) J O'Hare, (25 to 1) 9
92³ NATIVE BORN [-] 11-9-5 (2*) J Butler, ...(12 to 1) ur
Dist: 2½l, 2½l, 1½l, 10l. 4m 45.70s. (10 Ran).

(T Curran), Noel Meade

196 Mullacrew I.N.H. Flat Race (5-y-o and up) £2,226 2½m 153yds.......(8:30)

140² YOUNG DUBLINER (Ire) (bl) 7-11-7 (7*) Mr R Walsh,
....(13 to 8 fav) 1
133³ STRADBALLY JANE (Ire) 6-11-2 (7*) Mr Mark Walsh, (8 to 1) 2
177 DAWN INFIDEL (Ire) 6-11-9 Mr J A Nash, ...(4 to 1) 3
SUNSET DAZZLE (Ire) 8-11-11 (3*) Mr B M Cash, (100 to 30) 4
172⁶ BOREEN BOY (Ire) 6-11-7 (7*) Mr J D O'Connell, ..(10 to 1) 5
GALE GRIFFIN (Ire) 7-11-9 Mr A J Martin, ...(8 to 1) 6
34 YOUR WORSHIP (Ire) 6-11-7 (7*) Mr J Bright, ...(33 to 1) 7
95⁴ ZUZUS PETALS (Ire) 6-11-2 (7*) Mr A J Dempsey, (33 to 1) ur
Dist: 2l, 6l, ½l, 25l. 4m 45.30s. (8 Ran).

(John A Cooper), E Bolger

DOWN ROYAL (IRE) (good to firm (race 1), firm (2))
Saturday July 13th

197 Cory Towage Ltd. Maiden Hurdle (4-y-o and up) £1,370 2m...............(2:30)

180* JOHNNY'S DREAM (Ire) 6-11-9 (5*) G Cotter, ...(5 to 2 on) 1
173⁵ CORMAC LADY (Ire) 5-11-8 J K Kinane, ...(4 to 1) 2
119⁷ BENALF (Ire) 6-11-11 (3*) D T Evans, ...(33 to 1) 3
160⁵ MC CLATCHEY (Ire) 5-11-6 (7*) C Rae, ...(12 to 1) 4
DUNDORE FLASH (Ire) 4-11-7 F Woods, ...(50 to 1) 5
169 OG'S DESIRE (Ire) 5-11-8 P McWilliams, ...(50 to 1) 6
139 ASHLEY'S PRINCESS (Ire) 4-10-13 (3*) B Bowens, (10 to 1) f
Dist: 6l, 15l, 20l, 1l. (Time not taken) (7 Ran).

(Mrs James Nicholson), D T Hughes

198 Northern Ireland Tourist Board Handicap Chase (4-y-o and up) £2,740 2½m ....(4:00)

204 ANY PORT [-] 6-9-7 P L Malone, ...(14 to 1) 1
SWALLOWS NEST [-] 9-11-7 W T Slattery, ...(4 to 1) 2
TRYFIRION [-] 7-11-11 L P Cusack, ...(3 to 1 fav) 3
BALYARA (Ire) [-] (bl) 6-10-9 (3*) Mr B M Cash, ...(5 to 1) 4
136* BALD JOKER [-] 11-9-81 F Woods, ...(8 to 1) 5
63⁵ YOUNG ENTRY [-] 10-9-7 P McWilliams, ...(14 to 1) 6
138³ MIDNIGHT HOUR (Ire) [-] 7-10-10 C O'Dwyer, ...(4 to 1) 7
BALLINABOOLA GROVE [-] 9-9-2 (5*) T Martin, ...(12 to 1) 8
94* CABBERY ROSE [-] 8-9-11 (5*) G Cotter, ...(10 to 1) 9
Dist: 4l, nk, ½l, 8l. (Time not taken) (9 Ran).

(J H Lowry), A J Martin

GOWRAN PARK (IRE) (good to yielding)
Saturday July 13th

199 Mill Wheel I.N.H. Flat Race (4-y-o and up) £2,740 2m...................(8:30)

MAGS DWYER (Ire) 6-11-9 Mr P Fenton, ...(10 to 1) 1
159⁴ GALE HAMSHIRE (Ire) 7-11-9 Mr A J Martin, ...(6 to 1) 2
115⁵ FRESHFIELD GALE (Ire) 6-11-2 (7*) Mr A C Coyle, (14 to 1) 3
120³ CARNACREEVA GANE (Ire) 5-11-5 (3*) Mr B M Cash,
....(5 to 1) 4
MY BLACKBIRD (Ire) 4-11-3⁸ (7*) Mr D L Bolger, (3 to 1 fav) 5
GOOD VISIBILITY (Ire) 5-11-8 Mr D Marnane, ...(8 to 1) 6
BLAZING ARROW (Ire) 5-11-6 (7*) Mr T N Cloke, ...(14 to 1) 7

```
120  EASTERN CUSTOM (Ire) 5-11-5 (3*) Mr R O'Neill, ... (7 to 1)     8
144  MALICE 10-11-2 (7*) Miss U Corcoran, ..........(12 to 1)         9
     LOCAL RACE (Ire) 7-11-7 (7*) Mr B N Doyle, ......(20 to 1)      10
     PRYZON (Ire) 4-10-13 (3*) Mr K Whelan, ..........(20 to 1)      11
120⁹ RAHANINE MELODY (Ire) 4-10-9 (7*) Mr P J Crowley,
     ......................................(20 to 1)                 12
     CUBAN SHOES (Ire) 6-11-7 (7*) Mr M G Coleman, ...(8 to 1)       13
177  LISCAHILL BREEZE (Ire) 7-11-9 Mr H F Cleary, ... (12 to 1)      14
     HAND CARE (Ire) 5-11-1 (7*) Mr K M Roche, ......(14 to 1)       15
133  SARAH'S VISION (Ire) 5-11-5 (3*) Mr E Norris, ......(8 to 1)    16
144⁷ JOLLY SIGNAL (Ire) 5-11-1 (7*) Mr J Cullen, ......(20 to 1)     pu
Dist: 1½l, 5l, 7l, 1½l. 3m 42.70s. (17 Ran).
```
(M Wynne), J J Lennon

200 Prix du Lion d'Angers Handicap Hurdle (0-116 4-y-o and up) £2,740 2m (9:00)

```
     AN MAINEACH (Ire) [-] 7-11-0 (5*) J M Donnelly, ....(6 to 1)     1
     NANNAKA (USA) [-] 6-11-5 T P Treacy, ..........(5 to 4 on)       2
     KAWA-KAWA [-] 9-11-1 C F Swan, ................(4 to 1)          3
96³  PHARDY (Ire) [-] 5-10-7 C O'Dwyer, ............(5 to 2)          4
Dist: 5l, 15l, 15l. 3m 46.20s. (4 Ran).
```
(W T Tootgill), Capt D G Swan

SOUTHWELL (firm)
Saturday July 13th
Going Correction: NIL

201 BBC Radio Lincolnshire Novices' Chase Class D (5-y-o and up) £4,354 3m 110yds. (6:40)

```
     NOTABLE EXCEPTION 7-11-0 P Niven, al prmnt, led tenth,
     drvn out, fnshd lme...............(3 to 1 tchd 100 to 30)       1
164⁵ CUCHULLAINS GOLD (Ire) 8-11-0 R Dunwoody, mid-div,
     hdwy to chase ldrs 8th, rdn 3 out, wknd r-in.
     ..........................................(11 to 1 op 10 to 1)  2
     THE WEST'S ASLEEP 11-11-0 D Morris, prmnt, drvn alng 3
     out, wknd.........................................(12 to 1)     3
147⁴ DUSTYS TRAIL (Ire) 7-10-7 (7*) Mr R Thornton, hld up, hdwy
     7th, wkng whn blun 2 out.................(14 to 1 op 10 to 1)   4
     STRONG CASE (Ire) 8-11-0 D Bridgwater, prmnt, hit 4th,
     disputing ld whn f 6th. (5 to 4 fav op 6 to 4 tchd 13 to 8)     f
164³ BUCKANEER BAY 9-11-0 J Osborne, hld up, hdwy hlwy,
     wknd 14th, tld off whn pld up bef 4 out. (20 to 1 op 16 to 1)   pu
     PACIFIC POWER 6-11-0 D Byrne, beh hlwy, pld up bef 13th.
     ..........................................(40 to 1 op 33 to 1)  pu
168  SPANISH MONEY (Ire) 9-10-11 (3*) K Gaule, led to 6th, wknd
     8th, tld off whn pld up bef tenth.......(50 to 1 op 33 to 1)    pu
153⁹ PRIESTHILL (Ire) 7-10-7 (7*) Miss S Higgins, prmnt, led 6th to
     tenth, wknd quickly appr 3 out, beh whn pld up bef last.
     ..........................................(50 to 1 op 33 to 1)  pu
     THE GALLOPIN'MAJOR (Ire) 6-11-0 N Smith, hld up, mode-
     rate prog hlwy, beh whn pld up bef 4 out.
     ..........................................(10 to 1 op 8 to 1)   pu
     PENDIL'S DELIGHT 7-10-9 C Llewellyn, tld off hlwy, pld up
     bef 13th..................................(6 to 1 tchd 11 to 2) pu
Dist: 7l, 5l, 8l. 6m 32.20s. a 38.20s (11 Ran).
```
(Roland Hope), Mrs M Reveley

202 East Midlands Electricity Lincoln Handicap Chase Class E (0-110 5-y-o and up) £4,445 2½m 110yds. (7:10)

```
127* NOCATCHIM [90] 7-10-8 A S Smith, prmnt, led 3rd to 7th, led
     tenth, wnt clr aftr 4 out, styd on wl..............(5 to 1)     1
154³ ANDRELOT [110] (bl) 9-11-12 R Dunwoody, ran in snatches,
     mstk and lost pl 8th, hdwy 3 out, styd on r-in.....(100 to 30 jt-
     fav op 7 to 2 tchd 3 to 1)                                      2
     PIMS GUNNER (Ire) [110] 8-12-0 A Dobbin, mid-div, hdwy
     hlwy, no extr appr last................(6 to 1 op 5 to 1)       3
     ARCTIC LIFE (Ire) [100] 7-11-4 J Osborne, led to 3rd, led 7th
     to tenth, rdn and wknd 3 out.............(100 to 30 jt-
     fav op 3 to 1 tchd 7 to 2)                                      4
106⁴ BEAT THE RAP [82] 10-10-0 Richard Guest, not jump wl, al
     beh, tld off..............................(33 to 1 op 25 to 1)  5
165⁴ SWORD BEACH [105] 12-11-9 P Niven, prmnt till wknd 11th,
     wl beh whn f last...................(4 to 1 op 7 to 2 tchd 9 to 2) f
188  TRUSS [87] 9-10-5 R Supple, hld up, al rear, tld off whn pld up
     bef 3 out.................................(9 to 1 op 7 to 1)    pu
154  SEAL KING [90] 11-10-8 A P McCoy, prmnt, rdn 11th, sn lost
     pl, beh whn pld up bef 3 out.
     ......................................(11 to 1 op 10 to 1 tchd 12 to 1) pu
Dist: 2l, 2½l, 20l, 24l. 5m 15.20s. a 15.20s (8 Ran).
```
(R E Gray), K A Morgan

203 Promota Novices' Hurdle Class E (4-y-o and up) £2,326 3m 110yds. (7:40)

```
145² ORDOG MOR (Ire) 7-10-12 D Byrne, keen, led 5th, sn clr,
     eased r-in...............(3 to 1 op 7 to 2 tchd 11 to 4)        1
168* RIVER MOON 6-11-12 J Osborne, led to 5th, rdn 3 out, styd
     on same pace.......(9 to 1 jt-fav op 2 to 1 tchd 5 to 2)       2
145* WYNBEG 5-11-5 S Wynne, prmnt, rdn 4 out, kpt on one
     pace....................................(3 to 1 tchd 4 to 1)   3
163³ TREMBLE 7-10-9 (3*) D Parker, prmnt to 9th, tld off r-in.
     .................................................(25 to 1)     4
```

```
153  COOLMOREEN (Ire) 8-10-7 (5*) Chris Webb, hld up in tch, rdn
     8th, sn beh, tld off.......................(50 to 1 op 33 to 1) 5
164  QUIXALL CROSSETT 11-10-7 (5*) Mr M H Naughton, beh
     whn hmpd 3rd, tld off when pld up bef 9th..........(50 to 1)    pu
155* TIPPING THE LINE 6-11-2 D Bridgwater, in tch, lost pl 6th,
     sn pld up...........(9 to 4 jt-fav op 2 to 1 tchd 5 to 2)       pu
129  SWEET TALKER (Ire) 4-10-8 D Leahy, prmnt, hit 4th, sn lost pl,
     tld off whn pld up bef 9th...............(50 to 1 op 33 to 1)   pu
Dist: 14l, 9l, 30l, dist. 6m 14.40s. a 32.40s (8 Ran).
```
(M R Johnson), M G Meagher

204 Ian Loftus Printing Handicap Hurdle Class D (0-125 4-y-o and up) £2,835 2½m 110yds. (8:10)

```
106⁵ FLUIDITY (USA) [89] 8-10-5 R Supple, hld up, gd hdwy appr
     last, ran on wl to ld cl hme.
     ......................(14 to 1 op 10 to 1 tchd 16 to 1)         1
70*  SUPERHOO [91] 5-10-4 B Fenton, led 3rd, rdn and hdd 2 out,
     led r-in, ct cl hme......................(4 to 1 op 7 to 2)     2
105² SHIKAREE (Ire) [111] 12-11-4 A Thornton, chsd ldrs, rdn
     hlwy, led 2 out, hdd r-in, kpt on.......(9 to 4 fav op 3 to 1)  3
150⁴ GOVERNOR DANIEL [97] 5-10-5 (5*) Michael Brennan, chsd
     ldrs, rdn 2 out, styd on r-in..................(9 to 2)         4
     ELFLAA (Ire) [115] 5-12-0 R Dunwoody, prmnt, ev ch whn hit 2
     out, hrd rdn appr last, wknd r-in........(5 to 1 op 7 to 2)     5
82³  GONE BY [101] (bl) 8-11-3 A P McCoy, hld up, styd on 3 out,
     nvr rch ldrs............................(11 to 2 tchd 6 to 1)   6
     GEORGE ASHFORD (Ire) [88] 6-10-4 A S Smith, led to 3rd,
     beh hlwy, tld off..................(14 to 1 op 12 to 1 tchd 16 to 1) 7
148⁶ HACKETTS CROSS [105] 8-11-7 Richard Guest, hld up,
     effrt 7th, wknd 3 out, pld up bef nxt...............(20 to 1)   pu
Dist: Nk, ¾l, 1½l, 12l, 6l, 20l. 5m 13.90s. a 27.90s (8 Ran).
```
(DSM (Demolition Services (Midlands) Ltd)), J G M O'Shea

205 Paper Rose Greeting Cards Selling Handicap Hurdle Class G (0-95 4-7-y-o) £2,419 2m (8:40)

```
128  DENOMINATION (USA) [81] 4-11-6 D Bridgwater, hld up,
     hdwy 3 out, led last, ran on wl...............(4 to 1)          1
152⁵ SIAN WYN [82] 6-11-10 R Dunwoody, chsd ldrs, led 2 out to
     last, sn outpcd........(9 to 4 fav op 5 to 2 tchd 3 to 1)       2
166  IRIE MON (Ire) [80] 4-11-2 (3*) K Gaule, hld up, drvn alng 3 out,
     kept able to chal.............................(16 to 1)         3
101³ MINNESOTA FATS [67] 4-10-6 Gary Lyons, mid-div, rdn 3
     out, ran on one pace frm nxt...........(9 to 1 op 7 to 1)       4
45⁴  HIGH FLOWN (USA) [77] 4-11-2 W Fry, in tch, rdn 3 out, no
     imprsn.................................(14 to 1 op 12 to 1)     5
106⁶ THE EXECUTOR [76] 6-11-4 D Skyrme, hld up, styd on frm 2
     out..............................................(5 to 1)      6
150  BOOST [65] 4-10-4 S Wynne, hld up in tch, rdn 3 out, styd on
     same pace.......................................(33 to 1)      7
     HERETICAL MISS [75] 6-11-3 A P McCoy, led to second, led
     5th to 2 out, wknd......(4 to 1 op 8 to 1 tchd 10 to 1)         8
     PACIFIC OVERTURE [61] 4-10-0 P McLoughlin, nvr trble ldrs.
     ........................................(33 to 1)              9
101² BETABETCORBETT [77] 5-11-2 T Eley, led second to 5th,
     wknd appr last.........(13 to 2 op 5 to 1 tchd 7 to 1)          10
49   JAVA SHRINE (USA) [79] (bl) 5-11-4 S McNeill, prmnt to 4th,
     sn tld off....................(20 to 1, beh whn uns rdr appr last) ur
146  ARROGANT BOY [58] 7-9-9² (7*) Miss R Clark, chsd ldrs, rdn
     and wknd 3 out, beh whn uns rdr appr nxt...........(14 to 1 op 16 to 1) ur
     RAGAMUFFIN ROMEO [68] 7-10-7 (3*) R Massey, al rear, tld
     off whn pld up bef last, dismounted.....(14 to 1 op 16 to 1)    pu
Dist: 2l, 3½l, 3l, 1l, nk, 3l, 1½l, 2l, ½l, dist. 3m 56.70s. a 10.70s (13 Ran).
```
(Martin Pipe Racing Club), M C Pipe

206 Oak Handicap Hurdle Class F (0-100 4-y-o and up) £2,558 3m 110yds (9:10)

```
     DAWN FLIGHT [87] (bl) 7-11-4 J Osborne, al prmnt, led 2 out,
     styd on wl.................(11 to 1 op 10 to 1 tchd 12 to 1)    1
128⁴ WORDY'S WIND [69] 7-10-0 B Fenton, hld up, hdwy 4 out, kpt
     on r-in..............................(33 to 1 op 20 to 1)       2
125⁷ SCRABO VIEW (Ire) [96] (bl) 8-11-13 R Supple, al prmnt, ev ch
     2 out, no extr r-in................(9 to 1 op 6 to 1)           3
     BAHRAIN QUEEN (Ire) [89] 8-11-6 M Ranger, hld up, effrt
     3 out, no imprsn.............(9 to 1 op 7 to 1 tchd 10 to 1)    4
144⁶ MISS SOUTER [70] (v) 7-10-1 D Bridgwater, prmnt, mstk and
     wknd 2 out..............(11 to 1 op 10 to 1 tchd 12 to 1)       5
155  DERRING BRIDGE [91] 6-11-8 A P McCoy, chsd ldrs, led 3
     out to nxt, sn wknd.....(9 to 4 fav op 7 to 2 tchd 4 to 1)      6
146  THEY ALL FORGOT ME [69] 9-10-0 Miss C Dyson, beh hlwy,
     tld off.................................(9 to 1 op 25 to 1)     7
     GUNMAKER [82] 7-10-13 Mr J L Llewellyn, hld up in tch, effrt
     6th, wknd 4 out.......................(5 to 1 tchd 6 to 1)      8
146* MILZIG (USA) [74] 7-10-5 C Llewellyn, al rear.
     .................................................(7 to 2 op 4 to 1) 9
146⁶ RIVA'S BOOK (USA) [86] 5-10-13 D Byrne, made most to 4
     out, sn wknd...........(9 to 1 op 7 to 1 tchd 10 to 1)          10
125  STRONG JOHN (Ire) [85] 8-10-13 (3*) K Gaule, prmnt, led 4
     out to nxt, wknd.......................(9 to 1 op 10 to 1)      11
Dist: 1¼l, 4l, 10l, 3½l, ¾l, 6l, sht-hd, 1½l, 8l, 1¼l. 6m 16.60s. a 34.60s (11
Ran).
```
(Mrs Carol Davis), J R Jenkins

LES LANDES (JER) (good)
Sunday July 14th

207 Carling Channel Islands Champion Hurdle (4-y-o and up) £1,050 2m 1f
.... (3:00)

141*	WOLLBOLL 6-12-0 V Smith, ...(6 to 4 on)	1
	MAPLE DANCER 10-12-0 G Shenkin, ...(6 to 4)	2
141³	CLEAR HOME 10-12-0 B Powell, ...(6 to 1)	3

Dist: 10l, nk. 4m 0.70s. (3 Ran).

(M J Weaver), J S O Arthur

DOWN ROYAL (IRE) (firm)
Monday July 15th

208 Oriel Training Services (Mares) Novices' Hurdle (4-y-o and up) £1,370 2m
.... (3:00)

89³	LIMAHEIGHTS (Ire) 6-11-3 (3") D T Evans, ...(4 to 1)	1
161³	TIFFANY VICTORIA (Ire) 6-11-0 T J Mitchell, .. (7 to 4 fav)	2
169⁵	CLAIRE ME (Ire) 7-11-1 (5") T Martin, ...(8 to 1)	3
33⁵	PETITE MEWS (Ire) 5-11-2 (3") Mr B R Hamilton, .. (10 to 1)	4
	RATHNALLY STAR (Ire) 5-10-12 (7") J M Maguire, .(33 to 1)	5D
	BEASTY MAXX (Ger) 4-10-8 (5") G Cotter, ...(8 to 1)	5
	WINDMILL STAR (Ire) 5-11-5 P McWilliams, ...(16 to 1)	6
	KNOCANS PRIDE (Ire) 7-11-6 P L Malone, ...(33 to 1)	7
162⁴	BETTER STYLE (Ire) 5-11-9 L P Cusack, ...(4 to 1)	pu

Dist: 7l, 8l, 3l, 20l. (Time not taken) (9 Ran).

(Ivy Syndicate), Michael Flynn

209 Johnnie Walker Beginners Chase (5-y-o and up) £1,370 2m.......... (4:00)

93⁶	BALLYVERANE 10-11-7 (7") C Rae, ...(12 to 1)	1
158⁴	CUBAN QUESTION (bl) 9-11-9 (5") G Cotter, ... (7 to 4 fav)	2
131⁴	BALLINAGREEN (Ire) 6-12-0 H Rogers, ...(7 to 2)	3
20³	JUMPING FOR JOY (Ire) 7-11-11 (3") U Smyth, ...(9 to 4)	4
94	TREENS FOLLY (Ire) 7-11-7 (7") Mr G Elliott, ...(14 to 1)	5
195⁵	SPECTACLE (Ire) (bl) 6-11-11 (3") D Bromley, ...(20 to 1)	f
	JESSIE'S BOY (Ire) 7-11-7 (7") Mr G Gallagher, ...(16 to 1)	ur

Dist: 1½l, 6l, 5l, dist. (Time not taken) (7 Ran).

(R Rae), P F Graffin

210 Satzenbrau INH Flat Race (4-y-o and up) £1,370 2m................. (5:30)

159⁶	TWENTYFIVEQUID (Ire) 5-11-13 Mr P F Graffin, ...(6 to 1)	1
	SHARP ELVER (Ire) 4-10-9 (7") Mr A J Dempsey, ... (6 to 1)	2
180³	FANE PATH (Ire) 4-11-7 Mr G J Harford, ...(4 to 4 fav)	3
172³	MONTE'S EVENING (Ire) 8-11-11 (3") Mr P J Casey, (3 to 1)	4
23⁵	KITZBERG (Ire) 5-11-1 (7") Mr G Clugston, ...(8 to 1)	5
159	PROUDSTOWN LADY (Ire) 5-11-3 (5") Mr D McGoona,	
	....	6
	FLUMERI (Ire) 6-11-2 (7") Mr W Ewing, ...(12 to 1)	7
	RUN SPARKY (Ire) 4-10-9 (7") Mr G Elliott, ...(10 to 1)	8
159	SUPER SECRETARY (Ire) (bl) 5-11-1 (7") Mr S J Mahon,	
	....	9
	STRONG HOPE (Ire) 6-11-11 (3") Mr B R Hamilton, (10 to 1)	10
	DUNMORE SUNSET (Ire) 4-11-0 (7") Mr M P Browne,	
	....(25 to 1)	pu

Dist: 1½l, 4l, 3l, 20l. (Time not taken) (11 Ran).

(P F Graffin), P F Graffin

KILLARNEY (IRE) (good to firm)
Monday July 15th

211 Bourne Vincent Memorial Park Maiden Hurdle (4-y-o and up) £3,425 2m 1f
.... (6:00)

	TARAJAN (USA) (bl) 4-11-7 J Shortt, ...(100 to 30)	1
	ALLATRIM (Ire) 6-11-9 R Dunwoody, ...(9 to 4 fav)	2
	JANE DIGBY (Ire) 4-11-2 C F Swan, ...(7 to 2)	3
192³	PHARDANTE GIRL (Ire) 5-11-0 M P Hourigan, ...(10 to 1)	4
	CHERRYGARTH (Ire) 5-11-5 T P Rudd, ...(12 to 1)	5
	PERFECT TIMMER 6-10-13 (7") S P Kelly, ...(10 to 1)	6
133⁷	MUSKERRY KING (Ire) 5-11-5 W T Slattery, ...(7 to 1)	7
181⁵	DIAMOND CLUSTER 6-11-3 (3") Mr K Whelan, ...(20 to 1)	8
132⁷	HONEY TRADER 4-11-2 J P Broderick, ...(12 to 1)	9
173⁶	SOLAR CASTLE (Ire) (bl) 6-10-8 (7") A O'Shea, ...(33 to 1)	10
183	NUAN (Ire) 6-11-1 C O'Dwyer, ...(20 to 1)	11
173⁴	BRIGHT SHARES (Ire) 6-11-1 K F O'Brien, ...(10 to 1)	f
90⁵	BURGEES HILL VI 11-11-6 F Woods, ...(14 to 1)	pu

Dist: 1½l, 1l, 6l, 1l. 3m 59.90s. (13 Ran).

(Ms Maura Horan), Patrick Prendergast

212 Muckross Park Hotel Bi-Centenary Beginners Chase (5-y-o and up) £3,425 2¾m.................(8:00)

KILLARNEY (IRE) (good (races 1,2,3), good to firm (4))
Tuesday July 16th

214 Smirnoff Handicap Chase (4-y-o and up) £3,575 2m 1f............... (6:00)

131³	NATALIES FANCY [-] 10-9-10⁶ P Carberry, ...(5 to 2)	1
	ANABATIC (Ire) [-] 8-10-7 T P Rudd, ...(5 to 2)	2
	HOLIWAY STAR [-] 6-9-9⁴ C F Swan, ...(5 to 4 on)	f

Dist: Dist. 4m 8.30s. (3 Ran).

(Michael Dixon), James Joseph Mangan

215 Hotel Europa Novice Chase (4-y-o and up) £3,425 2½m.............. (6:30)

	SAVUTI (Ire) 7-11-1 (7") M D Murphy, ...(12 to 1)	1
65⁵	NORDIC THORN (Ire) 6-12-0 K F O'Brien, ...(5 to 2)	2
94	DORANS WAY (Ire) 5-11-1 J P Broderick, ...(5 to 2)	3
114⁷	KING TYRANT (Ire) 7-11-8 P Carberry, ...(25 to 1)	4
	WINTER BELLE (USA) (bl) 8-11-8 J Shortt, ...(10 to 9 on)	ur

Dist: 11l, nk, 20l. 5m 5.10s. (5 Ran).

(Mrs David V Tipper), W J Burke

216 Great Southern Hotel Long Distance Handicap Hurdle (4-y-o and up) £3,425 2¾m.......................... (7:00)

130⁷	LE GRANDE BARD (Ire) [-] 7-11-3 T P Treacy, ...(4 to 1)	1
158²	MERRY PEOPLE (Ire) [-] 8-12-0 T Horgan, ... (11 to 10 fav)	2
	BETH'S APPARITION (Ire) [-] 6-11-8 C F Swan, ...(9 to 2)	3
118³	THE SOUTH POLE INN (Ire) [-] 4-9-0 (7") A O'Shea, (16 to 1)	4
113⁴	ANDROS DAWN (Ire) [-] (bl) 6-10-0 P Carberry, ...(4 to 1)	5

Dist: 2l, ¾l, 12l, 15l. 5m 33.40s. (5 Ran).

(Mrs D J Tarrant), Mrs F M O'Brien

217 Whitegates Hotel Ladies QR INH Flat Race (6-y-o and up) £3,082 2m 1f
.... (8:30)

177³	OX EYE DAISY (Ire) 8-11-2 (7") Miss A L Crowley, (9 to 4 fav)	1
	PLEASE NO TEARS 9-11-9 Mrs C Barker, ...(5 to 1)	2
	QUIET ONE 11-11-2 (7") Miss U Corcoran, ...(14 to 1)	3
	GAIN CONTROL (Ire) 7-11-2 (7") Miss O Hayes, ...(20 to 1)	4
177⁴	GALATASORI JANE (Ire) 6-11-2 (7") Mrs H O'Keeffe-Daly,	
	....	5
142⁸	HE'S NO ANGEL (Ire) 6-12-0 Miss M Olivefalk, ...(4 to 1)	6
	CHESTNUT SHOON 10-11-2 (7") Miss C Gould, ...(25 to 1)	7
183	GOLD DEVON (Ire) 6-11-7 (7") Mrs C Doyle, ...(16 to 1)	8
91⁶	DUCHESS OF PADUA (Ire) 6-11-2 (7") Mrs R Hickey,	
	....	9
	SPEEDY DAN (Ire) 8-11-2 (7") Miss S J Leahy, ...(10 to 1)	10
	LEZIES LAST (Ire) 6-11-8⁶ (7") Mrs S O'Connor, ..(14 to 1)	11
	BOTHA BOCHT 9-11-2 (7") Miss J Lee, ...(25 to 1)	12
	NEARHAAN 6-11-7 (7") Miss A Sloane, ...(20 to 1)	13

Dist: ¾l, 7l, 14l, 2l. 3m 59.10s. (13 Ran).

	BLAZING SPECTACLE (Ire) 6-12-0 R Dunwoody,	
	....(11 to 8 on)	1
	PEAFIELD (Ire) 7-11-6 P M Verling, ...(16 to 1)	2
63⁴	FRIDAY THIRTEENTH (Ire) 7-11-6 A Powell, ...(16 to 1)	3
114⁴	RASCAL STREET LAD (Ire) 8-11-1 J F Titley, ...(14 to 1)	4
65³	COOLGREEN 8-11-6 S H O'Donovan, ...(10 to 1)	5
136³	SPINDANTE (Ire) 6-11-1 J Shortt, ...(7 to 1)	6
171⁷	ICANTELYA (Ire) 7-12-0 T P Treacy, ...(6 to 1)	7
	HAVE A DROP (Ire) 6-10-8 (7") A O'Shea, ...(25 to 1)	8
	TINERANA BOY (Ire) 6-11-6 C F Swan, ...(8 to 1)	9
93⁴	MURPHY'S LADY (Ire) (bl) 7-11-1 T J Murphy, ...(14 to 1)	10
94	SIMPLY PERKY (Ire) 5-11-2 J P Broderick, ...(10 to 1)	11
65	NAGLE RICE (Ire) 7-10-8 (7") M D Murphy, ...(33 to 1)	12
	JULY SCHOON 11-10-13 (7") Miss C Gould, ...(33 to 1)	pu

Dist: 5l, 5½l, 2l, 8l. 5m 47.70s. (13 Ran).

(Michael W J Smurfit), D K Weld

213 Manny Bernstein INH Flat Race (4 & 5-y-o) £3,082 2m 1f............. (9:00)

	THAT'S THE SUSS (Ire) 4-10-9 (7") Mr D A Harney, (8 to 1)	1
175⁷	TELL THE COUNTRY (Ire) 4-10-9 (7") Mr A C Coyle,	
	....(4 to 1)	2
	ROSIE FLYNN (Ire) 4-10-9 (7") Mr Sean O O'Brien.. (6 to 1)	3
	WILL I OR WONT I (Ire) 5-11-1 (7") Mr M J Walsh, ..(9 to 1)	4
77⁷	PERAMBIE (Ire) 4-10-9 (7") Miss A L Crowley, ...(11 to 2)	5
	PAUL (Ire) 4-11-0 (7") Mr John P Moloney, ...(20 to 1)	6
	KINCORA (Ire) 5-11-13 Mr J A Nash, ...(7 to 1)	7
	AMERICAN CONKER (Ire) 5-11-1 (7") Mr J T McNamara,	
	....(14 to 1)	8
	MORNING MIST (Ire) 4-11-0 (7") Mr S M Duffy, ...(10 to 2)	9
	SEXTON'S MIRROR (Ire) 4-11-7 Miss M Olivefalk, ..(8 to 1)	10
	BRINNY PRINCESS (Ire) 5-11-5 (3") Mr K Whelan, (16 to 1)	11
	INCH VALLEY (Ire) 7-11-1 Mr I M Burke, ...(14 to 1)	12
	MORNINGNOONANDNITE (Ire) 4-11-1 (7") Mr B N Doyle,	
	....(12 to 1)	13

Dist: Sht-hd, 3½l, 3½l, 1l. 4m 4.80s. (13 Ran).

(Mrs John W Nicholson), John W Nicholson

(L Hayden), E Sheehy

KILLARNEY (IRE) (good to firm)
Wednesday July 17th

218 Doyle Brothers' Chase (5-y-o and up) £4,042 2½m..................(2:30)

KELLY'S PEARL 9-11-6 C F Swan, ... (9 to 4)	1
138⁴ MICKS DELIGHT (Ire) 6-11-4 N Williamson, ...(Evens to 1)	2
138⁷ LOFTUS LAD (Ire) 8-11-6 (5*) Mr W M O'Sullivan, ...(5 to 2)	3

Dist: 1½l, 8l. 5m 7.50s. (3 Ran).

(Seamus O'Farrell), A P O'Brien

219 Whitbread Handicap Chase (0-102 4-y-o and up) £3,082 2m 1f.... (3:00)

NOBODYS SON [-] 10-11-3 P Carberry, ...(8 to 1)	1
98 SILENTBROOK [-] 11-9-1 (7*) A O'Shea, ...(9 to 2)	2
143⁵ SANDY FOREST LADY (Ire) [-] 7-10-5 T P Treacy, ...(8 to 1)	3
177 BARNAMIRE BAY (Ire) [-] 7-9-11 (7*) M D Murphy, (20 to 1)	4
AON DOCHAS (Ire) [-] 7-10-7¹ D H O'Connor, ..(14 to 1)	5
116² HANNIES GIRL (Ire) [-] 7-10-7 (7*) L J Fleming, ...(9 to 2)	6
98⁴ COOLADERRA LADY [-] 10-9-7 F Woods, ...(8 to 1)	7
116⁴ NO SIR ROM [-] 10-9-10 T Horgan, ...(12 to 1)	8
SISTER ROSZA (Ire) [-] (bl) 8-11-8 T J Murphy, ...(12 to 1)	9
136⁷ GREEK MAGIC [-] 9-10-7 A Powell, ...(14 to 1)	10
116* RATES RELIEF (Ire) [-] 6-11-4 (7*) Mr G Elliott, ...(7 to 2 fav)	f
BEST VINTAGE [-] 12-11-7 (7*) Mr J G Sheehan, ..(20 to 1)	ur

Dist: 2½l, hd, 9l, 2½l. 4m 11.50s. (12 Ran).

(R A Browne), Daniel O'Connell

220 Murphy's Irish Stout Handicap Hurdle (4-y-o and up) £12,900 2m 1f....(3:30)

KHAYRAWANI (Ire) [-] 4-10-1 C O'Dwyer, ...(2 to 1)	1
162² NORTHERN FANCY (Ire) [-] 5-9-7 F Woods, ...(13 to 2)	2
143² BOB THE YANK (Ire) [-] 6-9-12 N Williamson, ...(7 to 1)	3
JUST LITTLE [-] 4-10-5 C F Swan, ...(5 to 4 fav)	4
161⁷ WESPERADA (Ire) [-] 4-10-7 P Carberry, ...(7 to 1)	5

Dist: 4l, 8l, 8l, dist. 4m 13.20s. (5 Ran).

(John P McManus), P Burke

KILLARNEY (IRE) (good to firm)
Thursday July 18th

221 Dawn Fresh Cream Novice Hurdle (4-y-o and up) £3,767 2m 1f.......(2:30)

COLM'S ROCK 5-11-1 C F Swan, ...(10 to 9 on)	1
194² FRASER CAREY (Ire) (bl) 4-11-2 C O'Dwyer, ...(5 to 4)	2
211¹⁰ HONEY TRADER 4-10-9 J P Broderick, ...(12 to 1)	3
MULTIPIT (Ire) 4-10-9 N Williamson, ...(12 to 1)	4
BEN ORE 6-10-9 (7*) A O'Shea, ...(25 to 1)	5

Dist: 1l, 12l, dist, ¾l. 4m 4.70s. (5 Ran).

(R Finnegan), A P O'Brien

222 Evening Echo Handicap Hurdle (0-109 4-y-o and up) £3,082 2m 1f..... (3:00)

134⁷ BRIGHT PROJECT (Ire) [-] 4-9-11 (7*) A O'Shea, ...(8 to 1)	1
160² DANCING CLODAGH (Ire) [-] 4-10-8 J Shortt, ...(6 to 1)	2
135* MASCOT [-] 5-11-6 P L Malone, ...(9 to 2 fav)	3
184² TEMPLEROAN PRINCE [-] 9-11-11 M Duffy, ...(9 to 2 fav)	4
176⁴ SUDDEN STORM (Ire) [-] 5-10-8 T P Treacy, ...(8 to 1)	5
142⁵ LOUGH N UISCE (Ire) [-] 6-10-3 C F Swan, ...(10 to 1)	6
182 DEGO DANCER [-] 9-9-7 T Horgan, ...(16 to 1)	7
174⁷ DONERAILE PARK [-] 9-10-12 (7*) Mr B Walsh, ...(14 to 1)	8
182 FLYING IN THE GALE [-] 5-9-7 F Woods, ...(33 to 1)	9
131 I REMEMBER IT WELL (Ire) [-] 4-9-11 J P Broderick, (8 to 1)	f
193⁴ FAIR SOCIETY (Ire) [-] (bl) 5-9-7 N Williamson, ...(13 to 2)	bd

Dist: ½l, 2l, 1l, 8l. 4m 1.90s. (11 Ran).

(Sean Geary), Donal Hassett

223 Kerry Spring Water Handicap Hurdle (0-109 4-y-o and up) £3,082 2¾m
.... (3:30)

99³ MARGUERITA SONG [-] 6-10-8 T P Treacy, ...(6 to 1)	1
MAJESTIC JOHN (Ire) [-] 5-10-8 C F Swan, ...(10 to 1)	2
140* VAIN PRINCESS (Ire) [-] 7-11-2 M P Hourigan, ..(7 to 2 fav)	3
112* FORCE THIRTEEN (Ire) [-] 5-11-2 C O'Dwyer, ...(9 to 1)	4
173⁹ RUN ROSE RUN (Ire) [-] (bl) 6-9-7 T Horgan, ...(33 to 1)	5
182⁷ RUNABOUT (Ire) [-] 4-9-13 F Woods, ...(14 to 1)	6
140³ MISS BERTAINE (Ire) [-] 7-10-4 J P Broderick, ...(8 to 1)	7
32⁵ DANGEROUS REEF (Ire) [-] 8-11-2 T P Rudd, ...(8 to 1)	8
176 THE BRIDGE TAVERN (Ire) [-] 7-10-12 (3*) J R Barry,	
........................(20 to 1)	pu

Dist: 3½l, 3l, 5½l, ¾l. 5m 42.80s. (9 Ran).

(Mrs N Mitchell), Edward P Mitchell

224 Killarney Racegoers Club INH Flat Race (4-y-o and up) £3,425 2m 1f
.... (5:00)

193³ FRAU DANTE (Ire) 6-11-10 (3*) Mr K Whelan, ...(7 to 2 fav)	1
EXPEDIENT OPTION (Ire) 6-12-1 (3*) Mr B M Cash, (6 to 1)	2
BARRIGAN'S HILL (Ire) 6-11-4 (7*) Mr John P Moloney,	
........................(33 to 1)	3
177* CELIO LUCY (Ire) (bl) 6-11-6 (7*) Mr R Walsh, ...(11 to 2)	4
144³ ROLL OVER (Ire) 6-11-11 (7*) Mr A C Coyle, ...(5 to 1)	5
173² SLAVE GALE (Ire) 5-11-5 (7*) Mr Sean O O'Brien, ...(5 to 1)	6
THAI ELECTRIC (Ire) 5-11-5 (7*) Mr A Fleming, ...(8 to 1)	7
STRICT TEMPO (Ire) 7-11-4 (7*) Mr G Elliott, ...(14 to 1)	8
99² MAJOR GALE (Ire) 7-11-4 (7*) Mr M D Hennessy, ...(8 to 1)	9

Dist: 5l, 2½l, ¾l, 11l. 3m 56.80s. (9 Ran).

(Mrs Austin Fenton), Austin Fenton

WORCESTER (good to firm)
Thursday July 18th
Going Correction: MINUS 0.50 sec. per fur.

225 Steve Rhodes Benefit Selling Handicap Hurdle Class G (0-90 4-y-o and up) £2,129 2½m....................(6:00)

70³ JENNYELLEN (Ire) [90] 7-12-0 P Carberry, hld up in tch, hit 5th, led appr 2 out, sn clr.	
........................(5 to 2 fav op 11 to 4 tchd 7 to 2)	1
YACHT CLUB [77] 14-11-1 O Pears, trkd ldrs, led 4 out, hdd appr 2 out, one pace, btn whn hit last....(9 to 1 op 5 to 1)	2
100⁵ MYLORDMAYOR [62] 9-10-0 R Farrant, in tch, styd on one pace 3 out...........(13 to 2 op 7 to 1 tchd 4 to 1)	3
206⁷ THEY ALL FORGOT ME [67] 9-10-5 Miss C Dyson, led to 1st, lost pl 5th, styd on one pace frm 3 out. (33 to 1 op 25 to 1)	4
163⁴ NORDIC CROWN (Ire) [81] (bl) 5-11-2 D Bridgwater, led 1st to 6th, rdn 3 out, sn btn............(4 to 1 op 2 to 1)	5
VEXFORD MODEL [65] 6-10-3³ W McFarland, mid-div, nvr nr to chal........................(10 to 1 op 25 to 1)	6
163⁵ SOVEREIGN NICHE (Ire) [83] 8-11-4 (3*) D Walsh, prmnt, led 6th to nxt, sn wknd...........(8 to 1 op 9 to 2)	7
153⁷ SANDFORD THYNE (Ire) [70] 6-10-8 S Wynne, in tch to 5th, wl beh aftr........................(33 to 1 op 20 to 1)	8
146⁸ MARYJO [72] 7-10-10 B Fenton, mid-div, lost tch 4 out. ....(14 to 1 op 10 to 1)	9
150 SLIGHTLY SPECIAL (Ire) [65] 4-10-0 V Slattery, al beh, tld off........................(20 to 1 op 14 to 1)	10
GORT [63] 8-9-8 (7*) J Prior, prmnt till hit 4th, sn beh, tld off. ....(16 to 1 op 10 to 1)	11
COEUR BATTANT (Fr) [65] 6-10-3 B Powell, al rear, tld off. ....(14 to 1 op 20 to 1)	12
155 KHAZARI (USA) [69] 8-10-7 L Harvey, rear whn pld up bef 6th. ....(16 to 1 op 10 to 1)	pu
40⁶ LIABILITY ORDER [72] 7-10-10 M Moloney, prmnt early, tld off whn pld up bef 3 out. ...(33 to 1 op 20 to 1)	pu

Dist: 8l, 3½l, 8l, ¾l, 10l, 2½l, 3½l, nk, 10l, 21l. 4m 39.20s. a 3.20s (14 Ran).

(Liam Mulryan), F Murphy

226 Tom Moody Captain's Novices' Hurdle Class E (4-y-o and up) £2,442 2m (6:30)

150* SHAHRANI 4-11-2 D Bridgwater, made all, jumed rght and badly 5th and far, drvn out.	
........................(11 to 8 fav op 5 to 4 tchd Evens and 6 to 4)	1
107³ ZINE LANE 4-10-9 R Farrant, al in tch, second 5th, hrd rdn to press wnr frm 2 out......(11 to 4 op 7 to 2 tchd 4 to 1)	2
CHANCEY FELLA 5-10-12 R Davis, pld hrd, trkd wnr to 5th, one pace aftr.........(20 to 1 op 16 to 1)	3
SORISKY 4-10-9 Richard Guest, hld up in rear, effrt 5th, one pace frm out........................(33 to 1)	4
BACKVIEW 4-10-9 A P McCoy, prmnt, chsd wnr aftr second, wknd 5th, tld off........................(10 to 1 op 7 to 1)	5
50⁴ GENERAL SHIRLEY (Ire) 5-11-5 M Richards, hld up, hdwy 4th, wknd appr 3 out, tld off..........(10 to 1 op 6 to 1)	6
FENWICK'S BROTHER 6-10-12 O Pears, chsd ldrs till wknd 5th, tld off........................(16 to 1 op 12 to 1)	7
ROCKANGE (Ire) 7-10-7 W Marston, al beh, lost tch aftr mstk 5th, tld off........................(33 to 1 tchd 50 to 1)	8
HAND OF STRAW (Ire) 4-10-6 (3*) J Culloty, al beh, tld off. ....(14 to 1 op 7 to 1)	9
KETABI (USA) 5-10-7 (5*) S Ryan, hld up in tch, wknd aftr 4th, tld off........................(10 to 1 op 5 to 1)	10

Dist: ¾l, 14l, 5l, 16l, 19l, 6l, ¾l, dist. 3m 38.20s. b 1.80s (10 Ran).

SR: 26/18/7/-/-/-/ (A S Helaissi And Mr S Helaissi), M C Pipe

227 Tom Shervington Stag Handicap Hurdle Class E (0-115 4-y-o and up) £2,798 2½m....................(7:00)

61⁵ COAST ALONG (Ire) [89] 4-10-10 W Worthington, hld up, hdwy to ld sn aftr 3 out, rdn out. ...(8 to 1 op 7 to 1)	1
HOSTILE WITNESS (Ire) [98] 6-11-8 R Dunwoody, al prmnt, ev ch frm 5th, chlgd last, no extr.......(9 to 4 op 3 to 1)	2
152⁴ STAPLEFORD LADY [86] 8-10-10 W McFarland, hld up, mstk 5th, hdwy 4 out, one pace aftr nxt. (4 to 1 jt-fav tchd 9 to 2)	3
58⁶ FIRST CRACK [85] 11-10-9 P Carberry, hld up in rear, hdwy aftr 5th, wknd 2 out........(16 to 1 op 10 to 1)	4
OZZIE JONES [90] 5-10-11 D Bridgwater, in chasing grp, no hdwy aftr 3 out........(11 to 2 op 6 to 1 tchd 5 to 1)	5

105 BEAM ME UP SCOTTY (Ire) [88] 7-10-12 C Llewellyn, *in chasing grp till wknd appr 3 out* .... (20 to 1) 6
105³ CALL THE GUV'NOR [96] (bl) 7-11-6 J Osborne, *al towards rear, rdn 6th, nvr on terms* .... (4 to 1 jt-fav op 3 to 1) 7
81⁵ SYDNEY BARRY (NZ) [93] (bl) 11-11-3 B Powell, *sn clr, wknd quickly and hdd soon aftr 3 out, tld off.* (14 to 1 op 12 to 1) 8
155⁵ JOHNNY WILL [104] 11-12-0 J Ryan, *mstks, in chasing grp till wknd aftr 4 out, pld up r-in, dismounted.*
.... (16 to 1 op 14 to 1) pu
CAPTAIN MY CAPTAIN (Ire) [87] 8-10-11 L Harvey, *beh frm 5th, tld off whn pld up aftr 4 out.* .... (50 to 1 op 25 to 1) pu
RIVA ROCK [83] 6-10-7 A P McCoy, *in tch, wkng whn mstk 3 out, pld up lme bef last.* .... (6 to 1 tchd 7 to 1) pu
Dist: 1¾l, 6l, 3½l, 1¼l, 10l, 2½l, 20l. 4m 42.50s. a 6.50s (11 Ran).
(Peter J Douglas Engineering), P J Bevan

228 Tayhire 10th Anniversary Novices' Handicap Chase Class E (0-100 5-y-o and up) £3,556 2m .... (7:30)

152² WILLIE MAKEIT (Ire) [71] 6-10-10 (3*) J Culloty, *hld up, hdwy 6th, led appr 2 out, sn drw clr ...* (11 to 1 op 2 to 1) 1
41⁷ BIT OF A DREAM (Ire) [62] 6-10-4² Richard Guest, *in tch, hdwy to dispute ld 4 out, outpcd frm nxt.*
.... (12 to 1 tchd 14 to 1) 2
156⁹ EXCLUSION [80] 7-11-8 R Marley, *led second till aftr 3rd, lft in ld 5th, hdd appr 2 out, wknd.*
.... (11 to 1 op 10 to 1) 3
ALDINGTON CHAPPLE [77] 8-11-5 Gary Lyons, *not jump wl, hdwy 6th, ev ch whn blun 4 out, no chance aftr.*
.... (9 to 1 op 10 to 1) 4
156⁴ DUKE OF DREAMS [71] (bl) 6-10-13 B Powell, *prmnt, rdn 5 out, wknd 3 out.* .... (7 to 1 op 6 to 1) 5
167⁴ FORGETFUL [82] 7-11-10 D J Burchell, *in tch till blun 7th, sn beh.* .... (11 to 4 jt-fav op 9 to 4 tchd 3 to 1) 6
156⁸ LOFTY DEED (USA) [60] 6-9-13 (3*) K Gaule, *sn wl beh, tld off.*
.... (12 to 1 op 10 to 1) 7
WARNER FORPLEASURE [82] 10-10-3² (3*) D Walsh, *beh frm hfwy, tld off.* .... (33 to 1) 8
156 GEORGE LANE [68] 8-10-10 P Carberry, *led to second, led aftr nxt till blun and uns rdr 5th.* .... (8 to 1 op 10 to 1) ur
Dist: 14l, 3l, 8l, 2½l, 10l, 27l, dist. 3m 54.90s. a 5.90s (9 Ran).
(Old Berks Three), R T Phillips

229 Man Worcester Truck Services Novices' Hurdle Class E (4-y-o and up) £2,425 2½m .... (8:00)

150³ PRUSSIA 5-10-12 A P McCoy, *trkd ldr, led aftr 4 out, hdd appr 2 out, hrd rdn and rallied to ld cl hme.*
.... (3 to 1 fav op 100 to 30) 1
STAGE FRIGHT 5-10-12 P Carberry, *trkd ldrs, led appr 2 out, hrd rdn and edgd lft r-in, hdd cl hme.*
.... (14 to 1 op 10 to 1 tchd 16 to 1) 2
POLISH CONSUL 5-10-9 (3*) J Culloty, *hld up, mstk 4th, hdwy 6th, dsptd ld appr 3 out, one pace aftr ...* (9 to 1 op 7 to 1) 3
153* SEARCHLIGHT (Ire) (bl) 8-11-5 B Bridgwater, *led till sn aftr 4 out, rdn nxt, kpt on one pace ....* (7 to 2 op 4 to 1) 4
166⁴ POSITIVO 5-10-12 I Lawrence, *hld up, outpcd frm 4 out.*
.... (20 to 1 op 16 to 1 tchd 25 to 1) 5
103* SIGMA WIRELESS (Ire) 7-11-5 S Wynne, *hld up, hdwy 5th, rdn appr 3 out, sn btn...*(100 to 30 op 5 to 2 tchd 7 to 1) 6
153⁴ MIRAMARE 6-10-12 G Upton, *trkd ldrs till wknd appr 3 out.*
.... (50 to 1 op 33 to 1) 7
103⁷ DICKIES GIRL 6-10-7 B Fenton, *al beh, tld off.....* (50 to 1) 8
150² BIRTHDAY BOY (v) 4-11-2 J Osborne, *hld up in tch, wknd 4 out, tld off.* ...... (4 to 1 op 7 to 2 tchd 9 to 2) 9
GOODNIGHT VIENNA (Ire) 6-10-8¹ Mr M Munrowd, *al beh, tld off.* .... (33 to 1 tchd 40 to 1 and 25 to 1) 10
168 TEETER THE PEETH 6-10-12 P McLoughlin, *sn rdn, in rear whn blun 5th, tld off when pld up bef 3 out.*
.... (50 to 1 op 66 to 1 tchd 100 to 1) pu
OUR BARNY 4-10-9 O Pears, *mstk 5th, sn wl beh, tld off whn pld up bef 3 out.* .... (50 to 1 op 33 to 1) pu
Dist: Nk, 3l, 4l, 1½l, 6l, 5l, 19l, dist, dist. 4m 40.30s. a 4.30s (12 Ran).
(The Prussia Partnership), W Clay

230 Worcestershire County Cricket Club Handicap Chase Class F (0-100 5-y-o and up) £3,057 2m 7f .... (8:30)

154⁶ HURRYUP [90] 9-11-1 (3*) J Culloty, *lft in ld 1st, hdd aftr 5th, led 5 out, clr nxt, kpt on gmely und pres.*
.... (20 to 1 op 14 to 1) 1
153⁵ PHARRAGO (Ire) [72] 7-10-0 D J Burchell, *hld up in tch, cld on ldrs 4 out, hrd rdn and ran on strly to take second r-in.*
.... (20 to 1) 2
188² THE BLUE BOY [100] (bl) 8-12-0 R Johnson, *beh several ls strt, hdwy to ld aftr 5th, hdd 5 out, rallied 2 out, kpt on.*
.... (3 to 1 fav op 11 to 4) 3
188⁵ JIM VALENTINE [93] 10-11-7 W Marston, *hld up, hdwy hfwy, rdn appr 4 out, kpt on one pace ...* (10 to 1 tchd 9 to 1) 4
EVENING RAIN [80] 10-10-8 R Dunwoody, *hld up in rear, hdwy appr 4 out, sn rdn, wknd nxt.*
.... (10 to 1 op 11 to 1 tchd 14 to 1) 5
188 FATHER DOWLING [82] (v) 9-10-10 B Fenton, *beh, hdwy appr 4 out, nvr nr to chal.* .... (10 to 1 op 8 to 1) 6

188⁴ RUSTBIG BRIDGE [88] 9-10-9 (7*) Mr R Thornton, *prmnt, led briefy 5th, rdn hfwy, one pace 4 out ...* (14 to 1 op 10 to 1) 7
165³ BITACRACK [82] 9-10-10 L O'Hara, *in tch till wknd 12th.*
.... (8 to 1 op 7 to 1 tchd 9 to 1) 8
146⁷ BRAVO STAR (USA) [80] 11-10-8 R Greene, *al towards rear.*
.... (20 to 1) 9
COOL CHARACTER (Ire) [72] 8-10-0 B Powell, *beh, tld off frm hfwy....* .... (12 to 1) 10
154⁵ ARTFUL ARTHUR [73] 10-10-1 R Supple, *al beh, tld off hfwy.*
.... (33 to 1) 11
TURPIN'S GREEN [72] 13-10-0 J Osborne, *beh behind, tld off.* .... (16 to 1 op 14 to 1) 12
MAGSOOD [95] (v) 11-11-9 S Curran, *hld up, hdwy hfwy, wknd quickly and pld up, virtually pld up r-in.*
.... (9 to 1 op 7 to 1) 13
124⁴ REGARDLESS [72] 14-9-11 (3*) K Gaule, *in tch till blun tenth, sn beh, tld off.* .... (20 to 1) 14
164 MORNING BLUSH (Ire) [86] (bl) 6-11-0 D Bridgwater, *led till blun and uns rdr 1st....* (13 to 2 op 5 to 1 tchd 7 to 1) ur
PALACE YARD [78] 14-10-6⁶ Miss A Embiricos, *mid-div till lost tch tenth, tld off bef 5 out.* .... (33 to 1) pu
110⁴ TANGO'S DELIGHT [75] 8-10-3 D Leahy, *tld off hfwy, pld up bef 13th.* .... (16 to 1 op 10 to 1) pu
Dist: ¾l, 1½l, 3l, 1½l, 5l, ½l, 3l, 11l, 9l, 14l. 5m 59.50s. a 21.50s (17 Ran).
(Allan Bennett), R Dickin

231 Durham County Cricket Club Standard Open National Hunt Flat Class H (4,5,6-y-o) £1,269 2m .... (9:00)

129* ULTIMATE SMOOTHIE 4-11-8 D Bridgwater, *hld up in tch, hdwy hfwy, led o'r 2 fs out, drvn out.*
.... (2 to 1 op 11 to 10 tchd 9 to 4) 1
MR LURPAK 4-11-1 P Niven, *hld up, hdwy 5 fs out, ev ch 2 out, kpt on ins last.* .... (7 to 2 op 5 to 2) 2
PRIDEWOOD FUGGLE 6-11-4 A P McCoy, *set slow pace till hld aftr 4 fs, styd in tch, led briefly four out, rallied und pres ins last.* .... (25 to 1 op 16 to 1) 3
191⁸ OATS FOR NOTES 6-10-13 M R Rimell, *hld up in rear, hdwy o'r 3 fs out, nvr nr to chal.........* (33 to 1 op 20 to 1) 4
SUMMERWAY LEGEND 4-10-10 A Procter, *mid-div, hdwy 6 fs out, one pace fnl 3...* (12 to 1 op 10 to 1 tchd 14 to 1) 5
157* REGAL GEM (Ire) 5-11-13 B Fenton, *hld up, hdwy 5 fs out, sn rdn, wknd o'r 2 out ...* (15 to 8 fav op 9 to 4 tchd 5 to 2) 6
TWO HEARTS 4-10-10 G Upton, *trkd ldr, wknd 4 fs out.*
.... (25 to 1 tchd 33 to 1) 7
157³ SMART REMARK 4-11-1 P McLoughlin, *prmnt, rdn 6 fs out, wknd o'r 3 out.* .... (10 to 1 op 6 to 1) 8
WHERES SARAH 6-10-8 (5*) Michael Brennan, *led aftr 4 fs till four out, wknd quickly.* ..... (33 to 1 op 25 to 1) 9
COMMANDO DANCER (Ire) 4-10-8 (7*) Shaun Graham, *al beh.* .... (33 to 1) 10
NOBI E ACT (Ire) 5-11-1 (3*) J Culloty, *prmnt till wknd quickly 6 fs out.* .... (33 to 1 op 20 to 1) 11
157 FINAL SCORE (Ire) 6-10-13 R Greene, *slwly away, al beh.*
.... (33 to 1 op 25 to 1) 12
PRINCELY CHARM (Ire) 4-11-1 D Leahy, *in tch till wknd o'r 5 fs out, tld off.* .... (33 to 1 op 20 to 1) 13
Dist: ¾l, ¾l, 5l, 5l, 4l, 6l, 4l, ¾l, 1½l, 3l. 3m 55.20s. (13 Ran).
(Isca Bloodstock), M C Pipe

KILBEGGAN (IRE) (good to firm)
Friday July 19th

232 Tyrrellspass Maiden Hurdle (4-y-o and up) £2,226 2m 3f .... (6:00)

THE BOULD VIC (Ire) 4-11-7 P Carberry, ... (10 to 9 on) 1
176⁵ BISHOP'S HILL (Ire) 7-12-0 T P Treacy, ... (4 to 1) 2
178⁷ FOREST LADY (Ire) 4-10-8 (3*) D T Evans, ... (16 to 1) 3
181³ BALLY UPPER (Ire) 8-11-6 C O'Dwyer, ... (5 to 1) 4
133⁴ BIDDY HUNT (Ire) 5-11-0 J P Broderick, ... (10 to 1) 5
183 KIDSTUFF (Ire) 5-11-5 J F Titley, ... (14 to 1) 6
NINE OUT OF TEN (Ire) 5-11-0 M P Hourigan, ... (12 to 1) 7
119⁶ PHANTOMS GIRL (Ire) 5-11-0 D H O'Connor, ... (20 to 1) 8
183⁰ US FOUR (Ire) 6-11-6 W T Slattery, ... (12 to 1) 9
Dist: 3l, 2l, 5l, 4l. 4m 36.70s. (9 Ran).
(Ms P Haselden), Noel Meade

233 Tom McCormack Memorial Cup Maiden Hurdle (4-y-o and up) £2,226 2m 3f .... (6:30)

SLEETMORE GALE (Ire) 6-11-2 (7*) Mr B Hassett, .. (8 to 1) 1
178⁴ LEMOIRE (Ire) 5-11-5 (3*) D T Evans, ... (9 to 4 fav) 2
LADY DESART (Ire) 6-11-6 (3*) D J Casey, ... (7 to 1) 3
91⁴ PUNGAYNOR (Ire) 6-11-9 (5*) J M Donnelly, ... (8 to 1) 4
183⁸ DOCUMMINS (Ire) 6-11-4 K O'Brien, ... (25 to 1) 5
LISHILLAUN (Ire) 6-11-4 (5*) Susan A Finn, ... (7 to 1) 6
182⁶ ROSSI (Ire) 7-12-0 A Powell, ... (10 to 1) 7
175⁶ LOSLOMOS (Ire) 4-11-0 (7*) Mr D Duggan, ... (20 to 1) 8
175⁹ MOON-FROG 9-12-0 J H Burke, ... (25 to 1) 9
210⁵ KITZBERG (Ire) (bl) 5-11-8 T P Treacy, ... (10 to 1) 10
217⁹ DUCHESS OF PADUA (Ire) 6-11-9 W T Slattery, .. (14 to 1) 11
ASK THE FAIRIES (Ire) 8-11-6 (3*) J V Slattery, ... (20 to 1) 12
MISS MAGILLS (Ire) 5-11-8 J P Broderick, ... (25 to 1) 13

BRACKER (Ire) 4-11-7 C O'Dwyer, ... (12 to 1) 14
192⁷ TIGERALI (Ire) 6-11-9 C F Swan, ... (10 to 1) 15
192⁹ MOSHER (Ire) 4-11-0 (7") Mrs C Harrison, ... (20 to 1) 16
FIX THE SPEC (Ire) 6-11-9 (5") G Cotter, ... (16 to 1) 17
ERACLES II (Ire) 4-11-7 F Woods, ... (12 to 1) pu
Dist: Nk, 5½l, 6l, 4l. 4m 31.90s. (18 Ran).

(Donal Hassett), Donal Hassett

234 Valmet Tractors Handicap Hurdle (0-102 4-y-o and up) £2,740 3m (7:00)

173ᵃ LAURA GALE (Ire) [-] 7-11-2 T P Treacy, ... (9 to 4 j-fav) 1
195ᵃ WILD COUNTRY (Ire) [-] 5-11-1 P Carberry, ... (9 to 4 jt-fav) 2
176⁶ RATHER RECTOR (Ire) [-] 7-11-9 T Horgan, ... (8 to 1) 3
195 NATIVE BORN [-] 11-9-7 F Woods, ... (12 to 1) 4
158⁷ THE TOM'S ERROR (Ire) [-] 6-10-11 (3") J R Barry, (16 to 1) 5
195² PLOUGH THE LEA [-] 6-10-5 (3") U Smyth, ... (5 to 1) 6
171⁴ DANCING POSER (Ire) [-] (bl) 4-10-9 K F O'Brien, . . (8 to 1) 7
173⁷ JONATHAN'S ROSE (Ire) [-] 7-10-12 J K Kinane, . . (14 to 1) 8
159⁸ CLOVER MOR LASS (Ire) [-] 7-11-0 T J Mitchell, . . (12 to 1) pu
Dist: 3l, 16l, 13l, 20l. 5m 46.30s. (9 Ran).

(J M Foley), S J Treacy

235 Leinster Petroleum Handicap Hurdle (0-109 4-y-o and up) £2,740 2m 3f . . . . (7:30)

182² LEGITMAN (Ire) [-] 6-9-7 P Carberry, ... (3 to 1 fav) 1
JATINGA (Ire) [-] 8-11-1 C F Swan, ... (12 to 1) 2
118⁸ TISRARA LADY (Ire) [-] 6-11-5 C O'Dwyer, ... (9 to 2) 3
126⁶ TIBOULEN (Ire) [-] 6-10-12 (3") D T Evans, ... (8 to 1) 4
WAREZ (Ire) [-] 8-9-4 (3") D J Casey, ... (20 to 1) 5
HARVEYSLAND [-] 13-11-1 T Kinane Jnr, ... (20 to 1) 6
PASSER-BY [-] 9-11-1 (7") M P Cooney, ... (9 to 1) 7
179 RUNNING SLIPPER (Ire) [-] (bl) 6-10-5 L P Cusack, (20 to 1) 8
KUMA CHAN [-] 9-9-9 (5") J Butler, ... (20 to 1) 9
SMOOTH COUP [-] 10-11-11 F Woods, ... (8 to 1) 10
200² NANNAKA (USA) [-] 6-11-12 T P Treacy, ... (9 to 2) f
161⁵ FRENCH LADY (Ire) [-] 4-9-12 J P Broderick, ... (10 to 1) pu
Dist: 4½l, 2½l, 1½l, 25l. 4m 25.70s. (12 Ran).

(E Kavanagh), Noel Meade

236 Coola Handicap Chase (0-102 4-y-o and up) £2,911 3m 1f . . . . (8:00)

138² ROSSBEIGH CREEK [-] 9-11-6 F J Flood, ... (9 to 4 fav) 1
WATERLOO BALL (Ire) [-] 7-12-0 C F Swan, ... (8 to 1) 2
198⁵ BALD JOKER [-] 11-10-7 F Woods, ... (10 to 1) 3
93ᵃ FAYS FOLLY [-] 7-9-10 (7") R P Hogan, ... (5 to 1) 4
212 MURPHY'S LADY [-] 7-9-1 (7") Mr John P Moloney,
. . . . (12 to 1) 5
93⁵ BALLYBRIKEN CASTLE [-] 9-9-0 (7") M D Murphy, (14 to 1) 6
BALLINAVEEN BRIDGE [-] 9-9-8 P L Malone, ... (20 to 1) f
98² TIPTODICKS (Ire) [-] 6-9-0 (7") A O'Shea, ... (8 to 1) f
BEAU GRANDE [-] (bl) 8-10-12 L P Cusack, ... (4 to 1) pu
GOT NO CHOICE (Ire) [-] 6-10-1 T Horgan, ... (14 to 1) pu
Dist: ½l, 6l, 13l, 3l. 6m 22.90s. (10 Ran).

(Mrs Anne Marie Ferguson), F Flood

237 Ealan Beginners Chase (5-y-o and up) £2,740 2m 5f . . . . (8:30)

114³ BEET STATEMENT (Ire) 7-10-11 (7") Mr B Valentine,
. . . . (5 to 2 jt-fav) 1
215⁴ KING TYRANT (Ire) 7-11-9 K F O'Brien, ... (10 to 1) 2
98⁷ LET THE RIVER RUN 10-10-11 (7") R P Hogan, . . . (14 to 1) 3
MELDANTE VI (Ire) (bl) 5-10-8 (7") Mr John P Moloney,
. . . . (4 to 1) 4
BEAUFORT LASS 10-11-9 C F Swan, ... (4 to 1) 5
209 JESSIE'S BOY (Ire) 7-11-9 (5") T Martin, ... (14 to 1) 6
176 SWINGER (Ire) 7-11-2 P Carberry, ... (5 to 1) pu
Dist: 1½l, 1½l, 25l, 6l. 5m 27.70s. (7 Ran).

(W M Sheehy), W T Murphy

238 Coola Mills I.N.H. Flat Race (4-y-o and up) £2,226 2m 3f . . . . (9:00)

196³ DAWN INFIDEL (Ire) 6-11-2 (7") Mr R Walsh, ... (9 to 4 fav) 1
196² STRADBALLY JANE (Ire) 6-11-2 (7") Mr Mark Walsh, (7 to 2) 2
TIMEFORGOING (Ire) 5-11-1 (7") Mr T J Farrell, . . . (12 to 1) 3
135⁵ MARIE'S PRIDE (Ire) (bl) 5-11-7 (7") Mr John P Moloney,
. . . . (10 to 1) 4
JOSH'S FANCY (Ire) 5-11-5 (3") Mr K Whelan, ... (11 to 2) 5
RING O'ROSES (Ire) 8-11-2 (7") Mr T N Cloke, ... (12 to 1) 6
181⁷ CASTLE ELLEN BOY (Ire) 4-11-0 (7") Mr P J Gilligan,
. . . . (20 to 1) 7
MISTRESS KATE (Ire) 5-11-8 Mr A J Martin, ... (6 to 1) 8
WHAT ABOUT GARRY (Ire) 5-11-1 (7") Mr J P McNamara,
. . . . (7 to 1) 9
SWAPING LUCK (Ire) 4-11-9 Mr H F Cleary, ... (20 to 1) 10
WILLIE THE LION (Ire) 5-11-6 (7") Mr E Sheehy, . . . (20 to 1) 11
BLACKIE CONNORS (Ire) 5-11-6 (7") Miss W Oakes,
. . . . (20 to 1) 12
34⁸ FANORE (Ire) 5-11-6 (7") Mr M O'Connor, ... (20 to 1) 13
177⁶ GUILLIG LADY (Ire) 6-11-2 (7") Mr N Walsh, ... (12 to 1) 14
172⁷ CHARLIEADAMS (Ire) 6-11-11 (3") Mr B M Cash, . (20 to 1) 15
Dist: 12l, 2½l, ½l, sht-hd. 4m 21.00s. (15 Ran).

(Laurence Byrne), W P Mullins

SOUTHWELL (good to firm)
Friday July 19th
Going Correction: NIL

239 Fisherton Novices' Handicap Chase Class E (0-100 5-y-o and up) £4,425 2 ½m 110yds. (2:20)

80⁷ SASSIVER (USA) [87] 6-11-13 A P McCoy, led to 5th, cl up and hit 7th, reminders 9th and dsptd ld nxt till hit 4 out, sn drvn alng and led nr finish.
. . . . (13 to 8 fav op 11 to 10 tchd 7 to 4) 1
SAXON MAGIC [64] 6-10-4 L Harvey, hld up in tch, hdwy 9th, led 3 out, rdn appr last, hdd and no extr nr finish.
. . . . (5 to 1 op 7 to 2) 2
SAINT BENE'T (Ire) [65] (v) 8-10-5 R Farrant, prmnt, effrt 4 out, sn rdn and one pace frm nxt.
. . . . (4 to 1 op 7 to 2 tchd 5 to 1) 3
202⁵ BEAT THE RAP [70] (v) 10-11-7 N Mann, ...
. . rdn, rdn and hdd 3 out, sn btn. . . . . (8 to 1 tchd 10 to 1) 4
164⁴ DEAR EMILY [77] (v) 8-11-3 R Johnson, prmnt, rdn alng 9th, sn wknd. . . . . (9 to 2 op 4 to 1 tchd 5 to 1) 5
MR SOX [64] 5-10-0 R Davis, f 1st. . . . (20 to 1 op 14 to 1) f
Dist: ½l, 16l, 9l, 1l. 5m 26.90s. a 26.90s (6 Ran).

(P A Kelleway), P A Kelleway

240 Leeds Handicap Chase Class E (0-110 5-y-o and up) £4,498 2m. . . . . (2:50)

167³ NOBLELY (USA) [100] 9-11-6 R Farrant, cl up, led 7th till 3 out, sn hrd rdn, rallied to ld last, styd on. . . . . (11 to 8 jt-fav op 11 to 8 tchd 6 to 4) 1
43⁶ FULL O'PRAISE (NZ) [108] 9-12-0 A P McCoy, in tch, hit 6th and reminders, cl up nxt, sn rdn alng, led 3 out, jmpd badly lft next, hrd drvn and hdd last. . . . . (11 to 8 jt-fav op 7 to 4 tchd 2 to 1) 2
72⁵ MAGGOTS GREEN [80] 9-10-0 R Johnson, led to 7th, rdn alng and outpcd whn hit 4 out, kpt on frm 2 out.
. . . . (7 to 1 op 6 to 1 tchd 8 to 1) 3
CIRCULATION [80] 10-10-0 B Harding, in tch, rdn alng hfwy, sn wknd. . . . . (10 to 1 op 7 to 1) 4
Dist: 3½l, 2½l, dist. 4m 9.90s. a 15.90s (4 Ran).

(D H Cowgill), N J H Walker

241 Iggesund Timber Handicap Hurdle Class F (0-105 4-y-o and up) £2,566 2 ½m 110yds. . . . . (3:20)

156 GIMME (Ire) [97] (v) 6-11-7 (5") Michael Brennan, led aftr 1st, rdn betw last 2, ran on wl. . . . . (6 to 1 op 5 to 1) 1
206 STRONG JOHN (Ire) [85] 8-10-11 (3") D Parker, hld up, steady hdwy 4 out, chsd wnr aftr nxt, rdn betw last 2, kpt on.
. . . . (10 to 1 tchd 12 to 1 and 14 to 1) 2
LAWFUL LOVE (Ire) [80] 6-10-4 (5") Mr M H Naughton, hld up in tch, effrt 3 out, sn rdn and one pace. . (4 to 1 op 5 to 1) 3
202⁴ ARCTIC LIFE (Ire) [94] 7-11-9 J Osborne, led till aftr 1st, hit 3rd, prmnt till rdn appr 3 out, sn wknd.
. . . . (3 to 1 op 5 to 2 tchd 9 to 4) 4
CHIEFTAIN'S CROWN (USA) [94] 5-11-6 P McLoughlin, trkd ldrs, effrt 4 out, rdn nxt, sn wknd.
. . . . (2 to 1 fav op 13 to 8 tchd 5 to 2) 5
168 LEVEL EDGE [92] 5-10-11 (7") Mr T Thornton, chsd ldrs, rdn alng 4 out, sn wknd. . . . . . (4 to 1 op 7 to 2 tchd 9 to 2) 6
Dist: 1½l, 11l, 20l, sht-hd, 6l. 5m 14.00s. a 28.00s (6 Ran).

(Brian O'Kane), J G M O'Shea

242 Qualvis Packaging Maiden Hurdle Class E (4-y-o and up) £2,346 2m (3:50)

150⁵ PEGASUS BAY 5-11-5 R Garritty, hld up, steady hdwy 3 out, rdn to chal last, styd on to ld last 100 yards.
. . . . (4 to 1 op 5 to 1) 1
WAR WHOOP 4-11-2 M Foster, trkd ldrs, hdwy 4 out, led appr 2 out, rdn and jmpd slwly last, hdd and no extr last 100 yards.
. . . . . . (9 to 4 fav op 11 to 8 tchd 5 to 2 and 11 to 4) 2
THE LITTLE FERRET 6-11-5 R Johnson, prmnt, led 3rd, rdn 3 out and sn hdd, one pace. . . . . (7 to 1 tchd 8 to 1) 3
166⁶ SARACEN PRINCE (USA) 4-11-2 P Niven, led to 3rd, lost pl 5th, rdn and styd on frm 2 out. . . . . (4 to 1 op 5 to 2) 4
166 SMOCKING 6-11-0 P McLoughlin, jmpd slwly 1st, in tch till rdn and outpcd frm 4 out. . . . . (33 to 1 op 25 to 1) 5
150⁹ SPECIALIZE 4-11-2 A P McCoy, chsd ldrs, reminders 5th, wknd appr 3 out. . . . . (7 to 1 op 12 to 1) 6
TONY'S DELIGHT (Ire) 8-11-5 J Osborne, chsd ldrs, rdn and hit 6th, sn lost pl and beh, pld up aftr 3 out.
. . . . (4 to 1 op 5 to 2) pu
Dist: 1½l, 5l, 6l, 5l, ¾l. 4m 3.30s. a 17.30s (7 Ran).

(R P Dineen), W W Haigh

243 B.M.I. Park Hospital Selling Hurdle Class G (4-y-o and up) £2,012 2m . . . . (4:20)

TRADE WIND (v) 5-11-0 (5*) Michael Brennan, *trkd ldrs, hit 5th and lost pl, hdwy 3 out, chlgd and hmpd nxt, swtchd rght and rdn to ld last*..............................(3 to 1 op 9 to 4) 1

101* NIGHT TIME 4-10-9 (7*) Mr G Shenkin, *hld up, steady hdwy 3 out, effrt 2 out, rdn to ld and hng lft appr last, hdd and not quicken*..........................(7 to 2 op 5 to 2 tchd 4 to 1) 2

101⁵ LANCER (USA) 4-10-9 W Marston, *prmnt, led 3 out, rdn and hdd nxt, one pace....* (9 to 4 fav op 11 to 4 tchd 3 to 1) 3

KENYATTA (USA) 7-10-5 (7*) M Batchelor, *hld up, hdwy 4 out, effrt and lft in ld 2 out, sn hdd and wknd appr last.*
.............................(10 to 1 op 14 to 1 tchd 16 to 1) 4

PILLOW TALK (Ire) (bl) 5-10-7 Richard Guest, *prmnt, rdn along 3 out, wknd appr nxt.*............................(8 to 1) 5

DR DAVE (Ire) 5-10-9 (3*) T J Murphy, *hld up, rapid hdwy 3rd, cl up nxt, effrt to ld whn f 2 out.*.........................(25 to 1) f

NOBLE SOCIETY 8-11-12 J Ryan, *hld up, hdwy 3 out, rdn nxt and sn wknd, pld up lft.*.................(5 to 1 op 7 to 1) pu

FINE TIMING 9-10-12 Mr M Rimell, *led to 3 out, sn wknd and beh whn pld up bef last*.............(33 to 1 tchd 50 to 1) pu

150 TOP BANK 8-10-12 Miss S Sharratt, *prmnt, lost pl and beh frm 4 out, pld up bef last.*
........................(33 to 1 op 20 to 1 tchd 50 to 1) pu

KAJOSTAR 6-10-7 A S Smith, *al beh, pld up bef last.*
........................(33 to 1 op 20 to 1) pu

Dist: 2l, 5l, 3l, 3l. 4m 4.20s. a 18.20s (10 Ran).

(Gary Roberts), J G M O'Shea

244 Edingley Handicap Hurdle Class F (0-100 4-y-o and up) £2,589 2m (4:50)

152² ISLAND VISION (Ire) [99] (v) 6-11-9 (5*) Michael Brennan, *hld up, hdwy 3 out, chlgd nxt, rdn to ld appr last, ran on, fnshd lme*......................(9 to 4 fav op 2 to 1 tchd 5 to 2) 1

VERDE LUNA [80] 4-10-6 A P McCoy, *hld up, hdwy 3 out, rdn and ev ch appr last, kpt on*............ (5 to 1 op 4 to 1) 2

127⁹ STAY WITH ME (Fr) [95] 6-11-10 J Osborne, *in tch, hdwy to ld 3 out, rdn nxt, hdd and one pace appr last.*
..................................(9 to 2 op 3 to 1) 3

61⁶ NORTHERN TRIAL (USA) [93] (v) 8-11-8 A Larnach, *in tch, effrt and hdwy 3 out, rdn and one pace nxt.*
........................(4 to 1 op 7 to 2 tchd 9 to 2) 4

105⁵ RAY RIVER [93] 4-11-5 J Ryan, *hld up, hdwy 3 out, rdn nxt, one pace.*............(11 to 1 op 8 to 1 tchd 12 to 1) 5

152⁹ SHELLHOUSE [88] 8-11-0 (3*) T J Murphy, *pld hrd, chsd ldrs till led 3rd, hdd 3 out, drvn and wknd nxt.*
..................................(13 to 2 op 5 to 1) 6

40⁴ FLINTLOCK [84] 6-10-6 (7*) Mr R Thornton, *not fluent, led second to 3rd, prmnt till jmpd slwly 6th, sn lost pl.*
.............................(5 to 1 tchd 6 to 1) 7

AIDE MEMOIRE (Ire) [82] 7-10-11 A S Smith, *led to second, prmnt till wknd 5th, beh whn pld up bef 2 out.......*(16 to 1) pu

Dist: 2l, 1½l, 8l, 1l, sht-hd, 26l. 4m 2.60s. a 16.60s (8 Ran).

(Gary Roberts), J G M O'Shea

LEOPARDSTOWN (IRE) (good to firm)
Saturday July 20th

245 Kileview Co-Operative I.N.H. Flat Race (4-y-o and up) £4,110 2m....... (5:30)

CONNIES BUCK (Ire) 4-11-0 (7*) Mr A J Dempsey, ..(4 to 1) 1
LOLLIA PAULINA (Ire) 5-11-1 (7*) Mr Edgar Byrne, ..(6 to 1) 2
QILLA (Ire) 4-11-4 (3*) Mr B M Cash, ...(10 to 9 on) 3
647 RED RADICAL (Ire) 6-11-7 (7*) Mr P E I Newell, ...(12 to 1) 4
LADY LAUDER (Ire) 6-11-9 Mr H F Cleary, ...(14 to 1) 5
GLENREEF BOY (Ire) 7-11-11 (3*) Mr P Henley, ... (10 to 1) 6
PRINCESS TOUCHEE (Ire) 5-11-1 (7*) Mr D P Coakley,
..................................(14 to 1) 7
SUSIE'S DELIGHT (Ire) 6-11-2 (7*) Mr M S Hayden, ..(8 to 1) 8
CRABTREEJAZZ (Ire) 4-11-2 Mr D Marnane, ...(5 to 1) 9
Dist: 3½l, 1l, 5½l, ¾l. 3m 39.70s. (9 Ran).

(T J Culhane), D T Hughes

STRATFORD (good to firm)
Sunday July 21st
Going Correction: MINUS 0.15 sec. per fur.

246 West Midland Travel Selling Handicap Hurdle Class G (0-90 4 - 7-y-o and up) £1,982 2m 110yds.................... (2:10)

45 SET-EM-ALIGHT [62] 6-10-3 I Lawrence, *gd hdwy 5th, lft in ld 2 out, drvn out*..................(7 to 2 op 5 to 1 tchd 9 to 1) 1

205⁴ MINNESOTA FATS (Ire) [67] 4-10-2¹ Gary Lyons, *gd hdwy 3 out, lft second nxt, ev ch last, wknd.*
..................................(8 to 1 op 6 to 1 tchd 9 to 1) 2

KING OF BABYLON (Ire) [75] 4-10-10 P Carberry, *led to 3 out, one pace.*.............(15 to 1 op 7 to 1 tchd 9 to 1) 3

CLANCY'S EXPRESS [66] 5-10-2¹ S Fox, *nvr nr to chal.*
..................................(8 to 1) 4

153⁸ LASER LIGHT LADY [65] 4-10-0 B Powell, *chsd ldr 4th to 6th, wknd 3 out.*.........(40 to 1 op 33 to 1 tchd 50 to 1) 5

BUYERS DREAM (Ire) [76] (v) 6-11-3 A Dobbin, *chsd ldr to 4th, wknd nxt.*..............(7 to 2 op 5 to 1 tchd 11 to 2) 6

SWEDISH INVADER [86] 5-11-10 A P McCoy, *wl beh 6th, tld off.*..............................(5 to 1 tchd 11 to 2) 7

166 ON THE LEDGE (USA) [59] 6-9-7 (7*) A Dowling, *mstk 1st, wl beh 4th, tld off whn f 6th.*............(66 to 1 op 50 to 1) f

100⁸ STAY HAPPY (Fr) [59] 7-10-0 B Fenton, *hdwy 5th, led 3 out till f nxt, dead.*......................(9 to 4 fav op 9 to 4) f

Dist: 6l, 6l, 3l, 10l, 3l, 23l. 3m 53.50s. a 7.50s (9 Ran).

(R A Hughes), B Smart

247 DTZ Debenham Thorpe Novices' Chase Class D (5-y-o and up) £4,029 3m.................................. (2:40)

105⁶ STICKY MONEY 8-10-9 C Maude, *lft second 4th, led 13th, clr four out, hit last, easily*................(7 to 1 op 5 to 1) 1

147 HIZAL 7-11-0 Mr A Charles-Jones, *hdwy 6th, one pace frm 3 out, no ch wth wnr.*...........(33 to 1 op 20 to 1) 2

147 WAKT 6-10-9 B Fenton, *hdwy 13th, chsd wnr frm 4 out till wknd afr last.*........(6 to 1 op 5 to 1 tchd 13 to 2) 3

ABALENE 7-11-0 T Eley, *7th whn blun 12th, hdwy 4 out, nrst finish.*..............................(3 to 1 op 7 to 2) 4

DINO MALTA (Fr) 5-10-9 A Maguire, *hdwy tenth, rdn 14th, 4th whn blun four out, no ch aftr.*
..................................(5 to 4 fav op 11 to 8 tchd 6 to 4) 5

230 ARTFUL ARTHUR 10-11-0 Mr J Grassick, *in tch till wknd 4 out.*....................(66 to 1 op 33 to 1) 6

201⁴ DUSTYS TRAIL (Ire) 7-10-7 (7*) Mr R Thornton, *al beh, tld off frm 8th.*............(20 to 1 op 16 to 1 tchd 25 to 1) 7

201 PRIESTHILL 7-11-0 P Holley, *3rd whn f 5th.*
..................................(66 to 1 op 33 to 1) f

188 STORM WARRIOR (bl) 11-10-11 (3*) R Massey, *chsd ldr till blun and uns rdr 5th.*..............(66 to 1 op 25 to 1) ur

103 SAXON BLADE 8-11-0 W McFarland, *led till wknd 13th, beh whn pld up bef 4 out*...............(66 to 1 op 33 to 1) pu

SIGNE DE MARS (Fr) 5-10-9 K Jones, *tld off 7th, pld up bef 12th.*...................(16 to 1 op 7 to 1 tchd 20 to 1) pu

Dist: 12l, 1¼l, 3l, 1¼l, 11l, dist. 5m 53.40s. a 8.40s (11 Ran).

(Mrs D Jenks), M C Pipe

248 Millennium Copthorne Hotels Plc Stratford Summer Salver Handicap Hurdle Class D (0-125 4-y-o and up) £5,377 2m 110yds............... (3:10)

STAR MARKET [115] (bl) 6-12-0 A P McCoy, *al prmnt, led appr 6th, drvn clr approaching 2 out, all out.*
..................................(14 to 1 op 10 to 1) 1

40² SARMATIAN (USA) [95] 5-10-5 N Williamson, *hld up in rear, steady hdwy 6th, hit 3 out, quickened to chal last, no extr cl hme..........*(4 to 1 op 9 to 2 tchd 5 to 1 and 7 to 2) 2

FIELDRIDGE [103] 7-11-2 B Powell, *al prmnt, ran on one pace frm 2 out.*...........(9 to 1 op 8 to 1 tchd 10 to 1) 3

189⁵ LADY CONFESS [92] 6-10-5 R Supple, *led till appr 6th, 3rd and btn whn mstk last.*................(11 to 1 op 8 to 1) 4

60* ROLFE (NZ) [114] (bl) 6-11-13 A Maguire, *hdwy 5th, second whn blun 3 out, wknd 2 out.*.........(9 to 4 fav op 15 to 2) 5

189⁸ WAMDHA (Ire) [102] 6-11-1 A S Smith, *hdwy 5th, wknd appr 3 out.*..................................(16 to 1 op 12 to 1) 6

189* ROUTING [112] 8-11-11 C Maude, *in tch till wknd appr 3 out.*..................................(7 to 2 tchd 4 to 1) 7

152⁶ COMMANCHE CREEK [87] 6-9-9 (5*) Sophie Mitchell, *tld off 5th, pld up bef 3 out.*...............(11 to 1 op 8 to 1) pu

189 SHIFTING MOON [93] (bl) 4-10-3 P Carberry, *chsd ldr till wknd 5th, tld off whn pld up bef 3 out.*
..................................(16 to 1 op 14 to 1 tchd 20 to 1) pu

Dist: 1l, 7l, ¾l, 2½l, 4l, 1¼l. 3m 51.30s. a 5.30s (9 Ran).

SR: 23/-/3/-/10/2/

(Mrs P Joynes), J L Spearing

249 Richardson Developments Oldbury Stratford Summer Cup Handicap Chase Class D (0-125 5-y-o and up) £7,058 2½m.................... (3:40)

207² MAPLE DANCER [89] 10-10-11 R Greene, *al prmnt, chsd 3 out, lft clr last, drvn out.*...........(14 to 1 op 8 to 1) 1

202² ANDRELOT [110] (bl) 9-11-8 R Dunwoody, *chsd ldr 5th till rdn and outpcd appr 3 out, rallied last, ran on.*
..................................(4 to 1 tchd 5 to 1) 2

102² HENLEY REGATTA [94] 8-10-6 S Burrough, *gd hdwy 4 out, ev ch appr 2 out, lft second and hmpd last, wknd fnl 100 yards.*
..................................(12 to 1 op 8 to 1) 3

124 MAGIC BLOOM [100] 10-10-12 Richard Guest, *hdwy 9th, one pace frm 3 out.*..................(14 to 1 op 10 to 1) 4

188⁶ MANAMOUR [88] 9-10-0 C Llewellyn, *led, blun 9th, hdd and wknd appr 3 out.*........(12 to 1 op 10 to 1 tchd 16 to 1) 5

377 WISE ADVICE (Ire) [102] 6-11-0 R Garritty, *nvr nr to chal.*
..................................(12 to 1 op 8 to 1) 6

165* NORDIC SUN (Ire) [116] 8-12-0 M Dwyer, *chsd ldrs, wkng whn blun 4 out.*..............................(5 to 1) 7

149³ FLYING ZIAD (Can) [88] 13-9-7 (7*) A Dowling, *lost tch tenth.*..................(20 to 1 op 12 to 1) 8

149* SASKIA'S HERO [112] 9-11-10 D Byrne, *steady hdwy 4 out, slightly hmpd appr 2 out, second and clsg whn f last.*
..................................(2 to 1 fav op 5 to 2 tchd 11 to 4) f

POACHER'S DELIGHT [94] 10-10-6 B Fenton, *tld off 9th, pld up bef 11th.*...........(16 to 1 op 20 to 1 tchd 25 to 1) pu

Dist: 3l, 4l, 1¼l, 6l, ¾l, 1½l, 6l. 4m 50.30s. a 10.30s (10 Ran).

(Dr Ian R Shenkin), F Jordan

250 96.4 FM BRMB Novices' Hurdle Class E (4-y-o and up) £2,192 2¾m 110yds
.... (4:10)

229[6] SIGMA WIRELESS (Ire) 7-11-5 S Wynne, led to second, led appr 6th, clr 2 out, easily.
.... (Evens fav op 5 to 4 on tchd 11 to 10) 1
145[4] DANCING AT LAHARN (Ire) 6-10-12 A P McCoy, al prmnt, hrd rdn appr 4 out, chsd wnr 3 out, blun nxt, no imprsn.
.... (6 to 5 op 6 to 4) 2
CHAPS 6-10-12 P McLoughlin, led second till appr 6th, ev ch 4 out, wknd 3 out.........(25 to 1 op 14 to 1 tchd 33 to 1) 3
MISTER GENEROSITY (Ire) 5-10-12 M Richards, tld off frm 7th.....................(11 to 1 op 7 to 1 tchd 12 to 1) 4
Dist: 9l, 2½l, dist. 5m 27.50s. a 15.50s (4 Ran).

(Mrs Richard Strachan & Mrs David Lewis), Capt T A Forster

251 Richardsons Happy Family Novices' Handicap Hurdle Class E (0-100 4-y-o and up) £2,262 2m 110yds...... (4:40)

205[*] DENOMINATION (USA) [89] 4-11-4 C Maude, hdwy 5th, led appr 2 out, drvn out.............(2 to 1 jt-fav op 7 to 4) 1
126[*] ZAHID (USA) [96] 5-12-0 R Johnson, hdwy 6th, led 3 out, sn hdd, wth wnr whn slpd landing 2 out, rallied last, ran on.
.... (2 to 1 jt-fav tchd 5 to 2) 2
DESERT CHALLENGER (Ire) [75] (bl) 6-10-10 A P McCoy, led, sn clr, hdd 3 out, one pace.........(9 to 1 op 5 to 1) 3
150[6] LITTLE ROUSILLON [65] 8-10-0 W Humphreys, chsd ldrs, rdn appr 2 out, one pace. (9 to 1 op 8 to 1 tchd 10 to 1) 4
SWEET DISORDER [80] 6-10-8 (7") A Dowling, prmnt till wknd appr 3 out.........(11 to 2 op 4 to 1 tchd 6 to 1) 5
PRINCE OF SPADES [71] 4-9-11 (3") J Culloty, hdwy 5th, wknd appr 2 out.........(9 to 1 op 10 to 1 tchd 14 to 1) 6
152 COUNTRYWIDE LAD [65] 7-10-0 B Fenton, tld off frm 4th.
.... (33 to 1 op 25 to 1) 7
128 MARKETING MAN [65] 6-9-9[2] (7") D Bohan, chsd tar till wknd quickly 5th, beh whn f last.
.....................(33 to 1 op 14 to 1 tchd 50 to 1) f
Dist: 4l, 4l, 6l, 4l, 2l, 16l. 3m 55.00s. a 9.00s (8 Ran).

(Martin Pipe Racing Club), M C Pipe

TIPPERARY (IRE) (good to firm)
Sunday July 21st

252 Aer Rianta Shannon Handicap Chase (5-y-o and up) £6,850 2½m..... (4:00)

162[3] OPEN MARKET (USA) [-] 7-10-3 A Powell,........(8 to 1) 1
219[*] NOBODYS SON [-] 10-9-2 (5",3ex) G Cotter,......(10 to 1) 2
HIGH-SPEC [-] 10-9-4 (7") A O'Shea,............(10 to 1) 3
160[3] BOLD FLYER [-] 13-10-12 K F O'Brien,...........(8 to 1) 4
STEEL DAWN [-] 9-9-7 F Woods,................(7 to 1) 5
214[2] ANABATIC (Ire) [-] 8-12-0 T P Rudd,.............(4 to 1) ur
200[*] AN MAINEACH (Ire) [-] 7-10-8 C F Swan,..........(4 to 1) ur
BORO VACATION (Ire) [-] 7-11-5 T P Treacy,...(7 to 2 fav) su
Dist: 2l, 2l, dist, dist. 4m 45.20s. (8 Ran).

(S Creaven), D K Weld

253 Shannon Airport Marketing Flat Race (4-y-o and up) £2,397 2m....... (4:30)

180[2] NATIVE BABY (Ire) 6-11-2 (7") Mr R Walsh,........(11 to 4) 1
177[2] STANSWAY (Ire) 8-12-0 Mr P Fenton,..........(9 to 4 fav) 2
MAGICAL WAY (Ire) 6-11-7 (7") Mr B Hassett,......(14 to 1) 3
199[3] FRESHFIELD GALE (Ire) 6-11-2 (7") Mr A C Coyle,...(6 to 1) 4
185[7] ATTACK AT DAWN (Ire) 5-11-1 (7") Mr J P McNamara,
.... (10 to 1) 5
122 GALACTUS (Ire) 5-11-13 Mr D Marnane,..........(10 to 1) 6
199[8] EASTERN CUSTOM (Ire) 5-11-5 (3") Mr R O'Neill,....(12 to 1) 7
199[9] MALICE 10-11-6 (3") Mr E Norris,...............(14 to 1) 8
144[8] SHADOW CHASER (Ire) 4-10-9 (7") Mr G Elliott, ...(14 to 1) 9
183 GARLAND ROSE (Ire) 6-11-9 Mr J A Nash,.........(10 to 1) 10
DO THE BART (Ire) 4-11-0 (7") Mr Sean O O'Brien,..(10 to 1) 11
TIME TO GO (Ire) 4-10-9 (7") Mr J T McNamara,...(10 to 1) 12
INK BOTTLE (Ire) 6-11-7 (7") Mr N P Walsh,........(8 to 1) 13
SEE FOR FREE (Ire) 6-11-2 (7") Mr Patrick O'Keeffe,
.... (8 to 1) 14
BOTHAR GARBH (Ire) 5-11-6 (7") Mr John P Moloney,
.... (8 to 1) su
Dist: 15l, ¾l, ½l, 4l. 3m 45.10s. (15 Ran).

(W P Kerwin), W P Mullins

254 Aer Rianta Shannon Catering Handicap Hurdle (0-130 4-y-o and up) £3,425 2½m...................... (5:00)

CROSSFARNOGUE (Ire) [-] 7-12-0 C F Swan, ..(10 to 9 on) 1
184[3] INNOVATIVE (Ire) [-] 5-9-7 F Woods,.............(9 to 1) 2
LADY DAISY (Ire) [-] 7-10-5 (7") A O'Shea,.......(4 to 1) 3
130[3] MOUNTHENRY STAR (Ire) [-] 8-9-4[2] (7") C B Hynes, (10 to 1) 4
179[4] CULLENSTOWN LADY (Ire) [-] 5-11-2 A Powell, ...(5 to 2) 5
Dist: 2l, 20l, 25l. 4m 45.80s. (5 Ran).

(G Stafford), A P O'Brien

255 Shannon Aviation Fuels Novice Hurdle (4-y-o and up) £2,226 2½m..... (5:30)

192[*] FONTAINE LODGE (Ire) 6-10-10 (7") A O'Shea, ..(100 to 30) 1
BULWARK HILL (Ire) 6-11-2 T P Treacy,........(6 to 4 fav) 2
144[*] ERRAMORE (Ire) 4-10-3 C F Swan,..............(9 to 4) 3
GERAY LADY (Ire) 6-10-11 F Woods,.............(5 to 1) 4
Dist: 1½l, 2½l, dist. 5m 3.40s. (4 Ran).

(ABC Syndicate), Anthony Mullins

BALLINROBE (IRE) (good)
Monday July 22nd

256 Derks Maiden Hurdle (5-y-o and up) £2,226 2m...................... (6:00)

192[2] HAY DANCE 5-11-0 (5") Mr W M O'Sullivan,........(5 to 1) 1
177[1] SUPAMORE (Ire) [-] 5-11-1 T Horgan,..............(7 to 1) 2
182[5] RUSHEEN BAY (Ire) (bl) 7-10-13 (7") A O'Shea,....(7 to 1) 3
193[6] MONTETAN (Ire) 5-11-8 K F O'Brien,............(10 to 1) 4
182[4] THE BOURDA 10-11-7 (7") S P McCann,...........(8 to 1) 5
122 RADICAL ACTION (Ire) 5-11-8 T P Treacy,........(14 to 1) 6
194[5] DEARMISTERSHATTER (Ire) 5-11-5 M Duffy,......(20 to 1) 7
EOINS LAD (Ire) 5-11-5 C F Swan,..............(20 to 1) 8
178 BUBBLY PROSPECT (USA) 5-11-10 (3") C Everard, (4 to 1) f
Dist: 4l, ¾l, 6l, 12l. 4m 6.20s. (9 Ran).

(Mrs Fiona O'Sullivan), Eugene M O'Sullivan

257 George Moore Beginners Chase (5-y-o and up) £2,226 2m 1f.......... (7:30)

CLAHADA ROSE (Ire) 6-11-9 C F Swan,..........(11 to 4) 1
219[3] SANDY FOREST LADY (Ire) 7-11-9 J P Broderick, ..(6 to 1) 2
200[4] PHARDY (Ire) 5-11-7 G M O'Neill,...............(10 to 1) 3
BEAKSTOWN (Ire) 7-12-0 T P Treacy,......(11 to 10 fav) 4
198[8] BALLINABOOLA GROVE 9-11-9 (5") T Martin, ...(9 to 1) 5
212[8] HAVE A DROP (Ire) 6-11-2 (7") A O'Shea,.........(20 to 1) 6
WHAT IS THE PLAN (Ire) 7-11-7 (7") Mr B Hassett, (16 to 1) 7
Dist: 1½l, 1½l, 1l, 13l. 4m 24.60s. (7 Ran).

(Mrs P Ryan), A P O'Brien

258 Loughcarra INH Flat Race (5-y-o and up) £2,226 2m................... (9:00)

NEIPHIN BOY (Ire) 6-12-0 Mr H F Cleary,.........(4 to 1) 1
199[2] GALE HAMSHIRE (Ire) 7-11-9 Mr J A Nash, ..(11 to 10 fav) 2
NAKURU (Ire) 7-11-2 (7") Mr A C Coyle,.........(12 to 1) 3
115[3] BERCLUB (Ire) 5-11-6 (7") Mr Mark Walsh,........(8 to 1) 4
199[4] CARNACREEVA GANE (Ire) 5-11-5 (3") Mr B M Cash,
.... (4 to 1) 5
183 MOY VALLEY (Ire) 6-11-2 (7") Mr A Daly,........(25 to 1) 6
FRED OF THE HILL (Ire) 5-11-13 Mr P F Graffin, ...(14 to 1) 7
Dist: 2l, sht-hd, 3l, 5l. 4m 5.20s. (7 Ran).

(M V Walsh), F Flood

BALLINROBE (IRE) (good to firm)
Tuesday July 23rd

259 Robe Maiden Hurdle (4-y-o and up) £2,226 3m...................(6:00)

170[2] BUGGSY BLADE 10-11-6 L P Cusack,.............(4 to 1) 1
196[*] YOUNG DUBLINER (Ire) (bl) 7-12-0 J F Titley, (11 to 10 fav) 2
232[5] BIDDY HUNT (Ire) 5-11-0 J P Broderick,........(12 to 1) 3
132[5] BRAVE COMMITMENT (Ire) 5-11-8 C F Swan, ...(9 to 2) 4
WEAVER SQUARE (Ire) 7-11-3 (3") B Bowens,.....(6 to 1) 5
SUIRFONTAINE (Ire) 8-11-6 K F O'Brien,.........(25 to 1) 6
173 BABY WHALE (Ire) 6-11-1 T J O'Sullivan,.......(25 to 1) 7
233[5] DOCCUMMINS (Ire) (bl) 6-11-8 T P Treacy,......(20 to 1) 8
FORGIVENESS (Ire) 6-10-13 (7") A O'Shea,......(33 to 1) ur
Dist: 1½l, 25l, 6l, 6l. 6m 10.30s. (9 Ran).

(Mrs D J Coleman), Mrs D J Coleman

260 West Handicap Hurdle (0-109 4-y-o and up) £2,226 2½m.......... (6:30)

181[*] PRECEPTOR (Ire) [-] 7-11-2 (3") B Bowens,........(6 to 1) 1
235[*] LEGITMAN (Ire) [-] 6-9-13 (6ex) P Carberry,.......(7 to 1) 2
171[3] SANDRA LOUISE (Ire) [-] 6-9-9[2] C F Swan, ... (11 to 8 fav) 3
222 FAIR SOCIETY (Ire) [-] (bl) 5-9-11 J P Broderick, ...(9 to 2) 4
Dist: 2l, 5l, 2½l. 5m 3.90s. (4 Ran).

(P A McMahon), Victor Bowens

261 Corrib Spring Water Handicap Chase (0-109 4-y-o and up) £2,568 2m 1f
.... (7:30)

CARAGH BRIDGE [-] 9-9-13 C F Swan,...........(3 to 1) 1
219[6] HANNIES GIRL (Ire) [-] 7-9-13 (7") L J Fleming, (9 to 4 fav) 2
NEBRASKA [-] 10-11-4 P Carberry,..............(10 to 1) 3
NATIVE VENTURE (Ire) [-] 8-11-8 J F Titley,......(6 to 1) 4
DRINDOD (Ire) [-] 7-10-7 (7") D A McLoughlin, ...(11 to 2) f
177 DEEP REFRAIN (Ire) [-] (bl) 6-9-10 J P Broderick, (5 to 1) ur

Dist: 3½l, 4½l, dist. 4m 21.90s. (6 Ran).

(P Moriarty), Martin Michael Lynch

WORCESTER (good to firm)
Tuesday July 23rd
Going Correction: MINUS 0.10 sec. per fur.

262 Lincomb Maiden Hurdle Class D (4-y-o and up) £2,973 2½m............ (2:00)

50²	BORN TO PLEASE (Ire) 4-11-2 A P McCoy, hld up in tch, jmpd slwly 4 out, led 2 out, rdn out and wndrd r-in. ....(11 to 8 fav op 5 to 4 tchd 6 to 4)	1
186⁵	EWAR IMPERIAL 4-11-2 D Gallagher, hld up in tch, led 3 out, hdd nxt, one pace appr last..........(20 to 1 op 12 to 1)	2
153³	MURBERRY (Ire) 6-11-0 L Harvey, prmnt, led appr 5th, hdd 3 out, one pace nxt........(13 to 2 op 5 to 1 tchd 7 to 1)	3
78³	BIG TREAT (Ire) 4-10-13 (3°) E Husband, led till appr 5th, ev ch 3 out, 3rd and btn whn mstk nxt. ....(11 to 4 tchd 5 to 2 and 3 to 1)	4
47	UP THE TEMPO (Ire) 7-10-11 (3°) J Culloty, hld up, hdwy 6th, rdn alng and outpcd aftr nxt, kpt on one pace r-in. ....(16 to 1 op 8 to 1 tchd 20 to 1)	5
	SOMMERSBY (Ire) 5-11-5 R Dunwoody, hld up, mstk 5th, hdwy nxt, drvn alng frm 4 out, wknd appr next, tld off. ....(16 to 1 op 12 to 1)	6
157⁶	CARNIVAL CLOWN 4-11-2 R Greene, in tch to 6th, jmpd slwly and beh frm nxt, tld off..........(16 to 1 op 20 to 1)	7
	BOWLAND PARK 5-11-0 P Niven, blun and uns rdr 1st. ....(20 to 1 op 8 to 1)	ur
	LIBERTY JAMES 9-11-5 G Upton, mstk and beh frm 5th, tld off whn pld up bef 3 out..........(33 to 1 op 20 to 1)	pu
	ITS A MYTH 7-11-0 B Powell, mstk 4th, al beh, tld off whn pld up bef four out........(66 to 1 op 33 to 1 tchd 100 to 1)	pu

Dist: 7l, 2l, nk, 1l, dist, 4l. 4m 50.20s. a 14.20s (10 Ran).

(A B S Racing), P J Hobbs

263 Huddington Novices' Hurdle Class D (4-y-o and up) £2,910 2m...... (2:30)

	MILLION DANCER 4-10-9 D Bridgwater, made all, drw clr appr 3 out, unchlgd..................(3 to 1 op 5 to 2)	1
168⁴	SUPERMODEL (v) 4-10-11 R Dunwoody, chsd wnr to 5th, wnt moderate second appr 2 out, no imprsn. ....(4 to 1 fav op 5 to 2 tchd 3 to 1)	2
	COUNT OF FLANDERS (Ire) 6-10-12 A S Smith, in tch, chsd wnr frm 5th till appr 2 out, fdd..........(7 to 2 op 5 to 2)	3
205	BETABETCORBETT 5-10-12 T Eley, prmnt, reminder aftr 3rd, wknd quickly 5th, tld off..........(33 to 1 op 25 to 1)	4
	AT THE ACORN (Ire) 5-10-12 R Johnson, hld up, rdn and dived 5th, al beh, tld off..........(9 to 2 tchd 5 to 1)	5
	WET PATCH (Ire) 4-10-9 N Williamson, hld up, mstk 5th, wknd quickly, tld off..........(7 to 2 op 3 to 1)	6
	MARONETTA 4-10-4 J Ryan, al beh, tld off whn pld up bef 3 out..................(25 to 1 op 16 to 1 tchd 33 to 1)	pu

Dist: 11l, 17l, 9l, 12l, 24l. 3m 44.30s. a 4.30s (7 Ran).
SR: 22/13/-/-/ (Martin Pipe Racing Club), M C Pipe

264 Racing Channel Handicap Chase Class D (0-125 5-y-o and up) £4,185 2m 7f..............................(3:00)

188⁴	EVANGELICA (USA) [110] 6-11-10 D Bridgwater, chsd ldr, led appr 4 out, drw clr frm 2 out, eased r-in. ....(11 to 8 on tchd 5 to 4 on)	1
154⁴	WATERFORD CASTLE [109] 9-11-6 (3°) T J Murphy, hld up, rdn alng frm 14th, effrt whn mstks last 2, one pace. ....(9 to 4 op 7 to 4 tchd 5 to 2)	2
82⁵	TOUR LEADER (NZ) [87] 7-10-1 B Powell, led till appr 4 out, wknd nxt..........................(4 to 1 tchd 9 to 2)	3

Dist: 5l, 21l. 6m 14.60s. a 36.60s (3 Ran).

(Martin Pipe Racing Club), M C Pipe

265 Hawkers Investment Capitol Ltd Handicap Hurdle Class D (0-125 4-y-o and up) £2,726 3m..................... (3:30)

	STORMTRACKER (Ire) [105] 7-10-10 (5°) Michael Brennan, prmnt, chsd ldr frm 3rd, lft in ld appr 8th, sn clr, unchlgd. ....(11 to 4 op 5 to 2 tchd 3 to 1)	1
	THE BLACK MONK (Ire) [95] 8-10-5 D Bridgwater, hld up, hdwy 7th, chsd wnr appr 4 out, wknd 2 out, tld off. ....(5 to 2 fav op 11 to 4 tchd 3 to 1)	2
148⁷	GREEN LANE (USA) [112] 8-11-8 C Llewellyn, hld up, lost tch frm 8th, tld off..........(12 to 1 op 10 to 1)	3
	JAWANI (Ire) [118] 8-12-0 R Dunwoody, chsd ldr to 3rd, wknd frm 8th, tld off..........(11 to 4 op 5 to 2 tchd 3 to 1)	4
	SAME DIFFERENCE (Ire) [103] 8-10-13 A Larnach, hld up, tld off frm 3rd..................(12 to 1 op 10 to 1)	5
	QUIET DAWN [90] 10-10-0 A P McCoy, jmpd rght, led, pld up and dismouted bef 8th..........(10 to 1 tchd 11 to 1)	pu
164²	DARINGLY [90] 7-10-0 D Morris, hld up, hdwy 6th, wknd frm 8th, tld off whn pld up bef 3 out..................(20 to 1)	pu

Dist: 20l, dist, 15l. 5m 46.20s. a 10.20s (7 Ran).

(Tim Davis), C Weedon

266 Hereford And Worcester Chamber Of Commerce Handicap Chase Class F (0-100 5-y-o and up) £3,468 2m (4:00)

240³	MAGGOTS GREEN [72] 9-10-0 A P McCoy, chsd ldeer, led aftr 8th, clr frm 4 out, eased r-in.....(3 to 1 fav op 4 to 1)	1
227⁸	SYDNEY BARRY (NZ) [90] 11-11-4 B Powell, in tch, outpcd aftr 8th, styd on to chase wnr frm 2 out, no imprsn. ....(5 to 1 op 6 to 1 tchd 7 to 1)	2
79²	MICHERADO (Fr) [92] 6-11-6 R Johnson, led till aftr 8th, wknd 2 out..........................(7 to 2 op 3 to 1)	3
	CYRILL HENRY (Ire) [77] 7-10-5 C Maude, nvr nr to chal. ....(4 to 1 op 3 to 1 tchd 9 to 2)	4
	ASTOUNDED [76] 9-10-4 W Marston, nvr nr to chal. ....(10 to 1 tchd 12 to 1)	5
100	HUGH DANIELS [83] 8-10-11 Gary Lyons, al beh. ....(16 to 1 op 12 to 1)	6
	MERLINS WISH (USA) [100] 7-12-0 D Bridgwater, reminders aftr 3rd, al beh, tld off whn pld up bef 4 out. ....(5 to 1 op 3 to 1 tchd 11 to 2)	pu

Dist: 16l, 5l, 6l, 3½l, 28l. 3m 55.90s. a 6.90s (7 Ran).

(E A Hayward), J M Bradley

267 Champagne Handicap Hurdle Class F (0-105 4-y-o and up) £2,267 2m (4:30)

189³	OUT RANKING (Fr) [100] 4-11-8 D Bridgwater, made all, rdn whn jmpd rght fnl 2, all out..........(4 to 1 op 3 to 1)	1
189²	EL GRANDO [83] 6-10-8 D Gallagher, prmnt, hrd rdn frm 2 out, ran on wl r-in..........(4 to 1 op 3 to 1)	2
	MR SNAGGLE (Ire) [95] 7-11-6 C Maude, hld up, rdn appr 3 out, str run frm last, ran on. ....(14 to 1 op 10 to 1 tchd 20 to 1)	3
189⁶	KING'S SHILLING (USA) [95] 9-11-1 (5°) Michael Brennan, hld up, rdn appr 3 out, kpt on same pace....(9 to 2 op 3 to 1)	4
	PAIR OF JACKS (Ire) [83] 6-10-8 A P McCoy, prmnt, rdn appr 3 out, btn approaching last. ....(11 to 8 fav op 7 to 4 tchd 2 to 1)	5
105	BATTY'S ISLAND [103] 7-11-7 (7°) D Finnegan, chsd wnr till rdn 4th, sn wknd, tld off..........(11 to 1 op 12 to 1)	6

Dist: Nk, sht-hd, 10l, sht-hd, 30l. 3m 45.70s. a 5.70s (6 Ran).
SR: 21/7/19/9/-/-/ (Knight Hawks Partnership), M C Pipe

NAAS (IRE) (good)
Wednesday July 24th

268 Halfway House Handicap Hurdle (0-116 4-y-o and up) £3,082 2m (7:00)

210⁴	MONTE'S EVENING (Ire) [-] 8-9-10 P L Malone, ... (16 to 1)	1
113⁷	KATES CHOICE (Ire) [-] 4-11-8 T P Treacy, ... (2 to 1 fav)	2
	HIGHLANDER (Ire) [-] 7-11-9 (5°) G Cotter, ...(7 to 2)	3
194⁴	WHEREWILLITALL END (Ire) [-] 5-11-5 (3°) U Smyth, (4 to 1)	4
176³	DIFFICULT TIMES (Ire) [-] 4-11-10 S C Lyons, ...(13 to 2)	5
	BOLERO DANCER (Ire) [-] 8-10-8 F Woods, ...(9 to 1)	6
	L'ORAGE (Ire) [-] 8-11-7 K F O'Brien, ...(20 to 1)	7
219	RATES RELIEF (Ire) [-] 6-11-12 C F Swan, ...(8 to 1)	8

Dist: 2½l, 2l, ¾l, nk. 3m 45.50s. (8 Ran).

(Mrs T J Moore), Peter Casey

269 Kill I.N.H. Flat Race (4-y-o) £2,740 2m .... (9:00)

115	FRANCOSKID (Ire) 11-2 (7°) Mr J P McNamara, .. (12 to 1)	1
	MIDDLE MOGGS (Ire) 11-1 (3°) Mr K Whelan, ...(10 to 1)	2
213⁵	PERAMBIE (Ire) (bl) 10-11 (7°) Miss A L Crowley, ...(6 to 1)	3
	PARSEE (Ire) 11-10 (7°) Mr J D Moore, ...(7 to 2)	4
210²	SHARP ELVER (Ire) 10-11 (7°) Mr A J Dempsey, ..(3 to 1 jt-fav)	5
	HELLO MR JOHNSON (Ire) 11-2 (7°) Mr M A Cahill, (12 to 1)	6
	BALLYLENNON BAVARD (Ire) 10-13 (5°) Mr R Walsh, ...(3 to 1 jt-fav)	7
137⁴	GRAPHIC LADY (Ire) 10-11 (7°) Mr J Cash, ...(4 to 1)	8
	ACCOUNTANCY PERK (Ire) 10-11 (7°) Mr J M O'Brien, ...(8 to 1)	9
	DUNMORE SUPREME (Ire) 11-2 (7°) Mr M P Browne, ...(20 to 1)	10
	MARBLE QUEST (Ire) 10-11 (7°) Mr D P Coakley, ..(14 to 1)	11

Dist: Sht-hd, 2l, 1½l, ½l. 3m 43.60s. (11 Ran).

(T J Kidd), S J Treacy

WEXFORD (IRE) (good)
Thursday July 25th

270 Paddy Irish Whiskey Maiden Hurdle (4-y-o) £2,568 2¼m.............. (6:00)

169²	CLASSIC SILK (Ire) 11-0 L P Cusack, ...(4 to 1)	1
178²	MAGICAL FUN (Ire) 11-2 (3°) Mr P M Kelly, ... (100 to 30)	2
211³	JANE DIGBY (Ire) 11-0 C F Swan, ...(5 to 4 on)	3
34⁸	JARSUN QUEEN (Ire) 10-2 (7°) L J Fleming, ...(16 to 1)	4
208²	TIFFANY VICTORIA (Ire) 10-11 (5°) C O'Dwyer, ...(7 to 1)	5
	HARRY WELSH (Ire) 11-5 T P Treacy, ...(16 to 1)	6

Dist: ¾l, 7l, 5½l, 25l. 4m 21.80s. (6 Ran).

(Mrs D J Coleman), Mrs D J Coleman

271 West Coast Cooler Novice Hurdle (5-y-o and up) £2,756 2½m...... (6:30)

193* RATHGIBBON (Ire) 5-11-6 T P Treacy, ... (7 to 2 on) 1
224⁴ CELIO LUCY (Ire) 6-10-13 (3") D J Casey, ...(4 to 1) 2
259⁵ WEAVER SQUARE (Ire) 7-11-4 (3") B Bowens, ... (8 to 1) 3
94 COZY COTTAGE (Ire) 6-11-2 J P Broderick, ... (25 to 1) pu
Dist: 1l, 5l. 5m 5.60s. (4 Ran).

(Mrs Margaret Marshall), S J Treacy

272 Powers Gold Label Handicap Hurdle (0-102 5-y-o and up) £2,568 3m (7:00)

REGAL GROVE (Ire) [-] 7-11-7 C F Swan, ...(12 to 1) 1
234³ FATHER RECTOR (Ire) [-] 7-11-5 T Horgan, ... (6 to 1) 2
179² BITRAN [-] 6-10-11 P Carberry, ...(7 to 1) 3
170* KILCARAMORE (Ire) [-] 5-11-1 Mr P J Healy, ... (5 to 1) 4
217* OX EYE DAISY (Ire) [-] 8-11-3 (3") J R Barry, ... (8 to 1) 5
223* MARGUERITA SONG [-] 6-11-1 T P Treacy, ... (5 to 2 fav) 6
120⁵ NON MUSE RUN (Ire) [-] (bl) 6-9-7 F Woods, ... (14 to 1) 8
182⁹ CANDY IS DANDY (Ire) [-] 7-10-5¹ L P Cusack, ... (33 to 1) 9
SPANISH FAIR (Ire) [-] 8-11-2 C O'Dwyer, ...(6 to 1) pu
213⁸ AMERICAN CONKER (Ire) [-] 5-10-7 K F O'Brien, ..(14 to 1) pu
Dist: 2l, 15l, 11l, 11l. 5m 58.40s. (11 Ran).

(Coosan Syndicate), A P O'Brien

273 Bisquit Cognac Handicap Hurdle (0-109 4-y-o and up) £2,568 2½m .... (7:30)

195⁶ CHUCK (Ire) [-] 6-9-12 (7") D McCullagh, ... (8 to 1) 1
143³ PERSIAN MYSTIC (Ire) [-] 4-11-1 G M O'Neill, .. (5 to 2 fav) 2
175* ADARAMANN (Ire) [-] 4-10-6 (5") Mr R Walsh, ... (3 to 1) 3
235² JATINGA (Ire) [-] 8-11-1 C F Swan, ... (100 to 30) 4
MANETTI (Ire) [-] 4-10-9 (7") Mr S P Hennessy, ... (8 to 1) 5
235⁶ HARVEYSLAND [-] 13-10-12 T Kinane Jnr, ... (16 to 1) 6
234⁵ THE TOM'S ERROR (Ire) [-] 6-10-1 P Carberry, ...(12 to 1) 7
Dist: 8l, 1l, hd, 3½l. 4m 52.60s. (7 Ran).

(Mrs Sheila McCullagh), Michael McCullagh

274 Huzzar Vodka INH Flat Race (5-y-o and up) £2,568 2½m...................... (8:30)

238² STRADBALLY JANE (Ire) 4-11-2 (7") Mr Mark Walsh, (4 to 1) 1
99⁴ CRAZY DREAMS (Ire) 8-12-0 Mr P J Healy, ... (4 to 1) 2
GREAT SHAUN (Ire) 7-11-9 (5") Mr R Walsh, ...(6 to 4 fav) 3
238⁴ MARIE'S PRIDE (Ire) 7-11-9 (7") Mr John P Moloney,
.... (8 to 1) 4
217⁸ GOLD DEVON (Ire) 6-12-0 Mr T Doyle, ... (25 to 1) 5
WILDLIFE RANGER (Ire) 8-11-11 (3") Mr B M Cash, (9 to 1) 6
31⁵ BALLYDUFF ROSE (Ire) 6-11-2 (7") Mrs C Doyle, ..(9 to 1) 7
177⁸ CROCHAUN (Ire) 6-11-9 Mr A R Coonan, ...(14 to 1) 8
199 LOCAL RACE (Ire) 7-11-7 (7") Mr B N Doyle, ...(20 to 1) 9
NEEBURNS (Ire) 5-11-11 (3") Mr K Whelan, ...(12 to 1) 10
213 INCH VALLEY (Ire) 5-11-2 (7") Miss I M Burke, ..(33 to 1) 11
Dist: 13l, 2½l, 1½l, 3½l. 4m 51.40s. (11 Ran).

(The Curraghs Syndicate), Thomas G Walsh

WEXFORD (IRE) (good)
Friday July 26th

275 Guinness Handicap Hurdle (0-102 4-y-o and up) £2,740 2m............ (6:00)

NIYAMPOUR (Ire) [-] (bl) 5-11-11 T P Rudd, ...(7 to 2) 1
222² DANCING CLODAGH (Ire) [-] 4-11-8 P Carberry, (9 to 4 fav) 2
174⁴ THE WICKED CHICKEN (Ire) [-] 7-11-0 T Horgan, ...(7 to 1) 3
222 I REMEMBER IT WELL (Ire) [-] 4-10-7 M P Hourigan, (7 to 1) 4
258² GALE HAMSHIRE (Ire) [-] 7-10-5 (3") D J Casey, ..(9 to 1) 5
169² SLIEVROE (Ire) [-] 5-10-1 F Woods, ...(10 to 1) 6
118 RADIF (USA) [-] 5-10-5 J P Byrne, ...(10 to 1) 7
161⁶ JEWEL OF THE NIGHT (Ire) [-] 4-9-13 (3") J R Barry, (20 to 1) 8
175³ TRIPLE ACTION (Ire) [-] 7-10-7 (7") D Duggan, ...(16 to 1) 9
213 BRINNY PRINCESS (Ire) [-] (bl) 5-10-3 W T Slattery, (33 to 1) 10
CAREFORMENOW (USA) [-] (bl) 7-11-0 M Duffy, ...(33 to 1) 11
MISS MERENTI (Ire) [-] (bl) 5-9-7 P L Malone, ...(20 to 1) 12
Dist: 2½l, nk, 2l, 4l. 3m 50.60s. (12 Ran).

(D P Sharkey), M J P O'Brien

276 Club Orange Maiden Hurdle (4-y-o and up) £2,740 2m..................... (6:30)

133⁶ FATHER MICHAEL (Ire) 6-11-6 T P Treacy, ...(6 to 1) 1
211⁶ PERFECT TIMMER 6-11-6 C F Swan, ...(9 to 4) 2
192⁶ NEW WAY (Ire) 6-10-13 (7") S P McCann, ...(25 to 1) 3
PORT QUEEN (Ire) 5-11-1 T P Rudd, ...(6 to 4 fav) 4
192⁸ TENDER LASS (Ire) 5-11-0 P L Malone, ...(14 to 1) 5
176 CROGHAN BRIDGE (Ire) 7-11-6 J H Kavanagh, ...(33 to 1) 6
SAN SIRO (Ire) 6-10-13 (7") Mr Edgar Byrne, ...(16 to 1) 7
KUDOS (Ire) 5-11-0 (5") G Cotter, ...(16 to 1) 8
233⁸ LOSLOMOS (Ire) 4-10-9 (7") D Duggan, ...(20 to 1) 9
161⁴ SAWAALEFF (Ire) 4-11-2 H Rogers, ...(8 to 1) 10

(Politically Correct Syndicate), P Mullins

170 NOBODYWANTSME (Ire) 5-10-12 (7") Mr J Creighton,
....(20 to 1) 11
SLANEY CHOICE (Ire) 5-11-6 C O'Dwyer, ...(8 to 1) 12
Dist: ¾l, 20l, ½l, hd. 3m 52.80s. (12 Ran).

277 Noonan Developments Ferrycarrig Hotel Maiden Hurdle (5-y-o and up) £2,740 2m......................(7:00)

211⁴ PHARDANTE GIRL (Ire) 5-11-5 M P Hourigan, .. (4 to 1) 1
173 LANTINA (Ire) 5-11-5 D H O'Connor, ...(14 to 1) 2
229⁹ FLYING IN THE GALE (Ire) 5-11-2 (3") J R Barry, ...(25 to 1) 3
CROHANE PRINCESS (Ire) 7-11-6 S H O'Donovan, (20 to 1) 4
86⁶ HELORHIWATER (Ire) 5-11-13 T P Treacy, ...(5 to 4 on) 5
232⁸ PHANTOMS GIRL (Ire) 5-11-5 P L Malone, ... (16 to 1) 6
170⁸ DOTTIE'S DOUBLE (Ire) 5-11-5 T P Rudd, ...(9 to 1) 7
160⁴ VIENNA WALTZ (Ire) 6-11-6 H Rogers, ...(20 to 1) 8
173⁵ DUSTY ROSE (Ire) 7-11-6 M Moran, ...(9 to 1) 9
208 RATHNALLY STAR (Ire) 5-11-5 J P Broderick, ...(25 to 1) 10
HIGH PARK LADY (Ire) 5-11-5 P M Verling, ...(10 to 1) 11
173 UNDERSTANDING (Ire) 7-10-13 (7") Mr P J McGarry,
....(25 to 1) 13
Dist: 7l, 1½l, hd, 5l. 3m 54.90s. (13 Ran).

(D O'Leary), Michael Hourigan

278 Corkys Alcoholic Fruit Drink Flat Race (4-y-o and up) £2,740 2m...... (9:00)

180⁶ MIDNIGHT CYCLONE (Ire) 5-11-8 Mr J A Nash, ...(5 to 2) 1
PRINCESS GLORIA (Ire) 5-11-8 Mr P Fenton, ...(14 to 1) 2
LADY RICHENDA (Ire) 8-11-2 (7") Mr J T McNamara, (8 to 1) 3
213³ ROSIE FLYNN (Ire) 4-10-9 (7") Mr Sean O O'Brien,
....(7 to 4 fav) 4
88 MOLLY WHACK (Ire) 5-11-1 (7") M P Dunne, ...(16 to 1) 5
RACHEL'S SWALLOW (Ire) 4-10-13 (3") Mr R O'Neill,
....(12 to 1) 6
224⁸ STRICT TEMPO (Ire) 7-11-7 (7") Mr G Elliott, ...(10 to 1) 7
OWEN GOWLA (Ire) 4-11-0 (7") Mr J D Moore, ...(8 to 1) 8
173 RIVERRUNSTHROUGHIT (Ire) (bl) 5-11-1 (7") Mr J P Brennan,
....(16 to 1) 9
BAYVIEWLADY (Ire) 6-11-2 (7") Mr P Cashman, ...(16 to 1) 10
LADY CONDUCTOR (Ire) 5-11-8 Mr J A Berry, ...(7 to 1) 11
233 MISS MAGILLS (Ire) 5-11-1 (7") Mr D O'Meara, ...(14 to 1) 12
Dist: 6l, 5½l, 1½l, 1l. 3m 54.70s. (12 Ran).

(David Duane), W P Mullins

STRATFORD (good to firm)
Saturday July 27th
Going Correction: NIL

279 Richardsons Oldbury King George 'Surfers Paradise' Novices' Hurdle Class E (4-y-o and up) £2,276 2m 110yds.........................(2:25)

107* COUREUR 7-11-5 R Garritty, hld up, steady hdwy to chal 2
out, led and blun last, drvn out.
..................(6 to 5 fav op 7 to 4 tchd 15 to 8) 1
83* KARINSKA 6-11-0 W Worthington, strted slwly, ran in
snatches, hdwy hfwy, outpcd entering strt, kpt on ag'n betw
last 2...........................(5 to 1 op 4 to 1) 2
I HAVE HIM 9-10-12 B Powell, led, jmpd rght thrght, mstk 4th,
hdd and hit last, no extr...(5 to 1 op 4 to 1 tchd 11 to 2) 3
FLEET CADET 5-10-12 D Bridgwater, hld up, improved to
chase ldrs hfwy, outpcd whn jmpd slwly 3 out, one pace frm
nxt...........................(5 to 1 op 7 to 1) 4
MARIO'S DREAM (Ire) 8-10-12 D Gallagher, unruly strt, sn wl
beh, tld off hfwy.......(66 to 1 op 33 to 1 tchd 100 to 1) 5
128 DAN DE LYON 8-10-9 (3") J Magee, chsd ldr, 3rd and drvn
alng whn blun and uns rdr 6th.......(50 to 1 op 33 to 1) ur
Dist: 2½l, 1½l, 7l, 9l, dist. 4m 1.70s. a. 15.70s (7 Ran).

(Frank Hanson), M D Hammond

280 King Edward 'Great Barrier Reef' Novices' Chase Class E (5-y-o and up) £3,051 2m 1f 110yds.......... (3:00)

190* STATELY HOME (Ire) 5-11-2 R Johnson, cl up, jmpd wl, led
7th, drvn clr aftr 3 out, styd on strly.
..................(11 to 10 on op Evens tchd 11 to 10) 1
DISTANT MEMORY (bl) 7-10-12 A P McCoy, nvr far away,
chsd wnr fnl circuit, jmpd slwly and outpcd 3 out, kpt on ag'n
frm nxt...........(7 to 2 op 5 to 1 tchd 4 to 1) 2
156⁵ TELMAR SYSTEMS 7-10-12 B Fenton, chsd ldrs, reminders
and outpcd 6th, beh frm nxt......(20 to 1 op 12 to 1) 3
228² BIT OF A DREAM (Ire) 6-10-12 Richard Guest, hld up, mstk
and lost tch 8th, no dngr aftr.
....(33 to 1 op 25 to 1) 4
247 SAXON BLADE 8-10-12 W McFarland, sn led, hdd whn blun
and unseated rdr 7th............(33 to 1 op 25 to 1) ur

34

POND HOUSE (Ire) 7-11-5 D Bridgwater, *jmpd poorly, reminders in rear 5th, tld off whn pld up bef 9th.*
....(5 to 1 op 3 to 1) pu
Dist: 3½l, 14l, 1¼l. 4m 12.90s. a 10.90s (6 Ran).

(P Bowen), P Bowen

281 King Charles Warrnambool Trophy Class D Handicap Hurdle (0-120 4-y-o and up) £2,786 2m 110yds......(3:35)

148* IVY EDITH [116] 6-11-10 D Bridgwater, *early to post, led, quickened 4 out, strly pressed whn hit 2 out, ran on gmely.*
.............................(4 to 1 op 7 to 2 tchd 9 to 2) 1
FAUSTINO [110] 4-11-1 A P McCoy, *hld up, chlgd hfwy, not fluent and outpcd 4 out, rallied and ev ch whn hit last, kpt on und pres.*................................(5 to 4 fav tchd 6 to 4) 2
248* STAR MARKET [120] (bl) 6-12-0 R Dunwoody, *chsd ldr, mstk 5th, cl 3rd whn hit last, no extr.*
...........................(11 to 4 op 3 to 1 tchd 7 to 2) 3
VAIN PRINCE [107] 9-11-1 M Dwyer, *midfield, rdn and outpcd appr 4 out, no dngr aftr*....(10 to 1 op 6 to 1) 4
189 AMAZON EXPRESS [105] 7-10-13 R Johnson, *not fluent, struggling in rear 4 out, wl beh aftr*....(14 to 1 op 10 to 1) 5
CAXTON (USA) [92] 9-10-0 B Fenton, *hld up in rear, lost tch appr 4 out, sn beh*.....................(33 to 1 op 25 to 1) 6
266 MERLINS WISH (USA) [114] 7-11-1 (7*) B Moore, *chsd ldrs, reminders 5th, sn beh*.................(20 to 1 op 10 to 1) 7
Dist: ½l, 2½l, 20l, 12l, 3l, 2l. 3m 59.00s. a 13.00s (7 Ran).

(Glen Antill), T G Mills

282 Gerard Mann Mercedes Benz Handicap Chase Class E (0-110 5-y-o and up) £3,626 3m............(4:10)

249* MAPLE DANCER [92] 10-10-3 (7*) Mr G Shenkin, *cl up, jmpd ahead 5 out, clr nxt, drvn out.*.............(9 to 1 op 6 to 1) 1
249⁴ MAGIC BLOOM [98] 10-11-2 Richard Guest, *hld up, hdwy 12th, rdn to go second last, styd on.*
..........................(13 to 2 op 5 to 1 tchd 7 to 1) 2
165² CHANNEL PASTIME [93] 12-10-8 (3*) Guy Lewis, *midfield, hdwy to chase wnr 4 out, no imprsn*....(11 to 1 op 8 to 1) 3
249⁶ WISE ADVICE (Ire) [100] 6-11-4 R Garritty, *hld up, hdwy 6th, rdn and pld up appr 3 out*...................(10 to 1 op 8 to 1) 4
188⁷ BOXING MATCH [82] 9-10-0 A P McCoy, *hndy, led tenth, hdd 5 out, fdd frm nxt.*..................(14 to 1 op 12 to 1) 5
51⁶ VICTORY ANTHEM [82] 10-10-0 B Fenton, *beh, some hdwy 11th, mstk 12th, no dngr aftr*.....(25 to 1 op 16 to 1) 6
202* NOCATCHIM [95] 7-10-13 A S Smith, *chsd ldrs, mstk and reminders 5th, in tch till mistake and fdd 5 out, tld off.*
...........................(8 to 1 op 7 to 1 tchd 9 to 1) 7
188 JIMMY O'DEA [95] (v) 9-10-13 J Railton, *midfield, jmpd slwly 6th, struggling in rear fnl circuit, tld off.* (20 to 1 op 14 to 1) 8
HARRISTOWN LADY [108] (v) 9-11-12 N Williamson, *hld up, gd hdwy tenth, lost pl quickly 13th, tld off.*
...........................(9 to 2 op 6 to 1 tchd 7 to 1) 9
230⁷ RUSTY BRIDGE [85] 9-10-3 W Marston, *sn rdn in rear, tld off whn blun badly and uns rdr 4 out...*(16 to 1 op 12 to 1) ur
230³ THE BLUE BOY (Ire) [102] (bl) 8-11-6 R Johnson, *cl up, lost tch quickly 8th, tld off whn pld up 2 out.*
..........................(4 to 1 fav op 7 to 2 tchd 9 to 2) pu
230 MORNING BLUSH (Ire) [86] (bl) 6-11-0 D Bridgwater, *reminders and sn led, drvn and hdd tenth, wknd quickly and pld up bef 12th*.............(9 to 1 op 8 to 1 tchd 10 to 1) pu
Dist: 7l, 2½l, 20l, 8l, ½l, 5l, 1¼l, 14l. 5m 54.10s. a 9.10s (12 Ran).

(Dr Ian R Shenkin), F Jordan

283 King Henry 'Walkabout' Handicap Hurdle Class E (0-110 4-y-o and up) £2,262 3m 3f..............(4:45)

ELITE REG [106] (v) 7-12-0 D Bridgwater, *chsd ldrs, blun 5th, led 9th, clr whn hit 3 out, jmpd slwly last, hld on wl und pres.*
................................(3 to 1 jt-fav op 9 to 4 tchd 11 to 4) 1
155³ SANTELLA BOY (USA) [100] 4-11-4 R Dunwoody, *hld up, hdwy hfwy, chalg whn hit 2 out, rallied wl r-in, jst fld.*
.......................(2 to 1 jt-fav tchd 7 to 4 and 11 to 5) 2
155⁴ MISS PIMPERNEL [78] 6-10-0 A P McCoy, *trkd ldrs, not fluent 7th, blun nxt, wknd appr 2 out.*
...........................(11 to 2 op 5 to 1 tchd 6 to 1) 3
206² WORDY'S WIND [78] 7-9-7 (7*) C Rae, *hld up, hit 9th, wl beh appr 4 out.*..........................(8 to 1 op 5 to 1) 4
206⁶ DERRING BRIDGE [90] 6-10-12 R Johnson, *sn led, hdd 9th, struggling appr 4 out, tld off.*......(13 to 2 op 5 to 1) 5
247 STORM WARRIOR [78] (bl) 11-9-11 (3*) R Massey, *cl up, reminders 9th, tld off appr 4 out, fnshd lme.*
................................(40 to 1 op 16 to 1) 6
164 LITTLE THYNE [78] (bl) 11-10-0 Dr P Pritchard, *hld up, drvn and mstk 6th, tld off whn pld up aftr tenth.*
................................(40 to 1 op 25 to 1) pu
225 GORT [78] 8-9-8¹ (7*) J Prior, *not jump wl, reminders 5th, tld off whn pld up 4 out, fnshd lme*......(25 to 1 op 16 to 1) pu
Dist: Sht-hd, 27l, 23l, 17l, dist. 6m 42.10s. a 24.10s (8 Ran).

(Martin Pipe Racing Club), M C Pipe

284 Richardsons King Arthur 'Fair Dinkum' Novices' Handicap Hurdle Class E

(0-100 4-y-o and up) £2,178 2m 3f
................................(5:20)

SILVER SLEEVE (Ire) [77] (bl) 4-10-8 R Dunwoody, *hld up, gd hdwy to ld 3 out, rdn and ran on strly appr last.*
...........................(5 to 1 op 4 to 1 tchd 6 to 1) 1
186* SPARTS FAULT (Ire) [75] 6-10-12 Richard Guest, *hld up gng wl, chsd wnr frm 2 out, no extr r-in.*
...........................(9 to 2 op 4 to 1 tchd 5 to 1) 2
186² MUTLEY [65] 6-10-2² C Maude, *early to post, settled rear, pushed alng and unbl to quicken 3 out, sn one pace.*
..............(100 to 30 co-fav op 11 to 4 tchd 3 to 1) 3
IDIOM [63] 9-9-11 (3*) J Culloty, *cl up, drvn alng appr 2 out, sn outpcd.*....................(20 to 1 op 12 to 1) 4
111 SPANISH BLAZE (Ire) [64] 8-10-1 A P McCoy, *chsd ldr, led 6th, hdd and outpcd 3 out, fdd.*.........(100 to 30 co-fav op 4 to 1 tchd 7 to 2) 5
78⁵ PEMBRIDGE PLACE [94] 5-12-0 A Thornton, *led, hdd 6th, fdg whn slightly hmpd entering strt, sn beh.*.....(100 to 30 co-fav op 2 to 1 tchd 7 to 2) 6
Dist: 3l, 11l, nk, 9l, 6l. 4m 38.60s. a 18.60s (6 Ran).

(The Outside Nine), M D Hammond

LES LANDES (JER) (good to firm)
Sunday July 28th

285 BJ O'Connor Anniversary Handicap Hurdle (4-y-o and up) £720 2m...(3:00)

207³ CLEAR HOME 10-10-0 A McCabe, ...(9 to 4) 1
141⁴ FOOLS OF PRIDE (Ire) 4-10-5 B Powell, ...(6 to 1) 2
244⁴ NORTHERN TRIAL (USA) 8-12-0 A Larnach, ...(5 to 2 on) f
Dist: 10l. 3m 51.00s. (3 Ran).

(T J Bougourd), T J Bougourd

GALWAY (IRE) (good)
Monday July 29th

286 GPT Sligo Maiden Hurdle (6-y-o and up) £4,110 2m.................(5:10)

VICAR STREET (Ire) 6-12-0 C F Swan, ...(10 to 9 on) 1
243 TALE GAIL (Ire) 6-12-0 A P McCoy, ...(5 to 1) 2
142³ HIGH MOAT (Ire) 6-11-6 T Horgan, ...(12 to 1) 3
253³ MAGICAL WAY (Ire) 6-11-6 J F Titley, ...(12 to 1) 4
169³ BENNY THE BISHOP (Ire) 6-11-3 (7*) Mr A Ross, (14 to 1) 5
181 REAL TAOISEACH (Ire) 6-11-7 (7*) Mr A K Wyse, ..(7 to 1) 6
64³ SYNIEYOURMISSED (Ire) 7-10-13 (7*) Mr B Hassett,
....(10 to 1) 7
181⁶ NO DIAMOND (Ire) 7-11-6 .I P Broderick, ...(14 to 1) 8
172⁴ SIR GANDOUGE (Ire) 7-11-6 J Shortt, ...(12 to 1) 9
195³ PIONE SABI (Ire) (bl) 6-11-6 P L Malone, ...(33 to 1) 10
211 BRIGHT SHARES (Ire) 6-11-1 K F O'Brien, ...(33 to 1) 11
197³ DEE VALUE (Ire) 6-11-3 (3*) D T Evans, ...(33 to 1) 12
Dist: Nk, 5½l, 2l, 4½l. 3m 53.00s. (12 Ran).

(John P McManus), A P O'Brien

287 GPT Dublin Handicap Hurdle (0-130 4-y-o and up) £4,110 2m........(5:45)

RUPERT BELLE (Ire) [-] 5-10-1 (3*) Mr P Henley, (5 to 2 fav) 1
232* THE BOULD VIC (Ire) [-] 4-10-0 P Carberry, ...(7 to 1) 2
33* FINCHPALM (Ire) [-] 6-10-8 F J Flood, ...(4 to 1) 3
29* GALLETINA (Ire) [-] 6-11-3 R Dunwoody, ...(3 to 1) 4
PHARDANAIRE (Ire) [-] 5-10-9 D H O'Connor, ...(7 to 1) 5
131² BALMYRA (Ire) [-] (bl) 4-9-7 W T Slattery, ...(11 to 1) 6
184⁷ MISTER CHIPPY (Ire) [-] 4-10-13 C F Swan, ...(8 to 1) 7
Dist: 3l, 5l, 6l, 1½l. 3m 52.40s. (7 Ran).

(Mrs E Donoghue), C P Donoghue

288 GPT Contractors Plant INH Flat Race (4-y-o and up) £4,110 2m.......(8:35)

LEWISHAM (Ire) 4-11-4 (3*) Mr B M Cash, ... (5 to 4 fav) 1
KERANI (USA) 4-11-7 Mr P Fenton, ...(3 to 1) 2
217² PLEASE NO TEARS 9-11-9 Mrs C Barker, ...(14 to 1) 3
ELECTRIC RYMER (Ire) 6-11-7 Mr D Marnane, (11 to 2) 4
DUNEAVEY (Ire) 5-11-3 (5*) Mr R Walsh, ...(10 to 1) 5
238⁷ CASTLE ELLEN BOY (Ire) 4-11-7 J Culloty, ...(20 to 1) 6
LIMIT THE DAMAGE (USA) 4-11-0 (7*) G T Hourigan,
....(25 to 1) 7
ARCTIC CLOVER (Ire) 5-11-6 (7*) Mr A J Dempsey, (16 to 1) 8
JACK DORY (Ire) 4-11-4 (3*) Mr K Whelan, ...(10 to 1) 9
213 SEXTON'S MIRROR (Ire) 4-11-7 Miss M Olivefalk, (25 to 1) 10
213⁷ KINCORA (Ire) 5-11-13 Mr J A Nash, ...(14 to 1) 11
183⁴ JACKIE'S PERSIAN (Ire) 7-11-2 (7*) M P Dunne, ..(33 to 1) 12
SIAMSA REATHA (Ire) 5-11-3 (5*) G Cotter, ...(33 to 1) 13
258³ NAKURU (Ire) 7-11-2 (7*) Mr A C Coyle, ...(14 to 1) 14
ACTIVE LADY (Ire) 4-10-9 (7*) Mr B Walsh, ...(25 to 1) 15
OWEN BOLISCA (Ire) 4-10-9 (7*) Miss A L Moore, (16 to 1) 16
SHARLENE (Ire) 5-11-8 Mr A J Martin, ...(12 to 1) 17
MERRY CHANTER (Ire) 4-11-0 (7*) Mr G Elliott, ...(25 to 1) 18
Dist: Nk, 1½l, 5½l, 1½l. 3m 46.90s. (18 Ran).

(John P McManus), A P O'Brien

GALWAY (IRE) (good)
Tuesday July 30th

289 Albatross N-Rich Maiden Hurdle (4 & 5-y-o) £4,110 2m. . . . . (5:10)

CELTIC LORE (bl) 4-11-7 R Dunwoody, ... (Evens fav) 1
245^* CONNIES BUCK (Ire) 4-11-2 (5*) G Cotter, ... (20 to 1) 2
SENTOSA STAR (Ire) 5-11-13 A Maguire, ... (7 to 1) 3
DROMINEER (Ire) 5-11-13 M P Dwyer, ... (10 to 1) 4
BLAZING STORM (Ire) 4-11-7 J Shortt, ... (12 to 1) 5
31^2 LISS DE PAOR (Ire) 5-11-8 C F Swan, ... (7 to 1) 6
224^7 THAI ELECTRIC (Ire) 5-11-8 F Woods, ... (33 to 1) 7
CAITRIONA'S CHOICE (Ire) 5-11-13 A P McCoy, . . (11 to 1) 8
MULLOVER 5-11-5 C O'Dwyer, ... (16 to 1) 9
MADARAKA (USA) 5-11-5 (3*) Mr P Henley, ...(25 to 1) 10
BUNOWEN 4-11-2 K F O'Brien, ...(33 to 1) 11
181^2 DON'T LOOSE FAITH (Ire) 4-10-11 S C Lyons, ... (14 to 1) f
LIFE SUPPORT (Ire) 4-11-2 P Carberry, ... (5 to 1) f

Dist: 1½l, sht-hd, nk, 9l. 3m 57.10s. (13 Ran).
(Michael W J Smurfit), D K Weld

290 Albatross Chase (4-y-o and up) £5,137 2¾m. . . . . (5:45)

97^* STROLL HOME (Ire) 6-11-12 P Carberry, ...(12 to 1) 1
63^2 MILE A MINUTE (Ire) (bl) 5-11-5 A P McCoy, ... (5 to 1) 2
VERY LITTLE (Ire) 8-11-3 K P Gaule, ... (25 to 1) 3
218^2 MICKS DELIGHT (Ire) 6-11-12 M P Dwyer, ... (6 to 1) 4
97 THE OUTBACK WAY (Ire) (bl) 6-11-8 D H O'Connor, (7 to 1) 5
STEEL MIRROR (bl) 7-11-12 C F Swan, ... (5 to 4 fav) 6
237^4 MELDANTE VI (Ire) (bl) 5-11-1 J P Broderick, ... (33 to 1) 7
237^* BEET STATEMENT (Ire) 7-11-0 (7*) Mr B Valentine, (12 to 1) 8
114^8 NATURAL ABILITY 11-11-8 C N Bowens, ... (12 to 1) f
257^* CLAHADA ROSE (Ire) 6-11-7 T Horgan, ... (5 to 1) f

Dist: 1½l, 10l, 4l, 2½l. 5m 34.20s. (10 Ran).
(Mrs M Mangan), James Joseph Mangan

GALWAY (IRE) (good)
Wednesday July 31st

291 Digital European Software Centre Hurdle (4-y-o and up) £4,110 2m. . . . (2:00)

289 LIFE SUPPORT (Ire) 4-10-9 P Carberry, ... (5 to 2) 1
KALDAN KHAN 5-11-13 C F Swan, ...(11 to 10 fav) 2
221^* COLM'S ROCK (Ire) 5-11-13 T Horgan, ...(5 to 2) 3
256^* HAY DANCE 5-11-10 A Maguire, ...(10 to 1) 4
86^3 GHALAYAN 4-11-0 C O'Dwyer, ...(16 to 1) pu

Dist: 6l, 3½l, 1l. 3m 56.00s. (5 Ran).
(Mrs A S O'Brien), Noel Meade

292 C.K. Business Electronics Handicap Hurdle (0-116 4-y-o and up) £5,480 2½m. . . . . (2:35)

96^* KEPHREN (USA) [-] 7-11-2 C O'Dwyer, ...(7 to 1) 1
254^3 LADY DAISY (Ire) [-] 7-10-13 (7*) A O'Shea, ...(9 to 1) 2
223^3 VAIN PRINCESS (Ire) [-] 7-10-9 M P Hourigan, ... (10 to 1) 3
273^3 ADARAMANN (Ire) [-] 4-10-4 (5*) Mr R Walsh, ...(10 to 1) 4
182^8 JUST AN ILLUSION (Ire) [-] 4-11-3 A Maguire, ...(5 to 1) 5
171^* SHOREWOOD (Ire) [-] 5-10-8 R Dunwoody, ... (5 to 2 fav) 6
208^3 CLAIRE ME (Ire) [-] 7-9-7 P McWilliams, ...(20 to 1) 7
158^6 RISING BREEZE (Ire) [-] 7-10-7 C F Swan, ...(11 to 1) 8
209^2 CUBAN QUESTION [-] 9-9-7 (5*) G Cotter, ...(14 to 1) 9
179^2 MAKING THE POINT (Ire) [-] 5-11-6 K F O'Brien, . . . (8 to 1) 10
161^2 SPANKY (Ire) [-] 4-11-5 L P Cusack, ...(13 to 2) 11

Dist: 4l, 8l, 1l, hd. 4m 57.70s. (11 Ran).
(Paul Davis), V Kennedy

293 Digital Galway Plate (Grade 2) (Handicap Chase) (4-y-o and up) £31,125 2¾m. . . . . (4:00)

LIFE OF A LORD [-] 10-12-0 C F Swan, *wl plcd, trkd ldr 5 out, hrd rdn to chal r-in, led ins fnl furlong, ran on strly cl hme.* . . . .(9 to 2) 1
BISHOPS HALL [-] $10-10-2^1$ R Dunwoody, *wl plcd, prog to track ldrs aftr 6th, dsptd ld 3 out, led nxt, hdd r-in, wknd cl hme.* . . . . (14 to 1) 2
KING WAH GLORY (Ire) [-] 7-9-13 C O'Dwyer, *mid-div, jmpd slwly 8th, gd prog bef 3 out, kpt on, not trble 1st 2.* (9 to 4 fav) 3
SECOND SCHEDUAL [-] 11-10-6 M P Dwyer, *rear, gd prog bef 4 out, styd on wl.* . . . .(20 to 1) 4
198^3 TRYFIRION (Ire) [-] 7-9-7 B Powell, *rear early, some prog bef 7th, styd on wl r-in.* . . . .(10 to 1) 5
198^2 SWALLOWS NEST [-] 9-9-7 W T Slattery, *trkd ldr early, wl plcd till wkng aftr 2 out.* . . . .(20 to 1) 6
218^* KELLY'S PEARL [-] 9-9-7 T Horgan, *mid-div, prog bef 3 out, wknd aftr last.* . . . . (12 to 1) 7
85^7 ANOTHER GROUSE [-] $9-9-8^1$ J P Broderick, *al mid-div, rdn bef 3 out, not quicken.* . . . . (50 to 1) 8
252 BORO VACATION (Ire) [-] 7-9-10 P Carberry, *led till appr 5 out, sn wknd.* . . . .(8 to 1) 9
218^3 LOFTUS LAD (Ire) [-] $8-9-9^2$ J Culloty, *al rear, rdn aftr 4 out, no extr.* . . . .(66 to 1) 10
252^2 NOBODYS SON [-] 10-9-7 (3ex) T J Murphy, *trkd ldr early, wl plcd till wknd 5 out.* . . . .(66 to 1) 11
252^* OPEN MARKET (USA) [-] 7-9-7 (4ex) N Williamson, *rear, gd prog bef 4 out, trkd ldrs and rdn nxt, f 2 out.* . . . . (9 to 1) f
252 AN MAINEACH (Ire) [-] 7-9-4 (3*) D J Casey, *trkd ldr, slpd appr 6 out, prog to ld nxt, hdd 2 out, uns rdr last.* . . . .(20 to 1) ur
236^6 BALLYBRIKEN CASTLE [-] 9-9-7 P L Malone, *al rear, lost tch 3rd, pld up bef 8th.* . . . . (200 to 1) pu
JASSU [-] 10-10-10 J F Titley, *al rear, pld up bef 3 out.* . . . .(25 to 1) pu
252 ANABATIC (Ire) [-] 8-10-5 T P Rudd, *wl plcd early, wknd aftr 7th, pld up bef nxt, broke blood vessel.* . . . . (14 to 1) pu
76^7 MINISTER FOR FUN (Ire) [-] 8-9-7 F Woods, *wl plcd, wknd bef 4 out, pld up before 2 out.* . . . . (10 to 1) pu

Dist: 1½l, 8l, 3l, 3½l, 11l, 3l. 5m 20.40s. (17 Ran).
(M J Clancy), A P O'Brien

STRATFORD (good to firm)
Wednesday July 31st

Going Correction: MINUS 0.10 sec. per fur.

294 A.H.P. Trailers Wombourne Conditional Jockeys' Selling Handicap Hurdle Class G (0-90 4-y-o and up) £1,884 2m 110yds. (6:15)

205 RAGAMUFFIN ROMEO [66] 7-10-11 R Massey, *hld up, mstk second and 6th, hdwy to chase ldrs appr nxt, hrd rdn, hng rght and led nr finish.* . . . . . . (14 to 1 op 16 to 1 tchd 25 to 1) 1
INDIAN MINOR [60] 12-10-5 D J Kavanagh, *chsd clr ldr, led 3 out, rdn betw last 2, wknd and hdd nr finish.* . . . . (40 to 1 op 25 to 1) 2
205^8 HERETICAL MISS [75] 6-11-6 B Fenton, *hld up, hdwy aftr 4 out, drvn alng appr 2 out, kpt on one pace.* . . . .(4 to 1 op 5 to 1) 3
246^3 KING OF BABYLON (Ire) [72] 4-11-0 L Aspell, *chsd clr ldr, led aftr 5th, hdd 3 out, sn rdn and no imprsn.* . . . .(7 to 2 op 3 to 1 tchd 9 to 2 and 5 to 1) 4
100 DOCTOR-J (Ire) [82] 6-11-10 (3*) D Finnegan, *hld up, hdwy to chase ldr aftr 5th, rdn and wknd 3 out.* . . . . (11 to 2 op 7 to 2 tchd 6 to 1) 5
205^7 BOOST [65] 4-10-7 E Husband, *chsd clr ldr, ev ch 3 out, sn rdn and wknd.* . . . .(13 to 2 op 8 to 1 tchd 9 to 1 and 10 to 1) 6
246^* SET-EM-ALIGHT [69] 6-10-7 (7*) K Hibbert, *hld up, pld hrd, hard rdn and no imprsn aftr 4 out, sn btn.* . . . .(11 to 4 fav op 2 to 1) 7
243 KAJOSTAR [55] 6-10-0 O Burrows, *hld up, lost tch aftr 5th, tld off after 4 out.* . . . . (50 to 1 op 25 to 1) 8
279 DAN DE LYON [67] (bl) 8-10-12 J Magee, *led, sn clr, hit 3rd, hrd rdn and hdd aftr 5th, soon tld off, f 2 out.* . . . .(14 to 1 op 10 to 1 tchd 16 to 1) f

Dist: 1l, 2½l, 3l, ½l, 1¾l, 8l, dist. 4m 1.80s. a 15.80s (9 Ran).
(Mrs D Sawyer), H Sawyer

295 Richardson Novices' Hurdle Class E (4-y-o and up) £2,192 2¾m 110yds . . . . (6:45)

203^* ORDOG MOR (Ire) 7-11-5 D Byrne, *led aftr second, jmpd wl, drw clr after 3 out, easily.* . . . . (5 to 2 on op 2 to 1 on) 1
262^3 MURBERRY (Ire) 6-10-7 L Harvey, *hld up in tch, chsd ldr frm 7th, outpcd aftr 4 out, styd on ag'n after 2 out, no ch wth wnr.* . . . . (5 to 1 op 3 to 1 tchd 11 to 2) 2
TUG YOUR FORELOCK 5-10-12 A Thornton, *chsd ldg pair, wnt second 4 out, sn rdn and no imprsn.* . . . . (20 to 1 op 10 to 1) 3
284^2 SPARTS FAULT (Ire) 6-11-5 Richard Guest, *hld up, rdn and hdwy aftr 5 out, wknd after 3 out.* . . . .(6 to 1 op 5 to 1 tchd 7 to 1) 4
229^8 DICKIES GIRL 6-10-7 W Marston, *led til aftr second, pushed alng after 7th, sn lost tch, tld off 4 out.* . . . . (20 to 1 op 33 to 1 tchd 50 to 1) 5
FLASHING SABRE 4-10-9 Mr A Charles-Jones, *jmpd slwly 3rd, hld up, lost tch aftr 6th, tld off whn pld up after nxt.* . . . . (100 to 1 op 33 to 1) pu

Dist: 20l, 9l, nk, dist. 5m 31.20s. a 19.20s (6 Ran).
(M R Johnson), M G Meagher

296 Barry Ordish-Property Handicap Chase Class D (0-120 5-y-o and up) £3,847 2m 1f 110yds. . . . . (7:15)

NATIONAL HUNT RESULTS 1996-97

280* STATELY HOME (Ire) [105] 5-10-10 (7ex) R Johnson, *jmpd wl,*
made sl, styd on well frm 2 out . . . . . (11 to 8 op 11 to 10) 1
240* NOBLELY (USA) [100] 9-10-8 A P McCoy, *pressed ldr, ev ch 4
out, sn drvn alng, kpt on frm 2 out, no imprsn.*
. . . .(5 to 4 fav op 6 to 4 tchd 13 to 8) 2
249[8] FLYING ZIAD (Can) [92] 13-9-7 (7*) A Dowling, *hld up in last
pl, beh til hdwy aftr 4 out, styd on frm 2 out.*
. . . . (16 to 1 op 25 to 1) 3
NUCLEAR EXPRESS [92] 9-10-0 B Fenton, *chsd ldg pair til
pushed alng and lost pl aftr 6th, hdwy after 4 out, wknd after
nxt* . . . . (50 to 1 op 25 to 1) 4
SNITTON LANE [120] 10-12-0 B Storey, *hld up, wnt 3rd 5th,
chsd ldg pair til wknd 4 out, tld off.*
. . . . (5 to 1 op 7 to 2 tchd 11 to 2 and 6 to 1) 5
Dist: 5l, ¾l, 10l, dist. 4m 7.10s. a 5.10s (5 Ran).
SR: 14/7/   (P Bowen), P Bowen

297 Promota Maiden Hurdle Class E (4-y-o and up) £2,262 2m 110yds . . . . . . (7:45)

226[3] CHANCEY FELLA 5-11-0 A P McCoy, *led, drvn alng aftr 3 out,
hdd appr nxt, hrd rdn and rallied betw last 2, led nr finish.*
. . . . (7 to 2 op 3 to 1) 1
SAMBA SHARPLY 5-11-0 P Hide, *hld up in tch, trkd ldrs frm
4th, mstk four out, led gng wl appr 2 out, mistake last, sn rdn,
hdd nr finish.* . . . . (7 to 4 fav tchd 9 to 4) 2
226[4] SORISKY 4-10-11 Richard Guest, *trkd ldr, ev ch but drvn
alng aftr 4 out, styd on one pace frm nxt.*
. . . . (11 to 2 op 6 to 1 tchd 7 to 1) 3
229[7] MIRAMARE 6-11-0 G Upton, *hld up, beh 4th, chsd ldr aftr four
out, sn no imprsn* . . . . (14 to 1 op 12 to 1 tchd 16 to 1) 4
CANARY FALCON 5-11-0 V Smith, *hld up and beh, hdwy aftr
3 out, no imprsn* . . . . (8 to 1 op 5 to 1) 5
SAINT AMIGO 4-10-11 J A McCarthy, *hld up, hdwy aftr 5th,
rdn 4 out, sn btn* . . . . (12 to 1 op 10 to 1) 6
PEUTETRE (bl) 4-10-11 R Greene, *chsd ldr, in tch and drvn
alng 4 out, sn btn* . . . (20 to 1 op 12 to 1 tchd 25 to 1) 7
CANESTRELLI (USA) 11-10-7 (7*) Mr A Wintle, *chsd ldrs to
5th, sn beh* . . . .(100 to 1 op 50 to 1) 8
CORALCIOUS (Ire) 5-10-11 (3*) J Magee, *beh 4th, jmpd slwly
nxt, sn tld off* . . . . (66 to 1 op 33 to 1) 9
COLT D'OR 4-10-11 D Gallagher, *prmnt frm 3rd, stumbled
and broke leg aftr 5th, destroyed* . . . . (20 to 1 op 12 to 1) pu
MINIDIA 4-9-13 (7*) A Dowling, *al last, not fluent, tld off aftr
3rd, pld up bef 5th* . . . . (50 to 1 op 33 to 1) pu
Dist: ½l, 13l, 2½l, 2½l, 14l, 2½l, 2l, dist. 3m 58.60s. a 12.60s (11 Ran).
                                          (Mrs H E Haynes), H E Haynes

298 J. Round Machinery Ltd., Wednesbury Novices' Chase Class E (5-y-o and up) £3,051 2½m . . . . (8:15)

SONIC STAR (Ire) 7-10-12 A Maguire, *hld up, wnt second 9th,
stumbled badly and rdr lost iron aftr nxt, sn reco'red, pressed
ldr til slight l2 2 out, drvn out.*
. . . .(9 to 4 op 7 to 4 tchd 5 to 2) 1
204[3] SHIKAREE (Ire) 5-10-8 D Bridgwater, *trkd ldrs, cl up and ev ch
wth mstk 4 out, sn reco'red, every chance frm nxt, rdn 2 out,
not quicken* . . . .(11 to 8 fav op 6 to 4 tchd 13 to 8) 2
SYDMONTON 10-10-12 R Johnson, *led til hdd 2 out, wknd
betw last two* . . . .(20 to 1 op 12 to 1 tchd 25 to 1) 3
FOREST FEATHER (Ire) 8-10-12 M Richards, *not fluent
early, hld up, hdwy aftr tenth, ev ch 4 out, rdn and wknd after
nxt* . . . . . (2 to 1 op 9 to 4 tchd 5 to 2 and 11 to 4) 4
156[6] JAMESWICK 6-10-12 P Holley, *chsd ldg pair til wknd aftr 5
out* . . . .(33 to 1 op 14 to 1) 5
190[5] MASTER ART 6-10-12 G Upton, *chsd ldr, mstks 5th and 8th,
wknd aftr tenth, tld off, pld up bef 3 out.* (50 to 1 op 20 to 1) pu
Dist: 8l, 5l, 4l, 16l. 4m 52.70s. a 12.70s (6 Ran).
                                          (R F Nutland), D Nicholson

299 Richardson Oldbury Handicap Hurdle Class E (0-110 4-y-o and up) £2,234 2m 3f . . . . (8:45)

JENZSOPH (Ire) [103] 5-11-6 (5*) D J Kavanagh, *led, clr aftr
3rd, hdd after 3 out, rdn and rallied, to ld ag'n last, styd on wl.*
. . . . (11 to 4 op 4 to 1 tchd 5 to 2 op 3 to 1) 1
241[2] STRONG JOHN (Ire) [88] 8-10-10 (3*) D Parker, *hld up, hdwy
to chase ldr aftr 5th, led 3 out, hdd last, not quicken.*
. . . . (4 to 1 op 7 to 2) 2
44[6] CIRCUS COLOURS [96] 6-11-7 S Fox, *very slwly away, hdwy
4th, ev ch four out, rdn and wknd aftr 2 out, flashed tail and not
quicken betw last 2* . . . . (7 to 1 op 9 to 2) 3
206[9] MILZIG (USA) [75] 7-10-0 C Llewellyn, *wl beh aftr 5th, styd on
after 3 out, nvr nrr* . . . . . .(6 to 1 op 7 to 1 tchd 6 to 1) 4
204 HACKETTS CROSS (Ire) [103] 8-11-7 (7*) Mr R Thornton,
chsd ldr, ev ch 5 out, rdn and wknd aftr 4 out.
. . . . (25 to 1 op 20 to 1) 5
244[5] RAY RIVER [91] 4-10-13 J Ryan, *chsd ldr, drvn alng and
outpcd aftr 5th, sn lost tch* . . . . . . (7 to 1 tchd 8 to 1) 6
105[9] HOLY JOE [100] 14-11-11 D J Burchell, *lost tch and pushed
alng aftr 5th, sn tld off* . . . . (20 to 1 op 16 to 1) 7
LORCANJO [78] 5-10-0 A P McCoy, *chsd ldr, pushed alng
and lost pl aftr 5th, staying on ag'n whn pld up lme appr 2 out.*
. . . .(9 to 2 op 5 to 1 tchd 4 to 1) pu

37

Dist: 2l, 1¾l, 12l, 6l, 1¾l, dist. 4m 34.90s. a 14.90s (8 Ran).
                                          (Superset Two), P J Hobbs

GALWAY (IRE) (good)
Thursday August 1st

300 Guinness Novice Chase (4-y-o and up) £4,110 2m 1f . . . . (2:00)

290* STROLL HOME (Ire) 6-12-7 P Carberry, ... (3 to 1) 1
291[2] KALDAN KHAN 5-11-1 C F Swan, ... (7 to 4 fav) 2
RYE FONTAINE (Ire) 7-11-7 R Dunwoody, ... (9 to 2) 3
215* SAVUTI (Ire) 7-11-7 (7*) M D Murphy, ... (6 to 1) 4
20* IRISH FOUNTAIN (Ire) 8-12-0 J P Broderick, ... (11 to 2) f
65[7] PAT THE HAT (Ire) 6-11-7 T J Murphy, ... (33 to 1) pu
Dist: ¾l, dist, 1l. 4m 25.80s. (6 Ran).
                                          (Mrs M Mangan), James Joseph Mangan

301 Harp Lager Novice Hurdle (4-y-o and up) £4,110 2½m . . . . (2:35)

193[2] CLONAGAM (Ire) 7-11-0 C F Swan, ... (9 to 2) 1
TARTHOOTH (Ire) 5-11-0 F Woods, ... (10 to 9 on) 2
270* CLASSIC SILK (Ire) 4-10-9 N Williamson, ... (8 to 1) 3
185[3] WELL ARMED (Ire) 5-11-0 P Carberry, ... (16 to 1) 4
262[5] UP THE TEMPO (Ire) 7-10-9 R Dunwoody, ... (25 to 1) 5
260* PRECEPTOR (Ire) 7-11-7 (3*) B Bowens, ... (8 to 1) 6
271[2] CELIO LUCY (Ire) 6-10-6 (3*) D J Casey, ... (14 to 1) 7
269[2] MIDDLE MOGGS (Ire) 4-10-2 K F O'Brien, ... (20 to 1) 8
255[3] BULWARK HILL (Ire) 6-11-0 G Bradley, ... (6 to 1) 9
233 BRACKER (Ire) 4-10-11 (7*) Mr C A Murphy, ... (66 to 1) 10
261 DEEP REFRAIN (Ire) 6-11-0 J F Titley, ... (25 to 1) 11
178[6] GROVE VICTOR (Ire) (bl) 5-11-0 C O'Dwyer, ... (50 to 1) 12
Dist: 2½l, 3l, 9l, ½l. 4m 54.50s. (12 Ran).
                                          (R Galvin), A P O'Brien

302 St James's Gate Handicap Hurdle (0-123 4-y-o and up) £5,137 3m (3:10)

254 CULLENSTOWN LADY (Ire) [-] 5-11-8 R Dunwoody, (7 to 2) 1
GLENGARRIF GIRL (Ire) [-] (bl) 6-10-12 D Bridgwater,
. . . . (7 to 4 fav) 2
259* BUGGSY BLADE [-] 10-10-0 M Duffy, ... (7 to 1) 3
76[5] FINAL TUB [-] 13-10-1 T Horgan, ... (16 to 1) 4
222[5] SUDDEN STORM (Ire) [-] 6-10-3 D J Casey, ... (12 to 1) 5
273* CHUCK (Ire) [-] 6-9-11 (7*) D McCullagh, ... (10 to 1) 6
MARLAST (Ire) [-] 8-9-3 J Shortt, ... (14 to 1) 7
230* BRAVO STAR (USA) [-] (bl) 11-9-7 F Woods, ... (25 to 1) 8
273[8] MANETTI [-] 4-10-9 A P McCoy, ... (12 to 1) 9
222[8] DONERAILE PARK [-] 9-10-11 N Williamson, ... (20 to 1) 10
272[f] VALAMIR (Ire) [-] 6-9-7 B G Powell, ... (66 to 1) 11
252[5] STEEL DAWN [-] 9-11-7 (7*) Mr R J Curran, ... (12 to 1) pu
DERBY HAVEN [-] 9-10-6 S C Lyons, ... (10 to 1) pu
224[2] EXPEDIENT OPTION (Ire) [-] 6-10-12 C F Swan, . . (10 to 1) pu
Dist: ¾l, 15l, 1½l, 5½l. 5m 45.90s. (14 Ran).
                                          (P Hughes), P Hughes

303 Guinness Galway Hurdle Handicap (Grade 2) (4-y-o and up) £27,750 2m
. . . . (4:00)

MYSTICAL CITY (Ire) [-] 6-10-1 (3*) D J Casey, *mid-div, steady
prog aftr 4th, led bef last, rdn r-in kpt on wl* . . . . (20 to 1) 1
SPACE TRUCKER (Ire) [-] 5-10-11 N Williamson, *rear early,
some prog 3rd, trkd ldrs 2 out, chlgd aftr last, no extr fnl
furlong* . . . . (20 to 1) 2
220* JUST LITTLE [-] 4-10-3 C F Swan, *rear till prog aftr 4th, rdn
second last, slightly hmpd bef last, kpt on und pres.* (14 to 1) 3
220* KHAYRAWANI (Ire) [-] 4-10-6 (8ex) C O'Dwyer, *trkd ldr till led
aftr second, rdn and hdd bef last, wknd* . . . . (6 to 1) 4
220[2] NORTHERN FANCY [-] 5-9-7 F Woods, *towards rear,
some prog bef 3rd, trkd ldrs second last, rdn, no extr.*
. . . . (25 to 1) 5
DREAMS END [-] 8-11-3 R Farrant, *wl plcdd, trkd ldrs, 3rd,
rdn and wknd aftr second last* . . . . (20 to 1) 6
ALASAD [-] 6-10-11 P Carberry, *fst away, wl plcd, rdn bef
second last, hmpd and wknd before last* . . . . (7 to 1) 7
DANCE BEAT (Ire) [-] 5-11-7 J Shortt, *fst away, trkd ldrs till
lost pos 4th, rdn bef second last, not quicken* . . . . (14 to 1) 8
257[3] PHARDY (Ire) [-] 5-9-7 B G Powell, *rear till some prog aftr
last* . . . . (50 to 1) 9
182* WEST ON BRIDGE ST (Ire) [-] 6-9-12[1] D Bridgwater, *wl plcd
till rdn and lost pos bef second last* . . . . (10 to 1) 10
148[2] SUIVEZ [-] 6-10-11 J Osborne, *rear, some prog aftr 3rd last.*
. . . . (20 to 1) 11
287* RUPERT BELLE [-] 5-9-13 (3*,5ex) Mr P Henley, *towards
rear, some prog bef second last, trkd ldr* . . . . . . (20 to 1) 12
NO TAG (Ire) [-] 8-11-8 J F Titley, *wl plcd, prog to track ldr
second last, sn wknd* . . . . (20 to 1) 13
TALINA'S LAW (Ire) [-] (bl) 4-10-12 G Bradley, *trkd ldrs, dsptd ld
briefly 3rd, rdn nxt, wknd aftr second last* . . . . . (10 to 1) 14
TREBLE BOB (Ire) [-] 6-12-0 R Dunwoody, *al rear, rdn bef
second last, not quicken* . . . . (40 to 1) 15
200[3] KAWA-KAWA [-] 9-9-12 S H O'Donovan, *mid-div, some prog
bef 3rd, wknd aftr third last* . . . . (50 to 1) 16

254* CROSSFARNOGUE (Ire) [-] 7-11-10 (7ex) T Horgan, *led bef 1st, hdd aftr nxt, lost pos before 4th, sn wknd*......(33 to 1) 17
ROS CASTLE [-] (bl) 5-11-1 A P McCoy, *trkd ldrs, dsptd ld briefly 3rd, then tracked leader till lost pos and wknd bef second last*..........(14 to 1) 18
LADY ARPEL (Ire) [-] 4-10-12 K F O'Brien, *al towards rear, rdn bef second last, not quicken*..........(20 to 1) 19
STATE PRINCESS (Ire) [-] 6-10-9 A Maguire, *mid-divison till rdn and wknd aftr last*..........(20 to 1) 20
ROYAL ALBERT (Ire) [-] 7-10-9 M Duffy,........(9 to 2 fav) su
Dist: 2½l, nk, 3½l, 3l, hd, 7l. 3m 39.20s. (21 Ran).
(Phantom Syndicate), W P Mullins

304 Arthur Guinness INH Flat Race (5-y-o and up) £4,110 2¼m............(5:40)

ASK THE BUTLER (Ire) 5-11-9 (5*) Mr J Connolly, (5 to 4 on) 1
BABY JAKE (Ire) 6-11-7 (7*) Mr B Hassett,.........(7 to 1) 2
WRITTEN (Ire) 6-12-0 Mr P Fenton,..........(20 to 1) 3
245^{6} GLENREEF BOY (Ire) 7-11-11 (3*) Mr P Henley,.... (16 to 1) 5
224^{3} BARRIGAN'S HILL (Ire) 6-11-7 (7*) Mr John P Moloney, ...(14 to 1) 6
DEAR CHRIS (Ire) 5-11-4 (5*) Mr R Walsh,.........(10 to 1) 7
HIGHEST CALL (Ire) 5-12-0 Mr M Halford,.........(10 to 1) 8
CASTLEROYAL (Ire) 7-12-0 Mr D Marnane,........(12 to 1) 9
274^{4} MARIE'S PRIDE (Ire) (bl) 5-11-2 (7*) Mr D O'Meara, (12 to 1) 10
DAWN CALLER (Ire) 5-11-7 (7*) Mr M W Carroll,...(10 to 1) 11+
DIAMOND DOUBLE (Ire) 5-11-6 (3*) Mr B M Cash,..(8 to 1) 11+
197^{4} MC CLATCHEY (Ire) 5-12-0 Mr P F Graffin,........(20 to 1) 12
256^{8} EOINS LAD (Ire) 5-12-0 Mr A J Martin,..........(20 to 1) 13
271^{3} WEAVER SQUARE (Ire) 7-12-0 Mr J A Nash,.......(10 to 1) 14
259 FORGIVENESS (Ire) 6-11-7 (7*) Mr G Monroe,.....(50 to 1) 15
175^{5} CORKERS FLAME (Ire) 5-11-11 (3*) Mr K Whelan, (20 to 1) 16
191^{6} MORECEVA (Ire) 6-12-0 Mr J P Dempsey,.......(14 to 1) 17
HOWESSHECUTTING (Ire) 6-11-2 (7*) Mr G Elliott, (25 to 1) 18
62 CARNMORE CASTLE (Ire) (bl) 8-11-7 (7*) Mr K N McDonagh, ...(33 to 1) 19
THE BREASER FAWL (Ire) 8-11-7 (7*) Mr D Hassett, (20 to 1) 20
MYSTICAL RYE (Ire) 5-11-2 (7*) Mr A Daly,........ (33 to 1) 21
Dist: 5½l, 3½l, 1l, 1½l. 4m 11.40s. (21 Ran).
(Barry Lee McCoubrey), P Burke

BANGOR (good to firm)
Friday August 2nd
Going Correction: PLUS 0.15 sec. per fur.

305 M.F.M. And Marcher Gold Juvenile Novices' Claiming Hurdle Class F (3-y-o) £2,234 2m 1f...............(3:10)

FRIENDLY DREAMS (Ire) (bl) 10-0 T Eley, *led second, made rst, rdn clr r-in*..........(50 to 1 op 33 to 1) 1
FOUR WEDDINGS (USA) (bl) 11-12 D Bridgwater, *led aftr 1st to nxt, reminder after 3rd, jmpd slwly 5th, sn outpcd, drvn to chase wnr bef last, no imprsn.*
..........(6 to 5 fav op Evens tchd 5 to 4) 2
BALMORAL PRINCESS (bl) 10-6 R Bellamy, *led till aftr 1st, remainded hndy, wth wnr 4 out, ev ch whn mstk nxt, sn drvn and btn*..........(66 to 1 op 33 to 1) 3
MY KIND 10-0 J Osborne, *hld up in tch, effrt and hdwy 3 out, chsd wnr briefly bef nxt, wknd betw last 2.*
..........(11 to 4 op 3 to 1 tchd 7 to 2) 4
SHE'S SIMPLY GREAT (Ire) 10-13 (5*) R McGrath, *al beh, struggling frm 4 out*..........(4 to 1 op 3 to 1) 5
INCA BIRD 9-11 (3*) R Massey, *hld up, mstk 4th, sn wl beh, nvr a factor*..........(50 to 1 op 33 to 1) 6
ALL IN GOOD TIME 11-0 M Foster, *in tch, und pres frm 4 out, wl beh whn mstk nxt, tld off.*
..........(11 to 1 op 8 to 1 tchd 12 to 1) 7
IMAGE MAKER (Ire) 9-7 (7*) D Finnegan, *beh, blun and uns rdr 4th*..........(25 to 1 op 50 to 1 tchd 20 to 1) ur
SONG FOR JESS (Ire) 10-9 R Greene, *jmpd badly rght and uns rdr 1st*..........(25 to 1 op 16 to 1) ur
Dist: 6l, 3½l, 12l, 23l, 19l, 21l. 4m 8.50s. a 18.50s (9 Ran).
(J W Ellis), P T Dalton

306 Chronicle Newspapers Novices' Chase Class D (5-y-o and up) £3,517 3m 110yds.................... (3:40)

247* STICKY MONEY 8-11-1 D Bridgwater, *led second to 5th, rgned ld tenth, drw clr frm 4 out, very easily.*
..........(13 to 8 on op 5 to 4 on) 1
230^{2} PHARRAGO (Ire) 7-11-0 D J Burchell, *hld up, chsd wnr frm 11th, no imprsn from 4 out*..........(6 to 1 op 4 to 1) 2
206^{3} SCRABO VIEW (Ire) 8-11-0 R Supple, *hld up, feeling pace frm 4 out, nvr dngrs*....(4 to 1 op 3 to 1 tchd 9 to 2) 3
164* MANOR RHYME 9-11-6 B Powell, *led to second, led 5th to tenth, drvn and lost grnd quickly frm nxt, sn wl beh.*
..........(6 to 1 op 4 to 1) 4
Dist: 4l, 4l, 16l. 6m 13.40s. a 28.40s (4 Ran).
(Mrs D Jenks), M C Pipe

307 New Season Conditional Jockeys' Selling Handicap Hurdle Class G (0-95 4-y-o and up) £1,952 2m 1f..... (4:15)

PETER MONAMY [92] 4-11-8 D Walsh, *trkd ldrs, wnt second aftr 4th, gng wl upsides frm four out, led on bit r-in, cheekily.*
.....(5 to 4 on op 11 to 8 on tchd 6 to 4 on and 11 to 10 on) 1
GREEN'S SEAGO (USA) [67] 8-10-0 J Culloty, *trkd ldr, led aftr 4th, drvn whn hrd pressed frm 3 out, mstk nxt, hdd r-in, one pace*..........(2 to 1 op 3 to 1 tchd 7 to 2) 2
228^{6} FORGETFUL [95] 7-11-7 (7*) J Prior, *jmpd rght, led till aftr 4th, sn drvn and beh, tld off*..........(4 to 1 op 3 to 1) 3
OUR MICA [67] 6-9-11 (3*) D J Kavanagh, *hld up, drvn bef 4 out, sn tld off*..........(12 to 1 op 14 to 1 tchd 16 to 1) 4
166 PIMSBOY [67] (v) 9-10-0 G Cahill, *hld up in rear whn slpd up on bend aftr 3rd*..........(33 to 1) su
Dist: 2½l, dist, 2½l. 4m 2.70s. a 12.70s (5 Ran).
(Richard Green (Fine Paintings)), M C Pipe

308 Wrexham Lager Handicap Hurdle Class D (0-120 4-y-o and up) £2,723 2½m.......................... (4:45)

DIAMOND CUT (Fr) [114] 8-11-13 D Bridgwater, *made all, sn clr, slight mstk 7th, drvn bef last, ran on wl.*
..........(4 to 1 op 5 to 2) 1
DANCING DOVE (Ire) [115] 8-12-0 A Dobbin, *midfield, steady hdwy frm 6th, chsd wnr aftr 3 out, drvn betw last 2, no extr r-in.*
..........(4 to 1 op 3 to 1) 2
227^{4} FIRST CRACK [87] 11-10-0 S Wynne, *hld up, effrt and hdwy 3 out, sn chasing ldrs, one pace bef last*... (9 to 2 op 8 to 1) 3
267^{4} KING'S SHILLING (USA) [95] 9-10-5 (3*) J Culloty, *midfield, pushed alng 4 out, drvn aftr nxt, sn no imprsn.*
.... (8 to 1 tchd 9 to 1 and 10 to 1) 4
44^{3} BLUE RAVEN [93] 5-10-3 A P McCoy, *chsd wnr, drvn and mstk 7th, wknd appr 2 out.*
..........(2 to 1 fav op 9 to 4 tchd 5 to 2) 5
127^{3} PLAYFUL JULIET (Can) [88] 8-10-1^{1} T Kent, *chsd ldrs till wknd bef 7th*.......... (14 to 1 op 10 to 1 tchd 16 to 1) 6
267^{6} BATTY'S ISLAND [99] 7-10-5 (7*) D Finnegan, *beh, struggling 7th, tld off*..........(25 to 1 op 20 to 1) 7
Dist: 3l, 1¼l, 7l, 9l, 13l, 23l. 4m 40.40s. a 10.40s (7 Ran).
SR: 25/23/-/-/ (Martin Pipe Racing Club), M C Pipe

309 Erbistock Novices' Handicap Chase Class E (0-100 5-y-o and up) £2,996 2½m 110yds.....................(5:20)

280 POND HOUSE (Ire) [84] 7-10-12 D Bridgwater, *made all, clr frm 9th, eased dwn to walk r-in*........ (13 to 2 op 5 to 1) 1
MINERS REST [72] 8-10-0 A P McCoy, *trkd ldrs, chsd clr wnr frm 9th, no imprsn*...(11 to 2 op 5 to 1 tchd 6 to 1) 2
298^{4} FOREST FEATHER (Ire) [87] (bl) 8-11-1 M Richards, *in rear, niggled alng frm 9th, styd on from 3 out, nvr nrr.*
..........(6 to 4 fav op 2 to 1) 3
127 NORTHERN NATION [84] 8-10-12 R Johnson, *in tch to tenth, sn struggling, tld off*..........(16 to 1 op 12 to 1) 4
228 GEORGE LANE [73] 8-10-1^{1} R Greene, *in tch, some hdwy aftr 9th, 3rd whn blun badly 11th, und pres when blundered and uns rdr nxt.*
..........(10 to 1 op 12 to 1 tchd 14 to 1 and 9 to 1) ur
228^{8} WARNER FORPLEASURE [72] (bl) 10-10-0 B Harding, *prmnt, reminders aftr 7th, lost grnd quickly after 9th, sn wl beh, tld off whn pld up bef 2 out*..........(50 to 1 op 33 to 1) pu
241^{4} ARCTIC LIFE (Ire) [100] 7-12-0 J Osborne, *beh, some hdwy to chase ldrs appr 4 out, sn und pres and wknd, pld up bef 2 out, dismounted, lme*........(11 to 4 op 5 to 2 tchd 3 to 1) pu
Dist: 3½l, 1¼l, dist. 5m 4.20s. a 18.20s (7 Ran).
(C R Fleet), M C Pipe

310 Llangollen Novices' Hurdle Class E (4-y-o and up) £2,626 2m 1f........(5:50)

243^{3} LANCER (USA) 4-10-9 W Marston, *chsd clr ldr frm second, cld 5th, mstk 3 out, led jst aftr last, all out.*
..........(11 to 2 op 5 to 1 tchd 6 to 1) 1
263* MILLION DANCER 4-11-2 D Bridgwater, *led, clr frm 3rd to 5th, mstk 3 out, mistake ag'n last, sn hdd, rallied cl hme.*
..........(7 to 2 op 5 to 1 on tchd 30 to 2) 2
157 SEVEN WELLS 4-10-9 R Greene, *wl beh, hdwy frm 4th, sn chasing ldrs, no ch wth ldg pair from four out, tld off*. (33 to 1) 3
107 MERELY MORTAL 5-10-12 R Johnson, *in tch, und pres frm 4 out, wknd quickly, tld off.*
..........(33 to 1 op 20 to 1 tchd 50 to 1) 4
157^{8} DISCO'S WELL 5-10-12 T Kent, *al towards rear, pckd 3rd, struggling frm 5th, tld off*..........(20 to 1 op 10 to 1) 5
157 TIPSY QUEEN 5-10-4 (3*) J Culloty, *chsd ldr till mstk second, wknd quickly 4 out, eased whn btn aftr nxt, tld off.*
..........(14 to 1 op 12 to 1 tchd 16 to 1) 6
186^{8} ADMIRAL'S GUEST (Ire) 4-10-9 T Eley, *beh, struggling aftr 3rd, tld off whn pld up bef 2 out.*
..........(20 to 1 op 14 to 1 tchd 25 to 1) pu
INTEABADUN 4-10-9 S Wynne, *took no part.*
..........(50 to 1 op 33 to 1) l
Dist: Hd, dist, 23l, 8l, 3l. 3m 59.30s. a 9.30s (8 Ran).
SR: 13/20/-/-/-/ (A C W Price), R T Juckes

GALWAY (IRE) (good to firm)

NATIONAL HUNT RESULTS 1996-97

Friday August 2nd

311 Budweiser Q.R. Handicap Hurdle (0-116 4-y-o and up) £4,110 2¼m
.... (5:15)

303⁵ NORTHERN FANCY (Ire) [-] 5-10-13 (7") Mr G Elliott, (3 to 1) 1+
197¹ JOHNNY'S DREAM (Ire) [-] 6-11-0 Mr P Fenton, ... (6 to 1) 1+
260⁴ FAIR SOCIETY (Ire) [-] (bl) 5-9-11 (7") Mr John P Moloney,
.... (14 to 1) 3
232⁴ BALLY UPPER (Ire) [-] 8-10-10 Mr H F Cleary, ... (12 to 1) 4
162⁵ KENTUCKY BABY (Ire) [-] 6-11-7 (5") Mr R Walsh, . (13 to 2) 5
287² THE BOULD VIC (Ire) [-] 4-11-7 Mr G J Harford, (7 to 4 fav) 6
HAKKINEN (Ire) [-] 5-11-11 (7") Mr J T McNamara, (12 to 1) 7
260³ SANDRA LOUISE (Ire) [-] 6-9-11 (7") Mr A Ross, ... (8 to 1) 8
Dist: Dd-ht, 1l, ½l, 2l. 4m 15.80s. (8 Ran).

(Gerard McClure & Mrs James Nicholson), A J Martin & D T Hughes

312 Tony O'Malley Memorial Handicap Chase (4-y-o and up) £5,780 2m 1f
.... (5:50)

293⁵ TRYFIRION (Ire) [-] 7-11-10 (3") B Bowens, ... (9 to 4 fav) 1
THE RIDGE BOREEN [-] 12-11-11 M P Dwyer, ... (16 to 1) 2
WHO'S TO SAY [-] 10-11-13 N Williamson, ... (13 to 2) 3
215² NORDIC THORN [-] 6-11-1 K F O'Brien, ... (9 to 1) 4
286⁷ SYNIEYOURMISSED (Ire) [-] 7-9-8 T Horgan, ... (12 to 1) 5
257² SANDY FOREST LADY [-] 7-9-7 J P Broderick, ... (9 to 1) 6
116³ LA MODE LADY [-] 11-9-7 (5") G Cotter, ... (8 to 1) 7
SHANKORAK [-] 9-10-13 C O'Dwyer, ... (5 to 2) 8
Dist: 1½l, 5½l, 2½l, ½l. 4m 21.70s. (8 Ran).

(Mrs M T Quinn), Victor Bowens

GALWAY (IRE) (good to firm)
Saturday August 3rd

313 Jockeys Association Beginners Chase (4-y-o and up) £4,452 2m 1f. . . . (2:30)

257⁴ BEAKSTOWN (Ire) 7-12-0 R Dunwoody, ... (Evens fav) 1
292⁹ CUBAN QUESTION 9-11-9 (5") G Cotter, ... (11 to 2) 2
170⁴ MAIASAURA (Ire) 7-11-9 C O'Dwyer, ... (20 to 1) 3
290⁷ MELDANTE VI (Ire) (bl) 5-11-3 J P Broderick, . (20 to 1) 4
91¹ BOBSVILLE (Ire) 8-12-0 F Woods, ... (5 to 2) f
MAJESTIC MARINER (Ire) 5-11-3 M P Dwyer, ... (9 to 1) f
Dist: Nk, 25l, dist. 4m 26.60s. (6 Ran).

(Mrs P J O'Meara), P Mullins

314 Low Low Galway Blazers Handicap Chase (0-116 4-y-o and up) £4,110 2 ¾m. . . . . (3:00)

290⁸ BEET STATEMENT (Ire) [-] 7-9-12 T J Mitchell, ... (16 to 1) 1
293⁸ ANOTHER GROUSE [-] 9-12-0 J P Broderick, ... (10 to 1) 2
136⁴ CASTALINO [-] 10-10-6 K F O'Brien, ... (10 to 1) 3
198⁴ BALYARA (Ire) [-] (bl) 6-11-10 C F Swan, ... (15 to 2) 4
130⁴ FIXED ASSETS [-] 9-9-6 (7") A O'Shea, ... (20 to 1) 5
138⁵ SPRINGFORT LADY (Ire) [-] 7-10-7 N Williamson, . . (7 to 1) 6
302⁸ BRAVO STAR (USA) [-] 11-9-2 (5") T Martin, ... (33 to 1) 7
261³ NEBRASKA [-] 10-11-1 R Dunwoody, ... (10 to 1) 8
PHAIRY MIRACLES (Ire) [-] 7-10-7 P M Verling, . . . (14 to 1) f
90⁹ TIMELY AFFAIR (Ire) [-] (bl) 7-9-11 F Woods, ... (8 to 1) f
198⁷ ANY PORT (Ire) [-] 6-10-9 P L Malone, ... (6 to 1) ur
KINGSTON WAY [-] 10-11-2 (5") G Cotter, ... (12 to 1) bd
136⁵ ANOTHER COQ HARDI (Ire) [-] 8-10-8 P Carberry, (10 to 1) pu
236³ BALD JOKER [-] 11-9-13 T Horgan, ... (14 to 1) pu
290⁴ MICKS DELIGHT (Ire) [-] (bl) 6-11-8 M P Dwyer, . . . (10 to 1) pu
198⁷ MIDNIGHT HOUR (Ire) [-] 7-11-8 C O'Dwyer, . . . (4 to 1 fav) pu
Dist: Hd, 1l, 2l, 5l. 5m 28.40s. (16 Ran).

(W M Sheehy), W T Murphy

315 Dawn Milk Handicap Hurdle (4-y-o and up) £9,675 2m 5f 190yds. . . . . . . (3:30)

272² FATHER RECTOR (Ire) [-] 7-9-8 T Horgan, ... (12 to 1) 1
286¹ VICAR STREET (Ire) [-] 6-10-0 (3ex) C F Swan, . . . (5 to 1) 2
BAMAPOUR (Ire) [-] 6-10-11 P Carberry, ... (7 to 1) 3
302¹ CULLENSTOWN LADY (Ire) [-] 5-11-0 (5ex) R Dunwoody,
.... (7 to 2 fav) 4
HUNCHEON CHANCE (Ire) [-] 6-11-4 M P Dwyer, . . . (9 to 2) 5
162¹ SLANEY GLOW (Ire) [-] 5-10-12 K F O'Brien, ... (8 to 1) 6
179¹ ARCTIC KATE [-] 10-10-10 C O'Dwyer, ... (8 to 1) 7
292² LADY DAISY (Ire) [-] 7-9-7 (7") A O'Shea, ... (7 to 1) 8
194³ PINGO HILL (Ire) [-] 4-10-4 N Williamson, ... (12 to 1) f
311⁴ BALLY UPPER (Ire) [-] 8-9-0 (7") L J Fleming, ... (25 to 1) pu
Dist: ¾l, 2½l, 5l, 4l. 5m 3.20s. (10 Ran).

(Paddy Fennelly), Paddy Fennelly

316 Kerry Maid Festival INH Flat Race (4-y-o and up) £4,110 2m. . . . . (5:30)

185¹ REEVES (Ire) 4-11-8 (5") Mr R Walsh, ... (10 to 9 on) 1
224⁴ FRAU DANTE (Ire) 6-11-9 (7") Mr G Elliott, ... (5 to 2) 2
210⁴ TWENTYFIVEQUID (Ire) 5-12-4 Mr P F Graffin, ... (10 to 1) 3
269¹ FRANCOSKID (Ire) 4-11-6 (7") Mr P P Curran, ... (15 to 2) 4

INHERITIS (Ire) 4-10-8 (7") Mr D A Harney, ... (25 to 1) 5
199¹ MAGS DWYER (Ire) 6-11-13 Mr H F Cleary, ... (6 to 1) 6
Dist: 1l, 13l, 3½l, 10l. 3m 40.20s. (6 Ran).

(Alexander McCarthy), W P Mullins

MARKET RASEN (good to firm)
Saturday August 3rd
Going Correction: MINUS 0.10 sec. per fur.

317 Premiere Placements Amateur Riders' Novices' Handicap Hurdle Class F (0-100 4-y-o and up) £2,110 2m 1f 110yds. . . . . (6:10)

205³ IRIE MON (Ire) [79] 4-11-4 (7") Mr A Wintle, strted slwly, hld up, prog and mstk 5th, gd hdwy aftr 3 out, led after last, hng lft and drvn out. . . . . (3 to 1 op 7 to 2) 1
284¹ SILVER SLEEVE (Ire) [82] (bl) 4-11-1 (3") Mr C Bonner, trkd ldrs, led aftr 3 out, rdn and hdd after last, unbl to quicken.
.... (11 to 10 on op 5 to 4) 2
168 POPLIN [76] 5-11-4 (7") Mr R Thornton, wth ldr, led 4th till aftr 3 out, ev ch appr last, not quicken.
.... (6 to 1 op 11 to 2 tchd 13 to 2) 3
TONY'S MIST [74] 6-11-2 (7") Mr N H Oliver, trkd ldrs, lost pl aftr 3 out, shaken up appr last, fnshd strly.
.... (5 to 1 op 9 to 2 tchd 11 to 2) 4
NOTED STRAIN (Ire) [65] 8-10-7 (7") Miss K Di Marte, led to 4th, prmnt till one pace appr 2 out. . . . . (50 to 1 op 33 to 1) 5
AVRIL ETOILE [63] 6-10-5 (7") Miss B Small, hld up, pld hrd, in tch till wknd aftr 3 out. . . . . (50 to 1 op 33 to 1) 6
203 QUIXALL CROSSETT [70] 11-11-0 (5") Mr M H Naughton, chsd ldrs, lost pl 4th, sn wknd. . . . . (66 to 1 op 50 to 1) 7
205 ARROGANT BOY [59] 7-10-8¹³ (5") Mr N Wilson, strted slwly, hld up, lost tch bef 4th, no ch aftr. . . (66 to 1 op 33 to 1) 8
Dist: 3l, nk, 1½l, 5l, 10l, 19l, 1¼l. 4m 17.40s. a 16.40s.8 Ran).

(Sotby Farming Company Limited), M P Bielby

318 United Friendly Selling Handicap Hurdle Class G (0-95 4-y-o and up) £1,576 2m 5f 110yds. . . . . (6:40)

163⁹ JOLI'S GREAT [66] (bl) 8-10-0 J Ryan, trkd ldrs, led 7th, rdn 2 out, styd on wl. . . . . (14 to 1 op 12 to 1) 1
228⁷ LOFTY DEED (USA) [88] (bl) 6-10-0 L Harvey, wtd wth, prog 6th, chsd wnr aftr 3 out, ev ch last, not quicken.
.... (12 to 1 op 9 to 1) 2
204⁷ GEORGE ASHFORD (Ire) [88] (v) 6-11-8 A S Smith, led to 7th, rdn and not quicken aftr 3 out, styd on wl appr last.
.... (7 to 2 op 5 to 1) 3
146³ WHISTLING GIPSY [67] 11-10-1 Jacqui Oliver, strted slwly, hld up, hmpd bend appr 6th, ran on frm nxt, nrst finish.
.... (5 to 1 op 9 to 2) 4
225² YACHT CLUB [77] 14-10-11 O Pears, keen hold, trkd ldrs, rdn and one pace aftr 3 out. (3 to 1 fav op 7 to 2 tchd 4 to 1) 5
RARE PADDY [66] (v) 7-10-0 R Supple, hld up, prog appr 3 out, styd on one pace frm nxt. . . . . . (5 to 1 tchd 33 to 1) 6
MISTROY [70] 6-10-1 (3") G Cahill, hld up, effrt 7th, nvr rchd ldrs. . . . . (14 to 1 op 12 to 1) 7
LAMBSON [69] 9-10-3 C Llewellyn, hld up, outpcd frm 3 out, nvr able to chal. . . . . (13 to 2 op 6 to 1 tchd 7 to 1) 8
THARSIS [76] 11-10-5 (5") S Taylor, chsd ldr to 6th, sn wknd, wl beh aftr 3 out. . . . . (10 to 1 op 8 to 1) 9
CATTON LADY [66] 6-9-11 (3") G Lee, mstk second, chsd ldrs to 6th, sn wknd. . . . . (50 to 1 op 33 to 1) 10
FIVE FROM HOME (Ire) [90] 8-11-10 C Maude, prmnt till wknd rpdly 6th, tld off and pld up bef 3 out.
.... (9 to 2 op 7 to 2 tchd 5 to 1) pu
Dist: 2l, 2l, 5l, hd, hd, 2½l, 1¼l, 17l, 13l. 5m 21.10s. a 18.10s (11 Ran).

(Enterprise Markets Ltd), M J Ryan

319 Grahame Liles Novices' Chase Class D (5-y-o and up) £3,793 2½m. . . . . (7:10)

247² HIZAL 7-11-0 Mr A Charles-Jones, pressed ldr, rdn 3 out, lft in ld nxt, hld on. . . . . (5 to 2 op 7 to 4) 1
239⁷ SASSIVER (USA) 6-11-6 R Johnson, rdn thrght and jmpd slwly, led, blun and hdd 2 out, blunded last, not quicken.
.... (7 to 4 on op 2 to 1 on) 2
GHEDI (Pol) 5-10-10 C Llewellyn, not fluent, cl up, pushed alng 8th, wknd 11th, tld off. . . . . . (7 to 1 op 14 to 1) 3
MR ORIENTAL 6-11-0 D Byrne, immediately tld off.
.... (20 to 1 op 14 to 1) 4
Dist: 2l, dist, dist. 5m 9.00s. a 20.00s.(4 Ran).

(H J Manners), H J Manners

320 Fastnet Fish Juvenile Novices' Hurdle Class D (3-y-o) £2,745 2m 1f 110yds. . . . . (7:40)

KERNOF (Ire) 10-12 R Garritty, chsd ldg pair, cld 3 out, led and mstk nxt, drvn out.
.... (5 to 4 fav op 7 to 4 tchd 11 to 10) 1
HOME COOKIN' 10-7 C Maude, wth ldr, led 4th, hdd and blun 2 out, ev ch whn mstk last, not quicken... (4 to 1 op 5 to 2) 2

39

KILLMESSAN-TOWN (Ire) 10-9 (3*) F Leahy, *mid-div, prog 5th, rdn to chase ldrs nxt, btn 2 out, blun last.* ....(5 to 1 op 12 to 1 tchd 4 to 1) 3
NORTHERN FALCON 10-7 Mr N Wilson, *beh, hrd rdn aftr 5th, ran on frm 2 out, nrst finish*..........(20 to 1 op 14 to 1) 4
ANOTHER QUARTER (Ire) 10-7 P Hide, *not jump wl, led to 4th, chsd ldr till aftr 3 out, wknd.* ....(7 to 2 op 5 to 2 tchd 4 to 1) 5
COWBOY DREAMS (Ire) (bl) 10-9 (3*) K Gaule, *mid-div, pushed alng 5th, effrt nxt, wknd and eased appr 2 out.* ....(10 to 1 op 8 to 1) 6
RECALL TO MIND 10-9 (3*) D Parker, *al rear, rdn 4th, sn beh.* ....(25 to 1 op 16 to 1) 7
LIMYSKI 10-9 (3*) J Supple, *al rear, rdn aftr 4th, sn lost tch.* ....(50 to 1 op 33 to 1) 8
Dist: 4l, 14l, 1¼l, 1l, 19l, 1l, 2¼l. 4m 10.70s. a 9.70s (8 Ran).
(J M Gahan), M D Hammond

321 Liles Racing Handicap Chase Class E (0-115 5-y-o and up) £3,418 2½m .... (8:10)

165^{7} DRUMSTICK [89] 10-11-5 J Railton, *jmpd wl, led 3rd, pushed clr aftr 2 out, cmftbly*..................(10 to 1 op 7 to 1) 1
YAAKUM [92] 7-11-8 R Garritty, *hld up gng easily, trkd wnr appr 3 out, rdn and not quicken nxt*......(5 to 1 op 3 to 1) 2
266^{*} MAGGOTS GREEN [77] 9-10-7 R Johnson, *led to 3rd, pushed alng hfwy, lost pl 12th, kpt on one pace frm 3 out.* .... (9 to 4 op 5 to 2 tchd 11 to 4) 3
240^{4} CIRCULATION [70] 10-10-0 B Harding, *cl up, chsd wnr 12th, sn hrd rdn and wknd*...............(14 to 1 tchd 16 to 1) 4
WAKE UP LUV [90] 11-11-6 J Ryan, *wtd wth, prog 7th, cl 3rd whn f tenth*...................... (25 to 1 tchd 33 to 1) f
167^{*} RHOSSILI BAY [98] 8-12-0 P Niven, *4th whn f second.* .... (11 to 10 fav op 5 to 4 tchd 11 to 8) f
Dist: 5l, 1¼l, 25l. 4m 54.50s. a 5.50s (6 Ran).
SR: 16/14/-/ (Sarah Lady Allendale,E Hawkings,M Harris), K C Bailey

322 Weightlifter Maiden Hurdle Class E (4-y-o and up) £2,629 2m 1f 110yds (8:40)

FIELD OF VISION (Ire) 6-10-13 (3*) J Supple, *mstk 1st, cl up, trkd ldr appr 2 out, led last, drvn out*..... (4 to 1 op 3 to 1) 1
SILVERDALE LAD 5-11-2 S Wynne, *hld up, prog 5th, chlgd last, ev ch r-in, unbl to quicken*...... (16 to 1 op 12 to 1) 2
35^{2} FORGOTTEN EMPRESS 4-10-8 R Johnson, *hld up, prog 3 out, chsd ldrs nxt, styd on one pace*.....(4 to 1 op 5 to 1) 3
OTTAVIO FARNESE 4-10-13 P Hide, *hld up, prog aftr 4th, led 3 out till last, one pace*...............(10 to 1 op 8 to 1) 4
166^{2} SEA GOD 5-11-2 W Worthington, *hld up, prog 3rd, sddl slpd nxt, effrt 2 out, one pace.* .... (9 to 4 fav op 5 to 2 tchd 11 to 4 and 2 to 1) 5
LITTLE REDWING 4-10-8 R Garritty, *hld up mid-div, prog 3 out, eased whn btn aftr nxt*............ (12 to 1 op 8 to 1) 6
279^{4} FLEET CADET (bl) 5-11-2 C Maude, *prmnt, led 5th to nxt, wknd appr last*..................... (4 to 1 tchd 5 to 1) 7
COURT JESTER 5-11-2 J Railton, *hld up, prog to track ldrs 3 out, wknd nxt*......................(10 to 1 op 20 to 1) 8
SCALLYMILL 6-10-11 M Foster, *pld hrd, prmnt to 4th, wkng whn mstk nxt, tld off*.................. (50 to 1 op 33 to 1) 9
74^{7} OUSEFLEET BOY 4-10-13 A Thornton, *chsd ldrs to 5th, sn wknd tld off*........................(50 to 1 op 33 to 1) 10
HUTCEL BELL 5-10-11 P Niven, *chsd ldr to 4th, sn wknd, tld off*....................................(50 to 1 op 33 to 1) 11
BARGIN INN 6-11-2 D Gallagher, *al beh, blun 4th, tld off.* ....(50 to 1 op 33 to 1) 12
166 WOODBINE 6-11-2 D Byrne, *clr ldr, mstk 4th, hdd and wknd nxt, pld up bef 2 out*................ (50 to 1 op 25 to 1) pu
Dist: ½l, 2½l, ½l, 3½l, 9l, 3½l, 3½l, dist, 8l, 1¼l. 4m 7.90s. a 6.90s (13 Ran).
SR: 2/1/-/-/-/-/ (Mrs K Morrell), Mrs A Swinbank

NEWTON ABBOT (good to firm)
Saturday August 3rd
Going Correction: MINUS 0.05 sec. per fur.

323 Thoroughbred Clothing Company Presents Scudamore Juvenile Novices Hurdle Class D (3-y-o) £2,699 2m 1f .... (2:25)

ALWAYS HAPPY 10-7 D Bridgwater, *trkd ldr, led aftr 3 out, sn clr, unchlgd*.....(3 to 1 on op 5 to 2 on tchd 2 to 1 on) 1
BULLPEN BELLE 10-7 B Powell, *led till aftr 3 out, sn outpcd.* ....(5 to 1 op 3 to 1) 2
BEN BOWDEN 10-12 J Osborne, *towards rear, hdwy appr 3 out, wknd bef 2 out, disputing poor second whn f last, rmntd, tld off*.................................(11 to 2 op 7 to 2) 3
SAUCY SOUL 10-5 (7*) J Power, *not fluent, sn wl beh, tld off whn pld up bef last*....................(20 to 1 op 10 to 1) pu
OUR ADVENTURE 10-7 S Curran, *prmnt, reminders and lost pl aftr 3rd, tld off whn mstk 5th and nxt, pld up bef last.* ....(25 to 1 op 12 to 1 tchd 33 to 1) pu
Dist: 10l, dist. 4m 0.50s. a 11.50s (5 Ran).
(Knight Hawks Partnership), M C Pipe

324 Clive Morgan Selling Hurdle Class G (4 - 7-y-o) £1,783 2m 1f........... (2:55)

INDRAPURA (Ire) 4-10-9 D Bridgwater, *wtd wth, prog to ld appr 2 out, wndrd fnl two, readily*.......(5 to 1 op 5 to 2) 1
243^{*} TRADE WIND (v) 5-11-7 (5*) Michael Brennan, *hld up, hdwy appr 2 out, ev ch whn bumped approaching last, unbl to quicken*..................(9 to 2 op 4 to 1 tchd 5 to 1) 2
55^{4} DOUBLE PENDANT (Ire) 5-10-12 A P McCoy, *reluctant ldr till aftr second, tucked in beh ldrs after, rdn appr 2 out, sn one pace*...........................(7 to 4 fav op 5 to 2) 3
246^{4} CLANCY'S EXPRESS 5-10-12 S Fox, *hld up beh ldrs, ev ch appr 2 out, wknd bef last.* ....(16 to 1 op 12 to 1 tchd 20 to 1) 4
BURNT SIENNA (Ire) 4-10-4 W McFarland, *chsd ldr, led aftr second, hdd bef nxt, rgned ld after 3 out, headed appr 2 out, sn btn*.............................. (14 to 1 op 8 to 1) 5
251^{5} SWEET DISORDER (Ire) 6-10-0 (7*) A Dowling, *prmnt till wknd appr 3 out*...........................(6 to 1 op 4 to 1) 6
243 DR DAVE (Ire) 5-10-12 B Powell, *pld hrd in rear, hdwy to ld appr 3rd, hit nxt, hdd aftr 3 out, sn wknd.* (4 to 1 op 3 to 1) 7
Dist: ½l, 5l, 5l, 4l, 2l, 4l. 4m 6.60s. a 17.60s (7 Ran).
(Martin Pipe Racing Club), M C Pipe

325 Francis Kearns 70th Birthday Novices' Chase Class E (5-y-o and up) £2,845 2m 110yds..................... (3:30)

227^{3} STAPLEFORD LADY 8-10-7 W McFarland, *al hndy, led aftr 9th, hrd pressed frm 3 out, all out.* ....(4 to 1 op 5 to 1 tchd 11 to 2) 1
190^{3} NORDIC VALLEY (Ire) 5-10-9 D Bridgwater, *hld up, took clr order 4th, ev ch frm 3 out, ran on*.......(9 to 4 op 7 to 4) 2
228^{5} DUKE OF DREAMS 6-10-12 B Powell, *wtd wth, rdn aftr 9th, moderate hdwy fnl 2, no imprsn.* ....(11 to 1 op 10 to 1 tchd 14 to 1) 3
HERESTHEDEAL (Ire) 7-10-12 B Clifford, *made most till aftr 9th, wknd appr 3 out*.......... (5 to 4 on op 11 to 10 on) 4
GREAT UNCLE 8-10-12 G Upton, *dsptd ld till jmpd slwly 4th, rdn 8th, sn lost tch, tld off.* ....(25 to 1 op 12 to 1 tchd 33 to 1) 5
Dist: Hd, 12l, 6l, dist. 4m 4.00s. a 6.00s (5 Ran).
SR: 11/13/4/-/-/ (C Kyriakou), J S Moore

326 Fort George Conditional Jockeys' Novices' Handicap Hurdle Class F (4-y-o and up) £1,929 2¾m............(4:05)

103^{4} DREAM HERE [95] 8-12-0 B Fenton, *patiently rdn, prog 4 out, led appr 2 out, drvn out.* ....(11 to 4 fav op 9 to 4 tchd 3 to 1) 1
284^{4} IDIOM [67] 9-10-0 J Culloty, *hld up towards rear, hdwy 3 out, ev ch nxt, unbl to quicken last*...........(3 to 1 op 4 to 1) 2
CASHFLOW CRISIS (Ire) [78] 4-10-8 T J Murphy, *hld up in rear, hdwy and ev ch 2 out, sn hrd rdn, one pace last.* ....(7 to 2 tchd 4 to 1) 3
309^{2} MINERS REST [74] 8-10-7 D J Kavanagh, *dsptd ld, led 5th till appr 2 out, fdd*.........................(6 to 1 op 4 to 1) 4
111 LAC DE GRAS (Ire) [72] 5-10-2[2] D Walsh, *prmnt, ev ch appr 2 out, sn wknd*......... (20 to 1 op 16 to 1 tchd 25 to 1) 5
47 AKIYMANN (USA) [87] 6-11-2 (4*) B Moore, *made most to 5th, wknd quickly aftr nxt, tld off*.............(4 to 1 op 9 to 4) 6
Dist: 2l, 2½l, 22l, nk, dist. 5m 19.20s. a 18.20s (6 Ran).
(The Will To Win Partnership), J C Fox

327 Newton Abbot Town Day Handicap Chase Class D (0-120 5-y-o and up) £3,458 2m 5f 110yds........... (4:40)

SOHAIL (USA) [99] 13-10-8 J Culloty, *wtd wth, prog 4 out, led last, ran on wl*........ (14 to 1 op 10 to 1 tchd 16 to 1) 1
249^{3} HENLEY REGATTA [97] 8-10-6[5] S Burrough, *hld up, hdwy 6th, mstk 11th, led 3 out to last, no extr*.....(11 to 2 op 9 to 2) 2
48^{5} MUSKORA (Ire) [119] (bl) 7-12-0 A P McCoy, *led, not fluent and hdd 3 out, still ev ch nxt, btn appraoching last.* ....(7 to 4 fav tchd 2 to 1 and 13 to 8) 3
249^{2} ANDRELOT [110] (bl) 9-11-5 M A Fitzgerald, *prmnt, rdn appr 4 out, wknd bef nxt*.......................(9 to 4 tchd 2 to 1) 4
230^{4} JIM VALENTINE [91] (bl) 10-10-0 W Marston, *hld up, blun 3rd, mstk 6th, rdn appr 4 out, wknd*........(13 to 2 op 5 to 1) 5
188 THE LORRYMAN (Ire) [92] 8-10-1 S McNeill, *in tch, wknd appr 11th, tld off whn pld up bef 2 out*........(9 to 1 op 12 to 1) pu
Dist: 3½l, 3l, 16l, 13l. 5m 11.70s. a 9.70s (6 Ran).
(Mrs Carrie Janaway), J S King

328 Phoenix Print Handicap Hurdle Class E (0-110 4-y-o and up) £2,200 2m 1f .... (5:10)

COUNTRY STAR (Ire) [110] 5-12-0 G Bradley, *made all, sn clr, given breather appr 5th, quickened ag'n frm 2 out, unchlgd.* ....(5 to 4 on op 6 to 4 on) 1
ROCA MURADA (Ire) [97] 7-11-4 A P McCoy, *hld up, wnt second appr 5th, cld on wnr 3 out, sn rdn, outpcd nxt.* ....(3 to 1 op 2 to 1) 2

RE ROI (Ire) [92] 4-10-4 (3*) T J Murphy, *hld up, hdwy appr 3 out, outpcd bef nxt*..................(20 to 1 op 16 to 1) 3
PUSEY STREET BOY [79] 9-10-0 I Lawrence, *nvr nr to chal*.
..................................(14 to 1 op 12 to 1) 4
248 COMMANCHE CREEK [79] 6-9-9 (5*) Sophie Mitchell, *chsd wnr to 4th, beh frm 3 out*. (7 to 1 op 8 to 1 tchd 10 to 1) 5
COOLEY'S VALVE (Ire) [104] 8-11-11 S McNeill, *hld up, wnt second briefly hfwy, wknd appr 2 out*... (11 to 2 op 5 to 1) 6
Dist: 11l, 1¾l, nk, 2l. 3m 55.00s. a 6.00s (6 Ran).
SR: 32/11/-/-/-/11/ (H R H Prince Fahd Salman), C P E Brooks

LEOPARDSTOWN (IRE) (good)
Monday August 5th

329 Scalp I.N.H. Flat Race (4-y-o and up) £2,740 2½m....................(5:30)

DAFFODIL GLEN (Ire) 4-10-13 (3*) Mr B M Cash, ... (5 to 2) 1
210³ FANE PATH (Ire) 4-11-7 Mr G J Harford, ... (6 to 1) 2
274⁵ GOLD DEVON (Ire) 6-11-7 (7*) Mrs C Doyle, ... (20 to 1) 3
288³ PLEASE NO TEARS 9-11-9 Mrs C Barker, ... (9 to 4 fav) 4
245² LOLLIA PAULINA (Ire) 5-11-2 (7*) Mr Edgar Byrne, .. (6 to 1) 5
140⁴ CLEVER JACK (Ire) 6-11-7 (7*) Mr M O'Connor, ... (12 to 1) 6
ALL FOR MAX (Ire) 7-12-0 Mr J A Berry, ... (11 to 1) 7
238⁵ JOSH'S FANCY 5-11-9 Mr H F Cleary, ... (10 to 1) 8
245⁷ PRINCESS TOUCHEE (Ire) 5-11-2 (7*) Mr D P Coakley,
....(33 to 1) 9
235⁵ WAREZ (Ire) 8-11-7 (7*) Miss L E A Doyle, ... (20 to 1) 10
BALALTRAMA (Ire) 5-11-2 (7*) Mr T J Beattie, ... (25 to 1) 11
Dist: 4l, 3l, 1½l, 4l. 4m 49.30s. (11 Ran).
(Mrs E Slevin), A P O'Brien

NEWTON ABBOT (good to firm)
Monday August 5th
Going Correction: MINUS 0.50 sec. per fur.

330 Holsworthy Novices' Selling Hurdle Class G (4-y-o and up) £1,893 2m 1f
....(2:15)

324⁴ INDRAPURA (Ire) 4-11-2 (7ex) D Bridgwater, *hld up, hdwy to track ldr 3 out, led sn aftr nxt, wndrd in frnt, hrd held r-in.*
...............(11 to 8 fav op Evens tchd 11 to 10 on) 1
ALMAPA 4-10-6 (3*) T Dascombe, *hld up, hdwy appr 5th, led 3 out, rdn and hdd sn aftr nxt, no imprsn r-in.*
.....................(10 to 1 op 7 to 1 tchd 12 to 1) 2
243² NIGHT TIME 4-10-9 (7*) G Shenkin, *hld up, hdwy 5th, rdn appr nxt, no headway aftr*............ (2 to 1 tchd 5 to 2) 3
246² MINNESOTA FATS 4-10-9 Gary Lyons, *hld up, hdwy appr 5th, rdn and wknd approaching 2 out.*
...............................(6 to 1 op 7 to 1 tchd 8 to 1) 4
GALLOPING GUNS (Ire) 4-10-6 (3*) Guy Lewis, *chsd ldrs till wknd 5th, tld off*...................(33 to 1 op 25 to 1) 5
KAMA SIMBA (bl) 4-10-9 A P McCoy, *pld hrd, not fluent, in cl tch whn I 5th*...................(7 to 1 tchd 8 to 1) f
MARIO'S DREAM (Ire) 8-10-12 D Gallagher, *led till 1st, sec-ond whn ran out 5th*... (40 to 1 op 33 to 1 tchd 50 to 1) ro
246 ON THE LEDGE (USA) 6-10-5 (7*) A Dowling, *led 1st till hdd 3 out, wknd quickly, pld up bef nxt*.... (100 to 1 op 33 to 1) pu
Dist: ¾l, 8l, nk, dist. 3m 59.90s. a 10.90s (8 Ran).
(Martin Pipe Racing Club), M C Pipe

331 Newton Abbot Racecourse Car Boot Sales Handicap Hurdle Class F (0-100 4-y-o and up) £1,958 2¾m......(2:45)

SPRINGFIELD DANCER [94] 5-11-7 A P McCoy, *trkd ldr, led 4th, clr 3 out, unchlgd*......(9 to 2 op 4 to 1 tchd 5 to 1) 1
CELESTIAL FIRE [80] 4-10-7 D Gallagher, *hld up, hdwy to go second 3 out, no ch wth wnr, all out to stay second.*
.....................(11 to 1 op 8 to 1 tchd 12 to 1) 2
227⁶ BEAM ME UP SCOTTY (Ire) [84] 7-11-0 C Llewellyn, *led till 4th, wth wnr till 6th, wknd 3 out*......(5 to 1 op 10 to 1) 3
265² THE BLACK MONK (Ire) [95] (v) 8-11-11 D Bridgwater, *hld up, clsg whn hmpd by faller 5th, lost interst aftr, tld off.*
...............................(6 to 4 fav op 7 to 4) 4
225 COEUR BATTANT (Fr) [70] 6-10-0 B Powell, *wl beh till hdwy appr 2 out, chalg for second whn f last.*
.....................(40 to 1 op 7 to 1 tchd 50 to 1) f
225⁵ JENNYELLEN (Ire) [98] 7-12-0 R Johnson, *chsd ldrs till f 5th.*
....f
Dist: 18l, 1½l. 5m 18.30s. a 17.30s (6 Ran).
(Mr & Mrs J A Northover), P J Hobbs

332 Midsummer Novices' Chase Class E (5-y-o and up) £2,852 3¼m 110yds
....(3:15)

247³ WAKT 6-10-7 A P McCoy, *trkd ldrs, wnt second appr 6 out, led 4 out, sn clr, easily*....................... 1
124⁴ SOUTHERLY GALE 9-11-12 D Bridgwater, *led till hdd 4 out, sn btn*.........(Evens fav op 11 to 10 tchd 5 to 4) 2
DUKE OF LANCASTER (Ire) (v) 7-10-12 R Bellamy, *trkd ldr, dsptd ld 13th, wknd 6 out, tld off*........ (9 to 2 op 4 to 1) 3

264³ TOUR LEADER (NZ) 7-10-12 B Powell, *hld up, 4th whn blun and uns rdr tenth*...............(6 to 1 op 9 to 2) ur
262 LIBERTY JAMES 9-10-12 G Upton, *al beh, lost tch tenth, tld off whn pld up bef 14th*............(40 to 1 op 25 to 1) pu
Dist: 11l, dist. 6m 30.20s. a 10.20s (5 Ran).
(John R White), J White

333 Les Fletcher Memorial Challenge Trophy Class F Handicap Hurdle (0-100 4-y-o and up) £1,948 2m 1f.....(3:45)

244² VERDE LUNA [82] 4-10-12 A P McCoy, *hld up, hdwy 5th, rdn to ld appr 2 out, drvn out.*
.....................(100 to 30 op 3 to 1 tchd 7 to 2) 1
MISSED THE BOAT (Ire) [79] 6-10-12 A Thornton, *nvr far away, rdn appr 2 out, sddl slpd whn chalg last, not reco'r.*
.....................(3 to 1 op 7 to 4 tchd 100 to 30) 2
GAME DILEMMA [78] 5-10-8 R Greene, *hld up, gd hdwy 3 out, ev ch nxt, one pace*............(8 to 1 tchd 11 to 1) 3
SIRTELIMAR (Ire) [92] 7-11-8 (3*) T J Murphy, *wl beh till hdwy aftr 5th, rdn and no imprsn frm 2 out*...(9 to 1 op 10 to 1) 4
267³ MR SNAGGLE (Ire) [95] 7-12-0 C Maude, *dsptd ld, led 5th, hdd appr 2 out, one pace*..................(3 to 1 jt-
fav op 4 to 1 tchd 9 to 2) 5
244³ STAY WITH ME (Fr) [95] 6-12-0 J McCarthy, *al in tch, led briefly appr 2 out, wknd quickly bef last, eased, tme.*
.....................................(6 to 1 op 4 to 1) 6
MADRAJ (Ire) [77] 8-10-10 W McFarland, *beh frm 4th, tld off.*
.....................................(33 to 1 op 25 to 1) 7
206⁸ GUNMAKER [80] 7-10-13 Mr J L Llewellyn, *led till hdd 5th, drpd out quickly, tld off whn pld up bef 2 out.*
.....................................(12 to 1 op 10 to 1) pu
Dist: ¾l, 1½l, 1¾l, 1½l, 16l, dist. 3m 55.10s. a 6.10s (8 Ran).
(J A Leek), D W P Arbuthnot

334 August Novices' Handicap Hurdle Class E (0-100 4-y-o and up) £2,190 2m 1f..........................(4:15)

166⁷ KINDERGARTEN BOY (Ire) [80] 5-11-0 (3*) T J Murphy, *hld up, hdwy to go second 5th, led appr 2 out, clr whn hit last, easily.*
.....................(6 to 1 op 5 to 1 tchd 13 to 2) 1
SOUTHERN RIDGE [75] 5-10-12 Mr A Holdsworth, *led, clr second, rallied whn hdd appr 2 out, one pace.*
.....................(25 to 1 op 12 to 1 tchd 33 to 1) 2
284³ MUTLEY [64] 6-10-11 C Maude, *hld up, hdwy aftr 5th, one pace appr 2 out*...................(11 to 2 op 5 to 1) 3
189⁷ COURAGEOUS KNIGHT [84] 7-11-7 B Fenton, *trkd ldrs, wknd appr 2 out.*...................(11 to 4 op 2 to 1) 4
251⁴ DENOMINATION (USA) [94] 4-12-0 D Bridgwater, *hld up, beh 5th, sn btn, tld off*...... (10 to 1 op 11 to 10) 5
186⁹ DON TOCINO [69] 6-10-8 S Curran, *trkd ldr till 5th, wknd 3 out, tld off*.............(11 to 1 op 10 to 1 tchd 16 to 1) 6
Dist: 8l, 1¾l, 3½l, 2½l. 3m 58.70s. a 9.70s (6 Ran).
(Mrs E A Lerpiniere), K C Bailey

335 North Bank Highbury Handicap Chase Class E (0-110 5-y-o and up) £2,818 2m 110yds...................(4:45)

249⁵ MANAMOUR [78] 9-10-6 C Llewellyn, *trkd ldrs, rdn to ld sn aftr 2 out, ran on wl*................(11 to 4 op 7 to 2) 1
296² NOBLELY (USA) [100] 9-12-0 R Farrant, *jmpd wl, trkd ldr, led 6 out, hdd sn aftr 2 out, one pace.*
.....................(5 to 1 op 7 to 2 tchd 2 to 1) 2
296³ FLYING ZIAD (Can) [77] 13-10-5⁵ Mr A Charles-Jones, *hld up in tch, hdwy to go second 5 out, wknd 2 out.*
.....................(5 to 1 op 7 to 2 tchd 11 to 2) 3
GABISH [72] 11-9-7 (7*) Mr R Thornton, *in rear, hdwy 5 out, nvr nr to chal*.....(66 to 1 op 50 to 1 tchd 100 to 1) 4
230 TANGO'S DELIGHT [75] 8-10-3 B Powell, *al in rear, jmpd rght, tld off hfwy*...................(16 to 1 op 8 to 1) 5
PRUDENT PEGGY [76] (bl) 9-10-4⁴ J Frost, *beh, tld off hfwy.*
.....................................(20 to 1 op 14 to 1) 6
43⁵ RAMSTAR [99] 8-11-13 A P McCoy, *hld till hdd 6 out, sn wknd, tld off*..............(100 to 30 op 5 to 2 tchd 7 to 2) 7
Dist: 3½l, ¾l, 11l, 16l, 2l, dist. 3m 57.60s. b 0.40s (7 Ran).
SR: -/18/-/-/ (R L C Hartley), R Lee

336 Who's Who Standard Open National Hunt Flat Class H (4,5,6-y-o) £1,138 2m 1f.........................(5:15)

191⁴ KAILASH (USA) 5-12-4 D Bridgwater, *hld up in tch, led 5 fs out, very easily.* (7 to 2 on op 3 to 1 on tchd 5 to 2 on) 1
RED TEL (Ire) 4-11-1 C Maude, *hld up in rear, hdwy to chase wnr ins fnl 2 fs*..........(9 to 1 op 4 to 1 tchd 13 to 2) 2
191 KATHARINE'S SONG (Ire) 6-10-13 B Powell, *led till hdd 5 fs out, in tch till ran wide trng into strt, one pace aftr.*
.....................(50 to 1 op 33 to 1) 3
LUCKY MO 6-10-8 (5*) D Salter, *in tch, beh fnl 3 fs.*
.....................(16 to 1 op 25 to 1) 4
LATE ENCOUNTER 5-11-1 (3*) Guy Lewis, *prmnt early, wknd 5 fs out*....................(50 to 1 op 20 to 1) 5
157⁴ DRAGON FLY (Ire) 5-11-4 B Clifford, *sn trkd ldr, ran wide on bend wth circuit to go, al beh aftr*......(11 to 1 op 9 to 2) 6

ROYAL SALUTE 4-10-8 (7*) Mr G Shenkin, *trkd ldrs till lost tch*
hfwy ....(33 to 1 op 20 to 1) 7
Dist: 8l, 6l, 16l, 6l, 2½l, 2½l. 4m 1.20s. (7 Ran).

(Mick Fletcher), M C Pipe

TIPPERARY (IRE) (soft)
Monday August 5th

337 Ferndale Novice Hurdle (4-y-o and up)
£3,082 2m......................(3:35)

211⁷	MUSKERRY KING (Ire) 5-11-2 W T Slattery, ...(8 to 1)	1
276²	PERFECT TIMMER 6-11-2 C F Swan, ...(6 to 4)	2
256⁴	MONTETAN (Ire) 5-10-11 K F O'Brien, ...(12 to 1)	3
271*	RATHGIBBON 5-11-9 C O'Dwyer, ...(Evens fav)	4
194⁴	RONDELLI (Ire) 6-11-2 J K Kinane, ...(6 to 1)	5
Dist: ¾l, 3l, 7l, 20l. 4m 1.70s. (5 Ran).

(Model Farm Syndicate), T J O'Mara

338 Golden Handicap Chase (0-102 5-y-o
and up) £2,740 2¾m............(4:05)

236	TRIPTODICKS (Ire) [-] 6-9-2 (5*) T Martin, ...(6 to 1)	1
252³	HIGH-SPEC [-] 10-12-0 J F Titley, ...(11 to 2)	2
236	GOT NO CHOICE (Ire) [-] (bl) 6-9-13 T Horgan, ...(14 to 1)	3
219²	SILENTBROOK [-] 11-9-2 (7*) A O'Shea, ...(6 to 1)	4
312⁶	SANDY FOREST LADY (Ire) [-] 7-10-10 J P Broderick,
	....(8 to 1)	5
236⁵	MURPHY'S LADY (Ire) [-] 7-9-1¹ (7*) Mr John P Moloney,
	....(14 to 1)	6
314³	CASTALINO [-] 10-10-13 K F O'Brien, ...(7 to 2 fav)	7
212²	PEAFIELD (Ire) [-] 7-10-11 P M Verling, ...(10 to 1)	8
219⁹	SISTER ROSZA (Ire) [-] 8-11-5 C O'Dwyer, ...(14 to 1)	9
98	WALKERS LADY (Ire) [-] 8-10-9 (3*) D T Evans, ...(12 to 1)	10
293	NOBODYS SON [-] 10-11-4 (7*) M D Murphy, ...(7 to 1)	ur
Dist: 7l, 5l, hd, 1l. 5m 37.80s. (11 Ran).

(M G O'Huallachain), David A Kiely

339 Tipperary Directors Golf Classic Mdn
Hurdle (4 & 5-y-o) £3,253 2m....(4:35)

255³	ERRAMORE (Ire) 4-11-4 C F Swan, ...(7 to 4 fav)	1
173	DREAM ETERNAL (Ire) 5-11-11 W T Slattery, ...(6 to 1)	2
232³	FOREST LADY (Ire) 4-11-4 (3*) D T Evans, ...(7 to 1)	3
	SWINGS'N'THINGS (USA) 4-11-4 C O'Dwyer, ...(5 to 1)	4
221⁴	MULTIPIT (Ire) 4-11-2 (7*) Mr J Creighton, ...(12 to 1)	5
277	HIGH PARK LADY (Ire) 5-11-1 P M Verling, ...(14 to 1)	6
	BUNKER (Ire) 4-11-9 J K Kinane, ...(14 to 1)	7
258⁷	FRED OF THE HILL 5-11-6 T Horgan, ...(16 to 1)	8
	TEMPLARS INN (Ire) 4-10-13 J F Titley, ...(10 to 1)	9
	KINGS RUN 4-10-13 Mr M Phillips, ...(14 to 1)	10
Dist: 1½l, 3½l, ½l, 20l. 4m 6.10s. (10 Ran).

(J J Byrne), A P O'Brien

340 Tipperary Directors Golf Classic Flat
Race (5-y-o and up) £3,425 2m..(5:35)

233⁶	LISHILLAUN (Ire) 6-11-2 (7*) Miss J M Lee, ...(14 to 1)	1
	GRAIGUE HILL (Ire) 7-11-2 (7*) Mr R Walsh, ...(12 to 1)	2
278³	LADY RICHENDA (Ire) 8-11-2 (7*) Mr J T McNamara, (8 to 1)	3
253⁸	MALICE 10-11-6 (3*) Mr E Norris, ...(12 to 1)	4
213⁴	WILL I OR WONT I (Ire) 5-11-2 (7*) Mr M J Walsh, ..(6 to 1)	5
	DARING DAY (Ire) 7-11-9 Mr D Marnane, ...(20 to 1)	6
	MACK'S HOLLOW (Ire) 5-12-0 Mr P Fenton, ...(4 to 1)	7
	NICOLA MARIE (Ire) 7-11-2 (7*) Mr Sean O O'Brien, (14 to 1)	8
177⁷	PRINCESS LENA (Ire) (bl) 6-11-4 (5*) Mr W M O'Sullivan,
	....(20 to 1)	9
258⁴	BERCLUB 5-11-7 (7*) Mr Mark Walsh, ...(8 to 1)	10
	CULRUA ROSIE 5-11-2 (7*) Mr C O'Muireagain,
	....(12 to 1)	11
	ROSE OF STEEL 7-11-2 (7*) Mr John P Moloney,
	....(20 to 1)	12
	BANNPARK 6-11-7 (7*) Mr E Sheehy, ...(12 to 1)	13
274	INCH VALLEY (Ire) 5-11-2 (7*) Miss I M Burke, ...(20 to 1)	su
275⁵	GALE HAMSHIRE (Ire) 7-11-9 Mr J A Nash, ...(6 to 4 fav)	f
Dist: 6l, nk, 4l, 4l. 3m 53.70s. (15 Ran).

(Thomas Dunican), Mrs Edwina Finn

ROSCOMMON (IRE) (good)
Tuesday August 6th

341 Sallymount 3-Y-0 Maiden Hurdle
£2,397 2m......................(5:30)

	RHUM DANCER (Ire) 10-10 C O'Dwyer, ...(7 to 2)	1
	EVRIZA (Ire) 10-5 C F Swan, ...(100 to 30 fav)	2
	GREENHUE (Ire) 10-10 T P Rudd, ...(7 to 2)	3
	MISS ROBERTO (Ire) 10-5 K F O'Brien, ...(10 to 1)	4
	QUILL PROJECT (Ire) 9-12 (7*) M W Martin, ...(8 to 1)	5
	DUNEMER (Ire) 10-0 (5*) Mr R Walsh, ...(6 to 1)	6
	STONE HEAD (Ire) 10-10 J Shortt, ...(12 to 1)	7
	COMRADE CHINNERY (Ire) 10-10 M Duffy, ...(8 to 1)	8
	SPIONAN (USA) 10-10 T P Treacy, ...(12 to 1)	9
	WAAJ-U-SAY (Ire) 10-3¹ (3*) D T Evans, ...(20 to 1)	10
	RAINERY (Ire) 10-0 (5*) J Butler, ...(16 to 1)	11

ALTHOUGH 10-10 S W Kelly, ...(12 to 1) 12
PALLISTER (Ire) 10-10 T Horgan, ...(16 to 1) 13
Dist: Nk, 12l, 8l, 12l. 3m 52.60s. (13 Ran).

(Exors Late Mrs G W Jennings), D K Weld

342 Londis Handicap Hurdle (0-109 4-y-o
and up) £3,596 3m..............(6:00)

272*	REGAL GROVE (Ire) [-] 7-11-5 C F Swan, ...(Evens fav)	1
286	PRINCE SABI (Ire) [-] (bl) 6-9-7 P L Malone, ...(14 to 1)	2
235⁴	TIBOULEN (Ire) [-] 6-10-11 (3*) D T Evans, ...(12 to 1)	3
292⁴	ADARAMANN (Ire) [-] 4-10-6 (5*) Mr R Walsh, ...(9 to 2)	4
292³	VAIN PRINCESS (Ire) [-] 7-10-11 J P Broderick, (100 to 30)	5
234	CLOVER MOR LASS (Ire) [-] 7-10-0 C O'Dwyer, ...(16 to 1)	pu
Dist: 4l, nk, dist. 6m 1.20s. (6 Ran).

(Coosan Syndicate), A P O'Brien

343 Roscommon INH Flat Race (4-y-o and
up) £2,397 2m..................(8:30)

269³	PERAMBIE (Ire) (bl) 4-10-11 (7*) Miss A L Crowley,
	....(9 to 4 fav)	1
	CARRICK GLEN (Ire) 5-11-2 (7*) Mr T J Farrell, ...(8 to 1)	2
253⁷	EASTERN CUSTOM (Ire) 5-11-6 (3*) Mr R O'Neill, ..(8 to 1)	3
	YOU MAKE ME LAUGH (Ire) 4-11-2 (7*) Mr D W Cullen,
	....(14 to 1)	4
	LADY OF GRANGE 4-11-4 Mr H F Cleary, ...(6 to 1)	5
	MOSSA NOVA 8-11-11 (3*) Mr B M Cash, ...(12 to 1)	6
	TINERANA GLOW 4-11-4 Mr D Marnane, ...(14 to 1)	7
185⁸	PROPHETS FIST (Ire) 5-11-7 (7*) Mr D A Harney, ...(14 to 1)	8
	PERPETUAL PROSPECT (Ire) 4-11-2 (7*) Mr S M Duffy,
	....(3 to 1)	9
	HOSEA (Ire) 5-11-2 (7*) Mr J P McNamara, ...(8 to 1)	10
210⁹	SUPER SECRETARY (Ire) (bl) 5-11-2 (7*) Mr S J Mahon,
	....(33 to 1)	11
304	THE BREASER FAWL (Ire) 8-11-7 (7*) Mr D J Hassett,
	....(14 to 1)	12
Dist: 1½l, 5l, 1½l, 3l. 3m 50.30s. (12 Ran).

(Joseph Crowley), A P O'Brien

SLIGO (IRE) (soft)
Wednesday August 7th

344 Templeboy Handicap Hurdle (0-102
4-y-o and up) £2,226 2½l......(5:35)

195⁴	TABU LADY (Ire) [-] (bl) 5-10-0 T P Treacy, ...(100 to 30)	1
209	SPECTACLE (Ire) [-] 6-9-3 (7*) A O'Shea, ...(14 to 1)	2
	TARA'S TRIBE [-] 9-10-4 TJ Mitchell, ...(12 to 1)	3
208⁴	PETITE MEWS (Ire) [-] 5-10-2 P L Malone, ...(14 to 1)	4
	PUB TALK (Ire) [-] 6-9-2 (5*) J Butler, ...(7 to 1)	5
235⁷	PASSER-BY [-] 9-11-7 (7*) M P Cooney, ...(10 to 1)	6
275³	THE WICKED CHICKEN (Ire) [-] 7-10-10 T Horgan,
	....(7 to 4 fav)	7
158	BARNISH DAWN (Ire) [-] 6-9-3 (7*) M D Murphy, ..(33 to 1)	8
	LEADING TIME (Fr) [-] 7-9-11¹ J P Broderick, ...(20 to 1)	9
197²	CORMAC LADY (Ire) [-] 5-9-13 J K Kinane, ...(6 to 1)	10
	THE BROWN BEAR (Ire) [-] 5-10-10 D H O'Connor, (14 to 1)	11
Dist: 2½l, 2½l, 4l, 6l. 5m 12.50s. (11 Ran).

(P McWilliams), W Rock

345 Harridge Slates Beginners Chase (5-
y-o and up) £2,740 2½m........(7:05)

212³	FRIDAY THIRTEENTH (Ire) 7-12-0 A Powell, ...(6 to 1)	1
	CHOISYA (Ire) 8-11-9 T P Treacy, ...(8 to 1)	2
	THE ODIN LINE (Ire) 7-12-0 C O'Dwyer, ...(5 to 2)	3
	MUSICAL DUKE (Ire) 7-11-11 (3*) G Kilfeather, ...(14 to 1)	4
313	BOBSVILLE (Ire) 8-12-0 J Shortt, ...(Evens fav)	ur
	SINERGIA (Ire) 6-12-0 J P Broderick, ...(33 to 1)	pu
219⁴	BARNAMIRE BAY (Ire) 7-11-7 (7*) M D Murphy, ..(12 to 1)	pu
133	MAC-DUAGH (Ire) 6-11-7 (7*) A O'Shea, ...(33 to 1)	pu
Dist: 15l, 10l, dist. 5m 29.60s. (8 Ran).

(Derek Pugh), Derek Pugh

346 Summer I.N.H. Flat Race (4-y-o and up)
£2,226 2½m....................(8:05)

185²	CROSSCHILD 5-11-9 Mr J A Berry, ...(7 to 4 on)	1
224	MASK RIVER (Ire) 7-11-2 (7*) Mr A Daly, ...(14 to 1)	2
213⁶	PAUL (Ire) 4-11-0 (7*) Mr John P Moloney, ...(9 to 1)	3
269⁶	SHARP ELVER (Ire) 4-11-2 Mr A R Coonan, ...(11 to 4)	4
	MADDY KEEL 6-11-7 (7*) Mr R Myers, ...(14 to 1)	5
Dist: 11l, 1l, 7l, dist. 5m 23.90s. (5 Ran).

(Not For Friends Syndicate), J A Berry

SLIGO (IRE) (heavy)
Thursday August 8th

347 Strandhill Maiden Hurdle (4-y-o and
up) £2,226 2m.................(5:30)

142²	SHANRUE (Ire) 6-12-0 T Horgan, ...(11 to 10 fav)	1
316³	TWENTYFIVEQUID (Ire) 5-11-7 (7*) C Rae, ...(4 to 1)	2
269⁸	GRAPHIC LADY (Ire) 4-10-13 K F O'Brien, ...(10 to 1)	3

KARAWARA (Ire) 5-11-1 P L Malone, ...(14 to 1) 4
PIGEON HILL BUCK (Ire) 5-11-6 T P Treacy, ...(20 to 1) 5
KING'S MANDATE (Ire) 7-11-6 J K Kinane, ...(9 to 2) 6
ELYSIAN HEIGHTS (Ire) 4-10-8 (5*) J Butler, ...(12 to 1) 7
DANGAN LAD (USA) 4-11-4 C O'Dwyer, ...(7 to 1) 8
Dist: 3½l, 3½l, 7l, sht-hd. 4m 25.40s. (8 Ran).

(Joseph Crowley), A P O'Brien

348 Heineken Handicap Hurdle (0-109 4-y-o and up) £2,740 2m. . . . . (6:00)

184⁴ LOUGH ATALIA [-] 9-10-2 T Horgan, ...(7 to 2) 1
288 SHARLENE (Ire) [-] 5-10-1 T P Treacy, ...(4 to 1) 2
288⁸ ARCTIC CLOVER (Ire) [-] 5-9-13 C O'Dwyer, ...(10 to 1) 3
222¹ BRIGHT PROJECT (Ire) [-] 4-10-3 (7*) A O'Shea, ...(7 to 2) 4
268¹ MONTE'S EVENING (Ire) [-] 8-9-13 P L Malone, (9 to 4 fav) 5
NATURE PERFECTED (Ire) [-] 7-10-2 K F O'Brien, (12 to 1) 6
235⁹ KUMA CHAN [-] 9-9-6 (5*) J Butler, ...(16 to 1) pu
Dist: 13l, 5½l, 9l, 10l. 4m 11.80s. (7 Ran).

(P J O'Brien), V T O'Brien

349 Heineken Sligo Handicap Chase (0-102 4-y-o and up) £3,253 2m 1f . . . . (7:00)

261⁴ CARAGH BRIDGE [-] 9-10-10 C O'Dwyer, ...(6 to 4 fav) 1
219⁸ NO SIR ROM [-] 10-9-8 T Horgan, ...(12 to 1) 2
290² MILE A MINUTE (Ire) [-] (bl) 5-12-0 A Powell, ...(5 to 2) 3
219 GREEK MAGIC [-] 9-10-3 T P Treacy, ...(10 to 1) 4
209¹ BALLYVERANE [-] 10-10-0 (7*) C Rae, ...(6 to 1) pu
219⁵ AON DOCHAS (Ire) [-] (bl) 7-10-5 D H O'Connor, ...(7 to 1) pu
Dist: 20l, 20l, 15l. 4m 49.50s. (6 Ran).

(P Moriarty), Martin Michael Lynch

350 Mullaghmore INH Flat Race (4-y-o and up) £2,226 2m. . . . . (8:30)

GLADIATORIAL (Ire) 4-11-9 Mr P Fenton, ... (11 to 8 on) 1
159 STRONG EDITION (Ire) 5-11-9 Mr J A Berry, ...(9 to 2) 2
288 MUTUAL DECISION (Ire) 5-11-9 Mr P F Graffin, ...(12 to 1) 3
A SLIDER (Ire) 4-10-11 (7*) Mr J P McNamara, ...(12 to 1) 4
288 MERRY CHANTER (Ire) 4-11-9 Mr G J Harford, ...(12 to 1) 5
CHURCH ROCK (Ire) 4-11-9 Mr J P Dempsey, ...(12 to 1) 6
BELGROVE STAR (Ire) 4-11-2 (7*) Mr A Ross, ...(16 to 1) 7
SINGERS CORNER 4-10-11 (7*) Mr Edgar Byrne, (10 to 1) 8
169 EMYGUY (Ire) 4-11-2 (7*) Mr S McGonagle, ...(20 to 1) 9
ASTRID (Ire) 5-11-2 (7*) Mr A Jordan, ...(25 to 1) 10
REENIE (Ire) 5-11-2 (7*) Mr D A Harney, ...(12 to 1) 11
258⁶ MOY VALLEY (Ire) 6-11-2 (7*) Mr A Daly, ...(25 to 1) 12
269 DUNMORE SUPREME (Ire) 4-11-2 (7*) Mr M P Brown,
. . . .(33 to 1) 13
Dist: 20l, 9l, sht-hd, ¾l. 4m 13.60s. (13 Ran).

(Mrs John Magnier), M J Grassick

CLAIREFONTAINE (FR) (soft)
Friday August 9th

351 Prix Jacques Pemillon (Hurdle) (5-y-o and up) £6,588 2m 1f. . . . . (5:09)

PROFLUENT (USA) 5-10-6 D Bressou, ...1
RAIDER (Fr) 7-10-6 L Gerard, ...2
C'EST TRES BIEN (Fr) 6-10-12 T Roche, ...3
KING UBAD (USA) 7-10-2 N Milliere, rcd in second till wknd
hfwy. 5
Dist: 1½l, 5l, dist, dist. 3m 53.82s. (5 Ran).

(P A Leonard), J Bertran de Balanda

KILBEGGAN (IRE) (good)
Friday August 9th

352 Dysart Maiden Hurdle (4-y-o and up) £2,226 2m 3f. . . . . (5:30)

311³ FAIR SOCIETY (Ire) (bl) 5-10-8 (7*) Mr John P Moloney,
. . . .(3 to 1) 1
301⁷ CELIO LUCY (Ire) 6-11-2 (7*) P Morris, ...(9 to 2) 2
301 BRACKER (Ire) 4-10-11 (7*) Mr C A Murphy, ...(33 to 1) 3
ANSAL BOY 4-11-9 J P Byrne, ...(14 to 1) 4
MR MATCHIT (Ire) 4-10-11 (7*) M D Murphy, ...(20 to 1) 5
337² PERFECT TIMMER (Ire) 4-10-6 C F Swan, ...(6 to 4 on) pu
Dist: Dist, 8l, dist, 1½l. 4m 36.30s. (6 Ran).

(Fair Society Syndicate), Michael Hourigan

353 Tullamore Mares Maiden Hurdle (4-y-o and up) £2,226 2m 3f. . . . . (6:00)

270³ JANE DIGBY (Ire) 4-11-9 C F Swan, ...(3 to 1) 1
211² ALLATRIM (Ire) 6-12-0 Mr R Power, ... (11 to 10 fav) 2
339³ FOREST LADY 4-11-1 (3*) D T Evans, ...(7 to 1) 3
253 GARLAND ROSE (Ire) 6-10-13 (7*) P Morris, ...(14 to 1) 4
277⁷ DOTTIE'S DOUBLE (Ire) (bl) 5-11-6 T P Rudd, ...(10 to 1) 5
289⁷ THAI ELECTRIC (Ire) 5-11-6 K F O'Brien, ...(10 to 1) 6
272⁵ OX EYE DAISY (Ire) 8-12-0 T P Treacy, ...(8 to 1) 7
277⁸ VIENNA WALTZ (Ire) 6-11-6 H Rogers, ...(25 to 1) 8

192²⁵ SPRINGWELL MAY (Ire) (bl) 4-11-4 T Horgan, ...(12 to 1) 9
253⁹ SHADOW CHASER (Ire) (bl) 4-10-13 (5*) J Butler, . .(25 to 1) 10
DEVINE THYME (Ire) 5-11-6 S H O'Donovan, ...(33 to 1) ur
66⁴ NORDIC QUEEN (Ire) 6-11-7 (7*) Mr B Hassett, ...(8 to 1) pu
Dist: ¾l, 15l, 12l, 6l. 4m 31.90s. (12 Ran).

(New Road Syndicate), A P O'Brien

354 Sean Graham Handicap Hurdle (0-109 4-y-o and up) £2,740 2m 3f. . . . . (6:30)

275⁴ NIYAMPOUR (Ire) [-] (bl) 5-11-4 T P Rudd, ...(3 to 1) 1
342³ TIBOULEN (Ire) [-] 6-10-11 (3*) D T Evans, ...(7 to 1) 2
224⁴ TEMPLEROAN PRINCE [-] 9-11-11 M Duffy, ...(6 to 1) 3
223³ MASCOT [-] 5-11-6 P L Malone, ...(6 to 1) 4
235³ TISRARA LADY (Ire) [-] 5-11-7 T P Treacy, ...(5 to 2 fav) 5D
PORT NOBLE [-] 5-10-7 C F Swan, ...(12 to 1) 5
277¹ PHARDANTE GIRL (Ire) [-] (bl) 5-10-2 J P Broderick, (9 to 2) 6
Dist: 2l, 1½l, 8l, 3½l. 4m 30.30s. (7 Ran).

(D P Sharkey), M J P O'Brien

355 Sean Graham Handicap Hurdle (0-102 4-y-o and up) £2,740 3m. . . . . (7:00)

302⁵ SUDDEN STORM (Ire) [-] 5-10-12 T P Treacy, ...(7 to 2) 1
92¹ DUNDOCK WOOD [-] 8-10-12 K F O'Brien, ...(6 to 4 fav) 2
302⁹ MANETTI (Ire) [-] 4-11-0 (7*) Mr S P Hennessy, ...(12 to 1) 3
292⁸ RISING BREEZE (Ire) [-] 7-11-1 C F Swan, ...(11 to 2) 4
302 VALAMIR (Ire) [-] 6-9-0 (7*) D McCullagh, ...(25 to 1) 5
96⁵ INGMAR [-] 10-10-7 T Horgan, ...(14 to 1) 6
MAGIC ROYALE (Ire) [-] 6-9-0 (7*) J Butler, ...(25 to 1) 7
272⁴ KILCARAMORE (Ire) [-] 5-11-1 Mr P J Healy, ...(4 to 1) f
Dist: ½l, 1l, 3l, 20l. 6m 3.80s. (8 Ran).

(G Kingston), P Mullins

356 Joe Cooney Memorial Handicap Chase (0-109 4-y-o and up) £2,740 3m 1f . . . . (7:30)

216² MERRY PEOPLE (Ire) [-] 8-11-9 T Horgan, ...(9 to 4) 1
314⁴ BEET STATEMENT (Ire) [-] 7-10-2 (4ex) T J Mitchell, (13 to 2) 2
314⁵ FIXED ASSETS (Ire) [-] 9-9-5 (7*) A O'Shea, ...(10 to 1) 3
236² WATERLOO BALL (Ire) [-] 7-11-8 C F Swan, ...(2 to 1 fav) 4
236⁴ FAYS FOLLY (Ire) [-] 7-9-1 (7*) R P Hogan, ...(8 to 1) 5
236⁸ ROSSBEIGH CREEK [-] 9-11-3 F J Flood, ...(100 to 30) 6
Dist: ½l, 2½l, 1½l, 2l. 6m 32.20s. (6 Ran).

(Karl Casey), John Queally

357 Michael Moore Beginners Chase (4-y-o and up) £2,740 2m 5f. . . . .(8:00)

290³ VERY LITTLE (Ire) 8-11-9 C O'Dwyer, ...(4 to 1) 1
COSHLA EXPRESSO (Ire) 8-12-0 P L Malone, ...(14 to 1) 2
SANDY JAY 9-11-9 T P Treacy, ...(12 to 1) 3
237³ LET THE RIVER RUN 10-11-2 (7*) R P Hogan, ...(4 to 1) 4
MOOHONO (Ire) 7-11-9 C F Swan, ...(5 to 4 fav) f
257⁷ WHAT IS THE PLAN (Ire) 7-11-7 (7*) Mr B Hassett, (10 to 1) f
105 HOW'S IT GOIN (Ire) 5-11-1 (7*) P Morris, ...(9 to 2) ur
Dist: 6l, dist, 1½l. 5m 26.60s. (7 Ran).

(Dermot Lynch), P J Lally

358 Tom Birmingham Menswear I.N.H. Flat Race (6-y-o and up) £2,568 2m 3f . . . . (8:30)

286⁵ BENNY THE BISHOP (Ire) 6-11-7 (7*) Mr A Ross, . . .(4 to 1) 1
329⁷ ALL FOR MAX (Ire) 7-12-0 Mr J A Berry, ...(10 to 1) 2
304⁶ BARRIGAN'S HILL (Ire) 6-11-11 (3*) Mr K Whelan, . .(4 to 1) 3
340 GALE HAMSHIRE (Ire) 7-11-9 Mr J A Nash, . .(2 to 1 fav) 4
274⁶ WILDLIFE RANGER (Ire) 8-11-7 (7*) Mr R M Walsh, (10 to 1) 5
304⁹ CASTLEROYAL (Ire) 7-12-0 Mr D Marnane, ...(7 to 1) 6
238⁶ RING O'ROSES (Ire) 8-11-2 (7*) Mr T N Cloke, ...(12 to 1) 7
PALEFOOT (Ire) 8-11-2 (7*) Miss C O'Neill, ...(16 to 1) 8
245⁸ SUSIE'S DELIGHT (Ire) 6-11-6 (3*) Mr P M Kelly, . .(25 to 1) 9
Dist: 3l, 3l, hd, 7l. 4m 27.60s. (9 Ran).

(Mrs Salome Brennan), Cecil Ross

PLUMPTON (firm)
Friday August 9th
Going Correction: MINUS 0.35 sec. per fur.

359 Hove Novices' Hurdle Class E (4-y-o and up) £2,343 2½m. . . . .(2:30)

145⁵ LIMOSA 5-10-7 M Richards, chsd ldrs, lft second bend appr
6th, rdn alng 9th, led approaching last, styd on.
. . . .(7 to 2 op 5 to 2 tchd 4 to 1) 1
297⁵ CANARY FALCON 5-10-12 V Smith, beh till hdwy 7th, led
briefly 2 out, not quicken r-in.
. . . .(7 to 4 op 4 to 1 tchd 9 to 2) 2
SIR GALEFORCE (Ire) 6-10-12 D Morris, not fluent, chsd ldr,
led aftr 5th, slpd and lft clr bend appr 6th, hdd 2 out, wknd
approaching last. . . . .(13 to 2 op 5 to 1 tchd 7 to 1) 3
64¹ ARCTIC RED RIVER (Ire) 7-10-12 A Maguire, mstks second
and 6th, chsd ldg trio frm 8th, no imprsn.
. . . .(5 to 4 on tchd Evens) 4

FATTASH (USA) (bl) 4-10-4 (5*) S Ryan, *chsd ldrs till rdn and wknd 7th, tld off 9th*.....(33 to 1 op 20 to 1 tchd 50 to 1) 5
SHALIK (Ire) 6-10-12 J Railton, *led till aftr 5th, cl second whn slpd up bend appr nxt.* (33 to 1 op 20 to 1 tchd 40 to 1) su
BRIGADIER SUPREME (Ire) 7-10-12 B Fenton, *mid-div, sn pushed alng, hrd rdn and lost tch 7th, pld up bef 9th.*
.... (33 to 1 op 16 to 1) pu
Dist: 4l, 8l, 17l, dist. 4m 54.80s. a 17.80s (7 Ran).
(Mrs Lydia Richards), Mrs L Richards

360 Streat Conditional Jockeys' Selling Handicap Chase Class G (0-95 5-y-o and up) £2,259 2m..............(3:00)

SAFETY (USA) [81] (bl) 9-11-5 T J Murphy, *led aftr 1st, made rst, easily*..........................(2 to 1 fav op 2 to 1) 1
AFALTOUN [70] 11-10-8 P Henley, *led till aftr 1st, rgned second tenth, hrd rdn appr last, no imprsn.*
.... (13 to 2 op 8 to 1 tchd 12 to 1) 2
296^{4} NUCLEAR EXPRESS [72] 9-10-10 Guy Lewis, *in tch, chsd wnr 9th to tenth, sn hrd rdn and btn*
.........................(3 to 1 op 4 to 1 tchd 9 to 2) 3
DAYS OF THUNDER [90] 8-12-0 B Fenton, *mstk second, al beh, no ch whn mistake 2 out.*
...................(100 to 30 op 11 to 4 tchd 7 to 2) 4
282^{6} VICTORY ANTHEM [74] 10-10-12 Michael Brennan, *chsd wnr second to 9th, 4th and wkng whn mstk and uns rdr nxt.*
.... (7 to 2 op 3 to 1 tchd 4 to 1 and 9 to 2) ur
LAVALIGHT [70] 9-10-8 J Culloty, *al rear, no ch whn jmpd rght and uns rdr last*.........................(16 to 1 op 8 to 1) ur
Dist: 4l, 9l, 30l. 3m 54.50s. a 2.50s (6 Ran).
SR: 10/-/-/ (Keith Sturgis), J White

361 Berwick Handicap Hurdle Class E (0-110 4-y-o and up) £2,280 2m 1f .... (3:30)

267^{5} PAIR OF JACKS (Ire) [80] 6-10-3 C Llewellyn, *chsd ldr, led aftr 3 out, hld on gmely r-in*................ (2 to 1 op 6 to 4) 1
109^{8} NO LIGHT [100] 9-11-9 L Harvey, *trkd ldg pair, effrt 2 out, str chal r-in, kpt on wl*..........................(5 to 1 op 5 to 2) 2
ZABARGAR (USA) [108] 5-12-0 A Maguire, *hld up rear, hdwy to press ldrs 2 out, one pace r-in*.... (5 to 4 fav op 2 to 1) 3
IKHTIRAA (USA) [87] (bl) 6-10-10 D O'Sullivan, *not fluent, led till aftr 3 out, hrd rdn and wknd nxt.*
.... (6 to 1 op 4 to 1 tchd 13 to 2) 4
Dist: Hd, 2½l, 19l. 4m 14.00s. a 17.00s (4 Ran).
(D A Wilson), G L Moore

362 Chailey Novices' Handicap Chase Class E (0-100 5-y-o and up) £2,906 2m 5f..........................(4:00)

309^{*} POND HOUSE (Ire) [91] 7-11-6 (7ex) D Bridgwater, *made all, drw clr 4 out, easily*................. (5 to 4 fav op Evens) 1
106^{2} SIMPLY (Ire) [99] 7-12-0 A Maguire, *in tch, outpcd 11th, styd on to take second appr last, no ch wth wnr.*
.... (11 to 8 op 6 to 4 tchd 7 to 4) 2
147 CALL ME ALBI (Ire) [92] (v) 5-11-3 M Richards, *chsd wnr 4th, rdn and btn appr 3 out, lost second approaching last.*
.... (11 to 1 op 6 to 1 tchd 12 to 1) 3
280^{3} TELMAR SYSTEMS [71] (bl) 7-10-0 D Gallagher, *in tch till rdn and wknd tenth*......... (11 to 1 op 6 to 1 tchd 12 to 1) 4
JIMMY THE JACKDAW [71] 9-10-0 B Fenton, *rdn and lost tch 9th*.....................(25 to 1 op 12 to 1 tchd 33 to 1) 5
CARDAN [71] 10-10-0 R Greene, *sn tld off.*
.... (16 to 1 op 14 to 1 tchd 20 to 1) 6
Dist: 8l, 7l, 10l, 17l, 12l. 5m 7.10s. a 1.10s (6 Ran).
SR: 8/8/-/ (C R Fleet), M C Pipe

363 Jevington Juvenile Novices' Hurdle Class E (3-y-o) £2,217 2m 1f.... (4:30)

GALWAY BLADE 10-7 (3*) J Culloty, *made all, slpd bend appr 2 out, hld on gmely r-in*.........(2 to 1 jt-fav tchd 9 to 4) 1
VERULAM (Ire) 10-10 G Bradley, *pld hrd and beh, hdwy 4th, hard rdn appr last, ev ch r-in, kpt on.*
.... (11 to 4 op 4 to 1 tchd 9 to 2) 2
AGAIN TOGETHER 10-5 D Gallagher, *hld up, smooth chal 3 out, no extr r-in*.....(2 to 1 jt-fav op 5 to 2 tchd 11 to 4) 3
AMBER RING 10-5 D Skyrme, *hld up, jnd ldrs 7th, one pace appr nxt*............. (33 to 1 op 16 to 1 tchd 40 to 1) 4
KINGS NIGHTCLUB 10-5 B Fenton, *chsd ldrs, jmpd slwly 3rd, lost pl 6th, 5th and no ch whn slpd up bend appr 2 out.*
.... (16 to 1 op 7 to 1 tchd 20 to 1) su
LAST BUT NOT LEAST 10-5 D Bridgwater, *rear, mstk and nrly uns rdr 1st, tld off aftr, pld up after 3rd.*
.... (8 to 1 op 4 to 1 tchd 10 to 1) pu
Dist: ¾l, 1¼l, 1½l. 4m 20.80s. a 23.80s (6 Ran).
(T Blade), Miss H C Knight

GOWRAN PARK (IRE) (soft)
Saturday August 10th

364 Old Leighlin Maiden Hurdle (4-y-o and up) £2,397 2m.................. (4:30)

SHARATAN (Ire) 4-11-9 T P Treacy,..............(9 to 4 on) 1
286^{6} REAL TAOISEACH (Ire) 6-11-7 (7*) Mr A K Wyse, (100 to 30) 2
276^{7} SAN SIRO (Ire) 6-10-13 (7*) Mr Edgar Byrne,......(14 to 1) 3
276^{6} CROGHAN BRIDGE (Ire) 7-10-13 (7*) Mr C A Murphy,
....(33 to 1) 4
120^{*} TURRAMURRA GIRL (Ire) 7-11-2 (7*) L J Fleming, . . (7 to 1) 5
IRVINE (Ire) 4-11-4 G M O'Neill,................. (14 to 1) 6
274^{9} LOCAL RACE (Ire) 7-11-6 D H O'Connor,.........(33 to 1) 7
Dist: 1½l, 20l, ¾l, 4l. 4m 12.60s. (7 Ran).
(Mrs Dorothy Weld), Thomas Foley

365 Fenniscourt I.N.H. Flat Race (4-y-o and up) £2,740 2½m................ (6:00)

289^{6} LISS DE PAOR (Ire) 5-11-10 (3*) Mr B M Cash, . . (5 to 4 on) 1
304^{8} HIGHEST CALL (Ire) 5-11-11 Mr M Halford,.........(8 to 1) 2
253^{*} NATIVE BABY (Ire) 6-11-8 (5*) Mr R Walsh,..........(9 to 4) 3
[illegible] [illegible] (Ire) 7-10-10 (7*) Miss [illegible], . . (16 to 1) 4
274^{*} STRADBALLY JANE (Ire) 6-11-6 (7*) Mr Mark Walsh, (9 to 2) 5
253 TIME TO GO (Ire) 4-10-8 (7*) Mr J T McNamara, . . .(20 to 1) 6
270^{4} JARSUN QUEEN (Ire) 4-11-1 Mr H F Cleary, ... (16 to 1) 7
Dist: Dist, 3l, ½l, ¾l. 5m 3.00s. (7 Ran).
(J C Dempsey), A P O'Brien

MARKET RASEN (good)
Saturday August 10th
Going Correction: PLUS 0.25 sec. per fur.

366 Tote Combination Dual Forecast Novices' Chase Class D (5-y-o and up) £3,867 2½m..................(5:50)

155^{2} CATS RUN (Ire) 8-11-0 R Supple, *made all, clr aftr 4 out, ran on strly fnl 2*........................ (7 to 4 tchd 2 to 1) 1
325^{2} NORDIC VALLEY (Ire) 5-10-10 D Bridgwater, *pressed ldrs, wnt second 9th, rdn 4 out, one pace whn hit 2 out.*
...................(11 to 10 on op Evens tchd 11 to 10) 2
319^{2} SASSIVER (USA) 6-11-6 P Niven, *pressed ldr, jmpd slwly and outpcd 9th, tld off last 4*...............(4 to 1 op 7 to 2) 3
247 SIGNE DE MARS (Fr) 5-10-7 (3*) D Walsh, *not jump wl, sn lost tch, tld off whn pld up bef 5 out.*
........................(25 to 1 op 20 to 1 tchd 33 to 1) pu
Dist: 20l, dist. 5m 6.50s. a 17.50s (4 Ran).
(Mrs Ann Key), John R Upson

367 Singleton/Richardson Handicap Hurdle Class F (0-105 4-y-o and up) £1,954 2m 1f 110yds........... (6:20)

248^{6} WAMDHA (Ire) [100] 6-11-11 A S Smith, *keen hold, made all, ran on wl whn pressed fnl 2*......................(13 to 8 jt-fav op 11 to 8 tchd 7 to 4) 1
JOHN TUFTY [86] 5-10-8 M Dwyer, *chsd ldrs, smooth hdwy and ev ch 2 out, swtchd appr last, kpt on.*
......................................(7 to 2 tchd 4 to 1) 2
69^{2} ELITE JUSTICE [85] (bl) 4-10-7 A Dobbin, *cl up, rdn 4th, outpcd 2 out, btn whn blun last*... (13 to 8 jt-fav op 6 to 4) 3
GAVASKAR (Ire) [75] (bl) 7-10-0 B Powell, *cl up, ev ch 3 out, sn rdn and outpcd*..........................(12 to 1 op 7 to 1) 4
Dist: 1l, 11l, 26l. 4m 18.50s. a 17.50s (4 Ran).
(T R Pryke), K A Morgan

368 Freshney Place Handicap Chase Class E (0-115 5-y-o and up) £3,851 2¾m 110yds........................ (6:50)

282^{2} MAGIC BLOOM [99] 10-11-8 (5*) E Callaghan, *hndy, mstks 5th and 4 out, sn rdn, effrt 3 out, led aftr nxt, drvn out frm last.*
......................................(11 to 8 fav op 6 to 4) 1
321^{*} DRUMSTICK [96] 10-11-10 A Thornton, *led till mstk and hdd 5 out, rgned ld appr 3 out, headed aftr nxt, one pace r-in.*
....(2 to 1 op 6 to 4) 2
321 WAKE UP LUV [90] 11-11-4 G Bradley, *chsd ldr, led 5 out, hdd appr 3 out, sn struggling*..............(9 to 2 op 5 to 1) 3
202 TRUSS [85] 9-10-13 R Supple, *in tch, outpcd 9th, btn last 5.*
.............................(13 to 2 op 7 to 1 tchd 8 to 1) 4
230 REGARDLESS [72] 14-10-0 B Powell, *sn wl beh, tld off whn pld up bef tenth*...................(33 to 1 op 25 to 1) pu
Dist: 1½l, 23l, dist. 5m 41.00s. a 14.00s (5 Ran).
SR: 15/10/ (Peter Nelson), J M Jefferson

369 Singleton Birch Handicap Chase Class D (0-120 5-y-o and up) £4,075 2m 1f 110yds........................ (7:20)

321^{2} YAAKUM [91] 7-11-0 M A Fitzgerald, *settled in last pl, lft 3rd aftr 8th, smooth hdwy to ld after 2 out, pushed out.*
....(9 to 4 op 7 to 4) 1
325^{*} STAPLEFORD LADY [78] 8-10-1 W McFarland, *nvr far away, drvn alng and outpcd 3 out, rallied frm last.*
....(7 to 4 fav op 2 to 1) 2

282[4] WISE ADVICE (Ire) [95] 6-11-4 R Garritty, *chsd clr ldr, lft in ld aftr 8th, hdd after 2 out, hit last, no extr.*
....(5 to 1 op 9 to 2 tchd 6 to 1) 3
279[3] I HAVE HIM [101] 9-11-10 B Powell, *jmpd badly rght, led and clr, ran out jst aftr 8th.....*(11 to 4 op 5 to 2 tchd 3 to 1) ro
Dist: 2l, ½l. 4m 27.80s. a 13.80s (4 Ran).

(Ian Thompson), S E Kettlewell

370 Freshney Place Novices' Hurdle Class D (4-y-o and up) £2,804 2m 1f 110yds .... (7:50)

226* SHAHRANI 4-11-9 D Bridgwater, *made all, reminders second, hrd rdn to go clr 3 out, eased r-in.*
....(5 to 4 on tchd 11 to 10 on) 1
CHINA MAIL (Ire) 4-10-11 T J Murphy, *hndy, drvn 3 out, nvr able to chal...............*(8 to 1 op 7 to 1 tchd 9 to 1) 2
322[2] SILVERDALE LAD 5-11-0 M A Fitzgerald, *in tch, chsd wnr 4th, blun nxt, no ch with winner fnl 2.*
....(3 to 1 op 5 to 2 tchd 100 to 30) 3
MARBLE MAN (Ire) 6-11-0 R Garritty, *in tch, pushed alng whn blun badly 3 out, sn lost touch...........*(9 to 2 op 7 to 2) 4
329[9] SCALLYMILL 6-10-9 M Foster, *chsd wnr till 4th, hit and struggling nxt, tld off..* (40 to 1 op 33 to 1 tchd 50 to 1) 5
322 HUTCEL BELL 5-10-9 P Niven, *beh, lost tch fnl circuit, tld off.*
....(100 to 1 op 33 to 1) 6
Dist: 11l, 2½l, dist, 8l, 16l. 4m 19.50s. a 18.50s (6 Ran).

(A S Helaissi And Mr S Helaissi), M C Pipe

371 Interflora Novices' Handicap Hurdle Class F (0-95 4-y-o and up) £1,954 2m 5f 110yds.......................(8:20)

83[3] PLINTH [75] 5-11-0 G Bradley, *not fluent, cl up, drvn and ev ch 2 out, hit last, styd on to ld nr finish.*
....(13 to 8 fav op 7 to 4 tchd 15 to 8) 1
187* LITTLE TINCTURE (Ire) [65] 6-10-2 (5*) Sophie Mitchell, *led, rdn aftr 3 out, hdd nr finish...........*(9 to 2 op 4 to 1) 2
294* RAGAMUFFIN ROMEO [67] 7-10-9 N Mann, *beh, effrt and pushed alng appr 2 out, one pace frm last.*
....(9 to 2 op 4 to 1 tchd 4 to 1) 3
317[2] SILVER SLEEVE (Ire) [82] (bl) 4-11-4 R Garritty, *hndy, drvn 3 out, struggling betw last 2 ....*(7 to 2 op 5 to 2) 4
RIVER CHALLENGE (Ire) [89] 5-12-0 R Supple, *chsd ldrs, struggling 6th, pld up bef nxt............*(5 to 1 op 4 to 1) pu
Dist: ½l, 5l, 11l. 5m 35.70s. a 32.70s (5 Ran).

(T H Chadney), N A Graham

WORCESTER (good (races 1,2,3,4), good to soft (5,6))
Saturday August 10th
Going Correction: PLUS 0.10 sec. per fur.

372 Polly Garter Selling Handicap Hurdle Class G (0-95 4-y-o and up) £1,905 2m .... (6:00)

317[4] TONY'S MIST [73] 6-11-2 R Johnson, *hld up beh ldrs, wnt second 3 out, led nxt, clr r-in, cmftbly.* (9 to 2 tchd 11 to 2) 1
263[4] BETABETCORBETT [76] (bl) 5-11-2 T Eley, *led to 2 out, rdn and no extr....................*(14 to 1 op 10 to 1) 2
79 COLWAY PRINCE (Ire) [81] 8-11-10 S Curran, *hld up in rear, lost tch 5th, rdn and hdwy frm 3 out, not rch ldrs.*
....(8 to 1 op 7 to 1) 3
225[3] MYLORDMAYOR [59] 9-10-2 R Farrant, *pressed ldr to 3 out, 4th and btn whn blun last...*(8 to 1 op 7 to 1 tchd 9 to 1) 4
318[2] LOFTY DEED (USA) [66] (bl) 6-10-9 L Harvey, *hld up, hdwy 5th, wknd 3 out....*(4 to 1 fav tchd 9 to 2 and 7 to 2) 5
AL SKEET (USA) [57] 10-10-0 N Williamson, *towards rear, moderate hdwy frm 3 out, no imprsn.*
....(11 to 1 op 14 to 1 tchd 20 to 1) 6
309 GEORGE LANE [73] 8-10-11 (5*) L Aspell, *in tch, rdn alng 4th, wknd nxt...............*(13 to 2 op 6 to 1 tchd 7 to 1) 7
TRYPH [83] 4-11-9 A Maguire, *hld up, hdwy 5th, mstk 3 out, fdd.....................*(13 to 2 op 4 to 1) 8
BEAUFAN [78] 9-11-7 Gary Lyons, *mid-div, beh hfwy, sn tld off....................*(11 to 2 op 7 to 1 tchd 12 to 1) 9
328[4] PUSEY STREET BOY [80] 9-11-9 M Bosley, *hld up, f 3rd.*
....(9 to 1 op 7 to 1 tchd 10 to 1) f
Dist: 6l, 10l, 2½l, 6l, 3l, 9l, 5l, 30l. 3m 49.00s. a 9.00s (10 Ran).
SR: 14/8/6/-/-/-/

(Robert Bailey), J M Bradley

373 Edgar Thompson Novices' Chase Class E (5-y-o and up) £3,136 2m (6:30)

296* STATELY HOME (Ire) 5-12-2 R Johnson, *made all, clr frm 7th, canter....................*(5 to 4 and 11 to 8 and Evens) 1
307[2] GREEN'S SEAGO (USA) 8-10-9 (3*) J Culloty, *chsd wnr to 4th, lft in second nxt, rdn aftr 7th, no imprsn.*
....(11 to 1 op 8 to 1 tchd 12 to 1) 2
215 WINTER BELLE (v) 8-10-12 N Williamson, *hld up, chsd wnr 4th, blun and uns rdr nxt......*(11 to 8 on tchd Evens) ur
Dist: 18l. 4m 4.30s. a 15.30s (3 Ran).

(P Bowen), P Bowen

374 Weatherbys' Sponsorship In Racing Handicap Hurdle Class D (0-120 4-y-o and up) £2,763 2m..............(7:00)

WADADA [104] 5-10-9 D J Burchell, *al prmnt, led appr 5th, hdd briefly last, drvn out............*(5 to 1 op 4 to 1) 1
SAMANID (Ire) [110] 4-11-1 A Maguire, *wtd wth, hdwy 5th, ev ch 2 out, led briefly last, not quicken r-in.*
....(9 to 4 fav op 3 to 1) 2
281[3] STAR MARKET [120] (bl) 6-12-0 N Williamson, *in tch, led aftr second till appr 5th, rdn and ev ch 3 out, wknd nxt.*
....(3 to 1 op 5 to 2) 3
PREROGATIVE [105] 6-10-13 D Gallagher, *hld up, beh 5th, no imprsn aftr....................*(20 to 1 op 14 to 1) 4
295[5] DICKIES GIRL [92] 6-10-0 W Marston, *set steady pace, hdd aftr second, rdn 5th, sn wknd.*
....(33 to 1 op 20 to 1 tchd 50 to 1) 5
ASTERIX [96] 8-9-13 (3*) Guy Lewis, *hld up, hdwy 5th, rdn and wknd appr nxt.................*(7 to 1 op 11 to 2) 6
281[2] FAUSTINO [112] (bl) 4-10-12 (5*) D J Kavanagh, *hld up beh ldrs, not fluent 3rd and nxt, rdn aftr 5th, sn wknd.*
....(11 to 4 op 2 to 1) 7
Dist: 3l, 12l, 6l, 2l, 4l, 10l. 4m 7.40s. a 27.40s (7 Ran).

(Mrs Ruth Burchell), D Burchell

375 Back Up Staff 6th Anniversary Handicap Chase Class D (0-125 5-y-o and up) £3,591 2m 7f.............. (7:30)

108[2] HILLWALK [117] 10-12-0 D Morris, *hld up, lost pl 9th, mstk nxt, rdn 4 out, rallied 2 out, led cl hme...* (7 to 1 op 5 to 1) 1
24[2] THE YANK [100] (bl) 10-10-11 A Maguire, *made most till rdn and hdd cl hme..........*(11 to 2 op 4 to 1 tchd 6 to 1) 2
102* COMEDY ROAD [97] 12-10-8 R Johnson, *hld up, mstk 8th, wnt prmnt 12th, ev ch 2 out, one pace...*(8 to 1 op 7 to 1) 3
282[3] CHANNEL PASTIME [93] 12-10-1 (3*) Guy Lewis, *hld up, hdwy 8th, outpcd appr 4 out, rnwd effrt 2 out, one pace frm last.....................*(8 to 1 tchd 10 to 1) 4
264* EVANGELICA (USA) [115] 6-11-12 C Maude, *nvr a factor.*
....(9 to 2 op 4 to 1 tchd 5 to 1) 5
188 GILSTON LASS [95] 9-10-6 J R Kavanagh, *dsptd ld, mstks 1st and 12th, wknd....*(25 to 1 op 20 to 1 tchd 33 to 1) 6
CELTIC LAIRD [89] 8-10-0 W Marston, *trkd ldrs to tenth, ben 12th.....................*(10 to 1 op 8 to 1) 7
230[*] HURRYUP [93] 9-10-1 (3*) J Culloty, *hld up, mstk second, hdwy 9th, wknd 12th........*(7 to 1 op 6 to 1 tchd 8 to 1) 8
72 WINNIE LORRAINE [99] 11-10-5 (5*) P Henley, *chsd ldrs to 11th, beh whn pld up bef 4 out.......*(20 to 1 op 14 to 1) pu
Dist: ½l, 2l, 3½l, 26l, 2½l, 9l, 17l. 6m 0.10s. a 22.10s (9 Ran).

(M L Shone), R Curtis

376 Welsh Dragon Novices' Handicap Hurdle Class E (0-100 4-y-o and up) £2,320 2½m...................... (8:00)

83[4] BOURDONNER [84] 4-10-9 A Maguire, *made all, sn clr, mstks 4th and 7th, rdn out, ran on wl.*
....(11 to 2 op 9 to 4 tchd 3 to 1) 1
250* SIGMA WIRELESS (Ire) [100] 7-12-0 S Wynne, *hld up, rdn and hdwy 7th, chsd wnr frm 3 out, ev ch r-in, no extr.*
....(3 to 1 op 9 to 4) 2
262* BORN TO PLEASE (Ire) [92] 4-11-3 R Johnson, *trkd ldrs, rdn alng frm 5th, wknd appr 2 out....*(7 to 4 fav tchd 2 to 1) 3
153[6] CHEER'S BABY [72] 6-10-0 N Williamson, *nvr on terms.*
....(20 to 1 op 33 to 1) 4
322[8] COURT JESTER [79] 5-10-4 D Gallagher, *chsd wnr, mstks second and 3rd, wknd 3 out........*(8 to 1 tchd 10 to 1) 5
MUTUAL MEMORIES [72] 8-10-0 J R Kavanagh, *al beh, tld off 7th, pld up bef 2 out.* (14 to 1 op 10 to 1 tchd 16 to 1) pu
Dist: 1¾l, 22l, 1¾l, 2½l. 4m 53.00s. a 17.00s (6 Ran).

(Cornelius Lysaght), M D Hammond

377 Cheltenham And Three Counties Club Novices' Hurdle Class E (4-y-o and up) £2,407 2m.....................(8:30)

LORD TOMANICO (Fr) 4-10-9 J Railton, *made all, clr frm 2 out, unchlgd............*(100 to 30 op 2 to 1) 1
310* LANCER (USA) 4-11-2 W Marston, *keen hold early, chsd wnr, ev ch appr 3 out, sn rdn, btn nxt.*
....(5 to 2 op 2 to 1 tchd 11 to 4) 2
JEBI (USA) 4-10-9 (3*) K Gaule, *wtd wth, mstk 3rd, prog 5th, wknd nxt, third and no ch whn mistake last.*
....(9 to 1 op 8 to 1) 3
RAVEN'S ROOST (Ire) 5-10-12 P McLoughlin, *al prmnt, ev ch appr 3 out, sn rdn and wknd........*(16 to 1 op 8 to 1) 4
183[3] BELLE PERK 5-10-7 A Maguire, *hld up, effrt whn mstk 5th, wknd bef nxt, virtually pld up r-in, tld off.*
....(7 to 4 fav op 2 to 1 tchd 9 to 4) 5
SOCCER BALL 6-10-12 O Pears, *pld hrd in tch, wknd appr 3 out, tld off whn pulled up bef 2 out...*(33 to 1 op 16 to 1) pu
MARTELLO GIRL (Ire) 4-10-4 T Eley, *al beh, tld off whn pld up bef 2 out...........*(14 to 1 op 10 to 1 tchd 16 to 1) pu
Dist: 9l, 5l, 15l, dist. 3m 56.00s. a 16.00s (7 Ran).

(The Izz That Right Partnership), C J Mann

LES LANDES (JER) (good to soft)
Sunday August 11th

378 **Cater Allen Summer Handicap Hurdle (4-y-o and up) £720 2½m . . . . . . (3:00)**

207* WOLLBOLL 6-12-0 V Smith . . . . (5 to 4 on) 1
285* CLEAR HOME 10-9-7 A McCabe, ... (5 to 4) 2
285² FOOLS OF PRIDE (Ire) 4-9-7 B Powell, ... (6 to 1) 3
Dist: 7l, 20l. 5m 1.00s. (3 Ran).

(Mike Weaver), J S O Arthur

WORCESTER (good)
Monday August 12th
Going Correction: PLUS 0.15 sec. per fur.

379 **Enigma Security 71 71 Jolup Handicap Hurdle Class G (0-95 4-y-o and up) £1,849 3m . . . . (2:15)**

RAMPANT ROSIE (Ire) [66] (v) 8-11-4 G Cahill, hld up, chsd ldr frm 9th, led appr 2 out, clr approaching last, eased r-in . . . . (2 to 1 op 7 to 4) 1
PENIARTH [54] 10-10-6 B Fenton, chsd ldr, led appr 9th, hdd bef 2 out, sn btn . . . . (11 to 2 op 5 to 1) 2
205⁵ MISS SOUTER [65] 7-11-3 Guy Lewis, wtd wth, bent 8th, wknd frm 3 out . . . . (13 to 8 fav op 6 to 4 tchd 7 to 4) 3
146⁵ CROMABOO CROWN [76] 5-11-10 T J Murphy, led, hdd appr 9th, sn wknd, tld off . . . . (4 to 1 op 3 to 1) 4
Dist: 9l, dist. 5m 58.60s. a 22.60s (4 Ran).

(George J H Kemp), G Richards

380 **Pomp And Circumstance Novices' Chase Class E (5-y-o and up) £3,101 2m 7f. . . . . (2:45)**

306* STICKY MONEY 8-11-7 D Bridgwater, chsd ldr, led 6th, clr appr 4 out, canter . . . . (7 to 2 on op 4 to 1 on tchd 10 to 3 on and 3 to 1 on) 1
306² PHARRAGO (Ire) 7-10-12 D J Burchell, hld up, not fluent second, chsd wnr frm tenth, rdn aftr twelfth, sn outpcd . . . . (3 to 1 tchd 7 to 2 and 4 to 1) 2
319³ GHEDI (Pol) 5-10-7 B Powell, led to 6th, wkng whn mstk 11th, tld off . . . . (33 to 1 op 14 to 1) 3
Dist: 16l, dist. 6m 11.20s. a 33.20s (3 Ran).

(Mrs D Jenks), M C Pipe

381 **Nimrod Handicap Hurdle Class E (0-110 4-y-o and up) £2,267 2½m . . . . (3:15)**

168² CLEAN EDGE (USA) [97] 4-11-2 (3*) E Husband, chsd clr ldr, led appr 4th, rdn out . . . . . (5 to 2 op 9 to 4 tchd 11 to 4) 1
308³ FIRST CRACK [84] 11-10-9 S Wynne, hld up, chsd wnr 2 out, effrt last, one pace . . . . (5 to 2 op 9 to 4 tchd 11 to 4) 2
227* COAST ALONG (Ire) [94] 4-11-2 W Worthington, hld up, chsd wnr frm 7th till 2 out, fdd . . . . (5 to 4 fav tchd 11 to 8) 3
307³ FORGETFUL [92] 7-11-3 D J Burchell, jmpd rght, led, sn clr, hdd appr 7th, soon wknd, tld off . . . . (14 to 1 op 10 to 1 tchd 16 to 1) 4
Dist: 2l, 10l. 2l. 4m 46.90s. a 10.90s (4 Ran).
SR: 12/

(Mrs Sue Adams), J Mackie

382 **Plumb Center Handicap Hurdle Class C (0-130 4-y-o and up) £3,468 2m . . . . (3:45)**

ROYAL THIMBLE (Ire) [99] 5-11-10 R Johnson, set modest pace, hdd appr 3rd, styd hndy, rdn to rgn ld last one hundred yard, ran on wl . . . . (5 to 2 op 9 to 4) 1
377² LANCER (USA) [85] 4-10-7 W Marston, hld up, led 2 out, hdd last one hundred yards, unbl to quicken . . . . (100 to 30 op 5 to 2 tchd 7 to 2) 2
330³ NIGHT TIME [85] 4-10-0 (7*) Mr G Shenkin, prmnt, led appr 3rd, hdd bef nxt, rdn 3 out, one pace next . . . . (100 to 30 op 5 to 2 tchd 7 to 2) 3
299³ CIRCUS COLOURS [94] 6-11-8 A Maguire, took str hold, hld up, led appr 4th, hdd 2 out, no extr . . . . (9 to 4 fav op 5 to 4 tchd 11 to 4) 4
Dist: 1½l, 1½l, sht-hd. 4m 20.00s. a 40.00s (4 Ran).

(Mrs M Chance), Noel T Chance

383 **Gerontius Novices' Handicap Chase Class E (0-100 5-y-o and up) £2,877 2m. . . . . (4:15)**

228* WILLIE MAKEIT (Ire) [66] 6-11-3 (3*) J Culloty, wtd wth beh ldrs, led 4 out, mstk nxt, rdn out . . . . (11 to 8 fav op 5 to 4 tchd 11 to 10) 1
SCARABEN [82] 8-11-10 R Johnson, hld up, chsd wnr frm 3 out, mstk last, styd on one pace . . . . (13 to 8 op 5 to 4 tchd 7 to 4) 2

HARROW WAY (Ire) [69] 6-10-11 S McNeill, chsd ldr, ev ch 4 out, btn appr 2 out . . . . (10 to 1 op 7 to 1 tchd 11 to 1) 3
281⁶ CAXTON (USA) [81] 9-11-9 B Fenton, hld up in rear, rdn appr 4 out, no dngr . . . . (12 to 1 op 20 to 1) 4
266⁵ ASTOUNDED [76] 9-11-1 (3*) D Walsh, led to 4 out, sn wknd . . . . (12 to 1 op 20 to 1 tchd 10 to 1) 5
Dist: 1½l, 9l, 11l, ¾l. 4m 0.70s. a 11.70s (5 Ran).

(Old Berks Three), R T Phillips

384 **Chanson Mares' Only Novices' Hurdle Class E (4-y-o and up) £2,390 2m (4:45)**

322⁵ FORGOTTEN EMPRESS 4-10-7 R Johnson, hld up, wnt second appr 2 out, ran on to ld last fifty yards . . . . (2 to 1 tchd 5 to 2 and 11 to 4) 1
324⁵ BURNT SIENNA (Ire) (v) 4-10-7 W McFarland, led, sn clr, wnt lft und pres r-in, hdd and no extr last fifty yards . . . . (20 to 1 op 14 to 1) 2
231⁶ REGAL GEM (Ire) 5-10-10 B Fenton, wtd wth, chsd ldr frm 5th till appr 2 out, sn wknd . . . (11 to 4 op 5 to 2 tchd 3 to 1) 3
LAUGH DEADLY 4-10-7 R Dunwoody, hld up, hmpd 5th . . . . (16 to 1 op 20 to 1 tchd 25 to 1) 4
LAST LAUGH (Ire) 4-10-7 T J Murphy, jmpd slwly 3rd, chsd clr ldr till 5th, wknd nxt, tld off . . . . (6 to 4 fav op 5 to 4 tchd 13 to 8) 5
55 SISTER JIM 6-10-10 J R Kavanagh, al beh, tld off frm hlwy . . . . (66 to 1 op 50 to 1) 6
Dist: 1½l, 16l, 6l, dist, 14l. 3m 52.50s. a 12.50s (6 Ran).

(R Fenwick-Gibson), S E Kettlewell

SOUTHWELL (good)
Tuesday August 13th
Going Correction: PLUS 0.40 sec. per fur.

385 **Cromer Novices' Handicap Chase Class E (0-100 5-y-o and up) £3,812 3m 110yds. . . . . (2:15)**

318³ GEORGE ASHFORD (Ire) [82] 6-12-0 A S Smith, nvr far away, rdn to ld bef 3 out, drw clr . . . . (4 to 1 op 5 to 2) 1
308⁵ BLUE RAVEN [85] 5-11-12 A P McCoy, not fluent, cl up, chlgd fnl circuit, outpcd last 2. . . . . (11 to 4 fav op 5 to 2 tchd 3 to 1) 2
317⁷ QUIXALL CROSSETT [61] 11-10-7 P McLoughlin, in tch, rdn and struggling 12th, no dngr aftr . . . . (10 to 1 op 16 to 1) 3
ABITMORFUN [54] 10-10-0 L Harvey, led, hdd bef 3 out, sn struggling . . . . (20 to 1 op 16 to 1 tchd 33 to 1) 4
239³ SAINT BENE'T (Ire) [65] (v) 8-10-11 R Farrant, cl up, struggling fnl circuit, tld off . . . . (9 to 2 op 4 to 1 tchd 5 to 1) 5
284⁵ SPANISH BLAZE (Ire) [62] 8-10-8 J F Titley, settled in tch, f 11th . . . . (9 to 2 op 7 to 2 tchd 5 to 1) f
201 THE GALLOPIN'MAJOR (Ire) [75] 6-11-7 N Smith, hld up, mstk 12th, sn pld up . . . . (5 to 1 op 4 to 1) pu
Dist: 20l, 13l, ½l, 6l. 6m 38.70s. a 44.70s (7 Ran).

(B Leatherday), K A Morgan

386 **Skegness Handicap Chase Class E (0-110 5-y-o and up) £3,882 2½m 110yds. . . . . (2:45)**

321³ MAGGOTS GREEN [75] 9-10-1 R Johnson, led, hdd 9th, rgned ld 5 out, drvn out . . . . (11 to 4 co-fav op 5 to 2) 1
335² NOBELLY (USA) [98] 9-11-10 R Farrant, nvr far away, drvn to chase wnr 4 out, kpt on same pace frm last . . . . (11 to 4 co-fav op 2 to 1) 2
282⁷ NOCATCHIM [92] 7-11-4 A S Smith, chsd ldrs, reminders aftr 9th, sn outpcd, no dngr after . . . . (11 to 4 co-fav op 3 to 1) 3
THE COUNTRY TRADER [102] (bl) 10-12-0 A P McCoy, not fluent, cl up, led 9th, hdd 5 out, btn bef 3 out . . . (11 to 4 co-fav op 2 to 1) 4
Dist: 4l, 18l, dist. 5m 22.40s. a 22.40s (4 Ran).

(E A Hayward), J M Bradley

387 **Yarmouth Novices' Hurdle Class E (4-y-o and up) £2,448 2m. . . . . (3:15)**

GLENVALLY 5-10-7 G Bradley, chsd clr ldr, ev ch bef 2 out, led appr last, drvn out . . . . . (5 to 2 op 3 to 1 tchd 7 to 2) 1
317* IRIE MON (Ire) 4-10-9 (7*) Mr A Wintle, in tch, improved to ld appr 2 out, hdd approaching last, no extr. . . . . (15 to 8 on op 11 to 4 on tchd 7 to 4 on) 2
359 SHALIK (Ire) 6-10-12 J Railton, led and sn wl clr, hdd appr 2 out, soon wknd . . . . . (5 to 1 op 10 to 1) 3
CHADLEIGH WALK (Ire) 4-10-9 A S Smith, hld up, hit 4 out, not fluent nxt, sn outpcd . . . . (12 to 1 op 10 to 1) 4
Dist: 6l, 13l, 2l. 4m 5.20s. a 19.20s (4 Ran).

(Mrs M Lingwood), B W Murray

388 **Southend Maiden Hurdle Class E (4-y-o and up) £2,259 2½m 110yds (3:45)**

LONGCROFT 4-10-11 R Johnson, nvr far away, smooth hdwy to ld 3 out, clr nxt, eased considerably r-in . . . . (Evens fav op 5 to 4 tchd 11 to 10 on) 1

251³ DESERT CHALLENGER (Ire) (bl) 6-11-5 A P McCoy, *led, hdd 5th, blun 8th, sn hrd drvn and outpcd, no imprsn whn blunded last*.......(5 to 4 op 5 to 4 on tchd 11 to 8 and 6 to 4) 2
PERTEMPS FLYER 5-11-2 (3") J Magee, *sn cl up, led 5th, hdd 3 out, btn nxt*..........................(14 to 1 op 8 to 1) 3
SKIPLAM WOOD 10-11-0 A Dobbin, *chsd ldrs, outpcd fnl circuit*................................(20 to 1 op 14 to 1) 4
ARRANGE A GAME 9-11-2 (3") T Dascombe, *in tch, jmpd slwly second, reminders 5th, struggling fnl circuit*.
....(33 to 1 op 20 to 1) 5
Dist: 12l, 6l, 4l, 22l. 5m 25.80s. a 39.80s (5 Ran).

(J S Calvert), S E Kettlewell

389 Brighton Selling Handicap Hurdle Class G (0-95 4 - 7-y-o) £1,842 2½m 110yds........................(4:15)

324² TRADE WIND [92] (v) 5-11-9 (5") Michael Brennan, *hld up, improved to chase wnr 7th, chalg whn blun badly last, styd on wl to ld nr finish*...(5 to 4 fav op 5 to 4 on tchd 11 to 8) 1
ANTIGUAN FLYER [67] 7-10-6 R Farrant, *led, jnd appr last, hdd nr finish*.........................(8 to 1 op 7 to 1) 2
246⁵ LASER LIGHT LADY [67] (bl) 4-10-0 B Powell, *settled in tch, effrt aftr 3 out, struggling nxt*........(25 to 1 op 20 to 1) 3
299⁶ RAY RIVER [88] 4-11-0 (7") Mr A Wintle, *hld up, struggling bef 3 out, nvr on terms*.........................(10 to 4 op 3 to 1) 4
283⁴ WORDY'S WIND [67] 7-10-6 B Fenton, *pressed ldr, outpcd bef 7th, struggling whn blun and uns rdr 3 out*.
....(3 to 1 tchd 4 to 1) ur
Dist: Nk, 26l, sht-hd. 5m 17.60s. a 31.60s (5 Ran).

(Gary Roberts), J G M O'Shea

390 Blackpool Handicap Hurdle Class E (0-110 4-y-o and up) £2,427 2m (4:45)

RUDI'S PRIDE (Ire) [98] 5-11-4 N Smith, *nvr far away, led 5th, hrd pressed fnl 2. gmely*.............(3 to 1 tchd 7 to 2) 1
333³ GAME DILEMMA [80] 5-10-0 R Greene, *hndy, improved to chal last, kpt on finish*. (13 to 8 fav op 2 to 1 tchd 6 to 4) 2
281⁴ VAIN PRINCE [105] (bl) 9-12-0 M Dwyer, *chsd ldrs, effrt bef 2 out, one pace aftr last*.................(4 to 1 op 5 to 2) 3
61⁸ WORDSMITH (Ire) [88] 6-10-11 D Gallagher, *made most till jmpd slwly and hdd 5th, rallied and ev ch 2 out, outpcd last*.
.................................(5 to 1 op 4 to 1 tchd 11 to 2) 4
CHEAP METAL [79] (bl) 11-10-2² M Ranger, *hld up, hng badly lft 2 out, sn struggling*..............(25 to 1 op 20 to 1) 5
TIP IT IN [88] 7-10-11 M Brennan, *wth ldr till 4th, drvn aftr 3 out, struggling nxt*......................(11 to 1 op 8 to 1) 6
Dist: Nk, 3l, 3l, 12l, dist. 4m 13.60s. a 27.60s (6 Ran).

(Mrs Cheryl L Owen), S B Bell

WEXFORD (IRE) (good)
Tuesday August 13th

391 Enniscorthy Opportunity Handicap Hurdle (4-y-o and up) £2,740 2¼m ....(5:15)

216⁴ THE SOUTH POLE INN (Ire) [-] 4-9-6 (2") J Butler, (11 to 2) 1
276* FATHER MICHAEL (Ire) [-] 6-11-7 (4") A O'Shea,
....(11 to 8 fav) 2
275⁷ RADIF (USA) [-] 5-10-0³ D T Evans, ...(14 to 1) 3
302⁶ CHUCK (Ire) [-] 6-10-13 (4") D McCullagh, ...(5 to 2) 4
275⁸ JEWEL OF THE NIGHT (Ire) [-] 4-9-3 (4") M D Murphy,
....(20 to 1) 5
277⁹ DUSTY ROSE (Ire) [-] 7-9-9 (4") P Morris, ...(10 to 1) 6
275⁶ SLIEVROE (Ire) [-] 5-9-7 (2") T Martin, ...(8 to 1) ur
Dist: 1l, 1½l, 4l, 7l. 4m 20.30s. (7 Ran).

(St Brendan Syndicate), Ms E C Holdsworth

392 Nicky Rackard Maiden Hurdle (4-y-o and up) £2,740 2¼m ....(5:45)

224⁶ SLAVE GALE (Ire) 5-11-9 C F Swan, ...(11 to 8 on) 1
277³ FLYING IN THE GALE (Ire) 5-10-8 (7") A O'Shea,. (10 to 1) 2
352² CELIO LUCY (Ire) 6-11-2 (7") P Morris, ...(100 to 30) 3
365⁷ JARSUN QUEEN (Ire) 4-10-6 (7") L J Fleming, ...(12 to 1) 4
278⁸ OWEN GOWLA (Ire) 4-10-11 (7") D W O'Sullivan, .(8 to 1) 5
HOLLY LAKE (Ire) 6-11-1 P A Roche, ...(16 to 1) 6
RONETTE (Ire) 5-11-6 J P Broderick, ...(20 to 1) f
Dist: 3l, 20l, 2½l, 25l. 4m 25.50s. (7 Ran).

(G Merrigan), A P O'Brien

393 Nick O'Donnell Memorial Maiden Hurdle (4-y-o and up) £2,740 2¼m.. (6:15)

NO NEWS (Ire) 5-12-0 T P Treacy, ...(3 to 1 fav) 1
340³ LADY RICHENDA (Ire) 8-11-9 J P Broderick, ...(13 to 2) 2
353⁴ GARLAND ROSE (Ire) 6-11-2 (7") P Morris, ...(8 to 1) 3
347⁷ ELYSIAN HEIGHTS (Ire) 4-10-13 (5") J Butler, ...(12 to 1) 4
358⁵ WILDLIFE RANGER (Ire) 8-12-0 T Horgan, ...(14 to 1) 5
343⁷ LANTERN GLOW (Ire) 4-11-1 (3") D T Evans, ...(14 to 1) 6
277² LANTINA (Ire) 5-11-9 D H O'Connor, ...(9 to 2) 7
199 RAHANINE MELODY (Ire) 4-11-4² P McWilliams, ...(20 to 1) 8
286 BRIGHT SHARES (Ire) 6-11-9 K F O'Brien, ...(14 to 1) 9
238 WILLIE THE LION (Ire) 5-12-0 M Moran, ...(16 to 1) 10

288 OWEN BOLISCA (Ire) 4-11-4 C O'Brien, ...(14 to 1) 11
304 DAWN CALLER (Ire) 5-12-0 J Shortt, ...(10 to 1) 12
66 MILLA'S DELIGHT (Ire) 5-12-0 C O'Dwyer, ...(14 to 1) pu
Dist: 2½l, nk, 3l, ¾l. 4m 19.90s. (13 Ran).

(Mrs P Mullins), P Mullins

394 Jim Whitty Memorial INH Flat Race (5-y-o) £2,740 2m.................(7:45)

253⁵ ATTACK AT DAWN (Ire) 11-2 (7") Mr J P McNamara, (10 to 1) 1
343² CARRICK GLEN (Ire) 11-2 (7") Mr T J Farrell, ...(6 to 1) 2
278² PRINCESS GLORIA (Ire) 11-9 Mr P Fenton, ...(11 to 2) 3
TEMPLEORUM (Ire) 11-7 (7") Mr Mark Walsh, ...(8 to 1) 4
288⁵ DUNEAVEY (Ire) 11-4 (5") Mr R Walsh, ...(5 to 4 fav) 5
PHARADISO (Ire) 12-0 Mr J P Dempsey, ...(10 to 1) 6
340 CULRUA ROSIE (Ire) 12-2 (7") Mr E Sheehy, ...(25 to 1) 7
SERRANA BANK (Ire) 11-9 Mr D Marnane, ...(12 to 1) 8
MINOGUE LADY (Ire) 11-2 (7") Mr P Cashman, ...(20 to 1) 9
MUSIC MAN (Ire) 12-0 Mr H F Cleary, ...(16 to 1) 10
343³ EASTERN CUSTOM (Ire) 11-6 (3") Mr R O'Neill, ..(10 to 1) 11
340⁵ WILL I OR WONT I (Ire) 11-2 (7") Mr M J Walsh, ..(12 to 1) 12
STRONG DANCER (Ire) 11-7 (7") Mr M D Hennessy, (16 to 1) ro
TINNOCK (Ire) 11-2 (7") Miss Olivia Forrestal, ...(25 to 1) pu
Dist: Hd, sht-hd, hd, ¾l. 3m 49.00s. (14 Ran).

(Alex Heskin), S J Treacy

DUNDALK (IRE) (firm)
Thursday August 15th

395 Cullaville Maiden Hurdle (4-y-o and up) £2,226 2½m 153yds............(5:00)

329⁶ CLEVER JACK (Ire) 6-11-6 K F O'Brien, ...(11 to 2) 1
NOELEENS DELIGHT (Ire) 7-11-1 T P Treacy, .. (5 to 4 fav) 2
CHAPEL CHAT (Ire) 6-11-3 (3") U Smyth, ...(25 to 1) 3
133* SOUTHERN MARINER (Ire) 6-11-4 (5") J Butler, ...(11 to 4) 4
257⁵ BALLINABOOLA GROVE 9-11-6 J Shortt, ...(10 to 1) 5
233 FIX THE SPEC (Ire) (bl) 6-11-3 (3") D T Evans, ...(10 to 1) 6
344² SPECTACLE (Ire) (bl) 6-11-6 H Rogers, ...(8 to 1) 7
253⁶ GALACTUS (Ire) 5-11-6 J K Kinane, ...(10 to 1) 8
352⁴ ANSAL BOY 4-11-7 J P Byrne, ...(16 to 1) 9
342² PRINCE SABI (Ire) (bl) 6-11-6 P L Malone, ...(10 to 1) pu
Dist: 1l, dist, 2l, 2½l. 4m 43.20s. (10 Ran).

(Lady Prichard-Jones), Gerard Stack

396 Warrenpoint Handicap Hurdle (0-102 4-y-o and up) £2,226 2m 135yds(5:30)

268⁴ WHEREWILITALL END (Ire) [-] 5-11-8 (3") U Smyth, (7 to 2) 1
348 KUMA CHAN [-] 9-9-8 (5") J Butler, ...(25 to 1) 2
348⁵ MONTE'S EVENING (Ire) [-] 8-10-5 P L Malone, (100 to 30) 3
WILD ROSE OF YORK [-] 5-10-11 J Shortt, ... (3 to 1 fav) 4
NIGHTSCENE (Ire) [-] 4-10-3 (5") J M Donnelly, ...(10 to 1) 5
347⁴ KARAWARA (Ire) [-] 5-9-12 J P Broderick, ...(12 to 1) 6
135⁹ DEABHAILIN (Ire) [-] 6-9-12 (3") D Bromley, ...(10 to 1) 7
348³ ARCTIC CLOVER (Ire) [-] 5-10-5 K F O'Brien, ...(10 to 1) 8
194⁶ LADY PHARDANTE (Ire) [-] (bl) 6-9-2 (7") L J Fleming,
....(25 to 1) 9
67 CHIEF RANI (Ire) [-] 6-10-12 T P Treacy, ...(8 to 1) 10
120 GENNY'S SERENADE (Ire) [-] 5-9-9 (3") B Bowens, (10 to 1) 11
348⁶ NATURE PERFECTED (Ire) [-] 7-10-3 (3") D T Evans,
....(14 to 1) 12
Dist: ½l, ½l, 5½l, 3l. 3m 51.20s. (12 Ran).

(S P Mahon), Peter McCreery

397 Carnlough I.N.H. Flat Race (4-y-o and up) £2,226 2m 135yds.........(8:00)

286⁸ NO DIAMOND (Ire) 7-11-7 (7") Mr D W Cullen, ...(5 to 1) 1
329² FANE PATH (Ire) 4-11-9 Mr G J Harford, ...(11 to 10 fav) 2
AN SEABHAC (Ire) 4-11-2 (7") Mr T J Beattie, ...(10 to 1) 3
245⁴ RED RADICAL (Ire) 6-11-7 (7") Mr P E I Newell, ...(7 to 1) 4
347⁵ PIGEON HILL BUCK (Ire) 5-11-7 (7") Mr M Madden, (10 to 1) 5
BULA DELA (Ire) (bl) 6-11-2 (7") Mr A Fleming, ...(16 to 1) 6
POWERCUT PRINCESS (Ire) 5-11-9 Mr A J Martin, (12 to 1) 7
346⁵ MADDY KEEL 6-11-7 (7") Mr R Marrs, ...(20 to 1) 8
343⁶ MOSSA NOVA (Ire) 8-12-0 Mr J A Nash, ...(7 to 1) 9
MOOR HILL LASS (Ire) 6-11-2 (7") Mr G T Cuthbert, (20 to 1) 10
KILBOGGAN EXPRESS (Ire) 5-11-7 (7") Mr J A Hayes,
....(7 to 1) 11
Dist: ½l, 15l, 6l, sht-hd. 3m 44.40s. (11 Ran).

(John O'Meara), Niall Madden

NEWTON ABBOT (good to firm)
Thursday August 15th
Going Correction: MINUS 0.40 sec. per fur.

398 Jerzees Amateur Riders' Selling Handicap Hurdle Class G (0-95 4-y-o and up) £1,838 2m 1f...................(5:50)

NORD LYS (Ire) [68] 5-10-2 (7") Miss E J Jones, *hld up, rapid hdwy 4th, led appr nxt, wndrd approaching 2 out and last, drvn out*..............(10 to 1 op 14 to 1 tchd 16 to 1) 1

334² SOUTHERN RIDGE [78] 5-10-12 (7*) Mr A Holdsworth, *led till aftr 4th, mstk nxt, rallied after 2 out, kpt on r-in.*
.... (6 to 5 fav op Evens tchd 5 to 4) 2
AIR COMMAND (Bar) [56] 6-9-7 (7*) Mr P Phillips, *hld up, pushed alng aftr 5th, styd on frm 2 out, not rch wnr.*
.... (7 to 1 op 6 to 1 tchd 8 to 1) 3
333 GUNMAKER [80] 7-11-5 (5*) Mr J L Llewellyn, *hld up, pushed alng aftr 4th, wnt second 3 out, rdn and wknd appr nxt.*
.... (9 to 2 op 9 to 1) 4
294² INDIAN MINOR [63] 12-10-0 (7*) Mr L Jefford, *chsd ldr, mstk 5th, rallied aftr 3 out, wknd after nxt.*
.... (100 to 30 op 3 to 1 tchd 7 to 2) 5
MISS NORWAIT [57] 6-10-1⁸ (7*) Mr S Davis, *prmnt till wknd rpdly aftr 4th, sn tld off, mstk last, fnshd lme.*
.... (50 to 1 op 25 to 1) 6
Dist: 1½l, hd, 11l, 3½l, dist. 3m 58.80s. a 9.80s (6 Ran).

(N Heath), B J Llewellyn

399 August Evening Juvenile Novices' Hurdle Class E (3-y-o) £2,148 2m 1f (6:20)

323² BEN BOWDLIN 10-10-0 *ᴅɪ̄ɾᴜᴏᴜ̄ᴜʜʜ, hld up ṉᴜᴄᴏᴜᴜᴜᴜᴜ out.*
.... (11 to 2 op 4 to 1) 1
323* ALWAYS HAPPY 10-12 D Bridgwater, *chsd ldg pair, mstk 4th, pushed alng and ev ch 3 out, rdn and not quicken r-in.*
.... 2
ARCH ENEMY (Ire) 10-10 D Skyrme, *hld up, rapid hdwy to ld 4th, hdd aftr 3 out, wknd quickly, tld off.*
.... (12 to 1 op 10 to 1 tchd 14 to 1) 3
WATER MUSIC MELODY 10-5 W Humphreys, *led to 4th, mstk and wknd quickly nxt, sn tld off, pld up bef last.*
.... (5 to 1 op 12 to 1 tchd 33 to 1) pu
Dist: ¾l, dist. 4m 1.20s. a 12.20s (4 Ran).

(The Lower Bowden Syndicate), M Blanshard

400 Mission Impossible Novices' Chase Class E (5-y-o and up) £2,818 2m 5f 110yds. (6:50)

280² DISTANT MEMORY (bl) 7-10-12 A P McCoy, *led to 4th, led 6th, drw clr aftr 5 out, unchlgd.* (7 to 4 on tchd 13 to 8 on) 1
ANOTHER COMEDY 6-10-12 R Johnson, *chsd ldr, wnt second aftr 9th, mstk 11th, sn rdn, no imprsn frm 5 out.*
.... (5 to 1 op 4 to 1) 2
319* HIZAL 7-11-5 Mr A Charles-Jones, *hld up, pushed aftr 9th, wnt poor 3rd aftr nxt, no ch frm 5 out.*
.... (7 to 2 op 5 to 1) 3
SARACEN'S BOY (Ire) 8-10-12 Mr L Jefford, *led 4th to 6th, wkng whn mstk tenth, tld off six out.*
.... (40 to 1 op 33 to 1 tchd 50 to 1) 4
325⁸ GREAT UNCLE 8-10-7 (5*) P Henley, *jmpd slwly 3rd and 4th, al rdn, tld off aftr tenth.* (33 to 1 op 20 to 1 tchd 40 to 1) 5
Dist: 30l, 6l, 8l, 10l. 5m 16.60s. a 14.60s (5 Ran).

(Mrs Ann Weston), P J Hobbs

401 Midsummer Maiden Hurdle Class E (4-y-o and up) £2,190 2¾m. (7:20)

326² IDIOM 9-11-2 (3*) J Culloty, *hld up, hdwy 4 out, ev ch aftr nxt, led 2 out, pushed out.*
.... (5 to 2 fav tchd 4 and 11 to 4) 1
301⁵ UP THE TEMPO 9-11-0 R Greene, *hld up, cld on ldr aftr 6th, led appr 2 out, sn hdd, rallied last, not quicken.*
.... (3 to 1 op 5 to 2 tchd 7 to 2) 2
60⁶ CROWN IVORY (NZ) 8-11-5 S Fox, *chsd ldr frm 5th, drvn alng 4 out, kpt on one pace.* (25 to 1 op 16 to 1 tchd 33 to 1) 3
297⁴ MIRAMARE 6-11-0 (5*) P Henley, *mid-div, drvn alng aftr 6th, sn no imprsn.* .... (8 to 1 op 5 to 1 tchd 5 to 1) 4
MR POPPLETON 7-11-5 L Harvey, *chsd ldr, rdn and wknd aftr 4 out.* .... (6 to 1 op 4 to 1 tchd 13 to 2) 5
FATHER POWER 8-11-5 R Johnson, *led till aftr 3 out, wknd quickly.* .... (6 to 1 op 4 to 1 tchd 13 to 2) 6
KERRIER 4-11-2 Mr A Charles-Jones, *chsd ldr, wkng whn mstk 3 out, sn lost tch, tld off when pld up bef 2 out.*
.... (14 to 1 op 10 to 1 tchd 16 to 1) pu
POLLYANNA 5-11-0 S Curran, *chsd ldr, mstk 3rd, wnt second 6th, wknd quickly aftr 4 out, tld off whn pld up bef 2 out.*
.... (20 to 1 op 14 to 1) pu
Dist: 2l, 11l, 2½l, 2l, 1¼l. 5m 15.20s. a 14.20s (8 Ran).

(Mrs J Carrington), Mrs J G Retter

402 Night Is Young Handicap Chase Class E (0-115 5-y-o and up) £2,859 2m 110yds. (7:50)

325³ DUKE OF DREAMS [76] 6-10-0 B Powell, *hld up, pushed alng aftr 7th, led 3 out, drvn out.*
.... (8 to 1 op 10 to 1 tchd 12 to 1) 1
335* MANAMOUR [85] 10-10-9 (7ex) C Llewellyn, *chsd ldr, rdn aftr 4 out, chlgd betw last 2, no quicken.* .... (6 to 4 jt-fav op 7 to 4 tchd 5 to 4) 2
TOOMUCH TOOSOON (Ire) [100] 8-11-10 A P McCoy, *led, mstk second, mistake 9th, sn drvn alng, hdd aftr 3 out, wknd nxt.* .... (6 to 4 jt-fav op 5 to 4) 3
FENWICK [88] 9-10-9 (3*) T Dascombe, *chsd ldg pair, ev ch 4 out, wknd aftr nxt.* .... (6 to 1 op 9 to 2) 4

335⁴ GABISH [76] 11-9-7 (7*) Mr R Thornton, *mstk 3rd, pushed alng aftr 8th, sn lost tch.* (20 to 1 op 16 to 1 tchd 25 to 1) 5
Dist: 4l, 8l, 3½l, 9l. 3m 57.60s. b 0.40s (5 Ran).
SR: 10/15/22/6/-/

(Mrs V W Jones), R J Baker

403 Birdie Handicap Hurdle Class D (0-120 4-y-o and up) £2,699 2¾m. (8:20)

248³ FIELDRIDGE [103] 7-10-12 B Powell, *hld up, pushed king aftr 6th, led appr 2 out, sn clr, cmftbly.*
.... (7 to 2 op 11 to 4 tchd 4 to 1) 1
299* JENZSOPH (Ire) [108] 5-11-0 A P McCoy, *chsd ldr, led 4 out, mstk nxt, hdd appr 2 out, sn rdn and one pace.* .... (7 to 4) 2
308* DIAMOND CUT (Fr) [119] 8-12-0 R Johnson, *led to 4 out, sn drvn alng, one pace 2 out.*
.... (6 to 4 fav op 11 to 10 tchd 13 to 8) 3
331³ BEAM ME UP SCOTTY (Ire) [91] 7-9-11 (3*) J Culloty, *hld up, pushed alng and lost tch aftr 6th, sn beh.*
.... (8 to 1 op 6 to 1 tchd 10 to 1) 4
BIT OF A TOUCH [98] 10-10-7 J Frost, *lost tch aftr 4th, tld off after 6th, pld up bef 2 out.* .... (7 to 1 op 16 to 1) pu
Dist: 12l, 4l, 16l. 5m 7.30s. a 16.70s *(lᴜᴀᴏᴏ̄ɾ̄ᴏ̄ʜ̄ l and up), ᴜᴜᴜ ᴜᴜᴜᴜᴜᴜ̄*

TRAMORE (IRE) (good)
Thursday August 15th

404 Riverstown Q.R. Maiden Hurdle (4-y-o and up) £2,226 2½m. (5:15)

THE COBH GALE 9-11-1 Mr P Fenton, ... (7 to 2) 1
355³ MANETTI 4-10-9 (7*) Mr S P Hennessy, ... (5 to 4 fav) 2
364⁵ TURRAMURRA GIRL (Ire) 7-11-9 Mr H F Cleary, .. (11 to 2) 3
221³ HONEY TRADER 4-10-9 (7*) Mr John P Moloney, .. (4 to 1) 4
121⁶ COLONIA SKY (Ire) 5-10-8 (7*) Mr R Lenihan, ... (10 to 1) 5
340⁹ PRINCESS LENA (Ire) 6-10-8 (7*) Mr J T McNamara,
.... (16 to 1) 6
339⁷ BUNKER (Ire) 4-11-4 (3*) Mr K Whelan, ... (16 to 1) 7
SCOTCH ROSE (Ire) 6-11-8⁷ (7*) Mr B N Doyle, ... (10 to 1) 8
GALE DUBH (Ire) 5-10-13 (7*) Mr J G Sheehan, .. (14 to 1) pu
Dist: ½l, 13l, 2l, 6l. 4m 50.60s. (9 Ran).

(Mrs Angela Crowley), John Crowley

405 Power Handicap Hurdle (0-109 4-y-o and up) £2,568 2m. (5:45)

BAJAN QUEEN (Ire) [-] 6-10-6 (5*) T Martin, ... (8 to 1) 1
220³ BOB THE YANK (Ire) [-] 6-11-6 C F Swan, ... (5 to 4 fav) 2
339⁴ SWINGS'N'THINGS (USA) [-] 4-10-4 C O'Dwyer, ... (8 to 1) 3
BRAZEN ANGEL (Ire) [-] 6-11-2 (7*) A O'Shea, ... (9 to 1) 4
344⁷ THE WICKED CHICKEN (Ire) [-] 7-10-5 T Horgan, ... (5 to 1) 5
121⁷ GRANNY'S COTTAGE (Ire) [-] 5-9-13 W T Slattery, .. (16 to 1) 6
349 AON DOCHAS (Ire) [-] 7-10-1 T J Mitchell, ... (14 to 1) 7
337⁵ RONDELLI (Ire) [-] 6-10-9 A Powell, ... (12 to 1) 8
268⁸ RATES RELIEF (Ire) [-] 6-11-8 S H O'Donovan, ... (9 to 1) 9
87⁵ NORDIC RACE [-] 9-10-12 (7*) J E Casey, ... (10 to 1) 10
Dist: 3½l, ½l, sht-hd, 13l. 3m 55.30s. (10 Ran).

(Charles Johnston), Patrick Martin

406 Woodstown Beginners Chase (5-y-o and up) £2,226 2¾m. (6:15)

290⁵ THE OUTBACK WAY (Ire) (bl) 6-12-0 D H O'Connor,
.... (5 to 2 jt-fav) 1
313 MAJESTIC MARINER 5-11-0 C O'Dwyer, ... (100 to 30) 2
212 JULY SCHOON 11-11-2 (7*) Miss C Gould, ... (20 to 1) 3
KILCULLYS-PRIDE (Ire) (bl) 6-11-2 (7*) A O'Shea, .. (20 to 1) 4
98 EVEN CALL 10-11-9 S H O'Donovan, ... (14 to 1) 5
336⁵ MURPHY'S LADY (Ire) 7-11-1 (3*) Mr K Whelan, ... (10 to 1) 6
257⁶ HAVE A DROP (Ire) 6-10-11 (7*) Mr J A Collins, ... (16 to 1) f
338⁸ PEAFIELD (Ire) 7-11-9 P M Verling, ... (13 to 2) f
345² CHOISYA (Ire) 8-11-9 C F Swan, ... (5 to 2 jt-fav) pu
Dist: 15l, 6l, dist, hd. 5m 20.70s. (9 Ran).

(E O'Dwyer), James Joseph O'Connor

407 Cunningham I.N.H. Flat Race (4-y-o and up) £2,911 2m. (7:45)

183² MURPHY'S MALT (Ire) 4-11-3 (7*) Mr B M Cash, (7 to 4 on) 1
WILLIE BRENNAN (Ire) 4-11-2 (7*) Mr Sean O O'Brien,
.... (16 to 1) 2
358⁴ GALE HAMSHIRE (Ire) 7-11-4 (5*) Mr R Walsh, ... (9 to 2) 3
340⁴ MALICE 10-11-6 (3*) Mr J Connolly, ... (12 to 1) 4
224⁸ MAJOR GALE (Ire) 7-12-0 Mr P Fenton, ... (7 to 1) 5
394 EASTERN CUSTOM (Ire) 5-11-6 (3*) Mr R O'Neill, (12 to 1) 6
278⁷ STRICT TEMPO (Ire) 7-11-7 (7*) Mr John P Moloney,
.... (20 to 1) 7
PRINCESS HENRY (Ire) 6-11-2 (7*) Mr J T McNamara,
.... (20 to 1) 8
ZIGGY THE GREAT (Ire) 4-11-2 (7*) Mr J T Murphy, (16 to 1) 9
211 SOLAR CASTLE (Ire) 6-11-2 (7*) Mr T J Nagle-Jnr, (20 to 1) 10
NAHRANAH 4-11-1 (3*) Mr K Whelan, ... (10 to 1) 11
253 BOTHAR GARBH (Ire) 5-11-7 (7*) Mr P Moloney, (20 to 1) 12
Dist: Sht-hd, 4½l, 7l, 1½l. 3m 58.10s. (12 Ran).

(James Hennessy), A P O'Brien

TRAMORE (IRE) (good)
Friday August 16th

408 **Tramore (Q.R.) Handicap Hurdle (0-102 4-y-o and up) £2,226 2½m...... (5:15)**

344³	TARA'S TRIBE [-] 9-11-1 Mr H F Cleary, ...(13 to 2)	1
352⁴	FAIR SOCIETY (Ire) [-] (bl) 5-10-11 (7") Mr John P Moloney,	
	....(6 to 4 fav)	2
273⁷	THE TOM'S ERROR (Ire) [-] 6-11-2 Mr F Fenton, ...(12 to 1)	3
391⁴	THE SOUTH POLE INN (Ire) [-] 4-10-3 (7",6ex) Mr A C Coyle,	
	....(100 to 30)	4
355⁴	RISING BREEZE (Ire) [-] 7-11-8 (3") Mr B M Cash, ..(6 to 1)	5
131⁶	CROOM ABU (Ire) [-] 5-10-5³ (7") Mr P P O'Brien, ..(20 to 1)	6
355⁶	INGMAR [-] 10-10-8 (7") Mr T N Cloke, ...(10 to 1)	7
256⁷	DEARMISTERSHATTER (Ire) [-] 5-10-8 Mr J P Dempsey,	
	....(20 to 1)	8

Dist: Hd, 6l, 1½l, 3½l. 4m 48.20s. (8 Ran).

(J M Wilson), J A Berry

409 **John O'Brien Memorial Handicap Chase (0-109 4-y-o and up) £2,568 2m .... (6:15)**

261²	HANNIES GIRL (Ire) [-] 7-10-1 (7") L J Fleming, (4 to 1 fav)	1
345	BARNAMIRE BAY (Ire) [-] 7-9-3 (7") M D Murphy, ..(10 to 1)	2
338	NOBODYS SON [-] 10-11-5 J P Broderick, ...(5 to 1)	3
338⁴	SILENTBROOK [-] 11-9-0 (7") A O'Shea, ...(9 to 2)	4
	SIR L MUNNY [-] 12-9-9 C F Swan, ...(8 to 1)	5
349²	NO SIR ROM [-] 10-9-2 (5") J Butler, ...(8 to 1)	6
	CAPTAIN BRANDY [-] 11-10-13 K F O'Brien, ...(12 to 1)	7
	EVER SO BOLD [-] 9-12-0 T P Treacy, ...(8 to 1)	f
219	BEST VINTAGE [-] 12-11-7 T Horgan, ...(12 to 1)	pu

Dist: 3l, 6l, 1½l, 11l. 3m 53.10s. (9 Ran).

(Michael L Flynn), F Flood

410 **T & C Peugeot I.N.H. Flat Race (4-y-o and up) £2,568 2½m............ (7:45)**

253²	STANSWAY (Ire) 4-11-0 (7") Mr P Fenton, ...(9 to 4 fav)	1
213⁹	MORNING MIST (Ire) 4-11-0 (7") Mr S M Duffy, ...(7 to 1)	2
	SUP A WHISKEY (Ire) 5-11-2 (7") Mr Sean O O'Brien, (8 to 1)	3
	HOLY GROUNDER (Ire) 7-11-7 (7") Mr J T Nolan, ..(14 to 1)	4
393³	GARLAND ROSE (Ire) 6-11-2 (7") P Morris, ...(5 to 2)	5
288⁷	LIMIT THE DAMAGE (USA) 4-11-0 (7") G T Hourigan, (6 to 1)	6
22⁶	ORCHARD SUNSET (Ire) 6-11-7 (7") Mr D M Fogarty,	
	....(10 to 1)	7
329⁹	PRINCESS TOUCHEE (Ire) 5-11-2 (7") Mr D P Coakley,	
	....(33 to 1)	8
346³	PAI II (Ire) 4-11-0 (7") Mr John P Moloney, ...(14 to 1)	9
199	CUBAN SKIES (Ire) 6-11-7 (7") Mr M G Coleman, ..(14 to 1)	10
159⁷	TROJAN OAK (Ire) (bl) 5-11-7 (7") Mr S O'Gorman, (12 to 1)	11
212	NAGLE RICE (Ire) 7-11-2 (7") Mr J A Collins, ...(33 to 1)	12
340	ROSE OF STEEL (Ire) 7-11-6 (3") Mr K Whelan, ...(33 to 1)	13

Dist: Sht-hd, 2½l, 4l, 3½l. 4m 43.10s. (13 Ran).

(Michael O'Connor), Michael O'Connor

BANGOR (good to firm)
Saturday August 17th
Going Correction: PLUS 0.10 sec. per fur.

411 **EQE International Juvenile Novices' Hurdle Class E (3-y-o) £2,584 2m 1f .... (2:25)**

305³	BALMORAL PRINCESS (bl) 10-5 R Bellamy, hld up, trkd ldrs 4th, outpcd four out, chlgd frm 2 out, mstk last, rallied to ld cl hme.............................. (6 to 1 tchd 13 to 1)	1
	STILL HERE (Ire) 10-10 N Williamson, hld up, cl up 4th, upsides whn lft clr 3 out, hrd pressed nxt, mstk last, hdd and no extr close hme.............. (9 to 2 op 4 to 1 tchd 5 to 1)	2
320⁷	RECALL TO MIND (Ire) 10-7 (3") D Parker, prmnt, rdn and lost pl 4th, no dngr aftr................ (50 to 1 op 33 to 1)	3
320³	KILLMESSAN-TOWN (Ire) 10-12 (3") F Leahy, prmnt, drvn alng 4th, wknd appr four out, eased bef 2 out, tld off.	
	.... (9 to 4 op 6 to 1)	4
305⁴	FRIENDLY DREAMS (Ire) (bl) 10-12 D Bridgwater, towards rear, drvn alng aftr 3rd, wl beh 5th, eased bef 2 out, tld off.	
	.... (2 to 1 fav op 5 to 2 tchd 3 to 1)	5
	MILL HOUSE BOY (Ire) 10-10 R Supple, not jump wl, al beh, tld off whn f last............ (50 to 1 op 33 to 1)	f
	SKRAM 10-10 A Maguire, led, stumbled appr 4th, jnd whn f 3 out.............. (12 to 1 op 14 to 1)	f
305	SONG FOR JESS (Ire) 10-5 R Greene, towards rear whn f 1st.	
	.... (50 to 1 op 33 to 1)	f

Dist: ½l, 20l, dist, 29l. 4m 7.40s. a 17.40s (8 Ran).

(Mrs S K Maan), J H Peacock

412 **Prestatyn Novices' Handicap Chase Class E (0-100 5-y-o and up) £2,801 2m 1f 110yds................ (2:55)**

373²	GREEN'S SEAGO (USA) [68] 8-10-2 (5") P Henley, cl up, led 7th, drw clr aftr 3 out, easily..................(7 to 2)	1
228³	EXCLUSION [80] 7-11-5 R Marley, in rear, blun second, mstk 5th (water), upsides frm 7th, niggled alng and mistake 3 out, btn whn mistake 2 out. (2 to 1 fav op 7 to 4 tchd 9 to 4)	2
79	SHERWOOD BOY [85] 7-11-10 C Llewellyn, led, mstk 5th (water), hdd 7th, sn wknd, jmpd slwly 3 out, tld off.	
	.... (5 to 2 op 7 to 4)	3
309⁴	NORTHERN NATION [77] 8-11-2 A Maguire, in tch whn f 4th.	
	.... (6 to 1 op 5 to 1 tchd 13 to 2)	f
334⁶	DON TOCINO [64] (bl) 6-10-3 R Bellamy, hld up, struggling and lost tch frm 7th, mstk 3 out, 3rd and tld off whn f last.	
	.... (12 to 1 op 8 to 1)	f

Dist: Dist, 14l. 4m 20.20s. a 18.20s (5 Ran).

(Mrs S Kavanagh), H M Kavanagh

413 **Construction Services Novices' Chase Class D (5-y-o and up) £4,538 2½m 110yds........................ (3:25)**

	ALQAIRAWAAN 7-10-12 C Llewellyn, lft alone frm 1st, slight mstk 8th (water), fnshd alone....(7 to 4 on op 2 to 1 on)	1
266³	MICHERADO (Fr) 6-11-5 T Eley, led till f 1st........(6 to 4)	f

Won by 4m 55.30s. a 9.30s (2 Ran).

SR: 11/-/

(Jack Joseph), C J Mann

414 **Royal Welch Fusiliers Trophy Handicap Hurdle Class E Amateur Riders' (0-120 4-y-o and up) £2,746 2½m...... (3:55)**

	ROYAL CIRCUS [90] 7-10-5 (7") Mr P Scott, trkd ldr, led aftr 1st, pressed 2 out, styd on wl frm last....(3 to 1 op 2 to 1)	1
376⁷	BOURDONNER [87] 4-10-3 (3") Mr C Bonner, led till aftr 1st, continued to track ldr, mstk 7th, ev ch 2 out, sn drvn, mistake last, no extr.... (11 to 8 on op 5 to 4 on tchd 6 to 4)	2
204⁶	GONE BY (Ire) [102] (bl) 8-11-3 (7") Mr R Thornton, chsd ldrs, outpcd by ldg pair frm 7th, sn drvn, no dngr aftr.	
	.... (4 to 1 op 3 to 1 tchd 9 to 2)	3
308⁷	BATTY'S ISLAND [89] (bl) 7-10-4 (7") Miss L Boswell, strted slwly, beh, blun and uns rdr 6th.	
	.... (20 to 1 op 16 to 1 tchd 25 to 1)	ur

Dist: 3l, 13l. 4m 49.50s. a 19.50s (4 Ran).

(P W Hiatt), P W Hiatt

415 **Telegraph Service Stations Novices' Hurdle Class E (4-y-o and up) £2,612 2½m........................ (4:25)**

73³	TUKANO (Can) 5-11-5 G Bradley, hndy, narrow ld 4 out, styd on strly to go clr appr last.	
	.... (Evens fav op 11 to 10 tchd 6 to 5)	1
53⁴	PROFIT AND LOSS 5-10-7 A Maguire, chsd ldr, narrow ld 7th, hdd nxt, ev ch whn mstk 3 out, sn one pace.	
	.... (11 to 8 op 5 to 4 tchd 6 to 4)	2
	FIRST BEE 5-10-7 R Supple, hld up, mstk second, cld appr 4 out, sn und pres, one pace frm 2 out, not flnsht last.	
	.... (33 to 1 op 25 to 1)	3
	MELLOW YELLOW 5-10-12 T Eley, keen hold, hld up, hdwy appr 4 out to track ldrs, wknd quickly bef nxt.	
	.... (10 to 1 op 8 to 1)	4
310	ADMIRAL'S GUEST (Ire) (v) 4-10-9 N Williamson, led, clr till 3rd, slight mstk nxt, reminders and hdd 7th, wknd quickly, jmpd slwly 3 out, tld off.............. (20 to 1 op 25 to 1)	5

Dist: 9l, 2½l, 24l, dist. 4m 50.80s. a 20.80s (5 Ran).

(Mrs T McCoubrey), J R Jenkins

416 **Showtime Novices' Handicap Hurdle Class E (0-100 4-y-o and up) £2,584 2m 1f........................ (5:00)**

377⁴	RAVEN'S ROOST (Ire) [54] 5-10-0 P McLoughlin, keen hold, hld up, improved 4 out, led appr last, rdn out.	
	.... (16 to 1 op 14 to 1)	1
	TAWAFIJ (USA) [75] 7-11-7 R Garritty, hld up in rear, improved to track ldrs appr 3 out, sn chalg, no extr r-in.	
	.... (5 to 4 fav op 6 to 5 tchd 13 to 8)	2
263³	COUNT OF FLANDERS (Ire) [78] 6-11-10 A S Smith, cl up, led appr 2 out, drvn and hdd approaching last, one pace.	
	.... (3 to 1 op 9 to 2)	3
318⁶	RARE PADDY [60] (v) 7-10-6 R Supple, prmnt, led 3rd till 5th, led nxt till appr 2 out, sn wknd.	
	.... (8 to 1 op 6 to 1 tchd 9 to 1)	4
251	MARKETING MAN [55] 6-10-1 R Bellamy, keen hold, led till 3rd, led 5th till nxt, wkng whn mstk 3 out, tld off.	
	.... (33 to 1 op 25 to 1)	5
382³	NIGHT TIME [85] 4-11-7 (7") Mr G Shenkin, hndy, drvn alng and lost pl 5th, sn wl beh, tld off........(7 to 2 op 5 to 2)	6

Dist: 1¾l, 7l, 8l, 20l, ½l. 4m 3.60s. a 13.60s (6 Ran).

(G Elwyn Jones), G E Jones

STRATFORD (good to firm)
Saturday August 17th
Going Correction: MINUS 0.15 sec. per fur.

417 **Richardsons Fort Retail Park Claiming Hurdle Class F (4-y-o and up) £2,360 2¾m 110yds.....................(2:20)**

VIARDOT (Ire) 7-11-5 P Niven, *hld up, chsd clr ldr aftr 6th, wnt second 4 out, second and btn whn lft in ld 2 out.*

.........................(9 to 4 fav op 2 to 1 tchd 5 to 2) 1
ACROW LINE 11-10-7 D J Burchell, *not fluent, beh and pushed along aftr 5th, hdwy 7th, wnt 3rd after 4 out, lft second 2 out......................(6 to 1 tchd 9 to 2)* 2
206 RIVA'S BOOK (USA) 5-10-13 A P McCoy, *hld up, rdn to chase clr ldr aftr 6th, lost tch after 4 out, tld off.*

.........................(14 to 1 op 10 to 1 tchd 16 to 1) 3
299⁴ MILZIG (USA) 7-11-2 D Skyrme, *lost pl aftr 3rd, sn tld off.*

.........................(20 to 1 op 14 to 1) 4
281⁷ MERLINS WISH (USA) 7-10-6 (7*) G Supple, *prmnt till 4th, sn lost tch, tld off aftr 6th..............(14 to 1 op 8 to 1)* 5
359⁵ FATTASH (USA) 4-10-0 (5*) S Ryan, *mstks, reminders aftr 4th, tld off after 7th.................(100 to 1 op 33 to 1)* 6
403¹⁰ DIAMOND EDGE (Ire) 6-11-11 (7*) B Moore, *led, clr aftr second,*

.........................(11 to 4 op 3 to 1 tchd 7 to 2 and 5 to 1) f
331 JENNYELLEN (Ire) 7-11-0 R Johnson, *hld up, chsd clr ldr aftr 6th, 4th and wkng whn f four out.......(7 to 2 tchd 4 to 1)* f
229 GOODNIGHT VIENNA (Ire) 6-10-9¹ Mr M Munrowd, *beh, mstk 5th, sn lost tch, tld off aftr 7th, pld up bef 3 out.*

.........................(100 to 1 op 33 to 1) pu
Dist: 6l, 21l, dist, ½l, 8l. 5m 30.60s. a 18.60s (9 Ran).

(The Mary Reveley Racing Club), Mrs M Reveley

418 **Monks Cross Richardsons Retail Development Handicap Chase Class F (0-105 5-y-o and up) £2,770 3m (2:50)**

282* MAPLE DANCER [99] 10-11-3 (7*) Mr G Shenkin, *hld up, chsd clr ldr frm 8th, cld 4 out, led appr 2 out, hng rght approaching last, drvn out.........(7 to 4 fav op 2 to 1 tchd 5 to 1)* 1
SOME DAY SOON [100] 11-11-11 P Holley, *led, clr aftr 3rd til after 4 out, hdd 2 out, sn btn.*

.........................(13 to 2 op 5 to 1 tchd 7 to 1) 2
327* SOHAIL (USA) [103] 13-12-0 R Dunwoody, *hld up, chsd clr ldr aftr twelfth, wnt 3rd 4 out, no imprsn.*

.........................(5 to 4 op 1 to 1 tchd 11 to 1) 3
282 THE BLUE BOY [102] (bl) 8-11-13 R Johnson, *al rdn alng, no ch frm 6 out..........(6 to 1 op 5 to 1 tchd 13 to 2)* 4
282⁵ BOXING MATCH [75] 9-10-8 B Fenton, *lost pl 6th, beh and pushed along aftr 11th, hdwy 13th, wnt 4th 3 out, sn btn.*

.........................(8 to 1 op 10 to 1 tchd 7 to 1) 5
PAPER STAR [103] 9-12-0 B Powell, *jmpd slwly and lost pl 4th, hdwy to chase clr ldr aftr 8th, lost place after twelfth, sn tld off.................(10 to 1 op 8 to 1 tchd 11 to 1)* 6
375⁸ HURRYUP [91] 9-10-13 (3*) J Culloty, *chsd clr ldr frm 7th, mstk 13th, sn wknd, tld off whn pld up bef 3 out.*

.........................(13 to 2 op 10 to 1) pu
327 THE LORRYMAN (Ire) [85] (bl) 8-10-10 G Upton, *mstks, 4th whn jmpd slwly 8th, lost tch and drvn alng aftr nxt, tld off when pld up bef 6 out......(20 to 1 tchd 33 to 1 and 50 to 1)* pu
Dist: 6l, 9l, 17l, 11l, 22l. 5m 49.60s. a 4.60s (8 Ran).

SR: 14/9/3/-/-/ *(Dr Ian R Shenkin), A G Hobbs*

419 **Stratford-on-Avon Foods Maiden Hurdle Class E (Div I) (4-y-o and up) £1,926 2m 110yds.....................(3:20)**

226² ZINE LANE 4-11-2 R Farrant, *trkd ldr, led aftr 4 out, lft clr nxt, unchlgd.......(9 to 4 on op 7 to 4 on tchd 13 to 8 on)* 1
100 KUTAN (Ire) 6-11-5 E Byrne, *slwly away, hld up and beh, steady hdwy aftr 4 out, styd on to take second pl after 2 out.*

.........................(33 to 1 op 20 to 1) 2
DANTEAN 4-11-2 D O'Sullivan, *hld up, hdwy aftr 5th, lft poor second 3 out, wknd after nxt..........(12 to 1 op 8 to 1)* 3
TIGH-NA-MARA 8-10-9 (5*) E Callaghan, *chsd ldr frm 4th, wnt 3rd 5th, outpcd aftr nxt, no ch whn mstk 2 out.*

.........................(33 to 1 op 25 to 1) 4
297⁶ SAINT AMIGO 4-11-2 J A McCarthy, *jmpd slwly 1st, pressed ldr til rdn and wknd aftr 5th, tld off after 4 out.*

.........................(6 to 1 op 12 to 1) 5
ATHENIAN ALLIANCE 7-10-11 (3*) Guy Lewis, *hld up, lost tch aftr 4th, tld off after nxt..............(100 to 1 op 66 to 1)* 6
PRINCE DE BERRY 5-11-5 A P McCoy, *led, hdd aftr 4 out, second and wkng whn blun and uns rdr nxt.*

.........................(11 to 4 op 9 to 4) ur
330 ON THE LEDGE (USA) 6-10-12 (7*) A Dowling, *lost tch aftr 5th, tld off whn pld up bef 2 out.....(200 to 1 op 66 to 1)* pu
LILAC RAIN 4-10-11 W McFarland, *not fluent, lost tch aftr 5th, tld off whn pld up bef 3 out..........(25 to 1 tchd 33 to 1)* pu
297 MINIDIA 4-10-11 Mr A Charles-Jones, *not fluent, lost tch aftr 3rd, sn tld off, pld up after 5th......(150 to 1 op 66 to 1)* pu
Dist: 19l, 1l, 11l, dist, 15l. 3m 59.20s. a 13.20s (10 Ran).

(The Hopeful Partnership), Major W R Hern

420 **Stevenage Richardsons Retail Novices' Hurdle Class D (4-y-o and up) £2,775 2¾m 110yds...........(3:50)**

203³ WYNBERG 5-11-6 S Wynne, *led aftr second, stdly drw clr after 4 out, unchlgd...........(11 to 4 on op 9 to 4 on)* 1
ROSKEEN BRIDGE (Ire) 5-11-0 M Richards, *chsd ldr, pushed aftr 7th, lost tch after 3 out........(7 to 2 op 5 to 2)* 2
55 HATTA RIVER (USA) 6-11-0 R Johnson, *chsd ldr, drvn alng aftr 8th, 3rd whn mstk 4 out, sn tld off, blun 2 out.*

.........................(11 to 1 op 14 to 1 tchd 10 to 1) 3
CROSSING THE STYX 10-11-0 Miss A Embiricos, *led til aftr second, lost tch after 6th, sn tld off, pld up after 4 out.*

.........................(14 to 1 op 10 to 1) pu
Dist: 28l, dist. 5m 41.40s. a 29.40s (4 Ran).

(Mrs D Pridden), Capt T A Forster

421 **Parkway Richardsons Wednesbury Handicap Chase Class D (0-120 5-y-o and up) £3,731 2m 1f 110yds...(4:20)**

373* STATELY HOME (Ire) [108] 5-12-0 R Johnson, *led, blun 7th, sn reco'red, rdn aftr 4 out, styd on wl.*

.........................(6 to 4 on op 13 to 8 on tchd 11 to 8 on) 1
335³ FLYING ZIAD (Can) [77] 13-9-7 (7*) A Dowling, *chsd ldg pair, 3rd whn blun 7th, sn wknd, tld off after 4 out.*

.........................(4 to 1 op 7 to 2) 2
369³ WISE ADVICE (Ire) [95] 6-11-4 A Thornton, *chsd ldr, rdn whn mstk 4 out, sn wknd, eased when btn aftr 2 out.*

.........................(5 to 2 op 9 to 4 tchd 11 to 4) 3
Dist: 2l, 14l. 4m 9.20s. a 7.20s (3 Ran).

(P Bowen), P Bowen

422 **Atlantic Wharf Richardsons Cardiff Conditional Jockeys' Handicap Hurdle Class F (0-105 4-y-o and up) £2,192 2m 110yds....................(4:55)**

307* PETER MONAMY [99] 4-12-0 D Walsh, *set steady pace til quickened 3 out, drvn alng aftr nxt, hit last, styd on wl.*

.........................(11 to 10 fav op 6 to 4 on) 1
333⁴ SIRTELIMAR (Ire) [92] 7-11-10 T J Murphy, *chsd ldr, rdn to chal appr last, unbl to quicken r-in......(5 to 4 op 7 to 4)* 2
376⁶ ASTERIX [92] 8-11-10 B Fenton, *hld up, chsd ldg pair frm 5th, drvn aftr 3 out, no imprsn from nxt.....(9 to 2 tchd 5 to 1)* 3
Dist: 1¾l, 6l. 4m 5.80s. a 19.80s (3 Ran).

(Richard Green (Fine Paintings)), M C Pipe

423 **Stratford-on-Avon Foods Maiden Hurdle Class E (Div II) (4-y-o and up) £1,926 2m 110yds.....................(5:25)**

328³ RE ROI (Ire) 4-11-2 T J Murphy, *hld up, hdwy aftr 4 out, wnt fourth after nxt, quickened to ld last, drvn out r-in.*

.........................(5 to 2 tchd 7 to 2) 1
ANABRANCH 5-10-7 (7*) M Newton, *chsd clr ldr frm 4th, led 3 out, hdd nxt, rdn and unbl to quicken.*

.........................(Evens fav tchd 11 to 8) 2
300⁴ MINNESOTA FATS (Ire) 4-11-2 Gary Lyons, *led, clr aftr second, hdd 3 out, led ag'n nxt, headed last, sn btn.*

.........................(14 to 1 op 12 to 1 tchd 16 to 1) 3
RISKY ROMEO 4-11-2 R Dunwoody, *chsd clr ldr, jmpd slwly 4 out, ev ch nxt, sn rdn, wknd appr 2 out.*

.........................(4 to 1 tchd 3 to 1) 4
FLAIR LADY 5-10-7 (7*) J Power, *chsd clr ldr til wknd aftr 4 out.....................(33 to 1 op 20 to 1)* 5
CHIEF'S LADY 4-10-11 R Johnson, *chsd ldr, mstk 5th, sn wknd.............(50 to 1 op 33 to 1 tchd 66 to 1)* 6
330⁵ GALLOPING GUNS (Ire) 4-10-13 (3*) Guy Lewis, *hld up, pushed along aftr 5th, sn lost tch.*

.........................(100 to 1 op 66 to 1 tchd 150 to 1) 7
100⁹ AGAINST THE CLOCK 4-11-2 S Curran, *hld up, lost tch and drvn alng aftr 5th, sn beh............(25 to 1 op 14 to 1)* 8
295 FLASHING SABRE 4-10-9 (7*) A Dowling, *al last, mstk 4th, pld up bef nxt.................(200 to 1 op 100 to 1)* pu
Dist: 6l, 8l, 4l, 18l, 12l, 7l, 12l. 4m 2.20s. a 16.20s (9 Ran).

(J C Fox), J C Fox

TRAMORE (IRE) (good)
Saturday August 17th

424 **Richardson Brokers Maiden Hurdle (4-y-o and up) £2,568 2m.........(2:35)**

STONELEIGH TURBO (Ire) 7-11-7 (7*) M P Dunne, (12 to 1) 1
353³ FOREST LADY (Ire) 4-10-10 (3*) D T Evans, ...(11 to 2) 2
347⁶ KING'S MANDATE (Ire) 7-11-6 J K Kinane, ...(8 to 1) 3
169⁸ NEW LEGISLATION (Ire) (bl) 6-11-1 C F Swan, ...(13 to 2) 4
JODESI (Ire) 6-11-6 J P Broderick, ...(10 to 1) 5
339² DREAM ETERNAL (Ire) 5-11-1 W T Slattery, ...(6 to 4 fav) 6
JENBRO (Ire) 5-11-4 (5*) T Martin, ...(7 to 2) 7
174³ CARRAIG-AN-OIR (Ire) 7-11-7 (7*) J D Pratt, ...(6 to 1) 8
193⁸ DRUMELLA (Ire) 4-11-4 T P Treacy, ...(6 to 1) 9
Dist: 4l, ¾l, nk, 4l. 3m 56.40s. (9 Ran).

(John G Doyle), P A Fahy

425 **Richard Power Maiden Hurdle (3-y-o) £2,568 2m....................(3:05)**

IACCHUS (Ire) 10-5 C F Swan, ...(6 to 4 on) 1

```
        LUDDEN CHIEF (Ire) 10-5 J P Broderick, . . . . . . . . . . (6 to 1)    2
341  RAINERY (Ire) 10-0 T Horgan, . . . . . . . . . . . . . . . . . (5 to 1)    3
     JUST MIMI (Ire) 9-7 (7") Mr Edgar Byrne, . . . . . . . . (10 to 1)         4
     MAIDEN MIST (Ire) 9-7 (7") A O'Shea, . . . . . . . . . . . (6 to 1)        5
341  ALTHOUGH 10-0 (5") J Butler, . . . . . . . . . . . . . . . . .(10 to 1)    6
Dist: 5l, 2½l, 9l, 25l. 4m 5.70s. (6 Ran).
```
(Mrs A M O'Brien), A P O'Brien

426 Gain Beginners Chase (4-y-o and up) £2,740 2m . . . . (4:05)

```
303⁹  PHARDY (Ire) 5-11-8 G M O'Neill, . . . . . . . . . . . . . . (5 to 2)    1
391²  FATHER MICHAEL (Ire) 6-12-0 T P Treacy, . . . . . (2 to 1 fav)          2
338⁵  SANDY FOREST LADY (Ire) 7-11-9 J P Broderick, . . (5 to 1)             3
344⁶  PASSER-BY 9-12-0 K F O'Brien, . . . . . . . . . . . . . . . (7 to 1)     4
356³  FIXED ASSETS 9-11-9 C F Swan, . . . . . . . . . . . . . . (9 to 2)       5
406³  JULY SCHOON 11-11-7 (7") Miss C Gould, . . . . . . (14 to 1)            6
      FULL MOON FEVER (Ire) 7-12-0 T Horgan, . . . . . . . (20 to 1)          7
Dist: 1l, 8l, 6l, 9l. 3m 54.70s. (7 Ran).
```
(Gan Ceann Syndicate), Augustine Leahy

ROSCOMMON (IRE) (good to firm)
Sunday August 18th

427 Dermot Hughes Toyota Car Sales Novice Hurdle (4-y-o and up) £3,425 2½m . . . . (2:30)

```
268⁵  DIFFICULT TIMES (Ire) 4-11-1 S C Lyons, . . . . . . . . .(6 to 1)       1
301*  CLONAGAM (Ire) 7-11-8 C F Swan, . . . . . . . . . . (11 to 10 fav)      2
315³  BAMAPOUR (Ire) 6-11-8 A P McCoy, . . . . . . . . . . . . .(6 to 4)       3
337³  MONTETAN (Ire) 5-10-11 K F O'Brien, . . . . . . . . . (12 to 1)         4
160*  SIBERIAN TALE (Ire) 6-11-5 (3") Mr P J Casey, . . . (8 to 1)           5
Dist: 2l, dist, 10l, 9l. 4m 27.00s. (5 Ran).
```
(P M Dowling), G M Lyons

428 Flemings Super Valu Handicap Hurdle (4-y-o and up) £3,425 2m . . . . (3:00)

```
303³  JUST LITTLE [-] 4-11-0 C F Swan, . . . . . . . . . . . . .(5 to 4 on)    1
      PRACTICE RUN (Ire) [-] 8-11-6 A P McCoy, . . . . . . . (10 to 1)        2
      LA CIENAGA [-] 12-10-2⁵ J P Broderick, . . . . . . . . . (33 to 1)      3
275²  DANCING CLODAGH (Ire) [-] 4-9-4 (7") R Burke, . . (11 to 2)            4
303   WEST ON BRIDGE ST (Ire) [-] 6-10-8 C O'Dwyer, . . (5 to 2)            5
      PYR FOUR [-] 9-10-2 (7") D A McLoughlin, . . . . . . . (20 to 1)        6
      TOUCHING MOMENT (Ire) [-] 6-9-11 (7") Mr J Keville,
      . . . . . . . . . . . . . . . . . . . . . . . . . . . . . . . . . . . . . .(20 to 1)    pu
Dist: 4½l, 1½l, 3l, 5½l. 3m 43.30s. (7 Ran).
```
(Seamus O'Farrell), A P O'Brien

429 T.V. O'Brien Memorial Handicap Chase (0-116 4-y-o and up) £3,767 2m (4:00)

```
293   AN MAINEACH (Ire) [-] 7-12-0 C F Swan, . . . . . . . . (9 to 4)        1
312⁴  NORDIC THORN (Ire) [-] 6-11-6 K F O'Brien, . . . . . . (4 to 1)        2
349*  CARAGH BRIDGE [-] 9-10-6 C O'Dwyer, . . . . . . . (2 to 1 fav)         3
409³  NOBODYS SON [-] 10-10-2 J P Broderick, . . . . . . . . (7 to 1)        4
261   DRINDOD (Ire) [-] 7-10-2 (7") D A McLoughlin, . . . . (10 to 1)        5
409⁷  CAPTAIN BRANDY [-] 11-10-8 A P McCoy, . . . . . . . (12 to 1)          6
Dist: Sht-hd, 25l, 1½l, 10l. 3m 50.10s. (6 Ran).
```
(C H Pettigrew), Capt D G Swan

430 Midland Oil Company I.N.H. Flat Race (4-y-o and up) £3,425 2m . . . . (5:30)

```
364²  REAL TAOISEACH (Ire) 6-11-11 (7") Mr A K Wyse, . . (4 to 1)           1
      ROYAL ZIERO (Ire) 5-11-13 Mr J T McNamara, . (7 to 2)                 2
365³  NATIVE BABY (Ire) 6-11-13 Mr J A Nash, . . . . . . . . . (9 to 2)      3
358*  BANEY THE BISHOP (Ire) 6-11-11 (7") Mr A Ross, . . (5 to 1)           4
343*  PERAMBIE (bl) 4-11-1 (7") Miss A L Crowley, (3 to 1 fav)             5
256⁶  RADICAL ACTION (Ire) 6-11-4 (7") Miss S McDonogh,
      . . . . . . . . . . . . . . . . . . . . . . . . . . . . . . . . . . . . . .(14 to 1)    6
      HOLLY LADY (Ire) 5-11-3 (3") Mr B R Hamilton, . . . .(20 to 1)         7
      DESERT WAR (Ire) 5-10-13 (7") Mr D Naughton, . . . (20 to 1)          8
Dist: ¾l, 1½l, 2l, ¾l. 3m 50.80s. (8 Ran).
```
(A P Wyse), E J O'Grady

TRAMORE (IRE) (good)
Sunday August 18th

431 Mary O'Shaughnessy Memorial Handicap Chase (0-109 4-y-o and up) £3,425 2¾m . . . . (3:35)

```
313*  BEAKSTOWN (Ire) [-] 7-12-0 T P Treacy, . . . . . . . . . .(7 to 2)     1
338*  TRIPTODICKS (Ire) [-] 6-9-2 (5") T Martin, . . . . . (11 to 4 fav)     2
338³  GOT NO CHOICE (Ire) [-] 6-9-0 (7") M D Murphy, . . (10 to 1)          3
293   LOFTUS LAD (Ire) [-] 8-10-3 (7") A O'Shea, . . . . . . . . (7 to 1)    4
338²  HIGH-SPEC [-] 10-11-8 J F Titley, . . . . . . . . . . . . (100 to 30)   5
      CLONEENVERB [-] 12-9-2 (5") J Butler, . . . . . . . . . . (25 to 1)    6
364⁴  WATERLOO BALL (Ire) [-] (bl) 7-11-7 T Horgan, . . . . .(6 to 1)       7
235   SMOOTH COUP [-] 10-10-11-13 J Shortt, . . . . . . . .(12 to 1)        8
Dist: 1½l, 13l, 15l, 3l. 5m 16.80s. (8 Ran).
```
(Mrs P J O'Meara), P Mullins

432 W.L.R. FM Handicap Hurdle (0-109 4-y-o and up) £2,740 2½m . . . . (4:05)

```
315*  FATHER RECTOR (Ire) [-] 7-11-12 T Horgan, . . . (5 to 4 fav)         1
      BRONICA (Ire) [-] 4-11-3 J F Titley, . . . . . . . . . . . . . . (7 to 4)   2
      TEARDROP (Ire) [-] 4-10-6 (5") J Butler, . . . . . . . . . (10 to 1)    3
342   VAIN PRINCESS (Ire) [-] 7-10-11 (7") S FitzGerald, (11 to 2)          4
391⁴  CHUCK (Ire) [-] 6-10-11 (7") D McCullagh, . . . . . . . (6 to 1)       5
Dist: 2l, 11l, 3l, 6l. 4m 42.80s. (5 Ran).
```
(Paddy Fennelly), Paddy Fennelly

433 Richard Power Handicap Hurdle (0-130 4-y-o and up) £4,795 2m (4:35)

```
303*  MYSTICAL CITY (Ire) [-] 6-11-7 (7") P Morris, . . (6 to 4 on)         1
311²  HAKKINEN (Ire) [-] 5-11-3 G M O'Neill, . . . . . . . . . (10 to 1)     2
      LEGGAGH LADY (Ire) [-] 5-11-4 (5") J M Donnelly, . (12 to 1)         3
214*  NATALIES FANCY [-] 10-11-12 J F Titley, . . . . . . . . (10 to 1)      4
216³  BETH'S APPARITION (Ire) [-] 6-11-3 T Horgan, . . . . (10 to 1)        5
405⁵  THE WICKED CHICKEN (Ire) [-] (bl) 7-9-4 (5") T Martin,
      . . . . . . . . . . . . . . . . . . . . . . . . . . . . . . . . . . . . . .(12 to 1)    6
      RAMDON ROCKS [-] 9-10-12 J Shortt, . . . . . . . . . . .(20 to 1)     7
268²  KATES CHOICE (Ire) [-] 4-10-12 T P Treacy, . . . . . . .(5 to 1)       f
405²  BOB THE YANK (Ire) [-] 6-10-3 (7") A O'Shea, . . . . . (7 to 1)       ur
Dist: 14l, 1½l, 3l, 5l. 3m 52.80s. (9 Ran).
```
(Phantom Syndicate), W P Mullins

434 Morris Oil Mares I.N.H. Flat Race (4-y-o and up) £2,740 2m . . . . (5:35)

```
407³  GALE HAMSHIRE (Ire) 7-11-9 (5") Mr R Walsh, . . . . (3 to 1)          1
407⁴  MALICE 10-11-11 (3") Mr J Connolly, . . . . . . . . . . . (10 to 1)    2
      MONDEO ROSE (Ire) 4-11-2 (7") Mr C A Murphy, . . (8 to 1)            3
329⁴  PLEASE NO TEARS 9-12-0 Mrs C Barker, . . . . . (2 to 1 fav)          4
      FELICITY'S PRIDE (Ire) 5-11-7 (7") Mr D P Coakley, (10 to 1)         5
340⁶  DARING DAY (Ire) 7-12-0 Mr D Marnane, . . . . . . . . (10 to 1)       6
350   REENIE (Ire) 5-11-9 (5") T Martin, . . . . . . . . . . . . . . (12 to 1)   7
410⁸  PRINCESS TOUCHEE (Ire) 5-11-7 (7") Mr Edgar Byrne,
      . . . . . . . . . . . . . . . . . . . . . . . . . . . . . . . . . . . . . .(12 to 1)    8
301⁸  MIDDLE MOGGS (Ire) (bl) 4-11-6 (3") Mr K Whelan, (9 to 2)           9
258⁵  CARNACREEVA GANE (Ire) 5-11-7 (7") Mr R M Walsh,
      . . . . . . . . . . . . . . . . . . . . . . . . . . . . . . . . . . . . . .(10 to 1)   10
358²  PALEFOOT (Ire) (bl) 8-11-7 (7") Miss C O'Neill, . . . (12 to 1)      11
      GEEGEE (Ire) 5-11-7 (7") Mr J P Moloney, . . . . . . . (12 to 1)     12
31    FORD CLASSIC (Ire) 4-11-2 (7") Mr D Atkinson, . . (16 to 1)         pu
      LAUDANUM (Ire) 6-11-7 (7") Mr J P McNamara, . . (12 to 1)           pu
      LOULISSARO (Ire) 4-11-2 (7") M P Dunne, . . . . . . . .(16 to 1)     pu
Dist: Sht-hd, 2l, nk, 9l. 3m 51.20s. (15 Ran).
```
(Bernard Madden), W P Mullins

PLUMPTON (firm)
Monday August 19th
Going Correction: MINUS 0.70 sec. per fur.

435 Peacehaven Mares' Only Novices' Handicap Hurdle Class E (0-100 4-y-o and up) £2,238 2m 1f . . . . (5:30)

```
111²  SCAMALLACH (Ire) [85] (bl) 6-12-0 G Bradley, led aftr 1st,
      made rst, clr last, rdn out.
      . . . . . . . (11 to 8 on op 6 to 4 on tchd 9 to 4 on and 5 to 4 on)    1
      MISTY VIEW [72] 7-11-1 A P McCoy, cl up, chsd wnr 3 out, rdn
      and not quicken aftr nxt, btn whn hit last.
      . . . . . . . . . . . . . . . . . . . . . .(7 to 1 op 9 to 2 tchd 8 to 1)   2
45    SIESTA TIME (USA) [57] 6-10-0 N Williamson, not jump wl,
      chsd wnr second to 3 out, hrd rdn, not quicken.
      . . . . . . . . . . . . . . . . . . . . . . . (9 to 1 op 3 to 1 tchd 5 to 2)   3
      CLUB ELITE [73] 4-10-13 Ann Stokell, pld hrd, reluctant ldr
      till aftr 1st, lost pl 5th, btn 7th.
      . . . . . . . . . . . . . . . . . . . . (12 to 1 op 8 to 1 tchd 16 to 1)   4
389³  LASER LIGHT LADY [60] (bl) 4-10-0 B Powell, al rear, rdn aftr
      6th, outpcd nxt. . . . . . . . . .(16 to 1 op 8 to 1 tchd 20 to 1)   5
Dist: 4l, 7l, 8l, 16l. 4m 20.40s. a 23.40s (5 Ran).
```
(Mrs Susan McCarthy), J R Jenkins

436 Leicester Dyers And Rip-off Clothing Company Juvenile Novices' Hurdle Class E (3-y-o) £2,259 2m 1f . . . . (5:55)

```
363²  VERULAM (Ire) 10-10 G Bradley, reminder aftr 1st, chsd ldrs,
      led after 3 out, rdn out. . . . . . . . . . . .(9 to 4 op 9 to 4)       1
      BRIGHT ECLIPSE (USA) 10-10 C Llewellyn, wtd wth, jmpd
      slwly 3rd, prog aftr 7th, chsd wnr after 3 out, rdn and found nil
      nxt. . . . . . . . . . . . . . . .(4 to 1 op 9 to 2 tchd 3 to 1)       2
320²  HOME COOKIN' 10-5 D Bridgwater, led, jmpd slwly and
      several reminders, hrd rdn and hdd aftr 3 out, wknd.
      . . . . . . . . . . . . . . . . . . . . . . . .(11 to 8 fav op 5 to 4)   3
363³  AGAIN TOGETHER 10-5 D Gallagher, chsd ldr, mstk 5th, ev
      ch whn mistake 3 out, wknd.
      . . . . . . . . . . . . . . . . . . . .(9 to 2 op 7 to 2 tchd 5 to 1)   4
      GOVERNOR'S BID 10-10 J Railton, al beh, rdn hfwy, tld off
      and hmpd bef 3 out. . . .(50 to 1 op 20 to 1 tchd 66 to 1)   pu
Dist: 7l, 25l, ½l. 4m 14.20s. a 17.20s (5 Ran).
```
(R M Ellis), J R Jenkins

437 **Dr. Bernard Abeysundera Handicap Chase Class E (0-110 5-y-o and up) £2,906 2m.....................(6:25)**

386² NOBLELY (USA) [98] 9-11-10 R Farrant, *led to 8th, led tenth, clr 2 out, easily*.................(5 to 4 tchd 11 to 10) 1
360* SAFETY (USA) [88] (bl) 9-11-0 T J Murphy, *pressed wnr 3rd, led 8th to tenth, rdn and wknd appr 2 out.*
..................(Evens fav op 11 to 10 on tchd 11 to 10) 2
360 LAVALIGHT [74] 9-9-11² (5*) P Henley, *mstk second, sn beh, tld off 8th, kpt on one pace frm 2 out.*
..............(33 to 1 op 5 on 1 op 14 to 1 and 50 to 1) 3
360 VICTORY ANTHEM [74] 10-10-0 B Fenton, *pressed wnr to 3rd, struggling frm 5th, tld off from 8th.*
.......................(10 to 1 op 8 to 1 tchd 11 to 1) 4
Dist: 25l, 14l, dist. 3m 48.30s. b 3.70s (4 Ran).
SR: 21/ (D H Cowgill), N J H Walker

438 **London Racing Club Handicap Hurdle Class F (0-105 4-y-o and up) £2,029 2 ½m.........................(6:55)**

414³ GONE BY (Ire) [101] (v) 8-11-12 G Bradley, *hld up last, prog aftr 8th, led 3 out, drvn out r-in.*
..................(11 to 2 op 4 to 1 tchd 6 to 1) 1
361¹² NO LIGHT [103] 9-12-0 L Harvey, *hld up, prog 9th, trkd wnr aftr 3 out, edn and ev ch whn mstk last, not quicken.*
..........(13 to 8 tay op 5 to 1 tchd 7 to 4 and 15 to 8) 2
447 MR GENEAOLOGY (USA) [94] (bl) 6-11-5 A Maguire, *clr ldr, mstk 7th, rdn and hdd 3 out, wknd appr nxt.*
..................(7 to 2 tchd 4 to 1) 3
331² CELESTIAL FIRE [80] 4-10-2 A P McCoy, *chsd clr ldr, cld 9th, hrd rdn and ev ch 3 out, sn wknd.*
..................(9 to 4 op 5 to 2 tchd 3 to 1) 4
EMALLEN (Ire) [75] (bl) 8-9-9 (5*) Sophie Mitchell, *chsd clr ldr till wknd aftr 8th, sn beh.*.........(16 to 1 op 12 to 1) 5
Dist: 1¾l, 25l, 5l, 2½l. 4m 47.70s. a 10.70s (5 Ran).
(Mrs T McCoubrey), J R Jenkins

439 **Trans World Exhibitions Novices' Handicap Chase Class E (0-100 5-y-o and up) £3,087 3m 1f 110yds... (7:25)**

332* WAKT [87] 6-11-10 A P McCoy, *led 6th to 7th and frm 8th, clr 2 out, very easily.* (9 to 2 on op 4 to 1 on tchd 7 to 2) 1
362⁵ JIMMY THE JACKDAW [63] (bl) 9-10-0 B Fenton, *led to 6th and 7th to 8th, rdn and ev ch appr 3 out, no chance whn wnr...* (5 to 1 op 7 to 2 tchd 11 to 2 and 6 to 1) 2
247 PRIESTHILL (Ire) [65] 7-10-2² P Holley, *jmpd badly, tld off and reluctant to race frm 12th, refused 4 out, continued, f four out, rmntd, pld up bef 2 out.*...(10 to 1 op 8 to 1 tchd 12 to 1) pu
Dist: 5l. 6m 29.70s. a 15.70s (3 Ran).
(John R White), J White

440 **Buxted Novices' Hurdle Class E (4-y-o and up) £2,343 2½m......................(7:55)**

387³ SHALIK (Ire) 6-10-12 J Railton, *led second, made rst, drw clr last, pushed out.*.........(2 to 1 op 7 to 4 tchd 9 to 4) 1
326⁵ LAC DE GRAS (Ire) 5-10-12 D Morris, *chsd wnr 3rd, rdn and ev ch 2 out, wknd appr last.* (3 to 1 op 2 to 1 tchd 3 to 1) 2
359 BRIGADIER SUPREME (Ire) (bl) 7-10-12 T J Murphy, *mstks, led to second, beh frm 8th, tld off whn blun 2 out and last.*
..................(14 to 1 op 7 to 1 tchd 16 to 1 and 20 to 1) 3
330 KAMA SIMBA 4-10-9 A P McCoy, *not jump wl, hld up, rdn and prog aftr 8th, wknd after 3 out, pld up bef nxt, dismounted, dead.*..................(13 to 8 fav op 11 to 10) pu
Dist: 9l, dist. 5m 1.80s. a 24.80s (4 Ran).
(S Curran), J R Jenkins

ROSCOMMON (IRE) (good)
Monday August 19th

441 **Roscommon Handicap Chase (0-123 4-y-o and up) £2,740 3m 100yds (5:00)**

357* VERY LITTLE (Ire) [-] 8-9-12 J P Broderick, ...(7 to 1) 1
312* TRYFIRION (Ire) [-] 7-11-11 (3*) B Bowens, ...(13 to 4 fav) 2
345* FRIDAY THIRTEENTH (Ire) [-] 7-10-10 A Powell, ...(8 to 1) 3
314⁸ NEBRASKA [-] 10-10-1 C F Swan, ...(10 to 1) 4
312⁸ SHANKORAK (Ire) [-] 9-10-10 C O'Dwyer, ...(7 to 1) 5
STRADBALLEY (Ire) [-] 6-10-2 P Woods, ...(10 to 1) 6
293⁶ SWALLOWS NEST (Ire) [-] 9-11-8 W T Slattery, ...(3 to 1) pu
Dist: 2½l, 9l, 1l, ¾l. 6m 14.30s. (7 Ran).
(Dermot Lynch), P J Lally

442 **Elphin 3-y-o Maiden Hurdle £2,397 2m ....(5:30)**

341⁴ MISS ROBERTO (Ire) 10-5 K F O'Brien, ...(7 to 4 fav) 1
341⁹ SPIONAN (USA) (bl) 10-10 R Dunwoody, ...(10 to 1) 2
RENATA'S PRINCE (Ire) 10-10 J Shortt, ...(2 to 1) 3
TOY'S AWAY (Ire) 10-10 F Woods, ...(12 to 1) 4
HENCARLAM (Ire) 10-10 C O'Dwyer, ...(12 to 1) 5
DISPOSEN (Ire) 10-5 F Woods, ...(7 to 1) 6

IMAGINE THE CHAT (Ire) 10-3 (7*) J M Maguire, ...(14 to 1) 7
KILLARY (Ire) 10-3 (7*) M P Dunne, ...(10 to 1) 8
MINGLE (Ire) 10-5 C F Swan, ...(8 to 1) pu
Dist: 15l, 3½l, 8l, 2l. 3m 54.00s. (9 Ran).
(Mrs T Dalton), Martin Brassil

443 **Castle Handicap Hurdle (0-116 4-y-o and up) £2,740 3m.............(6:00)**

344* TABU LADY (Ire) [-] (bl) 5-10-0 F Woods, ...(8 to 1) 1
392³ CELIO LUCY (Ire) [-] 6-9-11 (7*) P Morris, ...(14 to 1) 2
292⁷ CLAIRE ME (Ire) [-] 7-9-8 P McWilliams, ...(20 to 1) 3
WICKLOW WAY (Ire) [-] 6-10-1 C O'Dwyer, ...(4 to 1) 4
355* SUDDEN STORM (Ire) [-] 5-10-10 R Dunwoody,
..................(100 to 30 fav) 5
302⁴ FINAL TUB [-] 13-10-6 T Horgan, ...(15 to 2) 6
301⁶ PRECEPTOR (Ire) [-] 7-11-5 B Bowens, ...(6 to 1) 7
355² DUNDOCK WOOD [-] 8-10-8 K F O'Brien, ...(9 to 2) pu
Dist: 2l, ½l, 4½l, 1l. 5m 51.80s. (8 Ran).
(P McWilliams), W Rock

444 **Castlerea INH Flat Race (4-y-o and up) £2,397 2m......................(7:30)**

SPIN THE WHEEL (Ire) 5-11-7 (7*) Mr A C Coyle, .. (4 to 1) 1
393⁶ TINERANA GLOW (Ire) 4-11-4 Mr D Marnane, ...(12 to 1) 2
286⁹ SIR GANDOUGE (Ire) 7-12-0 Mr M Halford, ...(3 to 1) 3
316⁵ INHERITIS (Ire) 4-10-11 (7*) Mr D A Harney, ...(14 to 1) 4
ANN'S DESIRE (Ire) 5-11-9 Mrs C Barker, ...(8 to 1) 5
394² CARRICK GLEN (Ire) 5-11-2 (7*) Mr A Ross, ...(7 to 4 fav) 6
238 CHARLIEADAMS (Ire) 6-11-7 (7*) Mr A G Cash, ...(25 to 1) 7
NEWBOG LAD (Ire) 5-11-7 (7*) Mr C P Donnelly, ...(20 to 1) 8
DERRYOWEN (Ire) 6-12-0 Mr A J Martin, ...(14 to 1) 9
LORD KNOCKEMSTIFF (Ire) 5-11-7 (7*) Miss S McDonogh,
..................(14 to 1) 10
MAID OF BENBRADAGH (Ire) 5-11-2 (7*) Mrs A Torrens,
..................(25 to 1) pu
Dist: 11l, 7l, hd, 3l. 3m 46.20s. (11 Ran).
(John Joseph Hanlon), P Mullins

EXETER (firm)
Wednesday August 21st
Going Correction: MINUS 0.15 sec. per fur.

445 **Bramble Conditional Jockeys' Selling Handicap Hurdle Class G (0-95 4-y-o and up) £1,781 2m 1f 110yds... (2:25)**

497 BUGLET [86] 6-11-6 D Walsh, *al prmnt, led appr 2 out, ran on wl.*..................(5 to 1 op 3 to 1) 1
225⁵ NORDIC CROWN (Ire) [75] (bl) 5-10-9 R Massey, *al prmnt, chsd wnr and hrd rdn frm 2 out, one pace.*.......(3 to 1 jt-fav op 11 to 4 tchd 7 to 2) 2
334⁵ DENOMINATION (USA) [93] 4-11-5 (5*) G Supple, *hld up in rear, mstk 4th, hdwy appr 2 out, one pace frm last.*
..................(4 to 1 op 3 to 1 tchd 9 to 2) 3
331 COEUR BATTANT (Fr) [66] 6-10-0 T Dascombe, *led, drvn clr 3 out, hdd and wknd bef nxt.* (6 to 1 op 7 to 1 tchd 8 to 1) 4
STARSHADOW [66] 7-9-9 (5*) J Power, *in tch till hrd rdn and wknd 4th, tld off frm 3 out.*
..................(33 to 1 tchd 40 to 1 and 50 to 1) 5
CHELWORTH WOLF [70] 4-10-1 Michael Brennan, *wl beh frm 5th, tld off.*..................(12 to 1 op 10 to 1) 6
403⁴ BEAM ME UP SCOTTY (Ire) [81] (v) 7-11-1 J Culloty, *in tch to 4th, 6th and rdn whn f 3 out.....* (3 to 1 jt-fav op 4 to 1) f
Dist: 2½l, 3l, 1¼l, dist, ¾l. 4m 1.10s. a 5.10s (7 Ran).
SR: 15/1/13/-/ (Mrs Helen L Stoneman), M C Pipe

446 **Interlink Express Delivery Maiden Hurdle Class E (4-y-o and up) £2,232 2m 1f 110yds...................(2:55)**

MISS FOXY 6-11-0 J Frost, *chsd ldr, led appr 2 out, ran on wl.*..................(5 to 1) 1
327⁷ FLEET CADET (bl) 5-11-5 D Bridgwater, *hld up, hdwy 3 out, ev ch nxt, hrd rdn and not quicken appr last.*
..................(2 to 1 op 2 to 1 tchd 7 to 4 and 9 to 4) 2
330² ALMAPA 4-10-13 (3*) T Dascombe, *al prmnt, ev ch appr 2 out, wknd approaching last.*
..................(6 to 4 fav op 2 to 1 tchd 9 to 4) 3
384³ REGAL GEM 5-11-0 B Fenton, *hld up, hdwy 3 out, rdn and one pace frm nxt....* (3 to 1 op 1 to 1 tchd 7 to 2) 4
FALCONS DAWN 9-11-5 Miss L Blackford, *led till wknd appr 2 out.*..................(33 to 1 op 25 to 1) 5
334³ MUTLEY 6-11-2 (3*) J Culloty, *pld hrd in rear, effrt 3 out, sn rdn and wknd.*..................(5 to 1 op 9 to 2) 6
Dist: 6l, 3½l, ¾l, 10l, 11l. 4m 7.50s. a 11.50s (6 Ran).
(P A Tylor), R G Frost

447 **City Of Exeter Challenge Bowl Handicap Chase Class D (0-120 5-y-o and up) £4,215 2m 3f...................(3:30)**

327² HENLEY REGATTA [94] 8-11-7 S Burrough, *led 9th, clr appr 4 out.*..........(9 to 4 op 2 to 1 tchd 11 to 4 and 3 to 1) 1

362* POND HOUSE (Ire) [97] 7-11-10 D Bridgwater, *led to 9th, wknd quickly appr 4 out, jmpd slwly 3 out, pld up bef nxt.*
....(3 to 1 on op 3 to 1 on) pu
Won by 4m 41.90s. a 13.90s (2 Ran).
SR: -/-/
(E T Wey), P R Rodford

448 Interlink Express Parcels Novices' Hurdle Class D (4-y-o and up) £2,707 2m 3f.............................(4:05)

370* SHAHRANI 4-12-1 D Bridgwater, *made virtually all, hrd rdn appr 2 out, all out.*
...............(2 to 1 on tchd 13 to 8 on and 6 to 4 on) 1
376³ BORN TO PLEASE (Ire) 4-11-3 A P McCoy, *mstk 3rd, chsd wnr, ev ch and hng lft frm 2 out, no extr nr finish.*
.......................(7 to 4 op 13 to 8 tchd 15 to 8) 2
ON MY TOES 5-10-9 J Frost, *al last, tld off frm 5th.*
.....................................(12 to 1 op 16 to 1) 3
Dist: 1¼l, dist. 4m 21.60s. a 5.60s (3 Ran).
SR: 16/2/-/
(A S Helaissi And M S Helaissi), M C Pipe

449 Interlink Express Data Novices' Chase Class D (5-y-o and up) £3,550 2m 3f ....(4:35)

DUBELLE 6-10-4 (3*) J Culloty, *al prmnt, led 5 out, jmpd rght last 4, ran on wl.*..............(16 to 1 op 12 to 1) 1
BISHOPS CASTLE (Ire) 8-10-12 J Frost, *al prmnt, chsd wnr frm 3 out, hrd rdn from last, no imprsn.*
.................................(12 to 1 op 10 to 1 tchd 14 to 1) 2
400* DISTANT MEMORY (bl) 7-11-5 A P McCoy, *led to 7th, led 8th to 5 out, wknd 3 out.*
..............(Evens fav op 5 to 4 tchd 11 to 8 and 6 to 4) 3
156 OUR NIKKI 6-10-7 S Burrough, *sn wl beh, hdwy appr 4 out, nvr on terms.*......................(25 to 1 op 33 to 1) 4
OCTOBER BREW (USA) (bl) 6-10-9 (3*) D Walsh, *led 7th to nxt, wknd 5 out, tld off.....(6 to 1 op 7 to 1 tchd 10 to 1) 5
123 ROBERT'S TOY (Ire) (bl) 5-11-8 D Bridgwater, *jmpd stickily in midfield, wknd 5 out, tld off frm nxt.*
.................................(7 to 4 op 6 to 4 tchd 15 to 8) 6
335⁵ TANGO'S DELIGHT 8-11-5 B Powell, *6th whn f sixth.*
..........................(25 to 1 op 16 to 1 tchd 33 to 1) f
332 LIBERTY JAMES 9-10-12 G Upton, *sn tld off, pld up bef 4 out.*
.................................(66 to 1 op 50 to 1) pu
Dist: 5l, 23l, 12l, dist, 3½l. 4m 36.20s. a 8.20s (8 Ran).
(W J Lee), J S King

450 Interlink Express Freight Novices' Handicap Hurdle Class E (0-100 4-y-o and up) £2,232 2¾m............(5:05)

326⁰ AKIYMANN (USA) [81] (bl) 6-11-10 D Bridgwater, *led appr 5 out, clr approaching 2 out, unchlgd.*
........(7 to 4 on op 5 to 2 on tchd 13 to 8 on and 6 to 4 on) 1
EMBLEY BUOY [60] 8-10-3 S Curran, *led till appr 5 out, wknd approaching 2 out.*..................(9 to 4 op 5 to 2) 2
WISSYWIS (Ire) [65] 4-10-5 B Fenton, *tld off frm 6th.*
....(7 to 1 op 5 to 1) 3
Dist: 16l, dist. 5m 19.00s. a 22.00s (3 Ran).
(Martin Pipe Racing Club), M C Pipe

HEREFORD (firm)
Wednesday August 21st
Going Correction: PLUS 0.10 sec. per fur.

451 Much Marcle Conditional Jockeys' Handicap Hurdle Class F (0-100 4-y-o and up) £2,570 2m 3f 110yds... (5:40)

370² CHINA MAIL (Ire) [90] 4-11-8 T J Murphy, *hld up in rear, hdwy 5th, mstk and reminder nxt, rdn appr 3 out, led approaching last, drvn out.*.......(3 to 1 op 5 to 2 tchd 100 to 30) 1
SLIPPERY MAX [72] 12-10-7 R Massey, *prmnt, led aftr 3 out, hdd appr last, one pace.*.................(20 to 1 op 12 to 1) 2
377* LORD TOMANICO (Fr) [92] 4-11-10 J Magee, *led to 3rd, rgned ld 7th, hdd aftr 3 out, wknd bef last.*
.....................................(2 to 1 on tchd 9 to 4 on) 3
SUKAAB [80] 11-11-1 T Dascombe, *hld up, hdwy 5th, wknd frm 7th.*....................................(9 to 1 op 8 to 1) 4
414 BATTY'S ISLAND [89] (bl) 7-11-7 (3*) D Finnegan, *prmnt, led 3rd, hdd 7th, wknd 4 out.*
......................(16 to 1 op 10 to 1 tchd 20 to 1) 5
Dist: 5l, 10l, 10l, 16l. 4m 43.90s. a 25.90s (5 Ran).
(The Merlin Syndicate), K C Bailey

452 Malvern Link Handicap Chase Class F (0-105 5-y-o and up) £3,186 2m 3f ....(6:10)

386* MAGGOTS GREEN [82] 9-10-13 (7ex) R Johnson, *led to second, rgned ld aftr tenth, clr 3 out, blun nxt, eased r-in.*
....(9 to 4 op 7 to 2) 1
368² DRUMSTICK [96] 10-11-13 J Railton, *led second till aftr nxt, wnt second after 3 out, no ch wth wnr.* (7 to 4 tchd 2 to 1) 2

402² MANAMOUR [82] 9-10-13 C Llewellyn, *prmnt, led aftr 3rd, hdd after tenth, second and wkng whn mstk 3 out.*
....(6 to 4 fav op 7 to 4) 3
Dist: 5l, 30l. 4m 42.50s. a 17.50s (3 Ran).
(E A Hayward), J M Bradley

453 Hendre Handicap Hurdle Class E (0-110 4-y-o and up) £2,822 3¼m ....(6:40)

302² GLENGARRIF GIRL (Ire) [108] (v) 6-12-0 D Bridgwater, *al hndy, led aftr 3 out, hdd last, rallied und pres to rgn ld cl hme.*
....(6 to 4 on op 11 to 8 on) 1
FOX CHAPEL [87] 9-10-7 M A Fitzgerald, *hld up, lft in second 2 out, led last, hdd cl hme.*...........(20 to 1 op 14 to 1) 2
STORM DRUM [95] (bl) 7-11-1 T J Murphy, *prmnt, rdn frm 4 out.*...............................(7 to 1 op 6 to 1) 3
420* WYNBERG [106] 5-11-8 (7ex) S Wynne, *led till aftr 3 out, still ev ch whn f nxt.*.........(15 to 8 op 6 to 4 tchd 2 to 1) f
Dist: ½l, 14l. 6m 20.70s. a 18.70s (4 Ran).
(David L'Estrange), M C Pipe

454 Wormbridge Novices' Hurdle Class E (4-y-o and up) £2,276 2m 1f.... (7:10)

297⁵ CHANCEY FELLA 5-11-5 A P McCoy, *made all, sn clr, unchlgd.*.......(11 to 2 on op 7 to 1 on tchd 5 to 1 on) 1
423⁷ GALLOPING GUNS (Ire) 4-10-9 B Powell, *took str hold, chsd wnr, no ch frm 3 out.*..............(8 to 1 op 12 to 1) 2
186⁷ PATS FOLLY 7-11-0 P McLoughlin, *pld hrd, hld up, dsptd poor second frm 4 out, wknd bef nxt.*..........(10 to 1 op 6 to 1) 3
129 LITTLE DERRING 5-10-7 R Johnson, *not fluent, tld off sn aftr 3rd.*.................................(16 to 1 tchd 20 to 1) 4
Dist: 25l, 19l, dist. 3m 58.00s. a 12.00s (4 Ran).
(Mrs H E Haynes), H E Haynes

455 Aconbury Novices' Handicap Chase Class E (0-100 5-y-o and up) £2,860 3m 1f 110yds.................(7:40)

201² CUCHLLAINS GOLD (Ire) [80] 8-11-9 N Williamson, *hld up, led appr 4 out, hdd bef nxt, rgned ld aftr 2 out, lft clr last.*
....(6 to 4 fav op 2 to 1) 1
362⁶ CARDAN [62] 10-10-5 B Powell, *keen hold, chsd ldr, led 5th till appr 8th, led ag'n 11th till approaching 4 out, sn wknd, tld off.*...................(12 to 1 op 10 to 1 tchd 14 to 1) 2
323³ DUKE OF LANCASTER (Ire) [85] (v) 7-12-0 R Bellamy, *led till appr 3rd, jmpd slwly 5th, led ag'n approaching 8th, mstk tenth, hdd out, wknd 12th, tld off.*
....(8 to 1 tchd 10 to 1) 3
MUTUAL AGREEMENT [73] 9-11-2 A P McCoy, *hld up, not fluent 8th, hdwy 4 out, led bef nxt, hdd aftr 2 out, second and held whn f last.*..........(5 to 2 op 2 to 1 tchd 11 to 4) f
106⁸ MISS DOTTY [64] 6-10-7 D Bridgwater, *sn wl beh, tld off whn pld up bef tenth.*
.....................(9 to 2 op 3 to 1 tchd 5 to 1 and 11 to 2) pu
Dist: Dist, 1¼l. 6m 26.70s. a 20.70s (5 Ran).
(M A McEvoy), J White

456 Border Standard Open National Hunt Flat Class H (4,5,6-y-o) £1,315 2m 1f ....(8:10)

336² RED TEL (Ire) 4-11-1 D Bridgwater, *wtd wth, prog on inner aftr 6 fs, led 4 out, edgd lft frm o'r one out, all out.*
.......................(2 to 1 fav op 5 to 4 tchd 5 to 2) 1
157 RARE SPREAD (Ire) 6-11-1 (3*) D Walsh, *mid-div, hdwy frm hfwy, hmpd 5 fs out, ev ch whn crrd lft from o'r one out, ran on.*.......(4 to 1 op 5 to 2 tchd 9 to 2 and 5 to 1) 2
191³ POWERFUL SPIRIT 4-10-10 (5*) Michael Brennan, *towards rear, hdwy o'r 6 fs out, effrt 3 out, no extr fnl 2 furlongs.*
.......................(5 to 2 tchd 9 to 4 and 11 to 4) 3
336³ KATHARINE'S SONG (Ire) 6-10-13 B Powell, *hld up beh ldrs, led 6 fs out, hdd 4 out, wknd appr fnl 2. (20 to 1 op 16 to 1) 4
SIERRA NEVADA 5-11-4 A P McCoy, *hld up beh ldrs, effrt 4 fs out, btn 3 out.* (6 to 1 op 5 to 1 tchd 7 to 1 and 8 to 1) 5
304 MORECEVA (Ire) 6-11-4 W Marston, *prmnt, wknd 5 fs out.*
....(25 to 1 op 16 to 1) 6
231 COMMANDO DANCER (Ire) 4-10-8 (7*) Shaun Graham, *hld up, detached hfwy, styd on one pace frm 3 out.*
....(33 to 1 tchd 50 to 1) 7
231³ PRIDEWOOD FUGGLE 6-11-4 A Maguire, *hld up beh ldrs, rdn 6 fs out, wknd o'r 4 out.* (7 to 2 op 3 to 1 tchd 4 to 1) 8
ABBEYDORAN 5-10-13 M Bosley, *no imprsn on ldrs.*
....(33 to 1 op 25 to 1) 9
336⁵ LATE ENCOUNTER 5-11-4 R Johnson, *hld up beh ldrs, drvn alng frm hfwy, wknd o'r 5 fs out.....(50 to 1 op 25 to 1) 10
TAILORMADE FUTURE 4-10-8 (7*) D Finnegan, *nvr dngrs.*
....(33 to 1 op 20 to 1) 11
EMMA'S JEWEL (Ire) 5-10-6 (7*) T C Murphy, *pld hrd, prmnt till wknd appr fnl 5 fs...* (25 to 1 op 20 to 1 tchd 33 to 1) 12
FRIZZBALL (Ire) 4-10-10 D Gallagher, *led, hdd 6 fs out, sn wknd.*.........(12 to 1 op 8 to 1 tchd 14 to 1) 13
191 OVERSEAS INVADER (Ire) 4-11-1 N Williamson, *al beh, tld off frm hfwy.*.........................(25 to 1 op 33 to 1) 14
Dist: ½l, 2l, 10l, 1½l, 1½l, 4l, hd, 1½l, 18l, 9l. 3m 50.20s. (14 Ran).
(Terry Neill), M C Pipe

NATIONAL HUNT RESULTS 1996-97

CARTMEL (good to firm)
Thursday August 22nd
Going Correction: MINUS 0.30 sec. per fur.

457 Burlington Slate Claiming Hurdle Amateur Riders' Class F (4-y-o and up) £1,892 2m 1f 110yds........... (5:45)

80	BURES (Ire) (v) 5-10-12 (7*) Mr R Wakley, *led aftr 1st, rdn clr r-in...*..........(5 to 4 fav op 5 to 4 on tchd 11 to 8)	1
295[5]	HACKETTS CROSS (Ire) 8-10-6 (7*) Mr R Thornton, *chsd clr ldrs, pckd 1st, hdwy to chase wnr last, no imprsn*...(5 to 1)	2
372[2]	BETABETCORBETT (bl) 5-10-6 (7*) Mr A Wintle, *led till aftr 1st, chsd ldr, not fluent nxt, mstk 4th, rdn and wknd last*..........................(11 to 2 op 6 to 1)	3
371[4]	SILVER SLEEVE (Ire) (bl) 4-11-0 (3*) Mr C Bonner, *beh, struggling 4 out, nvr a factor*.. (11 to 4 op 3 to 1 tchd 5 to 2)	4
167	OLD MORTALITY 10-10-8 (5*) Mr R Hale, *beh, drvn alng and lost tch 4 out, tld off*..........................(33 to 1)	5
	TOLL BOOTH 7-9-9 (7*) Miss P Robson, *beh, not fluent second, pld up bef nxt, broke dwn*....(33 to 1 op 25 to 1)	pu

Dist: 8l, 14l, 4l, dist. 4m 2.30s. a 2.30s (6 Ran).
SR: 16/2/-/
(John Wimbs), M H Tompkins

458 Nirex Handicap Chase Class E (0-115 5-y-o and up) £3,006 2m 5f 110yds .... (6:15)

	EARLYMORNING LIGHT (Ire) [115] 7-12-0 A Dobbin, *jmpd wl, trkd ldr, led 4 out, clr aftr last, eased finish.*..........(11 to 10 on op 6 to 4 on)	1
37[3]	BLAZING DAWN [87] 9-10-0 B Storey, *led, jmpd slwly 5th, hdd 4 out, outpcd frm last and lost second, rgned second fnl 100 yards, no ch wth wnr*..........(4 to 1 tchd 5 to 1)	2
167[2]	THE TOASTER [97] 9-10-10 M Dwyer, *trkd ldrs, struggling 4 out, chsd clr lder aftr last, lost second fnl 100 yards.*...................(7 to 4 tchd 2 to 1)	3
124	MISS ENRICO [91] 10-10-4[2] A Thornton, *rear, mstk second, jmpd slwly nxt, niggled alng 9th, lost tch 4 out, tld off.*..........................(25 to 1 op 14 to 1)	4

Dist: 2l, 1¼l, dist. 5m 21.70s. a 11.70s (4 Ran).
(Mrs Ann Starkie), G Richards

459 Oxley Developments Novices' Chase Class E (5-y-o and up) £2,338 3¼m .... (6:45)

306[3]	SCRABO VIEW (Ire) 8-10-12 R Supple, *al prmnt, mstk 13th, led nxt, hdd 3 out, led next, kpt on und pres.*..........(11 to 10 fav op 6 to 4 tchd 13 to 8)	1
	DEFINITE MAYBE (Ire) (bl) 6-10-12 A P McCoy, *trkd ldrs, drvn 14th, narrow ld 3 out, tried to refuse and hdd nxt, chlgd r-in, no extr finish*..........................(6 to 4 op 5 to 4)	2
	DONOVANS REEF 10-11-2 A Thornton, *led, mstk 4th, hdd 14th, sn wknd, tld off whn almost refused last.*..........(28 to 1 op 20 to 1 tchd 33 to 1)	3
	SAND KING (NZ) (bl) 10-10-12 D Bentley, *beh, mstk 7th, jmpd slwly nxt, lost tch, tld off whn pld up bef 13th.*..........................(13 to 2 op 6 to 1 tchd 7 to 1)	pu
247[7]	DUSTYS TRAIL (Ire) [7] 7-10-12 R Johnson, *not jump wl, sn drvn alng, lost tch 8th, tld off whn pld up aftr 14th.*..........................(12 to 1 op 8 to 1)	pu

Dist: 1l, dist. 6m 40.20s. a 23.20s (5 Ran).
(Robin Mellish), P Beaumont

460 Colony Candle Handicap Hurdle Class D (0-120 4-y-o and up) £2,532 2¾m .... (7:15)

281[5]	AMAZON EXPRESS [94] 7-11-10 R Johnson, *trkd ldr till appr 4 out, drvn and outpcd nxt, effrt last, led fnl half-furlong, styd on.*..........................(5 to 1 op 7 to 2)	1
	TAKE TWO [92] 8-11-8 A Dobbin, *hld up, hdwy aftr 7th, led after nxt to 3 out, led after 2 out, hdd and no extr fnl half-furlong*..........................(11 to 4 op 9 to 2)	2
	VALIANT DASH [86] 10-10-13 (3*) G Cahill, *led till aftr 4 out, sn outpcd, effrt last, wide strt, one pace.* (11 to 2 op 9 to 2)	3
25[3]	MASTER OFTHE HOUSE [90] 10-11-6 R Garritty, *trkd ldrs to 4 out, lost nxt till aftr 2 out, sn rdn, outpcd frm last.*..........................(Evens fav op 5 to 4 on)	4

Dist: 1l, 3l, 1½l. 5m 33.40s. a 26.40s (4 Ran).
(T M Morris), P Bowen

461 B.N.F.L. Novices' Handicap Chase Class E (0-100 5-y-o and up) £2,381 2m 1f 110yds .... (7:45)

	SEAHAWK RETRIEVER [65] 7-10-9 A P McCoy, *chsd ldrs, mstk 6th, lft clr nxt, mistake 9th, fnshd alone.*..........................(7 to 4 op 6 to 4)	1
	ANOTHER NICK [68] 10-10-12 B Storey, *jmpd slwly second, f nxt.*.......... (25 to 1 op 20 to 1 tchd 33 to 1)	f
412[3]	GREEN'S SEAGO (USA) [75] 8-11-0 (5*,7ex) P Henley, *chsd ldr till f 7th.*..........(5 to 4 fav tchd 6 to 4)	f
412[2]	EXCLUSION [80] 7-11-10 R Marley, *rcd freely, led till f 7th.*..........................(9 to 2 op 5 to 1)	f
26	BOETHIUS (USA) [80] 7-11-10 P Waggott, *not jump wl, beh, lost tch 5th, tld off whn refused last.* (12 to 1 tchd 14 to 1)	ref

Dist: 4m 37.30s. a 26.30s (5 Ran).
(Mrs Robert Blackburn), P F Nicholls

462 Hospice Of St Mary Of Furness Maiden Hurdle Class E (4-y-o and up) £2,532 3¼m........................... (8:15)

	GOOD HAND (USA) 10-11-5 R Johnson, *not fluent, hld up, hdwy to chal appr 3 out, mstk nxt, led approaching last, sn clr, eased cl hme.*..........(11 to 8 on op 6 to 4 on tchd 11 to 10 on)	1
385	THE GALLOPIN'MAJOR (Ire) (bl) 6-11-5 N Smith, *hld up, led 4 out, hdd briefly bef nxt, headed appr last, sn btn.*..................(100 to 30 op 4 to 1 tchd 11 to 4)	2
	MEGAMUNCH (Ire) 8-11-5 W Marston, *prmnt, led briefly appr 3 out, outpcd nxt*......(16 to 1 op 12 to 1 tchd 20 to 1)	3
226[7]	FENWICK'S BROTHER 6-11-5 O Pears, *keen hold, led at slow pace, hdd appr 4 out, sn drvn and wknd, tld off.*..........................(11 to 4 tchd 3 to 1)	4

Dist: 3l, 2l, dist. 6m 36.40s. a 38.40s (4 Ran).
(Uncle Jacks Pub), S E Kettlewell

TIPPERARY (IRE) (yielding)
Thursday August 22nd

463 I.T.B.A./Breeders Supporting Tipperary Novice Hurdle (4-y-o and up) £3,596 2m...........................(6:10)

211[*]	TARAJAN (USA) (bl) 4-11-2 J Short, ...(5 to 1)	1
316[2]	FRAU DANTE (Ire) 6-10-9 C O'Dwyer, ...(7 to 1)	2
	PRYS PAUPER (Ire) 8-11-0 F Woods, ...(50 to 1)	3
337[*]	MUSKERRY KING (Ire) 5-11-7 W Slattery, ...(10 to 1)	4
347[*]	SHANRUE (Ire) 6-11-7 C F Swan, ...(6 to 1)	5
329[*]	LOLLIA PAULINA (Ire) 5-10-2 (7*) Mr Edgar Byrne, (16 to 1)	6
340[*]	LISHILLAUN (Ire) 6-10-4 (5*) Susan A Finn, ...(16 to 1)	7
364[6]	IRVINE (Ire) 4-10-9 G M O'Neill, ...(33 to 1)	8
339[8]	FRED OF THE HILL (Ire) 5-11-7 K F O'Brien, ...(50 to 1)	9
	NATIVE SUCCESS (Ire) 5-10-9 T J O'Sullivan, ...(50 to 1)	10
291[*]	LIFE SUPPORT (Ire) 4-10-11 P Carberry, ...(11 to 8 on)	pu

Dist: 1l, 15l, 3l, 15l. 4m 1.10s. (11 Ran).
(Ms Maura Horan), Patrick Prendergast

464 Kilmurry I.N.H. Flat Race (4-y-o and up) £2,397 2m...........................(8:10)

	ABORIGINAL (Ire) 4-11-2 (7*) Mr A C Coyle, ... (Evens fav)	1
434[4]	PLEASE NO TEARS 9-11-9 Mrs C Barker, ...(12 to 1)	2
340[2]	GRAIGUE HILL (Ire) 7-11-2 (7*) Mr R M Walsh, ...(10 to 1)	3
	BESSMOUNT LEADER (Ire) 4-11-6 (3*) Mr B M Cash, ...(9 to 2)	4
288[6]	CASTLE ELLEN BOY (Ire) 4-11-2 (7*) Mr P J Gilligan, ...(25 to 1)	5
365[4]	GAIN CONTROL (Ire) 7-11-2 (7*) Miss O Hayes, ...(14 to 1)	6
434[2]	MALICE 10-11-6 (3*) Mr J Connolly, ...(12 to 1)	7
	SILKEN SECRETARIAT (Ire) 5-11-11 (3*) Mr P English, ...(14 to 1)	8
144[6]	BARLEY COURT (Ire) 6-11-9 (5*) Mr P A Deegan, ..(16 to 1)	9
	BALMY NATIVE (Ire) 4-11-9 Mr J P Dempsey, ...(14 to 1)	10
	BALLYLENNON LADY (Ire) 6-11-4 (5*) Mr R Walsh, (33 to 1)	11
430[6]	RADICAL ACTION (Ire) 6-11-7 (7*) Miss S McDonogh, ...(20 to 1)	12
407[9]	ZIGGY THE GREAT (Ire) (bl) 4-11-9 Mr R Maране, (33 to 1)	13
407	NAHRANAH (Ire) 4-10-11 (7*) Mr John P Moloney, (33 to 1)	14
	PHAR'N'WIDE (Ire) 5-11-9 Mr P Fenton, ...(12 to 1)	15
	STRAIGHTFORWARD (Ire) 8-11-7 (7*) Mr P Cody, (14 to 1)	16
	O'SULLIVANS CHOISE (Ire) 8-11-7 (7*) Mr D P Quinn, ...(33 to 1)	17
407[2]	WILLIE BRENNAN (Ire) 4-11-2 (7*) Mr Sean O O'Brien, ...(11 to 2)	su
	OPTIMISM REIGNS (Ire) 5-11-7 (7*) Mr J T McNamara, ...(14 to 1)	pu

Dist: 4½l, 2l, 4l, 1½l. 3m 59.30s. (19 Ran).
(Mrs P Mullins), P Mullins

CLAIREFONTAINE (FR) (soft)
Friday August 23rd

465 Prix des Troenes (Hurdle) (5-y-o and up) £6,588 2m 1f........................... (3:36)

328[*]	COUNTRY STAR (Ire) 5-10-4[2] G Bradley, *made all, quickened clr 2 out, ran on wl*...........................	1
	LEON DES PERRETS (Fr) 5-10-2 L Gerrard, ...	2
	DARRA (Fr) 5-9-11 F Menard, ...	3

Dist: 3l, sht-hd, 2½l, 6l, 8l, 4l, 10l, 15l, 10l. 3m 57.50s. (11 Ran).
(H R H Prince Fahd Salman), C P E Brooks

KILBEGGAN (IRE) (good)

NATIONAL HUNT RESULTS 1996-97

Friday August 23rd

466 Loughnagore Maiden Hurdle (5-y-o and up) £2,226 3m............(5:00)

358²	ALL FOR MAX (Ire) 7-11-6 P A Roche,............ (6 to 4)	1
	BLACK BOREEN (Ire) 6-12-0 C F Swan,........(Evens fav)	2
233⁹	MOON-FROG 9-11-6 F Woods,....................(20 to 1)	3
395⁶	FIX THE SPEC (Ire) 6-11-6 R Dunwoody,......... (7 to 1)	4
	ATTYSLANEY (Ire) 5-10-13 (7") A O'Shea,........ (20 to 1)	5
304	CORKERS FLAME (Ire) 5-11-6 W Slattery,........ (8 to 1)	6
	PRIME PAPERS 11-11-6 C O'Dwyer,............. (25 to 1)	7
	BALLYGRANT 9-11-7 (7") Mr B Valentine,........(20 to 1)	pu

Dist: 25l, 7l, 9l, 3½l. 6m 4.50s. (8 Ran).

(Gerard Halley), Gerard Halley

467 Tullamore Mares Maiden Hurdle (4-y-o and up) £2,226 2m 3f...........(5:30)

353²	ALLATRIM (Ire) 6-12-0 R Dunwoody,............(7 to 4 on)	1
424²	FOREST LADY (Ire) 4-11-1 (3") D T Evans,........ (8 to 1)	2
392²	FLYING IN THE GALE (Ire) 5-10-13 (7") A O'Shea,.. (8 to 1)	3
410⁵	GARLAND ROSE (Ire) 6-11-3 (3") D J Casey,...... (7 to 1)	4
	BIT OF A SET TOO (Ire) 5-11-6 C F Swan,........ (9 to 1)	5
407	SOLAR CASTLE (Ire) 6-10-13 (7") Mr T J Nagle Jnr, (33 to 1)	6
277	RATHNALLY STAR (Ire) 5-11-6 J P Broderick,......(14 to 1)	7
185⁹	ROSEY BUCK 4-11-1 (3") G Kilfeather,........... (14 to 1)	8
397⁶	BULA DELA (Ire) (bl) 6-10-13 (7") Mr A Fleming, ...(33 to 1)	9
365⁵	STRADBALLY JANE (Ire) 6-12-0 T Horgan,........ (8 to 1)	10
	BALLYHAYS LODGE (Ire) 7-11-3 (3") B Bowens, ...(14 to 1)	ref
404⁸	SCOTCH ROSE (Ire) 6-11-6 K F O'Brien,.........(16 to 1)	pu
350	ASTRID (Ire) 5-11-6 C O'Dwyer,................(20 to 1)	pu

Dist: 3½l, 2l, 7l, 13l. 4m 32.70s. (13 Ran).

(E R Madden), E J O'Grady

468 Tara Meats Maiden Hurdle (4-y-o and up) £2,740 2m 3f..............(6:00)

	LOUGHLOONE (Ire) 5-11-9 C F Swan,.........(9 to 2 co-fav)	1
404⁵	COLONIA SKY (Ire) 5-11-2 (7") Mr P R Lenihan, ...(10 to 1)	2
396⁷	DEABHAILIN (Ire) 6-12-0 C O'Dwyer,............ (12 to 1)	3
	CREGG ROSE 6-11-9 T Horgan,................(14 to 1)	4
21⁷	MANTON GIRL (Ire) 5-11-6 J P Broderick,........ (7 to 1)	5
276	NOBODYWANTSME (Ire) (bl) 5-11-9 (5") T Martin, (25 to 1)	6
392	RONETTE (Ire) 5-12-0 R Dunwoody,...........(9 to 2 co-fav)	7
347⁸	DANGAN LAD (USA) 4-11-9 S H O'Donovan,...... (5 to 1)	8
404⁶	PRINCESS LENA (Ire) 6-11-3¹ (7") Mr T J Nagle Jnr, (14 to 1)	f
392⁴	JARSUN QUEEN (Ire) 4-10-11 (7") L J Fleming, ...(5 to 1)	pu
233⁴	PUNGAYNOR (Ire) 6-12-0 K F O'Brien,...... (9 to 2 co-fav)	pu

Dist: 11l, 25l, 3½l, 15l. 4m 36.50s. (11 Ran).

(P B Hyland), A P O'Brien

469 Pat Doyle Memorial Handicap Hurdle (0-116 4-y-o and up) £2,226 2m 3f ....(6:30)

275⁴	I REMEMBER IT WELL (Ire) [-] 4-9-8 J P Broderick, (11 to 1)	1
353⁷	JANE DIGBY (Ire) [-] 4-10-13 C F Swan,........ (4 to 1 jt-fav)	2
260²	LEGITMAN (Ire) [-] 6-9-10¹ P Carberry,........(4 to 1 jt-fav)	3
432⁷	FATHER RECTOR (Ire) [-] 7-11-9 (6ex) T Horgan, .. (9 to 2)	4
408⁴	TARA'S TRIBE [-] 9-9-13 T J Mitchell,............(12 to 1)	5
315⁷	ARCTIC KATE [-] 10-12-0 C O'Dwyer,........... (8 to 1)	6
315⁸	LADY DAISY (Ire) [-] 7-11-8 A Powell,........... (7 to 1)	7
396⁴	WILD ROSE OF YORK [-] 5-9-12 (5") P D Carey, ... (8 to 1)	8
408²	FAIR SOCIETY (Ire) [-] (bl) 5-9-7 (7") Mr John P Moloney,	
	....(8 to 1)	f

Dist: Hd, 4l, 3l, 2½l. 4m 35.80s. (9 Ran).

(I Remember It Well Syndicate), Michael Hourigan

470 Cleaboy Stud Handicap Chase (0-109 4-y-o and up) £2,740 2m 5f..... (7:00)

431³	GOT NO CHOICE (Ire) [-] (bl) 6-9-0 (7") M D Murphy, (13 to 2)	1
356⁵	FAYS FOLLY (Ire) [-] 7-9-0 (7") R P Hogan,...... (7 to 1)	2
395⁵	IMANIABOOLA GROVE [-] 9-10-0 P Carberry,.....(11 to 2)	3
429⁶	CAPTAIN BRANDY [-] 11-10-11 K F O'Brien,......(10 to 1)	4
236	BALLINAVEEN BRIDGE [-] 9-9-7 P L Malone,.....(20 to 1)	5
356⁴	MERRY PEOPLE (Ire) [-] 8-11-12 T Horgan,...... (6 to 4 fav)	6
406⁵	THE OUTBACK WAY (Ire) [-] 6-11-9 D H O'Connor,	
	....(7 to 2)	7
138⁶	GLEN OG LANE [-] (bl) 13-9-9² F Woods,........(20 to 1)	ur

Dist: 2½l, 9l, 13l, 4l. 5m 21.80s. (8 Ran).

(Mrs B McCarthy), Donal Hassett

471 Hackett Bookmakers Beginners Chase (4-y-o and up) £2,740 2m 5f..... (7:30)

313²	CUBAN QUESTION 9-12-0 R Dunwoody,........ (7 to 1)	1
311⁵	KENTUCKY BABY (Ire) 6-11-9 C O'Dwyer,........(9 to 1)	2
426⁴	PASSER BY 9-12-0 K F O'Brien,................ (13 to 2)	3
432⁴	VAIN PRINCESS (Ire) 7-11-9 M P Hourigan,...... (4 to 1)	4
357⁴	LET THE RIVER RUN 10-11-9 (7") R P Hogan,.....(14 to 1)	5
391⁶	DUSTY ROSE 7-11-9 M Moran,................ (16 to 1)	6

Dist: 5½l, 4½l, dist, ½l. 5m 25.70s. (6 Ran).

(Laurence Byrne), D T Hughes

472 Moate I.N.H. Flat Race (4-y-o and up) £2,226 2m 3f.................. (8:00)

410³	SUP A WHISKEY (Ire) 5-11-2 (7") Mr Sean O O'Brien, (6 to 1)	1
397²	FANE PATH (Ire) 4-11-9 Mr G J Harford,.........(9 to 2)	2
	HILLTOP BOY (Ire) 7-11-11 (3") Mr B M Cash, ...(9 to 1)	3
394⁵	DUNEAVEY (Ire) 5-11-4 (5") Mr R Walsh,........(7 to 4 fav)	4
311⁸	SANDRA LOUISE (Ire) 6-11-2 (7") Mr A Ross,...... (8 to 1)	5
410⁹	PAUL (Ire) 4-11-2 (7") Mr John P Moloney,.......(25 to 1)	6
304⁷	DEAR CHRIS (Ire) 5-11-2 (7") Mr P J Gilligan,..... (8 to 1)	7
424⁵	JODESI (Ire) 6-12-0 Mr P Fenton,...............(6 to 1)	8
410	CUBAN SKIES (Ire) 6-11-7 (7") Mr M G Coleman, ..(25 to 1)	9
396	GENNY'S SERENADE (Ire) 5-11-2 (7") Mr A J Dempsey,	
	....(12 to 1)	su

Dist: Sht-hd, 14l, 2½l, 6l. 4m 30.40s. (10 Ran).

(Walter James Purcell), A P O'Brien

CARTMEL (good to firm)
Saturday August 24th
Going Correction: NIL

473 Bookmaker & Punter Novices' Hurdle Class E (4-y-o and up) £2,232 2¾m ....(2:25)

	RED SPECTACLE (Ire) 4-10-9 M Foster, made all, jmpd wl, pushed clr 3 out, styd on strly........(3 to 1 tchd 7 to 2)	1
	COMMANDER GLEN (Ire) 4-10-9 R Garritty, patiently rdn, hdwy whn not fluent 3 out, chasing wnr when hit last, unbl to quicken........................(11 to 1 op 7 to 1)	2
	WHAT'S SECRETO (USA) 4-10-9 A Maguire, hld up, not fluent, drvn and outpcd 4 out, sn beh... (13 to 2 op 5 to 1)	3
262	BOWLAND PARK 5-10-7 J Culloty, chsd ldrs, struggling whn not fluent 4 out, sn wl beh.................(5 to 1)	4
388²	LONGCROFT 4-10-11 R Johnson, pressed ldr, not fluent 6th, drvn alng 3 out, wknd quickly nxt, eased.	
	....(11 to 8 on op 11 to 10)	5
	BOYO (Ire) 5-10-12 L Wyer, beh, mstks 5th and 6th, sn lost tch, tld off whn pld up bef 2 out...........(9 to 1 op 7 to 1)	pu

Dist: 8l, dist, 2l, dist, dist. 5m 26.80s. a 19.80s (6 Ran).

(David H Morgan), P C Haslam

474 Lindale Inn Steaks Handicap Hurdle Class G For Conditional Jockeys (0-90 4-y-o and up) £2,206 2¾m ....(2:55)

	HUSO [86] 8-11-7 (3") S Taylor, hld up, steady hdwy to ld 2 out, strly pressed r-in, held on gmely.........(2 to 1 op 9 to 4)	1
379*	RAMPANT ROSIE (Ire) [76] (v) 8-11-0 G Cahill, led, hdd 6th, led ag'n whn slight mstk 3 out, headed nxt, kpt on strly r-in.	
	....(11 to 10 on op 5 to 4 on tchd Evens)	2
	TONY'S FEELINGS [64] 8-10-2 R McGrath, pld hrd, hdwy to ld 6th, rdn and hdd 3 out, sn btn.........(6 to 1 op 5 to 1)	3
368⁴	TRUSS [80] (bl) 9-11-4 D Parker, str hold, chsd ldr, drvn alng 7th, sn wknd, tld off.....................(6 to 1 op 5 to 1)	4

Dist: Sht-hd, dist, dist. 5m 39.70s. a 32.70s (4 Ran).

(Mrs C Barclay), P C Haslam

475 Carling Premier Handicap Chase Class D (0-120 5-y-o and up) £3,457 3¼m ....(3:30)

42*	ROYAL VACATION [100] 7-10-8 J Callaghan, gd hdwy 7th, led tenth, slight mstk 2 out, pushed clr frm last, easily.	
	....(5 to 4 fav op 6 to 4)	1
418⁴	THE BLUE BOY (Ire) [100] (bb) 8-10-8 R Johnson, pushed alng in rear frm 5th, chlgd 2 out, hit last, sn one pace.	
	....(4 to 1 op 4 to 1)	2
375*	HILLWALK [120] 10-12-0 D Morris, in tch, wnt second 14th, rdn and outpcd 2 out, no extr...........(5 to 2 op 11 to 4)	3
	KUSHBALOO [115] 11-11-9 B Storey, led 2nd to 6th, drpd rear and mstk tenth, beh frm 3 out...........(4 to 1 op 3 to 1)	4
124³	UPWELL [92] 12-10-0 K Johnson, led to 3rd, led ag'n 6th to tenth, lost pl 14th, sn beh, tld off.	
	....(25 to 1 op 20 to 1 tchd 33 to 1)	5

Dist: 15l, 6l, 6l, 22l. 6m 29.20s. a 12.20s (5 Ran).

(G P Edwards), G M Moore

476 Sunlight Services Handicap Hurdle Class D (0-120 4-y-o and up) £2,805 2m 1f 110yds...................(4:05)

49	HAVE A NIGHTCAP [95] (bl) 7-10-9 P Niven, pressed ldr, led 5th, drvn and ran on wl und pres frm last. (5 to 1 op 9 to 2)	1
109⁵	MAN N'EGGS [110] 5-11-7 R Garritty, hld up, reminders 5th, effrt to chase ldr 2 out, kpt on wl.....(6 to 4 fav op 2 to 1)	2
	ZAJIRA (Ire) [113] 6-11-13 A Maguire, led, hdd 5th, lost pl nxt, styd on stdly frm last...............(5 to 2 op 6 to 4)	3
	LATIN LEADER [86] (bl) 6-9-11 (3") D Parker, in tch, reminders 3 out, sn btn.......................(11 to 2 op 4 to 1)	4
244⁷	FLINTLOCK [86] 6-9-9 (5") R McGrath, not fluent in rear, struggling 6th, sn wl beh..............(10 to 1 op 8 to 1)	5

55

TASHREEF [86] (bl) 6-10-0 M Moloney, *in tch, chsd ldr 5th, mstk and lost touch 3 out, sn wl beh...*(20 to 1 op 16 to 1) 6
Dist: 1½sl, 20l, 7l, 15l, 3l. 4m 7.80s. a 7.80s (6 Ran).
SR: 3/13/-/ (Mrs G A Jennings), N P Littmoden

477 Grant Thornton Novices' Chase Class E (5-y-o and up) £3,038 2m 1f 110yds
.... (4:40)

264 REVE DE VALSE (USA) 9-10-12 K Johnson, *led, drvn and hdd last, rallied to ld ag'n r-in, driven out.*
.......................(5 to 2 on op 5 to 4 on) 1
366 SIGNE DE MARS (Fr) 5-10-9 R Farrant, *chsd ldr, ev ch frm 3 out, slight ld last, hdd r-in, eased whn btn cl hme.*
...........................(8 to 1 op 7 to 1) 2
461 ANOTHER NICK 10-10-12 B Storey, *keen hold, blun badly 4th, jmpd slwly aftr, tld off whn f four out (water).*
...........................(7 to 2 op 5 to 1 tchd 6 to 1) f
Dist: 11l. 4m 33.10s. a 22.10s (3 Ran).
(Robert Johnson), R Johnson

478 Racing Channel Saturday Service Novices' Hurdle Class E (4-y-o and up) £2,337 2m 1f 110yds........... (5:10)

TEMPTED (Ire) 8-10-4 (3") D Parker, *chsd ldrs, not fluent 3rd, led nxt, hit last, drvn out.*...........(33 to 1 op 20 to 1) 1
3822 LANCER (USA) 4-11-2 M A Fitzgerald, *hld up, steady hdwy to chase wnr betw last 2, kpt on, no imprsn cl hme.*
...........................(7 to 2 op 4 to 1 tchd 9 to 2) 2
322* FIELD OF VISION 6-11-2 (3") J Supple, *wl plcd, jmpd rght and pushed alng 6th, outpcd betw last 2, no extr.*
...........................(11 to 8 on op 11 to 10 on) 3
387* GLENVALLY 5-11-0 A Maguire, *blun 1st, chsd ldrs, hdwy and ev ch 3 out, hit nxt, fdd appr last.*
...........................(3 to 1 op 9 to 4 tchd 7 to 2) 4
HAUGHTON LAD (Ire) 7-10-12 A Dobbin, *beh, struggling fnl circuit, sn no dngr.*...........(25 to 1 op 14 to 1) 5
PATTERN ARMS 4-10-9 D J Moffatt, *hld up, hdwy to track ldrs hfwy, wknd frm 2 out, eased whn btn.*...........(16 to 1) 6
JARVEY (Ire) 4-10-4 (5") D J Kavanagh, *sn clr, jmpd slwly second and 3rd, hdd 4th, wknd frm four out, tld off.*
...........................(33 to 1 op 20 to 1) 7
Dist: 3l, ¾l, 14l, 9l, 5l, dist. 4m 19.80s. a 19.80s (7 Ran).
(J C Haynes), J C Haynes

HEREFORD (good to firm)
Saturday August 24th
Going Correction: PLUS 0.15 sec. per fur.

479 Tarrington Amateur Riders' Handicap Hurdle Class E (0-120 4-y-o and up) £2,206 2m 1f................. (5:30)

382* ROYAL THIMBLE (Ire) [101] 5-10-12 (7") Mr E James, *in tch, rdn alng appr 5th, mstk whn chalg 3 out, led approaching last, ridden out.*...........(15 to 8 fav op 2 to 1 tchd 7 to 4) 1
3983 AIR COMMAND (Bar) [82] 6-9-7 (7") Mr P Phillips, *chsd ldr, led 3rd till appr 5th, rgned ld approaching 2 out, hdd approaching last, no extr.*
...........................(14 to 1 op 20 to 1 tchd 12 to 1) 2
AMLAH (USA) [113] 4-11-7 (7") Mr J Creighton, *hld up, improved bef 4th, hdwy appr nxt, hdd approaching 2 out, ev ch whn mstk last, one pace.*...........(2 to 1 op 7 to 4) 3
4222 SIRTELIMAR (Ire) [92] 7-10-3 (7") Mr R Wakley, *hld up, effrt to chase ldrs appr 3 out, wknd aftr nxt.*.....(9 to 4 op 2 to 1) 4
3726 AL SKEET (USA) [82] 10-9-7 (7") Miss E J Jones, *cl up, drvn alng and wknd appr 4 out.*...........(33 to 1 op 20 to 1) 5
POCONO KNIGHT [82] 6-9-7 (7") Miss B Small, *al in rear, struggling frm 5th, mstk nxt, sn lost tch.*(33 to 1 op 20 to 1) 6
FINAL ACE [82] 9-9-7 (7") Mr R Thornton, *not fluent, led to 3rd, drvn and wknd quickly aftr nxt, tld off whn pld up bef 2 out.*
...........................(66 to 1 op 20 to 1) pu
Dist: 3½l, 1l, 16l, 9l, 8l. 3m 56.40s. a 11.40s (7 Ran).
SR: 2/-/13/-/ (Mrs M Chance), Noel T Chance

480 Whitecross Selling Handicap Chase Class G (0-95 5-y-o and up) £2,864 2m 3f................................. (6:00)

3264 MINERS REST [66] 8-10-0 A P McCoy, *wth ldr, lft in ld 7th, sn clr, unchlgd.*...........(11 to 4 fav op 9 to 4) 1
4024 FENWICK [88] 9-11-5 (3") T Dascombe, *in tch, hdwy 5th, chsd wnr frm 8th, drvn appr 3 out, no imprsn whn hit last.*
...........................(9 to 2 op 3 to 1) 2
4025 GABISH [66] 11-9-7 (7") Mr R Thornton, *towards rear, hdwy 7th, drvn alng tenth, no imprsn on ldrs.*
...........................(20 to 1 tchd 33 to 1) 3
3603 NUCLEAR EXPRESS [72] 9-10-6 B Fenton, *beh, hdwy to chase ldrs 9th, rdn alng appr 3 out, sn btn.*
...........................(12 to 1 tchd 14 to 1) 4
4185 BOXING MATCH [73] 9-10-7 N Williamson, *led 3rd til f 7th.*
...........................(9 to 2 op 4 to 1 tchd 11 to 2) f
3835 ASTOUNDED [73] 9-10-4 (3") D Walsh, *chsd ldrs, rdn alng and f three out.*...........(16 to 1 op 8 to 1) f

360² AFALTOUN [70] 11-9-13 (5") P Henley, *keen hold, led till 3rd, rdn alng and wknd 8th, tld off whn pld up bef 2 out.*
...........................(5 to 1 op 4 to 1) pu
3683 WAKE UP LUV [86] 11-11-6 G Bradley, *mstk 1st, sn wl beh, tld off whn pld up bef 2 out....*(9 to 2 op 4 to 1 tchd 5 to 1) pu
266² SYDNEY BARRY (NZ) [90] 11-11-10 B Powell, *hld up, mstk tenth, struggling frm nxt, 5th and wl beh whn pld up bef 2 out, dismounted.*...........(5 to 1 op 4 to 1) pu
Dist: 8l, 8l, 3½l. 4m 49.90s. a 24.90s (9 Ran).
(P J Hobbs), P J Hobbs

481 Yarsop Juvenile Novices' Hurdle Class E (3-y-o) £2,444 2m 1f.......... (6:30)

CHIEF MOUSE 10-12 J F Titley, *led till aftr 1st, remained prmnt, rgned ld 2 out, ran on wl.*
.....(5 to 4 on op 11 to 8 on tchd 6 to 4 on and 11 to 10 on) 1
ROYAL RAPPORT 10-7 (5") Michael Brennan, *in tch, hdwy to track ldrs 4 out, ev ch 2 out, chsd wnr appr last, one pace.*
...........................(10 to 1 op 8 to 1 tchd 11 to 1) 2
ANDSOME BOY 10-12 B Clifford, *hld up, improved 3 out, ev ch 2 out, one pace aftr.*...........(?? to 1 op ?? to 1) 3
411² BALMORAL PRINCESS (bl) 11-0 R Bellamy, *led aftr 1st, jmpd slwly 4th, mstk and hdd 2 out, sn wknd.*
...........................(9 to 4 op 5 to 2 tchd 3 to 1) 4
MY BEAUTIFUL DREAM 10-9² F Jousset, *chsd ldrs, prmnt 4th, mstk nxt, sn wknd, tld off whn mistake 2 out.*
...........................(20 to 1 tchd 33 to 1) 5
COPPER DIAMOND 10-7 D J Burchell, *wl beh, tld off whn pld up bef 5th.*...........(11 to 1 op 12 to 1 tchd 16 to 1) pu
Dist: 3½l, 3½l, 11l, dist. 4m 5.00s. a 20.00s (6 Ran).
(Lady Vestey), Miss H C Knight

482 BBC Hereford & Worcester Handicap Hurdle Class D (0-125 4-y-o and up) £2,864 2m 3f 110yds.......... (7:00)

3477 FAUSTINO [111] 4-12-0 A P McCoy, *trkd ldr, not fluent 7th, chlgd 3 out, led appr nxt, drvn out r-in.*
...........................(11 to 10 tchd 6 to 5 and 5 to 4) 1
LA MENORQUINA (USA) [102] 6-11-8 J A McCarthy, *led, rdn alng 3 out, hdd appr nxt, one pace bef last.*
...........................(11 to 8 on op 6 to 4 on tchd 5 to 4 on) 2
MABTHUL (USA) [80] 8-10-0 S Curran, *wnt to post early, reluctant to race, jmpd slwly 1st and second, tld off thrght.*
...........................(9 to 1 op 25 to 1 tchd 33 to 1) 3
Dist: 5l, dist. 4m 49.20s. a 31.20s (3 Ran).
(The Bilbrook '4'), P J Hobbs

483 Hole In The Wall Novices' Chase Class E (5-y-o and up) £3,035 3m 1f 110yds
.... (7:30)

439* WAKT 6-11-7 A P McCoy, *cl up, led appr 5th, sn clr, drvn whn pressed bef 2 out, styd on wl frm last.*
...(6 to 4 on op 5 to 4 on tchd 11 to 10 on and Evens) 1
332 TOUR LEADER (NZ) 7-12-0 B Powell, *hld up, hdwy 8th, sn chasing wnr, chlgd 2 out, ev ch last, no extr fnl 100 yards.*
...........................(5 to 2 op 3 to 1 tchd 7 to 2) 2
4003 HIZAL 7-11-5 Mr A Charles-Jones, *chsd ldrs, lost pl quickly 5th, sn beh, struggling fnl circuit, wnt poor 3rd appr 3 out, tld off.*...........(7 to 1 op 5 to 1 tchd 9 to 1) 3
2836 STORM WARRIOR (bl) 11-10-9 (3") R Massey, *in tch, jmpd lft second, mstk 5th, chsd wnr briefly 6th, sn lost grnd, beh fnl circuit, tld off.*...........(40 to 1 op 25 to 1 tchd 50 to 1) 4
147 MUSIC SCORE 10-10-12 A Thornton, *led, iron broke 1st, hdd appr 5th, wl beh frm 11th, pckd badly 14th, tld off whn pld up bef nxt.*...........(16 to 1 tchd 20 to 1) pu
LORD ANTRIM (Ire) 7-10-12 P Holley, *unruly and broke loose bef strt, started slwly, blun 1st, nvr gng wl and beh, tld off whn pld up before 9th.*...........(4 to 1 op 9 to 4) pu
Dist: 1½l, dist. distance. 6m 33.30s. a 27.30s (6 Ran).
(John R White), J White

484 Abergavenny Novices' Handicap Hurdle Class F (0-95 4-y-o and up) £2,108 2m 1f............................(8:00)

416* RAVEN'S ROOST (Ire) [62] 5-10-4 P McLoughlin, *in tch, hdwy 5th, led and jinked lft appr 2 out, styd on strly to go clr approaching last.*...........(3 to 1 op 7 to 4) 1
4015 MR POPPLETON [61] 7-10-6 L Harvey, *nvr far away, rdn alng and slightly outpcd 3 out, chsd wnr appr last, no imprsn.*
...........................(9 to 4 op 5 to 1 tchd 5 to 1) 2
2944 KING OF BABYLON (Ire) [71] 4-10-8 (5") L Aspell, *strted slwly, hld up in rear, hdwy to track ldrs 4 out, one pace frm 2 out.*
...........................(8 to 1 op 6 to 1 tchd 9 to 1) 3
372* TONY'S MIST [79] 6-11-10 R Johnson, *in tch, hdwy to go cl up 4 out, sn rdn alng, ev ch 2 out, soon outpcd.*
...........................(9 to 4 fav op 5 to 2 tchd 11 to 4) 4
3475 DICKIES GIRL [65] 6-10-10 T J Murphy, *led appr second, hdd approaching 2 out, tdd.*(10 to 1 tchd 8 to 1 and 8 to 1) 5
3765 COURT JESTER [74] 5-11-2 D Gallagher, *led, blun 1st, hdd appr nxt, lost pl quickly, sn beh.*...........(6 to 1 op 5 to 1) 6
4196 ATHENIAN ALLIANCE [55] 7-9-11 (3") Guy Lewis, *pld hrd, sn prmnt, wkng whn mstk 5th, losing tc whn hit nxt, tld off.*
...........................(33 to 1) 7

PALIAPOUR (Ire) [65] 5-10-7 W Marston, hld up, struggling
frm 4 out, eased bef nxt, tld off.
.................................(9 to 2 op 4 to 1 tchd 5 to 1)   8
Dist: 10l, 5l, 4l, 1½l, 10l, dist, 23l. 3m 58.50s. a 13.50s (8 Ran).

(G Elwyn Jones), G E Jones

TRALEE (IRE) (yielding to soft)
Sunday August 25th

485 Tralee Vintners Belvedere Trophy Beginners Chase (5-y-o and up) £3,575 2m............(3:10)

406² MAJESTIC MARINER (Ire) 5-11-8 C O'Dwyer, ...(8 to 1)   1
426³ SANDY FOREST LADY (Ire) 7-11-9 J P Broderick, . . (6 to 1)   2
       HOTEL MINELLA 9-12-0 R Dunwoody, ... (3 to 1 on)   ur
357 HOW'S IT GOIN (Ire) 5-11-5 (3") D J Casey, ...(4 to 1) ur
Dist: Dist. 4m 26.00s. (4 Ran).

(John Hackett), G T Hourigan

486 Mount Brandon Hotel Handicap Hurdle (4-y-o) £4,795 2m..............(3:40)

184⁵ KATIYMANN (Ire) [-] 10-13 T Horgan, ...(11 to 4)   1
270² MAGICAL FUN (Ire) [-] (bl) 10-11 C O'Dwyer, ...(7 to 2)   2
221² FRASER CAREY (Ire) [-] (bl) 11-0 R Dunwoody, (5 to 2 fav)   3
405³ SWINGS'N'THINGS (USA) [-] 10-0 T P Treacy, ...(7 to 1)   4
119² EARP (Ire) [-] 11-7 J Shortt,.......................(7 to 2)   5
Dist: 25l, 20l, nk, 25l. 4m 2.50s. (5 Ran).

(Frank Hardy), Thomas J Taaffe

487 Ballygarry House Hotel I.N.H. Flat Race (4-y-o and up) £3,425 2m 1f.....(4:10)

407* MURPHY'S MALT (Ire) 4-11-10 (3") Mr B M Cash,
430³ NATIVE BABY (Ire) 6-11-8 (5") Mr R Walsh, ... (11 to 4)   2
430⁵ PERAMBIE (Ire) (bl) 4-11-1 (7") Miss A L Crowley, . . (6 to 1)   3
316⁴ FRANCOSKID (Ire) 4-11-6 (7") Mr J P McNamara, ... (7 to 1)   4
430⁷ HOLLY LADY (Ire) 5-10-13 (7") Mr John P Moloney, (16 to 1)   5
       JUST A CHAT (Ire) 4-10-13 (7") Mr L Hennessy, ... (14 to 1)   6
343⁴ YOU MAKE ME LAUGH (Ire) 4-10-13 (7") Mr D W Cullen,
.................................(7 to 1)   7
Dist: 13l, 5½l, 9l, 15l. 4m 27.80s. (7 Ran).

(James Hennessy), A P O'Brien

CARTMEL (good)
Monday August 26th
Going Correction: PLUS 0.35 sec. per fur.

488 BBC Radio Cumbria Juvenile Novices' Hurdle Class E for the Army Benevolent Challenge Cup (3-y-o) £2,215 2m 1f 110yds......................(2:00)

PRELUDE TO FAME (USA) 10-10 A Dobbin, al cl up, slight ld
5th, rdn clr r-in...................(7 to 1 op 8 to 1)   1
GO-GO-POWER-RANGER 10-7 (3") G Cahill, cl up, dsptd ld
5th, pressed ldr aftr till no extr r-in...... (9 to 4 op 2 to 1)   2
MANOY 10-10 R Marley, hld up rear, cld up hfwy, ch 2 out, sn
rdn and wknd...........(9 to 1 op 8 to 1 tchd 10 to 1)   3
DOWN THE YARD 10-5 W Worthington, in tch, cld up hfwy,
wknd 2 out...................... (6 to 1 op 8 to 1)   4
RUSSIAN RASCAL (Ire) 10-10 L Wyer, hld up beh ldrs, cld up
hfwy, wknd frm 3 out. (2 to 1 fav op 5 to 2 tchd 11 to 4)   5
411³ RECALL TO MIND (bl) 10-7 (3") D Parker, led to 5th, sn rdn,
wknd aftr nxt....................... (10 to 1 op 12 to 1)   6
       VILLAGE OPERA 10-5 N Bentley, in tch, cld up hfwy, wknd 3
out...............................(25 to 1 op 20 to 1)   7
Dist: 8l, 8l, 6l, 12l, 13l, 17l. 4m 16.00s. a 16.00s (7 Ran).

(Jumbo Racing Club), Miss M K Milligan

489 Hampsfell Selling Handicap Hurdle Class G (0-90 4-y-o and up) £2,278 2m 1f 110yds.....................(2:35)

STEADFAST ELITE (Ire) [86] 5-11-10 A Roche, trkd ldrs, prog
5th, wnt second nxt, led last, rdn clr....... (9 to 4 fav op 9 to 2)   1
CLOVER GIRL [70] (v) 5-10-5 (3") G Cahill, hld up rear, prog
5th, effrt frm 2 out, ch last, no extr r-in.
.....................................(9 to 4 fav op 9 to 2)   2
RED MARCH HARE [69] 5-10-7 D J Moffatt, in tch, prog to
track ldr 5th, led nxt to last, sn wknd.....(7 to 2 op 3 to 1)   3
27   ON THE MOVE [73] 5-10-11 L O'Hara, in tch till rdn and wknd
3 out.............................(16 to 1 op 14 to 1)   4
167⁵ RUPPLES [79] 9-11-6 W Worthington, rear till styd on one
pace frm 3 out, nvr dngrs......................(8 to 1)   5
       CRIMINAL RECORD (USA) [65] 6-10-6 R Johnson, trkd ldr,
led 4th to 3 out, sn wknd............ (10 to 1 op 8 to 1)   6
457⁵ OLD MORTALITY [64] 10-10-5 B Storey, led to 4th, rdn and
wknd aftr nxt..................................(7 to 1)   7
       SEE YOU ALWAYS (Ire) [66] 6-10-7⁷ P Waggott, trkd ldrs,
reminder aftr 4th, rdn and wknd after nxt........ (12 to 1)   8

388⁴ SKIPLAM WOOD [59] 10-10-0 K Johnson, in tch to hfwy, tld
off frm 3 out....................(25 to 1 op 20 to 1)   9
Dist: 6l, 4l, 28l, 18l, 7l, 13l, 8l, 12l. 4m 16.20s. a 16.20s (9 Ran).

(Clayton Bigley Partnership Ltd), J J O'Neill

490 John Calvert Deb's Ball Handicap Chase Class C (0-130 5-y-o and up) £4,419 2m 1f 110yds..........(3:10)

421* STATELY HOME (Ire) [113] 5-10-13 R Johnson, mstk second,
led 4th, drw wl clr, eased well bef line. ....(7 to 4 jt-
fav tchd 2 to 1)   1
       BEAUCADEAU [105] 10-11-8 P Waggott, trkd ldrs, wnt sec-
ond 7th, no ch frm 2 out.............. (4 to 1 tchd 9 to 2)   2
458² BLAZING DAWN [97] 9-10-8 B Storey, led to 4th, wknd frm
8th, kpt on one pace.......(9 to 2 op 6 to 1 tchd 4 to 1)   3
312³ WHO'S TO SAY [122] 10-11-1 N Williamson, beh, cld up
hfwy, blun 7th, no ch aftr......(7 to 4 jt-fav tchd 15 to 8)   4
Dist: 8l, 1¼l, dist. 4m 23.20s. a 12.20s (4 Ran).
SR: 23/10/-/-/

(P Bowen), P Bowen

491 Tote Credit Handicap Hurdle Class F (0-100 4-y-o and up) £2,238 3¼m ....(3:45)

460⁵ AMAZON EXPRESS [101] 7-12-7 (7ex) R Johnson, hld up
mid-div, mstk 8th, gd prog to track ldr 3 out, led nxt, sn clr,
easily.........................(6 to 1 op 5 to 1)   1
       RECORD LOVER (Ire) [74] 6-10-8 W Worthington, rear, prog
to track ldrs 3 out, kpt on one pace frm nxt..........(4 to 1)   2
       BALLINDOO [84] 7-11-4 Mr R Armson, mid-div, prog to track
ldrs 3 out, no imprsn frm nxt.........(14 to 1 op 10 to 1)   3
56* CRAZY HORSE DANCER (USA) [84] 8-11-4 M Dwyer, trkd ldr
till wknd quickly aftr 4 out............ (3 to 1 op 11 to 4)   4
474² RAMPANT ROSIE (Ire) [76] (bl) 8-10-10 A Dobbin, led and clr
till blun 3 out, hdd nxt, sn beh.
.......................(7 to 4 fav op 9 to 4 tchd 6 to 4)   5
246⁶ BUYERS DREAM (Ire) [76] 6-10-6 (3") G Cahill, beh, nvr
dngrs................(5 to 1 op 11 to 1 tchd 12 to 1)   6
225⁴ THEY ALL FORGOT ME [66] 9-10-0 Miss C Dyson, trkd ldrs
till wknd and beh frm hfwy...........(25 to 1 op 20 to 1)   7
Dist: 10l, 13l, 1½l, ¾l, 27l, dist. 6m 32.30s. a 34.30s (7 Ran).

(T M Morris), P Bowen

492 Crowther Homes Novices' Chase Class E (5-y-o and up) £2,877 2m 5f 110yds............................(4:20)

459² DEFINITE MAYBE (Ire) (bl) 6-10-12 R Johnson, chsd ldrs, rdn
alng and not fluent lnl circuit, hit 3 out, ridden to ld hfwy up
r-in, sn clr................... (5 to 4 fav tchd 11 to 10)   1
477² SIGNE DE MARS (Fr) 5-10-8 B Storey, jmpd wl, led 4th, wndrd
2 out, rdn and hdd hfwy up r-in, eased whn btn.
......................(5 to 1 op 7 to 1 tchd 8 to 1)   2
36³ WHITE DIAMOND 8-10-12 M Foster, chsd ldrs, no ch frm 5
out...............................(6 to 4 op 5 to 4)   3
459³ DONOVANS REEF 10-11-2 D Bentley, led till mstk 4th, tld off
frm 9th............................(10 to 1 op 14 to 1)   4
Dist: 22l, 18l, dist. 5m 36.60s. a 26.60s (4 Ran).

(B C Kilby), P F Nicholls

493 Bet With The Tote Maiden Hurdle Class E (4-y-o and up) £2,320 2m 1f 110yds ....(4:55)

ETERNAL CITY 5-11-5 A Dobbin, wl beh in chasing grp till
prog frm 2 out, led frm lnl 50 yards. (11 to 4 tchd 5 to 2)   1
322⁵ SEA GOD 5-11-5 W Worthington, sn wl clr, rdn 2 out,
mstk last, hdd and no extr lnl 50 yards.
..................(5 to 4 fav op 6 to 4 tchd 13 to 8)   2
       FATEHALKHAIR (Ire) 4-10-13 (3") G Cahill, wl beh in chasing
grp, wnt second 3 out, prog frm nxt, ev ch r-in, no extr.
.... 3
       INGRAM VALLEY 6-11-0 D J Moffatt, led chasing grp till rdn
and wknd 3 out.....................(12 to 1 op 10 to 1)   4
       SHAA SPIN 4-10-11 M Moloney, prmnt chasing grp to hfwy,
sn drvn alng, wknd....(8 to 1 op 10 to 1 tchd 14 to 1)   5
       STONE CROSS (Ire) 4-11-2 M Dwyer, prmnt chasing grp till
rdn and wknd 3 out................(5 to 1 op 5 to 2)   6
Dist: 2½l, 1¼l, 23l, 5l, dist. 4m 22.20s. a 22.20s (6 Ran).

(R Tyrer), G Richards

DOWNPATRICK (IRE) (good)
Monday August 26th

494 Newcastle Maiden Hurdle (4-y-o and up) £1,370 2m 1f 172yds.......(2:30)

427⁴ MONTETAN (Ire) 5-11-9 K F O'Brien, ...(12 to 1)   1
430* REAL TAOISEACH (Ire) 6-11-7 (7") Mr A K Wyse, (5 to 4 on)   2
424⁴ NEW LEGISLATION (Ire) (bl) 6-11-1 F Woods, ...(12 to 1)   3
358⁶ CASTLEROYAL (Ire) 7-11-6 P McWilliams, ...(14 to 1)   4
347² TWENTYFIVEQUID (Ire) 5-11-7 (7") C Rae, ...(6 to 1)   5
289 DON'T LOOSE FAITH (Ire) 4-10-13 S C Lyons, ...(5 to 1)   6
364³ SAN SIRO (Ire) 6-10-13 (7") Mr Edgar Byrne, ...(20 to 1)   7

396 NATURE PERFECTED (Ire) (bl) 7-11-3 (3*) D T Evans,
....(33 to 1)   8
234⁸ JONATHAN'S ROSE (Ire) 7-11-1 J K Kinane, ...(16 to 1)   9
397⁵ PIGEON HILL BUCK (Ire) 5-11-6 H Rogers, ...(25 to 1)   10
Dist: 3l, 2l, 6l, 3½l. (Time not taken) (10 Ran).

(L T Reilly), L T Reilly

495 Ardglass Handicap Hurdle (0-102 4-y-o and up) £1,370 2¾m...........(3:00)

237⁶ JESSIE'S BOY (Ire) [-] 7-10-12 J K Kinane, ...(16 to 1)   1
344⁴ PETITE MEWS (Ire) [-] 5-10-2 P L Malone, ...(3 to 1)   2
234⁶ PLOUGH THE LEA (Ire) [-] 6-10-1 (3*) Mr J Connolly,
....(Evens fav)   3
396⁹ LADY PHARDANTE (Ire) [-] 6-9-3³ (7*) A O'Shea, ..(20 to 1)   4
349 BALLYVERANE [-] 10-10-8 (7*) C Rae, ...(4 to 1) pu
     BLUEHILL LAD [-] 9-10-3 K F O'Brien, ...(16 to 1) pu
Dist: 8l, 9l, dist. (Time not taken) (6 Ran).

(Luke Comer), Luke Comer

496 Farrie Puer Stimulus Beginners Chase (5-y-o and up) £1,370 2½m....(4:30)

470³ BALLINABOOLA GROVE 9-11-9 (5*) T Martin, ...(4 to 1)   1
357² COSHLA EXPRESSO 8-12-0 P L Malone, ...(4 to 1)   2
345³ THE ODIN LINE (Ire) 7-12-0 F Woods, ...(9 to 4 fav)   3
208¹ LIMAHEIGHTS (Ire) 6-11-6 (3*) D T Evans, ...(11 to 4)   4
     TALL ORDER (Ire) 7-11-11 (3*) U Smyth, ...(12 to 1)   5
313³ MAIASAURA (Ire) 7-11-7 (7*) C Rae, ...(6 to 1) pu
169 CHOICE COMPANY (Ire) 7-12-0 S C Lyons, ...(20 to 1) pu
Dist: 5l, 3l, dist. (Time not taken) (7 Ran).

(D Kinsella), Donal Kinsella

497 O.T.C. Building Contractors Flat Race (4-y-o and up) £1,370 2m 1f 172yds ....(5:00)

117³ CHANOBLE (Ire) 4-11-2 (7*) Mr A J Dempsey, ...(6 to 1)   1
397⁸ MADDY KEEL 6-11-7 (7*) Mr R Marrs, ...(20 to 1)   2
444⁵ ANN'S DESIRE (Ire) 5-11-2 (7*) Mr J Keville, ...(7 to 1)   3
     FENIAN COURT 5-11-9 Mr A J Martin, ...(6 to 4 fav)   4
396⁸ ARCTIC CLOVER (Ire) 5-11-2 Mr J P Dempsey, ...(11 to 2)   5
     HARLEY-D (Ire) 7-11-7 (7*) Mr John A Quinn, ...(14 to 1)   6
     FARM LODGE (Ire) 5-12-0 Mr D Marnane, ...(14 to 1)   7
196⁸ ZUZUS PETALS (Ire) 6-11-2 (7*) Mr F King, ...(20 to 1)   8
245⁹ CRABTREEJAZZ (Ire) 4-11-4 Mr A R Coonan, ...(8 to 1)   9
397 MOOR HILL LASS (Ire) 6-11-2 (7*) Mr G T Cuthbert, (33 to 1) pu
304 MC CLATCHEY (Ire) 5-12-0 Mr P F Graffin, ...(9 to 1) pu
     BOBBY BLAZER (Ire) 5-11-6 (3*) Mr B R Hamilton, (20 to 1) pu
Dist: 3l, 10l, 11l, 6l. (Time not taken) (12 Ran).

(Mrs Deirdre McMahon), Norman Cassidy

FONTWELL (good to firm)
Monday August 26th
Going Correction: NIL

498 Chichester Novices' Handicap Hurdle Class E (0-100 4-y-o and up) £2,237 2¾m 110yds.....................(2:30)

FEELING FOOLISH (Ire) [60] 7-10-3 (7*) M Moran, chsd ldr,
  led appr last, hrd drvn r-in, all out.
.........................(12 to 1 op 10 to 1 tchd 14 to 1)   1
371⁴ PLINTH [79] 5-11-12 A Maguire, led till appr last, hrd rdn and
  no extr r-in......(6 to 5 on op 5 to 4 tchd 5 to 4 on)   2
359⁴ LIMOSA [81] 5-12-0 M Richards, chsd ldrs, rdn 6th, lost tch
  8th, styd on r-in.................(7 to 2 op 7 to 1)   3
326³ CASHFLOW CRISIS (Ire) [78] 4-11-3 (5*) S Ryan, hld up rear,
  effrt 8th, hrd rdn and outpcd 3 out.
........................(11 to 4 op 3 to 1 tchd 7 to 2)   4
Dist: 3l, 4l, 9l. 5m 30.40s. a 16.40s (4 Ran).

(Miss L V Bacon), P J Hobbs

499 Bow Hill Selling Hurdle Class G (4-y-o and up) £1,825 2¼m 110yds....(3:00)

384² BURNT SIENNA (Ire) (v) 4-10-4 W McFarland, chsd ldr, led
  5th, sn clr, hrd rdn and edgd lft r-in, all out.
.........................(13 to 8 fav op 6 to 4 tchd 2 to 1)   1
438⁴ CELESTIAL FIRE 4-11-2 A Maguire, hdwy 6th, chsd wnr appr
  2 out, hrd rdn and ev ch r-in, no extr nr finish.
.........................(100 to 30 op 3 to 1 tchd 7 to 2)   2
     LADY POLY (bl) 8-11-7 Leesa Long, in tch, chsd wnr 5th till
  wknd appr 2 out......(40 to 1 op 20 to 1 tchd 50 to 1)   3
     SCALP 'EM (Ire) 8-10-12 Dr P Pritchard, hdwy 3rd, wknd 5th.
.........................(14 to 1 op 20 to 1)   4
417⁶ FATTASH (USA) (bl) 4-10-4 (5*) S Ryan, lost tch 6th.
.........................(40 to 1 op 25 to 1 tchd 50 to 1)   5
423⁸ AGAINST THE CLOCK (v) 4-10-9 J R Kavanagh, in tch to 3rd,
  tld off frm 5th.....................(10 to 1 tchd 12 to 1)   6
     CAST THE LINE (bl) 6-11-5 J A McCarthy, led to 5th, wknd
  quickly appr nxt, tld off whn pld up bef 3 out.
.........................(7 to 1 tchd 9 to 4) pu
Dist: 2½l, 19l, 14l, 12l, 4l. 4m 25.90s. a 8.90s (7 Ran).

(B & E Bloodstock Limited), J S Moore

500 News Handicap Chase Class E (0-115 5-y-o and up) £3,097 2m 3f.....(3:30)

HENLEY WOOD [92] 11-10-8 (3*) G Tormey, made all, blun 2
  out and last, clr r-in.....(5 to 2 op 11 to 4 tchd 3 to 1)   1
437⁴ NOBLELY (USA) [105] 9-11-10 (7ex) R Farrant, chsd wnr frm
  9th, ev ch 3 out, one pace.........(11 to 8 fav op 6 to 4)   2
     ARMALA [107] 11-11-7 (5*) L Aspell, chsd ldrs till outpcd 11th.
.........................(9 to 4 op 7 to 4 tchd 11 to 4)   3
437³ LAVALIGHT [81] 9-10-0 J Culloty, sn prmnt, jmpd slwly 3rd
  and tenth, third whn f 11th.
.........................(50 to 1 op 33 to 1 tchd 25 to 1)   f
     SAFFAAH (USA) [109] 9-12-0 M Richards, in tch to 5th, sn
  beh, tld off whn pld up bef 3 out.
.........................(14 to 1 op 10 to 1 tchd 16 to 1) pu
Dist: 10l, 28l. 4m 50.60s. a 15.60s (5 Ran).

(A J Scrimgeour), P J Hobbs

501 Fishbourne Juvenile Novices' Hurdle Class E (3-y-o) £2,175 2¼m 110yds ....(4:00)

411 SKRAM 10-3 J Culloty, set moderate pace, made all, ran on
  strly frm 2 out, readily..........(2 to 1 jt-fav op 7 to 4)   1
363⁴ AMBER RING 10-5 J R Kavanagh, al prmnt, one pace frm 3
  out........(2 to 1 jt-fav op 7 to 4 tchd 9 to 4)   2
     YELLOW DRAGON (Ire) 10-10 Leesa Long, hld up rear, mstk
  second, hdwy whn not much room and lost pl bend aftr 3 out,
  styd on frm nxt........(7 to 1 op 8 to 1 tchd 10 to 1)   3
363 KINGS NIGHTCLUB 10-5 A Maguire, hdwy 3 out, wknd appr
  last..................(11 to 4 op 4 to 1 tchd 9 to 2)   4
     OLD GOLD N TAN 10-5 (5*) L Aspell, prmnt to 3 out, 5th and
  btn whn bumped nxt....(25 to 1 op 12 to 1 tchd 33 to 1)   5
Dist: 5l, ¾l, 6l, 17l. 4m 34.80s. a 17.80s (5 Ran).

(W P Evans), R Dickin

502 Stane Street Novices' Chase Class E (5-y-o and up) £2,933 2¼m.....(4:30)

383³ HARROW WAY (Ire) 6-10-12 A Maguire, made all, ran on wl
  frm 3 out, comftbly.....(3 to 1 tchd 11 to 4 and 7 to 2)   1
362³ CALL ME ALBI (Ire) (v) 5-10-9 M Richards, in tch, rdn and ev
  ch appr 3 out, one pace..............(2 to 1 op 7 to 4)   2
369² STAPLEFORD LADY 8-11-0 W McFarland, chsd wnr till rdn
  and outpcd tenth, rallied 3 out, sn btn.
.........................(6 to 4 fav op 11 to 8)   3
298⁸ JAMESWICK 6-10-12 P Holley, in tch, mstks second and 4th,
  wknd 9th, beh whn hit tenth.
.........................(14 to 1 op 12 to 1 tchd 16 to 1)   4
     SANDRO (bl) 7-10-12 L Harvey, rear, lost tch 8th, tld off whn
  pld up aftr 12th........(20 to 1 op 16 to 1 tchd 25 to 1) pu
Dist: 2½l, 14l, 14l. 4m 49.60s. a 29.60s (5 Ran).

(Mrs Carrie Zetter-Wells), L Wells

503 Fons Handicap Hurdle Class E (0-110 4-y-o and up) £2,259 2¼m 110yds ....(5:00)

382⁴ CIRCUS COLOURS [95] 6-11-1 A Maguire, hld up rear, hdwy
  frm 2 out, ran on to 1½ out, drvn out...(7 to 2 tchd 5 to 1)   1
361* PAIR OF JACKS (Ire) [84] 6-10-4 C Llewellyn, chsd ldrs, led
  appr last, hdd r-in, ran on.
.........................(6 to 4 fav op 2 to 1 tchd 9 to 4)   2
     AMAZE [108] 7-11-7 (7*) Mr R Thornton, chsd ldr, led 2 out,
  hrd rdn and hdd appr last, kpt on.
.........................(9 to 2 op 4 to 1 tchd 9 to 4)   3
333⁶ STAY WITH ME (Fr) [93] 6-10-13 J A McCarthy, hld up, rdn
  and hdwy 2 out, styd on r-in........(9 to 1 op 6 to 1)   4
361⁴ IKHTIRAA (USA) [84] 6-10-4 P Holley, led, sn clr, hdd 2 out,
  one pace..............(12 to 1 op 8 to 1 tchd 14 to 1)   5
Dist: ½l, 1½l, ½l, 1¼l. 4m 23.80s. a 6.80s (5 Ran).
SR: 19/7/29/13/2/

(S Powell), J R Jenkins

HUNTINGDON (good to firm)
Monday August 26th
Going Correction: MINUS 0.45 sec. per fur.

504 March Conditional Jockeys' Selling Handicap Hurdle Class G (0-90 4-y-o and up) £1,849 2½m 110yds....(2:15)

318* JOLI'S GREAT [67] (bl) 8-11-3 B Fenton, made all, clr to 5th,
  quickened clear ag'n aftr 3 out, eased r-in.
.........................(Evens fav op 5 to 4 on tchd 11 to 8)   1
45   SAKBAH (USA) [57] 7-10-7 P Henley, rear till chsd wnr aftr
  5th, rdn and outpcd frm 3 out, fnshd tired.
.........................(9 to 2 op 3 to 1)   2
389⁴ RAY RIVER [84] (bl) 4-11-11 (3*) D Finnegan, dsptd second pl
  till aftr 5th, mstk nxt, lost tch frm 7th...(7 to 2 op 5 to 2)   3
246⁷ SWEDISH INVADER [81] 5-12-0 D J Kavanagh, dsptd second
  pl till drpd rear appr 6th, sn tld off....(3 to 1 tchd 4 to 1)   4
Dist: 16l, 28l, dist. 4m 44.60s. a 9.60s (4 Ran).

(Enterprise Markets Ltd), M J Ryan

505 Yelling Handicap Chase Class F (0-100 6-y-o and up) £3,140 2m 110yds (2:45)

FAR EAST (NZ) [70] 7-10-0 J Osborne, *led 4th, clr 6th, shaken up appr 2 out, lft wl clear last.*............. (8 to 1 op 6 to 1) 1

321⁴ CIRCULATION [70] 10-10-0 R Supple, *led to 4th, not fluent nxt, in 3rd pl whn lft second aftr last, no imprsn on wnr.*
....(5 to 1 op 4 to 1) 2

369° YAAKUM [97] 7-11-13 M A Fitzgerald, *hld up, chsd wnr frm 6th, cl second and rdn whn blun and uns rdr last, rmntd to finish, not officially plcd 3rd.*
............(13 to 8 on op 7 to 4 on tchd 6 to 4 on) ur

360⁴ DAYS OF THUNDER [90] 8-11-6 B Fenton, *beh, outpcd whn mstk 5th and nxt, tld off when pld up bef 3 out.*
....(7 to 2 tchd 4 to 1) pu

Dist: 10l. 4m 3.80s. a 9.80s (4 Ran).

(The Padrino Partnership), B de Haan

506 Offord Maiden Hurdle Class E (4-y-o and up) £2,320 2m 110yds...... (3:15)

WOTTASHAMBLES 5-11-5 D Morris, *hld up rear, prog 5th, led appr 2 out, sn clr, not extended.*..............(5 to 2 jt-
fav 9p to 4 tchd 3 to 1) 1

WANSTEAD (Ire) (v) 4-11-2 G Bradley, *al handily plcd, rdn to chase wnr appr 2 out, no imprsn last.*
............(7 to 2 op 3 to 1 tchd 4 to 1) 2

WITNEY-DE-BERGERAC (Ire) 4-10-13 (3°) J Magee, *wl in tch til lost pl 4th, styd on ag'n appr 2 out, not rch wnr.* (5 to 2 jt-
fav 9p to 4 tchd 3 to 1) 3

484⁶ COURT JESTER (bl) 5-11-5 B Fenton, *wth ldr, led 5th, hdd appr 2 out, sn wknd and tld off.*
....(9 to 1 op 14 to 1 tchd 16 to 1) 4

445⁶ CHELWORTH WOLF 4-11-2 R Supple, *hld up towards rear, rdn and lost tch frm 5th, tld off.*.......(33 to 1 op 20 to 1) 5

ACQUITTAL (Ire) (v) 4-11-2 T Eley, *in tch til rdn and wknd appr 5th, tld off whn pld up bef 2 out.*....(6 to 1 op 4 to 1) pu

KIRKIE CROSS 4-10-4 (7°) D Finnegan, *not jump wl, lost tch aftr mstks second and 3rd, tld off whn pld up bef 5th.*
....(33 to 1 op 16 to 1) pu

BABA AU RHUM (Ire) 4-11-2 J Osborne, *led til hdd and pckd 5th, lost pl quickly, tld off whn pld up bef 2 out.*
....(6 to 1 op 4 to 1) pu

Dist: 12l, nk, 28l, dist. 4m 40.90s. b 0.10s (8 Ran).

SR: 18/3/2/-/-/ (Dream On Racing Partnership), L Montague Hall

507 BBC Radio Cambridgeshire Novices' Chase Class D (5-y-o and up) £3,474 2 ½m 110yds......................(3:45)

298³ SYDMONTON 10-10-12 M A Fitzgerald, *trkd ldrs, pckd 12th, dsptd ld aftr 3 out, led nxt, rdn clr frm last.*
............(11 to 10 fav op 5 to 4 tchd 11 to 8) 1

333⁵ MR SNAGGLE (Ire) 7-10-12 C Maude, *took keen hold, hdwy 12th, wth wnr aftr 3 out till hit nxt, jmpd badly lft last, sn btn.*
....(2 to 1 op 6 to 4) 2

362⁴ TELMAR SYSTEMS (bl) 7-10-12 B Fenton, *not fluent, made most of rng till hdd aftr 3 out, sn tld off.*
....(8 to 1 tchd 10 to 1 and 12 to 1) 3

400² ANOTHER COMEDY 6-10-12 Richard Guest, *jmpd badly lft and mstks, lost tch aftr blund 9th, tld off whn pld up bef 12th.*
....(9 to 2 op 7 to 2 tchd 5 to 1) pu

Dist: 3½l, dist. 5m 2.50s. a 15.50s (4 Ran).

(Peter Oldfield), N J Henderson

508 Bank Holiday Handicap Hurdle Class E (0-110 4-y-o and up) £2,320 2m 110yds........................(4:15)

438° GONE BY (Ire) [108] (v) 8-12-0 (7ex) G Bradley, *hld up wl in tch, jnd ldr 3 out, slight ld last, drvn out.*
....(11 to 4 op 9 to 4 tchd 3 to 1) 1

367² JOHN TUFTY [87] 5-10-4 P Hide, *hld up in rear, hit 3rd, jnd ldrs 2 out, ev ch last, not quicken r-in.*
....(11 to 4 op 3 to 1 tchd 7 to 2) 2

390³ VAIN PRINCE [104] (bl) 9-11-10 M A Fitzgerald, *hld up chas-ing ldr, led 3 out, hdd nxt, sn btn.*.......(5 to 2 op 2 to 1) 3

LAYHAM LOW (Ire) [103] 5-11-6 J Osborne, *led til hdd 3 out, sn wknd and tld off.*....(9 to 4 fav op 7 to 4 tchd 5 to 2) 4

Dist: 1¼l, 3½l, dist. 3m 42.80s. a 1.80s (4 Ran).

(Mrs T McCoubrey), J R Jenkins

509 St Neots Novices' Hurdle Class E (4-y-o and up) £2,192 2½m 110yds (4:45)

283² SANTELLA BOY (USA) (bl) 4-11-2 J Railton, *chsd ldr gng wl, led last, quickened clr.*
............(13 to 8 on op 7 to 4 on tchd 2 to 1 on and 6 to 4 on) 1

KINGSLAND TAVERNER 5-10-12 J Osborne, *reluctant to line up and uns rdr bef strt, led till hdd last, outpcd r-in.*
....(11 to 8 op 6 to 4 tchd 2 to 1) 2

BALLAD RULER 10-10-12 R Supple, *hld up in last pl, rdn and effrt appr 3 out, lost tch bef nxt, tld off.*
....(12 to 1 op 16 to 1 tchd 20 to 1) 3

Dist: 4l, dist. 4m 47.00s. a 12.00s (3 Ran).

(The Link Leasing Partnership), C J Mann

NEWTON ABBOT (good)
Monday August 26th
Going Correction: PLUS 0.20 sec. per fur.

510 Bank Holiday Monday Selling Hand-icap Hurdle Class G (0-95 4-y-o and up) £1,893 2¾m....................(2:30)

163² NORTH BANNISTER [73] 9-10-6 D Gallagher, *chsd ldrs, steadied 3rd, chased lders 7th, led 3 out, sn drvn, kpt on wl.*
............(15 to 8 fav op 5 to 2 tchd 11 to 4 and 7 to 4) 1

314⁷ BRAVO STAR (USA) [67] 11-10-0 W Marston, *led 3 out, rdn and styd wth wnr til outpcd aftr 2 out.*
....(12 to 1 op 10 to 1 tchd 14 to 1) 2

419² KUTAN (Ire) [67] 6-10-0 E Byrne, *hld up, hdwy frm 3 out, styd on from 2 out, nrst finish.*....(6 to 1 op 5 to 1 tchd 13 to 2) 3

445⁴ COEUR BATTANT (Fr) [67] 6-10-0 B Powell, *pld hrd, hld up, hdwy 6th, rdn and one pace frm 3 out...*(8 to 1 op 5 to 1) 4

LAWBUSTER (Ire) [70] (bl) 4-9-10¹ (5°) D Salter, *chsd ldrs till drpd rear 6th, nvr dngrs aftr.*
....(40 to 1 op 25 to 1 tchd 50 to 1) 5

AUVILLAR (USA) [82] (bl) 8-11-1 T J Murphy, *chsd ldr aftr second to 7th, sn wknd.* (10 to 1 op 16 to 1 tchd 20 to 1) 6

331⁴ THE BLACK MONK (Ire) [94] 8-11-13 D Bridgwater, *chsd ldrs, rdn aftr 6th, jmpd slwly 7th and sn btn.*
....(2 to 1 op 9 to 4 tchd 3 to 1) 7

ROWHEDGE [71] 10-10-4 S Curran, *drpd rear 3rd, lost tch aftr 7th, tld off whn pld up bef 2 out....*(12 to 1 op 10 to 1) pu

Dist: 2l, 1l, 14l, 21l, 12l, 3½l. 5m 17.90s. a 16.90s (8 Ran).

(T P McGovern), T P McGovern

511 Sannacott Novices' Hurdle Class E (4-y-o and up) £2,211 2m 1f.......(3:00)

423° RE ROI (Ire) 4-11-2 T J Murphy, *hld up in rear, steady hdwy frm 3 out, chlgd 2 out, sn led, blun last, ran on wl....*(2 to 1) 1

310² MILLION DANCER 4-11-2 D Bridgwater, *led, sn clr, hdd 4th, rdn aftr 3rd, headed after 3 out, drvn to ld 2 out, soon headed, found no extr.*
............(2 to 1 on op 6 to 4 on tchd 11 to 8 on and 5 to 4 on) 2

446³ ALMAPA 4-10-6 (3°) T Dascombe, *beh, hdwy 4th, led aftr 3 out, hdd 2 out, sn one pace und pres...*(11 to 1 op 5 to 1) 3

DRY SEA 5-10-12 J Frost, *chsd ldr to 3 out, wknd appr 2 out.*
....(11 to 1 op 7 to 1 tchd 12 to 1) 4

446⁵ FALCONS DAWN 9-11-2⁴ Miss L Blackford, *beh frm 5th.*
....(50 to 1 op 16 to 1) 5

Dist: 1½l, 1¼l, 14l, 16l. 3m 59.60s. a 10.60s (5 Ran).

SR: 16/14/5/-/-/ (J C Fox), J C Fox

512 Clock End Novices' Chase Class E (5-y-o and up) £2,859 3¼m 110yds (3:30)

CLIFTON SET (bl) 5-10-7 R Dunwoody, *wth ldr till led 3rd to nxt, styd with lder till led 9th, hdd 12th, led 14th, sn clr, easily.*
....(5 to 2 on op 3 to 1 on tchd 9 to 4 on) 1

403 BIT OF A TOUCH 10-10-12 J Frost, *led to 3rd, led ag'n 4th, hdd 8th, styd with ldrs till led 12th, headed 14th, sn outpcd.*
....(25 to 1 op 16 to 1) 2

MANOR BOUND 6-10-7 S McNeill, *in tch, hit tenth, rdn 14th, styd on same pace.*..............(10 to 1 op 10 to 1) 3

104 BRORA ROSE (Ire) (bl) 8-10-7 S Burrough, *jmpd slwly in rear, tld off frm 6th.*...........(20 to 1 op 10 to 1) 4

MASTER KIWI (NZ) 9-10-7 (5°) D Salter, *in tch, led 8th, hdd nxt, wknd 11th, tld off whn pld up bef 3 out.*
....(11 to 2 op 9 to 2 tchd 6 to 1) pu

455 MISS DOTTY (bl) 6-10-4 (3°) D Walsh, *jmpd slwly in rear, rdn 6th, tld off 8th, pld up bef 14th.*
....(8 to 1 op 6 to 1 tchd 10 to 1) pu

Dist: 11l, 1½l, dist. 6m 36.20s. a 16.20s (6 Ran).

(Mrs Christine Fennell), C J Mann

513 Newton Abbot Annual Members Claiming Hurdle Class G (4-y-o and up) £1,893 2m 1f.................(4:00)

422° PETER MONAMY (bl) 4-11-3 (3°) D Walsh, *trkd ldrs, dsptd aftr 3 out, led appr 2 out, drvn out.*
....(7 to 4 fav op 6 to 4 tchd 2 to 1) 1

390² GAME DILEMMA 5-10-7 (7°) O Burrows, *hdwy aftr 4th, hmpd and lost pl bend appr 5th, styd on frm 2 out, kpt on r-in.*
....(7 to 1 op 7 to 1) 2

362² SIMPLY (Ire) 7-11-2 D Gallagher, *led till hdd appr 2 out, kpt on one pace und pres.*............(11 to 4 op 3 to 1) 3

328⁶ COOLEY'S VALVE (Ire) 8-11-5 S McNeill, *hld up, gd hdwy 5th, pressed ldrs aftr 3 out, blun 2 out, sn btn.*
....(9 to 2 op 4 to 1 tchd 5 to 1) 4

83⁶ REEFA'S MILL (Ire) (bl) 4-11-0 W Marston, *wth ldr aftr 4th, rdn 3 out, wknd appr 2 out.*.......(10 to 1 op 12 to 1) 5

LITTLE HOOLIGAN (bl) 5-11-2 B Powell, *in tch, chsd ldrs frm 3 out to 2 out, wknd quickly.*.......(12 to 1 op 10 to 1) 6

AMBER LILY 4-10-0 T J Murphy, *effrt aftr 4th, wknd after 5th.*
....(50 to 1 op 33 to 1) 7

123⁴ EMERALD MOON 9-10-10 S Burrough, *beh frm 4th.*
....(25 to 1 op 16 to 1) 8

417⁵ MERLINS WISH (USA) 7-10-13 D Bridgwater, *beh, rdn 4th, sn wknd, tld off frm 3 out*....(12 to 1 op 10 to 1 tchd 14 to 1) 9
DAZZLE ME 4-10-5⁵ F Jousset, *prmnt to 4th, tld off whn pld up bef 3 out*......................(50 to 1 op 33 to 1) pu
Dist: 3l, 2l, 1¼l, ½l, 12l, 8l, 2½l, dist. 4m 3.00s. a 14.00s (10 Ran).

(Richard Green (Fine Paintings)), M C Pipe

514 South West Racing Club Handicap Chase Class F (5-y-o and up) £2,691 2m 5f 110yds................... (4:30)

452* MAGGOTS GREEN [86] 9-11-0 (7ex) T J Murphy, *led to appr 3rd, led ag'n 12th, clr frm 4 out, easily.*
.........................(13 to 8 fav op 2 to 1 tchd 9 to 4) 1
402* DUKE OF DREAMS [79] 6-10-7 B Powell, *hit 4th, hdwy 9th, chsd wnr frm four out, no imprsn.*
.........................(4 to 1 op 9 to 4 tchd 5 to 1) 2
WINGSPAN (USA) [97] 12-11-11 A Thornton, *trkd ldrs, hit 11th, styd chasing ldrs till fdd frm 3 out.*
.........................(11 to 2 op 10 to 1 tchd 5 to 1) 3
30? SPEAK KINDLY [91] 11-11-4 R Gallagher, *drpd rear 9th, rallied* (*9 to 2 op 4 to 1 tchd 7 to 1*) ¡
335⁶ PRUDENT PEGGY [75] (bl) 9-10-3³ J Frost, *led appr 3rd, clr nxt, hdd 12th, sn wknd.* (14 to 1 op 12 to 1 tchd 16 to 1) 5
402³ TOOMUCH TOOSOON (Ire) [100] 8-12-0 D Bridgwater, *beh, hdwy and hit tenth, sn rdn, lost tch aftr nxt.*
.........................(3 to 1 op 2 to 1 tchd 100 to 30) 6
NICK THE DREAMER [100] 11-12-0 R Dunwoody, *chsd ldrs till wknd aftr 7th, tld off...*(13 to 2 op 6 to 1 tchd 7 to 1) 7
Dist: 9l, 10l, 7l, 6l, 4l, dist. 5m 15.40s. a 13.40s (7 Ran).

(E A Hayward), J M Bradley

515 J C Milton Electricals Handicap Hurdle Class E (0-115 4-y-o and up) £2,232 2 ¾m................... (5:00)

BLASKET HERO [95] (bl) 8-10-13 S McNeill, *hld up, rdn 7th, chsd ldr but plenty to do aftr 3 out, styd on wl to chal 2 out, sn led, pushed out.*........ (3 to 1 tchd 7 to 2 and 4 to 1) 1
THE MINDER (Fr) [88] (bl) 9-10-1 (5*) D Salter, *trkd ldrs, quickened to ld appr 7th, clr 3 out, wknd 2 out, sn hdd, no extr.*
.........................(7 to 1 op 5 to 1) 2
375⁵ EVANGELICA (USA) [103] 6-11-7 D Bridgwater, *hdwy and jmpd slwly 3rd, rdn aftr 6th, effrt 7th, found nothing, sn btn.*
.........................(13 to 8 jt-fav op 6 to 4 tchd 7 to 4) 3
FANTASTIC FLEET (Ire) [101] 4-11-2 S Curran, *chsd ldr to 7th, wknd aftr 3 out.....* (13 to 8 jt-fav op 2 to 1 tchd 9 to 4) 4
PASSED PAWN [109] 9-11-13 Miss S Vickery, *led, clr 4th, hit nxt, hdd appr 7th, sn wknd.*
.........................(12 to 1 op 8 to 1 tchd 14 to 1) 5
Dist: 13l, 20l, 4l, 5l. 5m 14.60s. a 13.60s (5 Ran).

(Miss H J Flower), Mrs S D Williams

SOUTHWELL (good)
Monday August 26th
Going Correction: PLUS 0.40 sec. per fur.

516 Canada Life Proud To Protect Novices' Handicap Chase Class D (0-105 5-y-o and up) £4,150 2½m 110yds.... (2:30)

383* WILLIE MAKEIT (Ire) [85] 6-11-10 J Railton, *cl up, led aftr second till hdd tenth, led after 4 out, clr after nxt, rdn appr last, ran on.*........................(6 to 5 on op 5 to 4 on) 1
461* SEAHAWK RETRIEVER [72] 7-10-11 (7ex) A P McCoy, *trkd ldg pair, hdwy to ld 3rd, sn clr, jnd and rdn 4 out, soon hdd, drvn 2 out, kpt on.*......................(6 to 4 op 5 to 4) 2
483³ HIZAL [72] 7-10-11 Mr A Charles-Jones, *led till aftr second, cl up till hit 9th and sn pushed alng, beh frm 11th.*
.........................(5 to 1 op 4 to 1) 3
Dist: 2l, dist. 5m 31.10s. a 31.10s (3 Ran).

(Old Berks Three), R T Phillips

517 Canada Life Champion Handicap Chase Class C (0-130 5-y-o and up) £5,287 3m 110yds................ (3:00)

327⁴ ANDRELOT [107] (bl) 9-11-10 A P McCoy, *made all, quickened clr aftr 12th, rdn alng 4 out, clear whn hit last, eased r-in.*
.........................(9 to 4 op 7 to 4) 1
368* MAGIC BLOOM [100] 10-10-12 (5*) E Callaghan, *hld up in tch, hit 4th, hdwy to chase wnr 5 out, rdn aftr last, no imprsn frm 3 out.*..............(7 to 4 op 2 to 1) 2
385* GEORGE ASHFORD (Ire) [90] (v) 6-10-7 A S Smith, *hld up in tch, reminders 6th, sn rdn alng, drvn and styd on frm 3 out, nvr dngrs.*............(13 to 8 fav op 9 to 4 tchd 15 to 8) 3
SPIKEY (Ire) [92] 10-10-4 (7*) N T Egan, *chsd wnr, hit 6th, sn rdn alng, wknd 5 out.*..........(16 to 1 op 10 to 1) 4
Dist: 4l, nk, 12l. 6m 27.50s. a 33.50s (4 Ran).

(H Jones), P Bowen

518 Canada Life Pension Claiming Hurdle Class F (4-y-o and up) £2,047 2½m 110yds................... (3:30)

ALWAYS GREENER (Ire) 5-10-3 (5*) Michael Brennan, *trkd ldrs, hdwy 4 out, cl up nxt, led appr 2 out, blun last, hld on.*
.........................(8 to 1 tchd 9 to 1) 1
417³ RIVA'S BOOK (USA) 5-10-13 A P McCoy, *hld up, reminders 6th, hdwy nxt, led 3 out, sn rdn and hdd next, drvn and kpt on.*
.........................(9 to 4 fav op 6 to 4 tchd 5 to 2) 2
412 NORTHERN NATION 8-10-13 A S Smith, *hld up, hit 4th, shaken up and hdwy 6th, rdn and hit nxt, wknd aftr four out.*
.........................(5 to 1 op 4 to 1) 3
389² ANTIGUAN FLYER 7-10-6 (7*) Mr A Coe, *led, rdn alng and hit 7th, hdd 3 out, wknd 4th.* ...(5 to 2 op 7 to 2) 4
451² SLIPPERY MAX 12-10-7 (3*) R Massey, *in tch, rdn alng 7th, wknd bef 3 out, tld off whn pld up bef last.*........(4 to 1) pu
SMOKEY TRACK 11-10-6 (5*) S Taylor, *chsd ldr, rdn alng 7th, sn wknd, tld off whn pld up bef nxt.*
.........................(40 to 1 op 33 to 1 tchd 50 to 1) pu
ANOTHERONE TO NOTE 5-10-0 (7*) A Dowling, *chsd ldrs till rdn and hit 6th, wknd quickly, pld up bef nxt.*
.........................(50 to 1 op 25 to 1) pu
Dist: 1¼l, dist, 5l. 5m 19.90s. a 33.90s (7 Ran).

(Peter Houghton), J W Mullins

519 A-Z Insurance Services Novices' Hurdle Class D (4-y-o and up) £2,794 3m 110yds................... (4:00)

295* ORDOG MOR (Ire) 7-11-12 A P McCoy, *made all, clr 9th, unchlgd.*..................(6 to 1 on op 4 to 1 on) 1
388⁵ ARRANGE A GAME (bl) 9-10-9 (5*) S Taylor, *in tch till rdn alng and outpcd 8th, sn beh, styd on frm 2 out, wnt remote second appr last.*..........(40 to 1 op 25 to 1 tchd 50 to 1) 2
401³ CROWN IVORY (NZ) 8-11-0 S Fox, *chsd wnr, rdn appr 4 out, sn one pace.*.................(5 to 1 op 4 to 1) 3
CRUISE FREE 7-11-0 Mr A Charles-Jones, *not fluent, beh frm 6th, tld off from 8th.*
.........................(16 to 1 op 14 to 1 tchd 20 to 1 and 25 to 1) 4
Dist: Dist, 6l, dist. 6m 24.00s. a 42.00s (4 Ran).

(M R Johnson), M G Meagher

520 Arthur Anderson Selling Hurdle Class G (4 - 7-y-o) £2,029 2m........ (4:30)

SIMAND 4-10-4 J Callaghan, *hld up in tch, hdwy 5th, led 4 out, clr 2 out, rdn last, ran on.*.................(4 to 1) 1
423³ MINNESOTA FATS (Ire) 5-10-4 Gary Lyons, *hld up, hdwy 7th, effrt 2 out an chasing wnr, drvn and ch last, not quicken r-in.*.................................(5 to 1) 2
SUMMER VILLA 4-10-4 O Pears, *in tch, pushed alng and outpcd 5th, hdwy aftr 3 out, rdn and hit nxt, kpt on one pace.*
.........................(6 to 1 op 7 to 1) 3
TRUMBLE 4-10-9 A P McCoy, *al prmnt, ev ch 4 out, rdn nxt, btn whn blun 2 out, wknd.......*(3 to 1 jt-fav tchd 11 to 4) 4
ROSE CHIME (Ire) 4-10-4 P McLoughlin, *chsd ldrs, rdn 5th, blun 3 out and sn wknd.*.........(12 to 1 op 8 to 1) 5
387² IRIE MON (Ire) 4-10-13 (3*) K Gaule, *hld up, hit second, not fluent aftr, beh frm 3 out.......* (3 to 1 jt-fav tchd 7 to 2) 6
294⁶ BOOST 4-10-9 S Wynne, *led, rdn 5th, hdd nxt, sn wknd.*
.........................(12 to 1) 7
387⁴ CHADLEIGH WALK (Ire) 4-10-9 A S Smith, *cl up, rdn 5th, wknd nxt, tld off whn pld up bef 2 out.* (20 to 1 op 16 to 1) pu
423 FLASHING SABRE 4-10-9 Mr A Charles-Jones, *pld hrd, al rear, tld off 5th, pulled up bef 3 out.....*(33 to 1 op 25 to 1) pu
Dist: 3l, 14l, 18l, ½l, 13l, 8l. 4m 4.60s. a 18.60s (9 Ran).

(Ms Sigrid Walter), G M Moore

521 Canada Life Assurance Handicap Hurdle Class E (0-115 4-y-o and up) £2,924 2½m 110yds........... (5:00)

49 FRONTIER FLIGHT (USA) [87] 6-11-3 S Wynne, *hld up, steady hdwy 5th, sn tracking ldrs, led appr 2 out, ran on.*
.........................(7 to 1 op 6 to 1) 1
TEL E THON [80] (v) 9-10-9 I Lawrence, *cl up, led 3rd, rdn 3 out, hdd appr nxt, one pace.*.........(8 to 1 op 5 to 1) 2
333* VERDE LUNA [86] 4-10-12 A P McCoy, *trkd ldrs, hdwy 7th and ev ch till rdn and wknd bef 2 out.*
.........................(7 to 4 fav tchd 6 to 4) 3
414* ROYAL CIRCUS [94] 7-11-6 (3*) E Husband, *led to 3rd, cl up till rdn alng aftr 6th and sn lost pl.....* (7 to 2 op 5 to 2) 4
TRUMPET [95] 7-11-5 (5*) Michael Brennan, *chsd ldrs to 4th, sn lost pl and tld off frm 7th.* (5 to 2 op 4 to 1 tchd 9 to 2) 5
Dist: 15l, 22l, 25l, 29l. 5m 18.70s. a 32.70s (5 Ran).

(Miss L C Siddall), Miss L C Siddall

TRALEE (IRE) (soft)
Monday August 26th

522 I.C.C. Bank Hurdle (3-y-o) £3,425 2m .... (5:05)

341* RHUM DANCER (Ire) 10-10 C O'Dwyer, ...(5 to 2 fav) 1
341² EVRIZA (Ire) 10-10 (5*) J Butler,...................(3 to 1) 2
THREE RIVERS 10-7 (3*) D J Casey,..................(3 to 1) 3
425² LUDDEN CHIEF (Ire) 10-5 T J Mitchell,..........(12 to 1) 4
SIMPLY RUN (Ire) 10-5 W Slattery,..................(16 to 1) 5
OH DOE (Ire) 10-0 T Horgan,........................(25 to 1) 6

TIP YOUR WAITRESS (Ire) 10-5 T J O'Sullivan, ...(33 to 1) 7
4423 RENATA'S PRINCE (Ire) 10-10 J Shortt, ... (12 to 1) 8
KILBAHA (Ire) 10-5 J P Broderick, ... (5 to 1) f
DILLON'S TAXI (Ire) 10-10 T P Treacy, ...(12 to 1) f
Dist: 9l, 3½l, dist, sht-hd. 4m 10.80s. (10 Ran).

(Exors Late Mrs G W Jennings), D K Weld

523 Barrett Bookmakers Q.R. Handicap Hurdle (0-123 4-y-o and up) £3,425 3m
. . . . (5:35)

4042 MANETTI [-] 4-10-13 (7") Mr S P Hennessy, ...(4 to 1) 1
392* SLAVE GALE (Ire) [-] 5-11-0 (7") Mr C A Murphy, (10 to 30) 2
4432 CELIO LUCY (Ire) [-] 6-10-5 (5") Mr R Walsh, ...(7 to 2) 3
3543 TEMPLEROAN PRINCE [-] 9-12-4 Mr G J Harford,
. . . . (9 to 4 fav) 4
4085 RISING BREEZE (Ire) [-] 7-10-10 (3") Mr B M Cash, (6 to 1) 5
3523 BRACKER (Ire) [-] 4-9-11 (7") Mr Jonn P Moloney, (20 to 1) 6
Dist: 9l, 6l, 15l, 20l. (Time not taken) (6 Ran).

(Peter Piller), T Stack

LES LANDES (JER) (good to soft)
Monday August 26th

524 Supporters' Handicap Hurdle (4-y-o and up) £720 2m. . . . .(2:30)

378* WOLLBOLL 6-12-0 V Smith, ...(5 to 2 on) 1
3782 CLEAR HOME 10-9-7 A McCabe, ... (9 to 4) 2
KNOT TRUE 6-9-7 S Fothergill, ... (12 to 1) 3
Dist: 2l, dist. 4m 0.00s. (3 Ran).

(Mike Weaver), J S O Arthur

TRALEE (IRE) (good to yielding)
Tuesday August 27th

525 W.H.Giles & Co.A.Blennerhassett Beginners Chase (4-y-o and up) £3,425 2½m. . . . .(5:35)

4714 VAIN PRINCESS (Ire) 7-11-9 M P Hourigan, ...(6 to 1) 1
3154 CULLENSTOWN LADY (Ire) 5-11-3 J Shortt, ...(4 to 1) 2
UP TRUMPS (Ire) 7-12-0 J P Broderick, ...(16 to 1) 3
MISS ELIZABETH (Ire) 6-11-9 K F O'Brien, ...(12 to 1) 4
2592 YOUNG DUBLINER (Ire) 7-12-0 C F Swan, ...(11 to 8 fav) 5
TOM THE BOY VI (Ire) 7-12-0 S H O'Donovan, . . .(25 to 1) f
345 MAC-DUAGH (Ire) 6-11-7 (7") Mr R D Lee, ...(33 to 1) f
DENNY'S GUESS (Ire) 8-12-0 G M O'Neill, ...(16 to 1) bd
THE GOPHER (Ire) 7-12-0 L P Cusack, ...(9 to 1) bd
357 WHAT IS THE PLAN (Ire) 7-11-7 (7") M R Murphy, (12 to 1) l
Dist: 6l, 15l, 12l. 5m 27.10s. (10 Ran).

(D O'Leary), Michael Hourigan

526 Nash's Mineral Waters Handicap Hurdle (Listed) (4-y-o and up) £6,850 2m 1f
. . . . (6:35)

TAITS CLOCK (Ire) [-] 7-9-13 T Horgan, trkd ldr, prog to ld
appr 7th, rdn approaching 2 out, jst hld on. . . . . . .(10 to 1) 1
3032 SPACE TRUCKER (Ire) [-] 5-11-6 J Shortt, wl plcd, jmpd slwly
4 out, sn prog, rdn aftr nxt, chlgd 2 out, jst flt. . .(5 to 4 fav) 2
BLACK QUEEN (Ire) [-] 5-10-5 K F O'Brien, wtd wth, rdn and
prog aftr 3 out, styd on wl. . . . .(100 to 30) 3
162* NEAR GALE (Ire) [-] 6-11-2 T P Treacy, wl plcd, lost pos appr 3
out, sn rdn, wknd aftr nxt. . . . .(11 to 2) 4
4283 LA CIENAGA [-] 12-9-92 J P Broderick, al rear, rdn bef 3 out,
not quicken. . . . .(20 to 1) 5
3156 SLANEY GLOW (Ire) [-] 5-10-10 F Woods, al rear, rdn aftr 3
out, no ext. . . . .(8 to 1) 6
JO JO BOY (Ire) [-] 7-10-9 F J Flood, led till appr 7th, rdn aftr 3
out, sn wknd. . . . .(14 to 1) 7
Dist: Hd, 3l, 2l, 11l. 4m 15.60s. (7 Ran).

(F Costello), Donal Hassett

527 Earl Of Desmond Hotel Mares Flat Race (4-y-o and up) £3,425 2m. .(8:05)

ACCOUNTANCY NATIVE (Ire) 4-11-2 (7") Mr J P McNamara,
. . . . (14 to 1) 1
1767 ANTICS (Ire) 4-11-2 (7") Mrs C Harrison, ...(14 to 1) 2
304 DIAMOND DOUBLE (Ire) 5-11-11 (3") Mr R M Cash,
. . . .(Evens fav) 3
4642 PLEASE NO TEARS 9-12-0 Mrs C Barker, ...(11 to 2) 4
3435 LADY OF GRANGE (Ire) 4-11-9 Mr H F Cleary, . . . (10 to 1) 5
ANJLORE (Ire) 5-11-7 (7") Mr K Taylor, ...(10 to 1) 6
PRIZE LADY (Ire) 6-11-7 (7") Mr J A Stack, ...(20 to 1) 7
21 WARLOCKFOE (Ire) 5-11-7 (7") Mr Sean O O'Brien, (9 to 1) 8
2748 CROCHAUN (Ire) (bl) 6-11-9 (5") Mr R Walsh, ...(20 to 1) 9
4078 PRINCESS HENRY (Ire) 6-11-7 (7") Mr John P Moloney,
. . . . (20 to 1) 10
159 ROMANCEINTHEDARK (Ire) 6-11-7 (7") Mr Edgar Byrne,
. . . . (14 to 1) 11
FLORIA (Ire) 4-11-2 (7") Miss A L Crowley, ...(12 to 1) 12
MARIAN'S OWN (Ire) 5-12-0 Mr J A Nash, ...(16 to 1) 13

340 INCH VALLEY (Ire) 5-11-7 (7") Miss I M Burke, ...(33 to 1) 14
3977 POWERCUT PRINCESS (Ire) 5-11-7 (7") Mr A J Dempsey,
. . . . (16 to 1) 15
217 LEZIES LAST (Ire) 6-11-7 (7") Mrs S O'Connor, . . .(25 to 1) ur
2747 BALLYDUFF ROSE (Ire) 6-11-7 (7") Mrs C Doyle, . . (16 to 1) pu
Dist: Hd, 5½l, 2l, 4l. 3m 58.00s. (17 Ran).

(Mrs Geraldine Treacy), S J Treacy

UTTOXETER (good to firm)
Tuesday August 27th
Going Correction: MINUS 0.20 sec. per fur.

528 Houghton Vaughan 'National Hunt' Novices' Hurdle Class D (4-y-o and up) £2,731 2½m 110yds. . . . .(2:15)

KNUCKLEBUSTER (Ire) 6-10-10 A P McCoy, al gng wl, quickened ahead bef 6th, clr whn jmpd rght last 3, easily.
. . . .(2 to 1 on op 6 to 4 on) 1
4464 REGAL GEM (Ire) 5-10-5 B Fenton, patiently rdn, improved to
chase wnr frm 4 out, effrt last 2, one pace.
. . . .(11 to 2 op 5 to 1 tchd 7 to 1) 2
3103 SEVEN WELLS 4-10-7 R Bellamy, led till hdd bef 6th, styd
second till rdn and outpcd 3 out.
. . . .(50 to 1 op 33 to 1 tchd 66 to 1) 3
2953 TUG YOUR FORELOCK 5-10-10 A Thornton, settled to track
ldrs, struggling whn pace quickened aftr one circuit, tld off.
. . . .(14 to 1 op 8 to 1) 4
SQUIRRELLSDAUGHTER 9-9-12 (7") Miss S Beddoes, wl
plcd for one circuit, sn lost tch, tld off. (20 to 1 op 16 to 1) 5
LILLY THE FILLY 5-10-5 E Byrne, chsd ldrs for one circuit, sn
lost tch, tld off whn l 3 out. . . . .(66 to 1 op 50 to 1) f
KINGSWELL BOY 10-10-10 D Bridgwater, refused to race,
took no part. . . . .(8 to 1 op 5 to 1) ref
Dist: 8l, 9l, 21l, 18l. 4m 48.90s. a 9.90s (7 Ran).

(Mrs D Poore), P J Hobbs

529 Caffrey's Handicap Hurdle Class D (0-120 4-y-o and up) £2,773 2½m 110yds. . . . .(2:45)

3744 PREROGATIVE [97] (v) 6-10-11 A P McCoy, wth ldr, jmpd
ahead second, clr frm hfwy, unchlgd. (14 to 1 op 10 to 1) 1
381* CLEAN EDGE (USA) [101] 4-10-6 (3") E Husband, patiently
rdn, improved to chase wnr frm hfwy, ridden and no imprsn
from 3 out. . . . .(6 to 5 fav op Evens tchd 5 to 4) 2
4572 HACKETTS CROSS (Ire) [96] 8-10-3 (7") Mr R Thornton, led
till mstk and hdd second, styd in tch, drvn alng bef 4 out, one
pace frm nxt. . . . .(8 to 1 tchd 9 to 1) 3
SHERIFF [117] 5-12-0 C Llewellyn, last and hld up, niggled
alng hfwy, no imprsn whn olumsy 3 out, tld off.
. . . .(5 to 4 tchd 11 to 8) 4
Dist: 7l, 7l, dist. 4m 41.80s. a 2.80s (4 Ran).
SR: 15/6/-/-/ (The Secret Partnership), H S Howe

530 Wellman Plc Novices' Handicap Chase Class E (0-100 5-y-o and up) £2,814 3¼m. . . . .(3:15)

WARNER'S SPORTS [72] 7-10-11 A P McCoy, al gng best,
led 7th, drw clr frm hfwy, unchlgd.
. . . .(11 to 8 on op 5 to 4 on tchd 7 to 4 on and 5 to 4 on) 1
483 MUSIC SCORE [82] 10-11-7 A Thornton, narrow ld to 4th, lost
tch hfwy, styd on und pres to take second r-in.
. . . .(8 to 1 op 6 to 1 tchd 9 to 1) 2
4553 DUKE OF LANCASTER (Ire) [85] (v) 7-11-10 W Marston, wth
ldrs, led 4th to 7th, chsd wnr aftr, blun last, lost second r-in.
. . . .(7 to 2 op 3 to 1 tchd 4 to 1) 3
3856 SAINT BENE'T (Ire) [63] (v) 8-10-2 J Culloty, blun and rdr lost
irons second, reco'red aftr 4th, struggling frm hfwy, nvr a
factor. . . . .(7 to 1 tchd 8 to 1) 4
3854 ABITMORFUN [61] 10-10-0 L Harvey, struggling and lost tch
bef hfwy, tld off, blun last. . . . .(16 to 1 op 10 to 1) 5
Dist: 13l, nk, 2l, dist. 6m 35.80s. a 23.80s (5 Ran).

(Terry Warner Sports), P J Hobbs

531 Strebel Boilers & Radiators Handicap Hurdle Class C (0-130 5-y-o and up) £3,403 3m 110yds. . . . .(3:45)

NIRVANA PRINCE [113] 7-11-10 A Maguire, wtd wth, not
fluent 3rd, given time to reco'r, jnd ldr 2 out, sn led, ran on
strly. . . . .(11 to 4 op 5 to 2 tchd 3 to 1) 1
283* ELITE REG [110] (v) 7-11-7 D Bridgwater, tried to make all,
jnd and rdn alng 3 out, hdd aftr 2 out, one pace.
. . . .(11 to 8 fav op 5 to 4 tchd 6 to 4) 2
2275 OZZIE JONES [93] 9-10-4 W Marston, lft second 4th, effrt 5
out, struggling aftr nxt, fdd last 3. . . . . . .(7 to 1 tchd 6 to 1) 3
584 TALLYWAGGER [117] 9-11-7 (7") T Hogg, tracking ldr whn f
4th. . . . .(11 to 4 op 5 to 2) f
Dist: 4l, 23l. 5m 41.40s. a 4.40s (4 Ran).

(D Portman), B Preece

532 Square And Compass Handicap Chase Class C (0-130 5-y-o and up) £4,686 2

½m. . . . . (4:15)

413 MICHERADO (Fr) [94] 6-10-0 R Johnson, *made all, hrd pressed frm 4 out, jmpd lft nxt 3, all out.*
. . . . (9 to 1 op 8 to 1 tchd 10 to 1) 1
CONTI D'ESTRUVAL (Fr) [122] 6-12-0 A P McCoy, *patiently rdn, improved to draw level 4 out, ridden betw last 2, rallied r-in.* . . . . (Evens fav tchd 11 to 10) 2
327³ MUSKORA (Ire) [116] (bl) 7-11-5 (3*) G Tormey, *mstks, trkd ldr, hit 4th and 5 out, wkng quickly whn blun and uns rdr 3 out.*
. . . . (11 to 10 op Evens tchd 6 to 5) ur
Dist: ¾l. 4m 58.10s. (3 Ran).

(Stanley W Clarke), S A Brookshaw

533 Caffrey's Conditional Jockeys' Novices' Hurdle Class F (4-y-o and up) £1,997 2m. . . . . (4:45)

511² MILLION DANCER 4-11-2 D Walsh, *made all, sn clr, rdn 6th, in control whn blun last, hld on.* . . . . . . (7 to 4 fav op 5 to 4) 1
KYMIN (Ire) 4-10-4 R Painter, *settled in rear, steady hdwy frm 2*
. . . . 2
335⁷ RAMSTAR 8-10-12 G Tormey, *chsd wnr, dsptd ld frm 6th, rdn 3 out, wknd from nxt.* . . . . (8 to 1 op 7 to 1) 3
478² LANCER (USA) 4-11-2 R Massey, *chsd ldrs, outpcd 6th, styd on ag'n frm 2 out.* . . . . (4 to 1 op 3 to 1) 4
307 PIMSBOY (y) 9-10-12 P Midgley, *settled mid-div, shaken up 3 out, no imprsn.* . . . . (40 to 1 op 33 to 1) 5
420³ HATTA RIVER (USA) 6-11-2 D Parker, *nvr better than mid-div.* . . . . (20 to 1 op 9 to 1) 6
415⁴ MELLOW YELLOW 5-10-12 E Husband, *hld up in rear, al beh.* . . . . (14 to 1 tchd 16 to 1) 7
SHARP HOLLY (Ire) 4-10-4 Sophie Mitchell, *al beh and outpcd.* . . . . (50 to 1) 8
CHESTERS QUEST 4-10-9 J Culloty, *mstk 1st, sn wl beh.*
. . . . (33 to 1 op 25 to 1) 9
GOOD (Ire) 4-10-9 B Fenton, *hld up in rear, effrt 6th, rdn appr 3 out, sn wknd, tld off.* . . . . . . (50 to 1 op 33 to 1) 10
Dist: 1½l, 6l, 1¾l, 20l, sht-hd, 3l, 3l, 1¾l, 9l. 3m 43.10s. a 6.10s (10 Ran).

(Martin Pipe Racing Club), M C Pipe

WAREGEM (BEL) (firm)
Tuesday August 27th

534 Prix Felix de Ruyck (Handicap Hurdle) (4-y-o and up) £6,566 2m 1f. . . . . (2:45)

BAGAREUR (Bel) (bl) 7-10-9 F Cheyer, ... 1
CELIBATE (Ire) 5-11-10 R Dunwoody, *hdwy 4 fs, led and mstk 2 out, hdd aftr last, one pace.* 2
LE MIRABEAU (Fr) 6-9-7 E Schepens, ... 3
294³ HERETICAL MISS 6-10-11 P Carberry, *prmnt, rdn and outpcd fnl circuit.* 5
DO BE WARE 6-9-12 J Joli, *mid-div early, sn tld off.* 8
Dist: 6l, 15l, 3l, 2l, 15l, 15l, dist. (Time not taken) (9 Ran).

(Marc Nuyttens), J Martens

535 Grand Steeplechase de Flandres (5-y-o and up) £32,830 2m 7f. . . . . . (3:15)

BEAU NOIR (Fr) 6-10-6 H Blois, ... 1
IRISH STAMP (Ire) 7-11-7 P Carberry, *jmpd wl, prog into 3rd 5 out, second last, kpt on r-in.* 2
LINE LAWYER (Fr) 5-10-8 P Corsi, ... 3
Dist: 3l, 3l, 4l, 2l, 2l, 3l. (Time not taken) (3 Ran).

(L Fertillet), Y Fertillet

TRALEE (IRE) (good to yielding)
Wednesday August 28th

536 Grand Hotel/Boyle Brothers Ltd Maiden Hurdle (5-y-o and up) £3,425 2 ½m. . . . . (2:35)

365⁴ LISS DE PAOR (Ire) 5-11-6 T Horgan, ... (7 to 4) 1
301² TARTHOOTH (Ire) 5-11-11 F Woods, ... (11 to 8 fav) 2
395² NOELEENS DELIGHT (Ire) 7-10-12 T P Treacy, ... (10 to 1) 3
LINDA'S BOY (Ire) 6-11-3 J Shortt, ... (12 to 1) 4
175² DROMINAGH (Ire) 8-10-10 (7*) R P Hogan, ... (14 to 1) 5
ALIGHIERI (Ire) 5-11-3 M P Dwyer, ... (14 to 1) 6
463⁷ LISHILLAUN (Ire) 6-11-1 (5*) Susan A Finn, ... (14 to 1) 7
CALL HER LIB (Ire) 6-10-12 J P Broderick, ... (50 to 1) 8
464⁶ GAIN CONTROL (Ire) 7-10-7 (5*) G Cotter, ... (20 to 1) 9
LAUGHING FONTAINE (Ire) 6-10-10 (7*) M H Murphy,
. . . . (25 to 1) 10
468⁷ RONETTE (Ire) 5-11-3 K F O'Brien, ... (33 to 1) 11
ROSETOWN GIRL (Ire) 5-10-12 M P Hourigan, ... (25 to 1) 12
466⁶ CORKERS FLAME (Ire) 5-11-3 W Slattery, ... (33 to 1) 13
410⁴ STANSWAY (Ire) 8-11-11 Mr P Fenton, ... (12 to 1) 14
66 LISS NA MAOL (Ire) 5-10-5 (7*) M D Murphy, ... (50 to 1) 15
Dist: 4l, 5l, 10l, 5l. 5m 1.20s. (15 Ran).

(J C Dempsey), A P O'Brien

537 McElligotts Garage/Mercedes Benz Handicap Chase (0-109 4-y-o and up) £3,425 2m. . . . . (3:05)

JAZZY REFRAIN (Ire) [-] 6-10-11 (7*) R P Hogan, . . . (5 to 1) 1
WACKO JACKO (Ire) [-] 7-10-11 J P Broderick, ... (9 to 2) 2
409* HANNIES GIRL (Ire) [-] 7-10-4 (7*) L J Fleming, (4 to 1 fav) 3
485² SANDY FOREST LADY (Ire) [-] 7-10-0 T P Treacy, . . (9 to 1) 4
314 MICKS DELIGHT (Ire) [-] 6-11-7 M P Dwyer, ... (7 to 1) 5
409⁵ SIR L MUNNY [-] 12-9-0 (7*) M D Murphy, ... (7 to 1) 6
BALLYBODEN [-] 9-10-7 M P Hourigan, ... (20 to 1) 7
426* PHARDY (Ire) [-] 5-11-6 G M O'Neill, ... (5 to 1) f
Dist: ½l, 15l, ¾l, 5½l. 4m 6.10s. (8 Ran).

(Mrs Mary M Hayes), John J Walsh

538 Garry Dillon Waste Disposal Flat Race (5-y-o and up) £3,425 2m 1f. . . . . (5:45)

COMAN'S JET (Ire) 6-12-0 Mr P Fenton, ... (9 to 2) 1
286⁴ MAGICAL WAY (Ire) 6-11-7 (7*) Mr B Hassett, ... (6 to 1) 2
HOLY GROUND (Ire) 6-11-7 (7*) Mr I T Nolan, ... (7 to 1) 3
394⁶ PHARADISO (Ire) 5-12-0 Mr J P Dempsey, ... (7 to 1) 3+
329³ GOLD DEVON (Ire) 6-11-7 (7*) Mrs C Doyle, ... (12 to 1) 5
CURRAGH RANGER (Ire) 6-11-7 (7*) Mr A J Dempsey,
. . . . (8 to 1) 6
APPLAUSE (Ire) 5-11-11 (3*) Mr B M Cash, ... (2 to 1 fav) 7
286³ HIGH MOAT (Ire) 6-11-7 (7*) Miss J M Lee, ... (11 to 2) 8
Dist: 13l, ¾l, dd-ht, 11l. 4m 8.30s. (8 Ran).

(M Vaughan), W J Burke

WORCESTER (good to firm)
Wednesday August 28th
Going Correction: NIL

539 Newland Maiden Hurdle Class F (4-y-o and up) £2,213 2m. . . . . (2:00)

178³ ALPINE MIST (Ire) 4-10-11 (5*) Michael Brennan, *patiently rdn, steady hdwy frm 4 out, ridden to draw level aftr nxt, led after 2 out, drvn clr.* . . . . (3 to 1 jt-fav op 2 to 1) 1
LEAR DANCER (USA) 5-11-5 Gary Lyons, *trkd ldrs, improved to jump ahead 3 out, jnd bef nxt, hdd aftr 2 out, btn whn almost f last.* . . . . (3 to 1 jt-fav op 5 to 1 tchd 11 to 2) 2
PYTCHLEY DAWN 6-11-0 V Slattery, *settled off the pace, struggling to keep in tch hfwy, some hdwy frm 3 out, nvr dngrs.* . . . . (33 to 1 op 25 to 1) 3
423⁵ FLAIR LADY 5-10-7 (7*) J Power, *settled to chase ldrs, struggling bef 4 out, rdn nxt, tld off.* . . . . . (25 to 1 tchd 33 to 1) 4
TRIPLE TIE (USA) 4-11-2 D Gallagher, *led, clr 3rd, wknd and hdd 3 out, lost tch, tld off.* (7 to 2 op 11 to 4 tchd 4 to 1) 5
310⁵ DISCO'S WELL (bl) 5-11-5 T Kent, *rcd freely, stopped pulling and lost pl quickly hfwy, tld off.* . . (20 to 1 tchd 33 to 1) 6
ORINOCO VENTURE (Ire) 5-11-5 D J Burchell, *chsd ldrs, struggling to keep in tch hfwy, tld off whn pld up bef 3 out.*
. . . . (6 to 1 tchd 5 to 1) pu
MASRUF (Ire) 4-11-2 M A Fitzgerald, *struggling bef hfwy, tld off whn hmpd and pld up before 3 out.*
. . . . (8 to 1 op 4 to 1 tchd 9 to 1) pu
Dist: 11l, 19l, 6l, 7l, dist. 3m 48.10s. a 8.10s (8 Ran).
SR: 7/-/-/-/-/ (Catch-42), J G M O'Shea

540 Levy Board Novices' Handicap Hurdle Class E (0-100 4-y-o and up) £2,234 3m. . . . . (2:30)

451⁴ CHINA MAIL (Ire) [90] 4-11-0 T J Murphy, *settled off the pace, gd hdwy frm 4 out, poised to chal whn lft in ld 2 out, sn clr.*
. . . . (100 to 30 op 5 to 2 tchd 7 to 1) 1
376² SIGMA WIRELESS (Ire) [100] 7-12-0 S Wynne, *patiently rdn promising effrt appr 3 out, sn ridden, not quicken frm betw last 2.* . . . . (3 to 1 jt-fav tchd 7 to 2) 2
371² LITTLE TINCTURE (Ire) [72] 6-9-9 (5*) Sophie Mitchell, *led, jnd hfwy, hdd 4 out, tld off and pres frm nxt.* . . . (9 to 2 op 4 to 1) 3
401² UP THE TEMPO (Ire) [72] 7-9-9 (5*) Michael Brennan, *sn struggling to go pace, drvn alng bef hfwy, tld off.*
. . . . (5 to 1 tchd 11 to 2) 4
WRITTEN AGREEMENT [72] 8-9-10¹ (5*) Chris Webb, *trkd ldr, drw level hfwy, led 4 out, one and a half ls clr but tiring whn f 2 out.* . . . . (25 to 1 op 33 to 1 tchd 50 to 1) f
ST KITTS [82] 5-10-6 R Dunwoody, *settled wth chasing grp, struggling fnl circuit, tld off whn pld up aftr 4 out.* (3 to 1 jt-fav op 7 to 2) pu
376⁴ CHEER'S BABY [72] (v) 6-10-0 R Johnson, *settled off the pace, last whn pld up lme aftr 6th.*
. . . . (40 to 1 op 33 to 1 tchd 50 to 1) pu
Dist: 9l, 11l, 17l. 5m 46.80s. a 10.80s (7 Ran).

(The Merlin Syndicate), K C Bailey

541 Stanford Marsh Group Handicap Chase Class D (0-120 5-y-o and up) £3,777 2½m 110yds. . . . . (3:00)

375³ COMEDY ROAD [98] 12-11-5 R Johnson, *al hndy, nosed ahead aftr 8 out, styd on strly to go clr frm last, eased.*
. . . . (5 to 4 fav tchd 6 to 4) 1

MERLINS DREAM (Ire) [103] 7-11-10 J Osborne, *wtd wth, improved to ld 9th (water), hdd aftr 6 out, ev ch till rdn betw last 2, sn btn*................ (6 to 4 op 5 to 4 tchd 13 to 8) 2

3757 CELTIC LAIRD [85] 8-10-6 W Marston, *dictated pace till hdd 9th (water), sn outpcd, rallied aftr 5 out, fdd nxt, tld off*.
.... (100 to 30 op 3 to 1) 3

Dist: 8l, dist. 5m 4.20s. a 7.20s (3 Ran).

SR: 19/16/-/- (Winsbury Livestock), R Lee

542 BBC Hereford & Worcester Juvenile Novices' Hurdle Class E (3-y-o) £2,302 2m...................................... (3:30)

SHEATH KEFAAH 10-10 G Bradley, *patiently rdn, steady hdwy appr 3 out, led betw last 2, jmpd lft last, drvn clr.* (3 to 1) 1

399* BEN BOWDEN 11-3 D Gallagher, *al frnt rnk, ev ch frm 3 out, rdn and crrd lft last, no extr*........ (5 to 2 fav op 2 to 1) 2

LEBEDINSKI (Ire) 10-5 R Marley, *settled in tch, jmpd slwly 3rd, rallied to chal 2 out, rdn and one pace.*
.... (9 to 1 op 10 to 1 tchd 12 to 1) 3

BATH KNIGHT 10-10 S McNeill, *led, rdn and hdd 2 out, wknd quickly.*........................ (6 to 1 op 4 to 1) 4

411 SONG FOR JESS (Ire) 10-5 S Wynne, *chsd ldrs, effrt aftr 4 out, wknd quickly appr 2 out.*............ (50 to 1 op 25 to 1) 5

REMEMBER STAR 10-5 F Jousset, *tucked away midfield, effrt aftr 4 out, wknd quickly, tld off.*
.... (20 to 1 op 25 to 1 tchd 33 to 1) 6

INDIAN SUNSET 10-10 J Osborne, *not fluent, settled mid-field, effrt 4 out, wknd quickly nxt, tld off.*
.... (11 to 4 tchd 3 to 1) 7

SANS PERE 10-10 W Marston, *struggling to keep up hfwy, sn tld off*.................... (20 to 1 op 8 to 1) 8

Dist: 3l, 4l, 11l, 10l, dist, 2l, 1l. 3m 54.80s. a 14.80s (8 Ran).

(K C Payne), J R Jenkins

543 Grandstand Conditional Jockeys' Handicap Hurdle Class E (0-110 4-y-o and up) £2,250 2½m............ (4:00)

3812 FIRST CRACK [81] 11-10-7 L Aspell, *settled travelling wl, poised to chal whn lft in ld 3 out, sn clr, easily.*
.... (100 to 30 op 3 to 1 tchd 7 to 2) 1

TAP ON TOOTSIE [94] 4-11-0 R Massey, *trkd ldr, ev ch 3 out, sn rdn, outpcd frm betw last 2.*
.... (7 to 2 op 3 to 1 tchd 4 to 1) 2

SCRIPT [80] 5-9-12 (5*) N T Egan, *settled to track ldrs, strug-gling whn pace quickened appr 3 out, sn btn, tld off.*
.... (8 to 1 op 7 to 1 tchd 9 to 1) 3

4032 JENZSOPH (Ire) [105] 5-12-0 D J Kavanagh, *tried to make all, hrd pressed whn f 3 out.*
.... (15 to 8 fav op 7 to 4 tchd 2 to 1) f

CLASH OF CYMBALS [80] 7-10-6 J Magee, *last and hld up till pld up lme aftr 4th*.............. (9 to 2 op 100 to 30) pu

Dist: 15l, 21l. 4m 49.80s. a 13.80s (5 Ran).

(D Pugh), F Jordan

544 Sonny Somers Novices' Handicap Chase Class E (0-100 5-y-o and up) £2,945 2m 7f................ (4:30)

LUCKY DOLLAR (Ire) [95] 8-11-13 A Thornton, *made all, gng clr whn jmpd lft 4 out, styd on strly.*
.... (9 to 4 fav op 5 to 2 tchd 11 to 4) 1

3852 BLUE RAVEN [85] 5-10-13 A P McCoy, *al pressing wnr, drvn alng bef 4 out, rdn and btn nxt.*
.... (11 to 4 op 5 to 2 tchd 3 to 1) 2

4004 SARACEN'S BOY (Ire) [68] (bl) 8-10-0 Mr L Jefford, *chsd ldrs, struggling whn hit tenth, tld off aftr*.... (33 to 1 op 20 to 1) 3

GLENFINN PRINCESS [96] 8-12-0 J F Titley, *wtd wth, effrt whn blun and uns rdr 8 out.* (7 to 2 op 3 to 1 tchd 4 to 1) ur

TIPPING ALONG (Ire) [74] 7-11-6 R Dunwoody, *settled to track ldrs, effrt whn hmpd and brght dwn 8 out.*
.... (11 to 4 op 9 to 4 tchd 3 to 1) bd

Dist: 23l, dist. 5m 58.60s. a 20.60s (5 Ran).

(G P D Milne), K C Bailey

545 Wichenford Mares' Only Intermediate National Hunt Flat Class H (4,5,6-y-o) £1,196 2m........................ (5:00)

NORTH END LADY 5-10-7 (7*) Mr R Thornton, *settled in rear, took clr order 6 fs out, led o'r one out, ran on wl.*
.... (33 to 1 op 14 to 1) 1

1912 MARLOUSION (Ire) 4-10-4 (7*) M Berry, *nvr far away, effrt and hrd rdn o'r one furlong out, hng lft and ran on wl furlong.*
.... (7 to 4 on op 9 to 4 on tchd 6 to 4 on) 2

GABRIELLE GERARD 4-10-4 (7*) R Wilkinson, *hld up in rear, hdwy hfwy, led 3 fs out till o'r one out, rallied und pres.*
.... (33 to 1 op 20 to 1) 3

4564 KATHARINE'S SONG (Ire) 6-11-0 J Culloty, *led till hdd and wknd 3 fs out.*......... (5 to 1 op 4 to 1 tchd 6 to 1) 4

HALAM BELL 4-10-4 (7*) J Power, *chsd ldrs, rdn o'r 5 fs out, grad lost tch*................. (9 to 1 op 6 to 1) 5

4569 ABBEYDORAN 5-11-0 T J Murphy, *chsd ldr, reminders o'r 5 fs out, sn wknd, tld off.* (25 to 1 op 20 to 1 tchd 40 to 1) 6

3364 LUCKY MO 6-10-9 (5*) D Salter, *hld up in rear, tld off fnl 6 fs.*
.... (5 to 1 tchd 8 to 1 and 4 to 1) 7

52 DERRING COURT 6-10-9 (5*) P Henley, *chsd ldrs till rdn and wknd o'r 5 fs out, tld off*.............. (40 to 1 op 20 to 1) 8

ORCHARD GENERATION 5-11-0 Mr L Jefford, *al wl beh, tld off last 6 fs*.................... (33 to 1 op 16 to 1) 9

Dist: ¾l, 1l, 18l, 18l, 10l, 16l, 10l, dist. 3m 46.80s. (9 Ran).

(Mrs Vicky Cunningham), W S Cunningham

SEDGEFIELD (good to firm) Thursday August 29th
Going Correction: MINUS 0.30 sec. per fur.

546 Welcome To A New Season Claiming Hurdle Class F (4-y-o and up) £2,059 2m 1f............................ (2:10)

BRAMBLES WAY (bl) 7-10-10 P Niven, *hld up, hdwy frm 3 out, led and slight mstk last, drvn out*........ (9 to 1 op 8 to 1) 1

457* BURES (Ire) (v) 5-11-1 (7*) Mr R Wakley, *chsd ldr, ducked lft 4th, led nxt, clr 3 out, hdd and slight mstk last, one pace.*
.... (7 to 4 on tchd 13 to 8 on and 6 to 4 on) 2

ANORAK (USA) 6-10-13 J Callaghan, *not fluent, hld up, blun 5th, struggling nxt, kpt on stdly.*........ (9 to 1 op 8 to 1) 3

GENESIS FOUR 6-10-4 (3*) G Cahill, *mstk 1st, hdwy to chase ldrs 3 out, sn no extr*.... (12 to 1 op 8 to 1 tchd 14 to 1) 4

25 CANDID LAD 9-10-7 B Storey, *in tch till 3 out, sn rdn and outpcd*........................ (16 to 1 op 14 to 1) 5

1277 MCGILLYCUDDY REEKS (Ire) 5-10-5 J Osborne, *pld hrd, led, hdd appr 5th, wknd quickly 3 out, tld off.* (5 to 1 op 4 to 1) 6

461 BOETHIUS (USA) 7-10-7 P Waggott, *struggling hfwy, sn tld off*.................................. (33 to 1) 7

RED TRIX 4-10-6 A Thornton, *lost tch 3rd, tld off whn pld up bef 5th*.......................... (66 to 1 op 50 to 1) pu

Dist: 3l, 8l, 6l, 17l, 22l, dist. 3m 48.80s. a 2.80s (8 Ran).

SR: 3/12/-/-/-/ (Nigel E M Jones), Mrs M Reveley

547 Landform Novices' Hurdle Class E (4-y-o and up) £2,318 2m 1f........ (2:40)

1072 BRAVE PATRIARCH (Ire) 5-11-5 M A Fitzgerald, *keen in mid-field, smooth hdwy to ld betw last 2, drvn out clr hme.*
.... (2 to 1 on op 9 to 4 on tchd 5 to 2 on) 1

4933 FATEHALKHAIR (Ire) 4-10-6 (3*) G Cahill, *hld up, pushed alng and hdwy appr 2 out, ev ch last, ran on.* (14 to 1 op 10 to 1) 2

HERE COMES HERBIE 4-10-9 M Moloney, *rcd freely, al hndy, led and slight mstk 5th, rdn and hdd whn mistake last, kpt on stdly.*............. (9 to 1 op 10 to 1 tchd 8 to 1) 3

ROBSERA (Ire) 5-10-12 L West, *hld up, hdwy to chase ldrs 3 out, reminders and one pace betw last 2.* (7 to 1 op 5 to 1) 4

4733 WHAT'S SECRETO (USA) (bl) 4-10-9 A Maguire, *led to 4th, ev ch whn drvn alng 3 out, fdd frm nxt*.............. (20 to 1) 5

2296 POSITIVO 5-10-12 I Lawrence, *in tch, not fluent 3rd, rdn and outpcd appr 2 out, sn btn*................. (12 to 1) 6

IHTIMAAM (Fr) 4-10-9 J Railton, *hld up, blun 4th, pushed alng 3 out, no dngr frm nxt.* .(14 to 1 op 10 to 1 tchd 16 to 1) 7

THE COTTONWOOL KID 4-10-9 A Thornton, *cl up, led 4th to nxt, sn struggling, tld off frm 3 out.* .(100 to 1 op 66 to 1) 8

PALLIUM (Ire) 8-10-12 M Foster, *not fluent in rear, lost tch frm 3 out, tld off whn pld up bef last*................. (25 to 1) pu

Dist: ¾l, 2l, 3½l, 7l, 5l, 2l, dist. 3m 55.90s. a 9.90s (9 Ran).

(Peter S Winfield), N J Henderson

548 Barclays Bank Handicap Chase Class E (0-115 5-y-o and up) £3,049 2m 5f...................................... (3:10)

230 TURPIN'S GREEN [71] 13-10-0 J Culloty, *chsd ldr, led 4 out, clr o'r 2 out, cmftbly*.............. (4 to 1 op 6 to 1) 1

STAIGUE FORT (Ire) [91] 8-11-6 P Niven, *led, jmpd rght, hdd 4 out, no oth wnr frm 2 out*........(7 to 2 fav op 3 to 1) 2

TRESIDDER [99] 14-12-0 R Garritty, *beh, pushed alng and hdwy tenth, lost tch appr 3 out, styd on stdly betw last 2.*
.... (4 to 1 op 11 to 4) 3

MIRAGE DANCER [71] 13-10-0 I Lawrence, *hld up, drvn and lost tch frm 4 out, sn no dngr*................(10 to 1) 4

263 BORING (USA) [80] 7-10-4 (5*) R McGrath, *in tch, drvn and outpcd appr 3 out, no dngr frm nxt*...... (4 to 1 op 3 to 1) 5

4584 MISS ENRICO [89] 10-11-4 A Thornton, *midfield, reminders 6th, blun in rear 11th, sn tld off*....... (12 to 1 op 10 to 1) 6

MORE JOY [80] 8-10-9 D Bentley, *hld up, reminders frm 5th, tld off 9th, pld up bef 5 out.*
.... (8 to 1 op 10 to 1 tchd 12 to 1) pu

Dist: 14l, 11l, hd, 1¾l, dist. 5m 6.30s. a 10.30s (7 Ran).

(Mrs P M King), J S King

549 Sharps Bedroom Maiden Chase Class E (5-y-o and up) £2,905 2m 110yds...................................... (3:40)

PRINCE SKYBURD 5-10-11 (5*) E Callaghan, *jmpd wl, made all, drvn clr frm 2 out, easily.*
.... (2 to 1 op 9 to 4 tchd 9 to 4) 1

4916 BUYERS DREAM (Ire) (v) 6-11-2 (3*) G Cahill, *cl up, not jump wl, drvn alng frm 3 out, 5 ls beh and hld whn blun badly last.*
.... (5 to 4 on op 6 to 4 on tchd 6 to 5 on) 2

385³ QUIXALL CROSSETT 11-11-5 P McLoughlin, *niggled alng frm 6th, tld off from 4 out*.............. (4 to 1 op 9 to 2) 3
Dist: 17l, dist. 4m 1.20s. a 9.20s (3 Ran).

(Mrs P M A Avison), Mrs P M A Avison

550 Dickens Home Improvements Handicap Hurdle Class F (0-100 4-y-o and up) £2,250 2m 5f 110yds.......(4:10)

308⁶ PLAYFUL JULIET (Can) [77] 8-10-10 S Wynne, *chsd ldr, led 8th, stumbled badly last, sn hdd, rallied gmely to ld cl hme*
...........................(7 to 1 op 6 to 1) 1
474* HUSO [86] 8-11-5 M Foster, *in tch, chlgd 2 out, lft in ld sn aftr last, kpt on, hdd cl hme*............(6 to 4 fav op 7 to 4) 2
163* RED JAM JAR [95] 11-12-0 K Johnson, *sn led, hit 7th, hdd nxt, outpcd appr 2 out*.............(5 to 2 op 2 to 1) 3
SHELTON ABBEY [67] (bl) 10-10-0 A Maguire, *hld up, struggling 7th, wl beh frm nxt, tld off*.... (11 to 2 op 5 to 1) 4
COPPERHURST (Ire) [80] 5-10-10 S McDougall, *hld up, 4th and in tch whn f 8th*............. (6 to 1 tchd 7 to 1) f
[illegible] *led by 6th*.....................(100 to 1 op 50 to 1) pu
4th, *pld up by 6th*.....
Dist: Sht-hd, 7l, dist. 4m 55.50s. a 7.50s (6 Ran).

(Mrs P Hewitt), A Bailey

551 Milton Keynes Surveys 'National Hunt' Novices' Hurdle Class E (4-y-o and up) £2,180 2m 5f 110yds.........(4:40)

242² WAR WHOOP 4-10-9 M Foster, *hld up, not fluent 5th, gd hdwy to ld 2 out, styd on str.*
.............(2 to 1 on tchd 9 to 4 on and 15 to 8 on) 1
462⁵ THE GALLOPIN'MAJOR (Ire) (bl) 6-10-12 N Smith, *wth ldr, led 6th, rdn and hdd 2 out, kpt on.*
...........(7 to 2 op 3 to 1 tchd 4 to 1) 2
OVER STATED (Ire) 6-10-12 R Supple, *hld up, not fluent, struggling whn hit 3 out, sn btn.*.....(16 to 1 tchd 20 to 1) 3
379² PENIARTH 10-10-7 A Maguire, *in tch, pushed alng frm hfwy, lost touch 3 out, sn beh.*...............(7 to 1 op 5 to 1) 4
473 BOYO (Ire) 5-10-12 L Wyer, *in tch, mstk 6th, effrt 8th, wknd frm 3 out.*.....................(20 to 1 op 14 to 1) 5
AHBEJAYBUS (Ire) 7-10-12 A Thornton, *led, hdd 6th, sn lost tch, tld off.*...............(100 to 1 op 33 to 1) 6
Dist: 2l, 22l, nk, 2½l, dist. 5m 6.80s. a 18.80s (6 Ran).

(Guy Reed), C W Thornton

TRALEE (IRE) (good to yielding) Thursday August 29th

552 O'Donnell Liston Centenary Maiden Hurdle (5-y-o and up) £3,425 2m 1f ....(2:25)

289⁴ DROMINEER (Ire) 5-12-0 M P Dwyer, ...(11 to 8 fav) 1
289⁵ CAITRIONA'S CHOICE (Ire) 5-12-0 R Dunwoody, . (11 to 2) 2
304* ASK THE BUTLER (Ire) 5-12-0 C O'Dwyer, ...(13 to 8) 3
393⁵ WILDLIFE RANGER (Ire) 8-12-0 T Horgan, ...(10 to 1) 4
MACAUNTA (Ire) 6-11-6 J P Broderick, ...(25 to 1) 5
424³ KING'S MANDATE (Ire) 7-11-6 J K Kinane, ...(20 to 1) 6
STAND ALONE (Ire) 7-11-6 P A Roche, ...(25 to 1) 7
MAJOR GALE (Ire) 7-10-13 (7*) M D Murphy, ...(16 to 1) 8
463⁹ FRED OF THE HILL (Ire) 5-11-6 F Woods, ...(50 to 1) 9
FUNNY HABITS (Ire) 5-11-1 P Carberry, ...(33 to 1) 10
221⁵ BEN ORE (Ire) 6-10-13 (7*) A O'Shea, ...(50 to 1) 11
THE GOTHIC (Ire) 5-11-6 N Williamson, ...(33 to 1) 12
KELLY'S MONEY (Ire) 7-11-6 K F O'Brien, ...(20 to 1) 13
Dist: 5l, 2½l, 20l, 2½l. 4m 7.80s. (13 Ran).

(Christopher Cashin), Thomas J Taaffe

553 Denny Gold Medal Handicap Chase (Listed) (4-y-o and up) £12,900 2½m ....(3:35)

429* AN MAINEACH (Ire) [-] 7-10-6 (5*) J M Donnelly, *dsptd ld till hdd 8th, mstk 6th last, rdn aftr 4 out, led last, kpt on wl whn chlgd*.......................(8 to 1) 1
293⁴ SECOND SCHEDUAL [-] 10-10-2 M P Dwyer, *wnt wth, prog 6 out and ag'n bef last, chlgd r-in, no extr cl hme.*.....(7 to 1) 2
865² HEIST [-] 7-10-11 P Carberry, *trkd ldrs, rdn aftr 3rd last, no extr r-in.*......................(4 to 1) 3
293⁵ BISHOPS HALL [-] 10-11-13 R Dunwoody, *dsptd ld till led 8th, rdn aftr 4 out, hdd bef last, wknd r-in.*...........(7 to 2 fav) 4
349³ MILE A MINUTE (Ire) [-] (bl) 5-9-10 F Woods, *rear till some prog bef 6 out, rdn before 4 out, kpt on.*.........(14 to 1) 5
431⁵ HIGH-SPEC [-] 10-9-4 (7*) A O'Shea, *rear till some prog aftr 6 out, kpt on.*....................(12 to 1) 6
MINELLA LAD [-] 10-11-6 T Horgan, *wl plcd early, rcd mid-div aftr 6th, rdn and wknd 4 out, nvr nrr, mstk nxt, wknd.*....(25 to 1) 7
429⁴ NOBODYS SON [-] 10-9-7 T P Treacy, *trkd ldrs, rdn bef 6 out, f 3 out, dead.*....................(20 to 1) f
441⁵ SHANKORAK [-] 9-9-11 T J Mitchell, *al towards rear, pld up bef 3 out.*....................(16 to 1) pu
LORD SINGAPORE (Ire) [-] 8-11-2 N Williamson, *mid-div till prog bef last r-in, wknd aftr 9th, pld up before 6 out.* (8 to 1) pu
Dist: Nk, 5½l, 5l, 11l. 5m 10.40s. (10 Ran).

(C H Pettigrew), Capt D G Swan

PERTH (good to firm) Friday August 30th
Going Correction: NIL

554 Abtrust Inverness Novices' Hurdle Class E (4-y-o and up) £2,190 2½m 110yds.....................(2:20)

ANCHORENA 4-10-4 R Johnson, *hld up in tch, took clr order aftr 3 out, shaken up betw last 2, led r-in, styd on.*
.......................(7 to 2 op 5 to 2 tchd 4 to 1) 1
448² BORN TO PLEASE (Ire) 4-11-2 A P McCoy, *trkd ldrs, rdn to chal 2 out, slight ld aftr last, hdd r-in, no extr.*
.............(11 to 10 fav tchd 5 to 4 and 11 to 8) 2
494⁴ CASTLEROYAL (Ire) 7-10-12 A Maguire, *led second, hrd pressed frm 2 out, hdd aftr last, rdn and no extr.*
.......................(6 to 1 tchd 7 to 1) 3
322⁶ LITTLE REDWING 4-10-6² R Garritty, *led to second, cl up, hit 3 out, lost tch frm nxt, tld off.*......(4 to 1 tchd 9 to 2) 4
Dist: 2l, ½l, 25l. 4m 52.10s. a 12.10s (4 Ran).

(A C & D S Partnership), Miss Venetia Williams

555 Abtrust Fort Lauderdale Novices' Handicap Chase Class E (0-100 5-y-o and up) £3,214 2½m 110yds....(2:55)

480* MINERS REST [72] 8-11-2 (7ex) A P McCoy, *led 3rd, jmpd lft 5th and 6th, styd on und pres r-in.* (7 to 4 on op 7 to 4 on) 1
477* REVE DE VALSE (USA) [87] 9-12-3 (7ex) K Johnson, *in tch, wnt second 9th, rdn aftr 12th, ch last, no extr.*
.............(100 to 30 op 3 to 1 tchd 4 to 1) 2
492³ WHITE DIAMOND [84] 8-12-0 A Thornton, *led, jmpd badly lft second, hdd nxt, cl up and drvn alng aftr 9th, grad lost tch frm 12th, tld off...* (4 to 1 op 3 to 1 tchd 9 to 2 and 5 to 1) 3
Dist: 3l, 27l. 5m 10.10s. a 18.10s (3 Ran).

(P J Hobbs), P J Hobbs

556 Aberdeen Trust Plc Handicap Chase Class E (0-115 5-y-o and up) £3,338 3m.......................(3:30)

375² THE YANK [102] (bl) 10-11-9 R Garritty, *cl up, led 6th, clr whn faltered bend bef 3 out, sn rdn, styd on.*
.......................(6 to 4 on tchd 11 to 10 on) 1
REAL PROGRESS (Ire) [107] 8-12-0 A P McCoy, *led to 6th, cl up, reminders hfwy, outpcd aftr 14th, rallied bef 3 out, no imprsn frm nxt.*........(6 to 4 op 5 to 4 tchd 13 to 8) 2
KELPIE THE CELT [79] 9-10-0 L O'Hara, *blun 1st, hld up in tch, rdn aftr 13th, sn lost touch, tld off whn pld up lme bef 3 out.*.................(8 to 1 op 6 to 1 tchd 12 to 1) pu
Dist: 6l. 6m 7.80s. a 12.80s (3 Ran).

(Mrs A Kane), M D Hammond

557 Abtrust Singapore Selling Handicap Hurdle Class G (0-90 4-y-o and up) £2,211 2m 110yds.......................(4:00)

VINTAGE RED [59] 6-10-4 A Dobbin, *trkd ldrs, chlgd 2 out, rdn to ld appr last, styd on*.... (6 to 1 op 7 to 1 tchd 8 to 1) 1
489* STEADFAST ELITE (Ire) [93] 5-12-2 (5*,7ex) R McGrath, *settled in tch, hrd rdn aftr last, styd on to take second cl hme.*
.......................2
457⁴ SILVER SLEEVE (Ire) [82] (v) 4-11-7 R Garritty, *chsd ldr, led aftr 3 out, hdd appr last, no extr.* (8 to 1 op 5 to 1) 3
CLASSY KAHYASI (Ire) [73] 6-10-13 (5*) Michael Brennan, *hld up, some hdwy aftr 3 out, sn hrd rdn, no further prog frm nxt.*
.......................4
294⁵ DOCTOR-J [77] (bl) 6-11-8 A P McCoy, *hld up, pushed alng aftr 3 out, sn btn.* (9 to 4 fav op 11 to 4 tchd 3 to 1) 5
39⁴ CARDENDEN (Ire) [70] 8-11-1 A Thornton, *led, hdd aftr 3 out, wknd quickly, tld off....* (20 to 1 op 12 to 1 tchd 25 to 1) 6
Dist: 2½l, ½l, 5l, 10l, 22l. 3m 49.70s. a 8.70s (6 Ran).
SR: -/17/-/

(Special Reserve Racing), G Richards

558 North Sound Radio Novices' Chase Class E (5-y-o and up) £2,957 2m (4:30)

45⁶ SPEAKER'S HOUSE (USA) 7-10-12 A Thornton, *hld up in tch, led gng wl aftr 3 out, styd on well.*
.......................(3 to 1 op 5 to 2 tchd 7 to 2) 1
383⁴ CAXTON (USA) 9-10-12 A Maguire, *prmnt, lft in ld aftr 8th, sn hdd, ev ch 2 out, rdn and no extr.*
.............(6 to 4 fav op 2 to 1 tchd 9 to 4) 2
RICHMOND (Ire) 8-10-12 B Storey, *in tch, led 9th, hdd aftr 3 out, wknd quickly, tld off.*............(8 to 1 op 4 to 1) 3
ISLANDREAGH (Ire) 5-10-4 A Dobbin, *led till sddl slpd and pld up aftr 8th.*..........(11 to 4 op 9 to 4 tchd 7 to 2) pu
Dist: 2l, 20l. 4m 3.60s. a 12.60s (4 Ran).

(Mrs C G Greig), Miss Lucinda V Russell

559 Famous Grouse Handicap Hurdle Class E (0-110 4-y-o and up) £3,048

NATIONAL HUNT RESULTS 1996-97

3m 110yds................... (5:05)

4142 BOURDONNER [87] 4-10-6 R Garritty, *led till aftr second, led 6th, hit nxt, clr 3 out, rdn betw last 2, styd on.*
.... (11 to 4 tchd 3 to 1 and 100 to 30) 1
4603 VALIANT DASH [82] 10-10-6 (3*) G Cahill, *mstks, led aftr second till hdd 6th, wh wnr till outpcd after 9th, styd on frm 2 out.* .... (5 to 1 op 7 to 2 tchd 11 to 2) 2
38* BLOOMING SPRING (Ire) [75] 7-10-2 L O'Hara, *sn wl beh, took clr order 6th, some hdwy aftr 3 out, one pace frm nxt.*
.... (15 to 2 op 8 to 1 tchd 7 to 1) 3
PRIDE OF MAY (Ire) [105] 5-12-0 J Callaghan, *sn wl beh, took clr order 6th, lost tch frm 8th, tld off.*....(13 to 2 op 5 to 1) 4
28* TOUGH TEST (Ire) [97] 6-11-10 B Fenton, *f 1st.*
.... (13 to 8 fav op 5 to 4 tchd 7 to 4) f
Dist: 4l, ½l, dist. 5m 54.60s. a 12.60s (5 Ran).
(Cornelius Lysaght), M D Hammond

TRALEE (IRE) (good to yielding)
Friday August 30th

560 Brownes Supersave Maiden Hurdle (4-y-o) £3,425 2m 1f............... (2:35)

350* GLADIATORIAL (Ire) 11-9 P L Malone, ...(7 to 2) 1
4638 IRVINE (Ire) 10-11 (7*) J E Casey, ...(25 to 1) 2
PALETTE (Ire) 11-1 (3*) D J Casey, ...(7 to 1) 3
PERMIT ME (Ire) 10-6 (7*) A O'Shea, ...(25 to 1) 4
288* LEWISHAM (Ire) 11-9 T Horgan, ...(11 to 8 on) 5
MACCABAEUS (Ire) 11-4 F Woods, ...(25 to 1) 6
SHAWAHIN 11-9 P Carberry, ...(12 to 1) 7
4044 HONEY TRADER 11-4 J P Broderick, ...(16 to 1) 8
4873 PERAMBIE (Ire) 10-13 (5*) J Butler, ...(12 to 1) 9
2706 HARRY WELSH (Ire) 11-9 C O'Dwyer, ...(10 to 1) 10
4047 BUNKER (Ire) 11-4 (5*) G Cahill, ...(25 to 1) 11
SUPREME CHANTER (Ire) 11-4 S H O'Donovan, ..(14 to 1) 12
SUGGS RUN (Ire) 10-13 Mr M Phillips, ...(33 to 1) pu
Dist: 1l, 3½l, 6l, ¾l, 4l. 4m 16.50s. (13 Ran).
(Mrs John Magnier), M J Grassick

561 Tom McGiff Plumbing/Slieve Mish Bar Mares Maiden Hurdle (5-y-o and up) £3,425 2m 1f.................. (3:05)

4632 FRAU DANTE 6-12-0 C O'Dwyer, ...(5 to 4 on) 1
4673 FLYING IN THE GALE (Ire) 5-10-13 (7*) A O'Shea, (12 to 1) 2
3932 LADY RICHENDA (Ire) 8-11-6 D H O'Connor, ...(10 to 1) 3
3396 HIGH PARK LADY (Ire) 5-11-6 P M Verling, ...(20 to 1) 4
4246 DREAM ETERNAL (Ire) 5-11-6 W Slattery, ...(14 to 1) 5
3482 SHARLENE (Ire) 5-11-6 R Dunwoody, ...(10 to 1) 6
394* ATTACK AT DAWN (Iro) 5-12-0 T P Treacy, ...(7 to 1) 7
472* SUP A WHISKEY (Ire) 5-12-0 T Horgan, ...(7 to 1) 8
LISNAGAR LADY (Ire) 7-11-6 S H O'Donovan, ...(20 to 1) 9
527 INCH VALLEY (Ire) 5-10-13 (7*) M D Murphy, ...(33 to 1) 10
COMING SOON (Ire) 6-10-13 (7*) Mr B Hassett, ..(16 to 1) 11
4347 REENIE (Ire) 5-11-6 K F O'Brien, ...(20 to 1) f
527 PRINCESS HENRY (Ire) 6-11-6 F Woods, ...(20 to 1) pu
Dist: 2½l, 9l, 25l, hd, 3l. 4m 11.80s. (13 Ran).
(Mrs Austin Fenton), Austin Fenton

562 Barrys Bakery Novice Hurdle (4-y-o and up) £6,850 2m............. (3:35)

316* REEVES (Ire) 4-10-10 (3*) D J Casey, ...(4 to 1) 1
4273 BAMAPOUR (Ire) 6-11-11 P Carberry, ...(11 to 2) 2
467* ALLATRIM (Ire) 6-11-3 R Dunwoody, ...(7 to 1) 3
2862 TALE GAIL (Ire) 4-11-4 C O'Dwyer, ...(6 to 1) 4
315² VICAR STREET (Ire) 6-11-11 T Horgan, ...(3 to 1 fav) 5
424* STONELEIGH TURBO (Ire) 7-11-8 F Woods, ...(16 to 1) 6
PROVEN SCHEDULE (Ire) 4-11-4 J P Broderick, ..(20 to 1) 7
4058 RONDELLI (Ire) 6-11-4 J K Kinane, ...(16 to 1) 8
COLLEGE LAND (Ire) 4-10-13 M P Hourigan, ...(20 to 1) 9
UNO NUMERO (Ire) 5-11-4 L P Cusack, ...(20 to 1) 10
ONEDAYATATIME (Ire) 6-11-4 S H O'Donovan, ...(14 to 1) 11
HEALING THOUGHT (Ire) 5-11-4 K F O'Brien, ...(50 to 1) pu
Dist: 2l, 1l, sht-hd, 6l, 11l. 4m 0.00s. (12 Ran).
(Alexander McCarthy), W P Mullins

563 WinElectric Paget Cup Handicap Chase (4-y-o and up) £6,165 2¾m
.... (4:05)

3142 ANOTHER GROUSE (Ire) [-] 9-10-7 T P Treacy, ...(8 to 1) 1
3146 SPRINGFONT LADY (Ire) [-] 7-9-4 (3*) D J Casey, ...(6 to 1) 2
5372 WACKO JACKO (Ire) [-] 7-9-103 J P Broderick, ...(9 to 2) 3
98* THERE TIS FOR YA (Ire) [-] 8-9-0 (7*) M D Murphy, (12 to 1) 4
4317 WATERLOO BALL (Ire) [-] 7-9-12 T Horgan, ...(11 to 1) 5
293 ANABATIC (Ire) [-] 8-12-0 T P Rudd, ...(11 to 1) 6
441* VERY LITTLE (Ire) [-] 8-9-103 P Carberry, ...(4 to 1 fav) 7
KALONA [-] 9-10-2 F Woods, ...(7 to 1) 8
43114 LOFTUS LAD (Ire) [-] 8-9-0 (7*) A O'Shea, ...(12 to 1) ur
Dist: Sht-hd, 7l, 2½l, 7l, 2l. 5m 42.00s. (9 Ran).
(M Kelly), Edward P Mitchell

564 Lixnaw Fabrications Ltd Handicap Hurdle (0-109 4-y-o and up) £3,425 2m

.... (4:35)

255* FONTAINE LODGE (Ire) [-] 6-10-10 (7*) A O'Shea, (4 to 1 jt-fav) 1
434* GALE HAMSHIRE (Ire) [-] 7-9-7 (3*) D J Casey, ... (13 to 2) 2
311* JOHNNY'S DREAM (Ire) [-] 6-10-7 (5*) G Cotter, ..(4 to 1 jt-fav) 3
ULTRA MAGIC [-] 9-11-5 (5*) J Butler, ...(14 to 1) 4
4335 BETH'S APPARITION (Ire) [-] 6-11-11 T Horgan, ...(7 to 1) 5
THE WISE KNIGHT (Ire) [-] 5-11-0 J P Broderick, ..(14 to 1) 6
354² TIBOULEN (Ire) [-] 6-10-13 (3*) D T Evans, ...(6 to 1) 7
DOUBLE JIG TIME (Ire) [-] 4-9-31 (5*) T Martin, ...(25 to 1) 8
4634 MUSKERRY KING (Ire) [-] 5-9-11 W Slattery, ...(12 to 1) f
NISHAYA (Ire) [-] 5-9-11 M P Hourigan, ...(33 to 1) pu
CLAHANE (Ire) [-] 5-11-1 G M O'Neill, ...(10 to 1) pu
Dist: 1l, 15l, ½l, 20l, 3½l. 3m 57.40s. (11 Ran).
(ABC Syndicate), Anthony Mullins

565 Ballybeggan Racegoers Club Paddy Kearns Memorial H'cap Hdle (0-102 4-y-o and up) £3,425 2½m...... (5:05)

3536 THAI ELECTRIC (Ire) [-] 5-10-6 T J Mitchell, ...(16 to 1) 1
VALMAR (Ire) [-] 8-9-10 F Woods, ...(20 to 1) 2
4692 JANE DIGBY (Ire) [-] 4-11-10 T Horgan, ...(4 to 1) 3
2726 MARGUERITA SONG [-] 6-11-3 T P Treacy, ...(9 to 2) 4
463* TARAJAN (USA) [-] 6d 11-11 J Shortt, ...(5 to 2 fav) 5
395* CLEVER JACK [-] 6-11-12 K F O'Brien, ...(7 to 1) 6
469 FAIR SOCIETY (Ire) [-] (bl) 5-10-3 (7*) Mr John P Moloney,
.... (9 to 2) 7
PROPHET'S THUMB (Ire) [-] 7-9-0 (7*) M D Murphy, (50 to 1) 8
4683 DEABHAILIN (Ire) [-] 6-10-1 C O'Dwyer, ...(16 to 1) 9
RIVERSTOWN LAD [-] 9-10-10 J P Broderick, ...(20 to 1) 10
Dist: 3½l, 6l, 3l, 2½l, sht-hd. 5m 4.30s. (10 Ran).
(Mrs Brenda Byrne), Sean Byrne

566 Abbeygate Hotel INH Flat Race (4 & 5-y-o) £3,425 2m 1f............. (5:35)

BROWNES HILL LAD (Ire) 4-11-9 Mr P Fenton, ...(7 to 1) 1
COSHEL LEADER (Ire) 5-11-7 (7*) Mr J P McNamara,
.... (6 to 1) 2
2884 ELECTRIC RYMER (Ire) 4-11-9 Mr D Marnane, ...(7 to 1) 3
EXECUTIVE HEIGHTS (Ire) 4-11-2 (7*) Mr P Cody, (10 to 1) 4
MISTY MOMENTS (Ire) 5-11-7 (7*) Mr A J Dempsey,
.... (11 to 2) 5
4102 MORNING MIST (Ire) 4-11-2 (7*) Mr S M Duffy, (4 to 1 fav) 6
MAJOR JAMIE (Ire) 5-11-7 (7*) Mr J D Moore, ...(9 to 2) 7
MILLTOWN LEADER (Ire) 5-11-9 (5*) Mr R Walsh, ..(10 to 1) 8
288 KINCORA (Ire) 5-12-0 Mr J A Nash, ...(10 to 1) 9
JANICE PRICE (Ire) 5-11-2 (7*) Mr M J Walsh, ...(14 to 1) 10
464 PHAR'N'WIDE (Ire) 5-11-2 (7*) Mr N C Kelleher, ..(16 to 1) 11
Dist: 4l, 2½l, 6l, 5l. 4m 9.50s. (11 Ran).
(Patrick Walsh), Patrick Walsh

PERTH (good to firm)
Saturday August 31st
Going Correction: MINUS 0.35 sec. per fur.

567 Scania 4-Series 'Horsepower' Juvenile Novices' Hurdle Class E (3-y-o) £2,190 2m 110yds............. (2:20)

ROSSEL (USA) 10-10 A Dobbin, *cl up in chasing grp, closed 3 out, led bef nxt, styd on und pres.*
.... (7 to 4 op 2 to 1 tchd 9 to 4) 1
RET FREM (Ire) 10-10 B Storey, *led chasing grp, cld 3 out, rdn to chal nxt, kpt on same pace.*... (5 to 4 on op 6 to 4 on) 2
PHAR CLOSER (bl) 10-5 S McDougall, *mstks, led and sn clr, blun 4th, hdd bef 2 out, hrd rdn, kpt on.* (25 to 1 op 10 to 1) 3
SKYLIGHT 10-7 (3*) G Cahill, *beh, rdn and lost tch aftr 3 out, tld off.* ....(10 to 1 op 7 to 1) 4
3054 MY KIND 10-5 J Osborne, *beh, lost tch aftr 3 out, tld off.*
.... (10 to 1 op 7 to 1) 5
Dist: 5l, 1¼l, 13l, 1¼l. 3m 53.10s. a 12.10s (5 Ran).
(Underwoods (1996) Ltd), P Monteith

568 James Halstead Novices' Chase Class D (5-y-o and up) £3,772 3m..... (2:50)

4493 DISTANT MEMORY (bl) 7-11-5 A P McCoy, *led to second, chsd ldr, reminders aftr 11th, rdn after 14th, crrd lft 3 out, sn led, styd on und pres.*
.... (Evens fav op 5 to 4 on tchd 6 to 4 on) 1
459* SCRABO VIEW (Ire) 8-11-5 R Supple, *hld up, rdn and lost tch aftr 12th, rallied and ch 2 out, no extr und pres.*
.... (6 to 4 op 7 to 4 tchd 2 to 1) 2
NATIONAL CHOICE 10-10-12 A Thornton, *jmpd lft, led second, jumped badly left 3 out, sn hdd, wl beh whn f last, rmntd.*
.... (5 to 1 op 4 to 1 tchd 11 to 2) 3
Dist: 2½l, dist. 6m 1.30s. a 6.30s (3 Ran).
(Mrs Ann Weston), P J Hobbs

569 Scania 1996 Truck Of The Year Novices' Hurdle Class E (4-y-o and up)

£2,178 3m 110yds. . . . . (3:20)

462* GOOD HAND (USA) 10-11-5 R Johnson, *hld up, hit 6th and 8th, cld 9th, led on bit betw last 2, eased nr finish, not extended*. . . . . (7 to 4 on op 2 to 1 on tchd 13 to 8 on) 1
559^{3} BLOOMING SPRING (Ire) 7-11-0 L O'Hara, *led to 1st, led 9th till betw last 2, kpt on, no ch wth wnr*. . . . . (7 to 4 op 2 to 1 tchd 13 to 8) 2
KRALINGEN 4-9-10 (7*) Miss C Metcalfe, *led 1st, sn clr, hdd 9th, wknd bef 2 out*. . . . . (10 to 1 op 7 to 1) 3
Dist: ½l, 11l. 5m 57.20s. a 15.20s (3 Ran).
(Uncle Jacks Pub), S E Kettlewell

570 Reliable Vehicles For Scania Chase Handicap Class F (0-100 5-y-o and up) £4,338 2m. . . . . (3:55)

110^{3} SUPER SHARP (NZ) [79] 8-10-7 Jacqui Oliver, *made all, mstk 4th, clr aftr 3 out, styd on wl*. . . . . (4 to 1 op 3 to 1) 1
BELDINE [100] 11-12-0 A Dobbin, *hld up, drvn alng whn hmpd 3 out, sn chasing wnr, rdn, no imprsn*. . . . . (6 to 1 on op 6 to 4 on) 2
BLAZING TRAIL (Ire) [103] 8-12-3 A Thornton, *chsd wnr, drvn alng and no imprsn whn blun 3 out, no ch aftr*. . . . . (9 to 2 op 5 to 2) 3
Dist: 14l, 11l. 3m 51.90s. a 0.90s (3 Ran).
SR: 14/21/13/ (Mrs Sue Careless), H Oliver

571 Heather Pre-Packs Handicap Hurdle Class D (0-120 4-y-o and up) £3,022 2m 110yds. (4:25)

248^{2} SARMATIAN (USA) [95] 5-11-0 R Garritty, *hld up, hdwy on bit bef 2 out, led and mstk last, drvn clr*. . . . . (5 to 2 jt-fav tchd 3 to 1) 1
367* WAMDHA (Ire) [102] 6-11-7 A S Smith, *in tch, jnd ldr 3 out, led nxt, hdd last, no extr*. . . . . (4 to 1 op 7 to 2 tchd 9 to 2) 2
EDEN DANCER [108] 4-11-10 P Niven, *prmnt, led 5th to 2 out, sn wknd*. . . . . (5 to 2 jt-fav op 2 to 1) 3
381^{4} FORGETFUL [85] 7-10-4 D J Burchell, *led to 5th, wkng whn blun 2 out*. . . . . (8 to 1 op 6 to 1 tchd 9 to 1) 4
508^{3} VAIN PRINCE [104] (bl) 9-11-9 J Osborne, *chsd ldrs, rdn aftr 3 out, sn wknd*. . . . . (8 to 1 op 7 to 1 tchd 9 to 1) 5
HEE'S A DANCER [105] 4-11-2 (5*) E Callaghan, *hld up, lost tch 3 out, tld off*. . . . . (7 to 1 op 4 to 1) 6
Dist: 5l, 12l, 5l, 2½l, 15l. 3m 44.30s. a 3.30s (6 Ran).
SR: 4/6/-/ (S T Brankin), M D Hammond

572 Scania 4-Series 'King Of The Road' Hurdle Handicap Class E (0-110 4-y-o and up) £2,710 2½m 110yds. . . . (4:55)

554^{2} BORN TO PLEASE (Ire) [87] 4-11-0 A P McCoy, *made all, reminders and chsd alng hfwy, clr whn hit 3 out, unchlgd*. . . . . (7 to 4 fav op 6 to 4 tchd 2 to 1) 1
476^{6} TASHREEF [77] (bl) 6-10-7 M Moloney, *in tch, outpcd bef 3 out, no dngr aftr*. . . . . (20 to 1 op 6 to 1 tchd 25 to 1) 2
460^{2} TAKE TWO [94] 8-11-10 A Dobbin, *hld up, rdn aftr 7th, no real hdwy*. . . . . (3 to 1 op 7 to 2 tchd 4 to 1) 3
SOUSON (Ire) [89] (bl) 8-11-5 K Jones, *chsd wnr till wknd aftr 7th*. . . . . (7 to 1 op 5 to 1) 4
521* FRONTIER FLIGHT (USA) [94] 6-11-7 (3*,7ex) E Husband, *hld up, hdwy to chase wnr 3 out, ten ls beh and no imprsn whn f nxt*. . . . . (2 to 1 tchd 9 to 4) f
Dist: 18l, sht-hd, 12l. 4m 53.10s. a 13.10s (5 Ran).
(A B S Racing), P J Hobbs

HEXHAM (firm)
Monday September 2nd
Going Correction: NIL

573 Buchanan Original Juvenile Novices' Hurdle Class E (3-y-o) £2,322 2m (2:00)

481^{2} ROYAL RAPPORT (v) 10-5 (5*) Michael Brennan, *hmpd 1st, keen hold wth ldr, led 6th, slpd betw last 2, edgd lft and drvn clr r-in*. . . . . (15 to 8 op 7 to 4 tchd 2 to 1 and 9 to 4) 1
320* KERNOF (Ire) 11-3 R Garritty, *not fluent, led to 6th, jmpd slwly 2 out, ev ch last, one pace*. . . . . (7 to 4 on tchd 2 to 1 on) 2
MISS IMPULSE 10-2 (3*) T Dascombe, *hld up, pushed alng appr 3 out, cl up beh ldrs whn slpd up bef nxt*. . . . . (10 to 1 op 8 to 1) su
Dist: 5l. 4m 2.40s. a 13.40s (3 Ran).
(Gary Roberts), J G M O'Shea

SLIGO (IRE) (yielding to soft)
Monday September 2nd

574 Yeats (3-y-o) Maiden Hurdle £2,226 2m . . . . (4:00)

GO SASHA (Ire) 10-4 (5*) T Martin, ... (16 to 1) 1
522^{2} EVRIZA (Ire) 10-9 T Horgan, ... (13 to 8) 2
522^{3} THREE RIVERS 10-11 (3*) D J Casey, ... (11 to 8 fav) 3
HOLLYMOUNT LADY 10-4 K F O'Brien, ... (12 to 1) 4
DOUBLE SEEKER (Ire) 10-9 (5*) J Butler, ... (10 to 1) 5
THE GENT (Ire) 10-9 P L Malone, ... (14 to 1) 6
KOKO NOR (Ire) 10-9 L P Cusack, ... (16 to 1) 7
442^{5} HENCARLAM (Ire) 10-9 C O'Dwyer, ... (14 to 1) 8
442 MINGLE (Ire) 10-4 S H O'Donovan, ... (33 to 1) 9
PLAYPRINT 10-9 T P Treacy, ... (7 to 1) f
RUN TO THE ACE (Ire) 10-9 J K Kinane, ... (20 to 1) pu
Dist: 1½l, 15l, 3½l, 8l. 4m 1.50s. (11 Ran).
(E A Keogh), Patrick Martin

575 Strandhill Handicap Hurdle (0-109 4-y-o and up) £2,226 2½m. . . . . (4:30)

427* DIFFICULT TIMES (Ire) [-] 4-12-0 S C Lyons, ... (100 to 30) 1
527^{7} PRIZE LADY (Ire) [-] 6-10-0 M P Hourigan, ... (14 to 1) 2
523^{2} SLAVE GALE (Ire) [-] 5-11-6 T Horgan, ... (3 to 1) 3
302^{3} BUGGSY BLADE [-] 10-10-12 L P Cusack, ... (9 to 2) 4
348* LOUGH ATALIA [-] 9-11-1 C O'Dwyer, ... (5 to 2 fav) 5
BROOKVILLE STAR (Fr) [-] 9-10-9 J K Kinane, ... (14 to 1) 6
RUN MY ROSIE (Ire) [-] 6-9-7 F Woods, ... (20 to 1) pu
Dist: 3½l, 9l, dist, 11l. 5m 14.50s. (7 Ran).
(P M Dowling), G M Lyons

576 Londis Beginners Chase (5-y-o and up) £2,911 2½m. . . . . (6:00)

BROOK HILL LADY (Ire) 7-11-9 T Horgan, ... (5 to 4 on) 1
BANNER GALE (Ire) 7-12-0 C O'Dwyer, ... (5 to 1) 2
238 BLACKIE CONNORS (Ire) 5-11-8 P L Malone, ... (33 to 1) 3
639 DROP THE ACT (Ire) 6-12-0 S H O'Donovan, ... (14 to 1) 4
525^{4} MISS ELIZABETH (Ire) 6-11-9 K F O'Brien, ... (12 to 1) 5
GARABAGH (Ire) 7-12-0 J Shortt, ... (6 to 1) 6
CORRIBLOUGH (Ire) 8-12-0 F Woods, ... (20 to 1) 7
345^{4} MUSICAL DUKE (Ire) 7-11-11 (3*) G Kilfeather, ... (8 to 1) f
Dist: 2½l, 11l, hd, ¾l. 5m 28.90s. (8 Ran).
(James Foxe), A P O'Brien

577 Grange INH Flat Race (4-y-o and up) £2,226 2m. (7:00)

YOUR SORRY NOW (Ire) 6-12-0 Mr J P Dempsey, (11 to 2) 1
527^{5} LADY OF GRANGE (Ire) 4-10-11 (7*) Mr A J Dempsey, ... (2 to 1 fav) 2
COURSING GLEN (Ire) 8-12-0 Mr A J Martin, ... (6 to 1) 3
SARAH BLUE (Ire) 6-11-9 Mr P Fenton, ... (5 to 1) 4
MATTORIA (Ire) 5-11-4 (5*) Mr R Walsh, ... (11 to 2) 5
444^{4} INHERITIS (Ire) 4-10-12^{1} (7*) Mr D A Harney, ... (8 to 1) 6
ARDFARNA LAD 13-11-7 (7*) Miss A L Crowley, . . . (14 to 1) 7
SHALOM (Ire) 4-11-2 (7*) Mr John P Moloney, ... (10 to 1) 8
350^{5} MERRY CHANTER (Ire) 4-11-9 Mr G J Harford, ... (8 to 1) 9
KATOUCHE (Ire) 5-11-7 (7*) Mr J P McNamara, ... (16 to 1) 10
ORANGE LIL (Ire) 4-11-1 (3*) Mr J Connolly, ... (14 to 1) 11
Dist: 2½l, hd, 3l, 11l. 4m 3.80s. (11 Ran).
(Mrs J H Scott), J H Scott

DUNDALK (IRE) (good to firm)
Wednesday September 4th

578 Carnlough Maiden Hurdle (4-y-o and up) £2,226 3m. . . . . (2:30)

536^{4} LINDA'S BOY (Ire) 6-11-6 J Shortt, ... (5 to 2 fav) 1
466^{2} BLACK BOREEN (Ire) 6-12-0 T Horgan, ... (7 to 2) 2
466^{3} MOON-FROG 9-11-6 F Woods, ... (16 to 1) 3
523^{3} CELIO LUCY (Ire) 6-11-2 (7*) P Morris, ... (7 to 2) 4
467 STRADBALLY JANE (Ire) 6-11-9 K F O'Brien, ... (10 to 1) 5
LAURA'S PURSUIT (Ire) 7-11-4 (5*) J Butler, ... (100 to 30) 6
393^{8} RAHANINE MELODY (Ire) 4-10-4 (7*) Mr P J Crowley, ... (33 to 1) 7
536 RONETTE (Ire) 5-11-6 J P Broderick, ... (20 to 1) 8
Dist: 7l, 2½l, 13l, 11l. 5m 58.30s. (8 Ran).
(Patrick Kearns), E Bolger

579 Cooley Handicap Hurdle (0-109 4-y-o and up) £2,226 2m 135yds. . . . . (3:00)

428^{4} DANCING CLODAGH (Ire) [-] (bl) 4-11-2 S C Lyons, (5 to 1) 1
396* WHEREWILITALL END (Ire) [-] 5-11-10 (3*) U Smyth, ... (4 to 1 fav) 2
354^{4} MASCOT [-] (bl) 5-11-10 P L Malone, ... (13 to 2) 3
405* BAJAN QUEEN (Ire) [-] 6-11-2 (5*) T Martin, ... (5 to 1) 4
564^{7} TIBOULEN (Ire) [-] 6-11-3 (3*) D T Evans, ... (7 to 1) 5
SHY GAL (Ire) [-] 8-10-2 (5*) J Butler, ... (16 to 1) 6
396^{2} KUMA CHAN [-] 9-9-9 (3*) D J Casey, ... (7 to 1) 7
444 LORD KNOCKEMSTIFF (Ire) [-] 5-10-1 T P Treacy, (20 to 1) 8
396^{5} NIGHTSCENE (Ire) [-] 4-10-1 (5*) J M Donnelly, ... (9 to 1) 9
CIARA CANE (Ire) [-] 5-10-5 L P Cusack, ... (12 to 1) 10
276^{5} TENDER LASS (Ire) [-] 5-9-4 (7*) R P Hogan, ... (9 to 1) 11
Dist: Nk, sht-hd, 1½l, 2l. 3m 57.40s. (11 Ran).
(Sportsmans Inn Syndicate), G M Lyons

580 Howandale Services Rossbracken Handicap Chase (0-102 4-y-o and up) £2,740 2½m. . . . . (3:30)

314 ANY PORT (Ire) [-] 6-11-2 P L Malone, ... (3 to 1) 1
314 TIMELY AFFAIR (Ire) [-] 7-10-5 F Woods, ... (5 to 2 jt-fav) 2
STRONG HURRICANE [-] 9-12-0 J Shortt, ... (5 to 1) 3
441⁴ NEBRASKA [-] (bl) 10-11-4 C O'Dwyer, ... (7 to 1) 4
563³ WACKO JACKO (Ire) [-] 7-11-6 J P Broderick, (5 to 2 jt-fav) 5
Dist: 5l, 3½l, 4½l, 13l. 5m 2.00s. (5 Ran).

(J H Lowry), A J Martin

581 Rostrevor I.N.H. Flat Race (4-y-o and up) £2,226 2m 135yds. . . . . (5:30)

397⁴ RED RADICAL (Ire) 6-11-7 (7") Mr P E I Newell, ...(14 to 1) 1
WEST OF WAIKIKI (Ire) 4-11-4 (5") Mr R Walsh, ...(9 to 2) 2
180⁴ SABANIYA (Fr) 4-11-1 (3") Mr J Connolly, ... (6 to 4 fav) 3
BRASSIS HILL (Ire) 5-11-7 (7") A O'Shea, ...(12 to 1) 4
BUNINOO (Ire) 4-11-4 Mr J A Nash, ...(10 to 1) 5
497⁴ FENIAN COURT (Ire) 5-11-9 Mr D Marnane, ...(8 to 1) 6
MISTY PEARL (Ire) 5-12-0 Mr A R Coonan, ...(14 to 1) 7
KERRIA'S GIFT (Ire) 5-11-9 (5") J Butler, ...(12 to 1) 8
ROSE'S PERK (Ire) 4-11-4 Mr P Fenton, ...(10 to 1) 9
GARAMOY (Ire) 5-11-2 (7") Mr M O'Connor, ...(20 to 1) 10
467⁹ BULA DELA (Ire) (bl) 6-11-2 (7") Mr A Fleming, ...(33 to 1) 11
PERFECT (Ire) 4-11-9 Mr G J Harford, ...(7 to 2) 12
RATH NA SIDHE (Ire) 4-11-9 Mr H F Cleary, ...(10 to 1) 13
ARCTIC PARTY (Ire) 4-11-4 Mr M McNulty, ...(16 to 1) 14
EDELS FIRST (Ire) 7-11-2 (7") J P Deegan, ...(20 to 1) 15
Dist: 1l, 7l, 1½l, 4½l. 3m 53.30s. (15 Ran).

(P E I Newell), P E I Newell

NEWTON ABBOT (good)
Wednesday September 4th
Going Correction: MINUS 0.30 sec. per fur.

582 MHV Selling Hurdle Class G (4 - 7-y-o) £1,774 2¾m. . . . .(2:30)

510³ KUTAN (Ire) 6-10-12 E Byrne, hld up, hdwy 4th, trkd ldrs 6th till
led on bit aftr 3 out, easily. . . . .(7 to 2 tchd 9 to 4) 1
379³ MISS SOUTER (v) 7-11-7 A P McCoy, led, sn clr, rdn 7th, hdd
aftr 3 out, soon btn. . . . . . .(5 to 1 op 7 to 2 tchd 11 to 2) 2
450* AKIYMANN (USA) 6-11-5 D Bridgwater, beh, rdn 4th, lost
pl aftr 6th, ran on to take poor 3rd frm 2 out.
. . . .(3 to 1 op 7 to 4 tchd 100 to 30) 3
510⁴ COEUR BATTANT (Fr) 6-11-5 B Powell, beh, lost tch aftr 6th,
styd on to take modest 4th frm 2 out. . . .(12 to 1 op 8 to 1) 4
JUST-MANA-MOU (Ire) 4-10-10 R Dunwoody, chsd ldr till hrd
rdn aftr 6th, wknd nxt. . . . .(9 to 4 op 2 to 1) 5
446⁶ MUTLEY 6-10-12 C Maude, steadied strt, keen hold and beh,
effrt 4th, sn btn, tld off whn pld up bef 2 out.
. . . .(12 to 1 op 8 to 1) pu
448³ OH MY TOES 5-10-7 J Frost, chsd ldrs to 5th, wknd aftr 6th,
tld off whn pld up bef last. . . . .(16 to 1 tchd 25 to 1) pu
Dist: 13l, 13l, 1¼l, 2l. 5m 16.60s. 15.60s (7 Ran).

(E S Chivers), Mrs Barbara Waring

583 Cooper Callas Kitchen And Bathroom Distributors Novices' Chase Class E (5-y-o and up) £2,831 2m 110yds (3:00)

512² BIT OF A LASS 10-10-12 J Frost, made all, clr 7th, hrd drvn
whn chlgd 2 out, ran on wl. . . . .(4 to 1 op 7 to 2) 1
514² DUKE OF DREAMS 6-11-5 B Powell, hit 1st, hdwy 5th, hrd
rdn to chal 2 out, sn one pace, dismounted.
. . . .(7 to 4 fav op 10 to 11 to 8) 2
CHICKABIDDY 8-10-7 M A Fitzgerald, beh till hdwy 8th, kpt
on frm 2 out, not rch ldrs. . .(9 to 4 op 5 to 2 tchd 100 to 30) 3
STORMY SUNSET 9-10-5 (7") Mr T Dennis, chsd ldrs till
wknd and hit 8th, tld off. . . . .(9 to 2 op 5 to 1 tchd 5 to 1) 4
400⁵ GREAT UNCLE (bl) 8-10-7 (5") P Henley, jmpd slwly in rear
4th, rdn and lost tch 6th, tld off. . . . . .(50 to 1 op 20 to 1) 5
544³ SARACEN'S BOY (Ire) 8-10-10 Mr L Jefford, chsd wnr, hit 8th,
wkng whn blun badly and came to 4 out.
. . . .(33 to 1 op 20 to 1 tchd 50 to 1) ur
Dist: 4l, 6l, dist, 12l. 4m 0.50s. a 2.50s (6 Ran).
SR: 9/12/-/ *(A E C Electric Fencing Ltd (Hotline)), R G Frost*

584 Chefs Larder Juvenile Novices' Hurdle Class D (3-y-o) £2,725 2m 1f. . . . (3:30)

NOBLE LORD 10-10 B Powell, hld up, hdwy on bit aftr 4th, led
5th, clr 3 out, easily. . .(9 to 2 op 4 to 1 tchd 5 to 1) 1
TABLETS OF STONE 10-10 M Bosley, not fluent, chsd ldr
aftr second, chlgd 5th, outpcd 3 out, styd on ag'n to take poor
second appr last. . . . .(14 to 1 op 5 to 1 tchd 16 to 1) 2
SPRING CAMPAIGN (Ire) 10-10 D Bridgwater, chsd ldrs, rdn
5th, chased wnr aftr 3 out to 2 out, sn wknd.
. . . .(7 to 4 on op 5 to 4 on tchd 11 to 10 on) 3
PREMIER SON 10-10 R Dunwoody, al beh, wknd appr 5th, tld
off. . . . .(11 to 1 op 9 to 2 tchd 12 to 1) 4
TAUREAN FIRE 10-5 (5") D J Kavanagh, sn tld off, pld up bef
5th, dismounted. . . . .(66 to 1 op 33 to 1) pu
305² FOUR WEDDINGS (USA) (bl) 10-10 C Maude, led, rdn 3rd,
hdd 5th, wknd quickly aftr 3 out, tld off whn pld up bef 2 out.
. . . .(9 to 2 op 11 to 4 tchd 5 to 1) pu
Dist: 21l, 14l, dist. 4m 0.70s. a 11.70s (6 Ran).

(The Old Timers Partnership), R H Buckler

585 Cooper Callas Kitchen And Bathroom Distributors Novices' Hurdle Class E (4-y-o and up) £2,200 2¾m. . . . . (4:00)

STORM RUN (Ire) 6-10-12 A P McCoy, trkd ldrs, led appr 7th,
clr 3 out, readily. . . . .(6 to 4 jt-fav tchd 7 to 4) 1
401* IDIOM 9-11-5 J Culloty, beh till hdwy to chase ldrs 6th, chsd
wnr frm 3 out, hrd rdn and no imprsn from 2 out.
. . . .(100 to 30 op 5 to 2 tchd 4 to 1) 2
540* CHINA MAIL (Ire) 4-11-3 T J Murphy, hld up, pushed alng aftr
6th, no imprsn on ldrs frm 3 out. . . . . .(6 to 4 jt-fav op 11 to 10) 3
THE LAST MISTRESS (Ire) 9-10-7 R Farrant, chsd ldrs to 6th, tld
off. . . . .(40 to 1 op 20 to 1 tchd 50 to 1) 4
HEATON (Ire) 5-10-12 B Powell, led to second, chlgd 4th, led
5th to appr 7th, sn wknd, tld off. . . . . .(66 to 1 op 25 to 1) 5
BANKS OF THE BRIDE 6-10-12 E Byrne, al beh, hit 6th, tld
off. . . . .(100 to 1 op 33 to 1) 6
PIONEER PRINCESS 4-10-5 M A Fitzgerald, al beh, hit 6th,
tld off whn pld up bef 2 out.
. . . .(100 to 1 op 16 to 1 tchd 40 to 1) pu
TAMARS COUSIN 6-10-12 G Upton, led second to 4th, styd
wth ldr till wknd rpdly bend appr 7th, tld off whn pld up bef 2
out. . . . .(100 to 1 op 33 to 1) pu
Dist: 8l, 10l, dist, 22l, 25l. 5m 16.80s. a 15.80s (8 Ran).

(J W Aplin), P F Nicholls

586 Booker Cash And Carry Handicap Chase Class D (0-120 5-y-o and up) £3,441 3¼m 110yds. . . . . (4:30)

RAINBOW CASTLE [95] 9-10-3 A P McCoy, beh till hdwy 7th,
chsd ldr 14th, rdn aftr 4 out, chlgd 2 out, sn led, styd on wl.
. . . .(2 to 1 fav op 6 to 4) 1
375³ GILSTON LASS [92] 9-10-0 J Culloty, led, clr 4th, jmpd slwly
6th, hit frm 15th, hit 2 out, sn hdd, one pace.
. . . .(10 to 1 op 7 to 1) 2
475³ HILLWALK [120] 10-12-0 D Morris, hdwy 7th, chsd ldr 11th to
14th, sn outpcd. . . . .(4 to 1 op 3 to 1) 3
517* ANDRELOT [113] (bl) 9-11-7 (6ex) R Dunwoody, chsd ldrs,
hdwy tenth, chasing ldrs whn hmpd 11th, rdn 13th, nvr dngrs
aftr. . . . .(9 to 4 op 2 to 1) 4
375 WINNIE LORRAINE [97] 11-10-5 C Llewellyn, chsd ldr till blun
and uns rdr tenth. . . . . ur
BANNTOWN BILL (Ire) [95] (v) 7-10-3 D Bridgwater, sn tld off,
pld up bef 13th. . . . .(9 to 1 op 7 to 1 tchd 10 to 1) pu
Dist: 4l, 24l, 22l. 6m 26.30s. a 6.30s (6 Ran).

(Jeffrey Hordle), P F Nicholls

587 Armitage Shanks Better Bathrooms Handicap Hurdle Class E (0-110 4-y-o and up) £2,221 2m 1f. . . . . (5:00)

419* ZINE LANE [98] 4-11-5 R Farrant, trkd ldr till badly hmpd 4th,
styd wth new ldr till led 3 out, drvn and ran on wl r-in.
. . . .(2 to 1 fav op 7 to 4 tchd 9 to 4) 1
MARCHMAN [88] 11-10-11 J Culloty, hdwy 5th, str chal frm 2
out till mstk last, no extr. . . . .(7 to 1 op 5 to 1) 2
479⁴ SIRTELIMAR (Ire) [88] 7-10-11 T J Murphy, hld up, hdwy 5th,
str chal 2 out, sn rdn and wknd.
. . . .(8 to 1 op 7 to 1 tchd 9 to 1) 3
205² SIAN WYN [83] 6-10-6 R Dunwoody, trkd ldrs, led 4th to 3
out, sn rdn and wknd. . . . .(6 to 1 op 11 to 2 tchd 13 to 2) 4
513⁶ LITTLE HOOLIGAN [88] (bl) 5-10-9 A P McCoy, hdwy 5th,
chsd ldrs 3 out, wknd appr 2 out.
. . . .(6 to 1 op 9 to 2 tchd 13 to 2) 5
480³ GABISH [77] 11-9-7 (7") Mr R Thornton, in tch to 5th, tld off.
. . . .(66 to 1 op 33 to 1 tchd 100 to 1) 6
JEWEL THIEF [87] 6-10-10 B Fenton, rdn and effrt appr 5th,
sn wknd, tld off. . . . .(14 to 1 op 8 to 1 tchd 16 to 1) 7
GOLD MEDAL (Fr) [105] 8-12-0 D Bridgwater, led, clr 3rd, f
4th. . . . .(10 to 1 op 6 to 1) f
267² EL GRANDO [83] 6-10-6 A Maguire, trkd ldrs till badly hmpd
and pld up sn aftr 4th. . . . . .(3 to 1 op 7 to 2 tchd 4 to 1) pu
Dist: 2½l, 6l, 9l, ½l, dist, 22l. 3m 58.20s. a 9.20s (9 Ran).

(The Hopeful Partnership), Major W R Hern

CLONMEL (IRE) (good)
Thursday September 5th

588 Tipp FM Handicap Chase (0-102 4-y-o and up) £2,226 2m 1f. . . . . (5:30)

563² SPRINGFORT LADY (Ire) [-] 7-11-1 N Williamson,
. . . .(9 to 4 fav) 1
431² TRIPTODICKS (Ire) [-] 6-9-11 (7") A O'Shea, ...(4 to 1) 2
431⁶ CLONEENVERB [-] 9-9-2 (5") J Butler, ...(25 to 1) 3
409⁶ NO SIR ROM [-] 10-9-9 T Horgan, ...(14 to 1) 4
85⁶ QUATTRO [-] 6-11-5 S H O'Donovan, ...(10 to 1) 5
409 BEST VINTAGE [-] (bl) 12-11-6 (7") Mr E Gallagher, (20 to 1) 6
537⁴ SANDY FOREST LADY (Ire) [-] 7-10-8 T P Treacy, . .(8 to 1) 7
537³ HANNIES GIRL (Ire) [-] 7-10-13 (7") L J Fleming, . . .(5 to 1) f
MONOKRATIC (Ire) [-] 7-11-4 (3") Mr K Whelan, ...(6 to 1) f
537⁶ SIR L MUNNY [-] 12-10-1 J P Broderick, ...(10 to 1) pu
Dist: 20l, 3½l, 10l, dist. 4m 6.90s. (10 Ran).

(Patrick Cagney), John J Walsh

589 Clonmel Oil Handicap Hurdle (0-109 4-y-o and up) £3,082 2m........ (6:00)

432⁵ CHUCK (Ire) [-] 6-10-5 (7") D McCullagh, ... (3 to 1)　1
　　ALLARACKET (Ire) [-] 7-10-6 (7") A O'Shea, ... (4 to 1)　2
536⁷ LISHILLAUN (Ire) [-] 6-9-8 (5") Susan A Finn, ... (7 to 2)　3
　　ROSCOLVIN (Ire) [-] 4-11-7 J Shortt, ... (2 to 1 fav)　4
　　HIGH PILGRIM (Ire) [-] 5-10-7 J P Broderick, ...(6 to 1)　5
Dist: 8l, 15l, 8l, 2l. 3m 58.40s. (5 Ran).

(Mrs Sheila McCullagh), Michael McCullagh

590 Clonmel Oil Maiden Hurdle (4-y-o) £2,740 2m......................(6:30)

434⁹ MIDDLE MOGGS (Ire) 10-11 P A Roche, ... (12 to 1)　1
　　JACK YEATS (Ire) 11-4 (3") Mr P M Kelly, ... (5 to 1)　2
　　DUBLIN TREASURE (Ire) 11-2 R Dunwoody, ... (9 to 4 fav)　3
　　DIGADUST (Ire) 11-7 M Duffy, ... (11 to 4)　4
347³ GRAPHIC LADY (Ire) 10-11 K F O'Brien, ... (8 to 1)　5
　　FOREST PRINCESS (Ire) 10-11 P Carberry, ... (12 to 1)　6
393⁴ ELYSIAN HEIGHTS (Ire) 10-6 (5") J Butler, ... (7 to 1)　7
560 HARRY WELSH (Ire) 11-7 C O'Dwyer, ... (16 to 1)　8
339⁸ TEMPLARS INN (Ire) 10-4 (7") A O'Shea, ... (20 to 1)　9
　　LADY WAAJIB (Ire) 10-11 F Woods, ... (14 to 1)　10
339⁵ MULTIPIT (Ire) 11-2 (5") T Martin, ... (16 to 1)　f
434 LOULISSARO (Ire) 10-4 (7") L A Hurley, ... (33 to 1)　pu
Dist: Nk, 1½l, 1½l, 10l. 3m 54.50s. (12 Ran).

(John Mansergh-Wallace), David Wachman

591 Tipperary I.N.H. Flat Race (5-y-o and up) £2,397 2m.................. (7:00)

　　KING OF THE DAWN 5-11-9 (5") Mr R Walsh, ... (5 to 4 fav)　1
538³ HOLY GROUNDER (Ire) 7-11-7 (7") Miss M Horgan, (12 to 1)　2
463⁶ LOLLIA PAULINA (Ire) (bl) 5-11-2 (7") Mr Edgar Byrne,
　　.. (10 to 1)　3
　　ACES AND EIGHTS (Ire) 6-12-0 Mr P Fenton, ... (11 to 4)　4
566 JANICE PRICE (Ire) 5-11-2 (7") Mr M J Walsh, ...(20 to 1)　5
407⁶ EASTERN CUSTOM (Ire) 5-11-6 (3") Mr R O'Neill, (12 to 1)　6
487⁵ HOLLY LADY (Ire) 5-11-2 (7") Mr John P Moloney, (25 to 1)　7
464⁷ MALICE 10-11-6 (3") Mr J Connolly, ... (11 to 1)　8
　　BOARDROOM BELLE (Ire) 5-11-6⁴ (7") Mr A McNamara,
　　.. (25 to 1)　9
464³ GRAIGUE HILL (Ire) 7-11-2 (7") Mr R M Walsh, ... (6 to 1)　10
　　GOLLY MISS MOLLY (Ire) 5-11-2 (7") Mr R Flavin, (25 to 1)　11
464⁸ SILKEN SECRETARIAT (Ire) 5-11-11 (3") Mr P English,
　　.. (12 to 1)　12
　　MARDON (Ire) 5-11-9 Mr J A Flynn, ... (10 to 1)　13
　　WILD BROOK (Ire) 6-11-7 (7") Mr J Cullen, ... (20 to 1)　14
217⁷ CHESTNUT SHOON 10-11-2 (7") Miss C Gould, .. (33 to 1)　15
　　CHASEYOURARM (Ire) 5-11-2 (7") Mr M W Carroll, (33 to 1)　16
Dist: 6l, 2½l, ½l, 9l. 3m 45.00s. (16 Ran).

(George Mullins), P Mullins

PLUMPTON (good to firm)
Thursday September 5th
Going Correction: MINUS 0.30 sec. per fur.

592 Patcham Conditional Jockeys' Handicap Hurdle Class F (0-105 4-y-o and up) £2,138 2m 1f.............. (2:30)

521² TEL E THON [78] (v) 9-10-7 D Fortt, *made all, rallied whn chlgd appr last, kpt on.....* (7 to 1 op 5 to 1 tchd 8 to 1)　1
503² PAIR OF JACKS (Ire) [82] 6-10-11 B Fenton, *hld up, hdwy 4 out, wknd appr nxt, chlgd appr last, no extr finish.*
　　...................(7 to 4 fav tchd 2 to 1 and 9 to 4)　2
437² SAFETY (USA) [93] (bl) 9-11-8 T J Murphy, *trkd wnr till one pace aftr 3 out.........* (11 to 2 op 5 to 2 tchd 6 to 1)　3
543³ SCRIPT [79] (v) 5-10-1 (5") N T Egan, *hld up in rear, effrt 4 out, sn btn.....................* (12 to 1 op 10 to 1 tchd 16 to 1)　4
438⁵ EMALLEN (Ire) [71] (bl) 8-10-0 Sophie Mitchell, *trkd ldrs till wknd 4 out...........* (25 to 1 op 12 to 1 tchd 33 to 1)　5
　　ANTONIO MARIANO (Swe) [97] 5-11-10 L Aspell, *mid-div, gd hdwy aftr 6th, wknd rpdly appr 3 out, tld off.*
　　........................(7 to 2 tchd 3 to 1)　6
　　ARAMON [75] (bl) 6-10-4 Michael Brennan, *chsd ldrs, 4th whn f four out.............*(10 to 1 tchd 8 to 1 and 12 to 1)　f
Dist: 2½l, 20l, 5l, 1½l, 26l. 4m 8.50s. a 11.50s (7 Ran).

(Miss C J E Caroe), Miss C J E Caroe

593 Lindfield Selling Hurdle Class G (4-y-o and up) £1,859 2½m........... (3:00)

529³ HACKETTS CROSS 8-11-5 A Maguire, *hld up in trh, hdwy 4 out, wnt second aftr nxt, rdn to ld r-in.* ..(13 to 8 jt-fav op 2 to 1)　1
528⁴ TUG YOUR FORELOCK 5-10-12 A Thornton, *hld up, hdwy to go second 5th, led 4 out, hrd rdn and hdd r-in.*
　　...........................(12 to 1 op 8 to 1)　2
528 KINGSWELL BOY 10-10-12 D Bridgwater, *trkd ldr, lft in ld 4th, hdd four out, wknd nxt.....*(5 to 1 op 4 to 1)　3
　　ROGER'S PAL 9-11-5 (7") M Batchelor, *hld up, lost tch 4 out.*
　　.......................(33 to 1 op 20 to 1)　4

509³ BALLAD RULER 10-10-12 R Supple, *in tch till wknd 4 out, tld off.....................*(33 to 1 op 12 to 1 tchd 50 to 1)　5
　　KESANTA 6-10-7 A P McCoy, *led, clr whn blun and uns rdr 4th.......................*(13 to 8 jt-fav op 5 to 4)　ur
　　DUDWELL VALLEY (Ire) 4-10-5 J Railton, *beh frm 3rd, tld off whn pld up bef 8th..............* (33 to 1 op 25 to 1)　pu
Dist: ½l, 8l, 6l, dist. 5m 5.00s. a 28.00s (7 Ran).

(Brian A Lewendon), P Eccles

594 Doug Wood Novices' Handicap Chase Class E (0-100 5-y-o and up) £2,933 2m............................. (3:30)

502* HARROW WAY [76] 6-10-7 (7ex) A Maguire, *hld up beh ldr, led 4 out, sn clr cmftbly.......* (7 to 4 on op 6 to 4 on)　1
325² HERESTHEDEAL [97] (v) 7-12-0 B Clifford, *led, mstk 4th, jmpd slwly and hdd four out, no imprsn aftr.*
　　............(9 to 4 op 6 to 4 tchd 11 to 4 and 3 to 1)　2
　　SEASAMACAMILE [69] 9-10-0 B Powell, *al same pl, blun 6th, no ch aftr.............* (8 to 1 op 8 to 1)　3
500 LAVALIGHT [70] 9-9-10 (5") P Henley, *al last, nvr on terms.*
　　.......................(33 to 1 op 20 to 1 tchd 40 to 1)　4
Dist: 5l, 8l, 19l. 3m 55.40s. a 3.40s (4 Ran).
SR: -/13/-/-/　　　　　　　　　　　　*(Mrs Carrie Zetter-Wells), L Wells*

595 Haywards Heath Novices' Claiming Hurdle Class F (4-y-o and up) £2,247 2m 1f........................(4:00)

　　COURBARIL 4-11-6 A P McCoy, *al prmnt, slight ld 4 out, wnt clr appr 2 out, cmftbly.* (3 to 1 fav op 4 to 1 tchd 5 to 1)　1
499* BURNT SIENNA (Ire) (v) 4-10-9 W McFarland, *al prmnt, led 6th, hdd nxt, (4 out), outpcd appr 2 out.*
　　.......................(5 to 1 op 4 to 1 tchd 11 to 2)　2
445³ DENOMINATION (USA) 4-11-3 D Bridgwater, *hld up, hdwy 4 out, one pace frm 2 out...* (9 to 2 op 3 to 1 tchd 5 to 1)　3
　　PAPER CLOUD 4-10-3 J Railton, *hld up, hdwy to track ldrs appr 3 out, wknd bef nxt.* (13 to 2 op 8 to 1 tchd 12 to 1)　4
　　LUCKY DOMINO 6-10-7 R Johnson, *mid-div, lost tch 4 out.*
　　.......................(33 to 1 op 20 to 1 tchd 40 to 1)　5
513⁵ REEFA'S MILL (Ire) (bl) 4-11-0 W Marston, *chsd ldrs till hit 6th, sn in rear...........*(12 to 1 op 10 to 1 tchd 14 to 1)　6
　　MORE BILLS (Ire) 4-9-12 (7") M Batchelor, *al beh, lost tch 4 out.................*(12 to 1 op 8 to 1 tchd 14 to 1)　7
419 ON THE LEDGE (USA) 6-10-0 (7") A Dowling, *prmnt till wknd quickly appr 4 out, tld off........*(100 to 1 op 33 to 1)　8
　　GONE FOR LUNCH 5-10-13 J Culloty, *hld up, lost tch appr 4 out, tld off.........* (4 to 1 op 3 to 1 tchd 9 to 2)　9
　　WOODLANDS ELECTRIC 6-10-7 R Supple, *al beh, tld off whn pld up bef 3 out.................*(100 to 1 op 33 to 1)　pu
　　SOLO VOLUMES 7-11-2 B Powell, *led to 6th, wknd quickly, tld off whn pld up bef 3 out.*
　　.......................(50 to 1 op 20 to 1 tchd 66 to 1)　pu
231⁷ TWO HEARTS 4-9-12 (5") P Henley, *al beh, tld off whn pld up bef 2 out.................*(33 to 1 op 20 to 1)　pu
　　RADICAL EXCEPTION (Ire) 6-10-10 P Holley, *sn beh, tld off 6th, pld up bef 4 out....* (50 to 1 op 20 to 1 tchd 66 to 1)　pu
Dist: 10l, hd, 2½l, 18l, 3½l, 3l, 16l, 1½l. 4m 8.10s. a 11.10s (13 Ran).

(G Steinberg), S Dow

596 George Poole Novices' Chase Class E (5-y-o and up) £2,976 2m 5f.....(4:30)

　　MILL O'THE RAGS (Ire) 7-10-12 J F Titley, *trkd ldr, lft clr 4th, nvr trbld aftr........* (6 to 4 fav tchd 5 to 4 and 13 to 8)　1
449⁴ OUR NIKKI 6-10-7 S Burrough, *hld up, hdwy to track ldrs tenth, wnt second 5 out, rdn whn hit 2 out, not trble wnr.*
　　.......................(20 to 1 op 10 to 1 tchd 25 to 1)　2
510* NORTH BANNISTER 9-10-12 G Crone, *lft second 4th, cld 6 out, mstks nxt 2, sn btn.*
　　.......................(33 to 1 op 20 to 1)　3
　　STRAIGHT LACED (USA) 9-10-12 B Fenton, *al beh, tld off 6th.*
　　.......................(33 to 1 op 20 to 1)　4
516³ HIZAL 7-11-5 Mr A Charles-Jones, *hld up, hmpd and uns rdr 5th.............*(7 to 2 op 3 to 1 tchd 4 to 1)　ur
　　FORT GALE (Ire) 5-10-9 G Bradley, *made most till blun and uns rdr 4th....* (5 to 1 op 7 to 2 tchd 6 to 1)　ur
401¹⁴ MIRAMARE 6-10-7 (5") P Henley, *beh frm 6th, tld off whn pld up bef 3 out.....*(12 to 1 op 7 to 1 tchd 14 to 1)　pu
Dist: 8l, 6l, dist. 5m 15.50s. a 9.50s (7 Ran).

(E J Fenaroli), Mrs D Haine

597 Pease Pottage Novices' Handicap Hurdle Class E (0-100 4-y-o and up) £2,280 2½m...................(5:00)

　　BRASSIC LINT [73] 6-10-7 D Bridgwater, *made all, hld 3rd and 7th, clr 4 out, tired appr last, kpt on gmely.*
　　.......................(9 to 4 op 2 to 1)　1
359² CANARY FALCON [84] 5-11-2 V Smith, *hld up, hdwy to go second 4 out, cld 2 out, rdn and no imprsn r-in.*
　　.......................(7 to 2 op 6 to 1 tchd 4 to 1)　2
547⁶ POSITIVO [87] 5-11-5 I Lawrence, *chsd wnr to 7th, wknd 3 out.....*(10 to 1 op 7 to 1 tchd 11 to 1 and 12 to 1)　3
166* EFHARISTO [92] (bl) 7-11-12 A Maguire, *al poor 4th, tld off.....................*(2 to 1 fav op 6 to 4)　4

105⁴ FIRST CLASS [94] 6-12-0 B Fenton, *in tch, chsd wnr 7th to 4 out, sn wknd, pld up bef 2 out.*
.................................(6 to 1 op 5 to 1 tchd 6 to 1) pu
Dist: 3l, 8l, 28l. 4m 57.30s. a 20.30s (5 Ran).

(K M Stanworth), J Neville

KILBEGGAN (IRE) (good)
Friday September 6th

598 **Foster And Allen Handicap Hurdle**
(0-116 4-y-o) £2,740 2m 3f......(4:30)

469* I REMEMBER IT WELL (Ire) [-] (bl) 10-6 J P Broderick,
....(11 to 8 fav) 1
467² FOREST LADY (Ire) [-] (bl) 10-4 (3*) D T Evans, ... (11 to 4) 2
342⁴ ADARAMANN (Ire) [-] (bl) 10-13 (5*) Mr R Walsh, ... (4 to 1) 3
408⁴ THE SOUTH POLE INN (Ire) [-] 9-7 (5*) J Butler, ... (5 to 1) pu
Dist: 3½l, 8l. 4m 33.30s. (4 Ran).

(I Remember It Well Syndicate), Michael Hourigan

599 **Innkeepers Novice Hurdle (4-y-o and up) £2,740 2m 3f..............(5:00)**

565³ JANE DIGBY (Ire) 4-11-4 T Horgan, ...(3 to 1) 1
562³ ALLATRIM (Ire) 6-11-9 R Dunwoody, ...(9 to 4) 2
560³ PALETTE (Ire) 4-10-9 (3*) D J Casey, ...(Evens fav) 3
119² RUDDS HILL (Ire) 8-11-6 F Woods, ...(25 to 1) 4
562⁹ COLLEGE LAND (Ire) 4-11-3 M P Hourigan, ...(33 to 1) 5
Dist: 5½l, hd, 9l, dist. 4m 28.60s. (5 Ran).

(New Road Syndicate), A P O'Brien

600 **Brusna Maiden Hurdle (4 & 5-y-o) £2,226 2m 3f.................(5:30)**

233² LEMOIRE (Ire) 5-10-12 (3*) D T Evans, ...(9 to 2) 1
142⁷ WOODY 5-12-0 P Carberry, ...(9 to 2) 2
561⁷ ATTACK AT DAWN (Ire) 5-11-9 T P Treacy, ...(8 to 1) 3
304 EOINS LAD (Ire) 5-11-6 R Dunwoody, ...(12 to 1) 4
468² COLONIA SKY (Ire) 5-10-8 (7*) Mr P R Lenihan, ... (10 to 1) 5
66 SPANISH CASTLE (Ire) 6-11-6 J P Broderick, ... (20 to 1) 6
ARRIENZIO (Ire) 4-11-4 T J Mitchell, ...(20 to 1) 7
467⁵ BIT OF A SET TOO (Ire) 5-10-10 (5*) J M Donnelly, ..(8 to 1) f
561³ FLYING IN THE GALE (Ire) 5-10-8 (7*) A O'Shea, (2 to 1 fav) f
MOTTO GUZZI (Ire) 5-10-8 (7*) D McCullagh, ... (25 to 1) f
JAKE CHOICE (Ire) 4-10-13 P M Verling, ...(25 to 1) f
Dist: 2½l, 15l, 2l, 8l. 4m 36.50s. (11 Ran).

(F J Lacy), F J Lacy

601 **Loughnagore Maiden Hurdle (6-y-o and up) £2,226 2m 3f..........(6:00)**

430⁴ BENNY THE BISHOP (Ire) 6-11-7 (7*) Mr A Hoss, (6 to 4 fav) 1
494³ NEW LEGISLATION (Ire) (bl) 6-11-1 F Woods, ... (5 to 1) 2
552⁴ WILDLIFE RANGER (Ire) 8-12-0 T Horgan, ...(4 to 1) 3
SLANEY STANDARD (Ire) 8-12-0 C O'Dwyer, ... (10 to 1) 4
536 STANSWAY (Ire) 9-12-0 Mr P Fenton, ...(10 to 1) 5
304 FORGIVENESS (Ire) 6-11-6 P M Verling, ...(33 to 1) 6
DERRY SAND (Ire) 6-11-1 (5*) P D Casey, ...(12 to 1) 7
AWAY IN A HACK (Ire) 6-11-6 D H O'Connor, ... (33 to 1) 8
494⁷ SAN SIRO (Ire) 6-10-13 (7*) Mr Edgar Byrne, ... (12 to 1) f
495 BLUEHILL LAD 9-11-6 K F O'Brien, ...(33 to 1) pu
253 INK BOTTLE (Ire) 6-11-6 T P Treacy, ...(14 to 1) pu
Dist: 8l, 5l, 2½l, 20l. 4m 34.10s. (11 Ran).

(Mrs Salome Brennan), Cecil Ross

602 **Lockes Whiskey Handicap Chase (0-109 4-y-o and up) £3,425 3m 1f**
....(6:30)

470⁶ MERRY PEOPLE (Ire) [-] 8-12-0 T Horgan, ... (5 to 2 fav) 1
470² FAYS FOLLY (Ire) [-] 7-9-2 (7*) R P Hogan, ...(7 to 1) 2
563⁴ THERE TIS FOR YA (Ire) [-] 8-10-10 C O'Dwyer, ..(6 to 1) 3
338 WALKERS LADY (Ire) [-] 8-10-0 (3*) D T Evans, ...(12 to 1) 4
470* GOT NO CHOICE (Ire) [-] (bl) 6-9-6 (7*) M D Murphy, (6 to 1) 5
563⁶ WATERLOO BALL (Ire) [-] 7-11-7 R Dunwoody, ...(5 to 1) 6
496* BALLINABOOLA GROVE [-] 9-10-4 P Carberry, ... (7 to 1) ur
470⁴ CAPTAIN BRANDY [-] 11-10-11 K F O'Brien, ...(12 to 1) pu
470 GLEN OG LANE [-] 13-9-7 F Woods, ...(20 to 1) pu
GENERALANAESTHETIC [-] 11-9-2 (5*) J Butler, ... (20 to 1) pu
Dist: 5l, 6l, 15l, 15l. 6m 23.30s. (10 Ran).

(Karl Casey), John Queally

603 **Bridge House Tullamore I.N.H. Flat Race (4-y-o and up) £2,740 2m 3f**
....(7:00)

472² FANE PATH (Ire) 4-11-9 Mr G J Harford, ... (11 to 8 fav) 1
329⁸ JOSH'S FANCY (Ire) 5-11-9 Mr P Fenton, ...(14 to 1) 2
MONTELISA (Ire) 4-11-1 (3*) Mr B M Cash, ...(100 to 30) 3
169 FREE AND EQUAL (Ire) 5-12-0 Mr J P Dempsey, ..(20 to 1) 4
KARA'S DREAM (Ire) 8-11-2 (7*) Mr A J Dempsey, (16 to 1) 5
ROMEO'S BROTHER (Ire) 5-12-0 Mr P J Healy, ... (20 to 1) 6
SLANEY CHARM (Ire) 6-11-7 (7*) Miss L E A Doyle, (11 to 1) 7
WOODROW (Ire) 7-11-11 (3*) Mr K Whelan, ... (20 to 1) 8
278⁴ ROSIE FLYNN (Ire) 4-10-11 (7*) Mr Sean O O'Brien, (5 to 1) 9
527 FLORIA (Ire) 4-10-11 (7*) Miss A L Crowley, ... (14 to 1) 10

EIMEARS DELIGHT (Ire) 5-11-9 Miss M Olivefalk, (10 to 1) 11
SCOTCH STONE GIRL (Ire) 4-10-11 (7*) Miss A Croke,
....(12 to 1) 12
779 LITTLE DUCHESS (Ire) 4-10-11 (7*) Mr F Nesbitt, .. (20 to 1) 13
MURGASTY (Ire) 4-10-11 (7*) Mr J T Murphy, ... (12 to 1) 14
STONEY WAY (Ire) 5-11-7 (7*) Mr J J Maguire, ... (20 to 1) 15
Dist: Hd, 12l, 2l, 5l. 4m 27.40s. (15 Ran).

(N Coburn), Noel Meade

604 **Breeders Supporting Kilbeggan Beginners Chase (4-y-o and up) £2,740 2m 5f.............................(7:30)**

496² COSHLA EXPRESSO (Ire) 8-12-0 P L Malone, .. (9 to 4 fav) 1
495* JESSIE'S BOY (Ire) 7-12-0 J K Kinane, ...(10 to 1) 2
STRONG BOOST (USA) 5-11-8 R Dunwoody, .. (100 to 30) 3
BORRISMORE FLASH (Ire) 8-12-0 J P Broderick, (12 to 1) 4
471⁵ LET THE RIVER RUN 10-11-2 (7*) R P Hogan, ... (8 to 1) 5
171⁸ STRAIGHT ON (Ire) 5-11-8 J Shortt, ...(9 to 2) 6
Dist: 1½l, 20l, 1½l, 1l. 5m 32.80s. (6 Ran).

(Thomas Heffernan), A J Martin

SEDGEFIELD (good to firm)
Friday September 6th
Going Correction: MINUS 0.25 sec. per fur.

605 **Winter Rape Novices' Handicap Chase Class E (0-100 5-y-o and up) £2,914 3m 3f.......................(2:25)**

551² THE GALLOPIN'MAJOR (Ire) [75] (bl) 6-10-9 N Smith, *trkd ldr frm 5th, led 17th, clr whn blun last.*
.......................(7 to 2 op 3 to 1 tchd 4 to 1) 1
517³ GEORGE ASHFORD (Ire) [90] (v) 6-11-10 A S Smith, *made most till aftr 4th, in tch, reminder after 9th, rdn to chase wnr frm 17th, no imprsn.*..................(9 to 4 op 7 to 4) 2
459 DUSTYS TRAIL (Ire) [67] 7-10-1 R Johnson, *prmnt, sn drvn alng, grad wknd frm 3 out.*
.......................(14 to 1 op 10 to 1 tchd 16 to 1) 3
492⁴ DONOVANS REEF [68] 10-10-2 D Bentley, *in tch, drvn alng aftr 16th, wknd aftr nxt.*.........(50 to 1 op 66 to 1) 4
549³ QUIXALL CROSSETT [66] 11-10-0 K Johnson, *in tch till rdn and wknd aftr 16th, tld off.*........(50 to 1 op 33 to 1) 5
455* CUCHULLAINS GOLD (Ire) [86] (bl) 8-11-6 N Williamson, *keen, hld up, hdwy to ld aftr 4th, hdd whn blun badly and uns rdr 17th.*........................(5 to 4 fav op 6 to 4) ur
319⁴ MR ORIENTAL [66] 6-10-0 J Culloty, *beh, tailing off whn blun 15th, pld up bef 2 out.*..(50 to 1 op 33 to 1) pu
Dist: 4l, 10l, 10l, 13l. 6m 49.90s. a 16.90s (7 Ran).

(R W S Jevon), Mrs M Reveley

606 **Federation Brewery Handicap Hurdle Class E (0-115 4-y-o and up) £2,355 2m 5f 110yds............(2:55)**

44² RED VALERIAN [114] (v) 5-11-9 (5*) Michael Brennan, *trkd ldrs, led on bit appr last, pushed out.* (2 to 1 op 6 to 4) 1
559 TOUGH TEST (Ire) [99] 6-11-8 B Fenton, *cl up, led 7th, rdn aftr 2 out, hdd appr last, no extr.* (7 to 2 op 3 to 1 tchd 4 to 1) 2
299² STRONG JOHN (Ire) [88] 8-10-1 (3*) D Parker, *hld up, hdwy to track ldrs 3 out, wknd aftr nxt.*.....(11 to 2 op 5 to 1) 3
491⁴ CRAZY HORSE DANCER (USA) [84] 8-10-0 R Johnson, *chsd ldrs till wknd aftr 3 out.*..........(9 to 1 op 8 to 1) 4
244 AIDE MEMOIRE (Ire) [84] 7-10-0 K Johnson, *towards rear, lost tch frm 7th.*........(25 to 1 op 20 to 1 tchd 33 to 1) 5
521⁴ ROYAL CIRCUS [93] 7-10-9 A P McCoy, *led till hdd 7th, wknd aftr 3 out.*.....(5 to 1 op 4 to 1 tchd 11 to 2) 6
390* RUDI'S PRIDE (Ire) [97] 5-10-11 N Smith, *towards rear, lost tch frm 6th, tld off whn pld up bef 2 out.*
.......................(11 to 2 op 9 to 2 tchd 6 to 1) pu
Dist: 4l, 11l, 12l, 9l, 8l. 4m 50.40s. a 2.40s (7 Ran).
SR: 23/6/-/-/

(Mrs Alurie O'Sullivan), G M Moore

607 **Raisby Quarries Handicap Chase Class D (0-120 5-y-o and up) £3,457 2m 5f.......................(3:25)**

517² MAGIC BLOOM [100] 10-11-0 (5*) E Callaghan, *sn chasing ldrs, blun 8th, led 2 out, styd on und pres, jst hld on.*
.......................(5 to 2 fav op 2 to 1) 1
475² THE BLUE BOY (Ire) [100] (bl) 8-11-5 R Johnson, *in tch, outpcd aftr 8th, chalg whn lost w8 cloth betw last 2, styd on wl, jst fld, fnshd second, disqualified.*.......(7 to 1 op 5 to 1) 2D
548² STAIGUE FORT (Ire) [91] 8-10-10 P Niven, *chsd ldr, mstk 11th, outpcd aftr 13th, rallied to chal 2 out, wknd appr last, fnshd 3rd, plcd second.*........(5 to 4 op 9 to 2 tchd 11 to 2) 2
CRACKLING FROST (Ire) [81] 8-10-0 N Williamson, *led to 2 out, fdd, fnshd 4th, plcd 3rd.*(4 to 1 op 5 to 1 tchd 7 to 2) 3
490² BEAUCADEAU [105] 10-11-10 P Waggott, *hld up, cld, rdn and wknd aftr 13th, fnshd 5th, plcd 4th.* (3 to 1 op 7 to 2) 4
CLARES OWN [100] 12-11-5 K Jones, *sn beh, lost tch frm hfwy, fnshd 6th, plcd 5th.*.............(7 to 1 op 6 to 1) 5
Dist: Sht-hd, 10l, 7l, 13l, 7l. 4m 59.70s. a 3.70s (6 Ran).
SR: 2/-/-/

(Peter Nelson), J M Jefferson

608 Sam Berry Novices' Chase Class E (5-y-o and up) £3,208 2m 5f........(4:00)

VAL DE RAMA (Ire) 7-10-12 P Niven, *trkd ldrs, blun and almost uns rdr 7th, led 11th, mstk nxt, hrd pressed frm 3 out, all out*.......... (11 to 10 on op 7 to 4 on tchd Evens) 1
549^{2} BUYERS DREAM (Ire) (v) 6-10-9 (3*) G Cahill, *nvr far away, drvn alng whn mstk 9th, drw clr wth wnr frm 13th, ev ch till no extr und pres r-in*........ (13 to 2 op 8 to 1 tchd 6 to 1) 2
CARDINAL SINNER (Ire) 7-10-12 K Jones, *led till hdd 9th, sn wknd, tld off*.................. (20 to 1 op 16 to 1) 3
474^{3} TONY'S FEELINGS 8-10-12 A Thornton, *mstk second, in tch till outpcd aftr tenth, tld off*..........(12 to 1 tchd 14 to 1) 4
489^{8} SEE YOU ALWAYS (Ire) 6-10-12 P Waggott, *in tch till wknd aftr tenth, tld off*.....................(20 to 1 op 16 to 1) 5
518 SMOKEY TRACK 11-10-2 (5*) S Taylor, *beh, lost tch frm tenth, tld off*.. (33 to 1) 6
558^{3} RICHMOND (Ire) 8-10-12 B Storey, *in tch till wknd aftr tenth, tld off*............................... (7 to 1 tchd 6 to 1) 7
CHILDSWAY 8-10-12 M A Fitzgerald, *prmnt, led 9th, hdd 11th, wknd aftr 13th, tld off*...... (11 to 1 op 8 to 1 tchd 12 to 1) 8
DURHAM HORNET 9-10-12 M Foster, *prmnt till outpcd aftr tenth, tld off whn blun and uns rdr 2 out.*
.... (20 to 1 op 16 to 1) ur

Dist: Nk, dist, 5l, 3l, 3l, 1l, 8l. 5m 5.20s. a 9.20s (9 Ran).

(D Morland), Denys Smith

609 Stanley Racing Novices' Hurdle Class E (4-y-o and up) £2,302 2m 5f 110yds .... (4:30)

78^{4} SUJUD (Ire) 4-10-6^{1} R Garritty, *settled midfield gng wl, steady hdwy to ld 2 out, ran on well, cmftbly*... (5 to 2 tchd 3 to 1) 1
547^{5} WHAT'S SECRETO (USA) (bl) 4-10-10 P Niven, *mid-div, hdwy hfwy, led 3 out, sn hdd, chsd wnr frm nxt, no imprsn.*
.... (9 to 1 op 8 to 1 tchd 10 to 1) 2
384* FORGOTTEN EMPRESS 4-10-12 R Johnson, *hld up, hdwy aftr 7th, rdn bef 2 out, no further prog, fnshd lme.*
...............(13 to 8 fav op 7 to 4 tchd 6 to 4) 3
YOUNG STEVEN (bl) 5-10-12 S McDougall, *prmnt, led 6th, hdd 3 out, sn rdn and btn*.........(9 to 1 op 8 to 1) 4
78^{9} CLASSIC CREST (Ire) (v) 5-11-5 N Bentley, *chsd ldrs, rdn aftr 3 out, sn wknd*.................... (8 to 1 op 6 to 1) 5
533^{5} PIMSBOY (v) 9-10-9 (3*) P Midgley, *hld up, mstk 7th, sn drvn alng and wknd*.................................. (20 to 1) 6
554^{4} LITTLE REDWING 4-10-2 (3*) Mr C Bonner, *beh, lost tch frm 7th*.. (7 to 1 op 6 to 1) 7
419^{4} TIGH-NA-MARA 8-10-3^{1} (5*) E Callaghan, *mid-div, hdwy aftr 7th, led after 3 out, jst hdd whn crashed through wing and ran out nxt*...............................(12 to 1 op 10 to 1) ro
WHIRLWIND ROMANCE (Ire) 5-10-8^{1} K Jones, *tld off whn pld up bef 6th*..(50 to 1) pu
473^{4} BOWLAND PARK 5-10-7 J Culloty, *led, wndrd badly into hurdles, hdd 6th, wknd bef 3 out, tld off whn pld up before nxt.*
.... (25 to 1 op 20 to 1) pu
322 OUSEFLEET BOY 4-10-7 (3*) G Cahill, *in tch till wknd aftr 7th, tld off whn pld up bef 2 out*.......... (50 to 1 op 33 to 1) pu
MOUNT KEEN 4-10-10 M Dwyer, *lost tch frm 6th, tld off whn pld up bef 2 out*.................(16 to 1 op 12 to 1) pu

Dist: 7l, 7l, 5l, 12l, 3½l, 2½l. 4m 56.50s. a 8.50s (12 Ran).

(D J Lever), M D Hammond

610 Sedgefield Maiden Hurdle Class E (4-y-o and up) £2,495 2m 1f........(5:05)

126^{3} SUAS LEAT (Ire) 6-10-12 (7*) M Newton, *in tch, chsd ldr frm 4th, led bef 2 out, styd on wl*.......... (13 to 2 op 6 to 1) 1
416^{2} TAWAFIJ (USA) 7-11-5 R Garritty, *hld up in rear, steady hdwy frm 5th, chsd wnr from 2 out, rdn aftr last, no imprsn.*
...............................(6 to 4 fav op 2 to 1) 2
546^{4} GENESIS FOUR 6-11-5 A P McCoy, *settled midfield, hdwy und pres to chase ldrs aftr 5th, kpt on same pace frm 2 out.*
.... (14 to 1 op 12 to 1) 3
FUNNY ROSE 6-10-11 (3*) G Cahill, *hld up and beh, hdwy bef 3 out, rdn aftr nxt, no further prog*.................(14 to 1) 4
TRUMPED (Ire) 4-10-12 A Dobbin, *led till hdd bef 2 out, fdd.*
....................................(5 to 1 op 3 to 1) 5
60^{6} LEAP IN THE DARK (Ire) 7-11-5 A Thornton, *chsd ldrs, drvn alng aftr 3 out, fdd*..............(33 to 1 op 25 to 1) 6
THALEROS 6-11-5 J Callaghan, *slwly into strd, beh, hdwy into midfield hfwy, rdn aftr 3 out, sn btn.* (8 to 1 op 6 to 1) 7
RULE OUT THE REST 5-11-5 M Foster, *mid-div till grad wknd frm 3 out*...............................(14 to 1 op 10 to 1) 8
478^{5} HAUGHTON LAD (Ire) 7-11-5 R Supple, *chsd ldrs to 5th, wknd bef 3 out*.............................. (33 to 1 op 25 to 1) 9
KANONA 5-11-5 J Supple, *beh frm 5th*..........(33 to 1) 10
GOLF BALL 6-11-5 M A Fitzgerald, *beh frm 5th.*
.... (16 to 1 op 12 to 1 tchd 25 to 1) 11
DARK MIDNIGHT (Ire) 7-11-5 J Burke, *in tch, rdn aftr 5th, sn wknd, tld off*....................................(33 to 1) 12
478^{6} PATTERN ARMS 4-11-3 D J Moffatt, *towards rear whn f 5th.*
.... (25 to 1 op 20 to 1) f
KASHANA (Ire) 4-10-12 M Moloney, *towards rear whn ran out 4th*................................. (8 to 1 op 16 to 1) ro
TINKLERS FOLLY 4-11-3 P Niven, *chsd ldrs to hfwy, sn wknd, tld off whn pld up bef 2 out*........... (8 to 1 op 11 to 2) pu

Dist: 1¾l, 7l, 1½l, 3½l, 3l, ¾l, 4l, 1¾l, 19l, 6l. 3m 52.30s. a 6.30s (15 Ran).

(Mrs J M Davenport), J M Jefferson

FAIRYHOUSE (IRE) (good to firm) Saturday September 7th

611 Rathbeggan I.N.H. Flat Race (4-y-o and up) £3,082 2¼m................ (5:30)

464* ABORIGINAL (Ire) 4-11-8 (5*) Mr R Walsh,...... (7 to 4 on) 1
464 OPTIMISM REIGNS (Ire) 5-11-11 Mr P Fenton,.... (14 to 1) 2
358^{3} BARRIGAN'S HILL (Ire) 6-11-8 (3*) Mr K Whelan,... (8 to 1) 3
KASSERINE PASS (Ire) 6-11-8 (3*) Mr P English,.. (14 to 1) 4
527* ACCOUNTANCY NATIVE (Ire) 4-11-1 (7*) Mr J P McNamara,
....(6 to 1) 5
AMBITIOUS FELLOW (Ire) 8-11-11 (7*) Miss L E A Doyle,
....(8 to 1) 6
358^{9} SUSIE'S DELIGHT (Ire) 6-10-13 (7*) Mr M S Hayden,
....(33 to 1) 7
560^{9} PERAMBIE (Ire) (bl) 4-11-1 (7*) Miss A L Crowley .... (8 to 1) 8
101 JUST A CHAT (Ire) 4-10-13 (7*) Mr L Hennessy, ... (33 to 1) 9
394 TINNOCK (Ire) 5-10-13 (7*) Miss Olivia Forrestal, .. (33 to 1) 10
BIT OF MARS (Ire) 5-11-4 (7*) Mr M A O'Dwyer, ... (14 to 1) 11

Dist: 4l, 6l, 1½l, 1l. 4m 14.20s. (11 Ran).

(Mrs P Mullins), P Mullins

STRATFORD (good) Saturday September 7th

Going Correction: MINUS 0.25 sec. per fur.

612 Richardsons Black Prince Conditional Jockeys' Selling Handicap Hurdle Class G (0-95 4-y-o and up) £2,052 2¾m 110yds....................(2:20)

299^{7} HOLY JOE [93] 14-11-5 (7*) J Prior, *trkd ldrs, wnt 3rd 7th, led 4 out, drvn out r-in*...... (25 to 1 op 20 to 1 tchd 33 to 1) 1
484^{3} KING OF BABYLON (Ire) [70] 4-10-1 L Aspell, *hld up, hdwy to track ldg grp 5 out, ev ch aftr 3 out, chlgd nxt, rdn and unbl to quicken r-in*.............(8 to 1 op 6 to 1 tchd 10 to 1) 2
491^{2} RECORD LOVER (Ire) [75] 6-10-8 G Hogan, *chsd ldrs, styd on und pres aftr 4 out, kpt on one pace*
.... (100 to 30 fav op 7 to 2 tchd 9 to 2) 3
504^{2} SAKBAH (USA) [67] 7-10-0 P Henley, *hld up, beh til styd on und pres aftr 3 out, nvr nrr*......... (25 to 1 tchd 33 to 1) 4
163^{7} EASY OVER (USA) [69] 10-10-2 R Massey, *led to second, chsd ldr til wknd aftr 3 out*
.... (20 to 1 op 10 to 1 tchd 25 to 1) 5
510^{2} BRAVO STAR (USA) [67] 11-10-0 Michael Brennan, *hld up, pushed alng aftr 8th, kpt on one pace frm 3 out*
.... (11 to 2 op 6 to 1 tchd 13 to 2) 6
TO BE FAIR [77] 9-10-10 G Tormey, *led second, mstk 6th, hdd and mistake 4 out, rdn and rallied nxt, wknd appr 2 out*
.... (9 to 1 op 4 to 1 tchd 10 to 1) 7
510^{6} AUVILLAR (USA) [80] 8-10-13 T J Murphy, *hld up, wl beh aftr 7th, kpt on one pace frm 3 out*
.... (20 to 1 op 14 to 1 tchd 25 to 1) 8
SIR PAGEANT [82] 7-11-1 J Culloty, *hld up, beh aftr 7th, nvr rchd ldrs*......................... (12 to 1 op 16 to 1) 9
CANARY BLUE (Ire) [80] 5-10-11 E Husband, *mstk 1st, hld up, pushed alng aftr 7th, lost tch after nxt*... (5 to 1 op 4 to 1) 10
146^{2} ERLEMO [78] (v) 7-10-11 Guy Lewis, *pressed ldrs til lost pl and drvn alng aftr 8th, sn beh*
.... (11 to 2 op 3 to 1 tchd 6 to 1) 11
551^{4} PENIARTH [67] 10-10-0 B Fenton, *prmnt til lost pl and pushed alng aftr 6th, tld off whn pld up after 3 out, broke leg, dead*
.... (33 to 1 op 20 to 1) pu

Dist: 3l, 6l, 4l, ½l, nk, 5l, 17l, ½l, sht-hd, 5l. 5m 30.70s. a 18.70s (12 Ran).

(Simon T Lewis), D Burchell

613 City Of Coventry Trophy Handicap Chase Class D (0-120 5-y-o and up) £3,899 3m......................(2:55)

514* MAGGOTS GREEN [93] 9-10-1 R Johnson, *led to 3rd, led ag'n 6th to 8th, led nxt, til aftr tenth, hrd rdn after 3 out, led r-in, all out*.................(9 to 1 op 6 to 1 tchd 10 to 1) 1
475* ROYAL VACATION [107] 7-11-1 J Callaghan, *not fluent early, hld up, rapid hdwy to ld aftr tenth, rdn after 3 out, hdd r-in, unbl to quicken*..........(3 to 1 op 2 to 1 tchd 7 to 2) 2
418* MAPLE DANCER [106] 10-10-7 (7*) Mr G Shenkin, *hld up, wnt 3rd 6 out, ev ch appr 2 out, rdn and kpt on one pace*
.........................(7 to 2 op 4 to 1 tchd 5 to 1) 3
458* EARLYMORNING LIGHT (Ire) [120] 7-12-0 A Dobbin, *trkd ldrs, pushed alng and outpcd aftr 5 out, eased whn btn after 3 out*................(7 to 4 fav op 15 to 8 tchd 6 to 4) 4
264^{2} WATERFORD CASTLE [109] 9-11-3 T J Murphy, *trkd ldrs, lost pl and pushed alng aftr 13th, no ch whn blun 4 out, pld up and dismounted after nxt, lme*. .(8 to 1 op 5 to 1 tchd 9 to 1) pu
532 MUSKORA (Ire) [116] (bl) 7-11-10 R Dunwoody, *led 3rd and jmpd slwly and hdd 6th, led 8th to nxt, wknd quickly aftr 11th, tld off whn pld up bef 13th*.............(16 to 1 op 8 to 1) pu

Dist: 1¼l, 5l, 28l. 5m 45.70s. a 0.70s (6 Ran).
SR: 6/18/12/ (E A Hayward), J M Bradley

614 Pertemps Juvenile Novices' Hurdle Class E (3-y-o) £2,458 2m 110yds
.... (3:25)

	SIBERIAN MYSTIC 10-5 W McFarland, chsd ldrs frm 4th, rdn to ld 2 out, hit last, drvn out. . . . . (7 to 1 op 4 to 1)	1
542⁵	SONG FOR JESS (Ire) 10-5 S Wynne, hld up, mstk 4th, hdwy aftr 3 out, kpt on wl r-in. . . . . . (100 to 1 op 25 to 1)	2
488⁴	DOWN THE YARD 10-5 W Worthington, wtd wth, steady hdwy aftr 4 out, mstk last, kpt on wl r-in. . . . . (20 to 1 op 10 to 1)	3
501*	SKRAM 11-3 J Culloty, led, hdd briefly 3 out, sn led ag'n, headed 2 out, rdn and unbl to quicken .... (9 to 1 op 7 to 1 tchd 10 to 1)	4
	UNCLE GEORGE (v) 10-10 A Maguire, chsd ldr, cld up 3 out, ev ch whn pckd nxt, rdn and unbl to quicken .... (4 to 1 op 3 to 1 tchd 9 to 2)	5
	ORANGE ORDER (Ire) 10-10 A P McCoy, chsd ldr, led and mstk 3 out, sn wknd (5 to 4 fav tchd 11 to 8 and 6 to 4)	6
	KENTFORD CONQUISTA 10-5 S Curran, beh 4th, some hdwy aftr four out, sn rdn and unbl to chal .... (50 to 1 op 25 to 1 tchd 66 to 1)	7
	LITTLE KENNY 10-2 (3*) R Massey, hld up, beh 4th, no imprsn frm four out. . . . . (16 to 1 op 10 to 1 tchd 20 to 1)	8
411²	STILL HERE (Ire) 10-10 N Williamson, prmnt, second whn mstk 4th, drvn alng aftr appr nxt, mistake 6th, wknd quickly .... (13 to 2 op 6 to 1 tchd 15 to 1)	9
481	COPPER DIAMOND (bl) 9-13¹ (7*) J Prior, mstks, al beh, tld off aftr 4th. . . . . (66 to 1 op 20 to 1)	10
	RAPID LINER 10-10 Jacqui Oliver, mstks, al beh, tld off aftr 4th. . . . . (50 to 1 op 20 to 1 tchd 66 to 1)	11
	SUPERMISTER 10-10 L Wyer, hld up, lost tch aftr 4th, tld off whn pld up bef 2 out. . . . . (25 to 1 op 16 to 1)	pu
	CASHAPLENTY 10-10 B Powell, chsd ldrs, mstk 5th, sn wknd, tld off whn pld up bef 3 out .... (40 to 1 op 20 to 1 tchd 50 to 1)	pu

Dist: 1¾l, ½l, 1¼l, 3l, 8l, 11l, 4l, 16l, dist, 16l. 4m 4.10s. a 18.10s (13 Ran).

(The Merry Men), P G Murphy

615 Dick Francis 'To The Hilt' Novices' Chase Class D (5-y-o and up) £4,110 2m 5f 110yds. . . . . (3:55)

298*	SONIC STAR 7-11-6 A Maguire, hld up, hdwy whn jmpd lft 9th, trkd ldr frm 11th, led 3 out, clr when jumped left and mstk 3 out, unchlgd. . . . . (7 to 4 on tchd 6 to 4)	1
516²	SEAHAWK RETRIEVER 7-11-6 A P McCoy, led, clr 6th, mstk and hdd 3 out, lft btn second nxt .... (15 to 2 op 8 to 1 tchd 9 to 1)	2
507²	MR SNAGGLE (Ire) 7-11-0 C Maude, hld up, pushed alng aftr 11th, no ch after nxt, lft poor 3rd 2 out. . . (7 to 2 op 3 to 1)	3
	RAPID FIRE (Ire) 8-11-0 M Dwyer, chsd ldrs, styd on frm 4 out, second and btn whn f 2 out .... (20 to 1 op 14 to 1 tchd 25 to 1)	f
401⁶	FATHER POWER (Ire) 8-11-0 R Johnson, prmnt to 9th, wkng whn mstk 11th, sn tld off, jmpd very slwly aftr, pld up bef 3 out .... (25 to 1 op 14 to 1)	pu
	ENNISTYMON (Ire) 5-10-6 S Curran, chsd ldr til wknd 7th, tld off whn pld up bef 12th. . . . . (50 to 1 op 25 to 1)	pu
483	LORD ANTRIM (Ire) (bl) 7-11-4² P Holley, whipped around strt, mstk 4th, beh whn pld up bef 6th .... (33 to 1 op 16 to 1 tchd 40 to 1)	pu

Dist: 19l, 6l. 5m 11.10s. a 11.10s (7 Ran).

(R F Nutland), D Nicholson

616 William Hill Handicap Hurdle Class D (0-120 4-y-o and up) £2,901 2m 110yds. . . . . (4:25)

	FINE THYNE (Ire) [106] 7-11-2 M A Fitzgerald, hld up, hdwy 4th, led four out, drw clr aftr 2 out, styd on wl .... (14 to 1 op 8 to 1)	1
513*	PETER MONAMY [101] (bl) 4-10-4 (3*) D Walsh, chsd ldrs, rdn alng 3 out, kpt on appr nxt, no imprsn .... (11 to 4 fav op 9 to 4)	2
511*	RE ROI (Ire) [97] 4-10-3 T J Murphy, lost pl aftr 3rd, beh til rdn and hdwy aftr 4 out, kpt on appr 2 out, no imprsn .... (3 to 1 tchd 7 to 2)	3
479*	ROYAL THIMBLE (Ire) [104] 5-10-12 R Johnson, hld up, hdwy 5th, sn drvn alng, no imprsn appr 2 out .... (3 to 1 op 11 to 4 tchd 10 to 3)	4
484*	RAVEN'S ROOST (Ire) [92] 5-10-0 P McLoughlin, hld up, pushed alng aftr 5th, wknd after 3 out, btn whn mstk last .... (16 to 1 op 14 to 1)	5
	SHOOFK [120] 5-12-0 R Dunwoody, led to 4 out, rdn and wknd aftr nxt, fnshd lme.. (13 to 2 op 5 to 1 tchd 7 to 1)	6
	WINDWARD ARIOM [106] 10-11-2 R Supple, hld up, blun and uns rdr second. . . . . (10 to 1 op 7 to 1 tchd 12 to 1)	ur

Dist: 8l, 4l, ¾l, 2l, 10l. 3m 58.90s. a 12.90s (7 Ran).

(Peter Wiegand), G Harwood

617 Hartshorne Motor Services Ltd Walsall Handicap Chase Class D (0-125 5-y-o and up) £3,795 2m 1f 110yds. . . (4:55)

500²	NOBELY (USA) [105] 9-10-8 R Farrant, prmnt, pressed ldr frm 6th, led 3 out, rdn and hld on wl nr finish .... (6 to 1 tchd 7 to 1)	1
	CAPTAIN KHEDIVE [125] 8-12-0 A P McCoy, hld up, wnt 3rd 9th, chlgd 2 out, rdn and unbl to quicken nr finish .... (2 to 1 fav tchd 9 to 4)	2
	REX TO THE RESCUE (Ire) [100] 8-9-12 (5*) P Henley, trkd ldrs, pushed alng aftr 4 out, rallied after 2 out, styd on r-in, better for race. . . . . (9 to 2 op 3 to 1)	3
490*	STATELY HOME (Ire) [120] 5-11-7 R Johnson, led to 3 out, rdn and unbl to quicken betw last 2. . . . . . . (9 to 4 op 2 to 1)	4
514³	WINGSPAN (USA) [97] 12-10-0 J R Kavanagh, hld up, lost tch aftr 4th, sn tld off. . . . . . (11 to 1 op 10 to 1 tchd 12 to 1)	5
79⁴	LOWAWATHA [103] 8-10-6 A Thornton, pressed ldr, ev ch til wknd quickly aftr 9th, tld off .... (16 to 1 op 12 to 1 tchd 20 to 1)	6
167⁶	SHREWD JOHN [100] 10-10-3³ M Dwyer, hld up, hdwy aftr 8th, cl 5th whn f 4 out.. (14 to 1 op 10 to 1 tchd 20 to 1)	f

Dist: Nk, 2l, 1¼l, dist, 1¼l. 4m 9.70s. a 7.70s (7 Ran).

(D H Cowgill), N J H Walker

618 Bird Groupage Services Ltd Oldbury 'National Hunt' Novices' Hurdle Class E (4-y-o and up) £2,318 2m 110yds
.... (5:25)

423²	ANABRANCH 5-10-0 (7*) M Newton, wnt 3rd 4th, led four out, clr aftr 3 out, hit last 2, cmftbly .... (11 to 10 fav op 6 to 5 tchd 11 to 8)	1
	DACELO (Fr) 5-10-12 J Osborne, hld up, hdwy aftr 5th, wnt second after 4 out, styd on appr 2 out, no imprsn .... (5 to 8 op 6 to 4 tchd 2 to 1)	2
	SMART LORD 5-10-12 M Bosley, chsd ldr and ev ch til rdn and wknd aftr 4 out. . . . (40 to 1 op 14 to 1 tchd 50 to 1)	3
435*	SCAMALLACH (Ire) (bl) 6-11-0 G Bradley, led to 4 out, sn wknd, no ch whn blun last (4 to 1 tchd 9 to 2 and 5 to 1)	4
	MILLCROFT RIVIERA (Ire) 5-10-7 (5*) P Henley, trkd ldrs frm 4th, drvn alng and outpcd aftr nxt, sn lost tch .... (16 to 1 op 10 to 1)	5
551⁵	BOYO (Ire) 5-10-12 L Wyer, hld up, wl beh whn jmpd slwly 5th, ran out bef nxt. . . . . . . (25 to 1 op 20 to 1 tchd 33 to 1)	ro
	ALBERT THE LION (Ire) 4-10-10 J Culloty, pressed ldr to 5th, wknd quickly, sn tld off, pld up bef 2 out .... (40 to 1 op 20 to 1 tchd 50 to 1)	pu

Dist: 7l, 28l, 12l, 18l. 4m 4.00s. a 18.00s (7 Ran).

(Mrs M Barker), J M Jefferson

BALLINROBE (IRE) (good)
Sunday September 8th

619 Ballinrobe Water Towers Beginners Chase (5-y-o and up) £3,425 2m 1f
.... (4:15)

	LIFE SAVER (Ire) 7-12-0 T Horgan, ... (2 to 1)	1
471²	KENTUCKY BABY (Ire) 6-11-9 C O'Dwyer, ... (5 to 4 fav)	2
496⁴	LIMAHEIGHTS (Ire) 6-11-9 D T Evans, ... (5 to 1)	3
466⁷	PRIME PAPERS 11-12-0 T P Treacy. . . . . (33 to 1)	4
	LONG SHOT JOHN (Ire) 5-11-6 (3*) U Smyth, ... (33 to 1)	5
408⁶	CROOM ABU (Ire) (bl) 5-11-2 (7*) Mr P P O'Brien, (20 to 1)	6
391	SLIEVROE (Ire) 5-11-4 J Shortt, ... (12 to 1)	7
343	THE BREASER FAWL (Ire) 8-12-0 J P Broderick,. . (20 to 1)	8

Dist: 4l, 20l, 20l, ½l. 4m 27.30s. (8 Ran).

(Mrs H A Hegarty), J A Berry

620 Ballinrobe Maiden Hurdle (3-y-o) £2,740 2m. . . . . (4:45)

574²	EVRIZA (Ire) 10-5 T Horgan, ... (9 to 4 jt-fav)	1
	FAIRLY SHARP (Ire) 10-5 J Shortt, ... (4 to 1)	2
574⁷	KOKO NOR (Ire) 10-10 L P Cusack, ... (20 to 1)	3
574⁵	DOUBLE SEEKER (Ire) 10-5 (5*) J Butler, ... (14 to 1)	4
425⁵	MAIDEN MIST (Ire) 10-2³ D T Evans, ... (25 to 1)	5
	NYMPH IN THE SKI (Ire) 10-5 F Woods, ... (25 to 1)	6
	LOVE HEART (Ire) 10-5 (5*) T Martin, ... (12 to 1)	7
	RIVER VALLEY LADY (Ire) 10-5 T P Treacy, . . (9 to 4 jt-fav)	8
522⁴	LUDDEN CHIEF (Ire) 10-10 C O'Dwyer, ... (12 to 1)	9
	PENZITA (Ire) 10-0 (5*) G Cotter, ... (33 to 1)	10
522	KILBAHA (Ire) 10-5 J P Broderick, ... (5 to 1)	11
425⁶	ALTHOUGH 10-3 (7*) S P Kelly, ... (16 to 1)	12
	GALICI (Ire) 10-10 D J Doran, ... (20 to 1)	13
	QUEEN OF SILVER (Ire) 10-5 P A Roche, ... (12 to 1)	pu

Dist: 20l, 15l, hd, 4l. 3m 53.20s. (14 Ran).

(Mrs Sally Carey), A P O'Brien

621 A.C.C. Bank Handicap Hurdle (0-116 4-y-o and up) £3,253 2m. . . . . . . (5:15)

433	BOB THE YANK (Ire) [-] 6-11-10 C O'Dwyer, ... (5 to 1)	1
538²	MAGICAL WAY (Ire) [-] 6-10-5 P A Roche, ... (5 to 1)	2
579⁴	BAJAN QUEEN (Ire) [-] 6-11-1 (5*) T Martin, (9 to 2 co-fav)	3
561⁶	SHARLENE (Ire) [-] 5-10-5 F Woods, ... (10 to 1)	4
564⁴	ULTRA MAGIC [-] 9-11-9 (5*) J Butler, ... (8 to 1)	5
405⁴	BRAZEN ANGEL (Ire) [-] 6-11-7 (5*) J M Donnelly, ... (9 to 2 co-fav)	6
468⁴	CREGG ROSE (Ire) [-] 6-9-7 T Horgan, ... (20 to 1)	7

579* DANCING CLODAGH (Ire) [-] (bl) 4-11-8 (6ex) S C Lyons,
.... (9 to 2 co-fav) 8
433⁶ THE WICKED CHICKEN (Ire) [-] (bl) 7-10-7 T P Treacy,
.... (8 to 1) 9
526⁵ LA CIENAGA [-] 12-11-2 J P Broderick, ... (10 to 1) 10
Dist: 3l, 2½l, 15l, 3l. 3m 54.80s. (10 Ran).
(R Phelan), P T Flavin

622 Lough Carra I.N.H. Flat Race (5-y-o and up) £2,740 2½m.............(5:45)

536³ NOELEENS DELIGHT (Ire) (bl) 7-11-2 (7*) Mr G Elliott,
.... (2 to 1 fav) 1
552⁹ FRED OF THE HILL (Ire) 5-11-7 (7*) Mr A Daly, ... (20 to 1) 2
527⁴ PLEASE NO TEARS 9-11-9 Mrs C Barker, ... (3 to 1) 3
472⁷ DEAR CHRIS (Ire) 5-11-9 Mr P F Graffin, ... (12 to 1) 4
353⁵ DOTTIE'S DOUBLE (Ire) 5-11-2 (7*) Miss K Rudd, .. (7 to 1) 5
467 BALLYHAYS LODGE (Ire) 7-11-2 (7*) Mr M G Whyte,
.... (14 to 1) 6
527 BALLYDUFF ROSE (Ire) 6-11-2 (7*) Mrs C Doyle, .. (14 to 1) 7
472³ HILLTOP BOY (Ire) 7-11-11 (3*) Mr B M Cash, ... (7 to 2) 8
MASTER FINBAR (Ire) 5-11-9 (7*) Mr B Cantillon, (11 to 1) 9
100 DELLUE WARRIOR (Ire) 5-11-7 (7*) Mr D Naughton, .(25 to 1) 10
577⁷ ARDFARNA LAD 13-11-7 (7*) Miss A L Crowley, ...(20 to 1) pu
RAYCATLOR (Ire) 6-11-7 (7*) Mr A Fleming, ...(20 to 1) pu
Dist: 5½l, 1l, 1½l, 6l. 5m 3.30s. (12 Ran).
(J-A-P Syndicate), Michael Cunningham

GALWAY (IRE) (good to firm)
Monday September 9th

623 Connacht Tribune Beginners Chase (4-y-o and up) £3,767 2¾m....... (4:00)

525³ UP TRUMPS (Ire) 7-12-0 N Williamson, ...(5 to 1) 1
471³ PASSER-BY 9-12-0 K F O'Brien, ...(5 to 2) 2
ROYAL STAR (Ire) 7-11-9 H Rogers, ...(10 to 1) 3
525 MAC-DUAGH (Ire) 6-11-7 (7*) K Bourke, ...(33 to 1) ur
345 BOBSVILLE (Ire) 8-12-0 F Woods, ...(11 to 8 on) pu
Dist: Dist, 7l. 5m 48.20s. (5 Ran).
(Mrs Mary Halpin), John J Walsh

624 Kenny Development Group Maiden Hurdle (4-y-o and up) £3,425 2m (4:30)

LOGSTOWN (Ire) 4-11-4 F Woods, ...(13 to 8 fav) 1
ABACO (USA) 4-11-4 R Dunwoody, ...(100 to 30) 2
FRANCES STREET (Ire) 4-11-9 T Horgan, ...(7 to 2) 3
560⁴ PERMIT ME (Ire) 4-10-8 (5*) G Cotter, ...(9 to 1) 4
442² TINERANA GLOW (Ire) 4-10-13 N Williamson, ...(10 to 1) 5
SPRITZER (Ire) 4-10-13 C O'Dwyer, ...(14 to 1) 6
COMMANDER JOHN (Ire) 6-11-6 W Slattery, ...(33 to 1) 7
GOLD DEPOSITOR (Ire) 4-10-11 (7*) J M Sullivan, .(10 to 1) ur
TAZ (Ire) 4-10-6 (7*) K Bourke, ...(33 to 1) ur
552 BEN ORE (Ire) 6-11-6 P M Verling, ...(33 to 1) pu
Dist: 15l, sht-hd, 6l, dist. 3m 52.00s. (10 Ran).
(Matthew Dunlea), C Collins

625 Gerald Naughton Memorial Handicap Hurdle (0-123 4-y-o and up) £3,767 3m
.... (5:00)

575* DIFFICULT TIMES (Ire) [-] 4-11-7 S C Lyons, ...(9 to 2) 1
525² CULLENSTOWN LADY (Ire) [-] 5-11-12 R Dunwoody,
.... (9 to 4 fav) 2
443⁵ SUDDEN STORM (Ire) [-] 5-10-0 T P Treacy, ...(5 to 1) 3
467⁴ GARLAND ROSE (Ire) [-] 6-9-6 (3*) D J Casey, ...(14 to 1) 4
562⁶ STONELEIGH TURBO (Ire) [-] 7-10-11 F Woods, ...(14 to 1) 5
469⁴ FATHER RECTOR (Ire) [-] 7-11-2 T Horgan, ...(9 to 2) 6
428² PRACTICE RUN (Ire) [-] 8-12-0 C O'Dwyer, ...(9 to 2) 7
Dist: 15l, 3½l, 1½l, 15l. 5m 54.00s. (7 Ran).
(P M Dowling), G M Lyons

GALWAY (IRE) (good to firm)
Tuesday September 10th

626 Uttoxeter And Newcastle Racecourses Novice Chase (5-y-o and up) £3,425 2m 1f...... (4:00)

471* CUBAN QUESTION 9-11-11 R Dunwoody, ...(5 to 2) 1
557 PHARDY 5-11-6 G M O'Neill, ...(5 to 2) 2
619² KENTUCKY BABY (Ire) 6-11-0 N Williamson, ...(11 to 4) 3
300* STROLL HOME (Ire) 6-12-9 C O'Dwyer, ...(9 to 4 fav) 4
Dist: 15l, dist. 4m 30.90s. (4 Ran).
(Laurence Byrne), D T Hughes

627 C.T. Electric E.B.F. Handicap Hurdle (Listed) (0-140 4-y-o and up) £5,480 2m......................... (4:30)

526⁴ NEAR GALE (Ire) [-] 6-11-2 T P Treacy, ...(9 to 2) 1
BLAZE OF HONOUR (Ire) [-] 5-10-8 M Moran, ...(12 to 1) 2
562² BAMAPOUR (Ire) [-] (bl) 5-10-9 R Dunwoody, ...(5 to 1) 3
526³ BLACK QUEEN (Ire) [-] 5-10-6 P A Roche, ...(5 to 1) 4

303 NO TAG (Ire) [-] 8-11-11 C O'Dwyer, ...(9 to 2) 5
526* TAITS CLOCK (Ire) [-] 7-10-5 T Horgan, ...(100 to 30 fav) 6
96⁴ TEXAS FRIDAY (Ire) [-] 6-9-4 (5*) T Martin, ...(10 to 1) 7
564⁶ THE WISE KNIGHT (Ire) [-] 5-9-10³ J P Broderick, (12 to 1) f
Dist: 5l, 4l, 10l, 12l. 3m 48.00s. (8 Ran).
(Patrick F Kehoe), P Mullins

628 Cunningham I.N.H. Flat Race (5-y-o and up) £3,425 2m.............(7:00)

MERCHANTS QUAY (Ire) 5-11-7 (7*) Mr G Kearns, ..(9 to 4) 1
STORM GEM (Ire) 5-11-4 (5*) Mr R Walsh, ...(5 to 1) 2
536 LAUGHING FONTAINE (Ire) 5-11-7 (7*) Mr H Murphy, (7 to 1) 3
BYPHARBEANRI (Ire) 5-11-7 (7*) Mr B Hassett, (7 to 4 fav) 4
591⁸ MALICE 10-11-9 Mr P Fenton, ...(5 to 1) 5
527 LEZIES LAST (Ire) 6-11-2 (7*) Mr R D Lee, ...(16 to 1) 6
Dist: 12l, 4½l, 15l, 8l. 3m 48.30s. (6 Ran).
(Andrew Redmond), D T Hughes

EXETER (firm)
Wednesday September 11th
Going Correction: MINUS 0.30 sec. per fur.

629 Devon County Cars Maiden Hurdle Class E (4-y-o and up) £2,347 2m 3f
.... (2:20)

KILLING TIME 5-11-5 D J Burchell, trkd ldr till lft in ld aftr 4th,
came clr appr 2 out, easily..............(12 to 1 op 6 to 1) 1
456² RARE SPREAD (Ire) 6-11-5 D Bridgwater, chsd ldrs, not fluent, chased wnr frm 5th, hrd rdn 2 out, no response.
.... (2 to 1 on op 5 to 4) 2
330 MARIO'S DREAM (Ire) 8-11-5 T J Murphy, prmnt, keen hold,
lost pos aftr 5th, moderate prog, not a dngr frm 2 out.
.... (100 to 1 op 25 to 1) 3
MY HARVINSKI 6-10-12 (7*) Miss E J Jones, beh 4th, brief
effrt 6th, sn wknd...........................(12 to 1 op 6 to 1) 4
499⁴ SCALP'EM (Ire) 8-11-5 Dr P Pritchard, keen hold, prmnt to
5th, mstk and wknd 6th. (33 to 1 op 14 to 1 tchd 50 to 1) 5
CROWNHILL CROSS 5-11-0 (5*) D Salter, beh frm 3rd.
.... (100 to 1 op 33 to 1 tchd 150 to 1) 6
545² MARLOUSION (Ire) 4-10-12 G Bradley, keen hold, led till hng
badly lft and pld up aftr 4th.
.... (5 to 2 op 7 to 4 tchd 11 to 4) pu
Dist: 29l, 5l, 11l, ½l, 3½l. 4m 27.40s. a 11.40s (7 Ran).
(Simon T Lewis), D Burchell

630 Scania 4-series 'Horsepower' Novices' Chase Class E (5-y-o and up) £2,827 2m 1f 110yds.................(2:55)

366² NORDIC VALLEY (Ire) 5-10-10 D Bridgwater, in tch 5th, chsd
ldrs 4 out, chlgd last, hrd rdn to ld cl hme.
.... (3 to 1 op 9 to 4 tchd 100 to 30 and 7 to 2) 1
449² BISHOPS CASTLE (Ire) 8-10-8 J A Frost, led thrchout, rdn along,
chasing ldr, wnt rght frm 4 out, led last and rdn, ct cl hme.
.... (100 to 30 op 11 to 4) 2
449* DUBELLE 6-11-0 J Culloty, sn chasing ldr, led 6th, wnt rght
frm 4 out, narrowly hdd last, rallied r-in, no extr cl hme.
.... 3
596 FORT GALE (Ire) 5-10-10 G Bradley, keen hold, hld up, jmpd
slwly 3rd, hdwy 8th, wknd frm 4 out.
.... (10 to 1 op 6 to 1 tchd 12 to 1) 4
596 HIZAL 7-11-5 Mr Charles-Jones, chsd ldrs 5th, wknd 8th.
.... (40 to 1 op 16 to 1 tchd 50 to 1) 5
594³ SEASAMACAMILE 9-10-7 B Powell, prmnt to 4th, beh frm
nxt..(14 to 1 op 10 to 1) 6
Dist: ½l, sht-hd, 12l, 29l, 14l. 4m 12.90s. a 7.90s (6 Ran).
(Pond House Racing), M C Pipe

631 Two Rivers Securities Handicap Hurdle Class F (0-105 4-y-o and up) £2,027 2m 1f 110yds.......... (3:30)

267* OUT RANKING (Fr) [101] 4-11-10 D Bridgwater, made all, clr
appr 2 out, drvn and ran on wl whn chlgd approaching last.
.... (7 to 2 op 3 to 1 tchd 5 to 1) 1
524* WOLLBOLL [79] 6-10-4 V Smith, keen hold, prmnt, chsd wnr
frm 4th, str chal appr last, no extr r-in.
.... (2 to 1 op 5 to 4 tchd 11 to 4) 2
587⁵ LITTLE HOOLIGAN [83] (bl) 5-10-8 A P McCoy, sn tracking
ldrs, rdn and outpcd frm 2 out.
.... (8 to 1 op 6 to 1 tchd 9 to 1) 3
587² MARCHMAN [81] 11-10-13 J Culloty, hld up, rdn and wknd 3
out..(15 to 8 fav op 7 to 4 tchd 2 to 1) 4
416⁶ NIGHT TIME [80] 4-9-10 (7*) Mr G Shenkin, beh, rdn 5th, sn
wknd..(16 to 1 op 8 to 1) 5
595⁸ ON THE LEDGE (USA) [75] 6-9-7 (7*) A Dowling, chsd wnr till
wknd appr 4th, tld off whn pld up bef 2 out.
.... (100 to 1 op 33 to 1) pu
503⁴ STAY WITH ME (Fr) [92] 6-11-3 J Osborne, hld up, brief effrt
5th, sn wknd, tld off whn pld up bef 2 out.
.... (4 to 1 tchd 6 to 1) pu
Dist: 2l, 5l, 29l, 21l. 3m 57.80s. a 1.80s (7 Ran).
SR: 25/3/2/-/
(Knight Hawks Partnership), M C Pipe

632 Scania 1996 Truck Of The Year Chase Handicap Class F (0-100 5-y-o and up) £3,344 2¾m 110yds............(4:00)

327⁵ JIM VALENTINE [84] 10-11-8 W Marston, *jmpd slwly second and beh, pushed alng and hdwy tenth, styd on to ld 3 out, clr frm nxt, easily*........................(7 to 1 op 15 to 2) 1
124⁷ DRUMCULLEN (Ire) [84] 7-11-8 W McFarland, *led till hdd briefly appr 4 out, sn led ag'n, headed 3 out, soon outpcd*............................(6 to 1 tchd 7 to 1) 2
480 BOXING MATCH [73] 9-10-11 R Johnson, *prmnt, ev ch 4 out, sn rdn, btn aftr nxt*.................(15 to 2 op 8 to 1) 3
548⁸ TURPIN'S GREEN [74] 13-10-12 J Culloty, *prmnt, chlgd 12th to 13th, led briefly appr 4 out, sn hdd and wknd*................................(7 to 1 op 8 to 1) 4
555⁷ MINERS REST [76] 8-11-4 P McCoy, *chsd ldrs, chlgd 12th to 13th, ev ch appr 4 out, sn wknd*............... (3 to 1 fav op 11 to 4 tchd 100 to 30) 5
380³ GHEDI (Pol) [65] (bl) 5-10-0 S Curran, *beh frm 7th, no ch whn f 12th*..................................(66 to 1) f
587⁶ GABISH [62] 11-9-7 (7*) Mr R Thornton, *hdwy to chase ldrs 5th, wknd 13th, tld off whn pld up bef 2 out*..................................(25 to 1 tchd 50 to 1) pu
483² TOUR LEADER (NZ) [86] 7-11-10 B Powell, *beh, rdn alng tenth, no ch whn blun 3 out and pld up*. (15 to 2 op 7 to 1) pu
282 MORNING BLUSH (Ire) [86] (v) 6-11-10 D Bridgwater, *prmnt, rdn 6th, hit 8th, sn drvn and effrt, wknd quickly 13th, tld off whn pld up bef 3 out*.............. (10 to 1 op 7 to 1) pu
380² PHARRAGO (Ire) [72] 7-10-10 D J Burchell, *beh and jmpd slwly tenth, tld off whn pld up bef 3 out*. (5 to 1 tchd 6 to 1) pu
Dist: 6l, 8l, 25l, 14l. 5m 35.50s. a 15.50s (10 Ran).

(R H L Barnes), D J Wintle

633 Westrucks For Scania Hurdle Handicap Class E (0-110 4-y-o and up) £2,611 2¾m............(4:30)

509* SANTELLA BOY (USA) [103] (bl) 4-11-10 J Railton, *hld up, trkd ldrs, chlgd last, sn led, pushed out*...............................(11 to 10 fav op 5 to 4 on) 1
445* BUGLET [93] 6-10-13 (3*) D Walsh, *al tracking ldrs, slight ld 2 out, hdd r-in, one pace*... (2 to 1 tchd 9 to 4 and 5 to 2) 2
491⁷ THEY ALL FORGOT ME [77] 9-10-0 Miss C Dyson, *led till hdd 2 out, sn outpcd*.............(66 to 1 op 25 to 1) 3
CHUCKLESTONE [85] 13-10-8 J Culloty, *chsd ldr, rdn alng 6th, outpcd frm 2 out*. (3 to 1 tchd 100 to 30 and 7 to 2) 4
582⁴ COEUR BATTANT (Fr) [77] 6-10-0 B Powell, *pld hrd, hld up in rear, mstk 5th and sn wl beh, hdwy to chase ldrs appr 2 out, soon wknd*.................(25 to 1 op 20 to 1) 5
Dist: Nk, 9l, sht-hd, 5l. 5m 22.50s. a 25.50s (5 Ran).

(The Link Leasing Partnership), C J Mann

634 Cox Of Devon Juvenile Novices' Hurdle Class E (3-y-o) £2,211 2m 1f 110yds .... (5:00)

584* NOBLE LORD 11-3 B Powell, *rcd keenly, made all, drw wl clr frm 4th, heavily eased fnl*..................(9 to 4 on op 5 to 2 on tchd 2 to 1 on) 1
411⁵ FRIENDLY DREAMS (Ire) (v) 10-12 D Bridgwater, *hld up and drvn, reluctant to race and not jump wl aftr, wknd rpdly after 3rd, sn well tld off and eased*............(13 to 2 op 6 to 1) 2
Won by Dist. 4m 14.90s. a 18.90s (2 Ran).
SR: -/-/   (The Old Timers Partnership), R H Buckler

GALWAY (IRE) (good to firm)
Wednesday September 11th

635 Nortel Enterprise Maiden Hurdle (5-y-o and up) £3,425 2m......... (2:30)

IDEAL PLAN (Ire) 6-12-0 R Dunwoody,..........(9 to 4) 1
552² CAITRIONA'S CHOICE (Ire) 5-11-7 (7*) Mr G Elliott,...............................(2 to 1 jt-fav) 2
552³ ASK THE BUTLER (Ire) 5-12-0 C O'Dwyer,.. (2 to 1 jt-fav) 3
BAY COTTAGE (Ire) 7-11-9 N Williamson,.........(20 to 1) 4
NA HUIBHEACHU (Ire) 5-11-1 (5*) G Cotter,........(8 to 1) 5
464 RADICAL ACTION (Ire) 6-11-6 K F O'Brien,.....(20 to 1) 6
PAR FOUR (Ire) 6-11-6 T P Rudd,...............(14 to 1) 7
ALLWAN (Ire) 7-11-1 S H O'Donovan,.........(33 to 1) 8
Dist: 10l, 1l, hd, 8l. 3m 47.30s. (8 Ran).

(Michael W J Smurfit), D K Weld

636 Nortel Applications E.B.F. Handicap Chase (Listed) (4-y-o and up) £5,780 2¾m...............................(3:30)

431⁵ BEAKSTOWN (Ire) [-] 7-10-8 T P Treacy,.....(11 to 10 fav) 1
293 JASSU [-] 10-12-0 R Dunwoody,..............(5 to 1) 2
563⁶ ANABATIC (Ire) [-] 8-11-6 T P Rudd,...............(7 to 1) 3
537⁵ MICKS DELIGHT (Ire) [-] 6-9-8¹ N Williamson,....(10 to 1) 4
580³ STRONG HURRICANE [-] 9-9-7 T J Mitchell,.....(6 to 1) 5
588⁵ QUATTRO [-] 6-9-4² (5*) G Cotter,.............(16 to 1) 6
VISIBLE DIFFERENCE [-] (bl) 10-10-7 C O'Dwyer,. (9 to 1) 7
CARRICKMINES [-] 11-9-11⁴ J P Broderick,......(20 to 1) su

Dist: 1l, 2½l, ½l, 12l. 5m 28.50s. (8 Ran).

(Mrs P J O'Meara), P Mullins

637 Anglo Printers I.N.H. Flat Race (4-y-o and up) £3,767 2m.............(5:30)

NO PRECEDENT (Ire) 4-10-8 (7*) Mr A C Coyle,.... (10 to 1) 1
SADALLAH (Ire) 4-10-13 (7*) Mr A Ross,..........(9 to 2) 2
464⁵ CASTLE ELLEN BOY (Ire) 4-11-7¹ Mr P F Graffin,.. (6 to 1) 3
487² NATIVE BABY (Ire) 6-11-8 (5*) Mr R Walsh,.... (2 to 1 fav) 4
MASTER EXECUTIVE (Ire) 4-10-13 (7*) Mr S P Hennessy,..................................(7 to 2) 5
581⁹ ROSE'S PERK (Ire) 4-10-8 (7*) Miss A Reilly,.....(20 to 1) 6
PYLON (Ire) 4-11-6 Miss M Olivefalk,........(10 to 1) 7
JOHN'S LAD (Ire) 8-11-11 (7*) Miss A L Crowley,... (5 to 1) pu
Dist: 3l, 6l, 3½l, 13l. 3m 40.70s. (8 Ran).

(G Meaney), P A Fahy

NEWTON ABBOT (good)
Thursday September 12th
Going Correction: MINUS 0.30 sec. per fur.

638 Coca-Cola Selling Hurdle Class G (4-y-o and up) £1,965 2m 1f........(2:20)

593* HACKETTS CROSS (Ire) 8-11-12 A Maguire, *al prmnt, led 3 out, pushed out*.............(5 to 2 fav op 2 to 1) 1
105 TWICE THE GROOM (Ire) (bl) 6-11-5 R Johnson, *hdwy 4th, ev ch last, ran on*...............(8 to 1 op 6 to 1) 2
PRESTIGE LADY 5-10-7 C Llewellyn, *strted slwly, gd hdwy 3 out, ev ch appr last, not quicken*....... (10 to 1 op 8 to 1) 3
479⁶ POCONO KNIGHT 6-10-5 (7*) M Keighley, *strted slwly, gd hdwy 5th, ev ch appr 2 out, sn wknd*... (25 to 1 op 20 to 1) 4
205 JAVA SHRINE (USA) 5-11-5 S McNeill, *al prmnt, led 5th to 3 out, wknd 2 out*.............(14 to 1 op 6 to 1) 5
595² BURNT SIENNA (Ire) (v) 4-10-12 W McFarland, *strted slwly, gd hdwy to ld aftr 4th, hdd and wknd 5th*...................(10 to 4 op 7 to 2 tchd 9 to 2) 6
513⁹ MERLINS WISH (USA) 7-11-12 (7*) G Supple, *hrd rdn 5th, nvr nr to chal*............(14 to 1 op 12 to 1 tchd 20 to 1) 7
539 ORINOCO VENTURE (Ire) 5-10-12 D J Burchell, *hld up, ev ch appr 2 out, wknd quickly*..........(14 to 1 op 12 to 1) 8
513⁷ AMBER LILY 4-10-5 A P McCoy, *wl beh frm 5th*...................................(20 to 1 op 8 to 1) 9
MASIMARA MUSIC 5-10-7 B Fenton, *wl beh frm 5th*......................(50 to 1 op 25 to 1) 10
595 SOLO VOLUMES 7-10-12 B Powell, *led to aftr 4th, wknd quickly 5th*..............(66 to 1 op 25 to 1) 11
317⁶ AVRIL ETOILE 6-10-7 G Upton, *tld off whn pld up and dismounted bef 2 out*..............(50 to 1 op 25 to 1) pu
ANNA BANNANNA 4-9-12 (7*) B Moore, *reluctant to race, tld off till pld up bef 2 out*...............(33 to 1 op 14 to 1) pu
511⁴ DRY SEA 5-10-12 J Frost, *prmnt till pld up and dismounted bef 4th*....................(5 to 1 op 4 to 1) pu
538⁸ SHARP HOLLY (Ire) (v) 4-10-5 L Harvey, *prmnt till wknd appr 5th, tld off whn pld up bef 2 out*....... (50 to 1 op 25 to 1) pu
Dist: 1¼l, 3l, 10l, 7l, 20l, 1¾l, 5l, 1l, 6l, 8l. 4m 2.00s. a 13.00s (15 Ran).

(Brian A Lewendon), P Eccles

639 Tetley Bitter Conditional Jockeys' Handicap Chase Class F (0-100 5-y-o and up) £2,703 2m 110yds.....(2:55)

570² SUPER SHARP (NZ) [85] 8-10-9 (5*) G Supple, *second till led 5th, made rst, drvn out*.................(5 to 2 jt-fav op 3 to 1 tchd 100 to 30) 1
480² FENWICK [88] 9-11-3 T Dascombe, *hdwy 7th, hrd rdn appr 2 out, ev ch approaching last, not quicken*.... (10 to 1 op 7 to 1) 2
615² SEAHAWK RETRIEVER [75] 7-10-4 O Burrows, *strted slwly, wl beh till hdwy 7th, sn drvn out, wknd 2 out*.............(6 to 1 op 4 to 1) 3
514⁵ PRUDENT PEGGY [71] (bl) 9-10-0 T J Murphy, *led to 5th, wknd 4 out*..................(20 to 1 op 16 to 1) 4
480 AFALTOUN [71] 11-10-0 P Henley, *chsd ldrs, hrd rdn and wknd 4 out, died aftr race*....... (33 to 1 op 16 to 1) 5
516* WILLIE MAKEIT (Ire) [90] 6-11-5 J Culloty, *nvr gng wl, al beh, hrd rdn 8th, no response*....... (5 to 2 jt-fav tchd 3 to 1) 6
514⁶ TOOMUCH TOOSOON (Ire) [95] 8-11-10 D Walsh, *not jump wl, prmnt till mstk and wknd 9th*........... (11 to 2 op 5 to 1 tchd 7 to 1) 7
502³ STAPLEFORD LADY [79] 8-10-8 J Magee, *al beh, tld off*................(13 to 2 op 5 to 1 tchd 7 to 1) 8
Dist: 5l, 5l, 6l, 3l, 5l, ½l, 15l. 4m 0.00s. a 2.00s (8 Ran).
SR: 16/14/-/-/-/   (Mrs Sue Careless), H Oliver

640 Dry Blackthorn Novices' Chase Class E (5-y-o and up) £2,913 2m 5f 110yds .... (3:30)

366* CATS RUN (Ire) 8-11-5 R Johnson, *led to second, led 5th to 7th, led 4 out, drvn out*......(Evens fav op 5 to 4 on) 1
544* LUCKY DOLLAR (Ire) 8-11-5 A Thornton, *led second, mstk 3rd, led 7th to 4 out, ran on one pace*...............(11 to 8 op 6 to 4 tchd 13 to 8 and 7 to 4) 2

73

544² BLUE RAVEN 5-10-9 A P McCoy, *reminders second, chsd ldrs, hrd rdn tenth, wknd 4 out.*
.............(6 to 1 op 5 to 1 tchd 8 to 1 and 9 to 1) 3
502⁴ JAMESWICK 6-10-12 P Holley, *4th whn blun tenth, tld off frm nxt.*.......................(50 to 1 op 16 to 1) 4
BELLS WOOD 7-10-12 C Maude, *lost tch 9th, tld off whn pld up bef 12th.*..........(25 to 1 op 16 to 1 tchd 33 to 1) pu
Dist: 1½l, 15l, dist. 5m 15.90s. a 13.90s (5 Ran).

(Mrs Ann Key), John R Upson

641 **Thurlestone Hotel Centenary/100 Years Celebrations Novices' Hurdle Class E (4-y-o and up) £2,326 2m 1f**
.... (4:00)

398² SOUTHERN RIDGE 5-10-12 Mr A Holdsworth, *al prmnt, led appr 2 out, ran on wl*................(12 to 1 op 10 to 1) 1
CADDY'S FIRST 4-10-10 N Mann, *hld up mid-div, hdwy 3 out, styd on, not trble wnr*.....(11 to 2 op 4 to 1 tchd 6 to 1) 2
SECOND COLOURS (USA) 6-10-12 D Bridgwater, *steady hdwy 5th, ev ch appr 2 out, wknd approaching last.*
...............................(6 to 4 fav tchd 7 to 4) 3
511³ ALMAPA 4-10-7 (3*) T Dascombe, *hld up mid-div, hdwy 3 out, hrd rdn 2 out, one pace*................(7 to 2 op 5 to 1) 4
533³ RAMSTAR 8-10-9 (3*) G Tormey, *led till wknd appr 2 out.*
..................................(11 to 1 op 8 to 1) 5
COLIN'S PRIDE 5-10-7 S McNeill, *wl beh till some hdwy 3 out, nvr nr to chal*......(12 to 1 op 10 to 1 tchd 16 to 1) 6
LANDLORD (bl) 4-10-10 J Railton, *chsd ldrs, hrd rdn 3rd, mstk 5th, wknd aftr 3 out.*(14 to 1 op 9 to 1 tchd 20 to 1) 7
423⁶ CHIEF'S LADY 4-10-5 R Johnson, *nvr trble ldrs.*
..................................(50 to 1 op 20 to 1) 8
SHARP THRILL 5-10-12 C Llewellyn, *nvr on terms.*
..................................(25 to 1 op 10 to 1) 9
FAIR ATTRACTION 4-10-5 (5*) P Henley, *wl beh 5th, tld off.*..................(25 to 1 op 20 to 1 tchd 33 to 1) 10
BATH TIMES 4-10-0 (5*) D Salter, *prmnt till wknd quickly appr 5th, tld off.*...................(40 to 1 op 33 to 1) 11
539⁵ TRIPLE TIE (USA) 5-10-7 D Gallagher, *very slwly away, tld off whn pld bef 2 out.*............(20 to 1 op 12 to 1) pu
Dist: 15l, 3l, nk, 12l, 11l, 1½l, 9l, 3l, 28l, ¾l. 4m 1.30s. a 12.30s (12 Ran).

(R G Frost), R G Frost

642 **Pure Genius Handicap Chase Class D (0-120 5-y-o and up) £3,458 2m 5f 110yds.**..................... (4:30)

HERBERT BUCHANAN (Ire) [93] 6-11-6 A P McCoy, *hld up, chsd ldr 11th, led appr 2 out, drvn out.*
..................(15 to 8 fav op 2 to 1 tchd 9 to 4) 1
TIME ENOUGH (Ire) [97] 7-11-10 G Bradley, *led, sn clr, hdd appr 2 out, rallied last, ran on.*
..................................(11 to 2 op 7 to 2 tchd 6 to 1) 2
CLEAR LEAD (Ire) [94] 8-11-7 J Frost, *chsd ldr to 11th, hrd rdn 3 out, ralied appr last, ran on.*
..................(13 to 2 op 6 to 1 tchd 7 to 1 and 8 to 1) 3
447⁵ HENLEY REGATTA [94] 8-11-7 S Burrough, *hdwy tenth, wknd 12th.*.............(4 to 1 op 7 to 2 tchd 9 to 2) 4
514⁴ SEAL KING [85] 11-10-12 R Johnson, *cl 5th whn blun tenth, sn wknd.*.........(5 to 1 op 6 to 1) 5
FAIRY PARK [96] 11-11-9 Jacqui Oliver, *sn wl in rear, reminders 8th, tld off tenth, pld up bef 2 out.*
..................(11 to 2 op 3 to 1 tchd 6 to 1) pu
Dist: 1¼l, ½l, 20l, dist. 5m 14.40s. a 12.40s (6 Ran).

(Five For Fun), P F Nicholls

643 **Teachers Whisky Challenge Handicap Hurdle Class D (0-120 4-y-o and up) £2,778 3m 3f.**.................. (5:00)

417² ACROW LINE [108] 11-12-0 D J Burchell, *hdwy 4 out, hrd rdn to ld appr 2 out, ran on wl*.........(8 to 1 tchd 10 to 1) 1
515⁵ BLASKET HERO [102] (bl) 8-11-8 S McNeill, *hld up in rear, hdwy 4 out, ev ch 2 out, not quicken*...(7 to 2 tchd 9 to 2) 2
453⁵ GLENGARRIF GIRL (Ire) [108] (v) 6-12-0 D Bridgwater, *hdwy 4 out, ev ch appr 2 out, wknd approaching last.*
..................(2 to 1 fav op 5 to 2 tchd 11 to 4) 3
453³ STORM DRUM [95] (bl) 7-11-7 T J Murphy, *al prmnt, led appr 7th, hdd and wknd approaching 2 out*...(16 to 1 op 8 to 1) 4
L'UOMO PIU [80] 12-10-0 B Powell, *led to 4th, led 5th till appr 7th, wknd aftr 4 out*......(50 to 1 op 20 to 1) 5
491⁵ AMAZON EXPRESS [106] 7-11-12 R Johnson, *hld up, ev ch 3 out, rdn and wknd bef nxt, 5th and no chance whn pld up before last.*..............(5 to 1 op 4 to 1 tchd 500 to 30) pu
ANSTEY GADABOUT [80] 10-10-0 Mr A Holdsworth, *led 4th to 5th, wkng whn mstk 7th, tld off when pld up bef four out.*
..................................(200 to 1 op 66 to 1) pu
331⁵ SPRINGFIELD DANCER [102] 5-11-5 A P McCoy, *hld up, chsd ldr 8th till wknd quickly aftr 3 out, pld up bef 2 out.*
..................(4 to 1 op 3 to 1 tchd 9 to 2) pu
Dist: 1½l, 11l, 12l, dist. 6m 35.00s. a 19.00s (8 Ran).

(Rhys Thomas Williams), D Burchell

DOWNPATRICK (IRE) (firm)
Friday September 13th

644 **Sean Graham Maiden Hurdle (5-y-o and up) £1,712 2m 1f 172yds... (4:45)**

601² NEW LEGISLATION (Ire) (bl) 6-11-1 F Woods,.. (5 to 4 fav) 1
472⁵ SANDRA LOUISE (Ire) 6-10-8 (7*) M A Ross,.........(7 to 2) 2
579⁸ LORD KNOCKENSTIFF (Ire) (bl) 5-11-6 K F O'Brien,
..................................(10 to 1) 3
579 TENDER LASS (Ire) 5-11-1 P L Malone,.........(7 to 1) 4
112⁴ ELLE CARVOEIRO (Ire) 5-10-10 (5*) T Martin,.....(10 to 1) 5
497⁷ FARM LODGE (Ire) 5-11-6 P McWilliams,.........(25 to 1) 6
600⁴ EOINS LAD (Ire) 5-11-6 T P Treacy,.............(10 to 1) 7
619⁷ SLIEVROE (Ire) 5-11-1 D T Evans,................(8 to 1) 8
LINDA'S PARADISE (Ire) 5-11-6 J Shortt,.........(12 to 1) 9
Dist: 4½l, 8l, 20l, 1½l. (Time not taken) (9 Ran).

(Michael Bergin), M Halford

645 **Sean Graham Handicap Hurdle (0-102 4-y-o and up) £1,712 2m 1f 172yds**
.... (5:15)

604⁶ STRAIGHT ON (Ire) [-] (bl) 5-10-13 J Shortt,.......(10 to 1) 1
270⁵ TIFFANY VICTORIA (Ire) [-] 4-10-8 K F O'Brien,.. (13 to 2) 2
557⁴ CLASSY KAHYASI (Ire) [-] 6-9-7 P McWilliams,.....(9 to 2) 3
579³ MASCOT [-] (bl) 5-12-0 P L Malone,.........(11 to 10 fav) 4
621⁴ SHARLENE (Ire) [-] 5-10-9 T P Treacy,............(10 to 1) 5
589⁴ ROSCOLVIN (Ire) [-] 4-11-6 (5*) T Martin,.........(8 to 1) 6
494⁹ JONATHAN'S ROSE (Ire) [-] 7-10-5 J K Kinane,...(20 to 1) 7
564 NISHAYA (Ire) [-] 5-9-13 J P Broderick,.........(33 to 1) 8
497⁵ ARCTIC CLOVER (Ire) [-] 5-10-5 F Woods,.........(14 to 1) 9
FILL MY GLASS [-] 12-11-1 D T Evans,.........(25 to 1) pu
Dist: Sht-hd, 2l, 3½l, 10l. (Time not taken) (10 Ran).

(M Hamilton), J G Coogan

646 **Sean Graham Handicap Chase (0-102 5-y-o and up) £1,712 2¼m... (6:45)**

429⁵ DRINDOD (Ire) [-] 7-11-6 J P Broderick,.............(9 to 2) 1
580* ANY PORT (Ire) [-] 6-11-10 P L Malone,........(4 to 1) 2
588⁴ NO SIR ROM [-] 10-9-7 F Woods,................(7 to 1) f
Dist: 12l. (Time not taken) (3 Ran).

(Sir John Thomson), J T R Dreaper

647 **Sean Graham I.N.H. Flat Race (4-y-o and up) £1,712 2m 1f 172yds... (7:15)**

581³ SABANIYA (Fr) 4-10-11 (7*) Mr A J Dempsey,.....(11 to 8) 1
566³ ELECTRIC RYMER 4-11-9 Mr D Marnane,
..................................(11 to 10 fav) 2
497³ ANN'S DESIRE (Ire) 5-11-2 (7*) Mr J Keville,.....(12 to 1) 3
603⁵ KARA'S DREAM (Ire) 8-11-2 (7*) Mr G Elliott,.....(8 to 1) 4
IRISH OATS (Ire) 6-11-7 (7*) Mr R Marrs,.........(33 to 1) 5
434⁸ PRINCESS TOUCHEE (Ire) 5-11-2 (7*) Mr D P Coakley,
..................................(40 to 1) 6
HUNTERS ISLAND (Ire) 4-10-11 (7*) Mr J T McNamara,
..................................(33 to 1) pu
Dist: Nk, 2l, 7l, 15l. (Time not taken) (7 Ran).

(H Donnelly), D Carroll

WORCESTER (firm (races 1,3,5,6), good to firm (2,4))
Friday September 13th
Going Correction: MINUS 0.55 sec. per fur. (races 1,3,5,6), MINUS 0.40 (2,4)

648 **New Street Novices' Hurdle Class E (4-y-o and up) £2,547 2½m....... (2:20)**

506* WOTTASHAMBLES 5-11-5 D Morris, *in tch, led 3 out, readily.*
..................(11 to 10 fav op 5 to 4 tchd 11 to 8 and 6 to 4) 1
BASIL STREET (Ire) 4-10-8 R Dunwoody, *hld up, gd hdwy 4 out, chsd wnr aftr 3 out, rdn and no imprsn last.*
...............(5 to 1 op 9 to 2 tchd 11 to 2 and 6 to 1) 2
610⁶ LEAP IN THE DARK (Ire) 7-10-12 A Thornton, *chsd ldrs, chlgd 4 out, sn lost pl, btn nxt.*......(50 to 1 op 33 to 1) 3
629 MARLOUSION (Ire) 4-10-5 D Gallagher, *prmnt, lost pl 5th and ran in snatches, moderate prog frm 2 out.*
..................................(16 to 1 op 8 to 1) 4
539* ALPINE MIST (Ire) 4-10-12 (5*) Michael Brennan, *prmnt, chsd ldrs appr 3 out, sn rdn and btn.*.......(5 to 1 op 9 to 2) 5
JEAN DE FLORETTE (USA) 5-10-9 (3*) E Husband, *in tch till wknd frm 4 out.*...............(66 to 1 op 50 to 1) 6
DANE ROSE 10-10-7 R Johnson, *jmpd slwly 5th, al beh.*
..................................(50 to 1 op 33 to 1) 7
HYDEMILLA 6-10-4 (3*) G Hogan, *led till hdd sn aftr 4 out, wknd rpdly, tld off.*..........(16 to 1 op 10 to 1) 8
415* TUKANO (Can) 5-11-12 G Bradley, *beh, rdn 6th, lost tch 3 out, pld up bef nxt.*...........(9 to 2 op 7 to 2 tchd 5 to 1) pu
Dist: 3½l, 3l, 10l, 4l, 2½l, 1½l, dist. 4m 34.50s. b 1.50s (9 Ran).

(Dream On Racing Partnership), L Montague Hall

649 **Bull Ring Novices' Chase Class D (5-y-o and up) £3,591 2m 7f.......(2:55)**

FATHER SKY 5-10-8 J Osborne, *led second till aftr 5th, chlgd ag'n frm 9th till led 14th, pushed out* ...... (5 to 2 op 5 to 4) 1

512* CLIFTON SET (bl) 5-11-1 R Dunwoody, *jmpd slwly 1st, chlgd frm 4th till led aftr 5th, hdd 14th, rallied and chald from four out till no extr r-in.*
.... (6 to 4 on op Evens tchd 11 to 10 and 5 to 4) 2

544 GLENFINI PRINCESS 8-10-7 M A Fitzgerald, *hld up and wl beh, hdwy to go 3rd 11th, no imprsn on ldrs frm 4 out.*
.... (5 to 1 tchd 6 to 1 and 13 to 2) 3

512³ MANOR BOUND 6-10-7 S McNeill, *al beh, tld off frm tenth.*
.... (20 to 1 op 25 to 1) 4

530² MUSIC SCORE 10-10-12 A Thornton, *led to second and mstk, mistakes aftr, hit 12th, tld off whn pld up bef 14th.*
.... (50 to 1 op 25 to 1) pu

GIORGIONE (Fr) 7-10-12 J Culloty, *chsd ldrs, wknd 10th, tld off whn pld up bef 13th.*
.... (66 to 1 op 50 to 1 tchd 100 to 1) pu

Dist: 7l, 5l, dist. 5m 44.70s. a 6.70s (6 Ran).

(Kenneth Kornfeld), O Sherwood

650 Selly Oak Novices' Handicap Hurdle Class E (0-100 4-y-o and up) £2,302 3m .... (3:25)

540³ LITTLE TINCTURE (Ire) [70] 6-10-4³ G Upton, *hld up, hdwy 5th, led appr 7th, hdd 2 out, hrd rdn and rallied r-in to ld nr finish* .... (9 to 1 op 8 to 1 tchd 10 to 1) 1

HYLTERS CHANCE (Ire) [69] 5-10-0 A P McCoy, *al chasing ldrs, hrd rdn frm 2 out, rallied und pres r-in, jst fld.*
.... (9 to 2 op 3 to 1) 2

453 WYNBERG [97] 5-12-0 S Wynne, *hdwy 6th, chsd ldr 4 out, chlgd nxt, led 2 out, wnt lme and hdd nr finish.*
.... (15 to 8 fav op 2 to 1 tchd 9 to 4 and 7 to 4) 3

582³ AKIYMANN (USA) [79] (bl) 6-10-13 D Bridgwater, *drpd rear 7th, sn dnvr and nvr dngrs aftr.* .... (16 to 1 op 12 to 1) 4

554* ANCHORENA [83] 4-10-11 N Williamson, *hld up and mstk 4th, hdwy into fourth whn pld up bef 8th, lme.*
.... (9 to 4 op 7 to 4) pu

440* SHALIK (Ire) [69] 6-10-3³ J Railton, *led, sn clr, hdd and wknd quickly appr 7th, tld off whn pld up bef 3 out.*
.... (16 to 1 op 10 to 1) pu

Dist: Sht-hd, 3l, 4l. 5m 38.90s. a 2.90s (6 Ran).

(Mrs T J McInnes Skinner), Mrs T J McInnes Skinner

651 Snow Hill Handicap Chase Class C (0-130 5-y-o and up) £4,745 2m (3:55)

617² CAPTAIN KHEDIVE [125] 8-12-0 A P McCoy, *hld up, lft second at 7th, quickened into slight ld frm 2 out, cleverley.*
.... (7 to 4 on tchd 13 to 8 on) 1

HOUGHTN [113] 10-10-9 (7*) Mr R Burton, *chsd ldr till led 4l, narrowly hdd 2 out, kpt on but no ch wth wnr.*
.... (12 to 1 op 10 to 1 tchd 14 to 1) 2

617* NOBELEY (USA) [111] 9-11-0 (6ex) R Farrant, *led to 4th, chsd ldr till blun badly and una rdr 7th.* .... (7 to 4 op 6 to 4) ur

Dist: 1¼l. 3m 49.20s. a 0.20s (3 Ran).

SR: 34/20/-/ (Khedive Partnership), P F Nicholls

652 Moor Street Maiden Hurdle Class F (4-y-o and up) £2,353 2m .... (4:30)

BLOWN WIND (Ire) 5-11-5 J Osborne, *prmnt till lost pos aftr 4th, gd hdwy to track ldrs after nxt, chlgd and slpd 3 out, led next, easily.* .... (7 to 2 jt-fav op 7 to 1 tchd 9 to 1 and 10 to 1) 1

419³ DANTEAN 4-11-3 P Holley, *hld up, hdwy 5th, ev ch 2 out, outpcd appr last.* .... (20 to 1 op 12 to 1) 2

384⁵ LAST LAUGH (Ire) (bl) 4-10-12 T J Murphy, *wth ldrs till led 3 out, hdd nxt, sn one pace.* ...... (50 to 1 op 50 to 1) 3

MATAMOROS 4-11-3 R Dunwoody, *chsd ldrs, rdn 3 out, outpcd frm nxt.* .... (4 to 1 op 7 to 2 tchd 9 to 2) 4

DIFFICULT DECISION (Ire) 5-11-5 M A Fitzgerald, *prmnt till wknd aftr 3 out.* .... (16 to 1 op 6 to 1) 5

520⁵ ROSE CHIME (Ire) 4-10-12 P McLoughlin, *hdwy frm 3 out, nrst finish.* .... (50 to 1 op 33 to 1) 6

CAMDEN'S RANSOM (USA) 9-11-5 B Powell, *led to 3 out, sn wknd.* .... (66 to 1 op 50 to 1) 7

SPRING LOADED 5-11-0 (5*) Michael Brennan, *beh till some prog frm 3 out.* .... (33 to 1) 8

HIGHLY CHARMING (Ire) 4-11-3 J F Titley, *hdwy 4th, chsd ldrs nxt, mstk 3 out and sn wknd.* .... (7 to 2 jt-fav tchd 11 to 4) 9

NORTHERN LAW 4-11-3 I Lawrence, *nvr rch ldrs.*
.... (16 to 1 op 10 to 1 tchd 20 to 1) 10

MARTHA'S DAUGHTER 7-11-0 A Thornton, *wnt prmnt 3rd, wknd 3 out.* .... (20 to 1 op 14 to 1) 11

CELESTIAL DOLLAR 5-11-5 R Johnson, *al in rear.*
.... (20 to 1 op 50 to 1 tchd 66 to 1) 12

506² WANSTEAD (Ire) (v) 4-11-3 G Bradley, *al beh.*
.... (8 to 1 op 7 to 1 tchd 10 to 1) 13

115* MISTER GIGI (Ire) 5-11-5 Gary Lyons, *prmnt till mstk and wknd 5th.* .... (14 to 1 op 7 to 1) 14

PUNCH (bl) 4-11-0 (3*) E Husband, *prmnt to hfwy.*
.... (50 to 1 op 33 to 1) 15

533 GOOD (Ire) 4-11-3 B Fenton, *al beh...* (66 to 1 op 33 to 1) 16

RAGTIME SONG 7-10-12 (7*) D Yellowlees, *beh, no ch whn f last.* .... (66 to 1 op 50 to 1 tchd 100 to 1) f

520 FLASHING SABRE 4-10-10 (7*) A Dowling, *prmnt early, tld off whn pld up bef 3 out.* .... (100 to 1) pu

Dist: 8l, 3l, 1½l, 3l, 1¼l, ¾l, 8l, 3½l, 2½l, 5l. 3m 38.10s. b 1.90s (18 Ran).

SR: 22/12/4/7/6/-/ (B T Stewart-Brown), O Sherwood

653 Birmingham Handicap Hurdle Class D (0-120 4-y-o and up) £2,726 2m (5:00)

513* COOLEY'S VALVE (Ire) [95] 8-10-8 (5*) Sophie Mitchell, *hld up, wnt second at 4th, led gng wl aftr 2 out, sn clr, readily.*
.... (15 to 8 op 9 to 4 tchd 5 to 2) 1

503⁵ IKHTIRAA (USA) [82] 6-10-0 P Holley, *led, rdn and hit 2 out, sn hdd and found nil.* .... (11 to 4 op 9 to 4 tchd 3 to 1) 2

508* GONE BY (Ire) [110] (v) 8-12-0 G Bradley, *chsd ldr to 4th, rdn aftr nxt, no response, al hld frm 2 out.*
.... (6 to 5 fav op 11 to 10) 3

Dist: 4l, 1½l. 3m 38.80s. b 1.80s (3 Ran).

SR: 9/-/17/ (Christopher & Shirley Brasher), Mrs S D Williams

BANGOR (good)
Saturday September 14th
Going Correction: MINUS 0.30 sec. per fur.

654 Long Shot 'National Hunt' Novices' Hurdle Class E (4-y-o and up) £2,472 2m 1f .... (2:10)

DANNY GALE (Ire) 5-10-12 G Bradley, *trkd ldrs, led appr 2 out, drvn and styd on wl r-in.*
.... (7 to 2 op 5 to 1 tchd 13 to 2) 1

COUNTRY MINSTREL (Ire) 5-10-12 S McNeill, *hld up, hdwy appr 3 out, ev ch nxt, one pace frm last.*
.... (40 to 1 op 33 to 1 tchd 50 to 1) 2

FOLLOW DE CALL 6-10-9 (3*) D Walsh, *in tch, improved to chase ldrs 5th, drvn and ev ch appr 2 out, no extr betw last two.* .... (100 to 1 op 50 to 1) 3

RAGOSA 5-10-7 A P McCoy, *prmnt, rcd wide and led 4th, hdd and bustd appr 2 out, hdd.* .... (20 to 1 op 12 to 1) 4

493* ETERNAL CITY 5-11-5 A Maguire, *in tch, effrt 4 out, sn imprsn, eased whn btn bef 2 out.*
.... (11 to 8 on op 5 to 4 on tchd 6 to 4 on) 5

SHADY EMMA 4-10-5 S Wynne, *sn beh, struggling frm 4 out, nvr on terms.* .... (66 to 1 op 25 to 1) 6

HYMOSS 5-10-7 T Jenks, *led to 4th, drvn and wknd appr 3 out, tld off.* .... (33 to 1 op 20 to 1) 7

456³ POWERFUL SPIRIT 4-10-5 (5*) Michael Brennan, *hld up, struggling frm 5th, sn drvn, tld off.* ...... (7 to 2 op 5 to 2) 8

Dist: 3½l, 6l, 4l, 8l, 2l, dist, 5l. 4m 3.20s. a 13.20s (8 Ran).

(Robert Cox), G M McCourt

655 Tote Credit Club Novices' Chase Class D (4-y-o and up) £3,517 2½m 110yds .... (2:40)

615* SONIC STAR (Ire) 7-12-4 A Maguire, *not fluent, trkd ldr, narrow ld 4 out, clr 2 out, easily.*
.... (9 to 4 on op 2 to 1 on tchd 15 to 8 on) 1

596* MILL O'THE RAGS (Ire) 7-11-12 J F Titley, *led till narrowly hdd aftr 4 out, wknd 2 out.* .... (2 to 1 tchd 9 to 4) 2

LITTLE BY LITTLE 6-11-6 A Thornton, *hld up, chsd ldrs frm 5th to 9th, sn lost tch, took poor 3rd cl hme, tld off.*
.... (33 to 1 op 20 to 1) 3

ON THE TEAR 10-11-6 S McNeill, *chsd ldrs, pckd second, rear frm 5th, mstk nxt, chased clr lders from 9th but lost tch, lost 3rd cl hme, tld off.* .... (33 to 1 op 20 to 1) 4

Dist: 29l, dist, sht-hd. 5m 6.60s. a 20.60s (4 Ran).

(R F Nutland), D Nicholson

656 Dick Francis Handicap Hurdle Class C (0-130 4-y-o and up) £3,371 2m 1f .... (3:10)

374³ STAR MARKET [117] (bl) 6-12-0 A P McCoy, *made all, clr 4 out, drvn bef last, eased cl hme.* .... (7 to 1 op 5 to 1) 1

571* SARMATIAN (USA) [100] 5-10-9 R Garritty, *hld up, hdwy appr 4 out, pushed aling to chase wnr aftr nxt, drvn and no imprsn betw last 2.* .... (9 to 4 fav op 11 to 4) 2

606* RED VALERIAN [117] (v) 5-12-0 M A Fitzgerald, *hld up, some hdwy und pres 4 out, not rch ldrs.* ...... (5 to 2 op 2 to 1) 3

449⁶ ROBERT'S TOY (Ire) [118] (bl) 5-11-13 A Maguire, *cl up, chsd wnr appr 4th till aftr 3 out, sn wknd.*
.... (9 to 2 op 3 to 1 tchd 5 to 1) 4

DON DU CADRAN (Fr) [104] 7-11-1 A Thornton, *trkd wnr till appr 4th, wknd nxt.* ...... (10 to 1 op 8 to 1 tchd 16 to 1) 5

476* HAVE A NIGHTCAP [98] (bl) 7-10-9 M Richards, *hndy, pushed alng 5th, sn lost pl and beh.* .... (10 to 1 op 6 to 1) 6

616 WINDWARD ARIOM [106] 10-11-3 A Larnach, *hld up, hdwy to chase ldrs 4th, 5th and wkng whn f 3 out.*
.... (20 to 1 op 14 to 1) f

Dist: 8l, 6l, 17l, 15l, 9l. 3m 52.10s. a 2.10s (7 Ran).

SR: 28/1/14/-/ (Mrs P Joynes), J L Spearing

657 Greenalls Inns Novices' Handicap Chase Class E (0-100 5-y-o and up)

£3,403 3m 110yds.............(3:40)

530* WARNER'S SPORTS [79] 7-10-10 A P McCoy, wth ldr, not
fluent 4th, led 9th, drvn clr 3 out, hrd pressed frm nxt, edgd
rght cl hme, all out..................(6 to 4 on op Evens) 1

492* DEFINITE MAYBE (Ire) [95] (bl) 6-11-12 M A Fitzgerald, chsd
alng thrght, chased ldrs, outpcd and plenty to do 4 out, cld 2
out, chlgd r-in, not keen and bumped close hme.
..........................(9 to 1 op 3 to 1) 2

RENT DAY [69] 7-10-0 S Curran, in tch, lft chasing wnr 12th,
outpcd by winner whn not fluent 3 out, rallied nxt, btn r-in, sn
eased............................(40 to 1 op 16 to 1) 3

SAN GIORGIO [90] 7-11-7 C Llewellyn, mstk second (water),
sn beh, reminder bef 11th, soon lost tch, tld off.
..........................(5 to 1 op 4 to 1) 4

483* WAKT [97] 6-11-11 (3*) Guy Lewis, keen hold, led to 9th, sn
niggled alng, second whn blun and uns rdr 12th.
..........................(5 to 1 op 3 to 1 tchd 11 to 2) ur

Dist: Nk, 10l, dist. 6m 10.10s. a 25.10s (5 Ran).
(Terry Warner Sports), P J Hobbs

658 Gordon Mytton Homes Juvenile Novices' Hurdle Class D (3-y-o) £2,827 2m
1f...........................(4:10)

SILVERDALE KNIGHT 10-10 M Foster, chsd ldrs, improved to
ld appr 2 out, clr bef last, easily.
..........................(8 to 1 op 5 to 1) 1

FLYING GREEN (Fr) 10-7 (3*) Guy Lewis, chsd ldr, led appr 3
out, rdn alng and hdd approaching nxt, not fluent 2 out, sn btn.
..........................(5 to 2 op 3 to 1) 2

542⁴ BATH KNIGHT (bl) 10-10 S McNeill, led till appr 3 out, sn
wknd..........................(25 to 1 op 12 to 1) 3

614² SONG FOR JESS (Ire) 10-5 S Wynne, in tch til outpcd frm 4
out..........................(12 to 1 tchd 16 to 1) 4

WELCOME ROYALE (Ire) 10-10 A Maguire, midfield, jmpd
slwly 1st, effrt 5th, sn no imprsn.
..........................(5 to 1 op 7 to 2 tchd 6 to 1) 5

481⁴ BALMORAL PRINCESS (bl) 10-12 R Bellamy, midfield, struggling and no hdwy frm 5th.
..........................(16 to 1 op 14 to 1 tchd 20 to 1) 6

542⁴ SHEATH KEFAAH 11-3 G Bradley, in tch, wknd appr 4 out.
..........................(2 to 1 fav op 9 to 4 tchd 5 to 2) 7

FLOOD'S FANCY 10-5 C Llewellyn, beh, lost tch 4th, tld off.
..........................(33 to 1 op 25 to 1) 8

KRASNIK (Ire) 10-10 J F Titley, al in rear, struggling frm hfwy,
tld off..........................(14 to 1 op 8 to 1) 9

TALLULAH BELLE 10-5 M Richards, hld up, steady hdwy whn
f 5th..........................(33 to 1 op 20 to 1) f

PEYTON JONES 10-10 F Jousset, midfield, wknd and lost tch
4th, tld off whn bef four out......(50 to 1 op 25 to 1) pu

Dist: 14l, 24l, 7l, 2½l, 1¼l, 9l, dist, hd. 3m 58.10s. a 8.10s (11 Ran).
(Auldyn Stud Ltd), K W Hogg

659 Dead Cert Handicap Hurdle Class F
(0-105 4-y-o and up) £2,967 2½m
...........................(4:40)

BELLROI (Ire) [94] 5-11-4 A Maguire, trkd ldrs, led appr 7th,
clr whn mstk last, easily....(9 to 2 op 3 to 1 tchd 5 to 1) 1

543³ FIRST CRACK [87] 11-10-13 S Wynne, midfield, hdwy appr
7th, drvn to chase wnr approaching 2 out, no imprsn.
..........................(7 to 2 fav op 3 to 1) 2

498² PLINTH [83] 5-10-7 M A Fitzgerald, trkd ldrs, outpcd by ldrs
frm 3 out..................(9 to 2 op 7 to 2 tchd 5 to 1) 3

ILEWIN [98] 9-11-10 G Bradley, hld up, hdwy to track ldrs 7th,
btn aftr 3 out..........(4 to 1 op 12 to 1 tchd 16 to 1) 4

PRIZE MATCH [80] 7-10-6 S McNeill, in rear, some hdwy 4
out, nvr able to chal..........................(33 to 1) 5

308⁴ KING'S SHILLING (USA) [90] 9-10-9 (7*) G Supple, towards
rear, effrt 4 out, not trble ldrs.
..........................(9 to 1 op 10 to 1 tchd 5 to 1) 6

SEVERN GALE [86] 6-10-12 A P McCoy, hld up, cl up 5th, wth
wnr 4 out, ev ch nxt, wknd bef 2 out....(4 to 1 op 7 to 2) 7

572² TASHREEF [75] (bl) 6-10-1 L O'Hara, in tch, hdwy 5th, sn cl up,
drvn and wknd aftr 4 out.
..........................(25 to 1 op 14 to 1 tchd 33 to 1) 8

EMPEROR CHANG (USA) [76] 9-10-2¹ T Kent, hndy, wknd
quickly 4 out, virtually pld up r-in.
..........................(33 to 1 op 25 to 1 tchd 50 to 1) 9

PLEASE CALL (Ire) [77] 7-10-3 J R Kavanagh, al beh, struggling frm 7th, nvr a factor............(50 to 1 op 25 to 1) 10

451⁵ BATTY'S ISLAND [82] 7-10-8 A Thornton, midfield, drvn and
wknd 7th, sn beh, tld off......(25 to 1 op 16 to 1) 11

IBN SINA (USA) [74] 9-10-0 S Curran, beh, niggled alng 5th,
tld off..........................(50 to 1 op 25 to 1) 12

LUSTREMAN [74] 9-10-0 R Bellamy, al beh, tld off whn pld up
bef 3 out..........................(40 to 1 op 25 to 1) pu

BUCKLEY BOYS [82] 5-9-13 (7*) Mr R Thornton, led till appr
7th, wknd aftr nxt, tld off whn pld up bef 2 out, dismounted.
..........................(33 to 1) pu

Dist: 4l, 15l, 2l, ¾l, 1½l, 3½l, 6l, 26l, 1l, 26l. 4m 41.10s. a 11.10s (14 Ran).
(Mrs G A E Smith), M H Tompkins

SEDGEFIELD (good to firm)
Saturday September 14th

Going Correction: MINUS 0.40 sec. per fur.

660 John Wade Hino Truck Novices' Selling
Handicap Hurdle Class G (4-y-o and
up) £1,891 2m 5f 110yds.......(1:50)

609² WHAT'S SECRETO (USA) [80] (bl) 4-11-9 P Niven, nvr far
away, led 4th, made rst, drvn and ran ungmely last 2.
..........................(11 to 10 fav op 6 to 4 tchd 13 to 8) 1

610⁹ HAUGHTON LAD (Ire) [68] 7-10-13 A Roche, cl up, hmpd 3rd,
chlgd 3 out, not quicken frm last.....(16 to 1 op 20 to 1) 2

612⁴ SAKBAH (USA) [60] 4-11-0 N Williamson, midfield, improved
hfwy, shaken up aftr 2 out, no imprsn last. (5 to 1 op 7 to 2) 3

609⁶ PIMSBOY [60] (bl) 9-10-4² [3*] P Midgley, chsd ldg grp, outpcd bef 3 out, no imprsn last..........(16 to 1 op 12 to 1) 4

609 BOWLAND PARK [72] 5-11-1 T J Murphy, hld up, steady
hdwy hfwy, struggling whn hng rght aftr 2 out.
..........................(40 to 1 op 20 to 1) 5

610 DARK MIDNIGHT (Ire) [60] 7-10-5 J Burke, hndy, challenged
4th, rdn aftr 3 out, outpcd nxt.....(40 to 1 op 33 to 1) 6

519² ARRANGE A GAME [55] (bl) 9-9-9 (5*) S Taylor, keen hold, sn
cl up, lft in ld 3rd, hdd nxt, struggling bef 3 out, soon btn.
..........................(5 to 1 op 20 to 1) 7

ANTHONY BELL [83] 10-11-7 (7*) T J Comerford, hld up, lost
tch fnl circuit, nvr on terms...........(12 to 1 op 9 to 1) 8

TOP FELLA (USA) [80] (bl) 4-11-9 D Bentley, in tch, struggling
4th, tld off..........................(8 to 1 op 6 to 1) 9

609⁵ CLASSIC CREST (Ire) [82] (v) 5-11-4 (7*) T Hogg, led till f 3rd.
..........................(5 to 1 op 4 to 1) f

Dist: 4l, 1l, 1¾l, 18l, 4l, 9l, 3½l, dist. 4m 58.00s. a 10.00s (10 Ran).
(A Atkinson), H Alexander

661 Shotton Novices' Hurdle Class E (4-y-o
and up) £2,477 2m 1f.........(2:20)

478³ FIELD OF VISION (Ire) 6-11-5 J Supple, made all, hrd pressed
4 out, hit last, gmely........(7 to 2 op 5 to 2 tchd 4 to 1) 1

547⁴ ROBSERA (Ire) 5-10-12 L Wyer, keen hold, hndy, chlgd 2 out,
one pace aftr last......(100 to 30 op 9 to 2 tchd 5 to 1) 2

547² FATEHALKHAIR (Ire) 4-10-7 (3*) G Cahill, al wl plcd, chlgd 2
out, kpt on same pace frm last.
..........................(5 to 5 fav op 5 to 4 tchd 6 to 4) 3

610⁵ TRUMPED (Ire) 4-10-5 B Harding, keen hold, hld up,
improved hfwy, outpcd fnl 2...........(7 to 1 op 6 to 1) 4

BLANC SEING (Fr) 9-10-12 Mr S Swiers, hld up, nvr nr to
chal..........................(20 to 1 op 10 to 1) 5

610 KASHANA 4-10-5 M Moloney, towards rear, effrt aftr 3
out, struggling nxt..........(9 to 1 tchd 10 to 1) 6

QUARTZ HILL (USA) 7-10-12 J Burke, nvr far away, chlgd
hfwy, one pace whn f 2 out............(66 to 1 op 33 to 1) f

RHYTHMIC DANCER 8-10-12 B Storey, pld very hrd in rear,
lost tch 4 out, pulled up 2 out, broke blood vessel.
..........................(14 to 1 op 12 to 1 tchd 16 to 1) pu

Dist: 3l, nk, 8l, 15l, 3l. 3m 53.10s. a 7.10s (8 Ran).
(Mrs K Morrell), Mrs A Swinbank

662 Johnny Ridley Memorial Handicap
Chase Class D (0-120 5-y-o and up)
£3,769 3m 3f..................(2:50)

605* THE GALLOPIN'MAJOR (Ire) [79] (bl) 6-10-2 N Smith, prmnt,
hit 5 out, drvn to ld last, hld on wl...(2 to 1 fav op 6 to 4) 1

607² STAIGUE FORT (Ire) [87] 8-10-10 P Niven, jmpd rght thrght,
led to tenth, led ag'in 13th, hit 17th, hdd nxt, rallied appr last.
..........................(5 to 1 op 9 to 2 tchd 11 to 2) 2

607 THE BLUE BOY (Ire) [99] (bl) 8-11-8 N Williamson, pressed
ldr, led tenth to 13th, led ag'n 4 out, clr aftr nxt, hdd and hit
last, no extr..........(7 to 1 op 5 to 1 tchd 8 to 1) 3

605² GEORGE ASHFORD (Ire) [90] 6-10-13 A S Smith, hndy,
struggling 14th, sn btn..........(4 to 1 op 7 to 2) 4

GO SILLY [105] (v) 10-11-11 (3*) G Cahill, not fluent, hld up,
outpcd 14th, pld up bef 5 out.
..........................(6 to 1 op 11 to 2 tchd 13 to 2) pu

Dist: 2½l, 3½l, dist. 6m 29.30s. a 3.70s (5 Ran).
SR: 3/8/16/-/-/ (R W S Jevon), Mrs M Reveley

663 Ramside Catering Services Handicap
Chase Class E (0-115 4-y-o and up)
£3,254 2m 5f..................(3:25)

MCGREGOR THE THIRD [112] 10-11-13 B Harding, jmpd wl,
cl up, led tenth, clr aftr 3 out, readily............(2 to 1 jt-
fav op 6 to 4) 1

REBEL KING [90] 6-10-5 P Waggott, nvr far away, chlgd
tenth, outpcd appr 2 out..........(8 to 1 op 6 to 1) 2

386³ NOCATCHIM [90] (v) 7-10-5 A S Smith, al cl up, drvn alng bef
4 out, struggling nxt.....(7 to 1 op 6 to 1 tchd 8 to 1) 3

JENDEE (Ire) [85] 8-9-12¹ (3*) G Cahill, beh, some hdwy bef 5
out, blun 2 out, nvr a factor............................. 4

LAURIE-O [90] (bl) 12-10-5³ J Burke, prmnt, led 4th, hit 8th,
hdd tenth, struggling nxt..........(33 to 1 op 20 to 1) 5

608⁶ SMOKEY TRACK [85] 11-9-9 (5*) S Taylor, beh, struggling
hfwy, tld off..........................(14 to 1 op 10 to 1) 6

421¹³ WISE ADVICE (Ire) [95] 6-10-10 N Williamson, in tch whn f
second..........(11 to 2 op 5 to 1 tchd 6 to 1) f

607* MAGIC BLOOM [100] 10-11-1 Richard Guest, *settled in tch, badly hmpd by faller second, sn pld up* .... (2 to 1 jt-
fav tchd 7 to 4) pu
Dist: 15l, 6l, 15l, 15l, 4l. 5m 0.00s. a 4.00s (8 Ran).

(Mrs D A Whitaker), G Richards

664 Partridge Juvenile Novices' Hurdle Class E (3-y-o) £2,425 2m 1f.... (4:05)

488² GO-GO-POWER-RANGER 10-7 (3*) G Cahill, *wth ldr, led 5th, ran on strly appr last* ..... (4 to 1 tchd 9 to 2 and 7 to 1) 1
COTTAGE PRINCE (Ire) 10-10 L Wyer, *settled midfield, smooth hdwy and ev ch 2 out, one pace last.*
.... (15 to 2 op 7 to 1 tchd 8 to 1) 2
488* PRELUDE TO FAME (USA) 11-3 A S Smith, *slight ld to 5th, prmnt, outpcd betw last 2* .... (2 to 1 fav tchd 7 to 4) 3
320⁴ NORTHERN FALCON (bl) 10-5 N Williamson, *prmnt, drvn 3 out, outpcd frm nxt* .... (12 to 1 op 10 to 1) 4
HOBBS CHOICE 10-5 N Bentley, *prmnt, lost pl hfwy, kpt on betw last 2* .... (12 to 1 op 8 to 1) 5
STOLEAMARCH 10-7 (3*) G Lee, *keen hold in midfield, effrt 3 out, outpcd nxt.* .... (25 to 1 op 16 to 1) 6
NO MORE HASSLE (Ire) 10-10 P Niven, *keen hold in rear, mstk second, nvr nr to chal.*
.... (11 to 2 op 4 to 1 tchd 6 to 1) 7
SLEEPY BOY 10-5 (5*) R McGrath, *mstk 1st, hld up, nvr nr to chal* .... (50 to 1 op 33 to 1) 8
THE BLACK DUBH (Ire) 10-10 B Storey, *keen hold in rear, struggling bef 3 out, no imprsn nxt* .... (20 to 1) 9
OXGANG (Ire) 10-10 M Dwyer, *mstk 1st, towards rear, struggling aftr 3 out, sn btn* .... (8 to 1 op 7 to 1) 10
HOT DOGGING 10-5 R Marley, *hld up, nvr on terms.*
.... (14 to 1 op 10 to 1) 11
573 MISS IMPULSE 10-0 (5*) S Taylor, *prmnt, rdn aftr 3 out, sn struggling* .... (20 to 1 op 14 to 1) 12
PHANTOM DANCER (Ire) 10-7 (3*) D Parker, *pressed ldrs, rdn bef 3 out, sn struggling* .... (25 to 1 op 20 to 1) 13
AMYLOU 9-12 (7*) S Melrose, *beh, struggling aftr 4 out, pld up bef 2 out* .... (40 to 1 op 16 to 1) pu
FIZZY BOY (Ire) 10-10 B Harding, *hld up, struggling aftr 4 out, pld up bef 2 out* .... (40 to 1 op 16 to 1) pu
Dist: 5l, 2½l, 1¼l, 3l, nk, 6l, 5l, 2½l, 6l, 7l. 3m 52.60s. a 6.60s (15 Ran).

(Kevin M L Brown), B Ellison

665 St Leger Conditional Jockeys' Handicap Hurdle Class F (0-105 4-y-o and up) £2,407 2m 1f............... (4:35)

606³ STRONG JOHN (Ire) [85] 8-10-13 D Parker, *al hndy, smooth hdwy to ld 2 out, hrd pressed last, hld on wl.*
.... (4 to 1 op 9 to 2 tchd 5 to 1) 1
610* SUAS LEAT (Ire) [85] 6-10-10 (3*) M Newton, *settled in tch, improved to chal last, kpt on und pres.*
.... (6 to 4 fav tchd 13 to 8) 2
BOLANEY GIRL (Ire) [78] 7-10-4 A Roche, *settled off the pace, gd hdwy to chase ldrs bef 2 out, sn rdn, one pace whn hit last.*
.... (16 to 1 op 12 to 1) 3
476⁵ FLINTLOCK (Ire) [77] 6-10-5 R McGrath, *led to 3rd, led ag'n 3 out, hdd nxt, no extr.* .... (12 to 1 op 9 to 1) 4
489² CLOVER GIRL [74] (v) 5-10-0 G Cahill, *hld up, improved to chase ldr 3 out, outpcd nxt.* .... (6 to 1 op 7 to 1) 5
WEE WIZARD (Ire) [88] 7-11-2 S Taylor, *prmnt, struggling fnl circuit, nvr able to chal.* .... (14 to 1 op 12 to 1) 6
610⁴ FUNNY ROSE [72] 6-10-0⁵ (5*) C McCormack, *beh, struggling 4 out, sn btn* .... (9 to 1 op 6 to 1 tchd 10 to 1) 7
461 EXCLUSION [83] 7-10-11 F Leahy, *wth ldr, led 3rd, hdd 3 out, fdd* .... (6 to 1 op 11 to 2) 8
FLY TO THE END (USA) [75] 6-9-10 (7*) S Ruddy, *beh, struggling frm hfwy* .... (16 to 1 op 10 to 1) 9
Dist: Nk, 5l, ¾l, 26l, 9l, 3l, 3½l, ¾l. 3m 46.10s. a 0.10s (9 Ran).
SR: 16/15/3/1/-/-/

(S Birkinshaw), M E Sowersby

WORCESTER (good to firm)
Saturday September 14th
Going Correction: MINUS 0.25 sec. per fur.

666 Polly Howes Conditional Jockeys' Selling Handicap Hurdle Class G (0-95 4-y-o and up) £2,129 2m........... (2:25)

520² MINNESOTA FATS (Ire) [70] 4-10-1 G Hogan, *hld up and confidently rdn, hdwy appr 3 out, led on bit approaching last, drvn out* .... (7 to 2 jt-fav op 3 to 1) 1
CORRIN HILL [95] 9-11-6 (8*) J Harris, *hld up in rear, hdwy 3 out, chlgd frm 2 out till outpcd r-in* ...... (7 to 1 op 4 to 1) 2
454² GALLOPING GUNS (Ire) [69] 4-10-0 Chris Webb, *prmnt till lost pl 4th, gd hdwy appr 3 out and mstk, ev ch 2 out, one pace.*
.... (25 to 1 op 14 to 1) 3
504³ RAY RIVER [76] (bl) 4-10-7 G Tormey, *rdn and hdwy 5th, ev ch frm 2 out till wknd r-in* .... (8 to 1 tchd 10 to 1) 4
390⁴ WORDSMITH (Ire) [86] 6-11-5 J Culloty, *prmnt, chlgd frm 3 out till wknd appr last.* .... (7 to 2 jt-
fav op 4 to 1 tchd 9 to 2) 5
520* SIMAND [80] 4-10-11 D J Kavanagh, *prmnt, led 5th till appr last, wknd r-in* .... (5 to 1 tchd 11 to 2 and 6 to 1) 6

CATWALKER (Ire) [69] 5-10-0 Sophie Mitchell, *beh, some hdwy whn hit 2 out, sn btn* .... (20 to 1 tchd 25 to 1) 7
56 LOVELARK [67] 7-10-0 B Fenton, *prmnt, led 3rd to 4th, wknd quickly aftr nxt* .... (40 to 1 op 20 to 1) 8
518 SLIPPERY MAX [70] (v) 12-10-3 R Massey, *pld hrd, led second to 3rd, wknd appr 2 out.*
.... (16 to 1 op 14 to 1 tchd 20 to 1) 9
518³ NORTHERN NATION [75] (v) 8-10-8 P Henley, *prmnt, rdn 5th, wknd 3 out* .... (16 to 1 op 10 to 1) 10
SHEDANSAR (Ire) [69] 4-10-0 E Husband, *led and hit 1st, hdd nxt, led 4th to 5th, wknd quickly appr 3 out.*
.... (40 to 1 op 20 to 1) 11
Dist: 3l, 3½l, sht-hd, 3½l, 2l, 1¼l, 4l, 10l, 3l, ½l. 3m 47.60s. a 7.60s (11 Ran).
(Miss M E Rowland), Miss M E Rowland

667 Queensway Maiden Hurdle Class F (4-y-o and up) £2,087 3m......... (2:55)

MISTER BLAKE 6-11-5 R Johnson, *beh till hdwy 9th, rdn 2 out, styd on to ld r-in, drvn out* ...... (12 to 1 tchd 16 to 1) 1
539² LEAR DANCER (USA) 5-11-5 Gary Lyons, *keen hold, hld up, steady hdwy frm 7th, led gng wl appr 3 out, clr nxt, hdd and wknd r-in* .... (6 to 4 fav op Evens tchd 13 to 8) 2
186 SALTIS (Ire) 4-11-2 T Eley, *hdwy aftr 6th, styd on same pace frm 3 out* .... (40 to 1 op 25 to 1 tchd 50 to 1) 3
FLYNN'S GIRL (Ire) 7-11-0 W Marston, *keen hold, hdwy 8th, chsd ldr 3 out, styd on same pace und pres frm nxt.*
.... (8 to 1 op 7 to 1 tchd 9 to 1) 4
DRAGONMIST (Ire) 6-10-7 (7*) Miss E J Jones, *prmnt, chlgd 8th, led nxt, hdd appr 3 out, sn wknd..* (33 to 1 op 16 to 1) 5
519³ CROWN IVORY (NZ) 8-11-5 S Fox, *hdwy aftr 6th, wknd after 3 out* .... (14 to 1 op 10 to 1) 6
KAREN'S TYPHOON (Ire) 5-11-5 J Osborne, *dsptd ld till led aftr 6th, hdd appr 3 out, wknd quickly, tld off.*
.... (100 to 30 op 7 to 2 tchd 4 to 1) 7
585⁵ HEATON (NZ) 9-11-5 B Powell, *made most till hdd aftr 6th, wknd 8th, tld off* .... (50 to 1 op 25 to 1 tchd 66 to 1) 8
585⁶ BANKS OF THE BRIDE 6-11-5 E Byrne, *not fluent, sn beh, blun 3 out, tld off* .... (50 to 1 op 33 to 1 tchd 66 to 1) 9
PADDITATE (Ire) 7-11-2 (3*) T Dascombe, *wth ldrs to 7th, sn wknd, tld off whn pld up bef 3 out*...(33 to 1 op 16 to 1) pu
544 TIPPING ALONG (Ire) (v) 7-11-5 R Dunwoody, *prmnt till wknd quickly aftr 6th, tld off whn pld up after 9th.*
.... (7 to 2 tchd 3 to 1) pu
Dist: 4l, 2l, 4l, 1½l, 1½l, dist, 2½l, 20l. 5m 49.30s. a 13.30s (11 Ran).
(W D Edwards), R Lee

668 Dowelanco Handicap Chase Class C (0-130 5-y-o and up) £4,467 2m 7f .... (3:30)

TARTAN TRADEWINDS [125] 9-12-0 R Dunwoody, *al gng wl, trkd ldr on bit frm 3 out, quickened to ld last, cmftbly.*
.... (7 to 2 op 4 to 1 tchd 5 to 2) 1
613* MAGGOTS GREEN [99] 9-10-2 R Johnson, *led, hit 9th, rdn 3 out, hdd last, kpt on but no ch wth wnr.*
.... (9 to 4 op 2 to 1 tchd 5 to 2) 2
613² ROYAL VACATION [111] 7-11-0 J Callaghan, *chsd ldr, chlgd tenth till hit 13th, ev ch 4 out, wknd appr 2 out.*
.... (11 to 8 fav op 7 to 4) 3
STAUNCH RIVAL (USA) [120] 9-11-9 B Powell, *in tch till hit tenth, rdn and lost touch, hdwy to chase ldrs 4 out, wknd nxt.*
.... (11 to 2 op 4 to 1 tchd 6 to 1) 4
Dist: 6l, 7l, 24l. 5m 51.40s. a 13.40s (4 Ran).
(Mackinnon Mills), G Richards

669 Solihull Handicap Hurdle Class C (0-130 4-y-o and up) £3,864 2½m .... (4:00)

403* FIELDRIDGE [110] 7-10-13 B Powell, *hld up, hdwy 5th, chlgd on bit frm 2 out, rdn to ld r-in.* .... (11 to 4 jt-
fav op 5 to 2 tchd 7 to 2) 1
374* WADADA [106] 5-10-7 D J Burchell, *steadied early, hdwy to chal 6th, led nxt, rdn frm 2 out, hdd and wknd r-in.*
.... (11 to 4 jt-fav op 5 to 2 tchd 3 to 1) 2
529² PREROGATIVE [110] (v) 6-10-13 C Maude, *led to 7th, sn wknd, lft poor 3rd 3 out, tld off.*
.... (15 to 2 op 5 to 1 tchd 8 to 1) 3
303 SUIVEZ [125] 6-12-0 R Dunwoody, *chsd ldrs, rdn and 3rd whn f 3 out* .... (11 to 2 op 7 to 2) f
543 JENZSOPH (Ire) [107] 5-10-3 (5*) D J Kavanagh, *hld up in tch till f 5th* .... (7 to 1 op 11 to 2) f
515⁴ FANTASTIC FLEET (Ire) [100] 4-10-1 R Johnson, *chsd ldrs, 4th and wkng whn brght dwn 3 out...*(10 to 1 tchd 12 to 1) bd
508⁴ LANHAM LOW (Ire) [102] 5-10-3 J Osborne, *hld up in rear till badly hmpd and pld up 5th* .... (7 to 1 op 5 to 1) pu
Dist: 2l, dist. 4m 37.40s. a 1.40s (7 Ran).
SR: 21/13/-/-/

(The Charleston Partnership), M P Muggeridge

670 Corporation Street Novices' Chase Class D (5-y-o and up) £3,562 2m .... (4:35)

534² CELIBATE (Ire) 5-10-10 R Dunwoody, *al gng wl beh ldrs, bumped 4 out, quickened to chal frm 3 out, led last, easily.*
.... (11 to 8 fav op 5 to 4 tchd 6 to 4) 1

594² HERESTHEDEAL (Ire) (v) 7-10-12 B Clifford, led, clr 4th, rdn 3
out, hdd appr last, kpt on but no ch wth wnr.
.....................................(7 to 2 tchd 4 to 1) 2
MR CONDUCTOR (Ire) 5-10-5 (5⁰) P Henley, beh, rdn 8th,
hdwy and hmpd 4 out, sn wknd.
.....................................(11 to 2 op 5 to 1 tchd 6 to 1) 3
457³ BETABETCORBETT (bl) 5-10-10 T Eley, prmnt, rdn and wnt lft
4 out, sn wknd.........(20 to 1 op 14 to 1 tchd 25 to 1) 4
191 WOTANITE 6-10-12 V Slattery, al beh, hmpd 5th, lost tch frm
nxt...................................(66 to 1 op 33 to 1) 5
280 SAXON BLADE 8-10-12 L Harvey, keen hold, prmnt early,
beh whn hmpd 5th, sn lost tch........(50 to 1 op 33 to 1) 6
HOLY WANDERER (USA) 7-10-9 (3⁰) G Hogan, in rear, some
prog whn f 5th...........................(3 to 1 tchd 100 to 30) f
Dist: 2½sl, 10l, 20l, 24l, 1¼l. 3m 52.30s. a 3.30s (7 Ran).

SR: 9/8/-/-/   (Stamford Bridge Partnership), C J Mann

671 Edgbaston Standard Open National Hunt Flat Class H (4,5,6-y-o) £1,385 2m..............................(5:05)

NEVER IN DEBT 4-10-9 (7⁰) Mr G Shenkin, mid-div, gd hdwy 3
fs out, chlgd o'r one out, led ins last, hld on wl.
.....................................(33 to 1 op 25 to 1) 1
MADHAZE (Ire) 5-11-4 W McFarland, beh, gd hdwy o'r 3 fs
out, str chal o'r one out, wknd ins last......(33 to 1 op 20 to 1) 2
SOLAR MOON 5-10-13 B Powell, beh, gd hdwy 6 fs out, str
chal o'r one out, wknd ins last...........(12 to 1 op 8 to 1) 3
CHIEF GALE (Ire) 4-10-11 (5⁰) Michael Brennan, chsd ldr, led
7 fs out, clr 3 out, rdn 2 out, hdd and wknd ins last.
........(7 to 2 fav op 3 to 1 tchd 9 to 2 and 5 to 1) 4
CAPTAIN FELIX (NZ) 6-11-4 C Maude, sn prmnt, rdn 3 fs,
wknd 2 out...............(16 to 1 op 14 to 1 tchd 20 to 1) 5
CELTIC FIREFLY 4-10-11 R Johnson, beh till styd on fnl 3 fs.
.....................................(6 to 1 op 4 to 1) 6
TERRANO STAR (Ire) 5-11-4 D J Burchell, pld hrd, led, hdd 7
fs out, wknd o'r 3 out...............(11 to 2 op 7 to 1) 7
LAKESIDE LAD 4-10-9 (7⁰) J Prior, chsd ldrs till wknd 4 fs out.
.....................................(20 to 1 op 16 to 1) 8
ROSEHALL 5-10-10 (3⁰) G Hogan, beh, modest hdwy o'r 4 fs
out, sn btn...........(25 to 1 op 20 to 1 tchd 33 to 1) 9
ALL SEWN UP 4-11-2 L Harvey, beh frm hfwy, nvr dngrs.
.....................................(16 to 1 op 14 to 1) 10
KLOSTERS 4-10-8 (3⁰) T Dascombe, in tch till wknd 3 fs out.
.....................................(8 to 1 op 10 to 1 tchd 12 to 1) 11
EYE OF THE STORM (Ire) 5-11-4 R Dunwoody, sn prmnt,
wknd 3 fs out.
.....................................(9 to 2 op 7 to 2 tchd 5 to 1 and 11 to 2) 12
LEOPARD LADY 4-10-4 (7⁰) N Willmington, prmnt to hfwy.
.....................................(20 to 1 op 10 to 1) 13
POLLIFUMAS 6-10-13 D Gallagher, sn beh.
.....................................(14 to 1 tchd 16 to 1) 14
NANJIZAL 4-11-2 T Eley, al beh...........(33 to 1 op 20 to 1) 15
WHITE AXLE (Ire) 6-11-4 B Fenton, al beh, tld off.
.....................................(25 to 1 op 20 to 1 tchd 33 to 1) 16
456 TAILORMADE FUTURE 4-10-9 (7⁰) D Finnegan, sn beh.
.....................................(25 to 1 op 33 to 1) 17
MISS NONNIE 4-10-11 D Leahy, hdwy aftr 6 fs, wknd rpdly
and brght dwn 5 furlongs out.
.....................................(16 to 1 op 25 to 1 tchd 33 to 1) bd
TEDDY EDWARD 6-10-11 (7⁰) R Wilkinson, prmnt 7 fs, beh
whn slpd up 5 furlongs out............(25 to 1 op 20 to 1) su
Dist: ¾l, 4l, 2l, 5l, 2l, 19l, ¾l, 4l, 6l, 2½l. 3m 39.80s. (19 Ran).

(M R Clough), A G Hobbs

FONTWELL (good to firm)
Monday September 16th
Going Correction: MINUS 0.05 sec. per fur.

672 Rank Challenge Cup Juvenile Novices' Hurdle Class E (3-y-o) £2,406 2¼m 110yds........................(2:15)

THE LEGIONS PRIDE 10-10 J Osborne, made most till hdd
r-in, rallied und pres to ld ag'n cl hme.
..........(100 to 30 op 3 to 1 tchd 5 to 2 and 7 to 2) 1
HOW COULD-I (Ire) 10-5 A Maguire, hld up, hdwy 5th, lft
second 2 out, hrd rdn to ld r-in, hdd cl hme.
.....................................(5 to 1 op 7 to 2) 2
501³ YELLOW DRAGON (Ire) 10-7 (3⁰) K Gaule, al prmnt, mstk 3rd,
sn trkd wnr, ev ch whn blun 2 out, not reco'r.
.....................................(6 to 1 tchd 7 to 1) 3
LORD EL LANGOWAN (Ire) 10-10 D Gallagher, hld up, hdwy 2
out, nvr nr to chal...................(20 to 1 op 14 to 1) 4
614⁴ SKRAM 11-3 J Culloty, prmnt till outpcd 6th, sn beh.
.....................................(13 to 2 op 5 to 1 tchd 7 to 1) 5
FURTHER FUTURE (Ire) 10-10 I Lawrence, al in rear.
.....................................(12 to 1 op 10 to 1) 6
501⁴ KINGS NIGHTCLUB (bl) 10-2 (3⁰) Guy Lewis, hld up, wknd
appr 6th............(25 to 1 op 20 to 1 tchd 33 to 1) 7
436⁷ VERULAM (Ire) 11-3 G Bradley, in rear till f 5th.
.....................................(3 to 1 fav tchd 5 to 2 and 100 to 30) f
501² AMBER RING 10-5 J R Kavanagh, al prmnt, rdn frm 4 out,
disputing second whn f 2 out..........(12 to 1 op 8 to 1) f

SCENE STEALER 10-5 F Jousset, in rear, tld off whn pld up
bef 6th...........................(50 to 1 op 33 to 1) pu
Dist: Nk, 6l, 2½l, 7l, 8l, 15l. 4m 28.20s. a 11.20s (10 Ran).
(Royal British Legion Racing Club), J W Hills

673 Arundel Selling Handicap Hurdle Class G (0-95 4-y-o and up) £1,943 2¼m 110yds........................(2:45)

NAHRAWALI (Ire) [89] 5-12-0 A P McCoy, al led 5th,
clr nxt, unchlgd.....................(9 to 4 fav op 4 to 1) 1
CREDIT CONTROLLER (Ire) [60] 7-10-1 B Fenton, hld up in
mid-div, hdwy to chase wnr appr 3 out.
.....................................(11 to 1 op 10 to 1 tchd 12 to 1) 2
596 MIRAMARE [60] 6-9-11¹ (5⁰) P Henley, mid-div, rdn 6th, some
hdwy appr 3 out, nvr dngrs.
.....................................(11 to 1 op 2 op 4 to 1 tchd 6 to 1) 3
518⁴ ANTIGUAN FLYER [70] 7-10-11 A Maguire, led till 5th, sn
wknd.....................(5 to 1 op 9 to 2 tchd 4 to 1) 4
631 ON THE LEDGE (USA) [59] 6-9-7 (7⁰) A Dowling, chsd ldrs till
wknd 6th.........................(50 to 1 tchd 66 to 1) 5
417⁴ MILZIG (USA) [71] 7-10-12 C Llewellyn, wl beh frm second, tld
off...................................(7 to 1 op 4 to 1) 6
593⁴ ROGER'S PAL [59] 9-9-7 (7⁰) M Batchelor, uns rdr 1st.
.....................................(9 to 1 op 6 to 1 tchd 10 to 1) ur
502 SANDRO [59] (bl) 7-10-0 L Harvey, trkd ldr early, beh frm 4th,
tld off whn pld up bef last...........(33 to 1 op 20 to 1) pu
440² LAC DE GRAS (Ire) [63] 5-10-2 D Morris, al beh, tld off whn pld
up bef 6th, broke blood vessel.........(10 to 1 op 7 to 1) pu
WHAT'S THE JOKE [63] 7-10-4 C Maude, prmnt till 4th, sn
beh, tld off whn pld up bef last........(5 to 1 op 10 to 1) pu
Dist: 13l, 7l, 9l, 20l, dist. 4m 24.60s. a 7.60s (10 Ran).
SR: 15/-/-/-/-/-/   (C F Sparrowhawk), A Moore

674 Elton Vehicle Contracts Handicap Chase Class F (0-105 5-y-o and up) £2,721 2m 3f................(3:15)

452³ MANAMOUR [82] 9-10-8 C Llewellyn, hld up, hdwy to track
ldrs 8th, lft second 12th, led and edgd right appr last, styd on.
.....................................(7 to 2 tchd 4 to 1) 1
452² DRUMSTICK [96] 10-11-8 J Railton, led 3rd till aftr 9th, lft in ld
12th, wkng and crossed whn hdd appr last, not reco'r last
fence blund........(5 to 2 op 2 to 1 tchd 11 to 4) 2
500⁴ HENLEY WOOD [98] 11-11-7 (3⁰) G Tormey, led till 3rd, mstk
6th, led aftr 9th, blun and uns rdr 12th.
.....................................(11 to 8 on op 6 to 5 on op 5 to 4 on) ur
TOP MISS [74] 7-9-12⁵ (7⁰) W Greatrex, jmpd slwly 5th, sn tld
off, refused 3 out.......(66 to 1 op 33 to 1 tchd 100 to 1) ref
Dist: 10l. 4m 54.00s. a 19.00s (4 Ran).
(R L C Hartley), R Lee

675 Strebel Boilers And Radiators Handicap Hurdle Series Qualifier Class E (0-110 4-y-o and up) £2,385 2¾m 110yds........................(3:45)

KALASADI (USA) [100] 5-11-6 J Culloty, al prmnt, led 4 out, sn
clr, unchlgd........................(6 to 1 op 4 to 1) 1
503³ CIRCUS COLOURS [98] 6-11-6 A Maguire, hld up in rear,
hdwy 4 out, wnt second appr 2 out, no ch wth wnr.
.....................................(5 to 2 op 2 to 1 tchd 11 to 4) 2
CABOCHON [102] 9-11-10 C Llewellyn, al rear, lost tch appr
4 out, tld off...................(10 to 1 op 10 to 1 tchd 20 to 1) 3
606⁶ ROYAL CIRCUS [93] 7-11-1 D Bridgwater, led till hdd 4 out,
sn btn, tld off whn pld up bef last.
.....................................(7 to 1 op 6 to 1 tchd 15 to 2) pu
283³ MISS PIMPERNEL [78] (v) 6-10-0 A P McCoy, prmnt early,
beh 4th, sn rdn, tld off whn pld up aftr 7th.
.....................................(7 to 1 op 6 to 1 tchd 10 to 1) pu
227² HOSTILE WITNESS (Ire) [100] 6-11-8 D J Burchell, chsd ldrs,
cl 3rd whn pld up 4 out, lme.........(7 to 4 fav op 2 to 1) pu
Dist: 20l, dist. 5m 27.00s. a 13.00s (6 Ran).
(G A Libson), V Soane

676 Fontwell Handicap Chase Class D (0-120 5-y-o and up) £3,460 3¼m 110yds........................(4:15)

FROZEN DROP [96] 9-11-11 S Fox, al prmnt, led 7th till 9th,
led 11th, wnt clr aftr 4 out, eased r-in.
.....................................(9 to 4 op 3 to 1 tchd 2 to 1) 1
568⁴ DISTANT MEMORY [99] (bl) 7-12-0 A P McCoy, trkd ldr, mstk
5th, chsd wnr 14th, mistake 4 out, no ch aftr.
.....................................(11 to 8 fav op 5 to 4 on tchd 13 to 8) 2
643⁵ L'UOMO PIU [80] (v) 12-10-9 B Powell, led till 7th, led 9th till
11th, 3rd whn mstk 4 out, sn btn.
.....................................(10 to 1 op 8 to 1 tchd 12 to 1) 3
630⁶ HIZAL [77] 7-10-6⁵ Mr A Charles-Jones, al beh, tld off.
.....................................(14 to 1 op 8 to 1) 4
632 GHEDI (Pol) [75] (bl) 5-10-0 S Curran, 4th whn blun and uns
rdr 13th.....................(50 to 1 op 33 to 1 tchd 66 to 1) ur
530³ DUKE OF LANCASTER (Ire) [77] (v) 7-10-6 W Marston, beh
3rd, tld off 6th, pld up aftr 15th........(4 to 1 tchd 5 to 1) pu
Dist: 5l, 7l, dist. 7m 1.60s. a 31.60s (6 Ran).
(Jock Cullen), P C Ritchens

677 Cowfold Swimming Pool Novices' Hurdle Class E (4-y-o and up) £2,364 2¾m 110yds.....................(4:45)

SUPREME STAR (USA) 5-10-12 M Richards, *not fluent, in in tch, rdn to go second appr 2 out, chalg whn blun badly last, rallied to ld r-in.*

.............(6 to 4 on tchd 13 to 8 on and 11 to 8 on) 1
510⁵ LAWBUSTER (Ire) (bl) 4-10-5 (5*) D Salter, *trkd ldr, led 4 out, hrd rdn 2 out, hdd r-in.*.............(50 to 1) 2
618⁴ SCAMALLACH (Ire) (bl) 6-11-0 G Bradley, *hld up, cld on ldrs 3 out, rdn and wknd appr nxt*.............(3 to 1 op 3 to 1) 3
479² AIR COMMAND (Bar) 6-10-5 (7*) Mr P Phillips, *led till hdd 4 out, wknd quickly, tld off*....(4 to 1 op 3 to 1 tchd 9 to 2) 4
ADILOV 4-10-10 D Gallagher, *mstks, tld off frm 5th.*
.............(16 to 1 tchd 20 to 1) 5
Dist: 1¼l, 6l, dist, dist. 5m 35.60s. a 21.60s (5 Ran).

(J J Whelan), P R Hedger

ROSCOMMON (IRE) (good to firm (races 1,2,4), firm (3))
Monday September 16th

678 Lough Ree Maiden Hurdle (6-y-o and up) £2,397 2m.................(4:00)

591⁴ ACES AND EIGHTS (Ire) 6-11-6 R Dunwoody, ...(5 to 2) 1
31³ JAY MAN (Ire) 6-11-9 (5*) Mr E J Kearns Jnr, ...(5 to 1) 2
OMAR (USA) 7-12-0 C O'Dwyer, ...(11 to 10 fav) 3
397¹ NO DIAMOND (Ire) 7-12-0 J P Broderick, ...(7 to 1) 4
635⁶ RADICAL ACTION (Ire) 6-11-6 K F O'Brien, ...(16 to 1) 5
410⁷ ORCHARD SUNSET (Ire) 6-10-13 (7*) Mr D M Fogarty,
.............(16 to 1) 6
645⁷ JONATHAN'S ROSE (Ire) (bl) 7-11-1 J K Kinane, ...(16 to 1) 7
INDEXIA (Ire) 6-11-6 L P Cusack, ...(25 to 1) 8
Dist: 7l, 25l, ¾l, 11l. 3m 44.90s. (8 Ran).

(P Hughes), P Hughes

679 Villiger Handicap Hurdle (0-123 4-y-o and up) £3,253 2m.............(4:30)

598* I REMEMBER IT WELL (Ire) [-] (bl) 4-10-0 J P Broderick,
.............(100 to 30 fav) 1
469⁵ TARA'S TRIBE [-] 9-9-11 F Woods, ...(12 to 1) 2
575³ SLAVE GALE (Ire) [-] 5-10-11 T Horgan, ...(9 to 2) 3
625⁵ STONELEIGH TURBO (Ire) [-] 7-9-9 R Dunwoody, (7 to 1) 4
433³ LEGGAGH LADY (Ire) [-] 5-11-9 (5*) J M Donnelly, ...(7 to 2) 5
575⁵ LOUGH ATALIA (Ire) [-] 9-10-4 C O'Dwyer, ...(7 to 1) 6
348⁴ BRIGHT PROJECT (Iro) [-] 4-10-6 T P Treacy, ...(4 to 1) 7
Dist: 4l, nk, 6l, 3½l. 3m 46.10s. (7 Ran).

(I Remember It Well Syndicate), Michael Hourigan

680 Carrolls Beginners Chase (4-y-o and up) £3,425 2m 5f........... (6:30)

625² CULLENSTOWN LADY 5-11-3 R Dunwoody,
.............(5 to 4 fav) 1
525 YOUNG DUBLINER (Ire) 7-12-0 J Shortt, ...(2 to 1) 2
525 WHAT IS THE PLAN (Ire) 7-12-0 C O'Dwyer, ...(14 to 1) 3
536⁵ DROMINAGH (Ire) 8-11-7 (7*) R P Hogan, ...(14 to 1) 4
604³ STRONG BOOST (USA) 5-11-8 F Woods, ...(6 to 1) 5
565⁸ PROPHET'S THUMB 7-11-7 (7*) M D Murphy, ...(14 to 1) 6
619⁴ PRIME PAPERS 11-12-0 T P Treacy, ...(25 to 1) 7
PALMURA 9-11-9 (5*) J M Donnelly, ...(16 to 1) 8
604⁴ BORRISMORE FLASH (Ire) 8-12-0 J P Broderick, ... f
137⁸ MISS TOP (Ire) 6-11-2 (7*) R Burke, ...(33 to 1) f
Dist: 2½l, 8l, 11l, 20l. 5m 5.80s. (10 Ran).

(P Hughes), P Hughes

681 Silver Bawn I.N.H. Flat Race (4-y-o and up) £2,397 2m.............(7:00)

340⁸ NICOLA MARIE (Ire) 7-11-2 (7*) Mr Sean O O'Brien, (25 to 1) 1
628² STORM GEM (Ire) 5-11-4 (5*) Mr R Walsh, ...(5 to 1) 2
591⁶ EASTERN CUSTOM (Ire) 5-11-6 (3*) Mr R O'Neill, (12 to 1) 3
591³ LOLLIA PAULINA (Ire) (bl) 5-11-2 (7*) Mr Edgar Byrne,
.............(7 to 1) 4
624⁵ TINERANA GLOW (Ire) 4-10-11 (7*) Mr A J Dempsey,
.............(10 to 1) 5
581⁵ BUNINOO (Ire) 4-10-11 (7*) Mr Edgar Byrne, ...(5 to 2 fav) 6
603² JOSH'S FANCY (Ire) 5-11-9 Mr P Fenton, ...(4 to 1) 7
444⁶ CARRICK GLEN (Ire) 5-11-2 (7*) Mr A Ross, ...(8 to 1) 8
611⁷ SUSIE'S DELIGHT (Ire) 6-11-2 (7*) Mr M S Hayden, (16 to 1) 9
CAILIN CHUINNE (Ire) 4-11-4 Mr D Marnane, ...(10 to 1) 10
BLAKESONIA (Ire) 6-12-0 Mr G J Harford, ...(12 to 1) 11
603 FLORIA (Ire) 4-11-1 (3*) Mr B M Cash, ...(14 to 1) 12
GONE ALL DAY (Ire) 6-11-2 (7*) Mr D G McHale, .. (33 to 1) 13
NO SPOKEN WORD (Ire) 5-11-2 (7*) Mr R M Walsh, (20 to 1) 14
LISBAND LADY (Ire) 6-11-2 (7*) Mr Joss Saville, ...(9 to 1) 15
Dist: 2l, hd, 7l, 2½l. 3m 40.40s. (15 Ran).

(Ms M Flynn), Ms M Flynn

AUTEUIL (FR) (soft)

Wednesday September 18th

682 Prix de L'Orleanais (Hurdle) (5-y-o and up) £13,175 2¼m.............(4:25)

84² AL CAPONE II (Fr) 8-10-1 J-Y Beaurain, *rear early, steady hdwy to ld 6 out, drw clr 2 out, easily*.................... 1
465* COUNTRY STAR (Ire) 5-10-5 G Bradley, *led, pckd and hdd 6 out, rdn r-in, styd on, no ch wth wnr*.................... 2
465² LEON DES PERRETS (Fr) 5-10-5 L Gerrard, ... 3
Dist: 10l, 6l, 6l, ¾l, ½l, 2l, 20l. 4m 21.00s. (9 Ran).

(R Fougedoire), B Secly

GOWRAN PARK (IRE) (good)
Thursday September 19th

683 Gowran Handicap Hurdle (0-102 4-y-o and up) £2,740 3m.............(4:00)

565* THAI ELECTRIC (Ire) [-] 5-11-0 T J Mitchell, ...(4 to 1 fav) 1
254² INNOVATIVE (Ire) [-] 5-10-13 C O'Dwyer, ...(7 to 1) 2
575⁴ BUGGSY BLADE [-] 10-10-13 L P Cusack, ...(7 to 1) 3
443⁴ WICKLOW WAY (Ire) [-] 6-10-7 K F O'Brien, ...(13 to 2) 4
497* CHANOBLE (Ire) [-] 4-9-8 (7*) B D Murtagh, ...(12 to 1) 5
578³ MOON-FROG [-] 9-10-7 F Woods, ...(12 to 1) 6
625⁴ GARLAND ROSE (Ire) [-] 6-10-7 (3*) D J Casey, ...(8 to 1) 7
64 FRISKY THYNE (Ire) [-] 7-10-7 P A Roche, ...(25 to 1) 8
565⁴ MARGUERITA SONG [-] 6-11-2 J P Broderick, ...(5 to 1) 9
536⁹ GAIN CONTROL (Ire) [-] 7-9-9 (5*) G Cotter, ...(20 to 1) 10
600⁶ COLONIA SKY (Ire) [-] 5-10-4 T Horgan, ...(16 to 1) 11
598 THE SOUTH POLE INN (Ire) [-] 4-9-8 (5*) J Butler, (16 to 1) pu
625³ SUDDEN STORM (Ire) [-] 5-11-2 T P Treacy, ...(9 to 2) pu
Dist: 1l, 2l. 6m 4.40s. (13 Ran).

(Mrs Brenda Byrne), Sean Byrne

684 Milford Handicap Hurdle (0-109 4-y-o and up) £2,397 2m.............(4:30)

599⁴ RUDDS HILL (Ire) [-] 8-10-10 F Woods, ...(14 to 1) 1
600 FLYING IN THE GALE (Ire) [-] 5-9-11 J P Broderick, (8 to 1) 2
396³ MONTE'S EVENING (Ire) [-] 8-9-13 P L Malone, ...(6 to 1) 3
BALLYQUIN BELLE (Ire) [-] 6-10-13 (3*) J R Barry, ..(7 to 1) 4
581⁶ FENIAN COURT (Ire) [-] 5-9-8† T J Mitchell, ...(10 to 1) 5
303 KAWA-KAWA [-] 9-10-13 (5*) G Cotter, ...(14 to 1) 6
LAURENS FANCY (Ire) [-] 6-10-3 S H O'Donovan, (14 to 1) 7
601 SAN SIRO (Ire) [-] 6-9-6 (7*) Mr Edgar Byrne, ...(20 to 1) 8
486³ FRASER CAREY (Ire) [-] 6-10-0 4-11-3 T P Treacy, (6 to 1) 9
635⁴ BAY COTTAGE (Ire) [-] 7-9-6 (3*) D J Casey, ...(5 to 1 jt-fav) 10
621⁸ DANCING CLODAGH (Ire) [-] (bl) 4-11-1 S C Lyons, (6 to 1) 11
161⁷ SERGEANT BILL (Ire) [-] 4-9-7† D Fisher, ...(33 to 1) 12
589* CHUCK (Ire) [-] 6-10-8 (7*) D McCullagh, ...(6 to 1) 13
643³ LORD KNOCKEMSTIFF (Ire) [-] (bl) 6 9-3 (5*) T Martin
.............(16 to 1) 14
268⁷ L'ORAGE (Ire) [-] 8-11-1 K F O'Brien, ...(20 to 1) 15
562⁸ RONDELLI (Ire) [-] 6-10-5 J K Kinane, ...(14 to 1) 16
Dist: 2½l, 8l, hd, sht-hd. 3m 50.20s. (16 Ran).

(Patrick John Murphy), Patrick John Murphy

685 Bagenalstown Maiden Hurdle (5-y-o) £2,397 2m.................(5:00)

566⁷ MAJOR JAMIE (Ire) 11-6 F Woods, ...(6 to 1) 1
MARTYS STEP (Ire) 10-13 (7*) D McCullagh, ...(20 to 1) 2
538³ PHARADISO (Ire) 11-3 (3*) D J Casey, ...(10 to 1) 3
66 CRUCIAL MOVE (Ire) 11-1 D H O'Connor, ...(5 to 1) 4
561⁵ DREAM ETERNAL (Ire) 11-1 W Slattery, ...(12 to 1) 5
277⁵ HELORHIWATER (Ire) 11-2 (7*) Mr E Sheehy, ...(6 to 1) 6
SUITE CITY LASS (Ire) 10-10 (5*) G Cotter, ...(14 to 1) 7
536⁶ ALIGHIERI (Ire) 11-6 T Horgan, ...(8 to 1) 8
393 DAWN CALLER (Ire) 11-6 J Shortt, ...(16 to 1) 9
591 MARDON (Ire) 10-8 (7*) M D Murphy, ...(20 to 1) 10
HOTSCENT (Ire) 11-1 P A Roche, ...(25 to 1) 11
444* SPIN THE WHEEL (Ire) 12-0 T P Treacy, ...(7 to 2) 12
MISSED CONNECTION (Ire) 10-10 (5*) J Butler, ...(50 to 1) 13
619⁵ LONG SHOT JOHN (Ire) 11-3 (3*) U Smyth, ...(20 to 1) 14
NOBLE SHOON (Ire) 12-0 C O'Dwyer, ...(3 to 1 fav) pu
600 MONTO GUZZI (Ire) 11-6 S H O'Donovan, ...(50 to 1) pu
Dist: Sht-hd, 3½l, 2½l, ½l. 3m 54.70s. (16 Ran).

(C Nolan), A L T Moore

686 Dungarvan I.N.H. Flat Race (4-y-o and up) £2,397 2m.................(5:30)

KNOCKAROO (Ire) 5-12-0 Mr P Fenton, ...(2 to 1 fav) 1
SPENDID (Ire) 4-11-2 (7*) Miss A L Crowley, ...(8 to 1) 2
647³ ANN'S DESIRE (Ire) 5-11-2 (7*) Mr J Keville, ...(10 to 1) 3
394⁴ TEMPLEORUM (Ire) 5-11-7 (7*) Mr Mark Walsh, ...(7 to 1) 4
566⁴ EXECUTIVE HEIGHTS (Ire) 4-11-2 (7*) Mr P Cody, (11 to 2) 5
337 LAKE MAJESTIC (Ire) 5-11-2 (7*) Mr P J Crowley, ..(20 to 1) 6
TEXARKANA (Ire) 8-11-2 (7*) Mr W Ross, ...(33 to 1) 7
581⁴ BRASSIS HILL (Ire) 5-11-7 (7*) Mr A C Coyle, ...(8 to 1) 8
611⁴ KASSERINE PASS (Ire) 6-11-11 (3*) Mr P English, ...(6 to 1) 9
591 SILKEN SECRETARIAT (Ire) 5-11-9 (5*) Mr R Walsh, (12 to 1) 10
STAR HAND (Ire) 5-12-0 Mr J A Berry, ...(8 to 1) 11
CAPTAIN ARTHUR (Ire) 5-11-7 (7*) Mr D M Loughnane,
.............(20 to 1) 12

79

NATIONAL HUNT RESULTS 1996-97

350[8]	SINGERS CORNER 4-10-11 (7*) Mr Edgar Byrne, (14 to 1)	13
464	BALMY NATIVE (Ire) 4-11-9 Mr J P Dempsey, ...(12 to 1)	14
467[8]	ROSEY BUCK (Ire) 4-10-11 (7*) Mr J P Kilfeather, . .(33 to 1)	15
34[5]	PEACEFULL RIVER (Ire) 7-11-2 (7*) Mr D Delaney, (12 to 1)	16
343[8]	PROPHETS FIRST (Ire) 5-11-7 (7*) Mr D A Harney, . .(14 to 1)	17
603	SCOTCH STONE GIRL (Ire) (bl) 4-10-11 (7*) Miss A Croke,	
	. . . .(14 to 1)	18
444[8]	NEWBOG LAD (Ire) 5-11-7 (7*) Mr C P Donnelly, . . .(20 to 1)	19
581	RATH NA SIDHE (Ire) 4-11-9 Mr H F Cleary, ...(12 to 1)	20

Dist: 1l, 3l, 2l, 6l. 3m 57.10s. (20 Ran).

(D Delahunty), K O'Sullivan

HUNTINGDON (firm (races 1,3,5,7), good to firm (2,4,6)) Friday September 20th
Going Correction: MINUS 0.60 sec. per fur.

687 Upwood Selling Handicap Hurdle Class G (0-95 4-y-o and up) £1,905 1f . . . . (2:20)

660[7]	ARRANGE A GAME [67] 9-9-9 (5*) S Taylor, handily plcd, led appr 3 out, rdn out frm last, kpt on wl.	
	. . . .(33 to 1 op 20 to 1 tchd 50 to 1)	1
438[3]	MR GENEAOLOGY (USA) [88] (bl) 6-11-7 A P McCoy, hld up, not fluent 3rd, hrd rdn 8th, not quicken 3 out, styd on und pres frm last. . . . .(9 to 2 op 5 to 2 tchd 5 to 1)	2
612[3]	RECORD LOVER (Ire) [75] 6-10-8 W Worthington, hld up towards rear till cld one ldrs 8th, rdn and one pace frm 2 out. . . . .(7 to 2 op 4 to 1 tchd 3 to 1)	3
660[3]	SAKBAH (USA) [67] 7-10-0 N Williamson, hld up in rear, gd hdwy 8th, chsd wnr frm 3 out till r-in, no extr . . . . (7 to 1)	4
318[5]	YACHT CLUB [75] 14-10-8 O Pears, with ldrs, led aftr 7th, hdd appr 3 out, btn bef nxt. . . . .(5 to 1 op 4 to 1 tchd 9 to 2)	5
612[2]	KING OF BABYLON (Ire) [73] 4-9-12 (5*) L Aspell, lost many ls at strt, in tch hfwy, effrt 9th, not run on appr 2 out. . . . .(9 to 2 tchd 5 to 1 and 4 to 1)	6
633[3]	THEY ALL FORGOT ME [67] 9-10-0 Miss C Dyson, led till hdd aftr 7th, wknd 9th. . . . .(25 to 1 op 10 to 1)	7
593[2]	TUG YOUR FORELOCK [75] 5-10-5 A Thornton, pressed ldrs till lost pl appr 3 out. . . . .(8 to 1 op 5 to 1 tchd 9 to 1)	8
612[9]	SIR PAGEANT [79] 7-10-12 D Bridgwater, mid-div till lost pl 3rd, rear 7th, lost tch 9th, tld off whn pld up bef 2 out. . . . .(13 to 2 op 10 to 1 tchd 9 to 1)	pu

Dist: 1¼l, 3½l, 1¼l, 7l, 19l, 3½l, 3l. 6m 13.30s. a 21.30s (9 Ran).

(A M McArdle), Miss J Bower

688 Owl End Novices' Chase Class E (5-y-o and up) £2,899 2m 110yds. . . . . .(2:55)

	STRONG PROMISE (Ire) 5-10-7 (3*) K Gaule, hld up in 3rd pl, chsd ldr aftr 3 out, led and hit last, quickened r-in, pushed out. . . . .(5 to 2 on op 13 to 8 on)	1
650	SHALIK (Ire) 6-10-5 (7*) N T Egan, led till hdd 7th, lft in ld aftr 3 out, headed and outpcd appr last, fnshd 3rd, plcd second. . . . .(25 to 1 op 20 to 1 tchd 33 to 1)	2
	RYTON RUN 11-11-2 B Fenton, jmpd lft, al beh, fnshd 4th, plcd 3rd . . . .(25 to 1 op 20 to 1 tchd 33 to 1)	3
	HANG'EM OUT TO DRY (Ire) 5-10-10 G Bradley, jmpd wl, chsd ldr, led 7th till pld up lme aftr 3 out. . . . .(9 to 1 op 6 to 1 tchd 10 to 1)	pu
670	HOLY WANDERER (USA) 7-10-9 (3*) G Hogan, hld up in 4th pl, lft 3rd aftr 3 out, with wnr hit last, outpcd r-in, fnshd second, disqualified. . . .(100 to 30 op 5 to 2 tchd 7 to 2)	0

Dist: 6l, 17l, 28l. 4m 5.40s. a 11.40s (5 Ran).

(G A Hubbard), G A Hubbard

689 Diddington Novices' Hurdle Class E (4-y-o and up) £2,722 2m 110yds. . (3:25)

	MR PERCY (Ire) 5-10-12 P Hide, wl plcd, led 2 out, rdn clr appr last. . . . .(7 to 2 op 3 to 1 tchd 4 to 1)	1
595*	COURBARIL 4-11-3 D Bridgwater, prmnt, led 3 out to nxt, sn rdn and outpcd. . . . . . .(9 to 4 fav op 3 to 1 tchd 7 to 2)	2
	NASHAAT (USA) 8-10-12 W Worthington, hld up towards rear, ran on frm 5th, styd on one pace from 3 out, not trble wnr. . . . .(10 to 1 op 5 to 1)	3
618[2]	DACELO (Fr) 5-10-12 J Osborne, trkd ldg grp, rdn and effrt appr 3 out, sn outpcd. . .(100 to 30 op 3 to 1 tchd 4 to 1)	4
454*	CHANCEY FELLA 5-11-12 A P McCoy, chsd ldr, led 4th, hdd 3 out, sn outpcd, fnshd lme. . . . .(12 to 1 op 10 to 1 tchd 14 to 1)	5
	ALCOVE 5-10-12 A Thornton, towards rear hfwy, kpt on one pace frm 3 out, no impsn on ldrs. . . . .(10 to 1 op 8 to 1 tchd 12 to 1)	6
	SHUTTLECOCK 5-10-12 A Maguire, wl in tch till wknd appr 3 out. . . . .(20 to 1 op 12 to 1 tchd 25 to 1)	7
	SPUMANTE 4-10-10 B Powell, rear most of way. . . . .(20 to 1 op 12 to 1)	8
641[2]	CADDY'S FIRST 4-10-10 N Mann, mid-div, rdn and no prog aftr 5th. . . . .(12 to 1 op 8 to 1)	9
	MANDYS ROYAL LAD 8-10-7 (5*) L Aspell, rear hfwy, nvr on terms aftr. . . . .(33 to 1 op 16 to 1)	10
	FERENS HALL 9-10-12 P McLoughlin, led to 4th, wknd aftr nxt. . . . .(33 to 1 op 16 to 1)	11

520	CHADLEIGH WALK (Ire) 4-10-7 (3*) P Midgley, al beh. . . . .(33 to 1 op 20 to 1)	12
610[3]	GENESIS FOUR 6-10-9 (3*) G Cahill, beh hfwy, nvr dngrs aftr. . . . .(20 to 1 op 12 to 1)	13
652	RAGTIME SONG 7-10-5 (7*) D Yellowlees, mstk 3rd, nvr nr ldrs aftr, tld off. . . . .(33 to 1 op 20 to 1)	14
	TITANIUM HONDA (Ire) 5-10-12 D Gallagher, mid-div, mstk 4th, sn wknd, pld up bef last. . . . .(33 to 1 op 20 to 1)	pu
	CLIFTON 7-10-12 D Morris, prmnt to 4th, wknd nxt, pld up and dismounted 2 out, destroyed . . . . (33 to 1 op 16 to 1)	pu

Dist: 8l, 14l, 4l, 3½l, 9l, 1¼l, 3l, ½l, nk, 1¼l. 3m 36.70s. b 4.30s (16 Ran).

SR: 28/25/6/2/12/-/ (Felix Rosenstiel's Widow & Son), J T Gifford

690 Sindall Construction Handicap Chase Class D (0-125 5-y-o and up) £3,594 2m 110yds. . . . .(3:55)

641[5]	RAMSTAR [99] 8-10-11 A P McCoy, chsd ldr, hit 6th and 8th, lft in ld 3 out, unchlgd. . . . .(6 to 1 op 7 to 2)	1
639*	SUPER SHARP (NZ) [88] 8-10-0 Jacqui Oliver, rcd in last nl outpcd frm 9th. ll . . . .(Evens fav tchd 11 to 10 and 11 to 10 on)	2
617[4]	STATELY HOME (Ire) [118] 5-12-0 R Johnson, led, blun badly hit 8th, blunded and uns rdr 3 out.	ur

Dist: Dist. 4m 0.50s. a 6.50s (3 Ran).

(A Loze), P J Hobbs

691 Goodliff Handicap Hurdle Class E (0-115 4-y-o and up) £2,442 2m 110yds. . . . .(4:25)

	PRIZEFIGHTER [99] 5-11-1 O Pears, hld up in 4th pl, cld on ldr appr 3 out, led aftr nxt, quickened clr r-in. . . . .(13 to 8 fav op 7 to 4 tchd 2 to 1)	1
109[6]	VUBRALEE (USA) [109] 4-11-11 D Bridgwater, made most of rng till hdd aftr 2 out, sn outpcd. . . . .(4 to 1 op 3 to 1 tchd 9 to 2)	2
587*	ZINE LANE [104] 4-11-6 R Farrant, trkd ldrs, rdn and no extr appr 2 out. . . . .(100 to 30 op 2 to 1 tchd 7 to 2)	3
	KING WILLIAM [93] 11-10-11 D Gallagher, hld up towards rear, rdn and outpcd appr 3 out. . . . .(14 to 1 op 10 to 1 tchd 16 to 1)	4
388[2]	DESERT CHALLENGER (Ire) [82] 6-10-0 S Fox, trkd ldr, dsptd ld 4th, rdn and outpcd appr 3 out, btn whn blun 2 out. . . . .(16 to 1 op 8 to 1)	5
438[2]	NO LIGHT [103] 9-11-7 L Harvey, settled in rear, rdn appr 3 out, nvr able to chal. . . . .(4 to 1 op 5 to 2 tchd 9 to 2)	6

Dist: 7l, 1¾l, 6l, 12l, 2½l. 3m 40.40s. b 0.60s (6 Ran).

(Diamond Racing Ltd), J L Eyre

692 Knapwell Amateur Riders' Handicap Chase Class E (0-110 5-y-o and up) £3,607 3m. . . . .(4:55)

632[2]	DRUMCULLEN (Ire) [84] 7-9-12 (7*) Mr R Wakley, made all, mstk and lft clr 2 out, styd on easily. . . . .(5 to 2 op 2 to 1 tchd 3 to 1)	1
642	FAIRY PARK [96] 11-10-10 (7*) Mr N H Oliver, hld up in rear, lost tch 14th, styd on 2 out, hit last, fnshd wl. . . . .(9 to 1 op 4 to 1 tchd 10 to 1)	2
556*	THE YANK [103] (bl) 10-11-7 (3*) Mr C Bonner, chsd wnr till mstk 9th, jmpd slwly and lost tch 14th, hit 16th, tld off. . .(11 to 10 fav op Evens tchd 11 to 10 on and 6 to 5)	3
	FINKLE STREET (Ire) [90] 8-10-6 (7*) Mr M Rimell, nvr on terms. . . . .(20 to 1 op 12 to 1)	4

(Martyn Booth), K C Bailey

693 September Intermediate Open National Hunt Flat Class H (4,5,6-y-o) £1,311 2m 110yds. . . . .(5:25)

	PROTOTYPE 5-11-4 A Thornton, hld up, hdwy 5 out, led o'r one out, pushed clr, not extended. . (10 to 1 tchd 14 to 1)	1
	ARDENBAR 4-11-A Maguire, chsd ldrs, not quicken 3 out, rallied o'r one out, ran on same pace. (100 to 30 op 4 to 1)	2
231*	ULTIMATE SMOOTHIE 4-11-12 D Bridgwater, trkd ldrs, led 5 out, hdd o'r one out, sn outpcd.	3
	SOUTHERNCROSSPATCH 5-11-4 S Curran, hdwy frm rear 5 fs out, kpt on one pace from 2 out. . .(33 to 1 op 20 to 1)	4
	LADY FOLEY (Ire) 4-10-4 (7*) D Kiernan, cld on ldrs frm hfwy, rdn and no extr o'r 3 fs out. . . . .(5 to 2 op 3 to 1)	5
	CAPTAIN NAVAR (Ire) 6-11-4 V Smith, rcd keenly, wth ldrs till lost pl 11 fs out, styd on one pace last 3 furlongs. . . . .(12 to 1 op 8 to 1 tchd 14 to 1 and 16 to 1)	6
	PAPERWORK PETE (Ire) 4-10-11 (5*) R McGrath, hld up in mid-div, rdn and no hdwy frm 4 out. . . . .(10 to 1 op 12 to 1 tchd 16 to 1)	7
	KOMASEPH 4-11-2 A S Smith, led aftr 5 fs, hdd 9 furlongs out, wknd quickly 6 out, tld off. . . . .(10 to 1 op 7 to 1 tchd 14 to 1 and 16 to 1)	8
	HAVANA EXPRESS 4-11-2 I Lawrence, al beh, tld off. . . . .(12 to 1 op 7 to 1 tchd 14 to 1 and 16 to 1)	9

80

74^4 GENERAL MONTY 4-11-2 N Williamson, *led for 5 fs, led ag'n 9 furlongs out till five out, tld off.* ....(8 to 1 op 5 to 1 tchd 10 to 1 and 11 to 1) 10
BERTIE 6-10-13 (5*) S Taylor, *rcd keenly, prmnt till drpd rear hfwy, tld off.*........................(33 to 1 op 25 to 1) 11
AUTUMN FLAME (Ire) 5-10-6 (7*) S Porritt, *trkd ldrs till wknd frm hfwy, tld off.*.........................(16 to 1 op 12 to 1) 12
Dist: 5l, 4l, 8l, 5l, 7l, 5l, dist, 9l, 1½l, 21l. 3m 40.20s. (12 Ran).
(Mrs H Johnson Houghton), G F Johnson Houghton

CARLISLE (firm)
Saturday September 21st
Going Correction: MINUS 0.40 sec. per fur.

694 Ullswater Novices' Hurdle Class E (4-y-o and up) £1,660 2½m 110yds (1:40)

609^* SUJUD (Ire) 4-10-12 R Garritty, *hld up and beh, hdwy 4 out, rdn to ld appr last, styd on wl.* ....(Evens fav op 5 to 4 tchd 11 to 8) 1
610^7 THALEROS 6-10-12 J Callaghan, *hld up gng wl, hdwy 4 out, ev ch nxt, sn rdn and one pace appr last.* (14 to 1 op 7 to 1) 2
533^* MILLION DANCER (bl) 4-11-3 D Bridgwater, *led and sn clr, hit 4th, jnd 3 out, rdn nxt and soon hdd, wknd.* ....(9 to 4 op 2 to 1 tchd 5 to 2) 3
PANGERAN (USA) 4-10-10 J Supple, *prmnt, rdn 3 out, wknd nxt.*...............(16 to 1 op 10 to 1 tchd 20 to 1) 4
551^* WAR WHOOP 4-11-3 M Foster, *in tch, rdn alng 4 out, wknd quickly and tld off.*........ (7 to 2 op 5 to 2 tchd 4 to 1) 5
370^5 SCALLYMILL 6-10-7 Mr K Whelan, *chsd ldrs, rdn and wknd 4 out, tld off.*.........................(50 to 1 op 25 to 1) 6
POLLY CINDERS 5-10-7 B Fenton, *beh frm 5th, tld off nxt.* ....(50 to 1 op 33 to 1) 7
609 OUSEFLEET BOY 4-10-10 A Dobbin, *al rear, beh whn pld up bef 6th.*............................(50 to 1 op 33 to 1) pu
Dist: 7l, 3½l, 1¼l, dist, dist, dist. 4m 45.40s. a 3.40s (8 Ran).
(D J Lever), M D Hammond

695 Thirlmere Novices' Chase Class E (5-y-o and up) £2,099 2m.......... (2:15)

TO BE THE BEST 6-10-12 J Burke, *pld hrd, made all and sn clr, rdn alng 3 out, kpt on wl frm nxt.*... (6 to 1 op 12 to 1) 1
558^2 CAXTON (USA) 9-10-12 N Williamson, *not fluent, hld up, hdwy hfwy, hit 7th and 8th, mstk 4 out and sn rdn, no imprsn frm nxt.*......................(2 to 1 on op 5 to 2 on) 2
546^7 BOETHIUS (USA) 7-10-12 P Waggott, *chsd wnr till wknd bef 4 out.*...............................(12 to 1 op 7 to 1) 3
608^7 RICHMOND (Ire) 8-10-12 B Storey, *hld up and beh, outpcd and remindors hfwy, rdn 4 out, styd on frm 2 out.* ....(7 to 2 op 3 to 1) 4
Dist: 26l, 16l, nk. 3m 57.20s. a 3.20s (4 Ran).
(Exors Of The Late Mr R R Lamb), D A Lamb

696 Brotherswater Handicap Hurdle Class E (0-115 4-y-o and up) £2,188 2½m 110yds......................... (2:50)

448^* SHAHRANI [109] 4-11-9 D Bridgwater, *set steady pace, quickened appr 2 out, rdn approaching last, kpt on wl.* ....(6 to 4 on op 7 to 4 on tchd 11 to 8 on) 1
653^3 GONE BY (Ire) [109] (v) 8-11-11 G Bradley, *trkd wnr, chlgd 3 out, rdn alng aftr nxt, one pace.*......(5 to 4 tchd 11 to 8) 2
Won by 4l. 4m 55.00s. a 13.00s (2 Ran).
SR: -/-/ (A S Helaissi And Mr S Helaissi), M C Pipe

697 'Red Rum' Handicap Chase Class D (0-125 5-y-o and up) £2,801 3m (3:25)

662^3 THE BLUE BOY (Ire) [99] (bl) 8-10-8 N Williamson, *al chasing ldr, effrt 4 out, rdn nxt, drvn to ld last, ran on.* ....(2 to 1 tchd 5 to 2) 1
475^4 KUSHBALOO [115] 11-11-10 B Storey, *pld hrd, led, mstk tenth, rdn appr 2 out, tiring whn blun and hdd last, no extr.* ....(5 to 4 on op 5 to 4) 2
475^5 UPWELL [91] 12-10-0 K Johnson, *chsd ldg pair thrght, outpcd and beh frm 11th.*...............(33 to 1 op 25 to 1) 3
663^4 JENDEE (Ire) [91] 8-9-12^1 (3*) G Cahill, *al rear, pld up bef tenth.*........................(12 to 1 op 8 to 1) pu
586 BANNTOWN BILL (Ire) [95] (v) 7-10-4 D Bridgwater, *in tch, scrubbed alng 9th, beh whn pld up bef nxt.* ....(5 to 1 op 7 to 2 tchd 11 to 2) pu
Dist: 5l, dist. 5m 59.90s. a 7.90s (5 Ran).
(T M Morris), P Bowen

698 Rydal Water Handicap Hurdle Class F (0-100 4-y-o and up) £1,744 2m 1f .... (3:55)

665^3 BOLANEY GIRL (Ire) [80] 7-10-8 A Dobbin, *hld up and beh, smooth hdwy 3 out, chlgd on bit nxt, sn led and pushed clr, easily.*..............................(4 to 1 op 6 to 1) 1
STAGS FELL [72] 11-10-0 Carol Cuthbert, *chsd ldrs, hdwy 4 out, led briefly 2 out, sn hdd and one pace und pres.* ....(33 to 1 op 20 to 1) 2
572^4 SOUSON (Ire) [86] (bl) 8-11-0 K Jones, *chsd ldr, led aftr 4th till 3 out, kpt on und pres...* (10 to 1 op 6 to 1 tchd 12 to 1) 3
405^5 WELL APPOINTED (Ire) [96] 7-11-10 B Storey, *prmnt, effrt and led briefly 3 out, sn rdn, hdd and one pace nxt.* ....(9 to 2 op 4 to 1 tchd 5 to 1) 4
SHARP SENSATION [100] 6-12-0 P Niven, *pld hrd, trkd ldrs, effrt 4 out, ev ch nxt, sn rdn and btn.* ....(11 to 2 op 5 to 1 tchd 6 to 1) 5
572^3 TAKE TWO [92] 8-11-3 (3*) G Cahill, *prmnt, ev ch 3 out, sn rdn and wknd nxt.*........... (6 to 1 op 5 to 1 tchd 7 to 1) 6
557^3 SILVER SLEEVE (Ire) [80] (bl) 4-10-6 R Garritty, *hld up, effrt and hdwy appr 3 out, sn rdn and btn bef nxt.* ....(6 to 1 op 5 to 1) 7
633^2 BUGLET [93] 6-11-7 D Bridgwater, *led, rdn alng and hdd aftr 4th, lost pl quickly four out, sn pld up.* ....(2 to 1 fav op 11 to 4 tchd 3 to 1) pu
Dist: 6l, sht-hd, 10l, 3l, ½l, 5l. 4m 2.80s. b 0.20s (8 Ran).
SR: 14/-/14/14/15/6/-/-/ (J Proudfoot), F P Murtagh

699 Bassenthwaite Lake Novices' Chase Class E (5-y-o and up) £2,060 3m (4:30)

GERMAN LEGEND 6-10-12 J Burke, *trkd ldrs, hdwy 12th, led briefly nxt, cl up till dsptd ld 3 out, sn rdn, drvn and led r-in, kpt on wl.*........(9 to 1 op 8 to 1 tchd 10 to 1) 1
605 CUCHULLAINS GOLD (Ire) 8-11-5 N Williamson, *hld up, gd hdwy 12th, led appr 14th, rdn 3 out, drvn last, hdd and no extr r-in.*.......................(11 to 10 on op 5 to 4 on) 2
608^2 BUYERS DREAM (Ire) (v) 6-10-9 (3*) G Cahill, *chsd ldr, led 11th, blun 13th and sn hdd, rdn and ev ch 4 out, wknd nxt.* ....(7 to 4 tchd 2 to 1) 3
548 MORE JOY (bl) 8-10-12 D Bentley, *led to 11th, mstk nxt, sn rdn, wknd appr 4 out.*....(9 to 1 op 8 to 1 tchd 10 to 1) 4
459 SAND KING (NZ) (v) 10-10-12 A Dobbin, *mstk 1st, prmnt till pld up bef 6th, dismounted.* ....(10 to 1 op 12 to 1 tchd 16 to 1) pu
Dist: 2l, 9l, dist. 6m 8.50s. a 16.50s (5 Ran).
(D G Pryde), D A Lamb

700 Derwent Intermediate Open National Hunt Flat Class H (4,5,6-y-o) £1,224 2m 1f.........................(5:05)

DURAID (Ire) 4-11-9 Richard Guest, *hld up, smooth hdwy 6 fs out, led 4 furlongs out, sn clr.* ....(2 to 1 on op 5 to 4 on tchd Evens) 1
SIOUX WARRIOR 4-10-9 (7*) N Horrocks, *chsd ldrs, effrt o'r 4 fs out, sn rdn, no ch wth£ wnr.* ....(6 to 1 op 4 to 1 tchd 7 to 1) 2
HENPECKED (Ire) 5-11-4 R Garritty, *hld up and beh, hdwy hfwy, rdn 4 out, kpt on same pace.*...... (6 to 1 op 5 to 2) 3
BEST FRIEND 4-10-11 Mr N Wilson, *led and clr, rdn alng 6 fs out, hdd 4 furlongs out, grad wknd.* ....(9 to 1 op 5 to 1 tchd 10 to 1) 4
FOUR FROM HOME (Ire) 4-11-2 A Roche, *chsd ldrs, rdn 4 fs out, sn wknd.*................................(8 to 1) 5
GRACE AND FAVOUR 5-10-13 J Burke, *chsd ldrs till rdn and outpcd 5 fs out.*........................(20 to 1 op 12 to 1) 6
THE KNITTER 4-11-2 M Moloney, *chsd ldrs till rdn and wknd 6 fs out.*...............................(20 to 1 op 12 to 1) 7
JOE'S BIT OF GOLD 4-10-11 P Niven, *al rear.* ....(14 to 1 tchd 12 to 1) 8
VALE OF OAK 5-10-13 B Harding, *mid-div tilllost pl hfwy, sn beh.*............. (25 to 1 op 12 to 1 tchd 33 to 1) 9
IN THE FUTURE (Ire) 5-10-10 (3*) G Cahill, *al beh.* ....(16 to 1 op 12 to 1) 10
GREEN AN CASTLE 6-10-13 Mr T Morrison, *chsd ldr to hfwy, sn lost pl, tld off fnl 4 fs.*........ (25 to 1 op 14 to 1) 11
WERE'S ME MONEY 6-10-13 Miss Sue Nichol, *al beh, tld off fnl 4 fs.*...........................(16 to 1 op 12 to 1) 12
Dist: 6l, 6l, 1½l, 16l, 3l, 3½l, nk, 5l, 1l, 20l. 4m 3.30s. (12 Ran).
(A Suddes), Denys Smith

DOWN ROYAL (IRE) (good to firm)
Saturday September 21st

701 Moira Maiden Hurdle (5-y-o and up) £1,370 2½m.....................(2:30)

686 PEACEFULL RIVER (Ire) 7-10-8 (7*) B D Murtagh, (14 to 1) 1
554^3 CASTLEROYAL (Ire) 7-11-6 P McWilliams,......(5 to 2 fav) 2
644^2 SANDRA LOUISE (Ire) 6-10-8 (7*) Mr A Ross,......(11 to 4) 3
622^5 DOTTIE'S DOUBLE (Ire) 5-11-1 T P Rudd,..........(6 to 1) 4
CAIRNCROSS (Ire) 5-10-13 (7*) R Burke,..........(8 to 1) 5
TERESIAN GIRL (Ire) 6-11-9 J P Broderick,........(10 to 1) 6
622^6 BALLYHAYS LODGE (Ire) 7-11-1 C N Bowens,.....(12 to 1) 7
622^8 HILLTOP BOY (Ire) 7-11-1 (5*) J Butler,............(9 to 2) pu
Dist: 1l, 4½l, 13l, 8l. 4m 45.50s. (8 Ran).
(Mrs B Carty), Norman Cassidy

702 James Nicholson 'Any Excuse Will Do' Novice Chase (5-y-o and up) £1,370 2½m.................................. (3:30)

576^3 BLACKIE CONNORS (Ire) 5-11-8 P L Malone,.. (5 to 4 on) 1
496^5 TALL ORDER (Ire) 7-11-11 (3*) U Smyth,...........(7 to 2) 2

680⁸ PALMURA 9-12-0 J P Broderick, ... (9 to 2) 3
680 MISS TOP (Ire) 6-11-2 (7*) R Burke, ... (10 to 1) 4
Dist: 25l, 2l, dist. 5m 15.40s. (4 Ran).

(Miss I T Oakes), Miss I T Oakes

703 James Nicholson Wine Merchants Flat Race (4 & 5-y-o) £1,370 2m . . . . . (5:30)

577² LADY OF GRANGE (Ire) 4-10-11 (7*) Mr G Elliott, . . . (2 to 1) 1
REGGIE'S HONOUR (Ire) 4-11-1 (3*) Mr B M Cash,
. . . . (7 to 4 fav) 2
BRADLEYS CORNER (Ire) 5-11-7 (7*) Mr L J Gracey,
. . . . (10 to 1) 3
397³ AN SEABHAC (Ire) 4-11-2 (7*) Mr T J Beattie, ... (7 to 2) 4
BOYNE VIEW (Ire) 4-10-11 (7*) Mr C Barnwell, ... (16 to 1) 5
497 MC CLATCHEY (Ire) 5-12-0 Mr P F Graffin, ... (10 to 1) 6
SECRET PRINCE (Ire) 5-11-7 (7*) Mr G J McKeever, (16 to 1) 7
Dist: 7l, 3l, 4½l, 11l. 3m 36.10s. (7 Ran).

(Raymond McConn), F Flood

MARKET RASEN (good to firm)
Saturday September 21st
Going Correction: NIL

704 Scania 4-series 'Horsepower' Hurdle Novices' Handicap Class E (0-100 4-y-o and up) £2,792 2m 1f 110yds. . (2:10)

330⁴ INDRAPURA (Ire) [91] 4-11-10 C Maude, hld up last to 5th,
quickened betw last 2, sn led r-in, rdn out
. . . . . . (15 to 8 fav op 6 to 4 tchd 5 to 2 and 11 to 4) 1
371³ RAGAMUFFIN ROMEO [70] 7-10-5 N Mann, chsd ldr til led 2
out, blun last, sn hdd, not reco'r . . . . . . (9 to 1 op 8 to 1) 2
416³ COUNT OF FLANDERS (Ire) [75] 6-10-10 A S Smith, jmpd
awkwardly in ld, hdd 2 out, ev ch appr last, not quicken
. . . . (9 to 4 op 5 to 2 tchd 2 to 1) 3
493² SEA GOD [88] 5-11-9 W Worthington, hld up gng wl, effrt aftr
3 out, drvn and little response appr last. (4 to 1 op 7 to 2) 4
520⁸ IRIE MON (Ire) [80] 4-10-13 R Dunwoody, hld up, effrt aftr 3
out, hit nxt, sn btn. . . . . (7 to 1 op 6 to 1) 5
MERRYHILL GOLD [71] 5-10-6 L Wyer, swrvd lft strt, chsd
ldrs til lost pl aftr 3 out (10 to 1 tchd 12 to 1 and 8 to 1) 6
294⁸ KAJOSTAR [65] 6-9-7 (7*) O Burrows, mid-div, wnt 3rd and ev
ch 3 out, sn rdn and btn . . . . (50 to 1 op 33 to 1) 7
533⁶ HATTA RIVER (USA) [66] (bl) 6-10-1 A Maguire, chsd ldg pair
til jmpd slwly 5th, lost pl quickly, tld off 2 out
. . . . (20 to 1 op 12 to 1) 8
Dist: 1¼l, 1¼l, ¾l, 4l, 1¼l, ¾l, dist. 4m 15.20s. a 14.20s (8 Ran).

(Martin Pipe Racing Club), M C Pipe

705 BBC Radio Lincolnshire Selling Hurdle Class G (3-y-o) Novices' £2,136 2m 1f 110yds. . . . . (2:45)

IN A TIZZY 10-5 A P McCoy, led aftr 1st, jmpd wl and sn clr, 20
ls ahead appr 2 out, kpt on well r-in
. . . . (13 to 2 op 8 to 1 tchd 9 to 1) 1
436³ HOME COOKIN' 10-5 C Maude, chsd ldrs, wnt second 5th,
hrd rdn and not rch wnr frm 2 out, hit last
. . . . (5 to 2 fav op 7 to 2 tchd 4 to 1 and 9 to 2) 2
584² TABLETS OF STONE (Ire) 10-10 M Bosley, mid-field, moderate hdwy frm 3 out, hit last, styd on . . . . (7 to 1 op 9 to 2) 3
614⁵ UNCLE GEORGE (v) 10-10 A Maguire, chsd ldrs, wnt 3rd 5th,
disputing second pl whn hit 2 out, drvn and not keen aftr
. . . . (3 to 1 op 7 to 4 tchd 7 to 2) 4
HANNAHS BAY 10-2 (3*) F Leahy, wl beh til some hdwy 5th,
drvn and not quicken 2 out. . . . . (25 to 1 op 16 to 1) 5
488⁶ RECALL TO MIND (bl) 10-7 (3*) D Parker, led til aftr 1st, chsd
ldr til rdn and mstk 4th, reminders and wknd appr 2 out
. . . . (25 to 1 op 14 to 1) 6
KAI'S LADY (Ire) 9-12 (7*) O Burrows, sn towards rear, tld off 3
out. . . . . (40 to 1 op 33 to 1 tchd 50 to 1) 7
ON THE HOME RUN 9-12 (7*) N T Egan, mid-field to 4th, tld
off 3 out. . . . . (25 to 1 op 14 to 1 tchd 33 to 1) 8
EARLY WARNING 10-5 J Osborne, chsd ldrs to 3rd, tld off 3
out. . . . . (13 to 2 op 4 to 1 tchd 7 to 1) 9
EURO EXPRESS (bl) 10-10 L Wyer, sn wl beh, tld off 3 out,
moderate hdwy aftr nxt (14 to 1 op 10 to 1 tchd 16 to 1) 10
SIZZLING SERENADE 10-5 P McLoughlin, mstks, no ch frm
4th, tld off 3 out. . . . . (25 to 1 tchd 33 to 1) 11
SEEKING DESTINY 10-10 W Worthington, jmpd badly,
no ch aftr blun 3rd, tld off 3 out
. . . . (20 to 1 op 14 to 1 tchd 25 to 1) 12
FERGAL (USA) 10-10 O Pears, al rear, no ch frm 4th, tld off 3
out, mstk last . . . . (40 to 1 op 33 to 1 tchd 50 to 1) 13
542²⁶ REMEMBER STAR 10-5 F Jousset, chsd ldrs til wknd 5th, sn
wl tld off. . . . . (33 to 1 tchd 50 to 1) 14
GHOSTLY APPARITION 10-10 R Supple, jmpd badly, sn tld
off. . . . . (5 to 1 op 10 to 1) 15
FLORRIE'N 10-5 D Gallagher, jmpd badly, sn tld off
. . . . (40 to 1 op 20 to 1 tchd 50 to 1) 16
ECCENTRIC DANCER (bl) 10-5 A S Smith, jmpd badly, sn tld
off, pld up bef 2 out. . . . . (5 to 1 op 10 to 1) pu
Dist: 7l, ¾l, ½l, 1¼l, 19l, 3½l, 6l, 1¾l, 1¾l, 8l. 4m 16.80s. a 15.80s (17 Ran).

(B & J Racing And Breeding Syndicate), P C Haslam

706 Scania 1996 Truck Of The Year Chase Class D Handicap (0-120 5-y-o and up) £4,497 2½m. . . . . (3:15)

584⁴ ANDRELOT [113] (bl) 9-11-12 A P McCoy, jmpd boldly, led
second, sn ten ls clr, rdn appr 3 out, lft wl clear nxt, blun and
pckd badly last, eased r-in. . . . . . . (5 to 1 tchd 11 to 2) 1
541² MERLINS DREAM (Ire) [103] 7-11-2 J Osborne, sn wl beh, rdn
8th, moderate hdwy 11th, 30 ls 4th aftr nxt, rapid prog 2 out,
wnt second r-in, not rch wnr
. . . . (2 to 1 fav tchd 9 to 4 and 5 to 2) 2
668² MAGGOTS GREEN [99] 9-10-12 R Johnson, not fluent, led til
jmpd slwly second, hit 9th, nvr dngrs aftr, lft second 2 out, until
mstk last, lost second r-in. . . . . . . (13 to 1 tchd 14 to 1) 3
DARK OAK [110] 10-11-9 L Wyer, sn tld off, mstk 12th, kpt on
stdly frm 3 out. . . . . (13 to 2 op 5 to 1 tchd 7 to 1) 4
607⁵ CLARES OWN [95] 12-10-8 A Thornton, chsd ldrs til rdn and
wknd 8th, 40 ls 5th aftr 12th, no imprsn (25 to 1 op 16 to 1) 5
651² HOUGHTON [113] 10-11-5 (7*) Mr R Burton, mstk 9th, rdn
ch 3 out, 4 ls second and hld whn f nxt. . . (8 to 1 op 13 to 2) 6
663 WISE ADVICE (Ire) [95] 6-10-8 A Maguire, chsd ldr frm 5th, ev
ch 3 out, 4 ls second and hld whn f nxt. . (8 to 1 op 13 to 2) f
Dist: 8l, 1¼l, 12l, ¾l, 20l. 4m 56.90s. a 7.90s (7 Ran).
SR: 19/1/-/-/ (H Jones), P Bowen

707 Audrey Buttery Reunion Handicap Hurdle Class C (0-130 4-y-o and up) £3,795 3m. (3:45)

531 TALLYWAGGER [116] 9-12-0 N Bentley, hld up, mstk 7th and
lost pl, rallied aftr 3 out, led last, drvn and ran on gmely
. . . . (7 to 1 op 9 to 2) 1
519⁴ ORDOG MOR (Ire) [102] 7-11-0 A P McCoy, led, wnt clr 8th,
rdn appr 2 out, hdd last, drvn and no extr fnl 100 yards
. . . . (Evens fav op 5 to 4) 2
550³ RED JAM JAR [93] 11-10-5 N Smith, trkd ldg pair, cld 6th, wnt
second 8th, hit nxt, ran on one pace aftr 2 out
. . . . (8 to 1 op 6 to 1 tchd 9 to 1) 3
585³ CHINA MAIL (Ire) [94] 4-10-13 T J Murphy, sn pushed alng in
rear, hdwy 8th, 3rd and clsr 3 out, unbl to chal aftr
. . . . (9 to 2 op 4 to 1) 4
572 FRONTIER FLIGHT (USA) [95] 6-10-4 (3*) E Husband, beh,
last frm 8th, tld off 3 out. . . . . . . (33 to 1 op 14 to 1) 5
125 MOOBAKKR (USA) [95] 5-10-4 A S Smith, chsd ldr to 8th, sn
wknd, tld off and pld up bef 2 out
. . . . (3 to 1 op 5 to 1 tchd 11 to 2) pu
Dist: 1l, 2½l, 27l, 12l. 5m 58.70s. a 19.70s (6 Ran).

(Mrs Susan Moore), G M Moore

708 Scanlink For Scania Novices' Chase Class D (5-y-o and up) £3,873 3m 1f . . . . (4:20)

640⁴ CATS RUN 8-11-12 R Supple, led to 4th, led tenth to 13th,
dsptd ld 15th til led 3 out, clr appr last eased r-in
. . . . (4 to 1 op 3 to 1 on) 1
DEISE MARSHALL (Ire) 8-11-0 A S Smith, led aftr 4th to tenth,
led 13th, jnd 15th, hdd 3 out, sn outpcd
. . . . (7 to 2 op 5 to 2 tchd 4 to 1) 2
608 DURHAM HORNET 9-11-0 N Smith, al last, struggling whn
jmpd slwly 6th, tld off and eased frm 15th
. . . . (14 to 1 op 10 to 1) 3
Dist: 10l, dist. 6m 22.60s. a 22.60s (3 Ran).

(Mrs Ann Key), John R Upson

709 Scania 4-series 'King Of The Road' Hurdle Class D Handicap (0-120 4-y-o and up) £3,103 2m 3f 110yds. . . (4:50)

659⁴ BELLROI (Ire) [100] 5-11-2 A Maguire, pressed ldr, mstk 5th,
rdn to ld 2 out, mistake last, styd on
. . . . (13 to 8 fav op 6 to 4 tchd 7 to 4) 1
631² WOLLBOLL [82] 6-10-0 V Smith, led til hdd 2 out, drvn and
one pace whn blun last. . . . . (7 to 1 op 6 to 1) 2
SCUD MISSILE (Ire) [102] 5-11-4 A Thornton, chsd ldrs, wnt
3rd 7th, pushed alng and lost tch wth lders aftr 3 out, kpt on
stdly. . . . . (10 to 1 tchd 12 to 1) 3
546² BURES (Ire) [112] 5-11-7 (7*) B Grattan, hld up and beh,
outpcd 3 out, some hdwy nxt. . . . . . (20 to 1 op 10 to 1) 4
571² WAMDHA (Ire) [100] 6-11-4 A S Smith, beh, effrt 7th, lost tch
aftr 3 out. . . . . (7 to 1 op 6 to 1 tchd 9 to 1) 5
631 STAY WITH ME (Fr) [90] 6-10-1 (7*) Mr R Thornton, hld up,
hdwy 7th, lost tch aftr 3 out . . . . . . (14 to 1 op 10 to 1) 6
616² PETER MONAMY [103] (bl) 4-11-0 (3*) D Walsh, mstks, chsd
ldrs til blun 6th, mistake nxt and lost tch tld off
. . . . (5 to 1 op 3 to 1 tchd 11 to 2) 7
669 LAYHAM LOW (Ire) [100] 5-11-2 J Osborne, trkd ldrs to 6th, tld
off aftr 3 out, pld up bef nxt (4 to 1 op 5 to 1 tchd 7 to 1) pu
Dist: 3½l, 13l, 1¼l, 1¾l, 8l, dist. 4m 46.70s. a 16.70s (8 Ran).

(Mrs G A E Smith), M H Tompkins

LISTOWEL (IRE) (good to firm)
Monday September 23rd

710 Bank Of Ireland Handicap Hurdle (0-116 5-y-o and up) £4,795 2m (3:00)

684[3] MONTE'S EVENING (Ire) [-] 8-10-0 P L Malone, ..(7 to 2 jt-fav) 1
523[4] TEMPLEROAN PRINCE [-] 9-11-12 R Dunwoody, .. (4 to 1) 2
564[3] JOHNNY'S DREAM (Ire) [-] 6-10-8 (5") G Cotter, ..(7 to 2 jt-fav) 3
463[5] SHANRUE (Ire) [-] 6-11-4 C F Swan, ... (6 to 1) 4
565[7] FAIR SOCIETY (Ire) [-] (bl) 5-10-3 M P Hourigan, ...(8 to 1) 5
589[3] LISHILLAUN (Ire) [-] (bl) 6-9-4 (5") Susan A Finn, ...(14 to 1) 6
579[2] WHEREWILITALL END (Ire) [-] 5-11-7 (3") U Smyth, (4 to 1) f
Dist: 1½l, ½l, 10l, 2l. 4m 22.60s. (7 Ran).
(Mrs T J Moore), Peter Casey

711 Patsy Byrne Beginners Chase (4-y-o and up) £4,795 2¼m 110yds.... (4:20)

626[3] KENTUCKY BABY (Ire) 6-11-9 N Williamson, ...(5 to 4 fav) 1
680[5] STRONG BOOST (USA) 5-11-9 R Dunwoody, ...(9 to 2) 2
SILENT SNEEZE (Ire) (bl) 6-11-2 (7") Mr K Beecher, (12 to 1) 3
209[5] TREENS FOLLY (bl) 7-12-0 K F O'Brien, ...(33 to 1) 4
SANDYS GIRL (Ire) 8-11-9 J P Broderick, ...(16 to 1) 5
MORE BANTER 6-12-0 F Woods, ...(9 to 4) 6
525 TOM THE BOY VI (Ire) 6-11-7 (7") M D Murphy, ...(33 to 1) 7
Dist: 7l, 25l, 4l, 12l. 4m 42.30s. (7 Ran).
(P G Tierney), Thomas J Taaffe

712 Devon Inn 3-Y-O Hurdle £3,767 2m .... (4:50)

620* EVRIZA (Ire) 11-0 C F Swan, ...(5 to 2) 1
341[3] GREENHUE (Ire) 11-0 T P Rudd, ...(8 to 1) 2
522* RHUM DANCER (Ire) 11-3 C O'Dwyer, ...(11 to 8 fav) 3
620[2] FAIRLY SHARP (Ire) 10-9 J Shortt, ...(8 to 1) 4
TAKEAMEMO (Ire) 10-9 R Dunwoody, ...(5 to 1) 5
442[4] MISS ROBERTO (Ire) 11-0 T J Murphy, ...(20 to 1) 6
620[5] MAIDEN MIST (Ire) 10-9 N Williamson, ...(25 to 1) 7
620[3] KOKO NOR (Ire) 11-0 L P Cusack, ...(25 to 1) 8
620 ALTHOUGH 10-7 (7") S P Kelly, ...(25 to 1) 9
Dist: 7l, 6l, 12l, 1½l. 3m 57.10s. (9 Ran).
(Mrs Sally Carey), A P O'Brien

713 John F. McGuire (4-Y-O) I.N.H. Flat Race £3,767 2m............... (5:55)

527[2] ANTICS (Ire) 10-9 (7") Mrs C Harrison, ...(12 to 1) 1
581[2] WEST OF WAIKIKI (Ire) 11-2 (5") Mr R Walsh, ...(3 to 1) 2
288[2] KERANI (USA) 11-7 Mr P Fenton, ...(2 to 1 fav) 3
CHRISTINES GALE (Ire) 10-9 (7") Miss A O'Brien, (10 to 1) 4
288[9] JACK DORY (Ire) 11-4 (3") Mr K Whelan, ...(14 to 1) 5
TIRYAM (USA) 11-0 (7") Mr A J Dempsey, ...(14 to 1) 6
PHARDANTE LILLY (Ire) 10-9 (7") Miss S J Leahy, (20 to 1) 7
686[2] SPENDID (Ire) 11-0 (7") Miss A L Crowley, ...(5 to 1) 8
LUNAR LADY (Ire) 10-9 (7") Mr R F O'Gorman, ...(12 to 1) 9
434[3] MONDEO ROSE (Ire) 10-11 (5") Mr B M Cash, ...(14 to 1) 10
637[5] MASTER EXECUTIVE (Ire) 11-0 (7") Mr S P Hennessy,
........................(12 to 1) 11
TOM SAID (Ire) 10-9 (7") Mr J O'Hanlon, ...(33 to 1) 12
RHOMAN STAR (Ire) 11-0 (7") Mr B A Murphy, ...(14 to 1) 13
PEJAYS DUCA (Ire) 11-0 (7") Mr P J Colville, ...(33 to 1) 14
BOPTWOPHAR (Ire) 11-4 (3") Mr E Norris, ...(7 to 1) ro
VIKING BUOY (Ire) 11-0 (7") Mr J T McNamara, ...(25 to 1) su
Dist: ½l, ¾l, 14l, 2l. 3m 53.30s. (16 Ran).
(Mrs C Harrison), Mrs C Harrison

LISTOWEL (IRE) (good to firm)
Tuesday September 24th

714 Sean Graham Handicap Chase (0-102 4-y-o and up) £4,110 2½m.... (3:50)

CORYMANDEL [-] 7-11-8 R Dunwoody, ...(12 to 1) 1
602[2] FAYS FOLLY (Ire) [-] 7-9-9 (7") R P Hogan, ...(7 to 1) 2
580[5] WACKO JACKO (Ire) [-] 7-11-8 J P Broderick, ..(9 to 2 fav) 3
636[6] QUATTRO [-] 6-11-3 T P Treacy, ...(8 to 1) 4
580[4] NEBRASKA [-] 10-11-4 M P Dwyer, ...(12 to 1) 5
636[4] MICKS DELIGHT (Ire) [-] 6-12-0 C F Swan, ...(7 to 1) 6
588[2] TRIPTODICKS (Ire) [-] 6-9-11 (7") A O'Shea, ...(6 to 1) f
621 LA CIENAGA [-] 12-11-1 K F O'Brien, ...(16 to 1) ref
602 BALLINABOOLA GROVE [-] 9-10-11 J Shortt, ...(6 to 1) pu
680[3] WHAT IS THE PLAN (Ire) [-] 7-10-3 N Williamson,...(8 to 1) pu
604* COSHLA EXPRESSO [-] 8-11-4 P L Malone, ...(11 to 1) l
Dist: 5l, 2½l, 11l, 4l. 5m 28.20s. (11 Ran).
(M J E Thornhill), H de Bromhead

715 Listowel Races Lartigue Handicap Hurdle (Grade 2) (4-y-o) £16,250 2m .... (4:30)

303[4] KHAYRAWANI (Ire) [-] 11-2 C O'Dwyer, wl plcd, jmpd slwly 3 out, smooth prog to ld bef nxt, cmftbly.........(9 to 4 fav) 1
428* JUST LITTLE [-] 11-6 N Williamson, wtd wth, prog bef 4 out and aftr 2 out, veered lft r-in, fnshd second, plcd 3rd. (10 to 1) 2D

METASTASIO (Ire) 11-5 H Rogers, wtd wth, prog bef 6th, dsptd ld 4 out, sn led, hdd before 2 out, hmpd r-in, fnshd 3rd, plcd second..................(12 to 1) 2
TRADE DISPUTE (Ire) [-] (bl) 11-9 R Dunwoody, trkd ldr till led 6th, jnd 4 out, sn hdd, wknd bef 2 out............(100 to 30) 4
220[5] VESPERADA (Ire) [-] 10-11 J Shortt, wl plcd, rdn aftr 3 out, sn wknd...................................(16 to 1) 5
463 LIFE SUPPORT (Ire) [-] 11-1 M P Dwyer, rear, rdn bef 2 out, not quicken...................................(8 to 1) 6
562* REEVES (Ire) [-] 11-1 D J Casey, al rear, rdn aftr 3 out, not quicken...................................(7 to 1) 7
364* SHARATAN (Ire) [-] 11-8 T P Treacy, wl plcd till rdn and wknd aftr 4 out...................................(8 to 1) 8
486* KATIYMANN (Ire) [-] 10-9 T Horgan, led till hdd 6th, rdn and wknd bef 3 out...................................(8 to 1) 9
THEATREWORLD (Ire) [-] 12-0 C F Swan, wl plcd till f second.
...................................(8 to 1) f
Dist: 6l, ½l, 6l, 14l. 4m 4.30s. (10 Ran).
(John P McManus), P Burke

716 T.J.Cross Maiden Hurdle (4 & 5-y-o) £3,817 2m.....................(5:05)

289[3] SENTOSA STAR (Ire) 5-12-0 M P Hourigan, ...(Evens fav) 1
560[5] LEWISHAM (Ire) 4-11-9 C F Swan, ...(5 to 1) 2
185[2] HILL OF HOPE (Ire) 5-11-6 W Slattery, ...(33 to 1) 3
JOHN'S RIGHT (Ire) 5-11-6 T J Murphy, ...(25 to 1) 4
VASILIKI (Ire) 4-11-4 M P Dwyer, ...(33 to 1) 5
122 SLIGO CHAMPION (Ire) 5-11-6 J K Kinane, ...(66 to 1) 6
561[4] HIGH PARK LADY (Ire) 5-11-1 P M Verling, ...(25 to 1) 7
635[3] ASK THE BUTLER (Ire) 5-12-0 C O'Dwyer, ...(5 to 1) 8
MOUNTHENRY LADY (Ire) 5-10-8 (7") D Flood, ...(25 to 1) 9
624 TAZ (Ire) 4-10-13 J P Broderick, ...(100 to 1) 10
KING OF KERRY (Ire) 5-12-0 T Horgan, ...(5 to 2) f
464 ZIGGY THE GREAT (Ire) 4-11-4 K F O'Brien, ...(33 to 1) pu
Dist: 12l, 13l, 2½l, 3½l. 4m 13.80s. (12 Ran).
(C J Deasy), Michael Hourigan

717 M.J.Carroll I.N.H. Flat Race (5-y-o) £4,110 2m.....................(5:35)

BORO BOW (Ire) 11-2 (7") Mr B E Hill, ...(100 to 30) 1
681[3] EASTERN CUSTOM (Ire) 11-6 (3") Mr R O'Neill, ... (6 to 1) 2
SIMPLY ACOUSTIC (Ire) 11-9 Mr P Fenton, ...(Evens fav) 3
434[5] FELICITY'S PRIDE (Ire) 11-2 (7") Mr D P Coakley, ...(7 to 1) 4
KILKEA (Fr) 11-2 (7") Mr A Daly, ...(14 to 1) 5
192 LOCH WEE (Ire) 11-2 (7") Mr J T McNamara, ...(25 to 1) 6
CASTLE GAP (Ire) 11-7 (7") Mr A Ross, ...(7 to 1) 7
FORTYNINEPLUS (Ire) 11-7 (7") Mr J Creighton, ...(14 to 1) pu
Dist: 9l, 10l, 7l, 6l. 4m 4.60s. (8 Ran).
(J P Hill), P Mullins

LISTOWEL (IRE) (good to yielding (races 1,3,5), good (2,4))
Wednesday September 25th

718 Mallinckrodt Veterinary Hurdle (4-y-o and up) £4,110 2m..............(2:35)

HILL SOCIETY (Ire) 4-11-9 M P Dwyer, ...(5 to 4 fav) 1
635* IDEAL PLAN (Ire) 6-12-0 R Dunwoody, ...(9 to 4) 2
624* LOGSTOWN (Ire) 4-11-4 F Woods, ...(5 to 2) 3
494[2] REAL TAOISEACH (Ire) 6-11-0 (7") Mr A K Wyse, (11 to 1) 4
SACULORE (Ire) 8-11-9 (5") J M Donnelly, ...(33 to 1) 5
577[8] SHALOM (Ire) 4-11-2 M P Hourigan, ...(50 to 1) 6
Dist: 11l, 2l, 15l, 4½l. 4m 10.40s. (Flag start) (6 Ran).
(P Garvey), Noel Meade

719 Guinness Kerry National Handicap Chase (Grade 2) (4-y-o and up) £27,900 3m.....................(3:50)

553[4] BISHOPS HALL [-] 10-9-12 F Woods, led second to 5th, trkd ldr till prog to ld 5 out, sn rdn, hdd briefly bef 2 out and before last, kpt on wl...................................(9 to 1) 1
636[3] ANABATIC (Ire) [-] 8-9-7 T P Rudd, rear till prog aftr 6 out, led briefly bef last, wknd fnl furlong............(14 to 1) 2
553[2] SECOND SCHEDUAL [-] 11-10-1 M P Dwyer, wtd wth, prog bef 5 out, kpt on wl frm 2 out...................(9 to 1) 3
OPERA HAT (Ire) [-] 8-11-0 C O'Dwyer, wl plcd, prog to ld 5th, hdd 5 out, rgned lead briefly bef 2 out, sn headed and wknd.
...................................(12 to 1) 4
636[2] JASSU [-] 10-10-2 R Dunwoody, wl plcd, rdn bef 3 out, wknd before nxt...................................(9 to 1) 5
ROYAL MOUNTBROWNE [-] 8-10-4 A J O'Brien, mid-div till lost pl bef 5th, sn rear, kpt on...................(20 to 1) 6
636* BEAKSTOWN (Ire) [-] 7-9-7 T P Treacy, wl plcd till lost pos aftr 6 out, rdn 3 out, sn lost tch...........(8 to 1) 7
602[4] WALKERS LADY (Ire) [-] 8-9-0 (7") A O'Shea, rear till f 5th.
...................................(100 to 1) f
553 LORD SINGAPORE [-] 8-9-7 N Williamson, mid-div, wl plcd 9th, trkd ldr 5 out, rdn aftr nxt, f 3 out...........(5 to 1) f
293[3] KING WAH GLORY (Ire) [-] 7-9-8 T Horgan, wknd 9th, wl plcd 5 out, tracking ldrs whn sddl slpd and uns rdr bef 2 out.
...................................(5 to 2 jt-fav) ur

293* LIFE OF A LORD [-] 10-12-3 C F Swan, *led 1st, trkd ldr, lost pos bef 12th, pld up aftr nxt, broke leg, destroyed.* (5 to 2 jt-fav) pu

Dist: 1½l, 5½l, 1½l, dist, 14l. 6m 7.80s. (11 Ran).

(T J Carroll), H de Bromhead

720 Cliff House Hotel Maiden Hurdle (6-y-o and up) £3,767 2¾m............ (4:25)

PRIVATE PEACE (Ire) 6-12-0 C F Swan,	(13 to 0 on)	1
YOUNG MRS KELLY (Ire) 6-11-1 J Jones,	(33 to 1)	2
680² YOUNG DUBLINER (Ire) 7-12-0 J Shortt,	(7 to 2)	3
635⁷ PAR FOUR (Ire) 6-11-6 T P Rudd,	(9 to 1)	4
KOPAIN (Ire) 6-11-6 R Dunwoody,	(10 to 1)	5
538⁵ GOLD DEVON (Ire) 6-11-6 P A Roche,	(14 to 1)	6
OWNING (Ire) 6-11-6 M Moran,	(14 to 1)	7
680⁶ PROPHET'S THUMB (Ire) 7-10-13 (7") M D Murphy,	(33 to 1)	8
578² BLACK BOREEN (Ire) 6-12-0 T Horgan,	(10 to 1)	9
SUEMENOMORE (Ire) 7-11-1 F Woods,	(33 to 1)	10
GLEN GIRL (Ire) 6-11-1 K F O'Brien,	(33 to 1)	11
ERINSBOROUGH (Ire) 8-11-6 A Powell,	(40 to 1)	12
LISADORRER LADY (NZ) 7-11-1 J D Dwyer,	(11 to 1)	
UP THE HEDGE (NZ) 7-11-6 M P Dwyer,	(33 to 1)	bd
601⁶ FORGIVENESS (Ire) 6-11-6 P M Verling,	(66 to 1)	pu

Dist: 1l, 12l, 5½l, nk. 6m 1.70s. (15 Ran).

(Mrs A M Daly), A P O'Brien

721 Seamus Mulvaney Handicap Chase (0-102 4-y-o and up) £4,110 2m (5:05)

626* CUBAN QUESTION [-] 9-12-0 R Dunwoody,	(7 to 4 fav)	1
98³ KYLE HOUSE VI (Ire) [-] 7-9-7 N Williamson,	(7 to 2)	2
552⁵ MACAUNTA (Ire) [-] 6-10-1 J P Broderick,	(16 to 1)	3
409⁴ SILENTBROOK (Ire) [-] 11-9-4 (7") A O'Shea,	(10 to 1)	4
429³ CARAGH BRIDGE [-] 9-11-7 J Shortt,	(8 to 1)	5
714³ WACKO JACKO (Ire) [-] 7-11-9 C O'Dwyer,	(9 to 1)	6
426⁷ FULL MOON FEVER (Ire) [-] 7-10-4 T Horgan,	(25 to 1)	7
588⁷ SANDY FOREST LADY (Ire) [-] 7-10-9 T P Treacy,	(14 to 1)	8
714² FAYS FOLLY (Ire) [-] 7-9-10 (7") R P Hogan,	(8 to 1)	f
588 HANNIES GIRL (Ire) [-] 7-11-0 (7") L J Fleming,	(11 to 1)	pu

Dist: 2, 2½l, nk, ½l. 3m 58.20s. (10 Ran).

(Laurence Byrne), D T Hughes

722 Shannon House I.N.H. Flat Race (5-y-o and up) £3,767 2½m............ (5:35)

304⁵ GLENREEF BOY (Ire) 7-12-0 Mr J P Dempsey,	(10 to 1)	1
527³ DIAMOND DOUBLE (Ire) 5-11-6 (3") Mr B M Cash,	(3 to 1)	2
611³ BARRIGAN'S HILL (Ire) 6-11-11 (3") Mr K Whelan,	(4 to 1)	3
683⁸ FRISKY THYNE (Ire) 7-11-7 (7") Mr M G Drohan,	(20 to 1)	4
591² HOLY GROUNDER (Ire) 7-12-0 Mr J E Kiely,	(7 to 4 fav)	5
527⁸ WARLOCKFOE (Ire) 5-11-9 Mr P Fenton,	(12 to 1)	6
SKULLDUGERY (Ire) 6-11-7 (7") Mr J T McNamara,	(16 to 1)	7
120⁶ SEA BRETA (Ire) 5-11-2 (7") Mr R M Walsh,	(14 to 1)	8
622² FRED OF THE HILL (Ire) 5-11-2 (7") Mr R Walsh,	(10 to 1)	9
KINGDOM GLORY (Ire) 5-12-0 Miss M Olivefale,	(12 to 1)	10
DONTBENOSEYHONEY (Ire) 6-11-7 (7") Mr G Elliott,	(33 to 1)	11
COMELY MAIDEN (Ire) 5-11-2 (7") Mr J J Dullea,	(25 to 1)	12

Dist: 9l, 3l, 2l, 25l. 5m 35.10s. (12 Ran).

(Mrs E Donoghue), C P Donoghue

PERTH (good to firm)
Wednesday September 25th
Going Correction: PLUS 0.10 sec. per fur.

723 Ballathie House Hotel Novices' Hurdle Class D for the Tony Charlton Memorial Trophy (4-y-o and up) £2,736 3m 110yds....................... (2:10)

SMART APPROACH 6-10-9 P Niven, *in tch, hdwy to track ldr 3 out, chalg whn lft in ld bef nxt, wndrd appr last, drvn out.*
.... (4 to 1 op 5 to 1 tchd 11 to 2) 1
ANTARCTIC WIND (Ire) 6-11-0 R Garritty, *hld up, hdwy to track ldrs 3 out, chasing wnr bef nxt, rdn betw last 2, no imprsn.*....................(20 to 1 op 6 to 1) 2
JUBRAN (USA) 10-11-6 Richard Guest, *hld up in rear, hdwy aftr 3 out, no further prog nxt.*
.... (9 to 2 op 4 to 1 tchd 5 to 1) 3
569² BLOOMING SPRING (Ire) 7-11-1 L O'Hara, *in tch, rdn aftr 9th, sn wknd.*...................(7 to 1 op 4 to 1 tchd 9 to 1) 4
RUSHEN RAIDER 4-10-11 M Foster, *keen, cl up, led 9th, jst in frnt and gng wl whn slpd up bend bef 2 out.*
.... (11 to 10 fav op 5 to 4 tchd 11 to 8) su
HEDDON HAUGH (Ire) 8-11-0 R Supple, *led till 9th, wknd quickly aftr nxt, tld off whn pld up bef last.*
.... (66 to 1 op 25 to 1 tchd 100 to 1) pu
660 CLASSIC CREST (Ire) 5-11-6 N Bentley, *prmnt, wkng whn mstk 9th, sn tld off, pld up bef 2 out....* (33 to 1 op 16 to 1) pu

Dist: 6l, 3½l, 9l. 6m 6.70s. (a 24.70s (7 Ran).

(Mrs M B Thwaites), Mrs M Reveley

724 Greig Middleton Novices' Chase Class E for the Kilmany Cup (5-y-o and up)

£3,046 2m......................(2:40)

BLUE CHARM (Ire) 6-10-12 A Maguire, *jmpd wl, trkd ldrs, led 3 out, clr aftr nxt, styd on....* (4 to 1 tchd 9 to 2)		1
695* TO BE THE BEST 6-11-5 (7ex) J Burke, *led till 3 out, no ch wth wnr whn mstk last....*(2 to 1 fav tchd 9 to 4)		2
555² REVE DE VALSE (USA) 9-11-5 K Johnson, *chsd ldr, rdn and ev ch 3 out, sn wknd....*(5 to 1 op 4 to 1 tchd 11 to 2)		3
665⁶ WEE WIZARD (Ire) 7-10-12 P Waggott, *outpcd and beh 5th, nvr dngrs....* (14 to 1 op 10 to 1)		4
MUSIC BLITZ 5-10-18 B Storey, *hld up, hdwy hfwy, disputing second and no imprsn on wnr whn blun and uns rdr 2 out.*
.... (8 to 1 op 7 to 1)		ur
558² SPEAKER'S HOUSE (USA) 7-11-5 A Thornton, *beh hfwy, tld off whn pld up bef 3 out....* (7 to 2 op 3 to 1)		pu
STRATHTORE DREAM 6-10-5 L O'Hara, *mstks, sn beh, tld off whn pld up bef 9th....*(100 to 1 op 33 to 1)		pu

Dist: 7l, 4l, 4l. 3m 59.70s. a 8.70s (7 Ran).

SR: 13/13/9/-/ (Mrs M C Lindsay), Mrs S C Bradburne

725 Moulin Brewery Amateur Riders' Handicap Hurdle Class C (0-100 4-y-o and up) £2,788 2½m 110yds.... (3:10)

PEGGY GORDON [74] 5-10-6 Mrs A Farrell, *hld up in rear, lost tch hfwy, gd hdwy aftr 7th, led bef 2 out, sn clr.*
.... (12 to 1 op 10 to 1 tchd 14 to 1)		1
125⁶ ABLE PLAYER (USA) [86] 9-10-13 (7") Mr K Drewry, *towards rear, styd on und pres 2 out, nvr able to chal.*
.... (10 to 1 op 6 to 1 tchd 12 to 1)		2
659⁸ TASHREEF [72] (bl) 6-10-1 (5") Mr M H Naughton, *beh, hdwy bef 7th, wknd appr 2 out.*
.... (14 to 1 op 10 to 1 tchd 16 to 1)		3
665⁴ FLINTLOCK (Ire) [78] 6-10-5 (7") Mr R Thornton, *prmnt, led 3rd to 5th, rdn to ld bef 3 out, hdd before nxt, sn wknd.*
.... (7 to 2 tchd 4 to 1)		4
559⁷ BOURDONNER [90] 4-11-5 (3") Mr C Bonner, *led, jmpd slwly and hdd 3rd, prmnt till wknd aftr 7th.*
.... (6 to 5 fav op 5 to 4 tchd 11 to 10)		5
28² NICHOLAS PLANT [94] 7-11-7 (7") Mr O McPhail, *chsd ldrs, led 5th till bef 3 out, wkng whn mstk nxt.* (6 to 1 op 4 to 1)		6
GOOD TEAM [80] 11-10-7 (7") Miss D V Russell, *in tch till wknd aftr 7th....* (50 to 1 op 12 to 1)		7

Dist: 10l, 1½l, 16l, 3l, 1½l, 4l. 5m 1.60s. a 21.60s (7 Ran).

(Frank Flynn And Richard Madden), Mrs D Thomson

726 Royal Bank Of Scotland Handicap Chase Class F for The Perthshire Challenge Cup (0-100 5-y-o and up) £4,201 3m...................... (3:40)

FORWARD GLEN [73] (bl) 9-10-3 R Supple, *in tch, pushed alng bef 3 out, led aftr nxt, styd on und pres.*
.... (20 to 1 op 14 to 1)		1
SOLO GENT [92] 7-11-8 S Curran, *hld up in tch, steady hdwy to ld 14th, hdd aftr 2 out, no extr und pres.*
.... (100 to 30 op 7 to 2 tchd 4 to 1 and 3 to 1)		2
230⁸ BITACRACK [79] 9-10-9 L O'Hara, *in tch, effrt aftr 15th, styd on frm 2 out....* (10 to 1 op 8 to 1)		3
GRAND SCENERY (Ire) [90] 8-11-6 A Maguire, *mstks, hld up and wl beh, took clr order hfwy, blun 14th, ev ch nxt till wknd aftr 2 out....* (4 to 1 op 7 to 2)		4
COMMANDEER (Ire) [73] 6-10-3 A S Smith, *made most till hdd 14th, fdd....* (20 to 1)		5
663² REBEL KING [94] 6-11-6 P Waggott, *chsd ldrs, outpcd whn mstk 13th, no dngr aftr....* (5 to 2 fav tchd 9 to 1)		6
24 OFF THE BRU [94] 11-11-3 (7") Mr M Bradburne, *dsptd ld till wknd aftr 14th, tld off....* (11 to 2 op 8 to 1)		7
BRIGHT DESTINY [74] 5-9-11 (3") G Lee, *not jump wl, lost tch 6th, well tld off....* (66 to 1 op 50 to 1)		8
WILLIE SPARKLE [79] 10-10-2 (7") A Watt, *prmnt till wknd bef 3 out, 5th and no ch whn pld up before last.*
.... (15 to 2 op 8 to 1 tchd 7 to 1)		pu

Dist: 6l, 5l, sht-hd, 8l, 8l, 22l, dist. 6m 14.40s. a 19.40s (9 Ran).

(Steve Corbett), P Cheesbrough

727 Royal Bank Of Scotland Claiming Hurdle Class F (4-y-o and up) £2,721 2m 110yds....................... (4:10)

BRODESSA 10-10-13 P Niven, *made al, hit 5th, styd on wl frm 2 out....*(11 to 10 op 5 to 4 tchd Evens)		1
666⁶ SIMAND 4-10-0 J Callaghan, *nvr far away, chsd wnr frm 3 out....* (10 to 1 op 6 to 1)		2
100 PARISH WALK (Ire) 6-11-3 M Foster, *chsd ldrs, drvn alng and outpcd aftr 3 out, kpt on frm nxt....* (20 to 1 op 12 to 1)		3
638⁷ HACKETTS CROSS (Ire) 8-10-13 A Maguire, *in tch, ev ch 3 out, sn rdn, one pace....* (5 to 1 op 4 to 1 tchd 3 to 1)		4
606⁵ AIDE MEMOIRE (Ire) 7-10-5 K Johnson, *prmnt, rdn and outpcd aftr 5th, styd on frm 2 out....* (50 to 1 op 33 to 1)		5
666⁷ MINNESOTA (Ire) 4-11-3 Gary Lyons, *hld up, some hdwy aftr 3 out, rdn betw last 2, wknd...* (12 to 1 op 8 to 1)		6
372³ COLWAY PRINCE (Ire) 8-10-7 S Curran, *in tch till wknd aftr 3 out, tld off....*(14 to 1 op 10 to 1 tchd 16 to 1)		7
MARCO MAGNIFICO (USA) 6-10-10 A Thornton, *lost tch hfwy, tld off....* (16 to 1 op 12 to 1 tchd 20 to 1)		8

Dist: 7l, 1¼l, ¾l, 8l, 6l, 23l, ¾l. 3m 57.00s. a 16.00s (8 Ran).

(R W S Jevon), Mrs M Reveley

728 Highland Spring Novices' Hurdle Class E (4-y-o and up) £2,780 2m 110yds
. . . . . (4:40)

MITHRAIC (Ire) 4-10-5 (7*) L McGrath, *chsd ldrs, led 2 out,*
styd on . . . .(5 to 1 tchd 11 to 2) 1
SUPERTOP 8-11-0 M Foster, *hld up in tch, hdwy to chase ldrs*
3 out, rdn bef nxt, kpt on frm last.
. . . .(13 to 8 fav op 7 to 4 tchd 2 to 1) 2
DR EDGAR 4-10-12 R Supple, *led till 2 out, btn whn mstk last.*
. . . . (14 to 1 op 10 to 1) 3
610² TAWAFIJ (USA) 7-11-0 R Garritty, *hld up in tch, drvn alng bef 2*
out, sn btn . . . .(5 to 2 op 9 to 4 tchd 11 to 4) 4
I'M THE MAN 5-11-0 K Johnson, *wl beh frm hfwy.*
. . . . (20 to 1 op 16 to 1) 5
WELBURN BOY 4-10-12 L Wyer, *wl beh frm hfwy.*
. . . . (20 to 1 op 14 to 1) 6
LOGANI 6-10-6 (3*) D Parker, *wl beh frm hfwy, tld off.*
. . . . (100 to 1 op 200 to 1) 7
FLYAWAY BLUES 4-10-12 P Niven, *f 1st.*
. . . . (11 to 1 op 6 to 1) f
661 RHYTHMIC DANCER 8-11-0 B Storey, *tld off whn pld up bef 3*
out. . . . .(40 to 1 op 33 to 1 tchd 50 to 1) pu
COURT JOKER (Ire) 4-10-5 (7*) Mr R Thornton, *wth ldr to*
start, sn wknd, tld off whn pld up bef 2 out.
. . . .(9 to 1 op 10 to 1 tchd 8 to 1) pu
Dist: 1½l, 10l, 8l, 16l, 1½l, dist. 3m 55.80s. a 14.80s (10 Ran).
(C P M Racing), W S Cunningham

LISTOWEL (IRE) (good)
Thursday September 26th

729 Kevin McManus Beginners Chase (4-y-o and up) £4,110 2¾m . . . . (3:15)

525 THE GOPHER (Ire) 7-12-0 L P Cusack, ...(14 to 1) 1
BRAVE FOUNTAIN (Ire) 8-12-0 T Horgan, ...(9 to 4 fav) 2
578* LINDA'S BOY (Ire) 6-12-0 J Shortt, ...(3 to 1) 3
406 PEAFIELD (Ire) 7-11-4 (5*) G Cotter, ...(11 to 1) 4
PORT RISING (Ire) 7-11-7 (7*) Mr E Gallagher, ...(9 to 1) f
525 DENNY'S GUESS (Ire) 8-11-9 G M O'Neill, ...(20 to 1) f
426⁶ JULY SCHOON 11-11-2 (7*) Miss C Gould, ...(33 to 1) ur
576⁷ CORRIBLOUGH (Ire) 8-11-9 T P Treacy, ...(20 to 1) pu
580² TIMELY AFFAIR (Ire) 7-11-4 F Woods, ...(3 to 1) pu
Dist: 8l, 7l, dist. 5m 58.10s. (Flag start) (9 Ran).
(T F Lacy), T F Lacy

730 Smithwicks Beer Handicap Hurdle (5-y-o and up) £13,500 2m . . . .(4:25)

526² SPACE TRUCKER (Ire) [-] 5-11-7 J Shortt, ... (4 to 1 fav) 1
433* MYSTICAL CITY (Ire) [-] 6-11-8 D J Casey, ...(10 to 1) 2
428⁵ WEST ON BRIDGE ST (Ire) [-] 6-10-0 F Woods, ...(20 to 1) 3
268³ HIGHLANDER (Ire) [-] 7-10-1 (3*) Mr J Connolly, . . .(16 to 1) 4
303⁷ ALASAD (Ire) [-] 6-10-12 R Dunwoody, ...(13 to 2) 5
564* FONTAINE LODGE (Ire) [-] 6-9-10 (7*) A O'Shea, . . .(16 to 1) 6
354* NIYAMPOUR (Ire) [-] (bl) 5-10-3 T P Rudd, ...(16 to 1) 7
627⁶ TAITS CLOCK (Ire) [-] 7-10-2 T Horgan, ...(9 to 1) 8
627² BLAZE OF HONOUR (Ire) [-] 5-10-7 C F Swan, ...(6 to 1) 9
710² TEMPLEROAN PRINCE [-] 9-9-13 (3*) J R Barry, . . .(16 to 1) 10
87⁷ GLOWING LINES (Ire) [-] (bl) 6-11-4 N Williamson, . .(25 to 1) 11
627* NEAR GALE (Ire) [-] 6-11-6 T P Treacy, ...(7 to 1) 12
621* BOB THE YANK (Ire) [-] 6-10-2 C O'Dwyer, ...(20 to 1) 13
429² NORDIC THORN (Ire) [-] (bl) 6-11-0 K F O'Brien, . .(16 to 1) 14
621⁵ ULTRA MAGIC (Ire) [-] 9-9-13 J Butler, ...(16 to 1) 15
Dist: ½l, sht-hd, 1½l, sht-hd. 3m 55.50s. (Flag start) (15 Ran).
(Mrs E Queally), Mrs John Harrington

731 Coleman Tunnelling Maiden Hurdle (4-y-o) £4,110 2m . . . . (4:55)

599³ PALETTE (Ire) 10-11 (3*) D J Casey, ...(11 to 4) 1
624³ FRANCES STREET (Ire) 11-5 C F Swan, ...(7 to 2) 2
487* MURPHY'S MALT (Ire) 11-0 (5*) J Butler, ...(10 to 1) 3
624* PERMIT ME (Ire) 10-7 (7*) A O'Shea, ...(14 to 1) 4
624 GOLD DEPOSITOR (Ire) 10-7 (7*) J M Sullivan, ...(16 to 1) 5
611⁸ PERAMBIE (Ire) 11-0 T Horgan, ...(14 to 1) 6
590⁸ HARRY WELSH (Ire) 11-5 C O'Dwyer, ...(20 to 1) 7
VINTNERS VENTURE (Ire) 11-0 (5*) M J Holbrook, .(20 to 1) 8
176⁸ CHUCKAWALLA (Ire) 11-0 A J O'Brien, ...(33 to 1) 9
560 BUNKER (Ire) 11-5 J K Kinane, ...(33 to 1) 10
RIVER RUMPUS (Ire) 11-5 J P Broderick, ...(25 to 1) 11
TOPAD (Ire) 11-0 T Evans, ...(33 to 1) 12
LAHANA (Ire) 11-0 F Woods, ...(20 to 1) 13
TAKLIF (Ire) 11-5 T P Rudd, ...(5 to 4 fav) f
HEMERO (Ire) 11-5 M P Hourigan, ...(12 to 1) f
590⁷ ELYSIAN HEIGHTS (Ire) 11-0 N Williamson, ...(16 to 1) pu
Dist: 3½l, 7l, 1½l, 8l. 4m 1.00s. (Flag start) (16 Ran).
(Mayden Syndicate), W P Mullins

732 Spectra Photo Labs Handicap Hurdle (0-116 4-y-o and up) £4,452 2¾m
. . . . . (5:30)

565² VALMAR (Ire) [-] 8-9-7 F Woods, ...(9 to 2 fav) 1
NATIVE GALE (Ire) [-] 4-11-3 (5*) T Martin, ...(12 to 1) 2
579⁵ TIBOULEN (Ire) [-] 6-11-2 D T Evans, ...(12 to 1) 3
627⁴ BLACK QUEEN (Ire) [-] 5-11-13 P A Roche, ...(10 to 1) 4
FALCARRAGH (Ire) [-] 6-10-5 (3*) J R Barry, ...(14 to 1) 5
683* THAI ELECTRIC (Ire) [-] 5-11-1 T J Mitchell, ...(5 to 1) 6
ONTHEROADAGAIN (Ire) [-] 8-11-12 T P Rudd, . . .(16 to 1) 7
292⁵ JUST AN ILLUSION (Ire) [-] 4-11-8 R Dunwoody, . .(10 to 1) 8
433² HAKKINEN (Ire) [-] 5-12-0 N Williamson, ...(12 to 1) 9
622* NOELEENS DELIGHT (Ire) [-] (bl) 7-10-9 T P Treacy, (8 to 1) 10
683⁹ MARGUERITA SONG [-] 6-10-9 J P Broderick, ...(10 to 1) 11
SOMERSET PRIDE (Ire) [-] 6-11-1 J Shortt, ...(33 to 1) 12
679⁷ TARA'S TRIBE [-] 9-10-4 C O'Dwyer, ...(12 to 1) 13
589² ALLARACKET (Ire) [-] 7-10-6 (7*) A O'Shea, ...(20 to 1) 14
552 KELLY'S MONEY (Ire) [-] 7-9-9 (5*) G Cotter, ...(14 to 1) 15
468* LOUGHLOONE (Ire) [-] 5-10-10 T Horgan, ...(14 to 1) pu
315 PINGO HILL (Ire) [-] 4-11-5 (7*) L J Fleming, ...(14 to 1) pu
339* ERRAMORE (Ire) [-] 4-11-2 C F Swan, ...(5 to 1) pu
Dist: 5l, 3l, nk, 10l. 5m 36.90s. (Flag start) (18 Ran).
(O B P Carroll), D P Kelly

733 Paddy Cullagh Memorial I.N.H. Flat Race (4-y-o and up) £4,110 2m . .(6:00)

RADANPOUR (Ire) 4-11-8 (5*) Mr R Walsh, . . .(11 to 10 fav) 1
MOSCOW EXPRESS (Ire) 4-11-6 (7*) Miss A L Crowley,
. . . .(7 to 2) 2
635² CAITRIONA'S CHOICE (Ire) 5-11-11 (7*) Mr G Elliott, (5 to 1) 3
591* KING OF THE DAWN 5-11-11 (7*) Mr A C Coyle, . . .(5 to 2) 4
647* SABANIYA (Fr) 4-11-1 (7*) Mr A J Dempsey, ...(12 to 1) 5
637⁴ NATIVE BABY (Ire) 6-11-13 Mr J A Nash, ...(20 to 1) 6
213* THAT'S THE SUSS (Ire) 4-11-1 (7*) Mr D A Harney, (20 to 1) 7
Dist: 13l, 3½l, 3l, 20l. 3m 46.10s. (Flag start) (7 Ran).
(P P T Bridson), W P Mullins

PERTH (good (races 1,2,3,4,5), good to firm (6,7))
Thursday September 26th
Going Correction: PLUS 0.30 sec. per fur.

734 Murrayshall Hotel Juvenile Novices' Hurdle Class D (3-y-o) £2,806 2m 110yds
. . . . . (2:10)

TARRY 10-5 T Eley, *mid-div, hdwy bef 3 out, shaken up to ld*
aftr last, ran on wl.
. . . .(13 to 2 op 7 to 1 tchd 8 to 1 and 5 to 1) 1
GLOBE RUNNER 10-10 A Roche, *hld up, hdwy hfwy, ch 2 out,*
styd on und pres frm last. . . . .(25 to 1 op 12 to 1) 2
658* SILVERDALE KNIGHT 11-3 M Foster, *led till hdd aftr last, no*
extr . . . .(5 to 4 on op Evens tchd 11 to 8) 3
567* ROSSEL (USA) 11-3 A Dobbin, *chsd ldrs, rdn bef 2 out, sn btn.*
. . . .(6 to 1 op 4 to 1 tchd 7 to 1) 4
WHAT JIM WANTS (Ire) 10-10 P Niven, *hld up, outpcd bef 5th,*
no dngr aftr. . . . .(33 to 1 op 16 to 1) 5
567² RET FREM 10-10 B Storey, *in tch, effrt aftr 3 out, sn btn.*
. . . .(9 to 1 op 5 to 1 tchd 10 to 1) 6
THORNTOUN ESTATE (Ire) 10-10 M Dwyer, *prmnt till wknd*
aftr 3 out, tld off . . . .(16 to 1 op 10 to 1 tchd 20 to 1) 7
672² HOW COULD-I (Ire) 10-5 A Maguire, *beh, some hdwy hfwy,*
wknd bef 3 out, tld off . . . .(8 to 1 op 5 to 1) 8
ARROGANT HEIR 10-10 L Wyer, *prmnt, mstk 4th, sn wknd*
and lost tch, tld off whn pld up bef 2 out.
. . . .(33 to 1 op 20 to 1 tchd 50 to 1) pu
MINERAL WATER 10-10 L O'Hara, *beh, lost tch frm hfwy, tld*
off whn pld up bef 2 out. . . . .(66 to 1 op 33 to 1) pu
Dist: 2l, ½l, 15l, 2l, nk, 19l, 5l. 4m 0.70s. a 19.70s (10 Ran).
(Mrs Chris Lester), A Streeter

735 Travail Employment Group Maiden Hurdle Class E (4-y-o and up) £2,684 2½m 110yds . . . . (2:40)

SHONARA'S WAY 5-11-0 A Dobbin, *nvr far away, rdn to ld 2*
out, styd on wl. . . . .(4 to 1 op 5 to 2) 1
JABAROOT 5-11-2 (3*) G Cahill, *hld up, hdwy bef 7th, led*
and quickened 3 out, rdn and hdd nxt, kpt on same pace.
. . . .(9 to 1 op 8 to 1) 2
667² LEAR DANCER (USA) 5-11-5 Gary Lyons, *hld up towards*
rear, hdwy bef 3 out, rdn whn hit nxt, kpt on same pace.
. . . .(10 to 1 op 16 to 1) 3
JONAEM (Ire) 6-11-5 K Johnson, *led till hdd 3 out, fdd.*
. . . .(14 to 1 op 25 to 1) 4
473² COMMANDER GLEN 4-11-0 (3*) Mr C Bonner, *sn prmnt,*
wknd bef 3 out. . . . .(7 to 1 op 5 to 1 tchd 10 to 1) 5
MISS LAMPLIGHT 6-11-0 R Supple, *towards rear, hdwy aftr*
7th, wknd after 3 out. . . . . . .(7 to 1 op 5 to 1 tchd 33 to 1) 6
NEW CAPRICORN (USA) 6-11-2 (3*) D Parker, *nvr nr to chal.*
. . . .(20 to 1 op 14 to 1) 7
CALDER'S GROVE 6-11-5 L O'Hara, *in tch till wknd aftr 3 out.*
. . . .(100 to 1 op 33 to 1) 8
MURPHY'S RUN (Ire) 6-11-5 A Maguire, *in tch, wkng whn*
crrd wide bef 3 out, tld off when pld up before nxt.
. . . .(11 to 2 op 5 to 1 tchd 6 to 1) pu

BOSTON MAN 5-11-5 L Wyer, *prmnt, hit 7th, sn wknd, tld off whn pld up bef last*................(20 to 1 op 16 to 1) pu

Dist: 6l, 9l, 1¾l, 11l, 6l, 16l, sht-hd. 5m 7.50s. a 27.50s (10 Ran).

(Alan Guthrie), P Monteith

736 Clarendon Carpets Handicap Hurdle Class D (0-120 4-y-o and up) £3,371 2m 110yds..................... (3:10)

656² SARMATIAN (USA) [100] 5-11-10 R Garritty, *trkd ldrs, chlgd 2 out, led last, ran on und pres.*
...............(6 to 4 fav tchd 7 to 4 and 2 to 1) 1
557¹ VINTAGE RED [74] 6-10-0 A Dobbin, *set very slow pace, quickened aftr 5th, hdd last, no extr, eased whn btn nr finish.*
.......................(6 to 1 op 5 to 1) 2
476⁴ LATIN LEADER [83] (bl) 6-10-6 (3*) D Parker, *trkd ldr, chlgd 2 out, sn rdn and wknd*................(12 to 1 op 8 to 1) 3
661² ROBSERA (Ire) [90] 5-11-0 L Wyer, *hld up, effrt bef 2 out, rdn betw last two, sn btn*................(4 to 1 op 3 to 1) 4
557² STEADFAST ELITE (Ire) [90] 5-11-0 A Roche, *5th, hld up, pushed alng aftr 3 out, sn wknd.*
...............(3 to 1 tchd 100 to 30 and 11 to 4) 5

Dist: 2l, 6l, 8l, 3½l. 4m 22.70s. a 41.70s (5 Ran).

(S T Brankin), M D Hammond

737 Coopers & Lybrand Handicap Chase Class D (0-125 4-y-o and up) £3,420 2m.......................... (3:40)

607⁴ BEAUCADEAU [100] 10-10-12 P Waggott, *prmnt, led 9th, styd on wl, collapsed and died aftr race.*
.......................(9 to 1 op 5 to 1 tchd 10 to 1) 1
570² BELDINE [100] 11-10-12 A Dobbin, *hld up, hdwy bef 9th, chsd wnr frm 3 out, no imprsn.*...............(11 to 4 jt-fav op 2 to 1 tchd 5 to 2) 2
NEWHALL PRINCE [112] 8-11-10 T Eley, *nvr far away, rdn aftr 3 out, no imprsn whn mstk last.*...............(11 to 4 jt-fav op 3 to 1 tchd 5 to 2) 3
617 SHREWD JOHN [97] 10-10-9 M Dwyer, *hld up, effrt bef 3 out, sn rdn, no hdwy*...............(3 to 1 op 7 to 2) 4
490³ BLAZING DAWN [88] 9-10-0 B Storey, *cl up, led 5th till hdd 9th, one pace frm 3 out.*...............(8 to 1 op 7 to 1) 5
SURE METAL [111] 13-11-9 D McCain, *led to 5th, in tch whn f 8th.*...............(50 to 1 op 20 to 1) f
571⁵ VAIN PRINCE [95] 10-11-9 R Garritty, *mstk 1st, sn beh, tld off whn pld up bef 6th.*...............(8 to 1 op 7 to 1) pu

Dist: 7l, nk, 1¼l, hd. 4m 3.50s. a 12.50s (7 Ran).

SR: 7/-/12/-/

(T A Barnes), M A Barnes

738 Highland Spring Scottish Celebration Handicap Hurdle Class E (0-115 4-y-o and up) £3,436 3m 110yds...... (4:10)

559² VALIANT DASH [85] 10-10-4 (3*) G Lee, *cl up, led 9th, jnd 2 out, styd on wl und pres.*...............(6 to 1 op 5 to 1) 1
TWIN FALLS [101] 5-11-6 J Callaghan, *hld up in tch, gd hdwy to dispute ld 2 out, sn rdn and btn.*(4 to 1 tchd 5 to 1) 2
606² TOUGH TEST [101] 6-11-9 B Fenton, *trkd ldrs, rdn and outpcd aftr 9th, no dngr after.*
.......................(6 to 4 fav op 5 to 4 tchd 7 to 4) 3
656⁶ DON DU CADRAN (Fr) [104] 7-11-12 A Thornton, *led till hdd 9th, wknd quickly aftr 3 out, tld off.*......(5 to 2 op 2 to 1) 4

Dist: 8l, 12l, dist. 6m 7.50s. a 25.50s (4 Ran).

(L W Dunbar), J S Goldie

739 Press & Journal Novices' Chase Class D Tamerosia Series Qualifier (5-y-o and up) £3,436 2½m.... (4:40)

TIGHTER BUDGET (USA) 9-11-0 M Moloney, *hld to 3rd, led 7th, wl clr 3 out, easily....* (13 to 8 op 2 to 1 tchd 9 to 4) 1
BARDAROS 7-11-0 A Thornton, *led 3rd to 7th, chsd wnr aftr, wknd aftr 9th.*...............(11 to 10 tay op 11 to 10 on) 2
KINCARDINE BRIDGE (USA) 7-10-7 (7*) Mr M Bradburne, *beh, some hdwy aftr 9th, no further prog whn mstk 12th, wknd quickly, tld off...........*(9 to 1 op 8 to 1 tchd 12 to 1) 3
608¹ SEE YOU ALWAYS (Ire) 6-11-0 P Waggott, *prmnt early, slpd bend bef 5th, lost tch frm hfwy, blun 11th, wl tld off.*
...............(25 to 1 op 14 to 1 tchd 33 to 1) 4
608⁴ TONY'S FEELINGS 8-11-0 M Foster, *beh whn f 7th.*
...............(14 to 1 op 10 to 1) f

Dist: Dist, 21l, 29l. 5m 15.90s. a 23.90s (5 Ran).

(Mrs Dianne Sayer), Mrs H D Sayer

740 European Breeders Fund Haste Ye Back Standard National Hunt Flat Class H (4,5,6-y-o) £1,516 2m 110yds .... (5:10)

NISHAMIRA (Ire) 4-10-8 (3*) G Tormey, *hld up, hdwy 5 fs out, led 3 out, styd on wl und pres....* (5 to 4 on tchd 11 to 10) 1
GOLF LAND 4-10-11 (5*) Mr M H Naughton, *hld up, hdwy 6 fs out, ev ch o'r 2 out, sn chasing wnr, no imprsn.*
.......................(8 to 1 op 6 to 1) 2
DAMIEN'S CHOICE (Ire) 4-10-13 (3*) F Leahy, *hld up, hdwy hfwy, chlgd 3 fs out, kpt on same pace....* (9 to 1 op 8 to 1) 3

WATER FONT (Ire) 4-11-2 A Roche, *settled in tch, took clr order hfwy, kpt on same pace fnl 3 fs.*
...............(16 to 1 op 14 to 1 tchd 20 to 1) 4
545* NORTH END LADY 5-10-13 (7*) Mr R Thornton, *cl up, led aftr 6 fs till hdd 3 out, fdd*......(6 to 1 op 5 to 1 tchd 7 to 1) 5
MONSIEUR PINK 4-11-2 J Culloty, *hld up, hdwy hfwy, one pace fnl 3 fs...*...............(7 to 1 op 8 to 1) 6
671 MISS NONNIE 4-10-8 (3*) R Massey, *in tch, no hdwy fnl 3 fs.*
...............(20 to 1 op 14 to 1) 7
671 TEDDY EDWARD 6-11-4 J Supple, *led 6 fs, chsd ldr, outpcd whn slpd badly and almost f o'r 3 out, no ch aftr.*
...............(20 to 1 tchd 25 to 1) 8
SUPER GUY 4-10-13 (3*) G Cahill, *chsd ldrs till wknd o'r 5 fs out.*...............(25 to 1 op 20 to 1) 9
SMART IN SOCKS 5-11-4 B Fenton, *beh frm hfwy.*
...............(16 to 1 tchd 20 to 1) 10
THE VALE (Ire) 4-10-13 (3*) D Parker, *beh frm hfwy.*
...............(66 to 1 op 50 to 1) 11
RINUS MAGNUS (Ire) 4-10-13 (3*) D Walsh, *chsd ldrs till wknd 6 fs out.*...............(50 to 1 op 33 to 1) 12

Dist: 8l, 5l, 5l, nk, 12l, 9l, 10l, ½l, 4l, 15l. 4m 7.40s. (12 Ran).

(M P Burke Developments Limited), T D Barron

LISTOWEL (IRE) (good (races 1,2,5), good to firm (3,4)) Friday September 27th

741 John J Galvin Maiden Hurdle (5-y-o and up) £3,967 2½m............ (2:35)

BALLINLAMMY ROSE (Ire) 6-12-0 C F Swan, (9 to 2 jt-fav) 1
565⁵ MISTY MOMENTS (Ire) 5-11-6 R Dunwoody, ...(7 to 1) 2
LUCKY BUST (Ire) 6-11-7 (7*) Mr D A Harney, ...(6 to 1) 3
684² FLYING IN THE GALE (Ire) 5-10-8 (7*) A O'Shea, (9 to 2 jt-fav) 4
628³ LAUGHING FONTAINE (Ire) 6-11-6 J P Broderick, (16 to 1) 5
WELSH GRIT (Ire) 7-11-11 (3*) D J Casey, ...(5 to 1) 6
GREAT DANTE (Ire) 6-11-9 T Horgan, ...(8 to 1) 7
SHAWS CROSS (Ire) 5-11-6 W Slattery, ...(16 to 1) 8
536 ROSETOWN GIRL (Ire) 5-11-1 M P Hourigan, ...(20 to 1) 9
684 BAY COTTAGE (Ire) 7-11-9 N Williamson, ...(10 to 1) 10
552 FUNNY HABITS (Ire) 5-11-1 A Powell, ...(20 to 1) 11
NEON VALLEY (Ire) 7-11-6 S H O'Donovan, ...(33 to 1) 12
468⁶ NOBODYWANTSME (Ire) 5-10-13 (7*) Mr J Creighton,
...............(33 to 1) 13
685 HOTSCENT (Ire) 5-11-1 P A Roche, ...(20 to 1) 14
717 FORTYNINEPLUS (Ire) 5-11-6 K F O'Brien, ...(33 to 1) pu
463 NATIVE SUCCESS (Ire) 5-10-9¹ (7*) Mr P P O'Brien, (33 to 1) pu
716⁸ MOUNTHENRY LADY (Ire) 7 D Flood, ...(33 to 1) l

Dist: Hd, 3½l, dist, nk. 5m 29.00s. (17 Ran).

(John G Irish), A P O'Brien

742 Listowel Autos Opportunity Handicap Hurdle (0-109 4-y-o and up) £4,110 2m .... (3:15)

TIDJANI (Ire) [-] 4-10-10 (4*) R P Hogan, ...(14 to 1) 1
679* I REMEMBER IT WELL (Ire) [-] (bl) 4-10-9 (4*) S FitzGerald,
...............(7 to 4 fav) 2
432² BRONICA (Ire) [-] 4-10-9 (4*) A O'Shea, ...(7 to 1) 3
565⁵ TARAJAN (USA) [-] (bl) 4-11-4 D J Casey, ...(7 to 1) 4
590* MIDDLE MOGGS (Ire) [-] 4-10-2 (4*) R Burke, ...(16 to 1) 5
COLLON LEADER (Ire) [-] 7-10-7 (4*) J M Maguire, (25 to 1) 6
494* MONTETAN (Ire) [-] 5-10-13 (4*) D McCullagh, ...(14 to 1) 7
627⁷ TEXAS FRIDAY (Ire) [-] 6-10-12 (2*) T Martin, ...(14 to 1) 8
684⁴ BALLYQUIN BELLE (Ire) [-] 6-11-3 J R Barry, ...(7 to 1) 9
685⁷ SUITE CITY LASS (Ire) [-] 5-9-13 (2*) G Cotter, ...(16 to 1) 10
354⁵ PORT NOBLE (Ire) [-] 5-10-4 (4*) S P Kelly, ...(20 to 1) 11
CEILI QUEEN (Ire) [-] 4-11-12 (2*) J Butler, ...(12 to 1) 12
273² PERSIAN MYSTIC (Ire) [-] 4-11-0 (4*) J E Casey, ...(12 to 1) 13
710⁶ LISHILLAUN (Ire) [-] 6-9-8 (2*) Susan A Finn, ...(16 to 1) 14
277⁶ PHANTOMS GIRL (Ire) [-] 5-9-3 (4*) L J Fleming, ..(50 to 1) 15
OLD FONTAINE (Ire) [-] 8-9-6³ (4*) S O'Donnell, ...(25 to 1) 16
WHAT A CHOICE (Ire) [-] 6-9-5 (2*) M J Holbrook, (50 to 1) 17
PHARELLA (Ire) [-] 8-10-4 (4*) M D Murphy, ...(25 to 1) 18

Dist: ¾l, 2½l, 1½l, 1½l. 4m 4.70s. (18 Ran).

(John P McManus), Francis Berry

743 Southampton Goodwill Handicap Chase (0-123 4-y-o and up) £4,110 2½m.......................... (4:25)

537⁷ BALLYBODEN (Ire) [-] 9-11-3 M P Hourigan, ...(33 to 1) 1
338⁷ CASTALINO (Ire) [-] 10-9-13 T P Treacy, ...(10 to 1) 2
HURDY (Ire) [-] 9-11-1 A P McCoy, ...(4 to 1) 3
67 ANOTHER COURSE (Ire) [-] 8-10-6 (7*) Mr E Gallagher,
...............(16 to 1) 4
721* CUBAN QUESTION (Ire) [-] 9-11-3 (6ex) R Dunwoody,
...............(7 to 4 fav) pu
602* MERRY PEOPLE (Ire) [-] 8-11-12 T Horgan, ...(4 to 1) pu
588* SPRINGFORT LADY (Ire) [-] 7-10-7 N Williamson, . (9 to 2) pu

Dist: ½l, 15l, dist. 5m 20.60s. (7 Ran).

(Mrs Eleanor McCormack), Michael Hourigan

744 Louis O'Connell Memorial Novice Chase (5-y-o and up) £4,310 2m (5:05)

619* LIFE SAVER (Ire) 7-11-8 R Dunwoody, ... (Evens fav) 1
300^{4} SAVUTI (Ire) 7-11-1 (7*) M D Murphy, ... (14 to 1) 2
626 STROLL HOME (Ire) 6-11-7 (7*) Mr E Gallagher, ... (3 to 1) 3
626^{2} PHARDY (Ire) 5-11-3 T Horgan, ... (7 to 1) 4
711^{7} TOM THE BOY VI (Ire) (bl) 6-10-11 (7*) A O'Shea, . .(50 to 1) 5
711* KENTUCKY BABY (Ire) 6-11-6 N Williamson, ... (7 to 1) f
591 WILD BROOK (Ire) (bl) 6-11-4 A P McCoy, ... (20 to 1) f
604^{2} JESSIE'S BOY (Ire) 7-11-4 J K Kinane, ... (20 to 1) pu
Dist: 3l, 10l, 8l, dist. 4m 0.60s. (8 Ran).
(Mrs H A Hegarty), J A Berry

745 David Fitzmaurice INH Flat Race (4-y-o and up) £3,767 2m. .... (5:35)

713^{8} SPENDID (Ire) 4-11-2 (7*) Miss A L Crowley, ... (5 to 1) 1
VALLEY ERNE (Ire) 5-12-0 Mr P Fenton, ... (5 to 2 fav) 2
YELAPA PRINCE (Ire) 5-12-0 Mr J A Nash, ... (7 to 1) 3
SOUND ORCHESTRA (Ire) 5-11-7 (7*) Mr P A Farrell, ... (12 to 1) 4
SHECOULDNTBEBETTER (Ire) 5-11-2 (7*) Mr A C Coyle, ... (3 to 1) 5
CASTLE BAILEY (Ire) 5-11-7 (7*) Mr T N Cloke, ... (14 to 1) 6
637^{2} SADALLAH (Ire) 4-11-2 (7*) Mr A Ross, ... (5 to 1) 7
566 PHAR'N'WIDE (Ire) 5-11-3^{1} (7*) Mr N C Kelleher, .. (25 to 1) 8
IRELAND INVADER 4-10-11 (7*) Mr J L Cullen, ... (20 to 1) 9
681 NO SPOKEN WORD (Ire) 5-11-2 (7*) Mr G Elliott, .. (25 to 1) 10
BRAVE WARRIOR (Ire) 6-11-6 (3*) Mr E Norris, ... (16 to 1) 11
Dist: 14l, 11l, 4½l, dist. 4m 0.30s. (11 Ran).
(Joseph Crowley), A P O'Brien

LISTOWEL (IRE) (good to firm) Saturday September 28th

746 Edmond Whelan Memorial Cup Novice Hurdle (5-y-o and up) £5,137 2½m .... (3:35)

536* LISS DE PAOR (Ire) 5-11-3 T Horgan, ... (11 to 10 fav) 1
427^{2} CLONAGAM (Ire) 7-11-8 C F Swan, ... (2 to 1) 2
627^{3} BAMAPOUR (Ire) (bl) 6-11-8 R Dunwoody, ... (5 to 1) 3
355 KILCARAMORE (Ire) 5-11-8 Mr P J Healy, ... (16 to 1) 4
PRINCESS JENNIFER (Ire) 5-10-11 K F O'Brien, .. (66 to 1) 5
601^{5} STANSWAY (Ire) 8-11-2 F Woods, ... (20 to 1) 6
561* FRAU DANTE (Ire) 6-11-3 C O'Dwyer, ... (7 to 1) f
SWEETMOUNT LAD (Ire) 5-11-2 D H O'Connor, ... (50 to 1) pu
Dist: 15l, 3½l, dist, 8l. 5m 19.90s. (8 Ran).
(J C Dempsey), A P O'Brien

747 Kerry Petroleum Chase (4-y-o and up) £4,110 2½m. .... (4:05)

719^{2} ANABATIC (Ire) 8-12-0 T P Rudd, ... (Evens fav) 1
470^{7} THE OUTBACK WAY (Ire) (bl) 6-12-0 D H O'Connor, (6 to 1) 2
TIMBUCKTOO 9-12-0 C O'Dwyer, ... (6 to 4) 3
441^{6} STRADBALLEY (Ire) 6-12-0 F Woods, ... (14 to 1) 4
720^{8} PROPHET'S THUMB (Ire) 7-11-1 (7*) M D Murphy, (33 to 1) 5
Dist: 7l, 2½l, dist, 25l. 5m 24.90s. (5 Ran).
(William J Phelan), M J P O'Brien

748 Golden Vale Milk Handicap Hurdle (Listed) (5-y-o and up) £7,150 3m... (4:35)

625^{6} FATHER RECTOR (Ire) [-] 7-10-3 T Horgan, *wl plcd, trkd ldrs 11th, led nxt, rdn whn lft clr 2 out*.................. (8 to 1) 1
599^{2} ALLATRIM (Ire) [-] 6-9-13 F Woods, *mid-div, prog bef 5 out, trkd ldr 3 out, sn rdn, kpt on*.................. (8 to 1) 2
303 TREBLE BOB (Ire) [-] 6-12-0 R Dunwoody, *rear, rdn 5 out, gd prog und pres aftr 3 out, kpt on wl*.............. (11 to 2) 3
ALWAYS IN TROUBLE [-] (bl) 9-10-4 T P Rudd, *mid-div, prog bef 5 out, trkd ldr 3 out, wknd aftr nxt*.............. (6 to 1) 4
176^{2} FLY ROSEY (Ire) [-] 6-9-13 (5*) J Butler, *str hold early, led, jnd briefly 7th, joined 11th, hdd nxt, sn rdn and wknd*... (10 to 1) 5
BETTERBEBOB (Ire) [-] 5-10-3 (3*) D J Casey, *al rear, rdn bef 4 out, not quicken*.............................. (10 to 1) 6
744 JESSIE'S BOY (Ire) [-] 7-9-7 J K Kinane, *wl plcd, dsptd ld briefly 11th, sn rdn and wknd*.................. (33 to 1) 7
562^{5} VICAR STREET (Ire) [-] 6-10-1 C F Swan, *hld up, gd prog aftr 4 out, chalg whn f 2 out*...................... (13 to 8 fav) f
MAN OF ARRAN (Ire) [-] 6-11-1 (5*) T Martin, *wl plcd early, mid-div 7th, some prog whn mstk 5 out, brght dwn 2 out.* .... (7 to 1) bd
RUSTY COIN [-] (bl) 11-10-9 T J Mitchell, *trkd ldr, led briefly 7th, wl plcd till rdn and wknd bef 5 out, pld up before 3 out.* .... (20 to 1) pu
Dist: 5½l, 3l, 8l, dist. 6m 25.50s. (10 Ran).
(Paddy Fennelly), Paddy Fennelly

WORCESTER (good to firm) Saturday September 28th

Going Correction: MINUS 0.15 sec. per fur.

749 Boathouse 'National Hunt' Novices' Hurdle Class E (4-y-o and up) £2,460 2m......................... (2:30)

COME ON PENNY 5-10-7 M Dwyer, *hld up in rear, hdwy 5th, rdn to ld last, drvn out.* .... (11 to 4 fav op 3 to 1 tchd 7 to 2) 1
47 WINTER ROSE 5-10-12 B Powell, *jmpd rght and pld hrd, led to second, led appr 4th, hit 3 out, sn hdd, lost pl, rallied to go second r-in*............ (14 to 1 op 12 to 1 tchd 16 to 1) 2
652^{5} DIFFICULT DECISION (Ire) 5-10-12 D Byrne, *hld up in tch, hdwy 5th, ev ch 3 out till rdn and wknd r-in.* .... (3 to 1 op 7 to 2 tchd 4 to 1) 3
FAITHFUL HAND 6-10-12 Richard Guest, *hld up, hdwy 4th, led sn aftr 3 out, rdn and hdd last, wknd r-in.* .... (20 to 1 op 12 to 1) 4
VALLINGALE (Ire) 5-10-7 J F Titley, *chsd ldrs, one pace frm 3 out*............ (11 to 2 op 9 to 2 tchd 6 to 1) 5
528^{3} SEVEN WELLS 4-10-10 R Bellamy, *pld hrd, rdn appr 5th, no hdwy aftr*............ (20 to 1 op 16 to 1 tchd 25 to 1) 6
AYDISUN 4-10-10 D Morris, *hld up in rear, hdwy aftr 5th, blun nxt (3 out), not reco'r*... (33 to 1 op 20 to 1 tchd 50 to 1) 7
LADYMALORD 4-10-5 I Lawrence, *al beh, tld off.* .... (50 to 1 op 33 to 1) 8
PACIFIC RIDGE (Ire) 5-10-12 M A Fitzgerald, *al beh, tld off.* ....(12 to 1 tchd 8 to 1) 9
CAULKIN (Ire) 5-10-12 A Thornton, *trkd ldrs till wknd quickly 4th, tld off*............ (33 to 1 op 25 to 1) 10
EL CORDOBES (Ire) 5-10-12 T Jenks, *pld hrd, led second, hdd appr 4th, wknd quickly aftr nxt, tld off.* .... (8 to 1 op 6 to 1 tchd 5 to 1 and 10 to 1) 11
654^{2} COUNTRY MINSTREL (Ire) 5-10-12 S McNeill, *hit 1st, in rear and tld off whn f last*.................. (10 to 1 op 8 to 1) f
INSIOUXBORDINATE 4-10-10 Gary Lyons, *tld off 5th, pld up bef 3 out*.............................. (66 to 1 op 50 to 1) pu
Dist: 3½l, 1¾l, 1¾l, 3l, ¾l, 3½l, 29l, nk, 2½l, 1¾l. 3m 46.60s. a 6.60s (13 Ran).
(A E Frost), D R Gandolfo

750 Tolladine Handicap Chase Class C (0-130 5-y-o and up) £4,532 2m 7f .... (3:00)

IFFEEE [123] 9-11-7 A Maguire, *jmpd rght, made virtually all, kpt on gmely whn chlgd 4 out, rdn clr r-in.* .... (10 to 1 op 6 to 1) 1
HAVE TO THINK [130] 8-12-0 M A Fitzgerald, *hld up early, cld on ldrs tenth, hit 5 out, ev ch till outpcd 3 out, wnt second close hme*.................... (4 to 1 op 3 to 1 tchd 9 to 2) 2
57* CERTAIN ANGLE [111] 7-10-9 C Maude, *in tch, hit 11th, pressed wnr frm 5 out, hrd rdn 3 out, wknd r-in.* .... (6 to 4 fav op 7 to 4) 3
71^{2} WISE APPROACH [130] 9-12-0 A Thornton, *wth wnr till wknd appr 4 out, one pace.* (3 to 1 tchd 11 to 4 and 100 to 30) 4
COKENNY BOY [110] 11-10-8 W Marston, *hld up in rear, hit tenth, sn outpcd, tld off*.... (4 to 1 tchd 9 to 2 and 5 to 1) 5
Dist: 5l, ½l, 6l, dist. 5m 45.80s. a 7.80s (5 Ran).
(T M Morris), P Bowen

751 W & P Food Service Novices' Chase Class D (5-y-o and up) £3,884 2m 7f .... (3:35)

265* STORMTRACKER (Ire) 7-10-12 M Richards, *trkd ldr, led 5th, made rst, rdn out*.................. (3 to 1 op 4 to 1) 1
596^{2} OUR NIKKI 6-10-7 S Burrough, *hld up in rear, steady hdwy frm tenth, wnt second 4 out, ran on r-in.* .... (25 to 1 op 20 to 1 tchd 33 to 1) 2
640^{2} LUCKY DOLLAR (Ire) 8-11-5 A Thornton, *hld up in rear, hdwy twelfth, one pace frm 4 out.* .... (15 to 8 fav op 9 to 4 tchd 7 to 4) 3
WESTERLY GALE (Ire) 6-10-12 M A Fitzgerald, *led to 5th, trkd wnr till blun 4 out, sn btn.* .... (16 to 1 op 12 to 1 tchd 20 to 1) 4
657^{2} DEFINITE MAYBE (Ire) (bl) 6-11-5 A Maguire, *hld up in tch, hdwy to go second briefly hfwy, wknd appr 4 out.* .... (6 to 1 op 11 to 2 tchd 13 to 2) 5
540^{2} SIGMA WIRELESS (Ire) 7-10-12 S Wynne, *mstk 1st, hld up in rear, hdwy hfwy, wknd 5 out.* .... (6 to 1 op 5 to 1 tchd 13 to 2) 6
630^{4} FORT GALE (Ire) 5-10-8 G Bradley, *hld up in rear, blun 11th, tld off*................ (14 to 1 op 10 to 1 tchd 16 to 1) 7
215^{3} DORANS WAY (Ire) 5-10-3 (5*) Michael Brennan, *trkd ldrs, 4th whn f tenth*................ (16 to 1 op 10 to 1) f
WAR FLOWER (Ire) 8-10-7 W Marston, *blun and uns rdr 1st.* .... (66 to 1 op 33 to 1) ur
640 BELLS WOOD 7-10-12 B Powell, *trkd ldrs till wknd hfwy, tld off whn pld up bef 14th.* (40 to 1 op 33 to 1 tchd 50 to 1) pu
Dist: 1l, 5l, ½l, 15l, 8l, 23l. 5m 53.20s. a 15.20s (10 Ran).
(Tim Davis), C Weedon

752 John Whitt Memorial Handicap Hurdle Class B (4-y-o and up) £4,922 2½m .... (4:10)

FREDDIE MUCK [105] 6-10-3 C Llewellyn, *trkd ldr, led 4th, quickened clr 3 out, eased r-in*.......... (7 to 2 op 9 to 2) 1

669* FIELDRIDGE [115] 7-10-13 B Powell, hld up, hdwy 6th, rdn
appr 2 out, kpt on to chase wnr r-in. . . . .(5 to 2 jt-
fav op 11 to 4 tchd 100 to 30) 2
612* HOLY JOE [102] 14-10-0 A Maguire, set steady pace to 4th,
trkd wnr for most of way till last.
. . . .(12 to 1 tchd 10 to 1 and 14 to 1) 3
633* SANTELLA BOY (USA) [106] (bl) 4-10-2¹ J Railton, hld up,
hdwy 4 out, wknd 2 out, hit last. . . . .(7 to 2 op 11 to 4) 4
648* WOTTASHAMBLES [112] 5-10-8 D Morris, trkd ldrs, mstk 5th,
outpcd 3 out, wknd appr last. . . . .(5 to 2 jt-
fav op 9 to 4 tchd 7 to 1 and 11 to 4) 5
ECHO DE JANSER (Fr) [130] 4-11-5 (7*) Mr G Shenkin, in tch
till wknd quickly 4 out, tld off.
. . . .(20 to 1 op 12 to 1 tchd 25 to 1) 6
Dist: 6l, 1½l, 5l, 9l, dist. 4m 46.50s. a 10.50s (6 Ran).
(Mrs C Twiston-Davies), N A Twiston-Davies

753 Excelnir Novices' Handicap Chase Class E (0-100 5-y-o and up) £3,081 2m. . . . . (4:45)

549* PRINCE SKYBURD [79] 5-10-12 D Bridgwater, trkd ldrs, led 3
out, rdn out. . . . .(6 to 1 op 11 to 2 tchd 13 to 2) 1
THE YOKEL [70] 10-10-0 (5*) P Henley, hld up, rdn and lost pl
appr 4 out, ridden 2 out, styd on. . . . .(20 to 1 tchd 25 to 1) 2
639³ SEAHAWK RETRIEVER [72] 7-10-7 M A Fitzgerald, hld up in
tch, dsptd ld 3 out, rdn and wknd appr last.
. . . .(6 to 1 tchd 7 to 1) 3
652 MARTHA'S DAUGHTER [88] 7-11-9 A Thornton, hld up in
rear, hdwy aftr 3 out, nvr nrr.
. . . .(11 to 2 op 5 to 1 tchd 6 to 1) 4
594* HARROW WAY (Ire) [86] 6-11-7 A Maguire, led till wknd and
hdd 3 out. . . . .(5 to 2 fav tchd 3 to 1) 5
592⁴ SCRIPT [68] 5-10-1 W Marston, al in rear.
. . . .(25 to 1 op 20 to 1 tchd 33 to 1) 6
630³ DUBELLE [82] 6-11-3 J Culloty, jmpd rght, trkd ldr to 3rd,
wknd quickly 6th, sn tld off. . . . .(11 to 4 op 4 to 1) 7
LAURA LYE (Ire) [67] 6-10-2 J Railton, trkd ldr 3rd, mstk 7th,
wknd quickly appr 4 out, tld off whn pld up bef last.
. . . .(20 to 1 op 12 to 1) pu
Dist: 2½l, 2l, 2l, 5l, 2l, 5l, dist. 3m 53.60s. a 4.60s (8 Ran).
SR: 14/4/18/11/   (Mrs P M A Avison), Mrs P M A Avison

754 Ladbrokes Handicap Hurdle Class E (0-115 4-y-o and up) £2,823 2m (5:15)

503³ AMAZE [108] 7-11-7 (7*) Mr R Thornton, al gng wl, trkd ldr,
led aftr 3rd, shaken up appr last, ran on strly.
. . . .(2 to 1 fav op 7 to 2) 1
653* COOLEY'S VALVE (Ire) [100] 8-11-1 (5*) Sophie Mitchell, hld
up in mid-div, steady hdwy frm 4th, chlgd last, not quicken
r-in. . . . .(4 to 1 tchd 9 to 2) 2
521³ VERDE LUNA [86] 4-10-4 G A Bradley, hld up in rear, gd hdwy
frm 3 out, nvr nrr. . . . .(6 to 1 op 5 to 1 tchd 13 to 2) 3
126⁵ HAMADRYAD (Ire) [85] 8-10-5 D Gallagher, hld up in rear,
mstk 3rd, hdwy aftr out, kpt on one pace frm 3 out.
. . . .(14 to 1 op 12 to 1 tchd 16 to 1) 4
110⁵ FIERCE [90] 8-10-3 (7*) D Yellowlees, led till aftr 3rd, styd in cl
tch, rdn and ev ch 2 out, wknd r-in.
. . . .(14 to 1 op 10 to 1 tchd 16 to 1) 5
WAYFARERS WAY (USA) [91] 5-10-9 M A Fitzgerald, pld hrd,
prmnt till rdn and wknd appr last, eased r-in.
. . . .(100 to 30 op 7 to 2 tchd 3 to 1) 6
486⁴ SWINGS'N'THINGS (USA) [93] 4-10-11 R Farrant, hld up,
hdwy 4th, wknd appr 2 out. . . . .(20 to 1 op 12 to 1) 7
TIBBS INN [80] 7-10-0 A Thornton, al beh, lost tch appr 3 out.
. . . .(50 to 1 op 25 to 1) 8
372 PUSEY STREET BOY [80] 9-10-0 I Lawrence, prmnt till rdn
and wknd rpdly aftr 5th, sn tld off.
. . . .(14 to 1 op 12 to 1 tchd 16 to 1) 9
Dist: 1¾l, ½l, ½l, 2½l, 4l, 7l, 9l, dist. 3m 50.50s. a 10.50s (9 Ran).
(Lady Katharine Phillips), Lady Herries

NEWTON ABBOT (good)
Sunday September 29th
Going Correction: PLUS 0.40 sec. per fur.

755 Pauline Trundle Novices' Chase Class D (5-y-o and up) £3,940 2m 5f 110yds . . . . (2:30)

147* IMPERIAL VINTAGE (Ire) [115] 6-11-5 N Williamson, led 3rd, clr
whn hit 5 out, sn reco'red, unchlgd.
. . . .(7 to 2 op 2 to 1 tchd 4 to 1) 1
LANSDOWNE 8-10-12 M A Fitzgerald, hld up, jmpd slwly 6th,
chsd wnr frm six out, tired whn jumped rght last 2.
. . . .(11 to 8 fav op 5 to 4 tchd 6 to 4) 2
HE'S A KING (USA) 5-10-9 (3*) T Dascombe, trkd ldr early,
outpcd frm 6 out.
. . . .(6 to 1 op 4 to 1 tchd 13 to 2 and 7 to 1) 3
RIVER GALA (Ire) 6-10-12 R Dunwoody, led to 3rd, trkd wnr
till wknd 6 out. . . . .(20 to 1 op 10 to 1) 4
659⁶ KING'S SHILLING (USA) 9-10-12 Jacqui Oliver, hld up in
rear, lost tch tenth, tealied off.
. . . .(14 to 1 op 8 to 1 tchd 16 to 1) 5

PONGO WARING (Ire) 7-10-12 J F Titley, lost tch 7th, tld off
whn pld up aftr 9th. . . .(100 to 30 op 5 to 1 tchd 6 to 1) pu
Dist: 13l, 8l, 6l, dist. 5m 22.20s. a 20.20s (6 Ran).
(David M Williams), Miss Venetia Williams

756 Partyfare Ltd Selling Handicap Hurdle Class G (0-95 4-y-o and up) £1,928 3m 3f. . . . . (3:05)

BETTER BYTHE GLASS (Ire) [95] 7-11-11 (3*) D Walsh, trkd
ldrs, led appr 4 out, rdn approaching 2 out, kpt on.
. . . .(13 to 8 fav op 5 to 2 tchd 6 to 4) 1
398⁴ GUNMAKER [77] 7-10-16 N Williamson, hld up in tch, gd
hdwy to track wnr 4 out, chlgd nxt, no imprsn frm 2 out.
. . . .(10 to 1 op 7 to 2) 2
667⁵ DRAGONMIST (Ire) [67] 6-9-7 (7*) Miss E J Jones, nvr far
away, one pace frm 4 out. . . . . .(10 to 1 tchd 12 to 1) 3
643⁴ STORM DRUM [91] (bl) 7-11-10 T J Murphy, led to second,
rdn to ld appr 7th, hdd bef 4 out, sn btn.
. . . .(15 to 2 op 7 to 1 tchd 8 to 1) 4
639⁴ PRUDENT PEGGY [72] 9-10-5⁴ J Frost, led second, hdd appr
7th, wknd approaching 3 out. . . . .(7 to 1 op 8 to 1) 5
648⁷ DANE ROSE [72] 10-10-5 A Maguire, beh till effrt 4 out, wknd
aftr nxt. . . . .(14 to 1 op 10 to 1) 6
612⁸ AUVILLAR (USA) [78] (v) 8-10-11 C Llewellyn, prmnt till wknd
8th, tld off. . . . .(25 to 1 op 16 to 1) 7
453² FOX CHAPEL [87] 9-11-6 M A Fitzgerald, hld up, lost tch 8th,
tld off whn pld up bef 2 out. . . . .(9 to 2 op 3 to 1) pu
MERRYHILL MADAM [67] 9-11-0 T Eley, hld up, tld off 4 out,
pld up bef 2 out. . . . .(20 to 1 op 14 to 1) pu
635⁵ COEUR BATTANT (Fr) [67] 6-10-0 B Powell, tld off 5th, pld up
bef 2 out. . . . .(16 to 1 op 14 to 1 tchd 20 to 1) pu
Dist: 2½l, 8l, 16l, 12l, 1½l, 16l. 6m 46.00s. a 30.00s (10 Ran).
(N A Twiston-Davies), N A Twiston-Davies

757 In Touch Racing Ltd Handicap Chase Class F (0-100 5-y-o and up) £2,775 3¼m 110yds. . . . . (3:35)

586* RAINBOW CASTLE [100] 9-12-0 P Hide, patiently rdn in tch,
second 14th, cld 2 out, led last, cmftbly.
. . . .(2 to 1 fav op 6 to 4) 1
586² GILSTON LASS [89] 9-11-3 J Culloty, led second, clr 8th, rdn
appr 2 out, hdd last, no extr. . . . .(5 to 2 op 4 to 1) 2
649⁴ MANOR BOUND [76] 6-10-4 R Farrant, al beh, tld off 8th.
. . . .(16 to 1) 3
ITS A SNIP [91] (bl) 11-11-5 R Dunwoody, led to second, trkd
to 14th, sn wknd, tld off. . . . .(5 to 1 op 7 to 1) 4
FOXGROVE [80] 10-10-8 B Fenton, al beh, lost tch 13th, tld
off. . . . .(10 to 1 op 8 to 1 tchd 12 to 1) 5
632³ BOXING MATCH [73] 9-10-1 N Williamson, in tch till wknd
quickly 14th, tld off. . . . .(12 to 1 tchd 14 to 1) 6
676³ L'UOMO PIU [77] (v) 12-10-5 B Powell, al beh, tld off 8th, pld
up bef 14th. . . . .(16 to 1 op 12 to 1) pu
697 BANNTOWN BILL (Ire) [95] 7-11-9 D Bridgwater, tld off 4th,
pld up bef 9th. . . . .(14 to 1 op 12 to 1) pu
657⁴ SAN GIORGIO [90] (bl) 7-11-4 C Llewellyn, mstk 3rd, trkd ldrs
till outpcd 8th, tld off 13th, pld up 5 out.
. . . .(7 to 1 op 6 to 1 tchd 8 to 1) pu
Dist: 3l, dist, 14l, 11l, dist. 6m 38.60s. a 18.60s (9 Ran).
SR: 20/6/-/-/-/-/   (Jeffrey Hordle), P F Nicholls

758 Lavis Medical Systems Novices' Hurdle Class D (4-y-o and up) £2,814 2¾m . . . . (4:10)

HAND WOVEN 4-10-10 C Llewellyn, al prmnt, led 4 out, rdn
clr 2 out. . . . .(11 to 10 op 6 to 4 on tchd Evens) 1
593 KESANTA 6-10-0 (7*) J Power, hld up in rear, steady hdwy frm
4 out, styd on to go second last, no ch with wnr.
. . . .(16 to 1 op 12 to 1) 2
GARRYNISK (Ire) 6-10-9 (3*) D Fortt, trkd ldr, made most frm
4th to four out, ev ch till one pace appr 2 out.
. . . .(6 to 1 op 4 to 1 tchd 7 to 1) 3
648² BASIL STREET (Ire) 4-10-10 R Dunwoody, hld up in rear,
hdwy appr 4 out, wknd aftr nxt.
. . . .(3 to 1 op 7 to 2 tchd 5 to 2) 4
KONGIES MELODY 5-10-7 M A Fitzgerald, prmnt to 5th, lost
tch 4 out, tld off. . . . .(50 to 1 op 20 to 1) 5
DTOTO 4-10-10 B Powell, chsd ldrs, mstk 3rd, outpcd 4 out,
btn fourth whn f last. . . . .(25 to 1 tchd 33 to 1) f
BALLYHAYS (Ire) 7-10-12 W McFarland, led to 4th, wth ldr till
lost tch 6th, tld off whn pld up bef 3 out. (66 to 1 op 33 to 1) pu
585² IDIOM 9-11-5 J Culloty, chsd ldrs till wknd quickly 4 out, tld off
whn pld up bef 2 out. . . . .(6 to 1 op 8 to 1 tchd 10 to 1) pu
FLASHMANS MISTRESS 9-10-7 B Fenton, al beh, tld off whn
pld up bef 2 out. . . . . . .(66 to 1 op 50 to 1 tchd 100 to 1) pu
456 LATE ENCOUNTER 5-10-9 (3*) Guy Lewis, ran wide bend aftr
second, sn beh, rdn 5th, pld up after nxt.
. . . .(66 to 1 op 33 to 1 tchd 100 to 1) pu
Dist: 3½l, 2l, 9l, dist. 5m 24.00s. a 23.00s (10 Ran).
(Matt Archer & Miss Jean Broadhurst), N A Twiston-Davies

759 J. C. Milton Electricals Handicap Chase Class E (0-110 5-y-o and up) £5,451 2m 5f 110yds. . . . . (4:45)

583* BIT OF A TOUCH [82] 10-10-8 J Frost, *led to second, styd prmnt, led 9th, drw clr 2 out, cmftbly*
.... (7 to 2 op 11 to 2 tchd 6 to 1 and 13 to 2)   1

617⁵ WINGSPAN (USA) [94] 12-11-6 A Thornton, *hld up in tch, cld on ldrs 4 out, wnt second 2 out, no ch wth wnr*...... (8 to 1)   2

639² FENWICK [88] 9-10-11 (3*) T Dascombe, *in tch till wknd 6 out. 4 out, wknd aftr nxt*................. (12 to 1 op 8 to 1)   3

632 GABISH [74] 11-9-7 (7*) Mr R Thornton, *al beh, tld off*
.... (6 to 1 op 11 to 2 tchd 13 to 2)   4

CRAFTY CHAPLAIN [97] 10-11-9 A Maguire, *al beh, lost tch*
.... (40 to 1 op 33 to 1 tchd 50 to 1)   5

51³ CHARGED [97] 7-11-9 R Dunwoody, *prmnt till wknd tenth, tld 6th, tld off*...... (7 to 1 tchd 8 to 1)   6

642⁵ SEAL KING [83] 11-10-9 T J Murphy, *led second to 9th, jmpd off*.......... (7 to 2 op 4 to 1 tchd 9 to 2)   7

642* HERBERT BUCHANAN (Ire) [98] 6-11-10 J Culloty, *hld up, slwly nxt, f 11th, (6 out)*............ (25 to 1 op 16 to 1)   f

642* HERBERT BUCHANAN (Ire) [98] 6-11-10 J Culloty, *hld up, making hdwy and prmnt whn f 6 out.*
.... (11 to 4 fav op 2 to 1 tchd 3 to 1)   f

Dist: 9l, 10l, 20l, 16l, 17l, ¾l. 5m 23.20s. a 21.20s (9 Ran).

(A E C Electric Fencing Ltd (Hotline)), R G Frost

760   Devon And Cornwall Bookmakers Handicap Hurdle Class E (0-110 4-y-o and up) £2,801 2m 1f.......... (5:15)

587³ SIRTELIMAR (Ire) [88] 7-11-2 T J Murphy, *hld up in tch, wnt second 4 out, led appr 2 out, rdn out.*
.... (7 to 4 fav op 11 to 4 tchd 3 to 1)   1

ZINGIBAR [76] 4-10-2 N Williamson, *trkd ldr till hmpd and lost pl 4 out, hrd rdn to press wnr 2 out, no imprsn r-in.*
.... (9 to 1 op 5 to 1 tchd 10 to 1)   2

666² CORRIN HILL [96] 9-11-7 (3*) T Dascombe, *hld up in tch, outpcd 3 out, rallied nxt, kpt on*........... (3 to 1 op 7 to 4)   3

TORDO (Ire) [96] (bl) 5-11-5 (3*) J Magee, *led till hdd and wknd appr 2 out*................... (3 to 1 op 2 to 1)   4

LUCAYAN GOLD [82] 12-10-10 R Dunwoody, *al in rear, lost tch aftr 4th, tld off*...... (4 to 1 op 5 to 1 tchd 6 to 1)   5

484⁷ ATHENIAN ALLIANCE [72] 7-10-0 B Fenton, *beh whn reminders 3rd, sn tld off, pld up aftr nxt.*
.... (66 to 1 op 20 to 1 tchd 100 to 1)   pu

Dist: 1l, 4l, 2½l, dist. 4m 9.30s. a 20.30s (6 Ran).

(Quicksilver Racing Partnership), K C Bailey

SEDGEFIELD (good to firm)
Tuesday October 1st
Going Correction: MINUS 0.15 sec. per fur.

761   Stanley Racing Golden Numbers Series Novices' Hurdle Class E (4-y-o and up) £2,232 2m 5f 110yds... (2:20)

610⁸ RULE OUT THE REST 5-10-12 A Thornton, *hmpd by loose horse aftr 3rd, reco'red to ld bef nxt, sn clr, styd on wl frm betw last 2*........... (12 to 1 op 10 to 1 tchd 14 to 1)   1

609 TIGH-NA-MARA 8-10-7 M Dwyer, *patiently rdn, improved to chase wnr frm 3 out, bounded nxt, one pace frm betw last 2.*
.... (7 to 2 op 3 to 1)   2

610 KANONA 5-10-12 J Supple, *led, crrd wide by loose horse bend aftr 3rd, feeling pace and drvn alng bef 3 out, sn struggling*................ (50 to 1 op 33 to 1)   3

467 PAPA'S BOY (Ire) 5-10-7 (5*) S Taylor, *blun and uns rdr 1st.*
.... (16 to 1 op 12 to 1)   ur

723 RUSHEN RAIDER 4-10-11 M Foster, *not jump wl, chsd ldr early, reminders and lost tch quickly aftr 4 out, tld off whn pld up aftr nxt, broke blood vessel.*
.... (7 to 2 op 3 to 1 on tchd 11 to 4 on)   pu

Dist: 7l, 22l. 4m 58.80s. a 10.80s (5 Ran).

(Mrs Sarah Horner-Harker), Mrs Sarah Horner-Harker

762   Satley Punch Bowl Claiming Hurdle Class F (4-y-o and up) £2,442 2m 1f .... (2:50)

689⁷ SHUTTLECOCK 5-10-11 A Maguire, *made most, jnd and rdn 2 out, styd on to go clr whn jmpd lft last, stayed on.*
.... (13 to 2 op 5 to 1 tchd 7 to 1)   1

NONIOS (Ire) 5-11-12 J Callaghan, *settled to track ldrs, improved to draw level 2 out, sn rdn, one pace frm last.*
.... (9 to 2 tchd 5 to 1)   2

489³ RED MARCH HARE 5-10-6 D J Moffatt, *patiently rdn, smooth hdwy gng wl aftr 3 out, hng fire betw last 2, kpt on und pres r-in*.............. (11 to 2 op 9 to 2 tchd 6 to 1)   3

665⁵ CLOVER GIRL (v) 5-10-3 (3*) G Cahill, *nvr far away, effrt and drvn alng frm 3 out, one pace frm betw last 2.*
.... (9 to 1 op 8 to 1)   4

698² STAGS FELL 11-10-8 Carol Cuthbert, *settled in tch, jnd wnr hfwy, wknd quickly bef 2 out*.......... (9 to 1 op 8 to 1)   5

ELLTEE-ESS 11-10-4 (7*) C R Weaver, *chsd ldrs, feeling pace hfwy, tld off frm 3 out*............... (50 to 1 op 33 to 1)   6

670² HERESTHEDEAL (Ire) (v) 7-10-7 (7*) R Hobson, *wth wnr, bumped and lost grnd 4th, struggling 3 out, tld off.*
.... (5 to 4 fav op 7 to 4)   7

546⁵ CANDID LAD 9-10-5 B Storey, *chsd ldrs, struggling and lost pl quickly bef 3 out, tld off*............ (8 to 1 op 10 to 1)   8

Dist: 2½l, 4l, hd, 15l, 13l, 4l, 6l. 3m 51.60s. a 5.60s (8 Ran).

SR: 2/14/-/-/-/   (Mrs N Macauley), Mrs N Macauley

763   Lazenby And Wilson Handicap Chase Class E (0-115 5-y-o and up) £3,418 2m 5f................................ (3:25)

663 MAGIC BLOOM [100] 10-11-0 Richard Guest, *settled off the pace, relentles prog fnl circuit, styd on strly to ld r-in, drw clr.*
.... (3 to 1 op 5 to 2 tchd 100 to 30)   1

375 CHARMING GALE [90] (v) 9-10-4 A Maguire, *set str pace, niggled alng frm 2 out, hit last, hdd and no extr r-in.*
.... (9 to 1 op 8 to 1)   2

717 CROSS CANNON [114] 10-12-0 T Reed, *settled off the pace, improved fnl circuit, hit 6 out, effrt last 3, one pace appr last.*
.... (11 to 2 op 9 to 2 tchd 6 to 1)   3

697* THE BLUE BOY (Ire) [100] (bl) 8-11-0 A P McCoy, *mstks, pressed ldr, struggling bef 3 out, no extr betw last 2.*
.... (7 to 2 op 3 to 1)   4

632⁴ TURPIN'S GREEN [86] 13-10-0 J Culloty, *al struggling to keep in tch, tld off aftr one circuit*.....(16 to 1 op 12 to 1)   5

37* UNOR (Fr) [107] 10-11-7 A Dobbin, *patiently rdn, steady hdwy to take cl order fnl circuit, second and one pace whn pld up lme bef 2 out*........(9 to 4 fav tchd 5 to 2 and 7 to 4)   pu

Dist: 4l, 13l, 10l, dist. 5m 5.80s. a 9.80s (6 Ran).

(Peter Nelson), J M Jefferson

764   Spitfire Novices' Chase Class E (5-y-o and up) £2,877 2m 5f............ (3:55)

201* NOTABLE EXCEPTION 7-11-5 P Niven, *patiently rdn, wnt second and hit 8th, styd on to ld 2 out, gng clr whn blun last.*
.... (11 to 10 fav op 11 to 10 on tchd 6 to 5)   1

608* VAL DE RAMA (Ire) 7-11-5 Richard Guest, *wtd wth, steady hdwy to track ldg pair 3 out, rdn and one pace frm betw last 2.*
.... (9 to 4 op 5 to 2 tchd 11 to 4)   2

558 ISLANDREAGH (Ire) 5-10-5 A Dobbin, *led frm 3rd, jmpd rght 5th, quickened clr fnl circuit, blun badly 4 out, hdd 2 out, sn btn*..................... (11 to 2 op 5 to 1 tchd 6 to 1)   3

41⁶ GOLDEN SAVANNAH 6-10-9 (3*) D Parker, *niggled alng to keep up 1st circuit, sn tld off*.........(16 to 1 op 12 to 1)   4

608³ CARDINAL SINNER (Ire) 7-10-12 K Jones, *led to 3rd, hit 7th, struggling fnl circuit, tld off*..........(33 to 1 op 25 to 1)   5

615 RAPID FIRE (Ire) 8-10-12 M Dwyer, *sn struggling to keep in tch, tld off fnl circuit, pld up bef 2 out.*
.... (6 to 1 op 5 to 1 tchd 7 to 1)   pu

Dist: 10l, 23l, 8l, 16l. 5m 7.10s. a 11.10s (6 Ran).

(Roland Hope), Mrs M Reveley

765   Kier North East Handicap Hurdle Class D (0-120 4-y-o and up) £2,792 2m 5f 110yds........................ (4:30)

656³ RED VALERIAN [119] (v) 5-11-9 (5*) Michael Brennan, *patiently rdn, imprvg on bit to ld whn hit 2 out, gd jump last, quickened clr*........(11 to 10 op Evens tchd 5 to 4)   1

SCARBA [94] 8-9-11 (7*) M Newton, *wtd wth, improved gng wl to chal 2 out, rdn and one pace frm betw last two.*
.... (8 to 1 op 5 to 1 tchd 9 to 1)   2

204² SUPERHOO [92] 5-10-1 B Fenton, *al pressing ldrs, hrd at work 3 out, kpt on one pace frm betw last 2.*
.... (3 to 1 op 11 to 4)   3

738³ TOUGH TEST (Ire) [100] 6-10-7 (3*) G Cahill, *pressed ldr, drvn alng bef 2 out, not quicken*........... (11 to 2 op 4 to 1)   4

725⁴ FLINTLOCK (Ire) [90] 6-9-9 (5*) R McGrath, *last and hld up, effrt hfwy, rdn 3 out, sn outpcd*.......(25 to 1 op 20 to 1)   5

707⁵ FRONTIER FLIGHT (USA) [91] 6-9-12 (3*) E Husband, *tried to make al, jnd 3 out, hdd nxt, fdd.*
.... (9 to 1 op 6 to 1 tchd 10 to 1)   6

Dist: 3½l, 1¾l, 3l, 4l, 1½l. 4m 58.20s. a 10.20s (6 Ran).

(Mrs Alurie O'Sullivan), G M Moore

766   Hurricane Novices' Hurdle Class E (4-y-o and up) £2,302 2m 1f.......(5:00)

665² SUAS LEAT (Ire) 6-10-12 (7*) M Newton, *led frm second, hdd md 3 out, nosed ahead ag'n nxt, hrd pressed last, drifted lft, styd on*..................... (9 to 4 op 7 to 4)   1

CANTON VENTURE 4-10-11 P Hide, *led till jmpd slwly and hdd second, styd upsides, nosed ahead aftr 3 out, headed nxt, ev ch till and not quicken r-in.*
.... (2 to 1 on tchd 7 to 4 on and 13 to 8 on)   2

728 COURT JOKER (Ire) 4-10-11 P Niven, *trkd ldrs, struggling whn pace quickened aftr 3 out, styd on frm betw last 2, no imprsn*..................... (5 to 1 op 12 to 1)   3

652⁸ ROSE CHIME (Ire) 4-10-6 P McLoughlin, *trkd ldrs, struggling whn pace lifted aftr 3 out, rdn and no imprsn after.*
.... (16 to 1 op 10 to 1)   4

TOP SKIPPER (Ire) 4-10-11 A S Smith, *pressed ldrs, struggling to keep up whn pace quickened aftr 3 out, lost tch, tld off.*
.... (50 to 1 op 33 to 1)   5

SALKELD KING (Ire) 4-10-11 P Waggott, *chsd ldrs, hrd at work 3 out, lost tch, tld off*...............(50 to 1 op 33 to 1)   6

Dist: 1¼l, 12l, 3l, 16l, 3l. 3m 54.80s. a 8.80s (6 Ran).

(Mrs J M Davenport), J M Jefferson

EXETER (good)
Wednesday October 2nd
Going Correction: MINUS 0.10 sec. per fur.

767 South West Racing Club Juvenile Novices' Hurdle Class E (3-y-o) £1,969 2m 1f 110yds.................................(2:15)

DOCTOR GREEN (Fr) (v) 10-10 A P McCoy, *made all, drw clr frm 3 out, untidy last, unchlgd*..... (13 to 8 jt-fav op 6 to 4) 1
481* CHIEF MOUSE 11-3 J F Titley, *al in tch, chsd wnr aftr 3 out, sn rdn, no imprsn*..... (13 to 8 jt-fav op 6 to 4) 2
481³ ANDSOME BOY 10-10 B Clifford, *pld hrd, in tch till outpcd frm 3 out*........................... (10 to 1 op 5 to 1) 3
542² BEN BOWDEN 11-3 D Gallagher, *trkd ldrs, lost tch appr 2 out*.
.... (10 to 1 op 5 to 1) 4
705³ TABLETS OF STONE (Ire) 10-10 M Bosley, *mstk 1st, nvr on terms, tld off*.......... (10 to 1 tchd 12 to 1) 5
CITU LENE 11-3 L Harvey, *al towards rear, hdwy wnr 4th, wknd quickly 3 out, tld off*.....(16 to 1 op 7 to 1) 6
SEVEN CROWNS (USA) 10-10 N Williamson, *not jump wl, al beh, tld off 4th*........ (16 to 1 op 10 to 1) 7
658 PEYTON JONES 10-10 F Jousset, *tld off 4th*.
.... (80 to 1 op 25 to 1 tchd 100 to 1) 8
Dist: 12l, 5l, 4l, dist, 15l, 26l, dist. 4m 4.10s. a 8.10s (8 Ran).

(Jim Weeden), M C Pipe

768 Dominion Oils Novices' Selling Hurdle Class G (4 - 7-y-o) £1,829 2m 3f (2:45)

694³ MILLION DANCER (bl) 4-11-1 (3*) D Walsh, *made all, sn clr, hit last 2, unchlgd*............. (2 to 1 tchd 7 to 4 on) 1
498⁴ CASHFLOW CRISIS (Ire) 4-11-4 S Curran, *sn chsd wnr, tried to cl aftr 3 out, no imprsn*. (11 to 2 op 5 to 1 tchd 6 to 1) 2
666⁸ LOVELARK 7-10-7 A Maguire, *rear, mstk 6th, some hdwy appr 2 out, nvr dngrs*............ (25 to 1 op 20 to 1) 3
SECRET SERENADE (bl) 5-10-12 W Marston, *al abt same pl, no ch frm hfwy*........... (10 to 1 op 9 to 1 tchd 11 to 1) 4
673 WHAT'S THE JOKE 7-10-7 C Maude, *al beh*.
.... (33 to 1 op 25 to 1) 5
419 LILAC RAIN (v) 4-10-6 M A Fitzgerald, *prmnt early, wknd quickly appr 5th*.................. (50 to 1 op 33 to 1) 6
435³ SIESTA TIME (USA) 6-10-7 D J Burchell, *kicked strt, took no part*....................... (10 to 1 tchd 12 to 1) I
545⁷ LUCKY MO 6-10-2 (5*) D Salter, *refused to race, took no part*.
.... (16 to 1 op 10 to 1) I
671⁸ LAKESIDE LAD 4-10-11 N Williamson, *refused to race, took no part*.......................... (12 to 1) I
Dist: 16l, 16l, 3l, 2½l, nk. 4m 28.10s. a 12.10s (9 Ran).

(Martin Pipe Racing Club), M C Pipe

769 Dominion Oils Novices' Chase Class E (5-y-o and up) £2,762 2m 3f.....(3:15)

755 PONGO WARING (Ire) 7-10-12 J F Titley, *hld up, gd hdwy tenth, jnd 5 out, led bef nxt, rdn out*.
.... (12 to 1 op 8 to 1 tchd 14 to 1) 1
HARDY WEATHER (Ire) 7-10-12 R Dunwoody, *al prmnt, led 6th, hdd appr 4 out, hrd rdn 2 out, no imprsn*.
.... (4 to 1 op 11 to 2) 2
583² CHICKABIDDY 8-10-7 M A Fitzgerald, *hdwy whn mstk 9th, lost pl, rallied and one pace frm 3 out*.
.... (100 to 30 op 4 to 1 tchd 9 to 2) 3
298² SHIKAREE (Ire) 5-10-10 A P McCoy, *hld up, cld on ldrs 5 out, rdn 3 out, sn btn*.
.... (5 to 4 on op 13 to 8 on tchd 11 to 10 on) 4
I REMEMBER YOU (Ire) 6-10-12 J Culloty, *led to 4th, in cl tch till wknd appr four out, tld off*.
.... (20 to 1 op 25 to 1 tchd 33 to 1) 5
COOLTEEN HERO (Ire) 6-10-12 W McFarland, *rcd keenly, in tch whn mstk 7th, wknd appr 4 out, tld off*.
.... (20 to 1 op 10 to 1) 6
KARLOVAC 10-10-12 A Maguire, *in tch till wknd 9th, tld off*.
.... (33 to 1 op 20 to 1) 7
670⁶ SAXON BLADE 8-10-12 L Harvey, *led 4th to 6th, wknd appr 8th, tld off*....... (66 to 1 op 33 to 1) 8
CHUKKARIO 10-10-12 M Bosley, *al beh, tld off 7th*.
.... (100 to 1 op 33 to 1) 9
688³ RYTON RUN 11-11-2 B Fenton, *al beh, tld off 7th, pld up bef last*..................... (50 to 1 op 25 to 1) pu
Dist: 4l, 16l, 12l, 25l, ¾l, 5l, dist, 20l. 4m 38.40s. a 10.40s (10 Ran).

(Miss H Knight), Miss H C Knight

770 Scudamore Clothing 0800 301 301 Amateur Riders' Novices' Hurdle Class F (4-y-o and up) £2,051 2m 1f 110yds
.................................(3:45)

689² COURBARIL 4-11-7 (5*) Mr M Rimell, *mid-div whn mstk 5th, wnt second aftr 3 out, led aftr mext, sn clr*.
.... (11 to 8 fav op 6 to 4 tchd 2 to 1) 1
168³ POLITICAL PANTO (Ire) 5-11-7 (5*) Mr A Farrant, *led clr 3rd, reluctant and hdd 2 out, rallied to go second ag'n r-in*.
.... (4 to 1 op 2 to 1 tchd 5 to 1) 2

RITTO 6-10-12 (7*) Mr R Thornton, *in tch, rdn to ld 2 out, sn hdd, wknd r-in*.
.... (7 to 2 op 6 to 1 tchd 5 to 2 and 4 to 1) 3
652⁹ HIGHLY CHARMING (Ire) 4-10-12 (7*) Mr A Wintle, *chsd ldr till wknd appr 2 out*........(14 to 1 op 6 to 1 tchd 16 to 1) 4
652³ LAST LAUGH (Ire) (bl) 4-10-7 (7*) Mr R Wakley, *mstks, beh frm 4th, tld off*.........(100 to 30 op 9 to 2 tchd 3 to 1) 5
GAELIC MILLION (Ire) 5-10-7 (7*) Mr T P Young, *al beh, tld off 4th*......................... (33 to 1 op 12 to 1) 6
186 ARDEARNED 9-10-7 (7*) Mr A Charles-Jones, *al beh, tld off 4th, fnshd lme*.................. (100 to 1 op 50 to 1) 7
Dist: 9l, 7l, 4l, 26l, 14l, 18l. 4m 5.00s. a 9.00s (7 Ran).

(Richard Green (Fine Paintings), M C Pipe

771 Dominion Oils Handicap Chase Class E (0-115 5-y-o and up) £2,736 2m 1f 110yds.........................(4:15)

630* NORDIC VALLEY (Ire) [83] 5-10-0 A P McCoy, *chsd ldrs, wnt second 4 out, rdn and styd on to ld r-in*.
.... (100 to 30 op 3 to 1 tchd 4 to 1) 1
617³ HEX TO THE RESCUE (Ire) [100] 8-10-13 (5*) P Henley, *led, kpt on whn chlgd 4 out, rdn and hdd r-in*.
.... (100 to 30 op 3 to 1 tchd 4 to 1) 2
FLAPJACK LAD [95] 7-10-10 (3*) D Walsh, *not fluent, chsd ldr, ev ch whn mstks 4 out and nxt, no imprsn aftr*.
.... (2 to 1 fav op 2 to 1) 3
165 DAMAS (Fr) [110] 5-11-13 C Maude, *in tch to 5th, wl beh 5 out, tld off*.................... (25 to 1 op 16 to 1) 4
DAWN CHANCE [82] 10-9-12¹ (3*) T Dascombe, *f 1st*.
.... (10 to 1 op 16 to 1) f
LAKE OF LOUGHREA (Ire) [104] 6-11-8 T J Murphy, *hld up, hdwy 5 out, disputing 3rd and ev ch whn f 3 out*.
.... (7 to 2 tchd 9 to 2) f
449 TANGO'S DELIGHT [82] 8-10-0 B Powell, *sn tld off, pld up 5th*.
.... (66 to 1 op 25 to 1) pu
Dist: 1½l, 4l, 26l. 4m 10.30s. a 5.30s (7 Ran).
SR: 2/18/9/-/

(Pond House Racing), M C Pipe

772 Dominion Oils Handicap Hurdle Class D (0-120 4-y-o and up) £2,792 2m 3f
.................................(4:45)

631* OUT RANKING (Fr) [109] 4-11-12 C Maude, *al prmnt, led 5th, sn clr, kpt on gmely whn chlgd frm 2 out*.
.... (6 to 1 op 4 to 1 tchd 7 to 1) 1
631³ LITTLE HOOLIGAN [83] (bl) 5-10-0 A Maguire, *hld up, hdwy appr 5th, outpcd 3 out, styd on to go second r-in*.
.... (7 to 1 op 5 to 1) 2
FLEUR DE TAL [100] 5-10-10 (7*) J Power, *nvr far away, chsd wnr 6th till nr out r-in*............. (20 to 1 op 16 to 1) 3
MORSTOCK [110] 6-11-9 (5*) Mr M Rimell, *chsd ldrs, no hdwy frm 3 out*.......(12 to 1 op 16 to 1 tchd 20 to 1) 4
669³ PREROGATIVE [106] (v) 6-11-10 R Dunwoody, *led to 5th, wknd quickly 3 out*......(14 to 1 op 12 to 1 tchd 16 to 1) 5
572* BORN TO PLEASE (Ire) [90] 4-10-7 A P McCoy, *hld up, effrt 5th, wknd 3 out*.......... (6 to 1 op 5 to 1 tchd 7 to 1) 6
652³ IKHTIRAA (USA) [82] 6-10-0 P Holley, *chsd ldrs to 5th, wknd aftr nxt*........... (14 to 1 op 12 to 1 tchd 16 to 1) 7
LESSONS LASS (Ire) [102] 4-11-5 J Culloty, *in tch till rdn and wknd quickly appr 2 out*........... (5 to 2 fav op 3 to 1) 8
DOMINION'S DREAM [107] (v) 4-11-3 (7*) G Supple, *hld up in rear, lost tch 5th, tld off*......... (25 to 1 op 14 to 1) 9
533⁴ LANCER (USA) [86] 4-10-3 W Marston, *al beh, tld off 5th*.
.... (10 to 1 op 16 to 1 tchd 25 to 1) 10
587 GOLD MEDAL (Fr) [105] 8-11-2 (7*) B Moore, *beh frm 5th, sn tld off*.................. (14 to 1 op 8 to 1) 11
698 BUGLET [92] 6-10-7 (3*) D Walsh, *sn reminders, tld off whn pld up bef 4th*........... (16 to 1 op 8 to 1) pu
Dist: 2l, 1¾l, 15l, 6l, 3l, 8l, 15l, 7l, 13l. 4m 24.80s. a 8.80s (12 Ran).

(Knight Hawks Partnership), M C Pipe

NAVAN (IRE) (good)
Wednesday October 2nd

773 Garlow I.N.H. Flat Race (4-y-o and up) £3,082 2m.......................(5:30)

733² MOSCOW EXPRESS (Ire) 4-11-10 (3*) Mr B M Cash,
.... (5 to 4 on) 1
741⁶ WELSH GRIT (Ire) 7-12-4 Mr J A Nash............(6 to 1) 2
346* CROSSCHILD (Ire) 5-11-6 (7*) Mr P M Cloke,...... (7 to 1) 3
681* NICOLA MARIE (Ire) 7-11-6 (7*) Mr Sean O O'Brien, (12 to 1) 4
628* MERCHANTS QUAY (Ire) 5-11-11 (7*) Mr G Kearns, (9 to 2) 5
678⁴ NO DIAMOND (Ire) 7-11-11 (7*) Mr D W Cullen,.... (11 to 1) 6
THE TEXAS KID (Ire) 5-11-4 (7*) Mr S M Duffy, ... (14 to 1) 7
68⁹ POLLYROE (Ire) 5-11-6 Mr J A Berry,................ (20 to 1) 8
WHINNEY HILL (Ire) 6-10-13 (7*) Mr R F Coonan, ... (16 to 1) 9
SEAMAS AN FEAR (Ire) 5-11-4 (7*) Mr J S O'Haire, (25 to 1) 10
STEMAR (Ire) 5-11-4 (7*) Mr J P Kilfeather,.........(25 to 1) 11
622⁹ MASTER FINBAR (Ire) 5-11-4 (7*) Mr A C Coyle,...(14 to 1) su
Dist: 5½l, 1½l, 3½l, 4l. 3m 43.90s. (12 Ran).

(T Conroy), A P O'Brien

MARKET RASEN (good)

NATIONAL HUNT RESULTS 1996-97

Thursday October 3rd
Going Correction: PLUS 0.10 sec. per fur.

774 Burley Fuel Effect Conditional Jockeys' Handicap Chase Class E (0-130 5-y-o and up) £3,347 2m 1f 110yds.............................(2:10)

651* CAPTAIN KHEDIVE [130] 8-12-0 Guy Lewis, *trkd ldrs, wnt second 4 out, led aftr nxt, easily.*
............................(5 to 2 on op 3 to 1 on tchd 2 to 1 on) 1
753² THE YOKEL [102] 10-10-0 P Henley, *hld up, led aftr 6th, hdd 8th, drvn alng after six out, 3rd whn mstk 3 out, styd on to take 2nd pl after last*....................(16 to 1 op 14 to 1) 2
505² CIRCULATION [102] (v) 10-10-0 D Walsh, *led, clr aftr second, mstk and hdd 6th, led ag'n and mistake 8th, sn drvn alng, headed after 3 out, mistake nxt*......(25 to 1 tchd 50 to 1) 3
71⁵ BALLY PARSON [115] 10-10-13 J Culloty, *trkd ldrs, hit 3rd, drvn alng and wknd quickly aftr 4 out.*
............................(9 to 4 op 11 to 4 tchd 3 to 1 and 2 to 1) 4
Dist: 3½l, 13l, 18l. 4m 23.70s. a 9.70s (4 Ran).
SR: 20/   *(Khedive Partnership), P F Nicholls*

775 Burley Butler Heated Trolly Novices' Hurdle Class E (4-y-o and up) £2,388 2m 1f 110yds.....................(2:45)

MISTER RM 4-10-11 C Llewellyn, *led, mstks, drw clr aftr 3 out, hit nxt, easily*.........(6 to 4 op 9 to 4 tchd 5 to 4) 1
689³ NASHAAT (USA) 8-10-12 W Worthington, *chsd ldr, mstk second, pushed alng aftr 3 out, lft second and no ch wth wnr 2 out.*
............................(15 to 2 op 6 to 1 tchd 1 to 1 and 8 to 1) 2
JAVA RED (Ire) 4-10-11 M Dwyer, *chsd ldr, drvn alng aftr 3 out, sn no imprsn, lft 3rd 2 out.*........(8 to 1 op 7 to 1) 3
704⁵ IRIE MON (Ire) 4-10-11 (7*) Mr A Wintle, *hld up and beh, rdn and hdwy aftr 5th, kpt on one pace after 3 out, lft 4th 2 out.*
............................(20 to 1 op 12 to 1 tchd 25 to 1) 4
533⁷ MELLOW YELLOW 5-10-9 (3*) E Husband, *chsd ldr, in tch til drvn alng aftr 5th, wknd after 3 out.*.............(33 to 1) 5
728 FLYAWAY BLUES 4-10-11 P Niven, *hld up, rdn aftr 5th, sn beh.*.................(14 to 1 op 12 to 1 tchd 16 to 1) 6
SUVALU (USA) 4-10-11 L Wyer, *prmnt to 5th, sn rdn and wknd.*...............(14 to 1 op 12 to 1 tchd 16 to 1) 7
618* ANABRANCH 5-10-7 (7*) M Newton, *hld up, hdwy aftr 5th, wnt second after 3 out, weaand and held whn f nxt.*
............................(5 to 4 fav op Evens tchd 13 to 8) f
BALLYSOKERRY (Ire) 5-10-12 A Dobbin, *jmpd slwly 3rd, sn beh, ran out 5th*......(66 to 1 op 50 to 1 tchd 100 to 1) ro
FIERY FOOTSTEPS 4-10-6 J Culloty, *hld up, lost tch aftr 3rd, tld off after 5th, pld up bef 2 out*....(50 to 1 tchd 66 to 1) pu
704⁷ KAJOSTAR 6-10-0 (7*) O Burrows, *sddl slpd and pld up aftr 1st*...........................(100 to 1) pu
Dist: 16l, ½l, 8l, 1¾l, 7l, 14l. 4m 15.40s. a 14.40s (11 Ran).
(F J Mills), N A Twiston-Davies

776 Burley Visiflame Novices' Chase Class C (5-y-o and up) £4,394 2m 1f 110yds...............................(3:15)

JATHIB (Can) 5-10-11 D Byrne, *chsd clr ldr, jmpd wl, led 8th, sn drw clear, imprsv*..............(5 to 2 tchd 2 to 1) 1
688* STRONG PROMISE 5-10-13 (3*) K Gaule, *wtd wth, rdn and hdwy after 8th, wnt second 4 out, ridden and no imprsn frm nxt*.....(9 to 4 on op 5 to 2 on tchd 2 to 1 on and 5 to 8 on) 2
698⁵ SHARP SENSATION 6-10-12 P Niven, *beh, mstk and drpd rear pl 8th, rdn and hdwy aftr 4 out, styd on to take 3rd place after 2 out.*....................(12 to 1 op 10 to 1) 3
687³ RECORD LOVER (Ire) 6-10-12 W Worthington, *hld up, wl beh 8th, hdwy aftr 4 out, wknd after nxt.*
............................(33 to 1 op 25 to 1 tchd 50 to 1) 4
557⁵ DOCTOR-J (Ire) 6-10-12 B Fenton, *beh, drvn alng aftr 7th, sn lost tch.*...........(50 to 1 op 33 to 1 tchd 66 to 1) 5
688² SHALIK (Ire) 6-10-5 (7*) N T Egan, *led, hit second, clr to 6th, mstk 7th, mistake and hdd nxt.*
............................(5 to 1 op 14 to 1 tchd 33 to 1) 6
Dist: 27l, 13l, 2½l, 18l, 17l. 4m 21.60s. a 7.60s (6 Ran).
SR: 24/2/-/   *(Crown Pkg & Mailing Svs Ltd), Mrs Merrita Jones*

777 Air Products Gases Handicap Hurdle Class C (0-135 4-y-o and up) £3,355 2m 1f 110yds.....................(3:50)

80⁴ NON VINTAGE (Ire) [130] 5-12-0 W Worthington, *hld up, hdwy to chase ldrs aftr 3 out, ev ch nxt, gd jump to ld last, drvn out.*
............................(11 to 2 op 9 to 2) 1
661* FIELD OF VISION (Ire) [101] 6-10-0 J Supple, *mstks, pressed ldr, rdn and ev ch aftr 3 out, led nxt, hdd last, not quicken.*
............................(3 to 1 op 2 to 1) 2
571³ EDEN DANCER [108] 4-10-5 P Niven, *led to 5th, pressed ldr, led ag'n aftr 3 out, hdd nxt, rdn and one pace betw last 2.*
............................(5 to 2 op 2 to 1) 3
DISTANT ECHO (Ire) [117] 6-11-2 R Dunwoody, *hld up, reminders and no response aftr 5th, wl beh til styd on to take poor 4th after last.*............(7 to 4 fav tchd 9 to 4) 4

DEVILRY [106] (bl) 6-10-5 B Fenton, *prmnt, wnt second 4th, led nxt, hdd aftr 3 out, sn rdn and wknd.*
............................(12 to 1 op 10 to 1 tchd 16 to 1) 5
Dist: 3l, 3½l, 18l, ¾l. 4m 13.00s. a 12.00s (5 Ran).
(Alan Mann), M C Chapman

778 Burley Forge Range Novices' Handicap Chase Class D (0-110 5-y-o and up) £3,779 3m 1f...................(4:25)

662* THE GALLOPIN'MAJOR (Ire) [84] 6-11-10 N Smith, *hld up, mstks 6 out and nxt, ev ch 3 out, rdn to ld aftr last, drvn out.*
............................(13 to 8 fav op 7 to 4 tchd 9 to 4) 1
MOBILE MESSENGER (NZ) [80] 8-11-6 M A Fitzgerald, *led to second, led 7th to 9th, led ag'n 12th til rdn and hdd aftr last.*
............................(3 to 1 tchd 7 to 2) 2
CAMP BANK [81] 6-11-7 C Llewellyn, *trkd ldrs, pushed alng aftr 5 out, hrd rdn and kpt on one pace after 3 out.*
............................(9 to 4 op 2 to 1 tchd 13 to 8) 3
FINAL BEAT (Ire) [82] 7-11-8 A Thornton, *led 6th to nxt, led 9th to 12th, styd prmnt, rdn alng aftr 4 out, kpt on one pace.*
............................(9 to 2 op 3 to 1 tchd 5 to 1) 4
AUNTIE LORNA [60] 7-9-7 (7*) Mr R Wakley, *led second to 6th, wknd aftr 12th, tld off after 14th, pld up bef 4 out.*
............................(33 to 1 tchd 40 to 1 and 50 to 1) pu
Dist: 2l, 3½l, 2½l. 6m 19.00s. a 19.00s (5 Ran).
(R W S Jevon), Mrs M Reveley

779 Burley Electric Fire Handicap Hurdle Class C (0-130 4-y-o and up) £3,371 3m.................................(5:00)

752* FREDDIE MUCK [111] 6-11-2 (6ex) C Llewellyn, *trkd ldrs, pushed alng aftr 4 out, rdn to ld 2 out, sn drw clr, easily.*
............................(11 to 10 on op 5 to 4 on tchd 11 to 10) 1
JALCANTO [121] 6-11-12 P Niven, *led 4th, mstk 6th, hdd and mistake nxt, ch nxt four out, second and btn whn mistake 2 out.*
............................(3 to 1 op 3 to 1) 2
707² ORDOG MOR (Ire) [105] 7-10-10 D Byrne, *hld up in last pl, rapid hdwy to ld aftr 7th, hdd 2 out, sn btn.*
............................(3 to 1 op 11 to 4 tchd 7 to 2) 3
MASTER OF THE ROCK [110] (v) 7-10-12 (3*) E Husband, *led to 4th, wknd quickly aftr 8th, sn tld off....(8 to 1 op 5 to 1) 4
Dist: 13l, 3½l, 22l. 6m 1.00s. a 22.00s (4 Ran).
(Mrs C Twiston-Davies), N A Twiston-Davies

PUNCHESTOWN (IRE) (good)
Thursday October 3rd
Going Correction: PLUS 0.15 sec. per fur.

780 Ingoldsby Handicap Chase (0-123 5-y-o and up) £3,767 2m.............(3:30)

KING OF THE GLEN [-] 10-10-10 (7*) Mr J T McNamara,
............................(5 to 1) 1
PERKNAPP [-] 9-11-11 (7*) Mr G Elliott, ... (5 to 2 fav) 2
721 FAYS FOLLY [-] 7-9-11 (7*) Mr A Ross,........(5 to 1) 3
721 HANNIES GIRL [-] 7-10-9 (3*) Mr B M Cash,.... (5 to 1) 4
646 NO SIR ROM [-] 10-9-11 (7*) Mr John P Moloney, (14 to 1) f
ALLIGATOR JOE [-] 8-11-11 (5*) Mr R Walsh, ... (11 to 2) f
646* DRINDOD (Ire) [-] 7-10-9 (7*) Mr M O'Connor, ... (5 to 1) f
FAMBO LAD (Ire) [-] 8-10-11 (7*) Mr P M Cloke, ... (9 to 1) pu
Dist: 2l, 6l, dist. 4m 9.30s. a 10.30s (8 Ran).
SR: 10/23/-/-/-/   *(Michael J Walshe), A J McNamara*

781 Knockadoo Hurdle (5-y-o and up) £3,082 2½m.....................(4:00)

746² CLONAGAM (Ire) 7-11-12 C F Swan, ...(Evens fav) 1
135⁵ MAJESTIC PADDY (Ire) 6-11-9 F Woods, ...(11 to 2) 2
686⁷ TEXARKANA (Ire) 8-10-7 (7*) A O'Shea, ...(20 to 1) 3
337⁴ RATHGIBBON (Ire) 5-11-9 T P Treacy, ...(7 to 2) 4
404³ TURRAMURRA GIRL (Ire) 7-11-2² Mr H F Cleary, ..(14 to 1) 5
CLEARLY CANADIAN (Ire) 5-11-0 (5*) G Cotter, ... (20 to 1) 6
685³ PHARADISO (Ire) 5-11-5 C O'Dwyer, ...(8 to 1) 7
581⁷ RED RADICAL (Ire) 6-10-13¹ (7*) Mr P E I Newell, ..(12 to 1) 8
685⁵ DREAM ETERNAL (Ire) 5-11-0 W Slattery, ...(12 to 1) 9
ICED HONEY 9-11-9 L P Cusack, ...(10 to 1) 10
COOLREE LORD (Ire) 5-11-5 M P Hourigan, ...(20 to 1) 11
685 MISSED CONNECTION (Ire) 5-10-9 (5*) J Butler, ..(66 to 1) 12
681⁹ SUSIE'S DELIGHT (Ire) 6-11-0 P L Malone, ...(25 to 1) 13
Dist: 7l, 4l, 6l, hd. 5m 7.80s. a 25.80s (13 Ran).
(Mrs E Queally), A P O'Brien

782 Killashee I.N.H. Flat Race (4-y-o) £3,082 2m.....................(5:30)

RATHBAWN PRINCE (Ire) 11-2 (7*) Mr A J Dempsey,
............................(5 to 1) jt-fav) 1
DO YE KNOW WHA (Ire) 11-2 (7*) Mr J P McNamara,
............................(13 to 1) 2
MINISTER'S CROSS (Ire) 11-2 (7*) Mr D A Harney, (10 to 1) 3
NATIVE PLAYER (Ire) 11-6 (3*) Mr B M Cash, ...(6 to 1) 4
MEN OF NINETYEIGHT (Ire) 11-2 (7*) Mr P A Farrell, (8 to 1) 5
686 SINGERS CORNER 10-11 (7*) Mr Edgar Byrne, ... (16 to 1) 6
703² REGGIE'S HONOUR (Ire) 10-11 (7*) Mr G Elliott, .. (10 to 1) 7

91

MY HAND (Ire) 11-2 (7*) Mr C A Murphy, ...(12 to 1) 8
MONTYS DELIGHT (Ire) 11-9 Mr A J Martin, ... (10 to 1) 9
SPARKEY SMITH (Ire) 11-9 Mr A R Coonan, ... (14 to 1) 10
OXFORD LUNCH (USA) 11-9 Mr J P Dempsey, . .(5 to 1 jt-
fav) 11
SUM OF ALL FEAR (Ire) 11-9 Mr G J Harford, ...(16 to 1) 12
180 BEHY BRIDGE (Ire) 10-11 (7*) Mr D P Coakley, . . .(33 to 1) 13
185 FLY BY WIRE (Ire) 11-2 (7*) Mr S T Nolan, ...(20 to 1) 14
WESTERN GREY (Ire) 11-2 (7*) Mr R P McNalley, . .(16 to 1) 15
KARMAJO (Ire) 11-2 (7*) Mr M G Whyte, ... (16 to 1) 16
731 HEMERO (Ire) 11-2 (7*) Mr John P Moloney, ...(14 to 1) 17
STORM COURSE (Ire) 11-4 Mr J A Nash, ...(10 to 1) 18
OH MAY OH (Ire) 10-11 (7*) Mr A C Coyle, ... (14 to 1) 19
JER-MARIE (Ire) 11-9 Mr H F Cleary, ... (16 to 1) ref
713 BOPTWOPHAR (Ire) 11-9 Mr P Fenton, ... (11 to 2) ro
Dist: 2l, hd, 3½l, 2½l. 3m 46.80s. (21 Ran).

(James O'Keeffe), James O'Keeffe

TAUNTON (hard)
Thursday October 3rd
Going Correction: MINUS 0.65 sec. per fur.

783 Norman Reading Memorial Maiden Hurdle Class E (4-y-o and up) £2,295 2m 3f 110yds. . . . .(1:50)

754⁷ SWINGS'N'THINGS (USA) 4-10-13 R Farrant, hld up, hdwy to press ldrs 3 out, led last, ran on.
. . . .(6 to 1 op 9 to 2 tchd 8 to 1) 1
641³ SECOND COLOURS (USA) 6-11-5 A P McCoy, mstks, chsd ldr, rdn appr 3 out, led and hit 2 out, hdd last, no extr.
. . . .(7 to 2 op 2 to 1) 2
GENERAL MOUKTAR (bl) 6-11-5 C Maude, led, clr 4th, hit 7th, rdn and hdd 2 out, one pace aftr.
. . . .(2 to 1 on op 11 to 8 on tchd 5 to 4 on) 3
REINE DE LA CHASSE (Fr) 4-10-13 A McCabe, hld up, lost tch 3 out, tld off. . . . .(14 to 1 op 8 to 1) 4
Dist: 1½l, 4l, dist. 4m 27.70s. a 9.70s (4 Ran).

(D Brennan), B Palling

784 Taunton Castle Selling Hurdle Class G (4-y-o and up) £2,005 2m 1f. . . . .(2:20)

641⁴ ALMAPA 4-10-11 P Holley, hld up in tch, wnt second 3 out, led last, drvn out. . . . .(4 to 1 op 9 to 2) 1
446² FLEET CADET (bl) 5-10-12 C Maude, hld up in rear, steady hdwy 6th, ev ch last, rdn and one pace.
. . . .(3 to 1 fav tchd 7 to 2) 2
727⁴ HACKETTS CROSS (Ire) 8-11-12 (7*) Mr R Thornton, hld up, gd hdwy 3 out, ev ch 2 out, one pace aftr.
. . . .(5 to 1 op 4 to 1 tchd 11 to 2) 3
689 FERENS HALL 9-10-12 P McLoughlin, led second, rdn appr 2 out, hdd and hmpd last, wknd r-in. . . . .(14 to 1 op 25 to 1) 4
638³ PRESTIGE LADY 5-10-7 W Marston, mid-div, mstks, drvn up to chal appr 2 out, btn whn mistake last. (9 to 2 op 7 to 2) 5
631⁵ NIGHT TIME 4-10-11 (7*) Mr G Shenkin, hld up, hdwy 3 out, nvr dngrs. . . . .(14 to 1 op 8 to 1) 6
638⁶ BURNT SIENNA (bl) (v) 4-10-13 W McFarland, led to second, styd prmnt till blun 3 out, sn wknd. . . . . .(8 to 1 op 6 to 1) 7
638⁵ JAVA SHRINE (USA) (bl) 5-11-5 R Bellamy, hld up, nvr on terms. . . . .(20 to 1 op 10 to 1) 8
673⁵ ON THE LEDGE (USA) (bl) 6-10-5 (7*) A Dowling, chsd ldr early, wknd 6th, tld off. . . . .(66 to 1 op 50 to 1) 9
OLD MASTER (Ire) 5-10-12 B Powell, al beh, tld off 6th.
. . . .(50 to 1 op 33 to 1) 10
652 FLASHING SABRE 4-10-11 Mr A Charles-Jones, al beh, tld off. . . . .(100 to 1) 11
398⁵ INDIAN MINOR 12-10-12 N Williamson, prmnt, mstk 4th, wknd quickly appr 3 out, pld up sn aftr, lme.
. . . .(25 to 1 op 12 to 1) pu
Dist: 4l, 1½l, 3½l, 4l, 5l, hd, 1¾l, dist, 10l, dist. 3m 42.60s. b 0.40s (12 Ran).

(P Slade), R J Hodges

785 Curland Handicap Chase Class D (0-125 5-y-o and up) £3,526 2m 3f
. . . . (2:55)

690* RAMSTAR [103] 8-11-10 A P McCoy, led 3rd till mstk 6th, hit and lost jd 9th, rdn to go second 4 out, ran on und str pres to ld cl hme. . . . .(10 to 1 op 7 to 4 tchd 9 to 4) 1
666⁹ SLIPPERY MAX [79] 12-10-0 W Marston, led to 3rd, rdn 11th, outpcd appr 2 out, str brst r-in, jst fld. . .(10 to 1 op 8 to 1) 2
759⁵ GABISH [79] 11-9-7 (7*) Mr R Thornton, hld up, hdwy to ld 6th, hrd rdn appr 2 out, hdd nr finish. . . . .(20 to 1 op 33 to 1) 3
642³ CLEAR IDEA (Ire) [94] 8-11-1 J Frost, hld up, hit and uns rdr 5th, destroyed.
. . . . . .(6 to 5 fav op 11 to 10 tchd 5 to 4 and 11 to 8) ur
POWDER BOY [97] 11-11-4 B Powell, hld up in tch, cl 3rd whn pld up bef tenth, lme. (9 to 2 op 6 to 1 tchd 13 to 2) pu
Dist: Hd, 1l. 4m 38.40s. a 7.40s (5 Ran).

(A Loze), P J Hobbs

786 Summerfield Handicap Hurdle Class E (0-115 4-y-o and up) £2,253 2m 1f

. . . . (3:25)

INDIAN JOCKEY [114] 4-12-0 A P McCoy, made all, rdn clr appr 2 out, unchlgd. . .(7 to 4 fav op 6 to 4 tchd 2 to 1) 1
592³ SAFETY (USA) [90] (bl) 9-10-5 A Maguire, chsd wnr thrght, slpd on bend appr 4th, no imprsn frm 2 out.
. . . .(14 to 1 op 10 to 1) 2
760³ CORRIN HILL [96] 9-10-4 (7*) J Harris, hld up, mstk 4th, sn no hdwy appr 2 out. . . .(7 to 2 op 4 to 1 tchd 3 to 1) 3
760* SIRTELIMAR (Ire) [95] 7-10-10 (7ex) T J Murphy, hld up, gd hdwy 5th, hrd rdn appr 2 out, 3rd and held whn hit last, eased r-in. . . . .(4 to 1 tchd 9 to 2) 4
HARLEQUIN WALK [88] (bl) 5-10-3 P Holley, hmpd second, trkd ldrs till wknd quickly appr 2 out.
. . . .(5 to 1 op 11 to 2 tchd 7 to 1) 5
656⁶ HAVE A NIGHTCAP [99] (v) 7-11-0 B Powell, f second.
. . . .(9 to 1 op 8 to 1) f
Dist: 2½l, 7l, 8l, 9l. 3m 39.40s. b 3.60s (6 Ran).
SR: 26/-/-/

(Stuart M Mercer), M C Pipe

787 Thurlbear Novices' Handicap Chase Class F (0-95 5-y-o and up) £2,683 2m 3f. . . . .(4:00)

640³ BLUE RAVEN [83] 5-11-10 A Maguire, led 3rd, jmpd slwly whn chlgd tenth and 11th, definite advantage 4 out, lft clr nxt.
. . . .(5 to 2 op 9 to 4) 1
507³ TELMAR SYSTEMS [64] 7-10-6 S Curran, led to 3rd, mstks 4th and 6th, wknd appr four out, lft poor second nxt.
. . . .(9 to 1 op 10 to 1) 2
632⁵ MINERS REST [76] 8-11-4 A P McCoy, f second.
. . . .(6 to 4 fav op 11 to 8) f
755⁴ RIVER GALA (Ire) [68] 6-10-10 P Holley, in tch, dsptd ld tenth and 11th, cl second whn stumbled and uns rdr 3 out.
. . . .(5 to 2 op 5 to 2 tchd 11 to 4) ur
Dist: 14l. 4m 46.80s. a 15.80s (4 Ran).

(David Brace), D Brace

788 Wiveliscombe Juvenile Novices' Hurdle Class E (3-y-o) £2,295 2m 1f (4:35)

COINTOSSER (Ire) 10-5 S Wynne, confidently rdn, hld up, wnt second appr 2 out, quickened to ld r-in, readily.
. . . .(6 to 4 on op 7 to 4 on tchd 11 to 8 on) 1
INDIRA 10-5 W McFarland, led till hdd and outpcd r-in.
. . . .(3 to 1 op 3 to 1) 2
705 GHOSTLY APPARITION 10-10 R Supple, pld hrd, trkd ldr till appr 2 out, wknd approaching last. . .(50 to 1 op 25 to 1) 3
COLEBROOK WILLIE 10-10 M Bosley, al abt same pl, outpcd appr 2 out, btn whn hit last. . . . .(50 to 1 op 33 to 1) 4
TRIANNA 10-5 I Harvey, trkd ldrs till wknd quickly 3 out.
. . . .(12 to 1 op 8 to 1) 5
481⁵ MY BEAUTIFUL DREAM 10-5 F Jousset, al beh, tld off whn pld-up r-in, lme. . . . .(66 to 1 op 33 to 1) pu
658⁴ SONG FOR JESS (Ire) 10-0² (7*) Mr G Shenkin, pld hrd, blun 3rd, prmnt whn mstk 5th, sn tld off, pulled up 2 out.
. . . .(7 to 1 op 6 to 1) pu
Dist: 2½l, 11l, 5l, 16l. 3m 56.10s. a 13.10s (7 Ran).

(David Manning Associates), M C Pipe

HEXHAM (firm)
Friday October 4th
Going Correction: NIL

789 Federation Brewery Buchanan Original Conditional Jockeys' Novices' Hurdle Class F (4-y-o and up) £1,992 2½m 110yds. . . . . (2:15)

LATVIAN (v) 9-10-9 (3*) S Melrose, al hndy, jnd ldr 4 out, led 2 out, idled, crrd head high and jmpd slwly last, all out.
. . . .(11 to 4 op 5 to 2) 1
694⁴ PANGERAN (USA) 4-10-11 J Supple, tried to make all, jnd 4 out, hdd 2 out, hrd drvn bef last, rallied r-in.
. . . .(13 to 8 fav op 6 to 4 tchd 7 to 4) 2
660⁴ PIMSBOY 9-10-12 G Cahill, trkd ldrs, hrd at work bef 4 out, wknd quickly aftr nxt, tld off.
. . . .(14 to 1 op 12 to 1 tchd 16 to 1) 3
648⁵ ALPINE MIST 4-11-4 Michael Brennan, nvr far away, cl 3rd and niggled alng whn f on landing 3 out.
. . . .(7 to 4 op 5 to 4) f
Dist: 1½l, 27l. 5m 4.30s. a 13.30s (4 Ran).

(I Bell), R Allan

790 Pat Wakelin And British Red Cross Novices' Hurdle Class E (4-y-o and up) £2,730 3m. . . . .(2:45)

CROFTON LAKE 5-11-8 B Storey, dictated pace, hdd 2 out, rallied on ins to ld ag'n betw last two, kpt on und pres r-in.
. . . .(5 to 4 op Evens tchd 11 to 8) 1
CANONBIEBOTHERED 5-10-7 F Perratt, trkd wnr, improved and mstk 3 out, led nxt, wnt wide and hdd betw last 2, swtchd lft r-in, kpt on. (13 to 8 on op 7 to 4 on tchd 6 to 4 on) 2
Won by ¾l. 6m 16.10s. a 28.10s (2 Ran).

SR: -/-/   (Mrs E M Dixon), J E Dixon

791   Johnnie Marshall Handicap Chase Class F (0-100 5-y-o and up) £2,635 2m 110yds.................... (3:15)

660[8] ANTHONY BELL [89] 10-11-7 A Dobbin, *made all, quickened into gd ld hfwy, styd on strly betw last 2.*
.... (7 to 4 op 6 to 4 tchd 15 to 8)   1D
659[4] ILEWIN [92] 9-11-10 G Bradley, *jmpd slwly thrght, chsd wnr, drvn alng 2 out, no imprsn.*
.... (9 to 4 on op 5 to 2 on tchd 2 to 1 on)   1
Won by 9l. 4m 16.70s. a 18.70s (2 Ran).
SR: -/-/   (Middx Packaging Ltd), G M McCourt

792   LCL Pils Lager Selling Hurdle Class G (4-y-o and up) £2,067 2m........ (3:50)

728[2] SUPERTOP 8-10-12 M Dwyer, *al gng wl, smooth hdwy aftr 3 out, led on bit betw last 2, sn clr, easily.*
.... (6 to 4 on tchd 11 to 8 on)   1
652[8] SPRINGLOADED 5-10-7 (5*) Michael Brennan, *patiently rdn, gd hdwy to go hndy 4 out, drvn alng betw last 2, kpt on, no ch wth wnr.*...................... (9 to 2 op 7 to 2)   2
609[7] LITTLE REDWING (bl) 4-10-7[1] R Garritty, *al hndy, led aftr 4th till betw last 2, one pace.*...... (8 to 1 op 11 to 2)   3
766[5] TOP SKIPPER (Ire) 4-10-11 A S Smith, *hit 1st, al chasing ldrs, effrt aftr 3 out, no extr betw last 2.....* (25 to 1 op 16 to 1)   4
660[9] TOP FELLA (USA) (bl) 4-10-11 D Bentley, *chsd ldrs, reminders aftr 4th, drvn alng after 3 out, sn lost tch.*
.... (14 to 1 op 8 to 1 tchd 20 to 1)   5
660[6] DARK MIDNIGHT (Ire) 7-10-12 J Burke, *led till aftr 4th, styd hndy till wknd quickly betw last 2.....* (16 to 1 op 20 to 1)   6
520[4] TRUMBLE 4-10-11 P Hide, *wl plcd till tdd und pres 3 out, tld off.*.................... (7 to 1 op 6 to 1)   7
SWANK GILBERT 10-10-12 Carol Cuthbert, *chsd ldrs, hit 4th, struggling 3 out, tld off.*............. (50 to 1 op 33 to 1)   8
Dist: 7l, 5l, 2l, 15l, hd, 4l, 29l. 3m 57.20s. a 8.20s (8 Ran).
SR: 2/-/-/-/-/   (Mrs Barbara Lungo), L Lungo

793   Conway Robinson Handicap Chase Class F (0-100 5-y-o and up) £3,362 3m 1f......................... (4:25)

521[5] TRUMPET [96] 7-11-5 (5*) Michael Brennan, *led 3rd, awkward 7 out, sn clr, pressed aftr 3 out, styd on strly betw last 2.*
.... (11 to 10 fav op 6 to 4 on tchd 5 to 4)   1
697[3] UPWELL [72] 12-10-0 K Johnson, *led to 3rd, rallied 9th, reminders 7 out, gocd hdwy aftr 3 out, one pace betw last 2.*
.... (5 to 2 op 11 to 4 tchd 3 to 1)   2
663[5] LAURIE-O [77] (bl) 12-10-5[5] J Burke, *wth ldr till blun badly and lost grnd 8th, 3rd and drvn alng whn f 5 out.*
.... (11 to 4 tchd 3 to 1)   f
663[6] SMOKEY TRACK [72] 11-9-9 (5*) S Taylor, *struggling in last pl thrght, blun and uns rdr 4 out......* (20 to 1 tchd 25 to 1)   ur
Dist: 7l. 6m 26.30s. a 21.30s (4 Ran).
       (Costas Andreou), J G M O'Shea

794   John Hogg Haulage Novices' Hurdle Class E (4-y-o and up) £2,364 2m (4:55)

736[2] VINTAGE RED 6-11-5 A Dobbin, *al gng fast, led betw last 2, drw clr, readily.....*(15 to 8 jt-fav op 2 to 1 tchd 7 to 4)   1
736[4] ROBSERA (Ire) 4-10-12 L Wyer, *nvr far away, effrt and drvn alng 2 out, one pace in.*.....................(15 to 8 jt-fav op 13 to 8 tchd 2 to 1)   2
694[2] THALEROS 6-10-12 J Callaghan, *al hndy, led 4th till betw last 2, sn und pres, no extr last.*...... (9 to 4 op 2 to 1)   3
AMBER HOLLY 7-10-7 B Storey, *led till hdd and almost f 4th, reco'red to race tld off till pld up bef last.*
.... (10 to 1 tchd 12 to 1)   pu
Dist: 3½l, 2l. 3m 57.20s. a 8.20s (4 Ran).
SR: 9/   (Special Reserve Racing), G Richards

795   Hexhamshire Standard National Hunt Flat Class H (4,5,6-y-o) £1,306 2m .... (5:25)

700[2] SIOUX WARRIOR 4-10-10 (7*) N Horrocks, *patiently rdn, str run frm off the pace appr fnl furlong, ran on to ld last strd.*
.... (13 to 8 op 5 to 4)   1
671[4] CHIEF GALE (Ire) 4-10-12 (5*) Michael Brennan, *led aftr 3 fs till three furlongs out, railled to ld ag'n one out, ran on, ct last strd.*..............(6 to 4 fav op 11 to 8 tchd 13 to 8)   2
LINDAJANE (Ire) 4-10-9 (3*) G Cahill, *al wl plcd, quickened ahead 3 fs out, hdd o'r one out, rdn and ran on one pace.*
.... (7 to 2 op 5 to 1 tchd 6 to 1 and 11 to 4)   3
FARMERS SUBSIDY 4-11-3 D Parker, *led 3 fs, styd hndy till rdn last half m, sn outpcd.*...........(8 to 1 op 6 to 1)   4
700 GREEN AN CASTLE 6-10-13 Mr T Morrison, *chsd ldrs to 5th, sn lost tch, tld off.*.............(33 to 1 op 20 to 1)   5
Dist: Nk, 1¾l, 11l. dist. 3m 55.60s. (5 Ran).
       (Guy Reed), C W Thornton

CHEPSTOW (good)
Saturday October 5th

Going Correction: MINUS 0.25 sec. per fur. (races 1,3,5,6), MINUS 0.05 (2,4)

796   Starters Novices' Hurdle Class C (4-y-o and up) £3,715 2m 110yds.. (1:45)

LAKE KARIBA 5-10-12 A P McCoy, *settled mid-div, mstk 3rd, improved 4th, led nxt, clr appproaching last, readily.*
..... (6 to 4 on op 11 to 8 on tchd 5 to 4 on and 11 to 10 on)   1
JALAPENO (Ire) 5-10-12 C Llewellyn, *chsd ldr, led aftr 4th, hdd nxt, sn rdn alng, one pace frm 2 out.*
.... (15 to 2 op 6 to 1 tchd 8 to 1)   2
49[8] WHISTLING BUCK (Ire) 8-10-7 (5*) L Aspell, *wtd wth, prog appr 5th, styd on same pace frm 3 out.* (40 to 1 op 33 to 1)   3
RANGITIKEI (NZ) 5-10-12 R Dunwoody, *al wl plcd, rdn 3 out, no imprsn.*......................(11 to 2 op 9 to 2)   4
ALLOW (Ire) 5-10-12 M A Fitzgerald, *wl plcd till wknd appr 2 out.*.....................(33 to 1 op 20 to 1)   5
LOUGH TULLY (Ire) 6-10-12 S Wynne, *led till aftr 4th, wknd appr 3 out.*..........(16 to 1 op 20 to 1 tchd 25 to 1)   6
SAXON MEAD 6-10-12 A Maguire, *hld up, steady prog 4th, wknd nxt.*...................(8 to 1 op 6 to 1)   7
IRREPRESSIBLE (Ire) 5-10-12 I Lawrence, *settled towards rear, short lived effrt appr 5th.*........(50 to 1 op 33 to 1)   8
629[4] MY HARWINSKI 6-10-5 (7*) Miss E J Jones, *hld up, shrtlvd effrt appr 5th.*....................(50 to 1 op 33 to 1)   9
629[6] CROWNHILL CROSS 5-10-7 (5*) D Salter, *struggling frm hfwy, tld off.*...............(100 to 1 op 50 to 1)   10
638 MASIMARA MUSIC 5-10-7 B Fenton, *struggling frm 3rd, tld off.*....................(100 to 1 op 50 to 1)   11
HIGH HOLME 5-10-12 B Powell, *al beh, tld off frm 4th.*
.... (50 to 1 op 33 to 1)   12
539[3] PYTCHLEY DAWN 6-10-7 V Slattery, *hmpd and f 1st.*
.... (40 to 1 op 33 to 1)   f
758 LATE ENCOUNTER 5-10-12 G Bradley, *jmpd slwly 1st, sn tld off, pld up bef 5th....* (66 to 1 op 50 to 1 tchd 100 to 1)   pu
Dist: 5l, 1½l, 2½l, 8l, 12l, 3½l, ½l, 1l, dist, dist. 3m 53.60s. a 6.60s (14 Ran).
       (The Lake Kariba Partnership), P F Nicholls

797   Mercedes Benz Handicap Chase Class B (0-145 5-y-o and up) £7,103 3m .... (2:15)

GENERAL CRACK (Ire) [120] 7-11-4 A P McCoy, *al gng wl, led appr 5 out, sn quickened clr, easily.*..........(9 to 4 jt-fav op 9 to 4)   1
515[3] EVANGELICA (USA) [115] 6-10-13 C Maude, *hld up and sn beh, slightly hmpd 3rd, prog appr 8th, outpcd approaching 5 out, styd on to go second last.*.........(12 to 1 op 8 to 1)   2
750[*] IFFEEE [129] 9-11-13 A Maguire, *led aftr second, hdd 4th, led appr 8th till approaching 5 out, outpcd whn jmpd rght four out and nxt.....* (6 to 1 op 9 to 2 tchd 13 to 2 and 7 to 1)   3
GRANGE BRAKE [125] 10-11-6 (3*) D Walsh, *led till aftr second, led 4th till appr 8th, rdn and wknd 12th.*
.... (10 to 1 op 7 to 1)   4
668[*] TARTAN TRADEWINDS [130] 9-12-0 A Dobbin, *hld up, steady prog appr 8th, outpcd approaching 5 out.........*(9 to 4 jt-fav op 5 to 2)   5
FLORIDA SKY [109] 9-10-7 G Bradley, *wtd wth, f 6th.*
.... (10 to 1 tchd 14 to 1)   f
750[3] CERTAIN ANGLE [111] 7-10-9 R Dunwoody, *3rd whn f third.*
.... (7 to 1 op 6 to 1 tchd 15 to 2)   f
GOOD FOR A LAUGH [110] 12-10-8 M A Fitzgerald, *struggling frm 9th, tld off whn pld up bef 13th.*
.... (66 to 1 op 33 to 1 tchd 100 to 1)   pu
Dist: 21l, 2½l, 1¾l, 10l. 5m 53.90s. a 3.90s (8 Ran).
SR: 39/13/24/18/13/   (J A Keighley And Mr Paul K Barber), P F Nicholls

798   Free Handicap Hurdle Class B (4-y-o) £6,947 2m 110yds.............. (2:50)

HAMILTON SILK [115] 10-7 G Bradley, *patiently rdn, steady prog appr 5th, led and not fluent last, kpt on wl.*
.... (16 to 1 op 14 to 1 tchd 20 to 1)   1
MIM-LOU-AND [110] 10-2 J Culloty, *sluggish strt, sn wl plcd, mstk nxt, not quicken.................*(8 to 1 op 7 to 1)   2
691[12] YUBRALEE (USA) [109] 10-1 C Maude, *led till last, no extr.*
.... (14 to 1 op 12 to 1)   3
758[*] HAND WOVEN [122] 11-0 (4ex) C Llewellyn, *chsd ldr till 4th, styd ag'n frm 2 out.....* (11 to 2 op 5 to 1 tchd 6 to 1)   4
ALLTIME DANCER (Ire) [125] 11-3 J A McCarthy, *wtd wth, effrt appr 3 out, no extr frm nxt.................*(5 to 1 op 4 to 1)   5
RISING DOUGH (Ire) [108] 10-0 L Wyer, *wtd wth, improved appr 5th, no further prog frm 3 out...*(14 to 1 tchd 16 to 1)   6
LOVE THE BLUES [108] 10-0 A Maguire, *wl plcd till wknd appr 3 out.........* (9 to 2 jt-fav op 4 to 1 tchd 5 to 1)   7
REAGANESQUE (USA) [122] 10-4 R Farrant, *hld up, took clr order 3rd, wknd 5th, tld off.* (8 to 1 op 7 to 1 tchd 9 to 1)   8
482[*] FAUSTINO [114] 10-6 (4ex) R Dunwoody, *hld up, reminders hfwy, sn beh, tld off.*.............(8 to 1 op 7 to 1)   9
IKTASAB [110] (bl) 10-2 A P McCoy, *cl up, second whn f 5th.*
.... (8 to 1 op 7 to 1 tchd 11 to 2)   f
OUR KRIS [112] (bl) 11-0 M A Fitzgerald, *wl plcd till badly hmpd 5th, pld up bef 2 out.....*(8 to 1 tchd 10 to 1)   pu
Dist: 2l, ½l, 1l, 1½l, 2l, 3l, 20l, 6l. 3m 48.20s. a 1.20s (11 Ran).
SR: 26/19/17/29/30/11/8/-/-/   (Elite Racing Club), M C Pipe

799 Maryland Farmhouse Cheddar Novices' Chase Class B (5-y-o and up) £7,103 2m 3f 110yds........... (3:25)

CALL EQUINAME 6-11-0 R Dunwoody, *chsd ldr, led 7th, drw clr 3 out, pckd last, unchlgd.*.... (5 to 4 on op 11 to 8 on) 1
655* SONIC STAR (Ire) 7-11-8 A Maguire, *strted slwly, hit 1st, gd hdwy aftr 12th, wnt second and hit 5 out, hit nxt, no ch wth wnr.* .... (11 to 8 op 7 to 4 tchd 2 to 1) 2
769^{4} SHIKAREE (Ire) (bl) 5-10-12 C Maude, *hld up, improved to chase wnr 7th, 3rd whn f 5 out.* ....(11 to 2 op 6 to 1 tchd 13 to 2 and 7 to 1) f
PRIORY ROSE 9-10-9 R Farrant, *led till 7th, wknd quickly nxt, tld off whn pld up bef tenth.* ....(66 to 1 op 40 to 1 tchd 100 to 1) pu

Dist: 18l. 4m 56.50s. a 13.50s (4 Ran).
(Mick Coburn, P K Barber, C Lewis), P F Nicholls

800 South-West Racing Club Novices' Handicap Hurdle Class E (0-100 4-y-o and up) [illegible] 2m 1f 110yds.... (4:00)

450^{2} EMBLEY BUOY [68] 8-10-0 S Curran, *al cl up, led 6th, clr whn hit 2 out, styd on und pres.*...........(50 to 1 op 33 to 1) 1
543^{2} TAP ON TOOTSIE [91] 4-11-5 (3*) R Massey, *wl plcd, outpcd appr 8th, kpt on frm 2 out*..............(9 to 2 tchd 6 to 1) 2
MYBLACKTHORN (Ire) [92] 6-11-3 (7*) O Burrows, *patiently rdn, gd hdwy appr 8th, no extr frm 3 out.* (14 to 1 op 8 to 1) 3
CROHANE QUAY (Ire) [90] 7-11-2[1] (7*) Mr A Balding, *settled in rear, hit 7th, steady hdwy frm 8th, nvr plcd to chal.* .... (14 to 1 op 8 to 1) 4
667^{7} KAREN'S TYPHOON (Ire) [76] 5-10-7 C Maude, *cl up, mstk 4th, outpcd appr 8th, styd on ag'n und pres frm 2 out.* .... (12 to 1 op 8 to 1) 5
650* LITTLE TINCTURE (Ire) [73] 6-10-5 G Upton, *settled mid-div, rdn appr 8th, no imprsn*...............(10 to 1 op 7 to 1) 6
DAJRAAN (Ire) [90] 7-11-8 C Llewellyn, *trkd ldrs, improved appr 7th, wknd approaching 3 out, fnshd lme.* ....(5 to 4 fav op 2 to 1) 7
528^{2} REGAL GEM (Ire) [78] 5-10-9 B Fenton, *nvr a factor.* ....(14 to 1 op 12 to 1 tchd 16 to 1) 8
PAVLOVA (Ire) [85] 6-10-12 (5*) L Aspell, *cl up, mstk 6th, wknd und pres appr 8th*................ (12 to 1 tchd 14 to 1) 9
QUEEN'S AWARD (Ire) [68] 7-10-0 B Powell, *settled in rear, short lived effrt appr 8th*............ (33 to 1 op 20 to 1) 10
648^{8} HYDEMILLA [80] 6-10-9 (3*) G Hogan, *led till 6th, lost pl appr 8th*.................................. (25 to 1 op 16 to 1) 11
SANDS POINT [90] 6-11-8 M A Fitzgerald, *reminders aftr 3rd, struggling frm 5th, tld off whn pld up bef 8th.* .... (12 to 1 op 8 to 1) pu

Dist: 2½l, 4l, 2l, 2½l, 6l, 1¾l, 4l, 3½l, 1½l, ½l. 4m 45.90s. a 7.90s (12 Ran).
(Mrs Heather Bare), J W Mullins

801 Valets Handicap Hurdle Class E (0-110 4-y-o and up) £2,940 2m 110yds (4:35)

MYTTON'S CHOICE (Ire) [105] 5-11-6 (7*) Mr R Thornton, *trkd ldrs gng wl, led 5th, sn clr, ran on well.* (13 to 2 op 12 to 1) 1
592^{2} PAIR OF JACKS (Ire) [85] 6-10-8 R Dunwoody, *settled in rear, styd on frm 3 out, not trble wnr.* ....(11 to 4 fav op 9 to 2 tchd 5 to 1) 2
760^{2} ZINGIBAR [79] 4-10-0 B Fenton, *beh, pushed alng hfwy, kpt on frm 3 out, not rch ldrs*............ (10 to 1 tchd 8 to 1) 3
RAMSDENS (Ire) [101] 4-11-8 C Llewellyn, *cl up, led briefly appr 5th, one pace*........ (9 to 2 op 7 to 2 tchd 5 to 1) 4
KNIGHT IN SIDE [82] 10-10-5 C Maude, *hld up and beh, nvr rch ldrs*.................(13 to 2 op 5 to 1 tchd 7 to 1) 5
ZAITOON (Ire) [106] 5-12-0 A Maguire, *cl up till wknd appr 5th.* .... (10 to 1 op 6 to 1) 6
639^{7} TOOMUCH TOOSOON (Ire) [96] 8-11-5 B Powell, *struggling frm hfwy*........................ (20 to 1 op 16 to 1) 7
MINSTER'S MADAM [85] (v) 5-10-7 J Culloty, *wl plcd till wknd 5th*.................................. (10 to 1 op 7 to 1) 8
LIME STREET BLUES (Ire) [82] (bl) 5-10-4 G Bradley, *led till appr 5th, sn lost pl, tld off*.......... (10 to 1 op 7 to 1) 9
49 WILL JAMES [77] (bl) 10-10-0 S Curran, *wl plcd till 5th, tld off.* ....(33 to 1) 10
MEANUS MILLER (Ire) [81] 8-10-4 D Gallagher, *hld up in rear, 6th and no ch whn f last, dead*....... (16 to 1 op 12 to 1) f

Dist: 11l, 5l, 1½l, hd, ½l, 16l, sht-hd, 8l, 12l. 3m 49.40s. a 2.40s (11 Ran).
SR: 35/5/-/12/-/16/ (Gordon Mytton), D Nicholson

DOWN ROYAL (IRE) (good)
Saturday October 5th

802 Bank Of Ireland Maiden Hurdle (4-y-o and up) £1,370 2½m............(2:25)

742^{6} COLLON LEADER (Ire) 7-11-6 (3*) J R Barry, (100 to 30 fav) 1
603* FANE PATH (Ire) 4-11-8 Mr G J Harford, ...(6 to 1) 2
685^{4} CRUCIAL MOVE (Ire) 5-11-1 D H O'Connor, ... (4 to 1) 3
576^{5} MISS ELIZABETH (Ire) 6-10-8 (7*) A O'Shea, ...(20 to 1) 4
302 DERBY HAVEN 9-11-6 S C Lyons, ...(6 to 1) 5
701^{5} CAIRNCROSS (Ire) 5-11-6 J P Broderick, ...(16 to 1) 6
562 UNO NUMERO (Ire) 5-11-6 L P Cusack, ...(20 to 1) 7
601^{3} WILDLIFE RANGER (Ire) 8-12-0 C F Swan, ... (5 to 1) 8
703^{7} SECRET PRINCE (Ire) 5-11-1 (5*) T Martin, ... (33 to 1) 9
PROLOGUE (Ire) 5-11-6 J Shortt, ...(14 to 1) 10
731 BUNKER (Ire) 4-11-8 J K Kinane, ...(25 to 1) 11
624^{6} SPRITZER (Ire) 4-10-12 D P Fagan, ...(16 to 1) 12
701 HILLTOP BOY (Ire) 7-11-1 (5*) J Butler, ...(10 to 1) 13
561 REENIE (Ire) 5-11-1 F Woods, ...(20 to 1) 14
315 BALLY UPPER (Ire) 8-10-13 (7*) L J Fleming, ...(10 to 1) 15
WEE ANN (Ire) 5-10-12 (3*) Mr B R Hamilton, ... (33 to 1) 16
MANDY'S CONVINCED (Ire) 6-10-8 (7*) Mr L J Gracey, ...(33 to 1) 17
703^{5} BOYNE VIEW (Ire) 4-10-9 (3*) B Bowens, ...(14 to 1) 18
681 BLAKESONIA (Ire) 6-11-6 H Rogers, ...(25 to 1) 19
CARDINALS FOLLY (Ire) 5-11-2[3] (7*) Mr M McNeilly, ...(33 to 1) 20

Dist: 1½l, 1l, 7l, 1l. 4m 48.00s. (20 Ran).
(Mrs I M Murphy), A J Martin

803 I.T.B.A.Supporting Down Royal Handicap Hurdle (0-116 4-y-o and up) £1,370 2m (2:55)

683^{5} CHANOBLE (Ire) [-] 4-9-0 (7*) B D Murtagh, ...(10 to 1) 1
683^{4} WICKLOW WAY (Ire) [-] 6-9-12 T P Treacy, ...(11 to 2) 2
679^{3} SLAVE GALE (Ire) [-] 5-11-0 C F Swan, ... (2 to 1 fav) 3
684^{9} FRASER CAREY (Ire) [-] (bl) 4-11-0 F Woods, ... (11 to 2) 4
590^{3} DUBLIN TREASURE (Ire) [-] 4-10-13 (5*) G Cotter, .. (7 to 2) 5
FIDDLERS BOW VI (Ire) [-] 8-11-4 K F O'Brien, ... (7 to 1) 6
20^{7} AMME ENAEK (Ire) [-] 7-10-0 H Rogers, ...(16 to 1) 7
97^{3} BOBSTAR DANCER (Ire) [-] 5-12-0 J Shortt, ...(12 to 1) 8
BENBRADAGH GLOW (Ire) [-] 4-10-7[2] (7*) Mr L J Gracey, ...(25 to 1) 9

Dist: ½l, 5½l, ½l, 15l. 3m 43.30s. (9 Ran).
(Mrs Deirdre McMahon), Norman Cassidy

804 John Haldane Memorial Beginners Chase (4-y-o and up) £1,370 2m (3:25)

701^{2} CASTLEROYAL (Ire) 7-12-0 H Rogers, ... (11 to 2) 1
496^{3} THE ODIN LINE (Ire) 7-12-0 F Woods, ...(4 to 1) 2
ANN'S AMBITION 9-12-0 K F O'Brien, ...(14 to 1) 3
711^{2} STRONG BOOST (USA) 5-11-10 C F Swan, ... (Evens fav) 4
538^{6} CURRAGH RANGER (Ire) 6-11-7 (7*) B D Murtagh, (14 to 1) 5
577^{3} COURSING GLEN (Ire) 8-12-0 T P Treacy, ... (6 to 1) ur
256^{5} THE BOURDA 10-12-0 J P Broderick, ... (12 to 1) pu

Dist: 4l, 4½l, dist, 9l. 3m 59.30s. (7 Ran).
(Brian McNichol), I R Ferguson

805 Aga Rayburn I.N.H. Flat Race (4-y-o and up) £1,370 2m..............(4:55)

681^{2} STORM GEM (Ire) 5-11-4 (5*) Mr R Walsh, ... (6 to 4 fav) 1
703^{3} BRADLEYS CORNER (Ire) 5-11-7 (7*) Mr L J Gracey, ...(12 to 1) 2
581 GARAMOY (Ire) 5-11-2 (7*) Mr M O'Connor, ... (33 to 1) 3
276^{3} NEW WEST (Ire) 6-11-7 (7*) Mr J D O'Connell, ... (12 to 1) 4
PRAY FOR PEACE (Ire) 5-11-2 (7*) Mr P Fahey, ... (10 to 1) 5
ROCHE MENTOR (Ire) 6-11-7 (7*) Mr C P McGivern, (7 to 1) 6
577 ORANGE LIL (Ire) 4-11-4 Mr G J Harford, ...(20 to 1) 7
394^{9} MINOGUE LADY (Ire) 5-11-2 (7*) Mr P M Cloke, ... (25 to 1) 8
581^{7} MISTY PEARL (Ire) 5-11-7 (7*) Mr J Cash, ... (14 to 1) 9
782^{7} REGGIE'S HONOUR (Ire) 4-11-4 Mr J A Nash, ... (4 to 1) 10
BANNAGH MOR (Ire) 5-11-7 (7*) Mr M McNeilly, .. (25 to 1) 11
RED ACE (Ire) 4-10-11 (7*) Mr C A Murphy, ... (10 to 1) 12
J-R ASHFORD (Ire) 5-11-11 (3*) Mr B M Cash, ... (8 to 1) 13
INDIAN RESERVE (Ire) 4-11-1 (3*) Mr B R Hamilton, (20 to 1) 14
GRANNY BOWLY (Ire) 6-11-6[4] (7*) Mr J P McCreesh, ...(14 to 1) 15
ELECTRIC LAD (Ire) 5-11-7 (7*) Mr R Geraghty, ... (12 to 1) 16
BARORA GALE (Ire) 5-11-2 (7*) Mr G Elliott, ... (16 to 1) 17

Dist: 25l, ½l, 1½l, 1½l. 3m 38.90s. (17 Ran).
(Town And Country Racing Club), P A Fahy

UTTOXETER (good to firm)
Saturday October 5th

Going Correction: MINUS 0.10 sec. per fur. (races 1,3,5,7), MINUS 0.35 (2,4,6)

806 North Staffordshire Advertiser Novices' Hurdle Class E sponsored by Sentinel (4-y-o and up) £2,410 2m .... (2:30)

NORDIC BREEZE (Ire) 4-10-10 C O'Dwyer, *settled gng wl, smooth hdwy to nose ahead 2 out, drw clr last.* ....(11 to 10 fav op 11 to 8) 1
ELA MAN HOWA 5-10-11 T Kent, *al hndy, led aftr 4th, hdd 2 out, rdn and kpt on same pace.* .... (9 to 1 op 7 to 1 tchd 10 to 1) 2
CULRAIN 5-10-11 A Thornton, *settled wth chasing grp, improved appr 3 out, rdn and styd on same pace frm nxt.* .... (66 to 1 op 50 to 1) 3
IN GOOD FAITH 4-10-10 M Dwyer, *patiently rdn, steady hdwy appr 4 out, effrt bef nxt, one pace last 2.* ....(9 to 4 op 7 to 4 tchd 5 to 2) 4

DASH TO THE PHONE (USA) 4-10-10 A S Smith, *settled wth chasing bunch, effrt hfwy, drvn alng 3 out, one pace.* ....(8 to 1 tchd 10 to 1) 5
EUROLINK SHADOW 4-10-10 B Harding, *al wl plcd, led 3rd till aftr nxt, styd hndy, wkng quickly whn blun 2 out.* .... (20 to 1 op 16 to 1) 6
45^{9} NIGHT BOAT 5-10-11 T Eley, *wtd wth, took clr order hfwy, feeling pace appr 3 out, fdd.*.... (25 to 1 op 16 to 1) 7
TIMELY EXAMPLE (USA) (bl) 5-10-11 Gary Lyons, *struggling wth chasing grp hfwy, nvr able to rch chalg pos.* .... (50 to 1 op 40 to 1) 8
PENTLAND SQUIRE 5-10-11 Richard Guest, *settled off the pace, steady hdwy aftr 4 out, wknd and eased frm nxt.* ....(16 to 1 op 14 to 1 tchd 20 to 1) 9
JAIME'S JOY 6-9-13 (7*) Shaun Graham, *sn struggling in rear, nvr a factor.*....(66 to 1 op 50 to 1) 10
NUKUD (USA) 4-10-7 (3*) G Cahill, *sn beh and struggling, tld off.*....(50 to 1 op 40 to 1) 11
CHAIN SHOT 11-10-11 R Bellamy, *rcd wth chasing grp till lost tch hfwy, tld off.*.... (40 to 1 tchd 50 to 1) 12
CHRISTIAN WARRIOR 7-10-6 (5*) Chris Webb, *took keen hold in rear, tld off frm hfwy.*.... (66 to 1 op 50 to 1) 13
FION CORN 9-10-11 J R Kavanagh, *rcd freely, led to 3rd, pld up aftr nxt.*....(25 to 1 op 20 to 1) pu
Dist: 3½l, 9l, hd, 2l, ¾l, 2½l, 7l, 3l, ½l, 6l. 3m 46.70s. a 9.70s (14 Ran).
(Malcolm B Jones), M C Pipe

807 Staffordshire Yeomanry Challenge Cup Novices' Chase Class C sponsored by Sentinel (5-y-o and up) £5,067 3m....(3:00)

649* FATHER SKY 5-11-3 J Osborne, *led till hdd and nrly uns rdr second, jmpd carefully aftr, ev ch 4 out, rdn and 2 ls second whn lft clr last.* ....(11 to 4 on tchd 5 to 2 on and 9 to 4 on) 1
657 WAKT 6-11-10 (3*) Guy Lewis, *wtd wth, wnt hndy aftr one circuit, reminder 6 out, rallied 4 out, rdn and fdd nxt, lft second last.*....(9 to 2 op 4 to 1 tchd 5 to 1) 2
PHAEDAIR 6-11-0 J R Kavanagh, *al struggling to keep in tch, tld off aftr one circuit.*.... (25 to 1 op 20 to 1) 3
NEWTOWN ROSIE (Ire) 7-10-9 J Ryan, *led second, hdd bef nxt, rgned ld 5th, 2 ls clr whn f last, rmntd.* .... (6 to 1 op 7 to 1 tchd 15 to 2) 4
751 WAR FLOWER (Ire) 8-10-9 W Marston, *took keen hold, led bef 3rd, sn clr, hdd 5th, lost tch frm 6 out, tld off.*....(50 to 1) 5
Dist: 14l, dist, ¾l, 24l. 6m 8.60s. (5 Ran).
(Kenneth Kornfeld), O Sherwood

808 Sentinel Handicap Hurdle Class B (0-145 4-y-o and up) £5,135 2½m 110yds.... (3:30)

TULLYMURRY TOFF (Ire) [117] 5-10-9 (5*) E Callaghan, *patiently rdn, improved to draw level 3 out, led nxt, drvn clr last.*....(9 to 4 op 5 to 2 tchd 11 to 4) 1
CALL MY GUEST (Ire) [123] 6-11-7 N Williamson, *al hndy, lft in ld 5 out, jnd in strt, hdd 2 out, one pace.* ....(6 to 1 tchd 7 to 1) 2
SPARKLING YASMIN [120] 4-11-0 (3*) G Tormey, *trkd ldrs, feeling pace and lost grnd appr 4 out, styd on ag'n frm betw last 2.*.... (7 to 2 op 3 to 1) 3
OLYMPIAN [118] (bl) 9-11-2 W Marston, *ran in snatches, wnt second hfwy, rdn and lost pl fnl circuit, no imprsn frm 3 out.* .... (10 to 1 op 8 to 1) 4
656* STAR MARKET [126] (bl) 6-11-10 D Bridgwater, *led, niggled alng to quicken aftr one circuit, ran out appr 5 out.* ....(2 to 1 fav op 7 to 4 tchd 9 to 4) ro
Dist: 6l, 2½l, 7l. 4m 44.10s. a 5.10s (5 Ran).
SR: 15/16/9/1/-/ (John H Wilson And Mr J H Riley), J M Jefferson

809 Britannia Building Society Duke Of Edinburgh's Award Handicap Chase Class D (0-120 5-y-o and up) £7,002 3 ¼m.... (4:05)

663* MCGREGOR THE THIRD [117] 10-11-13 B Harding, *jmpd boldly, al gng wl, led frm 4 out, drw clr, imprsv.* ....(7 to 4 fav op 5 to 2) 1
ANDROS PRINCE [93] 11-10-3 J R Kavanagh, *sn tld off last, improved frm off the pace from betw last 2, styd on, no ch wth wnr.*.... (20 to 1 op 14 to 1) 2
706* ANDRELOT [118] (bl) 9-12-0 N Williamson, *al hndy, led 4th, hit 8th, hdd aftr 6 out, rdn last four, one pace.* .... (10 to 1 op 6 to 1) 3
708* CATS RUN (Ire) [110] 8-11-6 R Supple, *bustled alng to keep up aftr one circuit, styd on und pres frm 4 out, no imprsn.* .... (11 to 2 op 4 to 1) 4
556^{2} REAL PROGRESS (Ire) [105] 8-10-12 (3*) G Tormey, *pressed ldrs, reminders to hold pl fnl circuit, lost tch frm 5 out, tld off.* ....(10 to 1 tchd 12 to 1) 5
CHILDHAY CHOCOLATE [105] 8-11-1 P Hide, *slight ld to 4th, continued to chase ldrs, nosed ahead aftr 6 out, hdd four out, wl beh whn refused last.*...(8 to 1 op 5 to 1 tchd 9 to 1) ref

692^{2} FAIRY PARK [97] 11-10-7 Jacqui Oliver, *chsd alng to keep in tch aftr one circuit, reminders 5 out, tld off whn pld up bef 2 out.*....(16 to 1 op 12 to 1) pu
WREKENGALE (Ire) [110] 6-11-6 W Marston, *settled in tch, clsg whn pld up bef 5 out, dismounted, lme.* .... (11 to 4 op 3 to 1 tchd 4 to 1) pu
Dist: 8l, ¾l, 1l, 14l. 6m 23.60s. a 11.60s (8 Ran).
(Mrs D A Whitaker), G Richards

810 Staffordshire Regiment Challenge Cup Handicap Hurdle Class D sponsored by Sentinel (0-120 4-y-o and up) £3,399 2m.... (4:40)

736^{5} STEADFAST ELITE (Ire) [90] 5-9-9 (5*) R McGrath, *al travelling wl, improved to ld bef 2 out, easily.* ....(6 to 4 fav op 7 to 4) 1
659^{9} EMPEROR CHANG (USA) [91] 9-10-2^{2} T Kent, *sn tld off last, styd on frm 3 out, no imprsn on wnr.*....(20 to 1) 2
656^{4} ROBERT'S TOY (Ire) [116] 5-11-5 (7*) G Supple, *cl hndy, nosed ahead appr 3 out, hdd aftr nxt, rdn and fdd betw last 2.* ....(7 to 4 op 6 to 4) 3
709 LAYHAM LOW (Ire) [95] (bl) 5-10-5 J Osborne, *led, quickened pace hfwy, hdd appr 3 out, lost tch, tld off.* (5 to 2 op 2 to 1) 4
Dist: 10l, 8l, 19l. 3m 41.30s. a 4.30s (4 Ran).
SR: 13/5/21/-/ (Clayton Bigley Partnership Ltd), J J O'Neill

811 Queen's Royal Lancers Challenge Cup Handicap Chase Class D sponsored by Sentinel (0-125 5-y-o and up) £4,201 2 ½m.... (5:10)

BERTONE (Ire) [123] 7-12-0 C O'Dwyer, *settled gng wl, loomed up to ld 2 out, ran on strly r-in.* ....(6 to 4 fav op 11 to 8 tchd 7 to 4) 1
532* MICHERADO (Fr) [95] 6-10-0 J Osborne, *jmpd lft, tried to make all, hdd 2 out, no extr r-in.*.... (9 to 2 op 7 to 2) 2
155^{9} EAST HOUSTON [101] 7-10-6 A Roche, *hmpd by faller 4th, improved fnl circuit, rdn four out, outpcd frm nxt.* ....(7 to 1 op 6 to 1 tchd 8 to 1) 3
57 MUTUAL TRUST [105] 12-10-10 N Williamson, *chsd ldr to hfwy, struggling fnl circuit, tld off frm 5 out.* .... (20 to 1 op 10 to 1) 4
541* COMEDY ROAD [100] 12-10-0 (5*) P Henley, *tracking ldrs whn f 4th.*.... (7 to 2 tchd 4 to 1) f
CORRARDER [110] 12-11-1 J Railton, *struggling to keep in tch bef hfwy, tld off whn pld up before 2 out.* .... (9 to 1 op 10 to 1 tchd 8 to 1) pu
Dist: 4l, 14l, dist. 4m 42.60s. b 1.40s (6 Ran).
SR: 44/12/4/ (Mrs Harry J Duffey), K C Bailey

812 Green'un Sports Final 'National Hunt' Novices' Hurdle Class C sponsored by Sentinel (4-y-o and up) £4,151 2¾m 110yds.... (5:40)

SAMLEE (Ire) 7-10-11 D Bridgwater, *made all, shaken up frm 3 out, styd on strly to go clr betw last 2.* .... (5 to 4 on op 11 to 10) 1
203 TIPPING THE LINE 6-11-9 C O'Dwyer, *al hndy, ev ch and rdn aftr 3 out, ran on same pace frm betw last 2.* ....(9 to 4 op 6 to 4) 2
MADGE MCSPLASH 4-10-5 M Dwyer, *patiently rdn, took clr order fnl circuit, effrt 3 out, not quicken frm nxt.* ....(5 to 1 op 9 to 2) 3
RIVERBANK ROSE 5-10-6 T Eley, *nvr far away, reminders and lost grnd appr 4 out, lost tch frm nxt.* .... (14 to 1 op 10 to 1 tchd 16 to 1) 4
MUSICAL HIT 5-10-11 R Bellamy, *al tld off last, pld up aftr 4 out.*....(20 to 1 op 12 to 1) pu
Dist: 4l, 7l, 20l. 5m 16.60s. a 9.60s (5 Ran).
(White Lion Partnership), P J Hobbs

KELSO (firm)
Sunday October 6th
Going Correction: MINUS 0.60 sec. per fur.

813 Radio Borders Novices' Hurdle Class E (4-y-o and up) £1,884 2¼m.... (2:30)

735^{5} COMMANDER GLEN (Ire) 4-10-11 R Garritty, *hld up, took clr order 7th, hdwy 2 out, chlgd last, rdn to ld r-in, drvn clr.* ....(5 to 2 op 7 to 2) 1
661^{3} FATEHALKHAIR (Ire) 4-10-8 (3*) G Cahill, *al prmnt, effrt to ld aftr 3 out, hit nxt and sn rdn, hdd and no extr r-in.* ....(9 to 4 tchd 2 to 1) 2
MONACO GOLD (Ire) 4-10-11 P Niven, *hld up, hdwy 7th, rdn and outpcd 2 out, styd on r-in.* ....(13 to 8 fav op 6 to 4 tchd 7 to 4) 3
728^{5} I'M THE MAN 5-10-12 K Johnson, *led to 4th, cl up, effrt 3 out, ev ch till rdn nxt, sn one pace.* .... (7 to 1 op 8 to 1 tchd 11 to 1) 4
GRANDERISE (Ire) 6-10-12 Mr D Swindlehurst, *pld hrd in rear, rapid hdwy 3rd, led and hit nxt, hdd aftr 3 out, grad wknd.* .... (66 to 1 op 33 to 1) 5

814 Highland Park 12 Y.O. Single Malt Novices' Chase Class E (5-y-o and up) £2,125 3m 1f................... (3:00)

739⁸ TIGHTER BUDGET (USA) 9-11-5 M Moloney, *made all, lft wl clr 4 out, unchlgd*............ (6 to 4 on tchd 11 to 8 on) 1
605⁵ QUIXALL CROSSETT 11-10-5 (7") Mr P Murray, *al prmnt, rdn alng 13th, lft poor second 4 out, no ch wth wnr.*
................................(150 to 1 op 50 to 1) 2
699⁷ GERMAN LEGEND 6-11-2 (3") G Cahill, *in tch whn blun badly second, sn wl beh, steady hdwy tenth, chsd wnr aftr 3 out, soon drvn and one pace, hit last.*
................................(11 to 4 op 9 to 4 tchd 3 to 1) 3
700⁸ DDICUT DESTINY 8-10-0 D Parker, *hld up, hmm hffwl, rdn alng 13th, sn one pace.*........(66 to 1 op 50 to 1) 4
ROYAL SURPRISE 9-10-12 T Reed, *chsd ldrs, rdn alng tenth, beh frm 14th.*............(13 to 2 op 6 to 1 tchd 8 to 1) 5
739 TONY'S FEELINGS 8-10-12 M Foster, *al rear, wl beh frm hfwy.*................(20 to 1 op 16 to 1 tchd 33 to 1) 6
735⁶ MISS LAMPLIGHT 6-10-7 A Dobbin, *in tch, hdwy to chase wnr, hit 11th, cl second whn f 4 out.*..... (9 to 1 op 7 to 1) f
JAMARSAM (Ire) 8-10-12 K Johnson, *prmnt to 6th, sn lost pl and beh, tld off whn pld up aftr 13th.* (150 to 1 op 50 to 1) pu
Dist: 12l, 1¾l, ½l, 3½l, 1½l. 6m 23.60s. a 26.60s (8 Ran).

(Mrs Dianne Sayer), Mrs H D Sayer

815 Macallan 10 Year Old Single Malt Juvenile Novices' Hurdle Class E (3-y-o) £1,856 2m 110yds.............. (3:30)

573² KERNOF (Ire) (bl) 11-3 R Garritty, *made all, clr appr 3 out, hit nxt, unchlgd*...................... (6 to 1 op 9 to 2) 1
305⁵ SHE'S SIMPLY GREAT (Ire) 10-0 (5") R McGrath, *chsd ldrs pulling hrd, hdwy 3 out, chased wnr nxt, no imprsn.*
..............................(14 to 1 op 10 to 1) 2
BALLPOINT 10-10 J Callaghan, *hld up, hdwy and hit 5th, slpd appr nxt and sn drvn alng, blun 2 out and no imprsn aftr.*
.... (6 to 5 on op 5 to 4 on tchd 11 to 10 on) 3
705 EURO EXPRESS 10-10 L Wyer, *cl up, remainders aftr second, blun and lost pl 5th and sn drvn alng, nvr dngrs aftr.*
..............................(33 to 1 op 20 to 1) 4
705* IN A TIZZY 10-12 M Foster, *chsd wnr, rdn 3 out, wknd nxt.*
..............................(7 to 4 tchd 2 to 1) 5
Dist: 17l, 10l, nk, 8l. 3m 45.30s. a 2.30s (5 Ran).

(J M Gahan), M D Hammond

816 Famous Grouse Handicap Chase Class D (0-120 5-y-o and up) £3,403 3m 1f................... (4:00)

668³ ROYAL VACATION [110] 7-11-10 J Callaghan, *trkd ldg pair, hdwy to ld 4 out, clr aftr nxt, eased r-in.*
..............................(11 to 10 fav op Evens tchd 5 to 4) 1
726⁷ OFF THE BRU [92] 11-10-2³ (7") Mr M Bradburne, *led to 11th, prmnt and pushed alng whn hit 3 out, kpt on one pace.*
..............................(3 to 1 op 11 to 4) 2
692³ THE YANK [103] (bl) 10-11-3 R Garritty, *cl up, led 11th, hdd 4 out and sn rdn, one pace frm nxt.*....... (9 to 4 op 2 to 1) 3
793² UPWELL [86] 12-10-0 K Johnson, *beh frm 6th, tld off hfwy.*
..............................(20 to 1 op 12 to 1) 4
Dist: 6l, 15l, dist. 6m 10.40s. a 13.40s (4 Ran).

(G P Edwards), G M Moore

817 Coopers & Lybrand Amateur Riders' Handicap Hurdle Class F (0-105 4-y-o and up) £2,318 2¾m 110yds.... (4:30)

BRIDLE PATH (Ire) [81] 5-10-8 (3") Mr K Whelan, *trkd ldrs, smooth hdwy 7th, led appr 2 out, cmftbly.*
..............................(5 to 1 tchd 6 to 1) 1
491³ BALLINDOO [84] 7-10-8 (7") Mr R Armson, *trkd ldrs, hdwy 4 out, effrt 2 out and ev ch last, rdn and not quicken r-in.*
..............................(8 to 1 op 9 to 1) 2
TALL MEASURE [80] (bl) 10-10-11⁸ (7") Mr D Swindlehurst, *al prmnt, led 7th, rdn and hdd appr 2 out, one pace r-in.*
..............................(50 to 1 op 33 to 1) 3
687⁵ YACHT CLUB [71] 14-9-9 (7") Miss A Armitage, *led till appr 7th, rdn alng 3 out, kpt on one pace nxt.*... (9 to 1 op 7 to 1) 4
735² JABAROOT (Ire) [84] 5-10-9 (5") Mr R Hale, *hld up, hdwy 7th, rdn and outpcd appr 3 out.*........ (5 to 2 fav op 3 to 1) 5
477 ANOTHER NICK [77] 10-10-1 (7") Miss P Robson, *al rear.*
..............................(50 to 1 op 33 to 1) 6
738⁷ VALIANT DASH [88] 10-10-12 (7") Mr O McPhail, *in tch, pushed alng and hit 7th, f nxt.*
..............................(9 to 4 op 3 to 1) f
707³ RED JAM JAR [93] 11-11-5 (5") Mr N Wilson, *blun and uns rdr 1st.*.......................(9 to 2 op 4 to 1) ur
Dist: 3½l, nk, 3½l, dist, 5l. 5m 12.30s. a 3.30s (8 Ran).

(Fred Wilson), T D Easterby

818 Bunnahabhain 12 Year Old Malt Handicap Hurdle Class D (0-120 4-y-o and up) £2,248 2m 110yds......... (5:00)

691* PRIZEFIGHTER [106] 5-11-10 O Pears, *trkd ldrs gng wl, hdwy 5th, led last, quickened clr.*
..............................(2 to 1 on op 7 to 4 on tchd 13 to 8 on) 1
709⁴ BURES (Ire) [110] 5-11-7 (7") B Grattan, *cl up, led 5th, rdn 2 out, hdd last, not quicken.*............(12 to 1 op 8 to 1) 2
737 VAIN PRINCE [99] (bl) 9-11-4 R Garritty, *hld up, hdwy 4th, rdn alng 3 out, sn btn.*.................(8 to 1 tchd 7 to 1) 3
698⁴ WELL APPOINTED [94] 7-10-13 B Storey, *led, hdd 5th, sn rdn alng, wknd appr 2 out.*............. (3 to 1 op 5 to 2) 4
STYLISH INTERVAL [90] 4-10-7 Richard Guest, *prmnt, rdn alng 4th, sn lost pl and beh.*..........(33 to 1 op 20 to 1) 5
695⁴ RICHMOND (Ire) [83] 8-10-2 Mr K Whelan, *prmnt to 3rd, sn lost pl, beh frm hfwy.*............(33 to 1 op 20 to 1) 6
Dist: 8l, 2½l, 5l, 7l, dist. 3m 39.70s. b 3.30s (6 Ran).
SR: 30/26/13/3/-/-/ (Diamond Racing Ltd), J L Eyre

KEMPTON (good to firm (races 1,4,6), good (2,3,5))
Sunday October 6th
Going Correction: NIL (races 1,4,6), MINUS 0.15 (2,3,5)

819 Children's Choice Juvenile Novices' Hurdle Class D (3-y-o) £2,897 2m.................................... (2:10)

TRUANCY 10-10 J Railton, *keen hold, hld up, jmpd lft, prog 5th, led appr last where dived left, ran on wl.*
..............................(8 to 1 op 6 to 1) 1
658 TALLULAH BELLE 10-5 M Richards, *hld up, steady prog frm 5th, chsd ldr briefly 2 out, 3rd and btn whn lft second last.*
..............................(11 to 6 op 6 to 1 tchd 8 to 1) 2
734⁸ HOW COULD-I (Ire) (bl) 10-5 A Maguire, *prmnt, wth ldr 4th till wknd aftr nxt, tld off.*...... (9 to 1 op 7 to 1 tchd 10 to 1) 3
399 WATER MUSIC MELODY 10-5 W Humphreys, *not jump wl, hld up, tld off frm 3rd.*...............(50 to 1 op 25 to 1) 4
SOLDIER BLUE 10-10 A P McCoy, *wl beh and hrd rdn 4th, sn tld off.*.......................... (5 to 1 tchd 10 to 1) 5
KALAO TUA (Ire) 10-5 P Hide, *lft in ld 3rd, rdn and hdd appr last, second and btn whn hmpd and f last.*
..............................(9 to 1 tchd 10 to 1) f
CANONS PARK 10-10 J Osborne, *pld hrd, hld up, led aftr second till ran out nxt.*...(5 to 2 fav op 7 to 4) ro
BELOW THE RED LINE 10-10 M FitzGerald, *sn wl beh, tld off whn nrly refused 3 out, pld up bef nxt.* (33 to 1 op 20 to 1) pu
614⁶ ORANGE ORDER (Ire) 10-10 N Williamson, *led till aftr second, wknd after 4th, fourth whn pld up bef nxt.*
..............................(7 to 2 op 5 to 2) pu
Dist: 16l, dist, 4l, 14l. 3m 48.30s. a 8.30s (9 Ran).

(J E Funnell), C J Mann

820 Staines News & Leader Novices' Chase Class D (4-y-o and up) £3,436 2m................................... (2:40)

670* CELIBATE (Ire) 5-11-9 J Railton, *chsd ldr, cld 8th, led aftr 2 out, pushed out, cmftbly*..(11 to 8 op Evens tchd 6 to 4) 1
GREENBACK (Bel) 5-11-3 C Llewellyn, *led, jmpd slwly 6th and 8th, hdd aftr 2 out, until to quicken.*
..............................(5 to 4 fav op 6 to 4) 2
688 HOLY WANDERER (USA) 7-11-1 (3") G Hogan, *not fluent, hld up, prog 7th, 3rd and btn whn mstk 3 out.*
..............................(5 to 1 op 7 to 2 tchd 11 to 2) 3
NIGHT IN A MILLION 5-11-3 J F Titley, *mstk second, al beh, tld off frm tenth.*........(20 to 1 tchd 40 to 1) 4
695² CAXTON (USA) 9-11-4 N Williamson, *chsd ldr till wknd 6th, tld off and pld up bef 8th.*...........(20 to 1 op 10 to 1) pu
Dist: 2½l, 24l, dist. 3m 54.90s. a 8.90s (5 Ran).

(Stamford Bridge Partnership), C J Mann

821 Sunday Racing Handicap Chase Class C (0-135 5-y-o and up) £4,788 3m.................................. (3:15)

BIG BEN DUN [107] 10-10-2 J Osborne, *chsd ldr, pushed alng 13th, chlgd 3 out, led last, rdn out.*
..............................(7 to 2 tchd 3 to 1 and 4 to 1) 1
STRAIGHT TALK [133] 9-12-0 A P McCoy, *jmpd wl, led, kicked clr aftr 12th, rdn hdd last, kpt on well.*
..............................(7 to 2 op 2 to 1 tchd 11 to 4) 2
VICOSA (Ire) [112] 7-10-2 (5") P Henley, *in tch till outpcd aftr 12th, ran on 14th, ev ch whn mstk 3 out, wknd nxt.*
..............................(11 to 2 op 4 to 1) 3
BAS DE LAINE (Fr) [115] 10-10-7 (3") Mr C Bonner, *not fluent, chsd ldrs till mstk 12th, tld off 14th.*
..............................(4 to 1 op 7 to 2 tchd 9 to 2) 4
59* FACTOR TEN (Ire) [118] 8-10-13 J F Titley, *not jump wl, whn blun 5th, lost tch aftr mstk 9th, tld off and pld up aftr 12th.*
..............................(3 to 1 op 7 to 2 tchd 4 to 1) pu

Dist: 2l, 25l, dist. 5m 51.50s. a 2.50s (5 Ran).
SR: 13/37/   (Uplands Bloodstock), C P E Brooks

822 WWW.Racing.Press.Net Handicap Hurdle Class D (0-125 4-y-o and up) £3,598 2m 5f. . . . . (3:50)

643² BLASKET HERO [105] (bl) 8-11-0 N Williamson, hld up, prog
6th, rdn aftr 3 out, led nxt, jmpd lft last, all out.
. . . . (7 to 2 op 6 to 1 tchd 7 to 1)   1
754* AMAZE [111] 7-10-13 (7*) Mr R Thornton, wtd wth, cld 6th, rdn
to chase wnr appr last, ev ch r-in, not quicken.
. . . . (5 to 2 fav tchd 9 to 4 and 11 to 4)   2
MR COPYFORCE [101] 6-10-10 M Richards, wtd wth, mstk
3rd, chsd ldr aftr 6th, led after 3 out, hdd nxt, ev ch r-in, kpt on.
. . . . (7 to 1 op 6 to 1 tchd 8 to 1)   3
675³ CABOCHON [95] 9-10-4 C Llewellyn, led second to 5th, lost
pl and rdn 3 out, sn btn. (20 to 1 op 12 to 1 tchd 25 to 1)   4
CAVINA [108] 6-11-3 G Bradley, led to second, led 5th till aftr
3 out, wknd rpdly nxt. . . . . (3 to 1 tchd 7 to 2)   5
JIMMY'S CROSS (Ire) [115] 6-11-10 A P McCoy, hld up last,
lost tch aftr 6th, tld off and pld up bef 2 out.
. . . . (4 to 1 op 9 to 4 tchd 9 to 2)   pu
Dist: 1½l, ¾l, 17l, dist. 4m 57.60s. a 11.60s (6 Ran).
                                    (Miss H J Flower), Mrs S D Williams

823 Kempton Park Handicap Chase Class C (0-135 5-y-o and up) £4,459 2½m 110yds. . . . . (4:20)

GLEMOT [134] 8-11-13 J Osborne, led to 3 out, led nxt,
rdn and hdd last, rallied to ld nr finish. . (3 to 1 op 7 to 2)   1
SUPER TACTICS [116] 8-10-4 (5*) P Henley, trkd ldrs, rdn
aftr 3 out, led last, hdd nr finish. . . . . (6 to 1 op 5 to 1)   2
532² CONTI D'ESTRUVAL (Fr) [122] 6-11-1 A P McCoy, pressed
wnr, rdn to ld 3 out, hdd and btn nxt. . . . . (15 to 8 jt-
fav 6 to 1 tchd 2 to 1)   3
774* CAPTAIN KHEDIVE [130] 8-11-9 P Hide, hld up in tch, ev ch
whn f 13th. . . . . (15 to 8 jt-fav op 2 to 1 tchd 7 to 4)   f
Dist: Nk, 10l. 5m 0.70s. a 7.70s (4 Ran).
                                    (Dennis Yardy), K C Bailey

824 Kids Free Novices' Hurdle Class D (4-y-o and up) £2,840 2m. . . . . (4:50)

MAZZINI (Ire) 5-10-7 (5*) L Aspell, trkd ldrs, rdn to chal 2 out,
led last, drvn out. . . . . (20 to 1 op 12 to 1)   1
652 WANSTEAD (Ire) (bl) 4-10-12 A Maguire, trkd ldr, led appr 2
out, hrd rdn and hdd last, swtchd rght r-in, no extr nr finish.
. . . . (7 to 1 op 5 to 1)   2
ATH CHEANNAITHE (Fr) 4-10-12 D Bridgwater, led till appr 2
out, rdn and ev ch last. not quicken r-in. (4 to 1 op 5 to 1)   3
SAMAKA HARA (Ire) 4-10-12 N Williamson, keen hold, trkd
ldrs, rdn and effrt appr 2 out, 4th and btn whn mstk last.
. . . . (8 to 1 op 10 to 1 tchd 12 to 1)   4
JAAZIM 6-10-12 B Fenton, mstk 3rd, in tch till 5th, sn outpcd,
rdn and modest prog frm 2 out. . . . . . . (14 to 1 op 10 to 1)   5
WATER HAZARD (Ire) 4-10-12 A P McCoy, keen hold, prmnt,
mstk 3rd, wknd aftr 3 out, eased whn no ch appr last.
. . . . (8 to 1 tchd 9 to 1 and 7 to 1)   6
HUNTERS ROCK (Ire) 7-10-12 A Thornton, trkd ldrs, pushed
alng whn mstk 3 out, sn btn.
. . . . (11 to 10 fav op 5 to 4 on tchd 6 to 5)   7
641⁶ COLIN'S PRIDE 5-10-7 R Farrant, in tch, mstk 4th, rdn and
wknd aftr nxt. . . . . (50 to 1 op 33 to 1)   8
CULTURAL ICON (USA) 4-10-12 G Bradley, in tch, rdn 5th,
wknd nxt, tld off. . . . . (33 to 1 op 20 to 1)   9
MANNAGAR (Ire) 4-10-5 (7*) Mr P O'Keeffe, hld up, al beh, tld
off 5th. . . . . (50 to 1 op 33 to 1)   10
MILLFIELD MISS 7-10-12 G Upton, strted slwly, jmpd slowly,
al wl beh, tld off and pld up bef last. . (50 to 1 op 33 to 1)   pu
Dist: ¾l, 2l, 10l, 2½l, 6l, 2½l, 13l, 10l, 21l. 3m 46.60s. a 6.60s (11 Ran).
SR: 18/17/15/5/2/-/   (Nicholas Cooper), R Rowe

TIPPERARY (IRE) (good (races 1,3), good to yielding (2,4,5)) Sunday October 6th

825 Croom House Stud Chase (4-y-o and up) £4,110 2m. . . . . (2:30)

SOUND MAN (Ire) 8-12-0 R Dunwoody, ... (4 to 1 on)   1
744⁴ PHARDY 5-11-0 T Horgan, ... (12 to 1)   2
719⁵ JASSU 10-11-11 C F Swan, ... (4 to 1)   3
711⁵ SANDYS GIRL (Ire) 8-11-13 J P Broderick, ... (50 to 1)   4
742 WHAT A CHOICE (Ire) 6-10-9 (5*) M J Holbrook, . (66 to 1)   5
744² SAVUTI (Ire) 7-10-11 (7*) M D Murphy, ... (8 to 1)   6
Dist: 20l, 8l, 20l, 7l. 3m 53.60s. (6 Ran).
                                    (David Lloyd), E J O'Grady

826 Tipperary Natural Mineral Water Hurdle (4-y-o and up) £4,452 2½m. . (4:00)

WHAT A QUESTION (Ire) 8-11-6 (3*) D J Casey, ... (5 to 1)   1
PERSIAN HALO (Ire) 8-11-7 (7*) Miss S Kauntze, . . . (9 to 4)   2

NEW CO (Ire) 8-12-0 C O'Dwyer, ... (6 to 4 fav)   3
485* MAJESTIC MARINER (Ire) 5-11-2 C F Swan, ... (7 to 1)   4
678⁶ ORCHARD SUNSET (Ire) 6-10-10¹ (7*) Mr D M Fogarty,
. . . . (33 to 1)   5
GARRAUN NATIVE (Ire) 4-9-13 (7*) A O'Shea, ... (25 to 1)   6
174⁵ JUSTAWAY (Ire) 6-11-8 K P Gaule, ... (14 to 1)   7
628⁴ BYPHARBEANRI (Ire) 5-11-2 J P Broderick, ... (25 to 1)   8
713⁷ PHARDANTE LILLY (Ire) 6-10-6 T J O'Sullivan, . . . (66 to 1)   9
566⁹ KINCORA (Ire) 5-10-11 (5*) J M Donnelly, ... (50 to 1)   10
Dist: 10l, 6l, 15l, 11l. 4m 54.20s. (10 Ran).
                                    (Mrs Miles Valentine), M F Morris

827 Junction E.B.F. Beginners Chase (4-y-o and up) £3,767 2m. . . . . (4:30)

303⁸ DANCE BEAT 5-11-5 J Shortt, ... (2 to 1)   1
561⁹ LISNAGAR LADY (Ire) 7-11-9 S H O'Donovan, ... (40 to 1)   2
IRISH LIGHT (Ire) 8-12-0 J P Broderick, ... (40 to 1)   3
87² ANGAREB (Ire) 7-12-0 T P Treacy, ... (10 to 1)   4
485 HOTEL MINELLA 9-12-0 R Dunwoody, ... (7 to 4 on)   f
MYFAVOURITEMARTIAN (Ire) 6-11-11 (3*) D J Casey,
. . . . (8 to 1)   ur
PROSPECT STAR (Ire) 5-11-3 (7*) Mr J Motherway, (33 to 1)   ur
Dist: 10l, 1½l, 25l. 3m 57.30s. (7 Ran).
                                    (Mrs E Queally), Mrs John Harrington

828 Premier County Publicans Handicap Hurdle (0-123 4-y-o and up) £3,767 2½m. . . . . (5:00)

730 BOB THE YANK (Ire) [-] 6-11-4 R Dunwoody, ... (12 to 1)   1
732* VALMAR (Ire) [-] 8-9-7 F Woods, ... (5 to 1)   2
730⁹ BLAZE OF HONOUR (Ire) [-] 5-11-9 C F Swan, (2 to 1 fav)   3
730⁶ FONTAINE LODGE (Ire) [-] 6-10-12 (7*) A O'Shea,
. . . . (100 to 30)   4
701* PEACEFULL RIVER (Ire) [-] 7-9-1 (7*) B D Murtagh, (16 to 1)   5
OAKLER (Ire) [-] 6-10-13 (7*) J A Robinson, ... (16 to 1)   6
287³ FINCHPALM (Ire) [-] 6-11-5 F J Flood, ... (9 to 1)   7
732⁹ HAKKINEN (Ire) [-] 5-11-6 K F O'Brien, ... (11 to 1)   8
732⁵ FALCARRAGH (Ire) [-] 6-9-7 (7*) J M Maguire, . . . (12 to 1)   9
732⁴ BLACK QUEEN (Ire) [-] 5-11-6 J Shortt, ... (7 to 1)   10
469⁶ ARCTIC KATE [-] 10-11-5 (5*) G Cotter, ... (14 to 1)   11
679⁴ STONELEIGH TURBO (Ire) [-] 7-10-10 S H O'Donovan,
. . . . (16 to 1)   12
Dist: 3l, ½l, 1l, 2½l. 4m 56.30s. (12 Ran).
                                    (R Phelan), P T Flavin

829 Willie O'Rourke Memorial I.N.H.Flat Race (4-y-o and up) £3,425 2m. . (5:30)

IODER WAN (Ire) 4-10-11 (7*) Mr J P Moloney, ... (10 to 1)   1
BARHALE BOY (Iro) 4-11-6 (3*) Mr B M Cash, . . (5 to 4 fav)   2
WEST OF THE MOON (Ire) 5-11-9 (5*) Mr R Walsh, (10 to 1)   3
22³ PREMIER WALK 7-11-7 (7*) Mr S P Hennessy, ... (16 to 1)   4
142⁴ GRANUALE (Ire) 5-11-2 (7*) Mr B Hassett, ... (9 to 2)   5
WATT A BUZZ (Ire) 5-11-2 (7*) Mr J C McNamara, (12 to 1)   6
603⁴ FREE AND EQUAL (Ire) 5-12-0 Mr J P Dempsey, . . (14 to 1)   7
JACK CHAUCER 4-11-2 (7*) Mr M W Carroll, ... (10 to 1)   8
JACKY FLYNN (Ire) 5-11-7 (7*) Mr B Walsh, ... (10 to 1)   9
TOTALLY FRANK (Ire) 8-12-0 Miss M Olivefalk, . . . (14 to 1)   10
DREAM SOVEREIGN (Ire) 5-11-9 Mr G J Harford, (13 to 2)   11
PATRAY LAD (Ire) 5-11-7 (7*) Mr M P Madden, ... (10 to 1)   12
RING MAN (Ire) 5-11-2 (7*) Mr B M Clohessy, ... (16 to 1)   13
GOOD RECOVERY (Ire) 6-11-7 (7*) Mr M D Scanlon,
. . . . (33 to 1)   14
603⁶ ROMEO'S BROTHER (Ire) 5-12-0 Mr P J Healy, . . (16 to 1)   15
MAYDAY DREAM (Ire) (bl) 6-11-2 (7*) Mr R Geraghty,
. . . . (12 to 1)   16
681 GONE ALL DAY (Ire) 6-11-7 (7*) Mr D G McHale, . (33 to 1)   17
MYSTERY PAT (Ire) 5-11-12¹⁰ (7*) Mr M Monahan, (20 to 1)   18
Dist: 2l, 14l, 3½l, 4½l. 3m 49.50s. (18 Ran).
                                    (Ioder Wan Syndicate), Michael Hourigan

FONTWELL (good to firm) Monday October 7th
Going Correction: PLUS 0.30 sec. per fur.

830 Susan Cork Birthday Novices' Claiming Hurdle Class F (4-y-o and up) £2,138 2¾m 110yds. . . . . (2:30)

677³ SCAMALLACH (Ire) (bl) 6-11-4 G Bradley, hld up, prog 8th,
chsd ldr nxt, led last, pushed clr.
. . . . (11 to 2 op 7 to 2 tchd 6 to 1)   1
784⁴ FERENS HALL 9-10-8 P McLoughlin, clr ldr, rdn appr 2 out,
hdd and wknd last. . . . . . (10 to 1 op 8 to 1 tchd 12 to 1)   2
186⁶ COOLEGALE 10-10-8 A Maguire, chsd ldr 4th till 8th, rdn and
no prog aftr 3 out, kpt on frm last. . . (20 to 1 tchd 25 to 1)   3
707⁴ CHINA MAIL (bl) 4-11-3 C O'Dwyer, chsd ldrs, rdn and
lost tch 7th, tld off frm nxt. . . . . (13 to 8 jt-
fav op 5 to 4 tchd 15 to 8)   4
KEEP-ON 8-10-0 T J Murphy, in tch till rdn and wknd 7th, tld
off nxt. . . . . (50 to 1 op 20 to 1)   5
SHALHOLME 6-10-0 B Fenton, in tch till rdn and wknd 8th, tld
off. . . . . (40 to 1 op 20 to 1)   6

AERODYNAMIC 10-10-0 (5") Sophie Mitchell, chsd ldr till 4th, wknd 6th, tld off and pld up bef 8th.................(20 to 1) pu
GREENSIDE CHAT (Ire) 6-11-3 A P McCoy, trkd ldrs, prog to chase later 8th, wknd rpdly nxt, pld up bef 2 out. (13 to 8 jt-
......................................fav op 9 to 4) 9t-
CHURCHTOWN SPIRIT 5-10-12 G Crone, al bhd, tld off 4th, pld up bef 8th.........(33 to 1 op 20 to 1 tchd 40 to 1) pu
Dist: 12l, nk, dist, 18l, 23l. 5m 35.10s. a 21.10s (9 Ran).

(Mrs Susan McCarthy), J R Jenkins

831 Frank Cundell Challenge Trophy Handicap Chase Class D (0-120 5-y-o and up) £3,720 2m 3f.............. (3:00)

AEDEAN [93] 7-10-1 A Maguire, trkd ldrs, prog 11th, led aftr 4 out till nxt, led last, all out. (8 to 1 op 10 to 1 tchd 6 to 1) 1
500³ ARMALA [107] 11-10-10 (5") L Aspell, led 6th till aftr 4 out, led ag'n nxt, hdd last, rallied r-in, jst f'd....(7 to 2 tchd 4 to 1) 2
674 HENLEY WOOD [98] 11-10-3 (3") G Tormey, led second till 4th, lost pl 12th, rallied 3 out, ran on wl r-in.
......................(3 to 1 fav op 2 to 1 tchd 100 to 30) 3
490⁴ WHO'S TO SAY [120] 10-11-9 (5") Michael Brennan, led till second and rmn 4th till 6th, rdn and lost pl 12th, rallied 2 out, fourth and staying on whn mstk last.
................................(10 to 1 op 6 to 1 tchd 12 to 1) 4
48⁶ BLACK CHURCH [98] 10-10-6 R Dunwoody, hld up, prog to track ldg pair 4 out, mstk nxt, wknd 2 out.
................................(5 to 1 op 7 to 1 tchd 8 to 1) 5
KINDLE'S DELIGHT [105] 8-10-13 J F Titley, in tch till outpcd 4 out, wknd 2 out........(11 to 2 op 7 to 2 tchd 6 to 1) 6
759² WINGSPAN (USA) [94] 12-10-2 A Thornton, mstk 4th, al rear, lost tch 12th, tld off......(13 to 2 op 8 to 1 tchd 6 to 1) 7
Dist: Sht-hd, nk, 5l, 1¾l, 12l, dist. 4m 49.60s. a 14.60s (7 Ran).

(M B Orpen-Palmer), G P Enright

832 'Salmon Spray' Challenge Trophy Handicap Hurdle Class D (0-125 4-y-o and up) £2,846 2¼m 110yds.... (3:30)

707 CHRIS'S GLEN [85] (v) 7-10-0 N Williamson, trkd ldr, led 5th, quickened nxt, rdn and hdd 2 out, rallied r-in, led nr finish.
................................(10 to 1 op 6 to 1 tchd 11 to 1) 1
616³ RE ROI (Ire) [97] 4-10-6 (5") P Henley, wtd wth, trkd ldr aftr 5th, led gng easily 2 out, hrd rdn r-in, hdd nr finish.
................................(7 to 4 fav op 5 to 2) 2
BON VOYAGE (USA) [102] 4-11-2 J R Kavanagh, trkd ldrs, pushed alng frm 6th, rdn and one pace from 2 out.
................................(9 to 4 op 6 to 4) 3
696² GONE BY (Ire) [109] (v) 8-11-10 G Bradley, hld up, pushed alng and not quicken aftr 6th, no dngr after.
................................(4 to 1 tchd 5 to 1) 4
STAR OF DAVID (Ire) [103] 8-11-4 R Dunwoody, led, reluctant to race and reminders aftr 3rd, hdd 5th, sn drpd out, pld up bef nxt................................(5 to 1 op 4 to 1) pu
Dist: ½l, 8l, 4l. 4m 37.00s. a 20.00s (5 Ran).

(The Crown At Hambrook Racing Club), J M Bradley

833 Strebel Boilers And Radiators Handicap Hurdle Series Qualifier Class E (0-110 4-y-o and up) £2,490 2¾m 110yds...................... (4:00)

VICTOR BRAVO (NZ) [103] (bl) 9-11-7 C Llewellyn, prmnt, chsd ldr 6th till rdn 8th, rallied to ld 2 out, clr last, ran on wl.
................................(16 to 1 op 10 to 1 tchd 20 to 1) 1
SOPHIE MAY [97] 5-11-0 A P McCoy, mid-div, pushed alng 8th, prog 3 out, styd on one pace frm nxt.
................................(14 to 1 op 8 to 1 tchd 16 to 1) 2
615³ MR SNAGGLE (Ire) [94] 7-10-5 (7") B McGann, trkd ldrs gng easily, prog to ld aftr 3 out, hdd and hdd nxt, not quicken.
................................(6 to 1 op 8 to 1 tchd 10 to 1) 3
673 ROGER'S PAL [92] 9-9-7 (7") M Batchelor, prmnt till rdn and outpcd 8th, sn beh, kpt on ag'n appr last.
................................(66 to 1 op 33 to 1) 4
KARAR (Ire) [109] 6-11-8 (5") L Aspell, trkd ldrs, rdn 8th, one pace aftr 3 out................(6 to 1 op 4 to 1 tchd 13 to 2) 5
CAPTAIN COE [87] 6-10-5 D Morris, led till aftr 3 out, sn btn, fnshd lme................................(3 to 1 fav tchd 4 to 1) 6
751 DORANS WAY (Ire) [94] 5-10-6 (5") Michael Brennan, trkd ldrs gng easily, chsd ldr 8th, rdn and ev ch aftr 3 out, wknd rpdly.
................................(25 to 1 op 14 to 1 tchd 33 to 1) 7
PUNCH'S HOTEL [110] (bl) 11-12-0 N Williamson, mstk ldr till 3rd, prmnt till wknd appr 8th, sn no ch.
................................(12 to 1 op 9 to 2 tchd 14 to 1) 8
675² CIRCUS COLOURS [98] 6-11-2 A Maguire, hld up last, effrt and prog 8th, chsd ldrs 3 out, wknd rpdly nxt.
................................(11 to 2 op 7 to 1 tchd 6 to 1) 9
709³ SCUD MISSILE (Ire) [103] 5-11-6 A Thornton, pckd 4th, chsd ldr 3rd till 6th, rdn and lost pl nxt, no ch aftr.
................................(9 to 2 op 5 to 1 tchd 11 to 2) 10
Dist: 6l, hd, 5l, ¾l, 6l, 18l, 6l, 3l, nk. 5m 31.80s. a 17.80s (10 Ran).

(Mrs R W S Baker), N A Gaselee

834 Singleton Amateur Riders' Novices' Handicap Chase Class F (0-100 5-y-o and up) £2,527 3¼m 110yds.... (4:30)

630⁶ SEASAMACAMILE [71] 9-9-7 (7") Mr R Thornton, pressed ldr, pushed alng 5 out, led nxt, drvn out.
................................(9 to 4 op 5 to 2 tchd 3 to 1) 1
676² DISTANT MEMORY [99] (bl) 7-11-7 (7") Mr S Mulcaire, led, pckd 5 out, hdd nxt, rdn and not quicken 2 out.
................................(5 to 4 on op 2 to 1 tchd Evens) 2
247⁶ ARTFUL ARTHUR [71] 10-9-11⁴ (7") Mr J Grassick, reminder 6th, lost tch 15th, tld off 4 out..........(7 to 1 op 6 to 1) 3
615 ENNISTYMON (Ire) [74] 5-9-12⁶ (7") Mr G Weatherley, cl up whn mstk and uns rdr 4th. (8 to 1 op 7 to 2 tchd 9 to 1) ur
Dist: 2½l, dist. 7m 14.40s. a 44.40s (4 Ran).

(M West), R H Buckler

835 Langstone Conservative Club Novices' Hurdle Class E (4-y-o and up) £2,511 2¼m 110yds...................... (5:00)

MR EDGAR (Ire) 5-10-12 P Hide, trkd ldrs, mstk 5th, prog whn lft in ld aftr 3 out, left clr after last, pushed out.
................................(11 to 8 on op 2 to 1 on tchd 11 to 10 on) 1
689⁴ DACELO (Fr) 5-10-12 J Osborne, led 4th till and aftr nxt, tried irons after last, not run on. (2 to 1 op 9 to 4 tchd 7 to 4) 2
689⁹ CADDY'S FIRST 4-10-11 N Mann, rcd wide, prmnt, led 4th till aftr 5th, ev ch 3 out, rdn and not quicken last.
................................(9 to 1 op 5 to 1 tchd 10 to 1) 3
ZUNO FLYER (USA) 4-10-11 A P McCoy, in tch, rdn 3 out, sn pace nxt, 4th and btn whn mstk last.
................................(10 to 1 op 12 to 1 tchd 16 to 1) 4
ALLEZ PABLO 6-10-7 (5") L Aspell, prmnt till rdn and wknd 6th, tld off 3 out....(50 to 1 op 20 to 1 tchd 66 to 1) 5
RAVUS 6-10-12 A Dicken, mstk 1st, sn wl beh, tld off 5th.
................................(66 to 1 op 33 to 1) 6
183⁷ HOLLOW WOOD (Ire) 5-10-12 B Powell, not jump wl, in tch, rdn 5th, sn wknd, tld off..............(33 to 1 op 20 to 1) 7
Dist: 12l, 5l, 1l, dist, 8l, 4l. 4m 29.80s. a 12.80s (7 Ran).
SR: 11/-/-/-/   (Felix Rosenstiel's Widow & Son), J T Gifford

TOWCESTER (good to firm)
Wednesday October 9th
Going Correction: NIL

836 Ascote Selling Hurdle Class G (4,5,6-y-o) £1,989 2m 5f.................. (2:20)

534⁸ DO BE WARE (bl) 6-11-5 B Fenton, chsd ldr, hdwy 6th, rdn 4 out, styd on und pres to ld last, all out.
................................(16 to 1 op 14 to 1 tchd 20 to 1 and 25 to 1) 1
727³ PARISH WALK (Ire) 5-10-12 A Maguire, led, clr 4th, rdn and wknd 2 out, hdd last, sn btn.
................................(6 to 4 on op 2 to 1 on tchd 11 to 8 on) 2
667³ SALTIS (Ire) 4-10-11 T Eley, hdwy 6th, outpcd 4 out, styd on frm 2 out, not rch 1st two.
................................(9 to 4 op 2 to 1 tchd 5 to 2 and 11 to 4) 3
652 NORTHERN LAW (bl) 4-10-11 L Lawrence, hit 5th and beh, sn tld off, pld up bef 7th................(4 to 1 tchd 9 to 2) pu
Dist: 9l, nk. 5m 20.50s. a 21.50s (4 Ran).

(John Ffitch-Heyes), J Ffitch-Heyes

837 Old Stratford Novices' Hurdle Class D (4-y-o and up) £2,889 2m........ (2:50)

YOUNG RADICAL (Ire) 4-10-11 R Supple, 3rd till hdwy to track ldr 5th, chlgd frm 3 out till slight ld 2 out, rdn out r-in.
................................(6 to 4 on op 5 to 2 on) 1
TOMAL 4-10-11 A P McCoy, chsd ldr, hit 5th, str chal frm 2 out and ag'n whn mstk last, one pace...(13 to 8 op 2 to 1) 2
689 RAGTIME SONG (v) 7-10-12 G Bradley, led, clr 3rd, narrowly hdd 2 out, sn outpcd....(14 to 1 op 16 to 1 tchd 20 to 1) 3
BITE THE BULLET 5-10-12 B Powell, mstk second, effrt 5th, wknd aftr 3 out........(33 to 1 op 25 to 1 tchd 40 to 1) 4
PRINCE RICO 5-10-12 S Wynne, sn beh, tld off 4th.
................................(33 to 1 op 16 to 1 tchd 50 to 1) 5
Dist: 1¾l, 4l, 13l, dist. 3m 57.20s. a 14.20s (5 Ran).

(N Jones), John R Upson

838 Biddlesden Novices' Chase Class E (5-y-o and up) £2,877 2m 110yds.. (3:20)

655² MILL O'THE RAGS (Ire) 7-11-5 J F Titley, led, hit 4th, hdd 7th, led 9th, lft clr 3 out, ran on gmely und pres frm 2 out. (Evens jt-fav op 5 to 4 tchd 11 to 8) 1
753⁴ MARTHA'S DAUGHTER 7-10-7 A Thornton, hld up in 3rd, outpcd 7th, hdwy whn lft second 3 out, rdn 2 out, found no extr.
................................(Evens jt-fav op 2 to 1 on) 2
LARKS TAIL 8-10-7 R Bellamy, al beh, hit 9th, nvr dngrs.
................................(33 to 1 op 20 to 1 tchd 40 to 1) 3
ROYAL HAND 6-10-12 B Fenton, hit 1st, chsd wnr, hit 4th, led 7th, hdd 9th, cl second whn blun and uns rdr 3 out.
................................(16 to 1 op 12 to 1) ur
Dist: 3l, 22l. 4m 9.20s. a 12.20s (4 Ran).

(E J Fenaroli), Mrs D Haine

839 KPMG Pasas Handicap Hurdle Class F (0-100 4-y-o and up) £2,285 2m (3:50)

SNOW BOARD [65] 7-10-3[1] D Byrne, *quickened to ld 3 out, ran on wl und pres r-in*.....(9 to 2 op 5 to 2 tchd 5 to 1) 1
704[2] RAGAMUFFIN ROMEO [72] 7-10-10 N Mann, *chsd ldr till 3rd, styd prmnt, rdn and kpt on appr last, not pace of wnr*.
......................(2 to 1 op 9 to 4 tchd 5 to 2) 2
709[2] WOLLBOLL [86] 6-11-10 V Smith, *led appr 4th, outpcd nxt, rallied to chal 3 out, one pace und pres frm 2 out*.
.....................(15 to 8 fav op 6 to 4 tchd 9 to 4) 3
665[8] EXCLUSION [80] 7-11-4 R Marley, *hdwy to chase ldr 3rd, led appr 4th, hdd 3 out, wknd approaching 2 out*.
.......................(10 to 1 tchd 12 to 1) 4
754[3] VERDE LUNA [87] 4-11-10 A P McCoy, *hdwy to chase ldrs 4 out, ev ch 3 out, fourth and wkng whn 1 2 out*.
.....................(9 to 4 op 2 to 1 tchd 5 to 2) f
Dist: 2½l, ¾l, 26l. 3m 51.00s. a 8.00s (5 Ran).
SR: -/-/12/-/-/ *(F J Sainsbury), Mrs Merrita Jones*

840 Lillingstone Lovell Handicap Chase Class E (0-110 5-y-o and up) £3,197 3m 1f............................(4:20)

632* JIM VALENTINE [91] 10-11-0 W Marston, *al gng wl, hdwy 8th, hit 13th, led last, cmftbly*.
.....................(2 to 1 fav op 9 to 4 tchd 5 to 2) 1
676* FROZEN DROP [102] 9-11-11 S Fox, *led second till 4th, chlgd 8th and 9th, led tenth, hdd last, one pace*.
.......................(9 to 4 tchd 5 to 2) 2
727 K C'S DANCER [79] 11-10-2 J Culloty, *in tch, outpcd 9th, staying on whn hit 3 out, kpt on one pace*.
.....................(14 to 1 op 10 to 1 tchd 16 to 1) 3
TITUS ANDRONICUS [89] (bl) 9-10-12 C Llewellyn, *hdwy to track ldrs 8th, rdn 2 out, sn wknd*.
.....................(4 to 1 op 5 to 2 tchd 9 to 2) 4
514[7] NICK THE DREAMER [100] 11-11-9 R Dunwoody, *led till second, styd wth ldr till led 4th, hdd tenth, wknd aftr 3 out*.
.....................(10 to 1 op 7 to 1 tchd 11 to 1) 5
WOODLANDS GENHIRE [77] 11-10-0 A Maguire, *hdwy to chase ldrs 5th, hit 6th, wknd tenth*.
........(12 to 1 op 10 to 1 tchd 14 to 1 and 16 to 1) 6
POLAR REGION [105] 10-11-9 (5*) Mr C Vigors, *hit 3rd, wknd 9th, lid off whn blun 12th, pld up bef 3 out*.
.....................(7 to 1 op 4 to 1 tchd 8 to 1) pu
Dist: 4l, 15l, 2l, 1½l, dist. 6m 20.20s. a 8.20s (7 Ran).
SR: 4/11/-/-/ *(R H L Barnes), D J Wintle*

841 Cosgrove Novices' Handicap Hurdle Class E (0-100 4-y-o and up) £2,262 3m..............................(4:50)

650[2] HYLTERS CHANCE (Ire) [71] 5-10-10 A P McCoy, *made all, came clr frm 3 out, unchlgd* ..... (Evens fav op 5 to 4 on) 1
687* ARRANGE A GAME [70] 9-10-6 (5*) S Taylor, *chsd ldrs, hit 8th, outpcd 3 out, styd on und pres to take second r-in, not a dngr*.
.....................(100 to 30 op 7 to 2) 2
673[2] CREDIT CONTROLLER (Ire) [62] 7-10-3 A Maguire, *hdwy to track wnr 8th, rdn aftr 3 out, sn no ch, wknd and clr for second r-in*.....(7 to 2 op 3 to 1 tchd 9 to 2) 3
PENNANT COTTAGE (Ire) [59] 8-9-10[1] (5*) Chris Webb, *chsd ldrs till 8th, sn wknd*..............(16 to 1 op 12 to 1) 4
YOUNG TESS [83] 6-11-10 Mr A Brown, *rdn alng 3rd, lost tch 6th*.....................(7 to 1 op 5 to 1) 5
Dist: 20l, nk, 13l, 7l. 5m 58.70s. a 16.70s (5 Ran).
(Mrs Karola Vann), P J Hobbs

LUDLOW (firm)
Thursday October 10th
Going Correction: NIL

842 Scania 4-series 'Horsepower' Selling Hurdle Handicap Class G (0-90 4-y-o and up) £1,968 2m 5f 110yds... (2:20)

687[6] KING OF BABYLON (Ire) [70] 4-11-6 (3*) L Aspell, *chsd ldr, chlgd 4th to nxt, led 2 out, pushed out*.
.....................(9 to 4 fav tchd 5 to 2) 1
673 LAC DE GRAS (Ire) [64] 5-11-3 D Morris, *chsd ldrs, led 3 out, hdd nxt, chlgd last, sn one pace*......(8 to 1 op 6 to 1) 2
687[7] THEY ALL FORGOT ME [59] 9-10-13 Miss C Dyson, *led, mstk second, hdd 3 out, wknd appr last*......(5 to 1 op 10 to 1) 3
756[6] DANE ROSE [70] 10-11-10 A Maguire, *hld up, not fluent 4 out, rdn and effrt nxt, sn one pace und pres*.
.....................(5 to 2 tchd 11 to 4) 4
AWESTRUCK [52] (bl) 6-10-3 (3*) G Hogan, *beh, rdn and effrt appr 3 out, sn wknd, mstk 2 out*........(10 to 1 op 6 to 1) 5
768 SIESTA TIME (USA) [53] 6-10-7 D J Burchell, *very slwly away, refused 1st*.....................(7 to 1 op 6 to 1) ref
Dist: 3½l, 2½l, 1¼l, 16l. 5m 14.20s. a 19.20s (6 Ran).
(R A Hancocks), F Jordan

843 Knighton Trucks For Scania Novices' Chase Class E (4-y-o and up) £3,009 2m..............................(2:50)

TENAYESTELIGN 8-11-0 J A McCarthy, *slwly away, chsd ldr aftr 5th, lft in ld bend appr nxt, made most of remainder, cmftbly*............................(4 to 1 op 3 to 1) 1
769 RYTON RUN 11-11-9 B Fenton, *led to second, lft second bend appr 6th, chlgd 9th till slpd bend approaching 4 out, hit 3 out, sn one pace*............(20 to 1 op 16 to 1) 2
820[8] HOLY WANDERER (USA) 7-11-2 (3*) G Hogan, *keen hold, led second, slpd up bend appr 6th, rmntd, not reco'r, tld off*.
.......................(7 to 4 on tchd 13 to 8 on) 3
753 LAURA LYE (Ire) 6-11-0 J Railton, *refused to race*.
.......................(11 to 1 op 8 to 1) l
Dist: 3l, dist. 4m 9.60s. a 19.60s (4 Ran).
(G J King), D Marks

844 Radio Shropshire Stayers' Handicap Hurdle Class D (0-120 4-y-o and up) £2,787 3¼m 110yds............(3:20)

752[3] HOLY JOE [99] 14-10-7 D J Burchell, *led till hdd aftr 7th, outpcd after 4 out, quickened 2 out, led last, ran on wl*.
.......................(3 to 1) 1
NATHAN BLAKE [92] (bl) 11-9-7 (7*) J Power, *chsd wnr frm 3rd till led aftr 7th, drvn clr after 4 out, hdd last, styd on one pace*.....................(25 to 1 op 20 to 1) 2
738[4] DON DU CADRAN (Fr) [99] (bl) 7-10-7 A Thornton, *hld up, hdwy 8th, outpcd aftr 4 out, styd on frm 2 out, not rch ldrs*.
.......................(5 to 1 op 4 to 1 tchd 11 to 2) 3
707* TALLYWAGGER [120] 9-12-0 N Bentley, *in tch, hdwy 8th, outpcd 4 out, rdn and nvr dngrs aftr*.
.......................(5 to 4 fav tchd 11 to 8) 4
756[4] STORM DRUM [92] 7-9-3[2] (7*) Mr R Wakley, *hld up in rear, lost tch frm 8*.........(10 to 1 op 8 to 1 tchd 11 to 1) 5
662[4] GEORGE ASHFORD (Ire) [92] 6-10-0 A S Smith, *prmnt early, beh frm 5th, lost tch nxt*.......(7 to 1 op 6 to 1) 6
Dist: 2l, ½l, 9l, 5l, 23l. 6m 21.00s. a 16.00s (6 Ran).
(Simon T Lewis), D Burchell

845 Scania 1996 Truck Of The Year Trophy Novices' Handicap Chase Class E (0-100 5-y-o and up) £3,386 2½m
..............................(3:50)

655[4] ON THE TEAR [61] 10-10-4 C Llewellyn, *trkd ldr, chlgd frm tenth till led 13th, lft clr 4 out, drvn out*.
.......................(6 to 1 op 7 to 1 tchd 8 to 1) 1
655[3] LITTLE BY LITTLE [60] 6-10-3 A Thornton, *jmpd slwly 1st, hit 4th, chlgd 12th, lft second four out, chald last, hng left, no extr*.....................(7 to 1 tchd 8 to 1) 2
753[6] SCRIPT [63] 5-10-4 W Marston, *mstk 7th and beh, jmpd slwly tenth, drvn and hdwy appr 4 out, kpt on one pace frm 2 out*.
.....................(13 to 8 op 7 to 4 tchd 6 to 4) 3
787 BLUE RAVEN [00] 6 12 3 (7ox) A Maguire, *led to 13th, styd pressing wnr till l 4 out*...........(11 to 8 fav op Evens) f
Dist: 2l, 3l. 5m 14.10s. a 25.10s (4 Ran).
(F Lloyd), F Lloyd

846 Scania 4-series International Challenge Novices' Hurdle Class E (4-y-o and up) £2,192 2m............(4:20)

SIGMA RUN (Ire) 7-10-12 T Hazlett, *made all, sn clr, shaken up whn chlgd frm 3 out, quickened smartly r-in*.
..............(13 to 8 on op 9 to 4 on tchd 6 to 4 on) 1
SUPERENSIS 6-10-12 T Wheeler, *sn tracking wnr, rdn and chlgd frm 3 out till outpcd r-in*.........(4 to 1 tchd 7 to 2) 2
JON'S CHOICE 8-10-12 C Llewellyn, *hld up in 3rd, drvn to chal frm 3 out till one pace und pres r-in*.
.......................(7 to 2 tchd 4 to 1) 3
ANDY COIN 5-10-7 J Titley, *al 4th, rdn and lost tch appr 3 out*.
.......................(20 to 1) 4
Dist: 2½l, hd, 14l. 3m 50.90s. a 18.90s (4 Ran).
(B G S Racing Partnership), J A C Edwards

847 Knighton Trucks 'Scania Know-how' Trophy Handicap Chase Class F (0-100 5-y-o and up) £2,682 2½m......(4:50)

607[3] CRACKLING FROST (Ire) [74] 8-10-2 J F Titley, *led 4th, clr frm 8th, came clear ag'n from four out, very easily*.
..........(6 to 5 on op 5 to 4 on tchd 11 to 10 on) 1
674[2] DRUMSTICK [96] 10-11-10 J Railton, *led and jmpd hesitantly till hdd 4th, outpcd 8th, hdwy to cl on wnr appr four out, sn outpaced*...........(Evens op 5 to 4 on) 2
Won by 15l. 4m 55.80s. a 6.80s (2 Ran).
SR: 6/13/ *(The Unlucky For Some Partnership), Mrs D Haine*

848 Scania 4-series 'King Of The Road' Juvenile Novices' Hurdle Class E (3-y-o) £2,451 2m..............(5:20)

HEVER GOLF DIAMOND 10-12 N Williamson, *hld up, hdwy to track ldrs 5th, chlgd 3 out, led nxt, sn clr, easily*.
.......................(11 to 4 op 9 to 4) 1
788[3] GHOSTLY APPARITION 10-12 R Supple, *wth ldrs to 3rd, rdn and outpcd 3 out, styd on ag'n to take second cl hme, no ch with wnr*....................(4 to 1 op 5 to 1) 2

614[8] LITTLE KENNY (v) 10-4 (3") R Massey, *wth ldrs to 3rd, styd prmnt, led 4 out, hit nxt, hdd 2 out, sn outpcd.*
....(4 to 1 op 7 to 2) 3
658[3] BATH KNIGHT (bl) 10-12 J F Titley, *jmpd lft thrght, led, hdd 4 out, wknd 2 out.*...............(9 to 4 fav tchd 5 to 2) 4
FORMENTIERE 10-7 B Fenton, *in tch, rdn to chase ldrs 4 out, wknd nxt.*............................(33 to 1 op 20 to 1) 5
788[4] COLEBROOK WILLIE 10-12 M Bosley, *beh, rdn and effrt appr 4 out, sn btn.*....................(14 to 1 op 10 to 1) 6
CHILLINGTON 10-12 C Llewellyn, *sn beh.*
....(33 to 1 op 20 to 1) 7
Dist: 7l, ½l, 3l, 4l, 10l, 19l. 3m 42.60s. a 10.60s (7 Ran).

(Hever Racing Club l), T J Naughton

THURLES (IRE) (good to firm)
Thursday October 10th

849 Eliogarty Handicap Hurdle (0-102 4-y-o and up) £2,226 2m............ (2:30)

742[3] BRONICA (Ire) [-] 4-11-6 C F Swan, ...(100 to 30 fav) 1
742[5] MIDDLE MOGGS (Ire) [-] 4-11-0 D J Casey, ... (12 to 1) 2
621[3] BAJAN QUEEN (Ire) [-] 6-11-5 (5") T Martin, ...(7 to 1) 3
684 CHUCK (Ire) [-] 6-11-2 (7") D McCullagh, ... (12 to 1) 4
742[4] TARAJAN (USA) [-] (bl) 4-11-11 J Shortt, ...(8 to 1) 5
742[7] MONTETAN (Ire) [-] 5-11-9 K F O'Brien, ... (12 to 1) 6
718[5] SACULORE (Ire) [-] 8-11-9 (5") J M Donnelly, ...(16 to 1) 7
HEIGHT OF LUXURY (Ire) [-] 8-9-5 (7") M D Murphy, (25 to 1) 8
SMYTHS LADY [-] 4-10-4 S H O'Donovan, ... (16 to 1) 9
781 MISSED CONNECTION (Ire) [-] 5-9-2 (5") J Butler, (50 to 1) 10
781[9] DREAM ETERNAL (Ire) [-] 5-10-11 W Slattery, ...(7 to 1) 11
742 OLD FONTAINE (Ire) [-] 8-9-6[4] (7") S O'Donnell, ... (25 to 1) 12
684[7] LAURENS FANCY (Ire) [-] 6-10-9 M Duffy, ...(8 to 1) 13
732 ALLARACKET (Ire) [-] 7-10-9 (7") A O'Shea, ...(12 to 1) 14
600" LEMOIRE (Ire) [-] 5-10-13 (7") R P Hogan, ...(12 to 1) 15
BAKEMA (Ire) [-] 4-11-6 (3") J R Barry, ...(12 to 1) 16
FORT DEELY (Ire) [-] 5-9-12 J Jones, ...(33 to 1) 17
SWEET REALM [-] 7-9-8 (7") B J Geraghty, ...(20 to 1) 18
233 ASK THE FAIRIES (Ire) [-] 4-10-6[2] F Woods, ...(20 to 1) 19
621[9] THE WICKED CHICKEN (Ire) [-] 7-10-9 T P Treacy, ...f
598[2] FOREST LADY (Ire) [-] 4-10-8 D T Evans, ...(10 to 1) pu
746[6] STANSWAY (Ire) [-] 8-10-6 T Horgan, ...(14 to 1) pu
Dist: 2l, 2l, 4½l, 3l. 3m 48.90s. (22 Ran).

(Mrs Ranka Pollmeter), J E Kiely

850 Tipperary Novice Hurdle (4-y-o and up) £2,226 2¼m.................. (3:00)

IRISH BREEZE 5-11-0 T Horgan, ...(7 to 1) 1
562[4] TALE GAIL (Ire) 6-11-0 W Slattery, ...(4 to 1) 2
685[2] MARTYS STEP (Ire) 5-10-7 (7") D McCullagh, ... (10 to 1) 3
731[3] MURPHY'S MALT (Ire) 4-10-8 C F Swan, ... (6 to 4 fav) 4
714 BALLINABOOLA GROVE 9-10-7 (7") J M Maguire, (20 to 1) 5
31[4] DUISKE ABBEY (Ire) 6-10-4 (5") G Cotter, ...(10 to 1) 6
CELTIC WHO (Ire) 5-11-0 T J Mitchell, ...(20 to 1) 7
717[3] SIMPLY ACOUSTIC (Ire) 5-10-2 (7") A O'Shea, ... (12 to 1) 8
DINAN (Ire) 4-10-8 K F O'Brien, ...(33 to 1) 9
716[5] VASILIKI (Ire) 4-10-5 (3") D J Casey, ...(20 to 1) 10
782 HEMERO (Ire) 4-10-8 M P Hourigan, ...(14 to 1) 11
FOREST STAR (USA) (bl) 7-11-0 D T Evans, ...(16 to 1) 12
718[6] SHALOM (Ire) 4-10-8 J P Broderick, ...(25 to 1) 13
782 WESTERN GREY (Ire) 4-10-1 (7") S FitzGerald, ...(33 to 1) 14
STEP IN LINE (Ire) 4-10-1 (7") M D Murphy, ...(33 to 1) 15
CARA ALANNA 9-10-4 (3") J Butler, ...(25 to 1) 16
213 MORNINGNOONANDNITE (Ire) 4-10-8 A J O'Brien,
....(50 to 1) 17
686 PROPHETS FIST (Ire) 5-11-0 J Shortt, ...(33 to 1) 18
EARLYFOOT (Ire) 5-10-9 S H O'Donovan, ...(33 to 1) 19
393" NO NEWS (Ire) 5-11-7 T P Treacy, ...(6 to 1) su
Dist: 1l, 4½l, 5l, 5l. 4m 21.20s. (20 Ran).

(J Donovan), David J McGrath

851 Upperchurch Chase (5-y-o and up) £2,568 2¾m................... (3:30)

747[2] THE OUTBACK WAY (Ire) (bl) 6-11-11 D H O'Connor,
....(6 to 4 fav) 1
714[6] MICKS DELIGHT (Ire) 6-12-0 C F Swan, ...(4 to 1) 2
WALLYS RUN 9-11-11 L P Cusack, ...(6 to 1) 3
409 EVER SO BOLD 9-11-11 T P Treacy, ...(4 to 1) 4
729 JULY SCHOON 11-11-0 (7") M D Murphy, ...(20 to 1) 5
65 DOONEGA 8-11-7 T Horgan, ...(7 to 1) 6
444[7] CHARLIEADAMS (Ire) 6-11-4 (3") U Smyth, ...(25 to 1) pu
711[3] SILENT SNEEZE (Ire) (bl) 6-10-11[2] (7") Mr K Beecher,
....(7 to 1) pu
Dist: 12l, 4l, 25l, ½l. 5m 32.60s. (8 Ran).

(E O'Dwyer), James Joseph O'Connor

852 Thurles Handicap Chase (0-102 4-y-o and up) £2,226 2¾m........... (4:30)

743[2] CASTALINO [-] 10-11-1 J Shortt, ...(4 to 1 fav) 1
93 TEAL BRIDGE [-] 11-11-4 T J Mitchell, ...(10 to 1) 2
719 WALKERS LADY (Ire) [-] 8-10-8 D T Evans, ...(8 to 1) 3
827[3] IRISH LIGHT (Ire) [-] 8-10-9 J P Broderick, ...(7 to 1) 4
721[3] MACAUNTA (Ire) [-] 6-10-0 A Powell, ...(8 to 1) 5

714[4] QUATTRO [-] (bl) 6-11-2 T P Treacy, ...(5 to 1) 6
680[7] PRIME PAPERS [-] 11-10-0 W Slattery, ...(33 to 1) 7
743[4] ANOTHER COURSE (Ire) [-] 8-11-13 T Horgan, ... (10 to 1) 8
588[3] CLONEENVERB [-] 12-9-2 (5") J Butler, ...(14 to 1) 9
744[5] TOM THE BOY VI (Ire) [-] (bl) 6-9-0 (7") M D Murphy, (25 to 1) 10
602 GLEN OG LANE [-] 13-9-7 F Woods, ...(20 to 1) pu
602[6] WATERLOO BALL (Ire) [-] (bl) 7-11-12 C F Swan, ... (7 to 1) pu
Dist: 1½l, ½l, 1½l, 3l. 5m 26.90s. (12 Ran).

(Stephen Ryan), Stephen Ryan

853 Liscahill I.N.H. Flat Race (5 & 6-y-o) £2,226 2¼m................. (5:30)

139[5] DREAMCATCHER (Ire) 6-11-7 (7") Miss A Foley, .. (12 to 1) 1
BALLYRIHY BOY (Ire) 5-11-7 (7") Mr J Motley, ...(16 to 1) 2
NEVER DELAY (Ire) 5-11-7 (7") Mr Sean O O'Brien, (5 to 1) 3
686[8] BRASSIS HILL (Ire) 5-12-0 Mr P Fenton, ...(12 to 1) 4
717[2] EASTERN CUSTOM (Ire) 5-11-2 (7") Miss D O'Neill, (12 to 1) 5
716[3] HILL OF HOPE (Ire) 5-12-0 Mr A J Martin, ...(12 to 1) 6
ALICE BRENNAN (Ire) 5-11-6 (3") Mr E Norris, .. (9 to 4 fav) 7
686[9] KASSERINE PASS (Ire) 6-11-11 (3") Mr P English, (10 to 1) 8
117[4] THE SENATOR (Ire) 5-11-7 (7") Mr T N Cloke, ...(14 to 1) 9
720 LISADOBBER LADY (Ire) 6-11-4 (5") Mr R Walsh, ...(25 to 1) 10
392[6] HOLLY LAKE (Ire) 6-11-2 (7") Mr J P Moloney, ...(20 to 1) 11
KYLOGUE KING (Ire) 5-11-7 (7") Mr L B Murphy, .. (20 to 1) 12
SHAREZA RIVER (Ire) 6-11-7 (7") Mr J T McNamara,
....(20 to 1) 13
686 STAR HAND (Ire) 5-11-7 (7") Mr D Whelan, ...(20 to 1) 14
591 GOLLY MISS MOLLY (Ire) 5-11-2 (7") Mr B J Clohessy,
....(20 to 1) 15
686 CAPTAIN ARTHUR (Ire) 5-11-7 (7") Mr D M Loughnane,
....(20 to 1) 16
BIT OF PEACE (Ire) 5-11-9 Mr J A Berry, ...(20 to 1) 17
434 LAUDANUM (Ire) 6-11-2 (7") Mr J P McNamara, ...(20 to 1) 18
CLOUGHTEANA (Ire) 5-11-2 (7") Mr Mark Walsh, .. (20 to 1) 19
WILL BROOK (Ire) 5-11-7 (7") Mr N C Kelleher, ...(20 to 1) 20
825[5] WHAT A CHOICE (Ire) 6-11-2 (7") Mr S P Hennessy, (20 to 1) 21
BACK AND AT IT (Ire) 5-11-7 (7") Mr R P McNalley, (20 to 1) su
Dist: Sht-hd, 2l, 1l, 1½l. 4m 9.70s. (22 Ran).

(Thomas Foley), Thomas Foley

WINCANTON (firm)
Thursday October 10th
Going Correction: MINUS 0.35 sec. per fur.

854 Hatherleigh Mares' Only Maiden Hurdle Class E (4-y-o and up) £2,267 2¾m
.... (2:10)

533[2] KYMIN (Ire) 4-10-13 A P McCoy, *hld up beh ldr, jmpd slwly 6th, chlgd nxt, led and lft clr 2 out, cmftbly.*......(5 to 4 fav op 11 to 10 tchd 6 to 4) 1
217[5] GALATASORI JANE (Ire) 6-10-7 (7") O Burrows, *hld up beh ldr, jmpd slwly 7th, reminders whn lft second 2 out, no imprsn und pres.*.............(4 to 1 op 9 to 2 tchd 6 to 1) 2
758[2] KESANTA 6-11-0 R Dunwoody, *reluctant ldr, flashed tail thrght, jst hdd whn f 2 out.*......(5 to 4 jt-fav op 11 to 10) f
Dist: 1¾l. 5m 36.10s. a 30.10s (3 Ran).

(Ms Diana Wilder), D J G Murray Smith

855 Oak Conditional Jockeys' Handicap Chase Class F (0-105 5-y-o and up) £2,804 3m 1f 110yds........... (2:40)

692" DRUMCULLEN (Ire) [88] 7-11-0 T J Murphy, *trkd ldrs, lft clr 16th, easily.*....................(5 to 2 tchd 11 to 4) 1
763[5] TURPIN'S GREEN [74] 13-10-0 J Culloty, *hld up in rear, hdwy 13th, outpcd whn slightly hmpd 16th, chsd wnr frm 3 out, no imprsn.*.......................(12 to 1 op 8 to 1) 2
757[5] FOXGROVE [80] 10-10-6 D Fortt, *hld up, effrt 15th, poor 3rd whn blun last.*........(11 to 1 op 10 to 1 tchd 12 to 1) 3
757 L'UOMO PIU [77] (v) 12-10-3 T Dascombe, *strted slwly, sn hndy, lost pl 8th, tld off 12th.*.........(20 to 1 op 14 to 1) 4
757 BANNTOWN BILL (Ire) [95] (bl) 7-11-7 D Walsh, *rdn alng thrght, led to 6th, led ag'n 9th till nxt, lost pl 11th, tld off 15th.*
....(25 to 1 op 16 to 1) 5
332[2] SOUTHERLY GALE [100] 9-11-8 (4") G Supple, *hld up in tch, hdwy to ld tenth, f 16th, dead.*........(5 to 2 tchd 3 to 1) f
MAREMMA GALE (Ire) [98] (bl) 8-11-10 K Gaule, *led 6th to 9th, rdn 13th, poor 4th whn pld up whn bef 3 out.*
....(9 to 4 fav op 5 to 2 tchd 2 to 1) pu
Dist: 10l, 10l, dist, dist. 6m 28.20s. a 12.20s (7 Ran).

(Martyn Booth), K C Bailey

856 South-West Racing Club Novices' Handicap Hurdle Class E (0-100 4-y-o and up) £2,302 2m............ (3:10)

704" INDRAPURA (Ire) [95] 4-11-13 C Maude, *hld up, chsd ldr appr 2 out, sn h'rd rdn, ran on und pres to ld nr finish.*
....(11 to 8 on tchd Evens) 1
597" CANARY FALCON [82] 5-11-1 P Holley, *hld up, led 3 out, rdn and hdd nr finish.*..................(5 to 2 op 3 to 1) 2
SAILEP (Fr) [86] 4-11-1 (3") T Dascombe, *lft in ld aftr 3rd, hdd 3 out, btn appr nxt.*..................(5 to 1 op 3 to 1) 3

INDIAN CROWN [67] 6-10-0 J Culloty, *led, rcd very freely, clr whn ran out aftr 3rd.....................*(20 to 1 tchd 25 to 1) ro
754[8] TIBBS INN [67] 7-9-7 (7*) Mr R Thornton, *hld up, 3rd whn slpd up bend appr 4th.....* (14 to 1 op 20 to 1 tchd 12 to 1) su
Dist: ¾l, 27l. 3m 36.30s. a 2.30s (5 Ran).
SR: 20/7/ (Martin Pipe Racing Club), M C Pipe

857 Pot Black Handicap Chase Class D (0-120 5-y-o and up) £4,186 2m 5f
..................................(3:40)

759* BIT OF A TOUCH [89] 10-10-9 J Frost, *trkd ldr, led 13th to nxt, cl up whn hmpd 3 out, rallied and quickened to ld nr finish.*
..................................(2 to 1) 1
759 HERBERT BUCHANAN (Ire) [98] 6-11-4 A P McCoy, *hld up in cl tch, jmpd slwly tenth, lft in ld 3 out, rdn and hld nr finish.*
..................................(7 to 4 op 6 to 1) 2
785[3] GABISH [80] 11-9-7 (7*) Mr R Thornton, *led, jmpd wl, pushed alng 12th, hdd nxt, wknd appr 3 out, tld off.*
..................................(25 to 1 op 16 to 1) 3
771 LAKE OF LOUGHREA (Ire) [104] 6-11-10 C O'Dwyer, *hld up in cl tch, narrow advantage 4 out, blun and uns rdr nxt.*
..................................(13 to 8 fav op 7 to 4) ur
Dist: 1½l, dist. 5m 16.70s. a 12.70s (4 Ran).
(A E C Electric Fencing Ltd (Hotline)), R G Frost

858 Shaftesbury Juvenile Novices' Claiming Hurdle Class F (3-y-o) £2,320 2m
..................................(4:10)

788* COINTOSSER (Ire) 10-12 S Wynne, *hld up, hdwy aftr 3 out, led last, rdn and ran on wl.*
..................................(13 to 8 on op 6 to 4 on tchd 7 to 4 on) 1
767[4] BEN BOWDEN 10-13 J Osborne, *wth ldr, led 4th to 6th, ev ch frm 3 out to r-in, no extr fnl 100 yards.* (7 to 1 tchd 9 to 1) 2
788[2] INDIRA 10-6 W McFarland, *led, jmpd wl, hung ah 6th till last, one pace.....*(7 to 2 op 3 to 1 tchd 4 to 1) 3
PROVE THE POINT (Ire) 10-8 P Holley, *hld up, reminders 4th, outpcd 3 out.....................*(20 to 1 tchd 25 to 1) 4
672[3] YELLOW DRAGON (Ire) 10-12 (3*) K Gaule, *hld up, mstk second, hrd rdn 5th, sn btn.*
..................................(8 to 1 op 6 to 1 tchd 10 to 1) 5
705 REMEMBER STAR 10-6 F Jousset, *al beh, tld off.*
..................................(100 to 1 op 33 to 1) 6
Dist: 5l, 1¼l, 23l, 3l, 26l. 3m 39.80s. a 5.80s (6 Ran).
(David Manning Associates), M C Pipe

859 Wincanton Novices' Hurdle Class E (4-y-o and up) £2,232 2¾m........(4:40)

770* COURBARIL 4-11-12 C Maude, *trkd ldr, led 6th, sn clr, hit 2 out, very easily.................*(3 to 1 on op 5 to 2) 1
673[3] MIRAMARE 6-10-6 (3*) T Dascombe, *hld up, chsd wnr frm 4 out, sn rdn alng, no imprsn.*
..................................(12 to 1 op 10 to 1 tchd 14 to 1) 2
ASK HARRY (Ire) 5-10-4 (5*) P Henley, *hld up, effrt 4 out, hit last, nvr on terms......*(16 to 1 op 12 to 1 tchd 20 to 1) 3
759[7] CHARGED 7-10-9 A P McCoy, *led to 6th, chsd wnr till wknd 4 out, tld off................*(4 to 1 op 3 to 1 tchd 9 to 2) 4
LADY NESS 5-10-4 R Bellamy, *tld off 6th, pld up bef last.*
..................................(50 to 1 op 66 to 1) pu
Dist: 21l, 2½l, dist. 5m 7.70s. a 1.70s (5 Ran).
SR: 4/-/ (Richard Green (Fine Paintings)), M C Pipe

CARLISLE (firm)
Friday October 11th
Going Correction: MINUS 0.25 sec. per fur.

860 Shap Juvenile Novices' Hurdle Class E (3-y-o) £2,276 2m 1f............(1:50)

DOUBLE DASH (Ire) 10-12 D J Moffatt, *nvr far away, imprvg whn hit 3 out, not fluent last, styd on und pres to ld r-in.*
..................................(7 to 4 op 2 to 1) 1
734[6] RET FREM (Ire) 10-12 B Storey, *led to 4th, styd upsides, lft in ld betw last 2, hdd and no extr r-in.*
..................................(6 to 4 fav op 11 to 10 on) 2
LOMOND LASSIE (USA) 10-7 O Pears, *chsd ldrs, struggling hfwy, lost tch, tld off........*(20 to 1 op 8 to 1) 3
705[5] HANNAHS BAY 10-4 (3*) F Leahy, *al hndy, led 4th, hit four out, broke off hind and hdd betw last 2, pld up, destroyed.*
..................................(2 to 1 op 7 to 4) pu
Dist: 3l, dist. 4m 17.20s. a 14.20s (4 Ran).
(The Sheroot Partnership), D Moffatt

861 Durdar Novices' Chase Class D (5-y-o and up) £3,542 2½m 110yds....(2:20)

SHOW YOUR HAND (Ire) 8-10-12 M Foster, *mostly jmpd wl, made all, hit 4 out, styd on strly frm betw last 2.*
..................................(13 to 8 on op 6 to 4 on tchd 11 to 8 on) 1
735[8] CALDER'S GROVE 6-10-9 (3*) G Cahill, *patiently rdn, improved fnl circuit, feeling pace aftr 4 out, styd on to take second r-in........................*(14 to 1 op 10 to 1) 2

KILTULLA (Ire) 6-10-12 Richard Guest, *al wl plcd, effrt whn awkward 6 out, rallied, rdn and one pace frm last.*
..................................(2 to 1 op 6 to 4) 3
BONNY JOHNNY 6-10-12 D J Moffatt, *rcd wide, trkd ldrs till lost grnd aftr 4 out, rdn and no imprsn frm nxt.*
..................................(20 to 1 tchd 25 to 1) 4
Dist: 2½l, 1¼l, 4l. 5m 16.80s. a 21.80s (4 Ran).
(Strathayr Publishers Ltd), L Lungo

862 Harraby Novices' Handicap Hurdle Class E (0-100 4-y-o and up) £2,332 2 ½m 110yds.....................(2:55)

735[4] JONAEM (Ire) [80] 6-11-10 K Johnson, *patiently rdn, improved to nose ahead 4 out, hrd pressed last, ran on gmely.*
..................................(3 to 1 tchd 100 to 30) 1
660[2] HAUGHTON LAD (Ire) [72] 7-11-2 A Dobbin, *nvr far away, feeling pace halfway, rallied frm 3 out, ev ch last, no extr cl hme......................*(9 to 2 op 4 to 1 tchd 5 to 1) 2
704[6] MERRYHILL GOLD [71] 5-11-0 L Wyer, *led till aftr second, styd hndy till rdn alng 3 out, ridden and outpcd frm betw last 2.*
..................................(7 to 2 tchd 4 to 1) 3
794 AMBER HOLLY [70] 7-11-0 B Storey, *wtd wth, improved to draw level 3 out, drvn alng bef nxt, sn lost tch.*
..................................(14 to 1 tchd 20 to 1) 4
PALACE OF GOLD [73] 6-11-3 M Foster, *pld hrd, led briefly aftr second, led ag'n 7th to 4 out, wknd quickly after nxt, tld off.*
..................................(15 to 8 fav op 7 to 4 tchd 2 to 1) 5
CRUISING KATE [59] 8-10-0 (3*) G Lee, *led 3rd to 7th, struggling aftr 4 out, tld off whn pld up bef last.*
..................................(14 to 1 op 10 to 1) pu
Dist: 1l, 12l, 16l, 13l. 4m 50.60s. a 8.60s (6 Ran).
(Mrs Evelyn Slack), Mrs E Slack

863 City Of Carlisle Handicap Chase Class C (0-130 5-y-o and up) £4,303 2m
..................................(3:30)

763[2] CHARMING GALE [94] (v) 9-10-0 L Wyer, *jmpd boldly, made all, styd on strly to go clr appr last.*
..................................(11 to 4 op 9 to 4 tchd 3 to 1) 1
POLITICAL TOWER [122] 9-11-11 (3*) G Cahill, *patiently rdn, improved frm 4 out, drvn alng betw last 2, one pace.*
..................................(7 to 4 fav op 6 to 4 tchd 2 to 1) 2
737[2] BELDINE [100] 11-10-6 A Dobbin, *al hndy, ev ch whn jmpd path appr 4 out, rdn aftr nxt, wknd bef last.*
..................................(2 to 1 op 7 to 4) 3
FLASH OF REALM (Fr) [97] 10-10-3 B Storey, *wth ldrs, rdn alng and lost grnd bef 4 out, lost tch, tld off.*
..................................(6 to 1 op 5 to 1) 4
Dist: 7l, 8l, 16l. 3m 56.40s. a 2.40s (4 Ran).
3R. 8/29/-/-/ (Mrs John Etherton), Mrs S C Bradburne

864 Orton Conditional Jockeys' Handicap Hurdle Class E (0-125 4-y-o and up) £2,220 2m 1f.......................(4:00)

818[4] WELL APPOINTED (Ire) [93] 7-11-8 G Lee, *dictated pace, quickened hfwy, hrd pressed aftr 3 out, hld on grimly towards finish.....................*(3 to 1 op 5 to 2) 1
762[2] NONIOS (Ire) [96] 5-11-10 E Callaghan, *nvr far away, drvn alng 3 out, str chal bef nxt, eqgd rght r-in, hld nr finish.*
..................................(11 to 4 op 9 to 4 tchd 3 to 1) 2
736[3] LATIN LEADER [82] (bl) 6-10-11 D Parker, *al hndy, hrd at work appr 2 out, sn outpcd.....*(5 to 1 op 4 to 1 tchd 11 to 2) 3
698* BOLANEY GIRL (Ire) [84] 7-10-13 A Roche, *unruly strt, pld hrd in rear, effrt hfwy, rdn and wknd quickly aftr 3 out.*
..................................(15 to 8 fav op 6 to 4 tchd 2 to 1) 4
789* LATVIAN [95] (v) 9-11-7 (3*,7ex) S Melrose, *trkd ldrs, reminders and lost pl quickly aftr 4 out, tld off.*
..................................(10 to 1 op 7 to 1) 5
Dist: ½l, 15l, 1¾l, 19l. 4m 10.80s. a 7.80s (5 Ran).
(Drumlanrig Racing), B Mactaggart

865 Blackwell Handicap Chase Class E (0-115 5-y-o and up) £3,452 3m (4:35)

697[2] KUSHBALOO [114] 11-12-0 B Storey, *jmpd heasitantly 1st circuit, made all, styd on strly frm 3 out.*
..................................(6 to 4 fav op 11 to 10) 1
706[4] DARK OAK [109] 10-11-9 L Wyer, *pressed wnr thrght, ev ch till rdn and no extr r-in....*(5 to 1 op 7 to 2 tchd 6 to 1) 2
SUPPOSIN [92] 8-10-6 Richard Guest, *wtd wth, improved appr 4 out, ev ch till quicken r-in.*(10 to 1 tchd 16 to 1) 3
763* MAGIC BLOOM [107] 10-11-2 (5*,7ex) E Callaghan, *settled to track ldrs, ev ch appr 4 out, rdn alng nxt, one pace r-in.*
..................................(7 to 4 op 13 to 8 tchd 2 to 1) 4
662 GO SILLY [105] (v) 10-11-2 (3*) G Cahill, *jmpd stickily, in tch till wknd and blun 2 out, tld off whn pld up bef last.*
..................................(8 to 1 op 9 to 2 tchd 10 to 1) pu
Dist: 3l, 1½l, 1¾l. 6m 13.90s. a 21.90s (5 Ran).
(Mr & Mrs Raymond Anderson Green), C Parker

866 Tarn Crag Standard National Hunt Flat Class H (4,5,6-y-o) £1,646 2m 1f (5:10)

NORTHERN FUSILIER 4-11-3 (7*) M Newton, *al gng wl, nosed ahead 7 fs out, drw clr in strt, unchlgd.*
.... (6 to 4 on tchd 11 to 8 on) 1
LOOK SHARPE 5-10-11 (7*) B Grattan, *settled to track ldrs, chsd wnr in strt, no imprsn, better for race.*
.... (16 to 1 op 10 to 1) 2
795³ LINDAJANE (Ire) 4-10-12 Mr T Morrison, *wd wth, effrt 7 fs out, lost tch in strt, tld off...............* (4 to 1 tchd 9 to 2) 3
700⁸ JOE'S BIT OF GOLD 4-10-9 (3*) G Cahill, *last and hld up, effrt hfwy, tld off in strt.................* (25 to 1 op 100 to 1) 4
700⁴ BEST FRIEND 4-11-3 (7*) Michael Brennan, *led and sn clr, hdd 7 fs out, lost tch in strt, tld off........* (5 to 1 op 4 to 1) 5
700⁷ THE KNITTER 4-10-10 (7*) M Dunne, *chsd ldrs to hfwy, tld off bef strt..............* (40 to 1 op 100 to 1 tchd 33 to 1) 6
JED ABBEY 4-10-5 (7*) S Melrose, *refused to race, took no part.................* (14 to 1 op 10 to 1 tchd 16 to 1) I
Dist: 24l, 30l, 6l, 22l, dist. 3m 59.90s. (7 Ran).

(Joe Donald), J M Jefferson

HUNTINGDON (good to firm)
Friday October 11th
Going Correction: MINUS 0.15 sec. per fur.

867 Emerald Isle Novices' Hurdle Class E (4-y-o and up) £2,320 2½m 110yds
.... (2:10)

MONTEL EXPRESS (Ire) 4-10-11 C O'Dwyer, *hld up, hmpd by faller 5th, hdwy nxt, narrow advantage 2 out, all out*
.... (5 to 2 fav op 2 to 1 tchd 3 to 1) 1
THE LAD 7-10-12 D Morris, *hld up in tch, chsd ldr frm 6th, ev ch from 2 out to r-in, no extr nr finish.*
.... (9 to 2 op 5 to 1 tchd 6 to 1 and 4 to 1) 2
MINOR KEY (Ire) 6-10-12 J Osborne, *led to 5th, rallied and ev ch appr 2 out, one pace approaching last.*
.... (12 to 1 op 6 to 1 tchd 14 to 1) 3
735³ LEAR DANCER (USA) (bl) 5-10-12 A P McCoy, *trkd ldg pair, led 5th, mstk nxt, sn drvn alng, hdd appr 2 out, wknd.*
.... (11 to 4 op 3 to 1 tchd 7 to 2) 4
242* PEGASUS BAY 5-11-5 R Dunwoody, *hld up beh, hdwy aftr 6th, hrd rdn after nxt, sn btn, tld off.*
.... (9 to 1 op 6 to 1 tchd 10 to 1) 5
ERNEST WILLIAM (Ire) 4-10-8 (3*) K Gaule, *tracking ldr whn f 5th....................* (40 to 1 op 25 to 1) f
JARI (USA) 5-10-12 V Smith, *strted slwly, al beh, tld off whn pld up bef 2 out................* (50 to 1 op 25 to 1) pu
654² DANNY GALE 5-11-5 G Bradley, *chsd ldrs till outpcd 6th, btn quickly, tld off and pld up bef 2 out..* (7 to 2 op 5 to 2) pu
MASTER GOODENOUGH (Ire) 5-10-12 N Williamson, *hld up, beh 6th, tld off whn pld up bef 2 out.*
.... (14 to 1 op 25 to 1 tchd 33 to 1) pu
Dist: Nk, 7l, 11l, 18l. 4m 47.80s. a 12.80s (9 Ran).

(Mrs Jacqueline Conroy), K C Bailey

868 Jack Ramply Memorial Novices' Chase Class D (5-y-o and up) £3,562 2½m 110yds
.... (2:45)

776* JATHIB (Can) 5-11-3 D Byrne, *hld up, cld 8th, chsd ldr appr 4 out, led aftr nxt, sn clr, hrd held...*(4 to 1 on op 5 to 4) 1
212⁷ ICANTELYA (Ire) 7-10-12 P Hide, *trkd ldrs, rdn to ld 11th, hdd aftr 3 out, outpcd....................* (10 to 1 op 6 to 1) 2
MANOR MIEO 10-10-12 (7*) Mr A Coe, *jmpd wl, sn cl up, wknd appr 4 out, finshed tired, tld off.*
.... (6 to 1 op 7 to 2 tchd 7 to 1) 3
FABULOUS FRANCY (Ire) 8-10-12 J Ryan, *in tch, outpcd 11th, btn whn mstk nxt, tld off...........* (20 to 1 op 14 to 1) 4
SPORTING FIXTURE (Ire) 5-10-10 A Thornton, *in tch, hit 6th, outpcd 11th, tld off...........* (66 to 1 op 40 to 1) 5
769⁸ SAXON BLADE 8-10-12 B Powell, *led to 11th, sn outpcd, tld off.......................* (100 to 1 op 40 to 1) 6
ISHMA (Ire) 5-10-10 J Railton, *al beh, losing tch whn jmpd slwly 8th, pld up bef nxt.....* (100 to 1 op 40 to 1) pu
CLONATTIN LADY (Ire) 7-10-7 D Leahy, *mstk 3rd, al beh, reminders 5th, losing tch whn jmpd slwly 8th, pld up aftr nxt.*
.... (100 to 1 op 40 to 1) pu
Dist: 12l, dist, 12l, 1¾l. dist. 4m 57.70s. a 10.70s (8 Ran).

(Crown Pkg & Mailing Svs Ltd), Mrs Merrita Jones

869 Huntingdon International Challenge Handicap Hurdle Class E (0-110 4-y-o and up) £2,215 2m 5f 110yds... (3:15)

772⁶ BORN TO PLEASE (Ire) [90] 4-10-8 A Maguire, *made most to 3 out, sn hrd rdn, led ag'n r-in, edgd lft und pres.*
.... (Evens fav op 11 to 8 tchd 6 to 4) 1
725² ABLE PLAYER (USA) [86] 9-10-5 W Harnett, *wth ldr, led 3 out, hit nxt and rdr lost iron, hdd r-in, ran on.*
.... (2 to 1 op 6 to 4 tchd 9 to 4) 2
832⁴ GONE BY (Ire) [109] (v) 8-12-0 G Bradley, *hld up beh ldg pair, pushed alng aftr 4 out, sn outpcd.*
.... (5 to 2 op 9 to 4 tchd 11 to 4) 3
Dist: Nk, 22l. 5m 7.40s. a 18.40s (3 Ran).

(A B S Racing), P J Hobbs

870 Hartley's Jam Handicap Chase Class C (0-135 5-y-o and up) £4,337 2m 110yds........................ (3:50)

FINE HARVEST [110] 10-11-9 D Bridgwater, *made all, hrd rdn appr last, ran on wl.......*(7 to 2 op 4 to 1 tchd 9 to 2) 1
617⁶ LOWAWATHA [100] 8-10-13 A Thornton, *trkd wnr, ev ch 4 out, rallied and hit 2 out..*(7 to 2 tchd 100 to 30) 2
785* RAMSTAR [109] 8-11-8 (6ex) A P McCoy, *trkd ldrs, outpcd 4 out, rallied and hit 2 out, sn one pace und pres. ..(3 to 1 jt-fav op 5 to 2 tchd 100 to 30) 3
754⁵ FIERCE [92] (v) 8-10-5 J Osborne, *hld up, reminders 7th, outpcd 4 out, tld off...(3 to 1 jt-fav op 5 to 2 tchd 100 to 30) 4
774⁴ BALLY PARSON [115] 10-12-0 J Culloty, *hld up, mstk 8th, losing grnd whn blun and uns rdr nxt.* (4 to 1 tchd 9 to 2) ur
Dist: 2½l, ½l, dist. 4m 5.00s. a 11.00s (5 Ran).

(Miss A Shirley-Priest), J L Spearing

871 Australia Handicap Hurdle Class C (0-130 4-y-o and up) £3,439 2m 110yds........................ (4:25)

808 STAR MARKET [126] (bl) 6-12-0 A P McCoy, *made all, wnt clr 4 out, blun 2 out, ran on...............*(11 to 4 op 2 to 1) 1
709⁵ WAMDHA (Ire) [100] 6-10-2 A S Smith, *hld up, chsd wnr frm 4th, sn outpcd, one pace from 2 out.* (13 to 8 fav op 7 to 4) 2
754² COOLEY'S VALVE (Ire) [101] 8-10-3 N Williamson, *strted slwly, hld up in last pl, effrt aftr 4 out, no imprsn 2 out, sn eased.......................* (5 to 2 op 2 to 1 tchd 11 to 4) 3
616⁶ SHOOFK [119] 5-11-6 R Dunwoody, *trkd wnr to 4th, sn pushed alng and outpcd nxt.......*(7 to 2 tchd 4 to 1) 4
Dist: 6l, 4l, 2½l. 3m 45.50s. a 4.50s (4 Ran).
SR: 29/-/-/8/

(Mrs P Joynes), J L Spearing

872 Great British Handicap Chase Class C (0-135 5-y-o and up) £4,370 3m (4:55)

750⁴ WISE APPROACH [129] 9-12-0 C O'Dwyer, *jmpd wl, made all, rdn out.........*(5 to 2 co-fav op 7 to 4 tchd 11 to 4) 1
106² MERLINS DREAM (Ire) [103] 7-10-2 J Osborne, *hld up in cl tch, mstks 11th and 12th, ch whn hit last, rallied und pres.
.... (5 to 2 co-fav op 7 to 4 tchd 3 to 1) 2
108* CHANGE THE REIGN [107] 9-10-6 J R Kavanagh, *hld up in tch, jmpd slwly 5th, reminders nxt, chlgd 4 out, ran wide and wknd appr 2 out, tld off..............* (3 to 1 tchd 4 to 1) 3
GILPA VALU [115] 7-11-0 W Marston, *tracking wnr whn f heavily 8th.....................* (5 to 2 co-fav op 7 to 4 tchd 3 to 1) f
Dist: Nk, dist. 5m 55.50s. a 15.50s (4 Ran).

(Mrs S Gee), K C Bailey

873 Huntingdon Intermediate Open National Hunt Flat Class H (4,5,6-y-o) £1,763 2m 110yds.............. (5:30)

SCOUNDREL 5-11-4 C O'Dwyer, *chsd ldrs, al gng wl, led 2 fs out, pushed out......(13 to 8 fav op Evens tchd 5 to 4) 1
THE BREWMASTER (Ire) 4-11-3 J Osborne, *keen hold, chsd ldrs, rdn 2 fs out, ran on wl.
.... (8 to 1 op 12 to 1 tchd 14 to 1) 2
BOMBADIL 4-11-3 J Railton, *hld up, hdwy o'r 5 fs out, rdn over 3 out, kpt on.......* (25 to 1 op 16 to 1 tchd 33 to 1) 3
EL CRANK SENOR 4-11-3 D Byrne, *keen hold, trkd ldrs, led o'r 5 fs out to 2 out, one pace...*(12 to 1 op 33 to 1) 4
ARCTIC FLAME 5-10-13 A P McCoy, *mid-div, drvn alng hfwy, hdwy o'r 4 fs out, one pace frm 2 out.
.... (10 to 1 op 7 to 1 tchd 12 to 1) 5
693² ARDENBAR 4-10-12 A Maguire, *led 6 fs, cl up, one pace frm 2 out.....................* (5 to 1 op 6 to 4) 6
ERMYNS PET 5-11-10 (7*) M Attwater, *chsd ldrs, ev ch o'r 2 fs out, wknd over one out..............* (5 to 1 op 6 to 4) 7
WARRIO 6-11-4 M Bosley, *hld up beh, styd on frd 2 fs, nnst finish...................* (33 to 1) 8
GOBALINO GIRL (Ire) 4-10-12 R Farrant, *mid-div, styd on o'r 3 fs out, not rch ldrs...............* (33 to 1) 9
BABA SAM (Ire) 5-11-4 A Thornton, *mid-div, styd on o'r 3 fs out, not rch ldrs..............*(33 to 1 op 20 to 1) 10
DENIS COMPTON 5-11-4 B Powell, *beh, hdwy o'r 5 fs out, wknd quickly 4 out.................* (33 to 1 op 25 to 1) 11
A S JIM 5-11-4 V Slattery, *hld up, nvr on terms....*(33 to 1) 12
693⁴ SOUTHERNCROSSPATCH 5-11-4 S Curran, *hld up beh, rdn and hdwy o'r 6 fs out, wknd over 4 out.* (16 to 1 op 7 to 1) 13
THERMECON (Ire) 5-11-1 (3*) K Gaule, *trkd ldr, led aftr 6 fs till o'r 5 out, sn wknd................* (16 to 1 tchd 10 to 1) 14
BARTON BLADE (Ire) 4-10-10 (7*) Mr A Wintle, *hld up beh ldg grp, wknd quickly o'r 6 fs out.*
.... (8 to 1 op 7 to 1 tchd 12 to 1) 15
693⁶ CAPTAIN NAVAR (Ire) 6-11-4 I Lawrence, *al beh.
.... (20 to 1 op 14 to 1) 16
JUST BECAUSE (Ire) 4-11-3 C Llewellyn, *al beh...(33 to 1) 17
CATCH THE WIND 6-10-13 A S Smith, *hld up in last pl, pld very hrd, rapid hdwy 9 fs out, wknd o'r 6 out.
.... (14 to 1 op 10 to 1) 18
TORO LOCO (Ire) 4-11-3 N Williamson, *hld up in mid-div, o'r 6 fs out, wknd quickly over 4 out, tld off.
.... (20 to 1 op 12 to 1 tchd 25 to 1) 19
336⁷ ROYAL SALUTE 4-11-3 S Wynne, *al beh, tld off...(33 to 1) 20

SYDILLIUM 4-11-3 M A Fitzgerald, *chsd ldrs till wknd quickly o'r 6 fs out, tld off*.....................(12 to 1 op 8 to 1) 21
PACIFIST 5-10-6 (7*) D Creech, *mid-div to hfwy, beh whn pld up 2 fs out, dismounted*.........................(33 to 1) pu
Dist: 1¾l, 4l, sht-hd, 2l, 7l, 2l, hd, 4l, 1¼l, hd. 3m 42.70s. (22 Ran).
(Mrs J M Corbett), K C Bailey

BANGOR (good to firm)
Saturday October 12th
Going Correction: PLUS 0.10 sec. per fur.

874
BBC Radio Merseyside Novices' Hurdle Class E (4-y-o and up) £2,710 2½m.....................................(2:05)

ELA MATA 4-10-11 J Railton, *hld up, steady hdwy 6th, led appr 3 out and sn clr easily.*
.................................(9 to 4 fav op 5 to 2 tchd 3 to 1) 1
761² TIGH-NA-MARA 8-10-4² (5*) E Callaghan, *chsd ldrs, rdn alng 3 out, kpt on, no ch with wnr.*
.................................(11 to 2 op 5 to 1 tchd 6 to 1) 2
749⁵ VALLINGALE (Ire) 5-10-7 J F Titley, *prmnt, effrt appr 3 out, sn rdn and one pace.*...............(7 to 1 op 4 to 1) 3
JILLS JOY (Ire) 5-10-12 W Fry, *prmnt, rdn alng 3 out and sn one pace, 4th and wl btn whn stumbled last.*
.................................(40 to 1 op 25 to 1) 4
LE BARON 5-10-12 J Osborne, *mid-div, pushed alng and outpcd 6th, hdwy 4 out, rdn and btn nxt...*(4 to 1 op 5 to 1) 5
MIDNIGHT BOB 5-10-12 R Marley, *hld up and beh, effrt and some hdwy aftr 6th, sn rdn and wknd.* (25 to 1 op 20 to 1) 6
SISTER GALE 4-10-6 Richard Guest, *hld up, hdwy and hit 7th, blun nxt and sn beh.*................(25 to 1 op 16 to 1) 7
BOXIT AGAIN 6-10-12 T Eley, *made most to 7th, sn wknd and beh whn pld up bef 2 out.*
.................................(33 to 1 op 25 to 1 tchd 50 to 1) pu
JUST LIKE DAD 4-10-11 M Dwyer, *chsd ldr, led and hit 7th, hdd aftr nxt and sn wknd, beh whn pld up lme bef last.*
.................................(9 to 1 op 7 to 1) pu
FASHION LEADER (Ire) 5-10-12 M Richards, *al rear, reminders 5th, tld off whn pld up bef 3 out.*
.................................(12 to 1 op 9 to 1) pu
Dist: 5l, 4l, 4l, 17l, dist, 16l. 4m 48.80s. a 18.80s (10 Ran).
(F J Sainsbury), Mrs A Swinbank

875
Stadco Handicap Chase Class E (0-115 5-y-o and up) £3,818 2m 1f 110yds.......................................(2:35)

753* PRINCE SKYBURD [86] 5-10-0 A Maguire, *hld up, hdwy 6th, led 3 out cmftbly..* (11 to 8 on op 5 to 4 on tchd Evens) 1
759⁶ CRAFTY CHAPLAIN [97] 10-10-9 (3*) D Walsh, *cl up, hit 5th, led nxt, rdn and hdd 3 out, kpt on und pres.*
.................................(14 to 1 op 10 to 1) 2
REGAL ROMPER (Ire) [108] 8-11-9 Richard Guest, *hld up, hdwy 7th, hit 4 out and sn wknd.*
.................................(5 to 1 op 7 to 2 tchd 11 to 2) 3
706⁶ HOUGHTON [109] 10-11-3 (7*) Mr R Burton, *led, hit 5th, hdd nxt, rdn alng and wknd 4 out.*
.................................(7 to 1 op 4 to 1 tchd 12 to 1) 4
UNCLE BERT (Ire) [94] 6-10-9 B Clifford, *hld up, hit second, hdwy 7th, rdn aftr nxt, wknd 4 out..*.....(5 to 1 op 7 to 2) 5
Dist: 2l, 23l, 2½l, 2½l. 4m 16.40s. a 14.40s (5 Ran).
(Mrs P M A Avison), Mrs P M A Avison

876
Numark Handicap Hurdle Class E (0-110 4-y-o and up) £3,176 2m 1f.......................................(3:05)

709⁶ STAY WITH ME (Fr) [87] 6-11-4 J Osborne, *trkd ldrs, hdwy 3 out, appr 3 out and sn clr, easily.*..............(5 to 1) 1
PHARARE (Ire) [91] 6-11-8 M Dwyer, *chsd ldrs, rdn alng 3 out, chased wnr nxt, kpt on.*.............(4 to 1 tchd 9 to 2) 2
659 BATTY'S ISLAND [76] 7-10-4 (3*) G Hogan, *hld up, hdwy 4 out, rdn nxt and kpt on one pace.*......(20 to 1 op 16 to 1) 3
675 ROYAL CIRCUS [89] 7-11-3 (3*) E Husband, *led to 4th, cl up till led four out, rdn nxt and sn hdd, 3rd and btn whn hit last.*
.................................(8 to 1 op 7 to 1 tchd 9 to 1) 4
760⁴ TORDO (Ire) [94] (bl) 5-11-7 (3*) J Magee, *hld up pulling hrd, rapid hdwy to ld 4th, hit nxt, hdd four out and sn wknd.*
.................................(100 to 30 fav op 3 to 1 tchd 11 to 4) 5
749² WINTER ROSE [86] 5-11-2 B Powell, *prmnt, hit 3rd, outpcd aftr 5th, sn beh till some late hdwy....*(7 to 2 tchd 4 to 1) 6
SAYMORE [89] 10-11-6 T Eley, *hld up, effrt and some hdwy 5th, sn rdn and wknd..*.............(20 to 1 op 16 to 1) 7
RIVER WYE (Ire) [90] 4-11-5 B Fenton, *chsd ldrs, rdn alng 4 out, sn wknd..*.................(8 to 1 op 7 to 1) 8
659 LUSTREMAN [89] 9-10-0 R Bellamy, *beh, some hdwy 5th, sn rdn and wknd, behind whn pld up bef 2 out........*(50 to 1) pu
Dist: 2l, 2l, 13l, ½l, 3l, 21l. 4m 0.50s. a 10.50s (9 Ran).
SR: 2/1/-/-/-/-/ (Mrs Sandra A Roe), C R Egerton

877
Willis Corroon Handicap Chase Class D (0-120 5-y-o and up) £4,507 3m 110yds......................................(3:40)

821 FACTOR TEN (Ire) [118] 8-12-0 J F Titley, *trkd ldr, led 4 out, sn clr, easily*.......................(3 to 1 tchd 100 to 30) 1
ALI'S ALIBI [117] 9-11-13 P Niven, *jmpd big early, hld up and beh, hdwy 3 out, wnt second nxt, tenderly rdn and kpt on.*
.................................(6 to 5 on op 5 to 4 on tchd 11 to 10 on) 2
756⁷ AUVILLAR (USA) [93] (v) 8-10-3 C Llewellyn, *led, rdn 5 out, hdd and hit nxt, sn wknd...........*(25 to 1 op 20 to 1) 3
MILLIES OWN [93] 9-10-1¹ (3*) G Tormey, *chsd ldg pair, reminders 13th, rdn and blun badly 3 out, no ch aftr.*
.................................(3 to 1 op 5 to 2) 4
Dist: 4l, 19l, 29l. 6m 8.40s. a 23.40s (4 Ran).
(Premier Crops Limited), Miss H C Knight

878
Thelwall Memorial Trophy Novices' Chase Class D (5-y-o and up) £3,663 2½m 110yds...............................(4:20)

THE LAST FLING (Ire) 6-10-12 Richard Guest, *trkd ldr, hdwy to chal and hit 2 out, led last, quickened clr flt, cmftbly.*
.................................(11 to 10 on op 5 to 4 on tchd 11 to 10) 1
670³ MR CONDUCTOR (Ire) 5-10-10 M A Fitzgerald, *led, rdn 2 out, hmpd by loose horse and hdd last, not quicken.*
.................................(11 to 4 tchd 3 to 1 and 5 to 2) 2
BRIDEPARK ROSE (Ire) 6-10-7 B Clifford, *al prmnt, effrt 11th, rdn 4 out, one pace frm nxt..............*(7 to 1 tchd 8 to 1) 3
769⁷ KARLOVAC (bl) 10-10-12 A Maguire, *hit second, in tch till rdn 5th, wl beh frm 5 out.*............(33 to 1 op 25 to 1) 4
318⁷ MISTROY 6-10-7 A S Smith, *not fluent, blun 6th, beh frm hfwy.*.....................................(33 to 1) 5
659 IBN SINA (USA) 9-10-12 T Eley, *chsd ldrs, rdn alng hfwy, sn lost tch, tld off 5 out.*......................(50 to 1) 6
GLAMANGLITZ 6-10-12 C Llewellyn, *in tch till f 4th.*
.................................(33 to 1 op 20 to 1) f
HIGHLAND WAY (Ire) 8-10-12 M Dwyer, *f 1st.*
.................................(8 to 1 op 6 to 1) f
Dist: 6l, 22l, 18l, 11l, 19l. 5m 3.60s. a 17.60s (8 Ran).
(Michael Jackson Bloodstock Ltd), Mrs S J Smith

879
Cock Bank Novices' Hurdle Class E (4-y-o and up) £2,878 2m 1f.............(4:50)

CONTRAFIRE (Ire) 4-10-11 J Supple, *chsd ldr, led 4 out, clr aftr nxt, ran on..........*(3 to 1 op 9 to 4 tchd 100 to 30) 1
INN AT THE TOP 4-10-11 W Fry, *chsd ldrs, effrt 3 out, rdn nxt, one pace last.*................(16 to 1 op 12 to 1) 2
775 ANABRANCH 5-10-9 (5*) E Callaghan, *in tch, hdwy to chase ldrs hfwy, rdn appr 2 out, 3rd and btn whn blun last.*
.................................(4 to 1 op 3 to 1) 3
806² ELA MAN HOWA 5-10-12 T Kent, *led, rdn and hdd 4 out, wknd appr 2 out.......*(6 to 4 fav op 2 to 1 tchd 5 to 4) 4
STUDIO THIRTY 4-10-11 P Niven, *beh, hdwy hfwy, kpt on frm 3 out, not rch ldrs.....................*(25 to 1 op 16 to 1) 5
BEAU MATELOT 4-10-11 A S Smith, *hld up, hdwy 4th, rdn bef 3 out, nvr a factor........*(9 to 1 op 8 to 1 tchd 10 to 1) 6
NAKED FEELINGS 4-10-11 M Dwyer, *al rear, tld off 3 out.*
.................................(33 to 1 op 20 to 1) 7
BIYA (Ire) 4-10-8 (3*) D Walsh, *in tch, rdn alng 5th, sn wknd.*.................(25 to 1 op 16 to 1) 8
YOUNG BENSON 4-10-8 (3*) R Massey, *al beh, tld off 3 out.*.................(16 to 1 op 12 to 1) 9
BETHS WISH 7-10-7 B Fenton, *blun 1st, al beh, tld off 3 out.*.................(50 to 1 op 33 to 1) 10
NUNSON 7-10-12 R Bellamy, *mid-div till lost pl hfwy, sn tld off.*.................(50 to 1 op 33 to 1) 11
CAHERASS COURT (Ire) 5-10-4 (3*) G Hogan, *al beh, tld off whn f 4 out......................*(50 to 1 op 33 to 1) f
GALAFRON 4-10-11 T Eley, *hit 1st, al beh, tld off whn pld up after 4 out........*(50 to 1 op 33 to 1) pu
Dist: 3l, 12l, 18l, 5l, 24l, 2l, 8l, 3l, 27l, 18l. 3m 59.10s. a 9.10s (13 Ran).
SR: 9/6/-/-/-/-/ (G B Turnbull Ltd), Mrs A Swinbank

880
Bangor Mares' Only Standard Open National Hunt Flat Class H (4,5,6-y-o) £1,679 2m 1f.................(5:20)

LADY REBECCA 4-11-3 A Maguire, *in tch, hdwy on inner 6 fs out, swtchd rght and headway to ld one and a half furlongs out, sn rdn and hng badly lft, hld on.*
.................................(7 to 2 op 3 to 1 tchd 11 to 4) 1
740⁶ NISHAMIRA (Ire) 4-11-10 M Dwyer, *trkd ldrs gng wl, hdwy 3 fs out, ev ch whn not much room o'r one furlong out, swtchd and ran on, jst fld.*
.................................(2 to 1 fav op 7 to 4 tchd 11 to 8 and 9 to 4) 2
HUTCEL LOCH 5-11-4 A S Smith, *led, rdn alng 4 out, hdd one and a half fs out, not quicken............*(33 to 1 op 25 to 1) 3
NIGHT ESCAPADE (Ire) 4-11-3 M Richards, *hld up, hdwy hfwy, chsd ldrs 4 fs out, sn rdn and one pace fnl 2 furlongs.*
.................................(20 to 1 op 14 to 1) 4
LIPPY LOUISE 4-11-3 P Niven, *beh till styd on fnl 3 fs, nvr dngrs.................*(15 to 2 op 5 to 1 tchd 8 to 1) 5
129³ NENAGH GUNNER 6-11-4 L Wyer, *in tch, hdwy hfwy, ev ch 4 fs out, sn rdn and wknd o'r 2 furlongs out.*
.................................(12 to 1 op 8 to 1) 6
693⁵ LADY FOLEY (Ire) 4-10-10 (7*) D Kiernan, *beh till some late hdwy........*(16 to 1 op 14 to 1) 7

DISTANT HILLS 4-11-3 Richard Guest, *chsd ldrs, effrt and hdwy 4 fs out, sn rdn and wknd 3 furlongs out.*
.... (12 to 1 op 8 to 1) 8
545⁵ HALAM BELL 4-11-3 P Holley, *in tch, rdn alng hfwy, wknd 5 fs out*............................... (25 to 1 op 20 to 1) 9
CARLINGFORD GALE (Ire) 5-11-4 M A Fitzgerald, *chsd ldrs till rdn and wknd 4 fs out.* (5 to 1 op 14 to 1 tchd 25 to 1) 10
GREY DANTE (Ire) 5-10-11 (7⁷) Miss S Beddoes, *nvr rchd ldrs*.................................. (33 to 1 op 20 to 1) 11
BRIDEN 4-10-12 (5⁵) E Callaghan, *chsd ldrs, pushed alng hfwy, sn lost pl, beh fnl 4 fs.*......... (20 to 1 tchd 25 to 1) 12
545³ GABRIELLE GERARD 4-10-10 (7⁷) R Wilkinson, *beh frm hfwy.*
.... (16 to 1 op 14 to 1) 13
740⁷ MISS NONNIE 4-11-3 D Leahy, *cl up till rdn and wknd o'r 4 fs out*................................. (33 to 1) 14
BARLOT 4-11-3 T Eley, *al wl beh.....* (25 to 1 op 20 to 1) 15
BARONBURN 6-10-11 (7⁷) Mr R Burton, *unruly bef strt, al beh, tld off fnl 4 fs*.......................(33 to 1) 16
AFRICAN BRIDE (Ire) 6-11-4 Miss P Jones, *prmnt, rdn alng 6 fs out, sn wknd*.........................(14 to 1 op 10 to 1) 17
CASPIAN DAWN 6-10-11 (7⁷) Mr P Murray, *in tch, rdn hfwy*..... (100 to 1 op 12 to 1) lU
Dist: Nk, 15l, 2l, 5l, 1l, 3l, 15l, 15l, ½l. 3m 58.00s. (18 Ran).
(Kinnersley Optimists), Miss Venetia Williams

FAIRYHOUSE (IRE) (good to firm)
Saturday October 12th

881 Chestnut E.B.F. Beginners Chase (5-y-o and up) £4,110 2½m....... (3:00)

720³ YOUNG DUBLINER (Ire) 7-12-0 C F Swan, ... (9 to 4) 1
THE SUBBIE (Ire) 7-12-0 T P Treacy, ... (5 to 4 fav) 2
114⁵ CELTIC BUCK 10-11-7 (7⁷) Mr Patrick O'Keeffe, ...(8 to 1) 3
443 PRECEPTOR (Ire) 7-11-11 (3³) B Bowens, ... (7 to 2) 4
711⁴ TREENS FOLLY 7-12-0 K F O'Brien, ...(50 to 1) 5
Dist: 7l, 5½l, ½l, dist. 5m 10.40s. a 15.40s (5 Ran).
(John A Cooper), E Bolger

882 Birch Maiden Hurdle (3-y-o) £3,082 2m .... (4:00)

712⁴ FAIRLY SHARP (Ire) 10-5 C O'Dwyer, ...(5 to 1) 1
341⁵ QUILL PROJECT (Ire) 9-12 (7⁷) M W Martin, ...(8 to 1) 2
CARRANSPRAWN (Ire) 10-2 J P Byrne, ...(12 to 1) 3
CHOOSEY'S TREASURE (Ire) 10-5 C F Swan, ... (9 to 2) 4
KING OF PEACE (Ire) 10-10 H Rogers, ...(8 to 1) 5
MAGIC COMBINATION (Ire) 10-10 J Short, ...(13 to 8 fav) 6
341⁸ COMRADE CHINNERY (Ire) 10-3 (7⁷) Mr G Elliott, (12 to 1) 7
341⁶ DUNEMER (Ire) 10-0 (5⁵) Mr R Walsh, ...(10 to 1) 8
SWEET NATURE (Ire) 10-5 A Powell, ...(20 to 1) 9
712⁸ KOKO NOR (Ire) 10-0 L P Cusack, ...(20 to 1) 10
NORD VENTE (Ire) 10-0 (5⁵) J Butler, ...(20 to 1) 11
ODY MORODY (Ire) 10-2 (3³) D J Casey, ...(25 to 1) 12
RED SQUARE (Ire) 10-5 C N Bowens, ...(20 to 1) 13
NASHALONG (Ire) 10-10 S C Lyons, ...(14 to 1) 14
620 PENZITA (Ire) 10-5 S H O'Donovan, ...(50 to 1) 15
TARAKHEL (USA) 10-10 F Woods, ...(50 to 1) 16
REKONDO (Ire) 10-10 P L Malone, ...(25 to 1) 17
574 PLAYPRINT 10-10 T P Treacy, ...(16 to 1) 18
THAKI 10-10 D H O'Connor, ...(33 to 1) pu
574⁴ HOLLYMOUNT LADY 10-5 K F O'Brien, ...(12 to 1) pu
SHYFIRION (Ire) 9-12 (7⁷) J M Maguire, ...(25 to 1) pu
Dist: 5l, ½l, 13l, 4l. 3m 43.80s. b 0.20s (21 Ran).
(Mrs A Hughes), J G Coogan

883 Rossmore Hurdle (4-y-o and up) £3,425 2m....................(4:30)

715 JUST LITTLE 4-10-9 C F Swan, ...(5 to 2 op 1) 1
685 NOBLE SHOON (Ire) 5-11-5 C O'Dwyer, ...(6 to 1) 2
MULKEV PRINCE (Ire) 5-11-5 S C Lyons, ... (100 to 30) 3
731⁵ GOLD DEPOSITOR (Ire) 4-10-9 J Short, ...(20 to 1) 4
PERSIAN DANSER (Ire) 4-10-6 (3³) U Smyth, ...(16 to 1) 5
686 BALMY NATIVE (Ire) 4-11-0 A Powell, ...(50 to 1) 6
Dist: 12l, 4l, 2l, 8l. 3m 42.60s. b 1.40s (6 Ran).
(Seamus O'Farrell), A P O'Brien

884 Sycamore I.N.H. Flat Race (4-y-o and up) £3,082 2m................. (5:30)

ARD LANE (Ire) 5-11-7 (7⁷) Mr R M Walsh, ... (2 to 1 fav) 1
GENTRY (Ire) 5-12-0 Mr M McNulty, ...(8 to 1) 2
NATIVE SHORE (Ire) 4-11-0 (7⁷) Mr K R O'Ryan,...(6 to 1) 3
SHANNON OAK (Ire) 4-11-6 (3³) Mr P M Kelly, ...(5 to 1) 4
CHARMING DUKE (Ire) 6-11-7 (7⁷) Mr D Delaney, ..(33 to 1) 5
PANTOBEACH (Ire) 6-11-2 (7⁷) Mr Mark Walsh, ...(20 to 1) 6
581 BULA DELA (Ire) 6-11-2 (7⁷) Mr A Fleming, ...(33 to 1) 7
121⁸ TRY ONCE MORE (Ire) (bl) 5-11-7 (7⁷) Mr A J Dempsey,
....(14 to 1) 8
805 BANNAGH MOR (Ire) 5-11-7 (7⁷) Mr M McNeilly, .. (33 to 1) 9
JUST BEFORE DAWN (Ire) 7-11-7 (7⁷) Mr T J Beattie, (6 to 1) 10
KATE FARLY (Ire) 5-11-9 Mr A R Coonan, ...(16 to 1) 11
MOYDUFF LUCY (Ire) 6-11-2 (7⁷) Mr G Elliott, ...(16 to 1) 12
FRENCH RAMBLER (Ire) 5-11-7 (7⁷) Mr M O'Connor,
....(14 to 1) 13

SISTER CAMILLUS (Ire) 5-11-9 Mr P Fenton, ... (7 to 1) 14
Dist: 6l, 3l, nk, 1l. 3m 40.00s. (14 Ran).
(Mrs Monica Hackett), A P O'Brien

HEXHAM (good to firm)
Saturday October 12th
Going Correction: MINUS 0.45 sec. per fur.

885 Capital Shopping Centres Novices' Handicap Chase Class F (0-90 5-y-o and up) £2,491 2m 110yds...... (2:20)

792² SPRING LOADED [70] 5-10-3 (5⁵) Michael Brennan, *patiently rdn, improved to draw level 4 out, led nxt, pckd 2 out, kpt on wl frm last*....................(9 to 4 op 5 to 2 tchd 2 to 1) 1
MR REINER (Ire) [76] 8-11-1 K Jones, *nvr far away, feeling pace 3 out, rallied aftr nxt, styd on und pres r-in.*
.... (5 to 1 op 4 to 1 tchd 11 to 2) 2
724³ REVE DE VALSE (USA) [87] 5-11-5 (7⁷) B Harding, *led til aftr 3rd, improved to dispute ld 5 out, one pace 3 out.*
.........................(2 to 1 fav op 7 to 4 tchd 9 to 4) 3
HAZEL CREST [72] 9-10-11 D Parker, *pressed ldg trio, effrt 4 out, rdn nxt, fdd.*....................(12 to 1 op 7 to 1) 4
239⁵ DEAR EMILY [74] 8-10-13 Mr S Swiers, *al struggling to keep up, sn tld off.*......................(7 to 1 op 5 to 1) 5
695³ BOETHIUS (USA) [75] (bl) 7-11-0 P Waggott, *trkd ldrs, reminders hfwy, sn tch bef 3 out, tld off.*
.........................(20 to 1 op 14 to 1) 6
Dist: 1¼l, 4l, 12l, dist, 2l. 4m 1.00s. a 3.00s (6 Ran).
(Panther Racing), J G M O'Shea

886 Metro Centre Juvenile Novices' Hurdle Class E (3-y-o) £2,217 2m...... (2:50)

664⁵ HOBBS CHOICE 10-5 N Bentley, *al frnt rnk, dsptd ld frm hfwy, led betw last 2, wndrd and hit last, all out.*
.................(11 to 10 on op 5 to 4 on tchd Evens) 1
SILENT QUEST (Ire) 10-10 R Garritty, *led, jnd hfwy, hdd betw last 2, rallied r-in.*....................(3 to 1 op 5 to 2) 2
705⁷ KAI'S LADY (Ire) 10-5 (7⁷) Michael Brennan, *chsd clr ldg pair frm hfwy, nvr rch chalg pos.*........(20 to 1 op 8 to 1) 3
MOST WANTED (Ire) 10-10 (5⁵) R McGrath, *trkd ldrs, struggling to hold pl bef hfwy, sn tld off.*
.........................(9 to 2 op 7 to 2 tchd 5 to 1) 4
705⁶ RECALL TO MIND (bl) 10-10 D Parker, *jmpd slwly, trkd ldrs till reminders 4th, sn lost tch, tld off.*........(14 to 1 op 8 to 1) 5
VALES ALES 10-7 (3³) G Cahill, *al struggling, tld off whn pld up bef 4 out.*....................(20 to 1 op 8 to 1) pu
Dist: Nk, 30l, 26l, nk. 3m 53.80s. a 4.80s (6 Ran).
(Miss Liz Hobbs), G M Moore

887 Regional Railways Novices' Chase Class E (5-y-o and up) £2,961 3m 1f
.... (3:20)

568² SCRABO VIEW (Ire) 8-11-5 R Supple, *wtd wth, niggled alng frm hfwy, str run und pres appr last, led r-in, ran on wl.*
.........................(2 to 1 fav op 7 to 4) 1
814⁵ ROYAL SURPRISE 9-10-12 T Reed, *al frnt rnk, led 5 out till hdd r-in, kpt on und pres.*............. (7 to 1 tchd 8 to 1) 2
739² BARDAROS 7-10-12 A Thornton, *patiently rdn, took clr order fnl circuit, ev ch betw last 2, styd on one pace r-in.*
.........................(11 to 4 op 3 to 1) 3
699⁴ MORE JOY 8-10-12 D Bentley, *led till hdd 3rd, rgned ld 6th, headed 5 out, hrd drvn appr last, kpt on same pace.*
.........................(11 to 1 op 12 to 1) 4
764⁴ GOLDEN SAVANNAH 6-10-12 D Parker, *settled in tch, effrt hfwy, struggling fnl circuit, lost touch, tld off.*
.....................(16 to 1 op 12 to 1 tchd 20 to 1) 5
814³ GERMAN LEGEND 6-11-5 J Burke, *settled to chase ldrs, feeling pace whn blun 6 out, sn lost tch, tld off.*
.........................(7 to 2 op 3 to 1 tchd 4 to 1) 6
793 SMOKEY TRACK 11-10-2 (5⁵) S Taylor, *not jump wl, al struggling in rear, tld off fnl circuit.*
.....................(33 to 1 op 25 to 1 tchd 40 to 1) 7
CLONROCHE LUCKY (Ire) 6-10-12 K Jones, *wth ldrs, led 3rd to 6th, styd hndy till lost tch quickly and pld up appr 3 out, dismounted.*.........(20 to 1 op 16 to 1 tchd 25 to 1) pu
Dist: Nk, 2½l, ½l, 16l, 8l, dist. 6m 25.70s. a 20.70s (8 Ran).
(Robin Mellish), P Beaumont

888 Hennessy Cognac Special Novices' Hurdle Class B (4-y-o and up) £6,192 2m........................ (3:50)

792⁴ SUPERTOP 8-10-12 M Foster, *patiently rdn, improved frm betw last 2, led last, drvn out.*......(9 to 2 op 11 to 2) 1
766⁴ SUAS LEAT (Ire) 6-10-12 M Newton, *nvr far away, led 3 out, gd advantage betw last 2, blun last, sn hdd, rallied.*
.........................(9 to 2 op 7 to 2) 2
766² CANTON VENTURE 4-10-11 P Hide, *led, jmpd slwly 1st, wndrd nxt, hdd 3 out, rallied last, styd on one pace.*
.........................(2 to 1 fav op 5 to 2 tchd 11 to 4) 3

104

KING RAT (Ire) 5-10-12 Michael Brennan, *trkd ldg pair hfwy, effrt and drvn alng frm 2 out, no extr appr last.*
.... (15 to 2 op 7 to 1 tchd 8 to 1) 4
766³ COURT JOKER (Ire) 4-10-11 B Storey, *settled off the pace, nvr able to rch chalg pos..........* (16 to 1 tchd 20 to 1) 5
661⁵ BLANC SEING (Fr) 9-10-12 Mr S Swiers, *lost pl quickly hfwy, no dngr aftr......................* (33 to 1 op 25 to 1) 6
279* COUREUR 7-10-12 R Garritty, *patiently rdn, steady hdwy 3 out, ridden and hit nxt, virtually pld up r-in, lme.*
.... (9 to 4 op 7 to 4 tchd 5 to 2) 7
GENERAL MUCK (Ire) 7-10-12 S Taylor, *chsd ldrs, feeling pace and drvn alng 3 out, wknd quickly, tld off.....* (33 to 1) 8
609 WHIRLWIND ROMANCE (Ire) 5-10-7 S McDougall, *beh whn jmpd badly rght 3rd, pld up bef nxt.................* (66 to 1) pu
Dist: 2l, 1l, 10l, 6l, 5l, 6l, 12l. 3m 48.00s. b 1.00s (9 Ran).
SR: 22/20/18/9/2/-/   (Mrs Barbara Lungo), L Lungo

889 **Metro Centre 10th Birthday Handicap Chase Class E (0-110 5-y-o and up) £3,175 2½m 110yds............ (4:25)**

706 WISE ADVICE (Ire) [95] 6-11-2 R Garritty, *made virtually all, jmpd clr 2 out, readily drw clear.*
.... (6 to 5 on op 6 to 4 on tchd 11 to 10 on) 1
726 WILLIE SPARKLE [79] 10-10-0 A Dobbin, *dsptd ld, ev ch whn pckd on landing 5 out, rdn and outpcd last 2.*
.... (11 to 10 on op Evens tchd 11 to 10) 2
Won by 8l. 5m 7.50s. a 9.50s (2 Ran).
SR: -/-/   (A G Chappell), M D Hammond

890 **In Situ Handicap Hurdle Class F (0-100 4-y-o and up) £2,108 3m............ (4:55)**

550⁴ SHELTON ABBEY [63] (bl) 10-10-3 K Jones, *settled gng wl, improved on bit to ld betw last 2, slowed and fluffed last, sn hdd, rallied to lead r-in, drvn out.*
.... (13 to 2 op 5 to 1 tchd 7 to 1) 1
790* CROFTON LAKE [62] 8-10-2 B Storey, *last and hld up, improved frm 3 out, str chal last, kpt on one pace.*
.... (7 to 1 op 10 to 1 tchd 11 to 1) 2
817² BALLINDOO [84] 7-11-10 Mr R Armson, *al hndy, led aftr 6th till hdd betw last 2, rallied to ld ag'n briefly after last, no extr.*
.... (2 to 1 fav op 7 to 2) 3
794³ THALEROS [83] 6-11-9 J Callaghan, *trkd ldrs, ev ch appr 2 out, rdn betw last two, one pace.........* (3 to 1 op 5 to 2) 4
550 COPPERHURST (Ire) [75] 5-10-13 S McDougall, *led till aftr 6th, lost grnd quickly 4 out, tld off whn pld up betw last 2.*
.... (11 to 4 op 3 to 1) pu
Dist: 2½l, nk, 4l. 5m 46.00s. b 2.00s (5 Ran).
SR: -/-/5/-/-/   (John Wade), J Wade

WORCESTER (good to firm)
Saturday October 12th
Going Correction: PLUS 0.05 sec. per fur.

891 **Duncan Fearnley Amateur Riders' Selling Handicap Hurdle Class G (0-95 4-y-o and up) £2,087 2m....... (2:25)**

754⁴ HAMADRYAD (Ire) [85] 8-10-13 (7") Mr R Thornton, *hld up, smooth hdwy 4th, led on bit 2 out, pushed clr r-in.*
.... (100 to 30 fav op 7 to 2) 1
784⁷ BURNT SIENNA (Ire) [79] (v) 4-10-6 (7") Mr E James, *led to 2 out, one pace.....................* (11 to 1 op 7 to 1) 2
595³ DENOMINATION (USA) [90] 4-11-5 (5") Mr A Farrant, *hld up in rear, hdwy appr 3 out, styd on one pace frm 2 out.*
.... (13 to 2 op 6 to 1 tchd 7 to 1 and 8 to 1) 3
GLOWING PATH [77] 6-10-9 (3") Mr C Bonner, *hld up in mid-division, hdwy aftr 5th, 4th and held whn mstk 2 out.*
.... (8 to 1 op 12 to 1) 4
FORCING TWO (USA) [70] (bl) 5-9-12 (7") D Byrne, *in tch till not fluent and lost pl 3rd, styd on one pace frm 2 out.*
.... (7 to 1 op 9 to 1) 5
666³ GALLOPING GUNS (Ire) [69] 4-9-10 (7") Miss E J Jones, *in tch, ev ch 3 out, wknd nxt.*
.... (12 to 1 op 10 to 1 tchd 14 to 1) 6
784⁸ JAVA SHRINE (USA) [72] 5-10-2² (7") Mr A Wintle, *jmpd slwly 3rd and nxt, nvr better than mid-div....* (10 to 1 op 8 to 1) 7
666⁷ CATWALKER (Ire) [65] 5-9-7 (7") Mr O McPhail, *nvr nrr.*
.... (25 to 1 op 16 to 1) 8
629⁵ SCALP 'EM (Ire) [65] 8-9-10² (7") Dr P Pritchard, *chsd ldr till appr 5th, wknd bef nxt...........* (33 to 1 tchd 50 to 1) 9
595⁶ REEFA'S MILL (Ire) [78] 4-10-9 (3") Mr M Rimell, *chsd ldrs to 4th, beh frm nxt........* (11 to 1 op 9 to 1 tchd 14 to 1) 10
638⁴ POCONO KNIGHT [68] 6-9-10 (7") Miss B Small, *al beh.*
.... (16 to 1 op 14 to 1) 11
784⁶ NIGHT TIME [75] 4-10-2 (7") Mr G Shenkin, *nvr on terms.*
.... (12 to 1) 12
856 TIBBS INN [65] 7-9-10³ (7") Mr R Widger, *strted slwly, nvr trbld ldrs, tld off.........* (20 to 1 tchd 25 to 1) 13
DOC'S COAT [71] 11-9-13 (7") Mr E Babington, *nvr a factor, tld off......................* (20 to 1 op 14 to 1) 14
Dist: 6l, 2½l, ¾l, 3½l, sht-hd, 1l, 6l, 7l, 6l, 1l. 3m 48.50s. a 8.50s (14 Ran).
SR: 15/2/10/-/-/-/   (Mrs R F Key & Mrs V C Ward), Mrs V C Ward

892 **MEB Powerline Novices' Chase Class E (5-y-o and up) £2,945 2m 7f... (2:55)**

649³ GLENFINN PRINCESS 8-10-7 D Byrne, *hld up, mstk 11th, hdwy 14th, led 4 out, clr frm nxt.*
.... (7 to 4 op 2 to 1 tchd 9 to 4) 1
755* IMPERIAL VINTAGE (Ire) 6-11-12 A P McCoy, *led, mstk 11th, blun 4teenth, hdd four out, an outpcd by wnr.*
.... (13 to 8 fav op 5 to 4 tchd 7 to 4) 2
799 SHIKAREE (Ire) (bl) 5-10-7 C Maude, *not fluent, chsd ldr to 5th and ag'n frm 8th till appr 4 out, fdd, tld off, virtually pld-up r-in.*
.... (11 to 4 op 5 to 2 tchd 3 to 1 and 100 to 30) 3
CAPO CASTANUM 7-10-12 G Bradley, *chsd ldrs frm 5th till 8th, 3rd whn hmpd and uns rdr twelfth.*
.... (11 to 1 op 7 to 1 tchd 12 to 1) ur
Dist: 14l, dist. 5m 52.40s. a 14.40s (4 Ran).
                     (Patrick McGinty), Mrs Merrita Jones

893 **Pertemps Juvenile Novices' Hurdle Class E (3-y-o) £2,360 2m....... (3:25)**

AGDISTIS 10-7 L Harvey, *pld hrd, hld up beh ldrs, led on bit appr 3 out, sn clr, very easily.*
.... (5 to 4 fav op 5 to 4 on tchd 11 to 8) 1
658⁸ FLOOD'S FANCY 10-7 D Byrne, *mid-div, lost pl hfwy, hdwy appr 3 out, wnt second nxt, no ch wth wnr.*
.... (40 to 1 op 25 to 1) 2
672 AMBER RING 10-7 J R Kavanagh, *hd to 3rd, chsd wnr frm 3 out to 2 out, sn outpcd..........* (50 to 1 op 25 to 1) 3
CHIPALATA 10-12 P McLoughlin, *beh, not fluent 3rd, styd on frm 2 out, nvr nrr...................* (50 to 1 op 25 to 1) 4
INDIAN WOLF 10-12 I Lawrence, *in tch, not fluent 4th, wknd appr 3 out...............* (33 to 1 op 25 to 1 tchd 50 to 1) 5
614 COPPER DIAMOND (bl) 10-0 (7") J Prior, *prmnt to 5th, sn wknd...................* (50 to 1 op 33 to 1) 6
788 SONG FOR JESS (Ire) 10-7 S Wynne, *nvr on terms.*
.... (13 to 1 op 8 to 1 tchd 14 to 1) 7
672 VERULAM (Ire) 11-5 G Bradley, *hld up beh ldrs, rdn and wknd bef 3 out, eased.....* (5 to 1 op 7 to 2 tchd 11 to 2) 8
819⁴ WATER MUSIC MELODY 10-7 Gary Lyons, *steadied strt, took str hold in rear, al beh, tld off...........* (50 to 1 op 33 to 1) 9
ROYAL THEN (Fr) 10-12 D Bridgwater, *prmnt, led appr 5th, hdd bef 3 out, 4th and wkng whn f 2 out.*
.... (100 to 30 op 4 to 1) f
DESERT SCOUT 10-12 W Marston, *mid-div, lost pl quickly hfwy, wl beh whn pld up bef 5th.*
.... (25 to 1 tchd 33 to 1 and 50 to 1) pu
323 OUR ADVENTURE 10-7 S Curran, *wth ldr, led 3rd till appr 5th, sn wknd, tld off whn pld up bef 3 out..........* (50 to 1) pu
Dist: 7l, 8l, 2l, 1l, 25l, 3½l, 7l, 6l, dist. 3m 50.40s. a 10.40s (12 Ran).
                     (Whitting Commodities Ltd), H Thomson Jones

894 **Domestic Appliances Distributors' Handicap Chase Class B (0-140 5-y-o and up) £4,922 2½m 110yds.... (3:55)**

PHILIP'S WOODY [115] 8-10-10 J R Kavanagh, *pld hrd, hld up, hdwy appr 7th, rdn to chal aftr 3 out, led on pres to ld last fifty yards.......................* (2 to 1 tchd 9 to 4) 1
872* WISE APPROACH [129] 9-11-9 (7") Mr R Wakley, *led, hit 7th, rdn and hdd last 50 yards, no extr.*
.... (9 to 4 op 6 to 4 tchd 5 to 2) 2
771² REX TO THE RESCUE (Ire) [105] 8-9-9 (5") P Henley, *chsd ldr, ev ch appr 4 out, sn wknd, tld off whn blun last.*
.... (7 to 4 fav op 6 to 4 tchd 2 to 1) 3
375⁴ CHANNEL PASTIME [105] 12-10-0 D J Burchell, *hld up, wl beh frm 6th, tld off........* (9 to 1 op 7 to 1 tchd 10 to 1) 4
Dist: 1¼l, dist, 11l. 5m 6.10s. a 9.10s (4 Ran).
SR: 1/13/-/-/   (K G Knox), N J Henderson

895 **Apollo 2000 Handicap Chase Class F (0-100 5-y-o and up) £2,805 2m (4:30)**

759³ NORTHERN OPTIMIST [82] 8-11-4 A P McCoy, *chsd ldr frm 4th, led aftr 3 out, rdn out, ran on wl.*
.... (5 to 2 tchd 11 to 4) 1
774² THE YOKEL [72] 10-10-3 (5") P Henley, *chsd ldr to 4th, rdn appr four out, took second last, no ch wth wnr.*
.... (7 to 4 fav op 5 to 2) 2
690² SUPER SHARP (NZ) [88] 8-11-10 Jacqui Oliver, *led, pckd 7th, hdd aftr 3 out, wknd frm last.......* (11 to 2 op 5 to 1) 3
771 DAWN CHANCE [79] 10-10-12 (3") T Dascombe, *hld up, lost tch frm 8th, poor 4th whn mstk 3 out, tld off.*
.... (10 to 1 op 7 to 1 tchd 11 to 1) 4
RED MATCH [68] 11-10-4 N Mann, *not fluent, al beh, tld off 4th, pld up bef 4 out.....* (16 to 1 op 12 to 1) pu
LODESTONE LAD (Ire) [85] 6-11-7 D Byrne, *al beh, tld off 4th, pld up and dismounted bef 7th.*
.... (9 to 2 op 4 to 1 tchd 5 to 1) pu
Dist: 7l, 11l, dist. 3m 57.90s. a 8.90s (6 Ran).
SR: 9/-/-/   (Mackworth Snooker Club Pt), B J Llewellyn

896 **Asko Appliances Handicap Hurdle Class C (0-130 4-y-o and up) £3,673 2 ½m............................ (5:00)**

752⁵ WOTTASHAMBLES [109] 5-11-5 D Morris, *made all, clr 2 out,*
ran on strly..................(3 to 1 tchd 4 to 1 and 5 to 1) 1
772³ FLEUR DE TAL [101] 5-10-4 (7") J Power, *chsd wnr frm*
second, rdn aftr 2 out, btn whn hit last... (3 to 1 op 9 to 4) 2
482² LA MENORQUINA (USA) [100] 6-10-11 J A McCarthy, *chsd*
wnr to second, shaken up 6th, rdn 3 out, one pace.
....(5 to 2 fav op 11 to 4) 3
643ᵛ ACROW LINE [117] 11-12-0 D J Burchell, *hld up, reminders*
aftr 5th, sn beh.....................(10 to 1 op 6 to 1) 4
TIM (Ire) [111] 6-11-8 G Bradley, *hld up in rear, rdn aftr 7th, sn*
beh...............................(3 to 1 tchd 7 to 2) 5
Dist: 5l, 1½l, 13l, 17l. 4m 48.20s. a 12.20s (5 Ran).
(Dream On Racing Partnership), L Montague Hall

NAAS (IRE) (good)
Sunday October 13th

897 **Coughlan Handicap Hurdle (4-y-o and**
up) £4,795 3m..................(3:30)

599* JANE DIGBY (Ire) [-] 4-10-0 C F Swan, ...(8 to 1) 1
625* DIFFICULT TIMES (Ire) [-] 4-11-2 S C Lyons, ...(9 to 2) 2
730⁵ ALASAD [-] 6-10-12 M P Dwyer, ...(5 to 1) 3
828⁶ OAKLER (Ire) [-] 6-9-10¹ (7") J A Robinson, ...(16 to 1) 4
748⁴ ALWAYS IN TROUBLE [-] 9-10-1 T P Rudd, ...(7 to 1) 5
746³ BAMAPOUR (Ire) [-] 6-10-7 A P McCoy, ...(10 to 1) 6
826* WHAT A QUESTION (Ire) [-] 8-11-11 (3") D J Casey,
....(3 to 1 fav) 7
TROUVILLE LASS (Ire) [-] 4-9-11 (5") T Martin, ...(14 to 1) 8
748* FATHER RECTOR (Ire) [-] 7-10-7 T Horgan, ...(7 to 1) 9
302 STEEL DAWN [-] 9-10-7 (3") J H Barry, ...(12 to 1) 10
TELL THE HIPPER (Ire) [-] 5-10-10 C O'Dwyer, ...(10 to 1) 11
683⁶ MOON-FROG [-] 9-10-0 F Woods, ...(50 to 1) pu
SPANKERS HILL (Ire) [-] 7-11-0 T P Treacy, ...(10 to 1) pu
Dist: 2½l, 3l, 8l, 4½l. 5m 51.20s. (13 Ran).
(New Road Syndicate), A P O'Brien

898 **Tend-R-Leen Horse Feeds I.N.H. Flat**
Race (4-y-o) £3,425 2m........(5:30)

782² DO YE KNOW WHA (Ire) 11-2 (7") Mr J P McNamara,
....(13 to 2) 1
560 SUPREME CHANTER (Ire) 11-9 Mr P Fenton, ...(10 to 1) 2
CORYROSE (Ire) 10-11 (7") Mr A J Dempsey, ...(20 to 1) 3
CLOONE BRIDGE (Ire) 11-6 (3") Mr B M Cash, ..(5 to 4 on) 4
LANCA'S TRIX (Ire) 10-13 (5") Mr R Walsh, ...(10 to 1) 5
782³ MINISTER'S CROSS (Ire) 11-2 (7") Mr D A Harney, (13 to 2) 6
269⁷ BALLYLENNON BAVARD (Ire) 11-1 (3") Mr P English,
....(16 to 1) 7
COOKSGROVE ROSIE (Ire) 10-11 (7") Mr G Elliott, ..(14 to 1) 8
MR MAGGET (Ire) 11-2 (7") Miss A O'Brien, ...(12 to 1) 9
472⁶ PAUL (Ire) 11-2 (7") Mr J P Moloney, ...(25 to 1) 10
OLD MOTHER HUBBARD (Ire) 10-13 (5") Mr W M O'Sullivan,
....(16 to 1) 11
NOBLE JEWEL (Ire) 10-11 (7") Mr E Gallagher, ...(14 to 1) 12
782⁶ SINGERS CORNER 10-11 (7") Mr Edgar Byrne, ...(16 to 1) 13
LOCKBEG LASS (Ire) 10-11 (7") Mr J T McNamara, (12 to 1) 14
172⁵ BARLEY MEADOW (Ire) 11-2 (7") Mr A C Coyle, ..(33 to 1) 15
WAITNOW (Ire) 11-2 (7") Mr S M Duffy, ...(14 to 1) 16
ROBAZALA (Ire) 10-11 (7") Mr B A Murphy, ...(14 to 1) 17
782 JER-MARIE (Ire) 11-9 Mr H F Cleary, ...(16 to 1) 18
MARGALE (Ire) 10-11 (7") Mr C A Murphy, ...(20 to 1) 19
581 ARCTIC PARTY (Ire) 11-4 Mr M McNulty, ...(50 to 1) 20
SUBLIME SPIRIT (Ire) 11-2 (7") Mr D Buckley, ...(33 to 1) 21
DOUBLE OR NOTHING (Ire) 11-4 Mr G J Harford, (50 to 1) 22
199 PRYZON (Ire) 11-1 (3") Mr E Norris, ...(33 to 1) 23
350⁶ CHURCH ROCK (Ire) 11-9 Mr J P Dempsey, ...(50 to 1) bd
KENNY'S PRINCESS (Ire) 10-11 (7") Mr P Murphy, (14 to 1) su
Dist: 13l, 1½l, ¾l, 8l. 3m 48.50s. (25 Ran).
(D Brennan Accountants Synd), S J Treacy

PARDUBICE (CZE) (good)
Sunday October 13th

899 **Velka Pardubicka Ceske Pojistovny**
(Chase) (6-y-o and up) £24,155 4¼m
110yds..........................(2:45)

CIPISEK (Cze) 8-10-2 V Snitkovski, ...(12 to 1) 1
535² IRISH STAMP (Ire) 7-10-7 N Williamson, *al in tch, hdwy into*
3rd 4 fs out, chsd wnr frm 3 out, no imprsn........(3 to 1) 2
757⁴ ITS A SNIP 11-10-7 R Dunwoody, *led till 5 out, kpt on one*
pace...............................(5 to 2) 3
FURTADO (Fr) 7-10-8 V Spalek, ... f
Dist: 4½l, dist, dist, 2½l. 12l. 9m 35.10s. (21 Ran).
(Staj Luka), J Vana

NEWTON ABBOT (good (races 1,2,3,4), good to soft (5,6,7))
Monday October 14th
Going Correction: PLUS 0.80 sec. per fur. (races 1,4,6,7), PLUS 0.20 (2,3,5)

900 **Simpkins Edwards Accountants**
Maiden Hurdle Class E (Div I) (4-y-o
and up) £1,955 2m 1f..........(2:15)

336* KAILASH (USA) 5-11-5 A P McCoy, *hld up, steady hdwy 5th,*
led sn aftr 3 out, very easily.....(5 to 2 on op 7 to 4 on) 1
BLAZE OF OAK (USA) 5-11-5 B Fenton, *al prmnt, chlgd wnr*
aftr 3 out, sn outpcd.............(5 to 1 tchd 11 to 2) 2
QUAKER WALTZ 6-11-0 R Bellamy, *prmnt, lft in ld 4th, hdd*
aftr 3 out, sn btn...............................(50 to 1) 3
SOUTHSEA SCANDALS (Ire) 5-11-5 M A Fitzgerald, *hdwy*
5th, one pace frm 3 out. (11 to 1 op 10 to 1 tchd 14 to 1) 4
SMART IN VELVET 6-11-0 I Lawrence, *hdwy 4th, rdn aftr nxt,*
sn btn...........................(100 to 1 op 33 to 1) 5
667 PADDITATE (Ire) 7-11-2 (3") T Dascombe, *beh 3rd, tld off whn f*
3 out...............................(100 to 1 op 33 to 1) f
768 LUCKY MO 6-10-9 (5") D Salter, *led, sn clr, ran out through*
wing 4th..........(66 to 1 op 33 to 1 tchd 100 to 1) ro
POLO KIT 5-11-5 P Holley, *lft disputing ld frm 4th till blun*
badly nxt, not reco'r, tld off whn pld up bef 2 out.
....(7 to 1 op 4 to 1) pu
DANTE'S RUBICON (Ire) 5-11-5 C Maude, *al beh, tld off whn*
pld up bef 2 out.....(66 to 1 op 33 to 1 tchd 100 to 1) pu
MINNEOLA 4-10-6 (7") Mr R Thornton, *mstk 1st, beh frm 4th,*
tld off whn pld up bef 3 out.......(100 to 1 op 33 to 1) pu
BAXWORTHY LORD 5-11-5 J Osborne, *chsd ldrs to 3 out, sn*
wknd, tld off whn pld up bef 2 out.
....(50 to 1 op 33 to 1 tchd 100 to 1) pu
PARADE RACER 5-11-5 W McFarland, *al beh, tld off whn pld*
up bef 2 out........(14 to 1 op 8 to 1 tchd 16 to 1) pu
DECOR (Ire) 6-11-5 J Frost, *beh frm 4th, tld off whn pld up bef*
2 out...............................(16 to 1 op 10 to 1) pu
Dist: 7l, 1½l, 5l, ¾l. 4m 14.90s. a 25.90s (13 Ran).
(Mick Fletcher), M C Pipe

901 **Bowring Marsh And McLennan Ltd**
Handicap Chase Class D (0-125 5-y-o
and up) £3,508 2m 110yds......(2:45)

MERRY PANTO (Ire) [92] 7-10-3 J Osborne, *hld up in tch,*
chlgd 9th, outpcd and held togthr appr 3 out, hdwy and
bumped 2 out, led last, ran on wl......(5 to 1 op 7 to 2) 1
690 STATELY HOME (Ire) [118] 5-12-0 A Maguire, *led to 7th, chlgd*
and hit 3 out, led 2 out, hdd last, one pace.
....(4 to 1 op 7 to 2 tchd 9 to 2) 2
797 GOOD FOR A LAUGH [110] 12-11-7 S Burrough, *in tch, rdn*
9th, sn btn.......................(7 to 1 op 9 to 2) 3
759⁴ FENWICK [89] (bl) 9-9-12¹ (3") T Dascombe, *chsd ldrs, hit 7th,*
wknd 9th..........................(7 to 1 op 8 to 1) 4
JAMES THE FIRST [115] 8-11-12 A P McCoy, *not fluent, jmpd*
slwly 1st, drvn to chase ldrs 5th, led 7th, driven alng till hdd 2
out, sn btn........(6 to 5 fav op 11 to 8 tchd 6 to 4) 5
583² DUKE OF DREAMS [89] 6-10-0 B Powell, *tld off 3rd, drvn and*
hdwy to chase ldrs 6th, sn wknd, tailed off whn pld up bef 9th.
....(5 to 1 op 4 to 1 tchd 11 to 2) pu
Dist: 1¾l, 13l, 1½l, 3l. 4m 8.30s. a 10.30s (6 Ran).
SR: 5/28/8/-/8/-/ (Uplands Bloodstock), C P E Brooks

902 **Spa-Trans Ltd Novices' Chase Class E**
(5-y-o and up) £2,995 2m 5f 110yds
...........................(3:15)

STRONG TARQUIN (Ire) 6-10-12 A P McCoy, *in tch, hdwy*
tenth, chlgd frm 4 out, hrd drvn from 3 out, slight ld whn lft clr
last, easily.......................(5 to 1 op 3 to 1) 1
KEEP IT ZIPPED (Ire) 6-10-12 J Osborne, *not fluent, lost pl*
6th, rdn alng frm tenth, styd on to take poor second r-in.
....(5 to 4 fav op 7 to 4) 2
WILKINS 7-10-12 P Holley, *chsd ldrs, led 4th, hit four out, sn*
hdd, btn nxt....................(20 to 1 op 10 to 1) 3
583⁴ STORMY SUNSET 9-10-3³ (7") Mr T Dennis, *hit 4th, hdwy*
tenth, sn one pace.... (16 to 1 op 12 to 1 tchd 20 to 1) 4
DUKE OF APROLON 9-10-12 P Hide, *led to 4th, wknd aftr*
11th...............................(12 to 1 op 7 to 1 tchd 14 to 1) 5
CALL ME RIVER (Ire) 8-10-12 I Lawrence, *hdwy 9th, prmnt till*
wknd 11th.......................(25 to 1 op 14 to 1) 6
LA MEZERAY 8-10-7 M Bosley, *hdwy tenth, sn wknd.*
....(50 to 1 op 25 to 1) 7
SWING QUARTET (Ire) 6-10-7 C Llewellyn, *prmnt, led sn aftr*
4 out, rdn 2 out, narrowly hdd whn f last. (3 to 1 tchd 7 to 2) f
KINDLY LADY 8-10-7 M A Fitzgerald, *chsd ldrs to 11th, sn*
wknd and pld up bef 2 out.
....(12 to 1 op 8 to 1 tchd 20 to 1) pu
VARECK II (Fr) 9-10-12 C Maude, *al beh, tld off whn pld up bef*
4 out...............................(20 to 1 op 12 to 1 tchd 25 to 1) pu
502² CALL ME ALBI (Ire) (v) 5-10-10 M Richards, *in tch to tenth, tld*
off whn pld up bef 4 out...........(20 to 1 op 12 to 1) pu
Dist: 29l, 1¼l, 5l, 6l, 4l, 7l. 5m 28.00s. a 26.00s (11 Ran).
(Paul K Barber And Mr J A Keighley), P F Nicholls

903 **Co-operative Bank Plc Conditional**
Jockeys' Mares' Only Handicap Hurdle
Class F (0-100 4-y-o and up) £1,919
2m 1f............................(3:45)

HULLO MARY DOLL [73] 7-10-12 Chris Webb, *trkd ldrs, led 5th, clr 3 out, pushed out...* (8 to 1 op 6 to 1 tchd 9 to 1)   1
445² NORDIC CROWN (Ire) [76] (bl) 5-10-11 (3*) B Moore, *led till hdd appr 3rd, sn led ag'n, headed 5th, rdn 3 out, one pace.*
.... (4 to 1 op 11 to 4)   2
659⁷ SEVERN GALE [85] 6-11-10 O Burrows, *hld up in rear, hdwy 5th, staying on whn hit 3 out, sn btn......* (5 to 2 op 2 to 1)   3
801¹⁸ MINSTER'S MADAM [85] (v) 5-11-9 D Walsh, *prmnt, led appr 3rd, sn hdd, rdn approaching 5th, soon btn, tld off.*
.... (2 to 1 fav op 9 to 4)   4
SAFE SECRET [68] 5-10-6 T Dascombe, *al beh, lost tch 5th, tld off whn pld up bef 2 out.*
.... (16 to 1 op 12 to 1 tchd 20 to 1)   pu
FAME AND FANTASY (Ire) [85] 5-11-9 P Henley, *rdn and lost tch 4th, sn tld off, pld up bef 2 out.*
.... (9 to 2 op 4 to 1 tchd 5 to 1)   pu
Dist: 14l, 2½l, dist. 4m 18.80s. a 29.80s (6 Ran).

(Plough Twenty (Ashton Keynes)), A J Chamberlain

904 Bevan Ashford Solicitors Novices' Chase Class E (5-y-o and up) £2,859 2m 110yds..................... (4:15)

AMBASSADOR ROYALE (Ire) 8-10-12 M A Fitzgerald, *chsd ldrs, chlgd 4 out, hit 3 out, sn led, readily.*
.... (14 to 1 op 12 to 1 tchd 16 to 1)   1
THE LANCER (Ire) 7-10-9 (3*) D Fortt, *hdwy 6th, chsd ldrs 8th, jmpd slwly nxt and outpcd, ran on ag'n r-in, no ch wth wnr.*
.... (12 to 1 op 7 to 1)   2
LORD NITROGEN (USA) 6-10-12 B Powell, *led aftr second, rdn alng 4 out, hdd after 3 out, hit nxt, wknd r-in.*
.... (20 to 1 op 14 to 1)   3
MR PLAYFULL 6-10-12 J Frost, *drpd rear 6th, pushed alng nxt, hdwy 8th, kpt on frm 2 out.*
.... (2 to 1 fav op 9 to 4 tchd 5 to 2)   4
190⁴ LEGAL ARTIST (Ire) 6-10-12 L Harvey, *chsd ldrs 6th, hit nxt, chased ldrs 4 out, wknd 2 out........* (12 to 1 op 6 to 1)   5
799 PRIORY ROSE 9-10-7 S Burrough, *beh frm 4th, tld off whn pld up bef 2 out.*...................... (33 to 1 op 25 to 1)   pu
755³ HE'S A KING (USA) 6-10-9 (3*) T Dascombe, *chsd ldrs till wknd 7th, sn tld off, pld up aftr 2 out, lme.* (7 to 2 op 5 to 2)   pu
KING'S GOLD 6-10-12 M Richards, *al beh, tld off whn pld up bef 2 out.*......................... (10 to 1 op 7 to 1)   pu
762⁷ HERESTHEDEAL (Ire) (v) 7-10-12 B Clifford, *led till hdd aftr second, hit 3rd, blun 7th and wknd, pld up after nxt, broke leg, destroyed........* (3 to 1 op 5 to 2 tchd 100 to 30)   pu
Dist: 2½l, 1¼l, ½l, 2½l. 4m 16.60s. a 18.60s (9 Ran).

(Miss Alison Broyd), Miss A E Broyd

905 Simpkins Edwards Accountants Maiden Hurdle Class E (Div II) (4-y-o and up) £1,945 2m 1f.......... (4:45)

770³ RITTO 6-11-5 A P McCoy, *hdwy to track ldrs 4th, rdn to ld 2 out, edgd lft last and ag'n r-in, ridden out.*
.... (100 to 30 op 5 to 1 tchd 4 to 1)   1
DEVON PEASANT 4-10-9 Mr L Jefford, *hdwy 4th, trkd ldrs gng wl 2 out, ev ch and not much room last, bumped cl hme, no extr.*............................ (14 to 1 op 8 to 1)   2
SHIFT AGAIN (Ire) 4-10-13 J Osborne, *in tch, lft in ld 3rd, hdd 2 out, sn rdn, one pace..* (5 to 1 op 5 to 2 tchd 11 to 2)   3
LORD ROOBLE (Ire) 5-11-5 P Hide, *prmnt, wth ldr 3 out, sn rdn and wknd............* (9 to 2 op 7 to 2 tchd 5 to 1)   4
THE PROMS (Ire) 5-11-5 C Llewellyn, *prmnt, dsptd ld 3rd, styd frnt rnk till wknd quickly aftr 3 out.*
.... (5 to 2 fav tchd 3 to 1)   5
ARTHUR'S SPECIAL 6-10-7 (7*) G Supple, *al beh.*
.... (40 to 1 op 12 to 1)   6
107⁷ SEVEN BROOKS 6-11-5 S Fox, *in tch whn blun 4th, reco'red nxt, wknd 3 out.....* (50 to 1 op 33 to 1 tchd 66 to 1)   7
THE CHEESE BARON 5-11-0 (6*) Chris Webb, *al beh, tld off.*
.... (50 to 1 op 33 to 1)   8
GEORGE BULL 4-11-4 R Farrant, *keen hold, led, sn clr, f 3rd.*
.... (11 to 2 op 4 to 1 tchd 6 to 1)   f
WAR REQUIEM (Ire) 6-11-5 P Holley, *chsd ldrs to 5th, tld off whn pld up bef 2 out...*(10 to 1 op 12 to 1 tchd 16 to 1)   pu
TOPANGA 4-11-4 L Harvey, *beh and rdn 4th, tld off whn pld up bef 2 out....* (20 to 1 op 12 to 1 tchd 25 to 1)   pu
749⁸ LADYMALORD 4-10-13 M Bosley, *beh frm 3rd, tld off whn pld up bef 2 out....................* (100 to 1 op 33 to 1)   pu
Dist: ½l, 3l, 28l, 20l, 12l, nk, dist. 4m 9.20s. a 20.20s (12 Ran).
SR: 25/18/15/-/-/-/

(Park Industrial Supplies (Wales) Ltd), J Neville

906 Tru-Mark Financial Services Ltd. Novices' Handicap Hurdle Class E (4-y-o and up) £2,242 2¾m........... (5:15)

ROSIE-B [71] 6-9-7 (7*) Mr R Thornton, *hdwy 5th, led 7th, ran on wl whn chlgd appr 2 out, pushed out.*
.... (11 to 2 op 3 to 1 tchd 6 to 1)   1
LUKE WARM [71] 6-10-0 A Maguire, *hdwy and hit 6th, str chal frm 3 out, sn hrd rdn, no extr.*
.... (9 to 2 op 2 to 6 to 1 tchd 7 to 1)   2
667 TIPPING ALONG (Ire) [79] 7-10-3 (5*) Sophie Mitchell, *beh, pushed alng frm 7th, ran on from 2 out but not a dngr.*
.... (16 to 1 op 8 to 1)   3

MU-TADIL [72] 4-10-0 B Powell, *ran in snatches, hrd drvn frm 7th, one pace from 3 out.*
.... (16 to 1 op 12 to 1 tchd 20 to 1)   4
518* ALWAYS GREENER (Ire) [82] 5-10-6 (5*) Michael Brennan, *lost tch 4th, hdwy 7th, wknd 3 out......* (8 to 1 op 5 to 1)   5
768⁵ WHAT'S THE JOKE [71] 7-10-0 J Railton, *prmnt, jmpd slwly 3rd, wknd 6th, tld off whn pld up bef 2 out.*
.... (33 to 1 op 20 to 1)   pu
768* MILLION DANCER [96] (bl) 4-11-10 C Maude, *led, sn clr, hdd 7th, wknd quickly, tld off whn pld up bef last.*
.... (5 to 1 op 11 to 4)   pu
841* HYLTERS CHANCE (Ire) [76] 5-10-5 (7ex) A P McCoy, *mstk 1st, chsd ldrs, hrd rdn appr 7th and sn wknd, tld off whn pld up bef 2 out..........* (5 to 4 on op 5 to 4 tchd 11 to 8)   pu
Dist: 10l, 21l, 3½l, 25l. 5m 29.20s. a 28.20s (8 Ran).

(Internet Racing), N M Babbage

ROSCOMMON (IRE) (yielding (races 1,2,4), good (3)) Monday October 14th

907 Lustre Handicap Hurdle (0-109 4-y-o and up) £2,740 2m.............. (2:30)

849⁵ TARAJAN (USA) [-] (bl) 4-11-2 T Hazlett, ...(8 to 1)   1
742² I REMEMBER IT WELL (Ire) [-] (bl) 4-11-0 F Stockdale,
.... (5 to 1)   2
685* MAJOR JAMIE (Ire) [-] 5-11-11 C F Swan, ...(11 to 2)   3
828 STONELEIGH TURBO (Ire) [-] 7-10-13 J P Broderick,
.... (16 to 1)   4
715⁵ WESPERADA (Ire) [-] 4-11-9 W Harnett, ...(9 to 1)   5
710³ JOHNNY'S DREAM (Ire) [-] 6-10-6 (5*) G Cotter, ...(15 to 2)   6
781 ICED HONEY [-] 9-10-11 L P Cusack, ...(33 to 1)   7
803² WICKLOW WAY (Ire) [-] 6-9-13 T P Treacy, ...(8 to 1)   8
849 LEMOIRE (Ire) [-] 5-10-4 (7*) R P Hogan, ...(16 to 1)   9
773⁶ NO DIAMOND (Ire) [-] 7-9-5 (7*) J M Maguire, ...(16 to 1)   10
564⁸ DOUBLE JIG TIME (Ire) [-] 4-9-7 W Slattery, ...(50 to 1)   11
DULWICH GATE (Ire) [-] 4-9-13 (3*) D Bromley, ...(16 to 1)   12
684 DANCING CLODAGH (Ire) [-] (bl) 4-11-0 F Woods, (12 to 1)   13
443³ SIR GANDOUGE (Ire) [-] 7-10-6 C O'Dwyer, ...(14 to 1)   14
MAKE AN EFFORT (Ire) [-] 5-11-6 A Powell, ...(9 to 2 fav)   15
645⁶ ROSCOLVIN (Ire) [-] (bl) 4-10-7 (5*) T Martin, ...(25 to 1)   16
748 RUSTY COIN [-] 11-12-0 J Shortt, ...(25 to 1)   17
710⁴ SHANRUE (Ire) [-] 6-11-1 T Walsh, ...(25 to 1)   ur
Dist: 3½l, 4½l, 4½l, ¾l. 3m 57.40s. (18 Ran).

(Ms Maura Horan), Patrick Prendergast

908 Irish National Hunt Novice Hurdle (4-y-o and up) £4,110 2m.......... (3:00)

733³ CAITHIONA'S CHOICE (Ire) 5-11-2 M P Dwyer, ...(7 to 2)   1
SLUSH PUPPY (Ire) 8-11-2 L P Cusack, ...(10 to 1)   2
590⁶ FOREST PRINCESS (Ire) 4-10-6 A Powell, ...(20 to 1)   3
716² LEWISHAM (Ire) 4-10-11 C F Swan, ...(3 to 1)   4
678* ACES AND EIGHTS (Ire) 6-11-8 C O'Dwyer, ...(6 to 4 fav)   5
PTARMIGAN LODGE 5-10-13 (3*) G Kilfeather, ...(14 to 1)   6
601* BENNY THE BISHOP (Ire) 6-11-1 (7*) Mr A Ross, ...(8 to 1)   7
781⁸ RED RADICAL (Ire) 6-10-12³ (7*) Mr P E I Newell, ..(14 to 1)   8
197 ASHLEY'S PRINCESS (Ire) 4-10-3 (3*) B Bowens, (50 to 1)   9
ENTERTAINMENT 4-10-11 J Shortt, ...(7 to 1)   10
MYSTICAL LORD (Ire) 4-10-6 J P Broderick, ...(33 to 1)   11
SABINTA (Ire) 5-10-11 F Woods, ...(10 to 1)   12
LABAN LADY (Ire) 7-10-11 T P Treacy, ...(25 to 1)   13
850 FOREST STAR (Ire) 7-11-2 D T Evans, ...(20 to 1)   su
Dist: 6l, 4½l, 9l, 1½l. 4m 3.60s. (14 Ran).

(Exors Of The Late Seamus MacCrosain), Michael Cunningham

909 Kilbegnet Novice Chase (Listed) (5-y-o and up) £5,480 2m.............. (5:00)

827* DANCE BEAT (Ire) 5-10-13 J Shortt, ...(9 to 4 on)   1
576² BANNER GALE (Ire) 7-11-4 C O'Dwyer, ...(10 to 1)   2
744³ STROLL HOME (Ire) 6-11-7 (7*) Mr E Gallagher, ...(10 to 1)   3
LUCKY TOWN (Ire) 5-11-0 C F Swan, ...(8 to 1)   4
TIME AND CHARGES (Ire) 6-10-11 (7*) R P Hogan, (20 to 1)   5
20² ARISTODEMUS 7-11-4 F Woods, ...(11 to 2)   6
Dist: 15l, 3l, 8l, 4l. 4m 8.60s. (6 Ran).

(Mrs E Queally), Mrs John Harrington

910 Peter Casey & Sons Ford Dealers Flat Race (5-y-o) £3,425 2m........ (5:30)

ZIMULANTE (Ire) 12-0 Miss M Olivefalk, ...(6 to 4 fav)   1
LORD EDENBURY (Ire) 11-9 (5*) Mr R Walsh, ...(3 to 1)   2
PHARDANA (Ire) 11-7 (7*) Mr J P McNamara, ...(13 to 2)   3
CARRICKDALE BOY (Ire) 11-7 (7*) Mr G Elliott, ..(12 to 1)   4
745² VALLEY ERNE (Ire) 12-0 Mr P Fenton, ...(7 to 1)   5
HIDDEN HOLLOW (Ire) 12-0 Mr H F Cleary, ...(20 to 1)   6
745³ YELAPA PRINCE (Ire) 12-0 Mr J A Nash, ...(10 to 1)   7
802 PROLOGUE (Ire) 12-0 Mr P F Graffin, ...(20 to 1)   8
THE ZAFFRING (Ire) 11-7 (7*) Mr S M Duffy, ...(25 to 1)   9
829 PATPAY LAD (Ire) 11-7 (7*) Mr M Madden, ...(20 to 1)   10
FOYLE WANDERER (Ire) 11-2 (7*) Miss S McDonogh,
.... (16 to 1)   11
CNOCADRUM VI (Ire) 11-7 (7*) Mr D A Harney, ...(20 to 1)   12
OSCARS LINK (Ire) 11-11 (3*) Mr B M Cash, ...(8 to 1)   13

SAND EEL (Ire) 11-9 Mr G J Harford..............(20 to 1) 14
1214^{4} BUCK AND A HALF (Ire) 11-7 (7*) Mr C P Donnelly, (20 to 1) 15
278^{5} MOLLY WHACK (Ire) 11-2 (7*) Mr A C Coyle,.......(20 to 1) 16
773 SEAMAS AN FEAR (Ire) 11-7 (7*) Mr J S O'Haire,..(33 to 1) 17
STRONG AUCTION (Ire) 11-2 (7*) Mr John P Moloney, ...(33 to 1) 18

Dist: 13l, 6l, 1½l, 5l. 3m 57.90s. (18 Ran).

(Capt D G Swan), Capt D G Swan

SEDGEFIELD (good to firm)
Tuesday October 15th
Going Correction: PLUS 0.40 sec. per fur.

911 John Wade Haulage Conditional Jockeys' Selling Handicap Hurdle Class G (0-95 4-y-o and up) £1,835 2m 5f 110yds.......................(2:15)

817 RED JAM JAR [92] 11-12-0 G Cahill, made virtually all, drvn *clr betw last 2, rdn out*..................(7 to 2 op 9 to 4) 1
723 CLASSIC CREST (Ire) [76] (v) 5-10-11 Michael Brennan, *wtd wth, improved fnl circuit, effrt frm 2 out, kpt on one pace r-in.* ....(10 to 1 op 8 to 1) 2
890* SHELTON ABBEY [70] (bl) 10-10-6 (7ex) G Hogan, *patiently rdn, niggled alng fnl circuit, effrt aftr 3 out, one pace frm nxt.* ....(9 to 2 op 11 to 4 tchd 5 to 1) 3
698^{3} SOUSON (Ire) [86] (bl) 8-11-1 (7*) Mark Brown, *trkd ldrs, drvn alng aftr 3 out, one pace frm nxt.* (11 to 4 fav tchd 3 to 1) 4
205^{5} HIGH FLOWN (USA) [76] 4-10-11 G Lee, *al wl plcd, wth ldr 3 out, rdn and struggling frm nxt.*.......(14 to 1 op 10 to 1) 5
765^{5} FLINTLOCK (Ire) [77] 6-10-13 R McGrath, *patiently rdn, improved fnl circuit, ridden aftr 3 out, wknd quickly frm nxt.* ....(6 to 1 op 5 to 1 tchd 13 to 2) 6
761 PAPA'S BOY (Ire) [86] 5-11-7 S Taylor, *tracking ldrs whn f 5th.* ....(12 to 1 op 10 to 1) f
689 CHADLEIGH WALK (Ire) [65] 4-10-0 O Burrows, *reminders aftr 4th, badly hmpd by faller nxt, sn tld off, pld up after 3 out.* ....(50 to 1 op 33 to 1) pu
HEAVENS ABOVE [68] 4-10-3^{3} E Callaghan, *struggling to keep up aftr one circuit, tld off whn pld up after 3 out.* ....(33 to 1 op 25 to 1) pu

Dist: 2l, 5l, 3½l, 7l, 19l. 5m 8.10s. a 20.10s (9 Ran).

(C H P Bell), S B Bell

912 Six & Out Handicap Hurdle Class F (0-95 4-y-o and up) £2,101 2m 1f (2:45)

762^{4} CLOVER GIRL [70] (v) 5-10-6 (3*) G Cahill, *wtd wth, steady hdwy 3 out, led betw last 2, drvn clr*....(5 to 1 tchd 6 to 1) 1
FEN TERRIER [90] 4-12-0 A Dobbin, *settled gng wl, chlgd and hit 3 out, rdn betw last 2, kpt on same pace.* ....(11 to 2 op 3 to 1 tchd 6 to 1) 2
MARSDEN ROCK [85] 9-11-3 (7*) S Haworth, *patiently rdn, improved gng wl 3 out, led bef nxt, hdd and one pace betw last 2*......................(7 to 2 op 3 to 1 tchd 11 to 4) 3
727^{2} SIMAND [78] 4-11-2 J Callaghan, *al pressing ldrs, effrt and drvn alng bef 2 out, one pace betw last two.* ....(5 to 2 fav tchd 11 to 4) 4
665^{9} FLY TO THE END (USA) [73] (v) 6-10-12 D Byrne, *made most till hdd appr 2 out, fdd bef last*......(16 to 1 op 12 to 1) 5
727^{8} MARCO MAGNIFICO (USA) [74] (v) 6-10-13 A Thornton, *settled in tch, effrt hfwy, und pres aftr 3 out, wknd quickly.* ....(9 to 1 op 8 to 1 tchd 10 to 1) 6
792^{6} DARK MIDNIGHT (Ire) [61] 7-9-13^{2} (3*) D Walsh, *pressed ldrs to hfwy, struggling aftr 3 out, sn lost tch.* ....(20 to 1 op 14 to 1 tchd 25 to 1) 7
766^{6} SALKELD KING (Ire) [75] 4-10-13 P Waggott, *chsd ldrs, hmpd bend aftr 3rd, struggling bef 3 out, lost tch, tld off.* ....(25 to 1 tchd 33 to 1) 8
727^{5} AIDE MEMOIRE (Ire) [77] 7-11-2 K Johnson, *wth ldrs, feeling pace and losing grnd whn slpd and f appr 2 out.* ....(11 to 1 op 8 to 1 tchd 12 to 1) su
817^{6} ANOTHER NICK [70] 10-10-9 B Storey, *lost grnd quickly hfwy, tld off whn pld up bef 2 out*.....(50 to 1 op 25 to 1) pu

Dist: 1½l, nk, 3l, 1¾l, 11l, 25l, nk. 4m 3.30s. a 17.30s (10 Ran).

(Kevin M L Brown), B Ellison

913 Red Onion Handicap Hurdle Class D (0-125 4-y-o and up) £2,745 2m 5f 110yds.......................(3:15)

529^{2} CLEAN EDGE (USA) [102] 4-10-1 (3*) E Husband, *settled midfield, improved to ld bef 2 out, forged clr frm betw last two.* ....(15 to 2 op 7 to 1 tchd 8 to 1) 1
764* NOTABLE EXCEPTION [106] 7-10-10 P Niven, *nvr far away, jnd issue frm 3 out, rdn and one pace from betw last 2.* .... (2 to 1 fav op 9 to 4 tchd 5 to 2 and 7 to 4) 2
765^{2} SCARBA [96] 8-9-7 (7*) M Newton, *patiently rdn, improved appr 3 out, ridden bef nxt, one pace.* ....(5 to 1 op 6 to 1 tchd 9 to 2) 3
DOWN THE FELL [117] 7-11-7 N Williamson, *led till hdd 3 out, wknd quickly bef nxt, tld off*..........(8 to 1 op 7 to 1) 4
EXEMPLAR (Ire) [96] 8-9-10^{3} (7*) Mr P Murray, *hit second, lost tch hfwy, tld off*....... (20 to 1 op 16 to 1 tchd 25 to 1) 5

765* RED VALERIAN [125] (v) 5-11-9 (5*) Michael Brennan, *settled midfield, improved hfwy, led 3 out till bef nxt, broke dwn badly and pld up betw last 2*...................(5 to 2 op 7 to 4) pu
URBAN DANCING (USA) [111] 7-10-12 (3*) G Cahill, *patiently rdn, effrt appr 3 out, no imprsn, struggling whn pld up betw last 2*..........(11 to 1 op 10 to 1 tchd 12 to 1) pu

Dist: 9l, 5l, 30l, 28l. 5m 5.00s. a 17.00s (7 Ran).

(Mrs Sue Adams), J Mackie

914 Chilton Club Handicap Chase Class E (0-115 5-y-o and up) £2,990 2m 110yds........................(3:45)

774^{3} CIRCULATION [76] (v) 10-9-13^{2} (3*) D Walsh, *set str pace till blun badly and hdd 5th, chsd ldr aftr, styd on grimly und pres to ld nr finish*..........(12 to 1 op 10 to 1 tchd 14 to 1) 1
THUNDERSTRUCK [82] 10-10-6 N Williamson, *chsd clr ldr, lft in ld 5th, blun 8th, drvn alng frm betw last 2, worn dwn nr finish*...............................(11 to 2 op 4 to 1) 2
863^{3} BELDINE [100] 11-11-10 A Dobbin, *chsd clr ldg pair thrght,* [illegible] ....(7 to 4 fav tchd 15 to 8) 3
548^{3} TRESIDDER [99] 14-11-9 R Garritty, *al struggling in last pl, tld off*.................................(100 to 30 op 5 to 2) 4
791* ANTHONY BELL [90] 10-11-0 Richard Guest, *drvn alng to go pace, al beh, tld off whn pld up bef 3 out.* ....(100 to 30 op 5 to 2 tchd 7 to 2) pu

Dist: 1½l, 19l, 15l. 4m 7.40s. a 15.40s (5 Ran).

(John Singleton), D McCain

915 Scotmail Handicap Chase Class F (0-100 5-y-o and up) £2,823 3m 3f .... (4:15)

697 JENDEE (Ire) [82] 8-10-7 (3*) G Cahill, *wtd wth, improved to ld 7 out, jnd and jmpd rght 2 out, hdd last, rallied gmely to lead cl hme*..................(16 to 1 op 14 to 1 tchd 20 to 1) 1
778* THE GALLOPIN'MAJOR (Ire) [87] (bl) 6-11-1 N Smith, *nvr far away, improved to nose ahead last, idled and rdn r-in, worn dwn cl hme*..........(13 to 8 fav op 6 to 4 tchd 7 to 4) 2
726^{4} GRAND SCENERY (Ire) [90] 8-11-4 N Williamson, *patiently rdn, promissing effrt whn hit 6 out and 3 out, struggling frm betw last 2*.............. (7 to 2 op 4 to 1 tchd 3 to 1) 3
793* TRUMPET [100] 7-11-9 (5*) Michael Brennan, *al frnt rnk, led 3rd to 13th, styd hndy till fdd frm 2 out*....(6 to 1 op 5 to 1) 4
726* FORWARD GLEN [79] (bl) 9-10-7 R Supple, *nvr far away, ev ch 4 out, rdn aftr nxt, sn outpcd*......... (6 to 1 op 5 to 1) 5
816^{4} UPWELL [72] 12-10-0 K Johnson, *led to 3rd, rdn and lost pl quickly fnl circuit, tld off.* ....(20 to 1 op 16 to 1 tchd 25 to 1) 6
737^{5} BLAZING DAWN [84] 9-10-12 B Storey, *trkd ldrs, led 13th till blun badly and hdd 7 out, sn tld off, pld up bef 3 out.* ....(6 to 1 op 5 to 1) pu

Dist: Nk, 21l, 1¼l, 6l, 28l. 6m 50.30s. a 17.30s (7 Ran).
SR: 17/21/3/11/ (Ferrograph Limited), B Ellison

916 LBW Novices' Chase Class E (4-y-o and up) £3,036 2m 5f........... (4:45)

26 LE DENSTAN 9-11-5 T Reed, *settled off the pace, effrt whn nrly f 5 out, rallied gmely to ld last 50 yards.* ....(20 to 1 op 16 to 1) 1
724* BLUE CHARM (Ire) 6-11-12 A Maguire, *al hndy, led aftr 3rd, hrd pressed frm haflway, worn dwn last 50 yards.* ....(6 to 5 on op 5 to 4 on tchd Evens) 2
764^{2} VAL DE RAMA (Ire) 7-11-12 Richard Guest, *patiently rdn, drvn alng to improve frm 4 out, chlgd last, outpcd r-in.* ....(7 to 2 op 3 to 1) 3
699^{3} BUYERS DREAM (Ire) (v) 6-11-2 (3*) G Cahill, *led till aftr 3rd, styd upsides till hit 2 out, no extr*........ (8 to 1 op 6 to 1) 4
UP FOR RANSOME (Ire) 7-11-5 N Williamson, *chsd ldrs, effrt and reminders 9th, struggling aftr nxt, sn lost tch.* ....(14 to 1 op 8 to 1 tchd 16 to 1) 5
724^{4} WEE WIZARD (Ire) 7-11-5 P Waggott, *nvr gng wl, reminders bef hfwy, tld off*...................... (8 to 1 op 10 to 1) 6
FOREVER SHY (Ire) 8-10-12 (7*) Miss S Lamb, *f 1st.* (50 to 1) f
KARENASTINO 5-10-10 (7*) Mr P Murray, *chasing ldg pair whn blun and uns rdr 8th*............(50 to 1 op 33 to 1) ur
764 RAPID FIRE (Ire) 8-11-0 (5*) E Callaghan, *brght dwn 1st.* ....(14 to 1 op 10 to 1) bd
814^{6} TONY'S FEELINGS 8-11-5 A Thornton, *struggling to keep in tch hfwy, tld off whn pld up bef 2 out*...(33 to 1 op 20 to 1) pu

Dist: 1¾l, 8l, 1l, 20l, 30l. 5m 18.70s. a 22.70s (10 Ran).

(L Wright), Mrs D Thomson

917 100 Not Out Intermediate Open National Hunt Flat Class H (4,5,6-y-o) £1,259 2m 1f.................... (5:15)

700* DURAID (Ire) 4-11-13 Richard Guest, *settled gng wl, smooth hdwy to ld o'r 4 fs out, ran on readily.* ....(7 to 4 on tchd 2 to 1 on and 6 to 4 on) 1
BIG PERKS (Ire) 4-11-3 R Marley, *chsd ldrs, improved to go second strt, styd on same pace last 2 fs.* ....(9 to 1 op 4 to 1 tchd 10 to 1) 2
GAZANALI (Ire) 5-11-4 N Bentley, *chsd clr ldr, effrt entering strt, kpt on same pace last 2 fs*.........(12 to 1 op 6 to 1) 3

MR HATCHET (Ire) 5-10-13 (5*) G F Ryan, *rcd freely in ld, hdd o'r 4 fs out, struggling bef strt, tld off.* .... (16 to 1 op 10 to 1 tchd 20 to 1) 4
SILVER MINX 4-11-3 P Niven, *settled off the pace, nvr rch chalg pos.* .... (7 to 1 op 5 to 1 tchd 8 to 1) 5
WILD CAT BAY 4-10-12 (5*) E Callaghan, *chsd clr ldg pair till o'r 4 fs out, lost tch, tld off.* .... (33 to 1 tchd 50 to 1) 6
TOSHIBA HOUSE (Ire) 5-10-10 (3*) G Cahill, *last and reminders bef hfwy, tld off.* .... (33 to 1 op 12 to 1) 7
AIR BRIDGE 4-11-3 N Williamson, *beh and reminders hfwy, tld off.* .... (10 to 1 op 7 to 1 tchd 11 to 1) 8
740[4] WATER FONT (Ire) 4-11-3 A Roche, *settled off the pace, steady hdwy to chase ldg trio appr strt, pld up 2 fs out, dismounted.* .... (5 to 1 op 12 to 1 tchd 14 to 1) pu
Dist: 2½l, ½l, dist, 6l, 5l, 13l, 1¼l. 3m 56.80s. (9 Ran).
(A Suddes), Denys Smith

EXETER (good to firm)
Wednesday October 16th
Going Correction: PLUS 0.35 sec. per fur.

918 Dean & Dyball Conditional Jockeys' Selling Handicap Hurdle Class G (0-90 4-y-o and up) £1,829 2m 3f..... (2:10)

768[2] CASHFLOW CRISIS (Ire) [76] 4-10-10 (3*) S Ryan, *hld up, hdwy appr 5th, led sn aftr 3 out, clr nxt, heavily eased r-in.* ....(11 to 4 fav op 3 to 1) 1
FAWLEY FLYER [74] 7-10-7 (5*) J Power, *al prmnt, wnt second appr 2 out, ran on, no ch wth wnr.* .. (10 to 1 op 7 to 1) 2
891[8] CATWALKER (Ire) [63] (bl) 5-10-0 Sophie Mitchell, *hld up in rear, hdwy 2 out, nvr nr to chal.* .... (9 to 1 op 7 to 1 tchd 10 to 1) 3
877[3] AUVILLAR (USA) [70] (v) 8-10-8 Michael Brennan, *trkd ldr, led appr 6th, hdd sn aftr 3 out, wknd quickly.* (10 to 1 op 8 to 1) 4
629[3] MARIO'S DREAM (Ire) [65] 8-10-3 G Hogan, *unruly strt, al beh, tld off.* .... (12 to 1 op 14 to 1 tchd 10 to 1) 5
772 BUGLET [90] (v) 6-12-0 D Walsh, *led till hdd appr 6th, sn beh, tld off.* .... (15 to 2 op 9 to 2 tchd 8 to 1) 6
100 CELCIUS [71] 12-10-4 (5*) G Supple, *hld up, rdn 3 out, sn btn, tld off.* .... (11 to 1 op 8 to 1) 7
499[6] AGAINST THE CLOCK [63] 4-9-7 (7*) T O'Connor, *al beh, tld off.* .... (20 to 1 op 14 to 1) 8
842* KING OF BABYLON (Ire) [77] 4-11-0 (7ex) L Aspell, *slwly away, wl in rear whn f 4th.* .... (4 to 1 op 3 to 1) f
COLOUR SCHEME [77] 9-10-8 (7*) B McGann, *chsd ldrs till wknd 5th, tld off whn pld up bef last.* .. (20 to 1 op 33 to 1) pu
Dist: ¾l, 16l, 10l, 25l, 7l, 9l, 15l. 4m 31.60s. a 15.60s (10 Ran).
(C D Tilly), J W Mullins

919 Dean & Dyball Novices' Hurdle Class E (4-y-o and up) £2,305 2m 3f..... (2:40)

859* COURBARIL 4-11-11 (7*) G Supple, *hld up in tch, hdwy to join ldr 5th, led 3 out, lft clr last.* .... (5 to 4 fav op Evens) 1
RUM CUSTOMER 5-10-12 B Fenton, *hld up in rear, hdwy 6th, wnt 3rd 3 out, rdn whn lft second last.* .... (12 to 1 op 8 to 1) 2
667[6] CROWN IVORY (NZ) 8-10-12 S Fox, *hld up in rear, hdwy appr 5th, outpcd 3 out, nvr dngrs aftr.* .... (33 to 1 op 20 to 1) 3
CASTLECONNER (Ire) 5-10-12 J Frost, *hld up in rear, some hdwy 2 out, nvr dngrs.* .... (25 to 1 op 12 to 1) 4
846* SIGMA RUN (Ire) 7-11-5 M A Fitzgerald, *led 4th, hdd 6th, wknd appr 2 out.* .... (12 to 1 op 10 to 1) 5
689[8] SPUMANTE 4-10-11 B Powell, *chsd ldr to 4th, wknd aftr nxt.* .... (8 to 1 op 10 to 1 tchd 12 to 1) 6
837[4] BITE THE BULLET 5-10-12 L Harvey, *prmnt till wknd 6th.* .... (100 to 1 op 33 to 1) 7
796 CROWNHILL CROSS 5-10-7 (5*) D Salter, *in tch to 5th, sn beh, tld off.* .... (100 to 1 op 50 to 1) 8
CONNAUGHT'S PRIDE 5-10-7 A P McCoy, *chsd ldrs till wknd 6th, tld off.* .... (9 to 4 op 7 to 2) 9
FROME LAD 4-10-4 (7*) J Power, *prmnt till wknd aftr 5th, tld off.* .... (14 to 1 tchd 16 to 1) 10
TRAIL BOSS (Ire) 5-10-12 J F Titley, *al prmnt, led 6th, hdd 3 out, chsd wnr, tired whn f last.* .... (6 to 1 op 3 to 1) f
KIRBY MOORSIDE 5-10-12 J Railton, *al beh, tld off whn pld up bef last.* .... (100 to 1 op 33 to 1) pu
BICKLEIGH BELLE 6-10-4 (3*) T Dascombe, *slwly away, not jump wl, tld off whn pld up bef 2 out.* (100 to 1 op 50 to 1) pu
Dist: 10l, 8l, 4l, 2½l, 5l, ¾l, dist, ½l, dist. 4m 32.40s. a 16.40s (13 Ran).
SR: 7/-/-/-/-/-/ (Richard Green (Fine Paintings)), M C Pipe

920 Dean & Dyball Challenge Trophy Novices' Chase Class D (5-y-o and up) £3,758 2¾m 110yds............ (3:10)

769* PONGO WARING (Ire) 7-11-6 J F Titley, *al hndy, wnt second tenth, led 4 out, rdn clr r-in.* .... (13 to 8 fav op 7 to 4 tchd 6 to 4) 1
FRAZER ISLAND (Ire) 7-10-11 (3*) L Aspell, *hld up in rear, hdwy tenth, chlgd 4 out, sn rdn, eased whn held r-in.* .... (7 to 1 op 5 to 1 tchd 8 to 1) 2
753[7] DUBELLE 6-11-1 A P McCoy, *al prmnt, led tenth till hit and hdd 4 out, sn btn.* .... (15 to 2 op 6 to 1) 3
751[2] OUR NIKKI 6-10-9 S Burrough, *in rear, hit second, hdwy aftr 9th, one pace frm 5 out.* .... (8 to 1 op 7 to 1) 4
751[4] WESTERLY GALE (Ire) 6-11-0 M A Fitzgerald, *led to tenth, lost tch aftr nxt.* .... (7 to 2 op 4 to 1) 5
EMERALD KNIGHT (Ire) 6-10-9 (5*) P Henley, *hld up in rear, outpcd 11th, tld off.* .... (5 to 1 op 3 to 1) 6
585[4] THE LAST MISTRESS 9-10-9 W Marston, *chsd ldr till wknd quickly tenth, tld off.* ... (40 to 1 op 33 to 1 tchd 50 to 1) 7
Dist: 8l, 13l, 6l, 5l, dist, 4l. 5m 45.70s. a 25.70s (7 Ran).
(Miss H Knight), Miss H C Knight

921 William Hill 'Golden Oldies' Stakes Class H Invitation (4-y-o and up) £1,502 1m 5f.................. (3:40)

696* SHAHRANI 4-12-0 Peter Scudamore, *made all, sn clr, unchlgd.* ..... (7 to 2 on tchd 11 to 4 on and 5 to 2 on) 1
BRIGHT SAPPHIRE 10-12-0 Mark Caswell, *al prmnt in chasing grp, wnt second o'r 2 fs out, no ch wth wnr.* .... (14 to 1 op 12 to 1) 2
SAAFI (Ire) 5-12-0 Colin Brown, *slwly away, hdwy hfwy, one pace fnl 3 fs.* .... (25 to 1 op 12 to 1) 3
TRAUMA (Ire) 4-11-9 Gordon Holmes, *in tch, chsd wnr aftr 4 fs to o'r 2 out, one pace.* .... (33 to 1 op 16 to 1) 4
796[9] MY HARVINSKI 6-12-0 Simon Earle, *hld up, effrt o'r 2 fs out, sn btn.* .... (33 to 1 op 20 to 1 tchd 50 to 1) 5
CALOGAN 9-12-0 Bryan Smart, *chsd ldrs till wknd 5 fs out, tld off.* .... (20 to 1 op 14 to 1) 6
SCOTTISH PARK 7-12-2 Mike Gallemore, *al towards rear, tld off.* .... (10 to 1 op 8 to 1) 7
RISKY ROSE 4-11-13 Peter Smith, *slwly away, al beh, tld off.* .... (5 to 1 op 7 to 2 tchd 11 to 2) 8
758 BALLYHAYS (Ire) 7-12-4 Chris Broad, *slwly away, tld off hfwy.* .... (50 to 1 op 33 to 1 tchd 66 to 1) 9
Dist: 11l, 8l, hd, 6l, 19l, 2l, 19l, 20l. 3m 12.20s. (9 Ran).
(A S Helaissi And Mr S Helaissi), M C Pipe

922 Dean & Dyball Novices' Handicap Chase Class E (0-100 5-y-o and up) £3,235 2m 1f 110yds.......... (4:10)

630[2] BISHOPS CASTLE (Ire) [82] 8-11-10 J Frost, *led second, made rst, clr 2 out, cmftbly.* .... (11 to 4 op 9 to 4) 1
769[3] CHICKABIDDY [78] 8-11-6 M A Fitzgerald, *in tch till outpcd 5th, hdwy to go second 2 out, ran on r-in.* .... (5 to 2 fav tchd 11 to 4) 2
769[5] I REMEMBER YOU (Ire) [67] 6-10-4 (5*) D Salter, *prmnt whn hmpd second, hdwy to chase wnr 5 out, wknd 2 out.* ....(7 to 1 op 6 to 1) 3
SPEEDY SNAPSGEM (Ire) [70] 6-10-12 A P McCoy, *led till swrvd lft and hdd second, styd in tch till wknd appr 4 out, tld off.* .... (7 to 2 op 3 to 1 tchd 4 to 1) 4
771 TANGO'S DELIGHT [75] 8-11-3 B Powell, *al beh, tld off 5 out.* .... (25 to 1 op 16 to 1) 5
758 IDIOM [70] 9-10-12 J R Kavanagh, *hld up in tch, f 5 out.* ....(6 to 1 op 5 to 1) f
843 LAURA LYE (Ire) [62] 6-10-4 J Railton, *slwly away, in rear whn f 4th.* .... (20 to 1 op 12 to 1) f
Dist: 1¾l, 13l, dist, 9l. 4m 21.80s. a 16.80s (7 Ran).
(A E C Electric Fencing Ltd (Hotline)), R G Frost

923 Dean & Dyball Handicap Hurdle Class C (0-130 4-y-o and up) £2,717 2m 1f 110yds....................... (4:40)

CRACK ON [115] 6-12-0 A P McCoy, *al gng wl, hld up in tch, led on bit appr 2 out, very easily.* ....(7 to 4 jt-fav op 6 to 4 tchd 15 to 8) 1
772* OUT RANKING (Fr) [115] 4-11-13 C Maude, *led till hdd appr 2 out, sn rdn, one pace.* .... (7 to 4 jt-fav op 6 to 4) 2
772[2] LITTLE HOOLIGAN [88] (bl) 5-9-7 (7*) Mr R Thornton, *trkd ldr, rdn appr 3 out, btn bef nxt.* .... (9 to 4 op 5 to 2) 3
752[6] ECHO DE JANSER (Fr) [115] 4-11-6 (7*) Mr G Shenkin, *hld up in tch, rdn appr 5th, wknd quickly, tld off.* .... (12 to 1 op 14 to 1) 4
Dist: 9l, 20l, dist. 4m 8.10s. a 12.10s (4 Ran).
SR: 40/30/-/-/ (D R Peppiatt), P J Hobbs

924 Dean & Dyball Mares' Only Novices' Handicap Hurdle Class E (0-100 4-y-o and up) £2,169 2m 1f 110yds... (5:10)

770[5] LAST LAUGH (Ire) [79] (bl) 4-11-7 A P McCoy, *al prmnt, led appr 2 out, rdn and wknd r-in, jst hld on.* (4 to 1 op 7 to 2) 1
756[3] DRAGONMIST (Ire) [63] 6-10-6 D J Burchell, *hld up, hdwy to ld 4th, rdn and hdd appr 2 out, rallied r-in, jst fld.* ....(4 to 1 op 7 to 2 tchd 5 to 1) 2
800 HYDEMILLA [75] 6-11-1 (3*) G Hogan, *chsd ldrs, rdn and wknd appr 2 out.* ....(5 to 1 op 4 to 1 tchd 6 to 1) 3
891[2] BURNT SIENNA (Ire) [79] (v) 4-11-7 W McFarland, *pld hrd, led till hdd appr 2 out, sn wknd.* (7 to 2 op 3 to 1 tchd 4 to 1) 4
854 KESANTA [85] 6-11-7 (7*) J Power, *in tch till wknd 3 out.* ....(3 to 1 fav op 7 to 2 tchd 4 to 1) 5
WORTH THE WAIT [58] 5-10-0 S Wynne, *al beh, tld off, fnshd lme.* .... (33 to 1 op 25 to 1 tchd 50 to 1) 6
WELTON RAMBLER [57] 9-9-12[1] (3*) T Dascombe, *al beh, tld off 5th.* .... (66 to 1 op 33 to 1) 7

856 INDIAN CROWN [66] 6-10-2 (7*) J Harris, *second whn ran out*
 3rd . . . . (10 to 1 op 12 to 1 tchd 16 to 1)   ro
Dist: Sht-hd, 12l, 6l, 5l, dist, 11l. 4m 14.80s. a 18.80s (8 Ran).
(Charles Eden Limited), K C Bailey

NAVAN (IRE) (yielding)
Wednesday October 16th

925
**Virginia Chase (5-y-o and up) £3,425
2m 1f . . . . (3:00)**

553³ HEIST 7-11-8 M P Dwyer, ... (4 to 1 on)   1
804 THE BOURDA 10-11-4 J P Broderick, ... (8 to 1)   2
744 WILD BROOK (Ire) 6-10-11 (7*) Mr J L Cullen, . . (20 to 1)   3
 LE GINNO (Fr) 9-11-4 T P Treacy, ... (6 to 1)   4
Dist: 4l, 8l, 1l. 4m 17.20s. (4 Ran).
(Mrs G Mathews), Noel Meade

926
**Wilkinstown Handicap Chase (0-123
4-y-o and up) £3,082 2½m . . . . . . (4:00)**

 IF YOU BELIEVE (Ire) [-] 9-10-13 (3*) B Bowens, ... (7 to 1)   1
780 DRINDOD (Ire) [-] 7-10-3 (3*) D J Casey, ... (10 to 1)   2
743 SPRINGFORT LADY (Ire) [-] 7-10-7 T Hazlett, (5 to 1 co-fav)   3
441³ FRIDAY THIRTEENTH (Ire) [-] 7-11-1 F Stockdale, . . (6 to 1)   4
 TALK TO YOU LATER [-] 10-10-2 W Harnett, ... (25 to 1)   5
635⁶ STRONG HURRICANE [-] 9-10-12 C O'Dwyer, . . (5 to 1 co-
 fav)   6
729* THE GOPHER (Ire) [-] 7-11-0 T Wheeler, ... (5 to 1 co-fav)   7
679⁶ LOUGH ATALIA [-] 9-9-9 T P Treacy, ... (12 to 1)   f
743³ HURDY [-] 9-11-1 K F O'Brien, ... (5 to 1 co-fav)   pu
Dist: 9l, 2l, 2½l, 1½l. 5m 8.50s. (9 Ran).
(Harry Smyth), H Smyth

927
**Juvenile Hurdle (3-y-o) £3,082 2m
. . . . (4:30)**

712⁶ MISS ROBERTO (Ire) 10-13 K F O'Brien, ... (5 to 1)   1
574* GO SASHA (Ire) 10-13 (5*) T Martin, ... (15 to 8 fav)   2
442² SPIONAN (USA) 10-7 (7*) P J Dobbs, ... (16 to 1)   3
 TALLY-HO MAJOR (Ire) 11-0 M P Dwyer, ... (15 to 2)   4
 J J BABOO (Ire) 11-0 C O'Dwyer, ... (10 to 1)   5
 KIRIBATI (Ire) 10-7 (7*) B J Geraghty, ... (14 to 1)   6
425* IACCHUS (Ire) 11-4 C F Swan, ... (7 to 1)   7
574⁶ THE GENT (Ire) 11-0 P L Malone, ... (25 to 1)   8
 MAGICAL IMPACT (Ire) 11-0 A Powell, ... (33 to 1)   9
 SWEET SEPTEMBER (Ire) 10-4 (5*) G Cotter, ... (20 to 1)   10
442⁸ KILLARY (Ire) 11-0 J P Broderick, ... (14 to 1)   11
 TURKISHMAN (Fr) 11-0 F Woods, ... (14 to 1)   12
882 TARAKHEL (USA) 11-0 J Shortt, ... (16 to 1)   pu
 BALLALANIN (Ire) 11-0 T J Mitchell, ... (25 to 1)   pu
Dist: 6l, 12l, 6l, 13l. 3m 52.40s. (14 Ran).
(Mrs T Dalton), Martin Brassil

928
**Kingscourt Maiden Hurdle (4-y-o and
up) £3,082 2m . . . . (5:00)**

590⁴ DIGADUST (Ire) 4-11-9 M Duffy, ... (7 to 4 fav)   1
802² FANE PATH 4-11-9 Mr G J Harford, ... (10 to 1)   2
678³ OMAR (USA) 7-12-0 C O'Dwyer, ... (4 to 1)   3
741⁵ LAUGHING FONTAINE (Ire) 6-11-6 J P Broderick, (20 to 1)   4
 DOOK'S DELIGHT (Ire) 5-12-0 L P Cusack, ... (16 to 1)   5
 DASHING DOLLAR (Ire) 5-11-6 C F Swan, ... (16 to 1)   6
829⁸ JACK CHAUCER 4-11-4 J Shortt, ... (25 to 1)   7
 DOONE BRAES (Ire) 6-11-3 (3*) U Smyth, ... (25 to 1)   8
590² JACK YEATS (Ire) 4-11-4 T P Treacy, ... (6 to 1)   9
 OUR DUCHESS (Ire) 5-11-1 K F O'Brien, ... (25 to 1)   10
681⁵ TINERANA GLOW (Ire) 4-10-13 D T Evans, ... (16 to 1)   11
560⁷ SHAWAHIN 4-11-9 M P Dwyer, ... (25 to 1)   12
 MARINERS REEF (Ire) 5-10-8 (7*) D McCullagh, . . (20 to 1)   13
684⁸ SAN SIRO (Ire) 6-10-13 (7*) Mr Edgar Byrne, ... (25 to 1)   14
 FALLOW TRIX (Ire) 4-10-11 (7*) Mr J Keville, ... (16 to 1)   15
 WYN WAN SOON (Ire) 5-11-6 D H O'Connor, ... (25 to 1)   16
805² ROCHE MENTOR (Ire) 6-11-6 P L Malone, ... (25 to 1)   17
 HOLLYBANK BUCK (Ire) 6-11-6 A Powell, ... (25 to 1)   18
 DEERE REPH (Ire) 5-10-8 (7*) B J Geraghty, ... (14 to 1)   19
 STAR CLUB (Ire) 4-11-4 H Rogers, ... (12 to 1)   20
 MANNOORI (Ire) 4-10-13 (5*) G Cotter, ... (14 to 1)   21
 RAVEN'S CAVE (Ire) 5-10-8 (7*) M A Cooney, ... (25 to 1)   22
 CHUCK'S TREASURE (Ire) 7-11-7 (7*) A O'Shea, . . (25 to 1)   23
 TIME FOR A WINNER (Ire) 5-11-1 F Woods, ... (25 to 1)   24
716⁶ SLIGO CHAMPION (Ire) 5-11-6 J K Kinane, ... (33 to 1)   25
 KING PUCK (Ire) 4-10-13 (5*) T Martin, ... (25 to 1)   26
 JUST SUPREME (Ire) 5-11-6 J P Byrne, ... (16 to 1)   27
773 STEMAR (Ire) 5-11-6 T J Mitchell, ... (16 to 1)   28
 BELVOIR BELLE (Ire) 4-10-6 (7*) J M Maguire, ... (20 to 1)   ur
Dist: 2l, ¾l, ½l, nk. 3m 56.50s. (29 Ran).
(Mrs Patrick Flynn), Patrick Joseph Flynn

929
**Oristown I.N.H. Flat Race (6-y-o and
up) £2,740 2m . . . . (5:30)**

 CORAL SEA 6-11-7 (7*) Mr A Ross, ... (14 to 1)   1
 PULKERRY (Ire) 6-11-7 (7*) Mr E Sheehy, ... (5 to 2 fav)   2
 LANTURN (Ire) 6-11-9 (5*) Mr R Walsh, ... (8 to 1)   3
722⁵ HOLY GROUNDER (Ire) 7-11-7 (7*) Miss M Horgan, (4 to 1)   4

 FOLLY ROAD (Ire) 6-11-7 (7*) Mr D A Harvey, ... (10 to 1)   5
 TWO IN TUNE (Ire) 8-11-7 (7*) Mr K O'Sullivan, ... (10 to 1)   6
 WICKLOW SONG (Ire) 6-11-7 (7*) Mr G Elliott, ... (10 to 1)   7
 SWIFT GLIDER (Ire) 7-11-2 (7*) Mr C A Murphy, . . (14 to 1)   8
884⁵ CHARMING DUKE (Ire) 6-11-7 (7*) Mr D Delaney, . (10 to 1)   9
 VALLEY OF KINGS (Ire) 6-11-7 (7*) Mr D A Harney, (14 to 1)   10
464 BALLYLENNON LADY (Ire) 6-11-6 (3*) Mr P English,
 . . . . (10 to 1)   11
 HOME I'LL BE (Ire) 6-11-11 (3*) Mr B R Hamilton, (10 to 1)   12
396 CHIEF RANI (Ire) 6-11-7 (7*) Mr A C Coyle, ... (11 to 2)   13
 ARKDEL (Ire) 7-12-0 Mr A R Coonan, ... (16 to 1)   14
Dist: 1l, 1l, 2l, 2l. 4m 0.10s. (14 Ran).
(Cecil Ross), Cecil Ross

WETHERBY (good)
Wednesday October 16th
**Going Correction: MINUS 0.35 sec. per fur. (races
1,3,5,6), MINUS 0.25 (2,4)**

930
**Goldsborough Juvenile Novices' Hur-
dle Class D (3-y-o) £3,055 2m . . . (2:20)**

 LAGAN 10-12 A S Smith, *made all, quickened to go clr last 2,
 ran on wl* . . . . (20 to 1 op 16 to 1)   1
 FALCON'S FLAME (USA) 10-12 R Garritty, *patiently rdn,
 improved frm 3 out, styd on, not pace of wnr*
 . . . . (8 to 1 op 7 to 1)   2
 PHANTOM HAZE 10-12 N Bentley, *sn tracking ldrs, ev ch
 appr 3 out, one pace* . . . . (9 to 2 op 4 to 1)   3
734² GLOBE RUNNER 10-12 A Roche, *wtd wth, improved appr 3
 out, rdn and one pace frm nxt* . . . . . (4 to 1 fav op 3 to 1)   4
 JACKSON PARK 10-12 L Wyer, *nvr far away, ev ch appr 3 out,
 eased whn btn nxt* . . . . (9 to 2 op 4 to 1)   5
 ERIC'S BETT 10-12 Mr K Whelan, *settled to track ldrs, ev ch
 appr 3 out, fdd frm nxt* . . . (7 to 1 op 6 to 1 tchd 8 to 1)   6
664 PHANTOM DANCER 10-12 D Parker, *al wl plcd, ev ch
 appr 3 out, grad wknd* (40 to 1 op 33 to 1 tchd 50 to 1)   7
734 ARROGANT HEIR 11-1³ Mr A Rebori, *settled to track ldrs, ev
 ch appr 3 out, fdd* . . . . (66 to 1 op 50 to 1)   8
 LUCKY BEA 10-12 N Williamson, *patiently rdn, steady hdwy
 appr 3 out, grad wknd frm nxt* . . . . . (10 to 1 op 8 to 1)   9
614 CASHAPLENTY 10-12 Mr D Verco, *pressed ldrs till fdd appr 3
 out* . . . . (66 to 1 op 50 to 1)   10
 SON OF ANSHAN 10-12 J Supple, *chsd ldrs till wknd appr 3
 out* . . . . (33 to 1 op 25 to 1)   11
 ALZOTIC (Ire) 10-12 W Fry, *settled off the pace, nvr nr to chal*
 . . . . (25 to 1 op 20 to 1 tchd 33 to 1)   12
 MOST RESPECTFUL 10-12 P Niven, *chsd ldg bunch, fdd frm
 3 out* . . . . (14 to 1)   13
 GILLING DANCER (Ire) 10-12 B Storey, *settled off the pace,
 nvr dngrs* . . . . (12 to 1 op 10 to 1 tchd 14 to 1)   14
 PROPOLIS POWER (Ire) 10-12 A Thornton, *chsd ldrs to hfwy,
 wknd bef 3 out* . . . . (50 to 1 op 33 to 1)   15
 BRIDLINGTON BAY 10-12 O Pears, *midfield whn f 4th*
 . . . . (25 to 1)   f
819² TALLULAH BELLE 10-7 M Richards, *chasing ldrs whn blun
 and ran out 3rd* . . . . (10 to 1 op 8 to 1)   ur
 AUTOFYR 10-6² (3*) P Midgley, *tld off whn pld up bef 3 out*.
 . . . . (10 to 1 op 50 to 1)   pu
 COUNTESS OF CADIZ (USA) 10-7 A Dobbin, *struggling frm
 3 out, tld off whn pld up bef 3 out* . . . (66 to 1 op 50 to 1)   pu
Dist: 5l, 6l, 4l, 6l, 2l, 9l, 1¾l, nk, 1¼l, ½l. 3m 41.20s. a 0.20s (19 Ran).
SR: 26/21/15/11/5/3/
(Wild Racing), K A Morgan

931
**Bobby Renton Novices' Handicap
Chase Class D (0-105 5-y-o and up)
£3,636 3m 1f . . . . (2:50)**

 MONY-SKIP (Ire) [85] 7-11-9 Richard Guest, *settled gng wl,
 jmpd ahead 3 out, going clr whn hit last, ran on well.*
 . . . . (5 to 2 tchd 9 to 4)   1
726⁵ COMMANDEER (Ire) [73] 6-10-11 A S Smith, *tried to make all,
 hrd pressed frm 6 out, hdd 3 out, kpt on, no ch wth wnr.*
 . . . . (10 to 1 op 7 to 1)   2
708² DEISE MARSHALL (Ire) [80] 8-11-4 A Maguire, *pressed ldr, ev
 ch 4 out, hrd drvn nxt, no extr.*
 . . . . (11 to 8 fav op 13 to 8 tchd 7 to 4)   3
814² QUIXALL CROSSETT [62] 11-9-8¹ (7*) Mr P Murray, *wl plcd
 till lost grnd and reminders hfwy, rallied frm 4 out, staying on
 finish.* . . . . (25 to 1 op 14 to 1)   4
 COOL WEATHER (Ire) [86] 8-11-10 R Supple, *not fluent, chsd
 ldrs, mstk and reminders 6 out, struggling frm nxt.*
 . . . . (13 to 2 op 4 to 1 tchd 7 to 1)   5
 CARSON CITY [82] 9-11-6 P Niven, *patiently rdn, took clr
 order 5 out, drvn alng bef nxt, lost tch, tld off.*
 . . . . (9 to 1 op 7 to 1)   6
Dist: 11l, 7l, 1½l, 7l, 14l. 6m 16.90s. a 30.90s (6 Ran).
(Trevor Hemmings), Mrs S J Smith

932
**Yorkshire-Tyne Tees Television Hand-
icap Hurdle Class C (0-135 4-y-o and
up) £3,574 2m . . . . (3:20)**

110

DESERT FIGHTER [105] 5-10-11 P Niven, *nvr far away, nosed ahead 3 out, rdn and ran on wl frm betw last 2.*
.......................(4 to 1 tchd 9 to 2)   1
736² SARMATIAN (USA) [104] 5-10-10 R Garritty, *tucked away gng wl, str chal frm 3 out, rdn last, styd on.*
.......................(5 to 1 op 4 to 1 tchd 11 to 2)   2
818⁶ PRIZEFIGHTER [114] 5-11-6 O Pears, *wtd wth, improved appr 3 out, feeling pace and rdn nxt, rallied r-in.*
.......................(6 to 4 fav op 5 to 4)   3
DIRECT ROUTE (Ire) [122] 5-12-0 N Williamson, *nvr far away, effrt and mstk 3 out, rdn and one pace frm nxt.*
.......................(11 to 2 op 5 to 1 tchd 6 to 1)   4
DONE WELL (USA) [118] 4-11-9 A Dobbin, *last and hld up, effrt appr 3 out, feeling pace bef nxt, eased whn btn.*
.......................(8 to 1 op 7 to 1 tchd 9 to 1)   5
SHINING EDGE [115] 4-11-1 L Wyer, *al hndy, gd jump to ld 4th, hdd 3 out, fdd.*........(9 to 1 op 10 to 1)   6
ROI DU NORD (Fr) [96] 4-10-1 A Maguire, *pld hrd, led 3rd to nxt, lost tch frm 3 out, tld off.*.........(20 to 1 op 14 to 1)   7
390⁶ TIP IT IN [93] 7-10-0 M Brennan, *led to 3rd, styd hndy to hfwy, lost tch 4 out, tld off.*..........(100 to 1 op 50 to 1)   8
Dist: ¾l, 6l, ½l, 1l, ½l, dist, dist. 3m 44.60s. a 5.30s (8 Ran).
(A Frame), Mrs M Reveley

933 **Gordon Foster Handicap Chase Class C (0-135 5-y-o and up) £4,497 2½m 110yds............(3:50)**

GENERAL COMMAND [114] 8-10-7 R Dunwoody, *jmpd wl, dsptd ld till nosed ahead 6 out, hrd pressed last 3, ran on strly r-in.*....................(11 to 10 on tchd Evens)   1
823⁴ GLEMOT (Ire) [135] 8-12-0 J Osborne, *patiently rdn, steady hdwy aftr 6 out, drw level last 3, ran on one pace r-in.*
.......................(5 to 2 op 2 to 1)   2
DE JORDAAN [115] 9-10-8 N Williamson, *wtd wth, improved frm off the pace aftr 6 out, feeling pace 3 out, no extr frm nxt.*
.......................(20 to 1)   3
763³ CROSS CANNON [114] 10-10-7 A Maguire, *slight ld till hdd 6 out, wknd quickly entering strt, tld off.*.. (8 to 1 op 6 to 1)   4
39⁵ LOCHNAGRAIN (Ire) [111] 8-10-4¹ P Niven, *blun badly and lost grnd 1st, hit 3rd, tld off till pld up bef 2 out.*
.......................(11 to 2 op 6 to 1)   pu
Dist: 3l, 16l, 29l. 4m 53.70s. a 0.70s (5 Ran).
SR: 21/39/3/-/-/   (Robert Ogden), G Richards

934 **Hallfield Novices' Hurdle Class D (4-y-o and up) £3,107 2½m 110yds (4:20)**

SHARE OPTIONS (Ire) 5-10-12 L Wyer, *nvr far away, moved ahead 2 out, drvn out r-in.* (8 to 1 op 6 to 1 tchd 9 to 1)   1
723² ANTARCTIC WIND (Ire) 6-10-12 R Garritty, *al wl plcd, str chal und prss frm betw last 2, kpt on......* (9 to 2 tchd 11 to 2)   2
HIGHBEATH 5-11-5 P Niven, *settled wth chasing grp, improved appr 3 out, styd on same pace frm nxt.*
.......................(3 to 1 fav op 5 to 2 tchd 100 to 30)   3
PARKLIFE (Ire) 4-10-11 H Foster, *led till aftr second, rgn ld 4 out, hdd 2 out, no one pace.*........(9 to 2 tchd 5 to 1)   4
761⁵ RULE OUT THE REST 5-11-5 A Thornton, *al wl plcd, led aftr second till hdd 4 out, fdd bef nxt.*........(10 to 1 op 6 to 1)   5
789² PANGERAN (USA) 4-11-0 J Supple, *pld hrd early, improved frm off the pace bef 3 out, one pace from nxt.*
.......................(12 to 1 op 10 to 1)   6
724 MUSIC BLITZ 5-10-12 T Reed, *settled in tch, effrt appr 3 out, not pace of others.*........(6 to 1 op 10 to 1)   7
EURO THYNE (Ire) 6-10-12 R Dunwoody, *settled off the pace, some hdwy frm 3 out, no imprsn......* (20 to 1 op 16 to 1)   8
LIFEBUOY (Ire) 5-10-12 W Fry, *nvr far away, efrrt whn blun 5th, wknd nxt.*...................(33 to 1)   9
648⁶ JEAN DE FLORETTE (USA) 5-10-9 (3*) E Husband, *chsd ldrs, feeling pace bef 4 out, sn lost tch.*.............(33 to 1)   10
792⁴ TOP SKIPPER (Ire) 4-10-11 A Dobbin, *struggling to keep up hfwy, tld off bef 3 out.*...........(16 to 1 op 12 to 1)   11
EVEZIO RUFO 4-10-11 Mr D Verco, *chsd ldg bunch, struggling bef 4 out, tld off.*........(20 to 1 op 16 to 1)   12
129³ MILLENNIUM MAN 5-10-12 J Callaghan, *settled in tch, feeling pace hfwy, tld off bef 3 out.*......(14 to 1 op 12 to 1)   13
NELSON MUST 6-10-12 A S Smith, *al wl beh, tld off.*
.......................(50 to 1 op 33 to 1)   14
BARAQUETA 4-10-11 O Pears, *struggling bef hfwy, tld off before 3 out.*....................(20 to 1 tchd 25 to 1)   15
WILLIE WANNABE (Ire) 6-10-12 L O'Hara, *pld hrd, lost tch frm hfwy, tld off.*...................(50 to 1)   16
Dist: ¾l, 7l, 2l, 4l, 12l, 11l, 14l, 1¼l, ½l, nk. 4m 50.70s. a 8.70s (16 Ran).
(Steve Hammond), T D Easterby

935 **Askham Richard Novices' Handicap Hurdle Class D (0-105 4-y-o and up) £3,226 3m 1f.............(4:50)**

PEBBLE BEACH (Ire) [79] 6-11-0 J Callaghan, *nvr far away, led bef 3 out, forged clr frm betw last 2.*
.......................(5 to 1 op 4 to 1 tchd 11 to 2 and 6 to 1)   1
723² SMART APPROACH (Ire) [90] 6-11-11 P Niven, *settled gng wl, str chal appr 3 out, rdn bef nxt, not pace of wnr.*
.......................(Evens fav tchd 11 to 8 and 6 to 4)   2
800⁶ LITTLE TINCTURE (Ire) [71] 6-10-6 G Upton, *wth ldrs, led aftr 3rd till hdd 3 out, one pace after....* (7 to 1 op 3 to 1)   3

GARBO'S BOY [78] 6-10-13 W Fry, *led 1st till aftr 3rd, struggling whn pace quickened appr 3 out, fdd.*
.......................(4 to 1 tchd 7 to 1)   4
COOL STEEL (Ire) [77] 4-10-5 (5*) E Callaghan, *trkd ldrs, rdn 8th, struggling aftr nxt, lost tch, tld off.* (20 to 1 op 14 to 1)   5
723 HEDDON HAUGH (Ire) [70] 8-10-5 R Supple, *chsd ldrs, reminders 8th, lost tch bef 4 out, tld off.*
.......................(16 to 1 op 10 to 1 tchd 20 to 1)   6
OLE OLE [79] 10-11-0 T Reed, *led to 1st, jmpd slwly aftr reminders 5th, lost tch, tld off whn pld up betw last 2.*
.......................(33 to 1 op 1 tchd 25 to 1)   pu
Dist: 7l, 18l, 3l, dist, dist. 6m 0.20s. a 14.20s (7 Ran).
(The Pebble Beach Partnership), G M Moore

TAUNTON (good to firm)
Thursday October 17th
Going Correction: MINUS 0.40 sec. per fur.

936 **Watchet Juvenile Novices' Claiming Hurdle Class G (3-y-o) £1,836 2m 1f ....(1:50)**

858* COINTOSSER (Ire) 11-4 S Wynne, *hld up in rear, plenty to do 3 out, rdn and gd hdwy to ld r-in, wndrd, ran on.*
.......................(11 to 10 fav op 6 to 4 tchd Evens)   1
858² BEN BOWDEN 11-3 J Osborne, *chsd ldr, mstks 5th and 3 out, ev ch nxt, rdn and outpcd r-in.*........(9 to 1 op 7 to 1)   2
858³ INDIRA 10-0 W McFarland, *al prmnt, mstk second, led appr 2 out, rdn and hdd r-in......* (3 to 1 op 11 to 4 tchd 7 to 2)   3
848* HEVER GOLF DIAMOND 11-9 N Williamson, *hld up, hdwy 6th, ev ch 2 out, rdn and no extr r-in.*
.......................(15 to 2 op 5 to 1 tchd 8 to 1)   4
767³ ANSOME BOY 11-0 B Clifford, *led till hdd and wknd approoching 2 out.*...................(10 to 1 op 7 to 1)   5
672⁷ KINGS NIGHTCLUB 10-0 (3*) Guy Lewis, *hld up, hdwy 4th, wknd quickly 3 out, tld off.*......(50 to 1 op 25 to 1)   6
LUNAR GRIS 10-0 B Powell, *al beh, tld off.*
.......................(100 to 1 op 50 to 1)   7
RED TIME 11-3 P Holley, *al beh, tld off.* (20 to 1 op 12 to 1)   8
LADY MAGNUM (Ire) 10-9 D Bridgwater, *slwly away, al beh, tld off.*........(40 to 1 op 16 to 1 tchd 50 to 1)   9
BRIN-LODGE (Ire) 10-0 V Slattery, *blun 1st, al beh, tld off.*
.......................(100 to 1 op 33 to 1)   10
767⁸ PEYTON JONES (bl) 10-5 F Jousset, *hmpd second, beh frm hfwy, tld off.*............(100 to 1 op 66 to 1)   11
Dist: 3l, ¾l, ¾l, 13l, dist, 2½l, 3½l, 8l, dist, 5l. 3m 44.80s. a 1.80s (11 Ran).
SR: 4/-/-/4/-/   (M C Pipe), R G Frost

937 **Donyatt Selling Handicap Hurdle Class G (0-90 4-y-o and up) £1,920 2m 1f ....(2:25)**

MUTAWALI (Ire) [68] 6-10-11 D Leahy, *hld up in rear, gd hdwy 6th, rdn to ld r-in, drvn clr.*...........(12 to 1 op 8 to 1)   1
372⁴ MYLORDMAYOR [57] (bl) 9-10-0 R Farrant, *al prmnt, led appr 2 out, hdd last, kpt on......*(11 to 1 op 8 to 1 tchd 12 to 1)   2
784* ALMAPA [80] 4-11-5 (3*) T Dascombe, *mid-div, hdwy 6th, hrd rdn to ld last, sn hdd, kpt on......*(3 to 1 fav op 5 to 2)   3
784² FLEET CADET [77] (bl) 5-11-5 C Maude, *in rear, steady hdwy frm 5th, hrd rdn 2 out, no extr r-in.*..... (7 to 2 op 5 to 2)   4
641⁹ SHARP THRILL [68] 5-10-10 C Llewellyn, *al prmnt, ev ch whn hit 2 out, one pace aftr.* (14 to 1 op 12 to 1 tchd 20 to 1)   5
891⁹ SCALP 'EM (Ire) [60] 8-10-3 Dr P Pritchard, *hld up in mid-div, hdwy 6th, one pace aftr 3 out......*(66 to 1 op 50 to 1)   6
638⁷ MERLINS WISH (USA) [81] (bl) 7-11-10 A P McCoy, *led second, pushed alng frm 6th, hdd appr 2 out, sn btn.*
.......................(8 to 1 op 7 to 1 tchd 10 to 1)   7
824⁸ COLIN'S PRIDE [58] (bl) 5-9-12³ (5*) P Henley, *al towards rear.*...................(11 to 1 op 7 to 1 tchd 12 to 1)   8
859² MIRAMARE [62] 6-10-5 M A Fitzgerald, *led to second, beh frm 6th.*...................(9 to 1 op 7 to 1)   9
891 REEFA'S MILL (Ire) [78] (bl) 4-11-6 D Bridgwater, *chsd ldrs till wknd quickly 6th, tld off......*(20 to 1 op 10 to 1)   10
830⁶ SHALHOLME [57] 6-10-0 N Williamson, *al beh, tld off.*
.......................(40 to 1 op 12 to 1 tchd 50 to 1)   11
595⁵ LUCKY DOMINO [61] 6-10-4 A Maguire, *al beh, tld off.*
.......................(14 to 1 op 10 to 1)   12
Dist: 3½l, sht-hd, 2½l, sht-hd, 4l, 6l, 7l, 4l, 12l, 2½l. 3m 43.90s. a 0.90s (12 Ran).
SR: 6/-/13/7/-/-/   (John Warren), R J Baker

938 **Lansdowne Chemical Handicap Chase Class D (0-120 5-y-o and up) £3,533 3m..............................(3:00)**

763⁴ THE BLUE BOY (Ire) [99] (bl) 8-11-8 N Williamson, *hmpd second, hdwy to ld 6th, hdd 2 out, rallied to lead last, drvn out.*
.......................(11 to 2 op 4 to 1)   1
855* DRUMCULLEN (Ire) [88] 7-10-11 W McFarland, *mstks, wnt second 13th, hit 2 out, hdd last, one pace.*
.......................(11 to 10 on op 11 to 10)   2
831³ HENLEY WOOD [98] 11-11-4 (3*) G Tormey, *chsd ldr to 13th, mstk 5 out, ev ch 3 out till no extr r-in.* (10 to 1 op 5 to 2)   3
785² SLIPPERY MAX [77] 12-10-0 W Marston, *hit 1st, led to 6th, wknd quickly 14th, tld off 4 out.*......(20 to 1 op 12 to 1)   4

NATIONAL HUNT RESULTS 1996-97

840⁵ NICK THE DREAMER [100] 11-11-9 A Thornton, *f second.*
.... (11 to 1 op 7 to 1 tchd 12 to 1) f
771⁴ DAMAS (Fr) [107] (bl) 5-11-13 A P McCoy, *badly hmpd and uns rdr second.*......... (15 to 2 op 6 to 1 tchd 8 to 1) ur
Dist: 2l, nk, dist. 5m 43.20s. a 0.20s (6 Ran).

(T M Morris), P Bowen

939 Tiverton Novices' Hurdle Class E (4-y-o and up) £2,389 2m 1f.......(3:35)

824³ ATH CHEANNAITHE (Fr) 4-10-11 D Bridgwater, *made all, pushed out r-in, cmftbly.*.......... (6 to 4 fav tchd 7 to 4) 1
LONICERA 6-10-2 (5") P Henley, *al prmnt, chsd wnr 5th, hit 3 out, rdn nxt, ran on one pace.*....... (33 to 1 op 12 to 1) 2
783² SECOND COLOURS (USA) 6-10-12 A P McCoy, *not jump wl, chsd wnr 4th till hit nxt, no ch frm 3 out.*
.... (5 to 1 op 14 to 4 tchd 11 to 2) 3
641* SOUTHERN RIDGE 5-11-5 Mr A Holdsworth, *hld up, hdwy 4th, fourth whn blun 3 out, no ch aftr.* (4 to 1 op 100 to 30) 4
279⁵ DESERT CALM (Ire) 7-10-12 P Holley, *hld up, hdwy 6th, nvr on terms.*.................... (12 to 1 op 10 to 1) 5
671 LIL FERMIN 10-10-12 B Powell, *chsd ldrs till wknd 4th, wknd aftr blun nxt, tld off.*........ (66 to 1 op 25 to 1) 6
784 OLD MASTER (Ire) 5-10-12 D Leahy, *al beh, tld off.*
.... (100 to 1 op 20 to 1) 7
RUSSELLS RUNNER 5-10-12 S Burrough, *chsd ldrs till wknd 5th, tld off.*.................. (100 to 1 op 33 to 1) 8
MYSTIC LEGEND 4-10-11 P Hide, *al towards rear, lost tch appr 3 out, tld off.*.. (25 to 1 op 20 to 1 tchd 33 to 1) 9
MR CUBE (Ire) 6-10-12 N Williamson, *al beh, tld off.*
.... (11 to 1 op 8 to 1 tchd 12 to 1) 10
MR JASPER 4-10-11 D Morris, *al beh, tld off.*
.... (100 to 1 op 33 to 1) 11
ANOTHER HUBBLICK 5-10-5 (7") O Burrows, *f second.*
.... (33 to 1 op 16 to 1) f
Dist: 1¾l, 7l, 14l, 2l, 16l, 4l, 5l, 10l, 1l, 11l. 3m 43.80s. a 0.80s (12 Ran).
SR: 7/1/-/-/-/-/ (J Neville), J Neville

940 Cavendish Technology Handicap Hurdle Class E (0-110 4-y-o and up) £2,736 2m 3f 110yds..... (4:05)

709⁷ POER MONAMY [101] (bl) 4-11-10 A P McCoy, *hld up in tch, wnt second 2 out, strly rdn to ld cl hme.*...(4 to 1 op 5 to 2) 1
801³ ZINGIBAR [78] 4-10-1 N Williamson, *trkd ldrs, led and hit 3 out, hrd rdn and cl hme.*........... (3 to 1 op 5 to 2) 2
MUTAZZ (USA) [105] 4-12-0 R Farrant, *trkd ldr, rdn 3 out, wknd nxt.*................. (7 to 4 fav tchd 2 to 1) 3
TAKE A FLYER (Ire) [85] (bl) 6-10-6 (3") T Dascombe, *led, hit 4th, hdd 3 out, rdn and wknd bef nxt.*...(9 to 2 tchd 4 to 1) 4
810² EMPEROR CHANG (USA) [84] 9-10-8 T Kent, *al last, in tch till rdn 3 out, sn wl beh, virtually pld up r-in, tld off.*
.... (8 to 1 op 7 to 1 tchd 10 to 1) 5
Dist: Sht-hd, 6l, 5l, dist. 4m 22.90s. a 4.90s (5 Ran).
(Richard Green (Fine Paintings)), M C Pipe

941 Iseflo Iodine Challenge Cup Novices' Chase Class E (5-y-o and up) £2,828 2m 110yds.................. (4:35)

769⁶ COOLTEEN HERO (Ire) 6-10-12 W McFarland, *made all, clr 7th, mstk 4 out, lft dist clear 3 out.*.......(9 to 4 op 7 to 4) 1
838 ROYAL HAND 6-10-12 B Fenton, *chsd wnr to 4 out, wknd, lft poor second nxt.*.......... (2 to 1 op 7 to 4 tchd 9 to 4) 2
838³ LARKS TAIL 8-10-7 R Bellamy, *hld up in rear, outpcd 7th, wnt second 4 out, held whn f nxt.*......(16 to 1 op 10 to 1) f
843* TENAYESTELIGN 8-11-0 J A McCarthy, *hld up, hdwy and disputing second whn blun and uns rdr 8th.*
.... (13 to 8 fav op 6 to 4 tchd 7 to 4) ur
Dist: Dist. 3m 59.70s. a 7.70s (4 Ran).
(J P M & J W Cook), R H Alner

942 October Standard Open National Hunt Flat Class H (4,5,6-y-o) £1,194 2m 1f .... (5:10)

MRS EM 4-10-12 A P McCoy, *hld up, hdwy o'r 5 fs out, led wl over one out, ran on strly.*............ (7 to 1 op 5 to 1) 1
WOODSTOCK WANDERER (Ire) 4-11-3 A Maguire, *hld up in rear, gd hdwy 5 fs out, ran on to chase wnr ins fnl 2.*
.... (4 to 1 op 3 to 1 tchd 9 to 2) 2
193⁵ MOONLIGHT ESCAPADE (Ire) 5-11-8 (3") T Dascombe, *al prmnt, led hfwy, hdd wl o'r one furlong out, one pace.*
.... (10 to 2 op 3 to 1) 3
231⁵ SUMMERWAY LEGEND 4-10-12 G Bradley, *hld up, hdwy to chase ldrs 7 fs out, outpcd fnl 2.*
.... (4 to 1 op 6 to 1 tchd 8 to 1) 4
456* RED TEL (Ire) 4-11-10 C Maude, *pld hrd, hld up, lost pl on bend o'r 3 fs out, sn btn.*
.... (9 to 4 fav op 2 to 1 tchd 5 to 2) 5
671 LEOPARD LADY 4-10-12 M A Fitzgerald, *prmnt till wknd 3 fs out.*.......... (11 to 1 op 25 to 1) 6
WEATHER WISE 4-10-10 (7") N Willmington, *made most to hfwy, wknd 3 fs out.*.......... (20 to 1 op 10 to 1) 7
DON'T ARGUE 5-11-4 Miss L Blackford, *al in rear.*
.... (66 to 1 op 33 to 1) 8

HIDDEN VALLEY 4-11-3 J Frost, *mid-div, lost tch hfwy.*
.... (33 to 1 op 20 to 1 tchd 50 to 1) 9
LITTLE EMBERS 4-10-12 N Williamson, *al beh.*
.... (25 to 1 op 8 to 1) 10
JOSEPHINE GREY 5-10-13 A Thornton, *al beh.*
.... (66 to 1 op 33 to 1) 11
671 NANJIZAL 4-11-3 V Slattery, *trkd ldrs till wknd sn aftr hfwy.*
.... (33 to 1 op 25 to 1) 12
ROWBET JACK 4-11-3 B Fenton, *al beh, tld off hfwy, pld up ins fnl furlong.*.......... (20 to 1 op 12 to 1) pu
Dist: 5l, 4l, 4l, 9l, ¾l, 5l, 1l, 3½l, 12l, nk. 3m 41.50s. (13 Ran).
(G Z Mizel), P F Nicholls

TIPPERARY (IRE) (soft)
Thursday October 17th

943 Sandown Novice Hurdle (4-y-o and up) £2,740 2m...................(4:30)

731* PALETTE 4-10-9 (5") D R Fox, ... (5 to 4 fav) 1
LOU DELLTLÉCÓTE 4-11-0 R Hughes, ... (4 to 1) 2
731² FRANCES STREET (Ire) 4-10-11 C F Swan, ...(5 to 1) 3
715⁸ SHARATAN (Ire) 4-11-3 T P Treacy, ... (5 to 1) 4
722⁴ FRISKY THYNE (Ire) 7-11-2 P A Roche, ...(20 to 1) 5
MY IRON MAN (Ire) 5-11-2 C O'Dwyer, ... (12 to 1) 6
FLASH OF SPEED (Ire) 5-10-11 K F O'Brien, ...(10 to 1) 7
MAGS SUPER TOI (Ire) 7-10-9 (7") A O'Shea, ...(33 to 1) 8
849 MISSED CONNECTION (Ire) 5-10-6 (5") J Butler, ..(50 to 1) 9
LOTTOVER (Ire) 7-10-11 T Horgan, ...(20 to 1) 10
31⁶ DEEP BIT (Ire) 5-11-2 F Woods, ...(25 to 1) 11
68 BOSTON MELODY (Ire) 4-10-6 J P Broderick, ..(50 to 1) 12
850 STEP IN LINE (Ire) 4-10-4 (7") M D Murphy, ...(33 to 1) 13
Dist: 1l, 5l, 3l, 2½l. 4m 13.10s. (13 Ran).
(Mayden Syndicate), W P Mullins

944 Rosehill Handicap Hurdle (0-130 5-y-o and up) £2,740 2½m............(5:00)

781⁴ RATHGIBBON (Ire) [-] 5-10-7 T P Treacy, ... (6 to 1) 1
ROYAL ROSY (Ire) [-] 5-11-8 F Stockdale, ... (8 to 1) 2
828³ BLAZE OF HONOUR (Ire) [-] 5-11-8 L P Cusack, ..(4 to 1) 3
DANCING VISION (Ire) [-] 6-10-11 F Woods, ...(9 to 1) 4
MIROSWAKI (USA) [-] 6-11-10 T Horgan, ...(6 to 1) 5
DARK SWAN (Ire) [-] 6-11-6 C F Swan, ...(10 to 1) 6
746 FRAU DANTE (Ire) [-] 6-10-6 C O'Dwyer, ...(2 to 1 fav) 7
NAMELOC [-] 12-10-7 D T Wheeler, ...(10 to 1) 8
THATCH AND GOLD (Ire) [-] (bl) 8-11-5 W Harnett, (14 to 1) pu
Dist: 10l, 1½l, 6l, 15l. 5m 13.40s. (9 Ran).
(Mrs Margaret Marshall), S J Treacy

945 Doonben I.N.H. Flat Race (5-y-o and up) £2,740 2m.................(5:30)

ROCHER LADY (Ire) 5-11-4 (5") Mr R Walsh, .. (7 to 4 fav) 1
SLYGUFF ROVER (Ire) 5-11-7 (7") Mr J P McNamara, (9 to 1) 2
829⁴ PREMIER WALK 7-11-7 (7") Mr S P Hennessy, ...(12 to 1) 3
773* THE TEXAS KID (Ire) 5-11-7 (7") Mr S M Duffy, ..(10 to 1) 4
KAITHEY CHOICE (Ire) 5-11-2 (7") Mr J Boland, ..(16 to 1) 5
SITE MISTRESS (Ire) 5-11-9 Mr H F Cleary, ...(20 to 1) 6
829⁵ JACKY FLYNN (Ire) 5-11-7 (7") Mr B Walsh, ...(8 to 1) 7
722³ BARRIGAN'S HILL (Ire) 6-12-0 Mr M Phillips, ...(8 to 1) 8
ANTON THE THIRD (Ire) 5-12-0 Miss M Olivefalk, (14 to 1) 9
GENTLE EYRE (Ire) 5-11-2 (7") Mr D A Harney, ...(16 to 1) 10
853 CAPTAIN ARTHUR (Ire) 5-11-7 (7") Mr D M Loughnane,
.... (20 to 1) 11
JAFFA MAN (Ire) 5-12-0 Mr P Fenton, ...(4 to 1) 12
852 TOM THE BOY VI (Ire) 6-11-7 (7") Miss I M Burke, (50 to 1) 13
FOROLD (Ire) 7-11-7 (7") Mr M A Cahill, ...(20 to 1) 14
ANNIDA (Ire) 5-11-2 (7") Mr G Elliott, ...(10 to 1) 15
581⁸ KERRIA'S GIFT (Ire) 5-12-0 Mr J P Dempsey, ...(14 to 1) 16
DONNA KING (Ire) 6-11-7 (7") Mr J T McNamara, ..(8 to 1) l
Dist: 8l, 14l, ½l, 1l. 4m 7.00s. (17 Ran).
(Gerard Rochford), W P Mullins

DOWNPATRICK (IRE) (good to yielding)
Friday October 18th

946 Tina T-P Maiden Hurdle (5-y-o and up) £1,370 2m 1f 172yds.......... (3:00)

805² BRADLEYS CORNER (Ire) 5-10-13 (7") Mr L J Gracey,
.... (12 to 1) 1
718⁴ REAL TAOISEACH (Ire) 6-11-7 (7") Mr A K Wyse, (Evens fav) 2
GLENFIELDS CASTLE (Ire) 6-11-7 (7") Mr A Stronge, (6 to 1) 3
STAR TRIX (Ire) 5-11-1 H Rogers, ...(14 to 1) 4
CORALDA (Ire) 5-11-1 K F O'Brien, ...(20 to 1) 5
802⁹ SECRET PRINCE (Ire) 5-11-1 (5") T Martin, ...(33 to 1) 6
467 ASTRID (Ire) 5-11-1 W Slattery, ...(33 to 1) 7
EIRE (Ire) 7-11-7 (7") Mr M O'Connor, ...(9 to 1) 8
WINTER PRINCESS 5-10-8 (7") Mr K Ross, ...(25 to 1) 9
142⁶ SCOUTS HONOUR (Ire) 5-11-9 C F Swan, ...(11 to 4) 10
ENDAGOLD (Ire) 5-10-8 (7") L J Fleming, ...(20 to 1) 11
MORAN'S PET (USA) 8-10-12 (3") U Smyth, ...(20 to 1) pu
802 MANDY'S CONVINCED (Ire) 6-11-1 F Woods, ...(25 to 1) pu
Dist: Hd, 4½l, 11l, 15l. 4m 25.90s. (13 Ran).

112

(L O'Kane), Mervyn Torrens

947 Down (Opportunity) Handicap Hurdle (0-109 5-y-o and up) £1,370 2¾m
.... (3:30)

849	FORT DEELY (Ire) [-] 5-9-2 (5*) R P Hogan, ...(6 to 1)	1
443⁶	FINAL TUB [-] 13-10-8 D J Casey, ... (7 to 2)	2
565	RIVERSTOWN LAD [-] 9-9-10 (5*) L O'Shea, ... (16 to 1)	3
803⁷	AMME ENAEK (Ire) [-] (bl) 7-9-11 (5*) D M Bean, ...(7 to 1)	4
	NEW TRIBE (Ire) [-] 5-10-2 B Bowens, ...(5 to 2 jt-fav)	5
	THE THIRD MAN (Ire) [-] 7-9-12 (3*) T Martin, (5 to 2 jt-fav)	6

Dist: 4½l, 3l, 6l, 14l. 5m 47.20s. (6 Ran).

(Peter Dundon), Eric McNamara

948 Bar One Racing Handicap Hurdle (0-102 4-y-o and up) £1,370 2m 1f 172yds. .... (4:00)

644*	NEW LEGISLATION (Ire) [-] (bl) 6-10-13 C F Swan, (11 to 4)	1
645⁷	STRAIGHT ON (Ire) [-] (bl) 5-11-5 F Woods, ... (9 to 2)	2
	COLLIERS HILL (Ire) [-] 8-11-13 T Wheeler, ... (6 to 1)	3
849²	MIDDLE MOGGS (Ire) [-] 4-11-2 T Hazlett, ... (2 to 1 fav)	4
678⁵	RADICAL ACTION (Ire) [-] 6-9-13 T P Treacy, ...(14 to 1)	5
645³	CLASSY KAHYASI (Ire) [-] 6-9-9 P McWilliams, ...(5 to 1)	6

Dist: 9l, 12l, 25l, dist. 4m 26.20s. (6 Ran).

(Michael Bergin), M Halford

949 Bar One Racing Handicap Chase (0-102 5-y-o and up) £1,370 3m (4:30)

852²	TEAL BRIDGE [-] 11-11-10 F Stockdale, ...(5 to 4 fav)	1
63⁷	MASTER MILLER [-] 10-10-9 T Hazlett, ... (8 to 1)	2
25⁴	DALUSMAN (Ire) [-] 8-10-3 T Wheeler, ... (14 to 1)	3
349⁴	GREEK MAGIC [-] 9-10-7 C F Swan, ... (9 to 1)	4
	ARCTIC TREASURE (Ire) [-] 7-9-9 (5*) T Martin, ...(20 to 1)	5
850⁵	BALLINABOOLA GROVE [-] 9-11-2 W Harnett, ...(3 to 1)	6
	DIAMOND SPRITE (USA) [-] 9-11-0 H Rogers, ...(9 to 1)	pu
926⁵	TALK TO YOU LATER [-] 10-11-9 T P Treacy, ...(4 to 1)	pu
852⁷	PRIME PAPERS [-] 11-10-3 F Woods, ...(20 to 1)	pu

Dist: Dist, 1l, dist, hd. 6m 23.30s. (9 Ran).

(Mrs M Heffernan), Andrew Heffernan

950 Janssen Animal Health Beginners Chase (5-y-o and up) £1,370 2¼m
.... (5:00)

	WHITE OAK BRIDGE (Ire) 7-11-4 A Powell, ... (13 to 8 fav)	1
804	COURSING GLEN (Ire) 8-11-9 D H O'Connor, ...(5 to 1)	2
804²	THE ODIN LINE (Ire) 7-11-9 F Woods, ...(9 to 4)	3
	DARA KNIGHT (Ire) 7-11 (2*) G Martin, ...(25 to 1)	4
804³	ANN'S AMBITION 9-11-9 K F O'Brien, ...(5 to 1)	pu
	NORTON'S BRIDGE (Ire) 6-11-9 D T Evans, ...(12 to 1)	pu

Dist: 2½l, dist, dist. 4m 47.50s. (6 Ran).

(J M Foley), P Hughes

951 Anglo Printers I.N.H. Flat Race (4-y-o and up) £1,370 2m 1f 172yds... (5:30)

	NATIVE FLING 4-11-9 Mr A R Coonan, ...(5 to 2)	1
647²	ELECTRIC RYMER (Ire) 4-11-4 (5*) Mr R Walsh, (5 to 4 fav)	2
802⁴	MISS ELIZABETH (Ire) 6-11-2 (7*) Mr C Barnwell, ...(8 to 1)	3
	BUCKLEY BAY (Ire) 5-11-7 (7*) Mr A J Dempsey, ...(20 to 1)	4
745⁴	SOUND ORCHESTRA (Ire) 5-11-2 (7*) Mr P A Farrell, (3 to 1)	5
805⁷	ORANGE LIL 4-11-4 Mr G J Harford, ...(33 to 1)	6
805⁴	NEW WEST (Ire) 5-11-7 (7*) Mr J D O'Connell, ...(16 to 1)	7
	BOLD IRENE (Ire) 5-11-2 (7*) Mr M O'Connor, ...(25 to 1)	8
	BALLINDANTE (Ire) 4-10-11 (7*) Mr K Ross, ...(25 to 1)	9
884	MOYDUFF LUCY (Ire) 6-11-6 (3*) Mr P J Casey, ...(33 to 1)	pu

Dist: Nk, 20l, 7l, dist. 4m 23.70s. (10 Ran).

(T McKeever), Peter McCreery

HEREFORD (good to firm)
Friday October 18th
Going Correction: PLUS 0.10 sec. per fur.

952 European Breeders Fund 'National Hunt' Novices' Hurdle Qualifier Class E (4,5,6-y-o) £2,276 2m 1f. .... (1:50)

	SOUNDS LIKE FUN 5-11-0 J F Titley, chsd clr ldr, nosed ahead frm hfwy, ran on strly from last.	
	..............(2 to 1 on op 7 to 4 on tchd 13 to 8 on)	1
749⁶	SEVEN WELLS 4-10-13 R Bellamy, wnt hndy hfwy, dsptd ld appr 4 out, kpt on same pace frm last. (8 to 1 tchd 7 to 1)	2
795²	CHIEF GALE (Ire) 4-10-8 (5*) Michael Brennan, improved to press ldg pair hfwy, ev ch whn awkward jump 2 out, not handle bend into strt, one pace frm betw last two.	
	..............................(5 to 2 op 7 to 4)	3
	CRUISINFORABRUISIN 6-11-0 Mr M Jackson, rcd freely in clr ld, hdd hfwy, lost tch frm 4 out, tld off. ....(20 to 1)	4

Dist: 2½l, 2½l, dist. 4m 0.20s. (4 Ran).

(Mrs H Brown), Miss H C Knight

953 Ovrevoll Handicap Chase Class D (0-120 5-y-o and up) £3,533 3m 1f 110yds. .... (2:20)

418²	SOME DAY SOON [100] 11-11-5 P Holley, jmpd boldly, made all, clr most of way, unchlgd.	
	...............(11 to 8 fav op 6 to 4 tchd 7 to 4)	1
418⁶	PAPER STAR [103] 9-11-8 B Powell, chsd wnr fo'o'r a circuit, struggling whn hit 8 out, lost pl, styd on ag'n to take remote second 2 out. ....(7 to 1 op 9 to 2)	2
855³	FOXGROVE [81] 10-9-7 (7*) Miss E J Jones, chsd ldrs, struggling to go apce aftr one circuit, one slow pace frm 2 out.	
	..........................(11 to 1 op 10 to 1)	3
857	LAKE OF LOUGHREA (Ire) [104] 6-11-9 C O'Dwyer, wtd wth, nrly f 3rd, mstks aftr, chsd wnr 6 out, rdn and not keen.	
	...........(13 to 8 op 6 to 4 tchd 7 to 4 and 2 to 1)	4
840	POLAR REGION [105] 10-11-5 (5*) Mr C Vigors, struggling to keep up aftr one circuit, tld off............(7 to 1 op 9 to 2)	5

Dist: 20l, 11l, 14l, 22l. 6m 16.90s. a 10.90s (5 Ran).

SR: 7/-/ *(C Elgram), M Bradstock*

954 Scudamore Clothing 0800 301301 Novices' Chase Class E (5-y-o and up) £3,067 2m. .... (2:55)

	SUBLIME FELLOW (Ire) 6-10-12 M A Fitzgerald, jmpd lft, led till aftr second, continued upsides to rgn ld 4 out, readily drw clr. ....(5 to 2 on op 3 to 1 on)	1
	MEAD COURT (Ire) 6-10-12 R Johnson, led aftr second, awkward 4th, hdd and hit four out, sn struggling.	
	..............................(9 to 4 op 2 to 1)	2
	BILL OF RIGHTS 8-10-12 B Powell, unruly at strt, struggling to keep up whn jmpd slwly 4th, tld off aftr.	
	....................(50 to 1 tchd 66 to 1)	3
654³	FOLLOW DE CALL 6-10-9 (3*) D Walsh, chasing clr ldg pair whn f second...................(16 to 1 tchd 20 to 1)	f

Dist: Dist. 3m 57.60s. a 10.60s (4 Ran).

(Rory McGrath), N J Henderson

955 Sankey Vending Novices' Hurdle Class E (4-y-o and up) £2,276 3¼m. ...(3:25)

824⁷	HUNTERS ROCK (Ire) 5-11-2 C O'Dwyer, settled gng wl, quickened up to ld last, ran on strly. (7 to 4 fav op 5 to 4)	1
	COPPER COIL 6-10-5 (7*) J Power, chsd ldr, improved to ld appr 2 out, kpt on same pace frm last.	
	...........(11 to 2 op 4 to 1 tchd 13 to 2 and 5 to 1)	2
667¹	MISTER BLAKE 6-11-5 R Johnson, settled wth chasing grp, improved appr 4 out, rdn and one pace aftr nxt.	
	....................(5 to 1 op 7 to 2)	3
	SUMMER HAVEN 7-10-2 (5*) Chris Webb, tried to make all, jnd 8th, hdd appr 2 out, no extr........(20 to 1 op 16 to 1)	4
	MAYB-MAYB 6-10-12 N Williamson, settled to track ldrs, reminders 5th, struggling aftr 3 out, sn btn.	
	..............(9 to 2 op 5 to 1 tchd 8 to 1)	5
	SLIGHT PANIC 8-10-7 V Slattery, chsd ldrs, effrt appr 4 out, lost grnd aftr nxt, sn lost tch.	
	...........(10 to 1 op 10 to 1 tchd 14 to 1)	6
	MILLY LE MOSS (Ire) 7-10-2 (5*) Michael Brennan, unruly at strt, settled in tch, effrt hfwy, wknd quickly frm 3 out, tld off.	
	...........(12 to 1 op 14 to 1 tchd 16 to 1)	7
859³	ASK HARRY (Ire) 5-10-5 (7*) P Henley, nvr far away, struggling aftr 3 out, 5th and btn whn f nxt...(14 to 1 op 7 to 1)	f

Dist: 2½l, 11l, 1½l, 15l, 9l, dist. 6m 20.40s. a 18.40s (8 Ran).

(Mrs Harry J Duffey), K C Bailey

956 Friends Of Arthur Elliott Memorial Novices' Handicap Chase Class E (0-100 5-y-o and up) £2,845 2m 3f
.... (4:00)

878⁴	KARLOVAC [65] 10-10-0 A Maguire, trkd ldrs, hit 7th, struggling and outpcd 5 out, rallied to ld betw last 2, ran on und pres to go clr......................(7 to 2 tchd 4 to 1)	1
755⁵	KING'S SHILLING (USA) [84] 9-11-5 Jacqui Oliver, al hndy, led 7 out, gd jump to go clr 4 out, good advantage whn blun badly and hdd 2 out, unbl to reco'r.....(4 to 1 tchd 5 to 1)	2
843²	RYTON RUN [89] 11-11-10 B Fenton, made most to 7 out, styd hndy, rdn aftr 3 out, sn outpcd...... (6 to 1 op 4 to 1)	3
838²	MARTHA'S DAUGHTER [83] 7-11-4 A Thornton, trkd ldrs, effrt 7 out, rdn aftr 3 out, fdd.	4
	SUNGIA (Ire) [65] (v) 7-10-0 W Marston, wl plcd, led briefly second, 4th and one pace whn f 6 out............. (50 to 1)	f

Dist: 7l, 16l, hd. 4m 43.70s. a 18.70s (5 Ran).

(Richard Lee), R Lee

957 Fownhope Handicap Hurdle Class D (0-120 4-y-o and up) £2,717 2m 3f 110yds. .... (4:35)

869*	BORN TO PLEASE (Ire) [95] 4-10-11 (7ex) A P McCoy, wth ldr, led aftr 6th, clr whn hit 3 out, styd on strly r-in.	
	...........(3 to 1 op 5 to 2 tchd 100 to 30)	1

786^{3} CORRIN HILL [94] 9-10-8 (3*) T Dascombe, *settled off the pace, improved to chase wnr appr 3 out, no imprsn r-in.* ....(3 to 1 tchd 7 to 2) 2
832* CHRIS'S GLEN [91] (v) 7-10-8 (7ex) N Williamson, *settled to chase clr ldg pair, drvn alng frm 3 out, nvr able to chal.* ....(4 to 1 tchd 9 to 2 and 5 to 1) 3
LACKENDARA [107] 9-11-3 (7*) Mr A Wintle, *led til hdd aftr 6th, wknd quickly bef 4 out, tld off*........(5 to 1 op 5 to 2) 4
832^{2} RE ROI (Ire) [97] 4-10-8 (5*) P Henley, *settled wth chasing grp, und pres hfwy, lost tch quickly and pld up bef hree out, broke blood vessel*.................... (5 to 2 fav tchd 3 to 1) pu
Dist: 8l, 29l, 21l. 4m 40.70s. a 22.70s (5 Ran).
(A B S Racing), P J Hobbs

KELSO (firm)
Saturday October 19th
Going Correction: MINUS 0.40 sec. per fur.

958 Edinburgh City Football Club Amateur Riders' Handicap Hurdle Class [illegible] (4-y-o and up) £2,178 2¾m 110yds.... (2:00)

ILENGAR (Ire) 7-11-2 (5*) Mr R Hale, *led to second, cl up, rdn alng 3 out, styd on to ld flt, ran on*....(100 to 30 op 9 to 2) 1
TEACHER (Ire) 6-11-0 (7*) Mr A Robson, *pld hrd, trkd ldrs, hdwy 7th, led nxt, hit 2 out, rdn last, hdd and no extr r-in.* ....(6 to 1 op 7 to 4) 2
SIDE OF HILL 11-11-0 (7*) Miss P Robson, *cl up, led second to 8th, rdn nxt and one pace.* ....(7 to 4 fav op 9 to 4 tchd 5 to 2 and 6 to 4) 3
WEE TAM 7-11-2 (5*) Mr M H Naughton, *trkd ldrs, hit second, hdwy 7th, dsptd ld nxt, ev ch whn hit 2 out, wndrd and wknd last*..................................(9 to 2 op 7 to 1) 4
813^{6} WALK IN THE WILD 4-11-5½ (7*) Miss S Cassels, *slwly away, al beh, tld off 5th*...............(66 to 1 op 33 to 1) 5
OVERWHELM (Ire) (bl) 8-11-4 (3*) Mr M Thompson, *chsd ldrs, reminders 6th, lost tch aftr nxt, sn wl beh.* ....(33 to 1 op 20 to 1) 6
700^{6} GRACE AND FAVOUR 5-10-11½ (7*) Mr A Parker, *prmnt, hit 1st, mstk 4th, pushed alng aftr nxt, sn lost pl, tld off whn pld up bef 3 out*..............................(12 to 1 op 10 to 1) pu
Dist: 3½l, 18l, 3½l, 24l, dist. 5m 23.00s. a 14.00s (7 Ran).
(J D Goodfellow), Mrs J D Goodfellow

959 Rank Hovis Millers Rothbury Home Bakery Novices' Chase Class E (5-y-o and up) £2,762 3m 1f........... (2:30)

814* TIGHTER BUDGET (USA) 9-11-13 M Moloney, *made all, clr 3 out, easily*.....(7 to 4 on op 2 to 1 on tchd 13 to 8 on) 1
WOODFORD GALE (Ire) 6-10-13 A Thornton, *chsd wnr thrght, rdn appr 3 out, one pace*..............(4 to 1 op 11 to 4) 2
555^{3} WHITE DIAMOND (v) 8-10-13 M Foster, *chsd ldg pair, rdn 4 out, sn one pace*.........(6 to 1 op 8 to 1 tchd 10 to 1) 3
814^{4} BRIGHT DESTINY 5-10-10 D Parker, *beh 12th, tld off 4 out.* ....(16 to 1 op 20 to 1 tchd 14 to 1) 4
861^{2} CALDER'S GROVE 6-10-10 (3*) G Cahill, *beh 12th, tld off 4 out*...............(10 to 1 op 12 to 1 tchd 14 to 1) 5
739^{3} KINCARDINE BRIDGE (USA) 7-10-6 (7*) Mr M Bradburne, *beh 12th, tld off whn f 4 out*..........(50 to 1 op 20 to 1) f
Dist: 18l, 2½l, 17l, sht-hd. 6m 11.70s. a 14.70s (6 Ran).
(Mrs Dianne Sayer), Mrs H D Sayer

960 Weatherbys Information Technology Novices' Hurdle Class E (4-y-o and up) £2,402 2m 110yds.............. (3:05)

370^{4} MARBLE MAN (Ire) 6-10-12 D Bentley, *keen hold, trkd ldrs and hit 5th, hdwy 2 out, led r-in, rdn out.* ....(2 to 1 fav op 7 to 4 tchd 6 to 4) 1
ADAMATIC (Ire) 5-10-12 (7*) S Melrose, *hld up, hdwy 5th, led and hit last, sn rdn and hdd, rdr lost whip and no extr last 100 yards*..............................(11 to 4 op 2 to 1) 2
862^{4} AMBER HOLLY 7-10-7 F Perratt, *al prmnt, effrt 3 out, rdn nxt, hit last, kpt on same pace und pres*....(14 to 1 op 10 to 1) 3
775^{6} FLYAWAY BLUES 4-10-11 P Niven, *hld up, hdwy aftr 3 out, styd on wl frm last*.........(5 to 1 op 6 to 1 tchd 7 to 1) 4
661^{4} TRUMPED (Ire) 4-10-6 A Dobbin, *mid-div, hdwy 5th, ch and rdn 2 out, one pace appr last*...........(7 to 1 op 8 to 1) 5
VICTOR LASZLO 4-10-11 B Storey, *hld up, effrt and hdwy 3 out, no imprsn nxt*.......(20 to 1 op 16 to 1 tchd 14 to 1) 6
813^{4} I'M THE MAN 5-10-12 K Johnson, *chsd ldrs, rdn 3 out, wknd nxt*.......................................(8 to 1) 7
FORBES (Ire) 5-10-12 N Williamson, *hld up and beh, gd hdwy 3 out, rdn aftr nxt, sn one pace*........(20 to 1 op 16 to 1) 8
PERSUASIVE TALENT (Ire) 5-10-12 J Burke, *led 1st, rdn 3 out, hdd and wknd aftr nxt*...........................(100 to 1) 9
LUMBACK LADY 6-10-4 (3*) G Lee, *cl up till rdn and wknd 3 out*..................................(50 to 1 op 25 to 1) 10
BACKHANDER (Ire) 4-10-8 (3*) G Cahill, *al beh*....(33 to 1) 11
CROCKALAWN (Ire) 8-10-12 Mr M Thompson, *prmnt, rdn 3 out, wknd quickly appr nxt*.......(200 to 1 op 100 to 1) 12
740^{9} SUPER GUY 4-10-11 A Thornton, *led and blun badly 1st, chsd ldrs till wknd 5th, tld off appr 2 out.* ....(33 to 1 op 25 to 1) 13

866^{6} THE KNITTER 4-10-11 M Moloney, *al rear, tld off 3 out.* ....(200 to 1 op 100 to 1) 14
Dist: ¾l, 2½l, ½l, ¾l, 7l, 2l, hd, 10l, 6l, ½l. 3m 51.60s. a 8.60s (14 Ran).
(D J Lever), M D Hammond

961 Greenmantle Ale Anthony & Johnnie Marshall Trophy Handicap C (0-125 5-y-o and up) £3,452 3m 1f..... (3:40)

821^{4} BAS DE LAINE (Fr) [111] (bl) 10-11-2 P Niven, *made all, lft wl clr 4 out, blun nxt, easily*...............(7 to 2 op 3 to 1) 1
24^{4} ROCKET RUN (Ire) [107] 8-10-12 A Thornton, *chsd wnr till hit tenth, sn pushed alng, beh whn lft second 4 out, nvr a threat.* ....(6 to 4 fav op 7 to 4) 2
OVER THE DEEL [119] 10-11-10 N Williamson, *hld up, hdwy to chase wnr tenth, clsg and 4 ls dwn whn f four out.* ....(3 to 1 op 5 to 2) f
816^{2} OFF THE BRU [95] 11-10-0 B Storey, *chsd ldrs till blun badly and uns rdr 13th*......... (7 to 2 tchd 3 to 1 and 4 to 1) ur
Dist: Dist. 6m 2.00s. a 5.00s (4 Ran).

962 Extrordinair Handicap Hurdle Class E (0-115 4-y-o and up) £2,206 2m 110yds......................... (4:10)

TOM BRODIE [111] 6-12-0 N Williamson, *hld up gng wl, smooth hdwy 2 out, led last, rdn out.* ....(9 to 2 op 4 to 1 tchd 5 to 1) 1
864^{2} NONIOS (Ire) [98] (v) 5-11-0 N Bentley, *cl up gng wl, chlgd 2 out, ev ch last, rdn and no extr r-in*...............(3 to 1) 2
777^{3} EDEN DANCER [106] 4-11-8 P Niven, *led till ran wide paddock bend aftr 3rd, led 4th till appr last, one pace.* ....(3 to 1 tchd 7 to 2) 3
818^{3} VAIN PRINCE [99] (bl) 9-11-2 A Thornton, *trkd ldrs, effrt 3 out, sn rdn and one pace appr last*.......(11 to 2 op 5 to 1) 4
777^{2} FIELD OF VISION (Ire) [100] (bl) 6-11-3 J Supple, *cl up, jmpd slwly 1st, hit 3rd, lft in ld bend aftr third, almost refused 4th, sn rear, drvn alng, no imprsn*..........(5 to 2 fav op 9 to 4) 5
Dist: 1½l, 2½l, nk, ½l. 3m 44.10s. a 1.10s (5 Ran).
SR: 24/8/13/6/6/ (Mrs M W Bird), J Howard Johnson

963 W & T Harkin Handicap Hurdle Class D (0-120 4-y-o and up) £2,528 2¾m 110yds........................ (4:40)

725^{6} NICHOLAS PLANT [92] 7-11-7 (3*) G Lee, *chsd ldr, led 4 out, rdn 2 out, ran on strly*...............(7 to 2 op 9 to 4) 1
862* JONAEM (Ire) [83] 6-11-1 K Johnson, *trkd ldg pair, hit 4 out and reminders, rdn alng and hdwy nxt, ev ch till drvn and one pace last*............................(13 to 8 fav op 5 to 2) 2
890^{2} CROFTON LAKE [68] 8-10-0 B Storey, *in tch till outpcd 7th, styd on und pres appr last, nvr dngrs.* ....(11 to 2 op 6 to 1 tchd 5 to 1) 3
765^{6} FRONTIER FLIGHT (USA) [89] 6-11-7 A Dobbin, *hld up in tch, hdwy 6th, effrt 3 out, rdn and one pace nxt.* ....(5 to 1 op 3 to 1) 4
876^{4} ROYAL CIRCUS [89] 7-11-4 (3*) E Husband, *led, rdn 7th, hdd 4 out, sn wknd*........... (4 to 1 op 7 to 2 tchd 9 to 2) 5
Dist: 5l, 13l, 1¼l, 20l. 5m 15.30s. a 6.30s (5 Ran).
(Mrs M F Paterson), J S Goldie

KEMPTON (good (races 1,4,5), good to firm (2,3,6))
Saturday October 19th
Going Correction: MINUS 0.15 sec. per fur. (races 1,4,5), MINUS 0.05 (2,3,6)

964 Ferry Boat Handicap Chase Class B (0-145 5-y-o and up) £4,351 2m (2:15)

823^{2} SUPER TACTICS (Ire) [117] 8-9-9 (5*) P Henley, *hld up, hdwy 6th, chsd ldrs 7th, chlgd 3 out, led nxt, cmftbly.* ....(4 to 1 op 5 to 2) 1
CLAY COUNTY [145] 11-12-0 R Garritty, *led, rdn 3 out, hdd nxt, sn outpcd*.......... (13 to 8 op 7 to 4 tchd 2 to 1) 2
823 CAPTAIN KHEDIVE [130] 8-10-13 A P McCoy, *not fluent 1st to 3rd, hmpd bend appr 4th, nvr gng aftr and hrd drvn, effrt four out, sn wknd*......(6 to 5 fav op 5 to 4 on tchd 5 to 4) 3
LASATA [117] 11-10-0 D Morris, *hit 1st, chsd ldr to 6th, hit nxt, sn btn, tld off*.......... (25 to 1 op 12 to 1 tchd 33 to 1) 4
Dist: 10l, 22l, dist. 3m 48.70s. a 2.70s (4 Ran).
SR: 21/39/2/-/ (H V Perry), R H Alner

965 Riverdale Juvenile Novices' Hurdle Class D (3-y-o) £2,915 2m.......(2:50)

CLASSIC DEFENCE (Ire) 10-12 J Osborne, *led to 5th, sn led ag'n, clr appr 2 out, blun last, easily.* ....(3 to 1 fav op 7 to 2 tchd 5 to 1) 1
A CHEF TOO FAR 10-9 (3*) L Aspell, *hld up, plenty to do aftr 3 out, ran on to chase wnr after 2 out, no imprsn r-in.* ....(9 to 2 tchd 7 to 2) 2

NATIONAL HUNT RESULTS 1996-97

SQUIRE'S OCCASION (Can) 10-12 A P McCoy, *al chasing ldrs, one pace frm 2 out, eased whn hld r-in.*
.................(7 to 2 op 9 to 4 tchd 4 to 1) 3
TYPHOON LAD 10-12 A Dicken, *hld up, steady hdwy appr 2 out, kpt on r-in.*.....................(12 to 1 op 8 to 1) 4
SUNLEY SECURE 10-12 R Johnson, *hdwy 5th, sn rdn alng, wknd 2 out.*..............(7 to 1 op 4 to 1 tchd 15 to 2) 5
734* TARRY 10-12 G Bradley, *sn chasing ldrs, led 5th, soon hdd, wknd quickly appr 2 out....*(6 to 1 op 5 to 1 tchd 7 to 1) 6
819⁵ SOLDIER BLUE 10-7 (5*) D J Kavanagh, *wth wnr second to 4th, wknd 5th.*............(10 to 1 op 12 to 1 tchd 10 to 1) 7
PREMIER GENERATION (Ire) 10-12 R Dunwoody, *chsd ldrs till rdn and wknd aftr 3 out.....*.........(7 to 1 op 7 to 2) 8
Dist: 6l, 5l, sht-hd, 2½l, sht-hd, 21l, 1¼l. 3m 51.40s. a 11.40s (8 Ran).
(J W Robb), J W Hills

966 Captain Quist Hurdle Class B (4-y-o and up) £4,765 2m..............(3:20)

CHIEF'S SONG 6-11-8 R Dunwoody, *made all, rdn and hld 2 out, ran on gmely und pres r-in.*
.................(7 to 2 op 5 to 2 tchd 4 to 1) 1
WARM SPELL 6-11-8 A P McCoy, *al chasing ldrs, rdn frm 3 out, rallied gmely r-in, no exta nr finish. ....*(3 to 1 jt-
fav op 2 to 1) 2
HOME COUNTIES (Ire) 7-11-8 D J Moffatt, *hld up, hdwy appr 2 out, ran on to chase ldrs r-in, no extr nr finish. ..*(3 to 1 jt-
fav op 5 to 2 tchd 7 to 2) 3
798 OUR KRIS (v) 4-10-13 M A Fitzgerald, *wth wnr to 5th, still ev ch 2 out, sn rdn and btn............*(100 to 30 op 4 to 1) 4
CUMBRIAN CHALLENGE (Ire) 7-11-5 R Garritty, *hld up, hdwy 2 out, wknd appr 2 out................*(5 to 1 tchd 6 to 1) 5
Dist: 1l, nk, 14l, 22l. 3m 43.30s. a 3.30s (5 Ran).
SR: 53/52/51/28/12/ (Mrs Anne Devine), S Dow

967 Charisma Gold Cup Handicap Chase Class B (0-150 5-y-o and up) £10,260 3m............................(3:55)

797* GENERAL CRACK (Ire) [128] 7-11-2 A P McCoy, *hdwy to chase ldrs 9th, led 13th, hdd nxt, led 15th, wnt lft 3 out, ran on gmely und pres frm next.*
.................(11 to 8 op on 5 to 4 tchd 6 to 4 on) 1
811* BERTONE (Ire) [130] 7-11-4 C O'Dwyer, *hld up, hdwy 13th, str chal frm 3 out, ev ch last, no extr cl hme.*
.................(7 to 2 op 4 to 1 tchd 5 to 1) 2
413* ALQAIRAWAAN [112] 7-10-0 C Llewellyn, *led to 13th, led ag'n nxt, hdd 15th, ev ch frm 3 out till no extr r-in.*
.................(8 to 1 tchd 10 to 1) 3
BAVARD DIEU (Ire) [140] 8-12-0 R Dunwoody, *in tch, pushed alng frm 9th, wknd 15th, tld off.*
.................(8 to 1 op 5 to 1 tchd 9 to 1) 4
NEVADA GOLD [112] 10-10-0 P McLoughlin, *hit 6th, lost tch frm 9th, tld off.......*(33 to 1 op 14 to 1 tchd 40 to 1) 5
SIR PETER LELY [130] (bl) 9-11-1 (3*) Mr C Bonner, *prmnt till lost tch 13th, tld off.....*(16 to 1 op 8 to 1 tchd 20 to 1) 6
816* ROYAL VACATION [112] 7-10-0 J Callaghan, *hit 3rd, sn beh, tld off whn pld up bef 4 out.*
.................(12 to 1 op 6 to 1 tchd 14 to 1) pu
Dist: 1¾l, nk, 11l, 1¼l, 12l, 8l. 3m 52.80s. a 2.60s (7 Ran).
SR: 26/26/7/-/ (J A Keighley And Mr Paul K Barber), P F Nicholls

968 Thames Novices' Chase Class D (5-y-o and up) £3,685 2m................(4:30)

LAND AFAR 9-11-0 M Dwyer, *hld up in tch, hdwy to chal 3 out, sn led, ran on wl................*(13 to 8 fav op 2 to 1) 1
AMANCIO (USA) 5-10-13 R Dunwoody, *chsd ldr, hit second, str chal 3 out to 2 out, one pace appr last.*
.................(11 to 4 op 5 to 2 tchd 3 to 1) 2
820² GREENBACK (Bel) 5-10-13 C Llewellyn, *led, hit second, hit 3 out and hdd, sn outpcd................*(5 to 2 op 2 to 1) 3
WILDE MUSIC (Ire) 6-11-0 G Bradley, *hdwy 7th, chsd ldrs 4 out, wknd appr last......*(11 to 1 op 6 to 1 tchd 14 to 1) 4
ICE MAGIC (v) 9-11-0 P McLoughlin, *beh till hdwy and blun 8th, not reco'r........*(50 to 1 op 20 to 1 tchd 66 to 1) 5
NORDANSK 7-11-0 B Fenton, *hld up, hdwy 3 out, not fluent 6th and lost tch, sd hdwy whn blun 9th, styd on ag'n frm 2 out, not reco'r.*
.................(11 to 1 op 6 to 1 tchd 14 to 1) 6
Dist: 5l, 2l, 1¼l, 12l, 8l. 3m 52.80s. a 6.80s (6 Ran).
(T J Ford), P R Webber

969 Park Handicap Hurdle Class B (0-150 4-y-o and up) £4,697 2m 5f.....(5:00)

FIRED EARTH (Ire) [123] 8-10-11 J Osborne, *chsd ldr till outpcd 4th, steady hdwy frm 3 out, chlgd on btl 2 out, led appr last, easily...................*(6 to 1 op 4 to 1) 1
808² CALL MY QUEST (Ire) [123] 6-10-11 A P McCoy, chsd ldrs, *led appr 7th, rdn 2 out, hld approaching last, sn outpcd.*
.................(15 to 8 fav op 2 to 1 tchd 9 to 4 and 7 to 4) 2
GIVUS A CALL (Ire) [112] 8-9-12¹ (3*) L Aspell, *hld up, effrt 3 out and hmpd, sn fdd....*(12 to 1 op 8 to 1 tchd 14 to 1) 3
BARNA BOY [137] 8-11-11 M A Fitzgerald, *hld up, pld hrd to chase ldr 4th, chlgd nxt till led aftr 6th, hdd appr 7th, sn wknd, tld off..........*(9 to 1 op 2 to 1 tchd 5 to 2) 4

HOPS AND POPS [140] 9-11-9 (5*) P Henley, *led till hld aftr 6th, 3rd but wl in tch whn f 2 out.*
.................(3 to 1 op 2 to 1 tchd 100 to 30) f
Dist: 10l, 8l, dist. 4m 59.50s. a 13.50s (5 Ran).
(Mrs J Fanshawe), J R Fanshawe

STRATFORD (good)
Saturday October 19th
Going Correction: MINUS 0.20 sec. per fur.

970 Shottery Meadow Lady Riders' Handicap Hurdle Class F (0-100 4-y-o and up) £2,444 2m 110yds.........(2:25)

SIMONE'S SON (Ire) [80] 9-10-8 Jacqui Oliver, *settled to track ldrs, improved gng wl 4 out, led bef nxt, sn clr, drvn out.*
.................(10 to 1 tchd 12 to 1) 1
801² PAIR OF JACKS (Ire) [87] 6-10-10 (5*) Miss P Jones, *patiently rdn, steady hdwy appr 3 out, one pace betw last 2, not nr wnr.*
.................(13 to 8 fav op 6 to 4 tchd 15 to 8) 2
940² ZINGIBAR [78] 4-9-12 (7*) Miss P Gundry, *wl plcd, hit second, lost grnd whn pace quickened 3 out, rallied frm betw last 2.*
.................(7 to 2 op 3 to 1) 3
WEEHEBY (USA) [96] 7-11-10 Ann Stokell, *nvr far away, rdn whn pace quickened 3 out, no imprsn aftr.*
.................(11 to 2 op 4 to 1) 4
870⁴ FIERCE [89] 8-11-3 Leesa Long, *al frnt rnk, made most frm 5th to appr 3 out, sn struggling......*(12 to 1 op 8 to 1) 5
SAN DIEGO CHARGER (Ire) [85] 5-10-12 Sophie Mitchell, *wtd wth, slpd bend appr 5th, effrt aftr 4 out, wknd quickly nxt.*
.................(4 to 1 op 7 to 2 tchd 9 to 2) 6
123 QUICK DECISION (Ire) [73] 5-9-7 (7*) Miss E J Jones, *led to 5th, reminders and led briefly bef nxt, blun and wknd 3 out, tld off.................*(50 to 1 op 33 to 1) 7
Dist: 1¼l, 1¾l, 11l, ½l, sht-hd, 29l. 3m 56.40s. a 10.40s (7 Ran).
(George Barnett), G Barnett

971 Richardsons Selling Hurdle Class G (4 - 7-y-o) £2,556 2m 110yds......(2:55)

186³ PICKENS (USA) 4-10-11 L Wyer, *wtd wth, steady hdwy hfwy, chasing clr ldr whn lft in frnt 2 out, drw clear......*(3 to 1 jt-
fav tchd 4 to 1) 1
762* SHUTTLECOCK 5-11-5 A Maguire, *made most till appr 3 out, lft second nxt, one pace........*(3 to 1 jt-fav tchd 7 to 2) 2
RANGER SLOANE 4-10-11 R Farrant, *patiently rdn, improved 3 out, styd on same pace frm nxt.*
.................(20 to 1 op 14 to 1) 3
GRIFFIN'S GIRL 4-10-1 (5*) S Ryan, *settled off the pace, improved frm 3 out, styd on same pace from betw last 2.*
.................(50 to 1 op 33 to 1) 4
638² TWICE THE GROOM (Ire) (bl) 6-11-5 L Harvey, *wtd wth, steady hdwy hfwy, effrt 3 out, rdn and not quicken appr nxt.*
.................(10 to 1 tchd 12 to 1) 5
435² MISTY VIEW 7-10-7 J R Kavanagh, *chsd ldrs thrght, rdn and not quicken 3 out..................*(10 to 1 tchd 12 to 1) 6
806⁸ TIMELY EXAMPLE (USA) (bl) 5-10-12 Gary Lyons, *settled midfield, steady hdwy 2 out, nvr plcd to chal.*
.................(10 to 1 op 12 to 1 tchd 8 to 1) 7
DASHING DANCER (Ire) 5-10-12 T Eley, *pressed ldr, ev ch till fdd 3 out...............*(20 to 1 op 16 to 1 tchd 25 to 1) 8
842⁵ AWESTRUCK (USA) 6-10-9 (3*) G Hogan, *sn beh, effrt hfwy, no imprsn 3 out.................*(50 to 1 op 33 to 1) 9
796 PYTCHLEY DAWN 6-10-7 V Slattery, *settled off the pace, chsd alng bef 3 out, nvr dngrs.........*(20 to 1 op 16 to 1) 10
THEYDON PRIDE 7-10-9 (3*) D Walsh, *pressed ldrs till wknd quickly appr 3 out..............*(33 to 1 op 25 to 1) 11
776⁶ SHALIK (Ire) 6-10-12 (7*) N T Egan, *in tch, rdn appr 3 out, sn struggling.................*(20 to 1 op 14 to 1 tchd 25 to 1) 12
673 SANDRO (bl) 7-11-12 (7*) M Clinton, *rcd midfield, struggling and lost tch 4 out.................*(50 to 1 op 33 to 1) 13
MONKEY'S WEDDING 5-10-12 S Fox, *unruly at strt, al beh, tld off.....................*(66 to 1 op 33 to 1) 14
704⁸ HATTA RIVER (USA) 6-10-12 W Marston, *pressed ldg bunch till wknd quickly appr 4 out, tld off..*(33 to 1 op 20 to 1) 15
CHAPEL OF BARRAS (Ire) 7-11-12 Mr P Gee, *taken to post early, middled whn f 4th................*(20 to 1 op 14 to 1) f
RUB AL KHALI 5-10-12 T J Murphy, *wtd wth, 9th and drvn alng whn f 4th.................................*(33 to 1) f
297³ SORISKY 4-10-11 Richard Guest, *settled midfield, improved to ld bef 3 out, 5 ls clr whn f nxt, unlucky.*
.................(15 to 2 op 6 to 1 tchd 8 to 1) f
Dist: 7l, 1¼l, 2½l, 2½l, 5l, 3½l, 3½l, 10l, 6l, ¾l. 3m 56.10s. a 10.10s (18 Ran).
(Philip J Grundy), N Tinkler

972 Corstorphine & Wright Handicap Chase Class D For the Clairefontaine Trophy (0-120 5-y-o and up) £3,684 2m 1f 110yds........................(3:25)

EASTERN MAGIC [89] 8-10-0 R Farrant, *rdn midfield, improved frm the pace 4 out, led bef last, hdd r-in, rallied und str pres to ld post...............*(20 to 1 op 14 to 1) 1

115

901[2] STATELY HOME (Ire) [118] 5-12-0 A Maguire, *led till aftr 1st, styd upsides, slightly outpcd 3 out, rallied to ld r-in, drvn and ct post*.............(7 to 2 tchd 10 to 30 and 4 to 1) 2

895* NORTHERN OPTIMIST [89] 8-10-0 B Powell, *settled off the pace, steady hdwy to ld 3 out, bad mstk nxt, sn hdd, one pace r-in*.................................(6 to 1 op 50 to 1) 3

NEWLANDS-GENERAL [115] 10-11-12 P Hide, *led aftr 1st, set str pace till hdd 3 out, wknd quickly bef nxt*.
.........................(11 to 4 fav op 5 to 2 tchd 3 to 1) 4

737[4] SHREWD JOHN [95] 10-10-6 L Wyer, *sn struggling in last pl, nvr able to rch chalg pos*..............(6 to 1 tchd 10 to 2) 5

870[3] RAMSTAR [108] 8-11-2 (3*) G Tormey, *wl plcd till mstk and lost grnd quickly 3rd, reminders hfwy, tld off*.
.............................(12 to 1 op 10 to 1) 6

737[3] NEWHALL PRINCE [112] 8-11-7 T Eley, *hit 1st, reminders to keep up hfwy, tld off whn pld up bef 3 out*.
.........................(3 to 1 tchd 7 to 2) pu
Dist: Sht-hd, 2l, 15l, 14l, dist. 4m 11.20s. a 9.20s (7 Ran).
(Mrs Christine Smith), G Barnett

973 for the JOHN A. Kerry Memorial Cup William Hill Handicap Class C (0-135 4-y-o and up) £3,652 2m 3f
.............................(4:00)

MAKE A STAND [114] 5-11-10 C Maude, *made all, gd jump to go clr 3 out, hit last, ran on wl*........(5 to 4 fav op Evens) 1

BARFORD SOVEREIGN [104] 4-10-13 P Hide, *al hndy, effrt to chase wnr aftr 3 out, styd on one pace r-in*.
.................................(5 to 1 op 4 to 1) 2

798[8] REAGANESQUE (USA) [110] 4-11-5 R Farrant, *al wl plcd, dsptd ld 4 out, rdn and wknd quickly aftr nxt*.
.......................(7 to 1 op 6 to 1 tchd 8 to 1) 3

DALLY BOY [106] 4-11-1 L Wyer, *struggling and rdn alng 4th, hdwy hfwy, no imprsn 3 out.* (9 to 2 op 4 to 1 tchd 5 to 1) 4

STONEY VALLEY [112] 6-11-9 A Maguire, *settled off the pace, tld off*.................(10 to 1 tchd 11 to 1) 5

876[7] SAYMORE [89] 10-11-0 S Wynne, *struggling to go pace thrght, tld off*.....................(50 to 1 op 33 to 1) 6

RAFTERS [99] 7-10-10 T J Murphy, *sn chasing ldg trio, lost pl quickly 4 out, tld off whn pld up bef 2 out*.
.............................(12 to 1 op 14 to 1) pu
Dist: 3½l, 22l, 8l, 29l, 1l. 4m 21.90s. a 1.90s (7 Ran).
SR: 39/24/8/-/ (P A Deal), M C Pipe

974 A.H.P. Trailers Wombourne Handicap Chase Class C (0-135 5-y-o and up) £4,987 2m 5f 110yds............(4:35)

LARRY'S LORD (Ire) [117] 7-10-11 P Hide, *jmpd wl, dsptd ld, definite advantage 6th, drw clr last 3, ran on strly...*(11 to 4) 1

GARRYLOUGH (Ire) [113] 7-10-4 (3*) D Fortt, *settled to track ldrs, effrt whn mstk 4 out, rallied to chase wnr bef 2 out, kpt on same pace.*......(9 to 4 fav op 9 to 2) 2

797 CERTAIN ANGLE [111] 7-10-5 D Bridgwater, *early mstks, improved hfwy, ev ch till blun 3 out, sn struggling.*
.................................(5 to 1 op 9 to 2) 3

811 COMEDY ROAD [106] 12-10-0 R Johnson, *settled in tch, rdn alng to go pace hfwy, rallied 6 out, outpcd aftr nxt, sn btn.*
.............................(12 to 1 op 10 to 1) 4

797[3] IFFEEE [128] 9-11-8 A Maguire, *slight ld to 6th, reminders 8th, lost tch six out, tld off.*..........(11 to 2 op 5 to 1) 5

MASTER BOSTON (Ire) [130] 8-11-10 L Wyer, *wnt hndy 6th, struggling hfwy, tailing off whn blun badly 4 out, pld up bef nxt.*
.........................(10 to 1 op 4 to 1 tchd 11 to 1) pu
Dist: 5l, 17l, 5l, dist. 5m 9.50s. a 9.50s (6 Ran).
(John Blackwell, Terry Curry, Des Nichols), P F Nicholls

975 Barnsley Associates 'National Hunt' Novices' Hurdle Class D (4-y-o and up) £3,155 2¾m 110yds............(5:05)

TARRS BRIDGE (Ire) 5-11-0 J Railton, *settled midfield, improved hfwy, led bef 2 out, forged clr.*
.........................(12 to 1 op 6 to 1 tchd 14 to 1) 1

INNER TEMPLE 6-11-0 S Wynne, *tucked away in midfield, improved 4 out, chsd wnr last 2, stumbled last, no imprsn.*
.........................(14 to 1 op 12 to 1 tchd 16 to 1) 2

MR STRONG GALE (Ire) 5-11-0 P Hide, *nvr far away, effrt and drvn alng aftr 4 out, one pace frm nxt.*
.................................(9 to 2 op 3 to 1 tchd 5 to 1) 3

JHAL FREZI 8-10-7 (7*) Mr R Thornton, *nvr far away, effrt 4 out, rdn and outpcd nxt.*......(25 to 1 op 20 to 1) 4

COSA FUAIR (Ire) 6-11-0 W McFarland, *wth ldr, led appr 4 out till bef nxt, fdd*.........(9 to 1 op 10 to 1 tchd 12 to 1) 5

UP THE CREEK (Ire) 4-10-7 Gary Lyons, *patiently rdn, rapid hdwy to ld appr 3 out, hdd bef nxt, wknd quickly.*
.................................(66 to 1 op 50 to 1) 6

770[6] GAELIC MILLION (Ire) 5-10-9 J F Titley, *settled to chase ldg bunch, effrt hfwy, no imprsn frm 3 out.*
.........................(12 to 1 tchd 20 to 1) 7

420[2] ROSKEEN BRIDGE (Ire) 5-11-0 M Richards, *sn beh, drvn alng hfwy, nvr dngrs*..............(20 to 1 op 16 to 1) 8

CAREY'S COTTAGE (Ire) 6-11-0 L Harvey, *settled off the pace, drvn alng bef 4 out, nvr a threat.* (50 to 1 op 33 to 1) 9

749[3] DIFFICULT DECISION (Ire) 5-11-0 D Byrne, *settled midfield, struggling hfwy, nvr dngrs.* (5 to 1 op 3 to 1 tchd 6 to 1) 10

---

806 JAIME'S JOY 6-10-2 (7*) Shaun Graham, *sn last and outpcd, nvr a factor.*..................(66 to 1 op 50 to 1) 11

LINFORD (Ire) 6-11-0 Mr R Bevis, *chsd ldrs to hfwy, lost tch, tld off.*.....................(25 to 1 op 20 to 1) 12

528 LILLY THE FILLY 5-10-9 E Byrne, *al beh, tld off.*
.................................(66 to 1 op 50 to 1) 13

BITOFAMIXUP (Ire) 5-11-0 B Powell, *pressed ldrs, ev ch hfwy, lost 4 out, tld off...*(4 to 1 op 3 to 1 tchd 9 to 2) 14

867[3] MINOR KEY 6-11-0 A Maguire, *tried to make all, hdd aftr 5 out, 5th and wkng whn f nxt.*.......(3 to 1 fav op 4 to 1) f

B FIFTY TWO (Ire) 5-10-7 (7*) D Slattery, *chsd ldrs, hit 3rd, lost tch quickly and pld up bef 3 out....*............(66 to 1) pu
Dist: 7l, 15l, 2½l, 5l, 9l, 14l, 12l, sht-hd, 1½l, nk. 5m 25.10s. a 13.10s (16 Ran).
(The Tuesday Syndicate), C J Mann

976 Jones Lang Wootton Maiden Hurdle Class E (4-y-o and up) £2,757 2m 110yds.............................(5:40)

IRON N GOLD 4-11-4 D Bridgwater, *patiently rdn, steady [illegible]*
.........................(11 to 2 op 5 to 1 tchd 6 to 1) 1

297[2] SAMBA SHARPLY 5-11-5 P Hide, *wtd wth, improved gng wl 3 out, chlgd last, rdn and ran on.*
.........................(5 to 2 fav op 7 to 2 tchd 9 to 4) 2

FLYING FIDDLER (Ire) 5-11-5 B Powell, *al wl plcd, led 4 out till hdd last, rdn and kpt on.*...........(7 to 2 op 10 to 1) 3

SILLY MONEY 5-11-5 L Wyer, *settled midfield, improved to join issue 3 out, one pace frm betw last 2.*
.........................(14 to 1 op 12 to 1 tchd 16 to 1) 4

SWAN STREET (NZ) 5-11-5 J Railton, *settled off the pace, improved to join ldrs 3 out, no extr betw last 2.*
.................................(10 to 1 op 7 to 1) 5

900[2] BLAZE OF OAK (USA) 5-11-5 R Johnson, *settled to track ldrs, ev ch appr 3 out, wknd betw last 2.*
.........................(5 to 1 op 9 to 2 tchd 11 to 2) 6

618[3] SMART LORD 5-11-5 M Bosley, *wtd wth, took clr order hfwy, bustled alng aftr 3 out, no imprsn...*(33 to 1 tchd 50 to 1) 7

824[4] SAMAKA HARA (Ire) 4-11-4 Richard Guest, *shwd up wl in frnt rnk till fdd 2 out....*(10 to 1 op 8 to 1 tchd 12 to 1) 8

TOTAL ASSET 6-11-5 T Eley, *trkd ldrs, short of room bend appr 2 out, fdd.*...................(50 to 1) 9

SLOE BRANDY 6-11-0 Mr A Walton, *sn beh, nvr a factor.*
.........................(33 to 1 op 25 to 1) 10

671[9] ROSEHALL 5-10-11 (3*) G Hogan, *chsd alng hfwy, no imprsn frm 3 out.*..................(33 to 1 tchd 50 to 1) 11

RACING TELEGRAPH 6-11-5 J F Titley, *led, hit second, hdd 4 out, wknd quickly betw last 2.*......(10 to 1 op 14 to 1) 12

BRAYDON FOREST 4-11-4 W Marston, *f second.*
.........................(12 to 1 tchd 14 to 1 and 16 to 1) f

RIZAL (USA) 4-11-1 (3*) D Walsh, *slwly away, mstks, no ch whn f 2 out.*..................(16 to 1 op 14 to 1) f

NAGARA SOUND 5-11-5 A Maguire, *wtd wth, improved hfwy, ev ch 3 out, 4th and btn whn f last....*(8 to 1 tchd 10 to 1) f
Dist: Nk, sht-hd, 6l, 6l, 3½l, 1¼l, nk, 5l, 2l, 22l. 4m 1.50s. a 15.50s (15 Ran).
(A Family Affair Partnership), T Casey

LIMERICK (IRE) (yielding (races 1,2,3,4,5), yielding to soft (6,7,8)) Sunday October 20th

977 B.R.C. McMahon Reinforcements Maiden Hurdle (Div I) (5-y-o and up) £3,425 2½m.................................(2:15)

716 KING OF KERRY 5-12-0 C F Swan,......(3 to 1 jt-fav) 1
223[7] MISS BERTAINE (Ire) 7-11-1 N Williamson,.......(20 to 1) 2
850[3] MARTYS STEP (Ire) 5-10-13 (7*) D McCullagh,....(9 to 1) 3
289[9] MULLOVER 5-11-6 J Short,.................(25 to 1) 4
GO NOW (Ire) 6-12-0 T P Treacy,.........(3 to 1 jt-fav) 5
741[3] LUCKY BUST (Ire) 6-11-7 (7*) Mr D A Harney,.....(7 to 1) 6
ROSENWALD (Ire) 6-11-6 A Powell,.............(33 to 1) 7
SARADANTE (Ire) 6-11-6 K F O'Brien,.........(25 to 1) 8
720 TOP OF THE RIDGE (NZ) 7-11-6 R Dunwoody,...(33 to 1) 9
781 COOLREE LORD (Ire) 5-11-6 M P Hourigan,......(33 to 1) 10
TEN FOUR (Ire) 5-11-6 J F Titley,.............(33 to 1) 11
EAGLES WITCH (Ire) 7-10-8 (7*) Mr P J Crowley,...(33 to 1) 12
SHEER MYSTERY (Ire) 7-11-6 P L Malone,.......(33 to 1) 13
741 HOTSCENT (Ire) 5-11-1 P A Roche,.............(33 to 1) 14
PRINCE WOT A MESS (Ire) 5-11-6 J P Cusack,...(50 to 1) 15
538* COMAN'S JET (Ire) 6-12-0 T Horgan,.............(7 to 2) 16
826 KINCORA (Ire) 5-11-6 M P Dwyer,.............(33 to 1) 17
JACK VETTY (Ire) 5-11-6 J P Broderick,.......(33 to 1) 18
CASTLE TIGER BAY (Ire) 5-11-6 F Woods,.......(33 to 1) 19
SALMON POOL (Ire) 6-10-8 (7*) D K Budds,......(50 to 1) pu
Dist: Sht-hd, 2½l, 2l, nk. 5m 7.90s. (20 Ran).
(The Local Boys Syndicate), A P O'Brien

978 B.R.C. McMahon Reinforcements Maiden Hurdle (Div II) (5-y-o and up) £3,425 2½m.................................(2:45)

GALLOPEN GARRY (Ire) 6-11-11 (3*) J R Barry,...(6 to 1) 1
119[5] MATTS DILEMMA (Ire) 8-11-6 F Woods,.........(20 to 1) 2
678[2] JAY MAN (Ire) 6-11-9 (5*) Mr E J Kearns Jnr,.....(4 to 1) 3

850² TALE GAIL (Ire) 6-12-0 R Dunwoody, ... (5 to 4 fav) 4
802 HILLTOP BOY (Ire) 7-11-6 C F Swan, ... (12 to 1) 5
716⁴ JOHN'S RIGHT (Ire) 5-10-13 (7ᵉ) M D Murphy, . . (10 to 1) 6
741⁸ SHAWS CROSS (Ire) 5-11-6 W Slattery, ... (14 to 1) 7
THAT'S POLITICS (Ire) 7-10-13 (7ᵉ) A O'Shea, . . . (10 to 1) 8
853 KYLOGUE KING (Ire) 5-11-4 (5ᵉ) G Cotter, ... (20 to 1) 9
MILLSOFBALLYSODARE (Ire) 5-11-6 M P Hourigan,
. . . . (20 to 1) 10
20⁶ WHITBY 8-11-1 (5ᵉ) J M Donnelly, ... (16 to 1) 11
829 ROMEO'S BROTHER (Ire) 6-11-4 Mr P J Healy, . . (25 to 1) 12
722⁷ SKULLDUGERY (Ire) 6-11-6 J Jones, ... (20 to 1) 13
591⁷ HOLLY LADY (Ire) 5-11-1 P A Roche, ... (33 to 1) 14
ORIENTAL PEARL (Ire) 6-11-1 G M O'Neill, ... (20 to 1) 15
LITTLE CHIP (Ire) 7-11-1 S H O'Donovan, ... (33 to 1) 16
NORTHERN REEF (Ire) 6-11-6 Mr H F Cleary, ... (20 to 1) pu
850⁷ CELTIC WHO (Ire) 5-11-6 C O'Dwyer, ... (9 to 1) pu
716⁷ HIGH PARK LADY (Ire) 5-11-1 P M Verling, ... (20 to 1) pu
Dist: 9l, nk, 13l, 10.5m 9.10s. (19 Ran).

(Shuttle Syndicate), Sean O O'Brien

979 Lancer Boss (Ireland) Ltd Novice Hurdle (5-y-o and up) £3,425 2½m . . (3:15)

720⁴ PRIVATE PEACE (Ire) 6-11-6 C F Swan, ... (7 to 2 on) 1
850⁷ IRISH BREEZE (Ire) 5-11-6 T Horgan, ... (3 to 1) 2
THE HEARTY LADY (Ire) 6-10-9 F Woods, ... (25 to 1) 3
JOLLY JOHN (Ire) 5-10-11 (3ᵉ) D J Casey, ... (33 to 1) 4
FEAR CLISTE (Ire) 5-11-0 C O'Dwyer, ... (33 to 1) 5
RENNY (Ire) 5-10-7 (7ᵉ) J E Casey, ... (12 to 1) pu
802⁷ UNO NUMERO (Ire) 5-11-0 L P Cusack, ... (33 to 1) pu
COURT AMBER (Ire) 5-11-0 J P Broderick, ... (33 to 1) pu
Dist: 4l, 11l, 5½l, 2l. 5m 13.60s. (8 Ran).

(Mrs A M Daly), A P O'Brien

980 Garryowen Handicap Hurdle (0-130 4-y-o and up) £3,425 2m 1f . . . . . (3:45)

742 CEILI QUEEN (Ire) [-] 4-10-11 (5ᵉ) J Butler, ... (14 to 1) 1
ANNADOT (Ire) [-] 6-10-11 F J Flood, ... (12 to 1) 2
849² SACULORE (Ire) [-] 8-10-8 C F Swan, ... (5 to 1) 3
730³ WEST ON BRIDGE ST (Ire) [-] 6-10-12 F Woods, (7 to 2 fav) 4
730 TEMPLEROAN PRINCE [-] 9-10-13 R Dunwoody, . (8 to 1) 5
BEAU CYRANO [-] 4-10-8 T J O'Sullivan, ... (12 to 1) 6
FONTAINE FABLES (Ire) [-] 6-11-8 M P Dwyer, . . . (7 to 1) 7
732 PINGO HILL (Ire) [-] 4-10-12 J Shortt, ... (14 to 1) 8
730⁸ TAITS CLOCK (Ire) [-] 7-10-12 T Horgan, ... (8 to 1) 9
WHAT IT IS (Ire) [-] 7-9-13 N Williamson, ... (20 to 1) 10
826⁷ JUSTAWAY (Ire) [-] (bl) 6-10-11 K P Gaule, ... (20 to 1) 11
742 PERSIAN MYSTIC (Ire) [-] 4-9-12 (7ᵉ) M J Collins, . (16 to 1) 12
621² MAGICAL WAY (Ire) [-] 6-9-7 M Duffy, ... (12 to 1) 13
SHEREGORI (Ire) [-] 6-11-9 (3ᵉ) Mr D Valentine, . . (8 to 1) 14
944² DANCING VISION (Ire) [-] 6-10-6 J F Titley, ... (8 to 1) f
Dist: 2½l, 4l, sht-hd, 4½l. 4m 16.00s. (15 Ran).

(Michael H Keogh), A P O'Brien

981 Murphys Irish Stout Munster National Limited Handicap Chase (5-y-o and up) £12,900 3m . . . . (4:15)

THREE BROWNIES [-] (bl) 9-10-1 C O'Dwyer, ... (16 to 1) 1
719 LORD SINGAPORE (Ire) [-] 8-10-13 N Williamson,
. . . . (11 to 4 fav) 2
TWIN RAINBOW [-] 9-10-1 L P Cusack, ... (6 to 1) 3
719³ SECOND SCHEDUAL [-] 11-11-12 R Dunwoody, . . (5 to 1) 4
553⁷ MINELLA LAD [-] 10-11-3 T Horgan, ... (16 to 1) 5
BEAT THE SECOND [-] 8-10-0 F Woods, ... (16 to 1) 6
LOVE THE LORD (Ire) [-] 6-11-0 T P Treacy, ... (18 to 1) 7
925⁷ HEIST [-] 7-10-8 M Dwyer, ... (10 to 1) f
LISSELAN PRINCE (Ire) [-] 8-12-0 C F Swan, ... (10 to 1) f
ALBERT'S FANCY [-] 10-10-0 F J Flood, ... (50 to 1) pu
719⁶ ROYAL MOUNTBROWNE [-] 8-12-0 C F Swan, . . (12 to 1) pu
743⁷ BALLYBODEN [-] 9-10-0 M P Hourigan, ... (20 to 1) pu
Dist: 3l, 10l, 10l, 2l, 20l. 5m 58.70s. (12 Ran).

(Mrs A M Daly), M F Morris

982 Shannon Novice Chase (5-y-o and up) £3,425 2¾m . . . . (4:45)

DORANS PRIDE 7-11-8 J P Broderick, ... (4 to 1 on) 1
925⁴ LE GINNO (Fr) 9-11-8 T P Treacy, ... (20 to 1) 2
CREHELP EXPRESS 6-11-3 L P Cusack, ... (14 to 1) 3
827² LISNAGAR LADY (Ire) 7-11-3 S H O'Donovan, . . (14 to 1) 4
601⁴ SLANEY STANDARD 8-11-8 C O'Dwyer, ... (14 to 1) 5
576 MUSICAL DUKE 7-11-5 (3ᵉ) G Kilfeather, ... (16 to 1) 6
BIG BO (Ire) 7-11-1 (7ᵉ) D K Budds, ... (33 to 1) 7
729 CORRIBLOUGH (Ire) 8-11-8 F Woods, ... (25 to 1) 8
827 PROSPECT STAR (Ire) 5-10-10 (7ᵉ) Mr J Motherway,
. . . . (33 to 1) 10
CHALWOOD (Ire) 6-11-8 A Powell, ... (16 to 1) 11
CONSHARON (Ire) 8-11-3 C F Swan, ... (5 to 2) f
853 WHAT A CHOICE (Ire) 6-12-0 (5ᵉ) M J Holbrook, . (40 to 1) f
732⁷ ONTHEROADAGAIN (Ire) 8-11-8 T P Rudd, ... (33 to 1) bd
623² PASSER-BY 9-11-8 K F O'Brien, ... (14 to 1) pu
BAILE NA GCLOCH (Ire) 7-11-5 (3ᵉ) P Murphy, . . (25 to 1) pu
Dist: 6l, 3l, 8l, 6l. 5m 32.80s. (16 Ran).

(T J Doran), Michael Hourigan

983 Shannon Mares I.N.H. Flat Race (5-y-o and up) £2,740 2½m . . . . (5:15)

FLAMINGO FLOWER (Ire) 8-11-8 (3ᵉ) Mr P J Casey, (7 to 1) 1
722² DIAMOND DOUBLE (Ire) 5-11-8 (3ᵉ) Mr B M Cash,
. . . . (9 to 4 fav) 2
720² YOUNG MRS KELLY (Ire) 6-11-4 (7ᵉ) Mr J T McNamara,
. . . . (100 to 30) 3
MINELLA LASS (Ire) 5-11-4 (7ᵉ) Mr M A Cahill, . . (8 to 1) 4
591⁵ JANICE PRICE (Ire) 5-11-4 (7ᵉ) Mr M J Walsh, . . (10 to 1) 5
VIVIANS VALE (Ire) 7-11-4 (7ᵉ) Mr M Budds, ... (14 to 1) 6
GRACEMARIE KATE (Ire) 7-11-4 (7ᵉ) Mr E Gallagher,
. . . . (16 to 1) 7
MARILLO (Ire) 7-11-4 (7ᵉ) Mr John P Moloney, . . (10 to 1) 8
HOLLOW GOLD (Ire) 7-11-4 (7ᵉ) Mr D W Cullen, . (8 to 1) 9
781³ TEXARKANA (Ire) 5-11-4 (7ᵉ) Mr W Ross, ... (10 to 1) 10
KILLALOONTY ROSE (Ire) 5-11-4 (7ᵉ) Mr C A Murphy,
. . . . (10 to 1) 11
RECKLESS YOUTH (Ire) 6-11-4 Mr A J Dempsey,
. . . . (10 to 1) 12
745⁵ SHECOULDNTBEBETTER (Ire) 5-11-4 (7ᵉ) Mr A C Coyle,
. . . . (10 to 1) 13
683 GAIN CONTROL (Ire) 7-11-4 (7ᵉ) Miss O Hayes, . (33 to 1) 14
805⁵ PRAY FOR PEACE (Ire) 5-11-4 (7ᵉ) Mr P Fahey, . (14 to 1) 15
CREGG CASTLE (Ire) 5-11-4 (7ᵉ) Mr D A Harney, . (33 to 1) 16
PENNY BRIDE (Ire) 7-11-4 (7ᵉ) Mr S O'Callaghan, (14 to 1) 17
527 MARIAN'S OWN (Ire) 5-11-11 Mr J A Nash, ... (20 to 1) 18
Dist: 2½l, hd, 2l, 9l. 5m 12.40s. (18 Ran).

(Mrs M E McCann), Peter Casey

984 Newenham Mulligan I.N.H. Flat Race (4-y-o and up) £3,767 2m 1f . . . . (5:45)

566⁸ BROWNES HILL LAD (Ire) 4-11-13 Mr P Fenton, . (7 to 1) 1
566⁶ MORNING MIST (Ire) 4-10-13 (7ᵉ) Mr C J Swords, (10 to 1) 2
BERE HAVEN (Ire) 4-10-13 (7ᵉ) Mr J T McNamara, (4 to 1) 3
717⁵ BORO BOW (Ire) 5-11-6 (7ᵉ) Mr B E Hill, ... (9 to 4 fav) 4
713⁴ ANTICS (Ire) 4-11-1 (7ᵉ) Mrs C Harrison, ... (8 to 1) 5
HEN HANSEL (Ire) 5-11-11 (7ᵉ) Mr Sean O O'Brien, (9 to 1) 6
603⁷ SLANEY CHARM (Ire) 6-11-4 (7ᵉ) Mr T N Cloke, . (20 to 1) 7
829⁷ IODER WAN (Ire) 4-11-1 (7ᵉ) Mr John P Moloney, . (7 to 1) 8
611⁶ AMBITIOUS FELLOW (Ire) 8-11-11 (7ᵉ) Miss L E A Doyle,
. . . . (8 to 1) 9
910 PATRAY LAD (Ire) 5-11-11 Miss M Olivefalk, ... (20 to 1) 10
LORD OGAN (Ire) 5-11-11 Mr H F Cleary, ... (25 to 1) 11
THE ENGINEER (Ire) 7-11-11 (7ᵉ) Mr A Stafford, . . (16 to 1) 12
COMMITTED SCHEDULE (Ire) 5-11-11 Mr J A Nash, (7 to 1) 13
MAIRTINS BUCK (Ire) 5-11-4 (7ᵉ) Mr D A Harney, . (25 to 1) 14
BUMPER TO BUMPER (Ire) 4-10-13 (7ᵉ) Mr D J O'Mara,
. . . . (33 to 1) 15
SHIP OF SHAME (Ire) 4-10-13 (7ᵉ) Mr E Gallagher, (20 to 1) 16
HILL TOP LAD (Ire) 4-10-13 (7ᵉ) Mr A G Jordan, . (14 to 1) 17
EVE'S DAUGHTER (Ire) 5-10-13 (7ᵉ) Mr D P Daly, (25 to 1) 18
AS ROYAL (Ire) 5-11-4 (7ᵉ) Mr G Elliott, ... (14 to 1) su
Dist: 2l, sht-hd, 3l, 3½l. 4m 13.50s. (19 Ran).

(Patrick Walsh), Patrick Walsh

PLUMPTON (good to firm)
Tuesday October 22nd
Going Correction: PLUS 0.10 sec. per fur.

985 Joe & Co Maiden Hurdle Class E (4-y-o and up) £2,700 2m 1f . . . . (2:20)

REGAL PURSUIT (Ire) 5-11-0 M A Fitzgerald, trkd ldrs, rdn
and prog to ld appr 3 out, sn clr, ran on wl.
. . . . (7 to 2 op 3 to 1) 1
WAKEEL (USA) 4-11-4 R Dunwoody, hld up, steady prog frm
4th, chsd wnr appr 3 out, rdn and no imprsn nxt, btn whn mstk
last. . . . . (6 to 1 op 9 to 1 tchd 10 to 1) 2
DOCKLANDS COURIER 4-11-4 C Llewellyn, in tch, cld up
7th, rdn and outpcd 3 out. (14 to 1 op 8 to 1 tchd 16 to 1) 3
GREENWICH AGAIN 4-11-4 D Bridgwater, with ldr till led 6th,
hdd appr 3 out, sn btn. . . . (5 to 1 op 7 to 1 tchd 8 to 1) 4
835³ CADDY'S FIRST 4-11-4 M Mann, chsd ldrs, mstk 6th and rdn,
sn wknd, tld off. . . . . (7 to 1 op 8 to 1 tchd 14 to 1) 5
ZAMALEK (USA) 4-11-4 A Maguire, led to 6th, wknd rpdly 3
out, tld off. . . . . (33 to 1 op 12 to 1) 6
ZADOK 4-11-4 B Fenton, mstk 5th, al rear, tld off frm 7th.
. . . . (50 to 1 op 25 to 1) 7
837³ RAGTIME SONG (v) 7-10-12 (7ᵉ) N T Egan, rear, lost tch 6th,
tld off. . . . . (50 to 1 op 25 to 1) 8
835⁵ ALLEZ PABLO 6-11-2 (3ᵉ) L Aspell, whipped round strt, tld off
till pld up bef 7th. . . . . (100 to 1 op 66 to 1) pu
BARBRALLEN 4-10-13 D Leahy, taken dwn early, al beh, tld
off whn pld up bef 7th. . . . . (100 to 1 op 66 to 1) pu
HARDY BREEZE 5-11-5 J R Kavanagh, rear, lost tch 6th,
no ch whn pld up bef 3 out.
. . . . (40 to 1 op 25 to 1 tchd 50 to 1) pu
Dist: 10l, 17l, 1¾l, dist, 7l, 2½l, 7l. 4m 14.50s. a 17.50s (11 Ran).

(Larry Tracey), N J Henderson

986 Joe & Co Selling Handicap Chase Class G (0-90 5-y-o and up) £2,595 3m

1f 110yds. (2:50)

892 CAPO CASTANUM [80] 7-11-4 T J Murphy, *wtd wth gng easily, prog 12th, lft in ld 5 out, clr whn blun 2 out, drvn out.*
. . . .(4 to 1 fav op 7 to 2) 1

54[6] RAGLAN ROAD [84] 12-11-8 J Ryan, *chsd ldg pair to 7th, outpcd 14th, rallied 5 out, chased wnr last, no imprsn.*
. . . .(8 to 1 tchd 10 to 1) 2

104 BRINDLEY HOUSE [82] 9-11-6 D Morris, *trkd ldrs gng easily, led 14th, blun and hdd 5 out, mstk nxt, one pace und pres.*
. . . .(10 to 1 op 12 to 1 tchd 16 to 1) 3

757[3] MANOR BOUND [72] 6-10-10 N Williamson, *rear and not fluent, rdn frm 6th, effrt 14th, sn outpcd, nvr able to chal.*
. . . .(12 to 1) 4

OPAL'S TENSPOT [72] 9-10-10 R Johnson, *ran in snatches, outpcd whn mstk 15th, no prog aftr. . . .* (12 to 1 op 7 to 1) 5

FIGHTING DAYS (USA) [89] 10-11-13 B Powell, *hld up, prog 6th, wkng whn mstk 15th, no ch aftr.*
. . . . (14 to 1 op 8 to 1 tchd 16 to 1) 6

840[6] WOODLANDS GENHIRE [71] (v) 11-10-9 A Maguire, *rdn thrght, chsd ldr to 8th, lost pl tenth, sn struggling.*
. . . . (8 to 1 op 13 to 2 tchd 9 to 1) 7

530[4] SAINT BENE'T (Ire) [62] 8-9-10[1] (5[*]) Michael Brennan, *jmpd slwly second and 3rd, sn tld off. . . .*(16 to 1 tchd 20 to 1) 8

201[3] THE WEST'S ASLEEP [67] 11-10-5 B Fenton, *in tch till rdn and wknd 14th, tld off. . . . .*(9 to 2 op 5 to 1) 9

TELF [62] 16-9-9 (5[*]) D J Kavanagh, *rear, wkng whn tried to refuse and uns rdr 7th. . . . .*(50 to 1 tchd 66 to 1) ur

855[4] L'UOMO PIU [71] 12-10-6 (3[*]) T Dascombe, *led to 14th, wknd rpdly, tld off and pld up bef 2 out. . . . .*(20 to 1 op 16 to 1) pu

MR CLANCY (Ire) [81] 8-11-5 S Curran, *trkd ldr 8th till wknd rpdly aftr tenth, tld off and pld up bef 14th.*
. . . . (8 to 1 op 12 to 1) pu

Dist: 3½l, 5l, 20l, ½l, 20l, 4l, 1¼l, dist. 6m 27.10s. a 13.10s (12 Ran).

(D C G Gyle-Thompson), Miss H C Knight

987 Knight Frank Centenary Handicap Hurdle Class F (0-105 4-y-o and up) £2,047 2½m. . . . .(3:20)

918[2] FAWLEY FLYER [73] 7-10-13 R Dunwoody, *wth ldr, led 4th, wl clr 2 out, eased r-in. . . . . . .*(9 to 4 op 7 to 4 tchd 5 to 2) 1

841[3] CREDIT CONTROLLER (Ire) [60] 7-10-0 B Fenton, *rear, rdn and lost tch aftr 8th, sn wl beh, styd on strly appr last, took second nr finish. . . . .*(9 to 1 op 6 to 1 tchd 10 to 1) 2

891 TIBBS INN [60] 7-9-7 (7[*]) Mr R Thornton, *wtd wth in tch, chsd ldg pair 9th, rdn and no imprsn nxt, one pace.*
. . . . (33 to 1 op 25 to 1 tchd 40 to 1) 3

796[3] WHISTLING BUCK (Ire) [83] 8-11-6 (3[*]) L Aspell, *prmnt, chsd wnr aftr 8th, rdn and btn aftr 3 out, blun last, wknd r-in.*
. . . .(2 to 1 fav op 7 to 4 tchd 9 to 4) 4

DURSHAN (USA) [79] (v) 7-11-5 N Williamson, *wtd wth in tch, outpcd 9th, tld off. . . . . .*(11 to 2 op 4 to 1 tchd 6 to 1) 5

587 MACEDONAS [76] 8-11-2 B Powell, *in tch, mstk 5th and reminder, rdn and wknd aftr 7th, tld off.*
. . . . (20 to 1 op 16 to 1 tchd 25 to 1) 6

MADAME PRESIDENT (Ire) [88] 5-11-10 (3[*]) G Hogan, *led to 4th, wknd 8th, tld off whn pld up bef 2 out.* (5 to 1 op 4 to 1) pu

Dist: 11l, nk, ½l, 25l, 10l. 5m 5.90s. a 28.90s (7 Ran).

(David Chown), W G M Turner

988 Highway Motor Policies At Lloyds Handicap Chase Class D (0-120 5-y-o and up) £3,562 2m 5f. . . . . (3:50)

ZAMBEZI SPIRIT (Ire) [88] 7-10-0 D Byrne, *trkd ldr 6th, led aftr tenth, clr 4 out, easily. . . . .*(11 to 4 jt-fav op 2 to 1 tchd 7 to 4) 1

MINE'S AN ACE (NZ) [95] 9-10-7 N Williamson, *mstk 1st, in tch, reminder tenth, chsd wnr nxt, rdn and no imprsn 4 out, fnshd tired. . . . .*(4 to 1 op 5 to 1 tchd 11 to 2) 2

831[5] BLACK CHURCH [98] 10-10-10 R Dunwoody, *wtd wth in tch, pushed alng aftr 9th, chsd ldg pair aftr 11th, outpcd frm 4 out.*
. . . .(11 to 4 jt-fav op 5 to 2 tchd 100 to 30) 3

847[2] DRUMSTICK [94] (bl) 10-10-6 J Railton, *rcd freely, clr ldr till hdd aftr tenth, sn rdn and struggling.*
. . . .(15 to 2 op 5 to 1 tchd 9 to 1) 4

BE SURPRISED [88] 10-10-0 J R Kavanagh, *al beh, tld off whn pld up bef tenth. . . . .*(50 to 1 tchd 80 to 1) pu

953[2] PAPER STAR [103] 9-11-1 B Powell, *sn rdn, chsd ldr to 6th, wknd 9th, tld off and pld up bef 4 out. . . .*(3 to 1 op 7 to 2) pu

Dist: 11l, 4l, 13l. 5m 12.90s. a 6.90s (6 Ran).
SR: 24/20/19/2/-/-/

(P C Townsend), Mrs Merrita Jones

989 A. R. Dennis Novices' Hurdle Class E (4-y-o and up) £2,385 2½m. . . . . (4:20)

SLEEPITE (Fr) 6-10-12 R Dunwoody, *al prmnt, led aftr 9th, clr 2 out, drvn out. . . . .*(7 to 1 op 5 to 1) 1

677[*] SUPREME STAR (USA) 5-11-5 M Richards, *hld up, prog 9th, chsd wnr and wide bend appr 2 out, styd on und pres, nvr nrr.*
. . . .(9 to 4 jt-fav op 5 to 2 tchd 2 to 1) 2

824[2] WANSTEAD (Ire) (bl) 4-10-11 A Maguire, *in tch, effrt 9th, kpt on one pace und pres frm 2 out. . . . .*(9 to 4 jt-fav op 7 to 4 tchd 5 to 2) 3

835[4] ZUNO FLYER (USA) 4-10-11 N Williamson, *cl up, chsd ldr 9th, lost pl rpdly bef nxt, ran on ag'n r-in. .*(20 to 1 op 10 to 1) 4

900 POLO KIT (Ire) 5-10-12 P Holley, *keen hold, prmnt, led 8th till aftr nxt, hrd rdn and wknd appr 2 out.*
. . . .(11 to 4 op 5 to 2 tchd 3 to 1) 5

225 SOLLEGALE (Ire) 4-10-11 C Llewellyn, *led to 8th, wknd rpdly, tld off. . . . .*(50 to 1 tchd 66 to 1) 6

830[3] COOLEGALE (bl) 10-10-9 (3[*]) G Hogan, *hld up, prog 4th, wth ldr 7th, wknd rpdly and mstk nxt, tld off. (33 to 1 op 14 to 1) 7

NIGHT THYNE (Ire) 4-10-11 B Powell, *hld up, prog aftr 8th, effrt 3 out, 4th and btn whn pld up bef 2 out, dismounted.*
. . . .(16 to 1 op 50 to 1) pu

Dist: 3l, 11l, 5l, nk, dist, 7l. 5m 6.80s. a 29.80s (8 Ran).

(David Chown), W G M Turner

990 Joe & Co Novices' Handicap Hurdle Class E (0-100 4-y-o and up) £2,448 2m 1f. . . . .(4:50)

856[2] CANARY FALCON [82] 5-11-1 P Holley, *trkd ldrs, prog 7th, led aftr 3 out, clr last, rdn out.*
. . . .(15 to 8 fav op 2 to 1 tchd 9 to 4 and 13 to 8) 1

824[*] MAZZINI (Ire) [95] 5-11-11 (3[*]) L Aspell, *trkd ldrs, effrt 7th, rdn to chase wnr 2 out, no imprsn r-in.*
. . . .(4 to 1 op 5 to 2 tchd 9 to 2) 2

BLURRED IMAGE (Ire) [67] 5-10-0 T J Murphy, *last pair till prog aftr 6th, effrt and ran wide bend appr 2 out, not quicken und pres. . . . .*(33 to 1 op 20 to 1) 3

FIRST INSTANCE (Ire) [75] 6-10-9 B Fenton, *hld up in tch gng easily, effrt 7th, one pace aftr 3 out. . . .*(12 to 1 op 16 to 1) 4

824[6] WATER HAZARD (Ire) [82] 4-11-0 R Dunwoody, *trkd ldrs, prog 7th, led appr 3 out till aftr three out, rdn whn stumbled bend approaching nxt, wknd.*
. . . .(3 to 1 tchd 5 to 2 and 100 to 30) 5

DEPTFORD BELLE [69] 6-10-3 D Morris, *last pair till prog aftr 6th, no imprsn on ldrs 3 out. . . . .*(33 to 1 op 20 to 1) 6

BOWLES PATROL (Ire) [68] 4-10-0 R Supple, *keen hold, prmnt, led briefly aftr 7th, wknd nxt.*
. . . .(14 to 1 op 12 to 1 tchd 16 to 1) 7

FULL OF TRICKS [66] 8-10-0 L Harvey, *led to 6th, wknd rpdly, tld off. . . . .*(50 to 1) 8

JACKSONS BAY [69] 6-10-3 E Murphy, *keen hold, prmnt, led 6th till aftr 7th, wknd rpdly, tld off. . .*(33 to 1 tchd 40 to 1) 9

FARMER'S TERN (Ire) [84] 4-10-9 (7[*]) Mr R Thornton, *mstks 3rd, in tch, rdn and wknd 6th, tld off.*
. . . .(9 to 1 op 6 to 1 tchd 10 to 1) 10

JUST A BEAU [67] 5-9-9 (5[*]) Sophie Mitchell, *in tch to 6th, sn wknd, tld off. . . . .*(66 to 1 op 50 to 1) 11

Dist: 5l, 3l, 3l, 5l, 15l, 2½l, dist, 5l, 1¼l, 18l. 4m 18.70s. a 21.70s (11 Ran).

(L Pipe), R J O'Sullivan

WARWICK (firm)
Tuesday October 22nd
Going Correction: MINUS 0.70 sec. per fur.

991 Ragley Hall Juvenile Novices' Hurdle Class D (3-y-o) £3,109 2m. . . . .(2:10)

767[*] DOCTOR GREEN (Fr) (v) 11-4 A P McCoy, *made all, hit second, clr 5th, pushed out, easily. . . .*(6 to 4 on op Evens) 1

819 KALAO TUA (Ire) 10-7 P Hide, *chsd ldrs, mstk 4th, pressed wnr frm 3 out, hld up, blun nxt. . . . .*(7 to 1 op 5 to 1) 2

HAL HOO YAROOM 10-12 R Farrant, *not fluent, pressed wnr till 3 out, sn btn. . . . .*(7 to 1 op 5 to 1) 3

TOPAGLOW (Ire) 10-12 T Eley, *chsd ldrs, blun 1st, rdn 4th, no hdwy frm nxt. . . . .*(33 to 1) 4

893[2] FLOOD'S FANCY 10-7 Richard Guest, *hld up beh ldrs, lost tch frm 5th. . . . .*(12 to 1 op 20 to 1) 5

819[3] HOW COULD-I (Ire) (bl) 10-7 A Thornton, *nvr trble ldrs.*
. . . .(25 to 1 op 14 to 1) 6

COLOUR COUNSELLOR (bl) 10-12 J Osborne, *hld up, hdwy aftr 3rd, beh frm 5th, no ch whn blun 2 out.*
. . . .(20 to 1 op 16 to 1) 7

THE GREY WEAVER 10-5 (7[*]) J K McCarthy, *nvr trble ldrs.*
. . . .(66 to 1 op 50 to 1) 8

I SAY DANCER (Ire) 10-7 S Wynne, *keen hold, hld up, al beh.*
. . . .(66 to 1 op 50 to 1) 9

893[5] INDIAN WOLF 10-12 I Lawrence, *beh till f 5th.*
. . . .(66 to 1 op 50 to 1) f

EMBROIDERED 10-4 (3[*]) G Tormey, *hld up, blun and uns rdr 3rd. . . . .*(66 to 1 op 50 to 1) ur

Dist: 9l, 3½l, 2½l, 2½l, 2l, 24l, 5l, 29l. 3m 36.90s. a 2.10s (11 Ran).

(Jim Weeden), M C Pipe

992 Coughton Court Claiming Hurdle Class G (4-y-o and up) £1,920 2m. . . . . (2:40)

786[*] INDIAN JOCKEY 4-11-12 A P McCoy, *made most, blun 3rd, jnd nxt, rdn aftr 3 out, all out r-in.*
. . . .(7 to 1 on tchd 6 to 1 on) 1

770[4] HIGHLY CHARMING (Ire) 14-10-7 (7[*]) Mr A Wintle, *chsd wnr, dsptd ld frm 4th, ev ch r-in, ran on. . . . .*(11 to 4 op 5 to 1) 2

THE DEACONESS 9-10-3 Gary Lyons, *hld up, some hdwy aftr 3rd, nvr nr to chal. . . . .*(50 to 1 op 33 to 1) 3

52[5] ROC AGE 5-11-7 Mr J Nolan, *trkd ldrs, rdn appr hfwy, sn btn.*
. . . .(33 to 1 op 20 to 1) 4

297[8] CANESTRELLI (USA) 11-10-8 Mr P Scott, *al beh.*
. . . .(50 to 1 op 33 to 1) 5

COMMANCHE STORM (Ire) 4-10-2⁴ (7*) Mr P O'Keeffe, mid-
div, wknd aftr 3rd, tld off............(100 to 1 op 66 to 1) 6
Dist: Sht-hd, 19l, 6l, 20l, dist. 3m 35.10s. b 3.90s (6 Ran).
SR: 25/13/-/ (Stuart M Mercer), M C Pipe

993 Hatton Country World Novices' Chase Class D (5-y-o and up) £3,458 2½m 110yds......................... (3:10)

772⁵ PREROGATIVE (v) 6-11-0 A P McCoy, made all, rdn out, ran
on wl...............(15 to 8 op 6 to 4 tchd 2 to 1) 1
ELITE GOVERNOR (Ire) 7-11-0 J Osborne, mstk and lost pl
4th, reminders appr 11th, chsd wnr frm nxt, rdn aftr 3 out, no
imprsn...............(4 to 1 op 5 to 1 tchd 11 to 2) 2
941 LARKS TAIL 8-10-9 R Bellamy, hld up, hdwy 7th, wknd and
mstk 11th, wl beh whn blun 2 out......(20 to 1 op 12 to 1) 3
868² ICANTELYA (Ire) 7-11-0 P Hide, prmnt till bad blund and lost
pl second, hdwy 9th, wknd 11th....(7 to 4 fav op 11 to 8) 4
778 AUNTIE LORNA 7-10-2 (7*) Mr R Wakley, slwly into strd, al
beh, tld off whn f 4 out...............(50 to 1 op 33 to 1) f
878 GLAMANGLITZ 6-11-0 T Eley, prmnt, chsd wnr frm second till
blun and uns rdr 11th.................(11 to 2 op 4 to 1) ur
Dist: 12l, 27l, 18l. 5m 8.20s. a 13.20s (6 Ran).
(The Secret Partnership), H S Howe

994 Carlisle & Gough Novices' Hurdle Class D (4-y-o and up) £2,773 2m 3f .... (3:40)

806³ CULRAIN 5-11-0 A Thornton, hld up, hdwy 5th, chsd ldr frm
nxt, led aftr 3 out, sn clr, styd on strly... (9 to 4 op 7 to 4) 1
766⁴ ROSE CHIME (Ire) 4-10-8 P McLoughlin, hld up beh ldrs, mstk
3rd, chsd wnr appr 2 out, no ch whn mistake last.
...............(15 to 8 fav op 7 to 4 tchd 2 to 1) 2
KIROV ROYALE 5-10-9 J Osborne, hld up beh ldrs, lost pl
whn blun 5th, styd on ag'n one pace frm 2 out......(3 to 1) 3
CALLEVA STAR (Ire) 5-11-0 W McFarland, led to aftr 3 out,
fdd........................(4 to 1 op 7 to 2 tchd 9 to 2) 4
768⁶ LILAC RAIN (v) 4-10-5 (3*) D Walsh, dsptd ld to 6th, sn wknd,
wl beh whn blun 3 out...............(20 to 1 op 14 to 1) 5
Dist: 8l, 8l, 1¼l, 16l. 4m 21.90s. (5 Ran).
(A J McDonald), T H Caldwell

995 Warwick Castle Handicap Chase Class E (0-115 5-y-o and up) £3,282 3¼m .... (4:10)

797² EVANGELICA (USA) [115] 6-12-0 A P McCoy, hld up, hit tenth,
hdwy appr 2 out, led r-in, readily.
...............(13 to 8 fav op 5 to 4 tchd 7 to 4) 1
642⁷ TIME ENOUGH (Ire) [90] 7-10-11 G Bradley, chsd ldr, led appr
4th to 13th, rgned ld 2 out, hdd and no extr r-in.
...............(9 to 4 op 4 to 1) 2
CELTIC SILVER [89] 8-10-2 Richard Guest, led to appr 4,
rgned ld 13th, hdd 2 out, one pace.
...............(7 to 4 op 2 to 1 tchd 13 to 8) 3
(Martin Pipe Racing Club), M C Pipe

996 Lord Leicester Hospital Handicap Hurdle Class D (0-125 4-y-o and up) £2,731 2m......................(4:40)

798⁴ HAMILTON SILK [120] 4-12-0 J Osborne, chsd ldr to second,
hld up aftr, led bt appr last, easily.
...............(6 to 5 on op 6 to 4 on) 1
189⁴ KALZARI (USA) [91] 11-10-0 A P McCoy, steadied strt, pld
hrd, chsd ldr frm second, led 3 out, hit nxt, hdd bef last, one
pace....................(3 to 1 op 5 to 2 tchd 7 to 2) 2
DAYTONA BEACH (Ire) [103] 6-10-12 G Bradley, led to 3 out,
pld up and dismounted bef nxt, lme.
...............(2 to 1 op 9 to 4 tchd 5 to 2) pu
Dist: 6l. 3m 40.30s. a 1.30s (3 Ran).
(Elite Racing Club), M C Pipe

EXETER (good to firm)
Wednesday October 23rd
Going Correction: PLUS 0.40 sec. per fur.

997 Kraft Jacob Suchard Novices' Hurdle Class E (4-y-o and up) £2,326 2m 1f 110yds.........................(1:50)

EDGEMOOR PRINCE 5-10-12 R Dunwoody, trkd ldr, led
appr 4th, rdn frm 2 out, styd on wl r-in... (4 to 1 op 3 to 1) 1
798 IKTASAB (bl) 4-11-4 A P McCoy, in tch, chsd wnr 3 out, rdn to
chal 2 out, sn hrd ridden, ev ch last, soon btn.
...............(7 to 2 op 4 to 1 on tchd 3 to 1 on) 2
STEER POINT 5-10-12 Mr A Holdsworth, beh, lost tch 5th,
some hdwy frm 2 out, not a dngr......(33 to 1 op 20 to 1) 3
900 DECOR (Ire) 6-10-12 J Frost, led to appr 4th, wknd 3 out.
...............(20 to 1 op 10 to 1) 4
ARADIA'S DIAMOND 5-10-7 N Williamson, sn beh, lost tch
frm 5th.....................(33 to 1 op 16 to 1) 5

975 LILLY THE FILLY 5-10-7 E Byrne, hdwy 4th, chsd wnr 5th till
blun 3 out, no ch whn blunded last...(100 to 1 op 50 to 1) 6
939 MR JASPER 4-10-11 D Morris, beh frm 4th, tld off.
...............(150 to 1 op 50 to 1) 7
Dist: 5l, 21l, 4l, sht-hd, 28l, dist. 4m 18.10s. a 22.10s (7 Ran).
(The Racing Hares), P J Hobbs

998 Kitsons Selling Handicap Hurdle Class G (0-95 4-y-o and up) £1,887 2m 1f 110yds.........................(2:20)

ASLAR (Ire) [59] 7-10-3 W McFarland, al in tch, chlgd 2 out, sn
led, drvn out..................(8 to 1 op 6 to 1) 1
891⁴ GLOWING PATH [76] 6-11-3 (3*) T Dascombe, chsd ldrs, rdn
2 out, kpt on r-in but not rch wnr.......(8 to 1 op 11 to 2) 2
903² NORDIC CROWN (Ire) [76] (bl) 5-11-5 C Maude, wth ldr till led
5th, hdd 2 out, sn one pace...........(7 to 1 op 11 to 2) 3
918³ CATWALKER (Ire) [63] (bl) 5-10-6 R Dunwoody, beh till hdwy 3
out, styd on same pace frm 2 out.....(14 to 1 op 10 to 1) 4
612⁷ TO BE FAIR [77] 9-11-0 (7*) Mr S Durack, trkd ldrs, led and
mstk 2 out, sn hdd, wknd appr last.....(14 to 1 op 8 to 1) 5
919⁷ BITE THE BULLET [57] 5-10-0 B Powell, made most to 5th,
wknd nxt...................(20 to 1 tchd 25 to 1) 6
891⁶ GALLOPING GUNS (Ire) [67] 4-10-7 (3*) Guy Lewis, hdwy 4th,
chsd ldrs 3 out, wknd appr nxt.......(20 to 1 op 14 to 1) 7
784⁵ PRESTIGE LADY [69] 5-10-12 C Llewellyn, not fluent, al beh.
...............(12 to 1 op 8 to 1) 8
924⁷ WELTON RAMBLER [56] 9-10-0 P Holley, sn beh.
...............(100 to 1 op 33 to 1) 9
918⁵ MARIO'S DREAM (Ire) [65] 8-10-9 M A Fitzgerald, in tch till
wknd and 15th...............(14 to 1 op 20 to 1 tchd 40 to 1) f
918⁷ CASHFLOW CRISIS (Ire) [76] 4-11-0 (5*) S Ryan, hdwy 4th,
tracking ldrs whn mstk and uns rdr 3 out.
...............(5 to 4 fav op 6 to 4 tchd 15 to 8) ur
225⁷ SOVEREIGN NICHE (Ire) [80] (bl) 8-11-10 A P McCoy, refused
to race..................(11 to 1 op 6 to 1) ref
Dist: 4l, 4l, 1¾l, 1¾l, 7l, 18l, 6l, 6l. 4m 15.40s. a 19.40s (12 Ran).
(Mrs P M Ratcliffe), J S Moore

999 Booker Foodservice First For Service Duchy Of Cornwall Cup Novices' Chase Class D (5-y-o and up) £4,140 2 ¾m 110yds.....................(2:50)

904⁴ MR PLAYFULL 6-11-0 J Frost, prmnt, led 5th to 8th, led 9th to
tenth, led 13th, hdd 3 out, rallied to chal last, sn led, ran on wl.
...............(5 to 2 op 2 to 1) 1
GOLDENSWIFT (Ire) 6-10-9 A P McCoy, chsd ldrs, chlgd 4
out, led 3 out, hdd sn aftr last, wknd quickly.
...............(6 to 5 on op Evens tchd 5 to 4 on) 2
MINGUS (USA) 9-11-0 B Powell, beh, hdwy tenth, lost pl 11th,
rallied 4 out, wknd nxt...............(10 to 1 tchd 12 to 1) 3
920⁴ OUR NIKKI 6-10-9 S Burrough, prmnt, rdn and wknd 4 out.
...............(9 to 1 op 8 to 1 tchd 10 to 1) 4
657³ RENT DAY 7-10-9 S Curran, in tch, hit 12th, chsd ldrs nxt, rdn
4 out, still in touch whn blun and uns rdr 3 out.
...............(16 to 1 op 12 to 1) ur
YES WE ARE 10-10-9 M A Fitzgerald, beh frm 6th, tld off whn
pld up bef 3 out.............(33 to 1 op 12 to 1 tchd 40 to 1) pu
902 VARECK II (Fr) 9-10-7 (7*) B Moore, led to 5th, hdd nxt, led
tenth, wknd quickly appr 4 out, tld off whn pld up
bef 3 out..................(40 to 1 op 12 to 1) pu
Dist: 5l, 10l, 27l. 5m 53.30s. a 33.30s (7 Ran).
(P A Tylor), R G Frost

1000 Kitsons Handicap Hurdle Class F (0-105 4-y-o and up) £2,706 2m 3f .... (3:20)

839⁹ SNOW BOARD [77] 7-10-2² D Byrne, in tch, drvn alng and
one pace appr 2 out, styd on approaching last, quickened to ld
r-in, readily...............(7 to 4 fav tchd 6 to 4 op 11 to 10) 1
RELATIVE CHANCE [75] 7-10-0 N Williamson, hdwy 6th, chsd
ldr 2 out, led appr last, hrd rdn, hdd r-in, no extr.
...............(12 to 1 op 8 to 1) 2
HANDSON [88] 4-10-7 (5*) D Salter, hld up, hdwy 6th, led aftr
3 mout, hit 2 out, sn hdd and outpcd...(14 to 1 op 10 to 1) 3
923³ LITTLE HOOLIGAN [85] (bl) 5-10-10 A P McCoy, hld up, hdwy
5th, wknd appr 2 out.....(100 to 30 op 4 to 1 tchd 5 to 1) 4
921² BRIGHT SAPPHIRE [79] 10-10-4 D J Burchell, led to 4th, led
ag'n 6th, hdd aftr 3 out, sn wknd.......(8 to 1 tchd 9 to 1) 5
MR FLUTTS [78] 10-10-3 R Bellamy, hdwy 5th, rdn 3 out, sn
wknd....................(16 to 1 op 10 to 1) 6
896² FLEUR DE TAL [99] 5-11-3 (7*) J Power, trkd ldrs, led 5th to
6th, chlgd 3 out, sn wknd. (13 to 2 op 5 to 1 tchd 7 to 1) 7
772⁹ DOMINION'S DREAM [104] (v) 4-11-7 (7*) G Supple, al beh.
...............(25 to 1 op 10 to 1) 8
876⁶ WINTER ROSE [82] 5-10-7 B Powell, wth ldr, led 4th to 5th,
wknd 3 out.................(16 to 1 op 12 to 1) 9
940⁴ TAKE A FLYER (Ire) [85] (bl) 6-10-7 (3*) T Dascombe, prmnt to
6th, tld off whn pld up bef 2 out.............(10 to 1 op 8 to 1) pu
ALLAHRAKHA [75] 5-10-0 S Fox, prmnt early, beh frm 5th, tld
off whn pld up bef last...............(10 to 1 op 8 to 1) pu
Dist: 1¾l, 12l, 19l, 3l, 1¼l, hd, 2½l, 6l. 4m 33.00s. a 17.00s (11 Ran).
(F J Sainsbury), Mrs Merrita Jones

1001
Booker Foodservice First For Service Novices' Handicap Chase Class E (0-100 5-y-o and up) £2,971 2m 1f 110yds. . . . . (3:50)

PLAYING TRUANT [81] 8-11-10 R Dunwoody, hld up, hdwy 5th, hit 6th, drvn to chal last, led r-in, all out.
. . . . (4 to 1 tchd 9 to 2 and 5 to 1)   1
922² CHICKABIDDY [78] 8-11-7 M A Fitzgerald, chsd ldrs, str chal frm 3 out till slight ld last, hdd r-in, hrd rdn, kpt on.
. . . . (11 to 8 fav op 6 to 4 tchd 9 to 4)   2
5877 JEWEL THIEF [78] (v) 6-11-7 A P McCoy, reluctant into fences, rdn frm 4th, lost tch 7th, tld off . . . (9 to 2 op 3 to 1)   3
9043 LORD NITROGEN (USA) [85] 6-12-0 B Powell, led, propped 1st, clr 8th, rdn whn chlgd frm 3 out, narrowly hdd when l last, rmntd. (5 to 1 op 3 to 1)   4
7699 CHUKKARIO [57] 10-10-0 I Lawrence, jmpd poorly in rear till pld up aftr 5th . . . . (100 to 1 op 66 to 1)   pu
Dist: 1l, dist, 6l. 4m 27.80s. a 22.80s (5 Ran).

(David O Moon), D R Gandolfo

1002
Booker Foodservice First For Service Novices' Hurdle Class E (4-y-o and up) £2,305 2¾m. . . . . (4:20)

812* SAMLEE (Ire) 7-11-5 A P McCoy, made all, hit 3 out, drvn frm nxt, all out. . . . . (2 to 1 on op 5 to 4 on)   1
KENDAL CAVALIER 6-10-12 B Fenton, beh, tld off 6th, steady hdwy frm 3 out, chsd wnr aftr 2 out, ev ch last, one pace.
. . . . (7 to 2 op 5 to 2 tchd 4 to 1)   2
7833 GENERAL MOUKTAR (v) 6-10-12 C Maude, in tch, hdwy to chase ldrs 7th, rdn and one pace frm 2 out.
. . . . (7 to 1 op 3 to 1)   3
GLISTENING DAWN (bl) 6-11-0 R Johnson, in tch, jmpd slwly 6th, hdwy 7th, wknd appr 2 out. . . . . . . (20 to 1 op 14 to 1)   4
GERRY'S PRIDE (Ire) 5-10-12 S Curran, beh 4th, hdwy 7th, wknd aftr 3 out . . . . (25 to 1 op 12 to 1)   5
9378 COLIN'S PRIDE (bl) 5-10-2 (5*) Sophie Mitchell, wth wnr to 5th, wknd 7th, tld off whn pld up bef 4 out.
. . . . (10 to 1 op 20 to 1)   pu
PROFESSION 5-10-12 R Farrant, al beh, tld off whn pld up bef 4 out. . . . . (100 to 1 op 25 to 1)   pu
Dist: 1¼l, 7l, 22l, 4l. 5m 32.30s. a 35.30s (7 Ran).

(White Lion Partnership), P J Hobbs

GOWRAN PARK (IRE) (yielding (races 1,2), soft (3))
Wednesday October 23rd

1003
Wexford Handicap Chase (0-109 5-y-o and up) £2,740 2¾m. . . . . . . (4:30)

714* CORYMANDEL (Ire) [-] 7-11-9 F Woods, ... (11 to 2)   1
714 TRIPTODICKS (Ire) [-] 6-9-7 (7*) A O'Shea, ... (4 to 1 fav)   2
FAIR GO [-] 10-9-3 (7*) Mrs C Harrison, ... (12 to 1)   3
981 BALLYBODEN [-] 9-11-1 M P Hourigan, ... (12 to 1)   4
7474 STRADBALLEY (Ire) [-] 6-11-0 K F O'Brien, ... (12 to 1)   5
OLYMPIC D'OR (Ire) [-] 8-12-0 C O'Dwyer, ... (10 to 1)   6
852* CASTALINO [-] 10-11-1 J Shortt, ... (5 to 1)   7
ROSSI NOVAE (-] (bl) 13-9-11 T P Treacy, ... (25 to 1)   8
576* BROOK HILL LADY (Ire) [-] 7-11-10 C F Swan, ... (11 to 2)   f
729 PORT RISING (Ire) [-] 7-10-7 D H O'Connor, ... (12 to 1)   pu
314 PHAIRY MIRACLES (Ire) [-] 7-10-13 P M Verling, . . . (6 to 1)   pu
Dist: 7l, dist, 1½l, 3l. 5m 51.60s. (11 Ran).

(M J E Thornhill), H de Bromhead

1004
Careys Cottage Handicap Chase (5-y-o and up) £3,425 2¼m. . . . . . (5:00)

851* THE OUTBACK WAY (Ire) [-] (bl) 6-10-5² D H O'Connor,
. . . . (9 to 4)   1
747* ANABATIC (Ire) [-] 8-12-0 T P Rudd, ... (2 to 1 fav)   2
7804 HANNIES GIRL (Ire) [-] 7-9-0 (7*) L J Fleming, ... (16 to 1)   3
8526 QUATTRO [-] 6-9-2 (5*) G Cotter, ... (14 to 1)   4
FIFTYSEVENCHANNELS (Ire) [-] 7-11-6 C F Swan, (11 to 2)   5
8526 ANOTHER COURSE (Ire) [-] 8-9-7 T Horgan, ... (12 to 1)   6
BOB DEVANI [-] 10-10-12 C O'Dwyer, ... (8 to 1)   7
8514 EVER SO BOLD [-] 9-10-2 T P Treacy, ... (12 to 1)   8
Dist: 6l, 3½l, 3½l, 7l. 4m 43.40s. (8 Ran).

(E O'Dwyer), James Joseph O'Connor

1005
Kilkenny I.N.H. Flat Race (4-y-o and up) £2,740 2m . . . . (5:30)

4644 BESSMOUNT LEADER (Ire) 4-11-6 (3*) Mr B M Cash,
. . . . (100 to 30)   1
BLUE IRISH (Ire) 5-11-7 (7*) Mr J Cullen, ... (25 to 1)   2
9102 LORD EDENBURY (Ire) 5-11-9 (5*) Mr R Walsh, (10 to 9 on)   3
9106 HIDDEN HOLLOW (Ire) 5-12-0 Mr H F Cleary, ... (10 to 1)   4
GALLIC HONEY (Ire) 5-11-2 (7*) Mrs C Harrison, . . (14 to 1)   5
JOKING ASIDE (Ire) 4-11-2 (7*) Mr J P Moloney, ... (8 to 1)   6
9296 TWO IN TUNE (Ire) 8-11-7 (7*) Mr D Keane, ... (16 to 1)   7
910 MOLLY WHACK (Ire) 5-11-2 (7*) Mr D P Coakley, . . (25 to 1)   8
GODSROCK VI (Ire) 7-11-7 (7*) Miss A Foley, ... (20 to 1)   9

853⁵ EASTERN CUSTOM (Ire) 5-11-6 (3*) Mr R O'Neill, . . (8 to 1)   10
JOLLY LAD (Ire) 5-12-0 Mr P Fenton, ... (7 to 1)   11
TUROS (Ire) 6-11-7 (7*) Mr J Cash, ... (16 to 1)   12
884 SISTER CAMILLUS (Ire) 5-11-2 (7*) Mr P G Murphy, (14 to 1)   13
805³ GARAMOY (Ire) 5-11-2 (7*) Mr M O'Connor, ... (12 to 1)   pu
Dist: 1l, 8l, 13l, hd. 4m 11.20s. (14 Ran).

(Miss J Butler), A P O'Brien

LUDLOW (firm)
Thursday October 24th
Going Correction: MINUS 0.15 sec. per fur.

1006
Halford Novices' Hurdle Class E (4-y-o and up) £2,388 2m. . . . . (2:20)

8675 PEGASUS BAY 5-11-5 J Osborne, hld up, steady hdwy appr 3 out, led on bit nxt, cmftbly. . . . . (20 to 1 op 12 to 1)   1
TODD (USA) 5-10-12 G Bradley, mstks, pressed ldr, led appr 3 out, rdn and hdd nxt, no extr r-in. . (12 to 1 tchd 14 to 1)   2
DRAKESTONE 5-10-12 R Johnson, hld up, gd hdwy appr 3 out, styd on und pres. . . (11 to 1 op 8 to 1 tchd 12 to 1)   3
939* ATH CHEANNAITHE (Fr) 4-11-4 D Bridgwater, led till hdd appr 3 out, eased whn btn bef last. . . (6 to 4 fav op 9 to 4)   4
8884 KING RAT (Ire) 5-10-7 (5*) Michael Brennan, mid-div, one pace frm 3 out. . . . . . (11 to 4 op 3 to 1 tchd 7 to 2)   5
8462 SUPERENSIS 6-10-12 I Lawrence, slwly away, in rear, effrt 6th, nvr dngrs. . . . . (25 to 1 op 10 to 1)   6
8799 YOUNG BENSON 4-10-8 (3*) R Massey, chsd ldrs till wknd quickly aftr 6th, tld off. . . . . (33 to 1 op 16 to 1)   7
9196 SPUMANTE (bl) 4-10-11 B Powell, al beh, tld off.
. . . . (16 to 1 op 12 to 1 tchd 20 to 1)   8
924* LAST LAUGH (Ire) (bl) 4-10-13 A P McCoy, al beh, lost tch 5th, tld off. . . . . (6 to 1 op 4 to 1 tchd 13 to 2)   9
BARGASH 4-10-11 Gary Lyons, chsd ldrs till wknd 5th, tld off. . . . . (25 to 1 op 14 to 1)   10
873 BARTON BLADE (Ire) 4-10-11 J F Titley, in tch till wknd 5th, tld off. . . . . (25 to 1 op 14 to 1)   11
Dist: 4l, 2½l, 5l, 4l, 12l, 18l, 10l, 1½l, 5l, 7l. 3m 36.90s. a 4.90s (11 Ran).
SR: 18/7/4/5/-/-/

(Don Cantillon), D E Cantillon

1007
Castle Selling Handicap Chase Class G (0-90 5-y-o and up) £2,668 2m. (2:50)

901⁴ FENWICK [85] 9-11-8 (3*) T Dascombe, al prmnt in chasing grp, led 4 out, clr 2 out. . . . . . . (3 to 1 tchd 100 to 30)   1
5570 CARDENDEN (Ire) [73] 8-10-13 A Thornton, trkd ldr, led appr 6th, hdd 4 out, rdn and one pace aftr.
. . . . (14 to 1 op 10 to 1 tchd 16 to 1)   2
7862 SAFETY (USA) [88] (bl) 9-12-0 A Maguire, led till hdd appr 6th, lost pl 9th, kpt on frm 4 out. . . . . (5 to 2 jt-fav op 7 to 2 tchd 4 to 1)   3
43 MASTER SALESMAN [73] 13-10-13 J R Kavanagh, hld up, hdwy 6th, ev ch appr 4 out, wknd nxt.
. . . . (20 to 1 op 16 to 1 tchd 25 to 1)   4
8573 GABISH [60] 11-9-7 (7*) Mr R Thornton, in tch to 6th, nvr on terms aftr. . . . . (15 to 2 op 8 to 1 tchd 10 to 1)   5
2666 HUGH DANIELS [72] 8-10-9 (3*) G Hogan, al beh, tld off 6th.
. . . . (20 to 1 op 16 to 1)   6
102 SALCOMBE HARBOUR (NZ) [63] 12-10-3 Dr P Pritchard, not jump wl, beh 5th, tld off whn blun 7th. (33 to 1 tchd 50 to 1)   7
885* SPRING LOADED [78] 5-10-12 (5*) Michael Brennan, in rear till rdn and hdwy appr 4 out, fourth and btn whn blun and uns rdr 2 out. . . . . (5 to 2 jt-fav op 6 to 4)   ur
895 RED MATCH [68] 11-10-8 B Powell, chsd ldrs to 5th, sn beh, tld off whn pld up bef 9th. . . . . (25 to 1 tchd 33 to 1)   pu
Dist: 11l, 4l, 1¼l, 8l, 28l, 2½l. 3m 55.50s. a 5.50s (9 Ran).
SR: 18/-/6/-/-/-/

(Major A W C Pearn), R J Hodges

1008
Farmers Stores Handicap Hurdle Class D (0-120 4-y-o and up) £2,684 2m. . . . . (3:20)

7983 YUBRALEE (USA) [111] 4-11-10 A P McCoy, made all, sn clr, unchlgd. . . . . (11 to 8 fav op 5 to 4 tchd 6 to 4)   1
CYRUS THE GREAT (Ire) [105] 4-11-4 G Bradley, chsd wnr thrght, no ch frm 3 out. . . . . (9 to 4 tchd 5 to 2)   2
876* STAY WITH ME (Fr) [95] 6-10-9 J Osborne, chsd 1st 2, rdn 3 out, wknd and eased nxt. . . (9 to 4 op 7 to 4 tchd 5 to 2)   3
CABIN HILL [100] 10-11-0 M M Jackson, tld off 4th.
. . . . (20 to 1 op 16 to 1 tchd 28 to 1)   4
PETITJEAN (Fr) [98] 5-10-12 T Eley, beh whn f 4th.
. . . . (14 to 1 op 10 to 1 tchd 16 to 1)   f
Dist: 6l, 8l, 28l. 3m 60.60s. a 4.60s (5 Ran).
SR: 26/14/

(D A Johnson), M C Pipe

1009
Ludlow Motors Novices' Chase Class E (5-y-o and up) £3,035 2½m. . . . . (3:50)

892² IMPERIAL VINTAGE (Ire) 6-11-12 A P McCoy, made all, in control whn hit 3 out, clr and mstk last, easily.
. . . . (2 to 1 on tchd 9 to 4 on)   1

250² DANCING AT LAHARN (Ire) 6-10-12 G Lyons, *chsd wnr thrght, hld and wkng whn stumbled on landing 3 out, no ch aftr* ....(9 to 1 op 5 to 1 tchd 13 to 2) 2
845² LITTLE BY LITTLE 6-10-12 A Thornton, *al beh, tld off tenth* ....(10 to 1 tchd 12 to 1) 3
NATIVE RAMBLER (Ire) 6-10-12 Mr M Jackson, *al beh, tld off tenth* ....(50 to 1 op 33 to 1 tchd 66 to 1) 4
904 PRIORY ROSE 9-10-7 S Burrough, *pld hrd, chsd ldrs till f 4th.* ....(66 to 1 op 33 to 1) f
671⁷ TERRANO STAR (Ire) 5-10-7 (3") Guy Lewis, *3rd whn f 7th.* ....(8 to 1 op 7 to 2 tchd 9 to 1) f
Dist: 14l, dist, 20l. 4m 55.20s. a 6.20s (6 Ran).
SR: 6/-/-/   (David M Williams, Miss Venetia Williams)

1010 Hazlin Doors Novices' Handicap Hurdle Class E (0-100 4-y-o and up) £2,276 2m 5f 110yds......... (4:20)

919³ CROWN IVORY (NZ) [66] 8-10-9 S Fox, *hld up in rear, hdwy to go second appr 3 out, hrd rdn and styd on to ld r-in.* ....(100 to 30 op 7 to 2 tchd 4 to 1 tchd 3 to 1) 1
836³ SALTIS (Ire) [76] 4-11-4 G Lyons, *hld up, hdwy 6th, led sn aftr 8th, hit 3 out, soon rdn, hdd and no extr r-in.* ....(9 to 1 op 7 to 2) 2
111⁴ ONE MORE DIME [72] 6-10-8 (7") Mr R Thornton, *al beh, tld off.* ....(8 to 1 op 5 to 1 tchd 7 to 1) 3
800⁵ KAREN'S TYPHOON (Ire) [75] (bl) 5-11-3 A P McCoy, *led till wknd quickly and hdd sn aftr 8th, tld off.* ....(13 to 8 fav op 7 to 4 tchd 2 to 1) 4
CURRAGH PETER [81] 9-11-7 (3") Guy Lewis, *chsd ldr till wknd quickly appr 6th, tld off.* ....(25 to 1 op 12 to 1 tchd 33 to 1) 5
937² MYLORDMAYOR [57] (bl) 10-10-0 R Farrant, *chsd ldrs, wnt second appr 6th, blun badly nxt, sn pld up.* ....(9 to 4 op 3 to 1) pu
Dist: 1¾l, dist, 4l, dist. 4m 59.30s. a 4.30s (6 Ran).
SR: 7/14/-/   (Mrs B D Adams), P C Ritchens

1011 Court Of Hill Amateur Riders' Handicap Chase Class E (0-110 5-y-o and up) £2,886 2½m......... (4:50)

COOLREE (Ire) [105] 8-11-11 (7") Mr J Tizzard, *al in tch, wnt second tenth, led twelfth, blun 3 out, sn reco'red, styd on.* ....(2 to 1 op 6 to 4) 1
81⁶ OSCAIL AN DORAS (Ire) [108] 7-12-4 (3") Mr K Whelan, *hld up in rear, hdwy to go second 13th, no imprsn frm 3 out.* ....(6 to 4 fav tchd 7 to 4) 2
875⁴ HOUGHTON [105] 10-11-11 (7") Mr R Burton, *led to 1st, trkd ldr till blun tenth, wknd appr 4 out, tld off.* ....(5 to 1 op 5 to 1 tchd 8 to 1) 3
842³ THEY ALL FORGOT ME [80] 9-10-0 (7") Miss C Dyson, *al beh, tld off whn f 4 out.* ....(25 to 1 op 16 to 1) f
MR PRIMETIME (Ire) [90] 6-10-10 (7") Mr E James, *pld hrd, led 1st to twelfth, cl 3rd and rdn whn f 4 out.* ....(100 to 30 op 9 to 4 tchd 7 to 1) f
Dist: 5l, dist. 4m 55.00s. a 6.00s (5 Ran).
SR: 14/12/   (B T R Weston), P F Nicholls

1012 Clun Intermediate National Hunt Flat Class H (4,5,6-y-o) £1,316 2m (5:20)

873* SCOUNDREL 5-11-4 (7") Mr R Wakley, *hld up in tch, hdwy to ld 3 fs out, ran on strly.* ....(9 to 4 on op 2 to 1 on tchd 7 to 4 on) 1
GUNNER SID 5-10-11 (7") Miss L Boswell, *hld up, hdwy hfwy, chsd wnr fnl 2 fs.* ....(14 to 1 op 7 to 1) 2
TAFZAL 5-10-11 (7") S Fowler, *hld up in rear, hdwy 6 fs out, kpt on to press second fnl 2 furlongs.* ....(33 to 1) 3
STRIKE A LIGHT (Ire) 4-10-10 (7") Mr A Wintle, *hld up in rear, hdwy o'r 4 fs out, nvr dngrs.* (9 to 2 op 5 to 2 tchd 9 to 4) 4
GERGAASH 4-10-10 (7") Clare Thorner, *beh, hdwy 5 furlong out, no terms.* ....(16 to 1 op 10 to 1) 5
MILLING BROOK 4-10-10 (7") J Power, *hld up, hdwy 5 fs out, nvr dngrs.* ....(50 to 1) 6
942⁷ WEATHER WISE 4-10-10 (7") N Willmington, *prmnt to hfwy, no ch fnl 5 fs.* ....(50 to 1 op 33 to 1) 7
MR C-I-P (Ire) 5-10-13 (5") Michael Brennan, *prmnt, led 7 fs out, hdd and wknd 3 out.* ....(66 to 1 op 50 to 1) 8
942⁶ LEOPARD LADY 4-10-5 (7") Mr R Thornton, *chsd ldrs, wknd 5 fs out.* ....(50 to 1) 9
BARNETTS BOY 4-11-0 (3") D Walsh, *unruly strt, al beh, tld off.* ....(20 to 1 op 10 to 1) 10
DERRING KNIGHT (v) 6-11-4 Mr A Sansome, *al beh, tld off.* ....(100 to 1 op 50 to 1) 11
SYBAN 5-11-1 (3") G Hogan, *pld hrd, prmnt till wknd 6 fs out, tld off.* ....(66 to 1 op 50 to 1) 12
DEFERENCE DUE (Ire) 5-11-4 Mr M Jackson, *pld hrd, led aftr 6 fs, hdd 7 out, wknd rpdly o'r 4 out, tld off.* ......(33 to 1) 13
942 LITTLE EMBERS 4-10-9 (3") R Massey, *al beh, tld off.* ....(50 to 1) 14
TEETON TWO (bl) 5-10-11 (7") Mr B Dixon, *led for 6 fs, sn wknd, tld off.* ....(12 to 1 op 10 to 1 tchd 33 to 1) 15
Dist: 14l, nk, 6l, 1¼l, 3½l, 2½l, 3l, 6l, 4l, 7l. 3m 30.90s. (15 Ran).
                                   (Mrs J M Corbett), K C Bailey

PUNCHESTOWN (IRE) (good to yielding) Thursday October 24th
Going Correction: PLUS 0.50 sec. per fur.

1013 Gowran Grange Maiden Hurdle (5-y-o and up) £3,082 2½m...... (2:30)

BANGABUNNY 6-11-6 D Parker, ...(8 to 1) 1
773⁵ MERCHANTS QUAY (Ire) 5-11-9 (5") G Cotter, ...(9 to 1) 2
720⁷ OWNING (Ire) 6-11-6 C F Swan, ...(10 to 1) 3
COMMERCIAL HOUSE (Ire) 8-11-6 D T Evans, ...(20 to 1) 4
722* GLENREEF BOY (Ire) 7-12-0 A Powell, ...(10 to 1) 5
ETON GALE (Ire) 7-12-0 R Dunwoody, ...(2 to 1 on) 6
928 MARINERS REEF (Ire) 5-10-8 (7") D McCullagh, ...(33 to 1) 7
853⁶ HILL OF HOPE (Ire) 5-11-6 W Slattery, ...(12 to 1) 8
PRE-LET (Ire) 6-11-1 M P Dwyer, ...(25 to 1) 9
910⁸ PROLOGUE (Ire) 5-11-6 J Shortt, ...(14 to 1) 10
928 JUST SUPREME (Ire) 5-11-6 T P Treacy, ...(33 to 1) 11
STRONG RAIDER (Ire) 6-11-6 K F O'Brien, ...(25 to 1) 12
928 TIME FOR A WINNER (Ire) 5-11-1 T J Mitchell, ...(50 to 1) 13
884⁸ TRY ONCE MORE (Ire) 5-11-6 C O'Dwyer, ...(16 to 1) 14
MR CHATAWAY (Ire) 5-11-6 F Woods, ...(16 to 1) 15
945 JAFFA MAN (Ire) 5-11-6 J P Broderick, ...(25 to 1) 16
132⁹ PIXIE BLUE (Ire) 5-10-8 (7") Mr R Behan, ...(50 to 1) 17
943 DEEP BIT (Ire) 5-11-6 N Williamson, ...(20 to 1) pu
Dist: 2½l, 1l, 5l, 2l. 5m 19.10s. a 37.10s (18 Ran).
                          (D C A Bramall), Mrs S A Bramall

1014 Dunstown Wood Chase (5-y-o and up) £3,425 2½m...................... (3:00)

JOHNNY SETASIDE (Ire) 7-12-0 M P Dwyer, ...(5 to 4 on) 1
THE CRAZY BISHOP (Ire) 8-11-8 T P Treacy, ...(7 to 2) 2
STRONG HICKS (Ire) 8-11-8 F J Flood, ...(6 to 1) 3
949 DIAMOND SPRITE (USA) 9-10-11 (7") G Martin, ...(40 to 1) 4
20⁸ LISNAGREE BOY 8-11-4 T J Mitchell, ...(25 to 1) f
MACALLISTER (Ire) 6-11-1 (3") B Bowens, ...(7 to 2) ur
Dist: 5½l, 2½l, dist. 5m 25.10s. a 28.10s (6 Ran).
                                   (John O'Meara), Noel Meade

1015 Nine Tree Hill Maiden Hurdle (4-y-o) £3,082 2m.................... (3:30)

733* RADANPOUR (Ire) 11-6 (3") D J Casey, ...(5 to 4 fav) 1
773* MOSCOW EXPRESS (Ire) 11-9 C F Swan, ...(7 to 4) 2
ICY PROJECT (Ire) 11-2 (7") M W Martin, ...(12 to 1) 3
928 SHAWAHIN 11-9 R Dunwoody, ...(20 to 1) 4
MIDDLEOFTHENIGHT (Ire) 11-4 P L Malone, ...(33 to 1) 5
578⁷ RAHANINE MELODY (Ire) 10-11 (7") Mr P J Crowley, ...(33 to 1) 6
883⁵ PERSIAN DANSER (Ire) 11-1 (3") U Smyth, ...(20 to 1) 7
731 RIVER RUMPUS (Ire) 11-9 F Woods, ...(33 to 1) 8
343⁹ PERPETUAL PROSPECT (Ire) 11-9 C O'Dwyer, ...(20 to 1) 9
COLONEL GEORGE 11-9 D Parker, ...(5 to 1) 10
850 SHALOM (Ire) 11-9 M P Hourigan, ...(33 to 1) 11
898 BARLEY MEADOW (Ire) 11-9 H Rogers, ...(33 to 1) 12
782 OXFORD LUNCH (USA) 11-9 T P Treacy, ...(20 to 1) 13
928 KING PUCK 11-4 (5") T Martin, ...(20 to 1) 14
733⁵ SABANIYA (Fr) 10-13 (5") G Cotter, ...(14 to 1) 15
JACKSON'S PANTHER (Ire) 11-4 A Powell, ...(20 to 1) 16
SHANNON GALE (Ire) 11-9 L P Cusack, ...(20 to 1) 17
560⁶ MACCABAEUS (Ire) 11-9 N Williamson, ...(20 to 1) 18
FLORAL EMBLEM (Ire) 11-1 (3") B Bowens, ...(20 to 1) 19
850 WESTERN GREY (Ire) 11-2 (7") S FitzGerald, ...(33 to 1) 20
GARRYSPILLANE (Ire) 11-2 (7") Mr S P Hennessy, (33 to 1) 21
716 ZIGGY THE GREAT (Ire) 11-9 K F O'Brien, ...(33 to 1) 22
ROB MINE (Ire) 11-2 (7") L A Hurley, ...(33 to 1) 23
DEL MADERA (Ire) 11-9 J P Broderick, ...(33 to 1) 24
AJKNAPP (Ire) 11-9 M P Dwyer, ...(20 to 1) pu
Dist: 2l, 11l, 8l, 11l. 4m 1.00s. a 16.00s (25 Ran).
SR: 15/13/2/-/-/   (P P T Bridson), W P Mullins

1016 European Breeders Fund Beginners Chase (5-y-o and up) £4,110 2m................................... (4:00)

881² THE SUBBIE (Ire) 7-12-0 T P Treacy, ...(4 to 1) 1
DAWN ALERT (Ire) 7-12-0 R Dunwoody, ...(11 to 2) 2
DERRYMOYLE (Ire) 7-12-0 M P Dwyer, ...(12 to 1) 3
909⁴ LUCKY TOWN (Ire) 5-11-10 C F Swan, ...(14 to 1) 4
GALANT DES EPEIRES (Fr) 5-11-10 D Parker, ...(14 to 1) 5
881⁴ PRECEPTOR (Ire) 7-11-11 (3") B Bowens, ...(9 to 1) 6
950⁴ DARA KNIGHT (Ire) 7-11-7 (7") G Martin, ...(66 to 1) f
Dist: 3l, 9l, 11l, 13l. 4m 18.30s. a 19.30s (7 Ran).
                                   (T Power), Thomas Foley

1017 Dollandstown Wood Handicap Hurdle (0-123 4-y-o and up) £3,425 2m................................... (4:30)

849 THE WICKED CHICKEN (Ire) [-] 7-9-2 (5") G Cotter, (20 to 1) 1
JOHNNY HANDSOME (Ire) [-] 9-9-3 D J Casey, (12 to 1) 2
849⁶ MONTETAN (Ire) [-] 5-10-3 K F O'Brien, ...(12 to 1) 3
907³ MAJOR JAMIE (Ire) [-] 5-10-5 F Woods, ...(5 to 1) 4
131³ PRACTICIAN (Ire) [-] 6-9-4 (7") J M Maguire, ...(12 to 1) 5

908* CAITRIONA'S CHOICE (Ire) [-] 5-10-13 M P Dwyer, ... (9 to 4 fav) 6
7812 MAJESTIC PADDY (Ire) [-] 6-10-6 R Dunwoody, ... (4 to 1) 7
8493 BAJAN QUEEN (Ire) [-] 6-10-0 (5*) T Martin, ... (7 to 1) 8
NO DUNCE (Ire) [-] 6-11-5 T P Treacy, ... (6 to 1) 9
Dist: 3l, ¾l, hd, 3l. 4m 3.30s. a 18.30s (9 Ran).
(John J Foley), Martin M Treacy

1018 Rathmore Hurdle (4-y-o and up) £3,082 2¼m.................(5:00)

THE LATVIAN LARK (Ire) 8-12-0 M P Dwyer, ..(2 to 1 jt-fav) 1
PENNDARA (Ire) 7-11-3 (5*) J Butler, ...(14 to 1) 2
560* GLADIATORIAL (Ire) 4-11-9 P L Malone, ... (2 to 1 jt-fav) 3
8832 NOBLE SHOON (Ire) 5-11-8 C O'Dwyer, ...(7 to 1) 4
741* BALLINLAMMY ROSE (Ire) 6-12-0 C F Swan, ...(3 to 1) 5
MR BAXTER BASICS 5-11-8 N Williamson, ...(16 to 1) 6
ROSIE LIL (Ire) 5-11-2 (7*) L A Hurley, ...(12 to 1) 7
FRIARSTOWN DUKE 6-11-5 (3*) U Smyth, ... (14 to 1) 8
850 HEMERO (Ire) 4-11-3 M P Hourigan, ...(33 to 1) pu
Dist: 5½l, 6l, 15l, sht-hd. 4m 22.70s. a 15.70s (9 Ran).
SR: 33/21/16/-/6/-/ (Mrs Rosalind Kilpatrick), Noel Meade

1019 Arthurstown I.N.H. Flat Race (4 & 5-y-o) £2,740 2m............. (5:30)

7824 NATIVE PLAYER (Ire) 4-11-6 (3*) Mr B M Cash, ..(Evens fav) 1
7412 MISTY MOMENTS (Ire) 5-11-7 (7*) Mr A J Dempsey, (9 to 2) 2
8985 LANCA'S TRIX (Ire) 4-10-13 (5*) Mr R Walsh, ...(5 to 1) 3
BEHAMORE GIRL (Ire) 4-10-11 (7*) Mr J P McNamara, ...(14 to 1) 4
KILCOGY CROSS (Ire) 4-10-11 (7*) Miss A L Crowley, ...(12 to 1) 5
BAILEYS BRIDGE (Ire) 5-11-7 (7*) Mr J Cullen, ... (14 to 1) 6
JACKPOT JOHNNY (Ire) 5-11-10¹ (5*) Mr G Farrell, (20 to 1) 7
MALLARDSTOWN (Ire) 5-12-0 Mr P Fenton, ... (9 to 1) 8
CEOIL AGUS CRAIC (Ire) 5-12-0 Mr J P Dempsey, (14 to 1) 9
HEAD CHAPLAIN (Ire) 5-11-7 (7*) Mr R Geraghty, ..(12 to 1) 10
INISHLACKAN (Ire) 4-11-4 Miss M Olivefalk, ...(12 to 1) 11
898 MARGALE (Ire) 4-11-4 Mr G J Harford, ...(20 to 1) 12
686 SILKEN SECRETARIAT (Ire) 5-11-11 (3*) Mr P English, ...(14 to 1) 13
ALL AT IT (Ire) 5-11-2 (7*) Mr D W Cullen, ...(14 to 1) 14
MONTOHOUSE (Ire) 5-11-2 (7*) Mr R J Curran, ... (14 to 1) 15
9109 THE ZAFFRING (Ire) 5-11-7 (7*) Mr S M Duffy, ...(14 to 1) 16
VERYWELL (Ire) 5-11-7 (7*) Mr N Geraghty, ...(16 to 1) 17
910 SAND EEL (Ire) 5-11-2 (7*) Mr A Ross, ...(25 to 1) 18
7738 POLLYROE (Ire) 5-11-9 Mr J A Berry, ...(14 to 1) 19
Dist: Sht-hd, 5l, 2l, ¾l. 3m 55.80s. (19 Ran).
(Derek O'Keeffe), A P O'Brien

FAKENHAM (good)
Friday October 25th
Going Correction: PLUS 0.40 sec. per fur.

1020 Walsingham Selling Handicap Hurdle Class G (0-95 4-y-o and up) £2,713 2m....................(2:20)

891* HAMADRYAD (Ire) [89] 8-11-5 (7*) Mr R Thornton, *wtd wth, gd hdwy to ld betw last 2, clr whn blun last.* .... (15 to 8 op 5 to 4 tchd 2 to 1) 1
9769 TOTAL ASSET [65] 6-10-2 G Lyons, *dsptd ld, ev ch aftr 3 out, one pace frm betw last 2.* (12 to 1 op 6 to 1 tchd 14 to 1) 2
ALOSAILI [78] 9-11-1 V Slattery, *pld hrd, improved to ld 4 out, hdd betw last 2, rdn and one pace.* ....(20 to 1 op 16 to 1 tchd 33 to 1) 3
8392 RAGAMUFFIN ROMEO [72] 7-10-9 Richard Guest, *chsd ldrs, feeling pace and drvn alng aftr 3 out, one pace after.* ....(11 to 8 fav op 6 to 4 tchd 2 to 1) 4
TONDRES (USA) [85] 5-11-7 W Fry, *chsd ldg bunch, struggling whn pace quickened aftr 3 out, sn lost tch.* ....(33 to 1 op 16 to 1 tchd 50 to 1) 5
7549 PUSEY STREET BOY [74] 9-10-11 M Bosley, *chsd ldrs for a circuit, struggling 3 out, tld off.*........ (10 to 1 op 8 to 1) 6
BEN CONNAN (Ire) [63] 6-9-11⁴ (7*) Mr R Wakley, *chsd ldrs, struggling aftr one circuit, lost tch 3 out, tld off.* .... (100 to 1 op 33 to 1) 7
LOCK TIGHT (USA) [63] 6-10-0 D Leahy, *al struggling in rear, tld off frm hfwy.*....................(100 to 1 op 33 to 1) 8
9705 FIERCE [89] (bl) 8-11-12 G Bradley, *made most till hdd and blun 4 out, pld up bef nxt.*.............. (7 to 1 op 4 to 1) pu
Dist: 5l, ¾l, 7l, 15l, 15l, 5l, dist. 4m 1.50s. a 17.50s (9 Ran).
(Mrs R F Key & Mrs V C Ward), Mrs V C Ward

1021 Weatherbys Stud Book Conditional Jockeys' Handicap Chase Class E (0-110 5-y-o and up) £3,308 3m 110yds......................... (2:50)

SPROWSTON BOY [81] 13-10-4 (5*) Ross Berry, *patiently rdn, steady hdwy fnl circuit, drw level last, sn led, ran on wl.* ....(7 to 2 op 4 to 1) 1
7513 LUCKY DOLLAR (Ire) [100] 8-12-0 G Hogan, *led till hdd 6th, styd hndy, led ag'n aftr 3 out, jnd last, sn headed and one pace.*............................(5 to 4 fav op Evens) 2
JOKER JACK [72] 11-10-0 T Dascombe, *al wl plcd, led 6th, reminders to quicken 5 out, hdd aftr 3 out, kpt on same pace frm betw last 2*..........(40 to 1 op 33 to 1 tchd 50 to 1) 3
9154 TRUMPET [100] 7-12-0 Michael Brennan, *nvr far away, feeling pace fnl circuit, lost tch frm 3 out, tld off.* ....(4 to 1 op 2 to 1) 4
SOLOMAN SPRINGS (USA) [84] (v) 6-10-12 D Parker, *hmpd 1st, struggling aftr, tld off whn pld up bef 7th.* ....(9 to 2 op 4 to 1 tchd 5 to 1) pu
Dist: 2½l, 2l, dist. 6m 26.80s. a 29.80s (5 Ran).
(Geoff Whiting), M C Chapman

1022 Wimpey Homes Novices' Chase Class E (5-y-o and up) £3,321 2m 110yds........................ (3:20)

7775 DEVILRY 6-10-12 R Johnson, *wtd wth, pckd 3rd, improved aftr 2 out, styd on to ld after last, drw clr.* ....(3 to 1 op 5 to 2 tchd 7 to 2) 1
971 SHALIK (Ire) 6-10-5 (7*) N T Egan, *led aftr 1st, hrd pressed 5 out, quickened clr after nxt, hdd after last, one pace.* ....(25 to 1 op 12 to 1 tchd 33 to 1) 2
9684 WILDE MUSIC (Ire) 6-10-12 G Bradley, *settled off the pace, steady hdwy whn blun 5 out, gd headway betw last 2, hng rght and eased bef last..*............. (7 to 4 on op 6 to 4 on) 3
1007 SPRING LOADED 5-10-13 (5*) Michael Brennan, *led till aftr 1st, styd upsides, feeling pace frm 3 out, lost tch.* ....(9 to 2 op 4 to 1 tchd 5 to 1) 4
7765 DOCTOR-J (Ire) 6-10-12 B Fenton, *chsd ldrs, feeling pace aftr 6 out, lost tch, tld off.* ....(33 to 1 op 20 to 1 tchd 50 to 1) 5
6915 DESERT CHALLENGER (Ire) (bl) 6-10-12 S Fox, *settled to chase ldrs, effrt hfwy, fdg whn f 4 out.* (10 to 1 tchd 11 to 1) f
1001 CHUKKARIO 10-10-12 M Bosley, *struggling to go pace whn pld up bef 5th..*....................(66 to 1 op 50 to 1) pu
868 ISHMA (Ire) (bl) 5-10-11 T J Murphy, *settled off the pace, not jump wl, blun 6 out, tld off whn pld up aftr nxt.* .... (66 to 1 op 50 to 1) pu
Dist: 4l, 1l, 11l, 26l. 4m 14.70s. a 17.70s (8 Ran).
(A T McAllister & S Wilson), R Craggs

1023 Michael Scotney Turf Accountant Handicap Hurdle Class F (0-105 4-y-o and up) £3,355 2m.......... (3:50)

9702 PAIR OF JACKS (Ire) [87] 6-10-8 (3*) D Fortt, *nvr far away, quickened up to ld aftr 3 out, gng clr whn hit last, ran on.* ....(2 to 1 fav tchd 11 to 4) 1
9327 ROI DU NORD (Fr) [96] 4-11-2 (3*) P Midgley, *settled to chase ldrs, effrt hfwy, pressed wnr aftr 3 out, kpt on one pace frm last..*..........................(5 to 1 op 6 to 1) 2
83 RED LIGHT [82] (v) 4-9-12 (7*) N T Egan, *chsd ldrs, effrt hfwy, drvn alng whn pace quickened aftr 3 out, one pace.* ....(14 to 1 op 10 to 1 tchd 16 to 1) 3
7942 ROBSERA (Ire) [85] 5-10-9 L Wyer, *settled wth chasing grp, effrt hfwy, drvn alng aftr 3 out, no imprsn.* (9 to 4 op 3 to 1) 4
VIAGGIO [84] (v) 8-10-8 G Lyons, *tried to make all, reminders aftr 5th, hdd after 3 out, one pace.*.... (25 to 1 op 14 to 1) 5
WATCH MY LIPS [102] 4-11-8 (3*) K Gaule, *patiently rdn, slpd bend aftr second, moved up hfwy, feeling pace after 3 out, not quicken..*....................................(9 to 2 op 2 to 1) 6
SALISONG [85] 7-10-2 (7*) Mr R Wakley, *chsd ldr frm second, feeling pace aftr 4 out, no imprsn after..*.(9 to 1 op 6 to 1) 7
Dist: 2l, 6l, 1½l, ½l, ¾l, hd. 4m 0.70s. a 16.70s (7 Ran).
(D A Wilson), G L Moore

1024 Little Snoring Juvenile Novices' Hurdle Class D (3-y-o) £2,733 2m (4:20)

6642 COTTAGE PRINCE (Ire) 10-9 L Wyer, *al gng wl, led bef 3 out, ran on strly frm betw last 2.* ....(2 to 1 fav op 3 to 1 tchd 7 to 2) 1
9655 SUNLEY SECURE 10-12 R Johnson, *nvr far away, pressed wnr aftr 3 out, drvn alng betw last 2, kpt on same pace.* ....(3 to 1 tchd 7 to 2) 2
6646 STOLEAMARCH 10-9 G Lyons, *settled midfield, effrt hfwy, drvn alng whn pace quickened 2 out, styd on r-in.* .... (16 to 1 op 12 to 1 tchd 20 to 1) 3
THE GREAT FLOOD 10-9 Richard Guest, *settled to chase ldg bunch, effrt hfwy, feeling pace aftr 3 out, no imprsn after.* ....(10 to 1 tchd 12 to 1) 4
EUROBOX BOY 10-12 D Byrne, *settled midfield, effrt hfwy, struggling bef 3 out, no imprsn aftr.* ....(9 to 2 op 2 to 1 tchd 5 to 1) 5
4364 AGAIN TOGETHER 10-4 B Fenton, *tried to make all, hdd bef 3 out, wknd und pres frm nxt.*........ (10 to 1 tchd 12 to 1) 6
8938 VERULAM (Ire) 11-2 G Bradley, *hmpd by faller second, chsd alng to keep in tch hfwy, lost touch bef 3 out, tld off.* ....(13 to 2 op 6 to 1 tchd 8 to 1 and 9 to 1) 7
KULSHI MOMKEN 10-9 W Fry, *chasing ldrs whn jmpd rght and f second..*....................(25 to 1 tchd 33 to 1) f
NORDIC HERO (Ire) 10-9 A Larnach, *chasing ldrs whn hmpd and brght dwn second..*............... (12 to 1 op 8 to 1) bd

IT'S DAWAN 10-6 (3*) L Aspell, *chasing ldrs whn hmpd and brght dwn second.*
.........(14 to 1 op 12 to 1 tchd 16 to 1 and 20 to 1) bd
Dist: 3l, 1¾l, 7l, nk, 2½l, 9l. 4m 2.60s. a 18.60s (10 Ran).

(Mrs Kay Thomas), J J Quinn

1025 Dereham Handicap Chase Class F
(0-100 5-y-o and up) £4,031 2m 5f 110yds...................... (4:50)

875² CRAFTY CHAPLAIN [97] 10-11-8 (3*) D Walsh, *pressed ldr, jmpd ahead 6 out, gd jump to go clr 3 out, kpt on strly frm betw last 2*........(2 to 1 op 9 to 4 tchd 5 to 2 and 7 to 4) 1
847* CRACKLING FROST (Ire) [79] 8-10-7 G Bradley, *led and hit 1st, hdd 6 out, rallied last 2, one pace r-in.*
..........................(7 to 4 on tchd 11 to 8 on) 2
868⁴ FABULOUS FRANCY (Ire) [72] 8-10-0 J Ryan, *chsd ldg pair, hit 4th and nxt, sn a fence beh, tld off.*
..........................(8 to 1 op 6 to 1 tchd 9 to 1) 3
548⁴ MIRAGE DANCER [72] 13-10-0 I Lawrence, *last but in tch whn f 3rd*..........(16 to 1 op 12 to 1 tchd 20 to 1) f
Dist: 8l, dist. 5m 30.20s. a 18.20s (4 Ran).

(D McCain), D McCain

1026 Weatherbys 'Stars Of Tomorrow' Open National Hunt Flat Standard - Class H (4,5,6-y-o) £1,196 2m (5:20)

BOOTS MADDEN (Ire) 6-11-4 R Johnson, *nvr far away, led o'r 3 fs out, styd on strly*..............(4 to 1 op 7 to 4) 1
FIRST LIGHT 4-11-3 L Wyer, *slwly away, given time to reco'r, chsd wnr frm over 2 fs out, no imprsn*....(9 to 2 op 8 to 1) 2
BIG STAR'S BOY 5-11-4 G Bradley, *settled midfield, took clr order fnl circuit, rdn and one pace frm o'r 2 fs out.*
..........................(7 to 4 fav tchd 9 to 4) 3
873⁶ ARDENBAR 4-10-12 Richard Guest, *chsd ldr, improved to ld 6 fs out, hdd o'r 3 out, sn rdn and outpcd.* (4 to 1 op 5 to 2) 4
CRANBROOK LAD 4-11-3 D Morris, *settled in tch, effrt hfwy, struggling o'r 3 fs out, tld off.*
..........................(25 to 1 op 14 to 1 tchd 33 to 1) 5
873⁹ WARRIO 6-11-14 M Bosley, *chsd ldrs for o'r a m, lost tch, tld off.*.......................(20 to 1 op 25 to 1) 6
BARRIE STIR 4-11-0 (3*) Guy Lewis, *settled to chase ldg grp, struggling o'r 5 fs out, tld off.*
..........................(13 to 2 op 6 to 1 tchd 8 to 1) 7
COUNTER ATTACK (Ire) 5-10-13 J Ryan, *reminders in midfield hfwy, lost tch, tld off.*
..........................(16 to 1 op 12 to 1 tchd 20 to 1) 8
HOLKHAM BAY 4-10-12 (5*) Michael Brennan, *chsd ldrs for o'r a m, lost tch, tld off.*.....(8 to 1 op 10 to 1) 9
693⁹ HAVANA EXPRESS 4-11-3 I Lawrence, *struggling and reminders hfwy, sn tld off.*
..........................(20 to 1 op 14 to 1 tchd 25 to 1) 10
740 RINUS MAJESTIC (Ire) 4-11-0 (3*) D Walsh, *led, reminders hfwy, hdd 6 fs out, lost tch, tld off.*
..........................(20 to 1 op 14 to 1 tchd 25 to 1) 11
Dist: 6l, 14l, 1¼l, 21l, sht-hd, 2l, 3l, 5l, 17l, dist. 3m 53.60s. (11 Ran).

(L J A Phipps), Miss Venetia Williams

NEWBURY (good (races 1,2,4,6), good to firm (3,5))
Friday October 25th
Going Correction: MINUS 0.40 sec. per fur.

1027 Crux Easton Juvenile Novices' Hurdle Class C (3-y-o) £3,730 2m 110yds..................... (2:10)

KERAWI 11-0 C Llewellyn, *keen early, trkd ldr, shaken up appr last, hrd rdn to ld r-in, ran on wl.*
..........................(9 to 2 op 5 to 1 tchd 11 to 2) 1
LE TETEU (Fr) 11-0 D Bridgwater, *hld up, hdwy to track ldrs aftr 4 out, chlgd 2 out, led briefly r-in, ran on.*
..........................(7 to 1 tchd 10 to 1) 2
SERENUS (USA) 11-0 M A Fitzgerald, *led aftr 1st, rdn and mstk 2 out, hdd after last, no extr*........(4 to 1 op 5 to 1) 3
CIRCUS STAR 11-0 A Maguire, *led 1st, cl up, keen early, mstk 4 out, ev ch 2 out, rdn and one pace appr last.*
..........................(6 to 4 fav op 11 to 10) 4
LAUGHING BUCCANEER 11-0 B Powell, *beh, some moderate late prog, tld off..* (5 to 1 op 4 to 1 tchd 33 to 1) 5
RIVERCARE (Ire) 11-0 V Smith, *trkd ldrs, jmpd slwly second, sn beh, tld off*..........(20 to 1 op 10 to 1 tchd 25 to 1) 6
767⁷ SEVEN CROWNS (USA) 11-0 N Williamson, *in tch, rdn aftr 4th, sn beh, tld off*..........(33 to 1 op 20 to 1) 7
CLASSICAL JOKER 10-9 W McFarland, *hld up beh ldrs, wkng whn blun 3 out, btn quickly, tld off.*
..........................(25 to 1 op 12 to 1 tchd 33 to 1) 8
PETROS GEM 10-9 P Hide, *chsd ldrs to 4th, sn beh, tld off.*
..........................(50 to 1 op 20 to 1 tchd 66 to 1) 9
GOLD LANCE (USA) 11-0 P Holley, *jmpd slwly 3rd, al beh, tld off.*..........(16 to 1 op 10 to 1 tchd 20 to 1) 10
DISH THE DOSH 10-9 D J Burchell, *al beh, tld off appr 4th.*
..........................(33 to 1 op 14 to 1 tchd 50 to 1) 11

CAST A FLY (Ire) 10-9 B Clifford, *reluctant to race, tld off whn pld up bef 2nd last...* (50 to 1 op 20 to 1 tchd 100 to 1) pu
LOCKET 10-9 L Harvey, *beh whn hit 4th, tld off when pld up aftr 3 out*..............(33 to 1 op 20 to 1 tchd 50 to 1) pu
Dist: 1½l, 1¼l, 2l, dist, 17l, 3½l, 9l, 1l, 1l, dist. 3m 49.10s. a 0.10s (13 Ran).
SR: 20/18/16/14/-/-/   (Matt Archer & Miss Jean Broadhurst), N A Twiston-Davies

1028 Fleetlease Anniversary Handicap Hurdle Class B (0-145 5-y-o and up) £4,695 2m 110yds........... (2:40)

682² COUNTRY STAR (Ire) [123] 5-10-8 J Osborne, *jmpd wl, made all, shaken up and ran on well*..........(2 to 1 op 9 to 4) 1
801* MYTTON'S CHOICE (Ire) [118] 5-10-3 A Maguire, *chsd wnr thrght, not fluent second, blun nxt, ch 2 out, one pace whn mstk last.....*..(Evens fav op 6 to 4 on tchd 11 to 10) 2
OH SO RISKY [142] 9-12-0 P Holley, *hld up in last pl, cld 4 out, outpcd aftr nxt.*
..........................(100 to 30 op 3 to 1 tchd 9 to 4 and 7 to 2) 3
Dist: 1½l, 15l. 3m 47.80s. b 1.20s (3 Ran).
SR: 26/19/29/   (H R H Prince Fahd Salman), C P E Brooks

1029 Kone Lifts Handicap Chase Class B (5-y-o and up) £7,000 2½m... (3:10)

STRONG MEDICINE [126] 9-10-4 C O'Dwyer, *hld up in cl tch, led appr 2 out, all out*..............(11 to 4 tchd 3 to 1) 1
EASTHORPE [141] 8-11-5 J F Titley, *made most till hdd appr 2 out, sn drvn, ran on one pace.*
..........................(5 to 2 fav op 3 to 1 tchd 9 to 4) 2
COMMERCIAL ARTIST [150] 10-12-0 C Llewellyn, *hld up in cl tch, jmpd slwly 8th, blun 4 out, sn outpcd.*
..........................(12 to 1 op 10 to 1) 3
293⁹ BORO VACATION (Ire) [130] 7-10-8 A P McCoy, *blun 1st, mstk tch in tch whn blunded badly and uns rdr 11th.*
..........................(7 to 2 tchd 4 to 1) ur
EGYPT MILL PRINCE [149] 10-11-13 W Marston, *wth ldr, ev ch whn pld up lme bef 4 out.* (7 to 2 op 3 to 1 tchd 4 to 1) pu
Dist: 1½l, 20l. 4m 57.30s. a 9.30s (5 Ran).

(Dr D B A Silk), K C Bailey

1030 Newbury Autumn Four Year Old Hurdle Class B £4,796 2m 110yds (3:40)

MISTINGUETT (Ire) 10-12 C Llewellyn, *led aftr 1st, made nxt, rdn clr frm last, easily.* (3 to 1 op 9 to 4 tchd 100 to 30) 1
HATTA BREEZE 10-12 A Maguire, *hld up in last pl, cld 3 out, chsd wnr frm nxt, sn hrd rdn and no imprsn.*
..........................(13 to 2 op 3 to 1 tchd 7 to 1) 2
PADDY'S RETURN (Ire) 11-7 R Dunwoody, *led 1st, settled beh wnr, hrd rdn aftr 4 out, rallied briofly appr 2 out, an no extr.*..........(11 to 10 on op 5 to 4 tchd 5 to 4 on) 3
798⁵ ALLTIME DANCER (Ire) 11-3 J Osborne, *in cl tch, wknd quickly aftr 3 out, tld off*................(4 to 1 op 3 to 1) 4
Dist: 7l, 10l, dist. 3m 46.60s. b 2.40s (4 Ran).
SR: 42/35/34/-/   (John Duggan), N A Twiston-Davies

1031 Penwood Novices' Chase Class D (5-y-o and up) £3,809 2m 1f...... (4:10)

PLUNDER BAY (USA) 5-11-6 M A Fitzgerald, *hld up in cl tch, shaken up appr 2 out, hrd rdn to ld r-in, ran on gmely.*
..........................(6 to 4 on op 7 to 4 on tchd 6 to 5 on) 1
CLIFTON GAME (Ire) 6-11-2 A Thornton, *cl up, led 8th, hdd r-in, ran on und pres*..........(9 to 2 tchd 3 to 1 and 5 to 1) 2
904* AMBASSADOR ROYALE (Ire) 8-11-7 A Maguire, *led til blun and hdd 8th, mstk nxt, wknd appr 3 out, tld off.*
..........................(9 to 4 op 7 to 4 tchd 5 to 2) 3
Dist: Nk, dist. 4m 2.90s. a 2.90s (3 Ran).
SR: 5/1/-/   (W V & Mrs E S Robins), N J Henderson

1032 October Handicap Hurdle Class B (0-145 4-y-o and up) £4,919 3m 110yds...................... (4:40)

755² LANSDOWNE [118] 8-10-9 A P McCoy, *hld up, hdwy appr 2 out, chlgd last, led r-in, edgd rght und pres, ran on.*
..........................(7 to 2 op 6 to 1) 1
JACK BUTSON (Ire) [136] 7-11-13 D Bridgwater, *hld up, drpd rear 7th, smooth hdwy appr 3 out, hdd r-in, no extr.*
..........................(5 to 1 op 7 to 2 tchd 6 to 1) 2
YES MAN (Ire) [112] 7-10-3 J F Titley, *led, rdn and hdd appr last, kpt on und pres..........*(7 to 4 fav tchd 2 to 1) 3
NEWTON POINT [137] 7-12-0 A Maguire, *trkd ldr, rdn alng appr 4 out, ev ch 2 out, kpt on one pace approaching last.*
..........................(9 to 2 op 7 to 2 tchd 5 to 1) 4
896⁴ ACROW LINE [114] 11-10-5 D J Burchell, *trkd ldrs, pushed alng appr 8th, drvn and wknd approaching 3 out.*
..........................(14 to 1 op 12 to 1 tchd 16 to 1) 5
MR KERMIT [131] 5-11-6 L Harvey, *trkd ldrs till rdn and wknd aftr 3 out*..........(12 to 1 op 8 to 1) 6
752² FIELDRIDGE [118] 7-10-9 B Powell, *hld up beh, hdwy to track ldrs appr 8th, wknd quickly frm 3 out.*
..........................(9 to 1 op 8 to 1 tchd 10 to 1) 7
Dist: 1½l, 4l, sht-hd, 18l, 5l, 4l. 5m 45.40s. b 0.60s (7 Ran).
SR: -/5/-/2/

(R F Denmead), P F Nicholls

CARLISLE (good)
Saturday October 26th
Going Correction: PLUS 0.35 sec. per fur. (races 1,2,4,6,7), PLUS 0.25 (3,5)

1033 Great Gable Novices' Hurdle Class E (4-y-o and up) £2,486 2m 1f...(1:55)

879^* CONTRAFIRE (Ire) 4-11-4 J Supple, *chsd ldrs, improved to ld appr 5th, pushed out and ran on r-in.* ....(11 to 4 on op 7 to 4 on tchd 3 to 1 on) 1

813^3 MONACO GOLD (Ire) 4-10-8 (3*) G Cahill, *chsd ldr, chalg whn mstk 3 out, ev ch till one pace frm last...* (6 to 1 op 7 to 2) 2

806^9 PENTLAND SQUIRE 5-10-12 Richard Guest, *hld up, steady hdwy appr 3 out, not trble ldrs.* ....(16 to 1 op 14 to 1 tchd 20 to 1) 3

960^3 AMBER HOLLY 7-10-7 B Storey, *in tch, hdwy to chase ldrs 5th, und pres appr 2 out, fdd..........* (8 to 1 op 5 to 1) 4

810 PATTERN ARMS 4-10-11 D J Moffatt, *midfield, outpcd appr 3 out, eased whn btn frm nxt..........* (33 to 1 op 25 to 1) 5

HOMECREST 4-10-11 A Dobbin, *in rear, effrt appr 3 out, sn no imprsn..........* (25 to 1 op 50 to 1 tchd 100 to 1) 6

STINGING BEE 5-10-12 T Reed, *hld up, niggled alng 4 out, sn no imprsn, eased whn btn frm 2 out.* (100 to 1 op 50 to 1) 7

REGAL DOMAIN (Ire) 5-10-12 D Bentley, *chsd ldrs, lost pl 4th, lost tch frm four out, tld off..........* (33 to 1 op 16 to 1) 8

LE AMBER (Ire) 7-10-7 B Harding, *keen hold, led, clr to 4th, hdd appr nxt, sn drvn and wknd quickly, tld off.* ....(100 to 1 op 50 to 1) 9

Dist: 5l, 20l, 12l, 16l, 17l, 11l, 21l, 8l. 4m 16.20s. a 13.20s (9 Ran).
SR: 18/6/-/-/-/- (G B Turnbull Ltd), Mrs A Swinbank

1034 Saddleback Novices' Hurdle Class E (4-y-o and up) £2,556 2½m 110yds .... (2:25)

SHANAVOGH 5-10-12 J Callaghan, *in tch, hdwy 6th, led 3 out, mstk last, drvn out.................*(3 to 1 op 6 to 1) 1

874^* ELA MATA 4-11-4 J Supple, *midfield, hdwy to chase ldrs 7th, ev ch 3 out, not fluent nxt, one pace.* ....(6 to 4 fav op 5 to 4 tchd Evens) 2

934^5 RULE OUT THE REST 5-11-5 M Foster, *hndy, led appr 6th, hdd 3 out, sn outpcd..................*(8 to 1 op 7 to 1) 3

874^7 SISTER GALE 4-10-6 Richard Guest, *midfield, effrt and hdwy 4 out, not rch ldrs..............................*(50 to 1) 4

934^9 LIFEBUOY (Ire) 5-10-12 T Reed, *towards rear, effrt and some hdwy 4 out, nvr dngrs..........................*(33 to 1) 5

TRAP DANCER 8-10-12 A Dobbin, *midfield, niggled alng aftr 5th, hdwy 7th, chlgd 3 out, sn drvn, wknd nxt.* ....(33 to 1 op 25 to 1) 6

EMILYMOORE 5-10-7 R Supple, *strted slwly, in rear, rdn alng appr 6th, hdwy into midfield approaching 3 out, sn no imprsn............................*(16 to 1 op 12 to 1) 7

SIGNOR NORTONE 4-10-11 B Harding, *midfield, struggling frm 4 out, nvr dngrs..........* (20 to 1 op 16 to 1) 8

949^3 DALUSMAN (Ire) 8-10-12 R Dunwoody, *midfield, drvn 7th, sn struggling..........................*(10 to 1 tchd 12 to 1) 9

35^3 MULLINS (Ire) 5-10-12 D J Moffatt, *hld up, hdwy into midfield appr 3 out, btn bef nxt..............* (20 to 1 op 10 to 1) 10

890^4 THALEROS 6-10-12 N Bentley, *trkd ldrs, led 4th till appr 6th, wkng whn mstk four out..............*(14 to 1 op 8 to 1) 11

793 LAURIE-O (bl) 12-10-12 J Burke, *prmnt, lost pl quickly aftr 5th, sn beh......................*(100 to 1 op 50 to 1) 12

TO SAY THE LEAST 6-10-5 (7*) S Haworth, *nvr gng wl, al well beh, tld off..........................* (100 to 1 op 50 to 1) 13

KIRCHWYN LAD 8-10-12 B Storey, *led till 4th, beh frm 6th, tld off whn pld up bef last....* (9 to 1 op 8 to 1 tchd 10 to 1) pu

CLAIRABELL (Ire) 5-10-7 K Johnson, *in tch, mstk 1st, wknd quickly 7th, tld off whn pld up bef last............* (25 to 1) pu

795^4 FARMERS SUBSIDY 4-10-11 D Parker, *cl up early, wl beh aftr 5th, tld off whn pld up bef 3 out....* (50 to 1 op 33 to 1) pu

Dist: 5l, 3l, 24l, nk, 1½l, nk, dist, nk, 1l, 4l. 4m 55.70s. a 13.70s (16 Ran).
SR: 18/19/17/-/-/- (Sean Graham), G M Moore

1035 Helvellyn Novices' Chase Class D (4-y-o and up) £3,829 2½m 110yds .... (2:55)

SOLOMON'S DANCER (USA) 6-11-5 A Dobbin, *in tch, trkd ldrs 9th, chlgd on bit 4 out, led 2 out, rdn aftr last, ran on.* ....(11 to 10 on op Evens tchd 5 to 4 on) 1

804^* CASTLEROYAL (Ire) 7-11-11 R Dunwoody, *cl up, led appr 4th, hdd nxt, rgned ld 12th, headed 2 out, rallied briefly aftr last, no extr fnl 100 yards..........*(4 to 1 op 3 to 1 tchd 9 to 2) 2

SHAWWELL 9-11-5 B Storey, *midfield, mstk 8th, hdwy appr 4 out, not rch ldrs........*(25 to 1 op 20 to 1 tchd 33 to 1) 3

BOLD ACCOUNT (Ire) 6-11-5 N Bentley, *midfield, pckd tenth, hdwy to chase ldrs appr 4 out, und pres and no imprsn bef nxt.* ....(8 to 1 op 7 to 1) 4

DAWN LAD (Ire) 7-11-5 J Supple, *midfield, mstk 7th, struggling frm tenth, no dngr aftr..........* (20 to 1 op 14 to 1) 5

147^5 MOVAC (Ire) 7-11-11 M Foster, *cl up till wknd quickly aftr 12th.* ....(6 to 1 op 9 to 2 tchd 7 to 1) 6

KENMORE-SPEED 9-11-5 Richard Guest, *handily plcd, led 5th till 12th, wknd quickly, wl beh whn blun last.* ....(16 to 1 tchd 20 to 1) 7

885^2 MR REINER (Ire) 8-11-5 K Jones, *rear div, tld off whn pld up bef 11th..........*(20 to 1 op 16 to 1) pu

GARCALL 10-11-5 D Bentley, *led, hdd appr 4th, beh frm 7th, tld off whn pld up bef tenth..........* (33 to 1 op 20 to 1) pu

THE ENERGISER 10-11-5 J Burke, *al beh, tld off whn pld up bef tenth.........................*(200 to 1 op 100 to 1) pu

FOX ON THE RUN 9-11-5 B Harding, *hld up, hdwy into midfield 8th, pld up lme bef 11th, dismounted.* .... (50 to 1 op 33 to 1) pu

ALICHARGER 6-11-2 (3*) G Cahill, *in rear, struggling aftr 9th, tld off whn pld up bef 11th..........*(33 to 1 op 20 to 1) pu

814 JAMARSAM (Ire) 8-11-5 K Johnson, *al beh, tld off whn pld up bef 11th..........................*(200 to 1 op 100 to 1) pu

Dist: 2½l, 26l, 1½l, 16l, 4l, 13l. 5m 7.00s. a 12.00s (13 Ran).
SR: 22/25/-/-/-/- (J Hales), G Richards

1036 Ladbrokes Lucky Choice Handicap Hurdle Class E (0-115 5-y-o and up) £2,290 3m 110yds............(3:25)

JOCKS CROSS (Ire) [107] 5-12-0 A Dobbin, *hndy, outpcd 4 out, hdwy to ld appr 2 out, rdn out r-in.* ....(7 to 4 fav op 6 to 4) 1

GRATE DEEL (Ire) [85] 6-10-8 R Supple, *led at slow pace, hdd appr 5th, remained cl up, ev ch 3 out, kpt on same pace.* ....(4 to 1 op 7 to 2) 2

913^5 EXEMPLAR (Ire) [89] 8-10-12 Richard Guest, *hld up, effrt 4 out, ev ch nxt, not fluent 2 out, kpt on one pace.* ....(100 to 30 op 3 to 1 tchd 7 to 2) 3

940^5 EMPEROR CHANG (USA) [77] 9-9-13^2 (3*) J Cahill, *in rear, effrt 4 out, rdn and ev ch nxt, outpcd frm 2 out.* ....(16 to 1 op 8 to 1) 4

THE STITCHER (Ire) [101] 6-11-10 T Reed, *keen hold, cl up, led appr 5th, hdd approaching 2 out, sn wknd and eased.* ....(7 to 2 op 3 to 1) 5

Dist: 4l, 2½l, 8l, dist. 6m 13.10s. a 22.10s (5 Ran).
(Mrs Gill Harrison), G Richards

1037 Scafell Handicap Chase Class D (0-125 5-y-o and up) £3,576 3m .... (3:55)

933^* GENERAL COMMAND (Ire) [118] 8-11-10 R Dunwoody, *nvr far away, chlgd 3 out, led appr nxt, drw clr last, eased cl hme.* .....(11 to 8 on op 5 to 4 on tchd 11 to 10 on and 6 to 4 on) 1

865^3 SUPPOSIN [100] 8-10-2^2 Richard Guest, *hld up, rdn alng 14th, hdwy nxt, styd on to chase wnr appr last, no imprsn.* ....(7 to 1 op 6 to 1) 2

72^8 GALE AHEAD (Ire) [100] 6-10-6 N Bentley, *cl up, wth ldr tenth, rdn and chlgd 3 out, one pace frm nxt...*(10 to 1 op 7 to 1) 3

865^* KUSHBALOO [117] 11-11-9 B Storey, *keen hold, led, jmpd slwly 1st, hdd appr 2 out, wknd approaching nxt.....* (3 to 1) 4

865 GO SILLY [103] (v) 10-10-6 (3*) G Cahill, *al in rear, not fluent 6th, struggling and no ch frm 13th.....*(20 to 1 op 16 to 1) 5

GREENHILL RAFFLES [122] 10-12-0 M Foster, *hld up in tch, outpcd frm 12th, no dngr aftr.........* (20 to 1 op 12 to 1) 6

Dist: 7l, 4l, 13l, 20l, 14l. 6m 11.10s. a 19.10s (6 Ran).
(Robert Ogden), G Richards

1038 Old Man Of Coniston Handicap Hurdle Class E (0-110 4-y-o and up) £2,360 2m 1f................ (4:30)

962^5 FIELD OF VISION (Ire) [100] 6-11-10 J Supple, *trkd ldrs, rdn alng and outpcd 4 out, hdwy frm 2 out, ran on to ld fnl half furlong..............................*(7 to 2 tchd 4 to 1) 1

888^* SUPERTOP [98] 8-11-8 M Foster, *hld up, effrt to chase ldrs 3 out, led last, hdd fnl half furlong, no extr.* ....(2 to 1 fav op 7 to 4 tchd 9 to 4) 2

864^3 LATIN LEADER [81] (bl) 6-10-5 D Parker, *in tch, effrt 3 out, styd on r-in..............................*(14 to 1 op 10 to 1) 3

912^2 FEN TERRIER [92] 4-11-1 A Dobbin, *led till appr second, remained wth ldr, ev ch 2 out, kpt on one pace r-in.* ....(7 to 2 tchd 4 to 1) 4

864^* WELL APPOINTED (Ire) [97] 7-11-4 (3*) G Lee, *prmnt, led appr second, hdd last, no extr r-in..........* (4 to 1 op 7 to 2) 5

JUMBO STAR [84] 6-10-8 B Storey, *hndy, mstk 5th, sn lost pl and beh, tld off..........*(33 to 1 op 16 to 1) 6

ENVIRONMENTAL LAW [79] 5-9-13 (3*) G Cahill, *in rear, struggling frm 5th, tld off..............*(20 to 1 op 12 to 1) 7

Dist: 1¼l, 1¾l, ½l, ¾l, dist, sht-hd. 4m 17.90s. a 14.90s (7 Ran).
SR: 7/3/-/-/ (Panther Racing Ltd), Mrs A Swinbank

1039 Great Dodd Standard National Hunt Flat Class H (4,5,6-y-o) £1,070 2m 1f .... (5:00)

866^* NORTHERN FUSILIER 4-11-6 (7*) M Newton, *hld up, hdwy 6 fs out, led o'r 3 out, drw clr frm over one out, cmftbly.* ....(13 to 8 on op 7 to 4 on tchd 2 to 1 on) 1

NATURAL TALENT 4-11-3 D Parker, *led 2 fs, remained cl up, one pace fnl two..............* (14 to 1 op 10 to 1) 2

CHILL FACTOR 6-10-11 (7*) C McCormack, *cl up, chlgd 4 fs out, sn drvn and outpcd..............*(14 to 1 op 12 to 1) 3

OLD CAVALIER 5-11-4 A Roche, *hld up, styd on und pres fnl 2
fs, nvr nrr* .... (8 to 1 op 5 to 1) 4
QATTARA (Ire) 6-11-8 (3") G Cahill, *midfield, hdwy 5 fs out,
wknd o'r 3 out* .... (4 to 1 op 7 to 2 tchd 9 to 2) 5
FASTER RON (Ire) 5-10-11 (7") S Melrose, *in tch, struggling
fnl 5 fs* .... (50 to 1) 6
866² LOOK SHARPE 5-10-11 (7") B Grattan, *keen hold, prmnt, led
aftr 2 fs, hdd o'r 3 out, wknd quickly* .. (16 to 1 op 12 to 1) 7
866 JED ABBEY 4-10-5 (7") S Haworth, *hndy, wknd quickly 6 fs
out, tld off* .... (33 to 1 op 25 to 1 tchd 50 to 1) 8
MONICAS BUZZ 6-10-6 (7") M Dunne, *hld up, niggled alng
hfwy, tld off* .... (50 to 1 op 33 to 1) 9
BLOOM'IN JUNES (Ire) 4-10-12 Mr R Hale, *midfield early,
beh frm hfwy, tld off* .... (50 to 1 op 33 to 1) 10
Dist: 9l, 5l, 4l, 15l, 6l, 4l, dist, 7l, dist. 4m 11.10s. (10 Ran).

(Joe Donald), J M Jefferson

DOWN ROYAL (IRE) (good to yielding)
Saturday October 26th

1040 Down Royal Committee Handicap Hurdle (0-109 4-y-o and up) £1,370 2
½m .... (2:25)

948* NEW LEGISLATION (Ire) [-] (bl) 6-11-0 C F Swan, (9 to 4 fav) 1
828⁹ FALCARRAGH (Ire) [-] 6-10-2 (7") J M Maguire, ... (4 to 1) 2
803* CHANOBLE (tre) [-] 4-9-11 (7") B D Murtagh, ... (6 to 1) 3
946⁵ CORALDA (Ire) [-] 5-9-7 W Slattery, ... (33 to 1) 4
947⁴ AMME ENAEK (Ire) [-] (bl) 7-10-2 H Rogers, ... (16 to 1) 5
THE VILLAGE FANCY (Ire) [-] 6-11-5 F J Flood, ... (12 to 1) 6
741⁴ FLYING IN THE GALE (Ire) [-] 5-9-12 (7") A O'Shea, (12 to 1) 7
DEESIDE DOINGS (Ire) [-] 8-9-12 P L Malone, ... (33 to 1) 8
292 MAKING THE POINT (Ire) [-] 5-11-7 (7") R P Hogan, (10 to 1) 9
948³ COLLIERS HILL (Ire) [-] 8-11-6 L P Cusack, ... (10 to 1) 10
579⁶ SHY GAL (Ire) [-] 8-10-2 (5") J Butler, ... (33 to 1) 11
947⁶ THE THIRD MAN (Ire) [-] 7-10-3 P McWilliams, ... (10 to 1) 12
MILLBROOK LAD (Ire) [-] 8-11-8 D T Evans, ... (14 to 1) 13
731⁷ HARRY WELSH (Ire) [-] 4-10-9 T P Treacy, ... (33 to 1) 14
701⁶ TERESIAN GIRL (Ire) [-] 5-9-12³ J P Broderick, ... (20 to 1) 15
Dist: 1l, 3½l, 1l, 2½l. 4m 59.50s. (15 Ran).

(Michael Bergin), M Halford

1041 Ali And Mohamad Soudavar Memorial Trial Hurdle (4-y-o and up) £3,425 2m .... (2:55)

COCKNEY LAD (Ire) 7-12-0 C F Swan, ... (5 to 2 on) 1
826² PERSIAN HALO (Ire) 8-11-7 (7") Miss S Kauntze, ... (9 to 4) 2
946³ GLENFIELDS CASTLE (Ire) 6-10-13 T P Treacy, ... (14 to 1) 3
497⁸ ZUZUS PETALS (Ire) 0-10-1 (7") A O'Shea, ... (50 to 1) 5
804⁵ CURRAGH RANGER (Ire) 6-10-6 (7") B D Murtagh, (33 to 1) 6
Dist: ¾l, 20l, 6l, dist. 3m 50.80s. (6 Ran).

(D Daly), Noel Meade

1042 Archie Watson Memorial Corinthian Flat Race (4-y-o and up) £1,370 2m
.... (4:55)

577⁵ MATTORIA (Ire) 5-10-11 (5") Mr R Walsh, ... (10 to 1) 1
577⁷ YOUR SORRY NOW (Ire) 6-11-7 (7") Mr G Elliott, ... (7 to 2) 2
946⁹ WINTER PRINCESS 5-10-9 (7") Mr K Ross, ... (25 to 1) 3
946⁸ EIRE (Ire) 7-11-7 (7") Mr M O'Connor, ... (12 to 1) 4
HANDSOME ANTHONY (Ire) 5-11-4 (3") Mr B R Hamilton,
.... (6 to 1) 5
686³ ANN'S DESIRE (Ire) 5-10-9 (7") Mr J Keville, ... (6 to 1) 6
951⁶ ORANGE LIL (Ire) 4-10-8 (3") Mr B M Cash, ... (25 to 1) 7
137⁵ HARRY HEANEY (Ire) 7-12-0 Mr G J Harford, ... (10 to 1) 8
884 JUST BEFORE DAWN (Ire) 7-11-0 (7") Mr T J Beattie,
.... (10 to 1) 9
CAROLANNS CHOICE (Ire) 7-10-9 (7") Mr S McGonagle,
.... (14 to 1) 10
929* CORAL SEA (Ire) 6-11-7 (7") Mr A Ross, ... (1 to 1 fav) 11
WILLY WEE (Ire) 5-11-7 Mr A J Martin, ... (14 to 1) 12
LYNX MARINE (Ire) 5-11-0 (7") Mr J D O'Connell, .. (25 to 1) 13
ONLY ONE (Ire) 6-11-7 Mr M McNulty, ... (10 to 1) 14
DREW'S BUCK (Ire) 5-11-0 (7") Miss L Miskimmins, (20 to 1) 15
Dist: Hd, 8l, 4½l, 12l. 3m 50.30s. (15 Ran).

(Glencree Syndicate), H Kirk

LEOPARDSTOWN (IRE) (yielding)
Saturday October 26th

1043 Dundrum INH Flat Race (4-y-o) £3,082 2m .... (5:30)

FURNITUREVILLE (Ire) 11-8 (5") Mr D McGoona, ... (5 to 1) 1
898* DO YE KNOW WHA (Ire) 11-6 (7") Mr J P McNamara,
.... (9 to 4 fav) 2
745* SPENDID (Ire) 11-6 (7") Miss A L Crowley, ... (5 to 2) 3
782* RATHBAWN PRINCE (Ire) 11-6 (7") Mr A J Dempsey, (5 to 2) 4
782⁹ MONTYS DELIGHT (Ire) 11-6 Mr J A Nash, ... (12 to 1) 5
898 ARCTIC PARTY (Ire) 10-12 (3") Mr P J Casey, ... (10 to 1) 6
Dist: Hd, 3l, 14l, 11l. 3m 43.00s. (6 Ran).

(Mrs Kayoko Iwasaki), Joseph M Canty

MARKET RASEN (good)
Saturday October 26th
Going Correction: PLUS 0.30 sec. per fur.

1044 Associated British Ports Hurdle Selling Handicap Class G (0-95 4,5,6-y-o) £1,982 2m 1f 110yds..... (2:15)

704³ COUNT OF FLANDERS (Ire) [75] 6-11-2 A S Smith, *made all,
clr appr last, styd on wl* .... (11 to 4 fav op 6 to 1) 1
478⁴ GLENVALLY [81] 5-11-2 (5") E Callaghan, *hld up, hdwy 3 out,
kpt on flt* .... (12 to 1) 2
911⁶ FLINTLOCK (Ire) [70] 6-10-11 P Niven, *prmnt, lost pl 5th, sn
beh, lft 3rd last* .... (7 to 1 op 6 to 1) 3
704⁴ SEA GOD [88] 5-12-0 W Worthington, *hld up, hdwy hfwy,
wknd aftr 3 out* .... (15 to 2 op 6 to 1 tchd 8 to 1) 4
792³ LITTLE REDWING (Ire) [69] (bl) 4-10-8 R Garritty, *hld up, effft 3 out,
no imprsn* .... (8 to 1 op 6 to 1 tchd 9 to 1) 5
971³ RANGER SLOANE [83] 4-11-8 Gary Lyons, *hld up, hdwy 5th,
rdn 3 out, grad wknd*.....(15 to 2 op 5 to 1 tchd 8 to 1) 6
934 TOP SKIPPER (Ire) [68] 4-10-7 N Smith, *al in rear*.
.... (12 to 1 op 8 to 1) 7
912⁵ FLY TO THE END (USA) [71] (v) 6-10-12 D Byrne, *in tch, drvn
alng hfwy, sn lost pl*.............. (7 to 1 op 12 to 1) 8
665⁵ WORDSMITH (Ire) [84] 6-11-11 P McLoughlin, *hld up, pushed
alng 4th, sn beh*...................... (40 to 1 op 33 to 1) 9
775 KAJOSTAR [62] 6-10-3⁶ (3") D Walsh, *dwlt, hdwy 3rd, hit nxt,
sn beh*....................... (40 to 1 op 33 to 1) 10
454³ PATS FOLLY [62] 5-10-2² W McFarland, *hld up, beh frm 4th*.
.... (10 to 1 op 25 to 1 tchd 50 to 1) 11
684⁵ FENIAN COURT (Ire) [82] 5-11-8 N Williamson, *trkd ldrs, rdn 2
out, wkng whn blun and uns rdr last*.
.... (6 to 1 tchd 7 to 1 and 8 to 1) ur
370⁶ HUTCEL BELL [60] 5-10-0 L Wyer, *prmnt til wknd quickly 3
out, pld up bef nxt*................... (50 to 1 op 33 to 1) pu
Dist: 3½l, 13l, 4l, 1¾l, 3l, 4l, 4l, 6l, 19l, hd. 4m 14.40s. a 13.40s (13 Ran).
SR: 6/7/-/-/-/-/ *(K A Morgan), K A Morgan*

1045 Lincolnshire Beef Day Novices' Chase Class D (5-y-o and up) £3,968 2½m .... (2:45)

SIMPLY DASHING (Ire) 5-10-12 L Wyer, *al prmnt, led briefly
7th, led 4 out, quickened clr nxt, almost crrd out by loose
horse last*...................... (13 to 8 on tchd 7 to 4 on) 1
776⁴ RECORD LOVER (Ire) 6-11-0 W Worthington, *trkd ldrs, led 9th
to 4 out, outpcd nxt*....(12 to 1 op 16 to 1 tchd 20 to 1) 2
CADER IDRIS 7-11-0 P Niven, *in tch, hmprd 4th, led 8th, hdd
and hit 9th, grad wknd.*(12 to 1 tchd 14 to 1 and 16 to 1) 3
GEMS LAD 9-10-7 (7") R Wilkinson, *hld up, rdn hfwy, sn lost
tch*.......................... (66 to 1 op 50 to 1) 4
878⁵ MISTROY 6-10-9 A S Smith, *prmnt, lft in td 4th, hdd 7th, wknd
quickly 9th*.......................... (50 to 1) 5
UNCLE KEENY (Ire) 6-11-0 M Dwyer, *led til blun badly and
uns rdr 4th*...................... (5 to 2 op 2 to 1) ur
Dist: 21l, 11l, 1½l, dist. 5m 4.20s. a 15.20s (6 Ran).

(Steve Hammond), T D Easterby

1046 Howard Smith Towage And Salvage Handicap Chase Class C (0-130 5-y-o and up) £4,560 3m 1f....... (3:15)

865² DARK OAK [110] 10-11-0 L Wyer, *led to 4th, led appr last,
edgd rght r-in, rdn out*............ (9 to 2 op 5 to 1) 1
DEEP DECISION [100] 10-10-4 A S Smith, *in tch, hdwy
twelfth, led 4 out, hdd appr last, styd on und pres*.
.... (10 to 1 op 8 to 1) 2
865⁴ MAGIC BLOOM [105] 10-10-4 (5") E Callaghan, *hld up, hdwy
4 out, hit 3 out, kpt on r-in.*........... (13 to 2 op 5 to 1) 3
811³ EAST HOUSTON [101] 7-10-5 N Williamson, *hld up, hit 14th,
reminder nxt, hdwy 4 out, no extr frm 2 out.*
.... (7 to 2 op 5 to 1) 4
892* GLENFINN PRINCESS [99] 8-10-3 D Byrne, *chsd ldrs, led
4th, hdd four out, sn btn.*
.... (7 to 4 fav op 2 to 1 tchd 5 to 2 and 3 to 1) 5
586³ HILLWALK [110] 10-11-7 (3") D Walsh, *prmnt, hit 9th, mstk
11th, lost pl 14th, sn beh*.......... (12 to 1 op 10 to 1) 6
SON OF IRIS [103] 8-10-7 P Niven, *in tch, jmpd slwly 5th, sn
beh, tld off whn pld up bef 9th*............ (5 to 1 op 9 to 2) pu
Dist: Nk, 2½l, 3½l, 15l, 4l. 6m 26.10s. a 26.10s (7 Ran).
(Mrs M E Curtis), J W Curtis

1047 Global Shipping Services Maiden Hurdle Class D (4-y-o and up) £3,291 2m 1f 110yds.............. (3:45)

796⁴ RANGITIKEI (NZ) 5-11-5 J Railton, *trkd ldrs, led appr 2 out, sn
hdd, rdn and lft clr last.* (4 to 1 fav op 3 to 1 tchd 9 to 2) 1
PIP'S DREAM 5-11-0 J Ryan, *led, hdd appr 2 out, sn wknd, lft
second last.*.......................... (11 to 1 op 8 to 1) 2
775² NASHAAT (USA) 8-11-5 W Worthington, *al prmnt, rdn appr 2
out, sn wknd, lft 3rd last*............... (9 to 1 op 7 to 1) 3

EARLY PEACE (Ire) 4-11-5 V Smith, *prmnt, lost pl 5th, rallied 2 out, hmpd flt, kpt on* .... (33 to 1 op 20 to 1)   4
KILNAMARTYRA GIRL 6-10-11 (3*) P Midgley, *prmnt, rdn 4 out, styd on same pace* .... (12 to 1 op 10 to 1)   5
879⁴ ELA MAN HOWA 5-11-5 T Kent, *hld up, nvr rchd ldrs.* .... (9 to 1 op 8 to 1 tchd 10 to 1)   6
SHARED RISK 4-11-5 E Callaghan, *hld up, styd on frm 2 out, nvr dngrs* .... (33 to 1)   7
SEGALA (Ire) 5-11-5 M Dwyer, *hld up, nvr rchd ldrs.* .... (20 to 1 op 16 to 1)   8
REFLEX HAMMER 5-11-5 K O'Brien, *hld up, nvr dngrs.* .... (5 to 1 tchd 9 to 2 and 11 to 2)   9
728³ DR EDGAR 4-11-5 P Niven, *prmnt til wknd and eased appr 2 out* .... (8 to 1 op 7 to 1 tchd 9 to 1)   10
LADY SWIFT 5-11-0 R Garritty, *al in rear* .... (33 to 1)   11
PAST MASTER (USA) 8-11-5 A S Smith, *prmnt to 5th.* .... (13 to 2 op 5 to 1 tchd 7 to 1)   12
OTTER PRINCE 7-10-12 (7*) C Hynes, *blun 1st, al beh.* .... (50 to 1)   13
879⁷ NAKED FEELINGS 4-11-5 M Moloney, *hld up, beh frm 5th.* .... (50 to 1 op 33 to 1)   14
874⁸ MIDNIGHT BOB 5-11-5 R Marley, *prmnt til blun and lost pl 5th, sn beh, tld off* .... (50 to 1 op 33 to 1)   15
DURANO 5-11-5 L Wyer, *hld up in tch, led and hit 2 out, f last.* .... (11 to 2 op 5 to 1 tchd 6 to 1)   f
735 BOSTON MAN 5-11-0 (5*) D J Kavanagh, *hld up, beh frm 5th, pld up bef 3 out* .... (50 to 1)   pu
Dist: 8l, nk, 3l, 5l, 2l, 2¹/₂l, ³/₄l, ¹/₄l, 10l, 6l. 4m 15.60s. a 14.60s (17 Ran).

(Mrs J M Mayo), C J Mann

1048 United European Car Carriers Handicap Hurdle Class D (0-125 4-y-o and up) £2,921 3m.............. (4:20)

808⁴ OLYMPIAN [114] (bl) 9-11-11 N Williamson, *slwly into strd, led second to 4 out, led and mstk 2 out, drvn out.* .... (11 to 1 op 8 to 1)   1
757 SAN GIORGIO [96] 7-10-7 T Jenks, *chsd ldr, led 4 out, hdd 2 out, hit last, no extr.* ..... (6 to 1 tchd 13 to 2 and 7 to 1)   2
ELBURG (Ire) [95] 6-10-6 D Byrne, *strted slwly, hdwy 5 out, wknd 3 out* .... (10 to 1 op 16 to 1)   3
203² RIVER ROOM [107] 6-11-4 J Railton, *led til second, rdn and wknd 3 out* .... (11 to 4 fav op 5 to 2 tchd 3 to 1 and 100 to 30)   4
913* CLEAN EDGE (USA) [108] 4-11-0 (3*) E Husband, *al beh.* .... (3 to 1 op 2 to 1)   5
NICK THE BEAK (Ire) [103] 7-11-0 K O'Brien, *prmnt, chsd ldr 5 out till wknd aftr 3 out* .... (8 to 1 op 7 to 1)   6
DOCKMASTER [101] 5-10-10 A S Smith, *hld up, lost tch hfwy, tld off, pld up bef 2 out* ... (11 to 2 op 5 to 1 tchd 6 to 1)   pu
JUST SUPROSEN (Ire) [99] 5-10-8 M Dwyer, *hld up, beh and rdn 7th, tld off whn pld up bef 3 out* ... (20 to 1 op 16 to 1)   pu
Dist: 3l, 15l, 7l, 6l, 1¹/₂l. 6m 2.10s. a 23.10s (8 Ran).

(J Neville), J Neville

1049 Cobelfret / Exxtor Novices' Chase Class E (4-y-o and up) £3,496 2m 1f 110yds.................... (4:55)

913⁴ DOWN THE FELL 7-11-4 N Williamson, *led to second, lft in ld 8th, clr 4 out* .... (2 to 1 op 7 to 4 tchd 9 to 4)   1
878 HIGHLAND WAY (Ire) 8-11-4 M Dwyer, *hld up and beh, hdwy to chase wnr 4 out, wknd 2 out* ..... (7 to 1 op 10 to 1)   2
STORMHILL PILGRIM 7-11-4 P McLoughlin, *pld hrd, led second to 5th, mstk 9th, sn beh* ... (20 to 1 tchd 16 to 1)   3
916 KARENASTINO 5-10-10 (7*) R Wilkinson, *prmnt to 5th.* .... (50 to 1 op 33 to 1)   4
THORNTON GATE 7-11-4 L Wyer, *chsd ldr, led 5th til f 8th.* .... (6 to 5 fav op 11 to 8 on tchd 5 to 4)   f
WREN WARBLER 6-10-13 A S Smith, *f second.* .... (5 to 1 op 8 to 1 tchd 9 to 1)   f
Dist: 20l, dist, 9l. 4m 26.10s. a 12.10s (6 Ran).
SR: 21/1/-/

(J Howard Johnson), J Howard Johnson

1050 Park Social / Trimesh Guardians Maiden Open National Hunt Flat Class H (4,5,6-y-o) £1,238 1m 5f 110yds.................... (5:25)

917⁵ SILVER MINX 4-11-5 P Niven, *led, hdd o'r 2 fs out, rallied to ld appr last, rdn out* .... (8 to 1 op 7 to 1 tchd 9 to 1)   1
NIFAAF (USA) 4-11-0 A S Smith, *trkd ldrs, wnt second 4 fs out, led o'r 2 out, rdn and hdd appr last, kpt on.* .... (3 to 1 op 5 to 2 tchd 100 to 30)   2
LEPTON (Ire) 5-11-5 L Wyer, *in tch, chlgd 2 fs out, styd on same pace* .... (14 to 1 op 8 to 1)   3
PRIMITIVE HEART 4-11-5 A Larnach, *prmnt, drvn alng o'r 2 fs out, wknd* .... (6 to 1 op 5 to 1 tchd 7 to 1)   4
PHAR ENOUGH (Ire) 4-11-5 W Dwan, *prmnt, rdn o'r 3 fs out, styd on same pace* .... (4 to 1 op 7 to 2 tchd 9 to 2)   5
MARNIES WOLF 5-11-5 Mrs F Needham, *hld up, hdwy hfwy, wknd o'r 2 fs out* .... (50 to 1 op 33 to 1)   6
JACKHO 4-11-0 (5*) S Taylor, *in tch, effrt hfwy, wknd o'r 3 fs out* .... (33 to 1 op 25 to 1)   7
WELSH SPINNER (Ire) 5-11-5 W McFarland, *hld up, rdn 4 fs out, sn beh* .... (33 to 1 op 25 to 1)   8

---

873 BABA SAM (Ire) 5-11-5 N Williamson, *hld up, drvn alng hfwy, sn wknd* .... (14 to 1 op 16 to 1 tchd 20 to 1)   9
LORD OF THE LOCH (Ire) 5-11-5 M Dwyer, *jinked rght and lft, uns rdr strt* .... (2 to 1 fav op 4 to 1 tchd 7 to 4)   ur
Dist: ³/₄l, 5l, 4l, 4l, nk, 8l, ¹/₂l, 7l. 3m 17.50s. (10 Ran).
(Mrs E A Kettlewell), Mrs M Reveley

WORCESTER (good)
Saturday October 26th
Going Correction: PLUS 0.40 sec. per fur. (races 1,3,6), PLUS 0.15 (2,4,5)

1051 City And County Conditional Jockeys' Handicap Hurdle Class F (0-105 4-y-o and up) £2,087 2m .... (2:05)

810* STEADFAST ELITE (Ire) [95] 5-11-10 R McGrath, *hld up, hdwy 3rd, wnt second appr 3 out, plenty to do last, ran on to ld post.* .... (4 to 1 op 3 to 1)   1
789 ALPINE MIST (Ire) [90] (v) 4-11-4 Michael Brennan, *hld up, hdwy 3rd, led appr 5th, clr 3 out, tired r-in, hdd post.* .... (6 to 1 op 9 to 2 tchd 7 to 1)   2
970³ ZINGIBAR [79] 4-10-2 (5*) J Power, *led till hdd appr 5th, sn lost pl, rdn and hdwy 2 out, styd on r-in.* .... (100 to 30 fav op 7 to 2 tchd 9 to 1)   3
SCOTTISH WEDDING [76] 6-10-6 R Massey, *prmnt till rdn and lost pl 5th, rallied appr 3 out, one pace frm nxt.* .... (11 to 1 op 12 to 1 tchd 10 to 1)   4
SLIPMATIC [84] 7-10-11 (3*) C Rae, *pld hrd, in tch till wknd 4th* .... (11 to 2 op 9 to 2 tchd 10 to 1)   5
THUHOOL [86] 8-10-9 (7*) A Garritty, *beh, nvr on terms.* .... (9 to 1 op 8 to 1)   6
ANLACE [88] 7-10-13 Chris Webb, *al beh.* .... (6 to 1 op 4 to 1 tchd 13 to 2 and 7 to 1)   7
801 WILL JAMES [71] (bl) 10-10-1 Guy Lewis, *trkd ldr till jmpd slwly 5th, sn wknd, tld off.* .... (33 to 1 op 25 to 1)   8
BILL AND WIN [85] 5-11-0 G Hogan, *al beh, mstk 3rd, tld off whn pld up bef 2 out* .... (33 to 1 tchd 40 to 1)   pu
Dist: Hd, 1¹/₄l, 3l, 10l, sht-hd, 2¹/₂l, 9l. 3m 56.40s. a 16.40s (9 Ran).
(Clayton Bigley Partnership Ltd), J J O'Neill

1052 John Burke Memorial Handicap Chase Class D (0-125 5-y-o and up) £3,562 2m.................... (2:35)

ZEREDAR (NZ) [95] 6-10-4 C O'Dwyer, *hld up in rear, mstk 3rd, hdwy 6th, wnt second 4 out, hit nxt, rdn to ld r-in.* .... (11 to 4 fav op 5 to 2 tchd 3 to 1 and 100 to 30)   1
972⁴ NEWLANDS-GENERAL [115] 10-11-10 A P McCoy, *lft in ld 1st, distracted by loose horse 2 out, rdn and hdd r-in.* .... (7 to 2 op 5 to 2 tchd 4 to 1)   2
SEOD RIOGA (Ire) [114] 7-11-9 N Mann, *hld up, lost pl 5th, blun 5 out, nvr on terms aftr* .... (10 to 1 op 6 to 1)   3
240² FULL O'PRAISE (NZ) [105] 9-11-0 M A Fitzgerald, *al prmnt, wnt second briefly appr 4 out, wknd nxt.* .... (9 to 1 op 8 to 1 tchd 11 to 1)   4
MAN MOOD (Fr) [112] 5-11-6 G Bradley, *trkd ldr till wknd appr 4 out* .... (14 to 1 op 6 to 1 tchd 16 to 1)   5
THE CAUMRUE (Ire) [105] 8-11-0 B Clifford, *al beh, tld off.* .... (10 to 1 op 8 to 1)   6
901³ GOOD FOR A LAUGH [102] 12-10-4 (7*) Mr G Shenkin, *al beh, tld off* .... (12 to 1 op 16 to 1 tchd 10 to 1)   7
870* FINE HARVEST [115] 10-11-10 D Bridgwater, *led till f 1st.* .... (5 to 1 op 4 to 1 tchd 11 to 2)   f
MIAMI SPLASH [97] 9-10-6 C Maude, *beh frm 4th, last whn blun badly 6th, sn pld up* .... (10 to 1 op 8 to 1)   pu
Dist: ³/₄l, 24l, ³/₄l, 3l, 7l, nk. 3m 57.80s. a 8.80s (9 Ran).
SR: 12/31/6/-/-/-/

(I M S Racing), K C Bailey

1053 John Murphy 75th Birthday European Breeders Fund 'National Hunt' Novices' Hurdle Qualifier Class E (4,5,6-y-o) £2,477 2¹/₄m.......... (3:05)

BIETSCHHORN BARD 6-10-11 (3*) D Fortt, *hld up in rear, rapid hdwy appr 3 out, led approaching last, ran on.* .... (14 to 1 op 10 to 1 tchd 16 to 1)   1
MYTHICAL APPROACH (Ire) 6-11-0 A Maguire, *nvr far away, led appr 2 out, hdd bef last, no imprsn r-in.* .... (11 to 4 fav op 5 to 2 tchd 3 to 1)   2
62* DONTLEAVETHENEST (Ire) 6-11-10 D Morris, *hld up, hdwy 6th, ev ch 3 out till wknd appr last.* .... (16 to 1 op 14 to 1 tchd 20 to 1 and 25 to 1)   3
RHYTHM AND BLUES 6-11-0 B Powell, *hld up in tch, wnt second 6th, 4th and held whn hit last.* (20 to 1 op 16 to 1)   4
PENTLANDS FLYER (Ire) 5-11-0 C Llewellyn, *pld hrd, chsd ldrs till wknd appr 2 out* .... (6 to 1 op 5 to 1)   5
MESP (Ire) 5-10-9 R Johnson, *hld up, hdwy 5th, wkng whn blun 3 out* .... (50 to 1 op 33 to 1)   6
SYLVESTER (Ire) 6-11-0 M A Fitzgerald, *led till wknd and hdd appr 2 out* .... (50 to 1 op 33 to 1 tchd 66 to 1)   7
BOUND FOR GOLD 5-11-0 J F Titley, *chsd ldrs, wknd appr 3 out, one pace aftr* .... (16 to 1 op 10 to 1)   8

SIR DANTE (Ire) 5-11-0 P Hide, *in tch to 6th.*
..................(11 to 2 op 11 to 4 tchd 6 to 1) 9
939 ANOTHER HUBBLICK 5-10-7 (7") O Burrows, *al beh.*
.................................(66 to 1 op 33 to 1) 10
BEL-DE-MOOR 4-10-8 W Marston, *al beh.*
.................................(50 to 1 op 33 to 1 tchd 66 to 1) 11
456⁵ SIERRA NEVADA 5-11-0 A P McCoy, *al beh.*
.................................(16 to 1 op 14 to 1) 12
STORM TIGER (Ire) 5-11-0 N Mann, *lost tch 5th, tld off.*
.................................(33 to 1 tchd 50 to 1) 13
SOUTHERN NIGHTS 6-11-0 C O'Dwyer, *pld hrd, hld up, hdwy 5th, prmnt whn pulled up 3 out, lme.*
.................................(4 to 1 tchd 7 to 2 and 9 to 2) pu
HOLD THE FORT 5-11-0 L Harvey, *mid-div, lost tch 5th, tld off whn pld up bef 3 out...............*(100 to 1 op 50 to 1) pu
CEANNAIRE (Ire) 6-11-0 J Osborne, *prmnt, mstk 1st, wknd quickly 6th, tld off whn pld up bef 3 out.*
.................................(14 to 1 tchd 16 to 1) pu
OLDEN DAYS 4-10-13 T J Murphy, *mid-div till wknd 5th, tld off whn pld up bef 3 out.* (50 to 1 op 20 to 1 tchd 66 to 1) pu
545⁴ KATHARINE'S SONG (Ire) 6-10-9 G Bradley, *al beh, tld off whn pld up bef 3 out....*(50 to 1 op 33 to 1 tchd 66 to 1) pu
654⁸ POWERFUL SPIRIT 4-10-8 (5") Michael Brennan, *chsd ldr till jmpd slwly 4th, wknd aftr nxt, tld off whn pld up after 3 out.*
.................................(33 to 1 tchd 50 to 1) pu
Dist: 2l, 8l, 4l, 2l, 12l, 5l, 9l, 5l, 2½l, 1l. 4m 20.70s. a 13.70s (19 Ran).
SR: 21/19/21/7/5/-/   (A W F Clapperton), D R Gandolfo

1054 Fred Rimell Memorial Novices' Chase Class D (5-y-o and up) £4,337 2½m 110yds.................(3:35)

799* CALL EQUINAME 6-11-6 A P McCoy, *trkd ldr, led aftr 6th, found extr whn chlgd last.*
..................(13 to 8 on op 7 to 4 on tchd 6 to 4 on) 1
616* FINE THYNE (Ire) 7-11-0 M A Fitzgerald, *mstk 5th, hld up, lft second tenth, rdn to chal last, no imprsn r-in.*
..................(5 to 1 op 4 to 1 tchd 9 to 2) 2
COVERDALE LANE 9-10-13 Mr P Murray, *chsd ldrs till wknd 7th, tld off......*(66 to 1 op 33 to 1 tchd 100 to 1) 3
902 SWING QUARTET (Ire) 6-10-9 C Llewellyn, *mstk 6th, lost tch 9th, tld off..........................*(9 to 2 op 4 to 1) 4
973 RAFTERS 7-11-0 R Johnson, *chsd ldrs, wnt second appr 7th, f tenth...........................*(33 to 1 op 25 to 1) f
772⁴ MORSTOCK 6-11-0 J Frost, *blun and uns rdr 3rd.*
..................(12 to 1 op 10 to 1 tchd 14 to 1 and 16 to 1) ur
MILLFRONE (Ire) 6-11-0 P Hide, *led till aftr 6th, wknd quickly, tld off whn pld up bef tenth...........*(33 to 1 op 14 to 1) pu
EVENTSINTERNASHNAL 7-11-0 B Powell, *slwly away, sn tld off, pld up bef 3rd...................*(100 to 1 op 50 to 1) pu
Dist: 1½l, dist, dist. 5m 14.20s. a 17.20s (8 Ran).
(Mick Coburn, P K Barber, C Lewis), P F Nicholls

1055 Durr 25th Anniversary Celebration Novices' Handicap Chase Class E (0-100 5-y-o and up) £3,363 2m 7f ....(4:10)

EXPRESS TRAVEL (Ire) [72] 8-10-0 D Morris, *hld up in rear, hdwy 5 out, led nxt, ran on wl.........*(20 to 1 op 14 to 1) 1
IVY HOUSE (Ire) [88] 8-11-2 A Maguire, *blun second, mid-div till hdwy appr 4 out, ev ch 2 out till no imprsn r-in.*
.................................(11 to 2 op 7 to 1) 2
NOW WE KNOW (Ire) [83] 8-10-11 B Powell, *hld up, hdwy hfwy, outpcd 4 out, styd on frm 2 out...*(14 to 1 op 8 to 1) 3
902* STRONG TARQUIN (Ire) [100] 6-12-0 A P McCoy, *hld up in tch, pld hrd, led 12th, hit 14th, sn hdd, wknd 2 out.*
..................(11 to 4 fav op 5 to 2 tchd 3 to 1) 4
82 ITS GRAND [72] 7-10-0 T J Murphy, *al prmnt, led aftr 5 out, hdd nxt, wknd appr 2 out.*
.................................(40 to 1 op 20 to 1 tchd 50 to 1) 5
957³ CHRIS'S GLEN [83] (v) 7-10-11 R Johnson, *hld up, hdwy hfwy, hit 11th, rallied and ev ch 4 out, wknd appr 2 out.*
.................................(16 to 1 op 12 to 1) 6
834* SEASAMACAMILE [72] 9-9-7 (7") Mr R Thornton, *hit 7th, tld off tenth....................*(16 to 1 tchd 20 to 1) 7
SEYMOUR SPY [85] 7-10-13 S Wynne, *chsd ldrs to hfwy, beh 12th, tld off....................*(10 to 1 op 8 to 1) 8
COUNTRY KEEPER [75] 8-10-3 G Upton, *blun and uns rdr 1st.......................*(50 to 1 op 25 to 1) ur
GALLIC GIRL (Ire) [72] 6-9-11 (3") T Dascombe, *blun and uns rdr 1st...............*(40 to 1 op 25 to 1 tchd 50 to 1) ur
CARDINAL RULE (Ire) [72] 7-10-0 W Marston, *led till hmpd and uns rdr 1st........................*(12 to 1 op 10 to 1) ur
999 YES WE ARE [73] 10-10-11 P Holley, *al beh, mstks, tld off whn pld up bef tenth.................*(100 to 1 op 66 to 1) pu
FLAMING MIRACLE (Ire) [72] (bl) 6-10-0 R Farrant, *pld hrd, led aftr 5th, hdd 12th, wknd quickly, tld off whn pulled up bef 4 out......* (10 to 1 op 25 to 1 tchd 33 to 1 and 50 to 1) pu
SCRABBLE [72] 7-10-0 Mr P Murray, *blun 9th, tld off 11th, pld up bef 4 out..........*(40 to 1 op 25 to 1 tchd 50 to 1) pu
SPEARHEAD AGAIN (Ire) [89] 7-11-3 M A Fitzgerald, *prmnt, bl briefly 6th, mstk tenth, wknd 12th, tld off whn pld up bef 4 out......*(6 to 1 op 7 to 1 tchd 5 to 1) pu
DOMINIE (Ire) [95] (bl) 8-11-9 C O'Dwyer, *chsd ldrs, wkng whn mstk 14th, tld off when pld up bef 2 out.*
.................................(9 to 1 op 6 to 1 tchd 10 to 1) pu

---

THE GO AHEAD (Ire) [92] 6-11-6 A Thornton, *lft in ld 1st, hdd 5th, wknd 12th, tld off whn pld up bef 4 out.*
.................................(14 to 1 tchd 16 to 1) pu
Dist: 2½l, 1½l, ¾l, 1½l, 13l, dist, 8l. 6m 6.30s. a 28.30s (17 Ran).
(Michael J Low), R Curtis

1056 Ladbrokes Handicap Hurdle Class C (0-135 4-y-o and up) £3,731 2½m ....(4:40)

TEEN JAY [117] 6-11-7 V Slattery, *hld up, hdwy 5th, led 2 out, drvn out.................*(15 to 2 op 7 to 2 tchd 8 to 1) 1
NAHRI (USA) [111] 5-11-0 A P McCoy, *hld up, hdwy appr 3 out, pressed ldrs nxt, ran on to go second r-in.*
.................................(9 to 1 op 6 to 1) 2
BALANAK (USA) [121] 5-11-10 A Maguire, *hld up in rear, hdwy 6th, ev ch last, no extr r-in.*
.................................(8 to 1 op 7 to 1 tchd 9 to 1) 3
GO BALLISTIC [124] 7-12-0 M A Fitzgerald, *hld up, hdwy appr 3 out, one pace frm nxt.*
.................................(11 to 2 op 7 to 1 tchd 9 to 1) 4
896* WOTTASHAMBLES [114] 5-11-3 D Morris, *chsd ldrs, dsptd ld frm 6th, led appr 3 out, hdd nxt, sn btn.*
.................................(5 to 1 op 4 to 1 tchd 11 to 2) 5
896³ LA MENORQUINA (USA) [98] 6-10-2 J A McCarthy, *led aftr 1st, hdd 7th, wknd 3 out...........*(7 to 1 op 12 to 1) 6
CELTINO [99] 8-10-3 S Wynne, *al in rear, some hdwy frm 3 out.................*(14 to 1 op 12 to 1 tchd 16 to 1) 7
SPRING TO GLORY [104] 9-10-8 B Fenton, *pld hrd, al beh.*
.................................(25 to 1 tchd 33 to 1) 8
NEEDWOOD MUPPET [112] 9-11-2 L Harvey, *led till aftr 1st, led briefly 7th, wknd 3 out...........*(16 to 1 op 12 to 1) 9
ARITHMETIC [113] 6-11-3 W Marston, *prmnt till wknd quickly appr 3 out.................*(4 to 1 fav op 3 to 1) 10
DANZIG ISLAND (Ire) [104] 5-10-7 C Llewellyn, *prmnt till hit 6th, sn beh, tld off......*(16 to 1 op 12 to 1 tchd 20 to 1) 11
HELLO ME MAN (Ire) [103] 8-10-7 Mr J L Llewellyn, *chsd ldrs to 5th, sn wknd, tld off whn pld up bef 3 out.*
.................................(40 to 1 op 25 to 1 tchd 50 to 1) pu
JUST FOR A REASON [97] 4-10-0 R Johnson, *al beh, tld off whn pld up bef 2 out.................*(40 to 1 op 25 to 1) pu
Dist: 1½l, nk, 3½l, 2½l, nk, 1l, 2l, 8l, 12l, dist. 4m 54.40s. a 18.40s (13 Ran).
(Gemini Associates), J B Llewellyn

GALWAY (IRE) (yielding (race 1), soft (2,3,4)) Sunday October 27th

1057 Bank Of Ireland Excel Juvenile Hurdle (3-y-o) £3,425 2m.........(1:30)

882² QUILL PROJECT (Ire) 9-12 (7") M W Martin, ...(5 to 1) 1
927* MISS ROBERTO (Ire) 11-1 K F O'Brien, ...(7 to 4 fav) 2
927² GO SASHA (Ire) 10-10 (5") T Martin, ...(9 to 2) 3
574³ THREE RIVERS 10-3 (7") P Morris, ...(8 to 1) 4
927⁶ KIRIBATI (Ire) 10-10 M P Dwyer, ...(9 to 1) 5
620 KILBAHA (Ire) 10-5 M P Hourigan, ...(10 to 1) 6
882⁵ KING OF PEACE (Ire) 10-10 H Rogers, ...(8 to 1) 7
927⁷ IACCHUS (Ire) 10-5 J P Kelly, ...(8 to 1) 8
927 KILLARY (Ire) 10-10 J Shortt, ...(14 to 1) 9
882 ODY MORODY (Ire) 10-5 S H O'Donovan, ...(33 to 1) 10
KERRY REEL (Ire) 10-3 (7") J M Maguire, ...(20 to 1) 11
527⁷ TIP YOUR WAITRESS (Ire) 10-10 G M O'Neill, ...(25 to 1) 12
PEAK VIEW (Ire) 10-3 (7") S FitzGerald, ...(33 to 1) f
MIND ME BRODY (Ire) 10-10 M P Duffy, ...(10 to 1) ro
Dist: ¾l, 25l, 2l, 15l. 4m 7.20s. (14 Ran).
(Mrs J S Bolger), J S Bolger

1058 Bank Of Ireland Pass Point Handicap Hurdle (0-116 4-y-o and up) £3,425 2½m...................(2:00)

907* TARAJAN (USA) [-] (bl) 4-11-8 J Shortt, ...(7 to 2) 1
SHINING WILLOW [-] 6-11-5 K F O'Brien, ...(8 to 1) 2
732⁸ JUST AN ILLUSION (Ire) [-] 4-11-5 D T Evans, ...(6 to 1) 3
802* COLLON LEADER (Ire) [-] 7-10-8 (7") J M Maguire,
.................................(5 to 2 fav) 4
526⁷ JO JO BOY (Ire) [-] 7-12-0 F J Flood, ...(12 to 1) 5
729 TIMELY AFFAIR (Ire) [-] 7-10-1 C O'Brien, ...(8 to 1) 6
BOBBYJO (Ire) [-] 6-10-13 P L Malone, ...(7 to 1) 7
THE SCEARDEEN (Ire) [-] 7-10-12 M Duffy, ...(12 to 1) 8
OVER THE WALL (Ire) [-] 7-10-5 T J O'Sullivan, ...(20 to 1) 9
DAMODAR [-] 7-10-13 S H O'Donovan, ...(9 to 1) 10
LA PENNY VIOLA (Ire) [-] 4-9-2 (5") T Martin, ...(25 to 1) 11
237 SWINGER (Ire) [-] 7-11-4 M P Dwyer, ...(12 to 1) pu
Dist: 4½l, sht-hd, 1½l, 25l. 5m 22.90s. (12 Ran).
(Ms Maura Horan), Patrick Prendergast

1059 Ballybrit Novice Chase (Grade 3) (5-y-o and up) £6,850 2m 1f.....(4:00)

730 NORDIC THORN (Ire) 6-11-6 K F O'Brien, ...(10 to 1) 1
909² BANNER GALE (Ire) 7-11-2 M P Dwyer, ...(7 to 4 fav) 2
909³ STROLL HOME (Ire) 6-11-5 (7") Mr E Gallagher, ... (4 to 1) 3
DADDY DANCER (Fr) 5-11-2 C O'Brien, ...(10 to 1) 4

925² THE BOURDA 10-10-11 (5*) T Martin, ... (6 to 1) 5
926 LOUGH ATALIA 9-11-2 G M O'Neill, ... (7 to 1) f
980⁹ TAITS CLOCK (Ire) 7-11-2 J Shortt, ... (7 to 1) 6
Dist: 10l, 9l, 15l, 9l: 4m 52.50s. (7 Ran).

(Peter Malone), Martin Brassil

1060 Bank Of Ireland Golden Years Flat Race (4-y-o and up) £3,425 2m (4:30)

853² BALLYRIHY BOY (Ire) 5-12-0 Miss M Olivefalk, ... (3 to 1) 1
929 VALLEY OF KINGS (Ire) 6-11-7 (7*) Mr D A Harney, (12 to 1) 2
346² MASK RIVER (Ire) 7-11-2 (7*) Mr A Daly, ... (12 to 1) 3
984 PATRAY LAD (Ire) 5-11-7 (7*) Mr A K Wyse, ... (14 to 1) 4
STORM MAN 4-11-2 (7*) Mr Damien Murphy,
. . . . (2 to 1 fav) 5
THE TOLLAH (Ire) 4-11-2 (7*) Mr G Elliott, ... (7 to 1) 6
560² IRVINE (Ire) 4-11-2 (7*) Miss S J Leahy, ... (5 to 1) 7
RINEEN BREEZE (Ire) 5-11-2 (7*) Mr B Hassett, . . . (10 to 1) 8
JAIMIES DANCER (Ire) 5-11-9 Mr A R Coonan, ... (16 to 1) 9
MAIGUESIDE PRINCE (Ire) 5-11-7 (7*) Mr John P Moloney,
. . . . (10 to 1) 10
EXECUTIVE OPAL (Ire) 5-11-2 (7*) Mr R P McNalley, (12 to 1) 11
NOBLE IRIS (Ire) 4-10-11 (7*) Mr B A Murphy, ... (12 to 1) 12
Dist: 20l, 2l, 1½l, 15l. 4m 9.50s. (12 Ran).

(M J Collison), Capt D G Swan

HUNTINGDON (good)
Sunday October 27th
Going Correction: PLUS 0.40 sec. per fur.

1061 Henkel Conditional Jockeys' Selling Handicap Hurdle Class G (0-95 4-y-o and up) £1,919 3¼m. . . . . (2:00)

TIGER CLAW (USA) [81] 10-11-2 (3*) O Burrows, hld up in tch,
led appr 2 out, rdn out . . . . (10 to 1 op 6 to 1) 1
659 PLEASE CALL (Ire) [72] 7-10-5 (5*) T Hagger, hdwy frm rear
8th, led 3 out, hdd appr nxt, kpt on one pace.
. . . . (33 to 1 op 16 to 1) 2
971⁹ AWESTRUCK [62] (bl) 6-10-9 G Hogan, beh and reminders
4th, effrt 7th, styd on aftr 3 out, nrst finish.
. . . . (16 to 1 op 25 to 1 tchd 33 to 1) 3
906³ TIPPING ALONG (Ire) [78] 7-11-2 Sophie Mitchell, in tch, prog
7th, no extr frm 3 out . . . . (9 to 2 op 3 to 1 tchd 5 to 1) 4
844⁵ STORM DRUM [90] (bl) 7-11-9 (5*) W Walsh, mid-div,
improved 9th, rdn and btn 3 out . . . . (13 to 2 op 4 to 1) 5
SNOWY LANE (Ire) [67] (bl) 8-10-5 T Dascombe, wl plcd till
wknd 9th. . . . . (7 to 1 op 10 to 1 tchd 8 to 1) 6
989⁶ SLIGHTLY SPECIAL (Ire) [64] 4-10-0 K Gaule, led, mstk 9th,
hdd 3 out, sn wknd. . . . . (33 to 1 op 16 to 1) 7
845³ SCRIPT [75] 5-10-4 (7*) D Yellowlees, hld up in rear, nvr on
terms. . . . . (15 to 2 op 7 to 1 tchd 8 to 1 and 13 to 2) 8
762⁶ ELLTEE-ESS [65] 11-9-10 (7*) C R Weaver, al towards rear, tld
off whn pld up bef 2 out . . . . (33 to 1 op 25 to 1) pu
CHRISTIAN SOLDIER [62] (v) 9-10-0 D Walsh, al rear, tld off
whn pld up aftr 7th. . . . . (33 to 1 tchd 50 to 1) pu
504⁴ JOLI'S GREAT [75] (bl) 8-10-13 Michael Brennan, pressed ldr
till wknd 8th, sn lost tch, pld up bef 2 out.
. . . . (11 to 4 fav op 7 to 4 tchd 3 to 1) pu
836⁷ DO BE WARE [76] 6-11-2 D J Kavanagh, prmnt till wknd aftr
9th, pld up bef 2 out. . . . . (13 to 2 op 5 to 1) pu
Dist: 1¼l, 3l, ½l, 4l, dist, 20l, 6l. 6m 34.20s. a 42.20s (12 Ran).

(Unity Farm Holiday Centre Ltd), A G Hobbs

1062 Jaguar Novices' Handicap Chase Class F (0-95 5-y-o and up) £2,940 2 ½m 110yds. . . . . (2:30)

838⁴ MILL O'THE RAGS (Ire) [95] 7-12-0 J F Titley, prmnt, rdn alng
appr 3 out, led 2 out, clr last, fnshd tired. (3 to 1 op 7 to 4) 1
DALAMETRE [67] 9-10-0 W Marston, led till hdd 4 out, lft in ld
ag'n aftr nxt, headed appr 2 out, mstk last.
. . . . (11 to 1 op 10 to 1 tchd 14 to 1) 2
639⁶ WILLIE MAKEIT (Ire) [87] 6-11-4 J Railton, ldg grp, rdn alng 3
out, btn whn hit last. . . . . . . (6 to 1 op 7 to 2 tchd 13 to 2) 3
CASTLE CHIEF [90] 7-11-7 P Hide, in tch till beh frm 11th.
. . . . (5 to 2 fav op 2 to 1 tchd 11 to 4) 4
956² KING'S SHILLING (USA) [84] 9-11-3 Jacqui Oliver, mstks 1st
and 9th, beh frm 11th . . . . . . (11 to 2 op 7 to 1 tchd 5 to 1) 5
920⁵ WESTERLY GALE (Ire) [76] 6-10-9 M A Fitzgerald, trkd ldrs,
led 4 out till blun and uns rdr nxt.
. . . . (9 to 2 op 4 to 1 tchd 11 to 2) ur
845⁴ ON THE TEAR [67] 10-10-0 D Byrne, al rear, tld off whn pld up
bef 4 out. . . . . (11 to 1 op 6 to 1 tchd 12 to 1) pu
956 SUNGIA (Ire) [70] (v) 7-10-3³ T Jenks, rear till pld up bef 8th.
. . . . (50 to 1 op 33 to 1) pu
Dist: 7l, 10l, 10l, 1¼l. 5m 12.60s. a 25.60s (8 Ran).

(E J Fenaroli), Mrs D Haine

1063 Peugeot Novices' Hurdle Class E (4-y-o and up) £2,617 2½m 110yds
. . . . (3:00)

879² INN AT THE TOP 4-10-11 D Byrne, handily plcd, led 3 out,
tried to run out nxt, hit last, eased bef line.
. . . . . . (11 to 8 fav op 2 to 1 tchd 9 to 4 and 11 to 10) 1
SALMON BREEZE (Ire) 5-10-12 M A Fitzgerald, trkd ldrs, hit
7th and lost pl, kpt on ag'n frm 3 out, no extr last.
. . . . (100 to 30 op 6 to 4 tchd 7 to 2) 2
905⁴ LORD ROOBLE (Ire) 5-10-12 P Hide, led till hdd 3 out, wknd
nxt . . . . (3 to 1 op 2 to 1) 3
978⁸ SAMAKA HARA (Ire) 4-10-11 T Jenks, chsd ldrs till weakend
appr 3 out . . . . (20 to 1 op 12 to 1 tchd 25 to 1) 4
GOATSFUT (Ire) 6-10-9 (3*) G Hogan, refused and uns rdr 1st.
. . . . (14 to 1 op 8 to 1 tchd 16 to 1) ref
649 GIORGIONE (Fr) 7-10-5 (7*) Mr R Wakley, chsd ldrs till wknd
frm 5th, tld off whn pld up bef 2 out . . . (50 to 1 op 33 to 1) pu
GUNNER JOHN 5-10-12 D Bridgwater, beh frm 5th, tld off
whn pld up bef 3 out. . . . . (16 to 1 op 14 to 1) pu
53 ROSSLAYNE SERENADE 5-10-0 (7*) C R Weaver, effrt 4th,
wknd 7th, tld off whn pld up bef 2 out. (50 to 1 op 25 to 1) pu
Dist: 14l, 7l, dist. 4m 54.80s. a 19.80s (8 Ran).

(Mrs Sylvia Blakeley), J Norton

1064 Henkel Teroson Automotive Handicap Chase Class D (0-120 5-y-o and up) £3,915 3m. . . . . (3:30)

872² MERLINS DREAM (Ire) [103] 7-10-11 J A McCarthy, chsd ldr
frm 3rd, mstk 14th, jmpd lft 2 out, led last, rdn clr.
. . . . (2 to 1 tchd 9 to 4 and 5 to 2) 1
ROMANY CREEK (Ire) [120] (v) 7-12-0 D Bridgwater, led 3rd,
hit tenth, hdd last, no extr. (6 to 1 op 4 to 1 tchd 7 to 1) 2
821¹³ VICOSA (Ire) [112] 7-10-13 (7*) Mr R Thornton, not jump wl,
hld up in tch, effrt 13th, wknd 16th. (13 to 8 fav op 7 to 4) 3
SORBIERE [100] 9-10-8 M A Fitzgerald, led to 3rd, wl in tch till
wknd 3 out. . . . . (3 to 1 op 5 to 2) 4
Dist: 18l, 8l, nk. 6m 11.20s. a 31.20s (4 Ran).

(W S Watt), O Sherwood

1065 Ford European Breeders Fund 'National Hunt' Novices' Hurdle Qualifier Class E (4,5,6-y-o) £2,390 2m 110yds. . . . . (4:00)

BEACON FLIGHT (Ire) 5-11-0 C Llewellyn, made all, set moderate pace till quickened appr 2 out, drvn out.
. . . . (7 to 2 op 3 to 1 tchd 4 to 1) 1
PEACE LORD 6-11-0 G Bradley, hld up in tch, cld on wnr
3 out, ev ch last, not quicken r-in.
. . . . (2 to 1 op 7 to 4 tchd 9 to 4) 2
DARAKHSAN (Ire) 4-10-13 J F Titley, trkd wnr, ev ch 2 out, rdn
and not quicken appr last.
. . . . (11 to 8 fav op 11 to 10 tchd 6 to 4) 3
CYPHRATES (Ire) 5-11-0 W Marston, hld up in tch, effrt 3 out,
one pace frm nxt . . . . (6 to 1 op 4 to 1) 4
QUARE DREAM'S (Ire) 5-10-9 D Bridgwater, hld up in last pl,
rdn and wknd 3 out . . . . (25 to 1 op 20 to 1 tchd 33 to 1) 5
746 SABOTEUSE 4-10-8 T J Murphy, hld up, effrt 3 out, rdn and
outpcd appr nxt . . . . (50 to 1 op 33 to 1) 6
Dist: 1½l, ½l, 5l, 14l, 4l. 4m 10.00s. a 29.00s (6 Ran).

(The Heyfleet Partnership), B de Haan

1066 Rover Handicap Hurdle Class E (0-115 4-y-o and up) £2,267 2m 110yds. . . . . (4:30)

MENELAVE (Ire) [99] 6-10-13 J A McCarthy, hld up, hdwy 5th,
led appr 3 out, jmpd lft and sddl slpd nxt, kpt on wl frm last.
. . . . (11 to 2 op 7 to 1 op 2) 1
YOUBETTERBELIEVEIT (Ire) [110] 7-11-10 G Bradley, wl
plcd, ev ch frm 2 out, not quicken r-in.
. . . . (15 to 8 fav op 2 to 1 tchd 9 to 4) 2
871² WAMDHA (Ire) [100] 6-11-0 A S Smith, wth ldrs till lost pl aftr
5th, kpt on ag'n one pace 2 out.
. . . . (11 to 4 op 2 to 1 tchd 3 to 1) 3
832³³ BON VOYAGE (USA) [100] 4-10-13 J R Kavanagh, led till hdd
aftr 3rd, wknd 5th.
. . . . (100 to 30 op 3 to 1 tchd 4 to 1 and 9 to 2) 4
PORPHYRIOS [107] 5-11-6 C Llewellyn, prmnt, led aftr 3rd,
hdd appr 3 out, sn btn. . . . . . . (10 to 1 op 4 to 1) 5
CAPTAIN TANDY (Ire) [90] 7-10-4 M Ranger, rear frm 4th, tld
off whn pld up bef 3 out. . . . . . . (50 to 1 op 20 to 1) pu
Dist: 2½l, 21l, 14l, 18l. 3m 59.10s. a 18.10s (6 Ran).

(R B Holt), O Sherwood

WETHERBY (good)
Sunday October 27th
Going Correction: PLUS 0.10 sec. per fur. (races 1,2,4,5,7), PLUS 0.15 (3,6)

1067 Yorkshire Racing Club Novices' Hurdle Class C (4-y-o and up) £3,860 2m 7f. (1:20)

934³ HIGHBEATH 5-11-6 P Niven, trkd ldg pair, dsptd ld hfwy, led 4
out, rdn 2 out and ran on wl. . . . . . . (11 to 8 on op 5 to 4) 1

MOVIE MAN 4-10-12 A Dobbin, *hld up, hdwy 8th, rdn 3 out, one pace appr nxt, lft second last*..... (33 to 1 op 25 to 1) 2
916 RAPID FIRE (Ire) 8-10-7 (7*) M Newton, *led to 5th, rdn alng 7th, plugged on same pace frm 3 out.* (33 to 1 op 20 to 1) 3
HOTSPUR STREET 4-10-12 N Williamson, *hld up and beh, hdwy 7th, pushed alng appr 3 out, no imprsn.* ....(7 to 1 op 5 to 1 tchd 8 to 1) 4
787 YOUNG KENNY 5-11-6 R Supple, *cl up, led 5th, hdd 4 out, rdn 2 out, second and hld whn f last.* .... (15 to 2 op 6 to 1 tchd 8 to 1) f
8742 TIGH-NA-MARA 8-10-4 (5*) E Callaghan, *hld up and beh, blun and uns rdr second*... (7 to 2 op 3 to 1 tchd 4 to 1) ur
ELLIOTT'S WISH (Ire) 5-11-0 A Maguire, *hld up and beh, lost tch 4 out, tld off whn pld up bef 2 out*...(14 to 1 op 10 to 1) pu
Dist: 16l, 6l, 4l. 5m 45.00s. (7 Ran).
(A Sharratt), Mrs M Reveley

1068 Micky Hammond Owners Selling Handicap Hurdle Class G (0-95 4-y-o and up) £2,460 2½m 110yds. . (1:50)

BELLE ROSE (Ire) [67] 6-10-0 A Dobbin, *chsd ldrs, hdwy 3 out, chlgd, not much room and mstk 2 out, swtchd and led last, rdn out*.......................(10 to 1 op 8 to 1) 1
FURIETTO (Ire) [95] 6-12-0 R Garritty, *trkd ldr, led 4 out, clr appr nxt, wnt lft 2 out, hdd last, no extr*...(7 to 1 op 5 to 1) 2
HIGHLAND PARK [82] 10-11-1 A Maguire, *hld up and beh, hdwy appr 4 out, effrt and rdn 2 out, one pace bef last.* .... (4 to 1 jt-fav op 7 to 2) 3
911* RED JAM JAR [94] 11-11-10 (3*) G Cahill, *led, rdn and hdd 4 out, one pace frm nxt*...........................(4 to 1 jt-fav op 9 to 2 tchd 5 to 1) 4
9126 MARCO MAGNIFICO (USA) [72] (v) 6-10-5 A Thornton, *mid-div, hdwy 4 out, rdn nxt, kpt on one pace.* .... (16 to 1 op 14 to 1) 5
DANCING DANCER [73] 7-10-6 R Supple, *prmnt, rdn alng and hit 4 out, wknd bef nxt.* (9 to 1 op 7 to 1 tchd 10 to 1) 6
5463 ANORAK (USA) [93] 6-11-12 J Callaghan, *mid-div, hdwy to chase ldrs 4 out, sn rdn and wknd bef nxt.* ....(8 to 1 tchd 9 to 1) 7
612 CANARY BLUE (Ire) [77] 5-10-6 (3*) E Husband, *al beh.* ....(10 to 1 op 8 to 1) 8
888 WHIRLWIND ROMANCE (Ire) [68] 5-10-0 S McDougall, *nvr rchd ldrs*.........................(50 to 1 op 33 to 1) 9
9166 WEE WIZARD (Ire) [87] 7-11-6 N Williamson, *hld up, hdwy 6th, chsd ldrs and hit 4 out, sn wknd*......(16 to 1 op 12 to 1) 10
JOYRIDER [92] 5-11-10 A S Smith, *in tch till lost pl 4 out, beh frm nxt*.......................(14 to 1 op 10 to 1) 11
SECONDS AWAY [68] 5-9-11 (3*) G Lee, *al beh, tld off 2 out.* .... (50 to 1 op 33 to 1) 12
8174 YACHT CLUB [67] 14-10-0 O Pears, *chsd ldrs whn blun and uns rdr second*......... (15 to 2 op 7 to 1 tchd 8 to 1) ur
7893 PIMSBOY [70] (v) 9-10-33 Richard Guest, *chsd ldrs till wknd 6th and sn beh, tld off whn pld up bef 2 out.* .... (25 to 1 op 20 to 1) pu
Dist: 4l, 10l, 1½l, 3½l, 2½l, 5l, 1¼l, 2l, 1l, 5l. 4m 56.20s. a 14.20s (14 Ran).
(The Belles), G Richards

1069 J. E. Hartley Memorial Handicap Chase Class B (0-140 5-y-o and up) £4,471 3m 1f.................. (2:20)

SOUNDS STRONG (Ire) [114] 7-10-8 A Maguire, *hld up in rear, hit tenth, smooth hdwy nxt, chlgd 4 out, led next, blun 2 out, rdn and ran on wl.* ....(11 to 4 op 3 to 1 tchd 100 to 30 and 5 to 2) 1
809* MCGREGOR THE THIRD [124] 10-11-4 B Harding, *trkd ldg pair, hdwy 13th, chlgd 4 out, rdn aftr nxt, kpt on.* .... (5 to 4 fav op 11 to 10 tchd 11 to 8) 2
SILVER STICK [125] (v) 9-11-5 N Williamson, *led, rdn 4 out, hdd nxt, one pace*...................(14 to 1 op 12 to 1) 3
FIVELEIGH BUILDS [130] 9-11-10 A Thornton, *cl up, rdn alng 13th, wknd nxt*........... (9 to 1 op 7 to 1 tchd 10 to 1) 4
2023 PIMS GUNNER (Ire) [110] 8-10-4 A Dobbin, *hld up in rear, hit 11th, rdn alng and some hdwy 14th, sn wknd.* .... (11 to 1 op 9 to 1) 5
TOOGOOD TO BE TRUE [134] 8-12-0 L Wyer, *hld up in tch, hdwy and blun badly 14th, no ch aftr*.....(5 to 1 op 9 to 2) 6
Dist: 6l, 4l, 22l, 3½l, dist. 6m 16.10s. a 8.10s (6 Ran).
SR: 36/40/37/20/-/-/ (Mrs David Thompson), D Nicholson

1070 Sanderson Bramall Motor Group Novices' Handicap Hurdle Class D (0-105 4-y-o and up) £3,036 2m .... (2:50)

8882 SUAS LEAT (Ire) [96] 6-11-2 (7*) M Newton, *hld up, hdwy 4 out, chlgd 2 out, rdn and ev ch last, edgd lft and styd on to ld post.* ....(9 to 2 op 4 to 1 tchd 5 to 1) 1
728* MITHRAIC (Ire) [97] 4-11-2 (7*) L McGrath, *trkd ldrs, hdwy 4 out, led 3 out, rdn appr last, ct post.* .... (6 to 1 op 5 to 1 tchd 13 to 2) 2
272 TEEJAY'N'AITCH (Ire) [77] 4-10-0 (3*) G Lee, *hld up, hdwy 4 out, rdn 2 out, kpt on same pace appr last.* .... (11 to 1 op 8 to 1 tchd 12 to 1) 3
9764 SILLY MONEY [91] 5-11-3 L Wyer, *hld up, hdwy appr 3 out, rdn nxt, kpt on same pace*.............(9 to 2 op 7 to 2) 4

MONYMAN (Ire) [97] 6-11-10 R Garritty, *in tch, hdwy 3 out, ev ch nxt, sn rdn, one pace*....(5 to 1 op 7 to 1 tchd 9 to 2) 5
8065 DASH TO THE PHONE (USA) [74] 4-9-11 (3*) R Massey, *led, hdd 3 out, wknd aftr nxt*...............(12 to 1 op 8 to 1) 6
MR CHRISTIE [78] 4-10-4 A Thornton, *hld up, effrt and some hdwy 4 out, rdn and one pace frm nxt.* (20 to 1 op 16 to 1) 7
STORMING LORNA (Ire) [73] 6-9-121 (3*) G Cahill, *hit second, al rear*....................................... (33 to 1) 8
RAMBOLLINA [86] 5-10-12 N Williamson, *hld up in rear, al beh*....................................... (20 to 1 op 16 to 1) 9
794* VINTAGE RED [89] 6-11-2 A Dobbin, *in tch on inner, hdwy appr 3 out, ev ch till rdn and wknd 2 out.* ....(3 to 1 fav op 7 to 2 tchd 4 to 1) 10
8185 STYLISH INTERVAL [89] 4-11-1 Richard Guest, *prmnt till rdn and wknd 4 out, beh frm nxt*......... (20 to 1 op 16 to 1) 11
SAYRAF DANCER (Ire) [79] 7-10-6 M Foster, *chsd ldrs, blun 3rd, hdwy 5th, rdn and wknd bef 3 out, sn beh.* .... (20 to 1 op 16 to 1) 12
Dist: Sht-hd, 8l, 2l, 2l, 2l, 4l, 6l, ½l, 4l, 6l. 3m 49.80s. a 8.80s (12 Ran).
SR: 23/23/-/7/12/-/ (Mrs J M Davenport), J M Jefferson

1071 British Field Sports Society Amateur Riders' Maiden Hurdle Class E (4-y-o and up) £2,075 2½m 110yds. . (3:20)

KEEN TO THE LAST (Fr) 4-11-6 (3*) Mr C Bonner, *trkd ldrs on inner, hdwy to ld 3 out, rdn appr last, kpt on wl flt.* ....(9 to 4 op 3 to 1 tchd 7 to 2 and 2 to 1) 1
BAHER (USA) 7-11-3 (7*) Mr Chris Wilson, *prmnt, led second till hdd 3 out, rdn nxt, rallied r-in, no extr nr finish.* .... (33 to 1 op 25 to 1) 2
BEGGARS BANQUET (Ire) 6-11-10 Mrs A Farrell, *in tch, gd hdwy to dispute ld 6th, rdn appr 3 out, sn one pace.* .... (11 to 10 on op 11 to 8 on tchd Evens) 3
OUR RAINBOW 4-10-11 (7*) Miss L Allan, *chsd ldrs, rdn alng appr 3 out, one pace*............ (20 to 1 op 14 to 1) 4
2624 BIG TREAT (Ire) 4-11-2 (7*) Mr P Scott, *led to second, cl up till rdn alng 4 out, sn one pace.* .... (14 to 1 op 12 to 1 tchd 16 to 1) 5
TARTAN MIX (Ire) 5-11-5 (5*) Mr N Wilson, *not fluent and sn wl beh, tld off hfwy, some hdwy frm 3 out.* (66 to 1 op 33 to 1) 6
L'EGLISE BELLE 4-10-11 (7*) Mr L Corcoran, *hld up, hdwy 6th, rdn and wknd appr 3 out*...........(8 to 1 op 6 to 1) 7
POLO PONY (Ire) 4-11-2 (7*) Miss P Robson, *prmnt till lost pl 6th, sn wl beh*......................(33 to 1 op 20 to 1) 8
BARNSTORMER 10-11-5 (5*) Mr R Hale, *al beh.* .... (33 to 1 op 25 to 1) 9
LAST TRY (Ire) 5-11-10 Mr S Swiers, *hld up, hdwy 5th, sn rdn and wknd, lost tch aftr 4 out*......... (20 to 1 op 12 to 1) 10
ALLEXTON LAD 5-11-3 (7*) Mr J Apiafi, *prmnt till wknd 6th, wl beh frm 4 out*...................... (66 to 1 op 50 to 1) 11
Dist: 1¼l, 8l, 3l, 20l, ½l, 13l, 6l, 6l, 6l, 7l. 5m 0.80s. a 18.80s (11 Ran).
(D E Allen & Mr S Balmer), M D Hammond

1072 Robert Bowett Saab Ltd Novices' Handicap Chase Class D (0-105 5-y-o and up) £3,561 2m.......... (3:50)

1049 BALLYLINE (Ire) [79] 5-11-1 T Reed, *cl up, led appr 4th, shaken up 2 out, styd on strly.* .... (100 to 30 op 3 to 1 tchd 7 to 2) 1
8854 HAZEL CREST [72] 9-10-9 D Parker, *hld up in tch, hdwy 4 out, ev ch 2 out, rdn and one pace last.* .... (14 to 1 op 10 to 1 tchd 16 to 1) 2
CHORUS LINE (Ire) [79] 7-11-2 R Supple, *lft in ld 1st, hdd appr 4th, rdn alng four out, one pace 2 out*..........(7 to 2) 3
8853 REVE DE VALSE (USA) [87] 9-11-10 K Johnson, *trkd ldrs, reminders 8th, effrt 4 out, rdn and blun 2 out, sn wknd.* ....(4 to 1 op 7 to 2 tchd 9 to 2) 4
861* SHOW YOUR HAND (Ire) [80] 8-11-3 M Foster, *led till stumbled and uns rdr 1st.* .... (15 to 8 fav op 7 to 4 tchd 2 to 1 and 9 to 4) ur
7394 SEE YOU ALWAYS (Ire) [63] 6-10-0 N Williamson, *prmnt, rdn appr 4 out and ev ch 2 out, drvn and blun 2 out, pld up bef last, lme.* .... (25 to 1 op 20 to 1) pu
Dist: 4l, 2½l, 8l. 4m 2.10s. a 15.10s (6 Ran).
(The 49 Partnership), W T Kemp

1073 Robert Clark & Sons Steeplejacks And Engineering Ltd Intermediate Open National Hunt Flat Class H (4,5,6-y-o) £1,406 2m........ (4:20)

917* DURAID (Ire) 4-12-3 Richard Guest, *hld up, gd hdwy 5 fs out, led o'r one out, ran on.* .... (7 to 4 fav op 2 to 1 tchd 5 to 2 and 6 to 4) 1
GOOD VIBES 4-11-3 L Wyer, *in tch, hdwy 6 fs out, led o'r 2 out, sn rdn and hdd appr last, kpt on.* .... (11 to 2 op 3 to 1 tchd 6 to 1) 2
LITTLE CRUMPLIN 4-11-3 N Williamson, *prmnt, hdwy to ld o'r 4 fs out, rdn and hdd over 2 out, kpt on.* ....(20 to 1 op 16 to 1) 3
ROTHARI 4-11-3 R Supple, *hld up, steady hdwy o'r 6 fs out, kpt on fnl 3 furlongs, nrst finish*...................(20 to 1) 4
STRONG MINT (Ire) 5-11-4 P Niven, *beh till styd on fnl 2 fs, nrst finish*.........................(9 to 1 op 7 to 1) 5

GALE FORCE (Ire) 5-10-11 (7") B Grattan, *prmnt on outer, effrt 5 fs out, ev ch 3 out, sn rdn and btn 2 out.*
....(7 to 2 op 3 to 1 tchd 5 to 2) 6
DESERT DEVIL 4-11-3 A Dobbin, *beh, pushed alng 6 fs out, some late hdwy, nvr dngrs.*
............................(8 to 1 op 7 to 1 tchd 9 to 1 and 10 to 1) 7
740⁸ TEDDY EDWARD 6-11-4 J Supple, *hld up, hdwy o'r 5 fs out, rdn over 3 out, wknd 2 out*............(33 to 1 tchd 50 to 1) 8
700³ HENPECKED (Ire) 5-11-4 R Garritty, *led, rdn and hdd o'r 4 fs out, grad wknd.*
............(15 to 2 op 8 to 1 tchd 7 to 1 and 10 to 1) 9
917⁷ TOSHIBA HOUSE (Ire) 5-10-10 (3") G Cahill, *cl up, rdn alng 5 fs out, wknd 3 out*..................(50 to 1 op 33 to 1) 10
SELECTRIC (Ire) 5-11-4 K Jones, *al beh.*
..................................(50 to 1 op 33 to 1) 11
RAGDON 5-11-4 S Wynne, *chsd ldrs, rdn o'r 7 fs out, sn lost pl and beh*.......................................(50 to 1) 12
740⁵ NORTH END LADY 5-10-13 (7") L McGrath, *very slwly away, al beh, sddl slpd, tld off frm hlwy*......(20 to 1 op 16 to 1) 13
74² SUPREME COMFORT (Ire) 4-10-12 Mr P Murray, *slwly into strd, al rear, beh whn pld up 3 fs out..*(20 to 1 op 14 to 1) pu
Dist: 1½l, 2l, 2l, 5l, nk, 10l, 2l, 3½l, 1l, 16l. 3m 48.60s. (14 Ran).

(A Suddes), Denys Smith

WEXFORD (IRE) (soft)
Sunday October 27th

1074
People Newspapers Handicap Hurdle (0-109 4-y-o and up) £3,253 3m
....(12:55)

ROSIN THE BOW (Ire) [-] 7-10-9 (5") J Butler, ...(10 to 1) 1
947¹ FORT DEELY (Ire) [-] 5-9-7 J Jones, ...(7 to 1) 2
746⁴ KILCARAMORE (Ire) [-] 5-10-0 (7") A O'Shea, ...(8 to 1) 3
CASEY JANE (Ire) [-] 5-10-7 (3") D J Casey, ...(7 to 1) 4
983 TEXARKANA (Ire) [-] 8-9-12 (5") G Cotter, ...(10 to 1) 5
MARIES POLLY [-] 6-10-5 J P Broderick, ...(12 to 1) 6
598³ ADARAMANN (Ire) [-] 4-10-5 (3") Mr R Walsh, ...(10 to 1) 7
944² ROYAL ROSY (Ire) [-] 5-12-0 C F Swan, ...(6 to 4 fav) 8
404* THE COBH GALE (Ire) [-] 9-10-1 T P Treacy, ...(8 to 1) 9
853⁹ THE SENATOR (Ire) [-] 5-10-5 D H O'Connor, ...(10 to 1) 10
828⁵ PEACEFULL RIVER (Ire) [-] 7-9-4 (7") B D Murtagh, (7 to 1) 11
BOB BARNES (Ire) [-] 5-10-7 (7") Mr J J O'Gorman, (20 to 1) 12
929⁶ SWIFT GLIDER (Ire) [-] 7-10-4 F Woods, ...(20 to 1) 13
897 MOON-FROG [-] 9-9-10 J K Kinane, ...(16 to 1) pu
AISEIRI [-] 9-10-11 T Horgan, ...(20 to 1) pu
Dist: 1l, 15l, nk, 13l. 6m 19.80s. (15 Ran).

(F Fitzsimons), A P O'Brien

1075
I.N.H. Stallion Owners E.B.F. Maiden Hurdle (Div I) (5-y-o and up) £3,767 3m
....(1:25)

908² SLUSH PUPPY (Ire) 8-11-6 L P Cusack, ...(6 to 4 fav) 1
BITTER HARVEST (Ire) 6-12-0 T P Treacy, ...(6 to 1) 2
ROCK'N ROLL KID (Ire) 5-11-3 (3") D J Casey, ...(6 to 1) 3
781⁵ TURRAMURRA GIRL (Ire) 7-11-9 Mr H F Cleary, ..(10 to 1) 4
ISLAND CHAMPION (Ire) 7-10-10 (5") G Cotter, ...(20 to 1) 5
943⁸ MAGS SUPER TOI (Ire) 7-10-13 (7") A O'Shea, ..(16 to 1) 6
951³ MISS ELIZABETH (Ire) 6-11-1 J P Broderick, ...(12 to 1) 7
978 SKULLDUGERY (Ire) 6-11-6 J Jones, ...(20 to 1) 8
ARTIC PEARL (Ire) 6-10-8 (7") D Flood, ...(20 to 1) 9
984⁶ HEN HANSEL (Ire) 5-12-0 T Horgan, ...(6 to 1) 10
773⁹ WHINNEY HILL (Ire) 6-11-1 A Powell, ...(20 to 1) 11
ARCTIC GALE (Ire) 5-11-1 C F Swan, ...(6 to 1) 12
364⁴ CROGHAN BRIDGE (Ire) 7-11-6 J K Kinane, ...(16 to 1) pu
WHATFORSURPRISE (Ire) 5-11-6 M Moran, ...(20 to 1) pu
SHORT OF A BUCK (Ire) 6-10-8 (7") Mr P M Madden,
....(20 to 1) pu
Dist: 7l, 3½l, 4½l, 8l. 6m 34.40s. (15 Ran).

(Mrs D J Coleman), Mrs D J Coleman

1076
I.N.H. Stallion Owners E.B.F. Maiden Hurdle (Div II) (5-y-o and up) £3,767 3m
....(1:55)

977⁵ GO NOW (Ire) 6-12-0 T P Treacy, ...(Evens fav) 1
978² MATTS DILEMMA (Ire) 8-11-6 F Woods, ...(9 to 1) 2
1013³ OWNING (Ire) 6-11-6 C F Swan, ...(100 to 30) 3
910⁷ VELAPA PRINCE (Ire) 5-11-3 (3") D J Casey, ...(12 to 1) 4
983³ YOUNG MRS KELLY (Ire) 6-11-1 J Jones, ...(11 to 2) 5
929⁴ HOLY GROUNDER (Ire) 7-10-13 (7") A O'Shea, ...(10 to 1) 6
928 WYN WAN SOON (Ire) 5-11-6 D H O'Connor, ...(20 to 1) 7
983⁶ VIVIANS VALE (Ire) 7-10-8 (7") Mr M Budds, ...(10 to 1) 8
946⁶ SECRET PRINCE (Ire) 5-11-6 A Powell, ...(20 to 1) 9
274² CRAZY DREAMS (Ire) 8-11-6 Mr P J Healy, ...(14 to 1) 10
578⁶ LAURA'S PURSUIT (Ire) 7-11-4 (5") J Butler, ...(10 to 1) 11
983 PENNY BRIDE (Ire) 7-10-8 (7") Mr S O'Callaghan, (20 to 1) 12
853 LISADOBBER LADY (Ire) 6-11-1 J P Broderick, ..(10 to 1) 13
853 CLOUGHTEANA (Ire) 5-10-8 (7") J E Casey, ...(20 to 1) pu
AYLESBURY BEAU (Ire) 5-10-12 (3") J R Barry, ...(20 to 1) pu
Dist: 1½l, 9l, 2½l, 3½l. 6m 28.00s. (15 Ran).

(B Cordell-Lavarack), Thomas Foley

1077
Chandigar Maiden Hurdle (4-y-o) £3,253 2¼m 100yds.........(2:25)

603³ MONTELISA (Ire) 10-13 C F Swan, ...(3 to 1 co-fav) 1
850 VASILIKI (Ire) 11-1 (3") D J Casey, ...(12 to 1) 2
CHARLIE-O (Ire) 10-13 (5") G Cotter, ...(9 to 1) 3
713 MONDEO ROSE (Ire) 10-8 (5") J Butler, ...(6 to 1) 4
ROSEY ELLEN (Ire) 10-6 (7") M D Murphy, ...(20 to 1) 5
GENTLE MOSSY (Ire) 11-4 D H O'Connor, ...(16 to 1) 6
ROWAN TREE (Ire) 10-13 F Woods, ...(8 to 1) 7
908⁹ ASHLEY'S PRINCESS (Ire) 10-10 (3") B Bowens, ..(14 to 1) 8
DAISY EILE (Ire) 10-6 (7") A O'Shea, ...(16 to 1) 9
PENNY POT 10-10 (3") Mr K Whelan, ...(10 to 1) 10
CAHONIS (Ire) 11-4 J P Broderick, ...(16 to 1) 11
908 MYSTICAL LORD (Ire) 10-13 T P Treacy, ...(14 to 1) 12
TITATIUM (Ire) 11-4 J Jones, ...(16 to 1) f
803⁵ DUBLIN TREASURE (Ire) 11-4 A Powell, ...(3 to 1 co-fav) ur
928⁹ JACK YEATS (Ire) 11-9 T J Mitchell, ...(3 to 1 co-fav) pu
Dist: 6l, 2½l, 15l, 3l. 4m 36.50s. (15 Ran).

(P J Fortune), A P O'Brien

1078
Wexford Block Handicap Hurdle (0-123 4-y-o and up) £3,253 2¼m 100yds......................(2:55)

907⁴ STONELEIGH TURBO (Ire) [-] 7-10-7 J P Broderick, (13 to 2) 1
684⁶ KAWA-KAWA [-] 9-10-5 (5") G Cotter, ...(12 to 1) 2
980 DANCING VISION (Ire) [-] 6-10-10 F Woods, ...(100 to 30) 3
980* CEILI QUEEN (Ire) [-] 4-12-0 C F Swan, ...(6 to 4 fav) 4
ANNFIELD LADY (Ire) [-] 8-11-4 T P Treacy, ...(6 to 1) 5
BOHOLA PETE (Ire) [-] 5-9-8 T J Mitchell, ...(10 to 1) 6
THE DASHER DOYLE (Ire) [-] 8-11-7 Mr P J Healy, ..(8 to 1) 7
849 ALLARACKET (Ire) [-] 7-9-7 (7") A O'Shea, ...(12 to 1) 8
803⁸ BOBSTAR DANCER (Ire) [-] 5-11-7 T Horgan, ...(12 to 1) 9
275 BRINNY PRINCESS (Ire) [-] 5-9-7⁷ (7") D Flood, ..(20 to 1) pu
Dist: Hd, 6l, 12l, nk. 4m 35.90s. (10 Ran).

(John G Doyle), P A Fahy

1079
Bewleys Hotel At Newlands Cross Handicap Chase (4-y-o and up) £8,220 3m...................(3:25)

ANTONIN (Fr) [-] 8-10-8 (3") Mr K Whelan, ...(2 to 1 fav) 1
BELVEDERIAN [-] 9-11-8 (3") D J Casey, ...(13 to 2) 2
981⁷ LOVE THE LORD (Ire) [-] 6-10-13 T P Treacy, ...(4 to 1) 3
FISSURE SEAL [-] 10-11-9 F Woods, ...(7 to 1) 4
825³ JASSU [-] 10-11-11 C F Swan, ...(100 to 30) 5
LOVING AROUND (Ire) [-] 8-10-10⁷ Mr P Fenton, ..(7 to 1) 6
981 ALBERT'S FANCY [-] 10-9-7 T J Mitchell, ...(25 to 1) 7
NUAFFE [-] 11-12-0 J P Broderick, ...(14 to 1) 8
Dist: Dist, ½l, 25l, 15l. 6m 25.10s. (8 Ran).

(Mrs S A Bramall), Mrs S A Bramall

1080
Talbot Hotel Beginners Chase (5-y-o and up) £3,253 2½m.........(3:55)

982² LE GINNO (Fr) 9-12-0 T P Treacy, ...(11 to 4) 1
WOODVILLE STAR (Ire) 7-11-9 T Horgan, ...(5 to 2 fav) 2
SCOBIE BOY (Ire) 8-12-0 P A Roche, ...(12 to 1) 3
GALE TOI (Ire) 7-11-7 (7") A O'Shea, ...(10 to 1) 4
RYHANE (Ire) 7-12-0 F Woods, ...(20 to 1) 5
DUN BELLE (Ire) 7-11-9 T J Mitchell, ...(12 to 1) 6
982 BAILE NA GCLOCH (Ire) 7-11-11 (3") D P Murphy, (33 to 1) 7
303 CROSSFARNOGUE (Ire) 7-12-0 C F Swan, ...(3 to 1) 8
982⁶ JUST A BREEZE (Ire) 8-11-2 (7") Mr T N Cloke, ..(20 to 1) 9
748⁷ JESSIE'S BOY (Ire) 7-12-0 J K Kinane, ...(25 to 1) 10
M MACG (Ire) 7-11-7 (7") Mr A Fleming, ...(33 to 1) 11
76⁶ CLASHWILLIAM GIRL (Ire) 8-11-9 L P Cusack, ...(10 to 1) 12
1013 JAFFA MAN (Ire) 5-11-10 J P Broderick, ...(20 to 1) f
MICK O'DWYER 9-11-7 (7") L J Fleming, ...(16 to 1) pu
466⁴ FIX THE SPEC (Ire) 6-11-9 (5") G Cotter, ...(25 to 1) l
Dist: 11l, 12l, 12l, 6l. 5m 19.10s. (15 Ran).

(Irish World Partnership), Thomas Foley

1081
Bree Hunt I.N.H. Flat Race (4-y-o and up) £3,253 2m................(4:25)

829² BARHALE BOY (Ire) 4-11-6 (3") Mr B M Cash, ...(6 to 4 fav) 1
850⁸ SIMPLY ACOUSTIC (Ire) 5-11-2 (7") Mr A C Coyle, ..(8 to 1) 2
394³ PRINCESS GLORIA (Ire) 5-11-9 Mr P Fenton, ...(4 to 1) 3
ASFREEASTHEWIND (Ire) 5-11-9 Mr J P Dempsey, (11 to 4) 4
ELLENMAE ROSE (Ire) 5-11-2 (7") Mr J G Sheehan, (12 to 1) 5
ASK ME IN (Ire) 5-11-6 (3") Mr K Whelan, ...(10 to 1) 6
681 FLORIA (Ire) 4-10-11 (7") Mr R M Walsh, ...(20 to 1) 7
1005⁴ HIDDEN HOLLOW (Ire) 5-12-0 Mr H F Cleary, ...(12 to 1) 8
898⁷ BALLYLENNON BAVARD (Ire) 4-11-1 (3") Mr P English,
....(10 to 1) 9
TELL NO ONE (Ire) 4-10-11 (7") Mr Sean O'Brien, (10 to 1) 10
884⁷ BULA DELA (Ire) 6-11-2 (7") Mr A Fleming, ...(25 to 1) 11
NATIVE BLOOD VI 11-12-0 Mr M McNulty, ...(20 to 1) 12
782 BEHY BRIDGE (Ire) 4-10-11 (7") Mr D P Coakley, ..(16 to 1) 13
782 OH MAY OH (Ire) 4-11-1 (3") Mr R Walsh, ...(20 to 1) 14
DEEP ESTEE (Ire) 5-11-2 (7") Mr G A Kingston, ..(20 to 1) pu
Dist: 2½l, 4½l, nk, 15l. 4m 5.80s. (15 Ran).

(Dennis Curran), A P O'Brien

NATIONAL HUNT RESULTS 1996-97

WINCANTON (good to firm)
Sunday October 27th
Going Correction: NIL (races 1,4,6), PLUS 0.30 (2,3,5)

1082 Witchampton Novices' Hurdle Class E (4-y-o and up) £2,635 2m....(2:10)

ROSENCRANTZ (Ire) 4-11-4 R Johnson, *hld up, hdwy frm 3 out, chlgd from nxt, kpt on und pres to ld last strd.*
............................(5 to 1 op 5 to 1) 1
EL DON 4-11-4 J Ryan, *hld up, hdwy 3 out, led jst aftr last, hdd last strd.....* (8 to 1 op 7 to 1 tchd 9 to 1 and 10 to 1) 2
806* NORDIC BREEZE (Ire) 4-11-4 A P McCoy, *chsd ldr to second, remained hndy, led appr 2 out till jst aftr last, no extr.*
.....(11 to 4 fav op 3 to 1 tchd 100 to 30 and 7 to 2) 3
KILMINGTON (Ire) 7-10-9 (3*) L Aspell, *hld up, rdn appr 2 out, styd on one pace, not rch ldrs.*
..............................(20 to 1 op 14 to 1 tchd 25 to 1) 4
POLICEMANS PRIDE (Fr) 7-10-12 G Upton, *hld up in tch, led aftr 3 out, hdd bef nxt, sn wknd........*(66 to 1 op 33 to 1) 5
905³ SHIFT AGAIN (Ire) (bl) 4-10-9 J Osborne, *hld up, jmpd slwly and lost pl 4th, rdn and rallied aftr 3 out, nvr able to chal.*
..............................(4 to 1 op 7 to 2) 6
824⁵ JAAZIM 6-10-12 B Fenton, *hld up beh ldrs, improved 5th, chlgd aftr 3 out, wknd bef nxt........* (25 to 1 op 20 to 1) 7
638 SOLO VOLUMES 7-10-12 B Powell, *al beh, tld off frm 3 out.*
..............................(150 to 1 op 66 to 1 tchd 200 to 1) 8
905⁶ ARTHUR'S SPECIAL 6-10-0 (7*) G Supple, *prmnt, mstk 1st, wknd 4th, tld off..................*(50 to 1 op 25 to 1) 9
MAPENGO 5-10-12 V Slattery, *led till aftr 3 out, wknd bef nxt, tld off.......................*(100 to 1 op 50 to 1) 10
TROUBLE AT MILL 6-10-12 Mr J L Llewellyn, *in tch, wknd 4th, tld off...................*(66 to 1 op 50 to 1) 11
SHRIMP 5-10-7 W McFarland, *mstk second, al beh, tld off.*
..............................(50 to 1 op 33 to 1) 12
WISE 'N' SHINE 5-10-2 (5*) Chris Webb, *al beh, tld off 4th.*
..............................(100 to 1 op 50 to 1) 13
905* RITTO 6-11-5 R Dunwoody, *mid-div, hdwy 5th, ev ch appr 2 out, wkng whn pckd last, beh when pld up r-in.*
..................(7 to 2 op 9 to 2 tchd 5 to 1) pu
Dist: Sht-hd, 2l, 18l, 9l, 1¼l, 3l, 26l, ½l, 5l, 1l. 3m 40.80s. a 6.80s (14 Ran).
SR: 22/22/20/-/-/-/ (L J Fulford, Miss Venetia Williams)

1083 Nether Wallop Novices' Chase Class D (5-y-o and up) £3,658 3m 1f 110yds......................(2:40)

HANAKHAM (Ire) 7-11-0 R Dunwoody, *jmpd wl, dsptd ld, definite advantage 18th, clr frm 2 out, easily.*
..............................(9 to 4 op 11 to 4 tchd 3 to 1) 1
751² STORMTRACKER (Ire) 7-11-6 C O'Dwyer, *made most til 18th, sn rdn, wknd aftr nxt...............*(2 to 1 op 7 to 4) 2
807* FATHER SKY 5-11-9 J Osborne, *hld up, hdwy tenth, lost pl aftr nxt, rnwd effrt 15th, wknd 17th, tld off.*
..................(7 to 4 fav op 6 to 4 tchd 2 to 1) 3
751⁵ DEFINITE MAYBE (Ire) (bl) 6-11-6 A P McCoy, *trkd ldrs till slpd on bend and lost pl appr 4th, rdn bef nxt, sn beh, tld off whn pld up before twelfth.*
..................(10 to 1 op 6 to 1 tchd 11 to 1) pu
Dist: 17l, dist. 6m 34.70s. a 18.70s (4 Ran).
(M Brereton), R J Hodges

1084 Desert Orchid South Western Pattern Chase Limited Handicap Class A Grade 2 (5-y-o and up) £18,660 2m 5f.........................(3:10)

COULTON [168] 9-11-10 J Osborne, *made all, shaken up and ran on wl frm 2 out, readily...........*(2 to 1 op 11 to 8) 1
GALES CAVALIER (Ire) [160] 8-11-2 R Dunwoody, *chsd wnr, effrt appr 3 out, one pace nxt.*
..............................(11 to 10 fav op 11 to 8 tchd 6 to 4) 2
MARTOMICK [147] 9-10-3 C O'Dwyer, *hld up, mstk 7th, hdwy 13th, disputing second whn mistake nxt, sn btn.*
..............................(5 to 2 tchd 11 to 4) 3
972² STATELY HOME (Ire) [149] 5-10-3 R Johnson, *beh frm twelfth, tld off........................*(25 to 1 op 20 to 1) 4
Dist: 3l, 29l, 26l. 5m 12.80s. a 8.80s (4 Ran).
SR: 71/60/18/-/ (M G St Quinton), O Sherwood

1085 Portman Novices' Hurdle Class E (4-y-o and up) £2,512 2³⁄₄m...... (3:40)

JOLIS ABSENT (bl) 6-10-7 J Ryan, *hld up, lost pl 7th, rallied appr 2 out, led r-in, ran on.*
..................(12 to 1 op 10 to 1 tchd 14 to 1) 1
770* POLITICAL PANTO (Ire) 5-11-5 A P McCoy, *led, sn clr, mstk 3 out, wknd and hdd r-in............*(2 to 1 fav op 9 to 4) 2
867⁹ THE LAD 7-10-12 J Osborne, *chsd clr ldr till appr 2 out, wknd...................*(9 to 4 op 7 to 4 tchd 5 to 2) 3
IMPERIAL HONORS (Ire) 5-10-7 (5*) Chris Webb, *nvr on terms, tld off..................*(100 to 1 op 50 to 1) 4

942³ MOONLIGHT ESCAPADE (Ire) 5-10-12 R Dunwoody, *not fluent, hld up, beh frm 8th, tld off.........* (4 to 1 op 5 to 1) 5
997⁷ MR JASPER 4-10-10 S Burrough, *strted slwly, al beh, tld off.*
..............................(150 to 1 op 50 to 1 tchd 200 to 1) 6
942⁸ DON'T ARGUE 5-11-0² Miss L Blackford, *pckd 1st, wl beh whn blun 3rd, tld off when pld up aftr 3 out.*
..............................(100 to 1 op 50 to 1) pu
919 BICKLEIGH BELLE 6-10-7 L Harvey, *al beh, tld off whn pld up bef 8th...............*(150 to 1 op 50 to 1 tchd 200 to 1) pu
Dist: 6l, 26l, 4l, dist, 13l. 5m 25.40s. a 19.40s (8 Ran).
(Mrs Karola Vann), M J Ryan

1086 Blackdown Handicap Chase Class E (0-110 5-y-o and up) £4,224 3m 1f 110yds.....................(4:10)

SPECIAL ACCOUNT [94] 10-11-1 B Fenton, *hld up, reminder 13th, hdwy 16th, led 2 out, drvn out.*
..............................(14 to 1 op 10 to 1 tchd 16 to 1) 1
840² FROZEN DROP [102] 9-11-9 S Fox, *chsd ldr, mstk 11th, led 16th till 2 out, kpt on same pace.*
..............................(9 to 2 op 4 to 1 tchd 11 to 2) 2
757* RAINBOW CASTLE [107] 9-12-0 A P McCoy, *hld up, hdwy 16th, rdn 3 out, ev ch whn pckd last, one pace.*
..............................(11 to 10 on op Evens) 3
834² DISTANT MEMORY [99] (bl) 7-11-6 J Osborne, *prmnt, mstks 6th and 7th, beh frm 17th, tld off......* (7 to 1 op 8 to 1) 4
938 NICK THE DREAMER [94] 11-11-1 R Dunwoody, *hld up beh ldrs, 3rd whn f 9th...............*(12 to 1 op 10 to 1) f
811⁴ MUTUAL TRUST [100] 12-11-7 R Johnson, *led till 16th, wknd appr 3 out, beh whn f last.......................*(20 to 1) f
TEARFUL PRINCE [79] 12-10-0 B Powell, *hld up, hdwy 8th, badly hmpd and uns rdr nxt.*
..............................(9 to 1 op 10 to 1 tchd 12 to 1) ur
Dist: ¾l, 1¼l, dist. 6m 44.60s. a 28.60s (7 Ran).
(Tony Fiorillo), C R Barwell

1087 Blandford Handicap Hurdle Class D (0-120 4-y-o and up) £3,006 2m ....(4:40)

DARK NIGHTINGALE [92] 6-10-12 J Osborne, *made all, hrd hld...................*(6 to 5 fav op 6 to 4) 1
940* PETER MONAMY [103] (bl) 4-11-8 A P McCoy, *chsd wnr, hit 3rd, rdn 3 out, no ch whn hit last.*
..............................(13 to 8 op 11 to 8 tchd 7 to 4) 2
939⁵ DESERT CALM (Ire) [90] 7-10-10 P Holley, *hld up, rdn 3 out, wknd r-in......................*(9 to 1 op 5 to 1) 3
TOP WAVE [104] 8-11-10 J Ryan, *hld up, wknd frm 3 out, tld off......................*(5 to 1 op 4 to 1 tchd 6 to 1) 4
Dist: 3l, 5l, dist. 3m 47.70s. a 13.70s (4 Ran).
(Miss Liz Clark), O Sherwood

GALWAY (IRE) (soft)
Monday October 28th

1088 Bank Of Ireland Ascent Novice Hurdle (4-y-o and up) £4,110 2½m (1:25)

536² TARTHOOTH (Ire) 5-11-4 F Woods, ...(5 to 4 on) 1
977* KING OF KERRY (Ire) 5-11-10 C F Swan, ...(6 to 4) 2
908⁴ LEWISHAM (Ire) 4-10-12 M P Dwyer, ...(4 to 1) 3
1015 WESTERN GREY (Ire) 4-10-12 M P Hourigan, ...(20 to 1) 4
984 BUMPER TO BUMPER (Ire) 4-10-12 N Williamson, (20 to 1) 5
SWISS THYNE (Ire) 6-10-8² (7*) Mr R D Lee, ...(25 to 1) 6
Dist: 25l, dist, 11l, 20l. 5m 19.60s. (6 Ran).
(Mrs H de Burgh), A L T Moore

1089 Bank Of Ireland Asset Management Handicap Hurdle (4-y-o and up) £7,150 2m 5f 190yds.........(1:55)

980² ANNADOT (Ire) [-] 6-9-12 F J Flood, ...(4 to 1) 1
BOHEMIAN CASTLE (Ire) [-] 7-10-7 (7*) Mr J T McNamara, ...(8 to 1) 2
944* RATHGIBBON (Ire) [-] 5-9-4 (5*) G Cotter, ...(3 to 1) 3
NATIVE STATUS (Ire) [-] 6-9-8² F Woods, ...(12 to 1) 4
748 VICAR STREET (Ire) [-] 6-9-12 C F Swan, ...(9 to 4 fav) 5
897 TELL THE NIPPER (Ire) [-] 5-10-7 N Williamson, ..(10 to 1) 6
715² METASTASIO [-] 4-10-11 H Rogers, ...(5 to 1) 7
748⁶ BETTERBEBOB (Ire) [-] 5-9-12 (3*) D J Casey, ...(8 to 1) 8
553 SHANKORAK [-] 9-11-0 (7*) R P Hogan, ...(14 to 1) pu
Dist: 20l, 1l, 1l, 5½l. 5m 32.40s. (9 Ran).
(Leonard Kelly), F Flood

1090 Bank Of Ireland Lifetime Maiden Hurdle (4-y-o and up) £3,725 2m ....(2:25)

PRE ORDAINED (Ire) 4-11-4 F J Flood, ...(5 to 1) 1
850⁴ MURPHY'S MALT (Ire) 4-11-4 T Horgan, ...(7 to 2) 2
773² WELSH GRIT 5-11-11 (3*) D J Casey, ...(9 to 2) 3
CELTIC LOTTO (Ire) 5-10-8 (7*) Mr J T McNamara, (10 to 1) 4
980 MAGICAL WAY (Ire) 6-11-6 M Duffy, ...(10 to 1) 5
943⁵ FRISKY THYNE (Ire) 7-11-6 P A Roche, ...(8 to 1) 6
DUKY RIVER (Ire) 5-11-6 N Williamson, ...(12 to 1) 7

131

978 MILLSOFBALLYSODARE (Ire) 5-11-6 M P Hourigan,
.... (20 to 1) 8
928³ OMAR (USA) 7-12-0 A Powell, ... (3 to 1 fav) 9
     MICK MAN (Ire) 5-11-6 M P Dwyer, ... (12 to 1) 10
     MIDNIGHT JAZZ (Ire) 6-11-7 (7") S Fitzgerald, ... (12 to 1) 11
977 KINCORA (Ire) 5-11-1 (5") J M Donnelly, ... (20 to 1) 12
928 OUR DUCHESS (Ire) 5-11-1 K F O'Brien, ... (25 to 1) 13
     CHEEKY GENIUS (Ire) 5-11-6 J H O'Donovan, ... (25 to 1) 14
984 MAIRTINS BUCK (Ire) 5-11-1 (5") T Martin, ... (20 to 1) 15
826⁹ PHARDANTE LILLY (Ire) 4-10-13 T J O'Sullivan, .. (20 to 1) 16
     MILLICANS BEND (Ire) 4-11-4 T Hazlett, ... (20 to 1) 17
628⁶ LEZIES LAST (Ire) 6-10-8 (7") Mr R D Lee, ... (20 to 1) 18
908 SABINTA (Ire) 5-11-1 W Slattery, ... (20 to 1) 19
     BORNACURRA KATIE (Ire) 5-11-1 F Woods, ... (20 to 1) 20
731 LAHANA (Ire) 4-10-13 G M O'Neill, ... (20 to 1) 21
Dist: 2½l, 6l, 4l, 6l. 4m 4.70s. (21 Ran).

(Mrs H McParland), F Flood

1091 Bank Of Ireland I.C.S.Building Society Handicap Chase (4-y-o and up) £7,150 2m 1f.............. (3:25)

947² FINAL TUB [-] 13-10-1 C F Swan, ... (5 to 1) 1
1004³ HANNIES GIRL (Ire) [-] 7-9-0 (7") L J Fleming, ... (6 to 1) 2
537* JAZZY REFRAIN (Ire) [-] 6-10-9 N Williamson, ... (5 to 2) 3
     MINSTREL FIRE (Ire) [-] 8-10-10 M P Dwyer, ... (5 to 2) 4
     BACK BAR (Ire) [-] 8-11-6 F Woods, ... (7 to 4 fav) pu
Dist: 13l, 10l, 25l. 4m 57.00s. (5 Ran).

(Sean O'Brien), V T O'Brien

1092 B.O.I. Mortgage Centre Beginners Chase (5-y-o and up) £4,067 2¾m .... (3:55)

     ANOTHER POINT (Ire) 8-11-9 N Williamson, ... (8 to 1) 1
     WEST BROGUE (Ire) 7-12-0 C F Swan, ... (7 to 4 fav) 2
     ALWAYS A PAUPER (Ire) 7-11-9 M P Dwyer, ... (10 to 1) 3
     FAIRY MIST (Ire) 8-11-4 (5") G Cotter, ... (12 to 1) 4
1005⁷ TWO IN TUNE (Ire) 8-11-9 G M O'Neill, ... (4 to 1) 5
     KNOCKTHOMAS (Ire) 7-12-0 F J Flood, ... (8 to 1) 6
881³ CELTIC BUCK 10-11-7 (7") Mr Patrick O'Keeffe, ... (8 to 1) 7
     MAYPOLE FOUNTAIN (Ire) 6-11-4 (5") Mr W M O'Sullivan,
.... (10 to 1) 8
982 PASSER-BY 9-12-0 K F O'Brien, ... (8 to 1) pu
982⁹ CORRIBLOUGH (Ire) 8-11-9 F Woods, ... (12 to 1) pu
982 PROSPECT STAR (Ire) 5-11-7 J T Mitchell, ... (12 to 1) pu
Dist: 7l, 5½l, 15l, 15l, 11l. 6m 8.70s. (11 Ran).

(Michael A Burke), Michael Hourigan

1093 Bank Of Ireland Banking 365 Flat Race (5-y-o and up) £4,110 2m (4:25)

     ANOZIRA GOLD (Ire) 6-11-6 (3") Mr G Elliott, ... (5 to 1) 1
805* STORM GEM (Ire) 5-11-10 (3") Mr R Walsh, ... (2 to 1) 2
884* ARD LANE (Ire) 5-11-11 (7") Mr R M Walsh, .. (11 to 10 fav) 3
     PORT NA SON (Ire) 5-11-4 (7") D A Harney, ... (8 to 1) 4
945 DONNA KING (Ire) 6-11-4 (7") Mr J T McNamara, ... (8 to 1) 5
745 BRAVE WARRIOR (Ire) 6-10-13 (7") Mr A J Dempsey,
.... (20 to 1) 6
     ARAPAWAY 12-11-11 (7") Mr K N McDonagh, ... (14 to 1) 7
Dist: 5l, 4l, 5½l, dist. 4m 8.80s. (7 Ran).

(W J Austin), W J Austin

LEOPARDSTOWN (IRE) (yielding)
Monday October 28th

1094 Ideal Minimiser High Efficient Boiler Chase (5-y-o and up) £4,795 2m 5f .... (2:45)

981 ROYAL MOUNTBROWNE 8-12-0 T Horgan, ... (9 to 2) 1
     FEATHERED GALE 9-12-0 C O'Brien, ... (5 to 1) 2
719⁴ OPERA HAT (Ire) 8-11-9 C O'Dwyer, ... (7 to 4 on) 3
719⁷ BEAKSTOWN (Ire) 7-12-0 T P Treacy, ... (4 to 1) 4
Dist: Sht-hd, 9l, 15l. 5m 39.40s. a 30.40s (4 Ran).

(Mrs J O'Kane), A P O'Brien

1095 Flavel Leisure Rangemaster Oct. H'cap Hurdle (Listed) (4-y-o and up) £8,220 2m...................... (3:15)

715 THEATREWORLD (Ire) [-] 4-11-8 (5") J Butler, wl plcd, prog to track ldr second last, sn led, quickened clr, eased cl hme.
.... (7 to 4 fav) 1
907² I REMEMBER IT WELL (Ire) [-] (bl) 4-10-0 J P Broderick, wtd wth, rdn and prog aftr second last, kpt on after last. (4 to 1) 2
828⁴ FONTAINE LODGE (Ire) [-] 6-10-0 (7") A O'Shea, rear till prog bef second last, kpt on wl.......... (13 to 2) 3
730 NEAR GALE (Ire) [-] 6-11-11 T P Treacy, chsd ldr till prog to ld bef 4th last, rdn aftr second last, sn hdd, no extr.... (6 to 1) 4
849* BRONICA (Ire) [-] 4-10-2 C O'Dwyer, mid-div, some prog bef 3rd last, sn rdn and wknd............ (9 to 2) 5
428⁶ PYR FOUR [-] 9-9-12 (7") S P McCann, wl plcd, trkd ldr briefly 3rd last, wknd aftr nxt.......... (12 to 1) 6
715⁹ KATIYMANN (Ire) [-] 4-10-7 T Horgan, led, hdd bef 4th last, sn wknd, toot tch before second last............ (9 to 2) 7

Dist: 7l, 1l, hd, 3½l. 3m 48.70s. a 4.70s (7 Ran).
SR: 52/18/24/42/15/-/-/   (Mrs John Magnier), A P O'Brien

1096 Gas View Home I.N.H. Flat Race (5-y-o and up) £4,110 2½m...... (4:15)

     THE GREY MARE (Ire) 7-11-2 (7") Mr P Fahey, ... (14 to 1) 1
     SHEISAGALE (Ire) 5-11-2 (7") Mr A C Coyle, ... (9 to 2) 2
984⁷ SLANEY CHARM (Ire) 6-11-7 (7") Miss L E A Doyle, (8 to 1) 3
     CAMDEN EXPRESS (Ire) 6-11-7 (7") Mr M A Cahill, (14 to 1) 4
     YASHGANS VISION (Ire) 5-11-2 (7") Mr N Moran, .. (20 to 1) 5
     EQUIVOCATOR (Ire) 5-11-11 (3") Mr D Valentine, .. (10 to 1) 6
977 COOLREE LORD (Ire) 5-11-7 (7") Mr John P Moloney,
.... (12 to 1) 7
622³ PLEASE NO TEARS 9-11-9 Mrs C Barker, ... (7 to 10) 8
     ANCIENT HISTORIAN (Ire) 7-11-11 (3") Mr B R Hamilton,
.... (14 to 1) 9
     SHUIL LE LAOI (Ire) 6-11-2 (7") Miss A L Crowley, (10 to 1) 10
853⁴ BRASSIS HILL (Ire) 5-11-7 (7") A O'Shea, ... (12 to 1) 11
     OCTOBER SEVENTH 5-11-7 (7") Mr Paul J McMahon,
.... (10 to 1) 12
     BARNA GIRL (Ire) 6-11-4 (5") J Butler, ... (20 to 1) 13
717⁴ FELICITY'S PRIDE (Ire) 5-11-2 (7") Mr D P Coakley, (20 to 1) 14
     MEGABOY (Ire) 5-11-7 (7") Mr C A Murphy, ... (14 to 1) 15
     CELEBRITY STATUS (Ire) 5-11-7 (7") Mr D Delaney, (10 to 1) 16
     DARK MAGIC (Ire) 5-12-0 Mr D M O'Brien, ... (12 to 1) 17
     DUNBEACON (Ire) 7-11-11 (3") Mr T Lombard, ... (10 to 1) 18
     COPPER SAND (Ire) 7-11-7 (7") Mr J S O'Haire, .. (25 to 1) pu
884² GENTRY (Ire) 5-12-0 Mr M McNulty, ... (5 to 1) pu
945² SLYGUFF ROVER (Ire) 5-11-7 (7") Mr J P McNamara,
.... (5 to 2 fav) pu
Dist: 10l, 4l, 7l, hd. 4m 51.90s. (21 Ran).

(Seamus Fahey), Seamus Fahey

CHELTENHAM (good to firm)
Tuesday October 29th
Going Correction: PLUS 0.10 sec. per fur.

1097 Cheltenham And Three Counties Club Maiden Hurdle Class D (4-y-o and up) £2,801 2m 110yds.... (1:40)

     HERBERT LODGE (Ire) 7-11-6 C O'Dwyer, pld hrd, led second, quickened aftr last, cmftbly.
.... (11 to 8 op 6 to 4 on tchd 6 to 4) 1
     CHARLIE PARROT (Ire) 6-11-6 A P McCoy, hdwy 5th, ev ch appr last, not quicken..........(10 to 1 op 7 to 1) 2
976² SAMBA SHARPLY 5-11-6 P Hide, chsd wnr frm 3rd till wknd appr last...........(11 to 2 op 5 to 1 tchd 7 to 1) 3
     MR GORDON BENNETT 5-10-13 (7") X Aizpuru, pld hrd, beh frm 3rd, tld off...........(100 to 1 op 25 to 1) 4
     SET THE FASHION (v) 7-11-6 R Dunwoody, f 1st.
.... (8 to 1 op 4 to 1 tchd 9 to 1) f
879⁵ STUDIO THIRTY 4-11-5 P Niven, chsd ldrs, cl 4th whn f 3 out.
.... (25 to 1 op 14 to 1 tchd 33 to 1) f
     MARCHING MARQUIS (Ire) 5-11-6 R Johnson, badly hmpd and uns rdr 1st......... (7 to 4 op 5 to 2 tchd 11 to 4) ur
976 RIZAL (USA) 4-11-2 (3") D Walsh, refused to strt, took no part.
.... (100 to 1 op 25 to 1) ref
     THE KNITTER 4-11-5 P McLoughlin, led to second, wl beh frm 3rd, tld off whn pld up aftr 2 out. (100 to 1 op 33 to 1) pu
960 THE KNITTER 4-11-5 P McLoughlin, led to second, wl beh frm 3rd, tld off whn pld up aftr 2 out. (100 to 1 op 33 to 1) pu
Dist: 1½l, 8l, dist. 4m 4.90s. a 15.90s (9 Ran).

(Mrs David Thompson), K C Bailey

1098 Frenchie Nicholson Conditional Jockeys' Handicap Hurdle Class E (4-y-o and up) £2,220 2m 110yds .... (2:15)

775* MISTER RM [106] 4-11-13 D Walsh, made all, ran on wl.
............................(Evens fav op 5 to 4 on tchd 11 to 10) 1
963⁴ FRONTIER FLIGHT (USA) [85] 6-10-7 E Husband, hld up, hdwy 3 out, wnt second appr last, no imprsn.
.... (7 to 1 op 6 to 1 tchd 8 to 1) 2
996² KALZARI (USA) [90] 11-10-12 Michael Brennan, hld up, hdwy and ev ch 2 out, wknd appr last.
.... (7 to 1 op 5 to 1 tchd 8 to 1) 3
870 BALLY PARSON [86] 10-11-1 (7") X Aizpuru, chsd wnr till wknd appr 3 out....... (14 to 1 op 12 to 1 tchd 20 to 1) 4
837* YOUNG RADICAL (Ire) [92] 4-10-13 D Parker, chsd ldrs, ev ch 3 out, wknd quickly 2 out, tld off.
.... (5 to 2 op 2 to 1 tchd 11 to 4) 5
Dist: 4l, 3l, 6l, 26l. 3m 57.80s. a 8.80s (5 Ran).
SR: 27/3/5/-/-/   (F J Mills & Mr W Mills), N A Twiston-Davies

1099 Business To Business Direct Novices' Handicap Chase Class D (0-110 5-y-o and up) £3,988 2½m 110yds .... (2:50)

776² STRONG PROMISE (Ire) [106] 5-11-11 (3") K Gaule, hld up, led on bit 2 out, easily.
.... (6 to 4 on op 7 to 4 on tchd 11 to 8 on) 1

920* PONGO WARING (Ire) [103] 7-11-13 J F Titley, *led to 4th, led 11th to 2 out, no ch wth wnr.*
.... (11 to 8 op 11 to 10 tchd 6 to 4) 2
ASHMEAD RAMBLER (Ire) [77] 6-10-11 C Maude, *led 4th to 11th, 3rd and btn whn l 2 out.*
.... (11 to 1 op 8 to 1 tchd 14 to 1) f
Dist: 11l. 5m 18.20s. a 21.20s (3 Ran).

(G A Hubbard), G A Hubbard

1100 Business Market Analysis Novices' Hurdle Class C (4-y-o and up) £3,485 3¼m.................. (3:25)

955* HUNTERS ROCK (Ire) 7-11-5 C O'Dwyer, *al gng wl, led on bit appr last, very easily.*
.... (11 to 10 on op 11 to 8 on tchd Evens) 1
812² TIPPING THE LINE 6-11-10 A P McCoy, *wth ldr, hrd rdn 8th, led 9th to appr last, no ch whn wnr.*
.... (11 to 8 op 6 to 4 on tchd 2 to 1) 2
830* SCAMALLACH (Ire) (bl) 6-11-5 G Bradley, *wnt poor 3rd appr 3 out, tld off.*.................. (8 to 1 op 5 to 1 tchd 10 to 1) 3
WIN A HAND 6-10-9 G Upton, *hld to 9th, wknd nxt, beh whn pld up bef 3 out.*.......(14 to 1 op 12 to 1 tchd 16 to 1) pu
997⁶ LILLY THE FILLY 5-10-9 E Byrne, *al beh, tld off frm 8th, pld up bef 3 out.*.................. (100 to 1 op 25 to 1) pu
Dist: 10l, dist. 6m 37.40s. a 21.40s (5 Ran).

(Mrs Harry J Duffey), K C Bailey

1101 Enigma Nightclub Amateur Riders' Handicap Chase Class E (0-125 5-y-o and up) £3,493 m 1f...... (4:00)

COOME HILL (Ire) [124] 7-12-0 (7*) Mr T Dennis, *led to second, led 6th to 8th, led 14th, easily.*
.... (11 to 8 fav op Evens tchd 6 to 4) 1
809³ ANDRELOT [118] (bl) 9-11-8 (7*) Mr R Thornton, *led 8th, hrd rdn and hdd 14th, no ch wth wnr.*.......... (9 to 4 op 2 to 1) 2
809 CHILDHAY CHOCOLATE [105] 8-10-9 (7*) Mr J Tizzard, *led second, mstk 5th, hdd 6th, 3rd whn mistakes 3 out and 2 out, one pace.*.................. (3 to 1 op 5 to 2) 3
953³ FOXGROVE [96] 10-10-0 (7*) Mr P Scott, *same pl most of way, lost tch 11th.*...... (20 to 1 op 12 to 1 tchd 25 to 1) 4
840³ K C'S DANCER [96] 11-10-0 (7*) Mr R Wakley, *sn beh, lost tch 11th.*.................. (10 to 1 op 8 to 1 tchd 14 to 1) 5
834³ ARTFUL ARTHUR [96] (v) 10-10-7⁷ (7*) Mr A Wintle, *sn tld off, pld up bef 15th.*.................. (66 to 1 op 33 to 1) pu
Dist: 7l, 15l, 9l, 8l. 6m 23.50s. a 15.50s (6 Ran).

(Mrs Jill Dennis), W W Dennis

1102 Rosehill Juvenile Novices' Hurdle Class C (3-y-o) £3,468 2m 110yds .... (4:30)

991* DOCTOR GREEN (Fr) (v) 11-8 A P McCoy, *made all, sn clr, rdn appr last, styd on.*
.... (5 to 2 on tchd 9 to 4 on and 3 to 1 on) 1
936² BEN BOWDEN 11-3 J Osborne, *al prmnt, wnt second appr 2 out, no imprsn.*.......... (8 to 1 op 5 to 1 tchd 10 to 1) 2
YEZZA (Ire) 10-7 A Maguire, *hdwy 4th, ran on one pace frm 3 out.*.................. (7 to 1 op 8 to 1) 3
614* SIBERIAN MYSTIC 10-12 W McFarland, *al prmnt, second whn mstks 3 out, 4th when hit 2 out, one pace.*
.... (7 to 1 op 5 to 1 tchd 8 to 1) 4
QUIET MOMENTS (Ire) 10-12 W Marston, *al beh.*
.... (50 to 1 op 20 to 1) 5
965⁷ SOLDIER BLUE 10-12 R Dunwoody, *prmnt till hrd rdn and wknd 5th, tld off.*......(40 to 1 op 16 to 1 tchd 50 to 1) 6
930⁸ ARROGANT HEIR 10-13¹ Mr A Rebori, *in rear till ran out and uns rdr appr 5th.*.................. (66 to 1 op 33 to 1) ro
STARTINGO 10-12 T J Murphy, *strted slwly, rapid hdwy whn mstk second, wknd quickly 4th, pld up bef nxt.*
.... (66 to 1 op 20 to 1) pu
Dist: 11l, 15l, 8l, 13l, dist. 3m 59.70s. a 10.70s (8 Ran).

(Jim Weeden), M C Pipe

CHELTENHAM (firm)
Wednesday October 30th
Going Correction: MINUS 0.05 sec. per fur.

1103 Cheltenham Sponsorship Club 'National Hunt' Novices' Hurdle Class D (4-y-o and up) £2,787 2m 110yds.................. (1:10)

900* KAILASH (USA) 5-11-6 A P McCoy, *hld up in rear, hdwy 4th, led appr 2 out, easily.*........ (8 to 1 on op 7 to 1 on) 1
SHANNON LAD (Ire) 6-11-0 T J Murphy, *al prmnt, chsd wnr frm 2 out, no imprsn.*.......... (8 to 1 op 6 to 1) 2
939⁶ ALL SEWN UP 4-10-13 L Harvey, *led second till appr 2 out, one pace.*.................. (50 to 1 op 25 to 1) 3
1006 BARTON BLADE (Ire) 4-10-13 J F Titley, *not fluent, led to second, wknd 3 out.*.......... (16 to 1 op 10 to 1) 4
CHAN THE MAN 5-10-11 (3*) Guy Lewis, *drpd rear 4th, tld off frm 5th.*.................. (50 to 1 op 25 to 1) 5
Dist: 9l, 11l, 18l, dist. 4m 2.80s. a 13.80s (5 Ran).

(Mick Fletcher), M C Pipe

1104 Lloyds Bowmaker Novices' Chase Class D (5-y-o and up) £3,701 2m.................. (1:40)

820* CELIBATE (Ire) 5-11-11 A P McCoy, *hld up, led aftr 9th, mstks 3 out and 2 out, wnt rght after last, ran on.*.......... (Evens Jt-fav op 6 to 5) 1
868² JATHIB (Can) 5-11-11 Derek Byrne, *jmpd rght, al prmnt, ev ch whn mstk 2 out, no extr aftr last.*.................. (Evens Jt-fav op 5 to 4 on tchd 11 to 10) 2
CHEEKA 7-11-0 M Ranger, *hld up, rdn appr 3 out, one pace frm 2 out.*.................. (80 to 1 op 33 to 1) 3
870² LOWAWATHA 8-11-6 A Thornton, *led till aftr 9th, wknd 2 out, virtually pld up after last, tld off.*
.... (16 to 1 op 8 to 1 tchd 20 to 1) 4
Dist: 2½l, 18l, dist. 3m 58.90s. a 6.90s (4 Ran).
SR: 20/17/-/-/ *(Stamford Bridge Partnership), C J Mann*

1105 Tim Emanuel Handicap Hurdle Class B (0-145 4-y-o and up) £4,833 2m 5f.................. (2:15)

919* COURBARIL [115] 4-11-2 A P McCoy, *made all, clr 3 out, drvn out....* (2 to 1 op 6 to 4 tchd 85 to 40 and 9 to 4) 1
779⁷ FREDDIE MUCK [118] 6-11-4 (3*) D Walsh, *chsd wnr, hrd rdn frm 7th, ran on wl from last.*
.... (15 to 8 fav op 2 to 1 tchd 9 to 4) 2
BLAZE AWAY (USA) [122] 5-11-10 G Bradley, *hld up, effrt and rdn appr 2 out, 3rd and no imprsn whn blun last.*
.... (2 to 1 op 5 to 2) 3
PEATSWOOD [119] 8-11-8 A Thornton, *chsd ldrs till outpcd appr 3 out, no ch aftr...* (20 to 1 op 14 to 1 tchd 25 to 1) 4
TUG OF PEACE [119] 9-11-8 B Clifford, *lost tch 6th, tld off.*.................. (25 to 1 op 12 to 1 tchd 33 to 1) 5
Dist: 1¼l, 4l, 3l, 29l. 5m 1.30s. a 5.30s (5 Ran).
SR: 25/28/27/22/-/ *(Richard Green (Fine Paintings)), M C Pipe*

1106 Jewson Novices' Chase Class D (5-y-o and up) £3,759 3m 1f..... (2:50)

931⁵ MONY-SKIP (Ire) 7-11-12 Richard Guest, *hld up, blun 4 out, hdwy 3 out, led appr last, easily.*
.... (7 to 4 on op 6 to 4 on tchd 5 to 4 on) 1
986* CAPO CASTANUM 7-11-6 T J Murphy, *al prmnt, ev ch appr last, no imprsn.*.......... (5 to 2 op 2 to 1) 2
902⁷ LA MEZERAY 8-10-6 (3*) D Walsh, *second till led 13th, sn clr, mstk 2 out, soon hdd, one pace....* (20 to 1 op 10 to 1) 3
INCH EMPEROR (Ire) 6-11-0 W Marston, *hld to 13th, 4th and btn whn blun 3 out.*.................. (20 to 1 op 12 to 1) 4
902 KINDLY LADY 8-10-9 G Upton, *in tch till wknd 4 out.*
.... (20 lu 1 op 10 to 1) 5
999 VARECK II (Fr) 9-10-7 (7*) B Moore, *tld off frm tenth, pld up bef 4 out.*.................. (20 to 1 op 12 to 1 tchd 33 to 1) pu
Dist: 4l, 10l, 14l, 8l. 6m 23.70s. a 15.70s (6 Ran).

(Trevor Hemmings), Mrs S J Smith

1107 Neville Russell Novices' Hurdle Class D (4-y-o and up) £2,906 2m 5f.................. (3:25)

888³ CANTON VENTURE 4-10-13 A Maguire, *led second, quick-ened clr appr last, easily........* (6 to 1 on op 8 to 1 on) 1
PEATSVILLE (Ire) 4-10-13 A Thornton, *chsd ldrs, rdn 3 out, wknd 2 out.*.................. (5 to 1 tchd 11 to 2) 2
993 AUNTIE LORNA 7-11-0⁵ Mr A Sansome, *led to second, in tch till pld up lme appr 2 out.*...............(20 to 1 op 12 to 1) pu
Dist: Dist. 5m 28.10s. a 32.10s (3 Ran).

(Dr Frank S B Chao), S P C Woods

1108 Studd Challenge Cup Handicap Chase Class C (0-135 5-y-o and up) £4,394 2½m 110yds.......... (4:00)

894² WISE APPROACH [130] 9-12-0 C O'Dwyer, *jmpd wl, led till aftr 4 out, led 3 out till appr last, led r-in, ran on well.*
.... (7 to 4 fav op 6 to 4 tchd 2 to 1) 1
894* PHILIP'S WOODY [115] 8-10-13 J R Kavanagh, *hld up in rear, hdwy 4 out, led appr last to r-in, one pace.*
.... (9 to 4 op 13 to 8) 2
831⁴ WHO'S TO SAY [118] 10-10-11 (5*) Michael Brennan, *al prmnt, led aftr 4 out to 3 out, hrd rdn 2 out, ev ch whn blun last, not reco'r.*.................. (7 to 2 op 3 to 1) 3
894³ CHANNEL PASTIME [102] 12-9-11 (3*) Guy Lewis, *prmnt till hrd rdn and wknd appr 3 out, tld off.*
.... (25 to 1 op 14 to 1 tchd 33 to 1) 4
933³ DE JORDAAN [115] 9-10-13 A Maguire, *hld up, hdwy 4 out, hrd rdn 2 out, fourth and btn whn l last.*
.... (3 to 1 tchd 100 to 30 and 11 to 4) f
Dist: 1½l, 11l, 27l. 5m 6.70s. a 9.70s (5 Ran).

(Mrs S Gee), K C Bailey

1109 Weatherbys 'Stars Of Tomorrow' National Hunt Flat Standard - Class H (4,5,6-y-o) £1,604 2m 110yds.................. (4:30)

TIDAL FORCE (Ire) 5-10-13 (5*) D J Kavanagh, *al prmnt, led 3 fs out, cmftbly.
.... (6 to 4 fav op 11 to 8 tchd 5 to 4 and 7 to 4) 1
COUNTRYMAN (Ire) 5-10-13 P M Betts, *hdwy 3 fs out, ev ch and hrd rdn o'r one out, no imprsn.*
.... (9 to 4 op 2 to 1 tchd 100 to 30) 2
8807 LADY FOLEY (Ire) (bl) 4-10-9 (3*) J Magee, *hdwy 3 fs out, hrd rdn o'r one out, one pace.*............ (7 to 1 op 5 to 1) 3
WILLOWS ROULETTE 4-10-10 (7*) O Burrows, *hdwy aftr 4 fs, rdn and one pace hfl 3....* (7 to 1 op 5 to 1 tchd 8 to 1) 4
1012 DERRING KNIGHT (v) 6-11-4 Mr A Sansome, *hdwy aftr 4 fs, wth ldr and hrd rdn 3 furlongs out, wknd 2 out.*
.... (50 to 1 op 33 to 1 tchd 66 to 1) 5
BURFORDS FOR SCRAP 4-10-10 (7*) X Aizpuru, *tld off fnl m.*
.... (20 to 1 op 12 to 1) 6
STICKWITHTHEHAND 5-11-4 Mr J Jukes, *led till wknd quickly 3 fs out, tld off.*................ (33 to 1 op 16 to 1) 7
LUMO (Ire) 5-11-1 (3*) R Massey, *prmnt till ran out and uns rdr o'r 6 fs out.*................... (5 to 1 tchd 11 to 2) ro
Dist: 5l, 1¼l, ¾l, 13l, 12l, 20l. 4m 1.90s. (8 Ran).

(Ian S Steam) P J Hobbs

FONTWELL (good)
Wednesday October 30th
Going Correction: PLUS 0.40 sec. per fur.

1110 Fontwell Park Annual Members Selling Handicap Hurdle Class G (0-95 4-y-o and up) £2,010 2¼m 110yds
.... (1:30)

BURLINGTON SAM (NZ) 7-10-8 (7*) Mr G Shenkin, *trkd ldrs gng easily, mstk 3 out and reminder, led appr nxt, rdn out.*
.... (12 to 1 tchd 14 to 1) 1
9375 SHARP THRILL 7-10-1 J Osborne, *trkd ldrs, pushed alng 6th, chsd wnr 2 out, no imprsn, kpt on r-in.* ...(5 to 2 jt-fav op 9 to 4 tchd 3 to 1) 2
9872 CREDIT CONTROLLER (Ire) 7-10-3 B Fenton, *rear, pckd second, rdn 5th, effrt appr 2 out, kpt on one pace.*
.... (9 to 2 op 7 to 2 tchd 5 to 1) 3
989* SLEEPTITE (Fr) 6-11-10 (7*,7ex) J Power, *trkd ldrs, led 5th, rdn and hdd appr 2 out, sn wknd.*...........(5 to 2 jt-fav op 7 to 4) 4
1899 CAVO GRECO (USA) 7-11-2 D Skyrme, *hld up, effrt and pushed alng aftr 5th, outpcd frm nxt..* (25 to 1 op 12 to 1) 5
RUTH'S GAMBLE 6-9-10-1 (5*) Sophie Mitchell, *chsd ldr 3rd to 5th, sn outpcd....*(25 to 1 op 20 to 1 tchd 33 to 1) 6
6734 ANTIGUAN FLYER 7-11-0 R Johnson, *led to 5th, rdn nxt, wknd 3 out.*............... (14 to 1 op 12 to 1) 7
DAMCADA (Ire) 8-10-10 B Powell, *lost pl 3rd, sn struggling.*.................. (14 to 1 op 12 to 1 tchd 16 to 1) 8
9889 RAGTIME SONG 7-9-81 (7*) N T Egan, *pld hrd, wth ldr to 4th, sn wknd, tld off...* (12 to 1 op 8 to 1 tchd 14 to 1) 9
891 DOC'S COAT 11-10-8 M A Fitzgerald, *al beh, rdn aftr 5th, tld off.*..................... (33 to 1 op 16 to 1) 10
6736 MILZIG (USA) 7-10-12 C Llewellyn, *reluctant to race and sn tld off, pld up bef 4th.* (25 to 1 op 12 to 1 tchd 33 to 1) pu
Dist: 8l, 5l, 6l, 10l, hd, 2½l, 16l, 15l, 27l. 4m 33.60s. a 16.60s (11 Ran).

(Mrs Jackie Reip), A G Hobbs

1111 Derek Wigan Memorial Novices' Handicap Chase Class E (0-100 5-y-o and up) £3,036 2¼m....... (2:05)

9023 WILKINS 7-11-5 P Holley, *led aftr 1st to 3rd, led 5th to 7th, led 9th, made rst, drvn out.*
.... (5 to 2 fav op 2 to 1 tchd 3 to 1) 1
SUGAR HILL (Ire) 6-11-13 P Hide, *led to aftr 1st, led 3rd to 5th and 7th till blun nxt, pressed wnr aftr, no imprsn 2 out.*
.... (9 to 2 op 4 to 1 tchd 6 to 1) 2
9042 THE LANCER (Ire) 7-11-9 (3*) D Fortt, *wtd wth, jmpd slwly 4th and 5th, rdn and prog to chase ldg pair tenth, no imprsn 3 out.*....................... (3 to 1 op 2 to 1) 3
MASTER PANGLOSS (Ire) 6-12-6-9-13 (7*) C Rae, *keen hold, mstks, chsd ldrs, rdn 4 out, wl btn whn blun 2 out and last.*
.... (25 to 1 op 20 to 1 tchd 33 to 1) 4
8204 NIGHT IN A MILLION 7-10-10 R Johnson, *mstks, chsd ldg pair 7th to tenth, sn btn.*............ (12 to 1) 5
9909 JACKSONS BAY 6-10-6 (3*) G Hogan, *mid-div, effrt 9th, no prog frm nxt.*............. (33 to 1 tchd 50 to 1) 6
9563 RYTON RUN 11-12-0 B Fenton, *prmnt whn mstk second, sn lost pl, tld off frm 9th.* (14 to 1 op 7 to 1 tchd 16 to 1) 7
PRECIOUS WONDER 7-9-8 (7*) Mr R Thornton, *not jump wl, prmnt to 4th, wknd 8th, tld off whn f 3 out.*
.... (20 to 1 tchd 25 to 1) f
KENTAVRUS WAY (Ire) 7-10-0 B Powell, *beh till mstk and uns rdr 6th....*....... (12 to 1 op 16 to 1) ur
904 KING'S GOLD 6-11-8 M Richards, *beh and rdn 7th, nvr on terms aftr, tld off and pld up bef 2 out.*
.... (11 to 1 op 8 to 1 tchd 12 to 1) pu
674 TOP MISS 7-10-2 (7*) W Greatrex, *blun 1st, al beh, tld off and pld up bef 4 out...*(66 to 1 op 33 to 1 tchd 100 to 1) pu
LETS GO NOW (Ire) 6-10-4 D Leahy, *chsd ldg pair 1st to 7th, sn wknd, tld off and pld up bef 4 out.*
.... (33 to 1 op 20 to 1) pu

Dist: 2½l, 11l, 9l, 12l, hd, 21l. 4m 45.50s. a 25.50s (12 Ran).

(Fred Honour), R J O'Sullivan

1112 Strebel Boilers And Radiators Handicap Hurdle Series Final Class B (4-y-o and up) £6,775 2¾m 110yds
.... (2:40)

833* VICTOR BRAVO (NZ) [109] (bl) 9-12-0 C Llewellyn, *prmnt, rdn 8th, rallied to ld aftr 2 out, clr last, all out.* (8 to 1 op 7 to 1) 1
675* KALASADI (USA) [107] 5-11-11 M Richards, *wtd wth in rear, outpcd 8th, rdn and ran on 2 out, chsd wnr aftr last, styd on.*
.... (11 to 4 jt-fav op 4 to 1 tchd 5 to 2) 2
8334 ROGER'S PAL [81] 9-9-7 (7*) M Batchelor, *prmnt, chsd ldr 5th to 8th, sn rdn, kpt on gmely und pres frm 2 out.*
.... (33 to 1 op 14 to 1 tchd 50 to 1) 3
8335 KARAR (Ire) [109] 6-11-11 (3*) L Aspell, *led, rdn 3 out, hdd sn aftr nxt, wknd last...*....... (8 to 1 op 7 to 1 tchd 9 to 1) 4
OLD ARCHIVES (Ire) [92] 7-10-11 P Hide, *wtd wth in tch, trkd ldrs appr 2 out, sn rdn and not quicken. (20 to 1 op 10 to 1) 5
[illegible] .... *easily 6th, jnd ldr appr 2 out, sn rdn and wknd.*
.... (10 to 1 op 12 to 1 tchd 20 to 1) 6
8333 MR SNAGGLE (Ire) [94] 7-10-13 C Maude, *wtd wth in tch, trkd ldrs appr 2 out, sn rdn and wknd.* (14 to 1 op 10 to 1) 7
8332 SOPHIE MAY [97] 5-11-1 J Osborne, *in tch, pushed alng and lost pl aftr 7th, nvr on terms after, brook blood vessel.*
.... (11 to 4 jt-fav op 5 to 1 tchd 6 to 1) 8
MUNTAFI [103] 5-11-7 M A Fitzgerald, *chsd ldr to 5th and ag'n 8th, wknd rpdly aftr 3 out, tld off.*
.... (9 to 1 op 10 to 1 tchd 14 to 1) 9
Dist: 2½l, 1¾l, 3l, 3l, ½l, 2½l, 4l. dist. 5m 39.70s. a 25.70s (9 Ran).

(Mrs R W S Baker), N A Gaselee

1113 Action Research For Crippled Child Novices' Chase Class E (5-y-o and up) £2,688 3¼m 110yds...... (3:15)

9022 KEEP IT ZIPPED (Ire) (bl) 6-10-12 J Osborne, *chsd ldg trio frm 6th, mstk tenth, pushed alng 15th, ran on 17th, led 3 out, drvn out.*...................(7 to 4 fav op 6 to 4 tchd 2 to 1) 1
GREY GORDEN (Ire) 8-10-12 D Morris, *prmnt, mstk 5th, led nxt, mistake 12th, hdd 3 out, kpt on one pace.*
.... (11 to 2 op 5 to 1) 2
10557 JOKER JACK 11-10-9 (3*) T Dascombe, *chsd ldg pair frm 6th, mstk 14th, wknd appr 3 out....* (20 to 1 tchd 25 to 1) 3
8683 MANOR MIEO 10-11-5 R Johnson, *led aftr 1st to 6th, chsd ldr till aftr 9 out, 3rd and btn whn mstk nxt, wknd.*
.... (4 to 1 op 7 to 2 tchd 9 to 1) 4
7782 MOBILE MESSENGER (NZ) 8-10-12 M A Fitzgerald, *al beh, no ch frm 17th, tld off and pld up bef 3 out.*
.... (11 to 4 op 3 to 1 tchd 7 to 2 and 5 to 2) pu
PINOCCIO 9-10-12 B Fenton, *reluctant to race and lft strt, al beh, tld off and pld up bef 16th.......* (50 to 1 op 33 to 1) pu
HERBIDACIOUS (Ire) 6-10-7 B Powell, *wl beh whn mstk 3rd, pld up bef nxt....*...............(100 to 1 op 33 to 1) pu
868 CLONATTIN LADY (Ire) (bl) 7-10-7 D Leahy, *al beh, tld off and pld up bef 13th....*..................(100 to 1 op 33 to 1) pu
Dist: 6l, 18l, 1l, 26l. 7m 6.00s. a 36.00s (9 Ran).

(Mrs Luisa Stewart-Brown), O Sherwood

1114 Ford Amateur Riders' Handicap Chase Class F (0-105 5-y-o and up) £2,786 2m 3f................ (3:50)

8572 HERBERT BUCHANAN (Ire) [98] 6-11-2 (7*) Mr J Tizzard, *wtd wth in tch, trkd ldrs fnl circuit, chlgd on bit last, sn led, rdn and kpt on..........* (11 to 10 on op 6 to 4 on tchd Evens) 1
MASTER COMEDY [75] (bl) 12-9-9² (7*) Mr R Wakley, *led till mstk 3 out, rallied to ld last, sn hdd, kpt on r-in.*
.... (16 to 1 op 12 to 1 tchd 20 to 1) 2
9726 RAMSTAR [103] 8-11-7 (7*) Mr S Mulcaire, *chsd ldr 6th, mstk 9th, led 3 out till last, not quicken.......*(7 to 2 op 9 to 4) 3
FICHU (USA) [75] 8-9-7 (7*) Mr R Thornton, *hld up, effrt tenth, outpcd 4 out, wknd r-in.............*(7 to 1 op 12 to 1) 4
834 ENNISTYMON (Ire) [76] 5-9-7 (7*) Mr G Weatherley, *last frm 7th, lost to 9th, kpt on ag'n frm 2 out.*
.... (40 to 1 op 25 to 1 tchd 50 to 1) 5
DURRINGTON [82] 10-10-7² (3*) Mr M Rimell, *chsd ldr to 6th, wkng whn mstk 11th, 5th and btn when f nxt.*
.... (5 to 1 tchd 6 to 1) f
Dist: ¾l, 7l, 11l, 1¼l. 5m 3.50s. a 28.50s (6 Ran).

(Five For Fun), P F Nicholls

1115 Middleton Maiden Hurdle Class E (4-y-o and up) £2,595 2¾m 110yds
.... (4:20)

SPRING GALE (Ire) 5-11-6 J Osborne, *prog 4th, trkd ldrs aftr, led 2 out, shaken up last, ran on strly.*
.... (2 to 1 fav tchd 11 to 4) 1
DREAM LEADER (Ire) 6-11-6 J Railton, *in tch, prog 3 out, ev ch nxt, unbl to quicken.....* (6 to 1 op 5 to 1 tchd 8 to 1) 2

955² COPPER COIL 6-10-13 (7") J Power, *led aftr 1st till 3 out, hng lft und pres, kpt on* .... (4 to 1 op 5 to 2) 3
CORE BUSINESS 5-11-6 E Murphy, *strted slwly, rear till prog 6th, trkd ldrs 8th, styd on one pace frm 2 out, improve.*
.... (6 to 1 op 8 to 1) 4
677² LAWBUSTER (Ire) (bl) 4-11-0 (5") D Salter, *prmnt, led 3 out, rdn and hdd nxt, wknd..* (11 to 1 op 7 to 1 tchd 12 to 1) 5
SNOWY PETREL (Ire) 4-11-5 C Llewellyn, *trkd ldrs, mstk 8th, rdn and not quicken aftr 3 out* .... (9 to 2 op 6 to 1) 6
NODDADANTE (Ire) 6-11-6 Mr N R Mitchell, *strted slwly, hld up rear, prog and in tch 7th, no imprsn on ldrs frm 3 out, improve.* .... (50 to 1 op 20 to 1 tchd 66 to 1) 7
985 ALLEZ PABLO 6-11-3 (3") L Aspell, *rear, prog and in tch 7th, wknd nxt* .... (100 to 1 op 50 to 1) 8
989⁷ COOLEGALE 5-10-13 (7") D Slattery, *al rear, wl beh frm 8th.* .... (66 to 1 op 33 to 1) 9
SOLAR WARRIOR (bl) 6-11-6 B Fenton, *al rear, wl beh frm 8th.* .... (100 to 1 op 50 to 1) 10
ONE MORE MAN (Ire) 5-11-6 P Hide, *led till aftr 1st, pressed ldr till wknd 8th, tld off.* .... (20 to 1 op 10 to 1) 11
TRACEY TROOPER 5-11-1 B Powell, *mid-div to 7th, sn wknd, tld off.* .... (50 to 1 tchd 66 to 1) 12
HUMMINBIRDPRINCESS 5-11-1 A Dicken, *strted slwly, prog and in tch whn pld up bef 6th, dismounted.*
.... (50 to 1 tchd 66 to 1) pu
835⁶ RAVUS 6-11-6 G Crone, *last frm 4th, tld off and pld up bef 8th.*
.... (100 to 1 op 50 to 1) pu
874 FASHION LEADER 5-11-6 M Richards, *prmnt, mstk 4th, wknd 6th, tld off and pld up bef 2 out.*
.... (50 to 1 op 33 to 1 tchd 66 to 1) pu
Dist: 11, ¾l, 3l, 12l, 2½l, 6l, 3l, 10l, ½l, 12l. 5m 43.50s. a 29.50s (15 Ran).

(M Crabb, B Ead, M Moore), O Sherwood

GOWRAN PARK (IRE) (heavy)
Thursday October 31st

1116 Bennettsbridge Chase (5-y-o and up) £3,082 2¼m...............(1:45)

1004⁵ THE OUTBACK WAY (Ire) (bl) 6-11-11 D H O'Connor,
.... (9 to 4 fav) 1
1080² WOODVILLE STAR (Ire) 7-10-13 T Horgan, ... (7 to 2) 2
MOUSSAHIM (Ire) 6-11-4 L P Cusack, ... (6 to 1) 3
TIME FOR A RUN 9-11-4 R Dunwoody, ... (3 to 1) 4
1014³ STRONG HICKS (Ire) 8-11-4 F J Flood, ... (7 to 2) 5
Dist: 1½l, 4l, hd, 15l. 5m 6.40s. (5 Ran).

(E O'Dwyer), James Joseph O'Connor

1117 I.N.H. Stallion Owners E.B.F. Maiden Hurdle (5-y-o and up) £3,767 2¾m
.... (2:15)

928 HOLLYBANK BUCK (Ire) 6-11-6 A Powell, ... (20 to 1) 1
983⁴ FLAMINGO FLOWER (Ire) 8-11-6 (3") Mr P J Casey,
.... (3 to 1 fav) 2
LEAMHOG (Ire) 6-12-0 T Horgan, ... (4 to 1) 3
977⁶ LUCKY BUST (Ire) 6-11-7 (7") Mr D A Harney, ... (5 to 1) 4
983² DIAMOND DOUBLE (Ire) 5-11-1 C F Swan, ... (4 to 1) 5
FIGHTING FIDDLE 5-11-3 (3") Mr R Walsh, ... (12 to 1) 6
978⁶ JOHN'S RIGHT (Ire) 5-11-6 J P Broderick, ... (10 to 1) 7
EMERALD GALE (Ire) 6-11-6 F Woods, ... (8 to 1) 8
928 SAN SIRO (Ire) 6-10-13 (7") Mr Edgar Byrne, ... (14 to 1) 9
853 GOLLY MISS MOLLY (Ire) 5-10-8 (7") A O'Shea, ... (33 to 1) 10
910 BLACK AND A HALF (Ire) 5-11-6 D H O'Connor, ... (14 to 1) 11
REMAINDER STAR 5-11-6 T J Mitchell, ... (8 to 1) su
1019⁶ BAILEYS BRIDGE (Ire) 5-11-6 D Parker, ... (8 to 1) pu
91 LANGRETTA 5-10-8 (7") M D Murphy, ... (33 to 1) pu
DECIDING DANCE (Ire) 5-11-1 K F O'Brien, ... (25 to 1) pu
TRASNA NA CUINGAIM (Ire) 5-11-1 Mr H F Cleary, (20 to 1) pu
Dist: 5l, 10l, 6l, 8l. 6m 4.30s. (16 Ran).

(Mrs Sarah Warner), A J Martin

1118 Wexford Opportunity Handicap Hurdle (0-123 4-y-o and up) £2,740 2m 1f.................................. (2:45)

89⁴ ILLBETHEREFORYOU (Ire) [-] 5-9-3 (4") S FitzGerald,
.... (8 to 1) 1
1017⁴ THE WICKED CHICKEN (Ire) [-] 7-10-0 (2") G Cotter, (7 to 2) 2
908⁶ PTARMIGAN LODGE [-] 5-10-9 G Kilfeather, ... (7 to 1) 3
980³ SACULORE (Ire) [-] 8-10-12 (2") J M Donnelly, (100 to 30 jt-fav) 4
HERSILIA (Ire) [-] 5-10-2 (4") L J Fleming, ... (9 to 1) 5
76 TOMMY PAUD (Ire) [-] 7-11-10 J R Barry, (100 to 30 jt-fav) 6
DANGER FLYNN (Ire) [-] 6-9-9 (4") M D Murphy, ... (12 to 1) 7
VEREDARIUS (Fr) [-] 5-10-11 (4") D W O'Sullivan, ...(6 to 1) 8
Dist: ¾l, 8l, 9l, 25l. 4m 46.10s. (8 Ran).

(G Walsh), Michael Hourigan

1119 Thomastown Maiden Hurdle (Div I) (4-y-o and up) £2,740 2m.....(3:15)

943³ FRANCES STREET (Ire) 4-11-9 C F Swan, ... (5 to 4 fav) 1
946² REAL TAOISEACH (Ire) 6-11-7 (7") Mr A K Wyse, ... (6 to 1) 2
ROCKETTS CASTLE (Ire) 6-11-6 D Parker, ... (4 to 1) 3
ABBEY GALE 5-11-1 C O'Dwyer, ... (12 to 1) 4

DELPHI LODGE (Ire) 6-12-0 R Dunwoody, ... (3 to 1) 5
1015 JACKSON'S PANTHER (Ire) 4-10-13 A Powell, ... (12 to 1) 6
978⁷ SHAWS CROSS (Ire) 5-11-6 W Slattery, ... (20 to 1) 7
978 HOLLY LADY (Ire) 5-11-1 P A Roche, ... (20 to 1) 8
983 SHECOULDNTBEBETTER (Ire) 5-11-1 T P Treacy, (12 to 1) 9
1077⁵ ROSEY ELLEN (Ire) 4-10-13 T Horgan, ... (12 to 1) 10
WHO IS ED (Ire) 5-11-6 J P Broderick, ... (12 to 1) 11
MAVISANDPEDS (Ire) 7-10-13 (7") J P Deegan, ... (25 to 1) 12
SAM QUALE (Ire) 4-10-11 (7") A O'Shea, ... (20 to 1) 13
1088⁵ BUMPER TO BUMPER (Ire) 4-11-4 M P Hourigan, (20 to 1) pu
Dist: 4½l, 3l, 6l, 5½l. 4m 22.90s. (14 Ran).

(Philip J Reynolds), A P O'Brien

1120 Thomastown Maiden Hurdle (Div II) (4-y-o and up) £2,740 2m..... (3:45)

1018² PENNDARA (Ire) 7-12-0 C F Swan, ... (2 to 1 on) 1
552⁸ MAJOR GALE (Ire) 7-11-7 (7") M D Murphy, ...(5 to 1) 2
977⁷ ROSENWALD (Ire) 6-11-6 A Powell, ... (10 to 1) 3
TREANAREE (Ire) 7-10-13 (7") S P Kelly, ... (10 to 1) 4
MYSTICAL AIR (Ire) 6-11-6 F Woods, ... (10 to 1) 5
BOULABALLY 4-11-4 R Dunwoody, ... (8 to 1) 6
1005⁸ MOLLY WHACK (Ire) 5-11-1 T J Mitchell, ... (14 to 1) 7
1060 EXECUTIVE OPAL 5-11-1 M P Hourigan, ... (10 to 1) 8
CARRIGMORE LADY (Ire) 4-10-13 C O'Dwyer, ... (12 to 1) 9
FINCHLEY LEADER 4-10-13 (5") G Cotter, ... (12 to 1) 10
Dist: 15l, 2½l, 7l, 7l. 4m 29.70s. (10 Ran).

(All Gold Syndicate), A P O'Brien

1121 Clonegall I.N.H. Flat Race (4-y-o) £2,740 2m 1f................. (4:15)

898⁴ CLOONE BRIDGE (Ire) 11-6 (3") Mr B M Cash, (10 to 9 on) 1
GRAPHIC EQUALISER (Ire) 11-2 (7") Mr Edgar Byrne,
.... (7 to 1) 2
884³ NATIVE SHORE (Ire) 10-11 (7") Mr K R O'Ryan, ...(8 to 1) 3
AROUND THE STUMP (Ire) 11-1 (3") Mr P English, (10 to 1) 4
928⁷ JACK CHAUCER 11-9 Mr P F Graffin, ... (5 to 1) 5
MALADANTE (Ire) 10-11 (7") Mr J P Hayden, ... (12 to 1) 6
1015 SHALOM (Ire) 11-6 (3") Mr R Walsh, ... (16 to 1) 7
288 ACTIVE LADY (Ire) 10-11 (7") Mr B Walsh, ... (20 to 1) 8
IRISH FROLIC (Ire) 11-2 (7") Mr D Turner, ... (25 to 1) 9
COOLSHAMROCK (Ire) 10-12¹ (7") Mr B Hassett, (10 to 1) 10
RUSTIC LODGE (Ire) 10-11 (7") Mr K Beecher, ... (20 to 1) 11
ELECTRICFLAME (Ire) 10-11 (7") Mr P Noonan, .. (25 to 1) su
Dist: 3l, 20l, 7l, 2½l. 4m 44.40s. (12 Ran).

(Mrs Kathleen Gillane), A P O'Brien

SEDGEFIELD (good to firm)
Thursday October 31st
Going Correction: PLUS 0.40 sec. per fur.

1122 Stonegrave Aggregates Selling Handicap Hurdle Class G (0-90 3-y-o and up) £1,877 2m 1f........ (1:10)

1044⁸ FLY TO THE END (USA) [71] 6-11-4 L Wyer, *hld up and beh, steady hdwy appr 4 out, led aftr nxt, rdn approaching last, ran on.* .... (10 to 1 op 8 to 1) 1
912⁴ CLOVER GIRL [74] (v) 5-11-3 (3") G Cahill, *hld up and beh, hdwy appr 4 out, chsd wnr frm nxt rdn and ev ch whn hit last, kpt on, fnshd lme.* .... (5 to 4 fav op 6 to 4) 2
318 CATTON LADY [53] 6-9-11 (3") G Lee, *chsd ldrs, rdn aftr 3 out, wknd bef nxt.* .... (33 to 1 tchd 50 to 1) 3
1044⁷ TOP SKIPPER (Ire) [68] 4-10-13 A S Smith, *led second, rdn and hdd 3 out, sn wknd.* (10 to 1 op 9 to 1 tchd 12 to 1) 4
1044 FENIAN COURT (Ire) [82] 5-11-9 (5") S Taylor, *led to second, prmnt till rdn and led briefly 3 out, sn hdd and wknd.*
.... (7 to 2 op 11 to 4 tchd 4 to 1) 5
1068⁵ MARCO MAGNIFICO (USA) [71] (v) 6-11-4 A Thornton, *chsd ldrs till reminders 4th and sn lost pl, beh nxt.*
.... (11 to 1 op 10 to 1 tchd 12 to 1) 6
489⁴ ON THE MOVE [70] 5-11-2 L O'Hara, *in tch, rdn 4th, sn lost pl and beh.* ...... (16 to 1 op 14 to 1 tchd 20 to 1) 7
724 STRATHTORE DREAM (Ire) [54] 5-9-7 (7") M Dunne, *pld hrd, chsd ldrs, hdwy to dispute ld 3 out, sn rdn and wknd.*
.... (50 to 1) 8
NICK THE BILL [56] 5-10-2 A Dobbin, *al rear, pushed alng and lost pl 4th, tld off 3 out.* .... (9 to 1 op 7 to 1) 9
SHUT UP [57] 7-10-4 K Johnson, *chsd ldrs, wknd 4th, tld off 3 out.* .... (50 to 1 op 33 to 1) 10
Dist: 3l, 1¾l, 5l, 8l, 5l, 9l, 15l, ½l, ½l. 4m 5.50s. a 19.50s (10 Ran).

(Ian Muir), J J Quinn

1123 European Breeders Fund 'National Hunt' Novices' Hurdle Qualifier Class D (4,5,6-y-o) £2,889 2m 1f
.... (1:40)

FLAMING HOPE (Ire) 6-10-9 J Burke, *made all, rdn 2 out, hld on wl frm last.* .... (33 to 1) 1
960³ ADAMATIC (Ire) 5-11-3 (7") S Melrose, *hld up, gd hdwy 3 out, swtchd to chal nxt, rdn and ev ch last, kpt on.*
.... (11 to 8 fav op 5 to 4) 2

135

740[2] GOLF LAND (Ire) 4-10-13 M Dwyer, *hld up, hdwy 4 out, rdn and outpcd aftr nxt, effrt and ev ch 2 out till ridden and hit last, one pace*................(3 to 1 op 7 to 2 tchd 4 to 1) 3
749[4] FAITHFUL HAND 6-11-0 Richard Guest, *trkd wnr, effrt to chal 3 out, ev ch till drvn and wknd appr last.* ....(100 to 30 op 11 to 4 tchd 7 to 2) 4
ONE MORE BILL 6-11-0 A Dobbin, *in tch till rdn and wknd 3 out*..............................(25 to 1 op 20 to 1) 5
RYSANSHYN 4-10-8 K Johnson, *in tch to 4th, sn lost pl and wl beh*.................................(25 to 1 op 20 to 1) 6
JOE LUKE (Ire) 4-10-13 J Callaghan, *not fluent in rear, beh 5th, sn tld off*...................... (16 to 1 op 12 to 1) 7
POLLY STAR 6-10-9 M Foster, *in tch till pld up lme bef 3rd.* .... (50 to 1 op 33 to 1) pu
WHITEMOSS LEADER (Ire) 6-10-9 A Thornton, *prmnt, rdn 3 out, sn wknd, beh whn pld up lme last.* (14 to 1 op 12 to 1) pu

Dist: ½l, 2l, 5l, 22l, 7l, 4l. 4m 11.10s. a 25.10s (9 Ran).
(Exors Of The Late Mr J W Hope), Mrs N Hope

1124 Mitsubishi TV, Video And HiFi Handicap Hurdle Class F (0-100 4-y-o and up) £2,267 3m 3f 110yds......(2:10)

TROODOS [89] 10-11-10 J Supple, *hld up, pckd 5th, hdwy 4 out, led appr 2 out, rdn clr last*.......... (9 to 4 op 7 to 2) 1
890[3] BALLINDOO [84] 7-11-5 Mr R Armson, *set slow pace to 3rd, cl up till led and quickened 4 out, rdn and hdd appr 2 out, one pace*.............. (2 to 1 jt-fav op 7 to 4 tchd 9 to 4) 2
HUDSON BAY TRADER (USA) [80] 9-11-1 R Supple, *cl up, pushed alng and wknd 3 out.* .... (11 to 1 op 9 to 1 tchd 12 to 1) 3
963[3] CROFTON LAKE [65] 8-10-0 B Storey, *cl up, led 3rd, pushed alng 8th, hdd and hit 4 out, sn wknd*.............(2 to 1 jt-fav op 6 to 4 tchd 9 to 4) 4
SWISS GOLD [70] 6-10-5 A S Smith, *cl up till hit tenth, sn wknd*............................. (12 to 1 op 10 to 1) 5

Dist: 5l, 15l, 25l, sht-hd. 7m 6.00s. a 44.00s (5 Ran).
(Scotnorth Racing Ltd), Mrs A Swinbank

1125 Rowena Coleman Handicap Hurdle Class E (0-110 4-y-o and up) £2,860 2m 5f 110yds.................(2:40)

TRIBUNE [84] 5-10-12 M Foster, *cl up, led 5th, rdn 2 out, kpt on gmely*.....................................(20 to 1) 1
738[2] TWIN FALLS (Ire) [98] 5-11-12 J Callaghan, *hld up, hdwy 4 out, chlgd 2 out, sn rdn and ev ch, one pace last.* (7 to 2 jt-fav) 2
813* COMMANDER GLEN (Ire) [94] 4-11-7 R Garritty, *hld up, hdwy 4 out, chlgd 2 out, ev ch till rdn and one pace last.* (7 to 2 jt-fav op 3 to 1) 3
1034[3] RULE OUT THE REST [92] 5-11-6 A Thornton, *prmnt, rdn 3 out, wknd appr nxt*..............................(4 to 1) 4
MANETTIA (Ire) [85] 7-10-11 (3*) G Lee, *trkd ldrs, pushed alng 4 out, one pace frm nxt, fnshd lme*................ (10 to 1) 5
963[2] JONAEM (Ire) [82] 6-10-11 K Johnson, *led to 5th, cl up till rdn and wknd appr 3 out*..................(5 to 1 op 9 to 2) 6
725* PEGGY GORDON [80] 5-10-8 L O'Hara, *hld up in rear, pushed alng 7th, no hdwy*.............(4 to 1 tchd 9 to 2) 7

Dist: 4l, nk, 7l, 15l, 1¾l, 2l. 5m 10.00s. a 22.00s (7 Ran).
(Hexagon Racing), C W Thornton

1126 Alderclad Handicap Chase Class E (0-110 5-y-o and up) £2,976 3m 3f .... (3:10)

915 BLAZING DAWN [81] 9-10-3 B Storey, *jmpd wl, prmnt till lft in ld 6th, rdn appr last, hld on well*....... (9 to 2 tchd 5 to 1) 1
935 OLE OLE [82] 10-10-4 L Wyer, *al prmnt, rdn to chal 3 out, one pace aftr nxt, rallied r-in, jst hld*.......(20 to 1 op 25 to 1) 2
915* JENDEE (Ire) [88] 8-10-7 (3*) G Cahill, *not fluent, in tch, effrt 15th and sn rdn, drvn 2 out, no imprsn appr last.* .... (5 to 4 fav op Evens) 3
706[5] CLARES OWN [90] 12-10-12 K Jones, *in tch till rdn, blun and wknd 4 out*.......................... (12 to 1 op 10 to 1) 4
36* TEMPLE GARTH [102] 7-11-10 R Supple, *led till f 6th.* ....(7 to 4 op 6 to 4 tchd 2 to 1) f

Dist: Nk, 3½l, dist. 6m 58.90s. a 25.90s (5 Ran).
(J S Hubbuck), J S Hubbuck

1127 Jayne Thompson Memorial Novices' Chase Class E (5-y-o and up) £3,150 2m 5f..........................(3:40)

913[2] NOTABLE EXCEPTION 7-11-12 P Niven, *hld up in tch, smooth hdwy tenth, led 3 out, hdd aftr nxt, sn rdn, rallied to ld r-in*...............(6 to 5 fav op 5 to 4 tchd 11 to 10) 1
916* LE DENSTAN 9-11-5 T Reed, *hld up and beh, gd hdwy appr 4 out, led aftr 2 out, hit last, rdn, hdd and no extr r-in.* ....(4 to 1 tchd 9 to 2) 2
KENMARE RIVER (Ire) 6-10-12 A Thornton, *al prmnt, led 9th, rdn and hdd 3 out, wknd nxt*.......... (16 to 1 op 14 to 1) 3
916[5] UP FOR RANSOME (Ire) (bl) 7-10-7 (5*) G F Ryan, *hld up in rear, hit 5th, hdwy 9th, rdn and wknd appr 4 out.* ....(16 to 1 op 14 to 1 tchd 20 to 1) 4
OSGATHORPE 9-10-12 Mrs F Needham, *pld hrd, hit second, chsd ldrs till wknd 9th*............... (25 to 1 op 20 to 1) 5
1035 THE ENERGISER 10-10-12 J Burke, *prmnt, blun 8th, rdn nxt, sn wknd*......................................(100 to 1) 6
DESERT BRAVE (Ire) 6-10-12 Richard Guest, *hld up, hdwy 6th, mstk 9th, sn rdn, wknd bef 4 out*..... (9 to 1 op 8 to 1) 7
916[3] VAL DE RAMA (Ire) 7-11-5 R Garritty, *blun and uns rdr second*...(11 to 2 op 5 to 1) ur
862[3] MERRYHILL GOLD 5-10-5 (5*) D J Kavanagh, *hld up, blun and uns rdr 6th*................... (20 to 1 op 16 to 1) ur
764[5] CARDINAL SINNER (Ire) 7-10-12 K Jones, *led, blun 8th, hdd nxt, sn wknd, tld off whn pld up bef 3 out.* .... (50 to 1 op 33 to 1) pu

Dist: 1½l, 18l, 14l, 17l, 1l, 6l. 5m 18.10s. a 22.10s (10 Ran).
(Roland Hope), Mrs M Reveley

1128 Quarrington Standard National Hunt Flat Class H (4,5,6-y-o) £1,070 2m 1f .... (4:10)

BRIGHTER SHADE (Ire) 6-10-11 (7*) C McCormack, *trkd ldrs, smooth headawy 5 fs out, led wl o'r one out, rdn clr.* (7 to 2 op 5 to 2 tchd 4 to 1) 1
BLOOD BROTHER 4-10-10 (7*) N Horrocks, *led, quickened 4 fs out, rdn o'r 2 out, hdd wl over one out, one pace.* ....(3 to 1 op 2 to 1 tchd 7 to 2) 2
917[3] GAZANALI (Ire) 5-10-13 (5*) Michael Brennan, *trkd ldr, hdwy to chal 3 fs out, ev ch till rdn and wknd wl o'r one out.* ....(11 to 10 on op 5 to 4 tchd 11 to 8 on) 3
FARRIERS FANTASY 4-10-5 (7*) S Haworth, *prmnt till rdn and wknd o'r 4 fs out*.......................... (25 to 1 op 14 to 1) 4
SAFETY TIP 4-10-9 (3*) G Cahill, *hld up, hdwy o'r 6 fs out, rdn and wknd over 4 out, sn tld off.* ....(10 to 1 op 8 to 1 tchd 12 to 1) 5
NOT SO PRIM 4-10-12 Mr C Mulhall, *chsd ldrs, rdn and lost pl hfwy, sn tld off*............(50 to 1 op 25 to 1) 6

Dist: 7l, 2½l, 30l, dist, dist. 4m 1.20s. (6 Ran).
(D S Hall), Mrs M Reveley

STRATFORD (good)
Thursday October 31st
Going Correction: PLUS 0.20 sec. per fur.

1129 Richardson's Parkway Maiden Hurdle Class E (Div I) (4-y-o and up) £2,040 2¾m 110yds.......... (1:20)

CAROLE'S CRUSADER 5-10-11 (3*) D Fortt, *led, rdn 3 out, hdd briefly r-in, rallied to ld last strd, all out.* ....(5 to 1 op 4 to 1 tchd 11 to 2) 1
FLYING GUNNER 5-11-5 A Maguire, *hld up, hdwy aftr 6th, wnt second 3 out, sn rdn, led briefly after last, hdd last strd.* .... (13 to 8 on op 6 to 4 on tchd 11 to 8 on) 2
1002[3] GENERAL MOUKTAR (v) 6-11-5 A P McCoy, *hld up, hdwy aftr 8th, pushed alng frm nxt, 3rd and btn whn pckd badly 2 out.* ....(13 to 2 op 6 to 1 tchd 11 to 2 and 7 to 1) 3
LITTLE NOTICE (Ire) 5-11-5 S Wynne, *chsd ldr frm 4th, in tch till wknd aftr four out*.... (12 to 1 op 6 to 1 tchd 14 to 1) 4
JAVELIN COOL (Ire) 5-11-2 (3*) K Gaule, *chsd ldr, in tch till wknd quickly aftr 4 out, tld off*.........(66 to 1 op 33 to 1) 5
812 MUSICAL HIT 5-11-5 R Bellamy, *beh, some hdwy aftr 6th, sn wknd, tld off 3 out*...................... (66 to 1 op 50 to 1) 6
GAN AWRY 9-11-0 Mr P Scott, *pressed ldr till wknd aftr 5 out, tld off 3 out*........................ (50 to 1 tchd 66 to 1) 7
LA BELLA VILLA 6-11-0 D Bridgwater, *al beh, tld off whn pld up bef 3 out*........................ (50 to 1 op 33 to 1) pu
919 KIRBY MOORSIDE 5-11-5 B Powell, *slwly away, al beh, pld up bef 5 out*.......................(100 to 1 op 66 to 1) pu
SUPER BRUSH (Ire) 4-10-13 M Sharratt, *chsd ldr till 8th, wknd quickly, beh whn pld up bef 2 out.* ....(100 to 1 op 66 to 1) pu
DELIRE D'ESTRUVAL (Fr) (bl) 5-11-5 J Osborne, *pressed ldr till wknd quickly aftr 6th, beh whn pld up bef 4 out.* ....(14 to 1 op 6 to 1 tchd 16 to 1) pu

Dist: Sht-hd, 16l, 18l, dist, 15l, 5l. 5m 35.50s. a 23.50s (11 Ran).
(Mrs C Skipworth), D R Gandolfo

1130 Richardson Developments Ltd. Selling Hurdle Class G (4 - 7-y-o) £1,940 2m 110yds.................. (1:50)

903[3] SEVERN GALE 6-11-0 A P McCoy, *made all, clr aftr 3 out, cmftbly*..............(9 to 4 fav op 7 to 4 tchd 5 to 2) 1
971[4] GRIFFIN'S GIRL 4-10-1 (5*) S Ryan, *hld up, hdwy aftr 5th, wnt second and mstk 3 out, sn rdn, no imprsn.* ....(9 to 1 op 7 to 1 tchd 10 to 1) 2
921[5] MY HARVINSKI 6-10-5 (7*) Miss E J Jones, *pressed ldr, drvn alng aftr 4 out, mstk and wknd after nxt.* (20 to 1 op 16 to 1) 3
971* PICKENS (USA) 4-11-4 J Osborne, *in tch, drvn alng aftr 5th, sn no imprsn*.........(100 to 30 op 3 to 1 tchd 7 to 2) 4
971 PYTCHLEY DAWN 6-10-7 V Slattery, *chsd ldr to 5th, sn wknd, lost tch aftr nxt*.......................(33 to 1 op 20 to 1) 5
971 CHAPEL OF BARRAS (Ire) 7-11-12 Mr P Gee, *chsd ldr till wknd quickly aftr 5th, tld off 3 out*......(20 to 1 op 16 to 1) 6
OOZLEM (Ire) 7-10-9 (3*) K Gaule, *chsd ldr frm 5th till wknd quickly aftr 3 out, pld up bef nxt.* .... (5 to 1 op 4 to 1 tchd 11 to 2) pu

KOMIAMAITE 4-10-11 D J Burchell, *al beh, pushed alng aftr 3rd, tld off whn pld up bef 2 out*..........(8 to 1 op 5 to 1) pu
HARD TO BREAK 5-10-12 Gary Lyons, *al beh, drvn alng aftr 3rd, tld off pld up, bef 4 out*.......(50 to 1 op 33 to 1) pu
101[7] WOODLANDS ENERGY 5-10-7 R Bellamy, *al beh, drvn alng aftr 3rd, tld off whn pld up bef 4 out*...(33 to 1 op 20 to 1) pu
922 LAURA LYE (Ire) 6-10-7 J Railton, *not fluent, chsd ldr till wknd aftr 6th, beh whn pld up bef 2 out*...(12 to 1 tchd 14 to 1) pu
Dist: 15l, 6l, 10l, ½l, dist. 4m 5.20s. a 19.20s (11 Ran).
(R M Phillips), P F Nicholls

1131 PSM Computers Handicap Chase Class C for the Oslo Trophy (0-135 5-y-o and up) £4,815 2m 1f 110yds .... (2:20)

CALLISOE BAY (Ire) [135] 7-12-0 J Osborne, *trkd ldr, mstk 3rd, led 3 out, hdd 4 out, led to ag'n r-in, pushed out.*
.............(7 to 4 on op 6 to 4 on tchd 5 to 4 on) 1
SOUTHAMPTON [120] 6-10-13 A P McCoy, *hld up, rdn and hdwy 5 out, wth wnr aftr 3 out, led nxt, hdd r-in, not quicken.*
.................................(2 to 1 op 6 to 4) 2
THUMBS UP [130] 10-11-9 B Clifford, *led til hdd 3 out, sn wknd*.................(6 to 1 op 4 to 1 tchd 13 to 2) 3
Dist: 2l, 26l. 4m 11.30s. a 9.30s (3 Ran).
SR: 42/25/9/   (R Waters), O Sherwood

1132 Archie Scott Benevolent Fund Cup Handicap Hurdle Class E (4-y-o and up) £2,442 2¾m 110yds (2:50)

975* TARRS BRIDGE (Ire) [92] 5-10-7 J Railton, *trkd ldrs, led aftr 4 out, clr aftr nxt, wknd r-in, hld on nr finish*......(9 to 4 jt-fav op 5 to 2) 1
FORTUNES COURSE (Ire) [106] 7-11-1 (7*) Mr A Wintle, *led aftr 3rd, mstk 7th, blun 4 out, sn hdd, rdn and rallied betw last 2, kpt on nr finish*....................(7 to 1 op 11 to 2) 2
SILVER STANDARD [99] 6-11-1 S Wynne, *hld up and beh, pushed alng and hdwy aftr 7th, styd on aftr 3 out, one pace.*
.................(6 to 1 op 5 to 1 tchd 13 to 2) 3
NORTHERN VILLAGE [107] 9-11-9 A Dicken, *beh, mstk 4th, rdn alng aftr 5 out, kpt on frm 3 out, nvr nrr.*
...........(14 to 1 op 8 to 1 tchd 16 to 1) 4
973[2] BARFORD SOVEREIGN [106] 4-11-6 P Hide, *trkd ldrs, cl up and ev ch 5 out, rdn and wknd aftr 3 out*..........(9 to 4 jt-fav op 5 to 2 tchd 3 to 1) 5
PETTAUGH (Ire) [92] 8-10-5 (3*) K Gaule, *chsd ldrs, in tch til rdn and wknd aftr 4 out*.(12 to 1 op 10 to 1 tchd 14 to 1) 6
JOHN NAMAN (Ire) [86] 7-9-9 (7*) G Supple, *chsd ldrs, in tch til wknd aftr 5 out, tld off*............(20 to 1 tchd 25 to 1) 7
892[3] SHIKAREE (Ire) [112] (bl) 5-11-13 A P McCoy, *hld up in tch 7th, sn lost tch, tld off*.....(10 to 1 op 7 to 1) 8
687 SIR PAGEANT [84] 7-10-0 V Slattery, *al beh, pushed alng aftr 7th, sn lost tch, tld off aftr 5 out*...(66 to 1 op 50 to 1) 9
924[3] HYDEMILLA [84] 6-9-12[1] (3*) G Hogan, *led til aftr 3rd, wknd quickly aftr 7th, sn tld off, pld up bef 3 out.*
.........................(33 to 1 op 20 to 1) pu
Dist: ½l, 16l, 1l, ½l, ½l, dist, 1¼l, dist. 5m 33.70s. a 21.70s (10 Ran).
(The Tuesday Syndicate), C J Mann

1133 Reg Lomas Farewell Handicap Chase Class D (0-120 5-y-o and up) £3,684 3½m................(3:20)

CHURCH LAW [97] 9-10-6 A Maguire, *hld up in last pl, steady hdwy aftr 6 out, led 2 out, styd on wl*....(7 to 2 op 5 to 1) 1
COURT MELODY (Ire) [115] (bl) 8-11-10 A P McCoy, *trkd ldg trio, slightly outpcd aftr 4 out, rdn and styd on betw last 2, not rch wnr*......................(4 to 1 op 9 to 4) 2
821* BIG BEN DUN [112] 10-11-7 G Bradley, *trkd ldrs, wnt second 5 out, led 3 out, sn hdd and one pace.*
.................(6 to 4 fav tchd 11 to 8 and 7 to 4) 3
872[3] CHANGE THE REIGN [107] 9-11-2 J Ryan, *led aftr 6th, hdd 8th, led ag'n nxt to 3 out, sn wknd.*.......(7 to 1 op 5 to 1) 4
TIPP MARINER [98] 11-10-7 J Osborne, *led to 6th, led ag'n 8th, hdd nxt, pressed ldr til rdn six out, wkng whn mstk 4 out, pld up bef last*.........................(16 to 1 tchd 20 to 1) pu
Dist: 2½l, 5l, 4l. 7m 12.10s. a 27.10s (5 Ran).
(Mrs L C Taylor), Mrs L C Taylor

1134 Richardson's Parkway Maiden Hurdle Class E (Div II) (4-y-o and up) £2,022 2¾m 110yds..........(3:50)

JACK TANNER (Ire) 7-11-5 A Maguire, *hld up, steady hdwy aftr 5 out, led 2 out, sn clr, easily.*
.............(5 to 1 on op 6 to 1 on tchd 9 to 2 on) 1
LORD KHALICE (Ire) 5-11-2 (7*) N Rossiter, *led 4th till hdd 2 out, kpt on betw last two, no ch wth wnr.*
.................(4 to 1 op 5 to 1 tchd 40 to 1) 2
MADAM'S WALK 6-11-0 C Llewellyn, *not fluent, mid-div, hdwy to chase ldrs aftr 4 out, kpt on one pace.*
.................(11 to 1 op 10 to 1 tchd 12 to 1) 3
796[6] LOUGH TULLY (Ire) 6-11-5 S Wynne, *chsd ldrs frm 6th till wknd aftr 4 out*.......(20 to 1 op 16 to 1 tchd 33 to 1) 4
975 LINFORD (Ire) 6-11-5 Mr R Bevis, *hdwy 5th, in tch whn mstk 4 out, wknd*.......(50 to 1 op 33 to 1) 5

---

879 BETHS WISH 7-11-0 B Fenton, *wl beh 6th, styd on one pace frm 4 out*....................(100 to 1 op 50 to 1) 6
FLINTERS (bl) 9-10-12 (7*) Mr R Thornton, *led to 4th, wknd quickly aftr 7th, sn tld off, pld up bef 3 out.*
.......................(50 to 1 op 25 to 1) pu
SMART ACT 7-11-5 Mr A Brown, *wl beh 6th, mstk and pld up aftr nxt*....................(100 to 1 op 50 to 1) pu
654[4] RAGOSA 5-11-0 J R Kavanagh, *beh frm 6th, tld off whn pld up bef 3 out*.......(40 to 1 op 33 to 1 tchd 50 to 1) pu
GUTTERIDGE (Ire) 6-11-5 R Johnson, *hld up, hdwy aftr 5 out, in tch 3 out, sn wknd, beh whn pld up bef last.*
........................(10 to 1 op 20 to 1) pu
LADY NOSO 5-11-0 W Marston, *chsd ldrs frm 5th till wknd aftr 8th, tld off whn pld up bef 3 out*.....(10 to 1 op 8 to 1) pu
Dist: 11l, 6l, 3l, 8l, 6l. 5m 45.80s. a 33.80s (11 Ran).
(Lady Harris), D Nicholson

1135 Richardson's Forum Stevenage Novices' Handicap Hurdle Class E (0-100 4-y-o and up) £2,355 2m 110yds..........................(4:20)

1020[4] RAGAMUFFIN ROMEO [71] 7-10-11 A P McCoy, *al prmnt, led aftr 5th, clr aftr 3 out, mstk nxt, drvn out.*
.....................(9 to 2 op 6 to 1 tchd 4 to 1) 1
LETS BE FRANK [80] 5-11-5 R Johnson, *hld up, hdwy aftr 5th, chsd wnr frm 3 out, kpt on aftr last, nrst finish...(7 to 2 jt-fav op 4 to 1 tchd 9 to 2) 2
937[3] ALMAPA [82] 4-11-3 (3*) T Dascombe, *in tch, chsd ldrs frm 5th, rdn aftr 4 out, sn wknd, tld off*......(8 to 1 op 9 to 1) 3
754[6] WAYFARERS WAY (USA) [88] 5-11-13 M A Fitzgerald, *hld up, hdwy aftr 5th, mstk 4 out, sn rdn and wknd, tld off.*(7 to 2 jt-fav op 4 to 1 tchd 9 to 2) 4
GLENDOE (Ire) [75] 5-10-7 (7*) C Rae, *hld up, hdwy whn mstk 5th, sn reco'red, chsd wnr till wknd rpdly aftr 3 out, tld off.*
......................(12 to 1 op 10 to 1) 5
801[9] LIME STREET BLUES (Ire) [82] (bl) 5-11-7 G Bradley, *led till 5th, wknd quickly, tld off aftr 3 out*..(5 to 1 op 7 to 2) 6
971 SORISKY [87] 4-11-11 A Maguire, *hld up, beh 4th, sn lost tch, tld off*........(4 to 1 op 7 to 2 tchd 9 to 2) 7
PHARLY REEF [75] 4-10-13 D J Burchell, *pressed ldr till wknd rpdly aftr 5th, sn tld off*.........(10 to 1 op 8 to 1) 8
WOODLANDS LAD TOO [70] 4-10-8 R Bellamy, *sn beh, tld off aftr 4th, pld up bef four out*................(33 to 1) pu
Dist: 3l, dist, 2½l, 1½l, ½l, dist, 6l. 4m 10.10s. a 24.10s (9 Ran).
(Mrs D Sawyer), H J Collingridge

BANGOR (good to soft) Friday November 1st
Going Correction: PLUS 1.10 sec. per fur.

1136 Halliwell Landau Novices' Claiming Hurdle Class F (4-y-o and up) £2,850 2m 1f........................(1:10)

856* INDRAPURA (Ire) 4-11-12 A P McCoy, *al hdwy and gng wl, dsptd ld 2 out, shaken up to lead r-in, cheekily.*
.................(2 to 1 om op 9 to 4 on tchd 15 to 8 on) 1
806[7] NIGHT BOAT 5-10-8 T Eley, *hld up, steady hdwy appr 5th, led approaching 2 out, sn und pres and jnd, hdd r-in, one pace.*
................(11 to 1 op 12 to 1 tchd 10 to 1) 2
1012[6] MILLING BROOK 4-11-6 R Johnson, *al in tch, effrt 3 out, sn ev ch, no qckn frm 2 out*......................(50 to 1) 3
23[2] BIREQUEST 5-10-11 D J Moffatt, *in tch, beh and 3rd pressed four out, hdd nxt, sn wknd*.......(9 to 2 op 5 to 1) 4
1006[7] YOUNG BENSON 4-11-0 (3*) R Massey, *prmnt, led 3 out, hdd appr nxt, sn wknd*..........(33 to 1) 5
THE FENCE SHRINKER 5-10-11 (3*) D Walsh, *cl up, effrt 4 out, ev ch nxt, wkng whn mstk next*...............(50 to 1) 6
BLUE LUGANA 4-10-8 D Bentley, *al beh, rdn 4th, nvr dngrs.*
.....................(50 to 1 op 33 to 1) 7
1012 LITTLE EMBERS (bl) 4-10-0 B Fenton, *midfield, drvn 4 out, sn wknd*.......................(66 to 1 op 50 to 1) 8
IRISH PERRY 9-11-7 C Llewellyn, *beh, lost tch 5th, tld off.*
.......................(50 to 1 op 33 to 1) 9
HAIDO'HART 4-10-8 M A Fitzgerald, *midfield, struggling 5th, sn lost tch, tld off whn pld up bef 2 out.*
.......................(20 to 1 tchd 25 to 1) pu
874 BOXIT AGAIN 6-10-5 W Marston, *led to appr 4th, wknd quickly, tld off.*
.........(40 to 1 op 33 to 1 tchd 50 to 1) pu
671 TAILORMADE FUTURE 4-10-5 Gary Lyons, *beh, reminders aftr 3rd, jmpd badly rght nxt, tld off whn pld up bef 5th.*
.........................(66 to 1 op 50 to 1) pu
Dist: 1¼l, 21l, 12l, 4l, 20l, 15l, 6l, 6l. 4m 21.40s. a 31.40s (12 Ran).
(Martin Pipe Racing Club), M C Pipe

1137 Corbett Bookmakers Handicap Chase Class D (0-125 5-y-o and up) £4,667 2½m 110yds..........(1:40)

MAJOR BELL [123] 8-12-0 B Harding, *trkd ldr, mstk 8th (water), drvn to ld appr 2 out, styd on wl.*
.......................(9 to 2 op 4 to 1 tchd 5 to 1) 1

771³ FLAPJACK LAD [95] 7-9-12¹ (3*) D Walsh, led, mstk 3rd, mistake whn pressed 3 out, hdd appr nxt, kpt on same pace.
.................................(7 to 1 tchd 8 to 1) 2
RUSTIC AIR [105] 9-10-10 M Dwyer, trkd ldrs, chlgd 11th, rdn and ev ch whn blun 2 out, kpt on one pace.
.................................(12 to 1 op 8 to 1 tchd 14 to 1) 3
SAILOR JIM [110] 9-11-1 C Maude, hld up, hdwy 11th, sn tracking ldrs, rdn bef last, kpt on......(14 to 1 op 12 to 1) 4
TOO PLUSH [103] 7-10-8 L Harvey, hld up in tch, mstk 4th, hdwy 11th, sn pushed alng and wknd...(4 to 1 tchd 9 to 2) 5
974² GARRYLOUGH (Ire) [113] 7-11-4 R Dunwoody, cl up, mstk 11th, sn wknd and eased.
.................................(2 to 1 fav op 7 to 4 tchd 9 to 4) 6
REAL GLEE (Ire) [105] 7-10-10 M A Fitzgerald, hld up in rear, mstk 7th, mistake whn no imprsn 2 out, sn eased.
.................................(16 to 1 op 12 to 1) 7
831* AEDEAN [95] 7-10-0 J R Kavanagh, beh, lost tch tenth, tld off whn pld up bef 2 out.......(8 to 1 op 7 to 1) pu
Dist: 2½l, 1¼l, 2l, 10l, 8l, 20l. 5m 19.80s. a 33.80s (8 Ran).
(Ian T Middlemiss), A C Whillans

1138 Jones Peckover Novices' Chase
Class D (5-y-o and up) £4,032 2m 1f 110yds. (2:10)

AROUND THE GALE (Ire) 5-10-12 R Dunwoody, led to 3rd, rgned ld 6th, drw clr last, easily.
.................................(5 to 4 on op 11 to 10 tchd 11 to 8 on) 1
1054 RAFTERS 7-10-12 R Johnson, midfield, hdwy to go prmnt 6th., ev ch 3 out, chsd wnr nxt, no imprsn.
.................................(25 to 1 op 20 to 1) 2
MONYMOSS (Ire) 7-10-5 (7*) R Wilkinson, handily plcd, out-pcd 8th, styd on ag'n frm 2 out......(33 to 1 op 25 to 1) 3
614 NAIYSARI (Ire) 8-10-12 W Marston, hld up, outpcd whn mstk 8th, kpt on frm 2 out...........(10 to 1 tchd 11 to 1) 4
954* SUBLIME FELLOW (Ire) 6-11-5 M A Fitzgerald, prmnt, ev ch 3 out, rdn nxt, sn wknd...... (2 to 1 op 7 to 4 tchd 9 to 4) 5
HEATHYARDS BOY 6-10-9 (3*) D Walsh, cl up, pckd 3rd, lost pl 6th, pecked 7th, sn beh............(66 to 1 op 50 to 1) 6
670⁴ BETABETCORBETT (bl) 5-10-12 T J Murphy, cl up, led 3rd, hdd and hit 6th, wknd 8th, no ch whn mstk 3 out.
.................................(100 to 1 op 50 to 1) 7
1007⁶ HUGH DANIELS 8-10-12 V Slattery, al beh, tld off whn pld up bef 8th.................................(200 to 1 op 100 to 1) pu
CAPTAIN STOCKFORD 9-10-12 T Eley, midfield, mstk 5th (water), lost tch 7th, tld off whn pld up bef 3 out.
.................................(100 to 1 op 50 to 1) pu
JYMJAM JOHNNY (Ire) 5-10-12 M Dwyer, hld up, effrt to chase ldrs 4 out, pld up aftr nxt, lme.
.................................(12 to 1 op 10 to 1 tchd 14 to 1) pu
TWICE SHY (Ire) 5-10-12 B Powell, beh, mstk 4th, tld off whn pld up bef 7th.................(200 to 1 op 100 to 1) pu
Dist: 12l, 1¼l, 10l, 8l, 15l, 1¼l. 4m 26.90s. a 24.90s (11 Ran).
SR: 29/17/15/5/4/-/

1139 Neilson Cobbold Conditional Jockeys' Handicap Hurdle Class E
(0-110 4-y-o and up) £2,927 2½m (2:45)

CASSIO'S BOY [80] 5-10-6 D J Kavanagh, hld up, hdwy 3 out, sn drvn, ran on strly to ld cl hme.
.................................(10 to 1 op 8 to 1 tchd 11 to 1) 1
1051³ ZINGIBAR [79] 4-10-0 (5*) J Power, dsptd ld, definite lead 4 out, hdd and no extr cl hme.............(9 to 4 op 6 to 4) 2
876³ BATTY'S ISLAND [76] 7-10-16 (7*) W Greatrex, cl up, effrt 3 out, sn outpcd, no imprsn whn swrvd to avoid faller last.
.................................(25 to 1 op 16 to 1) 3
559⁴ PRIDE OF MAY (Ire) [96] v 5-11-3 (5*) N Horrocks, dsptd ld to 4 out, sn wknd............................(20 to 1 op 16 to 1) 4
973⁶ SAYMORE [85] 10-10-11 R Massey, hld up, hdwy to track ldrs 4 out, wknd 2 out, no ch whn swrvd to avoid faller last.
.................................(33 to 1) 5
912³ MARSDEN ROCK [86] 9-10-9 (3*) S Haworth, hld up, strug-gling 4 out, tld off.....................(8 to 1 op 7 to 1) 6
BRANCHER [91] 5-11-3 E Callaghan, midfield, hdwy 4 out, ev ch whn mstk 2 out, cl second and pres when f last.
.................................f
659² FIRST CRACK [90] 11-11-2 L Aspell, trkd ldrs, drvn appr 3 out, sn wknd, beh whn pld up bef nxt.
.................................(6 to 1 op 5 to 1 tchd 13 to 2) pu
903* HULLO MARY DOLL [82] 7-10-8 Chris Webb, hld up, hdwy 6th, sn cl up, wknd aftr 3 out, tld off whn pld up bef last.
.................................(9 to 2 op 4 to 1 tchd 5 to 1) pu
801⁴ RAMSDENS (Ire) [101] 4-11-13 D Walsh, in tch, sn drvn alng, hdwy to go prmnt 6th, wknd nxt, tld off whn pld up bef 3 out.
.................................(9 to 4 fav op 11 to 4) pu
Dist: Hd, 16l, 5l, 1½l, dist. 5m 6.80s. a 36.80s (10 Ran).
(Lyonshall Racing), R J Eckley

1140 Tarporley Hunt Handicap Chase
Class F (0-100 5-y-o and up) £3,582 3m 110yds. (3:20)

BASILICUS (Fr) [100] 7-11-7 (7*) R Wilkinson, in tch, cl up 11th, led 3 out, sn hrd pressed, lft clr last.
.................................(20 to 1 op 25 to 1) 1

BALLY CLOVER [100] 9-12-0 A P McCoy, prmnt, mstks tenth and 11th (water), led 14th till 3 out, sn drvn and btn, lft poor second last......................(11 to 2 op 5 to 1 tchd 6 to 1) 2
LEINTHALL PRINCESS [80] 10-10-8 B Fenton, hld up, reminders tenth, styd on 4 out, nvr nrr.
.................................(25 to 1 op 16 to 1) 3
ARDCRONEY CHIEF [90] 10-11-4 M A Fitzgerald, handily plcd, drvn and outpcd frm 3 out.
.................................(11 to 1 op 6 to 1 tchd 12 to 1) 4
918⁴ AUVILLAR (USA) [86] 9 8-11-0 C Llewellyn, rear thrght, struggling 11th, tld off..........(40 to 1 op 20 to 1) 5
986⁵ OPAL'S TENSPOT [72] 9-10-0 R Johnson, in tch, reminders 13th, wknd quickly, tld off.
.................................(25 to 1 op 20 to 1 tchd 33 to 1) 6
809² ANDROS PRINCE [94] 11-11-8 J Ryan, nvr gng wl and al beh, tld off..............(5 to 1 op 7 to 2 tchd 11 to 2) 7
ABSOLATUM [72] 9-10-0 W Marston, sn und pres and tld off.
.................................(50 to 1 op 33 to 1) 8
1055² IVY HOUSE (Ire) [88] 8-11-2 M Dwyer, in tch, cl up 13th, chalg 2 out, rdn and upsides whn blun badly and uns rdr last.
.................................(6 to 4 fav tchd 2 to 1) ur
372⁹ BEAUFAN [85] 9-10-13 Gary Lyons, cl up, blun 9th, sn niggled alng and beh, tld off whn pld up aftr 12th.
.................................(50 to 1 op 20 to 1) pu
809 FAIRY PARK [96] 11-11-10 Jacqui Oliver, rear, lost tch 12th, blun 4 out, not reco'r, tld off whn pld up bef nxt.
.................................(33 to 1 op 14 to 1) pu
986³ BRINDLEY HOUSE [82] 9-10-10 D Morris, midfield, drvn 13th, sn beh, tld off whn pld up bef 2 out... (14 to 1 op 10 to 1) pu
FLIMSY TRUTH [83] 10-10-11 Mr J Jukes, led to 14th, sn drvn, wkng whn blun 3 out, tld off whn pld up bef nxt.
.................................(14 to 1 op 20 to 1) pu
BENDOR MARK [90] 7-11-4 J F Titley, hld up, hdwy to go prmnt tenth, wknd 13th, tld off whn pld up bef 3 out.
.................................(10 to 1 op 12 to 1 tchd 16 to 1) pu
Dist: 13l, ¾l, 1½l, dist, 9l, ½l, dist. 6m 28.80s. a 43.80s (14 Ran).
(Mrs S Smith), Mrs S J Smith

1141 Stanley Leisure Handicap Hurdle
Class E (0-110 4-y-o and up) £3,176 2m 1f. (3:55)

CENTAUR EXPRESS [106] 4-11-10 T Eley, prmnt, led appr second, clr aftr 3 out, unchlgd.
.................................(100 to 30 fav op 7 to 2 tchd 4 to 1 and 3 to 1) 1
TANSEEQ [88] 5-10-6 B Harding, hld up, styd on und pres frm 3 out, chsd wnr appr last, no imprsn.
.................................(7 to 2 op 7 to 2 tchd 6 to 1) 2
871³ COOLEY'S VALVE (Ire) [101] 8-11-0 (5*) Sophie Mitchell, hld up, kpt on stdly frm 3 out, nvr nrr.
.................................(7 to 1 op 9 to 2 tchd 8 to 1) 3
UNITED FRONT [98] 4-11-2 D Bridgwater, led till appr second, remained cl up, chsd wnr 3 out till approaching last, wknd......................(8 to 1 tchd 9 to 1) 4
912 AIDE MEMOIRE (Ire) [82] 7-10-0 K Johnson, midfield, strug-gling 4 out, sn btn.................(20 to 1 tchd 33 to 1) 5
DAHLIA'S BEST (USA) [100] 6-11-4 Gary Lyons, midfield, chsd ldrs 4th, fdd nxt..............(25 to 1 op 16 to 1) 6
PRIDEWOOD PICKER [90] 9-10-8 A P McCoy, hld up, hdwy to chase ldrs 3 out, wknd bef nxt........(4 to 1 op 3 to 1) 7
784³ HACKETTS CROSS (Ire) [95] 8-10-13 R Johnson, rear, rdn 4 out, sn no imprsn... (13 to 2 op 6 to 1 tchd 7 to 1) 8
MUIZENBERG [83] 9-10-11 A Thornton, chsd ldrs, wknd 4 out, wl beh whn pld up bef 2 out..................(33 to 1) pu
248 SHIFTING MOON [89] (bl) 4-10-7 S Wynne, sn prmnt, cl second whn blun 4 out, wknd quickly, wl beh whn pld up bef 2 out......................(14 to 1 op 10 to 1 tchd 16 to 1) pu
Dist: 7l, 9l, ½l, 6l, 6l, 7l, 5l. 4m 17.80s. a 27.80s (10 Ran).
SR: 5/-/-/-/-/-/
(Centaur Racing), A Streeter

1142 Bangor Intermediate Open National Hunt Flat Class H (4,5,6-y-o) £1,721
2m 1f. (4:30)

JOHNNY-K (Ire) 5-11-8 (3*) R Massey, hld up, steady hdwy hfwy, trkd ldrs 4 fs out, led o'r 2 out, sn clr, easily.
.................................(13 to 8 fav op 9 to 4) 1
WELSH SILK 4-10-13 (5*) Sophie Mitchell, midfield, improved hfwy, led o'r 3 fs out, hdd over 2 out, one pace.
.................................(12 to 1 op 6 to 1 tchd 14 to 1) 2
ZANDER 4-10-11 (7*) L Suthern, midfield, hdwy 6 fs out, ev ch on bit 3 out, sn drvn, not quicken......(6 to 1 tchd 8 to 1) 3
CALLINDOE (Ire) 6-10-13 B Fenton, hld up in rear, styd on und pres fnl 4 fs, nvr nrr.....................(50 to 1) 4
THE CROPPY BOY 4-11-4 D Bridgwater, hld up, hdwy on outsd 6 fs out, drvn 3 out, not rch ldrs...(20 to 1 op 8 to 1) 5
MY SHENANDOAH (Ire) 5-11-4 Jacqui Oliver, keen hold, hndy, led hfwy till o'r 3 fs out, sn wknd.
.................................(10 to 1 op 20 to 1 tchd 25 to 1) 6
SOUNDPOST 4-11-4 D J Moffatt, midfield, niggled along hfwy, no hdwy.......................(12 to 1 tchd 16 to 1) 7
942⁵ RED TEL (Ire) 4-11-11 A P McCoy, hld up, hdwy und pres 7 fs out, not trble ldrs.......(4 to 1 op 9 to 4 tchd 10 to 1) 8
LARKSHILL (Ire) 5-11-4 M Dwyer, midfield, drvn and hdwy o'r 4 fs out, fdd und 2 out......(9 to 2 op 4 to 1 tchd 5 to 1) 9
HIGH HANDED (Ire) 5-11-4 A Thornton, trkd ldrs, pushed alng hfwy, wknd 4 fs out....................(33 to 1) 10

JEMARO (Ire) 5-11-4 T Jenks, *cl up, effrt o'r 4 fs out, wknd over 3 out*.......................(50 to 1 op 33 to 1) 11
THE SECRET GREY 5-11-1 (3*) D Walsh, *chsd ldrs, und pres o'r 4 fs out, sn wknd*.............................(50 to 1) 12
671 POLLIFUMAS 6-10-6 (7*) R Wilkinson, *al beh, struggling fnl 5 fs*...(50 to 1) 13
GLENDRONACH 4-10-13 Gary Lyons, *al rear, eased whn btn fnl 4 fs*..(50 to 1) 14
1012 BARNETTS BOY 4-11-4 T J Murphy, *led to hfwy, sn drvn and wknd, tld off*.......................(50 to 1 op 33 to 1) 15
SCHOLAR GREEN 4-11-4 R Johnson, *cl up, lost pl hfwy, sn beh, tld off*...(33 to 1) 16
KYLE DAVID (Ire) 4-11-4 S Wynne, *hld up, niggled alng aftr 4 fs, tld off*...............(25 to 1 op 20 to 1 tchd 33 to 1) 17
880 BARLOT 4-10-13 T Eley, *in tch, pushed alng hfwy, sn beh, tld off*...........................(50 to 1 op 33 to 1) 18
Dist: 9l, 4l, 1¾l, 3½l, 4l, 13l, ¾l, ½l, 23l, 10l. 4m 14.30s. (18 Ran).
(Norwood Partners), D Nicholson

CLONMEL (IRE) (yielding)
Friday November 1st

1143 Amsterdam Maiden Hurdle (4-y-o) £2,568 2m...................(1:15)

1077 DUBLIN TREASURE (Ire) 11-2 F Woods,.......(3 to 1 fav) 1
1077^3 CHARLIE-O (Ire) 10-11 (5*) G Cotter,.............(10 to 1) 2
731^8 VINTNERS VENTURE (Ire) 10-11 (5*) M J Holbrook, (20 to 1) 3
BOSS DOYLE (Ire) 11-2 C O'Dwyer,.............(12 to 1) 4
1077^4 MONDEO ROSE (Ire) 10-11 C F Swan,.............(7 to 1) 5
1015^4 SHAWAHIN (bl) 11-7 K F O'Brien,.................(4 to 1) 6
984^8 IODER WAN (Ire) 11-2 M P Hourigan,..............(8 to 1) 7
1015^8 RIVER RUMPUS (Ire) 10-9 (7*) Mr J T McNamara, (20 to 1) 8
908^3 FOREST PRINCESS (Ire) 10-11 A Powell,..........(6 to 1) 9
1040 HARRY WELSH (Ire) (bl) 11-7 T Horgan,..........(16 to 1) 10
984^5 ANTICS (Ire) 10-9 (7*) Mrs C Harrison,.............(8 to 1) 11
1015 ZIGGY THE GREAT (Ire) 11-2 P A Roche,.........(50 to 1) 12
898 OLD MOTHER HUBBARD (Ire) 10-11 M Duffy,.... (20 to 1) 13
776^6 DANTE'S MOON (Ire) 10-11 P McWilliams,.......(14 to 1) 14
984 HILL TOP LAD (Ire) 11-2 W Slattery,.............(33 to 1) 15
898 ROBAZALA (Ire) 10-4 (7*) S FitzGerald,...........(33 to 1) 16
CORDAL DREAM (Ire) 10-11 J P Broderick,......(33 to 1) 17
30^8 MEDIA MISS (Ire) 10-11 J K Kinane,...............(14 to 1) f
POISON IVY (Ire) 10-4 (7*) J A Robinson,..........(20 to 1) ur
1015 OXFORD LUNCH (USA) 11-2 T P Treacy,..........(8 to 1) bd
Dist: 2l, 5½l, 6l, nk. 4m 8.40s. (20 Ran).
(George Moore), Michael Flynn

1144 London Gatwick Handicap Hurdle (0-109 4-y-o and up) £2,568 3m ....(1:45)

1074^2 FORT DEELY (Ire) [-] 5-9-9 J Jones,...........(2 to 1 fav) 1
1060^2 VALLEY OF KINGS (Ire) [-] 6-9-7 T Horgan,.......(10 to 1) 2
1074^4 CASEY JANE (Ire) [-] 5-10-10 (3*) D J Casey,......(13 to 2) 3
977^2 MISS BERTAINE (Ire) [-] 7-10-3 J P Broderick,......(4 to 1) 4
432^3 TEARDROP (Ire) [-] 4-10-6 C F Swan,............(10 to 1) 5
944^6 DARK SWAN (Ire) [-] 6-11-7 (7*) D Flood,..........(10 to 1) 6
LETTERLEE (Ire) [-] 6-11-6 M Duffy,..............(10 to 1) 7
1003^3 FAIR GO [-] 10-9-4 (7*) Mrs C Harrison,...........(10 to 1) 8
977 HOTSCENT (Ire) [-] 5-9-0 (7*) A O'Shea,...........(25 to 1) 9
ECLIPTIC MOON (Ire) [-] 6-9-2 (5*) G Cotter,......(12 to 1) 10
ROCK THE LORD (Ire) [-] 8-10-3 T J O'Sullivan,....(14 to 1) 11
951^4 BUCKLEY BAY (Ire) [-] 5-9-8 (3*) B Bowens,......(14 to 1) 12
1096 MEGABOY (Ire) [-] 5-10-2 (5*) J Butler,............(16 to 1) 13
Dist: 4½l, 2l, 2½l, 2½l. 6m 10.50s. (13 Ran).
(Peter Dundon), Eric McNamara

1145 London Stansted Maiden Hurdle (5-y-o) £2,568 2m.............. (2:15)

977^4 MULLOVER 11-6 T J Mitchell,................(7 to 4 fav) 1
1018^4 NOBLE SHOON (Ire) 12-0 K F O'Brien,.............(4 to 1) 2
983^5 JANICE PRICE (Ire) 11-1 C F Swan,................(7 to 1) 3
979^4 JOLLY JOHN (Ire) 11-6 C O'Dwyer,................(4 to 1) 4
928 DEERE REPH (Ire) 10-10 (5*) G Cotter,...........(10 to 1) 5
745^6 CASTLE BAILEY (Ire) 11-6 T J O'Sullivan,.........(20 to 1) 6
910 CNOCADRUM VI (Ire) 11-6 F Woods,............(33 to 1) 7
1090 OUR DUCHESS (Ire) 11-1 M Duffy,..............(20 to 1) 8
946^7 ASTRID (Ire) 11-1 J P Broderick,..................(14 to 1) 9
ATLANTA FLAME (Ire) 11-1 W Slattery,...........(33 to 1) 10
TREMBLE VALLEY (Ire) 11-1 Mr H F Cleary,......(25 to 1) 11
CLOWATER BUCK (Ire) 11-1 S H O'Donovan,.....(14 to 1) 12
1090 CHEEKY GENIUS (Ire) 10-13 (7*) A O'Shea,.......(33 to 1) 13
MASTER VALENTINE (Ire) 10-13 (7*) J O'Shaughnessy, ...(33 to 1) 14
Dist: 7l, 6l, 3l, 12l. 4m 14.20s. (14 Ran).
(Adam Gurney), Mrs John Harrington

1146 London Heathrow Captain Christy Beginners Chase (5-y-o and up) £2,568 2½m.........................(2:45)

DANOLI (Ire) 8-11-12 Mr P Fenton,............(5 to 4 on) 1
982 CONSHARON (Ire) 8-11-7 C F Swan,.............(5 to 2) 2
1080^6 DUN BELLE (Ire) 7-11-2 T J Mitchell,.............(16 to 1) 3
ANOTHER DEADLY 9-11-12 J P Broderick,.......(16 to 1) 4
JORIDI LE FORIGE (Ire) 5-10-12 (3*) Mr K Whelan, (33 to 1) 5
SIR-EILE (Ire) 8-11-0 (7*) A O'Shea,.............(33 to 1) 6
DRAMATIC VENTURE (Ire) 7-11-9 (3*) D J Casey,...(8 to 1) 7
PRATE BOX (Ire) 6-11-12 J K Kinane,............(14 to 1) 8
851^6 DOONEGA (Ire) 8-11-12 T Horgan,..............(16 to 1) 9
909^6 ARISTODEMUS 7-11-7 F Woods,...............(12 to 1) 10
576^6 GARABAGH (Ire) 7-11-12 K F O'Brien,...........(16 to 1) 11
627^5 NO TAG (Ire) 8-11-12 C O'Dwyer,................(10 to 1) f
Dist: 6l, 14l, 3½l, 4l. 5m 8.80s. (12 Ran).
(D J O'Neill), Thomas Foley

1147 Belfast City I.N.H. Flat Race (5-y-o and up) £2,568 2m...........(4:15)

928^6 DASHING DOLLAR (Ire) 5-11-11 (3*) Mr B M Cash, ...(2 to 1 fav) 1
945^3 PREMIER WALK 7-11-7 (7*) Mr S P Hennessy,....(10 to 1) 2
RANDOM RING (Ire) 5-11-7 (7*) Mr J T McNamara, (7 to 1) 3
910^3 PHARDANA (Ire) 5-11-7 (7*) Mr J P McNamara,.... (4 to 1) 4
KILBRICKEN GOLD (Ire) 5-11-6 (3*) Mr P M Kelly, (20 to 1) 5
1005^9 GODSROCK VI (Ire) 7-11-7 (7*) Miss A Foley,..... (14 to 1) 6
MALABRACKA (Ire) 5-11-2 (7*) Mr N D Fehily,.....(14 to 1) 7
LISKILNEWABBEY (Ire) 5-11-9 Mr P Fenton,.......(7 to 1) 8
TARIYMA (Ire) 5-11-2 (7*) Mr B Hassett,.............(8 to 1) 9
HOLLY'S PRIDE (Ire) 6-11-9 (5*) Mr W M O'Sullivan, (13 to 2) 10
FILEO (Ire) 5-11-2 (7*) Mr B Walsh,...............(12 to 1) 11
MAJESTIC LORD (Ire) 6-11-7 (7*) Mr D J Duggan, (16 to 1) 12
1005 SISTER CAMILLUS (Ire) 5-11-2 (7*) Mr A C Coyle, (16 to 1) 13
Dist: 3½l, 10l, ¾l, 2l. 4m 9.70s. (13 Ran).
(Martyn J McEnery), A P O'Brien

WETHERBY (good)
Friday November 1st
Going Correction: PLUS 0.20 sec. per fur.

1148 Linton Four Year Old Handicap Hurdle Class B £4,825 2m.......(1:30)

1082^2 EL DON [101] 9-11 (3*) K Gaule, *trkd ldrs, hdwy on inner 3 out, led appr last, rdn and ran on flt.* ....(11 to 4 op 7 to 2 tchd 4 to 1) 1
HIGHBANK [103] 9-13 (3*) G Lee, *trkd ldrs, hdwy 3 out, led nxt, rdn and hdd appr last, kpt on flt.* ....(9 to 1 op 7 to 1 tchd 10 to 1) 2
ELPIDOS [119] 11-4 R Garritty, *hld up, hdwy appr 3 out, ev ch whn hit nxt, sn rdn and kpt on*........(4 to 1 tchd 7 to 2) 3
798^2 MIM-LOU-AND [113] 10-12 P Niven, *trkd ldrs, effrt and ev ch 3 out, sn rdn and one pace betw last 2.* ....(5 to 2 fav op 9 to 4) 4
1030^4 ALLTIME DANCER (Ire) [125] 11-10 J Osborne, *cl up, led aftr 1st, rdn alng and hdd appr 3 out, wknd nxt.* ....(10 to 1 op 8 to 1) 5
HOLDERS HILL (Ire) [114] 10-13 A Maguire, *hld up in rear, hdwy appr 3 out, sn ev ch, rdn 2 out and soon one pace.* ....(16 to 1 op 12 to 1) 6
DAWN MISSION [106] 10-5 L Wyer, *led and blun 1st, cl up till led appr 3 out, hdd nxt and sn btn.* ....(10 to 1 op 8 to 1 tchd 12 to 1) 7
Dist: ¾l, ¾l, 1¼l, 7l, 5l, 6l. 3m 51.30s. a 10.30s (7 Ran).
SR: 1/2/17/9/14/-/-/ (Don Morris), M J Ryan

1149 Wetherby Novices' Chase Class D (5-y-o and up) £3,809 2m..... (2:00)

GOLDEN HELLO 5-11-0 L Wyer, *trkd ldg pair, hdwy 5th, led appr 4 out, rdn alng and blun 2 out, strly pressed whn lft clr last*..........(13 to 8 on op 9 to 4 on tchd 6 to 4 on) 1
1072^3 CHORUS LINE (Ire) 7-10-9 R Supple, *led, rdn alng and hdd 5 out, one pace aftr*.........................(4 to 1 op 9 to 2) 2
861^3 KILTULLA (Ire) 6-11-0 Richard Guest, *chsd ldr, led 5 out, hdd appr nxt and sn rdn, one pace in 3rd whn blun 3 out and no ch aftr*.......................................(7 to 1 op 6 to 1) 3
FLAT TOP 5-11-0 A Maguire, *hld up, hdwy appr 4 out, chlgd 2 out and ev ch whn f last*..................(7 to 1 op 6 to 1) f
Dist: 16l, 21l. 4m 0.30s. a 13.30s (Flag start) (4 Ran).
(G E Shouler), T D Easterby

1150 Green Hammerton Handicap Hurdle Class C (0-135 4-y-o and up) £2,792 2½m 110yds................. (2:35)

BURNT IMP (USA) [115] 6-11-9 J Callaghan, *cl up, led 6th, rdn 3 out, hit nxt, hld on gmely nr finish.* (5 to 1 op 7 to 2) 1
TARA RAMBLER (Ire) [116] 7-11-10 N Bentley, *trkd ldrs, hdwy to chal 3 out, rdn betw last 2, kpt on nr finish, jst hld.* ....(13 to 2 op 9 to 2) 2
973^4 DALLY BOY [106] 4-11-0 L Wyer, *led, hdd 6th, cl up till rdn and outpcd aftr 3 out, kpt on appr last*....(4 to 1 op 5 to 2) 3
MASTER HYDE (USA) [113] 7-11-2 (5*) R McGrath, *hld up, hdwy appr 3 out, sn rdn and wkng whn hit last 2.* ....(3 to 1 op 7 to 2 tchd 4 to 1) 4
ADMIRALS SEAT [98] 8-10-6 A Maguire, *trkd ldrs, reminders aftr 4 out, rdn nxt and btn whn pld up bef 2 out.* ....(15 to 8 fav op 5 to 2 tchd 7 to 4) pu
Dist: Hd, 2l, 10l. 4m 59.70s. a 17.70s (5 Ran).

(N B Mason (Farms) Ltd), G M Moore

1151 Harry Wharton Memorial Handicap Chase Class C (0-135 5-y-o and up) £4,744 2m..................(3:10)

875³ REGAL ROMPER (Ire) [108] 8-10-2 Richard Guest, jmpd wl, made all, rdn 2 out and ran on strly......(6 to 1 op 7 to 2) 1
ALJADEER (USA) [110] (bl) 7-10-4 A Maguire, hld up, hit second and 5th, hdwy appr 4 out, effrt and hng rght approaching lft, drvn and styd on wl r-in.........(3 to 1 op 2 to 1) 2
863² POLITICAL TOWER [122] 9-11-2 A Dobbin, cl up, blun second, hit 7th, chlgd 4 out and ev ch till drvn and not quicken appr last............(3 to 1 op 11 to 8 tchd 7 to 4) 3
KONVEKTA KING (Ire) [130] 8-11-10 J Osborne, took keen hold, hld up, hdwy appr 4 out, sn rdn and btn, eased 3 out.
...................................(3 to 1 tchd 5 to 2) 4
Dist: ½l, 2½l, 30l. 3m 55.00s. a 8.00s (4 Ran).
SR: 26/27/36/14/ (Mrs S Smith), Mrs S J Smith

1152 Tockwith Novices' Chase Class C (5-y-o and up) £4,523 3m 1f......(3:45)

878* THE LAST FLING (Ire) 6-11-5 Richard Guest, hld up, smooth hdwy appr 4 out, hit nxt, led 2 out and quickened clr last.
...................(6 to 5 on op Evens tchd 5 to 4 on) 1
CHOPWELL CURTAINS 6-11-0 L Wyer, prmnt, chsd ldr frm 5th, hit 13th, chlgd and ev ch 3 out, sn rdn and one pace last.
...................................(11 to 4 op 2 to 1) 2
881* YOUNG DUBLINER (Ire) 7-11-5 A Maguire, cl up, led 4th till rdn and hdd 3 out, hit nxt and no ch aftr. (3 to 1 op 7 to 2) 3
931² COMMANDEER 6-11-0 A S Smith, not fluent, led to 4th, lost pl 7th and tld off frm hfwy.......(25 to 1 op 16 to 1) 4
Dist: 3l, 14l, dist. 6m 20.40s. a 12.40s (4 Ran).
SR: 17/9/-/-/ (Michael Jackson Bloodstock Ltd), Mrs S J Smith

1153 Hornshaw Conditional Jockeys' Novices' Handicap Hurdle Class F (0-105 5-y-o and up) £2,092 3m 1f ....(4:20)

800 QUEEN'S AWARD (Ire) [66] 7-9-9 (5*) M Griffiths, hld up, steady hdwy hfwy, led aftr 4 out, clr 2 out, ran on strly.
...................(20 to 1 op 16 to 1 tchd 25 to 1) 1
955³ MISTER BLAKE [84] 5-11-4 G Hogan, hld up in rear, pushed alng and hdwy appr 3 out, kpt on approaching last, no ch wnr....................(9 to 1 op 8 to 1 tchd 10 to 1) 2
935* PEBBLE BEACH (Ire) [87] 6-11-7 Michael Brennan, chsd ldr, rdn alng bef 3 out, drvn nxt and one pace.......(2 to 1 jt-fav tchd 9 to 4) 3
935² SMART APPROACH (Ire) [92] 6-11-5 (7*) T J Comerford, trkd ldrs, pushed alng and lost pl bef 5 out, beh whn blun 2 out.
...................(2 to 1 jt-fav tchd 9 to 4) 4
1085² JOLIS ABSENT [87] (bb) 6-11-7 (7ex) K Gaule, led, rdn alng and hdd aftr 4 out, wknd nxt...........(9 to 4 op 5 to 2) 5
931⁴ QUIXALL CROSSETT [66] (bl) 11-9-7 (7*) Tristan Davidson, lost pl 4th and sn beh, tld off frm hfwy...........(50 to 1) 6
Dist: 15l, 2l, 12l, 19l, dist. 6m 8.50s. a 22.50s (6 Ran).
(R H Buckler), R H Buckler

ASCOT (good to firm)
Saturday November 2nd
Going Correction: PLUS 0.35 sec. per fur. (races 1,2,5,7), NIL (3,4,6)

1154 Binfield Juvenile Novices' Hurdle Class C (3-y-o) £4,175 2m 110yds ....(12:50)

965³ SQUIRE'S OCCASION (Can) 11-0 A P McCoy, trkd ldr, led aftr 4 out, not fluent nxt, sn clr....(7 to 2 on op 4 to 1 on) 1
893³ AMBER RING 10-9 J R Kavanagh, led, mstks 3rd and 5th, hdd aftr 4 out, no extr.............(11 to 4 op 3 to 1) 2
Won by 12l. 4m 12.30s. a 26.30s (2 Ran).
SR: -/-/ (Chelgate Public Relations Ltd), R Akehurst

1155 United House Development Novices' Hurdle Class C (4-y-o and up) £3,468 2m 110yds..................(1:20)

CIPRIANI QUEEN (Ire) 6-10-9 P Hide, chsd ldr, outpcd 3 out, rallied nxt, led appr last, all out.
...................................(3 to 1 op 2 to 1 tchd 7 to 4) 1
RIDING CROP (Ire) 6-11-0 M A Fitzgerald, cl up, outpcd aftr 3 out, rallied nxt, styd on and pres. (Evens fav tchd 13 to 8) 2
SAHEL (Ire) 8-11-0 S Curran, led, keen early, quickened clr 3 out, wknd and hdd appr last, no extr und pres.
...................................(9 to 2 op 8 to 1) 3
867 ERNEST WILLIAM (Ire) 4-10-11 (3*) K Gaule, hld up in cl tch, rdn alng 3 out, sn btn......(12 to 1 op 7 to 1 tchd 14 to 1) 4
AL HELAL 4-11-0 A P McCoy, hld up in tch, mstk 3rd, jmpd slwly nxt, rdn 4 out, sn outpcd, tld off.
...................................(15 to 2 op 5 to 1 tchd 8 to 1) 5
LIZIUM 4-10-9 S Fox, mstk 1st, blun badly and uns rdr nxt.
...................................(33 to 1 tchd 40 to 1 and 50 to 1) ur

Dist: ¾l, 5l, 24l, 21l. 4m 3.00s. a 17.00s (6 Ran).
(Tor Royal Racing Club), J T Gifford

1156 Bagshot Handicap Chase Class B (5-y-o and up) £8,013 3m 110yds (1:55)

1056⁴ GO BALLISTIC [121] 7-10-4¹ M A Fitzgerald, hld up, cld 14th, trkd ldr frm nxt, led on bit appr last, not extended.
...................................(2 to 1 op 5 to 3) 1
821² STRAIGHT TALK [133] 9-11-2 A P McCoy, led to 12th, led ag'n 14th, rdn alng 4 out, hdd appr last, no extr.
...................................(6 to 4 fav op 5 to 4) 2
ARTHUR'S MINSTREL [128] 9-10-11 R Johnson, trkd ldrs, blun 13th, rdn alng appr 5 out, one pace frm 3 out.
...................................3
1029³ COMMERCIAL ARTIST [145] 10-12-0 W Marston, trkd ldr, led 12th to 14th, hit nxt, sn btn, tld off.
...................................(16 to 1 op 10 to 1 tchd 20 to 1) 4
SENOR EL BETRUTTI (Ire) [138] 7-11-7 G Bradley, hld up, blun 3rd, outpcd 14th, sn rallied, wknd 4 out, tld off, better for race.............(11 to 2 op 7 to 2 tchd 6 to 1) 5
Dist: 8l, 5l, 20l, 24l. 6m 8.50s. a 7.50s (5 Ran).
SR: 1/5/ (Mrs B J Lockhart), J G M O'Shea

1157 United House Construction Handicap Chase Class B (5-y-o and up) £16,693 2m..................(2:30)

STORM ALERT [142] 10-11-9 R Johnson, led to second, rstrained to track ldr, led 3 out, hrd rdn appr last, blun badly, all out...................(Evens fav op 11 to 8 tchd 6 to 4) 1
BIG MATT (Ire) [144] 8-11-11 M A Fitzgerald, hld up, rdn alng to chase wnr appr 2 out, ev ch last, styd on und pres.
...................................(2 to 1 op 7 to 4 tchd 9 to 4) 2
1131³ THUMBS UP [130] 10-10-11 B Clifford, led second, hdd 3 out, wknd nxt...........(14 to 1 op 12 to 1 tchd 20 to 1) 3
UNCLE ERNIE [147] 11-12-0 A P McCoy, hld up, effrt 4 out, sn btn, tld off..........(9 to 30 op 5 to 2 tchd 7 to 2) 4
Dist: Nk, 15l, 16l. 3m 51.80s. a 3.80s (4 Ran).
SR: 57/59/30/31/ (Mrs Dawn Perrett), D Nicholson

1158 Valley Gardens Novices' Handicap Hurdle Class D (0-105 4-y-o and up) £3,591 2½m.................(3:05)

CLOD HOPPER (Ire) [67] 6-10-0 M Richards, led 4th, cld alng whn lft clr appr 2 out.......(11 to 2 op 8 to 1 tchd 5 to 1) 1
800² TAP ON TOOTSIE [91] 4-11-10 A P McCoy, led to 4th, mstk, hmpd and lost pl nxt, ev ch four out, lft modest second appr 2 out..............(7 to 4 fav tchd 2 to 1 and 13 to 8) 2
597³ POSITIVO [80] 5-10-13 D Leahy, hld up, lft second 5th, wknd appr 4 out, tld off........(9 to 1 op 10 to 1 tchd 11 to 1) 3
LYPHARD'S FABLE (USA) [74] 5-10-7 R Johnson, tracking ldr whn f 5th...................(12 to 1 op 6 to 1) f
800* EMBLEY BUOY [73] 8-10-6 S Curran, in cl tch whn brght dwn 5th...................(5 to 1 op 7 to 2 tchd 11 to 2) bd
998* ASLAR (Ire) [69] 7-10-2 W McFarland, hld up, not fluent, mstk and drvn 3 out, sn rallied to chase wnr, pld up lme appr 2 out.
...................................(100 to 30 op 5 to 2 tchd 4 to 1) pu
Dist: 21l, 13l. 4m 2.10s. a 21.10s (6 Ran).
(T J Parrott), W R Muir

1159 Stanlake Novices' Chase Class D (5-y-o and up) £4,986 2m 3f 110yds ....(3:40)

1099² STRONG PROMISE (Ire) 5-11-5 (3*,4ex) K Gaule, made all, shaken up aftr 2 out, cmftbly.
...................................(8 to 1 op 7 to 1 on tchd 6 to 1 on) 1
975 MINOR KEY (Ire) 6-11-1 G Bradley, chsd wnr, mstk 8th, effrt appr 2 out, hld whn blun last..........(6 to 1 op 5 to 1) 2
Won by 27l. 5m 7.20s. a 26.20s (2 Ran).
SR: -/-/ (G A Hubbard), G A Hubbard

1160 Copper Horse Handicap Hurdle Class B (4-y-o and up) £4,992 2m 110yds...................(4:10)

SILVER GROOM (Ire) [132] 6-11-4 (5*) S Ryan, hld up, cld frm 4 out, led appr 2 out, eased nr finish.....(5 to 2 op 6 to 4) 1
871⁴ SHOOFK [115] 5-10-6 A P McCoy, led, rdn alng 4 out, hdd appr 2 out, no extr whn hit last.......(4 to 1 tchd 5 to 1) 2
969⁴ BARNA BOY (Ire) [133] 8-11-10 M A Fitzgerald, hld up, cld frm 4 out, outpcd aftr nxt, styd on.
...................................(8 to 1 op 7 to 1 tchd 11 to 1) 3
CHARMING GIRL (USA) [127] 5-11-4 J Osborne, trkd ldr gng wl, ev ch entering strt, shrtlvd effrt and btn quickly appr 2 out.
...................................(Evens fav op 7 to 4) 4
973⁵ STONEY VALLEY [110] 6-9-8 (7*) N T Egan, al beh, tld off aftr 5th...................(14 to 1 op 7 to 1) 5
Dist: 8l, 1¼l, nk, dist. 3m 56.60s. a 10.60s (5 Ran).
SR: 47/22/38/32/-/ (The Silver Darling Partnership), R Akehurst

KELSO (good to firm)
Saturday November 2nd
Going Correction: NIL (races 1,3,5), MINUS 0.20

(2,4,6,7)

1161 Isle Of Skye Blended Scotch Whisky Novices' Handicap Chase Class E (0-100 5-y-o and up) £2,944 3m 1f .... (1:00)

SEEKING GOLD (Ire) [72] 7-10-4 B Storey, *hld up, improved to ld 5 out, lft clr 3 out, unchlgd*.........(7 to 1 op 11 to 2) 1
1035 MR REINER (Ire) [80] 8-10-12 K Jones, *hld up, effrt aftr 5 out, lft second 3 out, no ch wth wnr*..........(7 to 1 op 6 to 1) 2
605⁴ DONOVANS REEF [68] 10-10-0 K Johnson, *cl up, lost pl tenth, rallied bef 3 out, struggling nxt.* (20 to 1 op 12 to 1) 3
959³ WHITE DIAMOND [79] (v) 8-10-11 P Niven, *prmnt, struggling fnl circuit, tld off*..........(4 to 1 op 5 to 1 tchd 6 to 1) 4
1035 ALICHARGER [70] 6-10-2 A Dobbin, *cl up, hit 6th, struggling 14th, sn btn*......................(20 to 1 tchd 16 to 1) 5
959⁴ BRIGHT DESTINY [70] 5-10-0 D Parker, *hndy, struggling tenth, sn btn*..........(25 to 1 op 16 to 1 tchd 33 to 1) 6
MISTER TRICK (Ire) [68] 6-10-0 M Foster, *hld up, improved to chase ldrs whn f 4 out*..............(3 to 1 jt-fav op 2 to 1) f
1035⁶ MOVAC (Ire) [90] 7-11-8 M Moloney, *jmpd rght, led till hdd 5 out, five ls second and rdn whn blun badly and uns rdr 3 out.* ....(3 to 1 jt-fav op 2 to 1 tchd 100 to 30) ur

Dist: 9l, dist, 13l, 14l, 16l. 6m 18.00s. a 21.00s (8 Ran).

(Gilry), J Barclay

1162 Rosalind Birthday 'National Hunt' Novices' Hurdle Class D (4-y-o and up) £2,762 2¾m 110yds...... (1:30)

934² ANTARCTIC WIND (Ire) 6-10-12 R Garritty, *nvr far away, led 6th, drvn out frm last.* ....(2 to 1 on tchd 9 to 4 on and 7 to 4 on) 1
1034⁶ TRAP DANCER 8-10-12 A Dobbin, *nvr far away, drvn 3 out, chsd wnr frm last, no imprsn.* ....(7 to 1 op 8 to 1 tchd 10 to 1) 2
960⁷ I'M THE MAN 5-10-12 K Johnson, *nvr far away, chlgd 6th, rdn 2 out, outpcd frm last*..... (8 to 1 op 7 to 1 tchd 10 to 1) 3
1068⁹ WHIRLWIND ROMANCE (Ire) 5-10-7 S McDougall, *cl up, lost pl 5th, rdn and no imprsn fnl 2.* ....(66 to 1 op 33 to 1 tchd 100 to 1) 4
415² PROFIT AND LOSS 5-10-7 Mr K Whelan, *hld up, improved on outer 6th, reminders 4 out, struggling last 2.* ....(5 to 1 op 7 to 2 tchd 6 to 1) 5
ETHICAL NOTE (Ire) 5-10-12 Richard Guest, *led to 6th, outpcd aftr nxt, sn no dngr.* (20 to 1 op 10 to 1 tchd 25 to 1) 6
1071⁹ BARNSTORMER 10-10-12 D Parker, *chsd ldg grp, struggling aftr 5 out, sn btn*.................... (50 to 1 op 33 to 1) 7
1039⁶ FASTER RON (Ire) 5-10-5 (7*) S Melrose, *hld up, effrt aftr 2 out, no imprsn whn blun two out*...... (66 to 1 op 33 to 1) 8
SELDOM BUT SEVERE (Ire) 6-10-12 K Jones, *beh, struggling fnl circuit, tld off*..................(33 to 1 tchd 50 to 1) 9
934 MILLENNIUM MAN 5-10-12 J Callaghan, *dsptd ld second to nxt, struggling aftr 5 out, sn btn.* ....(33 to 1 op 14 to 1 tchd 12 to 1) 10

Dist: 7l, 2½l, 3l, 6l, 11l, 2½l, 3½l, 16l, 2½l. 5m 23.30s. a 14.30s (10 Ran).

(Gordon Brown), M D Hammond

1163 Newton Investment Management Handicap Chase Class D (0-120 5-y-o and up) £4,006 2m 1f....... (2:00)

BRIAR'S DELIGHT [90] (v) 8-10-10 B Harding, *nvr far away, led aftr last, drvn out*..................(7 to 4 op 3 to 1) 1
WEAVER GEORGE (Ire) [100] 6-11-6 M Moloney, *led till aftr 6th, led ag'n 8th till after last, one pace.* ....(4 to 1 op 7 to 2 tchd 9 to 2) 2
875* PRINCE SKYBURD [93] 5-10-8 (5*) E Callaghan, *settled in last pl, mstk 3 out, effrt aftr nxt, no imprsn.* .... (6 to 4 fav op 5 to 4 on tchd 13 to 8) 3
863⁴ FLASH OF REALM (Fr) [97] (v) 10-11-3 B Storey, *cl up, led aftr 6th, hdd 8th, outpcd frm last*.........(8 to 1 tchd 10 to 1) 4

Dist: 3l, 4l, 6l. 4m 13.10s. a 8.10s (4 Ran).
SR: 1/8/-/-/

(A Clark), R Allan

1164 Harrow Hotel Dalkeith Novices' Selling Hurdle Class G (4,5,6-y-o) £2,316 2m 110yds.................. (2:30)

1070 STYLISH INTERVAL 4-10-12 A Dobbin, *nvr far away, led bef 3 out, hrd drvn frm last, jst hld on*.......(4 to 1 op 3 to 1) 1
960⁴ FLYAWAY BLUES 4-10-12 P Niven, *hld up in tch, effrt aftr 2 out, kpt on frm last, jst held.* ....(5 to 4 on tchd Evens and 11 to 10) 2
661⁶ KASHANA (Ire) (v) 4-10-7 M Moloney, *chsd ldg grp, reminders 3rd, kpt on frm last, no imprsn.* ....(11 to 1 op 7 to 1) 3
1044⁵ LITTLE REDWING (bl) 4-10-7 R Garritty, *led till hdd aftr 5th, blun 2 out, sn btn*.....(13 to 2 op 8 to 1 tchd 6 to 1) 4
1068 SECONDS AWAY 5-10-9 (3*) G Lee, *in tch, struggling aftr 3 out, fdd*..............(33 to 1 op 25 to 1 tchd 50 to 1) 5
MOOFAJI 5-10-12 J Callaghan, *al beh, nvr on terms.* ....(14 to 1 op 10 to 1 tchd 16 to 1) 6
BARIK (Ire) 6-10-12 B Storey, *hld up, improved to chase wnr bef 2 out, hit two out, sn outpcd*...... (33 to 1 op 20 to 1) 7
MARY'S CASE (Ire) 6-10-12 T Reed, *not fluent in rear, al beh.* ....(11 to 1 op 10 to 1 tchd 12 to 1) 8
958⁵ WALK IN THE WILD 4-10-7 S McDougall, *dsptd ld to 4th, sn struggling*..................................(100 to 1) 9

Dist: Sht-hd, 11l, 8l, 5l, 1¼l, 7l, 1l, dist. 3m 49.20s. a 6.20s (9 Ran).

(Mrs J Waggott), N Waggott

1165 Salvesen Food Services Handicap Chase Class D (0-120 5-y-o and up) £5,182 2¾m 110yds.......... (3:00)

967 ROYAL VACATION [110] 7-11-7 J Callaghan, *hld up, improved fnl circuit, led r-in, kpt on wl.* (6 to 1 tchd 7 to 1) 1
995³ CELTIC SILVER [92] 8-10-3³ Richard Guest, *settled beh ldg grp, effrt whn hit 3 out, styd on wl frm last.* (4 to 1 op 9 to 2) 2
961* BAS DE LAINE (Fr) [115] (bl) 10-11-12 R Garritty, *led, mstk 3 out, hdd r-in, rallied.* .... (100 to 30 fav op 3 to 1 tchd 7 to 2) 3
STOP THE WALLER (Ire) [114] 7-11-11 Mr K Whelan, *nvr far away, effrt 3 out, kpt on frm last, better for race.* ....(12 to 1 op 10 to 1 tchd 14 to 1) 4
314⁴ BALYARA (Ire) [105] 6-11-2 P Niven, *beh and detached, styd on fnl 2, nrst finish.* ....(8 to 1 op 6 to 1 tchd 9 to 1 and 10 to 1) 5
GOLDEN FIDDLE (Ire) [101] 8-10-12 B Storey, *chsd ldg bunch, outpcd bef 3 out, kpt on aftr last.* (14 to 1 op 8 to 1) 6
GALA WATER [89] 10-10-0 R Supple, *cl up, struggling 4 out, sn no dngr*.......................... (66 to 1 op 50 to 1) 7
959* TIGHTER BUDGET (USA) [104] 9-11-1 M Moloney, *nvr far away, blun 11th, ev ch 4 out, wknd last*.. (7 to 2 op 5 to 2) 8
933⁴ CROSS CANNON [111] 10-11-8 K Jones, *hld up, f 4th.* ....(16 to 1 op 12 to 1) f

Dist: ½l, ½l, 6l, 1¼l, ¾l, 5l, 4l. 5m 31.30s. a 7.30s (9 Ran).
SR: 20/1/23/16/5/-/

(G P Edwards), G M Moore

1166 Ooh Aah Daily Star Handicap Hurdle Class D (0-125 4-y-o and up) £3,387 2¾m 110yds................. (3:30)

1036³ EXEMPLAR (Ire) [93] 8-10-3³ Richard Guest, *hld up, improved 7th, mstk 2 out, led r-in, kpt on wl.* ....(100 to 30 op 3 to 1 tchd 7 to 2) 1
844⁴ TALLYWAGGER [118] 9-11-7 (7*) T Hogg, *cl up, outpcd 6th, effrt 3 out, kpt on frm last*...............(9 to 1 op 6 to 1) 2
963* NICHOLAS PLANT [96] 7-10-3 (3*) G Lee, *led 3rd, hit 5th, hdd r-in, kpt on*.........................(5 to 2 fav op 2 to 1) 3
RALITSA (Ire) [102] 4-10-12 R Garritty, *settled in tch, improved to chal 2 out, edgd lft r-in, no extr last 100 yards.* ....(3 to 1 tchd 7 to 2) 4
D'ARBLAY STREET (Ire) [90] 7-10-0 S McDougall, *nvr far away, outpcd 4 out, kpt on frm last.* ....(14 to 1 op 20 to 1 tchd 25 to 1) 5
MARLINGFORD [90] 9-9-9 (5*) S Taylor, *led to 3rd, prmnt, struggling 7th, sn lost tch*........... (66 to 1 op 33 to 1) 6
BARK'N'BITE [95] 4-10-5 P Niven, *hld up, effrt 7th, wknd nxt, tld off*..............................(6 to 1 op 7 to 2) 7

Dist: 1¾l, sht-hd, 1¼l, 1¾l, dist, dist. 5m 19.50s. a 10.50s (7 Ran).

(Mrs S Smith), Mrs S J Smith

1167 Levy Board Conditional Jockeys' Handicap Hurdle Class E (0-115 4-y-o and up) £2,220 2m 110yds.. (4:00)

1038⁴ FEN TERRIER [92] 4-10-10 E Callaghan, *hld up in tch, rdn aftr 4 out, improved to ld last, held on wl.* ....(4 to 1 op 7 to 2 tchd 9 to 2) 1
KEMO SABO [82] 4-10-0 D Parker, *prmnt, outpcd 3 out, rallied appr last, kpt on, jst hld*.......(33 to 1 op 14 to 1) 2
1070³ TEEJAY'N'AITCH (Ire) [82] 4-10-0 G Lee, *prmnt, hit 3 out, styd on frm last, no extr nr finish.* ....(5 to 1 op 6 to 1 tchd 13 to 2) 3
962² NONIOS (Ire) [98] (v) 5-10-11 (5*) T Hogg, *prmnt, outpcd bef 3 out, improved aftr nxt, no extr last 100 yards.* ....(100 to 30 op 3 to 1 tchd 7 to 2) 4
1038⁵ WELL APPOINTED (Ire) [97] 7-10-12 (3*) S Melrose, *cl up, led bef 2 out, hdd last, sn btn.* (11 to 2 op 7 to 2 tchd 6 to 1) 5
NOORAN [82] 5-10-0 S Taylor, *settled in tch, improved to chal bef 2 out, wknd last.* ....(14 to 1 op 10 to 1 tchd 20 to 1 and 25 to 1) 6
962³ EDEN DANCER [106] 4-11-5 (5*) C McCormack, *led till hdd bef 2 out, sn btn*..................(5 to 2 fav op 3 to 1) 7
913 URBAN DANCING (USA) [110] 7-12-0 D J Kavanagh, *al beh.* ....(16 to 1 op 10 to 1) 8

Dist: Hd, 3l, 4l, ¾l, 11l, 2½l, 10l. 3m 45.90s. a 2.90s (8 Ran).
SR: 20/10/7/19/17/-/12/6/

(K G Fairbairn), F P Murtagh

NAVAN (IRE) (yielding)
Saturday November 2nd

1168 Glenfield Handicap Hurdle (0-116 4-y-o and up) £3,082 3m...... (1:15)

1074* ROSIN THE BOW (Ire) [-] 7-11-2 (4ex) C F Swan, ...(11 to 10 fav) 1
1089⁸ BETTERBEBOB (Ire) [-] 5-11-5 (3*) D J Casey,.....(14 to 1) 2
907⁸ WICKLOW WAY (Ire) [-] 6-9-5 (5*) G Cotter,........(9 to 1) 3

748² ALLATRIM (Ire) 6-11-3 N Williamson, ... (4 to 1)   4
926* IF YOU BELIEVE (Ire) [-] 7-9-5 (3") B Bowens, ... (5 to 2)   5
947⁵ NEW TRIBE (Ire) [-] 5-9-8² F Woods, ... (20 to 1)   6
Dist: ¾l, 5½l, 7l, 4l. 5m 59.90s. (6 Ran).

(F Fitzsimons), A P O'Brien

1169 Fortria E.B.F. Handicap Chase (Grade 3) (4-y-o and up) £7,350 2m 1f
. . . . (1:45)

1004² ANABATIC (Ire) [-] 8-10-0 T P Rudd, sn trkd ldr, jmpd wl, prog
bef 3 out, chlgd nxt, soon led, quickened clr . . . . (100 to 30)   1
825* SOUND MAN (Ire) [-] 8-12-0 N Williamson, led, sn ls clr, not
fluent 5 out and nxt, hdd aftr 2 out, wknd and slow last.
. . . . (4 to 1 on)   2
CORSTON DANCER (Ire) [-] (bl) 8-10-0 T Horgan, sn rear, lost
tch bef 3rd, soon tld off . . . . (50 to 1)   3
Dist: 20l, dist. 4m 14.00s. (3 Ran).

(William J Phelan), M J P O'Brien

1170 Rathfield Beginners Chase (4-y-o and up) £3,082 2m 1f . . . . . . (2:15)

982 ONTHEROADAGAIN (Ire) 8-12-0 T P Rudd, ... (8 to 1)   1
1016² DAWN ALERT (Ire) 7-12-0 C F Swan, ... (7 to 4 fav)   2
1080³ SCOBIE BOY (Ire) 8-12-0 P A Roche, ... (10 to 1)   3
TAYLORS QUAY (Ire) 8-12-0 T Horgan, ... (20 to 1)   4
1016⁵ GALANT DES EPEIRES (Fr) 5-11-11 N Williamson, (10 to 1)   5
909⁵ TIME AND CHARGES (Ire) 6-11-7 (7") R P Hogan, (16 to 1)   6
ORANGE JUICE (Ire) 6-12-0 L P Cusack, ... (20 to 1)   7
KILLERK LADY (Ire) 5-11-6 K F O'Brien, ... (50 to 1)   8
PUNTING PETE (Ire) 6-11-11 (3") D J Casey, ... (5 to 1)   f
JEFFELL 6-12-0 F Woods, ... (5 to 1)   co
552⁶ KING'S MANDATE (Ire) 7-12-0 P P Kinane, ... (25 to 1)   pu
Dist: Nk, 10l, 4l, 8l. 4m 27.80s. (11 Ran).

(T C Conroy), M J P O'Brien

1171 'For Auction' Novice Hurdle (Grade 3) (4-y-o and up) £6,850 2m . . . (2:45)

1015* RADANPOUR (Ire) 4-11-0 (3") D J Casey, mstk 3rd, slow 6th,
rdn bef 3 out, lft in ld aftr last . . . . (7 to 4)   1
1017⁶ CAITRIONA'S CHOICE (Ire) 5-11-8 N Williamson, rear early,
sn wl pld, chlgd bef last, no extr r-in . . . . (12 to 1)   2
KNOCKAULIN (Ire) 5-11-4 F J Flood, sn rear, slow 4th, lost
tch bef nxt . . . . (33 to 1)   3
910⁷ ZIMULANTE (Ire) 5-11-4 C F Swan, hld up, mstk second, hdd bef
3 out, lft in ld aftr nxt, broke leg appr last, jmpd flight, f,
destroyed . . . . (4 to 1)   f
746⁷ LISS DE PAOR (Ire) 5-11-6 T Horgan, trkd ldr till prog to ld bef
3 out, f nxt . . . . (Evens fav)   f
Dist: 2½l, dist. 3m 58.60s. (5 Ran).

(P P T Bridson), W P Mullins

1172 Lismullen Hurdle (Grade 3) (4-y-o and up) £6,850 2½m . . . . (3:15)

URUBANDE (Ire) 6-12-0 C F Swan, made all, rdn bef last, jst
hld on . . . . (9 to 4 fav)   1
826³ NEW CO (Ire) 8-11-8 (3") D J Casey, wtd wth, rdn and prog bef
3 out, ran on strly aftr last, jst fld . . . . (7 to 1)   2
NOTCOMPLAININGBUT (Ire) 5-11-4 (5") G Cotter, rear, gd
prog to track ldr bef 3 out, kpt on und pres aftr last . . (7 to 2)   3
1041* COCKNEY LAD (Ire) 7-12-0 Mr G J Harford, wl plcd, rdn bef 3
out, kpt on well . . . . (9 to 2)   4
ULTRA FLUTTER 9-11-11 N Williamson, wl plcd, prog to track
ldr 6th, rdn and wknd bef 3 out . . . . (16 to 1)   5
GENTLE BUCK (Ire) 7-11-11 K F O'Brien, trkd ldr, slow 5th
last, wknd bef 3 out . . . . (3 to 1)   6
Dist: Sht-hd, nk, ½l, dist. 4m 54.40s. (6 Ran).

(M G St Quinton), A P O'Brien

1173 Navan Golf Course Maiden Hurdle (3-y-o) £3,082 2m . . . . (3:45)

882⁴ CHOOSEY'S TREASURE (Ire) 10-9 C F Swan, . . (5 to 2 fav)   1
NARROW FOCUS (USA) 11-0 J P Broderick, ... (10 to 1)   2
712² GREENHUE (Ire) (bl) 11-0 T P Rudd, ... (3 to 1)   3
1057⁴ THREE RIVERS 10-11 (3") D J Casey, ... (8 to 1)   4
MAJOR CRISIS 10-8¹ (7") C Eyre, ... (9 to 1)   5
882³ CARRANSPRAWN (Ire) 11-0 J P Byrne, ... (11 to 2)   6
MISS PENNYHILL (Ire) 10-9 F J Flood, ... (16 to 1)   7
WOODEN DANCE (Ire) 10-6 (3") U Smyth, ... (20 to 1)   8
1057 MIND ME BRODY (Ire) 10-7 (7") A O'Shea, ... (14 to 1)   9
SPIRIT DANCER (Ire) 11-0 T J Mitchell, ... (20 to 1)   10
1057⁵ KIRIBATI (Ire) 11-0 N Williamson, ... (12 to 1)   11
NO AVAIL (Ire) 10-2 (7") P Morris, ... (10 to 1)   12
LADY CIANA (Ire) 10-9 K F O'Brien, ... (33 to 1)   13
DOUBLEBACK (Ire) 10-2 (7") K A Kelly, ... (33 to 1)   14
GALE EIGHT (Ire) 10-9 L P Cusack, ... (20 to 1)   15
ABSTRACT VIEW (USA) 10-7 (7") Mr L J Gracey, . (33 to 1)   16
927 SWEET SEPTEMBER (Ire) (bl) 10-4 (5") G Cotter, . (25 to 1)   17
SUMMER DREAMER 11-0 A Powell, ... (10 to 1)   18
1057 KERRY REEL (Ire) 11-0 M P Hourigan, ... (33 to 1)   19
MOSCOW'S FLAME (Ire) 11-0 S H O'Donovan, . . . (33 to 1)   20
927 TURKISHMAN (Fr) 11-0 F Woods, ... (25 to 1)   21
882 NORD VENTE (Ire) 10-4 (5") J Butler, ... (25 to 1)   f
DUGGAN DUFF (Ire) 10-7 (7") Mr S McGonagle, . . (33 to 1)   bd

UNASSISTED (Ire) 10-6 (3") B Bowens, ... (20 to 1)   bd
THE TODDY TAPPER (Ire) 11-0 P L Malone, ... (50 to 1)   pu
Dist: 3½l, 2l, ½l, 4l. 3m 56.00s. (25 Ran).

(M Moloney), A P O'Brien

1174 Navan Driving Range I.N.H. Flat Race (5-y-o and up) £3,082 2m. . . . . (4:15)

MURLEYS CROSS (Ire) 6-12-0 Mr P Fenton, ... (5 to 1)   1
BRASS BAND (Ire) 5-11-2 (7") Mr R H Fowler, ... (10 to 1)   2
1096⁸ PLEASE NO TEARS 9-11-9 Mrs C Barker, ... (5 to 1)   3
ISOLETTE 8-11-2 (7") Mr P J Casey, ... (12 to 1)   4
910 FOYLE WANDERER (Ire) 5-11-2 (7") Miss S McDonogh,
. . . . (9 to 1)   5
577 KATOUCHE (Ire) 5-11-11 (3") M R Walsh, ... (12 to 1)   6
CESAR DU MANOIR (Fr) 6-11-11 (3") Mr B M Cash,
. . . . (7 to 4 fav)   7
COLOURED THYME (Ire) 5-11-2 (7") Mr K Ross, . . . (20 to 1)   8
HIDDEN SPRINGS (Ire) 5-11-7 (7") Mr M O'Connor, (20 to 1)   9
1019⁷ JACKPOT JOHNNY (Ire) 5-11-9 (5") Mr G Farrell, . . (13 to 2)   10
905 ELECTRIC LAD (Ire) 5-11-2 (7") Mr P Geraghty, . . . (20 to 1)   11
ASHLEY LANE (Ire) 8-11-2 (7") Mr E Doyle, ... (20 to 1)   12
LISDARA LADY (Ire) 5-11-2 (7") Mr S Daly, ... (20 to 1)   13
QUENNIE MO GHRA (Ire) 5-11-9 Mr H F Cleary, . . . (8 to 1)   14
PAPER CHASE VI (Ire) 6-11-2 (7") Mr T Gibney, . . . (20 to 1)   15
210⁶ PROUDSTOWN LADY (Ire) 5-11-4 (5") Mr D McGoona,
. . . . (20 to 1)   16
Dist: 11l, 3l, 7l, 1½l. 3m 56.10s. (16 Ran).

(James P O'Keeffe), J P O'Keeffe

WARWICK (good to firm)
Saturday November 2nd
Going Correction: MINUS 0.60 sec. per fur.

1175 James Higgins Conditional Jockeys' Handicap Hurdle Class F (0-100 4-y-o and up) £2,174 2m . . . . (12:40)

998² GLOWING PATH [76] 6-10-2 (8") J Harris, took keen hold in
tch, led betw fnl 2, rdn out . . . . (8 to 1 tchd 10 to 1)   1
SUPERMICK [80] 5-11-0 A Bates, hld up beh ldrs, prog hfwy,
effrt appr 2 out, chsd wnr approaching last, kpt on one pace
. . . . (11 to 2 op 4 to 1 tchd 6 to 1)   2
972 NEWHALL PRINCE [87] (bl) 8-11-7 L Aspell, led, clr hfwy, hdd
betw fnl 2, one pace . . . . (7 to 1 op 6 to 1)   3
1008³ STAY WITH ME (Fr) [94] 6-12-0 Michael Brennan, hld up in
tch, rdn 3 out, styd on same pace . . . . (7 to 1 op 6 to 1)   4
1023* PAIR OF JACKS (Ire) [92] 6-11-4 (8") M Attwater, hld up, hdwy
5th, kpt on one frm 2 out . . . . (6 to 1 tchd 7 to 1)   5
513² GAME DILEMMA [80] 5-10-11 (3") O Burrows, nvr nr to chal.
. . . . (10 to 1 op 5 to 1)   6
1006* PEGASUS BAY [94] 5-12-0 G Hogan, keen hold, hld up in
mid-div, rdn 3 out, no imprsn.
. . . . (9 to 2 fav op 4 to 1 tchd 5 to 1)   7
1000³ HANDSON [88] 4-11-5 (3") D Salter, nvr trbld ldrs.
. . . . (7 to 1 tchd 6 to 1)   8
OUT OF THE BLUE [66] 4-9-9 (5") J Mogford, prmnt, jmpd
slwly and rdn 5th, sn beh . . . . (25 to 1 tchd 33 to 1)   9
664⁴ RAY RIVER [76] (bl) 4-10-10 N Massey, nvr on terms.
. . . . (16 to 1 op 12 to 1 tchd 20 to 1)   10
970⁶ SAN DIEGO CHARGER (Ire) [84] 5-11-4 Sophie Mitchell, pld
hrd, hld up, beh whn blun 4th, no dngr aftr.
. . . . (12 to 1 op 8 to 1 tchd 14 to 1)   11
990⁵ WATER HAZARD (Ire) [79] 4-10-3 (10") R Elkins, beh till f 2 out.
. . . . (11 to 1 op 6 to 1 tchd 12 to 1)   f
Dist: 4l, 2½l, ½l, 4l, 1¼l, 2½l, 3l, 7l, 2½l, 16l. 3m 39.40s. a 0.40s (12 Ran).

(P Slade), R J Hodges

1176 Arnold Lodge School Handicap Chase Class E (0-110 5-y-o and up) £3,049 2m . . . . (1:10)

895³ SUPER SHARP (NZ) [86] 8-11-0 Jacqui Oliver, made all, rdn
out, ran on wl . . . . (6 to 1 op 5 to 1 tchd 13 to 2)   1
914* CIRCULATION [72] (v) 10-10-0³ (3") D Walsh, chsd wnr,
9th, blun 3 out, one pace nxt . . . . (6 to 1 tchd 7 to 1)   2
972³ NORTHERN OPTIMIST [87] 8-11-1 Mr L J Llewellyn, trkd ldrs,
not fluent 5th, no imprsn aftr.
. . . . (3 to 1 op 5 to 2 tchd 100 to 30)   3
1052* ZEREDAR (NZ) [100] 6-12-0 J Osborne, jmpd rght thrght, hld
up, lost tch frm 6th, tld off whn pld up bef 3 out.
. . . . (11 to 10 on tchd 5 to 4 on)   pu
Dist: 7l, 1¾l. 3m 49.10s. b 2.90s (4 Ran).
SR: 19/-/11/-/

(Mrs Sue Careless), H Oliver

1177 BSPH Handicap Chase Class C (0-130 5-y-o and up) £4,692 3¼m
. . . . (1:40)

995² TIME ENOUGH (Ire) [98] 7-10-3 J F Titley, led till not fluent
and hdd 3rd, mstk nxt, rgned ld appr 14th, styd on wl frm 2 out.
. . . . (5 to 4 on op Evens)   1
COPPER MINE [123] 10-12-0 J Osborne, in tch, outpcd aftr
13th, rallied nxt, chsd wnr frm 15th, eased whn no ch r-in.
. . . . (9 to 4 op 6 to 4)   2

142

CROPREDY LAD [97] 9-10-2¹ A Thornton, *led 3rd, hdd appr 14th, wknd 16th*..........(7 to 2 op 3 to 1 tchd 4 to 1) 3

1061 ELLTEE-ESS [95] (v) 11-9-9² (7") C R Weaver, *not fluent, al beh, sn tld off*........(66 to 1 op 50 to 1 tchd 100 to 1) 4

Dist: 18l, 30l, dist. 6m 23.60s. a 9.60s (4 Ran).

(The Lewis Partnership), C P E Brooks

1178 Tensator Handicap Hurdle Class C (0-130 4-y-o and up) £3,600 2m 3f ....(2:15)

RUNAWAY PETE (USA) [119] 6-11-7 (3") D Walsh, *made all, rdn alng aftr 6th, styd on.* ....(11 to 8 fav tchd 5 to 4 and 6 to 4) 1

1054 MORSTOCK [110] 6-10-12 (3") T Dascombe, *keen hold early, hld up, chsd wnr frm 5th, no imprsn from 2 out.* ....(11 to 4 op 3 to 1 tchd 9 to 2) 2

148 DJAIS (Fr) [119] 7-11-10 J F Titley, *hld up beh ldrs, wknd appr 2 out, eased approaching last.* ....(9 to 2 op 2 to 1 tchd 5 to 1) 3

1110⁴ SLEEPTITE (Fr) [95] 6-9-9² (7") J Power, *blun second, chsd wnr till grad lost tch frm 5th.*..........(12 to 1 op 8 to 1) 4

GRAND APPLAUSE (Ire) [103] 6-10-8 D Bridgwater, *strted slwly, reminders aftr 1st, jmpd rght 4th, tld off whn pld up bef nxt.* ....(6 to 1 op 9 to 2) pu

Dist: 4l, 17l, 18l. 4m 15.00s. (5 Ran).

(J D Smeaden), M C Pipe

1179 St Mary's Juvenile Novices' Selling Hurdle Class G (3-y-o) £1,691 2m ....(2:45)

936³ INDIRA 10-4 (3") T Dascombe, *made all, rdn and lft clr 2 out, ridden out*...........(7 to 4 fav op 9 to 4 tchd 5 to 2) 1

936³ LADY MAGNUM (Ire) 10-7 D Bridgwater, *hld up and beh, hdwy and mstk 3 out, hmpd nxt, ran on wl r-in.* ....(10 to 1 op 12 to 1) 2

991⁶ HOW COULD-I (Ire) (bl) 10-7 A Thornton, *chsd ldrs, lft second and hmpd 2 out, one pace.* (11 to 2 op 4 to 1 tchd 6 to 1) 3

BLUNTSWOOD HALL 10-12 Gary Lyons, *chsd ldrs, one pace appr 2 out.* ....(66 to 1 op 50 to 1) 4

FIJON (Ire) 10-7 V Smith, *mid-div, hdwy appr 4th, btn whn hmpd 2 out.* ....(9 to 1 op 6 to 1 tchd 10 to 1) 5

IN CAHOOTS 10-12 F Jousset, *hld up, hdwy 5th, btn whn hmpd 2 out.* ....(7 to 1 op 5 to 1 tchd 8 to 1) 6

542³ LEBEDINSKI (Ire) 10-7 R Marley, *hld up and beh, hdwy 4th, btn whn hmpd 2 out.* ......(5 to 1 op 4 to 1 tchd 11 to 2) 7

SHANOORA (Ire) 10-4 (3") E Husband, *pld hrd, chsd ldrs till 4th.*..................(25 to 1 op 20 to 1 tchd 33 to 1) 8

991⁸ THE GREY WEAVER 10-5 (7") J K McCarthy, *beh frm 4th.* ....(66 to 1 op 50 to 1) 9

STORM WIND (Ire) 10-12 A Larnach, *took keen hold, in tch till 4th, sn beh.*..............(20 to 1 op 16 to 1) 10

BITES 10-7 J Railton, *mstk 3rd, nvr on terms.* ....(33 to 1 op 20 to 1) 11

886³ KAI'S LADY (Ire) 10-6² (3") P Midgley, *nvr on terms.* ....(25 to 1 op 20 to 1 tchd 33 to 1) 12

848⁷ CHILLINGTON (bl) 10-12 S Wynne, *pld hrd, prmnt till 5th.* ....(50 to 1 op 25 to 1) 13

991⁷ COLOUR COUNSELLOR 10-9 (3") D Fortt, *hld up, hdwy appr 4th, disputing ld whn f 2 out.*..........(13 to 2 op 6 to 1) f

936 BRIN-LODGE (Ire) 10-7 V Slattery, *keen hold, hld up, mstk second, beh whn blun 4th, sn tld off, pld up bef last.* ....(66 to 1 op 50 to 1) pu

Dist: 3l, 1¾l, 4l, 8l, 5l, 7l, 2l, 5l, 2½l, 5l. 3m 40.40s. a 1.40s (15 Ran).

(M A Long), C L Popham

1180 Offchurch Novices' Chase Class D (5-y-o and up) £3,795 2½m 110yds ....(3:20)

878² MR CONDUCTOR (Ire) 5-10-13 A Thornton, *lft in ld second, made rst, clr frm tenth, eased rght dwn r-in, very easily.* ....(7 to 4 on op 11 to 8 on tchd 2 to 1 on) 1

HAWAIIAN SAM (Ire) 6-11-0 G Crone, *beh frm 8th, wnt poor second appr last.*........(11 to 4 op 7 to 4 tchd 3 to 1) 2

993² ELITE GOVERNOR (Ire) 7-10-9 (5") Chris Webb, *chsd wnr frm second, mstks 8th and 9th, blun and lost tch nxt.* ....(9 to 2 op 4 to 1 tchd 4 to 1) 3

868⁵ SPORTING FIXTURE (Ire) 5-10-13 J A McCarthy, *f 1st.* ....(66 to 1 op 50 to 1 tchd 100 to 1) f

LUCKNAM DREAMER 8-11-0 E Byrne, *led till blun badly second, beh whn mstk 5th, tld off whn pld up and dismounted bef 7th.*............(40 to 1 op 25 to 1 tchd 50 to 1) pu

Dist: 12l, 2½l. 5m 6.10s. a 11.10s (5 Ran).

(P M de Wilde), R H Alner

1181 Weatherbys 'Stars Of Tomorrow' National Hunt Flat Standard - Class H (4,5,6-y-o) £1,364 2m ....(3:55)

DANZANTE (Ire) 4-11-1 (3") D Walsh, *hld up, hdwy frm hfwy, lft in ld o'r 2 fs out, rdn out*..(11 to 4 op 2 to 1 tchd 5 to 2) 1

DITOPERO 4-10-11 (7") N Willmington, *trkd ldrs, led hfwy till ran wide on bend o'r 2 fs out, no extr ins last.* ....(7 to 4 fav op 2 to 1 tchd 5 to 2) 2

BECKY'S LAD 6-11-1 (3") Guy Lewis, *hld up beh ldrs, rdn and ev ch 2 fs out, btn o'r one out.* ....(40 to 1 op 33 to 1 tchd 50 to 1) 3

LAIRD O'PRHYNIE 4-10-11 (7") Mr A Wintle, *hld up, hdwy 7 fs out, wknd o'r 2 out.*..........(8 to 1 op 5 to 1) 4

ABYSS 4-11-4 Mr D Verco, *beh fnl 5 fs, tld off.* ....(8 to 1 op 5 to 1) 5

942 NANJIZAL 4-10-13 (5") Michael Brennan, *led 5 fs, wknd o'r six out, tld off.*.........(33 to 1 op 16 to 1 tchd 40 to 1) 6

HONEST GEORGE 5-11-1 (3") R Massey, *keen hold, prmnt, led aftr 6 fs, hdd hfwy, sn wknd, tld off....* (7 to 2 op 5 to 2) 7

Dist: 1¾l, 5l, 5l, dist, 2l, dist. 4m 0.50s. (7 Ran).

(David Hallums), R M Stronge

WETHERBY (good)
Saturday November 2nd
Going Correction: MINUS 0.05 sec. per fur. (races 1,3,5,7), PLUS 0.05 (2,4,6)

1182 Bolton Percy Novices' Hurdle Class C (4-y-o and up) £4,159 2m.. (12:50)

QUEEN OF SPADES (Ire) 6-10-9 C Llewellyn, *made all, drw clr aftr 6th, easily.*.............(Evens fav op 13 to 8) 1

ENDOWMENT 4-10-11 (3") G Cahill, *prmnt, drvn alng and lost pl bef 5th, rallied to chase wnr before 3 out, no imprsn.* ....(20 to 1 op 12 to 1) 2

1070² MITHRAIC (Ire) 4-11-10 (7") L McGrath, *mid-div, hdwy alng aftr 6th, kpt on same pace frm 3 out......*(8 to 1 op 7 to 1) 3

1047 DURANO 5-11-0 L Wyer, *prmnt, chsd wnr 6th till wknd bef 3 out.*....................(6 to 1 op 3 to 1) 4

374² SAMANID (Ire) 4-11-4 C Maude, *prmnt till wknd bef 3 out.* ....(9 to 1 op 1 to 2 tchd 10 to 1) 5

1071 LAST TRY (Ire) 5-11-0 B Powell, *mid-div, some hdwy aftr 6th, wkng whn hmpd 3 out.*............(50 to 1 op 33 to 1) 6

L'EQUIPE (Ire) 6-11-0 R Dunwoody, *hld up, some hdwy aftr 5th, rdn bef 3 out, sn btn.* (11 to 1 op 8 to 1 tchd 12 to 1) 7

PENROSE LAD (NZ) 6-11-0 A Maguire, *beh most of way.* ....(8 to 1 op 6 to 1) 8

888⁶ BLANC SEING (Fr) (bl) 9-11-0 Mr S Swiers, *beh 5th.* ....(50 to 1 op 33 to 1) 9

CLEVER BOY 5-10-11 (3") F Leahy, *prmnt till wknd aftr 6th.*....................(50 to 1 op 33 to 1) 10

DONT FORGET CURTIS (Ire) 4-11-0 N Bentley, *mid-div, wkng whn f 3 out.*..............(50 to 1 op 25 to 1) f

HOPEFUL LORD (Ire) 4-10-7 (7") Mr S P Hennessy, *f 1st.* ....(50 to 1 op 33 to 1) f

B THE ONE 5-11-0 Derek Byrne, *beh whn hmpd 1st, tld off when pld up aftr 3rd.*...........(14 to 1 op 10 to 1) pu

Dist: 18l, 5l, 1¼l, 1¼l, 7l, 7l, ½l, 9l, 13l. 3m 44.60s. a 3.60s (13 Ran).

SR: 37/24/23/17/19/8/1/-/-/ (Mrs R Vaughan), N A Twiston-Davies

1183 Arthur Stephenson Novices' Handicap Chase Class C (5-y-o and up) £4,589 2½m 110yds.........(1:20)

POTTER'S BAY (Ire) [105] 7-11-10 A Maguire, *hld up in rear, hdwy on bel 11th, led 2 out, drvn out.* ....(2 to 1 fav op 6 to 4) 1

RANDOM HARVEST (Ire) [92] 7-10-11 R Dunwoody, *trkd ldrs, hit 5th, led 4 out till 2 out, styd on.* ....(3 to 1 op 4 to 1 tchd 9 to 2) 2

RYE CROSSING (Ire) [96] 6-11-1 L Wyer, *sn beh, styd on frm 3 out, nvr able to chal.* ......(9 to 2 op 4 to 1) 3

TICO GOLD [81] 8-9-12¹ (3") G Cahill, *mstk 4th, beh, styd on frm 2 out, nvr dngrs.*........(16 to 1 op 14 to 1) 4

931⁵ COOL WEATHER (Ire) [86] 8-10-5 A S Smith, *prmnt, ev ch 4 out, sn rdn and btn.*..........(20 to 1 op 16 to 1) 5

GRUNDON (Ire) [84] (bl) 7-10-3¹ G Upton, *made most to 4 out, sn wknd.*.............(20 to 1 op 14 to 1 tchd 25 to 1) 6

778³ CAMP BANK [81] 6-10-0 C Llewellyn, *prmnt, pushed alng aftr 9th, wknd bef 4 out.*..........(11 to 2 op 4 to 1) 7

778⁴ FINAL BEAT (Ire) [82] 7-10-1 C O'Dwyer, *in tch till wknd bef 4 out.*....................(10 to 1) 8

971 THEYDON PRIDE [81] 7-10-0 T J Murphy, *sn prmnt, mstk tenth, wkng whn blun 4 out.......*(100 to 1 op 50 to 1) 9

Dist: 2l, 16l, hd, 1¾l, 11l, 1¼l, 10l, 2½l. 5m 6.10s. a 13.10s (9 Ran).

(Mrs J E Potter), D Nicholson

1184 Stanley Racing Handicap Hurdle Class C (0-135 4-y-o and up) £3,710 2m........................(1:50)

932⁴ DIRECT ROUTE (Ire) [122] 5-11-2 A Maguire, *hld up and beh, smooth hdwy to ld 3 out, ran on wl.* ....(11 to 8 fav op 6 to 4 tchd 13 to 8) 1

FOURTH IN LINE (Ire) [129] 8-11-9 R Dunwoody, *led till rdn and hdd 3 out, kpt on, no imprsn on wnr.* ....(6 to 5 op 5 to 4 tchd 7 to 1) 2

KAITAK (Ire) [121] 5-10-12 (3") F Leahy, *chsd 4th, chlgd 6th, rdn bef 3 out, btn.*....................(6 to 1 op 11 to 2) 3

932² DESERT FIGHTER [111] 5-10-2 (3") G Cahill, *prmnt, drvn alng bef 3 out, sn wknd, beh whn blun nxt.* ....(9 to 4 op 5 to 2 tchd 11 to 4) 4

966⁵ CUMBRIAN CHALLENGE (Ire) [134] 7-12-0 L Wyer, *hld up,*
effrt bef 3 out, sn btn.....(13 to 2 op 6 to 1 tchd 7 to 1) 5
Dist: 5l, 4l, 4l, ¾l. 3m 48.70s. a 7.70s (5 Ran).
SR: 3/5/ (Chris Heron), J Howard Johnson

1185 Peterhouse Group Handicap Chase Class B (0-145 5-y-o and up) £6,710 2½m 110yds............... (2:20)

1084⁴ STATELY HOME (Ire) [118] 5-10-6 R Dunwoody, *made all, lft*
clr 8th, blun 2 out, easily... (7 to 1 op 5 to 1 tchd 9 to 1) 1
JOE WHITE [119] 10-10-8 A S Smith, *hld up in tch, outpcd aftr*
11th, kpt on frm 3 out, no ch wth wnr.
.... (14 to 1 op 10 to 1 tchd 16 to 1) 2
967² BERTONE (Ire) [135] 7-11-10 C O'Dwyer, *hld up in tch, blun*
badly 4th, hmpd 8th, rallied to chase wnr frm 11th, no imprsn,
eased whn no ch aftr last. (11 to 8 op 6 to 4 tchd 5 to 4) 3
HILL OF TULLOW (Ire) [139] 7-12-0 A Maguire, *chsd wnr till f*
8th....................... (6 to 5 fav op Evens tchd 5 to 4) f
Dist: 10l, 14l. 5m 9.00s. a 16.00s (4 Ran).

(P Bowen), P Bowen

1186 Tote West Yorkshire Hurdle Class A Grade 2 (4-y-o and up) £12,500 3m 1f........................... (2:50)

TRAINGLOT 9-11-0 R Dunwoody, *settled in tch, hdwy to track*
ldr aftr 9th, led 2 out, styd on strly. (7 to 4 fav tchd 2 to 1) 1
897⁷ WHAT A QUESTION (Ire) 8-10-9 C O'Dwyer, *trkd ldrs, led 9th*
till 2 out, kpt on, no ch wth wnr.........(2 to 1 op 13 to 8) 2
897² DIFFICULT TIMES (Ire) 4-10-13 L Wyer, *led to second, dsptd*
ld till outpcd by 1st 2 bef 3 out......(5 to 1 tchd 11 to 2) 3
777⁷ NON VINTAGE (Ire) 5-11-0 W Worthington, *hld up, outpcd aftr*
9th, nvr dngrs........................ (16 to 1 op 12 to 1) 4
TREASURE AGAIN (Ire) 7-11-4 Derek Byrne, *made most to*
9th, wknd bef 3 out.....................(11 to 2 tchd 6 to 1) 5
966² OUR KRIS 4-10-13 A S Smith, *beh, lost tch 9th, tld off.*
.... (25 to 1 op 20 to 1 tchd 33 to 1) 6
1047 PAST MASTER (USA) 8-11-0 A Maguire, *sn beh, lost tch 8th,*
tld off whn pld up bef 3 out.........(100 to 1 op 66 to 1) pu
Dist: 8l, 14l, 20l, 12l, dist. 5m 58.00s. a 12.00s (7 Ran).

(Marquesa de Moratalla), J G FitzGerald

1187 Charlie Hall Chase Class A Grade 2 (5-y-o and up) £18,300 3m 1f.. (3:25)

ONE MAN (Ire) 8-11-10 R Dunwoody, *hld up, hdwy to track*
ldrs 14th, led on bit 4 out, drvn out aftr last.
.... (11 to 8 on op 13 to 8 on tchd 7 to 4 on) 1
BARTON BANK 10-11-10 A Maguire, *led second, hit 9th, hdd*
4 out, chsd wnr aftr, no imprsn..........(6 to 1 tchd 7 to 1) 2
YOUNG HUSTLER 9-11-2 C Maude, *led to second, prmnt till*
outpcd aftr 4 out, no dngr after.
.... (11 to 2 op 5 to 1 tchd 6 to 1) 3
SCOTTON BANKS 7-11-10 L Wyer, *hld up, hdwy to track*
ldr hfwy, lost pl tenth, pushed alng bef 4 out, sn btn.
.... (5 to 1 op 7 to 2) 4
Dist: 7l, 6l, 14l. 6m 11.40s. a 3.40s (4 Ran).
SR: 75/68/54/48/ (J Hales), G Richards

1188 Wensleydale Juvenile Novices' Hurdle Class A Grade 2 (3-y-o) £9,690 2m........................... (4:00)

BELLATOR 10-12 B Fenton, *settled midfield, steady hdwy to*
ld 3 out, ran on strly.....................(4 to 1 tchd 9 to 2) 1
930⁵ JACKSON PARK 10-12 L Wyer, *prmnt, led 4th till hit 3 out and*
hdd, kpt on und pres, no ch wth wnr... (16 to 1 op 12 to 1) 2
936⁴ HEVER GOLF DIAMOND 10-12 R Dunwoody, *hld up, hdwy*
aftr 5th, ev ch 3 out, sn rdn, kpt on same pace.
.... (16 to 1 op 12 to 1) 3
1027* KERAWI 11-2 C Llewellyn, *prmnt till drvn alng and lost pl aftr*
5th, no dngr after.
.... (4 to 1 op Evens tchd 11 to 10 on and 5 to 4) 4
930¹ LAGAN 11-2 A S Smith, *trkd ldrs, ev ch bef 3 out, sn rdn and*
wknd........................(7 to 2 op 4 to 1 tchd 5 to 1) 5
664³ PRELUDE TO FAME (USA) 12-4 A Maguire, *in tch till wknd*
aftr 6th.............. (14 to 1 op 12 to 1 tchd 16 to 1) 6
SIX CLERKS (Ire) 10-12 F Leahy, *mid-div, hmpd 4th, wknd bef*
3 out.......................(25 to 1 op 16 to 1) 7
886* HOBBS CHOICE 10-7 N Bentley, *hld up, hdwy to chase ldrs*
6th, wknd quickly bef 3 out.........(33 to 1 op 16 to 1) 8
SIZZLING SYMPHONY 10-12 Derek Byrne, *al beh, tld off.*
.... (66 to 1 op 33 to 1) 9
930⁷ PHANTOM DANCER (Ire) 10-12 G Cahill, *al beh, tld off whn*
pld up bef 3 out....................(50 to 1 op 33 to 1) pu
815* KERNOF (Ire) (bl) 11-2 C O'Dwyer, *made most till mstk and*
hdd 4th, prmnt till wknd quickly aftr 6th, tld off whn pld up bef
last.........................(14 to 1 op 8 to 1) pu
GULF OF SIAM 10-12 D Bentley, *in tch, blun 4th, sn beh, tld*
off whn pld up bef 2 out................(25 to 1 op 14 to 1) pu
Dist: 8l, 3l, 12l, ¾l, 1¼l, 7l, nk, dist. 3m 47.30s. a 6.30s (12 Ran).
SR: 13/5/2/-/-/-/ (P Richardson), G B Balding

PUNCHESTOWN (IRE) (yielding)
Sunday November 3rd

Going Correction: NIL (races 1,2,5,7), PLUS 0.90 (3,4,6)

1189 Elverstown Novice Hurdle (5-y-o and up) £3,425 2½m............. (1:15)

978* GALLOPEN GARRY (Ire) 6-11-3 (3*) J R Barry, ... (8 to 1) 1
979* PRIVATE PEACE (Ire) 6-11-9 C F Swan, ... (3 to 1 on) 2
1075* SLUSH PUPPY (Ire) 8-11-6 L P Cusack, ...(7 to 1) 3
929⁵ FOLLY ROAD (Ire) 6-11-2 N Williamson, ...(50 to 1) 4
LISBOY LEADER (Ire) 7-11-2 C O'Dwyer, ...(33 to 1) 5
949⁶ BALLINABOOLA GROVE 9-10-9 (7*) J M Maguire, (25 to 1) 6
1013* BANGABUNNY 6-11-3 (3*) Mr K Whelan, ...(10 to 1) 7
1013 TIME FOR A WINNER (Ire) 5-10-11 F Woods, ...(100 to 1) 8
ARCTIC GREY (Ire) 6-10-9 (7*) L A Hurley, ...(33 to 1) f
908⁸ RED RADICAL (Ire) 6-10-12³ (7*) Mr P E I Newell, ..(33 to 1) f
1078* STONELEIGH TURBO (Ire) 7-11-9 T J Mitchell, ...(12 to 1) pu
Dist: ¾l, 12l, 4l, 9l. 5m 19.50s. a 37.50s (11 Ran).
(Shuttle Syndicate), Sean O O'Brien

1190 Burtown Wood Handicap Hurdle (4-y-o and up) £6,850 2m........ (1:45)

1078² KAWA-KAWA [-] 9-9-2 (5*) G Cotter, ...(11 to 2) 1
BLESS ME SISTER (Ire) [-] 7-10-13 N Williamson, (Evens fav) 2
1058⁵ JO JO BOY (Ire) [-] 7-10-1 F J Flood, ...(10 to 1) 3
980⁴ WEST ON BRIDGE ST (Ire) [-] 6-9-11 F Woods, ...(6 to 1) 4
980 JUSTAWAY (Ire) [-] (bl) 6-9-8 K P Gaule, ...(16 to 1) 5
BALAWHAR (Ire) [-] 6-12-0 C F Swan, ...(9 to 2) f
Dist: 3½l, sht-hd, ¾l, 2½l. 3m 49.40s. a 4.40s (6 Ran).
SR: 21/37/25/20/14/-/ (R J Collier), P Delaney

1191 Narraghmore Handicap Chase (0-102 5-y-o and up) £3,082 2m 5f........................ (2:15)

1004⁵ QUATTRO [-] 6-10-10 (5*) G Cotter, ...(10 to 1) 1
949⁷ TEAL BRIDGE [-] 6-11-5 T J Mitchell, ...(8 to 1) 2
852⁵ MACAUNTA (Ire) [-] 6-9-13 J P Broderick, ...(12 to 1) 3
1003⁵ STRADBALLEY (Ire) [-] 6-11-4 C F O'Brien, ...(14 to 1) 4
721⁶ WACKO JACKO (Ire) [-] 7-11-2 (5*) T Martin, ...(12 to 1) 5
LE MINTER (Ire) [-] 7-10-4 (5*) L Flynn, ...(50 to 1) 6
851² MICKS DELIGHT (Ire) [-] 6-11-11 C O'Dwyer, ...(14 to 1) 7
852³ WALKERS LADY (Ire) [-] 8-10-8 D T Evans, ...(8 to 1) 8
1003 BROOK HILL LADY (Ire) [-] 7-12-0 C F Swan, ..(4 to 1 fav) 9
950² WHITE OAK BRIDGE (Ire) [-] 7-11-8 A Powell, ...(12 to 1) 10
949⁴ GREEK MAGIC [-] 9-9-10 (3*) D J Casey, ...(40 to 1) f
1003⁴ BALLYBODEN [-] 9-11-4 M P Hourigan, ...(14 to 1) f
1003⁷ TRIPTODICKS (Ire) [-] 6-9-11 (7*) A O'Shea, ...(8 to 1) f
646² ANY PORT (Ire) [-] 6-11-10 P L Malone, ...(12 to 1) ur
BALLYFIN BOY [-] 10-11-0 F Woods, ...(33 to 1) pu
721² KYLE HOUSE VI (Ire) [-] 7-9-8¹ N Williamson, ...(8 to 1) pu
Dist: 2½l, 10l, 7l, 13l. 5m 40.10s. a 28.10s (16 Ran).
SR: -/1/-/-/-/-/ (Donal Cullen), Martin M Treacy

1192 Irish Field Novice Chase (Grade 3) (5-y-o and up) £6,910 2½m... (2:45)

982* DORANS PRIDE (Ire) 7-11-6 J P Broderick, *jmpd wl, trkd ldr,*
led appr 4 out, quickened aftr nxt, jumped slwly last, unchlgd.
.... 1
1016* THE SUBBIE (Ire) 7-11-6 C O'Dwyer, *wtd wth, jmpd slwly 6*
out, rdn aftr 3 out, kpt on wl, not nrble wnr...........(3 to 1) 2
982³ CREHELP EXPRESS (Ire) 6-10-11 N Williamson, *rear, jmpd*
slwly 6th, rdn bef 3 out, wknd aftr nxt, mstk last.......(7 to 1) 3
VULPIN DE LAUGERE (Fr) 9-10-13 (3*) Mr K Whelan, *led till*
appr 4 out, sn rdn, wknd aftr 2 out................. (25 to 1) 4
924² FRIDAY THIRTEENTH (Ire) 7-11-6 A Powell, *trkd ldr, f 1st,*
rmntd, al tld off........................... (33 to 1) 5
Dist: 11l, 15l, 7l, dist. 5m 20.20s. a 23.20s (5 Ran).
SR: 40/29/5/3/-/ (T J Doran), Michael Hourigan

1193 Shamrock Classic Maiden Hurdle (4-y-o and up) £3,082 2m....... (3:15)

1015² MOSCOW EXPRESS (Ire) 4-11-9 C F Swan, ...(9 to 4 on) 1
929³ LANTURN (Ire) 6-11-6 T J Mitchell, ...(14 to 1) 2
1013⁴ COMMERCIAL HOUSE (Ire) 6-11-6 D T Evans, ..(12 to 1) 3
802 SPRITZER (Ire) 4-10-13 D P Fagan, ...(25 to 1) 4
928 FALLOW TRIX (Ire) 4-10-11 (7*) Mr J Keville, ...(25 to 1) 5
945⁷ JACKY FLYNN (Ire) 5-11-6 N Williamson, ...(20 to 1) 6
1075⁴ TURRAMURRA GIRL (Ire) 7-11-9 Mr H F Cleary, ..(14 to 1) 7
MONTANA KING (Ire) 5-11-6 F Woods, ...(16 to 1) 8
1015 SABANIYA (Fr) 4-11-1 (3*) U Smyth, ...(16 to 1) 9
1090 MIDNIGHT JAZZ (Ire) 6-12-0 M P Hourigan, ...(25 to 1) 10
CLASSPERFORMER (Ire) 4-11-4 L P Cusack, ...(16 to 1) 11
1015⁹ PERPETUAL PROSPECT (Ire) 4-11-4 C O'Dwyer, ..(16 to 1) 12
681⁸ CARRICK GLEN (Ire) 5-10-8 (7*) R P Hogan, ...(20 to 1) 13
945⁸ BARRIGAN'S HILL (Ire) 6-11-6 S H O'Donovan, ..(16 to 1) 14
1024⁴ EIRE (Ire) 7-11-7 (7*) Mr M O'Connor, ...(20 to 1) 15
826⁵ ORCHARD SUNSET (Ire) 6-10-13 (7*) Mr D M Fogarty,
.... (20 to 1) 16
898⁸ COOKSGROVE ROSIE (Ire) 4-10-13 P Leech, ...(33 to 1) 17
1075 ARCTIC GALE 5-10-10 (5*) J Butler, ...(33 to 1) 18
908 FOREST STAR (USA) 7-11-6 C F O'Brien, ...(33 to 1) 19
OVER ALICE (Ire) 4-10-13 F J Flood, ...(25 to 1) 20
122* VARTRY BOY (Ire) 5-11-7 (7*) M D Murphy, ...(25 to 1) 21

1015 ROB MINE (Ire) 4-10-11 (7") L A Hurley, ... (33 to 1) 22
    AVALIN (Ire) 5-11-1 K P Gaule, ... (33 to 1) 23
977³ MARTYS STEP (Ire) 5-10-13 (7") D McCullagh, ... (5 to 1) f
Dist: 1½l, 7l, sht-hd, 2½l. 3m 53.30s. a 8.30s (24 Ran).
SR: 12/7/-/-/-/-/   (T Conroy), A P O'Brien

1194 Copelands Handicap Chase (0-132 5-y-o and up) £3,082 3m...... (3:45)

981* THREE BROWNIES [-] (bl) 9-11-7 C O'Dwyer, ... (7 to 2) 1
92⁶⁷ GO GO GALLANT (Ire) [-] 7-11-1 K P C Swan, ... (6 to 4 fav) 2
    THE GOPHER (Ire) [-] 7-10-6 L P Cusack, ... (16 to 1) 3
    LA-GREINE (Ire) [-] 9-9-11 (7") Mr K Ross, ... (20 to 1) 4
    JOHNEEN [-] 10-10-12 J P Broderick, ... (16 to 1) 5
    LAURA'S BEAU [-] (bl) 10-13-5 (7") R P Hogan, ...(20 to 1) 6
    VELEDA II (Fr) [-] 9-10-6 (3") Mr K Whelan, ...(10 to 1) f
    LOVE AND PORTER (Ire) [-] 8-12-0 D H O'Connor, ..(9 to 1) f
926³ SPRINGFORT LADY (Ire) [-] 7-10-1 N Williamson, .. (9 to 1) f
981⁶ BEAT THE SECOND (Ire) [-] 8-10-8 F Woods, ... (14 to 1) ur
1003⁶ OLYMPIC D'OR (Ire) [-] 8-10-4 (3") D J Casey, ...(20 to 1) ur
Dist: 4½l, 1½l, 25l, 3l. 6m 32.10s. a 32.10s (11 Ran).
                              (Mrs A M Daly), M F Morris

1195 Baron's Bog I.N.H. Flat Race (4 & 5-y-o) £2,740 2m................ (4:15)

    BE MY PLEASURE (Ire) 4-10-11 (7") Mr Sean O O'Brien,
    ....(4 to 1) 1
    DR KING (Ire) 4-11-6 (3") Mr R Walsh, ... (8 to 1) 2
1081² SIMPLY ACOUSTIC (Ire) 5-11-2 (7") Mr A C Coyle, ..(8 to 1) 3
1019⁸ MALLARDSTOWN (Ire) 5-12-0 Mr P Fenton, ... (10 to 1) 4
1019⁵ KILCOGY CROSS (Ire) 4-10-11 (7") Miss A L Crowley,
    ....(11 to 2) 5
    PRINCE DANTE (Ire) 4-11-2 (7") Mr M Murray, ... (14 to 1) 6
1005² BLUE IRISH (Ire) 5-11-11 (3") Mr K Whelan, ... (13 to 2) 7
    REGENCY RAKE (Ire) 4-11-2 (7") Mr G Donnelly, .. (14 to 1) 8
    KILCAR (Ire) 5-11-7 (7") Mr P Carberry, ... (14 to 1) 9
722⁶ WARLOCKFOE (Ire) 5-11-2 (7") Mr A K Wyse, ... (14 to 1) 10
    LAS ALMANDAS (Ire) 5-11-2 (7") Mr G Elliott, ... (12 to 1) 11
    KILPATRICK (Ire) 5-11-2 (7") Mr C J Sweeds, ...(10 to 1) 12
805 REGGIE'S HONOUR (Ire) 4-10-13 (5") J Butler, ... (12 to 1) 13
805 RED ACE (Ire) 4-11-1 (3") Mr B M Cash, ... (12 to 1) 14
    TOCHAR BOY (Ire) 5-12-0 Mr D Marnane, ... (20 to 1) 15
    CHIEF DELANEY (Ire) 4-11-9 Mr A J Martin, ... (5 to 2) 16
    NICKELLI (Ire) 5-11-2 (7") Mr P M Cloke, ... (14 to 1) 17
    HARAS ROSE (Ire) 5-11-2 (7") Mr J P McNamara, .(20 to 1) 18
984 EVE'S DAUGHTER (Ire) 5-11-2 (7") E Stack, ... (20 to 1) 19
    GALE JOHNSTON (Ire) 5-11-2 (7") Mr John P Moloney,
    ....(12 to 1) pu
Dist: 2½l, 4l, 7l, ½l. 3m 48.70s. (20 Ran).
                    (Sean O O'Brien), Sean O O'Brien

NEWCASTLE (good to firm)
Monday November 4th
Going Correction: MINUS 0.15 sec. per fur.

1196 'Barbour' Northumbria Juvenile Novices' Hurdle Class E (3-y-o) £2,274 2m...............(1:25)

886² SILENT GUEST (Ire) 10-12 R Garritty, led, hit 3 out and nxt, sn
hdd, lft in ld and hmpd last, styd on und pres.
    ....(3 to 1) tchd 7 to 2) 1
    THE BOOZING BRIEF (USA) 10-12 D Parker, sn prmnt, dsptd
ld 5th till rdn and outpcd aftr nxt, rallied after 2 out, no extr frm
last.............................(6 to 4 fav op 5 to 4) 2
860* DOUBLE DASH (Ire) 11-5 D J Moffatt, mstks, lost tch hfwy, no
dngr aftr........................(7 to 1 op 5 to 1) 3
    RATTLE 10-12 A Roche, hld up in tch, rdn bef 6th, wknd
before 3 out...........................(20 to 1 op 14 to 1) 4
930⁹ LUCKY BEA 10-9 (3") P Midgley, hld up in tch, hdwy bef 3 out,
rdn to ld betw last 2, two ls lead whn f last. (4 to 1 op 3 to 1) f
    DUNTALKIN 10-9² Richard Guest, sn tld off, pld up bef last.
    ....(12 to 1 op 10 to 1 tchd 14 to 1) pu
Dist: 2l, 11l, 7l. 3m 52.80s. a 12.80s (6 Ran).
                 (Mrs Patricia M Wilson), M D Hammond

1197 'Barbour' Bedale Novices' Chase Class E (5-y-o and up) £2,918 3m .... (1:55)

    BILLSBROOK 6-10-12 K Johnson, sn cl up, blun 12th, led nxt,
hdd 4 out, led and hit next, styd on wl.
    ....(14 to 1 tchd 16 to 1) 1
1035⁴ BOLD ACCOUNT (Ire) 6-10-12 N Bentley, led 4th to 13th, led
four out to nxt, no extr................ (11 to 8 op 2 to 1) 2
    TRICKLE LAD (Ire) 7-10-9 (3") K Gaule, hld up, mstk 16th,
hdwy and ev ch 4 out, sn wknd.. (5 to 4 fav op 6 to 4 on) 3
    BROOMHILL DUKER (Ire) 6-10-12 N Williamson, led to 4th,
prmnt whn blun 13th, rallied to chase ldrs four out, sn wknd.
    ....(14 to 1) 4
1153⁶ QUIXALL CROSSETT 11-10-12 Mr P Murray, mstks, in tch till
outpcd aftr 13th, no dngr after........ (66 to 1 op 50 to 1) 5
887³ BARDAROS 7-10-12 A Thornton, in tch, blun 9th, wkng whn
blunded 16th, tld off whn pld up bef 2 out.
    ....(6 to 1 op 5 to 1 tchd 7 to 1) pu

---

Dist: 8l, 2l, 3l, 21l. 6m 17.00s. a 31.00s (6 Ran).
                        (R Brewis), R Brewis

1198 'Barbour' Burghley Novices' Hurdle Class E (4-y-o and up) £2,274 2½m ....(2:25)

    STAN'S YOUR MAN 6-10-9 (3") G Cahill, made virtually all,
styd on wl frm 3 out.......(7 to 1 op 6 to 1 tchd 8 to 1) 1
1034* SHANAVOGH 5-11-5 J Callaghan, trkd ldrs, hdwy and ev ch 3
out, sn rdn, kpt on, no imprsn on wnr.
    ....(9 to 4 on op 2 to 1 on tchd 7 to 4 on) 2
648³ LEAP IN THE DARK (Ire) 7-10-12 A Thornton, prmnt, ev ch 3
out, kpt on same pace.................. (14 to 1 op 10 to 1) 3
1067⁴ HOTSPUR STREET 4-10-12 L Wyer, hld up, pushed alng bef
3 out, staying on same pace whn blun nxt.
    ....(9 to 1 op 6 to 1) 4
64 FINGERHILL 7-10-12 Mr M Thompson, prmnt, dsptd ld
5th till wknd bef 3 out...........(100 to 1 op 50 to 1) 5
    JOE JAGGER (Ire) 5-10-12 R Garritty, trkd ldrs, pushed alng
aftr 8th, tld.........................(20 to 1 op 10 to 1) 6
    NOBLE MONARCH (Ire) 7-10-12 N Williamson, hld up rear,
mstk 7th, effrt bef 3 out, sn btn.........(50 to 1 op 20 to 1) 7
    CASTLE RED (Ire) 5-10-12 K Jones, chsd ldrs till rdn and
wknd aftr 8th.........................(9 to 1 op 6 to 1) 8
    TIBBI BLUES 9-10-7 M Moloney, beh most of way, tld off whn
pld up bef 3 out.........(20 to 1 op 10 to 1) pu
Dist: 3½l, 4l, 5l, 13l, 1½l, sht-hd, 4l. 4m 58.60s. a 20.60s (9 Ran).
          (Mrs J D Goodfellow), Mrs J D Goodfellow

1199 'Barbour' Durham Handicap Chase Class D (0-125 5-y-o and up) £3,501 3m................... (2:55)

    ALY DALEY (Ire) [97] 8-10-0 N Williamson, made most, sev-
eral reminders, styd on wl und pres frm 3 out, all out.
    ....(6 to 1 tchd 7 to 1) 1
24 CEILIDH BOY [120] 10-11-9 A S Smith, chsd ldrs, ev ch whn
mstk 2 out, styd on wl und pres frm last.
    ....(14 to 1 op 12 to 1) 2
    STRONG DEEL (Ire) [119] 8-11-8 M Foster, nvr far away, rdn
bef 3 out, ch whn blun last, not reco'r.... (4 to 1 op 5 to 1) 3
877² ALI'S ALIBI [117] 9-11-6 P Niven, beh, drvn alng aftr 15th, no
hdwy frm 4 out.....................(9 to 4 fav op 5 to 2) 4
    HIGH PADRE [125] 10-11-11 (3") F Leahy, in tch, drvn alng to
dispute ld tenth, mstk 13th, sn beh, no dngr aftr.
    ....(4 to 1 tchd 9 to 2) 5
1037⁶ GREENHILL RAFFLES [122] 10-11-11 A Thornton, prmnt,
pushed alng whn blun 15th, sn beh, tld off.
    ....(100 to 1 op 20 to 1) 6
1037³ GALE AHEAD (Ire) [100] 6-10-3² N Bentley, blun and uns rdr
1st.............................(7 to 2 op 3 to 1) ur
Dist: ¾l, 12l, 3½l, 2l, 26l. 5m 56.00s. a 10.00s (7 Ran).
          (Michael Tobitt), J Howard Johnson

1200 'Barbour' Billy Bow Handicap Hurdle Class D (0-125 4-y-o and up) £2,752 2m.......................... (3:25)

962* TOM BRODIE [115] 6-11-11 N Williamson, hld up, hdwy on bit
bef 3 out, led appr last, drvn out.
    ....(7 to 4 fav op 6 to 4 tchd 15 to 8) 1
932⁵ DONE WELL (USA) [118] 4-12-0 A Dobbin, hld up rear, hdwy
3 out, staying on whn mstk last, no imprsn on wnr. (3 to 1) 2
818² BURES (Ire) [110] 5-10-13 (7") B Grattan, led till appr last, kpt
on.............................(8 to 1 op 6 to 1) 3
932⁶ SHINING EDGE [110] 4-11-6 L Wyer, in tch, rdn aftr 2 out, sn
btn.............................(7 to 1 op 6 to 1 tchd 8 to 1) 4
    ONCE MORE FOR LUCK (Ire) [113] 5-11-9 P Niven, in tch,
mstk and lost pl 6th, mistake 3 out, losing touch whn blun nxt,
tld off.............................(5 to 2 tchd 11 to 4) 5
Dist: 1¼l, ¾l, 4l, 21l. 3m 50.20s. a 10.20s (5 Ran).
          (Mrs M W Bird), J Howard Johnson

1201 W. K. Backhouse Amateur Riders' Handicap Chase Class E (0-115 5-y-o and up) £2,801 2m 110yds. . (3:55)

1126² BLAZING DAWN [88] 9-10-10 (7",7ex) Miss P Robson, sn
chasing ldr, dsptd ld 3 out, led last, styd on wl und pres.
    ....(4 to 1 op 7 to 2 tchd 9 to 2) 1
914² THUNDERSTRUCK [82] 10-10-4 (7") Mr R Thornton, led,
3 out, beat last, no extr und pres.
    ....(5 to 2 op 9 to 4 tchd 11 to 4) 2
    VICARIDGE [95] 9-11-3 (7") Mr A Robson, in tch, mstks 6th
and tenth, no imprsn on 1st 2 frm 4 out.
    ....(9 to 4 fav op 7 to 4) 3
    AUBURN BOY [91] 9-11-3 (3") Mr C Bonner, not fluent, beh
most of way, tchd 9th................(5 to 2 op 6 to 4) 4
    MONAUGHTY MAN [85] 10-10-7 (7") Mr P Murray, in tch,
mstks 6th and nxt, tailing off whn blun and uns rdr 4 out.
    ....(40 to 1 op 25 to 1 tchd 50 to 1) ur
Dist: 4l, 7l, 14l. 4m 3.80s. a 4.80s (5 Ran).
SR: 17/7/13/-/-/   (J S Hubbuck), J S Hubbuck

PLUMPTON (soft)

Monday November 4th
Going Correction: PLUS 1.05 sec. per fur.

1202 Stanmer Maiden Hurdle Class F (4-y-o and up) £2,156 2½m..... (1:35)

BAYERD (Ire) 5-11-5 J Osborne, trkd ldrs, jnd 2 out, sn led,
drvn out....................(11 to 2 op 4 to 1 tchd 6 to 1)   1
976³ FLYING FIDDLER (Ire) 5-11-5 B Powell, hld up in rear, hdwy 4
out, wnt second appr last...(2 to 1 op 5 to 4 tchd 5 to 2)   2
SECOND STEP (Ire) 5-11-5 R Dunwoody, hld up, wnt second
3 out, wknd appr last....(6 to 1 op 3 to 1 tchd 13 to 2)   3
BELLA SEDONA 4-11-0 E Murphy, mid-div, hdwy 4th, wnt
second 8th, led appr 3 out, hdd nxt, wknd quickly.
....................(6 to 4 fav op 5 to 4 tchd 6 to 4)   4
997⁴ DECOR (Ire) 6-11-2 (3*) T Dascombe, led till hdd appr 3 out,
wknd quickly, tld off..................(10 to 1 op 7 to 1)   5
749 CAULKIN (Ire) 5-11-5 D Bridgwater, al beh, tld off.
....................(40 to 1 op 20 to 1 tchd 50 to 1)   6
UPHAM RASCAL 5-11-5 D Leahy, trkd ldr to 8th, sn wknd, tld
off..................(33 to 1 op 20 to 1)   7
Dist: 1¾l, 12l, 2½l, 17l, ½l, 1l. 5m 28.80s. a 51.80s (7 Ran).

(J J King), C R Egerton

1203 Balcombe Conditional Jockeys' Selling Handicap Hurdle Class G (0-95 4-y-o and up) £1,859 2m 1f... (2:05)

903⁴ MINSTER'S MADAM [81] (v) 5-11-9 T Dascombe, led 3rd,
drvn clr 6th, unchlgd...(9 to 4 fav op 2 to 1 tchd 5 to 2)   1
RACHAEL'S OWEN [85] 6-11-13 G Hogan, hld up, hdwy to
chase wnr 4 out, no imprsn..........(5 to 2 op 5 to 4)   2
BRESIL (USA) [58] 7-9-7 (7*) Mark Brown, chsd wnr 4th till
wknd four out, tld off..................(14 to 1 op 6 to 1)   3
918⁸ AGAINST THE CLOCK [58] (bl) 4-9-7 (7*) T O'Connor, hld up,
no ch frm 4 out, tld off. (20 to 1 op 10 to 1 tchd 16 to 1)   4
1020³ ALOSAILI [78] 9-11-6 D Fortt, al beh, tld off.
....................(3 to 1 tchd 11 to 4)   5
971⁵ TWICE THE GROOM (Ire) [86] (bl) 6-11-9 (5*) M Griffiths, lost
tch 6th, tld off..................(5 to 1 op 4 to 1 tchd 6 to 1)   6
1007 RED MATCH [61] 11-9-12 (5*) J Harris, led to 3rd, wth wnr till
wknd 6th, blun 4 out, sn tld off...(33 to 1 op 16 to 1)   7
Dist: Dist, 30l, 5l, 1¾l, 6l, dist. 4m 35.10s. a 38.10s (7 Ran).

(J Neville), J Neville

1204 Jolly Tanners At Staplefield Handicap Chase Class D (0-120 5-y-o and up) £3,661 2m 5f........... (2:35)

BEAU BABILLARD [110] (bl) 9-11-6 A P McCoy, trkd ldrs, led
5 out, styd on und pres..........(4 to 1 tchd 7 to 2)   1
988* ZAMBEZI SPIRIT (Ire) [95] 7-10-5 Derek Byrne, hld up, hdwy
to ld tenth, hdd 5 out, rallied appr 2 out, one pace.
....................(15 to 8 fav op 5 to 4 tchd 2 to 1)   2
MR MATT (Ire) [105] 8-11-1 B Fenton, pckd 1st, hld up, hdwy 6
out, wknd appr 3 out, tld off.
....................(16 to 1 op 12 to 1 tchd 20 to 1)   3
1101² ANDRELOT [118] 9-12-0 A Maguire, led, rdn 9th, hdd nxt,
wknd quickly, pld up aftr 6 out..........(6 to 1 op 4 to 1)   pu
WHIPPERS DELIGHT (Ire) [93] 8-10-3 D Bridgwater, trkd ldr
till wknd quickly 9th, tld off whn pld up bef 6 out.
....................(9 to 2 op 5 to 1)   pu
REALLY A RASCAL [105] 9-11-1 R Dunwoody, hld up in tch,
wknd 6 out, tld off whn pld up bef 2 out.
....................(5 to 2 op 11 to 4 tchd 3 to 1)   pu
Dist: 2l, dist. 5m 40.40s. a 34.40s (6 Ran).

(Mrs C I A Paterson), P F Nicholls

1205 Cuckfield Novices' Hurdle Class E (4-y-o and up) £2,574 2m 1f... (3:05)

856³ SAILEP (Fr) 4-10-9 (3*) T Dascombe, trkd ldr, led appr 2 out,
kpt on, fnshd tired........(7 to 2 op 4 to 1 tchd 9 to 2)   1
1082⁶ SHIFT AGAIN (Ire) (bl) 4-10-7 J Osborne, led, hit 4th, hdd appr
2 out, fnshd very tired. (9 to 4 fav op 6 to 4 tchd 5 to 2)   2
ZACAROON 5-10-7 A P McCoy, trkd ldrs, rdn 4 out, wknd nxt,
tld off..................(20 to 1 op 10 to 1)   3
990³ BLURRED IMAGE (Ire) 5-10-12 T J Murphy, hld up, brief effrt
hfwy, wknd nxt, tld off..................(14 to 1 op 10 to 1)   4
NOT TO PANIC (Ire) 6-10-7 R Johnson, chsd ldrs, lost tch
hfwy, tld off..................(7 to 1 op 8 to 1 tchd 10 to 1)   5
SPITFIRE BRIDGE (Ire) 4-10-12 B Clifford, al beh, tld off whn
pld up bef 3 out........(12 to 1 op 6 to 1 tchd 14 to 1)   pu
1006⁴ ATH CHEANNAITHE (Ire) (bl) 4-11-5 D Bridgwater, mid-div,
wknd hfwy, tld off whn pld up bef 4 out.
....................(11 to 4 op 2 to 1 tchd 7 to 2)   pu
BOLD CHARLIE 4-10-12 N Mann, al beh, tld off whn pld up
bef 3 out..................(33 to 1 op 16 to 1)   pu
Dist: 2l, dist, 24l, 21l. 4m 41.00s. a 44.00s (8 Ran).

(P Slade), R J Hodges

1206 Chailey Handicap Chase Class E (0-115 5-y-o and up) £2,906 2m
.... (3:35)

875⁵ UNCLE BERT (Ire) [94] 6-10-4 (3*) D Fortt, rcd 3rd, lost tch wth
1st 2 5 out, styd on frm two out to ld r-in.
....................(5 to 2 op 7 to 4 tchd 11 to 4)   1
941* COOLTEEN HENRY (Ire) [88] 6-10-11 W McFarland, led till hdd
appr 2 out, edgd lft and ev ch last, one pace.
....................(9 to 4 op 9 to 4 tchd 9 to 2)   2
901⁵ JAMES THE FIRST [115] 8-12-0 A P McCoy, trkd ldr, hit
second, rdn 7th, jnd ldr 5 out, led appr 2 out, ridden bef last,
wnt rght and hdd r-in..................(5 to 4 on tchd Evens)   3
1113⁴ JOKER JACK [87] 11-9-13² (3*) T Dascombe, al last, tld off
frm 6th..................(14 to 1 op 10 to 1 tchd 16 to 1)   4
Dist: 5l, sht-hd, dist. 4m 16.20s. a 24.20s (4 Ran).
SR: 5/-/21/-/
(Alec Tuckerman), G M McCourt

1207 Plumpton Autumn Handicap Hurdle Class F (0-100 4-y-o and up) £2,083 2½m...................... (4:05)

987⁵ FAWLEY FLYER [81] 7-10-11 R Dunwoody, al in tch, hit
second, led 2 out, styd on gmely.
....................(2 to 1 fav op 5 to 4 tchd 9 to 4)   1
TITAN EMPRESS [72] (v) 7-10-2 N Mann, led second, hit 7th,
hdd 2 out, no extr.
....................(11 to 4 op 5 to 2 tchd 3 to 1 and 9 to 4)   2
COUNTRY STORE [95] 7-11-11 S Curran, led to second, rdn
8th, wknd appr 3 out, tld off.
....................(13 to 2 op 4 to 1 tchd 5 to 1 and 11 to 4)   3
DARING KING [92] 6-11-8 P Hide, al beh, tld off.
....................(14 to 1 op 8 to 1)   4
SOLEIL DANCER (Ire) [83] 8-10-13 B Fenton, al beh, tld off.
....................(14 to 1 op 8 to 1)   5
905 TOPANGA [90] 4-11-6 L Harvey, wtd wth, rdn 7th, sn btn, tld
off..................(10 to 1 op 6 to 1)   6
Dist: 8l, dist, 3l, 30l, 7l. 5m 37.20s. a 60.20s (6 Ran).

(David Chown), W G M Turner

EXETER (good to soft)
Tuesday November 5th
Going Correction: PLUS 0.60 sec. per fur.

1208 William Hill Credit Novices' Hurdle Class E (4-y-o and up) £2,826 2m 1f 110yds..................... (1:15)

IT'S A GEM 7-10-9 (3*) L Aspell, hld up in mid-div, styd on frm
2 out, led sn aftr last, ran on..........(50 to 1 tchd 66 to 1)   1
905² DEVON PEASANT 4-10-7 Mr L Jefford, al prmnt, led appr 2
out, hdd sn aftr, lft in ld and hmpd last, soon header.
....................(9 to 1 op 4 to 1 tchd 10 to 1)   2
796* LAKE KARIBA 5-11-5 A P McCoy, al in tch, ev ch 2 out, one
pace aftr..................(2 to 1 fav op 11 to 8)   3
ROSS DANCER (Ire) 4-10-9 (3*) J Magee, hld up in rear, some
hdwy frm 3 out, nvr dngrs..................(100 to 1)   4
1098³ MISTER RM 4-11-5 C Llewellyn, led till wknd appr 2 out.
....................(3 to 1 tchd 4 to 1)   5
GENTLE BREEZE (Ire) 4-10-7 P Hide, chsd ldrs till wknd appr
2 out..................(25 to 1 op 20 to 1)   6
1053⁴ RHYTHM AND BLUES 6-10-12 B Powell, mid-div, wknd 3 out.
....................(16 to 1 op 20 to 1 tchd 25 to 1)   7
796⁷ SAXON MEAD 6-10-12 A Maguire, chsd ldrs till wknd 5th.
....................(16 to 1 op 10 to 1 tchd 20 to 1)   8
921³ SAAFI (Ire) 5-10-12 D Leahy, hld up, effrt 5th, wknd 3 out, tld
off..................(100 to 1 op 50 to 1)   9
ECU DE FRANCE (Ire) 6-10-12 S Fox, al beh, tld off 6th.
....................(100 to 1)   10
1082⁸ SOLO VOLUMES 7-10-12 M Brennan, al beh, blun 3rd, sn tld
off..................(200 to 1 op 100 to 1)   11
FILCH 5-10-7 B Fenton, al beh, tld off 3 out.
....................(100 to 1 tchd 200 to 1)   12
CREDO BOY 7-10-12 S Burrough, f 1st.
....................(33 to 1 tchd 50 to 1)   f
1097 MARCHING MARQUIS (Ire) 5-10-12 M A Fitzgerald, al prmnt,
led sn aftr 2 out, drawing clr whn blun and uns rdr last.
....................(5 to 2 op 2 to 1 tchd 11 to 4)   ur
900 PARADE RACER 5-10-12 W McFarland, pld nxt, prmnt till
wknd quickly 4th, tld off whn pulled up bef last...(100 to 1)   pu
1053 HOLD THE FORT 5-10-7 (5*) D J Kavanagh, al beh, tld off 6th,
pld up bef 2 out..................(100 to 1 op 100 to 1)   pu
Dist: ½l, 4l, 22l, 5l, ½l, 3l, ¾l, dist, hd, dist. 4m 14.00s. a 18.00s (16 Ran).
SR: 9/3/11/-/-/-/
(Capt F Tyrwhitt-Drake), J T Gifford

1209 William Hill Lucky Choice Juvenile Novices' Selling Hurdle Class G (3-y-o) £1,859 2m 1f 110yds..... (1:45)

STONE ISLAND 10-12 R Dunwoody, chsd ldrs, hdwy 4th, led
sn aftr 3 out, rdn nxt, ran on gmely.
....................(11 to 2 op 5 to 1 tchd 6 to 1)   1
BRYANSTON SQUARE (Ire) (bl) 10-12 J Osborne, al prmnt,
wnt second 5th, ev ch 2 out till rdn and no extr cl hme.
....................(9 to 1 op 5 to 1 tchd 10 to 1)   2
FLASH IN THE PAN (Ire) 10-7 W McFarland, hld up, hdwy to
press ldrs 3 out, ev ch till rdn and no extr r-in.
....................(10 to 1 op 6 to 1 tchd 11 to 1)   3

705^{2} HOME COOKIN' 10-7 A P McCoy, *led till second, led 4th till rdn and hdd sn aftr 3 out, soon btn, tld off.* ....(6 to 4 fav op 7 to 4 tchd 11 to 8) 4
BLOSSOM DEARIE 10-7 J Frost, *in rear, effrt 5th, wknd aftr 3 out, tld off*..................(14 to 1 op 10 to 1) 5
1027 DISH THE DOSH 10-7 D J Burchell, *beh frm 3rd, tld off whn refused 3 out*.........(11 to 1 op 16 to 1 tchd 10 to 1) ref
DRAMATIC ACT 10-7 B Fenton, *pld hrd, led second to 4th, wknd quickly 3 out, tld off whn pulled up bef nxt.* ....(6 to 1 op 4 to 1 tchd 7 to 1) pu
BUS WAY GIRL 10-7 C Llewellyn, *al beh, tld off whn pld up bef 3 out*.........................(25 to 1 op 12 to 1) pu
PAULTON 10-12 M A Fitzgerald, *al beh, tld off 3rd, pld up bef 3 out*..................(20 to 1 op 10 to 1 tchd 25 to 1) pu
Dist: ½l, 1l, dist, 4l. 4m 28.10s. a 32.10s (9 Ran).
(P J Hobbs), P J Hobbs

1210 William Hill Haldon Gold Challenge Cup Chase Limited Handicap Class A Grade 2 (5-y-o and up) £17,985 2m 1f 110yds.....................(2:15)

ABSALOM'S LADY [152] 8-10-7 D Bridgwater, *hld up in rear, hdwy frm 5th, led 5 out, stumbled 3 out, hit nxt, ran on wl.* ....(8 to 1 op 10 to 1 tchd 16 to 1) 1
1084* COULTON [169] 9-11-10 J Osborne, *led till 8th, rdn 3 out, ran on to chase wnr r-in.* (13 to 8 fav op 11 to 8 tchd 7 to 4) 2
PIMBERLEY PLACE (Ire) [152] 8-10-7 C Llewellyn, *nvr far away, outpcd appr 4 out, ran on frm nxt.* ....(66 to 1 op 33 to 1 tchd 100 to 1) 3
TRAVADO [159] 10-11-0 M A Fitzgerald, *wnt second 5th, lost pl 5 out, rallied appr nxt, hrd rdn and ev ch till wknd r-in.* ....(15 to 8 op 5 to 4 tchd 2 to 1) 4
NAKIR (Fr) [152] 8-10-7 A Maguire, *hld up in tch, lost pl 5 out, nvr dngrs aftr*..........(4 to 1 op 7 to 2 tchd 100 to 30) 5
TERAO [152] 10-10-7 A P McCoy, *chsd ldr to 5th, wknd sn aftr, tld off*.........(16 to 1 op 12 to 1 tchd 20 to 1) 6
Dist: 2½l, 1¼l, sht-hd, 11l, dist. 4m 19.90s. a 14.90s (6 Ran).
SR: 35/49/30/37/19/-/ (Whitcombe Manor Racing Stables Limited), Miss Gay Kelleway

1211 William Hill Debit Card Novices' Handicap Hurdle Class E (0-100 4-y-o and up) £2,547 2m 3f....... (2:45)

796^{5} ALLOW (Ire) [78] 5-10-11 M A Fitzgerald, *chsd ldrs, wnt second appr 2 out, styd on to ld r-in.* ....(9 to 2 op 6 to 1 tchd 7 to 1) 1
906 MILLION DANCER [95] (bl) 4-12-0 A P McCoy, *led, clr 4th till 2 out, wndrd appr last, wknd and hdd r-in.* ....(10 to 1 op 8 to 1 tchd 12 to 1) 2
CRACKING PROSPECT [85] 5-10-13 (5*) D Salter, *hld up, hdwy 3 out, styd on, no ch wth 1st 2*...............(20 to 1) 3
906^{2} LUKE WARM [72] 6-10-5[1] R Dunwoody, *chsd ldrs, wnt second 3 out, wknd appr last.* ....(7 to 2 fav tchd 4 to 1 and 9 to 2) 4
COOLE HILL (Ire) [87] 5-11-6 A Maguire, *hld up in rear, hdwy 3 out, nvr dngrs*..........(11 to 2 op 4 to 1 tchd 6 to 1) 5
1055 SPEARHEAD AGAIN (Ire) [80] 7-10-13 D Bridgwater, *al rear.* ....(16 to 1) 6
997^{3} STEER POINT [74] 5-10-7 J Frost, *hld up in rear, nvr on terms*..........................(16 to 1 op 12 to 1) 7
FRENCH BUCK (Ire) [92] 6-11-11 C Llewellyn, *trkd ldr till aftr 4th, wknd 3 out, tld off*.....(11 to 2 op 4 to 1 tchd 6 to 1) 8
939^{7} OLD MASTER (Ire) [67] 5-10-0 B Powell, *al beh, tld off.* ....(100 to 1 op 50 to 1) 9
659^{3} PLINTH [80] 5-10-13 J Osborne, *chsd ldrs to 5th, sn wknd, tld off*.....................(8 to 1 op 7 to 1 tchd 10 to 1) 10
1082^{5} POLICEMANS PRIDE (Fr) [80] 7-10-13 G Upton, *chsd ldrs till wknd 5th, tld off whn pld up bef last*....(20 to 1 op 20 to 1) pu
800 SANDS POINT [86] 6-11-2 (3*) T Dascombe, *chsd ldrs to 4th, beh whn pld up lme last.* ....(16 to 1 op 10 to 1 tchd 20 to 1) pu
FREELINE LUSTRE (Ire) [68] 6-10-1 W McFarland, *al beh, tld off whn pld up bef 6th.* (50 to 1 op 66 to 1 tchd 100 to 1) pu
Dist: 7l, 6l, 10l, 9l, 9l, 7l, 2l, 10l, 22l. 4m 39.80s. a 23.80s (13 Ran).
(Mrs M Llewellyn), B Llewellyn

1212 William Hill Devon & Exeter Handicap Chase Class C (0-135 5-y-o and up) £4,856 2¾m 110yds...... (3:15)

FOOLS ERRAND (Ire) [105] 6-10-5 A P McCoy, *al prmnt, hit tenth, second 12th, led aftr 5 out, clr 3 out, very easily.* ....(5 to 1 op 9 to 2 tchd 11 to 2) 1
CLASS OF NINETYTWO (Ire) [122] 7-11-8 R Dunwoody, *sn trkd ldr, led 11th, hdd aftr 5 out, no imprsn after.* ....(7 to 2 op 4 to 1 tchd 9 to 2) 2
DOM SAMOURAI (Fr) [117] (bl) 5-11-2 J Frost, *hld up in rear, styd on to take 3rd r-in*...(11 to 1 op 7 to 2 tchd 12 to 1) 3
OATIS REGRETS [128] 8-12-0 J Osborne, *led till mstk 11th, no hdwy frm 4 out*................. (9 to 4 fav op 5 to 2) 4
SPUFFINGTON [120] 8-11-6 P Hide, *in rear, some hdwy frm 4 out*..........(13 to 2 op 7 to 1 tchd 8 to 1) 5
668^{4} STAUNCH RIVAL (USA) [120] 9-11-6 M A Fitzgerald, *hld up, wl beh frm 7th, tld off*.... (14 to 1 op 8 to 1 tchd 16 to 1) 6
HARWELL LAD (Ire) [120] 7-11-6 Mr R Nuttall, *chsd ldrs to 6th, refused to race aftr, pld up bef tenth.* ....(6 to 1 op 13 to 2 tchd 7 to 1) pu
Dist: 7l, 2½l, 1l, 4l, dist. 5m 54.10s. a 34.10s (7 Ran).
(Mrs David Russell), G B Balding

1213 William Hill Index Mares' Only Handicap Hurdle Class D (4-y-o and up) £2,898 2m 3f................ (3:45)

SAIL BY THE STARS [99] 7-10-12 R Dunwoody, *al prmnt, led appr 2 out, styd on und pres.* ....(6 to 1 op 9 to 2 tchd 13 to 2) 1
1087* DARK NIGHTINGALE [99] 6-10-12 J Osborne, *hld up in rear, hdwy appr 3 out, ev ch nxt, sn rdn, no extr.* ....(13 to 8 fav op 13 to 8) 2
MARINERS MIRROR [104] 9-11-3 Mr M Rimell, *hld up, hdwy to chase ldr 5th, ev ch 2 out, wknd appr last.* ....(7 to 1 op 5 to 1 tchd 15 to 2) 3
923^{2} OUT RANKING (Fr) [114] 4-11-13 A P McCoy, *led till appr 2 out, eased whn btn bef last*............(3 to 1 op 7 to 2) 4
STAC-POLLAIDH [89] 6-10-2 J Railton, *not jump wl, hit 1st and 3rd, prmnt till wknd 3 out.* ....(8 to 1 op 6 to 1 tchd 9 to 1) 5
KOO'S PROMISE [87] 5-9-11 (3*) T Dascombe, *beh frm 4th, tld off*...........................(25 to 1 op 14 to 1) 6
1056^{6} LA MENORQUINA (USA) [97] 6-10-5 (5*) Sophie Mitchell, *hld up, hdwy 3 out, in tch whn f nxt.* ....(10 to 1 op 6 to 1 tchd 11 to 1) f
Dist: 5l, 11l, 7l, 3½l, 27l. 4m 38.00s. a 22.00s (7 Ran).
(T F F Nixon), Capt T A Forster

1214 Exeter Levy Board Mares Only Standard Open National Hunt Flat Class H (4,5,6-y-o) £1,259 2m 1f 110yds .... (4:15)

CURRADUFF MOLL (Ire) 5-10-11 (7*) L Suthern, *chsd ldr, led o'r 3 fs out, wndrd in frnt, kpt on*.......(14 to 1 op 6 to 1) 1
POTTER'S GALE (Ire) 5-11-11 A Maguire, *hld up in mid-div, hdwy to chase wnr o'r 3 fs out, no imprsn fnl 2.* ....(Evens fav op 6 to 4) 2
JUST JASMINE 4-11-4 J Osborne, *al prmnt, rdn and styd on one pace fnl 3 fs*.....(20 to 1 tchd 25 to 1 and 50 to 1) 3
KOSHEEN (Ire) 5-10-11 (7*) Mr A Wintle, *chsd ldrs, hdwy 6 fs out, wknd 2 out*........(12 to 1 op 7 to 1 tchd 14 to 1) 4
JAYDEEBEE 5-11-4 G Upton, *chsd ldrs, no hdwy fnl 4 fs.* ....(33 to 1 op 16 to 1) 5
671^{3} SOLAR MOON 5-11-4 B Powell, *hld up, hdwy aftr 6 fs, wknd o'r 3 out*..............(11 to 1 op 8 to 1 tchd 12 to 1) 6
DOLCE NOTTE (Ire) 6-11-4 A P McCoy, *led till o'r 3 fs out, wknd quickly*.........................(7 to 2 op 4 to 1) 7
LOTSCHBERG EXPRESS 4-11-4 R Dunwoody, *beh till effrt hfwy, wknd 4 fs out*.....(10 to 1 op 6 to 1 tchd 11 to 1) 8
MISS NIGHT OWL 5-11-4 J Frost, *al beh, tld off.* ....(33 to 1 op 25 to 1 tchd 50 to 1) 9
MISS STARTEAM 6-11-4 Mr A Holdsworth, *al beh, tld off.* ....(66 to 1 op 33 to 1) 10
PHARMOREFUN (Ire) 4-11-4 B Fenton, *beh frm hfwy, tld off.* ....(14 to 1 op 6 to 1 tchd 16 to 1) 11
ALICE SHORELARK 5-11-4 Mr T Greed, *prmnt to hfwy, wknd 7 fs out, tld off*.................... (100 to 1 op 50 to 1) 12
880^{9} HALAM BELL 4-11-4 P Holley, *al beh, tld off.* ....(50 to 1 op 33 to 1) 13
LET YOU KNOW (Ire) 6-11-4 M A Fitzgerald, *al beh, tld off.* ....(50 to 1 op 25 to 1) 14
Dist: 1½l, 3½l, 12l, 4l, 9l, 15l, 19l, hd, 1¼l, 3l. 4m 12.90s. (14 Ran).
(John Duggan), N A Twiston-Davies

WARWICK (good to firm)
Tuesday November 5th
Going Correction: MINUS 0.40 sec. per fur.

1215 John Pym Novices' Hurdle Class E (4-y-o and up) £2,477 2m..... (1:25)

CHICKAWICKA (Ire) 5-10-12 G Bradley, *made all, hng lft and tried to run out second, clr frm 5th, hung left ag'n appr 2 out, eased r-in*............(7 to 4 fav op 5 to 4 tchd 9 to 4) 1
ABOVE THE CUT (USA) 4-10-12 C Maude, *hld up, hdwy appr 4th, chsd wnr frm 3 out, sn no imprsn.* (33 to 1 op 16 to 1) 2
976^{7} SMART LORD 5-10-12 M Bosley, *hld up in mid-div, keen hold, styd on one pace frm 3 out.* ....(25 to 1 op 16 to 1 tchd 33 to 1) 3
992^{2} HIGHLY CHARMING (Ire) 4-10-12 R Johnson, *trkd ldrs till wknd 3 out*.............. (11 to 4 op 3 to 1 tchd 9 to 4) 4
992^{3} THE DEACONESS 5-10-7 Gary Lyons, *trkd ldrs, mstk 5th, sn btn*............................(33 to 1 op 14 to 1) 5
107^{5} IRISH WILDCARD (NZ) 8-10-12 Jacqui Oliver, *mid-div, outpcd frm 5th*...........(50 to 1 op 25 to 1 tchd 66 to 1) 6
992^{4} ROC AGE 5-10-0 (7*) Mr J Nolan, *cl up, rdn and btn appr 5th.* ....(50 to 1 op 25 to 1) 7
SCHWARTZNDIGGER (Ire) 6-10-12 T Eley, *al beh.* ....(50 to 1 op 25 to 1) 8

1053 KATHARINE'S SONG (Ire) 6-10-7 N Williamson, *trkd ldrs, pushed alng and wknd appr 4th*......(66 to 1 op 25 to 1) 9
THE BREWER 4-10-12 R Bellamy, *whipped round strt, sn wl beh, tld off*............(25 to 1 op 16 to 1 tchd 33 to 1) 10
LABURNUM GOLD (Ire) 5-10-12 W Marston, *cl up, keen hold, chasing wnr whn f 3 out*.............(4 to 1 tchd 5 to 1) f
DESIGN (Ire) 6-10-2 (5*) Michael Brennan, *settled beh ldrs, chasing pack whn hmpd by faller and uns rdr 3 out*. ....(7 to 1 op 5 to 1) ur
WEB OF STEEL 6-10-12 B Clifford, *strted slwly, tld off whn pld up bef 4th*...................(100 to 1 op 66 to 1) pu
1097 RIZAL (USA) (bl) 4-10-9 (3*) D Walsh, *reluctant to race, sn tld off, pld up bef 4th*...............................(66 to 1) pu
TUNGSTEN (Ire) 5-10-12 J R Kavanagh, *beh, reminders aftr 3rd, tld off and pld up bef 2 out*.........(14 to 1 op 6 to 1) pu
Dist: 7l, 6l, 15l, 2l, 11l, 1l, 5l, ¾l, 3l. 3m 39.00s. (15 Ran).
SR: 20/13/7/-/-/-/ (Merthyr Motor Auctions), B Palling

1216 Thomas Fairfax Novices' Chase Class D (5-y-o and up) £3,639 2m .... (1:55)

BRAZIL OR BUST (Ire) 5-11-0 M Dwyer, *hld up, hdwy 4 out, led last, rdn out*......................(5 to 2 op 3 to 1) 1
SLINGSBY (Ire) 6-11-0 A Thornton, *trkd ldr, led 7th, hdd last, ran on*..................................(9 to 4 fav op 7 to 4) 2
919[5] SIGMA RUN (Ire) 7-11-0 R Johnson, *led to 7th, blun nxt, btn whn mstk 3 out*.......................(5 to 1 op 4 to 1) 3
KINO'S CROSS 7-11-0 L Harvey, *chsd ldrs, btn whn hmpd by faller 3 out*..............(11 to 4 op 2 to 1 tchd 3 to 1) 4
COPPER CABLE 9-11-0 M Ranger, *trkd ldrs to 6th*. ....(33 to 1 op 20 to 1) 5
993[3] LARKS TAIL 8-10-9 R Bellamy, *hld up beh, pld hrd, mstk and lost tch 6th, tld off*....................(20 to 1 op 12 to 1) 6
968[5] ICE MAGIC (v) 9-11-0 P McLoughlin, *trkd ldrs, wkng whn f 3 out*...................................(10 to 1 op 8 to 1) f
STRANGE WAYS 8-11-0 Mr A Charles-Jones, *hld up, blun and uns rdr 5th*..................(25 to 1 tchd 33 to 1) ur
Dist: Nk, 19l, 19l, 2½l, dist. 3m 53.60s. a 1.60s (8 Ran).
SR: 6/-/-/-/-/ (Mrs C A Waters), P R Webber

1217 Earl Of Strafford Novices' Hurdle Class E (4-y-o and up) £2,302 2m 3f .... (2:25)

976 ROSEHALL 5-10-4 (3*) G Hogan, *cl up till drpd rear aftr 5th, hmpd 2 out, rallied und pres to ld r-in, styd on*. ....(33 to 1 op 25 to 1) 1
989[3] WANSTEAD (Ire) (bl) 4-10-12 G Bradley, *cl up, lost pl 6th, rallied appr last, styd on und pres*. ....(4 to 1 op 5 to 2 tchd 5 to 1) 2
994* CULRAIN 5-11-5 A Thornton, *hld up beh ldrs, cld 5th, sn rdn alng, led last, hdd r-in*..... (7 to 2 op 4 to 1 tchd 3 to 1) 3
1082 WISE 'N' SHINE 5-10-2 (5*) Chris Webb, *cl up, rdn alng and outpcd frm 6th, styd on appr last*....... (66 to 1 op 50 to 1) 4
CLUB CARIBBEAN 4-10-7 N Williamson, *pld hrd, hld up, cld 5th, lft in ld 2 out, hdd last, wknd*........ (3 to 1 op 7 to 2) 5
BROWN AND MILD 5-10-9 (3*) D Fortt, *led till hdd 4 out, rdn and btn aftr nxt*........ (33 to 1 op 14 to 1 tchd 40 to 1) 6
OPERETTO (Ire) 6-10-12 Mr E James, *pld hrd, cl up, lft in ld whn f 2 out*.......................(12 to 1 op 8 to 1) f
835[2] DACELO (Fr) 5-10-12 J A McCarthy, *hld up, hdwy 4th, led four out, clr whn cocked jaw and ran out bend appr 2 out*. ....(7 to 4 fav op 5 to 4 tchd 15 to 8) ro
ALI'S DELIGHT 5-10-12 L Wyer, *beh frm 5th, tld off whn pld up bef 3 out*.............(33 to 1 op 14 to 1 tchd 40 to 1) pu
Dist: Nk, 2l, hd, 3l, 8l. 4m 32.80s. (9 Ran).
(Mrs T D Pilkington), Mrs T D Pilkington

1218 Earl Of Warwick Handicap Hurdle Class F (0-105 4-y-o and up) £2,011 2m 3f..........................(2:55)

DESERT FORCE (Ire) [83] 7-11-8 G Bradley, *hld up, hdwy 4th, led 3 out, ran on strly*. (11 to 4 fav op 9 to 4 tchd 3 to 1) 1
975[5] COSA FUAIR (Ire) [85] 6-11-10 C O'Dwyer, *hld up gng wl, effrt to chase wnr frm 2 out, sn no imprsn und pres*. ....(9 to 2 op 4 to 1) 2
1139 HULLO MARY DOLL [82] 7-11-2 (5*) Michael Brennan, *hld up, outpcd appr 5th, styd on frm 2 out, no imprsn frm last*. ....(9 to 2 op 4 to 1 tchd 5 to 1) 3
1051[8] WILL JAMES [67] (bl) 10-10-3 (3*) Guy Lewis, *hld up, hdwy to hold ev ch 3 out, sn rdn, wknd appr last*. ....(14 to 1 tchd 20 to 1 and 25 to 1) 4
1000[4] LITTLE HOOLIGAN [82] (bl) 5-11-7 R Johnson, *trkd ldrs, lost pl aftr 4th, sn rallied, wknd after 3 out*. ....(9 to 2 op 4 to 1 tchd 5 to 1) 5
963[5] ROYAL CIRCUS [84] 7-11-6 (3*) E Husband, *led, hit 4th, rdn nxt, hdd 3 out, sn btn*....................(9 to 2 op 4 to 1) 6
1051[7] ANLACE [82] 7-11-2 (5*) Chris Webb, *hld up, slpd up flt aftr 4th*.................................. (9 to 2 op 7 to 2) su
Dist: 6l, 3l, 4l, 7l, 1¾l. 4m 20.80s. (7 Ran).
(G Fierro), A Streeter

1219 Oliver Cromwell Handicap Chase Class D (0-125 5-y-o and up) £4,086 2½m 110yds................. (3:25)

988[4] DRUMSTICK [92] 10-10-9 C O'Dwyer, *chsd ldr, blun second, led appr 11th, lft alone nxt*. (5 to 4 op 6 to 4 tchd 7 to 4) 1
1052[5] MAN MOOD (Fr) [112] 5-12-0 G Bradley, *led, lost action and hdd appr 11th, pld up bef nxt*. .... (7 to 4 on op 2 to 1 on tchd 9 to 4 on and 13 to 8 on) pu
Won by 5m 16.30s. a 21.30s (2 Ran).
SR: -/-/ (Sarah Lady Allendale), K C Bailey

1220 Earl Of Essex Novices' Handicap Hurdle Class E (0-100 4-y-o and up) £2,302 2m.....................(3:55)

PORTSCATHO (Ire) [85] 4-11-4 S Curran, *trkd ldr, led 4 out, all out*..................(100 to 30 op 7 to 2 tchd 4 to 1) 1
1023[3] RED LIGHT [82] (v) 4-10-8 (7*) N T Egan, *hld up, hdwy 4th, chlgd 2 out, rdn and hng lft, rallied und pres nr finish*. ....(5 to 1 tchd 6 to 1) 2
484[2] MR POPPLETON [67] 7-10-0 L Harvey, *led to 4th, cl up, rdn and outpcd aftr 3 out*......(4 to 1 op 3 to 1 tchd 9 to 2) 3
1098[4] BALLY PARSON [86] 10-10-12 (7*) X Aizpuru, *hld up, outpcd aftr 5th*................(10 to 1 op 7 to 1 tchd 11 to 1) 4
1051[2] ALPINE MIST (Ire) [92] (v) 4-11-6 (5*) Michael Brennan, *trkd ldrs, rdn and mstk 3 out, sn btn*. ....(9 to 4 fav op 2 to 1 tchd 5 to 2) 5
1044[6] RANGER SLOANE [78] 4-10-11 G Bradley, *hld up beh, lost tch frm 4 out*..............(9 to 2 op 3 to 1 tchd 5 to 1) 6
Dist: Nk, 11l, 3l, 12l, 7l. 3m 42.00s. a 3.00s (6 Ran).
(Miss Jacqueline S Doyle), A P Jones

HAYDOCK (good)
Wednesday November 6th
Going Correction: PLUS 0.45 sec. per fur.

1221 Birchfield Juvenile Novices' Hurdle Class D (3-y-o) £3,067 2m.....(1:15)

399[2] ALWAYS HAPPY 11-1 C Maude, *patiently rdn, hdwy to ld last, ran on und pres*. (Evens fav op 5 to 4 on tchd 11 to 10) 1
930[4] GLOBE RUNNER 11-0 A Roche, *slight mstk 1st, chsd ldrs frm 2 out, styd on und pres to go second cl hme*. ....(4 to 1 op 7 to 2) 2
930 SON OF ANSHAN 11-0 J Supple, *nvr far away, mstk 4th, ev ch appr 2 out, kpt on*...............(33 to 1 op 25 to 1) 3
KINGFISHER BRAVE 11-0 L Wyer, *led, strly pressed whn slight mstk 2 out, hdd last, no extr*.....(14 to 1 op 16 to 1) 4
WHOTHEHELLISHARRY 11-0 M Moloney, *in tch, chalg whn not fluent 2 out, sn rdn and one pace*.............(25 to 1) 5
893 ROYAL THEN (Fr) 11-0 N Williamson, *beh, styd on und pres frm 2 out, nvr a factor*.................(9 to 1 op 7 to 1) 6
STAR BLAKENEY 11-0 R Farrant, *chsd ldrs, reminders 3 out, not quicken*......................................(50 to 1) 7
MELTEMISON 10-11 (3*) Mr C Bonner, *hld up, pushed alng 3 out, kpt on same pace*.... (15 to 2 op 4 to 1 tchd 8 to 1) 8
SOUSSE 10-9 P Niven, *patiently rdn, hdwy on outsd 4 out, one pace aftr nxt*.........................(7 to 1 op 5 to 1) 9
RADMORE BRANDY 10-9 Gary Lyons, *in tch, pushed alng appr 2 out, no extr betw last two*..................(14 to 1) 10
SNOW DOMINO (Ire) 11-0 M Dwyer, *hld up rear, nvr plcd to chal*...(14 to 1) 11
GRASSHOPPER 10-9 (5*) Michael Brennan, *cl up, niggled alng 3 out, btn whn hit nxt*.................................. (16 to 1) 12
JOHN-T 11-0 L O'Hara, *nvr better than mid-div*. .... (20 to 1 op 16 to 1) 13
BALLYKISSANGEL 11-0 D Bentley, *chsd ldr, not fluent 3rd, wknd quickly 4 out, tld off*...................................(50 to 1) 14
858[4] PROVE THE POINT (Ire) 10-9 Mr L Jefford, *wl beh 4 out, tld off*..(25 to 1) 15
APPEAL AGAIN (Ire) 11-0 D J Burchell, *tld off 4 out*. (25 to 1) 16
1024[3] STOLEAMARCH 11-0 T Eley, *chsd ldrs, pushed alng 3 out, wknd nxt, broke dwn, pld up appr last*.................(10 to 1) pu
Dist: 1¼l, hd, 3½l, 1¼l, 4l, sht-hd, hd, 1½l, 1¼l, 4l. 3m 54.10s. a 16.10s (17 Ran).
(Knight Hawks Partnership), M C Pipe

1222 Preston Amateur Riders' Handicap Hurdle Class E (0-125 4-y-o and up) £2,759 2½m...................(1:45)

PALOSANTO (Ire) [118] 6-11-5 (5*) Mr A Farrant, *led, clr whn blun 3 out, mstk nxt, unchlgd*. ....(5 to 2 on op 9 to 4 on tchd 2 to 1 on) 1
389* TRADE WIND [96] 5-9-9 (7*) Miss K Di Marte, *beh, struggling 3 out, styd on betw last 2, no ch wth wnr*. (3 to 1 op 2 to 1) 2
ZIP YOUR LIP [94] 6-9-7 (7*) Miss C Townsley, *chsd ldr, not fluent 5th, outpcd 3 out, sn btn, tld off*. ....(15 to 2 op 8 to 1 tchd 9 to 1) 3
Dist: 10l, 23l. 4m 55.00s. a 19.00s (3 Ran).
(B A Kilpatrick), M C Pipe

1223 Radio City Handicap Chase Class C (0-130 5-y-o and up) £5,408 2m .... (2:15)

972* EASTERN MAGIC [99] 8-10-0 R Farrant, *nvr far away, not fluent 4th, str chal 2 out, led r-in, drvn out.* (4 to 1 op 9 to 2) 1
1185* STATELY HOME (Ire) [123] 5-11-3 (7*,5ex) Mr R Thornton, *led, hit 8th, strly pressed frm 2 out, kpt on gmely till hdd and no extr r-in.* . . . . (6 to 4 fav op 11 to 10 tchd 13 to 8) 2
PATS MINSTREL [113] (bl) 11-11-0 A Dobbin, *cl up, reminders 8th, lost tch appr 3 out, sn beh.* . . . .(7 to 1 op 6 to 1 tchd 9 to 1) 3
NO PAIN NO GAIN (Ire) [123] 8-11-10 B Storey, *hld up, mstk second, chasing ldrs whn f 7th.* . . . . (13 to 8 op 7 to 4 tchd 15 to 8) f
Dist: 4l, dist. 4m 10.30s. a 14.30s (4 Ran).
SR: 1/21/-/-/ (Mrs Christine Smith), G Barnett

1224 Warrington Novices' Hurdle Class D (4-y-o and up) £3,011 2m. . . . . (2:45)

ADVANCE EAST 4-10-12 R Supple, *patiently rdn, hdwy on bit 2 out, shaken up to ld r-in, cleverly.*
. . . .(14 to 1 op 12 to 1 tchd 16 to 1) 1
1082³ NORDIC BREEZE (Ire) 4-11-4 N Williamson, *led, rdn and not fluent last, hdd r-in, not quicken. . .* (6 to 4 fav tchd 7 to 4) 2
GRANDINARE (USA) 4-10-7 (5*) R McGrath, *pld hrd, nvr far away, not quicken whn slight mstk last, rallied and ran on cl hme.* . . . .(14 to 1 op 10 to 1) 3
GALEN (Ire) 5-10-12 P Niven, *hld up, shaken up and lost tch aftr 4 out, styd on wl frm 2 out, nvr plcd to chal.*
. . . .(12 to 1 op 10 to 1 tchd 14 to 1) 4
THREE WILD DAYS 4-10-12 R Garritty, *hld up, improved to track ldrs 5th, wknd aftr 3 out.* . . . . (5 to 1 op 9 to 2) 5
STAR SELECTION 5-10-9 (3*) E Husband, *pld hrd wth ldrs, chalg whn blun 5th, rdn and lost tch appr 2 out.*
. . . .(9 to 2 op 4 to 1 tchd 5 to 1) 6
HEIGHTH OF FAME 5-10-12 D J Burchell, *sn hndy, drvn alng aftr 5th, sn no dngr.* . . . . (16 to 1 op 14 to 1) 7
1053⁵ PENTLANDS FLYER (Ire) 5-10-12 C Maude, *chsd ldrs, outpcd aftr 5th, sn no dngr.* . . . . (6 to 1 op 9 to 2) 8
ROOD MUSIC 5-10-12 L Wyer, *midfield, mistakes 3rd and nxt, lost tch 3 out, sn beh.* . . . .(16 to 1 op 20 to 1) 9
SEGALA (Ire) 5-10-12 A Roche, *midfield, drvn to chase ldrs aftr 5th, wknd appr 2 out, sn btn.* . . . . . .(20 to 1 op 16 to 1) 10
CLIBURNEL NEWS (Ire) 6-10-7 T Eley, *beh, mstk 3rd, reminders aftr 5th, btn nxt.* . . . .(16 to 1 op 14 to 1) 11
ROYRACE 4-10-12 S Wynne, *beh, stumbled appr 3rd, tld off 5th.* . . . . (50 to 1 op 33 to 1) 12
SCOTT'S RISK 6-10-12 Richard Guest, *tld off 4th, pld up bef 3 out.* . . . . (50 to 1) pu
INTENDANT 4-10-12 M Dwyer, *mstk second, hdwy to chase ldrs hfwy, weakend quickly bef 3 out, tld off whn pld up before nxt.* . . . . (14 to 1 op 10 to 1) pu
Dist: 1¾l, nk, 19l, 8l, 2l, hd, 1l, nk, 1¾l, 7l. 3m 52.90s. a 14.90s (14 Ran).
SR: 7/11/4/-/-/-/ (A F Monk), M Dods

1225 Radio City Handicap Hurdle Class D (0-120 5-y-o and up) £2,745 2m . . . . (3:15)

CHAI-YO [104] 6-11-3 G Upton, *hld up, not fluent 3rd, hdwy to ld appr last, pushed out. . . . . . .*(5 to 2 fav tchd 11 to 4) 1
SAINT CIEL (USA) [104] 8-11-3 S Wynne, *wth ldr, ev ch 3 out, rdn and not quicken r-in.* . . . .(7 to 1 op 6 to 1) 2
LORD McMURROUGH (Ire) [110] 6-11-9 R Farrant, *hld up, effrt 2 out, ev ch whn slight mstk last, no extr.*
. . . .(5 to 1 op 4 to 1) 3
THURSDAY NIGHT (Ire) [108] 5-11-7 L Wyer, *set slow pace, quickened 3 out, hdd and no extr.*
. . . . (7 to 1 op 11 to 1) 4
SEASONAL SPLENDOUR (Ire) [115] 6-12-0 C Maude, *hld up, niggled alng whn ldrs quickened 3 out, no imprsn.*
. . . .(7 to 2 op 3 to 1) 5
COOL LUKE (Ire) [106] 7-11-5 N Williamson, *chsd ldrs, effrt gng wl appr 2 out, rdn and wknd last.*
. . . . (9 to 2 op 5 to 1 tchd 11 to 2) 6
Dist: 2l, 3l, 1¼l, 4l, 4l. 4m 7.10s. a 29.10s (6 Ran).
(Nick Viney), J A B Old

1226 Glengoyne Single Highland Malt Novices' Chase Class D Tamerosia Series Qualifier (5-y-o and up) £3,770 3m. . . . . (3:45)

1009² IMPERIAL VINTAGE (Ire) 6-11-12 N Williamson, *made all, pushed alng 3 out, jmpd lft last, styd on wl und pres.*
. . . . (100 to 30 op 7 to 4) 1
1138³ MONYMOSS (Ire) 7-10-9 (7*) R Wilkinson, *hld up, chsd wnr frm 13th, mstk 3 out, sn rdn, kpt on. . . . . .* (5 to 1 op 7 to 1) 2
ROYAL PARIS (Ire) 8-11-2 Richard Guest, *hld up, chsd ldr 5th, blun nxt, tld off 11th.* . . . . (12 to 1 op 10 to 1) 3
WISLEY WONDER (Ire) 6-11-2 C Maude, *cl up jumping wl, blun and uns rdr 13th.*
. . . . (13 to 8 on op 6 to 4 tchd 11 to 8 on) ur
CHERRY ORCHID 9-11-2 R Supple, *keen hold, tld off frm 7th, pld up bef 5 out.* . . . . (50 to 1 op 33 to 1) pu
Dist: 1¾l, dist. 6m 25.60s. a 20.60s (5 Ran).
(David M Williams), Miss Venetia Williams

1227 Weatherbys 'Stars Of Tomorrow' Mares Only Open National Hunt Flat Intermediate Class H (4,5,6-y-o) £1,208 2m. . . . . (4:15)

MARELLO 5-11-7 (3*) G Cahill, *steadied rear, smooth hdwy 3 fs out, led o'r one out, eased cl hme, readily.*
. . . .(11 to 4 on op 5 to 2 on tchd 3 to 1 on) 1
COUNTRY ORCHID 5-11-0 P Niven, *hld up, effrt o'r 3 fs out, styd on wl, not pace of wnr.* (8 to 1 op 7 to 1 tchd 9 to 1) 2
HURST FLYER 4-11-0 A Dobbin, *hld up, pushed alng and hdwy o'r 2 fs out, kpt on.* (16 to 1 op 12 to 1 tchd 25 to 1) 3
BRIDLED TERN 5-10-9 (5*) E Callaghan, *wth ldr, led and quickened 4 fs out, hdd o'r one out, no extr.*
. . . .(8 to 1 op 5 to 1) 4
LOVELY RASCAL 4-10-9 (5*) R McGrath, *in tch, drpd rear 4 fs out, some hdwy 2 out, one pace aftr.*
. . . . (9 to 1 op 5 to 1 tchd 10 to 1) 5
880⁵ LIPPY LOUISE 4-11-0 R Hodge, *set slow pace, hdd 7 fs out, rdn and one pace frm 2 out. . . . . . .*(10 to 1 op 8 to 1) 6
HERBALLISTIC 4-10-9 (5*) Michael Brennan, *chsd ldrs, drvn alng wl o'r 2 fs out, no imprsn. . .*(33 to 1 op 20 to 1) 7
LADY ROSEBURY 6-11-0 N Williamson, *cl up, led 7 fs out to 4 out, sn wknd, tld off. . . . .*(25 to 1 op 14 to 1) 8
Dist: 1¼l, sht-hd, 1l, 1l, 2½l, ½l, 16l. 4m 5.90s. (8 Ran).
(Mrs M Williams), Mrs L Reveley

KEMPTON (good)
Wednesday November 6th
Going Correction: PLUS 0.35 sec. per fur. (races 1,3,6), PLUS 0.50 (2,4,5)

1228 USM Bowl Class E Novices' Hurdle (4-y-o and up) £2,360 2m 5f. . . (1:35)

MILLERSFORD 5-10-10 J R Kavanagh, *hdwy 6th, led 2 out, drvn out. . . . .*(4 to 1 op 5 to 1 tchd 6 to 1) 1
QUAFF (Ire) 6-10-10 P Hide, *hdwy 4 out, lost pl appr 2 out, rallied approaching last, ran on.*
. . . .(7 to 2 op 3 to 1 tchd 4 to 1) 2
MOUNTAIN PATH 6-10-10 M A Fitzgerald, *hdwy 6th, ev ch 2 out, not quicken. . . . .*(11 to 2 op 4 to 1 tchd 6 to 1) 3
SPRING DOUBLE (Ire) 5-10-10 C Llewellyn, *led to 2 out, one pace. . . . .*(2 to 1 fav op 5 to 2) 4
WINNOW 6-9-12 (7*) C Rae, *hdwy 4 out, wknd appr 2 out.*
. . . . (66 to 1 op 33 to 1 tchd 100 to 1) 5
DOMINOS RING (Ire) 7-10-10 Mr A Walton, *prmnt till wknd appr 2 out. . . . .*(7 to 1 op 9 to 2 tchd 8 to 1) 6
KRATON GARDEN (USA) 4 10 10 E Murphy, *prmnt till wknd quickly appr 2 out. . . . .*(20 to 1 op 14 to 1) 7
CHECKS AND STRIPES (Ire) 5-10-10 M Richards, *prmnt till wknd quickly appr 4 out, tld off.*
. . . . (33 to 1 op 20 to 1 tchd 40 to 1) 8
989⁴ ZUNO FLYER (USA) 4-10-10 B Powell, *blun 4th, tld off frm 5th.* . . . . (33 to 1 op 20 to 1) 9
FAST FORWARD FRED 5-10-10 D Morris, *tld off frm 5th, pld up bef 4 out. . . . .*(14 to 1 op 6 to 1 tchd 16 to 1) pu
1065⁵ QUARE DREAM'S (Ire) 5-10-5 C O'Dwyer, *chsd ldr till weak-end 4 out, tld off whn pld up bef 2 out.*
. . . . (25 to 1 op 14 to 1 tchd 33 to 1) pu
Dist: 3l, 2½l, 15l, 2l, 16l, 14l, dist, 1½l. 5m 7.20s. a 21.20s (11 Ran).
(Mrs Derek Fletcher), N A Gaselee

1229 Johnsons International Novices' Chase Class D (5-y-o and up) £3,517 3m. . . . . (2:05)

BARONET 6-11-0 A Maguire, *al prmnt, led 14th to 15th, led appr 3 out, ran on wl.*
. . . .(13 to 8 on op 7 to 4 on tchd 6 to 4 on) 1
1062⁴ CASTLE CHIEF (Ire) 7-11-0 P Hide, *led to 8th, led 15th till appr 3 out, ev ch 2 out, not quicken. . . . . . .*(4 to 1 op 11 to 4) 2
OUROWNFELLOW (Ire) 7-11-0 D Morris, *led 8th, mstk 12th, hdd 14th, ev ch 2 out, wknd appr last. . . .*(5 to 1 tchd 11 to 2) 3
PARLIAMENTARIAN (Ire) 7-11-0 C O'Dwyer, *in rear whn mstk 14th, tld off frm nxt. . . . .*(16 to 1 op 14 to 1 tchd 20 to 1) 4
GLENTOWER (Ire) 8-11-0 M A Fitzgerald, *in tch till wknd 15th, poor 4th whn f 2 out. . . .*(12 to 1 op 10 to 1 tchd 14 to 1) f
Dist: 7l, 8l, dist. 6m 6.70s. a 17.70s (5 Ran).
SR: 29/22/14/-/-/ (Mrs David Thompson), D Nicholson

1230 Mirror Select Conditional Jockeys' Claiming Hurdle Class F (4,5,6-y-o) £2,234 2m. . . . . (2:35)

1175⁵ PAIR OF JACKS (Ire) 6-11-7 D Fortt, *chsd ldr frm second, hrd rdn appr last, led cl hme. . . . .*(3 to 1 op 4 to 1) 1
677⁵ ADILOV 4-10-7 Sophie Mitchell, *hld up, hdwy 2 out, ev ch last, ran on nr finish. . . . .*(33 to 1 op 25 to 1) 2
992* INDIAN JOCKEY 4-11-13 D Walsh, *led, hrd rdn frm 5th, hdd cl hme. . . . .*(11 to 8 on op 2 to 1 tchd 5 to 4 on) 3
1006⁹ LAST LAUGH (Ire) 4-9-13 (5*) W Walsh, *hld up, ev ch appr 2 out, sn rdn and wknd. . . . .*(4 to 1 op 3 to 1) 4

1111^{5} NIGHT IN A MILLION 5-11-1 K Gaule, *hld up, ev ch 3 out, wknd bef nxt*........ (16 to 1 tchd 14 to 1 and 20 to 1) 5
Dist: Nk, ½l, 13l, 14l. 3m 55.10s. a 15.10s (5 Ran).
(D A Wilson), G L Moore

1231 Sporting Life Trophy Class D Handicap Chase (0-120 5-y-o and up) £3,501 3m....................(3:05)

938^{2} DRUMCULLEN (Ire) [96] 7-11-0 C O'Dwyer, *led, mstk 12th, hdd appr 3 out, led in ld approaching last, styd on.* ....(4 to 1 op 7 to 2 tchd 9 to 2) 1
988 PAPER STAR [103] 9-11-7 B Powell, *chsd wnr to 11th, lost pl 13th, styd on ag'n frm 2 out.* ....(33 to 1 op 16 to 1 tchd 40 to 1) 2
188^{8} FUNCHEON GALE [92] 9-10-10 D Morris, *in rear, mstks 1st and 5th, staying on whn mistake last, nvr nr to chal.* .... (9 to 2 op 4 to 1 tchd 11 to 2) 3
974^{3} CERTAIN ANGLE [106] 7-11-10 A Maguire, *jnd wnr 12th, ev ch whn blun badly 4 out, not reco'r*...... (7 to 2 op 5 to 2) 4
967^{5} NEVADA GOLD [100] 10-11-4 P McLoughlin, *chsd ldrs, hrd rdn 9th, beh frm 12th*..... (7 to 1 op 8 to 1 tchd 10 to 1) 5
1064^{4} SORBIERE [100] (bl) 9-11-4 M A Fitzgerald, *nvr gng wl, in rear whn f 13th*...........(9 to 1 op 6 to 1 tchd 10 to 1) f
MASTER ORCHESTRA (Ire) [103] 7-11-7 J F Titley, *al prmnt, led appr 3 out, clr whn pld up lme approaching last.* ....(9 to 4 fav op 2 to 1 tchd 5 to 2) pu
Dist: 8l, 3l, 1¾l, nk. 6m 7.70s. a 18.70s (7 Ran).
SR: 19/18/4/16/9/-/-/ (Martyn Booth), K C Bailey

1232 Ace Cup Class D Novices' Chase (5-y-o and up) £3,550 2½m 110yds ....(3:35)

1054^{2} FINE THYNE (Ire) 7-11-0 M A Fitzgerald, *al gng wl, led appr last, lft well clr, easily*...(6 to 5 fav op Evens tchd 5 to 4) 1
MYSTIC ISLE (Ire) 6-11-0 C Llewellyn, *mstk 7th, prmnt till wknd 4 out, mistake 3 out, poor fourth whn lft second last.* .... (9 to 1 op 6 to 1 tchd 10 to 1) 2
SUNSET AND VINE 9-11-0 C O'Dwyer, *tld off frm 12th, lft poor 3rd last*....................... (20 to 1 tchd 25 to 1) 3
968^{6} NORDANSK 7-11-0 D Morris, *hdwy 11th, ev ch whn blun 2 out, 3rd and btn when f last.* ....(9 to 1 op 7 to 1 tchd 10 to 1) f
968^{3} GREENBACK (Bel) 5-10-13 A Maguire, *mstk 4th, hdwy tenth, led aftr 13th till after 2 out, second and btn whn f last.* ....(9 to 2 op 4 to 1 tchd 5 to 2) f
WIXOE WONDER (Ire) 6-11-0 P Holley, *led, hdd aftr 13th, 4th and btn whn f four out.* (66 to 1 op 33 to 1 tchd 100 to 1) f
KEY TO MOYADE (Ire) 6-11-0 I Lawrence, *in tch whn crrd out bef 9th*.......................(33 to 1 op 16 to 1) co
MR JERVIS (Ire) 7-11-0 P Hide, *in tch whn pld up bef 9th.* ....(4 to 1 op 9 to 2 tchd 5 to 1) pu
Dist: Dist, dist. 5m 11.60s. a 18.60s (8 Ran).
SR: 3/-/-/-/-/ (Peter Wiegand), Mrs A J Perrett

1233 Fiesta Magazine Handicap Hurdle Class C (0-135 4-y-o and up) £3,436 3m 110yds................... (4:05)

OCEAN HAWK (USA) [128] 4-11-11 C Llewellyn, *al prmnt, led 4 out, sn wl clr, eased aftr last.* ....(9 to 4 fav op 5 to 2 tchd 2 to 1) 1
1032^{7} FIELDRIDGE [115] 7-10-13 B Powell, *hld up, wnt poor second appr 2 out, no ch wth wnr*........... (14 to 1 op 10 to 1) 2
1048* OLYMPIAN [118] (bl) 9-11-2 M FitzGerald, *al prmnt, hrd rdn 4 out, one pace*...........(7 to 1 op 5 to 1 tchd 15 to 2) 3
969^{3} GIVUS A CALL (Ire) [109] 6-10-7 P Hide, *chsd ldrs, no hdwy frm 3 out*........................... (8 to 1 tchd 7 to 1) 4
HARDING [103] 5-10-0 N Mann, *chsd ldr, wknd appr 2 out.* ....(3 to 1 tchd 9 to 2) 5
DARK HONEY [130] 11-12-0 A Dicken, *tld off frm 6th.* ....(20 to 1 op 12 to 1) 6
JADIDH [107] 8-10-5 P Holley, *tld off frm 6th.* ....(14 to 1 tchd 12 to 1) 7
1056^{5} WOTTASHAMBLES [112] 5-10-9 D Morris, *prmnt till mstk and wknd 6th, tld off whn pld up bef 2 out.* ....(6 to 1 op 11 to 2 tchd 13 to 2) pu
921* SHAHRANI [113] 4-10-7 (3*) D Walsh, *led till wknd quickly 4 out, tld off whn pld up bef 2 out.* .... (6 to 1 op 5 to 1 tchd 13 to 2) pu
Dist: 13l, 6l, 3l, 7l, dist, 1¼l. 5m 59.20s. a 14.20s (9 Ran).
SR: 39/12/9/-/-/-/ (Matt Archer & Miss Jean Broadhurst), N A Twiston-Davies

NEWTON ABBOT (heavy)
Wednesday November 6th

Going Correction: PLUS 1.45 sec. per fur. (races 1,2,4,5,7), PLUS 1.95 (3,6)

1234 Anfield Novices' Hurdle Class E (4-y-o and up) £2,284 3m 3f......(1:25)

1002^{2} KENDAL CAVALIER 6-10-10 B Fenton, *wth ldr, led appr 7th, hdd sn aftr 3 out, came wide into strt, led last, all out.* ....(15 to 8 fav op 9 to 4 tchd 7 to 4) 1
DENISE'S PROFILES 6-10-10 D Bridgwater, *hld up in rear, hdwy 7th, led sn aftr 3 out, rdn and hdd last, kpt on.* ....(9 to 4 tchd 5 to 2) 2
BRAMBLEHILL BUCK (Ire) 7-10-10 A P McCoy, *al prmnt, jnd ldrs 4 out, wknd aftr nxt*............... (6 to 1 op 4 to 1) 3
1115^{3} COPPER COIL 6-10-3 (7*) J Power, *made most till hdd appr 7th, sn wknd, tld off*.....................(12 to 1 op 10 to 1) 4
919^{4} CASTLECONNER (Ire) 5-10-10 J Frost, *in tch till wknd 4 out, tld off*..................(20 to 1 op 12 to 1 tchd 25 to 1) 5
841^{4} PENNANT COTTAGE (Ire) 8-10-0 (5*) Chris Webb, *prmnt to 7th, tld off*............(50 to 1 op 33 to 1 tchd 66 to 1) 6
906^{4} MU-TADIL 4-10-10 D Leahy, *al beh, tld off whn pld up bef 3 out*................................(33 to 1 op 20 to 1) pu
540^{4} UP THE TEMPO (Ire) 7-10-5 W Marston, *al beh, tld off whn pld up aftr 8th*..............................(25 to 1 op 12 to 1) pu
KARICLEIGH MAN 6-10-10 R Dunwoody, *hld up, hdwy 5th, wknd 3 out, tld off whn pld up bef last.* .... (6 to 1 op 11 to 2 tchd 7 to 1) pu
629^{2} RARE SPREAD (Ire) 6-10-10 G Bradley, *al towards rear, tld off whn pld up bef last*.................(14 to 1 op 6 to 1) pu
HOPPERDANTE (Ire) 6-10-5 R Johnson, *in tch till wknd 4 out, tld off whn pld up bef last.* .... (20 to 1 op 14 to 1 tchd 25 to 1) pu
Dist: Hd, 25l, 25l, 15l, dist. 7m 2.20s. a 46.20s (11 Ran).
SR: 12/12/-/-/-/-/ (Michael Wingfield Digby), G B Balding

1235 Old Trafford Selling Handicap Hurdle Class G (0-95 4-y-o and up) £1,865 2m 1f.........................(1:55)

ROYAL STANDARD [70] (v) 9-9-13 (7*) D Finnegan, *made all, clr 3 out, unchlgd*....... (15 to 2 op 5 to 1 tchd 9 to 1) 1
ALICE'S MIRROR [73] 7-10-9 R Johnson, *in tch till lost pl appr 4 out, styd on approaching 2 out, wnt second r-in.* ....(7 to 1 op 8 to 1) 2
1175* GLOWING PATH [76] 6-10-5 (7*) J Harris, *chsd ldrs, lost tch 4 out, wnt poor second 2 out, wknd r-in, fnshd tired.* ....(7 to 4 fav op 7 to 4) 3
937^{6} SCALP 'EM (Ire) [64] 8-10-0 Dr P Pritchard, *hld up, hdwy 4th, rdn and wknd appr 3 out, tld off*...... (33 to 1 op 16 to 1) 4
AL HAAL (USA) [71] 7-10-7 A McCabe, *chsd wnr till wknd 3 out, tld off*...........(14 to 1 op 10 to 1 tchd 16 to 1) 5
937* MUTAWALI (Ire) [75] 6-10-11 D Leahy, *slwly away, al beh, tld off*........................(4 to 1 op 7 to 2 tchd 9 to 2) 6
784 INDIAN MINOR [64] (bl) 12-9-9 (5*) D J Kavanagh, *chsd ldrs till wknd aftr 4th, tld off*...............(20 to 1 op 14 to 1) 7
TOUCH SILVER [92] 6-11-7 (7*) A Dowling, *slwly away, jmpd slowly, tld off 4th*.........(15 to 2 op 7 to 1 tchd 8 to 1) 8
918 COLOUR SCHEME [68] (v) 9-9-11 (7*) B McGann, *ran out bend aftr second*......(20 to 1 op 14 to 1 tchd 25 to 1) ro
NITA'S CHOICE [64] 6-10-0 A Thornton, *al beh, tld off whn pld up bef last*........................(20 to 1 op 14 to 1) pu
998 SOVEREIGN NICHE (Ire) [80] 8-11-2 A P McCoy, *refused to race*..................................(10 to 1 op 7 to 1) I
Dist: 26l, ½l, 9l, 6l, 26l, dist, 6l. 4m 19.90s. a 30.90s (11 Ran).
SR: 15/-/-/-/-/-/ (P M Rich), P M Rich

1236 Rodgers Of Brixton Novices' Chase Class E (5-y-o and up) £3,077 2m 5f 110yds........................ (2:25)

PUNTERS OVERHEAD (Ire) 8-10-12 A P McCoy, *trkd ldr, led 9th, rdn appr last, pushed out.* ....(2 to 1 fav op 6 to 4 tchd 9 to 4) 1
SUPER COIN 8-10-12 R Johnson, *hld up in rear, hdwy 9th, wnt second 5 out, ev ch 2 out, no imprsn aftr.* .... (100 to 30 op 5 to 2 tchd 7 to 2) 2
AMBER SPARK (Ire) 7-10-12 R Dunwoody, *hit 4th, hld up in rear, hdwy 5 out, 3rd whn mstk 2 out, styd on.* .... (7 to 1 tchd 8 to 1 and 10 to 1) 3
999* MR PLAYFULL 6-11-5 J Frost, *led to 9th, wknd quickly 5 out.* .... (4 to 1 op 5 to 1 tchd 6 to 1 and 7 to 2) 4
PURBECK CAVALIER 7-10-12 W McFarland, *prmnt till wknd 5 out, tld off*.......... (12 to 1 op 10 to 1 tchd 14 to 1) 5
BOLD ACRE 6-10-12 T J Murphy, *chsd ldrs till wknd tenth, tld off*...............(12 to 1 op 8 to 1 tchd 14 to 1) 6
VOSNE ROMANEE II (Fr) 9-10-5 (7*) G Supple, *rcd in rear, f 4 out*....................................(25 to 1 op 33 to 1) f
902^{4} STORMY SUNSET 9-10-2² (7*) Mr T Dennis, *al in rear, f 4 out.* ....(14 to 1 op 16 to 1) f
COLETTE'S CHOICE (Ire) 7-10-7 S Burrough, *f 6th.* ....(33 to 1 op 25 to 1 tchd 50 to 1) f
1055 COUNTRY KEEPER 8-10-9 (3*) T Dascombe, *f second.* ....(33 to 1 op 25 to 1 tchd 50 to 1) f
751 BELLS WOOD 7-10-12 L Harvey, *prmnt till wknd 9th, blun 11th, beh whn f 4 out*............... (50 to 1 op 33 to 1) f
LOWER BITHAM 9-10-2 (5*) D J Kavanagh, *al beh, tld off whn hmpd 4 out, pld up sn aftr*......... (50 to 1 tchd 66 to 1) pu
PADDY BURKE (Ire) 6-10-12 A Thornton, *al beh, tld off whn pld up bef 2 out*..(33 to 1) pu
Dist: 2l, 3½l, 25l, 14l, 19l. 5m 49.40s. a 47.40s (13 Ran).
SR: 29/27/23/5/-/-/ (Mrs Elaine Hutchinson), P F Nicholls

1237 Barclays Bank 'National Hunt' Novices' Hurdle Class E (4-y-o and up) £2,400 2¾m..................(2:55)

SEYMOURSWIFT 6-10-5 R Dunwoody, *al in tch, smooth hdwy to go second appr 2 out, sn rdn, all out to ld line.*
.................................(11 to 1 op 12 to 1 tchd 10 to 1)   1
MR COTTON SOCKS 8-10-10 J Frost, *led 3rd, hrd pressed frm 2 out, hdd last strd...*.(11 to 4 op 2 to 1 tchd 3 to 1)   2
ONE FOR NAVIGATION (Ire) 4-10-10 A P McCoy, *hld up, rdn alng frm 6th, hit 4 out, ev ch nxt, sn wknd.*
...........(11 to 8 on op 5 to 4 on tchd 11 to 10 on)   3
1047 OTTER PRINCE 7-10-10 R Johnson, *al in tch, wnt second appr 4 out, wknd aftr nxt, tld off.......*(66 to 1 op 33 to 1)   4
MISS SECRET 6-10-5 D Bridgwater, *al beh, tld off.* (66 to 1)   5
975⁴ JHAL FREZI 8-10-10 A Procter, *prmnt till wknd appr 4 out, tld off.......................................*(12 to 1)   6
ASHLEY HOUSE 7-10-5 (5*) D Salter, *hld up, hdwy 4th, wknd appr 3 out, tld off whn pld up bef nxt.*(50 to 1 tchd 66 to 1) pu
RAINBOW FOUNTAIN 9-10-0 (5*) Chris Webb, *led to 3rd, wknd quickly 6th, pld up bef nxt..........*(20 to 1 op 25 to 1) pu
BLAKEWAY 9-10-5 S Burrough, *prmnt to 5th, tld off whn pld up bef 2 out..............................*(66 to 1 op 50 to 1) pu
937⁹ MIRAMARE 6-10-7 (3*) T Dascombe, *al beh, tld off whn pld up bef last...................................*(50 to 1) pu
BID FOR TOOLS (Ire) 4-10-10 A Thornton, *tld off 4th, pld up aftr 6th............................*(66 to 1 op 50 to 1) pu
TOLCARNE LADY 7-10-5 L Harvey, *al beh, tld off whn pld up bef 3 out..............*(50 to 1 op 33 to 1 tchd 66 to 1) pu
456⁶ MORECEVA (Ire) 6-10-10 W Marston, *al beh, tld off whn pld up aftr 6th..........................*(50 to 1 op 33 to 1) pu
ALONE HOME (Ire) 5-10-10 J Railton, *prmnt to 6th, tld off whn pld up bef 2 out......................*(8 to 1 op 6 to 1) pu
Dist: Sht-hd, dist, 1¾l, dist, 8l. 5m 44.60s. a 43.60s (14 Ran).
(Starlight Racing), D R Gandolfo

1238 William Hill Trial Handicap Hurdle Class C (0-130 4-y-o and up) 2m 1f...................................(3:25)

MOUSE BIRD (Ire) [116] 6-10-12 R Dunwoody, *patiently rdn, hdwy 4 out, led appr 2 out, sn clr, eased r-in........*(7 to 2)   1
1178² MORSTOCK [110] 6-10-5 (3*) T Dascombe, *chsd ldr, ev ch 3 out, one pace aftr.......*(4 to 1 op 3 to 1 tchd 9 to 2)   2
CADOUGOLD (Fr) [123] 5-11-7 A P McCoy, *chsd ldrs, hdwy to ld 3 out, hdd bef nxt, sn btn.......*(3 to 1 tchd 7 to 2)   3
HOLDIMCLOSE [110] 6-10-8 J Frost, *led till hdd 3 out, wknd quickly.....................*(5 to 1 op 6 to 1 tchd 7 to 1)   4
FROGMARCH (USA) [130] 6-12-0 J Railton, *al beh, lost tch 5th...........................*(7 to 2 op 11 to 4)   5
WORLD EXPRESS (Ire) [102] 6-9-11² (5*) D Salter, *al beh, lost tch hfwy................*(15 to 2 op 6 to 1 tchd 8 to 1)   6
Dist: 7l, sht-hd, 15l, 6l, 8l. 4m 22.30s. a 33.30s (6 Ran).
(Osbert Pierce), D R Gandolfo

1239 Stamford Bridge Handicap Chase Class E (0-110 5-y-o and up) 3¼m 110yds................(3:55)

BOND JNR (Ire) [110] 7-12-0 A P McCoy, *made all, clr 4 out, tired appr 2 out, unchlgd.*
.................................6 to 5 on op 6 to 4 on tchd 11 to 10)   1
ROCKY PARK [92] 10-10-10 B Fenton, *al prmnt, blun tenth, reco'red to chase wnr frm 5 out..........*(6 to 1 op 7 to 2)   2
SHAMARPHIL [93] 10-10-11 Miss S Barraclough, *wl in rear, styd on frm 4 out, nvr nrr................*(8 to 1 op 6 to 1)   3
STEEPLE JACK [85] 9-10-3 S Burrough, *trkd ldrs, wknd 5 out.........................*(5 to 1 tchd 6 to 1)   4
SCOTONI [95] 10-10-13 S Curran, *trkd wnr till wknd 5 out, tld off..................................*(16 to 1 op 10 to 1)   5
TAPAGEUR [95] 11-10-6 (7*) G Supple, *hld up, mstks in rear, tld off whn pld up bef 4 out.* (6 to 1 op 4 to 1 tchd 7 to 1) pu
Dist: 6l, 2½l, 3½l, 21l. 7m 23.20s. a 63.20s (6 Ran).
(Paul K Barber), P F Nicholls

1240 Highbury Standard Open National Hunt Flat Class H (4,5,6-y-o) £1,236 2m 1f...........................(4:25)

693³ ULTIMATE SMOOTHIE 4-12-0 G Bradley, *wtd wth in rear and rcd wide, hdwy 6 fs out, str chal o'r one out, quickened to ld ins last..................*(7 to 1 op 4 to 1 tchd 8 to 1)   1
LORD FOLEY (NZ) 4-11-1 (3*) J Magee, *al in tch, led o'r 2 fs out, rdn and hdd ins last.* (9 to 1 op 4 to 1 tchd 10 to 1)   2
IVORY COASTER (NZ) 5-11-4 J Osborne, *rcd wide, al in tch, led 3 fs out, sn hdd, kpt on.*
.................................9 to 4 fav op 4 to 1 tchd 2 to 1)   3
53⁹ ARCTIC CHANTER 4-10-13 (5*) D Salter, *al prmnt, wnt second hfwy, led 5 fs out, hdd 3 out, wknd.* (33 to 1 op 25 to 1)   4
DEFENDTHEREALM 5-11-4 Mr A Holdsworth, *in tch till wknd o'r 3 fs out...................*(50 to 1 op 20 to 1)   5
TAIN TON 4-10-11 (7*) M Keighley, *mid-div, no hdwy fnl 4 fs.*
.................................(14 to 1 op 8 to 1 tchd 16 to 1)   6
LUCKY CALL (NZ) 5-10-11 (7*) Mr G Shenkin, *mid-div, effrt 5 fs out, nvr nr to chal.......*(11 to 2 op 5 to 1 tchd 7 to 1)   7
DUKES CASTLE (Ire) 5-11-4 J Frost, *in tch till wknd 4 fs out.......................*(11 to 2 op 4 to 1 tchd 10 to 1)   8
671⁵ CAPTAIN FELIX (NZ) 4-10-13 (5*) D J Kavanagh, *prmnt till wknd quickly 4 fs out..............*(14 to 1 op 10 to 1)   9
FRANKIE MUCK 4-10-11 (7*) L Suthern, *al beh.*
.................................(6 to 1 op 4 to 1)   10

ZAGGY LANE 4-11-4 B Fenton, *al beh.*
.................................(50 to 1 op 33 to 1)   11
KIND CLERIC 5-11-4 A P McCoy, *in tch to hfwy, tld off.*
.................................(14 to 1 op 8 to 1 tchd 16 to 1)   12
MURRAY'S MILLION 4-11-4 T J Murphy, *al beh, tld off.*
.................................(50 to 1 op 33 to 1 tchd 66 to 1)   13
MINGAY 5-10-11 (7*) Miss E Jones, *pld hrd, led, sn clr, wknd quickly and hdd 5 fs out, tld off.......*(66 to 1 op 33 to 1)   14
Dist: 1¼l, 1¼l, 12l, ¾l, ¾l, 8l, ¾l, 2½l, 5l, 5l. 4m 20.20s. (14 Ran).
(Isca Bloodstock), M C Pipe

CLONMEL (IRE) (yielding to soft)
Thursday November 7th

1241 Cashel Maiden Hurdle (5-y-o and up) £2,226 2m...................(1:00)

1147* DASHING DOLLAR (Ire) 5-12-0 C F Swan, ...(6 to 4 fav)   1
1090³ WELSH GRIT (Ire) 7-11-11 (3*) D J Casey, ...(5 to 1)   2
1119² REAL TAOISEACH (Ire) 6-11-7 (7*) Mr A K Wyse, ..(4 to 1)   3
978⁴ TALE GAIL (Ire) 6-12-0 C O'Dwyer, ...(9 to 2)   4
977⁸ SARADANTE (Ire) 6-11-6 K F O'Brien, ...(14 to 1)   5
1117 REMAINDER STAR (Ire) 5-11-6 T J Mitchell, ...(12 to 1)   6
1081⁶ ASK ME IN (Ire) 5-10-12 (3*) K Whelan, ...(20 to 1)   7
278 LADY CONDUCTOR (Ire) 5-11-1 P McWilliams, ...(16 to 1)   8
133⁸ MUSKERRY EXPRESS (Ire) 6-11-6 N Williamson, ..(16 to 1)   9
BARNA LASS (Ire) 5-10-10 (5*) J M Donnelly, ...(16 to 1)   10
1096 BRASSIS HILL (Ire) 5-10-13 (7*) A O'Shea, ...(14 to 1)   11
945⁶ SITE MISTRESS (Ire) 5-10-10 (5*) G Cotter, ...(16 to 1)   12
1119³ SHECOULDNTBEBETTER (Ire) 5-11-1 T P Treacy, ..(14 to 1)   13
1119⁶ HOLLY LADY (Ire) 5-11-1 P A Roche, ...(25 to 1)   14
QUEEN OF ALL GALES (Ire) 5-10-10 (5*) P D Carey, (14 to 1)   15
1120² MAJOR GALE (Ire) 7-10-13 (7*) M D Murphy, ...(12 to 1)   16
TOBY'S FRIEND (Ire) 7-10-10 (5*) J Butler, ...(20 to 1)   17
OAKDALE GIRL (Ire) 6-11-1 G M O'Neill, ...(20 to 1)   18
829⁶ WATT A BUZZ (Ire) 5-10-8 (7*) K M O'Callaghan, ..(20 to 1)   19
142 GLENBEG GROVE (Ire) 6-11-1 F Woods, ...(33 to 1)   20
Dist: 2l, 2l, 25l, 3½l. 4m 16.20s. (20 Ran).
(Martyn J McEnery), A P O'Brien

1242 European Breeders Fund Beginners Chase (5-y-o and up) £3,253 2½m ....(1:30)

1146³ DUN BELLE 7-11-9 T J Mitchell, ...(11 to 2)   1
1018* THE LATVIAN LARK (Ire) 8-12-0 M P Dwyer, ...(5 to 4 on)   2
1074⁶ MARIES POLLY 6-11-9 D H O'Connor, ...(16 to 1)   3
1146⁷ DRAMATIC VENTURE (Ire) 7-11-11 (3*) D J Casey, ..(8 to 1)   4
1076⁸ HOLY GROUNDER (Ire) 7-11-7 (7*) A O'Shea, ...(14 to 1)   5
1080⁷ BAILE NA GCLOCH (Ire) 7-11-11 (3*) D P Murphy, (20 to 1)   6
RISZARD (USA) 7-12-0 N Williamson, ...(10 to 1)   7
925⁸ WILD BROOK (Ire) 6-11-11 (3*) K Whelan, ...(12 to 1)   8
983⁷ GRACEMARIE KATE (Ire) 7-11-2 (7*) M D Murphy, .(20 to 1)   9
1092² WEST BROGUE (Ire) 7-12-0 C O'Dwyer, ...(4 to 1)   10
851 CHARLIEADAMS (Ire) 6-11-11 (3*) U Smyth, ...(50 to 1)   11
1080 CLASHWILLIAM GIRL (Ire) 8-11-9 L P Cusack, ...(8 to 1)   12
CELTIC SUNRISE 8-12-0 F Woods, ...(8 to 1)   13
LET BUNNY RUN (Ire) 6-12-0 H Rogers, ...(33 to 1)   14
1080 MICK O'DWYER 9-12-0 F J Flood, ...(16 to 1) pu
Dist: 3½l, 14l, 1½l, 15l. 5m 16.50s. (15 Ran).
(Mrs A Connolly), P A Fahy

1243 Morris Oil Chase (Grade 2) (5-y-o and up) £12,900 2½m............(2:00)

1094* ROYAL MOUNTBROWNE 8-11-7 C F Swan, *made all, mstk 5 out, rdn 2 out, kpt on wl...................*(6 to 1)   1
1079² BELVEDERIAN 9-11-7 C O'Dwyer, *wl plcd, rdn appr 2 out, styd on well r-in.......................*(6 to 1)   2
1079³ LOVE THE LORD (Ire) 6-11-9 T P Treacy, *trkd ldr, rdn bef 2 out, sn no extr.....................*(3 to 1)   3
MERRY GALE (Ire) 8-12-0 M P Dwyer, *wl plcd, jmpd well, rdn appr 2 out, sn wknd...................*(9 to 4 fav)   4
1079* ANTONIN (Fr) 8-12-0 K Whelan, *trkd ldr, reminder aftr 6th, jmpd slwly nxt, sn rdn and wknd............*(5 to 2)   5
KING OF THE GALES 9-12-0 F Woods, *rear, mstk 3 out, wknd..........................*(8 to 1)   6
1194 LOVE AND PORTER (Ire) 8-11-2 D H O'Connor, *rear, prog aftr 8th, rdn and wknd bef 2 out............*(12 to 1)   7
1079⁸ NUAFFE 11-12-0 T J Mitchell, *al rear................*(33 to 1)   8
Dist: 4½l, ½l, 11l, 10l. 5m 16.00s. (8 Ran).
(Mrs J O'Kane), A P O'Brien

1244 Morris Oil Premium Petrol Handicap Hurdle (0-109 4-y-o and up) £2,740 2½m...................................(2:30)

1144³ CASEY JANE (Ire) [-] 5-10-13 (3*) D J Casey, ...(7 to 2)   1
SIR JOHN (Ire) [-] 7-10-13 C F Swan, ...(11 to 4 fav)   2
849 LAURENS FANCY (Ire) [-] 6-10-1 (3*) J R Barry, ...(7 to 1)   3
1144 ECLIPTIC MOON (Ire) [-] 6-9-1 (7*) A O'Shea, ...(14 to 1)   4
SIDCUP HILL (Ire) [-] 7-10-10 (5*) G Cotter, ...(10 to 1)   5
THE BOYLERMAN (Ire) [-] 7-11-3 (7*) Mr K O'Sullivan.
.................................(16 to 1)   6
1090⁴ CELTIC LOTTO (Ire) [-] 5-10-5 J P Broderick, ...(7 to 1)   7
1040⁴ CORALDA (Ire) [-] 5-9-7 W Slattery, ...(12 to 1)   8

151

1018⁷ ROSIE LIL (Ire) [-] 5-10-4 (7*) L A Hurley, ...(9 to 1) 9
FLAMEWOOD [-] 7-10-6 (7*) Mr M A Scanlon, ...(20 to 1) 10
1078⁵ ANNFIELD LADY (Ire) [-] 8-12-0 T P Treacy, ...(7 to 1) f
1095⁶ PYR FOUR [-] 9-11-11 M P Dwyer, ...(10 to 1) pu
Dist: Hd, 1½l, 6l, 20l. 5m 16.30s. (12 Ran).

(J Comerford), W P Mullins

1245 Morris Oil Unleaded Petrol Handicap Chase (0-102 5-y-o and up) £2,740 2½m. . . . . (3:00)

1191³ MACAUNTA (Ire) [-] 6-9-11 J P Broderick, ...(6 to 1) 1
1146⁹ DOONEGA (Ire) [-] 8-10-6 (7*) Mr E Gallagher, ...(12 to 1) 2
1191⁴ STRADBALLEY (Ire) [-] 13 K F O'Brien, ...(8 to 1) 3
897 STEEL DAWN [-] 9-11-7 (3*) J R Barry, ...(8 to 1) 4
721⁴ SILENTBROOK [-] 11-9-0 (7*) A O'Shea, ...(10 to 1) 5
1194 SPRINGFORT LAD (Ire) [-] 7-11-7 N Williamson,
. . . .(7 to 2 fav) 6
1191⁵ WACKO JACKO (Ire) [-] 7-11-0 (5*) T Martin, ...(10 to 1) 7
602⁵ GOT NO CHOICE (Ire) [-] 6-9-11 (7*) M D Murphy, . .(8 to 1) 8
CALL ME HENRY [-] 7-11-4 C F Swan, ...(9 to 1) 9
1004⁸ EVER SO BOLD [-] 9-12-0 T P Treacy, ...(14 to 1) f
1004⁶ ANOTHER COURSE (Ire) [-] (bl) 8-11-6 D H O'Connor,
. . . .(10 to 1) pu
1014 LISNAGREE BOY (Ire) [-] (bl) 8-10-7 T J Mitchell, . .(20 to 1) pu
Dist: 10l, 10l, nk, 3½l. 5m 18.80s. (12 Ran).

(Mrs F Whelan), A J McNamara

1246 Irish National Hunt Novice Hurdle (4-y-o and up) £4,110 2m. . . . . (3:30)

1018⁵ BALLINLAMMY ROSE (Ire) 6-11-4 J Butler, ...(6 to 1) 1
1060* BALLYRIHY BOY (Ire) 5-10-11 (5*) J M Donnelly, . . .(7 to 2) 2
1119* FRANCES STREET (Ire) 4-11-4 C F Swan, ...(9 to 4 on) 3
LOUISES FANCY (Ire) 6-10-11 P L Malone, ...(10 to 1) 4
979⁵ FEAR CLISTE (Ire) 5-11-2 C O'Dwyer, ...(12 to 1) 5
898 NOBLE JEWEL (Ire) 4-10-6 N Williamson, ...(25 to 1) 6
SUPREME LINK (Ire) 7-11-2 D H O'Connor, ...(33 to 1) 7
1143 CORDAL DREAM (Ire) 5-11-8 J P Broderick, ...(33 to 1) 8
1121 COOLSHAMROCK (Ire) 4-10-3 (3*) K Whelan, ...(33 to 1) 9
1120 FINCHLEY LEADER (Ire) 4-10-6 (5*) G Cotter, ...(25 to 1) 10
1143 ROBAZALA (Ire) 4-10-6 M P Hourigan, ...(33 to 1) su
Dist: 9l, 8l, 4l, 12l. 4m 21.00s. (11 Ran).

(John G Irish), A P O'Brien

1247 Cahir I.N.H. Flat Race (4-y-o) £2,226 2m. . . . . (4:00)

NICK DUNDEE (Ire) 11-2 (5*) Mr W M O'Sullivan, . . .(9 to 2) 1
898² SUPREME CHANTER (Ire) 11-4 P F Fenton, . . .(7 to 4 fav) 2
774 SOPHIE VICTORIA (Ire) 10-9 (7*) Mr G Elliott, ...(12 to 1) 3
KING OF THIEVES (Ire) 11-0 (7*) Mr Damien Murphy, (5 to 1) 4
SOME ORCHESTRA (Ire) 10-9 (7*) Mr M Budds, . . .(20 to 1) 5
LETTIR LAD (Ire) 11-0 (7*) Mr J T McNamara, ...(14 to 1) 6
1019⁴ BEHAMORE GIRL (Ire) 10-9 (7*) Mr J P McNamara, (10 to 2) 7
600 JAKE CHOICE (Ire) 11-2 Mr P J Healy, ...(33 to 1) 8
MIRACLE ME (Ire) 11-0 (7*) Mr E Gallagher, ...(9 to 1) 9
1121⁶ MALADANTE (Ire) 10-9 (7*) Mr J P Hayden, ...(12 to 1) 10
745⁹ IRELAND INVADER 10-9 (7*) Mr J Cullen, ...(14 to 1) 11
WONDERSHOE (Ire) 10-9 (7*) Mr M A Scanlon, ...(20 to 1) 12
RIMET (Ire) 10-9 (7*) Mr B O'Sullivan, ...(20 to 1) 13
Dist: 5½l, 8l, 5l, 7l. 4m 17.10s. (13 Ran).

(Denis Fehan), Eugene M O'Sullivan

MARKET RASEN (good)
Thursday November 7th
Going Correction: PLUS 0.80 sec. per fur.

1248 'Students In Free Today' Conditional Jockeys' Handicap Hurdle Class E (0-110 4-y-o and up) £2,250 2m 1f 110yds. . . . . (1:20)

932⁸ TIP IT IN [80] 7-9-12 (5*) N Horrocks, prmnt, improved to chal betw last 2, led aftr last, rdn out.
. . . .(9 to 1 op 20 to 1 tchd 8 to 1) 1
879³ ANABRANCH [98] 5-11-4 (3*) M Newton, hld up, improved to chase ldr hfwy, led bef 2 out aftr last, no extr.
. . . .(7 to 2 op 3 to 1 tchd 4 to 1) 2
1175³ NEWHALL PRINCE [87] (bl) 8-10-10 L Aspell, wth ldr, led bef 4th till before 2 out, fdd.
. . . .(9 to 4 fav op 2 to 1 tchd 11 to 4) 3
1047³ NASHAAT (USA) [89] 8-10-7 (5*) Ross Berry, keen hold early, chsd ldrs, struggling bef 3 out, tld off. . .(4 to 1 tchd 9 to 2) 4
MONDAY CLUB [102] 12-11-11 D Walsh, beh, struggling bef 4th, tld off whn pld up before 3 out.
. . . .(14 to 1 op 12 to 1 tchd 16 to 1) pu
MILL THYME [95] 4-11-4 G Lee, hld till bef 4th, wknd quickly, tld off whn pld up before 2 out. . . . . .(7 to 2 tchd 4 to 1) pu
Dist: 1½l, 11l, 7l. 4m 24.40s. a 23.40s (6 Ran).

(Mrs M Dunning), A Smith

1249 Daniel Crane Exhibition Juvenile Novices' Hurdle Class D (3-y-o) £3,148 2m 1f 110yds. . . . . (1:50)

767² CHIEF MOUSE 11-5 J F Titley, made virtually all, clr whn blun last. . . . .(11 to 4 fav op 4 to 1) 1
CRABBIE'S PRIDE 10-12 A Maguire, nvr far away, chlgd hfwy, no ch wth wnr frnl 2.
. . . .(12 to 1 op 10 to 1 tchd 14 to 1) 2
MOCK TRIAL (Ire) 10-12 R Garritty, hld up, improved aftr 3rd, effrt bef 2 out, sn no imprsn.
. . . .(5 to 1 op 3 to 1 tchd 11 to 2 and 6 to 1) 3
THE BUTTERWICK KID 10-12 P Niven, hld up, improved 5th, rdn bef 2 out, sn outpcd. . . . .(7 to 1 op 6 to 1) 4
1024* COTTAGE PRINCE (Ire) 11-5 L Wyer, prmnt, rdn bef 2 out, fdd betw last two. . . . .(11 to 2 op 4 to 1 tchd 6 to 1) 5
BAASM 10-7 (5*) E Callaghan, prmnt, rdn 3 out, struggling whn mstk nxt. . . . .(10 to 1 op 16 to 1) 6
BOY BLAKENEY 10-12 Richard Guest, in tch till outpcd aftr 3 out. . . . .(20 to 1 op 16 to 1) 7
ALWARQA 10-7 D Bentley, hld up and beh, steady hdwy last 2 fs, nvr plcd to chal. . . . .(10 to 1 op 6 to 1) 8
320⁵ ANOTHER QUARTER (Ire) 10-7 W Worthington, beh, effrt 3 out, struggling nxt. . . . .(20 to 1) 9
CRAIGMORE MAGIC (USA) 10-12 A S Smith, wth ldr, struggling whn hmpd and blun 3 out. . . . .(25 to 1 op 20 to 1) 10
FIASCO 10-7 J Osborne, pld hrd on outer, prmnt till wknd bef 2 out. . . . .(16 to 1 op 8 to 1 tchd 20 to 1) 11
EXTREMELY FRIENDLY 10-12 D Bridgwater, in tch, struggling appr 3 out, pld up bef last.
. . . .(5 to 1 op 12 to 1 tchd 14 to 1) pu
ROZEL BAY 10-7 W Marston, mid-div, struggling 4 out, pld up bef last. . . . .(25 to 1 op 16 to 1 tchd 33 to 1) pu
LANDFALL 10-9 (3*) F Leahy, mid-div, struggling hfwy, pld up bef last. . . . .(14 to 1 op 10 to 1 tchd 16 to 1) pu
Dist: 5l, nk, 4l, 5l, 3l, 1¾l, ¾l, 7l, 6l, sht-hd. 4m 31.60s. a 30.60s (14 Ran).

(Lady Vestey), Miss H C Knight

1250 Jolly Fisherman Novices' Chase Class D (4-y-o and up) £3,977 2½m. . . . . (2:20)

1045* SIMPLY DASHING (Ire) 5-11-10 L Wyer, cl up, chalg whn blun badly 4 out, led and drw clr frm nxt.
. . . .(13 to 8 on op 7 to 4 on tchd 11 to 8 on) 1
MR PICKPOCKET (Ire) 8-11-5 J F Titley, led, hdd 3 out, no ch wth wnr. . . . .(15 to 8 op 7 to 4 on tchd 20 to 1) 2
1035⁷ KENMORE-SPEED 9-11-5 Richard Guest, chsd ldrs, mstk 11th, sn outpcd, no dngr aftr.
. . . .(10 to 1 op 12 to 1 tchd 14 to 1 and 20 to 1) 3
1045² RECORD LOVER (Ire) 6-11-5 W Worthington, in tch, struggling 11th, tld off. . . . .(20 to 1 op 16 to 1) 4
FAIR ALLY 6-11-5 D Parker, hld up, steady hdwy 8th, no imprsn whn blun 2 out. . . . .(50 to 1 op 25 to 1) 5
1127 MERRYHILL GOLD 5-10-13 (5*) D J Kavanagh, beh frm 4th, tld off. . . . .(40 to 1 op 33 to 1 tchd 50 to 1) 6
MONYMAX (Ire) 7-10-12 (7*) R Wilkinson, mstks, sn beh, tld off frl crpcd. . . . .(50 to 1 op 33 to 1) 7
JAC DEL PRINCE 6-11-5 P Hide, in tch, struggling 11th, tld off whn pld up bef last. . . .(20 to 1 op 16 to 1 tchd 25 to 1) pu
Dist: Dist, 6l, 21l, 20l, 10l, 10l. 5m 11.90s. a 22.90s (8 Ran).
SR: 27/-/-/-/-/

(Steve Hammond), T D Easterby

1251 Robert Peak Bookmaker Handicap Hurdle Class E (0-115 4-y-o and up) £2,310 2m 5f 110yds. . . . . (2:50)

933 LOCHNAGRAIN (Ire) [108] 7-11-10 P Niven, led second, made rst, drw clr frm 2 out. (9 to 2 op 7 to 2 tchd 5 to 1) 1
SINGLESOLE [90] 11-10-6 R Marley, led to second, pressed wnr, ev ch 3 out, hit nxt, no extr.
. . . .(9 to 2 op 3 to 1 tchd 4 to 1) 2
1071* KEEN TO THE LAST (Fr) [102] 4-11-4 R Garritty, chsd ldrs, rdn aftr 3 out, no imprsn frm nxt. . . . . . .(9 to 4 fav op 7 to 4) 3
GYMCRAK TIGER (Ire) [91] 6-10-7 A Maguire, hld up and beh, steady hdwy 3 out, no imprsn frm nxt. (4 to 1 tchd 9 to 2) 4
1112⁶ SCUD MISSILE (Ire) [99] 5-11-11 Lawrence, sn prmnt, rdn and outpcd aftr 3 out. . . . .(11 to 2 op 4 to 1) 5
CUILLIN CAPER [84] 4-10-0 D Bridgwater, hld up, struggling 3 out, sn btn. . . . .(10 to 1 op 8 to 1) 6
1130⁶ CHAPEL OF BARRAS (Ire) [92] 7-10-8 Mr P Gee, pld hrd in tch, lost pl hfwy, struggling last 4.
. . . .(33 to 1 op 20 to 1 tchd 40 to 1) 7
Dist: 12l, 8l, 1½l, 4l, dist, dist. 5m 43.70s. a 40.70s (7 Ran).

(Lightbody Of Hamilton Ltd), Mrs M Reveley

1252 Jacksons Novices' Hurdle Class D (4-y-o and up) £3,232 2m 1f 110yds. . . . . (3:20)

ALABANG 5-10-12 J Osborne, pld hrd, hld up, improved to ld 3 out, hit nxt, sn clr... (6 to 4 fav op 7 to 4 tchd 11 to 8) 1
1047⁷ SHARED RISK 4-10-7 (5*) E Callaghan, nvr far away, improved to chase ldr bef 2 out, one pace last.
. . . .(12 to 1 tchd 10 to 1) 2
NORTH BEAR 4-10-12 Richard Guest, led till hdd 3 out, not quicken frm nxt. . . . .(7 to 1 op 10 to 1) 3
EFAD (Ire) 5-10-9 (3*) G Lee, in tch, effrt 3 out, no imprsn whn nrly f last. . . . .(20 to 1 op 16 to 1) 4
MURPHY'S GOLD (Ire) 5-10-12 L Wyer, nvr far away, rdn 3 out, outpcd nxt. . . . .(7 to 1 op 9 to 2) 5

MENALDI (Ire) 6-10-12 R Supple, *beh, nvr a threat.* (12 to 1) 6
880⁶ NENAGH GUNNER 6-10-7 B Fenton, *beh, struggling hfwy, nvr on terms.*........ (16 to 1 op 14 to 1 tchd 33 to 1) 7
FERRERS 5-10-12 R Marley, *settled on outer, effrt bef 3 out, struggling before nxt.....* (6 to 1 op 7 to 1 tchd 8 to 1) 8
1097 STUDIO THIRTY 4-10-12 W Marston, *cl up, struggling aftr 5th, sn btn.*...........................(15 to 2 op 10 to 1) 9
CORBLEU (Ire) 6-10-12 K Johnson, *pld hrd, in tch till aftr 3rd, sn btn.*............................. (12 to 1 op 8 to 1) 10
866⁵ BEST FRIEND 4-10-4 (3*) F Leahy, *cl up, struggling aftr 4 out, sn btn.*......................... (25 to 1 op 16 to 1) 11
MUBARIZ (Ire) 4-10-12 M Ranger, *hld up, struggling frm 4th, tld off whn pld up bef 3 out.*......... (14 to 1 op 10 to 1) pu
Dist: 9l, 1¼l, 10l, 13l, 1l, 4l, 1½l, 15l, 15l, 7l. 4m 29.30s. a 28.30s (12 Ran).
(Elite Racing Club), M J Camacho

1253 Market Rasen Chamber Of Trade And Commerce Handicap Chase Class F (0-105 5-y-o and up) £2,951 3m 1f.........................(3:50)

GRIFFINS BAR [79] 8-10-4 R Marley, *made most to 6th, led ag'n 3 out, ran on wl.* (12 to 1 tchd 16 to 1 and 20 to 1) 1
WESTWELL BOY [100] 10-11-11 R Supple, *cl up, led 6th to 3 out, one pace frm last....* (5 to 1 op 9 to 2 tchd 11 to 2) 2
840* JIM VALENTINE [98] 10-11-9 W Marston, *hld up, imprvg whn hit 11th, chsd ldrs 14th, one pace fnl 3.*
.... (2 to 1 fav op 5 to 2 tchd 11 to 4 and 3 to 1) 3
SPARROW HALL [92] 9-11-3 W Dwan, *al prmnt, rdn whn hit 4 out, one pace nxt.*.................... (20 to 1 op 10 to 1) 4
JUKE BOX BILLY (Ire) [86] 8-10-11 A Dobbin, *in tch, effrt aftr 4 out, fourth and hld whn blun last........* (9 to 1 op 10 to 1) 5
1046 SON OF IRIS [103] 8-12-0 P Niven, *hld up, shrtlvd effrt 12th, struggling frm 14th.*.................... (9 to 1 op 8 to 1) 6
1046² DEEP DECISION [101] 10-11-12 A S Smith, *in tch, hmpd aftr 4th, fdd after four out....* (9 to 2 op 3 to 1 tchd 5 to 1) 7
BOSWORTH FIELD (Ire) [75] 8-10-0 B Fenton, *hld up, struggling whn blun 5 out.*.................(33 to 1 op 20 to 1) 8
1037² SUPPOSIN [92] 8-11-3 Richard Guest, *hld up, struggling 13th, sn btn.*..............(9 to 2 tchd 11 to 2) 9
HURRICANE ANDREW (Ire) [88] 8-10-13 Mr N Wilson, *al beh, tld off whn pld up bef 13th.*...........(16 to 1 op 10 to 1) pu
Dist: 3½l, 3l, 1¼l, 13l, dist, nk, 26l, 7l. 6m 47.00s. a 47.00s (10 Ran).
(M S Smith), Mrs P Sly

HEXHAM (good to firm)
Friday November 8th
Going Correction: MINUS 0.10 sec. per fur. (races 1,3,5), NIL (2,4,6)

1254 Service Welding Group Conditional Jockeys' Handicap Chase Class F (0-105 5-y-o and up) £2,846 2½m 110yds.......................(1:20)

916⁴ BUYERS DREAM (Ire) [76] (v) 6-10-0 G Cahill, *prmnt, hit 9th, improved aftr 4 out, led appr last, rdn out.*
...................(9 to 2 op 7 to 2 tchd 5 to 1) 1
1025* CRAFTY CHAPLAIN [100] 10-11-10 D Walsh, *led to second, led ag'n 7th till appr last, no imprsn.....* (5 to 1 jt-fav op 5 to 2) 2
915⁵ FORWARD GLEN [76] (bl) 9-10-0 G Lee, *settled in tch, outpcd bef 2 out, styd on r-in.*......................... 3
LIE DETECTOR [104] 8-11-11 (3*) D Parker, *nvr far away, outpcd bef 3 out, no dngr aftr.*
.... (13 to 2 op 6 to 1 tchd 7 to 1) 4
1021⁴ TRUMPET [96] (v) 7-11-3 (3*) Michael Brennan, *led second to 7th, styd upsides, struggling aftr 2 out, sn btn.*
.... (11 to 2 op 4 to 1) 5
889² WILLIE SPARKLE [76] 10-9-9 (5*) A Watt, *blun and uns rdr 3rd.*...............(3 to 1 jt-fav op 7 to 2 tchd 4 to 1) ur
Dist: 4l, 1¾l, 6l, 2l. 5m 7.00s. a 9.00s (6 Ran).
(Brian Chicken), B Ellison

1255 Karnheath Novices' Hurdle Class E (4-y-o and up) £2,532 2½m 110yds .... (1:50)

1071³ BEGGARS BANQUET (Ire) 6-10-5 (7*) B Grattan, *trkd ldr, led 5th, jnd whn hng lft last, ran on.*
...................(11 to 10 on op 6 to 4 on tchd Evens) 1
PAPERISING 4-10-12 A Dobbin, *nvr far away, chalg whn short of room last, ran on.*..........(6 to 4 op 7 to 4) 2
THE NEXT WALTZ 5-10-12 M Foster, *settled in tch, outpcd aftr 3 out, no dngr frm nxt.*
...................(10 to 1 op 6 to 1 tchd 8 to 1) 3
790² CANONBIEBOTHERED 5-10-7 F Perratt, *hld up, improved to chase ldrs 5th, outpcd last 2........* (25 to 1 op 16 to 1) 4
1123⁵ ONE MORE BILL 4-10-12 K Jones, *chsd ldrs, struggling 3 out, fdd.*....................(5 to 1 op 14 to 1) 5
PROMISE TO TRY (Ire) 4-10-2 (5*) S Taylor, *prmnt, struggling 3 out, fdd.*.....................(50 to 1 op 33 to 1) 6
LEIGHTEN LASS 5-10-7 K Johnson, *beh, lost tch fnl circuit, tld off.*.................... (25 to 1 op 20 to 1) 7
ROYAL PALM 4-10-12 Mr M Thompson, *hld up in tch, struggling bef 3 out, sn btn.*...............(33 to 1 tchd 50 to 1) 8

SHILDON (Ire) 8-10-12 Mr C Mulhall, *led till hdd 5th, wknd quickly, tld off whn pld up bef 2 out.*...............(50 to 1) pu
Dist: 1¼l, 20l, 13l, dist, nk, 1¼l, dist. 4m 57.70s. a 6.70s (9 Ran).
SR: 17/15/-/-/-/-/ (E H Ruddock), P Beaumont

1256 Robson Brown Communico Maiden Chase Class F (5-y-o and up) £2,935 3m 1f........................(2:20)

1045⁴ GEMS LAD 9-11-5 Richard Guest, *blun second, cl up, led tenth, made rst, rdn out frm last.*
.....................(7 to 1 op 5 to 1 tchd 8 to 1) 1
1152²⁴ COMMANDEER (Ire) 6-11-5 A Dobbin, *made most to tenth, sn outpcd, rallied 14th, styd on wl frm last.*
.... (5 to 1 op 4 to 1 tchd 11 to 2) 2
PANTARA PRINCE (Ire) 7-11-5 N Williamson, *hld up, steady hdwy to chase wnr 3 out, wknd bef last.*
.....................(5 to 2 fav op 11 to 4 tchd 3 to 1) 3
887² ROYAL SURPRISE 9-11-5 T Reed, *hld up, improved and prmnt 9th, struggling whn blun 14th, styd on bef last, no imprsn.*...................(9 to 2 op 7 to 2) 4
887⁴ MORE JOY 8-11-2 (3*) G Cahill, *prmnt, blun 12th, hit 3 out, fdd.*...................... (5 to 1 tchd 11 to 2) 5
931³ DEISE MARSHALL (Ire) 8-11-5 K Jones, *cl up, mstks 13th and blun outpcd........* (4 to 1 op 9 to 1 tchd 9 to 2) 6
AYLESBURY LAD (Ire) 7-11-5 J Burke, *wth ldr, struggling 12th, sn btn.*....................(33 to 1 op 20 to 1) 7
SMALL'N SMART 6-11-5 K Johnson, *beh whn f 9th.* (33 to 1) f
Dist: 9l, 3½l, 2½l, 10l, 7l, 24l. 6m 29.70s. a 24.70s (8 Ran).
(Miss J Wood), Mrs S J Smith

1257 Building Maintenance Company Selling Handicap Hurdle Class G (0-90 4-y-o and up) £1,725 2½m 110yds.......................(2:50)

1068* BELLE ROSE (Ire) [74] 6-11-1 A Dobbin, *nvr far away, improved to ld last, rdn out.....* (Evens fav op 11 to 10) 1
KINGS MINSTRAL (Ire) [63] 6-10-4³ J Burke, *led aftr second, hdd last, no extr.*.......................(33 to 1) 2
565⁵ ANTARTICTERN (USA) [77] 6-11-1 (3*) G Cahill, *hld up, effrt 3 out, outpcd last........* (5 to 1 op 9 to 2 tchd 11 to 2) 3
CHUMMY'S SAGA [69] 6-10-10 M Foster, *hld up, improved and prmnt hfwy, outpcd aftr 2 out....* (12 to 1 tchd 14 to 1) 4
1122³ CATTON LADY [59] 6-9-11 (3*) G Lee, *al cl up, outpcd 2 out, sn btn.*....................(14 to 1 op 12 to 1) 5
HELENS BAY (Ire) [81] 6-11-8 Mr M Thompson, *sn beh, struggling fnl circuit, nvr dngrs.......* (20 to 1 op 16 to 1) 6
1044 KAJOSTAR [59] 6-9-7 (7*) O Burrows, *beh and struggling, nvr on terms.*...................(14 to 1 op 12 to 1) 7
MEADOWLECK [59] 7-10-0 B Storey, *led till aftr second, struggling 7th, fdd.*...................... (33 to 1) 8
1129⁹ NICK THE BILL [63] 5-10-4⁴ K Jones, *chsd ldg bunch, rdn aftr 6th, struggling nxt.*.............(20 to 1 op 16 to 1) 9
1034⁸ SIGNOR NORTONE [74] 4-11-1 B Harding, *cl up, struggling 3 out, fdd.*...............(10 to 1 op 6 to 1) 10
CIRCLE BOY [68] 9-10-4 (5*) R McGrath, *f second.*
.....................(5 to 1 op 4 to 1) f
911 PAPA'S BOY (Ire) [83] 5-11-5 (5*) G F Ryan, *in tch, effrt bef 2 out, wkng whn f last, dead.*...........(14 to 1 op 12 to 1) f
Dist: 3l, 10l, 7l, 12l, 10l, 4l, hd, 2½l, 9l. 4m 58.00s. a 7.00s (12 Ran).
SR: 17/3/7/-/-/-/ (The Belles), G Richards

1258 John Eustace Smith Trophy Novices' Handicap Chase Class F (0-95 4-y-o and up) £2,655 2m 110yds.... (3:20)

ABBEYLANDS (Ire) [81] 8-11-5 N Williamson, *made all, sn clr, unchlgd.*....................(7 to 2 co-fav tchd 4 to 1) 1
1072* BALLYLINE (Ire) [86] 5-11-10 T Reed, *hld up, steady hdwy bef 3 out, chsd wnr last, no imprsn...* (7 to 2 co-fav op 3 to 1) 2
1149³ KILTULLA (Ire) [65] 6-10-3³ Richard Guest, *nvr far away, chsd wnr 3 out, fdd bef last....* (5 to 1 tchd 11 to 2 and 6 to 1) 3
1072 SHOW YOUR HAND (Ire) [80] 8-11-4 M Foster, *chsd wnr, struggling bef 2 out, sn btn...* (7 to 2 co-fav tchd 4 to 1) 4
1072² HAZEL CREST [72] 9-10-10 D Parker, *sn beh, nvr a factor.*....................(12 to 1 op 10 to 1) 5
764³ ISLANDREAGH (Ire) [80] 5-11-4 A Dobbin, *chsd ldrs, blun 6th and 4 out, sn struggling....* (9 to 2 op 5 to 1 tchd 4 to 1) 6
NIJWAY [78] 6-11-2 M Maloney, *beh and not fluent, nvr on terms.*....................(14 to 1 op 12 to 1) 7
MOUNTAIN FOX (Ire) [72] 6-10-10⁹ Mr M Thompson, *in tch, blun badly 6th, struggling whn blunded 8th.*
.... (50 to 1 op 33 to 1) 8
FINE TUNE (Ire) [62] 6-10-0 B Harding, *uns rdr 4th.* (16 to 1) ur
1104³ CHEEKA [81] 7-11-5 M Ranger, *in tch, hit 8th, sn struggling, pld up 3 out.*.................(12 to 1 op 10 to 1) pu
492² SIGNE DE MARS (Fr) [81] 5-11-5 B Storey, *beh whn pld up bef 5th.*...............(16 to 1 op 14 to 1 tchd 20 to 1) pu
Dist: 3½l, 8l, 16l, 10l, 2½l, dist, hd. 4m 3.00s. a 5.00s (11 Ran).
SR: 24/25/-/-/-/ (Chris Heron), J Howard Johnson

1259 Muse And Company Handicap Hurdle Class F (0-100 4-y-o and up) £2,174 2m................. (3:50)

APOLLO'S DAUGHTER [65] 8-10-0 A Dobbin, *hld up,
improved 3 out, led r-in, ran on wl* ..... (6 to 1 tchd 7 to 1) 1
934⁶ PANGERAN (USA) [82] 4-11-3 J Supple, *pressed ldr, led 4
out, hdd r-in, no extr* .... (2 to 1 fav op 7 to 4) 2
TIOTAO (Ire) [70] 6-10-5 D Parker, *nvr far away, effrt and rdn
aftr 2 out, outpcd r-in* .... (6 to 1 tchd 7 to 1) 3
725³ TASHREEF [72] (bl) 6-10-7 M Moloney, *cl up, chlgd 2 out,
outpcd last* .... (3 to 1) 4
1068⁷ ANORAK (USA) [91] (v) 6-11-12 J Callaghan, *chsd ldrs, outpcd aftr 3 out, sn no dngr* .... (3 to 1 op 5 to 1) 5
61⁷ MARSH'S LAW [86] 9-11-7 Mr C Mulhall, *hld up, struggling 3
out, nvr on terms* .... (11 to 2 op 4 to 1 tchd 6 to 1) 6
GONE ASHORE (Ire) [65] 5-10-0 N Williamson, *led, hdd 4 out,
struggling aftr nxt, tld off* .... (16 to 1) 7
Dist: 2½l, 3l, 2l, 9l, 21l, dist. 4m 2.60s. a 13.60s (7 Ran).
(Mrs M Goulding), J L Goulding

UTTOXETER (good)
Friday November 8th
Going Correction: MINUS 0.05 sec. per fur.

1260 Houghton Vaughan Maiden Hurdle Class E (4-y-o and up) £2,484 2¾m 110yds. .... (1:10)

1129³ GENERAL MOUKTAR 6-11-5 A P McCoy, *hld up, hdwy 4 out,
led appr 2 out, sn clr* ...... (4 to 1 op 5 to 1 tchd 11 to 2) 1
VICTORIA DAY 4-11-0 R Dunwoody, *chsd ldrs, led 8th till
appr 3 out, ran on one pace* .... (16 to 1) 2
PRU'S PROFILES (Ire) 5-11-5 D Bridgwater, *beh, hdwy 3 out,
sn rdn, no imprsn* .... (12 to 1 op 14 to 1) 3
1071⁴ OUR RAINBOW 4-11-0 R Marley, *wth ldr, led appr 3 out,
mstk, sn hdd, no extr* .... (10 to 1 tchd 12 to 1) 4
BARTON WARD 5-11-5 R Johnson, *hld up, hdwy 6th, rdn and
hmpd 3 out, styd on same pace.*
.... (6 to 1 op 7 to 1 tchd 9 to 1) 5
1053⁶ MESP (Ire) 5-11-0 M A Fitzgerald, *hld up, nvr trble ldrs.*
.... (33 to 1 tchd 50 to 1) 6
FANCY NANCY (Ire) 5-11-0 L Harvey, *hld up, hdwy 7th, wknd
3 out* .... (100 to 1) 7
SUPREMO (Ire) 7-11-5 C Llewellyn, *hld up, nvr rch ldrs.*
.... (12 to 1 tchd 14 to 1) 8
BURNTWOOD MELODY 5-11-5 W Marston, *hld up in tch,
effrt appr 4 out, sn btn* .... (50 to 1) 9
ZAMORSTON 7-11-2 (3⁴) E Husband, *mid-div, drvn alng 4
out, sn wknd* .... (16 to 1 op 14 to 1 tchd 20 to 1) 10
976⁶ BLAZE OF OAK (USA) 5-11-5 T J Murphy, *mid-div, rdn 4 out,
wknd nxt* .... (16 to 1 op 14 to 1 tchd 20 to 1) 11
SEVEN POTATO MORE (Ire) 6-11-5 A S Smith, *hld up, beh 4
out* .... (40 to 1 op 33 to 1) 12
SOVEREIGN GRIT (Ire) 6-11-5 C O'Dwyer, *hld up, hdwy 4 out,
rdn and btn whn hmpd nxt.*
.... (9 to 4 fav op 11 to 4 tchd 3 to 1) 13
LASTOFTHEIDIOTS 7-11-2 (3⁴) R Massey, *led to 8th, wknd 4
out* .... (100 to 1) 14
GALES OF LAUGHTER 7-11-5 A Thornton, *trkd ldrs, ev ch
whn I 3 out* .... (9 to 2 op 100 to 30) f
654⁶ SHADY EMMA 4-11-0 S Wynne, *prmnt, lost pl 7th, sn beh, tld
off whn pld up bef 3 out* .... (50 to 1 tchd 66 to 1) pu
Dist: 7l, ½l, 1¼l, ½l, 8l, 2½l, ¾l, 3l, ¾l, 12l. 5m 34.90s. a 27.90s (16 Ran).
(A S Helaissi), M C Pipe

1261 Holsten Pils Novices' Selling Hurdle Class G (4-y-o and up) £1,931 2½m 110yds. .... (1:40)

906⁵ ALWAYS GREENER (Ire) 5-11-0 S Curran, *chsd ldrs, led 3 out,
edgd lft r-in, all out* .... (11 to 2 op 5 to 1 tchd 3 to 1) 1
924² DRAGONMIST (Ire) 6-10-7 D J Burchell, *al prmnt, rdn and ev
ch last, not much room r-in, ran on.*
.... (9 to 4 fav op 11 to 4 tchd 3 to 1) 2
874⁵ LE BARON 5-10-12 J Osborne, *prmnt, rdn appr 2 out, not clr
run r-in, kpt on* .... (3 to 1 op 2 to 1 tchd 100 to 30) 3
73⁶ OAKBURY (Ire) 4-10-12 A Thornton, *prmnt, lost pl 6th, rallied
nxt, ev ch 3 out, kpt on one pace r-in* .. (6 to 1 tchd 7 to 1) 4
1061³ AWESTRUCK (bl) 6-10-7 R Johnson, *mid-div, hdwy 4 out,
one pace frm nxt* .... (9 to 1 op 7 to 1) 5
415⁵ ADMIRAL'S GUEST (Ire) 4-10-12 T Eley, *nvr dngrs.*
.... (20 to 1 tchd 25 to 1 and 33 to 1) 6
1082⁹ ARTHUR'S SPECIAL 6-10-7 A P McCoy, *prmnt, mstk 1st, led
6th, hdd and wknd 3 out.*
.... (12 to 1 op 16 to 1 tchd 10 to 1) 7
1134⁶ BETHS WISH 7-10-7 B Fenton, *al in rear.*
.... (25 to 1 tchd 33 to 1) 8
768⁴ SECRET SERENADE 5-10-12 W Marston, *prmnt till pld up
bef 4th* .... (14 to 1 op 12 to 1 tchd 16 to 1) pu
992⁶ COMMANCHE STORM (Ire) (bl) 4-10-12 Mr P Scott, *led, hdd
6th, sn lost pl, tld off whn pld up bef 2 out.*
.... (50 to 1 op 66 to 1) pu
1134 SMART ACT 7-10-12 Mr A Brown, *hld up, al in rear, tld off
whn pld up bef 2 out* .... (50 to 1 op 66 to 1) pu
COOL MANDY 5-10-7 J R Kavanagh, *al beh, tld off whn pld
up bef 2 out* .... (50 to 1) pu
987³ TIBBS INN 7-10-5 (7⁴) Mr R Thornton, *refused to race.*
.... (14 to 1 op 10 to 1) I

Dist: Nk, 1½l, 4l, 4l, 17l, 6l, 12l. 5m 3.60s. a 24.60s (13 Ran).
(Peter Houghton), J W Mullins

1262 John Partridge Novices' Handicap Chase Class E (0-100 5-y-o and up) £3,113 2m 5f. .... (2:10)

811² MICHERADO (Fr) [96] 6-11-12 R Johnson, *made all, jmpd lft,
sn clr, blun last, all out* .... (4 to 1 op 7 to 2) 1
BIRONI [95] 7-11-11 S Wynne, *mid-div, hdwy 12th, chsd wnr 3
out, nvr able to chal.*
.... (3 to 1 fav op 5 to 2 tchd 100 to 30) 2
1127⁷ DESERT BRAVE (Ire) [77] 6-10-0 (7⁴) R Wilkinson, *prmnt, chsd
wnr 9th, no imprsn* .... (16 to 1 op 14 to 1) 3
GOLDEN DRUM (Ire) [77] 8-11-7 T J Fitzgerald, *chsd wnr,
mstk second, beh frm 5 out.*
.... (20 to 1 op 16 to 1 tchd 25 to 1) 4
1055⁶ CHRIS'S GLEN [83] (v) 7-10-13 T J Murphy, *prmnt, drvn alng
5 out, sn wknd* .... (8 to 1 op 5 to 1) 5
1055 DOMINIE (Ire) [95] (bl) 8-11-11 C O'Dwyer, *beh frm 5th.*
.... (10 to 1 op 8 to 1 tchd 11 to 1) 6
▮▮▮▮▮▮▮▮▮▮▮▮▮▮▮▮ .... (20 to 1 op 16 to 1) 7
PRUSSIAN STORM (Ire) [70] 7-10-0 P Holley, *al in rear, no ch
whn I 4 out* .... (40 to 1 op 33 to 1 tchd 50 to 1) f
878³ BRIDEPARK ROSE (Ire) [89] 8-11-5 B Clifford, *prmnt till blun
and uns rdr 6th* .... (5 to 1) ur
956* KARLOVAC [70] 10-10-0 A Maguire, *al beh, tld off whn pld up
bef 4 out* .... (5 to 1 tchd 11 to 2) pu
Dist: 4l, 4l, 15l, 9l, 21l, dist. 5m 11.40s. a 13.40s (10 Ran).
(Stanley W Clarke), S A Brookshaw

1263 Flint Bishop & Barnett Novices' Handicap Hurdle Class E (0-100 3-y-o and up) £2,347 2m. .... (2:40)

BASSENHALLY [83] 6-10-12 R Marley, *trkd ldrs, led 3 out,
drvn out* .... (13 to 2 op 5 to 1 tchd 7 to 1) 1
1135* RAGAMUFFIN ROMEO [79] 7-10-8 (6ex) A P McCoy, *prmnt,
rdn and ev ch 2 out, no extr nr finish.*
.... (9 to 4 fav op 11 to 4 tchd 3 to 1) 2
229² PRUSSIA [99] 5-12-0 R Johnson, *prmnt, outpcd 4 out, staying
on whn mstk 2 out* .... (9 to 2 tchd 4 to 1) 3
965⁶ TARRY [90] 3-10-3 T Eley, *mid-div, sn pushed alng, nvr able
to chal* .... (7 to 2 op 11 to 4 tchd 4 to 1) 4
672⁵ SKRAM [87] 3-10-0 A Maguire, *chsd ldr, led aftr 4 out, hdd
and wknd nxt* .... (10 to 1 op 6 to 1) 5
TIME LEADER [71] 4-10-0 B Powell, *hld up, nvr plcd to chal.*
.... (20 to 1 op 14 to 1 tchd 33 to 1) 6
952⁴ CRUISINFORABRUISIN [71] 6-10-0 J R Kavanagh, *al in rear.*
.... (25 to 1 op 16 to 1 tchd 33 to 1) 7
998⁷ GALLOPING GUNS (Ire) [71] 4-10-0 S Curran, *hld up, al in
rear* .... (20 to 1 op 14 to 1) 8
1070⁶ DASH TO THE PHONE (USA) [72] (v) 4-10-1 A S Smith, *led,
hdd aftr 4 out, sn wknd* .... (5 to 1 op 6 to 1) 9
Dist: 1¼l, 7l, 4l, 4l, 1¾l, 1½l, 16l, 4l. 3m 52.80s. a 15.80s (9 Ran).
(Thorney Racing Club), Mrs P Sly

1264 Undergear 'Terra Tire' Novices' Chase Class D (5-y-o and up) £3,826 2m. .... (3:10)

MULLIGAN (Ire) 6-10-12 A Maguire, *made all, jmpd wl, canter* ....(9 to 4 on op 5 to 2 on tchd 2 to 1 on) 1
1055 FLAMING MIRACLE (Ire) (bl) 6-10-12 R Farrant, *mid-div,
hdwy to go second 5 out, no ch wth wnr.*
.... (33 to 1 tchd 40 to 1) 2
SCOTTISH BAMBI 8-10-12 J Osborne, *hld up, mstk 5th, hdwy
7th, no imprsn frm 2 out* .... (10 to 1 op 14 to 1) 3
1020² TOTAL ASSET 6-10-12 Gary Lyons, *hld up, mstk 1st, hit 4th, al
in rear* .... (33 to 1) 4
904⁵ LEGAL ARTIST (Ire) 6-10-12 L Harvey, *prmnt to 7th.*
.... (12 to 1 op 8 to 1) 5
1107 LORD NITROGEN (USA) 6-10-12 A P McCoy, *chsd wnr till
wknd 5 out, no ch whn blun and uns rdr nxt.*
.... (9 to 2 op 4 to 1) ur
1138⁷ BETABETCORBETT (v) 5-10-12 T Eley, *prmnt to 6th, tld off
whn pld up bef 4 out* .... (33 to 1 op 25 to 1) pu
Dist: 6l, 3½l, 10l, 19l. 3m 52.10s. a 5.10s (7 Ran).
SR: 25/19/15/5/
(Lady Harris), D Nicholson

1265 Strebel Boilers And Radiators Handicap Hurdle Class D (0-120 4-y-o and up) £2,814 2½m 110yds. .... (3:40)

DEYMIAR (Ire) [114] 4-11-10 R Dunwoody, *hld up, hdwy 3 out,
led last, drvn out.*
.... (3 to 1 op 5 to 2 tchd 100 to 30 and 7 to 2) 1
HIGH GRADE [110] 8-11-6 A P McCoy, *chsd ldr, lft in ld aftr
5th, hdd 3 out, ran on und pres nr finish.* (10 to 1 op 7 to 1) 2
876² PHARARE (Ire) [92] 6-10-2 L Wyer, *trkd ldrs, led 3 out, rdn and
hdd last, no extr.*
.... (15 to 8 fav op 9 to 4 tchd 5 to 2 and 7 to 4) 3
TIGHT FIST (Ire) [113] 6-11-9 J F Titley, *hld up, eased whn btn
whn 2 out* .... (7 to 1 op 5 to 1 tchd 11 to 2) 4
940³ MUTAZZ (USA) [105] 4-11-1 R Farrant, *hld up in tch, rdn 4 out,
wknd nxt* .... (100 to 30 op 7 to 2) 5

155⁸ LAUGHING GAS (Ire) [97] 7-10-7 P Hide, *led till pld up aftr 5th.*
.... (25 to 1 op 14 to 1 tchd 33 to 1)   pu
Dist: Nk, 4l, 21l, 12l. 4m 58.70s. a 19.70s (6 Ran).

(T J Whitley), D R Gandolfo

1266 Holsten Pils Handicap Hurdle Class F (0-100 4-y-o and up) £2,379 3m 110yds...................... (4:10)

1048³ ELBURG (Ire) [93] 6-11-10 M A Fitzgerald, *hld up, hdwy 6th, led 3 out, sn clr, eased r-in.*
.... (14 to 1 op 12 to 1 tchd 16 to 1)   1
1124² BALLINDOO [84] 7-11-1 Mr R Armson, *hld up, hdwy 5 out, chsd wnr 2 out, no imprsn*............. (4 to 1 tchd 5 to 1)   2
1000⁶ MR FLUTTS [77] 10-10-8 S McNeill, *hld up, hdwy 4 out, not trble ldrs.*
...............(12 to 1 op 14 to 1 tchd 16 to 1 and 20 to 1)   3
812⁴ RIVERBANK ROSE [71] 5-10-1 T Eley, *wth ldr, led 7th, hdd 3 out, wknd nxt.*..........(16 to 1 op 14 to 1 tchd 20 to 1)   4
APACHEE FLOWER [77] 6-10-8 A P McCoy, *hld up, hdwy 6th, wknd 3 out.*....................(9 to 4 fav op 4 to 1)   5
1139³ BATTY'S ISLAND [75] 7-10-6 A Maguire, *chsd ldr 3rd, hit 5th, wknd appr 3 out.*....................(15 to 2 op 10 to 1)   6
1000⁵ BRIGHT SAPPHIRE [75] 10-10-6 D J Burchell, *in tch till rdn and wknd 3 out.*.......... (9 to 1 op 8 to 1 tchd 10 to 1)   7
1010² SALTIS (Ire) [77] 4-10-7 Gary Lyons, *hld up, hdwy 6th, wknd 4 out.*....................... (7 to 1 op 5 to 1)   8
PROVENCE [80] 9-10-11 W Marston, *prmnt, mstks, rdn 4 out, sn wknd*................ (25 to 1 op 16 to 1 tchd 33 to 1)   9
KAYFAAT (USA) [85] 8-10-9 (7*) B Moore, *led till aftr second, wknd 7th.* (10 to 1 op 6 to 1 tchd 11 to 1 and 12 to 1)   10
1010⁵ CURRAGH PETER [72] 9-10-0 (3*) Guy Lewis, *hld up, pld hrd, hdwy to ld aftr second, hit 6th, hdd nxt, tld off whn pulled up bef 4 out.*...................................(33 to 1)   pu
ASTRAL INVASION (USA) [87] 5-11-3 B Clifford, *al beh, tld off whn pld up aftr 8th....* (16 to 1 op 14 to 1 tchd 20 to 1)   pu
Dist: 10l, 6l, 1l, 5l, 13l, 15l, 7l, dist, 13l. 5m 57.20s. a 20.20s (12 Ran).

(Mrs Alison Gamble), T R George

CHEPSTOW (good to soft)
Saturday November 9th
Going Correction: PLUS 0.40 sec. per fur. (races 1,3), PLUS 0.85 (2,4,5,6)

1267 Osmington Mills Holidays And Permit Trainers Association Handicap Chase Class C (0-130 5-y-o and up) £6,905 2m 110yds........... (1:15)

BENJAMIN LANCASTER [98] 12-9-/ (/*) M Griffiths, *jmpd wl, chsd ldr, led 4 out, ran on well.*........(16 to 1 op 10 to 1)   1
1052² NEWLANDS-GENERAL [115] 10-11-3 A P McCoy, *set str pace, blun 3rd, blunded and hdd 4 out, hrd rdn 2 out, not quicken.*..........(11 to 10 fav op 5 to 4 tchd 11 to 8)   2
1138⁴ NAIYSARI (Ire) [108] 8-10-10 W Marston, *gd hdwy 8th, 3rd whn blun 4 out, no imprsn*.............(10 to 1 op 6 to 1)   3
NORTHERN SADDLER [122] 9-11-10 R Dunwoody, *gd hdwy 8th, rdn and wknd 4 out....* (2 to 1 op 7 to 4 tchd 9 to 4)   4
OLLIVER DUCKETT [100] 7-10-2² M Sharratt, *al wl beh.*
.... (50 to 1 op 33 to 1)   5
1176³ NORTHERN OPTIMIST [98] 8-10-0 R Johnson, *al wl beh.*
.... (8 to 1 op 5 to 1 tchd 9 to 1)   6
Dist: 2½l, 14l, 17l, 9l. 4m 8.40s. a 11.40s (6 Ran).

SR: 24/38/17/14/-/-/

(M Griffin), M A Griffin

1268 Tote Silver Trophy Handicap Hurdle Class B (4-y-o and up) £16,217 2½m 110yds...................... (1:45)

CASTLE SWEEP (Ire) [135] 5-10-10 R Johnson, *mstks, hdwy 6th, led and hit 2 out, clr whn hit last, easily.*
.... (9 to 4 fav op 7 to 4 tchd 5 to 2)   1
1028² MYTTON'S CHOICE (Ire) [125] 5-9-7 (7*) Mr R Thornton, *al prmnt, led 4 out to 2 out, not quicken.* (14 to 1 op 10 to 1)   2
SILVER SHRED [130] 5-10-5 R Dunwoody, *hdwy 7th, ran on one pace frm 3 out.*....... (9 to 2 op 7 to 1 tchd 5 to 1)   3
798⁴ HAND WOVEN [125] 4-10-0 C Llewellyn, *hdwy appr 4 out, one pace frm nxt.*
...........(9 to 1 op 10 to 1 tchd 12 to 1 and 8 to 1)   4
MUSE [149] 9-11-10 A Procter, *led till appr 4 out, one pace.*
.... (5 to 2 op 20 to 1 tchd 33 to 1)   5
1178* RUNAWAY PETE (USA) [125] 6-10-0 (3ex) S Wynne, *effrt and rdn appr 4 out, nvr nr to chal.*......... (20 to 1 op 12 to 1)   6
DR LEUNT (Ire) [136] 5-10-11 A P McCoy, *chsd ldrs, led appr 4 out, sn hdd and wknd...* (11 to 2 op 5 to 1 tchd 6 to 1)   7
1056* TEEN JAY [125] 6-10-0 (3ex) V Slattery, *al beh, tld off.*
.... (50 to 1)   8
JET RULES (Ire) [127] 6-10-2 W Marston, *prmnt till wknd quickly appr 4 out, tld off...* (14 to 1 op 20 to 1 tchd 25 to 1)   9
MEDITATOR [125] 12-10-0 B Fenton, *in tch till wknd appr 4 out, tld off.*..................... (50 to 1)   10
Dist: 10l, 6l, 6l, 10l, 2½l, 3l, 30l, 1¼l, 11l. 4m 57.90s. a 19.90s (10 Ran).

SR: 57/37/36/25/39/12/18/-/-/

(Lord Vestey), D Nicholson

1269 Rising Stars Novices' Chase Class A Grade 2 (5-y-o and up) £13,786 2m 3f 110yds..................... (2:15)

SEE MORE BUSINESS (Ire) 6-11-0 A P McCoy, *hld up, mstk 4th, quickened to ld front, easily.*
.... (13 to 8 on op 7 to 4 on tchd 11 to 8 on)   1
WEE WINDY (Ire) 7-11-0 R Dunwoody, *jmpd wl, led to 4 out, no ch wth wnr*............ (5 to 1 op 9 to 2 tchd 11 to 2)   2
BUCKHOUSE BOY 6-11-0 T Jenks, *chsd ldr, rdn 11th, wknd 4 out, beh whn hit last 2*.... (2 to 1 op 7 to 4 tchd 9 to 4)   3
Dist: 8l, 11l. 5m 2.20s. a 19.20s (3 Ran).

(Paul K Barber And Mr J A Keighley), P F Nicholls

1270 Remembrance 'National Hunt' Novices' Hurdle Class D (4-y-o and up) £3,233 2½m 110yds......... (2:50)

MINELLA DERBY (Ire) 6-10-12 R Johnson, *hdwy 4th, mstks four out and nxt, led last, all out.*........(4 to 1 op 5 to 4)   1
HURDANTE (Ire) 6-10-12 B Fenton, *led second to last, ran on.*
.... (9 to 1 op 12 to 1 tchd 14 to 1)   2
THE REVEREND BERT (Ire) 8-10-12 A P McCoy, *hdwy 7th, ev ch 3 out, wknd nxt.....* (5 to 2 fav op 4 to 1 tchd 9 to 2)   3
STORMY PASSAGE (Ire) 6-10-5 (7*) Mr R Thornton, *chsd ldr till wknd 3 out.*...................... (8 to 1 op 6 to 1)   4
ARTURO 5-10-12 S Wynne, *prmnt till wknd 4 out.*
.... (20 to 1 op 16 to 1)   5
LOGICAL STEP (Ire) 6-10-12 R Dunwoody, *hld up in rear, hdwy 7th, hrd rdn appr 4 out, no response.*
.... (3 to 1 op 5 to 2)   6
KING'S COURTIER (Ire) 7-10-12 N Mann, *led to second, beh frm 5th, tld off.*....................(25 to 1 op 16 to 1)   7
SUPREME KELLYCARRA (Ire) 5-10-0 (7*) Mr A Wintle, *hdwy 7th, wknd 3 out, tld off.*............ (12 to 1 op 10 to 1)   8
KEDGE ANCHOR MAN 5-10-12 W Marston, *prmnt till wknd 3 out, 5th and btn whn f last.*.........(14 to 1 op 50 to 1)   f
DUNNICKS COUNTRY 6-10-0 (7*) M Griffiths, *prmnt till wknd 5th, tld off whn pld up bef 4 out.....* (25 to 1 op 10 to 1)   pu
QUEEN OF THE SUIR (Ire) 7-10-7 V Slattery, *al beh, tld off whn pld up bef 4 out.*................(50 to 1 op 33 to 1)   pu
905⁸ THE CHEESE BARON 5-10-7 (5*) Chris Webb, *al wl beh, tld off whn pld up bef 4 out.*.......... (33 to 1 op 25 to 1)   pu
Dist: 1l, 8l, 3½l, 10l, 16l, 18l, 1l. 5m 9.10s. a 31.10s (12 Ran).

(B C Kilby), P F Nicholls

1271 Stayers Novices' Hurdle Class D (4-y-o and up) £2,823 3m........ (3:25)

1129² FLYING GUNNER 5-11-0 R Johnson, *al prmnt, led 3 out, easily.*..........(7 to 4 on op 5 to 4 on tchd Evens)   1
JET BOYS 6-11-0 W Marston, *hdwy appr 4 out, styd on frm 2 out, no ch wth wnr*.............(9 to 2 op 2 to 1)   2
MENDIP PRINCE (Ire) 6-11-0 R Dunwoody, *led to second, led 4th to 3 out, btn whn hit last 2.*
.... (5 to 1 op 9 to 2 tchd 11 to 2)   3
COUNTRY BLUE 5-11-0 A P McCoy, *hld up, ev ch appr 4 out, wknd 3 out, tld off...* (10 to 1 op 7 to 1 tchd 12 to 1)   4
LA CHANCE 6-11-0 Mr A Walton, *tld off frm 6th.*
.... (50 to 1 op 25 to 1)   5
975 JAIME'S JOY 6-10-9 T Jenks, *tld off frm 4th, pld up aftr 8th.*
.... (100 to 1 op 33 to 1)   pu
783⁴ REINE DE LA CHASSE (Fr) 4-10-8 A McCabe, *jnd ldrs 7th, wknd quickly aftr nxt, pld up bef 4 out.* (25 to 1 op 10 to 1)   pu
1054 EVENTSINTERNASHNAL (bl) 7-11-4² Mr J M Pritchard, *led second to 4th, wknd quickly 6th, tld off whn pld up bef four out.*
.... (100 to 1 op 25 to 1)   pu
Dist: 8l, ¾l, dist, dist. 6m 30.70s. a 55.70s (8 Ran).

(R Maryan Green), D Nicholson

1272 Nimble Handicap Hurdle Class D (0-120 4-y-o and up) £2,784 2m 110yds...................... (3:55)

POTENTATE (USA) [117] 5-12-0 A P McCoy, *made all, sn clr, strly pressed 3 out, ran on wl frm nxt.* (5 to 4 on op 5 to 4)   1
PHAR FROM FUNNY [105] 5-11-2 B Fenton, *hld up in rear, hdwy 3rd, ev ch 3 out, one pace nxt.* (9 to 2 op 3 to 1)   2
NOTHINGTODOWITHME [92] 6-10-3 S Wynne, *chsd wnr till one pace frm 3 out....* (5 to 1 tchd 8 to 1)   3
MOMENT OF GLORY (Ire) [114] (bl) 5-11-11 R Dunwoody, *hld up and beh, hdwy 3rd, hrd rdn 5th, no response.*
.... (8 to 1 op 4 to 1)   4
1175 SAN DIEGO CHARGER (Ire) [89] 5-9-7 (7*) Mr R Thornton, *wl beh frm 4th.*....................(33 to 1 op 20 to 1)   5
MONICASMAN (Ire) [116] 6-11-13 W Marston, *prmnt till wknd appr 5th, tld off.*..........(11 to 2 op 3 to 1 tchd 6 to 1)   6
Dist: 6l, 6l, 4l, 11l, 29l. 4m 11.90s. a 24.90s (6 Ran).

(Jim Weeden), M C Pipe

NAAS (IRE) (yielding to soft)
Saturday November 9th

1273 Kilwarden Handicap Hurdle (0-102

NATIONAL HUNT RESULTS 1996-97

4-y-o and up) £3,082 2m...... (1:00)

803[6]	FIDDLERS BOW VI (Ire) [-] 8-11-11 C F Swan, ...(8 to 1)	1
1040[2]	FALCARRAGH (Ire) [-] 6-10-12 M Duffy, ...(6 to 1)	2
	LEGAL AND TENDER (Ire) [-] 5-10-6 (7") R P Hogan,	
	....(12 to 1)	3
828[2]	VALMAR (Ire) [-] 8-10-2 (5") G Cotter, ...(5 to 1 jt-fav)	4
329	WAREZ (Ire) [-] 8-9-6 (5") J Butler, ...(25 to 1)	5
	KERCORLI (Ire) [-] 5-10-5 J P Broderick, ...(20 to 1)	6
1047	ADARAMANN (Ire) [-] 4-10-13 (3") Mr R Walsh, ...(12 to 1)	7
1118"	ILLBETHEREFORYOU (Ire) [-] 5-10-10 M P Hourigan,	
	......................................(5 to 1 jt-fav)	8
1015[6]	MIDDLEOFTHENIGHT (Ire) [-] 4-10-5 P L Malone, (14 to 1)	9
928[6]	DOONE BRAES (Ire) [-] 6-10-1 (7") C Rae, ...(8 to 1)	10
907	NO DIAMOND (Ire) [-] 7-9-12 (7") J M Maguire, ...(14 to 1)	11
	CLASHBEG (Ire) [-] 5-11-6 K F O'Brien, ...(14 to 1)	12
849[8]	HEIGHT OF LUXURY (Ire) [-] 8-9-4 (7") M D Murphy, (30 to 1)	13
1145[9]	ASTRID (Ire) [-] 5-9-7 W Slattery, ...(33 to 1)	14
1040[9]	MAKING THE POINT (Ire) [-] 5-10-10 M O'Connor,	
	....(14 to 1)	15
	DROMARA BREEZE (Ire) [-] 8-10-7 (3") D J Casey, (20 to 1)	16
1078[6]	BOHOLA PETE (Ire) [-] 5-10-6 T J Mitchell, ...(14 to 1)	17
	CRAIGARY [-] 5-10-7 P P Kinane, ...(14 to 1)	18
907[7]	ICED HONEY [-] 9-11-4 L P Cusack, ...(12 to 1)	19
	THE PARSON'S FILLY (Ire) [-] 4-10-0 (3") G Kilfeather,	
	....(12 to 1)	20
1118[5]	HERSILIA (Ire) [-] 5-10-10 (7") Mr P F O'Reilly, ...(12 to 1)	21
1118[9]	VEREDARIUS (Fr) [-] 5-11-12 F Woods, ...(14 to 1)	22
803[5]	BENBRADAGH GLOW (Ire) [-] 4-10-13 (7") Mr L J Gracey,	
	....(33 to 1)	23
	SLEWMORE (Ire) [-] 5-11-0 (3") U Smyth, ...(25 to 1)	24
849	BAKEMA (Ire) [-] 4-11-5 (3") J R Barry, ...(10 to 1)	f

Dist: ¾l, ¾l, 4l, hd. 4m 2.90s. (25 Ran).

(Mrs A T B Kearney), Noel Meade

1274 Paddy Cox Handicap Chase (0-130 4-y-o and up) £3,767 2m 3f... (1:30)

1041[2]	PERSIAN HALO (Ire) [-] 8-12-0 C F Swan, ...(9 to 4 fav)	1
	BARNAGEERA BOY (Ire) [-] 7-11-2 K F O'Brien, ...(7 to 1)	2
1078[3]	DANCING VISION (Ire) [-] 6-10-12 J Jones, ...(8 to 1)	3
851[3]	WALLYS RUN [-] 9-10-6 L P Cusack, ...(8 to 1)	4
1091	BACK BAR (Ire) [-] 8-11-12 F Woods, ...(14 to 1)	5
1091[2]	HANNIES GIRL (Ire) [-] 7-9-7 (7") L J Fleming, ...(6 to 1)	6
	EDENAKILL LAD [-] 9-10-2 H Rogers, ...(14 to 1)	7
1004[7]	BOB DEVANI [-] 10-11-10 T J Mitchell, ...(10 to 1)	ur
949	TALK TO YOU LATER [-] (bl) 10-9-6 (3") D Bromley, (14 to 1)	ur

Dist: 1½l, 6l, 10l, 1l. 5m 11.40s. (9 Ran).

(Tematron Racing Club), Noel Meade

1275 Weatherbys Ireland Maiden Hurdle (4-y-o) £3,767 2m.............(2:00)

1090[2]	MURPHY'S MALT (Ire) 11-12 C F Swan, ...(2 to 1 fav)	1
	SWIFT CERT (bl) 11-12 M Duffy, ...(4 to 1)	2
486[2]	MAGICAL FUN (Ire) 11-12 K F O'Brien, ...(7 to 1)	3
1121[5]	JACK CHAUCER 11-7 T J Mitchell, ...(10 to 1)	4
1077[7]	ROWAN TREE (Ire) 11-2 T P Treacy, ...(20 to 1)	5
1119[6]	JACKSON'S PANTHER (Ire) 10-9 (7") Mr R A Behan,	
	....(14 to 1)	6
1193[4]	SPRITZER (Ire) 11-2 D P Fagan, ...(8 to 1)	7
1193	CLASSPERFORMER (Ire) 11-7 L P Cusack, ...(16 to 1)	8
731[4]	PERMIT ME (Ire) 10-9 (7") A O'Shea, ...(8 to 1)	9
1143	OLD MOTHER HUBBARD (Ire) 10-11 (5") G Cotter, (33 to 1)	10
1081	BEHY BRIDGE (Ire) 10-11 (5") T Martin, ...(33 to 1)	11
1015[7]	PERSIAN DANSER (Ire) 11-7 J P Broderick, ...(14 to 1)	12
	FAIRY COURT (Ire) 11-4 (3") K Whelan, ...(6 to 1)	13
122[8]	THE HOLY PARSON (Ire) 11-0 (7") M P Cooney, ...(20 to 1)	14
1081[7]	FLORIA (Ire) 10-11 (5") J Butler, ...(16 to 1)	15
	FAHEEN'S BOY (Ire) 11-4 (3") G Kilfeather, ...(33 to 1)	16
	GREY GUY (Ire) 11-7 F Woods, ...(14 to 1)	17
883[4]	GOLD DEPOSITOR (Ire) 11-7 G M O'Neill, ...(14 to 1)	18
1193	PERPETUAL PROSPECT (Ire) 10-0 (7") M W Martin, (12 to 1)	19
951"	NATIVE FLING (Ire) 11-9 (3") U Smyth, ...(8 to 1)	20
1143	DANTE'S MOON (Ire) 11-2 P McWilliams, ...(33 to 1)	21
	KRIESLER (Ire) 11-0 (7") Mr M P Madden, ...(25 to 1)	22
1143	HILL TOP LAD (Ire) 11-7 W Slattery, ...(33 to 1)	23
	DON'T FORGET MIAMI (Ire) 11-7 A Powell, ...(33 to 1)	24
1077[9]	DAISY EILE (Ire) 10-9 (7") M D Murphy, ...(33 to 1)	25

Dist: 6l, 3l, 7l, 1l. 4m 6.90s. (25 Ran).

(James Hennessy), A P O'Brien

1276 Quinns Of Naas Novice Chase (5-y-o and up) £4,795 2m.............(2:30)

1146"	DANOLI (Ire) 8-11-7 T P Treacy, ...(7 to 2 on)	1
1080[6]	CROSSFARNOGUE (Ire) 7-10-9 (5") J Butler, ...(10 to 1)	2
980	WHAT IT IS (Ire) 7-10-9 P McWilliams, ...(20 to 1)	3
	HEADBANGER 9-11-0 D H O'Connor, ...(14 to 1)	4
1192[3]	CREHELP EXPRESS (Ire) 9-11-0 (3") B Bowens, ...(7 to 1)	5
	AMBLE SPEEDY (Ire) 6-11-0 F Woods, ...(14 to 1)	6
1170	PUNTING PETE (Ire) 6-10-11 (3") D J Casey, ...(6 to 1)	7
	PERSIAN POWER (Ire) 8-11-0 C F Swan, ...(10 to 1)	8
1170[6]	TIME AND CHARGES (Ire) 6-10-7 (7") R P Hogan, (25 to 1)	f

Dist: 2½l, 11l, 8l, 25l. 4m 14.90s. (9 Ran).

(D J O'Neill), Thomas Foley

1277 Brown Lad Handicap Hurdle (Listed) (4-y-o and up) £6,850 2½m... (3:00)

	MINELLA MAN [-] 9-11-9 (5") G Cotter, wl plcd, rdn and prog	
	aftr 3 out to ld bef nxt, styd on und pres............(14 to 1)	1
944[3]	BLAZE OF HONOUR (Ire) [-] 5-10-1 C F Swan, wtd wth, prog	
	bef 4 out, rdn aftr nxt, kpt on wl................(11 to 2)	2
1168[2]	BETTERBEBOB (Ire) [-] 5-9-11 (3") D J Casey, mid-div till prog	
	bef 6th, rdn aftr 3 out, kpt on......................(2 to 1 fav)	3
897[3]	ALASAD [-] 6-10-8 Mr G J Harford, led, clr 5th, rdn and hdd	
	bef 2 out, sn wknd..................................(4 to 1)	4
1078[4]	CEILI QUEEN (Ire) [-] 4-10-1 (5") J Butler, wl plcd, trkd ldr 5th	
	till rdn and wknd bef 4 out........................(8 to 1)	5
	APPELLATE COURT [-] 8-10-0 A Powell, al rear, rdn aftr 3	
	out, not quicken..................................(20 to 1)	6
	SLEEPY RIVER (Ire) [-] 5-10-0 F Woods, trkd ldr till wknd bef 5	
	out, sn lost tch.....................................(10 to 1)	7
	TRENCH HILL LASS (Ire) [-] 7-10-0 T J Mitchell, al rear, rdn	
	aftr 3 out, not quicken..............................(16 to 1)	8
1095[4]	NEAR GALE (Ire) [-] 6-11-0 T P Treacy, wl plcd till broke off	
	hind leg and f appr 4th, destroyed...............(5 to 1)	su

Dist: 3½l, 4½l, 8l, 7l. 5m 6.80s. (9 Ran).

(John J Nallen), John J Nallen

1278 I.N.H. Stallion Owners E.B.F. Novices Hurdle (5-y-o and up) £4,110 2½m
....(3:30)

1076[4]	YELAPA PRINCE (Ire) 5-10-13 (3") D J Casey, ...(9 to 1)	1
	CHRISTINES RUN (Ire) 6-11-1 T P Rudd, ...(9 to 2)	2
	GRANGE COURT (Ire) 6-11-6 K F O'Brien, ...(4 to 1)	3
1093[2]	STORM GEM (Ire) 5-10-11 T J Mitchell, ...(10 to 1)	4
1093"	ANOZIRA GOLD (Ire) 6-11-1 F Woods, ...(6 to 1)	5
1096[9]	ANCIENT HISTORIAN (Ire) 7-10-13 (7") P Morris, ...(16 to 1)	6
1075[2]	BITTER HARVEST (Ire) 6-11-6 C F Swan, ...(5 to 2 fav)	7
1041[4]	GLENFIELDS CASTLE (Ire) 6-10-13 (7") Mr A Stronge,	
	....(14 to 1)	8
1090	MICK MAN (Ire) 5-10-9 (7") B J Geraghty, ...(33 to 1)	9
	LOUIS THE LIP 6-11-6 J P Broderick, ...(12 to 1)	10
1090	MAIRTINS BUCK (Ire) 5-11-2 G M O'Neill, ...(33 to 1)	11
1120[7]	MOLLY WHACK (Ire) 5-10-11 T P Treacy, ...(33 to 1)	pu
1075	SHORT OF A BUCK (Ire) 6-11-1 A Powell, ...(50 to 1)	pu

Dist: 8l, 6l, ¾l, 12l. 5m 12.90s. (13 Ran).

(Donal O'Connor), W P Mullins

1279 Philip A. McCartan Memorial INH Flat Race (4-y-o and up) £2,740 2m
....(4:00)

984[4]	BORO BOW (Ire) 5-11-6 (7") Mr B E Hill, ...(13 to 2)	1D
	PAULS RUN (Ire) 7-11-11 (7") Mr T N Cloke, ...(8 to 1)	1
945"	ROCHER LADY (Ire) 5-11-10 (3") Mr R Walsh, ...(9 to 4 fav)	3
1117[3]	LEAMHOG (Ire) 6-12-1 (3") Mr B M Cash, ...(5 to 1)	4
	FATHER GERRY (Ire) 6-11-11 Mr J A Flynn, ...(8 to 1)	5
1096[2]	SHEISAGALE (Ire) 5-10-13 (7") Mr A C Coyle, ...(7 to 1)	6
686"	KNOCKAROO (Ire) 5-12-4 Mr P Fenton, ...(3 to 1)	7
	BALLYMACREVAN (Ire) 6-11-4 (7") Mr K Ross, ...(66 to 1)	8
1042	DREW'S BUCK (Ire) 5-11-4 (7") Miss L Miskimmins, (66 to 1)	9
	SIMPLY CLASS (Ire) 5-10-13 (7") Mr J Keville, ...(20 to 1)	10
	LOVELY LYNSEY (Ire) 4-10-8 (7") Mr A J Dempsey, (20 to 1)	11
	VALLEY PLAYER (Ire) 4-10-13 (7") Mr A G Jordan, (20 to 1)	12

Dist: 1½l, 2l, 11l, 1l. 4m 1.60s. (12 Ran).

(Diamond Syndicate), W J Lanigan

NEWCASTLE (good)
Saturday November 9th
Going Correction: PLUS 0.05 sec. per fur. (races 1,3,5), MINUS 0.25 (2,4,6)

1280 European Breeders Fund 'National Hunt' Novices' Hurdle Qualifier Class E (4,5,6-y-o) £2,295 2m (1:00)

1182	B THE ONE 5-11-0 R Garritty, al hndy, smooth hdwy bef 3 out,	
	rdn to ld last 50 yards.......................(6 to 1 tchd 7 to 1)	1
1123[4]	FAITHFUL HAND 6-10-7 (7") R Wilkinson, led to second,	
	rgned ld nxt, rdn whn hit 2 out, hdd last 50 yards.	
	......................................(4 to 1 tchd 7 to 2)	2
	NICK ROSS 5-11-0 A Dobbin, hld up, improved to chase ldrs	
	aftr 4 out, rdn 2 out, one pace.	
	.............................(11 to 2 op 6 to 1 tchd 7 to 1)	3
	KING PIN 4-11-0 R Supple, hld up, smooth hdwy bef 4 out,	
	rdn whn hit 2 out, fdd...............(9 to 4 fav op 13 to 8)	4
	SCOTTON GREEN 5-11-0 L Wyer, nvr far away, rdn 3 out, sn	
	outpcd..........................(8 to 1 op 10 to 1 tchd 14 to 1)	5
1050[4]	PRIMITIVE HEART 4-11-0 A Larnach, hndy, outpcd aftr 4 out,	
	no imprsn frm nxt...........................(9 to 1 op 5 to 1)	6
960[9]	PERSUASIVE TALENT (Ire) 5-11-0 B Harding, sn chasing	
	ldrs, outpcd aftr 4 out, no dngr after... (66 to 1 op 50 to 1)	7
1073[8]	TEDDY EDWARD 6-11-0 J Supple, pld hrd, mstk and led	
	second, jmpd rght and hdd nxt, outpcd bef 4 out.	
	..................................(50 to 1 op 33 to 1)	8
	AR AGHAIDH ABHAILE (Ire) 5-11-0 A S Smith, in tch, strug-	
	gling aftr 5 out, sn btn............................(14 to 1)	9

156

NATIONAL HUNT RESULTS 1996-97

UN POCO LOCO 4-11-0 P Niven, *beh, struggling whn blun*
4th, tld off.......................... (20 1 op 12 to 1)   10
Dist: 1¼l, 5l, 5l, 5l, 2½l, 18l, 10l, 15l, 13l. 3m 52.20s. a 12.20s (10 Ran).
(Andrew Page And Mr John Pollard), J J Quinn

1281 Top Of The North Novices' Chase Class E (4-y-o and up) £2,853 2m 110yds...................... (1:30)

1035* SOLOMON'S DANCER (USA) 6-11-9 A Dobbin, *nvr far away,
led 3 out, hit nxt, ran on wl und pres frm next.*
.... (6 to 5 on op 6 to 4 on tchd 11 to 10 on)   1
1049* DOWN THE FELL 7-11-9 N Williamson, *led, hdd 3 out, rallied
and ev ch last, hld towards finish.......*(3 to 1 op 11 to 4)   2
916² BLUE CHARM (Ire) 6-11-9 R Garritty, *pressed ldr, outpcd bef
3 out, styd on frm last...*(16 to 1 op 25 to 1 tchd 33 to 1)   3
1035³ SHAWWELL 9-11-3 B Storey, *in tch, outpcd 5th, rallied 4 out,
struggling nxt......................*(50 to 1 op 33 to 1)   4
1149* GOLDEN HELLO 5-11-9 L Wyer, *jmpd rght, hld up in tch, hit
7th, f nxt............*(3 to 1 op 5 to 2 tchd 100 to 30)   f
Dist: ¾l, 1¾l, 25l. 4m 2.40s. a 3.40s (5 Ran).
SR: 20/19/17/-/-/   (J Hales), G Richards

1282 Jackdaw Handicap Hurdle Class C (0-135 4-y-o and up) £3,355 3m .... (2:05)

1036* JOCKS CROSS (Ire) [113] 5-11-7 A Dobbin, *made all, quickened 7th, ran on strly fnl 2.*
.... (8 to 4 fav op 5 to 4 tchd 7 to 4)   1
1166² TALLYWAGGER [118] 9-11-13 J Callaghan, *pressed wnr, ev
ch appr 3 out, sn outpcd, one pace betw last 2.*
.................................*(5 to 2 op 3 to 1)   2
1127* NOTABLE EXCEPTION [107] 7-11-2 P Niven, *nvr far away,
effrt and ev ch 3 out, one pace nxt.*
...............(3 to 1 op 5 to 2 tchd 100 to 30)   3
ATTADALE [119] 8-12-0 M Foster, *chsd ldrs, outpcd 5 out, btn
last 3...............................* (9 to 1 op 9 to 2)   4
Dist: 5l, 3l, dist. 5m 45.30s. a 14.30s (4 Ran).
(Mrs Gill Harrison), G Richards

1283 Peaty Sandy Handicap Chase Class C (0-135 5-y-o and up) £4,463 3¾m .... (2:40)

INTO THE RED [120] 12-11-3 P Niven, *settled on inn,
improved 11th, led 5 out till bef 2 out, rallied to ld r-in, gmely.*
.... (14 to 1 op 10 to 1)   1
1165* ROYAL VACATION [112] 7-10-9 J Callaghan, *hld up,
improved 5 out, led bef 2 out, hdd r-in, kpt on.*
....(7 to 2 tchd 4 to 1)   2
KILCOLGAN [103] 9-9¹-12¹ (3²) G Cahill, *cl up, lost pl 9th,
rallied 13th, blun 4 out, kpt on bef 2 out, flashed tail and kept
on r-in.....................(9 to 2 op 4 to 1 tchd 5 to 1)   3
1185² JOE WHITE [119] 10-11-2 N Williamson, *settled in tch,
improved 13th, chlgd 5 out, outpcd appr 2 out.*
............................(5 to 1 fav op 5 to 2)   4
797⁴ GRANGE BRAKE [124] 10-11-4 (3²) D Walsh, *mstks, led till
hdd and blun 5 out, struggling 3 out.....* (7 to 2 op 4 to 1)   5
958³ SIDE OF HILL [103] 11-9-11 (3²) G Lee, *dsptd ld one circuit, sn
lost pl, no dngr aftr................* (50 to 1 op 33 to 1)   6
1165⁶ GOLDEN FIDDLE (Ire) [103] 8-10-0 B Storey, *in tch, blun 16th
and 5 out, struggling last 3............*(6 to 1 tchd 7 to 1)   7
961 OFF THE BRU [104] 11-10-1⁸ (7²) Mr M Bradburne, *cl up, blun
6 out, sn struggling...............*(25 to 1 op 20 to 1)   8
Dist: 1¾l, nk, 25l, 5l, ½l, ¾l, 2½l. 7m 37.30s. a 12.30s (8 Ran).
(J Huckle), Mrs M Reveley

1284 Ekbalco Handicap Hurdle Class B (0-145 4-y-o and up) £4,824 2m .... (3:10)

1184* DIRECT ROUTE (Ire) [128] 5-10-11 N Williamson, *led on bit 2 out, drvn out frm last.*
..........................(11 to 8 fav op 7 to 4)   1
1167⁸ URBAN DANCING (USA) [117] 7-9-11 (3²) G Cahill, *al prmnt,
drvn bef 3 out, rallied aftr nxt, kpt on.* (100 to 1 op 66 to 1)   2
MARCHANT MING (Ire) [130] 4-10-13 R Garritty, *led 3rd to
4th, led ag'n bef 3 out, hdd nxt, kpt on r-in.*
..........................(11 to 1 op 9 to 1)   3
1049 THORNTON GATE [127] 7-10-10 L Wyer, *hld up, improved
bef 3 out, rdn and no imprsn aftr nxt.*
..........................(9 to 2 op 4 to 1 tchd 5 to 1)   4
1200² DONE WELL (USA) [118] 4-10-1 A Dobbin, *hld up, imprvg
whn sddl slpd hfwy, fdd and eased last 3.*
..........................(7 to 2 tchd 4 to 1)   5
1186⁶ OUR KRIS [125] (bl) 4-10-8 D Parker, *cl up, led 4th, hdd bef 3
out, sn struggling......* (25 to 1 op 20 to 1 tchd 33 to 1)   6
JAZILAH (Fr) [140] 8-11-2 (7²) S Melrose, *led till mstk and hdd
3rd, struggling 5th, tld off............* (7 to 2 op 2 to 1)   7
RARFY'S DREAM [117] 8-10-0 B Storey, *chsd ldg bunch,
struggling whn f 5th............*(200 to 1 op 100 to 1)   f
966³ HOME COUNTIES (Ire) [145] 7-12-0 D J Moffatt, *f 1st.*
..........................(7 to 2 op 2 tchd 4 to 1)   f
Dist: ¾l, 1l, 7l, 10l, ½l, dist. 3m 45.50s. a 5.50s (9 Ran).
SR: 36/24/36/26/7/13/   (Chris Heron), J Howard Johnson

1285 Swift Handicap Chase Class D (0-125 5-y-o and up) £3,702 2½m .... (3:45)

EASBY JOKER [117] 8-12-0 P Niven, *trkd ldr, hit 3rd, led 5
out, pushed clr last................*(11 to 8 op 5 to 4 on)   1
863² CHARMING GALE [95] (v) 9-10-6 L Wyer, *led, hdd 5 out,
rallied and ev ch last 3, one pace r-in.*
..........................(Evens fav op 11 to 10)   2
1165 CROSS CANNON [111] 10-11-8 T Reed, *chsd ldrs, chlgd 3
out, rdn and no quicken last............*(5 to 1 op 3 to 1)   3
Dist: 5l, ½l. 5m 9.20s. a 22.20s (3 Ran).
(G R Orchard), S E Kettlewell

SANDOWN (good)
Saturday November 9th
Going Correction: PLUS 0.30 sec. per fur. (races
1,3,6,7), PLUS 0.10 (2,4,5)

1286 County Sound Radio Juvenile Novices' Hurdle Class D (3-y-o) £2,801 2m 110yds................. (12:55)

SHOOTING LIGHT (Ire) 11-3 C O'Dwyer, *trkd ldrs, led appr 2
out, clr last, ran on wl............*(12 to 1 op 8 to 1)   1
PLEASURELAND (Ire) 11-3 D Morris, *hld up, gd hdwy 3 out,
rdn to chase wnr aftr nxt............*(50 to 1 op 20 to 1)   2
1154* SQUIRE'S OCCASION (Can) 11-5 (5²) S Ryan, *hld up in tch,
ev ch 3 out till hrd rdn and wknd aftr nxt.* (8 to 1 op 6 to 1)   3
1102* DOCTOR GREEN (Fr) (v) 11-10 C Maude, *not fluent, made
most till hdd appr 2 out, sn rdn and btn.*
..........(13 to 8 fav op 5 to 4 tchd 7 to 4)   4
1027³ SERENUS (USA) 11-3 M A Fitzgerald, *not fluent, with ldr till
appr 2 out, wknd bef last............*(7 to 4 tchd 9 to 4)   5
HANBITOOH (USA) 11-3 G Bradley, *hld up in tch, rdn and
wknd quickly appr 2 out, tld off.*
..........................(10 to 1 op 7 to 1 tchd 12 to 1)   6
DEUX CARR (USA) 11-0 J F Titley, *al beh, lost tch 3rd, tld off.*
..........................(14 to 1 op 6 to 1 tchd 16 to 1)   7
STERLING FELLOW (bl) 11-0 (3²) K Gaule, *al beh, tld off.*
..........................(14 to 1 op 10 to 1 tchd 20 to 1)   8
Dist: 5l, 7l, ¾l, ¾l, dist, 26l, 9l. 4m 4.20s. a 17.20s (8 Ran).
(J M Brown), P G Murphy

1287 Aldaniti Novices' Chase Class D (5-y-o and up) £3,493 2m........ (1:25)

AARDWOLF 5-11-0 G Bradley, *jmpd wl, led to 8th, led 4 out,
drw clr 2 out, easily.....* (8 to 1 op 11 to 2 tchd 9 to 1)   1
968² AMANCIO (U3A) 5-11-0 C Maude, *hld up in tch, mstk 3rd, wnt
second 5th, led 8th to tenth, ev ch whn blun 3 out, rdn and no
hdwy frm nxt....* (5 to 4 fav op 5 to 4 on tchd 11 to 8)   2
990⁸ FULL OF TRICKS 8-11-0 D Morris, *jmpd slwly 4th, sn lost tch,
tld off.......................* (150 to 1 op 66 to 1)   3
1031* PLUNDER BAY (USA) 5-11-7 M A Fitzgerald, *trkd wnr to 5th, f
nxt.......................*(7 to 2 op 9 to 4 tchd 4 to 1)   f
GROOVING (Ire) 7-11-0 P Hide, *f 1st.....*(9 to 4 op 3 to 1)   f
Dist: 19l, dist. 3m 55.80s. a 6.80s (5 Ran).
SR: 34/-/   (Lady Camilla Dempster), C P E Brooks

1288 London Racing Club Handicap Hurdle Class B (0-145 4-y-o and up) £4,879 2m 110yds........... (1:55)

923* CRACK ON [123] 6-10-12 M A Fitzgerald, *hld up in tch, al gng
wl, led on bit last, shaken up, ran on well.*
..........................(Evens fav op 5 to 4 tchd 11 to 8)   1
LIGHTENING LAD [125] 8-11-0 C Maude, *led till mstk and
hdd briefly 3 out, headed last, rallied, not quicken.*
..........................(5 to 1 op 6 to 1 tchd 7 to 1)   2
996* HAMILTON SILK [128] 4-11-3 G Bradley, *hld up in rear, gd
hdwy appr 2 out, rdn approaching last, one pace.*
..........................(7 to 2 op 7 to 2 tchd 5 to 1)   3
1186⁴ NON VINTAGE (Ire) [132] 5-11-7 W Worthington, *hld up, hdwy
appr 2 out, rdn and one pace aftr.*
..........................(11 to 2 op 5 to 1 tchd 6 to 1)   4
LONESOME TRAIN (USA) [134] 7-11-9 M Richards, *trkd ldr,
led briefly 3 out, rdn and wknd appr nxt, eased, tld off.*
..........................(11 to 1 op 7 to 1 tchd 12 to 1)   5
MANEREE [111] 9-10-0 J F Titley, *al beh, tld off 4th.*
..........................(25 to 1 op 16 to 1)   6
KINGSFOLD PET [135] 7-11-10 D Skyrme, *trkd ldrs till f 3rd.*
..........................(12 to 1 op 7 to 1)   f
Dist: 2½l, 4l, 4l, 30l, dist. 3m 56.20s. a 9.20s (7 Ran).
SR: 41/40/39/39/11/-/-/   (D R Peppiatt), P J Hobbs

1289 South East Racecourse Of The Year Handicap Chase Class C (0-130 5-y-o and up) £4,810 2½m 110yds (2:30)

1029* STRONG MEDICINE [129] 9-12-0 C O'Dwyer, *hld up, hdwy to
chase ldr tenth to 12th, mstk 4 out, led last, rdn out.*
..........................(6 to 4 fav tchd 7 to 4)   1

GOLDEN SPINNER [122] 9-11-7 M A Fitzgerald, *hit 1st, led till hdd last, rdn and kpt on one pace*......(9 to 4 op 2 to 1) 2
71 SHAARID (USA) [112] 8-10-11 G Bradley, *trkd ldr 6th to tenth and ag'n 12th to 3 out, wknd aftr nxt*...... (8 to 1 op 7 to 1) 3
KING CREDO [120] 11-11-5 J F Titley, *trkd ldrs to 6th, mstk nxt, lost tch 8th, tld off*... (14 to 1 op 8 to 1 tchd 16 to 1) 4
823³ CONTI D'ESTRUVAL (Fr) [122] 6-11-7 P Hide, *hld up in tch, blun and uns rdr 5 out*............... (9 to 2 op 5 to 2) ur
Dist: 1¼l, 12l, dist. 5m 13.30s. a 13.30s (5 Ran).

(Dr D B A Silk), K C Bailey

1290 Gunpowder Plot Handicap Chase Class B (5-y-o and up) £6,742 3m 110yds....................... (3:00)

INCHCAILLOCH (Ire) [118] 7-10-1 C Maude, *hld up in tch, wnt second appr 3 out, quickened to ld r-in.*
.... (9 to 4 fav op 7 to 4 tchd 9 to 4) 1
GREY SMOKE [124] 6-10-7 J F Titley, *trkd ldr, led sn aftr 4 out, rdn 2 out, ran on, hdd r-in.*
.... (9 to 4 tchd 2 to 1 and 5 to 2) 2
BETTY'S BOY (Ire) [127] 7-10-10 C O'Dwyer, *hld up, hdwy to chase ldrs 17th, rdn and wknd 2 out.*
.... (11 to 4 op 7 to 2 tchd 4 to 1) 3
COOL DAWN (Ire) [137] 8-11-6 Miss D Harding, *led 4th till hdd sn aftr four out, wknd nxt.* (11 to 2 op 5 to 1 tchd 6 to 1) 4
WILLSFORD [145] 13-11-11 (3*) G Hogan, *led to 4th, outpcd 15th, stdly wknd, tld off.* (16 to 1 op 14 to 1 tchd 20 to 1) 5
Dist: ½l, 14l, 1½l, dist. 6m 16.20s. a 17.20s (5 Ran).

(F J Carter), J S King

1291 Surrey Racing Novices' Handicap Hurdle Class D (0-105 4-y-o and up) £2,840 2¾m................ (3:30)

1048⁴ RIVER ROOM [104] 6-11-7 (7*) W Walsh, *hld up in tch, led second appr 2 out, styd on grimly to ld nr finish.*
.... (11 to 1 op 6 to 1) 1
906 HYLTERS CHANCE (Ire) [76] 5-10-0 L Harvey, *tried to make all, clr 2 out, tired appr last, ct nr finish.*
.... (9 to 2 op 4 to 1 tchd 5 to 1) 2
EL FREDDIE [93] 6-11-3 G Upton, *hld up, hdwy 2 out, nvr nrr.*
.... (7 to 2 op 9 to 2) 3
1158 EMBLEY BUOY [76] 8-10-0 S Curran, *al prmnt, chsd ldrs 6th till appr 2 out, wknd approaching last.*
.... (15 to 2 op 7 to 1 tchd 8 to 1) 4
1158³ POSITIVO [77] 5-10-1 D Leahy, *hld up in rear, nvr on terms.*
.... (16 to 1 op 14 to 1 tchd 20 to 1) 5
ROVESTAR [85] 5-10-9 C Maude, *mid-div, rdn appr 2 out, sn wknd.*.................. (9 to 1 op 10 to 1 tchd 20 to 1) 6
975⁹ CAREY'S COTTAGE (Ire) [76] 5-10-0 M Richards, *slwly away, al beh.*.................. (50 to 1 op 50 to 1) 7
867* MONTEL EXPRESS (Ire) [100] 4-11-10 C O'Dwyer, *in rear, effrt whn mstk 3 out, sn btn.*......(5 to 2 fav tchd 11 to 4) 8
919 TRAIL BOSS (Ire) [98] 5-11-8 J F Titley, *trkd ldr to 6th, wknd 3 out.*.................. (13 to 2 op 4 to 1 tchd 7 to 1) 9
Dist: Nk, 9l, nk, 3l, 6l, 9l, 2½l, 10l. 5m 23.60s. a 20.60s (9 Ran).

(Douglas Allum), K C Bailey

1292 Weatherbys 'Stars Of Tomorrow' Open National Hunt Flat Standard - Class H (4,5,6-y-o) £1,997 2m 110yds....................... (4:00)

MR MARKHAM (Ire) 4-11-4 P Hide, *hld up in tch, hdwy o'r 2 fs out, rdn and styd on to ld ins last.*
.... (8 to 1 op 6 to 1 tchd 10 to 1) 1
WADE ROAD (Ire) 5-11-11 J F Titley, *hld up in mid-div, hdwy to ld o'r 2 fs out, rdn and bttd ins last.*
.... (Evens fav op 5 to 4 on tchd 6 to 5) 2
693¹ PROTOTYPE 5-11-11 M A Fitzgerald, *hld up, hdwy o'r 2 fs out, one pace............* (6 to 1 op 3 to 1 tchd 13 to 2) 3
FOREST MUSK (Ire) 5-10-13 (5*) D J Kavanagh, *chsd ldr, led o'r 3 fs out, hdd over 2 out, sn btn.*
.... (16 to 1 op 6 to 1 tchd 20 to 1) 4
AZTEC WARRIOR 5-11-11 (7*) Mr R Wakley, *al prmnt, rdn o'r 2 fs out, sn wknd.*.................. (33 to 1 op 10 to 1) 5
SAUCY NUN (Ire) 4-10-13 C Maude, *in rear, hdwy o'r 3 fs out, wknd over 2 out*.................. (50 to 1 op 14 to 1) 6
873² THE BREWMASTER (Ire) 4-11-4 G Bradley, *pld hrd, hdwy hfwy, wknd 3 fs out.* (11 to 2 op 4 to 1 tchd 6 to 1) 7
DIAMOND LADY 4-10-13 M Richards, *in rear, nvr on terms.*
.... (33 to 1 op 14 to 1 tchd 50 to 1) 8
KNIGHT'S CREST (Ire) 6-11-4 Derek Byrne, *mid-div, nvr on terms.*.................. (33 to 1 op 21 to 1 tchd 50 to 1) 9
STENCIL 4-10-13 (5*) S Ryan, *hld up, rdn o'r 3 fs out, sn btn.*
.... (33 to 1 op 20 to 1) 10
FRENO (Ire) 5-11-4 C O'Dwyer, *hld up, effrt o'r 4 fs out, sn wknd.*.................. (33 to 1 op 14 to 1 tchd 20 to 1) 11
BELLIDIUM 4-10-10 (3*) R Massey, *led and sn clr, hdd o'r 3 fs out, wkng whn hng badly lft over 2 out.* (50 to 1 op 20 to 1) 12
MISS BARTHOLOMEW 6-10-10 (3*) G Hogan, *in tch till wknd o'r 4 fs out, tld off.....* (33 to 1 op 12 to 1 tchd 50 to 1) 13
THUNDER ROAD (Ire) 5-11-4 R Bellamy, *chsd ldrs till wknd 6 fs out, tld off.........* (33 to 1 op 14 to 1 tchd 50 to 1) 14
Dist: 1l, 11l, ¾l, 6l, ½l, 8l, ½l, 5l, 6l, 6l. 3m 52.20s. (14 Ran).

(Felix Rosensteil's Widow & Son), J T Gifford

UTTOXETER (good to firm) Saturday November 9th
Going Correction: PLUS 0.40 sec. per fur.

1293 PRD Fasteners Maiden Hurdle Class E (Div I) (4-y-o and up) £1,987 2m .... (12:40)

GREEN GREEN DESERT (Ire) 5-11-5 D Bridgwater, *hld up, pld hrd, hdwy 5th, led and jmpd lft appr 3 out, cmftbly.*
.... (13 to 8 on op 6 to 4 on tchd 7 to 4 on) 1
976⁵ SWAN STREET (NZ) 5-11-5 J Railton, *hld up, hdwy to chase wnr 3 out, rdn appr last, no extr.*
.... (7 to 2 op 3 to 1 tchd 4 to 1) 2
837 CAVIL 4-11-5 A Thornton, *chsd ldrs, rdn appr 2 out, styd on same pace.*.................. (20 to 1 op 14 to 1) 3
BARTON SCAMP 4-11-5 T Eley, *hld up, hdwy 4 out, rdn and no imprsn whn mstk last.* (10 to 1 op 8 to 1 tchd 11 to 1) 4
FASTINI GOLD 4-11-2 (3*) F Leahy, *beh till styd on frm 2 out, nvr nrr.*.................. (25 to 1 op 20 to 1 tchd 33 to 1) 5
1136⁷ BLUE LUGANA 4-11-5 D Bentley, *hld up, effrt 4 out, rdn and nvr rchd ldrs.*.................. (50 to 1) 6
971⁸ DASHING DANCER (Ire) 5-11-5 Gary Lyons, *hld up, effrt 4 out, nvr able to chal.*.................. (50 to 1 op 33 to 1) 7
419⁵ SAINT AMIGO (v) 4-11-5 Derek Byrne, *led to 3rd, led appr 4 out, hdd and wknd nxt.*......... (50 to 1 op 33 to 1) 8
DICTATION (USA) 4-11-5 A Roche, *hld up, nvr plcd to chal.*
.... (16 to 1 op 12 to 1 tchd 20 to 1) 9
MONTY 4-11-0 (5*) Michael Brennan, *in tch till wknd 4 out.*
.... (50 to 1 op 33 to 1) 10
KNAVE OF DIAMONDS 4-11-5 W McFarland, *prmnt to 5th, sn beh.*.................. (25 to 1 op 12 to 1) 11
1155⁵ AL HELAL (v) 4-10-12 (7*) N T Egan, *blun and uns rdr 1st.*
.... (25 to 1 op 14 to 1) ur
SCBOO 7-11-2 (3*) D Fortt, *led 3rd to appr 4 out, wknd quickly, pld up bef nxt.*.......... (100 to 1 op 50 to 1) pu
MY HANDSOME PRINCE (v) 4-11-5 R Bellamy, *prmnt, wknd quickly 4 out, pld up bef nxt.*....... (50 to 1 op 33 to 1) pu
Dist: 3½l, 8l, 1¼l, 8l, 1½l, 2½l, 2l, 4l, 14l, dist. 3m 59.20s. a 22.20s (14 Ran).

(Darren C Mercer), O Sherwood

1294 Derby Evening Telegraph Handicap Chase Class B (0-145 5-y-o and up) £6,827 2m 5f....................... (1:10)

CALL IT A DAY (Ire) [135] 6-11-9 A Maguire, *chsd ldr, led 6th to 9th, led 5 out, drvn out.....*(11 to 8 on tchd 5 to 4 on) 1
LORD GYLLENE (NZ) [119] 8-10-7 T Eley, *hld up, hdwy to ld 6 out, hdd nxt, still ev ch last, no extr......* (9 to 4 op 2 to 1) 2
967⁴ BAVARD DIEU (Ire) [140] 8-12-0 A Thornton, *led to 6th, led 9th to six out, outpcd 4 out, styd on r-in.....* (5 to 1 op 4 to 1) 3
Dist: 2½l, 5l. 5m 15.70s. a 17.70s (3 Ran).
SR: 2/-/-/

(Mrs Jane Lane), D Nicholson

1295 PRD Fasteners Maiden Hurdle Class E (Div II) (4-y-o and up) £1,976 2m .... (1:40)

MYWEND'S (Ire) 6-11-5 D Gallagher, *trkd ldrs, led on bit 3 out, pushed out.............* (4 to 1 op 3 to 1 tchd 9 to 2) 1
1053 SOUTHERN NIGHTS 6-11-5 A Thornton, *hld up, hdwy 5th, rdn and hmpd appr 2 out, styd on wl r-in.*
.... (2 to 1 fav op 7 to 4 tchd 9 to 4) 2
SMOLENSK (Ire) 4-11-5 M Moloney, *chsd ldrs, ev ch 3 out till no extr appr last.....* (16 to 1 op 14 to 1 tchd 20 to 1) 3
CYPRESS AVENUE (Ire) 4-11-0 (5*) Michael Brennan, *slwly into strd, hdwy 3 out, ran on wl.*
.... (9 to 1 op 7 to 1 tchd 10 to 1) 4
VENDOON (Ire) 6-11-5 D Bridgwater, *chsd ldr, rdn and ev ch 3 out, wknd appr last..............* (12 to 1 op 10 to 1) 5
1023⁴ ROBSERA (Ire) (v) 5-11-2 (3*) F Leahy, *led till appr 3 out, grad wknd...............* (14 to 1 op 10 to 1 tchd 5 to 1) 6
DARING RYDE 5-11-5 T Eley, *beh 5th.* (50 to 1 op 25 to 1) 7
CHANTRO BAY 8-11-5 M Dwyer, *hld up, effrt 4 out, wknd nxt.*
.... (33 to 1 op 25 to 1) 8
806 NUKUD (USA) (v) 4-10-12 (7*) C McCormack, *mid-div, drvn alng 4 out, sn wknd.............* (50 to 1 op 25 to 1) 9
1129 SUPER BRUSH (Ire) 4-10-9 (5*) G E Smith, *hld up, al beh.*
.... (50 to 1 op 25 to 1) 10
1097⁴ MR GORDON BENNETT 5-10-12 (7*) X Aizpuru, *prmnt till rdn and wknd 4 out...............* (50 to 1 op 25 to 1) 11
THAT OLD FEELING (Ire) 4-11-5 A Maguire, *hld up, al rear, wl beh whn f last..........* (14 to 1 op 12 to 1 tchd 16 to 1) f
Dist: 5l, nk, sht-hd, 11l, 3l, 25l, nk, 21l, 26l, 10l. 3m 51.10s. a 14.10s (12 Ran).
SR: 14/9/9/9/-/-/

(Uplands Bloodstock), C P E Brooks

1296 Mason Richards Handicap Chase Class D For Tom Curran Memorial Trophy (0-125 5-y-o and up) £3,858 3 ¼m....................... (2:10)

IDIOT'S LADY [120] 7-11-9 M Dwyer, *hld up, hdwy 12th, led 3 out, hit last, styd on wl....* (4 to 1 op 3 to 1 tchd 9 to 2) 1

RECTORY GARDEN (Ire) [113] 7-11-2 A Thornton, *wth ldr, led 9th till 3 out, styd on same pace.*
.........................(11 to 4 fav op 5 to 2 tchd 3 to 1) 2
MUSTHAVEASWIG [125] 10-12-0 A Maguire, *trkd ldrs, ev ch 4 out, one pace frm nxt.*............(7 to 2 tchd 4 to 1) 3
1064² ROMANY CREEK (Ire) [120] (v) 7-11-9 D Bridgwater, *prmnt, mstk 1st, hit 11th, rdn 14th, wknd quickly 4 out.*
.................................(5 to 1 op 7 to 2) 4
797 FLORIDA SKY [109] 9-10-12 D Gallagher, *led to 9th, wknd 6 out, tld off.*...........(12 to 1 op 8 to 1 tchd 14 to 1) 5
1137⁴ SAILOR JIM [110] 9-10-13 J Railton, *hld up, f 13th.*
.................................(11 to 2 op 5 to 1 tchd 6 to 1) f
Dist: 5l, 8l, 18l, dist. 6m 39.30s. a 27.30s (6 Ran).

(Mrs J Ollivant), Mrs J Pitman

1297 Stainless Threaded Fasteners 10th Anniversary Classic Novices' Hurdle Class A Grade 2 (4-y-o and up) £9,675 2½m 110yds.........(2:45)

1134* JACK TANNER (Ire) 7-11-0 A Maguire, *trkd ldr, mstk 6th, led 4 out, clr nxt, eased r-in.*........(10 to 3 on op 11 to 4 on) 1
973* MAKE A STAND 5-11-4 M Dwyer, *led, rcd keenly, hdd 4 out, no ch wth wnr.*..........................(3 to 1 op 9 to 4) 2
MANASIS (NZ) 5-11-0 T Eley, *hld up, outpcd frm 4 out.*
.................................(20 to 1 op 12 to 1) 3
Dist: Dist, dist. 5m 0.20s. a 21.20s (3 Ran).

(Lady Harris), D Nicholson

1298 Eurofast Petrochemical Supplies Novices' Chase Class D (5-y-o and up) £3,858 3m...............(3:20)

844³ DON DU CADRAN (Fr) 7-11-0 A Thornton, *trkd ldr, led 5 out, lft wl clr 2 out.*...............(9 to 2 tchd 5 to 1) 1
LOCH GARMAN HOTEL (Ire) 7-11-0 T Eley, *led, jmpd rght 6th, hdd 5 out, wknd nxt.*..........(7 to 1 tchd 8 to 1) 2
PHARANEAR (Ire) 6-11-0 A Maguire, *mstks, hld up, mistake 1st, blun badly second, hdwy to chase wnr 4 out, rdn and cl second whn f 2 out, rmntd.*
.................................(11 to 4 on op 3 to 1 on tchd 5 to 2 on) 3
AINSI SOIT IL (Fr) 5-10-9 (3*) D Fortt, *beh 5th, tld off whn refused last, wnt back, continued.*
.................................(33 to 1 op 16 to 1 tchd 40 to 1) 4
Dist: 24l, dist, 20l. 6m 16.10s. (4 Ran).

(Lord Cadogan), Capt T A Forster

1299 Derby Express Conditional Jockeys' Handicap Hurdle Class E (0-120 5-y-o and up) £2,710 2m........(3:50)

1008* YUBRALEE (USA) [115] 4-12-0 E Husband, *made all, clr 3 out, eased r-in.*.................(5 to 4 fav op 7 to 4) 1
DOOLAR (USA) [87] 9-10-0 Michael Brennan, *chsd wnr, rdn appr 3 out, sn lost tch.*.........(25 to 1 op 12 to 1) 2
806⁶ EUROLINK SHADOW [87] 4-10-0 D Fortt, *tld off 5th.*
.................................(14 to 1 op 8 to 1) 3
1051* STEADFAST ELITE (Ire) [98] 5-10-11 R McGrath, *f 1st.*
.................................(9 to 4 op 2 to 1 tchd 5 to 2) f
JEMIMA PUDDLEDUCK [93] 5-9-13 (7*) W Greatrex, *hld up, blun and uns rdr 4th.*.................(7 to 2 op 5 to 2) ur
Dist: 5l, dist. 3m 55.40s. a 18.40s (5 Ran).

(D A Johnson), M C Pipe

WINCANTON (good)
Saturday November 9th
Going Correction: MINUS 0.15 sec. per fur. (races 1,4,6,7), PLUS 0.30 (2,3,5)

1300 European Breeders Fund 'National Hunt' Novices' Hurdle Qualifier Class E (4,5,6-y-o) £2,600 2m (1:05)

990² MAZZINI (Ire) 5-11-3 (7*) Mr P O'Keeffe, *made all, rdn and ran on wl frm 2 out.*........(10 to 1 op 7 to 1 tchd 11 to 1) 1
NEAT FEAT (Ire) 5-11-0 P Holley, *hld up, effrt appr 2 out, took second r-in, no ch wth wnr.* (5 to 2 op 3 to 1 tchd 2 to 1) 2
1097² CHARLIE PARROT (Ire) 6-11-0 J Osborne, *hld up beh ldrs, wnt second 3 out, effrt whn hng rght nxt, wknd r-in.*
.................................(5 to 2 op 4 to 1 tchd 11 to 4) 3
SILVER THYNE (Ire) 4-11-0 R Farrant, *beh, jmpd lft 3rd, rdn 3 out, no imprsn on ldrs.*............(9 to 4 fav op 7 to 4) 4
WEST BAY BREEZE 4-10-9 B Powell, *in tch, jmpd slwly 4th, beh 3 out.*.............(9 to 1 op 12 to 1 tchd 16 to 1) 5
GALE SPRING (Ire) 4-10-6 (3*) T Dascombe, *prmnt, chsd wnr frm 3rd till mstk 3 out, wknd bef nxt.*..(50 to 1 op 25 to 1) 6
ADMIRAL BRUNY (Ire) 5-11-0 J R Kavanagh, *pld hrd, hld up, mstk second, nvr on terms, tld off.*..(14 to 1 op 7 to 1) 7
PARAMOUNT LEADER 4-11-0 J A McCarthy, *sn beh, tld off whn pld up bef last.*..............(100 to 1 op 50 to 1) pu
Dist: 5l, 7l, 11l, 10l, 5l, dist. 3m 46.30s. a 12.30s (8 Ran).

(Nicholas Cooper), R Rowe

1301 Silver Buck Handicap Chase Class E (0-115 5-y-o and up) £4,328 2m 5f

.................................(1:35)

48⁴ MONKS JAY (Ire) [88] 7-10-4 I Lawrence, *hld up, not fluent 7th, hdwy 12th, led last, ran on wl.*....(10 to 1 op 12 to 1) 1
1108⁴ CHANNEL PASTIME [93] 12-10-6 (3*) Guy Lewis, *prmnt, lft in ld 3 out, hdd last, one pace.*.......(16 to 1 tchd 20 to 1) 2
1052⁶ THE CAUMRUE (Ire) [105] 8-11-7 B Clifford, *hld up, hdwy 12th, rdn nxt, one pace frm 3 out.*.............(5 to 1) 3
974⁴ COMEDY ROAD [100] 12-11-2 P McLoughlin, *wtd wth, improved 12th, rdn aftr nxt, one pace 2 out.*
.................................(9 to 1 op 7 to 1) 4
988³ BLACK CHURCH [96] 10-10-12 D O'Sullivan, *slwly into strd, hld up, mstk 8th, hdwy 13th, wknd 3 out, btn whn mistake last.*
.................................(9 to 1) 5
MAXXUM EXPRESS [87] 8-10-3² Richard Guest, *strted slwly, al beh, tld off.*.................(20 to 1) 6
DUHALLOW LODGE [110] 9-11-12 J R Kavanagh, *led to second, styd hndy, wkng whn f 4 out.*..(12 to 1 op 10 to 1) f
MISS MARIGOLD [96] (bl) 7-10-9 (3*) T Dascombe, *pld hrd, led 4th, blun 12th, hdd appr four out, wknd bef nxt, f 2 out.*
.................................(4 to 1 op 9 to 2) f
BEATSON (Ire) [95] 7-10-11 B Powell, *prmnt, led appr 4 out, f nxt.*.................(9 to 1 op 7 to 1) f
1114* HERBERT BUCHANAN (Ire) [101] 6-10-10 (7*) Mr J Tizzard, *blun and uns rdr 3rd.*..........(9 to 4 fav op 5 to 2) ur
JUMBEAU [100] 11-11-2 S McNeill, *led second to 4th, hit 8th, beh frm nxt, tld off from 12th, pld up bef 2 out.*....(12 to 1) pu
Dist: 2½l, 5l, nk, 11l, dist, 4l. 5m 20.70s. a 16.70s (11 Ran).

(J A Cover), G Thorner

1302 K. J. Pike & Sons Novices' Handicap Chase Class E (0-100 5-y-o and up) £3,834 3m 1f 110yds.........(2:05)

GOD SPEED YOU (Ire) [82] (bl) 7-11-9 J R Kavanagh, *led 5th, hdd appr 14th, led ag'n 4 out, clr nxt, styd on wl.*
.................................(7 to 1 op 8 to 1) 1
902⁶ CALL ME RIVER (Ire) [64] 8-10-5 I Lawrence, *hld up, hdwy 11th, hit 4 out, chsd wnr appr nxt, no imprsn.*
.................................(20 to 1 op 16 to 1) 2
1049³ STORMHILL PILGRIM [70] 7-10-11 P McLoughlin, *led second to 5th, led ag'n appr 14th, hdd 4 out, wknd quickly bef nxt.*.................(14 to 1 op 12 to 1 tchd 16 to 1) 3
1055⁵ ITS GRAND [69] 7-10-10 T J Murphy, *led to second, rdn 17th, wknd 4 out.*......(13 to 2 op 6 to 1 tchd 7 to 1) 4
CERIDWEN [74] 6-11-1 P Holley, *hld up, mstk tenth, no ch frm 13th.*.........(16 to 1 op 12 to 1 tchd 20 to 1) 5
999⁴ OUR NIKKI [72] 6-10-13 S Burrough, *al beh.*
.................................(16 to 1 op 14 to 1 tchd 20 to 1) 6
1061* TIGER CLAW (USA) [83] 10-11-3 (7*) O Burrows, *al beh, tld off 7th, pld up bef 15th.*.......(12 to 1 tchd 14 to 1) pu
999³ MINGUS (USA) [83] 9-11-10 B Powell, *beh, blun 9th, tld off whn pld up and dismounted bef 15th.*
.................................(8 to 1 op 7 to 1 tchd 9 to 1) pu
1086 TEARFUL PRINCE [74] 12-11-1 S McNeill, *al beh, tld off whn pld up bef 16th.*.......(7 to 1 op 6 to 1 tchd 8 to 1) pu
1106 VARECK II (Fr) [60] 9-9-8 (7*) B Moore, *beh 11th, tld off whn pld up bef 14th.*...............(33 to 1 op 25 to 1) pu
MARKET GOSSIP [63] 6-10-1 P Henley, *prmnt till mstk 12th, beh whn blun 14th, pld up bef nxt.*
.................................(3 to 1 fav op 7 to 2) pu
1055 CARDINAL RULE (Ire) [70] 7-10-11 R Farrant, *not fluent, hld up, rdn 12th. sn beh, tld off whn pld up bef 4 out, broke blood vessel.*.................(8 to 1 op 6 to 1) pu
Dist: 10l, 8l, 1½l, 14l, 17l. 6m 35.00s. a 19.00s (12 Ran).

(Wallop), C P Morlock

1303 West Country Handicap Hurdle Class C (0-130 4-y-o and up) £5,540 2¾m.........................(2:35)

GYSART (Ire) [113] (bl) 7-11-3 J Osborne, *made all, sn clr, rdn out.*.........(5 to 1 op 7 to 1 tchd 6 to 4) 1
1032* LANSDOWNE [124] 8-11-7 (7*) O Burrows, *hld up, rdn appr 8th, chsd wnr approaching 2 out, one pace aftr last.*
.................................(3 to 1 op 5 to 2 tchd 100 to 30) 2
822* BLASKET HERO [107] (bl) 8-10-11 S McNeill, *hld up, styd on one pace frm 3 out, nvr nrr.*......(7 to 2 op 9 to 2) 3
1233⁷ JADIDH [107] 8-10-6 (5*) D Salter, *nvr on terms, tld off.*
.................................(16 to 1 op 12 to 1 tchd 20 to 1) 4
973³ REAGANESQUE (USA) [108] 4-10-12 R Farrant, *chsd wnr till appr 2 out, sn wknd, tld off.*............(6 to 1 op 5 to 1) 5
PRINCE TEETON [105] 7-10-5³ (7*) Mr J Tizzard, *in tch whn f 3rd.*.............(14 to 1 op 12 to 1 tchd 16 to 1) f
Dist: 4l, 12l, dist, 9l. 5m 11.20s. a 5.20s (6 Ran).
SR: 4/11/-/   (The Hon Mrs R Cobbold), M C Pipe

1304 Badger Beer Handicap Chase Class B (0-145 5-y-o and up) £13,888 3m 1f 110yds.........................(3:10)

1101* COOME HILL (Ire) [130] 7-11-7 J Frost, *wtd wth, prog 12th, led 2 out, readily.*..........(2 to 1 fav op 9 to 4 tchd 5 to 2) 1
933² GLEMOT (Ire) [135] 8-11-12 J Osborne, *made most, jmpd lft 13th, hdd 2 out, btn whn blun last.*....(10 to 1 tchd 12 to 1) 2

1002* SAMLEE (Ire) [110] 7-10-1 J R Kavanagh, *hld up beh ldrs, reminders aftr 6th, btn appr 3 out.*
.......................(9 to 2 op 7 to 2 tchd 5 to 1) 3
RUN UP THE FLAG [122] 9-10-10 (3*) L Aspell, *hld up, hdwy 17th, effrt appr 3 out, btn nxt, eased r-in.*
.......................(5 to 1 op 6 to 1 tchd 13 to 2) 4
1156² STRAIGHT TALK [133] 9-11-3 (7*) Mr J Tizzard, *chsd ldr, rdn 14th, wknd nxt.*.....................(13 to 2 op 4 to 1) 5
1133³ BIG BEN DUN [112] (bl) 10-10-3 Richard Guest, *pld hrd, in tch, mstk 12th, wknd appr 3 out, 6th whn blun and uns rdr nxt.*
.......................(12 to 1 op 8 to 1) ur
GARRISON SAVANNAH [130] 13-11-7 R Farrant, *hld up, lost tch 14th, tld off whn pld up, bef 3 out.*
.......................(20 to 1 op 10 to 1 tchd 25 to 1) pu
WELL BRIEFED [122] 9-10-10 B Powell, *mstks 11th and 15th, al beh, tld off whn pld up bef 3 out.*
.......................(20 to 1 op 12 to 1 tchd 25 to 1) pu
1105⁵ TUG OF PEACE [113] 9-10-4 B Clifford, *mid-div, beh frm 15th, pld up bef 17th.*......(14 to 1 op 10 to 1 tchd 16 to 1) pu
Dist: 10l, 10l, hd, 1¾l. 6m 29.20s. a 13.20s (9 Ran).

SR: 50/45/10/22/31/-/   (Mrs Jill Dennis), W W Dennis

1305 Tanglefoot Elite Hurdle Class A Grade 2 (4-y-o and up) £12,860 2m
.... (3:45)

303⁶ DREAMS END 8-10-12 R Farrant, *in tch, led and mstk last, ran on wl....* (7 to 2 op 4 to 1 tchd 9 to 2 and 5 to 1) 1
730* SPACE TRUCKER (Ire) 5-10-12 J Osborne, *hld up, hmpd 5th, hdwy nxt, ev ch frm 2 out, not quicken r-in.*
.......................(9 to 2 op 5 to 1) 2
GROUND NUT (Ire) 6-10-12 B Powell, *led to 2 out, wknd bef last.*.............(20 to 1 op 14 to 1 tchd 25 to 1) 3
1030* MISTINGUETT (Ire) 4-10-7 C Llewellyn, *nvr nr to chal.*
.......................(2 to 1 fav tchd 5 to 2) 4
ESKIMO NEL (Ire) 5-10-7 Richard Guest, *hld up, hmpd 5th, hdwy nxt, wknd bef 2 out.* (9 to 4 tchd 5 to 2 and 11 to 4) 5
969 HOPS AND POPS 9-10-11 P Henley, *chsd ldr till aftr 4th, jmpd slwly nxt, sn beh....* (9 to 1 op 6 to 1 tchd 10 to 1) 6
ARABIAN BOLD (Ire) 8-10-12 P Holley, *beh frm 4th, tld off 3 out.*.......................(50 to 1 tchd 66 to 1) 7
HARD TO FIGURE 10-10-12 T Dascombe, *hld up beh ldrs, mstk 4th, sn wknd, tld off whn pld up bef 2 out.*
.......................(33 to 1 op 25 to 1 tchd 50 to 1) pu
Dist: 2½l, 8l, 6l, 2½l, 22l, dist. 3m 35.20s. a 1.20s (8 Ran).

SR: 48/45/37/26/23/5/-/-/   (T G Price), P Bowen

1306 Weatherbys 'Stars Of Tomorrow' Open National Hunt Flat Intermediate - Class H (4,5,6-y-o) £1,458 2m
.... (4:15)

880* LADY REBECCA 4-11-6 R Farrant, *al hndy, led o'r 2 ts out, rdn out, ran on strly.*
.......................(100 to 30 fav op 3 to 1 tchd 4 to 1) 1
QUINI EAGLE (Fr) 4-11-4 C Llewellyn, *led till o'r 2 fs out, one pace.*.............(6 to 1 op 4 to 1 tchd 7 to 1) 2
POT BLACK UK 5-10-11 (7*) M Moran, *hld up, hdwy hfwy, effrt 3 fs out, one pace fnl 2 furlongs...*(10 to 1 op 7 to 1) 3
WENTWORTH (USA) 4-10-11 (7*) Clare Thorner, *pld hrd, hld up, hdwy aftr 6 fs, wknd 4 furlongs out.*
.......................(13 to 2 op 8 to 1 tchd 6 to 1) 4
KYLAMI (NZ) 4-10-11 (7*) Mr G Shenkin, *mid-div, kpt on one pace frm 3 fs out, nvr nrr.*
.......................(20 to 1 op 14 to 1 tchd 25 to 1) 5
NIGEL'S BOY 4-10-11 (7*) O Burrows, *keen hold in tch, wknd 4 fs out.*.............(50 to 1 op 33 to 1 tchd 66 to 1) 6
ENDEAVOUR (Fr) 4-11-4 B Powell, *nrst finish.*
.......................(50 to 1 op 20 to 1) 7
BAVARDIER (Ire) 5-11-4 B Clifford, *swrvd lft strt, nvr nr to chal.*.............(14 to 1 op 10 to 1 tchd 12 to 1) 8
DARK CHALLENGER (Ire) 4-11-4 I Lawrence, *hld up, hdwy hfwy, wknd 5 fs out....*(13 to 2 op 10 to 1 tchd 12 to 1) 9
BORODINO (Ire) 4-11-4 D O'Sullivan, *nvr on terms.*
.......................(14 to 1 op 12 to 1 tchd 16 to 1) 10
STELLAR FORCE (Ire) 5-11-4 J Osborne, *hld up beh ldrs, wknd 6 fs out, eased fnl 2 furlongs.*
.......................(7 to 2 op 3 to 1 tchd 4 to 1) 11
MO'S BOY 5-11-4 S McNeill, *al beh...*(20 to 1 op 12 to 1) 12
MISSED THE MATCH 6-11-4 P McLoughlin, *chsd ldrs to hfwy....*.......................(66 to 1 op 33 to 1) 13
FAIR HAUL 5-11-4 J Frost, *mid-div, rdn 6 fs out, sn beh, tld off.*.......................(50 to 1 op 33 to 1 tchd 66 to 1) 14
SOPHIES DREAM 5-11-4 T J Murphy, *prmnt, wknd 6 fs out, tld off...*.............(50 to 1 op 33 to 1) 15
SPECIAL TOPIC 6-10-13 Richard Guest, *mid-div, lost tch frm hfwy, tld off....*.....(50 to 1 op 33 to 1 tchd 66 to 1) 16
BEWELDERED 4-11-4 Mr A Holdsworth, *al beh, tld off.*
.......................(50 to 1 op 33 to 1) 17
Dist: 6l, 2½l, 13l, 3l, 1l, 1l, nk, sht-hd, ¾l, 5l. 3m 35.80s. (17 Ran).
(Kinnersley Optimists), Miss Venetia Williams

LEOPARDSTOWN (IRE) (yielding)
Sunday November 10th

1307 Brewery Road I.N.H. Flat Race (4-y-o and up) £3,082 2m........... (3:00)

LOOSE CANNON (Ire) 4-11-9 Mr G J Harford, ...(9 to 4 fav) 1
WEST LEADER (Ire) 5-11-7 (7*) Mr J Keville, ...(6 to 1) 2
472⁸ JODESI (Ire) 6-12-0 Mr J A Nash, ...(6 to 1) 3
1174³ PLEASE NO TEARS (bl) 9-11-2 (7*) Mr A J Dempsey, (8 to 1) 4
1247² SUPREME CHANTER (Ire) 4-11-9 Mr P Fenton, ...(9 to 2) 5
1081⁴ ASFREEASTHEWIND (Ire) 5-11-9 Mr J P Dempsey, (8 to 1) 6
984 LORD OGAN (Ire) 5-11-7 (7*) Mr G Elliott, ...(25 to 1) 7
898⁹ MR MAGGET (Ire) 4-11-6 (3*) Mr D Valentine, ...(10 to 1) 8
MIDNIGHT JOY (Ire) 4-11-4 Mr D Marnane, ...(14 to 1) 9
1042⁹ JUST BEFORE DAWN (Ire) 7-11-7 (7*) Mr T J Beattie,
.......................(16 to 1) 10
TRUVARO (Ire) 5-12-0 Mr H F Cleary, ...(6 to 1) 11
1042 CAROLANNS CHOICE (Ire) 7-11-2 (7*) Mr S McGonagle,
.......................(20 to 1) 12
BALLYMACHUGH LADY (Ire) 5-11-6 (3*) Mr B M Cash,
.......................(20 to 1) 13
ROYAL BELLE (Ire) 5-11-2 (7*) Mr D W Cullen, ...(16 to 1) 14
Dist: 5l, 2l, nk, 4½l. 3m 50.40s. (14 Ran).

(Mrs John Magnier), Noel Meade

1308 Commology Handicap Chase (5-y-o and up) £4,410 2m 1f......... (3:30)

1004⁵ FIFTYSEVENCHANNELS (Ire) [-] 7-10-7 C F Swan, (14 to 1) 1
KLAIRON DAVIS (Fr) [-] 7-12-0 F Woods, ...(3 to 1 on) 2
BROCKLEY COURT [-] 9-10-7 C O'Dwyer, ...(5 to 2) 3
Dist: ½l, 20l. 4m 17.80s. a 4.80s (3 Ran).
SR: 31/51/10/   (John A Cooper), E Bolger

1309 Sandyford Hurdle (3-y-o) £3,082 2m
.... (4:00)

1173⁷ CHOOSEY'S TREASURE (Ire) 10-10 C F Swan, (6 to 4 fav) 1
1173³ GREENHUE (Ire) 10-9 T P Rudd, ...(5 to 1) 2
1174³ THREE RIVERS 10-6 (3*) D J Casey, ...(7 to 1) 3
HIGHLY MOTIVATED 9-13 (5*) J Butler, ...(14 to 1) 4
DADDY'S HAT (Ire) 10-4 P L Malone, ...(16 to 1) 5
PEGUS JUNIOR (Ire) 10-2 (7*) R Donnelly, ...(20 to 1) 6
882⁹ SWEET NATURE (Ire) 10-4 A Powell, ...(20 to 1) 7
882* FAIRLY SHARP (Ire) 10-10 C O'Dwyer, ...(5 to 2) 8
ERNE PROJECT (Ire) 9-11 (7*) M W Martin, ...(20 to 1) 9
1173 DUGGAN DUFF (Ire) 10-9 F Woods, ...(25 to 1) 10
1057⁸ IACCHUS (Ire) 10-8 (7*) S P Kelly, ...(14 to 1) 11
927⁴ TALLY-HO MAJOR (Ire) 10-9 T P Treacy, ...(16 to 1) 12
KRAKKIS 10-9 K F O'Brien, ...(25 to 1) 13
1173 KERRY REEL (Ire) 10-9 M P Hourigan, ...(33 to 1) 14
Dist: 1l, 6l, 8l, nk. 3m 51.60s. a 5.60s (14 Ran).
SR: 26/24/18/5/-/-/   (M Moloney), A P O'Brien

AUTEUIL (FR) (soft)
Sunday November 10th

1310 Prix la Haye Jousselin Chase (5-y-o and up) £105,402 3m 3f 110yds
.... (2:35)

682* AL CAPONE II (Fr) 8-10-4 J-Y Beaurain, ... 1
BACCARAT COLLONGES (Fr) 7-10-4 , ... 2
VAL D'ALENE (Fr) 9-10-4 A Kondrat, *mid-div, styd on wl flt, nvr plcd to chal.*............................. 3
ALGAN (Fr) 8-10-4 L Metals, *moved clr wth wnr on second circuit, btn aftr 3 out, wknd flt, fnshd tired...* 4
CUMBERLAND (Fr) 6-, ... 5
STAFF (Fr) 8-, ... 6
GRACKY (Fr) 8-, ... 7
CYBORG DE BEAUFAI (Fr) 7-, ... 8
Dist: 15l, 1½l, 3l, 8l, 6l. 7m 25.00s. (8 Ran).
(R Fougedoire), B Secly

CARLISLE (good)
Monday November 11th
Going Correction: PLUS 0.10 sec. per fur. (races 1,3,5,7), PLUS 0.35 (2,4,6)

1311 'Anzio' Novices' Hurdle Class E (4-y-o and up) £2,262 3m 110yds (1:00)

MILITARY ACADEMY 7-10-12 R Dunwoody, *led aftr 5th, shaken up and drw clr betw last 2, readily.*
.......................(7 to 2 op 11 to 4) 1
BEN CRUACHAN (Ire) 6-10-12 M Dwyer, *patiently rdn, hdwy to chase wnr 2 out, kpt on till eased slightly whn btn r-in.*
.......................(3 to 1 op 7 to 2) 2
1153³ PEBBLE BEACH (Ire) 6-11-5 J Callaghan, *chsd ldrs, ev ch whn pckd 3 out, one pace aftr........*(10 to 1 op 7 to 1) 3
1039⁹ CHILL FACTOR 6-10-12 P Niven, *in tch, pushed alng, jmpd slwly 5 out, sn outpcd........*.......(14 to 1 op 10 to 1) 4
164 RUBER 9-10-12 B Storey, *wth ldrs, niggled alng 3 out, sn wknd.*.......................(200 to 1 op 100 to 1) 5
SOUTH COAST STAR (Ire) 6-10-12 A Maguire, *hld up in rear, lost tch 3 out, sn no dngr...........*(33 to 1 op 14 to 1) 6

SWANBISTER (Ire) 6-11-5 M Foster, *midfield whn badly hmpd and sddl slpd, sn uns rdr*.
..................(11 to 4 fav op 3 to 1 tchd 4 to 1) ur
1067 YOUNG KENNY 5-11-5 R Supple, *cl up, slight ld whn blun and uns rdr 5th*...................(5 to 1 op 7 to 2) ur
KIRTLE MONSTAR 5-10-12 F Perratt, *sn led, hdd 5th, ran very wide soon aftr, wknd quickly 5 out, tld off whn pld up betw last 2*................(66 to 1 op 33 to 1 tchd 100 to 1) pu
Dist: 10l, 9l, 10l, 6l, 4l. 6m 10.00s. a 19.00s (9 Ran).

(Robert Ogden), G Richards

1312 EBF Tattersalls Ireland Mares' Only Novices' Chase Qualifier Class E (5-y-o and up) £3,403 2½m 110yds
.... (1:30)

1213³ MARINERS MIRROR 9-10-12 Mr M Rimell, *jmpd wl, led 4th, lft well clr appr four out, easily*.
..................(2 to 1 op 9 to 4 tchd 7 to 4) 1
1054³ COVERDALE LANE 9-11-2 Mr P Murray, *led, mstk 3rd, hdd nxt, pushed alng whn hit 7th, lft poor second 4 out*.
..................(15 to 2 op 7 to 1 tchd 8 to 1) 2
MISS COLETTE 8-10-12 L O'Hara, *hld up, outpcd frm 9th, poor 3rd whn f 2 out, rmntd*....................(25 to 1) 3
MISS TINO 8-10-12 A Thornton, *tld off frm 9th, badly hmpd last, continued*.................................(100 to 1) 4
198⁹ CABBERY ROSE (Ire) 8-11-5 R Dunwoody, *f 1st*.
..................(4 to 1 tchd 9 to 2) f
OWENS QUEST (Ire) 6-10-12 R Rourke, *jmpd slwly towards rear, outpcd hfwy, drvn alng and ten 1s 3rd whn f 12th*.
..................(16 to 1 op 14 to 1) f
RICH DESIRE 7-10-12 A Maguire, *cl up, chasing wnr whn broke dwn and pld up appr 4 out*. (13 to 8 fav op 11 to 8) pu
Dist: Dist, dist, 2½l. 5m 7.60s. a 12.60s (7 Ran).
SR: 29/-/-/-/

(F J Mills), N A Twiston-Davies

1313 Brown Cow At Cockermouth Novices' Handicap Hurdle Class E (0-100 4-y-o and up) £2,360 2½m 110yds
.... (2:00)

1034⁵ LIFEBUOY (Ire) [77] 5-10-12² T Reed, *midfield, hdwy to ld aftr 3 out, clr last, cmftbly*...............(8 to 1 op 6 to 1) 1
1071² BAHER (USA) [88] 7-11-9 J Supple, *led till hdd 3 out, sn drvn alng, styd on same pace*.
........(7 to 2 fav op 9 to 2 tchd 5 to 1 and 3 to 1) 2
1198³ LEAP IN THE DARK (Ire) [78] 7-10-13 A Thornton, *chsd ldr, slight ld 3 out, sn hdd, no extr*..........(4 to 1 op 7 to 2) 3
862² HAUGHTON LAD (Ire) [72] 7-10-7 A Roche, *chsd ldrs, reminders 7th, outpcd nxt, kpt on stdly betw last 2*.
..................(5 to 1 op 4 to 1) 4
MENSHAAR (USA) [86] 4-11-7 M Dwyer, *hld up, hdwy and in tch 5 out, rdn and outpcd aftr 3 out*.
..................(10 to 1 op 7 to 1 tchd 14 to 1) 5
1038⁷ ENVIRONMENTAL LAW [73] 5-10-5 (3⁶) G Cahill, *chsd ldrs, drvn alng 3 out, sn no imprsn*.........(16 to 1 op 20 to 1) 6
FENLOE RAMBLER (Ire) [89] 5-11-10 Mr P Johnson, *jmpd slwly in rear, hit 5th and 7th, sn drvn alng 2 out*.
..................(16 to 1 op 12 to 1) 7
CORSTON JOKER [87] 6-11-8 M Foster, *hld up, gd hdwy to chase ldrs 5 out, wknd aftr 3 out, 7th and wl held whn f last*.
..................(8 to 1 op 6 to 1) f
1067³ RAPID FIRE (Ire) [65] 8-9-7 (7⁶) M Newton, *hld up, lost tch frm 3 out, pld up bef nxt*................(7 to 1 op 10 to 1) pu
888⁵ COURT JOKER (Ire) [82] 4-11-3 P Niven, *hld up in rear, lost tch 3 out, pld up bef nxt*...(15 to 2 op 6 to 1 tchd 8 to 1) pu
Dist: 9l, 3½l, 2½l, ¾l, nk, dist. 5m 1.50s. a 19.50s (10 Ran).

(Miss S J Turner), J R Turner

1314 Scots Guards 'Lucius' Challenge Cup Handicap Chase Class D (0-125 5-y-o and up) £4,535 3m...... (2:30)

PARSONS BOY [114] 7-11-6 B Harding, *in tch, drvn alng frm 3 out, chlgd and hit last, ran on strly und pres to ld cl hme*.
..................(5 to 1 op 4 to 1) 1
UBU VAL (Fr) [118] 10-11-10 A S Smith, *jmpd wl, al hndy, led 5 out, kpt on strly und pres till ct cl hme*.
..................(16 to 1 op 12 to 1) 2
HOLY STING (Ire) [94] (bl) 7-11-0 D Llewellyn, *wth ldr, lost pos hfwy, led 12th, hdd and drvn alng 5 out, rallied and styd on ag'n frm betw last 2*....(7 to 1 op 6 to 1 tchd 8 to 1) 3
PENNINE PRIDE [94] 9-10-0 A Maguire, *led, hdd tenth, struggling and lost tch aftr nxt, styd on stdly frm 2 out*.
..................(14 to 1 op 8 to 1) 4
SEVEN TOWERS (Ire) [115] 7-11-7 P Niven, *midfield, pushed alng frm 11th, outpcd 4 out, no imprsn*. (4 to 1 tchd 9 to 2) 5
1165⁴ STOP THE WALLER (Ire) [118] 7-11-6 K Whelan, *chsd ldrs, led tenth till hdd 12th, ev ch till fdd frm 3 out, hit whn jmpd slwly nxt*........................(7 to 2 fav tchd 4 to 1) 6
1199 GALE AHEAD (Ire) [98] 6-10-4 N Bentley, *cl up, lost pl hfwy, rallied to chase ldrs aftr nxt, fdd aftr 4 out*.
..................(14 to 1 op 10 to 1) 7
1046⁴ EAST HOUSTON [100] 7-10-6 A Roche, *hld up in rear, clr order 11th, mstk 14th, lost tch frm nxt*.
..................(16 to 1 tchd 20 to 1) 8

1140* BASILICUS (Fr) [107] 7-10-13 Richard Guest, *midfield, reminders 8th, drvn alng appr 4 out, fdd*. (5 to 1 op 9 to 2) 9
HOWCLEUCH [103] 9-10-9 B Storey, *mstk second, hld up in rear, struggling and lost tch 5 out, sn tld off*.
..................(16 to 1 op 14 to 1) 10
Dist: Nk, 4l, 13l, 2½l, 1½l, 14l, 2l, 19l, 5l. 6m 10.20s. a 18.20s (10 Ran).

(B Ridge), G Richards

1315 Hyndburn Bridge At Clayton-le-Moors Handicap Hurdle Class E (0-110 4-y-o and up) £2,318 3m 110yds........................ (3:00)

HAILE DERRING [101] 6-11-5 C Llewellyn, *sn led, quickened clr appr 4 out, unchlgd*.
..................(11 to 10 fav op 6 to 4 tchd Evens) 1
1124* TROODOS [95] 10-10-13 J Supple, *hld up, hdwy gng wl to chase ldr 4 out, no imprsn whn hit 2 out*. (4 to 1 op 5 to 2) 2
STORMY CORAL (Ire) [92] 6-10-10 B Storey, *in tch, drvn alng 4 out, struggling whn not fluent nxt, unbl to chal*.
..................(7 to 1 op 9 to 2 tchd 8 to 1) 3
PLUMBOB (Ire) [91] 7-10-9 M Foster, *hld up, improved hfwy, shaken up and outpcd aftr 4 out, nvr plcd to chal*.
..................(20 to 1 op 14 to 1) 4
PERSIAN HOUSE [110] 9-12-0 M Dwyer, *midfield, drvn and wknd aftr 4 out, collapsed and died after race*.
..................(16 to 1 op 12 to 1) 5
QUIET MISTRESS [82] 6-10-0 A S Smith, *cl up, drvn alng and mstk 5 out, sn struggling*.......(14 to 1 tchd 20 to 1) 6
SHALLOW RIVER (Ire) [96] 5-10-13 A Thornton, *hld up, lost tch frm 4 out, sn beh*...(14 to 1 op 12 to 1 tchd 16 to 1) 7
1139⁴ PRIDE OF MAY (Ire) [94] (v) 5-10-11 J Callaghan, *chsd ldrs, outpcd aftr 5 out, sn no dngr*............(8 to 1 op 7 to 1) 8
1048 DOCKMASTER [95] 5-10-12 L Wyer, *in tch, wknd frm 4 out, tld off*........................(14 to 1 op 12 to 1) 9
MAYBE O'GRADY (Ire) [94] 7-10-5 (7⁶) L McGrath, *al beh, tld off*..................(14 to 1 tchd 16 to 1 and 20 to 1) 10
Dist: 9l, 10l, 7l, 14l, 1l, 1½l, ¾l, 10l, 5l. 5m 59.80s. a 8.80s (10 Ran).
SR: 27/12/-/-/-/

(Mrs V Stockdale), N A Twiston-Davies

1316 Greyhound At Halton Handicap Chase Class D (0-125 5-y-o and up) £3,458 2m............ (3:30)

1151* REGAL ROMPER (Ire) [110] 8-11-10 Richard Guest, *in tch, chlgd 4 out, sn led, strly pressed last, hld on wl*.
..................(6 to 4 fav tchd 13 to 8) 1
PAGLIACCIO [99] 8-10-13 R Garritty, *led till hdd 6th, styd hndy, ev ch whn not fluent last, ran on strly*.
..................(9 to 2 tchd 5 to 2) 2
SOLBA (USA) [110] 7-11-10 B Storey, *hld up, pushed alng 4 out, kpt on wl till no extr appr last*......(12 to 1 op 7 to 1) 3
1163² WEAVER GEORGE (Ire) [100] 6-11-0 M Moloney, *chsd ldr, led 6th till hdd 4 out, outpcd frm nxt*........(7 to 2 op 3 to 1) 4
SUPER SANDY [89] 9-10-3 D Parker, *cl up, chlgd 4 out, rdn and wknd frm 2 out*...(20 to 1 op 16 to 1 tchd 33 to 1) 5
POTATO MAN [100] 10-10-11 (3⁶) G Cahill, *hld up, mstk 7th and nxt, lost tch frm 4 out*.................(4 to 1) 6
Dist: ½l, 9l, 6l, 3l, 4l. 4m 6.60s. a 12.60s (6 Ran).
SR: 26/14/16/

(Mrs S Smith), Mrs S J Smith

1317 'Tumbledown' Standard Open National Hunt Flat Class H (4,5,6-y-o) £1,070 2m 1f............ (4:00)

COLOUR CODE 4-11-4 J Supple, *nvr far away, pushed alng 4 fs out, led wl o'r one out, ran on strly*. (13 to 2 op 14 to 1) 1
1073² GOOD VIBES 4-11-4 L Wyer, *pld hrd early, cl up till slight ld 4 fs out, hdd wl o'r one out, unbl to quicken*.
..................(4 to 1 op 11 to 4) 2
ARDRINA 5-10-13 A Maguire, *al hndy, pushed alng and ev ch 3 fs out, kpt on stdly*......(16 to 1 op 14 to 1) 3
THE CROOKED OAK 4-10-11 (7⁶) M Keighley, *cl up, led 6 fs out to 4 out, rdn and no extr fnl 2 furlongs*. ....(2 to 1 jt-fav op 6 to 1 tchd 7 to 1) 4
CHEATER (Ire) 5-11-4 N Williamson, *led, hdd 6 fs out, fdd frm 3 out*........................(14 to 1 op 12 to 1) 5
1128* BRIGHTER SHADE (Ire) 6-11-4 (7⁶) C McCormack, *midfield, improved to chase ldrs 4 fs out, wknd frm 2 out*.
..................(10 to 1 tchd 12 to 1) 6
BOLD STATEMENT 4-11-4 N Bentley, *midfield, hdwy to track ldrs 5 fs out, no imprsn whn jinked lft o'r 2 out*.
..................(16 to 1 op 12 to 1) 7
1142⁹ LARKSHILL 5-11-4 M Dwyer, *nvr better than midfield*.
..................(25 to 1 op 20 to 1) 8
MAGPIE MELODY (Ire) 5-11-4 M Foster, *settled in rear, shaken up and unbl to quicken 4 fs out, nvr plcd to chal*.
..................(14 to 1 op 12 to 1 tchd 20 to 1) 9
1039² NATURAL TALENT 4-11-4 D Parker, *pressed ldr, drvn alng 5 fs out, fdd stdly*............(16 to 1 op 14 to 1) 10
JESSICA ONE (Ire) 5-10-13 P Niven, *hld up, hdwy into midfield 6 fs out, wknd frm 3 out, better for race*.
..................(10 to 1 op 5 to 1) 11
JERVAULX (Ire) 5-11-4 R Dunwoody, *midfield, improved to chase ldrs o'r 4 fs out, wknd wl over 2 out*. ....(2 to 1 jt-fav op 6 to 4 tchd 5 to 2) 12

GENERAL PARKER 5-11-4 A S Smith, *nvr a factor*.
.................................(100 to 1 op 50 to 1) 13

JESSOLLE 4-10-13 B Harding, *hld up in rear, outpcd 5 fs out, sn no impr*............................(20 to 1) 14

JENNIE'S PROSPECT 5-10-13 (5*) R McGrath, *in tch, rdn and lost touch 4 fs out, sn btn*......(16 to 1 op 12 to 1) 15

NAUTILUS THE THIRD (Ire) 5-11-4 R Garritty, *nvr dngrs*.
.................................(20 to 1 op 12 to 1) 16

BROOK HOUSE 5-10-10 (3*) G Lee, *nvr a factor*.
.................................(200 to 1 op 100 to 1) 17

KARENA'S PRINCE 4-11-4 Richard Guest, *al rear, tld off*.
.................................(20 to 1 tchd 25 to 1) 18

BOYZONTOOWA (Ire) 4-11-4 A Thornton, *al rear, tld off*.
.................................(50 to 1) 19

SAMITE (Ire) 5-11-4 N Leach, *wl tld off frm hfwy*.
.................................(200 to 1 op 100 to 1) 20

Dist: 5l, 2l, 10l, 1¾l, nk, 1¼l, ½l, 14l, 1¾l, ¾l. 4m 4.30s. (20 Ran).
(Bill Walker), Mrs A Swinbank

LUDLOW (good to firm)
Tuesday November 12th
Going Correction: PLUS 0.20 sec. per fur. (races 1,3,5,7), PLUS 0.25 (2,4,6)

1318 **Norton Maiden Hurdle Class E (4-y-o and up) £2,332 2m 5f 110yds (1:10)**

MEDFORD 6-10-12 (7*) J Power, *nvr far away, drw level 2 out, sn led, ran on wl to go clr r-in*........(4 to 1 tchd 5 to 1) 1

1217 DACELO (Fr) 5-11-5 J Osborne, *patiently rdn, smooth run to join issue 3 out, hng lft and shaken up betw last 2, not keen.*
.................(6 to 5 on op 5 to 4 on tchd Evens) 2

1010³ ONE MORE DIME (Ire) 6-11-0 B Fenton, *set steady pace, jnd 3 out, hdd aftr nxt, one pace r-in.*.....(12 to 1 op 7 to 1) 3

1073 RAGDON 5-11-5 S Wynne, *trkd ldr, drvn alng whn pace quickened 4 out, sn struggling, tld off.* (20 to 1 op 16 to 1) 4

846³ JON'S CHOICE 8-11-5 V Slattery, *settled in tch, effrt hfwy, struggling bef 4 out, tld off.*............(12 to 1 op 8 to 1) 5

1097 SET THE FASHION (v) 7-11-5 P Holley, *reminders second, struggling frm hfwy, tld off whn pld up aftr 4 out.*
.................................(3 to 1 op 9 to 4) pu

Dist: 4l, ¾l, dist, 17l. 5m 9.70s. a 14.70s (6 Ran).
(P F Coombes), W G M Turner

1319 **Hugh Sumner Handicap Chase Class F (0-105 5-y-o and up) £3,048 2m**
.................................(1:40)

1114⁴ FICHU (USA) [72] 8-10-0 M Richards, *patiently rdn, improved to take clr order 6 out, chalg whn lft in ld 3 out, ran clr.* (6 to 1) 1

1007³ FENWICK [88] 9-10-13 (3*) T Dascombe, *chsd ldrs, effrt hfwy, rdn and styd on frm 3 out, no imprsn.* (2 to 1 fav op 7 to 4) 2

1062³ WILLIE MAKEIT (Ire) [86] 6-11-0 A Maguire, *chsd ldg pair, effrt and drvn alng frm 3 out, one pace betw last 2.*
.................................(11 to 2 op 4 to 1) 3

SPINNING STEEL [99] 9-11-13 S Burrough, *chsd clr ldr, hndy whn nrly t 7 out, reminders and lost grnd bef 4 out, no imprsn aftr.*........(4 to 1 op 3 to 1 tchd 9 to 2) 4

806 CHAIN SHOT [77] (bl) 11-10-5 R Bellamy, *settled off the pace, struggling and lost tch bef 6 out, tld off.* (25 to 1 op 14 to 1) 5

LOBSTER COTTAGE [88] 8-11-2 A Thornton, *led, clr 4th, not fluent 5 out, blun nxt, 2 ls clear whn f 3 out.*
.................................(9 to 4 op 7 to 4) f

Dist: 11l, 2l, 2l, 25l. 4m 1.80s. a 11.80s (6 Ran).
(B Seal), Mrs L Richards

1320 **Blandford Betting Conditional Jockeys' Selling Handicap Hurdle Class G (0-95 4-y-o and up) £2,010 2m**.........................(2:10)

1110* BURLINGTON SAM (NZ) [77] 8-10-9 (3*) O Burrows, *al gng best, cruised ahead 3 out, readily drw clr.* (7 to 2 op 2 to 1) 1

1141⁸ HACKETTS CROSS (Ire) [93] 8-12-0 P Henley, *co'red up beh ldrs, effrt and short of room aftr 4 out, styd on frm betw last 2, not rch wnr*...............(7 to 1 op 5 to 1 tchd 8 to 1) 2

1203⁶ TWICE THE GROOM (Ire) [86] 6-11-7 G Hogan, *trkd ldrs made all, jnd and drvn alng aftr 4 out, hdd nxt, one pace betw last 2*...3

970⁷ QUICK DECISION (Ire) [65] 5-9-9 (5*) N T Egan, *tucked away beh ldrs, steady hdwy appr 3 out, sn on same pace frm betw last 2*.................(50 to 1 op 33 to 1 tchd 66 to 1) 4

1211⁹ OLD MASTER (Ire) [65] 5-10-0 G F Ryan, *tucked away beh ldrs, effrt bef 3 out, rdn and one pace frm nxt.*
.................................(33 to 1 tchd 50 to 1) 5

1132⁹ SIR PAGEANT [70] (bl) 7-10-2 (3*) M Griffiths, *settled midfield, drvn alng to improve appr 3 out, effrt whn not fluent nxt, no extr*...........................(33 to 1 tchd 50 to 1) 6

1203³ BRESIL (USA) [65] 7-9-7 (7*) Mark Brown, *trkd ldrs, feeling pace appr 3 out, fdd*............................7

891² JAVA SHRINE (USA) [69] 5-10-4 D Fortt, *settled to track ldg bunch, feeling pace appr 3 out, fdd nxt..*(5 to 1 op 6 to 1) 8

1130⁵ PYTCHLEY DAWN [68] 6-10-3 D J Kavanagh, *trkd ldrs, und pres bef 3 out, fdd*...................(20 to 1 op 20 to 1) 9

1139⁵ SAYMORE [81] 10-11-2 E Husband, *sn in rear, drvn alng hfwy, no imprsn frm 3 out*........(9 to 2 op 10 to 1) 10

1263⁸ GALLOPING GUNS (Ire) [65] 4-10-0 Guy Lewis, *with ldrs, feeling pace bef 3 out, fdd*..............(20 to 1 op 16 to 1) 11

876 LUSTREMAN [65] 9-10-0 T Dascombe, *with ldg grp to 3 out, sn lost tch, tld off*....................(50 to 1 op 33 to 1) 12

1051 BILL AND WIN [78] 5-10-13 E Smith, *chsd ldrs, struggling to hold pl bef 4 out, tld off*.........(25 to 1 op 20 to 1) 13

TADELLAL (Ire) [90] 5-11-6 (5*) J Power, *slwly away, effrt second, last whn pld up aftr nxt, lme.*
.................................(100 to 30 fav op 3 to 1 tchd 7 to 2) pu

Dist: 3½l, 1¼l, 2½l, 1¼l, 2½l, 3l, ½l, ½l, nk, 11l. 3m 44.10s. a 12.10s (14 Ran).
SR: -/7/-/-/-/-/ (Mrs Jackie Reip), A G Hobbs

1321 **Bates & Hunt Group Novices' Chase Class D (5-y-o and up) £3,776 2½m** ....(2:40)

1264⁵ LEGAL ARTIST (Ire) 6-10-12 L Harvey, *nvr far away, jmpd ahead 6 out, styd on strly to go clr last 3.* (5 to 1 op 4 to 1) 1

1062 ON THE TEAR 10-11-4 S McNeill, *al hndy, ev ch 6 out, drvn alng last 3, no chance wth wnr*........(16 to 1 op 10 to 1) 2

41⁸ DORMSTON BOYO 6-10-5 (7*) Mr R Thornton, *held till aftr 1st, rgned ld aftr 9th (water), hdd 6 out, one pace frm 3 out.*
.................................(25 to 1 op 16 to 1) 3

902 CALL ME ALBI (Ire) 6-11-5 Mr T M Richards, *trkd ldrs, reminders to hold pl aftr 5 out, struggling frm 3 out.*
.................................(11 to 2 op 3 to 1 tchd 6 to 1) 4

1236⁸ BOLD ACRE 6-10-12 R Johnson, *al hndy, ev ch hfwy, feeling pace and fdg whn blun badly 2 out.*...(5 to 2 tchd 11 to 4) 5

SEACHEST 7-10-7 Miss V Stephens, *led aftr 1st, hit 3rd and nxt, hdd appr 9th (water), wknd quickly 5 out, tld off.*
.................................(20 to 1 op 12 to 1) 6

1056 DANZIG ISLAND (Ire) (bl) 5-10-12 T Jenks, *sn in rear, drvn alng whn f tenth*....................(15 to 8 fav op 6 to 1) f

Dist: 14l, 1½l, 1¾l, ¾l, dist. 5m 4.50s. a 15.50s (7 Ran).
(T A Johnsey), Miss C Johnsey

1322 **European Breeders Fund 'National Hunt' Novices' Hurdle Qualifier Class E (4,5,6-y-o) £2,262 2m (3:10)**

LADY PETA (Ire) 6-11-0 M A Fitzgerald, *settled gng wl, improved to draw level 2 out, sn led, drvn out r-in.*
(5 to 4 on op 11 to 8 on tchd 11 to 10 on and Evens) 1

1065³ DARAKSHAN (Ire) 4-11-0 J F Titley, *tried to make all, jnd 2 out, sn hdd, rallied r-in*.......(5 to 4 tchd 6 to 4) 2

WELSH LOOT (Ire) 5-11-0 J Osborne, *nvr far away, drvn alng whn ldg pair quickened frm 3 out, no imprsn.*
.................................(11 to 1 op 1 to 1 tchd 12 to 1) 3

OPTIMISTIC AFFAIR 5-11-0 T Eley, *pressed ldrs, struggling whn pace quickened 3 out, one pace frm nxt.*
.................................(50 to 1 op 33 to 1) 4

1012 DEFERENCE DUE (Ire) 5-11-0 A Thornton, *chsd ldrs, feeling pace hfwy, lost tch bef 3 out, tld off..* (100 to 1 op 33 to 1) 5

Dist: Nk, 17l, ½l, dist. 3m 41.20s. a 9.20s (5 Ran).
SR: 26/26/9/8/-/ (B M Collins), N J Henderson

1323 **Tote Credit Handicap Chase Class E (0-115 5-y-o and up) £3,501 3m** ....(3:40)

LORD OF THE WEST (Ire) [90] 7-10-8 A Maguire, *nvr far away, drw level 3 out, sn led, jmpd lft nxt, styd on to go clr.*
.................................(5 to 2 op 3 to 1) 1

1083² FATHER SKY [110] (bl) 5-11-2 J Osborne, *wl plcd till rdn and outpcd appr 4 out, rallied, one pace frm betw last 2.*
.................................(9 to 2 op 11 to 4) 2

1086³ RAINBOW CASTLE [107] 9-11-11 A P McCoy, *tried to make all, jnd 3 out, sn hdd, crrd lft nxt, no extr.*
.................(6 to 5 on op 11 to 10 on tchd 11 to 10 on) 3

811 CORRARDER [110] 12-12-0 W Marston, *trkd ldrs, hit 4th, wknd quickly frm 7 out, tld off.*
.................................(12 to 1 op 7 to 1 tchd 16 to 1) 4

1086 MUTUAL TRUST [95] 12-10-13 R Johnson, *chsd ldrs, blun and nrly f 7th, not reco'r, pld up bef tenth.*
.................................(12 to 1 tchd 16 to 1) pu

Dist: 8l, 4l, dist. 5m 59.80s. a 12.80s (5 Ran).
SR: 12/22/17/-/-/ (Anne Duchess Of Westminster), J J O'Neill

1324 **Shobdon Intermediate Claiming National Hunt Flat Class H (4,5,6-y-o) £1,305 2m. (4:10)**

POPPY'S DREAM 6-10-1 (7*) Mr R Thornton, *patiently rdn, improved to ld o'r 3 fs out, drw clr, easily.* (5 to 1 op 4 to 1) 1

873 A S JIM 5-10-4 (5*) D J Kavanagh, *wtd wth, improved o'r 3 fs out, rdn and hng lft over one out, no ch wth wnr.*
.................................(6 to 1 op 4 to 1) 2

FOROFIVETWOHUNDRED (Ire) 6-10-12 (7*) G Supple, *led sn aftr strt, quickened clr back strt, rdn and hdd o'r 3 fs out, wknd in straight*.......................(6 to 1 op 5 to 1) 3

DAYDREAM BELIEVER 4-10-3 (7*) N T Egan, *wtd wth, took clr order halfway, effrt entering strt, sn rdn and btn.*
.................................(12 to 1 op 6 to 1) 4

1012 SYBAN 5-9-12 (7*) Miss L Boswell, *settled off the pace, effrt halfway, lost tch bef strt, tld off.*......(50 to 1 op 20 to 1) 5

1181² DITOPERO 4-10-2 (7*) J Power, *led early stages, styd upsides ldr till lost palce o'r 5 fs out, tld off.*
.... (13 to 8 on op 5 to 4 on tchd 11 to 10 on) 6
Dist: 20l, 6l, 18l, 10l, 22l. 3m 39.40s. (6 Ran).

(John Wharton), J Wharton

SEDGEFIELD (good)
Tuesday November 12th
Going Correction: PLUS 0.40 sec. per fur.

1325 **John Wade Haulage Selling Handicap Hurdle Class G (0-95 4-y-o and up) £1,877 3m 3f 110yds.... (12:50)**

1122⁴ TOP SKIPPER (Ire) [63] 4-10-0 A S Smith, *beh, clr order fnl circuit, led and edgd rght aftr 2 out, styd on strly.*
.... (10 to 1 op 8 to 1) 1
1061⁶ SNOWY LANE (Ire) [64] (h,bl) 8-10-2 N Williamson, *made most, rdn and hdd aftr 2 out, swtchd lft and mstk last, styd on strly und pres*.................(7 to 1 op 6 to 1) 2
1182⁹ BLANC SEING (Fr) [74] (bl) 9-10-12 Mr S Swiers, *midfield, chsd ldrs fnl circuit, rdn and one pace appr 2 out.*
.... (9 to 1 op 7 to 1 tchd 10 to 1) 3
1166⁵ D'ARBLAY STREET (Ire) [86] (bl) 7-11-10 S McDougall, *jnd ldr 6th, ev ch whn mstk 4 out, wknd appr 2 out.*
.... (11 to 8 fav op Evens tchd 6 to 4) 4
1162⁷ BARNSTORMER [63] 10-10-1 D Parker, *in tch, reminders 5 out, sn struggling, tld off*............ (14 to 1 op 16 to 1) 5
318⁹ THARSIS [72] 11-10-5 (5*) S Taylor, *hld up, struggling fnl circuit, tld off.*.................(10 to 1 op 8 to 1) 6
958⁶ OVERWHELM (Ire) [72] (bl) 8-10-10³ Mr M Thompson, *in tch, struggling fnl circuit, tld off frm 4 out*.............(50 to 1) 7
1126³ JENDEE (Ire) [83] 8-11-4 (3*) G Cahill, *cl up whn blun 5th, drpd rear 8th, pld up bef nxt*........... (5 to 2 tchd 9 to 4) pu
912⁷ DARK MIDNIGHT (Ire) [62] 7-10-0 B Harding, *beh, reminders 8th, sn tld off, pld up 3 out*........... (20 to 1 op 16 to 1) pu
ARTHUR BEE [62] 9-9-11 (3*) G Lee, *cl up till drpd rear 8th, sn tld off, pld up 3 out*.................................(33 to 1) pu
Dist: ½l, 5l, 8l, dist, 7l, dist. 6m 50.50s. a 28.50s (10 Ran).

(Mrs H H Wane), Martyn Wane

1326 **Hennessy Cognac Special Series Novices' Hurdle Class B (4-y-o and up) £5,654 2m 1f............ (1:20)**

546* BRAMBLES WAY (bl) 7-11-0 P Niven, *midfield, hit 3rd, steady hdwy 3 out, led betw last 2, drvn out.*
.... (8 to 1 op 6 to 1 tchd 10 to 1) 1
1033* CONTRAFIRE (Ire) 4-11-0 J Supple, *rcd freely, led and clr 3rd, mstks 5th and 6th, hdd betw last 2, no extr und pres r-in.*
.... (5 to 4 on op Evens tchd 11 to 10 and 5 to 4) 2
1070* SUAS LEAT (Ire) 6-11-4 M Newton, *chsd clr ldrs, effrt 3 out, not fluent nxt, sn outpcd*...............(9 to 2 op 4 to 1) 3
BOLLIN FRANK 4-11-0 L Wyer, *pld hrd wth ldr, drvn and unbl to quicken whn not fluent 2 out, fdd.*
.... (11 to 2 op 6 to 1 tchd 7 to 1 and 5 to 1) 4
FASSAN (Ire) 4-11-0 R Garritty, *hld up, some hdwy hfwy, rdn and wknd appr 2 out*...........(9 to 2 op 7 to 1 tchd 8 to 1) 5
ONEOFTHEOLDONES 4-11-0 Derek Byrne, *pld hrd, towards rear whn hmpd aftr 3rd, beh when f 3 out*.........(33 to 1) f
1164⁷ BARIK (Ire) 4-11-0 B Storey, *beh frm hfwy, tld off whn pld up bef 2 out.*.................................(33 to 1) pu
1033⁶ HOMECREST 4-11-0 G Cahill, *beh, drvn alng frm hfwy, tld off whn pld up bef 2 out*.....................(33 to 1) pu
1073 SELECTRIC (Ire) 5-11-0 K Jones, *tld off hfwy, pld up bef 2 out.*
....(50 to 1) pu
Dist: 4l, 10l, 8l, 7l. 4m 4.00s. a 18.00s (9 Ran).

(Nigel E M Jones), Mrs M Reveley

1327 **Racing Channel Handicap Chase Class E (0-110 5-y-o and up) £2,922 2m 110yds................. (1:50)**

1052⁴ FULL O'PRAISE (NZ) [100] 9-12-0 L Wyer, *cl up, slight ld 5 out, lft clr 2 out, hld on wl und pres r-in.*
.... (11 to 2 op 9 to 2 tchd 6 to 1) 1
1127 VAL DE RAMA (Ire) [89] 7-11-3 P Niven, *beh, not fluent, plenty to do whn jmpd slwly 8th, ran on strly frm 2 out, not rch wnr.*
.... (5 to 1 tchd 6 to 1 and 7 to 1) 2
1201² THUNDERSTRUCK [82] 10-10-10 N Williamson, *cl up, hmpd 5th, lft second 2 out, sn no extr*......(5 to 2 fav op 7 to 2) 3
1007⁴ MASTER SALESMAN [72] 13-10-0 D Parker, *al beh, struggling frm 5 out*.................................(25 to 1) 4
1163⁴ FLASH OF REALM (Fr) [96] (v) 10-11-10 B Storey, *hld up towards rear, nvr a factor*...........(8 to 1 tchd 9 to 1) 5
PORT IN A STORM [88] 7-10-13 (3*) Mr C Bonner, *midfield, outpcd appr 5 out, sn no dngr.*
.... (12 to 1 op 10 to 1 tchd 14 to 1) 6
1176² CIRCULATION [72] (v) 10-9-11 (3*) D Walsh, *sn led, mstk 8th, hdd 5 out, 6 ls second and hld whn f 2 out.* (5 to 1 op 6 to 1) f
PARSON'S LODGE (Ire) [79] 8-10-7 M Foster, *pld hrd wth ldr, mstk 4th, f nxt.*.....................(12 to 1 op 9 to 1) f
972⁵ SHREWD JOHN [92] (bl) 10-11-6 M Dwyer, *midfield, struggling frm 5 out, tld off whn pld up bef nxt.*
.... (7 to 1 op 6 to 1) pu

Dist: 1½l, 16l, 11l, ¾l, 9l. 4m 13.10s. a 21.10s (9 Ran).

(Lord Zetland), P Calver

1328 **Dick Brewitt Memorial Handicap Chase Class F (0-100 5-y-o and up) £2,838 3m 3f................. (2:20)**

1140 IVY HOUSE (Ire) [92] 8-11-9 M Dwyer, *patiently rdn, steady hdwy fnl circuit, led and quickened clr 2 out, eased considerably r-in*............ (2 to 1 fav op 5 to 2 tchd 3 to 1) 1
1199* ALY DALEY (Ire) [104] 8-12-7 (7ex) N Williamson, *led till hdd 14th, drvn alng and mstk 6 out, styd on betw last 2, no ch wth wnr*.....................(4 to 1 op 7 to 2 tchd 9 to 2) 2
1126² OLE OLE [84] 10-11-1 L Wyer, *hld up, mstk and lost pos 8th, drvn alng and mistake 1 out, kpt on ag'n frm 2 out.*
.... (13 to 2 op 6 to 1) 3
CALL THE SHOTS (Ire) [90] 7-11-7 K Jones, *wth ldr, hit 13th, led nxt till hdd 4 out, one pace frm 2 out. (7 to 1 op 6 to 1) 4
887* SCRABO VIEW (Ire) [96] (bl) 8-11-13 R Supple, *chsd ldrs, mstk 6 out, sn pushed alng, btn appr 2 out.*
.... (7 to 1 op 5 to 1) 5
1201* BLAZING DAWN [91] 9-11-8 (7ex) B Storey, *midfield, improved travelling strly to ld 4 out, hdd 2 out, sn wknd, btn whn mstk last*...........(11 to 2 op 5 to 1 tchd 6 to 1) 6
1011⁴ FOXGROVE [77] 10-10-8 Richard Guest, *beh, in tch and reminders 13th, sn struggling, tld off whn pld up bef 2 out.*
.... (14 to 1 tchd 16 to 1) pu
1165⁷ GALA WATER [86] 10-11-3 T Reed, *chsd ldrs, jmpd slwly 7th, ev ch whn mstk and rdr lost irons 4 out, sn beh, pld up betw last 2*............... (9 to 1 op 10 to 1 tchd 8 to 1) pu
Dist: 3½l, ½l, 1l, 8l, 2l. 7m 5.10s. a 32.10s (8 Ran).

(Mrs L R Joughin), J J O'Neill

1329 **John Hellens Novices' Chase Class E (4-y-o and up) £2,945 2m 5f (2:50)**

1045³ CADER IDRIS 7-11-4 P Niven, *led till hdd appr tenth, mstk 5 out, lft in ld 3 out, clr whn hit last, drvn out.*
.... (6 to 1 op 5 to 1) 1
1183⁸ FINAL BEAT (Ire) (bl) 7-11-4 L Wyer, *hld up, chasing ldrs whn mstk 8th, outpcd frm tenth, styd on wl ag'n from 2 out.*
.... (6 to 1 op 5 to 1) 2
1198⁵ FINGERHILL (Ire) 7-11-4 Mr M Thompson, *al chasing ldrs, drvn alng frm tenth, lft 2nd 3 out, no imp*....(33 to 1 tchd 50 to 1) 3
1127⁶ THE ENERGISER 10-11-4 J Burke, *chsd ldrs, rdn and lost tch appr 4 out, sn beh.*.................... (50 to 1 op 33 to 1) 4
1142 HIGH HANDED (Ire) 5-10-12 (5*) S Taylor, *beh, mstk 4th, gd hdwy to ld appr tenth, 3 ls clr whn blun and uns rdr three out.*
.... (50 to 1 op 33 to 1) ur
1035⁵ DAWN LAD (Ire) 7-11-4 J Supple, *in tch, mstk 9th, cl up whn blun and uns rdr 6 out*................(6 to 1 op 5 to 1) ur
UNCLE KEENY (Irc) 6-11-4 M Dwyer, *cl up, blun 7th, ev ch whn broke dwn bef tenth, sn pld up.*
.... (7 to 4 on tchd 13 to 8 on and 6 to 4 on) pu
DEAR JEAN 6-10-13 D Parker, *tld off frm hfwy, pld up bef 11th.*
.... (20 to 1 op 14 to 1) pu
Dist: 4l, 19l, 26l. 5m 30.30s. a 34.30s (8 Ran).

(D R Wellicome), Mrs M Reveley

1330 **Stanley Racing Novices' Hurdle Class E (4-y-o and up) £2,285 2m 5f 110yds...................... (3:20)**

1034² ELA MATA 4-11-5 J Railton, *hld up, led 6th, mstk 3 out, jnd nxt, drvn clr frm last*......................(3 to 1 op 2 to 1) 1
1073* DURAID (Ire) 4-10-12 Richard Guest, *hld up, jmpd wl, smooth hdwy 4 out, jnd wnr 2 out, rdn and no extr appr last.*
.... (6 to 4 on tchd 7 to 4 on) 2
874⁴ JILLS JOY (Ire) 5-10-9 (3*) G Lee, *in tch, rdn and outpcd aftr 6th, styd on ag'n frm 2 out, unbl to chal.* (25 to 1 op 16 to 1) 3
1070⁴ SILLY MONEY 5-10-12 L Wyer, *led 3rd till 6th, ev ch till outpcd 3 out, btn nxt*...........(4 to 1 op 5 to 1 tchd 9 to 2) 4
1217³ CULRAIN 5-11-0 (5*) S Taylor, *chsd ldrs, outpcd aftr 6th, tld off frm 3 out*.................(12 to 1 op 8 to 1) 5
RUSTIC WARRIOR 6-10-12 K Jones, *pld hrd, led till 3rd, drpd rear hfwy, tld off whn pulled up bef 3 out.*
.... (100 to 1 op 50 to 1) pu
ALICAT (Ire) 5-10-12 R Garritty, *wth ldrs, mstk 5th, wknd nxt, tld off and pld up bef 3 out*.................(33 to 1) pu
Dist: 7l, 2½l, 10l, dist. 5m 14.60s. a 26.60s (7 Ran).

(F J Sainsbury), Mrs A Swinbank

1331 **Levy Board Mares' Only Handicap Hurdle Class F (0-105 4-y-o and up) £1,987 2m 5f 110yds......... (3:50)**

1067 TIGH-NA-MARA [86] 8-10-7 (7*) M Newton, *keen hold, led appr 2 out, slight mstk last, drvn out..* (5 to 2 tchd 3 to 1) 1
1139⁶ MARSDEN ROCK [82] 9-10-3 (7*) S Haworth, *al hndy, ev ch frm 3 out, one pace two last*...........(7 to 1 op 6 to 1) 2
1153⁴ SMART APPROACH (Ire) [90] 6-11-4 P Niven, *cl up, slight ld 4 out till hdd appr 2 out, btn whn mstk last.*
.... (13 to 8 fav op 5 to 4 tchd 7 to 4) 3
CHADWICK'S GINGER [100] 8-11-7 (7*) B Grattan, *chsd ldrs, led 5th till 4 out, outpcd frm nxt, sn btn.*
.... (9 to 2 op 7 to 2 tchd 5 to 1) 4

MILLIES IMAGE [72] 5-10-0 R Supple, *cl up, niggled alng
hfwy, wl beh frm 3 out.* .... (8 to 1 op 12 to 1) 5
1257⁶ HELENS BAY (Ire) [81] 6-10-9 Mr M Thompson, *made most
till 5th, fdd frm nxt, tld off.* .... (20 to 1) 6
1070⁸ STORMING LORNA (Ire) [72] 6-9-11 (3*) G Cahill, *hld up,
struggling whn mstk 3 out, tld off when pld up bef last.*
.... (25 to 1 tchd 33 to 1) pu
Dist: 6l, 2l, 4l, dist, 2½l. 5m 16.90s. a 28.90s (7 Ran).
(Bryan Gordon), J M Jefferson

KELSO (good)
Wednesday November 13th
Going Correction: NIL

1332 Scottish Sports Aid Foundation Novices' Handicap Chase Class E (0-100 5-y-o and up) £3,048 2m 1f... (1:10)

1070⁵ MONYMAN (Ire) [92] 6-11-13 R Garritty, *hld up, jmpd wl, gd
hdwy to chase ldr 2 out, led sn aftr last, drvn out.*
.... (13 to 8 fav op 7 to 4 tchd 5 to 4) 1
1258² BALLYLINE (Ire) [86] 5-11-7 M Dwyer, *led, quickened 2 out,
hdd sn aftr last, styd on und pres.*
.... (15 to 8 op 2 to 1 tchd 5 to 2) 2
1127² LE DENSTAN [84] 9-11-5 T Reed, *hld up, hdwy 2 out, ev ch
last, styd on stdly.* .... (7 to 2 op 11 to 4 tchd 4 to 1) 3
1197⁵ QUIXALL CROSSETT [65] 11-9-9 (5*) S Taylor, *chsd ldrs,
pushed alng 9th, outpcd frm 2 out...* (100 to 1 op 33 to 1) 4
1125² TWIN FALLS (Ire) [93] 5-12-0 J Callaghan, *beh, not fluent,
struggling appr 2 out, sn no dngr.*
.... (9 to 1 op 4 to 1 tchd 12 to 1) 5
1615 ALICHARGER [65] 6-9-11 (3*) G Cahill, *pressed ldr,
reminders appr 7th, wknd approaching 2 out.*
.... (33 to 1 op 25 to 1) 6
1201 MONAUGHTY MAN [85] 10-11-6 Mr P Murray, *cl up, drvn
alng appr 2 out, sn lost tch........* (66 to 1 op 33 to 1) 7
Dist: 1½l, 2½l, 14l, 5l, 2l, 2½l. 4m 14.50s. a 9.50s (7 Ran).
SR: 4/-/-/-/ (Trevor Hemmings), M D Hammond

1333 Scotdisc Line Dancer Novices' Hurdle Class E (4-y-o and up) £2,388 2m 110yds........................ (1:40)

1445 DEL PIERO (Ire) 5-10-12 R Garritty, *hld up, not fluent 4th and
5th, chlgd last, styd on strly to ld last 100 yards.*
.... (6 to 1 op 5 to 1 tchd 7 to 1) 1
1047⁵ KILNAMARTYRA GIRL 6-10-7 P Niven, *nvr far away, led sn
aftr 2 out, wndrd r-in, hdd and no extr last 100 yards.*
.... (7 to 1 op 5 to 1) 2
1182³ MITHRAIC (Ire) 4-10-12 (7*) L McGrath, *chsd ldrs, slightly
hmpd and brght wide strt, effrt betw last 2, no extr r-in.*
.... (2 to 1 fav op 7 to 4) 3
960 LUMBACK LADY 6-10-4 (3*) G Lee, *chsd ldrs, effrt betw last
2, no extr frm last.* .... (100 to 1 op 50 to 1) 4
958² TEACHER (Ire) 6-10-12 B Harding, *led aftr 3rd, mstk 2 out, sn
hdd, fdd r-in.* .... (4 to 1 tchd 9 to 2) 5
CALLERNISH DAN (Ire) 6-10-12 M Dwyer, *pressed ldrs, not
fluent 3 out, outpcd betw last 2, eased whn btn.*
.... (7 to 2 op 4 to 1) 6
1198⁷ NOBLE MONARCH (Ire) 7-10-12 N Williamson, *steadied in
rear, hdwy aftr 3 out, fdd appr last, eased whn btn.*
.... (16 to 1 op 14 to 1) 7
1050³ LEPTON (Ire) 5-10-12 L Wyer, *set slow pace, hdd aftr 3rd, cl
up till rdn and wknd betw last 2....* (10 to 1 op 7 to 1) 8
MY MISSILE 6-10-7 L O'Hara, *pld hrd, pushed alng in rear 4
out, sn beh.* .... (100 to 1 op 50 to 1) 9
1038⁸ REGAL DOMAIN (Ire) 5-10-12 D Bentley, *beh, mstk 4th, tld off
aftr nxt........* .... (66 to 1 op 33 to 1) 10
Dist: Nk, 6l, ½l, 3l, 11l, 2l, 2½l, dist, dist. 3m 55.90s. a 12.90s (10 Ran).
(Frank Hanson), M D Hammond

1334 Ashleybank Investments Reg Tweedie Novices' Chase Class D (5-y-o and up) £4,182 3m 1f.....(2:10)

1197³ TRICKLE LAD (Ire) 7-11-0 N Williamson, *hld up in rear, not
fluent 12th, reminders nxt, steady hdwy to chal last, led sn
aftr, ran on und pres........* .... (5 to 2 fav op 6 to 4) 1
1165⁸ TIGHTER BUDGET (USA) 9-12-4 M Moloney, *led, jmpd rght,
blundered 13th, mstk 3 out, hdd sn aftr last, kpt on wl.*
.... (7 to 2 op 3 to 1) 2
765⁴ TOUGH TEST (Ire) 6-10-11 (3*) G Cahill, *al hndy, ev ch frm 3
out, kpt on wl r-in........* (7 to 2 op 4 to 1 tchd 5 to 1) 3
1161* SEEKING GOLD (Ire) 7-11-1 B Storey, *chsd ldrs, rdn and
outpcd appr 3 out, styd on stdly frm nxt.*
.... (5 to 1 op 6 to 1 tchd 7 to 1) 4
1183⁵ COOL WEATHER (Ire) 6-11-0 R Supple, *in tch, reminders aftr
2 out, fdd frm last........* (11 to 2 op 5 to 1 tchd 6 to 1) 5
STRONGALONG (Ire) 6-11-0 T Reed, *tld off frm hfwy.*
.... (50 to 1 op 16 to 1) 6
Dist: 1½l, sht-hd, 8l, 2l, 30l. 6m 17.20s. a 20.20s (6 Ran).
(Mrs H F Prendergast), F Murphy

1335 Glenmuir Sportswear Handicap Hurdle Class D (0-125 4-y-o and up)

£2,736 2¼m................(2:40)

1123² ADAMATIC (Ire) [96] 5-10-0 L Wyer, *mstk 1st, chsd ldrs, chlgd
gng wl 2 out, led sn aftr last, hrd drvn, jst hld on...*(5 to 2 jt-
fav op 4 to 1) 1
STASH THE CASH (Ire) [98] 5-10-2 D Bentley, *hld up, pld hrd,
clr order 7th, pressed ldrs betw last 2, ran on strly.*
.... (3 to 1 op 5 to 2 tchd 100 to 30) 2
1038* FIELD OF VISION (Ire) [104] 6-10-8 J Supple, *chsd ldrs,
pushed alng 7th, ev ch till no extr r-in...........*(5 to 2 jt-
fav tchd 11 to 4) 3
1167⁵ WELL APPOINTED (Ire) [97] 7-9-12 (3*) G Lee, *set slow pace,
quickened hfwy, hdd jst aftr last, kpt on same pace.*
.... (9 to 1 op 7 to 1 tchd 10 to 1) 4
COMMON SOUND (Ire) [120] 5-11-10 M Dwyer, *hld up in
rear, rdn and outpcd appr 2 out, sn beh.*
.......................(9 to 2 op 7 to 2 tchd 5 to 1) 5
Dist: ½l, 2½l, ½l, 27l. 4m 30.70s. a 23.70s (5 Ran).
(Geoff Adam), R Allan

1336 Tavern Middlemas Handicap Chase Class C (0-135 5-y-o and up) £5,158 2¾m 110yds................. (3:10)

1165³ BAS DE LAINE (Fr) [115] 10-10-13 R Garritty, *led, quickened 4
out, clr last, drvn out..................*(3 to 1 op 5 to 2) 1
1069⁴ FIVELEIGH BUILDS [128] 9-11-9 (3*) G Cahill, *chsd ldrs, blun
5th, ev ch whn blunded ag'n 2 out, one pace appr last.*
.......................(7 to 1 op 6 to 1) 2
1046* DARK OAK [113] 10-10-11 L Wyer, *hld up, mstk 9th, hdwy to
chase ldrs 2 out, one pace appr last...* (5 to 1 tchd 6 to 1) 3
613⁴ EARLYMORNING LIGHT (Ire) [119] 7-11-3 B Harding, *chsd
ldrs, niggled alng and not fluent 3 out, btn appr last, eased
considerably........* (5 to 4 fav op 7 to 4 tchd 5 to 2) 4
1199³ STRONG DEEL (Ire) [119] 8-11-3 N Williamson, *hld up in rear,
mstk 9th, blun and uns rdr nxt........* (11 to 4 op 5 to 2) ur
Dist: 8l, 3l, dist. 5m 29.60s. a 5.60s (5 Ran).
SR: 29/34/16/-/-/ (R K Bids Ltd), M D Hammond

1337 Langholm Dyeing Company Novices' Handicap Hurdle Class E (0-100 4-y-o and up) £2,584 2¾m 110yds (3:40)

1182 CLEVER BOY (Ire) [64] 5-10-0 L Wyer, *hld up in rear, mstk 7th,
steady hdwy frm 3 out, ran on strly to ld cl hme.*
.... (10 to 1 op 16 to 1) 1
KASIRAMA (Ire) [73] 5-10-9 R Garritty, *hld up, hdwy 3 out, led
and stumbled last, sn hdd, kpt on.*
.... (11 to 2 op 5 to 1 tchd 6 to 1) 2
CASH BOX (Ire) [76] 8-10-12 N Smith, *hld up, chlgd 3 out, led
briefly betw last 2, led ag'n r-in, edgd lft, hdd cl hme.*
.... (12 to 1 op 10 to 1 tchd 16 to 1) 3
1067² MOVIE MAN [75] 4-10-11 T Reed, *chsd ldrs, slight ld aftr 3
out, mstk and hdd 2 out, fdd frm last.*
.... (7 to 1 op 6 to 1 tchd 8 to 1) 4
1071⁶ TARTAN MIX (Ire) [71] 5-10-7 J Supple, *made most till 4 out,
sn drvn alng, wknd frm nxt............*(6 to 1 tchd 7 to 1) 5
1067 ELLIOTT'S WISH (Ire) [64] 5-10-0 N Williamson, *pld hrd wth
ldrs, drvn alng appr 2 out, btn betw last two.*
.... (16 to 1 op 8 to 1 tchd 20 to 1) 6
1624 WHIRLWIND ROMANCE (Ire) [64] (bl) 5-10-0 S McDougall, *cl
up till wknd frm 3 out....* (8 to 1 op 7 to 1 tchd 16 to 1) 7
TWEEDSWOOD (Ire) [62] 6-11-7 (7*) B Grattan, *hld up, short
of room and drpd rear 7th, lost tch aftr 3 out, sn wl beh.*
.... (5 to 2 fav tchd 3 to 1) 8
1167⁶ NOORAN [58] 5-11-0 B Harding, *hld up, chsd ldrs 7th, pushed
alng nxt, wknd quickly appr 2 out, eased whn btn, tld off.*
.... (7 to 2 op 3 to 1 tchd 4 to 1) 9
Dist: ¾l, hd, 14l, 4l, 3l, 11l, nk, dist. 5m 27.10s. a 18.10s (9 Ran).
(Mrs M E Curtis), J W Curtis

NEWBURY (good)
Wednesday November 13th
Going Correction: PLUS 0.25 sec. per fur. (races 1,3,6), PLUS 0.10 (2,4,5)

1338 European Breeders Fund 'National Hunt' Novices' Hurdle Qualifier Class D (4,5,6-y-o) £3,135 2m 110yds........................ (1:20)

AERION 5-11-0 J Osborne, *confidently rdn in mid-div,
shaken up to ld appr last, quickened clr r-in.*
.... (11 to 8 on op 5 to 4 tchd 11 to 8) 1
TOWER STREET 5-10-11 (3*) L Aspell, *mid-div, hdwy appr 2
out, ran on strly r-in...* (20 to 1 op 10 to 1 tchd 25 to 1) 2
EVER BLESSED (Ire) 4-11-0 W Marston, *hld up in rear,
steady hdwy whn hit 2 out, mstk last, rallied and ran on wl r-in.*
.... (13 to 2 op 6 to 1 tchd 7 to 1) 3
THE CAPTAIN'S WISH 5-11-3 (7*) Mr R Thornton, *hld up in
tch, chsd ldr, ev ch, one pace r-in...........* (10 to 1 op 5 to 1) 4
TOMPETOO (Ire) 5-10-11 (3*) D Walsh, *trkd ldr, led 2 out, hdd
appr last, outpcd r-in.............* (10 to 1 op 5 to 1) 5
MAID FOR ADVENTURE (Ire) 5-10-9 B Fenton, *mid-div, styd
on frm 2 out, nvr nrr.................* (33 to 1 op 16 to 1) 6

SAFEGLIDE (Ire) 6-11-0 P Hide, *led till hdd 2 out, wknd appr last*.................... (20 to 1 op 14 to 1 tchd 33 to 1) 7
STRATHMINSTER 5-11-0 C O'Dwyer, *beh till hdwy aftr 3 out, nvr dngrs*.......................... (14 to 1 op 5 to 1) 8
KENTFORD TINA 5-10-9 S Curran, *beh till hdwy 3 out, wknd r-in*..................(25 to 1 op 14 to 1 tchd 33 to 1) 9
SNOWSHILL HARVEST (Ire) 5-11-0 M A Fitzgerald, *mid-div, ev ch 3 out, wknd appr last*........... (25 to 1 op 10 to 1) 10
CHINA GEM (Ire) 5-11-0 G Bradley, *al beh, tld off appr 3 out.* .... (33 to 1 op 20 to 1) 11
1053 STORM TIGER (Ire) 5-11-0 N Mann, *prmnt till appr 3 out, tld off*.................................(50 to 1 op 25 to 1) 12
RATHKEAL (Ire) 5-11-0 D Gallagher, *prmnt till appr 3 out, tld off*.................. (33 to 1 tchd 50 to 1 and 66 to 1) 13
MR GOONHILLY 6-11-0 A Thornton, *prmnt, wknd 3 out, tld off*......................................(50 to 1 op 25 to 1) 14
MILLCROFT REGATTA (Ire) 4-10-11 (3*) P Henley, *mid-div till wknd 5th, tld off*...................(33 to 1 op 12 to 1) 15
873^{7} ERMYNS PET 5-11-0 D O'Sullivan, *rcd wide, lost tch hfwy, tld off*...............................(33 to 1 op 25 to 1) 16
CLASSICACTION (Ire) 5-11-0 L Harvey, *in rear, rdn appr 3rd, tld off whn pld up bef 2 out, dismounted, lme.* .... (50 to 1 op 33 to 1) pu
Dist: 3½l, nk, sht-hd, sht-hd, 3½l, 3½l, nk, 2l, 1½l, 14l. 3m 59.00s. a 10.00s (17 Ran).
SR: 28/24/24/34/24/15/16/16/9/ (P Chamberlain, D Addiscott Partnership), O Sherwood

1339 Lionel Vick Memorial Novices' Handicap Chase Class D (0-110 5-y-o and up) £3,519 3m................ (1:50)

999^{2} GOLDENSWIFT (Ire) [86] 6-11-1 B Fenton, *patiently rdn, chlgd 3 out, sn led, ran on wl*........(2 to 1 fav op 9 to 4) 1
LOTTERY TICKET (Ire) [99] 7-12-0 J Osborne, *led till pckd 3rd, led 13th, hdd sn aftr 3 out, ran on one pace.* ....(7 to 1 op 4 to 1 tchd 8 to 1) 2
1021^{2} LUCKY DOLLAR (Ire) [99] 8-12-0 C O'Dwyer, *hld up, styd on one pace frm 3 out*.......... (13 to 2 op 9 to 2 tchd 7 to 1) 3
1055 THE GO AHEAD (Ire) [92] 6-11-7 A Thornton, *trkd ldr, led 3rd to 13th, rdn appr 3 out, wknd bef nxt*.... (12 to 1 op 5 to 1) 4
1111^{2} SUGAR HILL (Ire) [87] 6-11-2 P Hide, *hld up in rear, hdwy 9th, hit 12th, wknd 3 out*................................ (4 to 1) 5
1062 WESTERLY GALE (Ire) [76] 6-10-5 M A Fitzgerald, *blun and uns rdr 3rd*.......................... (9 to 2 op 5 to 2) ur
BALLYEDWARD (Ire) [88] 6-11-3 B Powell, *blun badly second, sn tld off, pld up bef 7th*.............. (12 to 1 op 5 to 1) pu
Dist: 2½l, 3l, 4l, nk. 6m 2.40s. a 17.40s (7 Ran).
(Mrs S Watts), G B Balding

1340 Tom Masson Trophy Hurdle Class B (4-y-o and up) £4,901 2m 5f... (2:20)

MANDYS MANTINO 6-11-8 P Hide, *trkd ldr, lft in ld aftr 4th, shaken up appr 2 out, kpt on r-in.* ....(Evens fav op 5 to 4 on tchd 11 to 10) 1
LITTLE BUCK (Ire) 8-11-4 C O'Dwyer, *hld up, dsptd second frm 7th, edgd lft appr last, no extr r-in.* .... (12 to 1 op 5 to 1 tchd 14 to 1) 2
1178^{3} DJAIS (Fr) 7-11-4 G Bradley, *hld up, lft second aftr 4th, wknd after 2 out*..............(10 to 1 op 6 to 1 tchd 12 to 1) 3
DANJING (Ire) 4-10-9 J Osborne, *set steady pace till ran out on bend aftr 4th*.......................... (6 to 4 tchd 13 to 8) ro
Dist: 4l, 5l. 5m 20.10s. a 26.10s (4 Ran).
(John Plackett), J T Gifford

1341 Hallowe'en Novices' Chase Class D (5-y-o and up) £3,899 2½m... (2:50)

REDEEMYOURSELF (Ire) 7-11-3 P Hide, *trkd ldr frm 5th, hit 8th, led 3 out, clr r-in.* (6 to 4 fav op 5 to 4 tchd 13 to 8) 1
MADISON COUNTY (Ire) 6-11-3 C O'Dwyer, *hld up, disputing ld whn blun 3 out, one pace aftr*........ (9 to 4 op 7 to 4) 2
COURT MASTER (Ire) 8-11-3 B Powell, *led till hdd 3 out, sn wknd*................. (12 to 1 op 7 to 1 tchd 14 to 1) 3
FELLOO (Ire) 7-11-3 W Marston, *trkd ldr to 5th, no hdwy frm 4 out*.....................(25 to 1 op 20 to 1 tchd 33 to 1) 4
SCORPION BAY 8-11-3 P Holley, *hld up, wkng whn hit 4 out, tld off when f nxt*.....(66 to 1 op 100 to 1 tchd 150 to 1) f
1100^{3} SCAMALLACH (Ire) (bl) 6-10-12 G Bradley, *al beh, poor 4th whn f last*............. (20 to 1 op 14 to 1 tchd 25 to 1) f
MACGEORGE (Ire) 6-11-3 P McLoughlin, *hld up in tch, gd hdwy whn blun 9th, rdr lost irons, out of control when uns rider 5 out*...............................(9 to 2 op 7 to 1) ur
Dist: 12l, 10l, 20l. 5m 13.50s. a 25.50s (7 Ran).
(Mrs T Brown), J T Gifford

1342 John Hugo Gwynne 50th Business Year Conditional Jockeys' Handicap Chase Class E (0-125 5-y-o and up) £3,395 2m 1f.................. (3:20)

964* SUPER TACTICS (Ire) [122] 8-12-0 P Henley, *hld up in tch, rdn to ld appr last, pushed out.* .... (2 to 1 op 6 to 4 tchd 9 to 4 and 5 to 2) 1
901* MERRY PANTO (Ire) [98] 7-10-1 (3*) M Berry, *hld up, wnt second 7th, rdn and no imprsn aftr 2 out.* ....(6 to 4 fav op 7 to 4) 2
1267^{4} NORTHERN SADDLER [122] 9-12-0 T Dascombe, *led 5th till hdd and wknd appr last*................ (4 to 1 op 7 to 2) 3
HIGH ALLTITUDE (Ire) [105] 8-10-11 D Fortt, *hld up, hdwy hfwy, ev ch whn f 4 out*....(9 to 1 op 7 to 1 tchd 10 to 1) f
1204 WHIPPERS DELIGHT (Ire) [94] 8-10-0 D Walsh, *led to 5th, weakenening whn hit 5 out, tld off when pld up bef 3 out.* ....(12 to 1 op 10 to 1 tchd 14 to 1) pu
Dist: 1¾l, 15l. 4m 8.40s. a 8.40s (5 Ran).
SR: 33/7/16/-/-/ (H V Perry), R H Alner

1343 Cold Ash Novices' Handicap Hurdle Class D (0-110 4-y-o and up) £2,765 3m 110yds.................. (3:50)

1153* QUEEN'S AWARD (Ire) [77] 7-9-7 (7*) M Griffiths, *hld up, hdwy 4th, led 8th, drw clr appr 2 out, eased r-in.* ....(9 to 4 fav op 7 to 2) 1
SPACEAGE GOLD [99] 7-11-8 G Upton, *hld up, wl beh 4 out, rdn and styd on to go second r-in*.........(6 to 1 op 4 to 1) 2
PERCY THROWER [105] 9-11-11 (3*) D Walsh, *led to 6th, chsd wnr 8th to r-in*.......(5 to 1 op 4 to 1 tchd 11 to 2) 3
998^{6} BITE THE BULLET [78] 5-9-7 (7*) O Burrows, *hld up, hdwy 5th, rdn 3 out, wknd aftr nxt.* ....(100 to 1 op 66 to 1 tchd 150 to 1) 4
1291* RIVER ROOM [110] 6-11-12 (7*,6ex) W Walsh, *trkd ldrs, led 6th till stumbled on landing and hdd 8th, wknd appr 3 out.* .... (11 to 2 op 9 to 2 tchd 6 to 1) 5
830^{4} CHINA MAIL (Ire) [90] 4-10-12 L Harvey, *al beh, tld off 3 out.* .... (20 to 1 op 14 to 1) 6
1158* CLOD HOPPER (Ire) [77] 6-10-0 B Powell, *hld up, hdwy 5th, wknd 4 out, tld off*.................. (6 to 1 op 5 to 1) 7
1115^{9} COOLEGALE [81] (bl) 10-10-4[11] (7*) D Slattery, *prmnt to 7th, tld off 9th*......... (66 to 1 op 33 to 1 tchd 100 to 1) 8
1107* CANTON VENTURE [98] 4-11-6 P Hide, *rcd wide, hld up, hdwy 8th, cl 3rd whn blun badly 3 out, not reco'r, poor third when f last*............... (4 to 1 op 9 to 2 tchd 5 to 1) f
Dist: 4l, hd, 23l, 20l, dist, 2½l, 3l. 5m 58.10s. a 12.10s (9 Ran).
SR: 12/30/36/-/-/-/ (R H Buckler), R H Buckler

WORCESTER (good)
Wednesday November 13th
Going Correction: PLUS 0.40 sec. per fur.

1344 Astley Novices' Hurdle Class E (4-y-o and up) £2,722 2½m.........(1:00)

MIGHTY MOSS (Ire) 5-10-5 (7*) Mr F Hutsby, *hld up, hdwy 5th, led 4 out, pushed clr r-in* (13 to 8 fav op 6 to 4) 1
DENHAM HILL (Ire) 5-10-12 J Railton, *hld up, pld hrd, hdwy 5th, ev ch 3 out, outpcd appr last*..... (50 to 1 op 33 to 1) 2
1132 HYDEMILLA 6-10-4 (3*) G Hogan, *led aftr 1st, hdd 4 out, sn rdn and wknd*........................(50 to 1 op 33 to 1) 3
1053* BIETSCHHORN BARD 6-11-5 R Dunwoody, *hld up, hdwy 4 out, rdn and wknd nxt*................(11 to 2 op 11 to 4) 4
WARNER FOR PLAYERS (Ire) 5-10-12 A P McCoy, *hld up, hdwy to chase ldrs 5th, rdn and wknd 3 out.* ....(2 to 1 op 3 to 1) 5
SAMMORELLO (Ire) 5-10-12 C Llewellyn, *mid-div, drvn alng 5th, wknd nxt*...................... (20 to 1 op 12 to 1) 6
1129^{5} JAVELIN COOL (Ire) 5-10-9 (3*) K Gaule, *chsd ldr to 5th, wknd 4 out*...............................(100 to 1 op 50 to 1) 7
1217^{4} WISE 'N' SHINE 5-10-2 (5*) Chris Webb, *trkd ldrs, drvn alng 5th, grad wknd*..........................(50 to 1 op 33 to 1) 8
1006^{3} DRAKESTONE 5-10-12 R Johnson, *mid-div til rdn and wknd 5 out, virtually pld up r-in.* ....(12 to 1 op 10 to 1 tchd 14 to 1) 9
MR MOTIVATOR 6-10-12 S McNeill, *chsd ldrs til wknd 5 out.* ....(100 to 1 op 50 to 1 tchd 150 to 1) 10
KALADROSS 5-10-12 T Jenks, *al in rear, tld off whn f 3 out.* .... (20 to 1 op 10 to 1) f
1208 CREDO BOY 7-10-12 R Greene, *mstk 3rd, sn beh, tld off whn pld up bef 3 out*........................ (50 to 1 op 33 to 1) pu
DEXTRA (Ire) 6-10-12 C Maude, *led, hdd aftr 1st, wknd quickly 4 out, tld off and pld up bef nxt.* (33 to 1 op 25 to 1) pu
SULA'S DREAM 7-10-7 S Burrough, *mstk 1st, al beh, tld off whn pld up bef 3 out*..............(100 to 1 op 50 to 1) pu
Dist: 11l, 20l, 2l, 1¾l, 29l, 16l, 17l. 4m 53.90s. a 17.90s (14 Ran).
(K Hutsby), D Nicholson

1345 Dunley Chase Limited Handicap Class C (0-135 5-y-o and up) £5,025 2m 7f 110yds.................(1:30)

CHERRYNUT [125] 7-10-13 A P McCoy, *trkd ldg pair, not fluent 3rd (water), swtchd lft to ld bef 2 out, gd jump to go clr last, ran on*.......................................(3 to 1 op 9 to 4) 1
BILLYGOAT GRUFF [133] 7-11-7 A Maguire, *made most, mstk 5th last, hdd bef 2 out, rallied und pres r-in.* ....(11 to 8 on op 5 to 4 on) 2
KING LUCIFER (Ire) [130] 7-11-4 R Johnson, *dsptd ld, not fluent 11th, rdn whn pace quickened aftr 3 out, one pace r-in.* ....(3 to 1 op 2 to 1) 3
Dist: 2½l, 4l. 6m 8.80s. (3 Ran).

(Hunt & Co (Bournemouth) Ltd), P F Nicholls

1346 Plumb Center Handicap Hurdle
Class C (0-130 4-y-o and up) £3,556
2m.............................(2:00)

TEINEIN (Fr) [121] 5-11-7 A P McCoy, hld up, hdwy 4 out, mstk
nxt, led appr 2 out, sn clr, eased nr finish. (4 to 1 op 3 to 1) 1
1238* MOUSE BIRD (Ire) [119] (bl) 6-11-5 (5ex) R Dunwoody, hld up,
hdwy 4 out, chsd wnr 2 out, no imprsn.
.........(5 to 2 fav op 9 to 4 tchd 11 to 4 and 3 to 1) 2
CHICODARI [128] 4-12-0 A Maguire, hmpd 1st, trkd ldrs, rdn
appr 2 out, styd on same pace.
..................(9 to 2 op 7 to 2 tchd 5 to 1) 3
KHALIDI (Ire) [115] 7-10-10 (5*) Sophie Mitchell, wth ldr, led 4
out, hdd appr 2 out, sn btn.
..........(11 to 1 op 8 to 1 tchd 12 to 1 and 14 to 1) 4
11417 PRIDEWOOD PICKER [100] 9-9-9 (5*) D J Kavanagh, hld up,
hdwy 5th, wknd appr 2 out.
.................(25 to 1 op 16 to 1 tchd 33 to 1) 5
INICH GATE (Ire) [110] 5-10-5 M Richards, prmnt, mstk and
lost pl 4th, wknd quickly 3 out.
..................(11 to 1 op 10 to 1 op 12 to 1) 6
11414 UNITED FRONT [100] 4-10-0 R Johnson, led to 4 out, rdn and
wknd appr nxt.....................(16 to 1 op 12 to 1) 7
SOCIETY GUEST [118] 10-10-11 (7*) C Rae, jmpd lft 1st,
prmnt, mstk and uns rdr 3rd.
..........(6 to 1 op 5 to 1 tchd 13 to 2) ur
Dist: 3l, 1l, 10l, 4l, 13l, dist. 3m 53.90s. a 13.90s (8 Ran).
SR: 18/13/21/-/-/ (Simon Sainsbury), Capt T A Forster

1347 Worcester Novices' Chase Class A
Grade 2 (5-y-o and up) £12,386 2m
7f 110yds.....................(2:30)

PLEASURE SHARED (Ire) 8-11-1 C Maude, hit 1st, given time
to reco'r, improved 4 out, rdn to ld aftr nxt, drvn out.
..................(9 to 2 op 3 to 1 tchd 5 to 1) 1
1138* AROUND THE GALE (Ire) 5-10-13 R Dunwoody, al wl plcd, ev
ch fnl circuit, rdn and ran on strly r-in.
.....(11 to 4 fav op 3 to 1 tchd 100 to 30 and 7 to 2) 2
1106* MONY-SKIP (Ire) 7-11-1 Richard Guest, trkd ldrs, blun second, improved to ld 9th, hdd aftr 3 out, one pace.
..................(16 to 1 op 14 to 1 tchd 20 to 1) 3
1226 WISLEY WONDER (Ire) 6-11-1 C Llewellyn, nvr far away, ev
ch appr 4 out, rdn frm nxt, no extr.
..................(13 to 2 op 5 to 1 tchd 7 to 1) 4
COOL RUNNER 6-11-1 R Bellamy, trkd ldg bunch, effrt whn f
7 out..........................(50 to 1 op 33 to 1) f
CASTLEKELLYLEADER (Ire) 7-11-1 A P McCoy, trkd ldrs, effrt
whn f 9th..........................(5 to 1 op 7 to 2) f
SEACHANGE 7-11-1 I Lawrence, wtd wth, improved to go
hndy aftr one circuit, blun 7 out, pld up bef nxt, destroyed.
..................(40 to 1 op 33 to 1) pu
TENNESSEE TWIST (Ire) 6-11-1 R Farrant, in tch for a circuit,
tld off whn pld up bef 5 out.........(12 to 1 op 8 to 1) pu
BUTTERCUP JOE 6-11-1 A Maguire, settled to track ldrs, pld
up lme aftr 5 out..........(9 to 2 op 5 to 1 tchd 4 to 1) pu
1106⁴ INCH EMPEROR (Ire) 6-11-1 T J Murphy, led till hdd 9th, lost
tch fnl circuit, pld up bef 7 out......(200 to 1 op 100 to 1) pu
Dist: Nk, 8l, 7l. 6m 6.30s. (10 Ran).
(Tony Eaves), P J Hobbs

1348 Levy Board Novices' Handicap Hur-
dle Class D (0-105 4-y-o and up)
£2,847 2m.....................(3:00)

1136¹ INDRAPURA (Ire) 4-12-0 A P McCoy, hld up, hdwy 5th,
chsd ldr 3 out, led last, drvn out....(9 to 4 fav op 7 to 4) 1
1135² LETS BE FRANK [82] 5-10-10 R Johnson, prmnt, led 4 out,
rdn and hdd last, kpt on..............(11 to 2 op 4 to 1) 2
1263⁶ TIME LEADER [72] 4-10-0 R Bellamy, beh, hdwy 3 out, nvr
plcd to chal......................(25 to 1 op 16 to 1) 3
BLAZING MIRACLE [72] 4-9-11² (5*) D Salter, mid-div, lost pl
5th, styd on frm 2 out..................(33 to 1) 4
FAIRIES FAREWELL [83] 6-10-11 J A McCarthy, hld up, hdwy
4 out, rdn and wknd 2 out.........(7 to 2 op 9 to 2) 5
COLWALL [74] 5-10-2 C Llewellyn, prmnt, drvn alng 3 out, sn
wknd..........................(16 to 1 op 8 to 1) 6
1044* COUNT OF FLANDERS (Ire) [82] 6-10-10 A S Smith, chsd ldr,
rdn and wknd 3 out...................(9 to 2 op 7 to 1) 7
SWEET TRENTINO (Ire) [83] 5-10-11 A Maguire, hld up, hdwy
and mstk 4th, wknd four out, pld up bef nxt.
..................(14 to 1 op 8 to 1) pu
1053⁷ SYLVESTER (Ire) [75] 6-10-3 D Bridgwater, led to 4 out, sn
wknd, pld up bef 2 out..........(20 to 1 op 16 to 1) pu
KINGS VISION [72] 4-10-0 S Wynne, al in rear, tld off whn pld
up bef 3 out..........................(33 to 1 op 14 to 1) pu
YOUNG TYCOON (Ire) [58] 5-10-11 R Greene, beh frm 4th,
tld off whn pld up bef 3 out.........(33 to 1 op 16 to 1) pu
Dist: 1¼l, 8l, 8l, 3½l, 12l, 8l. 3m 53.70s. a 13.70s (11 Ran).
SR: 27/7/-/-/-/-/ (Martin Pipe Racing Club), M C Pipe

1349 Talfab Trophy Handicap Chase Class
F (0-100 5-y-o and up) £3,731 2m
.............................(3:30)

1066⁵ PORPHYRIOS [98] 5-11-12 C Llewellyn, settled off the pace,
plenty to do hfwy, gd hdwy 4 out, mstk last and rdr lost irons,
styd on grimly to ld r-in..........(8 to 1 op 5 to 1) 1
REESHLOCH [88] (bl) 7-10-9 (7*) C Rae, settled midfield, gd
hdwy to ld 4 out, rdn last, hdd and one pace r-in.
..................(9 to 1 op 10 to 1 tchd 8 to 1) 2
THATS THE LIFE [77] 11-10-5 R Johnson, led to 3rd, styd
hndy, ev ch and drvn alng 4 out, one pace frm nxt.
..................(25 to 1 op 20 to 1) 3
BROWN ROBBER [72] 8-10-0 R Farrant, settled midfield, effrt
hfwy, drvn alng 4 out, no imprsn.
..................(20 to 1 op 16 to 1 tchd 25 to 1) 4
DRESS DANCE (Ire) [85] 6-10-8 (5*) Sophie Mitchell, struggling frm hfwy, sn lost tch, tld off....(16 to 1 tchd 20 to 1) 5
WHO AM I (Ire) [84] 6-10-12 A P McCoy, trkd ldg grp,
improved to ld aftr 7 out, hdd 4 out, wknd quickly frm nxt, tld
off..........................(11 to 2 co-fav op 5 to 1) 6
1052⁷ GOOD FOR A LAUGH [95] 12-11-2 (7*) Mr G Shenkin, settled
beh ldg grp, struggling frm hfwy, tld off frm 4 out.
....(11 to 2 co-fav op 8 to 1 tchd 9 to 1 and 10 to 1) 7
1001³ JEWEL THIEF [74] (v) 6-10-2 B Clifford, al wl beh, tld off.
..................(33 to 1) 8
1031³ AMBASSADOR ROYALE (Ire) [91] 8-11-5 D Gallagher, wth
ldrs, lost pl quickly and pld up lme bef 6 out....(11 to 2 co-
fav op 5 to 1) pu
1023⁶ VIAGGIO [75] (v) 8-10-3 T Eley, chsd ldg grp, struggling and
lost tch aftr 5 out, pld up bef nxt.............(20 to 1) pu
HIGH LOW (USA) [100] 8-12-0 T Jenks, wth ldrs, led 3rd till
hdd 7 out, wknd quickly and pld up bef 4 out.
..................(9 to 1 op 6 to 1 tchd 10 to 1) pu
THE MINISTER (Ire) [82] 7-10-10 A Maguire, chsd ldrs, struggling aftr 5 out, blun nxt, sn pld up............(11 to 2 co-
fav op 4 to 1 tchd 6 to 1) pu
Dist: 1¼l, 10l, 1¾l, 15l, nk, 18l. 4m 7.00s. a 18.00s (12 Ran).
(Ian Bullerwell), K C Bailey

1350 Wychbold Standard Open National
Hunt Flat Class H (4,5,6-y-o) £1,427
2m.............................(4:00)

1026* BOOTS MADDEN (Ire) 6-11-11 R Johnson, hld up, hdwy o'r 4
fs out, led over 2 out, drvn out.
..................(7 to 2 fav op 4 to 1 tchd 11 to 2) 1
ANOTHER COCKPIT 4-10-13 (5*) D J Kavanagh, made most
til hdd o'r 2 fs out, no extr ins last......(12 to 1 op 6 to 1) 2
RACHEL LOUISE 4-10-13 D Bridgwater, hld up, hdwy 7 fs out,
ev ch o'r 2 out til no extr appr last....(12 to 1 op 33 to 1) 3
SUPER RAPIER (Ire) 4-11-4 Richard Guest, hld up, styd on fnl
3 fs, nvr nrr..........(25 to 1 op 20 to 1 tchd 33 to 1) 4
SYMPHONY'S SON (Ire) 5-11-4 A Maguire, hld up, hdwy o'r 2
fs out, rdn and edgd rght appr last, nvr imprsn.
..................(6 to 1 op 5 to 1) 5
DOMINDROSS 4-11-4 A P McCoy, hld up, hdwy und pres o'r
2 fs out, nvr nrr..................(8 to 1 op 3 to 1) 6
EUROFAST PET (Ire) 6-11-4 C Maude, hld up, styd on fnl 2 fs,
not rch ldrs.
.........(14 to 1 op 10 to 1 tchd 16 to 1 and 20 to 1) 7
NEW LEAF (Ire) 4-10-13 (5*) Sophie Mitchell, mid-div, hdwy
o'r 5 fs out, one pace fnl 3..........(20 to 1 tchd 33 to 1) 8
SHARIAKANNDI (Fr) 4-11-4 C Llewellyn, hld up, hdwy hfwy,
nvr rchd ldrs..........(25 to 1 op 20 to 1 tchd 33 to 1) 9
LOCH NA KEAL 4-10-13 J R Kavanagh, hld up, hdwy hfwy,
rdn and wknd wl o'r one furlong out..(12 to 1 op 14 to 1) 10
HILLS GAMBLE 6-11-4 W Worthington, mid-div, pld hrd,
hdwy hfwy, chlgd 4 fs out, sn wknd................(33 to 1) 11
FIRECROWN 6-11-4 M Richards, nvr rchd chalg pos.
..................(33 to 1 op 20 to 1) 12
LOOK IN THE MIRROR 5-10-11 (7*) L Suthern, prmnt til rdn
and wknd o'r 4 fs out......(9 to 1 op 6 to 1 tchd 10 to 1) 13
SMALL FLAME (Ire) 5-10-13 M Brennan, hld up, hdwy o'r 6 fs
out, wknd over 4 out..........................(33 to 1) 14
ARCTIC FUSILIER 5-10-11 (7*) Mr A Wintle, wth ldrs til rdn
and wknd wl o'r 2 fs out..(9 to 1 op 6 to 1 tchd 10 to 1) 15
1109³ LADY FOLEY (Ire) (bl) 4-10-13 R Dunwoody, trkd ldrs, rdn 5 fs
out, grad wknd..................(12 to 1 tchd 14 to 1) 16
1181³ BECKY'S LAD 6-11-1 (3*) Guy Lewis, wth ldrs til lost pl
quickly o'r 6 fs out..................(66 to 1 op 50 to 1) 17
ABOVE SUSPICION (Ire) 4-11-4 S McNeill, hld up, pld hrd,
hdwy hfwy, chlgd 4 fs out, sn wknd..............(33 to 1) 18
HIGH STATESMAN 4-11-4 J Railton, hld up, pld hrd, hdwy o'r
7 fs out, wknd 5 out..............................(33 to 1) 19
SABRECOIN (Ire) 5-11-1 (3*) K Gaule, in rear whn stumbled
badly aftr 4 fs, al beh..............(50 to 1 op 25 to 1) 20
ARKLOW KING (Ire) 4-10-11 (7*) S Fowler, prmnt til rdn and
wknd quickly o'r 6 fs out..........(66 to 1 op 50 to 1) 21
Dist: 1¼l, 3l, 9l, ¾l, 1l, 2l, hd, nk, 1½l, 1½l. 3m 56.60s. (21 Ran).
(L J A Phipps), Miss Venetia Williams

TAUNTON (good to firm)
Thursday November 14th
Going Correction: MINUS 0.15 sec. per fur.

1351 South-West Amateur Riders' Hand-
icap Hurdle Class G (0-110 4-y-o and

NATIONAL HUNT RESULTS 1996-97

up) £1,941 2m 3f 110yds......(1:00)

NOVA RUN [100] 7-11-0 (5") Mr C Vigors, *prmnt, lft in second 7th, led 2 out, jmpd rght last, drvn out*....(4 to 1 op 3 to 1) 1
1130* SEVERN GALE [90] 6-10-2 (7") Mr N Bradley, *led aftr 1st till 2 out, no extr*............(17 to 2 op 5 to 1 tchd 9 to 1) 2
1139² ZINGIBAR [81] 4-9-7 (7") Mr R Thornton, *hld up, prog appr 7th, wknd approaching 2 out*......(15 to 8 fav op 3 to 1) 3
1272⁵ SAN DIEGO CHARGER (Ire) [82] 5-9-8 (7") Mr O McPhail, *hld up, rdn and styd on frm 3 out, nvr nrr*. (16 to 1 op 12 to 1) 4
939⁴ SOUTHERN RIDGE [85] 5-9-11 (7") Mr A Holdsworth, *prmnt till lost pl 3rd, rnwd effrt 7th, wknd last.* .... (8 to 1 op 7 to 1 tchd 15 to 2) 5
GLEN MIRAGE [84] 11-9-10 (7") Miss M Coombe, *nvr trble ldrs*...........................(14 to 1 op 10 to 1) 6
1222³ ZIP YOUR LIP [89] 6-10-1 (7") Miss C Townsley, *hld up, some hdwy 7th, wknd 3 out*...............(20 to 1 tchd 25 to 1) 7
ALBEIT [81] 6-9-9² (7") Miss C Evans, *al beh.* .... (50 to 1 op 25 to 1 tchd 66 to 1) 8
ALWAYS REMEMBER [100] 9-10-12 (7") Mr R Widger, *led to 1st, wknd appr 6th, tld off*...........(16 to 1 op 10 to 1) 9
1000⁷ FLEUR DE TAL [97] 5-10-9 (7") Mr G Shenkin, *prmnt, second whn f 7th*..........................(9 to 1 op 6 to 1) f
FEARLESS WONDER [109] (bl) 5-11-7 (7") Miss K Di Marte, *sn tld off, pld up bef 3 out.* ....(25 to 1 op 10 to 1 tchd 33 to 1) pu
Dist: 6l, 14l, hd, 2l, 8l, 2l, 26l, dist. 4m 21.70s. a 3.70s (11 Ran).
SR: 24/8/-/-/-/-/ (S Keeling), N J Henderson

1352 WSM Mercedes Benz 'Actros' Chase Novices' Handicap Class E (0-100 5-y-o and up) £2,918 2m 3f... (1:30)

1001² CHICKABIDDY [78] 8-11-0 R Johnson, *chsd ldr, led aftr 4 out, lft clr nxt*....(5 to 2 op 9 to 4 tchd 11 to 4) 1
1099 ASHMEAD RAMBLER (Ire) [67] 6-10-3 C Maude, *hld up, led 11th tll aftr 4 out, rdn whn lft second and hmpd 3 out.* ....(4 to 1 op 7 to 2) 2
1264 LORD NITROGEN (USA) [81] 6-11-3 Mr J L Llewellyn, *not fluent, led, reminders aftr 5th and nxt, hdd 9th, wknd next, tld off 4 out*.............(7 to 1 op 9 to 2 tchd 15 to 2) 3
OXFORD QUILL [72] 9-10-8 D Morris, *keen hold early, prmnt, led 9th to 11th, cl second whn f 3 out.*
.......................(12 to 1 op 10 to 1 tchd 14 to 1) f
771* NORDIC VALLEY (Ire) [88] 5-11-10 A P McCoy, *not fluent, hld up, rdn and cl 3rd whn f 3 out*.......(6 to 4 fav op 5 to 4) f
Dist: 23l, 15l. 4m 43.60s. a 12.60s (5 Ran).
(G F Edwards), G F Edwards

1353 Orchard Portman Selling Handicap Hurdle Class G (0-90 3-y-o and up) £2,004 2m 1f.............(2:00)

1218⁵ LITTLE HOOLIGAN [82] 5-11-10 R Johnson, *mid-div, outpcd appr 5th, sn rdn, rallied aftr 3 out, led r-in, all out.* ....(6 to 1 op 9 to 2) 1
1205⁴ BLURRED IMAGE (Ire) [67] 5-10-9 T J Murphy, *hld up, hdwy 5th, led, jmpd lft and hit 2 out, hdd and no extr r-in.* ....(8 to 1 op 10 to 1) 2
1235⁶ MUTAWALI (Ire) [75] 6-11-3 D Leahy, *hld up, hit 5th, hdwy 3 out, styd on one pace r-in*............(4 to 1 op 5 to 1) 3
1261 TIBBS INN [58] 7-9-7 (7") Mr R Thornton, *strted slwly, beh, hdwy 4th, mstks nxt 2, led briefly appr two out, one pace.* ....(16 to 1 tchd 20 to 1) 4
998⁵ TO BE FAIR [76] 9-10-11 (7") Mr S Durack, *mstk 3rd, chsd ldr till aftr 3 out, btn nxt*......(9 to 1 op 8 to 1 tchd 10 to 1) 5
1203⁵ ALOSAILI [78] 9-11-6 V Slattery, *nvr nr to chal.* ....(9 to 1 op 7 to 1 tchd 10 to 1) 6
858⁶ REMEMBER STAR [74] 3-10-0 F Jousset, *nvr on terms.* ....(66 to 1 op 50 to 1) 7
1235 COLOUR SCHEME [65] (v) 9-10-7 B Powell, *al beh.* ....(50 to 1 op 33 to 1 tchd 66 to 1) 8
1102⁶ SOLDIER BLUE [75] (bl) 3-10-1 A P McCoy, *led to appr 2 out, sn wknd*....................(7 to 1 tchd 8 to 1) 9
1179* INDIRA [84] 3-10-7 (3") T Dascombe, *3rd whn blun and uns rdr second*..................(11 to 4 fav op 2 to 1) ur
Dist: 2l, 1½l, 3½l, 3½l, 4l, 2l, 3l, 3l. 3m 51.90s. a 8.90s (10 Ran).
(G F Edwards), G F Edwards

1354 Weatherbys Statistical Record Novices' Hurdle Class E (4-y-o and up) £2,358 2m 1f.................(2:30)

1082* ROSENCRANTZ (Ire) 4-11-12 N Williamson, *confidently rdn, hld up, hdwy appr 6th, led, hit and lft clr last, unchlgd.* ....(Evens fav op 5 to 4 tchd 6 to 4) 1
1220* PORTSCATHO (Ire) (bl) 4-11-5 S McNeill, *pressed ldrs till lost pl 3 out, styd on frm nxt, no ch wth wnr.* ....(10 to 1 op 8 to 1 tchd 11 to 1) 2
MAGIC WIZARD 5-10-12 C Maude, *in tch, rdn 3 out, one pace*.........................(12 to 1 tchd 14 to 1) 3
ADONISIS 4-10-12 A Procter, *towards rear, styd on frm 3 out, nrst finish*.............(25 to 1 tchd 33 to 1) 4
QUESTAN (bl) 4-10-12 A P McCoy, *hld up, hdwy 5th, second 3 out, sn wknd*..(12 to 1 tchd 6 to 4 and 9 to 4) 5
1205 ATH CHEANNAITHE (Fr) 4-11-5 R Johnson, *led till appr 5th, wknd 3 out.*........................(12 to 1 tchd 10 to 1) 6

921⁴ TRAUMA (Ire) 4-10-0 (7") N Willimington, *pld hrd, sn hndy, wknd 5th, beh whn mstk nxt, tld off*.... (66 to 1 op 33 to 1) 7
671 KLOSTERS 4-10-4 (3") T Dascombe, *al beh, tld off.* ....(66 to 1 op 50 to 1) 8
1103² ALL SEWN UP 4-10-12 B Powell, *al beh, tld off.* ....(66 to 1 op 25 to 1) 9
OUT ON A PROMISE (Ire) 4-10-5 (7") D Finnegan, *pld hrd, prmnt, led appr 5th, clr 3 out, hdd and f last.* ....(10 to 1 op 7 to 1 tchd 14 to 1) f
900 MINNEOLA 4-10-0 (7") Mr R Thornton, *al beh, tld off whn pld up*......................(66 to 1 op 50 to 1) pu
1065⁶ SABOTEUSE 4-10-7 T J Murphy, *al beh, tld off whn pld up bef 6th*..........................(9 to 1 op 33 to 1) pu
NIGELS CHOICE 4-10-12 F Jousset, *beh, ran wide on bend appr 3rd and aftr nxt, pld up bef 5th*.. (66 to 1 op 20 to 1) pu
Dist: 11l, 3½l, hd, 14l, 3½l, dist, 3l, 7l. 3m 47.60s. a 4.60s (13 Ran).
SR: 27/9/-/-/-/-/ (L J Fulford), Miss Venetia Williams

1355 WSM Mercedes Benz 'Vito' Novices' Hurdle Class D (4-y-o and up) £2,801 3m 110yds..................(3:00)

HONEY MOUNT 5-10-12 N Williamson, *hld up and beh, hdwy appr 9th, led last, sn clr*....(9 to 4 fav op 7 to 2) 1
1234⁴ COPPER COIL 6-10-5 (7") J Power, *led to second, rgned ld 3 out, hdd last, no extr*......(9 to 2 op 4 to 1 tchd 5 to 1) 2
1261² DRAGONMIST (Ire) (h) 6-10-7 D J Burchell, *hld up towards rear, hdwy 8th, one pace appr 2 out.* ....(6 to 1 op 7 to 2 tchd 13 to 2) 3
854² GALATASORI JANE (Ire) 6-10-7 A P McCoy, *led second till appr 4th, rgned ld 8th, hdd 3 out, one pace.*.......................(7 to 2 op 11 to 4 tchd 4 to 1) 4
FRANK NAYLAR 5-10-5 (7") M Griffiths, *hld up beh ldrs, wknd appr 8th.*................(8 to 1 op 4 to 1) 5
1234 MU-TADIL 4-10-11 B Powell, *nvr gng wl, prmnt, led appr 4th to 8th, wknd nxt*........(40 to 1 op 16 to 1) 6
1215⁵ KATHARINE'S SONG (Ire) 6-10-7 B Fenton, *al beh, tld off.* ....(40 to 1 op 20 to 1) 7
1130 LAURA LYE (Ire) 6-10-7 J Railton, *hld up beh ldrs, ev ch 3 out, wknd aftr nxt*........(50 to 1 op 25 to 1 tchd 66 to 1) 8
1240⁸ DUKES CASTLE (Ire) 5-10-12 J Frost, *mstk 1st, hld up, rdn appr 3rd, wknd nxt, tld off.*...(8 to 1 op 7 to 1 tchd 9 to 1) f
Dist: 2l, 6l, 3l, 18l, ¾l, 20l, 10l. 5m 39.70s. a 11.70s (9 Ran).
(Paul Green), N J H Walker

1356 WSM Mercedes Benz 'Sprinter' Chase Handicap Class F (0-105 5-y-o and up) £2,801 3m..........(3:30)

1106³ LA MEZERAY [75] 8-10-0³ (3") D Walsh, *hld up in tch, mstk 14th, sn rdn, led last 50 yards, all out...* (5 to 1 op 6 to 1) 1
938³ HENLEY WOOD [98] 11-11-9 L Harvey, *led to out, rgned ld 2 out, hdd and no oxtr last 50 yards.......* (7 to 2 op 5 to 2) 2
1055 GALLIC GIRL (Ire) [75] 6-9-12¹ (3") T Dascombe, *hld up in tch, led 4 out to 2 out, wknd last.*
.......................(33 to 1 op 20 to 1 tchd 40 to 1) 3
1301 HERBERT BUCHANAN (Ire) [101] 6-11-12 A P McCoy, *hld up, mstk 6th, blun badly and lost pl nxt, rallied 14th, effrt whn mistake 3 out, sn btn*..........(7 to 4 fav tchd 9 to 4) 4
938* THE BLUE BOY (Ire) [103] (bl) 8-12-0 N Williamson, *chsd ldr to 13th, 3rd whn f nxt*.................(9 to 4 tchd 5 to 2) f
RHOMAN FUN (Ire) [75] 7-10-0 B Powell, *hld up beh ldrs, 3rd whn blun badly 11th, behind when pld up aftr nxt.* ....(11 to 1 op 7 to 1 tchd 12 to 1) pu
Dist: 1l, 6l, 11l. 6m 0.00s. a 17.00s (6 Ran).
(Mrs J E Hawkins), Mrs J E Hawkins

1357 Weatherbys 'Stars Of Tomorrow' Open National Hunt Flat Standard - Class H (4,5,6-y-o) £1,215 2m 1f ....(4:00)

SCORING PEDIGREE (Ire) 4-11-4 S Curran, *hld up and beh, rapid hdwy on ins to ld 6 fs out, drvn out fnl 2, fnshd 1st, disqualified.*...............(3 to 1 op 4 to 1 tchd 5 to 2) 1D
MIDAS 5-11-4 A P McCoy, *keen hold, hld up, hdwy hfwy, ev ch o'r 2 fs out, no extr fnl furlong, fnshd second, plcd 1st.* ....(3 to 1 tchd 4 to 1) 2
LITTLE JAKE (Ire) 6-11-4 R Johnson, *hld up in tch, ev ch 3 fs out, one pace 2 out, fnshd 3rd, plcd second.* ....(7 to 4 fav op 5 to 4 tchd 2 to 1) 2
KING OF THE BLUES 4-11-4 T J Murphy, *keen hold, prmnt, effrt 3 fs out, wknd 2 out, fnshd 4th, plcd 3rd.* ....(11 to 2 op 5 to 2) 3
1214 HALAM BELL 4-10-13 P Holley, *chsd ldr till 6 fs out, wknd o'r 2 out, fnshd 5th, plcd 4th*..........(33 to 1 op 14 to 1) 4
DUNNICKS TOWN 4-11-4 G Upton, *nvr nr to chal, fnshd 6th, plcd 5th*..........(20 to 1 op 16 to 1 tchd 25 to 1) 5
BOOZYS DREAM 5-11-4 S Burrough, *mid-div, rdn hfwy, sn beh, tld off.*........(16 to 1 op 20 to 1 tchd 12 to 1) 6
COUNTESS MILLIE 4-10-8 (5") Chris Webb, *led till 6 fs out, sn wknd, tld off.*.........(33 to 1 op 25 to 1 tchd 50 to 1) 7
AQUA AMBER 4-11-4 B Fenton, *al beh, tld off fnl 6 fs.* ....(50 to 1 op 20 to 1) 9
1214⁹ MISS NIGHT OWL 5-10-13 J Frost, *pld hrd, prmnt, hmpd 6 fs out, wknd rpdly 3 out, tld off.*...(16 to 1 op 12 to 1) 10
Dist: 1½l, 3½l, 5l, 7l, 5l, 27l, 6l, 1½l, 13l. 3m 51.10s. (10 Ran).

167

NATIONAL HUNT RESULTS 1996-97

(D G & D J Robinson), K R Burke

THURLES (IRE) (yielding)
Thursday November 14th

1358 Littleton Opportunity Handicap Hurdle (88-109 4-y-o and up) £2,637 2¼m................................ (1:00)

1058⁴ COLLON LEADER (Ire) [-] 7-10-13 J R Barry, ... (2 to 1 fav)	1
1118² THE WICKED CHICKEN (Ire) [-] 7-10-5 (2⁰) G Cotter, (9 to 4)	2
1118³ PTARMIGAN LODGE [-] 5-10-11 G Kilfeather, ... (5 to 1)	3
1058⁵ THE SCEARDEEN (Ire) [-] 7-10-4 (4⁰) A O'Shea, ... (10 to 1)	4
DASHING ROSIE [-] 8-11-6 (4⁰) B J Geraghty, ... (7 to 2)	5
1074 AISEIRI [-] 9-10-5 (2⁰) J Butler, ... (16 to 1)	6
Dist: 2½l, 2l, 1½l, hd. 4m 39.40s. (6 Ran).	

(Mrs I M Murphy), A J Martin

1359 Tipperary Maiden Hurdle (5-y-o) £2,226 2m.................. (1:30)

1013⁶ HILL OF HOPE (Ire) 12-0 W Slattery, ... (10 to 1)	1
1193 MARTYS STEP (Ire) 11-7 (7⁰) D McCullagh, ... (3 to 1)	2
1241⁷ ASK ME IN (Ire) 11-2 (7⁰) M D Murphy, ... (10 to 1)	3
1145³ JANICE PRICE (Ire) 11-6 (3⁰) D J Casey, ... (7 to 1)	4
1195³ SIMPLY ACOUSTIC (Ire) 11-2 (7⁰) A O'Shea, ... (6 to 1)	5
928⁵ DOOK'S DELIGHT (Ire) 12-0 P Cusack, ... (2 to 1 fav)	6
1241 SHECOULDNTBEBETTER (Ire) 11-2 (7⁰) P Morris, (20 to 1)	7
1042⁶ ANN'S DESIRE (Ire) 11-9 P L Malone, ... (10 to 1)	8
978⁹ KYLOGUE KING (Ire) 11-8¹ (7⁰) Mr L B Murphy, ... (16 to 1)	9
1145⁶ CASTLE BAILEY (Ire) 12-0 T J O'Sullivan, ... (20 to 1)	10
829⁵ GRANUALE (Ire) 11-4 (5⁰) G Cotter, ... (8 to 1)	11
1241 WATT A BUZZ (Ire) 11-9 K F O'Brien, ... (33 to 1)	12
945⁹ ANTON THE THIRD (Ire) 11-2 Miss M Olivefalk, ... (16 to 1)	13
1096⁷ COOLREE LORD (Ire) 12-0 M P Hourigan, ... (14 to 1)	14
DERRYAD (Ire) 11-9 T P Treacy, ... (14 to 1)	15
1013 PIXIE BLUE (Ire) 11-2 (7⁰) Mr R A Behan, ... (33 to 1)	16
OAKS PRIDE (USA) 12-0 M P Dwyer, ... (12 to 1)	17
1005 GARAMOY (Ire) 11-9 F Woods, ... (33 to 1)	18
1090 SABINTA (Ire) 11-9 S H O'Donovan, ... (50 to 1)	19
1060 MAIGUESIDE PRINCE (Ire) 12-0 J P Broderick, ... (20 to 1)	20
1119⁴ ABBEY GALE (Ire) 11-9 C O'Dwyer, ... (11 to 2)	su
Dist: Sht-hd, 9l, 1l, 1l. 4m 25.90s. (21 Ran).	

(Michael O Bourke), Daniel Bourke

1360 Holycross Hurdle (5-y-o and up) £2,226 2¾m 110yds........ (2:00)

1076² MATTS DILEMMA (Ire) 8-11-0 F Woods, ... (3 to 1)	1
1013² MERCHANTS QUAY (Ire) 5-10-9 (5⁰) G Cotter, ... (5 to 4 fav)	2
IT'S THE KLONDIKE (Ire) 6-10-11 (3⁰) D J Casey, ... (12 to 1)	3
1037¹ MARINERS REEF (Ire) 5-10-2 (7⁰) D McCullagh, ... (14 to 1)	4
1175⁵ DIAMOND DOUBLE (Ire) 5-10-9 C F Swan, ... (8 to 1)	5
1193 BARRIGAN'S HILL (Ire) 6-11-0 S H O'Donovan, ... (14 to 1)	6
1090⁶ FRISKY THYNE (Ire) 7-11-0 P A Roche, ... (14 to 1)	7
1145⁴ JOLLY JOHN (Ire) 5-11-0 C O'Dwyer, ... (8 to 1)	8
983⁸ MARILLO (Ire) 6-10-9 J P Broderick, ... (14 to 1)	9
1076⁸ VIVIANS VALE (Ire) 7-10-2 (7⁰) D K Budds, ... (20 to 1)	10
1013 STRONG RAIDER (Ire) 6-11-0 K F O'Brien, ... (20 to 1)	11
1042³ WINTER PRINCESS 5-10-2 (7⁰) Mr K Ross, ... (20 to 1)	12
91³ THE YELLOW BOG (Ire) 6-11-0 T J Mitchell, ... (12 to 1)	13
977 CASTLE TIGER BAY 5-11-0 T P Treacy, ... (33 to 1)	14
TORUS STAR (Ire) 7-10-11 (3⁰) K Whelan, ... (25 to 1)	15
1005⁵ GALLIC HONEY (Ire) 5-10-2 (7⁰) Mrs C Harrison, ... (20 to 1)	16
HIGHLAND SUPREME (Ire) 7-11-0 M P Dwyer, ... (14 to 1)	pu
Dist: 3½l, hd, 3l, nk. 5m 50.00s. (17 Ran).	

(Slaney Meats Group), P J P Doyle

1361 Loughmore Handicap Hurdle (0-102 5-y-o and up) £2,226 3m.... (2:30)

1244³ LAURENS FANCY (Ire) [-] 6-10-6 (3⁰) J R Barry, (3 to 1 jt-fav)	1
1147⁴ LETTERLEE (Ire) [-] 6-11-4 (7⁰) Mr M A Cahill, ... (12 to 1)	2
1168³ WICKLOW WAY (Ire) [-] 6-10-7 T P Treacy, ... (13 to 2)	3
1075⁵ ISLAND CHAMPION (Ire) [-] 7-9-13 (5⁰) G Cotter, ... (16 to 1)	4
1040 COLLIERS HILL (Ire) [-] 8-11-3 F Woods, ... (10 to 1)	5
1040 THE THIRD MAN (Ire) [-] 7-10-3 P McWilliams, ... (14 to 1)	6
1092⁵ ANOTHER POINT (Ire) [-] 8-10-12 J P Broderick, ... (7 to 1)	7
1096 SHUIL LE LAOI (Ire) [-] 6-10-7 C F Swan, ... (12 to 1)	8
1074³ KILCARAMORE (Ire) [-] 5-11-2 Mr P J Healy, ... (10 to 1)	9
1040⁵ AMME ENAEK (Ire) [-] (bl) 7-10-3 H Rogers, ... (12 to 1)	10
428 TOUCHING MOMENT (Ire) [-] 6-11-7 (7⁰) A O'Shea, (20 to 1)	11
1040⁶ THE VILLAGE FANCY (Ire) [-] 6-11-4 F J Flood, ... (10 to 1)	12
1142⁴ VALLEY OF KINGS (Ire) [-] 6-10-0 C O'Dwyer, (3 to 1 jt-fav)	f
1058² OVER THE WALL (Ire) [-] 7-10-8 P A Roche, ... (33 to 1)	pu
ERRIGAL ISLAND (Ire) [-] 8-10-6 (5⁰) J Butler, ... (14 to 1)	pu
Dist: 3l, 5l, 6l, ½l. 6m 19.30s. (15 Ran).	

(Noel Delahunty), Patrick Joseph Flynn

1362 Seskin Beginners Chase (5-y-o and up) £2,226 2m............... (3:00)

748 MAN OF ARRAN (Ire) 6-12-0 K F O'Brien, ... (6 to 1)	1
980⁷ FONTAINE FABLES (Ire) 6-12-0 M P Dwyer, ... (7 to 2)	2
393⁷ LANTINA (Ire) 5-10-12 D H O'Connor, ... (16 to 1)	3
1118⁴ SACULORE (Ire) 8-11-9 (5⁰) J M Donnelly, ... (10 to 1)	4

1170⁴ TAYLORS QUAY (Ire) 8-11-2 (7⁰) Mr E Gallagher, ... (6 to 1)	5
KHARASAR (Ire) 6-12-0 C O'Dwyer, ... (5 to 2 fav)	6
982⁵ SLANEY STANDARD (Ire) 8-11-9 F Woods, ... (10 to 1)	7
1146⁶ SIR-EILE (Ire) 8-11-2 (7⁰) A O'Shea, ... (16 to 1)	8
720 SUEMENOMORE (Ire) 7-11-4 J Jones, ... (25 to 1)	9
1059 TAITS CLOCK (Ire) 7-11-11 (3⁰) K Whelan, ... (7 to 1)	10
SHARONS PRIDE (Ire) 6-11-1 (3⁰) J R Barry, ... (16 to 1)	11
1242⁷ RISZARD (USA) 7-12-0 J P Broderick, ... (10 to 1)	12
741 BAY COTTAGE (Ire) 7-11-1 (3⁰) D J Casey, ... (14 to 1)	13
LISNAGAR LAKE (Ire) 6-11-9 S H O'Donovan, ... (20 to 1)	14
1170⁸ KILLERK LADY (Ire) 5-10-12 T P Treacy, ... (25 to 1)	15
1058 SWINGER (Ire) 7-12-0 G M O'Neill, ... (14 to 1)	16
Dist: 15l, ¾l, 4½l, ¾l. 4m 16.90s. (16 Ran).	

(Patrick O'Leary), Patrick O'Leary

1363 Thurles Handicap Chase (0-102 4-y-o and up) £2,226 2¾m....... (3:30)

1191⁹ BROOK HILL LADY (Ire) [-] 7-12-0 C F Swan, ... (11 to 2)	1
1003⁷ CASTALINO [-] 10-11-5 C O'Dwyer, ... (6 to 1)	2
1245⁴ STEEL DAWN [-] 9-11-7 (3⁰) J R Barry, ... (5 to 1)	3
1245* MACAUNTA (Ire) [-] 6-10-6 J P Broderick, ... (7 to 4 fav)	4
1003⁸ ROSSI NOVAE [-] (bl) 13-9-11 T P Treacy, ... (16 to 1)	5
ROSEEN (Ire) [-] 7-10-12 W Slattery, ... (20 to 1)	6
1245 ANOTHER COURSE (Ire) [-] 8-10-3 D H O'Connor, (12 to 1)	7
1191⁸ WALKERS LADY (Ire) [-] 8-10-6 D T Evans, ... (8 to 1)	8
BUCK CASTLE (Ire) [-] 8-10-5 S H O'Donovan, ... (10 to 1)	9
Dist: 1l, 10l, 1l, 12l. 5m 52.60s. (9 Ran).	

(James Foxe), A P O'Brien

1364 Toboradora I.N.H. Flat Race (4 & 5-y-o) £2,226 2m.................. (4:00)

1096⁵ YASHGANS VISION (Ire) 5-11-2 (7⁰) Mr E Sheehy, (12 to 1)	1
278⁶ RACHEL'S SWALLOW (Ire) 4-11-1 (3⁰) Mr R O'Neill, (9 to 1)	2
1143² CHARLIE-O (Ire) 4-11-2 (7⁰) Mr D P Daly, ... (9 to 2 fav)	3
782 BOPTWOPHAR (Ire) 4-11-9 Mr A J Martin, ... (6 to 1)	4
1246⁵ FEAR CISTE (Ire) 5-11-11 (3⁰) Mr R Walsh, ... (5 to 1)	5
1093⁴ PORT NA SON (Ire) 5-11-7 (7⁰) Mr D A Harney, ... (8 to 1)	6
1147⁷ MALABRACKA (Ire) 5-11-2 (7⁰) Mr N D Fehily, ... (20 to 1)	7
TALKALOT (Ire) 5-12-0 Mr P Fenton, ... (11 to 2)	8
1174⁵ FOYLE WANDERER (Ire) 5-11-2 (7⁰) Miss S McDonogh,	
.... (9 to 1)	9
SARAH SUPREME (Ire) 5-11-2 (7⁰) Mr J T Murphy, ... (8 to 1)	10
945⁵ KAITHEY CHOICE (Ire) 5-11-2 (7⁰) Mr J Boland, ... (10 to 1)	11
MELVILLE ROSE (Ire) 4-10-11 (7⁰) Mr V P O'Brien, (20 to 1)	12
RAMBLE ARIS (Ire) 5-11-2 (7⁰) Mr D J Kenneally, ... (16 to 1)	13
1195 HARAS ROSE (Ire) 5-11-2 (7⁰) Mr J P McNamara, (33 to 1)	14
DIVINE LILY (Ire) 5-11-2 (7⁰) Mr C A Murphy, ... (33 to 1)	15
1195 EVE'S DAUGHTER (Ire) 5-11-2 (7⁰) Mr John P Moloney,	
.... (33 to 1)	16
PHARAWAYDREAM (Ire) 4-11-9 Mr J P Dempsey, (10 to 1)	bd
1060⁶ THE TOLLAH (Ire) 4-11-2 (7⁰) Mr G Elliott, ... (10 to 1)	su
Dist: ¾l, sht-hd, 2l, hd. 4m 25.40s. (18 Ran).	

(Peter Moran), Peter Moran

TOWCESTER (good)
Thursday November 14th

Going Correction: PLUS 0.35 sec. per fur. (races 1,3,5,6), PLUS 0.20 (2,4)

1365 Flurry Knox Selling Hurdle Class G (4-7-y-o) £2,115 2m............ (1:20)

WILLY STAR (Bel) 6-10-12 Richard Guest, hld up, not fluent 1st 2, cld 5th, pushed alng aftr 3 out, hit nxt, sn mstk last, ran on.................... (4 to 1 op 5 to 1 tchd 6 to 1)	1
TAMANDU 6-11-0 Mr E James, led, hit 2 out, sn hdd, no extr. .... (11 to 4 op 7 to 4 tchd 3 to 1)	2
CROSS TALK (Ire) 4-10-12 J Osborne, not fluent, hld up, clsg whn mstk 5th, one pace appr 2 out.	
.... (6 to 5 fav op Evens tchd 5 to 4)	3
1130³ MY HARVINSKI 6-10-5 (7⁰) Miss E J Jones, trkd ldrs, rdn 5th, wkng whn mstk 3 out.... (12 to 1 op 8 to 1 tchd 14 to 1)	4
1056 JUST FOR A REASON 4-10-12 W Marston, chsd ldrs, wknd und pres appr 2 out...... (15 to 2 op 6 to 1 tchd 8 to 1)	5
BROWN EYED GIRL 4-10-7 C Llewellyn, chsd ldrs, cld 4th, rdn and wknd aftr 3 out. (20 to 1 op 10 to 1 tchd 25 to 1)	6
693 AUTUMN FLAME 5-10-7 M Brennan, pld hrd, hld up beh, outpcd aftr 5th....... (16 to 1 op 14 to 1 tchd 20 to 1)	7
53⁸ DERRYBELLE 5-10-7 M Clarke, cl up till wknd appr 3 out, tld off..................... (14 to 1 op 7 to 1 tchd 16 to 1)	8
MASTER UPEX 4-10-6¹ (7⁰) W Greatrex, not fluent, al beh, tld off.................. (12 to 1 op 16 to 1 tchd 33 to 1)	9
1053 OLDEN DAYS 4-10-12 J Lawrence, stried slwly, beh whn reminders 4th, tld off whn pld up bef 2 out.	
.... (20 to 1 op 8 to 1 tchd 25 to 1)	pu
Dist: 6l, ½l, 14l, 3½l, 5l, 2l, dist, 11l. 3m 55.50s. a 12.50s (10 Ran).	
SR: 15/11/8/-/-/-/	

(Mrs S Smith), Mrs S J Smith

1366 Tiffield Handicap Chase Class D (0-125 5-y-o and up) £3,738 3m 1f
.... (1:50)

168

BALLYEA BOY (Ire) [101] 6-11-6 A Maguire, *jmpd soundly, trkd ldrs, led tenth to last, rallied und pres to ld nr finish.*
................................(3 to 1 op 2 to 1) 1
1140⁴ ARDCRONEY CHIEF [90] 10-10-9 R Dunwoody, *cl up gng wl, led last, hrd rdn, hdd nr finish.*.........(5 to 1 op 4 to 1) 2
1165² CELTIC SILVER [93] 8-10-12 Richard Guest, *hld up in last pl, cld appr 12th, rdn and outpcd approaching 2 out, rallied and squeezed out last, one pace*......(7 to 4 fav tchd 2 to 1) 3
1231* DRUMCULLEN [102] 7-11-0 (7*,6ex) Mr R Wakley, *led to tenth, wknd 13th.*.........(4 to 1 op 3 to 1 tchd 9 to 2) 4
NICKLUP [105] 9-11-10 A Thornton, *f second.*
................................(9 to 2 op 4 to 1 tchd 5 to 1) f
Dist: Nk, 4l, dist. 6m 23.70s. a 11.70s (5 Ran).
SR: 25/14/13/-/-/ (Denis Barry), D Nicholson

1367 Keyline Builders' Merchants Novices' Handicap Hurdle Class E (0-100 4-y-o and up) £2,302 2m
.... (2:20)

1047* RANGITIKEI (NZ) [97] 5-12-0 R Dunwoody, *trkd ldr, led aftr 3 out, blun nxt, clr whn mstk last, eased nr finish.*
................................(13 to 8 fav op 6 to 4 tchd 7 to 4) 1
1220³ MR POPPLETON [69] 7-10-0 J Osborne, *led till aftr 3 out, one pace.*................................(5 to 1 op 5 to 2) 2
506³ WITNEY-DE-BERGERAC (Ire) [90] 4-11-7 W McFarland, *hld up, cld appr 3 out, one pace approaching nxt.*
................................(5 to 2 op 2 to 1) 3
60⁹ SHERS DELIGHT (Ire) [88] 6-11-5 M Brennan, *trkd ldrs, rdn and wknd aftr 3 out.*................(5 to 1 op 4 to 1) 4
1155⁴ ERNEST WILLIAM (Ire) [75] 4-10-3 (3*) K Gaule, *hld up, cld 3rd, blun nxt, not reco'r, tld off.*
................................(11 to 2 op 5 to 1 tchd 6 to 1) 5
SWING LUCKY [70] 11-10-11 D Skyrme, *hld up, lost tch 3rd, al beh, tld off.*................(16 to 1 op 10 to 1) 6
1205 BOLD CHARLIE [69] 4-10-0 N Mann, *cl up, lost pl 3rd, outpcd approaching 3 out, tld off.*
................................(9 to 1 op 16 to 1 tchd 33 to 1) 7
Dist: 6l, 3½l, 13l, 22l, 1½l, 6l. 3m 56.00s. a 13.00s (7 Ran).
SR: 26/-/9/-/ (Mrs J M Mayo), C J Mann

1368 Irish R M Novices' Chase Class E (4-y-o and up) £3,104 2m 110yds (2:50)

SECOND CALL 7-10-12 R Dunwoody, *made most to 7th, shaken up to ld 2 out, sn clr, easily.*...........(15 to 8 jt-fav op 9 to 4 tchd 7 to 4) 1
1232 KEY TO MOYADE (Ire) 6-11-3 I Lawrence, *trkd ldrs, led 7th to nxt, led 9th to 2 out, no extr und pres.*
................................(9 to 1 op 10 to 1 tchd 14 to 1) 2
THINKING TWICE (USA) 7-11-3 J Kavanagh, *rstrained in rear aftr 1st, pushed alng 4 out, btn nxt.*........(15 to 8 jt-fav op 5 to 4 tchd 7 to 4) 3
1216⁵ COPPER CABLE 9-11-3 M Ranger, *cl up till wknd aftr 4 out.*................(50 to 1 op 25 to 1 tchd 66 to 1) 4
1202⁷ UPHAM RASCAL 5-11-3 S Wynne, *f 1st.*
................................(50 to 1 op 20 to 1) f
248⁵ ROLFE (NZ) (Ire) 6-11-3 A Maguire, *hld up, blun 5th, hdwy to ld 8th, hdd nxt, not fluent and wknd quickly 3 out, pld up bef next, broke blood vessel.*........(2 to 1 op 5 to 4 tchd 9 to 4) pu
Dist: 14l, 13l, 5l. 4m 10.90s. a 13.90s (6 Ran).
(J H Day), Capt T A Forster

1369 Moonlighter Mares Only 'National Hunt' Novices' Hurdle Class B (4-y-o and up) £2,407 2m...........(3:20)

1214² POTTER'S GALE (Ire) 5-10-7 A Maguire, *pld hrd, hld up, hdwy appr 3 out, led nxt, cmftbly.*
................................(6 to 4 on op 5 to 4 on tchd 7 to 4 on) 1
648⁴ MARLOUSION (Ire) 4-10-7 D Gallagher, *al cl up, ev ch 3 out to nxt, one pace.*............(9 to 1 op 6 to 1 tchd 10 to 1) 2
LADY HIGH SHERIFF (Ire) 6-10-7 S Wynne, *led to 3rd, cl up till outpcd 3 out, kpt on.*
................................(16 to 1 op 12 to 1 tchd 20 to 1) 3
BRIDGE DELIGHT 7-10-0 (7*) D C O'Connor, *hld up, pld hrd, mstk 5th, hdwy and ev ch 3 out, one pace nxt.*
................................(40 to 1 op 33 to 1 tchd 50 to 1) 4
MOOR HALL LADY 5-10-7 W Marston, *wth ldrs, led 3 out to nxt, no extr.*................(12 to 1 tchd 16 to 1) 5
DARK PHOENIX (Ire) 6-10-7 M Brennan, *pld hrd, cl up, led 3rd to 3 out, ev ch appr nxt, sn wknd.*
................................(16 to 1 op 12 to 1 tchd 20 to 1) 6
RIVER BAY (Ire) 5-10-7 J Osborne, *mstk 1st, trkd ldrs till rdn and wknd aftr 3 out.*......(9 to 2 op 3 to 1 tchd 5 to 1) 7
MAYLIN MAGIC 5-10-7 R Dunwoody, *hld up beh ldrs, rdn and outpcd aftr 3 out.*......(5 to 1 op 3 to 1 tchd 11 to 2) 8
1053 BEL-DE-MOOR 4-10-7 C Llewellyn, *al beh.*
................................(50 to 1 op 25 to 1) 9
MISS MYLETTE (Ire) 5-10-7 R Bellamy, *al beh, tld off.*
................................(50 to 1 op 25 to 1) 10
SEPTEMBER BREEZE (Ire) 5-10-7 R Garritty, *chsd ldrs, outpcd 3 out, sn drvn, 6th and btn whn f last.*
................................(25 to 1 op 14 to 1) f
Dist: 5l, 1½l, ¾l, 2l, hd, 2½l, hd, 8l, 14l. 3m 59.70s. a 16.70s (11 Ran).
(J E Potter), D Nicholson

1370 Wicken Handicap Hurdle Class D (0-120 4-y-o and up) £2,951 2m 5f
.... (3:50)

EUPHONIC [92] 6-10-1 J Osborne, *settled beh ldrs, cld 4 out, led appr 2 out, pushed out.*
................................(11 to 4 fav op 2 to 1 tchd 7 to 2) 1
1132³ SILVER STANDARD [100] (bl) 6-10-9 S Wynne, *trkd ldrs, rdn 3 out, kpt on one pace und pres frm last.*
................................(3 to 1 op 7 to 2 tchd 4 to 1) 2
1132² FORTUNES COURSE (Ire) [111] 7-10-13 (7*) Mr A Wintle, *cl up, lft in ld appr 3 out, hdd approaching nxt, one pace.*
................................(3 to 1 tchd 7 to 2) 3
1141⁶ DAHLIA'S BEST (USA) [97] 6-10-6 Gary Lyons, *hld up, cld 4 out, hrd ridden and one pace appr 2 out.*
................................(33 to 1 op 20 to 1 tchd 40 to 1) 4
1213 LA MENORQUINA (USA) [97] 6-10-6 J A McCarthy, *hld up, hdwy 7th, rdn and one pace aftr 3 out.*
................................(8 to 1 tchd 10 to 1 and 13 to 2) 5
BRAES OF MAR [119] 6-11-7 (7*) T C Murphy, *trkd ldrs, pushed alng appr 7th, btn approaching 3 out.*
................................(9 to 1 op 5 to 1) 6
MERILENA (Ire) [91] 6-9-13⁶ (7*) N Rossiter, *led to 3rd, cl up till wknd quickly appr 3 out, tld off.*
................................(11 to 1 op 10 to 1 tchd 16 to 1) 7
PYRAMIS PRINCE (Ire) [103] 6-10-12 A Maguire, *led 3rd till hdd and pld up lme appr 3 out.*......(16 to 1 op 12 to 1) pu
1048⁵ CLEAN EDGE (USA) [105] 4-10-11 (3*) E Husband, *strted slwly, beh whn pld up aftr 7th, broke leg, destroyed.*
................................(6 to 1 op 7 to 1 tchd 8 to 1 and 5 to 1) pu
Dist: 2l, 2l, 3l, 2l, 11l, 29l. 5m 16.50s. a 17.50s (9 Ran).
(Paul Stamp), I A Balding

AYR (good)
Friday November 15th
Going Correction: PLUS 0.35 sec. per fur. (races 1,2,3,5,7), PLUS 0.25 (4,6)

1371 Galloway Hills Maiden Hurdle Class E (Div I) (4-y-o and up) £1,996 2m
.... (12:25)

1182² ENDOWMENT (bl) 4-11-5 P Niven, *made all, clr whn mstks 3 out and nxt, chlgd last, ran on wl.*
................................(5 to 4 fav op 11 to 10 on tchd 6 to 4) 1
1224³ GRANDINARE (USA) (bl) 4-11-5 M Dwyer, *chsd wnr thrght, ev ch whn slight mstk last, one pace.*......(9 to 2 op 4 to 1) 2
BILL'S PRIDE 5-11-0 A Dobbin, *beh, moderate hdwy appr 3 out, nvr a factor.*................................(50 to 1) 3
BOWCLIFFE 5-11-5 J Supple, *in tch, rdn and outpcd appr 3 out, sn no dngr.*................(20 to 1 op 8 to 1) 4
PUBLIC WAY (Ire) 6-10-12 (7*) Miss C Metcalfe, *midfield, struggling frm 4 out, sn beh.*........(100 to 1 op 33 to 1) 5
PERCY PARROT 4-11-5 B Harding, *beh, tld off frm 4 out.*
................................(20 to 1 op 12 to 1) 6
LOVEYOUMILLIONS (Ire) 4-11-5 L Wyer, *not fluent, hdwy into midfield hfwy, outpcd 4 out, sn tld off.*.(10 to 1 op 5 to 1) 7
35⁶ GRINNELL (v) 5-11-5 K Johnson, *hld up, tld off whn blun 4 out.*................(200 to 1 op 50 to 1) 8
740 SMART IN SOCKS 5-11-5 A Thornton, *mstk 3rd, tld off frm 4 out.*................................(33 to 1 op 14 to 1) 9
FILS DE CRESSON (Ire) 6-11-5 J Railton, *midfield, keen hold, hdwy to chase ldrs whn o'rjmpd and f 5th.*
................................(8 to 1 op 11 to 1 tchd 7 to 1) f
GALLANT MAJOR 4-11-5 J Burke, *pld hrd, blun 1st, tld off frm 4 out, pulled up appr 2 out.*...(100 to 1 op 33 to 1) pu
Dist: 3l, 27l, 3½l, 9l, 21½l, 27l, dist, 1l. 3m 47.90s. a 11.90s (11 Ran).
SR: 28/25/-/-/-/-/ (R Hilley), Mrs M Reveley

1372 Mossblown Conditional Jockeys' Selling Handicap Hurdle Class G (0-95 4-y-o and up) £1,982 2½m
.... (12:55)

1038³ LATIN LEADER [81] (bl) 6-11-5 D Parker, *midfield, hdwy on bit to chal 3 out, slight ld nxt, drvn out r-in...*(4 to 1 op 5 to 1) 1
817³ TALL MEASURE [85] (bl) 10-11-9 G Cahill, *led, strly pressed 3 out, hdd nxt, kpt on stdly.*.(5 to 1 tchd 9 to 2 and 6 to 1) 2
1068³ HIGHLAND PARK [82] 10-11-1 (5*) C McCormack, *in tch, pushed alng hfwy, unbl to quicken 2 out, styd on r-in.*
................................(9 to 2 op 5 to 1 tchd 6 to 1) 3
SKANE RIVER (Ire) [71] 5-10-6 (3*) M Dunne, *cl up, niggled alng 4 out, hld in 3rd whn mistake last.*
................................(7 to 2 fav tchd 3 to 1) 4
NAWTINOOKEY [62] 6-10-0 G Lee, *chsd ldrs, hit 4th, unbl to quicken appr 2 out, btn whn mstk last.*
................................(33 to 1 tchd 66 to 1) 5
1257⁴ CHUMMY'S SAGA [69] 6-10-0 (7*) I Jardine, *rear, hdwy to chase ldrs 5 out, drvn and no extr frm 2 out.*
................................(10 to 1 op 5 to 1 tchd 14 to 1) 6
WE'RE IN THE MONEY [62] 12-9-7 (7*) Miss C Froggitt, *beh, mstk 6th, nvr dngrs.*................(33 to 1 tchd 50 to 1) 7
TROY'S DREAM [76] 5-10-9 (5*) R Burns, *midfield, mstk 4 out, outpcd nxt, sn lost tch.*................(8 to 1 op 11 to 2) 8

1070 SAYRAF DANCER (Ire) [76] 7-11-0 J Supple, *mstk second, wnt prmnt 5th, wknd quickly frm 4 out, tld off.*
................................(14 to 1 op 12 to 1 tchd 16 to 1) 9
1257 CIRCLE BOY [68] 9-10-6 R McGrath, *al beh, lost tch appr 4 out, tld off.*.................(13 to 2 op 4 to 1 tchd 7 to 1) 10
864⁵ LATVIAN [86] (v) 9-11-7 (3*) S Melrose, *hld up, in tch whn hit 7th, wknd quickly, tld off.*...............(25 to 1 op 12 to 1) 11
Dist: 4l, 1l, 2l, 3½l, hd, 18l, 6l, 6l, ¾l, 15l. 4m 59.60s. a 21.60s (11 Ran).
(Mr & Mrs Raymond Anderson Green), C Parker

1373 Galloway Hills Maiden Hurdle Class E (Div II) (4-y-o and up) £1,982 2m
.... (1:30)

CLARE MAID (Ire) 7-11-0 A Dobbin, *chsd ldrs gng wl, led 3 out, clr betw last 2, readily.*.............(3 to 1 op 9 to 4) 1
JAUNTY GENERAL 5-11-5 B Storey, *sn led, hdd 3 out, kpt on, no ch wth wnr.*........................(7 to 1 op 5 to 1) 2
1122⁵ FENIAN COURT (Ire) 5-11-0 A S Smith, *settled rear, hdwy 3 out, outpcd nxt, kpt on r-in.*...........(16 to 1 op 14 to 1) 3
1034 MULLINS (Ire) 5-11-5 D J Moffatt, *chsd ldr, rdn and outpcd whn hit fluent 2 out, no extr.*.......(25 to 1 op 20 to 1) 4
SUNNY LEITH 5-11-2 (3*) G Cahill, *keen hold, rcd midfield till outpcd 3 out, sn one pace.*......................(50 to 1) 5
1123³ GOLF LAND (Ire) 4-11-5 M Dwyer, *chsd ldrs, mstk 4 out, ev ch whn hit nxt, fdd.*.........(9 to 4 fav op 5 to 2 tchd 3 to 1) 6
AKITO RACING (Ire) 5-11-0 P Niven, *pld hrd, drvn alng 5th, no dngr frm nxt.*.......................(50 to 1 op 25 to 1) 7
1016 DARA KNIGHT (Ire) 7-11-5 Gerard Martin, *hld up, effrt hfwy, blun 4 out, lost tch nxt, tld off.*...................(50 to 1) 8
JARROW 5-11-5 J Supple, *hld up, f 4th.*..........(20 to 1) f
JUDICIOUS NORMAN (Ire) 5-11-5 J Railton, *led till jinked sharply lft and uns rdr 1st.* (3 to 1 tchd 7 to 2 and 4 to 1) ur
Dist: 4l, 2½l, 5l, 7l, 6l, 8l, dist. 3m 54.20s. a 18.20s (10 Ran).
(Leslie Lowry), G Richards

1374 Glengoyne Highland Malt Tamerosia Series Qualifier Novices' Chase Class D (5-y-o and up) £3,675 2m
.... (2:05)

SPARKY GAYLE (Ire) 6-11-0 B Storey, *midfield, gd hdwy 8th, led and quickened 2 out, sn clr, imprsv.*..........(2 to 1 jt-fav op 6 to 4 tchd 5 to 2) 1
BOLD BOSS 7-11-0 N Bentley, *str hold, led 6th, pushed clr aftr 5 out, mstk nxt, hdd and no extr frm 2 out.*
.....................(11 to 2 op 6 to 1 tchd 5 to 1) 2
JACK DOYLE (Ire) 5-11-0 M Dwyer, *patiently rdn, hdwy gng wl fnl circuit, chasing ldrs whn blun 3 out, no imprsn aftr, better for race.*.........(8 to 1 op 4 to 1 tchd 9 to 1) 3
934⁷ MUSIC BLITZ 5-11-0 T Reed, *chsd ldrs thrght, rdn and one pace appr 3 out.*.....................(33 to 1) 4
1035² CASTLEROYAL (Ire) 7-11-6 L Wyer, *wth ldr, not fluent, rdn and outpcd 4 out, fnshd lme.*...................(2 to 1 jt-fav op 3 to 1 tchd 9 to 2) 5
1258⁷ NIJWAY 6-11-0 J Burke, *led, hit 5th, hdd nxt, jmpd poorly aftr, lost whn blun and rdr lost irons last.*...........(100 to 1) 6
864⁵ BOLANEY GIRL (Ire) 7-10-9 R Supple, *led in at strt, hld up, hdwy 7th, pushed alng whn blun 4 out, sn no extr.*
........................(33 to 1 op 16 to 1) 7
UK HYGIENE 6-11-0 R Garritty, *hld up, outpcd aftr 5 out, nvr a factor.*........................(20 to 1 op 14 to 1) 8
CROSSHOT 9-11-0 K Jones, *chsd ldrs, niggled alng appr 4 out, sn lost tch.*...................(50 to 1 op 33 to 1) 9
SINGING SAND 6-11-0 A Dobbin, *beh whn blun badly 7th, nvr dngrs.*......................(33 to 1 op 20 to 1) 10
GRAND AS OWT 6-11-0 K Johnson, *al towards rear.*
.....................(200 to 1 op 100 to 1) 11
1022⁴ DEVILRY 6-11-6 A S Smith, *hld up, mstk and drpd rear 4th, wl beh aftr.*..............................(17 to 1) 12
1258 FINE TUNE (Ire) 6-11-0 A Thornton, *wth ldrs, mstk 8th, sn lost tch, tld off.*........................(100 to 1 op 100 to 1) 13
PAINT YOUR WAGON 6-11-0 D J Moffatt, *sn tld off, blun and uns rdr 3rd.*...................(200 to 1 op 100 to 1) ur
Dist: 12l, 4l, 1¾l, 7l, 1l, nk, 3l, 3l, 1½l, 16l. 3m 55.20s. a 10.20s (14 Ran).
SR: 24/12/8/6/5/-/   (Mr & Mrs Raymond Anderson Green), C Parker

1375 Fiveways Handicap Hurdle Class C (0-130 4-y-o and up) £3,415 3m 110yds.
.... (2:40)

1251⁴ LOCHNAGRAIN (Ire) [113] 8-11-2 (5ex) P Niven, *chsd ldrs, led fluent, chlgd 3 out, jmpd lft last, ran on strly und press to ld post.*..........(6 to 4 on op 5 to 4 on tchd 11 to 10 on) 1
550² HUSO [97] 8-9-9 (5*) S Taylor, *in tch, hdwy whn hit 4 out, slight ld nxt, kpt on strly till st post.*...........(7 to 1 op 5 to 1) 2
1265³ PHARARE (Ire) [97] 6-10-0 L Wyer, *led, rdn and hdd 3 out, fdd betw last 2.*...................(3 to 1 tchd 7 to 2) 3
PALACEGATE KING [125] 7-11-9 (5*) E Callaghan, *steadied rear, niggled alng to chase ldrs appr 3 out, wknd aftr 2 out.*
.....................(11 to 1 op 5 to 1 tchd 12 to 1) 4
DIG DEEPER [104] 9-10-7 A Dobbin, *chsd ldr, pld hrd, lost pl appr 3 out, sn wl beh.*...............(20 to 1 op 16 to 1) 5
MARCHWOOD [97] 9-9-8¹ (7*) Miss C Metcalfe, *not fluent in rear, blun 8th, tld off appr 4 out.*...(25 to 1 op 10 to 1) 6
Dist: Sht-hd, 14l, 5l, 19l, 5l. 6m 3.50s. a 22.50s (6 Ran).
(Lightbody Of Hamilton Ltd), Mrs M Reveley

1376 Joan Mackay Novices' Handicap Chase Class D (0-105 5-y-o and up) £3,616 2½m
.................(3:15)

MONNAIE FORTE (Ire) [90] 6-11-0 J Railton, *midfield, outpcd 4 out, moderate 3rd whn lft clr last.*.....(12 to 1 op 8 to 1) 1
BELLS HILL LAD [83] 9-10-7 A Dobbin, *chsd ldr, drvn alng appr 3 out, sn no ch whn lft second last.*(14 to 1 tchd 16 to 1) 2
1014⁴ DIAMOND SPRITE (USA) [79] 9-10-3 Gerard Martin, *beh, not fluent 9th, tld off frm 6 out.*.........(25 to 1 op 20 to 1) 3
1138 JYMJAM JOHNNY (Ire) [100] 7-11-10 M Dwyer, *hld up, keen hold, chlgd gng wl whn mstk 3 out, cl up and ev ch when f last, rmntd.*.......................(2 to 1 op 7 to 4) 4
1258⁴ SHOW YOUR HAND (Ire) [80] 8-10-4 M Foster, *led, hit second, strly pressed 3 out, not fluent nxt, jst ahead whn f last.*
.....................(10 to 1 op 8 to 1 tchd 12 to 1) f
1281³ BLUE CHARM (Ire) [93] 6-11-3 R Garritty, *chsd ldrs, f 5th.*
.....................(10 to 1 op on Evens tchd 11 to 10) f
1072 SEE YOU ALWAYS (Ire) [76] 6-10-0 B Storey, *in tch, hmpd and uns rdr 5th.*.......................(33 to 1) ur
Dist: 10l, dist, dist. 5m 16.30s. a 29.30s (7 Ran).
(James R Adam), J R Adam

1377 Lagg 'National Hunt' Novices' Hurdle Class E (4-y-o and up) £2,402 3m 110yds.
.... (3:45)

1162² TRAP DANCER 8-10-12 A Dobbin, *in tch, led 4 out, pushed clr betw last 2, styd on strly.*
.....................(3 to 1 op 5 to 2 tchd 100 to 30) 1
BOLD FOUNTAIN 5-10-12 N Bentley, *hld up, not jump wl, chlgd 3 out, mstk nxt, btn whn hit last.*
.....................(Evens fav op 5 to 4 on) 2
PHAR ECHO (Ire) 5-10-12 M Foster, *beh, hdwy hfwy, chsd ldr 4 out, rdn and outpcd appr 2 out.*.....(10 to 1 op 6 to 1) 3
POCAIRE GAOITHE (Ire) 6-10-12 M Moloney, *pushed alng to track ldrs 7th, reminders and outpcd appr 3 out, styd on ag'n frm last.*......................(25 to 1 op 16 to 1) 4
ALNBROOK 5-10-12 K Johnson, *chsd ldrs, keen hold, mstk 5th, outpcd whn hit 2 out, sn btn.*
.....................(25 to 1 op 20 to 1 tchd 33 to 1) 5
1162⁶ ETHICAL NOTE (Ire) 5-10-5 (7*) R Wilkinson, *made most till hdd 4 out, rdn and wknd frm nxt.*.......(25 to 1 op 12 to 1) 6
934 WILLIE WANNABE (Ire) 6-10-12 T Reed, *midfield, drpd rear whn hit 7th, no dngr aftr.*...........(100 to 1 op 50 to 1) 7
JIGGINSTOWN 9-10-12 A Roche, *hld up towards rear, lost tch 5 out, sn wl beh.*.....(15 to 2 op 6 to 1 tchd 8 to 1) 8
1257⁸ MEADOWLICK 7-10-7 B Storey, *wth ldr, led briefly 7th, wknd quickly frm 4 out, tld off.*.........(100 to 1 op 50 to 1) 9
1162⁵ PROFIT AND LOSS 5-10-7 M Dwyer, *hld up, lost tch appr 4 out, tld off whn pld up bef nxt.*.........(12 to 1 op 7 to 1) pu
SMART IN SATIN 6-10-12 A Thornton, *jmpd slwly, al towards rear, pld up bef 4 out.*............(33 to 1 op 20 to 1) pu
Dist: 7l, 10l, sht-hd, 3l, 14l, 3½l, 12l, 11l. 6m 12.90s. a 31.90s (11 Ran).
(A Dawson), P Monteith

CHELTENHAM (good to firm)
Friday November 15th
Going Correction: PLUS 0.10 sec. per fur. (races 1,3,5), PLUS 0.30 (2,4,6)

1378 Coln Valley Fish And Game Company Amateur Riders' Handicap Chase Class E (0-130 5-y-o and up) £3,160 2½m 110yds.
.................(1:15)

1274³ DANCING VISION (Ire) [105] 6-10-1¹ (7*) Mr J T McNamara, *hld up rear, chalg whn hmpd and mstk 3 out, rallied to ld last, pushed out.*......................(4 to 1 tchd 9 to 2) 1
1011⁷ COOLBEE (Ire) [109] 8-10-4 (7*) Mr J Tizzard, *not fluent, hld up, hdwy 6th, jmpd rght and mstk 3 out, led briefly appr last, hng rght r-in, no imprsn.*............(9 to 4 fav op 6 to 4) 2
1219 MAN MOOD (Fr) [112] 5-10-6 (7*) Mr E James, *hld up, hdwy 8th, led aftr 2 out till appr last, wknd r-in.*
.....................(16 to 1 op 10 to 1) 3
1177³ CROPREDY LAD [98] 9-9-10³ (7*) Mr P Scott, *led to 5th, led 11th till aftr 2 out, wknd.*(11 to 1 op 10 to 1 tchd 12 to 1) 4
1011² OSCAIL AN DORAS (Ire) [108] 7-10-5 (5*) Mr R Thornton, *prmnt to 8th, rallied tenth, rdn appr 3 out, wknd bef nxt.*
.....................(11 to 4 op 2 to 1 tchd 3 to 1) 5
SPANISH LIGHT (Ire) [122] 7-11-8⁵ (7*) Mr D Barlow, *pld hrd, trkd ldr, led 5th to 11th, wknd quickly aftr 4 out, tld off whn pulled up bef last.*................(4 to 1 tchd 9 to 2) pu
Dist: 1¾l, 8l, 6l, 10l. 5m 9.20s. a 12.20s (6 Ran).
(James Carey), Eric McNamara

1379 Scudamore Clothing 0800 301 301 Novices' Hurdle Class C (4-y-o and up) £3,680 2m 5f.............. (1:50)

HUNTING LORE 5-11-8 M A Fitzgerald, *not fluent, trkd ldrs, outpcd 7th, styd on frm 2 out, led fnl 50 yards.*
.....................(9 to 4 op 5 to 4) 1

263² SUPERMODEL 4-10-8 (5*) Mr R Thornton, *hld up early, hdwy 5th, rng on whn lft second 3 out, led nxt, wknd quickly appr last, hdd fnl 50 yards, tired.*
..............................(20 to 1 op 14 to 1 tchd 25 to 1) 2
1313³ LEAP IN THE DARK (Ire) 7-11-0 A Maguire, *mid-div, hdwy 6th, one pace frm 3 out.*.................(66 to 1 op 25 to 1) 3
1217 OPERETTO (Ire) 6-11-0 Mr E James, *wl beh frm 3rd.*
..............................(66 to 1 op 25 to 1) 4
BLAAZIING JOE (Ire) 5-11-0 P Holley, *mstk 4th, mid-div till wknd 6th, tld off.*..................(66 to 1 op 25 to 1) 5
1105* COURBARIL 4-11-8 A P McCoy, *led, clr till stumbled and f on landing 3 out.*...................(11 to 8 on op 5 to 4) f
997* EDGEMOOR PRINCE 5-11-4 R Dunwoody, *trkd ldr, lft in ld 3 out, hdd nxt, cl 3rd whn slpd on landing last, not reco'r, pld up.*
..............................(7 to 1 op 6 to 1 tchd 8 to 1) pu
Dist: 1¼l, 9l, 1¾l, dist. 5m 14.60s. a 18.60s (7 Ran).
(Milton Ritzenberg), N J Henderson

1380 Mitsubishi Shogun Handicap Chase Class B (0-145 5-y-o and up) £6,827 2m............................(2:25)

1514⁴ KONVEKTA KING (Ire) [125] 8-11-2 J Osborne, *led to 3rd, trkd ldr till blun 4 out, rallied und pres aftr 2 out, led last, ran on.*
..............................(10 to 1 op 8 to 1 tchd 11 to 1) 1
1131² SOUTHAMPTON [120] (v) 6-10-11 A P McCoy, *hld up, hdwy and wnt second 4 out, chalg whn pckd 2 out, ev ch till one pace r-in.*..............................(11 to 8 fav op Evens) 2
LORD DORCET (Ire) [133] 6-11-10 R Dunwoody, *jmpd wl, led and wknd r-in.*.....(6 to 4 op 2 to 1 tchd 11 to 8) 3
964³ CAPTAIN KHEDIVE [130] 8-11-7 A Maguire, *al last, hit second and 7th, nvr on terms.*....(9 to 2 op 4 to 1 tchd 5 to 1) 4
Dist: 2½l, 4l, 29l. 3m 58.20s. a 6.20s (4 Ran).
SR: 42/34/43/11/ (Konvekta Ltd), O Sherwood

1381 Murphy's 'In A Bottle' Hurdle Class B (4-y-o) £5,512 2m 110yds.....(3:00)

883* JUST LITTLE 10-12 C F Swan, *confidently rdn, hld up, hdwy on bit to ld last, sn clr.*..........(13 to 8 on op 11 to 8 on) 1
1148⁴ MIM-LOU-AND 11-0 J Osborne, *trkd ldr, chalg whn jmpd slwly 3 out, led aftr nxt, hdd last, one pace.*
..............................(9 to 2 op 6 to 1 tchd 13 to 2) 2
1182⁵ SAMANID (Ire) 11-3 A Maguire, *led till aftr 2 out, wknd quickly.*...................(25 to 1 op 14 to 1 tchd 33 to 1) 3
1340 DANJING (Ire) (bl) 11-3 A P McCoy, *refused to race, took no part.*.......................(3 to 1 op 6 to 4) r
Dist: 7l, 21l. 3m 58.80s. a 9.80s (4 Ran).
SR: 36/31/13/-/ (Seamus O'Farrell), A P O'Brien

1382 Steel Plate And Sections Novices' Chase Class B (5-y-o and up) £6,940 3m 1f....................(3:35)

1083² STORMTRACKER (Ire) 7-11-5 M Richards, *chsd ldr to 4th, led aftr 15th, hit four out, clr nxt, unchlgd.*
..............................(8 to 1 op 6 to 1 tchd 9 to 1) 1
877* FACTOR TEN (Ire) 8-11-8 A Maguire, *led, hit 15th, sn hdd, wknd appr 3 out, broke blood vessel.*
..............................(15 to 8 op 9 to 4 tchd 5 to 2) 2
1159² MINOR KEY (Ire) 6-11-0 J Osborne, *chsd ldr 4th till f 9th.*
..............................(25 to 1 op 20 to 1 tchd 33 to 1) f
1152* THE LAST FLING (Ire) 6-11-5 Richard Guest, *hld up, head-wawy 7th, hit nxt, lft second 9th, blun and uns rdr 14th.*
..............................(13 to 8 on tchd 6 to 4 on and 7 to 4 on) ur
Dist: Dist. 6m 34.40s. a 26.40s (4 Ran).
(Tim Davis), C Weedon

1383 Eurobale Conditional Jockeys' Handicap Hurdle Class E (0-130 4-y-o and up) £2,847 2m 5f......(4:05)

1238⁶ WORLD EXPRESS (Ire) [100] (bl) 6-10-6 D Salter, *trkd ldr, chalg whn hit 3 out, led nxt, ran on.*......(5 to 2 op 2 to 1) 1
1139 RAMSDENS (Ire) [100] (bl) 4-10-6 D Walsh, *led, rdn 3 out, hdd nxt, no extr r-in.*.. (11 to 10 on op 5 to 4 on tchd Evens) 2
1212⁶ STAUNCH RIVAL (USA) [118] 9-11-5 (5*) Clare Thorner, *al rear, lost tch 4 out, tld off whn hit rail aftr 2 out.*
..............................(7 to 1 op 8 to 1) 3
1160⁵ STONEY VALLEY [105] 6-10-6 (5*) N T Egan, *hld up rear, hit 3rd, hdwy appr 3 out, third and held whn f last.*
..............................(5 to 1 tchd 7 to 1) f
Dist: 7l, 12l. 5m 15.30s. a 19.30s (4 Ran).
(The Dragisic Partnership), B R Millman

AYR (good)
Saturday November 16th
Going Correction: PLUS 0.50 sec. per fur. (races 1,3,5,7), PLUS 0.55 (2,4,6)

1384 Sean Graham Juvenile Novices' Hurdle Class E (3-y-o) £2,346 2m (12:35)

734⁴ ROSSEL (USA) 11-4 A Dobbin, *chsd ldr, led 3 out, clr nxt, easily.*..............................(8 to 1 op 10 to 1) 1

1196² THE BOOZING BRIEF (USA) (bl) 10-12 D Parker, *led, not fluent, hdd 3 out, sn wndrd and outpcd...*(7 to 2 op 5 to 2) 2
SWYNFORD SUPREME 10-12 Derek Byrne, *al hndy, pushed alng 3 out, sn no extr.*..............(25 to 1 op 33 to 1) 3
734⁷ THORNTOUN ESTATE (Ire) 10-12 M Dwyer, *not fluent, in tch till outpcd appr 3 out, sn btn.*................(50 to 1) 4
1196⁴ RATTLE 10-7 (5*) R McGrath, *hld up, shaken up and outpcd appr 3 out, nvr dngrs.*............(66 to 1 op 33 to 1) 5
MAPLETON 10-5 (7*) R Wilkinson, *mstk 3rd, hdwy and prmnt 4 out, fdd aftr nxt.*......(14 to 1 op 10 to 1 tchd 16 to 1) 6
SOUNDS DEVIOUS 10-7 B Storey, *not fluent in rear, some hdwy appr 3 out, sn lost tch, tld off...* (33 to 1 op 25 to 1) 7
CRY BABY 10-12 M Foster, *in tch, pushed alng 4 out, fdg whn mstk nxt, tld off.*...................(14 to 1 op 12 to 1) 8
PRECIOUS GIRL 10-7 D J Moffatt, *settled rear, lost tch aftr 4 out, tld off.*............(15 to 2 op 6 to 1 tchd 8 to 1) 9
NORTHERN MOTTO 10-9 (3*) G Lee, *blun and uns rdr 1st.*
..............................(11 to 4 fav op 7 to 2 tchd 4 to 1) ur
1221² GLOBE RUNNER 10-12 A Roche, *hld up, chasing ldrs whn hit 4 out, sn drvn alng, pld up appr nxt.*
..............................(3 to 1 op 5 to 2 tchd 7 to 2) pu
Dist: 13l, 2½l, 5l, nk, 3l, 12l, 5l, 15l. 3m 50.70s. a 14.70s (11 Ran).
SR: 23/4/1/-/-/-/ (Allan W Melville), P Monteith

1385 Sean Graham Novices' Chase Class D (5-y-o and up) £3,714 3m 1f (1:05)

NAUGHTY FUTURE 7-11-0 A Roche, *hld up, not fluent tenth and 11th, chlgd 5 out, led nxt, sn clr, eased considerably r-in.*
..............................(11 to 2 op 5 to 1 tchd 9 to 2 and 6 to 1) 1
1256³ PANTARA PRINCE (Ire) 7-11-0 A Dobbin, *al chasing ldrs, drvn and outpcd 4 out, sn no extr.*
..............................(20 to 1 op 10 to 1 tchd 25 to 1) 2
KINGS SERMON (Ire) 7-11-0 R Supple, *led, mstk 3rd, blun nxt, hdd aftr tenth, hit 12th, fdd frm 4 out.*
..............................(33 to 1 op 16 to 1) 3
1197² BOLD ACCOUNT (Ire) 6-11-0 N Bentley, *chsd ldr, led aftr tenth till hdd 12th, lost tch 4 out.*
..............................(13 to 2 op 6 to 1 tchd 10 to 1) 4
841² ARRANGE A GAME 9-10-9 (5*) S Taylor, *jmpd slwly in rear, tld off frm 6 out.*................(100 to 1 op 33 to 1) 5
1226³ ROYAL PARIS (Ire) 8-11-0 T Reed, *cl up, led 12th, hdd whn f 4 out.*.......(16 to 1 op 10 to 1 tchd 20 to 1) f
THE BIRD O'DONNELL 10-10-7 (7*) Mr T J Barry, *struggling 13th, blun nxt, tld off whn pld up bef 3 out.*
..............................(4 to 1 tchd 7 to 2) pu
CROWN JEWELRY (Ire) 6-11-0 N Williamson, *virtually f and rdr lost irons 1st, sn pld up.*.........(5 to 4 fav op Evens) pu
Dist: 7l, 3l, 23l, 2l. 6m 36.00s. a 36.00s (8 Ran).
(A K Collins), J J O'Neill

1386 Sean Graham Bookmakers Handicap Hurdle Class E (0-110 4-y-o and up) £2,668 2m.....................(1:35)

932² SARMATIAN (USA) [108] 5-11-12 R Garritty, *patiently rdn, steady hdwy 3 out, led betw last 2, ran on strly und.pres.*
..............................(4 to 1 op 7 to 2 tchd 9 to 1) 1
1148² HIGHBANK [103] 4-11-4 (3*) G Lee, *hld up gng wl, hdwy and slight ld 3 out, hdd betw last 2, rallied well.*
..............................(7 to 4 fav tchd 2 to 1) 2
MISS GREENYARDS [84] 5-10-2 D Parker, *cl up, mstks sec-ond and 4th, ev ch whn not fluent 3 out, one pace frm nxt.*
..............................(7 to 2 tchd 4 to 1) 3
CITTADINO [102] 6-11-6 M Foster, *hld up, hdwy and slight ld aftr 4 out, blun and hdd nxt, fdd frm 2 out.*
..............................(4 to 1 op 9 to 2 tchd 5 to 1) 4
274⁴ TRIENNIUM (USA) [82] 7-10-0 A Dobbin, *hld up, clr order hfwy, rdn alng appr 2 out, fdd.*
..............................(17 to 2 op 10 to 1 tchd 12 to 1) 5
1141⁵ AIDE MEMOIRE (Ire) [82] 7-9-11 (3*) G Cahill, *hld up, outpcd nvr able to chal.*............(50 to 1 op 25 to 1) 6
1166⁶ MARLINGFORD [82] 9-9-9 (5*) S Taylor, *led till hdd 4th, drvn alng frm nxt, lost tch from 3 out.*.....(100 to 1 op 33 to 1) 7
FAMILIAR ART [89] 5-10-7 D J Moffatt, *wth ldr, led 4th till hdd aftr nxt, sn btn, tld off.*........(50 to 1 op 33 to 1) 8
1284 RARFY'S DREAM [110] 8-12-0 K Johnson, *midfield, strug-gling appr 4 out, tld off whn pld up bef nxt.*
..............................(100 to 1 op 50 to 1) pu
Dist: ½l, 10l, 6l, 2½l, ½l, 23l. 3m 50.50s. a 14.50s (9 Ran).
SR: 33/27/-/10/-/-/ (S T Brankin), M D Hammond

1387 Sean Graham Chase Limited Handicap Class B (5-y-o and up) £10,065 3m 1f..........................(2:10)

THE GREY MONK (Ire) [144] 8-10-5 A Dobbin, *jmpd wl, chsd ldr, led briefly aftr tenth, led ag'n appr 4 out, drvn clr frm 2 out, eased cl hme....*(5 to 4 on tchd 11 to 10 on and Evens) 1
JODAMI [165] 11-11-12 M Dwyer, *chsd ldrs, reminders and outpcd 6 out, shaken up and styd on strly frm 2 out, nrst finish.*
..............................(11 to 2 op 5 to 1 tchd 6 to 1) 2
MORCELI [153] 8-11-0 N Williamson, *made most, jmpd boldly, hdd appr 4 out, kpt on wl till no extr betw last 2.*
..............................(3 to 1) 3

MORGANS HARBOUR [144] 10-10-5 P Niven, *hld up, pushed alng and outpcd 13th, sn wl beh, styd on frm 2 out.*
............................(25 to 1 op 14 to 1) 4
BETTER TIMES AHEAD [144] 10-10-5 L O'Hara, *hld up in rear, not fluent 11th and 12th, sn lost tch, styd on frm 2 out.*
............................(11 to 1 op 8 to 1 tchd 12 to 1) 5
Dist: 5l, nk, 7l, 1¼l. 6m 23.90s. a 23.90s (5 Ran).

(Alistair Duff), G Richards

1388 Sean Graham Handicap Hurdle Class D (0-120 4-y-o and up) £3,629 2½m.....................(2:40)

1150* BURNT IMP (USA) [120] 6-12-0 J Callaghan, *chsd ldrs, mstk 5th, niggled alng 3 out, led jst aftr last, ran on und pres.*
............................(7 to 2 fav op 3 to 1 tchd 4 to 1) 1
CRYSTAL GIFT [100] 4-10-5 (3*) G Cahill, *chsd ldr, not fluent 7th, chlgd 3 out, slight ld last, sn hdd and one pace.*
............................(11 to 1 op 8 to 1) 2
1166³ NICHOLAS PLANT [96] 7-10-1 (3*) G Lee, *led, not fluent, mstk 6th, slvly pressed frm 3 out, hdd last, no extr.*
............................(4 to 1 op 9 to 2) 3
MR KNITWIT [114] 9-11-8 A Dobbin, *settled rear, pushed alng and hdwy to chase ldrs 3 out, rdn and no imprsn frm nxt.*
............................(33 to 1 op 20 to 1) 4
1125³ COMMANDER GLEN (Ire) [94] 4-9-13 (3*) Mr C Bonner, *beh, pushed alng 6th, styd on stdly frm 3 out, nvr a factor.,*
............................(15 to 2 op 6 to 1 tchd 8 to 1) 5
1225⁶ COOL LUKE (Ire) [104] 7-10-12 N Williamson, *hld up, smooth hdwy to chase ldrs 4 out, pushed alng appr nxt, sn outpcd.*
............................(4 to 1 op 3 to 1 tchd 9 to 2) 6
609⁴ YOUNG STEVEN [92] 5-10-0 M Foster, *cl up, hit 6th, wknd appr 3 out.*
............................(100 to 1 op 50 to 1) 7
GRANDMAN (Ire) [94] 5-10-2 D J Moffatt, *midfield, some hdwy 4 out, lost tch frm nxt.*...........(14 to 1 op 10 to 1) 8
ROYAL CITIZEN (Ire) [98] 7-10-6 Derek Byrne, *hld up towards rear, some hdwy 5 out, blun nxt, tld off whn pld up 3 out.*
............................(16 to 1 op 12 to 1) pu
BEND SABLE (Ire) [114] 6-11-8 B Storey, *hld up, some hdwy hfwy, struggling frm 4 out, tld off whn pld up bef 2 out.*
............................(16 to 1 op 12 to 1) pu
Dist: 2½l, 1l, 7l, 1¾l, 3½l, ¾l, 5l. 4m 55.90s. a 17.90s (10 Ran).
SR: 21/-/-/4/-/-/   (N B Mason (Farms) Ltd), G M Moore

1389 Sean Graham Bookmakers Handicap Chase Class C (0-135 5-y-o and up) £4,744 2m.....................(3:10)

1151³ POLITICAL TOWER [122] 9-11-2 A Dobbin, *mstk 4th, trkd ldrs till led four out, jmpd slwly and strly pressed 2 out, kpt on gmely und pres...* (9 to 4 jt-fav op 5 to 2 tchd 11 to 4) 1
1059* NORDIC THORN (Ire) [117] 6-10-11 N Williamson, *in tch, mstk 5 out, rallied and ev ch last, kpt on.* ....(9 to 4 jt-fav op 2 to 1 tchd 5 to 2) 2
1316* REGAL ROMPER (Ire) [115] 8-10-2 (7*,5ex) R Wilkinson, *blun second, cl up till led 8th, mstk and hdd 4 out, rallied and ev ch last, until to quicken.*.............(5 to 2 tchd 11 to 4) 3
MONTRAVE [106] 7-9-11 (3*) G Cahill, *chsd ldrs, pushed alng and outpcd appr 3 out, no imprsn aftr.*.............(14 to 1) 4
ALL THE ACES [134] 9-12-0 M Dwyer, *hld up, beh whn jmpd rght 7th, sn lost tch.*.............(16 to 1 op 10 to 1) 5
ONE FOR THE POT [110] 11-10-4 M Foster, *sn led, hdd 8th, wknd quickly 4 out, tld off.*............(12 to 1 tchd 14 to 1) 6
Dist: 2½l, sht-hd, 8l, 22l, sht-hd. 3m 58.90s. a 13.90s (6 Ran).
SR: 37/29/27/10/16/-/   (G R S Nixon), R Nixon

1390 Sean Graham Standard Open National Hunt Flat Class H (4,5,6-y-o) £1,070 2m..............(3:40)

ARDARROCH PRINCE 5-11-4 P Niven, *hld up, pushed alng and hdwy 4 fs out, drvn and styd on strly to ld ins last.*
............................(9 to 4 fav op 2 to 1 tchd 3 to 1) 1
1050 LORD OF THE LOCH (Ire) 5-11-4 M Foster, *pld hrd, chsd ldrs till led 3 fs out, kpt on strly till hdd wi ins last.*
............................(10 to 1 op 5 to 1 tchd 12 to 1) 2
ARDRONAN (Ire) 6-11-6 (5*) R McGrath, *hld up, improved frm hfwy, kpt on ins last, unbl to chal.*
............................(6 to 1 op 14 to 1 tchd 16 to 1) 3
1073⁵ STRONG MINT (Ire) 5-11-1 (3*) G Lee, *hld up, shaken up and outpcd 3 fs out, ran on strly ins last, better for race.*
............................(1 to 4 to 1 tchd 8 to 1) 4
1128² BLOOD BROTHER 4-10-11 (7*) N Horrocks, *made most, hdd 3 fs out, ev ch till fdd entering fnl furlong.*
............................(25 to 1 op 20 to 1 tchd 33 to 1) 5
917⁸ AIR BRIDGE 4-11-4 Derek Byrne, *keen hold, chsd ldrs, chlgd entering strt, one pace appr fnl furlong.*.........(100 to 1) 6
SKIDDAW KNIGHT (Ire) 5-11-1 (3*) G Cahill, *hld up, hdwy 5 fs out, rdn and no extr frm 2 out.*........(33 to 1 tchd 50 to 1) 7
THE STUFFED PUFFIN (Ire) 4-11-4 M Dwyer, *hld up, hdwy on ins hfwy, no extr frm o'r 2 fs out.*
............................(10 to 1 op 6 to 1 tchd 12 to 1) 8
HARFDECENT 5-11-10 (7*) T J Comerford, *hld up, hdwy on outsd 6 fs out, outpcd fnl 3 furlongs...*(33 to 1 op 25 to 1) 9
TEELIN BAY (Ire) 4-11-4 D Parker, *pld hrd, hdwy to chase ldrs hfwy, wknd o'r 2 fs out...*.............(16 to 1 op 12 to 1) 10

CHINOOK'S DAUGHTER (Ire) 4-10-13 A Dobbin, *hld up, clr order hfwy, rdn and outpcd o'r 2 fs out...*(8 to 1 op 6 to 1) 11
POLITICAL MILLSTAR 4-11-4 N Bentley, *nvr a factor.*
............................(100 to 1) 12
1142⁷ SOUNDPOST 4-11-4 D J Moffatt, *chsd ldrs, drvn alng o'r 3 fs out, fdd.*........................(20 to 1 op 14 to 1) 13
1050⁷ JACKHO 4-11-4 J Callaghan, *in tch, rdn and wknd fnl 4 fs.*
............................(50 to 1) 14
1073⁶ GALE FORCE (Ire) 5-10-11 (7*) B Grattan, *wth ldr, drvn alng o'r 3 fs out, fdd.*.........(13 to 2 op 7 to 2 tchd 7 to 1) 15
CARNANEE (Ire) 6-11-4 Mr B R Hamilton, *nvr better than midfield.*........................(100 to 1) 16
TADPOLE (Ire) 4-11-4 D Bentley, *nvr better than midfield.*
............................(33 to 1 op 25 to 1) 17
ROADWAY JOKER 5-11-4 J Burke, *midfield, struggling o'r 4 fs out, sn lost tch, tld off...*.................(100 to 1) 18
MOVISA 6-10-8 (5*) S Taylor, *tld off fnl 6 fs........*(100 to 1) 19
YOUNG ENDEAVOUR 4-11-4 A Roche, *al beh, pld up appr hfwy...*.............(10 to 1 op 4 to 1 tchd 12 to 1) pu
Dist: 1¼l, 3½l, 6l, ½l, ½l, 6l, 3l, nk, nk, 2½l. 3m 50.0s. (20 Ran).
(W G McHarg), Mrs M Reveley

CHELTENHAM (good to firm)
Saturday November 16th
Going Correction: PLUS 0.55 sec. per fur. (races 1,3,6), PLUS 0.10 (2,4,5)

1391 Fuggles Imperial Handicap Hurdle Class B (4-y-o and up) £6,645 3¼m ....(1:10)

1112* VICTOR BRAVO (NZ) [113] (bl) 9-10-5 C Llewellyn, *hld up rear, hdwy 4 out, led appr 2 out, sn clr, ran on wl.*
............................(15 to 8 op 2 to 1 tchd 7 to 4) 1
643³ GLENGARRIF GIRL (Ire) [108] (v) 6-10-0 A P McCoy, *chsd ldrs, lft in ld 3 out, sn hdd and hrd rdn, one pace.*
............................(13 to 8 fav op 11 to 8 tchd 7 to 4) 2
1048² SAN GIORGIO [109] 7-10-1 T Jenks, *led to 4th, led 7th, slpd on landing and hdd 3 out, no ch aftr.*
............................(5 to 1 op 6 to 1 tchd 8 to 1) 3
1305⁶ HOPS AND POPS [136] 9-12-0 R Dunwoody, *wth ldr, led 4th to 7th, wknd 9th, tld off nxt...........*(5 to 1 op 4 to 1) 4
Dist: 2½l, dist, dist. 6m 37.00s. a 21.00s (4 Ran).
(Mrs R W S Baker), N A Gaselee

1392 Wadworth 6x Novices' Chase Class C (5-y-o and up) £4,800 2½m 110yds ....(1:45)

1183* POTTER'S BAY (Ire) 7-11-5 A Maguire, *hld up rear, mstk 4th, smooth hdwy to ld appr last, rdn out.*
............................(7 to 2 on op 4 to 1 on tchd 3 to 1 on) 1
1140 FLIMSY TRUTH 10-11-6⁶ Mr M Harris, *led till appr last, ran on one pace...*........................(10 to 1 op 8 to 1) 2
GENERAL PONGO 7-11-0 R Dunwoody, *chsd ldr till hrd rdn and wknd appr last...............*(9 to 2 op 11 to 2) 3
Dist: 3½l, 13l. 5m 16.90s. a 19.90s (3 Ran).
(Mrs J E Potter), D Nicholson

1393 Murphy's Draughtflow Hurdle Handicap Class B (4-y-o and up) £27,126 2m 110yds..................(2:20)

1305² SPACE TRUCKER (Ire) [136] 5-11-11 J Osborne, *steady hdwy 3 out, led on bit last, shaken up and quickened clr...........................*(7 to 1 op 6 to 1) 1
730² MYSTICAL CITY (Ire) [135] 6-11-7 (3*) D J Casey, *hld up, steady hdwy 3 out, ev ch last, ran on one pace.*
............................(9 to 1 op 7 to 1 tchd 10 to 1) 2
1160³ BARNA BOY (Ire) [130] 8-11-5 M A Fitzgerald, *al prmnt, hrd rdn appr last, ran on one pace.*
............................(25 to 1 op 20 to 1 tchd 33 to 1) 3
1028* COUNTRY STAR (Ire) [128] 5-11-3 G Bradley, *chsd ldr, led aftr 2 out to last, not quicken...........*(9 to 2 tchd 5 to 1) 4
1297² MAKE A STAND [123] 5-10-12 A Maguire, *led till aftr 2 out, styd on...........................*(10 to 1 op 8 to 1) 5
966* CHIEF'S SONG [139] 6-12-0 R Dunwoody, *chsd ldrs, 3rd whn mstk 3 out, sn hrd rdn, wknd appr last.*
............................(7 to 1 op 6 to 1 tchd 8 to 1) 6
1288* CRACK ON [130] 6-11-5 A P McCoy, *drpd rear aftr 4th, mstk 5th, no ch after..........*(9 to 1 op 4 to 1 tchd 7 to 2) 7
1305* DREAMS END [137] 8-11-12 R Farrant, *in tch till wknd appr 2 out.........................*(15 to 2 op 6 to 1 tchd 8 to 1) 8
1381* JUST LITTLE [131] 4-11-6 (6ex) C O'Dwyer, *hld up rear, hdwy whn mstk 3 out, prmnt and gng wl when f nxt.*
............................(7 to 1 op 6 to 1) f
Dist: 3½l, ½l, 1¼l, 1l, 7l, 17l, 13l. 3m 54.00s. a 5.00s (9 Ran).
SR: 55/50/44/40/34/43/17/11/-/ (Mrs E Queally), Mrs J Harrington

1394 Murphy's Gold Cup Handicap Chase Class A Grade 3 (5-y-o and up) £38,270 2½m 110yds........(2:55)

CHALLENGER DU LUC (Fr) [142] (bl) 6-10-12 R Dunwoody, *hld up, hdwy 4 out, jnd ldr on bit last, led r-in, sn hrd rdn, jst held on*.................................(7 to 1 op 11 to 2) 1
1159* STRONG PROMISE (Ire) [141] 5-9-11 (3*) K Gaule, *al prmnt, lft in ld appr 3 out, hdd r-in, ran on wl.* (14 to 1 op 16 to 1) 2
ADDINGTON BOY (Ire) [150] 8-10-10 B Harding, *al prmnt, ev ch 2 out, hrd rdn appr last, not quicken.*
....(5 to 1 tchd 11 to 2) 3
1169* ANABATIC (Ire) [146] 8-10-6 T P Rudd, *hld up, hdwy 4 out, ev ch 2 out, wknd last.*.................(11 to 1 op 10 to 1) 4
11872 BARTON BANK [159] 10-11-5 A Maguire, *chsd ldr, ev ch 2 out, short of room and slpd appr last, not reco'r.*
....(12 to 1 tchd 14 to 1) 5
11572 BIG MATT (Ire) [144] 8-10-4 M A Fitzgerald, *lost pl 7th, hdwy 3 out, wknd last.*.......(9 to 2 fav op 5 to 1 tchd 11 to 2) 6
1289* STRONG MEDICINE [140] 9-10-0 (3ex) C O'Dwyer, *nvr nr to chal.*...............................(20 to 1 op 16 to 1) 7
12943 BAVARD DIEU (Ire) [140] 8-10-0 C Llewellyn, *tld off till styd on frm 2 out.*............(40 to 1 op 33 to 1 tchd 50 to 1) 8
10292 EASTHORPE [141] 8-10-1 J Osborne, *not fluent, chsd ldrs till wknd appr 4 out.*........(10 to 1 op 9 to 1 tchd 11 to 1) 9
KIBREET [146] 9-10-6 A P McCoy, *in tch till wknd appr 3 out.*
....(8 to 1 tchd 9 to 1) 10
DUBLIN FLYER [168] 10-12-0 B Powell, *led till slpd up appr 3 out.*...............................(7 to 1 op 8 to 1) su
1210* ABSALOM'S LADY [141] 8-10-1 (6ex) D Bridgwater, *tld off frm 7th, pld up bef 3 out.*... (11 to 1 op 10 to 1 tchd 12 to 1) pu
Dist: hd, 3½l, 5l, 5l, 11l, 14l, ¾l, ½l, 4l. 4m 59.90s. a 2.90s (12 Ran).
SR: 65/63/69/60/68/42/24/23/23/   (D A Johnson), M C Pipe

1395 Flowers Original Handicap Chase Class B (5-y-o and up) £10,130 3m 3f 110yds......................(3:30)

995* EVANGELICA (USA) [121] 6-10-0 A P McCoy, *hld up, led 3 out, easily.*................(13 to 8 fav op 6 to 4 tchd 15 to 8) 1
11772 COPPER MINE [123] 10-10-2 J Osborne, *led to 3 out, no ch wth wnr.*.............................(3 to 1 op 5 to 2) 2
10843 MARTOMICK [145] 9-11-10 C O'Dwyer, *not fluent, mstk 11th, al rear, effrt appr 3 out, sn wknd.*........ (2 to 1 op 7 to 4) 3
12905 WILLSFORD [135] 13-11-0 R Farrant, *chsd ldr till pld up aftr 16th.*.....................(15 to 2 op 5 to 1 tchd 8 to 1) pu
Dist: 5l, 17l. (Time not taken) (4 Ran).

(Martin Pipe Racing Club), M C Pipe

1396 Mackeson Novices' Hurdle Class A Grade 2 (4-y-o and up) £8,792 2m 110yds......................(4:05)

1103* KAILASH 5-10-12 A P McCoy, *made all, rdn clr appr 3 out, ran on wl.*...................(3 to 1 op 7 to 4) 1
1097* HERBERT LODGE (Ire) 7-10-12 C O'Dwyer, *hld up, hdwy 5th, chsd wnr and rdn appr 3 out, no imprsn.*
....(2 to 1 op 9 to 4 tchd 5 to 2) 2
1293* GREEN GREEN DESERT (Fr) 5-10-12 D Bridgwater, *same pl most of way, rdn appr 2 out, no hdwy.*
....(11 to 8 fav op 6 to 4 tchd 7 to 4) 3
FOXIES LAD 5-10-12 V Slattery, *al beh.*
....(20 to 1 op 25 to 1) 4
SOVIET BRIDE (Ire) 4-10-7 R Dunwoody, *chsd wnr, jmpd rght 3rd and 4th, wknd 5th.*...(10 to 1 op 6 to 1 tchd 11 to 1) 5
Dist: 7l, 15l, 3l, 8l. 4m 6.80s. a 17.80s (5 Ran).

(Mick Fletcher), M C Pipe

HUNTINGDON (good)
Saturday November 16th
Going Correction: PLUS 0.10 sec. per fur. (races 1,2,4,6), PLUS 0.25 (3,5)

1397 Kimbolton Novices' Hurdle Class E (4-y-o and up) £2,722 2m 110yds......................(1:00)

689* MR PERCY 5-11-5 P Hide, *prmnt, led 4th, shaken up last, rdn out nr finish.*..............(9 to 4 on op 6 to 4 on) 1
MENTMORE TOWERS (Ire) 4-10-12 W Marston, *prmnt, rdn to chase wnr aftr 3 out, chlgd last, unbl to quicken.*
....(5 to 1 op 4 to 1 tchd 8 to 1) 2
10652 PEACE LORD 6-10-9 (3*) G Hogan, *prmnt, chsd wnr aftr 4th till mstk 3 out, wknd appr last.*
....(7 to 1 op 6 to 1 tchd 8 to 1) 3
3224 OTTAVIO FARNESE 4-10-9 (3*) L Aspell, *chsd ldrs, one pace frm 3 out, btn whn mstk last.*........ (25 to 1 op 10 to 1) 4
LOOKINGFORARAINBOW (Ire) 8-10-12 V Smith, *keen hold, hld up, mstk 5th, prog bef nxt, sn no imprsn.*
....(10 to 1 op 7 to 1) 5
506 BABA AU RHUM (Ire) 4-10-12 D Gallagher, *hld up beh, prog 5th, no imprsn on ldrs 3 out.*..........(50 to 1 op 20 to 1) 6
12484 NASHAAT (USA) 8-10-12 W Worthington, *mid-div, effrt 5th, sn btn.*..............................(33 to 1 op 14 to 1) 7
12249 ROOD MUSIC 5-10-12 L Wyer, *led to 4th, rdn and btn aftr nxt.*
....(50 to 1 op 20 to 1) 8
MUDLARK 4-10-12 W Fry, *in tch till mstk 5th, wknd und pres.*
....(33 to 1 op 16 to 1 tchd 40 to 1) 9

9003 QUAKER WALTZ 6-10-7 S McNeill, *mid-div, wknd aftr 5th.*
....(50 to 1 op 20 to 1) 10
12525 MURPHY'S GOLD (Ire) 5-10-12 R Marley, *pld hrd, hld up, al beh, tld off.*.......................(25 to 1 op 12 to 1) 11
1063 ROSSLAYNE SERENADE 5-10-0 (7*) C R Weaver, *prmnt till f 3rd.*........................(50 to 1 op 20 to 1) f
ROSSELL ISLAND (Ire) 5-10-12 R Johnson, *prmnt whn hmpd and uns rdr 3rd.*.................(20 to 1 op 12 to 1) ur
12958 CHANTRO BAY 8-10-12 N Mann, *prmnt till kicked and broke leg 3rd, pld up, dead.*. (33 to 1 op 25 to 1 tchd 50 to 1) pu
12957 DARING RYDE (v) 5-10-12 A S Smith, *prmnt, wkng whn jmpd slwly 4th, tld off and pld up bef 2 out.*.. (50 to 1 op 25 to 1) pu
12158 SCHWARTZNDIGGER (Ire) 6-10-12 J R Kavanagh, *mstk second, al beh, tld off whn pld up bef 2 out.* (50 to 1 op 20 to 1) pu
Dist: 1l, 9l, 7l, 9l, 1l, 3l, hd, ½l, 7l. dist. 3m 48.30s. a 7.30s (16 Ran).
SR: 34/26/17/10/1/-/   (Felix Rosenstiel's Widow & Son), J T Gifford

1398 Southoe Juvenile Novices' Hurdle Class E (3-y-o) £2,547 2m 110yds......................(1:30)

11795 FIJON (Ire) 10-5 N Mann, *rear whn mstk second, prog to join ldrs 4th, hrd rdn to ld last, drvn out...* (33 to 1 op 16 to 1) 1
BELMARITA (Ire) 10-5 R Johnson, *prmnt, led aftr 3 out till last, no extr und pres.*.....................(4 to 1 tchd 5 to 1) 2
SOLDIER MAK 10-10 P Hide, *in tch, trkd ldrs gng easily 3 out, ev ch nxt, rdn and no extr.*........(12 to 1 op 10 to 1) 3
11887 SIX CLERKS (Ire) 10-7 (3*) F Leahy, *prmnt, led aftr 4th till aftr 3 out, hrd rdn and one pace.*
....(8 to 1 op 4 to 1 tchd 10 to 1) 4
PRECIOUS ISLAND 10-5 J Supple, *prmnt till outpcd appr 3 out, kpt on ag'n r-in....* (50 to 1 op 33 to 1 tchd 66 to 1) 5
12214 KINGFISHER BRAVE 10-10 L Wyer, *led to 4th, sn rdn, one pace frm 3 out.*.................(4 to 1 op 5 to 2) 6
12499 ANOTHER QUARTER (Ire) 10-5 W Worthington, *rear, kpt on frm 3 out, nvr dngrs.*...............(33 to 1 op 25 to 1) 7
11797 LEBEDINSKI (Ire) 10-5 R Marley, *mid-div, lost tch aftr 5th.*
....(50 to 1 op 16 to 1 tchd 66 to 1) 8
ALARICO (Fr) 10-10 D Gallagher, *in tch, effrt whn mstks 4th and 5th, wknd aftr 3 out.*......(50 to 1 op 25 to 1) 9
PONTEVEDRA (Ire) 10-5 A S Smith, *in tch to 5th, sn wknd.*
....(20 to 1 op 10 to 1) 10
FLINT AND STEEL 10-10 V Smith, *hld up, in tch 4th, wknd appr 3 out.*.....................(14 to 1 tchd 16 to 1) 11
6582 EUROBOX BOY 10-10 J A McCarthy, *hld up, prog and in tch 4th, wknd aftr nxt.*........ (3 to 1 fav tchd 7 to 2) 12
10245 EUROBOX BOY 10-10 W Marston, *prmnt, led briefly 4th, sn wknd.*.....................(14 to 1 op 12 to 1) 13
1024 KULSHI MOMKEN 10-10 W Fry, *hld up, losing tch whn mstk and uns rdr 4th.*...........(50 to 1 op 33 to 1) ur
CLASSIC DAISY 10-2 (3*) E Husband, *pld hrd, hld up, lost tch 4th, tried to refuse whn brght dwn by loose horse nxt.*
....(50 to 1 op 25 to 1) bd
12216 ROYAL THEN (Fr) 10-10 J R Kavanagh, *chsd ldrs to 5th, wl beh whn pld up bef 2 out.*
....(10 to 1 op 14 to 1 tchd 16 to 1) pu
Dist: 2l, 2l, 1¼l, 5l, 6l, 3½l, 3½l, 1¼l, 3½l, 13l, 1¾l. 3m 53.70s. a 12.70s (16 Ran).
(The Fijon Partnership), J Pearce

1399 Toseland Novices' Chase Class B (5-y-o and up) £3,825 2½m 110yds......................(2:00)

LIVELY KNIGHT (Ire) 7-10-12 P Hide, *prmnt, chsd ldr 11th, not quicken aftr 3 out, styd on to ld last, all out.*
....(5 to 2 op 7 to 4 tchd 11 to 4) 1
80* MISTER DRUM (Ire) 7-10-12 W Marston, *led, rdn clr aftr 3 out, hdd und pres last, kpt on r-in.*
....(7 to 2 tchd 4 to 1 and 3 to 1) 2
WILD WEST WIND (Ire) 6-10-12 R Johnson, *chsd ldr to 11th, cl up to 3 out, wknd...* (6 to 5 fav op 6 to 4 tchd 7 to 4) 3
3663 SASSIVER (USA) 6-11-2 (3*) G Hogan, *reminders aftr 3rd, chsd ldrs till pckd 12th and wknd.*
....(25 to 1 op 16 to 1 tchd 33 to 1) 4
MASTER HOPE (Ire) 7-10-12 R Bellamy, *hmpd 1st, chsd ldrs till rdn and wknd tenth, no ch whn mstk 12th.*
....(16 to 1 op 10 to 1) 5
12504 RECORD LOVER (Ire) 6-10-12 W Worthington, *chsd ldrs till wknd tenth.*.....(25 to 1 op 20 to 1 tchd 33 to 1) 6
104 ARR EFF BEE (bl) 9-10-12 A S Smith, *tld off frm 3rd.*
....(66 to 1 op 50 to 1) 7
STRONG STUFF (Ire) 5-10-12 S McNeill, *f 1st.*
....(8 to 1 op 4 to 1 tchd 10 to 1) f
971 HATTA RIVER (USA) 10-12 J Supple, *sn rdn and tld off, pld up bef 13th.*.......................(66 to 1 op 50 to 1) pu
1111 LETS GO NOW (Ire) 6-10-12 M Brennan, *wl beh frm 5th, tld off whn pld up bef 13th.*..........(50 to 1 op 50 to 1) pu
Dist: ½l, 29l, 17l, 7l, 16l, 14l. 4m 57.90s. a 10.90s (10 Ran).
SR: 26/25/-/-/-/-/   (A D Weller), J T Gifford

1400 Business Club Handicap Hurdle Class D (0-125 4-y-o and up) £2,931 3¼m......................(2:30)

1266* ELBURG (Ire) [102] 5-10-10 R Johnson, *hld up in tch, prog to ld 9th, clr 2 out, mstk last, easily.*
....(7 to 4 fav op 6 to 4 tchd 2 to 1) 1

1056 ARITHMETIC [113] 6-11-7 W Marston, *pld hrd, cl up, pressed wnr 9th till mstk 3 out, no imprsn aftr.*
.... (5 to 2 op 9 to 4 tchd 11 to 4) 2
ULURU (Ire) [117] 8-11-11 J R Kavanagh, *prmnt, led 8th to 9th, sn rdn and outpcd.* .... (3 to 1 op 4 to 1) 3
RUBINS BOY [92] 10-10-0 A S Smith, *hld up in tch, effrt and outpcd 9th, no prog aftr.* .... (20 to 1 op 14 to 1) 4
1266⁹ PROVENCE [92] 9-10-0³ (3*) G Hogan, *prmnt, led briefly aftr 4th, rdn and outpcd 9th, no ch after...* (50 to 1 op 33 to 1) 5
1251¹² SINGLESOLE [92] 11-10-0 R Marley, *made most to 8th, sn rdn and wknd, virtually pld up r-in.*
.... (11 to 2 op 7 to 2 tchd 6 to 1) 6
Dist: 6l, 17l, 2½l, nk, dist. 6m 24.90s. a 32.90s (6 Ran).
(Mrs Alison Gamble), T R George

1401 Macer Gifford Handicap Chase Class C (0-130 5-y-o and up) £4,597 2½m 110yds................. (3:00)

SHINING LIGHT (Ire) [100] 7-10-2 R Johnson, *trkd ldrs, prog 11th, led 2 out, edgd rght r-in, drvn out.*
.... (5 to 1 tchd 11 to 2) 1
MR PRESIDENT (Ire) [98] 7-10-0 D Gallagher, *hld up in tch, prog 12th, chlgd and hit 2 out, ev ch last, no extr nr finish.*
.... (4 to 1 op 7 to 2 tchd 9 to 2) 2
ACT OF PARLIAMENT (Ire) [105] (bl) 8-10-7 S McNeill, *prmnt, led 11th to 2 out, sn btn.* (7 to 2 fav op 3 to 1 tchd 9 to 2) 3
1137³ RUSTIC AIR [106] 9-10-8 W Dwan, *prmnt, ev ch whn mstk 4 out, wknd aftr nxt.* .... (4 to 1 op 9 to 1) 4
PURITAN (Can) [115] (bl) 7-11-3 Miss P Jones, *rear, lost tch 11th, no dngr aftr.* .... (14 to 1 op 10 to 1) 5
DENVER BAY [120] 9-11-5 (3*) L Aspell, *led to 11th, wknd aftr 3 out.* .... (9 to 2 tchd 11 to 2) 6
1289 CONTI D'ESTRUVAL (Fr) [122] 6-11-10 B Clifford, *not fluent, in tch, pushed alng whn jmpd slwly 12th, wknd, pld up bef 2 out.* .... (5 to 1 op 6 to 1 tchd 9 to 2) pu
Dist: 1¼l, 11l, 6l, 16l, 5l. 4m 58.60s. a 11.60s (7 Ran).
SR: 9/5/1/-/ (The Deeley Partnership), D Nicholson

1402 Willingham Handicap Hurdle Class D (0-120 4-y-o and up) £2,868 2m 110yds................. (3:35)

HENRIETTA HOWARD (Ire) [102] 6-10-12 (3*) G Hogan, *chsd ldr, led appr 2 out, clr last, shaken up r-in, cmftbly.*
.... (16 to 1 op 8 to 1) 1
1225³ LORD MCMURROUGH (Ire) [110] 6-11-9 W Marston, *led to appr 2 out, no ch wnr aftr.*
.... (8 to 1 op 7 to 1 tchd 12 to 1) 2
896⁵ TIM (Ire) [104] 6-10-10 (7*) D Yellowlees, *chsd ldrs till lost pl and rdn 4th, styd on wl frm 2 out, nrst finish.*
.... (8 to 1 op 7 to 1 tchd 12 to 1) 3
TEJANO GOLD (USA) [113] 6-11-12 R Johnson, *prmnt till rdn and outpcd aftr 5th, kpt on one pace frm 2 out.*
.... (8 to 1 tchd 12 to 1) 4
1141² TANSEEQ [88] 5-10-1 L Wyer, *strted very slwly, rear, effrt 5th, nvr on terms.* ....(11 to 2 op 7 to 2) 5
1066* MENELAVE (Ire) [108] 6-11-7 J A McCarthy, *hld up, prog aftr 4th, rdn and struggling bef 3 out.*
.... (9 to 4 fav op 2 to 1) 6
1175⁷ PEGASUS BAY [93] 5-10-6 S McNeill, *hld up beh, effrt 5th, nvr on terms.* ...... (12 to 1 op 10 to 1 tchd 14 to 1) 7
LUCY TUFTY [87] 5-10-0 V Smith, *wtd wth, progs 4th, chsd ldg pair 3 out, sn wknd.*...(4 to 1 op 5 to 1 tchd 7 to 2) 8
NAGOBELIA [97] 8-10-10 N Mann, *hld up, lost tch 5th, no ch aftr.*..................... (20 to 1 op 16 to 1 tchd 33 to 1) 9
Dist: 6l, 7l, 5l, 7l, 2l, 7l, 4l, 2l. 3m 51.50s. a 10.50s (9 Ran).
SR: -/1/-/-/-/-/ (Mrs Solna Thomson Jones), Mrs D Haine

PUNCHESTOWN (IRE) (soft)
Saturday November 16th
Going Correction: PLUS 0.35 sec. per fur. (races 1,2,4,5,7), PLUS 1.00 (3,6)

1403 Cullens Gorse Hurdle (3-y-o) £3,082 2m................. (12:45)

BROKEN RITES (Ire) 10-3 (5*) G Cotter, ... (3 to 1) 1
SARAH'S GUEST (Ire) 10-3 R Hughes, ... (13 to 2) 2
1309* CHOOSEY'S TREASURE (Ire) 10-11 C F Swan, (5 to 2 on) 3
1309 IACCHUS (Ire) 10-6 (7*) S P Kelly, ... (12 to 1) 4
1173 UNASSISTED (Ire) 10-8 (3*) B Bowens, ... (14 to 1) 5
882 REKONDO (Ire) 10-8 D T Evans, ... (25 to 1) 6
1173 GALE EIGHT (Ire) 10-3 T P Treacy, ... (20 to 1) 7
Dist: Sht-hd, 3l, sht-hd, 25l. 4m 59s. a 20.90s (7 Ran).
(N B Wachman), W M Roper

1404 Locks Restaurant Novice Hurdle (4-y-o and up) £3,767 2m........ (1:15)

NOBLE THYNE (Ire) 6-11-0 T P Treacy, ...(5 to 4 on) 1
ISTABRAQ (Ire) 4-10-9 C F Swan, ... (6 to 4) 2
SAVING BOND (Ire) 4-10-9 R Hughes, ... (8 to 1) 3
TULLABAWN (Ire) 4-10-9 T J Mitchell, ... (25 to 1) 4
1117* HOLLYBANK BUCK (Ire) 6-11-7 A Powell, ...(12 to 1) 5
1171³ KNOCKAULIN (Ire) 5-11-0 F J Flood, ...(25 to 1) 6

1015 SHANNON GALE (Ire) 4-10-9 L P Cusack, ...(25 to 1) 7
1015 BARLEY MEADOW (Ire) 4-10-9 H Rogers, ...(66 to 1) 8
CRISTYS PICNIC (Ire) 6-11-0 F Woods, ... (20 to 1) 9
1077 CAHONIS (Ire) 4-10-9 M P Hourigan, ... (33 to 1) 10
Dist: Hd, 20l, 11l, 2½l. 3m 57.20s. a 12.20s (10 Ran).
SR: 20/15/-/-/-/-/ (C Mayo), P Mullins

1405 Craddockstown Novice Chase (Grade 3) (4-y-o and up) £6,850 2m .... (1:45)

1170 JEFFELL 6-11-7 F Woods, *jmpd wl, made all, lft clr bef last, cmftbly.* .... (4 to 1) 1
1058⁷ BOBBYJO (Ire) 6-11-4 (3*) K Whelan, *wtd wth, some prog aftr 5 out, kpt on aftr 2 out.*..................... (2 to 1) 2
1116* THE OUTBACK WAY (Ire) (bl) 6-12-3 D H O'Connor, *trkd ldr, lost pl bef 4 out, rdn aftr nxt, not quicken.*........(4 to 1) 3
1094⁴ BEAKSTOWN (Ire) 7-12-3 T P Treacy, *wtd wth, some prog 3 out, sn no extr.*..................... (11 to 10 fav) 4
928 ROCHE MENTOR (Ire) 6-11-7 J F Broderick, *rear, jmpd slwly second and reminders, jumped slowly 4th, f 5 out.*(100 to 1) f
909* DANCE BEAT (Ire) 5-11-6 C F Swan, *wl plcd, jmpd slwly 5th, trkd ldr 5 out, rdn aftr 4 out, broke leg and pld up betw last 2.*
.... (11 to 10 fav) pu
Dist: 8l, 5½l, 1½l. 4m 21.00s. a 22.00s (6 Ran).
SR: 33/25/29/27/-/-/ (Thomas Bailey), A L T Moore

1406 Morgiana Hurdle (Grade 2) (4-y-o and up) £9,675 2m................. (2:15)

1172⁴ COCKNEY LAD (Ire) 7-12-0 C F Swan, *trkd ldr, led bef last, styd on wl.*..................... (5 to 4 fav) 1
718* HILL SOCIETY (Ire) 4-11-2 R Hughes, *trkd ldr, chlgd bef last, no extr.*..................... (6 to 1) 2
303 LADY ARPEL (Ire) 4-10-8 K F O'Brien, *led and clr second, wkng 3 out, rdn and hdd bef last.*..................... (10 to 1) 3
MAYASTA (Ire) 6-10-13 F Woods, *rear, rdn aftr 4 out, some prog after 2 out.*..................... (9 to 2 tchd 4 to 1) 4
PADASHPAN (USA) 7-10-11 (7*) P Morris, *trkd ldr till rdn and wknd bef 4 out.*..................... (10 to 1) 5
1016³ DERRYMOYLE (Ire) 7-12-0 J F Broderick, *rear till prog bef 4 out, rdn and wknd aftr 3 out.*..................... (7 to 2) 6
Dist: 1½l, 1½l, 25l, 4l. 3m 53.20s. a 8.20s (6 Ran).
SR: 74/60/50/30/31/-/ (D Daly), Noel Meade

1407 Rathsallagh House Handicap Hurdle (0-132 4-y-o and up) £4,795 2½m .... (2:45)

ANTAPOURA (Ire) [-] 4-10-11 C F Swan, ... (6 to 4 fav) 1
1089³ RATHGIBBON (Ire) [-] 5-10-5 T P Treacy, ... (7 to 1) 2
441² TRYFIRION (Ire) [-] 7-11-11 (3*) B Bowens, ...(14 to 1) 3
732⁶ THAI ELECTRIC (Ire) [-] 5-9-11 T J Mitchell, ...(10 to 1) 4
1089⁶ TELL THE NIPPER (Ire) [-] 7-11-2 J P Broderick, ...(11 to 1) 5
1146⁶ DARK SWAN (Ire) [-] 6-10-9 W Slattery, ... (20 to 1) 6
732² NATIVE GALE (Ire) [-] 4-10-2 (5*) T Martin, ...(6 to 1) 7
CIARA'S PRINCE (Ire) [-] 5-10-13 F J Flood, ... (6 to 1) 8
1189 STONELEIGH TURBO (Ire) [-] 7-10-2 F Woods, ...(12 to 1) 9
1823 FERRYCARRIG HOTEL (Ire) [-] 7-10-12 L P Cusack,
.... (11 to 1) 10
JOHNEEN [-] 10-11-11 K F O'Brien, ... (10 to 1) 11
HI KNIGHT (Ire) [-] 6-10-6 K F O'Brien, ...(12 to 1) pu
Dist: 1l, 6l, 5½l, 1½l. 5m 25.10s. a 43.10s (12 Ran).
(John Malone), A P O'Brien

1408 Watchhouse Cross Handicap Chase (0-109 4-y-o and up) £3,425 3m .... (3:15)

852⁴ IRISH LIGHT (Ire) [-] 8-10-0 J P Broderick, ... (7 to 2 fav) 1
1116⁵ STRONG HICKS (Ire) [-] 8-12-0 F J Flood, ... (8 to 1) 2
1194⁴ LA-GREINE [-] 9-10-8 (7*) Mr K Ross, ... (8 to 1) 3
1003* CORYMANDEL (Ire) [-] 7-11-11 F Woods, ...(9 to 2) 4
1194 VELEDA II (Fr) [-] 9-11-4 (3*) K Whelan, ...(13 to 2) 5
1192⁵ FRIDAY THIRTEENTH (Ire) [-] 7-11-6 A Powell, ...(14 to 1) 6
1191 GREEK MAGIC [-] 9-9-7² T P Treacy, ... (14 to 1) 7
1194 OLYMPIC D'OR (Ire) [-] 8-11-6 T J Mitchell, ...(14 to 1) f
1245² DOONEGA (Ire) [-] 8-10-0 (7*) Mr E Gallagher, ...(8 to 1) ur
1194³ THE GOPHER (Ire) [-] 7-11-5 L P Cusack, ... (5 to 1) pu
Dist: 9l, 25l, 10l, 15l. 6m 42.60s. a 42.60s (11 Ran).
(Michael J McDonagh), Michael J McDonagh

1409 Hatfield INH Flat Race (4-y-o) £2,740 2m................. (3:45)

1121² GRAPHIC EQUALISER (Ire) 11-2 (7*) Mr Edgar Byrne,
.... (5 to 4 fav) 1D
884⁴ SHANNON OAK (Ire) 11-6 (3*) Mr P M Kelly, ... (6 to 1) 1
898³ CORYROSE (Ire) 11-7 (7*) Mr A J Dempsey, ... (4 to 1) 2D
MR MONGOOSE (Ire) 11-2 (7*) Mr P J Prendergast, (7 to 1) 2
603⁹ ROSIE FLYNN (Ire) 10-11 (7*) Mr Sean O O'Brien, ...(5 to 1) 3
AUBURN ROILELET (Ire) 11-4 Mr A R Coonan, ...(10 to 1) 4
BRIEF CRUISE (Ire) 11-2 (7*) Mr T J Beattie, ...(14 to 1) 5
STRONG MARTINA (Ire) 10-11 (7*) Mr D W Cullen, (10 to 1) 6
CAHERMURPHY (Ire) 11-2 (7*) Mr G Elliott, ... (10 to 1) 7
1019 INISHLACKAN (Ire) 11-4 Miss M Olivefalk, ...(10 to 1) 8

Dist: 13l, 15l, 4l, 1l. 3m 58.60s. (10 Ran).
(Shannon Oak Syndicate), J C Hayden

WINDSOR (good (races 1,3,4,6,7), good to firm (2,5))
Saturday November 16th
Going Correction: MINUS 0.25 sec. per fur. (races 1,3,4,6,7), NIL (2,5)

1410 Scania 4-Series Novices' Hurdle Class E (Div I) (4-y-o and up) £2,110 2m........................(12:40)

SECRET SPRING (Fr) 4-10-12 M Richards, *hld up, hdwy appr 3 out, led 2 out, rdn clr*....(11 to 4 op 3 to 1 tchd 7 to 2) 1
DANEGOLD (Ire) 4-10-12 A Thornton, *al prmnt, ev ch 2 out, one pace*........................(7 to 1 tchd 10 to 1) 2
NO PATTERN 4-10-12 J Railton, *wtd wth, hdwy appr 3 out, ev ch nxt, one pace.* .... (9 to 4 fav op 2 to 1 tchd 7 to 4 and 5 to 2) 3
1215 LABURNUM GOLD (Ire) 5-10-12 I Lawrence, *chsd ldr, led appr 5th, hdd 2 out, 4th and btn whn mstk last.* ....(7 to 1 op 4 to 1) 4
1215² ABOVE THE CUT (USA) 4-10-12 C Maude, *led till appr 5th, wknd approaching last*...(10 to 1 op 8 to 1 tchd 11 to 1) 5
MUSEUM (Ire) 5-10-12 D Leahy, *nvr plcd to chal.* ....(33 to 1 op 20 to 1 tchd 50 to 1) 6
1182⁷ L'EQUIPE (Ire) 6-10-9 (3*) J Magee, *nvr nr to chal.* ....(12 to 1 op 6 to 1 tchd 14 to 1) 7
KUMARI KING (Ire) 6-10-12 D Morris, *nvr trbld ldrs.* ....(33 to 1 op 14 to 1 tchd 50 to 1) 8
1155³ SAHEL (Ire) 8-10-12 S Curran, *hld up and beh, hit 4th, hdwy appr 3 out, wknd bef nxt*....(4 to 1 op 7 to 2 tchd 9 to 2) 9
SEMINOLE WIND 5-10-12 B Fenton, *beh frm 5th.* ....(33 to 1 op 25 to 1) 10
AGANEROT (Ire) 6-10-12 R Greene, *trkd ldrs, hit second, wknd appr 3 out*...... (25 to 1 op 20 to 1 tchd 33 to 1) 11
NORTHERN SPRUCE (Ire) 4-10-12 W McFarland, *mid-div, jmpd slwly 5th, wknd bef nxt.* ....(33 to 1 op 12 to 1 tchd 50 to 1) 12

Dist: 3½l, 3½l, 5l, 10l, hd, 9l, 4l, 8l, 12l, 2½l. 3m 52.90s. a 7.90s (12 Ran).
(M K George), P R Hedger

1411 Scania Vehicle Management Novices' Chase Class E (5-y-o and up) £3,965 3m...................(1:10)

1303³ BLASKET HERO (bl) 8-10-12 B Fenton, *not fluent, hld up beh ldrs, led 12th, lft clr 4 out, jmpd left fnl 3, unchlgd.* ....(11 to 10 fav op 6 to 4 on tchd 5 to 4) 1
1110⁸ DAMCADA (Ire) 8-10-12 T J Murphy, *prmnt, rdn frm 14th, lft moderate second 2 out, no ch wth wnr.* (25 to 1 op 16 to 1) 2
THE HERBIVORE (Ire) 7-10-12 J Railton, *prmnt, wknd appr 4 out*..........................(33 to 1 op 25 to 1) 3
835⁷ HOLLOW WOOD (Ire) 5-10-10 A Thornton, *hld up, hdwy 9th, hit nxt, sn wknd, tld off.* (11 to 1 op 20 to 1 tchd 25 to 1) 4
1113² GREY GORDEN (Ire) 8-10-12 D Morris, *led, hit 8th, mstks tenth and nxt, hdd 12th, second and ev ch whn f 4 out.* ....(5 to 4 tchd Evens) f

Dist: 7l, 12l, dist. 6m 9.60s. a 16.60s (5 Ran).
(Miss H J Flower), Mrs S D Williams

1412 Scania 4-Series 'Horsepower' Juvenile Novices' Hurdle Class E (3-y-o) £2,687 2m...................(1:40)

FAR DAWN (USA) 10-12 C Maude, *led to 5th, rgned ld 3 out, clr betw fnl 2, cmftbly*............(6 to 4 fav tchd 2 to 1) 1
1286⁸ STERLING FELLOW (v) 10-12 M Clarke, *hld up, hdwy appr 2 out, chsd wnr r-in, no imprsn.* ....(16 to 1 op 14 to 1 tchd 20 to 1) 2
SAMARA SONG 10-5 (7*) J Power, *hld up, hdwy frm 5th, rdn 2 out, one pace*.........(25 to 1 op 20 to 1 tchd 33 to 1) 3
1179 COLOUR COUNSELLOR 10-12 D O'Sullivan, *hld up, hdwy 5th, rdn 2 out, one pace*...............(5 to 1 op 7 to 2) 4
STONECUTTER 10-12 P Holley, *hld up beh ldrs, rdn 3 out, no hdwy*...................(6 to 1 op 5 to 1 tchd 7 to 1) 5
1179⁶ IN CAHOOTS 10-12 F Jousset, *mid-div, effrt 3 out, one pace nxt*...................(12 to 1 op 10 to 1 tchd 14 to 1) 6
YOUNG MAZAAD (Ire) 10-12 T J Murphy, *in tch, wknd appr 2 out*...................(8 to 1 op 7 to 1 tchd 10 to 1) 7
HAWANAFA 10-7 W McFarland, *prmnt, led aftr 5th to 3 out, wknd bef nxt*......................(20 to 1 tchd 25 to 1) 8
ILLEGALLY YOURS 10-7 R Greene, *chsd ldrs to 3 out.* ....(10 to 1 tchd 8 to 1 and 12 to 1) 9
1024 IT'S DAWAN 10-12 L Harvey, *mid-div, mstks 3rd and 3 out, sn wknd*................(25 to 1 op 20 to 1 tchd 33 to 1) 10
IMPENDING DANGER 10-12 V Slattery, *hmpd 1st, mstk nxt, al beh*...............................(40 to 1 op 33 to 1) 11
848⁶ COLEBROOK WILLIE 10-12 M Bosley, *prmnt, led briefly 5th, wknd appr 3 out*..........................(20 to 1 op 12 to 1) 12
991 EMBROIDERED 10-0 (7*) J K McCarthy, *al beh.* ....(40 to 1 op 33 to 1 tchd 50 to 1) 13
HALF AN INCH (Ire) 10-12 D Leahy, *nvr on terms.* ....(25 to 1 op 16 to 1) 14
1179⁹ THE GREY WEAVER 10-9 (3*) T Dascombe, *hld up beh ldrs, mstk 5th, wknd 3 out*...(40 to 1 op 33 to 1 tchd 50 to 1) 15
DURALOCK FENCER 10-12 J Railton, *f 1st*.......(33 to 1) f
AAVASAKSA (Fr) 10-12 A Thornton, *hld up beh ldrs, wknd 5th, behind whn f 3 out*...........................(33 to 1) f
GENERAL HENRY 10-5 (7*) M Batchelor, *hld up, blun and uns rdr 3rd*.............. (40 to 1 op 33 to 1 tchd 50 to 1) ur
MOYLOUGH REBEL 10-12 B Fenton, *mid-div, rdn whn slpd up on bend appr 3 out.* (40 to 1 op 33 to 1 tchd 50 to 1) su

Dist: 4l, 3l, sht-hd, 5l, 2l, 2l, nk, 1¾l, ¾l, 1¼l. 3m 55.40s. a 10.40s (19 Ran).
(Peter Wiegand), Mrs A J Perrett

1413 Scania National Accounts Hurdle Class E Novices' Handicap (0-100 4-y-o and up) £2,798 2½m.... (2:15)

1115² DREAM LEADER (Ire) [85] 6-11-7 J Railton, *led till aftr 1st, rdn to rgn ld 2 out, hdd r-in, kpt on und pres to lead ag'n last strd.* ....(5 to 2 fav op 2 to 1) 1
1051⁵ SLIPMATIC [85] 7-11-0 (7*) C Rae, *prmnt, led aftr 1st to 2 out, hng lft appr last, rgned ld r-in, hdd last strd.* ....(7 to 1 op 11 to 2 tchd 8 to 1) 2
1291⁵ POSITIVO [76] 5-10-12 D Leahy, *hld up, rdn appr 3 out, styd on approaching last*.................(10 to 1 tchd 12 to 1) 3
BOSSYMOSS (Ire) [75] 7-10-11 T Eley, *prmnt, effrt 3 out, one pace nxt*..........................(6 to 1 tchd 13 to 2) 4
989² SUPREME STAR (USA) [89] 5-11-11 A Thornton, *hld up, hdwy and hit 7th, mstk nxt, wknd appr last.* ....(7 to 2 op 3 to 1 tchd 4 to 1) 5
998⁴ CATWALKER (Ire) [64] (bl) 5-9-9 (5*) Sophie Mitchell, *hld up, rdn appr 3 out, no imprsn*............ (14 to 1 op 12 to 1) 6
990⁴ FIRST INSTANCE (Ire) [76] 6-10-12 B Fenton, *hld up, rdn appr 3 out, no dngr*...........(7 to 1 op 10 to 1 tchd 6 to 1) 7
1002⁵ GERRY'S PRIDE (Ire) [79] 5-11-1 S Curran, *hld up in tch, ev ch 3 out, wknd appr nxt*............. (6 to 1 tchd 7 to 1) 8

Dist: Sht-hd, 4l, ½l, 3l, 3l, 1½l, 19l. 4m 47.70s. a 7.70s (8 Ran).
(Mike Roberts), M J Roberts

1414 Scania 1996 Truck Of The Year Handicap Chase Class D (0-120 5-y-o and up) £4,352 2m 5f....... (2:50)

1137⁵ TOO PLUSH [103] 7-10-13 L Harvey, *made all, rdn out.* ....(7 to 2 op 3 to 1 tchd 11 to 4 and 4 to 1) 1
953⁴ LAKE OF LOUGHREA (Ire) [104] 6-11-0 A Thornton, *hld up, hdwy 9th, chsd wnr frm 4 out, no extr 2 out.* ....(4 to 1 tchd 5 to 1) 2
1301 DUHALLOW LODGE [110] 9-11-6 B Fenton, *hld up, pckd 11th, one pace 4 out*.....(10 to 1 op 8 to 1 tchd 12 to 1) 3
831⁶ KINDLE'S DELIGHT [103] 8-10-13 T J Murphy, *prmnt, mstk 3rd, rdn 8th, wknd 4 out*... (9 to 2 op 4 to 1 tchd 5 to 1) 4
1301* MONKS JAY (Ire) [93] 7-10-3 I Lawrence, *hld up in tch, hdwy 7th, rdn 4 out, sn btn.* (5 to 2 fav op 7 to 4 tchd 11 to 4) 5
1108³ WHO'S TO SAY [118] 10-11-9 (5*) Mr R Thornton, *prmnt, rdn whn hit 3 out, sn wknd, beh when mstk last.* .... (5 to 1 op 7 to 2 tchd 11 to 2) 6

Dist: 5l, 3½l, 4l, 5l, 8l. 5m 15.80s. a 6.80s (6 Ran).
SR: 17/13/15/4/-/6/ (Mrs C C Williams), Andrew Turnell

1415 Scania 4-Series Novices' Hurdle Class E (Div II) (4-y-o and up) £2,092 2m.......................... (3:25)

673* NAHRAWALI (Ire) 5-10-12 (7*) M Batchelor, *al prmnt, mstk 1st 2, chsd ldr frm 5th, led and hit 3 out, rdn clr r-in.* ....(7 to 4 op 5 to 4 tchd 9 to 4) 1
BATTLESHIP BRUCE 4-10-7 (5*) S Ryan, *hld up, hdwy 5th, chsd wnr frm 3 out, ev ch appr nxt, second and btn whn mstk last*.....(13 to 8 fav op 2 to 1 tchd 9 to 4 and 6 to 4) 2
HAZAAF (USA) 7-10-12 F Jousset, *hld up, hdwy 3 out, outpcd bef nxt, 3rd and no ch whn hit last*.....(14 to 1 op 10 to 1) 3
LITTLE SHEFFORD 4-10-12 S Curran, *led to 3 out, sn wknd.* ....(25 to 1 op 20 to 1 tchd 33 to 1) 4
TREHANE 4-10-7 J Railton, *chsd ldrs to 5th, wknd bef nxt.* ....(9 to 1 op 6 to 1 tchd 10 to 1) 5
QUEEN OF SHANNON (Ire) 8-10-7 T J Murphy, *nvr on terms, tld off whn pld up bef 2 out.* ....(10 to 1 op 8 to 1 tchd 10 to 1) pu
1215 WEB OF STEEL 6-10-12 M Bosley, *chsd ldrs to 3rd, tld off whn pld up bef 2 out*....(25 to 1 op 20 to 1 tchd 33 to 1) pu
976 BRAYDON FOREST 4-10-9 (3*) Guy Lewis, *mstk second, nvr on terms, tld off whn pld up bef 2 out*.....(7 to 1 op 6 to 1) pu
LANESRA BREEZE 4-10-12 A Thornton, *al beh, tld off whn pld up bef 2 out*..................(20 to 1 op 14 to 1) pu
MISS THE BEAT 4-10-2 (5*) Chris Webb, *al beh, tld off whn pld up bef 2 out*........(25 to 1 op 14 to 1 tchd 33 to 1) pu

Dist: 12l, 5l, 14l, 7l. 3m 47.80s. a 2.80s (10 Ran).
SR: 23/4/-/-/-/ (C F Sparrowhawk), A Moore

1416 Scania 4-Series 'King Of The Road' Hurdle Handicap Class E (0-110 4-y-o and up) £2,997 2m......... (4:00)

1175² SUPERMICK [83] 5-11-1 M Richards, *prmnt, led 3rd to 3 out, kpt on gmely und pres to rgn ld cl hme.* ....(6 to 4 fav op 5 to 2 tchd 11 to 8) 1

DONTDRESSFORDINNER [81] 6-10-10 (3*) T Dascombe, hld up beh ldrs, led 3 out, hdd and no extr cl hme.
.......................(8 to 1 op 7 to 1 tchd 10 to 1) 2
KELLY MAC [88] 6-11-6 T J Murphy, led to 3rd, outpcd 3 out, rallied r-in, ran on wl......(7 to 1 op 4 to 1 tchd 8 to 1) 3
1230* PAIR OF JACKS (Ire) [92] 6-11-5 (5*) Mr R Thornton, al prmnt, ev ch 3 out, hit last, no extr.
.......................(100 to 30 op 3 to 1 tchd 4 to 1) 4
MUHTASHIM (Ire) [88] 6-11-7 B Fenton, hld up, hit 5th, one pace aftr nxt...........(14 to 1 op 8 to 1 tchd 16 to 1) 5
1218 ANLACE [82] 7-10-9 (5*) Chris Webb, hld up, rdn appr 3 out, no imprsn...............(9 to 2 op 5 to 1 tchd 11 to 2) 6
1218* WILL JAMES [68] (bl) 10-9-11 (3*) Guy Lewis, hld up, rdn 3 out, sn wknd........ (12 to 1 op 10 to 1 tchd 14 to 1) 7
ADDED DIMENSION (Ire) [91] 5-11-9 D Leahy, hld up, hdwy 5th, sn wknd.........(14 to 1 op 10 to 1 tchd 16 to 1) 8
Dist: Hd, nk, 2l, 4l, 7l, 2½l, 23l. 3m 51.30s. a 6.30s (8 Ran).
(Mrs J M Muir), W R Muir

CHELTENHAM (good)
Sunday November 17th
Going Correction: PLUS 0.50 sec. per fur.

1417 Carlton Refrigeration Fraser Digby Conditional Jockeys' Handicap Hurdle Class E (0-115 4-y-o and up) £2,316 2m 110yds...........(1:05)

1175⁶ HANDSON [87] 4-10-0 D Salter, hld up in rear, mstk 5th, plenty to do whn pckd 2 out, styd on, str brst r-in to ld cl hme.
.......................(7 to 2 op 4 to 1) 1
810³ ROBERT'S TOY (Ire) [113] 5-11-7 (5*) B Moore, pld hrd, trkd ldr, led appr last, rdn and ct cl hme.
.......................(7 to 1 op 4 to 1 tchd 8 to 1) 2
2914 HAY DANCE [95] 5-10-8 D J Kavanagh, hld up, gd hdwy 5th, led 2 out, rdn and hdd appr last, one pace r-in.
.......................(7 to 2 op 4 to 1) 3
1208⁵ MISTER RM [111] 4-11-10 D Walsh, led till hdd 2 out, rdn and sn btn...................(5 to 2 fav whn 8 to 1) 4
1218³ HULLO MARY DOLL [87] 7-10-0 Chris Webb, trkd ldrs till rdn quickly 5th, sn tld off..................(12 to 1 op 10 to 1 tchd 14 to 1) 5
1098³ KALZARI (USA) [87] 11-9-9 (5*) L Suthern, hld up in tch, wknd quickly 5th, sn tld off.................(6 to 1 op 5 to 1) 6
Dist: Nk, 1¼l, 11l, 1½l, dist. 4m 4.50s. a 15.50s (6 Ran).
SR: -/25/5/10/-/-/ (Burrow Racing), B R Millman

1418 Food Brokers-Gloystarne Handicap Chase Class C (0-135 5-y-o and up) £4,856 3m 1f..................(1:40)

1177* TIME ENOUGH (Ire) [105] 7-10-J Osborne, made all, drw clr frm 3 out, eased r-in... (9 to 4 fav op 2 to 1 tchd 5 to 2) 1
1108² PHILIP'S WOODY [115] 8-10-10 J R Kavanagh, hld up, hdwy 5 out, wnt second appr 3 out, sn rdn, no ch wth wnr.
.......................(3 to 1 op 5 to 2 tchd 100 to 30) 2
1086² FROZEN DROP [105] 9-10-0 S Fox, chsd wnr 3rd to tenth, mstk 4 out, btn whn blun nxt.
.......................(11 to 4 op 5 to 2 tchd 7 to 2) 3
1064³ VICOSA (Ire) [112] 7-10-4 (3*) P Henley, mstks in rear, hit 11th, sn rdn, some hdwy 4 out, nvr nr to chal.
.......................(9 to 2 op 4 to 1 tchd 7 to 2) 4
1231² PAPER STAR [105] 9-10-0 B Powell, trkd wnr to 3rd and ag'n tenth till aftr 4 out, wkng whn mstk nxt, tld off.
.......................(20 to 1 op 12 to 1 tchd 25 to 1) 5
Dist: 9l, 14l, 16l, 10l. 6m 34.80s. a 26.80s (5 Ran).
(The Lewis Partnership), C P E Brooks

1419 Murphy's Novices' Handicap Hurdle Class C (4-y-o and up) £4,856 3¼m ....(2:15)

1153² MISTER BLAKE [84] 6-10-0 R Johnson, hld up in rear, hdwy 9th, slight ld 2 out, sn hdd, led ag'n aftr last, styd on wl.
.......................(9 to 1 op 5 to 1 tchd 10 to 1) 1
1343* QUEEN'S AWARD (Ire) [84] 7-9-7 (7*,6ex) M Griffiths, hld up, hdwy to join ldrs 9th, led aftr 2 out, hdd and sn aftr last, one pace.............(2 to 1 fav tchd 9 to 4) 2
1211⁵ COOLE HILL (Ire) [88] 5-10-3 A Maguire, hld up in tch, hdwy appr 3 out, lft 3rd last, ran on one pace. (9 to 1 op 6 to 1) 3
1112⁵ OLD ARCHIVES (Ire) [89] 7-10-5 J Osborne, trkd ldrs, ev ch 4 out till wknd 2 out...............(7 to 1 op 6 to 1) 4
1291² HYLTERS CHANCE (Ire) [85] 5-10-0 L Harvey, led till hdd 2 out, wknd quickly, eased, tld off.
.......................(8 to 1 op 9 to 2 tchd 9 to 1) 5
1100² TIPPING THE LINE [108] 6-11-10 R Dunwoody, chsd ldr to 9th, wknd nxt (4 out), sn wl beh, tld off.
.......................(6 to 1 op 4 to 1) 6
1144* FORT DEELY (Ire) [94] 5-10-9 N Williamson, pld hrd, hld up, hdwy 8th, cld on ldrs 4 out, held and 3rd whn slpd on landing and f last..................(3 to 1 op 9 to 2) f
Dist: 3½l, 2l, 20l, 18l, 2l. 6m 56.00s. a 40.00s (7 Ran).
(W D Edwards), R Lee

1420 Sporting Index Chase Cross Country Chase Class B (5-y-o and up) £8,488

3m 7f........................(2:50)

1069² MCGREGOR THE THIRD 10-11-2 B Harding, al prmnt, led 12th to 15th, led 19th, drw clr 2 out, easily.
(6 to 5 on op 5 to 4 on tchd 6 to 4 on and 11 to 10) 1
899² IRISH STAMP (Ire) 7-11-5 N Williamson, hld up in rear, hdwy 12th, lft second 25th, ev ch 3 out, sn rdn, one pace.
.......................(11 to 4 op 5 to 2 tchd 3 to 1) 2
1113³ SEASAMACAMILE 9-10-5 A Maguire, in rear, hdwy 12th, lost pl 16th, headway 22nd, nvr nr to chal. (33 to 1 op 14 to 1) 3
230 COOL CHARACTER (Ire) 8-10-7 B Powell, in rear till hdwy 23rd, nvr nr to chal..................(33 to 1 op 14 to 1) 4
1239³ SHAMARPHIL 10-10-5 Miss S Barraclough, al beh, tld off.
.......................(11 to 1 op 10 to 1 tchd 16 to 1 and 20 to 1) 5
MARKETPLACE (Ire) 5-10-13 Pavel Slozil, prmnt till wknd 17th, tld off..................(33 to 1 op 14 to 1) 6
899³ ITS A SNIP (bl) 11-11-5 R Dunwoody, led, slpd on landing 3rd, hdd 6th, second whn pld up beh hme. (7 to 1 op 5 to 1) pu
FURTADO (Fr) 7-10-10 Josef Vana, pld hrd, prmnt whn mstk second, led 6th to 12th, led 15th to 19th, wknd 21st, pulled up bef 26th........................(100 to 1 op 14 to 1) pu
KENTUCKY GOLD (Ire) 11-10-3 Mr P Hacking, al beh, tld off whn pld up bef 27th.10s. (8 Ran).
(Mrs D A Whitaker), G Richards

1421 Stakis Casinos November Novices' Chase Class A Grade 2 (5-y-o and up) £11,780 2m..................(3:25)

1104² CELIBATE (Ire) 5-11-0 R Dunwoody, mostly jmpd wl, trkd ldr, led 6th, hit nxt, ran on well frm 2 out, cmftbly.
.......................(6 to 4 tchd 7 to 4) 1
968² LAND AFAR 9-11-0 M Dwyer, hld up, hdwy appr 3 out, wnt second approaching last, sn rdn, no imprsn r-in.
.......................(6 to 5 on op 6 to 4 on tchd 11 to 10 on) 2
HEDGEHOPPER (Ire) 8-11-0 M Richards, led till hit and hdd 6th, trkd wnr till wknd aftr 2 out.
.......................(9 to 1 op 5 to 1 tchd 10 to 1) 3
1031² CLIFTON GAME 6-11-0 A Thornton, hld up, hdwy 4 out, 3rd and rdn whn f 2 out, rmntd.
.......................(16 to 1 op 8 to 1 tchd 20 to 1) 4
Dist: 6l, 10l, dist. 4m 11.70s. a 19.70s (4 Ran).
(Stamford Bridge Partnership), C J Mann

1422 Tony Wright Benefit Juvenile Novices' Hurdle Class D (3-y-o) £2,829 2m 110yds..................(4:00)

634* NOBLE LORD 11-12 B Powell, made all, clr 3 out, unchlgd.
.......................(6 to 1 op 4 to 1) 1
1221* ALWAYS HAPPY 11-7 C Maude, hld up in rear, hdwy 2 out, styd on to go second r-in................(7 to 1 op 8 to 1) 2
1102² BEN BOWDEN 11-6 A Maguire, chsd wnr till mstk 3 out, second ag'n aftr nxt till wknd cl hme.
.......................(9 to 1 op 7 to 1 tchd 10 to 1) 3
991* TOPAGLOW (Ire) 11-0 T Eley, hld up, efrt appr 3 out, rdn and wknd nxt...................(25 to 1 op 20 to 1) 4
BRANDON MAGIC 11-0 R Dunwoody, not fluent, wknd 3 out, mstk nxt, tld off........ (2 to 1 fav tchd 9 to 4) 5
SEATTLE ALLEY (USA) 11-0 J Osborne, hld up, chsd wnr 3 out, wknd aftr nxt, virtually pld up r-in.
.......................(5 to 2 op 3 to 1 tchd 7 to 2) 6
788⁵ TRIANNA 10-9 L Harvey, al beh, tld off whn pld up bef 3 out.
.......................(50 to 1 op 33 to 1) pu
Dist: 15l, 1¼l, 7l, 30l, dist. 4m 6.10s. a 17.10s (7 Ran).
SR: 9/-/-/-/ (Mrs S Livesey), R H Buckler

FONTWELL (good (races 1,2), good to soft (3,4,5,6,7))
Sunday November 17th
Going Correction: PLUS 1.35 sec. per fur. (races 1,3,5,7), PLUS 1.25 (2,4,6)

1423 Richmond Park Conservative Club Maiden Hurdle Class E (Div I) (4-y-o and up) £2,490 2¼m 110yds (12:20)

GLORIANA 4-11-0 M A Fitzgerald, led to second, led 5th, pushed clr last, drvn out r-in.
.......................(11 to 4 fav op 7 to 4 tchd 3 to 1) 1
NORDIC SPREE (Ire) 5-11-5 P Holley, chsd ldrs, pushed alng 5th, prog und pres 3 out, styd on to take second nr finish.
.......................(10 to 1 op 16 to 1) 2
JAKES JUSTICE (Ire) 5-11-5 P Hide, hld up rear, prog aftr 5th, rdn to chase wnr appr last, no imprsn, wknd nr finish.
.......................(100 to 30 op 2 to 1 tchd 7 to 2) 3
1207⁶ TOPANGA (bl) 4-11-5 D Bridgwater, al prmnt, chsd wnr appr 2 where mstk, hrd rdn and sn btn.
.......................(14 to 1 op 12 to 1 tchd 16 to 1) 4
SAILS LEGEND 5-11-5 D Gallagher, mid-div, rdn aftr 5th, prog und pres to chase wnr after 3 out, sn btn.
.......................(5 to 1 tchd 6 to 1) 5
975³ MR STRONG GALE (Ire) 5-11-5 A P McCoy, led 3rd to 5th, sn rdn, whn wnr till wknd rpdly aftr 3 out....(3 to 1 op 4 to 1) 6
KAIFOON (USA) 7-11-5 B Fenton, al rear, tld off frm 6th.
.......................(14 to 1 op 12 to 1 tchd 16 to 1) 7

LITTLE LUKE (Ire) 5-11-5 T J Murphy, *mid-div, lost tch aftr 5th
sn tld off.* (40 to 1 op 33 to 1 tchd 25 to 1 and 50 to 1)   8
QUISTI 6-11-5 D O'Sullivan, *strted very slwly, at tld off.*
.... (33 to 1 op 10 to 1)   9
924   INDIAN CROWN (bl) 6-11-0 S Burrough, *pld hrd, led and slow
jump second, hdd nxt, wknd rpdly 5th, tld off.*
.... (50 to 1 op 33 to 1)   10
1136⁸   LITTLE EMBERS (v) 4-10-7 (7") J Power, *rear, 9th and rdn
whn blun and uns rdr 5th.*...........(50 to 1 op 20 to 1)   ur
Dist: 2½l, sht-hd, 5l, 6l, dist, dist, 8l, 14l, 8l. 4m 49.30s. a 32.30s (11 Ran).
SR: 12/14/14/9/3/-/   (D S W Blacker), Lady Herries

1424 Walberton Novices' Chase Class E (5-y-o and up) £3,263 2m 3f. .(12:50)

OBAN 6-10-12 G Bradley, *trkd ldrs, pushed alng frm tenth,
chlgd 3 out, led last, hrd rdn and jst hld on.*
.... (5 to 1 op 7 to 2 tchd 11 to 2)   1
HEADWIND (Ire) 5-10-11 P Hide, *wtd wth, trkd ldr aftr 6th, led
gng easily 2 out, hdd last, rallied, jst fld.*
.................................(Evens fav op 10 to 1 tchd 11 to 10 on)   2
1180*   MR CONDUCTOR (Ire) 5-11-4 A Thornton, *jmpd rght, led till
rdn and hdd 2 out, one pace.*
.... (15 to 8 op 2 to 1 tchd 9 to 4 and 7 to 4)   3
1302⁶   OUR NIKKI 6-10-7 S Burrough, *hmpd 1st, rear whn uns rdr
3rd.*...........................(33 to 1 op 25 to 1 tchd 40 to 1)   ur
VICTORY GATE (USA) 11-10-12 J Railton, *sn beh, tld off and
pld up bef tenth........(40 to 1 op 25 to 1 tchd 50 to 1)   pu
12873   FULL OF TRICKS 8-10-12 D Bridgwater, *mstk 5th, sn lost tch,
pld up bef 7th..........(50 to 1 op 33 to 1 tchd 66 to 1)   pu
1054   MILLFRONE (Ire) 6-10-12 D O'Sullivan, *jmpd lft, mstk 1st,
chsd ldr till aftr 6th, sn wknd, tld off and pld up bef 3 out.*
.... (33 to 1 tchd 50 to 1)   pu
Dist: Sht-hd, 13l. 5m 5.10s. a 30.10s (7 Ran).
SR: 21/20/14/-/   (Lord Hartington), Miss H C Knight

1425 Ford Selling Handicap Hurdle Class G (0-90 4-y-o and up) £2,075 2¼m 110yds..................... (1:25)

SPRINTFAYRE [61] 8-10-0 D Gallagher, *rcd wide, led to 3rd
and frm 5th, rdn 2 out, drvn out r-in....*(12 to 1 op 16 to 1)   1
KASHAN (Ire) [61] 8-10-0 B Fenton, *prmnt till rdn and outpcd
6th, rallied to chase wnr appr 2 out, kpt on und pres.*
.... (33 to 1 tchd 40 to 1)   2
1110²   SHARP THRILL [68] 5-10-7 C Llewellyn, *hld up in cl tch, chsd
wnr aftr 3 out till bef nxt, sn btn.....*(13 to 2 op 5 to 1)   3
1112⁸   ROGER'S PAL [79] 9-10-11 (7") M Batchelor, *mid-div, rdn and
struggling 5th, sn beh, kpt on frm 2 out...*(6 to 1 op 7 to 1)   4
1175⁶   GAME DILEMMA [80] 5-10-12 (7") O Burrows, *sn pushed alng
in roar, nvr nr ldrs........................*(7 to 1 op 5 to 1)   5
JONJAS CHUDLEIGH [81] 9-11-6 J Frost, *hld up rear, prog
aftr 5th, not rch ldrs, eased whn no ch 2 out.*
.... (16 to 1 tchd 20 to 1)   6
1135⁸   PHARLY REEF [72] 4-10-11 D J Burchell, *rear, prog frm mid-
div aftr 5th, rdn and wknd nxt.........*(14 to 1 op 10 to 1)   7
1110⁶   RUTH'S GAMBLE [61] (v) 8-10-0 D Leahy, *prmnt, led 3rd to
5th, rdn nxt, wknd rpdly aftr 3 out.....*(16 to 1 op 12 to 1)   8
1175   WATER HAZARD (Ire) [78] 4-11-3 A Dicken, *al beh, tld off 3
out...........................(12 to 1 op 7 to 1 tchd 14 to 1)   9
NATIONAL FLAG (Fr) [73] (v) 6-10-12 A P McCoy, *trkd ldrs till
rdn and wknd aftr 5th, tld off 3 out...*(7 to 2 fav op 4 to 1)   10
1111   PRECIOUS WONDER [68] 7-10-2 (5") Mr R Thornton, *mid-
div, rdn and btn 5th, tld off............*(14 to 1 op 25 to 1)   11
1115⁸   ALLEZ PABLO [61] 6-9-12¹ (3") L Aspell, *hld up beh, prog and
in tch 5th, wknd rpdly nxt, pld up bef 3 out.*
.... (14 to 1 tchd 16 to 1)   pu
652⁴   MATAMOROS [88] 4-11-13 M A Fitzgerald, *mid-div, rdn and
wknd 4th, tld off whn pld up bef 6th.*
.... (13 to 2 op 5 to 1 tchd 7 to 1)   pu
990   JUST A BEAU [61] 5-9-9 (5") Sophie Mitchell, *cl up to 4th,
wknd rpdly, tld off and pld up bef 6th.*
.... (33 to 1 op 25 to 1 tchd 40 to 1)   pu
955   ASK HARRY (Ire) [61] 5-10-0 D Bridgwater, *mstks, beh and
rdn 4th, tld off and pld up bef 6th.....*(16 to 1 op 20 to 1)   pu
Dist: 1l, 17l, 16l, 2½l, 16l, 1¾l, sht-hd, dist, 26l, sht-hd. 4m 47.90s. a 30.90s (15 Ran).
SR: 12/11/1/-/-/-/   (Mrs O C Foster), J E Long

1426 Tote Bookmakers Handicap Chase Class D (0-120 5-y-o and up) £4,355 3¼m 110yds.................. (2:00)

1140²   BALLY CLOVER [100] 9-11-5 R Farrant, *led second to 5th,
trkd ldr aftr, chlgd 3 out, lft wl clr nxt, eased to walk r-in.*
.................................(5 to 4 fav op 11 to 10 tchd 11 to 8 and 6 to 4)   1
1231   SORBIERE [100] (bl) 9-11-5 M A Fitzgerald, *pckd 4th, chsd
ldrs, mstk tenth, lost tch 18th, lft remote second 2 out.*
..................................(7 to 2 op 3 to 1 tchd 4 to 1)   2
1101³   CHILDHAY CHOCOLATE [105] 8-11-10 A P McCoy, *led to
second, led 5th, mstke 12th, blun 17th, hrd rdn 3 out, jnd and f nxt.*
...........................(2 to 1 tchd 9 to 4)   f
THE WIDGET MAN [105] 10-11-10 P Hide, *hld up last, in tch
whn blun 16th, tld off when blunded 18th and pld up.*
...............(9 to 1 op 10 to 1 tchd 12 to 1 and 8 to 1)   pu
Dist: Dist. 7m 36.70s. a 66.70s (4 Ran).
(James Williams), Miss Venetia Williams

1427 Bet With The Tote Handicap Hurdle Class E (0-115 4-y-o and up) £3,782 2³⁄₄m 110yds................. (2:35)

1272⁴   MOMENT OF GLORY (Ire) [112] 5-11-13 G Bradley, *rcd wide,
hld up beh, prog 8th, led aftr last, drvn out.*
.... (9 to 1 op 7 to 1 tchd 10 to 1)   1
1139*   CASSIO'S BOY [85] 5-11-0 D Gallagher, *trkd ldg pair 5th,
prog to ld 3 out, hdd aftr last, kpt on und pres.*
.... (4 to 1 op 5 to 1)   2
EULOGY (Ire) [113] 6-12-0 D O'Sullivan, *led to 3 out, shaken
up and not quicken aftr nxt........*(5 to 2 fav tchd 11 to 4)   3
SMUGGLER'S POINT (USA) [110] 6-11-11 D Bridgwater,
mstk 4th, pressed ldr to 8th, wknd aftr 3 out.
.... (10 to 1 op 7 to 1 tchd 12 to 1)   4
597   FIRST CLASS [90] 6-10-5 R Greene, *in tch to 7th, sn wknd, tld
off.*....................(25 to 1 tchd 33 to 1)   5
709*   BELLROI (Ire) [105] 5-11-6 A P McCoy, *wtd wth, rdn and btn
aftr 7th, sn tld off.................*(7 to 2 tchd 9 to 2)   6
1112²   KALASADI (USA) [106] 5-11-7 M A Fitzgerald, *chsd ldrs,
pushed alng 7th, wknd nxt, tld off whn pld up bef 2 out.*
.... (4 to 1 op 5 to 2)   pu
Dist: Nk, 19l, 17l, dist, dist. 5m 59.10s. a 45.10s (7 Ran).
(Mrs David Moon), D R Gandolfo

1428 Weatherbys 1997 Diary Handicap Chase Class D (0-125 5-y-o and up) £4,160 2¼m....................(3:10)

1267²   NEWLANDS-GENERAL [115] 10-12-0 A P McCoy, *made all,
mstk 8th, lft clr 12th, unchlgd.*
.... (5 to 4 fav tchd 6 to 5 and 11 to 8)   1
DEAR DO [104] 9-11-3 M A Fitzgerald, *wtd wth in last, lft
second aftr 12th, no imprsn on wnr......*(9 to 4 op 2 to 1)   2
THE CARROT MAN [107] 8-11-6 P Hide, *mstk second, chsd
wnr, in tch whn blun 12th (water), not reco'r, tld off.*
.... (4 to 1 op 7 to 2 tchd 9 to 2)   3
KYTTON CASTLE [99] 9-10-12 R Bellamy, *chsd ldg pair till f
11th.*..............................(6 to 1 op 8 to 1 tchd 10 to 1)   f
Dist: 22l, dist. 4m 56.30s. a 36.30s (4 Ran).
(C Murphy), P F Nicholls

1429 Richmond Park Conservative Club Maiden Hurdle Class E (Div II) (4-y-o and up) £2,469 2¼m 110yds.. (3:45)

CLAIRESWAN (Ire) 4-11-2 (3") K Gaule, *prmnt, led 6th, rdn clr
appr last, ran on wl................*(9 to 1 op 5 to 2)   1
DANCETILLYOUDROP (Ire) 5-11-5 A P McCoy, *wtd wth, prog
and mstk 6th, rdn and ev ch 2 out, unbl to quicken.*
.... (5 to 4 fav op 6 to 4 tchd 7 to 4 and 2 to 1)   2
1230²   ADILOV 4-11-0 (5") Sophie Mitchell, *in tch, prog 3 out, rdn and
one pace frm nxt........*(20 to 1 op 25 to 1 tchd 33 to 1)   3
1202²   FLYING FIDDLER (Ire) 5-11-5 M A Fitzgerald, *pressed ldr till
lost pl aftr 5th, ran on and ev ch aftr 3 out, sn btn.*
.... (11 to 2 op 5 to 1 tchd 6 to 1)   4
1208⁴   ROSS DANCER (Ire) 4-11-2 (3") J Magee, *in tch till outpcd 6th,
one pace frm 3 out.....*(7 to 1 op 10 to 1 tchd 12 to 1)   5
1293²   SWAN STREET (NZ) 5-11-5 J Railton, *hld up rear, prog, in
tch aftr 3 out, sn btn....*(7 to 1 op 6 to 1 tchd 8 to 1)   6
I RECALL (Ire) 5-11-5 B Fenton, *led till rdn and hdd 6th, wknd
rpdly aftr 3 out.........*(50 to 1 op 25 to 1 tchd 66 to 1)   7
CHARTER LANE (Ire) 6-11-5 D Leahy, *in tch in rear to 6th, tld
off.......................(66 to 1 op 50 to 1 tchd 100 to 1)   8
1260   BLAZE OF OAK (USA) (bl) 5-10-12 (7") J Power, *pld hrd, cl up
to 5th, wknd aftr nxt, tld off and pulled up bef last.*
.... (16 to 1 tchd 14 to 1)   pu
735   MURPHY'S RUN (Ire) 6-11-0 (5") Mr R Thornton, *cl up till
wknd aftr 5th, tld off and pld up bef last.*
.... (50 to 1 op 20 to 1 tchd 66 to 1)   pu
346⁴   SHARP ELVER (Ire) 4-11-0 P Hide, *cl up till wknd and ease 3
out, tld off whn pld up bef last.*
.... (40 to 1 op 25 to 1 tchd 66 to 1)   pu
Dist: 9l, 2½l, 13l, 18l, 2½l, 16l, 13l. 4m 49.10s. a 32.10s (11 Ran).
SR: 20/11/8/-/-/-/   (Claire And Beryl), M H Tompkins

NAVAN (IRE) (yielding (races 1,2,3,4,7), good to yielding (5,6)) Sunday November 17th

1430 Tara 3-Y-O Maiden Hurdle £2,740 2m .... (12:45)

1309⁴   HIGHLY MOTIVATED 10-9 C F Swan, ...(7 to 4 fav)   1
1173⁷   MISS PENNYHILL (Ire) 10-4 (5") T Martin, ...(14 to 1)   2
1173   SPIRIT DANCER (Ire) 11-0 S C Lyons, ...(20 to 1)   3
1173⁹   MIND ME BRODY (Ire) 10-7 (7") A O'Shea, ...(14 to 1)   4
882⁸   DUNEMER (Ire) 10-6 (3") Mr R Walsh, ...(14 to 1)   5
MARLONETTE (Ire) 10-6 (3") D J Casey, ...(12 to 1)   6
1173   KIRIBATI (Ire) (bl) 11-0 R Hughes, ...(14 to 1)   7
1309⁹   ERNE PROJECT (Ire) 10-9 H Rogers, ...(25 to 1)   8
1309   DUGGAN DUFF (Ire) 10-7 (7") Mr S McGonagle, ..(50 to 1)   9
1173²   NARROW FOCUS (USA) 11-0 J P Broderick, ...(14 to 1)   10
442⁶   DISPOSEN (Ire) 10-9 T J Mitchell, ...(33 to 1)   11

1173 LADY CIANA (Ire) 10-6 (3*) B Bowens, ... (50 to 1) 12
442[4] TOY'S AWAY (Ire) 11-0 F Woods, ...(13 to 2) 13
1309[6] PEGUS JUNIOR (Ire) 10-7 (7*) R Donnelly, ...(10 to 1) 14
DUNRALLY FORT (Ire) 10-11 (3*) K Whelan, ...(10 to 1) 15
1309[7] SWEET NATURE (Ire) 10-9 A Powell, ...(20 to 1) 16
1057[6] KILBAHA (Ire) 10-9 M P Hourigan, ...(12 to 1) 17
1173[8] WOODEN DANCE (Ire) 10-6 (3*) U Smyth, ...(20 to 1) 18
574 RUN TO THE ACE (Ire) 11-0 J K Kinane, ...(33 to 1) 19
1173 ABSTRACT VIEW (USA) 10-8[1] (7*) Mr L J Gracey, (50 to 1) 20
PRINCESS TYCOON (Ire) 10-2 (7*) J A Robinson, (25 to 1) 21
927[9] MAGICAL IMPACT (Ire) 11-0 D T Evans, ...(25 to 1) 22
PETASUS 10-9 (5*) J Butler, ...(14 to 1) 23
SPANISH CRAFT (Ire) 10-4 (5*) G Cotter, ...(20 to 1) 24
1057 PEAK VIEW (Ire) 10-7 (7*) S FitzGerald, ...(20 to 1) 25
WIRE MAN (Ire) 10-7 (7*) J O'Shaughnessy, ...(50 to 1) 26
Dist: 4½l, 2½l, 6l, ¾l. 3m 59.90s. (26 Ran).
(G Phelan), A P O'Brien

1431 Monksfield Novice Hurdle (Grade 3) (4-y-o and up) £6,850 2½m... (1:15)

1088* TARTHOOTH (Ire) 5-11-7 F Woods, [illegible] ....(5 to 2) 1
1171* RADANPOUR (Ire) 4-11-2 (3*) D J Casey, *trkd ldr, rdn bef 2 out, not quicken*.................................. (5 to 1) 2
1189* GALLOPEN GARRY (Ire) 6-11-10 J R Barry, *mid-div, prog bef 4 out, sn rdn, kpt on*..............................(10 to 1) 3
1145* MULLOVER 5-11-7 T J Mitchell, *wl plcd early, prog to track ldr 4th, rdn aftr four out, sn lost pos, kpt on after last.* (14 to 1) 4
1273[7] ADARAMANN (Ire) 4-10-13 (3*) Mr R Walsh, *rcd towards rear, last 5th, rdn bef 3 out, some prog*..........................(25 to 1) 5
1189[6] BALLINABOOLA GROVE 9-10-11 (7*) J M Maguire, *mid-div, rdn aftr 4 out, sn wknd*.............................. (50 to 1) 6
1119 WHO IS ED (Ire) 5-11-4 J P Broderick, *al rear, lost tch aftr 4 out*...(150 to 1) 7
1171 LISS DE PAOR (Ire) 5-11-5 C F Swan, *trkd ldr 1st 2 hurdles, then wl plcd, tracked lder whn f two out*.........(13 to 8 on) f
MONSIEUR DUPONT (Ire) 6-11-4 J K Kinane, *rear till pld up aftr 4th*..(200 to 1) pu
Dist: 5½l, 11l, 4l, 15l. 4m 55.30s. (9 Ran).
(Mrs H de Burgh), A L T Moore

1432 Crossakiel Maiden Hurdle (4-y-o and up) £3,082 2m................(1:45)

1119[5] DELPHI LODGE (Ire) 6-12-0 Mr A J Martin, ...(12 to 1) 1
1307 TRUVARO (Ire) 5-11-6 F J Flood, ...(20 to 1) 2
850[6] DUISKE ABBEY (Ire) 6-11-9 T P Treacy, ...(14 to 1) 3
FINNEGAN'S HOLLOW (Ire) 6-12-0 C F Swan, ..(9 to 4 on) 4
WYATT (Ire) 6-11-6 R Hughes, ...(20 to 1) 5
1042* MATTORIA (Ire) 5-11-6 (3*) Mr R Walsh, ...(16 to 1) 6
1120[4] TREANAREE (Ire) 7-10-13 (7*) S Kelly, ...(33 to 1) 7
1273 DOONE BRAES (Ire) 6-11-3 (3*) U Smyth, ...(20 to 1) 8
910[5] VALLEY ERNE (Ire) 5-10-13 (7*) D K Budds, ...(10 to 1) 9
CASTLE BLAKE 4-11-1 (3*) D J Casey, ...(25 to 1) 10
CLADY BOY (Ire) 5-11-6 J P Broderick, ...(66 to 1) 11
SEAN'S QUARTER (Ire) 4-11-4 D H O'Connor, ...(33 to 1) 12
ASK ME AGAIN (Ire) 6-11-6 H Rogers, ...(20 to 1) 13
1359 ABBEY GALE (Ire) 5-11-1 T J Mitchell, ...(14 to 1) 14
1193 MIDNIGHT JAZZ (Ire) 6-12-0 M P Hourigan, ...(33 to 1) 15
1193 COOKSGROVE ROSIE (Ire) 4-10-13 P Leech, ...(66 to 1) 16
RUM FUN (Ire) 5-11-1 (5*) G Cotter, ...(20 to 1) 17
1075 WHINNEY HILL (Ire) 6-11-1 D T Evans, ...(66 to 1) 18
1195 CHIEF DELANEY (Ire) 4-11-4 L P Cusack, ...(16 to 1) 19
1241[8] LADY CONDUCTOR (Ire) 5-11-1 P McWilliams, ...(33 to 1) 20
COULTERS HILL (Ire) 8-10-13 (7*) A O'Shea, ...(66 to 1) 21
DUN CARRAIG (Ire) 8-11-11 (3*) D Bromley, ...(50 to 1) 22
1193 CARRICK GLEN (Ire) 5-11-1 A Powell, ...(25 to 1) 23
32[9] COLOURED SPARROW (Ire) 6-10-10 (5*) T Martin, (33 to 1) 24
RAGGLEPUSS (Ire) 6-11-1 K F O'Brien, ...(66 to 1) 25
TINAMONA (Ire) 6-11-3 (3*) B Bowens, ...(33 to 1) 26
MYSTERY BREEZE (Ire) 6-11-3 (3*) K Whelan, ...(25 to 1) 27
1241[3] REAL TAOISEACH (Ire) 6-11-7 (7*) Mr A K Wyse, ...(8 to 1) f
978[3] JAY MAN (Ire) 6-11-9 (5*) Mr E J Kearns Jnr, ...(12 to 1) f
Dist: 2½l, 10l, 2l, 4½l. 3m 59.80s. (29 Ran).
(Mark Ferran), Thomas J Taaffe

1433 Beechmount Handicap Hurdle (4-y-o and up) £3,425 3m............(2:15)

1277[4] ALASAD [-] 6-11-10 R Hughes, ...(4 to 1) 1
1168* ROSIN THE BOW (Ire) [-] 7-11-2 C F Swan, ... (3 to 1 fav) 2
1058[2] SHINING WILLOW [-] 6-10-10 K F O'Brien, ...(11 to 2) 3
1089* ANNADOT (Ire) [-] 6-10-12 (7*) L J Fleming, ...(4 to 1) 4
1277[8] TRENCH HILL LASS (Ire) [-] 7-10-8 T P Treacy, ...(14 to 1) 5
1278[3] GRANGE COURT (Ire) [-] 6-11-7 T J Mitchell, ...(7 to 1) 6
TOTAL CONFUSION [-] 9-11-3 S C Lyons, ...(12 to 1) 7
WYLDE HIDE [-] 9-12-0 F Woods, ...(12 to 1) 8
JIMMY THE WEED (Ire) [-] 7-9-7 J R Barry, ...(14 to 1) 9
1193 ORCHARD SUNSET (Ire) [-] 6-9-1[1] (7*) A O'Shea, (25 to 1) 10
1189[8] TIME FOR A WINNER (Ire) [-] 5-9-0 (7*) R Burke, .. (50 to 1) 11
1244[5] SIDCUP HILL (Ire) [-] 7-9-7 (5*) G Cotter, ...(14 to 1) f
Dist: 2l, 25l, 2l, 10l. 5m 54.10s. (12 Ran).
(W Jameson), Noel Meade

1434 Troytown Handicap Chase (Grade 2) (4-y-o and up) £9,675 3m..... (2:45)

981[2] LORD SINGAPORE (Ire) [-] 8-10-8 (3*) D J Casey, *mid-div, prog aftr 7th, trkd ldr 3 out, dsptd ld nxt, sn led, styd on strly.* ....(5 to 1) 1
981 HEIST [-] 7-10-4 K F O'Brien, *wtd wth, some prog bef 7th, wl plcd 3 out, dsptd ld nxt, hdd before last, kpt on*..... (12 to 1) 2
1014* JOHNNY SETASIDE (Ire) [-] 7-11-8 C F Swan, *wl plcd, prog to track ldr aftr 6th, led after 4 out, sn rdn, hdd after 2 out, wknd.* ....(11 to 8 fav) 3
981[4] SECOND SCHEDUAL [-] 11-11-4 J P Broderick, *wtd wth, rdn aftr 3 out, styd on wl*..................................(10 to 1) 4
1243[3] LOVE THE LORD (Ire) [-] 6-11-2 T P Treacy, *mid-div till prog bef 5th, trkd ldr aftr 4 out, mstk nxt, wknd*..........(13 to 2) 5
1079[4] FISSURE SEAL [-] 10-11-6 F Woods, *strted slwly, mstk 1st, rear, rdn bef 3 out, no extr*.....................(14 to 1) 6
1243* ROYAL MOUNTBROWNE [-] 8-11-9 (5*) J Butler, *wl plcd, mstk 1st, led, mistakes 6th and 8th, slow 4 out, sn rdn and hdd, wknd*..(8 to 1) 7
897 SPANKERS HILL (Ire) [-] 7-10-5 (5*) G Cotter, *trkd ldrs 1st 2 fences, lost pos, rdn bef 3 out, no extr*..............(12 to 1) 8
1243[8] NUAFFE [-] 11-11-8 T J Mitchell, [illegible] *sn wknd, pld up bef 2 out*...... (33 to 1) pu
1243[7] LOVE AND PORTER (Ire) [-] 8-10-10 D H O'Connor, *led 1st, mstk, dsptd ld nxt, trkd ldr till wknd aftr 7th, pld up bef 2 out.* ....(14 to 1) pu
981[3] TWIN RAINBOW [-] 9-10-0 L P Cusack, *rear till pld up bef 7th.* ....(15 to 2) pu
Dist: 3½l, 14l, 11l, 9l. 6m 5.30s. (11 Ran).
(Mrs E Farrelly), John J Walsh

1435 Slane Beginners Chase (4-y-o and up) £3,082 2½m..............(3:15)

THE CARRIG RUA (Ire) 6-12-0 A Powell, ... (8 to 1) 1
1242[4] DRAMATIC VENTURE (Ire) 7-11-11 (3*) D J Casey, (12 to 1) 2
1170[3] SCOBIE BOY (Ire) 8-12-0 P A Roche, ...(12 to 1) 3
MACNAMARASBAND (Ire) 7-12-0 L P Cusack, ...(14 to 1) 4
1172[5] ULTRA FLUTTER 9-12-0 J P Broderick, ... (5 to 2 fav) 5
CURRENCY BASKET (Ire) 7-12-0 K F O'Brien, ... (8 to 1) 6
982[7] MUSICAL DUKE (Ire) 7-11-9 D H O'Connor, ... (20 to 1) 7
302[7] MARLAST (Ire) 5-11-7 T J Mitchell, ...(16 to 1) 8
897[6] BAMAPOUR (Ire) 6-12-0 F Woods, ...(14 to 1) 9
1276[8] PERSIAN POWER (Ire) 8-12-0 C F Swan, ...(16 to 1) 10
1146 GARABAGH (Ire) 7-12-0 P McWilliams, ...(25 to 1) 11
1014 MACALLISTER (Ire) 6-11-11 (3*) B Bowens, ...(7 to 2) 12
JOES DANTE (Ire) 5-11-12 F J Flood, ...(12 to 1) 13
978 NORTHERN REEF (Ire) 6-11-2 (7*) L J Fleming, ... (40 to 1) 14
FINAL RUN 9-11-9 (5*) G Cotter, ...(12 to 1) 15
NOELS DANCER (Ire) 6-11-7 (7*) D K Budds, ... (25 to 1) f
883[3] MULKEV PRINCE (Ire) 5-11-12 S C Lyons, ...(8 to 1) ro
SCARVEY BRIDGE (Ire) 5-10-11 (7*) D M Bean, ... (66 to 1) pu
Dist: 1l, hd, sht-hd, 2½l. 5m 21.20s. (18 Ran).
(George Moore), Michael Flynn

1436 Navan Races Golf Classic INH Flat Race (5-y-o and up) £2,740 2m (3:45)

GARRYS LOCK (Ire) 7-11-11 (3*) Mr P English, (9 to 2 jt-fav) 1
1147[4] PHARDANA (Ire) 5-11-7 (7*) Mr J P McNamara, ... (11 to 2) 2
MY LITTLE DOXIE (Ire) 6-11-9 Mr H F Cleary, ... (14 to 1) 3
1019[9] CEOIL AGUS CRAIC (Ire) 5-12-0 Mr J P Dempsey, (16 to 1) 4
1174[4] ISOLETTE 8-11-6 (3*) Mr P J Casey, ... (8 to 1) 5
1174[2] BRASS BAND (Ire) 5-11-2 (7*) Mr R H Fowler, (9 to 2 jt-fav) 6
RED OAK (Ire) 5-11-7 (7*) Mr J J Lennon, ...(25 to 1) 7
PHAREIGN (Ire) 5-12-0 Mr P Fenton, ...(7 to 1) 8
EMOTIONAL MAN (Ire) 6-11-11 (3*) Mr B M Cash, (10 to 1) 9
PERSIAN AMORE (Ire) 5-11-9 Mr G J Harford, ... (10 to 1) 10
HARBOUR BLAZE (Ire) 6-12-0 Mr J A Berry, ... (12 to 1) 11
1174[9] HIDDEN SPRINGS (Ire) 5-11-7 (7*) Mr M O'Connor, (20 to 1) 12
MEASURED STEP (Ire) 5-11-7 (7*) Mr A C Coyle, ..(16 to 1) 13
VESPER LADY (Ire) 5-11-2 (7*) Mr A K Wyse, ... (10 to 1) 14
ASTITCHINTIME 9-11-7 (7*) Mr C A Murphy, ...(10 to 1) 15
COLLON (Ire) 7-12-0 Mr D Marnane, ...(5 to 1) 16
1307 CAROLANNS CHOICE (Ire) 7-11-9 Mr A J Martin, (25 to 1) 17
NATIVE CHAMPION (Ire) 7-11-7 (7*) Mr P P O'Brien, ...(33 to 1) 18
RYTHM ROCK (Ire) (bl) 7-11-7 (7*) Mr M G Coleman, ...(20 to 1) 19
805[9] MISTY PEARL (Ire) 5-12-0 Mr A R Coonan, ... (20 to 1) 20
Dist: 3l, ¾l, 1l, 15l. 3m 57.40s. (20 Ran).
(Mrs Dorothy Weld), Thomas Foley

LEICESTER (good to soft (races 1,2,5,6,7), good to firm (3,4)) Monday November 18th

Going Correction: MINUS 0.10 sec. per fur. (races 1,2,5,6,7), NIL (3,4)

1437 Stoughton Novices' Hurdle Class E (4-y-o and up) £2,924 2m.... (12:55)

DARAYDAN (Ire) 4-10-12 A P McCoy, *made all, clr 4th, unchlgd*....(9 to 4 op 2 to 1 on tchd 13 to 8 on) 1
DANA POINT (Ire) 4-10-5 (7*) R Wilkinson, *chsd wnr, jmpd slwly and lost pl 4th, rallied to go second appr 3 out, no imprsn whn mstk nxt*... (16 to 1 op 14 to 1 tchd 20 to 1) 2

ELY'S HARBOUR (Ire) 5-10-12 J Osborne, beh, styd on frm 2
out, nrst finish..................... (10 to 1 op 5 to 1) 3
1026⁶ WARRIO 6-10-12 M Bosley, nvr rch chalg pos.
.... (66 to 1 op 50 to 1 tchd 100 to 1) 4
SEYMOUR'S DOUBLE 5-10-12 S Wynne, prmnt, mstk 1st,
chsd wnr 5th till wknd appr 3 out...... (66 to 1 op 33 to 1) 5
UPPER CLUB (Ire) 4-10-7 R Bellamy, mid-div, hdwy to chase
ldrs 4th, wknd 3 out................(66 to 1 op 33 to 1) 6
SMART CASANOVA 7-10-12 C Llewellyn, prmnt till wknd
appr 3 out.......... (66 to 1 op 33 to 1 tchd 100 to 1) 7
1039* NORTHERN FUSILIER 4-10-12 M Dwyer, hld up, 1 second,
destroyed...........(3 to 1 op 2 to 1 tchd 100 to 30) f
RIVERBANK RED 5-10-7 T Eley, beh 5th, tld off whn pld up bef
nxt...............................(33 to 1 op 20 to 1) pu
Dist: 16l, 20l, 2½l, 8l, 14l, ½l. 3m 46.40s. a 3.40s (9 Ran).
SR: 34/18/-/-/-/-/   (D A Johnson), M C Pipe

1438 Junior Selling Hurdle Class G (3 & 4-y-o) £2,952 2m............. (1:25)

1087² PETER MONAMY (bl) 4-12-0 A P McCoy, chsd ldrs,
reminders 5th, led 3 out, drvn out.. (11 to 8 fav op Evens) 1
1179⁴ BLUNTSWOOD HALL 3-10-5 Gary Lyons, hld up, hdwy 4 out,
chlgd nxt, no extr r-in................(12 to 1 op 8 to 1) 2
DARK TRUFFLE 3-10-11 T Kent, hld up, hdwy und pres 3 out,
nvr able to chal.........(9 to 1 op 6 to 1 tchd 10 to 1) 3
1249⁷ BOY BLAKENEY 3-9-12 (7*) R Wilkinson, beh, ran on frm 2
out, nrst finish............(20 to 1 op 10 to 1) 4
1221 PROVE THE POINT (Ire) 3-10-0 P Holley, mid-div, hdwy 5th,
styd on same pace frm 2 out..............(50 to 1) 5
658⁹ KRASNIK (Ire) (bl) 3-10-2 (3*) G Hogan, led, rdn and hdd 3 out,
sn btn...........................(50 to 1) 6
1179⁸ SHANOORA (Ire) 3-9-11 (3*) E Husband, beh, styd on frm 2
out, nvr nrr...........................(50 to 1) 7
1261⁶ ADMIRAL'S GUEST (Ire) 4-11-7 T Eley, nvr rch chalg pos.
..............................(50 to 1 op 33 to 1) 8
TEE TEE TOO (Ire) 4-11-7 C Llewellyn, mid-div, beh 4 out.
..............................(33 to 1) 9
1130² GRIFFIN'S GIRL 4-11-2 N Williamson, al rear.
.....................(11 to 1 op 8 to 1 tchd 12 to 1) 10
DUET 3-10-0 T J Murphy, chsd ldr, mstk 3rd, wknd quickly 3
out.............................(33 to 1) 11
1293⁸ SAINT AMIGO 4-11-7 Derek Byrne, beh 5th.
.....................(20 to 1 op 16 to 1) 12
OPEN AFFAIR 3-9-7 (7*) C Davies, prmnt till wknd 4 out.
.....................(20 to 1 op 14 to 1) 13
NORFOLK GLORY 4-11-7 D Gallagher, hld up, headway
5th, wkng whn f last...............(33 to 1 tchd 40 to 1) f
AIR WING 3-10-5 A Maguire, prmnt, rdn and wkng whn f 4 out.
.....................(10 to 1 tchd 12 to 1) f
1293 AL HELAL (v) 4-11-0 (7*) N T Egan, hld up, hdwy 4th, blun and
uns rdr nxt.....................(50 to 1) ur
ARCH ANGEL (Ire) 3-10-0 D Bridgwater, blun and uns rdr 1st.
.....................(33 to 1) ur
584 FOUR WEDDINGS (USA) (bl) 3-10-5 C Maude, beh 5th, tld off
whn pld up bef nxt...... (14 to 1 op 8 to 1 tchd 16 to 1) pu
1295⁹ NUKUD (USA) (v) 4-11-7 (7*) C McCormack, mid-div, mstk
second, beh whn pld up bef 2 out.............(50 to 1) pu
1 SNOW DOMINO (Ire) 3-10-5 M Dwyer, al rear, beh whn pld up
bef 2 out...................(8 to 1 op 5 to 1) pu
1024 NORDIC HERO (Ire) 3-10-5 R Johnson, al rear, tld off whn pld
up bef 2 out...................(8 to 1 op 5 to 1) pu
Dist: 2l, 7l, 2l, 3½l, 8l, ¾l, 1l, 3l, 4l, 2½l. 3m 55.10s. a 12.10s (21 Ran).
(Richard Green (Fine Paintings)), M C Pipe

1439 Leicester Novices' Chase Class E (5-y-o and up) £3,246 2m 1f......(1:55)

1216³ SIGMA RUN (Ire) 7-10-12 R Johnson, led, mstk 1st, sn hdd,
jmpd slwly 5th, led 2 out, pushed clr.. (7 to 4 tchd 2 to 1) 1
1138 CAPTAIN STOCKFORD 9-10-12 J R Kavanagh, led aftr 1st to
2 out, sn slkn and btn............(25 to 1 tchd 33 to 1) 2
1216⁵ LARKS TAIL 8-10-7 R Bellamy, hld up, rdn 3 out, wknd nxt.
.....................(14 to 1 op 10 to 1) 3
LOTHIAN JEM 7-10-2 (5*) Mr R Thornton, trkd ldrs, mstk 3rd,
jmpd slwly 5th, f nxt...................(2 to 1 op 10 to 1) f
1206² COOLTEEN HERO (Ire) 6-11-5 W McFarland, whipped round
and strtd nr strt... (5 to 4 fav op 5 to 4 on tchd 6 to 4) ur
Dist: 11l, 6l. 4m 17.60s. a 9.60s (5 Ran).
(B G S Racing Partnership), J A C Edwards

1440 Midland Handicap Chase Class E (0-110 5-y-o and up) £3,655 3m ....(2:25)

1226* IMPERIAL VINTAGE (Ire) [110] 6-12-0 N Williamson, made all,
clr 2 out, eased r-in.............(5 to 4 fav op Evens) 1
CELTIC TOWN [108] 8-11-12 J A McCarthy, chsd wnr, rdn 2
out, wknd appr last........(11 to 4 op 2 to 1 tchd 3 to 1) 2
FAR SENIOR [109] 10-11-13 J R Kavanagh, trkd ldrs, rdn 9th,
wknd 2 out..........(20 to 1 op 14 to 1 tchd 25 to 1) 3
1046³ MAGIC BLOOM [105] 10-11-4 (5*) E Callaghan, hld up, mstk
14th, hit 14th, wknd 3 out..........(2 to 1 tchd 9 to 4) 4
Dist: 3l, 2½l, 1¼l. 6m 13.70s. a 28.70s (4 Ran).
(David M Williams), Miss Venetia Williams

1441 Ladbrokes Steve Walsh Testimonial Handicap Hurdle Class C (0-130 4-y-o and up) £5,692 2m......... (2:55)

1056² NAHRI (USA) [112] 5-10-11 T Eley, hld up, reminders 5th,
hdwy 4 out, led and mstk last, drvn out.
.....................(7 to 2 op 3 to 1 tchd 4 to 1) 1
KINGDOM OF SHADES (USA) [121] 6-11-6 N Williamson,
trkd ldr, mstk 3 out, led nxt, rdn and hdd last, styd on same
pace.........................(4 to 1 op 5 to 2) 2
MIZYAN (Ire) [126] 8-11-11 Mr J G Townson, prmnt, lost pl 4th,
styd on frm 2 out........(16 to 1 op 12 to 1 tchd 20 to 1) 3
1299* YUBRALEE (USA) [115] 4-11-0 A P McCoy, led, sn clr, hdd
and wknd 2 out........(7 to 4 fav op 5 to 1 tchd 9 to 4) 4
1184² FOURTH IN LINE (Ire) [129] 8-12-0 C Llewellyn, chsd ldrs till
wknd 4 out.......................(6 to 1 op 5 to 1) 5
1272⁶ MONICASMAN (Ire) [115] 6-11-0 R Johnson, al rear, lost tch 4
out...................(12 to 1 op 7 to 1 tchd 14 to 1) 6
Dist: 3l, 7l, 2l, 18l, 2½l. 3m 46.60s. a 3.60s (6 Ran).
SR: 31/37/35/22/18/1/   (Mrs Sue Adams), J Mackie

1442 Desborough Mares' Only Novices' Handicap Hurdle Class E (0-100 4-y-o and up) £2,427 2½m 110yds (3:25)

1002⁴ GLISTENING DAWN [90] (bl) 6-11-13 S McNeill, al prmnt,
chsd ldr 7th, hit 3 out, sn led, drvn out.
.....................(10 to 1 tchd 11 to 1) 1
1153⁵ JOLIS ABSENT [91] (bl) 6-12-0 A P McCoy, hld up, hdwy 4
out, rdn and ev ch r-in, no extr nr finish.
.....................(4 to 1 op 7 to 2 tchd 9 to 2) 2
1266⁴ RIVERBANK ROSE [68] 5-10-5 T Eley, led, mstk 1st, hdd appr
2 out, mistake, one pace r-in............(6 to 1 op 8 to 1) 3
QUINAG [89] 5-11-12 J A McCarthy, prmnt, lost pl 5 out, styd
on one pace frm 2 out...........(8 to 1 op 6 to 1) 4
1331* TIGH-NA-MARA [93] 8-11-9 (7*,7ex) M Newton, hld up, hit
6th, effrt appr 2 out, no imprsn.............(7 to 2 jt-
fav op 5 to 2 tchd 4 to 1) 5
CHILDREN'S CHOICE (Ire) [73] 5-10-10 C Llewellyn, hld up,
hdwy 7th, wknd 3 out. (7 to 2 jt-fav op 3 to 1 tchd 4 to 1) 6
FORTUNES ROSE (Ire) [65] 4-10-2 T J Murphy, prmnt, mstk
5th, wknd quickly 3 out............(20 to 1 tchd 25 to 1) 7
687⁴ SAKBAH (USA) [63] 7-10-0 N Williamson, hld up, hdwy 4 out,
rdn and wknd nxt........................(14 to 1) 8
1251⁶ CUILLIN CAPER [79] 4-11-2 R Johnson, chsd ldrs, wknd
quickly 4 out......(12 to 1 op 10 to 1 tchd 16 to 1) 9
SHARMOOR [83] 4-11-6 A Thornton, hld up, pld hrd, hdwy
5th, wknd quickly 3 out...........(14 to 1 op 11 to 1) 10
Dist: 1½l, 1¼l, 6l, sht-hd, 25l, 2l, 7l, dist, 8l. 4m 55.90s. a 7.90s (10 Ran).
(David Milburn), T Keddy

1443 Levy Board Handicap Hurdle Class D (0-120 4-y-o and up) £3,054 2½m 110yds......................(3:55)

BARRYBEN [92] 7-10-0 (3*) R Massey, led, jmpd rght, hdd
4th, led 3 out, rdn out..............(11 to 1 op 14 to 1) 1
GENERAL TONIC [102] 9-10-8 (5*) Sophie Mitchell, hld up,
hdwy 3 out, styd on same pace r-in....(10 to 1 tchd 9 to 2) 2
EHTEFAAL (USA) [89] 5-10-0 T J Murphy, beh, styd on frm 3
out, nvr able to chal.....(6 to 1 op 5 to 1 tchd 13 to 2) 3
1132⁵ BARFORD SOVEREIGN [106] 4-11-3 J Osborne, prmnt, drvn
alng 3 out, wknd nxt. (5 to 2 fav op 9 to 4 tchd 11 to 4) 4
SUPER RITCHART [93] 8-10-4 R Farrant, hld up, hdwy and
not much room 3 out, rdn and wknd nxt.
.....................(20 to 1 op 14 to 1) 5
1233 SHAHRANI [113] 4-11-10 A P McCoy, led 4th to 3 out, sn rdn
and wknd...........(100 to 30 op 3 to 1 tchd 7 to 2) 6
779⁴ MASTER OF THE ROCK [108] (v) 7-11-2 (3*) E Husband, hld
up, pushed alng 5th, wknd 4 out.
.....................(9 to 2 op 4 to 1 tchd 5 to 1) 7
Dist: 3l, 8l, 6l, ¾l, 6l, 15l. 4m 52.20s. a 4.20s (7 Ran).
SR: 13/20/-/10/-/9/-/   (Mrs Mary Brisbourne), W M Brisbourne

PLUMPTON (good to soft)
Monday November 18th
Going Correction: PLUS 1.40 sec. per fur. (races 1,4,6), PLUS 1.10 (2,3,5)

1444 Ringmer Conditional Jockeys' Selling Handicap Hurdle Class G (0-95 4-y-o and up) £1,909 2½m.... (1:05)

987⁴ WHISTLING BUCK (Ire) [82] 8-11-1 (7*) A Garrity, cl up, chsd
ldr 9th, led 3 out, hld on r-in..........(5 to 1 tchd 6 to 1) 1
1207² FAWLEY FLYER [85] 7-11-6 (5*) J Power, pressed ldr till mstk
5th, lost pl 7th, rallied 9th, rdn and ev ch 2 out, not quicken.
.....................(4 to 1 op 7 to 4 fav op Evens) 2
1237 MIRAMARE [60] 6-10-0 T Dascombe, cl up, pushed alng 7th,
led and quickened nxt, hdd 3 out, one pace.
.....................(16 to 1 op 20 to 1) 3
1061 DO BE WARE [70] (bl) 6-10-10 D Walsh, led to 8th, outpcd nxt,
no ch aftr.......(11 to 1 op 8 to 1 tchd 12 to 1) 4

1228⁹ ZUNO FLYER (USA) [71] 4-10-4 (7*) M Batchelor, *last till rapid prog to join ldr 7th, wknd aftr nxt.* ....(9 to 1 op 7 to 1 tchd 10 to 1) 5
1110³ CREDIT CONTROLLER (Ire) [60] 7-10-0 P Henley, *in tch till outpcd aftr 8th, sn wl beh.*..............(4 to 1 op 5 to 1) 6
KALAKATE [84] 11-11-10 Guy Lewis, *prmnt till rdn 8th, sn wknd and beh.*.. (9 to 1 op 6 to 1 tchd 10 to 1) 7
Dist: 1l, 17l, 16l, 3½l, 18l, 4l. 5m 14.90s. a 37.90s (7 Ran).
(M P Sampson), R Rowe

1445 Sir Emile Littler Challenge Cup Handicap Chase Class E (0-115 5-y-o and up) £3,097 2m 5f....... (1:35)

WOODLANDS BOY (Ire) [96] 8-10-8 (3*) D Walsh, *in tch in rear, rdn frm 7th, kpt on und pres from 12th, led r-in, ran on wl.* ....(12 to 1) 1
1204³ MR MATT (Ire) [105] 8-11-6 B Fenton, *trkd ldrs, prog 11th, led 3 out, rdn appr last, hdd and no extr r-in.* ....(10 to 1 op 20 to 1) 2
CREDON [103] 8-11-4 R Dunwoody, *prmnt till outpcd and mstk 12th, kpt on und pres 2 out, styd on.* ....(13 to 2 op 6 to 1 tchd 7 to 1) 3
902⁵ DUKE OF APROLON [87] 9-10-2² P Hide, *led till blun and hdd 6th, led tenth, mstk nxt, headed 12th, ev ch 2 out, wknd.* ....(7 to 1 op 6 to 1 tchd 11 to 2) 4
1207² TITAN EMPRESS [85] (v) 7-10-0 N Mann, *prmnt, led 6th to tenth, lft in ld aftr 12th, hdd 3 out, wknd nxt.* .....(6 to 1 co-fav op 5 to 1 tchd 9 to 2) 5
JURASSIC CLASSIC [109] 9-11-10 M Richards, *rear, lost tch frm tenth, tld off.*..............(7 to 1 op 5 to 1) 6
KNOCKAVERRY (Ire) [102] 8-11-3 I Lawrence, *rear, rdn 9th, sn lost tch, tld off.*.............. (6 to 1 co-fav op 4 to 1) 7
1301⁵ BLACK CHURCH [92] 10-10-7 D O'Sullivan, *cl up, prog tenth, led and iron broke 12th, sn hdd and not reco'r, blun and uns rdr nxt.*..............(6 to 1 co-fav tchd 11 to 2) ur
THE MOTCOMBE OAK [95] 10-10-10 G Upton, *rear, wknd 9th, tld off and pld up bef 12th.*........(50 to 1 op 33 to 1) pu
1342 WHIPPERS DELIGHT (Ire) [93] 8-10-8 M A Fitzgerald, *not jump wl, beh whn blun 4th and pld up.* (20 to 1 op 16 to 1) pu
MIGHTY FROLIC [105] 9-11-6 Mr T Hills, *prmnt till wknd appr 12th, 6th and no ch whn blun 3 out, pld up bef nxt.* ....(12 to 1 op 14 to 1 tchd 16 to 1) pu
Dist: 1½l, 1l, 3½l, 6l, dist, ¾l. 5m 36.50s. a 30.50s (11 Ran).
SR: 9/16/13/-/-/-/ (Stan Moore), R Curtis

1446 George Ripley Memorial Challenge Trophy Handicap Chase Class F (0-105 5-y-o and up) £2,786 2m .... (2:05)

895⁴ DAWN CHANCE [77] 10-11-10 R Dunwoody, *led, blun tenth, sn hdd, 2 ls dwn and rdn whn lft wl clr two out.* ....(5 to 4 op Evens) 1
1206⁴ JOKER JACK [67] 11-10-11 (3*) T Dascombe, *mstk 4th, chsd wnr till outpcd 6th, tld off 8th, lft remote second 2 out.* .... (6 to 1 tchd 5 to 1 and 13 to 2) 2
1356³ GALLIC GIRL (Ire) [69] 6-11-2 M A Fitzgerald, *trkd wnr 6th, mstk tenth, sn led, 2 ls up and gng wl whn f two out, rmntd.* ....(11 to 10 fav op 5 to 4) 3
Dist: Dist, dist. 4m 25.00s. a 33.00s (3 Ran).
(G Small), R J Hodges

1447 Knight International 'National Hunt' Novices' Hurdle Class E (4-y-o and up) £2,616 2½m.............. (2:35)

SCOTBY (Bel) 6-10-12 B Powell, *led to 3rd and frm nxt, quickened 9th, rdn 2 out, drvn out.* ....(20 to 1 op 10 to 1 tchd 25 to 1) 1
DANTES CAVALIER (Ire) 6-10-12 R Dunwoody, *hld up, prog 8th, chsd wnr 3 out, rdn and not quicken frm nxt, kpt on.* ....(7 to 4 fav op 6 to 4 tchd 2 to 1) 2
1063³ LORD ROOBLE (Ire) 5-10-12 P Hide, *trkd ldrs gng wl, shaken up and effrt 2 out, chsd wnr and mstk last, too much to do.* ....(15 to 2 op 7 to 1 tchd 6 to 1 and 8 to 1) 3
CHILLED (Ire) 4-10-12 W Marston, *prmnt, chsd wnr 9th to 3 out, wknd nxt.*..........(12 to 1 op 10 to 1 tchd 14 to 1) 4
DUKES MEADOW (Ire) 6-10-12 C O'Dwyer, *trkd ldrs till rdn and outpcd aftr 8th, no prog after.* ....(11 to 4 op 3 to 1 tchd 7 to 2 and 5 to 2) 5
DICTUM (Ire) 5-10-12 G Bradley, *cl up, chsd wnr 6th to 9th, rdn and btn bef nxt.*...... (15 to 2 op 4 to 1 tchd 8 to 1) 6
BRACKENHEATH (Ire) 5-10-12 B Fenton, *mid-div, lost tch 8th, sn beh, kpt on frm 2 out.* (16 to 1 op 10 to 1 tchd 20 to 1) 7
LITTLE EARN 6-10-5 (7*) Mr A Wintle, *mid-div, mstk 5th, outpcd frm 8th, sn beh.* ....(66 to 1 op 25 to 1 tchd 100 to 1) 8
FLAMING ROSE (Ire) 6-10-7 D O'Sullivan, *al beh, tld off 6th, pld up bef 3 out.*......(66 to 1 op 33 to 1 tchd 100 to 1) pu
830 CHURCHTOWN SPIRIT 5-10-7 G Crone, *led 3rd to nxt, wknd rpdly 6th, tld off whn pld up bef 9th.* ....(66 to 1 op 50 to 1 tchd 100 to 1) pu
900⁵ SMART IN VELVET 6-10-7 I Lawrence, *rear, lost tch 8th, tld off whn pld up bef 2 out.*...(20 to 1 op 14 to 1 tchd 25 to 1) pu
WHITE IN FRONT 5-10-9 (3*) D Walsh, *rear, mstk 5th, wknd 7th, tld off and pld up bef 2 out.*......(100 to 1 op 25 to 1) pu
Dist: 1¾l, 2l, 16l, 22l, 10l, ¾l, 13l. 5m 10.70s. a 33.70s (12 Ran).
SR: 27/25/23/7/-/-/ (Mrs E B Gardiner), R H Buckler

1448 Trans World Exhibitions Maiden Chase Class F (4-y-o and up) £2,865 2m 5f..........................(3:05)

MAMMY'S CHOICE (Ire) 6-10-12 (3*) P Henley, *trkd ldr 6th, led 12th, jnd 2 out, drvn and styd on wl r-in.* ....(12 to 1 op 10 to 1 tchd 14 to 1) 1
1236³ AMBER SPARK (Ire) 7-11-6 R Dunwoody, *hld up, hmpd 1st, prog 9th, chsd wnr 4 out, ev ch frm 2 out till not quicken und pres r-in.*..............(6 to 4 fav tchd 2 to 1) 2
RAMSTOWN LAD (Ire) 7-11-6 C O'Dwyer, *wtd wth, prog aftr 11th, cl 3rd and rdn whn blun badly 2 out, not reco'r.* .... (10 to 1 op 6 to 1 tchd 12 to 1) 3
TELLICHERRY 7-11-1 G Bradley, *bumped 1st, trkd ldrs, ev ch 12th, rdn and wknd 3 out.* ....(5 to 2 op 9 to 4 tchd 2 to 1 and 11 to 4) 4
1113 PINOCCIO 9-11-6 P Hide, *chsd ldr to 6th, wknd appr 12th.* .... (66 to 1 op 25 to 1) 5
1129 DELIRE D'ESTRUVAL (Fr) (bl) 5-11-5 B Powell, *not fluent, led to 12th, sn wknd*....... (20 to 1 op 12 to 1 tchd 25 to 1) 6
THE WAYWARD BISHOP (Ire) 7-11-6 G Upton, *al beh, tld off tenth.*......(66 to 1 op 33 to 1 tchd 100 to 1) 7
JUST 'N ACE (Ire) 5-11-5 Mr T Hills, *f 1st.* ....(11 to 2 op 5 to 1 tchd 4 to 1 and 6 to 1) f
THE WEATHERMAN 8-11-6 N Mann, *pld hrd, blun, hmpd and uns rdr 1st*...........(66 to 1 op 33 to 1 tchd 100 to 1) ur
CRUISE CONTROL 10-11-6 D O'Sullivan, *prmnt to 8th, tld off whn pld up bef 4 out*....(16 to 1 op 10 to 1 tchd 20 to 1) pu
1025³ FABULOUS FRANCY (Ire) 8-11-6 J Ryan, *blun 1st, in tch to 11th, tld off whn pld up bef 2 out.* ....(33 to 1 op 16 to 1 tchd 50 to 1) pu
Dist: ¾l, 20l, ½l, 4l, 9l, dist. 5m 36.00s. a 30.00s (11 Ran).
SR: 18/22/2/-/-/-/ (David Young), R H Alner

1449 Pease Pottage Novices' Hurdle Class E (4-y-o and up) £2,364 2m 1f .... (3:35)

1082 RITTO 6-11-5 M A Fitzgerald, *made all, rdn clr appr last, drvn out.*.............. (9 to 4 op 6 to 4 tchd 3 to 1) 1
985³ DOCKLANDS COURIER 4-10-12 J Ryan, *keen hold, cl up, effrt 3 out, chsd wnr last, hrd rdn and kpt on.* ....(6 to 1 op 7 to 2 tchd 7 to 1) 2
MULLINTOR (Ire) 5-10-12 D O'Sullivan, *jmpd rght, hld up last, prog 7th, blun 3 out, kpt on und pres frm nxt.* ....(11 to 2 op 5 to 1 tchd 4 to 1 and 6 to 1) 3
MEMORY'S MUSIC 4-10-12 B Fenton, *pld hrd, hld up in tch, prog to chase wnr and mstk 2 out, wknd last.* ....(20 to 1 op 16 to 1 tchd 25 to 1) 4
1205³ ZACAROON 5-10-7 G Bradley, *wtd wth in rear, prog to chase wnr appr 3 out till nxt, rdn and wknd last.* ....(33 to 1 op 14 to 1 tchd 50 to 1) 5
1202³ SECOND STEP (Ire) 5-10-12 R Dunwoody, *wtd wth, effrt and cl up 3 out, sn rdn and wknd, virtually pld up r-in.* ....(2 to 1 fav op 5 to 2 tchd 7 to 4) 6
GALWAY BOSS (Ire) 4-10-12 B Powell, *prmnt, chsd wnr 7th till appr 3 out, wknd rpdly, tld off*...... (10 to 1 op 5 to 1) 7
FRANKS JESTER 5-10-12 W Marston, *chsd wnr till wknd rpdly 7th, tld off whn pld up bef 2 out.* ....(25 to 1 op 12 to 1 tchd 33 to 1) pu
Dist: 2½l, 3½l, 1½l, ½l, dist, 14l. 4m 40.00s. a 43.00s (8 Ran).
(Park Industrial Supplies (Wales) Ltd), J Neville

NEWTON ABBOT (heavy)
Tuesday November 19th
Going Correction: PLUS 1.80 sec. per fur.

1450 Philip Bowen 50th Birthday Selling Hurdle Class G (4 - 7-y-o) £1,783 2m 1f.......................... (1:00)

URBAN LILY (bl) 6-10-7 (7*) J Harris, *set modest pace, sn clr, hdd aftr 3 out, led ag'n 2 out, ran on wl*...(3 to 1 op 5 to 2) 1
YET AGAIN 4-10-12 D Bridgwater, *beh, jmpd slwly 5th, gd hdwy aftr 3 out, led appr 2 out, sn hdd, ev ch last, kpt on.* ....(13 to 2 op 3 to 1 tchd 7 to 1) 2
1293⁵ FASTINI GOLD 4-10-12 W McFarland, *chsd ldrs, jmpd slwly 5th, led aftr 3 out till appr nxt, sn wknd*... (4 to 1 op 4 to 1) 3
758⁵ KONGIES MELODY 5-10-7 R Greene, *al beh, jmpd slwly 5th, lost tch*.............. (11 to 1 op 12 to 1 tchd 16 to 1) 4
891³ DENOMINATION (USA) 4-11-12 A P McCoy, *chsd wnr, chlgd 3 out, sn rdn, wknd rpdly appr nxt.* ....(9 to 4 fav op 7 to 4 tchd 5 to 2) 5
1107² PEATSVILLE (Ire) 4-10-12 A Thornton, *jmpd slwly 1st, in tch till rdn and wknd 3 out, tld off whn pld up bef nxt.* ....(9 to 2 op 7 to 1 tchd 10 to 1) pu
Dist: ½l, 10l, 23l, 22l. 4m 43.40s. a 54.40s (6 Ran).
(Mrs C J Cole), R J Hodges

1451 South West Racing Club Novices' Handicap Chase Class E (0-100 4-y-

o and up) £2,982 2m 5f 110yds (1:30)

ORSWELL LAD [99] 7-11-13 R Dunwoody, *chsd ldrs, led 6th to tenth, chlgd 2 out, led last, hdd r-in, rallied to ld last strds.*
.... (11 to 4 op 7 to 2) 1
FOXTROT ROMEO [100] 6-12-0 D Gallagher, *chsd ldrs, chlgd 4th, led 6th to nxt, styd prmnt, led tenth to last, led r-in, ct last strds.*................... (9 to 2 op 5 to 2 tchd 5 to 1) 2
1236 COUNTRY KEEPER [75] 8-10-3³ G Upton, *beh, hdwy 9th, styd on same pace frm 3 out.*........(33 to 1 op 16 to 1) 3
1302⁴ ITS GRAND [72] 7-10-0 T J Murphy, *led aftr 1st to 3rd, chlgd 4th to wknd 9th.*......................(4 to 1 op 7 to 2) 4
1236 COLETTE'S CHOICE [82] 7-10-10 A Thornton, *led till aftr 1st, led 3rd to 5th, blun 11th, sn wknd.*
.... (14 to 1 op 10 to 1 tchd 16 to 1) 5
1055⁴ STRONG TARQUIN [76] 10-6-12-0 A P McCoy, *hld up, jmpd slwly 6th, rdn and lost tch 9th, tld off.*
..........................(9 to 4 fav op 7 to 4 tchd 5 to 2) 6
1302 VARECK II (Fr) [72] 9-9-7 (7*) B Moore, *chsd ldr, hit 3rd, sn lost tch, beh whn pld up 2 out.*........(33 to 1 op 16 to 1) 7
1234⁵ CASTLECONNER (Ire) [78] 5-10-5³ J Frost, *blun 8th and beh, tld off whn pld up bef 3 out.*
.... (16 to 1 op 10 to 1 tchd 20 to 1) pu
Dist: Sht-hd, 15l, sht-hd, dist, dist, 12l. 6m 2.60s. a 60.60s (8 Ran).
(R M E Wright), P J Hobbs

1452 Faucets Sirrus Shower Valves And Fittings Novices' Hurdle Class D (4-y-o and up) £2,845 2m 1f.....(2:00)

1208³ LAKE KARIBA 5-11-6 A P McCoy, *chlgd second, led 3rd, clr aftr nxt, styd on wl.*................... (2 to 1 fav op 6 to 4) 1
1208² DEVON PEASANT 4-10-9 Mr L Jefford, *al chasing wnr, hit 4th, effrt appr 2 out, no further prog.*
..........................(9 to 4 op 6 to 4 tchd 5 to 2) 2
NORDANCE PRINCE (Ire) 5-11-0 D Bridgwater, *beh, hdwy 5th, sn one pace.*................... (9 to 4 op 5 to 2) 3
1208 PARADE RACER 5-11-0 W McFarland, *al beh, wknd 5th.*
.... (25 to 1 op 33 to 1 tchd 50 to 1) 4
1056 HELLO ME MAN (Ire) 8-11-0 Mr J L Llewellyn, *al beh.*
.... (25 to 1 op 16 to 1 tchd 33 to 1) 5
COOL GUNNER 6-11-0 C Maude, *hdwy aftr 4th, wknd nxt.*
.... (20 to 1 op 16 to 1) 6
WALTER'S DESTINY 4-11-0 S McNeill, *chsd ldrs, hit 4th, sn wknd.*............... (25 to 1 op 33 to 1 tchd 20 to 1) 7
PALLADIUM BOY 6-11-0 R Dunwoody, *effrt 4th, sn wknd.*
.... (14 to 1 op 12 to 1 tchd 16 to 1) 8
IMALIGHT 7-10-9 J Frost, *beh till f 4th.*
.... (16 to 1 tchd 20 to 1) f
1208⁹ SAAFI (Ire) 5-11-0 B Powell, *al beh, no ch whn blun and uns rdr last.*.................. (66 to 1 op 33 to 1) ur
BRYAN ROBSON (USA) 5-11-0 C Curran, *al beh, tld off whn pld up bef 2 out.*...............(66 to 1 op 20 to 1) pu
1208⁸ SAXON MEAD 6-11-0 M A Fitzgerald, *hdwy 5th, wknd rpdly and pld up appr 2 out.*...........(16 to 1 op 10 to 1) pu
Dist: 15l, 18l, nk, 1½l, 9l, 1½l, 1l. 4m 28.30s. a 39.30s (12 Ran).
SR: 5/-/-/-/-/-/ (The Lake Kariba Partnership), P F Nicholls

1453 Claude Whitley Memorial Challenge Cup Handicap Chase Class D (0-120 5-y-o and up) £3,559 3¼m 110yds .... (2:30)

FLOW [92] 7-10-5 B Powell, *wth ldrs, chlgd tenth, hit 13th, led 4 out, clr frm nxt.*........ (7 to 1 op 11 to 2 tchd 8 to 1) 1
1243³ BRAMBLEHILL BUCK (Ire) [102] 7-11-1 A P McCoy, *led till aftr 4th, led 7t to 9th, chlgd and hit 13th, one pace four out.*..........................(7 to 2 op 4 to 1 tchd 100 to 30) 2
1212³ DOM SAMOURAI (Fr) [117] (bl) 5-12-0 C Maude, *wth ldrs, led aftr 4th, blun and hdd 7th, led to four out, sn one pace.*..........................(8 to 1 op 5 to 1) 3
1239² ROCKY PARK [92] 10-10-5 B Fenton, *in tch, rdn alng 12th, lost touch frm 4 out.*........................(100 to 30 jt-fav op 4 to 1 tchd 9 to 2) 4
SORREL HILL [100] 9-10-13 M A Fitzgerald, *chsd ldrs to 13th.*.......................... (10 to 1 op 7 to 1) 5
FAST THOUGHTS [114] 9-11-13 R Dunwoody, *chlgd and jmpd slwly 3rd, chald and blun 6th, not reco'r, tld off whn pld up bef 12th.*............... (10 to 1 op 11 to 2 tchd 10 to 1) pu
1133* CHURCH LAW [102] 9-11-1 D Bridgwater, *al beh, tld off whn pld up bef 12th.*............... (100 to 30 jt-fav op 5 to 2) pu
DESPERATE [100] 8-10-6 (7*) D Creech, *al beh, tld off whn pld up bef 12th.*...............(20 to 1 op 14 to 1 tchd 25 to 1) pu
Dist: 8l, nk, 20l, 2l, ½l. 7m 33.60s. a 73.60s (8 Ran).
(Mrs C J Dunn), R H Buckler

1454 William Hill Handicap Hurdle Class C (0-135 4-y-o and up) £3,485 2¾m .... (3:00)

808⁵ SPARKLING YASMIN [119] 4-11-8 B Powell, *chsd ldr, led 5th to 6th, led appr 7th to 3 out, str chal und pres frm 2 out, led last strds.*................... (6 to 1 op 5 to 2 tchd 13 to 2) 1
1238⁴ HOLDIMCLOSE [110] 6-10-13 J Frost, *beh, hdwy 7th, led 3 out, rdn aftr 2 out, ct last strds.*
.... (10 to 1 op 8 to 1 tchd 12 to 1) 2

OATIS ROSE [97] 6-10-0 C O'Dwyer, *chsd ldrs, chlgd 7th, outpcd 3 out.*...........(10 to 1 op 12 to 1 tchd 14 to 1) 3
1211* ALLOW (Ire) [57] 5-9-9 (5*) Mr R Thornton, *chsd ldrs, lost pl appr 5th, no dngr aftr.*...............(7 to 1 tchd 5 to 1) 4
1056³ BALANAK (USA) [121] (v) 5-11-10 R Dunwoody, *in tch, hdwy to chase ldrs 7th, sn wknd.*
..........................(9 to 4 fav op 11 to 4 tchd 2 to 1) 5
756* BETTER BYTHE GLASS (Ire) [100] 7-10-3 C Llewellyn, *led to 5th, led 6th, rdn and hdd 7th, wknd quickly.*
.... (10 to 1 op 8 to 1) 6
1270³ THE REVEREND BERT (Ire) [106] 8-10-9 A P McCoy, *hdwy to chase ldrs 6th, rdn nxt, wknd 3 out.*
.... (4 to 1 tchd 9 to 2 and 7 to 2) 7
1303⁴ JADIDH [99] 8-9-11 (5*) D Salter, *beh till f 6th.*
.... (14 to 1 op 16 to 1 tchd 20 to 1) f
1056⁹ NEEDWOOD MUPPET [110] 9-10-13 L Harvey, *al beh, tld off 6th, pld up bef 2 out.*...........(16 to 1 op 12 to 1) pu
Dist: Sht-hd, 18l, 15l, 22l. 5m 47.60s. a 46.60s (9 Ran).
SR: 24/15/-/-/-/ (Victor G Palmer), P J Hobbs

1455 Faucets A & J Gummers Handicap Chase Class E (0-115 5-y-o and up) £2,831 2m 110yds.......................... (3:30)

WELL TIMED [92] 6-10-5⁵ J Frost, *in tch, hdwy to chase ldr aftr 3 out, styd on und pres r-in to ld last strds.*
..........................(7 to 2 op 4 to 1 tchd 9 to 2) 1
1206³ JAMES THE FIRST [15] 8-12-0 A P McCoy, *led second, clr frm 2 out, rdn r-in, wknd and ct last strds.*
..........................(6 to 4 fav tchd 7 to 4) 2
894³ REX TO THE RESCUE (Ire) [100] 8-10-10 (3*) P Henley, *led to second, chsd ldr, hit 7th, hit 3 out, sn wknd.*
.... (3 to 1 op 2 to 1 tchd 100 to 30) 3
1319² FENWICK [88] 9-9-12 (3*) T Dascombe, *hdwy 6th, rdn 2 out, sn wknd.*...........(3 to 1 op 2 to 1 tchd 100 to 30) 4
Dist: Sht-hd, 7l, 20l. 4m 35.70s. a 37.70s (4 Ran).
SR: -/20/-/-/ (Mrs G A Robarts), R G Frost

1456 Bounderies Intermediate Open National Hunt Flat Class H (4,5,6-y-o) £1,201 2m 1f.......................... (4:00)

IRANOS (Fr) 4-11-4 A P McCoy, *made virtually all, clr frm 3 fs out.*...................(9 to 4 fav op 2 to 1 tchd 9 to 2) 1
671* NEVER IN DEBT 4-11-4 (7*) Mr G Shenkin, *hdwy 7 fs out, styd on to chase wnr o'r one out, no a dngr.* (10 to 1 op 5 to 1) 2
APRIL SEVENTH (Ire) 5-11-4 W Marston, *hdwy to chase ldrs 6 fs out, wknd wnr 3 out till o'r one out, sn one pace.*
.... (10 to 12 to 1 tchd 20 to 1) 3
COUNTRY TARQUIN 4-11-4 R Dunwoody, *al in tch, styd on same pace fnl 3 fs.*...................(3 to 1 op 2 to 1) 4
DOM BELTRANO (Fr) 4-10-11 (7*) L Suthern, *sn chasing ldrs, wknd 3 fs out.*.........(11 to 2 op 4 to 1 tchd 6 to 1) 5
GREENFIELD GEORGE (Ire) 5-11-4 L Harvey, *prmnt altr ten fs, wknd o'r 4 out.*........(15 to 2 op 9 to 2 tchd 8 to 1) 6
SPRIG MUSLIN 4-11-1 (5*) Sophie Mitchell, *prmnt early, beh hfwy.*.......... (9 to 2 op 4 to 1 tchd 5 to 1 and 5 to 1) 7
MR AGRIWISE 5-11-4 J Frost, *effrt hfwy, sn wknd.*
.... (20 to 1 op 8 to 1) 8
1240 ZAGGY LANE 4-10-13 (5*) D Salter, *with wnr to hfwy, sn wknd.*..................(66 to 1 op 33 to 1) 9
1240⁵ DEFENDTHEREALM 5-11-4 Mr A Holdsworth, *prmnt early, beh hfwy.*......(14 to 1 op 16 to 1 tchd 25 to 1) 10
SHE'S THE GOVERNOR 5-10-13 B Powell, *al beh, tld off whn pld up o'r 3 fs out.*...............(66 to 1 op 33 to 1) pu
Dist: 11l, 2l, sht-hd, ¾l, 25l, ¾l, 11l, 24l, 10l. 4m 25.00s. (11 Ran).
(B A Kilpatrick), M C Pipe

FAIRYHOUSE (IRE) (yielding to soft) Wednesday November 20th
Going Correction: PLUS 0.30 sec. per fur. (races 1,3,4,6,7), PLUS 0.45 (2,5)

1457 Kilbride Hurdle (4 & 5-y-o) £3,082 2m.......................... (12:45)

GUEST PERFORMANCE (Ire) 4-11-9 R Hughes, (Evens fav) 1
1406² HILL SOCIETY (Ire) 4-11-9 C F Swan, ... (6 to 4) 2
1246² BALLYRIHY BOY (Ire) 5-10-13 (5*) J M Donnelly, ... (8 to 1) 3
943⁴ SHARATAN 4-11-3 T P Treacy, ... (7 to 1) 4
NAZMI (Ire) 4-10-13 K F O'Brien, ... (8 to 1) 5
KAISER SOSA (Ire) 5-11-4 A Powell, ...(20 to 1) 6
1432 COOKSGROVE ROSIE (Ire) 4-10-8 P Leech, ... (50 to 1) 7
898 DOUBLE OR NOTHING (Ire) 4-10-8 H Rogers, ... (40 to 1) 8
JAKDUL (Ire) 5-11-4 T J Mitchell, ...(12 to 1) i
Dist: ½l, 8l, 6l, 13l. 3m 56.80s. a 12.80s (9 Ran).
SR: 15/14/-/-/-/-/ (S Mulryan), D T Hughes

1458 Donoughmore Handicap Chase (0-109 5-y-o and up) £3,082 2¼m .... (1:15)

HEMISPHERE (Ire) [-] 7-9-12 (5*) G Cotter, ...(4 to 1) 1
1274² BARNAGEERA BOY (Ire) [-] 7-12-0 K F O'Brien, (7 to 4 fav) 2
1091* FINAL TUB (Ire) [-] 13-11-12 C F Swan, ... (3 to 1) 3

1274⁶ HANNIES GIRL (Ire) [-] 7-10-2 (7*) L J Fleming, ... (5 to 1)   4
1191 BALLYFIN BOY [-] 10-10-5 F Woods, ... (14 to 1)   pu
 CARRICKROVADDY [-] 10-11-3 L P Cusack, ... (20 to 1)   pu
926² DRINDOD (Ire) [-] 7-11-2 J P Broderick, ... (5 to 1)   pu
Dist: 4½l, 15l, dist. 4m 39.30s. a 14.30s (7 Ran).
SR: 13/33/6/-/   (K F McNulty), D T Hughes

1459 Ward 3-Y-O Maiden Hurdle £3,082 2m. . . . . (1:45)

1309² GREENHUE (Ire) 11-0 T P Rudd, ...(13 to 8 fav)   1
1309³ THREE RIVERS 10-7 (7*) P Morris, ...(5 to 1)   2
 LOUGH SLANIA (Ire) 11-0 C F Swan, ... (10 to 1)   3
882⁷ COMRADE CHINNERY (Ire) 11-0 J P Broderick, . . .(10 to 1)   4
1430³ SPIRIT DANCER (Ire) 11-0 S C Lyons, ...(8 to 1)   5
 AUTOBABBLE (Ire) 10-7 (7*) Mr K Ross, ...(25 to 1)   6
1173⁶ CARRANSPRAWN (Ire) 11-0 R Hughes, ... (5 to 1)   7
 VINCITORE (Ire) 11-0 L P Cusack, ... (12 to 1)   8
 TAX REFORM (USA) 11-0 R Hogers, ... (10 to 1)   9
 IFTATAH 10-7 (7*) I Browne, ... (8 to 1)   10
 LUDGROVE 11-0 F Woods, ... (8 to 1)   11
 CHUIPHOGA 10-9 A Powell, ...(10 to 1)   12
 ROYAL MIDNIGHT (Ire) 10-7 (7*) L J Lmith, ...(10 to 1)   13
 CURRAGH COUNCIL (Ire) 10-9 K F O'Brien, ...(25 to 1)   14
 NORTH OF WHAT (Ire) 11-0 T P Treacy, ... (8 to 1)   f
 NAGILLAH (Ire) 10-2 (7*) K A Kelly, ...(33 to 1)   bd
 SNIFFLE (Ire) 10-9 R M Burke, ... (14 to 1)   ro
 SISTER BID (Ire) 10-9 P P Leech, ...(33 to 1)   pu
Dist: 2½l, 5½l, 4l, 1½l. 3m 54.80s. a 10.80s (18 Ran).
SR: 26/23/17/13/11/-/   (John F Newe), M J P O'Brien

1460 Curragha Maiden Hurdle (5-y-o) £3,082 2½m. . . . . (2:15)

1019² MISTY MOMENTS (Ire) 11-6 R Hughes, ...(5 to 4 fav)   1
1360⁵ DIAMOND DOUBLE (Ire) 11-1 C F Swan, ... (9 to 2)   2
1041³ THE CLIENT (Ire) 11-6 J P Broderick, ... (5 to 1)   3
1076⁷ WYN WAN SOON (Ire) 11-6 D H O'Connor, ...(16 to 1)   4
 IVERK'S PRIDE (Ire) 11-1 (5*) J Butler, ... (10 to 1)   5
1117⁶ FIGHTING FIDDLE (Ire) 11-3 (3*) Mr R Walsh, . . . (12 to 1)   6
 SORCERER'S DRUM (Ire) 11-6 C O'Brien, ...(14 to 1)   7
1195⁹ KILCAR (Ire) 11-3 (3*) K Whelan, ... (10 to 1)   8
1244⁸ CORALDA (Ire) 11-1 H Rogers, ... (14 to 1)   9
1074 BOB BARNES (Ire) (bl) 11-7 (7*) Mr J J O'Gorman, (16 to 1)   10
494⁵ TWENTYFIVEQUID (Ire) 12-0 Mr P F Graffin, ... (10 to 1)   11
1145⁷ CNOCADRUM VI (Ire) 11-6 T P Treacy, ... (16 to 1)   12
 COUNCILLOR (Ire) 11-6 S C Lyons, ... (16 to 1)   pu
1145⁸ OUR DUCHESS (Ire) 11-1 K F O'Brien, ...(16 to 1)   pu
 DUBLINTWELVE (Ire) 11-6 L P Cusack, ...(20 to 1)   pu
Dist: 3l, 6l, 15l. 4m 56.60s. a 12.60s (15 Ran).
SR: 26/18/17/14/-/-/   (Mrs T M Moriarty), D T Hughes

1461 Mulhuddart E.B.F. Novice Chase (5-y-o and up) £4,110 2¾m. . . . . . (2:45)

 PAPILLON 5-11-4 C F Swan, ... (3 to 1 fav)   1
1089⁴ NATIVE STATUS (Ire) 6-11-4 (3*) K Whelan, ... (10 to 1)   2
1276⁶ AMBLE SPEEDY (Ire) 6-11-7 F Woods, ... (10 to 1)   3
1080* LE GINNO (Fr) 9-11-11 T P Treacy, ...(7 to 2)   4
1059⁵ THE BOURDA 10-11-7 J P Broderick, ...(14 to 1)   5
1170* ONTHEROADAGAIN (Ire) 8-11-11 T P Rudd, ...(9 to 2)   6
 FINGAL BOY (Ire) 8-11-2 (5*) G Cotter, ...(20 to 1)   7
 BROWNRATH KING (Ire) 7-11-7 T J Mitchell, ...(20 to 1)   8
 SHUIL DAINGEAN (Ire) 6-11-0 (7*) Mr K Ross, ... (25 to 1)   9
1116³ MOUSSAHIM (USA) 6-11-11 L P Cusack, ... (7 to 1)   f
1242² THE LATVIAN LARK (Ire) 8-11-7 K F O'Brien, ...(4 to 1)   f
1362 SWINGER (Ire) 7-11-7 H Rogers, ...(20 to 1)   ur
 ALAMILLO (Ire) 7-10-13 (3*) U Smyth, ... (16 to 1)   bd
Dist: 2l, 15l, sht-hd, 25l. 5m 42.10s. a 15.10s (13 Ran).
SR: 38/39/24/28/-/-/   (Mrs J Maxwell Moran), T M Walsh

1462 Warrenstown Handicap Hurdle (0-123 4-y-o and up) £3,082 2m . . . . (3:15)

1017⁴ MAJOR JAMIE [-] 5-11-3 F Woods, ... (5 to 2 fav)   1
1275³ MAGICAL FUN (Ire) [-] 4-11-1 K F O'Brien, ... (10 to 1)   2
1273 ICED HONEY [-] 9-10-8 H Rogers, ...(12 to 1)   3
1273⁸ ILLBETHEREFORYOU (Ire) [-] 5-9-9 (7*) S FitzGerald,
 . . . . (10 to 1)   4
1273⁷ GREENHUE [-] 6-9-0 C F Swan, ... (3 to 1)   5
1190⁴ WEST ON BRIDGE ST (Ire) [-] 6-11-10 T P Treacy, (15 to 2)   6
1017² JOHNNY HANDSOME (Ire) [-] 6-9-13 (7*) M D Murphy,
 . . . .(6 to 1)   7
395⁷ SPECTACLE (Ire) [-] 6-9-0 (7*) A O'Shea, ... (16 to 1)   8
 COMMAND 'N CONTROL (Ire) [-] 7-10-9 (5*) G Cotter, (16 to 1)   9
744 KENTUCKY BABY (Ire) [-] 6-11-2 (5*) P D Carey, . . (10 to 1)   10
Dist: 9l, 2l, sht-hd, 5l. 3m 59.40s. a 15.40s (10 Ran).
 (C Nolan), A L T Moore

1463 Drumree I.N.H. Flat Race (5-y-o and up) £3,082 2¼m. . . . . (3:45)

611² OPTIMISM REIGNS (Ire) 5-12-0 Mr P Fenton, ...(4 to 1)   1
1013⁹ PRE-LET (Ire) 6-11-2 (7*) Mr G Elliott, ...(4 to 1)   2
1307³ JODESI (Ire) 6-12-0 Mr J A Nash, ... (3 to 1 jt-fav)   3
 BALLYCOPPIGAN (Ire) 5-11-2 (7*) Mr M Kavanagh, . .(14 to 1)   4
1279⁶ SHEISAGALE (Ire) 5-11-2 (7*) Mr A C Coyle, ...(5 to 1)   5

1018⁶ MR BAXTER BASICS 5-12-0 Mr A J Martin, . .(3 to 1 jt-fav)   6
1096 OCTOBER SEVENTH 5-12-0 Mr D Marnane, ... (8 to 1)   7
1019 HEAD CHAPLAIN (Ire) 5-11-7 (7*) Mr R Geraghty, . .(14 to 1)   8
945⁴ THE TEXAS KID (Ire) 5-11-7 (7*) Mr S M Duffy, ...(12 to 1)   9
1189 ARCTIC GREY (Ire) (bl) 6-11-11 (3*) Mr P English, . .(12 to 1)   10
1241 BARNA LASS (Ire) 5-11-9 Miss M Olivefalk, ...(12 to 1)   11
1019 VERYWELL (Ire) 5-11-7 (7*) Mr N Geraghty, ...(20 to 1)   12
 CARRIG BOY (Ire) 6-11-11 (3*) Mr D Valentine, ...(10 to 1)   13
929 ARKDEL (Ire) 7-12-0 Mr A R Coonan, ... (25 to 1)   14
1041⁵ ZUZUS PETALS (Ire) 6-11-6 (3*) Mr J Connolly, . . . (25 to 1)   15
1174 JACKPOT JOHNNY (Ire) 5-11-9 (5*) Mr G Farrell, . . (10 to 1)   16
1307⁶ ASFREEASTHEWIND (Ire) 5-11-9 Mr J P Dempsey, (8 to 1)   17
Dist: ¾l, hd, 2l, 4l. 4m 19.70s. (17 Ran).
 (John J McLoughlin), John J McLoughlin

HAYDOCK (good)
Wednesday November 20th
Going Correction: PLUS 0.30 sec. per fur. (races 1,2,4,6) PLUS 0.05 (3,5)

1464 Newton-Le-Willows Police Mares' Only Novices' Hurdle Class D (4-y-o and up) £2,885 2m. . . . . (1:10)

1227⁴ MARELLO 5-10-7 P Niven, patiently rdn, smooth hdwy hfwy,
 drw level 2 out, led last, ran on strly.
 . . . .(2 to 1 op 7 to 4 tchd 9 to 4)   1
1182* QUEEN OF SPADES (Ire) 5-10-7 C Llewellyn, led, quickened
 hfwy, jnd 2 out, hdd last, kpt on same pace.
 . . . .(2 to 1 on op 7 to 4 on tchd 13 to 8 on)   2
 ANGLESEY SEA VIEW 7-10-7 T Kent, al wl plcd, drvn alng
 whn ldg pair quickened 3 out, one pace aftr.
 . . . .(20 to 1 op 12 to 1)   3
1224 CLIBURNEL NEWS (Ire) 6-10-7 T Eley, settled midfield, bustled alng whn ldg trio drw clr appr 3 out, nvr dngrs. (33 to 1)   4
 SCALLY HICKS 5-10-7 Gary Lyons, pressed ldrs, feeling
 pace and rdn aftr 4 out, tld off. (66 to 1 op 50 to 1)   5
 MISS MONT 7-10-7 R Hodge, chsd ldrs, effrt hfwy, struggling
 aftr 4 out, tld off. . . . .(66 to 1)   6
 PRUSSIAN EAGLE (Ire) 4-10-7 R Dunwoody, struggling hfwy,
 tld off. . . . .(25 to 1 op 16 to 1)   7
 MEESONETTE 4-10-7 B Harding, pressed ldrs, struggling to
 hold pl aftr 4 out, lost tch, tld off. . . . .(66 to 1)   8
1255⁶ PROMISE TO TRY (Ire) 4-10-2 (5*) S Taylor, settled in tch,
 struggling hfwy, tld off. . . . .(66 to 1 op 50 to 1)   9
976 SLOE BRANDY 6-10-7 Mr A Walton, in tch to hfwy, tld off whn
 f 2 out. . . . .(66 to 1 op 50 to 1)   f
1227⁴ BRIDLED TERN 5-10-7 M Dwyer, settled rear, f 3rd.
Dist: 2½l, 28l, 16l, 28l, 6l, 17l, 1¼l, 14l. 3m 47.90s. a 9.90s (11 Ran).
SR: 28/32/-/-/-/-/   (Mrs M Williams), Mrs M Reveley

1465 Liverpool Handicap Hurdle Class D (0-120 4-y-o and up) £2,759 2m . . . . (1:40)

1225² SAINT CIEL (USA) [105] 8-11-6 R Supple, wtd wth, improved
 4 out, rdn and styd on gmely to ld r-in.
 . . . .(11 to 8 fav op 5 to 4 tchd 6 to 4)   1
 CIRCUS LINE [95] 5-10-10 M Dwyer, nvr far away, chlgd 3
 out, drw level nxt, kpt on same pace r-in.
 . . . .(7 to 2 op 4 to 1 tchd 9 to 2)   2
1184⁴ DESERT FIGHTER [111] 5-11-12 P Niven, trkd ldrs, effrt 3 out,
 rdn to ld last, hdd and not quicken r-in . . (5 to 1 op 7 to 2)   3
 NASHVILLE STAR (USA) [100] (v) 5-11-1 R Bellamy, led, mstk
 and reminder 3 out, jnd nxt, rdn and hdd last, no extr.
 . . . . (25 to 1 op 20 to 1)   4
 EUROTWIST [112] 7-11-10 (3*) G Lee, settled to track ldrs,
 effrt and drvn alng aftr 3 out, one pace betw last 2.
 . . . . (10 to 1 op 7 to 1)   5
 INNOCENT GEORGE [94] 7-10-9 R Dunwoody, pressed ldrs,
 drvn alng whn pace quickened 3 out, no imprsn frm nxt.
 . . . .(14 to 1 op 10 to 1)   6
1148⁶ HOLDERS HILL (Ire) [113] 4-12-0 L Wyer, patiently rdn,
 steady hdwy appr 3 out, ridden aftr nxt, 5th and tired whn f
 last. . . . .(9 to 1 op 7 to 1)   f
Dist: 1¾l, 2l, 2½l, 1¼l, nk. 3m 53.00s. a 15.00s (7 Ran).
 (Tam Racing), F Jordan

1466 Edward Hanmer Memorial Chase Limited Handicap Class B (5-y-o and up) £10,035 3m. . . . . (2:10)

 UNGUIDED MISSILE (Ire) [148] 8-11-0 R Dunwoody, jmpd wl,
 dsptd ld, led aftr tenth, pckd 6 out, styd on strly last 3.
 . . . .(11 to 10 on op 5 to 4 tchd 5 to 4 on)   1
 COULDNT BE BETTER [160] 9-11-12 G Bradley, settled to
 track ldg pair, chlgd 4 out, and pres whn hit 2 out, rallied frm
 last, ran on wl. . . . .(11 to 4 op 2 to 1)   2
1084² GALES CAVALIER (Ire) [160] 8-11-12 M Dwyer, made most till
 aftr tenth, drvn alng appr strt, rallied, wknd quickly frm last.
 . . . .(5 to 2 op 9 to 4)   3
1332⁴ QUIXALL CROSSETT [139] 11-10-0 (5*) S Taylor, sn one
 fence beh, al tld off. . . . .(500 to 1 op 200 to 1)   4
Dist: 4l, 20l, dist. 6m 15.90s. a 10.90s (4 Ran).

SR: 37/45/25/-/   (D E Harrison), G Richards

1467 Hindley Green Handicap Hurdle
Class C (0-135 4-y-o and up) £3,468
2½m. . . . . (2:40)

808* TULLYMURRY TOFF (Ire) [120] 5-11-0 (5*) E Callaghan, *nvr far away, led 2 out, quickened clr last, readily.*
. . . .(3 to 1 op 5 to 2)   1
1268² MYTTON'S CHOICE (Ire) [126] 5-11-6 (5*) Mr R Thornton, *al wl plcd, led hfwy, pckd and hdd 2 out, rallied r-in.*
. . . . (3 to 1 op 5 to 2 tchd 100 to 30)   2
TURNPOLE (Ire) [128] 5-11-13 P Niven, *trkd ldrs, hit 4th, effrt and hit 3 out, rdn and one pace aftr nxt.*
. . . . (5 to 2 fav op 9 to 4 tchd 11 to 4)   3
MR BUREAUCRAT (NZ) [119] 7-11-4 A Dobbin, *hld up last, improved appr 3 out, sn rdn, wknd quickly bef nxt.*
. . . . (11 to 1 op 10 to 1)   4
1222* PALOSANTO (Ire) [122] 6-11-7 C Llewellyn, *led, sn clr, hdd hfwy, hndy till reminders and wknd quickly appr 3 out, tld off.*
. . . . (11 to 4 op 5 to 2 tchd 3 to 1)   5
Dist: 3½l, 3l, 16l, 12l. 4m 54.60s. a 18.60s (5 Ran).
          (John H Wilson And Mr J H Riley), J M Jefferson

1468 Wargrave Handicap Chase Class C
(0-130 5-y-o and up) £4,349 2m
. . . . (3:10)

1157³ THUMBS UP [125] 10-12-0 R Dunwoody, *pressed ldr, led 5th to 5 out, upsides whn slpd bend bef 3 out, led aftr nxt, styd on.*
. . . . (13 to 8 fav op 11 to 8)   1
1378 SPANISH LIGHT (Ire) [122] 7-11-11 A Dobbin, *led to 5th, led 5 out till aftr 2 out, styd on same pace.*
. . . . (11 to 4 op 2 to 1 tchd 3 to 1)   2
726⁶ REBEL KING [97] 6-9-9 (5*) S Taylor, *chsd ldg pair, reminders frm hfwy, struggling and no imprsn from 3 out.*
. . . . (13 to 2 op 6 to 1)   3
1316⁵ POTATO MAN [100] 10-10-3 B Harding, *settled in tch, struggling to keep up hfwy, tld off.*
. . . . (9 to 4 op 5 to 2 tchd 11 to 4)   4
1332⁷ MONAUGHTY MAN [97] 10-10-0 Mr P Murray, *in tch till ran out and crashed through rail paddock bend aftr 4th.* (25 to 1)   ro
Dist: 7l, 11l, dist. 4m 5.90s. a 9.90s (5 Ran).
SR: 41/31/   (Mrs B Taylor), G M McCourt

1469 Earlestown Handicap Hurdle Class D
(0-120 4-y-o and up) £2,815 2m 7f
110yds. (3:40)

1315* HAILE DERRING [107] 6-12-2 (6ex) C Llewellyn, *led or dsptd ld thrght, narrow lead appr 2 out, kpt on wl to go clr r-in.*
. . . . (13 to 8 on op 2 to 1 on tchd 6 to 4 on)   1
1218² DESERT FORCE (Ire) [90] 7-10-13 G Bradley, *wtd wth, improved to draw level 2 out, rdn and kpt on same pace r-in.*
. . . . (4 to 1 tchd 9 to 2)   2
1207³ COUNTRY STORE [91] 7-11-0 S Curran, *led or dsptd ld till appr 2 out, rdn and wknd quickly betw last two.*
. . . . (16 to 1 op 10 to 1)   3
1149 FLAT TOP [99] 5-11-8 M Dwyer, *settled in tch, wnt hndy aftr 4 out, rdn nxt, wknd quickly, tld off.* . . . . (4 to 1 op 5 to 1)   4
Dist: 4l, 20l, 9l. 5m 57.80s. a 26.80s (4 Ran).
          (Mrs V Stockdale), N A Twiston-Davies

HEREFORD (good to soft)
Wednesday November 20th
Going Correction: PLUS 0.65 sec. per fur. (races 1,3,5,7), PLUS 0.50 (2,4,6)

1470 Marden Juvenile Novices' Hurdle
Class E (3-y-o) £2,486 2m 1f. . (1:00)

CROWN AND CUSHION 10-12 P Holley, *beh till hdwy appr 5th, lft second 3 out, left in ld bef nxt, rdn out.*
. . . . (100 to 1 op 50 to 1)   1
1102⁴ SIBERIAN MYSTIC 11-0 W McFarland, *hld up, hdwy 5th, lft 3rd 2 out and second nxt, no imprsn aftr.* (10 to 1 op 6 to 1)   2
WARNING REEF 10-12 R Johnson, *hld up, hdwy 4th, mstk nxt, poor 3rd whn blun 3 out and next, tld off.*
. . . . (5 to 1 op 5 to 2)   3
1209 PAULTON 10-12 R Greene, *nvr nr to chal, tld off.*
. . . . (100 to 1 op 66 to 1)   4
1179² LADY MAGNUM (Ire) 10-7 N Mann, *hld up, nvr on terms, tld off.* . . . . (10 to 1 tchd 12 to 1)   5
WORTH THE BILL 10-12 S Wynne, *al beh, tld off.*
. . . . (50 to 1 tchd 66 to 1)   6
IRISH KINSMAN 10-12 J R Kavanagh, *al beh, tld off.*
. . . . (33 to 1 op 14 to 1)   7
1221 GRASSHOPPER 10-9 (3*) D Walsh, *al beh, tld off.*
. . . . (33 to 1 op 16 to 1)   8
COME ON IN 10-5 (7*) X Aizpuru, *trkd ldr till f 3rd.*
. . . . (66 to 1 op 33 to 1)   f
1286⁷ DEUX CARR (USA) 10-12 V Smith, *prmnt, lft second 3rd, blun nxt, second whn f 3 out.* . . . . . . (40 to 1 op 16 to 1)   f
NOBLE COLOURS 10-12 Mr J Jukes, *hld up, brght dwn 3rd.*
. . . . (100 to 1 op 50 to 1)   bd

FURSAN (USA) 10-12 D Bridgwater, *led, clr 4th, rdn appr 3 out, wknd and pld up bef nxt.* . . . . (11 to 8 on op 11 to 10)   pu
848³ LITTLE KENNY (v) 10-7 B Powell, *pld up bef 3rd.*
. . . . (16 to 1 op 10 to 1)   pu
1102⁵ QUIET MOMENTS (Ire) 10-12 R Farrant, *trkd ldrs, wknd 5th, pld up bef 3 out.* . . . . . . (50 to 1 op 33 to 1 tchd 66 to 1)   pu
848⁵ FORMENTIERE 10-0 (7*) Mr A Wintle, *al beh, tld off whn pld up bef 3 out.* . . . . . (25 to 1 op 12 to 1 tchd 33 to 1)   pu
SECRET GIFT 10-4 (3*) G Hogan, *hit second, al beh, tld off whn pld up bef 2 out.* . . . . (10 to 1 op 7 to 1 tchd 12 to 1)   pu
Dist: 10l, dist, 3l, 25l, 14l, nk, dist. 4m 10.40s. a 25.40s (16 Ran).
          (Mrs S Greathead), T R Greathead

1471 Bacton Amateur Riders' Handicap
Chase Class F (0-100 5-y-o and up)
£2,878 2m 3f. . . . . (1:30)

POPPETS PET [86] 9-11-3 (7*) Mr A Balding, *led to 3rd, styd prmnt, lft in ld appr last, ran on.* . . . . . (11 to 1 op 6 to 1)   1
756⁵ PRUDENT PEGGY [69] 9-10-0 (7*) Mr A Holdsworth, *hld up, steady hdwy tenth, ran on one pace frm 3 out.*
. . . . (10 to 1 op 8 to 1 tchd 11 to 1)   2
WAYUPHILL [87] 9-11-4 (7*) Mr L Corcoran, *hld up, hdwy 9th, rdn appr 3 out, one pace aftr.* . . . . (4 to 1 co-fav op 5 to 1)   3
WHERE'S WILLIE (Fr) [97] 7-12-4 (3*) Mr M Rimell, *led 3rd, clr 3 out, wnt lme and hdd appr last.* . . . .(4 to 1 co-fav op 3 to 1 tchd 9 to 2)   4
1140⁶ OPAL'S TENSPOT [69] 9-10-0 (7*) Miss V Roberts, *beh, nvr nr to chal.* . . . . (20 to 1)   5
1267⁶ NORTHERN OPTIMIST [87] 8-11-6 (5*) Mr J. L Llewellyn, *prmnt till wknd 4 out.* . . . . . (4 to 1 co-fav op 7 to 2)   6
1356 RHOMAN FUN (Ire) [69] 7-10-0 (7*) Mr P Scott, *al beh.*
. . . . (6 to 1 op 11 to 2 tchd 13 to 2)   7
1140⁵ AUVILLAR (USA) [79] (v) 8-10-10 (7*) Mr A Wintle, *mstk 5th, beh frm 8th, tld off.* . . . . (20 to 1 op 14 to 1)   8
1114⁵ ENNISTYMON (Ire) [69] 5-10-0 (7*) Mr G Weatherley, *hld up, hdwy 9th, hit nxt, wknd appr 3 out, tld off whn f last.* (33 to 1)   f
1007⁴ SALCOMBE HARBOUR (NZ) [69] 12-10-0 (7*) Dr P Pritchard, *mid-div, lost tch 4 out, tld off whn pld up bef 2 out.* . .(50 to 1)   pu
1328 FOXGROVE [77] 10-10-8 (7*) Miss E J Jones, *prmnt to 7th, tld off whn pld up bef 3 out.* . . . . . (20 to 1 op 14 to 1)   pu
877⁴ MILLIES OWN [93] 9-11-10 (7*) Mr R Widger, *al beh, mstk 5th, tld off whn pld up bef 3 out.* . . . . . . (5 to 1 op 3 to 1)   pu
1216 STRANGE WAYS [69] 8-10-3³ (7*) Mr A Charles-Jones, *blun 4th, al beh, tld off whn pld up bef 3 out.*
. . . . (40 to 1 op 33 to 1 tchd 50 to 1)   pu
Dist: 1¾l, 7l, 1¾l, 16l, 2l, 6l, 20l. 4m 51.40s. a 26.40s (13 Ran).
          (Pipers Partnership), J W Mullins

1472 Bridstow Selling Handicap Hurdle
Class G (0-90 4-y-o and up) £1,940
2m 1f. . . . . (2:00)

1235³ GLOWING PATH [82] 6-11-2 (7*) J Harris, *al prmnt and gng wl, led and bit 3 out, rdn clr frm nxt.*
. . . . (3 to 1 op 7 to 4 tchd 100 to 30)   1
158³¹ LAWNSWOOD JUNIOR [87] 9-12-0 D Bridgwater, *hld up in rear, hdwy 5th, wnt second appr 2 out, one pace aftr.*
. . . . (7 to 2 op 11 to 4)   2
1235⁴ SCALP 'EM (Ire) [59] 8-11-0 Dr P Pritchard, *prmnt till lost pl 4th, rallied and styd on frm 3 out.* . . . . (14 to 1 op 8 to 1)   3
1365⁴ MY HARVINSKI [76] 6-10-10 (7*) Miss E J Jones, *led till hdd appr 4th, led ag'n nxt to 3 out, sn btn...* (12 to 1 op 8 to 1)   4
1235² ALICE'S MIRROR [73] 7-11-0 R Johnson, *prmnt early, rdn and lost pl 4th, nvr on terms aftr.*
. . . . (6 to 1 4v op 5 to 2 tchd 11 to 4)   5
1320⁷ BRESIL (Ire) [59] 7-9-7 (7*) Mark Brown, *chsd ldrs to 4th, wknd nxt.* . . . . (8 to 1 op 6 to 1)   6
THEM TIMES (Ire) [66] 7-10-7 S Wynne, *al beh, hit 5th, sn tld off.* . . . . (20 to 1 op 14 to 1)   7
1203⁴ AGAINST THE CLOCK [59] (bl) 4-9-7 (7*) T O'Connor, *prmnt, led appr 4th, hdd nxt, wkng whn hit next tld off.*
. . . . (25 to 1 op 16 to 1)   8
Dist: 13l, 1½l, 9l, 8l, 9l, 23l, 2l. 4m 4.20s. a 19.20s (8 Ran).
SR: 14/6/-/-/-/   (P Slade), R J Hodges

1473 Bogmarsh Novices' Chase Class E
(5-y-o and up) £3,009 3m 1f 110yds
. . . . (2:30)

1298* DON DU CADRAN (Fr) 7-11-5 A Thornton, *hld up, hdwy 12th, chlgd 3 out, lft clr nxt, ran on.* . . . . . . (6 to 1 op 9 to 2)   1
MOUNT SERRATH (Ire) 8-10-12 J A McCarthy, *hld up, hdwy to ld 11th, hdd 15th, rdn appr 3 out, lft poor second 2 out.*
. . . . (8 to 1 op 13 to 2 tchd 10 to 1)   2
1302 CARDINAL RULE (Ire) 7-10-12 R Farrant, *chsd ldrs, hit 14th, blun 4 out, lft 3rd nxt...*(25 to 1 op 20 to 1 tchd 33 to 1)   3
807⁴ NEWTOWN ROSIE (Ire) 7-10-7 J Ryan, *led 3rd to 11th, wknd 4 out.* . . . . (6 to 1 op 5 to 1)   4
BONNIFER (Ire) 7-10-12 I Lawrence, *f 7th.*
. . . . (50 to 1 tchd 66 to 1)   f
WHAT'S YOUR STORY (Ire) 7-10-12 R Johnson, *hld up, mstk tenth, hdwy nxt, led aftr 4 out, f 2 out.* (7 to 4 fav op 6 to 4)   f
JULTARA (Ire) 7-10-12 J R Kavanagh, *hld up in rear, steady hdwy frm 11th, led 15th, rdn and hdd aftr 4 out, 3rd whn blundeed and uns rdr nxt.* (7 to 2 op 5 to 1 tchd 11 to 2)   ur

SNOWDON LILY 5-10-2 (3*) E Husband, *brght dwn 7th.*
....(33 to 1 tchd 50 to 1) bd
1302 MINGUS (USA) 9-10-12 B Powell, *in tch till wknd 11th, tld off whn pld up bef 15th*................(50 to 1 op 33 to 1) pu
PICKETSTONE 9-10-12 Mr P Scott, *prmnt till wknd 13th, tld off whn pld up bef 15th.* (50 to 1 op 25 to 1 tchd 66 to 1) pu
1054⁴ SWING QUARTET (Ire) 6-10-7 T Jenks, *led to 3rd, wknd quickly 11th, sn tld off, pld up bef 15th.*
...............................(7 to 1 op 6 to 1 tchd 8 to 1) pu
Dist: 7l, 25l, 3½l. 6m 31.70s. a 25.70s (11 Ran).

(Lord Cadogan), Capt T A Forster

1474 Bishops Frome Novices' Handicap Hurdle Class E (0-100 4-y-o and up) £2,388 2m 3f 110yds........ (3:00)

1348² LETS BE FRANK [84] 5-11-10 R Johnson, *al prmnt, led appr 3 out, drw clr frm nxt....* (2 to 1 fav op 7 to 4 tchd 5 to 2) 1
615⁶ RAVEN'S ROOST (Ire) [76] 5-11-2 P McLoughlin, *hld up, hdwy appr 7th, pressed wnr 3 out, outpcd nxt.*
....(7 to 1 op 9 to 2) 2
1343⁷ CLOD HOPPER (Ire) [75] 6-10-10 (5*) A Bates, *al prmnt, led 6th till hdd appr 3 out, one pace aftr....* (10 to 1 op 8 to 1) 3
ARIOSO [62] 8-9-13 (3*) G Hogan, *hld up in tch, hdwy appr 7th, wknd bef 3 out....*..........(33 to 1 op 25 to 1) 4
629* KILLING TIME [78] 5-11-4 D J Burchell, *mid-div, nvr nr to chal....*...............................(7 to 1 op 4 to 1) 5
STEEL GEM (Ire) [76] 7-10-9 (7*) M Griffiths, *al beh.*
....(8 to 1 op 10 to 1 tchd 12 to 1) 6
1175⁹ OUT OF THE BLUE [63] (v) 4-9-10 (7*) J Mogford, *prmnt to 7th, sn wknd....*..........(16 to 1 op 25 to 1 tchd 50 to 1) 7
1237⁴ OTTER PRINCE [60] 7-10-0 R Farrant, *prmnt till mstk 7th, sn wknd, tld off....*.........(6 to 1 op 8 to 1) 8
PARISIAN [65] 11-10-5 L Harvey, *mid-div, effrt 7th, wknd nxt, tld off....*...............(20 to 1 op 16 to 1 tchd 25 to 1) 9
841⁵ YOUNG TESS [76] 6-11-2 Mr A Brown, *al beh, tld off.*
....(12 to 1 op 8 to 1) 10
INDIAN TEMPLE [75] 5-11-1 R Greene, *al beh, tld off.*
.....................................(20 to 1 op 12 to 1) 11
FORBURIES (Ire) [62] 7-10-2 B Powell, *al beh, tld off whn pld up bef 3 out.*..................(50 to 1 op 25 to 1) pu
NUNS LUCY [65] 5-10-5 S Wynne, *al beh, tld off whn pld up bef 7th.*...........(25 to 1 op 20 to 1 tchd 33 to 1) pu
ALTHREY ARISTOCRAT (Ire) [65] 6-10-5 S McNeill, *led to 6th, wknd appr nxt, tld off whn pld up bef 2 out.*
................................(50 to 1 op 33 to 1 tchd 66 to 1) pu
749 COUNTRY MINSTREL (Ire) [84] 5-11-7 (3*) D Walsh, *prmnt till wknd appr 7th, tld off whn pld up bef 3 out.* pu
Dist: 9l, 2l, 10l, 1¼l, 3½l, 2½l, 22l, ¾l, ¾l, 29l. 4m 52.40s. a 34.40s (15 Ran).

(Mrs M M Stobart), Noel T Chance

1475 Bridge Sollars Novices' Handicap Chase Class F (0-95 4-y-o and up) £2,814 2m.................. (3:30)

1264³ SCOTTISH BAMBI [78] 8-10-11 A Thornton, *hld up in tch, hdwy 7th, led appr 3 out, sn clr, easily.*
.............................(7 to 4 fav op 5 to 2 tchd 13 to 8) 1
POUCHER (Ire) [95] 6-12-0 S Wynne, *hld up, hdwy 8th, chsd wnr frm 2 out...........* (5 to 2 op 5 to 2 tchd 11 to 2) 2
NORTHERN SINGER [71] 6-10-4 P Holley, *wth ldr, led 4th, jmpd slwly nxt, hit 7th, hdd appr 3 out, wknd next.*
.................................(9 to 1 op 7 to 1 tchd 10 to 1) 3
1062⁵ KING'S SHILLING (USA) [84] 9-11-1 Jacqui Oliver, *prmnt till wknd 4 out, no ch whn blun 2 out......* (10 to 1 op 6 to 1) 4
941 TENAYESTELIGN [85] 8-11-4 J A McCarthy, *mstks in rear, nvr on terms.*..................(10 to 1 op 5 to 1) 5
KNOWING [76] 9-10-2 (7*) Mr A Wintle, *al beh, tld off.*
.................................(33 to 1 op 7 to 1) 6
1226 CHERRY ORCHID [67] 9-9-13² (3*) G Hogan, *al beh, tld off.*
.....................................(10 to 1 op 12 to 1) 7
1136⁶ THE FENCE SHRINKER [67] 5-10-0³ (3*) D Walsh, *hld up, hdwy 5th, wknd 7th, tld off....*....(33 to 1 op 25 to 1) 8
WOT NO GIN [67] 7-10-0 R Johnson, *in rear whn mstk 6th, hdwy nxt, f 4 out....*............(20 to 1 op 8 to 1) f
922* BISHOPS CASTLE (Ire) [87] 8-11-6 J Frost, *led to 4th, uns rdr nxt....*................(11 to 4 op 2 to 1 tchd 3 to 1) ur
900 BAXWORTHY LORD [67] 5-9-8¹ (7*) T O'Connor, *blun and uns rdr second.*.............(10 to 1 op 20 to 1) ur
1352² ASHMEAD RAMBLER (Ire) [68] 6-10-11 C Maude, *prmnt till crrd out by loose horse appr 4 out....*(7 to 1 op 9 to 2) co
Dist: 10l, 12l, 8l, 9l, 11l, 16l, 18l. 4m 1.90s. a 14.90s (12 Ran).
SR: 14/21/-/-/-/-/ (William J Kelly), P R Webber

1476 Weatherbys 'Stars Of Tomorrow' Mares' Only National Hunt Flat Standard - Class H (4,5,6-y-o) £1,395 2m 1f........................... (4:00)

MELSTOCK MEGGIE 6-10-11 (3*) G Hogan, *al gng wl, cruised into ld o'r 2 fs out, shaken up, cmftbly.*
.................................(8 to 1 op 7 to 2) 1
1227⁵ LOVELY RASCAL 4-10-9 (5*) R McGrath, *hld up, gd hdwy o'r 1 fs out, ran on to chase wnr ins 2 furlongs.*
.................................(9 to 4 fav op 3 to 1 tchd 2 to 1) 2

1214⁴ KOSHEEN (Ire) 5-10-7 (7*) Mr A Wintle, *hld up, hdwy hfwy, outpcd 5 fs out, rallied and styd on fnl 2 furlongs.*
.................................(9 to 2 op 3 to 1) 3
WHERE'S MIRANDA 4-10-7 (7*) R Hobson, *hld up, hdwy 3 fs out, ran on wl, nvr nrr....*......(20 to 1 op 14 to 1) 4
1214³ JUST JASMINE 4-10-7 (7*) G Supple, *prmnt, led 7 fs out, hdd o'r 2 out, wknd appr last...........*(5 to 2 tchd 7 to 2) 5
WINNETKA GAL (Ire) 4-10-7 (7*) L Suthern, *hld up, hdwy aftr 6 fs, wknd 2 out....*.......(13 to 2 op 11 to 4 tchd 7 to 1) 6
FUN WHILE IT LASTS 5-10-9 (5*) A Bates, *nvr on terms.*
.................................(11 to 1 op 7 to 1 tchd 12 to 1) 7
1227⁸ LADY ROSEBURY 6-10-7 (7*) M Griffiths, *chsd ldrs, rdn hfwy, sn btn....*...................(50 to 1 op 33 to 1) 8
TOMORROWS HARVEST 4-10-7 (7*) J Harris, *chsd ldrs, wknd 6 fs out....*..........(20 to 1 op 10 to 1 tchd 33 to 1) 9
TINKER'S CUSS 5-10-11 (3*) D Walsh, *al beh, tld off.*
.................................(33 to 1 tchd 40 to 1) 10
POLLERTON'S DREAM 6-10-11 (3*) Guy Lewis, *prmnt till wknd 7 fs out, tld off....*.............(50 to 1 op 33 to 1) 11
SILVER QUILL 5-10-13⁶ (7*) Mr A Balding, *hld up in mid-div, lost tch hfwy, tld off......*(12 to 1 op 5 to 1 tchd 14 to 1) 12
1214 LET YOU KNOW (Ire) 6-10-7 (7*) C Hynes, *led till hdd 7 fs out, wknd quickly, tld off.......*......(50 to 1 op 33 to 1) 13
Dist: 2l, 1¼l, nk, 7l, 2l, 20l, 16l, 15l, 9l, 1¼l. 4m 1.00s. (13 Ran).
(Mrs Kay Birchenhough), Mrs J Pitman

KEMPTON (good to soft)
Wednesday November 20th
Going Correction: PLUS 0.70 sec. per fur.

1477 Uxbridge Conditional Jockeys' Novices' Handicap Hurdle Class F (0-100 4-y-o and up) £1,960 2m..... (12:50)

990* CANARY FALCON [87] 5-10-12 (7*) N Willmington, *mid-div, hdwy 3 out, led appr nxt, rdn out r-in...*(13 to 2 op 6 to 1) 1
1205* SAILEP (Fr) [88] 4-11-6 T Dascombe, *hld up, hdwy to chase ldr 5th, chase wnr appr 2 out, rdn and unbl to quicken.*
.................................(7 to 1 op 6 to 1 tchd 8 to 1) 2
1263² RAGAMUFFIN ROMEO [82] 7-11-0 D J Kavanagh, *hld up, hdwy hfwy, rdn appr 2 out, one pace.*
.................................(6 to 1 op 5 to 1 tchd 7 to 1) 3
PRIME OF LIFE (Ire) [90] 6-11-5 (3*) C Rae, *hld up, hdwy fnl 2, nrst finish...........*(11 to 1 op 10 to 1 tchd 12 to 1) 4
1205² SHIFT AGAIN (Ire) [88] (bl) 4-10-12 (3*) D Thomas, *led aftr second, rgned ld 4th, hit 3 out, hdd bef nxt, one pace.*
.................................(13 to 2 op 5 to 1) 5
1024 BELLA SEDONA [96] 4-11-9 (5*) J Power, *hld up, rdn 3 out, no imprsn......................*(8 to 1 op 5 to 1) 6
NOTHING DOING (Ire) [68] 7-10-0 K Gaule, *keen hold, hld up, hdwy second, lft in ld nxt, hdd 4th, rdn appr 3 out, sn wknd.*
.................................(9 to 1 op 7 to 1 tchd 9 to 2) 7
1220² RED LIGHT [85] (v) 4-10-12 (5*) N T Egan, *al beh.*
.................................(9 to 1 op 6 to 1) 8
ALL OVER RED ROVER [70] 4-10-2 Chris Webb, *led aftr second till mstk and uns rdr nxt......*(14 to 1 op 25 to 1) ur
Dist: 2l, 3½l, ½l, 2l, 25l, 9l, 10l. 4m 0.80s. a 20.80s (9 Ran).

(L Pipe), R J O'Sullivan

1478 Staines Novices' Chase Class D (5-y-o and up) £3,566 2m.......... (1:20)

1264* MULLIGAN (Ire) 6-11-6 A Maguire, *led till aftr 3rd, rgned ld 8th, drw clr appr 3 out, unchlgd.*(6 to 4 op 5 to 4 tchd 13 to 8) 1
1022³ WILDE MUSIC (Ire) 6-11-0 D Gallagher, *wl beh frm 3rd, took moderate second last, no ch wth wnr.*
.................................(12 to 1 op 8 to 1 tchd 14 to 1) 2
FEEL THE POWER [Ire] 8-11-0 C O'Dwyer, *dsptd ld, led aftr 3rd, blun 6th, hdd 8th, second and hld whn mstk 3 out, wknd r-in...........................*(6 to 4 op 11 to 10) 3
MARKSMAN SPARKS 6-11-0 S Burrough, *blun 1st, al beh.*
.................................(50 to 1 op 20 to 1 tchd 66 to 1) 4
Dist: 11l, 6l, 16l. 4m 3.20s. a 17.20s (4 Ran).
SR: 32/15/9/-/ (Lady Harris), D Nicholson

1479 European Breeders Fund 'National Hunt' Novices' Hurdle Qualifier Class D (4,5,6-y-o) £2,969 2m (1:50)

NOT FOR TURNING (Ire) 5-11-3 J Osborne, *led till second, remained hndy, shaken up appr 3 out, hit nxt, led r-in, drvn out.*.................................(3 to 1 fav op 4 to 1) 1
ROYAL EVENT 5-11-0 A Maguire, *prmnt, led 5th, hdd r-in, kpt on..........................*(7 to 1 op 5 to 1 tchd 8 to 1) 2
HALONA 6-10-9 D Gallagher, *strted slwly, pld hrd in rear, hdwy appr 2 out, ran on wl r-in.*
.................................(11 to 2 op 7 to 2 tchd 6 to 1) 3
FAR SPRINGS (Ire) 5-11-0 C O'Dwyer, *hld up, hdwy 3 out, ev ch nxt, one pace last..........*(12 to 1 op 7 to 1) 4
BAY FAIR 4-10-9 M Richards, *hld up, hdwy frm 3 out, styd on fnl 2, nrst finish......*(12 to 1 op 10 to 1 tchd 14 to 1) 5
STRONG PALADIN 5-11-0 P Hide, *hld up beh ldrs, effrt 2 out, one pace..............*(12 to 1 op 10 to 1 tchd 14 to 1) 6
TREMPLIN (Ire) 5-10-9 M A Fitzgerald, *hld up beh ldrs, ev ch 2 out, btn appr last.......*(12 to 1 op 10 to 1 tchd 14 to 1) 7

1053⁹ SIR DANTE (Ire) 5-11-0 D O'Sullivan, *prmnt, wknd appr 2 out.*
............................(10 to 1 op 8 to 1 tchd 12 to 1) 8
LINE OF CONQUEST 6-11-0 N Williamson, *led second till 5th, wkng whn blun last*............. (8 to 1 tchd 10 to 1) 9
MR HEMP 4-11-0 Derek Byrne, *al beh.* (66 to 1 op 33 to 1) 10
PHYSICAL FUN 5-11-0 D Skyrme, *mid-div, wknd appr 5th.*
............................(66 to 1 op 50 to 1) 11
1103² SHANNON LAD (Ire) 6-11-0 D Morris, *wknd frm 3 out.*
............................(16 to 1 op 14 to 1) 12
1142⁸ RED TEL (Ire) 4-11-0 A P McCoy, *hld up beh ldrs, wknd 3 out.*
............................(14 to 1 op 10 to 1) 13
1142⁶ MY SHENANDOAH (Ire) 5-11-0 V Slattery, *strtd slwly, al beh.*
............................(20 to 1 op 14 to 1) 14
DERRING JACK 5-11-0 T J Murphy, *mid-div, rdn 3 out, sn wknd, beh whn f last...........*(66 to 1 op 50 to 1) f
TELUK (Ire) 5-11-0 W Marston, *al beh, tld off whn pld up bef 2 out...........*(33 to 1 op 20 to 1) pu
Dist: Hd, 3l, ¾l, 3½l, ½l, 3l, 2½l, 7l, 8l, 1¼l. 3m 57.50s. a 17.50s (16 Ran).
SR: 23/23/15/19/10/14/6/8/1/ (Charles F Engel), O Sherwood

1480 Limber Hill Chase Limited Handicap Class B (0-145 5-y-o and up) £4,715 2½m 110yds. .... (2:20)

TRYING AGAIN [140] 8-11-3 J Osborne, *prmnt, led 6 out, rdn out r-in, ran on wl...* (15 to 8 fav op 2 to 1 tchd 9 to 4) 1
OLD BRIDGE (Ire) [132] 8-10-9 N Williamson, *hld up, hdwy 6 out, chsd wnr appr 2 out, kpt on.......* (7 to 2 tchd 4 to 1) 2
957⁴ LACKENDARA [130] 9-10-7 B Fenton, *led till 6 out, rdn appr 3 out, wknr............*(50 to 1 op 33 to 1 tchd 66 to 1) 3
1342* SUPER TACTICS (Ire) [130] 8-10-4 (3*) P Henley, *hld up, blun 7th, wknd appr 3 out, 4th and btn whn blunded nxt.*
............................(9 to 2 op 5 to 1 tchd 6 to 1) 4
SUNY BAY (Ire) [144] 7-11-7 D Gallagher, *prmnt, mstk 5 out, wknd appr 3 out..........*(20 to 1 op 9 to 4) 5
BO KNOWS BEST (Ire) [130] 7-10-7 A P McCoy, *prmnt till f 5th.............*(20 to 1 op 12 to 1 tchd 25 to 1) f
1108* WISE APPROACH [132] 9-10-9 C O'Dwyer, *f 1st, broke neck, dead.............*(7 to 1 op 6 to 1) f
Dist: 7l, 4l, 22l, 5l. 5m 15.40s. a 22.40s (7 Ran).
SR: 9/-/-/-/ (W H Dore), D R Gandolfo

1481 Hanworth Handicap Hurdle Class C (0-130 4-y-o and up) £3,501 2m 5f .... (2:50)

1402³ TIM (Ire) [104] 6-10-6 J Osborne, *hld up towards rear, hdwy to chase ldr 3 out, led nxt, sn clr, readily.*
............................(15 to 2 op 5 to 1 tchd 8 to 1) 1
1265² HIGH GRADE [113] 8-11-1 N Williamson, *al prmnt, rdn appr 2 out, sn one pace r-in...* (8 to 1 op 6 to 1 tchd 9 to 1) 2
THE TOISEACH (Ire) [112] 5-11-0 P Hide, *chsd clr ldr till 3 out, rdn appr nxt, sn one pace.............* (3 to 1 op 2 to 1) 3
CHAPRASSI (Ire) [122] 7-11-10 A P McCoy, *led, sn clr, rdn aftr 3 out, hdd and mstk nxt, soon wknd.*
............................(11 to 8 on op Evens) 4
WELSHMAN [111] 10-10-13 D Gallagher, *al beh, tld off frm 4th.............*(20 to 1 op 14 to 1 tchd 25 to 1) 5
Dist: 5l, 2l, 9l, 3l. 5m 12.30s. a 26.30s (5 Ran).
(P W Piper), J R Jenkins

1482 Halliford Novices' Chase Class D (5-y-o and up) £3,566 3m........ (3:20)

1232* FINE THYNE (Ire) 7-11-6 M A Fitzgerald, *hld up, steady hdwy frm 13th, led last, hld rdn r-in, jnd post.*
............................(6 to 4 fav tchd 5 to 4) 1+
BERUDE NOT TO (Ire) 7-11-0 J Osborne, *not fluent 1st 2, chsd ldr, led appr 15th, hld last, rallied und pres to dead heat post.............*(7 to 4 op Evens tchd 15 to 8) 1+
APPLE JOHN 7-10-11 (3*) P Henley, *jmpd lft, led, clr frm 3rd till tenth, wknd aftr 3 out, tld off.........*(4 to 1 op 4 to 1) 3
1229³ OUROWNFELLOW (Ire) 7-11-0 D Morris, *jmpd lft, hld up, blun 13th, not reco'r, tld off.....*(6 to 1 op 5 to 1 tchd 7 to 1) 4
Dist: Dd-ht, dist, dist. 6m 18.90s. a 29.90s (4 Ran).
(Peter Wiegand & G Addiscott), Mrs A J Perrett & O Sherwood

1483 French Street Standard Open National Hunt Flat Class H (4,5,6-y-o) £1,416 2m............. (3:50)

1306² QUINI EAGLE (Fr) 4-11-4 A P McCoy, *made al, rdn frm 2 fs out, ran on wl.......*(11 to 4 fav op 3 to 1 tchd 4 to 1) 1
JACK GALLAGHER 5-11-4 M Richards, *hld up in tch, chsd wnr frm 5 fs out, effrt o'r 2 out, kpt on.* (12 to 1 op 10 to 1) 2
SHEKELS (Ire) 5-10-11 (7*) M Berry, *hld up in rear, hdwy o'r 3 fs out, styd on fnl 2.............*(16 to 1 op 14 to 1) 3
MILITARY LAW 5-11-4 T J Murphy, *al hndy, rdn and one pace fnl 2 fs.............*(16 to 1 op 20 to 1 tchd 14 to 1) 4
STANMORE (Ire) 4-11-4 D Gallagher, *hld up, hdwy hfwy, rdn o'r 2 fs out, one pace...* (14 to 1 op 10 to 1 tchd 16 to 1) 5
STORMYFAIRWEATHER (Ire) 4-11-4 M A Fitzgerald, *hld up, hdwy 7 fs out, rdn 3 out, sn one pace....* (7 to 2 op 5 to 1) 6
CHARLIE BANKER 4-11-4 A Larnach, *nvr nr to chal.*
............................(25 to 1 op 20 to 1 tchd 33 to 1) 7
QUICK BOWLER (Ire) 4-11-1 (3*) R Massey, *nvr nr to chal.*
............................(6 to 1 op 4 to 1 tchd 7 to 1) 8

SIDANORA (Ire) 6-11-4 C O'Dwyer, *mid-div, hdwy 6 fs out, wknd 2 out.............*(7 to 1 op 6 to 1 tchd 8 to 1) 9
MIKE'S MUSIC (Ire) 5-11-4 B Fenton, *nvr nrr.....* (33 to 1) 10
LIVELY ENCOUNTER (Ire) 5-11-4 Derek Byrne, *mid-div, badly hmpd o'r 3 fs out, not recvr.* (5 to 1 op 8 to 1 tchd 9 to 1) 11
NORMANDY DUKE (NZ) 4-11-1 (3*) J Magee, *beh, ran wide on bend o'r 4 fs out, nvr dngr....* (20 to 1 tchd 33 to 1) 12
FEEBEE FIVE 4-10-13 P Hide, *towards rear, hdwy and not much room on ins o'r 3 fs out, no imprsn.*
............................(12 to 1 op 8 to 1) 13
1390 JACKHO 4-11-1 (3*) T Dascombe, *hld up beh ldrs, wkng whn hmpd o'r 3 fs out.............*(33 to 1) 14
FIDDLER'S LEAP 4-11-4 J Osborne, *mid-div, wknd o'r 4 fs out.............*(6 to 1 op 5 to 1) 15
DERRYS PREROGATIVE 6-11-4 J Railton, *chsd ldrs, wkng whn hmpd o'r 3 fs out.............*(33 to 1) 16
SPRING BLADE 4-11-4 A Dicken, *mid-div, wknd 5 fs out.*
............................(33 to 1 op 25 to 1) 17
PERSIAN SUNSET (Ire) 4-10-10 (3*) K Gaule, *chsd wnr till 5 fs out, wknd o'r 3 out, tld off.............*(33 to 1) 18
SOU SOU WESTERLY (Ire) 5-11-4 N Williamson, *al beh, tld off.............*(16 to 1 op 14 to 1) 19
PRIVATE MEMORIES 6-11-4 W Marston, *beh fnl 6 fs, tld off.*
............................(33 to 1) 20
Dist: 1¾l, 6l, ½l, 2l, 4l, 4l, 3l, 6l, 5l, 1¼l. 3m 52.70s. (20 Ran).
(B A Kilpatrick), M C Pipe

TIPPERARY (IRE) (soft)
Thursday November 21st

1484 European Breeders Fund Mares Maiden Hurdle (Div I) (4-y-o and up) £3,767 2½m............... (12:45)

GLORIOUS GALE (Ire) 6-12-0 C F Swan, ...(7 to 2) 1
1143⁷ IODER WAN (Ire) 4-11-9 M P Hourigan, ...(7 to 1) 2
1193⁷ TURRAMURRA GIRL (Ire) 7-11-7 (7*) L J Fleming, . (7 to 1) 3
1144⁴ MISS BERTAINE (Ire) 7-12-0 J P Broderick, .. (13 to 8 fav) 4
NO BLUES (Ire) 5-11-9 (5*) G Cotter, ...(7 to 1) 5
1241 OAKDALE GIRL (Ire) 6-12-0 T Hazlett, ...(16 to 1) 6
1364 SARAH SUPREME (Ire) 5-12-0 J R Barry, ...(10 to 1) 7
908 LABAN LADY (Ire) 7-12-0 K F O'Brien, ...(12 to 1) 8
BESTERELLE (Ire) 5-12-0 M Duffy, ...(12 to 1) 9
RING HARRY 6-12-0 W Slattery, ...(8 to 1) 10
CITYJET (Ire) 6-12-0 P Carberry, ...(7 to 1) 11
HURRICANE GIRL (Ire) 7-11-11 (3*) K Whelan, ...(14 to 1) 12
Dist: 3l, 1½l, 1l, 4l. 5m 17.70s. (12 Ran).
(J G Leahy), A P O'Brien

1485 European Breeders Fund Mares Maiden Hurdle (Div II) (4-y-o and up) £3,767 2½m.................(1:15)

1117² FLAMINGO FLOWER (Ire) 8-11-11 (3*) Mr P J Casey, (5 to 2) 1
1435 MONDEO ROSE (Ire) 4-11-9 C F Swan, ...(7 to 1) 2
1244⁷ CELTIC LOTTO (Ire) 5-11-7 (7*) Mr J T McNamara, ..(8 to 1) 3
INDIAN MAGIC (Ire) 7-11-9 (5*) G Cotter, ...(8 to 1) 4
979³ THE HEARTY LADY (Ire) 6-12-0 J Jones, ...(5 to 1) 5
1143 ANTICS (Ire) 4-11-2 (7*) Mrs C Harrison, ...(7 to 1) 6
1076 LISADOBBER LADY (Ire) 6-12-0 J P Broderick, .. (10 to 1) 7
1075⁹ ARTIC PEARL (Ire) 6-11-7 (7*) D Flood, ...(20 to 1) 8
773⁴ NICOLA MARIE (Ire) 7-12-0 P A Roche, ...(7 to 1) 9
1090 PHARDANTE LILLY (Ire) 4-11-9 G M O'Neill, ..(16 to 1) 10
NOT A BID (Ire) 7-12-0 D H O'Connor, ...(20 to 1) 11
686 ROSEY BUCK (Ire) 4-11-6 (3*) G Kilfeather, ...(20 to 1) 12
1279³ ROCHER LADY (Ire) 5-11-7 (7*) P Morris, ...(7 to 1) ur
Dist: Nk, 8l, 4l, 3½l. 5m 21.10s. (13 Ran).
(Mrs M E McCann), Peter Casey

1486 Barronstown Maiden Hurdle (Div I) (5-y-o and up) £2,740 2m..... (1:45)

1278⁶ ANCIENT HISTORIAN (Ire) 7-10-8 (7*) P Morris, ... (11 to 2) 1
1147³ RANDOM RING (Ire) 5-10-8 (7*) Mr J T McNamara,
............................(9 to 4 fav) 2
ARABIAN SPRITE (Ire) 8-11-4 Mr P J Healy, ...(4 to 1) 3
1147 HOLLY'S PRIDE (Ire) 6-11-7 F Woods, ...(7 to 1) 4
741 NEON VALLEY (Ire) 7-11-1 S H O'Donovan, .•.... (20 to 1) 5
BUGGY (Ire) 7-11-9 K F O'Brien, ...(12 to 1) 6
CLONMEL COMMERCIAL (Ire) 5-10-8 (7*) D McCullagh,
............................(20 to 1) 7
1195 WARLOCKFOE (Ire) 5-10-10 J R Barry, ...(12 to 1) 8
1360 STRONG RAIDER (Ire) 6-11-7 A Powell, ...(10 to 1) 9
1360 GALLIC HONEY (Ire) 5-10-3 (7*) Mrs C Harrison, .. (16 to 1) 10
CROSSEROADS (Ire) 6-11-1 T J Mitchell, ...(10 to 1) 11
Dist: 5l, 6l, 9l, 15l. 4m 11.30s. (11 Ran).
(P W Mernagh), W P Mullins

1487 Barronstown Maiden Hurdle (Div II) (5-y-o and up) £2,740 2m..... (2:15)

STEP ON EYRE (Ire) 6-11-9 C F Swan, ...(11 to 8 on) 1
1005³ LORD EDENBURY (Ire) 5-11-1 A Powell, ...(6 to 1) 2
1193⁸ MONTANA KING (Ire) 5-11-1 F Woods, ...(6 to 1) 3
1120³ ROSENWALD (Ire) 6-10-10 (5*) J Butler, ...(8 to 1) 4
1432 JAY MAN (Ire) 6-11-4 (5*) Mr E J Kearns Jnr, ...(3 to 1) 5

HELL FOR LEATHER (Ire) 7-11-1 D H O'Connor, . . .(20 to 1) 6
1241 QUEEN OF ALL GALES (Ire) 5-10-5 (5*) P D Carey, (16 to 1) 7
978 WHITBY 8-11-1 J R Barry, ...(14 to 1) 8
1241 SITE MISTRESS (Ire) 5-10-5 (5*) G Cotter, ... (20 to 1) 9
1359 WATT A BUZZ (Ire) 5-10-12 P Broderick, ...(16 to 1) 10
DO-TELL-ME (Ire) 6-10-11 (7*) Mr John P Moloney, (14 to 1) 11
Dist: 3½l, ½l, 6l, 4l. 4m 16.80s. (11 Ran).

(Mrs J M Mullins), W P Mullins

1488 Kevin McManus Bookmaker Novice Hurdle (4-y-o and up) £5,480 2m
.... (2:45)

1088² KING OF KERRY (Ire) 5-11-7 C F Swan, ...(5 to 4 on) 1
THREE SCHOLARS 5-10-7 (7*) P Morris, ...(7 to 2) 2
1364³ CHARLIE-O (Ire) 4-10-4 (5*) G Cotter, ... (6 to 1) 3
742¹ TIDJANI (Ire) 4-11-2 F Woods, ...(3 to 1) 4
1143⁶ RIVER RUMPUS (Ire) 4-10-9 J P Broderick, ...(25 to 1) 5
1275 FAIRY COURT (Ire) 4-10-6 (3*) K Whelan, ...(25 to 1) 6
Dist: 6l, 3l, 20l, 9l. 4m 16.20s. (6 Ran).

(The Local Boys Syndicate), A P O'Brien

1489 Tipperary Handicap Hurdle (0-123 4-y-o and up) £2,740 2½m.... (3:15)

1407² RATHGIBBON (Ire) [-] 5-10-11 (5*) G Cotter, . . .(11 to 8 fav) 1
1273⁴ VALMAR (Ire) [-] 8-9-9 F Woods, ...(3 to 1) 2
1242 CLASHWILLIAM GIRL (Ire) [-] 8-10-13 (7*) Mr R M Walsh,
. . . .(8 to 1) 3
LISCAHILL FORT (Ire) [-] 7-10-12 (3*) K Whelan, . . .(10 to 1) 4
GLENBALLYMA (Ire) [-] 7-11-0 F J Flood, ...(6 to 1) 5
897¹ JANE DIGBY (Ire) [-] 4-11-10 C F Swan, ...(7 to 2) 6
980 PERSIAN MYSTIC (Ire) [-] 4-10-3 (7*) M J Collins, . .(12 to 1) 7
Dist: 9l, 12l, ½l, 20l. 5m 18.40s. (7 Ran).

(Mrs Margaret Marshall), S J Treacy

1490 Oola I.N.H. Flat Race (4-y-o) £2,740 2m.......................... (3:45)

1364² RACHEL'S SWALLOW (Ire) 11-1 (3*) Mr R O'Neill, . .(6 to 1) 1
TYLO STEAMER (Ire) 11-2 (7*) Mr J T McNamara, (16 to 1) 2
STRONTIUM (Ire) 11-9 Mr P Fenton, ...(4 to 1) 3
1247⁷ BEHAMORE GIRL (Ire) 10-11 (7*) Mr G Elliott, ...(8 to 1) 4
1409 CORYROSE (Ire) 10-11 (7*) Mr F J Crowley, ...(6 to 1) 5
1247² MIRACLE ME (Ire) 11-2 (7*) Mr E Gallagher, ...(12 to 1) 6
COOL N CALM 10-11 (7*) Mr A J Dempsey, ... (10 to 1) 7
1307⁹ MIDNIGHT JOY (Ire) 11-4 Mr D Marnane, ... (14 to 1) 8
1247⁵ SOME ORCHESTRA (Ire) 10-11 (7*) Mr M Budds, . .(12 to 1) 9
MIGHTY TERM (Ire) 11-6 (3*) Mr B M Cash, ...(8 to 1) 10
1364⁴ BOPTWOPHAR (Ire) 11-9 Mr J Martin, ... (3 to 1 fav) 11
1247⁸ JAKE CHOICE (Ire) 11-4 Mr P J Healy, ...(33 to 1) 12
1060 NOBLE IRIS (Ire) 10-11 (7*) Mr John P Moloney, . . .(20 to 1) 13
CARN LAKE (Ire) 11-2 (7*) Mr J P Kilfeather, ... (20 to 1) 14
1364 PHARAWAYDREAM (Ire) 11-9 Mr J P Dempsey, . . .(12 to 1) pu
Dist: Dist, 4½l, ¾l, 4½l. 4m 12.30s. (15 Ran).

(Ronald O'Neill), Ronald O'Neill

WARWICK (good)
Thursday November 21st
Going Correction: MINUS 0.15 sec. per fur.

1491 Ethelfleda's Mount Conditional Jockeys' Handicap Chase Class E (0-115 5-y-o and up) £3,148 2½m 110yds...................... (1:20)

EASTERN RIVER [74] 10-10-0 A Bates, hld up, cld 8th, led 11th, made rst, styd on wl.
. . . .(9 to 4 fav op 5 to 2 tchd 3 to 1) 1D
1137² FLAPJACK LAD [98] 7-11-10 D Walsh, cl up, led tenth to nxt, chsd wnr, ev ch aftr 3 out, wknd appr 2 out.
. . . .(5 to 2 op 6 to 4) 1
1301² CHANNEL PASTIME [93] 12-11-5 Guy Lewis, in tch, mstk 8th, hrd rdn tenth, outpcd frm 13th.
. . . .(6 to 1 op 7 to 2 tchd 13 to 2) 2
RIVER RED [79] 10-10-5 K Gaule, pushed alng in rear 7th, al beh, mstk 12th, tld off. . . . .(33 to 1 op 12 to 1) 3
1356² HENLEY WOOD [98] 11-11-10 D J Kavanagh, led till 3rd, cl up till wknd and mstk 9th, tld off whn pld up bef 11th.
. . . .(5 to 1 op 7 to 2 tchd 11 to 1) pu
1025² CRACKLING FROST [79] 8-10-3 G Hogan, led 3rd, hdd tenth, wknd appr 13th, tld off whn pld up bef 2 out.
. . . .(7 to 2 tchd 4 to 1) pu
Dist: 13l, 7l, dist. 5m 8.00s. a 13.00s (6 Ran).

(T H Ounsley), N A Twiston-Davies

1492 Harbury Selling Handicap Hurdle Class G (0-100 4-y-o and up) £1,691 2m 3f......................... (1:50)

1320⁶ SIR PAGEANT [71] (bl) 7-10-0 D Bridgwater, keen hold early, hld up beh ldrs, hrd drvn to chal aftr 3 out, led last, rdn out.
. . . .(10 to 1 tchd 12 to 1 and 14 to 1) 1
1266⁷ BRIGHT SAPPHIRE [71] 10-10-0 D J Burchell, hld up beh ldrs, led 5th, stumpled appr 2 out, hdd last, no extr.
. . . .(10 to 1 tchd 11 to 1) 2

KATBALLOU [71] 7-9-7 (7*) Mr O McPhail, beh, hdwy 5th, outpcd nxt, styd on frm 2 out.
. . . .(40 to 1 op 33 to 1 tchd 50 to 1) 3
1365² TAMANDU [78] 6-10-7 Mr E James, hld up in mid-div, pushed alng aftr 4th, hdwy nxt, outpcd frm 3 out, no ch whn hit last.
. . . .(5 to 1 tchd 6 to 1) 4
1320² HACKETTS CROSS (Ire) [88] 8-11-8 A P McCoy, hld up, pushed along and hdwy 6th, sn outpcd.
. . . .(11 to 1 op 8 to 1 tchd 9 to 2) 5
1175 RAY RIVER [74] (bl) 4-10-3 J Ryan, mid-div, effrt 6th, sn outpcd. . . . .(11 to 1 op 8 to 1) 6
756² GUNMAKER [79] 7-10-8 Mr J L Llewellyn, cl up till wknd aftr 4th. . . . .(9 to 1 op 7 to 1 tchd 10 to 1) 7
1132⁷ JOHN NAMAN (Ire) [84] 7-10-6 (7*) G Supple, chsd ldrs till wknd 5th, tld off. . . . .(14 to 1 op 20 to 1) 8
918 KING OF BABYLON (Ire) [74] 4-10-3 R Supple, al beh, tld off. . . . .(14 to 1 op 12 to 1 tchd 16 to 1) 9
971² SHUTTLECOCK [89] 5-11-4 A Maguire, led till 5th, sn wknd, tld off. . . . .(5 to 1 op 4 to 1 tchd 11 to 2) 10
COXWELL STEPTOE [95] 6-11-3 (7*) Mr A Wintle, prmnt till wknd 5th, no ch whn f 2 out.
. . . .(5 to 1 op 9 to 2 tchd 13 to 2) f
1353⁸ COLOUR SCHEME [71] (v) 9-10-0 B Powell, hld up, hdwy to track ldrs aftr 3rd, outpcd 5th, tld off whn pld up bef last, mismounted. . . . .(40 to 1 op 33 to 1) pu
Dist: 2l, 5l, hd, 10l, 2l, nk, 19l, 5l, 21l. 4m 24.30s. (12 Ran).

(The Dirty Dozen), K S Bridgwater

1493 Scottish Equitable / Jockeys Association Series Handicap Hurdle Qualifier Class D (0-125 4-y-o and up) £2,908 2m 3f........... (2:20)

DOMAPPEL [105] 4-10-11 T Kent, keen hold early, hld up beh ldrs, trkd lder frm 5th, shaken up to lead aftr 2 out, ran on wl. . . . .(7 to 2 op 4 to 1 tchd 9 to 2) 1
1268⁶ RUNAWAY PETE (USA) [122] 6-12-0 A P McCoy, led, drvn alng aftr 4th, hdd aftr 2 out, no extr.(7 to 4 fav op 6 to 4) 2
GROUSEMAN [114] (bl) 10-10-13 (7*) Mr A Wintle, with ldr to 5th, sn outpcd. . . . .(6 to 1 op 9 to 2 tchd 13 to 2) 3
WINSFORD HILL [94] 5-10-0 A Maguire, trkd ldrs till wknd und pres aftr 5th. . . . .(5 to 1 op 5 to 1) 4
1217² ROSEHALL [94] 5-9-12¹ (3*) G Hogan, al beh, lost tch appr 5th, tld off. . . . .(50 to 1 op 25 to 1) 5
1268⁸ TEEN JAY [122] 6-12-0 V Slattery, hld up beh, losing tch whn f 6th, dead. . . . .(4 to 1 op 3 to 1 tchd 9 to 2) f
Dist: 9l, 21l, 7l, 11l. 4m 22.60s. (6 Ran).

(M C Banks), Mrs J Cecil

1494 Shirley Maiden Chase Class D (5-y-o and up) £3,691 3¼m....... (2:50)

DROMHANA (Ire) 6-11-5 A P McCoy, trkd ldrs, led 3 out, all out............... (13 to 8 fav op 11 to 10 tchd 7 to 4) 1
THE SHY PADRE (Ire) 7-11-5 W Marston, mstk second, hld up beh, hdwy 8th, led aftr tenth, mistake and hdd 3 out, rallied frm last................ (5 to 1 op 11 to 2 tchd 6 to 1) 2
ANYTHINGYOULIKE 7-11-5 M Richards, hld up beh, hdwy to track ldrs 7th, mstk and outpcd 15th, styd on frm 2 out.
. . . .(25 to 1 op 20 to 1 tchd 33 to 1) 3
PEPTIC LADY (Ire) 6-11-0 C Maude, not jump wl, trkd ldrs, mstk 7th, drpd rear tenth, styd on aftr 3 out, blun last, kpt on. . . . .(16 to 1 op 12 to 1) 4
ARCTIC MADAM 7-10-7 (7*) O Burrows, hld up in tch, lost touch appr 14th........(14 to 1 op 6 to 1 tchd 16 to 1) 5
CONEY ROAD 7-11-5 G Bradley, hld up, hdwy aftr 13th, 3rd and rdn whn blun badly 3 out, not reco'r, tld off.
. . . .(7 to 2 op 3 to 1 tchd 5 to 1) 6
1229⁴ PARLIAMENTARIAN (Ire) 7-11-5 D Bridgwater, nvr on terms, lost tch 14th, tld off................(9 to 1 op 6 to 1) 7
THE BRUD 8-11-5 J Osborne, in tch whn hit 6th and uns rdr. . . . .(10 to 1 op 6 to 1 tchd 12 to 1) ur
1347 INCH EMPEROR (Ire) 6-11-5 T J Murphy, led till hdd aftr tenth, beh whn blun 15th, pld up bef nxt.
. . . .(33 to 1 tchd 40 to 1) pu
Dist: 2l, 7l, ½l, 9l, dist, 5l. 6m 36.60s. a 22.60s (9 Ran).

(J Blackwell, T Chappell, T Curry & D Nichols), P F Nicholls

1495 Shipston Handicap Chase Class B (0-145 5-y-o and up) £6,736 3¼m .... (3:20)

1212² CLASS OF NINETYTWO (Ire) [122] 7-11-5 A P McCoy, made all, jmpd slwly 5th and 8th, clr 16th, rdn alng appr 2 out, styd on wl.........(2 to 1 op 9 to 4 tchd 13 to 8 and 5 to 2) 1
1296¹ IDIOT'S LADY [127] 7-11-10 W Marston, jmpd rght, trkd wnr thrght, mstk 13th, allied aftr 3 out, no imprsn whn edgd lft r-in. . . . .(5 to 2 op 11 to 8 tchd 3 to 1) 2
1069¹ SOUNDS STRONG (Ire) [121] 7-11-4 A Maguire, hld up in last, gng easily whn f 14th.
. . . .(Evens fav op 5 to 4 tchd 11 to 8) f
Dist: 2l. 6m 30.50s. a 16.50s (3 Ran).

(Lord Cadogan), Capt T A Forster

1496 Ashorne Novices' Hurdle Class E (4-y-o and up) £2,721 2m........ (3:50)

HURRICANE LAMP 5-10-12 A Maguire, *keen hold beh ldrs, pushed alng aftr 4th, hdwy nxt, led after 3 out, styd on wl.*
.... (9 to 4 jt-fav op 6 to 4 tchd 5 to 2) 1
1295³ SMOLENSK (Ire) 4-10-12 M Moloney, *trkd ldrs, rdn appr 2 out, kpt on wl.* .... (16 to 1 tchd 25 to 1) 2
1215* CHICKAWICKA (Ire) 5-11-5 R Farrant, *led till aftr 3 out, one pace, lost second r-in.* .... (9 to 4 jt-fav op 2 to 1 tchd 3 to 1) 3
KILCARNE BAY (Ire) 6-10-12 G Bradley, *hld up, hdwy appr 2 out, rdn and no extr r-in.* ..(11 to 2 op 5 to 2 tchd 6 to 1) 4
934 EVEZIO RUFO (v) 4-10-12 J R Kavanagh, *beh, reminders 3rd and hdwy to track ldrs, outpcd aftr 4th, styd on.*
.... (66 to 1 op 33 to 1 tchd 100 to 1) 5
1410⁵ ABOVE THE CUT (USA) 4-10-12 C Maude, *keen hold early, chsd ldrs, wknd appr 4th.* ....(33 to 1 op 20 to 1) 6
MR DARCY 4-10-12 R Bellamy, *mid-div, outpcd frm 4th.*
.... (100 to 1 op 50 to 1) 7
BREAK THE RULES 4-10-12 A P McCoy, *trkd ldrs, wknd quickly aftr 3 out.* ....(9 to 2 op 5 to 2 tchd 5 to 1) 8
1215⁵ THE DEACONESS 5-10-7 Gary Lyons, *al beh.*
.... (150 to 1 op 50 to 1) 9
837² TOMAL 4-10-12 D Gallagher, *mstk 5th, al beh.*
.... (25 to 1 op 20 to 1) 10
DON'T MIND IF I DO (Ire) 5-10-12 Mr P Scott, *blun 1st, al beh, tld off.* ....(66 to 1 op 33 to 1) 11
WHITE CLARET 4-10-12 D Bridgwater, *chsd ldrs, wknd appr 4th, tld off.* ....(15 to 2 op 6 to 1 tchd 8 to 1) 12
BECKY'S GIRL 6-10-7 P Holley, *beh frm 4th, tld off.*
.... (150 to 1 op 50 to 1 tchd 200 to 1) 13
MR ROUGH 5-10-12 M Richards, *al beh, tld off whn pld up bef last.* ....(25 to 1 op 12 to 1 tchd 33 to 1) pu
PERSIAN BUTTERFLY 4-10-7 B Powell, *not jump wl, beh whn sddl slpd and pld up 3rd.* ....(150 to 1 op 50 to 1) pu
Dist: 5l, ½l, 4l, 7l, 1¾l, 1¾l, 8l, 7l, 14l. 3m 42.50s. a 3.50s (15 Ran).
SR: 25/20/26/15/11/4/2/-/-/ (Mr & Mrs F C Welch And Mr R A Barrs), D Nicholson

WINCANTON (good)
Thursday November 21st
Going Correction: PLUS 0.10 sec. per fur.

1497 U.W.E.S.U. Still Standing Novices' Hurdle Class E (0-100 4-y-o and up) £2,267 2m......... (1:30)

1135⁴ WAYFARERS WAY (USA) [87] 5-11-10 M A Fitzgerald, *hld up, hdwy frm 3 out, led appr last, rdn out.*
.... (4 to 1 op 3 to 1 tchd 9 to 2) 1
CALVARO (Ire) [69] 5-10-6 R Johnson, *keen hold early, prmnt, led briefly bef fnl 2, kpt on same pace.*
.... (25 to 1 op 10 to 1 tchd 33 to 1) 2
ASHBY HILL (Ire) [81] 5-11-4 D O'Sullivan, *keen hold, hld up, not fluent, hdwy 3 out, hit nxt, ev ch appr last, one pace.*
.... (6 to 4 on op 11 to 8 on tchd 11 to 10 on and 13 to 8 on) 3
49⁶ ELEANORA MUSE [70] 6-10-7 R Dunwoody, *led till appr last, wknd r-in.* ....(4 to 1 op 3 to 1 tchd 9 to 2) 4
1063⁴ SAMAKA HARA (Ire) [79] 4-11-2 T Jenks, *chsd 3 out, wknd quickly bef nxt, tld off, broke blood vessel.*
.... (11 to 1 op 8 to 1 tchd 12 to 1) 5
Dist: 1¾l, 1¾l, 9l, dist. 3m 45.60s. a 11.60s (5 Ran).
(Lady Tennant), N J Henderson

1498 Tote Bookmakers Novices' Handicap Chase Class D (0-105 5-y-o and up) £4,048 2m 5f............... (2:00)

HIGHLAND JACK [85] 6-10-10 R Dunwoody, *strted slwly, beh, gd hdwy tenth, wnt second 4 out, sn rdn, rallied to ld last 50 yards.* ....(6 to 1 tchd 7 to 1) 1
1262² BIRONI [97] 7-11-8 S Wynne, *jmpd rght, chsd ldr, led 11th, 3 ls clr whn blun last, hdd and not quicken last 50 yards.*
.... (9 to 4 fav op 5 to 2 tchd 3 to 1) 2
AT THE GROVE (Ire) [100] 6-11-11 C O'Dwyer, *hld up, hdwy tenth, wknd 4 out.* ....(10 to 1) 3
1321* LEGAL ARTIST (Ire) [83] 6-10-8 (6ex) L Harvey, *prmnt, blun 5th, lost pl 9th, rallied 4 out, wknd bef nxt.*
.... (10 to 1 op 8 to 1) 4
1302³ STORMHILL PILGRIM [75] (bl) 7-10-0 P McLoughlin, *led, hit 1st, mstk and hdd 11th, not fluent 13th, wknd 4 out.*
.... (14 to 1 op 9 to 1) 5
PURBECK RAMBLER [76] 5-10-0 B Clifford, *al beh, tld off.*
.... (25 to 1 op 16 to 1) 6
SWEET BUCK [75] 7-10-0 M Sharratt, *al beh, tld off.*
.... (66 to 1 op 33 to 1) 7
FERNY BALL (Ire) [78] 8-10-3³ A Thornton, *f second.*
.... (33 to 1 op 20 to 1) f
801⁶ ZAITOON (Ire) [101] 5-11-11 R Johnson, *hmpd and uns rdr second.* ....(11 to 2 op 4 to 1 tchd 6 to 1) ur
1211³ CRACKING PROSPECT [80] 5-9-13 (5⁰) D Salter, *pld hrd, hld up, lft in 3rd at 8th, wknd nxt, beh whn blun and uns rdr 13th.*
.... (10 to 1) ur
WHIRLY (Ire) [90] 7-11-1 S McNeill, *mstk 1st, prmnt, 3rd whn blun and uns rdr 8th.* ....(13 to 2 op 6 to 1 tchd 7 to 1) ur
1111⁴ MASTER PANGLOSS (Ire) [75] 6-9-7 (7⁰) C Rae, *mstk 1st, beh till blun and uns rdr 4th.* (25 to 1 op 20 to 1 tchd 33 to 1) ur

Dist: 2l, 12l, 9l, 3l, dist, dist. 5m 24.70s. a 20.70s (12 Ran).

(Karen Gibbons & Breda Cardiff), Andrew Turnell

1499 Hamilton Litestat Handicap Chase Class C (0-130 5-y-o and up) £6,775 3m 1f 110yds............... (2:30)

ANDRE LAVAL (Ire) [110] 7-10-11 C O'Dwyer, *hld up beh ldrs, not fluent 8th, hdwy 13th, led 16th to 2 out, led last, rdn out.*
.... (9 to 4 op 7 to 4 tchd 5 to 2) 1
BEAUREPAIRE (Ire) [108] 8-10-9 S McNeill, *led to 14th, lost pl 17th, rallied 4 out, led 2 out to last, no extr.*
.... (11 to 2 op 4 to 1) 2
1323² RAINBOW CASTLE [107] 9-10-8 P Hide, *chsd ldr, led 14th to 16th, one pace appr 3 out.*
.... (100 to 30 op 3 to 1 tchd 7 to 2) 3
LE MEILLE (Ire) [113] 7-11-0 R Johnson, *beh, blun second and tenth, hdwy 13th, mstk 16th, sn rdn and wknd, tld off.*
.... (6 to 4 fav op 11 to 8 tchd 7 to 4) 4
Dist: 1¼l, 4l, dist. 6m 39.50s. a 23.50s (4 Ran).

(Mrs Christopher Wright), K C Bailey

1500 Tote Betting Shop Handicap Hurdle Class C (0-135 4-y-o and up) £3,470 2m........................... (3:00)

1238² MORSTOCK [110] 6-10-7 (3⁰) T Dascombe, *made all, sn clr, mstk second, drvn out.* ....(3 to 1 tchd 7 to 2) 1
1272² PHAR FROM FUNNY [106] 5-10-6 B Fenton, *hld up, rdn to chase wnr appr 2 out, kpt on r-in.*
.... (5 to 4 on op 11 to 10 on) 2
1288³ HAMILTON SILK [128] 4-12-0 R Dunwoody, *chsd wnr frm 3rd till rdn and wknd appr 2 out, tld off.* ....(7 to 2 op 5 to 2) 3
VISION OF FREEDOM (Ire) [105] 8-10-5 A Thornton, *mstk 3rd, sn wl beh, tld off, broke blood vessel.*
.... (9 to 1 op 8 to 1 tchd 10 to 1) 4
Dist: 2l, dist, dist. 3m 41.00s. a 7.00s (4 Ran).

SR: 28/22/-/-/ (Mrs M Fairbairn), R J Hodges

1501 EBF Tattersalls Ireland Mares' Novices' Chase Qualifier Class D (5-y-o and up) £3,457 2m.............. (3:30)

1213⁶ KOO'S PROMISE 5-10-9 (3⁰) T Dascombe, *hld up beh ldrs, lost pl 9th, lft in second at fnl fence, kpt on to ld cl hme.*
.... (8 to 1 op 10 to 1 tchd 12 to 1) 1
1262 RIDEPARK ROSE (Ire) 8-10-12 S Fox, *wth ldr, led appr second till quickening 3 out, hdd cl hme, hdd cl hme....* (11 to 4 op 3 to 1 tchd 5 to 2) 2
1234 UP THE TEMPO (Ire) 7-10-12 A Thornton, *hld up, blun 9th, sn tld off.* ....(16 to 1 op 11 to 1) 3
1368* SECOND CALL 7-11-4 R Dunwoody, *al gng wl, led till appr second, led approaching 3 out, 20 ls clr whn f last, rmntd.*
.... (9 to 4 on op 5 to 2 on tchd 2 to 1 on) 4
Dist: Nk, dist, dist. 4m 2.80s. a 14.80s (4 Ran).

(G A Warren Limited), C L Popham

1502 Great Western Novices' Hurdle Class C (4-y-o and up) £3,834 2¾m........................... (4:00)

1082⁴ KILMINGTON (Ire) 7-11-0 P Hide, *al prmnt, led 8th, rdn betw fnl 2, ran on wl.* ....(11 to 2 op 4 to 1 tchd 6 to 1) 1
CAPTAIN JACK 6-11-0 R Dunwoody, *led to second, led 5th to 8th, ev ch 2 out, no extr....* (9 to 4 op 2 to 1 tchd 3 to 1) 2
ATAVISTIC (Ire) 4-11-0 M A Fitzgerald, *hld up, hdwy appr 7th, hit nxt, styd on one pace.*........(10 to 1 op 8 to 1) 3
MENESONIC (Ire) 6-10-11 (3⁰) P Henley, *chsd ldrs, rdn 3 out, one pace appr nxt.....*(12 to 1 op 10 to 1 tchd 14 to 1) 4
1100* HUNTERS ROCK (Ire) 7-11-10 C O'Dwyer, *hld up rear, hdwy 8th, effrt appr 2 out, wknd approaching last.*
.... (6 to 5 fav op 5 to 4 tchd 11 to 10) 5
1237⁵ MISS SECRET 6-10-9 A Thornton, *mid-div, hdwy 6th, wknd appr 2 out.* ....(66 to 1 op 33 to 1) 6
1348 YOUNG TYCOON (NZ) 5-11-0 L Harvey, *beh 7th.*
.... (66 to 1 op 33 to 1) 7
RED BRONZE (Ire) 5-11-0 B Fenton, *al beh.*
.... (20 to 1 op 16 to 1) 8
1215 THE BREWER 4-11-0 S McNeill, *al beh, tld off.*
.... (33 to 1 op 25 to 1) 9
1085⁶ MR JASPER (bl) 4-11-0 S Burrough, *pld hrd, led second to 5th, wknd nxt, tld off whn pulled up bef 8th.*
.... (100 to 1 op 50 to 1) pu

BLACK STATEMENT (Ire) 6-11-0 R Johnson, *prmnt to 8th, sn wknd, tld off whn pld up bef 2 out*.....(25 to 1 op 16 to 1) pu
Dist: 3l, sht-hd, 6l, 1¼l, 25l, 1½l, 2½l, dist. 5m 17.90s. a 11.90s (11 Ran).
(H T Pelham), J T Gifford

ASCOT (good to firm)
Friday November 22nd
Going Correction: PLUS 0.35 sec. per fur.

1503 Travelling The Turf Racecourse Of The Year Conditional Jockeys' Novices' Hurdle Class C (4-y-o and up) £3,517 2½m..................(1:00)

ROYAL RAVEN (Ire) 5-11-4 L Aspell, *hld up in tch, slight ld 8th, staying on wl whn not fluent last, cmftbly*.
.....................(100 to 30 op 2 to 1 tchd 7 to 2) 1
985* REGAL PURSUIT (Ire) 5-10-10 (7*) T Hagger, *prmnt, chlgd frm 5th till mstk 8th, styd on same pace from 2 out*.
.....................(6 to 5 on op Evens tchd 11 to 10) 2
1429³ ADILOV 4-11-4 Sophie Mitchell, *hld up rear, hdwy 8th, styd on wl frm 2 out, not pace to trble wnr*.
..........(9 to 1 op 12 to 1 tchd 14 to 1 and 7 to 1) 3
SATCOTINO (Ire) 5-10-13 K Gaule, *beh and pushed alng 6th, lost tch 7th*.....................(14 to 1 op 6 to 1) 4
1115 ONE MORE MAN (Ire) 5-10-8 (10*) W Greatrex, *wth ldr 1st to 5th, wknd 7th*.........(20 to 1 op 12 to 1 tchd 25 to 1) 5
952³ CHIEF GALE (Ire) 4-11-4 G Hogan, *led to 8th, sn wknd*.
.....................(8 to 1 op 4 to 1 tchd 9 to 1) 6
Dist: 4l, sht-hd, 24l, 8l, 15l. 5m 6.20s. a 25.20s (6 Ran).
(A D Weller), J T Gifford

1504 Charles Davis Novices' Handicap Chase Class C (5-y-o and up) £6,970 3m 110yds.................... (1:35)

1347³ MONY-SKIP (Ire) [99] 7-10-5 Richard Guest, *chsd ldr, hit 11th, led 15th, in command whn lft clr last*............(11 to 8 jt-fav op 6 to 4 tchd 5 to 4) 1
1339³ LUCKY DOLLAR (Ire) [99] 8-10-5 C O'Dwyer, *rcd in 4th, hit 7th, 11th and 13th, lft poor second at fnl fence*.
.................................(11 to 2 op 3 to 1) 2
1382 MINOR KEY (Ire) [94] 6-10-0 J Osborne, *led, slpd 1st, sn clr, hit 11th, hdd 15th, soon wknd, lft poor 3rd at fnl fence*.
.....................(14 to 1 op 10 to 1 tchd 16 to 1) 3
1183² RANDOM HARVEST (Ire) [94] 7-10-0 D Gallagher, *rcd in 3rd, hdwy to dispute second 12th to 15th, rdn 2 out, chalg but hld whn f last, rmntd*... (11 to 8 jt-fav op 5 to 4 tchd 6 to 4) 4
Dist: 7l, dist, dist. 6m 22.50s. a 21.50s (4 Ran).
(Trevor Hemmings), Mrs S J Smith

1505 Scudamore Clothing 0800 301 301 'National Hunt' Novices' Hurdle Class C (4-y-o and up) £3,631 3m .... (2:10)

1129* CAROLE'S CRUSADER 5-10-12 R Dunwoody, *made all, shaken up appr 2 out, sn clr, readily*.
.....................(100 to 30 op 3 to 1 tchd 7 to 2) 1
1271* FLYING GUNNER 5-11-3 A Maguire, *prmnt, chsd wnr frm 9th, rdn and hit 2 out, sn one pace*.
.....................(6 to 4 fav op 7 to 4 tchd 2 to 1) 2
1318² DACELO (Fr) 5-10-12 J Osborne, *beh, pushed alng and effrt aftr 3 out, sn one pace*..............(20 to 1 op 10 to 1) 3
172* SUPREME CHARM (Ire) 4-10-11 C O'Dwyer, *beh, hdwy 6th, rdn aftr 3 out, sn wknd*.... (8 to 1 op 5 to 1 tchd 10 to 1) 4
1300³ CHARLIE PARROT (Ire) 6-10-12 A P McCoy, *hld up, brief effrt frm rear aftr 3 out, sn fdd*. (16 to 1 op 7 to 1 tchd 20 to 1) 5
COOLE CHERRY 6-10-12 B Fenton, *chsd ldr to 5th, wknd 9th*.
.....................(33 to 1 op 20 to 1 tchd 50 to 1) 6
1237 ASHLEY HOUSE 7-10-7 (5*) D Salter, *beh 6th, tld off 8th, pld up bef 4 out*..................... (100 to 1 op 50 to 1) pu
1260³ PRU'S PROFILES (Ire) 5-10-12 D Bridgwater, *chsd ldr 5th to 9th, wknd tenth, tld off whn pld up aftr 3 out*.
.....................(12 to 1 op 7 to 1 tchd 20 to 1) pu
1295* MYWEND'S (Ire) 6-11-3 G Bradley, *blun 1st, hdwy 6th, 4th and wkng whn pld up aftr 3 out, dismounted*.
.....................(4 to 1 op 7 to 2 tchd 9 to 2) pu
Dist: 9l, 9l, 4l, 11l, 27l. 6m 2.50s. a 26.50s (9 Ran).
(Mrs C Skipworth), D R Gandolfo

1506 Coopers & Lybrand Ascot Hurdle Class A Grade 2 (4-y-o and up) £15,675 2½m................ (2:40)

1268⁵ MUSE 9-11-0 P Holley, *led, hdd aftr 3 out, sn drvn to ld ag'n, drw clr appr last, rdn out*............(13 to 8 op 11 to 10) 1
1305⁴ MISTINGUETT (Ire) 4-10-9 C Llewellyn, *dsptd second, chsd wnr 4 out, slight ld aftr nxt, sn hdd, outpcd appr last*.
.....(11 to 8 on op 5 to 4 on tchd 11 to 10 and 6 to 4 on) 2
1233² FIELDRIDGE 7-11-0 B Powell, *dsptd second to 4 out, one pace aftr 3 out*.......... (15 to 2 op 6 to 1 tchd 10 to 1) 3
Dist: 10l, 6l. 4m 58.50s. a 17.50s (3 Ran).
(White Horse Racing Ltd), D R C Elsworth

1507 Gerrard And National Handicap Chase Class B (4-y-o and up) £9,436 2m.......................... (3:10)

1157* STORM ALERT [145] 10-11-12 A Maguire, *led till aftr second, chsd ldr, chlgd 7th, led 4 out, kpt on wl r-in*.
.....................(6 to 5 fav op 11 to 10 on tchd 5 to 4) 1
1131* CALLISOE BAY (Ire) [137] 7-11-4 J Osborne, *led aftr 1st, hit 5th, hdd 4 out, not fluent nxt, rallied to chal last, sn one pace*.
.....................(11 to 8 op 5 to 4 tchd 6 to 4) 2
DANCING PADDY [147] 8-12-0 Richard Guest, *beh, hit 3rd, blun nxt, hdwy 7th, effrt appr 2 out, one pace last*.
.....................(5 to 1 op 7 to 2) 3
1319⁴ SPINNING STEEL [120] 9-10-1¹ S Burrough, *3rd till f 4th*.
.....................(50 to 1 op 33 to 1 tchd 66 to 1) f
Dist: 3½l, 4l. 3m 56.90s. a 8.90s (4 Ran).
SR: 65/53/59/-/ (Mrs Dawn Perrett), D Nicholson

1508 Ladbroke Trial Handicap Hurdle Class B (0-145 4-y-o and up) £6,589 2m 110yds.................. (3:40)

EXECUTIVE DESIGN [128] 4-11-3 P Niven, *hld up, steady hdwy 6th, chlgd 3 out, led nxt, readily*.
.....................(3 to 1 fav tchd 9 to 2) 1
1160⁴ CHARMING GIRL (USA) [127] 5-11-2 J Osborne, *hld up, hdwy 6th, chlgd 3 out, ev ch nxt, one pace r-in, eased whn held nr finish*...................(9 to 2 op 3 to 1) 2
1160² SHOOFK [114] 5-10-3 R Dunwoody, *chsd ldr, led aftr 4th, rdn 3 out, hdd nxt, sn one pace*.......... (7 to 1 tchd 8 to 1) 3
1184³ KAITAK (Ire) [120] 5-10-9 A Maguire, *chsd ldrs, chlgd 6th to 3 out, one pace nxt*.....................(6 to 1 op 4 to 1) 4
1305³ GROUND NUT (Ire) [125] 6-11-0 B Powell, *led till aftr 4th, outpcd 3 out, styd on r-in*..................(9 to 2 op 7 to 2) 5
1375⁴ PALACEGATE KING [125] 7-11-0 B Harding, *prmnt, rdn 6th, sn wknd*............ (16 to 1 op 12 to 1 tchd 20 to 1) 6
SOVEREIGNS PARADE [113] 4-10-2 M A Fitzgerald, *effrt 6th, wknd 3 out*............(9 to 1 op 6 to 1 tchd 10 to 1) 7
1288⁴ NON VINTAGE (Ire) [131] 5-11-6 W Worthington, *f second*.
.....................(10 to 1 op 7 to 1) f
Dist: 3l, hd, 1½l, 1¾l, 20l, 1¾l. 3m 59.20s. a 13.20s (8 Ran).
SR: 12/8/-/-/2/ (L T Foster), Mrs M Reveley

AINTREE (good)
Friday November 22nd
Going Correction: PLUS 0.40 sec. per fur.

1509 Southport Novices' Hurdle Class D (4-y-o and up) £3,009 2m 110yds .... (1:10)

TREMENDISTO 6-10-12 A Dobbin, *reluctant to line up, sn led, hdd 3 out, rallied to ld ag'n last, styd on und pres*.
.....................(4 to 1 op 11 to 4) 1
1224⁵ THREE WILD DAYS 4-10-12 R Garritty, *cl up, led 3 out, mstk nxt, hdd last, sn no extr*..........(3 to 1 jt-fav op 11 to 4) 2
1182⁸ PENROSE LAD (NZ) 6-10-12 R Johnson, *chsd ldrs, blun 3rd, hrd drvn appr 3 out, one pace frm nxt*............(3 to 1 jt-fav op 11 to 4) 3
1070⁷ MR CHRISTIE 4-10-12 A Thornton, *midfield, drvn alng frm hfwy, one pace appr 2 out*.......... (14 to 1 tchd 16 to 1) 4
1224 SEGALA (Ire) 5-10-12 N Williamson, *keen hold towards rear, not fluent 4th, rdn and outpcd 3 out, one pace frm nxt*.
.....................(16 to 1) 5
STAR MASTER 5-10-12 M Dwyer, *hld up, lost tch aftr 4 out, sn wl beh*..................(7 to 1 op 10 to 1 tchd 6 to 1) 6
1136⁵ YOUNG BENSON 4-10-9 (3*) R Massey, *chsd ldrs, wknd quickly appr 3 out, tld off*............(50 to 1 op 33 to 1) 7
BOLD STREET (Ire) 6-10-12 T Kent, *keen hold in rear, gd hdwy to chase ldrs 4 out, outpcd and hit nxt, btn whn pld up betw last 2*..................(20 to 1 op 14 to 1) pu
KINGS CAY (Ire) 5-10-12 L Wyer, *hld up, jmpd slwly in rear 5th, tld off whn pld up bef 2 out*.........(8 to 1 op 7 to 1) pu
1293⁹ DICTATION (USA) 4-10-12 A Roche, *hld up, mstk second, struggling 4 out, wl beh whn pld up bef nxt*.
.....................(20 to 1 op 16 to 1) pu
Dist: 6l, 1¼l, 1¼l, 2½l, dist, dist. 4m 10.80s. a 22.80s (10 Ran).
(Doug Marshall), Capt J Wilson

1510 Lydiate Conditional Jockeys' Novices' Handicap Hurdle Class E (0-110 4-y-o and up) £2,626 2½m .... (1:45)

1038² SUPERTOP [100] 8-11-7 (7*) I Jardine, *beh, smooth hdwy 4 out, not fluent nxt, led gng wl appr last, pushed clr*.
.....................(5 to 2 fav op 2 to 1) 1
KILLBALLY BOY (Ire) [86] 6-11-0 G F Ryan, *pressed ldr, blun 4th, led 7th till hdd appr last, sn one pace*.
.....................(11 to 4 op 5 to 2) 2
AUNTIE ALICE [80] 6-10-8 G Lee, *chsd ldrs, drvn alng 3 out, btn frm nxt*.....................(7 to 2) 3

NATIONAL HUNT RESULTS 1996-97

1266 CURRAGH PETER [72] 9-10-0 Guy Lewis, led, hit 5th, mstk
and hdd 7th, struggling appr 3 out, sn beh.
....(33 to 1 op 25 to 1)   4
1047⁶ ELA MAN HOWA [84] 5-10-9 (3*) D J Kavanagh, struggling 4
out, sn beh, tld off.............................(9 to 2 op 4 to 1)   5
1115⁵ LAWBUSTER (Ire) [78] (bl) 4-10-6 P Henley, hit 1st, pushed
alng to chase ldrs whn hit 6th, tld off when pld up aftr 4 out.
....(10 to 1 op 8 to 1)   pu
Dist: 13l, 6l, 15l, 9l. 5m 13.10s. a 35.10s (6 Ran).

(Mrs Barbara Lungo), L Lungo

1511 John Parrett Memorial Handicap Chase Class C (0-135 5-y-o and up) £6,742 3m 1f.................(2:20)

1336* BAS DE LAINE (Fr) [120] 10-11-4 (5ex) R Garritty, wth ldr,
jmpd slwly 3rd, led 11th, clr aftr 4 out, easily.....(9 to 4 jt-
fav tchd 5 to 2)   1
1336² FIVELEIGH BUILDS [128] 9-11-12 A Thornton, hmpd 3rd, led
5th till mstk and hdd 11th, chsd wnr till lost tch appr 3 out.
....(4 to 1 op 3 to 1)   2
WHAAT FETTLE [130] 11-12-0 A Dobbin, made most to 5th,
drpd rear 8th, tld off whn pld up bef 12th. (3 to 1 op 9 to 4)   pu
1296³ MUSTHAVEASWIG [125] 10-11-9 R Johnson, jmpd baldy,
drvn alng to chase ldrs hfwy, lost tch 6 out, tld off whn pld up
aftr 2 out.........................(9 to 4 jt-fav op 2 to 1)   pu
Dist: Dist. 6m 48.30s. a 43.30s (4 Ran).

(R K Bids Ltd), M D Hammond

1512 Croston Langenberger Handicap Hurdle Class D (0-120 4-y-o and up) £4,162 2m 110yds...........(2:50)

1225* CHAI-YO [110] 6-11-5 G Upton, settled rear, mstk 4th,
smooth hdwy appr 3 out, led on bit last, pushed clr.
..............................(13 to 8 fav op 6 to 4 tchd 7 to 4)   1
KING ATHELSTAN (USA) [108] 8-11-3 Derek Byrne, chsd clr
ldr, led 4th, pushed clear entering strt, hdd last, no extr.
......................................(9 to 1 op 3 to 1)   2
1386* SARMATIAN (USA) [114] 5-11-9 (6ex) R Garritty, str hold
towards rear, effrt to chase ldrs appr 2 out, no imprsn.
....(4 to 1 op 3 to 1)   3
HAWWAM [91] 10-10-0 L Wyer, chsd ldrs, drvn alng 3 out,
wknd und pres bef nxt...................(16 to 1 op 14 to 1)   4
1346⁵ PRIDEWOOD PICKER [91] 9-9-9 (5*) D J Kavanagh, pld hrd
towards rear, some hdwy 4 out, drvn and lost tch frm nxt.
...................................(12 to 1 op 10 to 1)   5
1284⁵ DONE WELL (USA) [119] 4-12-0 A Dobbin, settled rear, lost
tch appr 3 out, tld off...............(4 to 1 tchd 9 to 2)   6
1230³ INDIAN JOCKEY [112] 4-11-4 (3*) D Walsh, sn clr, hrd drvn
and hdd 4th, blun nxt, wknd quickly appr 3 out, tld off.
...........................(7 to 1 op 5 to 1 tchd 8 to 1)   7
Dist: 7l, 13l, 11l, 5l, dist, 17l. 4m 16.10s. a 28.10s (7 Ran).

(Nick Viney), J A B Old

1513 Liverpool Novices' Chase Class D (5-y-o and up) £4,464 3m 1f......(3:20)

1229* BARONET (Ire) 6-11-5 R Johnson, led, hit 9th, mstk and hdd
12th, led 5 out to nxt, rallied und pres betw last 2, led last 50
yards.........................(5 to 2 op 9 to 4 on)   1
1250³ KENMORE-SPEED 9-11-0 N Williamson, hld up, mstk 14th,
led 4 out, clr appr 2 out, not fluent last, hdd and no extr last 50
yards...............................(9 to 4 op 7 to 4 tchd 5 to 2)   2
SLOTAMATIQUE (Ire) 7-11-0 A Dobbin, wth ldr, led 12th till
mstk and hdd 5 out, rallied frm 2 out, no extr r-in.
....(9 to 2 op 9 to 2)   3
Dist: 2l, 3½l. 6m 50.60s. a 45.60s (3 Ran).

(Mrs David Thompson), D Nicholson

1514 Weatherbys 'Stars Of Tomorrow' Open National Hunt Flat Intermediate - Class H (4,5,6-y-o) £1,934 2m 110yds...................(3:50)

1317² GOOD VIBES 4-11-4 L Wyer, pld hrd, led till ran wide and hdd
briefly 5 fs out, edgd rght fnl furlong, styd on strly.
...............................(9 to 4 fav op 3 to 1 tchd 11 to 4)   1
1026² FIRST LIGHT 4-11-4 R Johnson, settled rear, improved frm
hfwy, chsd ldr and edgd lft entering fnl furlong, ran on.
..................(3 to 1 op 2 to 1 tchd 100 to 30)   2
MEADOW HYMN (Ire) 5-11-4 W Dwan, hld up, improved to
track ldrs 4 fs out, kpt on same pace frm o'r one out.
............................(20 to 1 op 16 to 1)   3
WHIP HAND (Ire) 5-11-11 M Dwyer, hld up, took clr order
hfwy, chsd wnr 3 fs out, no extr wi o'r one out.
.............................(100 to 30 op 3 to 1 tchd 7 to 2)   4
MAC'S SUPREME (Ire) 4-11-4 N Williamson, hld up towards
rear, shaken up o'r 4 fs out, no dngr fnl 3 furlongs.
..............................(12 to 1 op 8 to 1)   5
DASHANTI 5-11-1 (3*) R Massey, trkd ldrs, effrt 4 fs out, wknd
o'r 2 out, sn beh..................(10 to 1 op 8 to 1)   6
700⁵ FOUR FROM HOME 4-11-4 A Roche, pld hrd in midfield,
struggling o'r 3 fs out, sn beh............(20 to 1 op 12 to 1)   7
880⁴ NIGHT ESCAPADE (Ire) 4-10-13 M Richards, cl up, led briefly
5 fs out, wknd o'r 3 out...............(10 to 1 op 8 to 1)   8

1350 LOOK IN THE MIRROR 5-10-11 (7*) L Suthern, chsd ldr, wknd
quickly o'r 4 fs out, tld off.............(12 to 1 op 10 to 1)   9
CASHEL QUAY (Ire) 6-11-1 (3*) Guy Lewis, in tch, reminders
and lost touch o'r 4 fs out, tld off.....(33 to 1 op 20 to 1)   10
DANTES AMOUR (Ire) 5-11-4 R Garritty, al beh, tld off.
....(10 to 1 op 8 to 1)   11
Dist: 4l, 4l, 1l, 21l, 9l, 8l, 1¾l, 34l, 2l, dist. 4m 11.40s. (11 Ran).

(G E Shouler), T D Easterby

ASCOT (good to firm)
Saturday November 23rd
Going Correction: PLUS 0.30 sec. per fur.

1515 Holloways Gate Novices' Hurdle Class C (4-y-o and up) £3,517 2m 110yds...................(12:45)

RESIST THE FORCE (USA) 5-11-5 P Hide, hld up, steady
hdwy 6th, trkd ldrs 2 out, quickened to ld last, easily.
....(5 to 1 op 4 to 1)   1
CARLITO BRIGANTE 4-11-5 J Osborne, in tch, not fluent 6th,
chlgd and gng wl 2 out, rdn last, kpt on, not pace of wnr,
dismounted...........(9 to 4 fav op 7 to 4 tchd 5 to 2)   2
TAKE COVER (Ire) 5-11-5 A Maguire, led, rdn 2 out, hdd appr
last, one pace.........................(6 to 1 op 4 to 1)   3
THE STAGER (Ire) 4-11-5 G Bradley, hdwy 5th, chsd ldr aftr 3
out till appr nxt, sn wknd. (9 to 1 op 5 to 1 tchd 10 to 1)   4
BLUE AND ROYAL (Ire) 4-11-5 C Llewellyn, chsd ldr, chlgd
4th to 6th, wknd aftr 3 out.
.................................(40 to 1 op 33 to 1 tchd 50 to 1)   5
1354⁴ ADONISIS 4-11-5 A Procter, wnt lft strt and slwly away, keen
hold and sn reco'red, wknd 6th.
.................................(12 to 1 op 10 to 1 tchd 14 to 1)   6
SEVENTEENS LUCKY 4-11-5 V Smith, mid-div, shaken up
and effrt 3 out, wknd appr nxt, broke blood vessel.
.....................(9 to 2 op 3 to 1 tchd 5 to 1)   7
RIVER MONARCH 5-10-12 (7*) Mr P O'Keeffe, hld up rear,
lost tch 6th.............................(20 to 1 op 12 to 1)   8
NIGHT FLARE (Fr) 4-11-5 R Dunwoody, prmnt, mstks 3rd and
6th, sn wknd, tld off whn pld up bef 2 out.
............................(6 to 1 op 7 to 2 tchd 7 to 1)   pu
Dist: 7l, 6l, 8l, 4l, 8l, 2l, 1l. 4m 5.60s. a 19.60s (9 Ran).

(Mrs Barbara Hogan), J T Gifford

1516 Gardner Merchant Handicap Chase Class B (5-y-o and up) £9,987 3m 110yds......................(1:20)

1290* INCHCAILLOCH (Ire) 7-11-4 R Dunwoody, pressed ldr
5th to 7th and ag'n tenth, slpd 11th, led 15th, ran on wl frm 2
out...............................(Evens jt-fav tchd 6 to 5 on)   1
1156* GO BALLISTIC [129] 7-11-9 M A Fitzgerald, hld up in 3rd,
chsd wnr aftr 15th, not fluent 4 out, hit 2 out, sn rdn and no
extr.......................(Evens jt-fav op 5 to 4 on tchd 11 to 10)   2
1418⁶ PAPER STAR [106] 9-10-0 C Llewellyn, led to 15th, sn wknd,
tld off........................(22 to 1 op 14 to 1 tchd 25 to 1)   3
Dist: 3½l, dist. 6m 12.40s. a 11.40s (3 Ran).
SR: 49/50/-/

(F J Carter), J S King

1517 Aurelius Juvenile Novices' Hurdle Class B (3-y-o) £4,879 2m 110yds ....(1:55)

LEAR JET (USA) 11-3 R Dunwoody, chsd ldr appr 6th, chlgd 3
out till approaching nxt, rallied to ld last, all out.
.......................(9 to 1 op 6 to 1 tchd 10 to 1)   1
BLURRED (Ire) 11-3 A Maguire, hld up, steady hdwy frm 6th,
led on bit 2 out, hit last and hdd, sn btn.
...........................(5 to 4 fav tchd 6 to 4)   2
1286⁴ DOCTOR GREEN (Fr) (v) 11-7 C Llewellyn, led, sn clr, rdn 3
out, hdd nxt, styd on one paced..(4 to 1 op 3 to 1)   3
1286³ SQUIRE'S OCCASION (Can) 11-7 M A Fitzgerald, chsd ldr to
3 out, wknd appr nxt......(13 to 2 op 3 to 1 tchd 7 to 1)   4
1188³ HEVER GOLF DIAMOND 11-7 J Osborne, sn wl beh, modest
hdwy frm 2 out, not a dngr.
.............................(12 to 1 op 10 to 1 tchd 14 to 1)   5
SAM ROCKETT 11-3 K Gaule, not fluent and beh, tld off 4th.
...........................(50 to 1 op 25 to 1)   6
MR WILD (USA) 11-3 S Ryan, mstk and uns rdr second.
..........................(9 to 2 op 6 to 1 tchd 9 to 1)   ur
Dist: 2l, 4l, 5l, 6l, dist. 4m 4.10s. a 18.10s (7 Ran).

(Godorphal Racing Partnership), Bob Jones

1518 First National Bank Gold Cup Chase Class A Limited Handicap (5-y-o and up) £25,984 2m 3f 110yds... (2:30)

1394² STRONG PROMISE (Ire) [122] 5-10-5 (3*) K Gaule, jmpd wl,
chsd ldr till led 7th, kpt on frm 3 out, cmftbly.
.................................(11 to 8 fav op Evens tchd 6 to 4)   1
1137¹ MAJOR BELL [129] 8-11-1 B Harding, prmnt, chsd wnr frm
7th, effrt und pres frm 3 out, kpt on, not pace to chal frm 2
out.......................................(9 to 2 tchd 5 to 1)   2

189

1380² SOUTHAMPTON [120] (v) 6-10-6 B Fenton, beh, drvn alng
frm 11th, styd on und pres frm 3 out, not pace to trble ldrs.
.... (13 to 2 op 6 to 1 tchd 7 to 1)   3
1185³ BERTONE (Ire) [135] 7-11-7 J Osborne, hld up, hdwy 11th,
drvn to chal 3 out, wknd nxt.
.... (10 to 1 op 7 to 1 tchd 11 to 1)   4
1287 PLUNDER BAY (USA) [118] 5-10-4 M A Fitzgerald, hld up,
hdwy tenth, chsd ldrs 3 out, wknd appr nxt.
..........................(16 to 1 tchd 20 to 1)   5
1210³ PIMBERLEY PLACE (Ire) [125] 8-10-11 C Llewellyn, drvn into
strt, blun 6th, lost tch frm tenth, tld off.
..........................(20 to 1 tchd 25 to 1)   6
1184⁵ CUMBRIAN CHALLENGE (Ire) [129] 7-11-1 A Maguire, led till
jmpd slwly and hdd 7th, rallied and hit 3 out, sn wknd.
.... (9 to 1 tchd 8 to 1)   7
1156⁵ SENOR EL BETRUTTI (Ire) [138] 7-11-10 G Bradley, prmnt
early, lost tch frm 7th, tld off whn pld up bef tenth.
.... (9 to 1 op 10 to 1 tchd 8 to 1) pu
Dist: 4l, 5l, 12l, 9l, dist, 13l. 4m 51.50s. a 10.50s (8 Ran).
SR: 34/37/23/26/-/   (G A Hubbard), G A Hubbard

1519 Hurst Park Novices' Chase Class B (5-y-o and up) £6,825 2m..... (3:05)

1028³ OH SO RISKY 9-11-3 P Holley, trkd ldr 3rd, led 7th, clr 2 out,
readily.......................... (9 to 4 tchd 5 to 2)   1
DREAM RIDE (Ire) 6-11-3 A Maguire, blun 1st, chsd ldr aftr
second to nxt, disputing second whn lft chasing wnr 3 out, no
imprsn und pres..... (11 to 8 fav op 5 to 4 tchd 6 to 4)   2
1340³ DJAIS (Fr) 7-11-3 R Dunwoody, al beh, lost tch and tld off frm
8th.......................... (9 to 2 op 4 to 1 tchd 5 to 1)   3
1163³ PRINCE SKYBURD 5-11-3 M A Fitzgerald, led to 7th, disputing second and hrd drvn whn blun and uns rdr 3 out.
.... (4 to 1 op 7 to 2 tchd 6 to 1) ur
Dist: 7l, 22l. 3m 57.90s. a 9.90s (4 Ran).
SR: 38/31/9/-/   (M Tabor), D R C Elsworth

1520 Lion Gate Handicap Hurdle Class B (4-y-o and up) £5,414 3m..... (3:40)

1233³ OLYMPIAN [118] (bl) 9-10-7 M A Fitzgerald, trkd ldr, rdn aftr 3
out, chlgd nxt till styd on to ld nr finish. (14 to 1 op 8 to 1)   1
1233* OCEAN HAWK (USA) [140] 4-12-0 C Llewellyn, beh, drvn
alng frm 9th, plenty to do 3 out, rallied to chal nxt, slight ld r-in,
hdd and no extr nr finish.
..........................(11 to 8 on op Evens tchd 5 to 4)   2
1303* GYSART (Ire) [120] (bl) 7-10-9 A Maguire, led 1st, clr 3 out,
hdd r-in, one pace und pres.
.... (2 to 1 op 7 to 4 tchd 9 to 4)   3
1427* MOMENT OF GLORY (Ire) [115] 5-10-4 R Dunwoody, hld up,
jmpd slwly 3rd, hdwy whn not fluent 3 out, chlgd gng wl frm nxt
till wknd r-in.......................... (4 to 1 op 9 to 2)   4
Dist: Nk, hd, 2l. 6m 1.80s. a 25.80s (4 Ran).
    (J Neville), J Neville

CATTERICK (good to firm)
Saturday November 23rd
Going Correction: PLUS 0.05 sec. per fur. (races 1,2,4,6), PLUS 0.25 (3,5)

1521 Goathland Mares' Only Maiden Hurdle Class F (4-y-o and up) £1,793 2m 3f..... (1:10)

1464³ ANGLESEY SEA VIEW 7-11-0 T Kent, not fluent, prmnt, led
aftr 3 out, sn clr, easily.......... (10 to 1 on op 4 to 1 on)   1
997⁵ ARADIA'S DIAMOND 5-11-0 S McNeill, prmnt, outpcd hfwy,
rallied to chase ldrs 3 out, kpt on same pace.
.... (8 to 1 op 7 to 1)   2
APPEARANCE MONEY (Ire) 5-10-7 (7*) Miss Elizabeth Doyle,
in tch, hdwy to ld 4th, hdd aftr 3 out, kpt on same pace.
.... (33 to 1 op 25 to 1)   3
PHILBECKY 5-10-11 (3*) E Callaghan, chsd ldrs till outpcd
aftr 6th, no dngr aftr.................. (33 to 1 op 20 to 1)   4
1252 BEST FRIEND 4-11-0 J Callaghan, beh, hdwy to chase ldrs 3
out, wknd nxt.................. (25 to 1 tchd 33 to 1)   5
ABOUT MIDNIGHT 7-11-0 A Roche, led to 4th, wkng whn
blun 3 out.................. (66 to 1 op 33 to 1)   6
RINGRONE (Ire) 7-11-0 Mr M Thompson, mid-div till wknd bef
7th.................. (66 to 1 op 33 to 1)   7
RESTATE (Ire) 5-10-7 (7*) Mr T J Barry, beh, lost tch frm 7th, tld
off.................. (50 to 1 op 25 to 1)   8
1372⁵ NAWTINOOKEY 6-11-0 B Storey, in tch whn f 6th.
.... (6 to 1 op 10 to 1 tchd 5 to 1) f
1737 AKITO RACING (Ire) 5-11-0 M Moloney, beh, hmpd 6th, tld off
whn pld up bef 2 out..............(14 to 1 op 12 to 1) pu
Dist: 11l, 3l, 9l, 2½l, 30l, 1½l, dist. 4m 45.70s. a 25.70s (10 Ran).
    (Mrs P Hewitt), A Bailey

1522 Darlington And Stockton Times Novices' Handicap Hurdle Class E (0-100 4-y-o and up) £1,830 2m .... (1:40)

1182⁶ LAST TRY (Ire) [86] 5-11-4 (3*) G Cahill, cl up, led aftr 3 out, clr
betw last 2, eased towards finish........(4 to 1 op 7 to 2)   1
1280⁵ SCOTTON GREEN [74] 5-10-9 J Callaghan, trkd ldrs, chlgd
aftr 3 out, no extr und pres frm nxt........(6 to 1 op 4 to 1)   2
1371⁴ BOWCLIFFE [81] 5-11-2 J Supple, mid-div, effrt aftr 3 out,
styd on same pace frm nxt........... (12 to 1 op 9 to 1)   3
1198⁶ JOE JAGGER (Ire) [74] 5-10-9 D Bentley, chsd ldrs, drvn alng
and no imprsn whn mstk 2 out.
.... (9 to 5 on op 1 to 1 tchd 7 to 1)   4
1373⁴ MULLINS (Ire) [80] 5-11-1 D J Moffatt, beh, drvn alng and
outpcd aftr 3 out, no dngr after........(10 to 1 op 8 to 1)   5
1333² KILNAMARTYRA GIRL [89] 6-11-7 (3*) P Midgley, hld up,
mstk 5th, rdn aftr 3 out, sn beh........(9 to 1 op 7 to 1)   6
1123* FLAMING HOPE (Ire) [79] 6-11-0¹ J Burke, led, mstks 4th and
2 out, hdd, wknd bef nxt.
.... (9 to 4 fav op 9 to 4 tchd 3 to 1)   7
27⁸ COQUET GOLD [65] 5-10-0 B Storey, al beh.
.... (33 to 1 op 25 to 1)   8
Dist: 5l, ¾l, 1l, 10l, 2l, 9l, 13l. 3m 49.10s. a 9.10s (8 Ran).
SR: 10/-/-/-/-/   (H J Harenberg), B S Rothwell

1523 Northern Echo 'Racing North' Novices' Chase Class E (4-y-o and up) £2,816 2m..................(2:10)

1332⁵ TWIN FALLS (Ire) 5-11-3 J Callaghan, cl up, lft in ld bef 5th,
quickened clr aftr 8th, easily..........(10 to 1 op 6 to 1)   1
960* MARBLE MAN (Ire) 6-11-3 D Bentley, sn tracking ldrs, chsd
wnr frm 6th, outpcd aftr 8th, hit 3 out, no imprsn.
.... (11 to 4 op 7 to 4)   2
1327² VAL DE RAMA (Ire) 7-11-7 (3*) G Cahill, towards rear, blun
4th, hdwy to chase ldrs aftr 8th, wknd bef 3 out.
.... (5 to 1 op 7 to 2 tchd 6 to 1)   3
1329³ FINGERHILL (Ire) 7-11-3 Mr M Thompson, prmnt till wknd aftr
7th, tld off.......................... (5 to 1 op 33 to 1)   4
861¹⁴ BONNY JOHNNY 6-11-3 D J Moffatt, beh whn f 8th.
.... (100 to 1 op 50 to 1) f
1743¹ JACK DOYLE (Ire) 5-11-3 A Roche, hld up, steady hdwy whn f
8th..................(Evens fav op 11 to 10 tchd 5 to 4) f
1127 CARDINAL SINNER (Ire) 7-11-3 K Jones, led till took wrong
course bef 5th..................... (100 to 1 op 50 to 1) ro
Dist: 13l, 8l, 20l. 3m 57.60s. a 10.60s (7 Ran).
SR: 23/10/9/-/   (Mrs Susan Moore), G M Moore

1524 Calderprint Juvenile Novices' Claiming Hurdle Class G (3-y-o) £1,849 2m..................(2:40)

1024⁴ THE GREAT FLOOD 10-11 J Lawrence, chsd ldrs, led aftr 3
out, hdd nxt, rdn to ld last, styd on wl.... (4 to 1 op 5 to 2)   1
1249⁸ ALWARQA 10-9 D Bentley, hld up, hdwy hfwy, slight ld 2 out,
mstk and hdd last, no extr.
.... (15 to 8 fav op 9 to 2 tchd 5 to 4)   2
488⁵ RUSSIAN RASCAL (Ire) 11-12 S McNeill, in tch, hdwy and ch
aftr 3 out, kpt on same pace frm nxt...............(14 to 1)   3
1384⁴ THORNTOUN ESTATE (Ire) (bl) 10-5 (3*) E Callaghan, beh,
hdwy to chase ldrs aftr 3 out, no further prog frm nxt.
.... (8 to 1 op 7 to 1)   4
930 PROPOLIS POWER (Ire) 10-11 (3*) P Midgley, mid-div, kpt on
frm 3 out, nvr dngrs.......................... (50 to 1)   5
1412³ SAMARA SONG 10-10 (7*) N Willmington, chsd ldrs, drvn
alng aftr 3 out, fdd..........(9 to 2 op 4 to 1 tchd 5 to 1)   6
BROGANS BRUSH 9-12 (7*) N Horrocks, wl beh till some late
hdwy, nvr dngrs.......................... (200 to 1)   7
1249 FIASCO 10-2 (7*) M Newton, chsd ldrs till wknd quickly aftr 3
out.......................... (20 to 1)   8
815⁵ IN A TIZZY 10-12 M Foster, led and sn clr, hdd aftr 3 out, wknd
quickly..................(9 to 1 op 8 to 1 tchd 10 to 1) 9+
1353 INDIRA 10-3 (3*) T Dascombe, chsd ldrs till wknd quickly bef 3
out, tld off.......................... (33 to 1) 9+
WINN CALEY 10-9 J Callaghan, sn beh.......... (33 to 1) 10
930 BRIDLINGTON BAY 10-11 N Smith, in tch till wknd quickly bef
3 out.......................... (50 to 1) 11
1188 PHANTOM DANCER (Ire) 11-0 B Storey, chsd ldr till wknd
quickly bef 3 out.......................... (25 to 1) 12
NOIR ESPRIT 10-10 (7*) C McCormack, mid-div whn ducked
lft and ran out 3 out.......................... (33 to 1) ro
1221 BALLYKISSANGEL 11-6 M Moloney, in tch till wknd quickly
aftr 3 out, wl beh whn pld up bef nxt............ (100 to 1) pu
1249 CRAIGMORE MAGIC (USA) (bl) 10-5 A S Smith, towards rear,
mstk 3rd, wl beh whn pld up bef 2 out............ (25 to 1) pu
Dist: 2½l, 2l, 7l, 11l, 6l, 13l, 12l, 1l, 5l, 8l. 3m 47.90s. a 7.90s (16 Ran).
SR: 12/7/22/-/-/-/   (Richard Flood Bloodstock Ltd), C A Dwyer

1525 Dick Brewitt Memorial Challenge Cup Handicap Chase Class E (0-115 5-y-o and up) £2,851 2m 3f... (3:10)

1137⁷ REAL GLEE (Ire) [105] 7-11-4 T Reed, sn cl up, led 5th, mstks
7th (water) and 9th, hdd nxt, led last, soon headed, rallied to
ld post.......................... (7 to 2 op 9 to 4 tchd 5 to 1)   1
1163* BRIAR'S DELIGHT [95] (v) 8-10-8 B Storey, cl up, led tenth,
hdd last, sn led ag'n, ct post.
.... (15 to 8 fav op 9 to 2 tchd 7 to 4)   2
1327⁶ PORT IN A STORM [88] 7-10-1 D Bentley, led to 5th, prmnt till
drpd rear tenth, not trble ldrs aftr, styd on frm last.
.... (10 to 1 op 5 to 1)   3

1248³ NEWHALL PRINCE [112] (v) 8-11-11 T Eley, *in tch, hdwy to chal 3 out, ev ch whn hit last, sn wknd*.. (4 to 1 op 3 to 1) 4
1314⁸ EAST HOUSTON [97] 7-10-10 J Callaghan, *hld up in tch, f tenth*............... (3 to 1 tchd 100 to 30 and 7 to 1) f
Dist: Hd, 4l, hd. 4m 52.00s. a 22.00s (5 Ran).

(John Stone), J J Quinn

1526 Wood House Handicap Hurdle Class E (0-115 4-y-o and up) £2,247 3m 1f 110yds.............................. (3:40)

1150³ DALLY BOY [106] 4-11-7 (3*) E Callaghan, *made all, hit 2 out, shaken up and styd on wl*................. (5 to 2 op 9 to 4) 1
1315⁴ PLUMBOB (Ire) [90] 7-10-9 M Foster, *in tch, chsd wnr frm 7th, drvn alng aftr 3 out, no imprsn*............... (7 to 2) 2
1266² BALLINDOO [88] 7-10-7⁵ Mr R Armson, *hld up, effrt aftr 3 out, drvn alng bef last, kpt on same pace*..... (6 to 1 op 5 to 1) 3
1086 NICK THE DREAMER [97] 11-10-9 (7*) N Willmington, *jmpd slwly, lost tch frm 8th, tld off*........... (8 to 1 op 10 to 1) 4
1315² TROODOS [95] 10-11-0 J Supple, *cl up whn l 7th*.
.....................(6 to 4 fav op 5 to 4 tchd 7 to 4) f
Dist: 3½l, 1¼l, dist. (Time not taken) (5 Ran).

(T H Bennett), T D Easterby

AINTREE (good)
Saturday November 23rd
Going Correction: PLUS 0.90 sec. per fur.

1527 Tote Bookmakers Novices' Chase Class C (5-y-o and up) £5,251 2½m .... (1:05)

1281² DOWN THE FELL 7-11-8 N Williamson, *led, drvn clr 2 out, easily*........................(5 to 1 tchd 11 to 2) 1
1332* MONYMAN (Ire) 6-11-8 R Garritty, *hld up, improved to chase wnr 4 out, outpcd appr 2 out, btn whn jmpd slwly last.
.......................(6 to 1 op 5 to 1) 2
AH SHUSH (Ire) 8-11-3 A P McCoy, *chsd ldr, mstk and drpd rear 8th, drvn alng and jmpd slwly tenth, lost tch appr 3 out.
.......................(14 to 1 op 8 to 1) 3
1250* SIMPLY DASHING (Ire) 5-11-11 L Wyer, *chsd ldrs, jmpd slwly 3rd, chalg and gng wl whn f 12th.
................(5 to 2 on op 9 to 4 on tchd 2 to 1 on) f
Dist: 15l, 3½l. 5m 13.50s. a 25.50s (4 Ran).
SR: 20/5/-/-/

(The Sun Punters Club), J Howard Johnson

1528 Stanley Leisure Children In Need Handicap Hurdle Class B (0-140 4-y-o and up) £10,377 2m 110yds (1:35)

1200* TOM BRODIE [120] 6-11-0 N Williamson, *hld up, smooth hdwy appr 3 out, chalg whn slight mstk nxt, ran on strly und pres to ld cl hme*....................(7 to 2 tchd 4 to 1) 1
MASTER BEVELED [129] 6-11-9 A P McCoy, *chsd clr ldr, led 2 out, ran on wl und pres till ct cl hme*..........
.... fav op 7 to 2) 2
FORESTAL [108] 4-10-2 A Dobbin, *sn clr, not fluent 4th, rdn and hdd 2 out, no extr*.............. (12 to 1 op 10 to 1) 3
SURREY DANCER [130] 8-11-7 (3*) G Lee, *hld up, lost tch aftr 4 out, sn no dngr*........................(8 to 1 op 7 to 1) 4
1148³ ELPIDOS [119] 4-10-13 R Garritty, *hld up, not fluent second, slightly hmpd 5th, lost tch quickly 4 out, tld off whn blun 2 out.
.................(11 to 4 jt-fav op 5 to 2 tchd 3 to 1) 5
1284⁴ THORNTON GATE [127] 7-11-7 L Wyer, *midfield, hdwy and chasing ldr whn f 5th*...................(7 to 1 op 6 to 1) f
Dist: ¾l, 9l, 19l, dist. 4m 12.60s. a 24.60s (6 Ran).

(Mrs M W Bird), J Howard Johnson

1529 Crowther Homes Becher Chase Handicap Class B (6-y-o and up) £23,997 3m 3f................ (2:10)

1283* INTO THE RED [131] 12-10-0 A Dobbin, *hld up, steady hdwy fnl circuit, led 2 out, ran on strly*.............(7 to 4 op 2 to 1) 1
1187³ YOUNG HUSTLER [155] 9-11-10 C Maude, *led, jmpd rght, rdn and hdd 2 out, mstk last, kpt on same pace.
.......................(13 to 8 fav tchd 6 to 4) 2
1304² GLEMOT (Ire) [135] 8-10-4 C O'Dwyer, *mstk 3rd, al hndy, ev ch frm 3 out, rdn and wknd last 150 yards.
..................(7 to 1 tchd 8 to 1 and 6 to 1) 3
1187⁴ SCOTTON BANKS (Ire) [159] 7-12-0 R Garritty, *blun very badly second, chsd ldr 8th, lost pos 5 out, no dngr frm 3 out.
.................(4 to 1 op 7 to 2 tchd 9 to 2) 4
1283⁴ JOE WHITE [131] 10-10-0 N Williamson, *blun second, beh, some hdwy 9th, pushed alng whn f 13th.
..................(12 to 1 op 10 to 1) f
1199⁶ GREENHILL RAFFLES [131] 10-9-12¹ (3*) P Henley, *rdr lost irons second, al towards rear, beh whn f 14th (bechers).
.......................(66 to 1 op 50 to 1) f
1140⁷ ANDROS PRINCE [131] 11-10-0 J Ryan, *hld up, drvn alng tenth, tld off frm 14th, uns rdr last*.... (100 to 1 op 50 to 1) ur
1304⁵ STRAIGHT TALK [131] 9-10-0 A P McCoy, *chsd ldrs till outpcd 15th, hit 17th, struggling whn blun and uns rdr 4 out.
..................(11 to 2 op 5 to 1 tchd 6 to 1) ur
Dist: 3½l, 8l, 30l. 7m 15.70s. a 30.70s (8 Ran).

SR: 4/24/-/-/-/

(J Huckle), Mrs M Reveley

1530 Tote Credit Juvenile Novices' Hurdle Class B (3-y-o) £5,151 2m 110yds .... (2:45)

1188* BELLATOR 11-5 A P McCoy, *chsd clr ldr, led 6th, sn clear, hit last, easily*.. (6 to 5 on op 5 to 4 on tchd 11 to 10 on) 1
1422* NOBLE LORD 11-0 B Powell, *led till hdd 6th, outpcd appr 3 out, no oth wnr*.......................(7 to 4 tchd 2 to 1) 2
ONYOUROWN (Ire) 11-0 N Williamson, *hld up, not fluent 4th, outpcd and eased appr 3 out, sn wl beh*. (5 to 1 op 9 to 2) 3
STRETCHING (Ire) 11-0 J McLaughlin, *tld off frm hfwy.
.......................(66 to 1 op 50 to 1) 4
Dist: 15l, dist, dist. 4m 13.90s. a 25.90s (4 Ran).

(P Richardson), G B Balding

1531 Town Green Handicap Chase Class C (0-135 5-y-o and up) £5,546 2½m .... (3:15)

1301³ THE CAUMRUE (Ire) [105] 8-10-11 A P McCoy, *keen hold, led 9th, drvn alng 2 out, ran on wl und pres.
.............(15 to 8 on op 2 to 1 on tchd 7 to 4 on) 1
1289³ SHAARID (USA) [112] 8-11-1 (3*) Mr C Bonner, *led till hdd 9th, ev ch frm 3 out, no extr r-in*...........(6 to 4 op 11 to 8) 2
Won by 2½l. 5m 21.90s. a 33.90s (2 Ran).
SR: -/-/

(The On The Run Partnership), G B Balding

1532 European Breeders Fund 'National Hunt' Novices' Hurdle Qualifier Class C (4,5,6-y-o) £3,936 2m 110yds....................... (3:50)

LUCIA FORTE 5-10-9 C O'Dwyer, *keen hold, hld up, led betw last 2, sn clr*.......... (11 to 8 fav op 5 to 4 tchd 6 to 4) 1
1065* BEACON FLIGHT (Ire) 5-11-5 N Williamson, *sat modest pace, hit 3rd and 6th, quickened 3 out, hdd and outpcd betw last 2.
.......................(7 to 4 tchd 13 to 8 and 2 to 1) 2
HYDRO (Ire) 5-11-0 R Garritty, *chsd ldr, ev ch whn mstk 3 out, sn btn*...................(5 to 2 op 3 to 1 tchd 7 to 2) 3
Dist: 7l, 6l. 4m 20.10s. a 32.10s (3 Ran).

(Mrs Lucia Farmer), K C Bailey

NAAS (IRE) (yielding)
Saturday November 23rd

1533 Town Hurdle (4-y-o) £3,082 2m .... (12:45)

CHARLIE FOXTROT (Ire) 11-2 R Hughes,...... (2 to 1 fav) 1
1143⁴ BOSS DOYLE (Ire) 10-13 (3*) D J Casey,.........(20 to 1) 2
1275² SWIFT CERT (bl) 11-2 M Duffy,......................(7 to 1) 3
1015³ ICY PROJECT (Ire) (bl) 10-9 (7*) M W Martin,......(14 to 1) 4
611* ABORIGINAL (Ire) 11-2 M P Dwyer,..............(5 to 2) 5
KATSUKO (Ire) 10-11 H Rogers,.................(20 to 1) 6
TONI'S TIP (Ire) 11-2 K F O'Brien,................(16 to 1) 7
FISHIN JOELLA (Ire) 10-11 A Powell,............(5 to 1) 8
THINKERS CORNER (Ire) 10-13 (3*) G Cotter,.....(14 to 1) 9
FILL THE BILL (Ire) 11-2 C F Swan,...............(4 to 1) 10
THE BOY KING (Ire) 11-2 P A Roche,..............(8 to 1) 11
1275 FLORIA (Ire) 10-6 (5*) J Butler,....................(20 to 1) 12
MY BLUE 10-4 (7*) E F Cahalan,..................(14 to 1) 13
1246⁹ COOLSHAMROCK (Ire) 10-11 J P Broderick,....(20 to 1) 14
1275 PERPETUAL PROSPECT (Ire) 11-2 T J Mitchell,...(14 to 1) 15
1193 ROB MINE (Ire) 10-9 (7*) L A Hurley,.............(20 to 1) 16
1077⁶ GENTLE MOSSY (Ire) 11-2 D H O'Connor,.......(16 to 1) pu
Dist: ½l, 13l, 2l, 3½l. 3m 54.60s. (17 Ran).

(Mrs J Magnier), Noel Meade

1534 European Breeders Fund Beginners Chase (5-y-o and up) £4,452 2m 3f .... (1:15)

1276⁴ HEADBANGER 9-12-0 D H O'Connor,...........(6 to 1) 1
300² KALDAN KHAN 5-11-11 C F Swan,........... (7 to 2 fav) 2
MINELLA GOLD (Ire) 7-11-11 (3*) M B M Cash,....(4 to 1) 3
1435 MACALLISTER (Ire) 6-11-11 (3*) B Bowens,......(5 to 1) 4
1435 GARABAGH (Ire) 7-12-0 P McWilliams,..........(14 to 1) 5
DIORRAING (Ire) 6-12-0 F Woods,..............(14 to 1) 6
1276 TIME AND CHARGES (Ire) 6-12-0 T J Mitchell,....(16 to 1) 7
171² CONCLAVE (Ire) 6-11-11 (3*) G Cotter,..........(12 to 1) 8
EASTERN FOX (Ire) 7-12-0 D T Evans,...........(20 to 1) 9
1059² BANNER GALE (Ire) 7-12-0 M P Dwyer,..........(5 to 1) 10
1435 JOES DANTE (Ire) 5-11-11 F J Flood,..............(12 to 1) 11
1040⁸ DEESIDE DOINGS (Ire) 8-11-9 (5*) J Butler,.....(25 to 1) 12
TOUT VA BIEN 8-12-0 P L Malone,................(8 to 1) f
1242 LET BUNNY RUN (Ire) 6-12-0 K F O'Brien,......(33 to 1) f
KNOCKMUIRA (Ire) 6-11-11 (3*) D J Casey,......(14 to 1) ur
SHISOMA (Ire) 6-12-0 J P Broderick,.............(10 to 1) ur
APOLO ONE (Ire) 7-12-0 H Rogers,..............(20 to 1) pu
Dist: 3½l, 11l, 1½l, 7l. 5m 13.50s. (17 Ran).

(Mrs Beatrice Durkan), Martin Michael Lynch

1535 Sean Graham Handicap Hurdle (0-132 4-y-o and up) £6,850 2m .... (1:45)

1095^{3} FONTAINE LODGE (Ire) [-] 6-10-9 (7*) A O'Shea, ...(11 to 4) 1
1277^{5} CEILI QUEEN (Ire) [-] 4-11-11 C F Swan, ... (7 to 1) 2
1089^{7} METASTASIO [-] 4-12-0 H Rogers, ...(8 to 1) 3
1190* KAWA-KAWA [-] 9-11-0 (3*) G Cotter, ...(7 to 1) 4
1190^{3} JO JO BOY (Ire) [-] 7-11-6 F J Flood, ...(6 to 1) 5
1273^{3} LEGAL AND TENDER (Ire) [-] 5-10-0 R Hughes, ... (7 to 1) 6
1462^{7} JOHNNY HANDSOME (Ire) [-] 6-9-9 (3*) D J Casey, (10 to 1) 7
ARDSHUIL [-] 7-11-6 F Woods, ...(12 to 1) 8
928* DIGADUST (Ire) [-] 4-11-2 M Duffy, ...(5 to 2 fav) 9
1432^{8} DOONE BRAES (Ire) [-] 6-9-9^{2} T P Rudd, ...(14 to 1) 10
1407 FERRYCARRIG HOTEL (Ire) [-] 7-11-2 (3*) B Bowens, ...(12 to 1) 11
BUCKMINSTER [-] 9-11-11 J P Broderick, ...(16 to 1) 12
MAJESTIC MAN (Ire) [-] 5-12-0 T J Mitchell, ... (14 to 1) 13
Dist: Hd, 1l, 11l, ½l. 3m 56.10s. (13 Ran).
(ABC Syndicate), Anthony Mullins

1536 Kildare Maiden Hurdle (5-y-o and up) £3,082 2½m..................(2:15)

1189^{4} FOLLY ROAD (Ire) 6-11-6 P L Malone, ... (10 to 1) 1
1432^{5} WYATT (Ire) 6-11-6 R Hughes, ...(Evens fav) 2
1241^{5} SARADANTE (Ire) 6-11-6 M P Dwyer, ... (12 to 1) 3
1120^{5} MYSTICAL AIR (Ire) 6-11-6 D T Evans, ... (20 to 1) 4
1279^{4} LEAMHOG (Ire) 6-12-0 C F Swan, ... (9 to 4) 5
1076 LAURA'S PURSUIT (Ire) 7-11-6 (3*) G Cotter, ...(12 to 1) 6
1013^{5} GLENREEF BOY (Ire) 7-12-0 A Powell, ...(7 to 1) 7
984 COMMITTED SCHEDULE (Ire) 5-11-6 J P Broderick, ...(20 to 1) 8
YOUR CALL (Ire) 7-11-6 J Shortt, ... (10 to 1) 9
175^{4} THE ROAD TO MOSCOW (Ire) 5-11-6 J R Barry, .. (14 to 1) 10
BLACKTRENCH LADY (Ire) 8-11-9 H Rogers, ... (12 to 1) 11
1432 TINAMONA (Ire) 6-11-3 (3*) B Bowens, ...(20 to 1) 12
SUPREME ALLIANCE (Ire) 6-11-4 (5*) J Butler, ... (8 to 1) 13
1119 MAVISANDPEDS (Ire) 7-10-13 (7*) J P Deegan, ... (50 to 1) 14
NORE GLEN (Ire) 5-11-3 (3*) D J Casey, ... (14 to 1) ro
Dist: Sht-hd, 4l, 2l, 3½l. 5m 6.30s. (15 Ran).
(John Freaney), D Harvey

1537 Poplar Square Chase (5-y-o and up) £4,452 2½m..................(2:45)

1094^{3} OPERA HAT (Ire) 8-11-8 A Powell, ...(2 to 1) 1
1407^{3} TRYFIRION (Ire) 7-11-3 (3*) B Bowens, ...(11 to 1) 2
1274* PERSIAN HALO (Ire) 8-11-13 J Shortt, ... (8 to 1) 3
1243^{4} MERRY GALE (Ire) 8-11-13 M P Dwyer, ...(6 to 4 fav) 4
IDIOTS VENTURE 9-11-2 C F Swan, ...(6 to 1) 5
1243^{6} KING OF THE GALES 9-11-13 F Woods, ...(8 to 1) 6
1116^{4} TIME FOR A RUN 9-11-2 Mr P Fenton, ...(16 to 1) 7
1014^{2} THE CRAZY BISHOP (Ire) 8-10-13 (3*) D J Casey, (12 to 1) f
Dist: 7l, 1l, 2l, nk. 5m 26.40s. (8 Ran).
(Mrs T K Cooper), J R H Fowler

1538 Rathcoole Handicap Chase (0-102 4-y-o and up) £3,082 3m...... (3:15)

1194 BEAT THE SECOND (Ire) [-] 8-11-13 C F Swan, ... (5 to 2) 1
1408* IRISH LIGHT (Ire) [-] 8-10-11 (4ex) J P Broderick, (2 to 1 fav) 2
1191^{2} TEAL BRIDGE [-] 11-11-10 T J Mitchell, ...(5 to 1) 3
1144^{8} FAIR GO [-] 10-9-3 (7*) Mrs C Harrison, ...(14 to 1) 4
1092^{4} FAIRY MIST (Ire) [-] 8-9-4 (3*) G Cotter, ...(16 to 1) 5
1245^{7} WACKO JACKO (Ire) [-] 7-10-12 (5*) T Martin, ...(14 to 1) 6
1274^{7} EDENAKILL LAD [-] 9-11-3 M P Dwyer, ...(12 to 1) 7
BERMUDA BUCK [-] 10-12-0 F Woods, ...(12 to 1) 8
1363^{5} ROSSI NOVAE [-] (bl) 13-9-7 J R Barry, ...(20 to 1) 9
1274^{4} WALLYS RUN [-] 9-11-5 D T Evans, ...(10 to 1) 10
TOP RUN (Ire) [-] 8-11-1 T P Rudd, ...(20 to 1) 11
NOVELLO ALLEGRO (USA) [-] 8-10-9 (3*) D J Casey, ...(11 to 1) 12
780 FAMBO LAD (Ire) [-] 8-11-8 J Shortt, ... (14 to 1) ur
1274 TALK TO YOU LATER [-] (bl) 10-10-5 (3*) D Bromley, (16 to 1) pu
1168^{5} IF YOU BELIEVE (Ire) [-] 7-11-0 (3*) B Bowens, ... (8 to 1) pu
1169^{3} CORSTON DANCER (Ire) [-] (bl) 8-11-8 D H O'Connor, ...(14 to 1) pu
Dist: 4l, 8l, 25l, nk. 6m 36.90s. (16 Ran).
(Mrs P Corcoran), A P O'Brien

1539 Go Racing In Kildare I.N.H. Flat Race (5-y-o) £3,082 2m............(3:45)

984 AS ROYAL (Ire) 11-11 (3*) Mr P English, ... (4 to 1) 1
1436^{2} PHARDANA (Ire) 11-7 (7*) Mr J P McNamara, .. (2 to 1 fav) 2
STRONG SON (Ire) 12-0 Mr A R Coonan, ...(10 to 1) 3
FORTY SECRETS (Ire) 11-2 (7*) Mr J L Cullen, ... (14 to 1) 4
INTHEPITS (Ire) 11-11 (3*) Mr R Walsh, ...(10 to 1) 5
1307^{7} LORD OGAN (Ire) 12-0 Mr H F Cleary, ...(10 to 1) 6
KALORIEN 11-6 (3*) Mr E Norris, ...(6 to 1) 7
1081^{3} PRINCESS GLORIA (Ire) 11-9 Mr P Fenton, ...(7 to 1) 8
1436 VESPER LADY (Ire) 11-2 (7*) Mr A K Wyse, ...(12 to 1) 9
1195 GALE JOHNSTON (Ire) 11-2 (7*) Mr John P Moloney, (6 to 1) 10
ASK DOCK (Ire) 11-2 (7*) Mr G Elliott, ...(8 to 1) 11
1195 NICKELLI (Ire) 11-2 (7*) Mr P M Cloke, ...(14 to 1) 12
EXECUTIVE MERC (Ire) 11-7 (7*) Mr J F O'Shea, .. (14 to 1) 13
TINVACOOSH (Ire) 11-7 (7*) Mr G A Kingston, ...(20 to 1) 14
DAYVILLE (Ire) 11-11 (3*) Mr B R Hamilton, ... (10 to 1) 15
MONKEY LEAF (Ire) 11-2 (7*) Mr C A Cronin, ...(8 to 1) 16
TUDOR ROSE 11-7 (7*) Mr E Gallagher, ... (14 to 1) 17
HOLLOWDEE (Ire) 11-11 (3*) Mr B M Cash, ... (6 to 1) 18
1174 LISDARA LADY (Ire) 11-2 (7*) Miss L Agnew, ...(20 to 1) ro
Dist: 15l, 5l, ¾l, 2l. 3m 56.70s. (19 Ran).
(Michael O'Dowd), Thomas Foley

TOWCESTER (good)
Saturday November 23rd
Going Correction: PLUS 0.20 sec. per fur.

1540 Thomas Cook Maiden Hurdle Class F (Div I) (4-y-o and up) £1,849 2m 5f .... (12:30)

FOREST IVORY (NZ) 5-11-5 R Johnson, *hld up in tch, hdwy whn slightly hmpd appr 3 out, led sn aftr nxt, drw clr.* ....(11 to 8 on op 5 to 4 on) 1
FINE SIR 6-11-5 D Gallagher, *al prmnt, led appr 3 out till aftr nxt, sn btn*..............(11 to 2 op 7 to 2 tchd 6 to 1) 2
1291^{3} EL FREDDIE 6-11-5 G Upton, *al prmnt, led 7th till appr 3 out, one pace aftr*............. (3 to 1 op 7 to 2 tchd 9 to 2) 3
1012^{7} WEATHER WISE 4-11-5 A Thornton, *nvr far away, no hdwy frm 3 out*...(50 to 1) 4
1260^{9} BURNTWOOD MELODY 5-11-5 W Marston, *hld up, hdwy 6th, wknd appr 2 out*....... (33 to 1 op 25 to 1 tchd 50 to 1) 5
GEMMA'S WAGER (Ire) 6-11-0 L Harvey, *pld hrd, prmnt, led 5th to 7th, wknd appr 3 out*........... (50 to 1 op 33 to 1) 6
HIGH MOOD 6-10-12 (7*) C Hynes, *rcd wide in mid-div, nvr on terms*........ (100 to 1 op 66 to 1 tchd 150 to 1) 7
LOTHIAN COMMANDER 4-11-5 T Jenks, *chsd ldrs till wknd aftr 7th*..............................(50 to 1 op 20 to 1) 8
1071^{8} POLO PONY (Ire) 4-11-5 R Supple, *pld hrd, led to 5th, wknd quickly 7th*.....................................(50 to 1) 9
HIT THE BID (Ire) 5-11-5 J R Kavanagh, *al beh.* ....(66 to 1 tchd 100 to 1) 10
1369^{6} DARK PHOENIX (Ire) 6-11-0 M Brennan, *beh till hdwy 5th, wknd 7th, tld off*.................... (6 to 1 op 6 to 1) 11
HONEYBED WOOD 8-11-0 Mr A Brown, *prmnt, wkng whn hit 4 out, tld off when pld up bef 2 out.* ....(66 to 1 op 50 to 1 tchd 100 to 1) pu
NERO'S GEM 5-11-0 W McFarland, *al beh, tld off whn pld up bef 2 out*...................... (50 to 1 tchd 66 to 1) pu
CAMINO 9-11-5 D Bridgwater, *al beh, tld off whn pld up bef 2 out*..................................(33 to 1 op 20 to 1) pu
Dist: 6l, 11l, 14l, 11l, 1½l, 6l, 5l, 4l, 2l, dist. 5m 23.80s. a 24.80s (14 Ran).
(The Old Foresters Partnership), D Nicholson

1541 Akeley Novices' Selling Hurdle Class G (4-y-o and up) £2,185 2m... (1:00)

HARRY 6-10-12 D J Burchell, *hld up, hdwy 5th, led 2 out, sn clr*...(7 to 1) 1
1365* WILLY STAR (Bel) 6-10-12 (7*) R Wilkinson, *hld up, wnt second 5th, wknd appr 2 out*......... (11 to 8 fav op 6 to 4) 2
1425* SPRINTFAYRE 8-11-5 D Gallagher, *led to second, led briefly appr 2 out, sn btn*........ (8 to 1 op 7 to 1 tchd 9 to 1) 3
242^{4} SARACEN PRINCE (USA) 4-10-12 R Johnson, *hld up, some hdwy 3 out, nvr dngrs*.................(13 to 2 op 4 to 1) 4
1438 AL HELAL (v) 4-10-12 W Marston, *led second, wknd and hdd appr 2 out*........................(33 to 1 op 20 to 1) 5
NAUTICAL JEWEL 4-10-12 W McFarland, *in tch till wknd 3 out*......................(6 to 1 op 5 to 1 tchd 7 to 1) 6
1178^{4} SLEEPTITE (Fr) 6-11-5 A Thornton, *hld up, lost tch 5th.* ....(6 to 1 tchd 7 to 1) 7
1208 ECU DE FRANCE (Ire) 6-10-12 S Fox, *in tch till wknd aftr 4th, tld off*.............................(50 to 1 op 33 to 1) 8
954 FOLLOW DE CALL 6-10-12 T Jenks, *al beh, tld off.* .... (16 to 1 op 12 to 1 tchd 20 to 1) 9
1350 SMALL FLAME (Ire) 5-10-7 M Brennan, *al beh, tld off.* .... (25 to 1 op 20 to 1 tchd 33 to 1) 10
POLLI PUI 4-10-4 (3*) R Massey, *chsd ldrs to 3rd, beh whn f nxt*..................................... (20 to 1 op 14 to 1) f
1367^{6} SWING LUCKY 11-11-5 D Skyrme, *chsd ldrs till wknd 4th, tld off whn pld up bef 3 out.* (11 to 1 op 10 to 1 tchd 14 to 1) pu
1471 STRANGE WAYS 8-10-5 (7*) A Dowling, *al beh, tld off whn pld up bef 2 out*......... (50 to 1 op 25 to 1 tchd 66 to 1) pu
Dist: 8l, 5l, 2½l, 15l, 1½l, 3l, 19l, 2½l, dist. 3m 57.70s. a 14.70s (13 Ran).
(Simon T Lewis), D Burchell

1542 Alderton Novices' Chase Class D (5-y-o and up) £3,942 3m 1f......(1:30)

BANKHEAD (Ire) 7-11-0 D Bridgwater, *hld up, took clr order 7th, wnt second 14th, led appr 2 out, styd on gmely.* ....(3 to 1 tchd 4 to 1) 1
LITTLE MARTINA (Ire) 8-10-13 J R Kavanagh, *nvr far away, rdn to go second 2 out, one pace.* ....(3 to 1 op 7 to 2 tchd 9 to 2) 2
1180^{2} HAWAIIAN SAM (Ire) 6-11-0 G Crone, *al prmnt, lft in ld 9th, hdd appr 2 out, rallied und pres.* .... (11 to 1 op 6 to 1 tchd 12 to 1) 3
ROBSAND (Ire) 7-11-0 B Clifford, *hld up in rear, hdwy 4 out, nvr nr to chal*.......... (16 to 1 op 8 to 1 tchd 20 to 1) 4

	MAJORS LEGACY (Ire) 7-11-0 A Thornton, *hld up, hdwy 11th, wknd 4 out*..................... (14 to 1 op 8 to 1)	5
1250²	MR PICKPOCKET (Ire) 8-11-0 R Johnson, *led till blun badly 9th, sn beh, tld off*......................(7 to 4 fav op 2 to 1)	6
1298²	LOCH GARMAN HOTEL (Ire) 7-11-0 W Marston, *blun and uns rdr 1st*........................ (6 to 1 tchd 10 to 1)	ur
1448⁶	DELIRE D'ESTRUVAL (Fr) (bl) 5-10-12 L Harvey, *trkd ldrs, hit 9th, wkng whn blun and uns rdr 3 out.* (50 to 1 op 25 to 1)	ur
1237	RAINBOW FOUNTAIN 9-10-4 (5*) Chris Webb, *al beh, tld off 9th, pld up last.*....................(50 to 1 op 33 to 1)	pu

Dist: 3l, 1¾l, 15l, 7l, 5l. 6m 25.80s. a 13.80s (9 Ran).

(Mrs Liz Brazier), J L Spearing

1543 Thomas Cook Maiden Hurdle Class F (Div II) (4-y-o and up) £1,835 2m 5f .... (2:05)

1063²	SALMON BREEZE (Ire) 5-11-5 J R Kavanagh, *prmnt till lost pl appr 3 out, plenty to do till styd on to ld bef last.* ....(11 to 4 fav op 13 to 8 tchd 3 to 1)	1
1330³	JILLS JOY (Ire) 5-11-0 (5*) D J Kavanagh, *trkd ldrs, wnt second 6th, led appr 3 out bef last, no extr.* .... (6 to 1 op 7 to 1 tchd 11 to 1)	2
	FASHION MAKER (Ire) 6-11-5 L Harvey, *mid-div, hdwy 7th, styd on frm 2 out.*.....................(50 to 1 op 25 to 1)	3
1413³	POSITIVO 5-11-5 D Leahy, *in tch till lost pl 6th, rallied 3 out, one pace nxt.*........................(8 to 1 op 10 to 1)	4
1134⁴	LOUGH TULLY (Ire) 6-11-5 R Supple, *hld up, hdwy 4th, ev ch appr 2 out, rdn and sn wknd.* ....(8 to 1 op 7 to 1 tchd 10 to 1)	5
1228⁵	WINNOW 6-10-7 (7*) C Rae, *hld up, gd hdwy appr 7th, ev ch 3 out, rdn and sn wknd.*.... (8 to 1 op 5 to 1 tchd 10 to 1)	6
1129⁴	LITTLE NOTICE 5-11-5 S Wynne, *hld up in tch, hdwy appr 3 out, one pace aftr.*............... (3 to 1 op 3 to 1)	7
1211⁶	SPEARHEAD AGAIN (Ire) 7-11-5 D Bridgwater, *led till appr 3 out, wknd quickly, tld off.*..........(8 to 1 tchd 10 to 1)	8
	BARRISTERS BOY 6-11-5 G Upton, *mid-div, wknd appr 3 out, tld off.*........... (14 to 1 op 7 to 1 tchd 16 to 1)	9
	SURPRISE GUEST (Ire) 5-11-5 R Johnson, *trkd ldrs till wknd 7th, tld off.*.....................................	10
1271⁵	LA CHANCE 6-11-5 Mr A Walton, *al beh, tld off.*.. (50 to 1)	11
1115⁷	NODDADANTE (Ire) 6-11-5 Mr N R Mitchell, *in tch to 6th, tld off.*.................... (25 to 1 op 33 to 1 tchd 16 to 1)	12
	JOY FOR LIFE (Ire) 5-11-0 V Slattery, *al beh, tld off whn pld up bef 2 out.*................. (16 to 1 tchd 25 to 1)	pu

Dist: 4l, 4l, 2½l, 4l, 1l, 1l, 20l, hd, 16l, 13l. 5m 28.50s. a 29.50s (13 Ran).

(The Salmon Racing Partnership), N J Henderson

1544 National Letterbox Marketing Handicap Chase Class D (0-120 5-y-o and up) £3,591 2¾m................ (2:35)

1212⁷	FOOLS ERRAND (Ire) [112] 6-11-6 B Clifford, *hld up in tch, cld on ldrs tenth, led appr 2 out.* ....(9 to 4 fav op 7 to 4 tchd 5 to 2)	1
1366	NICKLUP [105] 9-10-13 A Thornton, *led to 12th, led 4 out to appr 2 out, rallied gmely r-in, jst fld.* .... (6 to 1 op 5 to 1 tchd 13 to 2)	2
1204	REALLY A RASCAL [105] 9-10-13 R Johnson, *hld up in rear, hdwy 4 out, ev ch appr last, no extr r-in.* ....(12 to 1 op 10 to 1 tchd 14 to 1)	3
1212⁵	SPUFFINGTON [120] 8-11-11 (3*) L Aspell, *al in tch, jnd ldrs 7th, led appr 12th till 4 out, wknd nxt.*.... (9 to 2 op 4 to 1)	4
	THREE SAINTS (Ire) [96] 7-10-4 S Wynne, *al in rear, lost tch 4 out.*....................... (9 to 2 op 3 to 1)	5
	MAKES ME GOOSEY (Ire) [98] 8-10-6 L Harvey, *hld up, hdwy 6th, wknd 4 out.*.......... (9 to 2 op 4 to 1 tchd 5 to 1)	6
	CALL HOME (Ire) [120] 8-12-0 Mr T Hills, *trkd ldrs to 7th, beh 11th, tld off.*..........(10 to 1 op 7 to 1 tchd 14 to 1)	7

Dist: Hd, 2½l, 17l, 10l, ¾l, dist. 5m 37.40s. a 11.40s (7 Ran).

SR: 22/15/12/10/

(Mrs David Russell), G B Balding

1545 Woodend 'National Hunt' Novices' Hurdle Class D (4-y-o and up) £3,351 3m...................... (3:10)

1295²	SOUTHERN NIGHTS 6-11-0 A Thornton, *hld up, gd hdwy to track ldrs 7th, led 4 out, clr whn mstk last, sddl slpd, veered badly lft r-in.*.................(8 to 1 op 5 to 1 tchd 9 to 1)	1
1338	CHINA GEM 5-11-0 O Gallagher, *hld up in rear, hdwy 7th, wnt second appr 2 out, ran on one pace.* ....(33 to 1 op 12 to 1)	2
1311	YOUNG KENNY 5-11-6 R Supple, *hld up, hdwy 7th, one pace frm 2 out.*.................(20 to 1 op 16 to 1 tchd 25 to 1)	3
1343²	SPACEAGE GOLD 7-11-0 G Upton, *hld up in tch, rdn 4 out, wknd nxt.*.......................(5 to 2 op 4 to 1)	4
1271²	JET BOYS (Ire) 6-11-0 W Marston, *hld up in tch, rdn appr 3 out, sn btn.*......................(11 to 8 fav op 6 to 4)	5
1270⁵	ARTURO 5-11-0 S Wynne, *beh till hdwy 4 out, wknd 2 out.* ....(12 to 1 op 8 to 1 tchd 16 to 1)	6
1318*	MEDFORD 6-10-13 (7*) J Power, *hld up, hdwy 7th, wknd appr 3 out.*...................(12 to 1 op 20 to 1 tchd 25 to 1)	7
	BAYLINE STAR (Ire) 6-11-0 J R Kavanagh, *always beh, tld off whn pld up bef last.*..... (4 to 1 op 5 to 2 tchd 9 to 2)	pu
	LUKER BOY 6-11-0 R Johnson, *al beh, tld off whn pld up bef 2 out.*...............(10 to 1 op 14 to 1 tchd 16 to 1)	pu

	SOUTHSEA SCANDALS (Ire) 5-11-0 R Greene, *al beh, tld off whn pld up bef 3 out.*...(20 to 1 op 16 to 1 tchd 25 to 1)	pu
900⁴		
1202⁶	CAULKIN (Ire) 5-10-9 (5*) Mr R Thornton, *prmnt till wknd aftr 7th, pld up bef 2 out, dismounted.*.....(66 to 1 op 33 to 1)	pu
1129⁶	MUSICAL HIT 5-11-0 L Harvey, *tld off 6th, pld up bef 9th.* ....(66 to 1 op 50 to 1)	pu
	MOONLIGHTER 6-10-9 W McFarland, *chsd ldrs till wknd 9th, tld off whn pld up bef 3 out.*......(50 to 1 op 33 to 1)	pu
975⁸	ROSKEEN BRIDGE (Ire) 5-11-0 M Richards, *led to second, wknd 7th, tld off whn pld up bef last.*..(66 to 1 op 33 to 1)	pu
1237	ALONE HOME (Ire) (bl) 5-11-0 J Railton, *led second to 4 out, wknd quickly, pld up bef 2 out.*...... (33 to 1 op 20 to 1)	pu

Dist: 5l, 1¼l, 5l, 8l, nk, 25l. 6m 7.80s. a 25.80s (15 Ran).

(J Perriss), K C Bailey

1546 Plumpton End Handicap Hurdle Class D (0-120 4-y-o and up) £2,910 2m............................ (3:45)

	JEFFERIES [91] 7-10-10 G Upton, *made all, rdn 2 out, clr last.* ....(5 to 2 op 5 to 1)	1
1228⁶	DOMINOS RING (Ire) [105] 7-11-5 (5*) Mr T Thornton, *hld up, hdwy 3rd, lost pl 3 out, rallied to chase wnr r-in.* .... (10 to 1 op 8 to 1)	2
1367⁴	SHERS DELIGHT [87] 6-10-6 M Brennan, *hld up in rear, gd hdwy 5th, chlgd wnr 3 out till wknd aftr nxt.* ....(9 to 2 op 7 to 2 tchd 5 to 1)	3
	TOO SHARP [100] 8-11-5 R Johnson, *in tch, chsd wnr appr 4th till wknd 3 out.*.............(10 to 1 op 6 to 1)	4
1272³	NOTHINGTODOWITHME [82] 6-10-11 S Wynne, *in tch till wknd 5th, tld off.*........(11 to 8 fav op 6 to 4)	5
1266	ASTRAL INVASION (USA) [81] (bl) 5-10-0 B Clifford, *trkd wnr till appr 4th, wknd nxt, tld off.*.......(8 to 1 op 5 to 1)	6

Dist: 2½l, 3½l, 14l, 15l, dist. 4m 3.80s. a 20.80s (6 Ran).

(Miss S Blumberg), J A B Old

CLONMEL (IRE) (heavy)
Sunday November 24th

1547 Clonmel Racecourse Supporters Club Juvenile Maiden Hurdle (3-y-o) £3,082 2m................... (12:15)

	RESCUE TIME (Ire) 10-11 C F Swan, ... (5 to 4 fav)	1
1403²	SARAH'S GUEST (Ire) 10-8 R Hughes, ... (9 to 4)	2
1430⁶	MARLONETTE (Ire) 10-3 (3*) D J Casey, ... (5 to 1)	3
1430	PRIONES TYCOON (Ire) 10-6 R Dunwoody, ... (14 to 1)	4
1173	NO AVAIL (Ire) 10-6 C O'Dwyer, ... (12 to 1)	5
1309⁵	DADDY'S HAT (Ire) 10-6 P L Malone, ...(8 to 1)	6
1430	WOODEN DANCE (Ire) 10-6 T J Mitchell, ... (20 to 1)	7
1057	TIP YOUR WAITRESS (Ire) 10-11 G M O'Neill, ... (20 to 1)	8
	KAYALIYNA (Ire) 10-6 J R Barry, ...(16 to 1)	f
1057†	KING OF PEACE (Ire) 10-11 H Rogers, ... (8 to 1)	co
1430*	MIND ME BRODY (Ire) 10-11 G Bradley, ... (8 to 1)	ro
	KUSSADAST (Ire) 10-11 T Hazlett, ...(20 to 1)	pu

Dist: 2l, 6l, 11l, 5l. 4m 25.40s. (13 Ran).

(G Berger), Kevin Prendergast

1548 I.N.H. Stallion Owners E.B.F. Maiden Hurdle (5-y-o and up) £3,767 3m .... (12:45)

1076⁵	YOUNG MRS KELLY (Ire) 6-11-1 J Jones, ...(100 to 30)	1
1360	VIVIANS VALE (Ire) 7-10-8 (7*) D K Budds, ...(20 to 1)	2
1075³	ROCK'N ROLL KID (Ire) 5-11-3 (3*) D J Casey, ..(5 to 2 fav)	3
1278⁷	BITTER HARVEST (Ire) 6-12-0 C F Swan, ...(5 to 1)	4
1436	ASTITCHINTIME 9-10-13 (7*) Mr C A Murphy, ...(14 to 1)	5
	DURKIN'S GIRL (Ire) (bl) 6-11-4 (5*) J Butler, ...(8 to 1)	6
1361⁸	SHUIL LE LAOI (Ire) 6-11-1 R Dunwoody, ...(20 to 1)	7
1075⁶	MAGS SUPER TOI (Ire) 7-11-6 F Woods, ...(20 to 1)	8
1145	CLOWATER BUCK (Ire) 5-11-1 S H O'Donovan, ...(16 to 1)	9
1359	CASTLE BAILEY (Ire) 5-11-6 T J O'Sullivan, ...(20 to 1)	10
	BALLYFORE (Ire) 7-11-6 (3*) G Cotter, ...(11 to 2)	ur
1278	MAIRTINS BUCK (Ire) 5-11-6 C O'Dwyer, ...(14 to 1)	pu
	BUCK RELATED (Ire) 5-11-6 G Bradley, ...(14 to 1)	pu
	LET HER RUN WILD (Ire) 5-11-1 F J Flood, ...(14 to 1)	pu

Dist: 1l, 4½l, 4l, 2½l. 6m 44.70s. (14 Ran).

(Mrs P G Kelly), E McNamara

1549 Bank Of Ireland Handicap Hurdle (88-116 4-y-o and up) £3,082 2m .... (1:15)

1273	CLASHBEG (Ire) [-] 5-10-6 R Dunwoody, ... (10 to 1)	1
1241*	DASHING DOLLAR (Ire) [-] 5-11-10 C F Swan, ..(6 to 4 fav)	2
828	BLACK QUEEN (Ire) [-] 5-11-6 A J O'Brien, ... (13 to 2)	3
1358²	THE WICKED CHICKEN (Ire) [-] 7-10-1 (3*) G Cotter, (5 to 1)	4
1358⁴	THE SCEARDEEN (Ire) [-] 7-10-5† G Bradley, ... (8 to 1)	5
	LADY NOBLE (Ire) [-] 6-11-4 JR Barry, ... (9 to 4)	6
720⁵	KOPAIN (Ire) [-] 6-10-12 M Duffy, ... (12 to 1)	7
	ST COLEMAN'S WELL [-] 13-10-7 J P Broderick, .. (20 to 1)	8

Dist: 3½l, 3l, 4l, 15l. 4m 26.90s. (8 Ran).

(P McLoughney), E J O'Grady

1550 Bank Of Ireland Handicap Hurdle (0-116 4-y-o and up) £3,082 3m
.... (1:45)

1244*	CASEY JANE (Ire) [-] 5-10-8 (3*) D J Casey,	(8 to 1)	1
1074⁸	ROYAL ROSY (Ire) [-] 5-11-10 C F Swan,	(7 to 1)	2
1273⁶	KERCORLI (Ire) [-] 5-9-4 (3*) G Cotter,	(10 to 1)	3
1273	BOHOLA PETE (Ire) [-] 5-9-7 R Hughes,	(16 to 1)	4
1077²	VASILIKI (Ire) [-] 4-10-4 R Dunwoody,	(8 to 1)	5
1360⁹	MARILLO (Ire) [-] 6-9-2 (7*) S FitzGerald,	(16 to 1)	6
1361*	LAURENS FANCY (Ire) [-] 6-10-2 J R Barry,	(11 to 2)	7
469⁷	LADY DAISY (Ire) [-] 7-10-9 (7*) A O'Shea,	(14 to 1)	8
	LADY QUAYSIDE (Ire) [-] 6-9-13 (7*) P Morris,	(14 to 1)	9
424⁸	CARRAIG-AN-OIR (Ire) [-] 9-9-12 J D Pratt,	(20 to 1)	10
1407⁶	DARK SWAN (Ire) [-] 6-11-3 M P Dwyer,	(16 to 1)	11
1244⁶	THE BOYLERMAN (Ire) [-] 7-10-3 (7*) Mr K O'Sullivan,		
		(11 to 1)	12
1489³	CLASHWILLIAM GIRL (Ire) [-] 8-10-13 (7*) Mr R M Walsh,		
		(14 to 1)	13
1360*	MATTS DILEMMA (Ire) [-] 8-10-11 F Woods,	(9 to 2 fav)	14
1360⁷	FRISKY THYNE (Ire) [-] 7-9-9 C O'Brien,	(16 to 1)	15
1360⁴	MARINERS REEF (Ire) [-] 5-9-7 (7*) D McCullagh,	(12 to 1)	16
897⁵	ALWAYS IN TROUBLE [-] 9-11-3 T P Rudd,	(7 to 1)	17

Dist: 4½sl, 3½l, 2l, 1l. 6m 45.00s. (17 Ran).

(J Comerford), W P Mullins

1551 Tipperary Racecourse Chase (Grade 3) (5-y-o and up) £6,850 2m.. (2:15)

1169²	SOUND MAN (Ire) 8-12-0 R Dunwoody,	(7 to 4 on)	1
1434⁷	ROYAL MOUNTBROWNE 8-11-7 C F Swan,	(5 to 1)	2
1243²	BELVEDERIAN 9-11-7 C O'Dwyer,	(11 to 2)	3
	ARCTIC WEATHER (Ire) 7-11-7 T P Rudd,	(10 to 1)	4
1434⁵	LOVE THE LORD (Ire) 6-11-9 J P Broderick,	(10 to 1)	5
1458⁴	HANNIES GIRL (Ire) 7-10-9 (7*) L J Fleming,	(50 to 1)	pu

Dist: 1l, 8l, 10l, 5l. 4m 4.40s. (6 Ran).

(David Lloyd), E J O'Grady

1552 Bank Of Ireland Beginners Chase (4-y-o and up) £3,082 2m....... (2:45)

1362⁶	KHARASAR (Ire) 6-12-0 C O'Dwyer,	(9 to 4 fav)	1
	MALACCA KING 5-11-8 (3*) D J Casey,	(12 to 1)	2
1362³	LANTINA (Ire) 5-10-12 D H O'Connor,	(10 to 1)	3
1276³	WHAT IT IS (Ire) 7-11-9 P McWilliams,	(10 to 1)	4
	MUSKIN MORE (Ire) 5-11-3 R Dunwoody,	(20 to 1)	5
1362	RISZARD (USA) 7-12-0 J P Broderick,	(14 to 1)	6
	THE NOBLE ROUGE (Ire) 7-11-11 (3*) G Cotter,	(16 to 1)	7
1362²	FONTAINE FABLES (Ire) 6-12-0 M P Dwyer,	(14 to 1)	8
1146⁸	PRATE BOX (Ire) 6-12-0 J K Kinane,	(14 to 1)	9
732	MARGUERITA SONG 6-11-4 (5*) T Martin,	(16 to 1)	10
	BALLYBERT BOY 10-12-0 D T Evans,	(20 to 1)	11
1362⁴	SACULORE (Ire) 8-12-0 C F Swan,	(11 to 1)	f
	GREAT SVENGALI (Ire) 7-12-0 J R Barry,	(4 to 1)	f
1435	MULKEV PRINCE (Ire) 5-11-11 S C Lyons,	(10 to 1)	f
1242⁵	HOLY GROUNDER (Ire) 7-11-9 G Bradley,	(14 to 1)	ur

Dist: 11l, 3l, 1½l, 2l. 4m 15.00s. (15 Ran).

(W Hennessy), Anthony Mullins

1553 Bank Of Ireland Handicap Chase (0-109 4-y-o and up) £3,425 2½m
.... (3:15)

	LOCAL STORY [-] 7-11-7 H Rogers,	(4 to 1)	1
1458³	FINAL TUB [-] 13-11-12 C O'Dwyer,	(9 to 1)	2
1408	DOONEGA (Ire) [-] 8-10-2 (7*) Mr E Gallagher,	(5 to 1)	3
1363³	SHOWEL DAWN [-] 9-11-3 R Dunwoody,	(5 to 1)	4
1363*	BROOK HILL LADY [-] 7-11-11 C F Swan,	(3 to 1 fav)	5
1363⁴	MACAUNTA (Ire) [-] 6-9-12 J P Broderick,	(5 to 1)	6
1363⁹	BUCK CASTLE (Ire) [-] 8-9-11 S H O'Donovan,	(14 to 1)	7
1191	BALLYBODEN [-] 9-10-11 M P Hourigan,	(10 to 1)	8

Dist: 3l, 2l, 2½l, 3l. 5m 30.20s. (8 Ran).

(C Donovan), W J Burke

1554 Bank Of Ireland I.N.H. Flat Race (5-y-o and up) £2,740 2m....... (3:45)

1147²	PREMIER WALK 7-11-4 (7*) Mr S P Hennessy,	(8 to 1)	1
	DOLITTLE BAY 5-11-11 (7*) Mr T N Cloke,	(10 to 1)	2+
1279	BORO BOW (Ire) 5-11-4 (7*) Mr B E Hill,	(11 to 10 fav)	2+
1075	HEN HANSEL (Ire) 5-11-11 (7*) Mr Sean O O'Brien,	(12 to 1)	4
4077	STRICT TEMPO (Ire) 7-11-4 (7*) Mr John P Moloney,		
		(16 to 1)	5
	PROUDANDAMBITIOUS (Ire) 5-12-1 (3*) Mr E Norris,		
		(3 to 1)	6
1436⁷	RED OAK (Ire) 4-11-4 (7*) Mr G A Kingston,	(16 to 1)	7
1096	BARNA GIRL 6-11-6 Mr P Fenton,	(20 to 1)	8
1358⁶	AISEIRI 9-11-11 (7*) Miss D O'Neill,	(20 to 1)	9
1436	NATIVE CHAMPION (Ire) 7-11-4 (7*) Mr P P O'Brien,		
		(33 to 1)	10

Dist: ½l, dd-ht, 3l. dist. 4m 31.70s. (10 Ran).

(Aidan Ryan), Malachy J Ryan

FOLKESTONE (good to soft (races 1,2,4,6), good (3,5))

Monday November 25th
Going Correction: PLUS 1.00 sec. per fur. (races 1,2,4,6), PLUS 0.55 (3,5)

1555 Brede Conditional Jockeys' Novices' Hurdle Class F (4-y-o and up) £2,138 2¾m 110yds.................... (1:00)

EMERALD STATEMENT (Ire) 6-10-12 G Hogan, *with ldrs in chasing grp, led aftr 5 out, clr after 2 out, easily.*
.................(5 to 1 op 6 to 1 tchd 7 to 1) 1
1292⁴ FOREST MUSK (Ire) 5-10-12 D J Kavanagh, *with ldrs in chasing grp, ev ch 2 out, sn outpcd.* (6 to 4 fav tchd 7 to 4) 2
1429⁵ ROSS DANCER (Ire) 4-11-2 J Magee, *with ldrs in chasing grp, ev ch 2 out, sn rdn and outpcd*
.................(10 to 1 op 12 to 1 tchd 14 to 1 and 8 to 1) 3
1134² LORD KHALICE (Ire) 5-10-6 (6*) N Rossiter, *with ldrs in chasing grp, outpcd frm 5 out, tld off........* (4 to 1 op 5 to 2) 4
1349⁶ WHO AM I (Ire) 6-10-12 P Henley, *hld up, cld 6th, wknd aftr 4 out, tld off.............* (13 to 2 op 6 to 1 tchd 7 to 1) 5
1115⁶ SNOWY PETREL (Ire) (bl) 4-10-9 (3*) W Walsh, *led, wl clr aftr second, hdd after 5 out, sn wknd, tld off.* (7 to 1 op 9 to 2) 6
1002 PROFESSION (v) 5-10-6 (6*) J K McCarthy, *hld up, cld 6th, wknd nxt, tld off.......*(50 to 1 op 20 to 1 tchd 66 to 1) 7
1180 SPORTING FELLOW (Ire) 5-10-12 G E Smith, *al beh, lost tch aftr 5th, tld off........* (50 to 1 op 14 to 1 tchd 66 to 1) 8
MADAM ROSE (Ire) 6-10-1 (6*) David Turner, *tld off aftr 5th, ran very wide bend and tried to run out after nxt, completed in own time.............* (33 to 1 op 20 to 1 tchd 50 to 1) 9
1365⁹ MASTER UPEX 4-10-6 (6*) W Greatrex, *jmpd big and awkwardly, wth ldr till aftr second, tld off whn pld up bef 6th.*
.................(66 to 1 op 33 to 1) pu

Dist: 24l, 8l, 27l, 14l, 18l, dist, 1½l, dist. 5m 42.30s. a 32.30s (10 Ran).

(The Hon Mrs C Yeates), D M Grissell

1556 European Breeders Fund 'National Hunt' Novices' Hurdle Qualifier Class E (4,5,6-y-o) £2,385 2m 1f 110yds..................... (1:30)

BOARDROOM SHUFFLE (Ire) 5-10-8 P Hide, *confidently rdn, hld up in cl tch, led appr last, sn clr, imprsv.*
.............(11 to 8 on tchd 5 to 4 on and 6 to 4 on) 1
SPLENDID THYNE 4-11-0 M A Fitzgerald, *trkd ldr, led 2 out till appr last, no ch wth wnr.............* (5 to 1 tchd 6 to 1) 2
FANTASY LINE 5-10-9 J Osborne, *hld up in cl tch, ev ch appr last, no extr.............* (8 to 1 op 4 to 1 tchd 10 to 1) 3
CHARLIE'S FOLLY 5-11-0 C Llewellyn, *hld up, pushed alng 5th, rallied nxt, outpcd frm 2 out.......*(20 to 1 op 10 to 1) 4
ARCTIC TRIUMPH 5-11-0 P Holley, *jmpd lft, led to 2 out, sn btn.............* (8 to 1 op 5 to 1 tchd 9 to 1) 5
1350⁴ SUPER RAPIER (Ire) 4-11-0 A P McCoy, *in tch, rdn and wknd aftr 2 out, tld off......* (9 to 2 op 7 to 2 tchd 5 to 1) 6
1026⁵ CRANBROOK LAD 4-11-0 D Morris, *hld up in tch, drpd rear 3 out, tld off whn pld up bef last.*
.................(50 to 1 op 20 to 1 tchd 66 to 1) pu

Dist: 10l, 1¾l, 10l, 22l, 3½l. 4m 20.90s. a 23.90s (7 Ran).
SR: 22/12/5/-/

(A D Weller), J T Gifford

1557 Daily Mail Novices' Handicap Chase Class E (0-100 5-y-o and up) £3,436 2m...................... (2:00)

SCORESHEET (Ire) [86] 6-11-0 P Hide, *al hndy, led 2 out, pushed clr, drifted lft r-in...* (4 to 1 op 4 to 1 tchd 7 to 2) 1
1349² REESHLOCH [93] 7-11-7 M A Fitzgerald, *hld up, reminders 6th, hrd rdn appr 2 out, kpt on to take second r-in.*
.................(100 to 30 op 6 to 4 tchd 7 to 2) 2
1425 NATIONAL FLAG (Fr) [77] 6-10-5⁵ A Larnach, *cl up, led appr 4 out, hdd 2 out, no extr und pres.*
.................(25 to 1 op 12 to 1 tchd 33 to 1) 3
1112⁸ SOPHIE MAY [91] 5-11-5 A P McCoy, *in tch, rdn alng 6th, btn aftr 3 out............* (7 to 1 tchd 8 to 1) 4
1439 COOLTEEN HERO (Ire) [88] 6-11-2 W McFarland, *led, mstk 4th, not jump wl aftr, hdd appr four out, sn btn.*
.................(7 to 1 op 6 to 1) 5
1416⁶ ANLACE [75] 7-9-12 (5*) Chris Webb, *hld up beh, rdn 7th, sn faller 5th, tld off.............* (6 to 1 op 25 to 1) 6
1399 LETS GO NOW (Ire) [72] 6-10-0 D Leahy, *al beh, hmpd by faller 5th, tld off.............* (6 to 1 op 25 to 1) 7
1111⁶ JACKSONS BAY [73] 6-9-12¹ (3*) G Hogan, *hld up in tch, rdn in rear whn f 3 out.* (33 to 1 op 25 to 1 tchd 40 to 1) f
1216* BRAZIL OR BUST (Ire) [100] 5-12-0 J Osborne, *hld up, f 5th.* ....(7 to 1 op 9 to 4 tchd 9 to 4) f

Dist: 13l, 1½l, 7l, nk, 5l, dist. 4m 6.30s. a 15.30s (9 Ran).
SR: 21/15/-/4/-/-/

(Pell-Mell Partners), J T Gifford

1558 David Cameron Memorial Handicap Hurdle Class F (0-105 4-y-o and up) £3,028 2¾m 110yds...........(2:30)

1048⁶ NICK THE BEAK (Ire) [100] 7-11-3 (7*) G Supple, *hld up beh ldrs, hdwy 4 out, led aftr 2 out, drvn out.*
.................(6 to 1 op 8 to 1 tchd 10 to 1) 1

1351⁶ GLEN MIRAGE [82] 11-10-6 Miss M Coombe, *sn settled towards rear, hdwy aftr 2 out, hrd rdn last, no imprsn r-in.*
........................(20 to 1 op 16 to 1 tchd 25 to 1) 2
1351 FLEUR DE TAL [95] 5-10-12 (7") J Power, *hld up, hdwy 4 out, drvn aftr 2 out, sn one pace.*
........................(14 to 1 op 10 to 1 tchd 16 to 1) 3
1132⁶ PETTALIGH (Ire) [93] 8-10-10 (7") N Rossiter, *wth ldrs till rdn and lost pl 6th, styd on frm 2 out.*
........................(9 to 2 tchd 4 to 1 and 5 to 1) 4
PADDYSWAY [91] 9-11-1 B Powell, *hld up beh ldrs, cld 7th, mstk wnt, sn btn............*(10 to 1 tchd 8 to 1) 5
1419⁴ OLD ARCHIVES (Ire) [86] (bl) 7-10-10 P Hide, *made most, kicked clr aftr 6th, hdd aftr 2 out, wknd.*
........................(9 to 1 tchd 10 to 1 and 8 to 1) 6
WHITEBONNET (Ire) [84] 6-10-8 J Osborne, *trkd ldrs, wknd quickly aftr 2 out, tld off..............*(10 to 1 op 7 to 1) 7
1266⁵ APACHEE FLOWER [76] (v) 6-10-0 A P McCoy, *chsd ldrs, rdn and btn 3 out, tld off..................*(9 to 2 op 7 to 2) 8
1087⁴ TOP WAVE [99] 8-11-9 J Ryan, *wth ldr, wknd appr 4 out, tld off.....................*(16 to 1 op 10 to 1 tchd 20 to 1) 9
1444* WHISTLING BUCK (Ire) [82] 8-10-6 D O'Sullivan, *hld up, steady hdwy 4 out, wknd appr 2 out, btn quickly, tld off whn pld up bef last..................*(7 to 2 fav op 5 to 2) pu
Dist: 3½sl, 9l, 1l, 1l, ¾l, dist, 20l, dist. 5m 50.30s. a 40.30s (10 Ran).
(Sir Nicholas Wilson), John R Upson

1559 Daily Mail Handicap Chase Class F In Memory of Lady Harmsworth Blunt (0-100 5-y-o and up) £4,302 3¼m
.... (3:00)

1231³ FUNCHEON GALE [92] 9-11-6 D Morris, *hld up, hdwy 11th, led appr 2 out, hng lft, rdn out.*
........................(6 to 4 fav tchd 11 to 8 and 13 to 8) 1
1471⁷ RHOMAN FUN (Ire) [72] 7-9-9 (5") Mr R Thornton, *hld up in cl tch, hrd rdn appr 3 out, styd on one pace frm nxt.*
........................(6 to 1 op 9 to 2 tchd 7 to 1) 2
1446² JOKER JACK [72] 11-9-12¹ (3") T Dascombe, *led 5th, drvn alng frm 14th, hdd appr 2 out and mstk, one pace.*
........................(20 to 1 tchd 25 to 1) 3
1114² MASTER COMEDY [75] (bl) 12-9-10 (7") Mr R Wakley, *at beh.*
........................(5 to 1 op 7 to 2) 4
1133 TIPP MARINER [98] (bl) 11-11-12 J Osborne, *not jump wl, led till mstk and hdd 5th, rdn and wknd 14th, tld off whn pld up bef 2 out.....................*(3 to 1 op 4 to 1 tchd 11 to 2) pu
1301 JUMBEAU [100] 11-11-11 (3") Mr C Bonner, *trkd ldrs till drpd rear 7th, tld off whn pld up aftr 12th......*(8 to 1 op 5 to 1) pu
DEEPENDABLE [90] (bl) 9-11-4 M Richards, *hld up, hdwy 11th, wknd 3 out, blun nxt, pld up.*
........................(12 to 1 op 7 to 1 tchd 14 to 1) pu
Dist: 1¾l, 3½l, 20l. 6m 54.30s. a 39.30s (7 Ran).
(Kings Of The Road Partnership), R Curtis

1560 Biggin Hill Mares' Only Intermediate Open National Hunt Flat Class H (4,5,6-y-o) £1,301 2m 1f 110yds
.... (3:30)

BULA VOGUE (Ire) 6-11-0 D O'Sullivan, *led, hdd and outpcd o'r 5 fs out, rallied over 2 out, led ins last, ran on wl.*
........................(11 to 1 op 10 to 1 tchd 12 to 1) 1
SUPREME TROGLODYTE (Ire) 4-11-0 J R Kavanagh, *hld up, hmpd o'r 6 fs out, sn cld, led wl over one furlong out till ins last, ran on............*(25 to 1 op 20 to 1 tchd 33 to 1) 2
PLAID MAID (Ire) 4-11-0 P Holley, *hld up, hdwy o'r 5 fs out, ev ch und pres ins last, one pace.*
........................(12 to 1 op 8 to 1 tchd 14 to 1) 3
ROYAL RULER (Ire) 5-11-0 P Hide, *hld up beh ldrs, led o'r 5 fs out till wl over one out, no extr......* (2 to 1 fav op 5 to 2) 4
GOOD THYNE GIRL 4-11-0 J Osborne, *hld up, hdwy to track ldrs o'r 5 fs out, wknd 2 out.*
........................(3 to 1 op 5 to 2 tchd 100 to 30) 5
1214⁶ SOLAR MOON 5-11-0 B Powell, *hld up in tch, cld o'r 5 fs out, wknd over 2 out........*(11 to 1 op 8 to 1 tchd 12 to 1) 6
YARSLEY JESTER 4-11-0 B Fenton, *chsd ldrs, lost pl o'r ten fs out, hdwy hfwy, wknd over 2 out.....* (14 to 1 op 10 to 1) 7
TAWNY WARBLER 4-11-0 M Richards, *pld hrd, cl up till lost pl o'r 5 fs out....................*(25 to 1) 8
CASTLE LYNCH (Ire) 4-10-11 (3") P Henley, *nvr nr to chal.*
........................(9 to 1 op 11 to 1 tchd 14 to 1) 9
AINTGOTWON 5-10-11 (3") L Aspell, *hld up beh, badly hmpd and almost uns rdr o'r 6 fs out, drvn and not much room over 3 out, sn btn.....*(12 to 1 op 12 to 1 tchd 20 to 1) 10
BLAMELESS 4-10-11 (3") G Hogan, *trkd ldr till o'r 6 fs out, sn wknd......................*(33 to 1 tchd 40 to 1) 11
BALLYQUINTET (Ire) 5-11-0 S McNeill, *hld up, al beh, tld off.*
........................(2 to 1 op 4 to 1 tchd 6 to 1) 12
REAL LUCILLE 4-11-0 M A Fitzgerald, *trkd ldrs till wknd hfwy, tld off......................*(20 to 1 op 14 to 1 tchd 25 to 1) 13
TABBITTS HILL 4-11-0 Mr P Scott, *trkd ldrs, hmpd o'r 6 fs out, sn lost pl, tld off.......*(10 to 1 op 6 to 1 tchd 14 to 1) 14
Dist: ¾l, 2½l, 6l, 4l, hd, 7l, 11l, 13l, 15l, hd. 4m 25.50s. (14 Ran).
(The In Vogue Partnership), R Rowe

CHELTENHAM (good to firm)

Tuesday November 26th
Going Correction: PLUS 0.40 sec. per fur. (races 1,4,6), PLUS 0.30 (2,3,5)

1561 Cheltenham Racecourse Of The Year Handicap Hurdle Class C (0-135 4-y-o and up) £3,468 2m 5f... (1:00)

1105³ BLAZE AWAY (USA) [122] 5-11-8 J Osborne, *trkd ldr frm 4th, steady hdwy 2 out, styd on to ld r-in, cmftbly.*
........................(13 to 8 op 7 to 4 tchd 6 to 4) 1
1379 COURBARIL [120] 4-11-6 A P McCoy, *led, clr aftr second, steadied 4th, pushed clear ag'n 6th, rdn appr 2 out, hng rght and hdd r-in, swshd tail und pres.*
........................(Evens fav op 5 to 4 on tchd 11 to 10) 2
1427⁶ BELLROI (Ire) [103] 5-10-3 A Maguire, *chsd ldr to 4th, remained in 3rd, lost tch 7th.*
........................(4 to 1 op 7 to 2 tchd 9 to 2) 3
BLAZER MORINIERE (Fr) [128] 7-12-0 S Fox, *al last, lost tch 5th, tld off nxt...................*(66 to 1 op 33 to 1) 4
Dist: 3l, 13l, dist. 5m 15.80s. a 19.80s (4 Ran).
(Paul Mellon), I A Balding

1562 Lansdown Novices' Handicap Chase Class D (0-110 5-y-o and up) £3,720 2½m 110yds................. (1:35)

1099² PONGO WARING (Ire) [103] 7-12-0 J Osborne, *jmpd wl, trkd ldr, quickened ahead 3 out, drvn and ran on well r-in.*
........................(11 to 4 fav op 2 to 1 tchd 3 to 1) 1
1392² FLIMSY TRUTH [91] 10-11-2 A Maguire, *led to 3 out, rallied nxt, chsd wnr appr last, one pace r-in.*
........................(8 to 1 op 6 to 1 tchd 9 to 1) 2
GLENALLA STAR (Ire) [100] 7-11-11 G Bradley, *in tch, steady hdwy to track ldrs 6th, chlgd 3 out, rdn aftr nxt, one pace und pres appr last...................*(3 to 1 op 7 to 2) 3
PEARL'S CHOICE (Ire) [88] 8-10-13 R Farrant, *in tch, drpd rear 7th, rallied 3 out, sn one pace.*
........................(25 to 1 op 20 to 1 tchd 33 to 1) 4
1062* MILL O'THE RAGS (Ire) [100] 7-11-11 N Williamson, *al rear, lost tch 12th, tld off.......*(9 to 2 op 4 to 1 tchd 5 to 1) 5
1332² BALLYLINE (Ire) [88] 5-10-12 M Dwyer, *lost pl 7th, hit nxt, staying on in 4th whn f 3 out.*
........................(3 to 1 op 7 to 2 tchd 4 to 1) f
Dist: 1l, 8l, 2l, dist. 5m 13.90s. a 16.90s (6 Ran).
(Miss H Knight), Miss H C Knight

1563 VFB Holidays Handicap Chase Class B (0-145 5-y-o and up) £6,762 3m 1f
.... (2:10)

YORKSHIRE GALE [130] 10-11-10 N Williamson, *hld up, wnt 3rd at 7th, hdwy to chase ldr 4 out, led nxt, drvn clr frm 2 out.*
........................(4 to 1 op 3 to 1) 1
1290³ BETTY'S BOY (Ire) [127] 7-11-7 C O'Dwyer, *dsptd 3rd till mstk 7th, styd wl in tch, quickened to ld 15th, hdd 3 out, one pace frm nxt...................*(11 to 4 op 5 to 2 tchd 3 to 1) 2
1395² COPPER MINE [120] 10-11-3 J Osborne, *led, rdn appr 12th, hdd and wknd aftr nxt, rallied to take poor 3rd approaching last...................*(8 to 1 op 5 to 1) 3
1290² GREY SMOKE [129] 6-11-9 G Bradley, *chsd ldr, chlgd 13th, sn led, hdd 15th, wknd 3 out, lost poor 3rd appr last.*
........................(11 to 10 fav op 5 to 4 tchd 11 to 8) 4
Dist: 21l, 15l, 8l. 6m 21.30s. 13.30s (4 Ran).
SR: 38/14/-/-/
(Bill Naylor), J T Gifford

1564 Newent Hurdle Class B for the Sport of Kings' Challenge (4-y-o and up) £7,335 2m 110yds........... (2:45)

1340* MANDYS MANTINO 6-11-4 P Hide, *led, clr second, hit 3 out, rdn appr last, hld on wl cl hme......*(11 to 8 fav op Evens) 1
SERENITY PRAYER (USA) 6-11-7 Chip Miller, *chsd ldr till mstk 3 out, lost pl appr nxt, rallied last, styd on wl, not rch wnr cl hme..................*(11 to 4 op 5 to 2 tchd 3 to 1) 2
1346³ CHICODARI 4-10-9 A Maguire, *in 3rd, hdwy to chase wnr aftr 3 out, rdn appr last, wknd cl hme.*
........................(7 to 4 tchd 13 to 8 and 15 to 8) 3
Dist: ½l, 7l. 3m 59.00s. a 10.00s (3 Ran).
SR: 56/58/39/
(John Plackett), J T Gifford

1565 Everyman Theatre Robin Hood Novices' Chase Class D (5-y-o and up) £5,789 3m 1f................. (3:20)

1440* HANAKHAM (Ire) 6-11-6 N Williamson, *chsd ldr till lft alone 4 out....................*(11 to 8 op 11 to 10) 1
1083* HANAKHAM (Ire) 7-11-6 J Osborne, *led till blun and uns rdr 4 out........*(13 to 8 on op 6 to 4 on tchd 11 to 8 on) ur
Won by 6m 56.60s. a 48.60s (2 Ran).
SR: -/-/
(David M Williams), Miss Venetia Williams

1566 Go Racing In Ireland 'National Hunt' Novices' Hurdle Class C (4-y-o and up) £3,501 3¼m............. (3:55)

1545[4] SPACEAGE GOLD 7-11-2 G Upton, *led, pushed alng aftr 8th, rdn 3 out, edgd lft und pres whn hdd bend appr last, hvt ridden to ld ag'n cl hme.*
..............................(5 to 4 fav op 11 to 8 tchd 6 to 4) 1

1132* TARRS BRIDGE (Ire) 5-11-10 J Railton, *hld up in 3rd, chsd wnr 4 out, chlgd 2 out,led and not much room bend appr last, rdn, hdd and no extr cl hme.*
..............................(11 to 8 op 11 to 10 on tchd 6 to 4) 2

1234 RARE SPREAD (Ire) 6-11-2 C Maude, *in 4th, lost tch 8th, steady hdwy four out, hng badly rght whn chasing ldrs frm 2 out, sn btn.*........(11 to 2 op 8 to 1 tchd 20 to 1) 3
NEWS FROM AFAR 5-11-2 A Maguire, *pressed wnr till aftr 7th, wknd 4 out, tld off.* (14 to 1 op 16 to 1 tchd 20 to 1) 4
Dist: 1l, 27l, dist. 6m 54.50s. 38.50s (4 Ran).
(Spaceage Plastics Limited), J A B Old

HUNTINGDON (good to soft)
Tuesday November 26th
Going Correction: PLUS 0.70 sec. per fur. (races 1,4,6), PLUS 0.95 (2,3,5)

1567 Houghton Selling Handicap Hurdle Class G (0-95 4-y-o and up) £2,031 3 ¼m...................... (12:40)

1266[3] MR FLUTTS [75] 10-10-10 S McNeill, *hld up, hdwy 8th, chsd ldr appr 3 out, led nxt, pushed out.* (4 to 1 jt-fav op 5 to 2) 1

1315[6] QUIET MISTRESS [80] (bl) 6-11-1 A S Smith, *led aftr second, made rst till hdd 2 out, no extr und pres.*
..............................(13 to 2 op 5 to 1 tchd 7 to 1) 2

1492[3] KATBALLOU [65] 7-9-7 (7*) Mr O McPhail, *mid div, hdwy 7th, ch 4 out, outpcd nxt.*......(8 to 1 op 5 to 1 tchd 10 to 1) 3

1302 TIGER CLAW (USA) [88] 10-11-2 (7*) O Burrows, *trkd ldrs till outpcd aftr 7th, tld off.*..........(7 to 1 tchd 8 to 1) 4
MARDOOD [80] 11-10-8 (7*) Miss R Clark, *led till aftr second, wth ldr till wknd quickly after 4 out, tld off.*
..............................(14 to 1 op 10 to 1 tchd 16 to 1) 5

1400[5] PROVENCE [73] 9-10-5 (3*) G Hogan, *trkd ldrs till wknd 7th, tld off.*..................(9 to 1 op 7 to 1 tchd 10 to 1) 6

1385[5] ARRANGE A GAME [69] 9-10-1 (3*) T Dascombe, *trkd ldrs, pushed alng 7th, sn wknd, tld off.*
..............................(10 to 1 tchd 12 to 1 tchd 9 to 1) 7

955* MILLY LE MOSS (Ire) [65] 7-10-0 R Johnson, *trkd ldrs till wknd 7th, tld off.*........(6 to 1 op 12 to 1 tchd 14 to 1) 8

1325[6] THARSIS [72] 11-10-2 (5*) S Taylor, *mid-div, reminders 6th, sn wknd, tld off.*..........(25 to 1 op 20 to 1 tchd 33 to 1) 9

1402[9] NAGOBELIA [93] 8-12-0 N Mann, *beh, lost tch 7th, tld off, completed in own time.* (14 to 1 op 10 to 1 tchd 16 to 1) 10

1474[9] PARISIAN [65] 11-10-0 L Harvey, *sn beh, tld off whn pld up bef 2 out.*...........(25 to 1 op 20 to 1 tchd 33 to 1) pu
FAST RUN (Ire) [76] 8-10-11 B Fenton, *al beh, tld off whn pld up bef last.*.....................(12 to 1 op 10 to 1) pu

1020[8] LOCK TIGHT (USA) [65] 6-10-0 D Leahy, *hrd rdn appr 5th, sn drpd out, pld up aftr 7th.* (50 to 1 op 20 to 1 tchd 66 to 1) pu

1260[4] OUR MURIEL [85] 4-11-5 R Marley, *mid-div, pushed alng 7th, sn wknd, tld off whn pld up bef 4 out.* ....(4 to 1 jt-fav 9 to 2 tchd 9 to 2) pu
Dist: 1¼l, 11l, dist, 5l, 1¼l, 18l, nk, 13l, dist. 6m 34.50s. a 42.50s (14 Ran).
(J C Tuck), J C Tuck

1568 Health-Spa Water Novices' Chase Class E (4-y-o and up) £3,994 2½m 110yds...................... (1:15)

1399[2] MISTER DRUM (Ire) 7-11-5 W Marston, *made all, mstks 5th and 12th, ran on wl.*
..............................(11 to 4 op 5 to 2 tchd 3 to 1 and 7 to 2) 1

1269[2] WEE WINDY (Ire) 7-11-5 R Dunwoody, *al hndy, rdn alng 2 out, outpcd appr last, kpt on und pres.*
..............................(5 to 4 on op 6 to 5 tchd 5 to 4) 2

1216[2] SLINGSBY (Ire) 6-11-5 A Thornton, *al hndy, mstk 11th (water), one pace frm 2 out.* (8 to 1 op 6 to 1 tchd 9 to 1) 3
HAUNTING MUSIC (Ire) 8-11-5 M A Fitzgerald, *trkd ldrs, outpcd 11th, rallied aftr 3 out, one pace frm nxt.*
..............................(12 to 1 op 8 to 1) 4

PEARL EPEE 7-11-0 R Bellamy, *hld up in mid-div, mstks 9th and 12th, sn btn.*........(16 to 1 op 12 to 1 tchd 20 to 1) 5

ANOTHER VENTURE (Ire) 6-11-5 B Fenton, *al beh, tld off.*
..............................(20 to 1 op 12 to 1 tchd 25 to 1) 6

1263* BASSENHALLY 6-11-5 R Marley, *hld up, wknd tenth, blun 12th, tld off.*..........(16 to 1 op 12 to 1 tchd 20 to 1) 7

MY WARRIOR 8-11-5 M Sharratt, *not jump wl, al beh, tld off.*
..............................(100 to 1 op 50 to 1) 8

RATHFARDON (Ire) 8-10-12 (7*) Mr T J Barry, *al beh, tld off.*
..............................(100 to 1 op 20 to 1) 9

HANCOCK 4-10-6 Derek Byrne, *mstks, t 4th.*
.... f

1402[7] PEGASUS BAY 5-11-4 S McNeill, *beh, hdwy aftr 8th, chasing ldrs whn f 3 out.*.......(33 to 1 op 20 to 1 tchd 50 to 1) f

1341 SCORPION BAY 8-11-5 P Holley, *beh whn blun and uns rdr 8th.*..............................(50 to 1 op 33 to 1) ur
OLD REDWOOD 9-11-5 L O'Hara, *trkd ldrs till wknd tenth, tld off whn pld up bef 2 out.*........(100 to 1 op 33 to 1) pu

1368 UPHAM RASCAL 5-11-4 D Leahy, *tld off whn tried to refuse 3rd, pld up aftr.*.....................(50 to 1 op 33 to 1) pu

---

Dist: 3½l, hd, 4l, 29l, 16l, ¾l, 10l, nk. 5m 12.00s. a 25.00s (14 Ran).
SR: 35/31/31/27/-/-/ (Malcolm Batchelor), M J Wilkinson

1569 Weatherbys VAT Service Handicap Chase Class E (0-110 5-y-o and up) £3,036 3m................... (1:50)

726[2] SOLO GENT [92] 7-11-6 S McNeill, *hld up beh ldrs, cld 4 out, led last, ran on wl.*..........(7 to 2 op 3 to 1 tchd 4 to 1) 1

1339[5] SUGAR HILL (Ire) [84] 6-10-9 (3*) L Aspell, *al hndy, led 15th till blun and hdd nxt, ev ch 2 out, no extr appr last.*
..............................(3 to 1 tchd 7 to 2 and 4 to 1) 2

DISTINCTIVE (Ire) [96] 7-11-10 R Dunwoody, *led, hit 12th, hdd 15th, led ag'n nxt, headed last, no extr.*
..............................(5 to 2 fav op 6 to 4) 3

1254[5] TRUMPET [96] (v) 7-11-10 R Johnson, *in tch, pushed alng and wknd appr 13th, tld off.*
..............................(12 to 1 op 8 to 1 tchd 14 to 1) 4

1301[6] MAXXUM EXPRESS (Ire) [85] 8-10-13 Richard Guest, *beh, hdwy 11th, outpcd aftr 3 out, tld off.*
..............................(15 to 2 op 8 to 1 tchd 10 to 1 and 7 to 1) 5
TIM SOLDIER (Fr) [79] 9-10-7 J R Kavanagh, *al beh, losing tch whn pld up bef 15th.*
..............................(20 to 1 op 16 to 1 tchd 25 to 1 and 33 to 1) pu
CARLINGFORD LAKES (Ire) [87] 8-11-1 M A Fitzgerald, *trkd ldrs, lost pl 11th, mstk nxt, losing tch whn pld up bef 15th.*
..............................(9 to 2 op 3 to 1 tchd 5 to 1 and 7 to 2) pu
Dist: 9l, 1½l, 27l, 8l. 6m 21.00s. a 41.20s (7 Ran).
(A A King), A P Jones

1570 Hoechst Roussel Panacur European Breeders Fund Mares' 'National Hunt' Novices' Hurdle Qualifier Class E (4-y-o and up) £2,460 2m 5f 110yds...................... (2:25)

GAYE FAME 5-10-12 S McNeill, *led 6th, mstk nxt, ran on wl frm 2 out.*......(9 to 4 op 7 to 4 tchd 5 to 2) 1

1369[2] MARLOUSION (Ire) 4-10-12 D Gallagher, *trkd ldrs, pushed alng appr 2 out, ev ch last, hrd rdn and no extr.*
..............................(6 to 1 op 5 to 1 tchd 7 to 1) 2

1369[3] LADY HIGH SHERIFF (Ire) 6-10-12 S Wynne, *in tch, outpcd 6th, hdwy frm 3 out, styd on.*
..............................(9 to 1 op 6 to 1 tchd 10 to 1) 3

1234 HOPPERDANTE (Ire) 6-10-12 R Johnson, *al beh, tld off.*
..............................(33 to 1 op 25 to 1 tchd 40 to 1 and 50 to 1) 4

1237* SEYMOURSWIFT 6-11-5 R Dunwoody, *cl up, ev ch 3 out, 3rd and wkng whn f nxt.*......(6 to 4 fav op 2 to 1 tchd 9 to 4) f
BRIERY GALE 6-10-12 A Thornton, *hld up, hdwy 6th, ev ch appr 3 out, sn btn, tld off whn pld up bef nxt.*
..............................(16 to 1 op 10 to 1) pu

1260[6] MESP (Ire) 5-10-12 M A Fitzgerald, *al beh, tld off whn pld up bef 6th.*..........(20 to 1 tchd 25 to 1 and 33 to 1) pu

1208[6] GENTLE BREEZE (Ire) 4-10-9 (3*) L Aspell, *hld up, drvn and wknd aftr 6th, tld off whn pld up bef 2 out.* (10 to 1 op 8 to 1) pu
PRIMITIVE PENNY 5-10-9 (3*) G Hogan, *led till hdd 6th, wknd nxt, tld off whn pld up bef 2 out.*....(14 to 1 op 12 to 1) pu
OFF PISTE SALLY 4-10-12 B Fenton, *al beh, tld off whn pld up bef 6th.*..........(33 to 1 op 20 to 1 tchd 50 to 1) pu
Dist: 1¼l, 13l, dist. 5m 21.00s. a 32.00s (10 Ran).
(Noel Cronin), K C Bailey

1571 Peterborough Chase Class A Grade 2 (5-y-o and up) £18,125 2½m 110yds...................... (3:00)

1394 DUBLIN FLYER 10-11-1 B Powell, *trkd ldr, shaken up to ld aftr 3 out, hit nxt, blun badly last, sn clr.*
..............................(9 to 4 on op 2 to 1 on tchd 2 to 1 on) 1

1466[3] GALES CAVALIER (Ire) 8-11-10 R Dunwoody, *led till hdd aftr 3 out, no extr, eased whn hld appr last.*
..............................(7 to 2 op 3 to 1 tchd 4 to 1) 2
KADI (Ger) 7-11-1 R Johnson, *chsd clr ldrs, mstk tenth, nvr on terms.*..........(5 to 1 op 9 to 2) 3

1466[4] QUIXALL CROSSETT 11-11-1 S Taylor, *in last pl whn blun badly and almost ran out tenth, styd on one pace frm 2 out, no ch wth 1st 3.*......(250 to 1 tchd 500 to 1 and 750 to 1) 4
STAGE PLAYER 10-11-1 J Lawrence, *al beh, mstk tenth, tld off.*..........................(100 to 1 op 50 to 1) 5

1468 MONAUGHTY MAN 10-11-1 Mr P Murray, *al beh, tld off.*
..............................(200 to 1 op 100 to 1 tchd 250 to 1) 6
Dist: 18l, 9l, dist, 10l, 3½l. 5m 11.90s. a 24.90s (6 Ran).
SR: 32/23/5/ (J B Sumner), Capt T A Forster

1572 Tote Handicap Hurdle Class C (0-130 4-y-o and up) £5,177 2m 110yds .... (3:35)

1346* TEINEIN (Fr) [128] 5-12-0 A P McCoy, *hld up in cl tch, led 2 out, hrd held.*
..............................(13 to 8 on op 5 to 4 on tchd 11 to 10 on and 7 to 4 on) 1

MARIUS (Ire) [112] 6-10-9 (3*) L Aspell, *trkd ldr, led 5th, hdd 2 out, no ch wth wnr.*
..............................(10 to 3 op 4 to 1 tchd 6 to 1 and 3 to 1) 2

NATIONAL HUNT RESULTS 1996-97

CHEF COMEDIEN (Ire) [120] 6-11-6 R Dunwoody, trkd ldrs, cld and ev ch 3 out, sn outpcd
.................................(15 to 2 op 8 to 1 tchd 7 to 1 and 9 to 1)   3
CAWARRA BOY [107] 8-10-7 Mr E James, hld up in tch, hit second, outpcd aftr 4 out.(14 to 1 op 6 to 1 tchd 16 to 1)   4
ALBEMINE (USA) [121] 7-11-7 T Kent, led til hdd 5th, sn btn.
....(10 to 1 op 5 to 1)   5
1288⁶ MANEREE [106] 9-10-6 D Gallagher, al beh, lost tch 4th, tld off...........................(20 to 1 op 8 to 1 tchd 25 to 1)   6
691¹³ ZINE LANE [103] 4-10-3¹ M A Fitzgerald, trkd ldrs till pushed alng and lost pl 5th, sn lost tch, tld off.
....(10 to 1 op 7 to 1 tchd 12 to 1)   7
Dist: 3½l, 17l, 17l, 1¾l, 6l, 18l, 28l. 3m 57.80s. a 16.80s (7 Ran).
SR: 48/28/19/4/12/-/-/ (Simon Sainsbury), Capt T A Forster

CHEPSTOW (soft (races 1,2,4,6), good to soft (3,5))
Wednesday November 27th
Going Correction: PLUS 1.20 sec. per fur. (races 1,2,4,6), PLUS 0.70 (3,5)

1573 Galway Novices' Hurdle Class C (4-y-o and up) £3,965 2½m 110yds
.... (1:25)

1344* MIGHTY MOSS (Ire) 5-10-12 (7*) Mr F Hutsby, al prmnt, led appr 5th, hit 4 out, clr 2 out, cmftbly.
...............(Evens fav op 5 to 4 on tchd 11 to 10)   1
GLITTER ISLE (Ire) 6-10-11 (3*) L Aspell, al in tch, wnt second appr 4 out, one pace frm nxt.
.......................(12 to 1 op 14 to 1 tchd 10 to 1)   2
1240 KIND CLERIC 5-11-0 R Dunwoody, hld up in rear, hdwy 7th, styd on frm 3 out, nvr nrr...............(66 to 1 op 33 to 1)   3
1447* SCOTBY (Bel) 6-11-5 B Powell, wth ldrs, rdn appr 4 out, btn whn mstk nxt....................(12 to 1 op 5 to 1)   4
KINGS CHERRY (Ire) 8-10-7 (7*) Mr G Baines, slwly away, in rear till some late hdwy...........(100 to 1 op 66 to 1)   5
1437* DARAYDAN (Ire) 4-11-5 A P McCoy, hld up in tch, wknd appr 3 out...................(5 to 4 op Evens tchd 6 to 4)   6
1348⁴ BLAZING MIRACLE 4-10-4 (5*) D Salter, mid-div, lost tch appr 4 out.........................(100 to 1 op 50 to 1)   7
1344⁹ DRAKESTONE 5-11-0 R Johnson, led till hdd appr 5th, second whn hit nxt, sn wknd.
.................................(66 to 1 op 33 to 1 tchd 100 to 1)   8
RED BRANCH (Ire) 7-11-0 T J Murphy, hld up, hdwy appr 7th, wknd bef nxt........................(100 to 1)   9
1479 MY SHENANDOAH (Ire) 5-11-0 V Slattery, al beh, tld off.
.................................(66 to 1 op 50 to 1)   10
HARRY THE HORSE 8-11-0 G Upton, mid-div till wknd 7th, tld off................(5 to 1 op 20 to 1 tchd 33 to 1)   11
1207 LUCKY CALL (NZ) 5-11-0 R Greene, chsd ldrs till wknd quickly appr 4 out, tld off...........(100 to 1 op 50 to 1)   12
1136⁹ IRISH PERRY 9-10-9 M Sharratt, very slwly away, tld off 5th.
....(100 to 1)   13
1208 FILCH 5-10-9 J R Kavanagh, in tch to 5th, tld off whn pld up bef 4 out.............(100 to 1 op 66 to 1)   pu
HAPPY JACK 5-11-0 D Leahy, al beh, mstk 5th, tld off whn pld up bef 4 out.........(100 to 1 op 50 to 1)   pu
Dist: 6l, 3l, 4l, 15l, 3½l, 4l, 1¼l, 9l, 5l, 3l. 5m 8.20s. a 30.20s (15 Ran).
SR: 35/24/21/22/2/3/ (K Hutsby), D Nicholson

1574 Sligo Selling Hurdle Class G (4 - 7-y-o) £1,940 2½m 110yds........(1:55)

1355³ DRAGONMIST (Ire) (h) 6-10-7 D J Burchell, hld up, hdwy 5th, wnt second aftr 7th, led 2 out, styd on....(8 to 1 op 6 to 1)   1
1452⁴ PARADE RACER 5-10-12 G Upton, led till hdd appr 4th, led 6th, lft clr nxt, jmpd rght 3 out, headed and hit next, one pace.
.................................(5 to 2 op 5 to 1)   2
1451 CASTLECONNER (Ire) (bl) 5-10-12 R Dunwoody, prmnt till one pace frm 4 out....(16 to 1 op 12 to 1 tchd 20 to 1)   3
1442⁷ FORTUNES ROSE (Ire) 4-10-7 T J Murphy, hld up in rear, hdwy 6th, no ch frm 4 out..........(33 to 1 op 25 to 1)   4
1082 TROUBLE AT MILL 6-10-12 P McLoughlin, in rear till hdwy 7th, wknd 4 out.............................(33 to 1)   5
1415 LANESRA BREEZE 4-10-12 C Maude, al towards rear, tld off.
.........................(50 to 1 op 33 to 1)   6
1343⁶ CHINA MAIL (Ire) 4-11-5 R Johnson, in rear, tld off.
...............................(20 to 1 op 12 to 1 tchd 25 to 1)   7
STRIKE-A-POSE 6-11-0 Mr J L Llewellyn, al beh, tld off.
..............................(16 to 1 op 12 to 1)   8
KADIRI (Ire) 5-10-12 W McFarland, hld up, hdwy whn mstk 6th, wknd nxt, tld off...(10 to 1 op 16 to 1 tchd 25 to 1)   9
1324³ FOROFIVETWOHUNDRED (Ire) 6-10-12 A P McCoy, chsd ldrs, mstk 5th, lft second and badly hmpd 7th, not reco'r, tld off...........................(12 to 1 op 6 to 1)   10
1068² FURIETTO (Ire) 6-11-5 A Maguire, prmnt, wnt second 6th, f nxt.............................(5 to 4 fav op Evens)   f
1320⁸ JAVA SHRINE (USA) 5-11-5 S McNeill, mid-div, hdwy 5th, wknd appr 4 out, tld off whn pld up bef 2 out.
.................................(25 to 1 op 16 to 1)   pu
1438 NORFOLK GLORY 4-10-5 (7*) Mr R Wakley, led appr 4th, hdd 6th, wknd quickly, tld off whn pld up bef four out.
.................................(33 to 1 op 20 to 1)   pu

1476 POLLERTON'S DREAM 6-10-4 (3*) Guy Lewis, mid-div till rdn and wknd 6th, tld off whn pld up bef 4 out.
.................................(66 to 1 op 50 to 1)   pu
Dist: 6l, 9l, 20l, 19l, 17l, 6l, 5l, 15l, dist. 5m 16.20s. a 38.20s (14 Ran).
(D Roderick), D Burchell

1575 Donegal Handicap Chase Class D (0-120 5-y-o and up) £3,484 2m 3f 110yds.....................(2:25)

BELLS LIFE (Ire) [120] 7-11-11 (3*) G Tormey, hld up, jmpd slwly 6th, mstk 11th, chlgd 3 out, lft clr nxt.
.................................(2 to 1 fav op 11 to 8 tchd 9 to 4)   1
1204² BEAU BABILLARD [115] (bl) 9-11-9 A P McCoy, hld up, hdwy appr 5 out, wknd nxt.................(11 to 4 op 5 to 2)   2
1267* BENJAMIN LANCASTER [100] 12-10-1 (7*) M Griffiths, led, reminder aftr 11th, rdn and hdd 5 out, wknd after nxt.
.................................(3 to 1 op 4 to 1)   3
831² ARMALA [108] 11-10-13 (3*) L Aspell, trkd ldr, led 5 out, hdd and f 2 out.........................(11 to 4 op 5 to 2)   f
Dist: 16l, 2½l. 5m 8.80s. a 25.80s (4 Ran).
(R Gibbs), P J Hobbs

1576 Independent Insurance Handicap Hurdle Class C (0-130 4-y-o and up) £3,715 3m.....................(2:55)

1443² GENERAL TONIC [102] 9-10-0 (5*) Sophie Mitchell, hld up, hdwy 7th, wnt second 4 out, led nxt, styd on wl.
.................................(11 to 1 op 10 to 1)   1
111²⁴ KARAR (Ire) [107] 6-10-10 D O'Sullivan, hld up, hdwy 6th, styd on to go second last, edgd lft r-in.
.................................(13 to 2 op 6 to 1 tchd 7 to 1)   2
MISS DISKIN (Ire) [110] 7-10-13 A Maguire, hld up, hdwy to track ldrs 7th, ev ch 3 out, one pace aftr. (14 to 1 op 8 to 1)   3
1303² LANSDOWNE [125] 8-11-7 (7*) O Burrows, hld up, hdwy 7th, wknd 3 out, btn whn mstk nxt...........(10 to 1 op 7 to 1)   4
1370³ FORTUNES COURSE (Ire) [111] 7-10-7 (7*) Mr A Wintle, led to second, prmnt till wknd 3 out..........(8 to 1 tchd 7 to 1)   5
TOP JAVALIN (NZ) [99] 9-9-9 (7*) M Griffiths, led second till hdd 3 out, wknd quickly.........(25 to 1 op 20 to 1)   6
1032⁵ ACROW LINE [110] 11-10-13 D J Burchell, al beh, tld off.
.................................(16 to 1 op 14 to 1 tchd 20 to 1)   7
ST VILLE [99] 10-10-2⁶ (5*) Mr R Thornton, chsd ldrs till wknd 8th....................(20 to 1 tchd 25 to 1)   8
ROYAL PIPER (NZ) [100] 9-10-5 R Greene, al beh, tld off.
.................................(14 to 1 tchd 10 to 1)   9
1032³ YES MAN (Ire) [112] 7-11-1 R Dunwoody, prmnt till rdn and wknd aftr 7th.......(3 to 1 fav op 4 to 1 tchd 9 to 2)   10
LITTLE GUNNER [118] 6-11-7 R Bellamy, brght dwn on bend aftr 5th....................(20 to 1 op 14 to 1)   bd
1391² GLENGARRIF GIRL (Ire) [108] (v) 6-10-11 A P McCoy, hld up, brght dwn on bend aftr 5th.
.................................(9 to 1 op 7 to 1 tchd 10 to 1)   bd
1454³ OATIS ROSE [97] 6-10-0 R Johnson, hit rail and slpd up on bend aftr 5th........(15 to 2 op 7 to 1 tchd 8 to 1)   su
LUCKY LANE [113] (bl) 12-11-2 C Maude, prmnt till wknd appr 5th, tld off whn pld up bef last....(33 to 1 op 25 to 1)   pu
SPRING HEBE [100] 6-10-3⁵ G Upton, hld up, badly hmpd on bend aftr 5th, not reco'r, tld off whn pld up bef 2 out.
.................................(25 to 1 op 16 to 1)   pu
Dist: 1¾l, 3½l, 7l, 2½l, 2½l, 22l, 2½l, dist, dist. 6m 25.50s. a 50.50s (15 Ran).
(Starlight Racing), D R Gandolfo

1577 Tipperary Novices' Chase Class E (5-y-o and up) £3,070 2m 110yds (3:25)

OR ROYAL (Fr) [11-5 A P McCoy, hld up in tch, al gng wl, wnt second 6th, led 3 out, pushed out. (11 to 10 on tchd 5 to 4)   1
1236² SUPER COIN 8-10-12 A Maguire, pld hrd, led 3rd, hit 5 out, mstk nxt, hdd 3 out, ev ch whn stumbled on landing last, rdn and ran on..........(11 to 4 op 2 to 1 tchd 3 to 1)   2
GORDON 5-10-12 C Maude, hld up, hdwy 5 out, nvr nr to chal................(40 to 1 op 33 to 1 tchd 50 to 1)   3
1349⁵ DRESS DANCE (Ire) 6-10-7 (5*) Sophie Mitchell, trkd ldrs to 7th, wknd 5 out.........(66 to 1 op 25 to 1)   4
1135⁵ GLENDOE (Ire) 5-10-12 G Upton, hld up, hdwy 7th, wknd appr 5 out, lft 3rd and btn whn blun tree out.
.................................(40 to 1 op 14 to 1 tchd 50 to 1)   5
MYSTIC COURT (Ire) 5-10-12 S McNeill, hld up, beh frm 7th, tld off.................(20 to 1 op 10 to 1 tchd 50 to 1)   6
BANKONIT (Ire) 6-10-12 T J Murphy, mstks, al beh, tld off.
.................................(66 to 1 op 33 to 1)   7
1346² MOUSE BIRD (Ire) 6-10-12 R Dunwoody, hld up in rear, hdwy 6th, rdn 3rd whn f 3 out.
..........(7 to 2 op 4 to 1 tchd 9 to 1 and 5 to 1)   f
1448⁷ THE WAYWARD BISHOP (Ire) 7-10-12 J R Kavanagh, led to 3rd, second whn hit 6th, blun and uns rdr nxt.
.................................(100 to 1 op 50 to 1)   ur
Dist: 1l, 18l, 1¼l, sht-hd, 30l, dist. 4m 13.90s. a 16.90s (9 Ran).
SR: 37/29/11/9/9/-/ (D A Johnson), M C Pipe

1578 Weatherbys 'Stars Of Tomorrow' Open National Hunt Flat Standard - Class H (4,5,6-y-o) £1,744 2m 110yds.....................(3:55)

197

1306* LADY REBECCA 4-11-9 A Maguire, *al in tch and gng wl, led on bit 4 out, quickened ins last, very easily.* ....(5 to 2 op 6 to 4) 1
SHORE PARTY (Ire) 4-10-11 (7*) L Suthern, *al prmnt, ev ch 4 out, hrd rdn ins fnl 2 fs, no imprsn.* ....(7 to 4 fav op 6 to 4 tchd 2 to 1) 2
STRONG TEL (Ire) 6-11-4 R Hughes, *hld up, gd hdwy 7 fs out, led briefly 5 out, rdn and one pace aftr.* (20 to 1 op 12 to 1) 3
REPEAT OFFER 4-11-4 C Maude, *hld up, hdwy 6 fs out, wknd 3 out*.... (33 to 1 op 20 to 1) 4
FINE SPIRIT 4-10-8 (5*) Chris Webb, *trkd ldrs, wknd 3 fs out.* .... (66 to 1 op 50 to 1) 5
MISTER CHIPS 5-11-4 R Dunwoody, *hld up in rear, nvr on terms*....(11 to 1 op 10 to 1 tchd 12 to 1) 6
ST MELLION LEISURE (Ire) 4-11-4 A P McCoy, *led for 2 fs, led ag'n hfwy, hng rght and hdd 5 out, sn btn.* .... (10 to 3 op 5 to 2 tchd 7 to 2) 7
1109[4] WILLOWS ROULETTE 4-10-11 (7*) O Burrows, *pld hrd, prmnt till wknd 6 fs out*....(12 to 1 tchd 14 to 1) 8
VANSELL 5-10-13 S McNeill, *prmnt till wknd 6 fs out.* ....(20 to 1 op 12 to 1) 9
COUNTRY KRIS 4-11-4 G Upton, *hld up, effrt hfwy, sn btn.* ....(66 to 1 op 50 to 1 tchd 100 to 1) 10
BABY LANCASTER 5-10-11 (7*) M Griffiths, *al beh, tld off* ....(66 to 1 op 50 to 1) 11
SAUCY'S WOLF 6-10-11 (7*) Mr J Tizzard, *prmnt till wknd 7 fs out, tld off*....(200 to 1 op 100 to 1) 12
1306 MISSED THE MATCH 6-11-4 P McLoughlin, *al beh, tld off.* ....(100 to 1 op 50 to 1) 13
FORTUNES GLEAM (Ire) 5-10-13 T J Murphy, *hld up, al beh, tld off*....(20 to 1 op 16 to 1 tchd 33 to 1) 14
1240 MINGAY 5-11-4 Mrs S Bosley, *sddl slpd, out of control and led aftr 2 fs, hdd hfwy, sn tld off*....(100 to 1) 15
Dist: 2½l, 12l, 2l, 12l, 6l, ½l, 1¼l, 10l, ½l, 25l. 4m 16.00s. (15 Ran).
(Kinnersley Optimists), Miss Venetia Williams

DOWNPATRICK (IRE) (heavy)
Wednesday November 27th

1579 Bishopscourt Maiden Hurdle (4-y-o) £1,370 2m 1f 172yds.... (1:15)

1193[5] FALLOW TRIX (Ire) 10-11 (7*) Mr J Keville, ...(9 to 4) 1
1404[7] SHANNON GALE (Ire) 11-4 L P Cusack, ...(9 to 2) 2
1273[9] MIDDLEOFTHENIGHT (Ire) 10-13 P L Malone, ...(8 to 1) 3
ABIGAIL ROSE (Bel) 10-13 D T Evans, ...(12 to 1) 4
1088[3] LEWISHAM (Ire) 11-9 C F Swan, ...(5 to 4 fav) 5
1143 ZIGGY THE GREAT (Ire) (bl) 11-4 P A Roche, ... (33 to 1) 6
1143 HARRY WELSH (Ire) (bl) 11-9 F Woods, ...(20 to 1) 7
468 JARSUN QUEEN (Ire) 10-6 (7*) L J Fleming, ...(14 to 1) 8
1533 MY BLUE 10-13 A Powell, ...(14 to 1) 9
SCATHACH (Ire) 10-13 H Rogers, ...(33 to 1) 10
NATIVE CAILIN (Ire) 10-6 (7*) G Martin, ...(33 to 1) 11
SKYLITE BOY (Ire) 10-13 (5*) J Butler, ...(33 to 1) 12
JIMMY JANE (Ire) 10-6 (7*) Mr J J Canavan, ...(66 to 1) 13
1275 BEHY BRIDGE (Ire) 10-13 T J Mitchell, ...(20 to 1) f
Dist: 2l, 3l, 12l, 1l. 4m 33.40s. (14 Ran).
(Laggallon Racing Syndicate), J R Cox

1580 Killyleagh Maiden Hurdle (5-y-o and up) £1,370 2½m.... (1:45)

1279[8] BALLYMACREVAN (Ire) 6-11-6 C F Swan, ...(10 to 1) 1
1484[3] TURRAMURRA GIRL (Ire) 7-11-2 (7*) L J Fleming, ...(9 to 2) 2
1278[4] STORM GEM (Ire) 5-11-9 T J Mitchell, ...(9 to 4 jt-fav) 3
1460 TWENTYFIVEQUID (Ire) 5-12-0 Mr P F Graffin, ...(12 to 1) 4
1432[9] VALLEY ERNE (Ire) 5-11-6 Mr A J Martin, ...(9 to 4 jt-fav) 5
EUROTHATCH (Ire) 8-11-6 J Shortt, ...(16 to 1) 6
1273 SLEWMORE (Ire) 5-11-3 (3*) U Smyth, ...(14 to 1) 7
1432 COLOURED SPARROW (Ire) 6-10-8 (7*) S M McGovern, ...(12 to 1) 8
1432 COULTERS HILL (Ire) 8-10-13 (7*) A O'Shea, ...(25 to 1) 9
1463 ZUZUS PETALS (Ire) 6-10-12 (3*) G Cotter, ...(25 to 1) 10
1536 BLACKTRENCH LADY (Ire) 8-11-9 H Rogers, ...(10 to 1) 11
BUCKAMERE (Ire) 5-11-1 P L Malone, ...(14 to 1) 12
1548 LET HER RUN WILD (Ire) 5-11-1 F J Flood, ...(12 to 1) 13
1373[8] DARA KNIGHT (Ire) 7-10-13 (7*) G Martin, ...(25 to 1) 14
1193 EIRE (Ire) 7-12-0 F Woods, ...(14 to 1) pu
Dist: 3½l, sht-hd, 20l, nk. 5m 38.00s. (15 Ran).
(Good Time Managers Syndicate), I A Duncan

1581 Irvinestown Handicap Hurdle (0-102 4-y-o and up) £1,370 2½m.... (2:15)

1407[9] STONELEIGH TURBO (Ire) [-] 7-11-2 (7*) A O'Shea, (9 to 1) 1
SONG FOR AFRICA (Ire) [-] (bl) 5-10-3 P L Malone, (12 to 1) 2
1278[8] GLENFIELDS CASTLE (Ire) [-] 6-11-4 D J Casey, ..(16 to 1) 3
209[3] BALLINAGREEN (Ire) [-] 6-11-10 C F Swan, ...(10 to 1) 4
946[4] STAR TRIX (Ire) [-] 5-10-3 H Rogers, ...(14 to 1) 5
1144 BUCKLEY BAY (Ire) [-] 5-9-9 (3*) B Bowens, ...(20 to 1) 6
1361[6] THE THIRD MAN (Ire) [-] 7-10-0 P McWilliams, ...(10 to 1) 7
1433[5] TRENCH HILL LASS (Ire) [-] 7-11-10 J Shortt, .. (2 to 1 fav) 8
1361[5] COLLIERS HILL (Ire) [-] 8-10-13 F Woods, ...(8 to 1) 9
1080 JESSIE'S BOY (Ire) [-] 7-11-1 J K Kinane, ...(16 to 1) 10
1460[9] CORALDA (Ire) [-] (bl) 5-9-7 W Slattery, ...(20 to 1) 11
1273[2] FALCARRAGH (Ire) [-] 6-10-13 M Duffy, ...(7 to 2) 12
344 CORMAC LADY (Ire) [-] 5-9-13 T J Mitchell, ...(20 to 1) 13
1550[4] BOHOLA PETE (Ire) [-] (bl) 5-9-13 (3*) G Cotter, ...(5 to 1) su
907 MAKE AN EFFORT (Ire) [-] 5-11-7 (7*) Mr G A Kingston, ...(10 to 1) pu
Dist: 2l, sht-hd, 10l, 2l. 5m 28.00s. (15 Ran).
(John G Doyle), P A Fahy

1582 Carryduff Shopping Centre Handicap Chase (0-102 4-y-o and up) £1,541 2¼m.... (2:45)

1040 MILLBROOK LAD (Ire) [-] 8-10-13 D T Evans, ...(7 to 1) 1
1551 HANNIES GIRL (Ire) [-] 7-10-8 (7*) L J Fleming, ...(7 to 2) 2
949[2] MASTER MILLER [-] 10-10-0 (3*) G Cotter, ...(6 to 1) 3
1408[3] LA-GREINE [-] 9-11-10 C F Swan, ... (2 to 1 fav) 4
1534 TOUT VA BIEN [-] 8-12-0 P L Malone, ...(5 to 2) 5
1376[3] DIAMOND SPRITE (USA) [-] (bl) 9-9-11 (7*) G Martin, ...(14 to 1) 6
JIMMYS DOUBLE [-] 10-9-8[8] (7*) Mr J J Canavan, (20 to 1) 7
Dist: ¾l, ¾l, hd, 4l. 4m 56.70s. (7 Ran).
(T J Topping), William Patton

1583 Toal Bookmakers E.B.F. Mares Novices' Chase (4-y-o and up) £3,425 2½m.... (3:15)

1242* DUN BELLE (Ire) 7-11-13 T J Mitchell, ... (7 to 4 on) 1
1075[7] MISS ELIZABETH (Ire) 6-11-7 C F Swan, ...(8 to 1) 2
1435[8] MARLAST (Ire) 5-11-4 J Shortt, ... (4 to 1) 3
1552[4] WHAT IT IS (Ire) 7-11-7 P McWilliams, ...(7 to 2) 4
Dist: 3½l, 20l, dist. 5m 37.10s. (4 Ran).
(Mrs A Connolly), P A Fahy

1584 H.S.S. Hire Shops I.N.H. Flat Race (4-y-o and up) £1,541 2m 1f 172yds.... (3:45)

1241[6] REMAINDER STAR (Ire) 5-11-7 (7*) Mr A C Coyle, ...(6 to 4 fav) 1
577[4] SARAH BLUE (Ire) 6-11-9 Mr P Fenton, ...(5 to 1) 2
929 HOME I'LL BE (Ire) 6-12-0 Mr P F Graffin, ...(8 to 1) 3
1195 KILPATRICK (Ire) 5-11-2 (7*) Mr C J Swords, ...(9 to 2) 4
WHAT EVER YOU WANT (Ire) 6-11-2 (7*) Mr M Callaghan, ...(25 to 1) 5
TOMMYS BAND (Ire) 5-12-0 Mr G J Harford, ...(4 to 1) 6
THAT'S LUCY (Ire) 5-11-2 (7*) Mr M O'Connor, ...(25 to 1) 7
1490[8] MIDNIGHT JOY (Ire) (bl) 4-11-4 Mr D Marnane, ... (10 to 1) 8
647[5] IRISH OATS (Ire) 6-11-7 (7*) Mr R Marrs, ...(16 to 1) 9
1360 WINTER PRINCESS 5-11-2 (7*) Mr A Stronge, ...(8 to 1) 10
SHINORA (Ire) 5-11-2 (7*) Mr G T Morrow, ...(20 to 1) 11
STORM DIEU (Ire) 4-10-11 (7*) Mr L Madine, ...(12 to 1) 0
DJENNE (Ire) 4-10-11 (7*) Mr W Ewing, ...(10 to 1) su
Dist: 1l, dist, 9l, 9l. 4m 32.70s. (13 Ran).
(P J W Byrne), P A Fahy

HEXHAM (good)
Wednesday November 27th

Going Correction: PLUS 0.25 sec. per fur. (races 1,3,5), PLUS 0.15 (2,4,6)

1585 Federation Brewery LCL Pils Novices' Chase Class E (5-y-o and up) £3,479 3m 1f.... (1:05)

1152[2] CHOPWELL CURTAINS 6-10-12 P Niven, *trkd ldrs, slight ld bef 2 out, hrd pressed last, styd on und pres.* ....(2 to 1 on op 7 to 4 on tchd 9 to 4 on) 1
MAMICA 6-10-12 N Smith, *in tch, hdwy aftr 12th, dsptd ld last, no extr und pres*.... (20 to 1 tchd 25 to 1) 2
1183[4] TICO GOLD 8-10-9 (3*) G Cahill, *cl up, chalg whn mstk 2 out, btn when mistake last*....(10 to 1) 3
1329 DAWN LAD (Ire) 7-10-12 J Supple, *in tch, hdwy to track ldrs aftr 15th, ev ch 2 out, sn wknd*....(9 to 1 op 8 to 1) 4
1256[7] AYLESBURY LAD (Ire) 7-10-12 J Burke, *cl up, led 8th till hdd bef 2 out, wknd betw last two*....(50 to 1) 5
SENORA D'OR 6-10-7 B Storey, *in tch, hdwy to track ldrs 12th, wknd aftr 2 out*.... (14 to 1 tchd 16 to 1) 6
1256[4] ROYAL SURPRISE 9-10-12 T Reed, *beh frm 12th, tld off.* .... (12 to 1 op 10 to 1) 7
1329 DEAR JEAN 6-10-7 D Parker, *sn beh, tld off*....(33 to 1) 8
1250[7] MONYMAX (Ire) 7-10-12 Richard Guest, *led till hdd 8th, prmnt till wknd aftr 13th*....(50 to 1 op 33 to 1) 9
1256 SMALL N SMART 6-10-12 K Johnson, *mstk 4th, al beh, tld off.* ....(50 to 1) 10
MONKSAAN (Ire) 7-10-12 R Garritty, *beh whn f 3rd.* ....(10 to 1 op 6 to 1) f
1374[6] NIJWAY 6-10-7 (5*) S Taylor, *chsd ldrs, mstk 4th, blun 12th, wkng whn blunded and uns rdr 14th*.. (20 to 1 op 14 to 1) ur
Dist: 1l, 11l, 6l, 1¼l, 9l, 27l, 9l, 11l, 4l. 6m 22.50s. a 17.50s (12 Ran).
(Durham Drapes Ltd), T D Easterby

1586 Federation Brewery Special Ale Novices' Handicap Hurdle Class E (0-100 3-y-o and up) £2,595 2½m

110yds.....................(1:35)

12572 KINGS MINSTRAL (Ire) [66] 6-10-5 J Burke, *hld up early, gd hdwy to ld aftr second, clr whn hit last, styd on wl.*
.........................(11 to 1 op 10 to 1 tchd 12 to 1) 1
DASHMAR [63] 9-10-2 D Bentley, *in tch, outpcd aftr 7th, rallied bef last, styd on, no ch wth wnr.*
.........................(20 to 1 op 14 tchd 25 to 1) 2
1337* CLEVER BOY [67] 5-10-6 N Williamson, *hld up in tch, effrt aftr 7th, kpt on same pace.......... (5 to 2 tchd 3 to 1) 3
1313* LIFEBUOY (Ire) [84] 5-11-9 T Reed, *hld up, gd hdwy to track ldrs aftr 7th, rdn and wknd bef last.. (2 to 1 fav op 5 to 2) 4
13136 ENVIRONMENTAL LAW [72] 5-10-8 (3*) G Cahill, *prmnt till wknd quickly bef last, tld off.*
.........................(11 to 1 op 7 to 1 tchd 12 to 1) 5
11885 LAGAN [100] 3-11-8 A S Smith, *led till hdd aftr second, prmnt till wknd quickly aftr 7th, tld off....(5 to 2 op 5 to 4) 6
14646 MISS MONT [61] 7-10-0 R Hodge, *lost tch aftr 7th, tld off whn pld up bef last...............(33 to 1 op 20 to 1) pu
Dist: 6l, nk, 1¾l, 28l, 18l. 5m 3.20s. a 12.20s (7 Ran).

(Exors Of The Late Mr R R Lamb), D A Lamb

1587 Keoghans Novices' Chase Class E (5-y-o and up) £3,206 2m 110yds ....(2:05)

13376 ELLIOTT'S WISH (Ire) 5-10-12 N Williamson, *in tch, hdwy hfwy, no imprsn on ldr whn lft in ld last, hld on und pres.*
.........................(16 to 1 tchd 20 to 1) 1
13748 UK HYGIENE (Ire) 6-10-12 R Garritty, *led till hdd 5th, prmnt, outpcd aftr 2 out, rallied after last, styd on und pres.*
.........................(4 to 1 op 6 to 1 tchd 7 to 2) 2
960 CROCKALAWN (Ire) 8-10-12 Mr M Thompson, *led 5th till hdd betw last 2, no extr................(50 to 1 op 33 to 1) 3
1523 BONNY JOHNNY 6-10-12 D J Moffatt, *beh till on wl frm betw last 2, nvr finish................(50 to 1 op 33 to 1) 4
DARK BUOY 7-10-12 B Storey, *mid-div, outpcd bef 2 out, styd on frm last.....................(33 to 1 op 25 to 1) 5
1068 WEE WIZARD (Ire) 7-10-7 (5*) S Taylor, *beh till some late hdwy, nvr dngrs...................(25 to 1 op 20 to 1) 6
1374 FINE TUNE (Ire) 6-10-12 A Thornton, *chsd ldrs till wknd appr 2 out.......................(33 to 1) 7
364 MISTER CASUAL 7-10-12 T Reed, *nvr on terms.*
.........................(25 to 1 op 20 to 1) 8
12505 FAIR ALLY 6-10-12 D Parker, *prmnt, ch whn slpd and f 2 out.*
.........................(33 to 1) f
10492 HIGHLAND WAY (Ire) 8-10-12 M Dwyer, *in tch whn f 7th.*
.........................(4 to 1 tchd 9 to 2 and 7 to 2) f
13776 ETHICAL NOTE (Ire) 5-10-12 Richard Guest, *in tch whn f 7th.*
.........................(20 to 1 op 16 to 1) f
1281 GOLDEN HELLO 5-11-5 P Niven, *hld up, hdwy hfwy, led betw last 2, 4 ls clr whn blun, swrvd rght and uns rdr last.*
.........................(7 to 4 fav op 11 to 10 tchd 2 to 1) ur
4624 FENWICK'S BROTHER 6-10-12 Mr P Murray, *prmnt whn blun and uns rdr second (water)...........(33 to 1) ur
13747 BOLANEY GIRL (Ire) 7-10-7 B Harding, *in tch, staying on whn slpd up betw last 2........(8 to 1 op 7 to 1 tchd 9 to 1) su
Dist: ½l, 2½l, 1l, 4l, 1½l, nk. 4m 8.90s. a 10.90s (14 Ran).

SR: 16/15/12/11/7/5/4/-/-/ (David M Fulton), J Howard Johnson

1588 Federation Brewery Handicap Hurdle Class F (0-105 4-y-o and up) £2,156 2m.............(2:35)

12482 ANABRANCH [98] 5-11-2 (7*) M Newton, *mid-div, hdwy hfwy, led 5th, clr last, easily..............(9 to 2 fav op 4 to 1) 1
1248* TIP IT IN [85] 7-10-3 (7*) N Horrocks, *hld up, rdn bef last, styd on, no ch wth wnr............(5 to 1 op 4 to 1) 2
1313 COURT JOKER (Ire) [77] 4-10-2 B Storey, *led to 3rd, chsd ldrs aftr, kpt on same pace frm bef last.....(13 to 1 op 10 to 1) 3
11674 NONIOS (Ire) [97] (v) 5-11-8 N Bentley, *prmnt, led 3rd till hdd 5th, wknd bef last..........(11 to 2 op 9 to 2 tchd 6 to 1) 4
20144 AUBURN BOY [103] 9-12-0 R Garritty, *hld up, hdwy aftr 5th, chsd wnr bef last, wknd und pres r-in.*
.........................(13 to 2 op 6 to 1 tchd 7 to 1) 5
IN A MOMENT (USA) [75] 5-10-0 J Callaghan, *beh, pushed aftr 4th, nvr dngrs...............(10 to 1 op 7 to 1) 6
1068 JOYRIDER [91] 5-11-2 A S Smith, *chsd ldrs till drvn alng and lost pl aftr 4th, no dngr after.*
.........................(10 to 1 tchd 11 to 1 and 12 to 1) 7
13354 WELL APPOINTED (Ire) [95] 7-11-3 (3*) G Lee, *trkd ldrs, alng aftr 5th, wknd bef last...........(11 to 2 op 5 to 1) 8
1122* FLY TO THE END (USA) [75] 6-10-0 N Williamson, *beh, drvn alng and some hdwy aftr 5th, wknd quickly bef last, tld off.*
.........................(6 to 1 op 5 to 1) 9
Dist: 12l, 1½l, hd, 4l, ¾l, ¾l, 3½l, 30l. 3m 58.90s. a 9.90s (9 Ran).

SR: 20/-/-/5/7/-/ (Mrs M Barker), J M Jefferson

1589 Federation Brewery Buchanan Handicap Chase Class F (0-95 4-y-o and up) £2,962 2½m 110yds.. (3:05)

1254* BUYERS DREAM (Ire) [81] (v) 6-10-11 (3*) G Cahill, *mid-div, drvn alng and hdwy bef 2 out, led last, styd on und pres.*
.........................(7 to 1 op 6 to 1) 1

1254 WILLIE SPARKLE [76] 10-10-9 M Foster, *mid-div, outpcd aftr 11th, rallied bef last, rdn and ev ch r-in, no extr clsg stages.*
.........................(14 to 1 op 12 to 1 tchd 16 to 1) 2
9153 GRAND SCENERY (Ire) [90] 8-11-9 N Williamson, *beh, hdwy aftr 10th, styd on same pace appr last.*
.........................(13 to 2 op 6 to 1 tchd 8 to 1 and 9 to 1) 3
12533 JUKE BOX BILLY (Ire) [86] 8-11-5 A Dobbin, *beh, hdwy to chase ldrs 10th, rdn to ld appr last, sn hdd, no extr. (6 to 1 jt-fav op 11 to 2) 4
14713 WAYUPHILL [87] 9-11-1 (5*) R McGrath, *in tch, hdwy to ld 10th, hdd appr last, sn btn. (7 to 1 op 5 to 1 tchd 8 to 1) 5
1253 HURRICANE ANDREW (Ire) [88] 8-11-7 Mr N Wilson, *sn beh, styd on frm 2 out, nvr dngrs.....(25 to 1 op 20 to 1) 6
1328 GALA WATER [86] 10-11-5 T Reed, *in tch till outpcd aftr 9th, no dngr after.....................(16 to 1) 7
1329* CADER IDRIS [86] 7-11-5 P Niven, *mid-div till outpcd aftr 9th, no dngr after...................(20 to 1 op 16 to 1) 8
1161 MOVAC (Ire) [90] 7-11-9 A Thornton, *prmnt, led 8th, hdd 10th, wknd aftr 2 out...............(13 to 2 op 4 to 1) 9
12543 FORWARD GLEN [76] (bl) 9-10-9 A S Smith, *beh most of way.*
.........................(10 to 1 op 10 to 1 tchd 12 to 1) 10
13165 SUPER SANDY [88] 9-11-7 K Johnson, *sn prmnt, wknd aftr 9th.....................(16 to 1 tchd 20 to 1) 11
12836 SIDE OF HILL [91] 11-11-7 (3*) G Lee, *led till hdd 8th, wkng whn blun 11th.......(14 to 1 op 12 to 1 tchd 16 to 1) 12
1376 SEE YOU ALWAYS (Ire) [67] 6-9-9 (5*) S Taylor, *chsd ldrs till wknd aftr 9th.....................(50 to 1 op 33 to 1) 13
12533 SUPPOSIN [92] 8-11-11 Richard Guest, *al beh.*
.........................(8 to 1 op 10 to 1) 14
Dist: Nk, 2½l, 2l, 2½l, 2½l, nk, ½l, 5l, 13l, 8l. 5m 12.40s. a 14.40s (14 Ran).
(Brian Chicken), B Ellison

1590 Federation Brewery Medallion Lager Intermediate Open National Hunt Flat Class H (4,5,6-y-o) £1,343 2m ....(3:35)

13177 BOLD STATEMENT 4-11-4 N Bentley, *made all, clr one furlong out, styd on.............(5 to 1 tchd 6 to 1) 1
FOR CATHAL (Ire) 5-11-4 P Niven, *in tch, styd on fnl 2 fs, no imprsn on wnr........(4 to 1 op 2 to 1 tchd 9 to 2) 2
BOBBY GRANT 5-11-4 N Williamson, *nvr far away, drvn alng 3 fs out, kpt on same pace..........(20 to 1 op 16 to 1) 3
13902 LORD OF THE LOCH (Ire) 5-11-4 M Foster, *hld up, hdwy hfwy, ev ch 2 fs out, sn rdn and btn......(11 to 8 fav op 5 to 4) 4
1317 NAUTILUS THE THIRD (Ire) 5-11-4 R Garritty, *prmnt till wknd 3 fs out..............(16 to 1 op 14 to 1 tchd 20 to 1) 5
RUN FOR THE MILL 4-10-11 (7*) M Newton, *chsd ldrs till wknd o'r 3 fs out........(7 to 1 op 8 to 1 tchd 14 to 1) 6
TARTAN JOY (Ire) 5-11-4 N Smith, *sn beh, nvr dngrs.*
.........................(25 to 1 op 16 to 1) 7
BORIS BROOK 5-10-11 (7*) S Melrose, *sn beh, nvr dngrs.*
.........................(50 to 1 op 33 to 1) 8
QUEENS BRIGADE 4-11-4 B Storey, *sn beh, nvr dngrs.*
.........................(50 to 1 op 33 to 1) 9
GUILE POINT 5-10-13 J Burke, *chsd ldrs till wknd 3 fs out.*
.........................(50 to 1 op 33 to 1) 10
1390 CHINOOK'S DAUGHTER (Ire) 4-10-13 A Dobbin, *mid-div till wknd 4 fs out.............(100 to 1 op 50 to 1) 11
ONLY A SIOUX 4-11-4 W Fry, *mid-div till wknd 4 fs out.*
.........................(50 to 1) 12
11285 SAFETY TIP 4-10-13 Miss P Robson, *in tch till wknd 5 fs out, tld off.....................(50 to 1 op 33 to 1) 13
MAGSLASS 4-10-8 (5*) R McGrath, *sn beh, tld off.*
.........................(20 to 1 op 33 to 1 tchd 50 to 1) 14
Dist: 4l, 1¼l, 3l, 8l, 5l, nk, 4l, ¾l, 4l, 4l. 3m 57.70s. (14 Ran).
(R I Graham), G M Moore

WINDSOR (good)
Wednesday November 27th
Going Correction: NIL (races 1,2,4,6,7), PLUS 0.10 (3,5)

1591 River Thames 'National Hunt' Novices' Hurdle Class D (Div I) (4-y-o and up) £2,602 2½m............(12:45)

1322* LADY PETA 6-11-4 M A Fitzgerald, *hld up, keen hold, led on bit aftr 2 out, idled and hrd rdn r-in, all out.*
.........................(Evens fav op 5 to 8 on tchd 11 to 10) 1
13697 RIVER BAY 5-10-7 B Fenton, *cl up, led 4 out, hit 2 out, sn hdd, blun last, rallied und pres, jst hld.. (9 to 2 op 3 to 1) 2
13069 DARK CHALLENGER (Ire) 4-10-12 W Marston, *in tch, cld appr 5th, pushed alng approaching 4 out, not fluent nxt, kpt on.....................(10 to 1 op 6 to 1 tchd 12 to 1) 3
879 NUNSON 7-10-12 C Llewellyn, *hld up, cld 4th, mstk 6th, sn outpcd.....................(33 to 1 op 14 to 1) 4
GROSVENOR (Ire) 5-10-12 J Osborne, *trkd ldrs, cld 5th, ev ch aftr 3 out, pushed alng and wknd quickly appr nxt.
.........................(2 to 1 op 9 to 4) 5
THE MILLMASTER (Ire) (bl) 5-10-12 R Supple, *trkd ldrs, mstk 4 out and drvn alng, sn wknd, tld off.. (40 to 1 op 14 to 1) 6
1477 ALL OVER RED ROVER 4-10-12 P Hide, *not fluent, led till hdd 4 out, wknd nxt, tld off. (20 to 1 tchd 25 to 1 and 16 to 1) 7
Dist: Hd, 9l, 14l, 2l, 19l, 19l. 4m 53.70s. a 13.70s (7 Ran).

(B M Collins), N J Henderson

1592 River Thames 'National Hunt' Novices' Hurdle Class D (Div II) (4-y-o and up) £2,581 2½m..........(1:15)

SPARKLING SPRING (Ire) 5-10-12 C O'Dwyer, *hld up beh, not fluent 6th, hdwy appr 3 out, led and hit last, ran on wl und pres*..................(11 to 1 op 5 to 1 tchd 12 to 1) 1
BEST OF FRIENDS (Ire) 6-10-12 B Fenton, *trkd ldrs, outpcd appr 3 out, rallied aftr nxt, not fluent last, ev ch, kpt on und pres*..........................(4 to 1 op 3 to 1) 2
NONE STIRRED (Ire) 6-10-12 P Hide, *hld up, hdwy aftr 6th, led after 4 out, hdd 2 out, hrd rdn and ev ch r-in, kpt on.*..................................(5 to 2 tchd 3 to 1) 3
1228* MILLERSFORD 5-11-4 C Llewellyn, *trkd ldrs, pushed alng appr 3 out, ev ch approaching nxt, kpt on one pace und pres.*..................................(2 to 1 fav op 9 to 4) 4
1413* DREAM LEADER (Ire) 6-11-4 J Railton, *led till hdd aftr 4 out, led ag'n 2 out to last, wknd und pres last 100 yards.*(9 to 1 op 6 to 1 tchd 10 to 1) 5
1379^{4} OPERETTO (Ire) 6-10-12 D Bridgwater, *cl up till wknd appr [illegible] out*..................(25 to 1 op 20 to 1 tchd 33 to 1) 6
1240^{3} IVORY COASTER (NZ) 5-10-12 J Osborne, *trkd ldrs, hrd rdn and wknd appr 2 out, eased.*............(15 to 2 op 6 to 1 tchd 8 to 1 and 9 to 1) 7
1026^{7} BARRIE STIR 4-10-12 D Gallagher, *hld up in rear, hit 5th, lost tch nxt, pld up bef 3 out.* (25 to 1 op 14 to 1 tchd 33 to 1) pu
1217 ALI'S DELIGHT 5-10-12 M A Fitzgerald, *hld up in tch, lost touch aftr 6th, pld up bef 3 out*......(100 to 1 op 50 to 1) pu

Dist: ½l, sht-hd, 2l, 2l, 13l, 20l. 4m 51.00s. a 11.00s (9 Ran).
(E Benfield), K C Bailey

1593 Windsor Novices' Handicap Chase Class E (0-100 5-y-o and up) £3,241 3m..........................(1:45)

1302^{2} CALL ME RIVER (Ire) [64] 8-10-1 I Lawrence, *jmpd wl, sn cl up, led 4 out, clr nxt, easily*...... (6 to 1 co-fav op 5 to 1) 1
1250 JAC DEL PRINCE [64] 6-10-1[1] P Hide, *led till hdd 4 out, kpt on same pace und pres, no ch wth wnr*... (33 to 1 op 20 to 1) 2
1473^{3} CARDINAL RULE (Ire) [70] 7-10-7 R Farrant, *trkd ldrs, outpcd 4 out, btn whn jmpd lft 2 out*.......... (14 to 1 op 12 to 1) 3
1473 MINGUS (USA) [83] 9-10-13 (7*) Mr B Dixon, *chsd ldg grp, blun 4th, pushed alng 12th, styd on same pace frm four out.*.................................(25 to 1 op 20 to 1) 4
1494 THE BRUD [80] 8-11-3 J A McCarthy, *hld up beh, styd on frm 2 out, nrst finish*......................(14 to 1 op 10 to 1) 5
1352 OXFORD QUILL [72] 9-10-9 D Morris, *mid-div, hdwy appr 4 out, sn outpcd*..........................(9 to 1 op 6 to 1) 6
1356* LA MEZERAY [76] 8-10-10 (3*) D Walsh, *chsd ldrs, mstk 13th, drvn aftr nxt, sn btn.* (6 to 1 co-fav op 5 to 1 tchd 7 to 1) 7
1451^{4} ITS GRAND [67] (bl) 7-10-1 (3*) T Dascombe, *cl up till pushed alng and lost pl 8th, sn beh, tld off*.....(10 to 1 op 12 to 1) 8
BOURNEL [83] 8-11-6 B Fenton, *al beh, tld off.*.................................(33 to 1 op 25 to 1) 9
1339 WESTERLY GALE (Ire) [76] 6-10-13 M A Fitzgerald, *trkd ldrs, hrd rdn aftr 5 out, f nxt*.........................(6 to 1 co-fav op 9 to 2 tchd 13 to 2) f
1498 MASTER PANGLOSS (Ire) [63] 6-10-0 L Harvey, *mid-div, hit 7th, no ch whn f 4 out*..............(16 to 1 op 12 to 1) f
ROMANY BLUES [63] 7-10-0 D Gallagher, *trkd ldrs, blun 13th, sn wknd, hld whn blunded and uns rdr last.*..........................(9 to 1 op 10 to 1 tchd 8 to 1) ur
THE WHOLE HOG (Ire) [78] 7-11-1 C O'Dwyer, *hld up in rear, blun 14th, beh whn blunded and uns rdr 4 out.*......................(16 to 1 op 12 to 1 tchd 20 to 1) ur
1298^{4} AINSI SOIT IL (Fr) [80] (bl) 5-11-1 B Clifford, *al beh, tld off whn blun and uns rdr 4 out*............. (33 to 1 op 20 to 1) ur
1411^{2} DAMCADA (Ire) [67] 8-10-4 W Marston, *al beh, reminders 9th, tld off whn pld up aftr 5 out*........... (12 to 1 op 8 to 1) pu
1399^{4} SASSIVER (USA) [87] 6-11-7 (3*) G Hogan, *not jump wl, al beh, tld off whn pld up aftr 5 out*.......(16 to 1 op 12 to 1) pu

Dist: 11l, 20l, 2½l, hd, 6l, 7l, 25l, 6l. 6m 0.40s. a 7.40s (16 Ran).
SR: 23/12/-/8/5/-/ (The Larkin Around Partnership), P R Hedger

1594 European Breeders Fund Sunninghill 'National Hunt' Novices' Hurdle Qualifier Class D (4,5,6-y-o) £3,078 2m....................(2:15)

READY MONEY CREEK (Ire) 5-11-0 J Osborne, *hld up beh ldrs, outpcd and pushed alng appr 3 out, hdwy nxt, hrd rdn to ld r-in, ran on wl.*............(11 to 10 on op 7 to 4 on tchd 11 to 10) 1
1322^{2} DARAKSHAN (Ire) 4-11-0 J Railton, *led to 5th, sn led ag'n, hdd r-in, kpt on und pres*............. (7 to 2 tchd 5 to 1) 2
HENRYS PORT 6-11-0 M Richards, *cl up till lost pl 3rd, styd on und pres appr last.* (66 to 1 op 40 to 1 tchd 100 to 1) 3
1300^{2} NEAT FEAT (Ire) 5-11-0 A Procter, *hld up beh ldrs, cld 5th, rdn whn mstk 2 out, one pace.* (3 to 1 op 4 to 1 tchd 9 to 2) 4
TREE CREEPER (Ire) 4-11-0 L Harvey, *pld hrd early, trkd ldrs till lost pl 3rd, styd on appr last.*......................(25 to 1 op 14 to 1 tchd 33 to 1) 5
55^{5} ILEWIN JANINE (Ire) 5-10-9 S Fox, *pld hrd, trkd ldr, led briefly 5th, wknd und pres aftr 2 out.*......................(33 to 1 op 16 to 1 tchd 40 to 1) 6
O MY LOVE 5-10-9 B Fenton, *hld up, effrt appr 3 out, sn btn, no ch whn mstk last*.. (50 to 1 op 40 to 1 tchd 100 to 1) 7
1292 FRENO (Ire) 5-11-0 C O'Dwyer, *al beh.*......................(20 to 1 op 12 to 1 tchd 25 to 1) 8
NISHAMAN 5-11-0 M A Fitzgerald, *al beh.*......................(25 to 1 op 14 to 1 tchd 33 to 1) 9
REACH THE CLOUDS (Ire) 4-11-0 R Supple, *pld hrd, trkd ldrs till wknd 7th, tld off*.... (14 to 1 op 20 to 1 tchd 12 to 1) 10
1338 MR GOONHILLY 6-11-0 I Lawrence, *mstk 3rd, in tch till wknd 5th, tld off whn pld up bef 2 out.*......................(66 to 1 op 40 to 1 tchd 100 to 1) pu

Dist: 2l, 2l, 2½l, 1¾l, 12l, 9l, 7l, 7l, 17l. 3m 52.60s. a 7.60s (11 Ran).
SR: 10/8/6/3/1/-/ (Roach Foods Limited), O Sherwood

1595 Datchet Handicap Chase Class E (0-110 4-y-o and up) £3,104 2m ....(2:45)

1176 ZEREDAR (NZ) [100] (bl) 6-11-4 C Llewellyn, *sn tracking ldrs, led appr 2 out, soon clr, very easily.*..............................(100 to 30 fav op 5 to 2) 1
904 [illegible] [101] [illegible] *hdwy 7th, led aftr 4 out, hdd appr 2 out, no ch wth wnr.*......................(20 to 1 op 14 to 1 tchd 25 to 1) 2
1319* FICHU (USA) [82] 8-10-0 M Richards, *hld up, hdwy appr 4 out, styd on one pace und pres*............. (6 to 1 op 4 to 1) 3
RED BEAN [100] 8-11-4 A Dicken, *trkd ldrs, outpcd 4 out, styd on appr last, kpt on*.................(8 to 1 op 14 to 1) 4
1327 CIRCULATION [82] (v) 10-10-0[3] (3*) D Walsh, *led till hdd aftr 4 out, hrd rdn after 2 out, no extr*.........(10 to 1 op 8 to 1) 5
338^{9} SISTER ROSZA (Ire) [96] 8-11-0 R Farrant, *chsd ldrs till lost pl 8th*............................(20 to 1 op 14 to 1) 6
PEGMARINE (USA) [82] 13-9-12[1] (3*) G Hogan, *trkd ldrs till lost pl 6th*......................(16 to 1 op 14 to 1) 7
1301 MISS MARIGOLD [96] (bl) 7-10-11 (3*) T Dascombe, *mstk 3rd, hdwy 7th, wknd 4 out, no ch whn blun 2 out.*...............(6 to 1 op 5 to 1 tchd 7 to 1) 8
THE FLYING FOOTMAN [97] 10-11-1 J Osborne, *hld up, effrt 4 out, no ch whn jmpd rght last*...... (16 to 1 op 12 to 1) 9
EARLY DRINKER [100] 8-11-4 J A McCarthy, *al beh, tld off.*.................................(7 to 2 op 5 to 2) 10

Dist: 4l, 3l, hd, ½l, 8l, ¾l, 2l, 2l, dist. 4m 1.90s. a 7.90s (10 Ran).
SR: 27/30/2/20/1/7/-/4/3/ (I M S Racing), K C Bailey

1596 White Hart Conditional Jockeys' Handicap Hurdle Class E (0-120 4-y-o and up) £2,320 2m..........(3:15)

1416^{2} DONTDRESSFORDINNER [87] 6-10-0 T Dascombe, *trkd ldrs, rdn to ld appr 2 out, drvn alng and ran on wl.*............... (3 to 1 fav op 11 to 4 tchd 100 to 30) 1
1416^{4} PAIR OF JACKS (Ire) [92] 6-10-5 D Fortt, *hld up, cld aftr 4th, ev ch appr 2 out, one pace*.. (9 to 2 tchd 5 to 1 and 4 to 1) 2
AUGUST TWELFTH [87] 8-10-0 D Walsh, *hld up beh, ran on strly frm last, nvr plcd to chal*...... (20 to 1 tchd 25 to 1) 3
1441^{4} YUBRALEE (USA) [115] 4-12-0 E Husband, *led, drvn appr 3rd, hdd approaching 2 out, one pace.*...................... (4 to 1 op 3 to 1 tchd 11 to 4) 4
TICKERTY'S GIFT [112] 6-11-6 (5*) M Attwater, *chsd ldrs, not fluent second, wknd appr 2 out.*......................(9 to 1 op 6 to 1 tchd 10 to 1) 5
SOMERSET DANCER (USA) [87] 9-9-11 (3*) D J Kavanagh, *al beh, tld off*......................(33 to 1 tchd 40 to 1) 6
1424 FULL OF TRICKS [87] 8-9-9 (5*) J Power, *cl up till wknd appr 5th, tld off*...................... (66 to 1 tchd 100 to 1) 7
1417^{6} KALZARI (USA) [87] 11-10-0 P Henley, *in tch, effrt 4th, losing touch whn mstk nxt, tld off when pld up bef 2 out.*...................... (10 to 1 op 8 to 1 tchd 11 to 1) pu
1346^{6} INCULCATE (Ire) [105] (bl) 5-11-4 G Hogan, *cl up till lost pl and rdn 4th, pld up bef nxt.* (5 to 1 op 9 to 2 tchd 4 to 1) pu

Dist: 4l, nk, 2l, 6l, dist, 22l. 3m 51.80s. a 6.80s (9 Ran).
SR: 4/5/-/26/17/-/ (A G Fear And Dontdressfordinner Partners), R J Hodges

1597 Cranbourne Handicap Hurdle Class D (0-125 4-y-o and up) £2,952 2¾m 110yds......................(3:45)

COPPER BOY [107] 7-11-9 B Powell, *keen hold early, made virtually all, hit 3 out, ran on wl.*..........................(7 to 2 op 3 to 1 tchd 4 to 1) 1
1427 KALASADI (USA) [104] (bl) 5-11-6 M Richards, *trkd ldrs, drvn to chal appr 3 out, kpt on one pace und pres.*......................(10 to 1 op 7 to 1 tchd 12 to 1) 2
772^{8} LESSONS LASS (Ire) [102] 4-11-4 J Osborne, *wth wnr, ev ch 3 out, one pace appr nxt.*.........(10 to 1 op 7 to 1 tchd 12 to 1 and 14 to 1) 3
987 MADAME PRESIDENT (Ire) [84] 5-9-11 (3*) G Hogan, *trkd ldrs, outpcd 4 out, kpt on frm last*.....(16 to 1 op 12 to 1) 4
1429* CLAIRESWAN (Ire) [99] 4-11-1 D Gallagher, *cl up, lost pl 6th, rallied 4 out, sn outpcd.* (9 to 4 fav op 2 to 1 tchd 5 to 2) 5
JACKSON FLINT [95] 8-10-11 M A Fitzgerald, *hld up, hdwy appr 3 out, sn btn*.................. (33 to 1 op 20 to 1) 6
RAQIB [109] 5-11-11 S Fox, *mid-div, outpcd frm 7th.*..................................(9 to 1 op 7 to 1) 7
SPINNAKER [105] 6-11-7 C Llewellyn, *hld up, mstk 5th, effrt appr 4 out, sn btn*...... (12 to 1 op 7 to 1 tchd 14 to 1) 8

1454 JADIDH [91] 8-10-2 (5") D Salter, hld up, reminder 5th, wknd
appr 4 out.........................(25 to 1 op 16 to 1) 9
    STROKESAVER (Ire) [94] 6-10-10 G Bradley, hld up, cld 5th,
wknd appr 3 out........................(8 to 1 op 5 to 1) 10
    DONT TELL THE WIFE [112] 10-11-9 (5") Mr R Thornton,
mstks, al beh........................... (20 to 1 tchd 25 to 1) 11
1207⁴ DARING KING [88] 6-10-4 P Hide, trkd ldrs to 7th, sn wknd, tld
off whn pld up bef 2 out...............(12 to 1 op 8 to 1) pu
Dist: 6l, 7l, nk, ¾l, 9l, ¾l, 2½l, 10l, 1½l, 3l. 5m 28.40s. a 13.40s (12 Ran).
                 (C Raymond), R H Buckler

TAUNTON (good to firm)
Thursday November 28th
Going Correction: PLUS 0.25 sec. per fur.

1598 Beech Novices' Hurdle Class C (4-y-o and up) £3,566 2m 1f......(1:25)

1450² YET AGAIN 4-11-0 D Bridgwater, hld up, hdwy appr 6th, hrd
rdn to ld r-in..........(16 to 1 op 14 to 1 tchd 20 to 1) 1
1410* SECRET SPRING (Fr) 4-11-6 M Richards, hld up, hdwy appr
5th, led 2 out, rdn and hdd r-in.
....(13 to 8 on op 11 to 10 on) 2
1354 OUT ON A PROMISE (Ire) 11-11-0 R Hughes, led to 3rd, ev ch 2
out, wknd appr last.........(4 to 1 op 7 to 2 tchd 9 to 2) 3
    RODERICK HUDSON 4-11-0 N Williamson, led 3rd, jmpd
slwly 5th, hdd and mstk 2 out, sn btn.
....(6 to 1 op 7 to 1 tchd 20 to 1) 4
    SPARKLING BUCK 4-10-9 J A McCarthy, hld up, hdwy aftr
4th, ev ch 3 out, wknd quickly appr nxt, tld off.
....(7 to 1 op 5 to 1 tchd 8 to 1) 5
    OFFICE HOURS 4-11-0 W McFarland, al towards rear, lost
tch 6th, tld off.........(40 to 1 op 14 to 1 tchd 50 to 1) 6
1215⁷ ROC AGE 5-10-2 (7") Mr J T Nolan, in tch till wknd 5th, tld off.
....(50 to 1 op 20 to 1) 7
    ANTIGUA'S TREASURE (Ire) 7-10-9 (5") Mr R Thornton, jmpd
slwly 1st, al beh, tld off.............(100 to 1 op 33 to 1) 8
1456⁴ COUNTRY TARQUIN 4-10-7 (7") J Harris, mstk 1st, al beh, tld
off..(16 to 1 op 10 to 1) 9
641⁷ LANDLORD 4-10-11 (3") D Walsh, al beh, tld off.
....(66 to 1 op 33 to 1 tchd 100 to 1) 10
1429 SHARP ELVER (Ire) 4-10-9 P Hide, prmnt till wknd quickly
appr 3 out...............(33 to 1 op 20 to 1 tchd 50 to 1) 11
    RACING HAWK (USA) (v) 4-11-0 P Holley, blun and uns refr
second....................(40 to 1 op 14 to 1 tchd 50 to 1) ur
1306 FAIR HAUL 5-11-0 B Powell, al beh, tld off 5th, pld up bef 2
out.......................................(100 to 1 op 33 to 1) pu
Dist: 1¼l, 10l, 1¾l, 26l, 6l, 1l, 7l, 1½l, 10l, 2½l. 3m 53.90s. a 10.90s (13 Ran).
SR: 19/23/7/5/-/-/   (A P Griffin), Miss Gay Kelleway

1599 Maple Juvenile Novices' Selling Hurdle Class G (3-y-o) £1,994 2m 1f ......(1:55)

    THEME ARENA 10-5 R Hughes, led to second, led appr 5th,
pckd 3 out, clr nxt, eased r-in.........(7 to 1 tchd 10 to 1) 1
    JAMMY JENNY 10-5 T Jenks, al prmnt, wnt second appr 6th,
ev ch aftr 3 out, one pace.............(7 to 1 op 4 to 1) 2
1438³ DARK TRUFFLE 10-5 J A McCarthy, hld up, rdn aftr 4th, hdwy
nxt, held whn mstk 2 out.
....(7 to 4 fav op 6 to 4 tchd 2 to 1) 3
    HAYLING-BILLY 10-3 (7") M Clinton, mid-div, some hdwy aftr
3 out.......................................(25 to 1 op 20 to 1) 4
1209* STONE ISLAND 11-3 N Williamson, pld hrd, hld up, mstk 5th,
hdwy nxt, rdn and wknd 3 out.
....(11 to 2 op 4 to 1 tchd 6 to 1) 5
1412 COLEBROOK WILLIE 10-10 M Bosley, al beh.
....(25 to 1 op 14 to 1) 6
1412⁶ IN CAHOOTS 10-10 F Jousset, pld hrd, prmnt till wknd 6th.
....(10 to 1 op 6 to 1) 7
936⁸ RED TIME 10-10 P Holley, led second, hdd and mstk 5th,
wknd nxt....................................(25 to 1) 8
1524⁶ SAMARA SONG 10-3 (7") N Willmington, chsd ldrs till wknd
quickly 3 out............(7 to 1 op 6 to 1) 9
    NANTGARW 10-5 A Procter, al beh, tld off.
....(12 to 1 op 10 to 1) 10
1221 APPEAL AGAIN (Ire) 10-10 D J Burchell, al beh, f 3 out.
....(20 to 1 op 14 to 1) f
    EWAR BOLD 10-10 B Fenton, blun and uns rdr 3rd.
....(14 to 1 tchd 16 to 1) ur
1209⁵ BLOSSOM DEARIE (bl) 10-5 B Powell, al beh, tld off whn pld
up bef 2 out..............................(33 to 1 op 16 to 1) pu
1422 TRIANNA 10-5 L Harvey, al beh, tld off whn pld up aftr 5th.
....(50 to 1 op 20 to 1) pu
Dist: 7l, 1¼l, 3½l, 15l, 7l, 1¾l, 3l, 5l, dist. 3m 56.50s. a 13.50s (14 Ran).
             (Antony Sofroniou), M C Pipe

1600 Mendip Plywood Novices' Chase Class C (5-y-o and up) £4,531 2m 3f ......(2:25)

1232 GREENBACK (Bel) 5-10-13 N Williamson, made most, jmpd
lft und pres last 3, drw clr r-in..................(Evens fav) 1

    JOVIAL MAN (Ire) 7-11-0 D Bridgwater, hld up, hdwy to track
wnr tenth, ev ch 4 out till wknd appr 2 out.
....(7 to 2 op 5 to 2 tchd 4 to 1) 2
    RAMALLAH 7-11-0 B Fenton, hld up, hdwy appr 9th, one
pace nxt..................(7 to 2 op 3 to 1 tchd 4 to 1) 3
994⁴ CALLEVA STAR (Ire) 5-10-10 (3") P Henley, hld up, outpcd 9th,
btn whn blun 3 out.....................(20 to 1 op 12 to 1) 4
1232 WIXOE WONDER (Ire) 6-11-0 P Holley, dsptd ld early, trkd
wnr till wknd tenth.......(10 to 1 op 8 to 1 tchd 7 to 1) 5
1236 PADDY BURKE (Ire) 6-10-11 (3") G Hogan, al beh, lost tch 9th,
tld off whn pld up bef 3 out.............(33 to 1 op 25 to 1) pu
1475 BAXWORTHY LORD 5-10-10 (3") T Dascombe, tld off 9th, pld
up bef 3 out..............................(50 to 1 op 20 to 1) pu
Dist: 11l, 4l, ½l, 4l. 4m 47.80s. a 16.80s (7 Ran).
             (Jack Joseph), P J Hobbs

1601 Oak Novices' Handicap Hurdle Class C (4-y-o and up) £3,533 2m 1f (2:55)

1417³ HAY DANCE [95] 5-10-3 (3") G Tormey, hld up, gd hdwy appr 2
out, led and jmpd rght last, edgd right r-in, drvn out.
....(11 to 4 op 5 to 2) 1
1354* ROSENCRANTZ (Ire) [108] 4-11-5 N Williamson, hld up in tch,
trkd ldr 5th, led 2 out, hdd and not much room last, not quicken
r-in.....................................(5 to 2 on tchd 2 to 1 on) 2
618⁵ MILLCROFT RIVIERA (Ire) [89] 5-9-11 (3") P Henley, led till hit
and hdd 2 out, one pace aftr.
....(25 to 1 op 16 to 1 tchd 33 to 1) 3
419 PRINCE DE BERRY [91] 5-10-2² P Holley, trkd ldr to 5th, wknd
appr 2 out.............(14 to 1 tchd 16 to 1) 4
1252⁹ STUDIO THIRTY [89] 4-10-0 D Bridgwater, beh till pld up aftr
4th.......................(20 to 1 op 16 to 1 tchd 25 to 1) pu
Dist: 2l, 1¼l, 10l. 3m 58.90s. a 15.90s (5 Ran).
        (Wessex Go Racing Partnership), P J Hobbs

1602 Mendip Plywood Handicap Chase Class D (0-125 5-y-o and up) £4,810 3m ......(3:25)

1414³ DUHALLOW LODGE [109] 9-11-10 B Fenton, hld up in rear,
hdwy 12th, rn to ld last, ran on.......(7 to 2 tchd 9 to 2) 1
1239⁵ SCOTONI [95] 10-10-10 B Powell, trkd ldr, led 12th, rdn and
hdd last, kpt on...........................(6 to 1 op 9 to 2) 2
1426* BALLY CLOVER [107] 9-11-8 N Williamson, led 6th to 12th, ev
ch whn hit 3 out, sn btn. (100 to 30 op 5 to 2 tchd 4 to 1) 3
1356⁴ HERBERT BUCHANAN (Ire) [101] 6-11-2 P Hide, hld up, blun
12th, wl beh aftr, tld off...............(4 to 1 op 3 to 1) 4
1231⁴ CERTAIN ANGLE [106] 7-11-7 D Bridgwater, led to 6th, dsptd
ld to 9th, wknd quickly appr 13th, pld up bef nxt.
....(9 to 4 fav op 5 to 2 tchd 11 to 4) pu
Dist: ½l, 9l, dist. 6m 5.80s. a 22.80s (5 Ran).
         (Robin Barwell), C R Barwell

1603 Walnut Handicap Hurdle Class D (0-120 4-y-o and up) £2,762 2m 3f 110yds......(3:55)

    ROAD TO AU BON (USA) [78] 8-10-2 B Powell, made most to
3 out, rdn to ld r-in, all out.
....(14 to 1 tchd 8 to 1 and 16 to 1) 1
    BEYOND OUR REACH [100] 8-11-7 (3") T Dascombe, al
prmnt, rdn appr 2 out, rallied and ev ch r-in, jst fld.
....(8 to 1 tchd 7 to 1) 2
1558³ FLEUR DE TAL [95] 5-10-12 (7") J Power, al prmnt, led 3 out,
hit last, rdn and hdd r-in. (3 to 1 op 5 to 1 tchd 7 to 1) 3
1353* LITTLE HOOLIGAN [85] 5-10-2 (7") J Harris, hld up in tch, rdn
and hdwy appr 2 out, kpt on r-in.
....(8 to 1 op 5 to 1 tchd 9 to 1) 4
1427⁵ FIRST CLASS [83] 6-10-7 R Greene, pld hrd, dsptd ld 5th to
6th, outpcd 3 out, styd on r-in.
....(5 to 1 op 7 to 1 tchd 9 to 1) 5
1351⁴ SAN DIEGO CHARGER (Ire) [80] 5-9-13 (5") Mr R Thornton,
hld up, rdn and outpcd whn mstk 7th, one pace aftr.
....(11 to 1 op 8 to 1 tchd 12 to 1) 6
1416* SUPERMICK [86] 5-10-10 M Richards, hld up, rdn and ev ch 3
out, fdd aftr nxt.......(13 to 8 fav op 7 to 4 tchd 9 to 4) 7
1413⁵ SUPREME STAR (USA) [88] (bl) 5-10-12 D Bridgwater, hld up
in tch, wknd 7th, btn appr 2 out, eased.
....(10 to 3 op 3 to 1 tchd 5 to 1) 8
Dist: Nk, ½l, 2½l, 1l, ½l, 5l, 25l. 4m 40.70s. a 22.70s (8 Ran).
         (M H Holland), R J Baker

BANGOR (good (race 1), good to soft (2,3,6), soft (4,5))
Friday November 29th
Going Correction: PLUS 1.20 sec. per fur. (races 1,3,6), PLUS 1.95 (2,4,5)

1604 Classic Racing Books Selling Hurdle Class G (4 - 7-y-o) £2,036 2m 1f ......(1:20)

1541² WILLY STAR (Bel) 6-11-5 Richard Guest, al cl up, led appr 4
out, drvn clr r-in, eased close hme. (11 to 4 fav op 9 to 4) 1

1510[5] ELA MAN HOWA 5-10-12 N Williamson, *hld up, steady hdwy appr 5th, chsd wnr bef 2 out, no imprsn.*
....(6 to 1 op 7 to 1 tchd 5 to 1) 2

1295[6] ROBSERA (Ire) 5-10-12 M Dwyer, *midfield, hdwy 5th, chsd wnr betw last 2, sn no imprsn, no extr r-in.*
..........................(8 to 1 op 7 to 1 tchd 10 to 1 and 14 to 1) 3

1442 SHARMOOR 4-10-7 A Thornton, *midfield, hdwy to go cl up 4th, ev ch 3 out, unid pres and fdd bef nxt.*
....(12 to 1 op 10 to 1 tchd 14 to 1) 4

THE FINAL SPARK 5-10-7 B Harding, *in tch, effrt bef 3 out, btn before nxt.*..............(12 to 1 op 8 to 1 tchd 14 to 1) 5

1425[7] PHARLY REEF 4-10-12 D J Burchell, *midfield, feeling pace 3 out, sn no dngr.*.......................(14 to 1 op 10 to 1) 6

TIRMIZI (USA) 5-11-5 J Supple, *prmnt, pushed alng aftr 3rd, wknd 3 out.*................................(5 to 1 op 3 to 1) 7

1450[5] DENOMINATION (USA) 4-11-5 (7*) B Moore, *in rear, drvn appr 4 out, nvr a factor.* (12 to 1 op 8 to 1 tchd 14 to 1) 8

879[8] BIYA (Ire) 4-10-9 (3*) D Walsh, *midfield, improved 4 out, ev ch nxt, sn drvn alng.*.............................(33 to 1) 9

1257[3] ANTARCTICTERN (USA) 6-10-12 A Dobbin, *cl up, pushed alng 3 out, wknd quickly.*..................(10 to 1 op 7 to 1) 10

1293[7] DASHING DANCER (Ire) 5-10-12 Gary Lyons, *keen hold, hld up in rear, struggling frm 4 out.*......(33 to 1 op 20 to 1) 11

912[4] SIMAND 4-11-0 J Callaghan, *beh, struggling 5th, eased whn btn 3 out.*......................(12 to 1 op 6 to 1 tchd 14 to 1) 12

1437 RIVERBANK RED 5-10-7 T Eley, *led till appr 4 out, wknd quickly nxt.*..(20 to 1) 13

1472[4] MY HARVINSKI (v) 6-10-5 (7*) Miss E J Jones, *prmnt, pushed alng 5th, wknd quickly.*.............(20 to 1 op 14 to 1) 14

1261[4] OAKBURY (Ire) 4-10-12 M Richards, *jmpd slwly 1st, in tch, niggled alng 4th, beh frm hdwy.*......(14 to 1 op 8 to 1) 15

GALLARDINI (Ire) 7-11-9 (3*) G Cahill, *not fluent, trkd ldrs, lost pl 4th, sn beh, tld off whn pld up bef last.*
...........................(12 to 1 op 8 to 1 tchd 16 to 1) pu

Dist: 3l, 1l, 9l, 3½l, 2l, 3½l, 14l, nk, 13l, nk. 4m 17.80s. a 27.80s (16 Ran).
SR: 17/7/6/-/-/-/

1605 **JPCS Novices' Handicap Chase Class E (0-100 4-y-o and up) £3,290 2½m 110yds................. (1:50)**

1392[3] GENERAL PONGO [90] 7-11-4 M Dwyer, *trkd ldrs, led 8th to 4 out, rallied to chal 2 out, styd on wl to rgn ld cl hme.*
....(10 to 1 op 8 to 1) 1

1498 WHIRLY (Ire) [90] 7-11-4 A Thornton, *in tch, improved 9th, led 4 out, hrd pressed frm 2 out, hdd and no extr cl hme.*
....(7 to 1 op 6 to 1) 2

1127[3] KENMARE RIVER (Ire) [72] 6-9-9 (5*) Mr R Thornton, *prmnt, drvn 3 out, sn outpcd.*............(20 to 1 op 16 to 1) 3

1226[2] MONYMOSS (Ire) [98] 7-11-12 Richard Guest, *in tch, lost pl 6th, no ch frm four out, eased 2 out.*..(9 to 2 op 3 to 1) 4

1001* PLAYING TRUANT [82] 8-10-7 (3*) D Fortt, *jmpd stickily, in tch early, beh frm 4 out.*......(4 to 1 jt-fav op 3 to 1) 5

CHOISTY (Ire) [92] 6-11-6 J Supple, *strted slwly, beh whn blun and uns rdr 1st.*.....................(4 to 1 jt-fav) ur

1321[2] ON THE TEAR [72] 10-10-0 S Wynne, *al beh, tld off whn pld up bef 3 out.*........................(25 to 1 op 16 to 1) pu

1098[2] FRONTIER FLIGHT (USA) [80] 6-10-5 (3*) E Husband, *al beh, tld off whn pld up bef 3 out.*....(16 to 1 op 14 to 1) pu

1138[6] HEATHYARDS BOY [72] 6-9-13[2] (3*) D Walsh, *cl up, led 4th, mstk 7th, hdd nxt, sn wknd, tld off whn pld up bef 3 out.*
....(33 to 1 op 25 to 1 tchd 40 to 1) pu

1321[3] DORMSTON BOYO [72] 6-10-0 D Bridgwater, *beh, lost tch 6th, tld off whn pld up bef nxt.*....(25 to 1 op 20 to 1) pu

1376* MONNAIE FORTE (Ire) 7-11-4 J Railton, *cl up, wknd 9th, beh whn pld up bef nxt.*...............(7 to 1 op 6 to 1) pu

1049[4] KARENASTINO [73] 5-10-0 Mr P Murray, *nvr gng wl, beh, tld off whn pld up bef last.*............(50 to 1 op 33 to 1) pu

Dist: 1½l, 28l, 3½l, 3½l. 5m 33.90s. a 47.90s (12 Ran).
SR: 11/9/-/-/-/-/

1606 **Ruabon Handicap Hurdle Class E (0-110 4-y-o and up) £2,814 2m 1f .... (2:20)**

1402[5] TANSEEQ [86] 5-10-7 Derek Byrne, *in tch, improved 4 out, ev ch and not fluent 2 out, led on bit last, cmftbly.*
....(9 to 2 fav op 7 to 2 tchd 5 to 1) 1

1175[4] STAY WITH ME (Fr) [94] 6-10-10 (5*) Mr R Thornton, *in tch, cl up 4th, led aftr 3 out, hdd appr last, one pace.*
....(6 to 1 op 9 to 2) 2

KINTAVI [82] 6-10-3 T Eley, *hld up, gd hdwy aftr 3 out, sn one pace.*........................(25 to 1 op 14 to 1) 3

COLORFUL AMBITION [106] 6-11-13 J Railton, *midfield, hdwy to chal aftr 3 out, no extr frm nxt...* (7 to 1 op 5 to 1) 4

1351[3] ZINGIBAR [79] 4-10-0 T J Murphy, *prmnt, lft in ld 4th, hdd aftr 3 out, sn wknd.*..................(6 to 1 tchd 8 to 1) 5

1266 KAYFAAT (USA) [81] (v) 8-9-9 (7*) B Moore, *cl up, drvn aftr 3 out, sn outpcd.*...........(16 to 1 op 12 to 1) 6

1388[8] GRANDMAN (Ire) [90] 5-10-11 D J Moffatt, *trkd ldrs, hmpd 4th, wknd appr 3 out.*
.............................(13 to 2 op 6 to 1 tchd 8 to 1) 7

1051[4] SCOTTISH WEDDING [79] 6-10-0 D Bridgwater, *hld up in rear, hdwy und pres 3 out, wknd bef 2 out, eased before last.*
...........................(8 to 1 op 7 to 1 tchd 10 to 1) 8

1346[7] UNITED FRONT [95] 4-11-2 N Williamson, *led till f 4th.*
....(8 to 1 op 10 to 1) f

DAILY SPORT GIRL [92] 7-10-13 Mr J L Llewellyn, *in tch, und pres 3 out, sn wknd, beh whn pld up bef nxt.*
...........................(9 to 1 op 5 to 1 tchd 10 to 1) pu

Dist: 1½l, 9l, nk, nk, 2½l, nk, 5l. 4m 20.70s. a 30.70s (10 Ran).
(Miss N C Taylor), M G Meagher

1607 **Maelor Handicap Chase Class C (0-130 4-y-o and up) £4,409 2½m 110yds...................... (2:50)**

RIVER MANDATE [120] 9-11-12 A Thornton, *trkd ldr, chlgd und pres 2 out, styd on to ld cl hme.*
.........................(15 to 8 fav op 7 to 4 tchd 9 to 4) 1

EVEN BLUE (Ire) [115] 8-11-4 (3*) D Walsh, *keen hold early, led, hrd pressed frm 2 out, hdd and no extr cl hme.*
....(2 to 1 op 7 to 4 tchd 9 to 4) 2

1204 ANDRELOT [118] (bl) 9-11-10 N Williamson, *drvn alng thrght, in rear, losing tch whn jmpd slwly 11th, wnt poor 3rd bef last, tld off...*...........(10 to 1 op 7 to 1 tchd 11 to 1) 3

1468[2] SPANISH LIGHT (Ire) [122] 7-12-0 A Dobbin, *hndy till wknd quickly 4 out, tld off........*(2 to 1 op 7 to 4 tchd 9 to 4) 4

Dist: ½l, dist, 24l. 5m 32.90s. a 46.90s (4 Ran).
SR: 29/23/-/-/
(Anne Duchess Of Westminster), Capt T A Forster

1608 **Malise Nicolson Memorial Novices' Chase Class D (5-y-o and up) £3,745 3m 110yds.......................... (3:20)**

1542* BANKHEAD (Ire) 7-11-5 D Bridgwater, *patiently rdn, cld aftr 12th, ridden to chal 2 out, sn led, ran on wl towards finish.*
....(10 to 3 op 5 to 2) 1

LANSBOROUGH 6-10-12 B Harding, *nvr far away, led on bit 3 out, stumbled whn pressed 2 out, sn hdd, rallied aftr last, no extr towards finish.* (11 to 10 on op Evens tchd 11 to 10) 2

1315[7] SHALLOW RIVER (Ire) 5-10-10 A Thornton, *led to 5th, led ag'n 11th till nxt, lft in ld 14th, hdd 3 out, wknd quickly, tld off.*
.............................(33 to 1 op 25 to 1 tchd 40 to 1) 3

GOLD PIGEON (Ire) 7-10-4 (3*) G Cahill, *not jump wl, cl up, lost pl 7th, sn beh, tld off.*
.............................(33 to 1 op 25 to 1 tchd 50 to 1) 4

1385* NAUGHTY FUTURE 7-11-5 M Dwyer, *hld up, mstk 1st, hdwy to go cl up 9th, led 12th, blun and uns rdr 14th.*
....(9 to 2 op 3 to 1) ur

ISLAND JEWEL 8-10-12 M Bosley, *hld up in tch, hdwy whn mstk 8th, wknd aftr tenth, tld off whn pld up bef 14th.*
..........................(9 to 1 op 5 to 1 tchd 10 to 1) pu

OVER THE WREKIN 9-10-12 Richard Guest, *hld up, lost tch 12th, tld off whn pld up bef 4 out.*
..........................(50 to 1 op 25 to 1 tchd 66 to 1) pu

BENBULBIN (Ire) 6-10-12 S Curran, *prmnt, led 5th till 11th, wknd nxt, tld off whn pld up bef 2 out.*
.............................(40 to 1 op 33 to 1 tchd 50 to 1) pu

Dist: 3l, dist, 26l. 6m 55.30s. a 70.30s (8 Ran).
(Mrs Liz Brazier), J L Spearing

1609 **Hanmer 'National Hunt' Novices' Hurdle Class D (4-y-o and up) £3,081 2m 1f......................(3:50)**

CRIMSON KING (Ire) 5-10-12 A Thornton, *cl up, led appr 3 out, mstk nxt, styd on strly to go clr frm last.*
.........................(7 to 2 op 4 to 1 tchd 5 to 2) 1

MARKET MAYHEM 6-10-12 Richard Guest, *hndy, drvn alng and outpcd 3 out, kpt on to take second r-in, no ch whn wnr.*
..........................(50 to 1 op 20 to 1) 2

1128[3] GAZANALI (Ire) 5-10-12 N Bentley, *midfield, hdwy to chase ldrs 3 out, sn one pace...*......(33 to 1 op 14 to 1) 3

1240* ULTIMATE SMOOTHIE 4-10-12 C Maude, *hld up beh, hdwy 3 out, drvn appr last, not rch ldrs.*
.............................(9 to 2 op 5 to 2 tchd 5 to 1) 4

1142* JOHNNY-K (Ire) 5-10-12 N Williamson, *midfield, hdwy to go cl up 4th, ev ch whn stumbled 2 out, tired when blun last, wknd r-in...*..........................(Evens fav op 11 to 10) 5

1047[9] REFLEX HAMMER 5-10-12 R Supple, *hndy, und pres 3 out, fdd bef nxt...*..............(20 to 1 op 12 to 1 tchd 25 to 1) 6

1136[3] MILLING BROOK 4-10-5 (7*) J Power, *in tch, jmpd slwly 4th, drvn and wknd 3 out...*..............(50 to 1 op 20 to 1) 7

KENTUCKY GOLD (Ire) 7-10-12 L O'Hara, *hld up, effrt 3 out, no hdwy...*.............................(100 to 1 op 33 to 1) 8

1123[7] JOE LUKE (Ire) 4-10-12 J Callaghan, *in rear, niggled alng appr 3 out, nvr a factor...*...............(50 to 1 op 20 to 1) 9

LUCKY TANNER 5-10-12 T J Murphy, *cl up, lost pl aftr 3rd, pushed alng appr 3 out, tld off...*...(33 to 1 op 10 to 1) 10

1373 JUDICIOUS NORMAN (Ire) 5-10-12 J Railton, *led till appr 3 out, wknd quickly, tld off.*
.............................(10 to 1 op 16 to 1 tchd 20 to 1) 11

1142 THE SECRET GREY 5-10-9 (3*) D Walsh, *prmnt, drvn and wknd quickly bef 3 out, tld off...*(100 to 1 op 50 to 1) 12

MANVULANE (Ire) 6-10-12 D Bridgwater, *al beh, lost tch 5th, tld off whn pld up before 2 out.*
.............................(100 to 1 op 50 to 1) pu

1306 SOPHIES DREAM 5-10-7 (5*) Mr R Thornton, *al rear div, tld off whn pld up bef 2 out...*..........(100 to 1 op 50 to 1) pu

1026 RINUS MAJESTIC (Ire) 4-10-12 B Harding, *hld up, struggling bef 5th, tld off whn pld up before 2 out.*
.............................(50 to 1 op 25 to 1 tchd 50 to 1) pu

Dist: 11l, 2½l, 3l, 1l, 8l, 7l, 3½l, 1l, 23l, 3l. 4m 19.60s. a 29.60s (15 Ran).
(Simon Sainsbury), Capt T A Forster

NEWBURY (good to soft (races 1,2,3,4,5), good (6))
Friday November 29th
Going Correction: PLUS 0.30 sec. per fur. (races 1,3,5,6), PLUS 0.85 (2,4)

1610 Freshman's Juvenile Novices' Hurdle Class C (3-y-o) £3,938 2m 110yds........................ (1:00)

WHITE SEA (Ire) 10-7 C F Swan, *trkd ldrs till led aftr 4th, pushed alng frm 2 out, ran on wl*...... (7 to 1 op 5 to 1) 1
1286* SHOOTING LIGHT (Ire) 11-3 G Bradley, *gd hdwy 3rd, chsd ldrs frm 5th, styd on one pace from 2 out.*
.... (5 to 1 op 6 to 1 tchd 13 to 2) 2
SUMMER SPELL (Ire) 10-12 M A Fitzgerald, *mid-div till hdwy 5th, rdn aftr 3 out, wknd r-in.*
.... (2 to 1 fav op 6 to 4 tchd 5 to 2) 3
SAMAKAAN (Ire) 10-12 A Maguire, *sn chasing ldrs, rdn 3 out, wknd appr last*........... (5 to 1 op 5 to 2 tchd 6 to 1) 4
1027² LE TETEU (Fr) 10-12 R Dunwoody, *prmnt, pushed alng aftr 5th, wknd 3 out*.......... (13 to 2 op 8 to 1) 5
1286² PLEASURELAND (bl) 10-12 D Morris, *jmpd slwly 3rd, hdwy to chase ldrs aftr 4th, wknd 2 out*.....(20 to 1 op 14 to 1) 6
1412² STERLING FELLOW (bl) 10-12 M Clarke, *beh, some hdwy 5th, wknd 3 out.*................... (33 to 1 op 20 to 1) 7
RED RAJA 10-12 D Gallagher, *some prog frm 3 out, not a dngr.*.................. (66 to 1 op 50 to 1) 8
APACHE PARK (USA) 10-12 C Llewellyn, *nvr better than mid-div.*..................... (50 to 1 op 14 to 1) 9
1249* CHIEF MOUSE 11-8 J Osborne, *led till aftr 1st, wknd 5th.*
.... (16 to 1 op 12 to 1 tchd 20 to 1) 10
1470³ WARNING REEF 10-12 S McNeill, *hdwy 4th, rdn to chase ldrs 5th, wknd 3 out*........ (50 to 1 op 25 to 1 tchd 66 to 1) 11
1027⁵ LAUGHING BUCCANEER 10-12 B Powell, *al beh.*
.... (66 to 1 op 50 to 1) 12
CLAIRE'S DANCER (Ire) 10-12 L Harvey, *prmnt to appr 5th.*
.... (33 to 1 op 25 to 1) 13
1024² SUNLEY SECURE 10-12 W Marston, *prmnt, rdn alng frm 3rd, wknd 5th.*.................. (33 to 1 op 25 to 1) 14
NORTHERN CLAN 10-5 (7*) O Burrows, *al beh.*
.... (66 to 1 op 33 to 1 tchd 100 to 1) 15
1398 FLYING GREEN (Fr) (bl) 10-12 R Farrant, *pld hrd, led aftr 1st, wknd aftr 4th, sn wknd*.......... (33 to 1 op 20 to 1) 16
1412⁸ HAWANAFA 10-7 W McFarland, *beh, no ch whn mstk 5th.*
.... (66 to 1 op 33 to 1 tchd 100 to 1) 17
965² A CHEF TOO FAR 10-12 D O'Sullivan, *rcd wide, lost tch frm 5th*..................... (16 to 1 op 10 to 1) 18
965⁸ PREMIER GENERATION (Ire) 10-12 I Lawrence, *chsd ldrs to 5th, sn wknd.*.................. (20 to 1 op 14 to 1) 19
PETROS PRIDE 10-7 P Hide, *al beh, tld off whn pld up bef 5th.*
.... (66 to 1 op 14 to 1 tchd 100 to 1) pu
436² BRIGHT ECLIPSE (USA) 10-7 (5*) Chris Webb, *al beh, tld off whn pld up bef 3 out*..(66 to 1 op 50 to 1 tchd 100 to 1) pu
Dist: 5l, 15l, ¾l, 3l, 19l, 18l, 7l, 1¼l, 2½l, 3½l. 3m 58.70s. a 9.70s (21 Ran).
SR: 32/37/17/16/13/-/ (T M Hely-Hutchinson), M C Pipe

1611 Oxfordshire Novices' Chase Class C (5-y-o and up) £4,627 3m..... (1:30)

HATCHAM BOY (Ire) 6-11-3 A Maguire, *hdwy to trkd ldrs 12th, chlgd 3 out, led nxt, rdn, wnt badly lft and ridd aftr last, rallied to ld ag'n cl hme*................ (8 to 1 op 6 to 1) 1
WELCOME CALL (Ire) 6-11-3 J Osborne, *trkd ldr frm 5th, led tenth, jmpd rght, remained in ld till hdd 2 out, wnt badly right last, sn led, rdn, headed cl hme...* (11 to 10 on op 5 to 4) 2
1347⁴ WISLEY WONDER (Ire) 6-11-3 C Llewellyn, *led till jmpd very slwly and hdd tenth, mstk nxt, drvn to stay with ldrs, kpt on wl und pres frm 3 out.*................... (7 to 1 op 6 to 1) 3
ACT OF FAITH 6-11-3 W Marston, *beh, hdwy appr 4 out, mstk 3 out, styd on frm 2 out.... (8 to 1 op 6 to 1 tchd 9 to 1) 4
1341² MADISON COUNTY (Ire) 6-11-3 R Dunwoody, *mid-div, hdwy 13th, trkd ldrs 4 out, wknd 2 out*....... (5 to 1 op 7 to 2) 5
1411* BLASKET HERO (bl) 8-11-7 B Fenton, *beh, mstks second and 3rd, wknd 8th, tld off whn pld up bef 3 out*
.... (20 to 1 tchd 25 to 1 and 33 to 1) pu
CLAYMORE LAD 6-11-3 P Hide, *wth ldr to 3rd, wknd tenth, tld off whn pld up bef 3 out*............ (100 to 1 op 50 to 1) pu
1473⁴ NEWTOWN ROSIE (Ire) 7-10-12 J Ryan, *prmnt early, lost tch 7th, mstk 8th, tld up nxt, lme.*
.... (33 to 1 op 16 to 1 tchd 50 to 1) pu
Dist: 1½l, 1l, 2l, 14l. 6m 11.60s. a 26.60s (8 Ran).
SR: 27/25/24/22/8/ (Robert Benton), D Nicholson

1612 Brimpton Handicap Hurdle Class B (0-140 4-y-o and up) £4,900 2m 110yds.................... (2:00)

MISTER MOROSE (Ire) [128] 6-11-4 C Llewellyn, *trkd ldr, drvn to ld 2 out, kpt on wl.*
.... (14 to 1 op 10 to 1 tchd 16 to 1) 1
1512* CHAI-YO [115] 6-10-5 (5ex) G Upton, *hld up in rear, steady hdwy frm 3 out, styd on appr last to take second r-in, not pace to rch wnr*....... (5 to 2 jt-fav tchd 11 to 4 and 3 to 1) 2

INTERMAGIC [110] 6-10-0 S Fox, *led, sn clr, rdn 3 out, hdd 2 out, one pace r-in, ct for second nr finish.*
.... (25 to 1 op 20 to 1 tchd 33 to 1) 3
1238³ CADOUGOLD (Fr) [123] 5-10-13 C F Swan, *beh, hdwy frm 3 out, one pace from nxt*........... (10 to 1 tchd 12 to 1) 4
BOLIVAR (Ire) [114] 4-9-13 (5*) S Ryan, *chaased ldrs, rdn 5th, wknd aftr 3 out.*.......... (6 to 1 op 5 to 1 tchd 9 to 1) 5
ABBEY STREET (Ire) [122] 4-10-12 J Osborne, *chsd ldrs till wknd frm 5th*.......... (5 to 2 op 7 to 1 tchd 8 to 1) 6
1288 KINGSFOLD PET [135] 7-11-11 D Skyrme, *al in rear.*
.... (12 to 1 tchd 14 to 1) 7
MASTER TRIBE (Ire) [120] 6-10-10 W Marston, *steady hdwy 5th, wknd aftr 3 out*...... (12 to 1 op 8 to 1 tchd 14 to 1) 8
1368³ THINKING TWICE (USA) [138] 7-12-0 M A Fitzgerald, *prmnt till wknd quickley appr 5th*...... (25 to 1 op 20 to 1) 9
EDELWEIS DU MOULIN (Fr) [127] 4-11-3 R Dunwoody, *hld up, some hdwy but plenty to do whn f 3 out*......(5 to 2 jt-fav op 7 to 4) f
Dist: 8l, 1¾l, 3½l, 18l, 6l, 16l, 21l, dist. 4m 3.00s. a 14.00s (10 Ran).
(Mrs J Mould), N A Twiston-Davies

1613 Jacky Upton Handicap Chase Class B (0-145 5-y-o and up) £7,488 2½m
.... (2:30)

1289² GOLDEN SPINNER [125] 9-11-0 M A Fitzgerald, *mstk 1st, sn prmnt, chlgd frm 8th till led 12th, styd on wl.*
.... (4 to 1 op 5 to 1 tchd 8 to 1) 1
AROUND THE HORN [135] 9-11-10 S McNeill, *in tch, hdwy 12th, chsd wnr frm 4 out, no imprssion.* (10 to 1 op 6 to 1) 2
1304 WELL BRIEFED [122] 9-10-11 B Powell, *led to 12th, hit 4 out, wknd 2 out, no ch whn blun last.....(25 to 1 op 14 to 1) 3
1394⁷ STRONG MEDICINE [134] 9-11-9 J A McCarthy, *beh, not fluent early, staying on whn f 4 out....* (6 to 1 op 3 to 1) f
GO UNIVERSAL (Ire) [134] 8-11-9 D Gallagher, *chsd ldr till mstk 9th, wknd 12th, f 4 out.*
.... (15 to 2 op 5 to 1 tchd 8 to 1) f
MAJOR SUMMIT (Ire) [134] 7-11-9 P Hide, *trkd ldrs, 3rd and gng wl whn mstk and uns rdr 12th.*
.... (11 to 10 on op Evens tchd 5 to 4 and 11 to 8) ur
RIVER BOUNTY [126] 10-11-1 G Bradley, *hld up in rear, blun 11th, staying on whn brght dwn 4 out....* (7 to 1 op 5 to 1) bd
Dist: 9l, 8l. 5m 12.30s. a 24.30s (7 Ran).
SR: 13/14/-/-/ (Mrs Hugh Maitland-Jones), N J Henderson

1614 Newbury Shopping Arcade Conditional Jockeys' Novices' Handicap Hurdle Class E (0-110 4-y-o and up) £2,880 2m 5f................ (3:00)

1454⁴ ALLOW (Ire) [86] 5-10-10 D J Kavanagh, *pushed alng and hdwy 8th, chsd ldrs 3 out, chlgd last, led und pres r-in.*
.... (6 to 1 op 9 to 2) 1
1338⁴ THE CAPTAIN'S WISH [102] 5-11-9 (3*) R Massey, *trkd ldrs till led 3 out, rdn appr last, hdd r-in, one pace.*
.... (3 to 1 fav tchd 5 to 2 and 7 to 2) 2
WRECKLESS MAN [84] 9-10-0 (8*) E Greehy, *beh, steady hdwy frm 3 out, trkd ldrs gng wl last, shaken up, swtchd lft and one pace r-in.*.......... (20 to 1 op 14 to 1) 3
1348³ TIME LEADER [76] 4-9-4 (10*) X Aizpuru, *hdwy 7th, ev ch 3 out till wknd aftr 2 out....* (4 to 1 op 14 to 1 tchd 20 to 1) 4
1355* HONEY MOUNT [90] 5-11-0 Guy Lewis, *hdwy 7th,str chalinge frm nxt, wknd aftr 2 out.....* (10 to 1 op 14 to 1) 5
1010* CROWN IVORY (NZ) [76] 8-10-0 T Dascombe, *hdwy 7th, rdn alng frm nxt, wknd aftr 3 out....* (16 to 1 tchd 14 to 1) 6
1202² BAYERD (Ire) [100] 5-11-10 L Aspell, *trkd ldrs, effrt 3 out, wknd nxt....*........(8 to 1 op 11 to 1 tchd 9 to 1) 7
1343³ HYDEMILLA [78] 6-10-2 G Hogan, *led to 3 out, sn wknd.*
.... (12 to 1 op 10 to 1 tchd 14 to 1) 8
1295⁵ VENDOON (Ire) [76] 6-10-0 K Gaule, *chsd ldr, mstk 6th, ev ch 3 out, wknd nxt.*.................. (9 to 2 op 5 to 1) 9
1158 LYPHARD'S FABLE (USA) [76] 5-9-4 (10*) C Hynes, *al beh, lost tch 6th, tld off...*.............. (25 to 1 op 20 to 1) 10
1343⁴ BITE THE BULLET [76] 5-10-0 O Burrows, *prmnt to 7th, tld off.*
.... (25 to 1 op 66 to 1) 11
DISSOLVE [77] 4-10-1 Chris Webb, *prmnt to 6th, tld off 7th.*
.... (50 to 1 op 25 to 1) 12
SMART REBAL (Ire) [76] 8-10-0³ (3*) M Berry, *pld up aftr 4th, broke leg,destroyed.*............. (66 to 1 tchd 100 to 1) pu
Dist: 3l, nk, 9l, 6l, nk, 10l, 14l, dist. 5m 16.70s. a 22.70s (13 Ran).
(Mrs M Llewellyn), B Llewellyn

1615 Sonning Novices' Hurdle Class C (4-y-o and up) £3,727 3m 110yds (3:30)

YAHMI (Ire) 6-11-0 J Osborne, *hld up and confidently rdn, smooth hdwy appr 3 out, quickened to ld last, easily.*
.... (5 to 2 tchd 11 to 4 and 2 to 1) 1
1502⁴ MENESONIC (Ire) 6-10-11 (3*) P Henley, *chsd ldrs, led 3 out, rdn nxt, hdd last, kpt on, not pace of wnr.*
.... (5 to 1 op 6 to 1) 2
1396² HERBERT LODGE (Ire) 7-11-5 G Bradley, *hld up, steady hdwy frm 3 out, chlgd last, sn btn.*
......(9 to 4 fav op 2 to 1 tchd 3 to 1 and 100 to 30) 3
JOBSAGOODUN 5-11-0 J R Kavanagh, *gd hdwy to chase ldrs 9th, rdn 2 out, sn btn.*
.... (50 to 1 op 33 to 1 tchd 66 to 1) 4

1155² RIDING CROP (Ire) 6-11-0 M A Fitzgerald, *prmnt, rdn 9th, wknd aftr 3 out* ....(12 to 1 op 8 to 1) 5
I'M A CHIPPY (Ire) 6-11-0 B Fenton, *in tch to 7th, hng lft and no ch frm 3 out* ......(16 to 1 op 14 to 1) 6
DEEL QUAY (Ire) 5-11-0 J A McCarthy, *effrt 9th, no hdwy frm 3 out* ....(50 to 1 op 20 to 1 tchd 66 to 1) 7
1343³ PERCY THROWER 9-11-10 C Llewellyn, *led aftr 1st to 6th, led ag'n aftr 9th to thre out, sn wknd.* (10 to 1 tchd 8 to 1) 8
MAURACHAS (Ire) 6-11-0 W Marston, *reluctant to race and lost a furlong at strt, al tld off* ......(20 to 1 op 14 to 1) 9
1343 CANTON VENTURE 4-11-5 A Maguire, *steady hdwy to chase ldrs 9th, wknd rpdly aftr 3 out, tld off.* ....(12 to 1 op 8 to 1 tchd 14 to 1) 10
1344 DEXTRA (Ire) 6-11-0 I Lawrence, *prmnt to 7th, tld off aftr 8th.* ....(66 to 1 op 33 to 1 tchd 100 to 1) 11
CHATERGOLD 4-11-0 C F Swan, *al beh, tld off.* ....(33 to 1 op 20 to 1) 12
1397⁵ LOOKINGFORARAINBOW (Ire) 8-11-0 V Smith, *keen hold, prmnt, led 6th, rcd wide aftr till hdd aftr 9th, sn wknd, tld off whn pld up bef 4 out....*(25 to 1 op 20 to 1 tchd 33 to 1) pu
DRUM BATTLE 4-11-0 G Upton, *led till aftr 1st, chlgd 4th to 5th, wknd 7th, tld off whn pld up bef 3 out.* ....(25 to 1 op 16 to 1) pu
1228² QUAFF (Ire) 6-11-0 P Hide, *hdwy 7th, rdn appr 3 out, sn wknd, pld up last.....................*(11 to 2 op 5 to 1 tchd 6 to 1) pu
BUTCHERS MINSTREL 4-11-0 W McFarland, *blun 6th and beh, tld off whn pld up bef 9th.*
Dist: 11l, 4l, 1¾l, 4l, 8l, 3l, 3l, dist, 10l, 12l. 6m 10.30s. a 24.30s (16 Ran).
(W E Sturt), J A B Old

FAIRYHOUSE (IRE) (yielding)
Saturday November 30th
Going Correction: PLUS 0.35 sec. per fur. (races 1,2,5,6,7), PLUS 0.25 (3,4)

1616
Juvenile Hurdle (Grade 3) (3-y-o) £6,850 2m............(12:30)

1459⁵ SPIRIT DANCER (Ire) 10-9 S C Lyons, *led till hdd briefly bef 2 out, ran on wl and pres.*......................(12 to 1) 1
1430* HIGHLY MOTIVATED 10-2 (5*) J Butler, *wl plcd, prog to ld bef 2 out, jmpd lft and hdd, dsptd lead last, not fluent and headed.* ....(4 to 1) 2
1459³ GREENHUE (Ire) 10-12 T P Rudd, *wl plcd, trkd ldrs 3 out, rdn and chlgd nxt, no extr r-in.*......................(7 to 1) 3
1430² MISS PENNYHILL (Ire) 9-13 (5*) T Martin, *trkd ldr till lost pos 4th, prog to track ldrs 3 out, no extr.*......(20 to 1) 4
712² EVRIZA (Ire) 10-10 P McWilliams, *wl plcd, rdn bef 2 out, no quicken.*......................(6 to 1) 5
CORN ABBEY (Ire) 10-2 (7*) A P Sweeney, *rear till ran on aftr 3 out, mstk nxt, kpt on.*......................(14 to 1) 6
1430 NARROW FOCUS (USA) 10-9 A Powell, *wl plcd till wknd bef 3 out.*......................(7 to 1) 7
1459³ TAX REFORM (USA) 10-9 H Rogers, *rear till prog to track ldrs bef 4 out, rdn and wknd aftr nxt.*......(20 to 1) 8
1459⁶ AUTOBABBLE (Ire) 10-9 T J Mitchell, *rear till some prog aftr 3 out.*......................(25 to 1) 9
1403* BROKEN RITES (Ire) 10-9 (3*) G Cotter, *rear, rdn bef 3 out, no extr.*......................(8 to 1) 10
1403³ CHOOSEY'S TREASURE (Ire) 10-7 (3*) R P O'Brien, *mid-div, wknd aftr 3 out.*......................(5 to 1) 11
DR BONES 10-6 (3*) K Whelan, *wl plcd till lost pos aftr 3rd, rdn bef 2 out, no extr.*......................(20 to 1) 12
1403⁴ IACCHUS (bl) 10-7 (5*) M J Holbrook, *wl plcd, rdn aftr 4 out, sn wknd.*......................(16 to 1) 13
RIVER ROCK 10-6 (3*) B Bowens, *al rear......*(20 to 1) 14
GRIMES 10-9 C O'Dwyer, *wl plcd till rdn and wknd aftr 3 out.* ....(2 to 1 fav) 15
BLUE BIT (Ire) 10-9 R Hughes, *mid-div, wknd aftr 4 out, pld up aftr nxt.*......................(8 to 1) pu
Dist: 1½l, hd, 3l, sht-hd. 3m 55.00s. a 11.00s (16 Ran).
SR: 27/23/28/17/23/-/ (Edward Campbell), G M Lyons

1617
J.C.'s Traditional Meat Hurdle (4 & 5-y-o) £3,425 2¼m............(1:00)

1457* GUEST PERFORMANCE (Ire) 4-11-9 R Hughes, ...(10 to 9 on) 1
RAWY (USA) 4-11-3 C O'Dwyer, ...(5 to 1) 2
EMBELLISHED (Ire) 4-11-6 D J Casey, ...(2 to 1) 3
BUKHARI (Ire) 4-10-13 L P Cusack, ...(12 to 1) 4
RAHEEN RIVER (Ire) 5-10-13 Mr A Daly, ...(50 to 1) 5
1432 CARRICK GLEN (Ire) 5-10-13 A Powell, ...(33 to 1) 6
THEPRINCESS MANHAR (Ire) 4-10-5 (7*) D M Bean, ...(16 to 1) 7
773³ CROSSCHILD (Ire) 5-10-13 D H O'Connor, ...(12 to 1) 8
1539 NICKELLI (Ire) 5-10-6 (7*) Mr P M Cloke, ...(66 to 1) 9
Dist: 3l, 14l, 14l, 4½l. 4m 25.10s. a 13.10s (9 Ran).
SR: 27/18/7/-/-/-/ (S Mulryan), D T Hughes

1618
Mullinam Beginners Chase (5-y-o and up) £3,425 2¾m............(1:30)

ROCKFIELD NATIVE (Ire) 6-11-11 (3*) Mr B M Cash, (5 to 1) 1
1435⁵ ULTRA FLUTTER 9-11-11 (3*) G Cotter, ...(9 to 2 fav) 2

1117⁸ EMERALD GALE (Ire) 6-11-9 D J Casey, ...(14 to 1) 3
1461 THE LATVIAN LARK (Ire) 8-12-10 Mr G J Harford, ...(5 to 1) 4
1435⁶ CURRENCY BASKET (Ire) 6-11-2 A Powell, ...(6 to 1) 5
1276⁵ CREHELP EXPRESS (Ire) 6-11-6 (3*) B Bowens, ...(7 to 1) 6
1435⁴ MACNAMARASBAND (Ire) 7-11-2 C O'Dwyer, ...(8 to 1) 7
1534⁶ DIORRAING (Ire) 6-11-9 D H O'Connor, ...(14 to 1) 8
1461⁸ BROWNRATH KING (Ire) 7-11-7 (7*) D M Bean, ...(25 to 1) 9
1534⁷ TIME AND CHARGES (Ire) 6-11-9 T J Mitchell, ...(10 to 1) 10
1461⁷ FINGAL BOY (Ire) 8-11-9 S C Lyons, ...(20 to 1) 11
1146⁴ ANOTHER DEADLY 9-12-0 G M O'Neill, ...(14 to 1) 12
1435 NORTHERN REEF (Ire) 6-11-2 (7*) L J Fleming, ...(20 to 1) 13
1242 WEST BROGUE (Ire) 7-11-9 (5*) J Butler, ...(14 to 1) 14
1362 LISNAGAR LAKE (Ire) 6-11-9 S H O'Donovan, ...(50 to 1) 15
1146⁵ JORIDI LE FORIGE (Ire) 5-11-3 T P Rudd, ...(12 to 1) 16
1362⁵ TAYLORS QUAY (Ire) 6-11-8 (3*) K Whelan, ...(12 to 1) f
1080⁵ RYHANE (Ire) 7-11-9 L P Cusack, ...(16 to 1) f
1405² BOBBYJO (Ire) 6-12-0 P L Malone, ...(13 to 2) ur
1242⁶ BAILE NA GCLOCH (Ire) 7-11-6 (3*) D P Murphy, ..(20 to 1) ur
LIVIN IT UP (Ire) 6-11-2 C O'Brien, ...(12 to 1) ur
DROICHEAD LAPEEN 9-11-2 (7*) Mr T J Beattie, ..(16 to 1) ref
Dist: 2l, 7l, 10l, 2½l. 5m 39.00s. a 12.00s (22 Ran).
SR: 35/33/21/16/13/-/ (M McKeon), A P O'Brien

1619
Pierse Porterstown Handicap Chase (Grade 3) (5-y-o and up) £9,675 3m 1f............(2:00)

1434³ JOHNNY SETASIDE (Ire) [-] 7-11-5 Mr G J Harford, *wl plcd, lft in ld and mstk 6 out, rdn and quickened aftr 4 out, styd on strly.* ....(7 to 4 jt-fav) 1
SON OF WAR [-] 9-11-11 (3*) U Smyth, *wtd wth till prog bef 5 out, rdn aftr nxt, styd on wl after 2 out.*......................(12 to 1) 2
1079⁵ JASSU [-] 10-11-3 A Powell, *wtd wth, some prog bef 8 out, rdn before 4 out, kpt on aftr 2 out.*......................(8 to 1) 3
TOPICAL TIP [-] 7-10-4 (3*) G Cotter, *wl plcd, trkd ldrs to track ldr 9th, rdn bef 4 out, no extr.*......................(7 to 1) 4
CARRIGEEN KERRIA (Ire) [-] 8-10-7 D J Casey, *mid-div till lost pos bef 8 out, rdn bef four out, lost tch aftr nxt.* ...(16 to 1) 5
BALLYHIRE LAD (Ire) [-] 7-10-8 L P Cusack, *al rear, mstk second, slow 4th, rdn bef four out, lost tch aftr nxt.* (16 to 1) 6
1434⁸ SPANKERS HILL (Ire) [-] 7-10-7 D H O'Connor, *trkd ldr till led 3rd, jnd 6th, hdd and mstk nxt, slow 9th, rdn bef 4 out, sn wknd.* ....(10 to 1) 7
1194* THREE BROWNIES [-] (bl) 9-10-7 C O'Dwyer, *led 1st 2, trkd ldr till dsptd ld 6th, led nxt till f six out....*(7 to 4 jt-fav) f
Dist: 10l, 5l, 4l, dist. 6m 33.90s. a 18.90s (8 Ran).
(John O'Meara), Noel Meade

1620
Sillogue Novice Hurdle (Grade 3) (5-y-o and up) £6,850 3m............(2:30)

1431⁵ TARTHOOTH (Ire) 5-11-10 C O'Brien, *slow 1st, dsptd ld to 4th, disputed lead 7th to nxt, led aftr four out, rdn and kpt on.* ....(3 to 1 on) 1
1485* FLAMINGO FLOWER (Ire) 8-10-13 (3*) Mr P J Casey, *hld up, prog bef 2 out, kpt on wl.*......................(14 to 1) 2
1168⁴ ALLATRIM (Ire) 6-11-2 R Hughes, *wl plcd, rdn bef 2 out, slight mstk, no extr.*......................(14 to 1) 3
1431⁴ MULLOVER 5-11-7 T J Mitchell, *wl plcd till rdn aftr 3 out, no extr.*......................(12 to 1) 4
1536⁵ LEAMHOG (Ire) 6-11-4 C O'Dwyer, *dsptd ld till led 4th, jnd briefly nxt, hdd and rdn aftr four out, sn wknd.....*(16 to 1) 5
1246* BALLINLAMMY ROSE (Ire) 6-11-5 (5*) J Butler, *al rear, lost tch aftr 2 out, fnshd lme.*......................(4 to 1) 6
Dist: 3l, 5½l, 6l, dist. 6m 3.60s. a 23.60s (6 Ran).
(Mrs H de Burgh), A L T Moore

1621
New Stand Handicap Hurdle (Grade 3) (4-y-o and up) £6,850 2m...(3:00)

DARDJINI (USA) [-] 6-12-0 R Hughes, ...(11 to 1) 1
FAMILY WAY [-] 9-10-11 (7*) D W O'Sullivan, ...(12 to 1) 2
1171² CAITRIONA'S CHOICE (Ire) [-] 5-10-6 L P Cusack, (10 to 1) 3
BOLINO STAR (Ire) [-] 5-11-8 (3*) G Cotter, ...(7 to 1) 4
1535³ METASTASIO [-] 4-11-3 H Rogers, ...(11 to 2) 5
1462* MAJOR JAMIE (Ire) [-] 5-10-6 D J Casey, ...(9 to 2 fav) 6
1488⁴ TIDJANI (Ire) [-] 4-10-4 T J Mitchell, ...(12 to 1) 7
303 TALINA'S LAW (Ire) [-] (bl) 4-10-10 (7*) A O'Shea, ..(7 to 1) 8
1537² TRYFIRION (Ire) [-] 7-11-8 (3*) B Bowens, ...(9 to 1) 9
1406³ LADY ARPEL (Ire) [-] 4-11-3 C O'Dwyer, ...(11 to 2) 10
1549² SHADING DOLLAR (Ire) [-] 5-10-5 (5*) J Butler, ...(9 to 1) 11
1535⁵ JO JO BOY (Ire) [-] 7-10-7 F J Flood, ...(10 to 1) f
Dist: Sht-hd, 3l, 2l, 2l. 3m 57.20s. a 13.20s (12 Ran).
SR: 24/14/-/16/6/-/ (The High Street Racing Synd), Noel Meade

1622
Fort William I.N.H. Flat Race (4-y-o and up) £3,082 2m............(3:25)

898⁶ MINISTER'S CROSS (Ire) 4-10-13 (7*) Mr D A Harney, ...(7 to 1) 1
1554² BORO BOW (Ire) 5-11-13 Mr T Mullins, ...(6 to 4 on) 2
1279⁵ FATHER GERRY 6-11-11 Mr J A Flynn, ...(5 to 1) 3
1436³ MY LITTLE DOXIE (Ire) 6-11-6 Mr H F Cleary, ...(9 to 2) 4
WALT (Ire) 6-11-11 Mr G J Harford, ...(20 to 1) 5
OLD FRIENDS (Ire) 5-11-11 Mr A R Coonan, ...(10 to 1) 6
1096³ SLANEY CHARM (Ire) 6-11-4 (7*) Miss L E A Doyle, ...(11 to 1) 7
1436 HARBOUR BLAZE (Ire) 6-11-11 Mr J A Berry, ...(20 to 1) 8

BEAUTY'S PRIDE (Ire) 4-10-8 (7*) Mr M Nakauchida,
....(20 to 1) 9
Dist: Sht-hd, nk, 4l, 7l. 4m 2.80s. (9 Ran).

(T W Nicholson), John W Nicholson

HAYDOCK (good)
Saturday November 30th
Going Correction: PLUS 0.70 sec. per fur. (races
1,3,6), PLUS 0.35 (2,4,5)

1623 White Lodge 'National Hunt' Novices' Hurdle Class C (4-y-o and up)
£3,875 2½m.................(1:10)

1198² SHANAVOGH 5-11-3 J Callaghan, trkd ldrs, hdwy 6th, led 2
out, sn rdn and kpt on wl. (9 to 1 op 10 to 1 tchd 12 to 1) 1
1311 SWANBISTER (Ire) 6-11-3 R Farrant, al prmnt, led appr 3 out,
hdd nxt, kpt on wl und pres..............(10 to 1 op 8 to 1) 2
1367* RANGITIKEI (NZ) 5-11-8 J Railton, chsd ldrs, hdwy 4 out, ev
ch nxt, rdn and one pace appr last.
....(11 to 2 op 4 to 1 tchd 6 to 1) 3
1255² PAPERISING 4-10-12 B Harding, hld up, hit 5th, hdwy appr 4
out, chsd ldrs frm nxt, sn rdn and one pace.
....(9 to 2 op 3 to 1 tchd 5 to 1) 4
1073⁴ ROTHARI 4-10-12 D Gallagher, prmnt, rdn alng 4 out, grad
wknd...............................(20 to 1 op 16 to 1) 5
GLENBOWER 4-10-9 (3*) Mr C Bonner, beh, hdwy hfwy, styd
on frm 3 out, hit nxt, not rch ldrs....(33 to 1 op 20 to 1) 6
1270² HURDANTE (Ire) 6-10-12 B Fenton, keen hold, led till rdn
alng and hdd appr 3 out, sn btn.... (11 to 8 fav op 5 to 4) 7
GRAND CRU 5-10-9 (3*) G Cahill, beh till styd on frm 3 out,
nvr a factor...........................(16 to 1 op 14 to 1) 8
1396⁴ FOXIES LAD 5-10-12 V Slattery, mid-div, hdwy and hit 6th, no
imprsn aftr..............(9 to 1 op 10 to 1 tchd 12 to 1) 9
ADIB (USA) 6-10-12 N Bentley, beh, hit 4th, nvr a factor.
....(33 to 1 op 20 to 1) 10
RELUCKINO 5-10-5 (7*) Mr J T Nolan, al beh.....(25 to 1) 11
1260 SEVEN POTATO MORE (Ire) 6-10-12 J Burke, beh frm halfway....................................(33 to 1 op 25 to 1) 12
THE OTHER MAN (Ire) 6-10-12 A Thornton, al rear, beh frm
hfwy....................................(33 to 1) 13
1540⁸ LOTHIAN COMMANDER 4-10-12 D Bridgwater, chsd ldrs to
5th, sn lost pl and beh frm hfwy.......(25 to 1 op 20 to 1) 14
NOQUITA (NZ) 9-10-12 M Sharratt, al beh.
....(25 to 1 op 25 to 1) 15
SILVER GROVE 6-10-7 (5*) R McGrath, beh frm hfwy, blun
and sn rdr last...........................(33 to 1 op 25 to 1) ur
Dist: ½l, 8l, 2½l, 13l, 3l, 7l, 9l, 6l, 5l, ¾l. 4m 56.60s. a 20.60s (16 Ran).
SR: 23/22/19/6/-/-/

(Sean Graham), G M Moore

1624 Rainford Handicap Chase Class E (0-115 5-y-o and up) £3,176 2½m
..................................(1:40)

1589⁵ WAYUPHILL [87] 9-10-9 (5*) R McGrath, hld up in tch, smooth
hdwy appr 5 out, led 2 out, clr last.
....(9 to 1 op 7 to 1 tchd 10 to 1) 1
1401² MR PRESIDENT (Ire) [102] 7-11-2 D Gallagher, whipped
round strt and lost 15 ls, hdwy and cl up 6th, rdn alng and hit 4
out, sn one pace..................................(Evens fav) 2
1296 SAILOR JIM [110] 9-11-10 B Harding, led, rdn and hdd appr 2
out, one pace approaching last........(4 to 1 op 7 to 2) 3
1254² CRAFTY CHAPLAIN [100] 10-11-0 D Bridgwater, cl up, hit
tenth, sn rdn and wknd 4 out..........(4 to 1 op 7 to 2) 4
NICKLE JOE [105] 10-11-5 W Marston, prmnt, hit second,
reminders 7th, drvn alng and wknd 4 out, sn tld off.
....(14 to 1 op 12 to 1 tchd 16 to 1) 5
Dist: 16l, ½l, 4l, dist. 5m 18.00s. a 21.00s (5 Ran).

(D Phelan), J J O'Neill

1625 Peter Richardson Half Century Claiming Hurdle Class F (4-y-o and up) £2,193 2½m.............(2:10)

1213⁴ OUT RANKING (Fr) 4-11-0 (7*) B Moore, jmpd rght, made all,
sn clr, rdn 2 out, kpt on wl...............(9 to 4 op 3 to 1) 1
ROBERTY LEA 8-11-9 (3*) G Cahill, chsd wnr frm 4th, rdn
appr 2 out, kpt on, not rch winner.
....(11 to 10 op 11 to 10 tchd 2 to 1) 2
1465⁵ EUROTWIST 7-10-11 (3*) G Lee, trkd ldrs, hdwy 4 out, rdn nxt,
kpt on same pace.....................(4 to 1 tchd 9 to 2) 3
1000⁸ DOMINION'S DREAM (v) 4-10-5 (7*) G Supple, beh till styd on
frm 3 out, nvr a factor....................(12 to 1 op 10 to 1) 4
IFALLELSEFAILS 8-10-10 (7*) I Jardine, hld up and beh, hdwy
hfwy, rdn bef 3 out, nvr a factor...(16 to 1 op 10 to 1) 5
KADARI (v) 7-10-6 A Thornton, prmnt, rdn alng 4 out, wknd
bef nxt....................................(15 to 2 op 7 to 1 tchd 8 to 1) 6
1348 SWEET TRENTINO (Ire) 5-10-11 W Marston, chsd ldrs,
pushed alng and blun badly 4 out, sn wl beh.
....(16 to 1 op 10 to 1) 7
Dist: 8l, 5l, 2½l, 14l, dist. 4m 57.90s. a 21.90s (7 Ran).
SR: 14/11/-/-/

(Knight Hawks Partnership), M C Pipe

1626 Tim Molony Memorial Chase Handicap Class B (0-140 5-y-o and up)

£6,729 3½m 110yds.........(2:40)

1314* PARSONS BOY [120] 7-10-8 B Harding, trkd ldr, effrt appr 3
out, rdn to chal nxt, led approaching last, ran on strly.
....(13 to 8 op 6 to 4 tchd 7 to 4) 1
1495* CLASS OF NINETYTWO (Ire) [125] 7-10-13 A Thornton, led,
rdn 3 out, jnd nxt, hdd appr last and wknd r-in.
....(11 to 8 fav op 6 to 4 tchd 13 to 8) 2
1199⁵ HIGH PADRE [125] 10-10-10 (3*) F Leahy, prmnt, hit tenth, rdn
alng and mstk 16th, sn one pace........(7 to 1 op 6 to 1) 3
DIAMOND FORT [112] 11-10-0 R Farrant, prmnt, hit 7th and
nxt, sn pushed alng, lost pl, tld off frm 16th.
....(16 to 1 op 14 to 1) 4
KILLESHIN [133] 10-11-7 S Curran, in tch, jmpd slwly 4th, hit
8th, pushed alng 14th, sn lost touch, tld off frm 16th.
....(11 to 2 op 5 to 1) 5
Dist: 9l, 1½l, dist, 16l. 7m 36.20s. a 24.20s (5 Ran).

(B Ridge), G Richards

1627 Makerfield Novices' Chase Class D (5-y-o and up) £3,740 2m.....(3:10)

OAT COUTURE 8-11-0 A Thornton, jmpd wl, chsd ldr, hdwy to
ld 2 out, pushed clr last. cmftbly....(10 to 1 tchd 11 to 1) 1
1267³ NAIYSARI (Ire) 8-11-0 W Marston, led, rdn 3 out, hdd nxt, no
extr und pres last.....................(6 to 1 op 8 to 1) 2
GAROLO (Fr) 6-11-0 D Gallagher, al prmnt, effrt to chal 3 out,
ev ch till rdn and one pace appr last.
....(10 to 3 op 5 to 2 tchd 7 to 2) 3
SPEEDWELL PRINCE (Ire) 6-11-0 D Bridgwater, not jump wl,
mstk 6th, pushed alng in tch whn blun badly nxt, no ch aftr.
....(9 to 4 op 7 to 2) 4
1374² BOLD BOSS 7-11-0 N Bentley, hld up and beh, mstk 4th,
hmpd 7th, no ch aftr. (15 to 8 fav op 2 to 1 tchd 9 to 4) 5
1475⁸ THE FENCE SHRINKER 5-11-0 B Harding, in tch, blun 5th, f
7th..............................(33 to 1 op 25 to 1) f
Dist: 1½l, 1½l, dist, dist. 4m 7.40s. a 11.40s (6 Ran).
SR: 28/26/24/

(Mackinnon Mills), L Lungo

1628 Haydock Gold Card Hurdle Handicap Class B (4-y-o and up) £4,992 2¾m
..................................(3:40)

ANZUM [130] 5-11-6 W Marston, chsd ldrs, blun badly 6th,
hdwy appr 4 out, rdn to chal 2 out, drvn r-in, kpt on to ld nr
finish..............................(13 to 2 op 4 to 1) 1
1388* BURNT IMP (USA) [125] 6-11-1 J Callaghan, in tch, gd hdwy
7th, effrt to chal 2 out, rdn and led nr finish, no extr r-in.
....(5 to 1 jt-
fav op 4 to 1 tchd 11 to 2) 2
1526* DALLY BOY [110] 4-9-11 (3*) F Leahy, prmnt, hdwy to ld 4 out,
rdn 2 out, wndrd appr drvn r-in, hdd and no extr nr finish.
....(5 to 1 jt-fav op 9 to 2 tchd 13 to 2) 3
OUTSET (Ire) [125] 6-10-12 (3*) Mr C Bonner, in tch gng wl,
smooth hdwy appr 4 out, ev ch 2 out, wknd last.
....(8 to 1 op 7 to 1) 4
IZZA [110] 5-9-9 (5*) R McGrath, hld up in rear, steady hdwy
8th, effrt 3 out, sn rdn and one pace nxt. (8 to 1 op 10 to 1) 5
ALLEGATION [137] (v) 6-11-6 (7*) B Moore, chsd ldrs, hdwy to
ld 7th, rdn and hdd 4 out, hit nxt, sn wknd.
....(20 to 1 op 10 to 1) 6
BEACHY HEAD [126] 8-11-2 A Thornton, hld up, some hdwy
7th, sn rdn, nvr a factor..................(16 to 1 op 12 to 1) 7
1467⁵ PALOSANTO (Ire) [119] 6-10-9 R Farrant, chsd ldrs, rdn alng
eigth, sn wknd...........................(9 to 1 op 6 to 1) 8
GIVE BEST [110] 5-10-0 B Harding, al beh.
....(16 to 1 op 12 to 1) 9
ARABIAN SULTAN [112] 9-9-9 (7*) G Supple, in tch, hdwy 7th,
dsptd ld nxt till rdn and wknd quickly 4 out, pld up bef next.
....(16 to 1 op 10 to 1) pu
VILLAGE REINDEER (NZ) [121] 9-10-11 Gary Lyons, al beh,
tld off whn pld up bef 4 out...........(11 to 1 op 8 to 1) pu
SUPERIOR RISK (Ire) [138] 7-12-0 D Bridgwater, led to 6th, cl
up till rdn and wknd 8th, beh whn pld up lme bef 3 out.
....(13 to 2 op 9 to 2 tchd 7 to 1) pu
Dist: Hd, hd, 10l, 17l, 20l, 5l, 8l, 1¾l. 5m 28.30s. a 21.30s (12 Ran).
SR: 35/30/15/20/-/-/ (The Old Foresters Partnership), D Nicholson

NEWCASTLE (good)
Saturday November 30th
Going Correction: PLUS 0.50 sec. per fur.

1629 Newcastle Building Society Juvenile Novices' Hurdle Class D (3-y-o)
£3,072 2m.................(12:10)

1188² JACKSON PARK 10-12 R Dunwoody, cl up, blun 6th, slight ld
bef 3 out, rdn and hdd last, sn led ag'n, all out.
....(2 to 1 fav op 7 to 4) 1
1221³ SON OF ANSHAN 10-12 Mr C Wilson, in tch, hdwy aftr 6th, ev
ch last till no extr und pres clsg stages.
....(12 to 1 op 10 to 1 tchd 14 to 1) 2
1384* ROSSEL (USA) 11-8 A Maguire, trkd ldrs, chlgd 3 out, slight ld
last, sn rdn and not extr...............(11 to 2 op 8 to 1) 3
1221⁸ MELTEMISON 10-5 (7*) R Burns, hld up in tch, steady hdwy
frm 3 out, fnshd wl, nvr plcd to chal...(33 to 1 op 25 to 1) 4

BOLD CLASSIC (Ire) 10-13[1] T Reed, *chsd ldrs, kpt on same pace frm 3 out*.....................(14 to 1 op 10 to 1) 5

1249[3] MOCK TRIAL (Ire) 10-12 Mr S Swiers, *chsd ldrs till outpcd aftr 6th, no dngr after*........(11 to 2 op 7 to 1 tchd 5 to 1) 6

664[4] NORTHERN FALCON (bl) 10-7 C Llewellyn, *made most till hdd bef 3 out, fdd*....................(33 to 1 op 20 to 1) 7

1249[5] COTTAGE PRINCE (Ire) 11-3 J Shortt, *chsd ldrs till grad wknd frm 3 out*........................(33 to 1 op 20 to 1) 8

734[5] WHAT JIM WANTS (Ire) 10-12 B Storey, *nvr nr to chal.*
..............................(50 to 1 op 25 to 1) 9

NEXSIS STAR 10-12 Richard Guest, *slwly into strd, nvr dngrs*...........................(50 to 1 op 33 to 1) 10

1196 LUCKY BEA 10-9 (3[*]) P Midgley, *nvr nr to chal.*
..............................(20 to 1 op 12 to 1) 11

MUA-TAB 10-7 D Bentley, *nvr better than mid-div, dead.*
..............................(33 to 1 op 20 to 1) 12

1530[3] ONYOUROWN (Ire) 10-7 (5[*]) G F Ryan, *nvr better than mid-div, no ch whn blun last*.............(12 to 1 op 10 to 1) 13

1384[5] RATTLE 10-5 (7[*]) D Jewett, *beh frm hfwy.*
..............................(100 to 1 op 25 to 1) 14

JOE SHAW 10-12 P Niven, *sn beh*.....(33 to 1 op 14 to 1) 15

1221[5] WHOTHEHELLISHARRY 10-12 M Moloney, *chsd ldrs till wknd bef 3 out*..................(20 to 1 op 25 to 1) 16

BANK ON INLAND 10-7 W Fry, *sn beh.*
..............................(100 to 1 op 50 to 1) 17

930[6] ERIC'S BETT 10-12 M Foster, *chsd ldrs till wknd aftr 6th.*
..............................(33 to 1 op 20 to 1) 18

1188[6] PRELUDE TO FAME (USA) 11-3 A S Smith, *in tch till wknd aftr 6th*...........................(33 to 1 op 20 to 1) 19

1188[8] HOBBS CHOICE 10-9 (3[*]) E Callaghan, *beh frm hfwy.*
..............................(33 to 1 op 25 to 1) 20

1438[4] BOY BLAKENEY 10-12 Mr P Murray, *slwly into strd, al beh.*
..............................(50 to 1 op 33 to 1) 21

OVERSMAN 10-12 M Dwyer, *chsd ldrs till wknd bef 6th.*
..............................(11 to 1 op 9 to 1) 22

1384[2] THE BOOZING BRIEF (USA) (bl) 10-12 D Parker, *prmnt whn blun and uns rdr 6th*....(20 to 1 op 14 to 1 tchd 25 to 1) ur

JUST RORY 10-12 K Johnson, *beh, tld off whn pld up bef 3 out*............................(100 to 1 op 33 to 1) pu

Dist: Nk, 1l, 5l, 10l, sht-hd, ¾l, 1¼l, sht-hd, nk, nk. 3m 53.60s. a 16.60s (24 Ran).

(C H Stevens), T D Easterby

1630 Tommy McNicholas Novices' Chase Class C (4-y-o and up) £5,340 2½m ....(12:40)

1374[*] SPARKY GAYLE (Ire) 6-11-9 B Storey, *sn tracking ldrs, led 11th, hrd pressed 3 out, styd on strly.*
..............(6 to 4 on op 5 to 4 on tchd 6 to 5 on) 1

1281[*] SOLOMON'S DANCER (USA) 6-11-13 R Dunwoody, *nvr far away, drvn alng bef 3 out, kpt on und pres frm last, no imprsn on wnr*.......................(9 to 4 op 2 to 1) 2

1376 BLUE CHARM (Ire) 6-11-9 A Maguire, *led 4th, mstk 7th, hdd 11th, ev ch 2 out, sn rdn, kpt on same pace.*
..............................(8 to 1 op 6 to 1) 3

CHIPPED OUT 6-11-4 M Dwyer, *blun 1st and second, beh, some hdwy aftr 12th, no further prog frm 3 out.*
..............(16 to 1 op 10 to 1 tchd 20 to 1) 4

1332[3] LE DENSTAN 9-11-9 T Reed, *nvr dngrs.*
..............................(20 to 1 op 14 to 1) 5

935[4] GARBO'S BOY 6-11-4 W Fry, *in tch till wknd aftr 10th.*
..............................(200 to 1 op 50 to 1) 6

1386[7] MARLINGFORD 9-10-11 (7[*]) L McGrath, *led to 4th, prmnt till wknd aftr 10th*..............(200 to 1 op 50 to 1) 7

1162[9] SELDOM BUT SEVERE (Ire) 6-11-4 K Johnson, *beh most of way*.............................(50 to 1 op 50 to 1) 8

MORE JOY 8-11-4 A S Smith, *al beh.* (200 to 1 op 50 to 1) 9

1523[4] FINGERHILL (Ire) 7-11-4 Mr M Thompson, *prmnt till blun and uns rdr 10th*.......(10 to 1 op 50 to 1 tchd 1000 to 1) ur

Dist: 2½l, 2½l, 20l, 12l, 12l, 2½l, 3l, 2½l. 5m 7.00s. a 20.00s (10 Ran).

(Mr & Mrs Raymond Anderson Green), C Parker

1631 Brulines Novices' Hurdle Class E (4-y-o and up) £2,536 3m.......(1:10)

AGISTMENT 5-10-12 M Dwyer, *in tch, smooth hdwy to dispute ld 2 out, led last, shaken up and styd on wl.*
..............................(100 to 30 op 4 to 1) 1

1268[4] HAND WOVEN 4-11-4 C Llewellyn, *led, jnd 2 out, hdd last, no extr und pres*.......(2 to 1 fav tchd 7 to 4 and 9 to 4) 2

1311[*] MILITARY ACADEMY 7-11-5 R Dunwoody, *al prmnt, drvn alng aftr 3 out, no extr whn mstk last*.............(4 to 1) 3

1419[3] COOLE HILL (Ire) 5-10-7 A Maguire, *in tch, ev ch 3 out, sn rdn and wknd*.........(12 to 1 op 10 to 1 tchd 14 to 1) 4

1371[2] GRANDINARE (USA) 4-10-11 Richard Guest, *beh, hdwy into midfield aftr 5th, staying on whn mstk 3 out, no further prog.*
..............................(11 to 1 op 6 to 1) 5

1388[2] CRYSTAL GIFT 4-11-1 (3[*]) E Callaghan, *chsd ldrs till wknd bef 2 out*....................(10 to 1 op 8 to 1) 6

1377[3] PHAR ECHO (Ire) 5-10-12 M Foster, *in tch, no hdwy frm 10th.*
..............................(50 to 1 op 25 to 1) 7

1311[4] CHILL FACTOR 6-10-12 P Niven, *nvr on terms.*
..............................(66 to 1 op 50 to 1) 8

1252[6] MENALDI (Ire) 6-10-12 A S Smith, *chsd ldrs aftr 10th.*
..............................(50 to 1) 9

1377[5] JIGGINSTOWN 9-10-5 (7[*]) L Cooper, *beh till some late hdwy, nvr dngrs*........................(200 to 1) 10

935[5] COOL STEEL (Ire) 4-10-11 Mr S Swiers, *nvr dngrs.*(200 to 1) 11

CLONGOUR (Ire) 6-10-5 (7[*]) Miss Elizabeth Doyle, *nvr on terms*.....................(33 to 1 tchd 50 to 1) 12

SEE MORE GHOSTS (Ire) 5-10-12 Mr C Wilson, *nvr dngrs.*
..............................(100 to 1) 13

ELEMENT OF RISK (Ire) 6-10-5 (7[*]) L McGrath, *beh most of way*...........................(25 to 1 op 33 to 1) 14

1227[6] LIPPY LOUISE 4-10-6 N Smith, *sn beh*.......(100 to 1) 15

1377[4] POCAIRE GAOITHE (Ire) 6-10-12 M Moloney, *chsd ldrs aftr 10th*..........................(50 to 1 op 33 to 1) 16

1311[5] RUBER 9-10-12 B Storey, *prmnt till wknd aftr 9th.* (200 to 1) 17

1313[7] FENLOE RAMBLER (Ire) 5-10-12 K Johnson, *sn beh.*
..............................(100 to 1) 18

1311[6] SOUTH COAST STAR (Ire) 6-10-7 (5[*]) G F Ryan, *nvr better than mid-div*...................(100 to 1 op 50 to 1) 19

1377[7] WILLIE WANNABE (Ire) 6-10-12 Miss P Robson, *nvr better than mid-div*.........................(300 to 1 op 200 to 1) 20

BLOND MOSS 6-10-12 D Bentley, *sn beh, tld off whn pld up bef 3 out*.........................(300 to 1 op 200 to 1) pu

TRIONA'S HOPE (Ire) 7-10-12 Mr P Murray, *in tch to hfwy, tld off whn pld up bef 3 out*.............(300 to 1 op 200 to 1) pu

CRAGNABUOY (Ire) 6-10-7 (5[*]) B Grattan, *towards rear, wl beh whn pld up bef last*................(25 to 1 op 16 to 1) pu

KNOCKBRIDE (Ire) 7-10-5 (7[*]) Mr T J Barry, *beh frm hfwy, tld off whn pld up bef last*......................(100 to 1) pu

1034 TO SAY THE LEAST 6-10-5 (7[*]) A K Smith, *chsd ldrs to hfwy, drvn alng and wknd, tld off whn pld up bef last, lme.*
..............................(300 to 1 op 200 to 1) pu

Dist: 4l, 1¼l, 11l, nk, 14l, 5l, ¾l, 3l, ½l, nk. 5m 55.30s. a 24.30s (25 Ran).

(Marquesa de Moratalla), J G FitzGerald

1632 MD Foods Handicap Chase Class C (0-130 5-y-o and up) £7,100 3m ....(1:45)

TURNING TRIX [123] 9-11-13 A Maguire, *trkd ldrs, led 2 out, mstk last, shaken up and styd on strly fnl 150 yards.*
..............(7 to 4 fav op 2 to 1 tchd 9 to 4) 1

ROAD BY THE RIVER [97] 8-10-1 B Storey, *hld up, steady hdwy to ld 11th, hdd 2 out, sn outpcd, kpt on frm last.*(33 to 1) 2

1199[4] ALI'S ALIBI [115] 9-11-5 P Niven, *towards rear, hdwy to track ldrs 9th, dsptd ld 2 out, ev ch till wknd quickly fnl 150 yards.*
..............................(9 to 2 tchd 4 to 1) 3

FRONT LINE [113] 9-11-3 M Moloney, *in tch, outpcd aftr 15th, no dngr after*..............(20 to 1 op 10 to 1 tchd 33 to 1) 4

1336 STRONG DEEL (Ire) [119] 8-11-9 C Llewellyn, *beh, outpcd aftr 15th, no dngr after*..............(13 to 2 op 6 to 1) 5

1199[2] CEILIDH BOY [124] 10-12-0 A S Smith, *in tch, reminder aftr 10th, rdn after 13th, wknd*........(6 to 1 op 7 to 1) 6

2544[4] LIE DETECTOR [104] 8-10-8 M Dwyer, *led to 4th, lost pl aftr 8th, beh after, tld off*.................(6 to 1 op 7 to 2) 7

MERRY MASTER [123] 12-11-13 Mr M Armytage, *jmpd rght, dsptd ld, led 7th, hdd 11th, fdg whn f 14th.*
..............................(20 to 1 op 16 to 1) f

1336[4] EARLYMORNING LIGHT (Ire) [119] 7-11-9 R Dunwoody, *led 4th to 7th, wth ldrs till wknd quickly and pld up aftr 3 out.*
..............................(10 to 1 op 5 to 1) pu

Dist: 8l, 2l, 16l, 16l, nk, 15l. 6m 3.50s. a 17.50s (9 Ran).
SR: 44/10/26/8/-/-/   (Mel Davies), D Nicholson

1633 Newcastle Building Society 'Fighting Fifth' Hurdle Limited Handicap Class A Grade 2 (4-y-o and up) £22,022 2m...................(2:15)

1393[*] SPACE TRUCKER (Ire) [140] 5-10-4 J Shortt, *settled in tch, hdwy on bit to ld 2 out, blun last and hdd, sn led ag'n, ran on wl*..........................(5 to 2 tchd 11 to 4) 1

1268[*] CASTLE SWEEP (Ire) [140] 5-10-4 A Maguire, *sn chasing ldr, led 5th, hit 3 out, hdd nxt, slight ld aftr last, soon headed and no extr und pres*...............(11 to 8 fav op 7 to 4) 2

DATO STAR (Ire) [140] 5-10-4 M Dwyer, *trkd ldrs, rdn and outpcd aftr 3 out, rallied after nxt, ev ch last, no extr und pres.*
..............................(9 to 1 op 8 to 1) 3

1284 HOME COUNTIES (Ire) [141] 7-10-5[1] D J Moffatt, *in tch, effrt aftr 5th, sn drvn alng, fdd*..(8 to 1 op 6 to 1 tchd 9 to 1) 4

1284[3] MARCHANT MING (Ire) [140] 4-10-4 D Bentley, *led till hdd 5th, wknd quickly aftr nxt*..................(33 to 1) 5

1284[7] JAZILAH (Fr) [140] 8-10-4 A S Smith, *sn beh, lost tch frm hfwy, tld off*..........................(33 to 1 op 20 to 1) 6

1508 NON VINTAGE (Ire) [140] 5-10-4 W Worthington, *hld up, drvn alng and outpcd aftr 5th, wl beh whn ran out bef 3 out.*
..............................(20 to 1 op 16 to 1 tchd 25 to 1) ro

GRANVILLE AGAIN [140] 10-10-4 M Foster, *lost tch frm hfwy, tld off whn pld up bef 6th*.................(100 to 1) pu

Dist: 1l, sht-hd, 17l, 21l, dist. 3m 46.30s. a 9.30s (8 Ran).
SR: 63/62/62/46/24/   (Mrs E Queally), Mrs J Harrington

1634 Douglas Smith Memorial Handicap Chase Class D (0-125 5-y-o and up) £3,810 2½m...................(2:45)

1285[*] EASBY JOKER [123] 8-12-0 P Niven, *hld up, hdwy hfwy, led gng wl betw last 2, clr aftr last, kpt on.* (4 to 1 tchd 9 to 2) 1

1253^{7} DEEP DECISION [100] 10-10-5 A S Smith, *al prmnt, ch 2 out, styd on wl towards finish*..............(10 to 1 op 7 to 1) 2
1151^{2} ALJADEER (USA) [110] (bl) 7-11-1 R Dunwoody, *hld up, hit 4th, hdwy hfwy, ch 2 out, kpt on same pace.* ....(5 to 2 fav op 2 to 1) 3
1316^{2} PAGLIACCIO [99] 8-10-4 A Maguire, *mstks, hld up in rear, hdwy hfwy, outpcd aftr 3 out, styd on frm last.* ....(4 to 1 op 7 to 2) 4
1401^{5} PURITAN (Can) [112] (bl) 7-11-3 Miss P Jones, *cl up frm 6th, rdn aftr 3 out, sn btn*....(16 to 1 op 14 to 1 tchd 20 to 1) 5
1201^{3} VICARIDGE [95] 9-10-0 K Johnson, *made most till hdd betw last 2, fdd*..........................(11 to 2 op 6 to 1) 6
1525 EAST HOUSTON [97] 7-10-2 M Moloney, *hld up, reminder aftr 9th, some hdwy after nxt, sn btn*. (12 to 1 tchd 14 to 1) 7
1401^{4} RUSTIC AIR [105] 9-10-10 M Dwyer, *chsd ldrs till wknd bef 3 out*....................................(7 to 1 op 6 to 1) 8
1328^{6} BLAZING DAWN [95] 9-10-0 Miss P Robson, *cl up, led aftr 5th, hdd 7th, wknd after 9th, broke blood vessel.* ....(20 to 1 op 12 to 1) 9
1571^{6} MONAUGHTY MAN [95] 10-10-0 Mr P Murray, *keen early, mstks, beh frm hfwy*..........(100 to 1 op 66 to 1) 10
Dist: 1½l, 4l, 3l, ¾l, 1l, 12l, 15l, 9l, nk. 5m 9.70s. a 22.70s (10 Ran).
(G R Orchard), S E Kettlewell

1635 Chisholm Bookmakers Handicap Hurdle Class D (0-125 4-y-o and up) £3,452 2m....................(3:15)

1465^{2} CIRCUS LINE [97] 5-10-5 M Dwyer, *mstks, made all, styd on wl frm 2 out*..........(2 to 1 fav op 9 to 4 tchd 5 to 2) 1
1512^{6} DONE WELL (USA) [118] 4-11-12 Richard Guest, *settled midfield, effrt bef 2 out, styd on und pres frm last*. ....(11 to 2 op 8 to 1) 2
1200^{4} SHINING EDGE [108] 4-11-2 A S Smith, *prmnt, ev ch 3 out, kpt on same pace frm nxt*..........(11 to 1 op 8 to 1) 3
1166^{4} RALITSA (Ire) [102] 4-10-3 (7*) R Burns, *in tch, pushed alng betw last 2, kpt on frm last.* ....(10 to 1 op 8 to 1 tchd 11 to 1) 4
1167* FEN TERRIER [95] 4-10-0 (3*) E Callaghan, *prmnt, ch 3 out, grad wknd*.........................(14 to 1 op 10 to 1) 5
1386^{4} CITTADINO [100] 6-10-8 M Foster, *mstks, beh, rdn aftr 5th, some late hdwy, nvr dngrs*..............(11 to 2 op 9 to 2) 6
1465^{3} DESERT FIGHTER [111] 5-11-5 P Niven, *hld up, effrt aftr 6th, wknd after 2 out, eased whn no ch*....(5 to 1 tchd 11 to 2) 7
1388^{6} COOL LUKE (Ire) [102] 7-10-7 (3*) L Aspell, *prmnt till wknd quickly bef 3 out*..................(10 to 1 op 12 to 1) 8
1150^{4} MASTER HYDE (USA) [112] 7-11-6 M Moloney, *in tch till wknd bef 3 out*.........(11 to 1 op 10 to 1 tchd 12 to 1) 9
DUAL IMAGE [108] 9-11-2 W Dwan, *al beh.* ....(25 to 1 tchd 33 to 1) 10
Dist: 3½l, 1l, 1¼l, ¾l, 16l, 1l, 8l, 6l, 12l. 3m 54.40s. a 17.40s (10 Ran).
(Mrs P A H Hartley), M W Easterby

NEWBURY (good)
Saturday November 30th
Going Correction: PLUS 0.35 sec. per fur. (races 1,4,5), PLUS 0.45 (2,3,6)

1636 Fulke Walwyn Chase Class C (5-y-o and up) £5,920 2½m.........(12:45)

1269^{3} BUCKHOUSE BOY 6-11-0 C Maude, *badly hmpd 1st, sn chasing clr ldr, lft in clear ld 9th, mstk 11th, unchlgd.* ....(5 to 2 fav op 2 to 1) 1
FOODBROKER STAR (Ire) 6-11-0 P Hide, *hld up, styd on to take moderate second last, no ch wth wnr.* ....(20 to 1 op 14 to 1 tchd 25 to 1) 2
TAKE THE BUCKSKIN 9-11-0 N Williamson, *hld up mstk 3rd not fluent 6th no imprsn frm twelfth* ....(9 to 2 op 5 to 1 tchd 11 to 2) 3
1341^{3} COURT MASTER (Ire) 8-11-0 B Powell, *hld up, lft in moderate second 9th, wkng whn mstk last*.......(10 to 1 op 7 to 1) 4
TWO JOHN'S (Ire) 7-11-0 C F Swan, *led till f 1st.* ....(6 to 1 op 5 to 1) f
133^{2} ART PRINCE (Ire) 6-11-0 S McNeill, *lft in ld 1st, sn wl clr, not fluent 6th, f 9th*..................(12 to 1 tchd 16 to 1) f
GARNWIN (Ire) 6-11-0 M A Fitzgerald, *brght dwn 1st.* ....(12 to 1 op 8 to 1 tchd 14 to 1) bd
1349^{4} BROWN ROBBER 8-11-0 G Upton, *al beh, mstks 5th and 7th, tld off whn pld up bef 12th*..........(66 to 1 op 50 to 1) pu
COLONEL IN CHIEF (Ire) 6-11-0 J Osborne, *wtd wth, mstk second, 5th and no ch whn hit 12th, pld up bef nxt.* ....(11 to 2 op 4 to 1 tchd 6 to 1) pu
PROUD TOBY (Ire) 6-11-0 B Clifford, *al beh, blun 9th, tld off whn pld up bef 12th*..... (16 to 1 op 8 to 1 tchd 20 to 1) pu
Dist: 25l, 3l, 6l. 5m 6.10s. a 18.10s (10 Ran).
(The Bawtry Boys), N A Twiston-Davies

1637 Equi Life Work Formula Long Distance Hurdle Class A Grade 2 (4-y-o and up) £12,380 3m 110yds...(1:15)

1186^{2} WHAT A QUESTION (Ire) 8-10-9 G Bradley, *wtd wth beh ldrs, led appr 2 out, rdn out, ran on wl.* ....(4 to 1 op 3 to 1 tchd 9 to 2) 1
1407* ANTAPOURA (Ire) 4-10-8 C F Swan, *hld up rear, improved appr 4 out, rdn and ev ch last, kpt on same pace.* ....(10 to 1 op 7 to 1) 2
1186* TRAINGLOT 9-11-7 N Williamson, *mid-div, hdwy 4 out, hit nxt, ev ch appr 2 out, edgd rght und pres bef last, not quicken.* ....(11 to 8 fav op 2 to 1 tchd 5 to 4) 3
1277* MINELLA MAN 9-11-0 F Woods, *trkd ldrs, led appr 3 out till bef nxt, btn whn short of room approaching last.* ....(10 to 1 op 6 to 1) 4
1340^{2} LITTLE BUCK (Ire) 8-11-0 S McNeill, *hld up beh, prog appr 3 out, ev ch nxt, wknd approaching last.* (25 to 1 op 20 to 1) 5
104 TOP SPIN 7-11-0 B Powell, *rear, gd hdwy appr 4 out, ev ch nxt, wknd approaching 2 out.* ....(40 to 1 op 33 to 1 tchd 50 to 1) 6
RULING (USA) 10-11-0 A Larnach, *wtd wth, wknd 4 out.* ....(40 to 1 op 33 to 1 tchd 50 to 1) 7
1032^{2} JACK BUTTON (Ire) 7-11-0 J Osborne, *led till appr 3 out, wknd bef last, eased*................(9 to 2 tchd 5 to 1) 8
HEBRIDEAN 9-11-0 M A Fitzgerald, *chsd ldr to 8th, rallied und pres 3 out, sn wknd*............(33 to 1 tchd 25 to 1) 9
1387^{5} BETTER TIMES AHEAD 10-11-7 A Dobbin, *chsd ldrs, rdn and wknd appr 4 out*..........................(10 to 1 op 6 to 1) 10
1233^{6} DARK HONEY 11-11-0 A Dicken, *mid-div, wknd 6th, tld off.* ....(66 to 1 tchd 50 to 1) 11
Dist: 1¾l, 6l, 7l, nk, 22l, 7l, ½l, 6l, 4l, dist. 6m 3.40s. a 17.40s (11 Ran).
SR: 17/14/21/7/6/-/ (Mrs Miles Valentine), M F Morris

1638 Bonusprint Gerry Feilden Hurdle Class A Grade 2 (4-y-o and up) £12,120 2m 110yds...........(1:50)

ZABADI (Ire) 4-11-6 N Williamson, *hld up, chsd ldr 5th, rdn appr last, kpt on gmely to ld cl hme.* ....(11 to 4 op 9 to 4 tchd 2 to 1) 1
1172* URUBANDE (Ire) 6-11-6 C F Swan, *led till aftr 1st, led 4th, rdn r-in, idled and hdd cl hme.* ....(6 to 4 on op 13 to 8 on tchd 11 to 10 on) 2
1276^{7} PUNTING PETE (Ire) 6-11-0 G Bradley, *led aftr 1st, hit 4th, sn hdd, wknd and eased appr 3 out*....... (12 to 1 op 6 to 1) 3
1397* MR PERCY (Ire) 5-11-0 P Hide, *hld up beh ldrs, 3rd whn f third*...............................(11 to 2 op 10 to 1) f
Dist: ½l, dist. 4m 3.50s. a 14.50s (4 Ran).
SR: 21/20/-/-/ (Lady Harris), D Nicholson

1639 Hennessy Cognac Gold Cup Handicap Chase Class A Grade 3 (5-y-o and up) £48,283 3¼m 110yds (2:25)

1304* COOME HILL (Ire) [136] 7-10-0 (4ex) J Osborne, *led to 6th, led aftr 11th to 13th, led appr last, rdn out, ran on wl.* ....(11 to 2 op 5 to 1 tchd 6 to 1) 1
1387* THE GREY MONK (Ire) [139] 8-10-3 (4ex) A Dobbin, *prmnt, hit 5th, led 13th till appr last, one pace.* ....(13 to 8 fav op 11 to 8 tchd 7 to 4) 2
LO STREGONE [150] (bl) 10-11-0 C F Swan, *sn chasing ldr, led 6th to nxt, rdn appr 4 out, wknd 2 out, lft 3rd at last.* ....(10 to 1 op 8 to 1 tchd 11 to 1) 3
MIDNIGHT CALLER [137] 10-10-1^{1} M A Fitzgerald, *mstks, hld up, hdwy 13th, wknd 4 out*............(20 to 1 op 33 to 1) 4
DEXTRA DOVE [137] 9-10-1 C Maude, *hld up, hdwy appr 17th, effrt approaching 3 out, wknd bef nxt, 4th and btn whn blun last*..............(12 to 1 op 14 to 1 tchd 16 to 1) 5
1094^{2} FEATHERED GALE [147] 9-10-11 F Woods, *hld up, hit 17th, btn whn mstk nxt*...................(14 to 1 op 12 to 1) 6
1480^{2} OLD BRIDGE (Ire) [136] 8-10-0 S McNeill, *mid-div, improved 11th, wknd 4 out, virtually pld up r-in.* ....(25 to 1 op 20 to 1 tchd 33 to 1) 7
1466^{2} COULDNT BE BETTER [160] 9-11-10 G Bradley, *hld up, rear rdn appr 4 out, sn btn, virtually pld up r-in, tld off.* ....(16 to 1 op 10 to 1 tchd 20 to 1) 8
1394* CHALLENGER DU LUC (Fr) [146] (bl) 6-10-10 (4ex) N Williamson, *hld up rear, f 14th*....(11 to 2 op 5 to 1 tchd 6 to 1) f
1283^{5} GRANGE BRAKE [136] (bl) 10-9-12^{1} (3*) D Walsh, *prmnt, led 7th till aftr 11th, ev ch 3 out, 3rd and hld whn blun and uns rdr last*.............................. (100 to 1 op 66 to 1) ur
967* GENERAL CRACK (Ire) [136] 7-10-0 P Hide, *hld up in tch, wknd 4 out, beh whn pld up bef 2 out.* ....(7 to 1 op 8 to 1 tchd 13 to 2) pu
Dist: 4l, 12l, 17l, ½l, 18l, 24l, ½l. 6m 40.60s. a 12.60s (11 Ran).
SR: 39/38/37/7/6/-/ (Mrs Jill Dennis), W W Dennis

1640 North Street Handicap Chase Class B (0-145 5-y-o and up) £6,845 2m 1f .... (2:55)

ASK TOM (Ire) [140] 7-11-9 R Garritty, *chsd ldr, led 4 out, clr 2 out, unchlgd*..................(7 to 4 fav tchd 15 to 8) 1
1210^{5} NAKIR (Fr) [140] 8-11-9 A Dobbin, *hld up, hdwy 9th, styd on to take second cl hme, no ch wth wnr*.....(5 to 1 tchd 6 to 1) 2
1157^{4} UNCLE ERNIE [145] 11-12-0 C F Swan, *wtd wth, kpt on to chase wnr frm 2 out till cl hme, no imprsn.* ....(5 to 1 op 9 to 2 tchd 4 to 1) 3
SOUND REVEILLE [145] 8-12-0 G Bradley, *led to 4 out, wknd appr 2 out, tld off whn pld up bef last, continued to finish fourth, tailed off*...........(9 to 1 op 6 to 1 tchd 10 to 1) 4
1480 BO KNOWS BEST (Ire) [121] 7-10-4 M A Fitzgerald, *tld off 5th, pld up bef 9th*................(12 to 1 tchd 14 to 1) pu

FRONT STREET [135] 9-11-4 J Osborne, *hld up, brief effrt appr 9th, sn wknd, beh whn pld up bef 2 out.*
.................................(3 to 1 op 9 to 4 tchd 100 to 30) pu
Dist: 27l, nk, dist. 4m 8.00s. a 8.00s (6 Ran).
SR: 75/48/52/ (B T Stewart-Brown), T P Tate

1641 Speen Novices' Hurdle Class C (4-y-o and up) £4,370 2m 110yds (3:25)

HOH WARRIOR (Ire) 5-11-0 G Bradley, *hld up, hdwy 5th, led aftr last, rdn out.*.......................(50 to 1 op 33 to 1) 1
1464² QUEEN OF SPADES (Ire) 6-11-5 C Maude, *led to 2 out, rdn whn short of room r-in, kpt on same pace.*.........(9 to 4 jt-fav op 7 to 4 tchd 5 to 2) 2
1452³ NORDANCE PRINCE (Ire) 5-10-9 (5*) A Bates, *hld up beh ldrs led 2 out hdd jst aftr last edgd rght and no extr und pres run in*
..............(20 to 1 op 14 to 1 tchd 25 to 1) 3
NASONE (Ire) 5-11-0 P Hide, *wtd wth, hdwy 3 out, one pace nxt.*.............................(7 to 1 op 5 to 1) 4
DONNINGTON (Ire) 6-11-0 J Osborne, *hld up, rdn and styd on one pace frm 3 out, nvr nrr.*........(9 to 4 jt-fav op 7 to 2) 5
1275* MURPHY'S MALT (Ire) 4-11-10 C F Swan, *trkd ldrs, ev ch 3 out, blun nxt, sn wknd.*....................(7 to 1 op 5 to 1) 6
FAIRY KNIGHT 4-11-0 S McNeill, *rear, prog 5th till wknd 2 out.*..................(10 to 1 op 12 to 1 tchd 16 to 1) 7
JOHN DRUMM 5-11-0 R Garritty, *hdwy to go hndy second, rdn to chal 3 out, fdd nxt.*
.....................(20 to 1 op 12 to 1 tchd 25 to 1) 8
1297⁷ I RECALL (Ire) 5-11-0 A Dobbin, *nvr nr to chal.*
.....................................(66 to 1 tchd 100 to 1) 9
HI MARBLE (Ire) 5-10-9 Derek Byrne, *nvr trble ldrs.*
......................(33 to 1 op 10 to 1) 10
1515⁶ ADONISIS 4-11-0 A Procter, *trkd ldrs till rdn and wknd appr 3 out.*......................(66 to 1 op 33 to 1) 11
ENGLISH INVADER 5-11-0 B Powell, *wtd wth, improved hfwy, tdd 3 out.*.........(25 to 1 op 14 to 1 tchd 33 to 1) 12
1155 LIZIUM 4-10-6 (3*) D Walsh, *hld up, wknd 5th.*
.... 13
GRAND CRACK (Ire) 4-11-0 P McLoughlin, *al beh.*
.....................................(50 to 1 op 33 to 1) 14
1452 BRYAN ROBSON (USA) (bl) 5-11-0 B Clifford, *prmnt to hfwy, tld off.*.........................(66 to 1 tchd 100 to 1) 15
CALON LAN 5-11-0 M A Fitzgerald, *chsd ldrs till l3rd.*
......................(12 to 1 op 10 to 1 tchd 14 to 1) f
MULTAN 4-10-7 (7*) M Attwater, *keen hold, al beh, tld off whn pld up bef last.*....................(50 to 1 op 33 to 1) pu
BOWCLIFFE COURT (Ire) 4-10-9 (5*) S Ryan, *trkd ldrs till pld up bef second, sddl slpd...* (7 to 1 op 5 to 1) pu
CROAGH HILL 4-11-0 S Fox, *hld up, wknd hfwy, tld off whn pld up bef last.*...............(50 to 1 op 25 to 1) pu
Dist: 3l, sht-hd, 4l, 14l, 5l, 1¾l, 20l, 10l, 3½l, 17l. 4m 1.40s. a 12.40s (19 Ran).
SR: 36/38/33/29/15/20/8/6/-/ (D F Allport), C P E Brooks

WARWICK (good)
Saturday November 30th
Going Correction: PLUS 0.10 sec. per fur. (races 1,3,5,7), MINUS 0.15 (2,4,6)

1642 North Leamington School Novices' Hurdle Class C (4-y-o and up) £4,302 2m................................(12:30)

IONIO (USA) 5-11-0 J R Kavanagh, *patiently rdn, improved hfwy, ridden to draw level last, sn led, ran on wl.*
..........................(10 to 1 op 8 to 1) 1
1479² ROYAL EVENT 5-10-11 (3*) D Fortt, *al wl plcd, quickened ahead bef 2 out, jnd last, sn hdd, kpt on same pace r-in.*
..................(7 to 4 fav tchd 6 to 4 and 2 to 1) 2
1224⁶ STAR SELECTION 5-10-11 (3*) E Husband, *al frnt rnk, led aftr 1st, rcd freely till hdd bef 2 out, rdn and one pace betw last two.*...........(14 to 1 op 10 to 1 tchd 16 to 1) 3
1496⁵ EVEZIO RUFO 4-11-0 L Harvey, *nvr far away, feeling pace and rdn aftr 3 out, one pace betw last 2.*
.....................(14 to 1 op 12 to 1 tchd 16 to 1) 4
MAZIRAH 5-11-0 D Morris, *wtd wth, improved frm off the pace hfwy, feeling pace aftr 4 out, no imprsn after.*
...............(66 to 1 op 50 to 1 tchd 100 to 1) 5
1292⁷ THE BREWMASTER (Ire) 4-10-11 (3*) G Hogan, *led till aftr 1st, styd hndy, hrd at work bef 3 out, fdd before nxt.*
..................(14 to 1 op 10 to 1 tchd 33 to 1) 6
SUN OF SPRING 6-11-0 T J Murphy, *settled in tch, effrt hfwy, struggling aftr 4 out, fdd nxt.*
..................(25 to 1 op 20 to 1 tchd 33 to 1) 7
1324² A S JIM 5-10-8¹ (7*) Mr A Mitchell, *patiently rdn, improved hfwy, struggling when ldrs quickened appr 3 out, sn btn.*
.................................(66 to 1 op 20 to 1) 8
1326 ONEOFTHEOLDONES 4-11-0 Derek Byrne, *sn outpcd in rear, tld off hfwy.*...........(100 to 1 op 25 to 1) 9
GALE WARGAME (Ire) 5-11-0 J A McCarthy, *settled in tch, feeling pace and losing grnd whn blun 3 out, tld off.*
.........................(11 to 4 op 4 to 1) 10
1357⁸ COUNTESS MILLIE 4-10-4 (5*) Chris Webb, *blun and uns rdr 1st.*.........................(100 to 1 op 50 to 1) ur
1415 WEB OF STEEL 6-11-0 M Bosley, *chsd ldrs to hfwy, wl beh whn pld up bef last.*.......(100 to 1 op 50 to 1) pu

OUR TOM 4-10-9 (5*) Mr R Thornton, *not fluent, tld off thrght, pld up aftr 4 out.*.......(40 to 1 op 16 to 1 tchd 50 to 1) pu
PENNY'S WISHING 4-10-9 M Ranger, *in tch to hfwy, wl beh whn pld up aftr 3 out.*...........(100 to 1 op 50 to 1) pu
TALK BACK (Ire) 4-11-0 M Richards, *wtd wth, effrt hfwy, struggling bef 3 out, tld off whn pld up before 2 out.*
Dist: 1¾l, 6l, 5l, 6l, 5l, 2l, 14l, 5l, 13l. 3m 46.60s. a 7.60s (15 Ran).
SR: 26/24/18/13/7/2/ (Mrs R F Key & Mrs V C Ward), Mrs V C Ward

1643 Tiltyard Bridge Handicap Chase Class D (0-125 5-y-o and up) £3,577 2m................................(1:00)

1052 FINE HARVEST [115] 10-11-10 T J Murphy, *made al, clr whn slpd aftr 5th, slipped ag'n bend after 3 out, hit nxt, styd on strly.*......................(11 to 4 op 5 to 2 tchd 7 to 2) 1
1220⁴ BALLY PARSON [112] 10-11-7 Derek Byrne, *settled wth chasing grp, imprvg whn blun 5th, rallied 3 out, styd on to chal second r-in.*........(6 to 1 op 9 to 2 tchd 13 to 2) 2
1378³ MAN MOOD (Fr) [112] 5-11-7 Mr E James, *al wl in tch, improved hfwy, chsd wnr 4 out, rdn nxt, no imprsn betw last 2.*
.................................(9 to 2 op 3 to 1) 3
1414² LAKE OF LOUGHREA (Ire) [105] 6-11-0 J A McCarthy, *settled wth chasing bunch, effrt hfwy, feeling pace bef 4 out, hit nxt, sn rdn and btn.*.........(5 to 2 fav op 9 to 4) 4
1248 MONDAY CLUB [112] 12-11-7 R Bellamy, *chsd wnr to 4 out, sn und pres, wknd quickly nxt.*
.......................(20 to 1 op 14 to 1 tchd 25 to 1) 5
1223³ PATS MINSTREL [110] 11-11-5 M Richards, *settled to track ldrs, und pres whn pace increased back strt, lost tch quickly, tld off 4 out.*..............(8 to 1 op 10 to 1 tchd 12 to 1) 6
COUNT BARACHOIS (USA) [96] 8-10-5 R Supple, *chsd ldrs, blun second, lost tch quickly hfwy, tld off.*
.........................(16 to 1 op 12 to 1 tchd 20 to 1) 7
Dist: 4l, 2l, 7l, 14l, 15l, 26l. 3m 56.40s. a 4.40s (7 Ran).
SR: 28/21/19/5/3/-/-/ (Miss A Shirley-Priest), J L Spearing

1644 Warwickshire College Of Agriculture Handicap Hurdle Class B (0-145 4-y-o and up) £5,052 2m 3f.......(1:35)

1454⁵ BALANAK (USA) [120] 5-10-1 (5*) Sophie Mitchell, *settled in last pl, gd hdwy frm off the pace appr 2 out, styd on strly to ld last 100 yards.*.................(14 to 1 op 12 to 1) 1
KARSHI [139] 6-11-11 M Richards, *dictated pace till hfwy, rallied to rgn ld betw last 2, ct last 100 yards.*
.................................(13 to 2 op 5 to 1 tchd 15 to 2) 2
1467² MYTTON'S CHOICE (Ire) [126] 5-10-7 (5*) Mr R Thornton, *al wl plcd, led hfwy till betw last 2, rdn and one pace r-in.*
.........................(9 to 4 jt-fav op 3 to 1) 3
HOODED HAWK (Ire) [114] 5-10-0 J R Kavanagh, *settled midfield, effrt and bustled alng hfwy, styd on one pace frm 2 out.*........................(16 to 1 tchd 14 to 1) 4
1493* DOMAPPEL [114] 4-10-0 T Kent, *nvr far away, ev ch hfwy, feeling pace whn ldg pair quickened 3 out, no imprsn aftr.*
......................(9 to 4 jt-fav op 2 to 1 tchd 5 to 2) 5
SUN SURFER (Fr) [136] 8-11-6 S Wynne, *chsd ldg bunch, und pres whn pace quickened 3 out, no imprsn after.*
.........................(6 to 1 op 5 to 1 tchd 13 to 2) 6
CASTLE COURAGEOUS [133] 9-11-5 E Murphy, *settled to track ldrs, hrd at work and lost grnd bef 3 out, no dngr aftr.*
...............(14 to 1 op 7 to 1 tchd 16 to 1) 7
1148⁵ ALLTIME DANCER (Ire) [124] 4-10-10 J A McCarthy, *settled to chase ldrs, lost grnd whn pace quickened 3 out, no dngr aftr.*........(12 to 1 op 8 to 1 tchd 14 to 1) 8
INDIAN QUEST [116] 7-9-13² (3*) G Hogan, *pressed ldrs, lost pl quickly whn pace quickened 3 out, sn btn.*
...............(25 to 1 op 20 to 1 tchd 33 to 1) 9
Dist: 1¼l, 1l, 5l, 8l, 1½l, 1½l, 2½l, 1½l. 4m 24.30s. (9 Ran).
(W H Dore), D R Gandolfo

1645 Stamina Test Handicap Chase Class D (0-125 5-y-o and up) £5,264 3¼m................................(2:05)

CHRISTMAS GORSE [113] 10-11-6 (3*) G Hogan, *nvr far away, str chal fnl circuit, led bef 2 out, styd on strongly r-in.*
.........................(10 to 1 tchd 12 to 1) 1
1453 CHURCH LAW [102] 9-10-12 R Supple, *al hndy, ev ch whn crowded bend appr 2 out, rdn bef last, styd on wl.*
.........................(9 to 2 op 3 to 1 tchd 5 to 1) 2
1314⁶ STOP THE WALLER (Ire) [114] 7-11-5 (5*) Mr R Thornton, *jmpd boldly, took keen hold, led 4th till bef 2 out, one pace r-in.*.....................(5 to 1 op 7 to 2) 3
1453 DESPERATE [100] 8-10-10 M Richards, *al hndy, ev ch fnl circuit, rdn aftr 3 out, eased whn btn betw last 2.*
.........................(20 to 1 op 16 to 1 tchd 25 to 1) 4
1304⁵ SAMLEE (Ire) [110] 7-11-3 (3*) G Tormey, *wth ldrs, led 3rd to nxt, jmpd slwly 5th, cl up whn blun and uns rdr next.*
.........................(100 to 30 op 3 to 1 tchd 4 to 1) ur
1440³ FAR SENIOR [108] 10-11-4 J R Kavanagh, *led to 3rd, lost pl and reminders 9th, tld off fnl circuit, pld up bef 6 out.*
......................(14 to 1 op 12 to 1 tchd 16 to 1) pu
1499² BEAUREPAIRE [108] 8-11-1 (3*) P Henley, *pressed ldrs for o'r a circuit, lost pl quickly bef 7 out, tld off whn pld up before 4 out.*.............(2 to 1 fav tchd 9 to 4) pu

Dist: 1l, 4l, 30l. 6m 42.70s. a 28.70s (7 Ran).

(D R Stoddart), N A Gaselee

1646 Emma Brazendale Novices' Handicap Hurdle Class E (0-100 3-y-o and up) £2,692 2m.............(2:35)

1291⁶	ROVESTAR [83] 5-11-4 T J Murphy, pushed alng to go early pace, improved 4 out, chalg whn lft in ld aftr last, drvn out. ....(5 to 1 fav op 8 to 1)	1
1263⁵	SKRAM [84] 3-9-10 (7") X Aizpuru, al frnt rnk, nosed ahead 4th till appr 3 out, rallied betw last 2, kpt on r-in. ....(14 to 1 op 12 to 1 tchd 16 to 1)	2
1367²	MR POPPLETON [67] 7-10-2 L Harvey, slight ld to 3rd, styd hndy, rdn betw last 2, kpt on same pace r-in. ....(7 to 1 op 5 to 1)	3
1412⁴	COLOUR COUNSELLOR [81] 3-10-0 R Supple, patiently rdn, improved hfwy, led 3 out till bef last, one pace. ....(6 to 1 op 4 to 1 tchd 13 to 2)	4
1215³	SMART LORD [87] 5-11-8 M Bosley, strted slwly, took clr order hfwy, rdn and outpcd 2 out......(12 to 1 op 8 to 1)	5
1410⁶	MUSEUM (Ire) [80] 5-11-1 D Leahy, settled midfield, feeling pace whn pace quickened 3 out, no imprsn frm nxt. ....(7 to 1 tchd 8 to 1 and 13 to 2)	6
	SCHNOZZLE (Ire) [90] 5-11-8 (3") R Massey, chsd ldg grp. effrt aftr 3 out, rdn bef nxt, fdd und pres. ....(12 to 1 tchd 14 to 1)	7
1295	THAT OLD FEELING (Ire) [75] 4-10-7 (3") Guy Lewis, settled in tch, hrd at work whn pace quickened 3 out, sn struggling, tld off..............................(16 to 1 op 12 to 1 tchd 20 to 1)	8
1367⁷	BOLD CHARLIE [65] 4-10-0 N Mann, settled midfield, feeling pace and drvn alng bef 3 out, sn lost tch, tld off. ....(50 to 1 op 33 to 1 tchd 66 to 1)	9
	DODGY DANCER [74] 6-10-9 L O'Hara, struggling to keep up hfwy, lost tch, tld off..............(50 to 1 tchd 20 to 1)	10
1367³	WITNEY-DE-BERGERAC (Ire) [89] 4-11-10 W McFarland, chasing ldrs whn f 3rd...(10 to 1 op 7 to 1 tchd 11 to 1)	f
867	MASTER GOODENOUGH (Ire) [73] 5-10-1⁸ (7") D Creech, led 3rd till hdd and f nxt... (50 to 1 op 33 to 1 tchd 66 to 1)	f
1496	TOMAL [70] 4-10-5 J R Kavanagh, wtd wth, gd hdwy 3 out, led betw last 2, o'rjmpd and uns rdr aftr last. (14 to 1 op 8 to 1)	ur
	ALPHA LEATHER [65] 5-10-0 Mr J Grassick, tracking ldrs whn brght dwn 3rd..................(66 to 1 op 33 to 1)	bd
749⁷	AYDISUN [64] 4-10-1 D Morris, wtd wth, imprvg whn ran out 4th........(6 to 1 op 5 to 1 tchd 10 to 1 and 5 to 1)	ro
	ETHBAAT [93] 5-12-0 M Richards, pld hrd, lost tch hfwy, tld off whn pulled up betw last 2. ....(17 to 2 op 8 to 1 tchd 10 to 1)	pu
153	DARING HEN (Ire) [85] 6-11-6 P Holley, struggling hfwy, tld off whn pld up betw last 2. (9 to 1 op 16 to 1 tchd 33 to 1)	pu

Dist: 2l, 4l, 2½l, hd, 6l, 18l, 13l, 1l, ¾l. 3m 48.40s. a 9.40s (17 Ran).

SR: 12/-/-/-/7/-/ (G Burr), J S King

1647 Sarah Dealtry Novices' Chase Class D (4-y-o and up) £3,951 2m... (3:05)

	FLIGHT LIEUTENANT (USA) 7-11-5 J A McCarthy, patiently rdn, steady hdwy to go hndy hfwy, lft in clr ld 4 out, hit 2 out, kpt on grimly to remain clear. ....(6 to 1 op 4 to 1 tchd 13 to 2)	1
1475*	SCOTTISH BAMBI 8-11-11 R Bellamy, settled to track ldrs, took clr order hfwy, hmpd 2 out, styd on betw last two, no ch wth wnr..............(5 to 2 op 9 to 4 tchd 3 to 1)	2
937	REEFA'S MILL (Ire) 4-10-7 P Holley, settled to track ldg grp, chsd alng whn lding trio quickened 3 out, kpt on, nvr trble ldrs. ....(50 to 1 op 33 to 1 tchd 66 to 1)	3
	NAUTICAL GEORGE (Ire) 6-11-5 R Supple, chsd ldrs, struggling whn hfwy, lost tch 4 out, tld off.	4
1264	BETABETCORBETT 5-11-5 T Eley, in tch to hfwy, sn lost pl, tld off 4 out......................(8 to 1 op 25 to 1 tchd 66 to 1)	5
	ODELL 6-11-5 W McFarland, led till aftr 5th, struggling to hold pl 5 out, tld off..............(7 to 1 op 5 to 1)	6
	EXTERIOR PROFILES (Ire) 6-11-5 Mr M Rimell, wth ldrs, led aftr 5th, clr whn pckd on landing 5 out, 4 l advantage whn f nxt......................(2 to 1 fav op 9 to 4 tchd 5 to 2)	f
1265⁴	TIGHT FIST (Ire) 6-11-5 M Richards, al chasing ldrs, second and staying on one pace whn blun and uns rdr 2 out. ....(4 to 1 op 7 to 2 tchd 9 to 2)	ur
1439²	CAPTAIN STOCKFORD 9-11-5 J R Kavanagh, pressed ldrs, blun 5th, lost tch quickly 5 out, tld off whn pld up aftr 3 out..............................(50 to 1 op 25 to 1)	pu
1439	LOTHIAN JEM 7-10-9 (5") Mr R Thornton, blun and nrly f second, jmpd badly lft 4th, wl beh whn pld up bef nxt. ....(40 to 1 op 20 to 1 tchd 50 to 1)	pu

Dist: 17l, 13l, 3l, 14l, 1½l. 3m 57.70s. a 5.70s (10 Ran).

SR: 9/-/-/-/-/ (Mrs Laura Pegg), T Casey

1648 Norton Lindsey Standard National Hunt Flat Class H (4,5,6-y-o) £1,374 2m.........................(3:35)

1240²	LORD FOLEY (NZ) 4-11-1 (3") J Magee, chsd ldg grp wl, improved frm midfield appr 3 out, quickened ahead jst o'r one furlong out, sprinted clr....(3 to 1 op 2 to 1 tchd 7 to 2)	1

1142³	ZANDER 4-10-11 (7") L Suthern, keen hold, made most till 4 fs out, rallied fnl furlong, not pace of wnr. ....(5 to 1 op 5 to 2 tchd 11 to 2)	2
	TRISTRAM'S IMAGE (NZ) 5-10-13 (5") Mr C Vigors, nvr far away, led 4 fs out till jst o'r one out, kpt on one pace. ....(6 to 4 fav op 7 to 2)	3
1142⁵	THE CROPPY BOY 4-11-1 (3") T Dascombe, nvr far away, ev ch 4 fs out, not quicken last 2. ....(11 to 1 op 8 to 1 tchd 12 to 1)	4
	OXBRIDGE LADY 5-10-6 (7") M Keighley, nvr far away, ev ch till rdn and one pace last 2 fs. ....(12 to 1 op 9 to 2 tchd 14 to 1)	5
1292	BELLIDIUM 4-10-10 (3") G Tormey, chsd ldg bunch, effrt hfwy, no imprsn last 2 fs... (66 to 1 op 33 to 1 tchd 100 to 1)	6
1142	SCHOLAR GREEN 4-11-1 (3") P Henley, struggling and beh aftr a m, styd on fnl 2 fs, nrst finish. ....(9 to 1 op 50 to 1 tchd 100 to 1)	7
	MISTRESS TUDOR 5-10-10 (3") E Husband, settled to track ldg grp, effrt aftr a m, struggling last quarter mile. ....(33 to 1 op 16 to 1)	8
	GAF 4-11-1 (3") R Massey, pressed ldrs for o'r a m, fdd und pres bef strt...................(66 to 1 op 25 to 1)	9
	MASTER HARRY 4-11-1 (3") G Hogan, settled aftr gd strt, nvr plcd to chal after.............(6 to 1 op 7 to 2)	10
	MOOR DANCE MAN 6-11-4 Mr D Verco, chsd ldrs for o'r a m, wknd quickly bef strt, tld off. ....(66 to 1 op 33 to 1 tchd 100 to 1)	11
	BYHOOKORBYCROOK (Ire) 4-10-8 (5") D J Kavanagh, sn in rear, tld off fnl m......(50 to 1 op 20 to 1 tchd 66 to 1)	12
	TATIBAG 4-10-13 (5") Sophie Mitchell, al beh, tld off aftr a m, ...(50 to 1 op 33 to 1)	13
873	TORO LOCO (Ire) 4-10-13 (5") Mr R Thornton, wth ldrs, nosed ahead briefly bef hfwy, wknd quickly last 4 fs, tld off. ....(66 to 1 op 33 to 1)	14
	TODDYS LASS 4-10-10 (3") D Fortt, wth ldrs early, lost tch quickly fnl m, tld off... (50 to 1 op 33 to 1 tchd 66 to 1)	15
52	ABER GLEN 6-10-6 (7") Mr A Wintle, chsd ldg bunch to hfwy, lost pl quickly and pld up bef strt, lme. ....(66 to 1 op 50 to 1 tchd 100 to 1)	pu

Dist: 5l, 7l, 2l, ¾l, 1l, 4l, 9l, 6l, 16l, 1¼l. 3m 48.50s. (16 Ran).

(Foley Steelstock), C J Mann

FAIRYHOUSE (IRE) (yielding)
Sunday December 1st
Going Correction: NIL (races 1,3,5,6,7), PLUS 0.55 (2,4)

1649 Ashbourne Maiden Hurdle (5-y-o and up) £3,082 2m.............(12:40)

710⁶	ACK THE BUTLER (Ire) 5 12 0 C O'Dwyer, ...(6 to 1)	1
1359⁸	ANN'S DESIRE (Ire) 5-11-1 P L Malone, ...(25 to 1)	2
	DIGIN FOR GOLD (Ire) 5-11-6 C O'Brien, ...(20 to 1)	3
1460⁴	WYN WAN SOON (Ire) 5-11-6 D H O'Connor, ...(20 to 1)	4
	EDUARDO (Ire) 6-12-0 R Dunwoody, ...(5 to 4 fav)	5
1359²	MARTYS STEP (Ire) 5-11-6 M P Dwyer, ...(20 to 1)	6
1580⁵	VALLEY ERNE (Ire) 5-11-6 L P Cusack, ...(16 to 1)	7
1457	JAKDUL (Ire) (bl) 5-12-0 J Shortt, ...(16 to 1)	8
1432	CLADY BOY (Ire) 5-11-6 C F Swan, ...(12 to 1)	9
	HEAVY HUSTLER (Ire) 5-11-6 F Woods, ...(14 to 1)	10
	KEEPITSAFE (Ire) 5-11-6 H Rogers, ...(25 to 1)	11
1193⁶	JACKY FLYNN (Ire) 5-11-6 C Llewellyn, ...(16 to 1)	12
	BRIAN'S DELIGHT (Ire) 5-10-8 (7") D K Budds, ...(20 to 1)	13
1554⁴	HEN HANSEL (Ire) 5-12-0 M Moran, ...(14 to 1)	14
	ATHA BEITHE (Ire) 5-12-0 R Hughes, ...(10 to 1)	15
1486⁷	CLONMEL COMMERCIAL (Ire) 5-10-13 (7") D McCullagh, ...(66 to 1)	16
	BLUSHING SAND (Ire) 6-11-7 (7") Mr T J Beattie, ..(12 to 1)	17
1364⁹	FOYLE WANDERER (Ire) 5-11-1 D T Evans, ...(16 to 1)	18
	DEIREADH AN SCEAL (Ire) 6-11-3 (3") G Cotter, ..(20 to 1)	19
62	STAR OF FERMANAGH (Ire) 7-11-6 T J Mitchell, (100 to 1)	20
	L'AMI DE ADAM (Ire) 5-11-1 A Powell, ...(50 to 1)	21
1359	DERRYAD (Ire) 5-11-1 T P Treacy, ...(50 to 1)	22
1145	MASTER VALENTINE (Ire) 5-10-13 (7") J O'Shaughnessy, ...(66 to 1)	23
1390	CARNANEE (Ire) 6-11-6 P McWilliams, ...(33 to 1)	24
1539	TUDOR ROSE 5-11-6 S H O'Donovan, ...(33 to 1)	25
1145²	HOLLYBUCK (Ire) 7-11-1 D J Casey, ...(50 to 1)	26
	NOBLE SHOON (Ire) 5-12-0 A P McCoy, ...(8 to 1)	f
1487⁶	HELL FOR LEATHER (Ire) 7-11-3 (3") K Whelan, ...(25 to 1)	pu

Dist: 6l, 1½l, shd-hd, 4l. 3m 51.40s. a 7.40s (28 Ran).

SR: 26/7/10/10/14/-/ (Barry Lee McCoubrey), C Roche

1650 Cottage Handicap Chase (4-y-o and up) £3,082 2m.............(1:10)

1458²	BARNAGEERA BOY (Ire) [-] 7-10-3 T J Mitchell, (4 to 1 co-fav)	1
1435³	SCOBIE BOY (Ire) [-] 8-10-12 L P Cusack, ...(12 to 1)	2
780²	PERKNAPP [-] 9-10-5 M P Dwyer, ...(4 to 1 co-fav)	3
1091⁴	MINSTREL FIRE (Ire) [-] 8-10-2 C Llewellyn, ...(12 to 1)	4
	SORRY ABOUT THAT [-] 10-9-7 P L Malone, ...(8 to 1)	5
1537⁷	TIME FOR A RUN [-] 9-10-13 R Dunwoody, ...(8 to 1)	6
1308*	FIFTYSEVENCHANNELS (Ire) [-] 7-11-8 C F Swan, ...(4 to 1 co-fav)	7

1091³ JAZZY REFRAIN (Ire) [-] 6-10-1 D J Casey, ... (14 to 1) 8
WHALE OF A KNIGHT (Ire) [-] 7-11-0 F Woods, ... (6 to 1) 9
1308³ BROCKLEY COURT [-] 9-12-0 J Shortt, ... (8 to 1) 10
COMMON POLICY (Ire) [-] 7-11-0 C O'Dwyer, ... (8 to 1) 11
1435 PERSIAN POWER (Ire) [-] 8-9-4 (3⁷) G Cotter, ... (16 to 1) ur
Dist: 6l, 1½l, 1l, 1l. 4m 6.90s. a 12.90s (12 Ran).
SR: 34/27/28/14/4/-/ (Anthony Kirwan), J T R Dreaper

1651 Avonmore Royal Bond Novice Hurdle (Grade 1) (4-y-o and up) £16,250 2m
. . . . (1:40)

1404² ISTABRAQ (Ire) 4-11-9 C F Swan, dsptd ld, wnt clr aftr 3 out,
imprsv. . . . . (11 to 8 fav) 1
943* PALETTE (Ire) 4-11-4 D J Casey, trkd ldrs, rdn aftr 4 out, styd
on wl aftr 2 out. . . . . (14 to 1) 2
1404* NOBLE THYNE (Ire) 6-12-0 T P Treacy, dsptd ld, rdn and wknd
aftr 3 out, jmpd slwly nxt. . . . . (13 to 8) 3
1533* CHARLIE FOXTROT (Ire) 4-11-9 R Hughes, wl plcd, rdn aftr 4
out, not quicken. . . . . (11 to 2) 4
1488² THREE SCHOLARS 5-12-0 R Dunwoody, rear, reminders
aftr 5th, rdn aftr 3 out, no extr. . . . . (14 to 1) 5
1452* LAKE KARIBA 5-12-0 A P McCoy, strted slwly, sn reco'red to
track ldrs 4th, wknd bef four out, soon lost tch. . . . . . (7 to 1) 6
1535 DOONE BRAES (Ire) 6-12-0 U Smyth, al rear. . . . . (200 to 1) 7
Dist: 4¼l, 15l, 11l, sht-hd. 3m 47.80s. a 3.80s (7 Ran).
SR: 57/47/42/26/31/-/-/ (John P McManus), A P O'Brien

1652 Chiquita Drinmore Novice Chase (Grade 1) (5-y-o and up) £22,750 2 ½m. . . . . (2:10)

1192* DORANS PRIDE 7-11-10 R Dunwoody, wl plcd, jmpd
slwly 4th, dsptd ld nxt to 6 out, prog to dispute lead 2 out, led
bef next, kpt on und pres. . . . . (5 to 4 fav) 1
1269* SEE MORE BUSINESS (Ire) 6-11-10 A P McCoy, wl plcd,
dsptd ld second, led nxt, jnd 5th, led 6 out, mstk 4 out, rdn aftr
next, joined 2 out, sn hdd, kpt on. . . . . (5 to 2) 2
EXECUTIVE OPTIONS (Ire) 7-11-5 C Llewellyn, wl plcd early,
mstk 4th, lost pl bef 7th, kpt on. . . . . (14 to 1) 3
1361⁷ ANOTHER POINT (Ire) 8-11-5 M P Hourigan, wl plcd till wknd
aftr 7th, sn no dngr. . . . . (66 to 1) 4
1276* DANOLI (Ire) 8-11-10 T P Treacy, wl plcd till f 3rd. (100 to 30) f
1435² DRAMATIC VENTURE (Ire) 7-11-5 D J Casey, rear till f 6th.
. . . . (20 to 1) f
1534⁴ MACALLISTER (Ire) 6-11-5 C O'Dwyer, led to 3rd, wl plcd till
wknd bef 4 out, rear whn hmpd and uns rdr last. . . (25 to 1) ur
1405³ THE OUTBACK WAY (Ire) (bl) 6-11-10 D H O'Connor, rear,
mstk 6th, wl beh whn refused last. . . . . (20 to 1) ref
Dist: 1l, dist, nk. 5m 11.80s. a 16.80s (8 Ran).
SR: 38/37/-/-/-/ (T J Doran), Michael Hourigan

1653 Avonmore Hatton's Grace Hurdle (Grade 1) (4-y-o and up) £26,000 2 ½m. . . . . (2:40)

LARGE ACTION 8-12-0 J Osborne, wl plcd, prog to ld
appr 3 out, kpt on strly. . . . . (9 to 4) 1
1406* COCKNEY LAD (Ire) 7-11-9 R Hughes, mid-div, rdn and prog
aftr 3 out, styd on after nxt. . . . . (8 to 1) 2
1095* THEATREWORLD (Ire) 4-11-4 C F Swan, mid-div, rdn and
hdwy appr 3 out, dsptd ld briefly aftr, wknd. . . . . . (6 to 4 fav) 3
1347 CASTLEKELLYLEADER (Ire) 7-11-9 A P McCoy, led, not fluent 1st, mstks 4th and nxt, hdd bef 3 out, sn wknd. . (6 to 1) 4
1406⁵ PADASHPAN (USA) 7-11-9 T P Treacy, al rear, rdn aftr 3 out,
no extr. . . . . (25 to 1) 5
1393² MYSTICAL CITY (Ire) 6-11-4 D J Casey, rear, rdn bef 3 out,
not quicken. . . . . (8 to 1) 6
1172⁵ NEW CO (Ire) 8-11-9 C O'Dwyer, rear, some prog bef 4 out, f 2
out. . . . . (8 to 1) f
1431² RADANPOUR (Ire) 4-11-4 R Dunwoody, trkd ldr, wknd bef 4
out, rear whn f last. . . . . (14 to 1) f
Dist: 6l, 1l, 25l, 4l. 4m 49.80s. a 5.80s (8 Ran).
SR: 42/31/25/5/1/ (B T Stewart-Brown), O Sherwood

1654 Bambury Bookmakers Handicap Hurdle (0-109 4-y-o and up) £4,110 2m. . . . . (3:10)

1462³ ICED HONEY [-] 9-10-6 L P Cusack, ... (8 to 1) 1
GRAVITY GATE [-] 7-10-12 (7⁷) S Laird, ... (16 to 1) 2
1404³ SAVING BOND [-] 4-11-6 R Hughes, ... (9 to 4 fav) 3
268⁶ BOLERO DANCER (Ire) [-] 8-10-3 D J Casey, ... (16 to 1) 4
DEARBORN TEC (Ire) [-] 7-11-5 C O'Brien, ... (20 to 1) 5
1273 CRAIGARY [-] 5-9-11 P P Kinane, ... (25 to 1) 6
1358* COLLON LEADER (Ire) [-] 7-11-4 M P Dwyer, ... (11 to 2) 7
1358³ PTARMIGAN LODGE [-] 5-10-7 (3⁷) G Kilfeather, . (10 to 1) 8
BEDFORD RAMBLER (Ire) [-] 7-9-13 T J Mitchell, . . (12 to 1) 9
1407⁸ CIARA'S PRINCE (Ire) [-] 5-12-0 A Powell, ... (16 to 1) 10
1246⁴ LOUISES FANCY (Ire) [-] 6-10-7 (7⁷) Mr J Keville, . (16 to 1) 11
1407 CONAGHER BOY (Ire) [-] 6-11-1 (7⁷) K A Kelly, . . . (33 to 1) 12
1275⁶ JACKSON'S PANTHER [-] 4-9-12 (3⁷) G Cotter, . . . (7 to 1) 13
1462² MAGICAL FUN (Ire) [-] 4-11-0 R Dunwoody, ... (6 to 1) 14
OWENDUFF (USA) [-] 6-11-5 (7⁷) D W O'Sullivan, . (20 to 1) 15
1246³ FRANCES STREET (Ire) [-] (bl) 4-11-11 C F Swan, . (7 to 1) 16
1535⁸ ARDSHUIL [-] 7-11-13 F Woods, ... (10 to 1) 17
1359 COOLREE LORD (Ire) [-] 5-9-0 (7⁷) S FitzGerald, . . (50 to 1) 18

258* NEIPHIN BOY (Ire) [-] 6-9-7 (7⁷) E Stack, ... (10 to 1) 19
1460 COUNCILLOR (Ire) [-] 5-11-1 S C Lyons, ... (20 to 1) 20
RUN BAVARD (Ire) [-] 8-11-1 T P Treacy, ... (20 to 1) 21
Dist: 2l, 1½l, hd, 4½l. 3m 52.50s. a 8.50s (21 Ran).
SR: -/4/3/-/-/-/ (Mrs D J Coleman), Mrs D J Coleman

1655 Narrow Neck I.N.H. Flat Race (4 & 5-y-o) £3,082 2m. . . . . (3:40)

DAVENPORT BANQUET (Ire) 5-12-0 Mr J A Nash,
. . . . (5 to 4 fav) 1
AONFOCALEILE (Ire) 4-11-2 (7⁷) Mr J P McNamara, (9 to 2) 2
PARI PASSU (Ire) 4-10-11 (7⁷) Mr A C Coyle, ... (8 to 1) 3
ANDREA COVA (Ire) 4-11-4 Mr J P Dempsey, ... (10 to 1) 4
BRACKENVALE (Ire) 5-11-2 (7⁷) Mr R J Barnwell, . . (16 to 1) 5
HEATHER VILLE (Ire) 4-11-4 Mr G J Harford, ... (8 to 1) 6
BRIDGES DAUGHTER (Ire) 5-11-6 (3⁷) Mr B R Hamilton,
. . . . (12 to 1) 7
1463⁸ HEAD CHAPLAIN (Ire) 5-11-7 (7⁷) Mr R Geraghty, . (12 to 1) 8
1436 MEASURED STEP (Ire) 5-11-7 (7⁷) Mr J T McNamara,
. . . . (33 to 1) 9
ROSE OF STRADBALLY (Ire) 5-11-2 (7⁷) Mr Sean O O'Brien,
. . . . (16 to 1) 10
MINSTRELS PRIDE (Ire) 5-12-0 Mr A R Coonan, . . (16 to 1) 11
MEADSIDE (Ire) 5-11-11 (3⁷) Mr B M Cash, ... (7 to 1) 12
CLONEE PRIDE (Ire) 5-11-9 Mrs O C Barker, ... (16 to 1) 13
RATHCORE LADY (Ire) 5-11-2 (7⁷) Mr A Ross, ... (16 to 1) 14
1539 DAYVILLE (Ire) 5-12-0 Mr H F Cleary, ... (33 to 1) 15
SMUGGLERS MOLL (Ire) 5-11-2 (7⁷) Mr W Ewing, . (33 to 1) 16
MAY BLOOM (Ire) 5-11-6 (3⁷) Mr E Norris, ... (16 to 1) 17
RED ISLAND GIRL (Ire) 5-11-9 Mr M McNulty, ... (14 to 1) 18
HOLLOW DAISY (Ire) 5-11-2 (7⁷) Mr J A Smith, . . . (33 to 1) 19
1539 LISDARA LADY (Ire) 5-11-2 (7⁷) Miss L Agnew, . . . (25 to 1) 20
1307 BALLYMACHUGH LADY (Ire) 5-11-9 Mr A J Martin, (25 to 1) 21
LINKS LADY 4-11-4 Mr M Murray, ... (16 to 1) 22
BELMONT DUKE (Ire) 5-11-11 (3⁷) Mr P English, . . (12 to 1) 23
Dist: 1l, 15l, 6l, 1l. 3m 47.40s. (23 Ran).
(Mrs M O'Callaghan), W P Mullins

KELSO (good)
Monday December 2nd
Going Correction: PLUS 0.45 sec. per fur. (races 1,2,4,6,7), PLUS 0.40 (3,5)

1656 John Hogg Novices' Hurdle Class D (Div I) (4-y-o and up) £2,502 2m 110yds. . . . . (12:30)

MISTER ROSS (Ire) 6-10-12 A S Smith, trkd ldrs, led bef 2 out,
drvn clr aftr last. . . . . (25 to 1 op 14 to 1) 1
SHINEROLLA 4-10-12 D Parker, trkd ldrs, effrt aftr 2 out, chsd
wnr aftr last, no imprsn. . . . . (6 to 1 op 5 to 1) 2
1280⁴ KING PIN 4-10-12 R Supple, in tch, hdwy aftr 2 out, styd on
frm last, nrst finish. . . . . (13 to 2 op 5 to 1 tchd 7 to 1) 3
1330² DURAID (Ire) 4-10-12 Richard Guest, trkd ldrs, effrt whn not
fluent last, sn rdn and wknd. . . . . (11 to 10 fav) 4
1371³ BILL'S PRIDE 5-10-7 A Dobbin, in tch till outpcd aftr 3 out, no
dngr after. . . . . (20 to 1 op 16 to 1) 5
CALDER KING 5-10-12 B Storey, mid-div whn hmpd 4th, kpt
on same pace frm 3 out. (12 to 1 op 10 to 1 tchd 14 to 1) 6
GREEK GOLD (Ire) 7-10-12 P Niven, beh, hdwy hfwy, chasing
ldrs bef 2 out, wknd appr last. . . . . (200 to 1) 7
JALMAID 4-10-2 (5⁷) R McGrath, beh most of way. (100 to 1) 8
NIZAAL (USA) 5-10-12 B Harding, beh most of way.
. . . . (20 to 1 op 16 to 1) 9
POLITICAL BILL 5-10-12 K Johnson, in tch till wknd aftr 3 out.
. . . . (100 to 1) 10
1326 BARIK (Ire) 6-10-9 (3⁷) G Lee, led till bef 2 out, sn wknd.
. . . . (500 to 1) 11
OBVIOUS RISK 5-10-12 Mr P Murray, chsd ldrs till wknd bef 3
out. . . . . (100 to 1) 12
KIERCHEM (Ire) 5-10-12 J Callaghan, chsd ldrs, wknd bef 3
out, tld off. . . . . (25 to 1 op 16 to 1) 13
806⁴ IN GOOD FAITH 4-10-12 M Dwyer, in tch whn f 4th.
. . . . (3 to 1 op 7 to 2 tchd 5 to 1) f
1255⁸ ROYAL PALM 4-10-12 Mr M Thompson, losing tch whn blun
and uns rdr 5th. . . . . (200 to 1) ur
Dist: 7l, 3l, 6l, 11l, 4l, 13l, nk, 16l, 1¾l, nk. 3m 56.50s. a 13.50s (15 Ran).
SR: 24/17/14/8/-/-/ (Gordon Brown), J Howard Johnson

1657 John Hogg Novices' Hurdle Class D (Div II) (4-y-o and up) £2,489 2m 110yds. . . . . (1:00)

1437² DANA POINT (Ire) 4-10-12 Richard Guest, hld up, hdwy bef 3
out, led last, rdn and styd on. . . . . (5 to 2 fav op 9 to 4) 1
MALTA MAN (Ire) 6-10-12 A S Smith, hld up, gd hdwy bef 2
out, dsptd ld last, sn chasing wnr, no imprsn.
. . . . (16 to 1 op 12 to 1) 2
1280³ NICK ROSS 5-10-12 K Johnson, chsd ldrs, slight ld aftr 2 out,
hdd last, sn rdn and wknd. . . . . (9 to 2 op 5 to 1) 3
DOUBLING DICE 5-10-5 (7⁷) S Melrose, beh, styd on frm 2
out, nvr dngrs. . . . . (16 to 1 op 12 to 1) 4
35 DRAKEWRATH (Ire) 6-10-12 D Parker, chsd ldrs, outpcd bef 3
out, no dngr aftr. . . . . (33 to 1 tchd 50 to 1) 5

1333* DEL PIERO (Ire) 5-11-5 R Garritty, *hld up, hdwy bef 3 out, ch nxt, sn rdn, wknd appr last*............ (3 to 1 op 5 to 2) 6
1373⁵ SUNNY LEITH 5-10-9 (3*) G Cahill, *trkd ldrs, chlgd 3 out, wknd aftr nxt*..................(25 to 1 tchd 33 to 1) 7
1047 DR EDGAR 4-10-12 R Supple, *led till aftr 2 out, sn wknd.* .... (20 to 1 op 14 to 1) 8
1522⁶ KILNAMARTYRA GIRL 6-10-7 P Niven, *in tch, effrt bef 3 out, sn wknd, tld off*....................(5 to 1 tchd 11 to 2) 9
1373 JARROW 5-10-12 M Foster, *mid-div, wknd aftr 5th, tld off.* ....(50 to 1) 10
960 SUPER GUY 4-10-12 B Storey, *beh most of way, tld off.* ....(100 to 1) 11
1371⁶ PERCY PARROT 4-10-12 B Harding, *in tch to hfwy, sn wknd, tld off.*..........(40 to 1 op 33 to 1 tchd 50 to 1) 12
1073⁷ DESERT DEVIL 4-10-12 A Dobbin, *beh hfwy, tld off.* .... (12 to 1 op 8 to 1 tchd 14 to 1) 13
GLINT OF AYR 6-10-7 J Callaghan, *f second*.... (100 to 1) f
1333 REGAL DOMAIN (Ire) 5-10-12 D Bentley, *prmnt, wknd quickly hfwy, tld off up bef 2 out*....................(100 to 1) pu
Dist: 4l, 10l, 2½l, ½l, 7l, ½l, nd, 20l, 2½l, 15l. 3m 57.00s. a 14.00s (15 Ran).
SR: 19/15/5/2/1/-/ (Mrs S Smith), Mrs S J Smith

1658 Jack Britton Memorial Novices' Chase Class C (5-y-o and up) £4,642 3m 1f........................(1:30)

1334⁴ SEEKING GOLD (Ire) 7-11-0 B Storey, *chsd ldrs, chalg whn lft in ld last, styd on wl*................. (10 to 1 op 8 to 1) 1
373 WINTER BELLE (USA) 8-11-0 A Dobbin, *beh, cld hfwy, hdwy to chal last, sn chasing wnr, no imprsn...*(7 to 2 op 4 to 1) 2
1334² TIGHTER BUDGET (USA) 9-12-1 M Moloney, *jmpd rght, made most to 3 out, wknd aftr 3 out.* ....(7 to 1 op 9 to 4) 3
1585 MONKSAAN (Ire) 7-10-11 (3*) Mr C Bonner, *lost tch tenth, tld off.*...........................(7 to 1 op 5 to 1) 4
1146 ARISTODEMUS 7-11-0 D Bentley, *tailing off whn f 12th.* ....(14 to 1 tchd 16 to 1) f
1334³ TOUGH TEST (Ire) 6-10-11 (3*) G Cahill, *prmnt, led 3 out, hrd pressed whn f last*................ (9 to 4 fav tchd 5 to 2) f
1334⁶ STRONGALONG (Ire) 6-11-0 A S Smith, *chsd ldrs, drvn aling whn f 12th*..(50 to 1) f
1253⁸ BOSWORTH FIELD 8-11-0 Richard Guest, *tld off whn pld up bef 12th*.........(50 to 1 op 100 to 1 tchd 200 to 1) pu
Dist: 6l, 21l, 30l. 6m 15.90s. a 18.90s (8 Ran).
(Gilry), J Barclay

1659 J. Rutherford Earlston Ltd. Handicap Hurdle Class D (0-125 4-y-o and up) £3,271 2¼m........................(2:00)

1335² STASH THE CASH (Ire) [99] 5-10-6 R Garritty, *hld up in tch, smooth hdwy to ld betw last 2, hrd pressed frm last, styd on und pres, all out*............... (11 to 8 on op 5 to 4 on) 1
1388⁴ MR KNITWIT [113] 9-11-6 A Dobbin, *nvr far away, hdwy to dispute ld last, sn rdn, ev ch till no extr clsg stages* ....(11 to 4 op 5 to 2) 2
COQUI LANE [121] 9-12-0 T Reed, *led, reminders aftr 5th, drvn aing and hdd betw last 2, sn wknd.* (7 to 2 op 5 to 2) 3
Dist: Hd, 24l. 4m 22.20s. a 15.20s (3 Ran).
SR: 7/21/5/ (G Shiel), M D Hammond

1660 John Hinchliffe Memorial Champion Chase (Handicap) Class B (5-y-o and up) £10,172 3½m...........(2:30)

1314⁵ SEVEN TOWERS (Ire) [115] 7-10-6 P Niven, *towards rear, drvn aing and outpcd aftr 3 out, rallied after last, styd on wl to ld cl hme*........................(11 to 4 fav op 2 to 1) 1
1504² MONY-SKIP (Ire) [114] 7-10-5 Richard Guest, *hld up, hdwy bef 3 out, ev ch to ld fnl 200 yards, ct cl hme* ....(3 to 1 op 5 to 2) 2
1253² WESTWELL BOY [109] 10-10-0 R Supple, *hmpd wl, cl up, led 6th till rdn and hdd fnl 200 yards, no extr*(11 to 4 op 3 to 1) 3
1069⁵ PIMS GUNNER (Ire) [109] 8-10-0 B Harding, *hld up, hdwy bef 3 out, ev ch last, wknd fnl 200 yards.*...(5 to 1 op 6 to 1) 4
1328² ALY DALEY (Ire) [109] 8-10-0 A Dobbin, *led to 6th, drvn aing aftr 11th, beh whn hmpd last*...........(8 to 1 op 6 to 1) 5
1589⁷ GALA WATER [109] 10-10-0 B Storey, *in tch till wknd bef 3 out.*..................................(5 to 1 tchd 66 to 1) 6
1283³ KILCOLGAN [109] 9-10-0 A S Smith, *nvr far away, 4th and no imprsn whn f last*.......(8 to 2 op 4 to 1 tchd 5 to 1) f
Dist: Hd, 4l, 1½l, 21l, 7l. 7m 2.30s. a 16.30s (7 Ran).
SR: 27/26/17/15/ (Mrs E A Murray), Mrs M Reveley

1661 E. Scarth & Son Handicap Hurdle Class C (0-130 4-y-o and up) £3,820 2¾m 110yds................ (3:00)

1375* LOCHNAGRAIN (Ire) [116] 8-11-9 P Niven, *beh, cld aftr 6th, effrt after 2 out, led fnl 200 yards, quickened clr.* ....(5 to 2 fav op 9 to 4 tchd 11 to 4) 1
1377* TRAP DANCER [93] 8-10-0 A Dobbin, *in tch chasing grp, slight ld 3 out, hdd nxt, ev ch till outpcd by wnr fnl 200 yards.* ....(11 to 4 op 5 to 2 tchd 3 to 1) 2
TRUMP [113] 7-11-6 D Parker, *in tch chasing grp, led 2 out till hdd fnl 200 yards, no extr.* ....(14 to 1 op 8 to 1 tchd 16 to 1) 3

1375⁵ DIG DEEPER [98] 9-10-5 B Harding, *led, clr to 7th, hdd 3 out, wknd aftr nxt*.......................(14 to 1 op 10 to 1) 4
1388³ NICHOLAS PLANT [96] 7-10-0 (3*) G Lee, *chsd clr ldr, mstk 7th, wknd aftr 3 out*....(100 to 30 op 3 to 1 tchd 7 to 2) 5
1282² TALLYWAGGER [117] 9-11-10 J Callaghan, *al beh.* ....(11 to 1 tchd 7 to 1) 6
1325⁴ D'ARBLAY STREET (Ire) [93] (bl) 7-10-0 S McDougall, *in tch till wknd bef 8th*........(16 to 1 op 14 to 1 tchd 25 to 1) 7
Dist: 8l, 1¼l, 11l, 5l, 1¼l, ½l. 5m 28.00s. a 19.00s (7 Ran).
SR: 6/-/-/-/ (Lightbody Of Hamilton Ltd), Mrs M Reveley

1662 Oswald Hughes Amateur Riders' Maiden Hurdle Class E (4-y-o and up) £2,346 2¾m 110yds..........(3:30)

PHARMISTEAC 5-11-3 (7*) Mr Chris Wilson, *in tch, effrt bef 2 out, styd on und pres to ld fnl 75 yards.* ....(5 to 1 op 14 to 1) 1
1337³ CASH BOX (Ire) 8-11-3 (7*) Mr C Mulhall, *hld up, gd hdwy bef 3 out, led appr last, hdd fnl 75 yards, no extr und pres.* .... (11 to 2 op 5 to 1 tchd 6 to 1) 2
BLACK ICE (Ire) 5-11-3 (7*) Mr W Burnell, *made appr 4th till appr last, ev ch till no extr fnl 200 yards.* ....(5 to 1 op 7 to 1) 3
MORE CHAMPAGNE 6-11-0 (5*) Miss P Robson, *al chasing ldrs, ch 2 out, kpt on same pace*.... (66 to 1 op 33 to 1) 4
1375⁵ CHEATER (Ire) 5-11-3 (7*) Miss P Jones, *trkd ldrs, ch 2 out, kpt on same pace frm last*....(7 to 2 op 4 to 1 tchd 9 to 2) 5
1253³ THE NEXT WALTZ (Ire) 5-11-5 (5*) Mr M H Naughton, *hld up, hdwy aftr 6th, kpt on same pace frm 3 out.* (7 to 1 op 5 to 1) 6
CRASHBALLOO (Ire) 5-11-3 (7*) Mr A Parker, *in tch till outpcd bef 3 out, no dngr aftr*.....(8 to 1 op 5 to 1 tchd 10 to 1) 7
1252⁷ NENAGH GUNNER 6-11-5 Mr S Swiers, *in tch, effrt bef 3 out, sn btn*................(10 to 1 op 7 to 1 tchd 11 to 1) 8
WOODSTOCK LODGE (USA) 8-11-7 (3*) Mr M Thompson, *prmnt till wknd quickly aftr 8th, tld off.* (66 to 1 op 33 to 1) 9
LA RIVIERA (Ire) 4-11-5 (5*) Mr N Wilson, *sn lost tch, wl tld off.* ....(33 to 1 op 25 to 1) 10
MARKS REFRAIN 12-11-3 (7*) Mr P Murray, *sn lost tch, tld off whn pld up aftr 8th*....................................(100 to 1) pu
LYFORD CAY (Ire) 6-11-3 (7*) Mr D Swindlehurst, *not jump wl, tld off whn pld up aftr 6th.* ....(40 to 1 op 33 to 1 tchd 50 to 1) pu
1332⁶ ALICHARGER 6-11-5 (5*) Mr R Hale, *led to 4th, in tch till wknd quickly bef 8th, tld off whn pld up before 3 out*......(50 to 1) pu
1337² KASIRAMA (Ire) 5-11-7 (3*) Mr C Bonner, *mid-div till wknd and lost tch bef 3 out, tld off whn pld up before nxt.* .... (5 to 2 fav tchd 3 to 1) pu
Dist: 1¼l, 6l, 1l, hd, 6l, 12l, 2½l, dist, 24l. 5m 35.00s. a 26.00s (14 Ran).
(John Halliday), Mrs A Swinbank

WINCANTON (good to firm)
Monday December 2nd
Going Correction: PLUS 0.15 sec. per fur.

1663 Cerne Abbas 'National Hunt' Novices' Hurdle Class E (4-y-o and up) £2,670 2¾m.................(1:20)

1355⁴ GALATASORI JANE (Ire) 6-10-0 (7*) L Cummins, *al hndy, led appr 2 out, ran on*. (14 to 1 op 12 to 1 tchd 16 to 1) 1
1413² SLIPMATIC 7-10-0 (7*) C Rae, *hld up, improved 7th, ev ch frm 2 out, hit last, unbl to quicken r-in*......(3 to 1 op 4 to 1) 2
1350² ANOTHER COCKPIT 4-10-12 A P McCoy, *hld up beh ldrs, rdn and outpcd frm 3 out, rallied and ran on r-in.* ....(4 to 1 op 5 to 2) 3
1442⁴ QUINAG 5-10-7 J A McCarthy, *prmnt, led 5th to 3 out, wknd frm nxt*.....................(9 to 1 op 7 to 1 tchd 10 to 1) 4
1355² COPPER COIL 6-10-5 (7*) J Power, *hld up in tch, rdn 3 out, wknd appr nxt*.......(11 to 1 op 10 to 1 tchd 12 to 1) 5
1502* KILMINGTON (Ire) 7-11-5 P Hide, *led to 5th, rgned ld 3 out, hdd bef nxt, sn btn*......................(7 to 4 fav op 6 to 4) 6
1502⁷ YOUNG TYCOON (NZ) 5-10-12 L Harvey, *midfield, lost tch frm 3 out, tld off*............................(66 to 1 op 25 to 1) 7
1437⁴ WARRIO 6-10-12 M Bosley, *al beh, tld off.* ....(50 to 1 op 25 to 1) 8
RAMBLING 10-10-9 (3*) P Henley, *nvr on terms, tld off whn pld up bef 2 out*........................(50 to 1 op 20 to 1) pu
1540 CAMINO (bl) 9-10-12 C Maude, *keen hold, beh till rapid hdwy 3rd, wknd 7th, tld off whn pld up bef 2 out.* ....(33 to 1 op 25 to 1) pu
STORMHILL HARPIE 5-10-7 S Burrough, *keen hold, in tch to 6th, tld off 8th, pld up bef 2 out.* ....(66 to 1 op 50 to 1 tchd 100 to 1) pu
1423⁶ MR STRONG GALE (Ire) 5-10-5 (7*) O Burrows, *hld up, prog 7th, in tch whn stumbled and rdr lost irons aftr 3 out, not reco'r, pld up bef nxt*....(14 to 1 op 8 to 1 tchd 16 to 1) pu
1464⁷ PRUSSIAN EAGLE (Ire) 4-10-7 P Holley, *strted slwly, al beh, tld off 8th, pld up bef 2 out*................(33 to 1 op 12 to 1) pu
1423⁹ QUISTI 6-10-12 M Richards, *al beh, tld off whn pld up bef 2 out*........................(33 to 1 op 20 to 1 tchd 50 to 1) pu
Dist: 5l, 4l, 1½l, 6l, 1¼l, dist. 5m 20.80s. a 14.80s (14 Ran).
(B L Blinman), P F Nicholls

1664 Somerset Conditional Jockeys' Handicap Chase Class E (0-120 5-y-o and up) £2,895 3m 1f 110yds (1:50)

BADASTAN (Ire) [110] (bl) 7-11-11 G Tormey, *made all, rdn out frm 3 out, styd on wl*..............(2 to 1 fav tchd 7 to 4) 1
PRICE'S HILL [107] 9-11-3 (5*) W Walsh, *hld up, hit second, chsd wnr frm 5th, ev ch whn pckd 3 out, hit nxt, kpt on r-in.*
..............................(4 to 1 op 5 to 2 tchd 9 to 2) 2
1499³ RAINBOW CASTLE [105] 9-11-3 (3*) O Burrows, *f second.*
..............................(5 to 2 op 3 to 1 tchd 100 to 30) f
1445³ CREDON [103] 8-11-4 P Henley, *chsd wnr to 5th, wknd appr 4 out, tld off whn pld up bef last.*......(100 to 30 op 5 to 1) pu
Dist: 2l. 6m 42.60s. a 26.60s (4 Ran).

(In Touch Racing Club), P J Hobbs

1665 Chard Juvenile Novices' Claiming Hurdle Class F (3-y-o) £2,372 2m
....(2:20)

1470⁵ LADY MAGNUM (Ire) 10-9 P Hide, *al hndy, led 4th, made rst, readily.*.................................(16 to 1 op 8 to 1) 1
1422² ALWAYS HAPPY 11-7 A P McCoy, *hld up rear, hdwy appr 2 out, chsd wnr approaching last, unbl to chal.*
..............................(11 to 8 on op 5 to 4 on) 2
1412⁵ STONECUTTER (v) 11-6 R Hughes, *hld up rear, improved appr 4th, outpcd frm 3 out, styd on one pace r-in.*
..............................(6 to 1 op 5 to 1 tchd 7 to 1) 3
1470² SIBERIAN MYSTIC 10-12 W McFarland, *hld up, hdwy hfwy, rdn and ev ch appr 2 out, sn wknd.*
..............................(13 to 2 op 5 to 1 tchd 7 to 1) 4
1524⁹ INDIRA 9-11 (3*) T Dascombe, *al prmnt, ev ch whn hit 2 out, wknd quickly.*........................(7 to 1 op 7 to 2) 5
1599⁵ STONE ISLAND (bl) 10-8 (3*) G Tormey, *hld up, prog hfwy, rdn and wknd appr 2 out*....(14 to 1 op 7 to 1 tchd 16 to 1) 6
1438 FOUR WEDDINGS (USA) (v) 10-5 C Maude, *led, reminder aftr 1st, hdd 4th, ev ch appr 2 out, sn wknd.*
..............................(20 to 1 op 12 to 1 tchd 25 to 1) 7
MISS PRAVDA 10-12 Mr J L Llewellyn, *al beh, tld off hfwy.*
..............................(16 to 1 op 16 to 1 tchd 33 to 1) 8
1438⁵ PROVE THE POINT (Ire) 10-3 P Holley, *chsd ldrs, lost pl hfwy, tld off whn pld up bef 2 out.*........(33 to 1 op 16 to 1) pu
Dist: 4l, 7l, nk, 2l, 3l, 17l, dist. 3m 43.50s. a 9.50s (9 Ran).
SR: 10/18/10/2/-/-/ (Magnum Construction Ltd), J Neville

1666 Nightingale Sings Handicap Chase Class D (0-120 5-y-o and up) £4,238 2m 5f........................(2:50)

1414* TOO PLUSH [109] 7-11-7 L Harvey, *prmnt, hit 6th, jmpd slwly tenth, wknd 13th,poor 3rd whn lft wl clr 2 out.*
..............................(5 to 2 op 2 to 1 tchd 11 to 4) 1
FIVE TO SEVEN (USA) [112] 7-11-10 A P McCoy, *led to 8th, rgned ld 12th, 6 ls clr whn badly hmpd by loose horse and refused 2 out, continued.*
..............................(2 to 1 fav op 7 to 4 tchd 9 to 4) 2
THE MINE CAPTAIN [98] 9-10-10 J A McCarthy, *prmnt, led 8th to 12th, 6 ls second whn lft in ld, badly hmpd by loose horse, refused and uns rdr 2 out, continued.*
..............................(5 to 2 op 9 to 4 tchd 11 to 4) 3
1531* THE CAUMRUE (Ire) [108] 8-11-6 B Clifford, *hld up, f 7th.*
..............................(4 to 1 op 3 to 1) f
Dist: Dist, 3l. 5m 31.50s. a 27.50s (4 Ran).

(Mrs C C Williams), Andrew Turnell

1667 Orchard FM Mares' Only Novices' Chase Class E (5-y-o and up) £2,856 2m.................................(3:20)

1501⁴ SECOND CALL 7-11-7 A P McCoy, *al gng wl, prmnt, led aftr 9th, lft clr nxt, hrd hld.*.........(2 to 1 on tchd 7 to 4 on) 1
JOSIFINA 5-11-0 C Maude, *hld up, hdwy 6th, lost tch 9th, lft in second nxt, no imprsn on wnr.*
..............................(9 to 2 op 7 to 2 tchd 5 to 1) 2
1501* KOO'S PROMISE 5-11-4 (3*) T Dascombe, *led to 3rd, pckd nxt, outpcd 9th, hmpd next, no imprsn aftr.*
..............................(12 to 1 op 8 to 1 tchd 14 to 1) 3
MISTRESS ROSIE 9-11-0 S Fox, *beh 7th, tld off.*
..............................(10 to 1 op 10 to 1) 4
RELKOWEN 6-11-0 M Richards, *dsptd ld, led 3rd till aftr 9th, one l second whn f 4 out.*...(9 to 2 op 4 to 1 tchd 5 to 1) f
1501³ UP THE TEMPO (Ire) 7-11-0 J R Kavanagh, *al beh, tld off 5th, pld up bef 4 out.*......(33 to 1 op 16 to 1 tchd 50 to 1) pu
Dist: 5l, 2l, dist. 4m 6.10s. a 18.10s (6 Ran).

(J H Day), Capt T A Forster

1668 Manston Handicap Hurdle Class E (0-115 4-y-o and up) £2,427 2¾m ....(3:50)

1260* GENERAL MOUKTAR [96] 6-11-0 A P McCoy, *wtd wth, prog frm 3 out, led aftr last, readily.*
..............................(7 to 4 fav op 5 to 2 tchd 11 to 4) 1
1500* MORSTOCK [110] 6-11-11 (3*) T Dascombe, *hld up, improved frm 3 out, ch nxt, no extr r-in.*
..............................(6 to 1 op 4 to 1 tchd 7 to 1) 2

1370² SILVER STANDARD [102] (bl) 6-11-6 C Maude, *trkd ldrs, led aftr 3 out till after last, no extr.*..........(2 to 1 op 7 to 4) 3
822⁵ CAVINA [108] 6-11-12 P Hide, *chsd ldr, lft in ld 3 out, sn hdd, wknd appr nxt, tld off.*......(7 to 2 op 3 to 1 tchd 4 to 1) 4
1355⁶ MU-TADIL [82] 4-9-7 (7*) N T Egan, *hld up, not fluent 4th and nxt, tld off 6th.*......................(50 to 1 op 25 to 1) 5
1481⁵ WELSHMAN [104] 10-11-8 J R Kavanagh, *led till pckd and hmpd 3 out, not reco'r, beh whn pld up bef nxt.*
..............................(16 to 1 op 10 to 1) pu
Dist: 1¼l, ½l, dist, dist. 5m 20.50s. a 14.50s (6 Ran).

(A S Helaissi), M C Pipe

WORCESTER (good to soft)
Monday December 2nd
Going Correction: PLUS 1.00 sec. per fur. (races 1,3,5,7), PLUS 0.85 (2,4,6)

1669 Rushock Mares' Only Novices' Hurdle Class E (4-y-o and up) £2,407 2m ....(12:40)

1476* MELSTOCK MEGGIE 6-10-12 W Marston, *trkd ldrs, led appr 3 out, edgd rght r-in, drvn out.*
..............................(3 to 1 op 9 to 4 tchd 100 to 30) 1
1369⁵ MOOR HALL LADY 5-10-12 A Maguire, *hld up, hdwy 5th, ev ch whn blun 2 out, mstk last, no extr.*
..............................(6 to 1 tchd 7 to 1 and 15 to 2) 2
SLIPPERY FIN 4-10-5 (7*) N Willmington, *hld up, hdwy 5th, rdn appr last, styd on same pace.*
..............................(25 to 1 op 20 to 1 tchd 50 to 1) 3
FAIRELAINE 4-10-5 (7*) Mr R Wakley, *hld up, hdwy 3 out, styd on.*...............................(16 to 1 tchd 20 to 1) 4
1397 QUAKER WALTZ 6-10-12 S McNeill, *hld up, hdwy 5th, wknd 2 out.*.....................(10 to 1 op 16 to 1 tchd 25 to 1) 5
1423* GLORIANA 4-11-5 M A Fitzgerald, *led, mstk second, hdd and wknd appr 3 out.*.............(9 to 4 fav op 6 to 4) 6
1496 PERSIAN BUTTERFLY 4-10-9 (3*) D Walsh, *chsd ldr till wknd appr 3 out.*........(66 to 1 op 33 to 1 tchd 100 to 1) 7
1365⁸ DERBY BELLE 5-10-12 M Clarke, *beh frm 4th, tld off.*
..............................(50 to 1 op 33 to 1 tchd 66 to 1) 8
1496 BECKY'S GIRL 6-10-12 N Mann, *beh frm 3rd, tld off.*
..............................(66 to 1 op 33 to 1 tchd 100 to 1) 9
1474 FORBURIES (Ire) (bl) 7-10-12 B Powell, *prmnt till mstk and wknd 3rd, tld off whn pld up bef 5th...(100 to 1 op 50 to 1) pu
CUPRONICKEL (Ire) 4-10-12 D J Burchell, *al in rear, tld off whn pld up bef 3 out.*...........(100 to 1 op 50 to 1) pu
KONVEKTA QUEEN (Ire) 5-10-12 J Osborne, *in tch, pckd 1st, lost pl 4th, beh whn pld bef 3 out.*
..............................(5 to 2 op 11 to 4 tchd 3 to 1) pu
1483 PERSIAN SUNSET (Ire) 4-10-12 D Bridgwater, *al in rear, tld off whn pld up bef 3 out.*
..............................(66 to 1 op 50 to 1 tchd 100 to 1) pu
Dist: 3l, 3l, 2½l, 5l, 13l, 10l, 17l, dist. 4m 5.40s. a 25.40s (13 Ran).

(Mrs Kay Birchenhough), Mrs J Pitman

1670 Bet With The Tote Novices' Chase Qualifier Class E (5-y-o and up) £3,605 2½m 110yds.........(1:10)

1298³ PHARANEAR (Ire) 6-10-12 A Maguire, *hld up, hdwy 7th, led last, hld briefly run in, drvn out.*......(5 to 1 op 3 to 1) 1
1186⁵ TREASURE AGAIN (Ire) 7-10-12 Derek Byrne, *hld up, hdwy 7th, led briefly run in, kpt on.*
..............................(11 to 4 fav op 5 to 2 tchd 7 to 2) 2
THREE PHILOSOPHERS (Ire) 7-10-12 S Wynne, *led 3rd, blun 5th,rdn and hdd last, no extr.*...........(6 to 1 op 4 to 1) 3
STAY LUCKY (NZ) 7-11-5 M A Fitzgerald, *chsd ldrs, mstk 8th, hit tenth, styd on same pace frm 2 out.* (8 to 1 op 11 to 2) 4
1341 MACGEORGE (Ire) 6-10-12 C Llewellyn, *sn wl beh, tld off.*
..............................(9 to 2 op 4 to 1 tchd 6 to 1) 5
1368² KEY TO MOYADE (Ire) 6-10-12 I Lawrence, *prmnt to 8th, tld off.*....................(16 to 1 op 12 to 1 tchd 20 to 1) 6
DOMAINE DE PRON (Fr) 5-10-12 M Sharratt, *mid -div, rdn 6th, sn beh, tld off.*............(50 to 1 op 33 to 1) 7
1473 BONNIFER (Ire) 7-10-12 W Marston, *hld up, hdwy 7th, wknd 9th, tld off.*...........(14 to 1 op 10 to 1) 8
THE BOOLEY HOUSE (Ire) 6-10-12 B Powell, *led to second, f 8th.*....................(14 to 1 op 10 to 1) f
1454⁷ THE REVEREND BERT (Ire) 8-10-12 B Fenton, *hmpd and uns rdr 5th.*.....................(25 to 1 op 20 to 1) ur
EASY BREEZY 6-10-12 J Railton, *hld up, bright dwn 5th.*
..............................(25 to 1 op 20 to 1 tchd 33 to 1) bd
1354⁷ TIBBS INN 7-10-7 (5*) Mr R Thornton, *refused 1st.*
..............................(66 to 1 op 50 to 1 tchd 100 to 1) ref
IL BAMBINO 8-10-5 (7*) A Dowling, *tld off frm 6th, pld up bef 9th.*..........................(50 to 1 op 33 to 1 tchd 66 to 1) pu
1636 TWO JOHN'S (Ire) 7-10-12 G Bradley, *chsd ldrs, rdn 2 out, btn whn pld up bef last, lme...(9 to 1 op 6 to 1 tchd 10 to 1) pu
1270 DUNNICKS COUNTRY 6-10-7 G Upton, *tld off frm 6th, pld up bef 8th.*..........(66 to 1 op 50 to 1 tchd 100 to 1) pu
BE BRAVE 6-10-12 N Mann, *tld off frm 6th, pld up bef 3 out.*
..............................(50 to 1 op 20 to 1) pu
CARACOL 7-10-12 D Bridgwater, *prmnt led second to 3rd, wknd 5 out, pld up bef nxt.*........(50 to 1 op 20 to 1) pu
Dist: Nk, 5l, hd, dist, 17l, 5l, dist. 5m 20.30s. a 23.30s (17 Ran).

SR: 25/24/19/26/-/-/ (Stainless Threaded Fasteners Ltd), D Nicholson

1671 River Severn Handicap Hurdle Class D (0-125 4-y-o and up) £3,120 2½m .... (1:40)

BIG STRAND (Ire) [107] 7-11-5 (3*) D Walsh, *hld up, hdwy 5th, led last, rdn out*........(5 to 1 op 5 to 2) 1

1303[5] REAGANESQUE (USA) [105] 4-11-6 R Farrant, *chsd ldr, led 5th, rdn and hdd last, styd on same pace.* .... (6 to 1 tchd 7 to 1 and 8 to 1) 2

1112[7] MR SNAGGLE (Ire) [91] 7-10-6 A Maguire, *hld up, hdwy 4 out, rdn and wknd 2 out*............................. (5 to 1) 3

1453 FAST THOUGHTS [109] 9-11-5 (5*) Sophie Mitchell, *led, sn clr, hdd 5th, wknd 4 out.* (16 to 1 op 12 to 1 tchd 20 to 1) 4

1442* GLISTENING DAWN [97] (bl) 6-10-12 S McNeill, *mid-div, effrt 4 out, wknd nxt, tld off*............(4 to 1 fav op 5 to 2) 5

MAJOR NOVA [100] 7-11-1 J Ryan, *sn wl beh, tld off whn pld up bef 3 out*........................(20 to 1 op 12 to 1) pu

MANOLETE [103] 5-11-4 Derek Byrne, *prmnt till 5th, tld off and pld up bef 2 out*..................(11 to 2 op 3 to 1) pu

NUNS CONE [93] 8-10-5 (3*) G Hogan, *prmnt till lost pl 5th, tld off whn pld up bef 4 out*..........(16 to 1 op 10 to 1) pu

TRECENTO [92] 5-10-7 W Marston, *hld up, hdwy 4th, wknd quickly aftr four out, pld up bef nxt.* ....(5 to 1 op 6 to 1 tchd 9 to 2) pu

Dist: 4l, 18l, 17l, dist. 5m 3.30s. a 27.30s (9 Ran).
SR: 21/15/-/-/-/-/ (E C Jones), M C Pipe

1672 Kempsey Handicap Chase Class C (0-135 4-y-o and up) £4,467 2m .... (2:10)

MISTER ODDY [123] 10-11-7 M A Fitzgerald, *prmnt, led 4 out, clr 2 out, eased r-in*.................(7 to 1 tchd 8 to 1) 1

1468* THUMBS UP [130] 10-11-11 (3*) D Fortt, *chsd ldrs, ev ch appr 4 out, styd on same pace frm nxt*..................(6 to 1) 2

RANDOM ASSAULT (NZ) [130] 7-12-0 A Maguire, *led and sn clr, blun 4th, hdd four out, soon btn*.................(4 to 1) 3

1428* NEWLANDS-GENERAL [118] 10-11-2 G Bradley, *prmnt, jnd ldr 5th, wkng whn blun 4 out*.................(9 to 4 jt-fav) 4

SEEK THE FAITH (USA) [107] 7-10-5 B Powell, *hld up, effrt appr 4 out, sn wknd*......................(9 to 4 jt-fav) 5

1428 KYTTON CASTLE [102] 9-10-0 R Bellamy, *al in rear, lost tch frm hfwy, tld off whn pld up bef 4 out*.. (7 to 1 tchd 8 to 1) pu

Dist: 6l, 6l, 1¼l, 8l. 4m 11.00s. a 22.00s (6 Ran).
SR: 9/10/4/ (Mrs R M Hill), J S King

1673 Spetchley 'National Hunt' Novices' Hurdle Class E (4-y-o and up) £2,915 2½m......................... (2:40)

1540* FOREST IVORY (NZ) 5-11-3 A Maguire, *hld up, hdwy 4 out, led nxt, styd on strly.* ....(Evens fav op 5 to 4 tchd 6 to 4 and 7 to 4) 1

1447[2] DANTES CAVALIER (Ire) 6-10-7 (3*) D Fortt, *hld up, hdwy 4 out, chsd wnr appr last, no imprsn.* ....(3 to 1 tchd 7 to 2 and 4 to 1) 2

AUT EVEN (Ire) 6-10-10 S Wynne, *hld up, hdwy 5 out, chsd wnr 3 out, one pace frm nxt.* ....(16 to 1 op 12 to 1 tchd 20 to 1) 3

1344[2] DENHAM HILL (Ire) 5-10-10 J Railton, *prmnt, rdn and mstk 3 out, sn wknd*...................(7 to 1 op 5 to 1 tchd 8 to 1) 4

1429[2] DANCETILLYOUDROP (Ire) 5-10-10 M A Fitzgerald, *mid-div, hdwy 5th, wknd appr 2 out*............(10 to 1 op 6 to 1) 5

1338 RATHKEAL (Ire) 5-10-10 D Gallagher, *hld up, hdwy 5th, wknd 3 out*...........................(50 to 1 tchd 66 to 1) 6

LOUGHDOO (Ire) 8-10-7 (3*) G Hogan, *hld up, nvr nr to chal.* ....(66 to 1 op 33 to 1) 7

CAST OF THOUSANDS 5-10-10 J Osborne, *nvr rchd chalg pos*.........................(20 to 1 op 12 to 1) 8

1496 DON'T MIND IF I DO (Ire) 5-10-10 Mr P Scott, *hld up, hdwy 5th, wknd 3 out*.................... (100 to 1 op 50 to 1) 9

CAREYSVILLE (Ire) 5-10-5 (5*) Mr R Thornton, *prmnt, led 5th till 4 out, wknd nxt*.................(66 to 1 op 50 to 1) 10

1300[5] WEST BAY BREEZE 4-10-5 B Powell, *in tch to 6th.* ....(50 to 1 op 33 to 1) 11

1228[4] SPRING DOUBLE (Ire) 5-10-10 C Llewellyn, *led aftr 1st till 5th, led ag'n 4 out, hdd and wknd nxt.* ....(9 to 1 op 6 to 1 tchd 10 to 1) 12

1456[6] GREENFIELD GEORGE (Ire) 5-10-5 (5*) D J Kavanagh, *prmnt, jnd ldrs 5th, wknd appr 3 out*.........(40 to 1 op 33 to 1) 13

1483 DERRYS PREROGATIVE 6-10-10 D Bridgwater, *beh frm hfwy*......................................(100 to 1) 14

1447[8] LITTLE EARN 6-10-3 (7*) Mr A Wintle, *beh frm 5th.* ....(100 to 1 op 50 to 1) 15

1479 DERRING JACK 5-10-10 T J Murphy, *al in rear, beh whn mstk and uns rdr 2 out*............................(100 to 1) ur

HANAFORD POINT (Ire) 7-10-5 W Marston, *al wl beh, tld off whn pld up bef 7th*................. (33 to 1 op 16 to 1) pu

1318[4] RAGDON 5-10-10 G Upton, *hld up, beh frm 5th, pld up bef 3 out*..................(66 to 1 op 50 to 1 tchd 100 to 1) pu

1474 ALTHREY ARISTOCRAT (Ire) 6-10-7 (3*) D Walsh, *wth ldrs, led 3rd to 5th, wknd 4 out, pld up bef 3 out*.........(100 to 1) pu

1134 GUTTERIDGE (Ire) 6-10-10 S McNeill, *in tch to 6th, beh whn pld up r-in*...................................(20 to 1) pu

1234 KARICLEIGH MAN 6-10-10 G Bradley, *beh frm 5th, pld up bef 3 out*............ (25 to 1 op 20 to 1 tchd 33 to 1) pu

1369 MISS MYLETTE (Ire) 5-10-5 T Jenks, *led till aftr 1st, wknd 5 out, pld up bef 2 out*...............(100 to 1 op 66 to 1) pu

Dist: 2½l, 10l, 1½l, 10l, 10l, ½l, 11l, 1½l, 1½l, 2l. 5m 1.40s. a 25.40s (22 Ran).
SR: 35/25/15/13/3/-/ (The Old Foresters Partnership), D Nicholson

1674 Malvern Handicap Chase Class F (0-100 4-y-o and up) £2,910 2m 7f 110yds...................... (3:10)

1323* LORD OF THE WEST (Ire) [98] 7-12-0 A Maguire, *beh, hdwy tenth, styd on und pres to ld r-in.* ....(5 to 2 tchd 11 to 4 and 9 to 4) 1

1491* EASTERN RIVER [80] 10-10-10 S Wynne, *hld up, hdwy 9th, led and blun badly 4 out, sn hdd, led ag'n 2 out, headed r-in, kpt on*............(7 to 4 fav op 11 to 8 tchd 15 to 8) 2

HANGOVER [75] 10-10-2 (3*) G Hogan, *al prmnt, led aftr 4 out, rdn and hdd 2 out, sn btn*........(20 to 1 op 14 to 1) 3

1046[5] GLENFINN PRINCESS [96] 8-11-12 Derek Byrne, *nvr rchd chalg pos*................. (5 to 1 op 9 to 2 tchd 6 to 1) 4

1140[3] LEINTHALL PRINCESS [80] 10-10-10 B Fenton, *prmnt, drvn alng tenth, sn lost pl*.....(12 to 1 op 8 to 1 tchd 14 to 1) 5

1445[5] TITAN EMPRESS [80] (v) 7-10-10 N Mann, *led 4th, hdd and wknd four out*..........(9 to 1 op 11 to 2 tchd 10 to 1) 6

1140 BEAUFAN [79] 9-10-9 Gary Lyons, *beh frm hfwy, hit 9th, pld up bef 6 out*............. (50 to 1 op 33 to 1 tchd 66 to 1) pu

COASTING [87] 10-11-3 J Railton, *led till 4th, wknd tenth, pld up bef 6 out*....................... (14 to 1 op 10 to 1) pu

1426[2] SORBIERE [98] (bl) 9-12-0 M A Fitzgerald, *chsd ldrs till wknd quickly appr 4 out, pld up bef last.* ....(14 to 1 op 12 to 1 tchd 16 to 1) pu

Dist: 1l, 11l, 3l, 12l, 3l. 6m 18.60s. (9 Ran).
(Anne Duchess Of Westminster), J J O'Neill

1675 Weatherbys 'Stars Of Tomorrow' National Hunt Flat Maiden - Class H (4,5,6-y-o) £1,448 2m......... (3:40)

BILLINGSGATE 4-10-12 (7*) N Willmington, *chsd ldrs, led o'r 3 fs out, rdn out*...................(50 to 1 op 33 to 1) 1

DARK ORCHARD (Ire) 5-11-0 (5*) A Bates, *hld up, hdwy hfwy, chsd wnr o'r 2 fs out, no imprsn*..................(33 to 1) 2

1317[3] ARDRINA 5-10-9 (5*) Mr R Thornton, *al prmnt, rdn o'r 3 fs out, styd on same pace*.....(3 to 1 fav op 5 to 2 tchd 7 to 2) 3

LANDA'S COUNSEL 5-10-9 (5*) Sophie Mitchell, *mid-div, hdwy o'r 5 fs out, nvr rchd ldrs*.........(7 to 2 op 9 to 4) 4

1240[6] TAIN TON 4-10-12 (7*) M Keighley, *nvr rchd chalg pos.* ....(16 to 1 op 14 to 1) 5

1575[5] IRISH DELIGHT 4-11-2 (3*) D Walsh, *chsd ldrs till wknd o'r 2 fs out*................(12 to 1 op 8 to 1 tchd 14 to 1) 6

1324[4] DAYDREAM BELIEVER 4-10-11 (3*) R Massey, *hld up, nvr nr to chal*...........................(100 to 1 op 50 to 1) 7

1476[3] KOSHEEN (Ire) 5-10-7 (7*) Mr A Wintle, *prmnt, jnd ldrs o'r 5 fs out, wknd over 3 out*.....(11 to 2 op 3 to 1 tchd 6 to 1) 8

CLASSIC CHAT 4-10-12 (7*) Miss C Spearing, *made most till hdd o'r 3 fs out, sn wknd*............(16 to 1 op 10 to 1) 9

OTAGO HEIGHTS (NZ) 4-11-2 (3*) G Hogan, *hld up, hdwy o'r ten fs out, wknd over 4 out.* ....(5 to 1 op 4 to 1 tchd 6 to 1 and 7 to 1) 10

NICANJON 5-10-12 (7*) X Aizpuru, *hld up, effrt hfwy, grad lost pl*...................(20 to 1 op 12 to 1 tchd 25 to 1) 11

SOCIAL INSECURITY (Ire) 5-11-0 (5*) D J Kavanagh, *nvr rchd chalg pos*...................... (50 to 1 tchd 66 to 1) 12

1476[6] WINNETKA GAL (Ire) 4-10-7 (7*) L Suthern, *prmnt, drvn alng o'r 5 fs out, sn wknd*................. (10 to 1 op 5 to 1) 13

1109[6] BURFORDS FOR SCRAP 4-10-12 (7*) Mr F Hutsby, *chsd ldrs, rdn o'r 6 fs out, wknd over 4 out*......(66 to 1 op 50 to 1) 14

1476 SILVER QUILL 5-11-0 R Arnold, *beh frm hfwy.* ....(20 to 1 op 16 to 1 tchd 25 to 1) 15

SPIRIT OF SUCCESS 6-11-5 Mr A Kinane, *mid-div, pushed alng hfwy, grad lost pl*............(100 to 1 op 50 to 1) 16

1483 PRIVATE MEMORIES 6-11-5 Miss C Dyson, *hld up, beh frm hfwy*........................(100 to 1 op 50 to 1) 17

BIT 'O' SUNSHINE 5-10-7 (7*) B Clarke, *prmnt to hfwy, tld off fnl 4 fs*........................(50 to 1 op 33 to 1) 18

ALRIGHT GUVNOR 6-10-9 (5*) G E Smith, *in tch to hfwy, tld off whn pld up fnl furlong*.........(100 to 1 op 33 to 1) pu

SUPREME CRUSADER (Ire) 5-11-2 (3*) D Fortt, *hld up in tch, hdwy hfwy, wknd quickly o'r 5 fs out tld off whn pld up ins last.* ....(100 to 1 op 50 to 1) pu

Dist: 4l, 12l, 4l, ¾l, 1½l, 20l, 1l, ¾l, ¾l, 10l. 3m 56.70s. (20 Ran).
(Dr D Chesney), Dr D Chesney

NEWCASTLE (good to soft)
Tuesday December 3rd

Going Correction: PLUS 1.05 sec. per fur. (races 1,2,4,5,7), PLUS 0.75 (3,6)

1676 Levy Board Conditional Jockeys' Handicap Hurdle Class E (0-110 4-y-o and up) £2,284 2m.........(12:30)

1167[2] KEMO SABO [84] 4-10-5 D Parker, *made all, drw clr bef 3 out, styd on wl*.........................(7 to 2 op 11 to 4) 1

1588⁵ AUBURN BOY [103] 9-11-10 P Midgley, *hld up, outpcd aftr 6th, styd on frm 2 out*..............(13 to 2 op 5 to 1) 2
BARTON HEIGHTS [90] 4-10-6 (5²) M Herrington, *sn chasing ldrs, drvn alng bef 3 out, fdd*............(4 to 1 op 3 to 1) 3
1386⁵ TRIENNIUM (USA) [79] 7-10-0 G Cahill, *in tch, hdwy aftr 6th, chasing wnr whn mstk 2 out, no imprsn, wknd clsg stages.*
....(7 to 1 op 5 to 1) 4
SKIDDAW SAMBA [84] 7-10-0 (5²) C McCormack, *in tch till outpcd aftr 6th, no dngr after*........(20 to 1 op 16 to 1) 5
1386³ MISS GREENYARDS [84] 5-10-5 S Taylor, *chsd ldrs till wknd bef 3 out, tld off*...............(7 to 4 fav op 2 to 1) 6
1521³ APPEARANCE MONEY (Ire) [81] 5-10-2⁸ (7²) F Bogle, *beh, lost tch aftr 6th, tld off*............(10 to 1 op 16 to 1) 7
DOON RIDGE [80] 5-9-12 (3²) M Newton, *chsd ldrs till wknd quickly aftr 5th, tld off whn pld up after nxt.*
....(33 to 1 op 25 to 1) pu

Dist: 8l, 2l, 1¼l, 2l, 22l, 8l. 4m 6.60s. a 29.60s (8 Ran).

(R Nichol), C Parker

1677 Polyflor And Newcastle Flooring Novices' Hurdle Class E (4-y-o and up) £2,536 2m...............(1:00)

1252* ALABANG 5-11-5 P Niven, *in tch, al gng wl, hdwy on bit to ld aftr 3 out, clr whn mstk last, very easily.*
....(11 to 10 on op 5 to 4 on) 1
1033³ PENTLAND SQUIRE 5-10-12 Richard Guest, *prmnt, dsptd ld aftr 6th, sn drvn alng, kpt on frm 2 out, no ch wth wnr.*
....(14 to 1 op 12 to 1) 2
1039⁵ QATTARA (Ire) 6-10-9 (3²) G Cahill, *prmnt, led aftr 6th, hdd after 3 out, no extr*.........................(20 to 1) 3
PAPPA CHARLIE (USA) 5-10-12 B Storey, *in tch, hdwy bef 6th, wknd before 3 out.*..................(10 to 1 op 8 to 1) 4
1509⁴ MR CHRISTIE 4-10-12 R Supple, *chsd ldrs, blun 4th, sn drvn alng, wknd aftr 6th*...............................(8 to 1) 5
PRINCE OF SAINTS (Ire) 5-10-12 R Garritty, *in tch till wknd aftr 6th*............................(20 to 1 op 16 to 1) 6
KILDRUMMY CASTLE 4-10-12 W Dwan, *mid-div till wknd aftr 6th*........................(7 to 1 op 5 to 1) 7
928⁴ LAUGHING FONTAINE (Ire) 6-10-12 K Whelan, *hld up, hdwy hfwy, wknd bef 3 out*...............(8 to 1 op 7 to 1) 8
1333⁷ NOBLE MONARCH (Ire) 7-10-12 N Williamson, *prmnt, led 6th, sn hdd and wknd*............(20 to 1 op 14 to 1) 9
EDSTONE (Ire) 4-10-12 J Callaghan, *wl beh frm 5th.* (33 to 1) 10
1374 PAINT YOUR WAGON 6-10-13¹ T Reed, *led till hdd 6th, wknd quickly*..(50 to 1) 11
HAWK HILL BOY 5-10-12 A S Smith, *al beh*..........(50 to 1) 12
PARRY 4-10-7 K Johnson, *in tch till wknd aftr 5th.* (100 to 1) 13
1464⁸ MEESONETTE 4-10-7 B Harding, *chsd ldrs till wknd quickly aftr 5th, tld off*..........................(100 to 1) 14
RUBISLAW 4-10-5 (7²) Miss S Lamb, *sn wl beh, tld off.*
....(100 to 1) 15
1590 SAFETY TIP 4-10-7 M Moloney, *sn wl beh, tld off.* (100 to 1) 16

Dist: 6l, 2l, 10l, 5l, 3l, 24l, 3l, ¾l, 9l, ¾l. 4m 1.90s. a 24.90s (16 Ran).

SR: 10/-/-/-/-/-/   *(Elite Racing Club), M J Camacho*

1678 Ramside Event Catering Handicap Chase Class C (0-135 5-y-o and up) £4,468 2m 110yds............(1:30)

1389* POLITICAL TOWER [125] 9-11-10 A Dobbin, *trkd ldr, hit 8th, led aftr 2 out, mstk last, hld on wl und pres.*
......................................(6 to 4 fav op 11 to 8 tchd 13 to 8) 1
747³ TIMBUCKTOO [115] 9-11-8 D Storey, *hld up in rear, effrt aftr 2 out, styd on und pres frm last, not rch wnr.*
......................................(4 to 1 tchd 5 to 1 and 6 to 1) 2
1389³ REGAL ROMPER (Ire) [115] 8-11-0 Richard Guest, *led till hdd aftr 2 out, wknd after last.*........(2 to 1 op 13 to 8) 3
1389⁶ ONE FOR THE POT [110] 11-10-9 M Foster, *prmnt frm 4th, ev ch bef 2 out, fdd*...........(5 to 1 op 9 to 2 tchd 11 to 4) 4
NOBODYS FLAME (Ire) [101] 8-9-13² (3²) G Cahill, *mstk 5th, beh aftr, lost tch quickly frm 8th, tld off whn pld up bef 2 out.*
....(100 to 1 op 66 to 1) pu

Dist: Nk, 7l, ½l. 4m 17.50s. a 18.50s (5 Ran).

SR: 35/25/18/12/-/   *(G R S Nixon), R Nixon*

1679 Newcastle Flooring And Halstead's Novices' Hurdle Class E (4-y-o and up) £2,589 2½m..............(2:00)

1255⁵ BEGGARS BANQUET (Ire) 6-10-12 (7²) B Grattan, *trkd ldrs, led 3 out, drvn out towards finish.*
...................................(9 to 2 op 7 to 2 tchd 5 to 1) 1
1063¹ INN AT THE TOP 4-11-5 W Fry, *sn tracking ldrs, led 8th, hdd 3 out, styd on wl*..............(9 to 2 op 3 to 1 tchd 5 to 1) 2
1162* ANTARCTIC WIND (Ire) 6-11-5 R Garritty, *chsd ldrs till outpcd by 1st 2 bef 3 out*..................(9 to 1 op 5 to 1) 3
1198³ STAN'S YOUR MAN 6-11-2 (3²) G Cahill, *led 3rd to 5th, cl up till wknd aftr 8th*.........(4 to 1 op 7 to 2 tchd 9 to 2) 4
1295⁴ CYPRESS AVENUE (Ire) 4-10-12 D Parker, *chsd ldrs, drvn alng aftr 7th, wknd after nxt*..........(7 to 1 op 6 to 1) 5
1509* TREMENDISTO 6-11-5 A Dobbin, *prmnt, led 5th, hdd 8th, sn wknd*......................(12 to 1 op 10 to 1 tchd 14 to 1) 6
LOSTRIS (Ire) 5-10-7 N Smith, *nvr dngrs.*
....(100 to 1 op 66 to 1) 7
1373² JAUNTY GENERAL 5-10-12 B Storey, *mstk 3rd, in tch till wknd aftr 8th*.......................(20 to 1 op 12 to 1) 8

1047 BOSTON MAN 5-10-12 J Callaghan, *in tch till wknd bef 8th.*
....(150 to 1) 9
1390 GALE FORCE (Ire) 5-10-12 R Supple, *sn beh.*
....(50 to 1 op 33 to 1) 10
1631 POCAIRE GAOITHE (Ire) 6-10-12 M Moloney, *beh frm hfwy.*
....(100 to 1) 11
887 CLONROCHE LUCKY (Ire) 6-10-12 F Perratt, *beh most of way*...(100 to 1) 12
BOLD'N 9-10-5 (7²) S Haworth, *tld off whn pld up bef 3 out.*
....(200 to 1) pu
MAGIC TIMES 5-10-12 J Railton, *led to 3rd, tld off whn pld up bef 3 out*..........................(100 to 1 op 66 to 1) pu
MOON CASTLE (Ire) 8-10-13¹ Mr M Thompson, *tld off whn pld up bef 3 out*.................................(500 to 1) pu
CLAVERING (Ire) 6-10-12 N Williamson, *chsd ldrs till wknd quickly aftr 7th, tld off whn pld up bef 3 out.*
...............................(7 to 2 fav tchd 3 to 1 and 4 to 1) pu
1333⁸ LEPTON (Ire) 5-10-12 P Niven, *tld off whn pld up bef 3 out.*
....(25 to 1 op 20 to 1) pu
1255⁷ LEIGHTEN LASS (Ire) 5-10-7 K Johnson, *sn wl beh, tld off whn pld up bef 3 out*................(100 to 1) pu
1317 GENERAL PARKER 5-10-12 A S Smith, *prmnt to hfwy, sn wknd, tld off whn pld up bef 3 out*.................(100 to 1) pu

Dist: 1½l, 26l, 11l, ½l, 3½l, nk, 7l, 10l, ½l, 10l. 5m 5.40s. a 27.40s (19 Ran).

SR: 27/26/-/-/-/-/   *(E H Ruddock), P Beaumont*

1680 Gosforth Park Handicap Hurdle Class C (0-135 4-y-o and up) £3,517 3m........................(2:30)

SEDVICTA [103] 4-10-0 (3²) G Cahill, *trkd ldrs, led 3 out, styd on wl*...........(6 to 5 fav op 11 to 10 tchd 5 to 4) 1
LEADING PROSPECT [100] 9-10-0 A S Smith, *made most till hdd 3 out, styd on wl*.................(25 to 1 op 14 to 1) 2
ACT THE WAG (Ire) [104] 7-10-4 B Harding, *nvr far away, ev ch 3 out, wknd aftr nxt*..............(10 to 3 op 3 to 1) 3
1315 MAYBE O'GRADY (Ire) [100] 7-9-7 (7²) L McGrath, *keen, hld up in rear, jnd ldrs 9th, outpcd bef 3 out, no dngr aftr.*
....(16 to 1 op 14 to 1) 4
UNCLE DOUG [128] 5-12-0 P Niven, *hld up in tch, effrt aftr 3 out, sn wknd*.......(9 to 4 op 7 to 4 tchd 5 to 2) 5

Dist: 1¾l, 9l, 2l, 8l. 6m 27.20s. a 56.20s (5 Ran).

(The Mary Reveley Racing Club), Mrs M Reveley

# 1681 Northern Racing Novices' Chase Class D (5-y-o and up) £3,663 3m
....(3:00)

MAJORITY MAJOR (Ire) 7-10-12 A S Smith, *hld up, steady hdwy hfwy, effrt aftr 2 out, led fnl 200 yards, styd on und pres.*
...............................(14 to 1 op 12 to 1) 1
1281⁴ SHAWWELL 9-10-12 B Storey, *prmnt, led 6th to 7th, led 2 out, hdd fnl 200 yards, no extr*.........(9 to 2 op 7 to 2) 2
1585⁷ ROYAL SURPRISE (bl) 9-10-12 T Reed, *styd badly 1st, led 3rd to 6th, led nxt, hdd 2 out, fdd*........(14 to 1 tchd 16 to 1) 3
CORPORAL KIRKWOOD (Ire) 6-10-12 A Dobbin, *in tch, hdwy hfwy, ev ch bef 3 out, wknd aftr nxt*.........(20 to 1 op 14 to 1) 4
1585⁸ MONYMAX (Ire) 7-10-12 Richard Guest, *chsd ldrs, wkng whn hmpd 12th, tld off*............(33 to 1 op 25 to 1) 5
1329⁴ THE ENERGISER 10-10-12 J Burke, *beh, some hdwy bef 13th, sn wknd, tld off*......................(50 to 1 op 50 to 1) 6
DISTILLERY HILL (Ire) 8-10-12 Mr M Thompson, *mstk 8th, beh whn hmpd 12th, tld off*............(20 to 1 op 16 to 1) 7
1329² FINAL BEAT (Ire) 7-10-12 P Niven, *chasing ldrs whn f 12th.*
....(8 to 1 op 7 to 1) f
1585³ TICO GOLD 8-10-9 (3²) G Cahill, *tracking ldrs whn f tenth.*
....(3 to 1 op 13 to 8) f
NIKI DEE (Ire) 6-10-12 R Supple, *led till f 3rd.*
....(5 to 2 fav op 6 to 4 tchd 11 to 4) f
1197⁴ BROOMHILL DUKER (Ire) 6-10-12 N Williamson, *blun 1st, mstks, beh, hdwy bef 13th, wkng whn blunded and uns rdr 2 out*.........................(7 to 1 op 6 to 1 tchd 8 to 1) ur

Dist: 1½l, 14l, 3l, 30l, 1½l, 22l. 6m 22.10s. a 36.10s (11 Ran).

(John R Jones), P Cheesbrough

1682 St. Modwen Standard Open National Hunt Flat Class H (4,5,6-y-o) £1,469 2m........................(3:30)

231² MR LURPAK 4-11-4 P Niven, *hld up in rear, steady hdwy hfwy, led o'r 2 fs out, quickened clr, easily.*
.........................(5 to 2 fav op 2 to 1 tchd 11 to 4) 1
CHERRY DEE 5-10-6 (7²) B Grattan, *al prmnt, ev ch o'r 2 fs out, sn chasing wnr, no imprsn*.......(10 to 1 op 7 to 1) 2
BILLY BUCKSKIN 4-11-4 W Fry, *mid-div, hdwy 6 fs out, chasing ldrs 3 out, kpt on*...........(16 to 1 op 10 to 1) 3
68¹ NUTTY SOLERA 6-11-11 B Storey, *sn tracking ldrs, led o'r 3 fs out, hdd over 2 out, fdd*.(8 to 1 op 7 to 1 tchd 9 to 1) 4
SOUTHERN CROSS 4-11-8 (3²) P Midgley, *chsd ldrs, outpcd 4 fs out, styd on fnl 2 furlongs*..............(12 to 1 op 8 to 1) 5
REVOLT 4-11-4 Richard Guest, *mid-div, kpt on fnl 3 fs, nvr dngrs*....................(10 to 1 op 8 to 1 tchd 12 to 1) 6
1514³ MEADOW HYMN (Ire) 5-11-4 W Dwan, *mid-div, kpt on fnl 3 fs, nvr dngrs*..........................(9 to 2 op 3 to 1) 7
DEERHUNTER 5-11-4 R Marley, *prmnt till wknd o'r 2 fs out.*
....(100 to 1) 8

214

EIRESPRAY (Ire) 5-11-4 R Garritty, *nvr dngrs.*
....(20 to 1 op 12 to 1) 9
ALAN'S PRIDE (Ire) 5-10-10 (3*) G Cahill, *led till hdd o'r 3 fs out, sn wknd.*........ (12 to 1 op 10 to 1 tchd 14 to 1) 10
SANTA BARBARA (Ire) 5-10-13 R Supple, *nvr dngrs.*
....(20 to 1) 11
SMIDDY LAD 5-11-4 D Bentley, *nvr better than mid-div.*
....(16 to 1) 12
TOP ACE 4-11-4 B Harding, *hld up and beh, gd hdwy 5 fs out, no further prog fnl 3 furlongs.*........ (16 to 1 op 14 to 1) 13
MILENBERG JOYS 4-11-4 D Parker, *in tch till wknd o'r 4 fs out.*...(100 to 1) 14
1390 POLITICAL MILLSTAR 4-11-4 N Bentley, *prmnt till wknd 4 fs out.*..(16 to 1) 15
SAM CHAMPAGNE (Ire) 4-11-4 K Whelan, *in tch, drvn alng hfwy, wknd 4 fs out.*..........................(16 to 1) 16
SALEM BEACH 4-10-10 (3*) G Lee, *in tch till wknd 4 fs out.*
....(16 to 1 op 12 to 1) 17
OTTADINI (Ire) 4-10-13 T Reed, *nvr better than mid-div.*
....(100 to 1) 18
MOUBEED (USA) 6-11-4 N Williamson, *in tch, pushed alng 6 fs out, sn wknd.*........................(10 to 1 op 8 to 1) 19
WHATYERONABOUT (Ire) 4-10-13 J Callaghan, *in tch to hfwy, sn beh.*..............................(14 to 1 op 10 to 1) 20
FLY EXECUTIVE 5-10-13 (5*) Mr M H Naughton, *al beh.*
....(100 to 1) 21
TIDAL RACE (Ire) 4-11-4 A Dobbin, *chsd ldrs to hfwy, sn wknd, tld off.*......................................(33 to 1) 22
MISS FORTINA 4-10-10 (3*) F Leahy, *al beh, tld off.* (100 to 1) 23
1317 SAMITE (Ire) 5-11-4 N Leach, *in tch till wknd 6 fs out, tld off.*
....(100 to 1) 24
Dist: 8l, ½l, 3l, 1l, 3½l, 6l, 2l, 1¾l, hd, 4l. 3m 59.80s. (24 Ran).
(MD Foods Plc), Mrs M Reveley

NEWTON ABBOT (heavy)
Tuesday December 3rd
Going Correction: PLUS 2.05 sec. per fur.

1683 Kerry Lady Riders' Novices' Handicap Hurdle Class E (0-100 4-y-o and up) £2,190 2m 1f.............(12:50)

1477⁵ SHIFT AGAIN (Ire) [82] (bl) 4-11-2 (5*) Sophie Mitchell, *trkd ldr frm 3rd, led 2 out, edgd lft appr last, kpt on.*
....(2 to 1 op 7 to 4) 1
TAP SHOES (Ire) [67] 6-10-6 Miss M Coombe, *hld up, hdwy 5th, ev ch 2 out, one pace but rallied r-in.*
....(9 to 2 op 5 to 1 tchd 6 to 1) 2
1235* ROYAL STANDARD [84] (v) 9-11-9 Ann Stokell, *led, clr second, tired and hdd 2 out, sn btn.*
....(6 to 5 fav op 5 to 4 on tchd 11 to 8) 3
CELTIC EMERALD [61] 8-9-7 (7*) Miss C Thomas, *chsd ldr to 3rd, reminders appr 5th, sn tld off.*
....(33 to 1 op 20 to 1 tchd 50 to 1) 4
1604⁸ DENOMINATION (USA) [89] 4-12-0 Miss S Vickery, *rcd wide, lost tch appr 3 out, tld off whn f nxt.*
....(10 to 1 op 5 to 1 tchd 11 to 1) f
1474 NUNS LUCY [61] (bl) 5-10-0 Jacqui Oliver, *hld up, lost tch hfwy, tld off whn pld up bef 3 out.*......(25 to 1 op 16 to 1) pu
Dist: 1¼l, 10l, dist. 4m 33.80s. a 44.80s (6 Ran).
(R J Bassett), O Sherwood

1684 Dublin Novices' Handicap Chase Class E (0-100 5-y-o and up) £2,913 2m 5f 110yds................(1:20)

1475² POUCHER (Ire) [95] 6-11-9 S Wynne, *hld up, hdwy 8th, chlgd 3 out, sn led and clr, eased nr finish.*
....(7 to 2 op 2 to 1 tchd 4 to 1) 1
1455* WELL TIMED [93] 6-11-7 B Powell, *jmpd wl, dsptd ld, led 5 out, hdd sn aftr 3 out, wknd.*........(9 to 2 op 7 to 2) 2
1451⁵ COLETTE'S CHOICE (Ire) [79] 7-10-2 (5*) Mr R Thornton, *hld up in rear, styd on one pace frm 3 out, nvr nrr.*
....(25 to 1 op 20 to 1) 3
1453⁵ SORREL HILL [100] (bl) 9-12-0 A P McCoy, *made most till hdd and wknd 5 out.*........................(5 to 1 tchd 6 to 1) 4
1498⁶ PURBECK RAMBLER [72] 5-10-0 B Fenton, *in tch, hdwy and pressing ldrs whn blun 3 out, not reco'r, tld off.*
....(20 to 1 op 12 to 1) 5
993⁴ ICANTELYA (Ire) [88] 7-11-2 P Hide, *trkd ldrs, hdwy 7th, wknd 5 out, tld off.*................................(10 to 1) 6
1448² AMBER SPARK (Ire) [94] 7-11-5 (3*) D Fortt, *in tch till f 5th.*
....(11 to 8 fav op 7 to 4) f
Dist: 13l, 14l, 3½l, 25l, 13l. 6m 10.60s. a 68.60s (7 Ran).
(Mrs A L Wood), Capt T A Forster

1685 Wexford 'National Hunt' Novices' Hurdle Class E (4-y-o and up) £2,221 2m 1f........................(1:50)

1270⁴ STORMY PASSAGE (Ire) 6-10-12 A Maguire, *trkd ldr, led 4th, hdd nxt, sn led ag'n, drw clr, cmftbly.*
....(11 to 10 fav op Evens tchd 5 to 4) 1

1452⁵ HELLO ME MAN (Ire) 8-10-12 Mr J L Llewellyn, *hld up, hdwy to ld briefly 5th, wknd aftr nxt.*
....(4 to 1 op 5 to 2 tchd 9 to 2) 2
1456 DEFENDTHEREALM 5-10-12 Mr A Holdsworth, *chsd ldrs, wknd 3 out.*...........................(33 to 1 op 20 to 1) 3
SHANAGORE WARRIOR (Ire) 4-10-12 N Mann, *beh till hdwy hfwy, wknd appr 3 out.*................(9 to 1 op 10 to 1) 4
1085⁵ MOONLIGHT ESCAPADE (Ire) 5-10-9 (3*) T Dascombe, *prmnt till wknd appr 5th.*..(8 to 1 op 6 to 1 tchd 9 to 1) 5
ZEN OR 5-10-7 S Curran, *al beh, tld off whn pld up bef 2 out.*
....(50 to 1 op 20 to 1) pu
1214⁷ DOLCE NOTTE (Ire) 6-10-7 A P McCoy, *al beh, tld off whn pld up bef 2 out.*........(3 to 1 op 9 to 4 tchd 7 to 2) pu
1354⁹ ALL SEWN UP 4-10-12 C Maude, *led till hdd and wknd quickly aftr 4th, tld off whn pld up bef 2 out.*
....(25 to 1 op 20 to 1) pu
1240⁹ CAPTAIN FELIX (NZ) 6-10-12 S McNeill, *al beh, tld off whn pld up bef 2 out.*...............(20 to 1 op 14 to 1) pu
Dist: 17l, 5l, 11l, 4l. 4m 30.40s. a 41.40s (9 Ran).
SR: 20/3/-/-/-/-/ (Peter Luff), P J Hobbs

1686 Cork Handicap Chase Class F (0-100 5-y-o and up) £2,628 2m 110yds............................(2:20)

1111³ THE LANCER (Ire) [82] 7-10-7 (3*) D Fortt, *al prmnt, led aftr 5th, drw clr frm 3 out.*..............(5 to 1 op 3 to 1) 1
HAWAIIAN YOUTH (Ire) [99] 8-11-13 A Maguire, *in tch, chsd wnr frm 6th, wknd aftr 3 out.*
....(5 to 2 fav tchd 3 to 1 and 2 to 1) 2
1455⁴ FENWICK [87] 9-10-12 (3*) T Dascombe, *hld up, hdwy 7th, ev ch 3 out, sn wknd.*..........(5 to 1 op 3 to 1) 3
1575³ BENJAMIN LANCASTER [100] 12-11-7 (7*) M Griffiths, *prmnt till wknd appr 3 out.*...........(13 to 2 op 9 to 1) 4
1352 NORDIC VALLEY (Ire) [88] 5-11-2 A P McCoy, *al beh, nvr nr to chal.*..............(11 to 2 op 9 to 1 tchd 6 to 1) 5
1471² PRUDENT PEGGY [72] 9-10-0 Mr A Holdsworth, *al beh, tld off frm 6th.*............................(11 to 2 op 9 to 1) 6
1319⁵ CHAIN SHOT [72] 11-10-0 R Bellamy, *led till hdd aftr 5th, sn wknd, tld off whn pld up bef last.*
....(50 to 1 op 20 to 1 tchd 66 to 1) pu
1349³ THATS THE LIFE [77] 11-10-5 M A Fitzgerald, *al beh, tld off whn pld up bef last.*..............(9 to 1 op 6 to 1) pu
Dist: 19l, 3½l, 4l, 2l, 18l. 4m 38.80s. a 40.80s (8 Ran).
SR: 12/10/-/-/-/ (A E Frost), D R Gandolfo

1687 Limerick Handicap Chase Class E (0-110 5-y-o and up) £2,954 3¼m 110yds......................(2:50)

1453² BRAMBLEHILL BUCK (Ire) [102] (bl) 7-11-6 A P McCoy, *al prmnt, led 12th, drw clr aftr 3 out.*
....(3 to 1 op 11 to 4 tchd 3 to 1 and 5 to 2) 1
1544⁵ THREE SAINTS (Ire) [96] 7-11-0 S Wynne, *hld up, hdwy 9th, hit 3 out, sn chsd wnr, fnshd tired.*
....(14 to 1 op 11 to 4 tchd 9 to 2) 2
A N C EXPRESS [110] 8-12-0 C Maude, *trkd ldrs, rdn and wknd 3 out.*..............(5 to 2 fav op 7 to 2 tchd 4 to 1) 3
JAILBREAKER [93] 9-10-6 (5*) D Salter, *chsd ldr till wknd quickly 3 out.*............................(10 to 1 op 7 to 1) 4
1239⁴ STEEPLE JACK [85] 9-10-3 R Greene, *al beh, tld off.*
....(9 to 1 op 7 to 1 tchd 10 to 1) 5
1420⁵ SHAMARPHIL [93] 10-10-11 Miss S Barraclough, *prmnt whn hit 6th, beh aftr tld off.*.............(10 to 1 op 6 to 1) 6
GOLDEN OPAL [90] 11-10-1 (7*) M Griffiths, *al beh, tld off whn pld up bef 2 out.*......(12 to 1 op 1 tchd 16 to 1) pu
1296⁵ FLORIDA SKY [105] 9-11-2 (7*) M Berry, *al beh, tld off to 12th, wknd quickly, tld off whn pld up bef 4 out....(14 to 1 op 10 to 1) pu
1451³ COUNTRY KEEPER [85] 8-10-3³ G Upton, *in rear, hdwy 8th, wknd 11th, tld off whn pld up bef last.*......(25 to 1 op 16 to 1) pu
Dist: 16l, 8l, 5l, 7l, 18l. 7m 43.20s. a 83.20s (9 Ran).
(T And J A Curry), P F Nicholls

1688 Sligo Handicap Hurdle Class D (0-125 4-y-o and up) £2,805 2¾m
....(3:20)

1213* SAIL BY THE STARS [105] 7-10-11 D Gallagher, *trkd ldr frm 4th, led four out, drw clr aftr nxt.*
....(5 to 4 on op Evens tchd 6 to 5) 1
1493² RUNAWAY PETE (USA) [122] 6-12-0 A P McCoy, *led till hdd 4 out, sn rdn and no imprsn.*............(8 to 1 op 5 to 1) 2
AMBLESIDE (Ire) [112] 5-11-4 S McNeill, *trkd ldr 4th, lost tch four out, tld off.*.............(5 to 2 op 9 to 4 tchd 2 to 1) 3
1213⁵ STAC-POLLAIDH [94] 6-9-7 (7*) W Walsh, *in tch till wknd quickly aftr 4th, tld off whn blun and uns rdr 3 out.*
....(12 to 1 op 10 to 1) ur
KILCORAN BAY [104] 4-10-10 R Greene, *hld up in tch till wknd aftr 4th, tld off whn refused 2 out.*
....(11 to 1 op 6 to 1 tchd 12 to 1) ref
Dist: Dist, 20l. 5m 56.40s. a 55.40s (5 Ran).
(T F F Nixon), Capt T A Forster

CATTERICK (good)
Wednesday December 4th

NATIONAL HUNT RESULTS 1996-97

Going Correction: PLUS 0.40 sec. per fur.

1689 Ellerton Juvenile Novices' Hurdle Class E (Div I) (3-y-o) £2,364 2m
.... (12:20)

PRIDDY FAIR 10-7 Richard Guest, *hld up in tch, lost pl aftr 3 out, smooth hdwy to ld after nxt, ran on wl.*
.... (16 to 1 op 14 to 1) 1
FRO 10-7 B Storey, *led 3rd till hdd aftr 2 out, kpt on wl und pres.* ....(9 to 2 op 4 to 1 tchd 5 to 1) 2
1422[4] TOPAGLOW (Ire) 10-12 N Williamson, *led to 3rd, wth ldr, ev ch 2 out, sn rdn, kpt on same pace.*
.......................(7 to 2 op 3 to 1 tchd 4 to 1) 3
1263[4] TARRY 11-0 T Eley, *prmnt, drvn alng whn mstk 2 out, fdd.*
.....................(5 to 2 fav op 7 to 4) 4
1384[3] SWYNFORD SUPREME 10-9 (3*) E Callaghan, *trkd ldrs, effrt bef 2 out, sn rdn and wknd.* (7 to 2 op 4 to 1 tchd 9 to 2) 5
1221 RADMORE BRANDY 10-7 A Dobbin, *hld up, hdwy bef 3 out, wknd before nxt.*.....................(5 to 1 op 4 to 1) 6
NEEDLE MATCH 10-7 (5*) R McGrath, *keen, hld up in tch, effrt bef 2 out, sn rdn and wknd.*.....(20 to 1 tchd 25 to 1) 7
GAUTBY HENPECKED 10-7 J Callaghan, *al beh.*
.........................(8 to 1 op 5 to 1) 8
860[3] LOMOND LASSIE (USA) 10-7 O Pears, *towards rear, rdn bef 5th, lost tch aftr 3 out, tld off.*.....................(100 to 1) 9
1196 DUNTALKIN 10-0 (7*) M Newton, *beh, mstk 3 out, sn lost tch, tld off.*..............................(50 to 1) 10
Dist: 1½l, 4l, 2½l, 7l, 5l, 3l, 4l, 19l, 4l. 3m 58.80s. a 18.80s (10 Ran).
(The Ebor Partnership), D W Barker

1690 Ellerton Juvenile Novices' Hurdle Class E (Div II) (3-y-o) £2,343 2m
.... (12:50)

1524[3] RUSSIAN RASCAL (Ire) 10-12 R Garritty, *trkd ldrs gng wl, led bef 2 out, ran on und pres.*..........(6 to 4 fav op 5 to 4) 1
1629 ERIC'S BETT 10-12 K Whelan, *mid-div, gd hdwy to chase wnr 2 out, rdn aftr last, no imprsn.*...............(20 to 1) 2
1524 NOIR ESPRIT 10-9 (3*) F Leahy, *trkd ldrs, led 3 out, hdd bef nxt, fdd.*..............(12 to 1 op 16 to 1 tchd 20 to 1) 3
1524[2] ALWARQA 10-7 D Bentley, *sn wth ldr, outpcd aftr 3 out, no imprsn aftr.*.....................(7 to 1 op 5 to 1) 4
1629 ONYOUROWN (Ire) 10-12 N Williamson, *beh, kpt on frm 2 out, nvr dngrs, fnshd distressed.*..........(10 to 1 op 7 to 1) 5
1196[3] DOUBLE DASH (Ire) 11-5 D J Moffatt, *in tch till outpcd aftr 3 out, no dngr after.*........................(20 to 1) 6
1249[2] CRABBIE'S PRIDE 10-12 A Dobbin, *made most till hdd 3 out, sn wknd.*.............(3 to 1 op 9 to 2 tchd 5 to 1) 7
PERPETUAL LIGHT 10-7 B Harding, *nvr dngrs.*
.......................(20 to 1 op 16 to 1) 8
DIAMOND BEACH 10-12 N Bentley, *beh, hdwy aftr 3 out, wknd bef nxt, tld off.*....................(12 to 1 op 10 to 1) 9
RECRUITMENT 10-12 T Reed, *al beh, tld off.*......(20 to 1) 10
NORTHERN DIAMOND (Ire) 10-12 Gary Lyons, *mid-div, pushed alng bef 2 out, wknd quickly, tld off.*....(100 to 1) 11
Dist: 3l, 9l, 2½l, 7l, ½l, 1¼l, ¾l, 17l, 2½l, ¾l. 3m 56.00s. a 16.00s (11 Ran).
(C H Stevens), T D Easterby

1691 Brompton Conditional Jockeys' Handicap Hurdle Class E (0-110 4-y-o and up) £2,427 2m 3f...... (1:20)

1588[2] TIP IT IN [85] 7-10-2 (5*) N Horrocks, *led 3rd to 4th, led 3 out, hrd pressed frm nxt, raon on wl.*........(5 to 1 op 4 to 1) 1
1635[4] RALITSA (Ire) [102] 4-11-5 (5*) R Burns, *settled midfield, hdwy aftr 3 out, ev ch frm nxt till no extr und pres r-in.*
.................(11 to 4 op 3 to 1 tchd 5 to 2) 2
SUDDEN SPIN [98] 6-11-3 (3*) B Grattan, *trkd ldrs, chlgd 3 out, no extr frm nxt.*......(7 to 1 tchd 8 to 1 and 6 to 1) 3
1259[5] ANORAK (USA) [88] 6-11-3 (7*) N Hannity, *hld up, hdwy to ld 4th, hdd 3 out, outpcd bef nxt, rallied appr last.*
.........................(33 to 1 op 20 to 1 tchd 50 to 1) 4
1510* SUPERTOP [106] 8-11-9 (5*) I Jardine, *hld up and beh, took clr order hfwy, hrd rdn bef 2 out, fdd.*
....................(9 to 4 fav op 7 to 4 tchd 5 to 2) 5
FRYUP SATELLITE [80] 5-10-2 G Cahill, *hld up, hdwy to chase ldrs aftr 3 out, kpt on same pace frm nxt.*
.........................(25 to 1 op 20 to 1) 6
1299[2] DOOLAR (USA) [91] 9-10-0 (3*) M Newton, *in tch, drvn alng and outpcd aftr 3 out, no dngr after.*
.........................(7 to 1 op 8 to 1 tchd 6 to 1) 7
DANBYS GORSE [94] 4-10-11 E Callaghan, *led to 3rd, prmnt till wknd aftr 3 out.*...............(16 to 1 op 12 to 1) 8
FRIENDLY KNIGHT [83] 6-10-5 F Leahy, *prmnt till wknd bef 3 out.*...........................(33 to 1 op 20 to 1) 9
1248 MILL THYME [95] 4-11-3 G Lee, *beh, drvn alng hfwy, tld off.*.....................(14 to 1 op 7 to 1 tchd 16 to 1) 10
RED BEACON [86] 9-10-8 J Supple, *chsd ldrs till wknd quickly bef 3 out, tld off.*...........(14 to 1 op 10 to 1) 11
Dist: ½l, 1l, 1l, 3½l, sht-hd, 15l, 6l, 16l, dist, 2l. 4m 50.20s. a 26.20s (11 Ran).
(Mrs M Dunning), A Smith

1692 Bobby Faulkner Memorial Challenge Trophy Handicap Chase Class F (0-105 4-y-o and up) £2,976 2m

..........................(1:50)

1072[4] REVE DE VALSE (USA) [85] 9-10-8 K Johnson, *al prmnt, led last, styd on und pres.*.................(7 to 1 op 6 to 1) 1
1206* UNCLE BERT (Ire) [99] 6-11-8 A Thornton, *in tch, hdwy aftr 9th, hmpd and lft in ld 3 out, hdd last, no extr.*
.........................(9 to 2 op 3 to 1) 2
1327* FULL O'PRAISE (NZ) [105] 9-12-0 T Reed, *hld up, hdwy aftr 9th, ch 3 out, wknd bef last 2.......(3 to 1 fav op 5 to 2) 3
247 POSITIVE ACTION [90] 10-10-8 (5*) S Taylor, *lost tch aftr 7th, tld off.*......................(14 to 1 op 10 to 1 tchd 16 to 1) 4
1262[3] DESERT BRAVE (Ire) [81] 6-10-4[4] Richard Guest, *hld pressed whn blun and uns rdr 3 out.....(4 to 1 op 7 to 2) ur
1587 BOLANEY GIRL (Ire) [77] 7-10-0 A Dobbin, *refused to race, took no part.*.............(9 to 2 op 4 to 1 tchd 5 to 1) ref
1327[3] THUNDERSTRUCK [82] 10-10-5 N Williamson, *not jump wl, beh whn pld up aftr 6th....(7 to 1 op 5 to 1 tchd 8 to 1) pu
Dist: 7l, 12l, 29l. 4m 2.50s. a 15.50s (7 Ran).
(Robert Johnson), R Johnson

1693 Calderprint Selling Handicap Hurdle Class G (0-95 4-y-o and up) £2,285 2m.......................... (2:20)

1164[2] FLYAWAY BLUES [84] 4-11-10 P Niven, *hld up in midfield, hdwy hfwy, chalg whn mstk 2 out, sn led, blun last, all out.*
.........................(3 to 1 fav op 5 to 1) 1
1372[6] CHUMMY'S SAGA [67] 6-10-7 M Foster, *hld up in midfield, hdwy hfwy, led aftr 3 out, hdd bef last 2, dsptd ld r-in, no extr und pres clsg stages.*.........(10 to 1 op 7 to 1) 2
1164[4] LITTLE REDWING [65] (v) 4-10-5[1] R Garritty, *mid-div, hdwy to chase ldrs aftr 3 out, kpt on same pace frm nxt.*
.........................(12 to 1 op 10 to 1) 3
1386[6] AIDE MEMOIRE (Ire) [75] 7-11-1 K Johnson, *beh, styd on frm 3 out, nrst finish.*................(20 to 1 op 14 to 1) 4
1325 ARTHUR BEE [60] 9-9-12[1] (3*) F Leahy, *beh, styd on frm 3 out, nrst finish.*...................(33 to 1 op 25 to 1) 5
911 HEAVENS ABOVE [60] 4-10-0 K Whelan, *in tch, hdwy aftr 3 out, no further prog frm nxt.*...............(20 to 1) 6
1386[8] FAMILIAR ART [80] 5-11-6 D J Moffatt, *beh, styd on frm 3 out, nvr dngrs.*....................(16 to 1 op 14 to 1) 7
367[3] ELITE JUSTICE [83] (bl) 4-11-9 A Dobbin, *led second till hdd aftr 3 out, fdd.*..............(10 to 1 op 8 to 1) 8
MY HANDY MAN [64] 5-10-4[2] Richard Guest, *hld up, gd hdwy to track ldrs aftr 3 out, wknd bef nxt.....(8 to 1 op 7 to 1) 9
1164[5] SECONDS AWAY [60] 5-9-11 (3*) G Lee, *heold up, gd hdwy aftr 3 out, wknd bef nxt..............(14 to 1 op 12 to 1) 10
551[3] OVER STATED (Ire) [63] 6-10-3 R Supple, *chsd ldrs, rdn bef 3 out, wknd.*......................(16 to 1 op 14 to 1) 11
1257[5] CATTON LADY [60] 6-10-0 P McLoughlin, *chsd ldrs till wknd aftr 3 out.*...................(50 to 1 op 25 to 1) 12
1325 DARK MIDNIGHT (Ire) [64] (bl) 7-10-4[4] J Burke, *chsd ldrs till wknd aftr 3 out.*.............(100 to 1 op 66 to 1) 13
RAGAZZO (Ire) [65] 6-10-5[8] (3*) P Midgley, *in tch till wknd bef 3 out.*....................(10 to 1 op 8 to 1) 14
1326 HOMECREST [60] (v) 4-9-13[2] (3*) G Cahill, *nvr better than mid-div*....................................(100 to 1) 15
1588[9] FLY TO THE END (USA) [75] 6-11-1 B Harding, *hld up in tch, hdwy aftr 3 out, wknd bef nxt.*......(9 to 1 op 6 to 1) 16
1122 SHUT UP [60] 7-9-7 (7*) C McCormack, *chsd ldrs till wknd bef 3 out.*...............................(50 to 1) 17
762[6] CANDID LAD [73] 9-10-13 B Storey, *beh most of way.*
.........................(7 to 1 op 5 to 1) 18
VINTAGE TAITTINGER (Ire) [68] 4-10-3 (5*) R McGrath, *in tch till wknd aftr 5th.*...............(25 to 1 op 20 to 1) 19
BATTUTA [77] 7-11-3 N Williamson, *led to second, chsd ldr to hfwy, sn wknd, tld off.* (16 to 1 op 14 to 1 tchd 20 to 1) 20
LADY KHADIJA [60] 10-9-11 (3*) E Husband, *sn beh, tld off whn pld up bef 4th.*........................(100 to 1) pu
27[3] CHARLISTONA [65] 5-10-5 A Thornton, *trkd ldrs till wknd aftr 3 out, beh whn pld up bef nxt.......(10 to 1 op 7 to 1) pu
Dist: Nk, 7l, ¾l, ½l, 4l, 13l, 2½l, sht-hd, 3½l, 1l. 3m 53.90s. a 13.90s (22 Ran).
SR: 21/3/-/2/-/-/ (Carnoustie Racing Club Ltd), Mrs M Reveley

1694 Charles Vickery Memorial Cup Handicap Chase Class E (0-110 5-y-o and up) £3,261 3m 1f 110yds (2:50)

1513[2] KENMORE-SPEED [95] 9-11-3 Richard Guest, *trkd ldrs, led tenth, mstk and hdd 15th, led last, styd on.*
.........................(6 to 4 fav tchd 11 to 8) 1
1314[7] GALE AHEAD (Ire) [97] 6-11-5 N Bentley, *mid-div, hdwy aftr 11th, led 15th, hdd last, no extr.*
.........................(8 to 1 op 7 to 1 tchd 10 to 1) 2
1283[8] OFF THE BRU [87] 11-10-2 (7*) Mr M Bradburne, *chsd ldrs, kpt on same pace frm 16th.*
.........................(16 to 1 op 10 to 1) 3
1589 FORWARD GLEN [78] (bl) 9-9-13[2] (3*) G Cahill, *towards rear, mstk 14th, nvr dngrs.*.............(9 to 1 op 8 to 1) 4
1301[4] COMEDY ROAD [100] 12-11-8 N Williamson, *beh, effrt whn blun 15th, sn lost tch.*.................(6 to 1 op 7 to 1) 5
TWIN STATES [98] 7-11-6 A Thornton, *in tch whn f 17th.*
.........................(10 to 1 op 8 to 1) f
1375[6] MARCHWOOD [105] 9-11-13 T Reed, *beh whn slpd and f 12th (water).*......................(50 to 1) f

216

1525[3] PORT IN A STORM [88] 7-10-7 (3*) Mr C Bonner, *cl up, led 7th to tenth, wknd aftr 14th, tld off whn pld up bef 2 out.* ....(7 to 1 op 4 to 1) pu
SNOOK POINT [82] 9-10-4[4] J Burke, *led to 7th, wknd quickly aftr 11th, lost tch and pld up bef nxt*....(25 to 1 op 16 to 1) pu
MULLINGAR (Ire) [93] 7-11-1 A Dobbin, *beh, lost tch aftr 13th, tld off whn pld up bef 15th*............(20 to 1 op 16 to 1) pu
Dist: 2l, 11l, 26l, 30l. 6m 40.20s. a 25.20s (10 Ran).
(K M Dacker), Mrs S J Smith

1695 Streetlam 'National Hunt' Novices' Hurdle Class E (4-y-o and up) £2,595 2m 3f........................(3:20)

LAGEN BRIDGE (Ire) 7-10-10 D J Moffatt, *mid-div, steady hdwy hfwy, led aftr 3 out, hng lft, mstk nxt, kpt on.* ....(25 to 1 op 16 to 1) 1
1280* B THE ONE 5-11-3 R Garritty, *trkd ldrs, drw clr wth wnr bef 2 out, ch last, no extr*.... (7 to 4 fav op 6 to 4 tchd 2 to 1) 2
1280[2] FAITHFUL HAND 6-10-10 Richard Guest, *trkd ldrs till lost pl aftr 3 out, rdn betw last 2, no imprsn.* ....(9 to 4 op 7 to 4 tchd 5 to 2) 3
ROBERT THE BRAVE 4-10-7 (3*) E Callaghan, *nvr dngrs.* ....(50 to 1 op 25 to 1) 4
1050* SILVER MINX 4-10-10 P Niven, *led till hdd aftr 3 out, sn wknd.* ....(9 to 4 op 5 to 2) 5
HADAWAY LAD 4-10-10 N Williamson, *beh most of way.* ....(14 to 1 op 20 to 1 tchd 33 to 1) 6
1514[7] FOUR FROM HOME (Ire) 4-10-5 (5*) R McGrath, *nvr dngrs.* ....(25 to 1 op 14 to 1) 7
RASIN LUCK 6-10-5 B Storey, *chsd ldrs to hfwy, sn wknd.* ....(25 to 1 op 20 to 1) 8
1280[6] PRIMITIVE HEART 4-10-10 A Larnach, *chsd ldrs till wknd quickly bef 3 out*..........(16 to 1) 9
1377 SMART IN SATIN 6-10-10 A Thornton, *sn beh*.... (100 to 1) 10
MAKE A BUCK 6-10-10 M Foster, *wl beh frm hfwy, tld off.* ....(33 to 1 op 20 to 1) 11
1073[9] HENPECKED (Ire) 5-10-7 (3*) Mr C Bonner, *in tch till wknd aftr 7th, wl beh whn f last*..........(16 to 1 op 12 to 1) f
Dist: 1l, 24l, 14l, 10l, 4l, 12l, 15l, 12l, 15l, 20l. 4m 44.50s. a 24.50s (12 Ran).
(Mrs Eileen M Milligan), D Moffatt

FONTWELL (good)
Wednesday December 4th
Going Correction: PLUS 0.50 sec. per fur. (races 1,2,4,5,7), PLUS 0.70 (3,6)

1696 Eartham Juvenile Novices' Hurdle Class E (Div I) (3-y-o) £2,364 2¼m 110yds......................(12:40)

1286[5] SERENUS (USA) 10-12 J R Kavanagh, *keen hold gng wl, slight ld frm 4th, clr aftr last, ran on well.* ....(3 to 1 op 9 to 4 tchd 100 to 30) 1
ACADEMY HOUSE (Ire) 10-12 A P McCoy, *in tch, hdwy to chase ldrs and jmpd slwly 6th, sn rdn, one pace r-in.* ....(5 to 4 on op 2 to 1 on tchd 6 to 5 on) 2
1422[3] BEN BOWDEN 11-5 J Osborne, *led aftr 1st to 4th, rdn 6th, wknd appr last*..........(8 to 1 op 6 to 1 tchd 9 to 1) 3
1286[6] HANBITOOH (USA) 10-12 C Maude, *led till aftr 1st, wknd 2 out*..........(16 to 1 op 14 to 1 tchd 20 to 1) 4
1470 QUIET MOMENTS (Ire) 10-12 W Marston, *keen hold, prmnt to 6th*..........(50 to 1 op 33 to 1) 5
PRINCELY AFFAIR 10-12 T J Murphy, *brief effrt 6th, sn wknd.* ....(25 to 1 op 12 to 1) 6
TATHMIN 10-12 M Bosley, *jmpd poorly, al beh.* ....(66 to 1 op 33 to 1) 7
1412[9] ILLEGALLY YOURS 10-7 D Morris, *prmnt till wknd quickly appr 6th*..........(33 to 1 op 14 to 1) 8
PRIVATE PERCIVAL 10-12 A Dicken, *mstk second, tld off 6th.* ....(66 to 1 op 33 to 1) 9
BOLD START LADY 10-0 (7*) M Griffiths, *slwly into strd, mstk 4th, beh whn f 5th*..........(66 to 1 op 33 to 1) f
1027 GOLD LANCE (USA) 10-12 D O'Sullivan, *prmnt to 5th, tld off whn pld up aftr 2 out*..........(14 to 1) pu
Dist: 14l, 7l, 1½l, 18l, 3½l, 1l, 6l, dist. 4m 36.30s. a 19.30s (11 Ran).
(W V & Mrs E S Robins), N J Henderson

1697 Selsey Selling Hurdle Class G (4 - 7-y-o) £2,010 2¼m 110yds....(1:10)

ZESTI 4-10-12 N Mann, *trkd ldrs 5th, chlgd 3 out, sn led, clr frm 2 out*....(5 to 1 op 8 to 1 tchd 10 to 1 and 9 to 2) 1
1574[6] LANESRA BREEZE 4-10-12 C Maude, *mstk 1st, reminder aftr second, prmnt nxt, styd on und pres frm 2 out.* ....(33 to 1 op 20 to 1 tchd 40 to 1) 2
1425[9] WATER HAZARD (Ire) 4-10-12 A Dicken, *trkd ldrs, led 6th till aftr 3 out, wknd after nxt*... (7 to 1 op 9 to 2 tchd 8 to 1) 3
1444[6] CREDIT CONTROLLER (Ire) 7-10-12 J R Kavanagh, *hld up rear, hdwy und pres 3 out, wknd aftr nxt.* ....(11 to 1 op 6 to 1 tchd 12 to 1) 4
1447 CHURCHTOWN SPIRIT 5-10-7 G Crone, *beh 5th, tld off.* ....(33 to 1 tchd 50 to 1) 5
MINI FETE (Fr) 7-10-7 D Bridgwater, *beh 5th, nvr dngrs.* ....(9 to 1 op 10 to 1 tchd 12 to 1 and 8 to 1) 6

1438 GRIFFIN'S GIRL 4-10-2 (5*) S Ryan, *keen hold, chsd ldrs, chlgd 3 out, sn wknd, tld off*............(6 to 1 op 3 to 1) 7
1447 FLAMING ROSE (Ire) 6-10-7 D O'Sullivan, *prmnt early, beh 5th, tld off*............(50 to 1 op 25 to 1 tchd 66 to 1) 8
1423[8] LITTLE LUKE (Ire) 5-10-12 T J Murphy, *led to 6th, wknd quickly 3 out, tld off*.... (33 to 1 op 25 to 1 tchd 40 to 1) 9
1449[4] MEMORY'S MUSIC 4-10-12 B Fenton, *hld up rear, rdn and hdwy 3 out, wknd aftr nxt, 5th and no ch whn f last.* ....(5 to 2 fav op 2 to 1 tchd 11 to 4) f
GEMINI MIST 5-10-7 P Holley, *prmnt to 5th, tld off whn pld up bef last*..........(12 to 1 tchd 14 to 1) pu
Dist: 8l, 1¼l, 3l, dist, hd, 8l, 22l, 1½l. 4m 41.10s. a 24.10s (11 Ran).
(Miss R J Bryant), T T Clement

1698 Norfolk Challenge Cup Novices' Handicap Chase Class E (0-100 4-y-o and up) £3,124 2¼m........(1:40)

1445[4] DUKE OF APROLON [82] 9-11-7 P Hide, *led to 3rd, styd tracking ldr, led appr 3 out, sn clr*....(5 to 2 fav op 9 to 4) 1
1319[3] WILLIE MAKEIT (Ire) [85] 6-11-10 J Railton, *hld up in tch, hdwy 8th, chsd wnr frm 3 out, no imprsn.* (5 to 1 op 4 to 1) 2
1557 JACKSONS BAY [63] 6-10-2 D Bridgwater, *beh, hdwy 4 out, styd on frm nxt, kpt on und pres r-in.* ....(12 to 1 op 20 to 1 tchd 25 to 1) 3
ALBURY GREY [61] 9-10-0 G Crone, *mstk 1st, wl beh 5th, some hdwy frm 4 out, nrst finish*..... (50 to 1 op 33 to 1) 4
1321[5] BOLD ACRE [84] 6-11-9 T J Murphy, *hdwy to chase ldrs 8th, hit tenth, wknd 2 out, no ch whn blun last.* (7 to 2 op 5 to 2) 5
1577[4] DRESS DANCE (Ire) [85] 6-11-5 (5*) Sophie Mitchell, *beh, rdn 8th, no ch whn mstk 4 out*..........(9 to 2 op 5 to 2) 6
1596[7] FULL OF TRICKS [69] 8-10-8 D Morris, *wth ldr, led 3rd, rdn 4 out, hdd appr nxt, sn wknd*.... (33 to 1 op 20 to 1) 7
HIDDEN PLEASURE [79] 10-11-4 D Leahy, *f 3rd.* ....(14 to 1 tchd 12 to 1 and 20 to 1) f
1448[5] PINOCCIO [80] 9-11-2 (3*) D Walsh, *chsd ldrs, rdn 8th, hit nxt and beh, tld off whn pld up bef 3 out*... (20 to 1 op 14 to 1) pu
1111 KENTAVRUS WAY (Ire) [61] 5-10-0 B Powell, *al beh, tld off 5th, pld up bef 3 out*.......... (20 to 1 tchd 25 to 1) pu
Dist: 16l, ¾l, 8l, 1½l, ½l, 16l. 4m 39.60s. a 19.60s (10 Ran).
SR: 23/10/-/-/-/-/ (The First Eleven Partnership), J T Gifford

1699 A & D Landscapes Handicap Hurdle Class D (0-125 4-y-o and up) £3,054 2¼m 110yds.................(2:10)

SUPREME LADY (Ire) [110] 5-11-8 J Osborne, *hld up rear, smooth hdwy to ld sn aftr 3 out, clr after nxt, cmftbly.* ....(9 to 4 fav tchd 5 to 2) 1
976* IRON N GOLD [97] 4-10-9 D Bridgwater, *hld up rear, hdwy to press wnr aftr 3 out, rdn nxt, sn one pace, no ch whn blun last.* ....(7 to 2 op 4 to 1 tchd 9 to 2) 2
1427[4] SMUGGLER'S POINT (USA) [100] 6-11-7 D Morris, *chsd ldr, chlgd 4th, outpcd 3 out, styd on r-in.* ....(10 to 1 op 8 to 1 tchd 12 to 1) 3
1596[5] TICKERTY'S GIFT [112] 6-11-3 (7*) M Attwater, *led till aftr 3 out, sn outpcd*.......... (9 to 1 op 7 to 1 tchd 10 to 1) 4
1066[4] BON VOYAGE (USA) [97] 4-10-9 J R Kavanagh, *in tch, rdn alng 6th, sn one pace*.....(9 to 1 op 7 to 1 tchd 10 to 1) 5
LUCKY EDDIE (Ire) [105] 5-11-3 C Maude, *hld up in tch, pushed alng appr 6th, wknd 3 out.* ....(9 to 2 op 4 to 1 tchd 5 to 1) 6
1416[5] MUHTASHIM (Ire) [89] 6-10-1 B Fenton, *mstk 3rd, tld off 5th.* ....(9 to 1 op 6 to 1 tchd 10 to 1) 7
RAAHIN (USA) [88] 11-10-0 M Richards, *prmnt early, mstk 4th, tld off nxt, pld up bef 3 out*........ (50 to 1 op 33 to 1) pu
Dist: 11l, 1l, nk, 3l, 12l, 14l. 4m 32.60s. a 15.60s (8 Ran).
SR: 30/6/17/19/1/ (The Supreme Lady Partnership), Miss H C Knight

1700 Sidlesham Conditional Jockeys' Handicap Hurdle Class E (0-110 4-y-o and up) £2,280 2¾m 110yds (2:40)

MIRADOR [88] 5-11-6 D Walsh, *hld up, confidently rdn, chlgd on bit aftr 3 out, led last, very easily.* ....(13 to 8 fav op 2 to 1 tchd 9 to 4) 1
1597 DARING KING [88] 6-11-6 L Aspell, *dsptd second, chsd ldr 5th, led 8th till aftr 2 out, sn no ch wth wnr*........ (10 to 1) 2
800[9] PAVLOVA (Ire) [82] 6-10-9 (5*) A Garrity, *beh, pushed alng 7th, styd on one pace frm 2 out.* ....(10 to 1 op 12 to 1 tchd 14 to 1) 3
1429[4] FLYING FIDDLER (Ire) [92] 5-11-10 P Henley, *chsd ldrs, rdn 3 out, wknd nxt*............ (7 to 1 op 9 to 2 tchd 8 to 1) 4
1425[4] ROGER'S PAL [77] 9-10-4 (5*) M Batchelor, *dsptd second to 5th, lost pl nxt, rdn 8th, sn rallied, chsd ldrs 3 out, wknd rpdly.* ....(10 to 1 op 8 to 1 tchd 12 to 1) 5
1427[2] CASSIO'S BOY [86] 5-11-4 D J Kavanagh, *hdwy 5th, lost pl 7th, ran on nxt, wknd 3 out.* (2 to 1 op 5 to 4 tchd 9 to 4) 6
1596[6] SOMERSET DANCER (USA) [80] 9-10-12 K Gaule, *sn rdn and beh, tld off 6th, pld up bef nxt*......(33 to 1 op 20 to 1) pu
1555[7] PROFESSION [70] 5-9-9[2] (7*) J K McCarthy, *led, sn clr, faltered 8th and hdd, soon wknd, tld off whn pld up bef 2 out.* ....(50 to 1 op 33 to 1 tchd 66 to 1) pu
Dist: 8l, 3½l, 5l, 6l, 18l. 5m 50.00s. a 36.00s (8 Ran).
(Mrs J Whitehead, J McGivern & Two Kates), R Curtis

1701 Mundham Novices' Chase Class E (5-y-o and up) £3,080 3¼m 110yds
.... (3:10)

FLAKED OATS 7-10-10 A P McCoy, *trkd ldr 9th, led 4 out, clr nxt, easily*..........(11 to 8 fav op 6 to 4 tchd 7 to 4) 1
PARAHANDY (Ire) 6-10-10 B Fenton, *mstk 3rd, trkd ldrs 8th, chsd wnr frm 3 out, no imprsn.*
..............................(13 to 2 op 5 to 1 tchd 8 to 1) 2
1411 GREY GORDEN (Ire) 8-10-10 D Morris, *led, mstk 15th, hdd aftr 4 out, kpt on same pace.*
..............................(6 to 1 op 9 to 2 tchd 13 to 2) 3
1113* KEEP IT ZIPPED (Ire) 6-11-7 J Osborne, *ran in snatches, sn drvn alng, chsd ldr to 4th, effrt four out, soon no response.*
..............................(4 to 1 op 7 to 2 tchd 5 to 1) 4
LANGTON PARMILL 11-10-3 (7*) N Willmington, *hit 8th and beh, no ch whn f 18th...*(40 to 1 op 20 to 1 tchd 50 to 1) f
APATURA HATI 7-10-2 (3*) P Henley, *beh 6th, lost tch 4 out, tld off whn pld up bef last....* (9 to 1 op 6 to 1 tchd 12 to 1) pu
LITTLE ROWLEY 7-10-10 M Richards, *blun second, tld off 13th, pld up bef 3 out.* (66 to 1 op 33 to 1 tchd 100 to 1) pu
ROLLED GOLD 7-10-10 D Bridgwater, *mstk 3rd, tld off 8th, pld up bef 9th.*........................(16 to 1 op 8 to 1) pu
Dist: 4l, 14l, 6l. 7m 2.60s. a 32.60s (8 Ran).

(E B Swaffield), P F Nicholls

1702 Eartham Juvenile Novices' Hurdle Class E (Div II) (3-y-o) £2,343 2¼m 110yds....................... (3:40)

JELALI (Ire) 10-12 D Gallagher, *hdwy 5th, chlgd 3 out, sn led, rdn out r-in*..............(11 to 4 op 5 to 1 tchd 6 to 1) 1
SIBERIAN HENRY 10-12 C Llewellyn, *trkd ldr, led 6th till sn aftr 3 out, one pace and pres frm nxt...*(9 to 1 op 20 to 1) 2
PROVINCE 10-12 J Railton, *trkd ldrs, chlgd and mstk 3 out, ev ch whn rdn and edgd rght nxt, sn btn.*
..............................(5 to 4 fav op 2 to 1 tchd 9 to 4) 3
VERONICA FRANCO 10-4 (3*) K Gaule, *beh,l ran on appr 2 out, not pace to trble ldrs*..........(33 to 1 op 14 to 1) 4
CLASSY CHIEF 10-12 T J Murphy, *gd hdwy to track ldrs appr 6th, wknd 2 out*..................(7 to 1 op 5 to 1) 5
EMBER 10-7 D Bridgwater, *beh, effrt appr 3 out, sn wknd.*
..............................(20 to 1 tchd 25 to 1 and 16 to 1) 6
1412 EMBROIDERED 10-0 (7*) J K McCarthy, *hdwy 5th, chsd ldrs nxt, led briefly aftr 3 out, wknd rpdly.*
..............................(33 to 1 op 20 to 1 tchd 50 to 1) 7
REEM FEVER (Ire) 10-7 A P McCoy, *prmnt to 5th, sn wknd, tld off...*..........(12 to 1 op 8 to 1 tchd 14 to 1) 8
RED RUSTY (USA) 10-12 M Richards, *mstk 3rd, wknd and pld up bef 5th, broke blood vessel.*
..............................(16 to 1 op 10 to 1 tchd 20 to 1) pu
1027⁹ PETROS GEM 10-7 P Hide, *led to 6th, wknd rpdly, tld off whn pld up bef last.*...................(33 to 1 tchd 50 to 1) pu
Dist: 4l, 3½l, 8l, 1¼l, 1½l, 24l, dist. 4m 48.20s. a 31.20s (10 Ran).

(The Fort Partnership), D J G Murray Smith

SOUTHWELL (good)
Wednesday December 4th
Going Correction: PLUS 0.10 sec. per fur. (races 1,3,6), MINUS 0.05 (2,4,5)

1703 European Breeders Fund Chasing In Mind 'National Hunt' Novices' Hurdle Qualifier Class E (4,5,6-y-o) £2,301 2 ½m 110yds.................(1:00)

LANCE ARMSTRONG (Ire) 6-11-0 A Maguire, *al gng best, jnd ldr hfwy, led 4 out, drw clr last 2, readily.*
..............................(6 to 4 on op 2 to 1 on tchd 5 to 4 on) 1
DRY HILL LAD 5-11-0 W Fry, *settled midfield, improved to join issue 4 out, rdn and one pace frm betw last 2.*
..............................(12 to 1 tchd 14 to 1) 2
1479 RED TEL (Ire) 4-11-0 M A Fitzgerald, *tucked away on ins, effrt and bustled alng aftr 3 out, kpt on same pace frm nxt.*
..............................(4 to 1 op 7 to 2 tchd 5 to 1) 3
CARLY-J 5-10-9 Mr N Kent, *co'red up beh ldrs, ev ch appr 4 out, aftr nxt, one pace frm betw last 2..........*(25 to 1) 4
1322⁴ OPTIMISTIC AFFAIR 5-11-0 A Larnach, *wtd wth, effrt aftr one circuit, rdn bef 4 out, lost tch, tld off last 2.*
..............................(6 to 1 op 7 to 1 tchd 8 to 1) 5
1034 FARMERS SUBSIDY 4-10-7 (7*) T Hogg, *wth ldrs for one circuit, feeling pace hfwy, lost tch bef 4 out, tld off.*
..............................(33 to 1 op 20 to 1 tchd 50 to 1) 6
1280⁹ AR AGHAIDH ABHAILE (Ire) 5-11-0 A S Smith, *made most till hdd 4 out, wknd quickly, tld off.......*(20 to 1 op 16 to 1) 7
989 NIGHT THYNE (Ire) 4-10-11 (3*) G Hogan, *settled to track ldrs, effrt aftr one circuit, 5th and btn whn f last.*
..............................(14 to 1 op 10 to 1) f
1357⁴ HALAM BELL 4-10-9 R Greene, *not jump wl, tried to refuse and uns rdr 3rd....................*(33 to 1 op 20 to 1) ur
Dist: 5l, 1l, nk, dist, 9l, dist. 5m 12.00s. a 26.00s (9 Ran).

(G L Porter), G M McCourt

1704 Welland Novices' Chase Class E (5-y-o and up) £3,206 2m........ (1:30)

1138⁵ SUBLIME FELLOW (Ire) 6-11-5 M A Fitzgerald, *al gng wl, led bef 7th, clr frm nxt, styd on well last 3, unchlgd....*(9 to 4 jt-fav op 2 to 1 tchd 5 to 2) 1
FORMAL INVITATION (Ire) 7-10-12 A Maguire, *patiently rdn, effrt and niggled alng aftr one circuit, styd on wl frm betw last 2, better for race........................*(9 to 4 jt-fav op 5 to 2) 2
1319 LOBSTER COTTAGE 8-11-5 C O'Dwyer, *last and hid up, gd hdwy to chase wnr 6 out, not fluent nxt, rdn and outpcd frm 3 out..............................*(9 to 2 tchd 5 to 1) 3
1022² SHALIK (Ire) 6-10-5 (7*) N T Egan, *led till hdd appr 7th, feeling pace and blun 5 out, reminders last 3, one pace.*
..............................(20 to 1 op 14 to 1) 4
1258 CHEEKA 7-10-12 M Ranger, *settled to chase ldrs, feeling pace and lost grnd frm 6 out, tld off bef strt.*
..............................(33 to 1 op 25 to 1) 5
1587 ETHICAL NOTE (Ire) 5-10-5 (7*) R Wilkinson, *settled wth chasing grp, struggling hfwy, tld off...* (33 to 1 op 25 to 1) 6
1203* MINSTER'S MADAM (v) 5-10-4 (3*) T Dascombe, *wth ldrs, clr 3rd and hndy whn f 7th..............*(16 to 1 op 14 to 1) 7
970⁴ WEEHEBY (USA) 7-10-12 S McNeill, *bad mstk 1st, struggling whn blun and uns rdr 3rd.*
..............................(10 to 1 op 8 to 1 tchd 12 to 1) ur
1264² FLAMING MIRACLE (Ire) (bl) 6-10-12 R Farrant, *settled in tch, struggling frm hfwy, tld off whn pld up aftr 4 out.*
..............................(4 to 1 op 8 to 1 tchd 10 to 1) pu
Dist: 8l, 23l, 10l, 3l, 24l. 3m 59.20s. a 5.20s (9 Ran).
SR: 31/16/-/-/-/-/   (Rory McGrath), N J Henderson

1705 Sail Inn Handicap Hurdle Class D (0-120 4-y-o and up) £2,888 2m
.... (2:00)

1606² STAY WITH ME (Fr) [94] 6-10-4 (5*) Mr R Thornton, *al wl plcd, led bef 5th, drw clr before 2 out, unchlgd.*
..............................(5 to 2 op 11 to 4 tchd 3 to 1) 1
1141 SHIFTING MOON [85] (bl) 4-10-0 S Wynne, *trkd ldr, led briefly 4th, rdn and chsd wnr appr 2 out, no imprsn.*
..............................(14 to 1 op 33 to 1) 2
1438* PETER MONAMY [103] (bl) 4-11-4 M A Fitzgerald, *trkd ldg pair, feeling pace hfwy, struggling whn 3 out, one pace after.*
..............................(7 to 2 op 5 to 2) 3
1354⁶ ATH CHEANNAITHE (Fr) [87] (h,bl) 4-10-2 A Maguire, *led till hdd 4th, struggling and lost tch aftr four out, tld off.*
..............................(10 to 1 op 8 to 1) 4
1512² KING ATHELSTAN (USA) [108] 8-11-9 Derek Byrne, *nvr gng wl, short lived effrt hfwy, blun and lost tch 3 out, tld off whn pld up bef nxt, lme..........* (2 to 1 fav op 6 to 4) pu
ISIAH [113] 7-12-0 T Kent, *patiently rdn, steady hdwy to take clr order hfwy, struggling bef 3 out, tld off whn pld up before 2 out.......................* (7 to 1 op 4 to 1 tchd 8 to 1) pu
Dist: 10l, 4l, dist. 3m 53.90s. a 7.90s (6 Ran).
SR: 19/-/14/   (Mrs Sandra A Roe), C R Egerton

1706 Grenville Chadwick Retirement Novices' Handicap Chase Class E (0-100 5-y-o and up) £3,479 3m 110yds
.... (2:30)

OCEAN LEADER [88] 9-11-3 A Maguire, *patiently rdn, steady hdwy fnl circuit, led 3 out, styd on gmely, clr frm last.*
..............................(7 to 4 fav op 6 to 4 tchd 15 to 8) 1
1399⁶ RECORD LOVER (Ire) [72] 6-10-0 W Worthington, *settled in tch, niggled alng to cl fnl circuit, str run frm betw last 2, kpt on same pace........................*(16 to 1 tchd 20 to 1) 2
1504² LUCKY DOLLAR (Ire) [99] 8-11-13 C O'Dwyer, *nvr far away, ev ch and bustled alng aftr 3 out, styd on one pace and pres frm betw last 2........................*(3 to 1 tchd 7 to 2) 3
TACTIX [72] 6-10-0 A S Smith, *not fluent, al wl in tch, effrt and bustled alng frm 3 out, kpt on one pace from betw last 2.*
..............................(50 to 1) 4
RING CORBITTS [84] 8-10-9 (3*) G Hogan, *al frnt rnk, lft in ld 12th, hdd 6 out, sn struggling, no imprsn last 3.*
..............................(20 to 1 op 16 to 1 tchd 25 to 1) 5
DUNLIR [75] 6-10-33 S Burrough, *nvr far away, blun and nrly uns rdr 5 out, not reco'r, tld off.......*(20 to 1 op 16 to 1) 6
1256* GEMS LAD [86] 9-11-0 M A Fitzgerald, *led till blun and hdd 12th, rdr lost iron, reco'red to rgn ld 6 out, headed 3 out, 3rd and one pace whn f nxt....................*(5 to 2 op 9 to 4) f
1113⁵ MANOR MIEO [90] 10-10-11 (7*) Mr A Coe, *took keen hold, al wl plcd, 5th and drvn alng whn blun and uns rdr 4 out.*
..............................(6 to 1 op 7 to 1) ur
Dist: 3l, ½l, 4l, 10l, dist. 6m 28.10s. a 34.10s (8 Ran).

(Sir Peter Gibbings), Mrs D Haine

1707 Thames Handicap Chase Class E (0-115 5-y-o and up) £4,290 2½m 110yds.......................... (3:00)

NETHERBY SAID [91] 6-11-1 A S Smith, *jmpd boldly, made all racing keenly, clr most of way, styd on strly frm 3 out, one to follow............................*(7 to 2 op 4 to 1) 1

218

1368⁴ COPPER CABLE [76] 9-10-0 M Ranger, *settled wth chasing grp, lft second 4 out, no imprsn on wnr whn nrly f last, fnshd tired* . . . . (25 to 1) 2
1011³ HOUGHTON [100] 10-11-3 (7") Mr R Burton, *trkd ldrs, hit 3rd, struggling bef hfwy, tld off fnl circuit* . . (12 to 1 op 14 to 1) 3
1056⁷ CELTINO [97] 8-11-7 S Wynne, *wtd wth, improved aftr one circuit, second and keeping on at one pace whn f 4 out.* . . . .(7 to 4 op 6 to 4 tchd 2 to 1) f
1204² ZAMBEZI SPIRIT (Ire) [98] 7-11-8 Derek Byrne, *hit 1st, chsd ldr for o'r a circuit, 3rd and rdn whn hmpd 4 out, lost tch and pld up bef nxt,broke blood vessel.* . . . .(Evens fav op 11 to 10 tchd 5 to 4) pu
Dist: Dist, 3¹⁄₂l. 5m 24.80s. a 24.80s (5 Ran).

(Mrs S Sunter), Miss M K Milligan

1708 Nene Conditional Jockeys' Handicap Hurdle Class E (0–110 4-y-o and up) £2,406 2½m 110yds. . . . . . (3:30)

1444² FAWLEY FLYER [86] 7-11-1 (5") J Power, *nvr far away, led 5th, rdn clr 3 out, wndrd nxt, kpt on und pres.* . . . .(7 to 2 op 2 to 1 tchd 4 to 1) 1
1469² DESERT FORCE (Ire) [90] 7-11-10 G Hogan, *patiently rdn, improved to take clr order 4 out, ridden frm nxt, effrt and swtchd 2 out, kpt on same pace.* . . . .(7 to 4 fav op 2 to 1 tchd 9 to 4) 2
1372⁷ WE'RE IN THE MONEY [66] 12-9-7 (7") Claudine Froggitt, *settled to track ldrs, lost grnd whn pace quickened aftr 3 out, styd on wl to take 3rd r-in* . . . .(33 to 1) 3
1139 FIRST CRACK [87] 11-11-7 G Tormey, *settled to chase ldrs, feeling pace and lost grnd quickly leaving backstrt, tld off frm 2 out.* . . . .(7 to 1 op 6 to 1 tchd 8 to 1) 4
TARGET LINE [73] 6-10-4 (3") R Wilkinson, *made most till hdd 5th, rdn to hold pl aftr 4 out, lost place quickly last 2, tld off.* . . . .(8 to 1 op 7 to 1) 5
PRECIPICE RUN [86] 11-11-6 R Massey, *pressed ldrs till lost pl quickly 5th, tld off frm 5 out.* . . . .(16 to 1 op 14 to 1 tchd 20 to 1) 6
1021 SOLOMAN SPRINGS (USA) [78] (v) 6-10-12 D Fortt, *struggling to keep up bef hfwy, lost tch quickly, tld off.* . . . .(12 to 1 op 10 to 1) 7
RAIN-N-SUN [84] 10-11-4 T Dascombe, *pressed ldrs till rdn and lost pl quickly hfwy, tld off aftr 3 out.* (10 to 1 op 8 to 1) 8
1259⁴ TASHREEF [72] (bl) 6-10-3 (3") S Melrose, *reluctant to race, refused 1st.* . . . .(11 to 1 op 8 to 1 tchd 12 to 1) ref
Dist: 1l, dist, 5l, 2l, sht-hd, 6l, 19l. 5m 4.00s. a 18.00s (9 Ran).

(David Chown), W G M Turner

THURLES (IRE) (yielding to soft)
Thursday December 5th

1709 Templemore Maiden Hurdle (3-y-o) £2,226 2m. . . . . (12:30)

HARD NEWS (USA) 10-8 (3") G Cotter, ...(20 to 1) 1
1459² THREE RIVERS 10-11 D J Casey, ...(2 to 1 fav) 2
1459 IFTATAH 10-4 (7") I Browne, ...(10 to 1) 3
1547⁹ TIP YOUR WAITRESS (Ire) 10-11 G M O'Neill, ...(20 to 1) 4
1547³ MARLONETTE 10-6 T P Treacy, ...(5 to 1) 5
1459 CURRAGH COUNCIL (Ire) (bl) 10-6 F Woods, ...(25 to 1) 6
1547⁴ PRINCESS TYCOON (Ire) 10-6 C F Swan, ...(7 to 1) 7
1430⁹ DUGGAN DUFF (Ire) 10-4 (7") Mr S McGonagle, . . .(20 to 1) 8
1547² SARAH'S GUEST (Ire) 10-6 K F O'Brien, ...(3 to 1) 9
927³ SPIONAN (Ire) 10-4 (7") J P Dobbs, ...(12 to 1) 10
1547 KING OF PEACE (Ire) 10-11 H Rogers, ...(10 to 1) 11
1430 DISPOSEN (Ire) 10-6 P L Malone, ...(25 to 1) 12
1430 PEAK VIEW (Ire) 10-11 J P Broderick, ...(20 to 1) 13
1547⁷ PETASUS 10-6 (5") J Butler, ...(12 to 1) 14
1459 SNIFFLE (Ire) 10-6 R M Burke, ...(10 to 1) 15
MARYSGROOM (Ire) 9-13 (7") A O'Shea, ...(25 to 1) 16
ARCTIC ZIPPER (USA) 10-11 A Powell, ...(20 to 1) 17
1459³ LOUGH SLANIA (Ire) 10-11 J Shortt, ...(5 to 1) f
Dist: Hd, dist, nk, 2¹⁄₂l. 4m 3.00s. (18 Ran).

(Denis S Curtin), D P Kelly

1710 Golden Maiden Hurdle (6-y-o and up) £2,226 2m. . . . .(1:00)

1487⁵ JAY MAN (Ire) 6-12-0 C F Swan, ...(6 to 1) 1
1013⁶ EIRON GALE (Ire) 7-12-0 T P Treacy, ...(11 to 8 on) 2
1241² WELSH GRIT (Ire) 7-12-0 D J Casey, ...(4 to 1) 3
1486³ ARABIAN SPRITE (Ire) 8-11-9 M J Healy, ...(8 to 1) 4
1436 RYTHM ROCK (Ire) 7-10-13 (7") A O'Shea, ...(20 to 1) 5
SCEAL SIOG (Ire) 7-11-1 K F O'Brien, ...(20 to 1) 6
CITY LOVE (Ire) 8-10-8 (7") D K Budds, ...(20 to 1) 7
TRUCKINABOUT (Ire) 6-11-6 F Woods, ...(14 to 1) 8
ANOTHER GALLOP (Ire) 8-11-6 L P Cusack, . . .(14 to 1) 9
SHOWBOAT MELODY (Ire) 6-10-8 (7") M D Murphy, ...(14 to 1) 10
1409⁹ CRISTYS PICNIC (Ire) 6-11-6 J Shortt, ...(10 to 1) 11
1075⁸ SKULLDUGERY (Ire) 6-11-6 J Jones, ...(25 to 1) 12
CASTLELAKE LADY (Ire) 7-11-1 D T Evans, ...(20 to 1) 13
977 SALMON POOL (Ire) 6-10-12 (3") G Cotter, ...(33 to 1) 14
1042 CORAL SEA (Ire) 6-11-7 (7") Mr A Ross, ...(12 to 1) 15
829 GONE ALL DAY (Ire) 6-11-6 J R Barry, ...(33 to 1) 16
1487⁸ WHITBY 8-10-13 (7") Mr P R Crowley, ...(20 to 1) f

1580 BLACKTRENCH LADY (Ire) 8-11-9 H Rogers, ...(16 to 1) su
Dist: 5l, 1¹⁄₂l, nk, ¹⁄₂l. 4m 6.20s. (18 Ran).

(Edward J Kearns), E J Kearns Jnr

1711 Kilsheelan Handicap Chase (0-109 4-y-o and up) £2,226 2½m. . . . (1:30)

1458* HEMISPHERE (Ire) [-] 7-10-13 (3") G Cotter, . .(11 to 10 fav) 1
1538⁶ WACKO JACKO (Ire) [-] 7-11-4 J P Broderick, ...(12 to 1) 2
FIFTH GENERATION (Ire) [-] 6-9-11 (3") K Whelan, . .(20 to 1) 3
1363² CASTALINO [-] 10-11-6 C F Swan, ...(4 to 1) 4
1538⁴ FAIR GO [-] 10-9-6 (7") Mrs C Harrison, ...(14 to 1) 5
1553⁸ BALLYBODEN [-] 9-11-2 M P Hourigan, ...(14 to 1) 6
1538⁵ FAIRY MIST (Ire) [-] 8-9-8¹ F Woods, ...(12 to 1) 7
1553³ DOONEGA (Ire) [-] 8-10-8 (7") Mr E Gallagher, ...(6 to 1) 8
PROGRAMMED TO WIN [-] 9-11-5 D T Evans, ...(14 to 1) 9
INTERIM ACCOUNT [-] 10-11-2 L P Cusack, ...(14 to 1) 10
1538⁹ ROSSI NOVAE [-] (bl) 13-9-11¹ T P Treacy, ...(25 to 1) 11
1582² HANNIES GIRL (Ire) [-] 7-10-8 (7") L J Fleming, . . .(11 to 1) 12
1538 NOVELLO ALLEGRO (USA) [-] 8-10-11 D H O'Connor, ...(16 to 1) 13
IF YOU SAY YES (Ire) [-] 8-11-3 D J Casey, ...(12 to 1) 14
ALL IN THE GAME (Ire) [-] 8-10-4 P A Roche, ...(16 to 1) 15
Dist: 4l, 1¹⁄₂l, 20l, 9l. 5m 27.20s. (15 Ran).

(K F McNulty), D T Hughes

1712 Cahir Hurdle (5-y-o and up) £2,226 2¾m. . . . . (2:00)

1620⁵ LEAMHOG (Ire) 6-11-2 C F Swan, ...(13 to 2) 1
1457³ BALLYRIHY BOY (Ire) 5-10-11 (5") J M Donnelly, (7 to 4 fav) 2
1550 MATTS DILEMMA (Ire) 8-11-8 F Woods, ...(7 to 1) 3
1433⁶ GRANGE COURT (Ire) 6-11-2 J Shortt, ...(9 to 4) 4
1536⁶ LAURA'S PURSUIT (Ire) 7-10-4 (7") A O'Shea, ...(10 to 1) 5
781⁶ CLEARLY CANADIAN (Ire) 5-10-13 (3") G Cotter, . .(14 to 1) 6
1536 NORE GLEN (Ire) 5-11-2 D J Casey, ...(14 to 1) 7
1360⁶ BARRIGAN'S HILL (Ire) 6-11-2 S H O'Donovan, ...(12 to 1) 8
1361 OVER THE WALL (Ire) 7-10-11 P A Roche, ...(33 to 1) 9
1013 PROLOGUE (Ire) 5-11-2 T P Treacy, ...(20 to 1) 10
OVER AGAIN (Ire) 8-11-2 A Powell, ...(20 to 1) 11
1486⁸ WARLOCKFOE (Ire) 5-10-11 T P Rudd, ...(25 to 1) 12
Dist: 1¹⁄₂l, 4l, nk, 2l. 5m 46.50s. (12 Ran).

(Walter James Purcell), A P O'Brien

1713 Munster Handicap Hurdle (0-109 4-y-o and up) £2,226 2m. . . . . . (2:30)

272⁸ RUN ROSE RUN (Ire) [-] (bl) 6-9-2 (5") J Butler, ...(20 to 1) 1
1077* MONTELISA (Ire) [-] 4-11-13 C F Swan, ...(7 to 1) 2
1486* ANCIENT HISTORIAN (Ire) [-] 7-11-10 D J Casey, . .(11 to 2) 3
1273 HEIGHT OF LUXURY (Ire) [-] 8-9-1 (7") M D Murphy, (33 to 1) 4
1549* CLASHBEG (Ire) [-] 7-11-2 T P Treacy, ...(6 to 1) 5
1273 HERSILIA (Ire) [-] 5-11-2 F J Flood, ...(8 to 1) 6
1462⁵ FIDDLERS BOW VI (Ire) [-] 8-12-0 J Shortt, ...(8 to 1) 7
WOODBORO LASS (Ire) [-] 6-10-4 C O'Brien, ...(14 to 1) 8
1361 TOUCHING MOMENT (Ire) [-] 6-11-0 (7") A O'Shea, .(20 to 1) 9
1654 COUNCILLOR (Ire) [-] 5-11-8 S C Lyons, ...(20 to 1) 10
15357 JOHNNY HANDSOME (Ire) [-] 6-10-10 J P Broderick, ...(10 to 1) f
1244⁴ ECLIPTIC MOON (Ire) [-] 6-9-3 (7") D McCullagh, . . .(8 to 1) f
1654⁴ BOLERO DANCER (Ire) [-] 8-10-10 F Woods, ...(5 to 1 fav) bd
9079 LEMOIRE (Ire) [-] 5-11-3 D T Evans, ...(14 to 1) bd
1462⁴ ILLBETHEREFORYOU (Ire) [-] 5-10-8 M P Hourigan, ...(10 to 1) bd
1654 JACKSON'S PANTHER (Ire) [-] 4-10-5 (3") G Cotter, (10 to 1) bd
Dist: Hd, 2l, 2¹⁄₂l, 6l. 4m 8.30s. (16 Ran).

(P Nunan), Timothy O'Callaghan

1714 Goodwill Beginners Chase (5-y-o and up) £2,226 2¼m. . . . .(3:00)

1461³ AMBLE SPEEDY (Ire) 6-12-0 C O'Brien, ...(7 to 1) 1
GLINT OF EAGLES (Ire) 7-12-0 D J Casey, ...(6 to 4 fav) 2
1581⁴ BALLINAGREEN (Ire) 6-12-0 C F Swan, ...(10 to 1) 3
1534 SHISOMA (Ire) 6-11-7 (7") Mr E Gallagher, ...(8 to 1) 4
14357 MUSICAL DUKE (Ire) 7-11-9 D H O'Connor, ...(14 to 1) 5
FARNAN (Ire) 8-11-6 (3") Mr B M Cash, ...(8 to 1) 6
1362 TAITS CLOCK (Ire) 7-11-11 (3") K Whelan, ...(20 to 1) 7
1461 SWINGER (Ire) 7-11-7 (7") Mr M Madden, ...(20 to 1) 8
1534⁸ CONCLAVE (Ire) 6-11-11 (3") G Cotter, ...(12 to 1) 9
1552 MARGUERITA SONG 6-11-4 (5") T Martin, ...(14 to 1) f
1362⁶ SUEMENDMORE (Ire) 7-11-4 J Jones, ...(20 to 1) f
1534 JOES DANTE (Ire) 5-11-12 F J Flood, ...(14 to 1) f
1552 SACULORE (Ire) 8-11-9 (5") J M Donnelly, ...(8 to 1) pu
GEALLAINNBAN (Ire) 6-12-0 A Powell, ...(14 to 1) pu
1583³ MARLAST (Ire) 5-11-7 T P Treacy, ...(12 to 1) pu
1552 MULKEV PRINCE (Ire) 5-11-12 J Shortt, ...(6 to 1) pu
Dist: 5l, 2¹⁄₂l, 7l, 7l. 4m 56.40s. (16 Ran).

(Robin Minnis), A L T Moore

1715 Liscahill I.N.H. Flat Race (6-y-o and up) £2,226 2m. . . . .(3:30)

1463³ JODESI (Ire) 6-12-0 Mr J A Nash, ...(Evens fav) 1
1463 ARCTIC GREY (Ire) (bl) 6-11-11 (3") Mr R Walsh, . .(12 to 1) 2
1436⁵ ISOLETTE-8 (3") Mr P J Casey, ...(8 to 1) 3
983⁹ HOLLOW GOLD (Ire) 7-11-2 (7") Mr D W Cullen, . . .(8 to 1) 4
1622⁷ SLANEY CHARM (Ire) 6-12-0 Mr H F Cleary, ...(10 to 1) 5

BARRED FROM ACTONS (Ire) 6-11-11 (3*) Mr D Valentine,
....(6 to 1) 6
1484[8] LABAN LADY (Ire) (bl) 7-11-2 (7*) Mr John P Moloney,
....(16 to 1) 7
1436[9] EMOTIONAL MAN (Ire) 6-11-11 (3*) Mr P English, . .(8 to 1) 8
929[9] CHARMING DUKE (Ire) 6-11-7 (7*) Mr D Delaney, . .(14 to 1) 9
COMINOLE (Ire) 7-11-2 (7*) Miss C O'Neill, ...(25 to 1) 10
929 BALLYLENNON LADY (Ire) 6-11-2 (7*) Miss Michelle McArdle, ...(14 to 1) 11
170[6] A THOUSAND DREAMS (Ire) 6-11-11 (3*) Mr B M Cash,
....(8 to 1) 12
NOBLE TUNE (Ire) 7-11-7 (7*) Mr E Sheehy, ...(10 to 1) 13
BALLINARD CASTLE (Ire) 6-11-7 (7*) Mr M A Cahill, (14 to 1) 14
1554 NATIVE CHAMPION (Ire) 7-11-7 (7*) Mr P P O'Brien,
....(20 to 1) 15
PUNTERS DREAM 6-11-7 (7*) Mr J P Murphy, ...(20 to 1) 16
NORTH TIPP (Ire) 7-11-7 (7*) Mr D A Harney, ...(8 to 1) 17
TRIBAL RIVER (Ire) 6-11-2 (7*) Mr J T McNamara, (25 to 1) pu
Dist: 6l, 3l, 2l, 8l. 4m 4.90s. (18 Ran).

(P J Dore), W P Mullins

WINDSOR (good)
Thursday December 5th
Going Correction: MINUS 0.10 sec. per fur. (races 1,2,4,7), NIL (3,5,6)

1716 Spital Novices' Hurdle Class E (Div I)
(4-y-o and up) £2,075 2m.... (12:30)

1410[2] DANEGOLD (Ire) 4-10-12 R Hughes, hld up, hdwy aftr 4th, ev ch 2 out, led last, drvn clr r-in.
..............................(3 to 1 fav op 4 to 1 tchd 5 to 1) 1
1477[2] SAILEP (Fr) 4-11-2 (3*) T Dascombe, led, rdn aftr 3 out, hdd last, not quicken.............(10 to 1 op 7 to 1 tchd 12 to 1) 2
1641[7] FAIRY KNIGHT 4-10-12 N Williamson, hld up, hdwy aftr 4th, ev ch 2 out, not quicken...(7 to 2 op 11 to 4 tchd 4 to 1) 3
NIGHT CITY 5-10-12 J Osborne, hld up, hdwy aftr 5th, ev ch 2 out, sn rdn and no imprsn.
..........................(100 to 30 op 6 to 4 tchd 7 to 2) 4
ILANDRA (Ire) 4-10-7 A P McCoy, chsd ldr frm 4th, ev ch whn mstk 3 out, sn wknd....(14 to 1 op 10 to 1 tchd 16 to 1) 5
MUSIC PLEASE 4-10-12 C O'Dwyer, hld up, hdwy to chase ldr aftr 4th, ev ch sn wknd.......(25 to 1 op 16 to 1) 6
JOVIE KING (Ire) 4-10-12 B Powell, chsd ldr aftr 4th, rdn appr 3 out, sn btn...............(25 to 1 op 8 to 1 tchd 33 to 1) 7
1449[6] SECOND STEP (Ire) 5-10-9 (3*) D Fortt, lost pl aftr 4th, beh frm 3 out...........................(11 to 1 op 10 to 1 tchd 16 to 1) 8
1479 MR HEMP 4-10-12 Derek Byrne, beh 3rd, no hdwy frm 4 out.
....(50 to 1 op 25 to 1) 9
1415[3] HAZAAF (USA) 7-10-12 F Jousset, chsd ldr till wknd quickly aftr 5th...................(14 to 1 op 8 to 1 tchd 16 to 1) 10
MANSUR (Ire) 4-10-12 M A Fitzgerald, led to 2 out, wknd quickly..............................(5 to 1 tchd 8 to 1) 11
1205[5] NOT TO PANIC (Ire) 6-10-7 A Larnach, tld off aftr 3rd.
....(50 to 1 op 33 to 1) 12
1515 NIGHT FLARE (Fr) 4-10-12 M Richards, chsd ldr 3rd till wknd quickly aftr 3 out.................(33 to 1 op 20 to 1) 13
1429 MURPHY'S RUN (Ire) 6-10-7 (5*) Mr R Thornton, chsd ldr, wknd quickly aftr 4 out...............(50 to 1 op 33 to 1) 14
129[7] CRUSTYGUN 6-10-9 (3*) G Hogan, sn beh, tld off aftr 3rd.
....(33 to 1 op 10 to 1) 15
Dist: 7l, hd, 6l, 4l, 4l, 10l, 4l, nk, ½l, 3l. 3m 49.90s. a 4.90s (15 Ran).

SR: 19/19/12/6/-/-/ (Circular Distributors Ltd), M R Channon

1717 Paley Street Mares' Only Handicap Hurdle Class D (0-120 4-y-o and up)
£2,747 2m.....................(1:00)

1351[2] SEVERN GALE [92] 6-9-13 (7*) X Aizpuru, made all, rdn 3 out, styd on strly..............(7 to 1 op 6 to 1 tchd 9 to 1) 1
1225[5] SEASONAL SPLENDOUR (Ire) [114] 6-11-0 A P McCoy, trkd ldr, ev ch appr 2 out, sn rdn, not quicken r-in.
..............................(9 to 2 op 3 to 1) 2
PEDALTOTHEMETAL (Ire) [90] 4-10-1 (3*) G Tormey, hld up in tch, wnt second aftr 4 out, ev ch nxt, sn rdn, not quicken r-in.
.........................(14 to 1 op 10 to 1 tchd 16 to 1) 3
1402[a] HENRIETTA HOWARD (Ire) [109] 6-11-6 (3*) G Hogan, hld up in tch, rdn to chal aftr 3 out, wknd after nxt. . . . . .(15 to 8 jt-fav op 6 to 4 tchd 2 to 1) 4
1606 DAILY SPORT GIRL [92] 7-9-13 (7*) Miss E J Jones, hld up, chsd ldr aftr 4th, sn rdn, wknd after 3 out.
.............................(12 to 1 op 10 to 1) 5
COSMIC STAR [86] 6-10-0 B Fenton, sn last, tld off aftr 4 out.
.............................(100 to 1 op 66 to 1) 6
1213[2] DARK NIGHTINGALE [100] 6-11-0 J Osborne, chsd ldr, rdn aftr 4 out, wknd quickly appr 2 out.............(15 to 8 jt-fav op 7 to 4 tchd 9 to 4) 7
Dist: 1½l, 1¾l, 20l, 13l, 1½l, dist. 3m 50.70s. a 5.70s (7 Ran).

SR: 5/25/-/-/ (Mrs Carol Allen), J Allen

1718 Woodside Novices' Chase Class E
(5-y-o and up) £3,104 3m..... (1:30)

1453* FLOW 7-11-0 B Powell, chsd ldr, ev ch 8th, led 5 out, rdn and styd on wl whn chlgd aftr last.
..............................(2 to 1 fav op 7 to 4 tchd 9 to 4) 1
SECRET BID (Ire) 6-10-9 (3*) P Henley, hld up, wl beh 7th, hdwy aftr 6 out, chlgd after 2 out, ev ch last, not quicken r-in.
....(10 to 1 tchd 16 to 1) 2
GARETHSON (Ire) 5-10-11 D Bridgwater, trkd ldr, ev ch 5 out, wknd 3 out...........................(4 to 1 op 3 to 1) 3
1339 BALLYEDWARD (Ire) 6-10-12 P Holley, chsd ldrs, wknd aftr 6 out................(14 to 1 op 10 to 1 tchd 20 to 1) 4
1498* HIGHLAND JACK 6-11-5 N Williamson, mstks 3rd and 9th, chsd ldrs til wknd 6 out.................(9 to 2 op 7 to 2) 5
1447[5] DUKES MEADOW (Ire) (bl) 6-10-12 C O'Dwyer, led to 6th, in tch whn f tenth...........(6 to 1 op 7 to 2 tchd 13 to 2) f
SHERIFFMUIR 7-10-9 (3*) G Hogan, chsd ldr, hmpd tenth, mstk nxt, sn wknd, beh whn pld up bef 4 out.
....(12 to 1 op 7 to 1) pu
1411[3] THE HERIGON (Ire) 7-10-12 J Railton, led frm 6th til hdd 5 out, sn wknd, beh whn pld up bef 3 out. (33 to 1 op 20 to 1) pu
615 LORD ANTRIM (Ire) 7-10-9 (3*) D Walsh, mstk 6th, lost tch aftr 13th, tld off whn pld up after 5 out.... (40 to 1 op 33 to 1) pu
Dist: 1½l, 25l, hd, 30l. (Time not taken) (9 Ran).

(Mrs C J Dunn), R H Buckler

1719 Spital Novices' Hurdle Class E (Div II)
(4-y-o and up) £2,057 2m..... (2:00)

PROTON 6-10-12 A P McCoy, al prmnt, led and not fluent 3 out, rdn and styd on wl whn chlgd aftr nxt, drw clr r-in.
..............................(7 to 1 op 6 to 1 tchd 8 to 1) 1
DESERT GREEN (Fr) 7-10-12 N Williamson, hld up, steady hdwy aftr 5th, chlgd after 3 out, ev ch nxt, sn rdn, wknd r-in.
......(15 to 8 fav op 2 to 1 tchd 9 to 4 and 13 to 8) 2
1415[2] BATTLESHIP BRUCE 4-10-12 D Bridgwater, chsd clr ldr, ev ch aftr 4 out, rdn and wknd after nxt.... (7 to 2 op 5 to 1) 3
985[7] ZADOK 4-10-9 (3*) P Henley, chsd clr ldr frm 3rd, ev ch appr 2 out, sn wknd...........................(66 to 1 op 33 to 1) 4
I'M A DREAMER (Ire) 6-11-5 Gary Lyons, mid-div, chsd ldr 5th till wknd appr 2 out.....(12 to 1 op 7 to 1 tchd 14 to 1) 5
1397[4] OTTAVIO FARNESE 4-10-9 (3*) L Aspell, chsd clr ldr in second pl, ev ch 3 out, wknd appr nxt....(7 to 1 op 5 to 1) 6
REVERSE THRUST 5-10-5 (7*) M Clinton, mid-div till wknd aftr 4 out.................(33 to 1 op 16 to 1 tchd 40 to 1) 7
1646 MASTER GOODENOUGH (Ire) 5-10-5 (7*) D Creech, led, sn clr, hdd 3 out, sn wknd.................(66 to 1 op 25 to 1) 8
1415 BRAYDON FOREST 4-10-12 J Railton, mid-div and reminders aftr 4th, sn beh..........(100 to 1 op 16 to 1) 9
ILSLEY STAR 6-10-12 Mr J Rees, beh 4th.
.............................(66 to 1 op 33 to 1 tchd 100 to 1) 10
KI CHI SAGA (USA) 4-10-12 D Morris, chsd clr ldr till wknd quickly aftr 3 out...............(20 to 1 op 5 to 1) 11
1410 SEMINOLE WIND 5-10-12 B Fenton, wl beh 3rd, tld off aftr 4 out...................(66 to 1 op 33 to 1 tchd 100 to 1) 12
ZAJKO (USA) 6-10-12 M A Fitzgerald, mid-div whn blun 4 out, not reco'r, pld up bef last...(7 to 1 op 4 to 1 tchd 8 to 1) pu
CALLONESCY (Ire) 4-10-9 (3*) D Walsh, lost tch aftr 4th, tld off whn pld up bef 3 out............(66 to 1 op 25 to 1) pu
Dist: 9l, 18l, 8l, 4l, 13l, 5l, 26l, 10l, 1½l. 3m 51.80s. a 6.80s (14 Ran).

(Persian War Racing), R Akehurst

1720 Wraysbury Handicap Chase Class D
(0-125 5-y-o and up) £3,591 2m
..................................(2:30)

1595* ZEREDAR (NZ) [107] (bl) 6-11-2 (7ex) C O'Dwyer, trkd ldr, led 6th, blun 3 out, sn reco'red, cmftbly.
.............................(5 to 4 on tchd 11 to 10 on) 1
1428[2] DEAR DO [104] 9-10-13 M A Fitzgerald, hld up, chsd ldr frm 5 out, rdn and no imprsn aftr 3 out........(9 to 4 op 2 to 1) 2
1414[6] WHO'S TO SAY [115] (v) 10-11-10 N Williamson, led to 6th, chsd ldr nxt till wknd aftr 3 out.
.............................(9 to 2 op 4 to 1 tchd 5 to 1) 3
1289[4] KING CREDO [119] (v) 11-12-0 J Osborne, hld up, mstk 6th, last whn pld up bef 5 out......(10 to 1 op 6 to 1) pu
Dist: 8l, 12l. 3m 59.70s. a 5.70s (4 Ran).

SR: 31/20/19/-/ (I M S Racing), K C Bailey

1721 Dorney Amateur Riders' Handicap
Chase Class E (0-115 4-y-o and up)
£3,059 2m 5f................ (3:00)

1401[3] ACT OF PARLIAMENT (Ire) [105] (bl) 8-11-7 (7*) Mr R Wakley, hld up beh, hdwy aftr 5 out, rdn and styd on after 3 out, led nr finish...................(100 to 30 op 5 to 2 tchd 7 to 2) 1
1455[3] REX TO THE RESCUE (Ire) [100] 8-11-4 (5*) Mr R Thornton, led to 4th, led and mstk nxt, hdd aftr 6th, led 8th, mistake 2 out, rdn and headed nr finish.............(6 to 1 tchd 8 to 1) 2
1378[2] COOLREE (Ire) [112] 8-12-0 (7*) Mr J Tizzard, hld up beh, hdwy aftr tenth, 3rd 4 out, rdn and kpt on one pace.
.............................(4 to 1 op 7 to 2 tchd 9 to 2) 3
1111* WILKINS [84] 7-10-0 (7*) Mr P O'Keeffe, chsd ldg pair, led aftr 6th to 8th, chased ldr, mstk 5 out, sn wknd.
.............................(11 to 4 fav op 4 to 1) 4
1445 WHIPPERS DELIGHT (Ire) [89] 8-10-5 (7*) Mr A Charles-Jones, led 3rd, mstk and hdd 5th, lost tch aftr tenth, sn beh.
.............................(33 to 1 tchd 40 to 1) 5

1342² MERRY PANTO (Ire) [102] 7-11-4 (7") Mr E James, hld up,
drvn alng aftr 5 out, no hdwy frm 3 out, 5th and btn whn f last.
........................(100 to 30 op 9 to 4 tchd 7 to 2) f
CALL ME EARLY [92] 11-10-8 (7") Mr J Rees, not fluent, last
whn blun 9th, sn tld off, pld up bef last.
........................(25 to 1 op 20 to 1 tchd 33 to 1) pu
Dist: 2l, 6l, 7l, 19l. 5m 16.30s. a 7.30s (7 Ran).
SR: 27/20/26/-/   (J Perriss), K C Bailey

1722 Pangbourne Handicap Hurdle Class F (0-105 4-y-o and up) £2,101 2½m
........................(3:30)

1474* LETS BE FRANK [90] 5-11-5 M A Fitzgerald, hld up, steady
hdwy aftr 6th, in tch 4 out, rdn to ld last, styd on wl.
........................(5 to 2 fav tchd 4 to 1) 1
1203² RACHAEL'S OWEN [84] 6-10-13 M Richards, trkd ldrs 4th,
led aftr four out to last, not quicken.
........................(12 to 1 op 10 to 1 tchd 14 to 1) 2
1000² RELATIVE CHANCE [77] 7-10-6 N Williamson, hld up, hdwy to
track ldg grp aftr 4 out, ev ch after nxt, sn rdn, styd on one
pace........................(7 to 2 op 4 to 1 tchd 9 to 2) 3
1596³ AUGUST TWELFTH [87] 8-10-13 (3") D Walsh, hld up beh,
hdwy to track ldg grp aftr 4 out, ev ch nxt, rdn and styd on one
pace........................(7 to 2 op 3 to 1 tchd 4 to 1) 4
1211 POLICEMANS PRIDE (Fr) [75] 7-10-4 B Fenton, led till aftr 4
out, rdn and kpt on one pace.
........................(50 to 1 op 25 to 1 tchd 66 to 1) 5
987⁵ DURSHAN (USA) [76] 7-10-5 J Osborne, trkd ldrs, ev ch 4 out,
no imprsn aftr nxt........(16 to 1 op 10 to 1 tchd 20 to 1) 6
1443⁵ SUPER RITCHART [90] 8-11-5 R Farrant, trkd ldr 4th, ev ch
four out, rdn and no imprsn.
........................(20 to 1 op 12 to 1 tchd 25 to 1) 7
CAMBO (USA) [95] 10-11-10 D Bridgwater, prmnt, lost pl aftr
4th, styd on one pace after 3 out.......(14 to 1 op 8 to 1) 8
659⁵ PRIZE MATCH [80] 7-10-9 R Bellamy, mid-div, effrt aftr 4 out,
sn wknd........................(25 to 1 op 20 to 1 tchd 33 to 1) 9
1596* DONTDRESSFORDINNER [83] 6-10-9 (3") T Dascombe, hld
up, brief effrt aftr 4 out, wknd quickly.
........................(5 to 1 op 3 to 1 tchd 5 to 2) 10
1370⁴ DAHLIA'S BEST (USA) [95] 6-11-10 Gary Lyons, lost pl aftr
3rd, beh 5th........(16 to 1 op 10 to 1 tchd 20 to 1) 11
PYRRHIC DANCE [79] 6-10-8 D Skyrme, chsd ldr till wknd
quickly aftr 4 out........................(50 to 1 op 25 to 1) 12
1416⁷ WILL JAMES [71] (bl) 10-9-12¹ (3") Guy Lewis, lost pl aftr 3rd,
sn beh........................(50 to 1 op 20 to 1 tchd 100 to 1) 13
Dist: 2½l, 11l, 3½l, 2l, 9l, 9l, 6l, 1¼l, 7l, 14l. 4m 5.80s. a 11.80s (13 Ran).
(Mrs M M Stobart), Noel T Chance

EXETER (good)
Friday December 6th
Going Correction: PLUS 1.10 sec. per fur. (races
1,5,6), PLUS 0.85 (2,3,4)

1723 Tripleprint Conditional Jockeys' Novices' Handicap Hurdle Class F (0-105 4-y-o and up) £2,156 2¼m
........................(12:50)

1320* BURLINGTON SAM (NZ) [83] 8-11-9 O Burrows, hld up in tch,
led appr 2 out, rdn sn aftr, all out.
........................(11 to 4 op 5 to 2 tchd 100 to 30) 1
1614⁴ TIME LEADER [70] 4-10-1 (9") X Aizpuru, hld up, steady hdwy
frm 3 out, went second aftr nxt, rdn and no imprsn r-in.
........................(7 to 4 fav op 9 to 4 tchd 5 to 2) 2
1010⁴ KAREN'S TYPHOON (Ire) [72] 5-10-9 (3") G Tormey, hmpd
strt, rear till some hdwy und pres 3 out, one pace.
........................(8 to 1 op 5 to 1 tchd 9 to 1) 3
1497⁴ ELEANORA MUSE [66] 6-10-6 Guy Lewis, led second, rdn
and hdd appr 2 out, wknd........(5 to 1 op 4 to 1 tchd 5 to 1) 4
1555⁹ MADAM ROSE (Ire) [60] 6-9-5 (9") David Turner, led to second,
hit 4th, wknd quickly 3 out, tld off........(20 to 1 op 12 to 1) 5
1450* URBAN LILY [84] (bl) 6-11-4 (6") J Harris, badly hmpd and uns
rdr strt........................(6 to 1 op 4 to 1 tchd 13 to 2) ur
1568 UPHAM RASCAL [63] 5-10-3⁶ (3") D Fortt, unruly strt, shied at
tape, uns rdr........(20 to 1 op 14 to 1 tchd 25 to 1) ur
Dist: 1½l, 3½l, 3½l, dist. 4m 37.70s. a 38.70s (7 Ran).
(Mrs Jackie Reip), A G Hobbs

1724 Bonusprint Selling Handicap Chase Class G (0-95 5-y-o and up) £2,469 2 ¼m
........................(1:20)

1574³ CASTLECONNER (Ire) [75] (bl) 5-10-8 Mr A Holdsworth, al
prmnt, led 4 out, rdn out. (12 to 1 op 8 to 1 tchd 14 to 1) 1
1593 THE WHOLE HOG (Ire) [78] 7-10-4 (7") Mr R Wakley, chsd
ldrs, styd on frm 4 out to chase wnr r-in. (14 to 1 op 7 to 1) 2
1686³ FENWICK [87] 9-11-3 (3") T Dascombe, hld up, hdwy 5th, ev
ch 4 out, wknd nxt........................(9 to 2 op 3 to 1) 3
1229 GLENTOWER (Ire) [90] 8-11-9 A Maguire, rear, some hdwy
frm 4 out, nvr nrr........(6 to 1 op 7 to 1 tchd 4 to 1) 4
1237⁶ JHAL FREZI [69] 8-10-2 A Procter, hld up, hdwy 5th, wknd aftr
8th........................(5 to 2 fav) 5
449⁵ OCTOBER BREW (USA) [86] (bl) 6-11-5 A P McCoy, led 4
out, rdn and sn wknd......(7 to 2 op 3 to 1 tchd 4 to 1) 6

650⁴ AKIYMANN (USA) [71] (bl) 6-9-11 (7") G Supple, beh whn
mstk second, sn lost tch, tld off........(16 to 1 op 8 to 1) 7
1349⁸ JEWEL THIEF [70] (v) 6-10-3 R Greene, al beh, tld off.
........................(14 to 1 op 12 to 1) 8
1239 TAPAGEUR [95] 11-11-7 (7") B Moore, chsd ldrs, wknd 4th,
pld up bef 7th........................(20 to 1 op 10 to 1) pu
1647 CAPTAIN STOCKFORD [67] 9-10-0 W Marston, trkd ldr, wknd
appr 4 out, beh whn pld up bef 2 out...(33 to 1 op 14 to 1) pu
1667 UP THE TEMPO (Ire) [67] 7-9-12¹ (3") Guy Lewis, al beh, tld off
whn pld up bef 3 out...(33 to 1 op 20 to 1 tchd 40 to 1) pu
Dist: 10l, 3½l, ½l, ¾l, dist, dist, 20l. 4m 35.40s. a 25.40s (11 Ran).
(Mrs G A Robarts), R G Frost

1725 Tripleprint Novices' Chase Class C (5-y-o and up) £5,047 2¼m... (1:50)

GUINDA (Ire) 6-10-9 C Llewellyn, hld up in tch, rdn whn lft
second 2 out, led r-in und pres.
........................(11 to 1 op 6 to 1 tchd 12 to 1) 1
1399⁷ LIVELY KNIGHT (Ire) 7-11-6 P Hide, led second to 4 out, hld
and und pres whn lft in ld 2 out, hrd rdn and hdd r-in.
........................(7 to 2 tchd 4 to 1) 2
1399³ WILD WEST WIND (Ire) 6-11-0 J Osborne, led to second, rdn
6th, lft 3rd 2 out, one pace. (9 to 1 op 6 to 1 tchd 10 to 1) 3
FLIPPANCE 6-11-0 W Marston, trkd ldrs till wknd appr 4 out.
........................(50 to 1 op 20 to 1 tchd 66 to 1) 4
1500² PHAR FROM FUNNY 5-11-0 A P McCoy, hld up, gd hdwy 7th,
led 4 out, gng wl whn stumbled and almost uns rdr 2 out, not
reco'r, tld off........................(8 to 1 op 6 to 1 tchd 9 to 1) 5
1236⁵ PURBECK CAVALIER 7-11-0 G Upton, al beh, tld off 5th.
........................(66 to 1 op 20 to 1) 6
SQUIRE SILK 7-11-0 R Dunwoody, hld up, mstk 3rd, gd hdwy
8th, second whn hmpd and uns rdr 2 out, mmtd, tld off.
........................(5 to 4 on tchd 6 to 4 on and 11 to 10 on) 7
ROBINS PRIDE (Ire) 6-10-11 (3") T Dascombe, mstk second,
chsd ldr 6th to 8th, wknd bef nxt, tld off whn pld up before last.
........................(33 to 1 op 20 to 1 tchd 50 to 1) pu
1216⁴ KINO'S CROSS 7-11-0 A Maguire, prmnt to 5th, tld off whn
pld up before 2 out...(20 to 1 op 14 to 1 tchd 25 to 1) pu
Dist: 1l, 10l, nk, 5l, dist, dist. 4m 31.60s. a 21.60s (9 Ran).
SR: 18/28/12/11/6/-/   (Mrs J K Powell), N A Twiston-Davies

1726 Bonusprint Handicap Chase Class D (0-120 5-y-o and up) £4,192 2m 7f 110yds........................(2:20)

1366* BALLYEA BOY (Ire) [106] 6-11-3 A Maguire, dsptd ld, led 3
out, idled r-in, pushed out......... (5 to 2 fav op 3 to 1) 1
1453⁴ ROCKY PARK [92] 10-10-3 B Fenton, prmnt till lost pl 3 out,
rallied r-in........................(14 to 1 op 12 to 1) 2
RED PARADE (NZ) [95] 8-10-6 R Greene, hld up, hdwy 11th,
ev ch 3 out, one pace aftr.
........................(9 to 1 op 12 to 1 tchd 14 to 1) 3
1451* ORSWELL LAD [105] 7-10-13 (3") G Tormey, hdwy 5 out, mstk
nxt, one pace........................(13 to 2 op 5 to 1) 4
1544⁴ SPUFFINGTON [114] 8-11-11 P Hide, made most to 3 out,
wknd nxt........................(10 to 1 op 8 to 1 tchd 11 to 1) 5
1499* ANDRE LAVAL (Ire) [113] 7-11-3 (7") Mr R Wakley, hld up, effrt
5 out, nvr nr to chal........(5 to 1 op 9 to 2 tchd 11 to 2) 6
1137⁶ GARRYLOUGH (Ire) [113] 7-11-10 R Dunwoody, beh, effrt
12th, nvr nr to chal........(6 to 1 op 5 to 1 tchd 13 to 2) 7
1086* SPECIAL ACCOUNT [97] 10-10-8 A P McCoy, in tch till wknd
appr 4 out........................(8 to 1 op 7 to 1) 8
GHIA GNEUIAGH [113] 10-11-10 C Llewellyn, al beh, tld off.
........................(20 to 1 op 16 to 1) 9
MR INVADER [102] 9-10-13 W Marston, al beh, tld off.
........................(16 to 1) 10
1414⁴ KINDLE'S DELIGHT [101] 8-10-12 J Osborne, prmnt to 5th,
appr 4 out, beh whn pld up bef last............(20 to 1) pu
Dist: ¾l, 3l, 4l, 1½l, ¾l, ½l, nk, dist, 2½l. 6m 8.70s. a 34.70s (11 Ran).
(Denis Barry), D Nicholson

1727 European Breeders Fund Tripleprint 'National Hunt' Novices' Hurdle Qualifier Class D (4,5,6-y-o) £4,020 2 ¼m........................(2:50)

1292² WADE ROAD (Ire) 5-11-0 R Dunwoody, al prmnt gng wl, wnt
second 4th, led appr 2 out, sn clr, easily.
........................(5 to 4 fav op 6 to 4 tchd 2 to 1 and 11 to 10) 1
THE LAND AGENT 5-11-0 S Curran, al prmnt, led 5th till appr
2 out, one pace aftr........................(5 to 2 op 9 to 4) 2
1479⁸ SIR DANTE (Ire) 5-11-0 D O'Sullivan, mstk 1st, sn chsd ldrs,
one pace 2 out........(12 to 1 op 8 to 1 tchd 14 to 1) 3
LEAP FROG 5-11-0 W Marston, hld up rear, hdwy 3 out, nvr
dngrs........................(25 to 1 op 20 to 1 tchd 33 to 1) 4
1483* QUINI EAGLE (Fr) 4-11-0 A P McCoy, led till jmpd slwly and
hdd 5th, prmnt till wknd appr 2 out.
........................(9 to 4 op 6 to 4 tchd 3 to 1) 5
FLAXLEY WOOD 5-11-0 B Fenton, al beh.
........................(66 to 1 op 20 to 1 tchd 100 to 1) 6
MASTER BOMBER (Ire) 5-11-0 J Osborne, beh 5th, tld off.
........................(66 to 1 op 20 to 1 tchd 100 to 1) 7
1082 SHRIMP 5-10-9 C Llewellyn, mid-div, lost tch 5th, tld off.
........................(66 to 1 op 33 to 1 tchd 100 to 1) 8
MYLINK (Ire) 6-11-0 A Maguire, hld up, hdwy 3rd, wknd
quickly appr 2 out, tld off. (10 to 1 op 6 to 1 tchd 12 to 1) 9

221

1452[8] PALLADIUM BOY 6-11-0 G Upton, *in tch till wknd 4th, tld off whn pld up bef 2 out*. ....(50 to 1 op 20 to 1) pu
1100 LILLY THE FILLY 5-10-9 P Hide, *al beh, tld off whn pld up bef 2 out*. ....(200 to 1 op 33 to 1) pu
1598 FAIR HAUL 5-11-0 Mr A Holdsworth, *trkd ldr to 4th, wknd nxt, pld up bef 2 out*. ....(200 to 1 op 50 to 1) pu
Dist: 23l, 4l, 2l, 3l, 4l, dist, ¾l, 6l. 4m 24.10s. a 25.10s (12 Ran).
SR: 33/10/6/4/1/-/ (Lord Chelsea), Miss H C Knight

1728 Bonusprint Handicap Hurdle Class F (0-105 4-y-o and up) £2,174 2¼m .... (3:20)

1625[4] DOMINION'S DREAM [98] (v) 4-11-0 (7*) G Supple, *led till bef 3rd, led before last, styd on*. .... (14 to 1 op 10 to 1 tchd 16 to 1) 1
1546* JEFFERIES [98] 7-11-7 G Upton, *hld up, hdwy 3rd, not pace to chal frm 2 out*. .... (6 to 5 fav op 2 to 1 tchd 9 to 4 and 11 to 10) 2
1291[4] EMBLEY BUOY [77] 8-10-0 S Curran, *trkd ldr, led bef 3rd till before last, wknd*...... (14 to 1 op 12 to 1 tchd 16 to 1) 3
1417* HANDCON [00] 4-10-0 (5*) D [illegible] *frm 3 out*. ....(4 to 1 op 3 to 1 tchd 9 to 2) 4
1603[2] BEYOND OUR REACH [100] 8-11-6 (3*) T Dascombe, *al rear*. ....(7 to 1 op 5 to 1) 5
1443* BARRYBEN [99] 7-11-5 (3*) R Massey, *chsd ldrs till wknd 5th*. ....(6 to 1 op 4 to 1 tchd 7 to 1) 6
FONTAINEROUGE (Ire) [85] 6-10-8 A P McCoy, *mstk 1st, al beh*. ....(7 to 1 op 4 to 1) 7
1474 INDIAN TEMPLE [77] 5-10-0 R Greene, *al beh*. ....(50 to 1 op 25 to 1) 8
FIRST CENTURY (Ire) [102] 7-11-11 R Dunwoody, *in tch till wknd 3 out, tld off*. ....(20 to 1 op 10 to 1) 9
CLASSIC PAL (USA) [79] 5-10-2[1] D Skyrme, *al beh, tld off whn pld up bef 2 out*...(25 to 1 op 16 to 1 tchd 33 to 1) pu
Dist: 2l, 2l, 3l, 2½l, 11l, 4l, hd, dist. 4m 27.40s. a 28.40s (10 Ran).
SR: 7/5/-/-/-/-/ (Martin Pipe Racing Club), M C Pipe

HEREFORD (good to soft)
Friday December 6th
Going Correction: PLUS 0.85 sec. per fur. (races 1,3,5,7), PLUS 0.95 (2,4,6)

1729 Widemarsh Novices' Hurdle Class E (4-y-o and up) £2,542 2m 3f 110yds .... (12:40)

1350* BOOTS MADDEN (Ire) 6-10-12 N Williamson, *hld up, hdwy 6th, led appr 2 out, drvn out*. ....(2 to 1 jt-fav op 11 to 10 tchd 9 to 4) 1
SUPREME FLYER (Ire) 6-10-12 C O'Dwyer, *hld up, prog 7th, ev ch frm 3 out, unbl to quicken r-in*.... (10 to 1 op 7 to 1) 2
BALLESWHIDDEN 4-10-12 I Lawrence, *towards rear, improved 6th, ev ch 3 out, wknd nxt*. .... (9 to 1 op 12 to 1 tchd 8 to 1) 3
1344[5] WARNER FOR PLAYERS (Ire) 5-10-12 B Powell, *trkd ldrs, lost pl 7th, styd on ag'n frm 2 out*..... (2 to 1 jt-fav op 2 to 1) 4
1540[5] BURNTWOOD MELODY 5-10-12 J Supple, *nvr nr to chal*. ....(33 to 1) 5
1573 MY SHENANDOAH (Ire) 5-10-12 V Slattery, *nvr nr to chal*. .... (50 to 1 op 33 to 1) 6
1039[4] OLD CAVALIER 5-10-12 M A Fitzgerald, *hld up in tch, led 4 out till appr 2 out, sn wknd*. .... (9 to 1 op 5 to 1 tchd 10 to 1) 7
1545[7] MEDFORD 6-10-12 (7*) J Power, *prmnt, chsd ldr frm 5th, led appr 7th, hdd 4 out, sn fdd*. ....(20 to 1 op 14 to 1) 8
1502[9] THE BREWER 4-10-12 S McNeill, *mid-div, lost pl 7th, no dngr aftr*. ....(50 to 1 op 33 to 1) 9
MADAM MUCK 5-10-7 T Jenks, *beh frm 7th*. .... (10 to 1 op 7 to 1) 10
1591[4] NUNSON 7-10-9 (3*) Mr C Bonner, *al beh, tld off*. ....(50 to 1 op 33 to 1) 11
ACHILL PRINCE (Ire) 5-10-12 W McFarland, *led, sn clr, hdd appr 7th, beh whn blun nxt, tld off*. ....(50 to 1) 12
CHILI HEIGHTS 6-10-12 D Bridgwater, *al beh, tld off whn pld up bef 3 out*. ....(25 to 1 op 16 to 1) pu
1573 FILCH (bl) 5-10-7 R Farrant, *chsd ldr to 5th, sn beh, tld off whn pld up bef 3 out*. ....(66 to 1 op 50 to 1) pu
1344 MR MOTIVATOR 6-10-12 D Leahy, *nvr on terms, tld off whn pld up bef 3 out*. .... (100 to 1) pu
ALTHREY GALE (Ire) 5-10-12 S Wynne, *not fluent, al beh, tld off whn pld up bef 3 out*. ....(100 to 1) pu
Dist: 2½l, 17l, 6l, 3l, ½l, nk, 13l, 3½l, 5l, 26l. 4m 47.70s. a 29.70s (16 Ran).
(L J A Phipps), Miss Venetia Williams

1730 Sidney Phillips For Pubs Handicap Chase Class E (0-110 5-y-o and up) £3,087 2m 3f................ (1:10)

1595[6] SISTER ROSZA (Ire) [96] 8-11-3 R Farrant, *wtd wth, improved 9th, kpt on und pres to ld last 75 yards*. (33 to 1 op 14 to 1) 1
1595[3] FICHU (USA) [79] 8-10-0 M Richards, *hld up beh ldrs, led appr 9th, rdn, hdd and no extr last 75 yards*. ....(4 to 1 op 5 to 2) 2
1595[2] LASATA [107] 11-12-0 D Morris, *patiently rdn, improved 9th, chsd ldr frm nxt, ev ch whn blun 3 out, hit next sn btn*. ....(3 to 1 jt-fav op 2 to 1) 3
1414[5] MONKS JAY (Ire) [91] 7-10-12 I Lawrence, *hld up, hdwy 9th, wknd appr 4 out*. ....(3 to 1 jt-fav op 9 to 4) 4
WINSPIT (Ire) [86] 6-10-4 (3*) P Henley, *hld up, hit 7th, prog 9th, 4th and in tch whn blun and uns rdr four out*. ....(9 to 2 op 3 to 1) ur
STAR OF ITALY [86] 9-10-7 L Harvey, *chsd ldr to 8th, beh tenth, tld off whn pld up bef 3 out*. ....(10 to 1 op 12 to 1 tchd 14 to 1) pu
OVER THE POLE [107] 9-11-11 (3*) Mr C Bonner, *jmpd lft, led till appr 9th, wkng whn blun nxt, tld off when pld up bef 3 out*. .... (9 to 1 op 10 to 1 tchd 12 to 1) pu
Dist: 1l, 14l, 18l. 4m 51.70s. a 26.70s (7 Ran).
SR: 2/-/-/-/ (P Lamyman), Mrs S Lamyman

1731 Pencoed Selling Hurdle Class G (4 - 7-y-o) £2,108 2m 1f.............(1:40)

1541* HARRY 6-11-5 D J Burchell, *keen hold, hld up, hdwy hfwy, led appr 2 out, sn clr, hrd held*. .... (11 to 10 fav op 5 to 4 tchd 6 to 4 and 7 to 4) 1
1135[6] LIME STREET BLUES (Ire) (bl) 5-10-12 G Bradley, *led to 4th, one pace frm 2 out*. ....(13 to 2 op 11 to 2) 2
PROUD IMAGE 4-10-12 B Clifford, *in tch, rdn and one pace appr 2 out*. ....(10 to 1 op 4 to 1) 3
COMEONUP 5-10-12 N Williamson, *beh, hdwy appr 5th, wknd approaching 2 out*. ....(25 to 1 op 20 to 1) 4
1574[8] STRIKE-A-POSE 6-11-0 Mr J L Llewellyn, *prmnt, led 4th till appr 2 out, sn wknd*. ....(14 to 1 op 10 to 1) 5
1397 DARING RYDE 5-10-12 A Thornton, *hld up, hmpd 5th, hdwy nxt, wknd appr 2 out*. ....(50 to 1 op 33 to 1) 6
1320[4] QUICK DECISION (Ire) 5-10-5 (7*) N T Egan, *mid-div, rdn appr 5th, wknd bef 3 out*. ....(33 to 1 op 20 to 1) 7
SMILEY FACE 4-10-12 P Holley, *hld up, hmpd 5th, rdn nxt, sn wknd*. ....(33 to 1 op 14 to 1) 8
1293 MONTY 4-10-9 (3*) P Henley, *keen hold, chsd ldrs to 5th, sn beh*. ....(50 to 1) 9
GLEN GARNOCK (Ire) 4-10-12 Gary Lyons, *nvr on terms*. ....(33 to 1 op 12 to 1) 10
921[9] BALLYHAYS (Ire) 7-10-12 R Farrant, *strted slwly, f 1st*. .... (50 to 1 op 33 to 1) f
1598[6] OFFICE HOURS 4-10-12 W McFarland, *prmnt till f 5th*. .... (8 to 1 tchd 10 to 1 and 12 to 1) f
AUDREY GRACE 5-10-7 D Bridgwater, *al beh, tld off whn blun 2 out, pld up bef nxt*. ....(7 to 1 op 4 to 1) pu
1476[9] TOMORROWS HARVEST 4-10-7 I Lawrence, *hdwy hfwy, wknd 6th tld off whn pld up bef last*.... (33 to 1 op 25 to 1) pu
Dist: 6l, 5l, 11l, 2½l, 1¼l, 4l, 2l, 9l, 2½l. 4m 10.40s. a 25.40s (14 Ran).
(Simon T Lewis), D Burchell

1732 Bet With The Tote Novices' Chase Qualifier Class E (5-y-o and up) £3,243 2m 3f................ (2:10)

1312* MARINERS MIRROR 9-11-0 Mr M Rimell, *bumped strt, hld up, hdwy 6th, led aftr 2 out, sn clr*..... (11 to 4 op 4 to 1) 1
1478[3] FEEL THE POWER (Ire) 8-10-12 C O'Dwyer, *hld up, hdwy 5th, led 4 out, hit and hdd nxt, hmpd and lft in ld briefly 2 out, sn btn*. ....(Evens fav op 11 to 10 on tchd 5 to 4) 2
1498 ZAITOON (Ire) 5-10-12 D Bridgwater, *hit 1st, wtd wth, prog 9th, effrt 3 out, sn btn*..... (8 to 1 op 4 to 1 tchd 9 to 1) 3
JOLLY BOAT 9-10-12 S Wynne, *in tch till 3 out, btn whn hit nxt*. .... (16 to 1 op 8 to 1) 4
1475[6] KNOWING 9-10-3[3] (7*) Mr A Wintle, *prmnt, pckd 4th, wknd four out*. .... (66 to 1 op 50 to 1) 5
1111 KING'S GOLD 6-10-12 M Richards, *al beh, tld off*. .... (33 to 1 op 20 to 1) 6
1573 IRISH PERRY 9-10-7 M Sharratt, *al beh, tld off*. .... (66 to 1 op 33 to 1) 7
1482[3] APPLE JOHN 7-10-9 (3*) P Henley, *wnt lft strt, f second*. ....(7 to 1 op 4 to 1 tchd 8 to 1) f
1475 WOT NO GIN 7-10-12 A Thornton, *hld up, hdwy frm 7th, led 3 out, one l clr whn f nxt*. ....(33 to 1) f
1475[4] KING'S SHILLING (USA) 9-10-12 Jacqui Oliver, *trkd ldrs, lost pl whn mstk tenth, tld off when pld up bef 3 out*. .... (50 to 1 op 20 to 1) pu
1577[7] BANKONIT (Ire) 8-10-12 I Lawrence, *al beh, tld off whn pld up bef 2 out*. ....(100 to 1 op 66 to 1) pu
ERNEST ARAGORN (v) 7-10-12 T J Murphy, *not fluent, led, sn clr, hdd and wknd 4 out, tld off whn pld up bef 2 out*. .... (100 to 1 op 66 to 1) pu
1329 HIGH HANDED (Ire) 5-10-12 B Clifford, *al beh, tld off whn pld up bef 9th*. ....(50 to 1 op 20 to 1) pu
Dist: 10l, 10l, 2½l, dist, 3l, 2½l. 4m 49.00s. a 24.00s (13 Ran).
SR: 27/15/5/2/-/-/ (F J Mills), N A Twiston-Davies

1733 Innplan Insurance Amateur Riders' Novices' Handicap Hurdle Class E (0-100 3-y-o and up) £2,486 2m 1f .... (2:40)

1497* WAYFARERS WAY (USA) [89] 5-11-5 (5*) Mr C Vigors, *hld up, hdwy appr 6th, led 3 out, easily*. ....(4 to 1 op 7 to 2 tchd 9 to 2) 1

1496[9] THE DEACONESS [70] 5-9-12 (7*) Mr O McPhail, *hld up, improved 6th, ev ch 3 out, chsd wnr frm nxt, no imprsn.* ....(25 to 1) 2

1215[6] IRISH WILDCARD (NZ) [67] 8-10-2[7] (7*) Mr N H Oliver, *wtd wth, hdwy appr 3 out, styd on fnl 2, broke blood vessel.* ....(9 to 2 op 5 to 2) 3

1474 COUNTRY MINSTREL (Ire) [78] 5-10-8 (5*) Mr J Jukes, *in tch, ev ch 3 out, sn btn*....................(20 to 1 op 16 to 1) 4

1474[2] RAVEN'S ROOST (Ire) [76] 5-10-6 (5*) Miss P Jones, *prmnt, led aftr 6th, hdd 3 out, sn btn.* ....(9 to 4 fav op 2 to 1 tchd 5 to 2) 5

1646 ALPHA LEATHER [65] 5-9-7 (7*) Mr J Grassick, *hld up, hdwy hfwy, wknd frm 3 out*.................... (50 to 1 op 33 to 1) 6

1215[4] HIGHLY CHARMING (Ire) [87] 4-11-1 (7*) Mr A Wintle, *hld up beh ldrs, led 5th till aftr nxt, wknd appr 2 out.* ....(15 to 2 op 6 to 1 tchd 8 to 1) 7

1509[5] SEGALA (Ire) [86] 5-11-0 (7*) Mr L Corcoran, *prmnt, effrt appr 3 out, wknd bef nxt*.................... (15 to 2 op 5 to 1 tchd 8 to 1) 8

1540 HONEYBED WOOD [70] 8-9-12 (7*) Mr A Brown, *al beh.* ....(20 to 1 op 25 to 1 tchd 33 to 1) 9

1527 ROYAL GLINT [70] 7-9-12 (7*) Mr P McAllister, *al beh.* ....(14 to 1 op 12 to 1) 10

ANALOGUE (Ire) [67] 4-9-9 (7*) Miss C Thomas, *prmnt, wknd frm hfwy*.................... (20 to 1 op 16 to 1) 11

1291[7] CAREY'S COTTAGE (Ire) [65] 6-9-7 (7*) Miss C Townsley, *al beh*....................(50 to 1) 12

1541[9] FOLLOW DE CALL [73] 6-10-1 (7*) Mr G Lake, *prmnt, wknd appr 5th*.................... (25 to 1 op 14 to 1) 13

1646[2] SKRAM [84] 3-10-2 (3*) Mr C Bonner, *led to 5th, sn wknd, tld off whn pld up bef last*....................(4 to 1) pu

Dist: 7l, 1l, 6l, 3½l, 4l, 13l, 1l, 4l, 19l, 10l. 4m 6.60s. a 21.60s (14 Ran).
SR: 24/-/-/-/-/ (Lady Tennant), N J Henderson

1734 Kings Caple Novices' Handicap Chase Class F (0-95 5-y-o and up) £2,866 3m 1f 110yds......... (3:10)

1302[5] CERIDWEN [74] 6-11-1 N Mann, *mid-div, hit 5th, hdwy and hmpd 3 out, lft second last, kpt on to ld r-in.* .... (20 to 1 op 16 to 1) 1

1600[5] WIXOE WONDER (Ire) [77] 6-11-4 P Holley, *hld up, hdwy tenth, lft in ld 2 out, hdd and no extr r-in*.................... (14 to 1) 2

1302 MARKET GOSSIP [63] 6-10-1 (3*) P Henley, *prmnt, effrt whn hit 3 out, kpt on same pace*....................(10 to 1 op 8 to 1) 3

1542[5] MAJORS LEGACY (Ire) [81] 7-11-8 A Thornton, *prmnt, one pace 3 out*....................(8 to 1 op 7 to 1) 4

1140[8] ABSOLATUM [62] 9-10-3 T J Murphy, *hld up, hdwy 14th, wkng whn hit 2 out*....................(33 to 1) 5

1420[4] COOL CHARACTER (Ire) [69] 8-10-10 B Powell, *in tch, blun 9th, wknd frm 15th*....................(10 to 1 tchd 8 to 1) 6

1262[4] GOLDEN DRUM (Ire) [70] 6-10-11 M A Fitzgerald, *not fluent, led to 14th, wknd 3 out*....................(16 to 1 op 14 to 1) 7

1542[4] ROBSAND (Ire) [83] 7-11-10 B Clifford, *al beh.* ....(8 to 1 op 5 to 1) 8

1413[4] BOSSYMOSS (Ire) [70] 7-10-11 Gary Lyons, *hld up, hit 4th, hdwy 15th, 2 ls second whn f last.* ....(7 to 1 op 6 to 1 tchd 8 to 1) f

RAGGED KINGDOM (Ire) [60] 7-10-1 J A McCarthy, *f 1st.* ....(33 to 1) f

1055* EXPRESS TRAVEL (Ire) [78] 8-11-5 D Morris, *hld up, hit tenth, hdwy nxt, wknd 14th, beh whn blun and uns rdr 4 out.* ....(2 to 1 fav op 4 to 1 tchd 7 to 4) ur

1312[2] COVERDALE LANE [82] 9-11-9 Mr P Murray, *beh, hdwy frm 10th, led 14th, 3 ls clr whn blun and uns rdr 2 out.* .... (16 to 1 op 14 to 1) ur

1674[3] HANGOVER [75] 10-10-13 (3*) G Hogan, *hld up beh ldrs, rdn 14th, sn wknd, tld off whn pld up bef 2 out.* ....(8 to 1 tchd 10 to 1) pu

BATHWICK BOBBIE [81] 9-11-8 S McNeill, *hit 8th, beh frm tenth, tld off whn pld up bef 4 out*.....(16 to 1 op 12 to 1) pu

1494[6] CONEY ROAD [75] 7-11-2 G Bradley, *beh frm 11th, tld off whn pld up bef 14th*....................(7 to 1 op 5 to 1) pu

Dist: 2l, 1¼l, ¾l, 7l, dist, 11l, 27l. 6m 39.80s. a 33.80s (15 Ran).
(Mrs S Greathead), T R Greathead

1735 Shepherds Meadow Standard Open National Hunt Flat Class H (4,5,6-y-o) £1,496 2m 1f............(3:40)

1456[5] DOM BELTRANO (Fr) 4-10-11 (7*) L Suthern, *prmnt, led 4 fs out, hdd 3 out, rgned ld appr last, pushed clr.* ....(6 to 1 op 5 to 1) 1

SUNDAY VENTURE (NZ) 4-11-4 M A Fitzgerald, *hld up, smooth prog appr hfwy, led 3 fs out, hdd approaching last, no extr*....................(5 to 2 fav op 9 to 4 tchd 3 to 1) 2

BOZO (Ire) 5-10-11 (7*) M Griffiths, *whipped round strt, beh, hdwy frm hfwy, styd on fnl 2 fs*.................... (50 to 1 op 25 to 1) 3

1292[9] KNIGHT'S CREST (Ire) 6-11-4 B Powell, *in tch, rdn and styd on same pace fnl 3 fs*....................(16 to 1 op 10 to 1) 4

JUST BAYARD (Ire) 4-11-4 I Lawrence, *hld up, hdwy 8 fs out, wknd 3 out*....................(50 to 1 op 20 to 1) 5

CROCKNAMOHILL (Ire) 5-11-4 D Bridgwater, *hdwy hfwy, wknd 3 fs out*.................... (16 to 1 op 12 to 1) 6

JACK (Ire) 4-11-4 S McNeill, *nvr nr to chal*....................(33 to 1) 7

JUST ONE QUESTION (Ire) 6-11-11 N Williamson, *prmnt, led hfwy till 4 fs out, sn wknd*....................(7 to 2 op 5 to 2) 8

1292[5] AZTEC WARRIOR 5-11-4 C O'Dwyer, *hld up beh ldrs, rdn 6 fs out, wknd 4 out*....................(4 to 1 op 3 to 1 tchd 9 to 2) 9

CAMP HEAD (Ire) 5-11-4 J A McCarthy, *mid-div, wknd 5 fs out*....................(5 to 1 op 4 to 1 tchd 11 to 2) 10

1240 MURRAY'S MILLION 4-11-4 T J Murphy, *prmnt, wknd 7 fs out*....................(33 to 1 op 20 to 1) 11

COOL HARRY (USA) 5-10-11 (7*) Mr A Wintle, *al beh.* .... (50 to 1 op 20 to 1) 12

ONE MORE RUPEE 5-11-4 J R Kavanagh, *al beh.* .... (50 to 1 op 20 to 1) 13

SURPRISE CITY 5-11-4 A Thornton, *al beh, tld off.* ....(33 to 1 op 14 to 1) 14

1590 MAGSLASS 4-10-13 G Bradley, *led to hfwy, wknd o'r 6 fs out, tld off*.................... (33 to 1) 15

Dist: 3½l, ¾l, ¾l, 17l, 2½l, ½l, 1¼l, 4l, 17l, 9l. 4m 2.20s. (15 Ran).
(Carl Wright), N A Twiston-Davies

MARKET RASEN (good)
Friday December 6th
Going Correction: PLUS 1.45 sec. per fur.

1736 Bob Kett Conditional Jockeys' Selling Handicap Hurdle Class G (0-95 4-y-o and up) £1,947 2m 3f 110yds .... (12:30)

1044[2] GLENVALLY [81] 5-11-8 E Callaghan, *settled in tch, drvn alng hfwy, rallied to ld aftr 3 out, styd on strly to go clr betw last 2.* ....(11 to 4 fav op 5 to 2 tchd 3 to 1) 1

WEATHER ALERT (Ire) [75] 5-10-13 (3*) M Newton, *ran in snatches, led briefly hfwy, rdn alng aftr 3 out, styd on und pres frm betw last 2*....................(8 to 1 op 7 to 1) 2

836[2] PARISH WALK (Ire) [78] 5-11-2 (3*) B Grattan, *al wl plcd, led 4th, clr 6th, hdd aftr 3 out, rdn and one pace frm betw last 2.* ....(9 to 2 tchd 5 to 1) 3

1567[9] THARSIS [67] 11-10-8 S Taylor, *led till hdd 4th, lost pl und pres hfwy, styd on ag'n frm 2 out, no imprsn*.................... (16 to 1) 4

1588[6] IN A MOMENT (USA) [73] 5-11-0 F Leahy, *niggled alng to keep up bef hfwy, effrt und pres appr 3 out, one pace frm nxt.* ....(4 to 1 op 7 to 2 tchd 9 to 2) 5

1313[4] HAUGHTON LAD (Ire) [72] 7-10-13 P Midgley, *reminders to keep up hfwy, struggling frm 4 out, sn lost tch.* .... (11 to 2 op 9 to 2) 6

1066 CAPTAIN TANDY (Ire) [83] 7-11-10 D J Kavanagh, *reluctant to race, jnd ldrs bef hfwy, led aftr 5th, clr nxt, hdd after 3 out, sn lost tch, tld off*....................(16 to 1 op 14 to 1) 7

STREPHON (Ire) [68] 6-10-9 K Gaule, *trkd ldrs, lost pl quickly frm hfwy, tld off from 3 out*....................(16 to 1 tchd 20 to 1) 8

1372[8] TROY'S DREAM [74] 5-10-10 (5*) R Burns, *chsd ldrs to hfwy, sn struggling, tld off whn pld up betw last 2.* ....(14 to 1 op 8 to 1 tchd 16 to 1) pu

TOUGH CHARACTER (Ire) [59] 8-10-0 D Parker, *sddl slpd 3rd, lost tch quickly and pld up bef nxt*....................(25 to 1) pu

Dist: 4l, 3l, 4l, 2l, 2½l, 27l, dist. 5m 14.80s. a 44.80s (10 Ran).
(Mrs M Lingwood), B W Murray

1737 Constant Security Juvenile Novices' Hurdle Class E (3-y-o) £2,758 2m 1f 110yds...................... (1:00)

664[7] NO MORE HASSLE (Ire) 10-12 P Niven, *wtd wth, improved to ld bef 3 out, blun and hdd nxt, rallied to rgn lead r-in.* ....(6 to 1 op 5 to 1) 1

1398[4] SIX CLERKS (Ire) 10-9 (3*) F Leahy, *nvr far away, chalg whn lft in ld 2 out, rdn last, hdd and one pace r-in.* ....(7 to 1 op 5 to 1) 2

PARROT'S HILL (Ire) 10-12 A Dobbin, *tucked away in mid-field, improved frm 3 out, rdn and kpt on same pace from three out*....................(12 to 1 op 8 to 1) 3

1249[6] BAASM 10-12 W Fry, *tucked away in midfield, took clr order 3 out, rdn and one pace frm nxt*.................... (16 to 1 op 12 to 1) 4

1398[6] KINGFISHER BRAVE 10-12 Derek Byrne, *co'red up in mid-field, effrt appr 3 out, rdn and no imprsn frm nxt.* .... (16 to 1 op 14 to 1) 5

1398[2] BELMARITA (Ire) 10-4 (3*) K Gaule, *led till hdd 3rd, lft in ld bef nxt, headed aftr 3 out, rdn and wknd next.* ....(11 to 8 fav op 5 to 4 tchd 13 to 8) 6

ARABIAN HEIGHTS 10-12 T Eley, *patiently rdn, improved on outsd bef 3 out, ridden and no imprsn frm nxt.* .... (16 to 1 op 14 to 1) 7

1398 PONTEVEDRA (Ire) 10-7 A S Smith, *pressed ldrs to hfwy, struggling bef 3 out, sn lost tch*.................... (20 to 1 op 12 to 1) 8

MR GOLD (Ire) 10-5 (7*) M Newton, *patiently rdn, took clr order 3 out, ridden and btn bef nxt*.... (20 to 1 op 14 to 1) 9

1249 EXTREMELY FRIENDLY 10-12 V Smith, *chsd ldrs till aftr 4 out, struggling frm nxt, sn btn*....................(10 to 1 op 14 to 1) 10

GENUINE JOHN (Ire) 10-9 (3*) P Midgley, *bustled alng to keep up bef hfwy, nvr rchd chalg pos .* .... (9 to 1 op 10 to 1 tchd 8 to 1) 11

1524[5] PROPOLIS POWER (Ire) 10-12 J Callaghan, *slow to strt, al struggling and beh*....................(25 to 1 op 20 to 1) 12

SHOJA 10-12 P McLoughlin, *sn beh, tld off bef 3 out.* ....(33 to 1 op 20 to 1) 13

1524 PHANTOM DANCER (Ire) (bl) 10-12 D Parker, *struggling and lost tch frm hfwy, tld off.* (20 to 1 op 16 to 1 tchd 25 to 1) 14

SOCIETY MAGIC (USA) 10-12 J Railton, *chasing ldrs whn slpd and uns rdr bend aftr 3rd*..........(9 to 1 op 8 to 1) ur
1398 CLASSIC DAISY 10-7 C Maude, *struggling to keep up whn pld up aftr 4th*....................................(33 to 1) pu
1629⁷ NORTHERN FALCON (bl) 10-7 R Garritty, *wth ldrs till checked bend and lost pl bend appr 4th, tld off whn pld up bef 2 out.*
....(12 to 1 op 8 to 1) pu

Dist: 2½sl, 8l, 3½sl, 1¾sl, 4l, 1l, ½sl, 5l, 3½sl, 18l. 4m 33.30s. a 32.30s (17 Ran).

SR: 15/12/4/-/-/-/ (The No Hassle Partnership), Mrs M Reveley

1738
Calderprint 'National Hunt' Novices' Hurdle Class D (4-y-o and up) £3,115 2m 1f 110yds.................(1:30)

1514* GOOD VIBES 4-10-12 R Garritty, *wth ldr, led 4 out, styaed on strly to go clr last 2, eased finish.*
................................(11 to 4 op 7 to 4 tchd 3 to 1) 1
ALZULU (Ire) 5-10-12 P Niven, *nvr far away, ev ch and bustled alng aftr 3 out, no imprsn on wnr last 2.*
................(13 to 8 on op 6 to 4 on tchd 5 to 4 on) 2
1369 SEPTEMBER BREEZE (Ire) 5-10-7 A S Smith, *tried to make all, hdd 4 out, drvn alng frm nxt, one pace from betw last 2.*
................................(25 to 1 op 16 to 1) 3
1540 DARK PHOENIX (Ire) 6-10-7 M Brennan, *chsd alng to keep up hfwy, feeling pace appr 3 out, nvr able to rch chalg pos.*
................................(10 to 1 op 14 to 1 tchd 16 to 1) 4
1252⁸ FERRERS 5-10-12 R Marley, *tucked away on ins, hrd at work whn ldrs quickened frm 3 out, fnshd tired.*
................................(14 to 1 op 7 to 1) 5
MINSTER BOY 5-10-12 A Dobbin, *last and struggling hfwy, tld off frm 3 out.*....................(25 to 1 op 20 to 1) 6
1483 JACKHO 4-10-7 (5*) S Taylor, *struggling to keep up thrght, tld off frm 3 out.*...................(66 to 1 op 50 to 1) 7
1367⁵ ERNEST WILLIAM (Ire) 4-10-9 (3*) K Gaule, *settled midfield, improved und pres 3 out, wknd quickly and eased bef nxt, tld off.*............(25 to 1 op 16 to 1 tchd 33 to 1) 8
1317 KARENA'S PRINCE 4-10-12 Richard Guest, *co'red up in midfield, struggling hfwy, tld off...* (33 to 1 op 25 to 1) 9
DOUGAL 5-10-12 R Supple, *co'red up on ins, struggling aftr 4 out, tld off whn pld up bef 2 out......* (50 to 1 op 33 to 1) pu

Dist: 9l, 1l, 23l, 8l, 17l, 13l, ¾l, dist. 4m 34.30s. a 31.00s (10 Ran).

SR: 29/20/14/-/-/-/ (G E Shouler), T D Easterby

1739
Alexandra Motors Handicap Chase Class E (0-110 5-y-o and up) £3,413 3½m 110yds.................(2:00)

1328* IVY HOUSE (Ire) [99] 8-10-12 (5*) R McGrath, *settled off the pace, blun 13th, improved 4 out, chalg whn lft in ld 3 out, styd on r-in.*........................(9 to 1 op 14 to 1 tchd 11 to 1) 1
1445* WOODLANDS BOY (Ire) [100] 8-11-1 (3*) F Leahy, *co'red up beh ldrs, effrt and drvn alng appr 3 out, styd on one pace und pres frm betw last 2.*.............(10 to 1 tchd 11 to 1) 2
1253⁴ SPARROW HALL [92] 9-10-10 P Niven, *nvr far away, jmpd ahead 7 out, hdd appr 4 out, rdn frm nxt, one pace.*
................................(14 to 1 op 8 to 1) 3
1366³ CELTIC SILVER [93] 8-10-11 Richard Guest, *settled to track ldrs, blun and lost pl 14th (water), rallied 6 out, rdn and one pace last 3.*.............(15 to 2 op 6 to 1 tchd 8 to 1) 4
1314⁴ PENNINE PRIDE [93] 9-10-11 R Garritty, *tucked away beh ldrs, feeling pace and drvn alng aftr 4 out, no imprsn frm nxt.*........................(15 to 2 op 6 to 1 tchd 8 to 1) 5
1021* SPROWSTON BOY [82] 13-10-0 W Worthington, *on chasing ldrs, feeling pace and rdn 7 out, lost tch frm 4 out, tld off.*........................(16 to 1 op 12 to 1) 6
1334⁵ COOL WEATHER (Ire) [82] (bl) 8-10-0 A S Smith, *patiently rdn, smooth hdwy to ld bef 4 out, strly chlgd whn f 3 out.*
................................(25 to 1 op 20 to 1) f
1328⁵ SCRABO VIEW (Ire) [95] (bl) 8-10-13 R Supple, *slpd, blun and uns rdr second.*........................(20 to 1) ur
1314³ HOLY STING (Ire) [95] (bl) 7-10-13 C Maude, *tracking ldrs whn hmpd and brght dwn paddock bend aftr 6th.*
................................(4 to 1 op 3 to 1) bd
1567⁷ ARRANGE A GAME [82] 9-9-9 (5*) S Taylor, *reluctant to race, tld off whn refused 4 out.*........(50 to 1 op 33 to 1) ref
1314 HOWCLEUCH [103] 9-11-7 B Storey, *chsd ldrs till pld up bef tenth.*................(16 to 1 op 14 to 1 tchd 20 to 1) pu
1253* GRIFFINS BAR [85] 8-10-13 R Marley, *led till hdd 7 out, lost tch quickly, tld off whn pld up bef 3 out....*(10 to 1 op 8 to 1) pu

Dist: 5l, 3l, 3l, 5l, 22l. 7m 54.30s. a 55.30s (12 Ran).

(Mrs L R Joughin), J J O'Neill

1740
Clugston Handicap Hurdle Class D (0-120 4-y-o and up) £2,945 2m 1f 110yds.....................(2:30)

1141⁵ CENTAUR EXPRESS [113] 4-11-12 T Eley, *made all, hrd pressed frm 2 out, styd on gmely r-in.*
................................(5 to 4 on op Evens tchd 11 to 10) 1
1546³ SHERS DELIGHT (Ire) [87] 6-10-0 M Brennan, *settled to track ldrs, improved to draw level 2 out, blun last, rdn and not quicken r-in.*...................(7 to 1 op 6 to 1) 2
1606⁴ COLORFUL AMBITION [106] 6-11-5 J Railton, *settled off the pace, improved hfwy, effrt and bustled alng aftr 3 out, not pace of ldg pair.*................(5 to 1 op 7 to 2) 3

1465⁶ INNOCENT GEORGE [93] 7-10-6 R Supple, *nvr far away, feeling pace and lost grnd aftr 3 out, no imprsn after.*
................................(10 to 1 op 8 to 1 tchd 11 to 1) 4
1370⁷ MERILENA (Ire) [87] 6-9-13⁶ (7*) N Rossiter, *settled to track ldrs, reminders hfwy, lost tch frm 3 out, tld off.*
................................(20 to 1 op 14 to 1) 5
NEW INN [115] 5-11-11 (3*) K Gaule, *tucked away beh ldrs, effrt hfwy, lost tch frm 3 out, tld off......*(7 to 1 op 5 to 1) 6
FRED'S DELIGHT (Ire) [87] 5-10-0 P McLoughlin, *struggling to keep up bef hfwy, sn lost tch, tld off.*
................................(40 to 1 op 33 to 1 tchd 50 to 1) 7

Dist: 2l, 18l, 2½sl, nk, 1¼l, dist. 4m 34.20s. a 33.20s (7 Ran).

SR: 22/-/-/-/ (Centaur Racing), A Streeter

1741
U.K. Hygiene Novices' Chase Class E (5-y-o and up) £3,299 2m 1f 110yds.............................(3:00)

1568* MISTER DRUM (Ire) 7-11-5 R Supple, *jmpd rght thrght, made all, rdn and styd on strly to go clr r-in.*
................................(Evens fav op 5 to 4 tchd 6 to 4) 1
1627⁵ BOLD BOSS 7-10-12 B Storey, *patiently rdn, improved frm hfwy, str chal from 3 out, ridden and outpcd from last.*
................................(9 to 1 op 6 to 1) 2
1587 GOLDEN HELLO 5-11-5 P Niven, *settled off the pace, pushed alng to improve frm 4 out, effrt whn hmpd by faller nxt, not quicken und pres....................*(9 to 2 op 3 to 1) 3
1587 FENWICK'S BROTHER 6-10-5 (7*) R Wilkinson, *settled off the pace, outpcd hfwy, styd on frm 3 out, nvr able to rch chalg pos.*................(40 to 1 op 33 to 1 tchd 50 to 1) 4
1587 FAIR ALLY 6-10-12 D Parker, *settled in midfield, feeling pace whn jmpd rght 6 out, sn lost tch, tld off.*
................................(25 to 1 op 20 to 1 tchd 33 to 1) 5
1225⁴ THURSDAY NIGHT (Ire) 5-10-12 A Dobbin, *nvr far away, str chal frm 4 out, disputing second and und pres whn f 3 out.*
................................(50 to 1 op 33 to 1) f
1523 CARDINAL SINNER (Ire) 7-10-12 A S Smith, *wth ldrs till lost tch quickly 6th (water), tld off whn pld up bef six out.*
................................(50 to 1 op 33 to 1) pu
1523 JACK DOYLE (Ire) 5-10-12 Richard Guest, *wl plcd till lost grnd quickly bef 4 out, tld off whn pld up before 3 out.*
................................(9 to 2 op 9 to 1) pu
1587² UK HYGIENE (Ire) 12-10-12 R Garritty, *chsd ldrs till lost tch quickly bef 4 out, tld off whn pld up appr nxt.*
................................(11 to 1 op 8 to 1 tchd 12 to 1) pu

Dist: 9l, 1l, 11l. 4m 44.60s. a 30.60s (9 Ran).

SR: 38/22/28/8/-/-/ (Malcolm Batchelor), M J Wilkinson

1742
'Christmas Is Coming' Intermediate Claiming National Hunt Flat Class H (4,5,6-y-o) £1,217 2m 1f 110yds.............................(3:30)

THE LADY CAPTAIN 4-10-1 (3*) K Gaule, *settled gng wl, led on bit 3 fs out, drvn alng appr fnl furlong, styd on.*
................................(8 to 1 op 7 to 1) 1
1456⁷ SPRIG MUSLIN (v) 4-10-1 (5*) Sophie Mitchell, *tried to make all, hdd 3 fs out, rallied appr last, no extr approaching finish.*................(11 to 2 op 7 to 2 tchd 6 to 1) 2
1324* POPPY'S DREAM 9-10-7 (5*) Mr R Thornton, *settled to track ldrs, struggling in grnd hfwy, rallied and ev ch 3 fs out, wndrd, one pace fnl furlong................*(6 to 4 fav tchd 5 to 2) 3
PUSH ON POLLY (Ire) 6-10-7 (3*) P Midgley, *wtd wth, effrt aftr a m, feeling pace bef strt, nvr rchd chalg pos.*
................................(10 to 1 tchd 12 to 1) 4
GAME DRIVE (Ire) 4-10-8 (3*) E Callaghan, *nvr far away, und pres whn ldrs quickened bef strt, sn rdn and btn.*
................................(4 to 1 tchd 9 to 2) 5
1390⁶ AIR BRIDGE 4-11-0 (5*) D J Kavanagh, *al tracking ldrs, struggling to hold pl bef strt, lost tch, tld off.*
................................(9 to 2 op 8 to 1 tchd 4 to 1) 6
1390 MOVISA 6-9-9 (5*) S Taylor, *settled beh ldg bunch, struggling aftr a m, lost tch, tld off.......................*(20 to 1) 7
1050⁵ PHAR ENOUGH (Ire) 4-11-6 (3*) F Leahy, *rcd keenly on heels of ldrs for o'r a m, sn lost tch, tld off.*
................................(11 to 2 op 5 to 1 tchd 6 to 1) 8
DONT TELL MARIE 6-9-12⁵ (7*) T J Comerford, *al wl beh, tld off aftr a m.......................................*(14 to 1) 9

Dist: 3l, 1¾l, 17l, 5l, 12l, 26l, 1¼l, dist. 4m 37.70s. (9 Ran).

(D T Thom), D T Thom

CHEPSTOW (soft (races 1,2,5,7), good to soft (3,4,6))
Saturday December 7th
Going Correction: PLUS 1.20 sec. per fur. (races 1,2,5,7), PLUS 0.75 (3,4,6)

1743
December Maiden Hurdle Class D (Div I) (4-y-o and up) £2,693 2m 110yds.....................(12:45)

1338⁵ TOMPETOO (Ire) 5-11-5 C Maude, *trkd ldr till led 3rd, pushed alng 5th, styd on to go clr frm 2 out.....*(5 to 2 op 5 to 2) 1

THREE FARTHINGS 6-11-5 G Upton, *in tch, hdwy to track wnr appr 5th, shaken up aftr 3 out, wknd nxt.*
.....................(9 to 4 fav op 2 to 1 tchd 5 to 2) 2
DANNICUS 5-11-5 V Slattery, *in tch, rdn alng and lost pos aftr 4th, styd on one pace und pres frm 3 out.*
.....................(13 to 2 op 11 to 2 tchd 7 to 1) 3
1449³ MULLINTOR (Ire) 5-11-5 D O'Sullivan, *beh, moderate hdwy appr 5th, sn one pace.*.............. (10 to 1 op 11 to 2) 4
REIMEI 7-11-5 A P McCoy, *mstk 1st, styd chasing ldrs till wknd 3 out, btn whn blun nxt.*
.....................(10 to 1 op 2 to 1 tchd 7 to 1) 5
1410⁸ KUMARI KING (Ire) 6-11-5 W Marston, *in tch till rdn aftr 4th, sn wknd.*.....................(66 to 1 op 20 to 1) 6
STEVIE'S WONDER (Ire) 6-11-5 Mr J L Llewellyn, *keen hold, led to 3rd, wknd aftr 4th.*...........(33 to 1 op 20 to 1) 7
KEVASINGO 4-11-5 D Bridgwater, *prmnt, hit 3rd, chsd ldrs appr 5th, sn wknd.*.................(33 to 1 op 16 to 1) 8
SOUTHERNHAY BOY 5-11-5 S McNeill, *chsd ldrs, rdn and wknd aftr 4th.*.........(11 to 1 op 10 to 1 tchd 14 to 1) 9
Dist: 10l, 9l, 20l, 11l, 22l, 1¼l, hd, ¾l. 4m 15.40s. a 28.40s (9 Ran).
SR: 5/-/-/-/-/-/ (Tom Pettifer Ltd), N A Twiston-Davies

1744 Timber Toppers Handicap Hurdle Class B (0-140 4-y-o and up) £4,935 2½m 110yds. .... (1:15)

1612⁴ CADOUGOLD (Fr) [123] 5-10-13 A P McCoy, *hld up and al gng wl, hdwy 6th, trkd ldr aftr 7th till led on bit 2 out, very easily.*...................(4 to 1 op 7 to 2 tchd 9 to 2) 1
1454ª SPARKLING YASMIN [125] 4-10-10 (5ª) D J Kavanagh, *led, not fluent 6th and 7th, rdn 3 out, hdd nxt, kpt on und pres but no ch wth wnr.*...............(7 to 2 op 5 to 2 tchd 4 to 1) 2
1558³ NICK THE BEAK (Ire) [110] 7-9-7 (7ª) G Supple, *in tch, hdwy to chase ldrs aftr 7th, styd on und pres frm 2 out.*
.....................(9 to 1 op 6 to 1 tchd 10 to 1) 3
1441⁵ FOURTH IN LINE [128] 8-11-4 W Marston, *mstk 1st, hdwy 6th, styd chasing ldrs till wknd 3 out.... (16 to 1 op 7 to 1) 4
1268 MEDITATOR [117] 12-10-7 S McNeill, *prmnt till lost pl 6th, rdn alng and rallied aftr 7th, wknd nxt...* (33 to 1 op 20 to 1) 5
1441⁸ KINGDOM OF SHADES (USA) [124] 6-11-0 C Maude, *hld up in tch, rdn and wknd rpdly aftr 7th, broke blood vessel.*
.....................(11 to 8 fav op 7 to 4) 6
1561⁴ BLAZER MORINIERE (Fr) [138] 7-12-0 S Fox, *prmnt till wknd quickly aftr 7th.*...................(100 to 1 op 33 to 1) 7
1576 LITTLE GUNNER [118] 6-10-8 D Bridgwater, *al beh, lost tch frm 6th.*...............(11 to 1 op 8 to 1 tchd 12 to 1) 8
Dist: 3l, 2l, 23l, 9l, 23l, 22l, 29l. 5m 6.90s. a 28.90s (8 Ran).
SR: 42/41/24/19/-/-/ (D A Johnson), M C Pipe

1745 Jack Brown Bookmaker Handicap Chase Class B (0-140 5-y-o and up) £7,126 3¼m 110yds. .... (1:45)

1645 SAMLEE (Ire) [110] 7-10-4 D Bridgwater, *beh till hdwy and mstk 12th,styd on ag'n frm 17th, chlgd nxt, led 4 out, drvn out r-in.*...................(20 to 1 op 8 to 1 tchd 12 to 1) 1
DAKYNS BOY [122] 11-11-2 C Maude, *trkd ldrs till lost pl 15th, rallied gmely und pres frm 3 out to take second place cl hme.*...................(20 to 1 op 14 to 1) 2
FULL OF OATS [119] 10-10-10 (3ª) D Fortt, *hld up in rear, styd on frm 3 out, no imprsn r-in.*...........(7 to 1 op 6 to 1) 3
1418ª TIME ENOUGH (Ire) [111] 7-10-5 S McNeill, *led, sn clr, quick-ened ag'n 14th, hdd 4 out, btn whn blun 3 out, hit nxt, soon wknd.*...................(4 to 1 op 3 to 1) 4
NAZZARO [125] 7-11-5 P Holley, *chsd ldr till wknd aftr 17th, sn and btn whn f nxt.*...................(14 to 1 op 10 to 1) f
1345² BILLYGOAT GRUFF [133] 7-11-13 W Marston, *mstks 4th and 5th, hdwy 7th, chsd ldrs till wknd 14th, 3rd and hld whn wnt rght, blun and uns rdr four out.*
.....................(6 to 4 fav op 5 to 4 tchd 13 to 8 and 7 to 4) ur
1239ª BOND JNR (Ire) [115] 7-10-9 A P McCoy, *not jump wl, effrt 12th, wknd quickly 17th, tld off whn pld up bef nxt.*
.....................(11 to 2 op 4 to 1 tchd 6 to 1) pu
Dist: 2½l, sht-hd, 1½l. 7m 8.70s. a 33.70s (7 Ran).
(White Lion Partnership), P J Hobbs

1746 Rehearsal Chase Limited Handicap Class A Grade 2 (5-y-o and up) £18,822 3m. .... (2:20)

BELMONT KING (Ire) [135] 8-10-8 A P McCoy, *hit second, led tenth, styd on und pres frm 3 out.*
.....................(6 to 1 op 7 to 1 tchd 11 to 1) 1
1480ª TRYING AGAIN [145] 8-11-1 (3ª) D Fortt, *al in tch, styd on wl frm 3 out, not rch wnr r-in.*...........(11 to 4 tchd 7 to 2) 2
ST MELLION FAIRWAY (Ire) [134] 7-10-7 W Marston, *beh, pushed alng 4 out, styd on frm nxt, gng on nr finish.*
.....................(5 to 1 op 4 to 1 tchd 11 to 2) 3
MR MULLIGAN (Ire) [153] 8-11-12 D Bridgwater, *led second to 4th, blun 6th, led 7th, hdd tenth, blunded 12th, styd pressing wnr till wknd 3 out....* (2 to 1 fav op 6 to 4 tchd 9 to 4) 4
1639 GRANGE BRAKE [132] 10-10-5 C Maude, *led to second, mstk 4th, wknd 11th.*...............(10 to 1 tchd 12 to 1) 5
SISTER STEPHANIE (Ire) [132] 7-10-5 B Clifford, *in tch 7th, mstk 9th, sn wknd.*...............(7 to 1 op 6 to 1) 6
1210⁶ TERAO [132] 10-10-2 (3ª) G Hogan, *al beh, tld off whn pld up bef 13th.*...............(20 to 1 op 25 to 1 tchd 33 to 1) pu

---

Dist: 1¼l, 11l, 1¼l, 3l, dist. 6m 10.70s. a 20.70s (7 Ran).
SR: 53/61/39/56/32/-/-/ (Mrs Billie Bond), P F Nicholls

1747 Scudamore Clothing 0800 301301 Novices' Selling Hurdle Class G (4 - 7-y-o) £1,954 2½m 110yds. ....(2:50)

1593 AINSI SOIT IL (Fr) 5-10-12 D Bridgwater, *trkd ldrs till led aftr 7th,sn wl clr, eased r-in...* (5 to 1 op 4 to 1 tchd 6 to 1) 1
1450⁴ KONGIES MELODY 5-10-7 R Greene, *sn prmnt, wnt distant second 3 out but no ch wth wnr...*.... (25 to 1 op 14 to 1) 2
1355⁸ LAURA LYE 6-10-7 G Upton, *led, sn clr, hdd aftr 7th, lost poor second 3 out...*.......(20 to 1 op 14 to 1 tchd 25 to 1) 3
1646 DARING HEN (Ire) 6-10-7 W Marston, *hit second, al beh.*
.....................(20 to 1 op 12 to 1) 4
1444³ MIRAMARE 6-10-9 (3ª) T Dascombe, *prmnt to 5th, wknd 7th.*
.....................(16 to 1 op 10 to 1) 5
1413⁶ CATWALKER (Ire) 5-10-9 (3ª) D Fortt, *al beh.*
.....................(16 to 1 op 10 to 1) 6
924⁵ KESANTA 6-10-0 (7ª) J Power, *sdd| slpd aftr 4th, pld up bef nxt...*...................(5 to 1 op 4 to 1) pu
TREAD THE BOARDS 5-10-7 A P McCoy, *hdwy 6th, wknd rpdly aftr nxt, tld off whn pld up bef nxt.*
.....................(2 to 1 fav op 5 to 4) pu
1557⁷ LETS GO NOW (Ire) 6-10-12 D Leahy, *chsd ldrs, rdn and wknd 7th, tld off whn pld up bef 4 out...*.(66 to 1 op 25 to 1) pu
1261³ LE BARON 5-10-12 C Maude, *in tch till wknd 7th, tld off whn pld up aftr 4 out....*...........(7 to 1 op 2 to 1) pu
Dist: 16l, 9l, 1l, 1½l, 2l. 5m 22.50s. a 44.50s (10 Ran).
(A-Men Partnership), G M McCourt

1748 Flurry Knox Novices' Chase Class D (5-y-o and up) £3,689 2m 3f 110yds .... (3:20)

1577ª OR ROYAL (Fr) 5-11-10 A P McCoy, *prmnt, chlgd 8th, hit tenth, led 11th, hdd nxt, styd wth ldr till slight ld and lft clr 2 out, easily...*.............(5 to 4 fav op 5 to 4 on tchd 11 to 8) 1
1519² DREAM RIDE (Ire) 6-10-12 W Marston, *hdwy 6th, hit tenth, trkd ldrs till lost pos aftr 4 out, mstk and lft second 2 out, no ch wth wnr...*.............(9 to 4 op 2 to 1 tchd 5 to 2) 2
1577² SUPER COIN 8-10-9 (3ª) G Hogan, *sn tracking ldr, led 8th, mstk nxt, led 12th, harrowly hdd but ev ch whn f 2 out.*
.....................(9 to 4 tchd 2 to 1 and 5 to 2) f
1578 SAUCY'S WOLF 6-10-12 R Greene, *f 1st.*
.....................(100 to 1 op 33 to 1) f
SAUSALITO BOY 8-10-12 D Bridgwater, *led to 6th, blun and uns rdr nxt...*.......(25 to 1 tchd 50 to 1 and 66 to 1) ur
1505 ASHLEY HOUSE 7-10-7 (5ª) D Salter, *prmnt, rdn 8th, sn wknd, tld off whn pld up bef 4 out....*.....(100 to 1 op 33 to 1) pu
Dist: 4l. 5m 19.70s. a 36.70s (6 Ran).
(D A Johnson), M C Pipe

1749 December Maiden Hurdle Class D (Div II) (4-y-o and up) £2,693 2m 110yds. .... (3:50)

1641 BOWCLIFFE COURT (Ire) 4-11-5 A P McCoy, *pushed alng to chase ldrs 4th, led aftr four out, drvn out.*
.....................(5 to 2 op 11 to 10 tchd 11 to 4) 1
SUPREME GENOTIN (Ire) 7-11-5 G Upton, *keen hold early, trkd ldrs till led aftr 4th, hdd aftr four out, rallied und pres aftr last, styd on, not rch wnr....*.(15 to 8 fav op 5 to 2) 2
1573ª DRAKESTONE 5-11-5 P McLoughlin, *led aftr 1st till aftr 4th, rallied und pres frm 2 out, styd on.....*.(20 to 1 op 12 to 1) 3
1452² DEVON PEASANT 4-11-0 Mr L Jefford, *prmnt, rdn to chase ldrs 2 out, sn wknd...*.(3 to 1 op 9 to 4 tchd 7 to 2) 4
1338 SNOWSHILL HARVEST (Ire) 5-11-5 S McNeill, *prmnt to 4th, sn wknd, tld off...*.............(11 to 1 tchd 6 to 1) 5
EMNALA (Ire) 4-10-7 (7ª) Mr R Wakley, *beh frm 3rd, tld off.*
.....................(50 to 1 op 25 to 1 tchd 66 to 1) 6
PRINCE OF PREY 8-11-5 W Marston, *beh frm 3rd, tld off whn pld up bef 4 out...*.......(50 to 1 op 25 to 1 tchd 66 to 1) pu
ASTRAL INVADER (Ire) 4-11-5 A McCabe, *beh frm 3rd, tld off whn pld up bef 4 out....*.(33 to 1 op 20 to 1 tchd 50 to 1) pu
1415 MISS THE BEAT 4-11-0 N Mann, *tld off aftr 1st, wknd quickly 4th, tld off whn pld up....*
.....................(66 to 1 op 25 to 1 tchd 100 to 1) pu
Dist: 1¾l, 1¼l, 3½l, dist, 7l. 4m 21.60s. a 34.60s (9 Ran).
(A D Spence), R Akehurst

PUNCHESTOWN (IRE) (yielding)
Saturday December 7th
Going Correction: PLUS 0.30 sec. per fur.

1750 MMI Stockbrokers Hurdle (3-y-o) £4,110 2m. .... (12:35)

1616⁸ TAX REFORM (USA) 10-9 H Rogers, ...(8 to 1) 1
1057³ GO SASHA (Ire) 10-10 (5ª) T Martin, ...(8 to 1) 2
1459⁴ COMRADE CHINNERY (Ire) 10-9 J P Broderick, ...(8 to 1) 3
1616⁴ MISS PENNYHILL (Ire) 10-4 C O'Dwyer, ...(4 to 1) 4
1459⁸ VINCITORE (Ire) 10-9 L P Cusack, ...(12 to 1) 5
1430 TOY'S AWAY (Ire) 10-9 A Powell, ...(10 to 1) 6
1547ª RESCUE TIME (Ire) 11-1 C F Swan, ...(6 to 4 on) 7

225

1403^{5} UNASSISTED (Ire) 10-1 (3*) B Bowens, ...(14 to 1) 8
620^{6} NYMPH IN THE SKI (Ire) 10-4 F Woods, ...(33 to 1) 9
MOFASA 10-9 T J Mitchell, ...(20 to 1) 10
620^{7} LOVE HEART (Ire) 10-2 (7*) B Halligan, ...(16 to 1) 11
1430 ABSTRACT VIEW (USA) 10-9 R M Burke, ...(33 to 1) 12
ROSY FUTURE (Bel) 10-4 T P Rudd, ...(33 to 1) 13
Dist: Hd, 6l, 4l, 1l. 3m 57.70s. a 12.70s (13 Ran).
SR: 2/8/-/-/-/-/ (D G McArdle), D G McArdle

1751 Londis, Manor Inn Naas Novice Hurdle (4-y-o and up) £3,767 2m..(1:05)

VITUS (USA) 4-10-9 J Shortt, ...(12 to 1) 1
1432* DELPHI LODGE (Ire) 6-11-7 Mr A J Martin, ...(13 to 8 fav) 2
1490* RACHEL'S SWALLOW (Ire) 4-10-4 C F Swan, ...(7 to 4) 3
1193^{3} COMMERCIAL HOUSE (Ire) 8-11-0 D T Evans, ...(12 to 1) 4
1580^{6} EUROTHATCH (Ire) 8-11-0 C O'Dwyer, ...(25 to 1) 5
1536^{8} COMMITTED SCHEDULE (Ire) 5-11-0 J P Broderick, ...(20 to 1) 6
1189^{3} SLUSH PUPPY (Ire) 8-11-7 L P Cusack, ...(4 to 1) 7
1486^{6} BUGGY (Ire) 7-11-0 T J Mitchell, ...(12 to 1) 8
1580^{4} TWENTYFIVEQUID (Ire) 5-11-3^{3} Mr P F Graffin, ...(16 to 1) 9
1649 KEEPITSAFE (Ire) 5-11-0 H Rogers, ...(33 to 1) 10
MOORE'S MELODIES (Ire) 5-11-0 F Woods, ...(20 to 1) 11
ISLE OF IONA (Ire) 5-11-0 T P Rudd, ...(25 to 1) f
Dist: 4l, 15l, 15l, ¾l. 3m 55.40s. a 10.40s (12 Ran).
SR: 25/33/1/-/-/-/ (D Kelly), D P Kelly

1752 Andrew J.Nolan Auctioneers Handicap Hurdle (0-127 4-y-o and up) £3,767 2½m..........(1:35)

1654^{2} GRAVITY GATE (Ire) [-] 7-10-6 C O'Dwyer, ... (5 to 1 jt-fav) 1
1549^{3} BLACK QUEEN (Ire) [-] 5-10-11 A J O'Brien, ...(11 to 1) 2
1621^{5} METASTASIO [-] 4-11-9 H Rogers, ...(11 to 2) 3
1535^{2} CEILI QUEEN (Ire) [-] 4-11-7 C F Swan, ...(6 to 1) 4
1277^{2} BLAZE OF HONOUR (Ire) [-] 5-11-2 M Moran, ...(10 to 1) 5
1433^{4} ANNADOT (Ire) [-] 6-10-9 (7*) L J Fleming, ...(8 to 1) 6
1277^{7} SLEEPY RIVER (Ire) [-] 5-10-8 F Woods, ...(9 to 1) 7
1407^{7} NATIVE GALE (Ire) [-] 4-10-3 (5*) T Martin, ...(14 to 1) 8
1550* CASEY JANE (Ire) [-] 5-10-12 T P Treacy, ... (5 to 1 jt-fav) 9
1433^{7} TOTAL CONFUSION [-] 9-10-12 S C Lyons, ...(14 to 1) 10
1654 CIARA'S PRINCE (Ire) [-] 5-11-1 F J Flood, ...(12 to 1) 11
292 SPANKY (Ire) [-] 4-10-9 L P Cusack, ...(12 to 1) 12
1535 MAJESTIC MAN (Ire) [-] 5-11-6 T J Mitchell, ...(25 to 1) 13
LIKE A LION (Ire) [-] 5-10-6 (5*) J M Donnelly, ...(12 to 1) 14
1617^{7} THEPRINCESS MANHAR (Ire) [-] 4-9-8 (7*) D M Bean, ...(33 to 1) 15
RISING WATERS (Ire) [-] 8-10-13 (3*) G Cotter, ...(25 to 1) 16
1535 BUCKMINSTER [-] 9-11-3 J P Broderick, ...(33 to 1) 17
1273 THE PARSON'S FILLY (Ire) [-] 6-9-2 (7*) R Burke, ..(25 to 1) f
1581 FALCARRAGH (Ire) [-] 6-9-0 (7*) J M Maguire, ...(12 to 1) ur
Dist: ½l, 2l, 2½l, 1l. 5m 27.80s. a 45.80s (19 Ran).
(Donald King), R H MacNabb

1753 MMI Stockbrokers Punchestown Chase (Grade 1) (5-y-o and up) £22,750 2½m.......... (2:05)

1551^{2} ROYAL MOUNTBROWNE 8-11-8 C F Swan, *trkd ldr till rdn and wknd aftr 4 out, ran on strly after last to ld last 50 yards.* ....(7 to 1) 1
1537^{4} MERRY GALE (Ire) 8-12-0 J P Broderick, *led, slow 6 out, jnd appr 4 out, rdn bef nxt, sn hdd, lft clr last, soon wknd, ct last 50 yards.*..........(8 to 1) 2
1650^{6} TIME FOR A RUN 9-11-8 J Shortt, *rear, wknd bef 5 out, kpt on aftr 2 out.*..........(25 to 1) 3
IMPERIAL CALL (Ire) 7-12-0 C O'Dwyer, *wl plcd, slow 7 out, prog to dispute ld 4 out, led aftr nxt, clr whn f last, rmntd to finish fourth.*..........(6 to 4 on) 4
1308^{2} KLAIRON DAVIS (Fr) 7-12-0 F Woods, *hld up, str hold early, prog to track ldrs whn f 4 out.*..........(5 to 2) f
1551^{5} LOVE THE LORD (Ire) 6-11-9 T P Treacy, *rear, mstk second and 3rd, reminders, lost tch 5th, tld off whn pld up aftr 5 out.* ....(16 to 1) pu
Dist: 3l, dist, 7l. 5m 23.40s. a 26.40s (6 Ran).
(Mrs J O'Kane), A P O'Brien

1754 Frank Ward & Co. Solicitors Cross Country Chase (5-y-o and up) £3,767 3½m.......... (2:35)

RISK OF THUNDER (Ire) 7-12-5 Mr E Bolger, .. (10 to 9 on) 1
DENNISTOWNTHRILLER (Ire) 8-11-4 Mr A J Martin, (6 to 1) 2
TEARAWAY KING (Ire) 6-10-11 (7*) Mr J Motherway, (4 to 1) 3
1408 OLYMPIC D'OR (Ire) 8-10-11 (7*) Mr W Ewing, ...(5 to 1) 4
1245^{8} GOT NO CHOICE (Ire) 6-10-11 (7*) Mr B Hassett, ...(8 to 1) 5
1092 PROSPECT STAR (Ire) 5-10-13 (3*) Mr R Walsh, ..(20 to 1) 6
WHY AILBHE (Ire) 6-10-12^{1} (7*) Mr S J Mahon, ...(20 to 1) 7
TAMER'S RUN 10-11-1 (3*) Mr B M Cash, ...(20 to 1) ur
Dist: 6l, 1½l, 6l, dist. 7m 35.50s. a 32.50s (8 Ran).
(Sean Connery), E Bolger

1755 Conyngham Cup (5-y-o and up) £6,850 3¼m 110yds.......... (3:05)

1619^{2} SON OF WAR [-] 9-12-4 Mr A J Martin, ...(9 to 4 fav) 1
1434^{4} SECOND SCHEDUAL [-] 11-11-4 Mr G J Harford, .. (4 to 1) 2
1538^{3} TEAL BRIDGE [-] 11-9-11 (7*) Mr G Elliott, ...(8 to 1) 3
1194^{6} LAURA'S BEAU [-] 12-10-1 (3*) Mr R Walsh, ...(20 to 1) 4
1274^{5} BACK BAR (Ire) [-] 8-10-3 (3*) Mr B M Cash, ...(11 to 4) 5
1408 JOHNEEN [-] 10-10-4 Miss M Olivefalk, ...(12 to 1) 6
1434^{6} FISSURE SEAL [-] 10-11-0 (7*) Mr W Ewing, ...(7 to 1) ur
Dist: 1l, hd, 4½l, 1l. 7m 31.20s. a 53.20s (7 Ran).
(Mrs Vera O'Brien), Peter McCreery

1756 Bawnogues (Pro-Am) I.N.H. Flat Race (4-y-o) £2,740 2m...... (3:35)

1409 GRAPHIC EQUALISER (Ire) 11-2 (7*) Mr Edgar Byrne, ...(Evens fav) 1
AGES AGO (Ire) 11-9 Mr J A Berry, ...(13 to 2) 2
1195^{6} PRINCE DANTE (Ire) 11-9 Mr M Murray, ...(12 to 1) 3
OUR-DANTE (Ire) 10-11 (7*) Mr Sean O O'Brien, ...(7 to 1) 4
1247^{3} SOPHIE VICTORIA (Ire) 10-11 (7*) Mr G Elliott, ... (12 to 1) 5
1404^{4} TULLABAWN (Ire) 11-9 Mr P F Graffin, ...(8 to 1) 6
1550^{5} VASILIKI (Ire) (bl) 11-2 (7*) G T Hourigan, ...(12 to 1) 7
1121^{4} AROUND THE STUMP (Ire) 11-1 (3*) Mr P English, (12 to 1) 8
1655^{4} ANDREA COVA (Ire) 11-1 (3*) B Bowens, ...(9 to 1) 9
DANNKALIA (Ire) 11-4 Mr J P Dempsey, ...(8 to 1) 10
898 SUBLIME SPIRIT (Ire) 11-2 (7*) Mr D Buckley, ...(33 to 1) 11
THE FLYING YANK (Ire) 11-4 Mr D Marnane, ...(7 to 1) 12
HI-LO PICCOLO (Ire) 10-11 (7*) Miss S McDonogh, (14 to 1) 13
MYGLASS (Ire) 11-1 (3*) G Cotter, ...(10 to 1) 14
CLARA ROCK (Ire) 10-11 (7*) Mr C J Radley, ...(20 to 1) 15
1409^{7} CAHERMURPHY (Ire) 11-9 Mr J A Nash, ...(33 to 1) 16
TEACH NA FINIUNA (Ire) 10-11 (7*) Mr T P Walsh, (25 to 1) 17
NICK OF TIME VI (Ire) 11-2 (7*) Mr J A Smith, ...(33 to 1) 18
1584 STORM DIEU (Ire) 10-11 (7*) Mr M O'Connor, ...(33 to 1) ro
ALVINE (Ire) 11-2 (7*) Mr S J Mahon, ...(33 to 1) su
Dist: 3l, 1l, 1½l, 3l. 3m 56.40s. (20 Ran).
(B R A S K Syndicate), F J Lacy

SANDOWN (good)
Saturday December 7th
Going Correction: PLUS 0.40 sec. per fur.

1757 Ewell Chase Class B (5-y-o and up) £6,872 3m 110yds..........(12:50)

1287* AARDWOLF 5-10-13 G Bradley, *led to 9th, led 12th to 17th, led appr 3 out, all out r-in.*..........(7 to 2 tchd 4 to 1) 1
1613 MAJOR SUMMIT (Ire) 7-11-7 P Hide, *chsd wnr to 9th, chlgd 3 out till mstk last, rallied and ev ch, ran on.* ....(11 to 10 fav op Evens tchd 6 to 5) 2
1185 HILL OF TULLOW (Ire) 7-11-10 A Maguire, *hld up, led 9th to 12th, led 17th till appr 3 out, sn wknd, beh whn blun nxt, tld off.* ....(7 to 2 op 9 to 4) 3
1395* EVANGELICA (USA) 6-11-0 R Dunwoody, *hld up in cl tch, f 17th, rmntd, tld off.*......(5 to 1 op 7 to 2 tchd 11 to 2) 4
Dist: Sht-hd, dist, dist. 6m 21.30s. a 22.30s (4 Ran).
(Lady Camilla Dempster), C P E Brooks

1758 Henry VIII Novices' Chase Class A Grade 2 (5-y-o and up) £11,848 2m.......... (1:20)

1478* MULLIGAN (Ire) 6-11-0 A Maguire, *made most, drvn out and ran on wl r-in.* (6 to 4 on op 11 to 8 on tchd 5 to 4 on and 13 to 8 on) 1
1421^{2} LAND AFAR 9-11-0 J Osborne, *patiently rdn, ev ch on bit last, ridden and ran on r-in.*.... (9 to 4 op 7 to 4 tchd 5 to 2) 2
1527* DOWN THE FELL 7-11-4 N Williamson, *pckd 1st, pressed wnr, ev ch 3 out, one pace appr last.*.... (5 to 1 op 3 to 1) 3
Dist: Nk, 5l. 4m 1.70s. a 12.70s (3 Ran).
SR: 23/22/21/ (Lady Harris), D Nicholson

1759 Thames Valley Eggs Novices' Handicap Hurdle Class C (4-y-o and up) £5,576 2m 110yds..........(1:55)

1338* AERION [107] 5-11-11 J Osborne, *al prmnt, led appr last, rdn out. ran on wl.*.....(7 to 4 fav tchd 13 to 8 and 15 to 8) 1
1601* HAY DANCE [96] 5-10-11 (3*) G Tormey, *str hold, hld up, hdwy frm 2 out, strong chal last, unbl to quicken r-in.* ....(16 to 1 op 10 to 1) 2
1217^{2} WANSTEAD (Ire) [84] 4-10-2 N Williamson, *trkd ldr, ev ch frm 2 out, kpt on same pace r-in.*.........(40 to 1 op 20 to 1) 3
1148* EL DON [105] 4-11-9 J Ryan, *hld up beh ldrs, lost pl appr 2 out, kpt on one pace r-in.* (6 to 1 op 5 to 1 tchd 13 to 2) 4
1591* LADY PETA (Ire) [105] 6-11-9 M A Fitzgerald, *wtd wth, prog appr 2 out, effrt approaching last, one pace.* ....(15 to 2 op 7 to 1 tchd 10 to 1) 5
1515* RESIST THE FORCE (USA) [110] 6-12-0 P Hide, *hld up, rdn and effrt 2 out, one pace appr last.* ....(5 to 2 op 3 to 1 tchd 100 to 30) 6
1344^{4} BIETSCHHORN BARD [90] 6-10-8 R Dunwoody, *hld up, mstk 2 out, sn btn.*..........(13 to 2 op 11 to 2 tchd 7 to 1) 7
1300* MAZZINI (Ire) [100] 5-10-11 (7*) Mr P O'Keeffe, *led till appr last, sn btn.*..........(16 to 1 op 12 to 1) 8
Dist: 1½l, ½l, ¾l, 1½l, 1¼l, 2l, 3l. 4m 4.10s. a 17.10s (8 Ran).
(P Chamberlain, D Addiscott Partnership), O Sherwood

1760 Mitsubishi Shogun Tingle Creek Trophy Chase Class A Grade 1 (5-y-o and up) £31,290 2m..........(2:30)

1551* SOUND MAN (Ire) 8-11-7 R Dunwoody, *in tch, led 3rd, hit 4 out, blun badly and hdd nxt, rallied to rgn ld last, rdn out.*
.... (11 to 10 on op 11 to 8 on tchd 11 to 10) 1
VIKING FLAGSHIP 9-11-7 A Maguire, *prmnt, chsd wnr frm 3rd, blun 9th, lft in ld 3 out, hdd and no extr last.*
.... (3 to 1 op 2 to 1 tchd 100 to 30) 2
1507* STORM ALERT 10-11-7 N Williamson, *led till hdd and blun badly 3rd, not reco´r, tld off.* (4 to 1 op 9 to 2 tchd 7 to 2) 3
1380³ LORD DORCET (Ire) 6-11-7 J Osborne, *hld up, f 3rd.*
.... (8 to 1 op 14 to 1 tchd 6 to 1) f

Dist: 5l, dist. 3m 59.10s. a 10.10s (4 Ran).

SR: 56/51/-/-/ (David Lloyd), E J O'Grady

1761 William Hill Handicap Hurdle Class B (0-150 4-y-o and up) £35,316 2m 110yds...................(3:05)

1393⁵ MAKE A STAND [123] 5-10-5 (3*) G Tormey, *made all, sn clr, rdn appr last, styd on gmely r-in.*
.... (9 to 1 op 8 to 1 tchd 10 to 1) 1
1528² MASTER BEVELED [132] 6-11-3 G Bradley, *mid-div, prog 3 out, chsd wnr appr last, kpt on.*
.... (20 to 1 op 16 to 1 tchd 25 to 1) 2
1621⁷ TIDJANI (Ire) [115] 4-10-0 J R Kavanagh, *mid-div, rdn aftr 3 out, styd on frm nxt, nrst finish.*
.... (50 to 1 op 33 to 1 tchd 66 to 1) 3
1160* SILVER GROOM (Ire) [137] 6-11-3 (5*) S Ryan, *midfield, rdn frm 3 out, chsd wnr nxt till approaching last, sn btn.*
.... (5 to 1 op 6 to 1 tchd 7 to 1) 4
1284* DIRECT ROUTE (Ire) [133] 5-11-4 N Williamson, *hld up, hdwy appr 2 out, wknd approaching last.*
.... (9 to 1 op 6 to 1 tchd 10 to 1) 5
1393³ BARNA BOY (Ire) [133] 8-11-4 M A Fitzgerald, *hld up in tch, chsd wnr aftr 3 out till styd appr nxt, sn btn.*
.... (16 to 1 op 14 to 1 tchd 20 to 1) 6
1653⁶ MYSTICAL CITY [139] 6-11-7 (3*) D J Casey, *hld up, styd on one pace fnl 2, nvr nrr.* .... (16 to 1 op 14 to 1) 7
1284² URBAN DANCING (USA) [115] 7-10-0 G Cahill, *prmnt to 3 out, wknd appr nxt.* .... (20 to 1 tchd 25 to 1) 8
1617³ EMBELLISHED (Ire) [133] 4-11-4 R Hughes, *nvr nr to chal.*
.... (9 to 1 op 10 to 1 tchd 11 to 2) 9
FLYING INSTRUCTOR [124] 6-10-9 R Bellamy, *nvr on terms.*
.... (12 to 1 op 10 to 1 tchd 8 to 1 tchd 14 to 1) 10
1305⁵ ESKIMO NEL (Ire) [137] 5-11-8 A Maguire, *hld up, rdn 3 out, no imprsn.* .... (10 to 1 tchd 12 to 1) 11
1572* TEINEIN (Fr) [137] 5-11-8 R Dunwoody, *hld up beh ldrs, hit 3 out, effrt appr nxt, sn wknd.*
.... (11 to 4 fav op 3 to 1 tchd 7 to 2) 12
1508² CHARMING GIRL (USA) [129] 5-11-0 J Osborne, *hld up rear, rdn appr 2 out, no imprsn.* .. (12 to 1 tchd 14 to 1) 13
1393⁸ DREAMS END [136] 8-11-7 P Hide, *in tch, wknd 3 out.*
.... (20 to 1 op 16 to 1 tchd 25 to 1) 14
1465⁴ NASHVILLE STAR (USA) [115] 5-9-11 (3*) R Massey, *chsd wnr till appr 2 out, wknd r-in.* .. (150 to 1 op 100 to 1) 15

Dist: 2l, 9l, 1¾l, 3l, ¾l, 1¼l, hd, 3l, 8l, 4l. 3m 56.90s. a 9.90s (15 Ran).

SR: 47/54/28/48/41/40/44/20/35/ (P A Deal), M C Pipe

1762 Doug Barrott Handicap Hurdle Class B (0-145 4-y-o and up) £5,347 2¾m .... (3:40)

750⁵ COKENNY BOY [103] 11-10-6 N Williamson, *chsd ldr, hit 3 out, led appr last, rdn out.*
.... (20 to 1 op 16 to 1 tchd 25 to 1) 1
1481* TIM (Ire) [110] 6-10-13 J Osborne, *hld up, hdwy appr 2 out, ev ch last, no extr r-in.* ...... (5 to 2 op 7 to 4 tchd 11 to 4) 2
1346⁴ KHALIDI (Ire) [113] 7-11-2 R Dunwoody, *led, not fluent 3 out, hdd appr last, one pace r-in.*
.... (100 to 30 op 3 to 1 tchd 7 to 2) 3
1150² TARA RAMBLER (Ire) [119] 7-11-8 A Maguire, *hld up, rdn appr 2 out, effrt bef last, wknd r-in.*
.... (11 to 10 on op Evens tchd 6 to 5) 4
1637 DARK HONEY [121] 11-11-10 A Dicken, *hld up, lost tch 8th, no dngr aftr.* ...... (16 to 1 op 6 to 1 tchd 20 to 1) 5

Dist: 2½l, 4l, 6l, 13l. 5m 31.20s. a 28.20s (5 Ran).

(S D Hemstock), Mrs J Pitman

TOWCESTER (good to soft (races 1,2,4,6,7), good (3,5))
Saturday December 7th
Going Correction: PLUS 0.75 sec. per fur. (races 1,2,4,6,7), PLUS 0.30 (3,5)

1763 European Breeders Fund Stoke Park 'National Hunt' Novices' Hurdle Qualifier Class D (4,5,6-y-o) £3,414 2m 5f...................... (12:25)

1545* SOUTHERN NIGHTS 6-11-8 A Thornton, *hdwy to track ldr 7th, chalg whn stumbled 2 out, led last, rdn out.*
.... (2 to 1 op 7 to 4 tchd 9 to 4) 1
1540² FINE SIR 6-10-12 D Gallagher, *dsptd ld, led 6th, rdn 2 out, untidy and hdd last, ran on.*
.... (15 to 8 fav op 6 to 4 tchd 2 to 1) 2
ABSOLUTLY EQUINAME (Ire) 5-10-12 B Powell, *hld up in mid-div, hdwy 6th, one pace frm 3 out.*
.... (9 to 1 op 5 to 1 tchd 10 to 1) 3
1502⁸ RED BRONZE (Ire) 5-10-12 B Fenton, *hld up in rear, styd on frm 3 out, nvr nrr.* ..(16 to 1 op 14 to 1 tchd 20 to 1) 4
1464 BRIDLED TERN 5-10-7 D Byrne, *chsd ldrs till wknd 3 out.*
.... (12 to 1 op 8 to 1) 5
BANK AVENUE 5-10-12 R Farrant, *mid-div, hdwy 6th, wknd 3 out.* .... (14 to 1 op 12 to 1) 6
1437⁵ SEYMOUR'S DOUBLE 5-10-12 S Wynne, *in tch till wknd 7th, tld off.* .... (33 to 1 tchd 50 to 1) 7
DINGLE WOOD (Ire) 6-10-9 (3*) P Henley, *made most to 6th, wknd nxt, tld off.* ...... (10 to 1 op 8 to 1 tchd 12 to 1) 8
1344⁶ SAMMORELLO (Ire) 5-10-12 C Llewellyn, *prmnt till wknd appr 7th, tld off.* .... (10 to 1 op 7 to 1) 9
1591⁶ THE MILLMASTER (Ire) 5-10-12 D Parker, *prmnt till wknd 7th, tld off.* .... (50 to 1 tchd 33 to 1) 10
52 SONRISA (Ire) 4-10-12 T J Murphy, *al beh, tld off.*
.... (50 to 1 op 33 to 1) 11
1545 MUSICAL HIT 5-10-12 L Harvey, *hit 1st, al beh, tld off whn pld up bef 2 out.* .... (50 to 1) pu
1109 LUMO (Ire) 5-10-12 T Jenks, *in tch to 6th, tld off whn pld up bef 2 out.* .... (16 to 1 op 8 to 1) pu
1573 HAPPY JACK (bl) 5-10-12 Mr A Kinane, *al beh, tld off 6th, pld up bef 3 out.* ...... (33 to 1 op 20 to 1 tchd 50 to 1) pu
COTTAGE JOKER 6-10-12 J Railton, *al beh, tld off whn pld up bef 2 out.* .... (33 to 1) pu
1355⁷ KATHARINE'S SONG (Ire) 6-10-2 (5*) Mr R Thornton, *prmnt to 5th, tld off whn pld up bef 2 out.* .... (50 to 1) pu

Dist: 1¼l, 19l, 7l, 1l, 17l, 5l, 16l, 1l, dist, 16l. 5m 26.20s. a 27.20s (16 Ran).

(J Perriss), K C Bailey

1764 Northants 96 Conditional Jockeys' Handicap Hurdle Class G (0-95 4-y-o and up) £2,094 2m..........(12:55)

1541³ SPRINTFAYRE [82] 8-10-12 (7*) A Irvine, *trkd ldr, led sn aftr 3 out, jmpd lft nxt, drw clr r-in.* .... (5 to 1) 1
AMBIDEXTROUS (Ire) [64] 4-9-10 (5*) L Cummins, *mid-div, gd hdwy frm 5th, wnt second 3 out, chlgd nxt, short of room and swtchd rght bef mstk last, one pace r-in.* (8 to 1 op 6 to 1) 2
1410⁷ L'EQUIPE (Ire) [87] (bl) 6-11-10 J Magee, *hld up, hdwy 3 out, sn rdn, one pace.* ...... (7 to 2 op 3 to 1 tchd 4 to 1) 3
1338 STORM TIGER (Ire) [67] 5-10-4 E Husband, *hld up in rear, some hdwy 3 out, nvr nr to chal.*
.... (11 to 1 op 6 to 1 tchd 12 to 1) 4
43³ DR ROCKET [90] 11-11-6 (7*) X Aizpuru, *chsd ldrs, wknd 3 out.* .... (8 to 1 op 5 to 1) 5
1609⁶ REFLEX HAMMER [83] 5-11-6 D Parker, *chsd ldrs till wknd appr 3 out.* .... (8 to 1 op 6 to 1) 6
1646 TOMAL [73] 4-10-10 G E Smith, *al in rear.*
.... (11 to 4 fav op 2 to 1) 7
1667 BARN'N'BITE [89] 4-11-12 G Cahill, *hld up in rear, hdwy 5th, wknd quickly nxt.* ...... (11 to 2 op 4 to 1 tchd 6 to 1) 8
GYMCRAK SOVEREIGN [86] 8-11-9 P Henley, *led, clr 3rd, wknd and hdd sn aftr 3 out.* ...... (16 to 1 op 10 to 1) 9

Dist: 6l, 4l, 19l, 3l, ½l, nk, ½l, 3½l. 4m 2.50s. a 19.50s (9 Ran).

SR: 16/-/11/-/-/-/ (Mrs O C Foster), J E Long

1765 Bet With The Tote Novices' Chase Qualifier Class D (5-y-o and up) £4,305 2¾m..................(1:25)

CREDO IS KING (Ire) 6-11-0 A Thornton, *in tch whn hit 4th, wnt second four out, led appr 2 out, all out.*
.... (12 to 1 op 10 to 1 tchd 16 to 1 and 10 to 1) 1
1611³ WISLEY WONDER 6-11-0 C Llewellyn, *prmnt till jmpd slwly and lost pl 9th, rdn frm nxt, styd on to press wnr r-in.*
.... (Evens fav op 11 to 8 tchd 6 to 4) 2
1542⁶ MR PICKPOCKET (Ire) 8-11-0 T J Murphy, *made most till hit and hdd 4 out, rdn and one pace aftr.* ..(4 to 1 op 7 to 2) 3
BROGEEN LADY (Ire) 6-10-9 R Farrant, *dsptd ld early, led 4 out, hdd appr 2 out, one pace aftr.* .. (12 to 1 op 6 to 1) 4
1339* GOLDENSWIFT (Ire) 6-11-2 B Fenton, *hld up, hdwy 7th, wknd 3 out.* .... (4 to 1 op 7 to 2) 5
1571⁵ STAGE PLAYER 10-11-0 I Lawrence, *in tch till wknd 5 out, tld off.* .... (25 to 1 op 16 to 1) 6
SNOWDON LILY 5-10-6 (3*) E Husband, *al beh, tld off.*
.... (50 to 1 op 25 to 1 tchd 66 to 1) 7
BIG ARCHIE 6-11-0 B Powell, *f 1st.*
.... (9 to 1 op 5 to 1 tchd 16 to 1) f
1540⁶ GEMMA'S WAGER (Ire) 6-10-9 L Harvey, *blun and uns rdr 3rd.* .... (50 to 1 op 25 to 1 tchd 66 to 1) ur
1636 PROUD TOBY (Ire) 6-11-0 J Railton, *al beh, tld off whn pld up bef 3 out.* .... (25 to 1 op 10 to 1) pu

Dist: 1½l, 5l, ½l, 20l, dist, 20l. 5m 39.60s. a 13.60s (10 Ran).

SR: 16/14/9/3/-/-/ (G L Porter), P R Webber

1766 Pattishall Handicap Hurdle Class E (0-115 4-y-o and up) £2,547 3m

. . . . . (1:55)

1000* SNOW BOARD [86] 7-10-2² Derek Byrne, *hld up in rear, steady hdwy 4 out, chlgd last, sn led, quickened wl.*
. . . .(5 to 1 op 3 to 1)   1

1443³ EHTEFAAL (USA) [87] 5-10-3 T J Murphy, *hld up in tch, hdwy appr 3 out, led briefly last, ran on one pace.*
. . . .(10 to 1 op 7 to 1)   2

869² ABLE PLAYER (USA) [86] 8-9-10-2 M Sharratt, *hld up, hdwy appr 7th, chlgd nxt, led approaching 3 out, rdn and hdd last, one pace.* . . . .(14 to 1 op 8 to 1)   3

1576 OATIS ROSE [97] 6-10-8 (5*) Mr R Thornton, *al prmnt, led 8th, hdd appr 2 out, no extr aftr.* . . . .(6 to 1 op 4 to 1)   4

1234* KENDAL CAVALIER [102] 6-11-4 B Fenton, *chsd ldrs, rdn and ev ch appr 2 out, wknd sn aftr.* . . . .(7 to 1 jt-
     fav op 4 to 1 tchd 5 to 1)   5

1597 STROKESAVER (Ire) [93] 6-10-9 D Gallagher, *hld up in rear, hdwy hfwy, wknd appr 2 out.* . . . . . .(12 to 1 op 10 to 1)   6

GRUNGE (Ire) [87] 8-10-3 A Thornton, *hld up, hdwy 8th, nvr on terms.* . . . .(10 to 1 op 8 to 1 tchd 12 to 1)   7

1469* HAILE DERRING [112] 6-12-0 C Llewellyn, *prmnt, rdn appr 8th, wknd approaching 3 out.* . . . .(7 to 2 jt-
     fav op 3 to 1 tchd 4 to 1)   8

1558⁴ PETTAUGH (Ire) [92] 8-10-5 (3*) K Gaule, *prmnt, led aftr 7th, hdd nxt, sn wknd, tld off.* . . . .(8 to 1 op 6 to 1)   9

RONANS GLEN [84] 9-9-10³ (7*) D C O'Connor, *al beh, tld off.*
. . . .(33 to 1 op 16 to 1)   10

1400⁴ RUBINS BOY [90] 10-10-6 R Farrant, *hld up in tch, wknd 4 out, tld off.* . . . .(20 to 1 op 10 to 1 tchd 25 to 1)   11

1400⁶ SINGLESOLE [86] 11-10-2 R Marley, *prmnt, led appr 7th, hdd bef nxt, sn wknd, tld off whn pld up before last.*
. . . . (14 to 1 op 8 to 1 tchd 16 to 1)   pu

1569 TIM SOLDIER (Fr) [84] 9-10-0 Ann Stokell, *al beh, tld off whn appr bef 2 out.* . . . .(25 to 1 op 20 to 1 tchd 33 to 1)   pu

955⁴ SUMMER HAVEN [84] 7-9-9 (5*) Sophie Mitchell, *led till hdd appr 7th, wknd nxt, tld off whn pld up bef 3 out.*
. . . .(33 to 1 op 20 to 1)   pu

Dist: 2l, ½l, 3l, 8l, 8l, 6l, 1½l, 5l, dist, dist. 6m 14.70s. a 32.70s (14 Ran).
       (F J Sainsbury), Mrs Merrita Jones

1767 Alderton Handicap Chase Class C
          (0-130 5-y-o and up) £5,150 3m 1f
. . . . . (2:25)

1212 HARWELL LAD (Ire) [120] 7-11-4 Mr R Nuttall, *led, jmpd wl, hdd briefly betw last 2, styd on well.*
. . . . (10 to 1 op 10 to 1 tchd 16 to 1)   1

1544³ REALLY A RASCAL [105] 9-10-3 R Farrant, *hit 1st, hld up, hdwy 11th, led briefly betw last 2, one pace r-in.*
. . . . (8 to 1 tchd 10 to 1)   2

1345⁵ KING LUCIFER (Ire) [130] 7-11-9 (5*) Mr R Thornton, *hld up, hdwy 11th, chsd wnr 4 out till wknd appr last.*
. . . . (4 to 1 tchd 9 to 2)   3

1133² COURT MELODY (Ire) [117] 10-11 B Powell, *al prmnt, chsd wnr 13th to 4 out, wknd nxt.* . . . . .(7 to 1 op 6 to 1)   4

1296² RECTORY GARDEN (Ire) [113] 7-10-11 A Thornton, *chsd wnr for most of way to 13th, till wknd 4 out.* . . . .(3 to 1 jt-
     fav op 9 to 4)   5

CHIEF RAGER [104] 7-10-2 C Llewellyn, *prmnt to 11th, rdn and sn beh.* . . . . (8 to 1 op 7 to 1)   6

1544⁶ MAKES ME GOOSEY (Ire) [102] 8-10-0 L Harvey, *prmnt to 11th, rdn and sn wknd.* (14 to 1 op 12 to 1 tchd 16 to 1)   7

986⁷ WOODLANDS GENHIRE [102] 11-10-0 T J Murphy, *al beh, tld off 8th.* . . . .(50 to 1 op 20 to 1)   8

1314² UBU VAL (Fr) [120] 10-11-4 J Railton, *in rear whn stumbled badly 12th, tld off when pld up bef 2 out.* . . . .(3 to 1 jt-
     fav op 9 to 2)   pu

1445⁷ KNOCKAVERRY (Ire) [102] 8-10-0 I Lawrence, *al beh, tld off whn pld up bef 2 out.* . . . . .(14 to 1 op 8 to 1 tchd 16 to 1)   pu

Dist: 2l, 2½l, 20l, 2½l, 1¾l, 11l, dist. 6m 25.50s. a 13.50s (10 Ran).
SR: 30/13/35/2/-/-/   (H Wellstead), R H Alner

1768 Weatherbys 'Stars Of Tomorrow'
         Open National Hunt Flat Standard -
         Class H (Div I) (4,5,6-y-o) £1,301 2m
. . . . . (3:00)

1483 LIVELY ENCOUNTER (Ire) 5-11-4 Derek Byrne, *nvr far away, led hfwy, drw clr ins fnl 2 fs, readily.*
. . . .(9 to 4 op 7 to 2 tchd 4 to 1)   1

1483⁷ JACK GALLAGHER 5-11-4 M Richards, *hld up in tch, prmnt frm hfwy, rdn 3 fs out, ran on to go second ins last.*
. . . .(9 to 4 op 6 to 4 tchd 9 to 4)   2

BROOKHAMPTON LANE (Ire) 5-11-4 B Powell, *al in tch, chsd wnr 3 fs out till wknd ins last.*
. . . . (16 to 1 op 6 to 1 tchd 20 to 1)   3

1306⁸ BAVARDIER (Ire) 5-11-4 B Fenton, *hld up in rear, hdwy 6 fs out, no ch fnl 3.* . . . .(8 to 1 op 6 to 1 tchd 9 to 1)   4

CLINKING 5-11-4 Mrs A Perrett, *settled in rear, nvr on terms.*
. . . .(9 to 2 op 4 to 1 tchd 9 to 4)   5

JUSTLIKEJIM 5-10-11 (7*) M Griffiths, *al beh.*
. . . .(20 to 1 op 12 to 1)   6

PEALINGS (Ire) 4-11-1 (3*) K Gaule, *pld hrd, led aftr 5 fs, hdd hfwy, wknd o'r 3 furlongs out.*
. . . .(9 to 1 op 12 to 1 tchd 14 to 1)   7

NORTHERN STAR 5-11-4 (7*) Miss J Wormall, *led for 5 fs, sn beh.* . . . .(10 to 1 op 6 to 1)   8

LUCRATIVE PERK (Ire) 4-10-13 I Lawrence, *in rear, effrt aftr 6 fs, sn btn, tld off.* . . . .(16 to 1 op 10 to 1 tchd 20 to 1)   9

SWEET MOUNT (Ire) 4-10-6 (7*) L Suthern, *prmnt to hfwy, tld off.* . . . . (11 to 2 op 7 to 2)   10

Dist: 9l, 3l, 11l, 12l, 1¼l, 1l, 1¼l, dist, 7l. 3m 56.70s. (10 Ran).
       (F J Sainsbury), Mrs Merrita Jones

1769 Weatherbys 'Stars Of Tomorrow'
         Open National Hunt Flat Standard -
         Class H (Div II) (4,5,6-y-o) £1,290 2m
. . . . . (3:35)

RED BROOK 4-11-1 (3*) E Callaghan, *al prmnt, rdn to go second o'r 2 fs out, led wl over one out, ran on.*
. . . .(10 to 1 op 6 to 1)   1

1142² WELSH SILK 4-10-13 (5*) Sophie Mitchell, *mid-div, rdn 3 fs out, styd on to go second on line.*
. . . . (3 to 1 op 5 to 2 tchd 100 to 30)   2

1306⁷ ENDEAVOUR (Fr) 4-11-4 J Railton, *hld up, hdwy hfwy, rdn to go second o'r 2 fs out, no extr cl hme.*(16 to 1 op 8 to 1)   3

JAYFCEE 4-11-4 B Powell, *led till hdd w'r o one furlong out, sn btn.* . . . . (33 to 1 op 12 to 1)   4

JET FILES (Ire) 5-11-4 R Farrant, *hld up, hdwy 4 fs out, wknd 2 out.* . . . .(9 to 2 op 11 to 4)   5

QUISTAQUAY 4-10-13 S Curran, *wl in rear, some hdwy fnl 2 fs, nvr dngrs.* . . . .(20 to 1 op 12 to 1 tchd 25 to 1)   6

1317⁴ THE CROOKED OAK 4-10-11 (7*) M Keighley, *wth ldr early, rdn and wknd o'r 3 fs out.*
. . . .(5 to 2 fav tchd 7 to 2 and 4 to 1)   7

1026³ BIG STAN'S BOY 5-10-11 (7*) M Berry, *chsd ldrs till wknd 4 fs out.* . . . .(6 to 1 op 3 to 1)   8

1456² NEVER IN DEBT 4-11-4 (7*) Mr A G Shenkin, *in tch to hfwy, tld off.* . . . .(4 to 1 op 3 to 1 tchd 6 to 1)   9

ROYAL DIVIDE (Ire) 4-11-4 C Llewellyn, *bolted bef strt, al beh, tld off.* . . . .(16 to 1 op 7 to 1 tchd 20 to 1)   10

Dist: 4l, nk, 7l, 6l, hd, 1½l, 1¼l, 22l, dist. 4m 0.10s. (10 Ran).
       (Dr B H Seal), J M Jefferson

WETHERBY (good to soft)
Saturday December 7th
Going Correction: PLUS 0.80 sec. per fur. (races 1,3,6), PLUS 0.60 (2,4,5)

1770 Thorp Arch Novices' Hurdle Class D
         (4-y-o and up) £2,684 2m 7f. .(12:40)

1311² BEN CRUACHAN (Ire) 6-11-0 Richard Guest, *mid-div, hdwy to track ldrs hfwy, led 3 out, styd on und pres.*
. . . .(3 to 1 op 11 to 4 tchd 100 to 30)   1

1333⁶ CALLERNISH DAN (Ire) 6-10-9 (5*) Michael Brennan, *led till hdd 3 out, kpt on, no imprsn on wnr..* (16 to 1 op 12 to 1)   2

1260⁵ BARTON WARD 5-11-0 A Dobbin, *chsd ldrs, ev ch bef 3 out, fdd.* . . . .(9 to 1 op 6 to 1 tchd 10 to 1)   3

1437³ ELY'S HARBOUR (Ire) 5-11-0 J A McCarthy, *chsd ldrs till wknd bef 3 out.* . . . .(10 to 1 op 7 to 1)   4

1317⁸ LARKSHILL (Ire) 5-10-11 (3*) F Leahy, *in tch, wkng whn mstk 3 out.* . . . .(25 to 1 op 20 to 1)   5

PILKINGTON (Ire) 6-11-0 A S Smith, *chsd ldrs till wknd quickly bef 3 out.* . . . .(16 to 1 op 14 to 1)   6

CELTIC DUKE 4-11-0 R Garritty, *beh most of way.*
. . . .(33 to 1 tchd 50 to 1)   7

934⁴ SHARE OPTIONS (Ire) 5-11-6 J Callaghan, *trkd ldrs till 9th.* . . . .(13 to 8 fav op 5 to 2 tchd 6 to 4)   f

1509⁶ STAR MASTER 5-11-0 M Foster, *beh, hdwy aftr 8th, wknd bef 3 out, behind whn blun and uns rdr last..* (20 to 1)   ur

CAIRO PRINCE (Ire) 6-11-0 A Roche, *sn beh, tld off whn pld up bef 3 out.* . . . .(10 to 1 op 5 to 1)   pu

1679 BOLD'N 9-10-7 (7*) S Haworth, *sn beh, tld off whn pld up bef 3 out.* . . . .(100 to 1 op 50 to 1)   pu

1260 ZAMORSTON 7-11-0 M Brennan, *lost tch and pld up bef 6th.* . . . .(33 to 1 op 25 to 1)   pu

1679 LEPTON (Ire) 5-11-0 B Storey, *prmnt till wknd quickly bef 9th, tld off whn pld up before last.* . . . .(50 to 1)   pu

THE ALAMO (Ire) 5-11-0 B Harding, *mid-div till lost tch and pld up aftr 7th, lme.* . . . .(100 to 1 op 50 to 1)   pu

PHARRAMBLING (Ire) 5-10-9 P Niven, *beh frm hfwy, tld off whn pld up bef 3 out.* . . . .(10 to 1 op 12 to 1)   pu

Dist: 7l, 12l, 2½l, 2½l, 10l, 2½l. 5m 51.70s. (15 Ran).
       (The Caledonian Racing Club), J M Jefferson

1771 Dick Warden Novices' Chase Class D
         (5-y-o and up) £4,107 2½m 110yds
. . . . . (1:10)

1527 SIMPLY DASHING (Ire) 5-11-10 R Garritty, *prmnt, led aftr tenth, clr 2 out, styd on strly.*
. . . .(11 to 10 on op 5 to 4 tchd 6 to 5 on)   1

1681 NIKI DEE (Ire) 6-11-0 R Supple, *led second to 6th, lost pl aftr tenth, styd on wl frm 3 out, no imprsn on wnr.*
. . . .(20 to 1 op 14 to 1)   2

RIVER UNSHION (Ire) 6-11-0 A S Smith, *keen early, led 6th till hdd aftr tenth, chsd wnr till wknd after 2 out.*
. . . .(12 to 1 op 8 to 1 tchd 14 to 1)   3

CATTLY HANG (Ire) 6-11-0 A Dobbin, *in tch till outpcd aftr tenth, no dngr after.* . . . .(33 to 1 op 20 to 1)   4

NATIONAL HUNT RESULTS 1996-97

BLACK BROOK (Ire) 7-10-11 (3*) Mr C Bonner, *towards rear, lost tch frm tenth* . . . . (50 to 1 op 20 to 1) 5

1608² LANSBOROUGH 6-11-0 B Harding, *led to second, prmnt till wknd aftr 4 out* . . . . . (2 to 1 op 7 to 4 tchd 9 to 4) 6

SIRERIC (Ire) 6-11-0 K Johnson, *keen early, in tch till wknd aftr tenth* . . . . (100 to 1 op 50 to 1) 7

ASLAN (Ire) 8-11-0 B Storey, *f second.*
. . . . (12 to 1 op 8 to 1 tchd 14 to 1) f

1469⁴ FLAT TOP 5-11-0 P Niven, *sn wl beh, tld off whn pld up bef 4 out* . . . . (20 to 1 op 14 to 1) pu

Dist: 10l, 9l, ¾l, 16l, 1¼l, 15l. 5m 14.90s. a 21.90s (9 Ran).

(Steve Hammond), T D Easterby

1772 ATS Handicap Hurdle Class C (0-135 4-y-o and up) £3,866 2m . . . . . . (1:40)

PENNY A DAY (Ire) [128] 6-11-10 P Niven, *trkd ldrs, chlgd 3 out, led nxt, styd on* . . . . (Evens fav op 6 to 4) 1

1326⁵ FASSAN (Ire) [105] 4-10-1 D Bentley, *in tch, effrt bef 3 out, styd on frm nxt.* . . . . (14 to 1 op 10 to 1 tchd 16 to 1) 2

1508⁴ KAITAK (Ire) [120] 5-10-13 (3*) F Leahy, *al prmnt, kpt on same pace frm 2 out.* . . . . (11 to 2 op 5 to 1 tchd 6 to 1) 3

1528⁵ ELPIDOS [119] 4-11-1 R Garritty, *towards rear, kpt on frm 3 out, nvr dngrs.* . . . . (8 to 1 op 7 to 1) 4

1467⁴ MR BUREAUCRAT (NZ) [117] 7-10-13 A Dobbin, *hld up, steady hdwy to ld 3 out, hdd nxt, fdd.* (10 to 1 tchd 11 to 1) 5

1633 NON VINTAGE (Ire) [130] 5-11-12 W Worthington, *hld up in tch, outpcd bef 3 out, no dngr aftr* . . . . (16 to 1 op 12 to 1) 6

1148⁷ DAWN MISSION [106] 4-10-2 A S Smith, *led till hdd 3 out, fdd.*
. . . . (16 to 1 op 14 to 1) 7

1528 THORNTON GATE [127] 7-11-9 J Callaghan, *nvr nr to chal.*
. . . . (10 to 1 op 8 to 1 tchd 12 to 1) 8

1388 BEND SABLE (Ire) [110] 6-10-6 B Storey, *mid-div, no hdwy frm 3 out.* . . . . (50 to 1 op 33 to 1) 9

1633⁶ JAZILAH (Fr) [130] 8-11-12 Richard Guest, *lost tch frm 4th.*
. . . . (33 to 1 op 20 to 1) 10

ELATION [119] 4-11-1 B Harding, *lost tch frm 4th.*
. . . . (10 to 1 op 7 to 1) 11

Dist: 3l, 2l, 1¼l, hd, 1¼l, 1¼l, 3½l, 5l, 11l, 1l. 3m 58.80s. a 17.80s (11 Ran).
SR: 46/20/33/30/28/39/13/30/8/ (J Good), Mrs M Reveley

1773 'Emmerdale' Handicap Chase Class B (0-145 5-y-o and up) £6,742 2½m 110yds. . . . . (2:10)

1518² THE LAST FLING (Ire) [118] 6-10-12 Richard Guest, *mstk 1st, sn tracking ldr, hit 9th, soon led, rdn aftr last, styd on.*
. . . . (11 to 10 fav op 11 to 8 tchd Evens) 1

1518⁷ CUMBRIAN CHALLENGE (Ire) [125] 7-11-5 R Garritty, *in tch, drvn alng aftr 4 out, rdn to chase wnr last, no imprsn.*
. . . . (6 to 1 op 5 to 1) 2

1401⁶ DENVER BAY [119] 9-10-10 (3*) L Aspell, *jmpd rght, led till hdd aftr 9th, drvn alng aftr 4 out, kpt on same pace.*
. . . . (4 to 1 op 3 to 1) 3

WEE RIVER (Ire) [125] 7-11-5 J Callaghan, *hld up, smooth hdwy to chase wnr 2 out, sn rdn and no extr.*
. . . . (7 to 1 op 9 to 2 tchd 8 to 1) 4

1389⁵ ALL THE ACES [134] 9-12-0 P Niven, *beh, effrt bef 4 out, no hdwy* . . . . (20 to 1 op 14 to 1) 5

1529 JOE WHITE [119] 10-10-13 A S Smith, *chsd ldrs till outpcd aftr 9th.* . . . . (10 to 1 op 7 to 1) 6

Dist: 1¼l, 7l, 2½l, 7l, 3l. 5m 18.20s. a 25.20s (6 Ran).

(Michael Jackson Bloodstock Ltd), Mrs S J Smith

1774 Wharfe Handicap Chase Class B (0-145 5-y-o and up) £6,944 3m 1f . . . . (2:40)

ISLAND CHIEF (Ire) [110] 7-10-0 R Supple, *jmpd wl, led second, made rst, styd on well* . . . . . (4 to 1 op 11 to 4) 1

1632³ ALI'S ALIBI [114] 9-10-4 P Niven, *beh, hdwy aftr 4 out, styd on to take second cl hme* . . . . (9 to 2 op 5 to 1) 2

1294² LORD GYLLENE (NZ) [120] 8-10-10 A Dobbin, *led 1st to second, wth wnr, drvn alng bef 4 out, kpt on same pace.*
. . . . (7 to 2 jt-fav) 3

1563* YORKSHIRE GALE [137] 10-11-10 (3*) L Aspell, *chsd ldrs till grad wknd frm 4 out.* . . . . . . (7 to 2 jt-fav tchd 4 to 1) 4

1336³ DARK OAK [113] 10-10-3 J Callaghan, *led to 1st, in tch till wknd bef 12th.* . . . . (10 to 1 op 8 to 1) 5

FLASHTHECASH [124] 10-11-0 J A McCarthy, *in tch, mstk 11th (water), sn wknd.* . . . . . (16 to 1 op 12 to 1) 6

ASTINGS (Fr) [116] 8-10-6 W Dwan, *blun and uns rdr 1st.*
. . . . (6 to 1 op 9 to 2) ur

URANUS COLLONGES (Fr) [118] 10-10-8 R Garritty, *lost tch aftr 11th, tld off whn pld up bef 4 out* . . (20 to 1 op 16 to 1) pu

1632⁵ STRONG DEEL (Ire) [116] 8-10-6 B Harding, *pld up aftr 4th, dead.* . . . . (12 to 1) pu

Dist: 5l, hd, 21l, 6l, 1¼l. 6m 27.40s. a 19.40s (9 Ran).
SR: 28/27/33/29/-/-/ (George Dilger), P Beaumont

1775 Walshford Novices' Handicap Hurdle Class D (0-105 4-y-o and up) £3,104 2½m 110yds. . . . . (3:15)

1330* ELA MATA [101] 4-11-3 (7*) B Grattan, *hld up in rear early, in clr ld aftr 5th, blun last, kpt on.* . . . . (6 to 1 op 4 to 1) 1

1115* SPRING GALE (Ire) [102] 5-11-11 J A McCarthy, *prmnt, chsd wnr frm 5th, kpt on, no imprsn.*
. . . . (7 to 2 tchd 4 to 1 and 3 to 1) 2

1182 DONT FORGET CURTIS (Ire) [84] 4-10-7 J Callaghan, *in tch, kpt on frm 2 out.* . . . . (14 to 1 tchd 16 to 1) 3

1275⁷ SPRITZER (Ire) [91] 4-11-0 W Dwan, *towards rear, styd on frm 3 out.* . . . . (12 to 1 op 12 to 1 tchd 16 to 1) 4

1198⁴ HOTSPUR STREET [78] (bl) 4-10-1 B Harding, *in tch, kpt on frm 3 out.* . . . . (12 to 1 op 8 to 1) 5

1313⁵ MENSHAAR (USA) [86] 4-10-9 M Foster, *nvr dngrs.*
. . . . (14 to 1 op 12 to 1) 6

1515³ TAKE COVER (Ire) [93] 5-11-2 A Dobbin, *chsd ldrs till wknd aftr 3 out.* . . . . (7 to 1 op 6 to 1) 7

1067* HIGHBEATH [98] 5-11-7 P Niven, *led early, wknd aftr 3 out.*
. . . . (7 to 2 tchd 9 to 2 and 4 to 1) 8

1252 CORBLEU (Ire) [77] 6-10-0 K Johnson, *keen early, prmnt, wknd bef 3 out.* . . . . (20 to 1 op 14 to 1) 9

1510³ AUNTIE ALICE [79] 6-9-13 (3*) F Leahy, *mid-div, chasing ldrs bef 3 out, sn wknd.* . . . . (14 to 1 op 12 to 1) 10

1524⁴ JOE JAGGER (Ire) [77] 5-10-0 D Bentley, *mid-div, drvn alng and wknd bef 3 out.* . . . . (16 to 1 op 12 to 1) 11

650 ANCHORENA [83] 4-10-6 Richard Guest, *nvr dngrs.*
. . . . (12 to 1 op 8 to 1) 12

1623 THE OTHER MAN (Ire) [77] 6-10-0 R Supple, *beh most of way.*
. . . . (50 to 1) 13

SKI PATH [77] 7-10-0 A S Smith, *beh most of way.*
. . . . (50 to 1 op 33 to 1) 14

BRAVE AND TENDER (Ire) [77] 7-9-9 (5*) G F Ryan, *pld up aftr 4th.* . . . . (33 to 1 op 25 to 1) pu

Dist: 2½l, 8l, 3½l, sht-hd, 9l, 3l, ½l, ½l, 2l, 2½l. (Time not taken) (15 Ran).

(F J Sainsbury), Mrs A Swinbank

CLONMEL (IRE) (soft)
Sunday December 8th

1776 Winter E.B.F. Mares Maiden Hurdle Qualifier (4-y-o and up) £3,767 2m . . . . (12:30)

1484² IODER WAN (Ire) 4-11-9 M P Hourigan, ... (5 to 1) 1
MARYOBEE (Ire) 6-11-6 C O'Dwyer, ... (10 to 1) 2

1485 ROCHER LADY (Ire) 5-12-0 D J Casey, ... (5 to 4 on) 3

1359⁴ JANICE PRICE (Ire) 5-11-6 N Williamson, ... (8 to 1) 4

1359³ ASK ME (Ire) 5-10-13 (7*) M D Murphy, ... (10 to 1) 5

1539⁸ PRINCESS GLORIA (Ire) 5-10-13 (7*) Mr M J Daly, (20 to 1) 6

1485⁷ LISADOBBER LADY (Ire) 6-11-6 J P Broderick, . . (14 to 1) 7

1247 MALADANTE (Ire) 4-11-4 F Woods, ... (20 to 1) 8

1617⁸ CROSSCHILD (Ire) 5-11-7 (7*) Mr P M Cloke, . . . (12 to 1) 9

1484⁹ BESTERELLE (Ire) 5-11-6 M Duffy, ... (12 to 1) 10

1174 QUENNIE MO GHRA (Ire) 5-11-6 F J Flood, ... (20 to 1) 11

1147 FILEO (Ire) 5-10-13 (7*) J E Casey, ... (33 to 1) 12

1/15* LABAN LADY (Ire) (bl) -/11-6 T P Treacy, ... (20 to 1) 13

1485⁸ ARTIC PEARL (Ire) 5-10-13 (7*) D Flood, ... (20 to 1) 14

BAR FLUTE (Ire) 5-11-6 C F Swan, ... (12 to 1) 15

RATHCOLMAN GALE (Ire) 6-11-3 (3*) K Whelan, . . (33 to 1) 16

983 GAIN CONTROL (Ire) 7-11-6 P A Roche, ... (33 to 1) 17

746⁵ PRINCESS JENNIFER (Ire) 5-11-6 C O'Brien, ... (33 to 1) 18

1432 LADY CONDUCTOR (Ire) 5-11-6 P McWilliams, . . (25 to 1) f

977 EAGLES WITCH (Ire) 7-11-6 J Shortt, ... (33 to 1) pu

Dist: 2l, 4l, ½l, 3l. 4m 10.40s. (20 Ran).

(Ioder Wan Syndicate), Michael Hourigan

1777 Tipperary Maiden Hurdle (4-y-o) £2,740 2m. . . . . (1:00)

TOAST THE SPREECE (Ire) 11-9 C F Swan, ... (9 to 4 fav) 1

1579⁶ ZIGGY THE GREAT (Ire) 10-11-4 P A Roche, ... (20 to 1) 2

1533⁷ TONI'S TIP (Ire) 11-1 (3*) K Whelan, ... (6 to 1) 3

1533 GENTLE MOSSY (Ire) 11-4 D H O'Connor, ... (14 to 1) 4

1457⁵ NAZMI (Ire) 11-9 J Shortt, ... (100 to 30) 5

1275⁹ PERMIT ME (Ire) 10-6 A O'Shea, ... (12 to 1) 6

1488³ CHARLIE-O (Ire) 11-1 (3*) G Cotter, ... (7 to 2) 7

MISTER AUDI (Ire) 11-4 J P Broderick, ... (16 to 1) 8

1432 CASTLE BLAKE 11-4 D J Casey, ... (12 to 1) 9

BLITZER (Ire) 11-9 S H O'Donovan, ... (14 to 1) 10

1120⁶ BOULABALLY (Ire) 11-4 N Williamson, ... (14 to 1) 11

1143 POISON IVY (Ire) 10-6 (7*) J A Robinson, ... (33 to 1) 12

1490⁴ BEHAMORE GIRL (Ire) 10-8 (5*) J Butler, ... (10 to 1) 13

1579 BEHY BRIDGE (Ire) 10-13 T J Mitchell, ... (25 to 1) 14

SPEED BOARD (Ire) 11-4 F J Flood, ... (8 to 1) 15

1579⁸ JARSUN QUEEN (Ire) 10-6 (7*) L J Fleming, ... (20 to 1) 16

MILLA'S MAN (Ire) 11-4 F Woods, ... (10 to 1) 17

1579⁹ MY BLUE 10-6 (7*) E F Cahalan, ... (20 to 1) 18

1409³ ROSIE FLYNN (Ire) 10-13 T P Treacy, ... (14 to 1) 19

1120⁹ CARRIGMORE LADY (Ire) 10-13 C O'Dwyer, ... (20 to 1) 20

Dist: 3½l, 2½l, 5l, 1l. 4m 12.50s. (20 Ran).

(Golden Step Racing Syndicate), A P O'Brien

1778 Ellickson Engineering Handicap Hurdle (0-109 4-y-o and up) £3,253 2 ½m. (1:30)

1548³ ROCK'N ROLL KID (Ire) [-] 5-10-11 D J Casey, ... (8 to 1) 1

1244² SIR JOHN (Ire) [-] 7-11-1 C F Swan, ... (Evens fav) 2

1581 BOHOLA PETE (Ire) [-] 5-9-11 T P Treacy, ... (10 to 1) 3

1713⁶ HERSILIA (Ire) [-] 5-10-4 (7*) L J Fleming, ... (12 to 1) 4

229

14844 MISS BERTAINE (Ire) [-] 7-10-2 N Williamson..... (10 to 1)   5
15811 STONELEIGH TURBO (Ire) [-] 7-11-1 (7") A O'Shea, (10 to 1)   6
13596 DOOK'S DELIGHT (Ire) [-] 5-11-0 L P Cusack, ... (10 to 1)   7
GLENA GALE (Ire) [-] 6-9-7 J Jones, ... (25 to 1)   8
15503 KERCORLI (Ire) [-] 5-9-13 J P Broderick, ... (10 to 1)   9
1242 CELTIC SUNRISE (Ire) 8-11-2 F Woods, ... (14 to 1)   10
15506 MARILLO (Ire) [-] 6-10-0 M P Hourigan, ... (14 to 1)   11
14856 THE HEARTY LADY (Ire) [-] 6-10-9 C O'Dwyer, .. (20 to 1)   12
1550 CARRAIG-AN-OIR (Ire) [-] 7-9-2 (7") J D Pratt, ... (20 to 1)   13
1621 JO JO BOY (Ire) [-] 7-12-0 F J Flood, ... (14 to 1)   14
15495 THE SCEARDEEN (Ire) [-] 7-10-9 M Duffy, ... (20 to 1)   15
14843 NO BLUES (Ire) [-] 5-10-3 (3") G Cotter, ... (16 to 1)   16
16546 CRAIGARY (Ire) [-] 5-9-11 P P Kinane, ... (14 to 1)   17
INDESTRUCTIBLE (Ire) [-] 8-11-0 G M O'Neill, ... (20 to 1)   18
11433 VINTNERS VENTURE (Ire) [-] 4-10-11 (5") M J Holbrook,
.... (20 to 1)   19
10156 RAHANINE MELODY (Ire) [-] 4-9-7 (5") J Butler, .. (33 to 1)   20
Dist: 3½l, 1l, 1l, 3½l. 5m 10.90s. (20 Ran).

(Early Bird Syndicate), W P Mullins

1779 Waterford Crystal Novice Chase (5-y-o and up) £3,425 2m........ (2:00)

14051 JEFFELL 6-11-11 F Woods, ... (10 to 9 on)   1
1362* MAN OF ARRAN (Ire) 6-11-11 J Shortt, ... (100 to 30)   2
14616 ONTHEROADAGAIN (Ire) 8-11-11 T P Rudd, ... (10 to 1)   3
1618 BAILE NA GCLOCH (Ire) 7-11-4 (3") D P Murphy, .. (25 to 1)   4
1618 RYHANE (Ire) 7-11-7 C O'Brien, ... (20 to 1)   5
MONALEE STATEMENT (Ire) 7-11-7 D H O'Connor, (33 to 1)   6
15525 MUSKIN MORE (Ire) 5-11-5 C O'Dwyer, ... (14 to 1)   7
1534 KNOCKMUIRA (Ire) 6-11-7 D J Casey, ... (25 to 1)   8
11922 THE SUBBIE (Ire) 7-11-11 T P Treacy, ... (7 to 2)   9
1170 KING'S MANDATE (Ire) 7-11-7 P P Kinane, ... (25 to 1)   f
Dist: 6l, 8l, 5l, 15l. 4m 7.30s. (10 Ran).

(Thomas Bailey), A L T Moore

1780 Tattersalls Ireland E.B.F. Mares Beginners Chase (5-y-o and up) £3,425 2½m.............. (2:30)

11162 WOODVILLE STAR (Ire) 7-11-11 (3") G Cotter, ... (Evens fav)   1
15502 ROYAL ROSY (Ire) 5-11-12 C F Swan, ... (100 to 30)   2
KILBRICKEN MAID (Ire) 6-11-7 (7") Mr C A Murphy, (20 to 1)   3
12423 MARES POLLY 6-12-0 D H O'Connor, ... (7 to 1)   4
COOLAFINKA (Ire) 7-12-0 C O'Dwyer, ... (16 to 1)   5
15523 LANTINA (Ire) 5-11-12 F Woods, ... (8 to 1)   6
1362 SHARONS PRIDE (Ire) 6-12-0 A Barry, ... (20 to 1)   7
ARTISTIC QUAY (Ire) 7-11-7 (7") Mr J A Collins, .. (20 to 1)   8
PILS INVADER (Ire) 8-12-0 D T Evans, ... (20 to 1)   9
FIELD OF DESTINY (Ire) 7-11-11 (3") K Whelan, .. (20 to 1)   10
1655 RATHCORE LADY (Ire) 5-11-12 N Williamson, ... (20 to 1)   11
1362 KILLERK LADY (Ire) 5-11-12 T P Treacy, ... (20 to 1)   12
1714 SUEMENOMORE (Ire) 7-12-0 J Jones, ... (20 to 1)   13
9824 LISNAGAR LADY (Ire) 7-12-0 S H O'Donovan, .. (12 to 1)   f
Dist: 10l, 5l, 7l, 14l. 5m 23.10s. (14 Ran).

(Sean Donnelly), W J Burke

1781 Merck Sharp & Dohme Eqvalan Handicap Chase (0-109 4-y-o and up) £3,938 2½m............. (3:00)

1710 WHITBY [-] 8-9-103 C F Swan, ... (14 to 1)   1
16524 ANOTHER POINT (Ire) [-] 8-11-11 N Williamson, ... (2 to 1)   2
1458 BALLYFIN BOY [-] 10-10-4 T P Treacy, ... (6 to 1)   3
1552 HOLY GROUNDER (Ire) [-] 7-10-4 (7") A O'Shea, ..(6 to 1)   4
1058 DAMODAR [-] 7-11-5 F J Flood, ... (13 to 8 fav)   5
12452 CALL ME HENRY [-] 7-11-0 J P Broderick, ... (7 to 1)   pu
Dist: 1l, 4l, 8l, 3l. 5m 29.50s. (6 Ran).

(Mrs Angela Crowley), John Crowley

1782 Golden I.N.H. Flat Race (5-y-o) £2,740 2m..................(3:30)

14635 SHEISAGALE (Ire) 11-6 (3") Mr R Walsh, ... (6 to 1)   1
14364 CEOIL AGUS CRAIC (Ire) 12-0 Mr J P Dempsey, .. (8 to 1)   2
13648 TALKALOT (Ire) 11-7 (7") Mr A C Coyle, ... (5 to 1)   3
CROMWELLS KEEP (Ire) 12-0 Mr J A Berry, ... (10 to 1)   4
14366 PHAREIGN (Ire) 11-11 (3") Mr B M Cash, ... (12 to 1)   5
15394 FORTY SECRETS (Ire) 11-2 (7") Mr J L Cullen, ... (10 to 1)   6
10425 HANDSOME ANTHONY (Ire) 11-11 (3") Mr R H Hamilton,
.... (5 to 1)   7
FAIR SET (Ire) 12-0 Mr H F Cleary, ... (7 to 1)   8
1539 GALE JOHNSTON (Ire) 11-2 (7") Mr John P Moloney,
.... (12 to 1)   9
1487 WATT A BUZZ (Ire) 11-2 (7") Mr J T McNamara, .. (20 to 1)   10
QUIPTECH (Ire) 11-11 (3") Mr P M Kelly, ... (6 to 1)   11
14873 MONTANA KING (Ire) 12-0 Mr A J Martin, ... (4 to 1 fav)   12
741 FORTYNINEPLUS (Ire) 11-7 (7") Mr A J Dempsey, (14 to 1)   13
13645 FEAR CLISTE (Ire) 11-7 (7") Mr W Ewing, ... (10 to 1)   14
SO DARING (Ire) 11-2 (7") Mr J P McNamara, ... (14 to 1)   15
10815 ELLENMAE ROSE (Ire) 11-2 (7") Mr J G Sheehan, (16 to 1)   16
1539 MONKEY LEAF (Ire) 11-2 (7") Mr C A Cronin, ... (20 to 1)   17
LOVE A CUDDLE (Ire) 11-2 (7") Mr G Elliott, ... (20 to 1)   18
394 WILL I OR WONT I (Ire) 11-2 (7") Mr M J Walsh, .. (16 to 1)   ur
Dist: Sht-hd, 7l, 2½l, 7l. 4m 10.40s. (19 Ran).

(Maurice Harrington), Thomas Foley

MUSSELBURGH (good to firm)
Monday December 9th
Going Correction: MINUS 0.45 sec. per fur. (races 1,2,4,5,7), MINUS 0.15 (3,6)

1783 Longniddry Mares' Only Maiden Hurdle Class F (4-y-o and up) £2,115 2m
.... (12:20)

16579 KILNAMARTYRA GIRL 6-11-0 A Thornton, cl up, led appr 2
out, drvn clr frm last..................... (3 to 1 fav op 5 to 2)   1
ARIAN SPIRIT (Ire) 5-11-0 B Storey, jmpd deliberately, al
hndy, rdn and one pace betw last 2......(7 to 2 op 2 to 1)   2
SOMETHING SPEEDY (Ire) 4-11-0 R Garritty, hld up, pushed
alng and lost tch 3 out, styd on stdly frm nxt.
.............................(16 to 1 op 12 to 1 tchd 20 to 1)   3
1586 MISS MONT 7-11-0 R Hodge, led, rdn and hdd appr 2 out, btn
whn hit last.................................(10 to 1)   4
HUTCHIES LADY 4-11-0 D Parker, hld up, pld hrd, outpcd 3
out, sn no dngr.................................(33 to 1)   5
16568 JALMAID 4-10-9 (5") R McGrath, not jump wl, drvn alng in
midfield hfwy, sn struggling............(12 to 1 op 33 to 1)   6
FAIRY-LAND (Ire) 4-11-0 A Dobbin, midfield, drvn and outpcd
3 out, sn wl beh...........(9 to 2 op 4 to 1 tchd 5 to 1)   7
1073 NORTH END LADY 5-10-7 (7") L McGrath, pld hrd, f 1st.
....(14 to 1)   f
MOONLIGHT CALYPSO 5-11-0 A S Smith, in tch, pushed
alng in 4th whn broke dwn aftr 2 out, dead.
.............................(5 to 1 op 6 to 1 tchd 7 to 1)   pu
SWIFT MOVE 4-11-0 G Cahill, beh, struggling whn blun 4 out,
tld off when pld up bef 2 out...............(50 to 1)   pu
CELTIC COMMA 5-11-0 T Reed, sn wl beh, tld off whn pld up
aftr 2 out.................(66 to 1 op 100 to 1)   pu
Dist: 5l, 10l, 3l, 11l, 2l, 25l. 3m 44.80s. a 7.80s (11 Ran).

(P J Cronin), J Parkes

1784 Prestonpans Conditional Jockeys' Selling Handicap Hurdle Class G (0-95 4-y-o and up) £2,290 3m
.... (12:50)

13255 BARNSTORMER [66] (bl) 10-10-0 D Parker, led to 3rd, styd
hndy, drvn to chal last, ran on strly und to pres to ld ag'n r-in.
.............................(50 to 1 tchd 66 to 1)   1
16612 TRAP DANCER [91] 8-11-11 G Cahill, chsd ldrs, rdn to ld 2
out, hdd r-in, no extr und pres...........(5 to 4 on)   2
16933 LITTLE REDWING [66] (v) 4-10-0 E Callaghan, hld up, hdwy to
chase ldrs 2 out, kpt on und pres...........(7 to 1 op 5 to 1)   3
17364 THARSIS [67] 11-10-1 S Taylor, midfield, reminders tenth, no
imprsn frm 2 out.........................(7 to 1 op 6 to 1)   4
1068 YACHT CLUB [67] 14-9-10 (5") C Elliott, led 3rd, blun nxt, rdn
and hdd 2 out, fdd...........................(9 to 1 op 8 to 1)   5
TANCRED MISCHIEF [78] 5-10-12 P Midgley, chsd ldrs,
pushed alng whn hit 3 out, fdd aftr nxt.
.............................(12 to 1 op 10 to 1 tchd 14 to 1)   6
1034 LAURIE-O [66] (bl) 12-9-7 (7") N Hannity, in tch, struggling
whn hit 4 out, tld off when pld up betw last 2.
.............................(66 to 1 op 50 to 1)   pu
11226 MARCO MAGNIFICO (USA) [66] 6-10-0 G Lee, al rear, hit
5th, sn wl beh, pld up bef 3 out.........(16 to 1 op 12 to 1)   pu
CHARLVIC [66] 6-9-9 (5") L McGrath, tld off hfwy, pld up bef
tenth.....................(20 to 1 op 16 to 1 tchd 25 to 1)   pu
Dist: 2l, 1¼l, 9l, ½l, 8l. 5m 42.90s. a 5.90s (9 Ran).

(Eric A Elliott), E A Elliott

1785 Wee Jimmy Mitchell Handicap Chase Class D (0-125 5-y-o and up) £3,550 3m..................(1:20)

12852 CHARMING GALE [95] (v) 9-10-2 M Foster, cl up, led 6 out,
strly pressed frm 4 out, kpt on gmely............(4 to 1 jt-
fav op 7 to 2)   1
16344 PAGLIACCIO [99] 8-10-6 R Garritty, led till blun 5th, styd
hndy, 2 ls second whn blunded last, kpt on wl.....(4 to 1 jt-
fav tchd 9 to 2)   2
16345 PURITAN (Can) [110] (bl) 7-11-3 B Storey, hld up, hit 11th,
pressed ldr appr 4 out, no extr betw last 2.
.............................(6 to 1 op 5 to 1)   3
16583 TIGHTER BUDGET (USA) [104] 9-11-11 M Moloney, led 5th,
hit nxt, blun and hdd 6 out, hit next, one pace frm 2 out.
.............................(10 to 2 op 5 to 1 tchd 6 to 1)   4
15893 GRAND SCENERY (Ire) [93] 8-10-0 A Dobbin, beh, not jump
wl, hdwy and in tch appr 4 out, one pace frm 2 out.
.............................(5 to 1 op 4 to 1)   5
4583 THE TOASTER [97] 9-10-4 A S Smith, hld up, gd hdwy and in
tch 5 out, blun 3 out, sn btn..........(12 to 1 tchd 14 to 1)   6
1529 GREENHILL RAFFLES [117] 10-11-10 A Thornton, reminders
and drpd rear 4th, wl beh fnl circuit.............(33 to 1)   7
CORNET [107] (v) 10-11-0 P Niven, chsd ldrs, pushed alng 5
out, hit nxt, beh whn blun and uns rdr next.
.............................(6 to 1 tchd 7 to 1)   ur
Dist: 3l, 6l, 1¼l, 5l, 22l, 9l. 5m 50.70s. a 1.70s (8 Ran).
SR: 21/22/27/19/3/

(Mrs John Etherton), Mrs S C Bradburne

NATIONAL HUNT RESULTS 1996-97

1786 Gorebridge Handicap Hurdle Class E (0-110 4-y-o and up) £2,584 2m
.... (1:50)

1659* STASH THE CASH (Ire) [106] 5-12-1 (7ex) R Garritty, *patiently rdn, steady hdwy 3 out, shaken up to chal last, sn led, drvn out*............. (6 to 4 jt-fav tchd 5 to 4 and 13 to 8) 1
1635⁵ FEN TERRIER [95] 4-11-4 A Dobbin, *chsd ldrs, led and hit 2 out, hdd sn aftr last, kpt on wl*................. (6 to 1 jt-fav op 2 to 1 tchd 9 to 4) 2
1125⁷ PEGGY GORDON [77] 5-10-0 G Cahill, *pressed ldr, chalg whn hit 5th, ev ch till no extr appr last*....(6 to 1 op 5 to 1) 3
571⁶ HEE'S A DANCER [102] 4-11-11 A Thornton, *made most till hdd 2 out, fdd appr last*. (12 to 1 op 10 to 1 tchd 14 to 1) 4
RAPID MOVER [88] (bl) 9-10-11 M Moloney, *midfield, pushed alng hfwy, chsd ldrs 2 out, sn outpcd.* (20 to 1 op 14 to 1) 5
1656 BARIK (Ire) [77] 6-10-0 B Storey, *hld up, mstk in rear 4th, hdwy to press ldrs appr 2 out, faded little*............... (66 to 1) 6
1676 DOON RIDGE [77] 5-10-0 R Supple, *hld up, drpd rear 4 out, sn tld off*..................................(50 to 1) 7

Dist: 4l, 12l, 3l, 6l, 4l, dist. 3m 36.80s. b 0.20s (7 Ran).

SR: 31/16/-/8/   (G Shiel), M D Hammond

1787 Levy Board Novices' Handicap Hurdle Class E (0-100 4-y-o and up) £2,542 2½m.................(2:20)

1388⁵ COMMANDER GLEN (Ire) [92] (v) 4-11-13 R Garritty, *settled 3rd, hdwy gng wl to ld last, drvn out*..... (5 to 2 op 2 to 1) 1
1379³ LEAP IN THE DARK (Ire) [80] 7-11-1 A Thornton, *reminder to chase ldr, chalg whn blun 2 out, sn led, hdd and not quicken last*....................................(3 to 1 op 5 to 2) 2
1586* KINGS MINSTRAL (Ire) [74] 6-10-9 J Burke, *led, mstks 4 out and nxt, hdd and one pace betw last 2.*
.....................................(6 to 4 fav op 7 to 4 tchd 2 to 1) 3
1677 RUBISLAW [65] 4-9-8! (7*) Miss S Lamb, *sn tld off.*
...................(50 to 1 op 33 to 1 tchd 100 to 1) 4
1604 ANTARCTICERN (USA) [73] 6-10-8 G Cahill, *hld up, jinked lft and refused to race bend aftr 6th*........(8 to 1 op 6 to 1) ref

Dist: 4l, 1½l, dist. 4m 45.30s. a 7.30s (5 Ran).

(Punters Haven Racing Club), M D Hammond

1788 Humbie Novices' Chase Class E (5-y-o and up) £2,953 2½m...... (2:50)

NOYAN 6-10-12 A Dobbin, *jmpd wl, chsd ldr hfwy, led aftr 5 out, lft clr nxt, easily.*
...................(11 to 8 fav op 5 to 4 on tchd 6 to 4) 1
935⁸ HEDDON HAUGH (Ire) 8-10-12 R Supple, *chsd ldrs, pckd 11th, outpcd 5 out, styd on stdly frm 2 out, no ch wth wnr.*
...............................(50 to 1 op 25 to 1) 2
1523² MARBLE MAN (Ire) 6-10-12 R Garritty, *cl up, blun 6th, drvn and lost tch appr 5 out, no dngr aftr.*
...........................(13 to 8 op 2 to 1 tchd 6 to 4) 3
1325⁷ OVERWHELM (Ire) 8-11-2 K Jones, *beh, drvn and lost tch 6 out, styd on stdly frm 3 out*..........(66 to 1 op 50 to 1) 4
1258⁸ MOUNTAIN FOX (Ire) 6-10-12 Mr M Thompson, *hld up, struggling tenth, sn wl beh*..............(100 to 1 op 50 to 1) 5
1161⁴ WHITE DIAMOND (v) 8-10-12 M Foster, *beh, not fluent, jmpd slwly tenth, sn tld off*.................(25 to 1 op 14 to 1) 6
1587 HIGHLAND WAY (Ire) 8-10-12 A S Smith, *chsd ldrs, hit beh aftr 3 out, 3 ls second and hld whn f nxt.* (9 to 2 op 5 to 1) f
CAMPTOSAURUS (Ire) 7-10-12 A Thornton, *cl up, outpcd 5 out, disputing 3rd and no ch whn uns rdr 4 out.*
............................(20 to 1 op 14 to 1) ur

Dist: 13l, sht-hd, ½l, 24l, 1½l. 4m 56.10s. a 9.10s (8 Ran).

(C H McGhie), R A Fahey

1789 Musselburgh Intermediate Open National Hunt Flat Class H (4,5,6-y-o) £1,196 2m.............. (3:20)

CARLISLE BANDITO'S (Ire) 4-11-4 M Moloney, *chsd ldr, led 3 fs out, drvn clr ins last*......(7 to 2 op 5 to 3 tchd 4 to 1) 1
COBLE LANE 4-11-1 (3*) G Parkin, *settled rear, came wide strt, hdwy to chase wnr appr fnl furlong, no imprsn.*
............................(3 to 1 op 4 to 1 tchd 5 to 1) 2
1590⁴ LORD OF THE LOCH (Ire) 5-11-4 R Garritty, *hld up, hdwy and chsd wnr, styd on same pace fnl 2 fs.*
.........................(6 to 4 fav tchd 2 to 1) 3
1682⁸ DEERHUNTER 5-11-4 R Marley, *pld hrd, hdwy to chase ldrs 4 fs out, no extr frm 2 out.*............. (5 to 1 op 5 to 1) 4
CAUGHT AT LAST (Ire) 5-11-4 G Cahill, *hld up, pushed alng and not quicken o'r 3 fs out, one pace aftr.*
.....................(16 to 1 op 12 to 1 tchd 20 to 1) 5
ATLANTIC SUNRISE 4-10-13 K Jones, *keen hold, chsd ldrs till outpcd o'r 3 fs out, sn btn.*
...................(50 to 1 op 33 to 1 tchd 66 to 1) 6
1390⁵ BLOOD BROTHER 4-10-11 (7*) N Horrocks, *led, rdn and hdd 3 fs out, sn wknd*...........(8 to 1 op 5 to 1) 7
BLUE CHEQUER 5-10-13 A Dobbin, *in tch, struggling 4 fs out, sn lost touch*.....(50 to 1 op 33 to 1 tchd 66 to 1) 8

Dist: 6l, 2½l, 2l, 1¼l, 11l, sht-hd, 4l. 3m 40.50s. (8 Ran).

(J Berry), J Berry

FOLKESTONE (good to soft)
Monday December 9th
Going Correction: PLUS 1.00 sec. per fur. (races 1,3,6), PLUS 0.75 (2,4,5)

1790 Ottinge Juvenile Novices' Hurdle Class E (3-y-o) £2,427 2m 1f 110yds
.... (1:00)

1610⁸ RED RAJA 10-12 J Osborne, *made all, drw clr appr last, very easily*............................(20 to 1 tchd 25 to 1) 1
NORTHERN FLEET 10-12 R Dunwoody, *trkd wnr for most of race, wknd appr last*...........(15 to 8 jt-fav op 6 to 4) 2
1610 A CHEF TOO FAR 10-12 D O'Sullivan, *hld up in rear, hdwy 3 out, nvr nr to chal*....................(15 to 2 op 8 to 1) 3
ROYAL DIVERSION (Ire) 10-7 A P McCoy, *trkd ldrs, wnt second briefly 2 out, sn wknd*.................(15 to 8 jt-fav op Evens tchd 2 to 1) 4
RIVERS MAGIC 10-12 J R Kavanagh, *al beh, lost tch 5th, tld off*.....................................(14 to 1 op 7 to 1) 5
1412 GENERAL HENRY 10-12 P Holley, *hld up, rdn appr 4th, sn tld off*.....................................(66 to 1 op 25 to 1) 6
DARK AGE (Ire) 10-12 N Williamson, *pld hrd, hld up, blun 5th, no ch aftr, tld off, fnshd distressed.*
..............................(4 to 1 op 3 to 1 tchd 9 to 2) 7

Dist: 14l, 3l, 16l, dist, 18l, 18l. 4m 21.10s. a 24.10s (7 Ran).

SR: 18/4/1/-/   (J R Ali), P Mitchell

1791 Stalisfield Green Novices' Chase Class E (5-y-o and up) £3,305 2m
.... (1:30)

1600* GREENBACK (Bel) 5-11-5 C Llewellyn, *jmpd lft thrght, hit 3rd, hdd 4 out, led ag'n aftr nxt, clr 2 out.*
...........................(11 to 8 on op 5 to 4 on) 1
1232³ SUNSET AND VINE 9-10-12 R Dunwoody, *trkd wnr frm 4th, led four out till aftr nxt, btn whn blun last.*
.....................(10 to 1 op 12 to 1 tchd 14 to 1) 2
1704 MINSTER'S MADAM (v) 5-10-4 (3*) T Dascombe, *in tch till jmpd slwly 5th and 6th, sn wl beh.*
........................(11 to 1 op 10 to 1 tchd 12 to 1) 3
1349⁷ PORPHYRIOS 5-11-5 A P McCoy, *hld up, making hdwy whn f 8th*...................(5 to 2 op 6 to 4 tchd 11 to 4) f
1503⁵ ONE MORE MAN (Ire) 5-10-12 P Hide, *trkd wnr early, wknd 6th, wl beh whn blun and uns rdr 2 out.*
..........................(12 to 1 op 8 to 1 tchd 14 to 1) ur

Dist: 11l, 8l. 4m 9.90s. a 18.90s (5 Ran).

SR: 22/4/   (Jack Joseph), P J Hobbs

1792 Minster Maiden Hurdle Class F (4-y-o and up) £2,411 2¾m 110yds
.... (2:00)

1673² DANTES CAVALIER (Ire) 6-11-5 R Dunwoody, *al prmnt, slightly hmpd and lft in ld on bend aftr 6th, steadied to avoid loose horse last, drvn out*...........(6 to 4 on op Evens) 1
KORBELL (Ire) 7-11-0 A P McCoy, *hld up in tch, rdn 7th, wnt second 3 out, ev ch appr last, ran on und pres.*
.............................(6 to 1 op 5 to 2) 2
1447³ LORD ROOBLE (Ire) 5-11-5 P Hide, *hld up, hdwy frm 2 out, nvr dngrs*.............(11 to 2 op 3 to 1 tchd 6 to 1) 3
MILLMOUNT (Ire) (bl) 6-11-0 N Williamson, *prmnt, led 6th, hmpd on bend and hdd bef nxt, rdn 3 out, wknd next.*
.....................(10 to 1 op 14 to 1 tchd 20 to 1) 4
985 HARDY BREEZE (Ire) 5-11-5 J R Kavanagh, *in tch till wknd 3 out*.............(40 to 1 op 20 to 1 tchd 50 to 1) 5
MEL (Ire) 6-11-5 B Powell, *chsd ldrs, rdn 7th, wknd nxt, tld off.*
.....................(14 to 1 op 33 to 1 tchd 50 to 1) 6
ALONGWAYDOWN (Ire) 7-11-2 (3*) D Fortt, *beh whn f second.*
.............................(50 to 1 op 20 to 1) f
GINGER MAID 8-11-0 C Maude, *trkd ldr to 6th, tld off whn pld up bef 3 out*..................(25 to 1 op 8 to 1) pu
1555 MASTER UPEX 4-11-5 B Fenton, *al beh, tld off whn pld up bef 4 out*...................(100 to 1 op 40 to 1) pu
1224 ROYRACE 4-11-5 C Llewellyn, *led to 6th, hmpd on bend sn aftr, weakend quickly, tld off whn pld up bef last.*
...................(6 to 1 op 5 to 2) pu
MOUNT LODGE (Ire) 5-11-5 D Leahy, *al beh, tld off whn pld up bef 7th*........(66 to 1 op 40 to 1 tchd 100 to 1) pu
IADES BOY (NZ) 5-11-5 J Railton, *al beh, tld off whn pld up bef last*.........................(20 to 1 op 25 to 1) pu
1476 TINKER'S CUSS 5-11-0 S Curran, *prmnt to 5th, tld off whn pld up bef 7th*...........(14 to 1 op 12 to 1) pu
1306 STELLAR FORCE (Ire) 5-11-5 J Osborne, *al beh, tld off whn pld up bef last*.......(14 to 1 op 8 to 1 tchd 16 to 1) pu

Dist: ½l, 10l, 4l, 12l, dist. 5m 46.10s. a 36.10s (14 Ran).

(W H Dore), D R Gandolfo

1793 White Horse Novices' Chase Class E (5-y-o and up) £3,752 3¼m... (2:30)

1542² LITTLE MARTINA (Ire) 8-10-11 J R Kavanagh, *led to 8th, led tenth to 14th, led 3 out, sn clr*......(2 to 1 fav op 11 to 8) 1

1576³ MISS DISKIN (Ire) 7-10-7 B Powell, *hld up, jmpd slwly 6th, rdn and jumped lft 14th, wnt second 2 out, no ch with wnr.*
............................(9 to 2 op 4 to 1 tchd 5 to 1) 2

1568⁴ HAUNTING MUSIC (Ire) 8-10-12 R Dunwoody, *trkd ldr, led 8th to tenth, led 14th, hdd 3 out, wknd quickly.*
..............................(5 to 2 tchd 3 to 1) 3

1494⁵ ARCTIC MADAM 7-10-7 A P McCoy, *in tch till rdn 13th, sn tld off.*.........................(6 to 1 op 5 to 1 tchd 13 to 2) 4

1545. ALONE HOME (Ire) 5-10-8 (3*) J Magee, *stumbled badly 7th, tld off seventh.*.......(40 to 1 op 20 to 1 tchd 50 to 1) 5

PENNCALER (Ire) 6-10-12 N Williamson, *f 1st.*
..........................(5 to 1 op 3 to 1 tchd 11 to 2) f

Dist: 8l, 30l, dist, dist. 6m 44.00s. a 29.00s (6 Ran).

(Christopher Newport), D M Grissell

1794 Denton Handicap Chase Class F (0-105 5-y-o and up) £2,736 2m 5f .... (3:00)

1448* MAMMY'S CHOICE (Ire) [90] 6-11-1 (3*) P Henley, *al prmnt, led 8th, hdd appr last, rallied to ld r-in.*
............................(11 to 10 fav tchd 5 to 4) 1

MAESTRO PAUL [99] 11-11-3 P Hide, *trkd ldrs, led appr last, rdn and hdd r-in.*....(3 to 1 op 11 to 4 tchd 7 to 2) 2

1595 EARLY DRINKER [100] 8-12-0 J A McCarthy, *hld up, hdwy 9th, nvr nr to chal.*..........(13 to 2 op 4 to 1 tchd 7 to 1) 3

RUMBLE (USA) [72] 8-10-0 B Fenton, *beh whn blun second and 5th, some hdwy 9th, sn lost tch, tld off.*.........(20 to 1) 4

1698 HIDDEN PLEASURE [79] 10-10-7 D Leahy, *led, jmpd lft, hdd 8th, wknd, f tenth.*...(16 to 1 op 12 to 1 tchd 20 to 1) f

1698³ JACKSONS BAY [72] 6-10-0 N Williamson, *hld up hdwy 8th, held and 4th whn f 2 out.*..(13 to 2 op 3 to 1 tchd 7 to 1) f

986⁶ FIGHTING DAYS (USA) [89] 10-11-3 P Holley, *jmpd lft, with ldr till wknd tenth, tld off 3 out, pld up bef last.*
............................(14 to 1 op 12 to 1 tchd 20 to 1) pu

Dist: 1½l, 6l, dist. 5m 35.60s. a 24.60s (7 Ran).

SR: 1/8/3/-/ *(David Young), R H Alner*

1795 Seabrook Handicap Hurdle Class E (0-110 4-y-o and up) £2,427 2¾m 110yds..................................... (3:30)

1668* GENERAL MOUKTAR [103] 6-11-7 (7ex) A P McCoy, *hld up in 3rd pl, wnt second last, led on bit sn aftr, very easily.*
........(11 to 8 on op 15 to 8 on tchd 2 to 1 on and 5 to 4 on) 1

1597⁶ JACKSON FLINT [93] 8-10-11 R Dunwoody, *trkd ldr, led appr last, hdd sn aftr, outpcd.*..(4 to 1 op 7 to 2 tchd 9 to 2) 2

1644⁹ INDIAN QUEST [110] 7-12-0 C Llewellyn, *led till hdd appr last, not quicken.*............(4 to 1 op 5 to 1 tchd 6 to 1) 3

1572⁶ MANEREE [101] 9-11-5 N Williamson, *rcd wide, al last, rdn 2 out, sn tld off.*............(6 to 1 op 7 to 2 tchd 13 to 2) 4

Dist: 3l, 5l, dist. 5m 54.60s. a 44.60s (4 Ran).

(A S Helaissi), M C Pipe

LUDLOW (good to firm)
Monday December 9th
Going Correction: PLUS 0.15 sec. per fur.

1796 Bircher Novices' Handicap Hurdle Class E (0-100 4-y-o and up) £2,430 2m 5f 110yds............... (12:40)

1348⁶ COLWALL [73] 5-10-4 (7*) K Hibbert, *trkd ldrs, chlgd frm 4 out, led sn aftr 3 out, hit nxt, ran on wl.*...........(10 to 1) 1

1603⁵ FIRST CLASS [82] 6-11-6 R Greene, *hld up, hdwy to track ldrs 6th, rdn and kpt on frm 2 out, not rch wnr r-in.*
..............................(7 to 2 fav op 3 to 1) 2

1266⁸ SALTIS (Ire) [75] 4-10-13 Gary Lyons, *trkd ldrs, led 7th, rdn alng aftr 4 out, hdd sn aftr 3 out.*(7 to 1 op 6 to 1) 3

687⁹ TUG YOUR FORELOCK [67] 5-10-5 A Maguire, *beh, gd hdwy 6th, chsd ldrs 3 out, one pace nxt.*.......(7 to 1 op 6 to 1) 4

QUITE A MAN [83] 8-11-0 (7*) T Mortimer, *wnt prmnt 5th, pressed ldrs 4 out till outpcd nxt.*......(25 to 1 op 16 to 1) 5

1555⁶ SNOWY PETREL (Ire) [86] 4-11-10 S McNeill, *hld up, hdwy 6th, chsd ldrs appr 3 out, sn one pace.*...(8 to 1 op 6 to 1) 6

1479 SHANNON LAD (Ire) [77] 6-11-1 D Morris, *prmnt till rdn and wknd appr 3 out.*............................(7 to 1) 7

1261⁵ AWESTRUCK [62] (bl) 6-9-7 (7*) J Mogford, *beh 5th.*
..............................(14 to 1 op 10 to 1 tchd 16 to 1) 8

1270 THE CHEESE BARON [65] 5-10-3 N Mann, *prmnt to 4 out, wknd bef nxt.*...................(33 to 1 op 25 to 1) 9

1498 FERNY BALL (Ire) [62] 8-10-0 S Wynne, *beh 5th.*
..............................(33 to 1 op 25 to 1) 10

CRAVATE (Fr) [62] 6-9-9 (5*) D J Kavanagh, *effrt 5th, sn wknd, tld off whn pld up bef 3 out.*......(14 to 1 op 10 to 1) pu

TANGO MAN (Ire) [66] 4-10-1 (3*) G Hogan, *pld hrd, led and sn wl clr, hdd 7th, wknd rpdly, tld off whn pulled up bef 3 out.*
..............................(33 to 1 op 25 to 1) pu

Dist: 3l, 3l, ¾l, nk, 7l, 17l, 8l, 2½l. 4m 25m. 5m 7.70s. a 12.70s (12 Ran).

(Mrs Yvonne Allsop), Miss P M Whittle

1797 P & T Jones Novices' Chase Class E (5-y-o and up) £3,035 2m..... (1:10)

1647² SCOTTISH BAMBI 8-11-5 A Maguire, *slwly into strd, rcd in 3rd till hdwy to track ldr 4 out, quickened to chal 2 out, led last, quickened smartly r-in.*..........(11 to 4 tchd 3 to 1) 1

CHERYL'S LAD (Ire) 6-10-12 M A Fitzgerald, *slwly away, last till smooth hdwy to chase ldrs 6th, chlgd nxt till led 4 out, rdn and hdd last, not quicken.*.......(3 to 1 on op 7 to 2 on) 2

1634 MONAUGHTY MAN 10-10-11 (5*) D J Kavanagh, *made most till appr 6th, lost tch approaching 4 out.*(25 to 1 op 16 to 1) 3

1627 THE FENCE SHRINKER 5-10-12 T Jenks, *keen hold, with ldr, led appr 6th to 4 out, wknd rpdly, no ch whn blun 2 out.*
..............................(50 to 1 op 33 to 1) 4

Dist: 1½l, 19l, 23l. 4m 6.90s. a 16.90s (4 Ran).

(William J Kelly), P R Webber

1798 Shropshire Building Supplies Conditional Jockeys' Handicap Hurdle Class F (0-105 4-y-o and up) £2,788 2m........................... (1:40)

1512⁵ PRIDEWOOD PICKER [88] 9-11-2 (3*) D J Kavanagh, *al gng wl, chlgd on bit 2 out, led last, cmftbly*
..............................(5 to 2 fav op 3 to 1 tchd 9 to 4) 1

1472* GLOWING PATH [87] 6-10-13 (5*) J Harris, *steady hdwy frm 5th, chlgd 3 out, led nxt, hdd last, kpt on same pace.*
..............................(11 to 4 op 9 to 4) 2

1646⁷ SCHNOZZLE (Ire) [89] 5-11-6 R Massey, *hld up, hdwy to track ldrs 4 out, gng wl wth ldrs frm nxt, rdn, hit last, sn one pace.*
..............................(12 to 1 op 10 to 1 tchd 14 to 1) 3

1365⁵ JUST FOR A REASON [73] 4-10-4 E Husband, *mstk second, hdwy 3 out, hrd drvn to chal nxt, one pace appr last.*
..............................(16 to 1 op 14 to 1) 4

1546⁵ NOTHINGTODOWITHME [89] 6-11-3 (3*) A Bates, *prmnt, wth ldrs whn ran wide bend appr 3 out, btn nxt.*
..............................(9 to 2 op 3 to 1) 5

1472⁷ THEM TIMES (Ire) [70] 7-10-11 L Aspell, *made most to 4th, styd wth ldr, led aftr four out to 2 out, wknd quickly.*
..............................(50 to 1 tchd 66 to 1) 6

1604⁹ BIYA (Ire) [73] 4-9-12¹ (7*) C Hoggart, *some hdwy 4 out, sn wknd.*..............(40 to 1 op 25 to 1 tchd 50 to 1) 7

1022⁴ SPRING LOADED [77] 5-10-5 (3*) Michael Brennan, *chsd ldrs till appr 3 out, sn wknd.*.....(10 to 1 op 7 to 1) 8

1492⁵ HACKETTS CROSS (Ire) [93] 8-11-10 G Hogan, *beh, brief effrt 4 out, sn wknd.*.....(10 to 1 op 6 to 1 tchd 11 to 1) 9

1474⁷ OUT OF THE BLUE [69] 4-9-9 (5*) J Mogford, *chsd ldrs, rdn 3 out, wknd nxt.*............(20 to 1 op 33 to 1) 10

BRITANNIA MILLS [76] 5-10-2 (5*) Ross Berry, *wth ldr, led 4th till aftr four out, wknd rpdly, tld off whn pld up bef nxt.*
..............................(14 to 1 op 10 to 1) pu

Dist: 1¾l, 2l, ¾l, 7l, 2½l, 2l, 1¼l, 4l, 1¾l. 3m 42.20s. a 10.20s (11 Ran).

SR: 13/10/10/-/2/-/ *(Mrs B Morris), R J Price*

1799 His Royal Highness The Prince Of Wales Challenge Trophy Amateur Riders' Handicap Chase Class F (0-100 5-y-o and up) £3,468 3m .... (2:10)

1471⁵ OPAL'S TENSPOT [72] 9-9-7 (7*) Miss V Roberts, *trkd ldrs, chlgd 14th to nxt, quickened to ld last, cmftbly.*
..............................(16 to 1 op 12 to 1 tchd 20 to 1) 1

1140 FAIRY PARK [91] (v) 11-10-12 (7*) Mr N H Oliver, *lft in ld second, rdn alng frm 4 out, hdd last, styd on.*
..............................(14 to 1 op 5 to 1) 2

JUST ONE CANALETTO [78] 8-9-13 (7*) Mr J Goldstein, *wth ldrs, ev ch 4 out to nxt, no extr appr last.*
..............................(4 to 1 op 3 to 1 tchd 9 to 2) 3

1558² GLEN MIRAGE [93] 11-11-0 (7*) Miss M Coombe, *trkd ldrs, chlgd 15th to 4 out, one pace aftr nxt.*....(4 to 1 op 3 to 1) 4

1498² BIRONI [97] 7-11-6 (5*) Mr J Jukes, *tld till took wrong course appr second, returned to continue tld off, reco'red to chase ldrs 4 out, fourth and btn whn f last.*
..............................(5 to 4 on op 6 to 4 on tchd 11 to 10 on) f

Dist: 4l, 1¼l, 2½l. 6m 25.30s. a 38.30s (5 Ran).

(Miss Joy Mailes), J M Bradley

1800 Michael Perrott Novices' Claiming Hurdle Class F (4-y-o and up) £2,486 2m............................ (2:40)

415³ FIRST BEE 5-10-3 S Wynne, *beh, steady hdwy aftr 4 out, chlgd nxt, led 2 out, ran on wl.*
..............................(10 to 1 op 7 to 1 tchd 11 to 1) 1

985⁶ DADDY'S FIRST (v) 4-11-0 N Mann, *in tch, rdn 2 out, chlgd last, edgd rght und pres r-in, jst fld.*...(10 to 1 op 7 to 1) 2

1464⁴ CLIBURNEL NEWS (Ire) 6-10-9 Gary Lyons, *jmpd slwly and lost pos 4th, rallied aftr 3 out, styd on same pace frm nxt.*
..............................(9 to 2 op 3 to 1 tchd 5 to 1) 3

1438⁹ TEE TEE TOO (Ire) 4-10-8 W Marston, *chsd ldrs, led appr 3 out to 2 out, sn outpcd.*(25 to 1 op 20 to 1 tchd 33 to 1) 4

3977 NASHAAT (USA) 8-10-11 W Worthington, *prmnt, led aftr 4 out till appr nxt, wknd last.*..........(2 to 1 fav op 5 to 2) 5

1353³ MUTAWALI (Ire) 6-10-11 (3*) G Hogan, *beh, some prog 5th, wknd aftr 3 out.*..........(7 to 2 op 3 to 2) 6

MILL DANCER (Ire) 4-9-9 (5*) Michael Brennan, *keen, led till aftr 4 out, wknd nxt.*............(25 to 1 op 20 to 1) 7

1646 DODGY DANCER 6-10-11 L O'Hara, *some prog 5th, wknd 3 out*.................(16 to 1 op 12 to 1 tchd 20 to 1) 8
971 RUB AL KHALI 5-10-5 T Eley, *al beh*.
.......................(33 to 1 op 20 to 1 tchd 50 to 1) 9
1541 POLLI PUI 4-9-11 (3*) R Massey, *slwly away, al rear*.
.......................(50 to 1 op 33 to 1 tchd 66 to 1) 10
1476 LET YOU KNOW (Ire) 6-10-3³ T Jenks, *nvr better than mid-div*.......................(50 to 1 op 33 to 1 tchd 66 to 1) 11
1731 OFFICE HOURS 4-10-8 W McFarland, *al beh, tld off whn pld up bef 3 out*..........................(8 to 1 op 6 to 1) pu
Dist: 1l, 3l, 1¼l, 3l, 8l, 9l, 5l, 19l, ½l, 19l. 3m 43.20s. a 11.20s (12 Ran).

(D Pugh), F Jordan

1801 Invershin Novices' Handicap Chase Class E (0-100 5-y-o and up) £3,126 3m........................(3:10)

1302* GOD SPEED YOU (Ire) [90] (bl) 7-11-7 A Maguire, *made virtually all, pushed alng frm 4 out, styd on wl.
.......................(7 to 4 fav op 2 to 1) 1
1494* DROMHANA (Ire) [95] 6-11-12 M A Fitzgerald, *mstk 1st, rdn alng and hdwy 12th, chsd wnr frm 4 out, no imprsn r-in*.
.......................(2 to 1 tchd 9 to 4) 2
1706² RECORD LOVER (Ire) [69] 6-10-0 W Worthington, *in tch, rdn and lost pos 15th, styd on for moderate 3rd frm 3 out*.
.......................(13 to 2 op 5 to 1) 3
1593⁶ OXFORD QUILL [69] 9-10-0 D Morris, *mstks 3rd and 5th, hdwy 12th, rdn appr 4 out, sn wknd*.
.......................(12 to 1 op 10 to 1 tchd 14 to 1) 4
CAPTIVA BAY [69] 7-10-0 S Wynne, *chsd ldrs till wknd 12th.
.......................(33 to 1 op 20 to 1) 5
1605 DORMSTON BOYO [72] 6-10-0 (3*) R Massey, *in tch till wknd 14th, no ch whn mstk 4 out*.......(33 to 1 op 20 to 1) 6
1593 ROMANY BLUES [69] 7-10-0 D Gallagher, *wth ldrs early, beh whn mstk and uns rdr 7th*...........(8 to 1 tchd 9 to 1) ur
1270⁷ KING'S COURTIER (Ire) [72] 7-10-3 N Mann, *sn wl beh, tld off whn pld up bef 12th*.............(33 to 1 op 20 to 1) pu
1614⁶ CROWN IVORY (NZ) [69] 8-10-0 S Fox, *sn wl beh, tld off whn pld up bef 12th*...................(10 to 1 op 12 to 1) pu
Dist: 1¾l, 24l, 10l, 17l, 14l. 6m 2.80s. a 15.80s (9 Ran).

(Wallop), C P Morlock

1802 Oldfield Standard Open National Hunt Flat Class H (4,5,6-y-o) £1,305 2m........................(3:40)

942* MRS EM 4-11-1 (5*) O Burrows, *in tch, quickened to ld o'r 3 fs out, clr over one out, readily.
.......................(11 to 8 fav op Evens tchd 2 to 1) 1
1357³ KING OF THE BLUES 4-10-11 (7*) L Suthern, *al chasing ldrs, str chal o'r 3 fs out till one pace frm 2 out*.(8 to 1 op 5 to 1) 2
MADAM POLLY 4-10-6 (7*) K Hibbert, *hdwy to chase ldrs 5 fs out, one pace frm 2 out*...........(50 to 1 op 33 to 1) 3
FLOOSY 5-10-13 M A Fitzgerald, *hdwy frm 6 fs out, styd on same pace from o'r 2 out*......................(3 to 1) 4
53⁶ SARENACARE (Ire) 4-11-1 (3*) G Tormey, *chsd ldrs, one pace fnl 3 fs*.......................(12 to 1 op 7 to 1) 5
BALLINA 4-10-13 (5*) Michael Brennan, *prmnt till wknd o'r 2 fs out*.......................(16 to 1 op 12 to 1) 6
1306⁵ KYLAMI (NZ) 4-10-11 (7*) Mr G Shenkin, *gd hdwy 6 fs out, wknd o'r 3 fs out*.......................(9 to 2 op 4 to 1) 7
CHAOS AND ORDER 4-11-4 S McNeill, *pld hrd, prmnt till wknd 3 fs out*.......................(20 to 1 op 10 to 1) 8
ELLY'S DREAM 5-10-13 S Fox, *al beh*.
.......................(40 to 1 op 33 to 1 tchd 50 to 1) 9
740⁶ MONSIEUR PINK 4-11-4 T Eley, *led till o'r 3 fs out, sn btn*.
.......................(16 to 1 op 12 to 1) 10
HANDS OFF MILLIE 5-10-13 Mr N Bradley, *sn beh, tld off hfwy*.......................(33 to 1 op 20 to 1) 11
Dist: 4l, 3l, nk, 2l, hd, 7l, ¾l, nk, 3½l, dist. 3m 46.80s. (11 Ran).

(G Z Mizel), P F Nicholls

HUNTINGDON (good to soft)
Tuesday December 10th
Going Correction: PLUS 0.65 sec. per fur. (races 1,3,5,7), PLUS 0.95 (2,4,6)

1803 Flat Jockeys Claiming Hurdle Class F (4-y-o and up) £2,185 2m 110yds........................(12:30)

1528⁴ SURREY DANCER 8-11-3 (3*) G Lee, *hld up, not fluent 4th, rdn alng aftr nxt, hdwy 3 out, led appr next, kpt on r-in, readily to 4 fav tchd 7 to 4) 1
FONTANAS (Ire) 8-10-11 B Clifford, *led 5th till appr nxt, outpcd and lost pl, kpt on wl to chase wnr appro aching last, ran on*.......................(7 to 1 op 4 to 1 tchd 8 to 1) 2
1416⁸ ADDED DIMENSION (Ire) 5-10-7 (7*) A Aizpuru, *trkd ldrs, pld hrd, ev ch 3 out, sn outpcd, kpt on*.
.......................(16 to 1 op 14 to 1 tchd 20 to 1) 3
EULOGY (Fr) 7-10-12 A A Larnach, *led second to 5th, one pace und pres 2 out*.......................(8 to 1 op 6 to 1) 4
QUILLWORK (USA) 4-10-3 V Smith, *hld up beh, hdwy appr 4th, led briefly approaching 3 out, wknd aftr nxt*.
.......................(20 to 1 op 12 to 1) 5

EUROLINK THE LAD 9-10-7 (7*) J Prior, *hld up beh, hdwy to ld 3 out, sn hdd and wknd...*(4 to 1 op 3 to 1 tchd 5 to 2) 6
1541 SWING LUCKY (bl) 11-10-5 D Skyrme, *led to second, cl up till lost pl 4th, tld off whn pld up bef 3 out*.
.......................(20 to 1 tchd 16 to 1 and 25 to 1) pu
1305⁷ ARABIAN BOLD (Ire) 8-11-6 P Holley, *trkd ldrs, wknd appr 3 out, pld up bef nxt...................(9 to 1 op 5 to 1) pu
1130 WOODLANDS ENERGY 5-10-6 R Bellamy, *hld up, keen hold early, tld off whn pld up bef 3 out*...(33 to 1 tchd 50 to 1) pu
Dist: 1¾l, 3½l, 4l, 1¾l, 4l. 4m 4.30s. a 23.30s (9 Ran).

(Laurel (Leisure) Limited), Mrs M Reveley

1804 What A Buck Maiden Chase Class F (5-y-o and up) £2,914 3m.....(1:00)

1569² SUGAR HILL (Ire) 6-11-0 P Hide, *made virtually all, styd on wl frm 2 out*....................(9 to 2 op 5 to 1 tchd 6 to 1) 1
SLIDEOFHILL (Ire) 7-11-0 A Thornton, *trkd ldrs, one pace frm 2 out, got up to take second on line.
.......................(8 to 1 op 5 to 1 tchd 10 to 1) 2
1684 AMBER SPARK (Ire) 7-11-0 R Dunwoody, *hld up, hdwy 14th, ev ch 2 out, sn hrd rdn and one pace, lost second on line.
.......................(3 to 1 fav tchd 11 to 4 and 7 to 2) 3
1399⁵ MASTER HOPE (Ire) 7-11-0 A Maguire, *hld up beh ldrs, blun 14th (water), mstk 3 out, sn one pace.
.......................(12 to 1 op 10 to 1 tchd 14 to 1) 4
1555² FOREST MUSK (Ire) 5-10-13 M A Fitzgerald, *hld up, hdwy 3rd, wth wnr, mstk 5th, blun 14th (water), rdn aftr 3 out, sn wknd....................(7 to 1 op 5 to 1 tchd 8 to 1) 5
BOLSHIE BARON 7-11-0 Mr M Harris, *mstk 4th, in tch, beh frm 14th, tld off*.................(20 to 1 op 14 to 1) 6
1442⁸ SAKBAH (USA) 7-10-9 W Marston, *mstks, in tch, pushed alng 11th, sn wknd, tld off*............(33 to 1 tchd 50 to 1) 7
1701 ROLLED GOLD 7-11-0 R Farrant, *trkd ldrs, mstk 7th, blun 12th, sn wknd, tld off*...................(33 to 1) 8
1571⁴ QUIXALL CROSSETT 11-10-9 (5*) D J Kavanagh, *al beh, tld off*.......................(33 to 1 tchd 50 to 1) 9
FULL SHILLING (USA) 7-11-0 Jan Raja, *f 6th.
.......................(33 to 1 op 25 to 1 tchd 50 to 1) f
1568⁵ PEARL EPEE 7-10-9 R Bellamy, *chsd ldrs, blun 12th, wkng whn f 5 out*.......................(14 to 1) f
1473² MOUNT SERRATH (Ire) 8-11-0 J Osborne, *blun and uns rdr 1st......................(4 to 1 op 7 to 2 tchd 5 to 1) ur
SWISS TACTIC (Ire) 7-11-0 V Smith, *beh, mstks 4th and 13th, behind whn blun and uns rdr four out.
.......................(33 to 1 tchd 50 to 1) ur
THE MARMALADE CAT 7-11-0 J R Kavanagh, *al beh, lost tch 9th, tld off whn pld up bef 4 out.
.......................(25 to 1 op 20 to 1 tchd 33 to 1) pu
1765 BIG ARCHIE 6-11-0 C Llewellyn, *mstk 8th, al beh, tld off whn pld up bef 4 out*........(12 to 1 op 10 to 1 tchd 14 to 1) pu
Dist: 3½l, sht-hd, 1¼l, 16l, 16l, 17l, 12l, 9l. 6m 26.50s. a 46.50s (15 Ran).

(Mrs Timothy Pilkington), J T Gifford

1805 Friends Of ISRT Novices' Hurdle Class E (4-y-o and up) £2,652 2m 110yds........................(1:30)

SHARPICAL 4-10-12 M A Fitzgerald, *hld up, cld 5th, quickened on bit to ld r-in, cheekily*.........(5 to 1 op 4 to 1) 1
MOONAX (Ire) 5-10-12 R Dunwoody, *cl up, led 3 out, hrd rdn and hdd r-in, kpt on, no ch wth wnr.
.......................(13 to 8 on op 5 to 4 on tchd Evens and 7 to 4 on) 2
1509³ PENROSE LAD (NZ) 6-10-7 (5*) Mr R Thornton, *chsd ldrs, ev ch frm 2 out, kpt on one pace und pres.
.......................(12 to 1 op 10 to 1 tchd 14 to 1) 3
NIGHT DANCE 4-10-12 G Tormey, *hld up beh ldrs, cld 4th, one pace appr 2 out.......(7 to 1 op 6 to 1 tchd 9 to 1) 4
TOTAL JOY (Ire) 5-10-12 J Railton, *hld up mid-div, cld 5th, hrd rdn and no imprsn appr last.
.......................(25 to 1 op 20 to 1 tchd 33 to 1) 5
1514⁶ DASHANTI 5-10-9 (3*) R Massey, *hld up beh, hrd rdn appr 2 out, styd on, nrst finish.........(33 to 1 op 20 to 1) 6
1514⁴ THE STAGER (Ire) 4-10-12 G Bradley, *beh, hdwy 5th, rdn and wknd aftr 3 out.................(25 to 1 op 20 to 1) 7
CLINTON (Ire) 5-10-12 C O'Dwyer, *hld up beh, hdwy appr 3 out, wknd 2 out.......................(33 to 1 op 20 to 1) 8
1350⁵ SYMPHONY'S SON (Ire) 5-10-12 A Maguire, *hld up, hdwy 4th, rdn 3 out, sn btn...............(14 to 1 op 12 to 1) 9
BOB'S PLOY 4-10-12 R Hughes, *cl up, led 4th till 3 out, sn drvn and btn, tld off*..............(12 to 1 tchd 25 to 1) 10
LATEST THYNE (Ire) 6-10-12 A Thornton, *hld up beh, tld off frm 3 out..........................(20 to 1 op 16 to 1) 11
1541⁵ AL HELAL (v) 4-10-12 W Marston, *keen hold, cl up till hrd rdn and wknd 2 out*.........(50 to 1 op 33 to 1) 12
LOCH GARMAN (Ire) 6-10-5 (7*) Miss Elizabeth Doyle, *mid-div, wknd aftr 4th, tld off*..................(50 to 1) 13
CADES BAY 5-10-12 C Llewellyn, *led to 4th, wknd nxt, tld off*.......................(33 to 1 op 16 to 1) 14
1560 BALLYQUINTET (Ire) 5-10-7 K Gaule, *cl up to 4th, sn wknd, tld off*.......................(50 to 1) 15
YOUNG ROSE 4-10-7 T Kent, *trkd ldrs till wknd quickly 4th, tld off*.......................(50 to 1) 16
1642 TALK BACK (Ire) 4-10-12 J Osborne, *hld up beh, blun 4th and pld up*..............(9 to 1 op 6 to 1 tchd 10 to 1) pu
1135 WOODLANDS LAD TOO 4-10-12 R Bellamy, *al beh, tld off whn pld up aftr 5th*.......................(50 to 1) pu

233

Dist: 1¼l, ¾l, 4l, 6l, 2½l, 1¾l, 7l, 2½l, 17l, 9l. 3m 58.40s. a 17.40s (18 Ran).
SR: 17/15/14/10/4/1/   (Thurloe Thoroughbreds II), N J Henderson

1806 Sir Peter Crossman ISRT Novices' Handicap Chase Class D (0-105 4-y-o and up) £3,855 2m 110yds.. (2:00)

	RIVER LEVEN [81] (bl) 7-10-5 R Dunwoody, chsd ldr, led appr last, rdn clr, eased nr finish.............. (12 to 1 op 10 to 1 tchd 16 to 1)	1
	AMBER VALLEY (USA) [97] 5-11-7 A Thornton, led, sn clr, hdd appr last, one pace................ (12 to 1 op 10 to 1 tchd 16 to 1)	2
1376⁴	JYMJAM JOHNNY (Ire) [100] 7-11-10 A Maguire, hld up, mstk 7th (water), effrt 3 out, kpt on one pace und pres frm nxt............ (11 to 2 op 4 to 1 tchd 5 to 1)	3
1568⁸	ANOTHER VENTURE (Ire) [92] 6-10-11 (5*) Mr R Thornton, hld up beh, outpcd frm 4 out, nvr nr to chal............ (20 to 1 op 10 to 1 tchd 33 to 1)	4
1264⁴	TOTAL ASSET [78] 6-10-2² Gary Lyons, hld up, nvr on terms............ (10 to 1 op 12 to 1 tchd 16 to 1)	5
1557	BRAZIL OR BUST [100] 5-11-10 J Osborne, chsd ldg .... fav op 2 to 1 tchd 7 to 2)	6
	SERIOUS [97] 6-11-7 C O'Dwyer, hld up, no hdwy whn mstk 3 out, sn btn and eased, tld off.... (3 to 1 co-fav op 2 to 1)	7

Dist: 9l, ¾l, 1½l, 9l, 30l, 5l. 4m 16.30s. a 22.30s (7 Ran).
SR: 11/18/20/10/   (R E Brinkworth), D R Gandolfo

1807 National Hunt Jockeys Handicap Hurdle Class D (0-125 4-y-o and up) £2,847 2m 110yds........... (2:30)

	MOST EQUAL [110] 6-11-5 R Hughes, hld up, hdwy 5th, led last, edgd lft, drvn out................(4 to 1 op 3 to 1)	1
1572⁵	ALBEMINE (USA) [119] 7-12-0 T Kent, hld up, hdwy 4th, led appr 2 out, hdd last, no extr und pres.... (9 to 1 op 7 to 1)	2
1402⁶	MENELAVE (Ire) [108] 6-11-3 J Osborne, trkd ldr frm 3rd, led 5th to appr 2 out, sn outpcd. (9 to 2 op 7 to 2 tchd 5 to 1)	3
1572²	MARIUS (Ire) [112] 6-11-7 P Hide, led, sn clr, hdd 5th, rdn and btn 3 out.................(15 to 8 fav op 5 to 2 tchd 3 to 1)	4
	GLANMERIN (Ire) [119] 5-12-0 G Bradley, beh, mstk 4th, tld off.......................(20 to 1 tchd 33 to 1)	5
	STORM DUST [110] 7-11-5 R Dunwoody, al beh, tld off	6
1299	JEMIMA PUDDLEDUCK [93] 5-10-2 T Eley, hld up, pushed alng appr 4th, sn btn, tld off............ (6 to 1 op 5 to 1 tchd 13 to 2)	7
1167⁷	EDEN DANCER [105] 4-10-11 (3*) G Lee, cl up till wknd aftr 4th, tld off............... (7 to 1 op 5 to 1)	8
	YOUNG AT HEART (Ire) [91] 5-10-0 D Skyrme, beh whn f 4th............ (20 to 1 op 16 to 1 tchd 25 to 1)	f

Dist: ¾l, 9l, 5l, 21l, 1l, 16l, ¾l. 3m 57.20s. a 16.20s (9 Ran).
SR: 36/44/14/13/-/-/   (Heeru Kirpalani), M C Pipe

1808 Horserace Writers Conditional Jockeys' Handicap Chase Class E (0-110 4-y-o and up) £2,968 2½m 110yds........................ (3:00)

1634⁷	EAST HOUSTON [96] 7-11-10 R McGrath, hld up, hdwy to ld 4 out, mstk and lft clr last...(4 to 1 op 7 to 2 tchd 9 to 2)	1
	JUDICIAL FIELD (Ire) [95] (bl) 7-11-9 E Husband, chsd ldrs, mstk 9th, rdn 4 out, lft modest second last.................(3 to 1 tchd 7 to 2)	2
1349	VIAGGIO [75] 8-10-3 Michael Brennan, hld up, not fluent tenth, hdwy and ev ch 3 out, sn outpcd. (20 to 1 op 14 to 1)	3
1643⁷	COUNT BARACHOIS (USA) [96] 8-11-10 K Gaule, dsptd ld, led 8th, hdd 4 out, sn btn............ (16 to 1 tchd 20 to 1)	4
1797³	MONAUGHTY MAN [72] 10-10-0 D J Kavanagh, dsptd ld to 8th, wth ldr whn f 12th...........(20 to 1 op 12 to 1)	f
1498³	AT THE GROVE (Ire) [96] 6-11-5 (5*) W Walsh, hld up, mstk 4th, f 9th.................(9 to 4 fav op 6 to 4)	f
1605⁵	PLAYING TRUANT [82] 8-10-10 L Aspell, hld up, hdwy to chase wnr aftr 3 out, held in second whn blun and uns rdr last........................(7 to 2 op 5 to 2)	ur

Dist: 21l, 13l, dist. 5m 22.50s. a 35.50s (7 Ran).
    (Highgreen Partnership), J J O'Neill

1809 Weatherbys 'Stars Of Tomorrow' National Hunt Flat Intermediate - Class H (4,5,6-y-o) £1,385 2m 110yds,................... (3:30)

1390⁴	STRONG MINT (Ire) 5-11-1 (3*) G Lee, hld up beh ldrs, hdwy o'r 4 fs out, led over 2 out, not extended............ (Evens fav op 5 to 4 tchd 2 to 1)	1
1483	FEEBEE FIVE 4-10-10 (3*) P Henley, hld up, hdwy 4 fs out, chsd wnr and hrd rdn o'r one out, no imprsn............ (14 to 1 op 16 to 1)	2
	BESSIE BROWNE (Ire) 4-10-13 K Gaule, cl up, drvn o'r 2 fs out, kpt on.............. (16 to 1 op 10 to 1 tchd 33 to 1)	3
1483	FIDDLER'S LEAP (Ire) 4-10-11 (7*) Mr A Wintle, al hndy, ev ch o'r 2 fs out, one pace............ (25 to 1 op 14 to 1 tchd 25 to 1)	4
	COSY RIDE 4-10-11 (7*) L Suthern, cl up, led 4 fs out to o'r 2 out, one pace................... (10 to 1 op 4 to 1)	5

	BENVENUTO 5-10-11 (7*) Mr R Wakley, al hndy, outpcd frm 3 fs out................(10 to 1 op 5 to 1 tchd 12 to 1)	6
1476²	LOVELY RASCAL 4-10-8 (5*) R McGrath, trkd ldrs, pushed alng 6 fs out, outpcd frm 4 out........(3 to 1 op 5 to 2 tchd 4 to 1)	7
	TRYMYPLY 4-10-13 (5*) Sophie Mitchell, beh, hdwy 4 fs out, wknd o'r 2 out...................(50 to 1)	8
	QUINCE BAY 4-10-13 (5*) Mr R Thornton, led to 4 fs out, sn btn....................... (33 to 1 tchd 50 to 1)	9
1675	SOCIAL INSECURITY (Ire) 5-10-13 (5*) D J Kavanagh, keen hold, cl up till rdn and wknd o'r 2 fs out..........(33 to 1)	10
1350	ABOVE SUSPICION (Ire) 4-11-4 Mr E James, hld up, al beh...................................(33 to 1)	11
1483	NORMANDY DUKE (NZ) 4-11-1 (3*) J Magee, hld up mid-div, hdwy o'r 7 fs out, wknd over 4 out..... (25 to 1 op 20 to 1)	12
1590⁶	RUN FOR THE MILL 4-10-11 (7*) M Newton, mid-div, pushed alng hfwy, wknd hfwy, tld off.............	13
1648	TODDYS LASS 4-10-8 (5*) Michael Brennan, hld up mid-div, beh frm hfwy, tld off...............(50 to 1 op 33 to 1)	14
	THAT MAN CARTER (Ire) 5-11-1 (3*) F Leahy, hld up, hrd rdn and wknd 6 fs out, tld off..........(16 to 1 op 12 to 1 tchd 20 to 1)	15
	ABFAB 4-10-11 (7*) A Watt, pld hrd, hld up beh ldrs, lost pl hfwy, tld off....................(33 to 1 op 20 to 1)	16

Dist: 2l, 5l, 1½l, 3½l, 1¼l, 3½l, 1½l, 5l, 2½l, nk. 4m 0.50s. (16 Ran).
    (J Good), Mrs M Reveley

PLUMPTON (good to soft)
Tuesday December 10th
Going Correction: PLUS 1.40 sec. per fur.

1810 Ditchling Novices' Hurdle Class E (4-y-o and up) £2,616 2½m...... (12:40)

1555*	EMERALD STATEMENT (Ire) 6-10-9 (3*) G Hogan, in tch and al sng wl, lft in ld 3 out, sn clr, easily............(7 to 4 on op 2 to 1 on tchd 6 to 4 on)	1
	SIOUX TO SPEAK 4-10-12 B Fenton, hld up in rear, hdwy appr 4 out, lft 3rd nxt, sn chsd wnr......(8 to 1 op 9 to 2)	2
1642⁵	MAZIRAH 5-10-12 D Morris, hld up, hdwy 6th, lft second 3 out, sn wknd...............(20 to 1 op 14 to 1 tchd 25 to 1)	3
1641	ENGLISH INVADER 5-10-12 A P McCoy, in tch whn mstk 4th, wknd four out, tld off....(7 to 1 op 10 to 1 tchd 6 to 1)	4
1573⁴	SCOTBY (Bel) 6-11-5 B Powell, prmnt, led 8th till f 3 out..................(7 to 2 op 3 to 1)	f
	KYBO'S REVENGE (Ire) 5-10-12 D O'Sullivan, in rear wen mstk 5th, uns rdr 7th... (25 to 1 op 14 to 1 tchd 33 to 1)	ur
1703	HALAM BELL 4-10-0 (7*) J Power, tried to refuse 1st 3 flights, refused 4th......................(66 to 1 op 33 to 1)	ref
	JACK OF DIAMONDS 8-10-12 A McCabe, led to 8th, sn wknd, tld off whn pld up bef 2 out... (50 to 1 op 20 to 1)	pu
1270	QUEEN OF THE SUIR (Ire) 7-10-7 S Curran, trkd ldr to 6th, sn wknd, pld up aftr 8th...............(100 to 1 op 50 to 1)	pu

Dist: 16l, ½l, dist. 5m 19.60s. a 42.60s (9 Ran).
    (The Hon Mrs C Yeates), D M Grissell

1811 Henfield Selling Handicap Hurdle Class G (0-90 4-y-o and up) £1,909 2m 1f........................(1:10)

1606⁶	KAYFAAT (USA) [78] 8-11-9 A P McCoy, pushed alng frm strt, led 4 out, drvn clr 2 out............(9 to 4 fav op 7 to 4 tchd 11 to 4)	1
1061⁷	SLIGHTLY SPECIAL (Ire) [59] 4-10-3 T J Murphy, led till hdd 4 out, ev ch nxt, rdn 2 out, eased whn hld............(33 to 1 op 12 to 1)	2
1697³	WATER HAZARD (Ire) [73] 4-11-3 A Dicken, al same pl, lost tch 4 out................(13 to 2 op 4 to 1 tchd 7 to 1)	3
1235⁵	AL HAAL (USA) [71] 7-11-1 D O'Sullivan, in tch whn mstk 4th, no ch frm four out.............(4 to 1 op 6 to 1)	4
	ALDWICK COLONNADE [80] 9-11-10 W McFarland, al towards rear....................(11 to 2 op 7 to 2 tchd 6 to 1)	5
	FRUIT TOWN (Ire) [70] 7-11-0 B Fenton, in rear whn hit 4th, effrt 6th, sn btn............(11 to 2 op 7 to 1)	6
	TRENDY AUCTIONEER [64] 8-10-8 D Leahy, al beh............ (20 to 1 op 16 to 1)	7
	PERSIAN BUD (Ire) [67] 8-10-11 M Bosley, al beh, tld off............(8 to 1 op 11 to 1 tchd 9 to 1)	8

Dist: 14l, 12l, 5l, ¾l, 4l, 5l, dist. 4m 35.90s. a 38.90s (8 Ran).
    (Crown Racing), M C Pipe

1812 Owl Holdings Handicap Chase Class D (0-120 4-y-o and up) £4,077 2m 5f......................(1:40)

1301	BEATSON (Ire) [95] 7-10-8 B Powell, trkd ldr frm 4th, disputing ld whn hit 5 out, rallied to lead 3 out, drvn clr.................(11 to 4 tchd 5 to 2)	1
1445²	MR MATT (Ire) [105] 8-11-4 B Fenton, trkd ldr, led 3rd to 7th, led 4 out, rdn and hdd nxt, hrd ridden and no further hdwy......................................(7 to 4 fav op 11 to 4)	2
1575²	BEAU BABILLARD [115] 9-12-0 A P McCoy, in tch till wknd appr 3 out..........(5 to 2 fav op 11 to 4 tchd 3 to 1)	3

1445 BLACK CHURCH [92] 10-10-5 D O'Sullivan, *in tch, led 7th till hdd 4 out, btn whn jmpd badly rght 2 out.* (3 to 1 op 9 to 4) 4
1559³ JOKER JACK [88] 11-9-12¹ (3*) T Dascombe, *led to 3rd, tld off 9th.* .... (40 to 1 op 33 to 1) 5
Dist: 9l, 7l, 2½l, dist. 5m 42.10s. a 36.10s (5 Ran).
SR: 13/14/17/-/-/ (Mrs E B Gardiner), R H Buckler

1813 Brighton Novices' Claiming Hurdle Class F (4 - 7-y-o) £1,992 2m 1f
.... (2:10)

1723 URBAN LILY 6-9-10 (7*) J Harris, *trkd ldr, led 4th, rdn clr appr 2 out.* .... (11 to 10 on op 5 to 4 on tchd Evens) 1
1669⁴ FAIRELAINE 4-11-1 A P McCoy, *hld up, hdwy to track wnr 6th, rdn 3 out, no imprsn aftr.* (5 to 4 op 11 to 10 tchd 6 to 4) 2
ROBIN ISLAND 4-10-1 (7*) M Clinton, *al abt same pl, lost tch 4 out, tld off.* .... (33 to 1 op 25 to 1 tchd 50 to 1) 3
WARSPITE 6-10-0 (5*) S Ryan, *al beh, rdn appr 4 out, sn btn, tld off.* .... (14 to 1 op 10 to 1 tchd 16 to 1) 4
SIR OLIVER (Ire) 7-11-0 T J Murphy, *led to 4th, sn wknd tld off whn pld up aftr 6th.* .... (50 to 1 op 25 to 1) 5
Dist: 24l, dist, 14l. 4m 37.20s. a 40.20s (5 Ran).
(Mrs C J Cole), R J Hodges

1814 'Galleano' Challenge Cup Class E Handicap Chase (0-110 5-y-o and up) £3,070 3m 1f 110yds..... (2:40)

1445⁶ JURASSIC CLASSIC [109] 9-12-0 M Richards, *al prmnt, led appr 14th, styd on wl whn chlgd frm 5 out.* ....(6 to 1 op 5 to 1 tchd 7 to 1) 1
1705² RING CORBITTS [84] 8-10-0 (3*) G Hogan, *hld up in rear, gd hdwy to go second 6 out, hit nxt 2, ev ch whn blun two out, no imprsn aftr.* .... (33 to 1 op 20 to 1) 2
1440² CELTIC TOWN [108] 8-11-13 J A McCarthy, *hld up, hdwy to go 3rd 14th, wknd 4 out, tld off.* (11 to 4 fav tchd 100 to 30) 3
1445 MIGHTY FROLIC [105] 9-11-10 Mr T Hills, *al beh and nvr on terms, tld off.* ....(14 to 1 op 16 to 1) 4
LAY IT OFF (Ire) [85] 7-10-4 S Curran, *chsd ldrs till rdn and lost tch 13th, tld off.* ....(11 to 2 op 8 to 1) 5
1426 CHILDHAY CHOCOLATE [105] 8-11-10 A P McCoy, *in tch whn f 6th.* ....(9 to 2 op 7 to 1 tchd 5 to 1) f
1664 CREDON [103] 8-11-8 N Williamson, *hld up in rear, hdwy 12th, wknd appr 6 out, tld off whn pld up bef 3 out.* ....(4 to 1 op 3 to 1 tchd 9 to 2) pu
1674⁶ TITAN EMPRESS [81] (v) 7-10-0 N Mann, *hit second, badly hmpd by faller 6th, pld up bef nxt.* ....(10 to 1 op 6 to 1) pu
1424 MILLFRONE (Ire) [83] 6-10-2² D O'Sullivan, *led till hdd appr 14th, wknd 6 out, tld off whn pld up bef tree out.* .... (66 to 1 op 50 to 1) pu
Dist: 2l, dist, 17l, 28l. 6m 58.70s. a 44.70s (9 Ran).
SR: 10/-/-/-/-/ (Brian Seal & Roger Rees), Mrs L Richards

1815 Chailey Novices' Handicap Hurdle Class E (0-100 4-y-o and up) £2,364 3m 110yds................ (3:10)

1663⁵ COPPER COIL [87] 6-11-4 (7*) J Power, *al prmnt, led aftr 9th, rallied und pres 2 out, all out.* ....(10 to 1 op 5 to 1) 1
1543⁵ LOUGH TULLY (Ire) [74] 6-10-12 S Wynne, *hld up in tch, gd hdwy 4 out, went second appr 2 out, kpt on und pres.* ....(4 to 1 fav op 10 to 1) 2
1502⁶ MISS SECRET [76] 6-11-0 D Bridgwater, *hld up in rear, hdwy wth circuit to go, ev ch appr 2 out, weakend bef last.* .... (25 to 1 op 33 to 1 tchd 50 to 1) 3
1614⁵ HONEY MOUNT [90] 5-12-0 N Williamson, *hld up, hdwy 4 out, ev ch 2 out, sn btn.* ....(5 to 1 op 7 to 2 tchd 6 to 1) 4
1663⁴ QUINAG [89] 5-11-13 S McNeill, *led till hdd aftr 6th, rdn 4 out, sn btn, tld off.* ....(10 to 1 op 9 to 2) 5
EQUITY'S DARLING (Ire) [79] 4-11-3 D Gallagher, *reluctant to race, al beh, tld off 4 out.* ....(14 to 1 op 6 to 1) 6
PLASSY BOY [75] 7-10-13 A P McCoy, *al beh, lost tch 6th, tld off.* ....(6 to 1 op 8 to 1 tchd 5 to 1) 7
1573⁹ RED BRANCH (Ire) [69] 7-10-7 T J Murphy, *al beh, tld off whn pld up bef 3 out.* ....(7 to 1 op 10 to 1 tchd 14 to 1) pu
1348⁵ FAIRIES FAREWELL [82] 6-11-6 J A McCarthy, *trkd ldrs till wknd bef 3 out, pld up before nxt.* ....(10 to 1 op 4 to 1) pu
975 DIFFICULT DECISION (Ire) [85] 5-11-9 Derek Byrne, *trkd ldr, led 6th, hdd aftr 9th, rdn and ev ch appr 2 out, tired quickly, pld up bef last.* ....(5 to 1 op 7 to 1 tchd 6 to 1) pu
Dist: 1½l, 12l, 8l, dist, 10l, 5l. 6m 44.80s. (10 Ran).
(R A Lloyd), W G M Turner

1816 Eastbourne Handicap Hurdle Class F (0-105 4-y-o and up) £1,974 2½m
.... (3:40)

ISMENO [97] 5-11-9 A Dicken, *led appr 4th, rdn approaching 2 out, styd on.* ....(8 to 1 op 6 to 1 tchd 9 to 1) 1
1383 STONEY VALLEY [102] 6-12-0 N Williamson, *hld up in rear, gd hdwy to go second appr 2 out, rdn bef nxt, no imprsn.* ....(7 to 1 op 5 to 1 tchd 8 to 1) 2
1795² GENERAL MOUKTAR [103] 6-12-1 (7ex) A P McCoy, *hld up in tch, outpcd 4 out, rdn and one pace aftr next.* .... (6 to 4 on op 11 to 8 on tchd 13 to 8 on) 3
1444⁴ DO BE WARE [74] 6-10-0 B Fenton, *led second to 3rd, styd in tch till wknd 3 out.* ......(33 to 1 op 20 to 1 tchd 40 to 1) 4

1699 RAAHIN (USA) [76] 11-10-2 S McNeill, *led to second, led 3rd to 4th, wknd 7th, tld off.* (25 to 1 op 20 to 1 tchd 33 to 1) 5
1558 WHISTLING BUCK (Ire) [86] 8-10-12 D O'Sullivan, *hld up, hdwy 4th, ev ch four out, wknd bef nxt.* .... (11 to 2 op 4 to 1 tchd 6 to 1) 6
1603⁴ LITTLE HOOLIGAN [84] 5-10-7 (3*) T Dascombe, *in tch till outpcd and wknd approahing 3 out, eased, tld off.* .... (8 to 1 op 6 to 1 tchd 10 to 1) 7
Dist: 4l, 5l, 17l, 26l, 1l, dist. 5m 33.40s. a 56.40s (7 Ran).
(Mrs A M Upsdell), S Dow

SEDGEFIELD (good)
Tuesday December 10th
Going Correction: PLUS 0.50 sec. per fur.

1817 Golden Lion 'National Hunt' Novices' Hurdle Class E (Div I) (4-y-o and up) £1,952 2m 5f 110yds........ (12:20)

SUTHERLAND MOSS 5-10-12 J Callaghan, *sn tracking ldrs, led bef 2 out, hit last, kpt on wl...* (13 to 8 fav op 11 to 10) 1
1623⁸ GRAND CRU 5-10-12 P Niven, *sn wth ldr, led bef 3 out, hdd before nxt, ch betw last 2, no extr.* .... (11 to 4 op 5 to 2 tchd 3 to 1) 2
BASINCROFT 6-10-5 (7*) A Todd, *sn wl beh, styd on frm 3 out, no ch wth 1st 2.* ....(50 to 1 tchd 66 to 1) 3
1631 SEE MORE GHOSTS (Ire) 5-10-12 J Supple, *beh, mstk 5th, sn drvn alng, kpt on frm 3 out, nvr dngrs.* .... (20 to 1 op 14 to 1 tchd 25 to 1) 4
PHILEAS FOGG (Ire) 7-10-12 B Storey, *made most till hdd bef 3 out, sn wknd.* ....(100 to 1) 5
1317 BOYZONTOOWA (Ire) 4-10-12 Richard Guest, *prmnt till wknd quickly aftr 3 out.* ....(66 to 1 op 50 to 1) 6
1390 SOUNDPOST 4-10-12 D J Moffatt, *mstk 4th, lost tch bef 3 out.* ....(16 to 1 op 12 to 1 tchd 20 to 1) 7
1521 AKITO RACING (Ire) 5-10-7 A Dobbin, *in tch till wknd quickly aftr 3 out.* ....(7 to 1 op 5 to 1) 8
1543² JILLS JOY (Ire) 5-10-5 (7*) B Grattan, *trkd ldrs, disputing ld whn f 3 out.* ....(9 to 1 op 7 to 1 tchd 10 to 1) f
Dist: 5l, 24l, 1¾l, 13l, 10l, 8l, 2½l. 5m 18.30s. a 30.30s (9 Ran).
(C E Whiteley), T P Tate

1818 Golden Lion 'National Hunt' Novices' Hurdle Class E (Div II) (4-y-o and up) £1,935 2m 5f 110yds........ (12:50)

1623⁴ PAPERISING 4-10-12 A Dobbin, *trkd ldrs, led aftr 3 out, clr after nxt, easily.* (11 to 8 on op 5 to 4 on tchd 11 to 10 on and Evens) 1
1525* REAL GLEE (Ire) 7-10-12 T Reed, *led 3rd till hdd aftr 6th, chsd wnr frm aftr 3 out, no imprsn.* .... (6 to 1 op 5 to 2) 2
ERNI (Fr) 4-10-6¹ (7*) R McCarthy, *in tch, some hdwy aftr 7th, kpt on same pace frm 3 out.* ....(16 to 1 op 14 to 1) 3
YEWCROFT BOY 4-10-12 F Perratt, *towards rear, kpt on frm 2 out, nvr dngrs.* ......(33 to 1 op 25 to 1 tchd 50 to 1) 4
MAITRE DE MUSIQUE (Fr) 5-10-12 B Harding, *led to 3rd, led aftr 6th till aftr 3 out, sn drvn alng and wknd.* .... (3 to 1 op 5 to 2 tchd 100 to 30) 5
IRISH BUZZ (Ire) 4-10-12 Mr Chris Wilson, *beh most of way.* ....(33 to 1 op 25 to 1) 6
1280⁷ PERSUASIVE TALENT (Ire) 5-10-12 J Burke, *beh, some hdwy hfwy, wknd bef 3 out.* ....(50 to 1 op 33 to 1) 7
THE MICKLETONIAN 5-10-12 K Johnson, *sn beh, lost tch bef 3 out, tld off.* ....(16 to 1 op 12 to 1) 8
WHITEGATES WILLIE 4-10-12 G Cahill, *in tch, drvn alng hfwy, wknd quickly aftr 7th, tld off whn pld up bef 2 out.* .... (50 to 1 op 25 to 1) pu
Dist: 9l, 7l, 8l, 1¼l, ½l, 8l, dist. 5m 14.00s. a 26.00s (9 Ran).
(The Jockeys Whips), G Richards

1819 Dickie Dods Memorial Handicap Hurdle Class E (0-115 4-y-o and up) £2,337 3m 110yds........ (1:20)

1526 TROODOS [95] 10-11-2 J Supple, *hld up, hdwy aftr 8th, led 2 out, sn rdn, styd on.* ....(9 to 4 fav op 7 to 4) 1
1125⁵ MANETTIA (Ire) [86] 7-10-7 G Cahill, *in tch, effrt bef 3 out, ch nxt till no extr und pres r-in.* ....(7 to 1 tchd 8 to 1) 2
1680³ ACT THE WAG (Ire) [104] 7-11-11 B Harding, *prmnt, led aftr 3 out, hdd nxt, kpt on same pace.* ....(9 to 1 op 7 to 1) 3
1661⁷ D'ARBLAY STREET (Ire) [86] (bl) 7-10-7 S McDougall, *made most till aftr 3 out, wknd bef last 2...* (14 to 1 op 16 to 1) 4
1375² HUSO [99] 8-11-6 M Foster, *hld up, hdwy aftr 8th, rdn aftr 3 out, sn btn.* ....(4 to 1 op 3 to 1) 5
1526² PLUMBOB (Ire) [87] 7-10-8 R Garritty, *chsd ldrs, drvn alng bef 3 out, sn wknd.* ....(6 to 1 op 5 to 1) 6
1576⁷ ACROW LINE [107] 11-12-0 D J Burchell, *al beh, lost tch aftr 3 out.* ....(10 to 1 op 7 to 1 tchd 9 to 1) 7
958* ILENGAR (Ire) [93] 7-10-11 (3*) E Callaghan, *lost tch frm 9th, tld off whn pld up bef 2 out.* .....(9 to 1 op 8 to 1) pu
WORLD WITHOUT END (USA) [79] 7-10-0 D Parker, *lost tch 8th, tld off whn pld up bef 2 out.....* (33 to 1 op 25 to 1) pu
Dist: 1½l, 9l, nk, 8l, 13l, dist. 6m 43.30s. a 21.30s (9 Ran).
SR: 12/1/10/-/-/-/ (Scotnorth Racing Ltd), Mrs A Swinbank

1820 Nags Head Maiden Chase Class E (5-y-o and up) £3,195 3m 3f.....(1:50)

1161 MISTER TRICK (Ire) 6-11-5 R Garritty, *hld up, hdwy aftr 13th, led betw last 2, styd on wl.* (7 to 1 op 6 to 1 tchd 8 to 1) 1
1585⁵ AYLESBURY LAD (Ire) (bl) 7-11-5 J Burke, *prmnt, led 12th, hdd betw last 2, no extr.*............(33 to 1 op 25 to 1) 2
1585⁶ SENORA D'OR 6-11-0 B Storey, *chsd ldrs, outpcd bef 17th, styd on frm 2 out.*.................(20 to 1 op 16 to 1) 3
SPRINGHILL QUAY (Ire) 7-11-5 A Dobbin, *trkd ldrs, drvn alng bef 18th, fdd.*.................(3 to 1 fav op 2 to 1) 4
1681 FINAL BEAT (Ire) 7-11-5 P Niven, *in tch, effrt bef 18th, sn btn.*
.........................(9 to 1 op 10 to 1 tchd 8 to 1) 5
1385³ KINGS SERMON (Ire) 7-11-5 R Supple, *led 4th till 12th, wknd bef 18th.*.................(7 to 1 op 11 to 2 tchd 8 to 1) 6
1679 CLONROCHE LUCKY (Ire) 6-11-5 K Jones, *beh frm 12th.*
....(50 to 1) 7
1312³ MISS COLETTE 8-11-0 L O'Hara, *sn beh, tld off...*(33 to 1) 8
814 MISS LAMPLIGHT 6-11-0 B Harding, *beh whn f 13th.*
....(12 to 1 op 10 to 1) f
1605 CHOISTY (Ire) 6-11-5 J Supple, *in tch, hdwy aftr 13th, cl up whn f 17th.*.................(9 to 2 op 4 to 1 tchd 5 to 1) f
1681 BROOMHILL DUKER (Ire) 6-11-5 G Cahill, *blun and uns rdr 1st.*.........................(12 to 1 op 10 to 1) ur
LIAM'S LOSS (Ire) 7-11-2 (3*) P Midgley, *sn tld off, pld up bef 13th.*...(100 to 1) pu
1658 BOSWORTH FIELD (Ire) 8-11-5 M Foster, *lost tch frm 17th, tld off whn pld up bef 3 out.*...........(66 to 1 op 50 to 1) pu
1605³ KENMARE RIVER (Ire) 6-11-5 K Johnson, *chsd ldrs, wknd bef 13th, tld off whn pld up before last.*............(16 to 1) pu
1161⁶ BRIGHT DESTINY (v) 5-11-5 D Parker, *beh, hdwy to chase ldrs hfwy, wknd aftr 17th, tld off whn pld up bef 2 out.*
....(50 to 1 op 33 to 1) pu
1385 ROYAL PARIS (Ire) 8-11-5 Richard Guest, *led to 4th, chsd ldrs, wkng whn blun 15th, tld off when pld up bef 3 out.*
....(6 to 1 op 5 to 1) pu
Dist: 6l, 10l, 18l, 1½l, nk, 3l, dist. 7m 2.30s. a 29.30s (16 Ran).
(Edward Birkbeck), L Lungo

1821 LMS Machine Services Handicap Chase Class E (0-115 4-y-o and up) £2,877 2m 110yds...........(2:20)

1316⁴ WEAVER GEORGE (Ire) [99] 6-11-3 M Moloney, *trkd ldrs, led 2 out, styd on wl.*......(4 to 1 op 9 to 2 tchd 7 to 2) 1
1468³ REBEL KING [90] 6-10-3 (5*) S Taylor, *prmnt, led 8th, hdd 2 out, kpt on.*...........(6 to 1 op 11 to 2) 2
1692* REVE DE VALSE (USA) [93] 9-10-11 (8ex) K Johnson, *led till 8th, outpcd aftr nxt, styd on frm 2 out.*............(7 to 2 jt-fav op 5 to 2 tchd 4 to 1) 3
1678⁴ ONE FOR THE POT [110] 11-12-0 M Foster, *hld up, hdwy and ev ch 3 out, fdd frm nxt.*.................(7 to 2 jt-fav op 5 to 2 tchd 4 to 1) 4
1327⁴ MASTER SALESMAN [82] 13-10-0 D Parker, *chsd ldrs till not much room and outpcd bef 7th, sn beh.* (50 to 1 op 33 to 1) 5
BISHOPDALE [85] 15-10-3³ F Perratt, *chsd ldrs, mstk 7th, sn beh.*.........................(25 to 1 op 16 to 1) 6
1692 BOLANEY GIRL (Ire) [82] 7-10-0 A Dobbin, *hld up in rear, smooth hdwy to track ldrs tenth, drvn alng aftr 3 out, 3rd and btn whn f last.*.................(8 to 1 op 7 to 1) f
1634⁹ BLAZING DAWN [91] 9-10-9 B Storey, *towards rear, lost tch bef tenth, tld off whn pld up before last.*..(5 to 1 op 9 to 2) pu
Dist: 4l, 8l, 2½l, 17l, ¾l. 4m 15.40s. a 23.40s (8 Ran).
(Regent Decorators Ltd), W Storey

1822 Hope Inn Handicap Chase Class F (0-105 4-y-o and up) £2,742 2m 5f .....(2:50)

1585⁴ DAWN LAD (Ire) [72] 7-10-0 J Supple, *hld up, hdwy to track ldrs hfwy, chlgd bef 2 out, styd on wl to ld aftr last, sn clr.*.........................(6 to 1 op 11 to 2) 1
1589⁴ JUKE BOX BILLY (Ire) [86] 8-11-0 A Dobbin, *prmnt, led 3 out, clr betw last 2, hdd aftr last, no extr.*
.........................(4 to 1 op 7 to 2 tchd 9 to 2) 2
1258³ KILTULLA (Ire) [72] 6-9-7 (7*) R Wilkinson, *mid-div, kpt on wl frm 2 out.*.................(14 to 1 op 12 to 1) 3
1374⁴ MUSIC BLITZ [80] 5-10-8 T Reed, *beh, effrt whn mstk 11th, styd on frm 2 out, nvr dngrs.*...........(5 to 1 op 3 to 1) 4
1253⁶ SON OF IRIS [100] 8-12-0 P Niven, *prmnt till rdn and wknd bef 2 out.*.................(3 to 1 fav op 4 to 1) 5
1589² WILLIE SPARKLE [79] 10-10-7 M Foster, *towards rear, some late hdwy, nvr dngrs.*.................(9 to 2 op 3 to 1) 6
RISKY DEE [76] 7-10-4 K Jones, *in tch till wknd aftr 13th.*
....(25 to 1) 7
1692 THUNDERSTRUCK [82] 10-10-10 B Harding, *led till 3 out, wkng whn blun nxt.*.................(20 to 1 op 16 to 1) 8
WALLS COURT [81] 9-10-9 L O'Hara, *prmnt till wknd aftr 3 out, btn whn blun nxt.*.................(20 to 1 op 16 to 1) 9
LAST REFUGE (Ire) [96] 7-11-10 N Smith, *beh most of way.*
....(20 to 1) 10
1605 KARENASTINO [72] 5-10-0 Mr P Murray, *mstks, al beh.*
....(50 to 1 op 40 to 1) 11
Dist: 7l, 3½l, 1¼l, 9l, 4l, 4l, 15l, 3l, 2½l, sht-hd. 5m 26.90s. a 30.90s (11 Ran).
(G A Swinbank), Mrs A Swinbank

1823 Hardwick Arms Novices' Handicap Hurdle Class E (0-100 4-y-o and up) £2,276 2m 1f................(3:20)

1588³ COURT JOKER (Ire) [77] 4-10-7 B Storey, *settled in tch, hdwy to ld aftr 3 out, sn hrd pressed, hdd appr last, rallied und pres to lead cl hme.*.........................(12 to 1) 1
1259² PANGERAN (USA) [84] 4-11-0 J Supple, *prmnt, led 5th, hdd aftr 3 out, rdn to ld and jmpd lft last, ct cl hme.*.....(10 to 1) 2
1522³ BOWCLIFFE [81] 5-10-11 M Foster, *chsd ldrs, outpcd by 1st 2 frm two out.*.................(12 to 1 op 10 to 1) 3
1733³ IRISH WILDCARD (NZ) [70] 8-10-0 V Slattery, *in tch, rdn and outpcd aftr 3 out, kpt on frm nxt.*
.........................(9 to 2 op 7 to 2 tchd 5 to 1) 4
1677⁵ MR CHRISTIE [78] 4-10-8 R Supple, *towards rear, kpt on frm 3 out, nvr dngrs.*.................(12 to 1 tchd 14 to 1) 5
1657⁴ DOUBLING DICE [70] 5-10-0 B Harding, *beh, some hdwy aftr 5th, no further prog frm 3 out.*
.........................(9 to 2 op 4 to 1 tchd 5 to 1) 6
1522⁵ MULLINS (Ire) [70] (v) 5-10-7 D J Moffatt, *hld up, some hdwy bef 3 out, sn wknd.*.................(20 to 1 op 14 to 1) 7
1313 CORSTON JOKER [86] 6-11-2 P Niven, *towards rear, some hdwy whn blun and lost pl 3 out, no dngr aftr.*
....(14 to 1 tchd 16 to 1) 8
1492 SHUTTLECOCK [85] 5-11-1 Richard Guest, *made most to 3rd, wknd bef 3 out.*.................(16 to 1 op 14 to 1) 9
1182⁴ DURANO [98] 5-12-0 R Garritty, *in tch, hdwy to track ldrs bef 3 out, wknd before nxt.* (5 to 2 fav op 3 to 1 tchd 11 to 4) 10
1070 VINTAGE RED [89] 6-11-5 A Dobbin, *chsd ldrs till wknd quickly bef 3 out.*.................(6 to 1 op 11 to 2) 11
1642⁹ ONEOFTHEOLDONES [70] 4-10-0³ (3*) E Callaghan, *keen early, led 3rd to 5th, sn wknd, wl beh whn f last.*
....(16 to 1 op 14 to 1 tchd 20 to 1) f
Dist: Hd, 13l, 2l, 1¼l, 4l, 8l, 10l, ¾l, 1l, 11l. 4m 6.50s. a 20.50s (12 Ran).
(James Kennedy), H Alexander

HEXHAM (good)
Wednesday December 11th
Going Correction: PLUS 0.30 sec. per fur. (races 1,3,4,6), PLUS 0.40 (2,5)

1824 Federation Brewery Special Ale Amateur Riders' Handicap Hurdle Class F (0-105 4-y-o and up) £2,480 3m.........................(12:50)

1124³ HUDSON BAY TRADER (USA) [79] 9-10-6 (5*) Miss P Robson, *prmnt, led tenth, hrd pressed frm 2 out, styd on wl und pres.*.........................(10 to 1 op 8 to 1) 1
1526³ BALLINDOO [83] 7-10-8 (7*) Mr R Armson, *hld up, hdwy bef 9th, chlgd aftr 2 out, no extr frm last.*.... (5 to 1 op 4 to 1) 2
1257* BELLE ROSE (Ire) [85] 6-10-10 (7*) Mr G Elliott, *settled mid-field, effrt aftr 2 out, ch whn mstk last, kpt on same pace.*
.........................(3 to 1 fav op 5 to 2) 3
913³ SCARBA [95] 8-11-8 (5*) Mr R Hale, *trkd ldrs, effrt aftr 2 out, kpt on same pace.*......(13 to 2 op 6 to 1 tchd 7 to 1) 4
1625⁵ IFALLELSEFAILS [94] 8-11-7 (5*) Mr M H Naughton, *hld up in rear, stumbled bend aftr 8th, gd hdwy bef 2 out, no extr appr last.*.........................(7 to 1 op 6 to 1) 5
GYMCRAK CYRANO (Ire) [90] 7-11-1 (7*) Miss C Metcalfe, *in tch, outpcd aftr 2 out, styd on frm last.* (16 to 1 op 14 to 1) 6
1771 FLAT TOP [95] 5-11-6 (7*) Mr M Watson, *hld up, hdwy aftr tenth, ch betw last 2, no extr whn blun last.*
.........................(12 to 1 op 16 to 1 tchd 25 to 1) 7
KINGS LANE [87] 7-11-2 (3*) Mr C Bonner, *nvr far away, dsptd ld 2 out, wknd appr last.*.................(10 to 1 op 8 to 1) 8
1331⁶ HELENS BAY (Ire) [79] 6-10-11⁷ (3*) Mr M Thompson, *in tch till wknd bef 2 out.*.................(33 to 1 op 20 to 1) 9
1567⁵ MARDOOD [76] 11-10-1 (7*) Miss R Clark, *chsd ldrs, outpcd bef 2 out, no dngr aftr.*.................(16 to 1 op 14 to 1) 10
1601 COOL STEEL (Ire) [74] 4-10-1² (7*) Miss J Eastwood, *led, mstk second, hdd 6th, wknd aftr tenth.*
.........................(25 to 1 op 20 to 1 tchd 33 to 1) 11
DAISY DAYS (Ire) [84] 6-10-11 (5*) Mr R Thornton, *prmnt, led 6th till hdd tenth, wkng whn hmpd aftr 2 out.*
....(6 to 1 op 5 to 1) 12
Dist: 1¾l, ¾l, ¾l, 1¼l, 2½l, 1½l, 1l, 1½l, 8l, 1¼l. 6m 5.30s. a 17.30s (12 Ran).
(P C N Curtis), P Beaumont

1825 Racing Channel Novices' Handicap Chase Class E (0-100 4-y-o and up) £3,452 3m 1f................(1:20)

1605⁴ MONYMOSS (Ire) [97] 7-11-11 Richard Guest, *prmnt, led 2 out, sn clr, kpt on und pres r-in.*
....1
1658* SEEKING GOLD (Ire) [86] 7-11-0 (7ex) B Storey, *in tch, mstk 14th, drvn alng and outpcd aftr 3 out, styd on wl frm betw last 2.*.........................(6 to 1 op 5 to 1) 2
1385⁴ BOLD ACCOUNT (Ire) [85] 6-10-13 N Bentley, *trkd ldrs, lft in ld 15th, hdd 2 out, no extr.*.........(10 to 1 op 8 to 1) 3
1513³ SLOTAMATIQUE (Ire) [94] 7-11-8 A Dobbin, *trkd ldrs, hmpd 15th, ev ch bef 2 out, kpt on same pace.*
.........................(7 to 4 fav op 2 to 1 tchd 9 to 4) 4

236

NOOSA SOUND (Ire) [72] 6-10-0 B Harding, *towards rear, styd on frm 2 out, nvr dngrs*........(25 to 1 tchd 33 to 1) 5
1608³ SHALLOW RIVER (Ire) [85] 5-10-7 (5*) Mr R Thornton, *sn pushed alng and beh, hdwy aftr 13th, chlgd 3 out, soon wknd*. ....(14 to 1 tchd 16 to 1) 6
DESPERATE DAYS (Ire) [72] 7-10-0 W Dwan, *beh most of way*..................................(16 to 1 op 50 to 1) 7
1681⁷ DISTILLERY HILL (Ire) [82] 8-10-10⁸ Mr M Thompson, *mstk second, cl up, lft in ld 12th, f 15th*......(50 to 1 op 33 to 1) f
1585² MAMICA [80] 6-10-8 R Supple, *mstks, chasing ldrs whn f 15th*................(100 to 30 op 2 to 1 tchd 7 to 2) f
1589⁸ CADER IDRIS [86] 7-11-0 P Niven, *led till f 12th*. ....(10 to 1 op 8 to 1) f
1608⁴ GOLD PIGEON (Ire) [72] 7-10-0 G Cahill, *beh most of way, tld off whn pld up bef last*...............(20 to 1 op 16 to 1) pu
AVOWHAT (Ire) [72] 6-9-9 (5*) R McGrath, *lost tch and pld up bef 14th*..............................(20 to 1 op 16 to 1) pu
Dist: 3½l, 4l, 1½l, ¾l, 13l, 8l. 6m 30.80s. a 25.80s (12 Ran).
(Mrs S Smith), Mrs S J Smith

1826 Buchanan Ales Novices' Selling Hurdle Class G (4 - 7-y-o) £1,794 2m .... (1:50)

1604³ ROBSERA (Ire) 5-10-12 R Garritty, *hld up, steady hdwy bef 2 out, led betw last two, styd on und pres*. ....(7 to 2 op 4 to 1 tchd 5 to 1) 1
1604* WILLY STAR (Bel) 6-11-12 Richard Guest, *settled midfield, hdwy bef 2 out, kpt on und pres frm last, no imprsn on wnr*. ....(11 to 10 fav op 6 to 4 tchd Evens) 2
1693 OVER STATED (Ire) 6-10-7 (5*) G F Ryan, *sn chasing ldrs, led bef 2 out, hdd betw last two, no extr und pres*...... (20 to 1) 3
LAST ROUNDUP 4-10-12 M Foster, *al chasing ldrs, kpt on same pace frm 2 out*.................(12 to 1 op 7 to 1) 4
1604 SIMAND 4-11-0 J Callaghan, *in tch, no hdwy frm 2 out*. .... (12 to 1 op 7 to 1) 5
1333⁹ MY MISSILE 6-10-7 L O'Hara, *beh, some hdwy frm 2 out, nvr nrr*..(33 to 1) 6
1677 MEESONETTE 4-10-7 G Cahill, *towards rear, kpt on frm 2 out, nvr dngrs*..................................(20 to 1) 7
1604⁵ THE FINAL SPARK 5-10-7 B Harding, *in tch, stumbled aftr 4th, wknd after 2 out*.....(13 to 2 op 5 to 1 tchd 7 to 1) 8
1255⁴ CANONBIEBOTHERED 5-10-7 F Perratt, *chsd ldrs till wknd aftr 6th*...........................(12 to 1 op 10 to 1) 9
TAJAR (USA) 4-10-12 R Supple, *hld up, hdwy hfwy, tracking ldr 2 out, sn rdn and wknd*............(10 to 1 op 8 to 1) 10
1377⁹ MEADOWLECK 7-10-7 B Storey, *led till hdd bef 2 out, sn wknd*..(33 to 1) 11
1521⁶ ABOUT MIDNIGHT 7-10-7 A Dobbin, *prmnt till wknd aftr 6th, tld off*....................................... (33 to 1) 12
1521⁷ RINGRONE (Ire) 7-10-11⁴ Mr M Thompson, *al beh, tld off*. ....(33 to 1) 13
1390 ROADWAY JOKER 5-10-7 (5*) S Taylor, *in tch till wknd bef 2 out, wl beh whn f last, dead*......................(33 to 1) f
FIRST IN THE FIELD 5-10-0 (7*) S Haworth, *blun and uns rdr 1st*...(25 to 1) ur
BLOW DRY (Ire) 6-10-12 P Niven, *beh most of way, tld off whn pld up bef last*................ (16 to 1 op 12 to 1) pu
1677 SAFETY TIP 4-10-2 (5*) R McGrath, *sn wl beh, tld off whn pld up bef 5th*...(33 to 1) pu
Dist: 2l, ¾l, 3½l, 8l, 11l, 8l, 1l, 1½l, 1l, 8l. 4m 2.20s. a 13.20s (17 Ran).
SR: -/12/-/-/-/- (Declan Kinahan), J J Quinn

1827 Federation Brewery Handicap Hurdle Class C (0-130 4-y-o and up) £3,460 2m.................... (2:20)

1635³ SHINING EDGE [108] 4-11-2 R Garritty, *hld up, took clr order 2 out, sn drvn alng, styd on wl und pres to ld close hme*. ....(9 to 2 op 4 to 1 tchd 5 to 1) 1
1588* ANABRANCH [107] 5-10-8 (7*) M Newton, *hld up, smooth hdwy to ld aftr 2 out, rdn r-in, ct cl hme*. ....(6 to 5 fav op 11 to 10 tchd 5 to 4) 2
1740³ COLORFUL AMBITION [106] 6-11-0 J Railton, *hld up, took clr order 2 out, sn drvn alng, kpt on same pace*. ....(6 to 1 tchd 7 to 1) 3
DUKE OF PERTH [92] 5-10-0 G Cahill, *chsd clr ldr, drvn to ld 2 out, sn hdd, no extr*...............(10 to 1 tchd 12 to 1) 4
1635² DONE WELL (USA) [119] 4-11-13 A Dobbin, *hld up, took clr order 2 out, sn drvn alng and wknd*. .... (5 to 2 op 2 to 1 tchd 11 to 4) 5
1635⁹ MASTER HYDE (USA) [110] 7-11-4 M Moloney, *led and sn clr, hdd 2 out, soon btn*.....(16 to 1 op 12 to 1 tchd 20 to 1) 6
Dist: ½l, 6l, 2½l, 7l, 1¼l. 4m 0.20s. a 11.20s (6 Ran).
SR: 24/22/15/-/18/7/ (G Graham), T D Easterby

1828 Border Counties Insurance Novices' Chase Class E (5-y-o and up) £3,261 2m 110yds................... (2:50)

DARING PAST 6-10-12 R Garritty, *settled in tch, hdwy bef 3 out, led betw last 2, sn clr*. ....(11 to 8 on op 5 to 4 on tchd 11 to 10 on) 1
CUSH SUPREME (Ire) 7-10-12 B Harding, *led till hdd betw last 2, kpt on, no ch wth wnr*..........(14 to 1 op 8 to 1) 2
1587⁴ BONNY JOHNNY 6-10-12 D J Moffatt, *beh, hdwy bef 3 out, styd on same pace frm nxt*. ....(13 to 2 op 5 to 1 tchd 7 to 1) 3
1587⁵ DARK BUOY 7-10-12 B Storey, *chsd ldrs, kpt on same pace frm 2 out*..(8 to 1) 4
1708⁵ TARGET LINE 6-10-5 (7*) R Wilkinson, *in tch till lost pl bef 3 out, no dngr aftr*.......................(16 to 1 op 12 to 1) 5
1630 FINGERHILL (Ire) 7-10-12 Mr M Thompson, *chsd ldrs, drvn alng aftr 3 out, fdd*.... (16 to 1 tchd 20 to 1 and 25 to 1) 6
1587⁶ WEE WIZARD (Ire) 7-10-7 (5*) S Taylor, *outpcd and drpd rear 7th, no dngr aftr*...........................(8 to 1 tchd 9 to 1) 7
1374 GRAND AS OWT 6-10-12 K Johnson, *prmnt, chlgd 3 out, wknd aftr nxt*..........................(50 to 1 op 33 to 1) 8
1033⁴ AMBER HOLLY 7-10-7 F Perratt, *in tch whn f 6th*. .... (12 to 1 op 8 to 1 tchd 14 to 1) f
1693 CHARLISTIONA 5-10-0 (7*) S Melrose, *beh whn blun and brght dwn 6th*..........................(33 to 1 op 20 to 1) bd
Dist: 6l, 4l, 1¾l, 7l, ¾l, hd, 1½l. 4m 10.80s. a 12.80s (10 Ran).
SR: 22/16/12/10/3/2/ (John A Petty), M D Hammond

1829 Federation Brewery Medallion Lager Novices' Hurdle Class E (4-y-o and up) £2,679 3m................ (3:20)

1775⁶ MENSHAAR (USA) 4-10-12 R Garritty, *in tch, drvn alng to dispute ld bef 2 out, led betw last two, styd on und pres*. ....(6 to 1 op 4 to 1 tchd 7 to 1) 1
1545³ YOUNG KENNY 5-11-5 R Supple, *trkd ldrs, led bef 2 out, hdd betw last two, no extr*...........................(2 to 1 jt-fav tchd 3 to 1 and 7 to 2) 2
1623 ADIB (USA) 6-10-12 N Bentley, *hld up, hdwy aftr 9th, styd on frm 2 out, no imprsn on 1st two*........................(20 to 1) 3
1325³ BLANC SEING (Fr) (bl) 9-10-12 Mr S Swiers, *towards rear, styd on frm 2 out, nvr dngrs*.......... (16 to 1 op 10 to 1) 4
CLONTOURA (Ire) 8-10-9 (3*) P Midgley, *chsd ldrs till wknd bef 2 out*.........................(33 to 1 op 16 to 1) 5
RAINING STAIRS (Ire) 5-10-12 B Harding, *hld up, styd on wl frm 2 out, nvr nr to chal, fnshd distressed*. .... (9 to 1 op 7 to 1 tchd 10 to 1) 6
1373* CLARE MAID (Ire) 7-11-0 A Dobbin, *in tch, hmpd bend bef 9th, wknd before 2 out*...............(2 to 1 jt-fav op 5 to 2) 7
1662* PHARMISTICE (Ire) 5-11-5 J Supple, *hld up in tch, some hdwy bef 9th, sn wknd*................ (9 to 2 op 4 to 1) 8
CARNMONEY (Ire) 8-10-12 T Reed, *made most till hdd bef 2 out, sn wknd*......................(50 to 1 op 25 to 1) 9
1609⁸ KENTUCKY GOLD (Ire) 7-10-12 L O'Hara, *chsd ldrs till wknd bef 2 out*.............(33 to 1 op 16 to 1 tchd 50 to 1) 10
1124⁴ CROFTON LAKE 8-11-5 F Perratt, *nvr on terms*. ....(20 to 1 op 16 to 1) 11
1662⁹ WOODSTOCK LODGE (USA) 8-10-12 Mr M Thompson, *chsd ldrs till wknd aftr 9th*................(50 to 1 op 33 to 1) 12
1631 RUBER 9-10-12 B Storey, *beh most of way*. ....(25 to 1 op 14 to 1) 13
1590⁸ BORIS BROOK 5-10-5 (7*) S Melrose, *in tch, reminder aftr 8th, wknd after nxt*..................(33 to 1 op 25 to 1) 14
1770 BOLD'N 9-10-5 (7*) S Haworth, *beh, tld off whn pld up bef 2 out*.. (50 to 1) pu
MEDERIC (Ire) 6-10-7 (5*) G F Ryan, *in tch till wknd aftr 9th, tld off whn pld up bef 2 out, lme*..........(33 to 1 op 16 to 1) pu
1703⁷ AR AGHAIDH ABHAILE (Ire) (bl) 5-10-12 G Cahill, *dsptd ld till wknd quickly aftr tenth, tld off whn pld up bef 2 out*. .... (25 to 1 op 20 to 1) pu
Dist: 3l, 3½l, 7l, 5l, 1½l, ½l, 9l, 1½l, 6l, sht-hd. 6m 2.80s. a 14.80s (17 Ran).
(G A Arthur), L Lungo

LEICESTER (good to soft (races 1,3,5,6), good to firm (2,4))
Wednesday December 11th
Going Correction: NIL

1830 Ash Mares' Only Novices' Hurdle Class E (4-y-o and up) £2,902 2m .... (1:00)

1369* POTTER'S GALE (Ire) 5-11-3 A Maguire, *hld up, hdwy to join ldrs 4 out, led and mstk last, drvn out*..........(5 to 4 fav) 1
1047² PIP'S DREAM 5-10-10 J Ryan, *chsd ldr, led 4th to four out, mstk 2 out, ev ch last, no extr r-in*. .... (14 to 1 op 7 to 1 tchd 16 to 1) 2
1669* MELSTOCK MEGGIE 6-11-3 W Marston, *trkd ldrs, outpcd 4 out, ran on und pres r-in*... (9 to 2 op 7 to 2 tchd 6 to 1) 3
QUICK QUOTE 6-10-10 L Harvey, *hld up, hdwy 5th, led 4 out to last, no extr*........(14 to 1 tchd 10 to 1 and 16 to 1) 4
1479⁵ BAY FAIR 4-10-10 M Richards, *hld up, hdwy 3 out, no imprsn frm nxt*.................(13 to 2 op 4 to 1 tchd 15 to 2) 5
1556³ FANTASY LINE 5-10-10 J Osborne, *prmnt till wknd appr 3 out*.......................................(5 to 1 tchd 7 to 1) 6
1350 LADY FOLEY (Ire) 4-10-7 (3*) J Magee, *in tch till wknd 3 out*. ....(50 to 1 op 33 to 1) 7
QUALITAIR PRIDE 4-10-10 G Bradley, *hld up, mstk 4 out, al rear*.......................(14 to 1 op 7 to 1 tchd 16 to 1) 8
1415⁵ TREHANE 4-10-10 N Williamson, *led to 4th, wknd 3 out*. ....(66 to 1 op 50 to 1) 9
NEPTUNES MISS 4-10-10 I Lawrence, *hld up, hdwy 5th, wknd 4 out*.........................(66 to 1 op 50 to 1) 10

Dist: 2½l, 1¼l, 1½l, 6l, 20l, 8l, 1½l, 10l, 14l. 3m 53.10s. a 10.10s (10 Ran).
(J E Potter), D Nicholson

1831 Spruce Novices' Chase Class E (5-y-o and up) £3,669 2½m 110yds
.... (1:30)

1568³ SLINGSBY (Ire) 6-10-12 R Dunwoody, led second to 4th, hit
7th, led last, drvn out.................(5 to 4 on op 6 to 4) 1
1501¹² BRIDEPARK ROSE (Ire) 8-10-7 S Fox, chsd ldrs, hit 5 out, led
nxt, rdn and hdd last, no extr.
....................(7 to 1 op 8 to 1 tchd 12 to 1) 2
1510⁴ CURRAGH PETER 9-10-9 (3") Guy Lewis, jmpd lft, led to
second, led 4th to four out, wknd nxt..(50 to 1 op 33 to 1) 3
1542 LOCH GARMAN HOTEL (Ire) 7-10-12 T Eley, prmnt, rdn 5 out,
sn wknd...................(8 to 1 op 5 to 1) 4
1670 THE BOOLEY HOUSE (Ire) 6-10-12 M Richards, hld up, al
rear, lft 8th, tld off.....................(11 to 2 op 7 to 2) 5
1429⁸ CHARTER LANE (Ire) 6-10-12 D Leahy, hld up, hit rls appr 6th,
sn tld off.....................(50 to 1 op 33 to 1) 6
TYPHOON (Ire) 6-10-12 M Sharratt, not jump wl, hit 1st, sn
well beh, tld off whn blun and uns rdr 9th.
.....................(50 to 1 op 20 to 1) ur
1519³ DJAIS (Fr) 7-10-12 G Bradley, not jump wl, sn well beh, tld off
whn pld up bef 3rd.........(5 to 1 op 4 to 1 tchd 11 to 2) pu
Dist: 2l, 24l, dist, 23l, 8l. 5m 8.90s. a 6.90s (8 Ran).
SR: 15/8/-/-/-/ (Simon Harrap Partnership), N A Gaselee

1832 Chestnut Conditional Jockeys' Selling Hurdle Class G (4 - 7-y-o) £2,012 2m.........................(2:00)

937⁴ FLEET CADET (v) 5-10-12 G Supple, hld up, hdwy 5th, led
appr last, pushed out......(4 to 1 op 5 to 2 tchd 9 to 2) 1
BEECHFIELD FLYER 5-10-12 G Tormey, chsd ldrs, rdn 3 out,
styd on same pace appr last.............(20 to 1 op 14 to 1) 2
1736³ PARISH WALK 5-10-12 B Grattan, led, rdn and hdd appr
last, no extr..................(7 to 2 op 3 to 1) 3
1450³ FASTINI GOLD 4-10-12 F Leahy, hld up, hdwy 5th, rdn 3 out,
no extr r-in..................(11 to 2 op 5 to 1 tchd 13 to 2) 4
1373³ FENIAN COURT (Ire) 5-10-7 K Gaule, prmnt, rdn 4 out, sn btn.
..................(11 to 4 fav op 9 to 4 tchd 3 to 1) 5
921⁷ SCOTTISH PARK 7-10-2 (5") B Moore, patiently rdn, effrt
appr 4 out, sn wl beh....(12 to 1 op 7 to 1) 6
ROSALEE ROYALE 4-10-7 G Hogan, hld up, tld off 4 out.
.....................(7 to 1 op 8 to 1 tchd 10 to 1) 7
1669⁷ PERSIAN BUTTERFLY 4-10-7 Michael Brennan, trkd ldrs,
sddl slpd aftr second, pld up bef 4th..(25 to 1 op 20 to 1) pu
Dist: 4l, 2l, 2l, 24l, 9l, 19l. 3m 56.50s. a 13.50s (8 Ran).
(Sir John Swaine), M C Pipe

1833 Sycamore Handicap Chase Class D (0-125 5-y-o and up) £4,449 3m
.... (2:30)

1674* LORD OF THE WEST (Ire) [104] 7-10-13 (6ex) A Maguire, sn
tracking ldr, lft in ld briefly 6th, lost pl nxt, led 2 out, blun last,
eased on finish........(7 to 1 fav op 9 to 4 tchd 7 to 4) 1
1418² PHILIP'S WOODY [115] 8-11-10 J R Kavanagh, hld up, led
aftr 6th, hmpd by loose horse tenth, hdd 4 out, slpd appr nxt,
ev ch 2 out, styd on same pace.
.....................(13 to 2 op 9 to 2 tchd 7 to 1) 2
1613³ WELL BRIEFED [114] 9-11-2 (7") M Griffiths, led, tried to
refuse and hdd 6th, led 4 out to 2 out, wknd.
.....................(9 to 1 op 7 to 1 tchd 10 to 1) 3
1494² THE SHY PADRE (Ire) [91] 7-10-0 W Marston, trkd ldr till f
second.....................(3 to 1 op 11 to 4 tchd 7 to 2) f
1565* IMPERIAL VINTAGE (Ire) [115] 6-11-10 N Williamson, f 1st.
.....................(11 to 4 op 5 to 2 tchd 3 to 1) f
Dist: 3½l, 7l. 6m 16.00s. a 31.00s (5 Ran).
(Anne Duchess Of Westminster), J J O'Neill

1834 Birch Handicap Hurdle Class D (0-120 4-y-o and up) £3,028 2½m 110yds.....................(3:00)

WASSL STREET (Ire) [95] 4-10-13 N Williamson, mid-div, cld
on ldrs 5 out, mstk nxt, led last, rdn out.(4 to 1 tchd 5 to 1) 1
DIWALI DANCER [110] 6-12-0 J Osborne, led, sn wl clr, hdd
last, unbl to quicken.................(7 to 2 op 9 to 4) 2
1402² LORD McMURROUGH (Ire) [110] 6-12-0 R Farrant, trkd clr
ldr, cld 5 out, ev ch whn mstk 3 out, btn appr last.
.....................(7 to 4 fav op 6 to 4 tchd 15 to 8) 3
VISCOUNT TULLY [82] 11-10-0 Miss S Jackson, nvr rch
chalg pos.....................(25 to 1 op 10 to 1) 4
1597² KALASADI (USA) [106] (bl) 5-11-10 M Richards, chsd ldrs,
drvn alng 4 out, sn wknd...(7 to 2 op 5 to 2 tchd 9 to 1) 5
227 CAPTAIN MY CAPTAIN (Ire) [82] 8-10-0 L Harvey, beh 5th, tld
off whn pld up bef 2 out............(50 to 1 tchd 66 to 1) pu
1388 ROYAL CITIZEN (Ire) [94] 7-10-12 G Bradley, hld up, al rear,
tld off whn pld up 2 out.........(12 to 1 op 10 to 1) pu
Dist: 4l, 9l, 9l, 23l. 4m 54.20s. a 6.20s (7 Ran).
SR: 23/34/25/-/ (B Leatherday), K A Morgan

1835 Oak Handicap Hurdle Class E (0-110 4-y-o and up) £2,544 2m...... (3:30)

1635* CIRCUS LINE [103] 5-11-8 M A Fitzgerald, al prmnt, led and
hit 4 out, mstk nxt, clr appr last.
.....................(13 to 8 fav op Evens tchd 2 to 1) 1
1606³ KINTAVI [82] 6-9-12 (3") G Hogan, strted slwly, hdwy 5th, wnt
second r-in, not rch wnr.............(7 to 1 op 6 to 1) 2
SHEPHERDS REST (Ire) [95] 4-10-7 (7") S Hearn, mid-div,
hdwy 5th, chsd wnr 2 out to r-in, no imprsn.
.....................(16 to 1 op 12 to 1) 3
1572⁴ CAWARRA BOY [105] 8-11-10 Mr E James, hld up, hmpd 1st,
nvr plcd to chal.........(15 to 2 op 4 to 1 tchd 8 to 1) 4
1625⁶ KADARI [92] 7-10-11 N Williamson, in tch, effrt 4 out, sn btn.
.....................(16 to 1 tchd 20 to 1) 5
1416³ KELLY MAC [90] 6-10-9 C Llewellyn, prmnt, rdn 5th, wknd 4
out.....................(7 to 2 tchd 4 to 1) 6
EURO SINGER [98] 4-11-3 J Osborne, led, sn clr, hdd 4 out,
wknd.....................(10 to 1 op 6 to 1) 7
SHEECKY [81] 5-10-0 D Bridgwater, prmnt till wknd appr 4
out.....................(33 to 1) 8
ERLKING (Ire) [96] 6-11-1 N Mann, hld up, al rear.
.....................(16 to 1 op 12 to 1) 9
ALASKAN HEIR [85] 5-10-4 T Eley, f 1st.
.....................(14 to 1 op 12 to 1) f
Dist: 5l, 7l, 2l, 5l, 2l, 4l, dist, 8l. 3m 52.10s. a 9.10s (10 Ran).
SR: 3/-/-/-/-/-/ (Mrs P A H Hartley), M W Easterby

CLONMEL (IRE) (yielding)
Thursday December 12th

1836 Cahir Maiden Hurdle (4 & 5-y-o) £2,226 2m.....................(12:30)

CLIFDON FOG (Ire) 5-12-0 T P Treacy.........(10 to 9 on) 1
1360² MERCHANTS QUAY (Ire) 5-11-11 (3") G Cotter,....(3 to 1) 2
1307² WEST LEADER (Ire) 5-11-6 T P Rudd,.............(4 to 1) 3
1090⁷ DUKY RIVER (Ire) 5-11-6 F Woods,.............(14 to 1) 4
TIDAL PRINCESS (Ire) 4-10-13 D T Evans,.......(20 to 1) 5
1119 ROSEY ELLEN (Ire) 4-10-6 (7") M D Murphy,.....(20 to 1) 6
1617⁵ RAHEEN RIVER (Ire) 5-11-1 C O'Dwyer,.........(10 to 1) 7
GRAIGNAMANAGH (Ire) 5-11-6 J R Barry,.......(16 to 1) 8
AHINDUCLINT (Ire) 4-11-4 T J O'Sullivan,.......(25 to 1) 9
238 FANORE (Ire) 5-10-13 (7") D A McLoughlin,.......(20 to 1) 10
1533 COOLSHAMROCK (Ire) 4-10-13 (3") K Whelan,...(20 to 1) 11
826⁸ BYPHARBEANRI (Ire) 5-11-6 J Shortt,.............(12 to 1) 12
POWER STEERING (Ire) 5-11-6 P L Malone,......(14 to 1) 13
SITE LADY (Ire) 5-11-9 D H O'Connor,.............(14 to 1) 14
BOCCACHERA (Ire) 4-10-13 A J O'Brien,.........(20 to 1) 15
IFIELD COURT HOTEL (Ire) 5-11-1 J P Broderick, (20 to 1) 16
ELECTRIC PRINCESS (Ire) 4-10-13 C F Swan,...(10 to 1) 17
MURKELBUR (Ire) 5-10-8 (7") R M Murphy,.....(25 to 1) 18
Dist: 3l, nk, 6l, 1l. 4m 3.30s. (18 Ran).
(J P Hill), J S Bolger

1837 Cashel Handicap Chase (0-102 4-y-o and up) £2,226 2¾m.........(1:00)

1711⁷ FAIRY MIST (Ire) [-] 8-9-5 (3") G Cotter,.........(7 to 1) 1
1711⁸ DOONEGA (Ire) [-] 8-10-9 (7") Mr E Gallagher,......(3 to 1) 2
1711³ FIFTH GENERATION (Ire) [-] 6-10-0 (3") K Whelan,
.....................(6 to 1 fav) 3
CAMINS CHOICE (Ire) [-] 7-11-3 J R Barry,......(12 to 1) 4
1781⁴ HOLY GROUNDER (Ire) [-] 7-11-5 C F Swan,.......(7 to 2) 5
1711 ROSSI NOVAE [-] (bl) 13-9-13⁶ T P Treacy,.......(14 to 1) 6
1780 FIELD OF DESTINY (Ire) [-] 7-11-11 C O'Dwyer,...(10 to 1) pu
Dist: Hd, 14l, 7l, 4l. 5m 52.00s. (7 Ran).
(John Patrick Ryan), John Patrick Ryan

1838 Nenagh Maiden Hurdle (5-y-o and up) £2,226 3m.............(1:30)

1712⁴ GRANGE COURT (Ire) 6-12-0 J Shortt,.........(3 to 1 fav) 1
1485⁴ INDIAN MAGIC (Ire) 7-10-12 (3") G Cotter,......(8 to 1) 2
1584* REMAINDER STAR (Ire) 5-12-0 T J Mitchell,......(6 to 1) 3
1548² VIVIANS VALE (Ire) 7-10-8 (7") D K Budds,......(5 to 1) 4
1536⁴ MYSTICAL AIR (Ire) 6-11-6 T P Treacy,...........(7 to 1) 5
1433 SIDCUP HILL (Ire) 7-11-1 A J O'Brien,...........(8 to 1) 6
TOUREEN GALE (Ire) 7-11-9 D J Casey,.........(4 to 1) 7
XANTHOS 6-11-6 J P Broderick,.................(20 to 1) 8
1618 DROICHEAD LAPEEN 9-11-7 (7") Mr T J Beattie,..(10 to 1) 9
1539⁶ LORD OGAN (Ire) 5-11-6 C O'Dwyer,.............(14 to 1) 10
1548⁶ DURKIN'S GIRL (Ire) (bl) 6-11-9 J R Barry,.......(6 to 1) 11
PRIZE OF PEACE (Ire) 6-11-1 F Woods,.........(12 to 1) 12
978 ORIENTAL PEARL (Ire) 6-11-1 T Hazlett,.........(33 to 1) 13
HAMSHIRE GALE (Ire) 6-11-1 A Powell,.........(14 to 1) 14
1618 NORTHERN REEF (Ire) (bl) 6-11-6 F J Flood,......(25 to 1) pu
1751⁴ COMMERCIAL HOUSE (Ire) 8-11-6 D T Evans,...(10 to 1) pu
1539 TINVACOOSH (Ire) 5-10-13 (7") S Kelly,.........(33 to 1) pu
1548⁷ SHUIL LE LAOI (Ire) 6-11-1 C F Swan,...........(12 to 1) pu
1360 TORUS STAR (Ire) 7-11-3 (3") K Whelan,.........(33 to 1) pu
1712 WARLOCKFOE (Ire) 5-11-1 T P Rudd,.............(25 to 1) pu
Dist: 2l, 2l, hd, 7l. 6m 16.50s. (20 Ran).
(Cronin Plc), Mrs John Harrington

1839 Ladbroke Handicap Hurdle (0-102 4-y-o and up) £2,740 2m..... (2:00)

1550⁸ LADY DAISY (Ire) [-] 7-11-5 (7") A O'Shea,..... (6 to 4 fav) 1

1654[7]	COLLON LEADER (Ire) [-] 7-11-10 J R Barry, ... (4 to 1)	2
1713[4]	HEIGHT OF LUXURY (Ire) [-] 8-9-0 (7") M D Murphy, (8 to 1)	3
1710	SKULLDUGERY (Ire) [-] 6-9-12 J Jones, ... (20 to 1)	4
1147[9]	TARIYMA (Ire) [-] 5-10-2 (3") K Whelan, ... (8 to 1)	5
1713[5]	CLASHBEG (Ire) [-] 5-10-13 (7") Mr A K Wyse, ... (5 to 1)	6
1584[2]	SARAH BLUE (Ire) [-] 6-10-7 P L Malone, ... (7 to 1)	7
1710[5]	RYTHM ROCK (Ire) [-] 7-11-0 (7") M W Martin, . . (12 to 1)	8
1649	CLONMEL COMMERCIAL (Ire) [-] 5-9-12 (7") D McCullagh,	
	. . . . (25 to 1)	9
1579[4]	ABIGAIL ROSE (Bel) [-] 4-10-2 (7") K A Kelly, ... (20 to 1)	10
1654	NEIPHIN BOY (Ire) [-] 6-10-5 J F Flood, ... (10 to 1)	11
	JIHAAD (USA) [-] 6-9-13 (7") J O'Shaughnessy, ... (20 to 1)	12
	KASELECTRIC (Ire) [-] 5-11-5 C O'Dwyer, ... (10 to 1)	13
1359[7]	SHECOULDNTBEBETTER (Ire) [-] 5-10-9 T P Treacy, (8 to 1)	14

Dist: 5l, 2½l, ½l, 4l. 4m 14.90s. (14 Ran).

(Patrick F Kehoe), Anthony Mullins

1840 Winter Novice Hurdle (4-y-o and up) £2,226 2½m. . . . . (2:30)

1752[5]	BLAZE OF HONOUR (Ire) 5-11-7 C F Swan, . . . (5 to 1)	1
1712[2]	BALLYRIHY BOY (Ire) 5-11-0 (5") J M Donnelly, ... (7 to 4)	2
	GLEBE LAD (Ire) 4-11-0 T P Rudd, ... (10 to 1)	3
1359*	HILL OF HOPE (Ire) 5-11-12 W Slattery, ... (8 to 1)	4
1244[9]	ROSIE LIL (Ire) (bl) 5-11-0 (7") L A Hurley, ... (10 to 1)	5
	DUKE OF HADES (Ire) 6-11-5 J Jones, ... (20 to 1)	6
	GLANTINE LAD (Ire) 6-11-5 C O'Dwyer, ... (20 to 1)	7
	BAYLINE LAD (Ire) 6-11-5 J P Broderick, ... (20 to 1)	8

Dist: 2l, 4l, 5l, 3l. 5m 22.00s. (8 Ran).

(Mrs Anne Leahy), A P O'Brien

1841 Templemore Beginners Chase (5-y-o and up) £2,226 2m 1f. . . . . (3:00)

1650[2]	SCOBIE BOY (Ire) 8-12-0 J P Broderick, ... (4 to 1)	1
1120*	PENNDARA (Ire) 7-12-0 C F Swan, ... (5 to 4 fav)	2
	IRISH PEACE (Ire) 8-12-0 C O'Dwyer, ... (12 to 1)	3
1170[5]	GALANT DES EPEIRES (Fr) 5-11-9 (3") K Whelan, (14 to 1)	4
1362[7]	SLANEY STANDARD (Ire) 8-12-0 D H O'Connor, . . (14 to 1)	5
1552[9]	PRATE BOX (Ire) 6-12-0 J K Kinane, ... (20 to 1)	6
1117[4]	LUCKY BUST (Ire) 6-11-7 (7") Mr D A Harney, ... (12 to 1)	7
1362[8]	SIR-EILE (Ire) 6-12-0 A O'Shea, ... (25 to 1)	8
	FERRYCARRIGCRYSTAL (Ire) 8-12-0 F Woods, . . (16 to 1)	9
1552[7]	THE NOBLE ROUGE (Ire) 7-11-11 (3") G Cotter, . . (12 to 1)	10
1583[4]	WHAT IT IS (Ire) 7-11-9 J Shortt, ... (12 to 1)	11
	KATIES HOLME (Ire) 5-11-7 T J Mitchell, ... (20 to 1)	12
1654	RUN BAVARD (Ire) 8-12-0 T P Treacy, ... (16 to 1)	f
1552[2]	MALACCA KING (Ire) 5-11-12 D J Casey, ... (3 to 1)	ur
1714[8]	SWINGER (Ire) 7-12-0 G M O'Neill, ... (25 to 1)	u

Dist: 7l, 1l, 1l, 3l. 4m 16.90s. (15 Ran).

(R V Shaw), R V Shaw

1842 Powerstown I.N.H. Flat Race (6-y-o and up) £2,226 2m. . . . . (3:30)

1554*	PREMIER WALK 7-11-11 (7") Mr S P Hennessy, ... (5 to 1)	1
1649[5]	EDUARDO (Ire) 6-12-4 Mr P Fenton, ... (Evens fav)	2
1715[2]	ARCTIC GREY (Ire) (bl) 6-11-8 (3") Mr B M Cash, . . (8 to 1)	3
1622[4]	MY LITTLE DOXIE (Ire) 6-10-13 (7") Mr G Elliott, . . . (5 to 1)	4
	CALL BOB (Ire) 6-11-4 (7") Mr T J Nagle Jnr, ... (12 to 1)	5
1484	RING HARRY (Ire) 6-10-13 (7") Mr T N Cloke, ... (12 to 1)	6
1433	ORCHARD SUNSET (Ire) 6-11-4 (7") Mr D M Fogarty,	
	. . . . (16 to 1)	7
1463	CARRIG BOY (Ire) 6-11-8 (3") Mr D Valentine, ... (16 to 1)	8
1536[9]	YOUR CALL (Ire) 7-11-4 (7") Mr M W Carroll, ... (8 to 1)	9
	ANOTHER CRACKER (Ire) 7-11-4 (7") Mr Eoghan J O'Grady,	
	. . . . (14 to 1)	10
316[6]	MAGS DWYER (Ire) 6-11-13 Mr J A Berry, ... (12 to 1)	11

Dist: 3l, 2½l, ½l, 14l. 4m 11.80s. (11 Ran).

(Aidan Ryan), Malachy J Ryan

FAKENHAM (good)
Thursday December 12th
Going Correction: PLUS 0.60 sec. per fur.

1843 Fitzwilliam Selling Handicap Hurdle Class G (0-95 4-y-o and up) £2,733 2m. . . . . (12:50)

1604[6]	PHARLY REEF [68] 4-10-11 A Dobbin, *hld up, improved to chase ldr aftr 3 out, led betw last 2, jmpd clr last, readily.*	
	. . . . (7 to 2 tchd 4 to 1 and 5 to 1)	1
1717[6]	COSMIC STAR [57] (bl) 6-10-0 J R Kavanagh, *led till aftr 1st, settled gng wl, led 3 out, hdd beteween last 2, kpt on one pace.* . . . . (40 to 1 op 20 to 1 tchd 50 to 1)	2
1693[8]	ELITE JUSTICE [83] (bl) 4-11-4 K Gaule, *nvr far away, effrt bef 3 out, feeling pace aftr nxt, styd on same pace betw last 2.* . . . . (10 to 1 op 6 to 1)	3
1425[8]	RUTH'S GAMBLE [57] (v) 8-10-0 D Leahy, *settled off the pace, rapid hdwy betw last 2, fnshd strly.*	
	. . . . (25 to 1 op 20 to 1 tchd 33 to 1)	4
1683[3]	ROYAL STANDARD [84] (v) 9-11-6 (7") M Griffiths, *keen hold, sn hndy, led 5th till hdd 3 out, rdn and outpcd nxt.*	
	. . . . (11 to 4 op 3 to 1 tchd 100 to 30 and 7 to 2)	5

1353[6]	ALOSAILI [72] 9-10-12 (3") G Hogan, *settled to chase ldrs, feeling pace and lost grnd 3 out, no extr frm nxt.*	
	. . . . (8 to 1 op 4 to 1 tchd 9 to 1)	6
1567[3]	KATBALLOU [62] 7-10-5 J Ryan, *al chasing ldrs, hit 4th, struggling 3 out, sn lost tch.*	
	. . . . (7 to 1 op 8 to 1 tchd 10 to 1)	7
1574	JAVA SHRINE (USA) [61] (bl) 5-10-4 R Bellamy, *pressed ldrs, und pres whn pace quickened frm 3 out, sn lost tch, tld off.*	
	. . . . (14 to 1 op 10 to 1 tchd 8 to 1)	8
1402[6]	LUCY TUFTY [84] 5-11-13 R Dunwoody, *patiently rdn, effrt fnl circuit, ridden and btn 3 out, tld off . . .* (5 to 2 fav op 7 to 4)	9
1425	JUST A BEAU [57] 5-9-9 (5") Sophie Mitchell, *led aftr 1st, hdd 5th, wknd quickly 4 out, tld off.* . . . . . . (66 to 1 op 33 to 1)	10

Dist: 3l, 1l, 2½l, 2l, 1¾l, 11l, 10l, 25l, dist. 4m 4.80s. a 20.80s (10 Ran).

(Vivian Guy), D Burchell

1844 New Smaller Size E.D.P. Juvenile Novices' Hurdle Class D (3-y-o) £2,720 2m. (1:20)

1610[5]	LE TETEU (Fr) 10-12 R Dunwoody, *wtd wth, improved 3 out, led and hit last, drvn out.* . . . . (6 to 4 fav op 11 to 10)	1
	DESERT MOUNTAIN (Ire) 10-12 C Llewellyn, *al frnt rnk, led 5th, quickened bef nxt, rdn and hdd last, kpt on one pace.*	
	. . . . (9 to 4 op 4 to 1 tchd 5 to 1)	2
	ROYAL ACTION 10-12 J R Kavanagh, *led aftr 1st, styd upsides till rdn and not quicken frm betw last 2.*	
	. . . . (11 to 4 op 7 to 2 tchd 4 to 1 and 2 to 1)	3
	FOREST BOY 10-9 (3") G Hogan, *settled to track ldrs, drvn alng whn pace quickened 3 out, fdd nxt.*	
	. . . . (12 to 1 op 7 to 1 tchd 14 to 1 and 16 to 1)	4
	HAUTE CUISINE 10-12 K Gaule, *settled midfield, und pres whn pace quickened 3 out, sn lost tch, tld off.*	
	. . . . (20 to 1 op 14 to 1 tchd 33 to 1)	5
	POETRY (Ire) 10-7 A Dobbin, *hld up, effrt whn not fluent 5th, struggling frm nxt, tld off.* (13 to 2 op 5 to 1 tchd 7 to 1)	6
1398*	FIJON (Ire) 10-13 V Smith, *unruly strt, settled in tch, struggling fnl circuit, tld off frm 3 out.* . . . . . (10 to 1 op 8 to 1)	7
1610	MAGIC ROLE 10-5 (7") N T Egan, *struggling to keep up bef hfwy, tld off aftr 4 out. . .* (16 to 1 op 8 to 1 tchd 20 to 1)	8
	BRIGHT ECLIPSE (USA) 10-12 T Jenks, *keen hold, led aftr 1st till hdd 5th, lost tch, tld off whn pld up aftr 3 out.*	
	. . . . (33 to 1 op 20 to 1)	pu

Dist: 2l, 10l, nk, 21l, 5l, 1¼l, 15l. 3m 59.70s. a 15.70s (9 Ran).
SR: 23/21/11/10/-/-/ *(Mrs Judit Woods), Bob Jones*

1845 Stephenson Smart Handicap Chase Class D (0-120 5-y-o and up) £4,307 3m 110yds. . . . . (1:55)

1597	DONT TELL THE WIFE [115] 10-11-13 J A McCarthy, *patiently rdn, improved to join ldg pair fnl circuit, drw level last, sn led, ran on strly.* . . . . (7 to 2 tchd 4 to 1)	1
1296[4]	ROMANY CREEK [116] 7-12-0 R Dunwoody, *nvr far away, hit 3rd, 7th and 4 out, led 2 out, jnd last, sn hdd, kpt on same pace.* . . . . (3 to 1 op 5 to 2)	2
1643[6]	PATS MINSTREL [108] 11-11-6 A Dobbin, *al wl plcd, lft in ld 9th, hdd 2 out, rdn betw last two, one pace.*	
	. . . . (8 to 1 tchd 10 to 1)	3
1424	VICTORY GATE (USA) [88] 11-10-0 D Leahy, *settled to track ldrs, struggling fnl circuit, lost tough and tld off 4 out.*	
	. . . . (50 to 1 op 20 to 1)	4
1812[5]	JOKER JACK [88] 11-9-12[1] (3") G Hogan, *wth ldrs, hit 4th, blun and lost grnd nxt, lost tch fnl circuit, tld off.*	
	. . . . (16 to 1 tchd 20 to 1)	5
	SPEAKER WEATHERILL (Ire) [108] 7-11-6 M Brennan, *led, gng wl whn o'rjmpd and f 9th.*	
	. . . . (Evens fav op 11 to 10 on tchd 11 to 10)	f
	GOOD OLD CHIPS [88] 9-10-0 J R Kavanagh, *struggling aftr one circuit, tld off whn pld up passing stands bef 6 out.*	
	. . . . (33 to 1 op 20 to 1)	pu

Dist: ½l, 5l, dist, ½l. 6m 33.50s. a 36.50s (7 Ran).

(Elite Racing Club), C R Egerton

1846 L. L. Firth Memorial Handicap Chase Class F (0-100 5-y-o and up) £4,307 2m 110yds. . . . . (2:30)

1686*	THE LANCER (Ire) [90] 7-11-8 (8ex) R Dunwoody, *nvr far away, drvn ahead betw last 2, styd on strly r-in.*	
	. . . . (6 to 4 fav tchd 9 to 4 and 5 to 2)	1
1764[5]	DR ROCKET [86] (bl) 11-11-4 C Llewellyn, *al wl plcd, ev ch and drvn alng 3 out, kpt on same pace r-in.*	
	. . . . (12 to 1 op 6 to 1)	2
1730	WINSPIT (Ire) [86] 6-11-4 J R Kavanagh, *al hndy, nosed ahead and lft a l clr 2 out, hdd betw last two, styd on same pace r-in.* . . . . (5 to 1 op 4 to 1 tchd 11 to 2)	3
843[3]	HOLY WANDERER (USA) [96] 7-11-11 (3") G Hogan, *patiently rdn, improved hfwy, effrt aftr 3 out, one pace betw last 2.*	
	. . . . (11 to 2 op 4 to 1 tchd 6 to 1)	4
	SOUNDS GOLDEN [68] 8-9-12[5] (7") Mr R Wakley, *pressed ldrs, reminders and lost gr ambition aftr 6 out, sn struggling, no imprsn after.* . . . . (33 to 1 tchd 50 to 1)	5
1349	THE MINISTER (Ire) [82] 7-11-0 A Dobbin, *al chasing ldrs, drvn alng whn blun and rdr lost reins, sn btn, tld off.*	
	. . . . (8 to 1 op 10 to 1 tchd 12 to 1)	6

1557³ NATIONAL FLAG (Fr) [72] 6-10-4 A Larnach, *hit 3rd, sn struggling, tld off frm hfwy*...................(8 to 1 tchd 10 to 1) 7
1595⁵ CIRCULATION [73] (v) 10-10-5⁶ (3*) D Walsh, *tried to make
all, hdd and rdn in second whn f 2 out*...(4 to 1 op 4 to 1) f
RUSTIC GENT [78] (v) 8-10-10 D Leahy, *trkd ldrs, struggling and losing tch rpdly whn jmpd slwly 4 out, pld up quickly
bef nxt*...................(33 to 1 op 20 to 1 tchd 50 to 1) pu
Dist: 2¹/₂l, 2l, 1¹/₂l, 10l, 18l, dist. 4m 17.00s. a 20.00s (9 Ran).

(A E Frost), D R Gandolfo

1847 Cottesmore Mares' Only Novices' Chase Class D (5-y-o and up) £3,352 2m 5f 110yds.................(3:00)

JASILU (bl) 6-11-2 C Llewellyn, *made all, pckd 6th, hrd
pressed fnl circuit, styd on strly to go clr appr last.*
.............(85 to 40 op 2 to 1 tchd 9 to 4 and 5 to 2) 1
1341 SCAMALLACH (Ire) (bl) 6-10-10 R Dunwoody, *al hndy, ev ch
fnl circuit, rdn and kpt on same pace frm betw last 2.*
.............................(2 to 1 op 5 to 4 on) 2
1722⁹ PRIZE MATCH 7-10-10 R Bellamy, *nvr far away, pckd 7th, ev
ch till blun 4 out, rdn and not quicken frm betw last 2.*
.....................(5 to 1 tchd 7 to 1 and 8 to 1) 3
1557⁴ SOPHIE MAY 5-10-10 A Dobbin, *nvr far away, effrt whn blun
tenth, rallied, rdn and bdd betw last 2.* ....(2 to 1 jt-
fav op 2 to 1 tchd 9 to 4 op Evens) 4
1234⁶ PENNANT COTTAGE (Ire) (bl) 8-10-10 T Jenks, *mstks, in tch
aftr one circuit, effrt whn nrly f 6 out, not reco'r, tld off after.*
.....................(33 to 1 op 20 to 1 tchd 50 to 1) 5
Dist: 3l, 5l, 2¹/₂l, dist. 5m 45.70s. a 33.70s (5 Ran).

(K C Bailey), K C Bailey

1848 Fakenham Racecourse Caravan Site Handicap Hurdle Class E (0-110 4-y-o and up) £3,386 2¹/₂m.......(3:30)

1443⁴ BARFORD SOVEREIGN [104] 4-11-12 A Dobbin, *led till aftr
second, continued to chase new ldr, rgned ld bef 4 out, drw clr
last 2, eased finish.*.......(4 to 1 op 5 to 1 tchd 8 to 1) 1
1717³ PEDALTOTHEMETAL (Ire) [90] 4-10-9 (3*) D Walsh, *settled
wth chasing grp, ev ch fnl circuit, rdn whn ldr quickened clr 2
out, no imprsn aftr*........(3 to 2 op 5 to 1 tchd 7 to 1) 2
669² WADADA [106] 5-11-7 (7*) J Prior, *settled wth chasing bunch,
improved to race in tch fnl circuit, und pres frm 3 out, no extr.*
.....................(6 to 1 op 4 to 1) 3
1766³ ABLE PLAYER (USA) [86] 9-10-8 M Sharratt, *settled midfield,
improved fnl circuit, und pres bef 3 out, sn outpcd.*
.....................(13 to 2 op 6 to 1 tchd 7 to 1) 4
1722⁶ DURSHAN (USA) [78] (bl) 7-10-0 J R Kavanagh, *in tch wth
chasing grp, effrt fnl circuit, struggling bef 3 out, lost grnd quickly
bef 4 out, styd on ag'n frm betw last 2.*
.....................(11 to 1 op 8 to 1 tchd 12 to 1) 5
1596² PAIR OF JACKS (Ire) [92] 6-11-0 R Dunwoody, *in tch in
midfield, effrt fnl circuit, struggling bef 3 out, lost touch, tld off.*
.....................(9 to 4 jt-fav op 3 to 1 tchd 7 to 2) 6
1567 NAGOBELIA [81] 8-10-3 K Gaule, *al wl in tch, feeling pace
whn pace quickened frm 3 out, lost touch, tld.*
.....................(25 to 1 op 16 to 1) 7
1615 LOOKINGFORARAINBOW (Ire) [83] 8-10-5 V Smith, *settled
off the pace, took clr order 7th, lost grnd quickly bef 3 out, tld
off.*.....................(9 to 4 jt-fav op 5 to 2) 8
AJDAR [88] 5-10-10 M Brennan, *rcd freely, led aftr second,
clr hfwy, hdd and wknd quickly bef 4 out, tld off.*
.....................(16 to 1 op 14 to 1) 9
Dist: 9l, 2l, 1³/₄l, nk, 16l, 2¹/₂l, 2¹/₂l, dist. 5m 14.50s. a 33.50s (9 Ran).

(Barford Bloodstock), J R Fanshawe

SANDOWN (good)
Thursday December 12th
Going Correction: PLUS 0.45 sec. per fur.

1849 European Breeders Fund 'National Hunt' Novices' Hurdle Qualifier Class D (4,5,6-y-o) £2,970 2m 110yds.................(1:00)

1496¹ HURRICANE LAMP 5-11-10 A Maguire, *hld up, steady hdwy
aftr 3 out, led 2 out, rdn appr last, drvn out.*
.....................(7 to 4 fav tchd 2 to 1 and 13 to 8) 1
1641⁴ NASONE (Ire) 5-11-0 P Hide, *hld up beh ldrs, hdwy to hold ev
ch frm 2 out, kpt on r-in....* (9 to 4 op 7 to 4 tchd 5 to 2) 2
FRIENDSHIP (Ire) 4-11-0 M A Fitzgerald, *hld up beh ldrs, not
fluent 3 out, ev ch appr nxt, kpt on und pres frm last.*
.....................(9 to 1 op 8 to 1) 3
AWARD (Ire) 5-11-0 D O'Sullivan, *hld up beh, hdwy 3rd, chsd
ldr nxt, led briefly appr 2 out, one pace frm last.*
.....................(50 to 1 op 33 to 1 tchd 66 to 1) 4
1594⁴ NEAT FEAT (Ire) 5-11-0 P Holley, *hld up mid-div, hdwy appr 2
out, sn outpcd........* (12 to 1 op 10 to 1 tchd 14 to 1) 5
1479 PHYSICAL FUN 5-11-0 D Skyrme, *hld up beh, outpcd aftr 4th,
some modest late prog, nvr nr to chal.*
.....................(66 to 1 op 50 to 1 tchd 100 to 1) 6
1350 LOCH NA KEAL 4-10-9 C Maude, *nvr on terms.*
.....................(40 to 1 op 16 to 1 tchd 50 to 1) 7

1397 ROSSELL ISLAND (Ire) 5-11-0 W Marston, *cl up, pushed alng
4th, wknd 3 out........* (50 to 1 op 33 to 1 tchd 66 to 1) 8
JAZZMAN (Ire) 4-11-0 D Gallagher, *hld up, al beh, styd on frm
last..................* (33 to 1 op 14 to 1 tchd 50 to 1) 9
1502 BLACK STATEMENT (Ire) 6-10-11 (3*) L Aspell, *cl up till
outpcd frm 3 out, tld off.* (50 to 1 op 33 to 1 tchd 66 to 1) 10
1497² CALVARO (Ire) 5-11-0 G Bradley, *cl up till wknd appr 5th, tld
off.....................* (25 to 1 op 16 to 1) 11
1642 GALE WARGAME (Ire) 5-11-0 J Osborne, *led to appr 2 out, sn
rdn and btn, tld off....* (16 to 1 op 14 to 1 tchd 25 to 1) 12
Dist: Nk, 3l, hd, 13l, 7l, 1l, 2l, 16l, 2l, 4m 2.40s. a 15.40s (12 Ran).
SR: 16/5/2/2/-/-/ (Mr & Mrs F C Welch And Mr R A Barrs), D Nicholson

1850 Bovis Lelliott Novices' Chase Class C (5-y-o and up) £4,844 2¹/₂m 110yds ....(1:35)

1392* POTTER'S BAY 7-11-7 A Maguire, *trkd ldr, led tenth,
mstk 13th, pushed out frm last....*(7 to 2 op 9 to 4 on) 1
TRIPLE WITCHING 10-11-0 M A Fitzgerald, *led to tenth,
shaken up and ev ch last, kpt on und pres.*
.....................(3 to 1 op 11 to 8) 2
Won by 1l. 5m 23.80s. a 23.80s (2 Ran).
SR: -/-/ (Mrs J E Potter), D Nicholson

1851 Bovis Crowngap Handicap Chase Class B (5-y-o and up) £6,775 2¹/₂m 110yds.................(2:10)

1223² STATELY HOME (Ire) [120] 5-10-0 A Maguire, *made all, clr 6th,
unchlgd...........* (9 to 4 jt-fav op 2 to 1 tchd 5 to 2) 1
1613 SWING MEDICINE [134] 9-11-0 J Osborne, *hld up, chsd
wnr frm tenth, no imprsn frm 3 out..............*(9 to 4 jt-
fav op 11 to 4) 2
BRADBURY STAR [148] 11-12-0 P Hide, *hld up, drpd rear
tenth, styd on frm 3 out, nvr able to chal.*
.....................(7 to 1 op 5 to 1 tchd 8 to 1) 3
1394⁹ EASTHORPE [141] 8-11-7 M A Fitzgerald, *chsd wnr to tenth,
wknd appr 12th, sn btn............* (3 to 1 op 9 to 4) 4
1401 CONTI D'ESTRUVAL (Fr) [121] 6-10-1 B Fenton, *hld up, effrt
appr 3 out, sn btn..........* (9 to 1 op 6 to 1 tchd 10 to 1) 5
Dist: 12l, 1¹/₄l, 1¹/₂l, 1³/₄l. 5m 12.60s. a 12.60s (5 Ran).
SR: 38/40/52/43/21/ (P Bowen), P Bowen

1852 Bovis Crowngap Winter Novices' Hurdle Class A Grade 2 (4-y-o and up) £9,645 2³/₄m.............(2:40)

1615* YAHMI (Ire) 6-11-4 J Osborne, *hld up in cl tch, chlgd 2 out, led
last, ran on wl und pres....* (4 to 1 op 5 to 2 tchd 9 to 2) 1
1297* JACK TANNER (Ire) 7-11-7 A Maguire, *not jump wl, hld up in
cl tch, led 2 out to last, rallied und pres, jst held.*
.....................(4 to 1 on op 9 to 4 on tchd 2 to 1 on) 2
1427³ EULOGY (Ire) 6-11-0 D O'Sullivan, *led briefly 5th, cl up, led
ag'n 3 out, sn hdd, ev ch appr nxt, one pace.*
.....................(25 to 1 op 14 to 1) 3
1379² SUPERMODEL 4-10-9 S Wynne, *hld up in cl tch, hrd rdn appr
last, sn no extr..........* (100 to 1 op 25 to 1) 4
1343⁶ RIVER ROOM 6-11-0 G Bradley, *wth ldr, led aftr 5th to 3 out,
sn led ag'n, hdd 2 out, wknd quickly.*
.....................(25 to 1 op 12 to 1 tchd 33 to 1) 5
1502³ ATAVISTIC (Ire) 4-11-0 M A Fitzgerald, *made most to 5th, cl
up, wknd quickly aftr 3 out, pld up bef nxt.*
.....................(33 to 1 op 12 to 1) pu
Dist: Hd, 5l, 2¹/₂l, dist. 5m 27.60s. a 24.60s (6 Ran).

(W E Sturt), J A B Old

1853 P & O Handicap Chase Class B (5-y-o and up) £6,677 3m 5f 110yds (3:10)

1516* INCHCAILLOCH (Ire) [128] 7-11-7 C Maude, *hld up, chsd ldr
frm 12th, led appr last, rdn out.*
.....................(6 to 4 on op 7 to 4 on tchd 11 to 8 on) 1
1645² CHURCH LAW [107] 9-10-0 A Maguire, *hld up, jmpd slwly
3rd, mstks tenth and 18th, cld 4 out, hrd rdn to chase wnr appr
last, no extr..........* (5 to 2 op 9 to 4 tchd 2 to 1) 2
1418³ FROZEN DROP [107] 9-10-0 S Fox, *led, rdn appr 4 out, hdd
approaching last, no extr...* (9 to 2 op 7 to 2 tchd 5 to 1) 3
1767⁸ WOODLANDS GENHIRE [107] (bl) 11-10-0 W Marston, *chsd
ldr to 12th, drpd rear 14th, sn lost tch, tld off.*
.....................(100 to 1 op 33 to 1) 4
Dist: 1³/₄l, 6l, dist. 7m 51.00s. a 38.00s (4 Ran).

(F J Carter), J S King

1854 Surrey Racing Juvenile Novices' Hurdle Class D (3-y-o) £2,905 2m 110yds.................(3:40)

1412* FAR DAWN (USA) 11-7 C Maude, *chsd ldg pair, cld 3 out, led
appr nxt, clr whn hit last, cmftbly.*
.....................(5 to 2 op 7 to 2 tchd 4 to 1) 1
FITZWILLIAM (USA) 11-3 J Osborne, *strted slwly, hld up,
hdwy appr 5th, mstk 3 out and lost plce, styd on frm approaching
2 out, kpt on one pace.* (6 to 5 fav op Evens tchd 11 to 8) 2
BARANOV (Ire) 11-3 D Gallagher, *pld hrd, led second till aftr
nxt, led 5th to appr 2 out, mstk, one pace.*
.....................(10 to 1 op 5 to 1) 3

SPIRAL FLYER (Ire) 10-12 W Marston, *trkd ldrs, outpcd frm 3 out*.................(33 to 1 op 20 to 1 tchd 50 to 1) 4
1398[3] SOLDIER MAK 11-3 P Hide, *led 1st, sn rstrained beh ldr, led aftr 3rd till 5th, mstk 3 out, soon btn*. ....(10 to 1 op 5 to 1 tchd 11 to 1) 5
GO WITH THE WIND 11-3 M Richards, *al beh*. ....(12 to 1 op 14 to 1) 6
1398[9] ALARICO (Fr) 11-3 A Maguire, *pld hrd, hld up, beh frm 3rd*. ....(66 to 1 op 50 to 1 tchd 100 to 1) 7
WHISPERING DAWN 10-12 G Bradley, *trkd ldrs, mstk 4th, sn wknd*..............................(8 to 1 op 6 to 1) 8
1702[4] VERONICA FRANCO 10-12 B Fenton, *al beh*. ....(33 to 1 op 20 to 1 tchd 50 to 1) 9
1517[6] SAM ROCKETT (bl) 10-12 (5*) S Ryan, *al beh, shrtlvd effrt aftr 3 out*..........(66 to 1 op 33 to 1 tchd 100 to 1) 10
1610 HAWANAFA 10-12 W McFarland, *mstk second, beh, lost tch aftr 3 out, tld off*......(66 to 1 op 33 to 1 tchd 100 to 1) 11
Dist: 12l, nk, 16l, 6l, 5l, nk, 3l, 6l, 6l, 9l. 4m 4.60s. a 17.60s (11 Ran).
(Peter Wiegand), Mrs A J Perrett

TAUNTON (good)
Thursday December 12th
Going Correction: PLUS 0.20 sec. per fur.

1855 West Hatch Novices' Hurdle Class C (4-y-o and up) £3,777 2m 1f...(1:10)

1598* YET AGAIN 4-11-6 D Bridgwater, *in tch, hdwy to track ldrs 3 out, chlgd nxt, led appr last, drvn out*. ....(11 to 4 op 5 to 2 tchd 3 to 1) 1
1532* LUCIA FORTE 5-11-1 S McNeill, *trkd ldrs, chlgd 2 out, ev ch last, not quicken r-in*..............(5 to 2 fav op 7 to 4) 2
EASY LISTENING (USA) 4-11-0 G Upton, *keen hold, wth ldr till led aftr 4th, hdd after 2 out, one pace und pres*. ....(8 to 1 op 5 to 1) 3
SHOW FAITH (Ire) 6-11-0 R Hughes, *steady hdwy frm 5th, rdn appr 2 out, found little*.... (15 to 2 op 5 to 1 tchd 8 to 1) 4
1429[6] SWAN STREET (NZ) 5-11-0 J Railton, *in tch to 5th, sn wknd*. ....(33 to 1 op 12 to 1) 5
1410[9] SAHEL (Ire) 8-11-0 S Curran, *made most to aftr 4th, styd wth ldr, hit 3 out, sn wknd*...(20 to 1 op 10 to 1 tchd 25 to 1) 6
1449[7] GALWAY BOSS (Ire) 4-11-0 N Williamson, *hdwy aftr 4th, wknd four out*..........................(50 to 1 op 20 to 1) 7
1749 ASTRAL INVADER (Ire) 4-10-11 (3*) T Dascombe, *not fluent, beh frm 5th*.......................(66 to 1 op 33 to 1) 8
1609 SOPHIES DREAM 5-11-0 T J Murphy, *al beh*. ....(100 to 1 op 50 to 1) 9
GWITHIAN 4-11-0 R Greene, *al beh*. ....(66 to 1 op 33 to 1 tchd 100 to 1) 10
DECEIT THE SECOND 4-11-0 S Burrough, *al beh*. ....(66 to 1 op 25 to 1) 11
997[2] IKTASAB 4-11-6 A P McCoy, *in tch, drvn alng to chase ldrs 5th, wknd 4 out, fifth and no ch whn f last*. ....(7 to 2 op 3 to 1 tchd 5 to 1) 12
MAETERLINCK (Ire) 4-10-7 (7*) Clare Thorner, *not fluent, al beh, no ch whn f 2 out*. (40 to 1 op 14 to 1 tchd 50 to 1) f
WESTERN PLAYBOY 4-11-0 R Farrant, *sn beh, tld off whn pld up bef 2 out*..........................(40 to 1 op 16 to 1) pu
Dist: 1¼l, 4l, 2½l, 10l, 15l, 12l, 8l, nk, ½l, 5l. 3m 53.80s. a 10.80s (14 Ran).
SR: 20/13/8/5/-/-/ (A P Griffin), Miss Gay Kelleway

1856 Chard Selling Hurdle Class G (4-y-o and up) £1,931 2m 3f 110yds (1:45)

1731* HARRY 6-11-12 D J Burchell, *steady hdwy to track ldrs aftr 5th, chlgd 3 out, sn led, kpt on wl* ....(Evens fav op 5 to 4 tchd 11 to 8) 1
1541[7] SLEEPTITE (Fr) 6-10-12 (7*) J Power, *wth ldrs to 3rd, styd prmnt, led 4 out, hdd aftr nxt, one pace und pres*. ....(16 to 1 op 8 to 1 tchd 20 to 1) 2
1541[4] SARACEN PRINCE (USA) 4-10-12 R Johnson, *rdn alng aftr 5th, hdwy und pres frm 2 out, styd on r-in*. ....(4 to 1 op 8 to 1 tchd 7 to 2) 3
TE AMO (Ire) 4-10-12 R Hughes, *led to 4 out, one pace und pres appr 2 out*.......... (7 to 2 op 2 to 1 tchd 4 to 1) 4
1320[5] OLD MASTER (Ire) 5-10-5 (7*) N Willmington, *dsptd ld to 3rd, beh frm 6th*......................(20 to 1 op 12 to 1) 5
1731[4] COMEONUP 5-10-12 N Williamson, *beh, rdn and lost tch frm 6th*..............................(20 to 1 op 12 to 1) 6
PERFECT BERTIE (Ire) 4-10-5 (7*) S O'Shea, *hdwy 6th, 4th and wkng whn mstk and uns rdr four out*. ....(16 to 1 op 14 to 1) ur
1237 BLAKEWAY 9-10-7 S Burrough, *beh frm 4th, tld off whn pld up bef last*..........................(50 to 1 op 16 to 1) pu
1747[5] MIRAMARE 6-10-9 (3*) T Dascombe, *beh frm 5th, tld off whn pld up bef for out*......(33 to 1 op 14 to 1 tchd 50 to 1) pu
Dist: 7l, 6l, 1¾l, 9l, dist. 4m 37.10s. a 19.10s (9 Ran).
(Simon T Lewis), D Burchell

1857 Stoke St Mary Novices' Handicap Chase Class E (0-100 5-y-o and up) £3,036 2m 3f...............(2:20)

1605 FRONTIER FLIGHT (USA) [80] 6-11-0 (3*) E Husband, *wl beh till hdwy 3 out, 5th whn lft 3rd at last, ran on well to ld nr finish*. ....(16 to 1) 1
1636 BROWN ROBBER [71] 8-10-8 R Farrant, *mstk and rdr lost irons 3rd, hdwy tenth, second and hld whn lft in ld last, rdn r-in, ct nr finish*........(16 to 1 op 10 to 1 tchd 20 to 1) 2
1498 CRACKING PROSPECT [80] 5-10-12 (5*) D Salter, *hdwy 9th, hld whn lft disputing ld last, one pace*..(11 to 1 op 8 to 1) 3
1262[5] CHRIS'S GLEN [80] (v) 7-11-3 N Williamson, *chsd ldr, led 7th to nxt, wknd 4 out*...... (10 to 1 op 7 to 1 tchd 11 to 1) 4
1667[3] KOO'S PROMISE [83] 5-11-3 (3*) T Dascombe, *nvr rchd ldrs*. ....(10 to 1 op 8 to 1 tchd 11 to 1 and 12 to 1) 5
1647[4] NAUTICAL GEORGE (Ire) [83] 6-11-6 R Supple, *blun 5th, al beh*..........................(12 to 1 op 10 to 1) 6
MASKED MARTIN [67] 5-10-4[4] S Burrough, *al beh*. ....(50 to 1 op 33 to 1) 7
1686[5] NORDIC VALLEY (Ire) [88] 5-11-11 T J Murphy, *in tch, pushed alng 9th, hmpd 3 out, 3rd and hld whn f last*......(7 to 2 jt-fav tchd 6 to 1 and 13 to 2) f
AFTER THE FOX [91] 9-12-0 G Upton, *led to 7th, led 8th, mstks tenth and nxt, hdd aftr 4 out, second whn f next*. ....(7 to 2 jt-fav tchd 9 to 2 and 3 to 1) f
1413[8] GERRY'S PRIDE (Ire) [68] 5-10-5 S Curran, *f 1st*. ....(12 to 1 op 10 to 1) f
1452 SAXON MEAD [63] (bl) 6-10-0 G Tormey, *mstk 8th, steady hdwy nxt, led aftr 4 out, mistake next, clr whn f last, unlucky*. ....(10 to 1 tchd 11 to 1) f
1498[4] LEGAL ARTIST (Ire) [79] 6-11-2 L Harvey, *al beh, tld off whn pld up bef 3 out*..........................(10 to 1) ur
1603[6] SAN DIEGO CHARGER (Ire) [74] 5-10-6 (5*) Mr R Thornton, *mstk and uns rdr second*. ....(16 to 1 op 10 to 1 tchd 20 to 1) ur
1557[6] ANLACE [70] 7-10-7 N Mann, *mstk second, sn tld off, pld up bef 4 out*..........................(16 to 1) pu
Dist: ½l, 1l, 10l, 1¾l, dist, 4l. 4m 49.10s. a 18.10s (14 Ran).
(Miss L C Siddall), Miss L C Siddall

1858 Gay Sheppard Memorial Challenge Trophy Handicap Hurdle Class D (0-120 4-y-o and up) £2,900 3m 110yds......................(2:50)

906* ROSIE-B [82] 6-9-9 (5*) Mr R Thornton, *sn in tch, chsd ldrs appr 2 out, quickened to ld r-in, all out*. ....(7 to 4 fav op 5 to 2 tchd 3 to 1) 1
1558[5] PADDYSWAY [90] 9-10-8 D Bridgwater, *led till aftr 5th, hrd drvn to ld ag'n after 3 out, hdd and one pace r-in*. ....(11 to 4 op 3 to 1 tchd 100 to 30) 2
LUGS BRANNIGAN (Ire) [93] 7-10-4 (7*) Katharine Hambidge, *beh, shaken up 2 out, ran on wl r-in, not rch ldrs*. ....(6 to 1 op 9 to 2) 3
1576[9] ROYAL PIPER (NZ) [100] 9-11-4 R Greene, *beh, pushed alng and hdwy 2 out, styd on und pres r-in*.... (8 to 1 op 9 to 2) 4
1383[3] STAUNCH RIVAL (USA) [109] (bl) 9-11-6 (7*) Clare Thorner, *beh, hdwy 3 out, kpt on same pace frm nxt*. ....(20 to 1 op 12 to 1 tchd 25 to 1) 5
1567[4] TIGER CLAW (USA) [84] 10-9-11 (5*) O Burrows, *in tch, rdn 3 out, wknd appr nxt*..........(16 to 1 op 8 to 1) 6
KHATIR (Can) [82] (bl) 5-10-0 N Williamson, *wth ldr till led aftr 5th, hdd after 3 out, wknd nxt*.......... (10 to 1 op 5 to 1) 7
1602 CERTAIN ANGLE [106] 7-11-10 G Tormey, *lost tch 8, tld off whn pld up bef 2 out*..........(8 to 1 op 5 to 1) pu
Dist: 1l, 5l, 1¾l, nk, 6l, 1¼l. 5m 49.40s. a 21.40s (8 Ran).
(Internet Racing), N M Babbage

1859 Dunster Handicap Chase Class F (0-105 5-y-o and up) £2,788 3m ....(3:20)

1593* CALL ME RIVER (Ire) [77] 8-10-0 I Lawrence, *sn in tch, chlgd 4 out, soon led, clr 2 out, readily*. ....(15 to 8 fav op 7 to 4 tchd 9 to 4) 1
1734[6] COOL CHARACTER (Ire) [77] 8-10-0 D Bridgwater, *beh, mstk 4 out, kpt on wl frm nxt to take second r-in, not rch wnr*. ....(12 to 1 tchd 14 to 1) 2
1516[3] PAPER STAR [99] 9-11-3 (5*) Mr R Thornton, *led to 5th, chsd ldr till led 12th, hdd aftr 4 out, styd on same pace*. ....(14 to 1 op 8 to 1) 3
1569* SOLO GENT [95] 7-11-4 S McNeill, *hld up, reminder 13th and some hdwy, one pace und pres frm 3 out*. ....(9 to 4 op 5 to 2 tchd 7 to 4) 4
1569[5] MAXXUM EXPRESS (Ire) [85] 8-10-8 Richard Guest, *led 5th to 12th, hit 14th wknd and blun nxt, sn weakened*. ....(16 to 1 op 12 to 1) 5
1664 RAINBOW CASTLE [105] 9-12-0 N Williamson, *beh till f 6th*. ....(7 to 1 op 4 to 1 tchd 15 to 2) f
ROYAL SAXON [95] 10-11-4 R Johnson, *prmnt to 9th, beh frm 11th, mstk nxt, tld off whn pld up bef 3 out*. ....(8 to 1 op 5 to 1 tchd 9 to 1) pu
1446[3] GALLIC GIRL (Ire) [77] 6-9-12[1] (3*) T Dascombe, *hdwy 13th, wknd 4 out, pld up bef 2 out, dismounted*. ....(12 to 1 op 8 to 1) pu
Dist: 2l, 2½l, 1¾l, 17l. 6m 9.70s. a 26.70s (8 Ran).
(The Larkin Around Partnership), P R Hedger

1860 Bicknoller Handicap Hurdle Class D (0-125 4-y-o and up) £2,794 2m 1f ....(3:50)

1625* OUT RANKING (Fr) [115] 4-11-10 R Hughes, *made all, drvn and ran on wl r-in*... (5 to 4 on op Evens tchd 11 to 10) 1
16996 LUCKY EDDIE (Ire) [105] 5-11-0 N Williamson, *trkd ldrs, chsd wnr aftr 2 out, kpt on wl und pres*........(6 to 1 op 4 to 1) 2
FABULOUS MTOTO [91] 6-10-0 P Holley, *keen hold, hdwy 4 out, chsd wnr 3 out till aftr nxt, sn outpcd.*
...................................(4 to 1 tchd 3 to 1) 3
16013 MILLCROFT RIVIERA (Ire) [91] 5-9-12[1] (3*) P Henley, *chsd wnr to 3 out, wknd*................. (11 to 2 op 4 to 1) 4
1641 ADONISIS [91] 4-10-0 A Procter, *al beh, mstk and lost tch 3 out*.................................(16 to 1 op 8 to 1) 5
Dist: 2½l, 8l, 9l, 10l. 3m 58.40s. a 15.40s (5 Ran).
(Knight Hawks Partnership), M C Pipe

CHELTENHAM (good to firm)
Friday December 13th
Going Correction: PLUS 0.40 sec. per fur.

1861 Letheby & Christopher Three Year Old Novices' Hurdle Class C £3,707 2m 1f..................... (12:15)

DISALLOWED (Ire) 10-9 M A Fitzgerald, *pressed ldrs till led appr 4th, pushed alng approaching last, ran on wl.*
...................................(4 to 1 fav op 3 to 1) 1
1737 SOCIETY MAGIC (USA) 11-0 R Dunwoody, *help up, steady hdwy appr 2 out, sn ev ch, one pace r-in*.........(10 to 1) 2
16106 PLEASURELAND (Ire) 11-0 D Morris, *gd hdwy appr 3 out, ev ch nxt, outpcd approaching last*........ (5 to 1 op 6 to 1) 3
MAZAMET (USA) 11-0 V Slattery, *in tch, mstk and outpcd 5th, styd on and ev ch 2 out, sn outpaced*....(6 to 1 op 8 to 1) 4
14225 BRANDON MAGIC 11-0 A Maguire, *led to 3rd, styd prmnt, ev ch 2 out, sn wknd*.........(11 to 2 op 5 to 1 tchd 6 to 1) 5
INFLUENCE PEDLER 11-0 C Llewellyn, *mstk 1st, led 3rd till appr nxt, ev ch 2 out, sn wknd.*
...................................(9 to 2 op 4 to 1 tchd 6 to 1) 6
17025 CLASSY CHIEF 11-0 T J Murphy, *hdwy to chase ldrs 6th, ev ch 2 out, sn wknd*.................(14 to 1 tchd 16 to 1) 7
1102 ARROGANT HEIR 11-0 Mr A Rebori, *not fluent, al in rear.*
...................................(100 to 1) 8
1470 NOBLE COLOURS 11-0 Mr J Jukes, *trkd ldrs, chsd wnr frm 6th, ev ch 2 out, wknd quickly*.................(100 to 1) 9
GET TOUGH 11-0 C Maude, *rear and mstk 6th, tld off.*
...................................(66 to 1 op 50 to 1) 10
BENKAROSAM 11-0 Gary Lyons, *tld off frm 4th.*
16893 TOPAGLOW (Ire) 11-0 N Williamson, *trkd ldrs, shaken up and ev ch whn f 2 out*...........................(5 to 1 op 6 to 1) f
Dist: 4l, 1l, 11l, 2½l, 2l, 2½l, 10l, nk, dist, 1½l. 4m 11.00s. a 17.00s (12 Ran).
(Million In Mind Partnership (6)), Miss H C Knight

1862 Chris Coley Racing Novices' Chase Class C (5-y-o and up) £4,980 3m 1f 110yds..................... (12:45)

15622 FLIMSY TRUTH 10-11-4 Mr M Harris, *trkd ldr, chsd 4th, led nxt, sn clr, hit 8th, pushed alng frm 3 out, hld on gmely r-in.*
...................................(9 to 1 op 6 to 1) 1
15682 WEE WINDY (Ire) 7-11-4 P Hide, *led to 5th, styd chasing wnr, shaken up 3 out, stayed on r-in, no imprsn.*
...................................(7 to 4 on op 5 to 4 on) 2
1833* LORD OF THE WEST (Ire) 7-11-8 A Maguire, *al 3rd, effrt frm 4 out, staying on whn mstk 2 out, sn btn.*
...................................(15 to 8 op 11 to 8 tchd 2 to 1) 3
Dist: 3l, 11l. 6m 43.70s. a 28.70s (3 Ran).
(M H Weston), M H Weston

1863 Chubb Fire Conditional Jockeys' Handicap Chase Class E (0-125 5-y-o and up) £3,160 2m 5f....... (1:20)

1812* BEATSON (Ire) [101] 7-10-9 (6ex) G Hogan, *trkd ldr till lft in ld 4th, hdd 6th, led aftr nxt, pushed alng after 2 out, cmftbly.*
...................................(5 to 4 fav op 5 to 10 tchd 11 to 8) 1
1589* BUYERS DREAM (Ire) [92] (v) 6-10-0 G Cahill, *chsd wnr frm tenth, hit 3 out, no imprsn appr last.*
...................................(9 to 2 op 6 to 1 tchd 4 to 1) 2
LINDEN'S LOTTO (Ire) [120] 7-12-0 Guy Lewis, *al in rear, jmpd slwly 11th, tld off 13th*............(9 to 2 op 7 to 1) 3
YEOMAN WARRIOR [102] 9-10-10 L Aspell, *led till slpd and uns rdr 4th*............................(9 to 2 op 7 to 2 tchd 5 to 1) ur
HALHAM TARN (Ire) [92] 6-9-9 (5*) A Dowling, *hdwy to chase ldr 5th, led 6th to nxt, sn hdd, wknd 11th, tld off whn blun and uns rdr 4 out*.....................(20 to 1 op 14 to 1) ur
Dist: 7l, dist. 5m 25.70s. a 21.70s (5 Ran).
(Mrs E B Gardiner), R H Buckler

1864 Marlborough Tiles Handicap Hurdle Class C (0-135 4-y-o and up) £3,468 2m 1f....................... (1:55)

16122 CHAI-YO [119] 6-11-3 G Upton, *hld up and took keen hold, smooth hdwy to track ldr aftr 2 out, str chal and gng wl whn lft clr last.*
...................................(5 to 1 fav op Evens tchd 5 to 4 on and 11 to 8) 1

1057 KIPPANOUR (USA) [115] 4-11-6 R Dunwoody, *wth ldr 5th to 3 out, outpcd frm nxt*......(9 to 1 op 8 to 1 tchd 10 to 1) 2
15087 SOVEREIGNS PARADE [113] (bl) 4-11-4 M A Fitzgerald, *rcd in 3rd, rdn 3 out, found nothing and sn btn.*
...................................(11 to 2 op 5 to 1 tchd 6 to 1) 3
15283 FORESTAL [108] 4-10-13 Mr J Jukes, *led, pushed alng frm 2 out, slight ld but rdn whn f last, rmntd.*
...................................(2 to 1 op 9 to 4 tchd 13 to 8) 4
Dist: 12l, 21l, dist. 4m 8.70s. a 14.70s (4 Ran).
SR: 17/1/-/-/ (Nick Viney), J A B Old

1865 Wragge & Co Challenge Handicap Chase Class B (5-y-o and up) £10,918 3m 1f 110yds........ (2:30)

17744 YORKSHIRE GALE [137] 10-11-10 N Williamson, *jmpd wl, made all, drvn alng frm 3 out, ran on well.*
...................................(11 to 10 op Evens tchd 6 to 5) 1
15293 GLEMOT (Ire) [135] 8-11-8 R Dunwoody, *nvr far off wnr, blun 8th, hit nxt, rdn aftr 3 out, no imprsn whn hit last.*
...................................(5 to 4 on op 11 to 8 on) 2
Won by 10l. 6m 41.70s. a 26.70s (2 Ran).
SR: -/-/ (Bill Naylor), J T Gifford

1866 Cheltenham Sponsorship Club Novices' Hurdle Class C (4-y-o and up) £3,810 2m 1f................... (3:05)

15736 DARAYDAN (Ire) 4-11-7 R Hughes, *led 3rd, drvn clr aftr 2 out, ran on wl*...............(6 to 4 fav tchd 7 to 4) 1
14967 MR DARCY 4-11-3 R Bellamy, *beh 4th, gd hdwy to track ldrs 3 out, styd on to chase wnr last, no imprsn und pres.*
...................................(40 to 1 op 25 to 1 tchd 50 to 1) 2
15322 BEACON FLIGHT (Ire) 5-11-7 C Llewellyn, *made most to 3rd, rdn and outpcd appr 2 out, styd on ag'n r-in.*
...................................(12 to 1 op 14 to 1 tchd 20 to 1) 3
15152 CARLITO BRIGANTE 4-11-3 M A Fitzgerald, *prmnt, chsd wnr 4th to last, wknd quickly*...............(5 to 2 op 9 to 4) 4
SHADIRWAN (Ire) 5-11-3 A Maguire, *chsd ldrs, rdn 3 out, wknd approaching last*.................(7 to 2 op 3 to 1) 5
14492 DOCKLANDS COURIER 4-11-3 N Williamson, *lost tch frm 5th, tld off*...................(16 to 1 op 12 to 1 tchd 33 to 1) 6
16427 SUN OF SPRING 6-11-3 T J Murphy, *lost tch frm 6th.*
...................................(33 to 1 op 25 to 1 tchd 40 to 1) 7
APOLLONO 4-11-3 R Johnson, *f 1st.*
...................................(20 to 1 op 16 to 1 tchd 25 to 1) f
AMAZON HEIGHTS 4-10-9 (3*) G Hogan, *sn beh, tld off whn pld up bef 2 out*..............(100 to 1 op 50 to 1) pu
Dist: 14l, 2½l, ¾l, 5l, dist, sht-hd. 4m 7.30s. a 13.30s (9 Ran).
SR: 28/10/11/6/1/-/ (D A Johnson), M C Pipe

1867 Gold Card Handicap Hurdle Qualifier Class B (4-y-o and up) £5,138 3m 110yds.................... (3:40)

1400* ELBURG (Ire) [111] 6-10-6 M A Fitzgerald, *in tch, quickened to chal 2 out, sn led, drvn out.* (7 to 2 op 4 to 1 tchd 5 to 1) 1
16882 RUNAWAY PETE (USA) [121] 6-11-2 R Dunwoody, *chsd ldrs till outpcd appr 2 out, styd on ag'n to chase wnr r-in, kpt on.*
...................................(12 to 1 op 8 to 1) 2
1520* OLYMPIAN [121] (bl) 9-11-2 N Williamson, *prmnt, chlgd 7th, ev ch 2 out, one pace r-in.* (8 to 1 op 5 to 1 tchd 9 to 1) 3
1576 GLENGARRIF GIRL (Ire) [106] (v) 6-10-1 R Hughes, *chsd ldrs, rdn appr 2 out, wknd aftr two out.*
...................................(8 to 1 op 6 to 1 tchd 9 to 1) 4
14003 ULURU (Ire) [116] 8-10-11 J R Kavanagh, *prmnt, chlgd frm 8th till rdn 3 out, sn hdd, wknd appr last.*
...................................(16 to 1 op 14 to 1 tchd 20 to 1) 5
1419* MISTER BLAKE [105] 6-10-0 R Johnson, *gd hdwy to chase ldrs 9th, ch 2 out, sn wknd*........(33 to 1 op 16 to 1) 6
ERZADJAN (Ire) [129] 6-11-10 G Cahill, *beh, outpcd 6th, effrt whn hit 9th, nvr dngrs*. (14 to 1 op 10 to 1 tchd 16 to 1) 7
1473 SWING QUARTET (Ire) [105] 6-10-0 C Llewellyn, *made most till hdd 2 out, wknd rpdly*..........(20 to 1 op 16 to 1) 8
1644* BALANAK (USA) [124] 5-11-0 (5*) Sophie Mitchell, *hld up, plenty to do 2 out, str run appr last, 3rd and gng wl whn f last.*
...................................(9 to 1 op 11 to 2 tchd 9 to 1) f
1661* LOCHNAGRAIN (Ire) [120] 8-11-1 (4ex) P Niven, *beh till hit 4th and uns rdr.*
...................................(15 to 8 fav op 2 to 1 tchd 5 to 2 and 7 to 4) ur
Dist: 1¾l, 7l, 2l, 2½l, 1½l, 9l, 7l. 6m 0.10s. a 21.10s (10 Ran).
(Mrs Alison Gamble), T R George

DONCASTER (good to firm)
Friday December 13th
Going Correction: PLUS 0.05 sec. per fur. (races 1,2,5,7), PLUS 0.35 (3,4,6)

1868 Saucy Kit Novices' Hurdle Class E (4-y-o and up) £2,847 2½m..... (12:05)

16792 INN AT THE TOP 4-11-5 W Fry, *cl up, led appr 3 out, clr nxt, edgd rght and styd on strly.*
...................................(6 to 4 op 7 to 4 tchd 15 to 8) 1

1615³ HERBERT LODGE (Ire) 7-11-5 C O'Dwyer, hld up, improved
hfwy, pressing ldr whn blun 3 out, hit nxt, unbl to quicken.
.............(11 to 10 fav op Evens tchd 11 to 10 on) 2
1337⁸ TWEEDSWOOD (Ire) 6-10-12 R Supple, led, ran wide bend
aftr 3rd, hdd appr 3 out, sn no extr.... (10 to 1 op 9 to 1) 3
1679⁵ CYPRESS AVENUE (Ire) 4-10-12 D Parker, not fluent, cl up till
outpcd 6th, no dngr aftr............ (16 to 1 tchd 20 to 1) 4
1570 MESP (Ire) 5-10-2 (5*) Michael Brennan, hld up, struggling
whn blun 4 out, sn tld off..........................(33 to 1) 5
1673 GUTTERIDGE (Ire) 6-10-12 S McNeill, wth ldrs, drvn and lost
tch aftr 4 out, sn wl beh...........................(33 to 1) 6
1073 TOSHIBA HOUSE (Ire) 5-10-7 B Harding, reminders 4th, tld
off frm four out....................(50 to 1 op 33 to 1) 7
1594³ HENRYS PORT 6-10-12 J Railton, beh, hdwy 7th, hit nxt, ten
ls 4th and one pace whn f last........ (8 to 1 op 10 to 1) f
1738 DOUGAL 5-10-12 B Storey, tld off hfwy, pld up bef 3 out.
.............................(50 to 1 op 33 to 1) pu
Dist: 3l, 13l, 13l, 14l, 14l, 18l, dist. 4m 47.80s. a 12.80s (9 Ran).
(Mrs Sylvia Blakeley), J Norton

1869 Glasgow Paddocks Selling Hurdle Class G (3 & 4-y-o) £2,228 2m 110yds.....................(12:35)

TOULSTON LADY (Ire) 4-10-11 (5*) Mr R Thornton, hld up, not
fluent, led and jmpd slwly 2 out, mde hdd last, ran on strly
und pres to ld ag'n cl hme. (8 to 1 op 7 to 1 tchd 9 to 1) 1
1610 LAUGHING BUCCANEER 3-10-7 S McNeill, hld up, hdwy 3
out, slight ld last, kpt on, hdd cl hme............ (4 to 1 co-
fav tchd 5 to 1) 2
1604 OAKBURY (Ire) 4-11-7 M Richards, hld up, niggled alng hfwy,
styd on frm 3 out, nrst finish.............. (8 to 1 op 7 to 1) 3
893⁷ SONG FOR JESS (Ire) 3-10-2 S Wynne, beh, hdwy to chase
ldrs 2 out, kpt on stdly.............(4 to 1 co-fav op 5 to 1) 4
BOLD TOP (v) 4-11-7 A Dobbin, sn led, not fluent 4th, rdn and
hdd 2 out, one pace.................(7 to 1 tchd 8 to 1) 5
1438 ARCH ANGEL (Ire) 3-10-2 D Bridgwater, settled rear, not
fluent 4 out, hdwy to chase ldrs whn blun last, no extr.
.............(16 to 1 op 14 to 1 tchd 20 to 1) 6
1397⁹ MUDLARK 4-11-0 (7*) B Grattan, hld up, hit second, pushed
alng 3 out, no imprsn frm nxt.. (4 to 1 co-fav tchd 9 to 2) 7
1438⁷ SHANOORA (Ire) 3-9-13 (3*) E Husband, in tch, drvn and no
imprsn 2 out, fdd appr last................ (9 to 1 tchd 7 to 1) 8
BEGGER'S OPERA 4-11-7 T Kent, chsd ldrs, wknd quickly
quickly aftr 3 out, pld up bef nxt..........(25 to 1 op 20 to 1) pu
1524 BALLYKISSANGEL (bl) 3-10-7 J Callaghan, wth ldr, wknd
quickly aftr 3 out, beh whn pld up betw last 2......(25 to 1) pu
DISPOL CONQUEROR (Ire) 3-10-7 B Storey, chsd ldrs, lost
tch appr 3 out, beh whn pld up last............ (12 to 1) pu
Dist: Nk, nk, 1¹⁄₄l, 3l, ³⁄₄l, ¹⁄₂l, 5l. 4m 6.20s. a 16.20s (11 Ran).
(W Wharton), J Wharton

1870 Red Rum Novices' Chase Class D (5-y-o and up) £3,756 3m.......(1:10)

1482* BERUDE NOT TO (Ire) 7-11-6 J Osborne, made most to 7th,
chlgd 4 out, led nxt, pushed alng and drw clr betw last 2.
.............(6 to 1 op 5 to 1 on tchd 9 to 2 on) 1
1670⁶ KEY TO MOYADE (Ire) 6-11-0 I Lawrence, led 7th, clr tenth,
reminders and hdd 3 out, btn whn mstk last.
.........................(8 to 1 op 5 to 1) 2
1765⁷ SNOWDON LILY 5-10-6 (3*) E Husband, mstk second, hld up,
lost tch 6 out, tld off whn blun 4 out... (50 to 1 op 25 to 1) 3
1180³ ELITE GOVERNOR (Ire) 7-11-0 D Bridgwater, hit 3rd, beh whn
pld up bef 7th..........................(10 to 1 op 7 to 1) pu
Dist: 4l, dist. 6m 9.30s. a 15.30s (4 Ran).
SR: 23/13/-/-/ (G Addiscott), O Sherwood

1871 Vulrory's Clown Chase Limited Handicap Class B (0-145 5-y-o and up) £4,526 2m 3f 110yds......(1:45)

1773² CUMBRIAN CHALLENGE (Ire) [126] 7-11-7 R Garritty, hld up,
improved to chal 2 out, led sn aftr last, drvn out.
.............(5 to 4 fav tchd 6 to 4) 1
1507² CALLISOE BAY (Ire) [138] 7-11-5 J Osborne, led 6th, strly
pressed whn not fluent 2 out, hdd sn aftr last, kpt on.
.....................(11 to 5 op Evens) 2
CRYSTAL SPIRIT [140] 9-11-7 G Bradley, led to 6th, not fluent
9th, unbl to quicken aftr, kpt on frm flt.
.............(9 to 2 op 7 to 2 tchd 5 to 1) 3
Dist: ¹⁄₂l, 2¹⁄₂l. 4m 55.80s. a 10.80s (3 Ran).
SR: 38/49/48/ (Cumbrian Industrials Ltd), T D Easterby

1872 Doorknocker Conditional Jockeys' Novices' Handicap Hurdle Class F (0-100 4-y-o and up) £2,102 2m 110yds......................(2:20)

1598³ OUT ON A PROMISE (Ire) [92] 4-11-8 (5*) D Finnegan, mstk
1st, hld up, gd hdwy hfwy, led and hit 2 out, clr whn not fluent
last, readily..........................(7 to 2 tchd 4 to 1) 1
1695³ FAITHFUL HAND [88] 6-11-6 (3*) R Wilkinson, keen hold, led
till hdd 2 out, sn one pace. (5 to 1 op 4 to 1 tchd 11 to 2) 2
1186 PAST MASTER (USA) [86] 8-11-7 K Gaule, midfield, niggled
alng frm hfwy, nvr able to chal.......(12 to 1 op 10 to 1) 3

1259³ TIOTAO (Ire) [70] 6-10-5 D Parker, chsd ldr, not fluent 3rd and
4th, lost pl appr 3 out, no dngr aftr.......(7 to 1 op 5 to 1) 4
1167³ TEEJAY'N'AITCH (Ire) [82] 4-11-3 G Lee, hld up, pushed alng
appr 3 out, no imprsn...................(5 to 1 op 4 to 1) 5
1477* CANARY FALCON [93] 5-11-9 (5*) N Willmington, settled
rear, drvn and no imprsn 3 out, btn whn blun last.
.........................(13 to 8 fav op 2 to 1) 6
1693 RAGAZZO (Ire) [70] (v) 6-10-5⁵ P Midgley, in tch, drpd rear
and reminders 4 out, sn tld off...................(20 to 1) 7
Dist: 9l, 7l, 4l, 10l, 8l, 23l. 3m 58.50s. a 8.50s (7 Ran).
SR: 22/9/-/-/ (Paul Green), N J H Walker

1873 Doncaster Racecourse Sponsorship Club Handicap Chase Class C (0-130 5-y-o and up) £4,531 2m 110yds...........................(2:55)

1720* ZEREDAR (NZ) [114] 6-11-2 (6ex) C O'Dwyer, led, jmpd
slwly 6th and 4 out, shaken up last, readily.
.............(8 to 3 fav op 6 to 4 tchd 7 to 4) 1
1525⁴ NEWHALL PRINCE [110] (v) 8-10-12 T Eley, in tch, not fluent
and reminder 7th, chsd wnr 3 out, no imprsn.
.........................(9 to 1 op 7 to 1) 2
1223* EASTERN MAGIC [98] 8-10-0 R Farrant, chsd ldr, outpcd
appr 3 out, sn btn......... (15 to 8 op 7 to 4 tchd 2 to 1) 3
Dist: 2l, 10l. 4m 6.80s. a 12.80s (3 Ran).
SR: 18/12/-/ (I M S Racing), K C Bailey

1874 Doncaster Mares' Only Standard Open National Hunt Flat Class H (4,5,6-y-o) £1,070 2m 110yds (3:30)

1227³ HURST FLYER 4-11-4 A Dobbin, al hndy, drvn to ld wl o'r one
furlong out, hld on gmely.................(7 to 1 op 5 to 1) 1
DERRING FLOSS 6-10-11 (7*) Miss J Wormall, beh, steady
hdwy 4 fs out, ev ch ins last, styd on strly.........(33 to 1) 2
1350³ RACHEL LOUISE 4-11-4 D Bridgwater, beh, hdwy 5 fs out,
styd on frm 2 out, nvr nrr... (9 to 2 op 5 to 2 tchd 5 to 1) 3
TULLOW LADY (Ire) 5-10-11 (7*) W Walsh, pld hrd, cl up, ev
ch 3 fs out, no extr entering last.......(12 to 1 op 10 to 1) 4
ARDROM 4-11-4 Mr P Scott, nvr far away, ev ch 3 fs out, unbl
to quicken o'r one out....................(7 to 1 op 5 to 1) 5
1227² COUNTRY ORCHID 5-10-11 (7*) C McCormack, chsd ldrs,
chlgd o'r 3 fs out, drvn and no extr frm 2 out.
.............(7 to 4 on op 5 to 4 tchd 6 to 4) 6
1682 SANTA BARBARA (Ire) 5-11-4 G Bradley, set slow pace,
quickened 4 fs out, hdd and no extr o'r one out, fdd.
.............(8 to 1 op 7 to 1 tchd 9 to 1) 7
PRIMITIVE LIGHT 6-11-1 (3*) P Midgley, hld up, improved to
chal o'r 3 fs out, hdd appr last.......(20 to 1 op 16 to 1) 8
1578⁵ FINE SPIRIT 4-11-1 (3*) T Dascombe, midfield, niggled alng 3
fs out, sn no dngr.......................(10 to 1 op 8 to 1) 9
CHIAPPELLI (Ire) 4-11-4 R Garritty, hld up, drpd rear entering
strt, sn no dngr........................(8 to 1 op 5 to 1) 10
RESTANDBEJOYFUL 4-11-4 R Farrant, hld up, struggling 3 fs
out, sn wl beh........................(33 to 1 op 25 to 1) 11
Dist: Nk, 5l, hd, nk, 1l, ¹⁄₂l, 6l, 7l, 4l, 5l. 4m 7.60s. (11 Ran).
(J Proudfoot), F P Murtagh

CHELTENHAM (good to firm)
Saturday December 14th
Going Correction: PLUS 0.45 sec. per fur.

1875 George Stevens Handicap Chase Class B (5-y-o and up) £6,714 2m 110yds....................(1:00)

1507³ DANCING PADDY [147] 8-11-10 A Dobbin, hld up in last pl,
hit 8th, wnt second nxt, led 4 out, sn clr, rdn out.
.............(15 to 8 op 6 to 4 tchd 2 to 1) 1
1394 KIBREET [146] 9-11-9 N Williamson, chsd ldr, lft in ld 9th, hdd
4 out, sn outpcd, hrd rdn and rallied appr last, one pace.
.............(11 to 10 on op Evens tchd 11 to 10) 2
1640⁴ SOUND REVEILLE [142] 8-11-5 G Bradley, led till blun and
hdd 9th, not reco'r...........(9 to 2 op 3 to 1 tchd 5 to 1) 3
Dist: 3¹⁄₂l, 25l. 4m 6.90s. a 13.90s (3 Ran).
SR: 31/26/-/ (Bychance Racing), K O Cunningham-Brown

1876 Bristol Novices' Hurdle Class A Grade 2 (4-y-o and up) £9,960 3m 110yds.......................(1:35)

1566² TARRS BRIDGE (Ire) (bl) 5-11-4 J Magee, hld up in cl tch gng
wl, chsd ldr 8th, led on bit last, not extended.
.............(10 to 1 op 7 to 1) 1
1763* SOUTHERN NIGHTS 4-11-4 A Thornton, hld up, hdwy aftr 3
out, led aftr nxt, pckd and hdd last, no ch wth wnr.
.............(5 to 1 op 9 to 2) 2
1505* CAROLE'S CRUSADER 5-10-13 R Dunwoody, led, mstk and
hdd 7th, led aftr 3 out, one pace.......(6 to 4 fav op 2 to 1) 3
1615⁶ I'M A CHIPPY (Ire) 6-11-0 B Fenton, hld up, rdn alng 7th, styd
on appr last.........................(33 to 1 op 20 to 1) 4
1566* SPACEAGE GOLD 7-11-4 G Upton, trkd ldrs, mstk 5th, drpd
last and reminders aftr nxt, no imprsn frm 3 out.
.............(12 to 1 op 10 to 1 tchd 14 to 1) 5

243

1663* GALATASORI JANE (Ire) 6-10-9 M A Fitzgerald, *trkd ldrs, led aftr 3 out till after nxt, wknd.*
...................................(16 to 1 op 11 to 1 tchd 20 to 1) 6
1735⁴ KNIGHT'S CREST (Ire) 6-11-0 N Williamson, *hld up, cld 7th, wknd 9th.*...........................(50 to 1 op 66 to 1) 7
1419² QUEEN'S AWARD (Ire) 7-11-0 M Griffiths, *hld up, cld 7th, wknd 3 out.*..........................(25 to 1 op 16 to 1) 8
1479* NOT FOR TURNING (Ire) 5-11-0 J Osborne, *cl up, wknd quickly aftr 3 out, pld up bef last.*
.................................(4 to 1 op 5 to 1 tchd 9 to 2) pu
Dist: 6l, 4l, 1½l, 12l, 1½l, nk, 9l. 5m 58.70s. a 19.70s (9 Ran).
SR: 3/-/-/-/-/-/ (The Tuesday Syndicate), C J Mann

1877 Bonusprint Bula Hurdle Class A Grade 2 (4-y-o and up) £22,085 2m 1f..........................(2:05)

1653* LARGE ACTION (Ire) 8-11-8 J Osborne, *cl up, outpcd and shaken up aftr 3 out, sn back on bit and led after nxt, edgd rght r-in, drvn out.*........(5 to 4 fav op Evens tchd 11 to 8) 1
BIMSEY (Ire) 6-11-0 G Bradley, *cl up, ev ch appr last, kpt on wl und pres.*...........................(3 to 1 op 7 to 2) 2
1653³ THEATREWORLD (Ire) 4-11-2 C F Swan, *trkd ldg trio, pushed alng aftr 3 out, sn rallied, outpcd appr last.*
..................................(11 to 2 op 6 to 1 tchd 13 to 2) 3
1506* MUSE 9-11-8 P Holley, *led, pushed alng aftr 6th, hdd after 2 out, outpcd.*..................(14 to 1 op 7 to 1 tchd 16 to 1) 4
PRIDWELL 6-11-4 C Maude, *reluctant to race, wl beh, some late prog, nvr on terms.*....................(7 to 2 op 3 to 1) 5
RIGHT WIN (Ire) 6-11-4 N Williamson, *hld up, effrt aftr 3 out, eased whn btn appr last.*............(16 to 1 op 10 to 1) 6
MOORISH 6-11-0 M A Fitzgerald, *strted slwly, beh, lost tch aftr 3 out.*......................(50 to 1 op 20 to 1) 7
Dist: ½l, 14l, 3½l, 4l, 9l. dist. 4m 5.70s. a 11.70s (7 Ran).
SR: 56/47/35/37/29/20/-/ (B T Stewart-Brown), O Sherwood

1878 Tripleprint Gold Cup Handicap Chase Class A Grade 3 (5-y-o and up) £37,690 2m 5f................(2:40)

1394³ ADDINGTON BOY (Ire) [152] 8-11-10 A Dobbin, *hit 1st, trkd ldrs, rdn to ld appr 2 out, drvn out.*............(7 to 4 fav) 1
1613 GO UNIVERSAL (Ire) [134] 8-10-6 G Bradley, *led to second, al cl up, ev ch appr 2 out, one pace.*
.................................(12 to 1 op 10 to 1 tchd 14 to 1) 2
NORTHERN HIDE (Ire) [129] 10-10-1 P Holley, *led second till appr 2 out, kpt on one pace.*...........(33 to 1 op 20 to 1) 3
1518⁴ BERTONE (Ire) [133] 7-10-5 J Osborne, *hld up, hdwy appr 4 out, one pace approaching 2 out, no imprsn whn not fluent last.*.........................(10 to 1 op 12 to 1) 4
1753* ROYAL MOUNTBROWNE [151] 8-11-9 (6ex) C F Swan, *trkd ldrs, lost pl and rdn alng 11th, rallied aftr 3 out, styd on.*
....(9 to 1 op 7 to 1) 5
1394⁴ ANABATIC (Ire) [145] 8-11-3 T P Rudd, *hld up, hdwy 12th, ev ch whn pckd 3 out, sn btn, tld off.*.......(7 to 1 op 5 to 1) 6
ALL FOR LUCK [133] 11-10-5 C Maude, *al beh, tld off 8th.*
.................................(16 to 1 op 12 to 1 tchd 20 to 1) 7
1639⁷ OLD BRIDGE (Ire) [132] 8-10-4 S McNeill, *hld up beh, effrt 4 out, sn btn, tld off.*......(13 to 2 op 11 to 2 tchd 7 to 1) 8
1551³ BELVEDERIAN [139] 9-10-11 N Williamson, *hld up, blun and uns rdr 4th.*......................(9 to 1 op 7 to 1) ur
1394⁶ BIG MATT (Ire) [144] 8-11-2 M A Fitzgerald, *hld up beh, struggling 9th, sn btn, tld of whn pld up bef 2 out.*
.................................(15 to 2 op 6 to 1 tchd 8 to 1) pu
Dist: 6l, 1¼l, ¾l, 3l, 22l, 15l, 2½l. 5m 16.30s. a 12.30s (10 Ran).
SR: 68/44/37/40/55/27/ (Gott Foods Limited), G Richards

1879 Doubleprint Novices' Chase Class C (5-y-o and up) £6,648 2m 5f...(3:15)

1833 IMPERIAL VINTAGE (Ire) 6-11-10 N Williamson, *mstk 1st, keen hold, trkd ldr, led 9th, clr 12th, mistake last, rdn out.*
.................................(11 to 8 on tchd 5 to 4 on) 1
1605* GENERAL PONGO 7-11-6 M A Fitzgerald, *led to 9th, hit 12th and lost grnd, rallied appr last, no imprsn r-in.*
..................................(6 to 5 op Evens tchd 5 to 4) 2
Won by 4l. 5m 32.00s. a 28.00s (2 Ran).
SR: -/-/ (David M Williams), Miss Venetia Williams

1880 Lonesome Glory Hurdle Class B for the Sport of Kings Challenge (4-y-o and up) £10,162 2½m........(3:45)

1644² KARSHI 6-10-12 J Osborne, *led, hdd r-in, rallied und pres to ld ag'n fnl 50 yards, ran on wl.*
..............(1 to 8 fav op 5 to 4 tchd 11 to 10 on 6 to 4) 1
1564* MANDYS MANTINO 6-11-7 P Hide, *trkd wnr, chlgd 2 out, led briefly r-in, sn no extr.*.............(7 to 2 op 5 to 2) 2
1564² SERENITY PRAYER (USA) 6-11-7 Chip Miller, *trkd ldg pair, wknd quickly aftr 3 out.*........(3 to 1 tchd 4 to 1) 3
ASHWELL BOY (Ire) 5-10-12 R Dunwoody, *hld up in last pl, in tch whn stumbled 2 out, sn btn.*.......(9 to 2 op 7 to 1) 4
Dist: 4l, 14l, 5l. 4m 55.30s. a 15.30s (4 Ran).
SR: 21/26/12/-/ (Lord Vestey), Miss H C Knight

DONCASTER (good to firm)

1881 Forgive'n Forget Maiden Chase Class D (4-y-o and up) £3,626 2m 3f 110yds.....................(12:15)

1636 ART PRINCE (Ire) 6-11-1 (7*) M Berry, *made all, drw wl clr frm 9th, mstk 3 out, easily.*.......(11 to 8 fav op 11 to 10) 1
1600⁴ CALLEVA STAR (Ire) 5-11-5 (3*) P Henley, *in tch, drvn alng aftr 8th, chsd wnr frm 3 out, no imprsn.*.......(9 to 2 op 7 to 2) 2
1670⁷ DOMAINE DE PRON (Fr) 5-11-8 M Sharratt, *mstks, chsd ldrs, drvn alng aftr 8th, no imprsn whn blun 4 out.*
....................................(33 to 1 op 25 to 1) 3
993 GLAMANGLITZ 6-11-8 T Eley, *in tch, effrt aftr 9th, sn chasing wnr, wknd after 4 out.*..........(8 to 1 op 12 to 1) 4
1718 DUKES MEADOW (Ire) 6-11-8 J A McCarthy, *lost tch frm 8th.*.............................(6 to 1 op 5 to 1) 5
941² ROYAL HAND 6-11-8 Mr R Armson, *sn beh, tld off whn l 3 out.*
....................................(16 to 1 op 14 to 1) f
1732 HIGH HANDED 5-11-8 Gary Lyons, *jmpd rght, blun 3rd, sn beh, tailing off whn blunded and uns rdr tenth.*
....................................(16 to 1 op 14 to 1) ur
1568 OLD REDWOOD 9-11-8 L O'Hara, *chsd ldrs till wknd aftr 8th, tld off whn pld up bef 4 out.*.......(33 to 1 op 25 to 1) pu
1647³ REEFA'S MILL (Ire) 4-10-7 (3*) T Dascombe, *chsd wnr till wknd aftr 9th, tld off whn pld up bef 2 out.*............(10 to 1) pu
Dist: Dist, 4l, 1½l, 21l. 4m 51.50s. a 6.50s (9 Ran).
SR: 29/-/-/-/-/-/ (Terry Neill), C P E Brooks

1882 Racecourse Medical Officers Association Novices' Hurdle Class E (4-y-o and up) £2,679 2m 110yds
..............................(12:45)

SEA VICTOR 4-10-9 (3*) R Massey, *hld up, hdwy aftr 5th, led appr last, hdd on wl und pres cl hme.*....(9 to 1 op 7 to 1) 1
1642* IONIO (USA) 5-11-5 B Storey, *hld up, smooth hdwy to ld bef 3 out, hdd appr last, styd on wl und pres.*
.................................(4 to 1 op 7 to 2 tchd 3 to 1) 2
TALATHATH (Fr) 4-10-7 (5*) Mr R Thornton, *towards rear, hdwy aftr 5th, styd on wl und pres frm 2 out.*
....(7 to 1 op 4 to 1) 3
1371* ENDOWMENT 4-11-5 P Niven, *led, hdd whn mstk 3 out, sn wknd.*...................(9 to 2 op 7 to 2 tchd 3 to 1) 4
1224* ADVANCE EAST 4-11-5 R Supple, *hld up, some hdwy aftr 5th, no prog frm 3 out.*.............(11 to 4 tchd 9 to 2) 5
TEN PAST SIX 4-10-12 L O'Hara, *chsd ldrs, drvn alng whn blun 3 out, sn wknd.*...............(16 to 1 op 10 to 1) 6
RISING MAN 5-10-12 K Gaule, *in tch till wknd aftr 5th.*
...................................(20 to 1 op 16 to 1) 7
1677⁷ KILDRUMMY CASTLE 4-10-9 (3*) F Leahy, *in tch till wknd aftr 5th.*..........................(10 to 1 op 8 to 1) 8
1623⁵ ROTHARI 4-10-12 J A McCarthy, *chsd ldr till wknd quickly bef 3 out.*..................(20 to 1 op 16 to 1) 9
FATHER GERARD 5-10-9 (3*) G Lee, *beh, lost tch frm hfwy, sn tld off.*............................(50 to 1) 10
1063 GOATSFUT (Ire) 6-10-9 (3*) G Hogan, *reluctant to race, refused 1st.*..........................(33 to 1) ref
TOSHIBA TALK (Ire) 4-10-12 G Cahill, *sn towards rear, wl beh whn pld up bef 3 out.*............(14 to 1 tchd 16 to 1) pu
Dist: Hd, 4l, 24l, 3½l, 21l, 9l, 21l, 5l, dist. 3m 54.20s. a 4.20s (12 Ran).
SR: 18/25/14/-/-/-/ (J David Abell), J L Harris

1883 Doncaster Racecourse Sponsorship Club Handicap Hurdle Class C (0-130 4-y-o and up) £3,626 2½m
..............................(1:20)

1561* BLAZE AWAY (USA) [125] 5-11-2 (7*) Mr A Balding, *hld up, smooth hdwy bef 3 out, led on bit nxt, sn wl clr, very easily.*
.................................(7 to 4 on op 5 to 4 on) 1
1441⁶ MONICASMAN (Ire) [113] 6-10-11 P Niven, *chsd ldr, drvn alng and outpcd bef 3 out, no dngr aftr.*..(7 to 1 op 5 to 1) 2
1772⁷ DAWN MISSION [105] 4-10-0 (3*) F Leahy, *led, mstk 1st, clr aftr 6th, mistake and hdd 2 out, wknd quickly.*
......................................(11 to 9 op 6 to 1) 3
1644⁷ CASTLE COURAGEOUS [130] 9-12-0 E Murphy, *hld up, drvn alng aftr 7th, lost tch bef 3 out.*........(4 to 1 op 7 to 2) 4
Dist: 17l, 3½l, 5l. 4m 49.90s. a 14.90s (4 Ran).
(Paul Mellon), I A Balding

1884 The Dikler Handicap Chase Class B (5-y-o and up) £6,909 3¼m... (1:50)

1511 MUSTHAVEASWIG [133] 10-9-9 (5*) Mr R Thornton, *cl up, led 9th, rdn aftr 3 out, styd on wl.*........(4 to 1 op 3 to 1) 1
1323² FATHER SKY [134] 5-10-0 J A McCarthy, *in tch, chsd wnr frm 15th, cls 2 out, kpt on und pres, no imprsn.*(9 to 1 op 7 to 1) 2
1529⁴ SCOTTON BANKS [157] 7-11-10 R Garritty, *led, hdd 9th, remider aftr nxt, rdn whn mstk 15th, sn wknd and lost tch, tld off.*...............(4 to 1 on tchd 5 to 2 on) 3
1660⁴ PIMS GUNNER (Ire) [135] 8-9-13² (3*) Mr C Bonner, *in tch whn blun and uns rdr 7th.*...............(14 to 1 op 10 to 1) ur
Dist: 1¼l, dist. 6m 27.70s. a 6.70s (4 Ran).

244

SR: 5/3/-/-/

(P R D Fasteners Ltd), D Nicholson

1885 Sea Pigeon Handicap Hurdle Class B (4-y-o and up) £4,831 2m 110yds
.... (2:25)

1740[6] NEW INN [113] 5-10-8 K Gaule, *set steady pace, quickened aftr 3 out, hrd pressed frm nxt, styd on wl, all out.*
................................(9 to 1 op 7 to 1 tchd 10 to 1) 1
1635[7] DESERT FIGHTER [110] 5-10-5 P Niven, *trkd ldr, drvn alng aftr 3 out, styd on wl und pres frm last. . .*(9 to 1 op 8 to 1) 2
1772[4] ELPIDOS [Ire] 4-11-0 R Garritty, *in tch, hdwy to chal 2 out, ev ch till no extr aftr last. . . . . .*(2 to 1 op 3 to 1 tchd 7 to 2) 3
1528* TOM BRODIE [127] 6-11-8 R Supple, *hld up, mstk 3 out, rdn betw last 2, no real hdwy. . . . .*(5 to 4 fav tchd 7 to 4) 4
1772[8] THORNTON GATE [125] 7-11-6 J Callaghan, *hld up in rear, hdwy on bit bef 3 out, ev ch nxt, sn rdn and wknd.*
................................(9 to 1 op 8 to 1 tchd 10 to 1) 5
1772[6] NON VINTAGE [Ire] [129] 5-11-10 W Worthington, *in tch, drvn alng aftr 3 out, wknd after nxt.*..........(10 to 1 op 7 to 1) 6
Dist: Nk, 3l, 2½l, nk, 2½l. 4m 2.40s. a 12.40s (6 Ran).

(Ian K I Stewart), S Gollings

1886 Burrough Hill Lad Novices' Chase Class D (4-y-o and up) £3,770 2m 110yds
.... (3:00)

1741[3] GOLDEN HELLO 5-11-7 R Garritty, *jmpd rght, trkd ldr, lft in ld 4 out, drw clr frm betw last 2. . . . .*(9 to 2 op 7 to 1) 1
1647* FLIGHT LIEUTENANT [Ire] 7-11-7 J A McCarthy, *in tch, ch aftr 4 out till wknd betw last 2. . . . .*(9 to 2 op 4 to 1) 2
1704 WEEHEBY [USA] 7-10-13 (3*) G Hogan, *mstk 3rd, sn lost tch, tld off. . . . .*(25 to 1 op 20 to 1) 3
1393[4] COUNTRY STAR [Ire] 5-11-2 D Gallagher, *led, 2 ls ahead whn blun and uns rdr 4 out.*
................................(11 to 8 on op Evens tchd 11 to 10) ur
Dist: 12l, dist. 4m 5.20s. a 11.20s (4 Ran).

(G E Shouler), T D Easterby

1887 Weatherbys 'Stars Of Tomorrow' National Hunt Flat Intermediate Class H (4,5,6-y-o) £1,259 2m 110yds
.... (3:30)

KING OF CAMELOT [Ire] 6-11-1 (3*) R Massey, *towards rear, hdwy 4 fs out, led o'r one out, styd on und pres. . .*(3 to 1 jt-fav op 5 to 2 tchd 100 to 30) 1
SHEBANG [Ire] 4-11-0[3] (7*) Mr H Dunlop, *beh, pushed alng 5 fs out, styd on wl fnl 2 furlongs, nvr able to chal. . .*(3 to 1 jt-fav op 6 to 4) 2
BOLD ACTION [Ire] 5-10-11 (7*) B Grattan, *cl up, led 7 fs out, hdd wl o'r 2 out, kpt on same pace. . . . . .*(6 to 1 op 4 to 1) 3
THE SHARROW LEGEND [Ire] 4-10-13 (5*) S Taylor, *in tch, hdwy to ld wl o'r 2 fs out, hdd over one out, no extr.*
................................(16 to 1 op 12 to 1) 4
1682[6] REVOLT 4-11-1 (3*) G Lee, *mid-div, rdn o'r 4 fs out, styd on fnl 2 furlongs. . . . .*(5 to 1 op 7 to 1 tchd 8 to 1) 5
BANKER COUNT 4-11-1 (3*) G Parkin, *hld up, hdwy to chal o'r 4 fs out, fdd fnl 2 furlongs. . . . .*(12 to 1 op 10 to 1) 6
PHAR SMOOTHER [Ire] 4-11-1 (3*) F Leahy, *in tch, hdwy and prmnt 6 fs out, wknd o'r 2. . . . .*(6 to 1 op 7 to 1) 7
1317 JENNIE'S PROSPECT 5-10-13 (5*) H McGrath, *in tch till wknd 5 fs out. . . . .*(16 to 1 op 25 to 1) 8
1590[7] TARTAN JOY [Ire] 5-11-4 Mr N Wilson, *led 6 fs, wknd six out.*
................................(33 to 1) 9
RASIN STANDARDS 6-11-1 (3*) G Hogan, *beh most of way, tld off. . . . .*(25 to 1) 10
CAHERLOW [Ire] 5-11-10 (7*) S Porritt, *cl up, led aftr 6 fs till hdd 7 out, sn wknd, tld off. . . . . .*(14 to 1 op 10 to 1) 11
EASTCLIFFE [Ire] 4-11-4 G Cahill, *pld hrd, trkd ldrs till crashed through wing and ran out 7 fs out.*
................................(14 to 1 op 12 to 1 tchd 16 to 1) ro
Dist: 2l, nk, 2l, 1½l, 2½l, 1l, 9l, sht-hd, 23l, 1¾l. 4m 0.60s. (12 Ran).

(Jerry Wright), D Nicholson

LINGFIELD (good to soft)
Saturday December 14th
Going Correction: PLUS 0.35 sec. per fur. (races 1,3,6,7), PLUS 0.85 (2,4,5)

1888 Tandridge District Council Handicap Hurdle Class C (0-130 4-y-o and up) £3,403 2m 110yds
..........(12:10)

1688[3] AMBLESIDE [Ire] [110] 5-10-10 A Maguire, *chsd ldr to 5th, rdn 2 out, rallied strly und pres r-in, led nr finish.*
................................(8 to 1 op 4 to 1) 1
KADASTROF [Fr] [128] 6-12-0 P Hide, *prmnt, chsd ldr 5th, rdn to chal last, sn led, hdd und pres nr finish.*(8 to 1 op 4 to 1) 2
1272* POTENTATE [USA] [124] 5-11-10 C Llewellyn, *not jump wl, led, rdn whn mstk last, sn hdd, ev ch r-in, no extr und pres.*
................................(7 to 4 on op 11 to 8 on tchd 5 to 4 on) 3
HAWTHORNE GLEN [102] 9-9-10[1] (7*) A Irvine, *jmpd rght, chsd ldrs, shaken up and not quicken 2 out, eased whn btn.*
................................(20 to 1 op 16 to 1) 4

COURT NAP [Ire] [113] 4-10-13 N Mann, *drpd last 3rd, no prog 3 out, 5th and no ch whn f nxt.*
................................(16 to 1 op 10 to 1 tchd 20 to 1) f
TARROCK [110] 6-10-10 Derek Byrne, *hld up, prog and in tch whn mstk 3 out, wknd rpdly and pld up bef nxt, lme.*
................................(9 to 2 tchd 5 to 1 and 4 to 1) pu
Dist: 1½l, sht-hd, 10l. 4m 2.20s. a 11.20s (6 Ran).
SR: 28/44/40/8/-/-/

(B M Yin), Mrs S D Williams

1889 Peak Handicap Chase Class D (0-120 5-y-o and up) £3,860 2½m 110yds
....................(12:40)

1627[2] NAIYSARI [Ire] [108] 8-11-4 T J Murphy, *al prmnt, led tenth, clr whn mstk 3 out, mistake last, pushed out.*
................................(6 to 1 op 7 to 2) 1
1666[2] FIVE TO SEVEN [USA] [112] 7-11-8 P Hide, *led till aftr second, prmnt after, ev ch 11th, rdn and styd on one pace frm 3 out.*........................(Evens fav op 7 to 4) 2
DANGER BABY [106] 6-11-1 J R Kavanagh, *chsd ldrs, blun 9th, sn struggling, lft modest 3rd 2 out .*
................................(9 to 1 op 6 to 1 tchd 10 to 1) 3
1559 DEEPENDABLE [90] (bl) 9-10-0 M Richards, *rear, prog and in tch 6th, wknd 8th, tld off 11th. . . . . .*(25 to 1 op 20 to 1) 4
1739[4] CELTIC SILVER [96] 8-10-6[3] Richard Guest, *led aftr second till tenth, sn rdn and wknd, tld off.*
................................(7 to 1 op 5 to 1 tchd 8 to 1) 5
1595[4] RED BEAN [100] 8-10-10 A Dicken, *al rear, mstk 9th, sn tld off. . . . .*(14 to 1 op 10 to 1) 6
1672 KYTTON CASTLE [99] 9-10-9 C Llewellyn, *trkd ldrs, rdn aftr 11th, 3rd and btn whn f 2 out. . . . .*(25 to 1 op 20 to 1) f
1640 BO KNOWS BEST [Ire] [118] 7-11-7 (7*) M Attwater, *cl up, mstk and lost pl 6th, rear whn blun and uns rdr nxt.*
................................(25 to 1 op 20 to 1) ur
1426 THE WIDGET MAN [105] 10-10-8 (7*) Mr R Wakley, *not jump wl, tld off frm 3rd till pld up bef 9th. . . .*(33 to 1 op 25 to 1) pu
988 BE SURPRISED [90] 10-10-0 N Mann, *prmnt to 6th, sn wknd, tld off and pld up bef 3 out. . . . .*(66 to 1 op 50 to 1) pu
1052[3] SEOD RIOGA [Ire] [114] 7-11-10 D Bridgwater, *strted slwly, hld up, effrt tenth, nvr rch ldrs, tld off and pld up bef 3 out.*
................................(13 to 2 op 7 to 1 tchd 8 to 1) pu
Dist: 3½l, 20l, 26l, 1¾l, 26l. 5m 24.80s. a 23.80s (11 Ran).
SR: 26/26/-/-/-/-/

(P M Rich), P M Rich

1890 TJH Group Summit Junior Hurdle Class A Grade 2 (3-y-o) £9,735 2m 110yds
....................(1:10)

1696* SERENUS [USA] 10-12 J R Kavanagh, *prmnt, led 5th, rdn aftr 2 out, styd on gmely r-in. . .*(5 to 2 op 2 to 1 tchd 7 to 4) 1
1027[4] CIRCUS STAR 10-12 A Maguire, *keen hold, hld up, prog aftr 3 out, hmpd nxt, swtchd rght to chal last, rdn and not quicken r-in. . . . .*(100 to 30 op 9 to 4 tchd 7 to 2) 2
SALLY'S TWINS 10-7 W McFarland, *trkd ldrs gng easily, effrt appr 2 out, rdn and one pace.*
................................(50 to 1 op 33 to 1 tchd 66 to 1) 3
1696[3] BEN BOWDEN 10-12 M Richards, *prmnt, rdn whn mstk 5th, sn btn. . . . .*(12 to 1 op 10 to 1 tchd 33 to 1) 4
1702[3] PROVINCE 10-12 J Railton, *led, mstk 3rd, hdd 5th, sn wknd.*
................................(20 to 1 op 12 to 1) 5
BIGWIG [Ire] 10-12 N Mann, *in tch to 4th, sn wknd, tld off.*
................................(66 to 1 op 50 to 1 tchd 100 to 1) 6
1517 MR WILD [USA] 10-12 D Bridgwater, *keen hold, hld up, gd prog aftr 5th, jnd wnr and f 2 out.*
................................(2 to 1 fav op 5 to 2 tchd 11 to 4) f
1188[4] KERAWI 11-2 C Llewellyn, *trkd ldrs, cl 3rd whn brght dwn 2 out. . . . .*(4 to 1 op 7 to 2 tchd 9 to 2) bd
APARTMENTS ABROAD 10-7 Derek Byrne, *keen hold, not jump wl, al beh, tld off 5th, pld up bef 2 out.*
................................(50 to 1 op 33 to 1 tchd 66 to 1) pu
Dist: 3l, 8l, 14l, 15l, dist. 4m 5.20s. a 14.20s (9 Ran).

(W V & Mrs E S Robins), N J Henderson

1891 Lowndes Lambert December Novices' Chase Class A Grade 2 (5-y-o and up) £13,280 3m
..........(1:40)

1636[2] FOODBROKER STAR [Ire] 6-11-0 L Aspell, *hld up, prog tenth, hmpd aftr 3 out, led last, drvn out.*
................................(33 to 1 op 25 to 1 tchd 40 to 1) 1
1670[4] STAY LUCKY [NZ] 7-11-0 J R Kavanagh, *led to 3rd, led 11th to 13th, rdn and lost pl 15th, rallied und pres 2 out, styd on r-in.*
................................(8 to 1 op 6 to 1 tchd 9 to 1) 2
1773* THE LAST FLING [Ire] 6-11-4 Richard Guest, *hld up, prog 8th, blun 11th, led 13th, blunded and rdr lost iron 3 out, hdd last, no extr.*........................(7 to 1 op 6 to 1 tchd 8 to 1) 3
THERMAL WARRIOR 8-11-0 L Harvey, *al beh, tld off whn pld up bef 3 out, continued.* (50 to 1 op 33 to 1 tchd 66 to 1) 4
1347* PLEASURE SHARED [Ire] 8-11-7 M Richards, *hld up, l second. . . . .*(3 to 1 fav tchd 7 to 2) f
1636* BLOCKHOUSE BOY 6-11-4 C Llewellyn, *led 4th till 9th.*
................................(5 to 1 tchd 6 to 1) f
1670* PHARANEAR [Ire] 6-11-4 A Maguire, *trkd ldrs, prog 15th, cl 4th and rng on whn f 3 out.*(13 to 2 op 5 to 1 tchd 7 to 1) f
1670[2] TREASURE AGAIN [Ire] (bl) 7-11-0 Derek Byrne, *hld up, in tch whn blun, swrvd lft, bumped and uns rdr 8th.*
................................(5 to 1 op 9 to 1 tchd 11 to 2) ur

1236* PUNTERS OVERHEAD (Ire) 8-11-0 J Railton, *led 3rd till blun 4th, lft in ld 8th, hdd 11th, mstk 14th, ev ch 3 out, sn btn, pld up aftr last*............................(10 to 1 op 7 to 1 tchd 11 to 1) pu
1608* BANKHEAD (Ire) 7-11-0 D Bridgwater, *not jump wl, well beh till prog tenth, rdn and wknd 13th, tld off and pld up bef 3 out.*
...............................(12 to 1 op 14 to 1 tchd 16 to 1) pu
1527³ AH SHUSH (Ire) 8-11-0 D Leahy, *not jump wl, al beh, blun 9th and pld up*...........................(33 to 1 op 25 to 1) pu
Dist: 1½l, 1¾l, dist. 6m 26.80s. a 32.80s (11 Ran).

(Food Brokers Ltd), J T Gifford

1892 TJH Group Chase Limited Handicap for the Lingfield Park Perpetual Trophy Class C (0-135 5-y-o and up) £4,878 3m....................(2:10)

1495 SOUNDS STRONG (Ire) 10-12-10 A Maguire, *hld up beh, mstk 3rd, prog 14th, mistake 3 out, led aftr last, ran on strly.*
.................(15 to 8 fav op 11 to 8 tchd 2 to 1) 1
FELLOW COUNTRYMAN [125] 9-11-0 C Llewellyn, *hld up, prog 15th, led 3 out till aftr last, ran on wl.*
........................(4 to 1 op 7 to 2 tchd 9 to 2) 2
750² HAVE TO THINK [130] (bl) 8-11-5 D Bridgwater, *led to 7th, rdn 15th, one pace frm 3 out.*..........(8 to 1 op 6 to 1) 3
1746 TERAO [132] 10-11-7 T J Murphy, *jmpd rght, led aftr 9th till 3 out, wknd appr last....*(16 to 1 op 14 to 1 tchd 20 to 1) 4
1223 NO PAIN NO GAIN (Ire) [123] 8-10-9 (3*) L Aspell, *mid-div, prog to track ldr 14th, wknd aftr 3 out...*(7 to 1 tchd 8 to 1) 5
1575* BELLS LIFE (Ire) [127] 7-11-2 G Tormey, *mid-div, mstk 13th, sn rdn and btn, wl beh frm 15th........*(9 to 4 tchd 5 to 2) 6
1576 LUCKY LANE [120] (bl) 12-10-9 I Lawrence, *prmnt, led 7th till hdd and rdn aftr 9th, wknd 13th......*(33 to 1 tchd 40 to 1) 7
SHEER ABILITY [128] 10-11-3 J Railton, *prmnt to 4th, last frm 8th, jmpd slwly tenth, tld off and pld up bef nxt.*
........................(25 to 1 op 20 to 1) pu
Dist: 1¼l, 18l, 1¾l, 5l, 17l, 2½l. 6m 24.30s. a 30.30s (8 Ran).

(Mrs David Thompson), D Nicholson

1893 Biffa Recycling Novices' Hurdle Class E (4-y-o and up) £2,952 2m 3f 110yds.......................(2:45)

905⁵ THE PROMS 6-10-12 C Llewellyn, *al prmnt, rdn 2 out, styd on to chal last, led r-in, drvn out.*
...............(14 to 1 op 8 to 1 tchd 16 to 1) 1
1208 MARCHING MARQUIS (Ire) 5-10-12 T J Murphy, *al prmnt, led aftr 3 out, hrd rdn nxt, hdd and unbl to quicken r-in.*
.......................(7 to 4 op 6 to 4) 2
CRANE HILL (bl) 6-10-12 G Tormey, *cl up, prog 6th, jnd ldr 2 out, ev ch last, no extr r-in...........*(8 to 1 tchd 10 to 1) 3
CUTHILL HOPE 5-10-12 Richard Guest, *mid-div, prog 6th, cl up 2 out, shaken up and one pace appr last, improve.*
........................(33 to 1 op 28 to 1) 4
1053² MYTHICAL APPROACH (Ire) 6-10-12 A Maguire, *hld up, prog aftr 4th, wth ldrs appr 2 out, sn one pace.*
.......................(5 to 2 tchd 3 to 1) 5
WRISTBURN 6-10-12 J Railton, *hld up, lost tch wth ldrs 7th, styd on stdly frm 2 out, improve.*
...............(12 to 1 op 10 to 1 tchd 14 to 1) 6
1479⁶ STRONG PALADIN (Ire) 5-10-7 (3*) L Aspell, *hld up, prog 7th, nvr rch ldrs............*(9 to 1 op 6 to 1 tchd 10 to 1) 7
1423³ JAKES JUSTICE (Ire) 5-10-5 (7*) Mr P O'Keeffe, *prmnt till fdd aftr 7th................*(14 to 1 op 8 to 1 tchd 16 to 1) 8
CHAPILLIERE (Fr) 6-10-12 M Richards, *cl up till lost pl 6th, nvr nr to chal aftr.....................*(50 to 1) 9
TIN PAN ALLEY 7-10-12 P McLoughlin, *mid-div, rdn aftr 6th, sn struggling................................*(50 to 1) 10
1641 HI MARBLE (Ire) 5-10-7 I Lawrence, *hld up, reminder aftr 6th, sn no ch...........*(20 to 1 op 12 to 1 tchd 25 to 1) 11
EAU SO SLOE 5-10-12 A Dicken, *mid-div, wknd 6th, sn beh.*
.....................................(50 to 1) 12
1697 GEMINI MIST 5-10-7 W McFarland, *al rear, tld off 3 out.*
.................(50 to 1 tchd 66 to 1) 13
NO MATTER (Ire) 5-10-12 D O'Sullivan, *mstks, hld up, al rear, tld off 3 out.........*(33 to 1 op 25 to 1 tchd 50 to 1) 14
1594⁸ NISHAMAN 5-10-12 J R Kavanagh, *led to 3rd, led 6th till aftr 3 out, wknd rpdly......*(33 to 1 op 25 to 1 tchd 50 to 1) 15
JEWEL TRADER (v) 4-10-12 D Leahy, *beh 5th, sn tld off.*
.................(66 to 1 op 50 to 1 tchd 100 to 1) 16
JOLTO 7-10-12 B Clifford, *led 3rd to 6th, sn wknd, tld off and pld up bef 2 out.*........(33 to 1 op 14 to 1) pu
1609² MARKET MAYHEM 6-10-12 D Bridgwater, *prmnt, mstk 4th, sn pld up and dismounted.*
.................(14 to 1 op 12 to 1 tchd 16 to 1) pu
Dist: 1¼l, 4l, 3l, 2l, 5l, 14l, 8l, 2½l, ½l, 4l. 4m 58.80s. a 25.80s (18 Ran).

(Mrs J Mould), N A Twiston-Davies

1894 Levy Board Handicap Hurdle Class D (0-120 4-y-o and up) £2,898 2m 3f 110yds.......................(3:20)

ROCKCLIFFE LAD [93] 7-10-5 C Llewellyn, *led till mstk and hdd 5th, mistake 7th, quickened to ld ag'n aftr 3 out, clr whn mistake last, eased nr finish.*
........................(3 to 1 op 7 to 2 tchd 9 to 2) 1

1816² STONEY VALLEY [102] 6-11-0 A Maguire, *hld up, prog to chase wnr aftr 3 out, mstk nxt, no imprsn.*
.................(7 to 2 op 3 to 1 tchd 4 to 1) 2
MORE DASH THANCASH (Ire) [92] 6-10-4 I Lawrence, *settled in 3rd, chsd ldr aftr 6th, ev ch 3 out, rdn and btn bef nxt.*
.................(9 to 4 op 11 to 4 tchd 7 to 2) 3
1699⁴ TICKERTY'S GIFT [110] (v) 6-11-1 (7*) M Attwater, *pressed ldr, led 5th till aftr 3 out, sn btn....*(2 to 1 fav op 11 to 8) 4
Dist: 10l, 4l, 6l. 5m 0.80s. a 27.80s (4 Ran).

(Simon Keswick), N A Twiston-Davies

NAVAN (IRE) (yielding to soft) Saturday December 14th

1895 Sherry Maiden Hurdle (5-y-o and up) £3,082 2¼m..............(12:35)

1751⁸ BUGGY (Ire) 7-12-0 T J Mitchell, ...(12 to 1) 1
31* NATIVE-DARRIG (Ire) 5-12-0 D J Casey, ...(9 to 4 fav) 2
1432⁶ MATTORIA (Ire) 5-11-6 (3*) Mr R Walsh, ...(10 to 1) 3
EBONY KING (Ire) 6-11-11 (3*) LJ Smyth, ...(8 to 1) 4
PAPO KHARISMA 6-11-6 F Woods, ...(10 to 1) 5
1279* PAULS RUN (Ire) 7-12-0 L P Cusack, ...(4 to 1) 6
1432⁷ TREANAREE (Ire) 7-10-13 (7*) S Kelly, ...(16 to 1) 7
1463⁷ OCTOBER SEVENTH 5-11-6 R Hughes, ...(12 to 1) 8
TEMPLEWOOD EXPRESS (Ire) 7-12-0 S H O'Donovan,
....(9 to 1) 9
BAHAO (Ire) 5-11-6 J P Broderick, ...(10 to 1) 10
MISS ORCHESTRA (Ire) 5-11-1 A Powell, ...(16 to 1) 11
1776 QUENNIE MO GHRA (Ire) 5-11-1 F J Flood, ...(14 to 1) 12
1649 FOYLE WANDERER (Ire) 5-11-1 D T Evans, ...(25 to 1) 13
1534 DEESIDE DOINGS (Ire) 8-11-1 (5*) J Butler, ...(20 to 1) 14
1432 RUM FUN (Ire) 5-11-3 (3*) G Cotter, ...(16 to 1) 15
KAVANAGHS DREAM (Ire) 7-12-0 H Rogers, ...(10 to 1) 16
1751⁵ EUROTHATCH (Ire) 8-11-6 T P Treacy, ...(20 to 1) 17
BERNESTIC WONDER (Ire) 7-11-6 J Jones, ...(20 to 1) 18
LADY ARGYLE (Ire) 5-10-8 (7*) L J Fleming, ...(20 to 1) 19
1463 ARKDEL (Ire) 7-11-1 (5*) T Martin, ...(50 to 1) 20
1019 THE ZAFFRING (Ire) 5-10-13 (7*) K A Kelly, ...(20 to 1) 21
1436 CAROLANNS CHOICE (Ire) 7-10-8 (7*) R P Hogan, (33 to 1) 22
KNOCKBOY QUAY (Ire) 6-11-6 J Shortt, ...(20 to 1) 23
1584⁶ TOMMYS BAND (Ire) 5-11-6 P Malone, ...(16 to 1) 24
THETHREETOMS (Ire) 5-11-13 (7*) Mr T Gibney, ...(33 to 1) 25
SECTION SEVEN (Ire) 6-12-0 C O'Dwyer, ...(6 to 1) pu
Dist: 3½l, 1l, 5l, 1½l. 4m 32.30s. (26 Ran).

(P Farrelly), K Farrelly

1896 Mince Pie Handicap Chase (0-123 4-y-o and up) £3,082 2½m....(1:05)

1653 NEW CO (Ire) [-] 8-11-8 C O'Dwyer, ...(3 to 1) 1
1711* HEMISPHERE (Ire) [-] 7-10-1 (3*) G Cotter, ...(11 to 4 fav) 2
1378* DANCING VISION (Ire) [-] 6-10-12 J Jones, ...(8 to 1) 3
1537 THE CRAZY BISHOP (Ire) [-] 8-11-5 (7*) A O'Shea, ..(8 to 1) 4
1538⁷ EDENAKILL LAD [-] 9-9-5 (3*) B Bowens, ...(16 to 1) 5
1274 BOB DEVANI [-] 10-11-3 Mr G J Harford, ...(14 to 1) 6
1458 DRINDOD (Ire) [-] 7-9-6 (7*) S P McCann, ...(14 to 1) 7
1537³ PERSIAN HALO (Ire) [-] 8-12-0 J Shortt, ...(6 to 1) 8
1538 IF YOU BELIEVE (Ire) [-] 7-9-13³ H Rogers, ...(14 to 1) 9
1538 TOP RUN (Ire) [-] 8-9-7 D J Casey, ...(16 to 1) 10
DEE ELL [-] 10-10-11 F Woods, ...(8 to 1) 11
1619⁴ TOPICAL TIP (Ire) [-] 7-11-5 T P Treacy, ...(8 to 1) 12
1461⁵ THE BOURDA [-] 10-10-0 J P Broderick, ...(16 to 1) 13
1712 OVER AGAIN (Ire) [-] 8-10-13 A Powell, ...(16 to 1) 14
1582⁷ JIMMYS DOUBLE [-] 10-9-8² (7*) Mr J J Canavan, (50 to 1) 15
THE REAL ARTICLE (Ire) [-] 7-11-10 T J Mitchell, ...(12 to 1) ur
Dist: 2l, 14l, 6l, 20l. 5m 18.30s. (16 Ran).

(Exors Of The Late Mrs L C Ronan), M F Morris

1897 Carol Maiden Hurdle (4-y-o) £3,082 2m........................(1:35)

1756* GRAPHIC EQUALISER (Ire) 11-9 D T Evans, ...(7 to 2) 1
1654³ SAVING BOND (Ire) 11-9 R Hughes, ...(11 to 4) 2
1307⁵ SUPREME CHANTER (Ire) 11-4 S H O'Donovan, ...(10 to 1) 3
1533 THE BOY KING (Ire) 11-4 C O'Dwyer, ...(10 to 1) 4
1535⁵ ABORIGINAL (Ire) 11-9 T P Treacy, ...(1 to 1 fav) 5
IMPERIAL PLAICE (Ire) 10-11 (7*) D M Bean, ...(25 to 1) 6
BLUE WAVE (Ire) 11-1 (3*) G Cotter, ...(20 to 1) 7
1533⁶ KATSUKO (Ire) 10-13 H Rogers, ...(12 to 1) 8
ARE YOU SAILING (Ire) 11-4 C O'Brien, ...(14 to 1) 9
WINTER MELODY (Ire) 11-4 L P Cusack, ...(16 to 1) 10
1088⁴ WESTERN GREY (Ire) 11-4 M P Hourigan, ...(16 to 1) 11
1409⁵ BRIEF CRUISE (Ire) 11-4 P L Malone, ...(33 to 1) 12
782 STORM COURSE (Ire) 10-6 (7*) D K Budds, ...(16 to 1) 13
NOT CLEVER (Ire) 10-11 (7*) R P Hogan, ...(20 to 1) 14
1077 JACK YEATS (Ire) 11-9 S C Lyons, ...(8 to 1) 15
1275 FAHEEN'S BOY (Ire) 11-1 (3*) G Kilfeather, ...(50 to 1) pu
Dist: 2l, 9l, 3½l, 1½l. 4m 0.80s. (16 Ran).

(B R A S K Syndicate), F J Lacy

1898 Navan European Breeders Fund Novice Chase (5-y-o and up) £4,110 2¾m........................(2:05)

1618² ULTRA FLUTTER 9-11-7 J P Broderick, ...(4 to 1) 1

1618* ROCKFIELD NATIVE (Ire) 6-11-11 C O'Dwyer, (11 to 10 fav) 2
1461* PAPILLON (Ire) 5-11-6 (3") G Cotter, ... (13 to 2) 3
1461¹⁴ LE GINNO (Fr) 9-11-11 T P Treacy, ... (12 to 1) 4
1461¹² NATIVE STATUS (Ire) 4-10-4 (3") K Whelan, ... (10 to 1) 5
1652 MACALLISTER (Ire) 6-11-4 (3") B Bowens, ...(10 to 1) 6
1435⁹ BAMAPOUR (Ire) 6-11-0 (7") D K Budds, ... (16 to 1) 7
1436 COLLON (Ire) 7-11-7 D T Evans, ... (25 to 1) 8
1652³ EXECUTIVE OPTIONS (Ire) 7-11-7 J Shortt, ...(8 to 1) 9
1618⁵ DIORRAING (Ire) 6-11-7 F Woods, ... (20 to 1) 10
1618⁹ BROWNRATH KING (Ire) 7-11-0 (7") D M Bean, ... (33 to 1) 11
       J J JACKSON (Ire) 7-11-7 D H O'Connor, ...(25 to 1) 12
       THE VENDOR (Ire) 6-11-2 D J Casey, ... (33 to 1) 13
1534⁵ GARABAGH (Ire) 7-11-7 T J Mitchell, ... (25 to 1) pu
1618 FINGAL BOY 8-11-2 (5") J Butler, ...(33 to 1) pu
       OVER THE MAINE (Ire) 6-11-11 H Rogers, ...(20 to 1) pu
       RADICAL GIRL (Ire) 8-11-2 P L Malone, ... (33 to 1) pu
       EXECUTIVE CHIEF (Ire) 5-11-5 A Powell, ... (33 to 1) pu
Dist: 10l, 3½l, 13l, 1l. 6m 4.10s. (18 Ran).

(Donal Higgins), Michael Hourigan

1899 Roast Turkey Handicap Hurdle (0-109 4-y-o and up) £3,082 2½m
. . . . (2:35)

1654⁸ PTARMIGAN LODGE [-] 5-10-4 (3") G Kilfeather, ...(9 to 1) 1
1407⁵ TELL THE NIPPER (Ire) [-] 5-12-0 J P Broderick, (7 to 2 fav) 2
1433³ SHINING WILLOW [-] 6-11-5 C O'Dwyer, ... (4 to 1) 3
1273 VEREDARIUS (Fr) [-] 5-11-0 F Woods, ...(8 to 1) 4
1581⁹ COLLIERS HILL (Ire) [-] (bl) 8-10-1 P L Malone, ...(14 to 1) 5
1361 AMME ENAEK (Ire) [-] (bl) 7-9-7 M Duffy, ... (16 to 1) 6
1581⁵ STAR TRIX (Ire) [-] 5-9-4 (3") B Bowens, ... (20 to 1) 7
1581³ GLENFIELDS CASTLE (Ire) [-] 6-10-11 D J Casey, (12 to 1) 8
1489⁵ GLENBALLYMA (Ire) [-] 7-11-2 F J Flood, ... (11 to 1) 9
1143⁶ SHAWAHIN [-] 4-10-13 R Hughes, ... (10 to 1) 10
1462⁸ SPECTACLE (Ire) [-] 6-9-0 (7") A O'Shea, ... (20 to 1) 11
1581⁷ THE THIRD MAN (Ire) [-] 7-9-11 (7") R P Hogan, . . . (20 to 1) 12
1433⁹ JIMMY THE WEED (Ire) [-] 7-10-1 J R Barry, ... (14 to 1) 13
1778 JO JO BOY (Ire) [-] 7-11-4 (7") L J Fleming, ... (14 to 1) 14
1581⁶ BUCKLEY BAY (Ire) [-] (bl) 5-9-0 (7") J M Maguire, (25 to 1) 15
1040 SHY GAL (Ire) [-] 8-9-5 (7") J Butler, ...(33 to 1) 16
443 DUNDOCK WOOD [-] 8-10-1 (5") T Martin, ... (14 to 1) 17
1654 CONAGHER BOY (Ire) [-] 6-10-12 (7") K A Kelly, . . . (10 to 1) 18
1778 VINTNERS VENTURE (Ire) [-] 4-10-8 (5") M J Holbrook,
. . . . (14 to 1) 19
1777 SPEED BOUND (Ire) [-] 4-10-7 A Powell, ... (20 to 1) 20
1649 DEIREADH AN SCEAL (Ire) [-] 6-9-12 T P Treacy, . . (25 to 1) 21
       TULLOLOUGH [-] 13-10-9 J Shortt, ...(25 to 1) 22
1359 PIXIE BLUE (Ire) [-] 5-9-4 (3") G Cotter, ... (33 to 1) 23
Dist: 9l, 2l, 3l, 2l. 5m 3.00s. (23 Ran).

(Francis J Davey), Martin Michael Lynch

1900 Christmas Pudding Handicap Hurdle (4-y-o and up) £6,850 2m . . . . (3:05)

1649* ASK THE BUTLER (Ire) [-] 5-10-5 C O'Dwyer, ...(3 to 1) 1
1621⁴ BOLINO STAR (Ire) [-] 5-11-5 R Hughes, ... (2 to 1 fav) 2
       GOOD GLOW [-] 6-9-11 F Woods, ... (14 to 1) 3
1535* FONTAINE LODGE (Ire) [-] 6-9-10 (7") A O'Shea, ...(8 to 1) 4
       SCENIC ROUTE (Ire) [-] 7-11-1 P A Roche, ... (10 to 1) 5
1172³ NOTCOMPLAININGBUT (Ire) [-] 5-12-0 T P Treacy, (5 to 1) 6
1190⁵ JUSTAWAY (Ire) [-] 6-9-3 (5") J Butler, ...(16 to 1) 7
1752 RISING WATERS (Ire) [-] 8-10-3 D T Evans, ...(16 to 1) 8
       REASILVIA (Ire) [-] 6-10-12 J Shortt, ... (12 to 1) 9
1462⁹ COMMAND 'N CONTROL [-] 7-9-4 (3") G Cotter, . . (20 to 1) 10
1090⁷ PRE ORDAINED (Ire) [-] 4-9-10 P L Malone, ...(12 to 1) 11
       SHANES HERO (Ire) [-] 6-11-3 J P Broderick, ... (14 to 1) 12
1406⁴ MAYASTA (Ire) [-] 6-11-0 (7") R P Hogan, ... (14 to 1) 13
Dist: Hd, 10l, 4½l, ¾l. 4m 10.00s. (13 Ran).

(Barry Lee McCoubrey), C Roche

1901 Yule Log Mares I.N.H. Flat Race (4,5,6-y-o) £3,082 2m . . . . (3:35)

1580³ STORM GEM (Ire) 5-11-11 (7") Mr J T McNamara, (12 to 1) 1
1364¹ YASHGANS VISION (Ire) 5-11-11 (7") Mr E Sheehy, (10 to 1) 2
1622² BORO BOW (Ire) 5-11-11 (7") Mr A C Coyle, ...(5 to 4 on) 3
1432³ DUISKE ABBEY (Ire) 6-11-11 (7") Mr J P McNamara, (5 to 1) 4
       ENNEL GALE (Ire) 6-11-11 Mr M McNulty, ... (12 to 1) 5
1655⁵ BRACKENVALE (Ire) 5-11-4 (7") Mr R J Barnwell, . . (12 to 1) 6
1756 DANNKALIA (Ire) 4-11-6 Mr J P Dempsey, ... (10 to 1) 7
       NEWPARK KATE (Ire) 6-11-4 (7") Mr P A Rattigan, (25 to 1) 8
       VICKYWIL (Ire) 4-10-13 (7") Mr L Madine, ... (25 to 1) 9
       MINE'S A PINT (Ire) 4-10-13 (7") Mr A J Dempsey, (14 to 1) 10
       DUSKY SOUND (Ire) 4-10-13 (7") Miss J Hyde, . . . (12 to 1) 11
1457⁷ COOKSGROVE ROSIE (Ire) 4-10-13 (7") Mr S J Mahon,
. . . . (33 to 1) 12
1539 ASK DOCK (Ire) 5-11-11 Mr H F Cleary, ... (14 to 1) 13
805 GRANNY BOWLY (Ire) 4-11-6 (7") Mr T P McCreesh,
. . . . (33 to 1) 14
91⁷ SHIR ROSE 6-11-11 (7") Mr T A Shirley, ... (14 to 1) 15
       SUPREME MISS (Ire) 5-11-4 (7") Mr G Elliott, ... (14 to 1) 16
       POLITICAL TROUBLES (Ire) 6-11-8 (3") Mr P J Casey,
. . . . (16 to 1) 17
1579 SCATHACH (Ire) 4-11-3 (3") Mr B R Hamilton, ...(33 to 1) 18
1584⁵ WHAT EVER YOU WANT (Ire) 6-11-4 (7") Mr M Callaghan,
. . . . (33 to 1) 19
       MIA LADY (Ire) 5-11-8 (3") Mr P English, ...(7 to 1) 20

1580 BUCKAMERE (Ire) 5-11-4 (7") Mr Philip Carberry, . .(20 to 1) 21
951 MOYDUFF LUCY (Ire) 6-11-4 (7") Mr N Geraghty, . .(33 to 1) 22
       BUN AN CHNOIC (Ire) 5-11-4 (7") Mr A K Wyse, . . (20 to 1) 23
Dist: 3l, 1l, 15l, 14l. 3m 59.10s. (23 Ran).

(Town And Country Racing Club), P A Fahy

THURLES (IRE) (yielding)
Sunday December 15th

1902 Munster INH Stallion Owners EBF Maiden Hurdle (4 & 5-y-o) £3,767 2m
. . . . (12:30)

1651⁵ THREE SCHOLARS 5-12-0 D J Casey, ...(2 to 1) 1
       BAI-BRUN KATE (Ire) 5-11-9 F J Flood, ... (11 to 2) 2
1485⁶ ANTICS (Ire) 4-10-11 (7") Mrs C Harrison, ...(12 to 1) 3
1777 BEHY BRIDGE (Ire) 4-11-4 T J Mitchell, ... (50 to 1) 4
857⁷ ALICE BRENNAN (Ire) 5-11-9 J Shortt, ...(10 to 1) 5
1751⁹ TWENTYFIVEQUID (Ire) 5-12-0 Mr P F Graffin, ...(12 to 1) 6
1776 BAR FLUTE (Ire) 5-11-9 C F Swan, ... (14 to 1) 7
1776 BESTERELLE (Ire) 5-11-9 M Duffy, ... (14 to 1) 8
1490⁶ MIRACLE ME (Ire) 4-11-2 (7") Mr J G Sheehan, . . . (20 to 1) 9
1536 THE ROAD TO MOSCOW (Ire) 5-12-0 J R Barry, . . (14 to 1) 10
1307⁸ MR MAGGET (Ire) 4-11-9 T P Rudd, ... (25 to 1) 11
1782⁵ PHAREIGN (Ire) 5-12-0 F Woods, ...(10 to 1) 12
1782 FORTYNINEPLUS (Ire) 5-11-11 (3") G Cotter, ... (25 to 1) 13
       PENNY POET (Ire) 4-11-9 J P Broderick, ... (33 to 1) 14
       CAN'T BE STOPPED (Ire) 4-11-2 (7") J P Deegan, (33 to 1) 15
1090 MILLICANS BEND (Ire) 4-11-9 T Hazlett, ... (25 to 1) 16
       STANDARA (Ire) 5-11-2 (7") J O'Shaughnessy, ... (33 to 1) ro
1777 BEHAMORE GIRL (Ire) 4-10-11 (7") A O'Shea, ...(14 to 1) pu
Dist: 1½l, 11l, 1l, 12l. 4m 1.00s. (18 Ran).

(Mrs J M Mullins), W P Mullins

1903 Garry Kennedy Handicap Chase (0-109 5-y-o and up) £2,740 3m
. . . . (1:00)

1711⁴ CASTALINO [-] 10-11-5 C F Swan, ...(11 to 4 jt-fav) 1
1618 TAYLORS QUAY (Ire) [-] 8-11-13 J P Broderick, ...(6 to 1) 2
1408 THE GOPHER (Ire) [-] 7-11-12 L P Cusack, ... (4 to 1) 3
1408⁵ VELEDA II (Fr) [-] 9-11-11 (3") K Whelan, ...(6 to 1) 4
1553⁴ STEEL DAWN [-] 9-11-7 F Woods, ...(11 to 4 jt-fav) 5
1711 ALL IN THE GAME (Ire) [-] 8-10-0 P A Roche, ... (12 to 1) 6
1312 CABBERY ROSE (Ire) [-] 8-11-0 (7") C Rae, ...(10 to 1) 7
Dist: 3l, 5l, 4½l, 15l. 6m 30.10s. (7 Ran).

(Stephen Ryan), Stephen Ryan

1904 Dromineer Handicap Hurdle (0-102 5-y-o and up) £2,740 2¾m 110yds
. . . . (1:30)

1361⁴ ISLAND CHAMPION (Ire) [-] 7-9-12 (3") G Cotter, . .(14 to 1) 1
1419 FORT DEELY (Ire) [-] 5-10-8 J Jones, ...(7 to 4 fav) 2
1654* ICED HONEY [-] 9-11-3 L P Cusack, ...(5 to 1) 3
1550⁸ LADY QUAYSIDE (Ire) [-] 6-10-10 (7") P Morris, . . .(12 to 1) 4
1713⁸ WOODBORO LASS (Ire) [-] 6-9-8 (7") L J Fleming, (10 to 1) 5
1778³ BOHOLA PETE (Ire) [-] 5-10-1 R Hughes, ...(6 to 1) 6
1548⁸ MAGS SUPER TOI (Ire) [-] 7-9-10 (7") M D Murphy, (20 to 1) 7
1712⁹ OVER THE WALL (Ire) [-] 7-9-11 (7") J O'Shaughnessy,
. . . . (33 to 1) 8
1710³ WELSH GRIT (Ire) [-] 7-12-0 D J Casey, ... (10 to 1) 9
1838⁶ SIDCUP HILL (Ire) [-] 7-10-13 A J O'Brien, ... (12 to 1) 10
1554⁹ AISEIRI [-] 9-10-7 C F Swan, ... (14 to 1) 11
1712⁵ LAURA'S PURSUIT (Ire) [-] 7-10-11 F Woods, ...(10 to 1) 12
1244 FLAMEWOOD [-] 7-10-13 J Shortt, ... (25 to 1) 13
1486⁹ STRONG RAIDER (Ire) [-] 6-10-5 T P Treacy, ... (6 to 1) 14
1581² SONG FOR AFRICA (Ire) [-] (bl) 5-10-3 P L Malone, (15 to 1) 15
       TAR AND CEMENT (Ire) [-] 8-10-0 P A Roche, ...(25 to 1) pu
1713* RUN ROSE RUN (Ire) [-] (bl) 6-9-2 (7") A O'Shea, . . .(9 to 1) pu
       BOWES LADY (Ire) [-] 5-10-0 (7") Miss S White, . . . (33 to 1) pu
Dist: 1l, hd, 2½l, ½l. 5m 40.00s. (18 Ran).

(M A O'Gorman Jun), M A O'Gorman Jun

1905 Carey Bros Vista/Therm Hurdle (5-y-o and up) £4,110 2m . . . . (2:00)

1488* KING OF KERRY 5-11-10 C F Swan, ...(9 to 2) 1
1621* DARDJINI (USA) 6-12-0 R Hughes, ...(9 to 4 on) 2
1752 LIKE A LION (Ire) 5-11-5 (5") J M Donnelly, ...(16 to 1) 3
1551¹⁴ ARCTIC WEATHER (Ire) 7-12-0 T P Rudd, ...(8 to 1) 4
1486² RANDOM RING (Ire) 5-11-2 J P Broderick, ... (25 to 1) 5
1638⁵ PUNTING PETE (Ire) 6-11-10 D J Casey, ... (6 to 1) 6
1751⁶ COMMITTED SCHEDULE (Ire) 5-11-2 F Woods, . . (33 to 1) 7
       UNYOKE RAMBLER (Ire) 6-10-8 (3") D P Murphy, (66 to 1) 8
       POWER CORE (Ire) 6-11-2 M Moran, ... (66 to 1) 9
       MR BOAL (Ire) 7-11-10 J Shortt, ... (33 to 1) pu
Dist: 1l, 3l, 2l, dist. 4m 3.10s. (10 Ran).

(The Local Boys Syndicate), A P O'Brien

1906 Nenagh Handicap Chase (0-102 4-y-o and up) £2,740 2m . . . . (2:30)

1711 HANNIES GIRL (Ire) [-] 7-10-8 (7") L J Fleming, ... (7 to 1) 1
       APPALACHEE BAY (Ire) [-] 6-11-3 (7") Mr C A Murphy,
. . . . (10 to 1) 2

1650⁵ SORRY ABOUT THAT [-] 10-11-11 P L Malone, ... (5 to 1) 3
1711² WACKO JACKO (Ire) [-] 7-11-7 J P Broderick, ...(7 to 2) 4
1781* WHITBY [-] 8-10-4 F Woods, ...(8 to 1) 5
1650 PERSIAN POWER (Ire) [-] 8-11-11 C F Swan, ...(5 to 2 fav) 6
1245⁵ SILENTBROOK [-] 11-9-3 (7") A O'Shea, ...(10 to 1) 7
881⁵ TREENS FOLLY [-] 7-10-2 (7") J O'Shaughnessy, ...(25 to 1) 8
1552 BALLYBRIT BOY [-] 10-7 P Cusack, ...(14 to 1) 9
1711 IF YOU SAY YES (Ire) [-] 8-11-3 D J Casey, ...(12 to 1) 10
Dist: 3l, 5½l, 4½l, 3l. 4m 21.30s. (10 Ran).

(Michael J Flynn), F Flood

1907 Puckane I.N.H. Flat Race (4-y-o) £2,740 2m....................(3:00)

1490³ STRONTIUM (Ire) 11-9 Mr P Fenton, ...(11 to 10 fav) 1
1533⁹ THINKERS CORNER (Ire) 11-2 (7") Mr A J Dempsey, (5 to 1) 2
1485² MONDEO ROSE (Ire) 10-11 (7") Mr C A Murphy, ...(8 to 1) 3
SUPER DEALER (Ire) 11-2 (7") Mr T J Nagle-Jnr, .. (16 to 1) 4
DICK MCCARTHY (Ire) 11-6 (3") Mr R Walsh, ...(3 to 1) 5
1777⁸ MISTER AUDI (Ire) 11-4 (5") Mr J T McNamara, ...(12 to 1) 6
1756⁵ SOPHIE VICTORIA (Ire) 10-11 (7") Mr G Elliott, ...(7 to 1) 7
THE TICK-TACK MAN (Ire) 11-2 (7") Mr D C Crinley,
....(16 to 1) 8
MARY DONT BE LONG (Ire) 10-11 (7") Mr G A Kingston,
....(20 to 1) 9
1756⁸ AROUND THE STUMP (Ire) 11-3 (3") Mr P English, (11 to 1) 10
288 SEXTON'S MIRROR (Ire) 11-9 Miss M Olivefalk, ..(16 to 1) 11
1490⁹ SOME ORCHESTRA (Ire) 10-11 (7") Mr M Budds, (20 to 1) 12
LAURAS ELECTRIC (Ire) 10-11 (7") Mr Sean O O'Brien,
....(10 to 1) 13
1015 AJKNAPP (Ire) (bl) 11-9 Mr A J Martin, ...(12 to 1) 14
1121⁸ ACTIVE LADY (Ire) 10-11 (7") Mr B Walsh, ...(20 to 1) 15
SHRAMORE LADY (Ire) 10-11 (7") Mr R J Cooper, (20 to 1) 16
TISNOTMYTURN (Ire) 11-4 Mr R O'Neill, ...(33 to 1) 17
1121 RUSTIC LODGE (Ire) 11-2³ (5") Mr W M O'Sullivan, (20 to 1) 18
Dist: 10l, ½l, sht-hd, 2l. 4m 2.90s. (18 Ran).

(Patrick Davern), John F Gleeson

1908 Portroe (Pro/Am) I.N.H. Flat Race (5-y-o) £2,740 2¼m............(3:30)

WINDY BEE (Ire) 11-2 (7") Aiden Nolan, ...(6 to 1) 1
1776⁶ PRINCESS GLORIA (Ire) 11-2 (7") Mr M J Daly, ...(8 to 1) 2
1364 KAITHEY CHOICE (Ire) 11-2 (7") Mr J Boland, ...(25 to 1) 3
1486 GALLIC HONEY (Ire) 11-2 (7") Mrs C Harrison, ...(8 to 1) 4
IADA (Ire) 11-2 (7") Mr Edgar Byrne, ...(8 to 1) 5
1584⁴ KILPATRICK (Ire) (bl) 11-2 (7") Mr C J Swords, ...(8 to 1) 6
1649⁶ MARTYS STEP (Ire) (bl) 11-7 (7") D McCullagh, (7 to 4 fav) 7
1463 BARNA LASS (Ire) 11-4 (5") J M Donnelly, ...(20 to 1) 8
1712⁶ CLEARLY CANADIAN (Ire) 11-11 (3") G Cotter, (13 to 2) 9
SAIL AWAY SAILOR (Ire) 11-2 (7") Mr R Hickey, ... (20 to 1) 10
1782 SO DARING (Ire) 11-2 (7") Mr J P McNamara, ...(20 to 1) 11
1463 MONKEY LEAF (Ire) 11-2 (7") Mr C A Cronin, ...(25 to 1) 12
1463 VERYWELL (Ire) 11-7 (7") Mr N Geraghty, ...(20 to 1) 13
ABLE LADY (Ire) 11-2 (7") K C Hartnett, ...(12 to 1) 14
1782 WILL I OR WONT I (Ire) 11-2 (7") Mr M J Walsh, ..(20 to 1) 15
DRUMASHELLIG LADY (Ire) 11-2 (7") J P Deegan, (25 to 1) 16
1655 MAY BLOOM (Ire) 11-6 (3") Mr R Walsh, ...(14 to 1) bd
MISCHIEF MAN (Ire) 11-11 (3") Mr P English, ...(14 to 1) su
Dist: 1½l, 1l, 8l, 1l. 4m 37.40s. (18 Ran).

(Brian Nolan), Brian Nolan

NEWCASTLE (good)
Monday December 16th
Going Correction: PLUS 0.30 sec. per fur.

1909 Newcastle Cultural Capital Of The North Juvenile Novices' Hurdle Class E (3-y-o) £2,337 2m....(12:40)

1629² SON OF ANSHAN 10-12 J Supple, chsd ldrs, pushed alng
aftr 5th, rdn bef 3 out, styd on wl und pres to ld chme.
....(6 to 4 fav op 7 to 4 tchd 5 to 4) 1
1629³ ROSSEL (USA) 11-5 (7") C McCormack, cl up, led 6th, clr 2
out, rdn bef last, wknd and ct close hme. (6 to 1 op 5 to 2) 2
1629* JACKSON PARK 11-5 R Dunwoody, cl up, chlgd 6th, sn drvn
alng, kpt on same pace frm 3 out.
....(9 to 4 op 5 to 2 tchd 3 to 1) 3
927⁵ J J BABOO (Ire) 10-12 R Garritty, in tch, effrt aftr 6th, kpt on
same pace frm 3 out....................(8 to 1 op 7 to 1) 4
1689² FRO 10-7 B Storey, in tch, drvn alng bef 6th, no hdwy.
....(14 to 1 op 10 to 1) 5
1690⁸ PERPETUAL LIGHT 10-7 Derek Byrne, nvr nr to chal.
....(20 to 1 op 16 to 1) 6
1221⁹ SOUSSE 10-7 P Niven, nvr dngrs....(14 to 1 op 12 to 1) 7
1689* PRIDDY FAIR 10-11 (3") P Midgley, settled midfield, effrt aftr
6th, sn tired.................................(20 to 1 op 14 to 1) 8
1629 NEXSIS STAR 10-5 (7") R Wilkinson, led till hdd 6th, sn rdn
and wknd...................................(25 to 1 op 20 to 1) 9
AMAZING SAIL (Ire) 10-12 A S Smith, in tch till wknd aftr 5th.
....(66 to 1 op 50 to 1 tchd 100 to 1) 10
WESTERN VENTURE (Ire) 10-12 A Dobbin, beh most of way.
....(50 to 1) 11
1629 BANK ON INLAND 10-7 W Fry, beh most of way. (100 to 1) 12
1629⁶ MOCK TRIAL (Ire) 10-12 S Swiers, prmnt, 5th and wkng
whn t 3 out.................................(14 to 1 op 12 to 1) f
248

BEACON HILL LADY 10-7 G Cahill, tld off whn pld up bef 3
out...(100 to 1) pu
BLAZING IMP (USA) 10-12 N Smith, tld off whn pld up bef 3
out...(66 to 1) pu
1384⁷ SOUNDS DEVIOUS 10-7 D Parker, tld off whn pld up bef 2 out.
....(100 to 1) pu
RAMOZRA 10-7 B Harding, tld off whn pld up bef 3 out.
....(100 to 1) pu
Dist: ½l, 7l, 12l, 10l, 10l, 3½l, 3l, 2l, 12l, 7l. 3m 55.90s. a 18.90s (17 Ran).

(G A Swinbank), Mrs A Swinbank

1910 Newcastle Tyne Bridge Illuminations Handicap Chase Class D (0-125 5-y-o and up) £3,452 3m.........(1:10)

1315³ STORMY CORAL (Ire) [97] 6-10-0 B Storey, hld up, gd hdwy to
track ldr 3 out, swtchd betw last 2, quickened to ld fnl 200
yards, pushed out... (13 to 8 fav op 2 to 1 tchd 6 to 4) 1
1774 ASTINGS (Fr) [116] 8-11-5 R Garritty, cl up, led 6th, hdd fnl 200
yards, no extr..............(2 to 1 op 7 to 4 tchd 9 to 4) 2
1632 EARLYMORNING LIGHT (Ire) [115] 7-11-4 A Dobbin, led to
6th, prmnt, rdn and one pace frm 3 out.
.....................................(10 to 1 op 6 to 1 tchd 11 to 1) 3
1634⁶ VICARIDGE [97] 9-10-0 K Johnson, beh, mstk 4th, hdwy to
track ldrs 11th, rdn aftr 15th, sn wknd. (5 to 2 tchd 11 to 4) 4
1821 BLAZING DAWN [97] 9-10-0 B Harding, in tch till wknd
quickly aftr 13th, tld off....................(25 to 1 op 16 to 1) 5
Dist: 3l, 30l, 7l, 30l. 6m 9.60s. a 23.60s (5 Ran).

(Mr & Mrs Raymond Anderson Green), C Parker

1911 Newcastle Initiative Claiming Hurdle Class F (4-y-o and up) £2,142 2m ....(1:40)

WHITE WILLOW (bl) 7-11-6 P Niven, made all, clr last, eased
towards finish...(11 to 10 on op 11 to 10 tchd 11 to 8) 1
1693⁴ AIDE MEMOIRE (Ire) 7-10-0 K Johnson, beh, hdwy to track
ldrs aftr 3rd, lost pl after 6th, styd on wl und pres frm 2 out,
swshd tail.................................(25 to 1 op 33 to 1) 2
1676² AUBURN BOY 9-11-12 R Garritty, hld up, hdwy bef 6th, chsd
wnr frm 3 out, no imprsn... (7 to 1 op 6 to 1 tchd 8 to 1) 3
1772 JAZILAH (Fr) 8-11-12 R Dunwoody, hld up, hdwy aftr 5th, rdn
aftr nxt, fdd......................................(20 to 1) 4
ARTWORLD (USA) 8-10-11 (3") P Midgley, trkd wnr, dsptd ld
aftr 6th, wknd after 3 out.
.....................................(40 to 1 op 33 to 1 tchd 66 to 1) 5
1588⁴ NONIOS (Ire) 5-10-13 (7") T Hogg, mid-div, no hdwy frm 6th.
.....................................(12 to 1 op 10 to 1 tchd 14 to 1) 6
1164* STYLISH INTERVAL 4-11-0 A Dobbin, towards rear, effrt aftr
6th, no hdwy whn hmpd 2 out........(25 to 1 op 20 to 1) 7
1693 FLY TO THE END (USA) 6-10-11 Derek Byrne, al beh, tld off.
.....................................(200 to 1 op 100 to 1) 8
824 MANNAGAR (Ire) 4-10-11 M Moloney, al beh, wl tld off.
.....................................(200 to 1 op 100 to 1) 9
1588⁷ JOYRIDER 5-10-5 A S Smith, chsd ldrs, 5th and wkng whn t 2
out...(8 to 1 op 6 to 1) f
1372 CIRCLE BOY 9-10-0 (5") R McGrath, chsd ldrs till wknd
quickly aftr 5th, tld off whn pld up bef 2 out.
.....................................(200 to 1 op 150 to 1) pu
1657 PERCY PARROT (bl) 4-10-5 B Harding, chsd ldrs to hfwy, sn
rdn and wknd, tld off whn pld up bef 3 out......(100 to 1) pu
Dist: 3½l, 1¼l, 11l, ½l, 3½l, 2½l, dist, dist. 4m 0.10s. a 23.10s (12 Ran).

(H North), Mrs M Reveley

1912 Newcastle Education Business Partnership Novices' Handicap Chase Class D (0-110 4-y-o and up) £3,452 2m 110yds.....................(2:10)

1374⁹ CROSSHOT [75] 9-10-9 K Jones, nvr far away, hdwy to
dispute ld 3 out, led last, kpt on und pres. (9 to 2 op 7 to 2) 1
COVER POINT (Ire) [90] 5-11-10 R Dunwoody, led, jnd 3 out,
hdd last, no extr und pres. (7 to 2 op 3 to 1 tchd 4 to 1) 2
1374 SINGING SAND [74] 6-10-8 G Cahill, hld up, smooth hdwy to
track ldr 8th, hit 3 out, sn outpcd.......(4 to 1 op 7 to 2) 3
1258⁶ ISLANDREAGH (Ire) [75] 5-10-9 A Dobbin, prmnt, wkng whn
mstk 9th, tld off...........................(8 to 1 op 4 to 1) 4
1808 MONAUGHTY MAN [69] 10-10-3 K Johnson, beh whn blun
4th, lost pl frm 7th, tld off.............(10 to 1 tchd 8 to 1) 5
1376 SHOW YOUR HAND (Ire) [77] 8-10-11 B Harding, prmnt whn f
5th...(2 to 1 fav op 9 to 4) f
COOLRENY (Ire) [76] 7-10-10⁴ Mr M Thompson, beh whn
blun badly and uns rdr 7th.
.....................................(40 to 1 op 33 to 1 tchd 50 to 1) ur
Dist: 7l, 5l, 30l, 10l. 4m 10.40s. a 11.40s (7 Ran).
SR: 16/24/3/-/

(R McDonald), R McDonald

1913 Newcastle City Of Energy Novices' Chase Class D (5-y-o and up) £3,517 2½m.....................(2:45)

1630⁶ GARBO'S BOY 6-11-0 W Fry, lft in ld 6th, blun 8th, styd on wl
frm 3 out...................(14 to 1 op 12 to 1 tchd 16 to 1) 1
GAELIC BLUE 6-10-7 (7") R Wilkinson, in tch, kpt on same
pace frm 3 out, no imprsn on wnr.....(12 to 1 op 10 to 1) 2
1568⁹ RATHFARDON (Ire) 8-10-7 (7") Mr T J Barry, in tch, dsptd ld
11th till rdn and no extr aftr 3 out.....(66 to 1 op 50 to 1) 3

1385² PANTARA PRINCE (Ire) 7-11-0 A Dobbin, *hmpd 1st, prmnt frm 6th till wknd from 3 out*.................(5 to 1 op 7 to 2) 4
CULLANE LAKE (Ire) 6-10-9 A S Smith, *hld up, lost tch frm bef 3 out*..................... (25 to 1 op 14 to 1 tchd 33 to 1) 5
1825 DISTILLERY HILL (Ire) 8-11-0 K Jones, *hld up*
.... (33 to 1 op 20 to 1) 6
1771 ASLAN (Ire) 8-11-0 W Dwan, *led 1st, clr whn refused 6th, continued tld off* ....(9 to 1 op 7 to 2) 7
CELTIC GIANT 6-11-0 R Garritty, *led and f 1st*.
....................................(7 to 4 op 6 to 4 on) f
Dist: 7l, hd, 17l, 4l, dist, 7l. 5m 18.10s. a 31.10s (8 Ran).

(J R Turner), J R Turner

1914 Newcastle Student City Handicap Hurdle Class D (0-120 4-y-o and up) £2,749 2½m................(3:15)

LIVIO (USA) [105] 5-11-5 A Dobbin, *in tch gng wl, led aftr 9th, clr 2 out, easily*.....................(5 to 1 op 9 to 2) 1
1139 BRANCHER [91] 5-10-5 W Fry, *in tch, drvn alng aftr 9th, wnt second appr last, no ch wth wnr*........(5 to 1 op 6 to 1) 2
PUREVALUE (Ire) [110] 5-11-10 R Dunwoody, *hld up in rear, hdwy und pres aftr 8th, chsd wnr frm 3 out, no imprsn*.
....................................(9 to 4 fav op 7 to 2 tchd 4 to 1) 3
1251³ KEEN TO THE LAST (Fr) [100] 4-11-0 R Garritty, *trkd ldrs, ev ch bef 3 out, sn rdn and btn*...........(8 to 1 op 5 to 1) 4
1166* EXEMPLAR (Ire) [96] 8-10-3 (7*) R Wilkinson, *led till hdd aftr 9th, rdn and wknd bef 3 out.* (8 to 1 op 5 to 1 tchd 9 to 1) 5
1635 DUAL IMAGE [106] 9-11-6 W Dwan, *nvr on terms*.
....................................(40 to 1 op 25 to 1) 6
1676³ BARTON HEIGHTS [90] 4-10-1 (3*) G Lee, *trkd ldrs, ev ch bef 3 out, sn rdn and wknd, eased whn no chance.*
....................................(3 to 1 op 9 to 4 tchd 7 to 2) 7
80⁶ GLENUGIE [102] 5-11-2 N Bentley, *chsd ldrs till wknd quickly aftr 7th, tld off*...................(10 to 1 op 8 to 1) 8
Dist: 7l, 4l, 7l, ½l, 2l, dist. 6l. 5m 17.50s. a 39.50s (8 Ran).

(The Low Flyers (Thoroughbreds) Ltd), P Monteith

NEWTON ABBOT (soft)
Monday December 16th
Going Correction: PLUS 1.15 sec. per fur. (races 1,3,5,7), PLUS 1.50 (2,4,6)

1915 Not So Red Selling Hurdle Class G (4-y-o and up) £1,793 2¾m.....(12:50)

1628⁸ PALOSANTO (Ire) [b] 6-11-12 A P McCoy, *made all, set steady pace till quickened appr 4 out, sn clr, hit 2 out, eased r-in.*.........................(6 to 5 op Evens tchd 5 to 4) 1
STAR PERFORMER 5-11-5 A Maguire, *pld hrd and hld up, mstk 5th, wnt second nxt, rdn and held whn mistake 3 out, no ch aftr*.....................(11 to 10 on op 5 to 4 on) 2
1731⁵ STRIKE-A-POSE 6-11-0 Mr J L Llewellyn, *hld up, lost tch appr 4 out*......................(12 to 1 op 8 to 1) 3
1697⁴ CREDIT CONTROLLER (Ire) [b] 7-10-12 B Fenton, *hld up early, chsd wnr appr 5th to nxt, rdn and sn wknd, tld off.*
....................(25 to 1 op 20 to 1 tchd 33 to 1) 4
BOWDEN SURPRISE 6-10-12 B Powell, *rcd wide, in tch till wknd 5th, tld off whn pld up bef 3 out.* (25 to 1 op 12 to 1) pu
Dist: 24l, 3l, dist. 5m 46.60s. a 45.60s (5 Ran).

(B A Kilpatrick), M C Pipe

1916 European Breeders Fund Tattersalls Ireland Mares' Only Novices' Chase Qualifier Class E (5-y-o and up) £2,995 2m 5f 110yds.........(1:20)

1793² MISS DISKIN (Ire) 7-10-10 B Powell, *hld up, hdwy to ld aftr 6th, hdd 5 out, led 3 out, rdn out.*
....................(2 to 1 fav op 5 to 2 tchd 11 to 4) 1
1469³ COUNTRY STORE 7-10-10 D Bridgwater, *hld up, hdwy to track ldrs 8th, ev ch 2 out, rdn one pace.*
....................(14 to 1 op 10 to 1 tchd 16 to 1) 2
1562⁴ PEARL'S CHOICE (Ire) 8-10-10 A Thornton, *al prmnt, led 3rd to nxt, led 5th till aftr next, led 5 out to 3 out, no extr frm next.*
....................(12 to 1 op 8 to 1 tchd 14 to 1) 3
WONDERFUL POLLY (Ire) 8-10-5 (5*) O Burrows, *hld up, hdwy 9th, blun 4 out, rallied and ev ch appr 2 out, one pace.*
....................(14 to 1 op 7 to 1) 4
LORNA-GAIL 10-10-7 (3*) P Henley, *hld up, hdwy 8th, wknd appr 2 out*..................(3 to 1 op 5 to 2) 5
ARDENT LOVE (Ire) 7-10-10 A Maguire, *hdwy 9th, rdn appr 2 out, one pace*... (11 to 1 op 7 to 1 tchd 12 to 1) 6
1593⁹ BOURNEL (v) 8-10-10 B Fenton, *al beh, tld off*.
....................................(33 to 1 op 16 to 1) 7
CARMEL'S JOY (Ire) 7-10-10 L Harvey, *chsd ldrs till blun 5 out, sn beh, tld off*............(9 to 2 op 7 to 2) 8
1793⁴ ARCTIC MADAM 7-10-3 (7*) Mr J Tizzard, *jmpd slwly 1st, blun 6th, tld off 9th*.............(25 to 1 op 12 to 1) 9
1667⁴ MISTRESS ROSIE 9-10-10 S Fox, *prmnt till wknd 9th, tld off whn pld up bef last*.............(25 to 1 op 16 to 1) pu
1732⁵ KNOWING 9-10-3 (7*) Mr A Wintle, *mid-div, beh 9th, tld off whn pld up bef 2 out*............(66 to 1 op 33 to 1) pu

KINGSMILL QUAY 7-10-10 G Upton, *led to 3rd led 4th nxt, blun 7th, sn beh, tld off whn pld up aftr 8th.*
....................(50 to 1 op 33 to 1 tchd 66 to 1) pu
Dist: 2½l, 1¼l, 1l, 2½l, 3½l, dist, nk, 26l. 5m 49.50s. a 47.50s (12 Ran).

(Martyn Forrester), R H Buckler

1917 Les Seward Memorial Challenge Trophy Handicap Hurdle Class E (0-110 4-y-o and up) £2,190 2m 1f ....(1:50)

FRIENDLY HOUSE (Ire) [91] 7-11-10 A P McCoy, *made all, strly rdn appr last, kpt on.*
....................(7 to 4 fav op Evens tchd 2 to 1) 1
1699⁷ MUHTASHIM (Ire) [87] 6-11-6 B Fenton, *in tch, rdn to go second sn aftr 3 out, ev ch appr last, no extr r-in.*
....................................(9 to 2 op 3 to 1) 2
1717⁵ DAILY SPORT GIRL [90] 7-11-9 Mr J L Llewellyn, *in rear, struggling 4th, styd on frm 3 out, nvr dngrs.*
....................................(9 to 2 op 3 to 1) 3
1417⁵ HULLO MARY DOLL [79] 7-10-7 (5*) Sophie Mitchell, *beh, some hdwy 3 out, nvr dngrs*...........(9 to 2 tchd 5 to 1) 4
1729 CHILI HEIGHTS [82] 6-11-1 R Greene, *chsd ldrs till wknd aftr 4th, hit 3 out, tld off.*......(14 to 1 op 10 to 1) 5
TILT TECH FLYER [82] 11-10-8 (7*) Miss E J Jones, *chsd wnr till wknd quickly 3 out, tld off*..........(7 to 1 op 5 to 1) 6
QUEENS CURATE [67] 9-10-0 B Powell, *rcd wide, tld off 5th.*
....................................(66 to 1 op 25 to 1) 7
Dist: 2½l, 24l, ¾l, dist, 7l, dist. 4m 21.30s. a 32.30s (7 Ran).

(Mrs Sarah Buckley), M C Pipe

1918 Weatherbys 1997 Diary Handicap Chase Class D (0-125 5-y-o and up) £3,424 2m 110yds...........(2:20)

1455² JAMES THE FIRST [115] [bl] 8-11-11 A P McCoy, *led till mstk second, jmpd lft nxt, led 4th to 5th, reminder to ld ag'n next, kpt up to work, clr 2 out.*
....................(6 to 5 fav op Evens tchd 11 to 8) 1
AAL EL AAL [105] 9-11-1 G Tormey, *hld up, wnt second aftr 5 out, tiring whn jmpd rght last.*
....................(9 to 4 op 7 to 4 tchd 5 to 2) 2
1730 STAR OF ITALY [90] 9-10-0 L Harvey, *led second to 4th, led 5th to nxt, rdn 4 out, wknd.* (16 to 1 op 10 to 1) 3
ALLO GEORGE [113] 10-11-9 A Thornton, *hld up, wknd quickly appr 6th, tld off.*...(11 to 4 op 9 to 4 tchd 3 to 1) 4
Dist: 22l, dist, dist. 4m 30.00s. a 32.00s (4 Ran).
SR: 25/

(B L Blinman), P F Nicholls

1919 Tom Holt And Reality Novices' Hurdle Class D (4-y-o and up) £2,911 2m 1f...............................(2:50)

DEANO'S BEENO 4-10-12 C Maude, *al prmnt, led appr 5th, clr 3 out, unchlgd.*
....................(100 to 30 op 6 to 4 tchd 7 to 2 and 4 to 1) 1
1651⁶ LAKE KARIBA 5-11-12 A P McCoy, *led to 1st, led 4th, hdd bef nxt, rdn and no ch frm 3 out.*
....................(Evens fav op 6 to 4 tchd 7 to 4) 2
RAFFLES ROOSTER 4-10-12 A Thornton, *chsd ldrs till wknd bef 5th, tld off*.............(12 to 1 op 6 to 1) 3
BLADE OF FORTUNE 8-10-5 (7*) Mr J Tizzard, *chsd ldrs till wknd appr 5th, tld off.*..(33 to 1 op 14 to 1 tchd 50 to 1) 4
SPIRIT LEVEL 8-11-2⁹ Mr R Payne, *tld off frm 3rd.*
....................(66 to 1 op 33 to 1 tchd 100 to 1) 5
LEES PLEASE (Ire) 4-10-12 G Upton, *tld off 3rd, pld up bef 3 out.*....................(66 to 1 op 20 to 1) pu
TYPHOON EIGHT (Ire) 4-10-12 B Powell, *in tch till mstk 4th, tld off whn pld up bef 2 out.*(5 to 1 op 3 to 1 tchd 11 to 2) pu
IL TRASTEVERE (Ire) 4-10-12 D Bridgwater, *led 1st to 4th, wknd quickly nxt, tld off whn pld up bef 3 out.*
....................(9 to 1 op 5 to 1 tchd 10 to 1) pu
157 JACKAMUS (Ire) 5-10-5 (7*) Mr M Frith, *al beh, tld off whn pld up bef 3 out*...............(100 to 1 op 20 to 1) pu
Dist: 25l, 30l, 24l, dist. 4m 13.50s. a 24.50s (9 Ran).
SR: 35/-/-/-/-/-/

(The Blue Chip Group), M C Pipe

1920 Pot Black Childcraft Handicap Chase Class E (0-110 5-y-o and up) £2,886 2m 5f 110yds........(3:20)

1814 TITAN EMPRESS [81] (v) 7-10-0 N Mann, *hld up, hdwy 9th, led 3 out, sn clr, tired nxt, kpt on one pace.*
....................(7 to 1 op 12 to 1 tchd 16 to 1) 1
1687 COUNTRY KEEPER [84] 8-10-3³ G Upton, *hld up in rear, steady hdwy 9th, styd on to go second 2 out, kpt on.*
....................(20 to 1 op 25 to 1 tchd 33 to 1) 2
1687⁴ JAILBREAKER [93] 9-10-7 (5*) D Salter, *led 4th till hdd 3 out, chsd wnr till wknd nxt.*.............(9 to 2 op 7 to 2) 3
GIVENTIME [105] 8-11-10 L Harvey, *prmnt till wknd 3 out.*............(4 to 1 op 7 to 2 tchd 9 to 2) 4
857* BIT OF A TIZZY [92] 10-10-11 C Maude, *in tch till wknd 5 out.*................(5 to 1 op 9 to 2 tchd 6 to 1) 5
1687* BRAMBLEHILL BUCK (Ire) [109] (bl) 7-12-0 A P McCoy, *prmnt till rdn and lost pl 7th, sn beh, tld off.*
....................................(5 to 2 fav op 6 to 4) 6

249

1602² SCOTONI [95] 10-11-0 B Powell, *led to 4th, lost tch 9th, tld off*
whn pld up bef four out.... (7 to 1 op 4 to 1 tchd 8 to 1) pu
1687 GOLDEN OPAL [90] 11-10-2 (7") M Griffiths, *in tch till wknd 5*
out, tld off whn pld up bef last........ (16 to 1 op 12 to 1) pu
Dist: 2l, 12l, 14l, 19l, dist. 5m 49.50s. a 47.50s (8 Ran).

(T D J Syder), S Mellor

1921 Bulpin Challenge Cup Handicap Hurdle For Amateur Riders Class E
(0-120 4-y-o and up) £2,305 2¾m
.... (3:50)

1576⁶ TOP JAVALIN (NZ) [98] 9-10-2 (7") Mr G Shenkin, *al prmnt, led*
sn aftr 3 out, hrd rdn appr last, kpt on... (13 to 2 op 5 to 1) 1
1671* BIG STRAND [112] 7-11-4 (5") Mr A Farrant, *hld up, hdwy*
appr 4 out, hrd rdn to hold ev ch last, kpt on.
.... (9 to 4 fav op 5 to 2 tchd 3 to 1) 2
TEXAN BABY (Bel) [115] 7-11-9 (3") Mr M Rimell, *trkd ldrs till*
wknd appr 2 out........................ (10 to 1 op 6 to 1) 3
1728⁷ FONTAINEROUGE (Ire) [89] 6-9-7 (7") Mr E Babington, *in tch*
till wknd 3 out....................... (20 to 1 op 16 to 1) 4
1762* COKENNY BOY [108] 11-10-12 (7") Mr P Cosgrave, *trkd ldrs,*
led briefly 3 out, wknd und pres bef nxt.
.... (15 to 2 op 5 to 1 tchd 8 to 1) 5
1766⁴ OATIS ROSE [97] (bl) 7-9-7 (7") Mr R Wakley, *in rear till effrt 4*
out, wknd nxt...................... (4 to 1 op 4 to 1) 6
1576⁸ ST VILLE [96] 10-10-0 (7") Miss M Coombe, *beh till effrt appr*
4 out.............................. (16 to 1 tchd 20 to 1) 7
1573⁵ KINGS CHERRY (Ire) [95] 8-9-13 (7") Mr G Baines, *in tch till*
wknd appr 4 out.......... (9 to 1 op 7 to 1 tchd 10 to 1) 8
1642 WEB OF STEEL [89] 6-9-7 (7") Miss A Dudley, *beh whn hit 5th,*
tld off............................ (200 to 1) 9
HIGHLY DECORATED [89] 11-9-12⁵ (7") Miss C J Elliott, *al*
beh................................ (100 to 1) 10
1685² HELLO ME MAN (Ire) [89] 8-9-7 (7") Miss E J Jones, *in tch, led*
aftr 6th till hdd 3 out, wknd, pld up bef nxt.
.... (8 to 1 op 14 to 1) pu
1671 MAJOR NOVA [95] 7-9-13 (7") Mr N Bradley, *led 3rd till hdd*
aftr 6th, sn wknd, tld off whn pld up bef 2 out.
.... (25 to 1 op 16 to 1) pu
PENNYMOOR PRINCE [101] 7-10-5 (7") Mr A Holdsworth,
led to 3rd, wknd aftr 6th, tld off whn pld up bef 2 out.
.... (12 to 1 op 14 to 1 tchd 20 to 1) pu
1351⁷ ZIP YOUR LIP [89] 6-9-7 (7") Miss C Townsley, *prmnt to 5th,*
tld off whn pld up bef 2 out......... (33 to 1 op 25 to 1) pu
Dist: ½l, 19l, 2½l, 4l, 4l, 6l, 8l, dist, dist. 5m 46.60s. a 45.60s (14 Ran).

(Mrs Valerie Thum), N J Hawke

WARWICK (good to firm)
Monday December 16th
Going Correction: NIL (races 1,2,4,6,7), PLUS 0.30 (3,5)

1922 Hampton Juvenile Novices' Hurdle Class E (3-y-o) £3,036 2m....(12:30)

NAME OF OUR FATHER (USA) 10-9 (3") D Walsh, *hld up beh*
ldrs, hdwy appr 4th, chsd lder approaching 3 out, rdn to lead
approaching last, drvn out.......... (33 to 1 op 20 to 1) 1
1599* THEME ARENA 11-0 R Hughes, *cl up, led appr 4th, clr 3 out,*
hdd betw last 2, no extr.............. (2 to 1 jt-
fav op 7 to 4 tchd 9 to 4) 2
658⁷ SHEATH KEFAAH (v) 11-5 G Bradley, *hld up beh, hdwy appr 3*
out, styd on.................... (14 to 1 op 10 to 1) 3
1412 IMPENDING DANGER 10-9 (3") R Massey, *hdwy to track ldrs*
aftr 3rd, outpcd after 3 out............ (50 to 1) 4
1610 WARNING REEF 10-9 (3") T Dascombe, *hld up, mstk second,*
cld 4th, rdn nxt, sn outpcd.......... (14 to 1 op 25 to 1) 5
658⁶ BALMORAL PRINCESS (bl) 11-0 R Bellamy, *beh, styd on firm*
2 out, nvr on terms................ (25 to 1 op 20 to 1) 6
CODE RED 10-12 J A McCarthy, *hld up in mid-div, rdn and*
outpcd aftr 4th........... (16 to 1 op 12 to 1 tchd 20 to 1) 7
1665* LADY MAGNUM (Ire) 11-0 P Hide, *cl up, rdn and wknd aftr 3*
out.................... (12 to 1 op 10 to 1 tchd 14 to 1) 8
ANGUS MCCOATUP (Ire) 10-12 D Bentley, *hld up, outpcd aftr*
4th, nvr on terms.......... (14 to 1 op 10 to 1 tchd 16 to 1) 9
1470* CROWN AND CUSHION 11-5 P Holley, *mid-div, pushed along*
appr 4th, sn beh................. (14 to 1 op 10 to 1) 10
1844 BRIGHT ECLIPSE (USA) 10-12 C Llewellyn, *mid-div, wknd*
aftr 4th, tld off.................. (33 to 1) 11
DECISION MAKER (Ire) 10-12 N Williamson, *mstk second,*
beh, hrd rdn appr 4th, sn lost tch, tld off.
.... (20 to 1 op 14 to 1 tchd 25 to 1) 12
RED TIE AFFAIR (USA) 10-12 D Gallagher, *led to second, tried*
to run out nxt, wknd appr 4th, tld off......... (33 to 1) 13
LOCH DANCER 10-7 S Wynne, *al beh, tld off frm 4th.*
.... (50 to 1 op 33 to 1) 14
SAUCY DANCER 10-7 S McNeill, *al beh, tld off frm 4th.*
.... (33 to 1 tchd 50 to 1) 15
SUPERGOLD (Ire) 10-12 K Gaule, *trkd ldrs, drvn alng aftr 3rd,*
wknd nxt, tld off.................. (33 to 1) 16
1702⁸ REEM FEVER (Ire) 10-8¹ M A Fitzgerald, *al beh, tld off frm 4th.*
.... (50 to 1) 17
TOBY BROWN 10-12 R Johnson, *beh whn f 3rd.*
.... (14 to 1 op 8 to 1 tchd 16 to 1) f

ALBAHA (USA) 10-12 J R Kavanagh, *whipped round strt,*
refused to race................. (2 to 1 jt-fav op 9 to 4) ref
EXTRA HOUR (Ire) 10-12 M Richards, *chsd ldrs, wknd quickly*
and pld up bef 5th................ (25 to 1 op 16 to 1) pu
1599² JAMMY JENNY (Ire) 10-7 T Jenks, *led second, hdd appr 4th, wknd*
quickly and pld up lme approaching nxt.
.... (8 to 1 op 6 to 1 tchd 10 to 1) pu
Dist: 3l, 4l, 6l, 10l, 1¾l, 6l, 2l, 7l, 1½l, 18l. 3m 46.10s. a 7.10s (21 Ran).
SR: 13/12/13/-/-/-/ (T M Morris), P Bowen

1923 Gog Brook Handicap Hurdle Class D (0-125 4-y-o and up) £2,786 2m
.... (1:00)

1717* SEVERN GALE [96] 6-10-7 (7") X Aizpuru, *hld up, led appr 4th,*
drvn approaching last, ran on wl....... (5 to 2 op 7 to 4) 1
1798⁷ PRIDEWOOD PICKER [88] 9-10-1 (5") D J Kavanagh, *hld up*
in last pl, cld 5th, ev ch 2 out, drvn and hng lft appr last, found
little.
.... (11 to 10 on op Evens tchd 11 to 10 and 5 to 4 on) 2
1705 ISAIAH [110] 7-12-0 T Kent, *chsd ldr, led briefly aftr 3rd, hit*
5th and sn drvn, btn after 2 out....... (10 to 1 op 6 to 1) 3
1835⁷ EURO SINGER [98] 4-11-2 M FitzGerald, *led till aftr 3rd, cl up,*
rdn and btn after 2 out.............. (9 to 2 tchd 5 to 1) 4
Dist: 8l, 1¾l, nk. 3m 45.40s. a 6.40s (4 Ran).
SR: 22/6/26/13/ (Mrs Carol Allen), J Allen

1924 Budbrooke Novices' Chase Class D (5-y-o and up) £3,769 3¼m... (1:30)

1520³ GYSART (Ire) (bl) 7-11-0 N Williamson, *made all, clr 14th, blun*
3 out, eased nr finish, unchlgd.
.... (15 to 8 on op 2 to 1 on tchd 7 to 4 on) 1
1327² IRISH PERRY 9-10-9 I Lawrence, *al beh, lft poor second 14th,*
no ch wth wnr......... (50 to 1 op 33 to 1 tchd 66 to 1) 2
1804 THE MARMALADE CAT 7-10-11 (3") G Hogan, *chsd wnr, hit*
11th, lost tch whn f 14th....... (40 to 1 op 20 to 1) f
1448³ RAMSTOWN LAD (Ire) 7-11-0 C O'Dwyer, *disputing second*
whn f 5th............... (7 to 4 op 6 to 4 tchd 2 to 1) f
Dist: Dist. 6m 52.50s. a 38.50s (4 Ran).

(The Hon Mrs R Cobbold), M C Pipe

1925 Ettington Handicap Hurdle Class D (0-120 4-y-o and up) £2,884 2m 3f
.... (2:00)

1671² REAGANESQUE (USA) [107] 4-11-8 J R Kavanagh, *trkd ldr,*
led appr 3 out, hit nxt, drvn out......... (3 to 1 op 9 to 4) 1
1834³ LORD MCMURROUGH (Ire) [110] 6-11-11 N Williamson, *hld*
up in last pl, cld 6th, pushed alng to chase wnr aftr 3 out, drvn
and hng lft appr last, no extr.......... (3 to 1 op 5 to 2) 2
1644⁵ DOMAPPEL [112] 4-11-13 T Kent, *trkd ldr, not fluent 4 out*
and sn struggling, rallied appr last, one pace.
.... (13 to 8 fav op 2 to 1 tchd 9 to 4) 3
1728* DOMINION'S DREAM [104] (v) 4-10-12 (7") G Supple, *led till*
appr 3 out, sn btn................. (7 to 2 op 9 to 4) 4
Dist: 2l, 6l, 12l. 4m 26.80s. (4 Ran).

(Mrs John Spielman), P G Murphy

1926 Stoneleigh Handicap Chase Class C (0-130 5-y-o and up) £4,599 2½m 110yds..................... (2:30)

1721² REX TO THE RESCUE (Ire) [100] 8-10-4 (5") Mr R Thornton,
led to 6th, led ag'n 4 out, clr 2 out, drvn out.
.... (4 to 1 op 7 to 2 tchd 9 to 2) 1
1624² MR PRESIDENT (Ire) [102] 7-10-11 G Bradley, *hld up, hit*
tenth, sn cld on ldrs, outpcd 3 out, hdwy nxt, styd on und pres.
.... (11 to 8 fav op 2 to 1) 2
1624⁴ CRAFTY CHAPLAIN [97] 10-10-3 (3") D Walsh, *keen hold, led*
6th, hdd 4 out, drvn and hit 2 out, one pace.
.... (10 to 1 op 8 to 1) 3
1643² BALLY PARSON [112] 10-11-7 N Williamson, *cl up, mstk 13th,*
blun 3 out, one pace whn hit last 2.
.... (5 to 1 op 3 to 1 tchd 11 to 2) 4
1643⁴ LAKE OF LOUGHREA (Ire) [104] 6-10-13 C O'Dwyer, *hld up,*
cld tenth, blun 3 out, sn btn.
.... (6 to 1 op 4 to 1 tchd 13 to 2) 5
1607³ ANDRELOT [115] (bl) 9-11-10 R Johnson, *slwly into strd and*
drvn alng, sn in tch, rdn 8th, struggling in rear 11th, tld off.
.... (10 to 1 op 5 to 1 tchd 12 to 1) 6
1624⁵ NICKLE JOE [102] 10-10-11 W Marston, *in tch, drvn to take*
clr order 7th, hrd rdn appr 11th, lost touch nxt, tld off.
.... (25 to 1 op 20 to 1 tchd 33 to 1) 7
Dist: 5l, 1¾l, 3l, 21l, dist, 21l. 5m 7.80s. a 12.80s (7 Ran).
SR: 18/15/8/20/ (Tony Thomas & Mr Stewart McDonald), R H Alner

1927 Hoechst Roussel Panacur European Breeders Fund Mares' 'National Hunt' Novices' Hurdle Qualifier Class E (4-y-o and up) £3,251 2½m 110yds..................... (3:00)

1669 KONVEKTA QUEEN (Ire) 5-10-10 J Osborne, *hld up beh,*
hdwy 7th, led on bit after 3 out, clr whn awkward last, easily.
.... (11 to 4 jt-fav op 2 to 1 tchd 3 to 1 and 7 to 2) 1

1543 JOY FOR LIFE (Ire) 5-10-7 (3") D Walsh, *cl up, pushed alng 7th, outpcd aftr 3 out, no imprsn und pres appr last.*
...................................(25 to 1 op 20 to 1 tchd 33 to 1) 2

1369⁸ MAYLIN MAGIC 5-10-10 M A Fitzgerald, *hld up beh ldrs, cld 7th, pushed alng aftr nxt, hrd rdn appr 2 out, one pace.*
....................................(7 to 2 op 3 to 1 tchd 4 to 1) 3

1570 BRIERY GALE 6-10-10 S Wynne, *trkd ldrs, lost pl 7th, styd wl frm last.*..........................(10 to 1 op 8 to 1) 4

DI'S LAST 6-10-10 R Hughes, *led, clr aftr 6th, hdd aftr 3 out, no extr.*..............(11 to 4 jt-fav op 2 to 1 tchd 3 to 1) 5

1344⁸ WISE 'N' SHINE 5-10-10 Mr A Kinane, *al beh, tld off frm 7th.*
....(50 to 1 op 33 to 1) 6

1540 NERO'S GEM 5-10-10 W McFarland, *hld up, rdn alng 6th, sn lost tch, tld off.*.....................(50 to 1 op 33 to 1) 7

1369⁴ BRIDGE DELIGHT 7-10-3 (7") D C O'Connor, *beh, mstk 6th, sn lost tch, tld off.*.........(9 to 2 op 5 to 2 tchd 5 to 1) 8

1306 SPECIAL TOPIC 6-10-10 S Curran, *trkd ldrs, hit 5th, wknd nxt, tld off whn pld up bef 7th.*...............(50 to 1 op 33 to 1) pu

1493⁵ ROSEHALL 5-11-0 (3") G Hogan, *chsd ldrs, lost pl 6th, tld off whn pld up bef nxt.*.......(14 to 1 op 8 to 1 tchd 16 to 1) pu
Dist: 10l, 6l, 2l, 2l, 12l, dist, nk. 5m 3.40s. a 18.40s (10 Ran).
(Konvekta Ltd), O Sherwood

1928 Temple Grafton Novices' Handicap Hurdle Class D (0-105 4-y-o and up) £2,999 2m 3f................(3:30)

1722⁶ LETS BE FRANK [95] 5-11-4 R Johnson, *trkd ldrs, led appr 2 out, drvn out.*......(6 to 5 fav op 5 to 4 tchd 11 to 10) 1

1614² THE CAPTAIN'S WISH [108] 5-11-12 (5") Mr R Thornton, *hld up, pushed alng and hdwy appr 5th, ev ch approaching 2 out, kpt on und pres frm last.*...(5 to 2 op 3 to 1 tchd 4 to 1) 2

1261* ALWAYS GREENER (Ire) [79] 5-10-2 S Curran, *led 3rd till appr 2 out, kpt on one pace und pres.*
................................(12 to 1 op 10 to 1 tchd 14 to 1) 3

1646⁵ SMART LORD [86] 5-10-9 M Bosley, *beh, effrt 3 out, styd on, nvr on terms.*...................(16 to 1 op 10 to 1) 4

1642⁴ EVEZIO RUFO [87] (v) 4-10-10 J R Kavanagh, *cl up, ev ch 3 out, sn wknd.*.............(10 to 1 op 7 to 1 tchd 11 to 1) 5

1625⁷ SWEET TRENTINO (Ire) [82] 5-10-5 W Marston, *beh, mstk 4th, styd on frm 2 out.*..................(25 to 1 op 16 to 1) 6

1477⁸ RED LIGHT [82] (bl) 4-10-5 G Bradley, *in tch, hdwy 5th, wknd appr 3 out.*...............(12 to 1 op 10 to 1 tchd 14 to 1) 7

1716 NOT TO PANIC (Ire) [77] 6-10-0 N Williamson, *al beh, btn whn blun 6th.*...................(13 to 1 op 25 to 1) 8

1515⁵ BLUE AND ROYAL (Ire) [84] 4-10-7 C Llewellyn, *hld up beh ldrs, wknd appr 5th.*.............(33 to 1 op 25 to 1) 9

1543⁴ POSITIVO [77] 5-10-0 D Leahy, *rdn alng 4th, al beh.*
................................(12 to 1 op 8 to 1) 10

1669⁹ BECKY'S GIRL [77] 6-10-0 P Holley, *led to 3rd, wknd quickly appr 5th.*.................(33 to 1 tchd 50 to 1) 11

1295 MR GORDON BENNETT [77] 5-9-7 (7") X Aizpuru, *pld hrd, beh frm 5th, pulled up bef 2 out.*.................(33 to 1) pu

SLEAZEY [77] 5-10-0 J Osborne, *trkd ldrs till wknd 6th, beh whn pld up bef 2 out.*.........(25 to 1 op 20 to 1) pu
Dist: 1l, ¾l, 4l, 10l, 1¾l, 2½l, ¾l, 8l, 6l, 7l. 4m 31.50s. (13 Ran).
(Mrs M M Stobart), Noel T Chance

MUSSELBURGH (firm)
Tuesday December 17th
Going Correction: MINUS 0.30 sec. per fur. (races 1,3,5,7), MINUS 0.15 (2,4,6)

1929 Table Maiden Hurdle Class E (4-y-o and up) £2,263 2½m..........(12:20)

INVEST WISELY 4-11-5 R Garritty, *sn disputing ld, led 8th, blun tenth, hdd 2 out, rallied und pres aftr last to lead cl hme.*
..................(6 to 5 on op Evens tchd 5 to 4 on) 1

1496² SMOLENSK (Ire) 4-11-5 M Moloney, *trkd ldrs, led 2 out, rdn aftr last, ct cl hme.*........(6 to 5 op Evens tchd 5 to 4) 2

1656⁹ NIZAAL (USA) 5-10-12 (7") S Melrose, *in tch, hit 7th, hdwy aftr tenth, wknd after 2 out.*...........(16 to 1 op 14 to 1) 3

1783 CELTIC COMMA 5-11-0 T Reed, *led till hdd 8th, wknd quickly aftr tenth.*..........................(66 to 1 op 50 to 1) 4

1657 SUPER GUY 4-11-5 A Dobbin, *dsptd ld early, lost tch frm hfwy.*..................................(33 to 1 op 33 to 1) 5

1656 ROYAL PALM 4-11-5 K Jones, *lost tch hfwy, tld off.*
..................................(66 to 1 op 50 to 1) 6
Dist: Nk, 18l, 20l, 3l, dist. 4m 47.10s. a 9.10s (6 Ran).
(A G Chappell), M D Hammond

1930 Bathing Coach Novices' Chase Class E (5-y-o and up) £2,831 3m ....(12:50)

1788² HEDDON HAUGH (Ire) 8-10-12 R Supple, *led 4th till hdd four out, rdn to ld ag'n fnl 50 yards.*
.....................(30 to 1 op 3 to 1 tchd 7 to 2) 1

1828⁶ FINGERHILL (Ire) 7-10-12 Mr M Thompson, *jmpd lft, in tch, hdwy aftr 12th, led 4 out, hdd and no extr fnl 50 yards.* (7 to 1) 2

1820 MISS LAMPLIGHT 6-10-7 A Dobbin, *hld up, hdwy aftr 12th, ev ch 2 out, rdn and no extr appr last.*...(7 to 1 op 6 to 1) 3

1788⁴ OVERWHELM (Ire) 8-11-2 K Jones, *in tch, wkng whn blun badly 3 out.*..................(5 to 1 tchd 9 to 2) 4

1681⁶ THE ENERGISER 10-10-12 J Burke, *hld up, hdwy aftr 12th, wknd bef 4 out.*....................(20 to 1 op 16 to 1) 5

36 ESTABLISH (Ire) 8-10-7 K Johnson, *prmnt, outpcd aftr 14th, staying on whn blun and uns rdr 4 out.*(16 to 1 op 10 to 1) ur

1681⁴ CORPORAL KIRKWOOD (Ire) 6-10-12 P Niven, *led till mstk 4th, mistake 9th, prmnt whn blun and uns rdr 11th.*
....................(3 to 1 fav tchd 7 to 2 and 4 to 1) ur

1587⁸ MISTER CASUAL 7-10-12 T Reed, *al beh, lost tch frm 13th, tld off whn pld up lme r-in.* (8 to 1 op 7 to 1 tchd 9 to 1) pu
Dist: ½l, 3l, 18l, 9l. 6m 5.70s. a 16.70s (8 Ran).
(I D Cheesbrough), P Cheesbrough

1931 Sea Hole Selling Handicap Hurdle Class G (0-95 4-y-o and up) £2,083 2m..........................(1:20)

1676⁴ TRIENNIUM (USA) [79] 7-11-13 A Dobbin, *in tch, steady hdwy to ld 2 out, kpt on wl.*
..................(11 to 10 on 11 to 10 tchd 5 to 4) 1

1693 SECONDS AWAY [53] 5-9-12 (3") G Lee, *hld up, hdwy aftr 6th, chsd wnr frm after 2 out, no imprsn.*...(7 to 1 op 5 to 1) 2

1693 CATTON LADY [52] 6-9-7 (7") B Grattan, *in tch, drvn alng bef 2 out, kpt on frm betw last two.*.......(16 to 1 op 12 to 1) 3

1736 TROY'S DREAM [67] 5-11-1 R Garritty, *hld up, hdwy bef 6th, ch 2 out, kpt on same pace.*..................(25 to 1) 4

SCHOOL OF SCIENCE [58] 6-10-6 S McDougall, *mid-div, kpt on same pace frm 3 out.*.........................(25 to 1) 5

1556⁷ GREEK GOLD (Ire) [54] 7-10-2 R Marley, *sn tracking ldr, led 6th, hdd 2 out, wknd quickly.*.......(5 to 1 tchd 6 to 1) 6

1693 DARK MIDNIGHT (Ire) [58] (bl) 7-10-6³ J Burke, *beh most of way.*..(33 to 1) 7

1786⁶ BARIK (Ire) [62] 6-10-10 B Storey, *led till hdd 6th, sn wknd.*
....................(12 to 1 op 14 to 1) 8

1783⁴ MISS MONT [53] 7-10-1 G Cahill, *prmnt whn blun and uns rdr 3rd.*.......................(12 to 1 op 8 to 1) ur
Dist: 3l, 1l, 1½l, 4l, 11l, 1¾l, 11l. 3m 40.40s. a 3.40s (9 Ran).
SR: 17/-/-/-/-/ (M C Boyd), P Monteith

1932 Musselburgh Links Handicap Chase Class D (0-120 5-y-o and up) £3,485 2½m..........................(1:50)

1389⁴ MONTRAVE [99] 7-11-3 A Dobbin, *hld up, hdwy to track ldrs 11th, led 4 out, styd on wl.*..................(5 to 2 op 4 to 1) 1

1785³ PURITAN (Can) [110] (bl) 7-12-0 Miss P Jones, *nvr far away, ev ch whn blun 2 out, styd on und pres frm last.*
....................(7 to 2 op 3 to 1 tchd 4 to 1) 2

1785² PAGLIACCIO [99] 8-11-3 R Garritty, *dsptd ld, led 7th till mstk and hdd 4 out, blun nxt, no dngr aftr.*
.....................(9 to 4 fav op 5 to 2 tchd 3 to 1) 3

1822⁷ RISKY DEE [85] 7-10-3³ K Jones, *beh, drvn alng bef 4 out, hit 2 out, kpt on same pace.*
.......................(66 to 1 op 33 to 1 tchd 100 to 1) 4

1285³ CROSS CANNON [110] 10-12-0 T Reed, *hld up, took clr order hfwy, wknd bef 4 out.* (5 to 1 op 9 to 2 tchd 6 to 1) 5

1785* CHARMING GALE [101] (v) 9-11-0 (5*,6ex) G F Ryan, *led to 7th, dsptd ld till wknd bef 3 out.*........(7 to 2 op 5 to 2) 6
Dist: ¾l, 6l, 6l, 1¾l, 4l. 4m 54.60s. a 7.60s (6 Ran).
(D St Clair), P Monteith

1933 Gas Handicap Hurdle Class D (0-125 4-y-o and up) £2,705 3m......(2:20)

1691⁵ SUPERTOP [105] 8-11-5 R Garritty, *hld up, took clr order 9th, led on bit aftr 2 out, pushed out.*.......(5 to 2 op 7 to 4) 1

1819⁴ D'ARBLAY STREET (Ire) [86] (bl) 7-10-0 S McDougall, *led till hdd aftr 2 out, kpt on, no ch wth wnr.*
....................(4 to 1 op 5 to 1 tchd 6 to 1) 2

1661⁶ TALLYWAGGER [114] 9-11-7 (7") T Hogg, *chsd ldr till lost pl bef 8th, in tch, kpt on same pace frm 2 out.*
.....................(2 to 1 fav op 7 to 4 tchd 9 to 4) 3

1372* LATIN LEADER [86] (bl) 6-10-0 D Parker, *hld up, drvn alng aftr tenth, wknd bef 2 out, tld off.*....(9 to 4 tchd 5 to 2) 4
Dist: 9l, 1¼l, dist. 5m 39.10s. a 2.10s (4 Ran).
(G A Arthur), L Lungo

1934 Hole Across Handicap Chase Class F (0-95 5-y-o and up) £2,734 2m (2:50)

1007² CARDENDEN (Ire) [68] 8-10-1 B Storey, *led till hdd 2 out, led ag'n aftr last, drvn out...* (5 to 2 op 9 to 4 tchd 11 to 4) 1

1786⁵ RAPID MOVER [91] (bl) 9-11-10 M Moloney, *sn tracking wnr, chlgd 4 out, slight ld 2 out till hdd aftr last, no extr.*
....................................(4 to 1 op 3 to 1) 2

1808² JUDICIAL FIELD (Ire) [95] (bl) 7-12-0 R Garritty, *hld up, blun 8th, rdn aftr 3 out, no imprsn on 1st 2.*
....................(11 to 10 fav op 6 to 5 tchd 11 to 8) 3

1327⁵ FLASH OF REALM (Fr) [95] 10-11-7 (7") I Jardine, *jmpd slwly, sn beh, tld off.*..................(8 to 1 op 4 to 1) 4
Dist: ½l, 6l, 13l. 3m 54.80s. a 5.80s (4 Ran).
SR: –/13/11/–/ (Kinneston Farmers), J Barclay

1935 Short Hole Standard Open National Hunt Flat Class H (4,5,6-y-o) £1,070 2m..........................(3:20)

1789* CARLISLE BANDITO'S (Ire) 4-11-11 M Moloney, *hld up, hdwy on bit to ld o'r one furlong out, shaken up and quickened clr.* ....(6 to 4 op 5 to 4) 1
795* SIOUX WARRIOR 4-11-8 (3*) E Husband, *led till hdd o'r one furlong out, no extr.*.......(7 to 2 op 3 to 1 tchd 4 to 1) 2
1682^{4} NUTTY SOLERA 6-11-11 B Storey, *trkd ldr, pushed alng o'r 2 fs out, fdd.*.................(5 to 4 fav tchd 11 to 8) 3
1682 SALEM BEACH 4-10-13 P Niven, *keen early, hld up, wknd 3 fs out.*..............................(20 to 1 op 14 to 1) 4
Dist: 6l, nk, 10l. 3m 38.00s. (4 Ran).
(Mrs J M Berry), J Berry

FOLKESTONE (good to soft (races 1,5,7), good (2,3,4,6))
Tuesday December 17th
Going Correction: PLUS 1.45 sec. per fur. (races 1,3,5,7), PLUS 1.10 (2,4,6)

1936 Levy Board Handicap Hurdle Class E (0-110 4-y-o and up) £2,259 2m 1f 110yds......................(12:30)

1606^{5} ZINGIBAR [78] 4-10-6 N Williamson, *made all, quickened 3 out, drvn clr appr last, kpt on.* ....(5 to 1 op 4 to 1 tchd 11 to 2) 1
1733* WAYFARERS WAY (USA) [96] 5-11-10 M A Fitzgerald, *hld up, prog to track wnr 2 out, rdn and not quicken appr last, wknd r-in.*............(Evens fav op 5 to 4 tchd 11 to 10 on) 2
1803^{2} FONTANAYS (Ire) [93] 8-11-7 D Bridgwater, *trkd wnr till rdn and outpcd 2 out, kpt on ag'n r-in.*.......(11 to 2 op 5 to 2) 3
1722^{4} AUGUST TWELFTH [86] 8-11-0 C Llewellyn, *wtd wth, outpcd and mstk 3 out, sn rdn and struggling.* ....(3 to 1 tchd 7 to 2 and 11 to 4) 4
Dist: 8l, 1l, 16l. 4m 29.40s. a 32.40s (4 Ran).
SR: 8/18/14/-/ (D Holpin), J M Bradley

1937 Heathfield Handicap Chase Class E (0-110 5-y-o and up) £3,590 3¼m ....(1:00)

1602^{3} BALLY CLOVER [107] 9-11-12 N Williamson, *trkd ldrs, mstks tenth and 13th, led 15th, clr 3 out, hrd rdn nxt, all out.* ....(7 to 4 fav op 2 to 1) 1
855^{5} BANNTOWN BILL (Ire) [90] (v) 7-10-9 C Maude, *led till jmpd slwly second, wth ldrs aftr, ev ch 15th, hrd rdn and not quicken nxt, styd on r-in.*......................(20 to 1 op 12 to 1) 2
1799^{4} GLEN MIRAGE [93] 11-10-12 Miss M Coombe, *jmpd lft, hld up, prog 11th, ev ch 15th, not quicken, kpt on one pace.* ....(9 to 1 op 6 to 1 tchd 10 to 1) 3
1814 CREDON [103] (v) 8-11-8 R Dunwoody, *wtd wth, mstk 6th, rdn and outpcd 4 out, kpt on frm 2 out.* ....(15 to 2 op 5 to 1 tchd 8 to 1) 4
1626^{4} DIAMOND FORT [109] 11-12-0 B Powell, *hld up, prog 11th, rdn and lost tch 13th, sn tld off, styd on ag'n frm 2 out.* ....(4 to 1 op 9 to 4) 5
1726 MR INVADER [99] 9-11-4 C Llewellyn, *wth ldr till rdn and wknd 15th, tld off.*...............(8 to 1 tchd 10 to 1) 6
1674 SORBIERE [95] (bl) 9-11-0 M A Fitzgerald, *in tch, mstk 5th and reminder, 6th whn f 9th.*............... (12 to 1 op 6 to 1) f
1845^{5} JOKER JACK [81] 11-9-13^{2} (3*) T Dascombe, *sn pushed alng, rdn and wknd 8th, tld off and pld up aftr 12th.* ....(40 to 1 op 16 to 1 tchd 50 to 1) pu
51 VICAR OF BRAY [90] 9-10-9 B Clifford, *lost tch rpdly 7th, tld off and pld up bef nxt.*.................. (20 to 1 op 8 to 1) pu
1801 KING'S COURTIER (Ire) [81] (v) 7-10-0 N Mann, *keen hold, led second to 15th, wknd rpdly, tld off and pld up bef 2 out.* ....(40 to 1 op 20 to 1 tchd 50 to 1) pu
Dist: 2½l, 3½l, 1¼l, 10l, dist. 7m 2.10s. a 47.10s (10 Ran).
(James Williams), Miss Venetia Williams

1938 Sellindge Handicap Hurdle Class F (0-105 4-y-o and up) £2,156 2¾m 110yds......................(1:30)

1747* AINSI SOIT IL (Fr) [94] (bl) 5-11-11 D Bridgwater, *trkd ldrs, led 2 out, hrd rdn and jnd last, styd on gmely r-in.* ....(7 to 2 tchd 4 to 1) 1
1566^{3} RARE SPREAD (Ire) [75] 6-10-6 C Maude, *wtd wth, steady prog 7th, jnd wnr on bit last, rdn and not run on.* ....(13 to 2 op 6 to 1 tchd 8 to 1) 2
1545 ROSKEEN BRIDGE (Ire) [69] 5-10-0 M Richards, *prmnt till rdn and outpcd 3 out, kpt on ag'n appr last.* ....(25 to 1 tchd 33 to 1) 3
1766 SUMMER HAVEN [70] 7-10-1 Mr A Kinane, *led aftr 1st till 2 out, rdn and no extr.*...............(25 to 1 tchd 33 to 1) 4
1747 LETS GO NOW (Ire) [69] 6-9-9 (5*) Sophie Mitchell, *wl beh till kpt on aftr 2 out, no dngr.*...........(100 to 1 op 50 to 1) 5
1592^{5} DREAM LEADER (Ire) [96] 6-11-13 J Railton, *led till aftr 1st, prmnt till hrd rdn 3 out, sn btn.*..........(6 to 1 op 4 to 1) 6
1816^{5} RAAHIN (USA) [85] 11-11-2 M Bosley, *in tch till wknd 6th, wl beh nxt.*........(25 to 1 op 20 to 1 tchd 33 to 1) 7
1593^{8} ITS GRAND [74] 7-10-5 R Johnson, *prmnt to 6th, sn rdn and struggling.*.........................(10 to 1 op 10 to 1) 8
1061^{8} SCRIPT [73] 5-9-11 (7*) N T Egan, *wtd wth in rear, rdn and no prog aftr 7th.*..........(25 to 1 op 20 to 1 tchd 33 to 1) 9
1492^{2} BRIGHT SAPPHIRE [75] 10-10-6 D J Burchell, *cl up till wknd 3 out.*..............(9 to 1 op 7 to 1 tchd 10 to 1) 10
1848^{5} DURSHAN (USA) [72] (bl) 7-10-3 J Osborne, *wtd wth, prog to press ldrs aftr 6th, wknd rpdly 3 out.* ....(10 to 1 op 7 to 1 tchd 11 to 1) 11
SWEETLY DISPOSED (Ire) [97] 8-11-7 (7*) T C Murphy, *strted very slwly, wl beh till cld up 6th, sn wknd, tld off whn f 3 out.* ....(20 to 1 op 12 to 1) f
1815^{6} EQUITY'S DARLING (Ire) [79] 4-10-10 C Llewellyn, *reluctant to race, tld off till brght dwn 3 out.* ....(20 to 1 op 12 to 1 tchd 25 to 1) bd
1540^{3} EL FREDDIE [90] 6-11-7 G Upton, *mid-div, rdn and lost pl rpdly 5th, tld off and pld up bef 7th.* ....(3 to 1 fav op 5 to 2 tchd 100 to 30) pu
Dist: 4l, 4l, 6l, 2½l, 10l, 2l, 1¾l, 14l, 4l, 13l. 5m 56.40s. a 46.40s (14 Ran).
(A-Men Partnership), G M McCourt

1939 Bet With The Tote Novices' Chase Qualifier Class E (5-y-o and up) £4,175 2m 5f................(2:00)

MELNIK 5-10-12 C Maude, *trkd ldr, led 2 out, shaken up appr last, ran on wl.*.........(9 to 1 op 6 to 1 tchd 10 to 1) 1
CONQUERING LEADER (Ire) 7-10-7 M A Fitzgerald, *trkd ldrs, effrt to chase wnr aftr 2 out, ev ch last, unbl to quicken.* ...(11 to 10 on op Evens tchd 11 to 10 and 5 to 4 on) 2
SIR LEONARD (Ire) 6-10-12 J Osborne, *led to 2 out, styd on one pace aftr.*..............................(5 to 1 op 5 to 2) 3
233* SLEETMORE GALE (Ire) 6-10-7 N Williamson, *hld up, prog 9th, blun nxt, cl up till wknd 2 out.* ....(16 to 1 op 10 to 1 tchd 20 to 1) 4
1233^{4} GIVUS A CALL (Ire) 6-10-12 P Hide, *hld up, in tch in rear whn hmpd tenth, nvr nr to chal aftr.* ....(12 to 1 op 8 to 1 tchd 14 to 1) 5
1600^{2} JOVIAL MAN (Ire) 7-10-12 D Bridgwater, *hld up, outpcd 11th, rdn and effrt aftr 3 out, 4th and staying on one pace whn blun badly last, not reco'r.*.......(4 to 1 op 5 to 1 tchd 7 to 1) 6
NIGHT FANCY 8-10-12 P McLoughlin, *prmnt till wknd rpdly aftr 3 out.*..........................(100 to 1 op 50 to 1) 7
1718 SHERIFFMUIR 7-10-9 (3*) G Hogan, *prmnt, wkng whn mstk tenth, sn tld off.*........(16 to 1 op 10 to 1 tchd 20 to 1) 8
1733 CAREY'S COTTAGE (Ire) 6-10-12 L Harvey, *al rear, rdn and wknd 9th, sn tld off.*...................(100 to 1 op 50 to 1) 9
LIFT AND LOAD (USA) 9-10-9 (3*) L Aspell, *rear, prog and in tch 9th, wknd 11th, tld off and pld up bef 2 out, dismounted.* ....(66 to 1 op 20 to 1 tchd 100 to 1) pu
Dist: 1¼l, 5l, 12l, 3l, 3l, 21l, 17l, 13l. 5m 39.70s. a 28.70s (10 Ran).
SR: 28/21/21/4/6/3/ (Peter Wiegand), Mrs A J Perrett

1940 Lympne Novices' Hurdle Class E (4-y-o and up) £2,805 2½m 110yds ....(2:30)

ROUGH QUEST 10-10-12 M A Fitzgerald, *hld up beh, prog 6th, sn chlgd on bit whn mistake last, rdn and quickened to ld nr finish.*.....(5 to 1 op 3 to 1 tchd 11 to 2) 1
DESTIN D'ESTRUVAL (Fr) 5-10-12 D Bridgwater, *trkd ldrs, led gng easily 2 out, rdn appr last, styd on wl, hdd nr finish.* ....(11 to 4 co-fav op 5 to 2 tchd 3 to 1) 2
1642^{2} ROYAL EVENT 5-10-12 R Dunwoody, *prmnt, led 6th till 2 out, wknd appr last.*..............(11 to 4 co-fav op 3 to 1) 3
1338^{7} SAFEGLIDE (Ire) 6-10-12 P Hide, *mstk 1st, prmnt till outpcd aftr 5th, rnwd effrt 3 out, wknd appr last.* ....(11 to 1 op 6 to 1 tchd 12 to 1) 4
1727^{6} FLAXLEY WOOD 5-10-12 B Powell, *sn wl beh, rdn and effrt aftr 7th, nvr rch ldrs.*................ (33 to 1 op 20 to 1) 5
1181* DANZANTE (Ire) 4-10-7 (5*) Mr R Thornton, *sn wl beh, rdn aftr 5th, nvr on terms.*...............(20 to 1 op 14 to 1) 6
1810 KYBO'S REVENGE (Ire) 5-10-12 D O'Sullivan, *mstks, sn wl beh, brief effrt aftr 7th, soon wknd.* ....(50 to 1 op 20 to 1 tchd 66 to 1) 7
1763^{8} DINGLE WOOD (Ire) 6-10-12 Mr A Kinane, *prmnt, led appr 5th till mstk and hdd nxt, wknd 3 out, tld off.* ....(16 to 1 tchd 20 to 1) 8
1502^{2} CAPTAIN JACK (bl) 6-10-12 R Hughes, *prmnt till hrd rdn and wknd aftr 6th, tld off and pld up bef 2 out.* ......(11 to 4 co-fav op 9 to 4 tchd 3 to 1) pu
SULLAMELL 5-10-5 (7*) J Harris, *clr ldr till wknd rpdly and hdd appr 5th, tld off and pld up bef 6th.* ....(33 to 1 tchd 40 to 1) pu
PETT LAD 8-10-12 M Richards, *al wl beh, tld off and pld up bef 6th.*.........................(50 to 1 tchd 100 to 1) pu
1623 NOQUITA (NZ) 9-10-12 J R Kavanagh, *mstks, al beh, tld off and pld up bef 6th.*.....(40 to 1 op 33 to 1 tchd 50 to 1) pu
1727^{7} MASTER BOMBER (Ire) 5-10-12 J Osborne, *chsd ldg grp till lost tch and eased aftr 6th, tld off and pld up bef last.* ....(50 to 1 op 25 to 1) pu
OVER THE WATER (Ire) 4-10-9 (3*) P Henley, *sn wl beh, effrt aftr 7th, nvr on terms, tld off and pld up bef last.* ....(20 to 1 tchd 5 to 1) pu
Dist: ½l, 25l, 5l, 10l, 8l, hd, dist. 5m 12.90s. a 37.90s (14 Ran).
SR: 2/1/-/-/-/-/ (A T A Wates), T Casey

1941 Shaddoxhurst Conditional Jockeys' Handicap Chase Class F (0-100 5-y-

o and up) £2,710 2m......... (3:00)

1595⁷ PEGMARINE (USA) [79] 4-11-7 G Hogan, *hld up beh, steady prog 8th, effrt to ld aftr 2 out, pushed out.*
.... (13 to 2 op 7 to 1 tchd 8 to 1) 1

1207⁵ SOLEIL DANCER (Ire) [84] 8-11-12 P Henley, *hld up, prog 8th, hrd rdn 3 out, styd on to chase wnr last, kpt on und pres.*
.... (11 to 1 op 8 to 1 tchd 12 to 1) 2

1730² FICHU (USA) [79] 8-11-4 (3*) M Clinton, *hld up in tch, chsd ldr 5th, led appr 2 out, mstk two out, sn hdd and wknd.*
.... (15 to 8 fav op 7 to 4 tchd 2 to 1) 3

1448 CRUISE CONTROL [81] 10-11-6 (3*) A Garrity, *strted slwly, wl beh, tld off 9th, ran on 2 out, nvr nrr.*
.... (20 to 1 op 8 to 1 tchd 33 to 1) 4

1704⁴ SHALIK (Ire) [76] 6-11-4 (3*) N T Egan, *clr ldr till wknd rpdly and hdd appr 2 out.*....... (7 to 1 op 9 to 2 tchd 8 to 1) 5

1446* DAWN CHANCE [79] 10-11-7 T Dascombe, *jmpd lft, chsd ldr to 5th, wknd aftr 7th, tld off.*
.... (5 to 1 op 2 to 2 tchd 11 to 2) 6

1698² WILLIE MAKEIT (Ire) [83] 6-11-11 Martin Smith, *uns rdr 1st.*
.... (7 to 2 op 9 to 4) ur

Dist: 1½l, 9l, ½l, 16l, dist. 4m 19.90s. a 28.90s (7 Ran).

(Mrs Ann Woodrow), Mrs A M Woodrow

1942 Weatherbys 'Stars Of Tomorrow' Open National Hunt Flat Standard - Class H (4,5,6-y-o) £1,322 2m 1f 110yds...................... (3:30)

GUIDO (Ire) 5-11-4 N Williamson, *hld up beh, prog hfwy, trkd ldr gng easily 3 fs out, shaken up to ln one out, drvn out and held on wl.*........... (12 to 1 op 16 to 1 tchd 20 to 1) 1

984* BROWNES HILL LAD (Ire) 4-12-0 D Bridgwater, *led, hrd rdn and hdd one furlong out, rallied gmely, jst hld.*
.... (4 to 1 tchd 9 to 2) 2

1483 MIKE'S MUSIC (Ire) 5-11-1 (3*) G Hogan, *keen hold, hld up in tch, effrt 3 fs out, sn rdn and btn.*
.... (20 to 1 op 25 to 1 tchd 33 to 1) 3

1560² SUPREME TROGLODYTE (Ire) 4-10-13 J R Kavanagh, *al prmnt, rdn and btn wl o'r 2 fs out.*
.... (3 to 1 fav tchd 7 to 2 and 11 to 4) 4

HURRICANE JANE (Ire) 4-10-13 J Railton, *rear of main grp, gd prog to press ldrs o'r 4 fs out, rdn and btn 3 out.* (33 to 1) 5

1214⁵ JAYDEEBEE 5-10-13 G Upton, *prmnt, chsd ldr 5 fs out till 3 out, sn wknd.*........................(25 to 1 op 33 to 1) 6

CHRISTCHURCH (Fr) 6-11-4 Mr Dennis Breen, *rcd wide, in tch till wknd wl o'r 2 fs out.*
.... (40 to 1 op 33 to 1 tchd 50 to 1) 7

BENJI 5-11-4 M A Fitzgerald, *trkd ldrs till wknd o'r 3 fs out, fnshd tired.*............(12 to 1 op 16 to 1 tchd 20 to 1) 8

KILSHEY 5-10-13 P Hide, *hld up, nvr nr to chal.*
.... (33 to 1 op 25 to 1 tchd 10 to 1) 9

ROMAN ACTOR 4-11-4 D O'Sullivan, *al rear, lost tch and beh hfwy.*..................(40 to 1 op 33 to 1 tchd 50 to 1) 10

FULL OF BOUNCE (Ire) 5-11-1 (3*) T Dascombe, *prmnt till rdn and wknd 5 fs out.*...(20 to 1 op 16 to 1 tchd 25 to 1) 11

EUROCHIEF 5-10-13 (5*) Mr R Thornton, *hld up beh, prog aftr 7 fs, rdn and wknd o'r 3 out.*............(33 to 1 op 20 to 1) 12

1675 SPIRIT OF SUCCESS 6-11-4 Mr A Kinane, *prmnt 4 fs, sn wknd, tld off hfwy.*............................(50 to 1) 13

1578⁷ ST MELLION LEISURE 4-11-4 C Maude, *pressed ldr till rdn and wknd 5 fs out.*....(5 to 1 op 5 to 2 tchd 11 to 2) 14

YOUNG MANNY 5-11-4 R Johnson, *al beh, tld off hfwy.*
.... (50 to 1 op 33 to 1) 15

SARAS DELIGHT 4-11-1 (3*) R Massey, *hld up, prog and in tch 7 fs out, sn wknd, tld off.* (4 to 1 op 2 to 1 tchd 9 to 2) 16

COLONEL JACK 4-10-11 (7*) J Harris, *hld up, al beh, tld off hfwy.*.....................(33 to 1 tchd 50 to 1) 17

Dist: Nk, 19l, ½l, 2l, 5l, 9l, 11l, ½l, 7l, 2l. 4m 26.00s. (17 Ran).

(T Pompsett), Miss Venetia Williams

BANGOR (good)
Wednesday December 18th
Going Correction: PLUS 1.05 sec. per fur. (races 1,3,5,7), PLUS 1.70 (2,4,6)

1943 Maesfen Novices' Selling Hurdle Class G (3,4,5-y-o) £2,088 2m 1f .... (12:30)

D'NAAN (Ire) (bl) 3-10-5 A P McCoy, *made all, clr frm 4th, styd on strly to remain clear frm betw last 2.*
.... (13 to 8 fav op 9 to 4 tchd 6 to 4) 1

1731² LIME STREET BLUES (Ire) (bl) 5-11-5 G Bradley, *wl plcd wth chasing grp, effrt and drvn alng frm 3 out, styd on from betw last 2, not rch wnr.*...............(11 to 4 op 2 to 1) 2

1832⁴ FASTINI GOLD (bl) 4-11-5 W McFarland, *settled wth chasing grp, improved and pres appr 3 out, kpt on, nvr able to chal.*
.... (10 to 1 tchd 9 to 1) 3

1731⁸ SMILEY FACE 4-10-12 (7*) J Harris, *beh whn blun 4th, styd on und pres frm 3 out, nvr able to rch chalg pos.......(33 to 1) 4

ANALOGICAL 3-10-0 S Wynne, *in tch in midield, struggling to go pace hfwy, nvr a factor, eased whn btn 3 out.* (33 to 1) 5

1438⁶ ADMIRAL'S GUEST (Ire) 4-11-5 R Farrant, *settled wth chasing grp, und pres to keep in tch sn aftr hfwy, nvr a threat.*
.... (33 to 1 op 25 to 1) 6

1205 SPITFIRE BRIDGE (Ire) 4-10-12 (7*) R Hobson, *sn struggling in rear, tld off frm hfwy.*......................(33 to 1) 7

1629 RATTLE (bl) 3-10-0 (5*) R McGrath, *settled in midfield, effrt hfwy, blun 3 out and last, sn lost tch, tld off.*
.... (5 to 1 op 4 to 1 tchd 11 to 2) 8

1136² NIGHT BOAT 5-11-5 T Eley, *al wl beh, tld off frm hfwy.*
.... (8 to 1 op 7 to 1) 9

1749 MISS THE BEAT 4-10-11 (3*) E Husband, *sn struggling in rear, tld off frm hfwy.*....................(50 to 1) 10

1179 CHILLINGTON (bl) 3-10-5 C Llewellyn, *drvn alng wth chasing grp, hit 3rd, lost tch quickly frm hfwy, tld off.......(33 to 1) 11

NAFERTITI (Ire) 4-11-0 S Curran, *al wl beh, tld off most of way.*
.... (25 to 1 op 20 to 1 tchd 33 to 1) 12

PERSIAN DAWN 3-10-0 R Johnson, *lost tch quickly bef hfwy, tld off whn pld up before 2 out......(20 to 1 tchd 25 to 1) pu

991 INDIAN WOLF (v) 3-10-5 I Lawrence, *wl plcd wth chasing grp till wknd rpdly 4th, tld off whn pld up aftr nxt......* (33 to 1) pu

Dist: 4l, 11l, 11l, 4l, hd, sht-hd, 3l, 13l, 3l, dist. 4m 15.80s. a 25.80s (14 Ran).

SR: -/8/-/-/-/-/ *(Mrs P B Browne), M C Pipe*

1944 St. Helens Ford Novices' Chase Class D (5-y-o and up) £4,357 2½m 110yds...................... (1:00)

1347² AROUND THE GALE (Ire) 5-11-6 R Dunwoody, *al wl plcd, led tenth, lft well clr 5 out, eased r-in.* (4 to 1 op 6 to 4 on) 1

1545 BAYLINE STAR (Ire) 6-11-0 G Bradley, *settled in tch, feeling pace hfwy, styd on und pres to take second nring finish.*
.... (14 to 1 op 8 to 1) 2

1636 GARNWIN (Ire) 6-11-0 J R Kavanagh, *trkd ldrs, lost pl appr hfwy, rallied und pres 3 out, one pace r-in.*
.... (10 to 1 op 12 to 1) 3

DECYBORG (Fr) 5-11-6 A P McCoy, *tried to make all, hdd tenth, lft poor second 5 out, wknd quickly frm 2 out, tld off.*
.... (8 to 1 op 6 to 1 tchd 10 to 1) 4

1630⁴ CHIPPED OUT 6-11-0 C Llewellyn, *settled in tch, drvn alng struggling hfwy, tld off aftr........* (8 to 1 tchd 9 to 1) 5

1670⁵ MACGEORGE (Ire) 6-11-0 R Johnson, *nvr far away, chalg and cl second whn f 5 out.*
.... (14 to 1 op 10 to 1 tchd 16 to 1) f

1608 NAUGHTY FUTURE 7-11-6 A Roche, *not jump wl, al well beh, tld off whn pld up aftr 4th, lme.*
.... (10 to 1 op 7 to 1 tchd 12 to 1) pu

VALLEY GARDEN 6-11-0 N Williamson, *sn beh, struggling hfwy, tld off whn pld up bef 2 out.......*(20 to 1 op 12 to 1) pu

Dist: 8l, 2l, 27l, dist. 5m 27.30s. a 41.30s (8 Ran).

SR: 27/13/11/-/-/ *(T J Whitley), D R Gandolfo*

1945 Astbury Wren Handicap Hurdle Class B (0-140 4-y-o and up) £4,765 3m........................ (1:30)

1105² FREDDIE MUCK [120] 6-11-0 C Llewellyn, *nvr far away, led bef 2 out, quickened clr betw last two, eased r-in, easily.*
.... (3 to 1 fav op 9 to 4 tchd 100 to 30) 1

1576 YES MAN (Ire) [110] 7-10-4 R Johnson, *tried to make all, hrd pressed 3 out, sn hdd, styd on same pace, no ch wth wnr.*
.... (8 to 1 op 6 to 1) 2

1644⁶ SUN SURFER (Fr) [134] 8-12-0 S Wynne, *settled to track ldrs, effrt whn hit 4 out, rallied frm betw last 2, one pace r-in.*
.... (5 to 1 op 7 to 2 tchd 11 to 2) 3

1576* GENERAL TONIC [109] 9-10-3 R Dunwoody, *tucked away beh ldrs, ev ch 4 out, drvn alng betw last 2, styd on towards finish.*................(100 to 30 op 2 to 1 tchd 7 to 2) 4

1744⁸ LITTLE GUNNER [112] 6-10-6 D Gallagher, *last and hld up, effrt fnl circuit, und pres frm 4 out, no imprsn on ldrs.*
.... (20 to 1 op 12 to 1 tchd 25 to 1) 5

NAHTHEN LAD (Ire) [130] 7-11-10 N Williamson, *settled to track ldrs, niggled alng fnl circuit, reminder 8th, sn btn, eased frm 2 out.....................*(7 to 2 op 5 to 1 tchd 9 to 2) 6

969² CALL MY GUEST (Ire) [125] 6-11-5 A P McCoy, *took keen hold, wth ldr till wknd quickly 4 out, tld off frm 3 out.* (14 to 1 op 10 to 1) 7

Dist: 3½l, 4l, ½l, 10l, 8l, 1½l. 6m 0.60s. a 31.60s (7 Ran).

SR: 22/8/28/2/-/5/-/ *(Cheltenham Racing Ltd), N A Twiston-Davies*

1946 Chalie Richards Malt Whisky Handicap Chase Class E (0-115 5-y-o and up) £4,162 4m 1f............. (2:00)

1739⁵ PENNINE PRIDE [91] (v) 9-10-1 N Williamson, *al frnt rnk, made most frm 9th, hit 7 out, styd on grimly to go clr frm betw last 2.*............................ (5 to 1 op 4 to 1) 1

1674⁴ GLENFINN PRINCESS [96] 8-10-6 Derek Byrne, *settled off the pace, gd hdwy fnl circuit, rdn and determined chal frm 3 out, kpt on one pace from betw last 2.*
.... (10 to 1 op 12 to 1 tchd 8 to 1) 2

1645³ STOP THE WALLER (Ire) [114] 7-11-5 (5*) Mr R Thornton, *wth ldrs, led 3rd till hdd 9th, styd hndy, struggling 3 out, no imprsn aftr..................................* (6 to 1) 3

1687⁶ SHAMARPHIL [90] 10-10-0 Miss S Barraclough, *settled to track ldrs, struggling to go pace fnl circuit, rallied, one pace frm 3 out.*..........................(20 to 1 op 16 to 1) 4

253

1739 HOLY STING (Ire) [95] (bl) 7-10-5 C Llewellyn, *led till jmpd rght and hdd 3rd, styd hndy, rdn aftr 4 out, lost tch, tld off.*
..................................(11 to 4 fav op 7 to 2) 5

1674⁵ LEINTHALL PRINCESS [90] 10-9-13³ (3*) G Hogan, *beh thrght, tld off whn hmpd by faller 5 out, l 3 out......* (33 to 1) f

1701⁴ KEEP IT ZIPPED (Ire) [99] (bl) 6-10-9 J A McCarthy, *settled midfield, hdwy fnl circuit, struggling and no imprsn whn f 5 out..................................* (10 to 1 op 8 to 1) f

1726² ROCKY PARK [95] 10-10-5 A P McCoy, *jmpd rght most of way, improved hfwy, midfield whn blun and uns rdr 6teenth.
..................................* (4 to 1 op 7 to 2) ur

1645⁴ DESPERATE [95] 8-10-5 M Richards, *chsd ldrs, feeling pace and lost grnd hfwy, rallied fnl circuit, struggling and pld up quickly aftr 4 out..................................* (7 to 1 op 10 to 1) pu

1632⁴ FRONT LINE [112] 9-11-8 M Moloney, *settled in tch, struggling fnl circuit, wl beh whn hmpd by faller 5 out, pld up bef nxt..................................* (12 to 1 op 10 to 1) pu

Dist: 7l, 18l, 1¼l, 24l. 9m 5.30s. a 65.30s (10 Ran).

(Mrs W A Beaumont), M D Hammond

1947
Red Coat Conditional Jockeys' Handicap Hurdle Class F (0-100 4-y-o and up) £2,640 2m 1f....... (2:30)

1835² KINTAVI [82] 6-10-13 G Hogan, *patiently rdn, improved 3 out, led bef nxt, drw clr betw last 2, readily.
..................................* (2 to 1 fav op 5 to 2 tchd 7 to 4) 1

1798² GLOWING PATH [87] 6-11-1 (3*) J Harris, *nvr far away, ev ch 3 out, rdn and one pace frm betw last 2, no imprsn.
..................................* (5 to 2 op 2 to 1) 2

1733⁴ COUNTRY MINSTREL (Ire) [76] 5-10-7 D Fortt, *al wl plcd, ev ch appr 3 out, one pace frm betw last 2.* (12 to 1 op 10 to 1) 3

1835⁵ KADARI [92] (v) 7-11-9 Guy Lewis, *al hndy, dsptd ld frm hfwy, led 3 out, hdd bef nxt, sn rdn and outpcd.
..................................* (12 to 1 tchd 14 to 1) 4

1798⁷ BIYA (Ire) [73] 4-10-4 D Walsh, *settled in tch, feeling pace and drvn alng bef 4 out, kpt on, not pace of ldrs.
..................................* (33 to 1 op 20 to 1) 5

1798³ SCHNOZZLE (Ire) [89] 5-11-6 R Massey, *last and beh, styd on und pres frm 3 out, nvr rchd chalg pos...* (5 to 1 op 7 to 2) 6

SHEEP STEALER [87] 8-11-4 Michael Brennan, *led, jnd hfwy, mstk 5th, reminder nxt, hdd 3 out, sn lost tch, tld off.
..................................* (14 to 1 op 12 to 1) 7

NEVER SO BLUE (Ire) [93] 5-11-10 D J Kavanagh, *chsd ldrs, struggling frm hfwy, tld off.
..................................* (16 to 1 op 14 to 1) 8

1796 TANGO MAN (Ire) [69] 4-10-0 T Dascombe, *in tch, struggling to go pace bef 4 out, sn lost touch, tld off.
..................................* (50 to 1 op 33 to 1) 9

1835 ALASKAN HEIR [85] 5-11-2 L Aspell, *swrvd and lost grnd strt, struggling frm hfwy, tld off.
..................................* (14 to 1 tchd 20 to 1) 10

Dist: 7l, 5l, 6l, 3½l, 10l, 10l, 1l, 3½l, 2½l. 4m 14.80s. a 24.80s (10 Ran).
SR: 15/13/-/7/-/-/

(S Taberner), T W Donnelly

1948
Clwyd Handicap Chase Class D (0-120 5-y-o and up) £4,065 2½m 110yds..................... (3:00)

1569³ DISTINCTIVE (Ire) [96] 7-10-9 C Llewellyn, *led, jnd and pckd 2 out, sn hdd, rdn and looking hld whn lft in ld last styd on wl r-in, eased finish..........* (5 to 1 op 9 to 2 tchd 11 to 2) 1

1544* FOOLS ERRAND (Ire) [115] 6-12-0 A P McCoy, *nvr far away, hit 6th, jmpd slwly 9th, hmpd by faller last, styd on one pace r-in..................................* (7 to 1 op 3 to 1) 2

1767² REALLY A RASCAL [106] 9-11-5 R Dunwoody, *patiently rdn, gd hdwy hfwy, ridden aftr 3 out, one pace frm betw last 2.
..................................* (11 to 4 fav tchd 3 to 1 and 5 to 2) 3

1316³ SOLBA (USA) [110] 7-11-9 B Storey, *settled in tch to chaser ldrs, und pres whn pace quickened frm 4 out, sn lost tch.
..................................* (9 to 2 op 7 to 2) 4

988² MINE'S AN ACE (NZ) [95] 9-10-8 N Williamson, *pressed ldr, struggling and lost grnd 4 out, 6th and wl btn whn f nxt.
..................................* (13 to 2 op 8 to 1) f

1730* SISTER ROSZA (Ire) [96] 8-10-9 R Farrant, *patiently rdn, smooth hdwy to go hndy frm hfwy, led aftr 2 out, two ls clr and gng wl whn f last..........* (11 to 1 op 8 to 1 tchd 12 to 1) f

1468⁴ POTATO MAN [100] 10-10-13 R Johnson, *wl plcd early, mstk 5th and nxt 2, lost tch frm hfwy, tld off whn pld up aftr 3 out.
..................................* (20 to 1) pu

DOLIKOS [98] 9-10-11 T Eley, *in tch, lost pl quickly whn pace increased hfwy, tld off whn pld up bef 3 out.
..................................* (40 to 1 op 33 to 1) pu

Dist: 4l, 2½l, 12l. 5m 30.20s. a 44.20s (8 Ran).
SR: -/2/-/-/-/

(Jeremy Hancock), M J Wilkinson

1949
Yellow Collar Intermediate Open National Hunt Flat Class H (4,5,6-y-o) £1,658 2m 1f............. (3:30)

1357 SCORING PEDIGREE (Ire) 4-11-4 S Curran, *al gng wl, led o'r 6 fs out, quickened clr, readily......* (5 to 4 fav op 5 to 2) 1

1142⁴ CALLINDOE (Ire) 6-10-13 N Williamson, *settled in midfield, improved to chase wnr in ins, no imprsn.
..................................* (7 to 1 tchd 8 to 1) 2

CHASING THE MOON (Ire) 4-11-4 A P McCoy, *patiently rdn, improved bef strt, styd on one pace in staight, no imprsn.
..................................* (9 to 2 op 5 to 2 tchd 5 to 1) 3

GOWER-SLAVE 4-11-4 R Johnson, *wth ldrs thrght, und pres whn pace quickened bef strt, one pace aftr.
..................................* (15 to 2 op 5 to 1) 4

THE EENS 4-11-1 (3*) D Walsh, *nvr far away, effrt und pres aftr a m, outpcd in strt, no imprsn aftr..........* (33 to 1) 5

MAGGIE STRAIT 4-10-6 (7*) Mr O McPhail, *settled off the pace, effrt hfwy, und pres bef strt, nvr dngrs.
..................................* (20 to 1 op 14 to 1) 6

1648⁸ MISTRESS TUDOR 5-10-10 (3*) E Husband, *tucked away on ins, struggling and lost tch.......* (33 to 1) 7

1648⁴ THE CROPPY BOY 4-11-1 (3*) T Dascombe, *led early, styd hndy till tld and pres appr strt........* (12 to 1 op 10 to 1) 8

917 WATER FONT (Ire) 4-11-4 A Roche, *wl plcd in frnt rnk till lost pl quickly bef nxt, no further dngr......* (12 to 1 op 9 to 1) 9

DANCING RANGER 5-11-4 T Eley, *co'red up on ins, feeling pace, no imprsn on ldrs last 2 fs..........* (50 to 1) 10

1357* MIDAS 5-11-11 R Dunwoody, *al frnt rnk, short lived effrt bef strt, sn struggling and lost tch.........* (6 to 1 op 4 to 1) 11

JUST ANDY 5-11-4 T Jenks, *settled midfield, feeling pace aftr a m, sn lost tch, tld off..........* (50 to 1 op 33 to 1) 12

1514 CASHEL QUAY (Ire) 6-11-1 (3*) Guy Lewis, *wtd wth, effrt hfwy, nvr dngrs, tld off..........* (100 to 1 op 66 to 1) 13

1142 GLENDRONACH 4-10-13 Gary Lyons, *an led, hdd o'r 6 fs out, lost tch quickly, tld off..........* (66 to 1 op 50 to 1) 14

Dist: 7l, 8l, 3½l, 4l, nk, ½l, 6l, 6l, nk, 3½l. 4m 18.10s. (14 Ran).
(Seamus Mullins), J W Mullins

CATTERICK (good)
Wednesday December 18th
Going Correction: PLUS 0.60 sec. per fur.

1950
Glebe Novices' Chase Class E (5-y-o and up) £3,042 2m.......... (12:50)

1527² MONYMAN (Ire) 6-11-5 R Garritty, *in tch, effrt aftr 3 out, rdn to ld last, styd on wl....* (11 to 8 fav op 6 to 4 tchd 7 to 4) 1

1523* TWIN FALLS (Ire) 5-11-5 J Callaghan, *trkd ldrs, led 8th, hdd last, no extr und pres..................* (3 to 1 op 5 to 2) 2

1741⁴ FENWICK'S BROTHER 6-10-12 Richard Guest, *beh, lost tch aftr 8th, hdwy bef 2 out, kpt on same pace frm last.
..................................* (14 to 1 op 10 to 1) 3

1806² AMBER VALLEY (USA) 5-10-12 P Holley, *led till hdd 8th, wknd quickly aftr 2 out, tld off..........* (2 to 1 op 13 to 8) 4

1691⁹ FRIENDLY KNIGHT 6-10-12 T Reed, *prmnt, ev ch whn f 3 out.
..................................* (40 to 1 op 33 to 1) f

1259⁷ GONE ASHORE (Ire) 5-10-7 (5*) S Taylor, *blun and uns rdr 1st.
..................................* (50 to 1 op 100 to 1) ur

Dist: 5l, 4l, 14l. (Time not taken) (6 Ran).

(Trevor Hemmings), M D Hammond

1951
Catterick Club 1997 'Join Up Now' Amateur Riders' Handicap Hurdle Class F (0-100 4-y-o and up) £2,120 2m 3f........................ (1:20)

1691⁶ FRYUP SATELLITE [79] 5-10-2 (5*) Miss P Robson, *in tch, hdwy hfwy, led 2 out, hrd pressed frm last, all out.
..................................* (9 to 2 op 5 to 2) 1

1827⁴ DUKE OF PERTH [90] 5-10-13 (5*) Miss P Jones, *trkd ldrs, chlgd last, dsptd ld till no extr aftr last.* (9 to 2 op 3 to 1) 2

1708* FAWLEY FLYER [91] 7-10-12 (7*) Mr E Babington, *led to second, led bef 6th till hdd 2 out, styd on wl frm last.
..................................* (5 to 1 op 4 to 1) 3

1824⁷ FLAT TOP [95] 5-11-2 (7*) Mr M Watson, *in tch, outpcd aftr 7th, hdwy whn mstk 2 out, styd on wl frm last.* (6 to 1 op 7 to 1) 4

HIGH PENHOWE [75] 8-10-0 (3*) Mr C Bonner, *beh, outpcd aftr 7th, no dngr after, tld off..........* (6 to 1 op 4 to 1) 5

1442⁹ CULLIN CAPER [75] 4-9-10 (7*) Miss R Clark, *chsd ldrs, ev ch 3 out, sn wknd, tld off..........* (50 to 1) 6

1775 SKI PATH [72] 7-9-11⁴ (7*) Mr P Murray, *sn beh, tld off.
..................................* (50 to 1) 7

1764⁹ GYMCRAK SOVEREIGN [84] 8-10-5 (7*) Miss C Evans, *led second till bef 6th, sn wknd, tld off..........* (25 to 1) 8

1787⁴ RUBISLAW [72] 4-9-7 (7*) Miss S Lamb, *al beh, tld off.
..................................* (200 to 1 op 100 to 1) 9

1372² TALL MEASURE [86] (bl) 10-10-13⁶ (7*) Mr D Swindlehurst, *beh whn f 4th..................* (12 to 1 op 8 to 1) f

1691³ SUDDEN SPIN [100] 6-11-9 (5*) Mr M H Naughton, *in tch whn f 6th..................................* (9 to 4 fav op 5 to 2) f

Dist: Hd, hd, ½l, dist, 16l, dist. 4m 46.00s. a 26.00s (11 Ran).

(John Lees), Mrs J Brown

1952
Good Luck Paul Alster Novices' Chase Class E (5-y-o and up) £3,179 3m 1f 110yds................ (1:50)

1706 GEMS LAD 9-11-5 Richard Guest, *made most frm 3rd till hdd 12th, rdn to chal whn mstk last, swtchd r-in, styd on wl to ld post..................................* (9 to 1 op 4 to 1) 1

1681 TICO GOLD 8-10-12 A S Smith, *in tch, blun 12th and 14th, gd hdwy to ld 3 out, mstk last, sn rdn, ct post.* (3 to 1 op 4 to 1) 2

1681² SHAWWELL 9-10-12 K Johnson, *led to 3rd, cl up, lft in ld 14th, mstk and hdd 3 out, sn wknd*.......(3 to 1 op 9 to 4) 3
1820⁷ CLONROCHE LUCKY (Ire) 6-10-12 K Jones, *blun second, lost tch aftr 11th, tld off*........................(33 to 1) 4
DORLIN CASTLE 8-10-12 T Reed, *hld up, gd hdwy to ld 12th, f 14th*..............................(7 to 4 fav op 11 to 10) f
1820 BROOMHILL DUKER (Ire) 6-10-12 A Dobbin, *tld off frm 9th, pld up bef 12th*......................(16 to 1 op 12 to 1) pu
Dist: Hd, 22l, 26l. 6m 49.30s. a 34.30s (6 Ran).

(Miss J Wood), Mrs S J Smith

1953 Raffyard House Selling Hurdle Class G (4,5,6-y-o) £1,943 2m 3f.... (2:20)

1604⁷ TIRMIZI (USA) 5-11-5 J Supple, *in tch, reminder aftr 4th, gd hdwy to ld bef 2 out, styd on wl.*
............(7 to 1 op 6 to 1 tchd 8 to 1 and 10 to 1) 1
1574 FURIETTO (Ire) 6-11-5 R Garritty, *trkd ldrs, led 3 out, hdd bef nxt, no extr....(2 to 1 on op 6 to 4 on tchd 11 to 8 on)* 2
1693⁶ HEAVENS ABOVE 4-10-12 K Whelan, *trkd ldrs, ev ch 3 out, kpt on same pace frm nxt.*............(25 to 1 op 10 to 1) 3
1736⁵ IN A MOMENT (USA) 5-11-5 J Callaghan, *in tch, outpcd aftr 7th, kpt on und pres frm 2 out.*
....................(14 to 1 op 10 to 1 tchd 20 to 1) 4
1824 COOL STEEL (Ire) 4-10-12 A Dobbin, *made most till hdd 3 out, wknd bef nxt.*................(20 to 1 op 14 to 1) 5
1691⁴ ANORAK (USA) 6-10-12 (7ᵉ) N Hannity, *mstks, led 4th to 5th, wknd aftr 7th.*....................(5 to 1 tchd 4 to 1) 6
1662⁸ NENAGH GUNNER 6-10-7 Richard Guest, *hld up, hdwy aftr 7th, lost pl aftr 3 out, tld off.*................(20 to 1) 7
1695⁴ ROBERT THE BRAVE 4-10-9 (3ᵉ) E Callaghan, *beh, lost tch frm 7th, tld off*........(25 to 1 op 16 to 1 tchd 33 to 1) 8
1826⁷ MEESONETTE (v) 4-10-7 A S Smith, *sn lost tch, tld off whn pld up bef 3 out.*..................(16 to 1 op 33 to 1) pu
1742⁸ PHAR ENOUGH (Ire) 4-10-12 P Niven, *prmnt to hfwy, sn wknd, tld off whn pld up bef 2 out.*
....................(20 to 1 op 10 to 1 tchd 25 to 1) pu
Dist: 5l, 5l, 7l, 6l, ½l, 26l, 20l. 4m 49.50s. a 29.50s (10 Ran).

(S Smith), Mrs A Swinbank

1954 Boville Handicap Chase Class F (0-105 4-y-o and up) £2,786 2m 3f .... (2:50)

1766 TIM SOLDIER (Fr) [79] 9-10-10 R Supple, *trkd ldrs, led 2 out, styd on wl.*...................(25 to 1 op 14 to 1) 1
1822 KARENASTINO [69] 5-10-0 Mr P Murray, *led, mstk 12th, hdd 2 out, no extr und pres.*...............(33 to 1 op 14 to 1) 2
1821¹² REBEL KING [90] 6-11-2 (5ᵉ) S Taylor, *nvr far away, ch 3 out, sn rdn, kpt on same pace.*.................(5 to 2 tchd 3 to 1) 3
1785⁶ THE TOASTER [97] 9-12-0 A C Smith, *in tch, ch 3 out, sn drvn aing, fdd.*.......................(9 to 2 tchd 5 to 1) 4
1822² JUKE BOX BILLY (Ire) [86] 8-11-3 A Dobbin, *in tch till wknd aftr 3 out.*.......................(7 to 4 fav tchd 2 to 1) 5
37 FUNNY OLD GAME [78] 9-10-9 K Johnson, *hld up, f 11th.*.................(20 to 1 op 12 to 1) f
1912 SHOW YOUR HAND (Ire) [77] 8-10-8 M Foster, *lost tch frm 7th, tld off whn pld up bef 2 out.*..(7 to 2 op 5 to 2) pu
Dist: 5l, ½l, 5l, 9l. 5m 0.90s. a 30.90s (7 Ran).

(Ken Dale), M F Barraclough

1955 Hutton Wandesley Novices' Handicap Hurdle Class F (0-95 4-y-o and up) £2,138 2m............ (3:20)

1522⁴ LAST TRY (Ire) [92] 5-12-0 A S Smith, *prmnt, led 3 out, ran on und pres frm last, all out.*............(4 to 1 op 3 to 1) 1
1586⁵ ENVIRONMENTAL LAW [67] (bl) 5-10-3 A Dobbin, *chsd ldrs, rdn to chal last, ev ch till no extr und pres cl hme.*
........................(11 to 2 op 10 to 1) 2
1737³ HIGHLY CHARMING (Ire) [84] 4-10-13 (7ᵉ) Mr A Wintle, *in tch, hdwy bef 3 out, rdn ch before nxt, kpt on same pace.*
......................(20 to 1 op 14 to 1) 3
1826⁵ SIMAND [74] 4-10-3 (7ᵉ) N Hannity, *beh, styd on frm 2 out, nvr nr to chal.*....................(20 to 1 op 14 to 1) 4
1872³ PAST MASTER (USA) [86] 8-11-8 K Gaule, *chsd ldrs till wknd bef 2 out.*......................(14 to 1 op 12 to 1 tchd 16 to 1) 5
1220⁶ RANGER SLOANE [75] 4-10-4 (7ᵉ) S Lycett, *in tch, drvn aing aftr 4th, one pace frm nxt.*..(25 to 1 op 16 to 1) 6
1823³ BOWCLIFFE [81] 5-11-3 M Foster, *mid-div, outpcd aftr 3 out, no dngr after.*.....(14 to 1 op 12 to 1 tchd 16 to 1) 7
1657⁸ DR EDGAR [80] 4-11-2 R Supple, *led till hdd 3 out, wknd appr nxt.*....................(16 to 1 op 12 to 1 tchd 16 to 1) 8
MAPLE BAY (Ire) [70] 7-10-3 (3ᵉ) Mr C Bonner, *hld up, some hdwy whn blun 2 out, no ch after.*
....................(15 to 2 op 9 to 2 tchd 8 to 1) 9
1125⁶ JONAEM (Ire) [80] 6-11-2 K Johnson, *nvr better than mid-div.*......................(16 to 1 op 14 to 1) 10
1729⁶ MY SHENANDOAH (Ire) [68] 5-10-4 V Slattery, *wl beh frm 4th.*........................(16 to 1 op 12 to 1 tchd 20 to 1) 11
1676⁷ APPEARANCE MONEY (Ire) [78] 5-10-7 (7ᵉ) Miss Elizabeth Doyle, *mid-div till wknd bef 3 out.*
..................(12 to 1 op 16 to 1 tchd 20 to 1) 12
1646 AYDISUN [64] 4-10-0 D Morris, *nvr better than mid-div, beh whn stumbled badly 2 out, tld off, swallowed tongue.*
....................(5 to 1 tchd 4 to 1) 13

1657 JARROW [65] 5-10-1 J Supple, *towards rear whn f 4th.*
......................(66 to 1 op 50 to 1) f
Dist: Hd, 6l, 2½l, hd, 2l, 1l, 15l, 1¼l, 4l, 2½l. 3m 57.80s. a 17.80s (14 Ran).
SR: 18/-/4/-/3/-/ (H J Harenberg), B S Rothwell

EXETER (soft)
Wednesday December 18th
Going Correction: PLUS 1.80 sec. per fur. (races 1,3,4,6), PLUS 1.45 (2,5)

1956 Gemini Radio Claiming Hurdle Class F (4,5,6-y-o) £2,102 2¼m.... (12:40)

1325* TOP SKIPPER (Ire) 4-10-7 (7ᵉ) Mr J Tizzard, *trkd ldrs, led aftr 3 out, styd on wl.*..................(12 to 1 op 8 to 1) 1
1705³ PETER MONAMY (bl) 4-11-3 C Maude, *prmnt, trkd ldrs gng wl 3 out, rdn and one pace frm nxt.*
....................(2 to 1 on op 5 to 2 on) 2
1574⁴ FORTUNES ROSE (Ire) 4-10-0 T J Murphy, *prmnt, rdn frm 5th, styd on und pres from 2 out.*
....................(20 to 1 op 12 to 1 tchd 33 to 1) 3
1858⁷ KHATIR (Can) (bl) 5-11-3 C O'Dwyer, *in tch, chlgd 3rd, led nxt, hdd aftr 3 out, btn next.*............(5 to 1 tchd 6 to 1) 4
BORJITO (Spa) 5-11-12 B Fenton, *wl beh till moderate hdwy aproaching 2 out.*....(25 to 1 op 20 to 1 tchd 33 to 1) 5
1574 NORFOLK GLORY 4-10-5 Mr A Holdsworth, *beh whn uns rdr second.*....................(66 to 1 op 33 to 1) ur
1604 MY HARVINSKI 6-10-5 M A Fitzgerald, *al beh, tld off whn pld up bef 2 out.*..................(14 to 1 op 8 to 1) pu
1000 ALLAHRAKHA 5-11-6 S Fox, *led to 4th, sn wknd, tld off whn pld up bef 2 out.*..................(14 to 1 op 8 to 1) pu
1813³ ROBIN ISLAND (bl) 4-9-12 (7ᵉ) M Clinton, *prmnt to 4th, tld off whn pld up bef 2 out.*.....(66 to 1 op 33 to 1) pu
Dist: 5l, 6l, nk, hd. 4m 42.30s. a 43.30s (9 Ran).

(V G Greenway), V G Greenway

1957 Childcraft Novices' Chase Class D (4-y-o and up) £4,958 2¼m... (1:10)

1287 GROOVING (Ire) 7-11-2 P Hide, *hdwy to chase 4th out, str run frm last to ld fnl strds...(7 to 2 op 9 to 2 tchd 5 to 1)* 1
1636⁴ COURT MASTER (Ire) 8-11-2 B Powell, *led, clr 4 out, rdn r-in, ct last strds.*............(11 to 1 op 10 to 1 tchd 14 to 1) 2
DANTE'S VIEW (USA) 8-11-2 D O'Sullivan, *mid-div, hdwy frm 3 out, styd on r-in.*...(50 to 1 op 25 to 1 tchd 66 to 1) 3
1448⁴ TELLICHERRY 7-10-11 J Osborne, *sn in tch, no hdwy frm 4 out.*......................(16 to 1 op 10 to 1) 4
DODGY DEALER (Ire) 6-11-2 C O'Dwyer, *chsd ldrs to 4 out, sn wknd.*....................(6 to 2 op 25 to 1) 5
BOOTS N ALL (Ire) 6-11-2 B Clifford, *chsd ldrs till mstk and wknd 6th.*................(40 to 1 op 20 to 1 tchd 50 to 1) 6
1667² JOSIFINA 5-10-11 A Thornton, *prmnt to 6th, sn wknd.*
......................(20 to 1 op 10 to 1) 7
1557² REESHLOCH 7-11-2 S McNeill, *in tch 5th, rdn nxt, tld off whn brght dwn 3 out.*......(12 to 1 op 6 to 1 tchd 14 to 1) bd
BULLANGUERO (Ire) 7-11-2 G Tormey, *tld off whn pld up bef 2 out.*......................(100 to 1 op 50 to 1) pu
KIMANICKY (Ire) 6-11-2 M A Fitzgerald, *hdwy 6th, tld off whn pld up bef 2 out.*...(6 to 4 fav tchd 11 to 8 and 7 to 4) pu
UNCLE ALGY 7-11-2 T J Murphy, *wth ldr to 3rd, tld off whn pld up bef 2 out....(25 to 1 op 14 to 1 tchd 33 to 1)* pu
1653⁴ CASTLEKELLYLEADER (Ire) 7-11-2 C Maude, *prmnt to 6th, tld off whn pld up bef 2 out.*(4 to 1 op 5 to 2 tchd 9 to 2) pu
Dist: Hd, 11l, 15l, 29l, ¾l, 3l. 4m 42.60s. a 32.60s (12 Ran).
SR: 23/23/12/-/-/-/ (Mrs T Brown), J T Gifford

1958 Henrietta Knight 50th Birthday Novices' Handicap Hurdle Class D (0-105 4-y-o and up) £3,129 2¼m .... (1:40)

1452⁶ COOL GUNNER [73] 6-10-0 C Maude, *in tch, chsd ldr 3 out, chlgd nxt, sn led, ran on wl.*
....................(8 to 1 tchd 10 to 1 and 7 to 1) 1
1749² SUPREME GENOTIN (Ire) [97] 7-11-10 G Upton, *led till hdd sn aftr 2 out, soon one pace.......*(6 to 4 fav tchd 7 to 4) 2
1543⁶ WINNOW [75] 6-10-2 L Harvey, *in tch, chsd ldrs appr 2 out, sn one pace.*....................(10 to 1 op 4 to 1) 3
TUDOR TOWN [77] 8-10-4⁴ S Burrough, *beh till ran on appr 2 out, kpt on r-in.*...............(7 to 1 op 6 to 1) 4
1573⁷ BLAZING MIRACLE [73] 4-9-11² (5ᵉ) D Salter, *prmnt, rdn 5th, nvr dngrs aftr.*....................(7 to 1 op 6 to 1) 5
1496⁶ ABOVE THE CUT (USA) [88] 4-11-1 A Maguire, *hdwy 5th, chsd ldrs 3 out, wknd appr nxt.*.........(6 to 1 op 7 to 2) 6
1683² TAP SHOES (Ire) [73] 6-10-0 B Powell, *sn beh, tld off.*
....................(7 to 2 op 4 to 1 tchd 9 to 2) 7
1749 PRINCE OF PREY [73] 8-10-0 S McNeill, *prmnt, chlgd 3rd to nxt, wknd 5th, tld off...(33 to 1 op 20 to 1 tchd 50 to 1)* 8
Dist: 6l, 3½l, 3½l, nk, dist, 1¾l, dist. 4m 38.60s. a 39.60s (8 Ran).
SR: -/18/-/-/-/ (Richard Peterson), J S King

1959 Scottish Equitable / Jockeys Association Handicap Hurdle Qualifier Class C (0-130 5-y-o and up) £3,590

2¼m...................... (2:10)

1379 EDGEMOOR PRINCE [96] 5-10-0 A Maguire, chlgd 3rd till led
5th, drvn out r-in................(4 to 1 op 5 to 2) 1
SPRING SAINT [107] 7-10-11 C Upton, hld up, hdwy 4th,
pressed ldrs nxt, rdn frm 2 out, not quicken r-in.
.....................(5 to 1 op 11 to 2 tchd 6 to 1) 2
BELL ONE (USA) [106] 7-10-10 S McNeill, sn chasing ldrs,
rdn and one pace frm 2 out.....(100 to 30 tav op 6 to 1) 3
1762³ KHALIDI (Ire) [113] 7-10-12 (5*) Sophie Mitchell, prmnt till
mstk second and lost pl, rallied frm 2 but no dngr.
..........................(4 to 1 op 3 to 1 tchd 9 to 2) 4
1603* ROAD TO AU BON (USA) [96] 8-10-0 B Powell, led to 5th,
wknd 3 out.....................(16 to 1 op 12 to 1) 5
SLEW MAN (Fr) [120] 5-11-10 C Maude, hdwy to press ldrs
3rd to 5th, sn wknd...............(11 to 2 op 3 to 1) 6
DECIDE YOURSELF (Ire) [102] 7-6-10-11 M A Fitzgerald, hld
up, effrt 4th, wknd 3 out, tld off whn pld up bef last.
...................(7 to 1 op 11 to 2 tchd 15 to 2) pu
Dist: 8l, 15l, 9l, 1¾l. 4m 39.50s. a 40.50s (7 Ran).

(The Racing Hares), P J Hobbs

1960 Edimbourg Handicap Chase Class C
(0-130 5-y-o and up) £4,867 2m 7f
110yds...................... (2:40)

FULL OF FIRE [111] 9-10-11 C O'Dwyer, hld up, steady hdwy
frm 4 out chlgd last, drvn to ld nr finish.
.....................(6 to 1 op 5 to 1 tchd 13 to 2) 1
1401* SHINING LIGHT [106] 7-10-6 A Maguire, hdwy 9th, chsd
ldr frm 13th, chlgd 2 out till led r-in, hdd nr finish.
.........................(2 to 1 fav op 11 to 8) 2
1212⁴ OATIS REGRETS [128] 8-12-0 J Osborne, led, clr appr 4 out,
drvn and not fluent frm 3 fences, hdd and wknd r-in.
...................(7 to 2 op 3 to 1 tchd 4 to 1) 3
SUNLEY BAY [123] 10-11-9 P Hide, in tch, mstk 6th, wknd 4
out.......................(8 to 1 tchd 12 to 1) 4
1453³ DOM SAMOURAI (Fr) [117] (bl) 5-11-3 C Maude, chsd ldr to
13th, wknd 3 out.
.........(7 to 2 op 4 to 1 tchd 9 to 2 and 100 to 30) 5
1602³ DUHALLOW LODGE [113] 9-10-13 B Fenton, in tch till wknd 8th,
wknd 12th, tld off whn pld up bef last...(12 to 1 op 6 to 1) pu
MASTER JOLSON [105] 8-10-5 M A Fitzgerald, prmnt till hit
9th, mstk and lost pl nxt, tld off whn pld up bef 2 out.
.......................(14 to 1 op 10 to 1 tchd 16 to 1) pu
Dist: 1½l, 9l, 10l, 1l. 6m 24.90s. a 50.90s (7 Ran).

(J Michael Gillow), K C Bailey

1961 Hoechst Roussel Panacur European
Breeders Fund Mares Only 'National
Hunt' Novices' Hurdle Qualifier (4-
y-o and up) £3,631 2m 3f 110yds
.... (3:10)

1591² RIVER BAY (Ire) 5-10-10 B Fenton,
......................(9 to 4 op 3 to 1 tchd 2 to 1) 1
FIDDLING THE FACTS (Ire) 5-10-10 M A Fitzgerald,
.....................(5 to 1 op 5 to 2 tchd 6 to 1) 2
1545 MOONLIGHTER 6-10-5 (5*) O Burrows, ...(100 to 1) 3
1570* GAYE FAME 5-11-3 C O'Dwyer, ...(2 to 1 fav op 5 to 4) 4
1594⁷ O MY LOVE 5-10-10 J Osborne, ...(20 to 1 op 14 to 1) 5
COUNTRY STYLE 7-10-7 (3*) P Henley,
..........................(33 to 1 op 25 to 1) 6
1792 GINGER MAID 8-10-3 (7*) G Supple, (100 to 1 op 33 to 1) 7
HALF MOON GIRL 4-10-10 Mr A Holdsworth,
..........................(100 to 1 op 66 to 1) 8
1578⁹ VANSELL 5-10-10 B Powell, ...(40 to 1 op 33 to 1) 9
BROWN WREN 5-10-10 G Tormey, ..(20 to 1 op 16 to 1) 10
COUNTRY TOWN 6-10-10 S McNeill,
..........................(100 to 1 op 66 to 1) 11
BONITA BLAKENEY 6-10-10 B Clifford,
.........................(50 to 1 op 33 to 1) 12
1685 ZEN OR 5-10-3 (7*) David Turner, ...(100 to 1) 13
1214 PHARMOREFUN (Ire) 4-10-10 T J Murphy,
.........................(50 to 1 op 33 to 1) 14
1727 LILLY THE FILLY 5-10-10 R Greene,
.........................(100 to 1 tchd 200 to 1) pu
1560⁴ ROYAL RULER 5-10-10 P Hide, ...(6 to 1 op 9 to 2) pu
1685 DOLCE NOTTE (Ire) 6-10-10 C Maude,
.........................(16 to 1 op 12 to 1) pu
Dist: Nk, 20l, 13l, 14l, 12l, ½l, 12l, 16l, ¾l, 2l. 5m 4.70s. a 43.70s (17 Ran).

(Riverwood Racing), Miss H C Knight

CATTERICK (soft)
Thursday December 19th
Going Correction: PLUS 1.20 sec. per fur. (races
1,3,5,7), PLUS 1.50 (2,4,6)

1962 Picton 'National Hunt' Novices' Hurdle Class E (4-y-o and up) £2,742 2m
3f...................... (12:20)

1656³ KING PIN 4-10-12 R Supple, settled midfield, hdwy aftr 3 out,
led last, easily.........(9 to 4 fav op 5 to 2 tchd 7 to 2) 1

1695* LAGEN BRIDGE (Ire) 7-11-5 D J Moffatt, sn tracking ldr, led
aftr 3 out, hng lft, hdd last, no extr.
......................(3 to 1 op 5 to 2 tchd 100 to 30) 2
MAJOR HARRIS (Ire) 4-10-12 R Garritty, hld up, hdwy hfwy,
chsd 1st 2 frm two out, no imprsn whn blun last and hit rail.
..........................(12 to 1) 3
DON'T TELL TOM (Ire) 6-10-12 K Jones, sn tracking ldrs,
dsptd ld aftr 3 out, fdd frm nxt.................(50 to 1) 4
1371 FILS DE CRESSON (Ire) 6-10-12 M Moloney, trkd ldrs, chlgd
aftr 3 out, fdd frm nxt.....(11 to 2 op 5 to 1 tchd 6 to 1) 5
1695⁵ SILVER MINX 4-10-12 R Hodge, led till hdd aftr 3 out, sn
wknd, tld off.........................(20 to 1 op 16 to 1) 6
1609³ GAZANALI (Ire) 5-10-12 N Bentley, mid-div, ch aftr 3 out, sn
wknd, tld off................(5 to 1 op 4 to 1 tchd 11 to 2) 7
1609⁹ JOE LUKE (Ire) 4-10-12 J Callaghan, al beh, tld off. (33 to 1) 8
654⁵ ETERNAL CITY 5-11-5 A Dobbin, in tch till wknd aftr 7th, tld
off.................................(14 to 1) 9
FORT ZEDDAAN (Ire) 6-10-12 Richard Guest, chsd ldrs till
wknd aftr 3 out, tld off........(33 to 1 op 25 to 1) 10
1631 ELEMENT OF RISK (Ire) 6-10-12 N Smith, chsd ldrs till wknd
aftr 7th, tld off................(16 to 1 op 14 to 1) 11
1631 BLOND MOSS 6-10-9 (3*) G Lee, chsd ldrs, hit 6th, sn wknd,
tld off.........................(100 to 1) 12
1677 EDSTONE (Ire) 4-10-12 B Storey, al beh, tld off....(100 to 1) 13
60 MATACHON 6-10-12 J Supple, chsd ldrs to hfwy, wknd
quickly, tld off.......................(100 to 1) 14
MEESONS EXPRESS 6-10-12 M Foster, tld off whn pld up bef
6th.................................(100 to 1) pu
1521⁴ PHILBECKY 5-10-4 (3*) E Callaghan, beh, lost tch and pld up
bef 7th.........................(50 to 1 op 33 to 1) pu
880³ HUTCEL LOCH 5-10-7 R Johnson, chsd ldrs till wknd bef 3
out, sn lost tch, pld up before 2 out..(12 to 1 op 10 to 1) pu
Dist: 1½l, 11l, 3½l, 4l, 26l, 1¼l, 6l, nk, 14l, ½l. 4m 58.50s. a 38.50s (17 Ran).
(Exors Of The Late Mr J N Hinchliffe), P Beaumont

1963 St Pauls Maiden Chase Class F (5-
y-o and up) £2,561 2m 3f.... (12:50)

1820 BOSWORTH FIELD (Ire) (bl) 8-11-5 M Foster, prmnt, led aftr
7th, styd on wl frm 3 out...................(10 to 1) 1
BRIGADIER JOHN (Ire) 7-11-5 M Moloney, blun 3rd, beh,
hdwy aftr 12th, styd on wl frm 2 out, nrst finish.
.........................(20 to 1 op 16 to 1) 2
1741⁵ FAIR ALLY 6-11-5 D Parker, impd rght, in tch, kpt on same
pace frm 3 out................(7 to 2 op 5 to 1 tchd 4 to 1) 3
1828² CUSH SUPREME (Ire) 7-11-5 R Johnson, prmnt, mstk 7th,
blun 12th, no imprsn on wnr frm 3 out, wknd appr last.
.......................(9 to 4 op 7 to 4 tchd 5 to 2) 4
1828⁸ GRAND AS OWT 6-11-5 K Johnson, chsd ldrs till wknd aftr
12th, tld off.........................(16 to 1) 5
1695 MAKE A BUCK (bl) 6-11-5 Richard Guest, blun 1st, f second.
.........................(16 to 1 op 12 to 1 tchd 20 to 1) f
1881 ROYAL HAND 6-11-5 Mr R Armson, mstk 11th, tld off whn f 3
out.........................(20 to 1 op 16 to 1) f
1741 CARDINAL SINNER (Ire) 6-11-5 K Jones, led, hit 3rd, hdd aftr
7th, wkng whn mstk 9th, tld off when pld up bef 3 out.
..........................(25 to 1 op 20 to 1) pu
1820⁴ SPRINGHILL QUAY (Ire) 7-11-5 A Dobbin, chsd ldrs till outpcd and drpd rear aftr 8th, tld off whn pld up bef 11th.
.........................(2 to 1 fav op 13 to 8) pu
PERIROYAL 6-10-12 (7*) R Wilkinson, beh, reminder aftr 7th,
gd hdwy to go prmnt nxt, f tenth.....(20 to 1 op 16 to 1) pu
Dist: 6l, 5l, 1l, 29l. 5m 12.60s. a 42.60s (10 Ran).
(Mrs Sarah Horner-Harker), Mrs Sarah Horner-Harker

1964 Ampleforth Handicap Hurdle Class F
(0-105 4-y-o and up) £2,065 2m
.... (1:20)

1786² FEN TERRIER [97] 4-11-13 A Dobbin, nvr far away, led bef 2
out, ran on wl, clr last, eased towards finish.
.........................(9 to 4 op 7 to 4 tchd 5 to 2) 1
OPERA FAN (Ire) [83] 4-10-13 A S Smith, pld hrd early, lost
tch aftr 4th, hdwy bef 2 out, chsd wnr appr last, no imprsn.
.........................(4 to 1) 2
1719⁵ I'M A DREAMER (Ire) [98] 6-11-7 (7*) R Wilkinson, trkd ldrs, ev
ch bef 2 out, sn rdn, wknd betw last two.
.........................(7 to 2 op 4 to 1 tchd 9 to 2) 3
1740⁷ FRED'S DELIGHT (Ire) [78] 5-10-8 B Storey, led to second, led
3 out, sn hdd, wknd frm nxt.
.........................(12 to 1 op 10 to 1 tchd 14 to 1) 4
1823² PANGERAN (USA) [84] 4-11-0 J Supple, led second till hdd 3
out, wknd quickly bef nxt, tld off.
.........................(7 to 4 fav op 6 to 4 tchd 15 to 8) 5
Dist: 5l, 10l, ½l, dist. 4m 7.00s. a 27.00s (5 Ran).
SR: 21/2/7/-/-/
(K G Fairbairn), F P Murtagh

1965 Happy Christmas Handicap Chase
Class F (0-105 5-y-o and up) £2,635
2m...................... (1:50)

1950² TWIN FALLS [93] 5-11-6 J Callaghan, in tch, dsptd ld frm
12th, rdn to lead last, all out.
.........................(13 to 8 op 5 to 4 on tchd 7 to 4) 1
1694 PORT IN A STORM [88] 7-10-12 (3*) Mr C Bonner, lft in ld aftr
4th, hrd pressed frm 12th, hdd last, no extr.
.........................(11 to 8 fav op 6 to 4 tchd 7 to 4) 2

1692⁴ POSITIVE ACTION [85] 10-10-7 (5*) S Taylor, *rdn and lost tch aftr 6th, tld off*............(7 2 op 4 to 1 tchd 9 to 2) 3
1912⁵ MONAUGHTY MAN [73] 10-10-0 K Johnson, *led till ran out aftr 4th*........................(12 to 1 tchd 14 to 1) ref
Dist: ¾l, dist. 4m 18.10s. a 31.10s (4 Ran).
SR: 21/15/-/-/   (Mrs Susan Moore), G M Moore

1966 Levy Board Handicap Hurdle Class E (0-115 4-y-o and up) £2,364 3m 1f 110yds...................... (2:20)

1375³ PHARARE (Ire) [93] 6-11-3 A Smith, *made all, quickened appr 2 out, styd on wl*............(1 to 1 fav op 5 to 2) 1
1331³ SMART APPROACH (Ire) [89] 6-10-6 (7*) C McCormack, *in tch, hdwy to chase wnr 2 out, styd on und pres, no imprsn.*
.................................(4 to 1 op 3 to 1) 2
1824⁵ IFALLELSEFAILS [94] 8-11-4 Richard Guest, *hld up, smooth hdwy to dispute ld aftr 3 out, wknd appr nxt.*
.................................(3 to 1 op 9 to 4 tchd 7 to 2) 3
707 MOOBAKKR (USA) [87] 5-10-8 (3*) E Callaghan, *chsd ldrs till wknd bef 2 out*...................... (20 to 1) 4
ABSALOM'S PILLAR [100] 6-11-10 T Eley, *keen early, in tch, mstk 3 out, wknd bef nxt...(9 to 2 op 3 to 1 tchd 5 to 1) 5
DENTICULATA [76] 8-10-0 D Parker, *chsd ldrs till outpcd aftr tenth, sn lost tch*...................(25 to 1) 6
1775 ANCHORENA [78] 4-10-2 A Dobbin, *mstks, lost tch frm tenth, tld off whn pld up bef 2 out*...............(8 to 1) pu
Dist: 1¾l, 19l, 15l, 7l, 2l. 6m 51.60s. a 50.60s (7 Ran).
(C F Colquhoun), R D E Woodhouse

1967 Catterick Club 1997 'Join Up Now' Handicap Chase Class D (0-120 5-y-o and up) £3,595 3m 1f 110yds (2:50)

HEAVENLY CITIZEN (Ire) [89] 8-10-2 B Storey, *led or dsptd ld till hdd 15th, led ag'n 3 out, styd on wl.*
.................................(16 to 1 tchd 14 to 1) 1
1694* KENMORE-SPEED [100] 9-10-13 Richard Guest, *dsptd ld frm 7th till led 15th, hdd 3 out, sn rdn, kpt on same pace.*
.................................(13 to 8 fav op 5 to 4 tchd 11 to 8) 2
1739³ SPARROW HALL [92] 9-10-5 R Johnson, *prmnt, mstk 8th, sn drvn alng, wknd bef 3 out, no ch whn mistake nxt...(9 to 2) 3
1845* DON'T TELL THE WIFE [121] 10-12-1 (5*,6ex) Mr R Thornton, *hld up, mstk 12th (water), wknd bef 3 out. (9 to 2 op 7 to 2) 4
1884 PIMS GUNNER (Ire) [107] 8-11-6 R Garritty, *in tch, rdn aftr 14th, wknd bef 3 out*...........(2 to 1 tchd 7 to 4) 5
1694 MARCHWOOD [98] 9-10-11 T Reed, *hld up, hdwy to track ldrs 12th, ev ch 3 out, 3rd and held whn f last*.....(25 to 1) f
Dist: 8l, 14l, 23l, 4l. 7m 5.10s. a 50.10s (6 Ran).
(J L Gledson), J L Gledson

1968 Garrison Intermediate National Hunt Flat Class H (4,5,6-y-o) £1,343 2m .... (3:20)

POINT REYES (Ire) 4-10-11 (7*) N Horrocks, *mid-div, effrt 3 out, sn rdn, ran on wl und pres to ld post.*
.................................(2 to 1 fav op 5 to 4 tchd 9 to 4) 1
1050² NIFAAF (USA) 4-10-8 (5*) Mr R Thornton, *led 2 fs, cl up, led 6 out, hrd pressed and rdn fnl two furlongs, gt post.*
.................................(10 to 1 op 6 to 1) 2
1390⁸ HARFDECENT 5-11-3 (3*) G Lee, *hdwy aftr 2 fs, hdd 6 out, remained cl up, dsptd ld frm two out, no extr und pres nr finish.*....................(9 to 4 op 5 to 2 tchd 3 to 1) 3
1390⁸ THE STUFFED PUFFIN (Ire) 4-10-11 (7*) I Jardine, *trkd ldrs, ev ch 2 fs out, sn rdn, kpt on wl fnl furlong.*
.................................(10 to 1 op 7 to 1) 4
MONSIEUR DARCY (Ire) 5-11-4 Mr T Storey, *chsd ldrs till wknd 2 fs out*........(20 to 1 op 16 to 1 tchd 25 to 1) 5
BRANDSBY MINSTER 5-10-11 (7*) B Grattan, *in tch, hdwy to track ldrs 6 fs out, wknd 2 out*.......(14 to 1 op 10 to 1) 6
1317 BROOK HOUSE 5-10-6 (7*) C McCormack, *beh, hdwy to chase ldrs 7 fs out, ev ch o'r 2 out, sn wknd.*
.................................(10 to 1 op 50 to 1) 7
1514 DANTES AMOUR (Ire) 5-10-11 (7*) R Burns, *nvr dngrs.*
.................................(25 to 1 op 14 to 1) 8
HUNTING SLANE 4-11-1 (3*) F Leahy, *mid-div, effrt o'r 3 fs sn wknd*............................(50 to 1) 9
1742⁴ PUSH ON POLLY (Ire) 6-10-10 (3*) E Callaghan, *prmnt to hfwy, sn wknd, tld off*.........(10 to 1 op 8 to 1) 10
RECCA (Ire) 4-11-1 (3*) Mr C Bonner, *beh, lost tch fnl 5 fs, tld off*....................(11 to 2 op 4 to 1) 11
1742⁷ MOVISA 6-10-8 (5*) S Taylor, *lost tch aftr 5 fs, tld off.*
.................................(200 to 1) 12
HENBRIG 6-10-10 (3*) G Parkin, *prmnt to hfwy, sn wknd, tld off*...............................(100 to 1) 13
Dist: Sht-hd, sht-hd, ¾l, 6l, 5l, ½l, 1¾l, 2½l, 21l, 6l. 4m 6.50s. (13 Ran).
(I Bray), C W Thornton

TOWCESTER (heavy (races 1,3,5,7), good to soft (2,4,6))
Thursday December 19th
Going Correction: PLUS 1.35 sec. per fur. (races 1,3,5,7), PLUS 1.10 (2,4,6)

1969 Turkey Selling Handicap Hurdle Class G (0-95 4-y-o and up) £2,094 2m................................. (12:40)

1764² AMBIDEXTROUS (Ire) [67] 4-10-5 (7*) L Cummins, *steady hdwy frm 4th, led sn aftr 5th, styd on wl.*
.................................(6 to 1 op 5 to 1 tchd 7 to 1) 1
1540⁹ POLO PONY (Ire) [66] 4-10-4 (7*) G Supple, *slwly into strd, hdwy 5th, styd on to chase wnr r-in but no imprsn.*
.................................(16 to 1 op 20 to 1 tchd 33 to 1) 2
1320 SAYMORE [74] 10-11-5 S Wynne, *hdwy 5th, chsd wnr frm 3 out till wknd r-in*.......(12 to 1 op 7 to 1 tchd 14 to 1) 3
1492* SIR PAGEANT [79] (bl) 7-11-10 D Bridgwater, *beh early, hdwy 5th, no imprsn frm 2 out*........(9 to 1 op 8 to 1) 4
1425² KASHAN (Ire) [64] 8-10-9 B Fenton, *prmnt, led 3rd to nxt, wknd 3 out*..............................(11 to 2 op 5 to 1) 5
1811² SLIGHTLY SPECIAL (Ire) [59] 4-10-4 T J Murphy, *prmnt, led 4th to nxt, wknd 3 out*...(15 to 8 fav op 7 to 4 tchd 2 to 1) 6
1843⁴ RUTH'S GAMBLE [57] (v) 8-10-2 D Leahy, *hdwy 4th, wknd 3 out*......................(12 to 1 op 10 to 1 tchd 14 to 1) 7
WICKENS ONE [69] 6-11-0 N Williamson, *al beh.*
.................................(16 to 1 op 25 to 1) 8
1697² LANESRA BREEZE [71] 4-11-2 C Maude, *nvr better than mid-div*.....................(14 to 1 op 7 to 1 tchd 16 to 1) 9
1110⁷ ANTIGUAN FLYER [68] 7-10-13 W Marston, *in tch, led and mstk 5th, sn hdd and wknd.*
.................................(25 to 1 op 14 to 1 tchd 33 to 1) 10
1736⁷ CAPTAIN TANDY (Ire) [78] 7-11-4 (5*) D J Kavanagh, *al beh.*
.................................(33 to 1 op 20 to 1 tchd 50 to 1) 11
1732 BANKONIT (Ire) [73] (bl) 8-11-4 I Lawrence, *al beh, tld off whn pld up bef 2 out*..................(16 to 1 op 10 to 1) pu
1320 BILL AND WIN [70] (v) 5-10-12 (3*) R Massey, *prmnt to 4th, sn wknd, tld off whn pld up bef 2 out*.....(33 to 1 op 20 to 1) pu
1604⁴ SHARMOOR [74] 4-11-5 A Thornton, *effrt 4th, chsd ldrs 5th, sn wknd, tld off whn pld up bef 2 out.*
.................................(10 to 1 op 5 to 1 tchd 12 to 1) pu
1763 COTTAGE JOKER [55] 6-10-0 A Maguire, *led to 3rd, wknd 5th, tld off whn pld up bef 2 out*..........(33 to 1 op 12 to 1) pu
Dist: 9l, 1¾l, 8l, 4l, 20l, 1¼l, 1¼l, 5l, 8l, 5l. 4m 11.50s. a 28.50s (15 Ran).
SR: 15/5/11/8/-/-/   (Mrs Carol P McPhail), E J Alston

1970 Holly Novices' Chase Class D (5-y-o and up) £4,059 2¾m.......... (1:10)

WHATTABOB (Ire) 7-10-12 M A Fitzgerald, *chlgd 6th till led and mstk tenth, hdd 12th, trkd ldr gng wl 2 out, led last, drvn out*.............................(7 to 2 op 5 to 2) 1
1600³ RAMALLAH 7-10-12 B Fenton, *beh, hdwy 3 out, styd on und pres frm 2 out, gng on at finish.*
.................................(10 to 1 op 7 to 1 tchd 12 to 1) 2
1831² BRIDEPARK ROSE (Ire) 8-10-7 S Fox, *trkd ldrs, led 3 out, mstk nxl, hdd last, one pace.*
.................................(10 to 1 op 12 to 1 tchd 14 to 1) 3
SEE ENOUGH 8-10-12 S McNeill, *pressed ldrs 4th till led 6th, hdd 8th, styd on und pres frm 2 out.*
.................................(12 to 1 op 8 to 1 tchd 14 to 1) 4
1725² LIVELY KNIGHT 7-11-5 P Hide, *beh, steady hdwy frm tenth, one pace from 2 out.*
.................................(11 to 4 fav op 5 to 2 tchd 3 to 1) 5
1804² SLIDEOFHILL (Ire) 7-10-12 C O'Dwyer, *nvr rch ldrs.*
.................................(7 to 2 op 3 to 1 tchd 4 to 1) 6
FURRY FOX (Ire) 8-10-12 D Morris, *nvr better than mid-div.*
.................................(25 to 1 op 16 to 1 tchd 33 to 1) 7
IVY BOY (Ire) 6-10-12 J Railton, *beh hfwy.*
.................................(20 to 1 op 12 to 1 tchd 25 to 1) 8
CHIAPPUCCI (Ire) 6-10-12 A Thornton, *led second to 6th, led 8th to tenth, led ag'n 12th to 3 out, wknd rpdly, tld off.*
.................................(33 to 1 op 20 to 1) 9
HUGE MISTAKE 7-10-12 C Llewellyn, *rdn and rear 7th, beh whn f tenth*..............(11 to 1 op 10 to 1 tchd 12 to 1) f
SAINT KEYNE 6-10-12 P Holley, *led to second, styd prmnt, mstk 4th, blun 13th, tld off whn pld up bef 3 out.*
.................................(33 to 1 op 20 to 1) pu
VOLLEYBALL (Ire) 7-10-12 M Richards, *beh 7th, blun 13th, tld off whn pld up bef 2 out*...........(20 to 1 op 16 to 1) pu
1766² STROKESAVER (Ire) 6-10-12 G Bradley, *mstk 1st, beh whn blun tenth, tld off when pld up bef 12th.*
.................................(14 to 1 op 10 to 1 tchd 16 to 1) pu
BUCKET OF GOLD 6-10-12 M Brennan, *chsd ldrs to tenth, wknd 12th, tld off whn pld up bef 2 out. (16 to 1 op 14 to 1) pu
1577³ GORDON 5-10-12 J Osborne, *sn beh, tld off whn pld up bef 2 out*..........................(8 to 1 op 10 to 1 tchd 7 to 1) pu
Dist: 3l, 2½l, nk, 2l, 17l, 15l, 3l, dist. 5m 56.30s. a 30.30s (15 Ran).
SR: 23/20/12/16/21/-/   (Mrs Margaret Turner), N J Henderson

1971 Plum Pudding Claiming Hurdle Class F (4-y-o and up) £2,199 2m 5f (1:40)

1625² ROBERTY LEA 8-11-12 P Niven, *trkd ldr till ld 6th, clr 3 out, blun last, readily. Cheekn, no ext tchd 11 to 10)* 1
1688 STAC-POLLAIDH 6-10-9 C O'Dwyer, *hdwy 6th, wnt 3rd 4 out, styd on to take remote second appr last.*
.................................(8 to 1 op 6 to 1 tchd 9 to 1) 2
1567² QUIET MISTRESS (bl) 6-10-6 A Maguire, *chsd ldrs, rdn alng whn cl second 4 out, wknd quickly appr 2 out, kpt on for poor 3rd r-in.*...................(5 to 1 tchd 4 to 1) 3

1325² SNOWY LANE (Ire) (h,bl) 8-10-11 N Williamson, *in tch, rdn aftr 6th, moderate hdwy und pres frm 2 out.*
.... (7 to 1 op 10 to 1 tchd 11 to 1)

1355⁵ FRANK NAYLAR 5-10-13 (7*) M Griffiths, *in tch, reminder appr 4th, sn beh.*.................... (16 to 1 op 8 to 1)   5

ESCADARO (USA) (v) 7-10-5 J R Kavanagh, *beh 5th, tld off whn pld up bef 4 out.*.............. (33 to 1 tchd 50 to 1)   pu

1719 SEMINOLE WIND (v) 5-10-11 B Fenton, *hdwy to 6th, wknd rpdly and pld up bef nxt.*................ (33 to 1 op 14 to 1)   pu

1796 FERNY BALL (Ire) (bl) 8-10-8 S Wynne, *al beh, tld off whn pld up bef 4 out.*.......... (20 to 1 op 10 to 1 tchd 25 to 1)   pu

1803⁵ QUILLWORK (USA) 4-10-3 V Smith, *slwly away, rear and rdn 5th, tld off whn blun 2 out, pld up bef nxt.* (14 to 1 op 7 to 1)   pu

1085⁴ IMPERIAL HONORS (Ire) 5-10-7 (7*) Mr L Baker, *beh 5th, tld off whn pld up bef 4 out.*.................................   pu

1675 BIT 'O' SUNSHINE 5-10-2⁹ (7*) B Clarke, *slwly into strd, lost tch 5th, tld off whn pld up bef 7th.* . . (33 to 1 tchd 50 to 1)   pu

Dist: 19l, 17l, 1¼l, 17l. 5m 49.80s. a 50.80s (11 Ran).

(Wentdale Const Ltd), Mrs M Reveley

1972 Christmas Cracker Handicap Chase Class D (0-125 5-y-o and up) £4,565 2m 110yds. . . . . (2:10)

1863* BEATSON (Ire) [101] 7-11-1 (6ex) B Powell, *sn tracking ldr, led aftr 3 out, in command whn lft wl clr nxt.*
.... (6 to 4 fav op 5 to 4 tchd 7 to 4)   1

JULEIT JONES (Ire) [90] 7-10-1 (3*) L Aspell, *keen hold, led aftr 3 out, third and no ch whn lft second nxt.*
....(4 to 1 op 7 to 2)   2

1846² DR ROCKET [86] 11-10-0 C Llewellyn, *hdwy 6th, hit 4 out and wknd, lft poor 3rd 2 out.*.......... (100 to 30 op 5 to 2)   3

1808⁴ COUNT BARACHOIS (USA) [96] 8-10-10 A Thornton, *made most to 3rd, wknd 7th, tld off.*.......... (14 to 1 op 8 to 1)   4

JACOB'S WIFE [106] 6-11-6 J Osborne, *beh, mstks 4th and nxt, hdwy 8th, chlgd and mistake 3 out, second and hld whn f 2 out.*................ (5 to 2 op 2 to 1 tchd 11 to 4)   f

Dist: 19l, 8l, dist. 4m 21.40s. a 24.40s (5 Ran).

SR: 25/-/   *(Mrs E B Gardiner), R H Buckler*

1973 Santa Claus Novices' Hurdle Class E (4-y-o and up) £2,897 2m. . . . . (2:40)

RED BLAZER 5-10-12 J Osborne, *steady hdwy 3 out, jmpd big and led nxt, gng wl whn lft clr last.*
.... (9 to 4 fav op 2 to 1 tchd 11 to 4)   1

1764* SPRINTFAYRE 8-10-12 (7*) A Irvine, *led till hdd but ev ch 2 out and wknd whn lft second at last.* (12 to 1 op 20 to 1)   2

1738⁵ FERRERS 5-10-12 R Marley, *hdwy to chase ldrs 4 out, rdn and kpt on und pres frm 2 out.*........ (33 to 1 op 20 to 1)   3

1503* ROYAL RAVEN (Ire) 5-10-9 (3*) L Aspell, *hdwy 5th, no prog appr 2 out.*........................ (5 to 1 op 3 to 1)   4

VITAMAN (Ire) 7-10-12 W Marston, *sn in tch, one pace frm 3 out.*................................ (33 to 1 op 20 to 1)   5

1338⁸ STRATHMINSTER 5-10-12 C O'Dwyer, *hdwy 5th, wknd appr 2 out.*...................... (9 to 1 op 6 to 1 tchd 10 to 1)   6

CAPTAIN WALTER (Ire) 6-10-12 G Upton, *prmnt to 3 out, sn wknd.*.................. (10 to 1 op 20 to 1 tchd 8 to 1)   7

EKEUS (Ire) 6-10-12 C Maude, *prominent to 5th, wknd 3 out.*
.... (33 to 1)   8

1641* HOH WARRIOR (Ire) 5-11-5 G Bradley, *hld up, effrt and mstk 5th, rdn aftr 3 out, no ch whn mistake nxt.*
.... (9 to 2 op 2 to 1 tchd 100 to 30)   9

1623⁹ FOXIES LAD 5-10-12 V Slattery, *chsd ldr to 5th, wknd rpdly.*
.... (25 to 1 op 20 to 1 tchd 33 to 1)   10

LEGIBLE 8-10-12 N Mann, *in tch to 5th.*
.... (9 to 1 op 14 to 1 tchd 20 to 1)   11

1792 ALONGWAYDOWN (Ire) 7-10-12 D Leahy, *al beh.*. . (33 to 1)   12

1830⁹ TREHANE 4-10-7 N Williamson, *al beh.*.......... (33 to 1)   13

MILWAUKEE (Ire) 7-10-7 M Brennan, *prmnt to 4th.*
.... (16 to 1 op 14 to 1 tchd 20 to 1)   14

77* MOTOQUA 4-10-7 A Maguire, *sn prmnt, chlgd 2 out, second and hld whn f last.*....... (8 to 1 op 6 to 1 tchd 10 to 1)   pu

1719 KI CHI SAGA (USA) 4-10-12 D Morris, *al beh, tld off whn pld up bef 2 out.*.............................. (33 to 1)   pu

Dist: 12l, ½l, 2l, 1¾l, nk, 18l, 8l, 16l, 5l, nk. 4m 10.30s. a 27.30s (16 Ran).

SR: 27/22/14/12/10/9/   *(T H Shrimpton), Miss H C Knight*

1974 Ladbroke Handicap Chase Class D (0-125 5-y-o and up) £7,262 3m 1f . . . . (3:10)

1664² PRICE'S HILL [107] 9-10-10 C O'Dwyer, *in tch, hdwy 9th, chlgd 12th, hit nxt, led 4 out, styd on wl frm 2 out.*
.... (4 to 1 op 5 to 1 tchd 11 to 2)   1

1607* RIVER MANDATE [125] 9-12-0 A Thornton, *chsd ldrs, rdn 3 out, one pace und pres frm nxt.*.................(5 to 2 jt-
fav op 2 to 1 tchd 11 to 4)   2

1726⁵ SPUFFINGTON [113] 8-11-2 P Hide, *prmnt, lost pos 11th, kpt on ag'n frm 3 out, styd on und pres r-in.*
.... (11 to 1 op 7 to 1 tchd 12 to 1)   3

1726⁸ SPECIAL ACCOUNT [97] 10-10-0 B Fenton, *mstk 5th, moderate hdwy frm 3 out.*.................(14 to 1 op 12 to 1)   4

1607² EVEN BLUE (Ire) [117] 8-11-6 R Dunwoody, *led to 4 out, str chal nxt, wknd quickly appr 2 out.*.................(5 to 2 jt-
fav op 2 to 1 tchd 11 to 4)   5

MWEENISH [97] 14-10-0 R Bellamy, *hit 3rd, beh whn blun 11th, tld off whn pld up bef 2 out.*.... (33 to 1 op 20 to 1)   pu

CELTIC BARLE [102] 12-10-5 A Maguire, *hit second, hdwy 12th, effrt und pres aftr 3 out, wknd quickly and pld up bef last.*
.... (10 to 1 tchd 12 to 1 op 14 to 1)   pu

1726⁹ GHIA GNEUIAGH [110] 10-10-13 C Maude, *nvr rch ldrs, tld off whn pld up bef 4 out.*............ (25 to 1 op 20 to 1)   pu

BRAVE BUCCANEER [105] 9-10-8 S McNeill, *hit 3rd, hdwy tenth, wknd 14th, tld off whn pld up bef last.*........ (16 to 1)   pu

1304 BIG BEN DUN [112] 10-11-1 G Bradley, *effrt and mstk 13th, sn wknd, tld off whn pld up bef 2 out.*
.... (11 to 1 op 7 to 1 tchd 12 to 1)   pu

1773⁵ ALL THE ACES [125] 9-12-0 P Niven, *al beh, tld off whn pld up bef 2 out.*.................. (16 to 1 op 12 to 1)   pu

SHEELIN LAD (Ire) [100] 8-10-3³ G Upton, *wth ldr till mstk 12th, wknd 4 out, tld off whn pld up bef 2 out.*
.... (25 to 1 op 20 to 1 tchd 33 to 1)   pu

Dist: 4l, sht-hd, dist, 1½l. 6m 45.00s. a 33.00s (12 Ran).

SR: 27/41/29/-/-/-/   *(G D W Swire), K C Bailey*

1975 Ivy Standard Open National Hunt Flat Class H (4,5,6-y-o) £1,416 2m . . . . (3:40)

PRINCEFUL (Ire) 5-11-8 (3*) G Hogan, *keen hold, made virtually all, drvn and kpt on wl frm 2 fs out.* (7 to 2 op 6 to 4)   1

1675* BILLINGSGATE 4-11-4 (7*) N Willmington, *chsd ldrs, rdn and on same pace fnl 2.*........... (7 to 1 op 7 to 2)   2

KING MOLE 5-11-4 G Upton, *steady hdwy frm 5 fs out, styd on same pace fnl 2.*............ (7 to 2 op 3 to 1)   3

MR MOONLIGHT (Ire) 4-11-4 G Bradley, *mid-div, hdwy 4 fs out, one pace fnl 3.*.............(12 to 1 op 6 to 1)   4

1578² SHORE PARTY (Ire) 4-10-11 (7*) L Suthern, *chsd ldrs till wknd 3 fs out.*.................. (7 to 4 fav op 9 to 4 tchd 6 to 4)   5

1768³ BROOKHAMPTON LANE (Ire) 5-11-4 B Powell, *prmnt, rdn alng hlwy, wknd 4 fs out...(9 to 1 op 6 to 1 tchd 10 to 1)   6

JOLLY HEART (Ire) 6-11-4 M Brennan, *steady hdwy to track ldrs 7 fs out, wknd 4 out.*............(20 to 1 op 12 to 1)   7

1578⁸ WILLOWS ROULETTE 4-11-4 R Greene, *keen hold, prmnt ten fs.*........................... (33 to 1 op 20 to 1)   8

BELVENTO (Ire) 4-11-4 P Hide, *al beh...* (8 to 1 op 4 to 1)   9

SHEET LIGHTNING 4-11-4 C Maude, *prmnt 9 fs.*
.... (25 to 1 op 16 to 1)   10

BARTHOLOMEW FAIR 5-11-4 I Lawrence, *effrt hfwy, wknd 5 out.*................... (9 to 1 op 14 to 1 tchd 20 to 1)   11

THETWOKAYS 5-10-11 (7*) S Porritt, *sn beh.*
.... (33 to 1 op 20 to 1)   12

MR ROBSTEE 5-11-4 L Harvey, *wth ldrs 5 fs, sn wknd.*
.... (33 to 1 op 20 to 1)   13

BENJAMIN JONES 4-11-4 B Fenton, *al beh.*
.... (33 to 1 op 1 tchd 33 to 1)   14

BIRDIETOO 4-10-13 R Marley, *al beh.* (33 to 1 op 20 to 1)   15

Dist: 2½l, 3l, 14l, hd, 27l, 4l, ½l, 18l, dist, 1¼l. 4m 12.40s. (15 Ran).

(Robert & Elizabeth Hitchins), Mrs J Pitman

HEREFORD (good to soft)
Friday December 20th
Going Correction: PLUS 1.00 sec. per fur. (races 1,2,3,5,7), PLUS 0.90 (4,6)

1976 Thyme Maiden Hurdle Class E (Div I) (4-y-o and up) £2,192 2m 1f. .(12:50)

1642³ STAR SELECTION 5-11-2 (3*) E Husband, *rcd keenly, made all, clr 3rd, steadied 6th, drw clear frm 3 out.*
.... (11 to 2 op 9 to 2 tchd 6 to 1)   1

1006⁵ KING RAT (Ire) (v) 5-11-0 (5*) Michael Brennan, *hld up, hdwy 5th, rdn to go second appr last, no ch whn wnr.*
.... (16 to 1 op 10 to 1)   2

1749³ DRAKESTONE 5-11-0 (5*) M R Thornton, *chsd wnr for most of race till rdn and wknd appr last.*...... (9 to 2 op 3 to 1)   3

919 FROME LAD 4-10-12 (7*) J Power, *prmnt till wknd appr 3 out.*
.... (33 to 1 op 20 to 1)   4

1716⁴ NIGHT CITY 5-11-5 J Osborne, *jmpd slwly 1st, hdwy aftr 4th, wknd quickly 3 out.*.................(2 to 1 fav op Evens)   5

LASTO ADREE (Ire) 5-11-5 B Powell, *hld up, mstk second, hdwy 4th, wknd 6th, tld off.* (7 to 1 op 4 to 1 tchd 8 to 1)   6

1716⁹ MR HEMP 4-11-5 Derek Byrne, *beh hfwy, tld off.*
.... (50 to 1 op 16 to 1)   7

50³ BRAMLEY MAY 6-11-5 A P McCoy, *prmnt, chsd wnr briefly betw 4th and 5th, wknd quickly appr 3 out, tld off.*
.... (5 to 2 op 3 to 1 tchd 4 to 2 to 1)   8

1805 WOODLANDS LAD TOO 4-11-5 R Bellamy, *al beh, tld off whn pld up bef 2 out.*............(100 to 1 op 50 to 1)   pu

1866 AMAZON HEIGHTS 4-10-11 (3*) G Hogan, *tld off 4th, pld up aftr 3 out.*...................(100 to 1 op 50 to 1)   pu

1260 SHADY EMMA 4-10-5 S Wynne, *beh frm strt, tld off whn pld up aftr 3rd, dismounted.*.........(66 to 1 op 50 to 1)   pu

1357⁹ AQUA AMBER 4-11-5 D Walsh, *mstks in rear, tld off whn pld up.*................................. (50 to 1 op 33 to 1)   pu

Dist: 12l, 4l, 23l, 7l, 26l, 10l, 1¼l. 4m 8.30s. a 23.30s (12 Ran).

SR: 28/16/12/-/-/-/   *(R M Mitchell), J Mackie*

1977 Thyme Maiden Hurdle Class E (Div II) (4-y-o and up) £2,178 2m 1f. . . (1:20)

MID DAY CHASER (Ire) 5-11-0 J Osborne, *hld up and al gng wl, wnt second 5th, led on bit appr 2 out, sn clr.
.................................(5 to 2 op 2 to 1 tchd 4 to 1)
1805⁵ TOTAL JOY (Ire) 5-11-5 J Railton, *hld up, hdwy 4th, led nxt, rdn and hdd appr 2 out, one pace*....... (4 to 1 op 9 to 4) 2
1743⁸ KEVASINGO 4-11-5 T J Murphy, *hld up in tch, rdn 3 out, one pace aftr*...........................(50 to 1 op 33 to 1) 3
TANTARA LODGE (Ire) 5-11-5 C O'Dwyer, *hld up in rear, hdwy whn mstk 6th, not rch ldrs.*
.................................(11 to 1 op 5 to 1 tchd 12 to 1) 4
1792 ROYRACE 4-11-5 S Wynne, *prmnt early, wknd 6th.*
.................................(100 to 1 op 50 to 1) 5
1609⁷ MILLING BROOK 4-11-2 (3*) T Dascombe, *chsd ldrs till wknd 6th*....................................(50 to 1 op 33 to 1) 6
1181⁶ NANJIZAL 4-11-2 (3*) R Massey, *al rear, tld off 6th.*
.................................(100 to 1 op 50 to 1) 7
DAUNT 4-11-5 A P McCoy, *pld hrd, not jump wl, led 3rd to 5th, wknd quickly, tld off.*
.................................(11 to 10 on op 2 to 1 on tchd Evens) 8
1299³ EUROLINK SHADOW (bl) 4-11-5 D Walsh, *led till hdd and hmpd 3rd, hrd rdn 6th, sn btn, tld off*. (50 to 1 op 33 to 1) 9
RED PHANTOM (Ire) 4-11-5 N Mann, *al beh, tld off 6th.*
.................................(25 to 1 op 20 to 1) 10
Dist: 10l, 4l, 26l, nk, hd, dist, 2½l, 1¼l, 3l. 4m 7.80s. a 22.80s (10 Ran).
SR: 28/23/19/-/-/-/ (Tavern Racing), P R Webber

1978 Cloves Conditional Jockeys' Novices' Handicap Hurdle Class F (0-100 4-y-o and up) £2,087 2m 3f 110yds
.... (1:50)

MAHLER [90] 6-11-7 (3*) D Walsh, *hld up in tch, pushed alng frm 7th, nosed ahead appr 2 out, fnshd tired.*
.................................(100 to 30 op 9 to 4 tchd 7 to 2) 1
1796* COLWALL [80] 5-10-4 (10*,7ex) K Hibbert, *al in tch, led appr 7th till approaching 2 out, kpt on one pace, fnshd tired.*
.................................(4 to 1 op 5 to 1) 2
1541⁸ ECU DE FRANCE (Ire) [66] 6-9-11 (3*) Michael Brennan, *beh and tld off till styd on strly frm 3 out, passed btn horses, nvr nrr*.................................(50 to 1 op 33 to 1) 3
1813* URBAN LILY [87] (bl) 6-10-11 (10*,7ex) J Harris, *in tch, rdn and lost pl 7th, plugged on one pace frm 3 out.*
.................................(2 to 1 fav op 6 to 4) 4
1723² TIME LEADER [75] 4-9-13 (10*) X Aizpuru, *mstk 3rd, ev ch 7th, wkng whn mistake nxt.* (100 to 30 op 9 to 4 tchd 5 to 1) 5
1614 LYPHARD'S FABLE (USA) [70] 5-9-8 (10*) C Hynes, *trkd ldr, led appr 6th till bef nxt, sn wknd*..... (14 to 1 op 10 to 1) 6
1723⁵ MADAM ROSE (Ire) [66] 6-9-4 (10*) David Turner, *led till appr 8th, sn wknd, tld off*...............(50 to 1 op 33 to 1) 7
1733 ANALOGUE (Ire) [66] 4-9-11 (3*) D J Kavanagh, *beh frm strt, tld off whn pld up bef 5th, dismounted.* (16 to 1 op 33 to 1) pu
1796⁹ THE CHEESE BARON [66] 7-9-4 (10*) S Hearn, *prmnt whn hmpd second, wknd 6th, tld off when pld up bef 3 out.*
.................................(50 to 1 op 33 to 1) pu
Dist: 2½l, 7l, 6l, 3l, 3½l, dist, ½l. dist. 5m 3.10s. a 45.10s (9 Ran).
(English Badminton Partnership), N A Twiston-Davies

1979 Caraway Novices' Handicap Chase Class E (0-100 5-y-o and up) £2,995 2m.................................. (2:20)

1724 CAPTAIN STOCKFORD [69] 9-10-0 S Wynne, *made all, hit and lft clr 2 out, unchlgd.*
.................................(33 to 1 op 25 to 1 tchd 50 to 1) 1
1797* SCOTTISH BAMBI [103] 8-12-6 (7ex) J Osborne, *hld up, mstk 6th, hdwy 3 out, ran on to chase wnr r-in.*.......(3 to 1 co-fav op 2 to 1) 2
1475³ NORTHERN SINGER [71] 6-9-13 (3*) T Dascombe, *hld up, hit second, hdwy 7th, lft second 2 out, rdn and wknd bef last.*
.................................(3 to 1 co-fav op 2 to 1) 3
1698⁵ BOLD ACRE [81] 6-10-12 N Williamson, *hld up, hdwy 7th, rdn aftr 4 out, one pace*....................(9 to 2 op 5 to 1) 4
1857 SAN DIEGO CHARGER (Ire) [74] 5-10-0 (5*) Mr R Thornton, *al beh, nvr on terms.*..............................(20 to 1) 5
1475 ASHMEAD RAMBLER (Ire) [70] 6-10-1¹ C Maude, *hld up in tch, hdwy 7th, btn whn hmpd 2 out.*.............(3 to 1 co-fav op 5 to 2) 6
PANDORA'S PRIZE [69] 10-10-0 T J Murphy, *al beh.*
.................................(50 to 1 op 33 to 1) 7
1670 IL BAMBINO [89] 8-11-6 Mr A Charles-Jones, *al beh, tld off 8th*....................................(14 to 1 op 10 to 1 tchd 16 to 1) 8
1670 CARACOL [69] 7-9-13² (3*) G Hogan, *hld up, hdwy 8th, in tch whn f 3 out*........(16 to 1 op 20 to 1 tchd 25 to 1) f
1577 THE WAYWARD BISHOP (Ire) [69] (bl) 7-9-9² (7*) D C O'Connor, *chsd wnr, hit 4th, rdn and ev ch whn f 2 out.*
.................................(33 to 1 tchd 50 to 1) f
DUNNICKS VIEW [72] 7-10-3¹ G Upton, *hit second, tld off 7th, pld up bef 3 out*.......... (10 to 1 op 11 to 1 tchd 12 to 1) pu
Dist: 4l, 6l, 5l, 11l, 5l, 1l, 22l. 4m 8.90s. a 21.90s (11 Ran).
SR: -/27/-/-/-/-/ (P Wegmann), P Wegmann

1980 Cowslip Selling Hurdle Class G (4-y-o and up) £2,052 2m 1f......(2:50)

MY MAN IN DUNDALK (Ire) 7-10-12 E Murphy, *wth ldr, led on bit appr 2 out, shaken up approaching last, cleverly.*
.................................(2 to 1 op 5 to 2) 1

1832* FLEET CADET (v) 5-10-12 A P McCoy, *hld up, hdwy appr 5th, rdn 2 out, ran on r-in.*
.................................(Evens fav op 7 to 4 on tchd 11 to 10) 2
1606⁸ SCOTTISH WEDDING 6-10-11 (3*) R Massey, *hld up, hdwy to chase ldrs 3rd, rdn and one pace frm 3 out.*
.................................(5 to 1 op 7 to 2) 3
1856⁶ COMEONUP 5-10-12 N Williamson, *made most till appr 2 out, wknd quickly.*..................(10 to 1 op 8 to 1) 4
1863 HALHAM TARN (Ire) 6-10-12 (7*) A Dowling, *hld up, hdwy aftr 4th, rdn and wknd appr 3 out.*
.................................(11 to 1 op 6 to 1 tchd 12 to 1) 5
LAJADHAL (Fr) 7-11-5 L Harvey, *prmnt, wkng whn mstk 6th.*
.................................(14 to 1 op 8 to 1) 6
NORDIC FLIGHT 8-10-7 (5*) D J Kavanagh, *al rear.* (50 to 1) 7
1743⁷ STEVIE'S WONDER (Ire) 6-10-12 Mr J L Llewellyn, *mid-div, lost tch 5th*...........................(25 to 1 op 20 to 1) 8
APPLIANCEOFSCIENCE 9-11-12 J Ryan, *al beh.*
.................................(33 to 1 op 25 to 1) 9
1803 WOODLANDS ENERGY 5-10-7 R Bellamy, *beh 4th, tld off.*
.................................(25 to 1 op 20 to 1) 10
1646⁹ BOLD CHARLIE 4-10-12 N Mann, *chsd ldrs till wknd aftr 4th, tld off*...........................(25 to 1 op 20 to 1) 11
1670 TIBBS INN (bl) 7-10-7 (5*) Mr R Thornton, *reluctant to race, tld off whn pld up bef 3 out*........(33 to 1 op 25 to 1) pu
Dist: Nk, 11l, 14l, 5l, 4l, nk, 9l, 4l, dist, 3½l. 4m 13.10s. a 28.10s (14 Ran).
(Mrs B J Curley), B J Curley

1981 Comfrey Maiden Chase Class E (5-y-o and up) £3,200 3m 1f 110yds.............................. (3:20)

INDIAN TRACKER 6-11-5 C Maude, *rcd on ins, made nrly all, drw clr appr 2 out*....................(5 to 1 op 3 to 1) 1
1765⁴ BROGEEN LADY (Ire) 6-11-0 A P McCoy, *rcd on outsd of wnr and jmpd wl, sometimes led, rdn appr 3 out, wknd bef nxt.*
.................................(9 to 4 fav op 7 to 2) 2
1494³ ANYTHINGYOULIKE 7-11-5 M Richards, *wl beh till hdwy 12th, badly hmpd 14th, passed btn horses frm 3 out.*
.................................(14 to 1 op 10 to 1) 3
1701 APATURA HATI 7-10-9 (5*) Mr R Thornton, *chsd ldrs, outpcd whn mstk 15th, wknd nxt.*
.................................(14 to 1 op 12 to 1 tchd 16 to 1) 4
1292 THUNDER ROAD 5-11-5 B Powell, *rear, nvr on terms.*
.................................(50 to 1 op 33 to 1) 5
1542 RAINBOW FOUNTAIN 9-11-0 Mr A Kinane, *prmnt, 3rd whn blun 14th, sn wknd*.................(50 to 1 op 33 to 1) 6
1673 GREENFIELD GEORGE (Ire) 5-11-5 N Williamson, *in tch early, rear whn jmpd slwly 9th, hmpd 14th, sn tld off.*
.................................(25 to 1 op 20 to 1) 7
WANDERING LIGHT (Ire) 7-11-5 S Wynne, *hld up, making gd hdwy and in cl tch whn badly hmpd on bend appr 14th, not reco'r, tld off*.................(9 to 2 op 5 to 1) 8
1352³ LORD NITROGEN (USA) 6-11-5 S Curran, *trkd ldrs till f 14th.*
.................................(20 to 1 op 16 to 1) f
MR LOVELY (Ire) 5-11-2 (3*) T Dascombe, *3rd whn f 1st.*
.................................(20 to 1 op 16 to 1) f
1732⁴ JOLLY BOAT 9-11-5 J R Kavanagh, *hit 5th, blun and uns rdr 8th*.................................(8 to 1 op 6 to 1) ur
605³ DUSTYS TRAIL (Ire) 7-11-5 D Walsh, *rdn 7th, tld off 10th, pld up bef 4 out*......................(20 to 1 op 16 to 1) pu
1701 LANGTON PARMILL 11-10-12 (7*) N Willmington, *mstk 11th, sn beh, tld off whn pld up bef 4 out*..........(33 to 1) pu
1804 MOUNT SERRATH (Ire) 8-11-5 J Osborne, *beh tenth, tld off whn pld up bef 4 out*......(13 to 2 op 4 to 1 tchd 7 to 1) pu
1748 SAUCY'S WOLF 6-11-5 L Harvey, *jmpd badly, tld off 6th, pld up aftr blun badly 9th*....................(50 to 1 op 33 to 1) pu
1924 RAMSTOWN LAD (Ire) 7-11-5 C O'Dwyer, *beh whn blun second, tld off when pld up bef 2 out.*
.................................(15 to 2 op 4 to 1 tchd 8 to 1) pu
Dist: 16l, 16l, 6l, 7l, 2½l, dist, 2l. 6m 39.60s. a 33.60s (16 Ran).
(Joe & Joanne Richards), M C Pipe

1982 Rosemary Handicap Hurdle Class D (0-120 4-y-o and up) £2,857 2m 1f.............................. (3:50)

1759² HAY DANCE [85] 5-10-11 N Williamson, *hld up in rear, steady hdwy frm 5th, wnt second appr 3 out, led approaching last, shaken up r-in*....................(5 to 2 fav tchd 11 to 4) 1
1759⁷ BIETSCHHORN BARD [88] 6-9-10 (5*) Sophie Mitchell, *wl in rear till rdn and gd hdwy 3 out, ran on and ev ch whn not fluent last, rallied r-in*....(3 to 1 op 11 to 4 tchd 7 to 2) 2
1716² SAILEP (Fr) [100] 4-10-10 (3*) T Dascombe, *trkd ldrs, led 6th, rdn 2 out, wknd and hdd appr last*.......(4 to 1 op 3 to 1) 3
1848³ WADADA [106] 5-11-5 D J Burchell, *hld up, hdwy 4th, led sn aftr nxt, hdd 6th, rdn and wknd 2 out*.... (5 to 1 op 4 to 1) 4
1761 NASHVILLE STAR (USA) [100] (v) 5-11-3 B Bellamy, *trkd ldr till aftr 4th, wknd appr 3 out*........(12 to 1 op 8 to 1) 5
RIVER ISLAND (USA) [103] 8-10-9 (7*) E Greehy, *hld up in rear, nvr on terms*..................(20 to 1 op 16 to 1) 6
1646 ETHBAAT (USA) [90] 5-10-3 M Richards, *hld up and pld hrd, hit second, tld off*.................(10 to 1 op 12 to 1) 7
1417² ROBERT'S TOY (Ire) [115] 5-12-0 A P McCoy, *led till sn aftr 5th, wknd appr 3 out, eased, tld off*.....(7 to 2 op 3 to 1) 8
Dist: ½l, 9l, 6l, 18l, 1¾l, 11l, 5l. 4m 11.50s. a 26.50s (8 Ran).
(Wessex Go Racing Partnership), P J Hobbs

259

HEXHAM (good to soft)
Friday December 20th

Going Correction: PLUS 0.70 sec. per fur. (races 1,2,4,5,7), PLUS 0.80 (3,6)

1983 Mince Pie Novices' Hurdle Class E (4-y-o and up) £2,700 2m.... (12:30)

1677[3] QATTARA (Ire) 6-10-12 G Cahill, *nvr far away, led aftr 2 out, styd on strly*.......................... (6 to 1 op 5 to 1) 1
ELASTIC 10-10-7 L O'Hara, *led till hdd 2 out, kpt on same pace*................. (16 to 1 op 12 to 1 tchd 20 to 1) 2
1772[2] FASSAN (Ire) 4-10-12 R Garritty, *hld up, hdwy hfwy, led 2 out, sn rdn and hdd, no extr.* ....(2 to 1 on op 6 to 4 on tchd 9 to 4 on) 3
1770 CAIRO PRINCE (Ire) 6-10-12 A Roche, *in tch, effrt bef 2 out, kpt on same pace*.................. (20 to 1 op 10 to 1) 4
1656[6] CALDER KING (bl) 5-10-12 B Storey, *hld up, hdwy aftr 6th, kpt on same pace frm 2 out.* (10 to 1 op 5 to 1 tchd 12 to 1) 5
STORM CALL 5-10-7 D Bentley, *in tch till wknd aftr 6th.* .... (20 to 1 op 16 to 1) 6
POSTED ABROAD (Ire) 4-10-12 A Dobbin, *beh, hdwy aftr 5th, wknd 2 out*........... (14 to 1 op 10 to 1 tchd 16 to 1) 7
1770 STAR MASTER 5-10-12 P Niven, *chsd ldrs till wknd bef 2 out, tld off*............................ (8 to 1 op 12 to 1) 8
ROBARA 6-11-5 N Leach, *beh frm 4th, tld off.* .... (20 to 1 op 10 to 1) 9
1330 RUSTIC WARRIOR 6-10-12 K Jones, *beh frm 5th, wl tld off.* .... (50 to 1 op 33 to 1) 10
1590 GUILE POINT 5-10-7 J Burke, *al beh, tld off whn pld up bef 2 out*.............................. (50 to 1 op 33 to 1) pu

Dist: 6l, 2l, 11l, sht-hd, 3l, 2l, dist, 16l, dist. 4m 6.60s. a 17.60s (11 Ran).
SR: 20/9/12/1/-/-/ (W McKeown), W McKeown

1984 Holly Novices' Hurdle Class E (4-y-o and up) £2,805 3m............(1:00)

1818* PAPERISING 4-11-5 A Dobbin, *nvr far away, smooth hdwy to ld bef 2 out, clr last, eased r-in*.........(3 to 1 op 2 to 1) 1
1623[2] SWANBISTER (Ire) 6-11-5 R Garritty, *hld up, hdwy to track ldrs 8th, slight ld 3 out, hdd bef nxt, kpt on, no ch wth wnr.* ....(5 to 4 fav tchd 6 to 4 and 7 to 4) 2
1679[9] BOSTON MAN 5-10-12 B Storey, *towards rear till drvn alng and styd on wl frm 2 out, nrst finish*................ (33 to 1) 3
1623[6] GLENBOWER 4-10-9 (3*) Mr C Bonner, *mid-div, some hdwy aftr 3 out, kpt on same pace frm nxt*.... (12 to 1 op 7 to 1) 4
1824[8] KINGS LANE 7-11-0 (5*) Mr M H Naughton, *trkd ldrs, effrt aftr 3 out, kpt on same pace*.............(12 to 1 op 16 to 1) 5
1729[7] OLD CAVALIER 5-10-12 P Niven, *prmnt, slight ld 9th, hdd 3 out, wknd appr nxt*...... (10 to 1 op 8 to 1 tchd 12 to 1) 6
1703[6] FARMERS SUBSIDY 4-10-12 N Bentley, *in tch, hdwy to chal 3 out, wknd bef nxt*............................ (33 to 1) 7
1826[6] MY MISSILE 6-10-7 L O'Hara, *in tch till outpcd bef 3 out, no dngr aftr*............................(50 to 1 op 33 to 1) 8
1631 SOUTH COAST STAR (Ire) 6-10-7 (5*) G F Ryan, *chsd ldrs till wknd bef 2 out*................................ (33 to 1) 9
1631 CLONGOUR (Ire) 6-10-12 K Whelan, *mid-div till wknd aftr 3 out*.............................. (6 to 1 op 12 to 1) 10
BARNEY RUBBLE 11-10-12 D Bentley, *led till hdd 9th, wknd aftr 3 out*.................................. (20 to 1) 11
1631 CRAGNABUOY (Ire) 6-10-12 T Reed, *al beh.* ....(14 to 1 tchd 16 to 1 and 20 to 1) 12
1662[7] CRASHBALLOO (Ire) 5-10-12 A S Smith, *sn beh.* ....(14 to 1 tchd 16 to 1) 13
1868[7] TOSHIBA HOUSE (Ire) 5-10-7 G Cahill, *chsd ldrs, hit 3 out, wknd quickly, pld up bef nxt*.......... (50 to 1 op 33 to 1) pu
1682 SAMITE (Ire) 5-10-12 N Leach, *tld off whn pld up bef 9th.* ....(33 to 1 tchd 50 to 1) pu

Dist: ¾l, 2½l, 2½l, 1¼l, 3½l, nk, 18l, 3l, 7l, hd. 6m 16.20s. a 28.20s (15 Ran).
(The Jockeys Whips), G Richards

1985 Roast Turkey Novices' Chase Class E (5-y-o and up) £3,234 2½m 110yds .... (1:30)

LIEN DE FAMILLE (Ire) 6-10-12 P Niven, *hld up, wnt second aftr 9th, led 3 out, styd on wl*.......... (4 to 1 tchd 5 to 1) 1
1913 CELTIC GIANT 6-10-12 R Garritty, *hld up, mstk 5th, hdwy aftr 11th, drvn alng after 3 out, chsd wnr frm betw last 2, no imprsn.* (5 to 4 on op 11 to 8 on tchd 6 to 5 on and 6 to 4 on) 2
1771[7] SIRERIC (Ire) 6-10-12 K Johnson, *led second, sn clr, mstk 4th, hdd 3 out, wknd betw last 2*..........(16 to 1 op 10 to 1) 3
1681[3] ROYAL SURPRISE (bl) 9-10-12 T Reed, *led to second, chsd clr ldr till aftr 9th, wknd bef 3 out*.......(12 to 1 op 6 to 1) 4
1828[3] BONNY JOHNNY 6-10-12 D J Moffatt, *beh, blun 9th, f nxt.* ....(7 to 1 op 5 to 1) f
1587* ELLIOTT'S WISH (Ire) 5-11-5 A Dobbin, *whipped round strt, beh whn blun 8th, hmpd tenth, tld off when pld up bef 12th.* ....(6 to 1 op 4 to 1) pu

Dist: 5l, 3½l, 20l. 5m 21.30s. a 23.30s (6 Ran).
SR: 15/10/6/ (Mrs Marie Taylor), J J Quinn

1986 St Nicholas Handicap Hurdle Class F (0-105 4-y-o and up) £2,259 2m .... (2:00)

BRUMON (Ire) [88] (bl) 5-11-7 D J Moffatt, *beh, took clr order 5th, led 2 out, kpt on und pres.* .... (14 to 1 op 8 to 1 tchd 20 to 1) 1
1676* KEMO SABO [92] 4-11-11 D Parker, *trkd ldr, chlgd bef 2 out, sn chasing wnr, rdn and no imprsn.* ....(6 to 4 fav op 5 to 4 on) 2
547[3] HERE COMES HERBIE [84] 4-11-3 M Moloney, *in tch, effrt bef 2 out, fdd*............ (9 to 2 op 6 to 1 tchd 4 to 1) 3
1733[8] SEGALA (Ire) [83] 5-11-2 P Niven, *led till hdd 2 out, sn wknd.* ....(6 to 1 tchd 7 to 1) 4
1788 HIGHLAND WAY (Ire) [95] 8-12-0 A S Smith, *hld up, effrt bef 2 out, sn wknd*............(13 to 2 op 5 to 1 tchd 7 to 1) 5
1708 TASHREEF [72] (bl) 6-10-5 B Storey, *reluctant to race, tld off whn pld up bef 3rd*..............................(20 to 1) pu
1693[7] FAMILIAR ART [75] 5-10-8 R Garritty, *in tch till wknd quickly aftr 3 out, tld off whn pld up bef nxt*.. (8 to 1 tchd 10 to 1) pu

Dist: 5l, 13l, ¾l, 9l. 4m 10.40s. a 21.40s (7 Ran).
(Mike Flynn), D Moffatt

1987 Christmas Bargain Conditional Jockeys' Selling Handicap Hurdle Class G (0-95 4-y-o and up) £1,725 2½m 110yds..................(2:30)

1708[6] PRECIPICE RUN [82] 11-11-10 G Cahill, *in tch, outpcd aftr 3 out, gd hdwy frm nxt, led after last, all out.* .... (16 to 1 op 10 to 1) 1
1784[5] YACHT CLUB [67] 14-10-4 (5*) C Elliott, *hld up, hit rail bef 4th, steady hdwy to ld 3 out, hit last, sn hdd, hrd rdn and kpt on.* ....(8 to 1 op 7 to 1) 2
1775[9] CORBLEU (Ire) [74] 6-11-2 E Callaghan, *made most till hdd 3 out, ev ch last, no extr*.... (5 to 1 op 4 to 1 tchd 11 to 2) 3
1784[4] THARSIS [65] 11-10-7 S Taylor, *in tch, drvn alng aftr 3 out, no hdwy*.............................. (12 to 1 op 7 to 1) 4
1586[2] DASHMAR [65] 9-10-7 D Parker, *led 3rd to 4th, outpcd and drpd rear aftr 6th, no dngr after.* .... (100 to 30 op 7 to 2 tchd 4 to 1) 5
MR SLOAN [58] 6-10-0 G Lee, *in tch till wknd bef 2 out.* ....(33 to 1) 6
1521 NAWTINOOKEY [60] (bl) 6-9-11 (5*) C McCormack, *in tch, hdwy to join ldrs 7th, rdn bef 2 out, wknd quickly, tld off.* ....(7 to 1 op 5 to 1 tchd 8 to 1) 7
1911 CIRCLE BOY [64] 9-10-6 R McGrath, *prmnt till wknd quickly aftr 3 out, tld off*........................ (7 to 1 op 9 to 2) 8
1829[4] BLANC SEING (Fr) [75] (bl) 9-11-3 F Leahy, *trkd ldrs till pld up lme bef 6th*.......... (5 to 2 fav tchd 3 to 1 and 9 to 4) pu

Dist: ¾l, 2l, 8l, 6l, 3½l, 30l, 15l. 5m 18.30s. a 27.30s (9 Ran).
(C Warwick), J J Birkett

1988 Santa Claus Handicap Chase Class E (0-110 5-y-o and up) £3,070 3m 1f .... (3:00)

1694[3] OFF THE BRU [85] 11-10-2[4] (7*) Mr M Bradburne, *led 5th till aftr 8th, drpd rear after 16th, hdwy to ld bef last, styd on wl.* ....(6 to 1 tchd 7 to 1) 1
1660[6] GALA WATER [90] 10-10-10[6] T Reed, *in tch, hdwy und pres to ld 3 out, hdd bef last, no extr*........ (7 to 1 tchd 8 to 1) 2
1632[2] ROAD BY THE RIVER (Ire) [97] 8-11-3 B Storey, *hld up, hdwy bef 14th, ch 3 out, wknd aftr nxt*.......... (3 to 1 op 2 to 1) 3
1325 JENDEE (Ire) [88] 8-10-5 (3*) Mr C Bonner, *hld up, hdwy aftr 16th, ev ch 3 out, sn wknd.* .... (10 to 1 op 8 to 1 tchd 12 to 1) 4
1845[3] PATS MINSTREL [108] 11-12-0 A Dobbin, *led to 5th, led aftr 8th to 11th, led 15th, hdd bef 3 out, sn wknd, tld off.* ....(8 to 1 tchd 10 to 1) 5
1660[3] WESTWELL BOY [107] 10-11-13 R Supple, *in tch, hdwy to dispute ld 11th, blun and uns rdr nxt.* ....(11 to 8 fav tchd 6 to 4 and 13 to 8) ur
1694 SNOOK POINT [84] 9-10-4[4] J Burke, *dsptd ld, led 11th to 15th, ev ch 3 out, wkng whn blun nxt, tld off when pld up bef last.* .... (20 to 1 op 14 to 1 tchd 25 to 1) pu

Dist: 8l, 14l, ½l, dist. 6m 37.60s. a 32.60s (7 Ran).
(The Fife Steeplechasing Partnership), Mrs S C Bradburne

1989 Levy Board Intermediate Open National Hunt Flat Class H (4,5,6-y-o) £1,406 2m.............. (3:30)

1590[3] BOBBY GRANT 5-11-4 P Niven, *prmnt, led 4 fs out, styd on wl frm 2 out*.............................(9 to 1 op 7 to 1) 1
1317[9] MAGPIE MELODY (Ire) 5-11-4 A Roche, *mid-div, hdwy 3 fs out, kpt on wl fnl furlong*..............(5 to 1 tchd 7 to 1) 2
ROMAN OUTLAW 4-11-4 D Bentley, *in tch, hdwy 3 fs out, not much room fnl furlong, styd on wl towards finish.* ....(16 to 1 tchd 20 to 1) 3
SIR BOB (Ire) 4-11-4 G Cahill, *prmnt, led hfwy, hdd 4 fs out, ev ch till no extr fnl 2 furlongs*............ (7 to 2 op 5 to 1) 4
1514[2] FIRST LIGHT 4-11-4 R Garritty, *mid-div, hdwy 3 fs out, kpt on same pace frm o'r one out.* ....(9 to 4 fav op 2 to 1 tchd 3 to 1) 5
DERANNIE (Ire) 4-11-4 A Dobbin, *mid-div, hdwy 3 fs out, no extr frm o'r one out*..........................(4 to 1 op 2 to 1) 6
1809[7] LOVELY RASCAL 4-10-8 (5*) R McGrath, *prmnt till wknd o'r 2 fs out*............................(16 to 1 op 12 to 1) 7

1682 TOP ACE 4-11-4 Mr A Robson, *chsd ldrs, ev ch 2 fs out, wknd
o'r one out* . . . .(33 to 1)   8
HOUSELOPE SPRING 4-10-13 (5*) G F Ryan, *prmnt till wknd
2 fs out* . . . .(20 to 1)   9
SNOOTY ESKIMO (Ire) 4-11-4 A S Smith, *towards rear, hdwy
into midfield hfwy, wknd 2 fs out* . . . . .(20 to 1 op 25 to 1)   10
1590⁹ QUEENS BRIGADE 4-11-4 B Storey, *nvr dngrs.*
. . . .(20 to 1 op 33 to 1)   11
JOHNNEYS SPIRIT 4-11-4 L O'Hara, *mid-div till wknd 3 fs
out, tld off* . . . .(16 to 1 op 33 to 1)   12
1682 ALAN'S PRIDE (Ire) 5-10-13 K Whelan, *in tch, hdwy hfwy,
wknd 3 fs out, tld off* . . . .(25 to 1 tchd 33 to 1)   13
THE BURGLAR (Ire) 4-11-4 R Supple, *al beh, tld off.* (33 to 1)   14
BANNER YEAR (Ire) 5-11-4 N Smith, *beh most of way, tld off.*
. . . .(33 to 1)   15
1682 OTTADINI (Ire) 4-10-13 T Reed, *led to hfwy, wknd 4 fs out, tld
off* . . . .(33 to 1)   16
1390 TEELIN BAY (Ire) 4-11-4 D Parker, *wl beh frm hfwy, tld off.*
. . . .(25 to 1)   17
MONTEIN 5-11-4 N Leach, *al beh, tld off* . . . .(33 to 1)   18
Dist: 2½l, 1l, hd, ¾l, 4l, 3½l, ½l, 6l, 2½l, ½l. 4m 5.50s. (18 Ran).
(John J Thompson), C Grant

UTTOXETER (soft)
Friday December 20th
**Going Correction: PLUS 1.05 sec. per fur. (races
1,3,6), PLUS 0.45 (2,4,5)**

1990 Strebel Boilers & Radiators Handicap Hurdle Class C (0-130 4-y-o and
up) £3,550 2m . . . . (1:10)

1402⁴ TEJANO GOLD (USA) [111] 6-11-0 R Dunwoody, *chsd clr ldr,
improved to ld 4 out, drw clear last 2, eased finish. .* (9 to 2)   1
1612⁸ MASTER TRIBE (Ire) [120] 6-11-9 W Marston, *settled wth
chasing grp, took clr order 4 out, ev ch and rdn nxt, kpt on one
pace r-in, no imprsn* . . . .(10 to 1 op 7 to 1)   2
1807* MOST EQUAL [115] 6-11-4 (5ex) R Hughes, *patiently rdn,
improved to go hndy 4 out, effrt and hit nxt, one pace frm betw
last 2* . . . .(3 to 1 op 5 to 2)   3
1772⁵ MR BUREAUCRAT (NZ) [117] 7-11-6 R Johnson, *wtd wth,
improved on outsd to go hndy 4 out, rdn alng frm nxt, btn betw
last 2* . . . .(7 to 1 op 5 to 1)   4
MOVING OUT [121] 8-11-7 (7*) Mr A Wintle, *tried to make all,
sn clr, hdd 4 out, rallied, fdd und pres frm betw last 2.*
. . . .(16 to 1 op 12 to 1)   5
1465* SAINT CIEL (USA) [110] 8-10-13 M A Fitzgerald, *settled in tch,
improved to join issue 4 out, rdn frm nxt, fdd und pres.*
. . . .(11 to 4 tchd 3 to 1)   6
1803⁶ EUROLINK THE LAD [106] 9-10-9 D J Burchell, *settled midfield, took clr order 4 out, und pres nxt, wknd quickly, tld off.*
. . . .(10 to 1 op 8 to 1)   7
Dist: 5l, 1½l, 6l, 1¼l, 3l, dist. 3m 59.80s. a 22.80s (7 Ran).
SR: 26/30/23/19/21/7/-/   (Paul Bradley), P Bradley

1991 Lefley's Hog Roast Novices' Chase
Class D (5-y-o and up) £3,826 2½m
. . . . (1:40)

1424* OBAN 6-11-6 G Bradley, *patiently rdn, steady hdwy appr 4
out, nosed ahead last, sprinted clr r-in.*
. . . .(100 to 30 fav op 3 to 1 tchd 7 to 2)   1
1791² SUNSET AND VINE 9-11-0 R Dunwoody, *wth ldrs, led aftr
second, lft clr 7th, rdn and hdd last, not quicken wth wnr.*
. . . .(4 to 1 op 3 to 1)   2
MAJOR LOOK (NZ) 8-11-4 R Johnson, *settled to track ldrs,
effrt appr 4 out, sn drvn alng, no imprsn frm betw last 2.*
. . . .(14 to 1)   3
1636³ TAKE THE BUCKSKIN 9-11-0 M A Fitzgerald, *wtd wth, hmpd
by faller 7th, rallied appr 4 out, rdn and wknd quickly last 2.*
. . . .(7 to 2 op 3 to 1 tchd 4 to 1)   4
1663³ SLIPMATIC 7-10-9 S McNeill, *wtd wth, unsighted whn f 1st.*
. . . .(10 to 1 op 20 to 1)   f
1732⁵ ZAITOON (Ire) 5-11-0 A Maguire, *nvr far away, ev ch appr 4
out, disputing second whn f four out.* . . . . .(8 to 1 op 7 to 1)   f
1741 THURSDAY NIGHT (Ire) 5-11-0 A Thornton, *led and jmpd
badly rght 1st, hdd aftr nxt, upsides whn f 7th.*
. . . .(4 to 1 op 7 to 2)   f
Dist: 6l, 5l, 4l. 5m 14.50s. a 30.50s (7 Ran).
(Lord Hartington), Miss H C Knight

1992 Burton Albion Football Club Juvenile
Novices' Selling Hurdle Class G (3-
y-o) £2,025 2m . . . . (2:10)

1665³ STONECUTTER (v) 10-10 R Hughes, *al wl plcd, led bef 3 out,
hrd pressed nxt 2, styd on grimly r-in.*
. . . .(9 to 4 fav op 5 to 2 tchd 11 to 4)   1
1629 BOY BLAKENEY 10-10 Richard Guest, *led. jmpd badly rght
nxt, hdd 3rd, styd hndy and ev ch frm 3 out, rdn and hmpd by
faller last, rallied.* . . . .(7 to 1 op 5 to 1)   2
1179³ HOW COULD-I (bl) (bl) 10-5 A Thornton, *patiently rdn, drvn
up frm midfield aftr 3 out, styd on from betw last 2, no imprsn.*
. . . .(6 to 1 op 5 to 1)   3

1470 COME ON IN 10-10 C Llewellyn, *settled off the pace,
improved frm 3 out, ran on from betw last 2, fnshd strly.*
. . . .(33 to 1 op 25 to 1)   4
1854⁴ SPIRAL FLYER (Ire) 10-5 W Marston, *settled to track ldrs, und
pres frm 3 out, no imprsn from betw last 2.*
. . . .(4 to 1 tchd 9 to 2)   5
1470⁴ PAULTON 10-10 R Greene, *co'red up in midfield, effrt hfwy,
feeling pace frm 3 out, no imprsn.* . . . .(50 to 1)   6
1696⁷ TATHMIN (v) 10-10 M Bosley, *settled midfield, hrd drvn bef 3
out, tdd frm nxt.* . . . .(25 to 1 op 20 to 1)   7
1869⁶ ARCH ANGEL (Ire) 10-5 D Gallagher, *beh whn hit 5th, struggling aftr, nvr a factor.* (12 to 1 op 10 to 1 tchd 14 to 1)   8
1599 APPEAL AGAIN (Ire) 10-7 (3*) Guy Lewis, *chsd ldg bunch, und
pres aftr 4 out, sn lost tch, tld off.*
. . . .(40 to 1 op 33 to 1 tchd 50 to 1)   9
1398⁸ LEBEDINSKI (Ire) (v) 10-5 R Marley, *struggling thrght, tld off
frm 4 out* . . . .(14 to 1 op 12 to 1)   10
1209³ FLASH IN THE PAN (Ire) 10-5 W McFarland, *nvr far away, str
chal frm 2 out, rdn and ev ch whn f last.* (7 to 1 op 5 to 1)   f
547²⁷ INDIAN SUNSET (bl) 10-10 J A McCarthy, *wth ldrs, led 3rd till
hdd appr 3 out, wknd quickly and pld up bef nxt.*
. . . .(12 to 1 op 7 to 1)   pu
1438 NORDIC HERO (Ire) 10-3 (7*) C Davies, *settled midfield,
struggling bef 4 out, tld off whn pld up bef 2 out.* (50 to 1)   pu
REBOUNDER 10-7 (3*) J Magee, *in tch to hfwy, wknd quickly
and pld up aftr 4 out.* . . . .(50 to 1 tchd 66 to 1)   pu
Dist: Nk, 12l, 3l, 2l, 1¼l, 2½l, 4l, 16l, 6l. 4m 3.50s. a 26.50s (14 Ran).
(Miss S Deburiatte), M R Channon

1993 St Modwen Chase Limited Handicap
Class C (0-135 5-y-o and up) £4,448
2m . . . . (2:40)

1480⁴ SUPER TACTICS (Ire) [128] 8-11-0 (3*) P Henley, *patiently
rdn, gd hdwy to draw level last, sn led, ran on strly to go clr.*
. . . .(9 to 2 op 4 to 1)   1
1672* MISTER ODDY [128] 10-11-3 M A Fitzgerald, *led to 4th,
continued to press new ldr, led aftr four out, hdd sn after last,
rdn and not pace of wnr . . . . . .(5 to 4 fav op 11 to 10 on)   2
NATIVE MISSION [132] 9-11-7 R Dunwoody, *nvr far away,
effrt and drvn alng aftr 4 out, one pace frm betw last 2.*
. . . .(3 to 1 op 11 to 4 tchd 7 to 2)   3
1672³ RANDOM ASSAULT (NZ) [132] 7-11-7 A Maguire, *took keen
hold, led 4th, quickened four out, hdd bef nxt, hit 3 out, wknd
quickly, eased whn btn . . . . .*(7 to 2 op 5 to 2 tchd 4 to 1)   4
Dist: 3l, 11¼l, 28l. 3m 59.10s. a 12.10s (4 Ran).
SR: 40/37/39/11/   (H V Perry), R H Alner

1994 Alan Povey Signs Novices' Handicap
Chase Class E (0-100 5-y-o and up)
£3,022 3¼m . . . .(3:10)

1734 COVERDALE LANE [82] 9-10-11 Mr P Murray, *settled off the
pace, drvn alng fnl circuit, styd on to ld last, kpt on strly to go
clr . . . .*(9 to 2 op 3 to 1)   1
1734⁴ MAJORS LEGACY (Ire) [81] 7-10-10 A Thornton, *al fron rnk,
ev ch frm 4 out, styd on same pace from last.*
. . . .(8 to 1 op 6 to 1 tchd 9 to 1)   2
1670 BE BRAVE [78] 6-10-7 R Rourke, *settled midfield, improved
fnl circuit, led 3 out till hdd last, one pace r-in . . . . .*(33 to 1)   3
1801 ROMANY BLUES [71] 7-10-0 D Gallagher, *settled wth chasing grp, improved to nose ahead 5 out, hdd 3 out, fdd und pres
nxt.* . . . .(25 to 1 op 20 to 1)   4
1706* OCEAN LEADER [95] 9-11-10 A Maguire, *settled off the pace,
struggling whn ldrs quickened 5 out, tld off.*
. . . .(5 to 2 fav op 9 to 4 tchd 11 to 4)   5
1262⁶ DOMINIE (Ire) [90] (bl) 8-11-5 C Llewellyn, *struggling and beh
aftr one circuit, tld off . . . . .*(20 to 1 op 14 to 1)   6
844⁶ GEORGE ASHFORD (Ire) [89] 6-11-4 M Sharratt, *lost tch aftr
one circuit, tld off . . . . .*(25 to 1 op 20 to 1)   7
OATS N BARLEY [88] 7-11-3 S Burrough, *struggling in mid-
field whn f 13th . . . .*(14 to 1 op 12 to 1)   f
1734 RAGGED KINGDOM (Ire) [71] 7-9-11 (3*) L Aspell, *al wl beh,
tld off whn f 13th . . . .*(50 to 1 tchd 66 to 1)   f
1739 GRIFFINS BAR [85] 8-11-0 R Marley, *made most till hdd 5 out,
lost tch quickly, tld off whn pld up betw last 2.*
. . . .(11 to 1 op 10 to 1 tchd 12 to 1)   pu
1593⁶ THE BRUD [76] 8-10-5 J A McCarthy, *al struggling in rear, tld
off whn pld up bef 4 out . .*(9 to 1 op 8 to 1 tchd 10 to 1)   pu
1734 BOSSYMOSS (Ire) [71] 7-10-0 T Eley, *settled midfield, struggling aftr one circuit, tld off whn pld up bef 2 out.*
. . . .(9 to 1 op 8 to 1)   pu
Dist: 6l, 1½l, 18l, 16l, dist, 10l. 7m 0.50s. a 48.50s (12 Ran).
(Jim Pilkington), Mrs S J Smith

1995 European Breeders Fund 'National
Hunt' Novices' Hurdle Qualifier
Class E (4,5,6-y-o) £2,536 2½m
110yds. . . . .(3:40)

1631* AGISTMENT 5-11-10 R Dunwoody, *nvr far away, led 4 out till
hdd 2 out, rallied to rgn ld sn aftr last, ran on gmely.*
. . . .(9 to 4 on op 5 to 4 tchd 11 to 4)   1
1573* MIGHTY MOSS (Ire) 5-11-3 (7*) Mr F Hutsby, *patiently rdn,
improved to join issue, 3 out, led nxt, hdd sn aftr last, ridden
and kpt on same pace.*
. . . .(6 to 4 on op 5 to 4 on tchd Evens)   2

261

1770³ BARTON WARD 5-11-0 R Johnson, *tucked away beh ldrs, effrt and drvn alng 3 out, no extr frm betw last 2.*
.... (25 to 1 op 20 to 1) 3
SEABROOK LAD 5-11-0 I Lawrence, *hld up and beh, styd on frm 3 out, nrst finish.*......................... (100 to 1) 4
1770 SHARE OPTIONS (Ire) 5-11-10 A Maguire, *al wl plcd, led 6th to 4 out, feeling pace aftr nxt, fdd und pres.*.........(8 to 1) 5
1673³ AUT EVEN (Ire) 6-11-0 A Thornton, *chsd ldg bunch, feeling pace and drvn alng bef 3 out, sn struggling.*
......................................14 to 1 op 12 to 1) 6
COLONEL BLAZER 4-11-0 M A Fitzgerald, *settled in tch, und pres appr 3 out, sn beh, tld off.*
.... (12 to 1 op 8 to 1 tchd 14 to 1) 7
1505⁶ COOLE CHERRY 6-11-0 B Fenton, *led till hdd 6th, wknd quickly aftr 4 out, tld off last 3.*...................(100 to 1) 8
1464⁵ SCALLY HICKS 5-10-9 Gary Lyons, *wl beh frm hfwy, tld off.*
....(100 to 1) 9
1703⁴ CARLY-J 5-10-9 Mr N Kent, *chsd ldg bunch, struggling and lost tch 4 out, tld off...*.......................(100 to 1) 10
1738⁶ MINSTER BOY 5-11-0 C Llewellyn, *struggling and beh frm hfwy, tld off...*...............................(100 to 1) 11
1615 CHATERGOLD (Ire) 4-10-7 (7*) C Davies, *wl plcd to hfwy, sn lost tch, tld off...*.............................(100 to 1) 12
1849 BLACK STATEMENT (Ire) 6-10-11 (3*) L Aspell, *wl plcd to hfwy, lost tch quickly, tld off...*....................(100 to 1) 13
Dist: ½l, 6l, 10l, 9l, 14l, 6l, nk, 7l, 11l, 4l. 5m 15.90s. a 36.90s (13 Ran).

(Marquesa de Moratalla), J G FitzGerald

ASCOT (good to firm)
Saturday December 21st
Going Correction: PLUS 0.25 sec. per fur. (races 1,4,5), PLUS 0.40 (2,3,6)

1996 'Book Of Music' Novices' Chase Class A formerly the Noel Steeple Chase Grade 2 (5-y-o and up) £12,320 2m 3f 110yds......(12:35)

1771* SIMPLY DASHING (Ire) 5-11-7 R Dunwoody, *al hndy, not fluent 4th and 3 out, led appr last, ran on well.*
......................(13 to 8 fav tchd 7 to 4 and 5 to 4) 1
1748* OR ROYAL (Fr) 5-11-10 A P McCoy, *al hndy, led 12th, sn pushed alng, hdd appr last, no extr.*
........................(7 to 2 op 2 to 1 tchd 4 to 1) 2
1519* OH SO RISKY 9-11-10 P Holley, *hld up in tch, shaken up aftr 12th, chsd ldg pair frm 4 out, rdn and one pace appr 2 out.*
.....................(5 to 1 op 9 to 2 tchd 6 to 1) 3
1797² CHERYL'S LAD (Ire) 6-11-3 M A Fitzgerald, *hld up, pushed alng and outpcd aftr tenth, nvr dngrs.*
........................(13 to 2 op 9 to 2 tchd 7 to 1) 4
1886 COUNTRY STAR (Ire) 5-11-3 G Bradley, *jmpd lft, led to 12th, sn outpcd, btn whn mstk 2 out.*
.................(7 to 1 op 5 to 1 tchd 15 to 2) 5
1804⁶ BOLSHIE BARON 7-11-3 Mr M Harris, *al beh, mstk 6th, sn lost tch, tld off....*.....(66 to 1 op 50 to 1 tchd 100 to 1) 6
1706³ LUCKY DOLLAR (Ire) 8-11-3 C Llewellyn, *hld up in tch, f heavily 8th.*
.........(25 to 1 op 20 to 1 tchd 33 to 1 and 50 to 1) f
1941⁵ SHALIK (Ire) 6-11-3 N T Egan, *al beh, lost tch 6th, tld off whn pld up bef 3 out.*..................(100 to 1 op 66 to 1) pu
Dist: 3l, 10l, 7l, 7l, dist. 4m 56.00s. a 15.00s (8 Ran).

(Steve Hammond), T D Easterby

1997 Mitie Group Kennel Gate Novices' Hurdle Class A Grade 2 (4-y-o and up) £9,212 2m 110yds........(1:10)

1761* MAKE A STAND 5-11-7 A P McCoy, *jmpd wl, made all, clr 3rd, eased nr finish, very easily.* (13 to 8 on op 11 to 10) 1
EAGLES REST (Ire) 5-11-0 M A Fitzgerald, *keen early, hld up, chsd wnr frm 3 out, kpt on wl, no ch with winner.*
...................(20 to 1 op 8 to 1 tchd 25 to 1) 2
1749* BOWCLIFFE COURT (Ire) 4-11-0 A Maguire, *hld up, mstk 3rd, effrt 5th, no hdwy frm 3 out.*
.............(8 to 1 op 5 to 1 tchd 9 to 1 and 10 to 1) 3
BAHAMIAN SUNSHINE (USA) 5-11-0 G Bradley, *sn chsd wnr, hit 5th, lost pl 3 out, soon btn.*
.......................(12 to 1 op 7 to 1 tchd 16 to 1) 4
1505⁴ SUPREME CHARM (Ire) 4-11-0 C Llewellyn, *hit 1st, sn hld up in rear, beh frm 5th.*.................(14 to 1 op 8 to 1) 5
SUPER HIGH 4-11-0 N Williamson, *hld up, beh frm 3rd.*
........................(50 to 1 op 33 to 1 tchd 66 to 1) 6
DANCES WITH HOOVES 4-11-0 S McNeill, *hit 1st and uns rdr.....* (33 to 1 op 20 to 1 tchd 40 to 1 and 50 to 1) ur
PERFECT PAL (Ire) 5-11-0 R Dunwoody, *pld hrd, hit 1st, mstk, hmpd and uns rdr second.* (7 to 1 op 4 to 1 tchd 8 to 1) ur
LATAHAAB (USA) 5-11-0 P Hide, *chsd ldrs, struggling whn mstk 6th, btn whn blun 2 out, pld up bef last.*
....................(10 to 1 op 6 to 1 tchd 12 to 1) pu
Dist: 5l, 16l, 10l, 8l, 3l. 2m 58.80s. a 12.80s (9 Ran).
SR: 31/19/3/-/-/-/

(P A Deal), M C Pipe

1998 Long Walk Hurdle Class A Grade 1 (4-y-o and up) £25,240 3m 1f 110yds

---

.... (1:45)

1520² OCEAN HAWK (USA) 4-11-7 C Llewellyn, *made all, clr 3rd, given breather hfwy, drvn clear appr 2 out, ran on gmely.*
...................(7 to 1 op 11 to 2 tchd 8 to 1) 1
1637³ TRAINGLOT 9-11-7 R Dunwoody, *hld up, cld 8th, rdn to chase ldg pair aftr 3 out, kpt on one pace und pres.*
................(9 to 4 fav op 2 to 1 tchd 5 to 2) 2
1891 PLEASURE SHARED (Ire) 8-11-7 N Williamson, *cl up, ev ch 3 out, hrd rdn and one pace appr nxt, hit last.*
..............................(5 to 2 op 7 to 4) 3
1637⁶ TOP SPIN 7-11-7 A Maguire, *hld up in last pl, cld 8th, effrt aftr 3 out, nvr able to chal...*...........(33 to 1 tchd 50 to 1) 4
1637* WHAT A QUESTION (Ire) 8-11-2 G Bradley, *cl up, hit 6th, ev ch 4 out, sn outpcd and btn quickly.*
........................(7 to 2 op 11 to 4 tchd 4 to 1) 5
1883* BLAZE AWAY (USA) 5-11-7 A P McCoy, *hld up, cld 8th, collapsed aftr tenth, dead.*
........................(9 to 1 op 10 to 1 tchd 12 to 1) f
Dist: 4l, 2l, 5l, 4l. 6m 22.70s. a 23.70s (6 Ran).

(Matt Archer & Miss Jean Broadhurst), N A Twiston-Davies

1999 Betterware Cup Class B Handicap Chase (5-y-o and up) £24,378 3m 110yds........................(2:20)

1516² GO BALLISTIC [128] 7-10-0 A P McCoy, *hld up in cl tch, mstks second and 6 out, led 2 out, rdn out.*
..............(4 to 1 op 9 to 2 tchd 5 to 1) 1
1466* UNGUIDED MISSILE (Ire) [153] 8-11-11 R Dunwoody, *led to 4th, cl up, mstk 11th, led four out, hdd 2 out, ev ch aftr last, no extr und pres.*.................(9 to 2 op 7 to 2) 2
1518² MAJOR BELL [135] 8-10-7 N Williamson, *trkd ldrs, mstk 11th, outpcd 4 out, sn drvn and no extr.*
.....................(9 to 2 op 4 to 1 tchd 5 to 1) 3
1632* TURNING TRIX [128] 9-10-0 A Maguire, *not fluent early, hld up in last pl, some prog 14th, btn whn blun 3 out.*
.......................(6 to 1 tchd 13 to 2) 4
1851² STRONG MEDICINE [134] 9-10-6 C Llewellyn, *led 4th, hdd four out, sn outpcd.*....................(25 to 1) 5
1853* INCHCAILLOCH (Ire) [133] 7-10-5 (5ex) G Maude, *hld up, pushed alng 13th, sn struggling, tld off...*(5 to 1 op 7 to 2) 6
1851³ BRADBURY STAR [148] 11-11-6 P Hide, *trkd ldrs, lost pl whn f heavily 5 out...*.................(33 to 1 op 25 to 1) f
1210⁴ TRAVADO [156] 10-12-0 M A Fitzgerald, *hld up, struggling and drpd rear 12th, tld off whn pld up bef last.*
...........................(25 to 1 op 16 to 1) pu
1639⁵ DEXTRA DOVE [137] 9-10-9 G Bradley, *mstk second, cl up till drpd rear 5th, hdwy appr 11th, led whn mistake and hdd 4 out, sn btn, pld up bef last.....(6 to 1 op 5 to 1 tchd 13 to 2) pu
Dist: 1¾l, 20l, 13l, 1¼l, dist. 6m 11.10s. a 10.10s (9 Ran).
SR: 32/55/17/-/1/-/

(Mrs B J Lockhart), J G M O'Shea

2000 Frogmore Handicap Chase Class B (5-y-o and up) £9,457 2m.....(2:50)

1760³ STORM ALERT [150] 10-11-11 A Maguire, *trkd ldr, lft in ld 4th, made rst, ran on wl und pres.*
.....................(3 to 1 op 7 to 2 tchd 11 to 4) 1
1640* ASK TOM (Ire) [152] 7-12-0 R Garritty, *hld up, pushed alng aftr 3 out, chsd wnr frm nxt, drvn and ev ch r-in, no extr nr finish.*
.....(Evens fav op 5 to 4 on tchd 11 to 10 and 6 to 5) 2
1613² AROUND THE HORN [135] 9-10-10 S McNeill, *cl up, ev ch whn mstk 2 out, sn btn...*(10 to 1 op 7 to 1 tchd 12 to 1) 3
SYBILLIN [140] 10-11-1 R Dunwoody, *hld up in last pl, pushed alng 4 out, no imprsn.*
........................(16 to 1 op 12 to 1 tchd 20 to 1) 4
1873* ZEREDAR (NZ) [125] (bl) 6-10-0 C Llewellyn, *led, f 4th.*
..................(4 to 1 op 7 to 2 tchd 9 to 2 and 5 to 1) f
Dist: ½l, 26l, 16l. 3m 54.20s. a 6.20s (5 Ran).
SR: 75/77/33/22/-/

(Mrs Dawn Perrett), D Nicholson

2001 Knights Royal Hurdle Class B (4 & 5-y-o) £8,559 2m 110yds.....(3:20)

1506² MISTINGUETT (Ire) 4-10-11 C Llewellyn, *made all, drvn out frm last.*.................(11 to 2 op 9 to 2 tchd 6 to 1) 1
1761 ESKIMO NEL (Ire) 5-10-11 R Garritty, *hld up, cld 5th, chsd wnr appr 2 out, ev ch last, sn no extr.......(8 to 1 op 6 to 1) 2
1638 MR PERCY (Ire) 5-10-12 P Hide, *hld up, shrtlvd effrt aftr 3 out, styd on same pace.*...........................(9 to 1 jt-
...................................fav tchd 10 to 1 op 10 to 1) 3
TIBETAN 4-11-2 M A Fitzgerald, *hit 1st, trkd wnr, mstk 4 out, btn appr 2 out.*...............(25 to 1 tchd 33 to 1) 4
1885⁶ NON VINTAGE (Ire) 5-11-5 W Worthington, *hld up beh, nvr on terms.*...................(25 to 1 tchd 33 to 1) 5
TRAGIC HERO (bl) 4-11-10 A P McCoy, *keen hold, trkd ldrs, pushed alng appr 4 out, wknd und pres aftr nxt....(9 to 1 jt-
.................................fav op 4 to 1 tchd 10 to 1) 6
1644⁸ ALLTIME DANCER (Ire) 4-11-2 G Bradley, *hld up beh, shrtlvd effrt aftr 3 out, no response.*
.........................(33 to 1 op 25 to 1 tchd 40 to 1) 7
1030³ PADDY'S RETURN (Ire) (bl) 4-11-10 R Dunwoody, *trkd ldg pair, drvn aftr 3 out, one pace and no imprsn whn f last.*
.....................(5 to 1 op 9 to 2 tchd 11 to 2) f

1880⁴ ASHWELL BOY (Ire) 5-11-2 N Williamson, *al beh, blun second, not fluent 4th, rdn alng nxt, tld off whn pld up bef 2 out.*
....(11 to 2 op 5 to 1 tchd 6 to 1) pu
Dist: 4l, 9l, 10l, 11l, 1¾l, 4l. 3m 55.30s. a 9.30s (9 Ran).
SR: 56/52/44/38/30/33/21/-/-/ (John Duggan), N A Twiston-Davies

HAYDOCK (good to soft)
Saturday December 21st
Going Correction: PLUS 0.55 sec. per fur. (races 1,3,5,7), PLUS 0.70 (2,4,6)

2002 Wirral Juvenile Novices' Hurdle
Class D (3-y-o) £2,955 2m... (12:15)

SHU GAA (Ire) 10-12 J Osborne, *made all, pushed clr 2 out, not fluent last, readily.*..........(11 to 10 fav op 5 to 4) 1
1629⁹ WHAT JIM WANTS (Ire) 10-7 (5*) R McGrath, *nvr far away, hdwy to chase wnr 2 out, no imprsn.*
....(12 to 1 op 10 to 1 tchd 14 to 1) 2
TAGATAY 10-9 (3*) E Callaghan, *pld hrd, cl up, rdn and not quicken appr 2 out, one pace.*........(14 to 1 op 10 to 1) 3
1737⁴ BAASM 10-12 W Fry, *in tch, pushed alng and outpcd 2 out, sn no extr.*...............(10 to 1 op 8 to 1) 4
1737⁷ ARABIAN HEIGHTS 10-9 (3*) E Husband, *cl up, niggled alng 3 out, outpcd frm nxt.*..........(10 to 1 op 8 to 1) 5
1737⁹ MR GOLD (Ire) 10-12 Richard Guest, *hld up, hdwy and in tch 5th, wkng whn mstk 2 out.*..............(14 to 1) 6
PALAMON (USA) 10-12 P Carberry, *midfield, rdn and lost tch 3 out, sn btn.*........(7 to 2 tchd 3 to 1 and 4 to 1) 7
1524⁴ THORNTOUN ESTATE (Ire) 10-12 A S Smith, *jmpd poorly, hmpd 3rd, tld off frm 4 out.*..........(16 to 1 op 20 to 1) 8
1470⁷ IRISH KINSMAN 10-12 W McFarland, *pckd 1st, hld up, in tch and reminders appr 3 out, sn wknd.*......(33 to 1) 9
1629 JOE SHAW 10-12 P Niven, *hld up, f 3rd.*
....(7 to 1 op 9 to 1 tchd 6 to 1) f
SHARP COMMAND 10-7 (5*) Michael Brennan, *pld hrd wth ldr, drvn alng and wkng whn ran clr 3 out.*
....(14 to 1 op 10 to 1) ur
1470⁶ WORTH THE BILL 10-12 S Wynne, *sn tld off, not jump wl, pld up bef 3 out.*..........(25 to 1 op 20 to 1) pu
Dist: 12l, 9l, 2l, ¾l, 21l, 8l, 5l, 5l. 3m 55.70s. a 17.70s (12 Ran).
SR: (Ali K Al Jafleh), O Sherwood

2003 Southport Novices' Chase Class C
(5-y-o and up) £4,485 2½m.. (12:45)

1825⁴ SLOTAMATIQUE (Ire) 7-11-0 A Dobbin, *cl up, lft in ld 5 out, strly pressed last, ran on wl und pres.* (9 to 2 tchd 4 to 1) 1
1597⁸ SPINNAKER 6-11-0 J Osborne, *hld up, clr order 5 out, chlgd last, kpt on wl till no extr close hme.*... (11 to 2 op 7 to 2) 2
CARIBOO GOLD (USA) 7-11-0 J Railton, *chsd ldr, pushed alng appr 2 out, drvn and wknd aftr last.*
....(9 to 2 op 4 to 1 tchd 5 to 1) 3
1771⁵ BLACK BROOK (Ire) 7-11-0 P Niven, *hld up, pushed alng and outpcd 7th, sn tld off.*........(12 to 1 op 8 to 1) 4
1627¹ OAT COUTURE 8-11-5 Richard Guest, *led, hit 5th, blun and hdd 5 out, blunded ag'n nxt, 4th and btn whn f 2 out.*
....(Evens fav tchd 6 to 5) f
Dist: ¾l, 18l, dist. 5m 17.50s. a 20.50s (5 Ran).
SR: 21/20/2/-/-/ (Slotamatics (Bolton) Ltd), G Richards

2004 Widnes Handicap Hurdle Class C
(0-135 4-y-o and up) £3,485 2m
.... (1:20)

1827* SHINING EDGE [111] 4-10-9 J Osborne, *chsd ldrs, not fluent 3rd, chlgd last, sn led, styd on strly.* (2 to 1 fav hdwy to 9 to 4) 1
1885* NEW INN [116] 5-11-0 K Gaule, *dsptd ld, led o'rall appr 2 out, rdn and hdd sn aftr last, kpt on.*
....(9 to 2 op 3 to 1) 2
HOUSE CAPTAIN [118] 7-10-13 (3*) F Leahy, *settled midfield, not fluent 5th, unbl to quicken whn hit 2 out, rallied strly flt, nrst finish.*..........(12 to 1 op 14 to 1) 3
1633⁸ MARCHANT MING (Ire) [130] 4-12-0 P Niven, *dsptd ld, pushed alng and unbl to quicken appr 2 out, sn no extr.*
....(3 to 1 tchd 7 to 2) 4
1023⁶ WATCH MY LIPS [102] 4-10-0 D Bridgwater, *hld up, hit second, clr order and fdg whn hit 2 out.*...(8 to 1 op 7 to 1) 5
ALBERTITO (Fr) [102] 9-10-0 S Wynne, *beh, tld off 4 out, no dngr aftr.*.......................(20 to 1 tchd 25 to 1) 6
1772 ELATION [119] 4-11-3 A Dobbin, *in tch, rdn and lost touch appr 2 out, eased considerably whn btn.*
....(13 to 2 op 6 to 1 tchd 7 to 1) 7
Dist: 2l, ½l, 6l, 18l, 14l, 4l. 3m 51.80s. a 13.80s (7 Ran).
SR: 31/34/35/41/ (G Graham), T D Easterby

2005 St Helens Handicap Chase Class B
(0-145 5-y-o and up) £6,684 4m 110yds..................... (1:55)

PINK GIN [107] 9-10-11 P Niven, *hld up, chsd ldr fnl circuit, led aftr 4 out, clr 2 out, cmftbly.*.........(7 to 1 op 6 to 1) 1
1937⁵ DIAMOND FORT [109] 10-12-0 S Wynne, *cl up, lost pos tenth, blun 14th, beh fnl circuit til styd on ag'n frm 3 out.*
....(11 to 2 op 5 to 1 tchd 6 to 1) 2

1859³ PAPER STAR [97] 9-10-1¹ W McFarland, *led, jmpd rght frm hfwy, hdd aftr 4 out, lost tch after nxt, fnshd tired.*
....(10 to 1 tchd 12 to 1) 3
1774 URANUS COLLONGES (Fr) [116] (bl) 10-11-6 A Dobbin, *in tch, rdn and outpcd 4 out, sn no dngr.* (10 to 1 tchd 12 to 1) 4
1804⁹ QUIXALL CROSSETT [96] 11-9-9 (5*) S Taylor, *hld up, struggling in rear frm hfwy, wl tld off whn f last.*
....(100 to 1 op 50 to 1) f
1645* CHRISTMAS GORSE [120] 10-11-0 J Osborne, *cl up, disputing ld whn f 13th.* (11 to 8 fav op 6 to 4 tchd 13 to 8) f
1767⁶ CHIEF RAGER [104] 7-10-8 D Bridgwater, *jmpd poorly in rear, tld off whn pld up aftr tenth.*
....(100 to 30 op 3 to 1 tchd 7 to 2) pu
Dist: 14l, 20l, 6l. 8m 56.80s. a 36.80s (7 Ran).
(Mrs Margaret Francis), M D Hammond

2006 European Breeders Fund 'National Hunt' Novices' Hurdle Qualifier
Class D (4,5,6-y-o) £3,025 2m (2:30)

1738² ALZULU 5-11-0 P Carberry, *hmpd strt, sn tracking ldrs, slight ld 3 out, hit nxt, strly pressed appr last, ran on wl und pres.*........(6 to 4 op 5 to 4 tchd 13 to 8) 1
1738¹ GOOD VIBES 4-11-10 J Osborne, *led till ran very wide bend aftr second, cl up till chlgd 3 out, drvn alng tehw last 2, kpt on till no extr close hme.*..........(Evens fav tchd 11 to 10) 2
1677² PENTLAND SQUIRE 5-11-0 Richard Guest, *lft in ld aftr second, not fluent 4 out, hdd nxt, hld whn blun last.*
....(9 to 1 op 8 to 1 tchd 10 to 1) 3
1682⁹ EIRESPRAY (Ire) 5-11-0 D Bentley, *hld up, hit second, lost tch 4 out, pushed alng and styd on stdly aftr nxt.*
....(33 to 1 op 25 to 1) 4
1224⁴ GALEN (Ire) 5-11-0 P Niven, *hld up, shaken up and lost tch 4 out, nvr a factor.*.........(12 to 1 op 10 to 1 tchd 14 to 1) 5
DAN DE MAN (Ire) 5-11-0 A Dobbin, *hld up, pld hrd, outpcd appr 4 out, sn no dngr.* (25 to 1 op 66 to 1 tchd 28 to 1) 6
1763⁷ SEYMOUR'S DOUBLE 5-11-0 S Wynne, *reluctant to jump off, beh till some hdwy 4 out, sn wknd.* (66 to 1 op 50 to 1) 7
Dist: 1¾l, 18l, 11l, 4l, 5l, 3l. 3m 53.00s. a 15.00s (7 Ran).
SR: 24/32/4/-/ (D Buckle), J G FitzGerald

2007 Boston Pit Handicap Chase Class C
(0-135 5-y-o and up) £4,711 2½m
.... (3:00)

1037* GENERAL COMMAND (Ire) [123] 8-11-2 P Carberry, *cl up, jmpd wl, not fluent 4 out, drw clr aftr nxt, easily.*
....(11 to 8 on tchd 11 to 10 on) 1
VALIANT WARRIOR [133] 8-11-12 P Niven, *cl up, pushed alng and outpcd 2 out, no ch wth wnr.*
....(2 to 1 op 13 to 8) 2
1851⁵ CONTI D'ESTRUVAL (Fr) [117] 6-10-10 A Dobbin, *cl up, hit 4th, outpcd aftr 3 out, eased whn btn after last.*
....(9 to 2 op 1 to 1 tchd 5 to 1) 3
Dist: 5l, 23l. 5m 19.30s. a 22.30s (3 Ran).
SR: 5/-/-/ (Robert Ogden), G Richards

2008 Thelwall Standard Open National Hunt Flat Class H (4,5,6-y-o) £1,292 2m........................... (3:30)

SLIDE ON 6-11-4 Gary Lyons, *midfield, gd hdwy hfwy, led 4 fs out, pushed clr o'r one out, styd on strly.*
....(16 to 1 op 10 to 1) 1
1682⁷ MEADOW HYMN (Ire) 5-11-4 W Dwan, *in tch, clr order hfwy, chsd wnr fnl 2 fs, kpt on.*..........(16 to 1 op 10 to 1) 2
MERRY MASQUERADE (Ire) 5-11-4 R Hodge, *ran green, sn pushed alng in rear, styd on wl fnl 3 fs, nrst finish.*
....(20 to 1 op 12 to 1) 3
1682³ BILLY BUCKSKIN 4-11-4 W Fry, *midfield, chlgd 6 fs out, drvn and one pace frm 2 out.*.......(14 to 1 op 10 to 1) 4
BEN EIGER (Ire) 4-11-4 D Bridgwater, *pushed alng toward rear aftr 5 fs, some hdwy appr strt, outpcd o'r 2 furlongs out.*
....(10 to 1 op 5 to 1) 5
BREATH OF SCANDAL (Ire) 5-11-4 J Osborne, *hld up gng wl, steady hdwy to track ldrs 4 fs out, outpcd o'r 2 out, better for race.*..........(9 to 4 fav op 7 to 4 tchd 5 to 2) 6
NO FINER MAN (Ire) 5-11-4 A Dobbin, *hld up, effrt and in tch 6 fs out, shaken up and lost touch o'r 3 furlongs out.*
....(4 to 1 op 6 to 1 tchd 7 to 1) 7
1874⁸ PRIMITIVE LIGHT 6-10-6 (7*) N Horrocks, *cl up, led 6 fs out till hdd 4 out, fdd.*..........(33 to 1 op 20 to 1) 8
BADGER'S LANE 5-11-11 J Railton, *led aftr 2 fs till ran wide and hdd after 4 furlongs, lost tch entering strt.*
....(5 to 1 op 4 to 1 tchd 7 to 1) 9
BACK ON THE LASH (Ire) 4-11-4 P Carberry, *hld up, lost tch entering strt, sn beh.*...........(20 to 1 op 12 to 1) 10
1809⁴ STRONG MINT (Ire) 5-11-11 P Niven, *hld up, effrt and in tch hfwy, wknd quickly entering strt, eased.*
....(11 to 4 op 7 to 2 tchd 5 to 2) 11
1735⁸ JUST ONE QUESTION (Ire) 6-11-11 Richard Guest, *made most till hdd 6 fs out, wknd quickly, tld off.*
....(16 to 1 op 10 to 1) 12
1809 SOCIAL INSECURITY (Ire) 5-11-4 K Gaule, *cl up till wknd quickly o'r 6 fs out, tld off.*......(20 to 1 op 16 to 1) 13
1648⁷ SCHOLAR GREEN 4-11-4 W McFarland, *tld off fnl 4 fs.*
....(33 to 1 op 20 to 1) 14

Dist: 5l, 13l, nk, 3l, 13l, 1l, ½l, 13l, 12l, 26l. 3m 46.70s. (14 Ran).
(P D Evans), P D Evans

LINGFIELD (good to soft)
Saturday December 21st
Going Correction: PLUS 1.05 sec. per fur.

2009 Brandy Butter Conditional Jockeys' Handicap Hurdle Class E (0-110 4-y-o and up) £2,364 2m 110yds (12:30)

1835³ SHEPHERDS REST (Ire) [95] 4-10-9 (7") S Hearn, wth ldr till led 2 out, sn clr, pushed out r-in.
...........................(100 to 30 op 3 to 1 tchd 4 to 1) 1
1646⁶ MUSEUM (Ire) [79] 5-9-10 (4") X Aizpuru, hld up, prog to chase ldg pair 3 out, not quicken bet nxt, styd on to go second appr last, not rch wnr..............(10 to 1 tchd 12 to 1) 2
1894⁴ TICKERTY'S GIFT [107] 6-11-10 (4") M Attwater, trkd ldrs, rdn and outpcd 3 out, kpt on frm nxt.
...........................(13 to 2 op 3 to 1 tchd 7 to 1) 3
1888⁴ HAWTHORNE GLEN [100] 9-11-3 (4") A Irvine, jmpd rght, made most till hdd and mstk 2 out, sn btn.
...........................(15 to 8 fav op 3 to 1 tchd 7 to 4) 4
1848² PEDALTOTHEMETAL (Ire) [90] 4-10-11 D J Kavanagh, hld up, rdn 5th, lost tch 3 out, one pace aftr.
...........................(9 to 2 op 11 to 4 tchd 5 to 1) 5
615 DERISBAY (Ire) [80] (bl) 8-10-1 Sophie Mitchell, prmnt to 4th, sn wknd, tld off..................(25 to 1 tchd 33 to 1) 6
FATHER POWER (Ire) [79] 8-10-0 C Rae, al rear, lost tch 4th, sn tld off...........................(50 to 1 op 33 to 1) 7
WIDE SUPPORT [90] 11-10-7 (4") M Batcholor, trkd ldrs, rdn 5th, wknd aftr nxt, poor 6th whn f last.
BALLYMGYR (Ire) [79] 7-9-10 (4") M Griffiths, prmnt to 3rd, sn wknd, tld off whn pld up aftr 3 out.
...........................(20 to 1 op 14 to 1 tchd 25 to 1) pu
Dist: 2½l, 5l, 8l, 10l, dist, sht-hd. 4m 15.80s. a 24.80s (9 Ran).
SR: 13/-/17/2/-/-/ (The Odd Dozen), S Mellor

2010 Port & Stilton Novices' Handicap Chase Class F (0-95 4-y-o and up) £2,584 2m (1:00)

1765⁶ STAGE PLAYER [82] 10-11-4 D Leahy, trkd ldrs, prog to ld aftr 9th, clr last, rdn out..........(16 to 1 tchd 20 to 1) 1
1806* RIVER LEVEN [88] (bl) 7-11-7 (3") D Fortt, chsd ldr 4th, mstk 6th and sn pushed alng, effrt und pres aftr 9th, ev ch 3 out, no extr...........................(11 to 8 fav op 5 to 4 on) 2
1722⁵ POLICEMANS PRIDE (Fr) [72] 7-10-8 B Fenton, set str pace and sn clr, mstk 7th and reminders, hdd aftr 9th, soon btn.
...........................(8 to 1 tchd 10 to 1) 3
BAYRAK (USA) [84] 6-11-1 (5") A Bates, al beh, tld off frm 4th.
...........................(7 to 2 op 6 to 1) 4
1732⁶ KING'S GOLD [78] 6-11-0 M Richards, mstk 1st, mistake and uns rdr nxt...........................(14 to 1 op 12 to 1) ur
1724* CASTLECONNER (Ire) [82] (bl) 5-11-4M A Holdsworth, beh, last whn mstk and uns rdr 5th..........(4 to 1 op 3 to 1) ur
1698 KENTAVRUS WAY (Ire) [64] 5-10-0 N Mann, refused to race.
...........................(33 to 1 op 25 to 1 tchd 40 to 1 and 50 to 1) l
Dist: 4l, 20l, dist. 4m 27.20s. a 33.20s (7 Ran).
(Miss C J E Caroe), Miss C J E Caroe

2011 H.B.L.B. Mares' Only Christmas Handicap Hurdle Class E (0-130 4-y-o and up) £3,492 2m 3f 110yds (1:35)

1688* SAIL BY THE STARS [115] 7-10-13 A Thornton, trkd ldr, led aftr 3 out, clr appr last, pushed out, cmftbly.
...........................(9 to 4 op 6 to 4) 1
1576⁵ FORTUNES COURSE (Ire) [110] 7-10-8 T J Murphy, led to aftr 3 out, sn rdn and outpcd, kpt on to go second ag'n last, no imprsn wnr...........................(6 to 1 op 4 to 1) 2
HANDY LASS [102] 7-9-7 (7") M Griffiths, hld up, prog 3 out, chsd wnr gng easily appr nxt, rdn and wknd approaching last.
...........................(9 to 4 jt-fav op 5 to 1 tchd 25 to 1) 3
1268³ SILVER SHRED [130] 5-11-9 (5") O Burrows, hld up, reminder appr 3 out, rdn 4 out...........(5 to 4 fav op 2 to 1) 4
1597³ LESSONS LASS (Ire) [103] 4-10-1 B Fenton, keen hold, trkd ldg pair till mstk 3 out, wknd rpdly, tld off.
...........................(9 to 2 op 5 to 1 tchd 11 to 2) 5
Dist: 4l, 5l, dist, dist. 5m 11.10s. a 38.10s (5 Ran).
(T F F Nixon), Capt T A Forster

2012 Jardine Insurance Services Juvenile Novices' Hurdle Class E (3-y-o) £2,616 2m 110yds (2:10)

ROSEBERRY AVENUE (Ire) 10-7 (5") S Ryan, al prmnt, led 2 out, hng lft appr last, hung rght and left r-in, all out.
...........................(9 to 4 op 6 to 4 tchd 3 to 1) 1
1790* HILL OF SPICE (Ire) 11-5 M Richards, led to 2 out, hmpd and swtchd rght appr last, rallied, no extr nr finish.
...........................(13 to 8 fav op 2 to 1) 2

1610⁷ STERLING FELLOW (v) 10-12 M Clarke, beh, rdn 3rd, tld off 5th, kpt on appr 2 out, took poor third nr finish.
...........................(12 to 1 op 10 to 1 tchd 14 to 1) 3
BRIGHTON ROAD (Ire) 10-12 B Clifford, prmnt, ev ch 3 out, sn wknd, lost poor 3rd nr finish..........(14 to 1 op 10 to 1) 4
1890⁶ BIGWIG (Ire) 10-12 N Mann, beh frm 3rd, tld off 5th, modest late prog...........(66 to 1 op 33 to 1 tchd 100 to 1) 5
SCOTTISH HERO 10-12 B Fenton, hld up, prog 4th, in tch nxt, wknd 3 out, tld off..(7 to 1 op 6 to 1 tchd 8 to 1) 6
1702⁷ EMBROIDERED 10-0 (7") J K McCarthy, strted slwly, hld up beh, some prog 5th, sn tld off.
...........................(66 to 1 op 33 to 1 tchd 100 to 1) 7
1696⁴ HANBITOOH (USA) 10-12 G Upton, prmnt, rdn aftr second, sn wknd, tld off 5th......(12 to 1 op 7 to 1 tchd 14 to 1) 8
1412 HALF AN INCH (Ire) (bl) 10-12 D Leahy, mid-div, rdn 3rd, sn wknd, tld off..........(33 to 1 op 20 to 1 tchd 40 to 1) 9
1854 SAM ROCKETT (bl) 10-7 (5") D J Kavanagh, hld up, prog and in tch aftr 4th, sn wknd, tld off.......(50 to 1 op 33 to 1) 10
BAILIWICK 10-12 S Curran, prmnt till rdn and wknd bef 5th, tld off...........................(25 to 1 op 14 to 1 tchd 33 to 1) 11
ESKIMO KISS (Ire) 10-7 A Thornton, mstk 1st, al beh, tld off 5th...........................(25 to 1 op 12 to 1 tchd 33 to 1) 12
JAMIES FIRST (Ire) 10-12 D O'Sullivan, al beh, tld off frm 5th.
...........................(25 to 1 op 10 to 1) 13
INDUNA MKUBWA 10-12 L Harvey, trkd ldrs to 5th, wkng whn mstk nxt, tld off..........(14 to 1 op 7 to 1 tchd 16 to 1) 14
1854⁹ VERONICA FRANCO 10-7 T J Murphy, prmnt, rdn 3rd, wknd mstk nxt, tld off......(50 to 1 op 25 to 1 tchd 66 to 1) 15
Dist: ¾l, dist, hd, 13l, 3l, 19l, 9l, 3l, 11l, 10l. 4m 14.60s. a 23.60s (15 Ran).
SR: 21/27/-/-/-/-/ (P D Savill), R Akehurst

2013 European Breeders Fund 'National Hunt' Novices' Hurdle Qualifier Class E (4,5,6-y-o) £2,532 2m 110yds (2:40)

1556* BOARDROOM SHUFFLE (Ire) 5-11-2 (3") L Aspell, keen hold, cl up, jnd ldr 3 out, led and hit nxt, sn clr, very easily.
...........................(15 to 8 on op 13 to 8 on tchd 6 to 4 on and 2 to 1 on) 1
1743² THREE FARTHINGS 6-11-0 G Upton, prmnt, led and mstk 4th, hdd 2 out, no ch wth wnr aftr.
...........................(9 to 2 op 7 to 2 tchd 5 to 1) 2
MASTER PILGRIM 4-11-0 B Fenton, keen hold, hld up, prog aftr 5th, not rch ldrs, lft modest 3rd 2 out.
...........................(33 to 1 op 25 to 1 tchd 50 to 1) 3
1792* DANTES CAVALIER (Ire) 6-11-2 (3") D Fortt, led to 4th, sn lost pl and struggling.........(4 to 1 op 3 to 1 tchd 9 to 2) 4
1641¹⁸ JOHN DRUMM 5-11-0 A Thornton, wth ldrs to 5th, sn rdn and wknd... (10 to 1 op 14 to 1 tchd 16 to 1 and 20 to 1) 5
1685⁴ SHANAGORE WARRIOR (Ire) 4-11-0 N Mann, keen hold, in tch to 4th, sn beh, tld off..........(33 to 1 tchd 50 to 1) 6
377⁵ BELLE PERK (Ire) 5-10-9 T J Murphy, hld up last, prog 5th, chsd ldg pair aftr 3 out, modest 3rd whn blun and uns rdr 2 out...........................(14 to 1 op 12 to 1) ur
Dist: 14l, 12l, 4l, 2½l, dist. 4m 13.90s. a 22.90s (7 Ran).
SR: 35/16/4/5/ (A D Weller), J T Gifford

2014 Mac Vidi Novices' Chase Class E (5-y-o and up) £3,425 3m (3:10)

1732* MARINERS MIRROR 9-11-7 Mr M Rimell, pressed ldr, led 7th, rdn and jst hdd whn lft clr 2 out, eased r-in.
...........................(5 to 2 op 9 to 4 tchd 11 to 4) 1
1766⁵ KENDAL CAVALIER 6-10-12 B Fenton, not fluent, chsd ldg pair, rdn 12th, effrt aftr 15th, one pace and no imprsn whn lft second and hmpd 2 out, kpt on.
...........................(5 to 2 op 9 to 4 tchd 11 to 4) 2
1765 GEMMA'S WAGER (Ire) 6-10-7 L Harvey, mstk 8th, al beh, rdn and struggling tenth, sn tld off.
...........................(40 to 1 op 33 to 1 tchd 100 to 1) 3
1765³ MR PICKPOCKET (Ire) 10-12 T J Murphy, led to 7th, pressed wnr aftr, mstk 11th, jst led whn f 2 out.
...........................(2 to 1 tchd 9 to 4) f
1608 BENBULBIN (Ire) 6-10-12 S Curran, al beh, rdn tenth, sn tld off, pld up bef 3 out......(33 to 1 op 25 to 1 tchd 50 to 1) pu
Dist: 4l, dist. 6m 44.10s. a 50.10s (5 Ran).
(F J Mills), N A Twiston-Davies

2015 Holly & Ivy Maiden Open National Hunt Flat Class H (4,5,6-y-o) £1,311 2m 110yds (3:40)

ARKLEY ROYAL 5-11-5 G Upton, wtd wth, prog 6 fs out, shaken up to ld 2 out, sn clr, cmftbly.
...........................(6 to 4 on op Evens tchd 7 to 4 on) 1
1350⁹ SHARIAKANNDI (Fr) 4-11-5 T J Murphy, hld up, prog 6 fs out, led and pres frm 3 out, took second nr finish.
...........................(10 to 1 op 6 to 1) 2
1578⁴ REPEAT OFFER 4-11-5 S Curran, keen hold, cl up, prog to ld 6 fs out, rdn and hdd 2 out, no extr...(4 to 1 tchd 6 to 1) 3
1675⁶ IRISH DELIGHT 4-11-5 D Morris, hld up, prog hfwy, no imprsn on ldrs o'r 4 fs out. (8 to 1 op 4 to 1 tchd 9 to 1) 4
PEACE INITIATIVE 4-11-5 A Dicken, prmnt, wth ldr 6 fs out, wknd 3 out...........................(14 to 1 op 10 to 1) 5
BEBE GREY (v) 5-10-7 (7") M Clinton, rear, pushed alng hfwy, sn lost tch...........(14 to 1 op 8 to 1 tchd 16 to 1) 6

HUISH (Ire) 5-11-5 Mr A Charles-Jones, *pld hrd, led to 6 fs*
out, wknd rpdly, tld off . . . . (25 to 1 op 20 to 1)   7
PITARRY 6-11-5 B Fenton, *prmnt till wknd 6 fs out, tld off.*
 . . . . (16 to 1 op 12 to 1 tchd 20 to 1)   8
CHEMIN-DE-FER 4-11-5 Mrs K Hills, *prmnt to hfwy, sn wknd,*
tld off . . . . (25 to 1 op 20 to 1 tchd 33 to 1)   9
1769 ROYAL DIVIDE (Ire) 4-11-5 M Richards, *taken dwn early, tld*
off aftr 5 fs . . . . (20 to 1) 10
Dist: 10l, ½l, 24l, 11l, 8l, dist, 18l, 11l, dist. 4m 14.90s. (10 Ran).
(John Bickel), J A B Old

NAVAN (IRE) (yielding to soft)
Saturday December 21st

2016 Reindeer Handicap Hurdle (0-102 4-y-o and up) £3,082 2m . . . . . (12:30)

1713³ ANCIENT HISTORIAN (Ire) [-] 7-11-5 (7*) P Morris, . . (3 to 1)   1
1550 MARINERS REEF (Ire) [-] 5-10-4 (7*) D McCullagh, (12 to 1)   2
1579⁵ LEWISHAM (Ire) [-] 4-11-9 C F Swan, ... (7 to 1)   3
946* BRADLEYS CORNER (Ire) [-] 5-10-13 (7*) Mr L J Gracey,
 . . . . (10 to 1)   4
THE QUADS [-] 4-10-1 (7*) D W O'Sullivan, ... (9 to 4 fav)   5
1579* FALLOW TRIX (Ire) [-] 4-11-3 (7*) Mr J Keville, ... (5 to 1)   6
KOOKABB (Ire) [-] 4-10-2 (5*) T Martin, ... (8 to 1)   7
1460 OUR DUCHESS (Ire) [-] 5-9-7 (7*) J M Maguire, . . (16 to 1)   8
1654 LOUISES FANCY (Ire) [-] 6-11-6 P L Malone, ... (10 to 1)   9
1900 COMMAND 'N CONTROL [-] 7-11-4 (3*) G Cotter, . . (7 to 1) 10
DOUBLE STRIKE (Ire) [-] 5-11-6 H Rogers, ... (12 to 1) 11
1580⁷ SLEWMORE (Ire) [-] 5-10-10 (3*) U Smyth, ... (20 to 1) 12
1777 MY BLUE [-] 4-9-4 (7*) E F Cahalan, ... (16 to 1) 13
1275 GOLD DEPOSITOR (Ire) [-] 4-10-12 J Shortt, ... (10 to 1) 14
1901 WHAT EVER YOU WANT (Ire) [-] 6-10-0 (7*) Mr M Callaghan,
 . . . . (33 to 1) 15
Dist: 9l, 3l, 1½l, nk. 4m 11.50s. (15 Ran).
(P W Mernagh), W P Mullins

2017 Irish National Hunt Novice Hurdle (4-y-o and up) £4,110 2m . . . . . . (1:00)

1777* TOAST THE SPREECE (Ire) 4-11-2 C F Swan, (11 to 8 on)   1
ALL THE VOWELS (Ire) 5-11-0 J P Broderick, ... (4 to 1)   2
1649 BLUSHING SAND (Ire) 6-10-7 (7*) Mr T J Beattie, . . (5 to 1)   3
THE DARGLE (Ire) 6-10-7 (7*) A O'Shea, ... (33 to 1)   4
DOUBLE COLOUR (Ire) 4-10-2 (7*) A P Sweeney, (14 to 1)   5
1751 KEEPITSAFE (Ire) 5-11-0 H Rogers, ... (20 to 1)   6
CLERICAL COUSIN (Ire) 7-11-0 F Woods, ... (14 to 1)   7
ISLAND ROCK (Ire) 5-10-4 (5*) T Martin, ... (14 to 1)   8
SINGLE OR BUST (Ire) 6-10-2 (7*) S M McGovern, (25 to 1)   9
1486 CROSSEROADS (Ire) 6-11-0 J Shortt, ... (20 to 1) 10
TAKE THE RAP (Ire) 6-10-9 A Powell, ... (33 to 1) 11
Dist: 3l, 15l, 1½l, 8l. 4m 12.90s. (11 Ran).
(Golden Step Racing Syndicate), A P O'Brien

2018 Christmas Presents Handicap Hurdle (4-y-o and up) £6,850 3m . . (1:30)

1433² ROSIN THE BOW (Ire) [-] 7-10-11 C F Swan, ... (9 to 2)   1
1904⁴ LADY QUAYSIDE (Ire) [-] 6-9-7 T Horgan, ... (10 to 1)   2
1489* LISCAHILL FORT (Ire) [-] 7-9-7 (7*) M D Murphy, . . (10 to 1)   3
1489* RATHGIBBON (Ire) [-] 5-10-10 T P Treacy, ... (4 to 1)   4
1778* ROCK'N ROLL KID (Ire) [-] 5-9-10 D J Casey, ... (7 to 1)   5
1752⁶ ANNADOT (Ire) [-] 6-10-4 (7*) L J Fleming, ... (8 to 1)   6
1620³ ALLATRIM (Ire) [-] 6-9-11 (3*) G Cotter, ... (9 to 1)   7
1434 NUAFFE [-] 11-10-1 T J Mitchell, ... (33 to 1)   8
BART OWEN [-] 11-10-10 (7*) A O'Shea, ... (33 to 1)   9
1433* ALASAD [-] 6-11-8 R Hughes, ... (3 to 1 fav) 10
Dist: 11l, 1l, sht-hd, 14l. 6m 0.90s. (10 Ran).
(F Fitzsimons), A P O'Brien

2019 Navan Hurdle (4-y-o and up) £3,425 2½m . . . . (2:00)

1840* BLAZE OF HONOUR (Ire) 5-11-6 C F Swan, . . . (5 to 2 fav)   1
GROUND WAR 9-11-2 M Moran, ... (12 to 1)   2
1436⁶ BRASS BAND (Ire) 5-10-11 D P Fagan, ... (12 to 1)   3
1896⁸ PERSIAN HALO (Ire) 6-12-0 C O'Dwyer, ... (3 to 1)   4
YUKON GOLD (Ire) (bl) 7-11-11 J Shortt, ... (8 to 1)   5
1905 MR BOAL (Ire) 7-11-11 K F O'Brien, ... (33 to 1)   6
1536* FOLLY ROAD (Ire) 6-11-8 P L Malone, ... (8 to 1)   7
COCK COCKBURN 10-11-7 (7*) J M Maguire, ... (14 to 1)   f
MAGICAL LADY (Ire) 4-11-4 T P Rudd, ... (7 to 2)   ur
KILMACREW 9-10-9 (7*) D W O'Sullivan, ... (50 to 1)   pu
Dist: 4l, 7l, 9l, 10l. 5m 19.00s. (10 Ran).
(Mrs Anne Leahy), A P O'Brien

2020 Santa Claus Handicap Chase (0-123 4-y-o and up) £3,082 3m . . . . . . (2:30)

1191* QUATTRO [-] 6-9-10 (3*) G Cotter, ... (5 to 1)   1
1779³ ONTHEROADAGAIN (Ire) [-] 8-11-1 T P Rudd, ... (13 to 2)   2
1896 TOPICAL TIP (Ire) [-] 7-11-4 J P Broderick, ... (10 to 1)   3
1903³ THE GOPHER (Ire) [-] (bl) 7-10-5 L P Cusack, ... (8 to 1)   4
1408² STRONG HICKS (Ire) [-] 8-11-1 F J Flood, ... (11 to 4 fav)   5
1652 DRAMATIC VENTURE (Ire) [-] 7-11-0 D J Casey, ... f
1898⁴ LE GINNO (Fr) [-] 9-11-3 T P Treacy, ... (6 to 1)   ur

---

1755⁶ JOHNEEN [-] 10-10-11 C O'Dwyer, ... (12 to 1)   pu
1538⁸ BERMUDA BUCK [-] 10-10-3 F Woods, ... (14 to 1)   l
Dist: ¾l, dist, 11l. 6m 30.70s. (9 Ran).
(Donal Cullen), Martin M Treacy

2021 Tattersalls Ireland EBF Mares Novice Chase (5-y-o and up) £3,767 2½m . . . . (3:00)

1583* DUN BELLE (Ire) 7-12-0 T J Mitchell, ... (11 to 2)   1
1780* WOODVILLE STAR (Ire) 7-11-8 T Horgan, ... (5 to 4 on)   2
1780² ROYAL ROSY (Ire) 5-11-0 C F Swan, ... (4 to 1)   3
1899³ SHINING WILLOW 6-11-2 C O'Dwyer, ... (8 to 1)   4
1780⁵ COOLAFINKA (Ire) 7-10-13 (3*) G Cotter, ... (16 to 1)   5
1780⁷ SHARONS PRIDE (Ire) 6-11-2 J R Barry, ... (25 to 1)   6
1780⁴ MARIES POLLY 6-11-2 D H O'Connor, ... (12 to 1)   7
WARKEY LADY (Ire) 6-10-13 (3*) D P Murphy, ... (50 to 1)   8
169⁹ RAHAN BRIDGE (Ire) 7-10-13 (3*) U Smyth, ... (12 to 1)   9
1898 THE VENDOR (Ire) 6-11-2 J P Broderick, ... (50 to 1) 10
1780³ KILBRICKEN MAID (Ire) 6-10-9 (7*) Mr C A Murphy, (16 to 1) pu
Dist: 6l, hd, 20l, 9l. 5m 28.50s. (11 Ran).
(Mrs A Connolly), P A Fahy

2022 Brandy Butter I.N.H. Flat Race (4 & 5-y-o) £2,740 2m . . . . (3:30)

1649⁷ VALLEY ERNE (Ire) 5-12-0 Mr A J Martin, ... (7 to 1)   1
1782 QUIPTECH (Ire) 5-11-7 (7*) Mr A C Coyle, ... (8 to 1)   2
1655⁶ HEATHER VILLE (Ire) 4-11-4 Mr G J Harford, . . . (7 to 4 fav)   3
1713 COUNCILLOR (Ire) 5-11-7 (7*) Mr M P Horan, ... (16 to 1)   4
MISS HOT TAMALLI (Ire) 5-11-6 (3*) Mr P M Kelly, (10 to 1)   5
BITOFAGLOW (Ire) 5-12-0 Mr A R Coonan, ... (10 to 1)   6
1756 ALVINE (Ire) 4-11-2 (7*) Mr S J Mahon, ... (6 to 1)   7
1655⁹ MEASURED STEP (Ire) 5-11-9 (5*) Mr J T McNamara,
 . . . . (12 to 1)   8
TOTAL SUCCESS (Ire) 4-11-2 (7*) Mr D Broad, ... (8 to 1)   9
1042 LYNX MARINE (Ire) 5-11-7 (7*) Mr J D O'Connell, . (33 to 1) 10
JAPAMA (Ire) 5-11-7 (7*) Mr R Geraghty, ... (8 to 1) 11
1174 ELECTRIC LAD (Ire) 5-12-0 Mr P F Graffin, ... (14 to 1) 12
NIANTIC BAY (Ire) 4-11-2 (7*) Mr J McNamara, ... (8 to 1) 13
STRATEGIC AFFAIR (Ire) 5-11-7 (7*) Miss A Reilly, (12 to 1) 14
1895 THETHREETOMS (Ire) 5-11-7 (7*) Mr T Gibney, . . . (25 to 1) 15
Dist: 8l, 5l, 5l, nk. 4m 7.60s. (15 Ran).
(S A M Syndicate), Michael Cunningham

UTTOXETER (good to soft)
Saturday December 21st
Going Correction: PLUS 0.75 sec. per fur.

2023 Technical High School Past Pupils Novices' Hurdle Class E (4-y-o and up) £2,631 2m . . . . (12:25)

1417⁴ MISTER RM 4-11-5 D Walsh, *hld up, hdwy 5th, led 3 out sn*
clr, cmftbly . . . . (4 to 1 tchd 9 to 2)   1
1685* STORMY PASSAGE (Ire) 6-11-5 G Tormey, *chsd ldrs, ev ch 3*
out, styd on same pace.
 . . . . (15 to 8 fav op 7 to 4 tchd 2 to 1)   2
1263³ PRUSSIA 5-11-5 D Gallagher, *chsd ldrs, led 5th to 3 out, styd*
on same pace. . . . . (8 to 1 op 7 to 1)   3
PERCY BRAITHWAITE (Ire) 4-10-5 (7*) K Hibbert, *rcd keenly,*
led 4th to nxt, wknd 2 out. (12 to 1 op 8 to 1 tchd 14 to 1)   4
1381³ SAMANID (Ire) 4-11-5 O Pears, *hld up, nvr plcd to chal.*
 . . . . (9 to 1 op 8 to 1 tchd 10 to 1)   5
BANNY HILL LAD 6-10-12 J R Kavanagh, *hld up, hdwy 3 out,*
eased whn btn nxt. . . . . (33 to 1 tchd 40 to 1)   6
1868⁶ GUTTERIDGE (Ire) 6-10-12 L Lawrence, *prmnt, pld ldrs*
whn jmpd slwly 4th, wknd 3 out. . . . . . (33 to 1 op 20 to 1)   7
1397⁸ ROOD MUSIC 5-10-12 Derek Byrne, *led to 4th, wknd appr 3*
out. . . . . (50 to 1 op 33 to 1)   8
1642 OUR TOM 4-11-5 (5*) Mr R Thornton, *al wl beh*. . (50 to 1)   9
1297³ MANASIS (NZ) 5-10-12 R Johnson, *prmnt till wknd 5th.*
 . . . . (14 to 1 op 8 to 1 tchd 16 to 1) 10
BALLYRANTER 7-10-9 (3*) Mr C Bonner, *hld up, beh frm 4th.*
 . . . . (12 to 1 op 8 to 1 tchd 14 to 1) 11
1260² VICTORIA DAY 4-10-4 (3*) T Dascombe, *prmnt, mstk 1st,*
wknd 4th. . . . . (12 to 1 op 10 to 1 tchd 14 to 1) 12
976 RACING TELEGRAPH 6-10-9 (3*) G Hogan, *strted slwly, hld*
up, al in rear, tld off whn pld up bef 3 out.
 . . . . (50 to 1 op 33 to 1) pu
Dist: 6l, 4l, 4l, 6l, 8l, 7l, 16l, sht-hd, 4l, nk. 3m 55.60s. a 18.60s (13 Ran).
SR: 25/19/15/4/5/-/   (F J Mills & Mr W Mills), N A Twiston-Davies

2024 Chris Talbot 39th Birthday Handicap Chase (0-120 5-y-o and up) £3,663 3m . . . . (12:55)

1774³ LORD GYLLENE (NZ) [119] 8-12-0 R Johnson, *hld up in tch,*
chsd ldr 6th, mstk 5 out, led appr 3 out, sn clr, eased r-in.
 . . . . (6 to 4 fav op 5 to 4)   1
1624³ SAILOR JIM [107] 9-11-2 W Marston, *led, mstk 4th, rdn and*
hdd appr 3 out, sn wknd. . . . . (9 to 2 op 4 to 1)   2
1569 CARLINGFORD LAKES (Ire) [91] 8-10-0 B Powell, *chsd ldr to*
6th, wknd six out. . . . . (9 to 1 op 8 to 1 tchd 10 to 1)   3

1370[6] BRAES OF MAR [110] 6-11-5 J R Kavanagh, *prmnt, jmpd slwly 11th, sn wknd*..................(6 to 1 op 5 to 1) 4
1814[3] CELTIC TOWN [108] 8-11-3 J A McCarthy, *hld up, rdn 8th, hit nxt, sn tld off*..................(11 to 2 op 5 to 1) 5
MY MAIN MAN [99] 8-10-8 D Walsh, *trkd ldrs, lost pl 4th, pld up aftr 6th*..............(10 to 1 op 8 to 1 tchd 11 to 1) pu
Dist: 16l, 5l, ½l, 29l. 6m 20.80s. (6 Ran).
(Stanley W Clarke), S A Brookshaw

2025 Manny Bernstein Bookmakers Novices' Handicap Hurdle Class E (0-100 4-y-o and up) £2,473 3m 110yds...................... (1:30)

1829* MENSHAAR (USA) [90] 4-11-4 R Supple, *al prmnt, led 2 out drvn out*.................... (7 to 2 jt-fav tchd 4 to 1) 1
1631[4] COOLE HILL (Ire) [93] 5-11-2 (5*) Mr R Thornton, *chsd ldrs, ev ch 3 out, styd on und pres r-in*... (7 to 2 jt-fav tchd 4 to 1) 2
TILTY (USA) [96] (v) 6-11-10 T Eley, *chsd ldrs, outpcd 4 out, ran on appr last*.
.........(12 to 1 op 14 to 1 tchd 16 to 1 and 20 to 1) 3
1928[5] EVEZIO RUFO [87] (v) 4-11-1 B Powell, *mid-div, hdwy 6th, led approching 3 out, hdd nxt, no extr r-in*.
.... (16 to 1 op 14 to 1 tchd 20 to 1) 4
1341[4] FELLOO (Ire) [91] 7-11-5 T Jenks, *lft in ld second, hdd appr 3 out, wknd last*......................(16 to 1 op 14 to 1) 5
1729[5] BURNTWOOD MELODY [72] 5-10-0 J Supple, *hld up, rdn 5 out, nvr nr ldrs*........ (14 to 1 op 16 to 1 tchd 20 to 1) 6
1796[5] QUITE A MAN [83] 8-10-4 (7*) T Mortimer, *hld up, hdwy 5th, sn chasing ldrs, wknd 4 out*.............. (20 to 1 op 14 to 1) 7
1775[5] HOTSPUR STREET [78] (bl) 4-10-6 W Marston, *led till mstk and uns rdr second*........(7 to 1 op 6 to 1 tchd 8 to 1) ur
1631 JIGGINSTOWN [84] 9-10-12 A Roche, *hld up, hdwy 5 out, wknd nxt, pld up bef 3 out*.................. (14 to 1 op 10 to 1) pu
1867[6] MISTER BLAKE [94] 6-11-8 R Johnson, *hld up, rdn 5 out, no ch whn pld up bef 3 out*... (5 to 1 op 9 to 2 tchd 11 to 2) pu
BALLYDOUGAN (Ire) [73] (v) 8-10-1 R Bellamy, *beh frm 6th, tld off whn pld up bef 3 out*.............. (25 to 1 tchd 33 to 1) pu
1442[3] RIVERBANK ROSE [72] 5-10-0 G Tormey, *prmnt till wknd 5 out, beh whn pld up bef 3 out*.
.... (12 to 1 op 10 to 1 tchd 14 to 1) pu
1729 NUNSON [72] 7-10-0 D Gallagher, *hld up, rdn hfwy, beh frm 5 out, pld up bef 3 out*.............. (50 to 1 op 25 to 1) pu
Dist: 3l, 1¼l, 2l, 7l, 5l, dist. 6m 14.80s. a 37.80s (13 Ran).
(G A Arthur), L Lungo

2026 Heathyards Engineering Novices' Handicap Chase Class E (0-100 5-y-o and up) £3,087 2m 5f....... (2:05)

1881* ART PRINCE (Ire) [100] 6-11-7 (7*) M Berry, *led second, clr tenth, unchlgd*. (11 to 8 on op 6 to 4 on tchd 5 to 4 on) 1
1815[7] PLASSY BOY (Ire) [72] 7-10-0 R Supple, *sn wl beh, nvr dngrs*.
.... (12 to 1 op 16 to 1) 2
BARONCELLI [72] 6-10-0 I Lawrence, *sn wl beh, nvr nrr*.
.... (14 to 1 op 12 to 1) 3
1804 PEARL EPEE [90] 7-11-4 R Johnson, *in tch, wnt second tenth, no imprsn*................(9 to 2 op 7 to 2 tchd 5 to 1) 4
1766 RONANS GLEN [77] 9-10-5 T J O'Sullivan, *beh whn f 7th*.
.....................................(12 to 1 tchd 14 to 1) f
1543[8] SPEARHEAD AGAIN (Ire) [89] (v) 7-11-0 (3*) R Massey, *led to second, hit 8th, sn wknd, tld whn f 4 out*.
.... (11 to 1 op 8 to 1 tchd 12 to 1) f
1605 HEATHYARDS BOY [72] (bl) 6-10-0 D Walsh, *prmnt, chsd wnr 8th, wknd 11th, tld off whn refused 3 out*.
.... (33 to 1 op 25 to 1 tchd 40 to 1) ref
1822[9] WALLS COURT [76] 9-10-4 L O'Hara, *al wl beh, tld off whn pld up bef 2 out*...................... (12 to 1 op 8 to 1) pu
Dist: Dist, 1½l, 4l. 5m 20.10s. a 22.10s (8 Ran).
SR: 36/-/-/-/- (Terry Neill), C P E Brooks

2027 Houghton Vaughan Handicap Hurdle Class B (0-145 4-y-o and up) £5,070 2½m 110yds................. (2:35)

1400[2] ARITHMETIC [115] 6-10-0 W Marston, *led to 3rd, led 5th, rdn appr last, all out*......... (5 to 2 op 2 to 1 tchd 11 to 4) 1
1628[3] DALLY BOY [115] 4-9-9 (5*) Mr R Thornton, *al prmnt, chlgd 3 out, rdn appr last, ran on*.....................(3 to 1 op 5 to 2) 2
EXPRESS GIFT [139] 7-11-10 N Smith, *hld up, lost grnd whn ldrs quickened 4 out, steady hdwy last 2, nvr plcd to chal*.
.... (11 to 2 op 4 to 1) 3
1628[4] OUTSET (Ire) [127] 6-10-9 (3*) Mr C Bonner, *chsd ldrs, led 3rd to 5th, wknd nxt*...... (2 to 1 fav op 11 to 4 tchd 3 to 1) 4
1268[7] DR LEUNT (Ire) [134] 5-11-5 G Tormey, *prmnt till wknd 4 out*.
.....................................(7 to 1 op 6 to 1) 5
1628[7] BEACHY HEAD [123] 8-10-8 A Roche, *prmnt, lost pl 4th, rdn nxt, sn beh*......... (25 to 1 op 10 to 1 tchd 33 to 1) 6
Dist: ¾l, 13l, 8l, nk, 3½l. 5m 5.60s. a 26.60s (6 Ran).
(Robert & Elizabeth Hitchins), Mrs J Pitman

2028 Wellman Plc Novices' Chase Class D (5-y-o and up) £3,598 2m..... (3:05)

1627[3] GAROLO (Fr) 6-11-0 D Gallagher, *let to 6th, led ag'n 2 out, styd on strly*....................(7 to 4 on op 5 to 2 on) 1
1725 ROBINS PRIDE (Ire) 6-10-11 (3*) T Dascombe, *chsd ldr, led 6th, rdn and hdd 2 out, btn whn mstk last*.
.... (8 to 1 tchd 16 to 1 and 20 to 1) 2
1368 ROLFE (NZ) (bl) 6-11-0 R Johnson, *al in rear, tld off frm 5th*.
.........................(2 to 1 op 7 to 4 tchd 9 to 4) 3
GLENMAVIS 9-11-0 Dr P Pritchard, *in tch till mstk and uns rdr 4th*................(40 to 1 op 33 to 1 tchd 100 to 1) ur
Dist: 12l, dist. 4m 5.50s. a 18.50s (4 Ran).
SR: 21/9/-/-/ (Lady Lloyd Webber), C P E Brooks

2029 Weatherbys 'Stars Of Tomorrow' Open National Hunt Flat Standard - Class H (4,5,6-y-o) £1,474 2m (3:35)

CHERRYMORE (Ire) 5-11-1 (3*) G Hogan, *chsd ldrs, led 3 fs out, styd on strly*.................. (Evens fav op 6 to 4) 1
BENEFIT-IN-KIND (Ire) 4-10-11 (7*) Mr A Wintle, *hld up, hdwy hfwy, ran on ins last, not rch wnr*.
.... (8 to 1 op 5 to 1 tchd 10 to 1) 2
1306[3] POT BLACK UK 5-11-4 G Tormey, *led till hdd 3 fs out, sn outpcd*.................(4 to 1 op 5 to 2 tchd 9 to 2) 3
MR MONTAGUE (Ire) 4-11-4 T Eley, *hld up, hdwy hfwy, rdn o'r 2 fs out, styd on same pace*...........(33 to 1 op 20 to 1) 4
BLOWING ROCK (Ire) 4-11-4 D Gallagher, *hld up in tch, rdn and wknd o'r 2 fs out*. (33 to 1 tchd 40 to 1 and 50 to 1) 5
LEDBURIAN 6-10-11 (7*) K Hibbert, *hld up, hdwy hfwy, rdn and wknd o'r 2 fs out*.................. (66 to 1 op 33 to 1) 6
1768[6] JUSTLIKEJIM 5-10-13 (5*) Mr R Thornton, *hld up, hdwy 5 fs out, wknd o'r 3 out*..... (33 to 1 op 25 to 1 tchd 50 to 1) 7
JUSTJIM 4-11-4 D Walsh, *prmnt, pushed alng 5 fs out, wknd o'r 3 out*................(15 to 2 op 5 to 1 tchd 8 to 1) 8
TOM TUGG (Ire) 6-11-4 R Johnson, *mid-div, took clr order hfwy, wknd o'r 4 fs out*. (20 to 1 op 12 to 1 tchd 33 to 1) 9
GO FOR THE DOCTOR 6-11-1 (3*) T Dascombe, *rcd keenly, chsd ldrs till wknd o'r 3 out*.
.... (50 to 1 op 33 to 1 tchd 66 to 1) 10
THE BUG 6-11-4 B Powell, *hld up, nvr rchd ldrs*.
.... (50 to 1 op 33 to 1) 11
PARK END 4-10-11 (7*) T O'Connor, *mid-div, shaken up hfwy, sn lost pl*...............(40 to 1 op 25 to 1 tchd 50 to 1) 12
MAY ROSE 6-10-6 (7*) Mr S Durack, *chsd ldrs pld hrd, wknd 5 fs out*...............(33 to 1 op 16 to 1 tchd 40 to 1) 13
GEM'S PRECIOUS 5-11-1 (3*) R Massey, *prmnt till wknd o'r 5 fs out*........................... (33 to 1 tchd 40 to 1) 14
THE MUCKLE QUINE 5-10-13 A Roche, *hld up, hdwy ten fs out, wknd 6 out, tld off*. (25 to 1 op 16 to 1 tchd 33 to 1) 15
Dist: 6l, nk, 3l, 8l, 5l, nk, 8l, 8l, 1¼l, 10l. 4m 1.00s. (15 Ran).
(Robert & Elizabeth Hitchins), Mrs J Pitman

LUDLOW (good to firm)
Monday December 23rd
Going Correction: MINUS 0.25 sec. per fur.

2030 Tanners Cava Conditional Jockeys' Selling Handicap Hurdle Class G (0-95 3-y-o and up) £2,146 2m 5f 110yds...................... (1:00)

1856[2] SLEEPTITE (Fr) [81] 6-11-0 (5*) J Power, *prmnt, led 4th till appr 6th, pckd four out, led approaching nxt, drvn out*.
.................................(3 to 1 fav op 4 to 1) 1
768[3] LOVELARK [62] 7-9-9 (5*) M Griffiths, *hld up beh ldrs, rdn aftr 4 out, styd on frm 2 out, not rch wnr*..............(33 to 1) 2
1938 BRIGHT SAPPHIRE [75] 10-10-8 (5*) J Prior, *prmnt, led appr 6th till approaching 3 out, one pace*.
.... (9 to 1 op 7 to 1 tchd 10 to 1) 3
1747 LE BARON [73] 5-10-11 Sophie Mitchell, *hld up beh ldrs, rdn 4 out, btn appr nxt*........(15 to 2 op 6 to 1 tchd 8 to 1) 4
1938[8] ITS GRAND [74] 7-10-12 T Dascombe, *al hndy, rdn and wknd appr 3 out*..........................(12 to 1 op 10 to 1) 5
1856 PERFECT BERTIE (Ire) [62] 4-9-10[1] (5*) M Keighley, *hld up, prog 6th, rdn appr 3 out, 4th and btn whn mstk nxt*.
.... (10 to 1 op 8 to 1) 6
1731[7] QUICK DECISION (Ire) [62] 5-9-9 (5*) N T Egan, *hld up beh ldrs, wknd 4 out*..........................(25 to 1 op 16 to 1) 7
1747[6] CATWALKER (Ire) [62] (bl) 5-9-9 (5*) C Rae, *hdwy aftr 6th, wknd 4 out*......................... (25 to 1 op 16 to 1) 8
1492[7] GUNMAKER [78] 7-10-13 (3*) D J Kavanagh, *nvr trble ldrs*.
.... (14 to 1 op 10 to 1) 9
1261[8] BETHS WISH [62] 7-10-0 Guy Lewis, *hld up beh ldrs, wknd 6th*...(33 to 1) 10
1796[4] TUG YOUR FORELOCK [67] 5-10-5 Michael Brennan, *mid-div, prog 6th, wknd 4 out*............... (9 to 2 op 4 to 1) 11
1747[4] DARING HEN (Ire) [69] (bl) 6-10-7 G Tormey, *nvr trble ldrs*.
....(16 to 1) 12
1492[9] KING OF BABYLON (Ire) [70] 4-10-8 L Aspell, *strted very slwly, al beh*..........................(16 to 1 op 14 to 1) 13
918[7] CELCIUS [67] (bl) 12-10-0 (5*) B Moore, *mid-div, improved 6th, wknd 4 out*.................. (20 to 1 op 12 to 1) 14
1614 BITE THE BULLET [62] 5-10-0 R Massey, *led to 4th, wknd four out*.. (20 to 1) 15
1798[9] HACKETTS CROSS (Ire) [90] 8-12-0 G Hogan, *al beh, tld off whn pld up bef 3 out*..................(10 to 1 op 5 to 1) pu
Dist: 4l, 1½l, 10l, 1¼l, 10l, 1¾l, 7l, 6l, nk, 3l. 5m 0.00s. a 5.00s (16 Ran).
(David Chown), W G M Turner

NATIONAL HUNT RESULTS 1996-97

2031 Tanners Champagne Handicap Chase Class D (0-120 5-y-o and up) £3,517 3m...................(1:30)

1721* ACT OF PARLIAMENT (Ire) [107] (bl) 8-11-2 C O'Dwyer, led till appr 3rd, rdn bef 4 out, rgned ld 2 out, all out.
................................(9 to 4 op 2 to 1 tchd 5 to 2) 1
1801* GOD SPEED YOU (Ire) [97] (bl) 7-10-6 A Maguire, led appr 3rd, pckd 3 out, hdd nxt, unbl to quicken r-in.
................................(13 to 8 on op 6 to 4 on) 2
282⁹ HARRISTOWN LADY [108] (bl) 9-11-3 A P McCoy, hld up, outpcd 12th, no imprsn aftr............(10 to 1 op 7 to 1) 3
1471 FOXGROVE [91] 10-9-9 (5*) Mr R Thornton, chsd ldrs, outpcd 12th, no imprsn aftr.. (66 to 1 op 50 to 1 tchd 100 to 1) 4
PANT LLIN [91] 10-10-0 S Wynne, nvr on terms.
................................(25 to 1 op 20 to 1) 5
1799² FAIRY PARK [91] (v) 11-9-7 (7*) Mr H J Oliver, mstk 7th, beh 12th.........................(16 to 1 op 8 to 1 tchd 20 to 1) 6
Dist: ½l, 30l, ½l, 14l, 4l. 5m 48.90s. a 1.90s (6 Ran).
SR: 9/-/-/ (J Perriss), K C Bailey

2032 Hoechst Roussel Panacur European Breeders Fund Mares' 'National Hunt' Novices' Hurdle Qualifier Class E (4-y-o and up) £2,724 2m 5f 110yds......................(2:00)

1338⁶ MAID FOR ADVENTURE 5-10-12 B Fenton, chsd ldrs, led and hit 3 out, sn clr...............(9 to 4 tchd 5 to 2) 1
1876⁶ GALATASORI JANE 6-11-5 A P McCoy, dsptd ld, led 7th till aftr 4 out, kpt on one pace frm 2 out, no ch wth wnr.
................................(11 to 4 op 2 to 1 tchd 3 to 1) 2
1927⁵ DI'S LAST 6-10-5 (7*) G Supple, hld up, prog 3rd, led aftr 4 out, hit 3 out and hdd, wknd nxt........(14 to 1 op 7 to 1) 3
1961 DOLCE NOTTE (Ire) 6-10-5 (7*) B Moore, hld up, hmpd and lft in ld briefly 5th, wknd appr 3rd.
................................(25 to 1 op 12 to 1 tchd 33 to 1) 4
GI MOSS (bl) 9-10-12 W Marston, led till appr 3rd, led aftr 5th to 7th, rdn 4 out, sn wknd..........(100 to 1 op 50 to 1) 5
1855² LUCIA FORTE 5-11-5 C O'Dwyer, chsd ldrs, led appr 3rd till f 5th.................(11 to 10 fav op Evens tchd 5 to 4) f
LUCY'S CHOICE 5-10-7 (5*) D Salter, hld up, rdn appr 6th, sn lost tch, tld off whn pld up bef 3 out..(100 to 1 op 50 to 1) pu
1675 ALRIGHT GUVNOR 6-10-12 J Ryan, al beh, tld off whn pld up bef 3 out.............................(100 to 1 op 50 to 1) pu
Dist: 10l, ¾l, 11l, 27l. 5m 3.80s. a 8.80s (8 Ran).
(Chris Brasher), Miss H C Knight

2033 Tanners Wines Novices' Chase Class C (5-y-o and up) £4,351 2m... (2:30)

1748 SUPER COIN 8-10-12 R Johnson, chsd ldrs, hit 1st, led 3rd to 5th, led 4 out, rdn whn lft clr last. (11 to 4 on op 5 to 2 on) 1
1803⁴ EULOGY (Fr) 9-10-12 A P McCoy, prmnt, led 5th, ran wide bend appr nxt, hdd 4 out, fdd.....(10 to 1 tchd 12 to 1) 2
1803 ARABIAN BOLD (Ire) 8-10-12 W Marston, led to 3rd, btn appr 4 out......................(25 to 1 op 16 to 1) 3
1846⁴ HOLY WANDERER (USA) 7-10-9 (3*) G Hogan, hld up, gd hdwy 8th, str chal whn blun and uns rdr last.
................................(3 to 1 op 9 to 4) ur
Dist: 15l, ½l. 3m 58.20s. a 8.20s (4 Ran).
(George Brookes), R Lee

2034 Tanners Burgundy Handicap Chase Class E (0-115 5-y-o and up) £3,100 2½m.......................(3:00)

1546⁴ TOO SHARP [100] 8-10-13 J F Titley, trkd ldrs, led sn aftr 3 out, drvn out.........(15 to 8 fav op 2 to 1 tchd 9 to 4) 1
1323⁴ CORRARDER [100] 12-10-13 J Railton, wtd wth, prog 13th, effrt last, no extr r-in.............(20 to 1 op 12 to 1) 2
1507 SPINNING STEEL [99] 9-10-12 S Burrough, led till sn aftr 3 out, fdd.........................(10 to 1 op 7 to 1) 3
1491³ CHANNEL PASTIME [88] 12-9-12 (3*) Guy Lewis, prmnt till wknd aftr 4 out......................(9 to 2 op 7 to 1) 4
1694⁵ COMEDY ROAD [93] 12-10-6 R Johnson, hld up, improved 9th, hit nxt, outpcd 13th, rallied and hit nxt, fdd.
................................(8 to 1 op 13 to 2) 5
1707 CELTINO [97] 8-10-10 S Wynne, not fluent, al beh, tld off whn pld up bef 3 out.........(2 to 1 op 7 to 4 tchd 11 to 8) pu
Dist: 1¾l, 20l, 2½l, 9l. 4m 50.70s. a 1.70s (6 Ran).
SR: 18/16/-/ (Sir Anthony Scott), Miss H C Knight

2035 Tanners Claret 'National Hunt' Novices' Hurdle Class E (4-y-o and up) £2,528 2m.....................(3:30)

1609⁴ ULTIMATE SMOOTHIE 4-10-12 A P McCoy, al hndy, led 2 out, ran on.........(5 to 4 jt-fav op 6 to 4 tchd 13 to 8) 1
JOSHUA'S VISION (Ire) 5-10-12 R Johnson, trkd ldrs, effrt 2 out, styd on r-in..........(6 to 1 op 7 to 1 tchd 8 to 1) 2
1609 MANVULANE (Ire) (v) 6-10-12 J Railton, led till hit 3 out and hdd, one pace.................(16 to 1 op 12 to 1) 3
952* SOUNDS LIKE FUN 5-11-5 J F Titley, trkd ldr, effrt 3 out, one pace nxt.....(5 to 4 jt-fav op 11 to 10 tchd 11 to 8) 4

SOUTH WEST EXPRESS (Ire) 4-10-12 W Marston, chsd ldrs till wknd appr 3 out..................(33 to 1) 5
1673 DERRYS PREROGATIVE 6-10-12 D Bridgwater, nvr on terms, tld off..............................(100 to 1 op 50 to 1) 6
1050⁹ BABA SAM (Ire) 5-10-12 B Fenton, al beh, tld off.
................................(50 to 1 op 33 to 1) 7
1673⁷ LOUGHDOO (Ire) 8-10-12 M Richards, al beh, tld off.
................................(33 to 1 op 20 to 1) 8
1675 PRIVATE MEMORIES 6-10-12 T J Murphy, al beh, tld off.
................................(100 to 1 op 33 to 1) 9
Dist: 1½l, 2l, 3½l, 10l, 22l, 1l, 17l, 13l. 3m 42.10s. a 10.10s (9 Ran).
(Isca Bloodstock), M C Pipe

DOWN ROYAL (IRE) (good)
Thursday December 26th

2036 Bet With The Tote Opportunity Handicap Hurdle (0-116 4-y-o and up) £1,370 2½m.....................(1:00)

1899⁵ COLLIERS HILL (Ire) [-] (bl) 8-9-12 (4*) R P Hogan, ...(9 to 2) 1
1899 THE THIRD MAN (Ire) [-] 6-9-7 (7*) D McCullagh, (12 to 1) 2
2016⁵ THE QUADS [-] 4-9-13 (4*) D W O'Sullivan, ...(3 to 1 jt-fav) 3
1778⁴ HERSILIA (Ire) [-] 5-10-7 (4*) L J Fleming, .. (3 to 1 jt-fav) 4
1899⁷ STAR TRIX (Ire) [-] 5-9-9 D Bromley, ...(12 to 1) 5
1713 BOLERO DANCER (Ire) [-] 8-10-2 (4*) D A McLoughlin,
................................(7 to 2) 6
495³ PLOUGH THE LEA (Ire) [-] 6-9-10 (4*) P J Dobbs, ..(12 to 1) 7
1901 COOKSGROVE ROSIE (Ire) [-] 4-9-7 (7*) D Fisher, (40 to 1) 8
1901 GRANNY BOWLY (Ire) [-] 6-9-6 (4*) R Burke, ...(25 to 1) 9
1580⁶ COLOURED SPARROW (Ire) [-] 6-9-9 (4*) S M McGovern,
................................(25 to 1) 10
SIR MOSS [-] 9-11-4 (7*) M W Martin, ...(9 to 1) 11
Dist: 2½l, 1l, 4l, 3½l. 5m 4.90s. (11 Ran).
(J Curran), D Harvey

2037 Calor Gas Maiden Hurdle (5-y-o and up) £1,370 3m...............(1:30)

1899⁸ GLENFIELDS CASTLE (Ire) 6-11-7 (7*) Mr A Stronge, (6 to 1) 1
1895 RUM FUN (Ire) 5-10-13 (7*) Mr A J Dempsey, ... (16 to 1) 2
1895³ MATTORIA (Ire) 5-11-2 (7*) P Morris, ...(5 to 2) 3
1839⁷ SARAH BLUE (Ire) 6-11-1 P L Malone, ...(5 to 1) 4
1908 VERYWELL (Ire) 5-10-13 (7*) B J Geraghty, ...(33 to 1) 5
1649⁶ CLADY BOY (Ire) 5-11-3 (3*) G Kilfeather, ...(7 to 1) 6
1902⁶ TWENTYFIVEQUID (Ire) 5-12-0 Mr P F Graffin, ...(10 to 1) 7
1655 SMUGGLERS MOLL (Ire) 6-10-8 (7*) R J Gordon, (33 to 1) 8
1838⁵ MYSTICAL AIR (Ire) 6-11-6 D T Evans, ...(7 to 1) 9
1895 QUENNIE MO GHRA (Ire) 5-10-8 (7*) L J Fleming, (10 to 1) 10
978⁵ HILLTOP BOY (Ire) 7-11-6 M Moran, ...(25 to 1) 11
1460⁸ KILCAR (Ire) 5-11-6 T P Rudd, ...(10 to 1) 12
PERSIAN RUG (Ire) 6-10-13 (7*) M Martin, ...(40 to 1) f
CRANNON BEAUTY (Ire) 6-10-13 (7*) A T Kelly, ...(12 to 1) f
802⁶ CAIRNCROSS (Ire) 5-10-13 (7*) Mr K Bourke, ...(14 to 1) ur
170 HANNAH'S PET (Ire) 6-10-8 (7*) Mr A Fleming, ...(40 to 1) pu
1838³ REMAINDER STAR (Ire) 5-11-7 (7*) M W Martin, (9 to 4 fav) pu
1279³ DREW'S BUCK (Ire) 5-10-13 (7*) R P Hogan, ...(33 to 1) pu
Dist: 7l, nk, 4l, 25l. 6m 3.00s. (18 Ran).
(T D Stronge), I A Duncan

2038 Harp Lager Handicap Chase (0-102 4-y-o and up) £1,370 2½m.... (2:00)

1899⁶ AMME ENAEK (Ire) [-] (bl) 7-11-1 (3*) D Bromley, ...(5 to 1) 1
1058⁶ TIMELY AFFAIR (Ire) [-] (bl) 7-10-7 (3*) Mr B R Hamilton,
................................(7 to 2 jt-fav) 2
1896⁹ IF YOU BELIEVE (Ire) [-] 7-11-7 T P Rudd, ...(4 to 1) 3
1582³ MASTER MILLER [-] 10-10-4 P L Malone, ...(4 to 1) 4
1903⁷ CABBERY ROSE (Ire) [-] 8-11-7 D T Evans, ...(12 to 1) 5
1896⁷ DRINDOD (Ire) [-] 7-11-2 (7*) D A McLoughlin, (7 to 2 jt-fav) 6
1896 JIMMYS DOUBLE [-] 10-9-9⁹⁹ (7*) Mr J J Canavan, (25 to 1) f
GREEN GLEN (USA) [-] 7-11-2³ (7*) Mr B Potts, ...(7 to 1) pu
Dist: 7l, 20l, 4l, 3½l. 5m 15.90s. (8 Ran).
(Mrs E Keane), Gerard Keane

2039 Major Lloyd Hall-Thompson Memorial Novice Chase (4-y-o and up) £1,370 2½m................(2:30)

1618 BOBBYJO (Ire) 6-12-0 P L Malone, ...(Evens fav) 1
1580* BALLYMACREVAN (Ire) 6-12-0 P McWilliams, ...(4 to 1) 2
1618 LIVIN IT UP (Ire) 6-11-7 (7*) Mr J Bright, ...(7 to 2) 3
1780⁹ PILS INVADER (Ire) 8-11-9 D T Evans, ...(33 to 1) 4
1898 BROWNRATH KING (Ire) 7-12-0 T P Rudd, ...(14 to 1) 5
1896 THE BOURDA 10-11-7 (7*) S P McCann, ...(7 to 1) pu
1649 STAR OF FERMANAGH (Ire) 7-11-7 (7*) Mr B Potts, (40 to 1) pu
Dist: 3l, 1½l, 20l, 15l. 5m 20.20s. (7 Ran).
(Robert Burke), Thomas Carberry

2040 Flocheck Valves Ltd (Mares) Flat Race (4-y-o and up) £1,541 2m (3:00)

COSALT (Ire) 4-11-6 (7*) Mr Edgar Byrne, ...(11 to 10 fav) 1
1842⁴ MY LITTLE DOXIE (Ire) 6-11-11 Mr H F Cleary, ...(3 to 1) 2
611⁵ ACCOUNTANCY NATIVE (Ire) 4-11-6 (7*) Mr J P McNamara,
................................(4 to 1) 3

267

	MISS CIRCLE (Ire) 7-11-8⁴ (7*) Miss C Woods, ... (8 to 1)	4
	LITE 'N EASY (Ire) 6-11-11 Mr D Marnane, ... (10 to 1)	5
1901⁹	VICKYWIL (Ire) 4-10-13 (7*) Mr L Madine, ... (14 to 1)	6
1756	STORM DIEU (Ire) 4-11-3⁴ (7*) Mr B Potts, ... (16 to 1)	7
1584	SHINORA (Ire) 5-11-4 (7*) Mr G T Morrow, ... (25 to 1)	8
	ANNIE OAKLEY (Ire) 4-11-1² (7*) Mr A Fleming, . . . (12 to 1)	9
	KATHERINE KATH 5-11-4 (7*) Miss E Hundman, . . (25 to 1)	10
1584⁷	THAT'S LUCY (Ire) 5-11-8 (3*) Mr B R Hamilton, . . . (16 to 1)	11
	HIDDEN PLAY (Ire) 8-11-4 (7*) Miss S L Kelly, ... (20 to 1)	12

Dist: 2½l, 2½l, 1½l, 6l. 3m 58.10s. (12 Ran).

(Exors Late Mrs G W Jennings), J G Burns

2041 Down Royal Bookmakers Flat Race (4-y-o and up) £1,370 2m. . . . . (3:30)

1195²	DR KING (Ire) 4-11-9 Mr P F Graffin, ... (5 to 4 on)	1
1539²	PHARDANA (Ire) 5-11-7 (7*) Mr J P McNamara, ... (5 to 1)	2
1782⁶	FAIR SET (Ire) 5-12-0 Mr H F Cleary, ... (5 to 1)	3
1584³	HOME I'LL BE (Ire) 6-12-0 Mr D Marnane, ... (8 to 1)	4
1405	ROCHE MENTOR (Ire) 6-11-7 (7*) Mr Philip Carberry,	
	. . . . (12 to 1)	5
	JUST 'R JAKE (Ire) 7-11-7 (7*) Mr P Cunckard, . . (50 to 1)	7
1584⁹	IRISH OATS (Ire) 6-11-7 (7*) Mr R Marrs, ... (16 to 1)	8
	LORD NOAN (Ire) 6-11-9 (5*) Mr R J Patton, ... (25 to 1)	9

Dist: 7l, 5½l, 10l, 4½l. 3m 51.00s. (9 Ran).

(Mrs George Donohoe), S Donohoe

KEMPTON (good to firm)
Thursday December 26th

Going Correction: MINUS 0.05 sec. per fur. (races 1,3,6), MINUS 0.20 (2,4,5)

2042 Good Job Novices' Hurdle Class B (4-y-o and up) £7,262 2m. . . . (12:40)

	SANMARTINO (Ire) 4-11-5 A Maguire, prmnt, mstk 3rd, led 2 out to last, rallied to ld nr finish.	
	. . . . (100 to 30 op 9 to 4 tchd 7 to 2)	1
1598²	SECRET SPRING (Fr) 4-11-5 M Richards, hld up gng wl, smooth hdwy frm 5th, led and quickened last, ct nr finish.	
	. . . . (6 to 1 op 5 to 1 tchd 13 to 2)	2
1719*	PROTON 6-11-5 R Dunwoody, chsd ldr, led 3 out to nxt, hrd rdn appr last, sn wknd. . . . (4 to 1 op 9 to 2 tchd 7 to 2)	3
1396*	KAILASH (USA) 5-11-10 A P McCoy, chsd ldrs, rdn 3 out, wknd nxt. . . . . (9 to 2 op 3 to 1 tchd 7 to 4)	4
	LEADING SPIRIT (Ire) 4-11-5 G Bradley, hdwy 4th, sir chal 3 out, wknd appr nxt. . . . . . (11 to 1 op 8 to 1 tchd 12 to 1)	5
1669²	MOOR HALL LADY 5-11-0 C Maude, sn beh, lost tch 3rd.	
	. . . . (50 to 1 op 33 to 1 tchd 66 to 1)	6
1716	MANSUR (Ire) 4-11-5 M A Fitzgerald, led, mstks 3rd and 4th, hdd 3 out, sn rdn and wknd. . . . . (33 to 1 op 20 to 1)	7
1719²	DESERT GREEN (Fr) 7-11-5 N Williamson, hld up in tch, 7th whn pld up lme bef 3 out.	
	. . . . (12 to 1 op 10 to 1 tchd 14 to 1)	pu

Dist: 1l, 9l, 2l, 11l, 15l, dist. 3m 44.50s. a 4.50s (8 Ran).

SR: 38/37/28/31/15/

(K Abdulla), D Nicholson

2043 Pertemps Recruitment Partnership Feltham Novices' Chase Class A Grade 1 (5-y-o and up) £23,100 3m
. . . . (1:10)

	DJEDDAH (Fr) 5-11-7 A Kondrat, cl up, pckd 13th, mstk nxt, led 16th, hld on wl r-in. . . (9 to 2 op 6 to 1 tchd 5 to 1)	1
1630²	SOLOMON'S DANCER (USA) 6-11-7 R Dunwoody, cl up frm 7th, led 15th to nxt, rdn and ev ch whn pckd last, kpt on.	
	. . . . (9 to 2 tchd 5 to 1)	2
1757*	AARDWOLF 5-11-7 G Bradley, led 3rd, hit 5th, mstk and hdd 15th, outpcd whn blun 3 out, styd on wl r-in.	
	. . . . (9 to 4 fav op 2 to 1 tchd 5 to 2)	3
1891	BUCKHOUSE BOY 6-11-7 C Maude, led to 3rd, mstks 4th and nxt, fourth and in tch whn f 8th.	
	. . . . (100 to 30 op 11 to 4 tchd 7 to 2)	f
1611*	HATCHAM BOY (Ire) 6-11-7 A Maguire, hld up rear, mstk and uns rdr 8th. . . . . (4 to 1 op 11 to 4)	ur

Dist: 1l, ¾l. 5m 51.60s. a 2.60s (5 Ran).

SR: 19/18/17/-/-/

(Mrs Stella Elkaim), F Doumen

2044 Network Personnel Handicap Hurdle Class B (4-y-o and up) £6,827 2m
. . . . (1:40)

1807²	ALBEMINE (USA) [122] 7-10-10 T Kent, made all, rdn appr 2 out, readily. . . . . (6 to 4 fav tchd 7 to 4)	1
1864*	CHAI-YO [124] 6-10-12 G Upton, hld up rear, hdwy 5th, chsd wnr 2 out, rdn and not quicken appr last. (7 to 4 op Evens)	2
1855*	YET AGAIN [112] 4-10-0 D Bridgwater, hld up, effrt 3 out, rdn and one pace nxt. . . . . (11 to 4 op 3 to 1)	3
1722	PYRRHIC DANCE [113] 6-10-11 D Skyrme, chsd wnr till mstk 3 out, rdn and wknd appr nxt, tld off.	
	. . . . (20 to 1 op 50 to 1 tchd 16 to 1)	4

Dist: 1¼l, 3l, dist. 3m 49.50s. a 9.50s (4 Ran).

(Mrs J Cecil), Mrs J Cecil

2045 Pertemps King George VI Chase Class A Grade 1 (5-y-o and up) £63,325 3m. . . . . (2:15)

1187*	ONE MAN (Ire) 8-11-10 R Dunwoody, hld up, hdwy 14th, chsd ldr nxt, led 3 out, rdn out.	
	. . . . (13 to 8 on op 2 to 1 on tchd 6 to 4 on)	1
1940*	ROUGH QUEST 10-11-10 M A Fitzgerald, hld up rear, effrt 15th, no imprsn on ldg pair, lft moderate second last.	
	. . . . (4 to 1 op 7 to 2 tchd 9 to 2)	2
1394⁵	BARTON BANK 10-11-10 A Maguire, chsd ldr till blun 15th, not reco'r. . . . . (10 to 1 op 7 to 1 tchd 11 to 1)	3
1518*	STRONG PROMISE (Ire) 5-11-10 K Gaule, chsd ldrs, rdn and wknd 14th, sn beh. . . . . . (6 to 1 op 5 to 1 tchd 13 to 2)	4
1746⁴	MR MULLIGAN 8-11-10 A P McCoy, led, mstks 6th and 15th, hdd 3 out, second and btn whn f last.	
	. . . . (13 to 2 op 12 to 1 tchd 6 to 1)	f

Dist: 12l, 1½l. 5m 45.30s. b 3.70s (5 Ran).

SR: 85/73/64/-/-/

(J Hales), G Richards

2046 Network Design International Wayward Lad Novices' Chase Class B (5-y-o and up) £10,308 2½m 110yds
. . . . (2:45)

1791⁵	GREENBACK (Bel) 5-11-7 N Williamson, in tch, jmpd lft 9th and nxt, led 2 out, hrd rdn, styd on.	
	. . . . (11 to 2 op 5 to 1 tchd 6 to 1)	1
1741⁵	MISTER DRUM (Ire) 7-11-7 R Dunwoody, led, mstk 11th, hdd 2 out, hrd rdn, kpt on. . . . (13 to 8 op 6 to 4 tchd 7 to 4)	2
1850⁷	POTTER'S BAY (Ire) 7-11-7 A Maguire, mstk 4th, hdwy 12th, hit four out, fourth and btn whn mistake last.	
	. . . . (11 to 8 fav op 6 to 4 tchd 13 to 8)	3
1704⁷	SUBLIME FELLOW 6-11-7 M A Fitzgerald, chsd ldr, mstk 8th, outpcd 13th, rallied appr 3 out, sn btn.	
	. . . . (6 to 1 op 9 to 2)	4

Dist: 1¾l, 10l, 5l. 5m 0.50s. a 7.50s (4 Ran).

(Jack Joseph), P J Hobbs

2047 Pertemps Crack Club Handicap Hurdle Class B (4-y-o and up) £6,911 3m 110yds. . . . . (3:15)

1762²	TIM (Ire) [112] 6-10-8 M A Fitzgerald, hld up gng wl, hdwy 3 out, led on bit last, rdn clr. . . . . (7 to 2 op 3 to 1)	1
1105⁴	PEATSWOOD [119] 8-11-1 G Bradley, chsd ldr, led 9th, hrd rdn and hdd last, sn outpcd.	
	. . . . (9 to 2 op 7 to 4 tchd 9 to 2)	2
	EALING COURT [107] 7-10-3³ G Upton, trkd ldrs, ev ch 3 out, wknd appr nxt. . . . . . . (16 to 1 op 10 to 1 tchd 20 to 1)	3
1644³	MYTTON'S CHOICE (Ire) [128] 5-11-10 A Maguire, hld up in tch, hit 6th, jnd ldr 3 out, rdn and btn appr nxt.	
	. . . . (11 to 4 op 7 to 4 tchd 3 to 1)	4
1867⁵	ULURU (Ire) [115] 8-10-11 R Dunwoody, led to 9th, hrd rdn and wknd nxt, tld off. . . (100 to 30 op 5 to 1 tchd 3 to 1)	5

Dist: 4l, 10l, nk, dist. 5m 54.10s. a 9.10s (5 Ran).

(The Crack Club), J R Jenkins

LEOPARDSTOWN (IRE) (yielding)
Thursday December 26th

Going Correction: PLUS 0.50 sec. per fur. (races 1,2,3,4,7), PLUS 0.10 (5,6)

2048 Waifos Maiden Hurdle (5-y-o and up) £4,110 2¼m. . . . . (12:25)

1432⁴	FINNEGAN'S HOLLOW (Ire) 6-12-0 C F Swan, . . (Evens fav)	1
	BE HOME EARLY (Ire) 6-11-7 (7*) A O'Shea, ... (9 to 1)	2
1649³	DIGIN FOR GOLD (Ire) 5-11-6 F Woods, ... (13 to 8)	3
1279⁷	KNOCKAROO (Ire) 5-11-13 (3*) G Cotter, ... (10 to 1)	4
1901⁴	DUISKE ABBEY (Ire) 6-11-9 T P Treacy, ... (8 to 1)	5
1836⁹	GRAIGNAMANAGH (Ire) 5-11-6 R Hughes, ... (20 to 1)	6
	DIAMANTINO (Fr) 5-11-3 (3*) K Whelan, ... (14 to 1)	7
1715	NORTH TIPP (Ire) 7-10-13 (7*) K C Hartnett, ... (16 to 1)	8
1436	HIDDEN SPRINGS (Ire) 5-11-6 K F O'Brien, ... (50 to 1)	9
	YOUNG CAL (Ire) 7-10-13 (7*) Mr P J Crowley, ... (33 to 1)	10
1655	CLONEE PRIDE (Ire) 5-10-12 (3*) B Bowens, ... (20 to 1)	11
1655	CLONEE PRIDE (Ire) 5-10-12 (3*) B Bowens, ... (33 to 1)	12
1710	CRISTYS PICNIC (Ire) 6-11-6 C O'Dwyer, ... (20 to 1)	13

Dist: 1½l, ½l, 6l, sht-hd. 4m 35.20s. a 23.20s (13 Ran).

(John P McManus), A P O'Brien

2049 Kerry Spring Maiden Hurdle (4-y-o) £4,110 2m. . . . . (12:55)

	I'M SUPPOSIN (Ire) 11-7 J Shortt, ... (6 to 4 fav)	1
1897²	SAVING BOND (Ire) 11-7 R Hughes, ... (4 to 1)	2
	SILVIAN BLISS (USA) 11-7 C O'Dwyer, ... (4 to 1)	3
1897	JACK YEATS (Ire) 11-7 S C Lyons, ... (20 to 1)	4
	INCHACOOLEY (Ire) 11-2 A Powell, ... (7 to 1)	5
1533	FILL THE BILL (Ire) 11-7 C F Swan, ... (6 to 1)	6
1622*	MINISTER'S CROSS (Ire) 11-7 F Woods, ... (14 to 1)	7
1756⁹	ANDREA COVA (Ire) 10-8 (3*) B Bowens, ... (25 to 1)	8
1275	NATIVE FLING (Ire) 11-4 (3*) U Smyth, ... (16 to 1)	9

268

2017[5]	DOUBLE COLOUR (Ire) 11-7 R M Burke, ...(16 to 1)	10
1015	COLONEL GEORGE 11-4 (3*) K Whelan, ...(16 to 1)	11
1897[5]	ABORIGINAL (Ire) 11-7 T P Treacy, ...(6 to 1)	12
898	SINGERS CORNER 10-8 (3*) G Cotter, ...(33 to 1)	13

Dist: 4l, nk, 6l, 5l. 3m 59.20s. a 15.20s (13 Ran).
SR: 21/17/16/10/-/-/ (A D Brennan), Kevin Prendergast

2050 Denny Juvenile Hurdle (Grade 2) (3-y-o) £9,675 2m.............. (1:30)

1616	GRIMES 10-9 C O'Dwyer, ...(9 to 1)	1
1616[3]	GREENHUE (Ire) 10-6 (3*) K L O'Brien, ...(7 to 1)	2
1750[7]	RESCUE TIME (Ire) 10-9 J Shortt, ...(8 to 1)	3
1616	CHOOSEY'S TREASURE (Ire) 10-6 (3*) R P O'Brien,	
	....(14 to 1)	4
1750[4]	MISS PENNYHILL (Ire) (bl) 9-11 (7*) J M Maguire, ..(14 to 1)	5
1057[2]	MISS ROBERTO (Ire) 10-9 K F O'Brien, ...(7 to 1)	6
1709*	HARD NEWS (USA) 10-6 (3*) G Cotter, ...(16 to 1)	7
1616*	SPIRIT DANCER (Ire) 11-0 S C Lyons, ...(10 to 1)	8
1616[6]	CORN ABBEY (Ire) 10-9 F Woods, ...(7 to 1)	9
1616	IAGCHUS (Ire) 10-4 (5*) J Butler, ...(20 to 1)	10
1750[2]	GO SASHA (Ire) 10-6 (5*) T Martin, ...(20 to 1)	11
1750*	TAX REFORM (USA) 10-9 H Rogers, ...(12 to 1)	12
	APACHE TWIST (Ire) 10-9 T P Treacy, ...(11 to 1)	13
1616[5]	EVRIZA (Ire) 10-9 J Osborne, ...(10 to 1)	f
	SLIGHTLY SPEEDY (Ire) 10-9 R Hughes, ...(16 to 1)	bd
1616[2]	HIGHLY MOTIVATED 10-4 C F Swan, ...(9 to 4 fav)	bd

Dist: Sht-hd, 5½l, hd, 1½l. 3m 57.10s. a 13.10s (16 Ran).
SR: 30/30/24/17/-/ (John P McManus), C Roche

2051 Low Low Handicap Hurdle (0-120 4-y-o and up) £6,850 2¼m.... (2:05)

1752[2]	BLACK QUEEN (Ire) [-] 5-11-1 A J O'Brien, ...(11 to 2)	1
1713[7]	FIDDLERS BOW VI (Ire) [-] 8-10-9 R Hughes, ...(12 to 1)	2
1752*	GRAVITY GATE (Ire) [-] 7-10-12 C O'Dwyer, ...(11 to 4 fav)	3
1058*	TARAJAN (USA) [-] (bl) 4-11-5 J Shortt, ...(6 to 1)	4
1752[7]	SLEEPY RIVER (Ire) [-] 5-10-9 F Woods, ...(7 to 2)	5
1752[4]	CEILI QUEEN (Ire) [-] 4-11-9 C F Swan, ...(9 to 2)	6
1752	FALCARRAGH (Ire) [-] 6-9-2 (7*) J M Maguire, ...(14 to 1)	7
118[9]	LORD BENTLEY [-] 6-9-6 (5*) J Butler, ...(25 to 1)	8
1752	MAJESTIC MAN (Ire) [-] 5-11-2 (3*) U Smyth, ...(16 to 1)	9
1900[8]	RISING WATERS (Ire) [-] 8-11-0 K F O'Brien, ...(14 to 1)	10
526[6]	SLANEY GLOW (Ire) [-] 5-10-12 (7*) Mr J S Cullen, (14 to 1)	11
	OWENBWEE (Ire) [-] 5-11-4 J Osborne, ...(10 to 1)	12

Dist: 1½l, 2½l, ½l, 2½l. 4m 30.80s. a 18.80s (12 Ran).
(Heinz Pollmeier), J E Kiely

2052 Denny Gold Medal Chase (Grade 1) (4-y-o and up) £22,750 2m 1f..(2:40)

1652	DANOLI (Ire) 8-11-6 T P Treacy, trkd ldr, mstk 4th, lft in ld aftr	
	6th, jnd four out, hdd whn jmpd slwly 3 out, led after nxt, ran	
	on strly...(5 to 2 jt-fav)	1
1758[2]	LAND AFAR 9-11-6 J Osborne, wl plcd, prog whn mstk 4 out,	
	kpt on aftr 2 out......................................(20 to 1)	2
1405[4]	BEAKSTOWN (Ire) 7-11-6 G Cotter, wl plcd, prog to dispute ld	
	4 out, hdd aftr 2 out, rdn and no extr................(20 to 1)	3
1534*	HEADBANGER (Ire) 6-11-6 D H O'Connor, hld up, prog aftr 4 out,	
	kpt on wl...(20 to 1)	4
1435*	THE CARRIG RUA (Ire) 6-11-6 A Powell, wtd with till some	
	prog aftr 4 out..(8 to 1)	5
1779*	JEFFELL 6-11-6 F Woods, wl plcd, rdn bef 3 out, wknd aftr	
	nxt...(5 to 2 jt-fav)	6
1841[2]	PENNDARA (Ire) 7-11-6 C F Swan, al rear............(14 to 1)	7
1552*	KHARASAR (Ire) 6-11-6 C O'Dwyer, wtd wth, prog bef 3 out,	
	clsg whn f 2 out.......................................(6 to 1)	f
1276[2]	CROSSFARNOGUE (Ire) 7-11-6 J Butler, led, jmpd right 1st,	
	not fluent, f 6th......................................(25 to 1)	f

Dist: 6l, 1l, 3½l, 3l. 4m 16.20s. a 6.20s (9 Ran).
SR: 47/41/40/36/33/-/ (D J O'Neill), Thomas Foley

2053 Paddy Power Dial-A-Bet Handicap Chase (0-116 4-y-o and up) £4,110 2m 5f........................(3:10)

1714*	AMBLE SPEEDY (Ire) 6-11-9 F Woods, ...(7 to 2)	1
1650[3]	PERKNAPP [-] 9-11-10 C F Swan, ...(9 to 2)	2
1896[2]	HEMISPHERE (Ire) [-] 7-10-12 (3*) G Cotter, ...(2 to 1 fav)	3
2020*	QUATTRO [-] 6-10-12 (4ex) T P Treacy, ...(5 to 1)	4
1408[4]	CORYMANDEL (Ire) [-] 7-11-5 C O'Dwyer, ...(9 to 1)	5
2020	STRONG HICKS (Ire) [-] 8-11-10 A Powell, ...(5 to 1)	6
1898[6]	MACALLISTER (Ire) [-] 6-11-4 (3*) B Bowens, ...(12 to 1)	7
1896[5]	BOB DEVANI [-] 10-11-10 Mr G J Harford, ...(16 to 1)	f
	BEAUCHAMP GRACE [-] 7-10-6 (3*) K Whelan, ...(9 to 1)	ur
1714[5]	MUSICAL DUKE (Ire) [-] 7-10-5 D H O'Connor, ...(14 to 1)	pu

Dist: 4½l, 7l, 11l, 20l. 5m 27.90s. a 18.90s (10 Ran).
(Robin Minnis), A L T Moore

2054 Ballyfree I.N.H. Flat Race (4-y-o) £4,110 2m........................(3:40)

	FLORIDA PEARL (Ire) 11-6 Mr J A Nash, ...(6 to 4 fav)	1
	PROMALEE (Ire) 10-13 (7*) Miss A L Crowley, ...(6 to 1)	2
	DUDLEY DO RIGHT (Ire) 11-6 Mr A J Martin, ...(5 to 1)	3
	FIRMOUNT CROSS (Ire) 10-13 (7*) Mr P J Prendergast,	
	....(6 to 1)	4
185[4]	CASTLE COIN (Ire) 11-3 (3*) Mr B M Cash, ...(8 to 1)	5

	UNCLE WAT 11-3 (3*) Mr D Valentine, ...(20 to 1)	6
1897[3]	SUPREME CHANTER (Ire) 10-13 (7*) Mr John P Moloney,	
	....(7 to 1)	7
1756[3]	PRINCE DANTE (Ire) 10-13 (7*) Mr M Murray, ...(7 to 1)	8
1756	HI-LO PICCOLO (Ire) 10-8 (7*) Miss S McDonogh, (33 to 1)	9
	SWIFT PICK (Ire) 11-6 Mr G J Harford, ...(10 to 1)	10
	WEE ICEMAN (Ire) 11-6 Mr P Fenton, ...(7 to 1)	11
1756[6]	TULLABAWN (Ire) 10-13 (7*) Mr Peter Fahey, ...(16 to 1)	12
1901[7]	DANNKALIA (Ire) 11-1 Mr J P Dempsey, ...(14 to 1)	13
487[7]	YOU MAKE ME LAUGH (Ire) 10-13 (7*) Mr D C Cullen,	
	....(33 to 1)	14
2022[7]	ALVINE (Ire) 10-13 (7*) Mr S J Mahon, ...(14 to 1)	15
1756	TEACH NA FINIUNA (Ire) 10-8 (7*) Mr T P Walsh, ..(33 to 1)	16
1901	MINE'S A PINT (Ire) 11-1 Mrs C Barker, ...(33 to 1)	17
	KING HAB (Ire) 10-13 (7*) Mr J Nolan, ...(25 to 1)	18
	PRIVATE BIT (Ire) 10-13 (7*) Mr W Ewing, ...(10 to 1)	19
	ETAT MAJOR (Fr) 10-13 (7*) Mr J Cullen, ...(14 to 1)	20
1622[9]	BEAUTY'S PRIDE (Ire) 10-8 (7*) Mr M Nakauchida, (33 to 1)	21
	TULLIBARDS FLYER (Ire) 10-13 (7*) Mr T N Cloke, (20 to 1)	22

Dist: 5l, 8l, 14l, ¾l. 3m 50.90s. (22 Ran).
(Mrs Violet O'Leary), W P Mullins

LIMERICK (IRE) (good to yielding) Thursday December 26th

2055 Craig Gardner Price Waterhouse Maiden Hurdle (4-y-o) £3,425 2m .... (1:05)

1195[8]	REGENCY RAKE (Ire) 10-13 C O'Brien, ...(8 to 1)	1
1777[7]	CHARLIE-O (Ire) 10-13 T Horgan, ...(6 to 1)	2
1897[4]	THE BOY KING (Ire) 10-13 L P Cusack, ...(5 to 2)	3
1902[9]	MIRACLE ME (Ire) 10-6 (7*) Mr J G Sheehan, ...(12 to 1)	4
1777	BLITZER (Ire) 11-7 S H O'Donovan, ...(14 to 1)	5
1121[7]	SHALOM (Ire) 10-13 M P Hourigan, ...(12 to 1)	6
1897[9]	IMPERIAL PLAICE (Ire) 10-6 (7*) D M Bean, ...(6 to 1)	7
1907	SEXTON'S MIRROR (Ire) 10-13 Miss M Olivefalk, ..(14 to 1)	8
1902	PENNY POET (Ire) 10-6 (7*) M D Murphy, ...(14 to 1)	9
1751[3]	RACHEL'S SWALLOW (Ire) 10-11 (5*) J M Donnelly,	
	....(9 to 4 fav)	10
1777[2]	ZIGGY THE GREAT (Ire) (bl) 10-13 P A Roche, ...(7 to 1)	11
716	TAZ (Ire) 10-8 P J Flood, ...(20 to 1)	12
	BRIGHT LANE (Ire) 11-2 M Duffy, ...(9 to 1)	13
	TOUGHERTHANTHEREST (Ire) 10-8 W Slattery, ...(20 to 1)	14
1902	MILLICANS BEND (Ire) 10-13 T Hazlett, ...(20 to 1)	15
	NIL FAIC (Ire) 10-8 J P Broderick, ...(14 to 1)	16
	SAMINA (Ire) 10-8 J R Barry, ...(10 to 1)	17
	LADY MINORCA (Ire) 10-7[6] (7*) Mr R J Curran, ..(12 to 1)	pu

Dist: 2½l, 14l, 8l, 3½l. 4m 6.00s. (18 Ran).
(Mrs J J McGettigan), A L T Moore

2056 Lane Leonard O'Reilly Costelloe Hurdle (5-y-o and up) £3,425 2m ....(1:35)

716*	SENTOSA STAR (Ire) 5-11-4 M P Hourigan, ...(10 to 9 on)	1
1752	CIARA'S PRINCE (Ire) 5-11-4 F J Flood, ...(5 to 1)	2
1710*	JAY MAN (Ire) 6-11-4 J P Broderick, ...(7 to 2)	3
1710[4]	ARABIAN SPRITE (Ire) 8-10-2 (7*) S FitzGerald, ...(10 to 1)	4
	MILLS PRIDE (Ire) 5-10-6 (7*) J O'Shaughnessy, ..(20 to 1)	5
	DOONANDORAS (Ire) 8-11-6 C O'Brien, ...(3 to 1)	f

Dist: 2l, 4½l, 9l, dist. 4m 0.00s. (6 Ran).
(C J Deasy), Michael Hourigan

2057 Bank Of Ireland Handicap Hurdle (0-116 4-y-o and up) £3,425 2½m ....(2:05)

1839	KASELECTRIC (Ire) [-] (bl) 5-10-8 T Horgan, ...(4 to 1)	1
1899	VINTNERS VENTURE (Ire) [-] 4-10-2 (5*) M J Holbrook,	
	....(10 to 1)	2
1839	JIHAAD (USA) [-] 6-9-4[4] (7*) J O'Shaughnessy, ...(14 to 1)	3
1902[3]	ANTICS (Ire) [-] 4-9-7 (7*) Mrs C Harrison, ...(9 to 2)	4
1776*	IODER WAN (Ire) [-] 4-10-12 M P Hourigan, ...(5 to 2 fav)	5
1752	BUCKMINSTER [-] 9-11-10 J P Broderick, ...(12 to 1)	6
1654[5]	DEARBORN TEC (Ire) [-] 7-10-13 C O'Brien, ...(11 to 4)	7
1488[5]	RIVER RUMPUS (Ire) [-] 4-9-3 (7*) M D Murphy, ...(14 to 1)	8
1902	THE ROAD TO MOSCOW (Ire) [-] 5-9-11 J R Barry, (12 to 1)	9
1777[9]	CASTLE BLAKE (Ire) [-] 4-10-4 D J Casey, ...(8 to 1)	pu

Dist: 4l, 3½l, 4l, 1l. 5m 28.00s. (10 Ran).
(J J Canty), E McNamara

2058 Murphys Irish Stout Novice Chase (Grade 3) (5-y-o and up) £6,850 2½m ....(2:35)

2021*	DUN BELLE (Ire) 7-11-9 T J Mitchell, ...(9 to 2)	1
1898*	ULTRA FLUTTER 9-11-9 J P Broderick, ...(Evens fav)	2
2021[2]	WOODVILLE STAR (Ire) 7-11-4 T Horgan, ...(3 to 1)	3
1841[3]	IRISH PEACE (Ire) 8-11-6 C O'Brien, ...(10 to 1)	4
1461	MOUSSAHIM (USA) 6-11-9 L P Cusack, ...(9 to 1)	5
1534[3]	MINELLA GOLD (Ire) 7-11-6 D J Casey, ...(6 to 1)	f

Dist: 1½l, nk, 20l, 15l. 5m 12.60s. (6 Ran).
(Mrs A Connolly), P A Fahy

269

2059 Holmes O'Malley & Sexton Handicap Chase (0-102 4-y-o and up) £3,425 2¾m.......................... (3:05)

1538² IRISH LIGHT (Ire) [-] 8-11-4 J P Broderick....... (5 to 4 fav)	1
1779⁴ BAILE NA GLOCH (Ire) [-] 7-11-5 (3") D P Murphy, (10 to 1)	2
1837² DOONEGA (Ire) [-] 8-10-6 (7") Mr E Gallagher, ...(100 to 30)	3
1711⁵ FAIR GO [-] 10-9-4 (7") Mrs C Harrison,............(7 to 1)	4
1552⁶ RISZARD (USA) [-] 7-11-13 D J Casey, ...(12 to 1)	5
1781³ BALLYFIN BOY [-] 10-10-2 (5") J M Donnelly, ... (10 to 1)	f
1837⁴ FAIRY MIST (Ire) [-] 8-9-7 W Slattery,..............(6 to 1)	f
1553⁶ MACAUNTA (Ire) [-] 6-9-11 (7") M D Murphy, ...(6 to 1)	bd
1711 INTERIM ACCOUNT [-] 10-11-0 L P Cusack, ... (10 to 1)	pu

Dist: 2½l, sht-hd, 9l, 25l. 5m 41.70s. (9 Ran).

(Michael J McDonagh), Michael J McDonagh

2060 Dunraven Arms Hotel I.N.H. Flat Race (4-y-o and up) £3,425 2m (3:35)

1622³ FATHER GERRY (Ire) 6-12-0 Mr J A Flynn,..........(5 to 2)	1
EMERALD PRINCE (Ire) 4-11-2 (7") Mr C A Murphy, (3 to 1)	2
ASHTALE (Ire) 4-11-1 (3") Mr R Walsh,.............(2 to 1 fav)	3
1782⁴ CROMWELLS KEEP (Ire) 5-12-0 Mr J A Berry,...... (7 to 1)	4
1484⁷ SARAH SUPREME (Ire) 5-11-4 (5") Mr T P Hyde, .. (10 to 1)	5
1655⁷ BRIDGES DAUGHTER (Ire) 5-11-9 Mr G Donnelly, ...(9 to 1)	6
WINDGAP HILL (Ire) 5-11-7 (7") Mr G Donnelly, ...(9 to 1)	7
SUPREME GAZETTE (Ire) 4-11-2 (7") Mr S P Hennessy,	
....(7 to 1)	8
1842³ ARCTIC GREY (Ire) (bl) 6-11-7 (7") Mr A G Cash, ... (6 to 1)	9
EARL OF NAAS (Ire) 5-12-0 Miss M Olivefalk, ... (16 to 1)	10

Dist: 1½l, sht-hd, 7l, 1l. 4m 10.00s. (10 Ran).

(Clashkin Syndicate), J A Flynn

MUSSELBURGH (good to firm)
Friday December 27th
Going Correction: MINUS 0.20 sec. per fur.

2061 Carberry Tower Juvenile Novices' Hurdle Class E (3-y-o) £1,815 2m .... (12:35)

1909² ROSSEL (USA) 11-12 A Dobbin, cl up, led bef 3rd, hdd before last, rallied to ld r-in, kpt on wl... (9 to 4 on op 7 to 4 on)	1
HONEYSCHOICE (Ire) 10-12 R Garritty, hld up, improved hfwy, chalg whn hit 2 out, led and 3 ls clr when blun last, sn hdd and no extr............(3 to 1 op 5 to 2 tchd 9 to 2)	2
1690³ NOIR ESPRIT 10-9 (3") F Leahy, hld up, effrt hfwy, ran on fnl 2, nrst finish............................(25 to 1 op 16 to 1)	3
1909⁸ PRIDDY FAIR 10-11 (3") P Midgley, mid-div, improved 3rd, not quicken fnl 2.....................(40 to 1 op 20 to 1)	4
CATHERINE'S CHOICE 10-9 (3") Mr C Bonner, not fluent, towards rear, pushed alng 3 out, nvr dngrs. ....(33 to 1 op 16 to 1)	5
MOUNTAIN DREAM 10-12 B Storey, hld up, nvr able to chal. ....(14 to 1 op 10 to 1 tchd 20 to 1)	6
MILETRIAN CITY 10-12 M Moloney, chsd ldg grp, blun 4 out, sn struggling.......................(20 to 1 op 12 to 1)	7
RESPECTING 10-12 N Smith, led till aftr second, fdd 3 out. ....(50 to 1 op 33 to 1)	8
1909 WESTERN VENTURE 10-12 D Parker, with ldr, led briefly aftr second, wknd quickly nxt......(200 to 1 op 100 to 1)	9
1524⁷ BROGANS BRUSH 10-12 G Cahill, al beh, struggling 3rd, tld off whn pld up bef 2 out..........(100 to 1 op 66 to 1)	pu

Dist: 3l, 1½l, 3l, 14l, 10l, 17l, ¾l, 4l. 3m 41.00s. a 4.00s (10 Ran).
SR: 26/9/7/6/-/-/

(Allan W Melville), P Monteith

2062 Rusty Nail Novices' Chase Class E (5-y-o and up) £2,455 3m..... (1:05)

1630³ BLUE CHARM (Ire) 6-11-5 R Garritty, made all, rdn and ran on wl fnl 3..........................(9 to 4 tchd 5 to 2)	1
1658² WINTER BELLE (USA) 8-10-9 (3") Mr C Bonner, hld up in tch, improved to chase wnr 3 out, kpt on frm last. ....(16 to 1 op 8 to 1)	2
1587⁷ FINE TUNE (Ire) 6-10-12 A Thornton, jmpd lft, nvr far away, hit 5 out, outpcd 3 out..................(100 to 1 op 66 to 1)	3
1930² FINGERHILL (Ire) 7-10-12 Mr M Thompson, in tch, hit 9th and nxt, hit 13th, sn struggling..........(33 to 1 op 25 to 1)	4
1788⁴ NOYAN 6-11-5 A Dobbin, hmpd and f 1st. ....(6 to 5 on op 5 to 4 on)	f
1930 ESTABLISH (Ire) 8-10-7 K Johnson, brght dwn 1st. ....(66 to 1 op 33 to 1)	bd
1930 HEDDON HAUGH (Ire) 8-11-5 R Supple, pld hrd early, wth wnr, hit 12th, sn struggling, pulled up bef 3 out. ....(33 to 1 op 25 to 1)	pu
1658 TOUGH TEST (Ire) 6-10-12 G Cahill, hmpd 1st, sn pld up. ....(8 to 1 op 6 to 1 tchd 9 to 1)	pu

Dist: 2½l, 19l, 19l. 6m 0.60s. a 11.80s (8 Ran).

(Mrs M C Lindsay), Mrs S C Bradburne

2063 Miller Hill Maiden Hurdle Class E (4-y-o and up) £1,878 2½m... (1:35)

1929² SMOLENSK (Ire) 4-11-5 M Moloney, hld up gng wl, smooth hdwy 5 out, led last, sn clr....... (7 to 4 fav tchd 2 to 1)	1

1662⁵ CHEATER (Ire) 5-11-5 A S Smith, nvr far away, led 3 out to last, no ch wth wnr...................(14 to 1 op 10 to 1)	2
1784³ LITTLE REDWING (v) 4-10-11 (3") Mr Bonner, al wl plcd, led 6th to 3 out, ev ch whn hit nxt, no extr. (50 to 1 op 33 to 1)	3
ARCTIC SANDY (Ire) 6-11-5 B Storey, hld up, improved 4 out, fdd last 2 .....(9 to 4 op 2 to 1 tchd 7 to 4 and 5 to 2)	4
1783³ SOMETHING SPEEDY (Ire) 4-11-0 R Garritty, hld up, gd hdwy on outsd 4 out, btn and eased fnl 2....(16 to 1 op 10 to 1)	5
CANAAN VALLEY 8-11-5 J Burke, mstks, led to 6th, struggling last 3.........................(25 to 1 op 20 to 1)	6
PENNY PEPPERMINT 4-11-0 N Smith, beh, struggling fnl circuit, tld off..................(200 to 1 op 100 to 1)	7
1826 RINGRONE (Ire) (bl) 7-11-0 Mr M Thompson, in tch to hfwy, sn btn.......................(200 to 1 op 100 to 1)	8
1509² THIRD WILD DAYS 4-11-5 A Thornton, settled midfield, imprvg whn f 5 out, dead...............(3 to 1 op 5 to 2)	f
1679⁸ JAUNTY GENERAL 5-11-5 D Parker, hndy, hmpd by faller 5 out, sn btn, pld up bef last...........(16 to 1 op 14 to 1)	pu

Dist: 11l, 4l, 7l, 2l, 10l, 11l, 23l. 4m 45.60s. a 7.60s (10 Ran).

(Mrs Chris Deuters), J Berry

2064 Pinkie Hill Handicap Hurdle Class D (0-125 4-y-o and up) £2,633 3m .... (2:05)

1661³ TRUMP [113] 7-11-10 D Parker, chsd clr ldr, rdn to ld aftr last, ran on wl. .....(6 to 5 fav op 5 to 4 tchd 11 to 8 and 11 to 10)	1
1933² D'ARBLAY STREET (Ire) [89] 7-10-0 S McDougall, led, sn wl clr, rdn bef 2 out, hdd aftr last, no extr. ....(6 to 1 op 9 to 2 tchd 7 to 1)	2
1966⁵ IFALLELSEFAILS [94] 8-10-5 R Supple, hld up beh, effrt 2 out, not quicken last.......................(7 to 2 op 3 to 1)	3
1824⁹ HELENS BAY (Ire) [89] (bl) 6-10-5 K Johnson, not fluent, cl up chasing grp, outpcd 8th, sn no dngr... (50 to 1 op 25 to 1)	4
1914⁷ BARTON HEIGHTS [90] 4-9-8 (7") C McCormack, hld up, rdn alng 3 out, btn betw last 2, virtually pld up r-in. ....(5 to 2 op 9 to 4)	5

Dist: 4l, 1¾l, 11l, dist. 5m 45.60s. a 8.60s (5 Ran).

(A Mrs Raymond Anderson Green), C Parker

2065 Col. W. L. M. Monteith Handicap Chase Class D (0-120 5-y-o and up) £2,697 3m.................... (2:40)

1589⁶ HURRICANE ANDREW (Ire) [87] 8-10-0 N Smith, made all, rdn and hld on gmely frm 2 out. ....(4 to 1 op 7 to 2 tchd 9 to 2)	1
1694⁴ FORWARD GLEN [87] (bl) 9-10-0 R Supple, hld up in tch, effrt 5 out, kpt on frm last............(16 to 1 op 14 to 1)	2
1624⁴ WAYUPHILL [92] 9-10-5 B Storey, hld up, improved and ev ch whn blun 3 out, hit nxt, kpt on wl frm last. ....(6 to 4 fav op 5 to 4 tchd 13 to 8)	3
1932⁴ RISKY DEE [87] 7-10-0 K Johnson, nvr far away, effrt bef 4 out, outpcd nxt.......(20 to 1 op 16 to 1 tchd 25 to 1)	4
1822⁶ WILLIE SPARKLE [87] 10-10-0 M Foster, jmpd lft, cl up, blun 13th, struggling last 4..............(7 to 1 op 5 to 1)	5
1821⁶ BISHOPDALE [87] 15-10-0 F Perratt, cl up, outpcd 11th, tld off whn pld up bef 4 out..............(25 to 1 tchd 33 to 1)	pu
1773⁶ JOE WHITE [115] 10-12-0 A S Smith, hndy, improved to chase ldrs 11th, struggling 5 out, pld up bef nxt. ....(11 to 4 op 7 to 2 tchd 4 to 1)	pu

Dist: ¾l, 1l, 19l, 7l. 6m 1.50s. a 12.50s (7 Ran).

(J A Moore), J A Moore

2066 Preston Tower Standard Open National Hunt Flat Class H (4,5,6-y-o) £1,138 2m.............. (3:15)

LORD LAMB 4-11-11 P Niven, hld up, smooth hdwy to ld o'r 2 fs out, shaken up, edgd rght and wnt clr ins last. ....(4 to 1 on op 9 to 2 on tchd 7 to 2 on)	1
1935³ NUTTY SOLERA 6-11-11 B Storey, nvr far away, led briefly 3 fs out, not pace of wnr ins last......... (6 to 1 op 4 to 1)	2
1935⁴ SALEM BEACH 4-10-13 A Dobbin, hld up, effrt entering strt, one pace last 2 fs.................(16 to 1 op 12 to 1)	3
1968⁸ DANTES AMOUR (Ire) 5-11-4 R Garritty, pressed ldr, ev ch 3 fs out, outpcd 2 out............(14 to 1 op 10 to 1)	4
THE EARLY BIRD 5-10-13 G Cahill, led to 3 fs out, sn btn. ....(14 to 1 op 33 to 1)	5
JIMMY SPRITE 5-11-4 N Smith, cl up, struggling o'r 4 fs out, sn btn.........................(10 to 1 op 50 to 1)	6

Dist: 3l, 9l, 1¼l, 5l, 10l. 3m 45.30s. (6 Ran).

(A Sharratt & Mr J Renton), Mrs M Reveley

LEOPARDSTOWN (IRE) (yielding (races 1,2,4,6,7), good to yielding (3,5))
Friday December 27th
Going Correction: PLUS 0.70 sec. per fur. (races 1,2,4,6,7), PLUS 0.35 (3,5)

2067 Tote Account Hurdle (3-y-o) £4,110 2m........................ (12:25)

FERN FIELDS (Ire) 9-9 (7") I Browne, ...(14 to 1)	1

CENTO (Ire) 10-7 R Dunwoody, ...(3 to 1 fav) 2
1709 LOUGH SLANIA (Ire) 10-7 J Shortt, ... (6 to 1) 3
VICTORY BOUND (USA) 10-7 F Woods, ...(20 to 1) 4
1709⁹ SARAH'S GUEST (Ire) (bl) 10-2 R Hughes, ...(9 to 2) 5
FALCON'S FIRE (Ire) 10-7 P L Malone, ...(12 to 1) 6
1709³ IFTATAH 10-7 A Powell, ...(10 to 1) 7
1750³ COMRADE CHINNERY (Ire) 10-7 J P Broderick, . . .(6 to 1) 8
1403⁷ GALE EIGHT (Ire) 10-2 T P Treacy, ...(20 to 1) 9
1750⁸ UNASSISTED (Ire) 9-13 (3") B Bowens, ...(16 to 1) 10
NASCIMENTO (USA) 10-7 C O'Dwyer, ... (7 to 1) 11
1459 ROYAL MIDYAN 10-7 D T Evans, ...(10 to 1) 12
1430⁸ ERNE PROJECT (Ire) 10-2 H Rogers, ...(16 to 1) 13
SIGMA COMMS (Ire) 10-7 P Carberry, ...(10 to 1) 14
NATIVE ECLIPSE (Ire) 10-7 C F Swan, ...(7 to 1) 15
Dist: Sht-hd, 3½l, hd, hd. 4m 8.20s. a 24.20s (15 Ran).

(Mrs Isobel Foley), Kevin Prendergast

2068 Cheltenham Gold Card Handicap Hurdle (Qualifier) (4-y-o and up) £5,480 3m . . . . (12:55)

MILTONFIELD [-] 7-10-4 C O'Dwyer, ...(3 to 1 fav) 1
1839² COLLON LEADER (Ire) [-] 7-9-8 J R Barry, ...(11 to 1) 2
1752⁹ CASEY JANE (Ire) [-] 5-10-0 D J Casey, ... (8 to 1) 3
1899² TELL THE NIPPER (Ire) [-] (bl) 5-10-5 J P Broderick, (5 to 1) 4
2053* AMBLE SPEEDY (Ire) [-] 4-10-1 F Woods, ...(5 to 1) 5
1653⁵ PADASHPAN (USA) [-] 7-11-6 T P Treacy, ...(14 to 1) 6
1778² SIR JOHN (Ire) [-] 7-9-2 (5") J Butler, ...(12 to 1) 7
2018³ LISCAHILL FORT (Ire) [-] 7-9-4 (3") B Bowens, ...(14 to 1) 8
1548* YOUNG MRS KELLY (Ire) [-] 6-9-7 J Jones, ...(12 to 1) 9
1550 DARK SWAN (Ire) [-] 6-9-9 R Hughes, ...(25 to 1) 10
1089⁵ VICAR STREET (Ire) [-] 6-9-13 C F Swan, ...(11 to 2) 11
1752 TOTAL CONFUSION [-] 9-10-2³ P Carberry, ...(10 to 1) 12
1190 BALAWHAR (Ire) [-] 6-12-0 R Dunwoody, ...(14 to 1) 13
1089 SHANKORAK [-] 9-10-12 (7") R P Hogan, ...(20 to 1) 14
2019⁶ MR BOAL (Ire) [-] 7-10-7 K F O'Brien, ...(33 to 1) 15
Dist: Hd, 7l, sht-hd, sht-hd. 6m 14.10s. a 37.10s (15 Ran).

(J C Savage), J E Mulhern

2069 McCain Handicap Chase (5-y-o and up) £6,850 2¼m. . . . . (1:25)

1753² MERRY GALE (Ire) [-] 8-10-13 R Dunwoody, ... (5 to 4) 1
1753 KLAIRON DAVIS (Fr) [-] 7-12-0 F Woods, ...(5 to 4 on) 2
1650⁷ FIFTYSEVENCHANNELS (Ire) [-] 7-10-0 C F Swan, (8 to 1) 3
1619³ JASSU [-] 10-10-1¹ A Powell, ...(14 to 1) 4
1244 PYR FOUR [-] 9-9-9 (5") J Butler, ...(25 to 1) 5
Dist: 8l, 13l, 3l, dist. (Time not taken) (5 Ran).

(Herb M Stanley), J T R Dreaper

2070 1st Choice Novice Hurdle (Grade 3) (4-y-o and up) £9,675 2¼m. . . (2:00)

1651* ISTABRAQ (Ire) 4-11-3 C F Swan, *wl plcd, prog to track ldr
  4th, jmpd slwly 3 out, dsptd ld nxt, sn led, easily.*(10 to 1 on) 1
1651² PALETTE (Ire) 4-11-1 D J Casey, *wtd wth, prog bef 3 out, kpt
  on wl, nt threaten wnr. . . . .*(100 to 30) 2
1751² DELPHI LODGE (Ire) 6-11-8 Mr A J Martin, *hld up, str hold
  early, rear 5th, some prog bef 2 out, kpt on. . . . . .*(33 to 1) 3
1902* THREE SCHOLARS 5-11-8 R Dunwoody, *led, clr 5th, jnd 2
  out, sn hdd and wknd. . . . .*(12 to 1) 4
2017² ALL THE VOWELS (Ire) 5-11-4 J P Broderick, *trkd ldr, lost pl 4
  out, rdn aftr nxt, sn wknd. . . . .*(25 to 1) 5
Dist: 5½l, 1l, 14l, 20l. 4m 28.30s. a 16.30s (5 Ran).
SR: 52/44/50/36/12/

(John P McManus), A P O'Brien

2071 Paddy Power Handicap Chase (Grade 2) (4-y-o and up) £44,050 3m . . . . (2:35)

1896* NEW CO [-] 8-10-6 C O'Dwyer, ...(11 to 4 fav) 1
1433⁸ WYLDE HIDE [-] 9-11-2 F Woods, ...(8 to 1) 2
1753³ TIME FOR A RUN [-] 9-10-4 R Dunwoody, ...(6 to 1) 3
1755⁵ BACK BAR (Ire) [-] 8-10-5 J P Broderick, ...(20 to 1) 4
1243⁵ ANTONIN (Fr) [-] 8-11-7 (3") K Whelan, ...(14 to 1) 5
1896³ DANCING VISION (Ire) [-] 6-9-12 J Jones, ...(25 to 1) 6
1639⁶ FEATHERED GALE [-] 9-11-9 (5") Mr J T McNamara,
  . . . .(16 to 1) 7
1434² HEIST [-] 7-10-9 K F O'Brien, ...(10 to 1) 8
1538* BEAT THE SECOND (Ire) [-] 8-9-13 C F Swan, ...(7 to 1) 9
1755² SECOND SCHEDUAL [-] 11-11-3 Mr G J Harford, . .(14 to 1) 10
1619⁸ WHALE OF A KNIGHT (Ire) [-] 7-10-7 P Carberry, . . .(7 to 1) 11
1619⁶ BALLYHIRE LAD (Ire) [-] 7-10-0 (3") Mr B M Cash, (33 to 1) 12
1434* LORD SINGAPORE (Ire) [-] 8-11-7 D J Casey, ...(8 to 1) 13
2020³ TOPICAL TIP (Ire) [-] 7-10-3 T P Treacy, ...(16 to 1) 14
1434 LOVE AND PORTER (Ire) [-] 8-10-9 D H O'Connor, (25 to 1) 15
2018⁸ NUAFFE [-] (bl) 11-11-4 T J Mitchell, ...(40 to 1) f
1621⁹ TRYFIRION (Ire) [-] 7-10-8 (3") B Bowens, ...(14 to 1) f
Dist: 1l, 7l, ½l, 6l, 11l. 6m 18.10s. a 11.10s (17 Ran).
SR: 51/60/41/41/54/17/

(Exors Of The Late Mrs L C Ronan), M F Morris

2072 Arboretum Garden Centre Maiden Hurdle (4-y-o) £4,110 2m. . . . .(3:10)

1617⁴ BUKHARI (Ire) 11-7 C O'Dwyer, ...(4 to 1) 1
1533² BOSS DOYLE (Ire) 11-2 C F Swan, ...(3 to 1) 2
HUMBEL (USA) 11-7 R Dunwoody, ...(11 to 8 on) 3

1897⁷ BLUE WAVE (Ire) 11-2 R Hughes, ...(33 to 1) 4
1777⁴ GENTLE MOSSY (Ire) 11-2 D H O'Connor, ...(20 to 1) 5
1836⁶ TIDAL PRINCESS (Ire) 10-11 D T Evans, ...(20 to 1) 6
1907⁵ DICK MCCARTHY (Ire) 11-2 D J Casey, ...(16 to 1) 7
CHATEAU MARTIN (Ire) 11-2 F Woods, ...(14 to 1) 8
TOURING-TURTLE (Ire) 11-2 K F O'Brien, ...(40 to 1) 9
IT'S HIMSELF 11-2 J Shortt, ...(33 to 1) 10
BRUSHETTA (Ire) 10-11 T P Treacy, ...(33 to 1) 11
1404⁸ BARLEY MEADOW (Ire) 11-2 H Rogers, ...(100 to 1) 12
Dist: 2l, 6l, 3½l, 14l. 4m 2.10s. a 18.10s (12 Ran).
SR: 24/17/16/7/-/-/

(John P McManus), C Roche

2073 Leopardstown Annual Badge INH Flat Race (4-y-o and up) £3,082 2m . . . . (3:40)

1579² SHANNON GALE (Ire) 4-10-13 (7") Mr G Elliott, ...(9 to 4) 1
1907* STRONTIUM (Ire) 4-11-13 Mr F Fenton, ... (2 to 1 fav) 2
1901³ BORO BOW (Ire) 5-11-13 Mr T Mullins, ...(7 to 2) 3
1195* BE MY PLEASURE (Ire) 4-11-1 (7") Mr Sean O O'Brien,
  . . . .(9 to 4) 4
1895 KAVANAGHS DREAM (Ire) 7-12-4 Mr H F Cleary, . .(25 to 1) 5
TEMPEST GALE (Ire) 7-11-4 (7") Mr A K Wyse, . . .(16 to 1) 6
1193 VARTRY BOY (Ire) 5-12-4 Mr D Marnane, ...(14 to 1) 7
Dist: ½l, 9l, 4l, dist. 4m 2.30s. (7 Ran).

(John P McManus), C Roche

LIMERICK (IRE) (good to yielding) Friday December 27th

2074 Bruff Maiden Hurdle (3-y-o) £2,740 2m. . . . . (12:30)

1709² THREE RIVERS 10-4 (7") P Morris, ... (5 to 4 on) 1
STRATEGIC PLOY 10-6 T P Rudd, ...(4 to 1) 2
AFARKA (Ire) 9-13 (7") A O'Shea, ...(3 to 1) 3
1750⁵ VINCITORE (Ire) 10-11 L P Cusack, ...(6 to 1) 4
1709⁸ DUGGAN DUFF (Ire) 10-4 (7") Mr S McGonagle, . . .(14 to 1) 5
1709⁶ CURRAGH COUNCIL (Ire) 10-1 (5") T Martin, . . .(12 to 1) 6
1309 KERRY REEL (Ire) 10-11 M P Hourigan, ...(14 to 1) 7
CEOTTHAS LASS (Ire) 10-12 (7") Mr R J Cooper, . .(25 to 1) 8
1430 PEGUS JUNIOR (Ire) 10-8 (3") G Cotter, ...(8 to 1) f
CALM BEAUTY (Ire) 9-13 (7") Mr C J Swords, ...(25 to 1) pu
Dist: 3l, 3½l, 4½l, 3½l. 4m 14.00s. (10 Ran).

(Mrs M Longton), W P Mullins

2075 Shannon Hurdle (4-y-o and up) £2,740 2½m. . . . . (1:00)

1777³ TONI'S TIP (Ire) 4-10-13 (3") G Cotter, ...(9 to 4 fav) 1
1840³ GLEBE LAD (Ire) 4-11-2 T P Rudd, ...(5 to 1) 2
PAS POSSIBLE (Ire) 4-11-8 T Hazlett, ...(12 to 1) 3
1776³ ROCHER LADY (Ire) 5-10-9 (7") P Morris, ...(11 to 4) 4
1712* LEAMHOG (Ire) 6-11-13 T Horgan, ...(7 to 2) 5
SUNSHINE BAY (Ire) 5-11-7 G M O'Neill, ...(10 to 1) 6
1904 TAR AND CEMENT (Ire) 8-11-7 A J O'Brien, ...(20 to 1) 7
1902 CAN'T BE STOPPED (Ire) 4-10-9 (7") J P Deegan, . .(25 to 1) 8
1838 HAMSHIRE GALE (Ire) 6-10-11 (5") J M Donnelly, . .(20 to 1) 9
SALLY SUPREME (Ire) 5-10-9 (7") Mr F P Cahill, . . .(20 to 1) 10
1246 ROBAZALA (Ire) 4-10-4 (7") Mr John P Moloney, . . .(25 to 1) 11
1897 WESTERN GREY (Ire) 4-11-2 M P Hourigan, ...(25 to 1) f
Dist: 7l, 2l, sht-hd, 6l. 5m 34.70s. (12 Ran).

(Mrs Toni S Tipper), W J Burke

2076 Hospital Handicap Hurdle (0-123 4-y-o and up) £2,740 2m. . . . (1:30)

1713 ILLBETHEREFORYOU [-] 5-9-10 M P Hourigan,
  . . . . (4 to 1 jt-fav) 1
1840⁴ HILL OF HOPE (Ire) [-] 5-10-13 W Slattery, ...(11 to 2) 2
980⁶ BEAU CYRANO (Ire) [-] 4-10-13 G M O'Neill, ...(7 to 1) 3
679⁵ LEGGAGH LADY (Ire) [-] 5-11-7 (5") M Donnelly, (4 to 1 jt-
  fav) 4
BE MY FOLLY (Ire) [-] 4-10-10 T Hazlett, ...(8 to 1) 5
1899 JO JO BOY (Ire) [-] 7-11-5 F J Flood, ...(5 to 1) 6
HOME PORT (Ire) [-] 4-11-11 (3") G Cotter, ...(5 to 1) 7
1650⁸ JAZZY REFRAIN (Ire) [-] 6-10-11 T Horgan, ...(10 to 1) 8
Dist: 1½l, ¾l, 1½l, 10l. 4m 18.00s. (8 Ran).

(G Walsh), Michael Hourigan

2077 Tattersalls Ireland EBF Mares Novice Chase (5-y-o and up) £3,425 2½m. . . . .(2:00)

2021³ ROYAL ROSY 5-11-12 T Horgan, ...(7 to 4 on) 1
2021⁵ COOLAFINKA (Ire) 7-11-11 (3") G Cotter, ...(7 to 1) 2
1904 LAURA'S PURSUIT (Ire) 7-11-9 (5") J M Donnelly, . .(7 to 1) 3
1780⁶ ARTISTIC QUAY (Ire) 7-11-7 (7") A O'Shea, ...(12 to 1) 4
1461 ALAMILLO (Ire) 7-11-11 (3") U Smyth, ...(6 to 1) 5
1776 LABAN LADY (Ire) 7-11-7 (7") M D Murphy, ...(10 to 1) 6
1714 MARGUERITA SONG 6-12-0 P A Roche, ...(7 to 1) 7
Dist: 3l, 2l, 8l, 1½l. 5m 21.90s. (7 Ran).

(Patrick M Sheehan), A P O'Brien

2078 Pat Chesser Handicap Chase (0-123 5-y-o and up) £3,425 2½m. . . . (2:30)

```
1896  THE REAL ARTICLE (Ire) [-] 7-11-11 L P Cusack, ... (7 to 1)     1
2020²  ONTHEROADAGAIN (Ire) [-] 8-11-3 T P Rudd, .... (5 to 2 fav)     2
1896⁴  THE CRAZY BISHOP (Ire) [-] 8-11-7 (7") A O'Shea, (11 to 4)     3
1619⁵  CARRIGEEN KERRIA (Ire) [-] 8-11-4 (3") G Cotter, .. (8 to 1)     4
1906⁴  WACKO JACKO (Ire) [-] 7-9-11 P A Roche, ........ (8 to 1)     5
        MONKEY AGO [-] 9-10-11 (7") Mr J L Cullen, ...... (12 to 1)     6
1896  OVER AGAIN (Ire) [-] 8-10-12 S H O'Donovan, .... (12 to 1)     7
1711⁶  BALLYBODEN [-] 9-9-2²² (7") M D Murphy, ........ (14 to 1)     f
1553⁸  BROOK HILL LADY (Ire) [-] 5-11-11 T Horgan, .....(7 to 1)     f
1781²  ANOTHER POINT (Ire) [-] (bl) 8-10-9 M P Hourigan, (7 to 1)     ur
Dist: 1l, ¾l, 15l, 3½l. 5m 17.60s. (10 Ran).
```

(William J Brennan), Gerard Stack

2079 Punchs Pub & Restaurant Mares Flat Race (4-y-o and up) £3,425 2m (3:00)

```
1490⁵  CORYROSE (Ire) 4-11-2 (7") Mr M T Hartrey, ....... (7 to 1)     1
1836⁷  RAHEEN RIVER (Ire) 5-12-0 Mr J A Berry, ......... (5 to 1)     2
1195⁵  KILCOGY CROSS (Ire) 4-11-2 (7") Miss A L Crowley, (5 to 1)     3
1756  CLARA ROCK (Ire) 4-11-2 (7") Mr C A Radley, ..... (14 to 1)     4
1908³  KAITHEY CHOICE (Ire) 5-11-7 (7") Mr J Boland, ... (10 to 1)     5
1710⁶  SCEAL SIOG (Ire) 7-11-7 (7") Mr J P McNamara, ... (8 to 1)     6
1995  MY BLACKBIRD (Ire) 4-11-8⁶ (7") Mr D L Bolger, ... (8 to 1)     7
        CLOSING THYNE (Ire) 5-11-7 (7") Mr P F O'Reilly, (12 to 1)     8
1778⁸  GLENA GALE (Ire) 6-11-7 (7") Mr John P Moloney, (10 to 1)     9
1902⁵  ALICE BRENNAN (Ire) 5-11-11 (3") Mr E Norris, (4 to 1 fav)     10
1279  LOVELY LYNSEY (Ire) 4-11-2 (7") Mr A J Dempsey,  (8 to 1)     11
1842⁶  RING HARRY (Ire) 6-11-7 (7") Mr T N Cloke, ...... (12 to 1)     12
1241  TOBY'S FRIEND (Ire) 7-11-7 (7") Mr D M D Scanlon, (14 to 1)     13
1756  THE FLYING YANK (Ire) 4-11-2 (7") Mr R J Curran, (12 to 1)     14
1901  MIA LADY 5-11-11 (3") Mr P English, ........(10 to 1)     15
        CLONCANNON BELL (Ire) 6-12-0 Miss M Olivefalk, (10 to 1)     16
        KITTYGALE 5-11-7 (7") Mr J L Cullen, ........ (12 to 1)     17
        TAR AN CARRAIG 4-11-9 Mrs C Barker, ........ (12 to 1)     18
        SISTER WEST (Ire) 4-11-2 (7") Mr K N McDonagh, (20 to 1)     19
1246⁸  CORDAL DREAM (Ire) 4-11-2 (7") Mr A English, ... (20 to 1)     20
Dist: 1½l, 13l, 10l, 1½l. 4m 9.90s. (20 Ran).
```

(M J E Thornhill), H de Bromhead

2080 Greenpark I.N.H. Flat Race (5-y-o) £2,740 2½m (3:30)

```
1782²  CEOIL AGUS CRAIC (Ire) 11-11 Mr J P Dempsey,
                                                    ........(100 to 30)     1
1908¹  WINDY BEE (Ire) 11-6 (7") Mr N D Fehily, ........ (4 to 1)     2
1902⁷  BAR FLUTE (Ire) 10-13 (7") Miss A L Crowley, ..... (6 to 1)     3
1776⁹  CROSSCHILD (Ire) 11-6 (7") Mr P M Cloke, ...... (13 to 2)     4
1901²  YASHGANS VISION (Ire) 11-6 (7") Mr E Sheehy, (9 to 4 fav)     5
1195⁷  BLUE IRISH (Ire) 11-4 (7") Mr J L Cullen, ........ (7 to 1)     6
        GALLIC BEAUTY (Ire) 10-13 (7") Mr R M Walsh, ... (16 to 1)     7
Dist: ¾l, 9l, 7l, 7l. 5m 28.40s. (7 Ran).
```

(S Bolger), Michael G Holden

LEOPARDSTOWN (IRE) (good to yielding)
Saturday December 28th
Going Correction: PLUS 0.70 sec. per fur. (races 1,2,4,6,7), PLUS 0.30 (3,5)

2081 William Neville & Sons Maiden Hurdle (5-y-o and up) £4,110 2½m (12:35)

```
1715*  JODESI (Ire) 6-12-0 D J Casey, ................ (5 to 2)     1
        KILCOO BOY 5-12-0 C F Swan, ................ (4 to 1)     2
1901*  STORM GEM (Ire) 5-11-9 T J Mitchell, .......... (6 to 1)     3
1649  HEAVY HUSTLER (Ire) 5-11-6 F Woods, ........ (8 to 1)     4
1460⁵  IVERK'S PRIDE (Ire) 5-10-13 (7") Mr C A Murphy, .. (20 to 1)     5
1536⁷  GREENREEF BOY (Ire) 7-12-0 D T Evans, ........ (12 to 1)     6
        BIT O'SPEED (Ire) 5-11-6 C O'Dwyer, ........ (14 to 1)     7
1653⁵  HEAD CHAPLAIN (Ire) 5-11-6 A Powell, ........ (20 to 1)     8
1895⁹  TEMPLEWOOD EXPRESS (Ire) 7-11-11 (3") B Bowens,
                                                    .............. (12 to 1)     9
1751  ISLE OF IONA (Ire) 5-11-6 T P Rudd, ............ (25 to 1)     10
1580²  TURRAMURRA GIRL (Ire) 7-11-2 (7") L J Fleming, (16 to 1)     11
1710²  ETON EAGLE (Ire) 7-12-0 T P Treacy, .......... (9 to 4 fav)     f
1715  PUNTERS DREAM 6-11-6 J P Broderick, ........ (66 to 1)     pu
977  PRINCE WOT A MESS (Ire) 5-11-6 L P Cusack, .. (66 to 1)     pu
Dist: 7l, 1½l, 1½l, 8l. 5m 10.00s. a 30.00s (14 Ran).
```

(P J Dore), W P Mullins

2082 O'Dwyers Stillorgan Orchard Novice Hurdle (4-y-o and up) £4,200 2¾m (1:05)

```
1651³  NOBLE THYNE (Ire) 6-11-8 T P Treacy, ........ (Evens fav)     1
1900*  ASK THE BUTLER (Ire) 5-11-11 C O'Dwyer, ......... (9 to 4)     2
1895*  BUGGY (Ire) 7-11-8 T J Mitchell, ............ (20 to 1)     3
1620*  TARTHOOTH (Ire) 5-12-0 F Woods, .............. (2 to 1)     f
Dist: Sht-hd, dist. 5m 45.00s. a 39.00s (4 Ran).
```

(C Mayo), P Mullins

2083 William Neville & Sons Novice Chase (Grade 3) (5-y-o and up) £6,850 3m (1:35)

```
1652*  DORANS PRIDE (Ire) 7-11-13 J P Broderick, made all, jmpd
        big 1st, quickened bef 8th and whn rdn aftr 2 out, easily.
                                                    ................(5 to 1 on)     1
2020  LE GINNO (Fr) 9-11-7 T P Treacy, trkd ldr, rdn bef 2 out, not
        quicken......................... (9 to 2)     2
1898  GARABAGH (Ire) 7-11-4 P Carberry, wl plcd till slow 4th, mstk
        7 out, sn lost tch........................(25 to 1)     3
        CAVALLO (Fr) 6-11-4 F Woods, rear, slow 3rd, mstk 8th, lost
        tch nxt, tld off 7 out.........................(25 to 1)     4
Dist: Dist, 25l, dist. 6m 24.50s. a 17.50s (4 Ran).
```

(T J Doran), Michael Hourigan

2084 Leopardstown Christmas Hurdle (Grade 3) (4-y-o and up) £6,850 3m (2:05)

```
1998⁵  WHAT A QUESTION (Ire) 8-11-7 C O'Dwyer, made all, wl clr
        second, rdn bef 2 out, kpt on strly.................(5 to 2)     1
1637²  ANTAPOURA (Ire) 4-10-8 C F Swan, trkd ldr, rdn aftr 3 out, gd
        prog after nxt, no extr r-in.................... (7 to 4 on)     2
2018⁴  RATHGIBBON (Ire) 5-11-2 T P Treacy, wl wth, rdn bef 2 out,
        kpt on without threatening.................... (20 to 1)     3
1896  DEE ELL 10-10-9 (7") Mr J D Moore, rear, mstk 1st, rdn bef
        7th, sn lost tch..................... (14 to 1)     4
1653  RADANPOUR (Ire) 4-10-13 D J Casey, trkd ldr till f 8th.
                                                    ................ (7 to 1)     f
Dist: 4l, 15l, dist. 6m 9.50s. a 32.50s (5 Ran).
```

(Mrs Miles Valentine), M F Morris

2085 Ericsson Chase (Grade 2) (5-y-o and up) £32,500 3m (2:40)

```
1619*  JOHNNY SETASIDE (Ire) 7-12-0 R Dunwoody, dsptd ld 1st 2,
        wl plcd, disputed lead 9th, led 6 out, jnd 4 out, hdd nxt, led two
        out, quickened clr. Collapsed, dead...........(2 to 1 fav)     1
1537⁶  KING OF THE GALES 9-12-0 F Woods, rear till some prog
        bef 8 out and ag'n before 4 out, styd on strly und pres.
                                                    .......................(16 to 1)     2
1537*  OPERA HAT (Ire) 8-11-9 A Powell, dsptd ld 1st 2, led, mstk 6th,
        jnd 9th, hdd six out, led 3 out, headed and mistake two out,
        mistake last, wknd........................ (7 to 2)     3
1878  BELVEDERIAN 9-12-0 C O'Dwyer, wl plcd till lost pos 3rd,
        slow 5th and 8 out, mstk 5 out, rdn bef 3 out, no extr. (8 to 1)     4
1755*  SON OF WAR 9-12-0 U Smyth, wl plcd, slow 7th, lost pos aftr
        nxt, sn rdn, no extr........................(15 to 2)     5
2053⁷  MACALLISTER (Ire) 6-11-11 B Bowens, rear till prog aftr 9th,
        mstk 6 out, no extr.........................(40 to 1)     6
1537⁵  IDIOTS VENTURE 9-12-0 C F Swan, wl plcd, prog to track
        ldrs 8 out, blun and uns rdr 4 out......... (5 to 2)     ur
Dist: 3l, 15l, 10l, 4½l. 6m 18.50s. a 11.50s (7 Ran).
SR: 57/54/34/29/24/-/-/
```

(John O'Meara), Noel Meade

2086 R.T.E. For Sport Handicap Hurdle (4-y-o and up) £6,850 2m (3:15)

```
1535⁶  LEGAL AND TENDER (Ire) [-] 5-9-11 (7") R P Hogan, (33 to 1)     1
1617²  RAWY (USA) [-] 4-11-5 C O'Dwyer, ........ (11 to 10 fav)     2
1836*  CLIFDON FOG (Ire) [-] 5-11-3 C F Swan, ......... (5 to 2)     3
1752³  METASTASIO [-] (bl) 4-11-5 H Rogers, ..........(6 to 1)     4
1654  OWENDUFF (USA) [-] 6-10-11 P Carberry, .........(10 to 1)     5
1905⁴  ARCTIC WEATHER (Ire) [-] 7-11-5 T P Rudd, ......(10 to 1)     6
1900⁴  FONTAINE LODGE (Ire) [-] 6-10-3 (7") A O'Shea, ...(10 to 1)     7
1905⁶  PUNTING PETE (Ire) [-] 6-11-11 T P Treacy, .....(12 to 1)     8
        MANHATTAN CASTLE (Ire) [-] 7-12-0 F Woods, ... (14 to 1)     9
1900⁹  REASILVIA (Ire) [-] 6-11-6 R Dunwoody, .........(14 to 1)     10
Dist: ½l, sht-hd, 6l, 2½l. 4m 1.30s. a 17.30s (10 Ran).
SR: 4/29/27/23/12/-/
```

(J P O'Flaherty), Francis Berry

2087 P.B. Bumper I.N.H. Flat Race (5-y-o and up) £8,220 2½m (3:45)

```
        CAILIN SUPREME (Ire) 5-11-9 Mr T Mullins, ..... (5 to 1)     1
1655⁷  DAVENPORT BANQUET (Ire) 5-12-0 Mr J A Nash,
                                                    ................... (5 to 4 on)     2
1539*  AS ROYAL (Ire) 5-11-11 (3") Mr P English, ....... (9 to 2)     3
        BELLS BRIDGE (Ire) 6-11-4 (3") Mr B M Cash, .... (11 to 1)     4
1096*  THE GREY MARE (Ire) 7-11-2 (7") Mr P Fahey, .... (14 to 1)     5
1463*  OPTIMISM REIGNS (Ire) 5-12-0 Mr P Fenton, .....(5 to 1)     6
        CHOCOLATE GIRL (Ire) 5-10-11 (5") Mr G Elliott, .. (40 to 1)     7
Dist: 4½l, 4l, 3l, 1l. 5m 9.80s. (7 Ran).
```

(E Morrissey), P Mullins

LIMERICK (IRE) (yielding)
Saturday December 28th

2088 I.N.H. Stallion Owners E.B.F. Maiden Hurdle (5-y-o and up) £3,767 2m 5f (1:20)

```
1895  MISS ORCHESTRA (Ire) 5-11-1 J Shortt, ......... (12 to 1)     1
1902²  BAI-BIRGHN KATE (Ire) 5-11-9 F J Flood, ......(11 to 10 fav)     2
        DESERTMORE (Ire) 6-10-13 (7") Mr N D Fehily, ...(10 to 1)     3
1904⁷  MAGS SUPER TOI (Ire) 7-10-13 (7") M D Murphy, (12 to 1)     4
1905⁷  COMMITTED SCHEDULE (Ire) 5-11-6 M P Hourigan, (7 to 1)     5
1838⁷  TOUREEN GALE (Ire) 7-11-4 (5") P Morris, ......(4 to 1)     6
1715⁵  SLANEY CHARM (Ire) 6-11-6 D H O'Connor, ......(8 to 1)     7
```

272

1776[2] MARYOBEE (Ire) 6-11-1 T Horgan, ...(7 to 2) 8
EXPEDIENT EXPRESS (Ire) 6-11-6 M Duffy, ...(12 to 1) 9
1840[7] GLANTINE LAD (Ire) 6-11-6 J Jones, ...(12 to 1) 10
978 CELTIC WHO (Ire) 5-11-6 N Williamson, ...(10 to 1) 11
1908[8] BARNA LASS (Ire) 5-10-10 (5*) J M Donnelly, ...(12 to 1) 12
1710 SALMON POOL (Ire) 6-10-12 (3*) K Whelan, ...(14 to 1) 13
1838 TORUS STAR (Ire) 7-10-13 (7*) Mr M P FitzGerald, (20 to 1) 14
1838[8] XANTHOS 6-11-6 S H O'Donovan, ...(12 to 1) 15
2037 CRANNON BEAUTY (Ire) 6-11-1 (5*) J Butler, ...(10 to 1) 16
1487[7] QUEEN OF ALL GALES (Ire) 5-10-10 (5*) P D Carey, (10 to 1) f
1649 TUDOR ROSE 5-11-6 K F O'Brien, ...(12 to 1) pu
Dist: ¾l, hd, 3l, 3½l. 5m 41.60s. (18 Ran).
(The B B Horse Racing Club), Mrs John Harrington

2089 Dromcollogher Handicap Hurdle (0-102 4-y-o and up) £2,740 2½m .... (1:50)

1839[4] SKULLDUGERY (Ire) [-] 6-10-0 J Jones, ...(3 to 1 fav) 1
2055[2] CHARLIE-O (Ire) [-] 4-11-2 (5*) Mr J T McNamara, (11 to 2) 2
1431[5] ADARAMANN (Ire) [-] 4-10-10 (3*) Mr R Walsh, ...(10 to 1) 3
2057[3] JIHAAD (USA) [-] 6-9-12 (7*) J O'Shaughnessy, ...(8 to 1) 4
1839 NEIPHIN BOY (Ire) [-] 6-10-6 F J Flood, ...(9 to 1) 5
1904* ISLAND CHAMPION (Ire) [-] 7-10-2 (5*) T Martin, ...(9 to 2) 6
1895[7] TREANAREE (Ire) [-] 7-10-9 (7*) S Kelly, ...(10 to 1) 7
1839[9] CLONMEL COMMERCIAL (Ire) [-] 5-9-11 (7*) D McCullagh, ...(16 to 1) 8
1776[4] JANICE PRICE (Ire) [-] 5-10-8 (7*) J E Casey, ...(10 to 1) 9
1904[5] WOODBORO LASS (Ire) [-] 6-9-11 (5*) J M Donnelly, (8 to 1) 10
742 LISHILLAUN (Ire) [-] 6-9-12 Miss M Olivefalk, ...(14 to 1) 11
1777[6] PERMIT ME (Ire) [-] 4-10-4 (7*) M D Murphy, ...(10 to 1) 12
1778 CARRAIG-AN-OIR (Ire) [-] 7-9-11 T Horgan, ...(14 to 1) 13
1489[7] PERSIAN MYSTIC (Ire) [-] 4-11-6 G M O'Neill, ...(10 to 1) 14
1904 RUN ROSE RUN (Ire) [-] (bl) 6-9-7 (5*) J Butler, ...(9 to 1) 15
1902[8] BESTERELLE (Ire) [-] 5-11-2 M Duffy, ...(10 to 1) 16
1715 NATIVE CHAMPION (Ire) [-] (bl) 7-10-8 K F O'Brien, (14 to 1) 17
Dist: 1l, 1½l, 3l, ½l. 5m 23.20s. (17 Ran).
(David Mann), E McNamara

2090 European Breeders Fund Beginners Chase (5-y-o and up) £3,767 2½m .... (2:20)

1712[3] MATTS DILEMMA (Ire) 8-12-0 D H O'Connor, ...(6 to 1) 1
1779[6] MONALEE STATEMENT (Ire) 6-12-0 N Williamson, ..(8 to 1) 2
1841 THE NOBLE ROUGE (Ire) 7-11-7 (7*) M D Murphy, ..(8 to 1) 3
1841[6] PRATE BOX (Ire) 6-12-0 J Shortt, ...(12 to 1) 4
980[5] TEMPLEROAN PRINCE 9-12-0 J R Barry, ...(6 to 1) 5
1900[5] SCENIC ROUTE (Ire) 7-11-9 (5*) Mr T P Hyde, ..(9 to 4 fav) f
CHESLOCK (Ire) 7-11-7 (7*) J O'Shaughnessy, ...(25 to 1) ur
1841 RUN BAVARD (Ire) 8-12-0 S H O'Donovan, ...(12 to 1) pu
2020 DRAMATIC VENTURE (Ire) 7-12-0 K F O'Brien, ...(5 to 2) pu
Dist: 3½l, ¾l, 8l, 10l. 5m 23.30s. (9 Ran).
(Slaney Meats Group), P J P Doyle

2091 Goggin Buckley Structural Steel Handicap Chase (0-109 5-y-o and up) £3,425 3m............... (2:50)

CANAILLOU II (Fr) [-] 6-10-5 (3*) K Whelan, ...(9 to 2) 1
1903* CASTALINO [-] 10-11-5 J Shortt, ...(2 to 1 fav) 2
2078 BALLYBODEN [-] 9-10-8 M P Hourigan, ...(8 to 1) 3
1618 WEST BROGUE (Ire) [-] 7-11-7 T Horgan, ...(5 to 1) 4
1906 IF YOU SAY YES (Ire) [-] 8-10-6 N Williamson, ...(10 to 1) 5
THRESA-ANITA (Ire) [-] 8-9-10 S H O'Donovan, ...(5 to 1) 6
1841[5] SLANEY STANDARD (Ire) [-] 8-11-2 D H O'Connor, ...(100 to 30) f
Dist: 3½l, 1l, 9l, 25l. 6m 44.70s. (7 Ran).
(M Stanners), Mrs S A Bramall

2092 A.I.B. Bank Ladies I.N.H. Flat Race (4 & 5-y-o) £3,425 2m........... (3:20)

1060[7] IRVINE (Ire) 4-11-2 (7*) Miss S J Leahy, ...(7 to 1) 1
KINGMAN (Ire) 4-11-2 (7*) Miss A M Kent, ...(20 to 1) 2
984[3] BERE HAVEN (Ire) 4-11-9 Mrs C Barker, ...(11 to 8 on) 3
1908[2] PRINCESS GLORIA (Ire) (bl) 5-11-2 (7*) Miss M Horgan, ...(6 to 1) 4
SUIR FIND (Ire) 4-11-2 (7*) Miss T S Dare, ...(12 to 1) 5
TORMOND PERK (Ire) 5-11-7 (7*) Miss A L Crowley, (5 to 1) 6
1019 SILKEN SECRETARIAT (Ire) 5-11-7 (7*) Miss A Foley, ...(20 to 1) 7
MR MAGNETIC (Ire) 5-11-7 (7*) Mrs C Doyle, ...(10 to 1) 8
1145 ATLANTA FLAME (Ire) 5-11-2 (7*) Miss L E A Doyle, (20 to 1) 9
1901 DUSKY SOUND (Ire) 4-10-11 (7*) Miss J Hyde, ...(12 to 1) 10
GO GO HENRY (Ire) 4-11-9 Miss M Olivefalk, ...(8 to 1) 11
Dist: 9l, 4l, 9l, 5l. 4m 7.40s. (11 Ran).
(Mrs Ellen Leahy), Augustine Leahy

2093 Rathbarry Stud I.N.H. Flat Race (6-y-o and up) £3,425 2½m..... (3:50)

1715[4] HOLLOW GOLD (Ire) 7-11-2 (7*) Mr D W Cullen, ...(7 to 1) 1
BUSH TELEGRAPH (Ire) 7-11-11 (3*) Mr R Walsh, ...(2 to 1 fav) 2
DESMARFRAN (Ire) 7-12-0 Mr J P Dempsey, ...(14 to 1) 3
1838 PRIZE OF PEACE (Ire) 6-11-2 (7*) Mr M T Hartrey, (12 to 1) 4
1776 ARTIC PEARL (Ire) 6-11-2 (7*) Mr John P Moloney, (16 to 1) 5
TEA-VINE (Ire) 7-11-2 (7*) Mr E Sheehy, ...(14 to 1) 6
1715[3] ISOLETTE 8-11-6 (3*) Mr P J Casey, ...(9 to 2) 7
1842[5] CALL BOB (Ire) 6-11-7 (7*) Mr T J Nagle-Jnr, ...(7 to 1) 8
TAXMAN WILLY (Ire) 6-11-7 (7*) Mr Sean O O'Brien, (14 to 1) 9
2060[9] ARCTIC GREY (Ire) (bl) 6-12-0 Mr J A Flynn, ...(8 to 1) 10
1360 THE YELLOW BOG (Ire) 6-11-7 (7*) Mr P J Gilligan, (8 to 1) 11
CHANCERY RIVER (Ire) 7-11-2 (7*) Mr R F O'Gorman, ...(12 to 1) pu
1905[9] POWER CORE (Ire) 6-11-7 (7*) Miss A L Crowley, ..(10 to 1) pu
WILLOW PARK (Ire) 6-11-7 (7*) Mr T N Cloke, ...(8 to 1) pu
CAMDEN ABBEY (Ire) 6-11-9 Mr T Doyle, ...(16 to 1) pu
Dist: 1½l, 15l, 2½l, hd. 5m 27.00s. (15 Ran).
(E Madden), Niall Madden

LEOPARDSTOWN (IRE) (yielding) Monday December 30th

Going Correction: PLUS 0.60 sec. per fur. (races 1,2,4,5,7), PLUS 0.20 (3,6)

2094 Three Rock Maiden Hurdle (5-y-o and up) £3,767 2m...........(12:45)

1463[6] MR BAXTER BASICS 5-11-6 N Williamson, ...(9 to 1) 1
1895[6] PAULS RUN (Ire) 7-12-0 L P Cusack, ...(5 to 1) 2
1895 FOYLE WANDERER (Ire) 5-11-1 D T Evans, ...(14 to 1) 3
1649 ATHA BEITHE (Ire) 5-12-0 R Hughes, ...(10 to 1) 4
TWO SHONAS (Ire) 5-11-6 (3*) D Bromley, ...(14 to 1) 5
1436* GARRYS LOCK (Ire) 7-12-0 T P Treacy, ...(7 to 4 fav) 6
CAVALIER D'OR (USA) 5-12-0 F Woods, ...(7 to 1) 7
1842[2] EDUARDO (Ire) 6-12-0 R Dunwoody, ...(9 to 4) 8
SAFRANE 8-11-6 Mr A R Coonan, ...(33 to 1) 9
1710 GONE ALL DAY (Ire) 6-11-6 J R Barry, ...(66 to 1) 10
MUDDY RAY (Ire) 5-11-6 A Powell, ...(40 to 1) 11
910 STRONG AUCTION (Ire) 5-11-1 J K Kinane, ...(50 to 1) 12
Dist: 4½l, 6l, 10l, 12l. 4m 5.50s. a 21.50s (12 Ran).
(Mrs Audrey Healy), Thomas J Taaffe

2095 December Festival Hurdle (Grade 2) (4-y-o and up) £9,675 2m..... (1:15)

1877[3] THEATREWORLD (Ire) 4-11-2 C F Swan, *made all, rdn and quickened bef 2 out, styd on strly, eased cl hme*.....(2 to 1) 1
1457[2] HILL SOCIETY (Ire) 4-11-2 R Dunwoody, *wl plcd, rdn aftr 2 out, kpt on well r-in*.................................(8 to 1) 2
1653[2] COCKNEY LAD (Ire) 7-11-7 P Carberry, *wl plcd, rdn aftr 2 out, not quicken*..............................(6 to 4 fav) 3
2051 SLANEY GLOW (Ire) 5-11-2 F Woods, *rear, rdn aftr 5th, lost tch after 3 out*..................................(33 to 1) 4
1900 MAYASTA (Ire) 6-11-2 C O'Dwyer, *rear, rdn aftr 3 out, lost tch after nxt*...(12 to 1) 5
1617* GUEST PERFORMANCE (Ire) 4-11-2 R Hughes, *trkd ldr till blun and uns rdr 4th*..............................(5 to 2) ur
Dist: 5l, 1½l, dist, 3½l. 3m 56.20s. a 12.20s (6 Ran).
SR: 62/57/60/ (Mrs John Magnier), A P O'Brien

2096 Dalkey Beginners Chase (4-y-o and up) £4,110 2m 3f............. (1:45)

828[7] FINCHPALM (Ire) 6-12-0 F J Flood, ...(7 to 1) 1
1714[2] GLINT OF EAGLES (Ire) 7-12-0 T P Treacy, ...(5 to 2 fav) 2
2021 THE VENDOR (Ire) 6-11-2 (7*) A O'Shea, ...(33 to 1) 3
1534[2] KALDAN KHAN 5-11-12 C F Swan, ...(5 to 1) 4
ARCTIC BUCK (Ire) 6-12-0 N Williamson, ...(20 to 1) 5
1779[7] MUSKIN MORE (Ire) 5-11-12 R Dunwoody, ...(14 to 1) 6
1189[7] BANGABUNNY 6-11-11 (3*) K Whelan, ...(12 to 1) 7
1552 GREAT SVENGALI (Ire) 7-12-0 C O'Dwyer, ...(4 to 1) 8
1779[8] KNOCKMUIRA (Ire) 6-12-0 L P Cusack, ...(16 to 1) 9
1074 MOON-FROG 9-12-0 J K Kinane, ...(50 to 1) f
1170[2] DAWN ALERT (Ire) 7-12-0 P Carberry, ...(7 to 2) f
RADIANT RIVER (Ire) 6-11-11 (3*) G Cotter, ...(14 to 1) pu
Dist: 2l, 14l, 3½l, 13l. 4m 49.70s. a 10.70s (12 Ran).
SR: 31/29/10/9/-/-/ (Finchpalm Limited), F Flood

2097 Ballinclea Handicap Hurdle (0-116 4-y-o and up) £3,767 2m..... (2:15)

2068[2] COLLON LEADER (Ire) [-] 7-10-12 (5*) Mr G Elliott, ..(3 to 1) 1
1839* LADY DAISY (Ire) [-] 7-11-7 (7*) A O'Shea, ...(2 to 1 fav) 2
2016[6] FALLOW TRIX (Ire) [-] 4-11-1 R Dunwoody, ...(8 to 1) 3
1017[5] PRACTICIAN (Ire) [-] 6-9-13 (7*) J M Maguire, ...(8 to 1) 4
1432 MIDNIGHT JAZZ (Ire) [-] 6-10-12 M P Hourigan, ...(20 to 1) 5
1654 FRANCES STREET (Ire) [-] (bl) 4-11-9 C F Swan, ...(5 to 1) 6
1900 PRE ORDAINED (Ire) [-] 4-11-5 F J Flood, ...(8 to 1) 7
SORALENA (Ire) [-] 5-9-10 (7*) R P Hogan, ...(14 to 1) 8
Dist: ½l, 20l, 5l, hd. 4m 7.70s. a 23.70s (8 Ran).
(Mrs I M Murphy), A J Martin

2098 Knocknashee I.N.H. Flat Race (4-y-o and up) £3,082 2m........... (2:45)

OLUMO (Ire) 5-12-0 Mr A J Martin, ...(8 to 1) 1
SCOUT AROUND (Ire) 4-11-9 Mr P Fenton, ...(5 to 4 on) 2
TIME TO LEAD (Ire) 6-11-7 (7*) Mr A K Wyse, ...(4 to 1) 3
KISSANE GALE (Ire) 4-10-11 (7*) Mr A J Dempsey, (8 to 1) 4
1195 TOCHAR BOY (Ire) 5-12-0 Mr D Marnane, ...(33 to 1) 5

SLIMLINE CAT (Ire) 4-11-6 (3ᵃ) Mr B M Cash, ... (4 to 1) 6
Dist: Nk, 7l, 3½l, 3½l. 4m 12.20s. (6 Ran).

(P A McGuinness), A J Martin

2099 Killiney Handicap Chase (0-109 4-y-o and up) £4,110 3m . . . . (3:15)

1534 BANNER GALE (Ire) [-] 7-11-9 C O'Dwyer, ...(5 to 1) 1
1192⁴ VULPIN DE LAUGERE (Fr) [-] 9-9-13 (3ᵃ) K Whelan,
. . . . (11 to 8 fav) 2
1618⁶ CREHELP EXPRESS (Ire) [-] 6-11-7 (3ᵃ) B Bowens, (5 to 1) 3
1538 WALLYS RUN [-] 9-10-11 L P Cusack, ... (6 to 1) 4
1754⁴ OLYMPIC D'OR (Ire) [-] 8-11-6 C F Swan, ...(5 to 1) 5
1896 TOP RUN (Ire) [-] 8-10-7 T P Treacy, ... (12 to 1) pu
Dist: 13l, 25l, dist, 15l. 6m 26.70s. a 19.70s (6 Ran).

(N O'Flaherty), Francis Berry

2100 Glenbourne I.N.H. Flat Race (4-y-o and up) £3,425 2m . . . . (3:45)

1043* FURNITUREVILLE (Ire) 4-11-11 (5ᵃ) Mr D McGoona, (5 to 1) 1
1096 CELEBRITY STATUS (Ire) 5-11-4 (7ᵃ) Mr D Delaney, (25 to 1) 2
1838⁹ DROICHEAD LAPEEN 9-12-0 (7ᵃ) Mr T J Beattie, . .(10 to 1) 3
CLAY AND WATTLES (Ire) 5-12-0 (7ᵃ) Mr A K Wyse,
. . . . (2 to 1 fav) 4
1842* PREMIER WALK 7-12-0 (7ᵃ) Mr S P Hennessy, . .(100 to 30) 5
RIPOSTE (Ire) 4-10-12 (3ᵃ) Mr B M Cash, ...(6 to 1) 6
Dist: 2l, 2l, 1l, 5l. 4m 12.20s. (6 Ran).

(Mrs Kayoko Iwasaki), Joseph M Canty

CAGNES-SUR-MER (FR) (very soft)
Tuesday December 31st

2101 Prix Jacques Pinel de Grandchamp (Hurdle) (4-y-o and up) £7,905 2m 55yds . . . . (1:45)

LA GOUGOULINE (Fr) 4-9-6 E Diard, wtd wth, late run to take
ld in fnl strds 1
2028* GAROLO (Fr) 6-10-4 G Bradley, led hfwy till fnl strds 2
FUNNY SPIRIT (Fr) 7-10-8 P Havas, ... 3
Dist: Nk, 6½l, ½l, 4l, 3l, 4l. 8m 0.50s. (13 Ran).

(R Notari), A Bosselet

CAGNES-SUR-MER (FR) (heavy)
Sunday January 5th

2102 Prix du Restaurant La Cravache d'Or - Roger Duchene (Hurdle) (5-y-o and up) £7,246 2¼m . . . . (2:52)

2101² GAROLO (Fr) 7-10-8 G Bradley, al prmnt, led appr last, hrd
rdn, jst hld on 1
BIKALAMOUN (Fr) 7-10-8 Y Bouche, ... 2
KARIVER (Fr) 6-10-1 F Cheyer, ... 3
Dist: Sht-hd, 7l, 6l, 3l, dist. (Time not taken) (9 Ran).

(Lady Lloyd Webber), C P E Brooks

THURLES (IRE) (good)
Monday January 6th

2103 Holiday Opportunity Handicap Hurdle (Div I) (0-102 4-y-o and up) £2,637 3m . . . . (1:20)

2018⁵ ROCK'N ROLL KID (Ire) [-] 6-11-3 (2ᵃ) P Morris, ...(5 to 1) 1
1778⁵ MISS BERTAINE (Ire) [-] (bl) 8-10-1 (4ᵃ) J E Casey, (15 to 2) 2
2093⁵ ARTIC PEARL (Ire) [-] 7-10-3 K Whelan, ...(20 to 1) 3
1713 ECLIPTIC MOON (Ire) [-] 7-9-9 J Butler, ... (6 to 1) 4
2036⁴ HERSILIA (Ire) [-] 6-10-8 (4ᵃ) L J Fleming, ...(8 to 1) 5
1550 THE BOYLERMAN (Ire) [-] 8-11-3 (3ᵃ) G Cotter, ...(14 to 1) 6
1838⁴ VIVIANS VALE (Ire) [-] 8-11-1 (4ᵃ) D K Budds, ... (13 to 2) 7
1548 CASTLE BAILEY (Ire) [-] 6-10-3 (2ᵃ) T Martin, ...(25 to 1) 8
2089⁸ CLONMEL COMMERCIAL (Ire) [-] 6-9-11 (4ᵃ) D McCullagh,
. . . .(14 to 1) 9
1840⁵ ROSIE LIL (Ire) [-] (bl) 6-10-8 (4ᵃ) L A Hurley, ...(9 to 1) 10
2068⁹ YOUNG MRS KELLY (Ire) [-] 7-11-1 (7ᵃ) R P Hogan,
. . . .(9 to 2 fav) 11
2055 MILLICANS BEND (Ire) [-] 5-9-5 (4ᵃ) M J Collins, . . .(33 to 1) 12
2057² VINTNERS VENTURE (Ire) [-] 5-11-2 (2ᵃ) M J Holbrook,
. . . .(13 to 2) pu
Dist: 2l, 1l, 2½l, 1l. 5m 55.90s. (13 Ran).

(Early Bird Syndicate), W P Mullins

2104 Holiday Opportunity Handicap Hurdle (Div II) (0-102 4-y-o and up) £2,637 3m . . . . (1:50)

2068 DARK SWAN (Ire) [-] 7-11-5 (4ᵃ) D Flood, ...(8 to 1) 1
1550⁷ LAURENS FANCY (Ire) [-] 7-10-13 G Cotter, ...(7 to 2) 2
2018² LADY QUAYSIDE (Ire) [-] 7-11-1 (2ᵃ) P Morris, . .(3 to 1 fav) 3
2016 DOUBLE STRIKE (Ire) [-] 6-11-4 D Bromley, ...(14 to 1) 4
1836⁶ ROSEY ELLEN (Ire) [-] 5-10-2 (4ᵃ) M D Murphy, ...(8 to 1) 5

1904⁸ OVER THE WALL (Ire) [-] 8-9-12 (4ᵃ) J M Maguire, (14 to 1) 6
2089⁴ JIHAAD (USA) [-] 7-9-13 (4ᵃ) J O'Shaughnessy, ...(8 to 1) 7
1904 SONG FOR AFRICA (Ire) [-] 6-10-2 (4ᵃ) R P Hogan, (14 to 1) 8
223² MAJESTIC JOHN (Ire) [-] 7-10-7 (4ᵃ) A T Kelly, ...(8 to 1) 9
2089* SKULLDUGERY (Ire) [-] 7-9-12 (4ᵃ) A O'Shea, ...(7 to 1) f
2088⁹ EXPEDIENT EXPRESS (Ire) [-] 7-10-1 K Whelan, . .(25 to 1) f
Dist: 4½l, 2l, 2l, 2½l, ½l. 6m 0.50s. (11 Ran).

(First Time Out Syndicate), T J O'Mara

2105 Killinan Hurdle (4-y-o) £2,226 2m . . . . (2:20)

2050⁵ MISS PENNYHILL (Ire) (bl) 9-11 (7ᵃ) J M Maguire, . . .(3 to 1) 1
2050 GO SASHA (Ire) (bl) 10-11 (5ᵃ) T Martin, ... (5 to 1) 2
2074* THREE RIVERS 11-2 D J Casey, ...(6 to 4 fav) 3
1709 KING OF PEACE (Ire) 10-6 (3ᵃ) D Bromley, ...(12 to 1) 4
2050 IACCHUS (Ire) 11-2 C F Swan, ...(8 to 1) 5
1709⁴ TIP YOUR WAITRESS (Ire) 10-9 G M O'Neill, ...(13 to 2) 6
KEAL RYAN (Ire) 10-6 (3ᵃ) G Cotter, ...(10 to 1) 7
2067 ERNE PROJECT (Ire) 10-4 H Rogers, ...(12 to 1) 8
1547⁵ NO AVAIL (Ire) 10-4 T P Treacy, ...(12 to 1) 9
Dist: 2l, 4½l, 2l, 4½l. 4m 6.30s. (9 Ran).

(A Sadik), A Sadik

2106 Cashel Hurdle (5-y-o) £2,226 2m . . . . (2:50)

2072² BOSS DOYLE (Ire) 11-0 C F Swan, ...(9 to 4 on) 1
2092* IRVINE (Ire) 10-7 (7ᵃ) Miss S J Leahy, ...(7 to 1) 2
2049⁷ MINISTER'S CROSS (Ire) 11-0 F Woods, ...(11 to 2) 3
2055⁴ MIRACLE ME (Ire) 10-7 (7ᵃ) Mr J G Sheehan, ...(12 to 1) 4
2055⁵ BLITZER (Ire) 11-0 S H O'Donovan, ...(12 to 1) 5
2055⁸ SEXTON'S MIRROR (Ire) 10-9 (5ᵃ) J M Donnelly, . .(25 to 1) 6
2055 BRIGHT LAKE (Ire) 10-9 M Duffy, ...(10 to 1) 7
2055³ THE BOY KING (Ire) 11-0 J P Broderick, ...(8 to 1) 8
2072⁹ TOURING-TURTLE (Ire) 10-9 (5ᵃ) P Morris, ... (25 to 1) 9
2072⁷ DICK MCCARTHY (Ire) 11-0 D J Casey, ...(12 to 1) 10
1907⁸ THE TICK-TACK MAN (Ire) 11-0 T J Mitchell, ... (20 to 1) 11
Dist: 4½l, 6l, 6l, 6l. 4m 6.90s. (11 Ran).

(Mrs A M Daly), M F Morris

2107 Irish National Hunt Novice Hurdle (5-y-o and up) £4,110 2m . . . . (3:20)

2070⁴ THREE SCHOLARS 6-11-7 D J Casey, ...(3 to 1) 1
1713² MONTELISA (Ire) 5-10-12 C F Swan, ...(5 to 2 fav) 2
1751* VITUS (Ire) 6-11-3 J Short, ...(3 to 1) 3
1840² BALLYRIHY BOY (Ire) 6-10-9 (5ᵃ) J M Donnelly, ...(6 to 1) 4
1649 HEN HANSEL (Ire) 6-11-0 T Horgan, ...(12 to 1) 5
1707⁷ ORANGE JUICE (Ire) 7-11-0 J P Broderick, ...(20 to 1) 6
1486⁵ NEON VALLEY (Ire) 8-11-0 S H O'Donovan, ... (25 to 1) 7
MICKS MAN (Ire) 6-11-0 J R Barry, ...(33 to 1) 8
2100⁵ PREMIER WALK 8-10-7 (7ᵃ) Mr S P Hennessy, ...(7 to 1) 9
HURRICANE DAVID (Ire) 8-11-0 K F O'Brien, ...(33 to 1) 10
2079 RING HARRY (Ire) 7-10-9 W Slattery, ... (16 to 1) 11
2075⁹ HAMSHIRE GALE (Ire) 7-10-9 A Powell, ...(25 to 1) 12
1836 IFIELD COURT HOTEL (Ire) 6-10-2 (7ᵃ) S FitzGerald,
. . . . 13
1842 MAGS DWYER (Ire) 7-9-10 T P Treacy, ...(14 to 1) 14
1895 KNOCKBOY QUAY (Ire) 7-11-0 C O'Dwyer, ... (33 to 1) pu
2088 GLANTINE LAD (Ire) 7-11-0 J Jones, ...(25 to 1) pu
Dist: 3l, ¾l, 15l, 12l. 4m 4.20s. (16 Ran).

(Mrs J M Mullins), W P Mullins

2108 Archerstown I.N.H. Flat Race (5 & 6-y-o) £2,226 2m . . . . (3:50)

2060⁶ BRIDGES DAUGHTER (Ire) 6-11-9 Mr D Marnane, . .(7 to 1) 1
CARROLLS ROCK (Ire) 6-12-0 Mr P Fenton, ...(7 to 1) 2
RING ALBERT (Ire) 5-11-10 Mr A J Nash, ...(11 to 8 fav) 3
1432² TRUVARO (Ire) 6-12-0 Mr H F Cleary, ...(5 to 2) 4
2055 LADY MINORCA (Ire) 5-10-12 (7ᵃ) Mr R J Curran, . .(14 to 1) 5
IRISH REEF (Ire) 6-12-0 Mr D M O'Brien, ...(14 to 1) 6
1907 ACTIVE LADY (Ire) 5-10-12 (7ᵃ) Mr B Walsh, ...(25 to 1) 7
MOONBIT (Ire) 6-11-7 (7ᵃ) Mr D A Harney, ...(10 to 1) 8
ST BARTS (Ire) 5-11-10 Miss M Olivefalk, ...(10 to 1) 9
Dist: 8l, 2l, 5l, 1l. 4m 3.50s. (9 Ran).

(Mrs O E Matthews), John Roche

CAGNES-SUR-MER (FR) (heavy)
Wednesday January 8th

2109 Grande Course de Haies de Cagnes (Hurdle) (5-y-o and up) £22,447 2½m . . . . (1:01)

PAMPAJIM (Fr) 8-10-7 T Pelerin, ... 1
MON DOMINO (Fr) 8-10-9 P Havas, ... 2
CHINESE GORDON (Fr) 7-10-7 H Blois, ... 3
2102* GAROLO (Fr) 7-10-6 G Bradley, rcd in 3rd till wknd quickly 3
out 7
Dist: 3½l, 4l, hd, 5½l, 2½l, dist. 5m 3.03s. (13 Ran).

(Ecurie Partners), T Civel

THURLES (IRE) (good)

Thursday January 9th

2110 Liffey Maiden Hurdle (Div I) (5-y-o and up) £3,082 2m 3f........ (1:15)

```
KINGS RETURN (Ire) 6-11-7 D J Casey, ........(6 to 4 on)      1
MAJESTIC RED (Ire) 6-11-7 C O'Dwyer, .........(20 to 1)      2
1908⁹ CLEARLY CANADIAN (Ire) 6-11-4 (3²) G Cotter, .....(5 to 1)  3
1895 BERNESTIC WONDER (Ire) 8-11-7 J Jones, .....(16 to 1)   4
2054 BEAUTY'S PRIDE (Ire) 5-10-7 (5²) T Martin, .......(25 to 1)  5
2048⁶ GRAIGNAMANAGH (Ire) 6-11-7 J R Barry, .........(9 to 4)   f
```
Dist: 8l, 1½l, dist, dist. 4m 37.20s. (6 Ran).

(Lilliten Syndicate), W P Mullins

2111 Liffey Maiden Hurdle (Div II) (5-y-o and up) £3,082 2m 3f........ (1:45)

```
1836⁴ DUKY RIVER (Ire) 6-11-7 F Woods, ..............(3 to 1)  1
LIVER BIRD (Ire) 7-11-7 C O'Dwyer, ......(5 to 2 on)   2
2072 BRUSHETTA (Ire) 5-10-12 T P Treacy, ..........(16 to 1)   3
2073⁵ KAVANAGHS DREAM (Ire) 8-11-7 H Rogers, .....(7 to 1)   4
2022⁶ BITOFAGLOW (Ire) 6-11-4 (3²) U Smyth, .........(12 to 1)  5
2048⁸ NORTH TIPP (Ire) 8-11-0 (7²) K C Hartnett, .......(12 to 1)  6
```
Dist: 3l, dist, 1l, 5½l. 4m 32.90s. (6 Ran).

(Miss E A Tierney), John Queally

2112 Barrow Maiden Hurdle (4-y-o) £3,082 2m........................(2:15)

```
1709⁵ MARLONETTE (Ire) 10-9 D J Casey, ............(9 to 1)   1
2074³ AFARKA (Ire) 10-6 (3²) G Cotter, .................(9 to 4)   2
2067² CENTO (Ire) 10-9 R Dunwoody, .............(6 to 4 fav)  3
2074 PEGUS JUNIOR (Ire) 10-9 K F O'Brien, .........(10 to 1)  4
RAINBOW ERA (Ire) 10-9 T Horgan, ...........(14 to 1)  5
2050 SLIGHTLY SPEEDY (Ire) 11-0 J Shortt, .............(9 to 2)  6
2067 NATIVE ECLIPSE (Ire) 10-9 C F Swan, ...........(12 to 1)  7
2067 SIGMA COMMS (Ire) (bl) 10-9 P Carberry, ........(12 to 1)  8
1547⁸ WOODEN DANCE (Ire) 10-4 T J Mitchell, .........(16 to 1)  f
2067⁹ GALE EIGHT (Ire) 10-4 T P Treacy, ............(12 to 1)  pu
```
Dist: 4l, 9l, ¾l, 2½l. 4m 3.90s. (10 Ran).

(J Doran), W P Mullins

2113 Slaney EBF Novice Hurdle (Grade 3) (5-y-o and up) £6,850 2½m... (2:45)

```
1431 LISS DE PAOR (Ire) 6-11-6 C F Swan, .......(11 to 10 fav)  1
1620⁴ MULLOVER 6-11-8 J Shortt, ................(16 to 1)   2
2084 RADANPOUR (Ire) 5-11-7 D J Casey, ...........(5 to 1)  3
2082² ASK THE BUTLER (Ire) 6-11-11 C O'Dwyer, .......(5 to 4)  pu
```
Dist: 2½l, sht-hd. 4m 51.40s. (4 Ran).

(J C Dempsey), A P O'Brien

2114 Slate Handicap Hurdle (0-123 4-y-o and up) £3,082 2m.............(3:15)

```
2097² LADY DAISY (Ire) [-] 8-11-7 (7²) A O'Shea, .....(2 to 1 fav)  1
1900³ GOOD GLOW [-] 7-11-5 F Woods, ............(9 to 4)   2
1900⁷ JUSTAWAY (Ire) [-] 7-11-2 C F Swan, ...........(6 to 1)   3
2076² HILL OF HOPE (Ire) [-] 6-11-3 W Slattery, .........(8 to 1)  4
1752 THEPRINCESS MANHAR (Ire) [-] 5-10-3 (7²) D M Bean,
.............................(14 to 1)  5
2076² ILLBETHEREFORYOU (Ire) [-] 6-10-3 M P Hourigan, (8 to 1)  6
1275 PERSIAN DANSER (Ire) [-] 5-9-12 J P Broderick, ...(14 to 1)  7
```
Dist: 8l, 1l, 4½l, 1l. 4m 6.10s. (7 Ran).

(Patrick F Kehoe), Anthony Mullins

2115 Dodder I N H Flat Race (5-y-o and up) £3,082 2m...................(3:45)

```
2054² PROMALEE (Ire) 5-11-3 (7²) Miss A L Crowley, ..(5 to 2 on)  1
GARRYHILL CHOICE (Ire) 6-11-11 (3²) Mr R Walsh, .(7 to 1)  2
THATS FINE BY ME (Ire) 5-11-5 (5²) Mr G Elliott, ...(11 to 4)  3
2054 YOU MAKE ME LAUGH (Ire) 5-11-3 (7²) Mr D W Cullen,
.............................(14 to 1)  4
AISLING ALAINN (Ire) 5-11-3 (7²) Mr Philip Carberry,
.............................(12 to 1)  5
ARDCARN PRINCESS (Ire) 5-10-12 (7²) Mr R J Cooper,
.............................(20 to 1)  6
1655 MINSTRELS RIDE (Ire) 6-10-12 A R Coonan, ...(10 to 1)  7
CLONLOO LADY (Ire) 5-10-12 (7²) Mr J P McNamara,
.............................(20 to 1)  8
```
Dist: 1l, 3l, 1l, 6l. 4m 5.00s. (8 Ran).

(Seamus O'Farrell), A P O'Brien

MUSSELBURGH (good to firm)
Friday January 10th
Going Correction: PLUS 0.15 sec. per fur. (races 1,2,3,5,7), PLUS 0.30 (4,6)

2116 Dyewater Maiden Hurdle Class F (Div I) (4-y-o and up) £1,928 2m
.... (12:40)

```
BEST OF ALL (Ire) 5-11-2 M Moloney, hld up, hdwy aftr 3 out,
led after last, ran on wl.............(16 to 1 tchd 20 to 1)  1
```

```
1656² SHINEROLLA 5-11-7 D Parker, hld up, hdwy aftr 3 out, led
betw last 2, hdd last, no extr und pres............(2 to 1 jt-
fav op 7 to 4 tchd 13 to 8 and 9 to 4)  2
930² FALCON'S FLAME (USA) 4-10-9 A P McCoy, pld hrd, trkd
ldrs frm 3rd, slight ld last, sn hdd, no extr und pres.
.............................(9 to 4 tchd 11 to 4)  3
1768* LIVELY ENCOUNTER (Ire) 6-11-7 Derek Byrne, hld up, gd
hdwy to dispute ld 5th, wkng whn not much room aftr 2 out.
.......................(2 to 1 jt-fav op 7 to 4 tchd 9 to 4)  4
1962⁷ GAZANALI (Ire) 6-11-7 N Bentley, prmnt, led 4th till betw last
2, sn wknd............(14 to 1 op 10 to 1 tchd 16 to 1)  5
1783⁶ JALMAID 5-10-11 (5²) R McGrath, in tch, outpcd aftr 3 out, no
dngr after...........................(50 to 1)  6
1524 BRIDLINGTON BAY 4-10-9 G Cahill, led aftr second to 4th,
wknd after 3 out.........................(200 to 1)  7
KINGS HIGH (Ire) 7-11-7 S McDougall, led till aftr second,
prmnt till wknd quickly after 3 out.............(100 to 1)  8
OUR WILMA 8-11-2 T Reed, in tch till wknd aftr 3 out.
.............................(200 to 1)  9
728⁶ WELBURN BOY 5-11-7 A S Smith, trkd ldrs till wknd bef 3
out.................(50 to 1 op 25 to 1) 10
DESERT LORE 6-11-7 M Moloney, al beh, tld off.
...................(100 to 1 op 66 to 1) 11
```
Dist: 4l, sht-hd, 12l, 6l, 4l, ¾l, 12l, 4l, 1¼l, dist. 3m 47.70s. a 10.70s (11 Ran).
SR: 5/6/-/-/-/-/ (Robert Aird), J Berry

2117 Dyewater Maiden Hurdle Class F (Div II) (4-y-o and up) £1,909 2m
.... (1:10)

```
1962 HUTCEL LOCH 6-11-2 A S Smith, made virtually all, hrd
pressed frm betw last 2, kpt on wl und pres clsg stages.
.............................(9 to 1 op 6 to 1)  1
1955⁹ MAPLE BAY (Ire) 8-11-7 G Cahill, hld up, hdwy aftr 3 out,
dsptd ld betw last 2, ev ch till no extr und pres clsg stages.
.............(12 to 1 op 10 to 1 tchd 14 to 1)  2
2066² NUTTY SOLERA 7-11-7 B Storey, hld up, hdwy aftr 3 out, kpt
on same pace und pres frm nxt.........(5 to 1 op 4 to 1)  3
1333⁴ LUMBACK LADY 7-10-13 (3²) G Lee, cl up frm 3rd, ev ch 2
out, sn wknd.............................(4 to 1)  4
1716⁶ MUSIC PLEASE 5-11-7 C O'Dwyer, mid-div, hdwy to track
ldrs aftr 2 out..........................(11 to 8 fav op Evens tchd 6 to 4)  5
UNPREJUDICE 6-11-7 R Garritty, hld up, some hdwy aftr 3
out, rdn after nxt, sn beh.................(5 to 1 op 7 to 2)  6
DECENT PENNY (Ire) 8-11-2 A Thornton, chsd ldrs till wknd
aftr 3 out.............(16 to 1 op 20 to 1 tchd 14 to 1)  7
1039⁸ JED ABBEY 5-11-2 D Bentley, beh most of way.... (50 to 1)  8
930 MOST RESPECTFUL 4-10-9 P Niven, chsd ldrs till wknd
quickly aftr 2 out, tld off. (11 to 1 op 12 to 1 tchd 14 to 1)  9
1826 ABOUT MIDNIGHT (bl) 8-11-2 A Dobbin, dsptd ld to 3rd, sn
wknd, tld off whn pld up bef 2 out...............(200 to 1)  pu
```
Dist: 4l, sht-hd, 4l, 4l, 1l, 11l, 9l, 25l. 3m 46.70s. a 9.70s (10 Ran).
SR: 15/20/11/2/3/2/ (W H Jackson), R D E Woodhouse

2118 Links Selling Handicap Hurdle Class G (0-95 4-y-o and up) £2,406 2m
.... (1:45)

```
1931* TRIENNIUM (USA) [85] 8-11-10 A Dobbin, in tch gng wl, led
aftr 3 out, cmftbly....................(2 to 1 fav op 5 to 2)  1
1872⁴ TIOTAO (Ire) [70] 7-10-9 D Parker, nvr far away, hit 5th, kpt on
wl frm last, no ch wh wnr.............................(11 to 1 op 8 to 1 tchd 12 to 1)  2
1931³ CATTON LADY [61] 7-9-7 (7²) B Grattan, prmnt, drvn alng bef
2 out, kpt on frm last...............(20 to 1 tchd 25 to 1)  3
BLUE DOMAIN [71] 6-10-10 N Smith, hld up, steady hdwy to
chase wnr aftr 2 out, wknd r-in..................(20 to 1)  4
1931⁵ SCHOOL OF SCIENCE [61] 7-10-0 S McDougall, prmnt, led
4th till aftr 3 out, sn outpcd, no dngr after.
.............................(25 to 1 op 20 to 1)  5
1931⁴ TROY'S DREAM [67] 6-10-6 R Garritty, hld up, drvn alng and
some hdwy aftr 3 out, no prog frm nxt.
.............................(8 to 1 op 6 to 1 tchd 10 to 1)  6
1823⁶ DOUBLING DICE [70] 6-10-2 (7²) S Melrose, hld up, some
hdwy aftr 3 out, no prog frm nxt.........(10 to 1 op 4 to 1)  7
61⁹ BUD'S BET (Ire) [77] 9-11-2 R Johnson, nvr on terms.
.............................(7 to 1 op 8 to 1)  8
1943⁸ RATTLE [73] 4-9-9 (5²) R McGrath, mid-div, outpcd bef 3 out,
no dngr after.............................(13 to 1)  9
1955⁴ SIMAND [74] 5-10-13 J Callaghan, chsd ldrs till wknd aftr 3
out.............................(33 to 1 op 25 to 1) 10
1589 SEE YOU ALWAYS (Ire) [62] (bl) 7-9-10 (5²) S Taylor, led to 4th,
wknd bef 2 out.............................(33 to 1 op 25 to 1) 11
1931 MISS MONT [61] 8-10-0 G Cahill, in tch till wknd aftr 3 out, lost
touch and pld up bef nxt.
.............(33 to 1 op 25 to 1 tchd 50 to 1)  pu
```
Dist: 4l, 1½l, 1½l, ½l, 12l, 6l, 3l, hd, 9l, 3½l. 3m 46.80s. a 9.80s (12 Ran).
SR: 22/3/-/1/-/-/ (M C Boyd), P Monteith

2119 Hopeswater Novices' Chase Class E (5-y-o and up) £3,097 2m..... (2:15)

```
1950* MONYMAN (Ire) 7-12-2 R Garritty, hld up, hdwy to track ldr
8th, hmpd 3 out, sn led, easily.
.............(11 to 8 on op Evens tchd 11 to 10)  1
```

1374 DEVILRY 7-11-10 N Smith, hld up, hdwy aftr 8th, blun last, kpt
on, no ch wth wnr.....(12 to 1 op 10 to 1 tchd 14 to 1) 2
1950 GONE ASHORE (Ire) 6-10-13 (5*) S Taylor, led till aftr 3 out, btn
whn blun nxt.........................(66 to 1 op 50 to 1) 3
1985 ELLIOTT'S WISH (Ire) (bl) 6-11-10 R Johnson, mstks, cl up,
blun 8th, sn lost tch, tld off...........(20 to 1 op 12 to 1) 4
1868² HERBERT LODGE (Ire) 8-11-4 C O'Dwyer, blun and uns rdr
second....................(7 to 4 op 5 to 4 tchd 2 to 1) ur
1662 ALICHARGER (v) 7-11-4 A Dobbin, sn beh, tld off whn pld up
bef 4 out....................................(50 to 1) pu
Dist: 10l, 6l, 26l. 4m 2.00s. a 13.00s (6 Ran).
SR: 20/4/-/   (Trevor Hemmings), M D Hammond

2120 Musselburgh 10th Anniversary Handicap Hurdle Class E (0-115 4-y-o and up) £3,692 3m.........(2:45)

1372³ HIGHLAND PARK [85] 11-10-0 A Dobbin, trkd ldrs, rdn to ld 2
out, sn hrd pressed, styd on wl.
....................(16 to 1 op 14 to 1 tchd 20 to 1) 1
1766* SNOW BOARD [91] 8-10-6 Derek Byrne, hld up, hdwy to track
ldrs 9th, rdn betw last 2, styd on wl finish.
....................(11 to 4 op 2 to 1 tchd 3 to 1) 2
1933* SUPERTOP [111] 9-11-12 R Garritty, hld up, effrt bef 2 out, ch
betw last two, kpt on same pace.
....................(6 to 4 fav op 2 to 1 tchd 5 to 4) 3
1829 RUBER [85] 10-10-0 D Parker, chsd ldrs, outpcd aftr 9th,
rallied betw last 2, kpt on same pace frm last...... (66 to 1) 4
2064² D'ARBLAY STREET (Ire) [86] 8-10-1 S McDougall, led to 4th,
led aftr 3 out to nxt, wknd appr last......(8 to 1 op 6 to 1) 5
1984³ BOSTON MAN [85] 6-10-0 B Storey, hld up, hdwy aftr 3 out,
chlgd nxt, ev ch till wknd after last.
....................(15 to 2 op 7 to 1 tchd 8 to 1) 6
1994⁶ DOMINIE (Ire) [99] (bl) 9-11-0 C O'Dwyer, hld up, effrt aftr 3
out, sn pushed alng, wkng whn mstk last, tld off.
....................(12 to 1 op 7 to 1) 7
1933³ TALLYWAGGER [113] 10-11-7 (7*) T Hogg, made most frm 4th
till aftr 3 out, wknd after nxt, tld off......(10 to 1 op 6 to 1) 8
Dist: Nk, 1l, sht-hd, ¾l, 2l, 24l, 5l. 5m 52.00s. a 15.00s (8 Ran).
(Ray Craggs), R Craggs

2121 Musselburgh 10th Anniversary Handicap Chase Class E (0-115 5-y-o and up) £3,535 2½m.......(3:15)

2065³ WAYUPHILL [92] 10-10-11 B Storey, trkd ldrs, chalg whn lft in
ld 3 out, styd on wl....................(5 to 1 tchd 11 to 2) 1
1932² PURITAN (Can) [109] (bl) 8-12-0 R Garritty, hld up, hdwy bef
12th, chsd wnr frm 3 out, no imprsn.
....................(9 to 4 op 5 to 2 tchd 11 to 4) 2
1523³ VAL DE RAMA (Ire) [89] 8-10-8 P Niven, prmnt till outpcd bef
12th, no dngr aftr..........(8 to 1 op 7 to 1 tchd 9 to 1) 3
1785² GRAND SCENERY (Ire) [89] 9-10-8 A P McCoy, hld up, hdwy
bef 12th, ev ch aftr........................(7 to 1) 4
1934² RAPID MOVER [91] (bl) 10-10-10 M Moloney, in tch till wknd
aftr 12th...................(14 to 1 op 10 to 1) 5
1954³ REBEL KING [90] 7-10-4 (5*) S Taylor, mstks, prmnt till wknd
bef 11th, tld off..........(14 to 1 op 12 to 1 tchd 16 to 1) 6
1932* MONTRAVE [99] 8-11-4 A Dobbin, led, jnd whn I 3 out.
....................(5 to 2 op 9 to 4 tchd 11 to 4) 7
Dist: 8l, 9l, nk, 17l, 24l. 5m 6.90s. a 19.90s (7 Ran).
(Mr & Mrs Raymond Anderson Green), C Parker

2122 Whitewater Novices' Handicap Hurdle Class E (0-100 4-y-o and up) £2,637 2½m..............(3:45)

KALISKO (Fr) [77] 7-10-4 (7*) S Melrose, sn mid-div, gd hdwy
to ld 2 out, styd on wl................(16 to 1 op 14 to 1) 1
1693² FLYAWAY BLUES [89] 5-11-9 P Niven, hld up, hdwy aftr 9th,
slightly hmpd after 3 out, chsd wnr frm nxt, kpt on, no imprsn.
....................(5 to 1 op 6 to 1 tchd 7 to 1) 2
1823⁵ MR CHRISTIE [77] 5-10-11 A Thornton, mid-div, outpcd bef
9th, styd on frm 2 out, nvr able to chal.
....................(25 to 1 op 20 to 1) 3
1823* COURT JOKER (Ire) [83] 5-11-3 B Storey, in tch, effrt aftr 3
out, kpt on same pace frm nxt..........(10 to 1 op 8 to 1) 4
1966 ANCHORENA [73] 5-10-7 R Johnson, towards rear, hdwy
whn badly hmpd aftr 3 out, styd on frm nxt, nvr able to chal.
....................(12 to 1 op 10 to 1) 5
2002⁵ WHAT JIM WANTS (Ire) [86] 4-10-2 (5*) R McGrath, chsd ldrs,
wkng whn mstk 2 out........................(6 to 1 op 5 to 1) 6
1775³ DONT FORGET CURTIS (Ire) [84] 5-11-4 J Callaghan, in tch,
no hdwy frm 3 out........(7 to 1 op 6 to 1 tchd 8 to 1) 7
1690⁴ ALWARQA [81] 4-10-2 D Bentley, in tch, effrt whn hmpd aftr 3
out, no imprsn whn blun nxt......(100 to 30 fav op 5 to 2) 8
1787³ KINGS MINSTRAL (Ire) [73] 7-10-7 J Burke, led till aftr 3 out,
wknd bef nxt..........(14 to 1 op 16 to 1 tchd 20 to 1) 9
2063⁶ CANAAN VALLEY [83] 9-11-3 F Perratt, cl up, wkng whn
hmpd aftr 3 out..............................(20 to 1) 10
1911⁷ STYLISH INTERVAL [90] 5-11-10 A P McCoy, chsd ldrs, led
aftr 3 out, rdn and hdd nxt, sn wknd... (10 to 1 op 16 to 1) 11
1331⁶ MILLIES IMAGE [66] 6-10-4 A Dobbin, wl beh frm hfwy.
....................(100 to 1 op 66 to 1) 12
1951* FRYUP SATELLITE [82] 6-10-13 (3*) E Callaghan, hld up,
hdwy into midfield hfwy, wknd aftr 3 out.
....................(12 to 1 tchd 14 to 1) 13

1815 DIFFICULT DECISION (Ire) [80] 6-11-0 C O'Dwyer, chsd ldrs,
blun 9th, sn wknd...................(10 to 1 op 14 to 1) 14
1662⁴ MORE CHAMPAGNE [66] 7-10-0 G Cahill, sn beh, lost tch
and pld up bef 9th..........................(14 to 1) pu
Dist: 2½l, 1l, 20l, hd, 1½l, hd, 1¼l, 9l, 2l, 6l. 4m 49.60s. a 11.60s (15 Ran).
SR: -/6/-/-/-/-/   (Miss Louise Davis), R Allan

SOUTHWELL (A.W) (std)
Friday January 10th
Going Correction: NIL

2123 Levy Board Standard Open National Hunt Flat Class H (4 - 7-y-o) £1,318 2m...................(12:55)

EDGE AHEAD (Ire) 7-11-4 M A Fitzgerald, hld up, pushed alng
and hdwy 4 fs out, drvn and str run to ld ins last.
....................(12 to 1 op 10 to 1) 1
IN THE VAN 5-11-4 J F Titley, settled towards rear, hdwy and
in tch hfwy, led briefly entering fnl furlong, kpt on stdly.
....................(9 to 2 op 2 to 1 tchd 5 to 1) 2
2008² MEADOW HYMN (Ire) 6-11-4 W Dwan, in tch, drvn and ev ch
o'r one furlong out, no extr ins last......(6 to 1 op 5 to 1) 3
1802⁴ MRS EM 5-11-4 (5*) O Burrows, hld up, chsd ldrs hfwy, slight
ld o'r 3 fs out till entering last, no extr....(9 to 2 op 2 to 1) 4
2008* SLIDE ON 7-11-11 Gary Lyons, hdwy to chase ldrs hfwy,
niggled alng 3 fs out, unbl to quicken o'r one out.
....................(11 to 4 fav op 5 to 2 tchd 7 to 2) 5
FERN LEADER (Ire) 7-11-4 J Supple, hld up, hdwy and in tch
frm hfwy, unbl to quicken fnl 2 fs......(10 to 1 op 7 to 1) 6
CYBER KING 4-10-6 N Williamson, pld hrd, cl up, jnd ldr gng
wl entering strt, fdd and eased entering fnl furlong, better for
race..................(20 to 1 tchd 25 to 1) 7
SUPER SAFFRON 5-10-13 C Llewellyn, cl up, led o'r 5 fs out
till over 3 out, fdd.................(10 to 1 tchd 12 to 1) 8
LOST IN THE POST (Ire) 4-9-13 (7*) N Horrocks, cl up, drvn
alng entering strt, fdd......(6 to 1 op 7 to 1 tchd 8 to 1) 9
MOON DEVIL (Ire) 7-11-4 M Richards, led till o'r 5 fs out,
wknd entering strt.................(10 to 1 op 7 to 1) 10
PORT VALENSKA (Ire) 4-10-6 D Gallagher, tld off fnl 5 fs
....................(40 to 1 op 33 to 1) 11
SILVER GULL (Ire) 6-11-4 G Tormey, tld off 6 fs out.
....................(40 to 1 op 33 to 1) 12
HYPERION LAD 5-11-4 J Railton, tld off 5 fs out...(33 to 1) 13
RUSH ME NOT (Ire) 4-10-1 (5*) Michael Brennan, beh, tld off 6
fs out.................(40 to 1 op 33 to 1) 14
IFAFA BEACH (Ire) 5-10-13 (5*) D J Kavanagh, tld off bef hfwy.
....................(16 to 1 op 14 to 1) 15
GYMCRAK PHAROAH 4-10-6 A Maguire, tld off 6 fs out.
....................(16 to 1 op 14 to 1) 16
Dist: 1l, 1½l, 2½l, 2l, 2½l, 2½l, 16l, 6l, dist, 15l. 3m 56.70s. (16 Ran).
(Mrs Carol Edge), T Thomson Jones

LEOPARDSTOWN (IRE) (good to yielding)
Saturday January 11th
Going Correction: PLUS 0.25 sec. per fur. (races 1,3,5,6,7), PLUS 0.55 (2,4)

2124 Fitzpatrick Castle Hurdle (5-y-o and up) £4,110 2m..........(12:35)

2086² RAWY (USA) (bl) 5-11-7 C O'Dwyer,...........(2 to 1 on) 1
2094* MR BAXTER BASICS 6-11-11 N Williamson,.......(9 to 2) 2
KILSPINDIE 6-11-11 F Woods,..................(5 to 1) 3
2060* FATHER GERRY (Ire) 7-11-7 R Dunwoody,.......(10 to 1) 4
2094³ FOYLE WANDERER (Ire) 6-11-2 D T Evans,.......(20 to 1) 5
1432 ASK ME AGAIN (Ire) 7-11-7 H Rogers,.......(33 to 1) 6
Dist: 5l, 1l, 25l, 6l. 3m 55.70s. a 11.70s (6 Ran).
SR: 16/15/14/   (John P McManus), C Roche

2125 Fitzpatrick Hotel Group Novice Chase (5-y-o and up) £5,480 2m 5f ....(1:05)

2058² ULTRA FLUTTER 10-11-8 A P McCoy,.......(5 to 4 fav) 1
MIRACLE MAN 9-11-4 N Williamson,.........(5 to 1) 2
2052⁵ THE CARRIG RUA (Ire) 7-11-8 R Dunwoody,....(5 to 2) 3
1779² MAN OF ARRAN (Ire) 7-11-4 K F O'Brien,.........(7 to 2) 4
2083³ GARABAGH (Ire) 8-11-4 P McWilliams,.........(33 to 1) 5
2096 RADIANT RIVER (Ire) 7-11-1 (3*) G Cotter,.......(33 to 1) 6
Dist: ½l, 6l, 25l, 20l. 5m 41.20s. a 32.20s (6 Ran).
(Donal Higgins), Michael Hourigan

2126 S.M.Morris Handicap Hurdle (4-y-o and up) £4,110 3m...........(1:35)

2018* ROSIN THE BOW (Ire) [-] 8-11-6 C F Swan,.. (11 to 10 on) 1
2113² MULLOVER [-] 6-10-5¹ J Shortt,...............(7 to 2) 2
2103* ROCK'N ROLL KID (Ire) [-] 6-10-0 (4ex) D J Casey, (5 to 1) 3
2068⁴ TELL THE NIPPER (Ire) [-] (bl) 6-10-12 R Dunwoody, (4 to 1) 4
1277⁶ APPELLATE COURT [-] 9-10-4 A Powell,.........(33 to 1) 5
2051 RISING WATERS (Ire) [-] 9-10-5 K F O'Brien,......(20 to 1) 6
Dist: Hd, 3l, 5½l, 5l. 5m 59.70s. a 22.70s (6 Ran).
(F Fitzsimons), A P O'Brien

2127 Pierse Leopardstown Handicap Chase (Grade 2) (5-y-o and up) £16,250 3m.......................(2:05)

2071³	TIME FOR A RUN [-] 10-10-0 N Williamson, wtd wth, prog to track ldr 2 out, led last, quickened wl.................(4 to 1)	1
2071	WHALE OF A KNIGHT (Ire) [-] 8-10-0 F Woods, wtd wth, prog bef 2 out to chal before last, not quicken.........(6 to 4 fav)	2
2085²	KING OF THE GALES [-] 10-11-7 C O'Brien, wtd wth, jmpd slwly 4 out, rdn, kpt on frm 2 out.................(9 to 2)	3
2078³	THE CRAZY BISHOP (Ire) [-] 9-10-3 A P McCoy, trkd ldrs, mstk 4th, hmpd 8th, rdn bef 3 out, led before nxt till hdd last, wknd................................(16 to 1)	4
2085	IDIOTS VENTURE [-] 10-11-11 C F Swan, wl plcd, rdn aftr 2 out, sn wknd.....................(5 to 1)	5
1878⁵	ROYAL MOUNTBROWNE [-] 9-12-0 T Horgan, led, jmpd slwly 3rd, mstk 7th, jumped slowly tenth, rdn bef 3 out, hdd and wknd before nxt............................(9 to 1)	6
1755	FISSURE SEAL [-] 11-10-13 R Dunwoody, trkd ldr till blun and uns rdr 8th...........................(20 to 1)	ur
2071	TRYFIRION (Ire) [-] 8-10-1 (3*) B Bowens, mid-div, mstk 5th, rdn aftr 5 out, mistake and unseated rdr 3 out....(14 to 1)	ur

Dist: 10l, 7l, ¾l, 12l. 6m 22.40s. a 15.40s (8 Ran).
SR: 50/40/54/35/45/ (John P McManus), E J O'Grady

2128 The Ladbroke (Grade 1) (4-y-o and up) £39,200 2m..............(2:35)

1990²	MASTER TRIBE (Ire) [-] 7-10-4 N Williamson, wl plcd, prog to track ldrs on bridle 2 out, led last, rdn, styd on strly. (18 to 1)	1
2051³	BLACK QUEEN (Ire) [-] 6-9-13 A J O'Brien, wtd wth, gd prog aftr 3 out to chal last, kpt on wl, jst fld.............(12 to 1)	2
1772*	PENNY A DAY (Ire) [-] 7-11-10 P Niven, mid-div, rdn and prog bef 2 out, kpt on wl...........................(7 to 1)	3
1621²	FAMILY WAY [-] 10-10-11 F Woods, rear, rdn and prog aftr 3 out, kpt on, not trble ldrs...................(15 to 2)	4
2086⁴	METASTASIO [-] (bl) 5-10-10 H Rogers, mid-div, rdn and prog bef 2 out, styd on wl........................(33 to 1)	5
715*	KHAYRAWANI (Ire) [-] 5-11-4 C O'Dwyer, wl plcd, prog to track ldr 3 out, led aftr nxt, hdd bef last, sn wknd. (5 to 1 fav)	6
1508*	EXECUTIVE DESIGN [-] 5-11-5 G Cahill, rear, rdn and some prog aftr 3 out, wknd bef nxt.................(16 to 1)	7
2095	GUEST PERFORMANCE (Ire) [-] 5-11-10 R Hughes, trkd ldrs frm 1st, wl plcd till wknd bef 3 out.................(14 to 1)	8
2019	MAGICAL LADY [-] 5-11-3 T P Rudd, trkd ldrs, prog to ld bef 4 out, rdn before 2 out, sn hdd and wknd.......(33 to 1)	9
2095²	HILL SOCIETY (Ire) [-] 5-11-6 R Dunwoody, wl plcd, prog to track ldrs 4 out, rdn and wknd bef 2 out.........(16 to 1)	10
1772³	KAITAK (Ire) [-] 6-10-4 F Leahy, mid-div, prog aftr 4th, wl plcd 3 out, rdn and wknd bef nxt.................(40 to 1)	11
1905*	KING OF KERRY (Ire) [-] 6-10-13 C F Swan, rear, rdn and prog aftr 3 out, wknd bef last.................(11 to 1)	12
1508⁶	PALACEGATE KING [-] 8-10-4 T Horgan, wl plcd till lost pos bef 4th, rdn aftr 3 out, no extr.................(40 to 1)	13
2050³	RESCUE TIME (Ire) [-] 4-9-12 G Cotter, rear, rdn aftr 3 out, no quicken............................(40 to 1)	14
2086⁷	FONTAINE LODGE (Ire) [-] 7-10-1 A Powell, wl plcd, rdn aftr 3rd, rdn after 3 out, not quicken.............(40 to 1)	15
2027³	EXPRESS GIFT [-] 8-11-10 N Smith, rear, rdn aftr 3 out, no quicken............................(20 to 1)	16
2086³	CLIFDON FOG (Ire) [-] (bl) 6-10-8 A P McCoy, trkd ldrs, rdn aftr 3rd, wknd after nxt...........................(7 to 1)	17
1900⁶	NOTCOMPLAININGBUT (Ire) [-] 6-11-12 T P Treacy, trkd ldrs 1st 2, wl plcd till lost pos bef 4 out, rdn and wknd aftr nxt.................................(25 to 1)	18
1900	SHANES HERO (Ire) [-] 7-10-13 J P Broderick, wl plcd, prog aftr 4th to track ldrs 3 out, rdn bef nxt, sn wknd...(50 to 1)	19
1740*	CENTAUR EXPRESS [-] 5-10-4 T Eley, fst away, dsptd ld till wknd bef 4 out..........................(25 to 1)	20
1621	LADY ARPEL (Ire) [-] 5-10-9 K F O'Brien, fst away, dsptd ld till wknd bef 4 out.........................(14 to 1)	21
2086	REASILVIA (Ire) [-] 7-10-10 G Bradley, al rear, lost tch 3rd............................(50 to 1)	22
2096²	GLINT OF EAGLES (Ire) [-] 8-10-9 D J Casey, wl plcd till drpd back and uns rdr aftr 3 out, broke leg, destroyed... (25 to 1)	ur

Dist: Hd, 6l, 1½l, 3l. 3m 50.00s. a 6.00s (23 Ran).
SR: 56/51/70/55/51/-/ (Jebel Ali Racing Stables), Mrs J Pitman

2129 Ashford I.N.H. Flat Race (5-y-o and up) £3,082 2m.......................(3:10)

	OUR BID (Ire) 6-11-8 (3*) Mr R Walsh,........(13 to 8 fav)	1
2081²	KILCOO BOY (Ire) 6-12-1 (3*) Mr B M Cash,.......(9 to 4)	2
2100⁴	CLAY AND WATTLES (Ire) 6-12-0 (7*) Mr A K Wyse, (11 to 2)	3
2022*	VALLEY ERNE (Ire) 6-12-4 Mr A J Martin,......(6 to 1)	4
2079*	CORYROSE (Ire) 5-11-2 (7*) Mr M T Hartrey,......(12 to 1)	5
	CONAGHER LEADER (Ire) 6-11-11 Mr P F Graffin, (12 to 1)	6
2100³	DROICHEAD LAPEEN 10-12-0 (7*) Mr T J Beattie, (12 to 1)	7
2054⁹	HI-LO PICCOLO (Ire) 5-10-9 (7*) Miss S McDonogh,	
	..................................(33 to 1)	8
	GROWTOWN LAD (Ire) 6-11-11 Mr J A Berry,.....(25 to 1)	9
1539	EXECUTIVE MERC (Ire) 4-11-4 (7*) Mr J F O'Shea, (33 to 1)	10
2107	MAGS DWYER (Ire) 7-11-6 (7*) Mr J P McNamara, (20 to 1)	11

Dist: 1½l, 3½l, 1l, 5½l. 3m 56.30s. (11 Ran).
(James McEvoy), Kevin Prendergast

2130 Taney I.N.H. Flat Race (4-y-o) £3,082 2m.......................(3:40)

	RAINBOW VICTOR (Ire) 11-0 (7*) Miss A L Crowley,	
	..................................(100 to 30)	1
	MYKON GOLD (Ire) 11-4 (3*) Mr R Walsh,.....(11 to 10 on)	2
	ALOTAWANNA (Ire) 11-7 Mr A J Martin,..........(4 to 1)	3
	DUE TO YOU (Ire) 11-7 Mr S J Mahon,........(16 to 1)	4
	CYBER MANOR (Ire) 11-2 (5*) Mr D McGoona,...(16 to 1)	5
	CAJUN ROSE (Ire) 10-9 (7*) Mr J P McNamara,...(6 to 1)	6
	COUNTY CAPTAIN (Ire) 11-0 (7*) Mr M P Horan,...(11 to 1)	7
	LOCH BAN (Ire) 11-7 (7*) Mr M T Hartrey,.....(16 to 1)	8

Dist: 4l, 15l, 20l, 4½l. 4m 1.80s. (8 Ran).
(Joseph Crowley), A P O'Brien

NAVAN (IRE) (good to yielding)
Sunday January 12th

2131 Mullacurry Maiden Hurdle (5 & 6-y-o) £3,082 2m....................(1:00)

1460⁷	SORCERER'S DRUM (Ire) 6-11-6 F Woods,.......(10 to 1)	1
	STAGALIER (Ire) 5-10-4 (7*) B J Geraghty,.........(20 to 1)	2
2055⁷	IMPERIAL PLAICE (Ire) 5-10-9 (7*) D M Bean,....(12 to 1)	3
2080³	BAR FLUTE 6-11-1 C F Swan,...................(7 to 1)	4
1782	MONTANA KING (Ire) 6-11-6 R Dunwoody,....(3 to 1 fav)	5
1908⁵	IADA (Ire) 6-11-1 D T Evans,...................(7 to 1)	6
	PINKPINKFIZZ (Ire) 6-11-6 N Williamson,.........(9 to 2)	7
	NUZUM ROAD MAKERS (Ire) 6-10-13 (7*) D K Budds,	
	..................................(16 to 1)	8
2079	ALICE BRENNAN (Ire) 6-11-1 J Shortt,..........(10 to 1)	9
179⁶	SHINDARAR (Ire) 6-11-6 H Rogers,.............(12 to 1)	10
1901	ASK DOCK (Ire) 6-10-8 (7*) L J Fleming,.........(25 to 1)	11
703*	LADY OF GRANGE (Ire) 5-11-5 F J Flood,........(8 to 1)	12
1908	ABLE LADY (Ire) 6-10-8 (7*) K C Hartnett,........(25 to 1)	13
2094⁵	TWO SHONAS (Ire) 6-11-6 (3*) D Bromley,.........(8 to 1)	14
1836	POWER STEERING (Ire) 6-11-6 P L Malone,......(20 to 1)	15
	FLOWERS OF MAY (Ire) 6-10-8 (7*) R P Hogan,...(20 to 1)	16
2040	THAT'S LUCY (Ire) 6-10-10 (5*) T Martin,.........(33 to 1)	17
1836	MURKELBUR (Ire) 6-10-8 (7*) R M Murphy,.......(50 to 1)	18

Dist: 1½l, 5½l, 5½l, 1l. 4m 5.80s. (18 Ran).
(Mrs A L T Moore), A L T Moore

2132 Navan Novice Hurdle (5-y-o and up) £3,082 2¼m....................(1:30)

2017*	TOAST THE SPREECE (Ire) 5-11-10 C F Swan, ...(7 to 4)	1
2082³	BUGGY (Ire) 8-11-8 T J Mitchell,..............(11 to 2)	2
2048²	BE HOME EARLY (Ire) 7-11-2 G Bradley,....(11 to 10 fav)	3
2107⁶	ORANGE JUICE (Ire) 7-11-2 J P Broderick,......(20 to 1)	4
	WELCOME DEAL (Ire) 9-11-2 L P Cusack,.......(33 to 1)	5
2036	COLOURED SPARROW (Ire) 7-10-8 (3*) D Bromley, (33 to 1)	6
2017⁴	THE DARGLE (Ire) 7-10-9 (7*) A O'Shea,.........(20 to 1)	7
2060⁷	WINDGAP HILL (Ire) 6-11-2 F Woods,..........(16 to 1)	8
2111⁴	KAVANAGHS DREAM (Ire) 8-11-2 H Rogers,.......(20 to 1)	9
2017⁹	SINGLE OR BUST (Ire) 7-10-4 (7*) S M McGovern, (50 to 1)	10
2019	KILMACREW 10-10-9 (7*) D W O'Sullivan,.........(66 to 1)	pu
2016⁴	BRADLEYS CORNER (Ire) 6-11-8 R Dunwoody,...(12 to 1)	pu

Dist: 1½l, 3½l, dist, 2l. 4m 31.80s. (12 Ran).
(Golden Step Racing Syndicate), A P O'Brien

2133 European Breeders Fund Beginners Chase (5-y-o and up) £4,110 2m 1f
..................................(2:00)

	CORKET (Ire) 7-12-0 C F Swan,............(15 to 8 fav)	1
1119³	ROCKETTS CASTLE (Ire) 7-11-6 (3*) K Whelan,..(10 to 1)	2
2090	SCENIC ROUTE (Ire) 8-11-9 (5*) Mr T P Hyde,....(4 to 1)	3
1552⁸	FONTAINE FABLES (Ire) 7-12-0 R Dunwoody,......(7 to 1)	4
1841⁴	GALANT DES EPEIRES (Fr) 6-12-0 N Williamson, (10 to 1)	5
907⁶	JOHNNY'S DREAM (Ire) 7-11-11 (3*) G Cotter,.....(12 to 1)	6
2090⁵	TEMPLEROAN PRINCE 10-12-0 J R Barry,.........(14 to 1)	7
2086⁸	PUNTING PETE (Ire) 7-12-0 T P Treacy,..........(8 to 1)	8
2111⁶	NORTH TIPP (Ire) 8-11-2 (7*) K C Hartnett,.......(33 to 1)	9
2096⁸	GREAT SVENGALI (Ire) 8-12-0 J Shortt,...........(5 to 1)	f
	LAKEVIEW LAD (Ire) 8-11-9 J P Broderick,.......(33 to 1)	pu
	QUICK LEARNER (Ire) 8-11-7 (7*) R P Hogan,....(14 to 1)	pu
1117⁹	SAN SIRO (Ire) 11-7 (7*) Mr Edgar Byrnes,......(33 to 1)	pu

Dist: 1l, 3½l, 5½l, 5l. 4m 27.30s. (13 Ran).
(S J O'Sullivan), A P O'Brien

2134 Proudstown Limited Handicap Hurdle (Listed) (4-y-o and up) £6,850 2½m...............(2:30)

2051³	GRAVITY GATE (Ire) [-] 8-9-10 (5*) T Martin, wl plcd, smooth prog to ld appr last, ran on wl.................(4 to 1 fav)	1
2051²	FIDDLERS BOW VI (Ire) [-] 9-10-0 R Hughes, wl plcd, prog bef 2 out, kpt on wl...........................(13 to 2)	2
2068³	CASEY JANE (Ire) [-] 6-10-2 D J Casey, wl plcd, rdn and prog aftr 2 out, kpt on.........................(8 to 1)	3
2018⁶	ANNADOT (Ire) [-] 7-10-6 F J Flood, dsptd ld till bef 3 out, rdn to lead before nxt, hdd before last, wknd.........(20 to 1)	4
2084³	RATHGIBBON (Ire) [-] 6-10-2 (3*) G Cotter, trkd ldrs, rdn 4 out to ld nxt, sn hdd, wknd bef last...........(6 to 1)	5

1778 CELTIC SUNRISE [-] 9-10-0 P Carberry, *wtd wth, prog aftr 3*
out, kpt on ....(20 to 1) 6
1186³ DIFFICULT TIMES (Ire) [-] 5-11-5 S C Lyons, *dsptd ld till wknd*
bef 2 out ....(12 to 1) 7
2050⁴ CHOOSEY'S TREASURE (Ire) [-] 4-9-12 (3") J Butler, *wl plcd,*
rdn bef 2 out, wknd ....(16 to 1) 8
2068 BALAWHAR (Ire) [-] 7-12-0 R Dunwoody, *rear, some prog aftr*
3 out ....(20 to 1) 9
1621⁸ TALINA'S LAW (Ire) [-] (bl) 5-10-12 T P Treacy, *mid-div, rdn*
and wknd bef 2 out ....(8 to 1) 10
2019* BLAZE OF HONOUR (Ire) [-] 6-10-13 T Horgan, *mid-div, prog*
5th, trkd ldrs 2 out, sn wknd ....(10 to 1) 11
1899* PTARMIGAN LODGE [-] 6-9-7 (7") R Burke, *rear, rdn bef 2 out,*
not quicken ....(8 to 1) 12
309³ FOREST FEATHER (Ire) [-] (bl) 9-10-12 N Williamson, *rear,*
rdn aftr 3 out, not quicken ....(14 to 1) 13
2051⁶ CEILI QUEEN (Ire) [-] 5-10-12 C F Swan, *al rear, rdn aftr 3 out,*
not quicken ....(7 to 1) 14
Dist: 5l, sht-hd, 1½l, 1l. 5m 3.90s. (14 Ran).

(Donald King), R H MacNabb

2135 I.N.H. Stallion Owners EBF Novice Hurdle (5-y-o and up) £4,110 2¾m
....(3:00)

2075² GLEBE LAD (Ire) 5-11-4 T P Rudd, ...(13 to 2) 1
2075* TONI'S TIP (Ire) 5-11-7 (3") G Cotter, ...(9 to 4) 2
2075⁵ LEAMHOG (Ire) 7-12-0 C F Swan, ...(9 to 1) 3
2075⁴ ROCHER LADY (Ire) 6-10-12 (5") P Morris, ...(8 to 1) 4
1460* MISTY MOMENTS (Ire) 6-12-0 R Hughes, ...(2 to 1 fav) 5
2037 CAIRNCROSS (Ire) 6-11-8 J P Broderick, ...(25 to 1) 6
1174⁷ CESAR DU MANOIR (Fr) 7-11-5 (3") K Whelan, ...(11 to 1) 7
2088* MISS ORCHESTRA (Ire) 6-11-9 J Shortt, ...(5 to 1) 8
2075⁵ VERYWELL (Ire) 6-11-1 (7") B J Geraghty, ...(25 to 1) 9
1751 MOORE'S MELODIES (Ire) 6-11-8 F Woods, ...(20 to 1) 10
Dist: 7l, 2½l, 2l, 2l. 5m 40.80s. (10 Ran).

(T B Conroy), M J P O'Brien

2136 Trim Handicap Chase (0-123 5-y-o and up) £3,425 2m 1f.........(3:30)

2086⁶ ARCTIC WEATHER (Ire) [-] 8-11-8 T P Rudd, ...(7 to 1) 1
1650* BARNAGEERA BOY (Ire) [-] 8-11-5 K F O'Brien,
....(11 to 8 fav) 2
2071 BALLYHIRE LAD (Ire) [-] 8-11-13 C F Swan, ...(9 to 2) 3
2056 DOONANDORAS (Ire) [-] 9-11-12 F Woods, ...(15 to 2) 4
2078* THE REAL ARTICLE (Ire) [-] 8-12-0 L P Cusack, ..(6 to 1) 5
YOUNG WOLF [-] 9-9-9² P L Malone, ...(20 to 1) 6
UNA'S CHOICE (Ire) [-] 9-10-11 F J Flood, ...(16 to 1) 7
1906⁶ PERSIAN POWER (Ire) [-] 9-10-0¹ P Carberry, ...(9 to 1) pu
1618 TIME AND CHARGES (Ire) [-] 7-9-4 (7") R P Hogan, (12 to 1) pu
Dist: 5½l, 6l, 5½l, 3l. 4m 26.10s. (9 Ran).

(Richard Bomze), M J P O'Brien

2137 Boyne I.N.H. Flat Race (5-y-o and up) £3,082 2m.................(4:00)

2072⁴ BLUE WAVE (Ire) 5-11-3 (7") Mr A J Dempsey, ...(4 to 1) 1
2022² QUIPTECH (Ire) 6-11-11 (3") Mr R Walsh, ...(5 to 1) 2
NATIVE ESTATES (Ire) 5-11-10 Mr G J Harford, ...(6 to 1) 3
1649 BRIAN'S DELIGHT (Ire) 6-11-9 Mr A J Martin, ...(6 to 1) 4
210⁸ RUN SPARKY (Ire) 5-11-0 (5") Mr R J Patton, ...(50 to 1) 5
2079 LOVELY LYNSEY (Ire) (bl) 5-10-12 (7") Mr A C Coyle,
....(50 to 1) 6
1901⁵ ENNEL GALE (Ire) 7-11-9 Mr M McNulty, ...(13 to 2) 7
2040⁴ MISS CIRCLE (Ire) 8-11-2 (7") Miss C Woods, ...(16 to 1) 8
TULIP (Ire) 6-11-2 (7") Miss A O'Brien, ...(12 to 1) 9
2022⁴ COUNCILLOR (Ire) 7-11-9 Mr M P Horan, ...(14 to 1) 10
88 ST CAROL (Ire) 6-11-9 Mr T Mullins, ...(3 to 1 fav) 11
SWIFT GALE (Ire) 6-12-0 Mr H F Cleary, ...(20 to 1) 12
SUDDEN INSPIRATION (Ire) (bl) 6-11-9 Mr J P Dempsey,
....(14 to 1) 13
BORLEAGH PILOT (Ire) 6-11-7 (7") Mr M Costello, (14 to 1) 14
2073⁶ TEMPEST GALE (Ire) 8-11-7 (7") Mr A K Wyse, ...(14 to 1) 15
DR DOLITTLE (Ire) 6-12-0 Mr D Marnane, ...(25 to 1) 16
2040 HIDDEN PLAY (Ire) 9-11-2 (7") Miss S L Kelly, ...(50 to 1) 17
Dist: 1l, 1l, 1l, 5½l. 3m 56.30s. (17 Ran).

(Mrs Pauline Donnelly), D T Hughes

PUNCHESTOWN (IRE) (yielding)
Monday January 13th
Going Correction: PLUS 0.30 sec. per fur.

2138 Punchestown E.B.F. Mares Maiden Hurdle (5 & 6-y-o) £4,110 2½m
....(12:15)

1907³ MONDEO ROSE (Ire) 5-11-2 C F Swan, ...(7 to 4 fav) 1
2080⁴ CROSSCHILD (Ire) 6-12-0 C O'Dwyer, ...(10 to 1) 2
1782* SHEISAGALE (Ire) 6-12-0 P Carberry, ...(9 to 2) 3
2040³ ACCOUNTANCY NATIVE (Ire) 5-11-10 T P Treacy, ..(5 to 1) 4
2080⁵ YASHGANS VISION (Ire) 6-12-0 R Dunwoody, ...(8 to 1) 5
2088 BARNA LASS (Ire) (bl) 6-11-1 (5") J M Donnelly, ..(20 to 1) 6
2092⁴ PRINCESS GLORIA (Ire) 6-10-13 (7") Mr M J Daly, (10 to 1) 7
PINTPLEASE PAT (Ire) 6-11-6 L P Cusack, ...(20 to 1) 8
2019³ BRASS BAND (Ire) 6-10-13 (7") Mr R H Fowler, ...(7 to 2) 9

2088 QUEEN OF ALL GALES (Ire) 6-11-3 (3") G Cotter, ..(14 to 1) 10
2049 SINGERS CORNER 5-10-13 (3") U Smyth, ...(33 to 1) 11
1432 ABBEY GALE (Ire) 6-11-6 J Shortt, ...(14 to 1) f
Dist: 3½l, 3½l, 15l, 1l. 5m 34.10s. a 52.10s (12 Ran).

(County Cork Syndicate), A P O'Brien

2139 Tattersalls Ireland EBF Mares Beginners' Chase (6-y-o and up) £3,767 2m.......................................(12:45)

2021⁴ SHINING WILLOW 7-12-0 C O'Dwyer, ...(7 to 4 fav) 1
2077² COOLAFINKA (Ire) 8-11-9 R Dunwoody, ...(3 to 1) 2
2077⁴ ARTISTIC QUAY (Ire) 8-11-2 (7") A O'Shea, ...(12 to 1) 3
2077⁵ ALAMILLO (Ire) 8-11-6 (3") U Smyth, ...(14 to 1) 4
DIVINITY RUN (Ire) 8-12-0 D T Evans, ...(7 to 2) f
CREATIVE BLAZE (Ire) 8-12-0 C F Swan, ...(3 to 1) ur
Dist: 11l, 15l, 25l. 4m 30.80s. a 31.80s (6 Ran).

(S P Tindall), J R H Fowler

2140 I.N.H. Stallion Owners EBF Novice Hurdle (5-y-o and up) £4,110 2½m
....(1:15)

2110* KINGS RETURN (Ire) 6-11-11 D J Casey, ...(6 to 4 on) 1
1895⁴ EBONY KING (Ire) 7-11-3 (3") U Smyth, ...(3 to 1) 2
2097⁶ FRANCES STREET (Ire) 5-11-7 C F Swan, ...(7 to 2) 3
2088⁶ TOUREEN GALE (Ire) 8-10-10 (5") P Morris, ...(8 to 1) 4
1902 PHAREIGN (Ire) 6-11-6 R Dunwoody, ...(16 to 1) 5
2054 TULLABAWN (Ire) 5-11-2 J Shortt, ...(14 to 1) 6
Dist: 3l, 14l, 3½l, 6l. 5m 28.70s. a 46.70s (6 Ran).

(Lilliten Syndicate), W P Mullins

2141 Carrick Hill Handicap Chase (0-109 5-y-o and up) £3,082 2m 5f... (1:45)

2039* BOBBYJO (Ire) [-] 7-12-0 P Carberry, ...(6 to 1) 1
2053⁴ QUATTRO [-] 7-11-5 T P Treacy, ...(4 to 1) 2
2084⁴ DEE ELL [-] 11-11-12 F Woods, ...(7 to 1) 3
2053 BEAUCHAMP GRACE [-] 8-10-13 (3") K Whelan,
....(11 to 4 fav) 4
2059 BALLYFIN BOY [-] 11-10-0¹ T J Mitchell, ...(12 to 1) 5
2091⁴ WEST BROGUE (Ire) [-] (bl) 8-11-4 C F Swan, ...(7 to 1) 6
2078⁵ WACKO JACKO (Ire) [-] 9-10-0 J P Broderick, ...(8 to 1) 7
1408⁷ GREEK MAGIC [-] 10-9-4 (3") G Cotter, ...(25 to 1) 8
1896⁵ EDENAKILL LAD [-] 10-10-9 R Dunwoody, ...(6 to 1) f
2078 ANOTHER POINT (Ire) [-] (bl) 9-11-9 M P Hourigan, (6 to 1) pu
Dist: Hd, 25l, 15l, 8l. 5m 49.70s. a 37.70s (10 Ran).

(Robert Burke), Thomas Carberry

2142 Fairyland Handicap Hurdle (0-116 5-y-o and up) £3,082 2m...... (2:15)

1621³ CAITRIONA'S CHOICE (Ire) [-] 6-11-7 R Dunwoody,
....(7 to 4 fav) 1
2016² MARINERS REEF (Ire) [-] 6-9-7 (7") D McCullagh, .(10 to 1) 2
2114³ JUSTAWAY (Ire) [-] 7-11-0 C F Swan, ...(5 to 1) 3
2055* REGENCY RAKE [-] 5-11-3 F Woods, ...(4 to 1) 4
2036* COLLIERS HILL (Ire) [-] (bl) 9-9-13 P L Malone, ...(13 to 2) 5
2037³ MATTORIA (Ire) [-] 6-10-1 (3") Mr R Walsh, ...(12 to 1) 6
2079⁶ SCEAL SIOG (Ire) [-] 8-9-7 (7") R P Hogan, ...(16 to 1) 7
2097⁷ PRE ORDAINED (Ire) [-] 5-11-1 F J Flood, ...(8 to 1) 8
2076⁴ LEGGAGH LADY (Ire) [-] 6-11-5 (5") J M Donnelly, ..(8 to 1) 9
1074 SWIFT GLIDER (Ire) [-] 8-9-6 (7") M J Cullen, ...(25 to 1) 10
SUPER FLAME (Can) [-] 10-11-13 A Powell, ...(10 to 1) 11
1581 MAKE AN EFFORT (Ire) [-] 6-10-10¹ (7") Mr G A Kingston,
....(14 to 1) pu
Dist: 2l, 4½l, 5l, 3½l. 3m 55.40s. a 10.40s (12 Ran).
SR: 37/14/23/21/-/-/

(Herb M Stanley), Michael Cunningham

2143 Barrettstown Beginners Chase (5-y-o and up) £3,082 3m....... (2:45)

2197⁷ FOLLY ROAD (Ire) 7-12-0 P L Malone, ...(8 to 1) 1
2058⁴ IRISH PEACE (Ire) 9-12-0 C O'Dwyer, ...(8 to 1) 2
1714⁴ SHISOMA (Ire) 7-12-0 J P Broderick, ...(8 to 1) 3
1582⁵ TOUT VA BIEN 9-12-0 P Carberry, ...(12 to 1) 4
2079 TOBY'S FRIEND (Ire) 8-11-4 W Slattery, ...(33 to 1) 5
2090² MONALEE STATEMENT (Ire) 7-11-9 L P Cusack, ..(8 to 1) 6
1779⁵ RYHANE (Ire) 8-11-9 F Woods, ...(14 to 1) 7
2093² BALLYMACREVAN (Ire) 7-12-0 T P Treacy, ...(10 to 1) 8
729² BRAVE FOUNTAIN (Ire) 8-12-0 C F Swan, ...(2 to 1 fav) 9
1898 J J ACKSON (Ire) 8-11-9 D H O'Connor, ...(12 to 1) 10
2096 DAWN ALERT (Ire) 8-12-0 Mr G J Harford, ...(6 to 1) f
SPIRE HILL (Ire) 8-11-6 (3") G Cotter, ...(25 to 1) f
1117 BAILEYS BRIDGE (Ire) 6-11-2 (7") Mr J S Cullen, ..(20 to 1) f
2092² VULPIN DE LAUGERE (Fr) 10-11-6 (3") K Whelan, ..(8 to 1) pu
1534⁹ EASTERN FOX (Ire) 8-11-9 D T Evans, ...(25 to 1) pu
2083⁴ CAVALLO (Fr) 7-11-9 D J Casey, ...(25 to 1) pu
1460⁶ FIGHTING FIDDLE (Ire) 6-11-9 K F O'Brien, ...(12 to 1) pu
1898⁵ COLLON (Ire) 8-11-9 T J Mitchell, ...(8 to 1) pu
Dist: 8l, 15l, dist, 1l. 6m 48.60s. a 48.60s (18 Ran).

(John Freaney), D Harvey

2144 Martinstown I.N.H. Flat Race (5-y-o and up) £3,082 2m............(3:15)

CORRACHOILL (Ire) 6-12-0 Mr A R Coonan, ...(6 to 1) 1
1404⁶ KNOCKAULIN (Ire) 6-12-0 Mr H F Cleary, ...(9 to 4) 2

2060³ ASHTALE (Ire) 5-11-2 (3") Mr R Walsh, ...(5 to 4 fav)   3
MISS PECKSNIFF (Ire) 7-11-9 Mr A J Martin, ...(14 to 1)   4
394⁷ CULRUA ROSIE (Ire) 6-11-2 (7") Mr E Sheehy, ...(12 to 1)   5
1174⁶ KATOUCHE (Ire) 6-11-7 (7") Mr A J Dempsey, ...(12 to 1)   6
1907⁹ MARY DONT BE LONG (Ire) 5-10-12 (7") Mr G A Kingston,
....(10 to 1)   7
MALLARDSTOWN LASS (Ire) 7-11-9 Mr R O'Neill, (20 to 1)   8
SUPREME FUEL (Ire) 7-11-6 (3") Mr P English, ...(8 to 1)   9
BEATRICE ALLEGRO (Ire) 5-10-12 (7") Mr J P McNamara,
....(8 to 1)   10
Dist: 1½sl, 5l, 6l, 15l. 3m 56.70s. (10 Ran).
(Mrs P D McCreery), Peter McCreery

CARLISLE (good)
Tuesday January 14th
Going Correction: PLUS 0.25 sec. per fur.

2145 Sean Graham Novices' Hurdle Class
E (Div I) (4-y-o and up) £2,108 2m 1f
.... (12:30)

QUANGO 5-11-5 P Carberry, settled midfield, hdwy on bit to
ld bef 2 out, sn clr, eased nr finish........(4 to 1 op 7 to 4)   1
CUMBRIAN MAESTRO 4-10-7 R Garritty, trkd ldrs, drvn alng
aftr 2 out, kpt on, no ch wth wnr.
....................................(11 to 4 op 3 to 1 tchd 5 to 2)   2
BUTTERWICK KING (Ire) 5-11-5 P Niven, hld up beh, hdwy
bef 3 out, drvn alng before nxt, styd on.
....................................(14 to 1 op 12 to 1 tchd 16 to 1)   3
1679 CLAVERING (Ire) 7-11-5 A Dobbin, trkd ldrs, led 6th till bef 2
out, no extr..............(5 to 2 fav op 7 to 2 tchd 9 to 4)   4
1682 POLITICAL MILLSTAR 5-11-5 B Storey, hld up, hdwy aftr 3
out, styd on frm nxt, nrst finish........................(50 to 1)   5
GAELIC CHARM (Ire) 9-11-0 K Johnson, trkd ldrs, ev ch 3 out,
rdn and wknd aftr nxt..................(33 to 1 op 20 to 1)   6
1882⁶ TEN PAST SIX 5-11-5 A S Smith, wth ldrs till wknd appr 2 out.
1962⁴ DON'T TELL TOM (Ire) 7-11-5 K Jones, led to second, prmnt
till wknd aftr 3 out.......(11 to 1 op 10 to 1 tchd 12 to 1)   8
1989 ALAN'S PRIDE (Ire) 6-11-0 G Cahill, stnyd slwly, made most
frm second to 6th, wknd 3 out........(20 to 1 op 33 to 1)   9
1629 HOBBS CHOICE 4-10-9 N Bentley, nvr dngrs.
....................................(14 to 1 op 10 to 1)   10
MEADOW BEE 5-11-5 T Reed, lost tch hfwy, tld off.
....................................(100 to 1 op 50 to 1)   11
MARTHA BUCKLE 8-10-11 (3") G Lee, beh most of way, tld
off.......................................(66 to 1 op 33 to 1)   12
HILTONS TRAVEL (Ire) 6-11-5 M Foster, losing tch whn blun
5th, pld up bef nxt....................(50 to 1 op 33 to 1)   pu
JOCK 5-10-12 (7") A Todd, in tch, wknd aftr 5th, tld off whn pld
up bef 3 out...(50 to 1)   pu
Dist: 3l, 1½sl, 4l, 1¾sl, 4l, 1¼sl, 3½sl, 6l, 2½sl, dist. 4m 19.20s. a 16.20s (14 Ran).
(L Milligan), J G FitzGerald

2146 Sean Graham Novices' Chase Class
D (5-y-o and up) £3,842 3m... (1:00)

1820 CHOISTY (Ire) 7-11-3 J Supple, al prmnt, chlgd 2 out, rdn to ld
fnl 200 yards, styd on.....(9 to 2 op 4 to 1 tchd 5 to 1)   1
BRANDY CROSS (Ire) 8-11-3 P Carberry, jmpd wl, made most
frm 4th till hdd fnl 200 yards, no extr.....(6 to 1 op 5 to 1)   2
1590² FOR CATHAL (Ire) 6-11-3 P Niven, hld up, hdwy to track ldrs
hfwy, ev ch 2 out, no extr appr last.
....................................(2 to 1 fav op 5 to 2 tchd 11 to 4)   3
1825 MAMICA 7-11-3 N Smith, beh, styd on frm 4 out, nvr dngrs.
....................................(9 to 1 op 8 to 1)   4
1944 NAUGHTY FUTURE 8-11-9 A Roche, prmnt, rdn whn mstk 3
out, sn wknd..............(11 to 2 op 5 to 1 tchd 6 to 1)   5
1739 COOL WEATHER (Ire) (bl) 9-11-3 A S Smith, in tch, some
hdwy bef 4 out, wkng whn blun 2 out..(12 to 1 op 10 to 1)   6
1256⁶ DEISE MARSHALL (Ire) 9-11-3 B Storey, in tch, mstk tenth, sn
lost pl, no dngr aftr..................(25 to 1 op 16 to 1)   7
1987⁶ MR SLOAN 7-11-0 (3") G Lee, beh most of way... (100 to 1)   8
1913³ RATHFARDON (Ire) 9-10-10 (7") Mr T J Barry, in tch, no hdwy
whn mstk 4 out.....................(25 to 1 op 20 to 1)   9
1952⁴ CLONROCHE LUCKY (Ire) 7-11-3 K Jones, in tch till wknd
12th.......................................(100 to 1 op 33 to 1)   10
959² WOODFORD GALE (Ire) 7-11-3 A Thornton, chsd ldrs till
wknd bef 4 out..................(14 to 1 op 12 to 1)   11
1703² DRY HILL LAD 6-11-3 W Fry, f 1st.......................(14 to 1)   f
1985⁴ ROYAL SURPRISE (bl) 10-11-3 T Reed, led to 4th, prmnt till
wknd bef 14th, wl beh whn pld up before last......(33 to 1)   pu
1913⁴ PANTARA PRINCE (Ire) 8-11-3 A Dobbin, tld off 12th, pld up
bef 4 out..............................(20 to 1 op 16 to 1)   pu
WILD GAME (Ire) 6-10-10 (7") A Todd, mstks, lost tch and pld
up aftr tenth...(100 to 1)   pu
Dist: 2½sl, 1½sl, 12l, 12l, 11l, ¾sl, 17l, ½sl, 1¼sl, 1½sl. 6m 15.60s. a 23.60s (15
Ran).
(Hotel Brokers International), Mrs A Swinbank

2147 Sean Graham Novices' Hurdle Class
E (Div II) (4-y-o and up) £2,122 2m 1f
.... (1:30)

1882⁴ ENDOWMENT (bl) 5-11-12 P Niven, made most, mstk 6th, lft
clr 3 out, sddl slpd nxt, styd on und pres.
....................................(3 to 1 tchd 7 to 2)   1
1679⁷ LOSTRIS (Ire) 6-11-0-8 B Storey, in tch, hdwy bef 3 out, chsd
wnr frm betw last 2, no imprsn.
....................................(16 to 1 op 20 to 1 tchd 25 to 1)   2
BAREFOOT LANDING (USA) 6-11-0 D Parker, sn beh, styd on
frm 3 out, nvr nr to chal........................(50 to 1)   3
2002⁶ MR GOLD (Ire) 4-10-4 (3") E Callaghan, wth wnr till wknd appr
3 out..................................(33 to 1 op 25 to 1)   4
1373⁶ GOLF LAND (Ire) 5-11-5 A Thornton, in tch, no hdwy frm 6th.
....................................(16 to 1 op 12 to 1)   5
1955 JARROW 6-11-5 M Foster, nvr better than mid-div.
....................................(200 to 1 op 100 to 1)   6
TSANGA 5-11-5 N Bentley, beh hfwy. (33 to 1 op 25 to 1)   7
1522⁸ COQUET GOLD 6-11-0 K Johnson, sn beh, tld off.
....................................(200 to 1 op 100 to 1)   8
1908 MONTEIN 5-11-5 N Leach, mstk 1st, sn beh, tld off.
....................................(200 to 1 op 100 to 1)   9
1909* SON OF ANSHAN 4-11-0 J Supple, chsd ldrs, rdn to chase
wnr aftr 6th, 5 ls beh whn f 3 out.
....................................(Evens fav op 5 to 4 on tchd 11 to 10)   f
1983* QATTARA (Ire) 7-11-12 G Cahill, chsd ldrs, wnt second 2 out,
broke leg and f betw last two, dead.
....................................(7 to 2 op 3 to 1 tchd 4 to 1)   su
1677 HAWK HILL BOY 6-11-5 A Dobbin, sn wl beh, tld off whn pld
up bef 3 out..........(100 to 1 tchd 200 to 1)   pu
Dist: 5l, 14l, 3l, 18l, 15l, 2l, dist, 3l. 4m 15.00s. a 12.00s (12 Ran).
SR: 20/3/-/-/-/-/
(R Hilley), Mrs M Reveley

2148 Sean Graham Handicap Chase Class
B (0-140 5-y-o and up) £6,963 3m
.... (2:00)

1910* STORMY CORAL (Ire) [103] 7-10-7 B Storey, hld up, hdwy to
join ldr 13th, led 4 out to nxt, led betw last 2, hdd last, styd on
wl to ld fnl 100 yards.....(13 to 8 fav op 6 to 4 tchd 7 to 4)   1
1774² ALI'S ALIBI [114] 10-11-4 P Niven, chsd ldrs, mstk 11th, led 3
out till betw last 2, led last, hdd fnl 100 yards, no extr und pres.
....................................(3 to 1 op 5 to 2)   2
1660⁵ ALY DALEY (Ire) [103] 9-10-7 A Dobbin, made most to 4 out,
wknd appr 2 out.............(7 to 1 op 5 to 1)   3
1957 UBU VAL (Fr) [120] 11-11-10 A S Smith, drpd rear 7th, no
hdwy whn slightly hmpd 4 out.........(4 to 1 op 3 to 1)   4
1946* PENNINE PRIDE [96] (v) 10-9-11 (3") Mr C Bonner, dsptd ld,
pushed alng frm hfwy, wkng und pres whn f 4 out.
....................................(4 to 1 op 7 to 2)   f
Dist: 2l, 13l, 8l. 6m 12.10s. a 20.10s (5 Ran).
(Mr & Mrs Raymond Anderson Green), C Parker

2149 Sean Graham Handicap Hurdle
Class C (0-135 5-y-o and up) £3,420
2m 1f...(2:30)

RALLEGIO [94] 8-10-0 A Dobbin, trkd ldrs, rdn and outpcd
aftr 3 out, hdwy to ld betw last 2, ran on wl.
....................................(10 to 1 op 8 to 1)   1
1635⁶ CITTADINO [98] 7-10-4 M Foster, towards rear, styd on und
pres frm 2 out, nvr able to chal........(10 to 1 op 8 to 1)   2
2004² NEW INN [118] 6-11-5 (5") Michael Brennan, led betw last
2, no extr...(4 to 1)   3
2004* SHINING EDGE [114] 5-11-6 R Garritty, trkd ldrs, ev ch 2 out,
sn rdn, kpt on same pace..........(11 to 4 fav op 9 to 4)   4
1951² DUKE OF PERTH [94] 6-10-0 P Carberry, trkd ldrs, ev ch 2
out, sn rdn, fdd...............(7 to 1 op 6 to 1 tchd 8 to 1)   5
1200⁵ ONCE MORE FOR LUCK (Ire) [112] 6-11-4 P Niven, in tch,
effrt aftr 3 out, no imprsn...(15 to 2 op 6 to 1 tchd 8 to 1)   6
1821 BOLANEY GIRL (Ire) [94] 8-10-0 A Roche, al beh..(33 to 1)   7
1827² ANABRANCH [110] 6-10-9 (7") M Newton, cl up, ev ch 3 out,
sn drvn alng, wknd aftr nxt, beh whn blun and uns rdr last.
....................................(3 to 1 op 11 to 4)   ur
Dist: 3½sl, 1l, 1l, 2l, 6l, 7l. 4m 12.70s. a 9.70s (8 Ran).
SR: 18/18/37/32/10/22/-/-/
(Guthrie Robertson), P Monteith

2150 Sean Graham Bookmakers Handicap
Chase Class D (0-120 5-y-o and up)
£3,566 2½m 110yds..........(3:00)

1504⁴ RANDOM HARVEST [93] 8-10-11 P Niven, trkd ldrs, led
7th, hit 3 out, styd on wl.
....................................(Evens fav op 11 to 10 tchd 6 to 5)   1
1634⁸ RUSTIC AIR [104] 10-11-8 P Carberry, trkd ldrs, rdn to chase
wnr 2 out, kpt on, no imprsn...........(9 to 1 op 7 to 1)   2
RUSSIAN CASTLE (Ire) [105] 8-11-9 K Jones, led to 7th,
prmnt till outpcd aftr 4 out, styd on frm betw last 2.
....................................(16 to 1 op 14 to 1)   3
1988³ ROAD BY THE RIVER (Ire) [96] 9-11-0 A S Smith, prmnt, ev ch
3 out, kpt on same pace frm nxt......(9 to 1 op 8 to 1)   4
1806³ JYMJAM JOHNNY (Ire) [99] 8-10-12 (5") R McGrath, beh,
mstk tenth, gd hdwy to chase ldrs 4 out, kpt on same pace frm
nxt......................................(8 to 1 op 6 to 1)   5
1589 SUPER SANDY [83] 10-10-1 K Johnson, nvr on terms.
....................................(33 to 1 op 25 to 1)   6
1948⁴ SOLBA (USA) [109] 8-11-13 B Storey, in tch till wknd bef 3 out.
....................................(6 to 1 tchd 13 to 2)   7
POPESHALL [110] 10-11-7 (7") A Todd, in tch, effrt bef 4 out.
wknd aftr nxt..........(20 to 1 op 14 to 1 tchd 25 to 1)   8

1806⁴ ANOTHER VENTURE (Ire) [90] 7-10-8 R Garritty, *beh, some hdwy bef 9th, wknd before 4 out, tld off whn pld up before 2 out*................................. (12 to 1 tchd 14 to 1) pu
Dist: 6l, 6l, 3½l, 3½l, 1¾l, nk, 3½l. 5m 9.10s. a 14.10s (9 Ran).
(C C Buckley), Mrs M Reveley

2151 Sean Graham Bookmakers Handicap Hurdle Class D (0-125 4-y-o and up) £2,997 2½m 110yds.........(3:30)

1914* LIVIO (USA) [115] 6-11-8 A Dobbin, *trkd ldrs, blun 6th, gd hdwy to ld 2 out, clr last, styd on wl*.
.......(13 to 8 fav op 6 to 4 tchd 11 to 8 and 7 to 4) 1
1867 LOCHNAGRAIN (Ire) [121] 9-11-7 P Niven, *hld up beh, hdwy aftr 8th, styd on wl und pres frm 2 out, no imprsn on wnr*.
.... (4 to 1 tchd 9 to 2) 2
1991 THURSDAY NIGHT (Ire) [108] 6-11-1 P Carberry, *settled midfield, effrt bef 3 out, styd on frm nxt*.... (7 to 1 tchd 8 to 1) 3
2064⁴ TRUMP [115] 8-11-8 D Parker, *trkd ldrs, led aftr 3 out to nxt, no extr*..................................(8 to 1) 4
1661⁵ NICHOLAS PLANT [93] 8-9-11 (3*) G Lee, *hld up, hdwy bef 8th, led 3 out, sn rdn and hdd, fdd*....(14 to 1 op 12 to 1) 5
1914⁸ GLENUGIE [100] 6-10-7 N Bentley, *hld up, hdwy bef 8th, ch 3 out, sn rdn and wknd*................(20 to 1 op 14 to 1) 6
1691⁸ DANBYS GORSE [93] 5-9-7 (7*) M Newton, *nvr dngrs*.
.... (33 to 1 op 25 to 1) 7
OLD HABITS (Ire) [108] 8-11-1 B Storey, *cl up till wknd aftr 3 out*..................................(14 to 1) 8
1951 SUDDEN SPIN [100] 7-10-4 (3*) E Callaghan, *beh hfwy*.
.......................(8 to 1 op 7 to 1 tchd 9 to 1) 9
FARNEY GLEN [95] 10-9-11 (5*) R McGrath, *in tch till wknd bef 3 out*..................................(66 to 1) 10
PEEP O DAY [100] 6-10-7 A Thornton, *made most to 3 out, wknd quickly, tld off*..............(14 to 1 op 12 to 1) 11
JOHNNY KELLY [110] 10-11-0 (3*) F Leahy, *al beh, lost tch and pld up bef 2 out*................(50 to 1 op 33 to 1) pu
Dist: 2½l, 5l, nk, 4l, 18l, 2l, 1l, 14l, 11l, 24l. 5m 2.70s. a 20.70s (12 Ran).
(The Low Flyers (Thoroughbreds) Ltd), P Monteith

LEICESTER (good to soft (races 1,2,5,7), good to firm (3,4,6)) Tuesday January 14th
Going Correction: PLUS 0.10 sec. per fur.

2152 Lyric Novices' Hurdle Class E (Div I) (5-y-o and up) £2,018 3m....(12:40)

1792² KORBELL (Ire) 8-10-7 A P McCoy, *al wl plcd, nosed ahead last, drvn out*..........(11 to 4 op 9 to 4 tchd 3 to 1) 1
1505² FLYING GUNNER 6-11-4 A Maguire, *nvr far away, ev ch frm 4 out, ran on wl und pres from last*.
.... (11 to 2 op 9 to 2 tchd 6 to 1) 2
1631² HAND WOVEN 5-11-4 C Llewellyn, *tried to make all, rdn and hdd last, one pace nring finish*.
.......................(7 to 4 fav op 5 to 4 tchd 2 to 1) 3
1727⁵ QUINI EAGLE (Fr) 5-10-12 C Maude, *al frnt rnk, drvn alng whn pace quickened frm 4 out, no extr from aftr nxt*.
.... (16 to 1 op 12 to 1 tchd 20 to 1) 4
MUSIC MASTER (Ire) 7-10-12 J Osborne, *settled in tch, effrt fnl circuit, feeling pace frm 4 out, no imprsn*.
.... (33 to 1 op 25 to 1) 5
1829³ ADIB (USA) 7-10-12 J Callaghan, *settled in rear, drvn alng whn pace quickened appr 4 out, no imprsn on ldrs*.
.... (16 to 1 tchd 20 to 1) 6
1849⁸ ROSSELL ISLAND (Ire) 6-10-12 W Marston, *settled to track ldrs, effrt fnl circuit, one pace bef 4 out, fdd*.
.... (14 to 1 op 10 to 1 tchd 16 to 1) 7
1615⁴ JOBSAGOODUN 6-10-12 M A Fitzgerald, *settled in midfield, effrt hfwy, drvn alng bef 4 out, no imprsn on ldrs*.
.... (7 to 1 op 5 to 1) 8
1868⁴ CYPRESS AVENUE (Ire) 5-10-12 J R Kavanagh, *chsd ldg bunch for o'r a circuit, und pres bef 4 out, sn rdn and btn*.
.... (20 to 1 op 14 to 1 tchd 25 to 1) 9
SERGENT KAY 7-10-9 (3*) P Midgley, *sn struggling to keep in tch, nvr able to rch chalg pos*..................(100 to 1) 10
1817* SUTHERLAND MOSS 6-11-4 N Williamson, *tucked away in midfield, feeling pace fnl circuit, lost tch, tld off*.
.... (12 to 1 op 10 to 1) 11
1350 HILLS GAMBLE 7-10-12 W Worthington, *wth ldrs for o'r a circuit, lost tch, tld off*..........................(50 to 1) 12
1675 BURFORDS FOR SCRAP 5-10-12 B Powell, *al wl beh, tld off*.
.... (100 to 1) 13
1980⁷ NORDIC FLIGHT 9-10-7 (5*) D J Kavanagh, *al struggling in rear, tld off*..............(100 to 1 tchd 200 to 1) 14
1928 BECKY'S GIRL 7-10-7 L Harvey, *sn struggling in rear, tld off*.
.... (100 to 1) 15
1142 KYLE DAVID (Ire) 5-10-12 S Wynne, *tailing off whn refused 5th*..................................(100 to 1) ref
SOVEREIGN PASS 5-10-12 D Gallagher, *al wl beh, tld off whn pld up bef 4 out*..................(100 to 1) pu
Dist: Nk, 4l, 10l, 5l, 10l, 6l, 5l, 3½l, 8l, 1l. 5m 55.60s. a 8.60s (17 Ran).
SR: 17/28/24/8/3/-/   (K J Mitchell), P F Nicholls

2153 Penwick Novices' Hurdle Class E (4-

---

y-o and up) £2,725 2m.......(1:10)

1973⁹ HOH WARRIOR (Ire) 6-11-11 G Bradley, *wtd wth, improved frm 4 out, drvn ahead aftr last, ran on wl*. (6 to 1 op 5 to 1) 1
AVANTI EXPRESS (Ire) 7-11-5 J Osborne, *al wl plcd, ev ch frm 4 out, led betw last 2, hdd aftr last, one pace and pres*.
.... (11 to 1 op 7 to 1 tchd 12 to 1) 2
46⁴ JUST BRUCE 8-11-5 D Gallagher, *made most, hrd pressed frm 4 out, hdd betw last 2, one pace*.
.... (20 to 1 op 16 to 1 tchd 25 to 1) 3
MILFORD SOUND 4-10-7 R Johnson, *settled midfield, effrt appr 4 out, kpt on last 2, no imprsn on ldrs*.
.... (10 to 1 op 8 to 1 tchd 12 to 1) 4
1300⁴ SILVER THYNE (Ire) 5-11-5 W Marston, *nvr far away, effrt hfwy, feeling pace aftr 4 out, no extr last 2*.
.... (6 to 1 op 5 to 1 tchd 7 to 1) 5
1743* TOMPETOO (Ire) 6-11-11 C Llewellyn, *al hndy, ev ch till fdd frm 3 out*..................(3 to 1 fav op 5 to 2) 6
MORPHEUS 8-11-5 A Maguire, *settled to track ldrs, ev ch aftr 4 out, rdn and no extr frm nxt*......(10 to 1 op 8 to 1) 7
1830⁶ FANTASY LINE 6-11-0 R Bellamy, *settled midfield, effrt appr 4 out, rdn and fdd aftr nxt*..................(16 to 1) 8
1410⁴ LABURNUM GOLD (Ire) 6-11-5 R Farrant, *chsd ldg grp, feeling pace 4 out, no imprsn frm nxt*.....(10 to 1 op 8 to 1) 9
1648³ TRISTRAM'S IMAGE (NZ) 6-11-5 M A Fitzgerald, *settled midfield, effrt hfwy, rdn and no imprsn on ldrs frm nxt*.
.... (10 to 1 op 8 to 1) 10
1805 CADES BAY 6-11-5 D Bridgwater, *beh and pushed alng hfwy, nvr able to rch chalg pos*..........(20 to 1 op 16 to 1) 11
1006² TODD (USA) 6-11-5 J A McCarthy, *beh and niggled alng hfwy, nvr able to rch chalg pos*......(20 to 1 tchd 25 to 1) 12
1109* TIDAL FORCE (Ire) 6-11-5 N Williamson, *settled in tch, feeling pace bef 4 out, no imprsn*... (9 to 2 op 6 to 1 tchd 7 to 1) 13
COTTESMORE 6-11-5 J R Kavanagh, *wth ldg grp till fdd appr 4 out*..................................(100 to 1) 14
2176 BROWN AND MILD 6-11-5 J Ryan, *wth ldrs, ev ch till wknd quickly aftr 4 out*..........(66 to 1 op 50 to 1) 15
1790⁴ ROYAL DIVERSION (Ire) 4-10-2 A P McCoy, *feeling pace and lost grnd hfwy, wl beh frm 4 out*.
.... (18 to 1 op 6 to 1 tchd 9 to 1) 16
1810³ MAZIRAH 6-11-5 D Morris, *struggling and lost tch hfwy, wl beh aftr*..................(20 to 1 op 14 to 1 tchd 25 to 1) 17
1689⁸ GAUTBY HENPECKED 4-10-2 J Callaghan, *sn wl beh, tld off*.
.... (50 to 1) 18
SERIOUS OPTION (Ire) 6-11-5 D Walsh, *struggling to keep in tch hfwy, tld off in strt*..................(50 to 1) 19
NEVER TIME (Ire) 5-11-0 (5*) Mr T Rornton, *lost tch hfwy, tld off whn pld up betw last 2*..................(50 to 1) pu
Dist: 1l, 10l, 2½l, 2½l, 1½l, ¾l, 2½l, ¾l, 5l, 3l. 3m 52.70s. a 9.70s (20 Ran).
SR: 16/9/-/-/-/-/   (D F Allport), C P E Brooks

2154 Danny Novices' Handicap Chase Class E (0-105 5-y-o and up) £3,057 2½m 110yds...............(1:40)

1944³ GARNWIN (Ire) [95] 7-11-4 M A Fitzgerald, *led to 3rd, nvr far away, nosed ahead 2 out, ran on gmely r-in*.
.... (9 to 4 op 2 to 1 tchd 5 to 2) 1
1857 NORDIC VALLEY (Ire) [86] 6-10-9 A P McCoy, *wtd wth, niggled alng hfwy, str chal frm 3 out, kpt on und pres r-in*.
.... (7 to 2 op 9 to 4) 2
2026 RONANS GLEN [77] 10-10-0 R Supple, *settled to track ldrs, led aftr 3rd to 8th, feeling pace 3 out, kpt on one pace frm betw last 2*..................(25 to 1 op 12 to 1) 3
GIPSY RAMBLER [77] 12-10-0 W Worthington, *al wl plcd, ev ch till rdn and no extr frm 2 out*......(50 to 1 op 33 to 1) 4
1793³ HAUNTING MUSIC (Ire) [105] 9-12-0 C Maude, *al frnt rnk, led 3rd, sn hdd, rgned ld 8th, headed 3 out, fdd betw last 2*.
.... (2 to 1 fav tchd 7 to 4) 5
1491⁴ RIVER RED [77] 11-10-0 P McLoughlin, *nvr far away, niggled alng 8th, rallied to ld 3 out, hdd and wknd quickly nxt*.
.... (25 to 1 op 16 to 1) 6
1913⁷ ASLAN (Ire) [95] 9-11-4 N Williamson, *tracking ldrs whn f 1st, dead*..................(4 to 1 op 6 to 1) f
1437⁷ SMART CASANOVA [77] 8-10-0 I Lawrence, *co'red up, unsighted whn brght dwn 1st*.......(50 to 1 op 33 to 1) bd
Dist: ¾l, 6l, 1½l, 3l, 10l. 5m 16.70s. a 14.70s (8 Ran).
(Pioneer Heat-Treatment), N J Henderson

2155 Maderia Queen Novices' Chase Class E (5-y-o and up) £2,901 2m 1f ....(2:10)

1287² AMANCIO (USA) 6-11-3 M FitzGerald, *al gng best, led bef 3rd (water), drw clr frm 4 out, very easily*.
.... (2 to 1 on op 9 to 4 on tchd 15 to 8 on) 1
1944⁸ DECYBORG (Fr) 6-11-9 A P McCoy, *led till hdd bef 3rd (water), pressed ldr till reminders 6th, rdn and outpcd 4 out, sn btn*..................(7 to 4 tchd 15 to 8) 2
1330 ALICAT (Ire) 6-11-3 Derek Byrne, *sn tld off last, plodded round a fence beh*..........................(50 to 1 op 33 to 1) 3
1729 MR MOTIVATOR 7-11-3 S McNeill, *chasing clr ldg pair whn f 1st*..........................(33 to 1 tchd 50 to 1) f
Dist: Dist, dist. 4m 19.00s. a 11.00s (4 Ran).
(Paul H Locke), Mrs A J Perrett

2156 Lyric Novices' Hurdle Class E (Div II)
(5-y-o and up) £2,018 3m.... (2:40)

1829²	YOUNG KENNY 6-11-4 R Supple, settled to track ldg grp, bustled alng bef 3 out, looked btn betw last 2, swtchd rght, rallied to ld cl hme............... (12 to 1 tchd 14 to 1)	1
	MONTECOT (Fr) 8-10-12 N Mann, settled gng wl, str chal frm 3 out, ev ch last, kpt on well und pres. (12 to 1 op 25 to 1)	2
1940²	DESTIN D'ESTRUVAL (Fr) 6-10-12 D Bridgwater, settled gng wl, led aftr 3 out, hrd pressed frm nxt, rdn and worn dwn cl hme............... (13 to 8 on op 5 to 4 on tchd 6 to 5 on)	3
1729*	BOOTS MADDEN (Ire) 7-11-4 N Williamson, wtd wth, improved to take clr order 4 out, drvn alng nxt, fdd bef 2 out. .... (9 to 2 op 11 to 4)	4
	PARIS FASHION (Fr) 6-10-7 T Jenks, tried to make all, hdd and rdn aftr 3 out, fdd bef nxt. .... (14 to 1 op 10 to 1 tchd 16 to 1)	5
1271³	MENDIP PRINCE (Ire) 7-10-12 A Maguire, wth ldrs thrght, rdn alng whn pace quickened 3 out, sn lost tch. .... (14 to 1 op 8 to 1)	6
1591³	DARK CHALLENGER (Ire) 5-10-12 W Marston, settled midfield, feeling pace and up nxt, wknd quickly bef nxt. .... (16 to 1 op 10 to 1)	7
1586³	CLEVER BOY (Ire) 6-11-4 Derek Byrne, tucked away beh ldrs, effrt hfwy, wknd bef 3 out, sn lost tch. .... (5 to 1 op 20 to 1 tchd 33 to 1)	8
1673⁶	RATHKEAL 6-10-12 D Gallagher, chsd ldg grp for o'r a circuit, lost pl quickly bef 3 out, tld off. .... (25 to 1 tchd 33 to 1)	9
1763⁶	BANK AVENUE 6-10-12 R Farrant, settled in tch, wknd quickly bef 3 out, tld off............... (25 to 1 op 20 to 1)	10
	BROWNSCROFT 9-10-0 (7*) K Hibbert, struggling to keep up aftr one circuit, tld off nxt, tld off. (100 to 1 op 50 to 1)	11
	ITSPENSHAMS 8-10-7 S McNeill, al beh, tld off. .... (100 to 1 op 50 to 1)	12
	SO FAR BOLD (Ire) 7-10-12 J Osborne, wth ldrs till wknd quickly bef 3 out, tld off. (16 to 1 op 12 to 1 tchd 20 to 1)	13
1995	MINSTER BOY 6-10-12 C Llewellyn, struggling to keep in tch aftr one circuit, tld off...........(100 to 1 op 50 to 1)	14
1855	DECEIT THE SECOND 5-10-12 G Burrough, lost tch frm hfwy, tld off whn pld up bef 3 out................(100 to 1)	pu
1648	MOOR DANCE MAN 7-10-12 Mr D Verco, wl plcd for one circuit, lost tch, tld off whn pld up bef 4 out. .... (25 to 1 op 50 to 1)	pu
	BALCONY BOY 5-10-12 J Callaghan, al beh, tld off whn pld up bef 3 out...............(50 to 1 tchd 66 to 1)	pu

Dist: Nk, hd, 15l, 5l, 13l, 3l, 3l, 14l, nk, 30l. 5m 58.60s. a 11.60s (17 Ran).

(J G Read), P Beaumont

2157 Thunderbolt Novices' Chase Class E
(5-y-o and up) £3,161 3m..... (3:10)

1801²	DROMHANA (Ire) 7-11-11 A P McCoy, jmpd boldly, led 6th, lft clr 7 out, styd on wl, unchlgd. .... (100 to 30 op 9 to 4 tchd 7 to 2)	1
1820⁵	FINAL BEAT 8-11-5 Derek Byrne, settled to track ldrs, chsd alng frm 6 out, styd on to take second r-in, no ch wth wnr. .... (5 to 1 op 16 to 1)	2
1870²	KEY TO MOYADE (Ire) 7-11-5 I Lawrence, nvr far away, reminders 9th, lft poor second 7 out, rdn and clr for second r-in....................... (8 to 1 op 7 to 1)	3
1793	PENNCALER (Ire) 7-11-5 R Johnson, sn struggling to keep up, tld off aftr one circuit............ (8 to 1 op 6 to 1)	4
1857⁷	MASKED MARTIN 6-11-5 S Burrough, wl 4th, sn lost tch, tld off....................... (100 to 1 op 50 to 1)	5
1924*	GYSART (Ire) 8-11-11 C Maude, al wl plcd, second and pushed alng whn l 7 out.........(11 to 4 op 2 to 1)	f
1765²	WISLEY WONDER (Ire) 7-11-5 C Llewellyn, led to 6th, 4th and bustled alng whn blun and uns rdr tenth. .... (2 to 1 fav op 9 to 4 tchd 5 to 2)	ur
	DISPOL DANCER 6-11-0 (5*) Mr R Thornton, tld off till pld up bef 11th...............(100 to 1 op 50 to 1)	pu
1482⁴	OUROWNFELLOW (Ire) 8-11-5 D Morris, tld off whn pld up bef 11th..................... (10 to 1 op 8 to 1)	pu

Dist: 25l, ½l, dist, 9l. 6m 3.10s. a 18.10s (9 Ran).

(J Blackwell, T Chappell, T Curry & D Nichols), P F Nicholls

2158 Major League Novices' Handicap
Hurdle Class E (0-105 4-y-o and up)
£2,473 2½m 110yds.........(3:40)

1909	MOCK TRIAL (Ire) [-] 4-10-0 B Fenton, nvr far away, led 3 out, ran on strly r-in...........(7 to 1 op 6 to 1 tchd 9 to 1)	1
1703*	LANCE ARMSTRONG (Ire) [-] 7-11-12 A Maguire, al frnt rnk, ev ch frm 4 out, styd on same pace frm betw last 2. .... (10 to 1 op 6 to 1)	2
1815²	LOUGH TULLY [-] 7-10-2 S Wynne, settled midfield, improved aftr 4 out, rdn and styd on frm betw last 2. .... (9 to 1 op 1 tchd 10 to 1)	3
1816³	GENERAL MOUKTAR [-] 7-12-0 A P McCoy, settled to track ldrs, effrt and drvn alng frm 3 out, kpt on one pace frm betw last 2...................... (6 to 1 op 4 to 1)	4
1830³	MELSTOCK MEGGIE [-] 7-10-13 W Marston, tucked away beh ldg grp, effrt and not much room appr 2 out, swtchd lft r-in, styd on........................ (9 to 4 fav op 7 to 2)	5

2 column (right)

1978²	COLWALL [-] 6-9-12 (7*) K Hibbert, co'red up in midfield, effrt aftr 4 out, rdn alng frm no nxt, not quicken........(14 to 1)	6
1978*	MAHLER [-] 11-4 D Walsh, led 3rd till hdd 3 out, fdd und pres frm betw last 2......... (5 to 1 op 7 to 1 tchd 8 to 1)	7
	SNOWSHILL SHAKER [-] 8-10-8 C Llewellyn, settled in tch, feeling pace and drvn alng bef 3 out, fdd........ (12 to 1)	8
1958²	SUPREME GENOTIN (Ire) [-] 8-11-6 G Upton, settled off the pace, effrt und pres appr 3 out, no extr. (10 to 1 op 6 to 1)	9
1646*	ROVESTAR [-] 6-10-12 T J Murphy, chsd ldg grp till wknd quickly und pres frm 4 out.........(14 to 1 op 12 to 1)	10
1978⁵	TIME LEADER [78] 5-10-0 B Powell, in tch till wknd quickly aftr 4 out................. (25 to 1 tchd 33 to 1)	11
1671⁵	GLISTENING DAWN [-] 7-11-4 S McNeill, wl plcd till fdd frm 4 out, sn lost tch................. (14 to 1 op 10 to 1)	12
1817²	GRAND CRU [-] 6-11-0 D Gallagher, settled midfield, feeling pace bef 4 out, sn lost tch.........(14 to 1 op 8 to 1)	13
1647	LOTHIAN JEM [-] 8-9-9 (5*) Mr R Thornton, led to 3rd, lost tch quickly bef 4 out, tld off whn pld up before 2 out. .... (50 to 1 tchd 66 to 1)	pu
1995	CARLY-J [-] 6-10-2² Mr N Kent, lost tch bef 4 out, tld off whn pld up before 2 out......................(33 to 1)	pu
	NO MORALS [-] 6-10-1 J Osborne, al beh, tld off whn pld up bef 2 out.................(33 to 1 op 20 to 1)	pu

Dist: 3l, 1½l, 2l, hd, 6l, 1¼l, 1¼l, nk, 4l, 8l. 5m 0.20s. a 12.20s (16 Ran).

(P A Leonard), Mrs J R Ramsden

TRAMORE (IRE) (yielding to soft)
Tuesday January 14th

2159 Fenor Opportunity Handicap Hurdle
(5-y-o and up) £2,637 2m..... (1:00)

	MONICA'S CHOICE (Ire) [-] 6-11-8 (4*) R P Hogan, ... (5 to 4 fav)	1
1273	BAKEMA (Ire) [-] 5-11-3 (2*) J M Donnelly, ... (8 to 1)	2
2076³	BEAU CYRANO (Ire) [-] 5-11-6 (4*) M J Collins, ... (6 to 1)	3
1839³	HEIGHT OF LUXURY (Ire) [-] 9-9-3 (4*) M D Murphy, (5 to 1)	4
1549⁴	THE WICKED CHICKEN (Ire) [-] 8-10-13 G Cotter, (11 to 2)	5
2055	ZIGGY THE GREAT (Ire) [-] (bl) 5-11-3 J Butler, ...(10 to 1)	6
1713	JOHNNY HANDSOME (Ire) [-] 7-10-5 (4*) A O'Shea, (8 to 1)	7
1245	EVER SO BOLD [-] 10-10-12 (4*) D McCullagh, ...(16 to 1)	8
683⁷	GARLAND ROSE (Ire) [-] 7-10-4 (2*) P Morris, ...(12 to 1)	9
2016	SLEWMORE (Ire) [-] 6-10-4 (4*) M P Cooney, ...(20 to 1)	10
1713	JACKSON'S PANTHER (Ire) [-] (bl) 5-10-2 (4*) J M Maguire, ... (10 to 1)	11
1359	GRANUAILE (Ire) [-] 6-10-7 K Whelan, ...(10 to 1)	12
2017⁸	ISLAND ROCK (Ire) [-] 6-10-0 (2*) T Martin, ...(10 to 1)	13

Dist: 2l, sht-hd, 1l, 7l. 4m 17.50s. (13 Ran).

(Mrs Noeleen Roche), C Roche

2160 Passage East Hurdle (5-y-o and up)
£2,226 2m...................(1:30)

2097⁵	MIDNIGHT JAZZ (Ire) 7-11-7 J P Broderick, ... (10 to 1)	1
2056³	JAY MAN (Ire) 7-12-0 C F Swan, ...(11 to 8 on)	2
1839⁵	RYTHM ROCK (Ire) 8-11-0 (7*) A O'Shea, ...(10 to 1)	3
1275	THE HOLY PARSON (Ire) 5-10-10 (7*) M P Cooney, (25 to 1)	4
2106	DICK MCCARTHY (Ire) 5-11-3 D J Casey, ...(12 to 1)	5
1838	LORD OGAN (Ire) 6-11-7 K F O'Brien, ...(20 to 1)	6
2092⁵	SUIR FIND (Ire) 5-11-3 J Shortt, ...(12 to 1)	7
2076⁵	BE MY FOLLY (Ire) 5-11-5 T Hazlett, ...(20 to 1)	8
2092⁸	ATLANTA FLAME (Ire) 6-11-2 W Slattery, ...(20 to 1)	9
1042⁸	HARRY HEANEY (Ire) 8-11-2 (5*) T Martin, ...(12 to 1)	10
	WINTER MELODY (Ire) 5-11-3 L P Cusack, ...(16 to 1)	11
216	OAMOOS (Ire) 7-11-0 (7*) D W O'Sullivan, ...(12 to 1)	12
1836	BOCCACHERA (Ire) 5-10-12 A J O'Brien, ...(20 to 1)	13
1359	OAKS PRIDE (USA) 6-11-7 F Woods, ...(20 to 1)	14
	AFGHANI (Ire) 8-11-2 (5*) P Morris, ...(8 to 1)	15

Dist: 1½l, 7l, 15l, 2½l. 4m 21.30s. (15 Ran).

(A Germano Terrinoni), Michael Hourigan

2161 Brownstown Maiden Hurdle (4-y-o)
£2,226 2m...................(2:00)

2105	NO AVAIL (Ire) 10-4 T P Treacy, ...(7 to 1)	1
2112⁷	NATIVE ECLIPSE (Ire) 10-9 C F Swan, ...(8 to 1)	2
	RED TONIC (USA) 10-9 L P Cusack, ...(8 to 1)	3
1430⁵	DUNEMER (Ire) 10-6 (3*) M R Walsh, ...(3 to 1 fav)	4
1547⁶	DADDY'S HAT (Ire) 10-9 P L Malone, ...(6 to 1)	5
2105⁷	KEAL RYAN (Ire) 10-6 (3*) G Cotter, ...(10 to 1)	6
1547	KAYALYNA (Ire) 10-4 T Horgan, ...(14 to 1)	7
2105⁴	KING OF PEACE (Ire) 11-0 H Rogers, ...(7 to 2)	8
	LOVELY PROSPECT 10-2 (7*) R P Hogan, ...(20 to 1)	9
	RAINBOW TIMES (Ire) 10-4 M P Hourigan, ...(14 to 1)	10
1459	CHUIPHOGA 10-4 K F O'Brien, ...(14 to 1)	11
	ACCOUNTANCY JEWEL (Ire) 10-9 J P Broderick, ...(8 to 1)	12
2074	CALM BEAUTY (Ire) 9-11 (7*) Mr C J Swords, ...(20 to 1)	13
	MAY BE SHALL (Ire) 10-2⁵ (7*) Mr N D Fehily, ...(20 to 1)	14

Dist: 2l, ¾l, nk, 1l. 4m 31.40s. (14 Ran).

(Mrs P Mullins), P Mullins

2162 Tramore Handicap Hurdle (0-102
5-y-o and up) £2,226 2¾m.... (2:30)

1778	INDESTRUCTIBLE [-] 9-11-3 G M O'Neill, ... (10 to 1)	1
2089³	ADARAMANN (Ire) [-] 5-10-7 (3*) Mr R Walsh, ...(10 to 1)	2

2103³ ARTIC PEARL (Ire) [-] 7-10-3 W Slattery, ... (7 to 1) 3
1778⁷ DOOK'S DELIGHT (Ire) [-] 6-11-2 L P Cusack, ... (7 to 1) 4
2104³ LADY QUAYSIDE (Ire) [-] 7-11-2 D J Casey, ... (5 to 1) 5
2103 ROSIE LIL (Ire) [-] (bl) 6-10-3 (7") L A Hurley, ... (10 to 1) 6
2037 VIVIANS VALE (Ire) [-] 8-10-11 (7") D K Budds, ... (10 to 1) 7
1901 SHIR ROSE (Ire) [-] 7-10-9 C F Swan, ... (3 to 1 fav) 8
2103⁶ HERSILIA (Ire) [-] (bl) 6-10-11 F J Flood, ... (6 to 1) 9
1839 SHECOULDNTBEBETTER (Ire) [-] 6-10-7 T P Treacy,
. . . . (10 to 1) 10
2088⁵ COMMITTED SCHEDULE (Ire) [-] 6-10-6 J P Broderick,
. . . . (14 to 1) 11
1361⁸ KILCARAMORE (Ire) [-] 6-10-5 (7") S FitzGerald, . . (10 to 1) 12
278⁸ KUDOS (Ire) [-] 6-10-0 (7") R P Hogan, ... (20 to 1) 13
1839⁵ TARIYMA (Ire) [-] 6-10-1 (3") K Whelan, ... (14 to 1) 14
1144⁵ TEARDROP (Ire) [-] 5-10-7 (3") J Butler, ... (20 to 1) 15
Dist: 2l, 2l, ½l, ¾l. 5m 43.60s. (15 Ran).

(John Quane), Augustine Leahy

2163 Dunmore East Handicap Chase (0-102 5-y-o and up) £2,226 2¾m . . . . (3:00)

2090⁴ MATTS DILEMMA (Ire) [-] 9-12-0 D H O'Connor, . . . (11 to 2) 1
2091³ BALLYBODEN [-] 10-10-12 M P Hourigan, ... (8 to 1) 2
1078⁷ THE DASHER DOYLE (Ire) [-] 9-11-4 Mr P J Healy, (10 to 1) 3
2059⁵ RISZARD (USA) [-] 8-11-9 D J Casey, ... (12 to 1) 4
HOTEL SALTEES (Ire) [-] 9-10-13 F Woods, ... (14 to 1) 5
2091⁴ CANAILLOU II (Fr) [-] 7-11-0 (3") K Whelan, . . (9 to 4 fav) 6
1906² APPALACHEE BAY (Ire) [-] 7-11-3 (3") J Butler, ... (7 to 2) f
2021⁷ MARIES POLLY [-] 7-11-1 J P Broderick, ... (12 to 1) f
2059³ DOONEGA (Ire) [-] 9-10-3 (7") Mr E Gallagher, ... (9 to 2) ur
1754⁵ GOT NO CHOICE (Ire) [-] (bl) 7-9-10 (7") M D Murphy,
. . . . (10 to 1) ur
Dist: 25l, ¾l, 2l, 6l. 5m 54.70s. (10 Ran).

(Slaney Meats Group), P J P Doyle

2164 Metal Man Beginners Chase (5-y-o and up) £2,226 2½m . . . . (3:30)

1841⁹ FERRYCARRIGCRYSTAL (Ire) 9-12-0 K F O'Brien, (12 to 1) 1
2134 BLAZE OF HONOUR (Ire) 6-11-9 C F Swan, ... (13 to 2) 2
2090³ THE NOBLE ROUGE (Ire) 8-11-11 (3") G Cotter, . . . (10 to 1) 3
2090⁴ PRATE BOX (Ire) 7-12-0 A Powell, ... (8 to 1) 4
2137⁷ TEMPLEROAN PRINCE 10-12-0 J R Barry, ... (8 to 1) 5
1550 ALWAYS IN TROUBLE 10-12-0 T P Rudd, ... (14 to 1) 6
2103⁶ THE BOYLERMAN (Ire) 8-11-7 (7") Mr K O'Sullivan, (12 to 1) 7
1903² TAYLORS QUAY (Ire) 9-12-0 J P Broderick, ... (6 to 1) 8
1841 MALACCA KING (Ire) 6-12-0 D J Casey, ... (9 to 4 fav) 9
SIOBHAILIN DUBH (Ire) 8-11-9 P A Roche, ... (20 to 1) 10
2077 MARGUERITA SONG 7-11-11 P Treacy, ... (16 to 1) 11
2091 SLANEY STANDARD (Ire) 9-12-0 D H O'Connor, . . . (8 to 1) 12
2141⁹ MUSKERRY EXPRESS (Ire) 7-11-7 (7") J E Casey, (20 to 1) 13
1242⁸ WILD BROOK (Ire) 7-11-11 (3") K Whelan, ... (14 to 1) 14
729³ LINDA'S BOY (Ire) 7-12-0 J Shortt, ... (10 to 1) 15
Dist: 7l, 3l, 1l, 3l. 5m 9.20s. (15 Ran).

(Mrs Mary Lambert), S J Lambert

2165 Garrarus I.N.H. Flat Race (6-y-o and up) £2,226 2m . . . . (4:00)

2107⁸ MICKS MAN (Ire) 6-11-11 (3") Mr E Norris, ... (10 to 1) 1
2093 ARCTIC GREY (Ire) (bl) 7-11-11 (3") Mr R Walsh, . . (8 to 1) 2
2108² CARROLLS ROCK (Ire) 6-12-0 Mr P Fenton, . . . (5 to 2 fav) 3
884⁶ PANTOBEACH (Ire) 7-11-2 (7") Mr Mark Walsh, . . (14 to 1) 4
1837⁵ FIFTH GENERATION (Ire) (bl) 7-11-7 (7") Mr B Hassett,
. . . . (7 to 1) 5
1908⁶ KILPATRICK (Ire) 6-11-2 (7") Mr C J Swords, ... (8 to 1) 6
2088 CRANNON BEAUTY (Ire) 7-11-11 (3") Mr B M Cash, (8 to 1) 7
FATHER PRESCOTT (Ire) 7-11-7 (7") Mr D Whelan, (20 to 1) 8
2088⁴ MAGS SUPER TOI (Ire) 8-11-7 (7") Mr K Beecher, (10 to 1) 9
2087⁷ CHOCOLATE GIRL (Ire) 6-11-2 (7") Mr C P Donnelly,
. . . . (16 to 1) 10
2075 SALLY SUPREME (Ire) 6-11-2 (7") Mr M G Coleman,
. . . . (25 to 1) 11
THE NOBLE REBEL (Ire) 6-12-0 Mr J A Flynn, ... (10 to 1) 12
2093⁴ PRIZE OF PEACE (Ire) 7-11-2 (7") Mr M T Hartrey, . . (6 to 1) bd
BORN TO WIN (Ire) 7-11-6 (3") Mr D Valentine, . . . (9 to 2) su
1776 LADY CONDUCTOR (Ire) 6-11-4 (5") Mr G Elliott, . . (14 to 1) su
Dist: 20l, 13l, 15l, 1½l. 4m 19.80s. (15 Ran).

(Curt Hill Syndicate), Patrick Joseph Flynn

FAIRYHOUSE (IRE) (good)
Wednesday January 15th
Going Correction: PLUS 0.35 sec. per fur.

2166 Fairyhouse E.B.F. Mares Maiden Hurdle (4-y-o and up) £4,110 2¼m . . . . (1:00)

2080² WINDY BEE (Ire) 6-11-7 (7") A Nolan, ... (4 to 1) 1
2073⁸ BORO BOW (Ire) 6-12-0 T P Treacy, ... (5 to 2 jt-fav) 2
EOIN'S ORCHESTRA (Ire) 8-12-0 C F Swan, ... (6 to 1) 3
1895 LADY ARGYLE (Ire) 6-11-6 F J Flood, ... (20 to 1) 4
2056⁴ ARABIAN SPRITE (Ire) 9-12-0 Mr P J Healy, ... (7 to 1) 5
MARKET LASS (Ire) 5-11-2 J Shortt, ... (14 to 1) 6
2079² RAHEEN RIVER (Ire) 6-11-6 C O'Dwyer, ... (5 to 2 jt-fav) 7

625⁵ THATS MY WIFE (Ire) 6-11-3 (3") J Butler, ... (10 to 1) 8
1901 POLITICAL TROUBLES (Ire) 7-11-6 K F O'Brien, . . (20 to 1) 9
SHE'S OUR MARE (Ire) 4-10-9 A Powell, ... (20 to 1) 10
2079⁸ CLOSING THYNE (Ire) 6-10-13 (7") L J Fleming, . . . (20 to 1) 11
2040⁹ ANNIE OAKLEY (Ire) 5-11-2 F Woods, ... (25 to 1) 12
1895 CAROLANNS CHOICE (Ire) 8-10-13 (7") R P Hogan,
. . . . (50 to 1) 13
1897 STORM COURSE (Ire) 5-10-9 (7") D K Budds, ... (20 to 1) 14
1905⁸ UNYOKE RAMBLER (Ire) 7-11-3 (3") D P Murphy, (25 to 1) 15
Dist: 1l, 7l, 1l, 10l. 4m 27.70s. a 15.70s (15 Ran).
SR: 6/5/-/-/-/-/ (Brian Nolan), Brian Nolan

2167 Widgeon Handicap Chase (0-120 5-y-o and up) £3,082 2m . . . . . . (1:30)

1841⁴ SCOBIE BOY (Ire) [-] 9-11-6 J P Broderick, ... (2 to 1) 1
2136² BARNAGEERA BOY (Ire) [-] 8-11-11 K F O'Brien, (Evens fav) 2
1650⁴ MINSTREL FIRE (Ire) [-] 9-11-2 P Carberry, ... (7 to 1) 3
1906¹ HANNIES GIRL (Ire) [-] 8-9-9 (7") L J Fleming, ... (11 to 2) 4
Dist: 7l, 11l, 25l. 4m 7.60s. a 13.60s (4 Ran).
SR: 12/10/-/-/ (R V Shaw), R V Shaw

2168 Goosander Maiden Hurdle (5-y-o) £3,082 2m. . . . . (2:00)

1275 GREY GUY (Ire) 11-2 F Woods, ... (4 to 1) 1
2049² SAVING BOND (Ire) 11-10 R Hughes, ... (11 to 10 fav) 2
2049⁶ FILL THE BILL (Ire) 11-10 C F Swan, ... (6 to 1) 3
2049⁴ JACK YEATS (Ire) 11-10 S C Lyons, ... (10 to 1) 4
2072⁵ GENTLE MOSSY (Ire) 11-2 D H O'Connor, ... (10 to 1) 5
2049⁹ NATIVE FLING (Ire) 11-7 (3") U Smyth, ... (12 to 1) 6
1907² THINKERS CORNER (Ire) 10-13 (3") G Cotter, ... (10 to 1) 7
2106⁹ TOURING-TURTLE (Ire) 11-2 D J Casey, ... (25 to 1) 8
GLEN CAMDEN (Ire) 11-2 K F O'Brien, ... (14 to 1) 9
1579³ MIDDLEOFTHENIGHT (Ire) 10-11 P Carberry, ... (20 to 1) 10
1756 CAHERMURPHY (Ire) 11-2 J Shortt, ... (33 to 1) 11
2054⁵ CASTLE COIN (Ire) 11-2 T Horgan, ... (12 to 1) 12
2054 WEE ICEMAN (Ire) 11-2 C O'Dwyer, ... (14 to 1) 13
1897⁹ ARE YOU SAILING (Ire) 11-2 C O'Brien, ... (33 to 1) 14
2131 LADY OF GRANGE (Ire) 11-5 F J Flood, ... (14 to 1) 15
Dist: 2½l, 2l, hd, 1l. 3m 55.50s. a 11.50s (15 Ran).
SR: 29/34/32/32/23/-/ (Frank Conroy), A L T Moore

2169 Eider Handicap Chase (0-109 5-y-o and up) £3,082 3m 1f. . . . . (2:30)

2059² BAILE NA GCLOCH (Ire) [-] 8-10-10 (3") D P Murphy, (9 to 2) 1
2091² CASTALINO [-] 11-11-2 C F Swan, ... (3 to 1 fav) 2
2099⁵ OLYMPIC D'OR (Ire) [-] 9-11-4 J Shortt, ... (10 to 1) 3
2059⁴ FAIR GO [-] 11-9-0 (7") Mrs C Harrison, ... (10 to 1) 4
2059 FAIRY MIST (Ire) [-] 9-9-4 (3") G Cotter, ... (11 to 1) 5
2078⁶ MONKEY AGO [-] 10-11-7 (7") Mr J L Cullen, ... (14 to 1) 6
1538 CORSTON DANCER (Ire) [-] (bl) 9-10-13 T Horgan, (12 to 1) 7
1903⁴ VELEDA II (Fr) [-] 10-11-1 (3") K Whelan, ... (11 to 2) 8
2141 EDENAKILL LAD [-] 10-10-7 C O'Dwyer, ... (4 to 1) 9
1363⁶ ROSEEN [-] 8-9-9 (7") A O'Shea, ... (12 to 1) ur
Dist: 7l, 2½l, 2l, 1½l. 6m 43.40s. a 28.40s (10 Ran).
(B & T Murphy Syndicate), John P Berry

2170 Teal Handicap Hurdle (0-123 4-y-o and up) £3,082 2¼m . . . . (3:00)

2134² FIDDLERS BOW VI (Ire) [-] 9-10-13 P Carberry, (6 to 1 fav) 1
1714 MULKEV PRINCE (Ire) [-] 6-11-8 J Shortt, ... (10 to 1) 2
2016³ LEWISHAM (Ire) [-] 5-10-6 C F Swan, ... (7 to 1) 3
2037² RUM FUN (Ire) [-] 6-9-12 R Hughes, ... (12 to 1) 4
2095⁴ SLANEY GLOW (Ire) [-] 6-11-6 C O'Dwyer, ... (8 to 1) 5
1836² MERCHANTS QUAY (Ire) [-] 6-10-9 (3") G Cotter, . . (8 to 1) 6
2051 OWENBWEE (Ire) [-] 6-11-5 F Woods, ... (9 to 1) 7
POWER PACK (Ire) [-] 9-11-7 (3") Mr B R Hamilton, (10 to 1) 8
715⁷ REEVES (Ire) [-] 5-11-6 D J Casey, ... (8 to 1) 9
2071 LOVE AND PORTER (Ire) [-] 9-12-0 D H O'Connor, (16 to 1) 10
2037 HANNAH'S PET (Ire) [-] 7-9-0 (7") R P Hogan, . . . (50 to 1) 11
GLENHAVEN ARTIST (Ire) [-] 7-11-1 F J Flood, . . . (14 to 1) 12
Dist: 3½l, ½l, sht-hd, 1l. 4m 25.80s. a 13.80s (12 Ran).
SR: 10/15/-/-/-/-/ (Mrs A T B Kearney), Noel Meade

2171 Tattersalls Ireland EBF Mares Novices' Chase (6-y-o and up) £3,767 2 ½m. . . . . (3:30)

2139⁴ SHINING WILLOW 7-11-8 C O'Dwyer, ... (3 to 1) 1
2038¹ AMME ENAEK (Ire) (bl) 8-11-8 H Rogers, ... (8 to 1) 2
2077⁴ ROYAL ROSY (Ire) 6-11-8 C F Swan, ... (7 to 4 fav) 3
2099³ CREHELP EXPRESS (Ire) 7-10-13 (3") B Bowens, . . (9 to 2) f
1901 BUCKAMERE (Ire) 6-11-2 P L Malone, ... (50 to 1) ur
2139 CREATIVE BLAZE (Ire) 8-11-2 P Carberry, ... (11 to 4) bd
Dist: 1½l, 12l. 5m 17.70s. a 22.70s (6 Ran).

(S P Tindall), J R H Fowler

2172 Merganser I.N.H. Flat Race (5-y-o and up) £3,082 2m. . . . . (4:00)

ARCTIC CAMPER 5-11-3 (7") Mr P J Crowley, ... (14 to 1) 1
THE RED SIDE (Ire) 5-10-12 (7") Mr P G Murphy, . . (12 to 1) 2
2060² EMERALD PRINCE (Ire) 5-11-7 (3") Mr B M Cash, . . (3 to 1) 3
DINES (Ire) 5-11-10 Mr P Fenton, ... (14 to 1) 4
2022 THETHREETOMS (Ire) 6-11-7 (3") Mr T Gibney, ... (33 to 1) 5

282

2137 COUNCILLOR (Ire) 6-11-7 (7*) Mr M P Horan, ...(20 to 1) 6
232⁹ US FOUR (Ire) 7-11-11 (3*) Mr R Walsh, ... (16 to 1) 7
ANTRIM TOWN (Ire) 6-12-0 Mr G J Harford, ... (10 to 1) 8
BUTLER'S GROVE (Ire) 5-11-10 Mr T Mullins, . . .(Evens fav) 9
1432 RAGGLEPUSS (Ire) 7-11-4 (5*) Mr G Elliott, ...(25 to 1) 10
PLATIN GALE (Ire) 5-11-3 (7*) Mr S J Mahon, ... (20 to 1) 11
2022⁸ MEASURED STEP (Ire) 6-11-9 (5*) Mr J T McNamara,
. . . .(25 to 1) 12
SHOW UP (Ire) 5-11-10 Mr J P Dempsey, ... (12 to 1) 13
2054 TEACH NA FINIUNA (Ire) 5-10-12 (7*) Mr T P Walsh, (33 to 1) 14
SAN FAIRY ANN (Ire) 6-11-2 (7*) Mr J Keville, ... (14 to 1) 15
WOOLPACKER (Ire) 6-11-7 (7*) Mr E Sheehy, ... (8 to 1) 16
2098⁶ SLIMLINE CAT (Ire) 5-11-10 Mr D Marnane, ... (14 to 1) 17
2041⁸ IRISH OATS (Ire) (bl) 7-11-7 (7*) Mr R Marrs, ... (33 to 1) 18
581 EDELS FIRST (Ire) 8-11-2 (7*) Mr J P McNamara, . .(50 to 1) 19
Dist: 9l, 1½l, ½l, 1½l. 3m 50.50s. (19 Ran).

(G J Burke), J E Kiely

LUDLOW (good to firm)
Thursday January 16th
Going Correction: PLUS 0.10 sec. per fur. (races 1,2,5,7), MINUS 0.10 (3,4,6)

2173 Marshbrook Maiden Hurdle Class E (4-y-o and up) £2,682 2m . . . . . (1:10)

2023⁴ PERCY BRAITHWAITE (Ire) 5-11-1 (7*) K Hibbert, hdwy appr
3 out, led 2 out, ran on wl. . . . .(8 to 1 op 4 to 1) 1
1854² FITZWILLIAM (USA) 4-10-10 G Bradley, al prmnt, led appr 3
to 2 out, ev ch whn blun last, hrd rdn, ran on.
. . . .(5 to 4 fav op 5 to 4 on) 2
1866² MR DARCY 5-11-8 R Bellamy, chsd ldrs, rdn and outpcd appr
3 out, styd on frm 2 out. . . .(3 to 1 op 7 to 2 tchd 9 to 2) 3
1496⁸ BREAK THE RULES 5-11-8 C Maude, gd hdwy appr 3 out,
one pace frm 2 out. . . . . (5 to 1 op 7 to 2) 4
MEG'S MEMORY (Ire) 4-10-5 T Eley, gd hdwy appr 3 out, not
quicken frm 2 out, better for race.
. . . .(50 to 1 op 33 to 1 tchd 66 to 1) 5
1521⁵ BEST FRIEND 5-11-3 Derek Byrne, led till wknd appr 3 out.
. . . .(66 to 1 op 33 to 1) 6
ALISTOVER 4-9-12 (7*) X Aizpuru, prmnt till wknd appr 3 out.
. . . .(100 to 1 op 50 to 1) 7
1354⁵ QUESTAN 5-11-1 (7*) G Supple, chsd ldr, wknd quickly appr 3
out, tld off. . . . .(12 to 1 op 8 to 1) 8
RED LANE 7-11-8 Mr A Dalton, jmpd stickily, al beh, tld off.
. . . . (100 to 1 op 50 to 1) 9
TIME GOES ON 5-11-0 (3*) T Dascombe, al beh, tld off.
. . . . (66 to 1 op 50 to 1) 10
1980⁶ STEVIE'S WONDER (Ire) 7-11-8 Mr J L Llewellyn, unruly,
refused to strt, took no part. I
Dist: 1¼l, 3l, 4l, ¾l, 7l, 1¼l, dist, 8l, 1¾l. 3m 40.70s. a 8.70s (11 Ran).
SR: 23/9/18/14/-/1/ (Glass Pig Racing Syndicate), Miss P M Whittle

2174 Neenton Selling Handicap Hurdle Class G (0-95 4-y-o and up) £2,024 2m . . . . (1:40)

1943³ FASTINI GOLD [70] 5-10-7 M A Fitzgerald, hdwy 3 out, quickened to ld cl hme. . . . . (4 to 1 jt-fav op 7 to 1) 1
1546⁶ ASTRAL INVASION (USA) [81] (bl) 6-10-11 (7*) R Hobson, led,
hrd rdn last, hdd nr finish . . . . (14 to 1 op 12 to 1) 2
1843² COSMIC STAR [63] (bl) 7-9-7 (7*) X Aizpuru, al prmnt, jnd ldr
on bit 3 out, hrd rdn and not quicken frm last.
. . . . (6 to 1 op 4 to 1) 3
1798⁶ THEM TIMES (Ire) [66] 8-10-3 S Wynne, chsd ldr to 3 out,
rallied appr last, one pace. . . . . (8 to 1 op 6 to 1) 4
1816⁷ LITTLE HOOLIGAN [81] 6-11-1 (3*) T Dascombe, hdwy and
ev ch appr 3 out, one pace frm 2 out. . . . .(4 to 1 jt-
fav op 9 to 1) 5
1800⁴ TEE TEE TOO (Ire) [76] 5-10-13 W Marston, prmnt till blun
3rd, one pace frm 3 out. . . . . (6 to 1 op 5 to 1) 6
1683 DENOMINATION (USA) [87] 5-11-10 C Maude, hld up and
beh, effrt and rdn appr 3 out, nvr nr ldrs.
. . . .(9 to 2 op 3 to 1 tchd 5 to 1) 7
1980⁶ LAJADHAL (Fr) [71] 8-10-8 L Harvey, al beh.
. . . . (14 to 1 op 10 to 1) 8
1472⁸ AGAINST THE CLOCK [63] 5-10-0 R Johnson, prmnt till wknd
appr 3 out. (14 to 1 op 10 to 1) 9
1472³ SCALP 'EM (Ire) [63] 9-10-0 Dr P Pritchard, wl beh frm 6th, pld
up bef last. . . . .(25 to 1 op 20 to 1) pu
Dist: 1½l, nk, 5l, nk, ¾l, 11l, 6l, 20l. 3m 42.60s. a 10.60s (10 Ran).

(G A Summers), M D I Usher

2175 Tenbury Handicap Chase Class D (0-125 5-y-o and up) £3,566 3m . . . . (2:10)

1879* IMPERIAL VINTAGE (Ire) [115] 7-11-5 N Williamson, mstks,
blun 4th, led twelfth, ran on gmely.
. . . .(7 to 2 op 4 to 1 tchd 9 to 2) 1
2011² FORTUNES COURSE (Ire) [96] 8-10-0 T J Murphy, chsd to 3rd,
second whn blun 13th, ev ch last, ran on.
. . . .(5 to 1 tchd 6 to 1) 2
1774⁵ DARK OAK [111] 11-11-1 Derek Byrne, hdwy 14th, jnd wnr
and ev ch frm 4 out, ran on . . . .(16 to 1 op 12 to 1) 3

1511² FIVELEIGH BUILDS [124] 10-12-0 A Thornton, hdwy twelfth,
ev ch 4 out, one pace frm 2 out.
. . . .(11 to 1 op 8 to 1 tchd 12 to 1) 4
1721³ COOLREE (Ire) [110] 9-11-0 M A Fitzgerald, al prmnt, ev ch 4
out, one pace frm nxt. . . . . (5 to 1 op 4 to 1) 5
2031² GOD SPEED YOU (Ire) [101] (bl) 8-10-5 J R Kavanagh, led
3rd, hit 5th, ran out aftr 11th, continued, tld off after.
. . . . (13 to 8 fav op 2 to 1) 6
1926⁶ ANDRELOT [113] (bl) 10-11-3 R Johnson, lft in ld aftr 11th,
hdd 12th, wknd 15th, tld off. . . . .(25 to 1 op 20 to 1) 7
1833³ WELL BRIEFED [113] 10-11-3 B Powell, blun and lost tch
twelfth, tld off whn pld up bef 3 out. . . . (16 to 1 op 14 to 1) pu
Dist: Hd, hd, 4l, nk, 25l, 30l. 5m 53.50s. a 6.50s (8 Ran).
SR: 2/-/-/-/-/ (David M Williams), Miss Venetia Williams

2176 Longmynd Novices' Handicap Chase Class E (0-105 5-y-o and up) £2,948 2m . . . . (2:40)

1979³ NORTHERN SINGER [77] 7-9-13² (3*) T Dascombe, al prmnt,
led 8th, ran on wl. . . . . (16 to 1 op 12 to 1) 1
1979⁴ BOLD ACRE [77] (bl) 7-10-0 R Johnson, chsd ldr, ev ch whn
hit 4 out, no imprsn. . . . (14 to 1 op 12 to 1 tchd 16 to 1) 2
1704³ LOBSTER COTTAGE [88] 9-10-11 S McNeill, jmpd lft, led to
8th, one pace frm 3 out. . . . .(11 to 2 op 4 to 1) 3
1741 UK HYGIENE (Ire) [82] 7-10-5² R Garritty, chsd ldrs, one pace
frm 3 out. . . . . (9 to 2 op 7 to 2 tchd 5 to 1) 4
1957³ DANTE'S VIEW (USA) [91] 9-11-0 D O'Sullivan, nvr nr to chal.
. . . . (tchd 9 to 2) 5
2093 HOLY WANDERER (USA) [96] 8-11-2 (3*) G Hogan, hld up in
rear, gd hdwy 9th, wknd 3 out. . . . .(7 to 2 fav tchd 4 to 1) 6
DARA'S COURSE (Ire) [77] 8-10-0 T J Murphy, prmnt till wknd
8th. . . . .(25 to 1 op 20 to 1) 7
1216 ICE MAGIC [77] (v) 10-10-0 B Fenton, tld off frm 4 out.
. . . . (33 to 1 op 20 to 1) 8
1979² SCOTTISH BAMBI [105] 9-12-0 A Thornton, hld up, effrt 8th,
sn wknd, pld up bef 2 out. . . . . (4 to 1 op 11 to 2) pu
2025 NUNSON [77] 8-10-0 B Powell, tld off frm 7th, pld up bef 4 out.
. . . . (50 to 1) pu
Dist: 3½l, 5l, nk, 3l, 20l, 8l. chsd. 3m 54.10s. a 4.10s (10 Ran).
SR: 15/11/17/11/17/2/ (Joe Panes), R J Hodges

2177 Welshpool Handicap Hurdle Class F (0-100 5-y-o and up) £2,528 3¼m 110yds . . . . (3:10)

2030⁹ GUNMAKER [72] 8-10-4 N Williamson, hdwy 9th, str run frm 2
out, led last hundred yards.
. . . . (5 to 1 op 9 to 2 tchd 11 to 2) 1
1140 BRINDLEY HOUSE [90] 10-11-8 D Walsh, led to 3 out, rallied
last, ran on. . . . .(25 to 1 op 16 to 1) 2
1708⁴ FIRST CRACK [84] 12-11-2 S Wynne, hld up, smooth hdwy 4
out, led 3 out, clr 2 out, wknd and hdd last hundred yards.
. . . . (10 to 1) 3
285⁵ DERRING BRIDGE [86] 7-11-4 A Thornton, chsd ldrs, outpcd
4 out, styd on frm 2 out. . . . . (12 to 1 tchd 14 to 1) 4
1796 CRAVATE (Fr) [68] 7-9-7 (7*) M Moran, hdwy 4 out, nvr nr to
chal. . . . .(50 to 1 op 33 to 1) 5
1796⁸ AWESTRUCK [70] (bl) 7-10-2² T Jenks, chsd ldr till rdn and
wknd aftr 4 out. . . . .(25 to 1 op 20 to 1) 6
1938² RARE SPREAD (Ire) [78] 7-10-10 C Maude, beh till hdwy 4, sn
rdn and wknd. . . . .(9 to 2 jt-fav tchd 5 to 1) 7
1858⁶ TIGER CLAW (USA) [81] 11-10-6 (7*) Mr G Shenkin, prmnt till
wknd 9th. . . . .(12 to 1 op 8 to 1 tchd 14 to 1) 8
1593 WESTERLY GALE (Ire) [86] 7-11-4 M A Fitzgerald, prmnt till
wknd quickly 4 out. . . . .(7 to 1 op 6 to 1) 9
2025⁴ EVEZIO RUFO [85] (v) 5-11-3 B Powell, prmnt till hrd rdn and
wknd 4 out. . . . .(9 to 2 jt-fav op 5 to 1) 10
2025 MISTER BLAKE [92] 7-11-10 R Johnson, lost tch 9th, pld up
bef 3 out. . . . .(5 to 1 op 3 to 1) pu
Dist: 1¼l, 1¼l, 20l, 1l, 1¼l, 3l, ¾l, 5l, 1½l. 6m 17.70s. a 12.70s (11 Ran).
(B J Llewellyn), B J Llewellyn

2178 Telford Novices' Chase Class E (5-y-o and up) £3,013 2½m . . . . . . (3:40)

1494 INCH EMPEROR (Ire) 7-11-5 T J Murphy, jmpd wl, made all,
quickened 3 out, easily. . . . . .(9 to 2 op 6 to 1 tchd 13 to 2) 1
1981 JOLLY BOAT 10-11-5 S Wynne, chsd wnr, ev ch 4 out, wknd
and hit 3 out. . . . . . .(11 to 8 fav op 5 to 4 tchd 6 to 4) 2
AEOLIAN 6-10-12 (7*) K Hibbert, hdwy 12th, styd on, blun last,
not rch 1st 2. . . . .(66 to 1 op 50 to 1) 3
1870³ SNOWDON LILY 6-11-0 R Bellamy, wl beh till some hdwy 4
out, nvr nr to chal. . . . .(20 to 1 op 12 to 1) 4
1250⁶ MERRYHILL GOLD 6-11-5 Derek Byrne, prmnt till wknd 12th.
. . . .(20 to 1 op 14 to 1) 5
1788⁶ WHITE DIAMOND (v) 9-11-5 M Foster, drpd rear and rdn 6th,
no ch aftr. . . . .(9 to 2 op 4 to 1) 6
2033³ ARABIAN BOLD 9-11-5 W Marston, wl beh frm 12th, tld
off. . . . .(4 to 1 op 5 to 2) 7
Dist: 3l, 20l, 13l, 1¼l, 2½l, 25l. 5m 0.60s. a 11.60s (7 Ran).
(T V Cullen), A W Carroll

2179 Weatherbys 'Stars Of Tomorrow' National Hunt Flat Intermediate - Class H (4,5,6-y-o) £1,413 2m (4:10)

MOUNTAIN STORM 5-10-12 (7*) T Hagger, *al prmnt, led o'r
one furlong out, ran on wl*..............(4 to 1 op 5 to 2) 1
1887² SHEBANG (Ire) 5-10-12 (7*) Mr H Dunlop, *chsd clr ldr, led 2 fs
out, hdd o'r one out, not quicken*...(7 to 4 fav tchd 9 to 4) 2
JIM'S QUEST 4-10-0 (7*) M Moran, *hdwy 5 fs out, one pace fnl
2 furlongs*............................(6 to 1 op 9 to 2) 3
CERTAIN SHOT 6-10-12 (7*) R Hobson, *hdwy fnl 2 fs., lost
finish*............................(14 to 1 op 10 to 1) 4
1802² KING OF THE BLUES 5-10-12 (7*) M Griffiths, *prmnt till wknd
o'r 2 fs out*................(6 to 1 op 4 to 1 tchd 13 to 2) 5
2029⁵ BLOWING ROCK (Ire) 5-10-12 (7*) X Aizpuru, *nvr nr to chal*.
...................(12 to 1 op 10 to 1 tchd 14 to 1) 6
ITSAHARDLIFE (Ire) 6-10-12 (7*) R Burns, *nvr trbld ldrs.*
.... 7
SOCIETY TIMES (USA) 4-10-0 (7*) G Supple, *pld hrd, led, sn
wl clr, hdd and wknd quickly 2 fs out*....(6 to 1 op 5 to 1) 8
1768 SWEET MOUNT (Ire) 5-10-7 (7*) L Suthern, *wl beh fnl 6 fs.*
......................(12 to 1 tchd 14 to 1) 9
1949 JUST ANDY 6-10-12 (7*) Miss L Boswell, *prmnt till wknd 7 fs
out, tld off*...................................... 10
VITA NUOVA (Ire) 6-11-0 Mr A Mitchell, *very slwly away, al
beh, tld off*..............................(20 to 1) 11
JIMSUE 6-11-5 Mr L Lay, *al beh, tld off*............(33 to 1) 12
Dist: 5l, 2l, 4l, 5l, 8l, 3l, 1l, 1¼l, 25l, 1l. 3m 33.10s. (12 Ran).
(Anthony Speelman), N J Henderson

TAUNTON (good to firm)
Thursday January 16th
Going Correction: PLUS 0.25 sec. per fur.

2180 Levy Board January Conditional
Jockeys' Handicap Hurdle Class E
(0-115 4-y-o and up) £2,221 2m 3f
110yds.....................(1:20)

1936* ZINGIBAR [95] 5-10-2 Michael Brennan, *rear and pushed
alng 5th, hdwy nxt, lft in ld 4 out, sn clr, drvn out r-in.*
.................................(8 to 1 op 6 to 1) 1
1723* BURLINGTON SAM (NZ) [89] 9-10-8 O Burrows, *chsd ldrs, lft
second 4 out, styd on und pres frm 2 out, not rch nxt*
...............................(9 to 2 op 3 to 1) 2
1603² FLEUR DE TAL [94] 6-10-8 (5*) J Power, *keen hold, led 4th till
appr 6th, wknd 3 out*......(9 to 2 op 5 to 1 tchd 4 to 1) 3
1923⁴ EURO SINGER [95] 5-11-0 E Husband, *led, mstk 3rd and sn
hdd, drvn to chase ldr 6th, soon rdn, wknd 3 out.*
...............................(13 to 2 op 7 to 1) 4
1500⁴ VISION OF FREEDOM (Ire) [105] 9-11-10 D J Kavanagh, *al
beh, lost tch 6th*........(13 to 2 op 5 to 1 tchd 8 to 1) 5
1224² NORDIC BREEZE (Ire) [102] (bl) 5-11-2 (5*) B Moore, *trkd ldr,
led aftr 3rd to nxt, led appr 6th, still gng wl whn mstk and uns
rdr 4 out*...............(7 to 4 fav op 6 to 4 tchd 2 to 1) ur
Dist: 2½l, 16l, 8l, 28l. 4m 37.60s. a 19.60s (6 Ran).
(D Holpin), J M Bradley

2181 Pickeridge Selling Hurdle Class G
(4,5,6-y-o) £1,857 2m 1f......(1:50)

2012 SAM ROCKETT (bl) 4-10-2 (5*) S Ryan, *trkd ldrs, led appr 2
out, readily*...........................(16 to 1 op 14 to 1) 1
1943* D'NAAN (Ire) (bl) 4-11-0 A P McCoy, *led, pld hrd, sn clr, rdn
alng frm 5th, hdd appr 2 out, soon one pace.*
...............(6 to 4 on op 7 to 4 on tchd 5 to 4 on and 6 to 5 on) 2
1992⁶ PAULTON 4-10-7 R Greene, *in tch, some prog frm 3 out, not a
dngr*....................(10 to 1 op 14 to 1 tchd 25 to 1) 3
ROSE OF GLENN 6-11-0 R Farrant, *very slwly away and beh,
moderate hdwy frm 3 out.*
.................(16 to 1 op 10 to 1 tchd 20 to 1) 4
CONTRACT BRIDGE (Ire) 4-10-3¹ W McFarland, *slwly away,
al beh*.....................(6 to 1 op 9 to 4 tchd 13 to 2) 5
1860⁵ ADONISIS 5-11-5 P Holley, *prmnt, rdn and wkng whn mstk 3
out*...........................(10 to 1 op 6 to 1) 6
1943⁴ SMILEY FACE 5-10-12 (7*) J Harris, *chsd ldrs, 3rd and wkng
whn mstk 3 out*.......(11 to 1 op 14 to 1 tchd 16 to 1) 7
1412 AAVASAKSA (Fr) 4-10-7 J Osborne, *hdwy 5th, rdn and wknd 4
out*...................(12 to 1 op 16 to 1 tchd 10 to 1) 8
2035⁷ BABA SAM (Ire) 6-11-0 (5*) Mr R Thornton, *hdwy 5th, wknd
and mstk 4 out*.......(40 to 1 op 33 to 1 tchd 50 to 1) 9
PRINCE RUDOLF (Ire) 5-10-12 (7*) N Willmington, *in tch whn f
3rd*.........................(20 to 1 op 10 to 1 tchd 25 to 1) f
1956 NORFOLK GLORY 5-11-5 Mr A Holdsworth, *slwly away, sn
reco'red, chasing ldrs whn uns rdr 3rd.*
.................................(100 to 1 op 50 to 1) ur
1980 WOODLANDS ENERGY 6-11-0 C Llewellyn, *beh frm 4th, tld
off whn pld up bef 2 out.*(50 to 1 op 33 to 1 tchd 66 to 1) pu
Dist: 9l, 8l, 6l, 5l, 1½l, 1½l, 8l, 15l. 3m 59.70s. a 16.70s (12 Ran).
(P M Mooney), P Mooney

2182 Stephen Little and Dick Reynolds
Bookmakers Handicap Chase Class
B for the Cecil Hunt Memorial Trophy
(0-145 5-y-o and up) £6,937 4¼m
110yds.....................(2:20)

1853⁴ WOODLANDS GENHIRE [105] (bl) 12-10-0 C Llewellyn, *trkd
ldr, led 23rd, drvn and hld on wl frm 2 out.*
.................................(100 to 1 op 66 to 1) 1
1757⁴ EVANGELICA (USA) [125] 7-11-6 A P McCoy, *hdwy to chase
ldrs tenth, rdn and styd on to chase wnr frm 3 out, kpt on.*
..................(11 to 4 jt-fav op 5 to 2 tchd 3 to 1) 2
1853³ FROZEN DROP [105] 10-10-0 S Fox, *chsd ldrs, hit 18th, styd
on und pres frm 4 out, not pace to chal r-in.*
.................................(9 to 1 op 8 to 1) 3
1960⁴ SUNLEY BAY [123] 11-11-4 P Hide, *chsd ldrs, mstk 13th, lost
pl 19th, ran on frm 21st, one pace r-in...*(13 to 2 op 9 to 2) 4
1664* BADASTAN (Ire) [115] (bl) 8-10-10 G Tormey, *led to 23rd,
rallied to chal 4 out, wknd quickly 2 out, collapsed aftr line.*
.........................(11 to 4 jt-fav op 3 to 1) 5
1626⁵ KILLESHIN [133] 11-11-7 (7*) A Dowling, *nvr gng wl, sn tld off,
pld up bef 17th*.............(9 to 1 op 6 to 1 tchd 10 to 1) pu
DISTILLATION [105] 12-9-9 (5*) Mr R Thornton, *hdwy und
pres 13th, blun 15th, tld off whn pld up bef 3 out.*
.................(66 to 1 op 50 to 1 tchd 100 to 1) pu
1892³ HAVE TO THINK [128] 9-11-9 D Bridgwater, *wnt prmnt 11th,
rdn and beh 20th, tld off whn pld up bef 4 out.*
.................(16 to 1 op 14 to 1 tchd 33 to 1) pu
1739² WOODLANDS BOY (Ire) [105] 9-10-0 D Morris, *hit 11th, rdn
alng frm 12th, hdwy 20th, mstk nxt and wknd, tld off whn pld up
bef 3 out*.................(13 to 2 op 6 to 1 tchd 11 to 2) pu
2157⁹ MASKED MARTIN [111] (bl) 6-10-6⁸ S Burrough, *mstks, beh
frm 11th, tld off 14th, pld up bef 21st.*(200 to 1 op 100 to 1) pu
Dist: 2½l, 1½l, sht-nd, 6l. 9m 1.50s. a 40.50s (10 Ran).
(Woodlands (Worcestershire) Ltd), P A Pritchard

2183 European Breeders Fund 'National
Hunt' Novices' Hurdle Qualifier
Class D (5,6,7-y-o) £3,137 2m 3f
110yds.....................(2:50)

1775² SPRING GALE (Ire) 6-11-10 J Osborne, *hld up gng wl, chlgd
frm 4 out, led 2 out, readily.*
.....................(6 to 5 fav op 6 to 4 tchd 13 to 8) 1
1959* EDGEMOOR PRINCE 6-11-10 A Maguire, *led, drvn alng frm
3 out, hdd nxt, sn one pace.* (2 to 1 op 6 to 4 tchd 9 to 4) 2
1540⁴ WEATHER WISE 5-10-7 (7*) J Power, *al chasing ldrs, rdn and
one pace frm 3 out*..........................(12 to 1) 3
2032³ DI'S LAST 7-10-9 A P McCoy, *sn chasing ldrs, rdn 5th, wknd 3
out*.........................(5 to 1 op 4 to 1) 4
1723⁴ ELEANORA MUSE 7-10-6 (3*) Guy Lewis, *mid-div, rdn alng
5th, wknd nxt*......(14 to 1 op 12 to 1 tchd 16 to 1) 5
1961 BROWN WREN 6-10-9 G Tormey, *beh 5th.*
.....................(10 to 1 op 12 to 1 tchd 20 to 1) 6
2035⁶ DERRYS PREROGATIVE 7-11-0 D Bridgwater, *mstk 6th, al
beh*...................(66 to 1 op 33 to 1 tchd 100 to 1) 7
1961 LILLY THE FILLY 6-10-9 R Greene, *al beh.*
.................(100 to 1 op 50 to 1 tchd 150 to 1) 8
1578 MISSED THE MATCH 7-11-0 P McLoughlin, *keen hold, prmnt
to 5th, sn wknd*.....................(10 to 1 op 50 to 1) 9
PICCOLINA 5-10-9 J Railton, *hit 4th, sn beh.*
.....................(14 to 1 op 12 to 1) 10
1053 SIERRA NEVADA 6-10-9 (5*) O Burrows, *beh 5th.*
.................(16 to 1 op 12 to 1 tchd 20 to 1) 11
1792 TINKER'S CUSS 6-10-9 S Curran, *beh 5th.*
.................(66 to 1 op 50 to 1 tchd 150 to 1) 12
BIG THEO 6-11-0 P Holley, *hdwy 6th, wknd and pld up bef 2
out*...................(20 to 1 op 12 to 1) pu
Dist: 2l, 3l, 11l, 9l, ¾l, 7l, 7l, 22l, ¾l, 5l. 4m 36.80s. a 18.80s (13 Ran).
(M Crabb, B Ead, M Moore), O Sherwood

2184 Bickenhall Novices' Handicap Chase
Class D (0-110 5-y-o and up) £3,550
2m 3f.....................(3:20)

1267⁵ OLLIVER DUCKETT [76] 8-10-6 G Tormey, *chsd ldrs, led aftr
4th, drvn alng frm 3 out, styd on gmely r-in.*
.................(14 to 1 op 12 to 1 tchd 16 to 1) 1
1666³ THE MINE CAPTAIN [98] 10-12-0 J Osborne, *hld up in tch,
improved 9th, reminder 3 out, sn chalg, still ev ch last, no extr.*
.....................(2 to 1 tchd 9 to 4) 2
1958³ WINNOW [70] 7-9-7 (7*) C Rae, *led till aftr 4th, outpcd tenth,
styd on frm 2 out*........(13 to 2 op 6 to 1 tchd 7 to 1) 3
1857⁴ CHRIS'S GLEN [77] (v) 8-10-2 (5*) Michael Brennan, *chsd
ldrs, hit 7th, wknd 3 out*.(13 to 2 op 10 to 1 tchd 7 to 1) 4
1970³ BRIDEPARK ROSE (Ire) [82] 9-10-12 S Fox, *hit 6th, drpd rear,
mstks 8th and tenth, hdwy appr 3 out, wknd nxt.*
.................(6 to 4 fav op 7 to 4 tchd 2 to 1) 5
1970 GORDON [90] 6-11-6 A Maguire, *beh, brief effrt 4 out, sn
wknd*.......................(8 to 1 op 6 to 1) 6
Dist: 1l, 7l, 6l, 5l, 17l. 4m 53.80s. a 22.80s (6 Ran).
(M A Long), C L Popham

2185 Yarcombe Novices' Handicap Hurdle
Class E (0-100 4-y-o and up) £2,475
2m 1f.....................(3:50)

1415⁴ LITTLE SHEFFORD [75] 5-10-6 I Lawrence, *led, clr appr 5th,
clear ag'n 2 out, drvn out.*
.................(20 to 1 op 10 to 1 tchd 25 to 1) 1
1733 SKRAM [87] 4-10-6 A Maguire, *al chasing ldrs, rdn and kpt on
wl appr last, not rch wnr r-in.*
.................(14 to 1 op 7 to 1 tchd 16 to 1) 2

1705[4] ATH CHEANNAITHE (Fr) [82] 5-10-13 D Bridgwater, *chsd ldrs, one pace aftr 3 out*.....(16 to 1 op 8 to 1 tchd 20 to 1) 3
1683* SHIFT AGAIN (Ire) [84] (bl) 5-10-10 (5*) Sophie Mitchell, *rapid hdwy to chase ldrs 5th, wknd 2 out.*
.... (13 to 2 op 9 to 2 tchd 7 to 1) 4
2035* ULTIMATE SMOOTHIE [97] 5-12-0 A P McCoy, *hdwy 5th, sn rdn, wknd appr 2 out.* (13 to 8 fav op 2 to 1 tchd 9 to 4) 5
1977[6] MILLING BROOK [75] 5-10-1 (5*) Michael Brennan, *wl beh 5th, moderate hdwy frm 3 out.*
.... (20 to 1 op 14 to 1 tchd 25 to 1) 6
1855[4] SHOW FAITH (Ire) [95] 7-11-12 J A McCarthy, *hdwy 4th, rdn four out, sn wknd*.........(5 to 1 op 7 to 2 tchd 11 to 2) 7
1135[3] ALMAPA [82] 5-10-6 (7*) J Harris, *nvr better than mid-div, mstk and wknd 3 out...* (14 to 1 op 10 to 1 tchd 16 to 1) 8
1855[6] SAHEL (Ire) [85] 9-11-2 S Curran, *prmnt to 5th.*
.... (14 to 1 op 10 to 1) 9
1917[5] CHILI HEIGHTS [77] (bl) 7-10-8 R Greene, *rdn alng 4th, sn beh.*......................(33 to 1 op 20 to 1) 10
SOBER ISLAND [69] 8-9-11 (3*) Guy Lewis, *slwly away, al beh.*.................... (66 to 1 op 33 to 1 tchd 80 to 1) 11
1947[3] COUNTRY MINSTREL (Ire) [76] 6-10-0 (7*) C Rae, *gd hdwy 5th, fifth and rdn whn stumbled and f aftr 2 out.*
.... (14 to 1 op 10 to 1) f
1574[2] PARADE RACER [72] 6-10-3 W McFarland, *beh till f 3 out.*
.... (10 to 1 op 7 to 1) f
Dist: 2½l, 8l, 4l, 5l, 1¾l, ½l, 2l, 3l, dist. 3m 53.80s. a 10.80s (13 Ran).
SR: 12/9/8/6/14/-/9/-/-/ (John Liddiard), M P Muggeridge

2186 Curland Handicap Hurdle Class D (0-120 4-y-o and up) £2,759 2m 1f (4:20)

LE KHOUMF (Fr) [110] 6-11-6 J Osborne, *trkd ldr 4th, led 5th, still gng wl whn wnt rght 2 out, readily.*
.... (100 to 30 op 3 to 1 tchd 7 to 2) 1
105* NINE O THREE (Ire) [105] 8-11-1 D Gallagher, *chsd ldr to 4th, chased wnr appr 2 out, one pace.*
.... (100 to 30 op 7 to 2 tchd 4 to 1) 2
1947[2] GLOWING PATH [90] 7-9-7 (7*) J Harris, *in tch 4th, styd on same pace appr 2 out....* (7 to 1 op 6 to 1) 3
1596[4] YUBRALEE (USA) [114] 5-11-10 A P McCoy, *set str pace, sn clr, hdd 5th, wknd appr 2 out....* (3 to 1 fav tchd 4 to 1) 4
CHANTRY BEATH [93] 6-9-12 (5*) Sophie Mitchell, *al beh.*
.... (16 to 1 op 8 to 1) 5
1728[9] FIRST CENTURY (Ire) [102] 8-10-12 A Maguire, *sn beh, tld off 5th.*....................(33 to 1 op 12 to 1) 6
1923[2] PRIDEWOOD PICKER [94] 10-9-13 (5*) D J Kavanagh, *some hdwy 5th, fifth and no ch whn f last....*(4 to 1 tchd 5 to 1) f
Dist: 5l, 7l, 6l, 5l, dist. 3m 53.90s. a 10.90s (7 Ran).
SR: 25/15/-/11/ (David S Lewis), J Neville

KELSO (good)
Friday January 17th
Going Correction: PLUS 0.35 sec. per fur. (races 1,3,5), PLUS 0.55 (2,4,6)

2187 European Breeders Fund Tattersalls Ireland Mares' Novices' Chase Qualifier Class E (6-y-o and up) £3,436 2 ¾m 110yds. (1:00)

1825[2] SEEKING GOLD (Ire) 8-11-8 B Storey, *led to second, cl up till outpcd and pushed alng 13th, rdn to ld last, styd on wl.*
.... (11 to 4 op 2 to 1) 1
1916[2] ARDENT LOVE (Ire) 8-10-10 A Maguire, *not fluent, chsd ldrs and pushed alng frm 4th, hrd drvn 2 out, kpt on r-in.*
.... (7 to 2 op 5 to 2 tchd 4 to 1) 2
CALL ME BLACK (Ire) 8-10-10 R Garritty, *hld up, hmpd 5th, steady hdwy 13th, ev ch whn blun last, no extr.*
.... (6 to 1 op 7 to 1 tchd 8 to 1) 3
1913[5] CULLANE LAKE (Ire) 7-10-10 A S Smith, *cl up, led second, rdn 2 out, hit last and hdd, sn no extr.* (20 to 1 tchd 16 to 1) 4
OLD BETSY 79-10-10 Richard Guest, *trkd ldrs, hdwy to chal 12th, ev ch whn blun 2 out, not reco'r.* (33 to 1 op 16 to 1) 5
2062 ESTABLISH (Ire) 9-10-10 K Johnson, *hld up, hmpd 5th, sn beh, f 13th.*............ (16 to 1 op 14 to 1 tchd 25 to 1) f
GAME POINT 8-10-10 J Burke, *prmnt till f 5th.*
.... (66 to 1 op 50 to 1 tchd 100 to 1) f
WEEJUMPAWUD 7-10-10 Mr C Storey, *f 1st.*
.... (33 to 1 op 20 to 1) f
1957[4] TELLICHERRY 8-10-10 B Fenton, *trkd ldrs till hmpd and uns rdr 5th*.................... (2 to 1 fav op 9 to 4 tchd 5 to 2) ur
Dist: 4l, 1l, 2l, 13l. 5m 49.40s. a 25.40s (9 Ran).
(Gilry), J Barclay

2188 Glassedin Scottish Juvenile Novices' Hurdle Class C (4-y-o) £3,582 2m 110yds. (1:30)

2061* ROSSEL (USA) 11-9 A Dobbin, *trkd ldrs, led 5th, rdn last, ran on gmely.*............................(5 to 1 op 9 to 2) 1
SOLDAT (USA) 11-9 D Bridgwater, *hld up, hdwy whn hit 3 out, rdn alng nxt, swtchd lft and drvn r-in, kpt on.*
.... (2 to 1 on op 6 to 4 on tchd 11 to 8 on) 2

1909[3] JACKSON PARK 11-5 A Maguire, *made most to 5th, cl up, rdn and ev ch last, no extr nr finish*........ (8 to 1 op 6 to 1) 3
1909[4] J J BABOO (Ire) 11-0 R Garritty, *chsd ldrs, effrt appr 2 out, sn rdn and kpt on same pace*..........(25 to 1 op 16 to 1) 4
1629[4] MELTEMISON 10-11 (3*) Mr C Bonner, *prmnt, rdn alng appr 2 out, wknd approaching last*..........(12 to 1 op 8 to 1) 5
DOUBLE AGENT 11-0 P Carberry, *hesitant, led to 1st, wl th till no extr last 2*.................... (25 to 1 op 20 to 1) 6
1909[7] SOUSSE 10-9 P Niven, *al rear......* (40 to 1 op 33 to 1) 7
1384[8] CRY BABY 10-9 (5*) S Taylor, *cl up, rdn alng appr 3 out, sn btn*.................... (200 to 1 op 100 to 1) 8
1690[6] DOUBLE DASH (Ire) 11-5 D J Moffatt, *al rear....* (100 to 1) 9
1909[6] PERPETUAL LIGHT 10-9 Derek Byrne, *in tch, pushed alng bef 3 out, sn lost pl*.................... (66 to 1 op 20 to 1) 10
2061[6] MOUNTAIN DREAM 11-0 B Storey, *al rear, tld off 3 out.*
.... (66 to 1 op 50 to 1) 11
1384[6] MAPLETON 11-0 Richard Guest, *mid-div, beh hfwy.*
.... (66 to 1 op 50 to 1) 12
Dist: Nk, ¾l, 4l, 3½l, 2l, 7l, 7½l, 18l, 10l, 5l. 3m 59.40s. a 16.40s (12 Ran).
SR: 21/21/16/7/3/-/ (Allan W Melville), P Monteith

2189 Scottish Borders National Handicap Chase Class B (5-y-o and up) £20,902 4m. (2:00)

1660* SEVEN TOWERS (Ire) [125] 8-10-0 B Storey, *hld up, steady hdwy 16th, chlgd 2 out, rdn to ld r-in, ran on strly.*
.... (11 to 2 op 5 to 1 tchd 6 to 1) 1
1660[2] MONY-SKIP (Ire) [128] 8-10-3[3] Richard Guest, *al hndy, hdwy 5 out, led and hit 2 out, rdn last, hdd and no extr r-in.*
.... (16 to 1 op 14 to 1) 2
1639[3] LO STREGONE [150] 11-11-11 C F Swan, *mid-div, pushed alng 6 out, gd hdwy to join ldrs 3 out, rdn nxt, one pace appr last*.................... (11 to 2 tchd 6 to 1) 3
1529* INTO THE RED [133] 13-10-8 P Niven, *hld up, hdwy to chase ldrs hfwy, rdn alng and hit 5 out, styd on und pres frm 2 out.*
.... (5 to 1 fav op 9 to 2 tchd 11 to 2) 4
1746[3] ST MELLION FAIRWAY (Ire) [134] 8-10-9 A Maguire, *hld up, hdwy to chase ldrs hfwy, blun 5 out, rdn nxt, one pace appr 2 out*.................... (11 to 2 op 6 to 1) 5
1910[2] ASTINGS (Fr) [125] 9-10-0 P Carberry, *in tch whn blun and lost pl 11th, hdwy 5 out, rdn nxt, one pace 2 out.*
.... (9 to 1 op 8 to 1 tchd 10 to 1) 6
1745 NAZZARO [128] (bl) 8-10-3[3] A Thornton, *led, rdn alng 4 out, hdd 2 out, wknd*.................... (16 to 1) 7
1632[6] CEILIDH BOY [125] 11-10-0 A S Smith, *chsd ldrs, blun 18th, beh aftr*.................... (25 to 1 op 20 to 1) 8
1511 WHAAT FETTLE [130] 12-10-5 A Dobbin, *cl up, rdn alng 19th, sn lost pl*.................... (20 to 1 op 14 to 1) 9
1589 SIDE OF HILL [125] 12-9-11 (3*) G Lee, *prmnt, rdn alng 18th, sn beh*.................... (200 to 1) 10
2005* PINK GIN [125] 10-10-0 D Bridgwater, *al beh, reminders 9th, tld off hfwy*.................... (14 to 1 tchd 16 to 1) 11
1745[3] FULL OF OATS [125] 11-10-0 B Fenton, *trkd ldrs till f 17th.*
.... (7 to 1 op 6 to 1) f
1785[7] GREENHILL RAFFLES [125] (v) 11-10-0 M Foster, *chsd ldrs, rdn alng and lost pl 8eenth, beh whn pld up aftr 3 out.*
.... (100 to 1) pu
Dist: 4l, 8l, 3½l, 5l, 4l, 4l, 20l, 6l, 12l, dist. 8m 7.50s. a 14.50s (13 Ran).
SR: 39/38/52/31/27/14/13/-/-/ (Mrs E A Murray), Mrs M Reveley

2190 Tim Doody White Line Morebattle Hurdle Class B Limited Handicap (4-y-o and up) £4,769 2m 110yds (2:30)

1761[5] DIRECT ROUTE (Ire) [133] 6-10-12 P Carberry, *hld up, smooth hdwy appr 3 out, chlgd on bit last, led r-in, hrd held.*
.... (100 to 30 jt-fav op 7 to 2 tchd 4 to 1 and 3 to 1) 1
1680[5] UNCLE DOUG [127] 6-10-6 P Niven, *al cl up, led 2 out, hrd drvn and hdd r-in, no ch wth wnr....*(16 to 1 op 14 to 1) 2
1885[5] THORNTON GATE [125] 8-10-4 J Callaghan, *hld up, hdwy appr 3 out, rdn r-in, one pace....*(10 to 1 op 8 to 1) 3
INGLETONIAN [121] 8-10-0 B Storey, *al prmnt, rdn 2 out, cl up whn hmpd last, kpt on*..........(150 to 1 op 100 to 1) 4
1633[4] HOME COUNTIES (Ire) [142] (v) 8-11-7 D J Moffatt, *prmnt, rdn whn hit 3 out, sn wknd*.............. (5 to 1 op 9 to 2) 5
2004[4] MARCHANT MING (Fr) [141] 5-10-8 R Garritty, *led, rdn and hdd 2 out, hng lft appr last, sn wknd and eased.*
.... (5 to 1 op 9 to 2) 6
ARAGON AYR [121] 9-10-0 A Dobbin, *in tch, pushed alng hfwy, beh frm 3 out....*.................... (9 to 1) 7
1335[5] COMMON SOUND (Ire) [121] 6-9-9 (5*) Mr R Thornton, *in tch to hfwy, sn beh..........................*(33 to 1) 8
1030[2] HATTA BREEZE [141] 5-10-8 A Maguire, *in tch, effrt and hdwy 5th, rdn 3 out, wkng whn f nxt....*..........(100 to 30 jt-fav op 7 to 2 tchd 4 to 1) f
1911[4] JAZILAH (Fr) [121] 9-10-0 D Bridgwater, *al rear, tld off whn pld up bef 3 out....*.................... (10 to 1 op 20 to 1) pu
Dist: 1l, ½l, 3½l, 9l, 30l, 4l, 7l. 3m 55.70s. a 12.70s (10 Ran).
SR: 47/40/37/29/41/-/ (Chris Heron), J Howard Johnson

2191 Andrew Hamilton & Co. Rutherford Handicap Chase Class C (0-135 5-y-o and up) £4,421 2m 1f. (3:00)

1773[4] WEE RIVER (Ire) [125] 8-11-4 J Callaghan, *hld up, hdwy and hit 8th, led aftr 2 out, rdn and ran on wl frm last.*
.................................(7 to 4 tchd 2 to 1) 1
1678[3] REGAL ROMPER (Ire) [112] 9-10-5 Richard Guest, *led,hit 5th and hdd, led 8th, rdn 2 out, sn headed, rallied last, no extr last 100 yards.*................................(9 to 2 op 4 to 1) 2
1760 LORD DORCET (Ire) [133] 7-11-12 A Dobbin, *hld up, beh 6th, hdwy 3 out, hit nxt, drvn to chal last, no extr.*
.................................(6 to 4 fav tchd 11 to 8) 3
1821[4] ONE FOR THE POT [107] 12-10-0 M Foster, *cl up, led 5th to 8th, rdn alng and hit 3 out, sn wknd....*(20 to 1 op 14 to 1) 4
2000[4] SYBILLIN [135] 11-12-0 P Carberry, *hld up, hdwy 3 out, rdn and hit nxt, sn wknd....*(10 to 1 op 8 to 1 tchd 12 to 1) 5
1692[2] UNCLE BERT (Ire) [111] 7-10-4[4] A Thornton, *chsd ldrs, hit 4th, wknd bef four out...*.............(5 to 1 op 33 to 1) 6
Dist: 2l, 3½l, 9l, 9l, 3½l. 4m 15.80s. a 10.80s (6 Ran).

SR: 42/27/44/9/28/-/ (Sean Graham), G M Moore

2192 European Breeders Fund 'National Hunt' Novices' Hurdle Qualifier Class E (5,6,7-y-o) £2,584 2¼m
......................................(3:30)

2006[4] ALZULU (Ire) 6-11-10 P Carberry, *cl up, led 7th, clr whn blun last, easily.*....................(5 to 4 on op 6 to 4 on) 1
1887[5] REVOLT 5-11-0 C F Swan, *chsd ldrs, hdwy 5th, chasing wnr whn hit 2 out and last, kpt on same pace und pres.*
...................................(12 to 1 op 14 to 1 tchd 16 to 1) 2
1893[5] MYTHICAL APPROACH (Ire) 7-11-0 A Maguire, *chsd ldrs, rdn appr 2 out, sn one pace....*(9 to 2 op 5 to 1 tchd 6 to 1) 3
1657[2] MATA MAN (Ire) 7-11-0 A S Smith, *hld up beh, steady hdwy 4 out, kpt on wl appr last.* (14 to 1 op 16 to 1 tchd 20 to 1) 4
1609 JUDICIOUS NORMAN (Ire) 6-11-0 T Reed, *hld up and wl beh, steady hdwy appr 3 out, nvr plcd to chal.*
.................................(33 to 1 op 25 to 1) 5
1829 BORIS BROOK 6-10-7 (7') S Melrose, *chsd ldrs, rdn alng 4 out, wknd bef 2 out...*........................(200 to 1) 6
NORDIC PRINCE (Ire) 6-11-0 R Garritty, *in tch, effrt 4 out, sn rdn, one pace frm 2 out...*............(6 to 1 tchd 5 to 1) 7
1456[3] APRIL SEVENTH (Ire) 6-11-0 D Bridgwater, *led to 7th, sn rdn, wknd nxt.*...........................(16 to 1 tchd 20 to 1) 8
1818[7] PERSUASIVE TALENT (Ire) 6-11-0 J Burke, *chsd ldrs, rdn alng 4 out, wknd nxt.*...............(200 to 1 op 100 to 1) 9
1682 SMIDDY LAD 6-11-0 D Bentley, *in tch till wknd 4 out.*
.................................(100 to 1) 10
SOLSGIRTH 6-11-0 A Thornton, *not fluent, in tch to hfwy, sn lost pl...*.................................(200 to 1) 11
1657[1] SUNNY LEITH 6-11-0 A Dobbin, *beh hfwy.........*(50 to 1) 12
MY MAVOURNEEN 5-10-9 M Foster, *beh hfwy....*(100 to 1) 13
1887[4] THE SHARROW LEGEND (Ire) 5-11-0 B Storey, *beh hfwy.*
.................................(33 to 1) 14
GREAT GABLE (Ire) 6-11-0 D J Moffatt, *chsd ldrs, rdn 4 out, sn wknd...*.................................(200 to 1) 15
1963 MAKE A BUCK (bl) 7-11-0 R Supple, *prmnt, rdn alng and reminders 4th, sn beh.*......................(200 to 1) 16
132[8] GLACIAL GIRL (Ire) 5-10-9 K Johnson, *beh hfwy.* (200 to 1) 17
2116[8] KINGS HIGH (Ire) 7-11-0 S McDougall, *beh hfwy, tld off whn pld up r-in, lme.*.......................(200 to 1) pu
1789[8] BLUE CHEQUER 6-10-9 P Niven, *al beh, tld off whn pld up bef 2 out.*.................................(100 to 1) pu
Dist: 7l, 1¼l, 1¼l, hd, ¾l, 1¼l, 9l, 8l, 1¼l, 2l. 4m 28.30s. a 21.30s (19 Ran).
(D Buckle), J G FitzGerald

KEMPTON (good to firm) Friday January 17th
Going Correction: PLUS 0.05 sec. per fur.

2193 Runnymede Conditional Jockeys' Novices' Handicap Hurdle Class E (0-110 5-y-o and up) £2,780 3m 110yds.........................(1:40)

1940 CAPTAIN JACK [103] 7-11-11 D Walsh, *drvn into 1st 4 flights to dispute ld, pressed ldr till led 7th, driven and kpt on wl frm 2 out.*.................................(6 to 4 fav op Evens) 1
1958[5] BLAZING MIRACLE [78] 5-10-0 D Salter, *dsptd 3rd most of way, ran on und pres to take second nr finish, no imprsn.*
.................................(13 to 2 op 7 to 1 tchd 8 to 1) 2
CARDINAL GAYLE (Ire) [78] 7-10-0 P Henley, *last but in tch, pushed alng 7th, styd on into second appr 2 out, wknd r-in.*
.................................(7 to 1 tchd 6 to 1) 3
895 LODESTONE LAD (Ire) [78] 6-10-0 (5') X Aizpuru, *narrow ld to 7th, chsd wnr till wknd aftr 3 out....* (10 to 1 op 7 to 1) 4
1759[3] WANSTEAD (Ire) [86] (bl) 5-10-3 (5') N T Egan, *hld up disputing 3rd, chsd wnr aftr 3 out till appr nxt, sn wknd.*
.................................(9 to 4 op 2 to 1 tchd 5 to 2) 5
Dist: 5l, 3l, 30l, 1½l. 6m 5.90s. a 20.90s (5 Ran).

(Clive D Smith), M C Pipe

2194 Easter Hero Handicap Chase Class C (0-135 5-y-o and up) £4,463 2m
......................................(2:10)

1993[*] SUPER TACTICS (Ire) [131] 9-11-9 (3') P Henley, *in tch, gd hdwy 9th, trkd ldr 3 out, led sn aftr nxt, styd on wl r-in.*
.................................(5 to 2 fav op 2 to 1 tchd 11 to 4) 1
1643[*] FINE HARVEST [122] 11-11-3 T J Murphy, *trkd ldrs, chlgd 6th, sn led, wnt badly lft 3 out, hdd soon aftr nxt, no extr r-in.*
.................................(7 to 2 op 5 to 2) 2
1518 SENOR EL BETRUTTI (Ire) [133] 8-12-0 G Bradley, *wl beh till took hold of bit and hdwy frm 9th, chsd ldrs from 3 out, no extr r-in...*.................................(9 to 1 op 10 to 1) 3
1720[2] DEAR DO [108] 10-10-3[3] M A Fitzgerald, *hit 5th, hdwy 4 out, one pace frm nxt...........*(4 to 1 op 3 to 1 tchd 9 to 2) 4
1926[4] BALLY PARSON [110] 11-10-5 N Williamson, *wth ldr till blun 3rd, dsptd ld till aftr 6th, hit 9th, wknd 3 out.*
.................................(6 to 1 tchd 5 to 1) 5
1575 ARMALA [108] 12-10-2[2] (3') L Aspell, *al beh, moderate improvement frm 4 out...*(6 to 1 op 5 to 1 tchd 13 to 2) 6
1972[4] COUNT BARACHOIS (USA) [105] 9-10-0 K Gaule, *made most till aftr 6th, chsd ldr till wknd appr 3 out.*
.................................(50 to 1 op 33 to 1 tchd 66 to 1) 7
Dist: 1¾l, 1¼l, 6l, 12l, 8l, 3l. 3m 53.80s. a 7.80s (7 Ran).

SR: 28/17/26/-/ (H V Perry), R H Alner

2195 Walton Juvenile Novices' Hurdle Class B (4-y-o) £6,246 2m.....(2:40)

1610[3] SUMMER SPELL (USA) 10-10 M A Fitzgerald, *hld up, steady hdwy aftr 4th, chlgd on bit frm 2 out till slight ld last, sn clr.*
.................................(11 to 4 fav op 3 to 1 tchd 4 to 1) 1
1890 MR WILD (USA) 10-10 A P McCoy, *trkd ldrs, led 5th, drvn clr 3 out, hrd rdn nxt, hdd last, one pace......*(9 to 2 op 5 to 2) 2
QUALITY (Ire) 10-10 R Dunwoody, *gd hdwy aftr 5th, chsd ldrs 2 out, one pace und pres.* (10 to 1 op 6 to 1 tchd 12 to 1) 3
1854[*] FAR DAWN (USA) 11-2 C Maude, *in tch, drvn alng aftr 3 out, one pace frm nxt....*(3 to 1 op 5 to 2 tchd 10 to 3) 4
SULAWESI (Ire) 10-5 C Llewellyn, *beh, mstk 3rd, styd on frm 3 out, not trble ldrs....* (33 to 1 op 20 to 1 tchd 50 to 1) 5
BRILLIANT RED 10-10 M Richards, *hdwy 4th, chsd ldrs 3 out, wkng whn mstk nxt......*(10 to 1 op 6 to 1 tchd 12 to 1) 6
1861[*] DISALLOWED (Ire) 10-10 J F Titley, *wth ldrs till led 4th, sn hdd, aftr 3 out.........*(7 to 1 op 5 to 1 tchd 9 to 1) 7
1422[6] SEATTLE ALLEY (USA) 10-10 J Osborne, *beh till moderate hdwy frm 3 out.........*(14 to 1 tchd 16 to 1) 8
1861[5] BRANDON MAGIC 10-10 G Bradley, *wth ldrs till led aftr 4th, hdd nxt, hit 3 out and wknd quickly.*
.................................(16 to 1 op 12 to 1 tchd 20 to 1) 9
BRECON 10-10 J R Kavanagh, *al in rear.*
.................................(100 to 1 op 33 to 1) 10
SCATHEBURY 10-10 A Larnach, *beh frm hfwy.*
.................................(6 to 1 op 5 to 1 tchd 100 to 1) 11
1844[8] MAGIC ROLE 10-10 J Railton, *in tch to 4th.*
.................................(100 to 1 op 50 to 1) 12
2012 BAILIWICK 10-10 N Williamson, *al in rear.*
.................................(100 to 1 op 50 to 1) 13
1922 SAUCY DANCER 10-5 S McNeill, *sn beh.*
.................................(100 to 1 op 50 to 1) 14
MR HACKER 10-10 B Powell, *sn in rear.*
.................................(100 to 1 op 50 to 1) 15
1854[3] BARANOV (Ire) 10-10 D Gallagher, *led till jmpd badly lft and hdd 3rd, wknd aftr 5th, tld off whn pld up bef 2 out.*
.................................(20 to 1 op 12 to 1 tchd 25 to 1) pu
Dist: 3l, 4l, 1¾l, 16l, 3½l, 3l, 12l, 15l, 1l, 6l. 3m 53.90s a 5.60s (16 Ran).

SR: 34/31/27/31/4/5/7/-/ (W V & Mrs E S Robins), N J Henderson

2196 Hanworth Handicap Chase Class B (0-140 5-y-o and up) £5,006 3m
......................................(3:10)

1999 DEXTRA DOVE [137] 10-11-11 C Maude, *chlgd frm 5th till led 9th, hdd nxt, str chal whn lft in ld 3 out, drvn out r-in.*
.................................(11 to 4 op 9 to 4 tchd 3 to 1) 1
1833[2] PHILIP'S WOODY [115] 9-10-3 J R Kavanagh, *rdn in 4th in tch, hdwy to chase ldrs whn lft cl second 3 out, ev ch frm nxt till one pace r-in.........*(100 to 30 op 5 to 2 tchd 7 to 2) 2
ROSE KING [114] 10-10-2[5] (3') L Aspell, *keen hold, rcd in 3rd till improved to chase ldr briefly 15th, one pace appr 3 out.*
.................................(16 to 1 op 33 to 1) 3
1499[4] LE MEILLE (Ire) [112] 8-10-0 N Williamson, *hld up in 5th, hdwy and hit 13th, one pace in 3rd whn blun 2 out.*
.................................(3 to 1 tchd 10 to 3) 4
1563[4] GREY SMOKE [129] 7-11-3 J F Titley, *made most, briefly hdd 9th, still slight ld and gng wl whn f 3 out.*
.................................(9 to 4 fav op 2 to 1) f
Dist: 3l, 8l, 2½l. 6m 5.20s. a 16.20s (5 Ran).

(Dextra Lighting Systems), Simon Earle

2197 Ashford Novices' Hurdle Class B (5-y-o and up) £6,376 2m.......(3:40)

2042[2] SECRET SPRING (Fr) 5-11-4 M Richards, *hld up, steady hdwy frm 5th, trkd ldrs 2 out, drvn into slight ld last, held on wl.*
.................................(3 to 1 op 5 to 2 tchd 7 to 2) 1
1805[*] SHARPICAL 5-11-4 M A Fitzgerald, *hld up and confidently rdn, smooth hdwy 3 out, chlgd on bit last, sn ridden, no imprsn.........*(5 to 2 op 2 to 1 tchd 11 to 4) 2
1866[*] DARAYDAN (Ire) 5-11-8 A P McCoy, *led, sn clr, reminder 5th, hdd last, soon btn....* (5 to 2 fav op 2 to 1 tchd 11 to 4) 3

1866⁴ CARLITO BRIGANTE 5-10-12 J Osborne, *al tracking ldrs, rdn 2 out, sn one pace* ..... (25 to 1 op 16 to 1 tchd 33 to 1) 4
1641³ NORDANCE PRINCE (Ire) 6-10-12 R Dunwoody, *hdwy to chase ldrs 4th, rdn 3 out, wknd appr 2 out.*
.... (10 to 1 op 8 to 1 tchd 11 to 1) 5
PEETSIE (Ire) 5-10-7 C Llewellyn, *prmnt, chsd ldr briefly aftr 4th, wknd after 3 out* ... (50 to 1 op 33 to 1 tchd 66 to 1) 6
BLOMBERG (Ire) 5-10-12 P Hide, *chsd ldr till wknd aftr 3 out.*
.... (9 to 2 op 7 to 2 tchd 5 to 1) 7
1719³ BATTLESHIP BRUCE 5-10-12 D Gallagher, *hmpd second, al beh* .... (50 to 1 op 33 to 1 tchd 66 to 1) 8
AT LIBERTY (Ire) 5-10-12 N Williamson, *effrt into mid-div 4th, wknd aftr nxt* .... (50 to 1 op 33 to 1 tchd 66 to 1) 9
CLOCK WATCHERS 9-10-12 D Morris, *hmpd second, al beh.*
.... (100 to 1 tchd 200 to 1) 10
1866⁵ SHADIRWAN (Ire) 6-10-12 G Bradley, *chasing ldr whn f second* .... (33 to 1 op 20 to 1) f
1759⁶ RESIST THE FORCE (USA) 7-11-8 L Aspell, *beh, effrt 5th, wknd 3 out, pld up bef nxt* .... (20 to 1 op 14 to 1) pu
ITANI 5-10-12 I Lawrence, *beh most of way, tld off whn pld up bef 2 out* .... (100 to 1 tchd 200 to 1) pu
Dist: 2½l, 1¾l, 2½l, 12l, 10l, 1¼l, 25l, 3l. 3m 45.60s. a 5.60s (13 Ran).
SR: 42/39/41/28/16/1/ (M K George), P R Hedger

2198 Royal Mail Handicap Hurdle Class C (0-135 4-y-o and up) £3,615 3m 110yds. .... (4:10)

1921⁵ COKENNY BOY [108] 12-10-11 N Williamson, *trkd ldrs gng wl, drvn into slight ld last, ran on well und pres.*
.... (5 to 1 op 9 to 2 tchd 11 to 2) 1
1867³ OLYMPIAN [121] (bl) 10-11-10 R Dunwoody, *led aftr second to 8th, styd pressing ldr, rdn 2 out, str chal last, one pace.*
.... (7 to 2 tchd 4 to 1) 2
1834² DIWALI DANCER [113] 7-11-2 A P McCoy, *led till aftr second, chlgd 7th, led ag'n 8th, hdd last, no extr und pres.*
.... (11 to 4 op 9 to 1) 3
2047¹ TIM (Ire) [115] 7-11-4 J Osborne, *hld up, hdwy to track ldrs aftr 3 out, rdn and hit 2 out, sn one pace.*
.... (2 to 1 fav tchd 7 to 4) 4
1937 SORBIERE [100] 10-10-3 M A Fitzgerald, *in tch till wknd aftr 3 out.* .... (20 to 1 op 16 to 1) 5
1945⁵ LITTLE GUNNER [100] 7-10-13 D Gallagher, *prominet, rdn aftr 3 out, wknd quickly appr nxt* ...... (10 to 1 op 14 to 1) 6
Dist: 1½l, 1¼l, 2l, 14l, 14l. 6m 5.10s. a 20.10s (6 Ran).
(S D Hemstock), Mrs J Pitman

SOUTHWELL (A.W) (std)
Friday January 17th
Going Correction: NIL

2199 Levy Board Standard Open National Hunt Flat Class H (4 - 7-y-o) £1,213 2m. .... (12:45)

THE KHOINOA (Ire) 7-11-4 J Supple, *settled in tch, improved to ld o'r 3 fs out, drvn clr in strt.*
.... (10 to 1 op 8 to 1 tchd 12 to 1) 1
2123⁵ SLIDE ON 7-11-6 (5ᵗ) Michael Brennan, *led early, styd hndy, rgned ld 5 fs out, hdd o'r 3 out, rdn and kpt on same pace.*
.... (6 to 4 fav op 5 to 4 tchd 7 to 4) 2
SIR BOSTON 4-10-6 R Johnson, *wtd wth, improved to go hndy 5 fs out, rdn and kpt on one pace fnl 2* .... (16 to 1) 3
RUDOLPHINE (Ire) 6-11-4 N Mann, *pld hrd on ins, improved to chal bef strt, came wide, one pace last 2 fs.*
.... (5 to 1 op 12 to 1) 4
ROLL AGAIN 6-10-11 (7ᵗ) G Supple, *settled midfield, und pres whn pace quickened entering strt, no imprsn.*
.... (4 to 1 op 5 to 2) 5
STONE THE CROWS (Ire) 7-11-4 W Dwan, *tucked away in midfield, wnt hndy hfwy, feeling pace bef strt, fdd last 2 fs.*
.... (7 to 2 op 5 to 2 tchd 4 to 1) 6
OUR CAROL (Ire) 5-10-13 V Smith, *trkd ldrs for o'r a m, wknd and lost tch quickly bef strt* .... (20 to 1) 7
1181⁵ ABYSS 5-11-4 L Harvey, *trkd ldg pair for a m, wknd quickly and lost tch bef strt* .... (20 to 1 op 16 to 1) 8
GIFT STAR (USA) 4-10-6 O Pears, *took keen hold, rcd wide, wknd and lost tch quickly bef strt* .... (12 to 1) 9
2015⁷ HUISH (Ire) 6-11-4 Mr A Charles-Jones, *sn led, hdd 5 fs out, wknd quickly, tld off* .... (20 to 1) 10
1026⁹ HOLKHAM BAY 5-10-11 (7ᵗ) C Rae, *pld hrd, lost tch quickly bef strt, tld off* .... (14 to 1) 11
RED OASSIS 6-10-11 (7ᵗ) Mr H Oliver, *last thrght, tld off.* .... (12 to 1 op 10 to 1) 12
Dist: 10l, 1l, 18l, 10l, 6l, 12l, 10l, 7l, 2½l, 19l. 3m 59.90s. (12 Ran).
(M Allison), Mrs A Swinbank

CATTERICK (good)
Saturday January 18th
Going Correction: PLUS 0.40 sec. per fur.

2200 Swale Novices' Hurdle Class E (5-y-o and up) £2,931 3m 1f 110yds (1:00)

1995⁵ SHARE OPTIONS (Ire) 6-11-4 J Callaghan, *trkd ldrs, in ld 3 out, hdd nxt, led last, styd on und pres.*
.... (7 to 4 fav tchd 9 to 4) 1
1966² SMART APPROACH (Ire) 7-10-6 (7ᵗ) C McCormack, *in tch, tracking ldrs 3 out, led nxt, hdd last, no extr und pres.*
.... (7 to 2 op 9 to 4 tchd 4 to 1) 2
1631⁶ CHILL FACTOR 7-10-9 (3ᵗ) G Lee, *towards rear early, styd on to go 3rd 2 out, no imprsn on 1st two.* (25 to 1 op 10 to 1) 3
1637⁷ PHAR ECHO (Ire) 5-10-12 R Supple, *chsd ldrs, rdn aftr 3 out, fdd* .... (20 to 1 op 10 to 1 tchd 25 to 1) 4
2063² CHEATER (Ire) 6-10-12 A S Smith, *chsd ldrs, outpcd bef 3 out, no dngr aftr* .... (13 to 2 op 7 to 1 tchd 10 to 1) 5
1818³ ERNI (Fr) 5-10-5 (7ᵗ) R McCarthy, *prmnt, rdn aftr 3 out, sn wknd* .... (11 to 1 op 10 to 1 tchd 33 to 1) 6
1984 CLONGOUR (Ire) 7-10-5 (7ᵗ) Miss Elizabeth Doyle, *nvr dngrs.*
.... (25 to 1 op 14 to 1) 7
1817 JILLS JOY (Ire) 6-10-12 W Fry, *in tch, chasing ldrs 3 out, sn wknd* .... (7 to 1 op 6 to 1) 8
KING FLY 7-10-12 M Foster, *trkd ldrs, ev ch 3 out, wknd quickly, tld off* .... (50 to 1 op 25 to 1) 9
1677⁶ PRINCE OF SAINTS (Ire) 6-10-12 A Dobbin, *in tch till wknd quickly aftr 3 out, tld off* .... (7 to 1 op 12 to 1) 10
1989 OTTADINI (Ire) 5-10-11⁴ T Reed, *led till f 1st.*
.... (200 to 1 op 50 to 1) f
1817³ BASINCROFT 7-10-5 (7ᵗ) A Todd, *brght dwn 1st.*
.... (100 to 1 op 33 to 1) bd
1820 LIAM'S LOSS (Ire) 8-10-12 V Smith, *beh frm hfwy, tld off whn pld up bef 2 out* .... (200 to 1 op 50 to 1) pu
MY YOUNG PET 8-10-12 K Jones, *sn beh, tld off whn pld up bef 2 out* .... (200 to 1 op 50 to 1) pu
103 CLASSIC JESTER (Ire) 6-10-12 M Moloney, *mid-div, wknd aftr 8th, tld off whn pld up bef 2 out* . (200 to 1 op 50 to 1) pu
2116 WELBURN BOY 5-10-12 B Storey, *nvr better than mid-div, tld off whn pld up bef 2 out* .... (50 to 1 op 33 to 1) pu
1829⁹ CARNMONEY (Ire) 9-10-12 G Cahill, *led 1st till aftr 7th, wknd bef 3 out, tld off whn pld up before last.* (66 to 1 op 33 to 1) pu
1570 OFF PISTE SALLY 5-10-2 (5ᵗ) Mr R Thornton, *sn beh, tld off whn pld up bef 8th* ..... (50 to 1 op 25 to 1 tchd 66 to 1) pu
1962 EDSTONE (Ire) 5-10-12 Derek Byrne, *in tch, hdwy to join ldrs 6th, wknd bef 3 out, tld off whn pld up before nxt.*
.... (200 to 1 op 50 to 1) pu
1656 POLITICAL BILL 6-10-12 K Johnson, *nvr better than mid-div, tld off whn pld up bef 2 out* ...... (100 to 1 op 33 to 1) pu
JUST POLLY 5-10-0 (7ᵗ) Mr T J Barry, *sn beh, tld off whn pld up bef 2 out* .... (100 to 1 op 33 to 1) pu
KAMBLETREE (Ire) 6-10-7 D Parker, *sn beh, tld off whn pld up bef 8th* .... (100 to 1 op 33 to 1) pu
DARING MAGIC 5-10-4 (3ᵗ) E Callaghan, *beh frm hfwy, tld off whn pld up bef 2 out* .... (200 to 1 op 50 to 1) pu
Dist: ½l, 18l, 9l, 9l, 1l, nk, 1¼l, 22l, 6l. (Time not taken) (23 Ran).
(Steve Hammond), T D Easterby

2201 Bedale Novices' Chase Class E (5-y-o and up) £3,336 2m. ...... (1:30)

2062 NOYAN 7-11-4 (5ᵗ) Mr R Thornton, *trkd ldrs, led 3 out, hdd nxt, rdn to ld last, ran on wl.*
.... (11 to 4 op 5 to 2 tchd 3 to 1) 1
1741² BOLD BOSS 8-11-3 B Storey, *prmnt, led 8th, hdd 3 out, led ag'n nxt, headed last, no extr und pres.*
.... (11 to 4 op 5 to 2 tchd 3 to 1) 2
873⁴ EL CRANK SENOR 5-10-7 Derek Byrne, *in tch, outpcd aftr 8th, styd on frm 3 out* .... (16 to 1 op 20 to 1) 3
1149² CHORUS LINE (Ire) 8-10-12 R Supple, *in tch, chasing ldrs 8th, no hdwy frm nxt.* ..(20 to 1 op 14 to 1 tchd 25 to 1) 4
ROYAL CRIMSON 6-1-0 (3ᵗ) Mr C Bonner, *nvr dngrs.*
.... (20 to 1 op 16 to 1 tchd 25 to 1) 5
1886³ WEEHEBY (USA) 8-11-3 T J Murphy, *chsd ldrs till wknd aftr 9th* .... (50 to 1 op 33 to 1) 6
1761⁸ URBAN DANCING (USA) 8-11-3 G Cahill, *nvr dngrs.*
.... (7 to 1 tchd 8 to 1) 7
608⁵ CHILDSWAY 9-10-12 (5ᵗ) Michael Brennan, *led 3rd till hdd 8th, sn wknd* .... (66 to 1 op 33 to 1) 8
1831³ CURRAGH PETER 10-11-0 (3ᵗ) Guy Lewis, *nvr dngrs.*
.... (50 to 1) 9
1828² DARING PAST 7-11-9 A Dobbin, *chsd ldrs, 3rd and rdn whn f 3 out* .... (5 to 2 fav op 5 to 2 tchd 9 to 2) f
1963 CARDINAL SINNER (Ire) 8-11-3 K Jones, *f 1st.*
.... (200 to 1 op 50 to 1) f
DIDDY RYMER 7-10-12 Mr P Murray, *f 1st.*
.... (66 to 1 op 33 to 1) f
1950³ FENWICK'S BROTHER 7-10-10 (7ᵗ) R Wilkinson, *beh whn f 7th* .... (12 to 1 op 10 to 1 tchd 16 to 1) f
DANDY DES PLAUTS (Fr) 6-11-3 K Johnson, *beh whn f 8th.*
.... (66 to 1 op 33 to 1) f
1732 ERNEST ARAGORN 8-11-3 B Clifford, *ran out 1st.*
.... (200 to 1 op 50 to 1) ro
1984⁹ SOUTH COAST STAR (Ire) 7-11-3 A S Smith, *tld off whn pld up bef 3 out* .... (100 to 1 op 33 to 1) pu
1770 LEPTON (Ire) 6-11-3 J Callaghan, *beh most of way, tld off whn pld up bef last* .... (50 to 1) pu
2119³ GONE ASHORE (Ire) 6-10-12 (5ᵗ) S Taylor, *led to 3rd, tld off whn pld up bef 3 out* .... (100 to 1 op 33 to 1) pu
Dist: 5l, 7l, 3½l, 14l, 1½l, 5l, 4l, 3½l. (Time not taken) (18 Ran).
(C H McGhie), R A Fahey

2202 Darlington Conditional Jockeys' Selling Handicap Hurdle Class G (0-90 4-y-o and up) £2,057 2m (2:00)

1656 KIERCHEM (Ire) [65] 6-10-5 Michael Brennan, mid-div, hdwy hfwy, drvn alng bef 2 out, led appr last, ran on wl.
.... (25 to 1 op 14 to 1) 1
1953⁶ ANORAK (USA) [88] 7-11-7 (7") N Hannity, prmnt, dsptd ld 5th till outpcd aftr 3 out, styd on frm betw last 2.
.... (25 to 1 op 12 to 1) 2
1693⁵ ARTHUR BEE [61] 10-9-11 (4") C McCormack, towards rear, hdwy hfwy, kpt on frm 2 out.
.... (16 to 1 op 20 to 1 tchd 25 to 1) 3
1955 APPEARANCE MONEY (Ire) [72] 6-10-8 (4") T Hogg, settled midfield, hdwy to ld aftr 3 out, hdd appr last, no extr.
.... (16 to 1 op 10 to 1) 4
1693² CHUMMY'S SAGA [73] 7-10-9 (4") I Jardine, mid-div, hdwy aftr 3 out, kpt on same pace frm nxt. . . . . (5 to 1 tchd 9 to 2) 5
2116⁶ JALMAID [66] 5-10-6 R McGrath, in tch, outpcd aftr 3 out, no dngr after. (12 to 1 op 10 to 1) 6
2118⁸ BUD'S BET (Ire) [77] 9-11-3 M Newton, sn beh, nvr dngrs.
.... (12 to 1 op 14 to 1) 7
1869⁵ BOLD TOP [67] 5-10-7 E Callaghan, led second till hdd 5th, aftr 3 out. . . . . (12 to 1 op 10 to 1 tchd 14 to 1) 8
1955² ENVIRONMENTAL LAW [72] 6-10-12 G Cahill, chsd ldrs till wknd aftr 5th. . . . . (7 to 2 fav op 6 to 1) 9
2118 SEE YOU ALWAYS (Ire) [60] 7-10-0 S Taylor, chsd ldrs till wknd aftr 3 out. . . . . (50 to 1 op 25 to 1) 10
1931² SECONDS AWAY [60] 6-10-0 G Lee, nvr on terms.
.... (20 to 1 op 12 to 1) 11
1736² WEATHER ALERT (Ire) [75] 6-11-1 R Massey, led to second, chsd ldrs till wknd aftr 5th. . . . . (5 to 1 op 6 to 1) 12
1992² BOY BLAKENEY [88] 4-11-2 R Wilkinson, prmnt, led 5th till hdd aftr 3 out, wknd quickly. . . . . (4 to 1 tchd 9 to 2) 13
1986 FAMILIAR ART [70] 6-10-3 (7") I Pike, strted slwly, mstk 1st, al beh. . . . . (33 to 1 op 20 to 1) 14
1736 TOUGH CHARACTER (Ire) [60] 9-9-10 (4") N Horrocks, sn beh, tld off. . . . . (200 to 1 op 50 to 1) 15
Dist: 3l, 1¼l, ¾l, 1¼l, ½l, 9l, ¾l, ¾l, 1¼l, 9l. 3m 55.10s. a 15.10s (15 Ran).
SR: -/10/-/-/-/-/ (Mrs M Hunter), C Grant

2203 Leeming Handicap Chase Class E (0-110 5-y-o and up) £3,159 3m 1f 110yds. (2:30)

1954* TIM SOLDIER (Fr) [84] 10-10-2 R Supple, chsd ldrs, led aftr 2 out, blun last, styd on wl, eased towards finish.
.... (4 to 1 op 5 to 1) 1
1820 KENMARE RIVER (Ire) [82] 7-9-9 (5") Mr R Thornton, led till hdd aftr 2 out, kpt on same pace. . . . . (100 to 1 op 20 to 1) 2
1988 SNOOK POINT [86] 10-10-4⁴ J Burke, sn tracking ldrs, ch whn blun 3 out, soon btn. . . . . (9 to 2 op 3 to 1) 3
1948 SISTER ROSZA (Ire) [97] 9-11-1 Derek Byrne, in tch, effrt and ch 16th, fdd. . . . . (9 to 2 op 3 to 1) 4
1967* HEAVENLY CITIZEN (Ire) [95] 9-10-13 B Storey, chsd ldrs, drvn alng aftr 11th, outpcd aftr 13th, styd on frm 3 out.
.... (6 to 1 op 5 to 1 tchd 7 to 1) 5
2150³ RUSSIAN CASTLE (Ire) [105] 8-11-6 (3") Mr C Bonner, cl up, hit 7th, rdn and wknd bef 16th.
.... (9 to 2 op 4 to 1 tchd 5 to 1) 6
1820 BRIGHT DESTINY [82] 6-9-11 (3") G Lee, nvr on terms.
.... (200 to 1 op 33 to 1 tchd 500 to 1) 7
1967 MARCHWOOD [98] 10-11-2 K Johnson, hld up, hdwy to track ldrs hfwy, wknd aftr 15th. . . . . (12 to 1 op 12 to 1) 8
1694² GALE AHEAD (Ire) [98] 7-11-2 N Bentley, in tch, drvn alng aftr 11th, wknd after 13th, tld off. . . . . . . (7 to 2 fav tchd 4 to 1) 9
I'M IN CLOVER (Ire) [82] 8-9-7 (7") B Grattan, beh whn blun and uns rdr 15th. . . . . (33 to 1 op 20 to 1) ur
1645 FAR SENIOR [108] 11-11-12 Gary Lyons, drvn alng and beh 9th, lost tch and pld up bef 13th. . . . . (33 to 1 op 14 to 1) pu
1988⁴ JENDEE (Ire) [85] 9-10-3 G Cahill, al beh, tld off whn pld up bef 2 out. . . . . (14 to 1 op 12 to 1 tchd 16 to 1) pu
1948 POTATO MAN [99] 11-11-3 A Dobbin, mstk 7th, sn beh, tld off whn pld up bef 12th. . . . . (20 to 1 op 6 to 1 tchd 33 to 1) pu
1328³ OLE OLE [82] 11-10-0 J Callaghan, mid-div till wknd aftr 14th, tld off whn pld up bef 16th. (9 to 1 op 8 to 1 tchd 10 to 1) pu
1954⁴ THE TOASTER [95] 10-10-13 A S Smith, al beh, tld off whn pld up bef 3 out. . . . . . (14 to 1 op 12 to 1 tchd 16 to 1) pu
1694 TWIN STATES [98] 8-11-2 W Fry, mid-div, lost tch and pld up bef 15th, broke blood vessel.
.... (12 to 1 op 10 to 1 tchd 14 to 1) pu
Dist: 3½l, 7l, 7l, 1¾l, 8l, 3l, hd, dist. 6m 47.20s. a 32.20s (16 Ran).
(Ken Dale), M F Barraclough

2204 Leyburn Handicap Hurdle Class E (0-110 4-y-o and up) £2,553 2m . . . . (3:00)

MR MORIARTY (Ire) [92] 6-11-0 M Foster, led 3rd, hdd 2 out, lft in ld last, kpt on. . . . (14 to 1 op 8 to 1 tchd 16 to 1) 1
1964² OPERA FAN (Ire) [83] 5-10-5 A S Smith, trkd ldrs, ev ch 2 out, sn rdn, kpt on. . . . . (6 to 1 op 11 to 2 tchd 8 to 1) 2
1807² JEMIMA PUDDLEDUCK [93] 6-11-1 T Eley, mid-div, sn pushed alng, styd on wl und pres frm 2 out, nvr able to chal.
.... (14 to 1 op 8 to 1 tchd 16 to 1) 3

1911³ AUBURN BOY [103] 10-11-6 (5") Michael Brennan, towards rear, effrt aftr 3 out, kpt on same pace frm nxt.
.... (10 to 1 op 7 to 1 tchd 12 to 1) 4
SHAHGRAM (Ire) [98] 9-10-13 (7") B Grattan, hld up, effrt bef 2 out, ran on frm last, nrst finish. . . . . . (10 to 1 op 16 to 1) 5
1690* RUSSIAN RASCAL (Ire) [95] 4-10-0 (5") Mr R Thornton, led second to 3rd, prmnt, ev ch bef 2 out, kpt on same pace.
.... (9 to 2 op 4 to 1) 6
TAPATCH (Ire) [91] 9-11-3 (3") P Midgley, settled midfield, hdwy to track ldrs 3 out, dsptd ld nxt, sn rdn, one-paced.
.... (25 to 1 op 20 to 1) 7
1826* ROBSERA (Ire) [84] 6-11-0 Derek Byrne, mid-div, ch bef 2 out, btn whn hmpd last. . . . . . . (14 to 1 op 16 to 1) 8
1976* STAR SELECTION [98] 6-11-3 (3") E Husband, mstk 1st, led to second, chsd ldrs till outpcd bef 3 out, no dngr aftr.
.... (3 to 1 fav tchd 7 to 2) 9
1986³ HERE COMES HERBIE [83] 5-10-5 M Moloney, chsd ldrs till wknd bef 2 out. . . . . (20 to 1 op 10 to 1) 10
1606⁷ GRANDMAN (ie) [88] 6-10-10 D J Moffatt, sn wl beh, some late hdwy, nvr dngrs. . . . . (16 to 1 tchd 20 to 1) 11
1827⁶ MASTER HYDE (USA) [106] 8-11-9 (5") R McGrath, chsd ldrs till wknd aftr 3 out. . . (25 to 1 op 14 to 1 tchd 33 to 1) 12
1604 GALLARDINI (Ire) [86] 8-10-8 R Supple, in tch, drvn alng aftr 3rd, lost touch frm 3 out, tld off. . . . . (33 to 1 op 25 to 1) 13
1705² SHIFTING MOON [84] 5-10-6 S Wynne, prmnt till wknd quickly aftr 3 out, tld off. (11 to 1 op 8 to 1 tchd 12 to 1) 14
1333³ MITHRAIC (Ire) [92] 5-11-3 (7") L McGrath, prmnt, wkng whn mstk 5th, sn beh, tld off. . . . . . . (10 to 1 op 12 to 1) 15
ALL CLEAR (Ire) [96] 6-11-4 D Parker, sn wl beh, tld off.
.... (33 to 1 op 20 to 1 tchd 50 to 1) 16
1772⁹ BEND SABLE (Ire) [105] 7-11-13 B Storey, hld up, gd hdwy to track ldrs 3 out, led nxt, 2 ls ahead whn f last.
.... (10 to 1 op 16 to 1) f
879⁶ BEAU MATELOT [85] 5-10-7 G Cahill, in tch to hfwy, sn beh, tld off whn pld up bef 2 out.
.... (33 to 1 op 20 to 1 tchd 50 to 1) pu
1657⁶ DEL PIERO (Ire) [96] 6-11-3 A Dobbin, pld up bef 3rd, broke leg, destroyed. . . . . . . (14 to 1 op 8 to 1 tchd 16 to 1) pu
Dist: 1½l, nk, 2½l, 1l, ½l, hd, hd, 6l, 2l, ¾l. 3m 55.30s. a 15.30s (19 Ran).
(D H Bowring), S R Bowring

2205 Seamer Novices' Handicap Chase Class E (0-105 5-y-o and up) £3,440 2m 3f. . . . . (3:30)

1630⁷ MARLINGFORD [78] 10-9-11⁴ (7") L McGrath, sn chasing ldrs, outpcd aftr 12th, rallied to chase lder betw last 2, got up und pres cl hme. . . . . . . (9 to 1 op 5 to 1 tchd 20 to 1) 1+
1605 MONNAIE FORTE (Ire) [90] 7-11-2 M Moloney, nvr far away, led 3 out, styd on und pres, jst hld on. (33 to 1 op 14 to 1) 1+
1822³ KILTULLA (Ire) [74] 7-9-7 (7") R Wilkinson, nvr far away, blun 12th, ev ch 3 out, kpt on same pace.
.... (14 to 1 op 7 to 1 tchd 16 to 1) 3
1954² KARENASTINO [74] 6-10-0 Mr P Murray, mstks, led 3rd till hit 3 out and hdd, no extr. . . . . . . (20 to 1 op 14 to 1) 4
1965* TWIN FALLS (Ire) [94] 6-11-6 J Callaghan, mid-div, outpcd aftr 12th, no dngr after. . . . (3 to 1 op 11 to 4 tchd 100 to 30) 5
1913* GARBO'S BOY [79] 7-10-5 W Fry, mstks, beh frm 8th.
.... (10 to 1 op 12 to 1) 6
1985* LIEN DE FAMILLE (Ire) [102] 7-12-0 B Storey, beh most of way. . . . . (5 to 1 op 4 to 1 tchd 11 to 2) 7
1788 CAMPTOSAURUS (Ire) [75] 8-10-1 K Johnson, sn wl beh.
.... (33 to 1 op 14 to 1) 8
1828⁷ WEE WIZARD (Ire) [74] 8-10-0 T Taylor, sn wl beh. (25 to 1) 9
KNOW-NO-NO (Ire) [83] 8-10-9 A Dobbin, chsd ldrs, ev ch 3 out, mstk nxt, 5th and wkng whn f last.
.... (10 to 1 op 8 to 1 tchd 12 to 1) f
1819 WORLD WITHOUT END (USA) [80] 8-10-6 D Parker, beh whn f 3rd. . . . . (50 to 1 op 25 to 1) f
1963* BOSWORTH FIELD (Ire) [78] 9-10-4 M Foster, chsd ldrs, wkng whn f 11th, dead. . . . . (11 to 1 op 7 to 1) f
1994 BOSSYMOSS (Ire) [74] 8-10-0 T Eley, blun 5th, beh whn blunded and uns rdr 11th. . . . . (14 to 1 op 10 to 1) ur
MOST RICH (Ire) [74] 9-10-0 G Cahill, in tch, wknd aftr 12th, beh whn pld up bef 2 out. . . . . (50 to 1 op 20 to 1) pu
1258* ABBEYLANDS (Ire) [91] 9-11-3 A S Smith, led to 3rd, pld up bef 5th, lme. . . . . (11 to 4 fav op 9 to 4 tchd 3 to 1) pu
Dist: Dd-ht, 9l, ½l, 12l, 8l, 8l, 9l, 15l. 4m 56.20s. a 26.20s (15 Ran).
(Miss J Seaton & James R Adam), Mrs J Jordan & J R Adam

2206 Catterick Maiden National Hunt Flat Class H (4 - 7-y-o) £1,360 2m (4:00)

AUTUMN LORD 4-10-5 (7") B Grattan, trkd ldrs, led gng wl 3 fs out, ran on well.
.... (6 to 1 op 12 to 1 tchd 3 to 1) 1
2008⁴ BILLY BUCKSKIN 5-11-5 (5") Mr R Thornton, trkd ldrs, chsd wnr fnl 3 fs, kpt on, no imprsn. . . . . . . (4 to 1 op 7 to 2) 2
1887⁷ PHAR SMOOTHER (Ire) 5-11-7 (3") F Leahy, chsd ldrs, outpcd o'r 3 fs out, styd on fnl 2 furlongs.
.... (6 to 1 op 5 to 1 tchd 7 to 1) 3
SUPREME TARGET (Ire) 5-11-2 (3") G Lee, trkd ldrs, ev ch o'r 3 fs out, sn rdn and btn. (2 to 1 fav op 9 to 4 tchd 5 to 2) 4
BUDDLEIA 4-10-0 (7") N Horrocks, chsd ldrs, rdn o'r 3 fs out, sn btn. . . . . (25 to 1 op 14 to 1 tchd 33 to 1) 5
NOSAM 7-11-3 (7") S Haworth, chsd ldrs till wknd o'r 3 fs out.
.... (14 to 1 op 25 to 1) 6

NATIONAL HUNT RESULTS 1996-97

1887 EASTCLIFFE (Ire) 5-11-10 G Cahill, *cl up, led aftr 6 fs till hdd 3 out, wknd quickly*........ (8 to 1 op 14 to 1 tchd 7 to 1) 7
SUNSTRIKE 5-11-3 (7") C McCormack, *in tch, hdwy 5 fs out, hrd rdn 3 out, sn wknd*.............(100 to 1 op 50 to 1) 8
1968⁴ THE STUFFED PUFFIN (Ire) 5-11-3 (7") I Jardine, *beh, some late hdwy, nvr dngrs*..................(6 to 1 op 7 to 2) 9
STONESBY (Ire) 5-11-3 (7") N Hannity, *beh, hdwy 5 fs out, wknd 3 out*...........(10 to 1 op 12 to 1 tchd 16 to 1) 10
HELPERBY (Ire) 5-11-5 (5") G F Ryan, *nvr dngrs.*
.........................(14 to 1 op 8 to 1 tchd 20 to 1) 11
1968⁹ HUNTING SLANE 5-11-5 (5") Michael Brennan, *in tch till wknd 4 fs out, tld off....* (12 to 1 op 25 to 1 tchd 33 to 1) 12
1968 RECCA (Ire) 5-11-3 (7") R Burns, *beh fnl 4 fs, tld off.*
............................(12 to 1 op 14 to 1 tchd 25 to 1) 13
1989 SNOOTY ESKIMO (Ire) 5-11-7 (3") E Callaghan, *beh fnl 4 fs, tld off*...........................(16 to 1 op 33 to 1) 14
JO LIGHTNING (Ire) 4-10-12 Mr R Hale, *sn lost tch, wl tld off.*
......................(33 to 1 op 25 to 1 tchd 50 to 1) 15
2029 THE MUCKLE QUINE 6-11-0 (5") R McGrath, *lost tch frm hfwy, wl tld off*.................(50 to 1 op 20 to 1) 16
1682 TIDAL RACE (Ire) 5-11-7 (3") P Midgley, *lost tch frm hfwy. wl tld off...*......................(100 to 1 op 50 to 1) 17
HAWKERS DEAL 4-10-9 (3") R Massey, *led 6 fs, wknd quickly, wl tld off...*.................(14 to 1 op 20 to 1) 18
1682 MISS FORTINA 5-10-12 (7") M Newton, *sn lost tch, wl tld off*....................(200 to 1 op 50 to 1) 19
Dist: 7l, 11l, ½l, 4l, 2½l, 4l, 5l, 3½l, sht-hd, 2½l. 3m 50.70s. (19 Ran).
(A R Boocock), P Beaumont

HAYDOCK (good to firm)
Saturday January 18th
Going Correction: PLUS 0.05 sec. per fur. (races 1,2,4,7), MINUS 0.10 (3,5,6)

2207 North West Racing Club Novices' Hurdle Class E (4-y-o and up) £2,778 2½m.....................(12:45)

HARBOUR ISLAND 5-11-6 C Maude, *chsd clr ldr, improved to nose ahead 4 out, drw clear aftr nxt, very easily.*
.........................(3 to 1 tchd 5 to 2) 1
2123³ MR CHRISTIE 5-11-6 A Thornton, *settled wth chasing grp, improved frm off the pace 3 out, styd on frm betw last 2, no ch wth nnr*........................(14 to 1 op 10 to 1) 2
1679⁶ TREMENDISTO 7-11-11 Richard Guest, *led, clr whn hit 3rd, hdd 4 out, sn drvn alng, one pace nxt...* (12 to 1 op 8 to 1) 3
1940⁵ FLAXLEY WOOD 6-11-6 B Powell, *settled midfield, effrt and bustled alng frm 4 out, nvr able to rch chalg pos.*
.........................(25 to 1 op 16 to 1) 4
1927" KONVEKTA QUEEN (Ire) 6-11-6 R Dunwoody, *tucked away wth chasing grp, effrt and bustled alng appr 3 out, no imprsn.*
.........................(5 to 2 fav op 9 to 4 tchd 11 to 4) 5
1792⁶ MEL (Ire) 7-11-6 L Harvey, *chsd ldg pair to hfwy, struggling to improve 4 out, no imprsn on ldrs....*(33 to 1 op 16 to 1) 6
1787² LEAP IN THE DARK (Ire) 8-11-6 O Pears, *bustled alng wth chasing grp hfwy, nvr able to rch chalg pos.*
.........................(25 to 1 op 16 to 1) 7
1217⁵ CLUB CARIBBEAN 5-11-1 N Williamson, *settled wth main grp, effrt and pres to chase ldg trio appr 3 out, lost tch, tld off.*
.........................(20 to 1 op 14 to 1) 8
2006⁵ GALEN (Ire) 6-11-6 P Niven, *struggling to keep up bef hfwy, sn beh, tld off...*...............(9 to 1 op 6 to 1) 9
BENFLEET 6-11-6 D Walsh, *struggling and drvn alng bef hfwy, lost tch, tld off*......................(11 to 1 op 8 to 1) 10
1861³ PLEASURELAND (Ire) 4-10-7 D Morris, *in tch, wknd quickly bef 4 out, tld off.........*(7 to 2 op 5 to 2 tchd 4 to 1) 11
LA MON DERE (Ire) 6-11-6 W Marston, *sn struggling to keep up, tld off hfwy..........*(16 to 1 op 10 to 1 tchd 20 to 1) 12
NIYAKA 10-11-6 J R Kavanagh, *lost tch quickly hfwy, tld off whn pld up aftr 3 out*.............(33 to 1 op 25 to 1) pu
GIVRY (Ire) 7-11-6 D Bridgwater, *lost tch hfwy, tld off whn pld up 4 out*...................(33 to 1 op 20 to 1) pu
Dist: 16l, 1¾l, 3l, ¾l, 6l, 8l, 24l, 4l, 4l, 11l. 4m 49.30s. a 13.30s (14 Ran).

(Malcolm B Jones), M C Pipe

2208 Bellcharm Mitsubishi Champion Hurdle Trial Class A Grade 2 (5-y-o and up) £18,860 2m.........(1:15)

2001² MISTINGUETT (Ire) 5-11-2 C Llewellyn, *made all, hrd pressed appr 3 out, styd on strly to go clr betw last 2.*
.........................(8 to 1 tchd 9 to 1) 1
1633³ DATO STAR (Ire) 6-11-7 Richard Guest, *settled travelling wl, chalg whn mstk 4 out, ev ch bef nxt, kpt on same pace betw last 2...*......... (7 to 2 op 3 to 1 tchd 4 to 1) 2
1877² BIMSEY (Ire) 7-11-3 R Dunwoody, *chsd ldr, hit second, rdn 4 out, rallied last 2, kpt on to take 3rd betw last two, no imprsn.*
.........................(5 to 4 fav op 6 to 4) 3
1877⁵ PRIDWELL 7-11-7 C Maude, *sn beh, styd on frm off the pace aftr 3 out, nvr rch chalg pos..*....................(5 to 1) 4
1877⁶ RIGHT WIN (Ire) 7-11-10 J A McCarthy, *settled wth chasing grp, feeling pace bef 4 out, nvr rch chalg pos.*
.........................(33 to 1 op 50 to 1) 5

2001² ESKIMO NEL (Ire) 6-10-12 D Bridgwater, *co`red up with chasing grp, feeling pace appr 4 out, lost tch, tld off.*
.........................(12 to 1 tchd 14 to 1) 6
EDIPO RE 5-11-3 P Carberry, *struggling and beh hfwy, tld off.*
.........................(40 to 1 op 33 to 1 tchd 50 to 1) 7
2001⁶ TRAGIC HERO 5-11-10 D Walsh, *tucked away midfield, struggling bef 4 out, tld off...*..........(25 to 1) 8
2128" MASTER TRIBE (Ire) 7-11-3 N Williamson, *settled gng wl, smooth hdwy frm 4 out, wnt 3rd aftr nxt, btn and eased betw last 2, pld up r-in....*.............(10 to 1 op 8 to 1) pu
Dist: 4l, 11l, 8l, 12l, 23l, 1¼l, 9l. 3m 41.00s. a 3.00s (9 Ran).
SR: 66/67/52/48/39/4/7/-/-/   (John Duggan), N A Twiston-Davies

2209 Peter Marsh Chase Limited Handicap Class A Grade 2 (5-y-o and up) £24,776 3m.................(1:45)

1387² JODAMI [162] 12-11-10 N Williamson, *patiently rdn, wnt hndy fnl circuit, reminders bef 3 out, hit last, swtchd lft and ran on gmely und pres to ld cl hme...........* (9 to 2 op 4 to 1) 1
1999² UNGUIDED MISSILE (Ire) [158] 9-11-6 R Dunwoody, *al wl plcd, made most frm 12th, hrd pressed last 3, ran on, ct cl hme.............*(11 to 8 on op 11 to 10 on tchd Evens) 2
AVRO ANSON [145] 9-10-7 P Niven, *nvr far away, str chal frm 3 out, ev ch r-in, ran on wl finish.......* (9 to 1 op 6 to 1) 3
1884³ SCOTTON BANKS (Ire) [153] 8-11-1 P Carberry, *led to 12th, losing tch whn blun 4 out, tld off....* (10 to 1 tchd 11 to 1) 4
1746⁵ GRANGE BRAKE [145] 11-10-7 D Walsh, *hit 1st, awkward 7th, lost tch tenth, tld off whn pld up bef 4 out.......* (33 to 1) pu
1945⁶ NAHTHEN LAD (Ire) [156] 8-11-4 W Marston, *trkd ldrs, reminders tenth, lost tch quickly and pld up bef 5 out.*
.........................(5 to 1 tchd 11 to 2) pu
Dist: Nk, ½l, dist. 6m 3.50s. b 1.50s (6 Ran).
SR: 87/83/69/   (J N Yeadon), P Beaumont

2210 Tote Premier Long Distance Hurdle Class A Grade 2 (5-y-o and up) £12,740 2m 7f 110yds.......(2:15)

1998" OCEAN HAWK (USA) 5-11-10 C Llewellyn, *clr to hfwy, hdd 5 out, rallied to ld 3 out, kpt on gmely r-in.*
.........................(Evens fav op 5 to 4 on tchd 11 to 10) 1
1998³ PLEASURE SHARED (Ire) 9-11-10 R Dunwoody, *al wl plcd, led 5 out 3 out, rallied betw last 2, kpt on.*
.........................(6 to 4 op 5 to 4 tchd 13 to 8) 2
1998⁴ TOP SPIN 8-11-3 P Carberry, *last and hld up, effrt and reminders 4 out, styd on last 2, no imprsn.*
MUDAHIM 11-11-3 W Marston, *nvr far away, reminders and lost grnd 5 out, struggling nxt, sn lost tch.*
.........................(10 to 1 op 6 to 1) 4
1637" RULING (USA) 11-11-3 N Williamson, *al wl plcd, disputing ld whn hit 4 out, reminders, wknd quickly aftr nxt.*
.........................(20 to 1 op 12 to 1) 5
Dist: ¾l, 15l, 2½l, 7l. 5m 48.80s. a 17.80s (5 Ran).
(Matt Archer & Miss Jean Broadhurst), N A Twiston-Davies

2211 St. Helens College Students Novices' Chase Class B (5-y-o and up) £11,715 2½m.................(2:45)

1996" SIMPLY DASHING (Ire) 6-11-2 R Dunwoody, *wth ldr, hit 5 out, led aftr 3 out, forged clr betw last 2, easily.*
.........................(7 to 2 on tchd 4 to 1 on) 1
1562 BALLYLINE (Ire) 6-11-9 N Williamson, *made most till aftr 3 out, kpt on pace frm nxt, no ch wth wnr.*
.........................(9 to 1 tchd 10 to 1) 2
1862" FLIMSY TRUTH 11-11-9 Mr M Harris, *nvr far away, effrt hfwy, bustled alng whn pace quickened 4 out, styd on last 2, no imprsn.*.........................(9 to 2 op 4 to 1) 3
1593" LA MEZERAY 9-11-4 D Walsh, *trkd ldrs, struggling to keep up 4 out, sn lost tch.* (25 to 1 op 20 to 1) 4
Dist: 10l, 3½l, 25l. 5m 13.20s. a 16.20s (4 Ran).
(Steve Hammond), T D Easterby

2212 Old Hall Country Club Handicap Chase Class B (5-y-o and up) £7,162 2m.........................(3:15)

1380" KONVEKTA KING (Ire) [128] 9-10-13 R Dunwoody, *nvr far away, rdn to ld aftr last, styd on wl.*
.........................(5 to 2 fav op 9 to 4 tchd 11 to 4) 1
1851⁴ EASTHORPE [138] 9-11-9 J F Titley, *dsptd ld, led aftr 4 out, hdd and rdn after last, kpt on one pace finish.*
.........................(11 to 1 tchd 7 to 2) 2
1678" POLITICAL TOWER [130] 10-11-1 P Niven, *al wl plcd, ev ch whn hit 2 out, one pace und pres r-in...* (7 to 2 op 11 to 4) 3
TIME WON'T WAIT (Ire) [137] 8-11-8 J Railton, *last and hld up, hit second, chalg whn nrly uns rdr last, not reco`r.*
.........................(9 to 2 op 4 to 1) 4
1875³ SOUND REVEILLE [139] 9-11-3 (7") M Berry, *made most, hrd pressed frm hfwy, hdd aftr 4 out, rdn and one pace betw last 2.*.........................(8 to 1 op 6 to 1) 5
Dist: 2½l, 2½l, 1½l, 2½l. 3m 58.40s. a 2.40s (5 Ran).
SR: 45/52/41/46/45/   (Konvekta Ltd), O Sherwood

289

2213 Haydock Standard Open National Hunt Flat Class H (4,5,6-y-o) £1,633
2m................................ (3:45)

1317* COLOUR CODE 5-11-11 J Supple, *made all, sn clr, styd on strly last 2 fs, imprsv.*
.............(11 to 10 on 5 to 4 tchd 5 to 4 on) 1

BALLAD MINSTREL (Ire) 5-11-11 P Carberry, *patiently rdn, improved to chase wnr appr strt, no imprsn last 2 fs.*
.............................(7 to 4 op 5 to 4) 2

INTO THE BLACK (Ire) 6-11-4 P Niven, *settled off the pace, styd on last 2 fs, nvr nrr.*.........(8 to 1 tchd 9 to 1) 3

1968⁵ MONSIEUR DARCY (Ire) 6-11-4 J Railton, *wth nvr early, feeling pace and lost grnd quickly leaving back strt, no dngr aftr.*........................(20 to 1 op 14 to 1) 4

1809⁵ COSY RIDE (Ire) 5-11-4 C Llewellyn, *chsd ldrs for o'r one m, lost tch bef strt, tld off.*............(8 to 1 tchd 10 to 1) 5

CHAMPS-GIRL (Ire) 4-10-1 W Dwan, *struggling and beh hfwy, tld off.*.......................(50 to 1 op 25 to 1) 6

Dist: 19l, 9l, 1¼l, 15l, dist. 3m 42.30s. (6 Ran).
(Bill Walker), Mrs A Swinbank

KEMPTON (good to firm)
Saturday January 18th
Going Correction: NIL (races 1,3,6,7), PLUS 0.15 (2,4,5,8)

2214 Twickenham Novices' Chase Class B (5-y-o and up) £9,240 2m.... (12:40)

2052² LAND AFAR 10-11-7 J Osborne, *hld up, pushed alng 8th, sn cld, led appr 2 out, pushed out.......* (5 to 4 fav op 6 to 5) 1

2046² MISTER DRUM (Ire) 8-11-7 A P McCoy, *led to 3rd, wth ldr, not fluent 5th, mstk nxt, led 8th, drvn 4 out, hdd appr 2 out, no extr whn blun last.*............(4 to 1 op 7 to 1 tchd 9 to 2) 2

1880* MANDYS MANTINO 7-11-3 P Hide, *hld up, cld appr 7th, jmpd slwly 4 out, sn lost pl, styd on und pres frm 2 out, mstk last.*
....................(100 to 30 op 7 to 4 tchd 7 to 2) 3

1758³ DOWN THE FELL 8-11-11 A Maguire, *led 3rd, mstk 6th, hdd 8th, drw level 4 out, btn appr nxt, no ch whn blun 2 out.*
.................................(7 to 1 op 5 to 1) 4

1886* GOLDEN HELLO 6-11-7 R Garritty, *hld up, mstk 3rd, f 7th.*
.............(10 to 1 op 7 to 1 tchd 11 to 1) f

Dist: 5l, 3l, 26l. 3m 51.10s. a 5.10s (5 Ran).
SR: 42/37/30/12/-/ (T J Ford), P R Webber

2215 John Court Of Margate Quality Decorators Novices' Hurdle Class B (5-y-o and up) £6,285 2m 5f.....(1:10)

1882* SEA VICTOR 5-11-4 D Gallagher, *keen early, hld up in tch, hdwy to chase ldr 3 out, led appr nxt, not fluent last, hrd rdn, ran on gmely.*.................(2 to 1 fav tchd 9 to 4) 1

2156² MONTECOT (Fr) 8-11-0 N Mann, *trkd ldrs, hit 7th, rdn and not quicken appr 2 out, kpt on one pace r-in.*
.................(11 to 2 op 4 to 1 tchd 6 to 1) 2

1561² COURBARIL 5-11-7 A P McCoy, *led, sn clr, hrd rdn and hdd appr 2 out, no extr r-in...........* (5 to 2 tchd 7 to 2) 3

1594* READY MONEY CREEK (Ire) 6-11-4 J Osborne, *sn chsd clr ldr to 3 out, wknd appr nxt.* (11 to 4 op 9 to 4 tchd 2 to 1) 4

1598* COUNTRY TARQUIN 5-11-0 T Dascombe, *prmpt appr 1st, in tch, drvn alng frm 6th, wknd aftr 3 out.* (50 to 1 op 25 to 1) 5

1503³ ADILOV 5-11-0 A Maguire, *in tch, hrd rdn and btn 7th, tld off.*
.........................(5 to 1 op 14 to 1 tchd 33 to 1) 6

1802⁵ SARENACARE 5-11-0 G Tormey, *chsd ldrs, reminders 5th, mstk nxt, sn lost tch, tld off.......*(100 to 1 op 33 to 1) 7

1855 GWITHIAN 5-11-0 R Greene, *pld hrd early, hld up, beh 5th, tld off nxt.*........................(100 to 1 op 33 to 1) 8

HONEST DAVE 7-11-0 K Gaule, *trkd ldrs, rdn alng appr 3rd, lost tch 6th, tld off.*............(25 to 1 op 33 to 1) 9

1927³ MAYLIN MAGIC 6-10-9 M A Fitzgerald, *al beh, lost tch 6th, tld off whn pld up 3 out....*(25 to 1 op 20 to 1 tchd 16 to 1) pu

Dist: 1¼l, 5l, 16l, 8l, dist, 6l, 3l, dist. 5m 5.40s. a 19.40s (10 Ran).
(J David Abell), J L Harris

2216 Sunbury Novices' Chase Class B (5-y-o and up) £8,165 3m........ (1:40)

1482* FINE THYNE (Ire) 8-11-10 M A Fitzgerald, *trkd ldr, led aftr 14th, easily....* (11 to 4 on op 3 to 1 tchd 9 to 4 on) 1

PAVI'S BROTHER 9-11-10 I Lawrence, *chsd ldg pair, lost tch 12th, blun 14th, styd on to chase wnr frm 2 out, no imprsn.*
............................(12 to 1 op 14 to 1 tchd 10 to 1) 2

1970 VOLLEYBALL (Ire) 5-11-5 M Richards, *mstks 1st and 5th, al beh, lost tch 12th, blun nxt, took modest 3rd at last.*
.................................(50 to 1 op 25 to 1) 3

1991² SUNSET AND VINE 10-11-5 A P McCoy, *led, mstks 1st, jmpd lft 4th, hdd aftr 14th, lost second 2 out, wknd quickly, virtually pld up, fnshd sore.*.............(11 to 4 op 5 to 2) 4

Dist: 6l, 27l, dist. 6m 12.30s. a 23.30s (4 Ran).
(Peter Wiegand), Mrs A J Perrett

2217 Victor Chandler Handicap Hurdle Class C (0-135 5-y-o and up) £3,745

2m 5f........................ (2:10)

1807⁶ STORM DUST [107] 8-10-5 B Fenton, *chsd ldrs, outpcd and pushed alng 4 out, chlgd 2 out, hrd rdn to ld last, jst hld on.*
.............................(25 to 1 op 16 to 1) 1

1858⁴ ROYAL PIPER (NZ) [102] 10-10-0 R Greene, *hld up beh, shaken up and hrd rdn, ran on wl nr finish, jst fld.*
.............................(25 to 1 op 20 to 1 tchd 33 to 1) 2

1668² MORSTOCK [112] 7-10-7 (3*) T Dascombe, *hld up in mid-div, hdwy to track ldrs 4 out, led appr 2 out, hrd rdn and hdd last, no extr...................*(8 to 1 op 7 to 1 tchd 9 to 1) 3

1848* BARFORD SOVEREIGN [109] 5-10-7 P Hide, *led, hdd appr 2 out, one pace..................*(7 to 2 jt-fav tchd 4 to 1) 4

1834⁵ KALASADI (USA) [104] (bl) 6-10-2 M Richards, *beh, styd on und pres frm 2 out, nvr nr to chal.*
.............................(16 to 1 op 14 to 1 tchd 20 to 1) 5

1699³ SMUGGLER'S POINT (USA) [107] 7-10-5 A Maguire, *cl up till 5th.*................(10 to 1 op 8 to 1 tchd 11 to 1) 6

1885⁵ ELPIDOS [118] 5-11-2 R Garritty, *hld up in rear, hrd rdn aftr 4 out, cld nxt, drvn alng and btn appr 2 out.*
.............................(7 to 1 op 6 to 1 tchd 15 to 2) 7

1945⁷ CALL MY GUEST (Ire) [123] 7-11-7 A P McCoy, *prmnt, hrd rdn appr 4 out, sn wknd.*(14 to 1 op 12 to 1 tchd 16 to 1) 8

1831 DJAIS (Fr) [119] (v) 8-11-3 G Bradley, *hdwy to track ldrs 3rd, drvn and wknd appr 2 out..................*(20 to 1) 9

1889 SECO RIOGA (Ire) [106] (v) 8-10-4 N Mann, *al beh, tld off.*
.............................(33 to 1 op 25 to 1 tchd 50 to 1) 10

2001⁷ ALLTIME DANCER (Ire) [119] 5-11-3 J Osborne, *hld up, hrd rdn appr 4 out, sn btn, tld off.....*(14 to 1 op 12 to 1) 11

1601² ROSENCRANTZ (Ire) [108] 5-10-6 R Johnson, *hld up, hdwy 4 out, cl 3rd and ev ch whn fld 4 out...*(7 to 2 jt-fav op 5 to 2) f

LUCKY BLUE [130] 10-12-0 M A Fitzgerald, *trkd ldrs, lost pl 6th, tld off whn pld up bef 3 out.*
.............................(16 to 1 op 12 to 1 tchd 20 to 1) pu

Dist: Nk, 1¼l, 8l, 6l, 4l, 4l, 20l, hd, 10l, 1l. 5m 2.50s. a 16.50s (13 Ran).
(R J Sunley Tice), Miss H C Knight

2218 Sun King Of The Punters Lanzarote Handicap Hurdle Class B (4-y-o and up) £14,278 2m.............. (2:40)

1997* MAKE A STAND [132] 6-10-3 A P McCoy, *made all, sn clr, hit 5th, shaken up appr 2 out, unchlgd.* (2 to 1 fav op 13 to 8) 1

1571² GALES CAVALIER (Ire) [129] 9-10-0 J Osborne, *hld up beh, shaken up and hdwy appr 2 out, styd on wl.*
.............................(10 to 1 op 8 to 1 tchd 11 to 1) 2

1761⁴ SILVER GROOM (Ire) [137] 7-10-3 (5*) S Ryan, *hld up, cld 5th, drvn to chase wnr appr 2 out, no extr und pres.*
.............................(10 to 1 op 7 to 1) 3

1885⁴ TOM BRODIE [129] 7-10-0 B Fenton, *hld up beh ldrs, shaken up aftr 3 out, sn hrd rdn and kpt on one pace.*
.............................(11 to 1 op 12 to 1 tchd 14 to 1) 4

1393⁶ CHIEF'S SONG [136] 7-10-7 D Gallagher, *chsd wnr to 4th, cl up till rdn and wknd frm 3 out......* (7 to 1 tchd 8 to 1) 5

2047⁴ MYTTON'S CHOICE (Ire) [129] 6-10-0 A Maguire, *in tch, hdwy second and 5th, hrd rdn 3 out, sn btn.*
.............................(11 to 1 op 10 to 1 tchd 12 to 1) 6

1761² MASTER BEVELED [139] 7-10-10 G Bradley, *cl up, chsd wnr frm 4th to appr 2 out, sn wknd.*
.............................(5 to 1 op 11 to 2 tchd 6 to 1) 7

1761 DREAMS END [134] 9-10-5 R Farrant, *in tch, pushed alng 5th, wknd und pres appr 2 out.........*(14 to 1 tchd 16 to 1) 8

KISSAIR (Ire) [134] 6-10-5 M A Fitzgerald, *al beh.*
.............................(25 to 1 tchd 33 to 1) 9

ROLL A DOLLAR [129] 11-10-0 P Holley, *keen early, hld up in tch, drvn and wknd frm 3 out.*
.............................(20 to 1 op 25 to 1 tchd 33 to 1) 10

303 ROS CASTLE [129] 6-10-0 I Lawrence, *al beh.*
.............................(33 to 1 tchd 40 to 1) 11

2001 ASHWELL BOY (Ire) [134] 6-10-5 R Johnson, *beh whn f 4th.*
.............................(25 to 1 tchd 33 to 1) f

Dist: 4l, 2l, 1¼l, 5l, 6l, 9l, 6l, 1l, 2l, 15l. 3m 44.10s. a 4.10s (12 Ran).
SR: 58/51/57/47/49/36/37/26/25/ (P A Deal), M C Pipe

2219 Victor Chandler Handicap Chase Class A Grade 2 (5-y-o and up) £21,560 2m................. (3:10)

2000² ASK TOM (Ire) [156] 8-10-10 R Garritty, *trkd ldr frm 4th, not fluent 8th, pushed alng aftr four out, lost pl appr nxt, hrd rdn, led r-in, gmely.......* (9 to 4 fav op 2 to 1 tchd 5 to 2) 1

964² CLAY COUNTY [146] 12-10-0 A P McCoy, *led, hit 9th, not fluent nxt, hrd rdn appr last, hdd r-in, ran on wl.*
.............................(11 to 1 op 8 to 1 tchd 12 to 1) 2

1878 BIG MATT (Ire) [148] 9-10-2² M A Fitzgerald, *hld up, hdwy appr 9th, shaken up aftr 4 out, rdn and mstk 2 out, kpt on.*
.............................(13 to 2 op 9 to 2 tchd 7 to 1) 3

1760² VIKING FLAGSHIP [170] 10-11-10 A Maguire, *trkd ldrs, shaken up aftr 4 out, chsd ldr appr nxt, ev ch approaching last, no extr.........* (4 to 1 op 9 to 2 tchd 5 to 1) 4

1875² KIBREET [146] 10-10-0 G Tormey, *trkd wnr to 4th, lost pl 6th, reminder appr 9th, sn btn.*
.............................(14 to 1 op 10 to 1 tchd 16 to 1) 5

2000* STORM ALERT [154] 11-10-8 R Johnson, *nvr gng wl, al beh, lost tch frm 7th, tld off....*(11 to 2 op 4 to 1 tchd 6 to 1) 6

1875* DANCING PADDY [148] 9-10-2 P Hide, *blun 1st, f nxt.*
.............................(6 to 1 op 10 to 1) f

1871² CALLISOE BAY (Ire) [146] 8-10-0 J Osborne, *blun and uns rdr*
1st..(14 to 1 op 16 to 1)　ur
Dist: ¾l, 2l, hd, 17l, 15l. 3m 46.50s. a 0.50s (8 Ran).
SR: 77/66/66/88/47/40/-/-/　　　　　　　(B T Stewart-Brown), T P Tate

2220 Sun Punters Club Fulwell Handicap Chase Class B (0-145 5-y-o and up) £7,080 2½m 110yds........(3:40)

1726⁷ GARRYLOUGH (Ire) [111] (bl) 8-10-1 A Maguire, *jmpd wl, made all, clr aftr 4 out, easily*...........(11 to 2 op 6 to 1)　1
1889² FIVE TO SEVEN (USA) [117] 8-10-7 A P McCoy, *cl up, reminders and chsd wnr frm 11th, ev ch 4 out, sn outpcd.*
....................................(3 to 1 fav op 11 to 4 tchd 7 to 2)　2
1480³ LACKENDARA [118] 10-10-8 B Fenton, *cl up, wknd 12th, no ch whn blun 4 out.*.........(5 to 1 op 9 to 1 tchd 11 to 2)　3
1972* BEATSON (Ire) [112] 8-9-13 (3*) G Hogan, *cl up, pushed alng aftr 12th, 3rd and ev ch whn blun 5 out, sn btn.*
....................................(100 to 30 op 5 to 2)　4
1999⁵ STRONG MEDICINE [134] 10-11-10 S McNeill, *hld up beh, blun 4th, btn 5 out, tld off.*...........(10 to 1 op 7 to 1)　5
1878² GO UNIVERSAL (Ire) [134] 9-11-10 G Bradley, *mstk 4th, hld up beh, struggling 13th, sn btn, tld off whn pld up bef 3 out.*
....................................(100 to 30 op 5 to 2 tchd 7 to 2)　pu
Dist: 14l, 19l, 10l, 21l. 5m 2.10s. a 9.10s (6 Ran).

(T J Whitley), D R Gandolfo

2221 Weatherbys 'Stars Of Tomorrow' Open National Hunt Flat Standard - Class H (4,5,6-y-o) £1,696 2m (4:10)

1768⁵ CLINKING 6-11-5 Mrs A Perrett, *pld hrd, trkd ldrs, led 2 fs out, ran on wl.*..............(8 to 1 op 5 to 1 tchd 10 to 1)　1
53² TANGLEFOOT TIPPLE 6-11-2 (3*) P Henley, *trkd ldrs, swtchd rght and chsd wnr wl o'r one furlong out, kpt on...*(2 to 1 jt-
fav op 5 to 2 tchd 3 to 1)　2
TEN TIMES (USA) 4-10-7 A P McCoy, *set steady pace, reminder and quickened 5 fs out; hdd 2 out, rallied briefly, sn outpcd...*(2 to 1 jt-fav op 6 to 4 tchd 5 to 4)　3
CURRER BELL 4-10-2 K Gaule, *trkd ldr, drw level 2 fs out, sn outpcd...*........(7 to 1 op 5 to 1 tchd 8 to 1)　4
EMBARGO (Ire) 5-10-12 (7*) Mr H Dunlop, *hld up, keen hold, outpcd 5 fs out, styd on ins last.*
....................................(13 to 2 op 2 to 1 tchd 7 to 1)　5
STAR ISLAND 4-10-0 (7*) Mr N Moran, *hld up beh, effrt 5 fs out, no imprsn o'r 2 out...*(7 to 1 op 5 to 1 tchd 9 to 1)　6
GREMATIC 6-11-5 R Greene, *hld up, outpcd fnl 5 fs, tld off.*
....................................(25 to 1 op 14 to 1 tchd 33 to 1)　7
SHAVANO 5-11-5 B Fenton, *hld up, outpcd 5 fs out, tld off.*
....................................(33 to 1 op 20 to 1 tchd 50 to 1)　8
Dist: 7l, 9l, 6l, 4l, 2½l, 12l, 30l. 3m 51.10s. (8 Ran).

(G Harwood), Mrs A J Perrett

PUNCHESTOWN (IRE) (yielding to soft) Saturday January 18th
Going Correction: PLUS 0.40 sec. per fur.

2222 Brannockstown Maiden Hurdle (5-y-o and up) £3,082 2m........(1:00)

1533⁸ FISHIN JOELLA (Ire) 5-11-2 (3*) G Cotter, ...(8 to 1)　1
BAWNROCK (Ire) 8-12-0 C F Swan, ...(12 to 1)　2
1836³ WEST LEADER (Ire) 6-11-6 T P Rudd, ...(8 to 1)　3
1895² NATIVE-DARRIG (Ire) 6-12-0 D J Casey, ...(7 to 4 fav)　4
1649 NOBLE SHOON (Ire) 6-12-0 K F O'Brien, ...(10 to 1)　5
2131¹³ IMPERIAL PLAICE (Ire) 5-10-9 (7*) D M Bean, ...(10 to 1)　6
635⁵ NA HUIBHEACHU (Ire) 6-11-6 R Hughes, ...(12 to 1)　7
2017³ BLUSHING SAND (Ire) 7-11-7 (7*) Mr T J Beattie, ..(10 to 1)　8
1899 CONAGHER BOY (Ire) 7-12-0 A Powell, ...(16 to 1)　9
2131 TWO SHONAS (Ire) 6-11-9 J Short, ...(16 to 1)　10
2106 THE TICK-TACK MAN (Ire) 5-10-9 (7*) K Kelly, ..(25 to 1)　11
2040⁵ LITE 'N EASY (Ire) 7-11-1 C O'Brien, ...(20 to 1)　12
2094⁶ GARRYS LOCK (Ire) 8-12-0 C O'Dwyer, ...(9 to 2)　13
2131¹⁴ BAR FLUTE (Ire) 6-11-1 T Horgan, ...(20 to 1)　14
1279³ MICK MAN (Ire) 6-10-13 (7*) B J Geraghty, ...(33 to 1)　15
2048 CLONEE PRIDE (Ire) 6-11-1 P L Malone, ...(33 to 1)　16
2094⁷ CAVALIER D'OR (USA) 6-12-0 F Woods, ...(10 to 1)　17
MONALEA (Ire) 6-10-13 (7*) A P Sweeney, ...(33 to 1)　18
DAN PATCH (Ire) 11-12-0 L P Cusack, ...(33 to 1)　19
2110⁴ BERNSTIC WONDER 8-11-6 J Jones, ...(33 to 1)　20
1432 WHINNEY HILL (Ire) 7-11-1 D T Evans, ...(50 to 1)　21
2092⁷ SILKEN SECRETARIAT (Ire) 6-11-6 T P Treacy, ...(50 to 1)　22
2129 MAGS DWYER (Ire) 7-11-4 (5*) T Martin, ...(20 to 1)　23
1193 FOREST STAR (USA) 8-11-11 (3*) K Whelan, ...(33 to 1)　24
2107 HURRICANE DROID (Ire) 8-11-7 (7*) R P Hogan, ..(33 to 1)　25
2079 CORDAL DREAM (Ire) 5-10-11 J P Broderick, ...(50 to 1)　26
717⁵ KILKEA (Ire) 6-11-1 J K Kinane, ...(33 to 1)　27
2131 MURKELBUR (Ire) 6-10-8 (7*) R M Murphy, ...(66 to 1)　28
Dist: 15l, 16l, 1½l, 1½l. 3m 56.50s. a 11.50s (28 Ran).
SR: 40/34/20/23/21/-/　　　　　(C A Bailey), Peadar Matthews

2223 Dunshane Handicap Chase (0-102 5-y-o and up) £3,767 2¾m....(1:30)

1903⁶ ALL IN THE GAME (Ire) [-] 9-9-13² P A Roche, ...(16 to 1)　1

2169* BAILE NA GCLOCH (Ire) [-] 8-11-7 (3*,4ex) D P Murphy, ...(6 to 4 fav)　2
2096⁶ MUSKIN MORE (Ire) [-] 6-11-3 C O'Dwyer, ...(7 to 1)　3
2141⁸ GREEK MAGIC [-] 10-9-4 (3*) G Cotter, ...(33 to 1)　4
2038² TIMELY AFFAIR (Ire) [-] (bl) 8-10-5 F Woods, ...(9 to 2)　5
2163² BALLYBODEN [-] 10-10-12 M P Hourigan, ...(8 to 1)　6
1755⁴ LAURA'S BEAU [-] 13-11-7 (7*) R P Hogan, ...(12 to 1)　7
1582⁴ LA-GREINE [-] 10-10-13 (7*) Mr K Ross, ...(7 to 1)　8
Dist: 3l, 25l, 11l, 5½l. 6m 12.30s. (8 Ran).

(Fiacre J Hensey), John Brassil

2224 The Sunday Times Novice Chase (5-y-o and up) £4,117 2½m......(2:00)

2057⁸ BUCKMINSTER 10-11-8 C O'Brien, ...(12 to 1)　1
2039³ LIVIN IT UP (Ire) 7-11-8 F Woods, ...(11 to 2)　2
2096⁷ BANGABUNNY 7-11-5 (3*) K Whelan, ...(12 to 1)　3
2143 DAWN ALERT (Ire) 8-11-8 C F Swan, ...(6 to 1)　4
2096⁴ KALDAN KHAN 6-11-8 C F Swan, ...(11 to 4 fav)　5
1779⁹ THE SUBBIE (Ire) 8-12-0 T P Treacy, ...(4 to 1)　6
2096⁵ ARCTIC BUCK (Ire) 7-11-8 C O'Dwyer, ...(14 to 1)　7
1899 SPECTACLE (Ire) (bl) 7-11-8 A Powell, ...(20 to 1)　8
1841⁷ LUCKY BUST (Ire) 7-11-1 (7*) Mr D A Harney, ...(12 to 1)　ur
2143 SPIRE HILL (Ire) 8-11-1 (7*) Mr K Ross, ...(33 to 1)　ur
2096³ THE VENDOR (Ire) 7-10-10 (7*) A O'Shea, ...(8 to 1)　ur
2036⁹ GRANNY BOWLY (Ire) 7-11-3 H Rogers, ...(33 to 1)　pu
Dist: 8l, 5½l, 2½l, 20l. 5m 38.20s. a 41.20s (12 Ran).

(A Lillingston), A Lillingston

2225 Blessington Novice Hurdle (4-y-o and up) £3,767 2½m.........(2:30)

2135* GLEBE LAD (Ire) 5-11-10 T P Rudd, ...(5 to 1)　1
2107² MONTELISA (Ire) 5-11-5 C F Swan, ...(9 to 1)　2
2105² GO SASHA (Ire) (bl) 4-10-7 (5*) T Martin, ...(8 to 1)　3
1018³ GLADIATORIAL (Ire) 5-11-10 P L Malone, ...(7 to 1)　4
2081* JODESI (Ire) 7-12-0 D J Casey, ...(5 to 4 fav)　5
2080⁶ BLUE IRISH (Ire) 6-11-5 (3*) K Whelan, ...(20 to 1)　6
1839 ABIGAIL ROSE (Bel) 5-10-13 D T Evans, ...(20 to 1)　7
2107 HAMSHIRE GALE (Ire) 7-11-3 A Powell, ...(50 to 1)　8
MAGIC MOONBEAM (Ire) 7-11-3 J P Broderick, ...(25 to 1)　pu
Dist: 4l, 3½l, dist, 15l. 5m 29.40s. a 47.40s (9 Ran).

(T B Conroy), M J P O'Brien

2226 Ballymore Eustace Handicap Chase (0-109 5-y-o and up) £3,767 2m
....(3:00)

2164⁴ PRATE BOX (Ire) [-] 7-11-3 A Powell, ...(9 to 2)　1
1906³ SORRY ABOUT THAT [-] 11-11-0 P L Malone, ...(5 to 2 fav)　2
2133 QUICK LEARNER (Ire) [-] 8-10-9 C O'Dwyer, ...(10 to 1)　3
2167³ MINSTREL FIRE (Ire) [-] 9-11-5 (7*) Mr B Hassett, ...(5 to 1)　4
2167⁴ HANNIES GIRL (Ire) [-] 8-10-5 (7*) L J Fleming, ...(7 to 1)　5
2076⁵ JAZZY REFRAIN (Ire) [-] 7-11-12 C F Swan, ...(8 to 1)　6
2136⁷ UNA'S CHOICE (Ire) [-] 9-12-0 F J Flood, ...(14 to 1)　f
Dist: 4l, 1l, 11l, 2l. 4m 49.10s. a 50.10s (7 Ran).

(Miss Heather Scully), P Hughes

2227 Landenstown Handicap Hurdle (0-137 4-y-o and up) £4,110 2m
....(3:30)

2114* LADY DAISY (Ire) [-] 8-10-9 (7*) A O'Shea, ...(7 to 4 fav)　1
2086* LEGAL AND TENDER (Ire) [-] 6-9-0 (7*) R P Hogan, (4 to 1)　2
2086⁵ OWENDUFF (USA) [-] 7-10-6 F Woods, ...(7 to 2)　3
2128 REASILVIA (Ire) [-] 7-10-13 C F Swan, ...(14 to 1)　4
2057⁵ IODER WAN (Ire) [-] 5-9-2 (7*) P G Hourigan, ...(10 to 1)　5
2016⁹ LOUISES FANCY (Ire) [-] 7-9-4 (3*) G Cotter, ...(20 to 1)　6
2126⁵ APPELLATE COURT [-] 9-10-13 A Powell, ...(16 to 1)　7
944⁵ MIROSWAKI (USA) [-] 7-10-7 C O'Dwyer, ...(14 to 1)　8
2133⁸ PUNTING PETE (Ire) [-] 7-11-5 T P Treacy, ...(10 to 1)　9
1650 BROCKLEY COURT [-] 10-12-0 J Short, ...(10 to 1)　10
Dist: 6l, 1½l, 8l, 3l. 3m 56.80s. a 11.80s (10 Ran).
SR: 34/5/16/15/-/-/　　　　　(Patrick F Kehoe), Anthony Mullins

2228 Rooske I.N.H. Flat Race (5-y-o and up) £3,082 2m.....(4:00)

NORTHERN GALAXY (Ire) 5-11-3 (7*) Mr G Donnelly,
....................................(10 to 1)　1
2108³ RING MAID (Ire) 7-11-3 (7*) Mr R Walsh, ...(5 to 1)　2
1756⁴ OUR-DANTE (Ire) 5-10-12 (7*) Mr Sean O O'Brien, ...(5 to 1)　3
1273 DROMARA BREEZE (Ire) 9-11-7 (7*) Mr A J Dempsey,
....................................(14 to 1)　4
CHOICE JENNY (Ire) 5-10-12 (7*) Mr A C Coyle, (9 to 4 fav)　5
TOBYS PAL (Ire) 7-11-9 (5*) Mr D McGoona, ...(14 to 1)　6
2129 EXECUTIVE MERC (Ire) 6-11-7 (7*) Mr J F O'Shea,
....................................(25 to 1)　7
2092⁶ TORMOND PERK (Ire) 6-11-11 (3*) Mr B M Cash, (10 to 1)　8
HOLLOW FINGER (Ire) 6-11-9 (5*) Mr G Elliott, ...(8 to 1)　9
561³ LADY RICHENDA (Ire) 9-11-2 (7*) Mr J P McNamara,
....................................(12 to 1)　10
DENNETT VALLEY (Ire) 8-11-7 (7*) Miss S McDonogh,
....................................(20 to 1)　11
ROSE ANA (Ire) 7-11-2 (7*) Mr T N Cloke, ...(12 to 1)　12
FAIRFIELD BRANDY (Ire) 6-11-4 (5*) Mr J T McNamara,
....................................(16 to 1)　13

304 MYSTICAL RYE (Ire) 6-11-2 (7*) Mr M T Hartrey, . . .(25 to 1) 14
Dist: 15l, 13l, 7l, 2½l. 3m 57.60s. (14 Ran).
(Mrs Sean M Collins), A L T Moore

LEOPARDSTOWN (IRE) (good to yielding)
Sunday January 19th

Going Correction: PLUS 0.15 sec. per fur. (races 1,2,4,6,7), PLUS 0.05 (3,5)

2229 Brownstown Handicap Hurdle (0-130 5-y-o and up) £3,082 2¾m .... (1:05)

2036[3] THE QUADS [-] 5-9-7 F Woods, ... (8 to 1) 1
1756[7] VASILIKI (Ire) [-] 5-10-2 D J Casey, ...(25 to 1) 2
2068[8] LISCAHILL FORT (Ire) [-] 8-10-8 (3*) B Bowens, . . . (12 to 1) 3
2057* KASELECTRIC (Ire) [-] (bl) 6-10-11 T Horgan, ... (8 to 1) 4
2097[3] FALLOW TRIX (Ire) [-] 5-10-2 (7*) Mr J Keville, ...(10 to 1) 5
2126[4] TELL THE NIPPER (Ire) [-] (bl) 6-11-8 R Dunwoody, ...(9 to 4 fav) 6
[illegible] [illegible] CASTLE (Ire) [-] 7-10-0 (7*) Mr A Stronge, ...(9 to 1) 7
2068[7] SIR JOHN (Ire) [-] 8-10-8 C F Swan, ...(3 to 1) 8
1838* GRANGE COURT (Ire) [-] 7-11-8 J Shortt, ...(8 to 1) 9
1489[6] JANE DIGBY (Ire) [-] 5-11-2 (7*) S P Kelly, ... (20 to 1) 10
1899[9] GLENBALLYMA (Ire) [-] 8-10-11 F J Flood, ...(6 to 1) pu
Dist: 1l, 1½l, 1½l, 3½l. 5m 14.10s. a 8.10s (11 Ran).
SR: 17/25/32/30/24/-/ (I Told You So Syndicate), A L T Moore

2230 Waterford Crystal Hurdle (4-y-o) £4,110 2m. . . . .(1:35)

1616 DR BONES (Ire) 10-7 T P Rudd, ...(25 to 1) 1
2112[2] AFARKA (Ire) 10-2 T P Treacy, ...(10 to 1) 2
2050[8] SPIRIT DANCER (Ire) 10-13 S C Lyons, ... (12 to 1) 3
SNOW FALCON 10-7 R Dunwoody, ... (14 to 1) 4
2112* MARLONETTE (Ire) 10-8 D J Casey, ... (8 to 1) 5
NAMOODAJ 10-7 P Carberry, ... (5 to 4 fav) 6
2050 HIGHLY MOTIVATED 10-8 C F Swan, ...(100 to 30) 7
FAMILY PROJECT (Ire) 9-9 (7*) M W Martin, ...(12 to 1) 8
THE SWAN 10-2 R Hughes, ... (12 to 1) 9
2067[4] VICTORY BOUND (USA) 10-7 F Woods, ...(6 to 1) 10
2067[3] LOUGH SLANIA (Ire) 10-7 J Shortt, ...(14 to 1) 11
2050 EVRIZA (Ire) 11-0 T Horgan, ...(10 to 1) 12
2067 NASCIMENTO (USA) 10-7 C O'Dwyer, ... (16 to 1) 13
Dist: Nk, 2½l, 2½l, 4l. 3m 53.10s. a 9.10s (13 Ran).
SR: 12/7/15/6/3/-/ (Mrs Denis Fortune), M J P O'Brien

2231 Baileys Arkle Perpetual Challenge Cup (Grade 2) (5-y-o and up) £9,675 2m 1f. . . . .(2:05)

1758* MULLIGAN (Ire) 7-12-0 A Maguire, *made all, jmpd wl, quickened aftr last.* . . . .(2 to 1) 1
2052[3] BEAKSTOWN (Ire) 8-11-11 (3*) G Cotter, *wl plcd, rdn and prog aftr 2 out, no extr r-in.* . . . .(14 to 1) 2
2052[7] PENNDARA (Ire) 8-11-7 C F Swan, *trkd ldr, travelling wl whn mstk 2 out, sn rdn, wknd r-in.* . . . .(20 to 1) 3
2052 KHARASAR (Ire) 7-11-7 C O'Dwyer, *rear, mstk 4 out, sn rdn, jmpd slwly nxt, wknd.* . . . .(5 to 1) 4
2052[4] HEADBANGER 10-11-7 D H O'Connor, *rear, mstk 5th, rdn aftr 3 out, not quicken.* . . . .(16 to 1) 5
2052* DANOLI (Ire) 9-12-0 T P Treacy, *wl plcd till mstk and f second.* . . . .(10 to 9 on) f
Dist: 9l, 1l, 9l, 1½l. 4m 16.00s. a 6.00s (6 Ran).
SR: 48/39/31/22/20/-/ (Lady Harris), D Nicholson

2232 A.I.G. Europe Champion Hurdle (Grade 1) (4-y-o and up) £34,000 2m .... (2:40)

2095[3] COCKNEY LAD (Ire) 8-11-10 R Hughes, *wtd wth, prog bef 2 out, sn rdn, ran on strly to ld last 20 yards.* . . . . (10 to 1) 1
2095* THEATREWORLD (Ire) 5-11-6 C F Swan, *led or dsptd ld, not fluent, rdn aftr 4 out, led 2 out till hdd fnl 20 yards.* . . . . (13 to 8 fav) 2
1905[2] DARDJINI (USA) 7-11-10 P Carberry, *trkd ldrs, rdn aftr 2 out, chalg whn mstk last, no extr.* . . . . (25 to 1) 3
1638[2] URUBANDE (Ire) 7-11-10 R Dunwoody, *dsptd ld, narrow advantage 4 out, rdn and hdd 2 out, sn wknd.* . . . .(4 to 1) 4
ESCARTEFIGUE (Fr) 5-11-6 D Bridgwater, *wl plcd, rdn and wknd appr 2 out.* . . . .(7 to 1) 5
2128 NOTCOMPLAININGBUT (Ire) 6-11-5 T P Treacy, *al rear, rdn aftr 3 out, not quicken.* . . . . (25 to 1) 6
1638* ZABADI (Ire) 5-11-6 A Maguire, *mid-div, rdn and prog bef 2 out, wknd before last.* . . . . (100 to 30) 7
Dist: 1l, 2l, 9l, 4½l. 3m 51.40s. a 7.40s (7 Ran).
SR: 46/41/43/34/25/-/-/ (D Daly), Noel Meade

2233 Foxrock Handicap Chase (Listed) (5-y-o and up) £5,480 2m 3f. . . . . .(3:10)

2086[9] MANHATTAN CASTLE (Ire) [-] 8-9-13 F Woods, *wtd wth, gd prog aftr 2 out to dispute ld last, sn clr.* . . . .(4 to 1) 1
2136* ARCTIC WEATHER (Ire) [-] 8-9-7 T P Rudd, *wtd wth, mstk 4th, rdn aftr 2 out to dispute ld last, no extr.* . . . . (5 to 1) 2
1294* CALL IT A DAY (Ire) [-] 7-10-3 A Maguire, *wl plcd, rdn and prog to track ldr 2 out, no extr frm last.* . . . . . .(100 to 30 fav) 3
2085[4] BELVEDERIAN [-] 10-10-5 P Carberry, *trkd ldr, led bef 6th, rdn and hdd aftr 2 out, no extr.* . . . . (10 to 1) 4
1571[3] KADI (Ger) [-] 8-10-4 R Johnson, *wl plcd, prog to track ldr 3 out, rdn bef nxt, wknd appr last.* . . . .(7 to 1) 5
2085[3] OPERA HAT (Ire) [-] 9-11-2 C O'Dwyer, *wl plcd, jmpd slwly 4 out, rdn bef 2 out, wknd before last.* . . . .(4 to 1) 6
2069[3] FIFTYSEVENCHANNELS (Ire) [-] 8-9-10 C F Swan, *rear, rdn and prog bef 2 out, wknd before last.* . . . . (7 to 1) 7
2127[6] ROYAL MOUNTBROWNE [-] 9-11-3 T Horgan, *led till bef 6th, mstk 3 out, sn wknd.* . . . .(10 to 1) 8
Dist: 1½l, ½l, 2l, 1½l. 4m 41.90s. a 2.90s (8 Ran).
SR: 51/43/52/52/49/ (P Fitzpatrick), A L T Moore

2234 Foxrock (Pro-Am) I.N.H. Flat Race (4-y-o) £3,082 2m. . . . . (3:40)

FAWN PRINCE (Ire) 11-2 (3*) Mr B M Cash, . . .(3 to 1 jt-fav) 1
SLANEY NATIVE (Ire) 11-2 (3*) Mr P English, ... (6 to 1) 2
DIVINE DANCER (Ire) 11-0 Mr J P Dempsey, ...(14 to 1) 3
KOHOUTEK 11-2 (3*) Mr R Walsh, ...(8 to 1) 4
GALLAHER'S WALK (Ire) 11-5 Mr P Fenton, . .(3 to 1 jt-fav) 5
FISHIN PRINT (Ire) 11-2 (3*) G Cotter, ...(11 to 2) 6
BILL BISHOP (Ire) 11-5 Mr D Marnane, ...(10 to 1) 7
GERRYS GIFT (Ire) 10-7 (7*) Mr Edgar Byrne, ... (7 to 2) 8
2130[6] CAJUN ROSE (Ire) 10-7 (7*) Mr J P McNamara, . . . (16 to 1) 9
Dist: 2½l, 1½l, ½l, 1½l. 4m 11.20s. (9 Ran).
(John P McManus), A P O'Brien

2235 Fairhaven I.N.H. Flat Race (5-y-o and up) £3,082 2¼m. . . . . (4:10)

2115* PROMALEE (Ire) 5-11-7 (7*) Miss A L Crowley, . .(7 to 4 fav) 1
2129[2] KILCOO BOY (Ire) 6-12-1 (3*) Mr B M Cash, ... (2 to 1) 2
2041* DR KING (Ire) 5-11-11 (3*) Mr R Walsh, ...(5 to 1) 3
2087[5] THE GREY MARE (Ire) 8-11-6 (7*) Mr P Fahey, ... (14 to 1) 4
2098[2] SCOUT AROUND (Ire) 5-11-7 Mr P Fenton, ...(3 to 1) 5
Dist: Sht-hd, 5½l, 20l, 6l. 4m 14.10s. (5 Ran).
(Seamus O'Farrell), A P O'Brien

CARLISLE (good to firm)
Monday January 20th

Going Correction: PLUS 0.30 sec. per fur. (races 1,3,6), PLUS 0.15 (2,4,5)

2236 Gossip Holme Novices' Hurdle Class E (4-y-o and up) £2,612 2m 1f (1:25)

1656* MISTER ROSS (Ire) 7-11-11 P Carberry, *led 3rd, hrd pressed 3 out, styd on wl to go clr betw last 2, eased considerably finish.* . . . .(Evens fav op 5 to 4 tchd 11 to 8) 1
NORTHERN UNION (Can) 6-11-5 D Parker, *cl up, chsd wnr frm 6th, ev ch 3 out, kpt on same pace.* (5 to 1 tchd 9 to 2) 2
FOREVER NOBLE (Ire) 4-10-7 R Garritty, *sn mid-div, hdwy bef 3 out, styd on wl und pres frm betw last 2, nrst finish.* . . . . (10 to 1 op 7 to 1) 3
2061[5] CATHERINE'S CHOICE 4-10-4 (3*) Mr C Bonner, *in tch, hdwy bef 3 out, kpt on same pace frm nxt.* . . .(33 to 1 op 20 to 1) 4
2117[4] LUMBACK LADY 7-10-11 (3*) G Lee, *hld up, hdwy bef 3 out, kpt on same pace frm nxt.* . . . .(20 to 1) 5
1818[4] YEWCROFT BOY 5-11-0 (5*) S Taylor, *prmnt, pushed alng bef 5th, kpt on same pace frm 3 out.* . . . . (50 to 1) 6
1690 RECRUITMENT 4-10-7 W Fry, *in tch, gd hdwy bef 3 out, wknd aftr nxt.* . . . . (100 to 1 op 50 to 1) 7
1690[7] CRABBIE'S PRIDE (bl) 4-10-7 Derek Byrne, *nvr better than mid-div.* . . . .(16 to 1 op 14 to 1) 8
1662[3] BLACK ICE (Ire) 6-11-5 P Niven, *led to 3rd, prmnt till wknd bef 3 out.* . . . . . . (15 to 2 op 8 to 1 tchd 10 to 1 and 7 to 1) 9
HENRY HOOLET 8-11-5 G Cahill, *nvr better than mid-div.* . . . .(25 to 1 op 16 to 1) 10
1629 WHOTHEHELLISHARRY (bl) 4-10-7 M Moloney, *chsd ldrs till wknd bef 3 out.* . . . .(20 to 1 op 14 to 1) 11
1326[4] BOLLIN FRANK 5-11-5 A S Smith, *chsd ldrs till wknd aftr 6th.* . . . . (11 to 1 op 8 to 1) 12
1826[8] THE FINAL SPARK 6-11-0 L O'Hara, *wl beh hfwy.* . . . .(50 to 1 op 33 to 1) 13
1631 TRIONA'S HOPE (Ire) 8-10-12 (7*) Tristan Davidson, *strted slwly, wl beh hfwy.* . . . .(1000 to 1) 14
MILLERS GOLDENGIRL (Ire) 6-11-0 Richard Guest, *wl beh hfwy.* . . . .(100 to 1 op 66 to 1) 15
AUNT PIQUEE 8-11-0 A Dobbin, *wl beh hfwy, tld off.* . . . .(25 to 1 op 14 to 1) 16
1689[7] NEEDLE MATCH 4-10-2 (5*) R McGrath, *f 1st.* . . . . . (33 to 1) f
2061[7] MILETRIAN CITY 4-10-0 (7*) S Haworth, *brght dwn 1st.* . . . .(50 to 1) bd
COEUR FRANCAIS (Fr) 5-11-0 (5*) Michael Brennan, *tld off whn ran out 5th.* . . . .(100 to 1) ro
Dist: 1¼l, hd, 9l, 1l, 4l, 11l, 3½l, nk, 5l, 4l. 4m 18.00s. a 15.00s (19 Ran).
(Gordon Brown), J Howard Johnson

NATIONAL HUNT RESULTS 1996-97

2237 Brick Kiln Novices' Chase Class E (5-y-o and up) £3,258 2½m 110yds
.... (1:55)

1385 CROWN EQUERRY (Ire) 7-11-4 P Carberry, sn tracking ldrs, hit 11th, led 4 out, clr last, eased finish.
.............(13 to 8 on op 5 to 4 on tchd 7 to 4 on) 1
1825³ BOLD ACCOUNT (Ire) 7-11-4 A Dobbin, led 4th to four out, kpt on same pace, no ch wth wnr..........(7 to 1 op 5 to 1) 2
1952² TICO GOLD 9-11-4 A S Smith, in tch, outpcd bef 12th, styd on wl und pres frm 2 out.....(6 to 1 op 4 to 1 tchd 13 to 2) 3
GONE AWAY (Ire) 8-11-4 R Garritty, towards rear, lost tch bef 12th, tld off..........(20 to 1 op 10 to 1 tchd 25 to 1) 4
1913² GAELIC BLUE 7-11-4 Richard Guest, in tch, hdwy to track ldrs 12th, 3rd and ch whn blun and uns rdr 4 out.
.................................(7 to 1 op 6 to 1) ur
1954 SHOW YOUR HAND (Ire) 9-11-10 M Foster, lad to 4th, prmnt, wknd quickly aftr four out, losing tch whn blun 2 out, pld up bef last............(16 to 1 op 10 to 1 tchd 25 to 1) pu
1828⁴ DARK BUOY 8-11-4 B Storey, beh, lost tch bef 12th, tld off whn pld up before last, broke blood vessel.
.................(14 to 1 op 12 to 1 tchd 20 to 1) pu
Dist: 2l, 1¼l, dist. 5m 14.30s. a 19.30s (7 Ran).
(Robert Ogden), G Richards

2238 Mary Brow Handicap Hurdle Class E (0-115 4-y-o and up) £2,416 2½m 110yds....................... (2:25)

1775* ELA MATA [110] 5-11-2 (7*) B Grattan, hld up and beh, steady hdwy to ld aftr 8th, clr last, easily.
....................(6 to 5 fav op 6 to 4 tchd 13 to 8) 1
1986² KEMO SABO [92] 5-10-5 D Parker, in tch, effrt aftr 8th, sn pushed alng, kpt on same pace, no ch wth wnr.
.................(11 to 2 op 9 to 2 tchd 13 to 2) 2
2151⁶ GLENUGIE [100] 6-10-13 N Bentley, in tch, pushed along aftr 8th, kpt on same pace....(13 to 2 op 6 to 1 tchd 7 to 1) 3
1914⁴ KEEN TO THE LAST (Fr) [99] 5-10-12 R Garritty, made most till aftr 8th, kpt on same pace.
.................(9 to 1 op 7 to 1 tchd 10 to 1) 4
1315⁹ DOCKMASTER [88] 6-10-1 A S Smith, in tch till outpcd aftr 7th, no chng after.............(12 to 1 op 10 to 1) 5
2004⁷ ELATION [115] 5-12-0 A Dobbin, chsd ldrs till wknd bef 3 out.
.......................(13 to 2 op 6 to 1 tchd 7 to 1) 6
1914⁵ EXEMPLAR (Ire) [95] 9-10-8 Richard Guest, dsptd ld to 5th, wknd aftr 8th....................(7 to 1 op 5 to 1) 7
EUROLINK THE REBEL (USA) [96] 5-10-2 (7*) Miss R Clark, hld up, outpcd and lost tch aftr 7th, tld off whn pld up bef 2 out.
..................................(66 to 1 op 50 to 1) pu
Dist: 16l, sht-hd, 3½l, 21l, 6l, 11l. 5m 0.50s. a 18.50s (8 Ran).
(F J Sainsbury), Mrs A Swinbank

2239 Todd Hills Handicap Chase Class D (0-120 5-y-o and up) £3,848 3m
.... (2:55)

1822⁵ SON OF IRIS [98] 9-11-3 P Niven, hld up, cld 13th, blun nxt, led 3 out, styd on wl.................(6 to 1 op 9 to 2) 1
1988 WESTWELL BOY [105] 11-11-10 R Supple, led to 8th, dsptd ld, led 4 out to nxt, sn rdn, kpt on same pace.
..............(6 to 5 fav op 5 to 4 tchd 11 to 10) 2
2003* SLOTAMATIQUE (Ire) [102] 8-11-7 A Dobbin, cl up, mstk 5th, made most frm 8th to 4 out, fdd aftr nxt...(2 to 1 op 6 to 4) 3
1589 SUPPOSIN [92] 9-10-11 Richard Guest, hld up, effrt bef 3 out, sn rdn and btn............(7 to 1 op 6 to 1 tchd 8 to 1) 4
2065² FORWARD GLEN [81] 9-10-10-0 A S Smith, hld up, effrt aftr 4 out, ch whn f nxt....................(9 to 1 op 7 to 1) f
Dist: 7l, 2½l, ½l. 6m 18.60s. a 26.60s (5 Ran).
(M H G Systems Ltd), Mrs M Reveley

2240 Hoary Tom Novices' Chase Class D (5-y-o and up) £3,707 2m..... (3:25)

1630* SPARKY GAYLE (Ire) 7-11-13 B Storey, beh, hdwy hfwy, led 2 out, styd on wl und pres.
.............(7 to 4 on op 6 to 4 on tchd 11 to 8 on) 1
CHIEF MINISTER (Ire) 8-11-3 R Garritty, hld up, steady hdwy to chase ldr 7th, chlgd 3 out, chsd wnr frm nxt, kpt on wl und pres.........................(9 to 4 op 4 to 6) 2
1912³ SINGING SAND 7-11-3 A Dobbin, chsd ldr, lft in ld 5th, mstk and hdd 2 out, wknd. (40 to 1 op 50 to 1 tchd 66 to 1) 3
1585 NIJWAY 7-10-12 (5*) S Taylor, in tch, rdn hfwy, wknd 4 out.
...................................(150 to 1 op 100 to 1) 4
2201 FENWICK'S BROTHER 7-11-3 Richard Guest, chsd ldrs, cl up 5th till fdd 8th.......(40 to 1 op 25 to 1 tchd 50 to 1) 5
1510² KILLBALLY BOY 7-11-3 P Carberry, led till f 5th.
.................(9 to 1 op 8 to 1 tchd 10 to 1) f
1589⁹ MOVAC (Ire) (v) 8-11-8 G Cahill, lost tch hfwy, tld off whn pld up bef 4 out...................(25 to 1 op 16 to 1) pu
Dist: 1¼l, 20l, 3l, 2l. 4m 2.50s. a 8.50s (7 Ran).
SR: 38/26/6/3/1/-/-/ (Mr & Mrs Raymond Anderson Green), C Parker

2241 Bells Field Novices' Handicap Hurdle Class E (0-105 4-y-o and up) £2,458 3m 110yds................. (3:55)

1197 BARDAROS [74] 8-10-8 M Foster, trkd ldrs, led 2 out, sn clr, easily...................(20 to 1 op 16 to 1) 1
1311³ PEBBLE BEACH [87] 7-11-7 N Bentley, trkd ldrs, led 9th, sn hrd pressed, hdd 2 out, kpt on same pace.
.................(11 to 2 op 5 to 1 tchd 6 to 1) 2
1736⁶ HAUGHTON LAD (Ire) [69] 8-10-3 V Smith, in tch, hdwy bef 9th, styd on same pace frm 3 out....(16 to 1 op 14 to 1) 3
2120⁴ RUBER [75] 10-10-9 D Parker, mid-div, pushed alng hfwy, styd on same pace frm 3 out.
.................(7 to 1 op 6 to 1 tchd 8 to 1) 4
1987⁵ DASHMAR [66] (v) 10-9-10¹ (5*) Michael Brennan, beh and pushed alng hfwy, styd on whn 3 out to go second aftr last, eased fnl 50 yards, fnshd lme........(25 to 1 op 20 to 1) 5
1337⁴ MOVIE MAN [76] 5-10-8 A Dobbin, hld up, hdwy bef 3 out, kpt on same pace frm nxt...............(16 to 1 op 12 to 1) 6
1631 FENLOE RAMBLER (Ire) [80] 6-11-0 K Johnson, prmnt, rdn to ld 8th, hdd nxt, sn outpcd, kpt on und pres frm 2 out.
.................(14 to 1 op 12 to 1) 7
1662⁶ THE NEXT WALTZ (Ire) [79] 6-11-0 R Supple, in tch, hdwy aftr 7th, chlgd 3 out, wknd appr nxt.........(8 to 1 op 6 to 1) 8
1679 POCAIRE GAOITHE (Ire) [72] (v) 7-10-6 M Moloney, mid-div, rdn hfwy, no hdwy frm 8th.
.................(12 to 1 op 20 to 1 tchd 25 to 1) 9
1984⁵ KINGS LANE [89] 8-11-4 (5*) Mr M H Naughton, in tch, some hdwy aftr 9th, wknd after 3 out.......(12 to 1 op 10 to 1) 10
1951⁶ CUILLIN CAPER [71] 5-10-3 O Pears, in tch till wknd bef 3 out, tld off........................(33 to 1) 11
1313² BAHER (USA) [90] 8-11-10 J Supple, in tch, hdwy hfwy, drvn alng to clsd 9th, ev ch whn f 3 out......(6 to 1 op 7 to 1) f
BUSY BOY [70] 10-10-4 J Burke, chsd ldrs till wknd quickly bef 9th, tld off whn pld up before 3 out............(20 to 1) pu
2122⁶ WHAT JIM WANTS (Ire) [85] 4-10-0 (5*) R McGrath, outpcd and drpd rear hfwy, some hdwy aftr 9th, pld up lme after nxt.
.................(7 to 1 op 6 to 1 tchd 8 to 1) pu
2120⁶ BOSTON MAN [84] 6-11-4 B Storey, not jump wl, sn beh, lost tch and pld up aftr 6th. (7 to 2 op 10 to 1 tchd 9 to 1) pu
1984⁷ FARMERS SUBSIDY [77] 5-10-9 R Garritty, made most to 8th, wknd quickly aftr nxt, tld off whn pld up bef 2 out.
.................(14 to 1 op 12 to 1) pu
Dist: 13l, ¾l, 1¼l, 3l, nk, ¾l, sht-hd, 3½l, 4l, 13l, dist. 6m 3.90s. a 12.90s (16 Ran).
SR: 24/24/5/9/-/7/13/4/-/ (Peter J S Russell), Miss Lucinda V Russell

NEWTON ABBOT (heavy)
Monday January 20th
Going Correction: PLUS 1.70 sec. per fur. (races 1,2,5,7), PLUS 1.90 (3,4,6)

2242 Teignmouth Maiden Hurdle Class F (4-y-o and up) £2,344 2m 1f... (1:35)

JUYUSH (USA) 5-11-8 J Osborne, prmnt, pressed wnr frm 3rd till led 5th, came wide into strt and pckd 2 out, cmftbly.
.............(Evens fav op 11 to 10 on tchd 11 to 10) 1
1973 MOTOQUA 5-11-3 A Maguire, in tch, styd on to chase wnr appr 2 out, sn one pace........................(11 to 4) 2
COUNTRY LOVER (v) 6-11-8 A P McCoy, hdwy to chase ldrs 4th, trkd wnr aftr till wknd appr 2 out..........(6 to 1) 3
ASHTAR (USA) 7-11-8 C Maude, in tch, blun 4th, drvn to stay chasing ldrs frm nxt, wknd 3 out.............(16 to 1) 4
FENCER'S QUEST (Ire) 4-10-10 N Williamson, steady hdwy to track ldrs aftr 4th, wknd 3 out............(33 to 1) 5
1919⁴ BLADE OF FORTUNE 9-11-1 (7*) Mr J Tizzard, led to 5th, sn btn........................(33 to 1) 6
ALPINE JOKER 4-10-10 R Dunwoody, in tch to 5th, sn wknd.
.................(16 to 1) 7
1977³ KEVASINGO 5-11-8 T J Murphy, hdwy 4th, rdn nxt, sn wknd.
.................(33 to 1) 8
PIPER'S ROCK (Ire) 6-11-8 B Clifford, al beh, tld off aftr 4th.
.................(33 to 1) 9
1976⁴ FROME LAD 5-11-1 (7*) J Power, prominent to 5th, sn wknd, tld off whn pld up bef 2 out.......................(25 to 1) pu
CHALCUCHIMA 4-10-10 R Greene, beh frm 4th, tld off whn pld up bef 3 out........................(33 to 1) pu
WIN I DID (Ire) 7-11-0 (3*) P Henley, beh frm 4th, tld off whn pld up bef 3 out..........................(33 to 1) pu
1354⁸ KLOSTERS 5-11-0 (3*) T Dascombe, chsd ldrs till wknd quickly 4th, tld off whn pld up bef 3 out.........(100 to 1) pu
1357 MISS NIGHT OWL 6-11-3 J Frost, al beh, tld off frm 4th, tailed off whn pld up bef 2 out.....................(33 to 1) pu
Dist: 7l, 10l, 20l, 2½l, 3l, ¾l, 25l, dist. 4m 23.50s. a 34.50s (14 Ran).
SR: 38/26/21/1/-/-/ (W E Sturt), J A B Old

2243 January 'National Hunt' Novices' Hurdle Class E (4-y-o and up) £2,652 2¾m........................ (2:05)

1810 SCOTBY (Bel) 7-11-10 B Powell, hld up, hit 4th, improved nxt, led appr 2 out, drvn out...........(9 to 2 op 9 to 2) 1
1685³ DEFENDTHEREALM 6-11-4 J Frost, hld up towards rear, hdwy 5th, rdn and ev ch appr 2 out, one pace.
.................(33 to 1 op 25 to 1) 2
2013⁶ SHANAGORE WARRIOR (Ire) 5-10-11 (7*) S Hearn, hld up beh ldrs, rdn alng 3 out, btn bef nxt....(33 to 1 op 20 to 1) 3

293

2015² SHARIAKANNDI (Fr) 5-11-4 T J Murphy, *hld up towards rear,
prog 6th, ev ch appr 2 out, sn btn*......(16 to 1 op 14 to 1) 4
ST MELLION DRIVE 7-11-4 A P McCoy, *led till appr 2 out, sn*
.........................(2 to 1 fav op 7 to 4 tchd 13 to 8) 5
1942 FULL OF BOUNCE (Ire) 6-11-1 (3") T Dascombe, *hld up, rdn
and hdwy appr 7th, wknd approaching 3 out, tld off.*
....(33 to 1 op 20 to 1) 6
1894* ROCKCLIFFE LAD 8-11-10 C Llewellyn, *trkd ldrs, hit 7th, sn
wknd, tld off.*
.........(11 to 4 op 5 to 2 tchd 100 to 30 and 7 to 2) 7
ALPINE SONG 12-10-13 Miss V Stephens, *nvr on terms, tld
off whn pld up bef 2 out*..............(33 to 1 tchd 40 to 1) pu
LADY OF MINE 7-11-3 R Johnson, *beh frm 6th, tld off whn
pld up bef 2 out*.....................(33 to 1 tchd 40 to 1) pu
1214 ALICE SHORELARK 6-10-13 Mr T Greed, *wl beh frm 6th, tld
off whn pld up bef 2 out*..........................(66 to 1) pu
VANCOUVER LAD (Ire) 8-10-11 (7") J Power, *trkd ldrs, wknd
appr 7th, tld off whn pld up bef 2 out...(66 to 1 op 33 to 1)* pu
1802³ MADAM POLLY 5-10-6 (7") K Hibbert, *beh frm 6th, tld off whn
pld up bef 2 out*......................................(33 to 1) pu
SUMMIT ELSE 6-10-13 T Jenks, *mid-div, hdwy 5th, wknd
appr 7th, tld off whn pld up bef 2 out*...(20 to 1 op 12 to 1) pu
1675⁹ CLASSIC CHAT 5-11-4 D Bridgwater, *beh frm 4th, tld off whn
pld up bef 2 out*.......................(33 to 1 op 25 to 1) pu
1237³ ONE FOR NAVIGATION (Ire) 5-11-4 P Hide, *chsd ldr till mstk
7th, wknd frm 3 out, 5th and no ch whn pld up bef 2 out.*
....(7 to 1 op 6 to 1) pu
CAMILLAS LEGACY 6-10-13 D Gallagher, *not fluent, al beh,
tld off whn pld up bef 2 out*.........(33 to 1 tchd 50 to 1) pu
Dist: 4l, 5l, nk, 19l, dist, 26l. 5m 44.70s. a 43.70s (16 Ran).
SR: 33/23/18/18/-/-/ (Mrs E B Gardiner), R H Buckler

2244 Newton Abbot Handicap Chase Class F (0-100 5-y-o and up) £2,696 2m 110yds.................... (2:35)

INDIAN ARROW (NZ) [90] 9-11-5 C Maude, *led to 5th, le ag'n
nxt, came clr appr 2 out, easily*.......(12 to 1 op 10 to 1) 1
1236⁴ MR PLAYFULL [91] 7-11-6 J Frost, *in tch, hdwy to track ldrs
8th, chsd wnr frm 2 out but no imprsn.* (6 to 1 tchd 7 to 1) 2
1349⁷ GOOD FOR A LAUGH [88] 13-10-10 (7") Mr G Shenkin, *in tch
till rdn and drpd rear 5th, rallied und pres frm 3 out, styd on.*
....(12 to 1 op 14 to 1) 3
1920² COUNTRY KEEPER [75] 9-10-4 G Upton, *beh, mstk 4th
(water) still wl in rear till styd on und pres frm four out.*
....(8 to 1 op 6 to 1) 4
1846* THE LANCER (Ire) [95] 8-11-10 R Dunwoody, *wth 1st, styd
tracking ldrs till lft second 4 out, rdn nxt, wknd 2 out.*
.......(5 to 2 fav op 9 to 4 tchd 3 to 1 and 100 to 30) 5
1916⁴ WONDERFULL POLLY (Ire) [87] 9-11-2 P Hide, *steady hdwy
7th, rdn whn hmpd and mstk 4 out, sn wknd.*
....(6 to 1 op 5 to 1) 6
1744⁷ BLAZER MORINIERE (Fr) [90] 8-11-5 S Fox, *beh frm 6th, mstk
8th, sn lost tch.*.....(25 to 1 op 20 to 1 tchd 33 to 1) 7
1684³ COLETTE'S CHOICE (Ire) [76] 8-10-0 (5") Mr R Thornton, *beh
frm 6th, tld off.*...................................(20 to 1) 8
HANSON STREET (NZ) [71] 10-10-0 N Williamson, *in rear till f
8th.*....................................(20 to 1 op 10 to 1) f
1724³ FENWICK [85] 10-10-11 (3") T Dascombe, *trkd ldrs, second
and pushed alng whn blun and uns rdr 4 out.*
..............................(16 to 1 op 12 to 1 tchd 14 to 1) ur
1686⁴ BENJAMIN LANCASTER [97] 13-11-5 (7") M Griffiths, *trkd ldr
till led 5th, hdd nxt, hit 8th, sn wknd, tld off whn pld up bef 2 out.*
.............................(14 to 1 op 10 to 1 tchd 16 to 1) pu
1916 MISTRESS ROSIE [72] 10-10-1 J R Kavanagh, *chsd ldrs to
7th, wknd, pld up bef 2 out*.......(33 to 1 op 20 to 1) pu
1595⁸ MISS MARIGOLD [93] 8-11-8 B Powell, *jmpd moderately in
rear till tld off whn pld up bef 9th*.....(20 to 1 op 14 to 1) pu
1725 KINO'S CROSS [98] 8-11-13 A Thornton, *in tch, rdn alng 6th,
hit nxt and wknd, tld off whn pld up bef last.*
.............................(10 to 1 op 12 to 1 tchd 14 to 1) pu
Dist: 9l, 6l, ½l, 3½l, 3½l, 13l, dist. 4m 35.50s. a 37.50s (14 Ran).
SR: 29/21/12/-/14/2/ (Joe & Joanne Richards), M C Pipe

2245 Bet With The Tote Novices' Chase Qualifier Class E (6-y-o and up) £3,121 3¼m 110yds.......... (3:05)

CYBORGO (Fr) 7-10-12 A P McCoy, *al prmnt, led 14th to 16th,
rgned ld 4 out, clr 2 out, cmftbly.*
.......(11 to 8 on op 7 to 4 on tchd 2 to 1 on and 5 to 4 on) 1
1684² WELL TIMED 7-11-5 J Frost, *chsd ldrs, led 16th to 4 out, one
pace appr 2 out, lft clr second last...(33 to 1 tchd 50 to 1)* 2
1970⁴ SEE ENOUGH 9-10-12 S McNeill, *mid-div, lost pl 13th, no
imprsn aftr, tld off.*.......................(5 to 1 op 10 to 1) 3
2014² KENDAL CAVALIER 7-10-12 B Fenton, *mid-div, no hdwy frm
15th, tld off.*.......................................(14 to 1) 4
1916* MISS DISKIN (Ire) 8-11-0 B Powell, *prmnt, led 4th to 14th,
wknd nxt, tld off*.................(14 to 1 tchd 16 to 1) 5
1701* FLAKED OATS 8-11-5 P Hide, *trkd ldrs, chlgd 4 out, second
and hld whn f last*.................(1 to 1 op 8 to 1) f
1473 WHAT'S YOUR STORY (Ire) 8-10-12 A Maguire, *f second.*
..............................(13 to 2 op 8 to 1) f
1970 HUGE MISTAKE 8-10-12 C Llewellyn, *hmpd second, al beh,
pckd 9th, mstk 14th, blun and uns rdr 15th.*
..............................(25 to 1 op 20 to 1 tchd 33 to 1) ur

1847* JASILU (bl) 7-11-0 (7") A Thornton, *led second to 4th, wknd
appr 12th, tld off whn pld up bef nxt*...(25 to 1 op 20 to 1) pu
1981³ ANYTHINGYOULIKE 8-10-12 M Richards, *mid-div, wknd
13th, tld off whn pld up bef 4 out*.....(33 to 1 tchd 50 to 1) pu
1726³ RED PARADE (NZ) 9-10-12 R Greene, *al beh, tld off whn pld
up bef 4 out*....................(14 to 1 op 12 to 1) pu
2025 BALLYDOUGAN (Ire) (v) 9-10-12 R Bellamy, *strted slwly, al
beh, tld off whn pld up bef 15th*.......(100 to 1 op 66 to 1) pu
GOLDEN DROPS (NZ) 9-10-12 C Maude, *beh frm 13th, tld off
whn pld up bef 4 out*..................(50 to 1 op 33 to 1) pu
1684⁴ SORREL HILL 10-10-12 M A Fitzgerald, *led to second, beh
frm 12th, tld off whn pld up bef 16th.*...............(33 to 1) pu
1891 BANKHEAD (Ire) 8-11-12 D Bridgwater, *not fluent 7th, sn tld
off, pld up bef 11th*....................(16 to 1 op 14 to 1) pu
1451² FOXTROT ROMEO 7-10-12 G Bradley, *in tch till 15th, beh
whn pld up bef 2 out*............(12 to 1 op 10 to 1) pu
Dist: 20l, 22l, 4l, 2½l. 7m 24.50s. a 43.50s (16 Ran).
(County Stores (Somerset) Holdings Ltd), M C Pipe

2246 Horserace Betting Levy Board Handicap Hurdle Class D (0-125 4-y-o and up) £3,039 3m 3f............. (3:35)

MAID EQUAL [97] 6-9-7 (7") G Supple, *in tch, hdwy to track
ldrs 7th, led aftr 3 out, drvn out.*
.........................(25 to 1 op 20 to 1 tchd 33 to 1) 1
2047³ EALING COURT [97] 8-10-0 N Williamson, *chsd ldrs 5th,
pressed ldrs frm 3 out, kpt on und pres frm nxt but not rch
wnr*.................................(8 to 1 op 7 to 1) 2
1767⁷ GRUNGE (Ire) 9-10-0 D Gallagher, *hdwy frm 8th, styd on
und pres frm 3 out, one pace frm nxt.*
....(25 to 1 op 16 to 1) 3
1766² EHTEFAAL (USA) [97] 6-10-0 T J Murphy, *hdwy 5th, outpcd
7th, styd on ag'n und pres frm 3 out.* (10 to 1 tchd 12 to 1) 4
RAKAZONA BEAU [116] 7-11-5 C Maude, *sn in tch, chsd ldrs
3 out, wknd appr nxt*....................(25 to 1 op 20 to 1) 5
1893³⁴ CRANE HILL [105] (bl) 7-10-8 G Tormey, *sn prmnt, pressed
ldr 6th, led 9th, hdd aftr 3 out, soon btn...(8 to 1 op 6 to 1)* 6
1921⁶ OATIS ROSE [97] 7-9-10¹ (5") Mr R Thornton, *beh till steady
hdwy to press ldrs 7th, hit 9th, sn wknd.*
.........................(9 to 1 op 8 to 1 tchd 10 to 1) 7
1576⁴ LANSDOWNE [125] 9-11-7 (7") L Cummins, *hdwy 7th, wknd 3
out.*............................(10 to 1 tchd 11 to 1) 8
1921³ TEXAN BABY (Bel) [115] 8-11-4 C Llewellyn, *chsd ldrs, rdn
9th and sn wknd*....(11 to 2 fav op 5 to 1 tchd 6 to 1) 9
1921⁷ ST VILLE [97] 11-10-0 B Powell, *prmnt early, beh frm 6th, tld
off 8th*.........................(7 to 1 tchd 8 to 1) 10
MONTAGNARD [97] 13-10-0 P Holley, *aftr second till after
8th, wknd rpdly, tld off whn pld up bef 2 out.*
....(25 to 1 op 20 to 1) pu
1744⁵ MEDITATOR [112] (bl) 13-11-1 S McNeill, *effrt 5th, mstk and
wknd nxt, tld off whn pld up bef 2 out*.............(20 to 1) pu
1597⁹ JADIDH [97] 9-9-11² (5") D Salter, *al beh, tld off 7th, pld up aftr
nxt*......................(20 to 1 op 16 to 1) pu
FLYER'S NAP [110] 11-10-10 (3") P Henley, *effrt 5th, beh frm
7th, tld off whn pld up bef 2 out.*
.........................(9 to 1 op 8 to 1 tchd 10 to 1) pu
1748 SAUSALITO BOY [99] 9-10-2 D Walsh, *prmnt, rdn and wknd
7th, tld off whn pld up aftr nxt.......(50 to 1 op 25 to 1)* pu
MOUNTAIN REACH [97] 7-10-0 J Osborne, *led till aftr second, wknd 8th, tld off whn pld up bef 2 out*
.......................(20 to 1 tchd 25 to 1) pu
1938* AINSI SOIT IL (Fr) [101] (bl) 6-10-4 D Bridgwater, *prmnt, rdn to
ld aftr 8th, hdd nxt, sn wekaned, tld off whn pld up bef 2 out.*
....(8 to 1 op 7 to 1) pu
Dist: 3l, 8l, 1¼l, 6l, 2l, 18l, 4l, 5l, 20l. 7m 9.80s. a 53.80s (17 Ran).
(Heeru Kirpalani), M C Pipe

2247 Argyle Bookmakers Of Plymouth Handicap Chase Class D (0-125 5-y-o and up) £3,696 2m 5f 110yds (4:05)

1726⁴ ORSWELL LAD [105] 8-10-8 N Williamson, *prmnt, hit 9th, led
nxt to 4 out, rgned ld last, drvn out...(10 to 1 tchd 11 to 1)* 1
MONTEBEL (Ire) [113] 9-11-2 D Walsh, *hld up, hdwy 4th, led
four out to last, no extr..........(11 to 2 jt-fav op 5 to 1)* 2
1892⁶ BELLS LIFE (Ire) [125] 8-12-0 G Tormey, *sn in tch, effrt 4 out,
one pace nxt.*.....................(12 to 1 op 10 to 1) 3
1921* TOP JAVALIN (NZ) [98] 10-10-1 R Greene, *trkd ldrs, hit 6th,
wknd 11th...(8 to 1 op 7 to 1 tchd 9 to 1 and 10 to 1)* 4
1948² FOOLS ERRAND (Ire) [115] 7-11-4 A P McCoy, *in tch, hit 4th,
sn beh*..............................(6 to 1 op 5 to 1) 5
1981² BROGEEN LADY (Ire) [100] 7-10-3 R Dunwoody, *led to tenth,
wknd 4 out*........(11 to 2 jt-fav op 5 to 1) 6
1672⁴ NEWLANDS-GENERAL [118] 11-11-2 (5") O Burrows, *pld
hrd, prog 7th, in tch whn blun and uns rdr 11th.*
....(16 to 1 op 14 to 1) ur
1724 TAPAGEUR [97] 12-9-7 (7") G Supple, *not fluent, al beh, tld off
9th, pld up bef 11th*..................(16 to 1 op 33 to 1) pu
SILVERINO [102] (bl) 11-10-5⁵ C Maude, *lost pl 3rd, tld off 9th,
pld up bef 4 out*......................(16 to 1 op 14 to 1) pu
1812³ BEAU BABILLARD [113] (bl) 10-11-2 P Hide, *in tch to tenth,
tld off whn pld up bef 4 out*.........(16 to 1 op 14 to 1) pu
1920 GOLDEN OPAL [97] 12-9-7 (7") M Griffiths, *beh frm 4th, tld off
whn pld up bef 9 out*.........(16 to 1 op 14 to 1) pu
CANTORIS FRATER [101] 10-10-4 W Marston, *mstk 4th, al
beh, tld off whn pld up bef four out*............(12 to 1) pu

294

1611⁵ MADISON COUNTY (Ire) [110] (v) 7-10-13 M A Fitzgerald, *al
beh, tld off whn pld up bef 3 out*...................(8 to 1)   pu
1972 JACOB'S WIFE [106] 7-10-9 J Osborne, *al beh, tld off whn pld
up bef 11th*......................................(6 to 1)   pu
1794* MAMMY'S CHOICE (Ire) [97] 7-9-13² (3ᵃ) P Henley, *hld up,
improved 5th, hit tenth, sn wknd, tld off whn pld up bef 2 out.*
....(10 to 1 op 8 to 1)   pu
Dist: 2l, 9l, 23l, 6l, 27l. 5m 57.00s. a 55.00s (15 Ran).

(R M E Wright), P J Hobbs

2248 Weatherbys 'Stars Of Tomorrow' Open National Hunt Flat Intermediate - Class H (4 - 7-y-o) £1,271 2m 1f .... (4:35)

1456* IRANOS (Fr) 5-11-12 A P McCoy, *led till hdd 3 ls out, styd
pressing ldr till slight ld ins last, all out.*
....(5 to 4 on op Evens)   1
1735* DOM BELTRANO (Fr) 5-11-5 (7ᵃ) L Suthern, *tracker ldrs,
pressed wnr frm hfwy till led 3 ls out, faltered o'r one out, hdd
and faltered ag'n ins last, jst fld*........(10 to 1 op 7 to 2)   2
ROYAL POT BLACK (Ire) 6-11-5 G Tormey, *wnt prmnt hfwy,
styd on same pace frm 2 ls out*........(10 to 1 op 7 to 1)   3
HOT 'N SAUCY 5-11-0 Mr S Bush, *sn in tch, styd on same
pace frm 3 ls out*..................................(66 to 1 op 20 to 1)   4
DUBLIN FREDDY 6-11-12 N Williamson, *hld up in tch, rdn
and effrt 3 ls out, sn btn.*
..................................(5 to 2 op 3 to 1 tchd 100 to 30 and 7 to 2)   5
COUNTRY BEAU 5-11-5 T J Murphy, *beh till hdwy hfwy,
wknd 4 ls out*..(20 to 1 op 12 to 1)   6
HEIDIQUEENOFCLUBS (Ire) 6-11-0 D Bridgwater, *beh,
reminders aftr 5 ls, tld off*
....(10 to 1 op 5 to 1 tchd 12 to 1)   7
1456⁸ MR AGRIWISE 6-11-5 J Frost, *beh frm hfwy, tld off.*
....(40 to 1 op 20 to 1)   8
BRAVE EDWIN (Ire) 7-11-5 J Osborne, *in tch till wknd 4 ls out,
tld off*..(10 to 1 tchd 12 to 1)   9
SLACK ALICE 6-11-0 D Walsh, *chsd ldrs till wknd 4 ls out.*
....(40 to 1 op 20 to 1 tchd 50 to 1)   10
SPLASH OF BLAKENEY 6-10-9 (5ᵃ) D Salter, *beh frm hfwy, tld
off*...(66 to 1 op 33 to 1)   11
JOYFUL PABS 5-11-0 R Greene, *al beh, tld off frm hfwy.*
....(66 to 1 op 33 to 1)   12
ST MABYN INN BOY 5-11-5 S Burrough, *slwly away, al beh,
tld off frm hfwy*..................................(66 to 1 op 33 to 1)   13
1802⁹ ELLY'S DREAM 5-11-5 E Fox, *prominet, rdn hfwy, sn wknd,
tld off*...(66 to 1 op 25 to 1)   14
1578 BABY LANCASTER 6-10-12 (7ᵃ) M Griffiths, *chsd wnr early,
wknd 9 ls out, tld off*..............................(66 to 1 op 25 to 1)   15
Dist: ¾l, 6l, 6l, 5l, 4l, dist, ½l, 2½l, nk, 2½l. 4m 22.50s. (15 Ran).

(B A Kilpatrick), M C Pipe

LEICESTER (good to soft (races 1,2,3,5,7), good to firm (4,6)) Tuesday January 21st
Going Correction: PLUS 0.30 sec. per fur.

2249 Stonesby Novices' Hurdle Class E (Div I) (4-y-o and up) £2,329 2½m 110yds.................... (1:00)

1623⁷ HURDANTE (Ire) 7-11-6 A P McCoy, *hld up in tch, led 4 out, clr
2 out, cmftbly*........................(10 to 1 op 8 to 1 tchd 12 to 1)   1
1397² MENTMORE TOWERS (Ire) 5-11-6 W Marston, *led, mstk 3rd,
hdd and slpd nxt, led 5 out to next, styd on same pace frm 2
out*.......................................(5 to 2 op 9 to 4 tchd 11 to 4)   2
1805³ PENROSE LAD (NZ) 7-11-6 A Maguire, *al prmnt, rdn appr 2
out, ran on same pace*.....(15 to 2 op 6 to 1 tchd 8 to 1)   3
2122⁷ DONT FORGET CURTIS (Ire) 5-11-6 N Bentley, *hld up, hdwy
6th, wknd 2 out*..(25 to 1)   4
1673 SPRING DOUBLE (Ire) 6-11-6 D Bridgwater, *hld up, hmpd 5th,
nvr rchd ldrs*...(20 to 1 op 16 to 1)   5
1997² EAGLES REST (Ire) 6-11-6 M A Fitzgerald, *hld up, hdwy 5 out,
rdn and btn 2 out.*
..................................(11 to 10 on op 11 to 8 on tchd Evens)   6
1260⁷ FANCY NANCY 6-11-1 L Harvey, *prmnt, hmpd 5th, wknd
appr 4 out*...(100 to 1)   7
WESTCOTE LAD 8-11-6 T Jenks, *chsd ldr, led 4th, hdd 5 out,
wknd 3 out*...(33 to 1)   8
1810² SIOUX TO SPEAK 5-11-6 B Fenton, *hld up, effrt 5 out, wkng
whn mstk nxt*...(20 to 1 op 16 to 1)   9
1995⁴ SEABROOK LAD 6-11-6 I Lawrence, *mid-div, taking clr order
whn f 5th*..(20 to 1)   f
1631 KNOCKBRIDE (Ire) 8-11-6 M Foster, *in rear, rdn appr 5th, sn
beh, tld off and pld up bef 4 out*...............(100 to 1)   pu
1350 FIRECROWN 11-11-6 M Richards, *rear, effrt 5 out sn beh, tld
off whn pld up bef nxt*...........................(100 to 1)   pu
Dist: 9l, hd, 10l, 1½l, ¾l, 24l, 18l, 14l. 5m 3.90s. a 15.90s (12 Ran).

(Tja Consultants Ltd), G B Balding

2250 Stonesby Novices' Hurdle Class E (Div II) (4-y-o and up) £2,329 2½m 110yds.................... (1:30)

SPECIAL BEAT 5-10-10 (5ᵃ) Mr C Vigors, *chsd ldr, ev ch 3 out,
sn outpcd, wl hld whn lft in ld last, rdn out.*(8 to 1 op 6 to 1)   1
EDREDON BLEU (Fr) 5-11-6 J Dunwoody, *led, quickened clr
6th, hdd 3 out sn rdn and btn, lft second last, kpt on.*
..................................(5 to 2 co-fav op 7 to 4 tchd 11 to 4)   2
1805⁹ SYMPHONY'S SON (Ire) 6-11-6 A Maguire, *hld up, hdwy 4
out, pckd 3 out, eased whn btn*.................(7 to 1 op 5 to 1)   3
2023⁶ BANNY HILL LAD 7-11-6 J R Kavanagh, *prmnt to 5th, nvr
dngrs aftr*...(33 to 1 op 20 to 1)   4
1997 LATAHAAB (USA) 6-11-6 P Hide, *mid-div, hdwy 5th, wknd
appr 4 out*..(12 to 1 op 10 to 1)   5
1260⁸ SUPREMO (Ire) 8-11-6 T J O'Sullivan, *hld up, al in rear.*
....(25 to 1 op 20 to 1)   6
1849⁴ AWARD (Ire) 6-11-6 D O'Sullivan, *hld up, hdwy 5 out, led 3 out,
sn clr til f last*..................(5 to 2 co-fav op 2 to 1)   f
BELGRAN (USA) 6-11-6 T Jenks, *in tch to 4th, tld off and
pld up bef four out*...............................(100 to 1)   pu
1973 ALONGWAYDOWN (Ire) 8-11-6 D Leahy, *hld up, mstk 5 out,
tld off and pld up bef 2 out*................(50 to 1 op 33 to 1)   pu
ANTARCTICA (USA) 5-10-8 (7ᵃ) M Newton, *hld up, effrt 5 out,
beh whn pld up bef 2 out*........................(100 to 1)   pu
1893⁹ CHAPILLIERE (Fr) 7-11-6 M A Fitzgerald, *prmnt to 5th, tld off
and pld up bef last*..........................(33 to 1 op 20 to 1)   pu
1496⁴ KILCARNE BAY (Ire) 7-11-6 J Osborne, *prmnt, rdn and wknd
3 out, pld up bef nxt.*...........................(5 to 2 co-
fav op 9 to 4 tchd 11 to 4)   pu
1673⁹ DON'T MIND IF I DO (Ire) 6-11-6 Mr P Scott, *in tch to 5th, tld
off whn pld up bef 3 out*.......................(25 to 1 op 20 to 1)   pu
Dist: 2½sl, 7l, 27l, 4l, dist. 5m 4.80s. a 16.80s (13 Ran).

(C Marner), N J Henderson

2251 Brook Conditional Jockeys' Selling Handicap Hurdle Class G (0-90 4-y-o and up) £2,145 2m........... (2:00)

1980² FLEET CADET [82] (v) 6-11-12 G Supple, *hld up, hdwy 5th, led
on bit appr last, cmftbly*..........(5 to 4 fav tchd 11 to 8)   1
1728⁸ INDIAN TEMPLE [69] 6-10-13 E Husband, *mid-div, hdwy 4th,
led aftr 5th, rdn and hdd appr last, no extr.*
....(9 to 1 op 8 to 1)   2
1969⁶ SLIGHTLY SPECIAL (Ire) [70] 5-10-2⁶ (5ᵃ) Gordon Gallagher,
led second, hdd aftr 5th, styd on same pace frm 2 out.
....(12 to 1)   3
1353⁷ REMEMBER STAR [68] 4-10-0 A Bates, *beh til styd on frm 2
out, nvr nrr.*...............(16 to 1 op 10 to 1 tchd 20 to 1)   4
1817⁷ TRENDY AUCTIONEER (Ire) [57] (v) 9-10-1 Sophie Mitchell,
nvr nr to chal............................(25 to 1 op 33 to 1)   5
BERTS CHOICE [65] 6-10-9 Michael Brennan, *al in rear.*
....(20 to 1 tchd 25 to 1)   6
1980 BOLD CHARLIE [68] (v) 5-9-9 (5ᵃ) S Hearn, *mid-div, took clr
order 4th, wknd four out*..........(25 to 1 op 33 to 1)   7
1943² LIME STREET BLUES (Ire) [79] (bl) 6-11-9 M Berry, *led to
second, wknd 3 out*.................(15 to 8 op 5 to 4 tchd 7 to 4)   8
1138 HUGH DANIELS [72] 9-10-11 (5ᵃ) J Mogford, *beh frm 4th, tld
off and pld up bef four out*........................(16 to 1)   pu
1697⁶ MINI FETE (Fr) [62] 8-10-6 R Painter, *al in rear, tld off and pld
up bef 2 out*..(20 to 1)   pu
2158 LOTHIAN JEM [67] (bb) 8-10-11 G Hogan, *chsd ldrs, mstk 4th,
wknd nxt, pld up bef four out*..................(33 to 1)   pu
Dist: 4l, 2½l, 2½l, 23l, 3l, 25l, dist. 4m 2.60s. a 19.60s (11 Ran).

(Sir John Swaine), M C Pipe

2252 Rabbit Handicap Chase Class F (0-105 5-y-o and up) £3,566 3m .... (2:30)

1140 BENDOR MARK [90] 8-11-1 A P McCoy, *hld up, hdwy tenth,
lft in ld 4 out, rdn out*...........................(10 to 1 op 8 to 1)   1
1863 YEOMAN WARRIOR [102] 10-11-13 D O'Sullivan, *chsd ldrs,
led 7th to nxt, led 12th, blun badly and hdd 5 out, rallied to
chase wnr 2 out, no extr run in*.......(16 to 1 op 14 to 1)   2
1859* CALL ME RIVER (Ire) [79] 9-10-4 I Lawrence, *hld up, hdwy
tenth, rdn and wknd appr last...*(2 to 1 fav tchd 5 to 2)   3
1794² MAESTRO PAUL [99] 11-11-10 P Hide, *hld up, hdwy 6 out,
chsd wnr 4 out to 2 out, sn wknd........*(8 to 1 op 6 to 1)   4
1799³ JUST ONE CANALETTO [78] 9-10-3 T J Murphy, *chsd ldrs,
rdn and hmpd 12th, wknd 4 out.......*(10 to 1 op 8 to 1)   5
1814⁵ LAY IT OFF (Ire) [85] 8-10-10 S Curran, *led to 5th, wknd 3 out.*
....(16 to 1)   6
1859⁴ SOLO GENT [95] 8-11-6 S McNeill, *nvr rchd chalg pos.*
....(8 to 1 op 7 to 1)   7
1937⁶ MR INVADER [90] 10-11-1 W Marston, *slwly into strd, hmpd
second, hdwy 7th, ev ch whn blun badly 5 out, sn wknd.*
....(16 to 1)   8
1707³ HOUGHTON [94] 11-10-12 (7ᵃ) M R Burton, *f second.*
..................................(16 to 1 op 12 to 1 tchd 20 to 1)   f
418 HURRYUP [91] 10-11-2 R Dunwoody, *chsd ldrs, led second
to 7th, led to 12th, lft in ld 5 out till f next.*
....(12 to 1 tchd 14 to 1)   f
1734 CONEY ROAD [75] 8-10-0 D Gallagher, *chsd ldrs till f 12th.*
....(10 to 1)   f
1721 CALL ME EARLY [92] 12-11-3 Mr J Rees, *blun and uns rdr
5th...................................*(5 to 2 op 25 to 1)   ur
1937 KING'S COURTIER (Ire) [75] (v) 8-9-13² (3ᵃ) E Husband, *blun
and uns 6th*...(33 to 1)   ur
2031⁵ PANT LLIN [80] 11-10-5 S Wynne, *al in rear, tld off whn pld up
bef 4 out*..(25 to 1 op 20 to 1)   pu

ROYAL SQUARE (Can) [95] 11-11-6 D Bridgwater, *not jump wl, sn beh, pld up bef 6th*..........(16 to 1 op 25 to 1) pu
1799* OPAL'S TENSPOT [75] 10-10-0 R Farrant, *al in rear, mstk 11th, tld off and pld up bef 4 out.*
.....................(11 to 1 op 8 to 1 tchd 12 to 1) pu
1994 GRIFFINS BAR [85] 9-10-10 R Marley, *prmnt to tenth, beh whn pld up bef 4 out*.................................(16 to 1) pu
Dist: 2l, 20l, 5l, 5l, 8l, dist. 6m 4.90s. a 19.90s (17 Ran).
(C J Courage), M J Wilkinson

2253 Daniel Lambert Handicap Hurdle Class D (0-120 5-y-o and up) £3,652 2½m 110yds................ (3:00)

1717^4 HENRIETTA HOWARD (Ire) [109] 7-11-2 (3*) G Hogan, *hld up, hdwy 5th, led appr last, rdn out.*
...............................(14 to 1 op 12 to 1 tchd 16 to 1) 1
1816* ISMENO [105] 6-11-1 A Dicken, *hld up, hdwy 5 out, led 3 out, hdd appr last, ran on one pace*........(10 to 1 op 7 to 1) 2
1668^3 SILVER STANDARD [102] (bl) 7-10-12 S Wynne, *mid-div, hdwy 4 out, styd on*..................(10 to 1 op 8 to 1) 3
1700^6 CASSIO'S BOY [90] 6-10-0 D Gallagher, *hld up, hdwy 6th, wknd 2 out*..........(16 to 1 op 14 to 1 tchd 20 to 1) 4
2011^3 HANDY LASS [98] 8-10-8 T J Murphy, *nvr rchd ldrs.* (20 to 1) 5
1925* REAGANESQUE (USA) [112] 5-11-8 R Farrant, *trkd ldrs, rdn 3 out, sn wknd*..........................(10 to 1 op 8 to 1) 6
SELATAN (Ire) [111] 5-11-4 (3*) D Fortt, *hld up in tch, lost pl 5 out, nvr dngrs aftr*..................(16 to 1 op 14 to 1) 7
1860* OUT RANKING (Fr) [118] 5-12-0 A P McCoy, *led, jmpd rght, hdd and wknd 3 out*.......(7 to 1 op 6 to 1 tchd 8 to 1) 8
1852^3 EULOGY (Ire) [112] 7-11-8 D O'Sullivan, *mid-div, hdwy 5th, wknd 3 out*..........(4 to 1 jt-fav op 6 to 1 tchd 7 to 1) 9
1722^8 CAMBO (USA) [91] 11-10-1 D Skyrme, *prmnt till wknd 4 out.*
..............................(20 to 1 op 14 to 1) 10
1835^4 CAWARRA BOY [105] 9-11-1 Mr E James, *hld up, hdwy 5th, wknd appr 3 out*......(16 to 1 op 14 to 1 tchd 20 to 1) 11
1864^2 KIPPANOUR (USA) [112] (bl) 5-11-8 R Dunwoody, *trkd ldrs till wknd 3 out*...........................(10 to 1 tchd 12 to 1) 12
MUSICAL MONARCH (NZ) [112] 11-11-8 M Richards, *hld up, hdwy 6th, wknd 4 out*.................................(33 to 1) 13
BOYFRIEND [90] 7-10-0 W Marston, *prmnt to 4 out.*
..............................(20 to 1 op 16 to 1) 14
GARAIYBA (Ire) [96] 6-10-6 A Maguire, *hld up, hdwy 4 out, wknd nxt, collapsed and f appr 2 out*............(4 to 1 jt-fav op 3 to 1) f
HOODWINKER (Ire) [110] 8-11-6 T Jenks, *prmnt to 6th, tld off and pld up bef 4 out*..................(16 to 1 op 12 to 1) pu
1383^2 RAMSDENS (Ire) [100] 5-10-10 D Bridgwater, *chsd ldr, mstk 5 out, sn rdn and lost pl, beh whn pld up bef 2 out.*
..............................(10 to 1 op 12 to 1 tchd 14 to 1) pu
Dist: 1¾l, 2l, 8l, 7l, 7l, 4l, nk, ¾l, hd, 16l. 5m 0.70s. a 12.70s (17 Ran).
SR: 25/19/14/-/-/2/ (Mrs Solna Thomson Jones), Mrs D Haine

2254 Dick Christian Novices' Chase Class E (5-y-o and up) £3,561 2½m 110yds .... (3:30)

1831* SLINGSBY (Ire) 7-11-10 A Thornton, *hld up, hdwy to ld 5 out, clr 3 out, eased r-in*.......................(3 to 1 op 9 to 4) 1
1957 UNCLE ALGY 8-11-4 B Fenton, *hld up, styd on frm 3 out, nvr plcd to chal*.....................................(20 to 1) 2
1722^7 SUPER RITCHART 9-11-4 R Farrant, *prmnt, blun tenth, wknd 4 out*...........................(20 to 1 op 16 to 1) 3
1576^2 KARAR (Ire) 7-11-4 D O'Sullivan, *hld up, nvr nr to chal.*
..........................(4 to 1 op 5 to 1 tchd 7 to 2) 4
1732 WOT NO GIN 8-11-4 M A Fitzgerald, *beh whn blun 4th, nvr nrr*..............................(13 to 2 op 4 to 1) 5
1570 PRIMITIVE PENNY 6-10-10 (3*) G Hogan, *al in rear.*
..............................(33 to 1 op 25 to 1) 6
1846^5 SOUNDS GOLDEN 9-10-11 (7*) P Hide, *chsd ldrs, lft in ld 8th, hdd 5 out, wkng whn hit 3 out*..................(50 to 1) 7
1847^5 PENNANT COTTAGE (Ire) 9-10-13 T Jenks, *al in rear, tld off whn f 2 out*......................................(50 to 1) f
1670^3 THREE PHILOSOPHERS (Ire) 8-11-4 S Wynne, *led and sn clr, f 8th*...............(11 to 8 fav op 5 to 4 tchd 6 to 4) f
2178^4 SNOWDON LILY 6-10-10 (3*) E Husband, *chsd ldr, hmpd 8th, f 5 out*..........................(66 to 1 op 50 to 1) f
Dist: 7l, 3l, 8l, 3½l, 3l, 29l. 5m 22.30s. a 20.30s (10 Ran).
(Simon Harrap Partnership), N A Gaselee

2255 Croxton Park Novices' Hurdle Class E (4-y-o and up) £3,372 2m....(4:00)

2042* SANMARTINO (Ire) 5-11-11 A Maguire, *trkd ldrs, led 2 out, rdn out.* (15 to 8 on op 9 to 4 on tchd 7 to 4 on and 13 to 8 on) 1
HIGH IN THE CLOUDS (Ire) 5-11-5 S Wynne, *hld up in tch, led briefly appr 2 out, styd on und pres*...(20 to 1 op 16 to 1) 2
1805^2 MOONAX (Ire) 6-11-5 R Dunwoody, *hld up, hdwy 5th, ev ch appr 2 out, styd on same pace.*
..............................(9 to 4 op 2 to 1 tchd 5 to 2) 3
1790^2 NORTHERN FLEET 4-10-7 M A Fitzgerald, *wth ldrs, led 3 out, sn hdd and wknd*...................(16 to 1 op 10 to 1) 4
1922^4 IMPENDING DANGER 4-10-4 (3*) R Massey, *prmnt, led 4th to 3 out, sn wknd*........................(25 to 1 op 20 to 1) 5
1610^9 APACHE PARK (USA) 4-10-7 D Gallagher, *made most to 3rd, wknd 3 out*...........................(66 to 1 op 33 to 1) 6
1977^8 DAUNT 5-11-5 A P McCoy, *hld up, hdwy 4 out, wknd nxt.*
..............................(14 to 1 op 12 to 1) 7
1769^2 WELSH SILK 5-11-2 (3*) D Fortt, *nvr nr to chal.*
..............................(33 to 1 op 20 to 1) 8
1743^5 REIMEI 8-11-5 D Bridgwater, *nvr rchd chalg pos.*
..............................(20 to 1 op 14 to 1) 9
1943^7 SPITFIRE BRIDGE (Ire) 5-10-12 (7*) R Hobson, *nvr rchd ldrs.*
..............................(66 to 1 op 50 to 1) 10
KNOCKBRIT LADY (Ire) 6-11-0 A Thornton, *nvr nrr.*
..............................(66 to 1 op 50 to 1) 11
2002 WORTH THE BILL 4-10-7 P Hide, *nvr better than mid-div.*
..............................(66 to 1 op 50 to 1) 12
MAN OF THE MATCH 7-11-5 R Farrant, *mid-div, hdwy 5th, wknd nxt*..............................(40 to 1 op 25 to 1) 13
1665^6 STONE ISLAND 4-10-6 (7*) L Harvey, *al in rear.*
..............................(66 to 1 op 50 to 1) 14
1977 RED PHANTOM (Ire) 5-11-2 (3*) E Husband, *al wl beh.*
..............................(66 to 1 op 50 to 1) 15
1928 SLEAZEY 6-11-5 S Curran, *prmnt, hrd rdn and wknd appr 4 out*..............................(66 to 1 op 50 to 1) 16
IT'STHEBUSINESS 5-11-5 G Upton, *hld up, hdwy 5th, wknd 3 out, f and broke leg nxt*..............(66 to 1 op 33 to 1) f
1893 NO MATTER (Ire) 6-11-5 D O'Sullivan, *trkd ldrs, rdn 5 out, wknd nxt, pld up bef 3 out*............(66 to 1 op 50 to 1) pu
Dist: 1½l, 4l, 13l, 11l, 7l, 2½l, ½l, 2½l, ½l, 20l. 3m 54.80s. a 11.80s (18 Ran).
SR: 27/19/15/-/-/-/ (K Abdulla), D Nicholson

MARKET RASEN (good)
Tuesday January 21st

Going Correction: PLUS 0.20 sec. per fur. (races 1,2,5,7), PLUS 1.05 (3,4,6)

2256 Middle Rasen Novices' Hurdle Class E (4-y-o and up) £2,559 2m 1f 110yds....................... (1:10)

1805^4 NIGHT DANCE 5-11-5 A S Smith, *made all, pushed clr aftr 2 out, rdn last, kpt on*.......(11 to 2 op 6 to 1 tchd 4 to 1) 1
1922 TOBY BROWN 4-10-7 R Johnson, *hit 1st and beh, steady hdwy 3 out, rdn and hit last, styd on strly.*
.........................(20 to 1 op 14 to 1 tchd 25 to 1) 2
1909^9 NEXSIS STAR 4-10-7 Richard Guest, *hld up, steady hdwy 5th, chsd wnr frm 2 out, rdn appr last, kpt on same pace.*
..............................(33 to 1 op 20 to 1) 3
1977^2 TOTAL JOY (Ire) 6-11-5 J Railton, *prmnt, rdn alng 3 out and one pace frm nxt*.....................(14 to 1 op 8 to 1) 4
1830^2 PIP'S DREAM 6-11-0 J Ryan, *in tch, hdwy 5th, effrt and rdn 2 out, wknd appr last*..................(12 to 1 op 10 to 1) 5
1293^4 BARTON SCAMP 5-11-5 N Williamson, *hld up, hdwy to chase ldrs 5th, rdn 2 out and sn one pace*....(33 to 1 op 25 to 1) 6
1922^9 ANGUS MCCOATUP (Ire) 4-10-7 D Bentley, *mid-div, hdwy whn hit 2 out, sn one pace*...........(50 to 1 op 33 to 1) 7
INDICATOR 5-11-5 P Niven, *hld up, hdwy aftr 3 out, kpt on, not rch ldrs*.........................(12 to 1 op 10 to 1) 8
WHITE PLAINS (Ire) 4-10-7 D Walsh, *prmnt, hdwy to chase wnr 5th, rdn and wknd 2 out.*
..........................(7 to 2 op 4 to 1 tchd 5 to 1) 9
1737^8 PONTEVEDRA (Ire) 4-9-11 (5*) Mr R Thornton, *al rear.*
..............................(33 to 1 op 20 to 1) 10
SKIP TO SOMERFIELD 5-11-0 A Dobbin, *prmnt till rdn and wknd bef 3 out*.........(33 to 1 op 25 to 1 tchd 50 to 1) 11
2061^2 HONEYSCHOICE (Ire) 4-10-7 R Garritty, *uns rdr and bolted strt, mid-div, hdwy 5th, rdn and btn bef 2 out.*
..............................(2 to 1 fav op 3 to 1) 12
1955^3 HIGHLY CHARMING (Ire) 5-10-12 (7*) Mr A Wintle, *beh frm hfwy*...(33 to 1) 13
SURANOM (Ire) 5-11-5 J F Titley, *chsd ldrs till wknd bef 3 out.*
..........................(6 to 1 op 4 to 1 tchd 7 to 1) 14
1855^3 EASY LISTENING (USA) 5-11-5 C Maude, *prmnt, rdn alng 5th, wknd bef 2 out.*
...............(6 to 1 op 7 to 1 tchd 8 to 1 and 9 to 1) 15
1689^5 SWYNFORD SUPREME 4-10-7 Derek Byrne, *al rear, tld off 3 out*..............................(25 to 1 op 20 to 1) 16
SHAAGNI ANA (USA) 6-11-5 R Supple, *al beh, tld off frm hfwy*..............................(50 to 1 op 33 to 1) 17
SHIRLEY'S TIME 6-11-5 P Carberry, *mid-div, rdn alng 3 out, no hdwy whn f nxt*....................(50 to 1 op 33 to 1) f
2202 TOUGH CHARACTER (Ire) 9-11-5 L O'Hara, *al rear, tld off whn pld up bef 5th*................(100 to 1 op 50 to 1) pu
Dist: ½l, 1½l, 8l, 1l, 3l, 4l, hd, 1¾l, 4l, 1¼l. 4m 11.80s. a 10.80s (19 Ran).
SR: 18/5/3/7/1/3/ (Racecourse Medical Officers Association), K A Morgan

2257 Scothern Handicap Hurdle Class D (0-120 4-y-o and up) £2,987 2m 1f 110yds....................... (1:40)

1835* CIRCUS LINE [114] 6-11-10 P Carberry, *trkd ldr gng wl, led on bit 2 out, sn clr, blun last, easily.*
..........................(2 to 1 fav op 7 to 4 tchd 9 to 4) 1
1923^3 ISAIAH [108] 8-11-4 T Kent, *trkd ldrs, hdwy 3 out, chsd wnr frm nxt, sn rdn and kpt on.*
.........................(16 to 1 op 12 to 1 tchd 20 to 1) 2
1736* GLENVALLY [91] 6-10-1^4 (3*) E Callaghan, *chsd ldrs, rdn alng aftr 3 out, kpt on appr last*...........(20 to 1 op 16 to 1) 3

1593 SASSIVER (USA) [92] 7-10-2 K Gaule, *in tch, rdn alng 5th, styd on frm 2 out, nvr a factor* . . . . (12 1 op 10 to 1)   4
1512⁷ INDIAN JOCKEY [105] (bl) 5-11-1 D Walsh, *led, rdn alng 3 out, hdd nxt and sn wknd.*
. . . . (11 to 1 op 10 to 1 tchd 12 to 1)   5
1251⁴ GYMCRAK TIGER (Ire) [90] 7-10-0 N Williamson, *hld up and beh, hdwy aftr 3 out, nvr rch ldrs* . . . . (14 to 1)   6
1807⁵ GLANMERIN (Ire) [116] 6-11-12 A S Smith, *hld up and beh, effrt and some hdwy 3 out, 8th and wl held whn hmpd last.*
. . . . (25 to 1 op 20 to 1)   7
1983³ FASSAN (Ire) [105] 5-11-1 R Garritty, *hld up, some hdwy 3 out, rdn and no imprsn frm nxt.*
. . . . (9 to 1 op 8 to 1 tchd 10 to 1)   8
1625³ EUROTWIST [104] 8-11-0 R Johnson, *al rear.*
. . . . (13 to 2 op 8 to 1 tchd 6 to 1)   9
1671 MANOLETE [99] 6-10-9 Derek Byrne, *mid-div, rdn alng 3 out and sn struggling* . . . . (12 to 1 op 10 to 1)   10
832 STAR OF DAVID (Ire) [103] 9-10-13 J Ryan, *prmnt till rdn alng and lost pl 4th, sn beh and tld off 3 out.* . . . . . . (33 to 1)   11
1381² MIM-LOU-AND [115] 5-11-4 (7ᵛ) Mr A Wintle, *chsd ldrs, rdn alng 5th, wknd aftr nxt.* . . . . (3 to 1 op 9 to 2)   12
MAJOR YAASI (USA) [93] 7-10-3 T Eley, *hld up and beh, hdwy 3 out, rdn nxt, 7th and wl held whn f last.* . . . . (33 to 1)   f
JUNGLE KNIFE [118] 11-12-0 A Dobbin, *al rear, beh whn pld up bef 3 out.* . . . . (33 to 1 op 25 to 1 tchd 50 to 1)   pu
Dist: 2l, ¾l, 3l, 3l, 2½l, 6l, 1l, 5l, 1l, 18l. 4m 10.70s. a 9.70s (14 Ran).
SR: 34/26/8/6/16/-/18/6/-/   (Mrs P A H Hartley), M W Easterby

2258 Eric & Lucy Papworth Handicap Chase Class E (0-110 5-y-o and up) £3,047 3½m 110yds. . . . . (2:10)

1937² BANNTOWN BILL (Ire) [90] (v) 8-10-8 D Walsh, *cl up, led briefly second, led 5 out, drvn last, styd on gmely.*
. . . . (6 to 1 op 5 to 1)   1
1328⁴ CALL THE SHOTS (Ire) [90] 8-10-8 N Williamson, *trkd ldrs, hdwy 6 out, rdn 2 out, chlgd last and ev ch till drvn and no extr last 100 yards.* . . . . . (4 to 1 fav op 9 to 2 tchd 5 to 1)   2
1133⁴ CHANGE THE REIGN [107] 10-11-6 (5ᵛ) Mr R Thornton, *chsd ldrs. rdn and hdwy 4 out, drvn nxt and styd on same pace.*
. . . . (14 to 1 op 12 to 1)   3
1967³ SPARROW HALL [90] (bl) 10-10-8 R Johnson, *cl up, led 3rd, hit 6 out, blun and hdd nxt, drvn whn blunded 3 out, sn wknd.*
. . . . (11 to 2 op 5 to 1)   4
1946⁵ HOLY STING (Ire) [95] (bl) 8-10-13 C Maude, *chsd ldrs till rdn and outpcd 6 out.* . . . . (9 to 2 op 4 to 1 tchd 7 to 2)   5
2146⁶ COOL WEATHER (Ire) [82] (bl) 9-10-0 A S Smith, *chsd ldrs, rdn 5 out, wknd quickly bef 3 out.* . . . . . (10 to 1 op 12 to 1)   6
1739⁶ SPROWSTON BOY [82] 14-9-7 (7ᵛ) Ross Berry, *al beh, no ch whn blun and uns rdr last.* . . . . (20 to 1 op 14 to 1)   ur
1994⁵ OCEAN LEADER [92] 10-10-10 J F Titley, *hld up and beh, steady hdwy 12th, pushed alng and blun 6 out, pld up bef nxt.*
. . . . (5 to 1 op 9 to 2 tchd 11 to 2)   pu
1801³ RECORD LOVER (Ire) [82] 7-10-0 W Worthington, *al beh, tld off whn pld up bef 4 out.* . . . . (33 to 1 op 25 to 1)   pu
2065ᵛ HURRICANE ANDREW (Ire) [88] 9-10-6 N Smith, *led to second, prmnt till blun and lost pl 11th, beh whn pld up bef 4 out.*
. . . . (13 to 2 op 6 to 1)   pu
Dist: 4l, 22l, 1½l, hd, dist. 7m 44.50s. a 45.50s (10 Ran).
                                    (Eric Scarth), M C Pipe

2259 Bet With The Tote Novices' Chase Qualifier Class E (6-y-o and up) £3,421 2¾m 110yds. . . . . (2:40)

KAMIKAZE (bl) 7-10-10 C O'Dwyer, *in tch gng wl, hdwy 5 out, led 3 out, clr nxt.* . . . . (6 to 1 op 5 to 1)   1
1825ᵛ MONYMOSS (Ire) 8-11-2 Richard Guest, *al prmnt, hit 6th, blun tenth, rdn 4 out, one pace frm nxt.* . . (7 to 2 op 9 to 2)   2
MISS OPTIMIST 7-10-5 R Johnson, *hld up, jmpd rght 4th, steady hdwy eigth, effrt and ch 3 out, sn rdn and one pace.*
. . . . (100 to 30 fav op 3 to 1 tchd 7 to 2)   3
1991³ MAJOR LOOK (NZ) 9-11-0 A Dobbin, *cl up, led 5th till aftr 4 out, sn wknd.* . . . . (4 to 1 op 7 to 2)   4
2152 SERGEANT JAY 7-10-10 P Carberry, *mid-div whn hmpd 4th, beh aftr.* . . . . (50 to 1 op 33 to 1)   5
1825⁷ DESPERATE DAYS (Ire) 8-10-10 W Dwan, *al beh.*
. . . . (66 to 1 op 33 to 1)   6
2205 WORLD WITHOUT END (USA) 8-10-5 (5ᵛ) S Taylor, *not jump wl, mid-div whn blun and uns rdr 5th.* . . (50 to 1 op 33 to 1)   ur
HAWKER HUNTER (USA) 6-10-10 J A McCarthy, *al beh, blun and uns rdr tenth.* . . . . (12 to 1 op 10 to 1 tchd 14 to 1)   ur
HALKOPOUS 11-10-10 N Williamson, *al prmnt, hit 4th, mstk tenth, led aftr four out to nxt, wknd quickly and pld up bef 2 out, dismounted.* . . . . (7 to 2 op 5 to 2)   pu
1804⁷ SAKBAH (USA) 8-10-2 (3ᵛ) P Henley, *mstk second, sn beh, pld up bef tenth.* . . . . (50 to 1)   pu
2157 DISPOL DANCER 6-10-5 (5ᵛ) Mr R Thornton, *not jump wl and al beh, tld off whn pld up bef 9th.* . . . . (66 to 1 op 33 to 1)   pu
GENERAL GIGGS (Ire) 9-11-0 K Gaule, *beh frm hfwy, blun 5 out, pld up bef 3 out.* . . . . (33 to 1 op 20 to 1)   pu
1963³ FAIR ALLY 7-10-10 D Parker, *whipped round strt, sn in tch, chsd ldrs till hit 9th and soon wknd, beh whn pld up bef 3 out.*
. . . . (25 to 1 op 16 to 1)   pu
2201 LEPTON (Ire) 6-10-10 Derek Byrne, *led to 9th, rdn alng and wknd 5 out, beh whn pld up bef 3 out.* (66 to 1 op 50 to 1)   pu
Dist: 11l, 2l, 15l, 7l, 6l. 5m 57.90s. a 30.90s (14 Ran).

SR: 3/-/-/-/-/-/   (Major B Gatensbury), K C Bailey

2260 European Breeders Fund 'National Hunt' Novices' Hurdle Qualifier Class E (5,6,7-y-o) £2,700 2m 3f 110yds. . . . . (3:10)

1043³ SPENDID (Ire) 5-11-0 R Johnson, *hld up in tch, smooth hdwy 3 out, led 2 out, quickened clr appr last.*
. . . . (9 to 1 op 6 to 1 tchd 10 to 1)   1
1397³ PEACE LORD (Ire) 7-11-0 J F Titley, *hld up in rear, hdwy 7th, effrt to chal and ev ch 2 out, rdn and not quicken appr last.*
. . . . (6 to 1 op 4 to 1 tchd 9 to 1)   2
1594² DARAKSHAN (Ire) 5-11-0 J Railton, *trkd ldr, led 5th, rdn and hdd 2 out, one pace.* . . . . (13 to 8 fav op 3 to 1)   3
1682⁵ SOUTHERN CROSS 5-11-0 P Carberry, *hld up in rear, hdwy on inner 4 out, chsd ldrs nxt, rdn alng 2 out and kpt on same pace.* . . . . (9 to 1 op 10 to 1)   4
1866³ BEACON FLIGHT (Ire) 6-11-5 N Williamson, *prmnt, rdn 3 out and wknd appr nxt.* . . . . (5 to 1 op 7 to 2)   5
1874² DERRING FLOSS 7-10-2 (7ᵛ) Miss J Wormall, *led to 5th, cl up till rdn 3 out and sn wknd.* . . . . (20 to 1)   6
1769⁷ THE CROOKED OAK 5-11-0 C Maude, *hld up and beh, some hdwy 3 out, sn rdn alng and no imprsn.* (14 to 1 op 12 to 1)   7
1817⁶ BOYZONTOOWA (Ire) 5-11-0 Richard Guest, *in tch till rdn and wknd 4 out.* . . . . (66 to 1 op 50 to 1)   8
1968³ HARFDECENT 6-11-0 P Niven, *al rear, hdwy 3 out, nvr nrr.* . . .   9
1631⁹ MENALDI (Ire) 7-11-0 A S Smith, *al rear.*
. . . . (33 to 1 op 25 to 1)   10
1769⁴ JAYFCEE 5-11-0 B Powell, *mid-div, hdwy to chase ldrs 5th, rdn and wknd 4 out.* . . . . (33 to 1 op 25 to 1)   11
1942 ST MELLION LEISURE (Ire) 5-11-0 D Walsh, *prmnt till rdn and wknd appr 4 out.* . . . . (14 to 1 op 12 to 1)   12
1887³ BOLD ACTION (Ire) 6-11-0 W Fry, *not jump wl, beh hfwy, sn tld off.* . . . . (14 to 1 op 12 to 1)   13
REDWOOD LAD 7-11-0 Derek Byrne, *mid-div till lost pl quickly bef 6th, tld off whn pld up before 4 out.*
. . . . (50 to 1 op 33 to 1)   pu
1673⁸ CAST OF THOUSANDS 6-11-0 J A McCarthy, *hld up in rear, steady hdwy 4 out, rdn alng and lost pl aftr nxt, pld up bef 2 out.* . . . . (8 to 1 tchd 10 to 1)   pu
Dist: 6l, 4l, 2l, 7l, 11l, ½l, 25l, hd, nk, 3½l. 4m 47.70s. a 17.70s (15 Ran).
           (Mrs Stewart Catherwood), D Nicholson

2261 Market Rasen Handicap Chase Class E (0-115 5-y-o and up) £2,891 2m 1f 110yds. . . . . (3:40)

1707ᵛ NETHERBY SAID [97] 7-11-1 R Supple, *cl up, led second, sn clr, rdn 3 out, blun last, kpt on wl.* . . (7 to 4 fav tchd 2 to 1)   1
1788³ MARBLE MAN (Ire) [85] 7-10-3 D Bentley, *led to second, chsd wnr, rdn 3 out, hit nxt and sn drvn, one pace.*
. . . . (9 to 1 op 8 to 1 tchd 10 to 1)   2
1634³ ALJADEER (USA) [110] (bl) 8-12-0 P Carberry, *hit second and beh, steady hdwy 8th, chsd wnr and blun 3 out, drvn and hit nxt, one pace.*
. . . . (5 to 1 op 5 to 1 tchd 2 to 1 and 11 to 4)   3
1818² REAL GLEE (Ire) [106] 8-11-10 C Maude, *chsd ldrs till outpcd 6th, hdwy whn blun 9th, styd on frm 4 out, not rch ldrs.*
. . . . (8 to 1 op 5 to 1)   4
1972³ DR ROCKET [86] 12-10-4 N Williamson, *chsd ldrs, rdn and wknd bef 4 out.* . . . . (12 to 1 tchd 14 to 1)   5
1821³ REVE DE VALSE (USA) [91] 10-10-9 K Johnson, *chsd ldrs to 6th, sn lost pl and beh frm 5 out.* . . . . . (14 to 1 op 10 to 1)   6
1926³ CRAFTY CHAPLAIN [94] 11-10-12 D Walsh, *chsd ldrs, blun 7th and 8th, sn wknd.* . . . . (10 to 1 tchd 11 to 1)   7
1730³ LASATA [107] 12-11-11 D Morris, *in tch, rdn and blun 5 out, sn wknd.* . . . . (14 to 1 op 12 to 1)   8
1726 KINDLE'S DELIGHT [98] 9-11-2 J F Titley, *al rear, tld off frm 5 out.* . . . . (10 to 1 op 8 to 1)   9
1707² COPPER CABLE [82] 10-10-0 M Ranger, *al beh, tld off whn pld up aftr 4 out.* . . . . (50 to 1 op 33 to 1)   pu
Dist: 4l, 2l, 12l, 19l, 8l, 21l, 18l, 13l. 4m 39.00s. a 25.00s (10 Ran).
SR: 21/5/28/12/-/-/   (Mrs S Sunter), P Beaumont

2262 West Rasen Standard Open National Hunt Flat Class H (4,5,6-y-o) £1,287 1m 5f 110yds. . . . . (4:10)

INVERCARGILL (NZ) 5-10-11 (7ᵛ) D Kiernan, *trkd ldrs, effrt and squeezed through on inner to ld one and a half fs out, sn rdn and ran on strly.* . . . . (10 to 1 op 6 to 1)   1
NOBLE TOM (Ire) 5-11-4 R Johnson, *chsd ldrs on outer, hdwy o'r 4 fs out, wide strt, rdn to chal appr fnl furlong, not quicken ins last.* . . . . (16 to 1 op 12 to 1)   2
ALISANDE (Ire) 5-10-10 (3ᵛ) Mr C Bonner, *al prmnt, effrt o'r 3 out, rdn 2 out, kpt on same pace.* . . . . (8 to 1 op 5 to 1)   3
1317 JESSICA ONE (Ire) 5-10-9 P Niven, *hld up in tch, hdwy on outer o'r 3 fs out, rdn 2 out and sn one pace.*
. . . . (7 to 4 fav op 2 to 1 tchd 6 to 4 and 3 to 1)   4
JUNIPER HILL 5-11-4 A S Smith, *al chasing ldrs, rdn 3 fs out, styd on onepace fnl 2.* . . . . (8 to 1 op 6 to 1)   5
DONNEGALE (Ire) 5-10-11 (7ᵛ) R McCarthy, *chsd ldrs on outer till rdn alng and outpcd 5 fs out, styd on fnl 2.*
. . . . (8 to 1 op 6 to 1)   6

BLASTER WATSON 6-11-4 M Ranger, *pld hrd, cl up till led 5 fs out, rdn o'r 2 furlongs out, sn hdd and wknd.*
................................(16 to 1 op 10 to 1) 7

2123³ LOST IN THE POST (Ire) 4-9-13 (7*) N Horrocks, *led, rdn alng and hdd 5 fs out, cl up and ev ch till ridden and wknd 2 furlongs out.*......................(8 to 1 op 6 to 1) 8

DIG FOR GOLD 4-10-6 N Bentley, *in tch, effrt o'r 3 fs out, sn rdn and wknd 2 out.*......(5 to 1 op 3 to 1 tchd 6 to 1) 9

MY VANTAGE 4-10-3 (3*) G Parkin, *hld up in rear, effrt and some hdwy 4 fs out, sn btn.*........(16 to 1 op 12 to 1) 10

GYMCRAK-GYPSY 5-10-13 R Garritty, *al rear.*
................................(14 to 1 op 10 to 1) 11

TYCOON PRINCE (bl) 4-10-6 M Brennan, *prmnt till rdn and wknd o'r 4 fs out.*....(16 to 1 op 14 to 1 tchd 20 to 1) 12

FARM TALK 5-11-4 D Parker, *mid-div, hdwy to chase ldrs hfwy, sn rdn and wknd quickly 5 fs out.* (25 to 1 op 20 to 1) 13

MAGNUS MAXIMUS 5-11-4 B Clifford, *al beh, tld off frm hfwy.*......................(25 to 1 op 14 to 1) 14

1648 BYHOOKORBYCROOK (Ire) 5-10-13 V Slattery, *al beh, tld off 5 fs out.*......................(33 to 1 op 20 to 1) 15

Dist: ¾l, 1¾l, 1¾l, 1¼l, 2l, 6l, 1¾l, ¾l, 8l, 2½l. 3m 20.30s. (15 Ran).
(Mrs P Dodd), C J Mann

LINGFIELD (soft)
Wednesday January 22nd
Going Correction: PLUS 1.05 sec. per fur. (races 1,2,3,5,7), PLUS 1.30 (4,6)

2263 Portcullis Amateur Riders' Novices' Hurdle Class E (4-y-o and up) £2,687 2m 7f......................(1:10)

1573³ KIND CLERIC 6-11-5 (7*) Mr S Mulcaire, *mid-div, rdn and steady hdwy 8th, led r-in, all out.*.......(8 to 1 op 5 to 1) 1

1810* EMERALD STATEMENT (Ire) 7-12-0 (5*) Mr R Thornton, *hld up, hdwy 4th, rdn 7th, led 3 out, hdd r-in, kpt on.*
................................(5 to 2 fav op 9 to 4) 2

2152⁴ QUINI EAGLE (Fr) 5-11-7 (5*) Mr A Farrant, *led 7th to 3 out, wknd nxt, tld off.*......(9 to 1 op 7 to 1 tchd 10 to 1) 3

CLARKES GORSE 6-11-5 (7*) Mr P O'Keeffe, *nvr on terms, tld off.*..................(7 to 1 op 10 to 1) 4

2158⁷ MAHLER 7-11-9 (3*) Mr M Rimell, *led to 7th, wknd appr 3 out.*
................................(16 to 1 op 14 to 1 tchd 20 to 1) 5

1615 DRUM BATTLE 5-11-5 (7*) Mr E Babington, *trkd ldrs, wknd 4 out, tld off.*......(25 to 1 op 20 to 1 tchd 33 to 1) 6

1270* MINELLA DERBY (Ire) 7-11-12 (7*) Mr J Tizzard, *in tch till wknd 4 out, tld off.*......(7 to 2 op 3 to 1 tchd 4 to 1) 7

1763² FINE SIR 7-11-12 Mr M Armytage, *hld up, steady hdwy 5th, wknd 8th, wknd rdn pld up bef 2 out.*
................................(7 to 1 op 5 to 1 tchd 8 to 1) pu

1578 FORTUNES GLEAM (Ire) 6-11-2 (5*) Mr A Sansome, *beh 4th, tld off whn pld up bef 3 out.*........(100 to 1 op 50 to 1) pu

1719⁴ ZADOK 5-11-5 (7*) Mr G Shenkin, *al beh, tld off whn pld up bef 3 out.*......................(50 to 1 op 33 to 1) pu

1609 LUCKY TANNER 6-11-5 (7*) Mr A Wintle, *prmnt to 9th, tld off whn pld up bef 2 out.*......(50 to 1 tchd 66 to 1) pu

1893 EAU SO SLOE 6-11-5 (7*) Mr J Goldstein, *beh 5th, tld off whn pld up bef 2 out.*........(100 to 1 op 50 to 1) pu

1614⁷ BAYERD (Ire) (bl) 6-11-12 (7*) Mr E James, *al beh, tld off whn pld up bef 2 out.*......(20 to 1 op 14 to 1) pu

RAKAPOSHI IMP 7-11-0 (7*) Miss B Small, *al beh, tld off whn hit 5th, pld up bef 7th.*............(100 to 1 op 50 to 1) pu

RYDER CUP (Ire) 5-11-7 (5*) Mr C Vigors, *prmnt early, beh 4th, tld off whn pld up bef 3 out.*
................................(10 to 1 op 5 to 1 tchd 12 to 1) pu

LETMO WARRIOR (Ire) 5-11-7 (5*) Mr L E Balogh, *al beh, tld off whn pld up bef 2 out.*(50 to 1 op 33 to 1 tchd 66 to 1) pu

Dist: ¾l, dist, 7l, ¾l, 18l, 10l. 6m 3.60s. a 37.60s (16 Ran).
(The Hammer Partnership), P J Hobbs

2264 Rampart 'National Hunt' Maiden Hurdle Class D (4-y-o and up) £3,091 2m 110yds..................(1:40)

1556² SPLENDID THYNE 5-11-7 M A Fitzgerald, *hld up in tch, rdn 2 out, led last, ran on.*(4 to 1 jt-fav op 3 to 1 tchd 9 to 2) 1

SURSUM CORDA 6-11-7 R Dunwoody, *hld up, improved 5th, led aftr 3 out to last, no extr.*....(4 to 1 jt-fav op 6 to 1) 2

1893⁸ JAKES JUSTICE (Ire) 6-11-7 P Hide, *prmnt, ev ch 2 out, wknd appr last.*..................(14 to 1 op 10 to 1) 3

1675² DARK ORCHARD (Ire) 6-11-7 M Richards, *hld up, hdwy hfwy, ev ch 2 out, wknd appr last.*
................................(10 to 1 op 7 to 1 tchd 12 to 1) 4

2116⁴ LIVELY ENCOUNTER (Ire) 6-11-7 Derek Byrne, *led to 4th, wknd 3 out.*..................(5 to 1 op 6 to 1) 5

1556⁴ CHARLIE'S FOLLY 6-11-7 J Osborne, *hld up, hdwy hfwy, btn 3 out.*......................

UPRISING (Ire) 7-11-7 S McNeill, *keen hold, led 4th till appr 3 out, wknd approaching nxt.*........(25 to 1 op 20 to 1) 7

1975⁶ BROOKHAMPTON LANE 6-11-7 B Powell, *prmnt, led briefly appr 3 out, wknd bef nxt.*.....(25 to 1 op 20 to 1) 8

1065⁴ CYPHRATIS (Ire) 6-11-7 W Marston, *mid-div, hdwy hfwy, lost tch 3 out.*........(9 to 1 op 5 to 1 tchd 10 to 1) 9

1648² ZANDER 5-11-7 D Bridgwater, *prmnt to 3 out.*
................................(12 to 1 op 10 to 1) 10

1942⁴ SUPREME TROGLODYTE (Ire) 5-11-2 J R Kavanagh, *nvr on terms, tld off.*..................(20 to 1 op 12 to 1) 11

1942⁸ BENJI 6-11-7 N Williamson, *nvr on terms, tld off.*
................................(50 to 1 op 20 to 1) 12

1743⁴ MULLINTOR (Ire) 6-11-7 D O'Sullivan, *mid-div, wknd 5th, tld off.*..................(20 to 1 op 12 to 1) 13

ZAISAN (Ire) 4-10-6 (3*) L Aspell, *al beh, tld off.*
................................(25 to 1 tchd 33 to 1) 14

THIRTY BELOW (Ire) 8-11-7 G Upton, *al beh, tld off.*
................................(25 to 1 op 20 to 1) 15

DOUBLE ACHIEVEMENT (Ire) 7-11-7 A P McCoy, *al beh, tld off.*..................(14 to 1 op 12 to 1) 16

ILEWINIT (Ire) 8-11-7 S Fox, *al beh, tld off.*......(50 to 1) 17

CALM DOWN (Ire) 6-11-7 A Thornton, *prmnt, reins broke and wknd rpdly aftr 3rd, tld off.*....(33 to 1 op 25 to 1) 18

SINGLE SOURCING (Ire) 6-11-7 J F Titley, *beh whn pld up bef 5th, broke blood vessel.*..(15 to 2 op 6 to 1 tchd 8 to 1) pu

SHOULDHAVESAIDNO (Ire) 6-11-2 P McLoughlin, *beh 5th, tld off whn pld up bef 3 out.*..........(50 to 1) pu

Dist: 1¼l, 11l, ¾l, 10l, 6l, ¾l, 2l, 9l, 18l, sht-hd. 4m 14.30s. a 23.30s (20 Ran).
SR: 33/31/20/19/9/3/2/-/-/ (John Galvanoni), T Casey

2265 Moat Selling Hurdle Class G (4 - 7-y-o) £2,219 2m 110yds..........(2:10)

1477⁶ BELLA SEDONA 5-11-0 R Dunwoody, *badly hmpd 1st, gd hdwy appr last, sstnd run to ld cl hme.*
................................(5 to 2 fav op 11 to 4) 1

ONE IN THE EYE 4-10-7 A Dicken, *hld up, hdwy 3rd, jmpd rght 2 out, led r-in, hdd cl hme.*.....(50 to 1 op 33 to 1) 2

1992⁸ ARCH ANGEL 4-10-3¹ Mr A Charles-Jones, *hdwy 5th, led last, hdd r-in, kpt on.*..................(20 to 1) 3

1747³ LAURA LYE (Ire) 7-11-0 G Upton, *hld up, led 2 out to last, no extr.*......................(20 to 1 op 16 to 1) 4

2181⁴ ROSE OF GLENN 6-11-0 R Farrant, *al prmnt, led 5th to 2 out, one pace r-in.*......(9 to 1 op 7 to 1 tchd 10 to 1) 5

1747 TREAD THE BOARDS 6-11-0 A P McCoy, *hld up, hdwy frm hfwy, ev ch 2 out, one pace frm last.*
................................(13 to 2 op 6 to 1 tchd 8 to 1) 6

CELTIC LILLEY (bl) 7-11-0 B Fenton, *nvr nr to chal.*
................................(50 to 1 op 33 to 1) 7

1922⁷ CODE RED 4-10-7 M Richards, *prmnt, wknd appr 2 out.*
................................(7 to 1 op 6 to 1 tchd 8 to 1) 8

1599 EWAR BOLD 4-10-7 D Gallagher, *jmpd rght 1st, no dngr aftr.*
................................(20 to 1 tchd 25 to 1) 9

56⁷ JOBBER'S FIDDLE 5-11-0 N Williamson, *nvr better than mid-div.*..................(20 to 1 op 33 to 1) 10

3247 DR DAVE (Ire) 6-11-5 A Thornton, *mid-div, rdn 3 out, sn wknd.*......(16 to 1 op 10 to 1 tchd 20 to 1) 11

1992 FLASH IN THE PAN 4-10-2 W McFarland, *beh 5th, tld off.*
................................(4 to 1 op 3 to 1) 12

2012⁹ HALF AN INCH (Ire) (bl) 4-10-7 B Powell, *led to 3rd, wknd 5th, tld off.*......(25 to 1 op 20 to 1 tchd 33 to 1) 13

ANOTHER FIDDLE 7-11-5 T J Murphy, *hld up, rdn 5th, sn beh, tld off.*......(20 to 1 op 14 to 1 tchd 33 to 1) 14

107 SAYITAGAIN 5-11-5 J Osborne, *pld hrd, beh 4th, tld off.*
................................(33 to 1 tchd 66 to 1) 15

1449 FRANKS JESTER 6-11-5 W Marston, *prmnt to 4th, sn beh, tld off.*..................(25 to 1 op 20 to 1) 16

1940 SULLAMELL 6-11-5 S Burrough, *beh 4th, tld off whn pld up 2 out.*..................(33 to 1 op 25 to 1) pu

1844⁵ HAUTE CUISINE 4-10-7 J R Kavanagh, *led 3rd to 5th, wknd 3 out, tld off whn pld up bef last.*............(14 to 1) pu

506 KIRKIE CROSS (bl) 5-11-0 J Ryan, *chsd ldrs to 5th, tld off whn pld up bef last.*......(50 to 1 op 33 to 1) pu

1922 SUPERGOLD (Ire) (bl) 4-10-7 K Gaule, *prmnt, pckd second, wknd appr 3 out, tld off whn pld up bef last.*.....(33 to 1) pu

1731 TOMORROWS HARVEST 5-10-11 (3*) T Dascombe, *tld off 3rd, pld up bef 2 out.*........(50 to 1 op 33 to 1) pu

Dist: Nk, ½l, 4l, nk, 2l, 8l, 12l, 3l, 3l, 2l. 4m 21.80s. a 30.80s (21 Ran).
(E Reitel), Lady Herries

2266 Fort Novices' Handicap Chase Class E (0-105 5-y-o and up) £3,570 2½m 110yds......................(2:40)

1847⁴ SOPHIE MAY [82] (bl) 6-10-13 A P McCoy, *hld up, hdwy 9th, led appr 3 out, ran on wl.*
................................(10 to 1 tchd 9 to 1 and 12 to 1) 1

1557* SCORESHEET [93] 7-11-10 P Hide, *prmnt, rdn 3 out, one pace nxt.*......(4 to 1 op 3 to 1) 2

1803³ AMBER SPARK (Ire) 8-11-5 R Dunwoody, *hdwy 9th, chsd wnr frm 3 out, wknd r-in.*
................................(3 to 1 fav op 5 to 2 tchd 7 to 2) 3

1670⁸ BONNIFER (Ire) [69] 8-10-0 W Marston, *hld up, hdwy 4 out, sn rdn and btn.*..................(20 to 1 tchd 25 to 1) 4

2026³ BARONCELLI [69] 7-10-0 I Lawrence, *mstk 8th, nvr nrr.*
................................(20 to 1 op 16 to 1) 5

1972² JULEIT JONES (Ire) [90] 8-11-4 (3*) L Aspell, *led till appr 3 out, wknd approaching nxt.* (14 to 1 op 12 to 1 tchd 16 to 1) 6

1957 REESHLOCH [90] 8-11-0 (7*) C Rae, *hld up, hdwy 4 out, wknd appr 3 out.*......................(7 to 1 op 6 to 1) 7

1990⁵ MOVING OUT [87] 9-11-4 G Bradley, *prmnt to 9th, rallied 4 out, wknd appr nxt, tld off.*.....(100 to 30 op 4 to 1) 8

1568⁷ BASSENHALLY [83] 7-11-0 R Marley, *mid-div till blun and uns rdr 5th.*......(11 to 1 op 8 to 1 tchd 12 to 1) ur

1845[4] VICTORY GATE (USA) [71] 12-10-2 D Leahy, *al beh, tld off*
whn pld up bef 9th .... (33 to 1) pu
1734 BATHWICK BOBBIE [81] 10-10-9 (3*) G Hogan, *mid-div whn*
hit 6th, beh tenth, tld off when pld up bef 3 out ..... (20 to 1) pu
2009 BALLYMGYR (Ire) [87] 8-11-4 D Gallagher, *hmpd 5th, tld off*
whn pld up bef 3 out .... (20 to 1 op 16 to 1 tchd 25 to 1) pu
1494[7] PARLIAMENTARIAN (Ire) [85] (bl) 8-11-2 M A Fitzgerald,
prmnt to 6th, tld off whn pld up bef 3 out.
.... (25 to 1 op 20 to 1 tchd 33 to 1) pu
ONEOFUS [69] 8-10-0 M Richards, *prmnt to 4 out, beh whn*
pld up bef out. .... (33 to 1) pu
Dist: 4l, 3l, 17l, 8l, ½l, 5l, 23l. 5m 34.80s. a 33.80s (14 Ran).
SR: 14/21/13/-/-/-/   (J Daniels), L Montague Hall

2267 Keep Novices' Handicap Hurdle
Class E (0-105 4-y-o and up) £2,407
2m 110yds. .... (3:10)

1592[3] NONE STIRRED (Ire) [98] 7-11-12 P Hide, *prmnt, effrt 2 out,*
hld whn lft in ld last. ....(6 to 1 op 5 to 1) 1
1982[3] SAILEP (Fr) [97] 5-11-8 (3*) T Dascombe, *in tch, rdn 2 out, lft in*
second pl fnl fence, kpt on one pace. .... (8 to 1 op 6 to 1) 2
FIONANS FLUTTER (Ire) [92] 9-11-6 P Holley, *styd on frm 2*
out, kpt on one pace. ....(12 to 1 op 10 to 1) 3
1570 GENTLE BREEZE (Ire) [80] 5-10-5 (3*) L Aspell, *hld up,*
improved appr 3 out, one pace nxt.
.... (14 to 1 op 10 to 1 tchd 16 to 1) 4
2010 KING'S GOLD [79] 7-10-7 M Richards, *rear early, hdwy 3 out,*
one pace nxt. .... (16 to 1 op 14 to 1 tchd 20 to 1) 5
1961[5] O MY LOVE [79] 6-10-7 J Osborne, *hld up, hdwy 3 out, one*
pace appr nxt. ....(12 to 1 op 8 to 1 tchd 16 to 1) 6
1648[8] THAT OLD FEELING (Ire) [72] 5-10-0 T J Murphy, *prmnt to 3rd.*
.... (16 to 1 op 14 to 1 tchd 20 to 1) 7
2009[2] MUSEUM (Ire) [82] 6-10-3 (7*) X Aizpuru, *nvr better than mid-*
div. ....(6 to 1 op 5 to 1) 8
1727[3] SIR DANTE (Ire) [85] 6-10-13 D O'Sullivan, *beh 4th.*
.... (11 to 2 op 5 to 1 tchd 6 to 1) 9
1854 HAWANAFA [86] (bl) 4-10-2[2] W McFarland, *hld up, wknd 5th.*
....(33 to 1) 10
1594[6] ILEWIN JANINE (Ire) [83] 6-10-11 S Fox, *led to 3 out, fdd*
quickly. .... (12 to 1 op 10 to 1 tchd 14 to 1) 11
1423[4] TOPANGA [84] (bl) 5-10-12 D Bridgwater, *al beh.*
.... (11 to 1 op 10 to 1 tchd 12 to 1) 12
1719[8] MASTER GOODENOUGH (Ire) [72] 6-9-13[6] (7*) D Creech,
blun 4th, sn wknd,tld off .... (33 to 1) 13
1733 ROYAL GLINT [72] 8-10-0 N Williamson, *al beh, tld off.*
.... (10 to 1 op 12 to 1) 14
1716 MURPHY'S RUN (Ire) [72] 7-9-9 (5*) Mr R Thornton, *al beh, tld*
off. .... (33 to 1) 15
1958[7] COOL GUNNER [81] 7-10-9 C Maude, *al prmnt, led 3 out till*
stumbled and uns rdr last.
.... (9 to 2 fav op 4 to 1 tchd 5 to 1) ur
Dist: 2½l, 4l, ¾l, 3l, hd, 3½l, 10l, 8l, 8l, 14l. 4m 18.30s. a 27.30s (16 Ran).
(Colin Frewin), J T Gifford

2268 Dave Freeman Memorial Handicap
Chase Class F (0-105 5-y-o and up)
£3,014 3m. ....(3:40)

1974 BRAVE BUCCANEER [105] 10-11-7 (7*) C Rae, *hld up, hdwy*
13th, hmpd 2 out, led r-in, rdn out. .... (25 to 1 op 20 to 1) 1
1674[2] EASTERN RIVER [85] 11-10-8 S Wynne, *al prmnt, led aftr 4*
out to r-in, no extr. .... (4 to 1 fav op 5 to 2 tchd 9 to 2) 2
1812[4] BLACK CHURCH [90] 11-10-13 D O'Sullivan, *hld up, hdwy 4*
out, rdn 2 out, ran on one pace. .... (14 to 1 op 10 to 1) 3
2024[3] CARLINGFORD LAKES (Ire) [87] 9-10-10 M A Fitzgerald,
hdwy 4 out, kpt on one pace frm 2 out.
.... (16 to 1 op 10 to 1 tchd 20 to 1) 4
DARREN THE BRAVE [100] 9-11-9 G Bradley, *al prmnt, ev ch*
whn stumbled 3 out, blun nxt, not reco'r.
.... (6 to 1 op 7 to 1 tchd 5 to 1) 5
1804[*] SUGAR HILL (Ire) [90] 7-10-13 P Hide, *led till appr 4 out, sn*
wknd. .... (11 to 2 op 5 to 1 tchd 9 to 2) 6
LITTLE-NIPPER [95] 12-11-4 C Maude, *hld up, hdwy 7th,*
wknd 4 out. .... (33 to 1 op 20 to 1 tchd 50 to 1) 7
KEANO (Ire) [93] 8-11-2 A P McCoy, *hld up, lost tch frm 4 out.*
.... (7 to 1 op 5 to 1 tchd 8 to 1) 8
1707 ZAMBEZI SPIRIT (Ire) [96] 8-11-5 Derek Byrne, *nvr on terms*
.... (10 to 1 op 7 to 1 tchd 12 to 1) 9
1994 OATS N BARLEY [88] 8-10-11 S Burrough, *nvr on terms*
.... (8 to 1 tchd 9 to 1) 10
VALNAU (Fr) [81] (bl) 10-9-11 (7*) G Supple, *beh whn f 8th.*
.... (16 to 1 op 12 to 1 tchd 20 to 1) f
1974 MWEENISH [86] 15-10-9 R Bellamy, *chsd ldrs, hit 12th, sn*
lost pl, pld up bef 3 out. .... (50 to 1 op 33 to 1) pu
517[4] SPIKEY (NZ) [85] 11-10-8 J Osborne, *beh till pld up bef 7th.*
.... (33 to 1 op 14 to 1) pu
1814[4] MIGHTY FROLIC [100] 10-11-9 Mr T Hills, *hdwy 6th, wknd*
appr 3 out, blun nxt, tld off whn pld up bef last.
.... (33 to 1 op 20 to 1 tchd 50 to 1) pu
1974 SHEELIN LAD (Ire) [86] 9-10-9 G Upton, *prmnt to 9th, tld off*
whn pld up bef 3 out ....(20 to 1 op 33 to 1) pu
2005 CHIEF RAGER [104] 8-11-13 D Bridgwater, *not fluent, tld off*
whn pld up bef tenth ...(14 to 1 op 12 to 1 tchd 16 to 1) pu
PROFESSOR STRONG (Ire) [103] 9-11-12 N Williamson, *tld*
off whn pld up bef tenth .... (8 to 1 op 9 to 1) pu

---

1701 LITTLE ROWLEY [77] 8-10-0 M Richards, *mstk 1st, beh 12th,*
tld off whn pld up bef 3 out .... (50 to 1 op 20 to 1) pu
Dist: 2½l, 1¼l, ¾l, 21l, 2l, 16l, 2½l, 3½l, 16l. 6m 43.20s. a 49.20s (18 Ran).
(R C Watts), Andrew Turnell

2269 Weatherbys 'Stars Of Tomorrow'
Open National Hunt Flat Standard -
Class H (4,5,6-y-o) £1,306 2m
110yds. ....(4:10)

2015[*] ARKLEY ROYAL 6-11-11 G Upton, *hld up, hdwy 6 fs out, led*
o'r one out, hdd ins last, rallied to ld last.
.... (13 to 8 fav op 5 to 4 tchd 2 to 1) 1
EDMOND (Fr) 5-11-4 A Thornton, *hld up, prog hfwy, led o'r 3*
out till over one out, led ins last, ct last strd.
.... (9 to 1 op 8 to 1 tchd 10 to 1) 2
MISTER ERMYN 4-10-6 D Morris, *hld up, improved hfwy, effrt*
2 fs out, kpt on. ....(33 to 1 op 20 to 1) 3
RASAK 5-11-4 E Murphy, *wtd wth, gd hdwy 6 fs out, rdn 2 out,*
kpt on. ....(100 to 30 op 2 to 1 tchd 7 to 2) 4
BIGSOUND (Ire) 5-11-4 N Williamson, *hld up in tch, rdn and*
ev ch o'r one furlong out, wknd entering last.
.... (8 to 1 op 4 to 1) 5
WISLEY WARRIOR 6-11-4 C Maude, *prmnt, led o'r 6 fs out till*
over 3 out, sn fdd. ..... (12 to 1 op 8 to 1 tchd 14 to 1) 6
BOLD LEAP 5-11-4 Mr A Sansome, *trkd ldrs, lost pl aftr 6 fs,*
styd on one pace frm 2 out. .... (33 to 1 op 20 to 1) 7
WELSH ASSET 6-10-11 (7*) Mr A Wintle, *nvr nr to chal.*
.... (40 to 1 op 33 to 1 tchd 50 to 1) 8
DANTE'S GOLD (Ire) 6-11-4 J Osborne, *hdwy hfwy, wknd o'r*
5 fs out. .... (14 to 1 op 10 to 1 tchd 16 to 1) 9
FRED MOTH 4-10-6 P McLoughlin, *led till o'r 6 fs out, fdd 3*
out. ....(40 to 1 op 33 to 1 tchd 50 to 1) 10
NORLANDIC (NZ) 5-11-4 M A Fitzgerald, *trkd ldrs till wknd 3*
fs out. ....(16 to 1 op 10 to 1 tchd 20 to 1) 11
1240 FRANKIE MUCK 5-11-4 D Bridgwater, *trkd ldrs, fdd fnl 3 fs.*
.... (20 to 1 op 14 to 1) 12
CALDEBROOK (Ire) 6-10-11 (7*) S Laird, *hld up, rdn and wknd*
appr fnl 3 fs. .... (20 to 1 op 8 to 1) 13
KAZ KALEM 5-11-4 G Tormey, *beh fnl 4 fs.*
.... (10 to 1 op 14 to 1 tchd 20 to 1) 14
GOOD TIME DANCER 5-10-13 Mr P Scott, *chsd ldrs, wknd*
hfwy. ....(16 to 1 op 10 to 1 tchd 20 to 1) 15
WHOD OF THOUGHT IT (Ire) 6-10-13 (5*) Mr C Vigors, *hdwy*
aftr 4 fs, wknd o'r 5 fs out. .... (100 to 1 op 33 to 1) 16
TEDROSS 6-10-13 (5*) Mr R Thornton, *prmnt till wknd hfwy.*
.... (40 to 1 op 25 to 1 tchd 50 to 1) 17
BECKAMERE 5-10-13 T J Murphy, *beh fnl ten fs, tld off.*
.... (66 to 1 op 33 to 1 tchd 100 to 1) 18
X-RAY (Ire) 4-10-6 G Bradley, *whipped round strt, pld very hrd*
early, al beh, tld off.... (33 to 1 op 14 to 1 tchd 50 to 1) 19
Dist: Sht-hd, 1l, 1½l, 5l, 6l, 21l, 2l, 2½l, 6l, 5l. 4m 14.80s. (19 Ran).
(John Bickel), J A B Old

GOWRAN PARK (IRE) (good)
Thursday January 23rd

2270 Burger King Cork Maiden Hurdle (4 &
5-y-o) £3,082 2m. .... (1:15)

WHAT'S THE VERDICT (Ire) 5-11-6 C F Swan, ... (6 to 1) 1
TEMPO (Ire) 5-11-6 C O'Dwyer, ...(5 to 4 on) 2
2106[4] MIRACLE ME (Ire) 5-11-6 L F Woods, ...(14 to 1) 3
2067[5] SARAH'S GUEST (Ire) (bl) 4-10-7[2] G Bradley, ... (8 to 1) 4
ORMOND JENNY (Ire) 5-10-8 (7*) R P Hogan, ...(50 to 1) 5
2222[6] IMPERIAL PLAICE (Ire) 5-10-5 (7*) D M Bean, ...(12 to 1) 6
PRAGUE SPRING 5-10-12 (3*) G Cotter, ...(20 to 1) 7
2072 IT'S HIMSELF 5-10-12 J Shortt, ...(25 to 1) 8
DA SILVA (Ire) 5-10-13 (7*) M W Martin, ...(12 to 1) 9
COULTHARD (Ire) 4-9-12 (7*) M J Collins, ...(33 to 1) 10
1777[5] NAZMI (Ire) 5-11-6 K F O'Brien, ...(6 to 1) 11
ST RITA 4-10-0 T P Rudd, ...(14 to 1) 12
ONE MORE SPIN (Ire) 4-10-5 R Dunwoody, ...(10 to 1) 13
2168 LADY OF GRANGE (Ire) 5-11-1 F J Flood, ...(20 to 1) 14
2055 NIL FAIC (Ire) 5-10-7 M P Hourigan, ...(66 to 1) 15
ZACOPANI (Ire) 5-10-12 D J Casey, ...(16 to 1) 16
1247 IRELAND INVADER 5-10-4 (3*) K Whelan, ...(50 to 1) 17
PEYTO LAKE (Ire) 5-10-12 T Horgan, ...(25 to 1) 18
LISARDBOULA (Ire) 5-10-5 (7*) A A O'Shea, ...(50 to 1) 19
COMKILRED (Ire) 5-11-1 D H O'Connor, ...(10 to 1) f
Dist: 7l, 15l, 4½l, 1½l. 3m 50.30s. (20 Ran).
(R W Huggins), M Johnston

2271 Burger King Limerick Maiden Hurdle
(6-y-o and up) £3,082 2m. .... (1:45)

2235[2] KILCOO BOY (Ire) 6-12-0 C F Swan, ... (2 to 1 fav) 1
2132[3] BE HOME EARLY (Ire) 7-11-7 (7*) A O'Shea, ... (9 to 4) 2
21074 BALLYRIHY BOY (Ire) 6-11-9 (5*) J M Donnelly, ... (10 to 1) 3
2094[2] PAULS RUN (Ire) 8-12-0 L P Cusack, ...(6 to 1) 4
2089[7] TREANAREE (Ire) 8-10-13 (7*) S Kelly, ...(25 to 1) 5
2138[5] YASHGANS VISION (Ire) 6-11-2 (7*) R P Hogan, ...(12 to 1) 6
1018[8] FRIARSTOWN DUKE 7-11-11 (3*) U Smyth, ...(14 to 1) 7
2107[9] PREMIER WALK 8-11-7 (7*) S O'Donnell, ...(12 to 1) 8
2108[6] IRISH REEF (Ire) 6-11-6 K F O'Brien, ...(33 to 1) 9
CURRAVARING (Ire) 7-11-6 W Slattery, ...(50 to 1) 10

NATIVE FLECK (Ire) 7-12-0 C O'Dwyer, ... (12 to 1) 11
4337 RAMDON ROCKS 10-12-0 P McWilliams, ... (33 to 1) 12
CASEY JUNIOR (Ire) 9-12-0 D J Casey, ... (20 to 1) 13
HAZY WALK (Ire) 6-11-9 T P Treacy, ... (25 to 1) 14
WHOSE YER WAN (Ire) 7-11-9 A Powell, ... (25 tc 1) 15
2165⁷ CRANNON BEAUTY (Ire) 7-11-3 (3ˣ) J Butler, ... (25 to 1) 16
2132⁴ ORANGE JUICE (Ire) 7-11-6 J P Broderick, ... (25 to 1) 17
BATTLE AIR (NZ) 9-11-11 (3ˣ) R P O'Brien, ... (20 to 1) 18
2094⁴ ATHA BEITHE (Ire) 6-12-0 G Bradley, ... (4 to 1) pu
2124⁴ FATHER GERRY (Ire) 7-12-0 R Dunwoody, ... (8 to 1) pu
Dist: 16d, 10l, 1½l, 1½l. 3m 49.30s. (20 Ran).

(Patrick G J Murphy), A P O'Brien

2272 Burger King Waterford Handicap Hurdle (0-116 4-y-o and up) £3,767 2m 1f. . . . . (2:15)

2140⁴ TOUREEN GALE (Ire) [-] 8-10-5 D J Casey, ... (9 to 1) 1
2128 LADY ARPEL (Ire) [-] 5-12-0 K F O'Brien, ... (8 to 1) 2
2142² MARINERS REEF (Ire) [-] 6-9-6 (7ˣ) D McCullagh, ... (5 to 1) 3
1899⁴ VEREDARIUS (Fr) [-] 6-10-9 F Woods, ... (100 to 30 fav) 4
2131⁶ IADA (Ire) [-] 6-10-4 D T Evans, ... (14 to 1) 5
2057⁴ ANTICS (Ire) [-] 5-9-5 (7ˣ) Mrs C Harrison, ... (12 to 1) 6
2134⁸ CHOOSEY'S TREASURE (Ire) [-] 4-11-3 C F Swan, (8 to 1) 7
2114⁶ ILLBETHEREFORYOU (Ire) [-] 6-9-5 (7ˣ) P G Hourigan, ... (8 to 1) 8
2170 GLENHAVEN ARTIST (Ire) [-] 7-11-2 F J Flood, ... (16 to 1) 9
2057⁹ THE ROAD TO MOSCOW (Ire) [-] 6-9-9 T M Duffy, . . (14 to 1) 10
2103² MISS BERTAINE (Ire) [-] (bl) 8-9-1 (7ˣ) J E Casey, . (10 to 1) 11
2114⁵ THEPRINCESS MANHAR (Ire) [-] 5-9-12 (7ˣ) D M Bean, ... (12 to 1) 12
PADDY'S PET (Ire) [-] 8-9-13 (7ˣ) K A Kelly, ... (16 to 1) 13
2159² BAKEMA (Ire) [-] 5-10-8 J R Barry, ... (9 to 1) 14
2142 SUPER FLAME (Can) [-] 10-11-8 A Powell, ... (14 to 1) 15
THURSDAY SWEEP [-] 11-9-12¹ J P Broderick, ... (25 to 1) 16
2162 SHECOULDNTBEBETTER (Ire) [-] 6-9-7 T P Treacy, (12 to 1) pu
2172⁶ COUNCILLOR (Ire) [-] (bl) 6-10-1 T J Mitchell, ... (25 to 1) pu
Dist: 2½l, 10l, ¾l, ¾l. 4m 7.40s. (18 Ran).

(E P Cogan), W P Mullins

2273 Burger King Thyestes Handicap Chase (Grade 2) (5-y-o and up) £16,125 3m. . . . . (2:45)

1639⁸ COULDNT BE BETTER [-] 10-12-0 G Bradley, hld up, hdwy 6 out, led and styd on wl r-in. . . . . (7 to 1) 1
2053⁵ CORYMANDEL (Ire) [-] 8-10-0 T P Rudd, led bef 3rd, mstk last, hdd and no extr r-in. . . . . (40 to 1) 2
2071⁴ NEW CO (Ire) [-] 9-10-5 C O'Dwyer, chsd ldrs, bad mstk tenth, hdwy 4 out, no extr r-in. . . . . (7 to 4 fav) 3
2058⁷ DUN BELLE (Ire) [-] 8-10-0 T J Mitchell, beh early, hdwy 5 out, nrst finish. . . . . (13 to 2) 4
2127⁴ THE CRAZY BISHOP (Ire) [-] (bl) 9-10-2² R Dunwoody, mid-div, hdwy 6 out, wknd aftr nxt, sn no dngr. . . . . (8 to 1) 5
2169⁶ MONKEY AGO [-] 10-9-7 (7ˣ) M D Murphy, beh, prog bef 5 out, nrst finish. . . . . (40 to 1) 6
2071⁴ BACK BAR (Ire) [-] 9-10-0 J P Broderick, mid-div, wknd aftr 6 out, sn btn. . . . . (14 to 1) 7
2127 FISSURE SEAL [-] (bl) 11-10-8 F Woods, al prmnt, wknd quickly aftr 3 out, sn no dngr after. . . . . (11 to 1) 8
2018⁹ BART OWEN [-] 12-10-0 T Horgan, al beh, tld off. . (40 to 1) 9
2071 NUAFFE [-] (bl) 12-10-4 (3ˣ) G Cotter, led early, hdd bef 3rd, wknd aftr 5 out, tld off. . . . . (14 to 1) 10
2069⁴ JASSU [-] 11-10-5 T P Treacy, al beh, tld off. . . . . . (14 to 1) 11
2127⁵ IDIOTS VENTURE [-] 10-11-5 C F Swan, beh whn f 11th. . . . . (9 to 1) f
1652 THE OUTBACK WAY (Ire) [-] (bl) 7-10-1¹ D H O'Connor, tld off whn pld up bef 2 out. (16 to 1) pu
SHANAGARRY (Ire) [-] 8-10-8 K F O'Brien, beh whn pld up bef 4 out. . . . . (14 to 1) pu
Dist: 2½l, ½l, 1½l, 3½l. 6m 9.90s. (14 Ran).

(R A B Whittle), C P E Brooks

2274 Burger King Grafton Street Handicap Chase (0-116 5-y-o and up) £3,082 2½m. . . . . (3:15)

2171³ ROYAL ROSY (Ire) [-] 6-10-11 C F Swan, ... (5 to 1) 1
2163 APPALACHEE BAY (Ire) [-] 7-10-12 (3ˣ) J Butler, ... (8 to 1) 2
2164 MARGUERITA SONG [-] 7-9-12 J P Broderick, ... (20 to 1) 3
MASTER MCCARTAN (Ire) [-] 8-10-11 (7ˣ) Mr Brian Moran, ... (11 to 1) 4
2099⁴ WALLYS RUN [-] 10-9-10 (3ˣ) G Cotter, ... (9 to 1) 5
2141² QUATTRO [-] 7-10-12 T P Treacy, ... (5 to 2 fav) 6
2053⁶ STRONG HICKS (Ire) [-] 9-11-7 F J Flood, ... (9 to 2) 7
2136⁶ YOUNG WOLF [-] 9-9-10 P L Malone, ... (14 to 1) 8
2143⁴ TOUT VA BIEN [-] 9-10-7 F Woods, ... (9 to 1) 9
2162¹ INDESTRUCTIBLE [-] (bl) 9-11-0 G M O'Neill, ... (9 to 1) pu
Dist: 3½l, 4l, 4½l, 2l. 5m 29.30s. (10 Ran).

(Patrick M Sheehan), A P O'Brien

2275 Burger King Jervis Street P.McCreery Memorial Hurdle (5-y-o and up) £3,082 2¼m. . . . . (3:45)

2166² BORO BOW (Ire) 6-11-2 T P Treacy, ... (11 to 8 on) 1

SYDNEY TWOTHOUSAND (NZ) 7-11-7 R Dunwoody, ... (7 to 1) 2
2160* MIDNIGHT JAZZ (Ire) 7-12-0 J P Broderick, ... (5 to 1) 3
MORAL SUPPORT (Ire) 5-11-3 C O'Dwyer, ... (12 to 1) 4
2140³ FRANCES STREET (Ire) (bl) 5-11-10 C F Swan, ... (7 to 2) 5
ROSDEMON (Ire) 9-11-7 P A Roche, ... (14 to 1) 6
2160 AFGHANI (Ire) 8-11-2 (5ˣ) P Morris, ... (14 to 1) 7
2079 SISTER WEST (Ire) 5-10-12 T P Rudd, ... (66 to 1) 8
2093⁶ TEA-VINE (Ire) 8-10-9 (7ˣ) R P Hogan, ... (33 to 1) pu
Dist: Nk, 15l, 8l, 11l. 4m 30.00s. (9 Ran).

(J P Hill), P Mullins

2276 Burger King O'Connell Street Flat Race (4-y-o and up) £3,082 2m (4:15)

2130* RAINBOW VICTOR (Ire) 4-10-11 (7ˣ) Miss A L Crowley, ... (11 to 8 fav) 1
MUSICAL WONDER (Ire) 6-11-6 Mr P Fenton, . . . (12 to 1) 2
2115² GARRYHILL CHOICE (Ire) 6-11-8 (3ˣ) Mr R Walsh, (15 to 8) 3
2107⁵ HEN HANSEL (Ire) 6-11-11 (7ˣ) Mr Sean O O'Brien, (14 to 1) 4
2165* MICKS MAN (Ire) 6-12-1 (3ˣ) Mr E Norris, ... (5 to 1) 5
2108* BRIDGES DAUGHTER (Ire) 6-11-13 Mr D Marnane, (8 to 1) 6
2129⁵ CORYROSE (Ire) 5-11-2 (7ˣ) Mr F J Crowley, ... (11 to 1) 7
2108⁷ ACTIVE LADY (Ire) 5-10-9 (7ˣ) Mr B Walsh, ... (50 to 1) 8
MARIA-NOELLE (Ire) 7-10-13 (7ˣ) Mr J P McNamara, ... (25 to 1) 9
DRUMCLIFFE (Ire) 6-11-4 (7ˣ) Mr J L Cullen, ... (25 to 1) 10
1780 RATHCORE LADY (Ire) 6-10-13 (7ˣ) Mr A Ross, . . . (40 to 1) 11
2222 MAGS DWYER (Ire) 7-11-6 (7ˣ) Mr G A Kingston, . . (40 to 1) 12
Dist: 3l, 15l, sht-hd, 5l. 3m 48.30s. (12 Ran).

(Joseph Crowley), A P O'Brien

HUNTINGDON (good to soft (races 1,2,3,4,5,7), good (6)) Thursday January 23rd
Going Correction: PLUS 0.85 sec. per fur. (races 1,3,5,7), PLUS 1.05 (2,4,6)

2277 Offord 'National Hunt' Novices' Hurdle Class E (4-y-o and up) £3,055 2m 110yds. . . . . (1:20)

1973 LEGIBLE 9-11-5 R Johnson, hld up behd, pushed alng and hdwy aftr 3 out, not fluent nxt and sn rdn, led r-in, jst held on. . . . . (14 to 1 op 12 to 1 tchd 16 to 1) 1
1805⁸ CLINTON (Ire) 6-11-5 A Thornton, not fluent 1st, hld up, hdwy aftr 3 out, hrd rdn appr last, str run flt, jst fld. . . . . (25 to 1 op 14 to 1) 2
SIERRA BAY 7-11-5 J Osborne, hld up, gng wl, steady hdwy frm 4th, led 2 out, hdd and no extr r-in, better for race. . . . . (15 to 8 fav op 7 to 4 tchd 9 to 4 and 5 to 2) 3
1483³ SHEKELS 6-11-5 D Gallagher, al hndy, ev ch 2 out, sn one pace and pres. . . . . (16 to 1 op 10 to 1) 4
1849² NASONE (Ire) 6-11-5 P Hide, led 3rd to nxt, led 5th to 2 out, sn one pace. . . . . (2 to 1 op 5 to 2) 5
1868 HENRYS PORT 7-11-5 M Richards, hld up in mid-div, styd on same pace frm 3 out, not pace to chal. (40 to 1 op 16 to 1) 6
2029* CHERRYMORE 6-11-5 W Marston, keen early, trkd ldrs, not fluent 5th an sn rdn alng, btn appr 2 out. . . . . (4 to 1 op 3 to 1) 7
1849⁶ PHYSICAL FUN 6-11-5 D Skyrme, al mid-div, effrt frm 3 out, no imprsn from nxt. . . . . (50 to 1 op 33 to 1) 8
HARLEQUIN CHORUS 7-11-5 G Upton, chsd ldrs, wknd frm 3 out. . . . . (25 to 1 op 20 to 1 tchd 33 to 1) 9
1940⁷ KYBO'S REVENGE 6-11-5 D O'Sullivan, beh, nvr rchd ldg grp. (50 to 1 op 33 to 1) 10
1719⁷ REVERSE THRUST 6-10-12 (7ˣ) M Clinton, chsd ldrs, wknd und pres appr 2 out. . . . . (50 to 1 op 33 to 1) 11
LIBERTARIAN (Ire) 7-11-2 (3ˣ) G Hogan, hld up beh, nvr on terms. . . . . (50 to 1 op 25 to 1) 12
2028 GLENMAVIS 10-11-5 Dr P Pritchard, hld up, mstk 4th, sn struggling in rear. . . . . (50 to 1 op 33 to 1) 13
1973³ FERRERS 6-11-5 R Marley, led to 3rd, led 4th to nxt, wknd 3 out. . . . . (20 to 1 op 14 to 1) 14
2153 TIDAL FORCE 6-11-5 M A Fitzgerald, hld up, cld aftr 5th. . . . . (12 to 1 op 8 to 1) 15
1997⁵ SUPREME CHARM 5m 5-11-5 S McNeill, prmnt to 5th, sn beh. . . . . (50 to 1 op 10 to 1 tchd 20 to 1) 16
1874⁴ TULLOW LADY (Ire) 6-11-0 M Brennan, al beh, tld off whn mstk 3 out. . . . . (33 to 1 op 16 to 1) 17
1805 LOCH GARMAN (Ire) 7-11-5 B Fenton, blun second and pld up, broke leg, dead. . . . . (50 to 1 op 33 to 1) pu
2179 JUST ANDY 6-11-5 T Jenks, chsd ldrs, pushed alng 3rd, losing tch whn mstks 4th and nxt, pld up bef 2 out. . . . . (50 to 1 op 25 to 1) pu
52⁷ BLUE HAVANA 5-11-0 J R Kavanagh, al beh, pld up bef 2 out. . . . . (50 to 1 op 33 to 1) pu
1594 REACH THE CLOUDS 5-11-5 C Maude, al towards rear, pld up bef 2 out. . . . . (33 to 1) pu
Dist: Hd, 1¾l, 3l, hd, 3l, 3l, 5l, 5l, nk, 1¼l. 4m 1.00s. a 20.00s (21 Ran).
SR: 31/31/29/26/26/23/20/15/10/

(S P Tindall), S Mellor

2278 Kitty Ward-Thomas Novices' Chase Class D (5-y-o and up) £4,142 2m

110yds. . . . . (1:50)

1288² LIGHTENING LAD 9-11-4 C Maude, *cl up, led aftr 5th, made rst, jmpd rght last, drvn out.* . . . . (3 to 1 op 7 to 2) 1

1725* GUINDA (Ire) 7-11-6 D Walsh, *cl up, wkn frm aftr 5th, mstk 4 out, ev ch, ran on one pace.*
. . . .(4 to 1 op 7 to 2 tchd 9 to 2) 2

1393⁷ CRACK ON 7-11-4 R Johnson, *hld up beh ldrs, cld frm 7th, not fluent 3 out and mstk nxt, drvn and awkward last, no extr.*
. . . .(9 to 4 fav op 2 to 1 tchd 5 to 2) 3

WHO IS EQUINAME (Ire) 7-11-4 M A Fitzgerald, *hld up, pckd 6th, outpcd frm 4 out, tld off.*
. . . .(11 to 1 op 10 to 1 tchd 12 to 1) 4

2153³ JUST BRUCE 8-11-4 K Gaule, *mid-divsion, pushed alng, outpcd frm 8th, tld off.* . . . .(33 to 1 op 16 to 1) 5

ALTHREY BLUE (Ire) 8-11-4 S McNeill, *al beh, tld off.*
. . . .(100 to 1 op 50 to 1) 6

2155 MR MOTIVATOR 7-11-4 l Lawrence, *outpcd, tld off.*
. . . . (50 to 1 op 33 to 1 tchd 66 to 1) 7

1813⁴ WARSPITE 7-10-13 (5*) S Ryan, *beh, rdn alng 5th, sn struggling, tld off.* . . . .(66 to 1 op 33 to 1) 8

BLAIR CASTLE (Ire) 6-11-4 B Fenton, *f 1st.*
. . . .(12 to 1 tchd 14 to 1) f

1957* GROOVING (Ire) 8-11-11 P Hide, *trkd ldrs, cl 3rd and ev ch whn f 8th.* . . . .(4 to 1 op 3 to 1) f

MHEANMETOO 6-11-1 (3*) G Hogan, *led to aftr 5th, sn lost pl, mstk 8th and pld up bef nxt.* . . . .(66 to 1 op 33 to 1) pu

Dist: 3½l, 2l, dist, 4l, 4l, 26l, 19l. 4m 17.40s. a 23.40s (11 Ran).

SR: 29/27/23/-/-/-/ (Richard Peterson), J S King

2279 Yelling Novices' Handicap Hurdle Class E (0-100 4-y-o and up) £2,582 2m 110yds. . . . . (2:20)

1969* AMBIDEXTROUS (Ire) [75] 5-10-1 (7*) L Cummins, *hld up, hdwy 3 out, led appr last, rdn out.* . . . . . . (9 to 1 tchd 9 to 2) 1

1764⁴ STORM TIGER (Ire) [67] (v) 6-9-11 (3*) E Husband, *trkd ldrs, led 2 out till appr last, no extr.* . . . .(10 to 1 op 14 to 1) 2

1953³ HEAVENS ABOVE [67] 5-10-0 B Fenton, *made most, hdd 2 out, one pace.* . . . .(20 to 1 op 16 to 1 tchd 25 to 1) 3

2002⁴ BAASM [80] 4-9-10 (5*) B Grattan, *hld up, hdwy appr 3 out, no imprsn und pres frm nxt.* . . . .(12 to 1 op 10 to 1) 4

1928⁷ RED LIGHT [80] (bl) 5-10-13 J Osborne, *beh, hrd rdn aftr 3 out, kpt on, nvr nrr.* . . . . .(16 to 1 op 12 to 1 tchd 14 to 1) 5

1731⁶ DARING RYDE [72] 6-10-5⁵ A Thornton, *not fluent 1st, styd on frm 3 out, nvr nrr.* . . . .(33 to 1 op 20 to 1 tchd 40 to 1) 6

1982² BIETSCHHORN BARD [90] 7-11-6 (3*) D Fortt, *hld up beh, drvn alng 5th, sn btn.* . . (9 to 4 fav op 2 to 1 tchd 5 to 2) 7

1719⁶ OTTAVIO FARNESE [91] 5-11-10 P Hide, *hld up, hdwy appr 3 out, sn no imprsn.* . . . .(8 to 1 op 6 to 1 tchd 9 to 1) 8

MILLENNIUM LASS (Ire) [93] 9-11-12 Gary Lyons, *trkd ldrs, 5th, wknd aftr 3 out.* . . . .(33 to 1 op 25 to 1) 9

1729³ THE BREWER [67] 5-10-0 S McNeill, *al beh, shrtlvd effrt 3 out.* . . . .(25 to 1 op 20 to 1) 10

976 NAGARA SOUND [87] 6-11-6 T Jenks, *mid-div, rdn and beh frm 5th.* . . . .(14 to 1 op 16 to 1) 11

1832 PERSIAN BUTTERFLY [67] 5-9-7 (7*) J Supple, *trkd ldr, wknd 3 out, tld off.* . . . . (40 to 1 op 25 to 1 tchd 50 to 1) 12

1928 MR GORDON BENNETT [67] 6-9-7 (7*) X Aizpuru, *trkd ldrs till wknd 4th, tld off.* . . . .(33 to 1 op 25 to 1) 13

2181* SAM ROCKETT [79] (bl) 4-9-9 (5*,7ex) S Ryan, *mid-div, drvn and wknd aftr 5th, tld off.* . .(3 to 1 tchd 7 to 2 and 4 to 1) 14

1846 RUSTIC GENT (Ire) [67] (v) 9-10-0 D Leahy, *chsd ldrs till hrd rdn and wknd aftr 5th, tld off.* 15

MARROWFAT LADY (Ire) [84] 6-10-10 (7*) S Melrose, *f 3rd.*
. . . .(33 to 1 tchd 40 to 1) f

Dist: 3l, 7l, 2½l, ½l, 1l, 3½l, 1½l, sht-hd, sht-hd, ½l. 4m 3.80s. a 22.80s (16 Ran).

(Mrs Carol P McPhail), E J Alston

2280 Bet With The Tote Novices' Chase Qualifier Class D (6-y-o and up) £4,141 3m. . . . . (2:50)

1939³ SIR LEONARD (Ire) 7-10-10 J Osborne, *cl up, led 9th to 14th, led nxt to 3 out, led last, rdn clr, styd on wl.*
. . . .(9 to 2 op 7 to 2 tchd 5 to 1) 1

1670 THE REVEREND BERT (Ire) 9-10-10 B Fenton, *hld up, hdwy 15th, led 3 out, blun last, one pace..* (10 to 1 tchd 14 to 1) 2

1862² WEE WINDY (Ire) 8-10-10 P Hide, *al hmpd, mstk and lost grnd 5 out, rallied nxt, one pace frm 2 out.*
. . . .(9 to 4 fav tchd 2 to 1 and 5 to 2) 3

2014 MR PICKPOCKET (Ire) 9-10-10 J F Titley, *mstk ldrs, lost pl 13th, rallied appr 2 out, one pace..* . . . . . (9 to 2 op 7 to 2) 4

1611 CLAYMORE LAD 7-10-10 T J Murphy, *led to 9th, led 14th to nxt, wknd appr 2 out.* . . . .(50 to 1 op 40 to 1) 5

1385 THE BIRD O'DONNELL 11-10-3 (7*) Mr T J Barry, *hld up beh ldrs, mstks 6th and 5 out, sn outpcd.*
. . . .(14 to 1 op 16 to 1 tchd 20 to 1) 6

1833 THE SHY PADRE (Ire) 8-10-10 R Farrant, *hld up, cld hfwy, wknd 14th.* . . . .(9 to 4 op 5 to 2 tchd 3 to 1) 7

1881⁵ DUKES MEADOW (Ire) 7-10-10 A Thornton, *trkd ldrs, jmpd slwly 4th, blun 13th, rdn nxt, sn btn..* (33 to 1 op 16 to 1) 8

1957⁶ BOOTS N ALL (Ire) 7-10-10 B Clifford, *al beh. . . . .*(33 to 1) 9

1970 SAINT KEYNE 7-10-10 J R Kavanagh, *al beh, lost tch frm 13th, tld off whn pld up bef 2 out.*. . . .(40 to 1 tchd 50 to 1) pu

---

1939* MELNIK 6-11-3 C Maude, *hld up, niggled alng 11th, struggling nxt, btn quickly and pld up bef 2 out.*(9 to 2 op 5 to 2) pu

2026⁴ PEARL EPEE 8-10-5 R Johnson, *mstk second, blun badly and almost uns rdr 5th, not jump wi in rear aftr, lost tch 13th, pld up bef 2 out.* . . . .(16 to 1 op 12 to 1) pu

1970 STROKESAVER (Ire) 7-10-10 D Gallagher, *chsd ldrs, wknd 14th, losing tch whn pld up bef 3 out.*
. . . . (25 to 1 op 20 to 1 tchd 33 to 1) pu

Dist: 5l, 3½l, 7l, nk, 12l, 3l, 2½l, 6l. 6m 24.70s. a 44.70s (13 Ran).

(Mrs Jean R Bishop), O Sherwood

2281 Sapley Conditional Jockeys' Handicap Hurdle Class F (0-105 5-y-o and up) £2,286 2m 5f 110yds. . . . . . (3:20)

1597⁴ MADAME PRESIDENT (Ire) [83] 6-10-10 D Fortt, *al cl up, drvn and outpcd aftr 3 out, rallied appr last, led r-in, rdn out.*
. . . . (12 to 1 op 9 to 1) 1

1614³ WRECKLESS MAN [86] 10-10-6 (7*) E Greehy, *beh, hdwy appr 2 out, styd on wl frm last.*
. . . .(5 to 1 op 9 to 2 tchd 6 to 1 and 7 to 1) 2

1211⁴ LUKE WARM [73] 7-9-11 (3*) Sophie Mitchell, *hld up beh ldrs, hdwy to ld 6th, clr aftr 3 out, mstk nxt, hdd r-in, no extr.*
. . . .(12 to 1 op 10 to 1 tchd 14 to 1) 3

1855⁵ SWAN STREET (NZ) [83] 6-10-7 (3*) J Magee, *mstk and drpd rear second, reco'red to chase ldrs 6th, cld appr 4 out, one pace frm 2 out.* . . . .(10 to 1 op 8 to 1) 4

1792³ LORD ROOBLE (Ire) [94] 6-10-11 (10*) W Greatrex, *hld up beh, hdwy 7th, outpcd appr 2 out.*
. . . . (13 to 2 op 7 to 2 tchd 7 to 1) 5

1914² BRANCHER [91] 6-11-4 E Callaghan, *hld up, hdwy to track ldrs aftr 5th, btn 3 out.* . . . .(4 to 1 fav op 5 to 2) 6

BIGWHEEL BILL (Ire) [89] 8-10-6 (10*) D Yellowlees, *keen early, prmnt till wknd 3 out.* . . . .(33 to 1 op 20 to 1) 7

1969² POLO PONY (Ire) [73] 5-10-8 B Grattan, *hld up in mid-div, beh frm 4th.* . . . .(16 to 1 tchd 20 to 1) 8

1927² JOY FOR LIFE (Ire) [73] 6-9-10 (4*) G Supple, *trkd ldrs, rdn aftr 6th, wknd appr 3 out.* . . . .(16 to 1 tchd 20 to 1) 9

1708³ WE'RE IN THE MONEY [73] 13-9-4 (10*) Claudine Froggitt, *keen hold, trkd ldrs to 3rd, sn beh, tld off.*
. . . . (10 to 1 op 20 to 1 tchd 50 to 1) 10

1867⁸ SWING QUARTET (Ire) [99] 7-11-9 (3*) D Walsh, *cl up, led aftr 5th to nxt, sn rdn alng and wknd quickly, tld off.*
. . . . (14 to 1 op 12 to 1) 11

1684⁶ ICANTELYA (Ire) [92] 8-11-5 P Henley, *rdn alng thrght, chsd ldrs till wknd 5th, tld off.* . . . . .(33 to 1 op 16 to 1) 12

1722 DAHLIA'S BEST (USA) [90] 7-11-3 G Hogan, *f 1st.*
. . . . (33 to 1 op 25 to 1) f

1795⁴ MANEREE [94] 10-11-7 Michael Brennan, *hmpd 1st, beh, hdwy 7th, sn rdn, wknd quickly and mstk 3 out, pld up bef nxt.*
. . . . pu

1664* MOOBAKKR (USA) [82] 6-10-9 R Massey, *led to aftr 5th, wknd after nxt, pld up bef last.* . . . . . . (8 to 1 op 12 to 1) pu

1266⁶ BATTY'S ISLAND [73] 8-9-10 (4*) J Mogford, *mid-div, pushed alng appr 6th, sn wknd, tld off whn pld up bef 2 out.*
. . . . (20 to 1 op 14 to 1) pu

1938⁵ LETS GO NOW (Ire) [73] 7-10-0 G Tormey, *mstk in rear 3rd, rdn aftr 5th, tld off whn pld up bef 2 out.*
. . . .(33 to 1 op 20 to 1 tchd 50 to 1) pu

Dist: 1½l, 1l, 15l, 6l, sht-hd, 2l, 7l, 2½l, 11l, 18l. 5m 22.40s. a 33.40s (17 Ran).

(Sir Peter Miller), C P Morlock

2282 March Handicap Chase Class D (0-120 5-y-o and up) £3,661 2m 110yds. . . . . (3:50)

1959⁴ KHALIDI (Ire) [106] 8-11-2 J Osborne, *hld up, hdwy to ld aftr 3 out, hdd last, rallied and pres to lead ag'n nr finish.*
. . . . (85 to 40 op 9 to 4 tchd 5 to 2 and 2 to 1) 1

1918² AAL EL AAL [105] 10-11-1 G Tormey, *hld up in rear, mstk 9th, hdwy to ld and blun last, hdd und pres nr finish.*
. . . .(2 to 1 fav op 6 to 4 tchd 9 to 4) 2

2194⁷ COUNT BARACHOIS (USA) [90] 9-10-0 K Gaule, *led second till aftr 3 out, outpcd frm nxt.*
. . . . (7 to 1 op 8 to 1 tchd 10 to 1) 3

1595⁵ THE FLYING FOOTMAN [97] 11-10-7 P Hide, *led to second, chsd ldr to 7th, wknd appr 2 out, pld up bef last.*
. . . .(9 to 1 op 11 to 1 tchd 10 to 1) pu

1643³ MAN MOOD (Fr) [110] (bl) 6-11-6 Mr E James, *in tch, hrd rdn and wknd 8th, pld up bef last.*
. . . .(85 to 40 op 6 to 4 tchd 9 to 4) pu

Dist: 1l, 12l. 4m 24.60s. a 30.60s (5 Ran).

(T J Whitley), D R Gandolfo

2283 Huntingdon Maiden Open National Hunt Flat Class H (4,5,6-y-o) £1,602 2m 110yds. . . . . (4:20)

1975³ KING MOLE 6-11-5 G Upton, *hld up, hdwy o'r 6 fs out, led 2 out, ran on wl.* . . . .(9 to 2 op 4 to 1 tchd 5 to 1) 1

1350⁸ NEW LEAF (Ire) 5-11-2 (3*) D Fortt, *hld up mid-div, hdwy o'r 5 fs out, rdn 4 out, kpt on wl frm 2 out.*
. . . .(11 to 1 op 10 to 1 tchd 12 to 1) 2

1975⁴ MR MOONLIGHT 5-11-5 D Gallagher, *hld up rear, hdwy 7 fs out, led 4 out to 2 out, one pace.* . . . .(14 to 1 op 7 to 1) 3

2008³ MERRY MASQUERADE (Ire) 6-11-5 R Hodge, *hld up beh, rdn and hdwy frm 2 fs out, kpt on und pres.*
....(6 to 1 op 7 to 1 tchd 8 to 1) 4
TAPPERS KNAPP (Ire) 5-11-5 J Osborne, *hld up beh, rdn alng hfwy, hdwy o'r 3 fs out, remained alone far side entering strt, sn one pace.* ....(4 to 1 op 2 to 1) 5
THE CLARSACH 5-11-0 S Wynne, *mid-div, steady hdwy frm 6 fs out, rdn alng o'r 2 out, one pace.*
.........................(20 to 1 op 16 to 1 tchd 25 to 1) 6
TAILORMADE 5-11-5 A Thornton, *hld up, hdwy 7 fs out, rdn 4 out, wknd wl o'r one out.* ....(16 to 1 op 10 to 1) 7
1942 EUROCHIEF 6-11-5 D Walsh, *prmnt, led 6 fs out to 4 out, wknd o'r 2 out.* ....(20 to 1) 8
ROYAL TEAM 5-11-5 M Sharratt, *hld up in rear grp, hdwy o'r 6 fs out, wknd over 2 out.* ....(33 to 1) 9
PEDLAR'S CROSS (Ire) 5-10-12 (7") R Studholme, *chsd ldg grp, pushed alng hfwy, wknd 4 fs out.* ....(33 to 1) 10
FOLDING 6-11-5 P Hide, *trkd ldrs till wknd 3 fs out.*
.... (33 to 1 op 20 to 1) 11
1809 ABOVE SUSPICION (Ire) 5-11-5 Mr E James, *hld up beh, effrt o'r 4 fs out, nvr nr to chal.* ....(33 to 1 op 20 to 1) 12
GREEN KING 5-11-5 M A Fitzgerald, *nvr on terms, tld off.*
....................................(20 to 1 op 12 to 1) 13
1809⁴ FIDDLER'S LEAP (Ire) 5-10-12 (7") M A Wintle, *cl up till wknd 4 fs out.* ....(20 to 1 op 14 to 1) 14
1874³ RACHEL LOUISE 5-11-0 S McNeill, *prmnt till then and wknd 6 fs out, tld off.* ....(12 to 1 op 7 to 1 tchd 14 to 1) 15
1549³ CHASING THE MOON (Ire) 5-11-5 B Fenton, *hld up in mid-div, beh fnl 6 fs, tld off.* ....(8 to 1 op 6 to 1) 16
STONEHENGE SAM (Ire) 5-11-5 S Curran, *hld up in mid-div, beh fnl 6 fs, tld off.* ....(33 to 1) 17
1975 BARTHOLOMEW FAIR 6-11-5 I Lawrence, *trkd ldrs, led hfwy, hdd 6 fs out, sn wknd, tld off.*
.....................(12 to 1 op 8 to 1 tchd 14 to 1) 18
ARDLEIGH VENTURE 4-10-2 K Gaule, *al beh, tld off.*
.........................(20 to 1 op 16 to 1 tchd 25 to 1) 19
1560 BLAMELESS 5-11-0 J F Titley, *al beh, tld off.*
...................................(25 to 1 op 14 to 1) 20
2029⁶ JUSTJIM 5-10-12 (7") L Suthern, *prmnt to hfwy, sn beh, tld off.*
.........................(16 to 1 op 14 to 1 tchd 20 to 1) 21
TUPENNY SMOKE 5-10-7 (7") Martin Smith, *led to hfwy, lost pl quickly, tld off.* ....(33 to 1) 22
Dist: 1¾l, 1l, 1¼l, 2l, ¾l, 14l, ¾l, nk, 3l, 2l. 4m 0.10s. (22 Ran).
(Mrs J Fowler), J A B Old

WETHERBY (good)
Thursday January 23rd
Going Correction: PLUS 0.40 sec. per fur.

2284 Arctic Tern Novices' Hurdle Class E
(4-y-o and up) £2,517 2m..... (1:35)

1514⁴ WHIP HAND (Ire) 6-11-5 P Carberry, *pld hrd early, trkd ldrs, led on bit 2 out, easily.* ....(7 to 2 tchd 5 to 1) 1
1823 DURANO 6-11-5 P Niven, *cl up, led 3 out to nxt, kpt on wl, no ch wth wnr.* ....(12 to 1 op 6 to 1) 2
KHALIKHOUM 4-10-7 A Dobbin, *keen early, trkd ldrs, effrt bef 3 out, kpt on same pace.* ......(14 to 1 op 12 to 1) 3
FUTURE'S TRADER 4-10-7 R Garritty, *in tch, effrt bef 3 out, sn drvn alng and btn.* ....(25 to 1 op 20 to 1) 4
1955⁷ BOWCLIFFE 6-11-5 M Foster, *led fo 3 out, sn wknd.*
..............................(20 to 1 tchd 25 to 1) 5
2023 BALLYRANTER 8-11-2 (3") Mr C Bonner, *in tch, outpcd bef 3 out, no dngr aftr...................*(50 to 1 tchd 33 to 1) 6
NOBLE CANONIRE 5-11-0 A S Smith, *sn beh......*(50 to 1) 7
PRINCE BALTASAR 8-11-5 O Pears, *beh hfwy.*
..................................(100 to 1 op 50 to 1) 8
PETRICO 5-11-5 R Supple, *sn beh, tld off.*
..................................(50 to 1 op 33 to 1) 9
1679 MAGIC TIMES 6-11-5 B Storey, *sn beh, tld off whn pld up bef last.* ....(50 to 1) pu
1890² CIRCUS STAR 4-10-7 A Maguire, *settled midfield, effrt whn blun 3 out, sn btn, pld up bef last.*
...........................(5 to 4 on tchd 7 to 4 on) pu
1326 SELECTRIC (Ire) 6-11-5 G Cahill, *prmnt, rdn and wknd quickly aftr 6th, lost tch and bef 3 out.* ....(50 to 1) pu
BONNY RIGG (Ire) 5-11-0 T Reed, *sn beh, tld off whn pld up bef last.* ....(50 to 1) pu
KING OF SPARTA 4-10-7 D Bridgwater, *in tch, mstk and drpd rear 4th, pld up bef nxt....*(11 to 2 op 7 to 2 tchd 6 to 1) pu
Dist: 3l, 25l, 1¼l, 1½l, 1¾l, 21l, 10l, dist. 4m 3.70s. a 22.70s (14 Ran).
(Lady Lloyd Webber), J G FitzGerald

2285 Woolly Mammoth Novices' Chase
Class E (5-y-o and up) £3,077 3m 1f
.... (2:05)

2146* CHOISTY 7-11-10 J Supple, *made all, sn clr, hrd pressed frm 4 out, styd on wl frm 2 out, all out...* (5 to 2 on tchd 11 to 8 on) 1
2043 HATCHAM BOY (Ire) 7-11-10 A Maguire, *chsd wnr aftr 5th, chlgd 4 out, sn rdn, ev ch whn mstk last, no extr und pres.*
..................(2 to 1 op 7 to 4 on tchd 15 to 8 on) 2
2146 CLONROCHE LUCKY (Ire) 7-11-5 B Storey, *sn wl beh, tld off.*
.....................................(50 to 1 op 40 to 1) 3

2178⁵ MERRYHILL GOLD 6-11-5 Derek Byrne, *chsd wnr till aftr 5th, sn wl beh, tld off.* ....(50 to 1 op 33 to 1) 4
1820 ROYAL PARIS (Ire) 9-11-5 T Reed, *sn wl beh, tld off.*
......................................(20 to 1 op 14 to 1) 5
1681⁵ MONYMAX (Ire) 8-11-5 Richard Guest, *beh whn f 6th.*
......................................(25 to 1 op 20 to 1) f
MANOR COURT (Ire) 9-11-5 J Burke, *beh, hdwy hfwy, wknd aftr 11th, tld off whn pld up 4 out.* (33 to 1 op 25 to 1) pu
Dist: Nk, dist, ¾l, dist. 6m 41.10s. a 33.10s (7 Ran).
(Hotel Brokers International), Mrs A Swinbank

2286 Arctic Fox Novices' Handicap Chase
Class D (0-110 5-y-o and up) £3,480
2½m 110yds.................. (2:35)

1944 MACGEORGE (Ire) [100] 7-11-12 A Maguire, *made virtually all, hrd pressed frm 4 out, styd on wl und pres frm last.*
...................................(11 to 2 tchd 6 to 1) 1
2150* RANDOM HARVEST (Ire) [99] 8-11-11 (6ex) P Niven, *nvr far away, chlgd 3 out, ev ch last, no extr und pres.*
.... (11 to 8 on op 5 to 4 on tchd 11 to 10 on) 2
1771⁴ CATTLY HANG (Ire) [98] 7-11-10 A Dobbin, *prmnt, chlgd 4 out, wknd bef 2 out........*(15 to 2 op 7 to 1 tchd 8 to 1) 3
1994³ BE BRAVE [79] 7-10-5 R Rourke, *mstk second, beh, lost tch hfwy, kpt on frm 4 out, nvr dngrs........* (12 to 1 op 8 to 1) 4
2205* MARLINGFORD [74] 10-9-7 (7",6ex) L McGrath, *hld up, effrt whn mstk 11th, sn rdn and wknd........* (8 to 1 op 5 to 1) 5
MASTER OF TROY [80] 9-10-6 D Parker, *beh whn hmpd 7th, sn lost tch, tld off.....................*(25 to 1 op 16 to 1) 6
2237 GAELIC BLUE [77] 7-10-3³ Richard Guest, *in tch whn f 7th.*
......................................(9 to 1 op 7 to 1) f
Dist: 2l, 18l, 13l, ¾l, 25l. 5m 23.10s. a 30.10s (7 Ran).
(J H Watson), R Lee

2287 Snow Leopard Handicap Chase
Class C (0-130 5-y-o and up) £4,337
2m........................... (3:05)

1873³ EASTERN MAGIC [100] 9-10-0 D Bridgwater, *cl up, made most frm 6th, hrd pressed and rdn from 2 out, hld on wl finish.*
...........................(6 to 1 op 11 to 2 tchd 13 to 2) 1
1821¹⁰ WEAVER GEORGE (Ire) [102] 7-10-2 M Moloney, *in tch, rdn aftr 8th, sn outpcd, rallied after 2 out, styd on wl und pres r-in.*
.....................(4 to 1 op 7 to 2 tchd 9 to 2) 2
2119⁹ MONYMAN (Ire) [105] 7-10-5 R Garritty, *trkd ldrs, effrt aftr 4 out, ev ch nxt till no extr und pres r-in.* (Evens fav op 5 to 4) 3
1993⁴ RANDOM ASSAULT (NZ) [128] 8-12-0 A Maguire, *led to 6th, cl up, rdn aftr 3 out, sn btn.................*(7 to 1 op 11 to 2) 4
1692³ FULL O'PRAISE (NZ) [101] 10-10-1 B Storey, *hld up, effrt bef 4 out, sn wknd and lost tch, tld off.*
.........................(13 to 2 op 11 to 2 tchd 7 to 1) 5
Dist: Hd, 2½l, 2½l, 23l. 4m 13.10s. a 26.10s (5 Ran).
(Mrs Christine Smith), G Barnett

2288 Yeti Novices' Hurdle Class E (5-y-o
and up) £2,587 2½m 110yds.. (3:35)

1989⁷ BOBBY GRANT 6-10-12 P Niven, *trkd ldrs, led appr 3 out, wndrd and styd on wl, hng rght r-in.*
....................................(9 to 1 op 12 to 1 tchd 14 to 1) 1
798⁷ LOVE THE BLUES 5-10-7 A Maguire, *mid-div, hdwy aftr 3 out, styd on und pres frm nxt, nvr able to chal.*
.......................(3 to 1 fav op 5 to 2 tchd 4 to 1) 2
CHEROKEE CHIEF 6-10-12 J A McCarthy, *hld up beh, steady hdwy frm hfwy, chlgd appr 3 out, kpt on same pace from nxt.*
....(12 to 1 op 8 to 1) 3
1326³ SUAS LEAT (Ire) 7-11-6 (7") M Newton, *mid-div, hdwy aftr 6th, ev ch appr 3 out, kpt on same pace......*(8 to 1 op 7 to 1) 4
1984⁴ GLENBOWER 5-10-9 (3") Mr C Bonner, *chsd ldrs, effrt aftr 7th, sn outpcd, kpt on 2 out..........* (14 to 1 op 12 to 1) 5
2145⁸ DON'T TELL TOM (Ire) 7-10-12 G Cahill, *chsd ldrs, outpcd aftr 7th, kpt on frm 3 out.......................*(9 to 1 op 6 to 1) 6
1679³ ANTARCTIC WIND (Ire) 7-11-3 R Garritty, *cl up, led bef 5th till appr 3 out, sn wknd........................*(11 to 8 op 6 to 1) 7
1598⁵ SPARKLING BUCK 5-10-0 (7") D Thomas, *rear, hdwy aftr 6th, no prog frm nxt........*(16 to 1 tchd 14 to 1 and 20 to 1) 8
1682² CHERRY DEE 6-10-7 R Supple, *nvr nr to chal.*
....(5 to 1 op 7 to 2) 9
1775 THE OTHER MAN (Ire) 7-10-12 O Pears, *nvr dngrs.* (50 to 1) 10
1770⁵ LARKSHILL (Ire) 6-10-12 P Carberry, *mid-div, effrt aftr 7th, sn btn.......................*(7 to 2 op 5 to 1 tchd 11 to 2) 11
1829 KENTUCKY GOLD (Ire) 8-10-12 L O'Hara, *prmnt till rdn and wknd aftr 7th...*(50 to 1) 12
2152 SOVEREIGN PASS 5-10-12 B Storey, *sn beh, tld off.* (50 to 1) 13
CORRIMULZIE (Ire) 6-10-12 A S Smith, *sn wl beh, tld off.*
......................................(25 to 1 op 20 to 1) 14
PERSIAN GRANGE (Ire) 7-10-12 J Burke, *led till bef 5th, sn wknd, tld off...*(50 to 1) 15
JOSS BAY 5-10-12 Richard Guest, *al beh, f 3 out.*
......................................(20 to 1 op 16 to 1) f
862⁵ PALACE OF GOLD 7-10-5 (7") W Dowling, *pld up aftr 4th, sddl slpd...*(25 to 1) pu
BLACK ICE BOY (Ire) 6-10-9 (3") H Bastiman, *al beh, tld off whn pld up bef last..*(50 to 1) pu
2145⁷ TEN PAST SIX 5-10-12 A Dobbin, *chsd ldrs till wknd aftr 6th, lost tch and tld off bef 3 out..........* (25 to 1 op 20 to 1) pu

1590 ONLY A SIOUX 5-10-12 W Fry, *nvr better than mid-div, tld off*
whn pld up bef last............................ (50 to 1) pu
Dist: 4l, 1½l, 2½l, 2½l, 2l, 10l, 5l, 2l, 2l, 4l. 5m 16.10s. a 34.10s (20 Ran).

(John J Thompson), C Grant

2289 Polar Bear Handicap Hurdle Class C
(0-135 4-y-o and up) £3,395 2m 7f
.... (4:05)

17443 NICK THE BEAK (Ire) [108] 8-10-5 R Supple, *trkd ldrs, led 3
out, sn hrd pressed, styd on wl und pres frm last.*
.... (12 to 1 op 10 to 1) 1
18677 ERZADJAN (Ire) [128] 7-11-7 P Niven, *hld up, hdwy aftr 9th,
chlgd 2 out, ev ch till no extr und pres nr finish.*
.............................(7 to 1 op 6 to 1) 2
14813 THE TOISEACH (Ire) [112] 6-10-9 A Maguire, *prmnt, led 9th to
3 out, kpt on same pace.*................ (11 to 2 op 9 to 2) 3
1282* JOCKS CROSS (Ire) [117] 6-11-0 A Dobbin, *trkd ldrs, ev ch
bef 3 out, sn rdn, fdd.*............... (9 to 2 jt-fav op 5 to 1) 4
20272 DALLY BOY [115] 5-10-12 R Garritty, *trkd ldrs, drvn alng aftr
9th, fdd.*................. (5 to 1 op 4 to 1 tchd 11 to 2) 5
DISCO DES MOTTES (Fr) [131] 6-12-0 P Carberry, *in tch, rdn
aftr 9th, sn wknd, tld off.*............ (25 to 1 tchd 33 to 1) 6
1966* PHARARE (Ire) [103] 7-10-0 B Storey, *led to 9th, sn wknd, tld
off.*............................(16 to 1 op 14 to 1) 7
16285 IZZA [108] 6-10-0 (5*) R McGrath, *hld up, f 7th, dead.*
.... (15 to 2 op 6 to 1 tchd 8 to 1) f
1971* ROBERTY LEA [118] 9-11-1 G Cahill, *drvn alng frm 6th, sn
beh, tld off whn pld up bef 3 out.*......(12 to 1 op 10 to 1) pu
1834* WASSL STREET (Ire) [103] 5-10-0 A S Smith, *hld up, lost tch
aftr 9th, tld off whn pld up bef 3 out.* ....(9 to 2 jt-
fav op 6 to 1 tchd 4 to 1) pu
Dist: Hd, 9l, 10l, 1¾l, 30l, 2l. 5m 53.90s. (10 Ran).

(Sir Nicholas Wilson), John R Upson

WINCANTON (good to firm)
Thursday January 23rd
**Going Correction: PLUS 0.10 sec. per fur. (races
1,3,6), PLUS 0.40 (2,4,5)**

2290 Painters Handicap Hurdle Class D
(0-125 4-y-o and up) £3,183 2m
.... (1:30)

1982* HAY DANCE [102] 6-10-5 N Williamson, *hld up and confidently rdn, hdwy on bit to track ldrs aftr 3 out, quickened to ld
nr finish, very easily.*
....................(11 to 8 op on op 11 to 10 tchd 5 to 4) 1
22173 MORSTOCK [112] 7-10-12 (3*) T Dascombe, *led, sn clr, rdn
appr 2 out, hdd and no ch whn wnr nr finish*
....................................(9 to 4 op 6 to 1) 2
21857 SHOW FAITH (Ire) [97] 7-10-0 R Hughes, *chsd ldr aftr
second, chlgd frm 3 out and ag'n nxt, sn outpcd.*
.... (5 to 1 op 4 to 1 tchd 11 to 2) 3
1982⁵ NASHVILLE STAR (USA) [97] (v) 6-10-0 R Bellamy, *chsd ldr till
aftr second, rdn to chal 3 out, sn wknd.*
.... (16 to 1 op 10 to 1 tchd 14 to 1) 4
656 WINDWARD ARIOM [108] (bl) 11-10-11 A Larnach, *al beh,
rdn and lost tch 4th.*.....(25 to 1 op 14 to 1 tchd 33 to 1) 5
Dist: 1¼l, 7l, 15l, 25l. 3m 40.90s. a 6.90s (5 Ran).

SR: 24/32/10/-/-/   (Wessex Go Racing Partnership), P J Hobbs

2291 Maurice Lister Maiden Chase Class
E (6-y-o and up) £3,847 3m 1f
110yds.......................(2:00)

1236 STORMY SUNSET 10-10-7 (7*) Mr T Dennis, *in tch, hmpd 1st,
led aftr 7th, styd on wl frm 3 out.*.......(8 to 1 op 10 to 1) 1
1996⁶ BOLSHIE BARON 8-11-5 Mr M Harris, *hdwy 12th, pressed
wnr and mstk 3 out, styd cl up till mistake last and wknd.*
.... (10 to 1 op 12 to 1) 2
GLENDINE (Ire) 7-11-5 J Railton, *gd hdwy to track ldrs 12th,
mstk nxt, styd prmnt till wknd 3 out.*..... (8 to 1 op 6 to 1) 3
1593² JAC DEL PRINCE 7-11-5 B Powell, *chsd ldr to 6th, wknd 4
out.*.................. (5 to 2 fav tchd 3 to 1 and 100 to 30) 4
2026² PLASSY BOY 8-11-5 A Larnach, *hdwy tenth, wknd 13th.*
...................................(9 to 1 op 7 to 1) 5
WITHYCOMBE HILL 7-10-12 (7*) Mr S Durack, *al beh.*
................................(50 to 1) 6
2182 MASKED MARTIN (bl) 6-11-5 S Burrough, *wl beh till 16th.*
..................................(50 to 1) 7
1810 JACK OF DIAMONDS 9-11-5 A McCabe, *prmnt early, beh
whn hit 9th, f nxt.*.................................(50 to 1) f
9224 SPEEDY SNAPSGEM (Ire) 7-11-5 A P McCoy, *f 1st.*
.... (7 to 1 tchd 8 to 1) f
19944 ROMANY BLUES 8-10-7 (7*) M Berry, *mstk and uns rdr 3rd.*
.... (8 to 1 tchd 9 to 1) ur
FORTRIA ROSIE DAWN 7-11-0 N Williamson, *beh whn uns
rdr 6th.*................................(20 to 1) ur
1804 FULL SHILLING (USA) (v) 8-11-2 (3*) Guy Lewis, *al beh, tld off
whn pld up bef 15th.*.............. (10 to 1 op 14 to 1) pu
WAIPIRO 7-11-5 L Harvey, *beh frm 7th, tld off whe pld up bef
16th.*..........................(20 to 1 op 14 to 1) pu

1347⁷ GOLDEN DRUM (Ire) (bl) 7-11-0 (5*) Mr R Thornton, *led but
jmpd very big, blun 3rd, hdd aftr 7th, wknd 11th tld off whn pld
up bef 17th.*..............(16 to 1 op 14 to 1 tchd 20 to 1) pu
1856 MIRAMARE 7-11-2 (3*) T Dascombe, *beh frm 5th, tld off whn
pld up bef 12th.*......................(33 to 1 op 20 to 1) pu
Dist: 9l, 6l, 26l, 9l, 2l. 6m 41.00s. a 25.00s (15 Ran).

(Mrs Jill Dennis), W W Dennis

2292 Elite Racing Club Juvenile Novices'
Claiming Hurdle Class F (4-y-o)
£2,197 2m.................(2:30)

19228 LADY MAGNUM (Ire) 10-12 N Mann, *trkd ldr, chlgd 3 out, sn
led, clr whn not fluent last, cmftbly.*
..........................(4 to 1 op 7 to 2 tchd 9 to 2) 1
21812 D'NAAN (Ire) (bl) 11-3 R Bellamy, *keen hold, led till hld aftr 3
out, styd on to chase wnr und pres, no imprsn frm nxt.*
..................(5 to 2 fav op 9 to 4 tchd 3 to 1) 2
2012 ESKIMO KISS (Ire) 10-6 J Railton, *prmnt, outpcd 5th, styd on
ag'n und pres frm 2 out.*...............(9 to 1 op 10 to 1) 3
EL BARDADOR (Ire) 10-10 (7*) J Harris, *in tch, rdn and kpt on
one pace frm 2 out.*.............. (9 to 1 op 10 to 1) 4
1992⁷ TATHMIN (v) 11-0 M Bosley, *beh, some hdwy frm 3 out, not a
dngr.*...........................(20 to 1 op 16 to 1) 5
18694 SONG FOR JESS (Ire) 10-6 R Greene, *al beh.*
...................(12 to 1 op 8 to 1 tchd 14 to 1) 6
18545 SOLDIER MAK 11-3 (3*) L Aspell, *in tch till outpcd frm 3 out.*
............................(100 to 30 op 7 to 2 tchd 5 to 1) 7
15998 RED TIME 10-11 P Holley, *hdwy 4th, mstk and wknd nxt.*
..........................(25 to 1 tchd 33 to 1) 8
1861 BENKAROSAM 10-5 L Harvey, *sn beh.*
...............(40 to 1 op 33 to 1 tchd 50 to 1) 9
2195 SCATHEBURY 11-6 N Williamson, *hdwy 4th, wknd 3 out.*
...........................(14 to 1 op 10 to 1) 10
17905 RIVERS MAGIC 11-3 (3*) T Dascombe, *beh till f 3 out.*
...........................(12 to 1 op 14 to 1 tchd 10 to 1) f
10277 SEVEN CROWNS (USA) 10-11 B Powell, *sn beh, mstk 4th, tld
off whn pld up bef 2 out.*............(25 to 1 op 20 to 1) pu
1412 IT'S DAWAN 11-12 R Hughes, *tld off till pld up bef 5th.*
.....................................(20 to 1) pu
1696 BOLD START LADY 11-0 (7*) M Griffiths, *mstk 3rd, al beh, tld
off whn pld up bef 2 out.*(33 to 1 op 25 to 1 tchd 50 to 1) pu
Dist: 7l, 11l, 5l, 3½l, 2l, ¾l, 11l, hd, 6l. 3m 45.60s. a 11.60s (14 Ran).

(Magnum Construction Ltd), J Neville

2293 Pat Ruthven And Guy Nixon Memo-
rial Vase Handicap Chase For Amateur Riders Class E (0-115 5-y-o and
up) £3,782 3m 1f 110yds......(3:00)

2031* ACT OF PARLIAMENT (Ire) [112] (bl) 9-11-4 (7*) Mr R Wakley,
*trkd ldr to 14th, styd frnt rnk and chlgd frm 3e out, drvn into
slight ld r-in, all out.*...........(9 to 4 op 7 to 4 tchd 5 to 2) 1
2157* DROMHANA (Ire) [10b] 7-11-1 (7*,6ex) Mr J Tizzard, *led,
drvn 3 out, hdd r-in, styd on.*......(11 to 10 on op 5 to 4) 2
1304 TUG OF PEACE [113] 10-11-5 (7*) Mr A Balding, *in tch, chsd
ldr frm 14th till dsptd ld from 3 out, wknd r-in.*
.......................(12 to 1 op 7 to 1 tchd 14 to 1) 3
1859² COOL CHARACTER (Ire) [87] 9-9-9 (5*) Mr R Thornton, *hit
6th,jmpd slwly nxt, mstk 12th and 14th, sn lost tch.*
...................................(10 to 1 op 8 to 1) 4
21823 FROZEN DROP [102] 10-10-8 (7*) Mr G Shenkin, *frnt rnk to
5th, hit nxt, tld off 12th, pld up bef 17th...* (6 to 1 op 4 to 1) pu
Dist: 1l, 7l, 19l. 6m 40.80s. a 24.80s (5 Ran).

(J Perriss), K C Bailey

2294 Artists Handicap Chase Class C
(0-135 5-y-o and up) £6,184 2m
.... (3:30)

2247 NEWLANDS-GENERAL [118] 11-11-4 B Powell, *made all, clr
whn wnt till 3 out, unchlgd.*..............(11 to 8 op Evens) 1
16724 THUMBS UP [128] 11-12-0 J Railton, *shaken up to chase wnr
4 out, found little and bln nxt...*(7 to 4 on tchd 6 to 4 on) 2
Won by 11l. 4m 0.10s. a 12.10s (2 Ran).

SR: 33/32/   (C Murphy), P F Nicholls

2295 Potters Handicap Hurdle Class F
(0-105 4-y-o and up) £2,372 2¾m
.... (4:00)

14743 CLOD HOPPER (Ire) [77] 7-9-9 (5*) A Bates, *made all, clr 3
out, hrd drvn whn chlgd last, hld on gmely*
...........................(10 to 1 op 8 to 1) 1
1663 MR STRONG GALE (Ire) [91] 6-10-8 (3*) L Aspell, *hld up,
steady hdwy aftr 3 out, shaken up nxt, chlgd last, kpt on.*
.......................(11 to 2 op 5 to 1 tchd 6 to 1) 2
1971² STAC-POLLAIDH [87] 7-10-4¹ (7*) Mr R Wakley, *mid-div,
pushed alng 5th, hdwy und pres frm 2 out, styd on one pace.*
...................................(9 to 1 op 8 to 1) 3
21584 GENERAL MOUKTAR [105] 7-10-2 J Railton, *hdwy to chase
ldrs 6th, styd on und pres frm 2 out.*
...................................(9 to 1 op 10 to 1) 4
17962 FIRST CLASS [85] 7-10-8 R Greene, *steady hdwy frm 3 out,
chsd ldrs appr nxt, sn wknd.*
...................(11 to 2 op 7 to 1 tchd 8 to 1) 5

1937³ GLEN MIRAGE [84] 12-10-7 Miss M Coombe, *beh, some hdwy frm 6th, rdn aftr 3 out, moderate headway 2 out.*
.... (11 to 1 op 8 to 1) 6
QUELQUE CHOSE [92] 7-11-1 R Hughes, *hld up, hdwy 7th, wknd aftr 3 out.*.................(25 to 1 op 20 to 1) 7
1978⁴ URBAN LILY [80] (bl) 7-9-10 (7*) J Harris, *chsd ldrs, wnt second briefly 3 out, wknd quickly appr nxt.*
.... (12 to 1 op 8 to 1) 8
1956⁷ TOP SKIPPER (Ire) [80] 5-10-3⁷ (7*) Mr J Tizzard, *chsd wnr to 3 out, sn wknd.*..........(13 to 2 op 8 to 1 tchd 6 to 1) 9
2181⁶ ADONISIS [93] 5-10-3 P Holley, *in tch 5th, sn wknd.*
.... (33 to 1 op 25 to 1 tchd 50 to 1) 10
2158 GLISTENING DAWN [95] (bl) 7-11-4 N Mann, *beh frm 5th.*
.... (14 to 1 op 10 to 1) 11
1959⁵ ROAD TO AU BON (USA) [80] 9-10-3 B Powell, *prominent to 6th, tld off frm 8th.*..............(14 to 1 op 12 to 1) 12
1857 LEGAL ARTIST (Ire) [98] 7-11-2 (5*) Mr R Thornton, *beh and mstk 7th, tld off.*..........(25 to 1 op 16 to 1 tchd 33 to 1) 13
FANE PARK (Ire) [85] 9-10-5 (3*) T Dascombe, *f 1st.*
.... (33 to 1 op 16 to 1 tchd 50 to 1) f
Dist: 1l, 8l, hd, 5l, 5l, 2l, 17l, 4l, 4l, dist. 5m 16.40s. a 10.40s (14 Ran).
(T J Parrott), W R Muir

DONCASTER (good)
Friday January 24th
Going Correction: PLUS 0.20 sec. per fur. (races 1,3,4,7), PLUS 0.40 (2,5,6)

2296 Selby Conditional Jockeys' Novices' Handicap Hurdle Class F (0-110 4-y-o and up) £2,156 2m 110yds.. (1:00)

1964³ I'M A DREAMER (Ire) [94] 7-11-9 P Midgley, *nvr far away, led bef 2 out, hld on gmely und pres r-in.....*(8 to 1 op 7 to 1) 1
1330⁴ SILLY MONEY [87] 6-11-2 E Callaghan, *al wl plcd, rdn to draw level appr 2 out, ran on, jst hld.*.........(6 to 1 op 9 to 2) 2
RARE OCCURANCE [80] 7-10-9 Michael Brennan, *patiently rdn, effrt and drvn alng frm 3 out, kpt on, no imprsn.*
.... (20 to 1 op 16 to 1) 3
1629 LUCKY BEA [84] 4-10-1 G Lee, *settled to track ldrs, effrt and swtchd lft betw last 2, not quicken.*
.... (9 to 2 op 3 to 1 tchd 5 to 1) 4
1738⁴ DARK PHOENIX (Ire) [87] 7-11-2 R Massey, *al hndy, drvn alng whn ldrs quickened 3 out, fdd und pres.*
.... (4 to 1 fav op 5 to 1 tchd 6 to 1) 5
1826² WILLY STAR (Bel) [95] 7-11-2 (3*) R Wilkinson, *settled mid-field, bustled alng whn pace quickened 3 out, outpcd nxt.*
.... (7 to 1 op 9 to 2) 6
1955⁵ PAST MASTER (USA) [83] 9-10-9 (3*) G Supple, *set modest pace, hrd pressed appr 3 out, fdd nxt...* (10 to 1 op 8 to 1) 7
2042⁶ MOOR HALL LADY [88] 6-11-3 G Tormey, *last and hld up, feeling pace bef 3 out, sn lost tch.*
.... (9 to 2 op 5 to 1 tchd 6 to 1) 8
1737 NORTHERN FALCON [87] (bl) 4-10-4 F Leahy, *in tch, wknd quickly aftr 4 out, tld off.*(11 to 1 op 10 to 1 tchd 14 to 1) 9
2147⁶ JARROW [71] 6-10-0 G F Ryan, *pressed ldrs, wknd quickly bef 3 out, tld off.*...................(50 to 1 op 33 to 1) 10
Dist: 6l, 6l, 1¾l, 2½l, 2½l, ½l, 12l, 13l, 7l. 4m 7.10s. a 17.10s (10 Ran).
(Miss M E Rowland), Miss M E Rowland

2297 Balby Novices' Chase Class D (6-y-o and up) £3,680 2m 110yds.... (1:35)

1104² JATHIB (Can) 6-11-12 Derek Byrne, *trkd ldr, led 6th, hdd briefly appr 4 out, ran on strly to go clr r-in.*
.... (5 to 4 on op Evens) 1
2214 GOLDEN HELLO 6-11-12 R Garritty, *jmpd rght thrght, nvr far away, effrt und pres frm 3 out, hng right and no extr r-in.*
.... (100 to 30 op 5 to 2 tchd 7 to 2) 2
1806⁶ BRAZIL OR BUST (Ire) 6-11-6 M A Fitzgerald, *patiently rdn, effrt und pres appr 4 out, ridden and outpcd betw last 2.*
.... (7 to 2 op 5 to 2) 3
1439* SIGMA RUN (Ire) 8-11-1 (5*) Michael Brennan, *led, blun and hdd 6th, rallied to ld briefly appr 4 out, second and drvn alng whn f nxt.*..............(14 to 1 op 8 to 1 tchd 16 to 1) f
Dist: 4l, 9l. 4m 7.30s. a 13.30s (4 Ran).
SR: 31/27/12/-/   (Crown Pkg & Mailing Svs Ltd), Mrs Merrita Jones

2298 Cusworth Novices' Hurdle Class D (5-y-o and up) £3,353 3m 110yds
.... (2:05)

1543* SALMON BREEZE (Ire) 6-11-4 M A Fitzgerald, *al frnt rnk, led bef 3 out, kpt on gmely und pres frm betw last 2.*
.... (7 to 1 op 5 to 1) 1
1763³ ABSOLUTLY EQUINAME (Ire) 6-10-12 D Gallagher, *nvr far away, str chal frm 3 out, kpt on und pres r-in.*
.... (12 to 1 op 10 to 1 tchd 14 to 1) 2
1503⁴ SATCOTINO (Ire) 6-10-7 K Gaule, *patiently rdn, improved frm 3 out, ridden and one pace betw last 2.* (16 to 1 op 12 to 1) 3
2025² COOLE HILL (Ire) 7-10-12 A Maguire, *al wl plcd, str chal 3 out, rdn and not quicken nxt.*............(7 to 1 op 6 to 1) 4
1961⁴ GAYE FAME 6-10-13 P Carberry, *al hndy, ev ch and bustled alng 3 out, one pace nxt.* (7 to 1 op 11 to 2 tchd 15 to 2) 5

2156⁸ CLEVER BOY (Ire) 6-11-4 Derek Byrne, *wtd wth, improved fnl circuit, feeling pace bef 3 out, fdd.*
.... (25 to 1 op 16 to 1 tchd 33 to 1) 6
1868⁵ MESP (Ire) (v) 6-10-2 (5*) Michael Brennan, *chsd ldg grp for o'r one circuit, struggling bef 3 out, sn lost tch.*
.... (50 to 1 op 33 to 1) 7
2152³ HAND WOVEN 5-11-4 C Llewellyn, *led till aftr 1st, led after 4th till bef 3 out, blun and sn wknd.*
.... (11 to 10 on op 11 to 10 tchd 6 to 5 and 6 to 5 on) 8
1763⁹ SAMMORELLO (Ire) 6-10-12 D Bridgwater, *struggling to keep up aftr one circuit, tld off 3 out.*........(25 to 1 op 16 to 1) 9
1743³ DANNICUS 6-10-12 V Slattery, *chsd ldrs for o'r one circuit, feeling pace bef 3 out, tld off.*.........(14 to 1 op 10 to 1) 10
761 RUSHEN RAIDER 5-10-12 M Foster, *pressed ldrs, wknd quickly bef 3 out, tld off.*........(10 to 1 op 8 to 1) 11
1735 ONE MORE RUPEE 6-10-5 (7*) M Handley, *led aftr 1st till after 4th, wkng whn nrly uns rdr 5th, continued tld off.*
.... (66 to 1 op 50 to 1) 12
KICKCASHTAL 8-10-12 W Fry, *tld off whn pld up bef 4 out.*
.... (100 to 1 op 50 to 1) pu
1800⁸ DODGY DANCER 7-10-12 L O'Hara, *lost tch aftr one circuit, tld off whn pld up bef 3 out.*........(66 to 1 op 33 to 1) pu
BOOK OF DREAMS (Ire) 9-10-12 Richard Guest, *al wl beh, tld off whn pld up bef 2 out.*............(100 to 1 op 50 to 1) pu
2183⁸ LILLY THE FILLY 6-10-7 R Greene, *lost tch bef hfwy, tld off whn pld up before 3 out.*............(14 to 1 op 10 to 1) pu
1590⁵ NAUTILUS THE THIRD (Ire) 6-10-12 R Garritty, *chsd ldrs for o'r one circuit, tld off whn pld up bef 2 out.*.......(20 to 1) pu
Dist: Nk, 7l, 2l, 11l, 11l, 5l, nk, 25l, 22l, 3l. 6m 0.70s. a 18.70s (17 Ran).
(The Salmon Racing Partnership), N J Henderson

2299 Rossington Main Novices' Hurdle Class A Grade 2 (4-y-o and up) £9,816 2m 110yds............(2:35)

1844* LE TETEU (Fr) 4-10-7 R Garritty, *al wl plcd, drw level 3 out, led nxt, clr last.*...........(5 to 2 op 3 to 1 tchd 100 to 30) 1
1849* HURRICANE LAMP 6-11-5 A Maguire, *chsd clr ldr hfwy, lft in ld 4 out, jnd and hit 3 out, hdd nxt, not pace of wnr.*
.... (11 to 8 fav op 5 to 4 tchd 6 to 4) 2
1396³ GREEN GREEN DESERT (Fr) 6-11-5 D Bridgwater, *patiently rdn, steady hdwy to join ldrs 3 out, ridden and no extr nxt.*
.... (5 to 1 op 4 to 1) 3
2023* MISTER RM 5-11-5 C Llewellyn, *nvr far away, feeling pace and rdn bef 3 out, wknd.*...........(10 to 1 op 7 to 1) 4
2119 HERBERT LODGE (Ire) (bl) 8-11-5 P Carberry, *sn clr, blun, hdd and nrly uns rdr 4 out, continued tld off.*
.... (10 to 1 op 8 to 1) 5
Dist: 5l, 7l, 6l, dist. 3m 58.20s. a 8.20s (5 Ran).
SR: 29/36/29/23/-/   (Mrs Judit Woods), Bob Jones

2300 Doncaster Sponsorship Club Handicap Chase Class C (0-135 5-y-o and up) £4,597 2m 3f 110yds......(3:10)

BELL STAFFBOY (Ire) [110] 8-10-9 (5*) Michael Brennan, *dsptd ld, led appr 8th, shaken up 5 out, drw clr nxt, cmftbly.*
.... (2 to 1 op 5 to 2) 1
2121² PURITAN (Can) [109] (bl) 8-10-13 R Garritty, *trkd ldg pair, ran in snatches frm hfwy, rdn and no imprsn from 3 out.*
.... (Evens fav op 5 to 4 on tchd 5 to 4) 2
IN TRUTH [119] 9-11-9 K Gaule, *slight ld till appr 8th, feeling pace whn hit 6 out, lost tch nxt, tld off.* (8 to 1 tchd 10 to 1) 3
1863³ LINDEN'S LOTTO (Ire) [120] 8-11-10 A Maguire, *sn wl beh, tld off.*............(5 to 1 op 4 to 1) 4
Dist: 7l, 28l, dist. 4m 57.60s. a 12.60s (4 Ran).
SR: 37/29/11/-/   (K W Bell & Son Ltd), J G M O'Shea

2301 Sandall Beat Novices' Handicap Chase Class D (0-115 5-y-o and up) £3,659 3m.................(3:40)

2175⁶ GOD SPEED YOU [101] (bl) 8-11-5 A Maguire, *mstks, made all, quickened clr aftr 6 out, styd on wl.*
.... (11 to 8 fav op 11 to 10 tchd 6 to 4) 1
1884² FATHER SKY [110] (bl) 6-12-0 P Niven, *settled wth chasing grp, wnt second and mstk 7 out, reminders 3 out, no imprsn on wnr...* (85 to 40 op 9 to 4 tchd 11 to 4 and 2 to 1) 2
1831³ THE BOOLEY HOUSE (Ire) [97] 7-11-1 Derek Byrne, *last and hld up, blun and rdr lost iron 8th, struggling fnl circuit, tld off.*
.... (13 to 2 op 5 to 1) 3
2154³ RONANS GLEN [82] 10-10-0 R Supple, *trkd ldrs, reminders 7th, struggling whn blun seven out, tld off.*
.... (5 to 1 tchd 11 to 2) 4
LORD VICK (Ire) [82] (bl) 8-10-0 J Ryan, *chsd ldr, reminders 7th, blun and reminders 9th, lost tch quickly fnl circuit, tld off.*
.... (14 to 1 op 12 to 1) 5
Dist: 16l, 19l, 5l, 25l. 6m 12.60s. a 18.60s (5 Ran).
(Wallop), C P Morlock

2302 Weatherbys 'Stars Of Tomorrow' Open National Hunt Flat Standard - Class H (4,5,6-y-o) £1,507 2m 110yds.................(4:10)

1682* MR LURPAK 5-11-12 P Niven, *patiently rdn, improved to ld on blr o'r 2 fs out, pushed clr, readily.*
..................................(6 to 5 fav op 5 to 4 tchd Evens) 1
POTTER AGAIN (Ire) 5-10-11 (3*) R Massey, *settled midfield, steady hdwy to draw level entering strt, kpt on same pace appr fnl furlong...................(4 to 1 tchd 7 to 2)* 2
THE SNOW BURN 4-10-7 J Callaghan, *nvr far away, drvn ahead o'r 3 ls out, hdd over 2 out, one pace und pres.*
....(20 to 1) 3
JACK ROBBO (Ire) 5-11-5 W Dwan, *settled midfield, effrt appr strt, rdn and no imprsn last 2 fs...* (10 to 1 op 6 to 1) 4
1306⁴ WENTWORTH (USA) 5-11-5 D Bridgwater, *wl plcd to strt, wknd...................*(12 to 1 op 8 to 1) 5
POLO RIDGE (Ire) 5-10-12 (7*) D Thomas, *wld wth, improved hfwy, no imprsn on ldrs last 2 fs........*(10 to 1 op 6 to 1) 6
MY BUSTER 5-11-5 A Maguire, *trkd ldrs gng wl, ev ch entering strt, wknd last 2 fs.*
..................................(6 to 1 op 5 to 1 tchd 10 to 1) 7
CHASING DREAMS 6-11-5 R Garritty, *wnt hndy hfwy, lost grnd entering strt, fdd...............*(20 to 1 tchd 25 to 1) 8
COROMANDEL 5-11-0 A S Smith, *settled off the pace, nvr rch chalg pos...............*(25 to 1 op 20 to 1) 9
BRIEF SUSPENCE (Ire) 4-10-7 Derek Byrne, *settled in tch, lost grnd entering strt, fdd.......................*(20 to 1) 10
1292³ PROTOTYPE 6-11-12 M A Fitzgerald, *wth ldr, led bef hfwy till o'r 3 ls out, fdd.....................*(7 to 1 op 4 to 1) 11
PEARL SILK 4-9-13 (3*) G Lee, *wl plcd, wknd bef strt, sn lost tch...........................*(33 to 1 op 20 to 1) 12
CONNEL'S CROFT 5-11-5 R Supple, *settled off the pace, nvr rch chalg pos...............*(33 to 1 op 20 to 1) 13
2008 SOCIAL INSECURITY (Ire) 6-11-5 K Gaule, *led till bef hfwy, fdd before strt, tld off...................*(50 to 1 op 33 to 1) 14
WOODHOUSE LANE 5-10-12 (7*) Miss C Metcalfe, *sluggish strt, nvr a factor, tld off.................*(50 to 1 op 33 to 1) 15
SEVEN FOUR SEVEN 6-11-0 L O'Hara, *sluggish strt, al beh, tld off.............................*(50 to 1 op 33 to 1) 16
Dist: 4l, 5l, 19l, 2l, 2¹/₂l, 2l, 1¹/₂l, 6l, 2¹/₂l, 7l. 3m 58.30s. (16 Ran).
(MD Foods Plc), Mrs M Reveley

FOLKESTONE (soft (races 1,3,5,7), good to soft (2,4,6)) Friday January 24th
Going Correction: PLUS 1.45 sec. per fur. (races 1,3,5,7), PLUS 0.70 (2,4,6)

2303 Valentine Gorton Juvenile Maiden Hurdle Class E (4-y-o) £2,749 2m 1f 110yds.....................(1:10)

1844² DESERT MOUNTAIN (Ire) 11-5 R Hughes, *al in tch, chlgd 2 out, led appr last, rdn out...*(3 lo 1 op 4 lo 1 tchd 9 to 2) 1
MELT THE CLOUDS (Can) 11-5 R Dunwoody, *hld up in rear, hdwy 4th, ev ch appr last, one pace r-in.*
..............................(10 to 30 op 5 to 1 tchd 9 to 1) 2
ANNA SOLEIL (Ire) 11-5 J A McCarthy, *wth ldr, led 3 out, wknd and hdd appr last....*(16 to 1 op 7 to 1 tchd 20 to 1) 3
2195² MR WILD (USA) 11-0 (5*) S Ryan, *in tch, rdn frm 5th, wknd last........................*(6 to 4 fav op 5 to 4 on) 4
ILLUMINATE 11-5 T J Murphy, *al in rear.*
....(33 to 1 op 16 to 1) 5
DAYDREAMER (USA) 11-5 B Powell, *in tch till rdn and wknd 5th........................*(25 to 1 op 14 to 1 tchd 33 to 1) 6
1610 CLAIRE'S DANCER (Ire) (bl) 11-5 L Harvey, *pld hrd, led till hdd 3 out, sn wknd......................*(50 to 1 op 20 to 1) 7
2181⁸ AAVASAKSA (Fr) 11-2 (3*) T Dascombe, *al beh, tld off whn f last......................*(100 to 1 op 50 to 1) 8
ELITE FORCE (Ire) 11-5 D Morris, *trkd ldrs to 3rd, sn beh, tld off whn pld up bef 3 out...........*(50 to 1 op 20 to 1) pu
PROSPERO 11-5 M Richards, *prmnt till rdn 2 out, sn wknd, pld up bef last..........*(7 to 1 op 7 to 2 tchd 8 to 1) pu
QUEENS FANCY 11-0 A Dicken, *al beh, tld off whn pld up bef last...................*(66 to 1 op 20 to 1 tchd 100 to 1) pu
2012 JAMIES FIRST (Ire) 11-5 D O'Sullivan, *lost tch 3rd, tld off whn pld up bef 3 out................*(100 to 1 op 66 to 1) pu
Dist: 1³/₄l, 5l, 12l, nk, 16l, dist. 4m 28.90s, a 31.90s (12 Ran).
SR: 26/24/19/7/7/-/ (Easy Monk Partnership), N A Callaghan

2304 Manston Novices' Handicap Chase Class E (0-100 5-y-o and up) £3,128 2m......................(1:45)

KEY PLAYER (Ire) [71] 8-10-4 D O'Sullivan, *trkd ldrs, lft 3rd 2 out, rdn to ld r-in.......*(16 to 1 op 20 to 1 tchd 25 to 1) 1
MR BEAN [87] 7-11-6 A Larnach, *in tch, lft second 2 out, sn led, rdn and hdd r-in...* (16 to 1 op 12 to 1 tchd 20 to 1) 2
2010³ POLICEMANS PRIDE (Fr) [67] 8-10-0 D Morris, *led till hdd appr 6th, und pres whn lft in ld 2 out, sn headed and wknd.*
..............................(12 to 1 op 6 to 1 tchd 14 to 1) 3
2010² RIVER LENNAS [91] (bl) 8-11-10 R Dunwoody, *sn pushed alng, one pace frm 3 out...*(5 to 2 fav op 9 to 4 tchd 11 to 4) 4
VIRBAZAR (Fr) [69] 10-10-2² G Upton, *hld up in tch, rdn and wknd appr 2 out.........*(16 to 1 op 33 to 1) 5
440³ BRIGADIER SUPREME (Ire) [72] 8-10-5 T J Murphy, *jmpd slwly in rear, sn tld off......................*(33 to 1 op 16 to 1) 6

2176² BOLD ACRE [76] (bl) 7-10-9 P Hide, *trkd ldr, led appr 6th, 2 ls up and gng wl whn f two out.........*(3 to 1 tchd 7 to 2) f
1979 CARACOL [67] 8-9-11 (3*) T Dascombe, *f 4th.*
..................................(6 to 1 tchd 5 to 1) f
1667 RELKOWEN [80] 7-10-13 M Richards, *f 1st.*
..........................(13 to 2 op 3 to 1 tchd 9 to 1) f
2154 SMART CASANOVA [67] 8-10-0 T J O'Sullivan, *al towards rear, 5th and btn whn uns rdr last.*
....................................(33 to 1 op 20 to 1 tchd 40 to 1) ur
1593 MASTER PANGLOSS (Ire) [67] 7-9-8¹ (7*) C Rae, *brght dwn 4th.......................*(33 to 1 op 20 to 1) bd
1698⁷ FULL OF TRICKS [67] 9-10-0 L Harvey, *al beh, tld off whn pld up bef 8th...............*(33 to 1 op 20 to 1) pu
1794 HIDDEN PLEASURE [76] 11-10-9 D Leahy, *slwly away, tried to refuse 3rd, tld off whn pld up bef 5th.*
....................................(33 to 1 op 16 to 1 tchd 40 to 1) pu
Dist: 1l, 10l, 6l, 2¹/₂l, dist. 4m 12.70s. a 21.70s (13 Ran).
(W Packham), R Rowe

2305 North Foreland Selling Hurdle Class G (4 - 7-y-o) £2,074 2m 1f 110yds
..................................(2:15)

858⁵ YELLOW DRAGON (Ire) 4-10-5 R Hughes, *hld up in tch, hdwy 5th, led on bit appr last, rdn clr.*
.................................(7 to 1 op 8 to 1 tchd 10 to 1) 1
CHOCOLATE ICE 4-10-5 D O'Sullivan, *trkd ldrs, hdwy to chase wnr appr last, no imprsn r-in.*
...........................(5 to 1 op 4 to 1 tchd 6 to 1) 2
1953² FURIETTO (Ire) 7-11-10 R Dunwoody, *led till hrd rdn and hdd appr last, sn btn.*
..........................(11 to 10 fav op 11 to 8 on tchd 6 to 5) 3
1669⁵ QUAKER WALTZ 7-10-12 S McNeill, *trkd ldrs, rdn and wknd aftr 2 out....*(5 to 1 op 9 to 2 tchd 11 to 2) 4
1697 MEMORY'S MUSIC 5-11-3 D Morris, *lost tch 5th, tld off whn pld up bef last.......*(8 to 1 op 5 to 1 tchd 9 to 1) pu
1800 OFFICE HOURS 5-11-3 W McFarland, *al beh, tld off whn pld up bef last..........*(14 to 1 op 10 to 1 tchd 20 to 1) pu
2265 SAYITAGAIN 5-10-10 (7*) N T Egan, *al beh, tld off whn pld up bef last..........*(12 to 1 op 12 to 1 tchd 40 to 1) pu
TENNYSON BAY 5-11-3 A Dicken, *al beh, tld off whn pld up bef last.........*(25 to 1 op 10 to 1 tchd 33 to 1) pu
1179 STORM WIND (Ire) 4-10-5 A Larnach, *chsd ldr 4th to 2 out, sn wknd, pld up bef last................*(33 to 1 op 16 to 1) pu
1354 SABOTEUSE 5-10-12 T J Murphy, *pld hrd, prmnt till wknd 5th, tld off whn pulled up bef 2 out.* (20 to 1 tchd 25 to 1) pu
Dist: 9l, 8l, 4l. 4m 28.10s. a 31.10s (10 Ran).
SR: 19/10/21/5/-/-/ (C M Kwai), B A Pearce

2306 Kent Handicap Chase Class D (0-125 5-y-o and up) £4,760 3¹/₄m... (2:45)

1767⁴ COURT MELODY (Ire) [115] (bl) 9-10-11 (7*) Mr J Tizzard, *hld up, hdwy tenth, led 13th, rdn and hit last, all out.*
................................(8 to 1 tchd 10 to 1) 1
1793* LITTLE MARTINA (Ire) [105] 9-10-8 J R Kavanagh, *trkd ldr, led 3rd to 7th, styd in tch, rallied appr last, stayed on gmely r-in.*
...........................(5 to 2 fav op 9 to 4 tchd 11 to 4) 2
1974³ SPUFFINGTON [113] 9-10-3 (3*) L Aspell, *al prmnt, wnt second 3 out, wknd appr last.*
......................................(13 to 2 op 6 to 1 tchd 7 to 1) 3
2024⁵ CELTIC TOWN [104] (bl) 9-10-7 J A McCarthy, *hld up in rear, lost pl 13th, made some late hdwy...*(20 to 1 tchd 25 to 1) 4
1645 BEAUREPAIRE (Ire) [108] 9-10-11 S McNeill, *prmnt, led 7th, hdd 13th, sn wknd, tld off.* (11 to 1 op 8 to 1 tchd 12 to 1) 5
1974 CELTIC BARLE [102] 13-10-5 A P McCoy, *in tch till wknd 3 out, tld off whn virtually pld up r-in....* (8 to 1 tchd 9 to 1) 6
1892 SHEER ABILITY [125] 11-12-0 R Dunwoody, *al beh, tld off hfwy....................*(12 to 1 op 10 to 1 tchd 14 to 1) 7
VERYVEL (Cze) [97] 6-9-12¹ (3*) N Mann, *f 1st.....*(20 to 1) f
2005² DIAMOND FORT [105] 12-10-8 R Farrant, *al beh, tld off hfwy, pld up bef 13th.........*(14 to 1 op 12 to 1 tchd 16 to 1) pu
1774⁶ FLASHTHECASH [122] 11-11-11 M Richards, *in rear till hdwy 13th, wknd quickly 3 out, pld up bef last.*
.................................(10 to 1 tchd 12 to 1) pu
TOP BRASS (Ire) [103] 9-10-6 T J Murphy, *led till hit 3rd, wknd tenth, tld off whn pld up bef 5 out.....*(9 to 1 op 8 to 1) pu
1718* FLOW [105] 8-10-8 B Powell, *hld up, hdwy 6th, wknd 13th, tld off whn pld up bef 3 out.......*(9 to 2 op 3 to 1) pu
Dist: ¹/₂l, 4l, 18l, dist, 6l, dist. 6m 50.90s. a 35.90s (12 Ran).
(J W Aplin, P K Barber & Mick Coburn), P F Nicholls

2307 H.B.L.B. Goodwins Handicap Hurdle Class F (0-105 4-y-o and up) £2,180 2m 1f 110yds................(3:20)

1803³ ADDED DIMENSION (Ire) [89] 6-10-8 (7*) X Aizpuru, *hld up, hdwy 2 out, led wl bef last, rdn clr r-in.*
.............................(11 to 1 op 12 to 1 tchd 16 to 1) 1
1728 CLASSIC PAL (USA) [75] 6-10-1¹ D Skyrme, *hld up towards rear, hdwy to chase wnr appr last.*
.................................(10 to 1 op 20 to 1 tchd 8 to 1) 2
1759⁸ MAZZINI (Ire) [76] 4-11-2 (7*) Mr P O'Keeffe, *trkd ldr, led 3rd, hdd 3 out, outpcd frm nxt.* (18 to 1 op 20 to 1) 3
1665² ALWAYS HAPPY [93] 4-10-7 S McNeill, *trkd ldrs, led 3 out, rdn and hdd wl bef last, wknd..........*(7 to 1 op 3 to 1) 4

2180* ZINGIBAR [83] 5-10-9 R Dunwoody, *led to tird, lost pl 3 out, rdn and nvr on terms aftr* ....(3 to 1 fav op 5 to 2)　5

833⁹ CIRCUS COLOURS [97] 7-11-9 R Hughes, *hld up, hdwy 3 out, wknd aftr nxt*......(14 to 1 op 12 to 1 tchd 16 to 1)　6

1697* ZESTI [80] 5-10-6 N Mann, *hld up in tch, wknd appr 2 out, tld off*..(5 to 1 op 7 to 2)　7

2009* SHEPHERDS REST (Ire) [101] 5-11-6 (7") S Hearn, *trkd ldrs, ev ch and gng wl whn hit and uns rdr 2 out.*

.................................(11 to 2 op 5 to 1 tchd 6 to 1)　ur

Dist: 6l, 1¾l, 4l, 4l, 10l, dist: 4m 33.80s. a 36.80s (8 Ran).

(N A Dunger), P Winkworth

2308 Canterbury Handicap Chase Class F
(0-100 5-y-o and up) £3,064 2m 5f
....(3:50)

1801⁴ OXFORD QUILL [71] 10-10-0 D Morris, *beh till hdwy 6th, led on long bend appr 2 out, rdn out.*

...........................(25 to 1 op 16 to 1 tchd 33 to 1)　1

1808 PLAYING TRUANT [81] 9-10-10 R Dunwoody, *hld up in rear, hdwy 7th, chsd wnr 2 out, one pace.*

.................................(9 to 2 fav op 7 to 2 tchd 5 to 1)　2

1916³ PEARL'S CHOICE (Ire) [87] 9-11-2 B Powell, *al prmnt, rdn appr 2 out, one pace*......(13 to 2 op 6 to 1 tchd 7 to 1)　3

2034⁴ CHANNEL PASTIME [85] 13-10-11 (3") Guy Lewis, *sn trkd ldrs, wknd appr 2 out*.....(9 to 1 op 7 to 1 tchd 10 to 1)　4

1700³ PAVLOVA (Ire) [75] 7-10-4 D O'Sullivan, *al abt same pl, one pace aftr 8th*......................(14 to 1 op 12 to 1)　5

2252 OPAL'S TENSPOT [71] 10-10-0 R Farrant, *prmnt till wknd 7th, tld off*.............................(25 to 1 op 16 to 1)　6

1847³ PRIZE MATCH [75] 8-10-4 S McNeill, *l 4th.*
.................................(12 to 1 op 10 to 1 tchd 14 to 1)　f

1920* TITAN EMPRESS [81] (v) 8-10-10 N Mann, *brght dwn 4th, dead.*....................(11 to 2 op 4 to 1 tchd 6 to 1)　bd

RETAIL RUNNER [90] 12-11-5 Mr T Hills, *led till hdd on long bend appr 2 out, wknd and pld up bef last.*

.................................(7 to 1 op 12 to 1)　pu

1941⁴ CRUISE CONTROL [78] 11-10-0 (7") A Garrity, *al beh, tld off whn pld up bef last*.....(14 to 1 op 12 to 1 tchd 16 to 1)　pu

1889⁴ DEEPENDABLE [88] (bl) 10-11-3 M Richards, *al beh, tld off whn pld up bef last*.............(12 to 1 tchd 14 to 1)　pu

2134 FOREST FEATHER (Ire) [87] (bl) 9-11-2 B Clifford, *beh whn pld up bef 7th*............(6 to 1 op 4 to 1 tchd 13 to 2)　pu

104⁵ SPY DESSA [71] 9-9-11 (3") P Henley, *blun badly 4th, tld off 6th, pld up bef last*....(12 to 1 op 25 to 1 tchd 16 to 1)　pu

Dist: 8l, 2l, 1¾l, 5l, 27l. 5m 31.70s. a 20.70s (13 Ran).

SR: 12/14/18/14/-/-/

(T F Parrett), R Curtis

2309 Ashford Mares' Only Standard
National Hunt Flat Class H (4,5,6-y-o) £1,266 2m 1f 110yds.....(4:20)

TARA GALE (Ire) 5-10-11 (7") X lazpuru, *hld up in rear, hdwy 4 fs out, styd on to ld one out, ran on.*

.................................(14 to 1 op 12 to 1 tchd 16 to 1)　1

1476⁴ WHERE'S MIRANDA 5-10-11 (7") R Hobson, *trkd ldrs, led wl o'r one furlong out, hdd entering last, kpt on.*

.................................(7 to 4 fav op 2 to 1 tchd 9 to 1)　2

1769⁶ QUISTAQUAY 5-11-1 (3") P Henley, *rcd keenly, prmnt till lost pl hfwy, rdn and styd on ins fnl 3 fs.*

.................................(9 to 1 op 5 to 1 tchd 10 to 1)　3

1942⁶ JAYDEEBEE 6-10-11 (7") J Power, *hld up in tch, chsd ldr 5 fs out till wknd o'r one out.* (14 to 1 op 10 to 1 tchd 20 to 1)　4

1942⁵ HURRICANE JANE (Ire) 5-11-4 Mrs A Perrett, *led aftr 7 fs, hdd wl o'r one out, wknd.*....(11 to 2 op 4 to 1 tchd 7 to 1)　5

2015⁸ BEBE GREY (v) 6-10-11 (7") M Clinton, *in tch to hfwy, one pace fnl 3 fs.*.......................(25 to 1 op 20 to 1)　6

1874⁵ ARDROM 5-11-4 Mr P Scott, *pld hrd early, sn prmnt, chsd ldrs 7 fs out till wknd 5 out.*

.................................(3 to 1 op 7 to 4 tchd 100 to 30)　7

FOLESCLAVE (Ire) 5-10-11 (7") Mr J Tizzard, *hld up, hdwy hfwy, wknd 3 fs out.*........(10 to 1 op 6 to 1)　8

1949⁷ MISTRESS TUDOR 4-10-11 (3") E Husband, *led, sn clr, hdd aftr 7 fs, soon beh*.....(20 to 1 op 14 to 1 tchd 25 to 1)　9

1560 AINTGOTWON 6-11-1 (3") L Aspell, *pld hrd, effrt hfwy, sn wknd, tld off*................(25 to 1 op 14 to 1)　10

1949⁸ MAGGIE STRAIT 5-10-11 (7") Mr O McPhail, *in rear, rdn hfwy, tld off*...........................(7 to 1 op 5 to 1)　11

NELLY BLANCHE 6-10-11 (7") Mr N Moran, *al beh, tld off.*

.................................(16 to 1 op 8 to 1 tchd 20 to 1)　12

Dist: 3l, 2l, 1¾l, 9l, 6l, 10l, 9l, 9l, 16l, 2l. 4m 34.30s. (12 Ran).

(A J Williams), J Neville

UTTOXETER (good)
Friday January 24th
Going Correction: PLUS 0.35 sec. per fur. (races 1,3,5), PLUS 0.15 (2,4,6)

2310 Brake Bros. Food Services Handicap
Chase Class D (0-125 5-y-o and up)
£3,647 3¼m.................(1:15)

2024* LORD GYLLENE (NZ) [125] 9-12-0 A Dobbin, *led to 3rd, led ag'n aftr 5th, clr frm 14th, in command whn not fluent last, cmftbly*...........................(8 to 1 op 5 to 1)　1

1745* SAMLEE (Ire) [115] 8-11-4 N Williamson, *hdwy 7th, chsd ldrs frm 15th, styd on to take second at last but no ch wth wnr.*
.................................(9 to 2 jt-fav op 5 to 1 tchd 11 to 2)　2

1767⁵ RECTORY GARDEN (Ire) [111] 8-11-0 A Thornton, *al frnt rnk, rdn alng frm 15th, styd on one pace frm 4 out.*
.................................(11 to 2 op 5 to 1 tchd 6 to 1)　3

1884* MUSTHAVEASWIG [123] 11-11-12 R Johnson, *prmnt, hit 13th, chsd wnr frm 14th, rdn from nxt, wknd last.*
.................................(9 to 1 op 7 to 1 tchd 10 to 1)　4

1974 BIG BEN DUN [107] 11-10-3 (7") M Berry, *steady hdwy to track ldrs 13th, rdn 15th, wknd appoaching 4 out.*
.................................(16 to 1 op 12 to 1)　5

1726* BALLYEA BOY (Ire) [113] 7-10-11 (5") R Thornton, *mid-div, hdwy 14th, hit 16th, wknd appr 4 out.*...........(9 to 2 jt-fav op 3 to 1)　6

2031³ HARRISTOWN LADY [107] (bl) 10-10-10 B Fenton, *beh, rdn alng 12th, sn lost tch*...........(20 to 1 op 14 to 1)　7

1831⁴ LOCH GARMAN HOTEL (Ire) [99] 8-10-2² C Maude, *prmnt early, beh frm 8th*..............(66 to 1 op 50 to 1)　8

1853² CHURCH LAW [105] 10-10-8 J Railton, *in tch 12th, effrt 15th, sn wknd*..................(8 to 1 op 7 to 1)　9

1563³ COPPER MINE [120] 11-11-9 J Osborne, *led 3rd till blun and hdd 5th, wknd quickly 15th.*
.................................(14 to 1 op 12 to 1 tchd 16 to 1)　10

1967⁴ DONT TELL THE WIFE [119] 11-11-8 J F Titley, *al beh, rdn and lost tch frm 13th*...(16 to 1 op 12 to 1 tchd 20 to 1)　11

Dist: 15l, 3l, 2½l, 18l, 6l, sht-hd, 1½l, 1½l, 17l, 12l. 6m 34.90s. a 22.90s (11 Ran).

(Stanley W Clarke), S A Brookshaw

2311 Addison Of Newport Novices' Hurdle
Class E (4-y-o and up) £2,652 2½m
110yds...........................(1:50)

1995³ BARTON WARD 6-11-5 A Dobbin, *hdwy 6th, pushed alng aftr 4 out, ld appr 2 out, ran on wl.*......(8 to 1 op 5 to 1)　1

1592* SPARKLING SPRING (Ire) 6-11-4 C O'Dwyer, *in tch 3rd, steady hdwy to track ldrs 6th, chlgd 3 out, kpt on same pace aftr nxt.*......................(13 to 2 op 9 to 2)　2

1729² SUPREME FLYER (Ire) 7-10-12 (7") Mr R Wakley, *prominent, chlgd frm 6th till outpcd from 2 out....* (20 to 1 op 10 to 1)　3

1928² THE CAPTAIN'S WISH 6-11-11 R Johnson, *prmnt, chlgd 7th to 3 out, sn rdn, wknd aftr 2 out*........(6 to 1 op 5 to 1)　4

THE BARGEMAN (NZ) 9-11-2 (3") D Fortt, *beh till ran on frm 3 out, nvr dngrs*.......(50 to 1 op 33 to 1 tchd 100 to 1)　5

2215² MONTECOT (Fr) 8-11-5 J Railton, *in tch, pushed alng to track ldrs 3 out, sn rdn and lost.*

.................................(15 to 8 fav op 2 to 1 tchd 5 to 2 and 7 to 4)　6

289⁵ BLAZING STORM (Ire) 5-11-0 (5") Mr R Thornton, *hdwy 5th, wknd 7th.*.....................(25 to 1 op 16 to 1)　7

2025⁶ BURNTWOOD MELODY 6-11-5 B Fenton, *promined to 7th, wknd frm 3 out*.........(66 to 1 op 50 to 1)　8

2023⁸ PRUSSIA 6-11-11 A Thornton, *keen hold, chsd ldr to 7th, sn wknd*.................(25 to 1 op 16 to 1)　9

1861 TOPAGLOW (Ire) 4-10-6 T Eley, *prmnt to 6th.*
.................................(33 to 1 op 25 to 1 tchd 50 to 1)　10

1769⁵ JET FILES (Ire) 6-11-5 W Marston, *not fluent, al in rear.*
.................................(20 to 1 op 16 to 1 tchd 25 to 1)　11

2002* SHU GAA (Ire) 4-10-12 J Osborne, *led, hit 5th, hdd appr 2 out, wknd rpdly, blun last.*

.................................(5 to 1 op 7 to 2 tchd 6 to 1 and 13 to 2)　12

2023 VICTORIA DAY 5-11-0 S Wynne, *beh frm 5th, tld off.* (33 to 1)　13

919⁹ CONNAUGHT'S PRIDE 6-11-0 N Williamson, *hdwy 6th, wknd quickly appr 3 out, tld off.*　14

1134³ MADAM'S WALK 7-11-0 C Maude, *jmpd poorly in rear, tld off frm 5th, tailed off whn pld up bef 2 out.* (25 to 1 op 20 to 1)　pu

1882 GOATSFUT (Ire) 7-11-5 T Jenks, *beh frm 5th, tld off whn pld up bef 2 out.*....................(100 to 1)　pu

Dist: 5l, 2½l, 2l, 3l, 1½l, 2½l, 9l, 6l, sht-hd, 6l. 4m 52.00s. a 13.00s (16 Ran).

(Mrs H J Clarke), S A Brookshaw

2312 Roger Aston Novices' Chase Class E
(5-y-o and up) £3,103 2m 5f...(2:20)

1725³ WILD WEST WIND (Ire) 7-11-4 J F Titley, *trkd ldr till chlgd frm tenth, led appr 4 out, rdn whn chald from 2 out, styd on wl.*
.................................(5 to 1 tchd 6 to 1)　1

1732² FEEL THE POWER (Ire) 9-11-4 C O'Dwyer, *hld up, steady hdwy appr 4 out, chlgd 2 out, sn rdn, ev ch last, found no extr.*
.................................(3 to 1 op 9 to 4 tchd 100 to 30)　2

HIM OF PRAISE (Ire) 7-11-4 J Osborne, *keen hold and sn led, hdd appr for out, fdd frm nxt.*
.................................(6 to 5 fav op 11 to 8 tchd 6 to 4)　3

1670 EASY BREEZY 7-11-4 J Railton, *in tch, hit 8th, wknd 4 out.*
.................................(20 to 1 op 14 to 1)　4

1706⁶ DUNLIR 7-10-7 (7") M Griffiths, *blun 3rd and 4th, tld off frm 6th.*...........................(50 to 1 op 20 to 1)　5

2003² SPINNAKER 7-11-4 A Thornton, *trkd ldrs, chlgd 4 out, sn rdn, 3rd and hld whn f 2 out*.........(9 to 2 op 7 to 2)　f

Dist: 3½l, 18l, 9l, 30l. 5m 10.70s. a 12.70s (6 Ran).

SR: 36/32/14/5/-/-/

(Lord Vestey), Miss H C Knight

2313 Jenkinsons Caterers Handicap Hurdle Class C (0-135 4-y-o and up)
£3,436 3m 110yds...........(2:50)

1766⁸ HAILE DERRING [112] 7-11-7 C Maude, *in tch, chlgd frm 6th till led aftr 4 out, drvn clr 2 out, readily*
.... (5 to 4 fav op 6 to 4 tchd 7 to 4) 1
RIMOUSKI [97] 9-10-6 N Williamson, *al in tch, chsd wnr frm 3 out, no imprsn*.................. (5 to 1 tchd 6 to 1) 2

21774 DERRING BRIDGE [91] 7-11-0 R Johnson, *drpd rear 7th, styd on one pace and pres frm 3 out*........ (8 to 1 op 6 to 1) 3

1671⁴ FAST THOUGHTS [106] 10-10-10 (5*) Sophie Mitchell, *chlgd frm 3rd till led aftr 4th, hdd after four out, wknd nxt.*
.... (14 to 1 op 10 to 1) 4
SPARKLING CONE [112] 8-11-7 J Osborne, *hld up, hdwy 6th, wnt 3rd approaching 3 out, wknd aftr nxt.*
.... (9 to 2 op 7 to 2 tchd 11 to 2 and 6 to 1) 5
SMITH TOO (Ire) [115] 9-11-7 (3*) G Hogan, *led till aftr 4th, wknd four out*........... (5 to 1 op 3 to 1 tchd 11 to 2) 6
Dist: 5l, 2½l, 5l, 2l, 12l. 5m 54.30s. a 17.30s (6 Ran).

(Mrs V Stockdale), N A Twiston-Davies

2314 John Partridge English Clothing Handicap Chase Class C (0-130 5-y-o and up) £4,435 2m 5f....... (3:25)

MELY MOSS (Fr) [126] 6-12-0 J Osborne, *made virtually all drvn alng 4 out, clr frm nxt, easily.*
.... (4 to 1 op 8 to 1 tchd 9 to 1) 1

1491² FLAPJACK LAD [98] 8-10-0 D Walsh, *chsd wnr, led briefly appr 4 out, one pace frm nxt*........ (6 to 1 tchd 13 to 2) 2

1613 RIVER BOUNTY [126] 11-11-7 (7*) M Berry, *al chasing ldrs, rdn 4 out, styd on same pace*........... (11 to 1 op 8 to 1) 3

2024² SAILOR JIM [107] 10-10-9 C Maude, *beh, drvn alng appr 4 out, no imprsn*....(11 to 4 fav op 5 to 1 tchd 100 to 30) 4

2034* TOO SHARP [105] 9-10-7 J F Titley, *in tch, rdn tenth, one pace frm 4 out*....... (4 to 1 op 7 to 2 tchd 9 to 2) 5

1666 THE CAUMRUE (Ire) [108] 9-11-0 B Fenton, *beh most of way, lost tch frm 12th, tld off*............ (10 to 1 op 7 to 1) 6

1948⁷ DISTINCTIVE (Ire) [98] 8-10-0 W Marston, *uns rdr strt.*
.... (8 to 1 op 6 to 1) ur
POSTMAN'S PATH [103] 11-10-5 A Thornton, *al beh, tld off whn pld up bef 11th*... (20 to 1 op 14 to 1 tchd 25 to 1) pu
Dist: 14l, ¾l, 1l, 2l, dist. 5m 11.30s. a 13.30s (8 Ran).

SR: 40/-/25/5/1/

(Darren C Mercer), C R Egerton

2315 Ram FM Novices' Hurdle Class E (4-y-o and up) £2,463 2m....... (3:55)

1641⁵ DONNINGTON (Ire) 7-11-5 J Osborne, *hld up in rear, steady hdwy frm 4 out, chlgd 2 out and sn led, drvn out.*
.... (3 to 1 tchd 4 to 1) 1

1727* WADE ROAD (Ire) 6-11-11 J F Titley, *in tch, chsd ldr 4 out, str chal frm nxt till not quicken und pres r-in.*
.... (7 to 4 on op 2 to 1 on tchd 9 to 4 on and 13 to 8 on) 2
BONJOUR 7-11-5 J Railton, *hld up, smooth hdwy frm 4 out, trkd ldrs from nxt, one pace from 2 out.*
.... (20 to 1 op 16 to 1 tchd 25 to 1) 3

2032 LUCIA FORTE 6-11-6 C O'Dwyer, *trkd ldr till led 5th, hdd sn aftr 2 out, soon btn*........ (6 to 1 op 8 to 1 tchd 9 to 1) 4

1977⁴ TANTARA LODGE (Ire) 6-11-5 A Thornton, *sn beh and nvr dngrs*................. (40 to 1 op 25 to 1 tchd 50 to 1) 5

1689⁴ TARRY 4-10-8 T Eley, *beh frm 4th*.....(33 to 1 op 25 to 1) 6

1350⁷ EUROFAST PET (Ire) 7-11-5 A Dobbin, *beh frm hfwy.*
.... (33 to 1) 7

1995⁹ SCALLY HICKS 6-11-0 Gary Lyons, *beh frm hfwy.*
.... (100 to 1 op 66 to 1) 8

2156 DECEIT THE SECOND (bl) 5-10-12 (7*) M Griffiths, *led to 5th, wknd rpdly, tld off*............ (100 to 1 op 66 to 1) 9
Dist: 2l, 6l, 4l, 27l, 5l, 9l, 4l, dist. 3m 45.50s. a 8.50s (9 Ran).

SR: 30/34/22/19/-/-/

(B T Stewart-Brown), O Sherwood

AYR (good)
Saturday January 25th
Going Correction: PLUS 0.65 sec. per fur.

2316 Albert Bartlett & Sons Handicap Hurdle Class D (0-125 4-y-o and up) £2,901 2m.................. (12:30)

1786* STASH THE CASH (Ire) [110] 6-11-6 R Garritty, *patiently rdn, smooth hdwy 3 out, led betw last 2, drvn clr.*
.... (100 to 30 op 3 to 1 tchd 7 to 2) 1
SUPREME SOVIET [92] 7-9-11 (5*) S Taylor, *chsd ldr, led 5th, drvn and hdd aftr 2 out, one pace und pres.*
.... (8 to 1 op 7 to 1 tchd 9 to 1) 2

1335⁴ ADAMATIC (Ire) [98] 6-10-8 J Callaghan, *in tch, mstk 5th, chsd ldr appr 3 out, sn no imprsn*...... (4 to 1 op 7 to 2) 3

2190⁸ COMMON SOUND (Ire) [114] 6-11-10 B Storey, *beh, not fluent 5th, hdwy to chase ldrs 3 out, sn one pace.*
.... (50 to 1 op 25 to 1) 4

2147² ENDOWMENT [105] (bl) 5-11-1 P Niven, *set gd pace, hdd 5th, wknd quickly nxt, wl beh whn hit 2 out, fnshd lme.*
.... (2 to 1 fav op 7 to 4 tchd 9 to 4) 5

2204 ALL CLEAR (Ire) [93] 6-10-3 D Parker, *keen hold, chsd ldrs till lost tch 4 out, tld off*............ (100 to 1 op 20 to 1) 6
FOX SPARROW [76] 7-11-3 A S Smith, *hld up, beh whn blun 4 out, tld off*.................. (25 to 1 tchd 16 to 1) 7

2118* TRIENNIUM (USA) [90] 8-10-0 G Cahill, *hld up, outpcd aftr 4 out, btn whn pld up bef nxt.* (6 to 1 op 7 to 1 tchd 8 to 1) pu
Dist: 5l, 6l, 8l, 28l, nk, 4l. 3m 51.60s. a 15.60s (8 Ran).

SR: 40/17/17/25/-/

(G Shiel), M D Hammond

2317 Stakis Casinos Handicap Chase Class C for the McAlpine Challenge Cup (0-130 5-y-o and up) £5,735 3m 1f.................. (1:00)

2175⁴ FIVELEIGH BUILDS [122] 10-11-6 M Foster, *made most till hdd 4 out, rallied to ld ag'n 2 out, styd on strly und pres.*
.... (4 to 1 tchd 9 to 2) 1
WHISPERING STEEL [127] 11-11-11 B Storey, *hld up, chlgd gng wl 6 out, led 4 out till hdd 2 out, kpt on well till no extr cl hme.*
.... (11 to 4 fav op 2 to 4) 2

2148² ALI'S ALIBI [114] 10-10-12 P Niven, *hld up, clr order fnl circuit, chasing ldrs whn mstk 6 out, drvn and one pace frm 3 out.*
.... (6 to 4 fav tchd 7 to 4) 3

2189⁶ CEILIDH BOY [120] (bl) 11-11-4 A S Smith, *hld up, reminder hfwy, pushed alng and outpcd 6 out, styd on frm 3 out, unbl to chal.*...................... (12 to 1 op 8 to 1) 4

2148³ ALY DALEY (Ire) [103] 9-10-1 G Cahill, *led to second, cl up till blun and lost pl tenth, lost tch appr 4 out, sn beh.*
.... (14 to 1 op 8 to 1) 5

2150⁷ SOLBA (USA) [106] 8-10-4 D Parker, *chsd ldrs, not fluent, pushed alng and mstk 5 out, fdd*..............(10 to 1) 6

1634² DEEP DECISION [102] 11-10-0 K Johnson, *hld up, drvn and outpcd 5 out, sn lost tch, tld off*........ (8 to 1 op 6 to 1) 7
Dist: 1½l, 4l, 7l, 16l, 1½l, 13l. 6m 34.20s. a 34.20s (7 Ran).

(Miss Lucinda V Russell), Miss Lucinda V Russell

2318 Client Entertainment Services European Breeders Fund 'National Hunt Novices Hurdle Qualifier (5,6,7-y-o) £4,988 2½m.................. (1:30)

1962* KING PIN 5-11-10 R Supple, *hld up, not fluent, edgd lft and slight ld 2 out, hit last, pushed clr, readily.*
.... (3 to 1 tchd 100 to 30) 1

1984* PAPERISINGS 5-11-10 B Storey, *nvr far away, led appr 3 out, hdd nxt, kpt on stdly.*.......................(5 to 2 jt-fav op 9 to 4 tchd 11 to 4) 2

2158² LANCE ARMSTRONG (Ire) 7-11-2 (3*) D Fortt, *led till rdn and hdd appr 3 out, unbl to quicken*........ (11 to 4 op 2 to 1) 3

1623* SHANAVOGH 6-11-10 J Callaghan, *chsd ldr, ev ch 4 out, outpcd nxt, fdd*.... (5 to 2 jt-fav op 9 to 4 tchd 11 to 4) 4
APOLLO COLOSSO 7-11-0 M Moloney, *hld up, wknd quickly 7th, tld off whn pld up bef 3 out.*.................. (100 to 1) pu

2192⁵ JUDICIOUS NORMAN 6-11-0 T Reed, *keen hold in rear, lost tch 4 out, beh whn pld up bef nxt.* (14 to 1 op 12 to 1) pu
Dist: 3l, 3l, 12l. 5m 4.70s. a 26.70s (6 Ran).

(J R Hinchliffe), P Beaumont

2319 Scottish Sun Made In Scotland For Scotland Novices' Chase Class B (6-y-o and up) £7,064 3m 1f..... (2:00)

SANTA CONCERTO (Ire) 8-10-12 R Supple, *nvr far away, chalg whn blun 5 out, led 3 out, steadied and jmpd slwly last, pushed clr fnl.*.............. (7 to 4 fav tchd 6 to 4) 1

2187* SEEKING GOLD (Ire) 8-10-12 G Cahill, *settled rear, pushed alng and lost tch fnl circuit, styd on strly frm 3 out, nrst finish.*
.... (16 to 1 op 12 to 1 tchd 20 to 1) 2

2211² BALLYLINE (Ire) 6-11-3 A S Smith, *hld up, hdwy 4 out whn hit circuit, hdd 3 out, one pace betw last 2*.....(14 to 1 tchd 16 to 1) 3
ASK ME LATER (Ire) 8-10-12 M Foster, *in tch, rdn and outpcd twelfth, sn no dngr.*.................. (50 to 1 op 25 to 1) 4

1659³ COQUI LANE 10-10-12 T Reed, *chsd ldr, jmpd wl, lost tch fnl circuit, tld off whn pld up 5 out.*........ (100 to 1 op 12 to 1) pu

1862³ LORD OF THE WEST (Ire) 8-11-3 P Niven, *blunds in rear 9th and tenth, sn wl beh, tld off whn pld up 5 out.*
.... (7 to 2 op 11 to 4 tchd 4 to 1) pu

2237* CROWN EQUERRY (Ire) 7-11-3 B Storey, *hld up, mstk 8th, struggling frm tenth, tld off whn pld up 4 out.*
.... (9 to 4 op 2 to 1 tchd 5 to 2) pu
Dist: 1¾l, 6l, dist. 6m 38.90s. a 38.90s (7 Ran).

(John Corr), L Lungo

2320 Highland Mary Novices' Handicap Hurdle Class D (0-110 5-y-o and up) £2,290 3m 110yds........... (2:35)

2152⁶ ADIB (USA) [85] 7-10-9 N Bentley, *in tch, ev ch whn mstk 9th, led appr 3 out, clr when hit last, ran on.*
.... (13 to 8 op 2 to 1 tchd 9 to 4) 1

1824³ BELLE ROSE (Ire) [85] 7-10-9 L O'Hara, *hld up, hdwy to ld 8th, rdn and hdd appr 3 out, one pace.*..... (4 to 1 op 5 to 2) 2

2025* MENSHAAR (USA) [100] 5-11-10 R Supple, *hld up, not fluent 4th, niggled alng four out, no extr frm 3 out.*
.... (5 to 4 fav op 11 to 10 tchd 11 to 8) 3

1826 MEADOWLECK [76] 8-10-0 G Cahill, *set steady pace, hdd 8th, outpcd appr 3 out, sn no extr....* (100 to 1 op 66 to 1) 4

1829 CROFTON LAKE [76] 9-10-0 B Storey, *beh, pushed alng frm 7th, wknd appr strt.*.....(25 to 1 op 16 to 1 tchd 33 to 1) 5

1784 CHARLVIC [76] 7-9-7 (7") L McGrath, chsd ldr, drvn alng 7th,
tld off whn blun 2 out.................(50 to 1 op 66 to 1) 6
Dist: 4l, 7l, 1¼l, 12l, 18l. 6m 29.80s. a 48.80s (6 Ran).
(N B Mason (Farms) Ltd), G M Moore

2321 Land Of Burns Handicap Chase Class E (0-115 5-y-o and up) £3,090 2½m. (3:10)

2121 MONTRAVE [99] 8-11-9 R Supple, mstk 3rd, nvr far away, led
12th, pushed clr 3 out, eased considerably r-in.
...................................(5 to 2 fav op 9 to 4) 1
1934³ JUDICIAL FIELD (Ire) [93] (bl) 8-11-3 R Garritty, hld up, jmpd
slwly 4th, chsd wnr 4th, mstk four out and nxt, styd on stdly,
no ch whn wnr..........(5 to 1 op 9 to 2 tchd 11 to 2) 2
1283⁷ GOLDEN FIDDLE (Ire) [100] 9-11-10 B Storey, chsd ldr, not
fluent, rdn and outpcd 5 out, rallied frm 2 out, gng on finish.
.....................................(5 to 1 op 9 to 2) 3
1954 FUNNY OLD GAME [78] 10-10-2 K Johnson, in tch, led 11th,
mstk and hdd nxt, outpcd 5 out, no dngr aftr.
...................................(25 to 1 op 20 to 1) 4
1954⁵ JUKE BOX BILLY (Ire) [84] 9-10-8 A S Smith, hld up, hdwy to
track ldrs 5 out, drvn alng whn hit 3 out.................
..................................(5 to 1 op 4 to 1) 5
2065⁵ WILLIE SPARKLE [77] 11-10-1 M Foster, mstk second, hld up,
outpcd 5 out, sn no dngr. (12 to 1 op 7 to 1 tchd 14 to 1) 6
1934* CARDENDEN (Ire) [76] 10-10-0 D Parker, set steady pace till
hdd 11th, wknd quickly, tld off
...........................(14 to 1 op 7 to 1 tchd 16 to 1) 7
2151⁵ NICHOLAS PLANT [87] 8-10-11 G Cahill, uns rdr second.
....................................(5 to 1) ur
Dist: 2½l, 5l, hd, hd, 1¾l, dist. 5m 24.20s. a 37.20s (8 Ran).
(D St Clair), P Monteith

2322 Ayrshire Post Standard National Hunt Flat Class H (4,5,6-y-o) £1,329 2m. (3:40)

LORD PODGSKI (Ire) 6-11-5 G Cahill, al hndy, led o'r 3 fs out,
rdn clr over one out, styd on strly.
...................................(9 to 4 fav op 2 to 1 tchd 11 to 4) 1
1989² MAGPIE MELODY (Ire) 6-11-0 (5") B Grattan, al hndy, led 5 fs
out till o'r 3 out, kpt on same pace.
...................................(11 to 4 op 2 to 1 tchd 3 to 1) 2
WOODFIELD VISION (Ire) 6-10-12 (7") C McCormack, midfield, chlgd gng wl o'r 3 fs out, sn rdn and no imprsn.
...................................(11 to 1 op 8 to 1 tchd 14 to 1) 3
PORTMAN 5-10-12 (7") N Horrocks, steadied rear, pushed
alng and outpcd entering strt, nvr able to chal.
...................................(14 to 1 op 12 to 1) 4
ANDY CLYDE 4-10-0 (7") S Melrose, hld up, niggled alng o'r 4
fs out, no imprsn......................(16 to 1 op 8 to 1) 5
WELLSWOOD (Ire) 4-10-0 (7") M Newton, chsd ldrs, struggling o'r 6 fs out, sn no dngr.........(11 to 4 op 4 to 1) 6
ROYAL SPRUCE (Ire) 6-10-12 (7") N Hannity, chsd ldrs, niggled alng and outpcd 6 fs out, sn bhn...(25 to 1 op 16 to 1) 7
1993³ SIR BOSTON 4-10-0 (7") G Supple, hld up, keen hold, rdn and
wknd entering strt.................(12 to 1 tchd 14 to 1) 8
COTTSTOWN BOY (Ire) 6-10-12 (7") Mr M Bradburne, pld
hrd, made most till hdd 5 fs out, wknd quickly 3 out.
...................................(100 to 1 tchd 200 to 1) 9
SUNSET FLASH 5-11-5 Mr R Hale, cl up, led briefly ten fs out,
lost tch quickly appr strt........(50 to 1 op 25 to 1) 10
740 THE VALE (Ire) 5-11-0 (5") R McGrath, wl beh fnl 5 fs, tld off.
...................................(200 to 1 op 100 to 1) 11
Dist: 6l, 7l, 3½l, 11l, 3½l, ½l, 1½l, 7l, 12l, 10l. 3m 52.40s. (11 Ran).
(Mrs G Smyth), P Monteith

CHELTENHAM (good to firm)
Saturday January 25th
Going Correction: PLUS 0.15 sec. per fur. (races
1,2,4,7), PLUS 0.20 (3,5,6)

2323 John Simpson Golden Jubilee Nov-ices' Handicap Hurdle Class D (0-120 5-y-o and up) £3,647 2m 1f
.....................................(1:00)

2013* BOARDROOM SHUFFLE (Ire) 6-12-0 P Hide, wtd wth,
prog aftr 5th, chlgd betw fnl 2, led r-in, rdn out
...................................(5 to 2 fav op 9 to 4 tchd 11 to 4) 1
1830¹ POTTER'S GALE (Ire) [98] 6-10-6 A Maguire, hld up beh ldrs,
hdwy 5th, led appr last, hdd r-in, kpt on same pace.
...................................(6 to 1 op 5 to 1 tchd 13 to 2) 2
1716⁴ DANEGOLD (Ire) [105] 5-10-13 J Osborne, mid-div, hit second, hdwy appr 2 out, ev ch last, wknd r-in.
...................................(12 to 1 op 16 to 1) 3
1623³ RANGITIKEI (NZ) [103] 6-10-11 R Dunwoody, trkd ldrs, led 3
out, hit nxt, hdd appr last, wknd r-in......(8 to 1 op 14 to 1) 4
2290* HAY DANCE [109] 6-11-3 (7ex) N Williamson, hld up, hdwy
and effrt appr 2 out, wknd approaching last.
.....................................(4 to 1 tchd 5 to 1) 5
1727 PALLADIUM BOY [92] 7-10-0 T J Murphy, mid-division, rdn
and wknd 2 out.....(100 to 1 op 50 to 1 tchd 200 to 1) 6

2197³ DARAYDAN (Ire) [120] (bl) 5-12-0 C Maude, led to 4th, wknd
aftr 2 out....................................(9 to 2 op 9 to 4) 7
2023⁵ SAMANID (Ire) [105] 5-10-13 O Pears, mid-div, lost pl 5th, tld
off...(25 to 1) 8
2185 COUNTRY MINSTREL (Ire) [92] 6-9-7 (7") C Rae, hld up beh
ldrs, rdn and wknd appr 2 out, behind whn f last.
...................................(100 to 1 op 50 to 1) f
1699² IRON N GOLD [95] 5-10-3 D Bridgwater, beh, hit second and
nxt, sn tld off, pld up bef 3 out.
...................................(20 to 1 tchd 25 to 1 and 33 to 1) pu
1759⁴ EL DON [105] 5-10-13 J Ryan, chsd ldr, led 4th, hit nxt, hdd 3
out, wknd quickly aftr next, beh whn pld up bef last.
...................................(11 to 1 op 12 to 1 tchd 10 to 1) pu
2035⁴ SOUNDS LIKE FUN [96] 6-10-4 J F Titley, al beh, tld off whn
pld up bef 2 out.................................(20 to 1) pu
Dist: 1½l, 5l, ½l, 3½l, 8l, 2½l, 19l. 4m 1.30s. a 7.30s (12 Ran).
SR: 52/28/30/27/29/4/29/-/-/   (A D Weller), J T Gifford

2324 Finesse Four Years Old Hurdle Class A Grade 2 £9,779 2m 1f. (1:35)

1610² SHOOTING LIGHT (Ire) 11-0 R Dunwoody, al hndy, led appr
2 out, ran on.
...................................(11 to 10 on op Evens tchd 5 to 4 and 11 to 8) 1
1530² NOBLE LORD 11-0 B Powell, led till appr last, one pace.
.....................................(7 to 1 op 6 to 1) 2
2012* ROSEBERRY AVENUE (Ire) 11-0 A Maguire, in tch, ev ch appr
2 out till one pace bef last.............(11 to 2 op 3 to 1) 3
1861⁴ MAZAMET (USA) 11-0 V Slattery, in tch, rdn and effrt appr 2
out, one pace bef last................(33 to 1 tchd 25 to 1) 4
1517⁵ LEAR JET (USA) 11-4 J Osborne, prmnt, mstk 5th, wknd aftr 2
out, tld off.........................(6 to 1 tchd 13 to 2) 5
1890³ SALLY'S TWINS 10-9 W McFarland, mstks second and 4th, al
beh, tld off frm 3 out...................(33 to 1 op 20 to 1) 6
1470 FURSAN (USA) 11-0 D Bridgwater, pld hrd, hld up, hdwy 3
out, wknd nxt, tld off whn pulled up bef last...(10 to 1) pu
MACMORRIS (USA) 11-0 P Holley, prmnt, wknd quickly 3 out,
tld off whn pld up bef last..........(20 to 1 op 16 to 1) pu
Dist: 6l, 1½l, 6l, 27l, ¾l. 4m 2.50s. a 8.50s (8 Ran).
SR: 26/20/18/12/-/   (J M Brown), P G Murphy

2325 Ladbroke Trophy Chase Handicap Class B (5-y-o and up) £16,937 2m 5f
.....................................(2:10)

1571* DUBLIN FLYER [168] 11-12-0 B Powell, made all, ran on
gmely r-in.
...................................(15 to 8 fav op 5 to 2 tchd 11 to 4 and 7 to 4) 1
1878* ADDINGTON BOY (Ire) [158] 9-11-4 A Dobbin, nvr far away,
lft second tenth, effrt 3 out, not quicken betw fnl 2.
...................................(2 to 1 op 11 to 8 tchd 9 to 4) 2
1757³ HILL OF TULLOW (Ire) [140] (bl) 8-10-0 A Maguire, beh, mstk
12th, styd on frm 2 out, nvr nrr.......(16 to 1 op 14 to 1) 3
2220 GO UNIVERSAL (Ire) [140] 9-10-0 N Williamson, chsd wnr till
blun tenth, wknd appr 2 out...........(16 to 1 op 12 to 1) 4
PASHTO [140] 10-10-0 J Osborne, trkd ldrs till wknd appr 2
out.......................................(50 to 1 op 33 to 1) 5
1639 CHALLENGER DU LUC (Fr) [153] (bl) 7-10-13 R Dunwoody,
towards rear, wknd whn jmpd slwly 12th, wknd 3 out.
...................................(11 to 4 op 9 to 4) 6
1999 BRADBURY STAR [145] 12-10-5 P Hide, beh frm 7th.
...................................(20 to 1 op 14 to 1) 7
Dist: 2l, 17l, 4l, ¾l, 7l, 5l. 5m 9.80s. a 5.80s (7 Ran).
SR: 84/72/37/33/32/38/25/   (J B Sumner), Capt T A Forster

2326 Cleeve Hurdle Class A Grade 1 (4-y-o and up) £25,640 2m 5f 110yds (2:45)

1877* LARGE ACTION (Ire) 9-11-8 J Osborne, chsd ldr, led jst aftr 2
out, ran on wl.
...................................(15 to 8 on op 7 to 4 on tchd 13 to 8 on and 2 to 1 on) 1
2208⁴ PRIDWELL 7-11-8 R Dunwoody, hld up in cl tch, ev ch aftr 2
out, ran on frm last.......................(7 to 1 op 6 to 1) 2
1633² CASTLE SWEEP (Ire) 6-11-8 A Maguire, hld up in cl tch, effrt
betw fnl 2, one pace...................(3 to 1 op 9 to 4) 3
1877⁴ MUSE 10-11-8 P Holley, led till jst aftr 2 out, sn wknd, virtually
pld up r-in, fnshd lme...(14 to 1 op 12 to 1 tchd 16 to 1) 4
Dist: 1¾l, 1¼l, dist. 5m 10.50s. a 12.50s (4 Ran).
SR: 1/   (B T Stewart-Brown), O Sherwood

2327 Pillar Property Investments Chase Class B (6-y-o and up) £16,775 3m 1f 110yds (3:20)

2045* ONE MAN (Ire) 9-11-12 R Dunwoody, hld up, prog 13th, chsd
ldr frm 5 out, led r-in, pushed out.
...................................(5 to 2 on op 11 to 4 on tchd 3 to 1 on and 9 to 4 on) 1
2045³ BARTON BANK 11-11-12 A Maguire, chsd ldr, led 3rd to r-in,
ran on wl.................(4 to 1 op 3 to 1 tchd 9 to 2) 2
1865* YORKSHIRE GALE 11-11-6 N Williamson, not fluent second
and 3rd, chsd ldr 6th to 5 out, wknd 3 out, tld off.
...................................(6 to 1 op 10 to 1) 3
1395³ MARTOMICK 10-11-5 J Osborne, led to 3rd, second whn
blun 6th, beh whn mstk tenth, sn tld off.
...................................(16 to 1 op 12 to 1 tchd 20 to 1) 4
Dist: Hd, dist, dist. 6m 24.20s. a 9.20s (4 Ran).
SR: 57/57/-/-/   (J Hales), G Richards

2328 '50 Years Of Timeform' Novices' Handicap Chase Class C (5-y-o and up) £7,520 2m 5f............ (3:55)

2184² THE MINE CAPTAIN [100] 10-10-5 J Osborne, *jmpd wl, sn in tch, led 3 out, drvn alng nxt, kpt on well whn chlgd r-in.*
.... (6 to 1 op 5 to 1 tchd 13 to 2) 1

2046³ POTTER'S BAY (Ire) [119] 8-11-10 A Maguire, *hld up rear, prog 11th, ev ch frm 2 out, ran on from last.*
.... (100 to 30 op 11 to 4) 2

1970⁵ LIVELY KNIGHT (Ire) [115] 8-11-6 P Hide, *hld up in tch, mstks 11th and 4 out, sn wknd....* (7 to 2 op 3 to 1 tchd 4 to 1) 3

2175* IMPERIAL VINTAGE (Ire) [118] 7-11-9 N Williamson, *led, mstks second, 3rd and 5th, hdd nxt, led 7th to 3 out, wknd next.*
.... (11 to 4 fav op 7 to 2 tchd 4 to 1) 4

2211⁴ LA MEZERAY [95] 9-10-0 W Marston, *chsd ldr, led 6th to nxt, wknd 3 out*.................... (50 to 1 op 33 to 1) 5

1886² FLIGHT LIEUTENANT (USA) [109] 8-11-0 R Dunwoody, *hld up, blun tenth, hit nxt, hdwy 3 out, 5th and btn whn mstk next, tld off.*.................... (11 to 2 op 9 to 2 tchd 6 to 1) 6

1857 AFTER THE FOX [95] 10-10-0 B Powell, *hld up, hit 4th, rdr lost irons and pld up aftr 8th...*(11 to 2 op 9 to 2 tchd 6 to 1) pu

Dist: Nk, 15l, 6l, 6l, dist. 5m 14.80s. a 10.80s (7 Ran).

SR: 11/30/11/8/ (Gerald W Evans), O Sherwood

2329 D. J. Equine Handicap Hurdle Class B (0-145 4-y-o and up) £5,589 2m 1f .... (4:30)

1864⁴ FORESTAL [109] 5-10-1 T J Murphy, *hld up beh ldrs, drpd towards rear aftr second, hdwy frm 2 out, led r-in, ran on wl.*
.... (10 to 1 op 8 to 1) 1

1612⁵ BOLIVAR (Ire) [114] 5-10-1 (5*) S Ryan, *hld up, hdwy 5th, led appr last to r-in, one pace....* (10 to 1 op 11 to 2 tchd 9 to 1) 2

STAR RAGE (Ire) [126] 7-11-4 D Gallagher, *in tch, led briefly appr last, one pace*................ (11 to 4 fav op 4 to 1) 3

1564³ CHICODARI [127] (bl) 5-11-5 A Maguire, *hld up beh ldrs, rdn 2 out, ran on one pace r-in.*(11 to 2 op 6 to 1 tchd 13 to 2) 4

1744⁴ FOURTH IN LINE (Ire) [125] 9-11-3 W Marston, *beh, hdwy appr 2 out, sn rdn, kpt on one pace.*
.... (16 to 1 op 14 to 1 tchd 20 to 1) 5

2027⁵ DR LEUNT (Ire) [130] 6-11-8 G Tormey, *led to second, wknd appr last*.................... (14 to 1 op 10 to 1) 6

2218 ROLL A DOLLAR [125] 11-11-3 P Holley, *nvr nr to chal.*
.... (25 to 1 op 20 to 1) 7

1990³ MOST EQUAL [117] 7-10-9 R Dunwoody, *hld up, hdwy 3 out, wknd frm nxt.*.................... (5 to 1 tchd 6 to 1) 8

1888² KADASTROF (Fr) [128] 7-11-6 B Powell, *keen hold, in tch, not fluent 5th, wknd 3 out.*............ (14 to 1 op 12 to 1) 9

2001⁵ NON VINTAGE (Ire) [126] 6-11-4 W Worthington, *beh frm 3 out.*.................... (14 to 1 op 12 to 1) 10

2290⁴ NASHVILLE STAR (USA) [108] (v) 6-10-0 D Bridgwater, *led second, hdd appr last, fdd.*.................... (50 to 1) 11

1612³ INTERMAGIC [111] 7-10-3 S Fox, *hld up, hdwy 3 out, weak-end appr last, eased.*............(10 to 1 op 8 to 1) 12

1612⁹ THINKING TWICE (USA) [134] 8-11-12 N Williamson, *keen hold early, prmnt, rdn aftr 3 out, eased betw frm 2.*
.... (25 to 1 op 20 to 1 tchd 33 to 1) 13

1612⁶ ABBEY STREET (Ire) [122] 5-11-0 J Osborne, *hld up, hdwy 5th, wknd frm 3 out, tld off whn pld up bef last, lme.*
.... (7 to 1 op 12 to 1) pu

Dist: 2½l, 4l, 2½l, 2½l, nk, 1¼l, 2l, 2½l, 6l, 9l. 4m 1.30s. a 7.30s (14 Ran).

SR: 25/27/35/33/28/33/26/16/24/ (S G Griffiths), S G Griffiths

DONCASTER (good)
Saturday January 25th
Going Correction: PLUS 0.15 sec. per fur. (races 1,5,6), PLUS 0.10 (2,3,4,7)

2330 'Great Yorkshire Meeting' Novices' Chase Class D (5-y-o and up) £4,029 2m 3f 110yds................(12:45)

WOODBRIDGE (Ire) 8-11-4 P Carberry, *led 1st till aftr 4th, rgned ld 5 out, styd on strly last 3, clr r-in.*
.... (20 to 1 op 16 to 1) 1

2003³ CARIBOO GOLD (USA) (bl) 8-11-4 A Thornton, *al hndy, chalg whn blun and nrly uns rdr 6 out, reco'red to chal 3 out, stumbled nxt, kpt on one pace....*(4 to 1 on op 6 to 1) 2

2201⁹ CURRAGH PETER 10-11-1 (3*) Guy Lewis, *led to 1st, styd upsides, led ag'n aftr 4th to 5 out, rdn and fdd last 3, tld off.*
.... (14 to 1) 3

1048 JUST SUPPOSEN (Ire) 6-11-1 (3*) E Callaghan, *settled to chase ldrs, efrt whn f 7th.*.......... (10 to 1 op 8 to 1) f

1881³ DOMAINE DE PRON (Fr) 4-11-4 T J O'Sullivan, *settled to track ldrs, rdn at work hlwy, last and struggling whn blun and uns rdr 4 out.*.................(10 to 1 op 8 to 1) ur

Dist: 2l, 24l. 5m 0.70s. a 15.70s (5 Ran).

(Sonny Purcell), F Murphy

2331 Bessacarr Handicap Hurdle Class C (0-135 4-y-o and up) £3,678 2m 110yds..................... (1:20)

2149⁴ SHINING EDGE [114] 5-10-12 G Bradley, *confidently rdn, smooth hdwy to draw level 2 out, shaken up to ld r-in, ridden out*.................... (11 to 1 op 10 to 1) 1

2149³ NEW INN [118] 6-11-2 K Gaule, *led, gd jump to go clr 3 out, jnd nxt, hdd and one pace r-in....*(14 to 1 op 12 to 1) 2

1923* SEVERN GALE [102] 7-9-7 (7*) X Aizpuru, *co'red up beh ldrs, efrt and drvn alng appr 3 out, styd on, no imprsn.*
.... (14 to 1 tchd 16 to 1) 3

2128 KAITAK (Ire) [119] 6-11-0 (3*) F Leahy, *settled midfield, efrt and bustled alng appr 3 out, kpt on same pace und pres frm nxt.*.................... (14 to 1 tchd 16 to 1) 4

1885² DESERT FIGHTER [112] 6-10-7 (3*) G Lee, *settled to track ldrs, rdn at work whn pace quickened frm 3 out, fdd.*
.... (14 to 1 op 12 to 1) 5

1761 CHARMING GIRL (USA) [129] 6-11-13 J A McCarthy, *strug-gling to go pace hfwy, lost tch bef 3 out, tld off.*
.... (14 to 1 tchd 16 to 1) 6

1990⁴ MR BUREAUCRAT (NZ) [115] 8-10-13 R Johnson, *al wl plcd, feeling pace and rdn 3 out, wknd quickly, tld off.*
.... (12 to 1 op 10 to 1) 7

NIJMEGEN [130] 8-12-0 P Carberry, *tucked away beh ldrs, hmpd by faller 4th, lost pl bef 3 out, tld off.*
.... (25 to 1 op 20 to 1) 8

2044* ALBEMINE (USA) [124] 8-11-8 T Kent, *tucked away in mid-field, efrt hfwy, lost tch frm 3 out, tld off.*
.... (11 to 2 op 6 to 1 tchd 13 to 2) 9

1990⁶ SAINT CIEL (USA) [108] 9-10-6 S Wynne, *chsd ldrs, und pres bef 3 out, lost tch, tld off.*............(20 to 1 op 16 to 1) 10

1990* TEJANO GOLD (USA) [119] 7-11-3 A Thornton, *settled to track ldrs, efrt whn f 4th.* (7 to 1 op 6 to 1 tchd 15 to 2) f

CELESTIAL CHOIR [114] 7-10-12 Richard Guest, *settled in tch, efrt whn f 4 out*.......(5 to 1 op 9 to 2 tchd 4 to 1) f

2186* LE KHOUMF (Fr) [117] 6-11-1 M A Fitzgerald, *patiently rdn, efrt hfwy, eased whn btn 3 out, pld up betw last 2.*
.... (11 to 4 fav op 4 to 1) pu

Dist: 1¼l, 9l, ¾l, 12l, 8l, 1l, 11l, 7l, 9l. 3m 56.30s. a 6.30s (13 Ran).

SR: 37/39/14/30/11/20/5/9/ (G Graham), T D Easterby

2332 Doncaster Sponsorship Club Handicap Hurdle Class C (0-135 4-y-o and up) £3,834 2½m............. (1:50)

1914⁶ DUAL IMAGE [104] 10-10-2 P Carberry, *confidently rdn, improved on bit to ld bef 2 out, drvn out r-in.*
.... (11 to 1 op 10 to 1 tchd 12 to 1) 1

1925³ DOMAPPEL [111] 5-10-9 T Kent, *led aftr 1st, clr 3rd, mstks 5th and nxt, hdd bef 2 out, one pace und pres r-in.*
.... (7 to 2 tchd 10 to 3) 2

2217 ALLTIME DANCER (Ire) [117] (bl) 5-11-1 J A McCarthy, *al wl plcd, ev ch and drvn alng frm 3 out, styd on same pace from betw last 2.*.................... (14 to 1 op 12 to 1) 3

1914³ PUREVALUE (Ire) [110] 6-10-8 R Johnson, *settled to track ldrs, efrt 6th, und pres whn pace quickened 3 out, lost tch, tld off.*.................... (7 to 4 fav tchd 15 to 8) 4

1284⁶ OUR KRIS [120] 5-11-4 J R Kavanagh, *nvr far away, und pres whn pace quickened appr 3 out, wknd quickly, tld off.*
.... (20 to 1) 5

2004⁶ ALBERTITO (Fr) [102] 10-10-0 S Wynne, *led till aftr 1st, styd hndy, struggling to keep in tch 4 out, lost touch, tld off.*
.... (33 to 1 op 25 to 1) 6

BLAST FREEZE (Ire) [126] 8-11-10 M A Fitzgerald, *patiently rdn, smooth hdwy to join issue aftr 3 out, upsides whn f nxt.*
.... (6 to 1 tchd 13 to 2) f

1691² RALITSA (Ire) [105] 5-9-10 (7*) R Burns, *settled to track ldg bunch, efrt whn hit 6th, lost pl quickly and pld up bef 4 out.*
.... (9 to 2 tchd 5 to 1) pu

Dist: 1¾l, 1½l, dist, 13l, 6l. 4m 49.90s. a 14.90s (8 Ran).

(Datum Building Supplies Limited), J G FitzGerald

2333 Napoleons Racing River Don Novices' Hurdle Class A Grade 2 (4-y-o and up) £9,883 2½m.........(2:25)

1868* INN AT THE TOP 5-11-6 Derek Byrne, *made all, quickened bef 3 out, hrd pressed last three, ran on frm last.*
.... (5 to 1 op 9 to 1) 1

1995² MIGHTY MOSS (Ire) 6-11-10 Mr F Hutsby, *nvr far away, rdn to chal 3 out, edgd lft und pres and blun nxt, one pace r-in.*
.... (11 to 10 fav op 6 to 4 tchd 13 to 8) 2

2153* HOH WARRIOR (Ire) 6-11-10 G Bradley, *al wl plcd, drvn level 3 out, one pace frm betw last 2.......*.(6 to 1 tchd 11 to 2) 3

1882² IONIO (USA) 6-11-10 J R Kavanagh, *settled in tch, feeling pace and lost grnd quickly bef 3 out, tld off.*
.... (9 to 4 op 2 to 1) 4

1517⁴ SQUIRE'S OCCASION (Can) 4-10-11 R Johnson, *chsd ldrs, reminders 4th, struggling bef 3 out, tld off.*
.... (16 to 1 op 12 to 1 tchd 20 to 1) 5

Dist: 2l, 2½l, 27l, dist. 4m 47.20s. a 12.20s (5 Ran).

(Mrs Sylvia Blakeley), J Norton

2334 Pertemps Great Yorkshire Chase Handicap Chase Class B (0-145 5-y-o and up) £23,315 3m.........(3:00)

2007⁴ GENERAL COMMAND (Ire) [130] 9-11-10 P Carberry, *sn dis-puting ld, definite advantage 8 out, styd on strly to go clr frm betw last 2.*.................... (5 to 2 fav op 3 to 1) 1

1767³ KING LUCIFER (Ire) [130] 8-11-5 (5*) Mr R Thornton, *nvr far away, blun 6 out, prmsg effrt frm 3 out, kpt on same pace from betw last 2* .... (14 to 1 op 12 to 1) 2

1613* GOLDEN SPINNER [130] 10-11-10 M A Fitzgerald, *al wl plcd, chlgd frm 5 out, rdn and no extr from 3 out* .... (9 to 2 op 4 to 1 tchd 5 to 1) 3

1999⁴ TURNING TRIX [127] 10-11-7 J R Kavanagh, *settled midfield, effrt whn blun 7 out, rdn appr strt, one pace last 3.* (10 to 1) 4

1563² BETTY'S BOY (Ire) [127] 8-11-7 A Thornton, *nvr far away, ev ch appr 4 out, kep on same pace frm nxt.* .... (14 to 1 tchd 16 to 1) 5

1892* SOUNDS STRONG (Ire) [127] 8-11-7 R Johnson, *al chasing ldrs, feeling pace fnl circuit, styd on frm 4 out, no imprsn.* .... (9 to 2 op 4 to 1 tchd 5 to 1) 6

1304⁴ RUN UP THE FLAG [122] 10-10-13 (3*) Mr C Bonner, *tucked away in midfield, improved and ev ch appr 5 out, rdn and one pace frm nxt.* .... (12 to 1 tchd 14 to 1) 7

1960 DUHALLOW LODGE [113] 10-10-7 B Fenton, *settled in tch, feeling pace and lost grnd fnl circuit, styd on ag'n frm 4 out, no imprsn* .... (33 to 1) 8

1967⁵ PIMS GUNNER (Ire) [106] 9-10-0 D Bentley, *settled to chase ldrs, feeling pace fnl circuit, rdn ag'n frm 4 out, no imprsn.* .... (13 to 2 op 6 to 1) 9

1032 MENAI MASTER (Ire) [91] 13-10-13 S McNeill, *led till hdd 8 out, lost tch quickly bef 4 out, tld off.* .... (33 to 1 op 25 to 1 tchd 40 to 1) 10

1845² ROMANY CREEK (Ire) [119] 8-10-13 K Gaule, *beh whn blun and uns rdr second.* .... (16 to 1) ur

1634* EASBY JOKER [129] 9-11-9 G Bradley, *last but in tch, short lived effrt fnl circuit, no ch whn pld up betw last 2.* .... (13 to 2 op 6 to 1) pu

Dist: 5l, 6l, ½sl, 4l, 1¼l, 3l, 1¾l, sht-hd, dist. 6m 1.50s. a 7.50s (12 Ran).
SR: 57/52/46/42/38/36/28/17/10/ (Robert Ogden), G Richards

2335 Mansion House Handicap Chase Class B (5-y-o and up) £6,932 2m 110yds .... (3:35)

2191³ LORD DORCET (Ire) [132] 7-11-6 R Johnson, *al frnt rnk, jnd ldr hfwy, jmpd ahead 5 out, hrd pressed frm 2 out, kpt on strly to go clr r-in* .... (7 to 2 op 3 to 1 tchd 4 to 1) 1

1993³ NATIVE MISSION [132] 10-11-8 P Carberry, *settled gng wl, improved 4 out, str chal last 2, edgd lft und pres, one pace.* .... (4 to 1 tchd 7 to 2) 2

2212⁴ TIME WON'T WAIT (Ire) [135] 8-11-11 J Railton, *patiently rdn, hit 6 out, effrt last 4, styd on one pace frm betw last 2.* .... (3 to 1 fav op 11 to 4) 3

2000³ AROUND THE FARM [130] 10-11-6 S McNeill, *nvr far away, effrt 4 out, rdn and one pace frm betw last 2.* .... (8 to 1 tchd 9 to 1) 4

2212³ POLITICAL TOWER [129] 10-11-5 Richard Guest, *al tracking ldrs, effrt and drvn aing frm 4 out, styd on one pace und pres.* .... (15 to 2 op 7 to 1 tchd 8 to 1) 5

2046⁴ SUBLIME FELLOW (Ire) [118] 7-10-8 M A Fitzgerald, *led, jnd hfwy, hdd and blun 5 out, feeling pace whn blunded 3 out, tld off.* .... (8 to 1 op 10 to 1 tchd 11 to 1) 6

2191⁵ SYBILLIN [125] 11-11-1 Derek Byrne, *chsd ldrs, reminders aftr 6 out, lost tch frm nxt, tld off...* (20 to 1 tchd 25 to 1) 7

2219 CALLISOE BAY [138] 8-12-0 J A McCarthy, *settled in tch, jmpd stickly 5th, lost touch bef strt, tld off last 3.* .... (9 to 1 op 10 to 1) 8

Dist: 1½l, 7l, ¾l, nk, 2l, 26l, 9l. 4m 2.50s. a 8.50s (8 Ran).
SR: 32/32/28/22/21/8/-/-/ (John Hogg), J I A Charlton

2336 South Yorkshire Times Brewers Juvenile Novices' Hurdle Class C (4-y-o) £4,588 2m 110yds .... (4:10)

2188³ JACKSON PARK 11-6 R Johnson, *trkd ldr, str chai frm 3 out, slightly hmpd and swtchd last, ran on to ld r-in, drw clr.* .... (13 to 8 op 7 to 4 tchd 15 to 8) 1

1844³ ROYAL ACTION 11-0 J R Kavanagh, *led, hrd pressed frm 3 out, hdd and rdn r-in, kpt on same pace.* .... (6 to 4 fav op 11 to 8 tchd 13 to 8) 2

2195⁸ SEATTLE ALLEY (USA) 11-0 A Thornton, *patiently rdn, improved to join tdg pair aftr 3 out, ridden and one pace frm betw last 2* .... (12 to 1 op 16 to 1) 3

1737³ PARROT'S HILL (Ire) 11-0 Richard Guest, *trkd ldrs, effrt und pres to chase ldg trio appr 3 out, no imprsn frm nxt.* .... (7 to 1 op 6 to 1) 4

APACHE LEN (USA) 10-7 (7*) R Burns, *settled midfield, feeling pace whn ldrs quickened bef 3 out, no imprsn, tld off.* .... (16 to 1 op 14 to 1) 5

MIGHTY KEEN 11-0 D Skyrme, *chsd ldrs to hfwy, lost tch quickly aftr 4 out, tld off...* (25 to 1 op 20 to 1) 6

SOCIETY GIRL 10-4 (5*) Michael Brennan, *keen hold, in tch in midfield till whnd quickly bef 3 out, sn lost touch, tld off.* .... (14 to 1 op 16 to 1 tchd 20 to 1) 7

CLASSIC COLOURS (USA) 11-0 K Gaule, *chsd ldrs, hrd at work frm hfwy, tld off bef 3 out.* .... (33 to 1 op 20 to 1) 8

LITTLE MURRAY 11-0 P Carberry, *chsd ldrs to hfwy, strug-gling bef 3 out, sn lost tch, tld off...* (33 to 1 op 20 to 1) 9

Dist: 1¼l, 3½l, 13l, 25l, 21l, 1½l, 14l, dist. 4m 0.10s. a 10.10s (9 Ran).
SR: 8/-/-/-/-/-/ (C H Stevens), T D Easterby

NAAS (IRE) (good)

2337 Sallins Maiden Hurdle (4-y-o) £3,082 2m .... (1:15)

2074² STRATEGIC PLOY 10-9 T J Mitchell, ... (5 to 1) 1
2050⁸ CORN ABBEY (Ire) 11-0 F Woods, ... (6 to 1) 2
2112³ CENTO (Ire) (bl) 11-0 A Powell, ... (6 to 1) 3
2112⁴ PEGUS JUNIOR (Ire) 10-7 (7*) S M McGovern, ... (12 to 1) 4
ALAMBAR (Ire) 10-7 (7*) B J Geraghty, ... (14 to 1) 5
MALDINION 10-9 A Powell, ... (8 to 1) 6
620⁸ RIVER VALLEY LADY (Ire) 10-9 T P Treacy, ... (14 to 1) 7
WELCOME PARADE 11-0 C O'Dwyer, ... (4 to 1 fav) 8
2161³ RED TONIC (USA) 11-0 L P Cusack, ... (10 to 1) 9
2230 NASCIMENTO (USA) 11-0 F J Flood, ... (14 to 1) 10
2161⁷ KAYALIYNA (Ire) 10-9 T Horgan, ... (20 to 1) 11
2067⁸ COMRADE CHINNERY (Ire) 11-0 J P Broderick, ...(10 to 1) 12
2161² NATIVE ECLIPSE (Ire) 11-0 C F Swan, ... (8 to 1) 13
2161⁹ LOVELY PROSPECT 10-2 (7*) R P Hogan, ...(33 to 1) 14
1616⁹ AUTOBABBLE (Ire) 10-11 (3*) K Whelan, ...(33 to 1) 15
1616 BLUE BIT (Ire) 11-0 K F O'Brien, ... (14 to 1) 16
GOLDSCENTED (Ire) 11-0 A J O'Brien, ... (16 to 1) 17
2161 CHUPHOGA (bl) 10-9 D J Casey, ... (33 to 1) 18
MY NIECE (Ire) 10-9 D T Evans, ... (25 to 1) 19
PICARD (Ire) 11-0 T P Rudd, ... (25 to 1) 20
2074⁸ CEOTTHAS LASS (Ire) 10-31 (7*) Mr R J Cooper, .. (50 to 1) f
2230 LOUGH SLANIA (Ire) 10-7 (7*) I Browne, ...(10 to 1) ur
2230⁸ FAMILY PROJECT (Ire) 10-2 (7*) M W Martin, ...(10 to 1) pu
2067⁶ FALCON'S FIRE (Ire) 11-0 P L Malone, ... (14 to 1) pu
1430 MAGICAL IMPACT (Ire) 11-0 P McWilliams, ...(33 to 1) pu
Dist: 12l, hd, 1l, 2½l. 4m 2.30s. (25 Ran).

(John McKay), John McKay

2338 Cedar Building Handicap Chase (0-116 5-y-o and up) £3,767 3m .... (1:45)

2059* IRISH LIGHT (Ire) [-] 9-11-0 J P Broderick, ... (5 to 2 fav) 1
1413 DEE ELL [-] 11-11-8 F Woods, ... (5 to 1) 2
2169³ OLYMPIC D'OR (Ire) 9-11-3 J Shortt, ... (9 to 1) 3
2020 BERMUDA BUCK [-] 11-11-0 D T Evans, ... (14 to 1) 4
2141⁶ WEST BROGUE (Ire) [-] (bl) 8-11-7 T Horgan, ...(12 to 1) 5
2169² CASTALINO [-] 11-11-2 C F Swan, ... (5 to 1) 6
2125⁵ GARABAGH (Ire) [-] 8-10-9 P McWilliams, ...(14 to 1) 7
2163⁵ HOTEL SALTEES (Ire) [-] 9-10-4 T P Rudd, ...(16 to 1) 8
2143 VULPIN DE LAUGERE (Fr) [-] 10-9-11 (3*) K Whelan, ... (10 to 1) 9
1755³ TEAL BRIDGE [-] 12-11-6 T J Mitchell, ... (5 to 1) f
2226³ QUICK LEARNER (Ire) [-] 8-10-6 C O'Dwyer, ...(5 to 1) f
2091⁵ IF YOU SAY YES (Ire) [-] (bl) 9-10-0 D J Casey, ...(14 to 1) pu
Dist: 9l, 20l, 12l, 6l. 6m 45.70s. (12 Ran).

(Michael J McDonagh), Michael J McDonagh

2339 Naas Maiden Hurdle (5-y-o and up) £3,082 2½m .... (2:15)

2111² LIVER BIRD (Ire) 7-12-0 C O'Dwyer, ...(11 to 10 fav) 1
2135⁶ CAIRNCROSS (Ire) 6-11-6 J P Broderick, ...(20 to 1) 2
1618 JORIDI LE FORIGE (Ire) (bl) 6-11-6 T P Rudd, ...(14 to 1) 3
MOUNT DRUID (Ire) 7-11-6 J Shortt, ... (16 to 1) 4
2088³ DESERTMORE (Ire) 7-10-13 (7*) Mr N D Fehily, ...(12 to 1) 5
2140² EBONY KING (Ire) 7-11-11 (3*) U Smyth, ...(6 to 1) 6
2138⁹ BRASS BAND (Ire) 6-10-91 (7*) Mr R H Fowler, ...(14 to 1) 7
2087³ AS ROYAL (Ire) 6-11-11 (3*) G Cotter, ... (8 to 1) 8
2135⁹ VERYWELL (Ire) 6-10-13 (7*) Mr R Geraghty, ...(33 to 1) 9
2162⁷ VIVIANS VALE (Ire) 6-11-0 (7*) D K Budds, ...(16 to 1) 10
2137 ST CAROL (Ire) 6-11-1 P L Malone, ... (16 to 1) 11
2129⁷ DROICHEAD LAPEEN 10-11-7 (7*) Mr T J Beattie, .. (14 to 1) 12
2081⁸ HEAD CHAPLAIN (Ire) 6-11-6 K F O'Brien, ...(25 to 1) 13
2075⁷ TAR AND CEMENT (Ire) 9-10-13 (7*) A O'Shea, ...(33 to 1) 14
2131 SHINDARAR (Ire) 6-11-6 H Rogers, ... (20 to 1) 15
2037⁹ MYSTICAL AIR (Ire) 7-11-6 D T Evans, ... (20 to 1) 16
2222 KILKEA (Fr) 6-11-1 J K Kinane, ... (66 to 1) 17
2049 DOUBLE COLOUR (Ire) 5-11-3 (7*) A P Sweeney, .(20 to 1) 18
2111³ BRUSHETTA (Ire) 5-10-11 T P Treacy, ... (12 to 1) 19
2222 DAN PATCH 11-12-0 L P Cusack, ... (33 to 1) 20
2137² QUIPTECH (Ire) 6-11-6 T J Mitchell, ... (12 to 1) 21
2054 MINE'S A PINT (Ire) 5-10-11 C N Bowens, ...(33 to 1) 22
2081⁶ GLENREEF BOY (Ire) 8-12-0 A Powell, ... (20 to 1) 23
2225⁸ HAMSHIRE GALE (Ire) 7-11-1 F Woods, ... (33 to 1) 24
EXPERT ADVICE (Ire) 6-11-6 D J Casey, ... (16 to 1) 25
2075⁸ CAN'T BE STOPPED (Ire) 5-10-9 (7*) J P Deegan, .(66 to 1) 26
2131 FLOWERS OF MAY (Ire) 6-10-8 (7*) R P Hogan, ...(33 to 1) 27
2135⁴ THE GREY MARE (Ire) 8-11-4 (5*) P Morris, ...(14 to 1) f
2166³ EOIN'S ORCHESTRA (Ire) 8-11-6 (3*) C F Swan, ...(9 to 2) pu
HOTCHPOT (Ire) 8-11-6 P A Roche, ... (25 to 1) pu
Dist: Hd, 15l, hd, 12l. 5m 6.90s. (30 Ran).

(G B F Clarke), J A Berry

2340 Celbridge Handicap Hurdle (4-y-o and up) £5,480 2m 3f .... (2:45)

2128⁵ METASTASIO [-] (bl) 5-11-3 H Rogers, ...(11 to 4 fav) 1
2128⁹ MAGICAL LADY (Ire) [-] 5-11-11 C O'Dwyer, ...(7 to 1) 2
2128 CLIFDON FOG (Ire) [-] 6-10-10 (7*) M W Martin, ...(6 to 1) 3
2227⁷ APPELLATE COURT [-] (bl) 9-9-8 (7*) B J Geraghty, (25 to 1) 4
2227⁴ REASILVIA (Ire) [-] 7-11-3 J Shortt, ... (8 to 1) 5

1278*	YELAPA PRINCE (Ire) [-] 6-11-1 D J Casey,	(9 to 1)	6
2134	TALINA'S LAW (Ire) [-] (bl) 5-11-1 T P Treacy,	(12 to 1)	7
2051⁵	SLEEPY HORN (Ire) [-] 6-10-2 F Woods,	(11 to 2)	8
2134	CEILI QUEEN (Ire) [-] 5-11-3 C F Swan,	(8 to 1)	9
2134⁵	RATHGIBBON (Ire) [-] 6-10-6 (3*) G Cotter,	(7 to 1)	10
2127	TRYFIRION (Ire) [-] 8-11-11 K F O'Brien,	(10 to 1)	11
	CHANCE COFFEY [-] 12-11-7 G M O'Neill,	(20 to 1)	12
	KARABAKH (Ire) [-] 8-10-13 (5*) P Morris,	(20 to 1)	13
2229	JANE DIGBY (Ire) [-] 5-10-11 T Horgan,	(16 to 1)	14
2051⁹	MAJESTIC MAN (Ire) [-] 6-10-10 T J Mitchell,	(20 to 1)	pu

Dist: 5½l, 2l, 9l, sht-hd. 4m 48.00s. (15 Ran).

(F Mallon), D G McArdle

2341 Naas Novice Chase (Grade 3) (5-y-o and up) £6,850 3m............(3:15)

2125*	ULTRA FLUTTER 10-11-11 J P Broderick,	(6 to 4 fav)	1
2068⁵	AMBLE SPEEDY (Ire) 7-11-11 F Woods,	(100 to 30)	2
2083²	LE GINNO (Fr) 10-11-8 T P Treacy,	(12 to 1)	3
1898⁹	EXECUTIVE OPTIONS (Ire) 8-11-5 J Shortt,	(7 to 1)	4
2143*	FOLLY ROAD (Ire) 7-11-8 P L Malone,	(7 to 1)	5
2164*	FERRYCARRIGCRYSTAL (Ire) 9-11-8 K F O'Brien,	(8 to 1)	6
2143²	IRISH PEACE (Ire) 9-11-5 C O'Dwyer,	(9 to 1)	7
2143	BAILEYS BRIDGE (Ire) 6-10-12 (7*) M D Murphy,	(66 to 1)	8
2143⁹	BRAVE FOUNTAIN (Ire) 9-11-5 C F Swan,	(8 to 1)	9
1077	PENNY POT 5-9-13¹ (7*) Mr J L Cullen,	(66 to 1)	10
2135⁷	CESAR DU MANOIR (Fr) 7-11-2 (3*) K Whelan,	(20 to 1)	ur
2125⁶	RADIANT RIVER (Ire) 7-11-2 (3*) G Cotter,	(25 to 1)	ur

Dist: 11l, 5½l, 9l, 2½l. 6m 45.00s. (12 Ran).

(Donal Higgins), Michael Hourigan

2342 Irish Racing Writers Novice Hurdle (4-y-o and up) £3,082 2m..... (3:45)

2049*	I'M SUPPOSIN (Ire) 5-11-7 J Shortt,	(5 to 4 on)	1
2048*	FINNEGAN'S HOLLOW (Ire) 7-11-11 C F Swan,	(4 to 1)	2
1897*	GRAPHIC EQUALISER (Ire) 5-11-7 D T Evans,	(7 to 2)	3
2132²	BUGGY (Ire) 8-11-11 T J Mitchell,	(12 to 1)	4
2070³	DELPHI LODGE (Ire) 7-11-11 Mr A J Martin,	(8 to 1)	5
2222⁸	BLUSHING SAND (Ire) 7-10-12 (7*) Mr T J Beattie,	(14 to 1)	6
2137⁷	ENNEL GALE (Ire) 7-10-7 (7*) D A McLoughlin,	(33 to 1)	7
2275⁷	AFGHANI (Ire) 8-11-0 (5*) P Morris,	(25 to 1)	8
2160	HARRY HEANEY (Ire) 8-11-0 (5*) T Martin,	(100 to 1)	9
2138	SINGERS CORNER 5-10-7 (3*) U Smyth,	(200 to 1)	10

Dist: 7l, nk, 1½l, 1l. 4m 6.80s. (10 Ran).

(Nicholas G Cooper), Kevin Prendergast

2343 Kilcullen I.N.H. Flat Race (5-y-o and up) £3,082 2m 3f............ (4:15)

	SARSFIELD THE MAN (Ire) 6-12-0 Mr D Marnane,		
		(7 to 4 fav)	1
2222	BAR FLUTE (Ire) 6-11-6 (3*) Mr B M Cash,	(4 to 1)	2
	JENSALEE (Ire) 6-11-2 (7*) Mr A C Coyle,	(10 to 1)	3
	BACK TO THE NEST (Ire) 6-11-6 (3*) Mr R Walsh,	(5 to 1)	4
2079⁴	CLARA ROCK (Ire) 5-10-12 (7*) Mr C J Radley,	(14 to 1)	5
2172⁵	THETHREETOMS (Ire) 6-11-7 (7*) Mr T Gibney,	(20 to 1)	6
	LADY ELISE (Ire) 6-11-2 (7*) Mr J M Roche,	(25 to 1)	7
2098⁵	TOCHAR BOY (Ire) 6-12-0 Mr P Fenton,	(12 to 1)	8
2228⁴	DROMARA BREEZE (Ire) 9-12-0 Mr J A Berry,	(12 to 1)	9
2093³	DESMARFRAN (Ire) 8-11-9 (5*) Mr G Elliott,	(12 to 1)	10
	SOUNDSGOODTOME 6-11-9 Mr P F Graffin,	(10 to 1)	11
2110³	CLEARLY CANADIAN (Ire) 6-11-7 (7*) Mr A J Dempsey,		
		(10 to 1)	12
2144⁵	CULRUA ROSIE (Ire) 6-11-2 (7*) Mr E Sheehy,	(16 to 1)	13
	CARRAIGMACLEIR (Ire) 6-11-2 (7*) Mr M A Cahill,	(12 to 1)	14
1895⁸	OCTOBER SEVENTH (Ire) 6-11-7 (7*) Mr Paul J McMahon,		
		(12 to 1)	15
	PRIDE OF TIPPERARY (Ire) 6-11-2 (7*) Ms W Fox,	(16 to 1)	16
527	ROMANCEINTHEDARK (Ire) 7-11-2 (7*) Mr S P Ryan,		
		(25 to 1)	17
1838	TINVACOOSH (Ire) (bl) 6-12-0 Mr H F Cleary,	(25 to 1)	18
2137⁶	LOVELY LYNSEY (Ire) (bl) 5-10-12 (7*) Mr J P McNamara,		
		(10 to 1)	19
2137⁹	TULIP (Ire) 6-11-2 (7*) Miss A O'Brien,	(20 to 1)	20
2049⁸	ANDREA COVA (Ire) 5-11-5 Mr J P Dempsey,	(8 to 1)	21
	CALELLA PARSONS (Ire) 7-11-2 (7*) Miss T Schmill,		
		(25 to 1)	22
1174	ASHLEY LANE (Ire) 9-11-2 (7*) Mr E E Doyle,	(33 to 1)	23
2079	MIA LADY (Ire) 6-11-6 (3*) Mr P English,	(20 to 1)	24
1908	DRUMASHELLIG LADY (Ire) 6-11-2 (7*) Mr J T Murphy,		
		(50 to 1)	pu

Dist: 4½l, ¾l, 12l, 15l. 4m 49.00s. (25 Ran).

(J A Stewart), Liam Browne

AYR (good)
Monday January 27th
Going Correction: PLUS 0.80 sec. per fur. (races 1,3,6), PLUS 0.85 (2,4,5)

2344 Alloway Village 'National Hunt' Novices' Hurdle Class E (4-y-o and up) £2,556 2m................... (1:40)

1317	JERVAULX (Ire) 6-11-5 P Carberry, prmnt, mstk 6th, led bef 3 out, styd on wl	(8 to 1 op 5 to 1 tchd 10 to 1)	1

1390*	ARDARROCH PRINCE 6-11-5 P Niven, hld up, gd hdwy to track ldrs 6th, ev ch 2 out, kpt on same pace.		
		(9 to 4 fav op 5 to 2 tchd 11 to 4 and 2 to 1)	2
1327	PARSON'S LODGE (Ire) 9-11-0 R Supple, hld up towards rear, hdwy aftr 3 out, styd on strly frm last, nrst finish.		
		(66 to 1 op 50 to 1)	3
1962⁵	FILS DE CRESSON (Ire) 7-11-5 M Moloney, settled midfield, hdwy aftr 6th, rdn after 3 out, kpt on same pace.		
		(5 to 1 op 4 to 1 tchd 6 to 1)	4
1818⁵	MAITRE DE MUSIQUE (Fr) 6-11-0 (5*) Michael Brennan, cl up, led 4th till bef 3 out, wknd betw last 2... (10 to 1 op 6 to 1)		5
2188	MAPLETON 4-11-7 Richard Guest, chsd ldrs, outpcd bef 3 out, styd on frm nxt.	(33 to 1)	6
1962³	MAJOR HARRIS (Ire) 5-11-5 R Garritty, mid-div, no hdwy frm 6th.	(100 to 30 op 5 tchd 7 to 2)	7
2236	HENRY HOOLET 8-11-5 G Cahill, in tch, kpt on frm 3 out, nvr dngrs.	(100 to 1 op 66 to 1)	8
1983⁶	STORM CALL 6-11-0 D Bentley, beh, hdwy hlwy, outpcd aftr 6th, no dngr after.	(25 to 1)	9
2192	MY MAVOURNEEN 5-11-0 M Foster, prmnt till wknd bef 3 out.		
		(200 to 1)	10
	SHARP SAND 7-11-5 T Reed, chsd ldrs till wknd aftr 6th.		
		(100 to 1)	11
2236	TRIONA'S HOPE (Ire) 8-10-12 (7*) Tristan Davidson, sn beh.		
		(500 to 1)	12
2236	AUNT PIQUEE 8-11-0 A Dobbin, sn beh, tld off... (200 to 1)		13
1935²	SIOUX WARRIOR 5-11-2 (3*) E Husband, sn beh, tld off.		
		(25 to 1 op 20 to 1)	14
1695	SMART IN SATIN 7-11-5 L O'Hara, chsd ldrs, rdn and wknd bef 6th, tld off.	(200 to 1 op 100 to 1)	15
1311	KIRTLE MONSTAR 6-11-5 F Perratt, led to 4th, wknd aftr nxt, tld off.	(100 to 1 op 66 to 1)	16
1789⁷	BLOOD BROTHER 5-11-5 A Thornton, in tch, wknd bef 6th, tld off.	(25 to 1 op 16 to 1)	17
1590⁷	BOLD STATEMENT 5-11-5 N Bentley, hmpd and uns rdr 1st.		
		(5 to 1 tchd 6 to 1)	ur
1909	SOUNDS DEVIOUS 4-10-2 D Parker, hmpd and uns rdr 1st.		
		(200 to 1 op 100 to 1)	ur

Dist: 4l, 1½l, nk, ½l, 1¼l, nk, 1¾l, 8l, 1l, 5l. 3m 55.70s. a 19.70s (19 Ran).
SR: 22/18/11/16/15/1/13/11/-/

(Robert Ogden), G Richards

2345 Tam O'Shanter Novices' Chase Class D (5-y-o and up) £3,688 2m .... (2:10)

2201²	BOLD BOSS 8-11-3 B Storey, hld up, hdwy und pres hfwy, led bef 2 out, styd on wl.	(5 to 4 on op Evens)	1
1337⁹	NOORAN 6-11-3 P Carberry, chsd ldr, led 6th, blun badly 8th, rdn and hdd bef 2 out, kpt on... (33 to 1 tchd 50 to 1)		2
2149*	RALLEGIO 8-11-3 A Dobbin, hld up, hdwy hfwy, chlgd 8th, ev ch till no extr frm 2 out.... (5 to 2 op 7 to 2 tchd 4 to 1)		3
1912*	CROSSHOT 10-11-9 K Jones, in tch, ev ch whn hmpd and stumbled aftr 8th, sn lost pl, no dngr after.		
		(11 to 1 op 7 to 1 tchd 12 to 1)	4
2240⁵	FENWICK'S BROTHER 7-11-3 Richard Guest, in tch till out-pcd and lost pl hfwy, no dngr aftr.		
		(11 to 1 op 10 to 1 tchd 12 to 1)	5
2205	KNOW-NO-NO (Ire) 8-11-3 R Garritty, sn chasing ldrs, ev ch bef 4 out, wkng whn blun 2 out.		
		(14 to 1 op 10 to 1 tchd 12 to 1)	6
1823⁸	CORSTON JOKER 7-11-3 R Supple, towards rear, mstk 5th, nvr dngrs.	(10 to 1 op 14 to 1)	7
1950	FRIENDLY KNIGHT 7-11-3 T Reed, sn wl beh.....(16 to 1)		8
2202	SEE YOU ALWAYS (Ire) 8-11-3 M Foster, sn pushed alng, beh frm hfwy.	(66 to 1)	9
	EMERALD SEA (USA) 10-11-3 A Thornton, in tch whn blun and lost pl 4th, sn beh, tld off.	(25 to 1)	10
1657	GLINT OF AYR 7-10-12 G Cahill, sn wl beh, tld off whn pld up bef 6th.	(200 to 1)	pu
	MOSS PAGEANT 7-11-3 K Johnson, sn clr, hdd 6th, wknd quickly aftr 8th, tld off whn pld up bef 2 out.		
		(66 to 1 tchd 100 to 1)	pu

Dist: 2½l, 2l, 1½l, nk, 1¼l, 3l, 14l, nk, dist. 4m 5.30s. a 20.30s (12 Ran).
SR: 20/17/15/5/-/-/

(John Robson), G M Moore

2346 Soutar Johnny Novices' Hurdle Class E (5-y-o and up) £2,430 3m 110yds.................... (2:40)

1984²	SWANBISTER (Ire) 7-11-4 R Supple, trkd ldrs, led bef 3 out, sn hrd pressed, rdn and styd on wl frm last.		
		(5 to 4 fav op 11 to 10)	1
2192	SMIDDY LAD 6-10-12 D Bentley, settled midfield, smooth hdwy aftr 9th, chalg whn mstk 3 out, sn rdn, ch last, no extr.		
		(50 to 1)	2
1770⁷	CELTIC DUKE 5-10-12 R Garritty, towards rear, effrt bef 9th, kpt on frm 3 out, nvr dngrs............(25 to 1 op 16 to 1)		3
	ALLERBANK 6-11-4 M C Storey, in tch, drvn alng aftr 9th, kpt on und pres frm 2 out.	(100 to 1)	4
2199*	THE KHOINOA (Ire) 7-10-12 J Supple, mstks, beh, hdwy hfwy, ch 9th, wknd bef 3 out....(4 to 1 op 9 to 2 tchd 5 to 1)		5
1695⁷	FOUR FROM HOME (Ire) 5-10-12 A Roche, cl up, led 8th till bef 3 out, sn wknd.................(50 to 1 op 33 to 1)		6
2177⁷	DECENT PENNY 8-10-7 A Thornton, led to 8th, sn wknd.		
		(50 to 1)	7
2147²	LOSTRIS (Ire) 6-10-7 B Storey, in tch, wknd quickly aftr 9th, tld off.............(9 to 2 tchd 4 to 1 and 5 to 1)		8

1656 OBVIOUS RISK 6-10-5 (7*) Tristan Davidson, *sn beh, tld off 8th*.. (200 to 1) 9

2241^{6} MOVIE MAN 5-10-12 T Reed, *in tch, wknd quickly aftr 9th, tld off*.......... (20 to 1 op 25 to 1 tchd 33 to 1) 10

2241^{2} PEBBLE BEACH (Ire) 7-11-4 J Callaghan, *chsd ldrs, wkng whn f 9th*............................ (6 to 1 tchd 7 to 1) f

2241 BUSY BOY 10-10-12 J Burke, *sn beh, lost tch frm 8th, tld off whn pld up bef 3 out*........(100 to 1 tchd 500 to 1) pu

2192^{6} BORIS BROOK 6-10-5 (7*) S Melrose, *sn beh, drvn alng hfwy, lost tch frm 8th, tld off whn pld up bef 3 out*.........(25 to 1) pu

2147 HAWK HILL BOY 6-10-12 A Dobbin, *lost tch frm 8th, tld off whn pld up bef 3 out*..............(100 to 1 op 50 to 1) pu

Dist: 2l, 16l, 3½l, 18l, 3½l, 4l, 21l, 4l, 2½l. 6m 20.90s. a 39.90s (14 Ran).

(Colonel D C Greig), L Lungo

2347 Happy Birthday May Millar Novices' Handicap Chase Class E (0-105 5-y-o and up) £3,281 3m 1f....... (3:10)

1820^{6} KINGS SERMON (Ire) [78] 8-10-5 R Supple, *mstks, cl up, lft in ld 13th, clr 4 out, kpt on*........... (10 to 1 tchd 12 to 1) 1

1825^{5} NOOSA SOUND (Ire) [73] 7-10-0 B Storey, *prmnt, chsd wnr frm 13th, kpt on wl towards finish*. ....(6 to 1 op 5 to 1 tchd 7 to 1) 2

1994* COVERDALE LANE [90] 10-11-3 Mr P Murray, *beh, drvn alng hfwy, hdwy aftr 13th, 3rd and no imprsn whn blun 2 out*. .... (3 to 1 fav tchd 7 to 2) 3

2205^{6} GARBO'S BOY [79] 7-10-6 W Fry, *mstks, in tch, kpt on same pace frm 15th*........................(14 to 1 op 12 to 1) 4

2203^{7} BRIGHT DESTINY [73] (v) 6-10-0 G Cahill, *chsd ldrs till grad wknd frm 15th*.......................(33 to 1 tchd 50 to 1) 5

ABBEY LAMP (Ire) [93] 8-11-6 A Thornton, *prmnt, rdn aftr tenth, sn wknd, tld off*..............(25 to 1 op 16 to 1) 6

2005 QUIXALL CROSSETT [73] 12-9-9^{2} (7*) Tristan Davidson, *sn lost tch, tld off*..................................(50 to 1) 7

2146^{8} MR SLOAN [73] 7-9-11 (3*) G Lee, *chsd ldrs, drvn alng whn f 14th*..........(66 to 1 op 100 to 1 tchd 200 to 1) f

1820* MISTER TRICK (Ire) [79] 7-10-6^{1} R Garritty, *in tch whn f 7th*. ....(7 to 2) f

2205^{9} WEE WIZARD (Ire) [73] (bl) 8-9-9 (5*) S Taylor, *sn pushed alng and beh, tld off whn pld up bef 14th*.............. (50 to 1) pu

1944 VALLEY GARDEN [97] (bl) 7-11-10 P Carberry, *prmnt, drvn alng whn blun 15th, sn lost tch, tld off when pld up bef 3 out*. .... (16 to 1 op 14 to 1) pu

1820^{2} AYLESBURY LAD (Ire) [75] (bl) 8-10-2^{2} J Burke, *led, blun 8th, blunded badly and pld up 13th, dead*... (10 to 1 op 8 to 1) pu

ANSURO AGAIN [78] 8-10-5 P Niven, *beh, some hdwy bef 11th, mstk nxt, sn lost tch, pld up before 14th*. ....(6 to 1 op 5 to 1) pu

2146^{4} MAMICA [80] 7-10-7 N Smith, *beh, hdwy whn blun 11th, sn no ch, tld off when pld up bef 3 out*..................(5 to 1) pu

Dist: 1l, 17l, 3l, 10l, dist, 25l. 6m 38.10s. a 38.10s (14 Ran).

(Mrs P A H Hartley), P Beaumont

2348 Burns' Cottage Novices' Chase Class D (5-y-o and up) £3,824 2½m .... (3:40)

1659^{2} MR KNITWIT 10-11-4 A Dobbin, *trkd ldrs, led 4 out, sn quickened clr, easily*.......................(6 to 1 op 4 to 1) 1

1771^{6} LANSBOROUGH 7-11-4 P Carberry, *hmpd second, in tch, hdwy to track ldrs whn slightly hampered 4 out, sn chasing wnr, no imprsn*.......................(4 to 1 op 5 to 2) 2

JUDICIOUS CAPTAIN 10-11-4 Mr C Storey, *in tch, outpcd aftr 12th, kpt on frm 4 out*..............................(66 to 1) 3

2003 OAT COUTURE 9-11-10 A Thornton, *towards rear, effrt whn blun 11th, no ch aftr, tld off*. (4 to 1 op 3 to 1 tchd 9 to 2) 4

1775^{8} HIGHBEATH 6-11-4 P Niven, *towards rear, lost tch aftr 12th, tld off*..................(14 to 1 op 10 to 1 tchd 16 to 1) 5

RIFAWAN (USA) 6-11-4 D Walsh, *trkd ldr, led aftr 13th, jnd whn f 4 out, dead*..... (5 to 4 fav op 2 to 1 tchd 9 to 4) f

2062^{3} FINE TUNE (Ire) 7-11-4 M Foster, *f second*........(100 to 1) f

2240^{3} SINGING SAND 7-11-4 R Supple, *led, mstk 11th, hdd aftr 13th, wknd quickly 4 out, fourth and no ch whn f last*. .... (33 to 1 op 25 to 1) f

1963^{5} GRAND AS OWT 7-11-4 K Johnson, *lost tch frm 9th, tld off whn pld up bef 13th*................. (50 to 1 op 66 to 1) pu

1704^{6} ETHICAL NOTE (Ire) 6-11-4 Richard Guest, *tld off 8th, pld up bef 3 out*........................(100 to 1 op 200 to 1) pu

Dist: 11l, 1¾l, dist, 20l. 5m 19.60s. a 32.60s (10 Ran).

(Coupar Capital Racing), P Monteith

2349 Auld Brig Novices' Handicap Hurdle Class D (0-110 4-y-o and up) £3,218 2½m......................... (4:10)

2200^{4} PHAR ECHO (Ire) [85] 6-11-6 R Supple, *chsd ldr, led 3 out, sn hdd, rallied to ld aftr last, styd on und pres*. ....(5 to 1 op 4 to 1) 1

1586^{4} LIFEBUOY (Ire) [83] 6-11-4 T Reed, *mid-div, steady hdwy to ld aftr 3 out, hdd after last, no extr und pres*. .... (100 to 30 fav op 7 to 2 tchd 4 to 1) 2

PARIAH (Ire) [89] 8-11-10 P Niven, *hld up, hdwy to chase ldrs 3 out, no imprsn on 1st 2 frm nxt*...... (20 to 1 op 16 to 1) 3

2192 SUNNY LEITH [78] 6-10-13 A Dobbin, *led to 3 out, sn hdd, grad wknd*.............. (9 to 1 op 7 to 1 tchd 10 to 1) 4

570^{3} BLAZING TRAIL (Ire) [89] 9-11-10 A Thornton, *chsd ldrs, rdn bef 3 out, sn btn*.......................(10 to 1 op 8 to 1) 5

1872^{5} TEEJAY'N'AITCH (Ire) [79] 5-10-11 (3*) G Lee, *in tch, effrt bef 3 out, sn btn*.............................. (10 to 1 op 14 to 1) 6

2147^{3} BAREFOOT LANDING (USA) [76] 6-10-11 D Parker, *hld up, hdwy aftr 8th, rdn bef 3 out, sn wknd*.....(5 to 1 op 4 to 1) 7

1662 KASIRAMA (Ire) [78] 6-10-13 R Garritty, *in tch, effrt aftr 8th, ch bef 3 out, sn wknd*........(11 to 2 op 5 to 1 tchd 6 to 1) 8

2122^{9} KINGS MINSTRAL (Ire) [73] 7-10-8 J Burke, *chsd ldrs, wknd quickly aftr 8th, lost tch and pld up bef 3 out*. .... (9 to 1 op 6 to 1 tchd 10 to 1) pu

2145 MARTHA BUCKLE [65] 8-10-0 G Cahill, *hld up in rear, rdn aftr 8th, sn lost tch, pld up bef 3 out*.....(50 to 1 op 33 to 1) pu

Dist: 1l, 3l, 10l, 3l, nk, 1l, ½l. 5m 8.00s. a 30.00s (10 Ran).

(S H C Racing), L Lungo

PLUMPTON (good)
Monday January 27th

Going Correction: PLUS 1.25 sec. per fur. (races 1,2,4,7), PLUS 0.85 (3,5,6)

2350 Hickstead Maiden Hurdle Class F (Div I) (6-y-o and up) £1,917 2m 1f .... (1:30)

POMME SECRET (Fr) 4-10-10 C Maude, *made virtually all, rdn appr last, ran on wl*............. (9 to 2 op 7 to 2) 1

2153^{2} AVANTI EXPRESS (Ire) 7-11-8 J Osborne, *al in tch, chlgd 3 out, ev ch till not quicken r-in*..... (11 to 10 fav op 5 to 4) 2

EAU DE COLOGNE 5-11-8 M Richards, *trkd wnr to 6th, prmnt till wknd appr 2 out*.....(20 to 1 op 14 to 1 tchd 25 to 1) 3

1592^{7} IVORY COASTER (NZ) 6-11-8 C Llewellyn, *in tch till rdn and wknd appr 3 out*....... (25 to 1 op 14 to 1 tchd 33 to 1) 4

2197 CLOCK WATCHERS 9-11-8 D Morris, *prmnt till outpcd appr 3 out*..................................(100 to 1 op 50 to 1) 5

BARBARY FALCON 7-11-8 S McNeill, *hld up, hdwy to chase wnr hfwy, wknd appr 3 out*. .... (25 to 1 op 12 to 1 tchd 33 to 1) 6

BURN OUT 5-11-8 R Dunwoody, *chsd ldrs till wknd appr 3 out*.....................(3 to 1 op 2 to 1 tchd 100 to 30) 7

2013 BELLE PERK (Ire) 6-11-3 M A Fitzgerald, *in rear till effrt appr 7th, sn btn*........... (20 to 1 op 33 to 1 tchd 50 to 1) 8

1735 MURRAY'S MILLION 5-11-8 T J Murphy, *al towards rear, rdn and wknd 7th, tld off*................(100 to 1 op 50 to 1) 9

THE BIZZO 6-11-0 (3*) P Henley, *al beh, tld off*. ....(100 to 1 op 50 to 1) 10

1997 PERFECT PAL (Ire) 6-11-8 D Bridgwater, *al towards rear, rdn and wknd 7th, tld off*..... (12 to 1 op 8 to 1 tchd 14 to 1) 11

2181 PRINCE RUDOLF (Ire) 5-11-1 (7*) N Willmington, *al in rear, tld off 6th*............................ (100 to 1 op 25 to 1) 12

Dist: 4l, 11l, 14l, 12l, nk, 12l, ½l, 18l, 21l, 8l. 4m 24.50s. a 27.50s (12 Ran).

SR: 20/28/17/3/-/-/ (Elite Racing Club), M C Pipe

2351 Poynings Selling Handicap Hurdle Class G (0-90 6-y-o and up) £2,042 2m 1f..........................(2:00)

1816^{4} DO BE WARE [69] 7-10-8 B Fenton, *hld up, gd hdwy 4 out, led aftr nxt, all out*...................... (20 to 1 op 12 to 1) 1

1843* PHARLY REEF [75] 5-11-0 D J Burchell, *hld up, hdwy frm 6th, chlgd 2 out, kpt on und pres*............. (9 to 2 op 4 to 1) 2

520^{3} SUMMER VILLA [65] (bl) 5-10-4 J Ryan, *hld up, hdwy appr 2 out, ev ch last, ran on*.....(9 to 1 op 8 to 1 tchd 10 to 1) 3

1938^{9} SCRIPT [68] 6-10-7 J Osborne, *chsd ldr, led briefly 2 out, ev ch till rdn appr last, one pace r-in*.... (16 to 1 op 12 to 1) 4

1811^{3} WATER HAZARD (Ire) [69] 5-10-8 A Dicken, *in tch till outpcd appr 3 out*.............................(10 to 1 op 7 to 1) 5

1791^{3} MINSTER'S MADAM [89] (v) 6-11-11 (3*) T Dascombe, *led till rdn and hdd 3 out, sn btn*. ....(7 to 2 fav op 3 to 1 tchd 4 to 1) 6

2174^{8} LAJADHAL (Fr) [68] 8-10-7 L Harvey, *nvr on terms*. .... (20 to 1 op 12 to 1) 7

2009^{6} DERISBAY (Ire) [76] (bl) 9-11-1 D Morris, *trkd ldrs till wknd 4 out*....................................(33 to 1 op 25 to 1) 8

1969^{7} RUTH'S GAMBLE [61] (v) 9-10-0 D Leahy, *hld up, gd hdwy appr 4 out, rdn and wknd bef nxt*..... (16 to 1 op 14 to 1) 9

1978^{3} ECU DE FRANCE (Ire) [65] 7-10-4 S Fox, *trkd ldrs till wknd 4 out*..................(12 to 1 op 14 to 1 tchd 16 to 1) 10

1843^{9} LUCY TUFTY [81] 6-11-6 R Dunwoody, *hld up, effrt 6th, wknd appr 3 out*................(7 to 1 op 6 to 1 tchd 8 to 1) 11

NEVER FORGOTTEN [86] 12-11-11 N Mann, *al beh, tld off*. .... (33 to 1 op 25 to 1) 12

1921 HIGHLY DECORATED [80] (bl) 12-10-12 (7*) J K McCarthy, *mid-div, weakend 4 out, tld off*......... (33 to 1 op 25 to 1) 13

1811^{5} ALDWICK COLONNADE [75] 10-11-0 W McFarland, *al beh, tld off*....................................(12 to 1 op 8 to 1) 14

2009 WIDE SUPPORT [84] 12-11-9 P Holley, *mid-div till wknd hfwy, tld off*.............................(33 to 1 op 25 to 1) 15

1665^{7} FOUR WEDDINGS (USA) [75] 4-10-2 J R Kavanagh, *al beh, tld off*.......................................(20 to 1 op 12 to 1) 16

Dist: ¾l, hd, 2½l, 14l, 1l, 7l, 5l, 1¼l, 1l, 6l. 4m 27.50s. a 30.50s (16 Ran).

(John Ffitch-Heyes), J Ffitch-Heyes

2352 Lewes Novices' Chase Class E (5-y-o and up) £3,157 2m............(2:30)

2155* AMANCIO (USA) 6-11-9 M A Fitzgerald, *made all, jmpd wl, shaken up appr 2 out, sn clr, very easily.*
.................(9 to 2 op 3 to 1 on tchd 5 to 1 on) 1
2028² ROBINS PRIDE (Ire) 7-11-0 (3*) T Dascombe, *rcd 3rd, clsg whn lft clr second 4 out, sn rdn, one pace.* (5 to 1 op 7 to 2) 2
1970⁷ FURRY FOX (Ire) 9-11-3 D Morris, *lost tch 6th, tld off.*
................(25 to 1 op 14 to 1 tchd 33 to 1 and 50 to 1) 3
2304⁶ BRIGADIER SUPREME (Ire) 8-11-3 T J Murphy, *al beh, tailing off whn f 5 out, rmntd.* (100 to 1 op 20 to 1 tchd 150 to 1) 4
1725⁶ PURBECK CAVALIER (Ire) 8-11-0 (3*) P Henley, *chsd wnr, jst lost second pl whn blun badly and uns rdr 4 out.*
................(33 to 1 op 20 to 1 tchd 50 to 1) ur
Dist: 10l, dist, dist. 4m 11.60s. a 19.60s (5 Ran).
SR: 35/19/ (Lady Harrison), Mrs A J Perrett

2353 Hickstead Maiden Hurdle Class F (Div II) (4-y-o and up) £1,917 2m 1f
.... (3:00)

1410³ NO PATTERN 5-11-8 D Gallagher, *al prmnt, led 2 out, rdn out.*
.................(7 to 2 op 7 to 4) 1
COTTIER CHIEF (Ire) 6-11-8 R Dunwoody, *hld up in rear, gd hdwy 6th, rdn appr 2 out, swtchd lft bef hit last, no extr r-in.*
.................(9 to 4 fav op 5 to 2 tchd 3 to 1) 2
1560* BULA VOGUE (Ire) 7-11-3 D O'Sullivan, *chsd ldrs, led 3 out, hdd nxt, rallied r-in.*.....(10 to 1 op 4 to 1 tchd 11 to 1) 3
PERSIAN ELITE 6-11-8 J Osborne, *led to 4th, rdn four out, ev ch till one pace frm 2 out.*
.................(12 to 1 op 10 to 1 tchd 14 to 1) 4
WORTHY MEMORIES 8-11-3 Derek Byrne, *nvr on terms.*
.................(100 to 1 op 33 to 1) 5
VOILA PREMIERE (Ire) 5-11-8 K Gaule, *al towards rear, lost tch hfwy.*...........(100 to 30 op 4 to 1 tchd 9 to 2) 6
2221² TANGLEFOOT TIPPLE 6-11-5 (3*) P Henley, *trkd ldr, led 4th till hdd and wknd quickly four out.*
.................(15 to 2 op 5 to 1 tchd 8 to 1 and 9 to 1) 7
1560⁷ YARSLEY JESTER 5-11-3 J R Kavanagh, *al beh.*
.................(50 to 1 op 20 to 1 tchd 66 to 1) 8
SPEEDY SNAPS PRIDE 5-11-8 L Harvey, *mstk 3rd, al beh.*
.................(50 to 1 op 20 to 1) 9
2215⁶ ADILOV 5-11-8 D Morris, *chsd ldrs till f 6th.*
.................(20 to 1 op 12 to 1 tchd 25 to 1) f
CRAMPSCASTLE (Ire) 7-11-8 R Johnson, *in tch till wknd appr 2 out, pld up bef last.*.................(20 to 1 op 12 to 1) pu
Dist: 1¾l, nk, ½l, 23l, 11l, 9l, 6l, 1¼l. 4m 32.30s. a 35.30s (11 Ran).
(K Higson), G L Moore

2354 Plumpton Novices' Handicap Chase Class E (0-100 5-y-o and up) £3,503 2m 5f..........................(3:30)

1593³ CARDINAL RULE (Ire) [66] 8-10-1 R Johnson, *al prmnt, led 10th, rdn clr r-in.*.................(10 to 1 op 8 to 1) 1
2184³ WINNOW [69] 7-9-11 (7*) C Rae, *hld up, hdwy 10th, wnt second 4 out, not quicken appr last.*
.................(15 to 2 op 6 to 1 tchd 8 to 1) 2
2176⁵ DANTE'S VIEW (USA) [89] 9-11-10 M A Fitzgerald, *hld up, steady hdwy 10th, rdn and one pace frm 2 out.*
.................(11 to 2 op 4 to 1 tchd 6 to 1) 3
1891⁴ THERMAL WARRIOR [79] 9-11-0 G Upton, *hld up in rear, hdwy 3 out, nvr nrr.*......(10 to 1 op 8 to 1 tchd 12 to 1) 4
1734 HANGOVER [75] 11-10-7 (3*) G Hogan, *hld up, hdwy 9th, wknd appr 2 out.*.....(16 to 1 op 12 to 1 tchd 20 to 1) 5
1684⁵ PURBECK RAMBLER [68] (v) 6-10-3 B Fenton, *mstks, in tch till outpcd 5 out.*.................(20 to 1 op 25 to 1) 6
1857⁵ KOO'S PROMISE [80] 6-10-12 (3*) T Dascombe, *in tch till wknd 4 out.*.................(12 to 1 op 10 to 1) 7
2207⁶ MEL [71] 7-10-6 B Powell, *led to 3rd, led 5th to tenth, mstk 6 out, sn btn.*.................(6 to 1 op 7 to 1) 8
ROLLESTON BLADE [79] 10-10-7 (7*) Mr P O'Keeffe, *chsd ldrs till wknd 6 out.*.................(20 to 1 op 14 to 1) 9
1262⁷ SENSE OF VALUE [87] 8-11-8 W Marston, *al beh, tld off.*
.................(25 to 1 op 20 to 1 tchd 33 to 1) 10
1857 GERRY'S PRIDE (Ire) [68] 6-10-3 S Curran, *hld up in rear, hdwy 6 out, wknd 3 out, f last.*
.................(20 to 1 op 14 to 1 tchd 25 to 1) f
1857 SAXON MEAD [65] 7-10-0 G Tormey, *hld up, hdwy 9th, 3rd and held whn f 2 out.* (5 to 1 tchd 11 to 1 op 7 to 2) f
1814² RING CORBITTS [84] 9-11-5 J Railton, *blun and uns rdr 7th.*
.................(11 to 2 op 4 to 1 tchd 6 to 1) ur
1504³ MINOR KEY [87] 7-11-8 G Bradley, *led 3rd to 5th, beh whn pld up bef 6 out.*.................(14 to 1 op 12 to 1) pu
2244 HANSON STREET (NZ) [65] 10-10-0 K Gaule, *beh frm 9th, tld off whn pld up bef 2 out.*.................(25 to 1) pu
Dist: 5l, 1l, 4l, 1¾l, 9l, 17l, 9l, 4l, 14l. 5m 34.70s. a 28.70s (15 Ran).
(Peter J Burch), Miss Venetia Williams

2355 Albourne Handicap Chase Class F (0-105 5-y-o and up) £2,733 2m..............................(4:00)

1721⁵ WHIPPERS DELIGHT (Ire) [87] 9-10-10 Mr A Charles-Jones, *trkd 6th to 4 out, rallied 2 out, led last, drvn out.*
.................(20 to 1 op 1 tchd 25 to 1) 1
1921⁸ KINGS CHERRY (Ire) [104] 9-11-13 G Upton, *hld up, hdwy appr 3 out, ran on.*.....(14 to 1 op 12 to 1 tchd 16 to 1) 2

2184* OLLIVER DUCKETT [82] 8-10-5 G Tormey, *set fst pace till hdd last, no extr r-in.*.....(2 to 1 fav op 9 to 4 tchd 5 to 2) 3
1846³ WINSPIT (Ire) [86] 7-10-9 J R Kavanagh, *nvr far away, chsd ldr 4 out till blun 2 out, not reco'r.*
.................(9 to 2 op 4 to 5 tchd 5 to 1) 4
1816⁶ WHISTLING BUCK (Ire) [81] 9-10-4 D O'Sullivan, *in rear, some hdwy 4 out, nvr dngrs.*.......(10 to 1 tchd 11 to 1) 5
1327 SHREWD JOHN [91] 11-11-0 D Gallagher, *mid-div, nvr nr to chal.*.................(20 to 1 op 16 to 1 tchd 25 to 1) 6
CHURCHTOWN PORT (Ire) [99] 7-11-8 M A Fitzgerald, *chsd ldrs till rdn and wknd 5 out.* (8 to 1 op 7 to 1 tchd 9 to 1) 7
2279 RUSTIC GENT (Ire) [78] (v) 9-10-1 D Leahy, *al beh,tld off.*
.................(50 to 1 op 33 to 1) 8
1941* PEGMARINE (USA) [81] 14-10-4 J A McCarthy, *al beh, tld off.*
.................(10 to 1 op 7 to 1 tchd 11 to 1) 9
1980⁵ HALHAM TARN (Ire) [90] 7-10-6 (7*) A Dowling, *al prmnt, chsd ldr 6th to 4 out, sn wknd, f 2 out.*
.................(20 to 1 op 16 to 1 tchd 25 to 1) f
1941² SOLEIL DANCER (Ire) [84] 9-10-4 (3*) P Henley, *al beh, tld off whn pld up bef 5 out.*.....(13 to 2 op 5 to 1 tchd 7 to 1) pu
YOUNG ALFIE [77] (bl) 12-9-13² (3*) G Hogan, *al beh, tld off whn pld up bef 4 out.*.......(50 to 1 op 33 to 1) pu
Dist: 4l, 1½l, 10l, 6l, ½l, 8l, 23l, 10l. 4m 14.30s. a 22.30s (12 Ran).
SR: -/8/-/-/-/-/ (S P Tindall), G F H Charles-Jones

2356 Pyecombe Handicap Hurdle Class E (0-110 4-y-o and up) £2,490 2½m..............................(4:30)

2207⁴ FLAXLEY WOOD [83] 6-10-4 B Powell, *led 5th, rdn and ran on wl frm 2 out.*...........(11 to 2 op 7 to 2 tchd 6 to 1) 1
1951³ FAWLEY FLYER [92] 8-10-6 (7*) J Power, *led to 3rd, styd prmnt, chsd wnr 3 out, rdn and no extr frm nxt.*
.................(8 to 1 op 6 to 1) 2
2256⁴ TOTAL JOY (Ire) [92] 6-10-13 R Dunwoody, *hld up, hdwy 4 out, ev ch nxt, rdn and one pace aftr.*
.................(4 to 1 fav op 9 to 2 tchd 5 to 1 and 11 to 2) 3
1597⁵ CLAIRESWAN (Ire) [98] 5-11-5 K Gaule, *al prmnt, wknd appr 2 out.*.................(7 to 1 op 5 to 1) 4
2217⁶ SMUGGLER'S POINT (USA) [105] 7-11-12 D Morris, *led 3rd to 5th, wknd appr 3 out.*..(14 to 1 op 8 to 1 tchd 16 to 1) 5
1795³ INDIAN QUEST [104] 8-11-11 C Llewellyn, *mid-div, hdwy 4 out, wknd aftr nxt.*.......(8 to 1 tchd 6 to 1 to 10 to 1) 6
1688 KILCORAN BAY [88] 5-11-5 R Greene, *beh frm 7th.*
.................(10 to 1 op 16 to 1 tchd 20 to 1) 7
1695⁵ BON VOYAGE (USA) [95] (bl) 5-11-2 J R Kavanagh, *hld up, hdwy 7th, wknd 4 out.* (16 to 1 op 14 to 1 tchd 20 to 1) 8
1792⁴ MILLMOUNT (Ire) [93] (bl) 7-11-0 M A Fitzgerald, *beh frm 7th.*
.................(9 to 2 op 8 to 1) 9
1938 EQUITY'S DARLING (Ire) [79] 5-9-9 (5*) Mr R Thornton, *virtually refused to race, tld off frm second.*
.................(33 to 1 op 50 to 1) 10
2253⁵ HANDY LASS [98] 8-11-5 T J Murphy, *al beh, virtually pld up r-in.*...............(12 to 1 op 10 to 1 tchd 14 to 1) 11
1948 MINE'S AN ACE (NZ) [96] 10-11-3 R Johnson, *hld up in tch, wknd appr 3 out, tld off whn pld up bef last.*
.................(16 to 1 op 14 to 1 tchd 20 to 1) pu
2246 SAUSALITO BOY [87] 9-10-8 D Bridgwater, *very slwly away, tld off whn pld up aftr 3rd.*
.................(20 to 1 tchd 25 to 1 and 33 to 1) pu
Dist: 1½l, 4l, 8l, 6l, nk, 3l, 7l, 10l, 1¾l, 23l. 5m 15.60s. a 38.60s (13 Ran).
(Mrs D A La Trobe), R H Buckler

MUSSELBURGH (good to firm)
Tuesday January 28th
Going Correction: NIL

2357 McEwans Export Novices' Hurdle Class E (4-y-o and up) £2,574 2m..............................(1:20)

2117² MAPLE BAY (Ire) 8-11-5 A Dobbin, *in tch, hdwy aftr 5th, led betw last 2, ran on and pres.*
.................(11 to 2 op 9 to 2 tchd 6 to 1) 1
2116* BEST OF ALL (Ire) 5-11-7 M Moloney, *in tch, hdwy to chase ldr 5th, ev ch frm 2 out, no extr und pres r-in.*
.................(3 to 1 op 11 to 4 tchd 7 to 2) 2
2116³ FALCON'S FLAME (USA) 4-10-7 P Carberry, *hld up, smooth hdwy bef 2 out, ev ch whn mstk last, no extr und pres.*
.................(11 to 4 fav tchd 3 to 1) 3
HIGH HOPE HENRY (USA) 4-10-7 R Garritty, *hld up, hdwy aftr 6th, kpt on same pace frm betw last 2.*
.................(10 to 1 op 8 to 1 tchd 11 to 1) 4
2116² SHINEROLLA 5-11-5 D Parker, *mid-div, hdwy aftr 6th, rdn aftr 2 out, no headway.*.................(7 to 2 op 3 to 1) 5
NANCYS CHOICE 7-11-5 J Burke, *led second, blun 2 out, sn hdd and wknd.*...........................(100 to 1) 6
2192 THE SHARROW LEGEND (Ire) 5-11-0 (5*) S Taylor, *chsd ldrs till rdn and wknd aftr 2 out.*...........(50 to 1) 7
KNAVE 4-10-7 G Cahill, *nvr on terms.*..........(25 to 1) 8
1695⁹ PRIMITIVE HEART 5-11-5 A S Smith, *led to second, chsd ldrs till wknd aftr 6th.*...........(25 to 1 op 20 to 1) 9
ON THE OFF CHANCE 5-11-5 R Supple, *beh most of way.*
.................(66 to 1 op 50 to 1) 10

1911⁹ MANNAGAR (Ire) 5-11-0 (5*) R McGrath, *beh most of way, fnshd distressed*................(100 to 1 tchd 150 to 1)   11
2116 DESERT LORE 6-11-5 B Storey, *chsd ldrs till wknd aftr 5th, tld off*............................(200 to 1)   12
Dist: 2l, ½l, 7l, nk, 9l, 2l, 12l, 7l, 12l, 5l. 3m 44.30s. a 7.30s (12 Ran).
SR: 18/18/3/-/8/-/   (Ferrograph Limited), B Ellison

2358 Beamish Red Irish Ale Novices' Chase Class E (5-y-o and up) £3,070 2m...........................(1:50)

22017 URBAN DANCING (USA) 8-11-3 K Johnson, *in tch, drvn alng bef 3 out, styd on und pres to ld fnl 100 yards.*
.........................(5 to 1 op 6 to 1 tchd 11 to 2)   1
22024 APPEARANCE MONEY (Ire) 6-10-12 P Carberry, *hld up, hdwy to track ldr 7th, led on bit 3 out, stumbled last, hdd fnl 100 no, extr.*.........(10 to 1 op 20 to 1 tchd 25 to 1)   2
20634 ARCTIC SANDY (Ire) 7-11-3 B Storey, *hld up, hdwy to chase ldr 5th, lft in ld 7th, mstk and hdd 3 out, sn rdn, kpt on same pace*..............(5 to 2 fav op 9 to 4 tchd 11 to 4)   3
2240 MOVAC (Ire) 8-11-10 M Moloney, *chsd ldrs till wknd aftr 7th, tld off*...............(10 to 1 op 8 to 1 tchd 12 to 1)   4
22047 TAPATCH (Ire) (bl) 9-11-3 R Garritty, *chasing ldr whn f 4th.*
...........................(11 to 2 op 4 to 1 tchd 6 to 1)   f
22014 CHORUS LINE (Ire) 8-10-12 R Supple, *led till blun badly and uns rdr 7th.*.......................(7 to 2 op 3 to 1)   ur
21496 BOLANEY GIRL (Ire) 8-10-12 A Dobbin, *refused to race, took no part.*...........................(10 to 1)   l
Dist: 2½l, 1½l, dist. 3m 55.00s. a 6.00s (7 Ran).
SR: 29/21/24/-/   (Ronald McCulloch), B Ellison

2359 Gillespie Malt Stout Novices' Handicap Hurdle Class E (0-100 4-y-o and up) £2,616 2½m.............(2:20)

22793 HEAVENS ABOVE [62] 5-10-1 P Carberry, *cl up, led on bit 2 out, drvn out r-in*..................(7 to 2 fav tchd 4 to 1)   1
1629 PRELUDE TO FAME (USA) [89] 4-11-1 A Dobbin, *cl up, led 5th to 2 out, rdn and kpt on wl*........(8 to 1 tchd 10 to 1)   2
2204 COMES HERBIE [80] 5-11-5 M Moloney, *sn chasing ldrs, kpt on wl frm betw last 2*......(14 to 1 tchd 16 to 1)   3
20028 THORNTOUN ESTATE (Ire) [74] (bl) 4-9-7 (7*) M McCormack, *mstks, in tch, hdwy aftr 9th, sn drvn alng, kpt on same pace frm 2 out*.................(9 to 2 op 8 to 1 tchd 10 to 1)   4
17832 ARIAN SPIRIT (Ire) [80] 6-11-5 B Storey, *in tch, no hdwy frm 2 out*................(13 to 2 op 11 to 2 tchd 7 to 1)   5
20633 LITTLE REDWING [69] (v) 5-10-8 R Garritty, *mid-div, pushed alng aftr 8th, nvr dngrs*...........(12 to 1 tchd 14 to 1)   6
19288 NOT TO PANIC (Ire) [65] 7-10-4 A S Smith, *chsd ldrs till wknd aftr 2 out*...........(14 to 1 op 12 to 1 tchd 16 to 1)   7
21187 DOUBLING DICE [68] 6-10-0 (7*) S Melrose, *nvr better than mid-div*..................(16 to 1 op 14 to 1)   8
19645 PANGERAN (USA) [88] 5-11-13 J Supple, *in tch till wknd aftr 9th*........................(8 to 1 op 6 to 1)   9
22418 THE NEXT WALTZ (Ire) [75] 6-11-0 R Supple, *in tch till wknd aftr 9th*..................(8 to 1 op 7 to 1)   10
21185 SCHOOL OF SCIENCE [61] (bl) 7-10-0 S McDougall, *made most to 5th, chsd ldrs till wknd aftr 9th*.....(50 to 1)   11
2202 SECONDS AWAY [61] 6-10-0 G Cahill, *sn beh*........(33 to 1)   12
15227 FLAMING HOPE (Ire) [78] (v) 7-11-3 J Burke, *chsd ldrs to 7th, sn wknd*......................(10 to 1)   13
GREENFIELD MANOR [72] 10-10-6 (5*) S Taylor, *sn beh.*
...............................(33 to 1)   14
19519 RUBISLAW [61] 5-9-7 (7*) Miss S Lamb, *sn beh, tld off*
...............................(100 to 1)   15
Dist: ¾l, 1l, 8l, ¾l, nk, 1¼l, 1¼l, 14l, 2l, 4l. 4m 45.30s. a 7.30s (15 Ran).
SR: -/13/16/-/7/-/   (R & G Leonard), F Murphy

2360 Kilmany Cup Handicap Chase Class D (0-120 5-y-o and up) £3,525 2½m ....(2:50)

2121* WAYUPHILL [98] 10-10-7 B Storey, *hld up, hdwy bef 11th, led 4 out, styd on wl*.....(13 to 8 fav op 6 to 4 tchd 7 to 4)   1
19104 VICARIDGE [93] 10-10-2 A S Smith, *jmpd lft, prmnt, made aftr 8th to 4 out, blun 2 out, no extr.*
...............................(7 to 1 op 8 to 1 tchd 9 to 1)   2
19326 CHARMING GALE [98] 10-10-7 M Foster, *led till aftr 8th, prmnt, drvn alng after 4 out, grad wknd.* (8 to 1 op 5 to 1)   3
21215 RAPID MOVER [91] (bl) 10-10-0 M Moloney, *trkd ldrs, rdn bef 4 out, sn wknd*..................(50 to 1 op 20 to 1)   4
16782 TIMBUCKTOO [119] 10-12-0 A Dobbin, *chsd ldrs till wknd aftr 4 out*...............(9 to 2 op 7 to 2)   5
23002 PURITAN (Can) [109] (bl) 8-11-2 P Jones, *beh, hdwy bef 4 out, 3rd and no imprsn whn hmpd and uns rdr last.*
...............................(9 to 2 op 4 to 1)   ur
21214 GRAND SCENERY (Ire) [91] 9-10-0 P Carberry, *blun and uns rdr second*....................(8 to 1 op 7 to 1)   ur
Dist: 10l, 3½l, 1¾l, 18l. 4m 57.90s. a 10.90s (7 Ran).
(Mr & Mrs Raymond Anderson Green), C Parker

2361 McEwans 70/- Handicap Hurdle Class D (0-125 4-y-o and up) £3,659 3m.........................(3:20)

22005 CHEATER (Ire) [86] (bl) 6-10-0 P Carberry, *made all, rdn aftr 2 out, styd on wl*...............(10 to 1 tchd 12 to 1)   1

2120* HIGHLAND PARK [86] 11-10-0 A Dobbin, *in tch, pushed alng aftr tenth, hdwy to chase wnr 2 out, ev ch after last, no extr und pres*...............(11 to 2 op 6 to 1 tchd 5 to 1)   2
21203 SUPERTOP [111] 9-11-11 R Supple, *hld up, hdwy aftr 11th, ev ch betw last 2, sn rdn, kpt on same pace.*
...............................(9 to 4 op 13 to 1)   3
1929* INVEST WISELY [97] 5-10-11 R Garritty, *chsd wnr, ev ch whn stumbled 2 out, sn rdn and btn.*
...............................(11 to 8 fav op Evens tchd 6 to 4)   4
21518 OLD HABITS (Ire) [108] 8-11-8 B Storey, *hld up, hdwy to chase ldrs 11th, outpcd bef 2 out, no dngr aftr.*
...............................(16 to 1 op 12 to 1)   5
2200 CARNMONEY (Ire) [86] 9-9-9 (5*) S Taylor, *chsd ldrs, rdn aftr 8th, wknd bef 2 out*............(100 to 1 op 200 to 1)   6
1680² LEADING PROSPECT [100] 10-11-0 A S Smith, *chsd ldrs, pushed alng frm 8th, wknd bef 2 out*...(10 to 1 op 12 to 1)   7
Dist: 4l, 1¾l, 4l, ¾l, 11l, 6l. 5m 48.40s. a 11.40s (7 Ran).
(Gordon Brown), J Howard Johnson

2362 McEwans Lager Novices' Chase Class E (5-y-o and up) £2,988 3m ....(3:50)

19634 CUSH SUPREME (Ire) 8-11-5 P Carberry, *keen, led 3rd, sn clr, styd on wl frm 2 out, cmftbly*.......(6 to 1 tchd 7 to 1)   1
2062 TOUGH TEST (Ire) 7-11-5 G Cahill, *led to 3rd, chsd wnr aftr, hdwy bef 4 out, no extr 2 out*..........(2 to 1 tchd 9 to 4)   2
21514 TRUMP 8-11-5 D Parker, *beh, some hdwy bef 4 out, no prog frm 2 out*.......(5 to 4 fav op 11 to 10 tchd 11 to 8)   3
KALAJO 7-11-5 B Storey, *prmnt early, outpcd and beh hfwy, no dngr aftr*.................(25 to 1 op 33 to 1)   4
17064 TACTIX 7-11-0 A S Smith, *cl up chasing grp, wknd bef 4 out, beh whn f last*...........................(16 to 1 op 14 to 1)   f
2120* D'ARBLAY STREET (Ire) 8-11-5 S McDougall, *in tch chasing grp whn blun and uns rdr 5th*.......(14 to 1 op 12 to 1)   ur
911² CLASSIC CREST (Ire) (v) 6-11-5 M Foster, *in tch chasing grp whn blun and uns rdr 8th*.........(16 to 1 tchd 20 to 1)   ur
1952 BROOMHILL DUKER (Ire) 7-11-5 A Dobbin, *tld off whn pld up bef 11th*...................(50 to 1 op 33 to 1)   pu
Dist: 4l, 14l, 3l. 6m 10.00s. a 21.00s (8 Ran).
(Robert Ogden), Martin Todhunter

2363 Weatherbys 'Stars Of Tomorrow' Open National Hunt Flat Standard Class H (4,5,6-y-o) £1,516 2m (4:20)

18744 COUNTRY ORCHID 6-11-0 P Niven, *hld up, hdwy 4 fs out, led o'r one out, ran on wl*..............(4 to 1 tchd 3 to 1)   1
ES GO 4-10-4 (3*) H Bastiman, *led aftr 5 fs, drvn alng 3 out, hdd o'r one out, no extr.*
...............................(11 to 4 fav op 5 to 2 tchd 3 to 1)   2
DELIGHTFOOL 6-11-0 A Dobbin, *hld up, hdwy o'r 3 fs out, styd on frm 2 out*...............(20 to 1 op 16 to 1)   3
JUST NED 6-11-5 A S Smith, *led 5 fs, prmnt, kpt on same pace frm 3 out*........................(100 to 1)   4
CASTLE BAY (Ire) 6-11-5 R Supple, *hld up, hdwy 4 fs out, hng rght o'r 2 out, nvr able to chal.*
...............................(3 to 1 tchd 4 to 1 and 11 to 4)   5
1789⁶ ATLANTIC SUNRISE 5-10-7 (7*) C McCormack, *mid-div, no hdwy fnl 3 fs*....................(50 to 1 op 33 to 1)   6
SUNRISE SENSATION 4-10-7 K Jones, *in tch, no hdwy fnl 3 fs*.............................(20 to 1)   7
74⁹ CHIEF OF KHORASSAN (Fr) 5-11-2 (3*) G Lee, *beh, some late hdwy, nvr dngrs*..........(12 to 1 op 10 to 1)   8
1949 MIDAS 6-11-12 P Carberry, *hld up, hdwy 4 fs out, wknd o'r 2 out*.........(7 to 1 op 5 to 1 tchd 8 to 1)   9
23229 COTTSTOWN BOY (Ire) 6-11-5 M Foster, *keen early, in tch, wknd 3 fs out*.................(100 to 1)   10
22065 BUDDLEIA 4-9-9 (7*) N Horrocks, *prmnt till wknd 3 fs out.*
...............................(20 to 1 op 14 to 1)   11
CHIEF CHIPPIE 4-10-7 S McDougall, *chsd ldrs till wknd 4 fs out*............................(33 to 1)   12
KATSAR 5-11-5 R Garritty, *nvr on terms.*
...............................(12 to 1 op 7 to 1)   13
BUSTER TWO (Ire) 4-10-7 M Moloney, *in tch to hfwy, sn wknd, losing touch whn slpd up 3 fs out*.............(100 to 1)   su
FAR PASTURE 5-11-0 J Burke, *prmnt to hfwy, sn wknd, tld off fnl 3 fs, pld up ins last*...................(100 to 1)   pu
Dist: 2½l, 9l, nk, hd, 1¼l, sht-hd, sht-hd, 1¼l, 9l, 6l. 3m 44.60s. (15 Ran).
(Mrs J V Kehoe), Mrs M Reveley

PUNCHESTOWN (IRE) (yielding) Tuesday January 28th
Going Correction: PLUS 0.50 sec. per fur.

2364 Red Bog Hurdle (4-y-o and up) £3,082 2½m.................(1:05)

21288 GUEST PERFORMANCE (Ire) 5-11-7 (3*) G Cotter,
...............................(11 to 10 fav)   1
14066 DERRYMOYLE (Ire) 8-12-0 J P Broderick,.........(4 to 1)   2
ANUSHA 7-11-9 D T Evans,...................(20 to 1)   3
20842 ANTAPOURA (Ire) 5-11-2 C F Swan,............(13 to 8)   f
Dist: 9l, dist. 5m 20.10s. a 38.10s (4 Ran).
(S Mulryan), D T Hughes

2365 Rathside Handicap Chase (0-123 5-y-o and up) £3,082 2½m.... (1:35)

2136³	BALLYHIRE LAD (Ire) [-] 8-11-¹³ C F Swan, ...(7 to 4 on)	1
2136⁵	THE REAL ARTICLE (Ire) [-] 8-12-0 L P Cusack, ... (4 to 1)	2
2223⁴	GREEK MAGIC [-] 10-9-11 (3") G Cotter, ...(20 to 1)	3
2078⁴	CARRIGEEN KERRIA (Ire) [-] 9-11-3 D J Casey, ... (5 to 1)	4
2053	BOB DEVANI [-] 11-10-13 C O'Dwyer, ...(8 to 1)	5
	PERSPEX GALE (Ire) [-] 9-10-1 F Woods, ...(12 to 1)	6
1781⁵	DAMODAR [-] 8-10-1 F J Flood, ...(5 to 1)	7

Dist: 2l, sht-hd, 10l, ¾l. 5m 38.40s. a 41.40s (7 Ran).

(Mrs Anna Foxe), A P O'Brien

2366 Ballintaggart Handicap Hurdle (0-102 5-y-o and up) £3,082 3m .... (2:05)

2229²	VASILIKI (Ire) [-] 5-11-1 C O'Dwyer, ...(6 to 1)	1
1654	COOLREE LORD (Ire) [-] 6-9-11 M P Hourigan, ...(12 to 1)	2
2271⁵	TREANAREE (Ire) [-] 8-10-5 (7") S Kelly, ...(14 to 1)	3
2162	KILCARAMORE (Ire) [-] 6-10-3 (7") S FitzGerald, ..(20 to 1)	4
1407	HI KNIGHT (Ire) [-] 7-11-13 K F O'Brien, ...(16 to 1)	5
2138⁴	MONDEO ROSE (Ire) [-] 5-11-7 C F Swan, ...(11 to 2 fav)	6
2162⁸	SHIR ROSE (Ire) [-] 7-10-8 T Horgan, ...(14 to 1)	7
2170⁴	RUM FLIN (Ire) [-] 6-10-10 (3") G Cotter, ...(10 to 1)	8
2134⁶	CELTIC SUNRISE [-] 9-11-6 F Woods, ...(12 to 1)	9
2104⁴	DARK SWAN (Ire) [-] 7-11-7 (7") D Flood, ...(10 to 1)	10
2162⁴	DOOK'S DELIGHT (Ire) [-] 6-11-0 L P Cusack, ...(10 to 1)	11
2162²	ADARAMANN (Ire) [-] (bl) 5-10-8 (3") Mr R Walsh, ..(10 to 1)	12
1899	JIMMY THE WEED (Ire) [-] 8-10-5 J R Barry, ...(20 to 1)	13
2104	EXPEDIENT EXPRESS (Ire) [-] 7-9-13 (3") K Whelan,	
	....(14 to 1)	14
2162	TEARDROP (Ire) [-] 5-10-6 (3") J Butler, ...(20 to 1)	15
2162⁵	LADY QUAYSIDE (Ire) [-] 7-11-1 D J Casey, ...(10 to 1)	16
2041⁴	HOME I'LL BE (Ire) [-] 7-9-4 (3") B Bowens, ...(10 to 1)	17
1752	THE PARSON'S FILLY (Ire) [-] 7-10-11 (3") G Kilfeather,	
	....(7 to 1)	18
1899	SPEED BOARD (Ire) [-] 5-10-11 F J Flood, ...(20 to 1)	19
2104⁴	DOUBLE STRIKE (Ire) [-] (bl) 6-11-3 H Rogers, ...(14 to 1)	20
2339	TAR AND CEMENT (Ire) [-] (bl) 9-9-7 (7") A O'Shea, (33 to 1)	f
	ROSEAUSTIN (Ire) [-] 7-9-10 (7") D McCullagh, ...(20 to 1)	f
2222	BERNESTIC WONDER (Ire) [-] 8-9-7 J Jones, ...(33 to 1)	f
1895	DEESIDE DOINGS (Ire) [-] (bl) 9-9-10 P L Malone, (40 to 1)	bd
2104⁷	JIHAAD (USA) [-] 7-10-2 J P Broderick, ...(14 to 1)	pu

Dist: 4l, 5½l, 1l, 1l. 6m 22.10s. a 37.10s (25 Ran).

(Delton Syndicate), G T Hourigan

2367 Grangebeg Beginners Chase (5-y-o and up) £3,082 2m...........(2:35)

2231³	PFNNDARA (Ire) 8-12-0 C F Swan, ...(5 to 4 on)	1
2133³	SCENIC ROUTE (Ire) 8-11-9 (5") Mr I P Hyde, ...(4 to 1)	2
2164⁸	TAYLORS QUAY (Ire) 9-11-9 J P Broderick, ...(10 to 1)	3
1654	ARDSHUIL 8-12-0 F Woods, ...(9 to 1)	4
2134⁴	FONTAINE FABLES (Ire) 7-12-0 J Shortt, ...(10 to 1)	5
2164	LINDA'S BOY (Ire) 7-12-0 K F O'Brien, ...(14 to 1)	6
2133⁶	JOHNNY'S DREAM (Ire) 7-11-11 (3") G Cotter, ...(12 to 1)	f
2133²	ROCKETTS CASTLE (Ire) 7-11-6 (3") K Whelan, ...(6 to 1)	f

Dist: 10l, 6l, 20l, 7l. 4m 28.60s. a 29.60s (8 Ran).

(All Gold Syndicate), A P O'Brien

2368 Tynte Park Maiden Hurdle (5-y-o) £3,082 2½m.................(3:05)

2137¹	BLUE WAVE (Ire) 12-0 J Shortt, ...(5 to 4 fav)	1
	IRIDAL (bl) 12-0 K F O'Brien, ...(6 to 1)	2
2168⁶	NATIVE FLING (Ire) 11-11 (3") U Smyth, ...(9 to 2)	3
928²	FANE PATH (Ire) 11-7 (7") B J Geraghty, ...(6 to 1)	4
2168	CASTLE COIN (Ire) 11-6 C F Swan, ...(10 to 1)	5
	ROYAL MARINE 11-6 F Woods, ...(10 to 1)	6
2055⁶	SHALOM (Ire) 11-6 M P Hourigan, ...(20 to 1)	7
2022³	HEATHER VILLE (Ire) 11-1 C O'Dwyer, ...(8 to 1)	8
1907	AROUND THE STUMP (Ire) 11-1 S H O'Donovan, ..(20 to 1)	9
	SECRET DREAMWORLD (Ire) 11-1 A Powell, ...(25 to 1)	pu

Dist: 2l, 5½l, ¾l, 5½l. 5m 37.80s. a 55.80s (10 Ran).

(Mrs Pauline Donnelly), D T Hughes

2369 Newtown Boy Handicap Hurdle (0-116 4-y-o and up) £3,082 2m .... (3:35)

2129⁴	VALLEY ERNE (Ire) [-] 6-10-5 J P Broderick, ...(7 to 2)	1
2114²	GOOD GLOW [-] 7-11-2 F Woods, ...(2 to 1 fav)	2
2142³	JUSTAWAY (Ire) [-] 7-10-12 C F Swan, ...(6 to 1)	3
2128	RESCUE TIME (Ire) [-] 4-11-2 J Shortt, ...(6 to 1)	4
	UPPER MOUNT STREET (Ire) [-] 7-10-4 T Horgan, (14 to 1)	5
2272⁶	ILLBETHEREFORYOU (Ire) [-] 6-9-5 (7") S P McCann,	
	....(10 to 1)	6
2142⁸	PRE (Ireland) (Ire) [-] 5-10-11 F J Flood, ...(8 to 1)	7
943²	CELTIC LORE [-] 5-12-0 D T Evans, ...(9 to 1)	8
	SOFT SPOT (Ire) [-] 5-9-9 M Duffy, ...(16 to 1)	9
355⁷	MAGIC ROYALE (Ire) [-] 7-9-4 (3") J M Hunter, ...(50 to 1)	f

Dist: ¾l, 3l, 2l, 4½l. 3m 58.30s. a 13.30s (10 Ran).

SR: 24/34/27/29/12/-/   (S A M Syndicate), Michael Cunningham

2370 Battlemount I.N.H. Flat Race (4-y-o) £3,082 2m...................(4:05)

	SIMONS CASTLE (Ire) 11-2 Mr A R Coonan, ...(12 to 1)	1
	ALL THE COLOURS (Ire) 11-2 Mrs C Barker, ...(14 to 1)	2
2234³	DIVINE DANCER (Ire) 10-11 Mr J P Dempsey, ...(8 to 1)	3
	COMMON MAN (Ire) 10-13 (3") Mr B M Cash, ...(10 to 1)	4
	SUPPORT ACT (Ire) 11-2 Mr D Marnane, ...(7 to 1)	5
	CAMDEN MOON (Ire) 10-9 (7") Mr J C Kelly, ...(14 to 1)	6
2130³	ALOTAWANNA (Ire) 11-2 Mr A J Martin, ...(10 to 1)	7
2234⁶	FISHIN PRINT (Ire) 10-9 (7") Mr A J Dempsey, ...(11 to 2)	8
	COULDN'T SAY (Ire) 11-2 Mr T Mullins, ...(9 to 1)	9
	THE BONGO MAN (Ire) 11-2 Mr P Fenton, ...(11 to 10 fav)	10
	TREDAGH MAN (Ire) 10-11 (5") Mr J T McNamara, (14 to 1)	11
2234⁴	KOHOUTEK 10-13 (3") Mr R Walsh, ...(10 to 1)	12
	TONIBEROLI (Ire) 10-4 (7") Mr J P McNamara, ...(14 to 1)	13
	KILCORDION (Ire) 10-4 (7") Miss G C Feighery, ...(14 to 1)	14

Dist: Nk, 5½l, hd, 6l. 3m 52.50s. (14 Ran).

(Mrs C Collins), Miss S Collins

WARWICK (good to firm)
Tuesday January 28th
Going Correction: NIL (races 1,2,4,7), MINUS 0.10 (3,5,6)

2371 'High Front' Novices' Hurdle Class E (4-y-o and up) £2,909 2m..... (1:10)

2197⁴	CARLITO BRIGANTE 5-11-5 J Osborne, al gng wl and in tch,	
	trkd ldr aftr 3 out, chlgd 2 out, sn led, cmftbly.	
	...............(11 to 10 on op Evens tchd 11 to 10)	1
2195⁷	DISALLOWED (Ire) 4-10-8 M A Fitzgerald, led, drvn alng aftr	
	thre out, hdd sn after 2 out, kpt on but not pace of wnr.	
	............(9 to 2 op 4 to 1 tchd 5 to 1)	2
2242³	COUNTRY LOVER (v) 6-11-5 R Dunwoody, al chasing ldrs,	
	rdn and one pace aftr 3 out.	
	................(4 to 1 op 3 to 1 tchd 9 to 2 and 5 to 1)	3
1594⁵	TREE CREEPER (Ire) 5-11-5 L Harvey, chsd ldrs, rdn and	
	outpcd appr 3 out, styd on ag'n frm nxt.	
	................(10 to 1 op 8 to 1 tchd 12 to 1)	4
2117⁵	MUSIC PLEASE 5-11-5 A Thornton, al in tch, rdn and one	
	pace frm 3 out. ....(16 to 1 op 12 to 1 tchd 20 to 1)	5
2029³	POT BLACK UK 6-11-5 G Tormey, chsd ldrs, mstk 4th, rdn	
	and mistake 3 out, sn wknd. ....(20 to 1 op 12 to 1)	6
1221⁷	STAR BLAKENEY 4-10-7 R Farrant, some hdwy 5th but not a	
	dngr. ....(25 to 1 op 20 to 1)	7
2002⁷	PALAMON (USA) 4-10-7 B Clifford, nvr rchd ldrs.	
	........................(20 to 1 op 12 to 1)	8
1855⁷	GALWAY BOSS (Ire) 5-11-5 B Powell, slwly away, some hdwy	
	frm 3 out. ....(100 to 1)	9
	FRED JEFFREY (Ire) 6-11-12 (7") C Rae, mid-division whn	
	blun 3rd, nvr dngrs aftr. (50 to 1 op 25 to 1 tchd 66 to 1)	10
2153	TODD (USA) 6-11-5 J A McCarthy, in tch rdn 5th, wknd	
	quickly appr 3 out.................(33 to 1 op 20 to 1)	11
2248⁸	MR AGRIWISE 6-11-5 J Frost, al in rear. ....(100 to 1)	12
191	MOLLIE SILVERS 5-10-7 (7") N T Egan, al in rear. (100 to 1)	13
	CLASSIC MODEL 6-11-5 S McNeill, al beh.	
	............(66 to 1 op 50 to 1)	14
	NICKY WILDE 7-11-5 G Bradley, chsd ldr rdn 4th, wknd	
	quickly nxt........................(25 to 1 op 12 to 1)	15
	CUILLIN 5-11-0 D Walsh, slwly away, al beh, tld off.	
	.....................................(100 to 1)	16
1683	NUNS LUCY 6-11-0 S Wynne, sn wl beh, tld off frm hfwy.	
	....(100 to 1)	17
	BRIGHTLING FAIR 5-10-7 (7") J M McCarthy, slwly away, tld	
	off............................(100 to 1 op 50 to 1)	18
1293	SCBOO 8-11-0 (5") Michael Brennan, prmnt to 3rd, sn wknd,	
	tld off whn pld up bef 2 out.	pu

Dist: 1¾l, 10l, 1l, 1l, 10l, 5l, 1¼l, 6l, 1l, 5l. 3m 44.40s. a 5.40s (19 Ran).

SR: 37/24/25/24/23/13/   (Lady Bamford), P R Webber

2372 'Low Pressure' Novices' Handicap Hurdle Class E (0-105 4-y-o and up) £2,447 2m................... (1:40)

	TROUVAILLE (Ire) [89] 6-11-3 L Harvey, trkd ldr till led 5th, rdn	
	alng whn chlgd appr 2 out, styd on wl.	
	.............(7 to 1 op 8 to 1 tchd 9 to 1 and 10 to 1)	1
2174⁴	FASTINI GOLD [75] 5-10-3 J Osborne, hdwy and rdn frm 4th,	
	styd on und pres from 3 out, not rcvr nxt.	
	...............(9 to 2 op 7 to 2 tchd 5 to 1)	2
	BEAUMONT (Ire) [96] 7-11-10 J R Kavanagh, prmnt, chlgd	
	appr 2 out, rdn, swtchd lft and stumbled approaching last, sn	
	one pace.............(3 to 1 fav tchd 7 to 2 and 4 to 1)	3
	TILAAL (USA) [88] 5-11-2 R Dunwoody, gd hdwy frm 4th, trkd	
	ldrs nxt, chlgd gng wl appr 2 out, sn rdn, last.	
	...............(9 to 2 op 5 to 1 tchd 11 to 2)	4
2158	TIME LEADER [73] 5-9-8 (7") X Aizpuru, hld up, some hdwy	
	frm 4th, one pace appr 2 out. (10 to 1 tchd 8 to 1 and 12 to 1)	5
2185⁶	MILLING BROOK [73] 5-10-1 R Johnson, chsd ldrs, rdn 3 out,	
	sn wknd.................(8 to 1 op 14 to 1)	6
1623	LOTHIAN COMMANDER [75] 5-10-3² D Walsh, rdn alng frm	
	3rd, some prog frm 2 out but not a dngr.	
	...............(33 to 1 op 25 to 1 tchd 50 to 1)	7

1733⁶ ALPHA LEATHER [72] 6-10-0 Mr J Grassick, *gd hdwy to chase ldrs aftr 3rd, wknd 3 out*...... (33 to 1 tchd 40 to 1) 8
1723 UPHAM RASCAL [72] 6-10-0 D Leahy, *in tch whn mstk 4th, sn wknd*........................(33 to 1 tchd 50 to 1) 9
1869² LAUGHING BUCCANEER [84] 4-10-0 B Powell, *chsd ldrs till rdn and wknd 5th*...... (12 to 1 op 10 to 1 tchd 14 to 1) 10
1976² KING RAT (Ire) [85] (v) 6-10-8 (5*) Michael Brennan, *sn chasing ldrs, rdn and wknd 3 out*........(7 to 2 op 5 to 2) 11
1348 KINGS VISION [75] 5-10-3³ T Jenks, *beh frm 3rd*.
.............................(50 to 1 op 33 to 1) 12
2279 MR GORDON BENNETT [72] (bl) 6-10-0 C Llewellyn, *keen hold, led till hdd 5th, sn wknd*........(50 to 1 op 33 to 1) 13
URSHI-JADE [76] 9-10-4¹¹ (7*) J T Nolan, *beh frm 3rd*.
.............................(50 to 1 op 33 to 1) 14
2185 SOBER ISLAND [72] 8-9-12¹ (3*) Guy Lewis, *prmnt early, beh frm 4th*..................................(50 to 1) 15
Dist: 3½l, ½l, 1¾l, 4l, 3½l, 2½l, 5l, sht-hd, 9l, 1¾l. 3m 46.90s. a 7.90s (15 Ran).
SR: 10/-/12/2/-/-/   (G Payne), Andrew Turnell

2373 Roscoe Harvey Memorial Novices' Chase Class D (5-y-o and up) £4,122 2½m 110yds.....................(2:10)

1748² DREAM RIDE (Ire) 7-11-4 R Johnson, *led second to 5th, chlgd 6th to 8th, dsptd ld 12th, led till hdd 3 out, sn led ag'n, easily*.
................(5 to 2 on op 9 to 4 on tchd 2 to 1 on) 1
1815 RED BRANCH (Ire) 8-11-4 T J Murphy, *chsd ldrs, led 5th till sn aftr 12th, led ag'n 3 out, soon hdd, kpt on but no ch wth wnr whn mstk last*.....................(33 to 1 op 20 to 1) 2
1973⁶ EKEUS (Ire) 7-11-4 C Maude, *led to second, styd in tch till wknd 12th*.........................(20 to 1 op 16 to 1) 3
2030⁷ QUICK DECISION (Ire) 6-10-11 (7*) N T Egan, *in tch, reminders tenth, lost touch 12th, mstk 14th*.
................(40 to 1 op 20 to 1 tchd 50 to 1) 4
1831 TYPHOON (Ire) 7-11-4 M Sharratt, *tld off frm 4th, blun and uns rdr 3 out, rmntd to finish*................(66 to 1 op 50 to 1) 5
STARLIGHT FOOL (bl) 8-11-4 A Thornton, *f second*.
.............................(20 to 1 op 12 to 1) f
1454² HOLDIMCLOSE 7-11-4 J Frost, *f 3rd*.
................(11 to 4 op 9 to 4 tchd 3 to 1) f
Dist: 10l, 19l, 20l. 5m 11.40s. a 16.40s (7 Ran).
(C G Clarke And G C Mordaunt), D Nicholson

2374 Mackenzie Consulting Novices' Hurdle Class E (4-y-o and up) £2,640 2½m 110yds.................(2:40)

2242⁸ MOTOQUA 5-11-0 R Johnson, *in tch, hdwy 7th, trkd ldrs 3 out, chlgd nxt, sn led, cmftbly*.
.............................(3 to 1 op 4 to 1 tchd 7 to 2) 1
1483⁶ STORMYFAIRWEATHER (Ire) 5-11-5 M A Fitzgerald, *hld up in rear, mstk 5th, rdn appr 2 out, styd on to take second r-in but not a dngr*..............(16 to 1 op 8 to 1 tchd 20 to 1) 2
1642⁶ THE BREWMASTER (Ire) 5-11-5 B Powell, *led, rdn alng whn chlgd frm 7th, hdd sn aftr 2 out, one pace*.
................(33 to 1 op 20 to 1) 3
SWEET LORD (Ire) 6-11-5 P Holley, *trkd ldr till chlgd frm 7th, rdn 2 out, wkng whn mstk last*.
.........(25 to 1 op 33 to 1 tchd 50 to 1 and 66 to 1) 4
1696⁵ QUIET MOMENTS (Ire) 4-10-6 R Farrant, *in tch till wknd 4 out*.
................(100 to 1 op 50 to 1) 5
1928⁶ SWEET TRENTINO (Ire) 6-11-5 W Marston, *al beh, lost tch frm 7th*.................(40 to 1 op 20 to 1 tchd 50 to 1) 6
2207¹ HARBOUR ISLAND 5-11-11 R Dunwoody, *stumbled, hmpd and uns rdr 1st*.
................(9 to 4 on op 2 to 1 on tchd 11 to 4 on) ur
1849 GALE WARGAME (Ire) 6-11-5 J Osborne, *chsd ldrs, rdn alng aftr 7th, wknd quickly 4 out, tld off whn pld up bef 2 out*.
................(25 to 1 op 12 to 1) pu
Dist: 6l, 1l, hd, 6l, 11l. 5m 2.20s. a 17.20s (8 Ran).
(Mrs Claire Smith), D Nicholson

2375 'Wind Chill' Novices' Chase Class D (5-y-o and up) £3,783 3¼m...(3:10)

2211³ FLIMSY TRUTH 11-11-10 Mr M Harris, *led to 14th, led ag'n 16th, sn drvn alng, hld on wl whn chlgd frm 2 out*.
.............(6 to 1 op 7 to 4 on tchd 11 to 10 on) 1
1473 JULTARA (Ire) 8-11-5 B Powell, *trkd wnr, hit 9th, slight ld frm 14th till blun and hdd 16th, rallied to chal from 2 out, no extr r-in*...................(6 to 5 op 5 to 4 tchd 11 to 10) 2
1763 MUSICAL HIT 6-11-5 R Bellamy, *blun 3rd and in rear, lost tch 8th and sn tld off*......(40 to 1 op 33 to 1 tchd 50 to 1) 3
1399⁷ ARR EFF BEE 10-11-5 A Thornton, *blun 6th and sn tld off, hit 8th*...........................(25 to 1 op 16 to 1) 4
WESSEX MILORD 12-11-5 L Harvey, *mstk 1st, lost tch 3rd and sn tld off, pld up bef 15th*.........(66 to 1 op 50 to 1) pu
Dist: 1l, dist, ½l. 6m 34.10s. a 20.10s (5 Ran).
(M H Weston), M H Weston

2376 'Long Range' Novices' Handicap Chase Class E (0-105 5-y-o and up) £2,849 2m...............(3:40)

1704 FLAMING MIRACLE (Ire) [72] (bl) 7-10-1 R Farrant, *hdwy 6th, chlgd 7th, outpcd 3 out, rallied frm nxt, styd on wl to ld nr finish*...........................(5 to 1 op 4 to 1) 1
2297³ BRAZIL OR BUST (Ire) [99] 6-12-0 J Osborne, *hld up, shaken up and hdwy 3 out, led 2 out, rdn, one pace and ct r-in*.
................(11 to 4 op 2 to 1) 2
1796⁶ SNOWY PETREL (Ire) [89] (bl) 5-10-8 A Thornton, *led aftr 5th, hdd 3 out, styd on same pace frm 2 out*. (10 to 1 op 7 to 1) 3
1912² COVER POINT (Ire) [92] 6-11-7 R Dunwoody, *prmnt, chlgd 5th, dsptd ld frm 8th till led 3 out, hdd nxt, wknd quickly last*.
................(2 to 1 fav op 5 to 4 tchd 9 to 4) 4
2026 HEATHYARDS BOY [71] (bl) 7-10-0 D Walsh, *led till aftr 5th, wknd 7th*.......................(50 to 1 op 33 to 1) 5
1860² LUCKY EDDIE (Ire) [99] 6-12-0 C Maude, *mstk second, lost tch frm 6th*...............(7 to 2 op 5 to 2 tchd 4 to 1) 6
1557⁵ COOLTEEN HERO (Ire) [83] 7-10-12 W McFarland, *mstks, drpd rear 6th, blun and uns rdr 8th*..... (10 to 1 op 8 to 1) ur
Dist: 1¾l, 7l, 4l, 9l, 15l. 3m 57.50s. a 5.50s (7 Ran).
SR: 2/27/-/9/   (George Barnett), G Barnett

2377 'Slow Thaw' Standard Open National Hunt Flat Class H (4,5,6-y-o) £1,476 2m.........................(4:10)

917² BIG PERKS (Ire) 5-11-4 C Maude, *gd hdwy frm 3 out, ran on und pres to ld ins last*..................(7 to 1 op 12 to 1) 1
SPUNKIE 4-10-6 R Johnson, *in tch, hdwy 3 fs out, ld wl o'r one out, hdd ins last, kpt on*..........(14 to 1 op 10 to 1) 2
1789² COBLE LANE 5-11-4 J Osborne, *hdwy 7 fs out, chsd ldr o'r 2 furlongs out, one pace fnl furlong*.
................(8 to 1 op 7 to 1 tchd 9 to 1) 3
SHEEPCOTE HILL (Ire) 6-11-1 (3*) R Massey, *hdwy 6 fs out, styd on same pace fnl 2*...(11 to 2 op 7 to 2 tchd 6 to 1) 4
MASTER PIP 5-11-4 S McNeill, *hdwy 5 fs out, one pace fnl 2*.
................(20 to 1 op 33 to 1) 5
SILENT CRACKER 5-11-4 B Powell, *led hfwy, rdn 3 fs out, hdd and wknd wl o'r one furlong out*............(33 to 1) 6
1648* LORD FOLEY (NZ) 5-11-6 (5*) Michael Brennan, *keen hold in tch, rdn 3 fs out, wknd o'r one out*.
................(14 to 4 fav op 5 to 2 tchd 5 to 2) 7
1483⁵ STANMORE (Ire) 5-11-4 G Bradley, *hld up and wl beh, hdwy 7 fs out, no headway fnl 3 furlongs*..........(16 to 1 op 50 to 1) 8
1975 SHEET LIGHTNING 5-10-11 (7*) L Suthern, *chsd ldrs till one pace fnl 3 fs*....................(20 to 1 op 33 to 1) 9
BULKO BOY (NZ) 5-11-4 D Bridgwater, *in tch, pushed alng hfwy, wknd o'r 2 fs out*...(8 to 1 op 7 to 1 tchd 10 to 1) 10
1768⁹ LUCRATIVE PERK (Ire) 5-10-13 I Lawrence, *nvever rchd ldrs*.
................(100 to 1 op 50 to 1) 11
BUCKS REEF 5-11-4 A Thornton, *al mid-div*.
................(33 to 1 op 25 to 1) 12
2221⁷ GREMATIC 6-11-4 R Dunwoody, *chsd ldrs 11 fs*.
................(50 to 1 op 33 to 1) 13
ROYAL MIST 6-11-1 (3*) G Hogan, *nvr better than mid-div*............................(7 to 1) 14
SANDVILLE LAD 5-11-1 (3*) Guy Lewis, *prmnt ten fs*.
................(50 to 1 tchd 100 to 1) 15
TINGRITH LAD 5-11-4 L Harvey, *beh frm hfwy*.
................(100 to 1 op 50 to 1) 16
SUPER NOVA 6-11-4 B Fenton, *beh frm hfwy, tld off*.
................(50 to 1) 17
MISS MIGHTY 4-10-11 R Bellamy, *led to hfwy, sn wknd, tld off*.
................(100 to 1 op 50 to 1) 18
Dist: ½l, 8l, nk, 1l, 2l, 1l, 3½l, 8l, sht-hd, 3l. 3m 51.10s. (18 Ran).
(R A H Perkins), P T Dalton

DOWN ROYAL (IRE) (good to yielding)
Wednesday January 29th

2378 Bet With The Tote Maiden Hurdle (5-y-o and up) £1,370 2m.......(2:00)

2037⁶ CLADY BOY (Ire) 6-11-6 J P Broderick, ...(7 to 1) 1
1895 BAHAO (Ire) 6-11-6 D J Casey, ...(10 to 1) 2
2172⁷ US FOUR (Ire) 7-10-13 (7*) K A Kelly, ...(16 to 1) 3
2271 CRANNON BEAUTY (Ire) 7-11-6 C F Swan, ...(14 to 1) 4
2222 MICK MAN (Ire) 6-10-13 (7*) B J Geraghty, ...(14 to 1) 5
2124⁵ FOYLE WANDERER (Ire) 6-11-1 D T Evans, ...(14 to 1) 6
2041⁶ JUST IN GAME (Ire) 8-10-13 (7*) A O'Shea, ...(40 to 1) 7
2041³ FAIR SET (Ire) 6-11-6 F J Flood, ...(7 to 1) 8
983 PRAY FOR PEACE (Ire) 6-10-8 (7*) Mr P Fahey, ...(14 to 1) 9
2342⁹ HARRY HEANEY (Ire) 8-11-9 (5*) T Martin, ...(14 to 1) 10
BOLD CAVALIER (Ire) 8-10-13 (7*) Mr A Ross, ...(16 to 1) 11
SAMBAGUIRE (Ire) 5-10-13 (3*) U Smyth, ...(33 to 1) 12
2132 SINGLE OR BUST (Ire) 7-10-8 (7*) D K Budds, ...(33 to 1) 13
1622⁸ HARBOUR BLAZE (Ire) 7-11-6 A Powell, ...(20 to 1) 14
1275 KRIESLER (Ire) 5-11-2 J Shortt, ...(16 to 1) 15
2132 KILMACREW 10-10-13 (7*) D W O'Sullivan, ...(50 to 1) 16
2222⁵ NOBLE SHOON (Ire) 6-12-0 K F O'Brien, ...(7 to 4 fav) 17
1649 L'AMI DE ADAM (Ire) 6-10-12 (3*) G Cotter, ...(33 to 1) f
2131⁵ MONTANA KING (Ire) 6-11-6 F Woods, ...(4 to 1) ur
2037⁷ TWENTYFIVEQUID (Ire) 6-12-0 Mr P F Graffin, ..(12 to 1) bd
Dist: 2½l, 7l, 3½l, 4l. 3m 56.60s. (20 Ran).
(K J Martin), S A Kirk

2379 Thoroughbred Insurances Ltd Handicap Hurdle (0-109 5-y-o and up) £1,370 2½m..................(2:30)

2339[2] CAIRNCROSS (Ire) [-] 6-11-5 J P Broderick,........(9 to 4) 1
2104[8] SONG FOR AFRICA (Ire) [-] (bl) 6-10-4 D J Casey, (14 to 1) 2
2103 VINTNERS VENTURE (Ire) [-] 5-11-9 C F Swan,.... (8 to 1) 3
2142[5] COLLIERS HILL (Ire) [-] 9-10-7 (7*) R P Hogan,.....(6 to 1) 4
1435 NOELS DANCER (Ire) [-] 7-11-7 (7*) D K Budds,...(14 to 1) 5
2079[9] GLENA GALE (Ire) [-] 7-10-1 F Woods,............(8 to 1) 6
2036[2] THE THIRD MAN (Ire) [-] (bl) 8-10-2 P McWilliams, (12 to 1) 7
1901 SCATHACH (Ire) [-] 5-9-8 (7*) R J Gordon,........(33 to 1) 8
2170 HANNAH'S PET (Ire) [-] 7-9-5 (5*) T Martin,.......(33 to 1) 9
2104 SKULLDUGERY (Ire) [-] 7-10-7 J Jones,....... (2 to 1 fav) 10
NORDIC SENSATION (Ire) [-] 8-11-3 (7*) Mr K Ross, (16 to 1) 11
2225[7] ABIGAIL ROSE (Bel) [-] (bl) 5-10-12 D T Evans,....(20 to 1) 12
2138 QUEEN OF ALL GALES (Ire) [-] 6-10-1 (7*) A O'Shea, ...(16 to 1) 13
2222 FOREST STAR (USA) [-] (bl) 8-10-0[1] (3*) K Whelan, (33 to 1) 14
1273 BENBRADAGH GLOW (Ire) [-] 5-10-13 (7*) Mr L J Gracey, ...(20 to 1) 15
JOSHUA TREE [-] 12-11-5 J K Kinane,...........(25 to 1) 16
WADABLAST (Ire) [-] 7-10-7 (7*) Mr G T Morrow,.. (14 to 1) 17
1579 JIMMY JANE (Ire) [-] 5-9-7[7] (7*) Mr J J Canavan,.. (66 to 1) 18
2016 WHAT EVER YOU WANT (Ire) [-] 7-10-0 (7*) Mr M Callaghan, ...(33 to 1) 19
2229[7] GLENFIELDS CASTLE (Ire) [-] 7-11-3 (7*) Mr A Stronge, ...(7 to 1) ur

Dist: 4½l, ½l, ½l, 8l. 5m 0.60s. (20 Ran).
(Philip White), K Woods

2380 European Breeders Fund Mares Maiden Hurdle (5-y-o and up) £2,055 2½m........................ (3:00)

2131[2] STAGALIER (Ire) 5-10-9 (7*) B J Geraghty,.....(11 to 8 on) 1
2037[4] SARAH BLUE (Ire) (bl) 7-11-6 D T Evans,.........(5 to 1) 2
2138[8] PINTPLEASE PAT (Ire) 6-11-6 L P Cusack,........(16 to 1) 3
2036[8] COOKSGROVE ROSIE (Ire) 5-11-2 P Leech,......(25 to 1) 4
2079[3] KILCOGY CROSS (Ire) 5-11-2 C F Swan,..........(7 to 2) 5
2166[9] POLITICAL TROUBLES (Ire) 7-11-6 J Shortt,......(10 to 1) 6
2339 KILKEA (Fr) 6-11-6 J K Kinane,..................(50 to 1) 7
805 BARORA GALE (Ire) 6-11-1 (5*) T Martin,.........(50 to 1) 8
2222 LITE 'N EASY (Ire) 7-10-13 (7*) A O'Shea,..........(8 to 1) f

Dist: 1l, 7l, 20l, 12l. 5m 9.90s. (9 Ran).
(Gerard Callaghan), Noel Meade

2381 Down Royal Handicap Chase (0-116 5-y-o and up) £1,370 3m 1f... (3:30)

2171[2] AMME ENAEK (Ire) [-] (bl) 8-11-0 H Rogers,........(4 to 1) 1
1581[8] TRENCH HILL LASS (Ire) [-] 8-11-3 (7*) Mr I Buchanan, ...(7 to 1) 2
2038[4] MASTER MILLER [-] 11-9-7 J Jones,............ (12 to 1) 3
136[2] PENNYBRIDGE (Ire) [-] 8-11-7 L P Cusack,........ (7 to 1) 4
2038[5] CABBERY ROSE (Ire) [-] 9-9-12 (7*) A O'Shea,.... (12 to 1) 5
2223[7] LAURA'S BEAU [-] 13-10-8 (7*) R P Hogan,.........(14 to 1) 6
2071[9] BEAT THE SECOND (Ire) [-] 9-12-0 C F Swan,.. (6 to 4 on) ur

Dist: 8l, sht-hd, 2l, 2½l. 6m 39.00s. (7 Ran).
(Mrs E Keane), Gerard Keane

2382 Capita Management Consultants Ltd Novice Chase (5-y-o and up) £1,370 2½m........................ (4:00)

2143[8] BALLYMACREVAN (Ire) 7-11-8 T P Treacy,.........(4 to 1) 1
2227[8] MIROSWAKI (USA) 7-11-8 T J Mitchell,.............(8 to 1) 2
2224[4] DAWN ALERT (Ire) 8-11-8 C F Swan,........(11 to 10 fav) 3
1898 OVER THE MAINE (Ire) 7-12-0 H Rogers,.........(10 to 1) 4
1461[9] SHUIL DAINGEAN (Ire) 7-11-5 (3*) K Whelan,..... (10 to 1) 5
2051[7] FALCARRAGH (Ire) 7-11-8 A Powell,..............(6 to 1) 6
1582[6] DIAMOND SPRITE (USA) 10-11-1 (7*) G Martin,...(33 to 1) f
2039[4] PILS INVADER (Ire) 9-11-3 D T Evans,........... (33 to 1) f
2224[8] SPECTACLE (Ire) (bl) 7-11-1 (7*) A O'Shea,....... (25 to 1) f
2171 BUCKAMERE (Ire) 6-11-3 F Woods,................(33 to 1) ur
2036 SIR MOSS 10-11-8 J P Broderick,................(12 to 1) pu

Dist: 5l, 6l, sht-hd, 1½l. 5m 17.20s. (11 Ran).
(Good Time Managers Syndicate), I A Duncan

2383 Lisburn I.N.H. Flat Race (4-y-o and up) £1,370 2m................ (4:30)

FRANKIE WILLOW (Ire) 4-11-2[2] Mr P F Graffin,.....(8 to 1) 1
2272 COUNCILLOR (Ire) 6-11-7 (7*) Mr M P Horan,......(7 to 1) 2
2137[5] RUN SPARKY (Ire) 5-11-0 (5*) Mr R J Patton,...... (3 to 1) 3
2137[8] MISS CIRCLE (Ire) (bl) 8-11-4[2] (7*) Miss C Woods,..(7 to 1) 4
2228 DENNETT VALLEY (Ire) 8-11-7 (7*) Miss S McDonogh, ...(20 to 1) 5
2040[8] SHINORA (Ire) 6-11-2 (7*) Mr G T Morrow,....... (20 to 1) 6
2115[5] AISLING ALAINN (Ire) 5-11-3 (7*) Mr Philip Carberry, ... (5 to 2 fav) 7
2137 HIDDEN PLAY (Ire) 9-11-2 (7*) Mr L D McBratney, (25 to 1) 8
CARA GAIL (Ire) 5-10-12 (7*) Mr M P Madden,..... (6 to 1) 9
2228[6] TOBYS PAL (Ire) 7-11-9 (5*) Mr D McGoona,........(5 to 1) 10
2172 RAGGLEPUSS (Ire) 7-11-4 (5*) Mr G Elliott,......(14 to 1) 11
2166 CAROLANNS CHOICE (Ire) 8-11-9 Mr A J Martin, (20 to 1) 12
1580 DARA KNIGHT (Ire) 8-11-11 (3*) Mr B R Hamilton, (20 to 1) 13
CINDERELLA'S DREAM (Ire) 4-10-2 (7*) Mrs A Doran, ...(20 to 1) 14
JOAN'S PRINCESS (Ire) 4-11-3[1]5 (7*) Mr J P McCreesh, ...(20 to 1) 15

Dist: 9l, 1½l, 1l, 7l. 3m 58.30s. (15 Ran).
(Mrs Bernadette McAtamney), P F Graffin

LEICESTER (good to soft (races 1,2,4,6), good to firm (3,5)) Wednesday January 29th

Going Correction: PLUS 0.55 sec. per fur. (races 1,2,4,6), PLUS 0.15 (3,5)

2384 European Breeders Fund 'National Hunt' Novices' Hurdle Qualifier Class D (5,6,7-y-o) £3,548 2½m 110yds...................... (1:40)

1973* RED BLAZER 6-11-10 J Osborne, *hld up in mid-div, hdwy 5th, mstk 7th, led appr last, ran on wl.* ....(5 to 4 fav op 6 to 4 tchd 7 to 4) 1
1673[4] DENHAM HILL (Ire) 6-10-11 (3*) J Magee, *led 4th, rdn and hdd appr last, kpt on wl.*....(14 to 1 op 10 to 1 tchd 16 to 1) 2
1609* CRIMSON KING (Ire) 6-11-10 A Thornton, *hld up, hdwy 7th, ev ch 2 out, one pace aftr.*..............(9 to 1 op 5 to 1) 3
1849[3] FRIENDSHIP (Ire) 5-11-0 M A Fitzgerald, *chsd ldrs, one pace frm 3 out.*........................(4 to 1 op 2 to 1) 4
1975* PRINCEFUL (Ire) 6-11-0 W Marston, *trkd ldrs, mstk 5th, wknd 3 out.*..................(11 to 2 op 9 to 2 tchd 6 to 1) 5
1849[9] JAZZMAN (Ire) 5-11-0 J F Titley, *hld up in rear, hdwy appr 4 out, styd on one pace.*..............(25 to 1 op 20 to 1) 6
2249 SEABROOK LAD 6-11-0 P Niven, *hld up, hdwy 5th, nvr nr to chal.*..(20 to 1) 7
1727[2] THE LAND AGENT 6-11-0 S Curran, *prmnt till wknd 4 out.* ....(11 to 1 op 7 to 1 tchd 12 to 1) 8
1770[4] ELY'S HARBOUR (Ire) 6-11-0 J A McCarthy, *nvr on terms.* .... (25 to 1 op 16 to 1) 9
2255[8] WELSH SILK 5-10-9 (5*) Sophie Mitchell, *al towards rear.* ....(33 to 1 op 25 to 1) 10
CHARLEY LAMBERT (Ire) 6-11-0 R Supple, *prmnt till wknd 7th, tld off.*......................(33 to 1 op 25 to 1) 11
2029[9] TOM TUGG (Ire) 7-11-0 C Maude, *led till hit and hdd 4th, styd prmnt till wknd 7th, tld off.*.......... (66 to 1 op 50 to 1) 12
1540 HIT THE BID (Ire) 6-11-0 P Carberry, *prmnt till wknd appr 4 out, tld off.*................................ (100 to 1) 13
AXO SPORT (Ire) 5-11-0 S Wynne, *chsd ldrs till wknd 7th, tld off.*..(100 to 1) 14
1594 MR GOONHILLY 7-10-9 (5*) Mr R Thornton, *al beh, tld off whn pld up bef 2 out.*..............(100 to 1 op 50 to 1) pu
1995 CHAIERGOLD (Ire) 5-10-7 (7*) C Davies, *prmnt till wknd 7th, tld off whn pld up bef 2 out.*......................(100 to 1) pu
TEAM PRINCESS 7-10-9 R Johnson, *tld off 5th, pld up bef 4 out.*..(100 to 1) pu

Dist: 3l, 1¼l, 6l, 6l, 1l, ½l, 10l, 2l, 8l, 17l. 5m 6.50s. a 18.50s (17 Ran).
SR: 23/10/18/2/-/-/ (T H Shrimpton), Miss H C Knight

2385 Burton Lazars Conditional Jockeys' Selling Handicap Hurdle C (0-90 4,5,6-y-o) £1,952 2m..........(2:10)

1832[2] BEECHFIELD FLYER [77] 6-11-9 G Tormey, *made virtually all, mstk 4 out, rdn clr appr last.*.......(7 to 2 tchd 4 to 1) 1
1835[8] SHEECKY [71] 6-11-3 S Ryan, *chsd ldrs, wnt second 4 out, ev ch till one pace appr 2 out.* (9 to 1 op 8 to 1 tchd 12 to 1) 2
2251* FLEET CADET [89] (v) 6-12-7 (7ex) G Supple, *hld up in rear, hdwy approching 4 out, rdn appr 2 out, found little.* .... (13 to 8 fav op 5 to 4 on tchd 7 to 4) 3
1947[9] TANGO MAN (Ire) [62] 5-10-8 B Grattan, *wl in rear till styd on frm 4 out, nvr dngrs.*..........................(33 to 1) 4
1798[8] SPRING LOADED [73] (v) 6-11-0 (5*) J T Nolan, *hld up, some hdwy 5th, wknd nxt.*..................(9 to 1 op 7 to 1) 5
2251[6] BERTS CHOICE [65] 6-10-11 G Lee, *wth wnr till wknd 4 out.* ....(33 to 1) 6
2181[7] SMILEY FACE [65] 5-10-6 (5*) J Harris, *al beh, effrt 5th, nvr on terms.*..........................(12 to 1 op 20 to 1) 7
2181[3] PAULTON [72] 4-10-6 E Husband, *in rear whn mstk 5th, sn wl beh.*................................(4 to 1 op 8 to 1) 8

Dist: 7l, 4l, 2l, 8l, 15l, 4l, 3l. 4m 4.70s. a 21.70s (8 Ran).
(Mrs M Robertson), W Clay

2386 Marshall Handicap Chase Class D (0-125 5-y-o and up) £3,850 2½m 110yds...................... (2:40)

1960[2] SHINING LIGHT (Ire) [109] 8-11-3 R Johnson, *hld up, hdwy appr 3 out, chalg whn mstk last, rallied and led r-in.* ....(7 to 2 op 5 to 2) 1
1926* REX TO THE RESCUE (Ire) [105] 9-10-8 (5*) Mr R Thornton, *sn led, not al fluent, hdd 7th, led 2 out till headed r-in.* ....(7 to 2 op 3 to 1) 2
2150[2] RUSTIC AIR [104] 10-10-12 P Carberry, *al prmnt, rallied 2 out, ran on.*.................(3 to 1 fav tchd 100 to 30) 3

1518^{5} PLUNDER BAY (USA) [115] 6-11-9 M A Fitzgerald, *hld up, hdwy whn jmpd slwly tenth, one pace frm 3 out.* ....(9 to 2 op 4 to 1 tchd 5 to 1) 4
1378^{4} CROPREDY LAD [96] 10-10-4 J Osborne, *al prmnt, led 7th till hdd 2 out, rdn and wknd r-in*..........(16 to 1 op 10 to 1) 5
51^{2} HOWGILL [94] 11-10-2 S Wynne, *hld up, making hdwy whn blun 4 out, nvr dngrs aftr*..............(14 to 1 op 12 to 1) 6
MUGONI BEACH [117] 12-11-11 C Maude, *al in rear, mstk 3rd, lost tch tenth*.........(9 to 1 op 5 to 1 tchd 10 to 1) 7
Dist: 2½l, 2½l, 3l, 5l, 7l, 2½l. 5m 10.80s. a 8.80s (7 Ran).
SR: 31/24/20/28/4/-/15/ (The Deeley Partnership), D Nicholson

2387 Charnwood Novices' Claiming Hurdle Class F (4-y-o and up) £2,679 2m .... (3:10)

1326* BRAMBLES WAY (bl) 8-11-12 P Niven, *hld up, smooth hdwy appr 4 out, led nxt, sn clr*........(6 to 4 fav op 7 to 4 on) 1
1438^{2} BLUNTSWOOD HALL 4-10-9 Gary Lyons, *led to 3rd, styd prmnt, outpcd frm 3 out*...(9 to 1 op 7 to 1 tchd 10 to 1) 2
1854^{8} WHISPERING DAWN 4-11-0 G Bradley, *trkd ldr, led 3rd, hdd 3 out, one pace aftr*....................(4 to 1 op 7 to 1) 3
SAHHAR 4-10-11 W Worthington, *hld up, hdwy 4th, rdn 3 out, kpt on one pace*..............................(50 to 1) 4
957 RE ROI (Ire) 5-10-13 (7*) J Power, *hld up in rear, hdwy 4 out, one pace frm 3 out*...................(7 to 1 tchd 8 to 1) 5
2023^{9} OUR TOM 5-11-3 (5*) Mr R Thornton, *prmnt, mstk 4th, one pace frm 3 out*.........................(66 to 1 op 50 to 1) 6
2032^{5} GI MOSS (bl) 10-11-1 W Marston, *chsd ldrs till wknd 3 out.* ....(66 to 1 op 50 to 1) 7
2174^{7} DENOMINATION (USA) 5-10-13 (7*) G Supple, *in tch, ev ch 4 out, rdn and sn btn*...............(20 to 1 op 12 to 1) 8
KAYE'S SECRET 4-10-8 R Supple, *rdn 4th, nvr nr to chal.* ....(50 to 1) 9
2002^{9} IRISH KINSMAN (bl) 4-10-11 V Slattery, *beh frm 4th, tld off.* ....(66 to 1 op 50 to 1) 10
1179 BITES 4-10-0 T Eley, *al beh, tld off*....(66 to 1 op 50 to 1) 11
1942 COLONEL JACK 5-10-13 (7*) J Harris, *al beh, tld off.* ....(66 to 1 op 50 to 1) 12
FIRST GOLD 8-11-8 R Johnson, *jmpd badly lft 3rd, al beh, tld off*..............................(20 to 1 op 14 to 1) 13
1599 TRIANNA 4-10-4 S Curran, *al beh, tld off.* ....(50 to 1 op 33 to 1) 14
THE ODDFELLOW 4-11-1 J Supple, *al beh, tld off.* ....(66 to 1 op 50 to 1) 15
A MILLION WATTS 6-10-9 (7*) R Hobson, *brght dwn 1st.* ....(66 to 1 op 50 to 1) bd
1844^{7} FIJON (Ire) 4-10-2 J Osborne, *brght dwn 1st.* ....(9 to 2 op 3 to 1) bd
539 MASRUF (Ire) 5-11-8 C O'Dwyer, *hld up, hdwy 4th, wknd appr 2 out, tld off whn pld up aftr nxt*.......(33 to 1 op 20 to 1) pu
1237 TOLCARNE LADY 8-10-13 R Greene, *chsd ldrs till wknd 5th, tld off whn pld up bef 2 out*..........(66 to 1 op 50 to 1) pu
Dist: 15l, ½l, sht-hd, 2l, nk, ½l, 12l, nk, 24l, ¾l. 4m 3.10s. a 20.10s (19 Ran).
(Nigel E M Jones), Mrs M Reveley

2388 Silver Bell Maiden Chase Class F (6-y-o and up) £3,195 3m........ (3:40)

2254^{6} PRIMITIVE PENNY 6-11-0 J F Titley, *hld up, hdwy 11th, led 15th, blun 2 out, sn reco'red, styd on und pres.* ....(16 to 1 op 14 to 1) 1
1615^{7} DEEL QUAY (Ire) 6-11-5 C O'Dwyer, *hld up in tch, hdwy 8th, styd on to go second r-in*...........(9 to 4 fav op 5 to 2) 2
1881^{2} CALLEVA STAR (Ire) 6-11-5 M A Fitzgerald, *hld up in tch, hdwy 9th, blun and lost pl 12th, styd on wl frm 2 out.* .... (6 to 1 op 5 to 1 tchd 13 to 2) 3
2310^{8} LOCH GARMAN HOTEL (Ire) 8-11-5 C Maude, *jmpd wl, led to 15th, ev ch till no extr r-in*...............(7 to 1 op 6 to 1) 4
1763 THE MILLMASTER (Ire) 6-11-5 R Supple, *trkd ldr to 8th, wknd 14th, tld off*........................ (25 to 1 op 20 to 1) 5
1981^{5} THUNDER ROAD (Ire) 6-11-5 P Niven, *hmpd 6th, al beh, tld off*..............................(16 to 1 op 10 to 1) 6
1963 ROYAL HAND 7-11-5 Mr R Armson, *hit 4th, al beh, tld off.* ....(50 to 1) 7
2291^{2} BOLSHIE BARON 8-11-5 Mr M Harris, *mstks, chsd ldrs, wknd appr 15th*............ (11 to 1 op 10 to 1 tchd 12 to 1) 8
999 RENT DAY 8-11-0 S Curran, *hld up in tch, badly hmpd 6th, hdwy 9th, btn in 5th pl whn ran out 2 out, continued, tld off.* ....(16 to 1 op 12 to 1) 9
1804^{4} MASTER HOPE (Ire) 8-11-5 R Johnson, *in tch whn f 6th, broke neck, dead*.........................(3 to 1 op 5 to 2) f
1600 PADDY BURKE (Ire) 7-11-5 A Thornton, *mid-div whn f 7th.* ....(50 to 1) f
1804^{8} ROLLED GOLD 8-11-0 (5*) Mr R Thornton, *prmnt, chsd ldr 8th till f 12th*..............................(33 to 1) f
2176^{8} ICE MAGIC (v) 10-11-5 J Supple, *mstks in rear, tld off whn refused 15th*.............................(25 to 1) ref
Dist: ½l, ¾l, nk, 29l, ½l, sht-hd, 13l. 6m 9.80s. a 24.80s (13 Ran).
(Mrs Peter Mason), Mrs D Haine

2389 Golden Miller Handicap Hurdle Class D (0-120 4-y-o and up) £3,054 2½m 110yds........................ (4:10)

2149^{2} CITTADINO [100] 7-10-10 M Foster, *al in tch, led appr 2 out, hrd rdn, all out*........................(6 to 1 op 7 to 1) 1
1520^{4} MOMENT OF GLORY (Ire) [114] 6-11-10 G Bradley, *hld up in rear, hdwy 4 out, one pace frm 3 out.* .... (9 to 1 op 6 to 1 tchd 10 to 1) 2
2217 ROSENCRANTZ (Ire) [108] 5-11-4 R Johnson, *hld up, hdwy 7th, ev ch appr last, one pace.* ....(11 to 4 fav op 3 to 1 tchd 4 to 1) 3
1614* ALLOW (Ire) [93] 6-9-12 (5*) Mr R Thornton, *hld up, hdwy appr 4 out, wknd approaching last*........... (8 to 1 op 6 to 1) 4
WINGS COVE [118] 7-12-0 J Osborne, *chsd ldrs, one pace frm 3 out*.........................(20 to 1 op 10 to 1) 5
1728^{2} JEFFERIES [101] 8-10-11 G Upton, *hld up in mid-div, one pace frm 3 out*........................ (7 to 1 op 6 to 1) 6
2198^{3} DIWALI DANCER [113] 7-11-2 (7*) G Supple, *led till hdd appr 2 out, sn wknd*.........................(9 to 1 op 6 to 1) 7
2253 KIPPANOUR (USA) [112] (bl) 5-11-5 (3*) J Magee, *hld up, hdwy 5th, ev ch 3 out, sn wknd*........(20 to 1 op 14 to 1) 8
THE GLOW (Ire) [106] 9-11-2 W Marston, *chsd ldrs till wknd appr 4 out*.........................(20 to 1 op 16 to 1) 9
CHILL WIND [91] 8-10-1 R Supple, *al beh, tld off 7th.* ....(50 to 1 op 33 to 1) 10
2203 FAR SENIOR [95] 11-10-5 Gary Lyons, *al beh, tld off 7th.* ....(66 to 1 op 50 to 1) 11
1966^{5} ABSALOM'S PILLAR [96] 7-10-6 T Eley, *hld up, f 5th.* ....(14 to 1 op 10 to 1) f
1762^{5} DARK HONEY [109] 12-11-5 A Dicken, *beh whn hmpd and uns rdr 5th*........................(25 to 1 op 20 to 1) ur
1959^{2} SPRING SAINT [107] 8-11-3 C Maude, *hld up, tld off whn pld up bef 2 out*.........................(20 to 1 op 14 to 1) pu
1889 KYTTON CASTLE [109] 10-10-12 (7*) X Aizpuru, *hld up in tch, wknd and pld up appr 4 out, collapsed, dead.* ....(33 to 1 op 20 to 1) pu
2257* CIRCUS LINE [120] 6-12-2 (6ex) M A Fitzgerald, *not fluent early, prmnt till pld aftr 7th, dismounted.* .... (13 to 2 op 4 to 1 tchd 7 to 1) pu
Dist: Hd, 2l, 3½l, 1¾l, 1l, 4l, 2½l, 7l, dist, dist. 5m 5.10s. a 17.10s (16 Ran).
SR: 23/37/29/10/33/15/23/19/6/ (D B Dennison), C W Thornton

WINDSOR (good to firm)
Wednesday January 29th
Going Correction: PLUS 0.20 sec. per fur. (races 1,3,5,7), NIL (2,4,6)

2390 Burnham Selling Hurdle Class G (4 - 7-y-o) £2,090 2m............ (1:30)

1731^{3} PROUD IMAGE 5-11-5 B Clifford, *trkd ldrs, chlgd and wnt rght 2 out, sn led, went badly right ag'n last, drvn out.* ....(5 to 1 op 7 to 2) 1
2185^{8} ALMAPA 5-11-9 (3*) T Dascombe, *hdwy to track ldrs 4th, styd on frm 3 out, one pace*..........(12 to 1 op 8 to 1) 2
2265^{6} TREAD THE BOARDS (bl) 6-11-0 B Powell, *sn prmnt, drvn alng to chase ldrs appr 3 out, styd on same pace.* ....(6 to 1 op 5 to 1) 3
2279 PERSIAN BUTTERFLY 5-11-0 P Hide, *trkd ldr, chlgd 3rd, led nxt, hdd sn aftr 2 out, one pace*...... (33 to 1 op 20 to 1) 4
2265 JOBBER'S FIDDLE 5-11-0 M Clarke, *wnt prmnt 5th, one pace 2 out*............................ (33 to 1 op 25 to 1) 5
2265^{9} EWAR BOLD 4-10-7 D Gallagher, *wl beh, drvn alng 3 out, moderate hdwy und pres frm nxt*.....(33 to 1 op 25 to 1) 6
CLASSIC DELIGHT (USA) 4-10-2 K Gaule, *beh, styd on frm 2 out, not a dngr*.................................... (33 to 1) 7
1969 SHARMOOR 5-11-0 M Richards, *beh, some hdwy frm 3 out.* .... (10 to 1 op 8 to 1 tchd 12 to 1) 8
ESPLA 6-11-5 W McFarland, *nvr nr ldrs.* ....(12 to 1 tchd 14 to 1) 9
2279 MARROWFAT LADY (Ire) 6-10-7 (7*) S Melrose, *hdwy to chase ldrs 4th, wknd appr 3 out.* .... (16 to 1 op 25 to 1 tchd 14 to 1) 10
1733 FOLLOW DE CALL 7-11-5 D Walsh, *hdwy 4th, chsd ldrs nxt, sn wknd*......................................(33 to 1) 11
TAUTEN (Ire) 7-11-0 I Lawrence, *al beh.* ....(25 to 1 op 20 to 1) 12
JUST FLAMENCO 6-11-5 J R Kavanagh, *sn beh.* ....(33 to 1 op 20 to 1) 13
2265^{5} ROSE OF GLENN 6-11-0 R Farrant, *hdwy 4th, chasing ldrs whn f nxt*...........................(8 to 1 op 6 to 1) f
2197^{8} BATTLESHIP BRUCE 5-11-5 D Bridgwater, *trkd ldrs, rdn alng appr 3 out, str chal nxt, 3rd and hld whn f last.* ....(15 to 8 fav op 7 to 4 tchd 9 to 4) f
ROCKVILLE PIKE (Ire) 5-11-0 (5*) Michael Brennan, *keen hold, led to 4th, wknd aftr nxt, beh whn f 2 out.* ....(20 to 1 op 14 to 1) f
2255 RED PHANTOM (Ire) (v) 5-11-5 N Mann, *hdwy 4th, chasing ldrs whn brght dwn nxt*............. (25 to 1 op 20 to 1) bd
STARK LOMOND (USA) 4-10-7 P McLoughlin, *al beh, tld off whn pld up bef 2 out*..................(12 to 1 op 10 to 1) pu
1992^{5} SPIRAL FLYER (Ire) 4-10-2 L Harvey, *sn beh, tld off whn pld up bef 2 out*............................(8 to 1 tchd 9 to 1) pu
Dist: 3½l, 3l, 5l, 5l, 10l, 1¾l, 2½l, 7l, 11l, 3l. 3m 55.70s. a 10.70s (19 Ran).
SR: 16/19/4/-/-/-/ (Town And Country Tyre Services Limited), G M McCourt

2391 Oakside Novices' Chase Class E (5-y-o and up) £3,614 3m........ (2:00)

1915* PALOSANTO (Ire) 7-11-5 D Walsh, *trkd clr ldr, led aftr 9th, sn wl clear, shaken up and blun 2 out, kpt on.*
................................(11 to 4 op 3 to 1 tchd 9 to 4) 1
1542³ HAWAIIAN SAM (Ire) 7-11-5 G Crone, *hdwy 12th, chsd wnr frm 14th, some headway till no imprsn from 4 out.*
................................(9 to 2 op 4 to 1) 2
2254³ SUPER RITCHART 9-11-5 Derek Byrne, *wl beh, moderate hdwy frm 12th, styd on to take poor 3rd 3 out, tld off.*
................................(14 to 1 op 12 to 1 tchd 16 to 1) 3
2266 BALLYMGYR (Ire) (bl) 8-11-5 D Gallagher, *chsd ldrs, no ch frm 12th, tld off.*..................(25 to 1 op 20 to 1) 4
2216³ VOLLEYBALL (Ire) 8-11-5 M Richards, *al wl beh, tld off whn blun last.*........................(33 to 1 op 20 to 1) 5
1814 MILLFRONE (Ire) 7-11-5 D O'Sullivan, *sn clr, hdd aftr 9th, wknd 11th, tld off.*......(50 to 1 op 33 to 1 tchd 66 to 1) 6
1718² SECRET BID (Ire) 7-11-5 J R Kavanagh, *jmpd poorly, al beh, blun 12th, tld off.*...................(5 to 2 fav tchd 3 to 1) 7
1961 BONITA BLAKENEY 7-11-0 B Clifford, *al beh, tld off.*
................................(33 to 1 op 20 to 1 tchd 50 to 1) 8
NAPOLEON'S GOLD (Ire) 7-10-12 (7*) D Creech, *tld off 3rd.*
................................(50 to 1 op 33 to 1 tchd 66 to 1) 9
1939⁵ GIVUS A CALL (Ire) 7-11-2 (3*) L Aspell, *beh till blun and uns rdr 8th.*..................(13 to 2 op 7 to 2 tchd 7 to 1) ur
MYSTIC MANNA 11-11-5 L Harvey, *al beh, tld off whn pld up bef 14th.*...............(20 to 1 op 12 to 1 tchd 25 to 1) pu
1938⁶ DREAM LEADER (Ire) 7-11-5 B Powell, *al beh, tld off whn pld up bef 14th.*......................(10 to 1 op 6 to 1) pu
1718 LORD ANTRIM (Ire) 8-11-5 P Hide, *al beh, tld off whn pld up bef 4 out.*.............(50 to 1 op 33 to 1 tchd 66 to 1) pu
Dist: 10l, dist, 14l, 18l, 2l, 20l, 21l. 5m 58.50s. a 5.50s (13 Ran).
SR: 36/26/-/-/-/-/   (B A Kilpatrick), M C Pipe

2392 Levy Board Novices' Handicap Hurdle Class E (0-100 4-y-o and up) £2,915 2¾m 110yds......... (2:30)

1291⁸ MONTEL EXPRESS (Ire) [95] 5-11-6 (7*) Mr R Wakley, *steady hdwy 7th, trkd ldr 2 out, chlgd last, sn led, all out.*
................................(10 to 1 op 6 to 1) 1
2295* CLOD HOPPER (Ire) [80] 7-10-7 (5*,7ex) A Bates, *led second, drvn alng frm 3 out, hdd sn aftr last, styd on und pres.*
................................(5 to 1 tchd 11 to 2) 2
2158⁶ COLWALL [82] 6-10-7 (7*) K Hibbert, *al tracking ldrs, shaken up 3 out, one pace frm nxt.*
................................(11 to 1 op 8 to 1 tchd 12 to 1) 3
1921 ZIP YOUR LIP [82] 7-11-0 Derek Byrne, *hdwy 5th, chsd ldrs and rdn 3 out, no headway frm nxt...*(33 to 1 op 25 to 1) 4
2207² MR CHRISTIE [83] 5-11-1 B Powell, *drvn and hdwy 6th, chsd ldrs 3 out, sn outpcd.* (9 to 2 op 5 to 1 tchd 11 to 2) 5
JAY EM ESS (NZ) [83] 8-10-8 (7*) Mr G Shenkin, *hdwy 3 out, kpt on frm nxt, not a dngr.*...........(3 to 1 tchd 4 to 1) 6
1423² NORDIC SPREE (Ire) [92] 5-11-10 P Holley, *hdwy 7th, hrd rdn appr 3 out, wknd nxt...*(14 to 1 op 10 to 1 tchd 16 to 1) 7
1723³ KAREN'S TYPHOON (Ire) [72] 6-10-4 D Gallagher, *beh, rdn and hdwy 3 out, n.d a dngr.*
................................(16 to 1 op 12 to 1 tchd 20 to 1) 8
1623 RELUCKINO [80] 7-10-7 (5*) Michael Brennan, *beh, some hdwy frm 3 out.*..............(16 to 1 tchd 20 to 1) 9
FARLEYER ROSE (Ire) [69] 8-10-1 M Richards, *rapid hdwy to chase ldrs 6th, chsd lder nxt till appr 3 out, sn wknd.*
................................(14 to 1 op 12 to 1 tchd 16 to 1) 10
1555³ ROSS DANCER (Ire) [86] 5-11-4 W McFarland, *nvr rch ldrs.*
................................(12 to 1 op 14 to 1 tchd 16 to 1) 11
2174 SCALP 'EM (Ire) [68] 9-10-0 Dr P Pritchard, *chsd ldrs to 7th, wknd appr 3 out.*..........(33 to 1 tchd 50 to 1) 12
2252 KING'S COURTIER (Ire) [74] (v) 8-10-6 C Llewellyn, *led to second, prmnt till wknd 4 out.*.....(33 to 1 tchd 40 to 1) 13
1663⁷ YOUNG TYCOON (NZ) [78] 6-10-10 L Harvey, *al rear.*
................................(33 to 1 op 20 to 1) 14
2193³ CARDINAL GAYLE (Ire) [68] 7-9-12¹ (3*) P Henley, *hdwy 7th, wknd aftr 4 out...*(11 to 1 op 10 to 1 tchd 12 to 1) 15
2193⁴ LODESTONE LAD (Ire) [68] 7-10-0 T J Murphy, *blun 4 out, al beh...*.......................(33 to 1 op 20 to 1) 16
1973 TREHANE [75] 5-10-7 K Gaule, *prmnt till rdn and wknd 4 out.*
................................(33 to 1 op 20 to 1) 17
2012⁸ STERLING FELLOW [88] (v) 4-10-7 D Bridgwater, *chsd ldrs, rdn alng 5th, wknd 7th...*(15 to 2 op 7 to 1 tchd 8 to 1) 18
2023⁷ GUTTERIDGE (Ire) [76] 7-10-8 D Walsh, *chsd ldrs, mstk and wknd 3 out, pld up bef nxt.*...........(5 to 1 op 8 to 1) pu
2152⁷ ROSSELL ISLAND (Ire) [81] 6-10-10 (3*) G Hogan, *al beh, tld off whn pld up bef 3 out.*(14 to 1 op 12 to 1 tchd 16 to 1) pu
1697⁸ FLAMING ROSE (Ire) [70] 7-10-2² D O'Sullivan, *sn beh, tld off whn pld up bef 3 out.*...........(33 to 1 tchd 50 to 1) pu
Dist: 1¾l, 9l, ¾l, 5l, 3l, 7l, 1½l, 8l, 9l, 5l. 5m 28.30s. a 13.30s (21 Ran).
SR: 11/-/-/-/-/-/   (Mrs Jacqueline Conroy), K C Bailey

2393 Scania Approved Used Vehicles Chase Handicap Class D (0-125 5-y-o and up) £4,053 3m......... (3:00)

2268⁹ ZAMBEZI SPIRIT (Ire) [97] 8-10-0 Derek Byrne, *trkd ldrs 7th, lost pos 11th, hdwy 14th, chlgd frm 2 out, led r-in, drvn out.*
................................(13 to 2 op 7 to 1 tchd 15 to 1) 1
2220² FIVE TO SEVEN (USA) [117] 8-11-6 D Bridgwater, *hit 1st, chsd ldr frm 12th, led 3 out, hit nxt, hdd r-in, rallied, no extr cl hme.*
................................(7 to 2 jt-fav tchd 4 to 1) 2

1511* BAS DE LAINE (Fr) [125] (v) 11-12-0 R Garritty, *led, hit 5th, blun and hdd 3 out, rallied last, no extr.*..........(7 to 2 jt-fav tchd 4 to 1) 3
1889³ DANGER BABY [105] 7-10-8 P Holley, *sn in tch, drvn alng appr 4 out, styd on same pace frm nxt.* (4 to 1 tchd 5 to 1) 4
2252⁸ MR INVADER [97] (bl) 10-10-0 C Llewellyn, *prmnt, hit 4th, chlgd 8th, rdn alng frm four out, styd on to chase ldrs till wknd aftr 2 out.*..................(16 to 1 op 14 to 1) 5
1948³ REALLY A RASCAL [105] 10-10-5 (3*) D Fortt, *beh, some hdwy 4 out, rdn and kpt on frm 2 out, lme.* (6 to 1 op 5 to 1) 6
CLAXTON GREENE [97] 13-10-0 D Gallagher, *beh 5th.*
................................(25 to 1) 7
1767 KNOCKAVERRY (Ire) [100] 9-10-3 I Lawrence, *beh, rapid hdwy to chase ldrs 9th, hit 14th, wknd.* (16 to 1 op 14 to 1) 8
2194⁵ BALLY PARSON [105] 11-10-8 T J Murphy, *with ldr to second, blun 6th, no ch whn blunded 12th...*(14 to 1 op 12 to 1) 9
1858⁵ STAUNCH RIVAL (USA) [115] (bl) 10-11-4 B Powell, *chsd ldrs 9th, wknd 13th.*..........(12 to 1 tchd 14 to 1) 10
2247⁵ FOOLS ERRAND (Ire) [115] 7-11-4 B Clifford, *hit 9th and beh, pld up bef nxt.*..........(7 to 1 op 12 to 1 tchd 14 to 1) pu
Dist: ½l, 5l, ¾l, ¾l, ½l, 17l, 22l, 2½l, 7l. 5m 59.60s. a 6.60s (11 Ran).
SR: 6/25/28/7/-/5/   (P C Townsend), Mrs Merrita Jones

2394 Exterior Profiles Novices' Hurdle Class E (4-y-o and up) £2,757 2½m .... (3:30)

1012* SCOUNDREL 6-11-4 S McNeill, *hld up, hdwy to track ldrs 5th, quickened to ld 3 out, ran on wl whn chlgd and not much room r-in...*..........(6 to 5 fav op 5 to 4 on tchd 11 to 8) 1
1768² JACK GALLAGHER 6-11-4 M Richards, *pressed ldr, led 5th to 3 out, styd chalg, rdn and hng badly lft r-in, no extr cl hme.*
................................(6 to 1 op 11 to 2 tchd 7 to 1) 2
1961* RIVER BAY (Ire) 6-11-5 B Fenton, *hdwy to track ldrs 4th, chlgd 3 out, sn outpcd.*..........(7 to 4 tchd 2 to 1) 3
1995⁸ COOLE CHERRY 7-11-4 J R Kavanagh, *led to 5th, rdn to chase ldrs 3 out, sn one pace.*
................................(25 to 1 op 20 to 1 tchd 33 to 1) 4
2197⁹ AT LIBERTY (Ire) 5-11-4 D Gallagher, *trkd ldrs till wknd 3 out.*........................(20 to 1 op 12 to 1) 5
873 CAPTAIN NAVAR (Ire) 7-10-13 (5*) Michael Brennan, *beh most of way...*(50 to 1 op 20 to 1 tchd 100 to 1) 6
1855 MAETERLINCK (Ire) 5-10-11 (7*) Clare Thorner, *keen hold, chsd ldrs till appr 3 out...*(50 to 1 op 33 to 1) 7
1675⁷ DAYDREAM BELIEVER 5-10-13 W McFarland, *hdwy 4th, lost tch four out...*(50 to 1 op 33 to 1 tchd 100 to 1) 8
1940⁶ DANZANTE (Ire) 5-11-4 D Walsh, *beh, blun 5th, tld off nxt, pld up bef 2 out...*(12 to 1 op 7 to 1 tchd 14 to 1) pu
Dist: Sht-hd, 9l, 2l, 10l, 6l, 2l, 16l. 4m 59.30s. a 19.30s (9 Ran).
(Mrs J M Corbett), K C Bailey

2395 Holyport Conditional Jockeys' Handicap Chase Class E (0-115 5-y-o and up) £3,068 2m 5f.......... (4:00)

1686² HAWAIIAN YOUTH (Ire) [99] 9-10-12 D Fortt, *prmnt, led aftr 7th to 11th, led appr 4 out, styd on wl frm nxt......*(5 to 2 jt-fav op 11 to 4) 1
2244³ GOOD FOR A LAUGH [88] 13-10-1 O Burrows, *hdwy 6th, prmnt whn mstk 9th, chsd winer frm 3 out, no imprsn.*
................................(10 to 1 tchd 12 to 1) 2
1424³ MR CONDUCTOR (Ire) [108] 6-11-7 P Henley, *hdwy 6th, hit tenth and beh, sn rdn, moderate headway frm 3 out.*
......(5 to 2 jt-fav op 9 to 4 tchd 2 to 1 and 11 to 4) 3
1920³ JAILBREAKER [87] 10-10-0 D Salter, *beh, some hdwy 4 out, one pace und pres nxt...*(5 to 1 op 7 to 1) 4
1889 BE SURPRISED [87] 11-10-0 M Batchelor, *led to 3rd, styd disputing ld, led 11th till appr 4 out, wknd nxt.*
................................(33 to 1 tchd 50 to 1) 5
2194⁶ ARMALA [105] 12-11-4 L Aspell, *led 3rd till aftr 7th, blun and wknd 11th.*........................(5 to 1 op 9 to 2) 6
2266 BATHWICK BOBBIE [87] 10-10-0 G Hogan, *beh, aftr 11th, wknd 4 out.*...............(33 to 1 op 25 to 1) 7
TRIBAL RULER [90] 12-10-3 D Walsh, *in tch, chsd ldrs 11th, drvn to go second appr for out, sn weakened.*
................................(20 to 1 op 16 to 1) 8
2247 BEAU BABILLARD [113] (bl) 10-11-12 L Cummins, *hdwy 7th, wknd 4 out...............*(10 to 1 op 8 to 1 tchd 11 to 1) 9
2291 FULL SHILLING (USA) [87] (bl) 8-10-0 Guy Lewis, *chsd ldrs to 4 out, sn wknd...........*(33 to 1 op 25 to 1 tchd 50 to 1) 10
1674 COASTING [87] 11-10-0 A Bates, *hit 9th, al beh.*
................................(33 to 1 op 25 to 1 tchd 50 to 1) 11
2291 ROMANY BLUES [89] 8-10-2² M Berry, *hdwy 11th, staying on and clsg on ldrs whn f 4 out.*
................................(33 to 1 op 25 to 1 tchd 50 to 1) f
Dist: 4l, 10l, 1¼l, nk, 10l, 7l, 1l, ½l, 1l, ½l. 5m 19.70s. a 10.70s (12 Ran).
(G Redford), G M McCourt

2396 Copper Horse Handicap Hurdle Class D (0-120 4-y-o and up) £2,945 2m................................ (4:30)

1940³ ROYAL EVENT [100] 6-10-5 (3*) D Fortt, *made most till held briefly aftr 4 out, ran on wl whn chlgd frm 2 out, hld on gmely.*
................................(2 to 1 fav op 9 to 4 tchd 5 to 2) 1

1728[4] HANDSON [92] 5-9-10[1] (5*) D Salter, *beh, hdwy appr 3 out, chlgd last, kpt on, not pace of wnr nr finish.*
....(6 to 1 op 4 to 1) 2
1603[7] SUPERMICK [92] 6-10-0 M Richards, *chsd ldrs, led briefly aftr 4 out, styd chasing wnr, ev ch frm 2 out till no extr r-in.*
....................(7 to 1 op 5 to 1 tchd 15 to 2) 3
2244 MISS MARIGOLD [96] (bl) 8-10-4 B Powell, *beh, rdn and hdwy 5th, chsd ldrs 3 out, sn fdd....* (33 to 1 op 20 to 1) 4
1835[6] KELLY MAC [92] 7-10-0 C Llewellyn, *wth wnr to 3rd, styd prmnt to 3 out...........*(8 to 1 op 6 to 1 tchd 9 to 1) 5
1722 DONTDRESSFORDINNER [92] 7-9-12[1] (3*) T Dascombe, *in tch, rdn and wknd 3 out.* (11 to 1 op 7 to 1 tchd 12 to 1) 6
1346 SOCIETY GUEST [118] 11-11-5 (7*) C Rae, *chsd ldrs to 3 out, sn wknd...................*(6 to 1 op 4 to 1 tchd 7 to 1) 7
1835[9] ERLKING (Ire) [93] (bl) 7-10-1 D Bridgwater, *hld up, gd hdwy to chase ldrs appr 3 out, sn fdd.....* (12 to 1 op 8 to 1) 8
FLYING EAGLE [108] 6-11-2 P McLoughlin, *chsd ldrs to 4 out, sn wknd.....................*(9 to 2 op 6 to 1 tchd 4 to 1) 9
9387 RAAHIN (USA) [93] 12-10-11 S McNeill, *al rear.*
....................(50 to 1 op 25 to 1 tchd 66 to 1) 10
Dist: ½l, 5l, ¾l, 6l, ¾l, 10l, 7l, 23l, 16l. 3m 54.20s. a 9.20s (10 Ran).
SR: 20/11/6/9/-/-/14/-/-/ (T J Whitley), D R Gandolfo

FOLKESTONE (good to soft (races 1,2,4,6), good (3,5))
Thursday January 30th
Going Correction: PLUS 1.05 sec. per fur. (races 1,2,4,6), PLUS 0.30 (3,5)

2397 Gibbons Brook Novices' Hurdle
Class E (4-y-o and up) £2,368 2m 1f 110yds........................(1:45)

SHADOW LEADER 6-11-3 J A McCarthy, *hld up, steady hdwy appr 3 out, led approaching last, rdn out.*
........................(3 to 1 fav op 5 to 2) 1
GRIEF (Ire) 4-10-7 P Holley, *hld up, took clr order 3rd, led briefly appr last, one pace r-in........*(10 to 1 op 7 to 1) 2
WISE KING 7-11-3 G Upton, *hld up, hdwy frm 5th, rdn aftr 2 out, one pace appr last...............*(7 to 2 op 5 to 2) 3
KINGS WITNESS (USA) 4-10-7 B Powell, *hld up beh ldrs, hit 4th, jmpd slwly 3 out, sn rdn, one pace appr last.*
........................(4 to 1 op 5 to 2) 4
FRESH FRUIT DAILY 5-10-12 D Gallagher, *keen hold early, led 3rd, hdd and wknd appr last.*
............................(12 to 1 op 10 to 1 tchd 14 to 1) 5
GEISWAY (Can) 7-11-3 R Farrant, *jmpd slwly 1st, prmnt till wknd betw fnl 2........*(16 to 1 op 8 to 1 tchd 20 to 1) 6
SALAMAN (Fr) 5-11-3 C Llewellyn, *not fluent, al beh.*
........................(4 to 1 op 12 to 1 tchd 16 to 1) 7
ENVOCAMANDA (Ire) 8-11-3 J R Kavanagh, *beh frm 6th.*
.......................(20 to 1 tchd 33 to 1) 8
COURTING DANGER 4-10-7 M A Fitzgerald, *beh frm 6th, tld off whn pld up bef last...............*(20 to 1 op 12 to 1) pu
451[3] LORD TOMANICO (Fr) 5-11-9 J Railton, *led to 3rd, wknd quickly appr 3 out, tld off whn pld up and dismounted bef last.*
....................(15 to 2 op 5 to 1 tchd 8 to 1) pu
Dist: 3l, 11½l, 8l, 24l, 24l, 6l, 19l. 4m 22.20s. a 25.20s (10 Ran).
SR: 21/8/16/2/-/-/ (James Blackshaw), C R Egerton

2398 Stelling Minnis Novices' Hurdle
Class E (4-y-o and up) £2,326 2¾m 110yds.......................(2:15)

1961[2] FIDDLING THE FACTS (Ire) 6-10-13 M A Fitzgerald, *nvr far away, led appr last, pushed clr, cmftbly.*
....................(7 to 4 fav op 6 to 4 tchd 5 to 4) 1
1973[4] ROYAL RAVEN (Ire) 6-11-1 (3*) L Aspell, *wtd wth, prog 6th, rdn to chase wnr appr last, no imprsn.*
........................(4 to 1 op 7 to 2 tchd 9 to 2) 2
UNSINKABLE BOXER (Ire) 8-11-4 I Lawrence, *hld up, led 7th, hdd appr last, sn wknd...................*(14 to 1) 3
2152[5] MUSIC MASTER 7-11-4 J A McCarthy, *hld up, hmpd bend aftr 1st, hdwy appr 8th, wknd bef 2 out, tld off.*
........................(7 to 2 op 5 to 2) 4
KINGSWOOD MANOR 7-11-4 R Farrant, *prmnt till wknd 3 out, tld off..................*(12 to 1 op 12 to 1) 5
1792[5] HARDY BREEZE (Ire) 6-11-4 J R Kavanagh, *prmnt till wknd 7th, tld off...........*(16 to 1 op 10 to 1 tchd 20 to 1) 6
1815[5] QUINAG 6-10-13 S McNeill, *hld up in tch, wknd 8th, tld off.*
....................(14 to 1 op 8 to 1 tchd 16 to 1) 7
UPHAM SURPRISE 9-11-4 G Upton, *beh frm 8th, tld off whn pld up bef last.............*(8 to 1 op 10 to 1) pu
2250 ALONGWAYDOWN (Ire) 8-11-4 D Leahy, *beh frm 8th, tld off whn pld up bef last......................*(66 to 1 op 50 to 1) pu
GENTLE TUNE (Ire) 7-10-11 (7*) Mr P O'Keeffe, *led till hdd and mstk 7th, sn wknd, tld off whn pld up bef 3 out.*
.......................(33 to 1 op 20 to 1) pu
Dist: 10l, 15l, 24l, 2½l, 3½l, 5l. 5m 56.30s. a 46.30s (10 Ran).
(Mrs E Roberts), N J Henderson

2399 Paddlesworth Novices' Chase Class
D (5-y-o and up) £3,550 2m 5f (2:45)

2280[2] THE REVEREND BERT (Ire) 9-11-3 B Fenton, *hld up, improved 10th, led 2 out, rdn whn lft clr last.*
....................(7 to 2 op 4 to 1 tchd 3 to 1) 1
920[2] FRAZER ISLAND (Ire) 8-11-3 D O'Sullivan, *in tch, rdn appr 3 out, wnt second r-in, no imprsn on wnr.* (14 to 1 op 10 to 1) 2
NORMARANGE (Ire) 7-11-3 M Richards, *hld up beh ldrs, hit 4th, rdn whn awkward four out, btn appr 2 out.*
....................(20 to 1 op 12 to 1) 3
1725[4] FLIPPANCE 7-11-3 C Llewellyn, *in tch, rdn and btn 3 out.*
....................(8 to 1 op 5 to 1) 4
1957[2] COURT MASTER (Ire) 9-11-3 B Powell, *made most, hit 8th, hdd 12th, wknd appr 2 out............*(6 to 1 op 6 to 1) 5
1573 HARRY THE HORSE 9-11-3 G Upton, *nvr on terms.*
....................(14 to 1 op 8 to 1) 6
WELSH COTTAGE 10-10-10 (7*) Mr P O'Keeffe, *hld up, lost tch frm 10th...................*(33 to 1 op 12 to 1) 7
1831[6] CHARTER LANE (Ire) 7-11-3 D Leahy, *hld up, wknd 4 out.*
....................(50 to 1 op 33 to 1) 8
1939[2] CONQUERING LEADER (Ire) 8-10-12 M A Fitzgerald, *al hndy, led 12th, hdd 2 out, rallying und pres whn f last.*
.......................(5 to 4 on tchd 11 to 8 on and 6 to 5 on) f
1794[4] RUMBLE (USA) 9-11-3 S McNeill, *prmnt till 6th, beh whn pld up bef 8th, broke blood vessel......*(33 to 1 op 20 to 1) pu
Dist: 9l, 1¼l, 6l, 13l, 10l, nk, hd. 5m 24.00s. a 13.00s (10 Ran).
SR: 22/13/11/5/-/-/ (The Bollie Club), G B Balding

2400 Six Mile Bottom Handicap Hurdle
Class E (0-115 4-y-o and up) £2,158 2m 1f 110yds.................(3:15)

1807[4] MARIUS (Ire) [110] 7-11-11 (3*) L Aspell, *chsd ldr, led appr 5th, clr frm 2 out, unchlgd..........*(9 to 4 fav op 7 to 4) 1
1936[4] AUGUST TWELFTH [85] 9-10-3 C Llewellyn, *hld up beh ldrs, outpcd 5th, rallied to chase wnr frm 2 out, no imprsn.*
....................(5 to 1 op 4 to 1 tchd 11 to 2) 2
2257[4] SASSIVER (USA) [92] 7-10-7 (3*) G Hogan, *hld up in tch, outpcd 5th, rallied 3 out, one pace 2 out.*
....................(7 to 2 op 5 to 2 tchd 4 to 1) 3
1982[6] RIVER ISLAND (USA) [98] 9-11-2 G Upton, *led till appr 5th, sn wknd, tld off...........*(10 to 1 tchd 12 to 1) 4
THEFIELDSOFATHENRY (Ire) [109] 7-11-13 J M McCarthy, *took keen hold, hld up, hdwy to chase wnr appr 5th till 2 out, sn wknd.................*(4 to 1 op 5 to 1 tchd 9 to 2) 5
PLAY GAMES (USA) [95] 9-10-13 D Gallagher, *beh frm 5th, tld off whn pld up bef 3 out.........*(5 to 1 op 8 to 1) pu
Dist: 17l, 8l, 26l, 17l. 4m 26.30s. a 29.30s (6 Ran).
(Mrs Anthony Andrews), J T Gifford

2401 Newington Peene Handicap Chase
Class E (0-115 5-y-o and up) £2,862 3¼m.......................(3:45)

SIMPSON [87] 12-10-6 G Upton, *in tch till lost pl 7th, rallied 12th, outpcd 4 out, rallied ag'n appr last, led r-in, ran on wl.*
....................(4 to 1 op 3 to 1) 1
1946 ROCKY PARK [95] 11-11-0 B Fenton, *jmpd lft, prmnt, led 5th, jumped badly left last, hdd r-in, no extr.*
....................(5 to 1 op 5 to 1 tchd 6 to 1 and 9 to 2) 2
1734 EXPRESS TRAVEL (Ire) [81] 9-10-0 D Morris, *hld up, hdwy 7th, hit 9th, rdn to chal 2 out, unbl to quicken r-in.*
....................(4 to 1 op 5 to 1 tchd 6 to 1) 3
2252[4] MAESTRO PAUL [99] 11-11-1 (3*) L Aspell, *hld up, prog 14th, rdn and wknd 3 out...................*(10 to 1 op 6 to 1) 4
1766 RUBINS BOY [81] 11-9-7 (7*) D Finnegan, *trkd ldrs till wknd 13th.............................*(25 to 1 op 16 to 1) 5
2252[2] YEOMAN WARRIOR [102] 10-11-7 D O'Sullivan, *led to 5th, lost pl frm 10th, no dngr aftr.....* (5 to 4 fav tchd 7 to 4) 6
1960 MASTER JOLSON [105] 9-11-10 J R Kavanagh, *hld up, not fluent 11th, improved 15th, wknd 3 out.* (16 to 1 op 10 to 1) 7
Dist: 2½l, 4l, 17l, 6l, 12l, 16l. 6m 43.50s. a 28.50s (7 Ran).
(John Bickel), J A B Old

2402 West Wood Standard Open National
Hunt Flat Class H (4,5,6-y-o) £1,182 2m 1f 110yds.......................(4:15)

TOP NOTE (Ire) 5-11-1 (3*) L Aspell, *hld up, drvn alng o'r 3 fs out, hdwy over 2 out, led ins last, ran on wl.......*(9 to 4 jt-fav op 6 to 4 tchd 5 to 2) 1
2269[9] DANTE'S GOLD (Ire) 6-11-4 J A McCarthy, *led aftr 2 fs, rdn and hdd ins last, kpt on same pace....*(14 to 1 op 10 to 1) 2
SQUADDIE 5-11-4 I Lawrence, *wtd wth, prog 6 fs out, effrt frm 2 furlongs out, kpt on one pace.*
....................(8 to 1 op 6 to 1 tchd 10 to 1) 3
1942[3] MIKE'S MUSIC (Ire) 6-11-1 (3*) G Hogan, *in tch, rdn and ev ch 2 fs out, one pace ins last.* (5 to 1 op 4 to 1 tchd 11 to 2) 4
YOUR FELLOW (Ire) 5-11-4 D Gallagher, *hld up, improved o'r 4 fs out, ev ch over 2 out, btn wl over one out.....*(9 to 4 jt-fav op 2 to 1 tchd 5 to 2) 5
1735[5] JUST BAYARD (Ire) 5-11-4 C Llewellyn, *in tch, effrt o'r 2 fs out, btn whn not much room one out.*
....................(13 to 2 op 10 to 1 tchd 10 to 1) 6
2221[6] STAR ISLAND 4-10-8 P Holley, *nvr dngrs.*
....................(7 to 1 op 5 to 1 tchd 10 to 1) 7
DON'TCALLMEGEORGE 6-10-11 (7*) Mr P O'Keeffe, *led 2 fs, remained prmnt till wknd 5 out........*(33 to 1 op 20 to 1) 8

UNFORGETABLE 5-11-4 J Railton, *trkd ldrs till wknd o'r 5 fs*
out.....................(11 to 1 op 10 to 1 tchd 14 to 1)　9
Dist: ¾l, 1¾l, 2½l, 7l, ½l, 18l, 17l, ½l. 4m 33.30s. (9 Ran).
(Mrs S N J Embiricos), J T Gifford

TOWCESTER (good to soft (races 1,3,5,7), good (2,4,6))
Thursday January 30th

Going Correction: PLUS 0.90 sec. per fur. (races 1,3,5,7), PLUS 0.70 (2,4,6)

2403 Canons Ashby Selling Handicap Hurdle Class G (0-95 4-y-o and up) £2,232 2m 5f................(1:30)

2185 PARADE RACER [70] 6-10-9 W McFarland, *steady hdwy to track ldrs 6th, chlgd 3 out, sn led, drvn out r-in.*
..........................(5 to 2 fav op 5 to 1)　1
1558⁷ WHITEBONNET (Ire) [82] (bl) 7-11-7 J Osborne, *al in tch, chlgd 3 out, chsd wnr appr nxt but no imprsn.*
..........................(6 to 1 tchd 7 to 1)　2
1834⁴ VISCOUNT TULLY [78] 12-11-3 Miss S Jackson, *beh till steady hdwy 6th, chsd ldrs 3 out, styd on.*
..........................(20 to 1 op 12 to 1)　3
1947⁴ KADARI [88] (v) 8-11-10 (3⁹) Guy Lewis, *chsd ldrs 3 out, sn outpcd*.....(9 to 1 op 12 to 1 tchd 14 to 1 and 8 to 1)　4
1956³ FORTUNES ROSE (Ire) [63] 5-10-2 T J Murphy, *chsd ldrs, rdn 3 out, one pace.*..........(14 to 1 op 10 to 1)　5
2030² LOVELARK [61] 8-9-7 (7⁹) M Griffiths, *lft in ld second, hdd sn aftr 3 out, soon wknd*......(8 to 1 op 7 to 1 tchd 9 to 1)　6
2152 NORDIC FLIGHT [62] (bl) 9-10-1 R Johnson, *in tch, rdn 7th, sn wknd*...........................(33 to 1)　7
2281⁸ POLO PONY (Ire) [67] 5-10-6 R Supple, *nvr better than mid-div*..................(9 to 1 op 7 to 1 tchd 10 to 1)　8
2183⁷ DERRYS PREROGATIVE [65] (v) 7-10-4 D Bridgwater, *nvr rchd ldrs*.......................(40 to 1 op 33 to 1)　9
ANNABEL'S BABY (Ire) [66] 8-10-W Marston, *hdwy 8th, chlgd 3 out, wknd rpdly*..........(33 to 1 op 20 to 1)　10
2201 DIDDY RYMER [80] 7-11-5 Richard Guest, *chsd ldrs till wknd quickly appr 3 out*.................(16 to 1 tchd 20 to 1)　11
1739⁹ HONEYBED WOOD [66] 9-10-5 Mr A Brown, *hdwy to track ldrs 7th, wknd 3 out*................(33 to 1 tchd 40 to 1)　12
2186⁵ CHANTRY BEATH [89] 6-12-0 E Murphy, *led till f second.*
..........................(12 to 1 op 10 to 1 tchd 7 to 1)　f
1766 SINGLESOLE [84] 12-11-4 (5⁹) Sophie Mitchell, *al beh, tld off whn pld up and dismounted last.*... (16 to 1 op 10 to 1)　pu
1472⁵ ALICE'S MIRROR [73] 8-10-9 (3⁹) P Henley, *chsd ldrs, mstk 6th, tld off whn pld up bef last.*.......(16 to 1 op 14 to 1)　pu
1474⁵ KILLING TIME [75] 6-11-0 D J Burchell, *sn beh, tld off whn pld up bef nxt*.....(8 to 1 op 7 to 1 tchd 9 to 1 and 10 to 1)　pu
CHILLY LAD [71] (v) 6-10-10 Gary Lyons, *chlgd 5th, sn wknd, tld off whn pld up bef 3 out*........(40 to 1 op 33 to 1)　pu
DUGORT STRAND (Ire) [77] 6-11-2 M Brennan, *blun 5th and beh, tld off whn pld up bef last*....(9 to 1 op 25 to 1)　pu
CORNS LITTLE FELLA [65] 9-9-11 (7⁹) T Hagger, *beh till pld up bef 6th*.....................(40 to 1 op 33 to 1)　pu
1747² KONGIES MELODY [74] 6-10-13 R Greene, *rdn 5th, sn beh, tld off whn pld up aftr nxt*.........(33 to 1 op 25 to 1)　pu
2030 DARING HEN (Ire) [63] 7-9-13 (3⁹) R Massey, *blun 3rd and beh, tld off whn pld up last*....(40 to 1 op 33 to 1)　pu
Dist: 5l, 10l, 7l, 1¾l, 26l, 1½l, hd, 4l, 30l. 5m 34.40s. a 35.40s (21 Ran).
(LM Racing), P G Murphy

2404 Lamport Hall Handicap Chase Class C (0-130 5-y-o and up) £4,647 3m 1f
.............................(2:00)

1746⁶ SISTER STEPHANIE (Ire) [123] 8-11-12 D Bridgwater, *neat and reminder aftr 4th, jmpd slwly 9th, hdwy and hit 12th, drvn and styd on frm 3 out, led last, rdn out...(6 to 4 op 5 to 4)　1
1974² RIVER MANDATE [125] 10-12-0 A Thornton, *wnt second 9th but pushed alng, chlgd 3 out, sn led, hdd last, rallied und pres, no extr cl hme*................(Evens fav tchd 5 to 4 on)　2
2245 RED PARADE (NZ) [98] 9-10-1 ⁹ C Maude, *led to 3rd, styd wth ldr till led ag'n 7th, hdd sn aftr 3 out, wknd last.*
..........................(9 to 1 op 4 to 1)　3
2024 MY MAIN MAN [99] 9-10-2 R Johnson, *led 3rd to 7th, jmpd slwly and wknd 4 out, tld off whn pld up bef 2 out.*
..........................(11 to 1 op 10 to 1 tchd 12 to 1)　pu
Dist: ½l, 7l. 6m 35.80s. a 23.80s (4 Ran).
SR: 35/36/-/-/　(The Antwick Partnership), G M McCourt

2405 Drayton House Novices' Hurdle Class E (4-y-o and up) £2,810 2m
.............................(2:30)

2242* JUYUSH (USA) 5-11-10 J Osborne, *led to 3rd, led ag'n aftr 4th, rdn frm 2 out, edgd rght appr last, styd on.*
.......(1 to 4 on op 2 to 1 on tchd 5 to 2 on and 1 to 3 on)　1
1657* DANA POINT 5-11-10 Richard Guest, *trkd ldrs, str chal 2 out, still nvr able to chal, no extr*.....(10 to 1 tchd 14 to 1)　2
1479³ HALONA 7-10-12 G Bradley, *pld hrd and hdwy to led 3rd, hdd aftr 4th, one pace appr 2 out.*
..........................(13 to 2 op 5 to 1 tchd 7 to 1)　3

ABSOLUTE LIMIT 5-11-3 P Hide, *in tch, one pace frm 3 out.*
..........................(33 to 1)　4
2197⁵ NORDANCE PRINCE (Ire) 6-11-3 D Bridgwater, *chsd ldrs, chlgd 5th to nxt, wknd appr 2 out*......(10 to 1 op 7 to 1)　5
1992⁴ COME ON IN 4-10-7 T J Murphy, *hdwy to chase ldrs 4th, wknd aftr 3 out*..............(66 to 1 op 50 to 1)　6
TIME TO PARLEZ 6-11-3 S Curran, *nvr rchd ldrs.*
..........................(66 to 1 op 33 to 1 tchd 100 to 1)　7
OVER ZEALOUS (Ire) 5-11-3 R Supple, *effrt 5th, wknd nxt.*
..........................(50 to 1 op 33 to 1 tchd 66 to 1)　8
231⁸ SMART REMARK 5-11-3 P McLoughlin, *hdwy 4th, wknd 3 out.*..........................(50 to 1 op 33 to 1)　9
2173⁷ ALISTOVER 4-9-9 (7⁹) X Aizpuru, *in tch to 5th*.....(50 to 1)　10
2277 REACH THE CLOUDS (Ire) 5-11-3 C Maude, *slwly away, al beh*................(66 to 1 op 50 to 1 tchd 100 to 1)　11
2181⁵ CONTRACT BRIDGE (Ire) 4-10-2 W McFarland, *hdwy 4th, wknd aftr nxt*.............................(50 to 1)　12
1673 RAGDON 6-11-3 S Wynne, *beh frm 5th.*
..........................(66 to 1 op 50 to 1 tchd 100 to 1)　13
2236 MILLERS GOLDENGIRL (Ire) 6-10-12 T Reed, *sn beh.*
..........................(66 to 1 op 50 to 1)　14
PARTY LADY (Ire) 8-10-12 L Harvey, *sn beh.*
..........................(66 to 1 op 50 to 1)　15
BALLY WONDER 5-10-12 A Thornton, *in tch to 4th, tld off whn pld up aftr 2 out*...........(66 to 1 op 33 to 1)　pu
50⁵ OUT FOR A DUCK 6-11-3 R Johnson, *sn beh, tld off whn pld up bef 2 out*.................(50 to 1 tchd 66 to 1)　pu
BALLADUR (USA) 4-10-7 R Dunwoody, *pld hrd, in tch mid-div 4th, sn wknd, tld off whn pulled up bef 2 out.*
..........................(12 to 1 op 8 to 1)　pu
Dist: 5l, 15l, 4l, 6l, 10l, 7l, 3l, 10l, 1¾l, 1l. 4m 3.80s. a 20.80s (18 Ran).
SR: 32/27/-/¹/-/-/　(W E Sturt), J A B Old

2406 Canons Ashby Novices' Chase Class E (5-y-o and up) £3,873 2¾m. (3:00)

DRUID'S BROOK 8-11-4 A Thornton, *hdwy 8th, chsd ldrs and rdn 3 out, styd on gmely r-in to ld last strds.*
..........................(6 to 1 op 5 to 1 tchd 13 to 2)　1
1718³ GARETHSON (Ire) 6-11-4 D Bridgwater, *led 3rd, clr 4 out, rdn whn lft clear 2 out, wknd r-in and ct last strds.*
..........................(6 to 1 tchd 13 to 2)　2
2187² ARDENT LOVE (Ire) 8-10-13 R Johnson, *beh, hit 7th, styd on frm 3 out but not rch ldrs*...........(8 to 1 op 10 to 1)　3
1734⁸ ROBSAND (Ire) 6-11-4 B Clifford, *in tch 5th, hit 8th and lost pl, styd on ag'n frm 3 out*..................(16 to 1)　4
1940⁴ SAFEGLIDE (Ire) 7-11-4 P Hide, *hit 3rd, prmnt, chlgd aftr 9th, wknd 3 out, no ch whn blun 2 out*...(12 to 1 op 10 to 1)　5
2014³ GEMMA'S WAGER (Ire) 7-10-13 L Harvey, *in tch whn hit 6th, nvr dngrs aftr*........................(50 to 1)　6
2285⁵ ROYAL PARIS (Ire) 9-11-4 T Reed, *effrt 5th, wknd 4 out.*
..........................(33 to 1 op 25 to 1)　7
2245 BALLYDOUGAN (Ire) (v) 9-11-4 R Bellamy, *keen hold, hdwy 8th, wknd 4 out*..............(50 to 1 op 33 to 1)　8
2178² JOLLY BOAT 10-11-4 S Wynne, *chsd ldrs to 4 out, wknd quickly*..........(14 to 1 op 16 to 1 tchd 20 to 1)　9
FORTYTWO DEE (Ire) 7-11-3 J Ryan, *beh frm 4th*. (50 to 1)　10
2187⁵ OLD BETSY 7-10-13 Richard Guest, *in tch 6th, blun and wknd 9th*...............(25 to 1 op 16 to 1)　11
1970* WHATTABOB (Ire) 8-11-10 J Osborne, *in tch, mstk 6th and 9th, quickened to chase ldr 4 out, staying on whn mistake and uns rdr 2 out.* (Evens fav tchd 11 to 10 on and 11 to 10)　ur
2014 BENBULBIN (Ire) 7-11-4 S Curran, *led to 3rd, chasing ldr whn mstk and uns rdr 7th.*..................(50 to 1)　ur
1857² BROWN ROBBER 9-11-4 Mr W Henderson, *tld off 7th, pld up bef 2 out.*..............(33 to 1 tchd 50 to 1)　pu
1973 MILWAUKEE (Ire) 8-10-13 M Brennan, *slwly away, jmpd moderately in rear, tld off whn pld up bef 2 out.*
..........................(33 to 1 op 25 to 1 tchd 50 to 1)　pu
Dist: Sht-hd, 3l, 1l, 2½l, 16l, 5l, hd, 5l, 24l, nk. 5m 49.80s. a 23.80s (15 Ran).
SR: 6/6/-/-/-/-/　(Racing Club KCB), K C Bailey

2407 Levy Board Handicap Hurdle Class E (0-110 4-y-o and up) £2,477 2m
.............................(3:30)

1737* NO MORE HASSLE (Ire) [95] 4-10-12 P Niven, *trkd ldrs, rdn and mstk 2 out, challnenged last, led r-in, all out.*
..........................(6 to 4 fav op 5 to 4 tchd 7 to 4)　1
2151⁷ DANBYS GORSE [86] 5-10-12 (3⁹) E Callaghan, *lost pos and drpd wl beh 4th, plenty to do aftr 3 out, styd on frm 2 out, not much room and ran on r-in, too much to do.*
..........................(12 to 1 tchd 14 to 1)　2
2279* AMBIDEXTROUS (Ire) [82] 5-10-4 (7⁹,7ex) L Cummins, *hld up, hdwy to track ldrs 3 out, str chal last, one pace nr finish.*
..........................(15 to 8 op 9 to 4 tchd 7 to 4)　3
1805 BOB'S PLOY [80] (v) 5-10-9 Richard Guest, *led, pushed alng 2 out, hdd sn aftr last, no extr*........(12 to 1 op 8 to 1)　4
1493⁴ WINSFORD HILL [90] 6-11-5 G Tormey, *trkd ldrs, chlgd 3 out, ev ch appr last, styd on one pace*......(12 to 1 op 8 to 1)　5
1708⁸ RAIN-N-SUN [78] 11-10-7 A Thornton, *chsd ldrs, chlgd 3 out, wknd frm 2 out*.................(12 to 1 op 10 to 1)　6
2257 MAJOR YAASI (USA) [93] 7-11-8 R Johnson, *jmpd slwly 3rd, some hdwy nxt, sn beh.*(16 to 1 op 14 to 1 tchd 20 to 1)　7
9907 BOWLES PATROL (Ire) [71] 5-10-0 R Supple, *al beh.*
..........................(33 to 1)　8

1848⁹ AJDAR [80] 6-10-9 M Brennan, hld up, keen hold in mid-
divsion 5th, sn wknd..................(20 to 1 op 14 to 1) 9
1947 ALASKAN HEIR [84] 6-10-13 T Eley, chsd ldrs to 5th.
.............................(16 to 1 op 14 to 1) 10
KARLINE KA (Fr) [95] 6-11-3 (7*) X Aizpuru, prmnt to 5th,
wknd, tld off...............................(25 to 1 op 33 to 1) 11
MRS JAWLEYFORD (USA) [88] 9-11-3 M Ranger, in tch early,
beh frm 5th, tld off whn pld up bef 2 out.
.............................(33 to 1 tchd 40 to 1) pu
Dist: Nk, ½l, 2½l, 5l, 2½l, 17l, 2½l, 3½l, 3l, dist. 4m 12.00s. a 29.00s (12 Ran).
(The No Hassle Partnership), Mrs M Reveley

2408 Althorp House Handicap Chase Class D (0-120 5-y-o and up) £3,497 2m 110yds.............................(4:00)

ARFER MOLE (Ire) [110] 9-11-11 J Osborne, trkd ldr till rdn,
outpcd and swtchd appr 2 out but sn quicken to ld, styd on wl
r-in.........(11 to 4 op 5 to 2 tchd 3 to 1 and 7 to 2) 1
1667* SECOND CALL [108] 8-11-9 R Dunwoody, hld up in tch,
quickened to chal 3 out, sn led, hdd 2 out, soon rdn and no
extr.............................(Evens fav op 5 to 4 on) 2
1519 PRINCE SKYBURD [93] 6-10-8 D Bridgwater, rcd in 3rd most
of way, chlgd 3 out, sn lost tch.
.............................(11 to 4 op 9 to 4 tchd 3 to 1) 3
2282³ COUNT BARACHOIS (USA) [86] 9-10-1 K Gaule, led till hdd
aftr 3 out, sn btn.........(10 to 1 op 6 to 1 tchd 12 to 1) 4
Dist: 2l, 25l, 2½l. 4m 16.40s. a 19.40s (4 Ran).
SR: 19/15/-/-/ (W E Sturt), J A B Old

2409 Castle Ashby Intermediate Open National Hunt Flat Class H (4,5,6-y-o) £1,371 2m.............................(4:30)

1769* RED BROOK 5-11-7 (3*) E Callaghan, gd hdwy 5 fs out, led 2
and a half out, hld on wl und pres.
.............................(5 to 1 op 4 to 1 tchd 6 to 1) 1
2248³ ROYAL POT BLACK (Ire) 5-11-3 G Tormey, hdwy to chase ldrs
hfwy, chlgd frm 2 and a half fs out till no extr wl ins last.
.............................(3 to 1 fav tchd 5 to 2) 2
CRACKON JAKE 4-10-7 W McFarland, steady hdwy 6 fs
out, ran on but no imprsn on ldrs fnl furlong.......(33 to 1) 3
SKYCAB (Ire) 5-10-10 (7*) W Greatrex, hld up in rear, ran on
fnl 3 fs but not a dngr.............(6 to 1 op 5 to 1) 4
1742* THE LADY CAPTAIN 5-11-5 K Gaule, chsd ldrs, drvn 3 fs out.
wknd 2 out.............................(14 to 1 op 8 to 1) 5
COOL AS A CUCUMBER (Ire) 6-11-3 J Osborne, keen hold,
chsd way into ld aftr 5 fs, hdd and wknd 2 and a half out.
.............................(6 to 1 op 4 to 1 tchd 7 to 1) 6
JUPITER PROBE (Ire) 6-11-3 W Marston, sn chasing ldrs,
wknd frm 3 fs out.............................(33 to 1) 7
HIJACK 6-11-3 J P Titley, pld hrd, sn led, hdd 9 fs out, wknd 4
out.............................(16 to 1 op 14 to 1) 8
FORBIDDEN WATERS (Ire) 6-11-3 A Thornton, hdwy hfwy,
wknd 4 fs out.............................(33 to 1 op 20 to 1) 9
LUDO'S ORCHESTRA 6-11-3 L Harvey, in tch ten fs.
.............................(33 to 1 op 20 to 1) 10
COLTIBUONO (Ire) 5-11-3 G Bradley, with ldr 5 fs, wknd five
out.............................(33 to 1 op 20 to 1) 11
BOMBA CHARGER 5-11-3 R Greene, prmnt ten fs.
.............................(33 to 1 op 20 to 1) 12
OLD MAN OF RAMAS 5-10-10 (7*) S O'Shea, al in rear.
.............................(13 to 2 op 20 to 1 tchd 25 to 1) 13
52³ BOUNDTOHONOUR (Ire) 5-11-3 R Dunwoody, al beh.
.............................(13 to 2 op 8 to 1 tchd 9 to 1) 14
2221⁵ EMBARGO (Ire) 5-10-10 (7*) M H Dunlop, in tch to hfwy.
.............................(8 to 1 op 6 to 1 tchd 9 to 1) 15
ORIENTAL BOY 5-11-3 R Johnson, beh frm hfwy.
.............................(20 to 1 op 14 to 1) 16
QUERY LINE 6-10-12 S Curran, tried to run out aftr 7 fs, al wl
beh.............................(33 to 1 op 20 to 1) 17
THE GADFLY 5-11-3 T J Murphy, sn in rear.......(33 to 1) 18
Dist: ¾l, 1l, 13l, 12l, 3½l, nk, 1l, 6l, 2½l, 5l. 4m 0.60s. (18 Ran).
(Dr B H Seal), J M Jefferson

TRAMORE (IRE) (yielding)
Thursday January 30th

2410 Dunmore East Beginners Chase (5-y-o and up) £2,226 2½m.....(1:30)

1904 SIDCUP HILL 8-11-9 T P Rudd,.............(12 to 1) 1
2164³ THE NOBLE ROUGE (Ire) 8-12-0 T Horgan,.........(5 to 1) 2
2164² BLAZE OF HONOUR (Ire) 6-11-9 C F Swan,.....(5 to 4 fav) 3
2057⁷ DEARBORN TEC (Ire) 8-12-0 C O'Brien,.............(8 to 1) 4
V'SOSKE GALE (Ire) 7-11-9 A Powell,.............(8 to 1) 5
SAM VAUGHAN (Ire) 8-11-9 (5*) W M W O'Sullivan, tld to 6
1241 MAJOR GALE (Ire) 8-11-7 (7*) M D Murphy,.......(14 to 1) 7
1534 LET BUNNY RUN (Ire) 7-12-0 D H O'Connor,.......(20 to 1) 8
2019 COCK COCKBURN 11-12-0 F Woods,.............(8 to 1) 9
2341 PENNY POT 5-10-11 (3*) K Whelan,.............(25 to 1) 10
1906⁹ BALLYBRIT BOY 11-12-0 L P Cusack,.............(14 to 1) 11
HAVE A BRANDY (Ire) 8-12-0 A J O'Brien,.......(14 to 1) 12
ONE EYED GER VI (Ire) 8-12-0 T J Mitchell,.......(14 to 1) 13
2171 CREATIVE BLAZE (Ire) 8-11-9 J P Broderick,.......(9 to 2) f
1710 CASTLELAKE LADY (Ire) 8-11-9 D T Evans,.......(25 to 1) f

Dist: 1½l, ¾l, 15l, 3½l. 5m 0.60s. (15 Ran).
(Mrs V O'Brien), Michael O'Connor

2411 Fenor Opportunity Handicap Chase (0-102 5-y-o and up) £2,637 2¾m.............................(2:00)

2059 MACAUNTA (Ire) [-] 7-9-13 (4*) M D Murphy,.......(8 to 1) 1
2274 INDESTRUCTIBLE (Ire) [-] 9-11-10 (4*) L J Fleming, (7 to 1) 2
2274² APPALACHEE BAY (Ire) [-] 7-11-7 J Butler,.....(3 to 1 fav) 3
2163 MARIES POLLY [-] (bl) 7-11-0 (2*) J M Donnelly,.....(7 to 1) 4
2163 DOONEGA (Ire) [-] 9-10-10 (2*) T Martin,.............(6 to 1) 5
1245³ STRADBALLEY (Ire) [-] 7-10-10 (4*) D Flood,.......(8 to 1) 6
2163 GOT NO CHOICE (Ire) [-] (bl) 7-10-0 (4*) S FitzGerald,
.............................(12 to 1) 7
1906⁷ SILENTBROOK [-] 12-9-3 (4*) S P McCann,.......(10 to 1) 8
RICH TRADITION (Ire) [-] 9-11-12 U Smyth,.......(10 to 1) 9
2169 ROSEEN (Ire) [-] 8-10-6 (4*) R P Hogan,.......(25 to 1) 10
2141⁴ BEAUCHAMP GRACE [-] 8-11-6 K Whelan,.......(5 to 1) f
LAKE TOUR (Ire) [-] 7-11-4 (4*) L A Hurley,.......(10 to 1) f
Dist: 4½l, ¾l, 11l, dist. 5m 40.70s. (12 Ran).
(Mrs F Whelan), A J McNamara

2412 Waterford Crystal Chase (5-y-o and up) £3,601 2m.............(2:30)

2273⁵ THE CRAZY BISHOP (Ire) (bl) 9-11-10 C F Swan,...(7 to 4) 1
2167* SCOBIE BOY (Ire) 9-11-5 J P Broderick,.........(5 to 4 on) 2
2226⁵ HANNIES GIRL (Ire) 8-10-7 (7*) L J Fleming,.......(10 to 1) 3
1363⁷ ANOTHER COURSE (Ire) 9-11-10 D H O'Connor,..(14 to 1) 4
2164 WILD BROOK (Ire) 7-10-11 (3*) K Whelan,.......(16 to 1) 5
2226⁶ JAZZY REFRAIN (Ire) 7-11-0 F Woods,.............(9 to 1) 6
1144 ROCK THE LORD (Ire) 9-10-11 (3*) J Butler,.......(25 to 1) 7
Dist: 8l, 5½l, 11l, 6l. 4m 11.50s. (7 Ran).
(John J Hanlon), Anthony Mullins

2413 Benvoy Lady Riders Maiden Hurdle (5-y-o and up) £2,226 2m..... (3:00)

2271³ BALLYRIHY BOY (Ire) 6-11-7 Miss M Olivefalk, (5 to 4 on) 1
2165 BORN TO WIN (Ire) 7-10-1 (7*) Miss K Rudd,.......(5 to 1) 2
2160³ RYTHM ROCK 8-10-6 (7*) Miss M Horgan,.......(12 to 1) 3
2131 ASK DOCK (Ire) 6-10-1 (7*) Miss C Gould,.......(20 to 1) 4
2089 WOODBORO LASS (Ire) 7-10-1 (7*) Miss A Sloane, (20 to 1) 5
2159⁶ ZIGGY THE GREAT (Ire) (bl) 5-10-9 Mrs C Barker, (10 to 1) 6
SASSY SALLY (Ire) 7-10-1 (7*) Miss E Doyle,.......(20 to 1) 7
2367 SHIR ROSE (Ire) 7-10-9 (7*) Miss C O'Neill,.......(12 to 1) 8
1777 POISON IVY (Ire) 5-9-11 (7*) Miss C O'Donovan, .. (33 to 1) 9
898 LOCKBEG LASS (Ire) 5-9-11 (7*) Mrs F A O'Sullivan,
.............................(25 to 1) 10
1715 NOBLE TUNE (Ire) 8-10-6 (7*) Miss E Peck,.......(20 to 1) 11
2089 LISHILLAUN (Ire) 7-10-9 (7*) Miss J M Lee,.......(16 to 1) 12
2164 SLANEY STANDARD (Ire) 9-11-0 (7*) Miss L E A Doyle,
.............................(12 to 1) 13
2166⁸ THATS MY WIFE (Ire) 6-10-3 (5*) Susan A Finn, ...(7 to 2) 14
2271 RAMDON ROCKS 10-11-0 (7*) Mrs H Somers, ...(16 to 1) 15
Dist: 3l, nk, 12l, 1½l. 4m 15.90s. (15 Ran).
(M J Collison), Capt D G Swan

2414 Annestown Maiden Hurdle (5-y-o) £2,226 2½m.................(3:30)

2270³ MIRACLE ME (Ire) 11-6 F Woods,.............(9 to 4) 1
1902 MR MAGGET (Ire) 11-6 T P Rudd,.............(12 to 1) 2
245³ GILLA (Ire) 11-6 C F Swan,.............(7 to 1) 3
2104⁵ ROSEY ELLEN (Ire) 10-12 (3*) K Whelan,.......(10 to 1) 4
2168⁵ GENTLE MOSSY (Ire) 11-6 D H O'Connor, .. (11 to 8 fav) 5
1776⁸ MALADANTE (Ire) 11-1 T P Treacy,.............(14 to 1) 6
2106⁸ THE BOY KING (Ire) 11-6 J P Broderick,.......(7 to 1) 7
2106⁶ SEXTON'S MIRROR (Ire) 11-1 (5*) J M Donnelly, .. (12 to 1) 8
ROYAL SANTAL (Ire) 11-1 M P Hourigan,.........(20 to 1) 9
1275 OLD MOTHER HUBBARD (Ire) 11-1 T Horgan,.....(14 to 1) 10
NEWBERRY ROSE (Ire) 11-2⁶ (5*) Mr W M O'Sullivan,
.............................(20 to 1) 11
2144⁷ MARY DONT BE LONG (Ire) 11-1 F J Flood,.......(14 to 1) 12
2270 IRELAND INVADER (bl) 10-8 (7*) Mr M Costello, ...(33 to 1) 13
2270 ZACOPANI (Ire) 11-6 C F Swan,.............(14 to 1) pu
Dist: 1½l, 3l, ¾l, 6l. 5m 4.70s. (14 Ran).
(Mrs D P Magnier), James Joseph Mangan

2415 Tramore Q.R. Handicap Hurdle (0-109 4-y-o and up) £2,226 2m.............................(4:00)

2272⁷ CHOOSEY'S TREASURE (Ire) [-] 4-11-8 (3*) Mr B M Cash,
.............................(3 to 1 fav*) 1
WITHOUT EQUAL (USA) [-] 10-11-9 (7*) Mr R J Curran,
.............................(10 to 1) 2
2160⁸ BE MY FOLLY (Ire) [-] 5-10-13 (3*) Mr R Walsh,.......(6 to 1) 3
2276⁴ HEN HANSEL (Ire) [-] 6-10-5 (7*) Mr Sean O O'Brien, (14 to 1) 4
2159 SLEWMORE (Ire) [-] 6-10-5¹ Mr A R Coonan,.......(20 to 1) 5
2097⁸ SORALENA (Ire) [-] 6-9-12 (7*) Mr A Ross,.......(14 to 1) 6
ZVORNIK [-] 10-11-5 (7*) Mr M G Drohan,.......(7 to 1) 7
2105⁶ TIP YOUR WAITRESS (Ire) [-] 4-10-1 (7*) Miss S J Leahy,
.............................(8 to 1) 8
RUTABAGA (Ire) [-] 8-9-12¹ (7*) Mr P A Farrell,.......(20 to 1) 9
2159⁹ GARLAND ROSE (Ire) [-] 7-9-11 (7*) Miss T Gilmour, (12 to 1) 10

2103⁸ CASTLE BAILEY (Ire) [-] (bl) 6-9-13² (7") Mr T N Cloke,
.... (14 to 1) 11
EMARRCEEVEESS [-] 10-11-4 (7") Mr P G Fahey, (16 to 1) pu
Dist: ¾l, 10l, sht-hd, 8l. 4m 19.60s. (12 Ran).
(M Moloney), A P O'Brien

2416 Woodstown INH Flat Race (5-y-o and up) £2,226 2m............. (4:30)

2228³ OUR-DANTE (Ire) 5-10-12 (7") Mr Sean O O'Brien, ..(5 to 1) 1
2165 PRIZE OF PEACE (Ire) 7-11-2 (7") Mr M T Hartrey, (12 to 1) 2
1836⁹ AHINDUCLINT (Ire) 5-11-10 Mr P Fenton, ... (11 to 4) 3
2172² THE RED SIDE (Ire) 5-10-12 (7") Mr P Murphy, ...(2 to 1 fav) 4
1554⁵ STRICT TEMPO (Ire) 8-11-7 (7") Mr John P Moloney,
.... (12 to 1) 5
1147⁸ LISKILNEWABBEY (Ire) 6-11-6 (3") Mr R Walsh, ...(14 to 1) 6
2342 SINGERS CORNER (bl) 5-10-12 (7") Mr A J Dempsey,
.... (14 to 1) 7
2144⁹ SUPREME FUEL (Ire) 7-11-6 (3") Mr P English, ...(14 to 1) 8
1490 BOPTWOPHAR (Ire) 5-11-7 (3") Mr E Norris, ... (8 to 1) 9
2160⁴ THE HOLY PARSON (Ire) 5-11-10 Mr J P Dempsey, (12 to 1) 10
MOREPORTER (Ire) 5-10-12 (7") Mr J M Barcoe, ..(16 to 1) 11
NAUL EXPRESS 12-11-9 (5") Mr J T McNamara, ..(33 to 1) 12
CHELSEA BELLE (Ire) 5-10-12 (7") Mr N D Fehily, ..(25 to 1) 13
AIMEES PRINCESS (Ire) 5-10-12 (7") Mr P J Faulkner,
.... (14 to 1) 14
THE MILLMAN (Ire) 6-11-11 (3") Mr B M Cash, ...(12 to 1) pu
Dist: ½l, 9l, 2l, sht-hd. 4m 15.30s. (15 Ran).
(Rathlin Syndicate), Sean O O'Brien

CATTERICK (good)
Friday January 31st
Going Correction: PLUS 0.50 sec. per fur.

2417 Hartlepool Juvenile Novices' Hurdle Class E (4-y-o) £2,565 2m..... (1:40)

2204⁶ RUSSIAN RASCAL (Ire) 11-5 P Niven, trkd ldrs, led on bit 2
out, sn quickened clr, easily............ (5 to 1 op 7 to 2) 1
2188⁴ J J BABOO (Ire) 10-12 R Garritty, led second till hdd 2 out, kpt
on, no ch wth wnr................... (5 to 2 fav op 6 to 4) 2
2002⁵ ARABIAN HEIGHTS 10-12 T Eley, hld up towards rear, hdwy
bef 2 out, rdn betw last two, styd on wl r-in.
.... (20 to 1 op 14 to 1) 3
734³ SILVERDALE KNIGHT 11-5 M Foster, trkd ldrs, ev ch bef 2
out, sn rdn, kpt on same pace............ (6 to 1 tchd 7 to 1) 4
2061⁴ PRIDDY FAIR 10-12¹ (3") P Midgley, settled midfield, hdwy
aftr 3 out, ch nxt, sn rdn and no extr................. (20 to 1) 5
FORMIDABLE PARTNER 10-7 (5") Mr R Thornton, led to
second, in tch, drvn alng and hdwy aftr 3 out, kpt on same
pace frm nxt....................... (25 to 1 op 16 to 1) 6
2061³ NOIR ESPRIT 10-9 (3") F Leahy, hdwy, efrrt aftr 3 out, no
real hdwy frm nxt................... (10 to 1 op 12 to 1) 7
2002³ TAGATAY 10-9 (3") E Callaghan, hld up, hdwy hfwy, pushed
alng aftr 3 out, kpt on same pace.......(14 to 1 op 12 to 1) 8
2256⁷ ANGUS MCCOATUP (Ire) 10-12 D Bentley, nvr better than
mid-div............................ (25 to 1 op 14 to 1) 9
1689⁶ RADMORE BRANDY 10-7 A Dobbin, in tch, efrrt aftr 3 out, sn
btn............................. (25 to 1 op 20 to 1) 10
2145 HOBBS CHOICE 11-0 J Callaghan, prmnt till wknd bef 2 out.
.... (50 to 1 op 33 to 1) 11
2256³ NEXSIS STAR 10-12 Richard Guest, in tch, efrrt bef 2 out, sn
btn............................. (6 to 1 op 5 to 1 tchd 7 to 1) 12
2296⁴ LUCKY BEA 10-12 P Carberry, sn beh, tld off.
.... (12 to 1 tchd 14 to 1) 13
1909 BANK ON INLAND 10-7 W Fry, sn beh, tld off......(100 to 1) 14
2116⁷ BRIDLINGTON BAY 10-12 G Cahill, dsptd ld early, sn beh, tld
off... (100 to 1) 15
1909 BEACON HILL LADY 10-7 K Johnson, sn beh, tld off.
.... (200 to 1) 16
1690⁹ DIAMOND BEACH 10-12 N Bentley, in tch whn blun and uns
rdr 5th........................... (50 to 1) ur
PRINCIPAL BOY (Ire) 10-12 R Rourke, pld hrd early, al beh,
tld off whn pulled up bef 2 out................... (50 to 1) pu
MATCH THE COLOUR 10-12 B Storey, blun 1st, al beh, tld off
whn pld up bef 2 out.......................... (50 to 1) pu
Dist: 8l, 1¼l, ¾l, nk, ¾l, 2½l, nk, nk, 8l, sht-hd. 3m 54.90s. a 14.90s (19 Ran).
SR: 22/7/5/11/6/3/   (C H Stevens), T D Easterby

2418 Stayers' Novices' Chase Class D (5-y-o and up) £3,678 3m 1f 110yds
.... (2:10)

2237³ TICO GOLD 9-11-5 A S Smith, trkd ldr, led 3 out, clr last, hrd
rdn r-in, all out.................. (6 to 4 fav tchd 13 to 8) 1
2280⁶ THE BIRD O'DONNELL 11-10-12 (7") Mr T J Barry, rcd wide,
led till hdd 3 out, mstk nxt, styd on und pres frm last.
.... (13 to 8 op 5 to 4 tchd 7 to 4) 2
2122 MILLIES IMAGE 6-11-0 A Dobbin, lost tch frm 15th, tld off.
.... (20 to 1 op 12 to 1) 3
1585⁸ DEAR JEAN 7-11-0 D Parker, lost tch frm 7th, wl tld off.
.... (33 to 1 op 16 to 1) 4
2146 DRY HILL LAD 6-11-5 W Fry, chsd ldrs, cl 3rd and drvn alng
whn f 15th............... (7 to 2 op 3 to 1 tchd 4 to 1) f
Dist: 1½l, dist, dist. 6m 53.50s. a 38.50s (5 Ran).
(Miss S J Turner), P Cheesbrough

2419 European Breeders Fund 'National Hunt' Novices' Hurdle Qualifier Class E (5,6,7-y-o) £2,477 2m 3f
.... (2:40)

1775⁴ SPRITZER (Ire) 5-10-6 (3") F Leahy, hld up, hdwy aftr 6th, led
bef 2 out, sn clr, easily...(5 to 1 op 4 to 1 tchd 11 to 2) 1
1775⁷ TAKE COVER (Ire) 6-11-0 Richard Guest, mid-div, hdwy aftr 3
out, chsd wnr frm betw last 2, no imprsn.(12 to 1 op 8 to 1) 2
2192⁷ NORDIC PRINCE (Ire) 6-11-0 J Callaghan, trkd ldrs, led aftr 3
out, sn hdd, kpt on same pace.
.... (5 to 1 op 4 to 1 tchd 11 to 2) 3
1738³ SEPTEMBER BREEZE (Ire) 6-10-9 A S Smith, chsd ldrs, ev ch
3 out, grad wknd.......................... (7 to 1 op 5 to 1) 4
1532³ HYDRO (Ire) 6-11-0 R Garritty, prmnt, led 7th, hdd aftr 3 out,
wknd frm nxt......................... (14 to 1 op 10 to 1) 5
1675³ ARDRINA 6-10-9 P Carberry, chsd ldrs till outpcd aftr 3 out,
no dngr after.................... (5 to 2 fav op 9 to 2) 6
2277 FERRERS 6-11-0 M Brennan, in tch, efrrt bef 3 out, no real
hdwy............................... (14 to 1 op 12 to 1) 7
1985 BONNY JOHNNY 7-11-0 D J Moffatt, nvr dngrs...(50 to 1) 8
1789⁵ CAUGHT AT LAST (Ire) 6-11-0 G Cahill, nvr dngrs.
.... (50 to 1 op 33 to 1) 9
2262⁶ DONNEGALE (Ire) 5-11-0 P Niven, beh most of way, tld off.
.... (14 to 1 op 12 to 1) 10
2117⁷ HUTCEL LOCH 6-11-0 A Dobbin, led till hdd 7th, wknd
quickly aftr 3 out, tld off...(11 to 2 op 7 to 2 tchd 6 to 1) 11
2147⁷ TSANGA 5-11-0 N Bentley, beh most of way, tld off. (66 to 1) 12
2288 ONLY A SIOUX 5-11-0 D Parker, chsd ldrs till wknd bef 3 out,
tld off.............................. (100 to 1) 13
FLORRIE GUNNER 7-10-9 B Storey, towards rear whn mstk,
stumbled and uns rdr 6th................... (50 to 1) ur
2145 MEADOW BEE 5-11-0 T Reed, sn wl beh, tld off whn pld up
bef last............................... (200 to 1) pu
Dist: 11l, 3½l, 1¾l, 2l, 14l, 1¼l, 2l, nk, 23l, 9l. 4m 47.80s. (15 Ran).
(Mrs R A G Haggie), J G FitzGerald

2420 Dinsdale Conditional Jockeys' Selling Handicap Hurdle Class G (0-95 4-y-o and up) £1,642 2m 3f... (3:10)

1987² YACHT CLUB [71] 15-10-0⁴ (4") C Elliott, mid-div, hdwy bef
7th, led aftr 3 out, ran on wl und pres frm nxt, all out.(10 to 1) 1
2202⁶ JALMAID [67] 5-10-0 R McGrath, mid-div, pushed alng aftr
6th, hdwy bef 2 out, styd on wl und pres frm last, not rch wnr.
.... (9 to 1 op 8 to 1 tchd 10 to 1) 2
1969³ SAYMORE [74] 11-10-7 R Massey, led to 3rd, led 6th till hdd
aftr 3 out, ev ch nxt, kpt on same pace..........(4 to 1 jt-
fav tchd 9 to 2) 3
1953⁴ IN A MOMENT (USA) [70] 6-10-3 Michael Brennan, sn pushed
alng and beh, styd on frm 2 out, nvr able to chal..(4 to 1 jt-
fav op 3 to 1) 4
IJAB (Can) [78] 7-10-11 E Callaghan, in tch till lost pl hfwy,
styd on frm 2 out, nvr dngrs..........(8 to 1 op 10 to 1) 5
2202³ ARTHUR BEE [68] 9-10-11¹ (4") C McCormack, prmnt,
pushed alng hfwy, ev ch 3 out, sn hrd rdn, fdd.
.... (11 to 1 op 10 to 1 tchd 12 to 1) 6
2202² ANORAK (USA) [90] 7-11-2 (7") N Hannity, in tch, lost pl hfwy,
some hdwy bef 7th, wknd aftr 3 out.....(6 to 1 op 5 to 1) 7
1911⁵ ARTWORLD (USA) [80] 9-10-13 P Midgley, hld up in midfield,
smooth hdwy to track ldrs 3 out, ev ch nxt, 4th and btn whn
blun badly last.................... (6 to 1 op 9 to 2) 8
KISMETIM [67] 7-10-0 B Grattan, towards rear, some hdwy
aftr 3 out, wknd after last.................... (50 to 1) 9
2259 WORLD WITHOUT END (USA) [72] 8-10-5 G Cahill, led 3rd till
hdd 6th, wknd bef 3 out, tld off...... (50 to 1 op 33 to 1) 10
791² ILEWIN [95] 10-12-0 H Bastiman, hld up, hdwy bef 7th, wknd
aftr 3 out, tld off................... (6 to 1 op 12 to 1) 11
1911 JOYRIDER [85] 6-11-4 M Newton, chsd ldrs till wknd bef 2
out, tld off....................... (10 to 1 op 8 to 1) 12
DOLLY PRICES [67] 12-10-0 S Taylor, sn wl beh, pld up and
dismounted bef 5th................ (33 to 1 op 25 to 1) pu
1737 PHANTOM DANCER (Ire) [79] 4-9-10 (4") N Horrocks, chsd
ldrs to hfwy, sn wknd, tld off whn pld up bef 2 out.
.... (100 to 1 op 50 to 1) pu
Dist: 1l, 3l, 11l, 1¾l, 1½l, 1½l, ½l, 6l, 30l, 15l. 4m 49.90s. a 29.90s (14 Ran).
(Ernest Spencer), J L Eyre

2421 Stokesley Handicap Chase Class D (0-120 5-y-o and up) £3,470 2m 3f
.... (3:40)

2287² WEAVER GEORGE (Ire) [102] 7-11-6 M Moloney, cl up, led
9th, rdn bef 3 out, styd on wl.
.... (11 to 8 fav op 6 to 4 tchd 13 to 8) 1
2203¹ TIM SOLDIER (Fr) [89] 10-10-7 R Supple, prmnt, drw clr wth
wnr frm 12th, rdn and no imprsn frm 3 out.
.... (9 to 4 op 2 to 1 tchd 5 to 2) 2
2205⁵ TWIN FALLS (Ire) [94] 6-10-12 J Callaghan, prmnt till wknd
quickly aftr 12th, tld off...(5 to 2 op 2 to 1 tchd 11 to 4) 3
1965² PORT IN A STORM [88] 8-10-3 (3") Mr C Bonner, led, hdd 9th,
blun nxt, lost tch and pld up bef 12th.....(7 to 1 op 9 to 2) pu
Dist: 2l, 25l. 4m 57.00s. a 27.00s (4 Ran).
(Regent Decorators Ltd), W Storey

2422 Cowton Handicap Hurdle Class E (0-115 5-y-o and up) £2,407 3m 1f 110yds...................... (4:10)

2025³ TILTY (USA) [97] (v) 7-11-2 T Eley, *made most, rdn frm hfwy, hrd pressed from 3 out, styd on wl appr last.*
.... (6 to 4 fav tchd 13 to 8) 1
1708² SOLOMAN SPRINGS (USA) [81] 7-9-9 (5*) Mr R Thornton, *sn beh, drvn alng and hdwy aftr 3 out, chlgd nxt, ev ch till no extr appr last.* .... (8 to 1 op 6 to 1 tchd 12 to 1) 2
1951⁵ HIGH PENHOWE [81] 9-9-10¹ (5*) Michael Brennan, *trkd ldrs, rdn bef 2 out, fdd.*.................... (7 to 1 op 9 to 2) 3
2064⁵ BARTON HEIGHTS [85] 5-10-4 P Niven, *cl up, slight ld 3 out, sn hdd, wknd quickly frm nxt, virtually pld up r-in, tld off.*
.... (13 to 8 op 5 to 4) 4
JOHNNY'S TURN [109] 12-12-0 Mr N Kent, *hld up, f 5th.*
.... (16 to 1 op 14 to 1) f
Dist: 8l, 11l, dist. 6m 34.00s. a 33.00s (5 Ran).
(Cheadle Racing), A Streeter

LINGFIELD (soft (races 1,2,4,6,7), good to soft (3,5))
Friday January 31st
Going Correction: PLUS 0.70 sec. per fur.

2423 Ashurst Juvenile Novices' Hurdle Class E (4-y-o) £2,279 2m 3f 110yds .... (1:30)

CHEERFUL ASPECT (Ire) 10-10 N Williamson, *hld up in tch, hit 5th, led appr last, sn clr.* (5 to 1 op 4 to 1 tchd 7 to 2) 1
ELA AGAPI MOU (USA) 10-10 P Holley, *wtd wth, prog appr 3 out, outpcd bef nxt, rallied approaching last, chsd wnr r-in, no imprsn.*.....................(33 to 1 op 20 to 1) 2
2207 PLEASURELAND (Ire) 10-10 D Morris, *hld up, hdwy appr 3 out, one pace 2 out.* .. (9 to 1 op 5 to 1 tchd 8 to 1) 3
CHABROL (Can) 10-10 V Smith, *in tch, rdn appr 3 out, one pace.*..................... (20 to 1 tchd 25 to 1) 4
2012² RED RAJA 11-3 J Osborne, *led, hit and hdd 5th, rgned ld appr 2 out, headed and btn bef nxt.*
.... (15 to 8 fav op 2 to 1 tchd 9 to 4 and 5 to 2) 5
MAJOR DUNDEE (Ire) 10-10 R Dunwoody, *chsd ldr, led 5th, hdd appr 2 out, sn wknd.*.............(3 to 1 op 5 to 2) 6
1398 ROYAL THEN (Fr) 10-10 J R Kavanagh, *al beh, tld off.*
.... (33 to 1 tchd 50 to 1) 7
2012⁵ BIGWIG (Ire) 10-10 N Mann, *hit 3rd, beh frm 6th, tld off.*
.... (66 to 1 op 50 to 1) 8
1599³ DARK TRUFFLE 9-12 (7*) C Hynes, *trkd ldrs till wknd bef 3 out, tld off.*........(25 to 1 op 33 to 1 tchd 50 to 1) 9
HARBET HOUSE (Fr) 10-10 D Bridgwater, *hld up, not fluent second, hdwy appr 3 out, 3rd and ev ch whn f 2 out.*
.... (25 to 1 op 20 to 1 tchd 33 to 1) f
1702² JELALI (Ire) 11-3 D Gallagher, *beh frm 6th, tld off whn pld up bef 2 out.*..................................... pu
674² LORD ELLANGOWAN (Ire) (bl) 10-10 K Gaule, *trkd ldrs, wknd frm 6th, tld off whn pld up bef 2 out.*
.... (33 to 1 op 14 to 1 tchd 50 to 1) pu
GULLIVER 10-10 I Lawrence, *hld up, hdwy 5th, wknd frm 7th, tld off whn pld up aftr 2 out.*
.... (16 to 1 op 14 to 1 tchd 20 to 1) pu
Dist: 10l, 2l, 1½l, nk, 22l, 25l, 3l, dist. 5m 6.10s. a 33.10s (13 Ran).
(Lady Pilkington), Capt T A Forster

2424 Worth Wood Selling Handicap Hurdle Class G (0-95 4-y-o and up) £1,852 2m 110yds..................... (2:00)

2351⁴ SCRIPT [68] 6-10-7 J Osborne, *pressed ldrs till outpcd aftr 3 out, rallied betw fnl 2, led r-in, drvn out.* (5 to 1 op 3 to 1) 1
2251³ SLIGHTLY SPECIAL (Ire) [61] 5-10-0 T J Murphy, *led hit 5th, hdd r-in, no extr.*...............(6 to 1 tchd 13 to 2) 2
2010 KENTAVRUS WAY (Ire) [61] 6-9-7 (7*) M Batchelor, *hld up, rdn 5th, lost pl appr 2 out, rallied bef last, sn one pace.*
.... (14 to 1 op 12 to 1 tchd 16 to 1) 3
2351⁸ DERISBAY (Ire) [76] (bl) 9-11-1 D O'Sullivan, *chsd ldr, ev ch aftr 3 out, disputing second but btn whn hit nxt.*
.... (20 to 1 op 14 to 1 tchd 25 to 1) 4
2186³ GLOWING PATH [89] 7-11-7 (7*) J Harris, *took clr order aftr second, rdn alng frm 5th, wknd appr 2 out.*
.... (9 to 4 fav tchd 5 to 2) 5
1719 CALLONESCCY (Ire) [61] 5-10-0 C Llewellyn, *beh frm 3rd.*
.... (33 to 1 op 20 to 1 tchd 40 to 1) 6
398⁷ NORD LYS (Ire) [69] 6-10-1 (7*) Miss E J Jones, *hld up, hdwy 4th, wknd frm 3 out.*.........(7 to 1 op 6 to 1) 7
1764⁷ TOMAL [70] 5-10-9 D Gallagher, *hld up beh ldrs, rdn whn hit 2 out, 3rd and wkng when f last.*
.... (5 to 2 op 9 to 4 tchd 11 to 4) f
Dist: 2l, 7l, 1l, 9l, 5l, 17l. 4m 14.30s. a 23.30s (8 Ran).
(Electronic & Software Publications Ltd), J R Jenkins

2425 Adventure Novices' Chase Class D (5-y-o and up) £3,597 2m..... (2:30)

1573² GLITTER ISLE (Ire) 7-11-4 P Hide, *led to second, chsd ldr frm 6th, led sn aftr 2 out, rdn out, ran on wl.* (13 to 2 op 6 to 1) 1
2109⁷ GAROLO (Fr) (bl) 7-11-10 G Bradley, *hld up in tch, effrt frm 3 out, kpt on one pace r-in.*
.... (11 to 2 op 4 to 1 tchd 6 to 1 and 13 to 2) 2
AS DU TREFLE (Fr) 9-11-4 J Osborne, *pckd 1st, led 3rd, hdd sn aftr 2 out, soon btn.*.................(14 to 1 op 7 to 1) 3
1647 EXTERIOR PROFILES (Ire) 7-11-4 T J Murphy, *led second to nxt, 4th whn blun badly fourth, not reco'r.*
.... (11 to 2 op 6 to 1) 4
1577 MOUSE BIRD (Ire) 7-11-4 R Dunwoody, *hld up, mstk 5th, shaken up and styd on fnl 3, nvr nr.*
.... (9 to 2 op 4 to 1 tchd 5 to 1) 5
1939⁶ JOVIAL MAN (Ire) 8-11-4 D O'Sullivan, *beh frm 4th, tld off.*
.... (12 to 1 op 14 to 1 tchd 16 to 1) 6
2304 FULL OF TRICKS 9-11-4 D Morris, *prmnt, rdn 8th, sn wknd, tld off.*..................... (100 to 1 op 50 to 1) 7
2267³ FIONANS FLUTTER (Ire) 9-11-4 P Holley, *beh till f 4th, dead.*
.... (12 to 1 op 14 to 1 tchd 16 to 1) f
1761 TEINEIN (Fr) 6-11-4 N Williamson, *hld up, hit 6th, prog appr 3 out, 4th and btn whn f 2 out.*
.... (9 to 4 fav op 7 to 4 tchd 5 to 2) f
2259 HAWKER HUNTER (USA) (bl) 6-11-4 J A McCarthy, *blun and uns rdr second.*.................... (33 to 1 op 25 to 1) ur
2201 ERNEST ARAGORN 8-11-4 B Clifford, *beh till pld up bef 5th.*
.... (100 to 1 op 50 to 1) pu
Dist: 2l, 5l, 1¾l, sht-hd, dist, 12l. 4m 12.20s. a 18.20s (11 Ran).
SR: 20/24/13/11/11/-/ (Mrs Timothy Pilkington), J T Gifford

2426 Holtye Maiden Hurdle Class E (4-y-o and up) £2,685 2m 110yds.... (3:00)

2013² THREE FARTHINGS 7-11-8 C Llewellyn, *hld up beh ldrs, rdn betw fnl 2, led r-in, ran on wl.*
.... (13 to 8 fav op 6 to 4 tchd 7 to 4) 1
MUTANASSIB (Ire) 4-10-10 R Dunwoody, *led second, hdd and no extr r-in.*.............(4 to 1 op 2 to 1) 2
882⁶ MAGIC COMBINATION (Ire) 4-10-7 (3*) L Aspell, *hld up beh ldrs, effrt betw fnl 2, one pace.*
.... (7 to 2 op 5 to 1 tchd 6 to 1 and 8 to 1) 3
2173³ MR DARCY 5-11-8 J Osborne, *hld up, styd on one pace frm 2 out, not rch ldrs.*............(9 to 2 op 7 to 1 tchd 4 to 1) 4
2013³ MASTER PILGRIM 5-11-8 B Fenton, *trkd ldrs, rdn appr 2 out, sn wknd.*...................(14 to 1 op 10 to 1) 5
1716 NIGHT FLARE (Fr) 5-11-8 N Williamson, *beh, hdwy 3 out, wknd bef nxt.*......... (50 to 1 op 20 to 1 tchd 66 to 1) 6
1961 ROYAL RULER (Ire) 6-11-3 P Hide, *led to second, wknd 3 out, tld off.*.........(16 to 1 op 12 to 1 tchd 20 to 1) 7
1893 NISHAMAN 6-11-8 J R Kavanagh, *al beh, tld off.*
.... (25 to 1 op 14 to 1) 8
BON LUCK (Ire) 5-11-8 L Harvey, *al beh, tld off.*
.... (14 to 1 op 20 to 1 tchd 25 to 1) 9
SHE SAID NO 5-10-10 (7*) M Attwater, *in tch till 3 out, tld off whn pld up bef last.*....(33 to 1 op 20 to 1 tchd 50 to 1) pu
Dist: 2l, 6l, 13l, 1l, 2½l, dist, 6l, 14l. 4m 9.30s. a 18.30s (10 Ran).
SR: 26/12/6/5/4/-/ (K R Britten), J A B Old

2427 Felcourt Handicap Chase Class D (0-125 5-y-o and up) £3,808 3m .... (3:30)

1920⁴ GIVENTIME [105] 9-11-2 L Harvey, *hld up beh ldrs, led sn aftr 4 out, ran on wl.*........(7 to 2 op 3 to 1 tchd 4 to 1) 1
1687³ A N C EXPRESS [110] 9-11-7 T J Murphy, *hld up, hdwy 7th, drvn alng 12th, outpcd appr 3 out, rallied 2 out, kpt on.*
.... (4 to 1 op 11 to 4) 2
PLASTIC SPACEAGE [115] 14-11-12 C Llewellyn, *hld up beh ldrs, lost pl 9th, rallied and ran on r-in.*
.... (9 to 1 op 13 to 1 tchd 9 to 1) 3
2203⁴ SISTER ROSZA (Ire) [96] 9-10-7 R Farrant, *trkd ldrs, hmpd second, hit 7th, effrt 3 out, one pace appr last.*
.... (8 to 1 op 14 to 1) 4
1814* JURASSIC CLASSIC [112] 10-11-9 M Richards, *lft in ld second, mstk 4 out, sn hdd, wknd betw fnl 2.* (7 to 1 op 5 to 1) 5
1767⁷ MAKES ME GOOSEY (Ire) [96] (bl) 9-10-7 P Hide, *hld up, not fluent 9th, effrt 3 out, wknd nxt.*
.... (16 to 1 op 14 to 1 tchd 20 to 1) 6
1960⁵ DOM SAMOURAI (Fr) [117] (bl) 6-12-0 R Dunwoody, *hmpd second, al beh, tld off...*(12 to 1 op 8 to 1 tchd 14 to 1) 7
2306 VERYVEL (Cze) [97] 6-10-8 N Williamson, *mstks, al beh tld off.*
.... (25 to 1 op 20 to 1 tchd 33 to 1) 8
2024⁴ BRAES OF MAR [106] (bl) 7-11-3 J Osborne, *led till f second.*
.... (10 to 1 op 7 to 1) f
1687² THREE SAINTS (Ire) [96] 8-10-7 S Wynne, *prmnt till blun and uns rdr 11th.*.............(5 to 1 op 7 to 2 tchd 11 to 2) ur
Dist: 2l, 4l, nk, 3l, nk, dist, 1½l. 6m 30.90s. a 36.90s (10 Ran).
(L G Kimber), Andrew Turnell

2428 Heddon Novices' Handicap Hurdle Class E (0-100 5-y-o and up) £2,419 2m 3f 110yds.................. (4:00)

2356 EQUITY'S DARLING (Ire) [74] (bl) 5-10-6 P Hide, *wtd wth, improved 6th, led aftr 2 out, drvn out.*
.... (20 to 1 tchd 16 to 1 and 25 to 1) 1

1570³ LADY HIGH SHERIFF (Ire) [72] 7-10-4 S Wynne, *hld up, prog 6th, led appr 2 out, hdd bef nxt, one pace.* ....(5 to 1 op 4 to 1 tchd 6 to 1) 2
1474⁶ STEEL GEM (Ire) [74] 8-9-13 (7*) M Griffiths, *hdwy appr 5th, led 7th, hdd bef 2 out, wknd approaching last.* ....(4 to 1 fav op 10 to 1 tchd 7 to 2) 3
2153⁸ FANTASY LINE [87] 6-11-5 J Osborne, *patiently rdn, steady hdwy frm 7th, btn appr 2 out.* ....(16 to 1 op 12 to 1 tchd 20 to 1) 4
1830⁴ QUICK QUOTE [85] 7-11-3 L Harvey, *hld up, hdwy appr 3 out, wknd bef 2 out*..........(6 to 1 tchd 7 to 1 and 11 to 2) 5
2158⁸ SNOWSHILL SHAKER [85] 8-11-3 C Llewellyn, *keen hold early, hld up beh ldrs, rdn and wknd appr 2 out.* ....(11 to 2 op 5 to 1 tchd 6 to 1) 6
2158 ROVESTAR [89] 6-11-7 T J Murphy, *prmnt, drvn alng 6th, wknd appr 2 out, tld off.* (12 to 1 op 10 to 1 tchd 14 to 1) 7
1474⁸ OTTER PRINCE [68] (bl) 8-9-7 (7*) C Hynes, *hld up beh ldrs, rdn 6th, sn wknd, tld off*..............(25 to 1 op 20 to 1) 8
KENNETT SQUARE (Ire) [70] 8-10-2 J A McCarthy, *prmnt, led 4th till hit and hdd 7th, sn wknd, tld off.* (33 to 1 op 25 to 1) 9
HANGING GROVE (Ire) [89] 7-11-7 N Mann, *in tch, led 3rd to 4th, wknd 6th, tld off*................ (14 to 1 tchd 16 to 1) 10
1921 HELLO ME MAN (Ire) [84] 9-11-2 Mr J L Llewellyn, *al beh, tld off whn pld up aftr 6th*..............................(20 to 1) pu
TORCH VERT (Ire) [92] 5-11-10 R Farrant, *led to 3rd, wknd 7th, tld off whn pld up bef 2 out.* ....(14 to 1 op 10 to 1 tchd 16 to 1) pu
1980* MY MAN IN DUNDALK (Ire) [84] 8-10-13 (3*) L Aspell, *beh frm 5th, tld off whn pld up bef 2 out.* ....(13 to 2 op 5 to 2 tchd 7 to 1) pu
1719⁹ BRAYDON FOREST [73] (bl) 5-10-5⁵ A Thornton, *al beh, tld off whn pld up bef 2 out*..............(33 to 1 op 25 to 1) pu
2025⁵ FELLOO (Ire) [90] 8-11-8 R Dunwoody, *trkd ldrs till lost pl aftr 4th, tld off whn pld up bef 2 out.* ....(10 to 1 op 12 to 1 tchd 14 to 1) pu
Dist: 1½l, 13l, 9l, 5l, 2l, 26l, 8l, 21l, dist. 5m 5.60s. a 32.60s (15 Ran).
(Mrs V O'Brien), D C O'Brien

2429 H.B.L.B. Edenbridge Handicap Hurdle Class E (0-110 4-y-o and up) £2,251 2m 3f 110yds......... (4:30)

2009³ TICKERTY'S GIFT [107] 7-11-7 (7*) M Attwater, *trkd ldr, led 5th, drw clr betw fnl 2, ran on wl.* ....(9 to 2 op 5 to 1 tchd 4 to 1) 1
2307 SHEPHERDS REST (Ire) [101] 5-11-8 A Thornton, *al hndy, rdn whn lft in second 2 out, wknd appr last.* ....(11 to 4 op 2 to 1 tchd 3 to 1) 2
1917³ DAILY SPORT GIRL [88] 8-10-9 Mr J L Llewellyn, *beh frm 5th, styd on ag'n one pace from 2 out.* ....(12 to 1 op 10 to 1 tchd 14 to 1) 3
2307⁵ ZINGIBAR [87] 5-10-8 N Williamson, *hld up in tch, reminders aftr 4th, wknd 3 out*.....(11 to 1 op 6 to 1 tchd 12 to 1) 4
1917* FRIENDLY HOUSE (Ire) [97] 8-11-4 R Dunwoody, *led, dived 1st, hdd 5th, wknd 7th, tld off.* ....(5 to 2 fav op 9 to 4 tchd 11 to 4 and 3 to 1) 5
2305* YELLOW DRAGON (Ire) [94] 4-9-10 (7*,6ex) Gordon Gallagher, *prmnt, chsd wnr frm 7th, chalg whn pckd 3 out, second and rdn when f nxt*....... (7 to 2 op 3 to 1 tchd 4 to 1) f
Dist: 8l, 7l, 20l, 24l. 5m 11.10s. a 38.10s (6 Ran).
(K Higson), G L Moore

TAUNTON (good)
Friday January 31st
Going Correction: PLUS 0.45 sec. per fur.

2430 Martin Pipe Winners Galore Novices' Hurdle Class E (4-y-o and up) £2,442 2m 1f.........................(1:45)

2256 EASY LISTENING (USA) 5-11-3 J Railton, *prmnt, trkd ldr aftr 4 out, drvn to ld 2 out, sn clr, hld on wl r-in.* ....(14 to 1 op 8 to 1) 1
2173⁴ BREAK THE RULES 5-10-10 (7*) G Supple, *hld up, steady hdwy frm 4 out, chsd wnr from 2 out, kpt on but no imprsn cl hme*..............................(16 to 1 op 8 to 1) 2
MERAWANG (Ire) 4-10-7 R Johnson, *in tch 5th, styd on to chase ldrs 2 out, ran on*...............(4 to 1 op 5 to 2) 3
2195⁶ BRILLIANT RED 4-10-7 B Powell, *trkd ldrs, hit 5th, ran on same pace frm 2 out*...............................(5 to 1) 4
1517³ DOCTOR GREEN (Fr) (v) 4-12-0 D Walsh, *led, sn clr, blun 3 out, hdd 2 out, soon wknd*...........(16 to 1 op 8 to 1) 5
1610 CHIEF MOUSE 4-11-7 J F Titley, *chsd ldr till aftr 4 out, wknd 2 out*.................................(20 to 1 op 8 to 1) 6
2303² MELT THE CLOUDS (Can) 4-10-7 C Maude, *hld up, hdwy aftr 3 out, sn rdn, wknd after 2 out*..... (5 to 4 fav tchd 6 to 4) 7
1743⁹ SOUTHERNHAY BOY 6-11-3 W McFarland, *hit 4th, mstk nxt, sn beh*...............(16 to 1 op 20 to 1 tchd 33 to 1) 8
MYSTIC HILL 6-11-3 J Frost, *blun 1st, al beh.* ....(14 to 1 op 8 to 1 tchd 16 to 1) 9
QU'APPELLE 4-10-7 S McNeill, *mstk 1st, al beh, tld off.* ....(100 to 1 op 20 to 1) 10
2173 TIME GOES ON 5-10-9 (3*) D Fortt, *al beh, tld off.* ....(100 to 1 op 50 to 1 tchd 200 to 1) 11
2242 CHALCUCHIMA 4-10-7 R Greene, *al beh, hit 5th, tld off.* ....(100 to 1 op 33 to 1) 12
1300⁶ GALE SPRING (Ire) 5-10-9 (3*) T Dascombe, *beh frm 4th, f 2 out*.................(50 to 1 op 25 to 1 tchd 100 to 1) f
Dist: 2l, 4l, ½l, sht-hd, 2l, 2½l, 18l, 1¼l, dist, 11l. 3m 57.50s. a 14.50s (13 Ran).
SR: 21/19/5/4/25/16/ (Derek Kacy Flint), N J Hawke

2431 Alison Farrant Pretty Woman Novices' Handicap Chase Class D (0-110 5-y-o and up) £3,517 2m 110yds .... (2:15)

2257⁵ INDIAN JOCKEY [108] 5-11-10 D Walsh, *made all, sn clr, unchlgd*................(6 to 1 op 3 to 1 tchd 13 to 2) 1
1857³ CRACKING PROSPECT [77] (bl) 6-9-12 (5*) D Salter, *mstk 1st, hdwy 7th, chsd wnr, no imprsn frm 4 out.* ....(5 to 1 tchd 11 to 2) 2
2154² NORDIC VALLEY (Ire) [86] 6-10-12 C Maude, *chsd wnr to 4th, lft second ag'n 9th to four out, hit 2 out, styd on same pace.* ....(7 to 2 op 9 to 4) 3
1724⁶ OCTOBER BREW (USA) [84] (bl) 7-10-3 (7*) G Supple, *chsd wnr 4th till blun 9th, sn wknd, tld off.* ....(9 to 1 op 10 to 1 tchd 8 to 1) 4
1475 BISHOPS CASTLE (Ire) [87] 9-10-13 J Frost, *wl beh frm 5th, tld off*.............................(9 to 2 op 4 to 1) 5
1978⁷ MADAM ROSE (Ire) [74] 7-10-0 S Curran, *hmpd second, al wl beh, tld off*........................(50 to 1 op 33 to 1) 6
1600 BAXWORTHY LORD [74] 6-10-0 G Tormey, *hit 5th, beh whn f 8th*.........................(66 to 1 op 33 to 1) f
2176* NORTHERN SINGER [81] 7-10-4 (3*) T Dascombe, *uns rdr second*.......... (3 to 1 fav op 11 to 4 tchd 100 to 30) ur
1748 ASHLEY HOUSE [74] 8-10-0 B Powell, *hmpd 1st, sn tld off, pld up bef 8th*......................(50 to 1 op 33 to 1) pu
Dist: 8l, 1l, dist, 4l, dist. 4m 6.00s. a 14.00s (9 Ran).
SR: 32/3/11/-/-/-/ (Stuart M Mercer), M C Pipe

2432 Martin Pipe Racing Is Life Novices' Handicap Hurdle Class E (0-105 4-y-o and up) £2,253 2m 1f....... (2:45)

2292² D'NAAN (Ire) [88] (bl) 4-10-7 C Maude, *made virtually all, sn clr, hrd rdn whn chlgd frm 3 out, ran on gmely.* ....(100 to 30 op 3 to 1 tchd 4 to 1) 1
2390² ALMAPA [80] 5-10-8 (3*) T Dascombe, *gd hdwy 3 out, str chal last, not quicken r-in*..............................(4 to 1) 2
2185⁵ ULTIMATE SMOOTHIE [97] 5-11-7 (7*) G Supple, *hld up in rear, hdwy 3 out, styd on same pace frm nxt.* ....(3 to 1 fav op 9 to 4 tchd 10 to 3) 3
2372 LAUGHING BUCCANEER [81] 4-10-0 B Powell, *wl beh till hdwy 5th, lost pl nxt, ran on ag'n frm 2 out.* ....(12 to 1 op 7 to 1) 4
939² LONICERA [89] 7-11-3 (3*) P Henley, *pld hrd, chsd wnr, str chal frm 3 out till wknd nxt*.............(11 to 2 op 4 to 1) 5
2267 ROYAL GLINT [69] 8-9-7 (7*) Mr L Baker, *in tch, rdn alng aftr 5th, wknd frm 3 out*..... (12 to 1 op 6 to 1 tchd 16 to 1) 6
2279 NAGARA SOUND [87] 6-11-4 T Jenks, *in tch, rdn 3 out, sn wknd*..................(11 to 2 op 5 to 1 tchd 6 to 1) 7
CONCINNITY (USA) [69] 8-9-7 (7*) Mr O McPhail, *tld off frm 5th*.......................(33 to 1 op 20 to 1) 8
Dist: 2l, 8l, 7l, 4l, 13l, 2½l, 22l. 3m 58.40s. a 15.40s (8 Ran).
SR: 2/4/13/-/-/ (Mrs P B Browne), M C Pipe

2433 Chester Barnes 50th Birthday 'National Hunt' Novices' Hurdle Class E (Div I) (4-y-o and up) £1,945 2m 3f 110yds..................(3:15)

1852 ATAVISTIC (Ire) 5-11-1 (3*) T Dascombe, *chsd ldrs, led 3 out, rdn and styd on wl frm nxt*......... (2 to 1 fav op 6 to 4) 1
1940 OVER THE WATER (Ire) 5-11-1 (3*) P Henley, *trkd ldr till led 4 out, hdd nxt, styd on same pace frm 2 out.* ....(33 to 1 op 12 to 1) 2
1505⁵ CHARLIE PARROT (Ire) 7-11-4 D Walsh, *hld up, steady hdwy frm 4 out, chsd wnr appr 2 out, sn rdn and one pace.* ....(3 to 1 op 2 to 1 tchd 100 to 30) 3
2183⁶ BROWN WREN 6-10-13 G Tormey, *beh till hdwy 5th, styd on ag'n frm 2 out*...............(13 to 2 op 6 to 1) 4
ANNIE RUTH (Ire) 6-10-10 (3*) G Hogan, *mstk 5th, sn beh.* ....(14 to 1 op 12 to 1) 5
2242⁴ ASHTAR (USA) 7-11-4 C Maude, *led, ran green into early hurdles, clr 4th, hdd four out, wknd frm 3 out.* ....(9 to 4 op 11 to 4 tchd 3 to 1) 6
2243 ALICE SHORELARK 6-10-13 Mr T Greed, *hit 6th, al beh, tld off*...................................(66 to 1 op 50 to 1) 7
1344 SULA'S DREAM 8-10-10 (3*) D Fortt, *al beh, tld off.* ....(50 to 1 op 33 to 1) 8
1350 BECKY'S LAD 7-11-1 (3*) Guy Lewis, *beh and rdn 5th, sn tld off*.................... (33 to 1 op 25 to 1 tchd 50 to 1) 9
1237 MORECEVA (Ire) 7-11-4 W Marston, *beh frm 5th, tld off.* .... (33 to 1 op 20 to 1) 10
Dist: 9l, 3½l, 15l, 13l, 1¾l, dist, 11l, 9l, 1¾l. 4m 41.60s. a 23.60s (10 Ran).
(Mrs Jill Emery, Mr A Staple, Mr E Morris), C L Popham

2434 David Johnson Challenger Handicap Chase Class E (0-110 5-y-o and up)

£2,887 3m.....................(3:45)

2258⁴ BANNTOWN BILL (Ire) [97] (v) 8-11-5 (7ex) D Walsh, *in tch, led 6th, hit nxt, hdd 8th, wth ldr to 13th, drvn to ld ag'n 3 out, ran on wl.............*(3 to 1 fav op 5 to 2 tchd 4 to 1) 1
MOZEMO [84] 10-10-6 C Maude, *trkd ldrs, quickened to ld 13th, hdd 3 out, sn one pace.*
.............................(7 to 2 op 4 to 1 tchd 11 to 4) 2
1814 CHILDHAY CHOCOLATE [102] 9-11-10 R Johnson, *led to 6th, wth ldr till led ag'n 8th, hdd 13th, wknd 3 out.*
.............................(6 to 1 op 4 to 1) 3
2293⁴ COOL CHARACTER (Ire) [78] 9-10-0 B Powell, *hdwy tenth, rdn and styd on ag'n frm 2 out.*
.............................(13 to 2 op 5 to 1 tchd 7 to 1) 4
1687⁵ STEEPLE JACK [82] 10-10-4 R Greene, *tld off frm 6th.*
.............................(6 to 1 op 5 to 1 tchd 9 to 1) 5
2295⁶ GLEN MIRAGE [90] 12-10-12 Miss M Coombe, *hdwy 11th, wknd quickly and pld up bef 14th.*.............(5 to 1) pu
1724⁴ GLENTOWER (Ire) [88] 9-10-10 G Tormey, *pld up aftr 5th, lme.*
.............................(5 to 1) pu
Dist: 11l, 6l, 1½l, dist. 6m 6.60s. a 23.60s (7 Ran).

(Eric Scarth), M C Pipe

2435
Martin Pipe Am I That Difficult? Handicap Hurdle Class E (0-110 5-y-o and up) £2,284 3m 110yds.. (4:15)

2246⁴ MAID EQUAL [93] 6-10-4 (7*,7ex) G Supple, *hld up, hdwy 5th, led 4 out, ran on gmely whn chlgd frm 2 out.*
.............................(2 to 1 op 7 to 4 tchd 9 to 4) 1
2295² MR STRONG GALE (Ire) [88] 6-10-6 R Johnson, *hld up, hdwy 8th, str chal frm 2 out, no extr und pres r-in.*
.............................(Evens fav op 7 to 4) 2
2177⁸ TIGER CLAW (USA) [82] 11-10-0 R Greene, *in tch till rdn and lost pos 8th, styd on ag'n frm 2 out....*(20 to 1 op 14 to 1) 3
2281 BATTY'S ISLAND [82] 8-9-7 (7*) J Mogford, *chsd ldrs till wknd frm 3 out...........*(20 to 1 op 16 to 1 tchd 25 to 1) 4
2177⁷ GUNMAKER [82] 8-10-0 S Curran, *prmnt, chlgd 6th, led aftr nxt, hdd 4 out, sn wknd............*(13 to 2 op 5 to 1) 5
2246 JADIDH [87] (v) 9-10-0 (5*) D Salter, *beh frm 5th.*
.............................(12 to 1 op 8 to 1 tchd 14 to 1) 6
515⁵ PASSED PAWN [107] 10-11-11 C Maude, *led till aftr 7th, wth ldrs till wknd quickly appr 4 out, tld off whn pld up bef 2 out.*
.............................(12 to 1 op 8 to 1) pu
Dist: 1l, 19l, 3l, 29l, 2½l. 5m 50.80s. a 22.80s (7 Ran).

(Heeru Kirpalani), M C Pipe

2436
Chester Barnes 50th Birthday 'National Hunt' Novices' Hurdle Class E (Div II) (4-y-o and up) £1,934 2m 3f 110yds.................(4:45)

1860⁴ MILLCROFT RIVIERA (Ire) 6-11-1 (3*) P Henley, *in tch till mstk and lost pl 7th, lft second 2 out, styd on pres to ld nr finish.*
.............................(7 to 1 op 4 to 1 tchd 15 to 2) 1
2155² DECYBORG (Fr) 6-11-4 C Maude, *led, sn wl clr, hdd and btn whn lft in ld ag'n 2 out, hrd rdn, headed and wknd nr finish.*
.............................(13 to 2 op 5 to 1 tchd 7 to 1) 2
446³ MISS FOXY 7-11-5 J Frost, *in tch 5th, wknd 7th, tld off.*
.............................(8 to 1 op 5 to 1 tchd 9 to 1) 3
LAUREN'S TREASURE (Ire) 6-11-4 W McFarland, *beh frm 3rd, tld off 5th.......*(20 to 1 tchd 16 to 1) 4
LANDSKER STAR 7-10-8 (5*) D Salter, *beh frm 6th, tld off.*
.............................(66 to 1 op 20 to 1) 5
1578 MINGAY 6-10-11 (7*) J Prior, *mstk 1st, tld off frm 3rd.*
.............................(100 to 1 op 33 to 1) 6
1961 ZEN OR 6-10-6 (7*) David Turner, *beh frm 6th, tld off.*
.............................(66 to 1 op 33 to 1 tchd 100 to 1) 7
2249⁹ SIOUX TO SPEAK 5-11-4 J F Titley, *trkd ldrs, pushed alng 3 out, led and staying on whn f 2 out......*(4 to 1 op 5 to 1) f
2123⁴ MRS EM 5-10-13 R Johnson, *hld up, hdwy 6th, str chal and gng wl whn f 2 out...............*(11 to 10 on op 5 to 4) f
103 RORY'M (Ire) 8-11-4 D Leahy, *jmpd slwly second and not fluent, tld off frm 6th, pld up bef 2 out.*
.............................(100 to 1 op 40 to 1) pu
Dist: 2l, dist, ¾l, 14l, 29l, 27l. 4m 41.90s. a 23.90s (10 Ran).

(John Carter), R H Alner

CHEPSTOW (good)
Saturday February 1st
Going Correction: PLUS 0.45 sec. per fur. (races 1,3,5), PLUS 0.40 (2,4,6)

2437
BBC Ceefax And Marcia-Ann Cooper Handicap Chase Class C (0-135 5-y-o and up) £7,555 2m 3f 110yds (1:15)

2247³ BELLS LIFE (Ire) [125] 8-11-4 G Tormey, *jmpd wl, hld up, hdwy 9th, led 3 out, sn in command, cmftbly.*
.............................(7 to 4 op 4 to 1 tchd 9 to 2) 1
1672⁵ SEEK THE FAITH (USA) [107] 8-10-0 B Powell, *hld up in rear, hdwy appr 5 out, chsd wnr frm 2 out...*(14 to 1 op 12 to 1) 2
2014⁴ MARINERS MIRROR [120] 10-10-13 Mr M Rimell, *chsd ldrs, hdwy to ld 4 out, hdd nxt, one pace aftr.* (11 to 2 op 9 to 2) 3

2007³ CONTI D'ESTRUVAL (Fr) [115] 7-10-8 B Clifford, *hld up in mid-div, hdwy 9th, one pace frm 3 out.*
.............................(10 to 1 op 12 to 1 tchd 9 to 1) 4
1773³ DENVER BAY [119] 10-10-9 (3*) L Aspell, *hld up, hdwy appr 5 out, one pace.......................*(11 to 2 op 9 to 2) 5
2194³ SENOR EL BETRUTTI (Ire) [133] 8-11-12 C Llewellyn, *in tch till no hdwy frm 3 out..............*(8 to 1 tchd 7 to 1) 6
2244 BENJAMIN LANCASTER [107] 13-9-7 (7*) M Griffiths, *prmnt till hit 8th, sn beh.......................*(33 to 1) 7
GENERAL PERSHING [135] 11-12-0 R Johnson, *led till hdd appr 8th, wknd bef 5 out......*(12 to 1 op 8 to 1) 8
1892⁴ TERAO [127] 11-11-6 T J Murphy, *jmpd rght, pld hrd, chsd ldr 5th, led appr 8th, hdd 4 out, wknd quickly.*
.............................(12 to 1 op 8 to 1) 9
2212⁵ SOUND REVEILLE [135] 9-11-7 (7*) M Berry, *prmnt till lost pl appr 6th, beh whn blun and uns rdr 4 out.*
.............................(12 to 1 op 10 to 1) ur
1889 BO KNOWS BEST (Ire) [115] 8-10-8 C Maude, *tld off 5th, pld up bef 5 out.............*(25 to 1 op 20 to 1) pu
Dist: 7l, 3l, hd, ½l, 11l, 6l, 1¾l, 6l. 4m 57.20s. a 14.20s (11 Ran).
SR: 35/10/20/15/18/21/-/15/1/ (R Gibbs), P J Hobbs

2438
**Prestige Novices' Hurdle Class A Grade 2 (5-y-o and up) £9,915 3m
.............................(1:45)**

2156⁴ YOUNG KENNY 6-11-0 R Supple, *hld up in rear, hdwy 8th, sn rdn, led 2 out, ran on wl..........*(11 to 2 op 5 to 1) 1
2152⁵ KORBELL (Ire) 8-10-9 R Johnson, *mid-div, rdn to go second 3 out, swtchd lft appr last, ran on r-in.....*(5 to 1 tchd 6 to 1) 2
1615² MENESONIC (Ire) 7-11-0 J Culloty, *hld up, hdwy 4 out, styd on one pace frm 2 out..................*(12 to 1 op 8 to 1) 3
2156³ DESTIN D'ESTRUVAL (Fr) 6-11-0 D Bridgwater, *trkd ldr, led 7th, clr appr 4 out, rdn and hdd 2 out, one pace aftr.*
.............................(100 to 30 op 4 to 1 tchd 9 to 2) 4
1729⁴ WARNER FOR PLAYERS (Ire) 6-11-0 C Llewellyn, *hld up in rear, hdwy 4 out, wkng whn mstk 2 out.*
.............................(20 to 1 op 16 to 1 tchd 25 to 1) 5
2249⁴ HURDANTE (Ire) 7-11-0 B Clifford, *hld up, hdwy 4th, hit 5th, chsd ldr aftr 8th till wknd 3 out.*
.............................(3 to 1 fav op 11 to 4 tchd 100 to 30) 6
2253⁹ EULOGY (Ire) 7-11-0 L Aspell, *mstk 4th, led to 7th, wknd appr four out, tld off..................*(12 to 1 op 10 to 1) 7
2243⁴ SCOTBY (Bel) 7-11-0 B Powell, *hld up, hdwy appr 6th, wknd 4 out..........................*(12 to 1 op 10 to 1) 8
2183² EDGEMOOR PRINCE 6-11-3 C Maude, *pld hrd, trkd ldrs till wknd 7th, tld off.................*(12 to 1 op 10 to 1) 9
1592² BEST OF FRIENDS (Ire) 7-11-0 J F Titley, *al beh, struggling 7th, tld off......................*(12 to 1 op 10 to 1) 10
Dist: 1¾l, 3l, 4l, 10l, 8l, 22l, 1¼l, 12l, dist. 5m 53.40s. a 18.40s (10 Ran).
(J G Read), P Beaumont

2439
John Hughes Grand National Trial Class B Handicap Chase £10,201 3m 5f 110yds.....................(2:15)

2246 FLYER'S NAP [130] 11-11-7 D Bridgwater, *hld up, hdwy 12th, led aftr 6 out, in command whn lft wl clr 2 out, eased r-in.*
.............................(11 to 1 op 8 to 1 tchd 12 to 1) 1
2182⁴ SUNLEY BAY [120] 10-11-0 R Johnson, *hld up, outpcd 15th, styd on frm 5 out, lft poor second 2 out..*(9 to 2 op 4 to 1) 2
2189 FULL OF OATS [120] 11-10-11 J Culloty, *mstk second, hld up, hdwy 15th, one pace 5 out, lft poor 3rd 2 out.*
.............................(13 to 8 fav op 7 to 4 tchd 15 to 8) 3
1745² DAKYNS BOY [124] 12-11-1 C Llewellyn, *led to 11th, outpcd frm 4 out........................*(7 to 2) 4
2182 KILLESHIN [133] 11-11-10 S Curran, *beh whn jmpd slwly 13th, tld off 17th..............*(16 to 1 op 12 to 1) 5
2245³ SEE ENOUGH [110] 9-10-1 S McNeill, *chsd ldr, led 11th, hdd aftr 6 out, second and btn whn f 2 out...*(10 to 1 op 8 to 1) f
2306³ SPUFFINGTON [113] 9-10-1 (3*) L Aspell, *beh till hdwy 6th, wnt second 14th, btn 3rd whn brght dwn 2 out.*
.............................(11 to 2 op 5 to 1 tchd 6 to 1) bd
2182 DISTILLATION [109] 12-9-11 (3*) T Dascombe, *al beh, lost tch 15th, tld off whn pld up bef 5 out...*(100 to 1 op 66 to 1) pu
Dist: 8l, 3l, 3½l, 29l. 7m 43.90s. a 17.90s (8 Ran).
SR: 46/28/25/25/5/ (R J Tory), R H Alner

2440
Poachers Selling Handicap Hurdle Class G (0-95 4-y-o and up) £2,192 2m 110yds.....................(2:50)

1980³ SCOTTISH WEDDING [75] 7-10-10 R Johnson, *jmpd slwly second, hdwy 4th, outpcd 3 out, rallied appr last, drvn out to ld r-in.......................*(7 to 1 op 6 to 1) 1
1936³ FONTANAYS (Ire) [89] 9-11-3 (7*) R Hobson, *hld up gng wl, steady hdwy frm 4th, led appr 2 out, four ls clr whn blun badly last, hdd r-in...........*(5 to 1 fav op 4 to 1) 2
1915³ STRIKE-A-POSE [76] 7-10-11 Mr J L Llewellyn, *al prmnt, led 4th till hdd appr 2 out, one pace aftr.*(14 to 1 op 12 to 1) 3
2267 HAWANAFA [75] (bl) 4-10-0 S McNeill, *al prmnt, chsd ldr frm 4th, ev ch 3 out, one pace aftr........*(20 to 1 op 14 to 1) 4
2295⁸ URBAN LILY [77] (bl) 7-10-5 (7*) J Harris, *al prmnt, ev ch 3 out, rdn and wknd appr last.................*(9 to 1 op 10 to 1) 5
2251⁸ LIME STREET BLUES (Ire) [79] (bl) 6-10-7 (7*) M Berry, *pld hrd, prmnt, ev ch whn mstk 3 out, sn btn.*(6 to 1 op 5 to 1) 6

326

1956^{4} KHATIR (Can) [78] (v) 6-10-13 C Maude, *sn beh, some hdwy 3 out, nvr on terms*.................. (8 to 1 tchd 10 to 1) 7
2174^{5} LITTLE HOOLIGAN [80] 6-10-12 (3*) T Dascombe, *hld up, jmpd slwly second, hdwy 4th, rdn and wknd appr 2 out.* ....(6 to 1 op 5 to 1) 8
1425^{6} JONJAS CHUDLEIGH [78] 10-10-13 J Frost, *wl beh second till some late hdwy, nvr dngrs*.........(10 to 1 op 8 to 1) 9
1947^{8} NEVER SO BLUE (Ire) [88] 6-11-4 (5*) Sophie Mitchell, *prmnt till wknd 3 out*........ (14 to 1 op 12 to 1 tchd 16 to 1) 10
MICK THE YANK (Ire) [73] 7-10-1 (7*) Mr H Oliver, *al beh.* .... (20 to 1 op 14 to 1) 11
2174^{6} TEE TEE TOO (Ire) [75] 5-10-3 (7*) M Griffiths, *prmnt till rdn and wknd hfwy*........ (16 to 1 op 20 to 1 tchd 14 to 1) 12
2351 WIDE SUPPORT [84] (v) 12-11-5 N Mann, *jmpd slwly second, beh frm 4th*.........................(33 to 1 op 25 to 1) 13
518 ANOTHERONE TO NOTE [65] 6-9-9^{2} (7*) A Dowling, *hld up in rear, hdwy whn mstk 4th, sn btn*..... (50 to 1 op 33 to 1) 14
DEEP ISLE [75] 11-10-10 R Supple, *prmnt, led second, hdd and mstk nxt, sn btn*.........................(33 to 1 op 25 to 1) 15
1969 BILL AND WIN [65] (v) 6-10-0 R Farrant, *in tch till wknd 4th, tld off*....................................(50 to 1 op 33 to 1) 16
GILBERT (Ire) [65] 9-10-0 B Powell, *led to 3rd, wknd aftr nxt, tld off whn pld up bef 2 out.* .... (33 to 1 op 25 to 1 tchd 50 to 1) pu
Dist: 2l, 2l, 3½l, ½l, 2½l, 6l, 2l, nk, ½l, 11l. 4m 5.20s. a 18.20s (17 Ran).
(G A Weetman, Reynolds & Dean), T Wall

2441 Tony Preston Aspiring Champions Novices' Chase Class C (5-y-o and up) £5,411 3m................ (3:20)

1347 TENNESSEE TWIST (Ire) 7-11-2 R Farrant, *chsd ldrs, outpcd 13th, rallied to go second 4 out, styd on gmely to ld sn aftr last, rdn out*...................(13 to 2 op 5 to 1 tchd 7 to 1) 1
1981* INDIAN TRACKER 7-11-7 C Maude, *rcd keenly and jmpd wl, clr 5 out, rdn and pckd last, sn hdd, no extr.* ....(2 to 1 fav op 5 to 2) 2
1513* BARONET (Ire) 7-11-11 R Johnson, *chsd ldrs, mstk 6th, rdn appr 5 out, wknd 3 out*................ (8 to 1 op 5 to 1) 3
1870* BERUDE NOT TO (Ire) 8-11-11 J A McCarthy, *mstk 1st, in tch, rdn appr 5 out, one pace frm nxt.* .... (100 to 30 op 5 to 2 tchd 7 to 2) 4
1765* CREDO IS KING (Ire) 7-11-7 A Thornton, *chsd ldr, blun 4th, rdn appr 5 out, wknd quickly nxt.* .... (11 to 2 op 6 to 1 tchd 13 to 2) 5
1891* FOODBROKER STAR (Ire) 7-11-8 (3*) L Aspell, *al mid-div, lost tch 13th, tld off*....................... (6 to 1 op 5 to 1) 6
2245^{4} KENDAL CAVALIER 7-11-2 B Clifford, *jmpd slwly 1st, al beh, tld off 8th. y*.......................(20 to 1 op 14 to 1) 7
2157^{4} PENNCALER (Ire) 7-11-2 C Llewellyn, *al beh, lost tch 8th, tld off*.......................................(33 to 1 op 20 to 1) 8
2268 OATS N BARLEY 8-11-2 B Powell, *al beh, tld off whn pld up bef 4 out*........................ (40 to 1 op 33 to 1) pu
1921 MAJOR NOVA 8-11-2 J Ryan, *al beh, tld off whn pld up bef 13th*................................. (50 to 1 op 33 to 1) pu
1615 DEXTRA (Ire) 7-11-2 S Curran, *al beh, tld off whn pld up bef 4 out*...................................(66 to 1 op 50 to 1) pu
SWIFT POKEY 7-11-2 M Clarke, *al beh, tld off whn pld up bef 12th*.....................................(66 to 1 op 20 to 1) pu
Dist: 2l, 17l, nk, 30l, 24l, 29l, dist. 6m 8.50s. a 18.50s (12 Ran).
SR: 11/14/2/2/-/-/ (Halewood International Ltd), Mrs J Pitman

2442 Gamekeepers Handicap Hurdle Class C (0-130 4-y-o and up) £3,715 2m 110yds.................. (3:55)

2329^{9} KADASTROF (Fr) [128] 7-11-5 (7*) X Aizpuru, *led 3rd, made rst, mstk 3 out, ran on wl*.............(12 to 1 op 8 to 1) 1
1888* AMBLESIDE (Ire) [112] 6-10-10 D Bridgwater, *trkd ldrs, lost pl 4th, rallied appr 2 out, no imprsn aftr.* .... (11 to 10 fav op 3 to 1 tchd Evens) 2
DOCTOOR (USA) [108] 7-9-13 (7*) B Moore, *hld up, steady hdwy 3 out, tenderly rdn r-in, nvr nrr.* (25 to 1 op 16 to 1) 3
2219^{5} KIBREET [118] 10-11-2 R Johnson, *al prmnt, chsd wnr frm 3rd, wknd appr last.* ....(9 to 1 op 8 to 1 tchd 10 to 1 and 11 to 1) 4
BRAVE TORNADO [125] 6-11-9 B Clifford, *hld up, hdwy appr 4 out, one pace frm nxt*.................. (20 to 1 op 10 to 1) 5
2218^{8} DREAMS END [130] 9-12-0 R Farrant, *hld up, hdwy 3rd, wknd 3 out*.............................. (16 to 1 op 10 to 1) 6
1921 PENNYMOOR PRINCE [110] 8-10-8^{8} J Frost, *beh, some hdwy 3 out, nvr dngrs*..............(40 to 1 op 20 to 1) 7
2218 ROS CASTLE [124] 6-11-1 (7*) J Harris, *beind, nvr on terms.* .... (20 to 1 op 14 to 1) 8
1959^{6} SLEW MAN (Fr) [120] 6-10-11 (7*) G Supple, *hld up, hdwy hfwy, wknd 4 out*......................(16 to 1 op 12 to 1) 9
1481^{4} CHAPRASSI (Ire) [121] 8-11-5 C Maude, *led to 3rd, hit nxt, wknd quickly appr 3 out*...(11 to 4 op 3 to 1 tchd 7 to 2) 10
2257 MANOLETE [102] 6-9-7 (7*) M Lane, *al beh, tld off.* .... (33 to 1 op 20 to 1) 11
1959^{3} BELL ONE (USA) [105] 8-10-3 S McNeill, *prmnt to 3rd, sn beh, tld off*..................................(7 to 1 op 5 to 1) 12
1888 COURT NAP (Ire) [112] 5-10-10 C Llewellyn, *al beh, tld off.* ....(14 to 1 op 12 to 1) 13
1911* WHITE WILLOW [125] (v) 8-11-6 (3*) R Massey, *beh frm 3rd, tld off*.................................(16 to 1 op 12 to 1) 14
Dist: 3l, hd, 6l, ¾l, 8l, 1¼l, 1l, 2½l, ½l, 12l. 3m 58.40s. a 11.40s (14 Ran).
SR: 50/31/27/31/37/34/12/25/18/ (A P Paton), R Dickin

FAIRYHOUSE (IRE) (good to yielding)
Saturday February 1st
Going Correction: PLUS 0.25 sec. per fur. (races 1,3,5,7), PLUS 0.55 (2,4,6)

2443 Fanmond Maiden Hurdle (5 & 6-y-o) £3,082 2¼m.................(1:30)

2072^{3} HUMBEL (USA) 5-11-11 D T Evans,...........(5 to 4 fav) 1
2048^{3} DIGIN FOR GOLD (Ire) 6-11-6 F Woods,...........(4 to 1) 2
2041^{2} PHARDANA (Ire) 6-11-6 J P Broderick,...........(14 to 1) 3
2144* CORRACHOILL (Ire) 6-11-11 (3*) U Smyth,.........(12 to 1) 4
1096^{6} EQUIVOCATOR (Ire) 6-11-6 T P Rudd,...........(12 to 1) 5
1359^{5} SIMPLY ACOUSTIC (Ire) 6-10-8 (7*) S P Kelly,......(20 to 1) 6
2339^{8} AS ROYAL (Ire) 6-12-0 T P Treacy,...............(12 to 1) 7
2131^{8} NUZUM ROAD MAKERS (Ire) 6-10-13 (7*) D K Budds, ...(33 to 1) 8
2160 WINTER MELODY (Ire) 5-11-3 L P Cusack,........(20 to 1) 9
2168^{9} GLEN CAMDEN (Ire) 5-11-3 A Powell,..............(50 to 1) 10
KEITHS CHOICE (Ire) 5-10-7 (5*) J M Donnelly,....(50 to 1) 11
PARTLY CLOUDY (Ire) 6-11-6 T Horgan,..........(25 to 1) 12
1836 FANORE (Ire) 6-10-13 (7*) D A McLoughlin,........(50 to 1) 13
2339 EXPERT ADVICE (Ire) 6-11-6 D J Casey,..........(33 to 1) 14
WALK ON MIX (Fr) 5-11-11 C F Swan,............(9 to 2) 15
1901^{6} BRACKENVALE (Ire) 6-11-1 D H O'Connor,.........(50 to 1) 16
1463 JACKPOT JOHNNY (Ire) 6-10-13 (7*) M D Murphy, (33 to 1) 17
2168 CAHERMURPHY (Ire) 5-10-12 (5*) T Martin,...... (50 to 1) 18
2293 POLISH CONSUL 6-11-3 (3*) K Whelan,...........(16 to 1) 19
2339 QUIPTECH (Ire) 6-11-6 T J Mitchell,.............(14 to 1) 20
2343 OCTOBER SEVENTH 6-11-6 J Shortt,.............(25 to 1) 21
GETTING CLOSER (Ire) 6-11-6 C O'Dwyer,........(14 to 1) 22
1655 DAYVILLE (Ire) 6-11-6 H Rogers,................(50 to 1) 23
HEART 'N SOUL-ON (Ire) 6-10-13 (7*) S M McGovern, ...(50 to 1) 24
THE SIDHE (Ire) 5-10-12 J R Barry,..............(50 to 1) 25
BALLYBANE LASSIE (Ire) 6-10-8 (7*) R M Murphy, (50 to 1) 26
1364 DIVINE LILY (Ire) 6-10-8 (7*) S FitzGerald,.........(50 to 1) 27
2048^{4} KNOCKAROO (Ire) (bl) 6-12-0 K F O'Brien,........(12 to 1) f
2271^{6} YASHGANS VISION (Ire) 6-11-2 (7*) Mr N Moran, ..(14 to 1) ur
2271 HAZY WALK (Ire) 6-11-2 (7*) M W Martin,.........(20 to 1) l
Dist: 8l, 4l, 3l, 7l. 4m 22.50s. a 10.50s (30 Ran).
SR: 37/24/20/25/10/-/ (Michael W J Smurfit), D K Weld

2444 Normans Grove Handicap Chase (5-y-o and up) £6,850 2m........ (2:00)

2233^{7} FIFTYSEVENCHANNELS (Ire) [-] 8-11-11 C F Swan, (5 to 1) 1
2231^{2} BEAKSTOWN (Ire) [-] 8-12-0 T P Treacy,.......(5 to 4 fav) 2
2226^{4} MINSTREL FIRE (Ire) [-] 9-10-5 C O'Dwyer,........(12 to 1) 3
2226^{2} SORRY ABOUT THAT [-] 11-9-11 (3*) K Whelan,....(8 to 1) 4
2233^{2} ARCTIC WEATHER (Ire) [-] 8-11-12 T P Rudd,.......(7 to 4) f
Dist: Sht-hd, 5l, 15l. 4m 10.90s. a 16.90s (5 Ran).
SR: 16/19/ (John A Cooper), E Bolger

2445 Irish National Hunt Novice Hurdle Series (5-y-o and up) £4,110 2½m .... (2:30)

1193* MOSCOW EXPRESS (Ire) 5-11-5 C F Swan,........ (3 to 1) 1
2135^{5} MISTY MOMENTS (Ire) 6-11-1 (7*) Mr A J Dempsey, (8 to 1) 2
2081 ETON GALE (Ire) 8-11-2 C O'Dwyer,...............(5 to 1) 3
2111* DUKY RIVER (Ire) 6-11-8 F Woods,................(9 to 2) 4
2140* KINGS RETURN (Ire) 6-12-0 D J Casey,........ (5 to 2 fav) 5
2107^{3} VITUS (USA) 5-11-5 J Shortt,...................... (6 to 1) 6
2276^{7} CORYROSE (Ire) 5-10-8 T P Rudd,.................. (16 to 1) 7
2340^{6} YELAPA PRINCE (Ire) 6-11-8 A J O'Brien,........ (10 to 1) 8
FLASHY LAD (Ire) 6-11-2 T Horgan,..............(25 to 1) 9
2132^{9} KAVANAGHS DREAM (Ire) 8-11-2 H Rogers,.......(20 to 1) 10
2070^{5} ALL THE VOWELS (Ire) 6-11-2 J P Broderick,......(14 to 1) 11
Dist: 2½l, 5½l, 1½l, 1l. 4m 54.90s. a 10.90s (11 Ran).
SR: 32/32/20/24/29/-/ (T Conroy), A P O'Brien

2446 Kilsallaghan Beginners Chase (5-y-o and up) £3,082 2½m.........(3:00)

1618^{4} THE LATVIAN LARK (Ire) 9-12-0 Mr B M Cash, (2 to 1 fav) 1
2341^{9} BRAVE FOUNTAIN (Ire) 9-12-0 C F Swan,........ (10 to 1) 2
2341^{7} IRISH PEACE (Ire) 9-12-0 C O'Dwyer,.............(7 to 1) 3
2339 MYSTICAL AIR (Ire) 7-11-9 D T Evans,........... (20 to 1) 4
1714^{9} CONCLAVE (Ire) 7-11-7 (7*) Mr A J Dempsey,..... (16 to 1) 5
2341^{4} EXECUTIVE OPTIONS (Ire) 8-12-0 J Shortt,.........(4 to 1) 6
2133 LAKEVIEW LAD (Ire) 8-11-9 J P Broderick,........ (40 to 1) 7
1780^{6} LANTINA (Ire) 6-11-4 D H O'Connor,............... (10 to 1) 8
2224 THE VENDOR (Ire) 7-11-4 A Powell,............... (6 to 1) 9
2017^{7} CLERICAL COUSIN (Ire) 8-11-9 F Woods,.......... (10 to 1) 10
1898 FINGAL BOY (Ire) 9-11-6 (3*) J Butler,............(20 to 1) 11
1842^{9} YOUR CALL (Ire) 8-11-9 T J Mitchell,............. (10 to 1) 12
2090 CHESLOCK (Ire) 8-11-6 (3*) U Smyth,.............(33 to 1) 13
2224 LUCKY BUST (Ire) 7-11-9 T Horgan,...............(12 to 1) f
159 LAERGY CRIPPERTY (Ire) 9-11-9 J K Kinane,.....(50 to 1) pu
2166 UNYOKE RAMBLER (Ire) 7-11-1 (3*) D P Murphy, (33 to 1) pu
2341 RADIANT RIVER (Ire) 7-11-9 T P Rudd,...........(25 to 1) pu
Dist: 15l, 8l, ½l, dist. 5m 12.10s. a 17.10s (17 Ran).
SR: 39/24/16/10/-/-/ (Mrs Rosalind Kilpatrick), Noel Meade

2447 Monaloe Handicap Hurdle (0-116 4-y-o and up) £3,082 2½m. . . . (3:30)

2379[4] COLLIERS HILL (Ire) [-] (bl) 9-9-6 (7*) R P Hogan, . . (10 to 1) 1
2170[5] SLANEY GLOW (Ire) [-] 6-11-11 C O'Dwyer, ... (7 to 1) 2
2229[4] KASELECTRIC (Ire) [-] (bl) 6-10-13 T Horgan, ... (4 to 1) 3
2170[2] MULKEV PRINCE (Ire) [-] 6-12-0 S C Lyons, ... (7 to 1) 4
2366[8] RUM FUN (Ire) [-] 6-10-3 C F Swan, ...(10 to 1) 5
2131* SORCERER'S DRUM (Ire) [-] 6-11-5 F Woods, ... (8 to 1) 6
2272 PADDY'S PET (Ire) [-] 8-9-13 (7*) K A Kelly, ... (25 to 1) 7
2162 TARIYMA (Ire) [-] 6-9-0 (7*) S FitzGerald, ...(16 to 1) 8
2272[6] ANTICS (Ire) [-] 5-9-6 (7*) Mrs C Harrison, ... (14 to 1) 9
2126[2] MULLOVER [-] 6-11-6 J Shortt, ...(13 to 8 fav) 10
2272[3] MARINERS REEF (Ire) [-] 6-9-12 (3*) B Bowens, ... (10 to 1) 11
2337 AUTOBABBLE (Ire) [-] 4-10-4 J P Broderick, ... (25 to 1) 12
2339 SHINDARAR (Ire) [-] 6-9-13 H Rogers, ... (25 to 1) 13
Dist: 5l, ½l, 6l, nk. 4m 56.40s. a 12.40s (13 Ran).
SR: -/18/5/14/-/-/ (J Curran), D Harvey

2448 Impudent Barney Handicap Chase (0-102 4-y-o and up) £3,082 3m 1f . . . . (4:00)

2338 TEAL BRIDGE [-] 12-11-12 T J Mitchell, ... (7 to 1) 1
2139[2] COOLAFINKA (Ire) [-] 8-11-0 C O'Dwyer, ... (7 to 1) 2
2226* PRATE BOX (Ire) [-] 7-12-0 A Powell, ...(8 to 1) 3
1898 DIORRAING (Ire) [-] (bl) 7-11-0 D H O'Connor, ...(14 to 1) 4
2169[4] FAIR GO [-] 11-9-0 (7*) Mrs C Harrison, ...(7 to 1) 5
2223* ALL IN THE GAME (Ire) [-] 9-10-5 P A Roche, ... (5 to 1) 6
2381* AMME ENAEK (Ire) [-] (bl) 8-11-13 (4ex) H Rogers, ...(11 to 4 fav) f
2165[5] FIFTH GENERATION (Ire) [-] 7-9-11 T Horgan, ...(12 to 1) f
2274[3] MARGUERITA SONG [-] 7-10-12 J P Broderick, . . . (10 to 1) f
2338[7] GARABAGH (Ire) [-] 8-10-13 P McWilliams, ... (16 to 1) pu
1754[7] WHY AILBHE (Ire) [-] 7-9-8[1] P Leech, ... (33 to 1) pu
Dist: 1l, 11l, 10l, 13l. 6m 41.30s. a 26.30s (11 Ran).
(Mrs M Heffernan), Andrew Heffernan

2449 Clonee I.N.H. Flat Race (4-y-o and up) £3,082 2m. . . . . (4:30)

MUSICAL MAYHEM (Ire) 4-11-2 Mr D Marnane, . . . (10 to 1) 1
COLONEL HENDERSON (Ire) 5-11-11 Mr B M Cash, ...(11 to 8 on) 2
1782[3] TALKALOT (Ire) 6-12-0 Mr J A Berry, ... (12 to 1) 3+
LANCASTRIAN PRIDE (Ire) 7-12-0 Mr J A Nash, . . .(14 to 1) 3+
LAFONTD'OR (Ire) 6-11-7 (7*) Mr M McLoughney, (14 to 1) 5
KING CORONA (Ire) 6-11-11 (3*) Mr P English, ... (20 to 1) 6
2228[2] RING ALBERT (Ire) 5-11-8 (3*) Mr R Walsh, ... (12 to 1) 7
2172[4] DINES (Ire) 5-11-11 Mr P Fenton, ...(10 to 1) 8
LOST ALPHABET (Ire) 4-10-9 (7*) Mr P G Fahey, . . (16 to 1) 9
2234[5] GALLAHER'S WALK (Ire) 4-10-9 (7*) Mr T N Cloke, (8 to 1) 10
2130[4] DUE TO YOU (Ire) 4-10-13[4] (7*) Mr S J Mahon, ...(25 to 1) 11
2081 PRINCE WOT A MESS (Ire) 6-11-7 (7*) Mr S McGonagle, ...(66 to 1) 12
NOBLE GESTURE (Ire) 5-11-4 (7*) Mr M P Madden, (14 to 1) 13
TOUGH TERMS (Ire) 5-11-11 Mr T Mullins, ... (12 to 1) 14
1776 RATHCOLMAN GALE (Ire) 7-11-2 (7*) Mr A Ross, . .(66 to 1) 15
2060[8] SUPREME GAZETTE (Ire) 5-11-4 (7*) Mr S P Hennessy, ...(16 to 1) 16
1539[3] STRONG SON (Ire) 6-12-0 Mr A R Coonan, ... (16 to 1) 17
2129[6] CONAGHER LEADER (Ire) 6-12-0 Mr P F Graffin, . .(14 to 1) 18
1554[8] BARNA GIRL (Ire) 7-11-2 (7*) Mr M J Daly, ... (33 to 1) 19
AMAZING ALL (Ire) 8-11-8[1] (7*) Mr I Buchanan, . . . (25 to 1) 20
2110[2] MAJESTIC RED (Ire) 6-11-11 (3*) Mr E Norris, ...(14 to 1) bd
2343[6] THETHREETOMS (Ire) 6-11-7 (7*) Mr T Gibney, . . . (25 to 1) su
Dist: 4l, ½l, dd-ht, 2l. 3m 47.20s. (22 Ran).
(D K Weld), D K Weld

SANDOWN (good to firm)
Saturday February 1st
Going Correction: PLUS 0.35 sec. per fur. (races 1,3,6), PLUS 0.40 (2,4,5,7)

2450 Scilly Isles Novices' Chase Class A Grade 1 (5-y-o and up) £22,032 2½m 110yds. . . . . (12:45)

1851* STATELY HOME (Ire) 6-11-6 N Williamson, *jmpd boldly, sn clr, hit twelfth, drvn alng frm 2 out, ran on gmely.* . . . . (5 to 1 op 4 to 1 tchd 11 to 2) 1
2214* LAND AFAR 10-11-6 J Osborne, *hld up, not fluent 6th and 11th (water), chsd wnr frm 5 out, drvn alng and mstk 2 out, unbl to quicken.* . . . . (11 to 4 op 5 to 2 tchd 3 to 1) 2
1950[4] AMBER VALLEY (USA) 6-11-6 A Thornton, *beh, lft poor 3rd 5 out, nvr a factor.* . . . . . (66 to 1 op 33 to 1 tchd 100 to 1) 3
2214[2] MISTER DRUM (Ire) 8-11-6 W Marston, *f 1st.* . . . . (14 to 1 op 7 to 1) f
2278 GROOVING (Ire) 8-11-6 P Niven, *hld up, clr order 7th, mstk tenth, 3rd and in tch whn f 6 out.* . . . . (12 to 1 op 10 to 1 tchd 14 to 1) f
2211* SIMPLY DASHING (Ire) 6-11-6 R Dunwoody, *chsd clr ldr, not fluent 8th, second and gng strly whn f heavily 5 out.* . . . . (6 to 5 on op 11 to 8 on tchd Evens) f
Dist: 1½l, dist. 5m 16.20s. a 16.20s (6 Ran).
SR: 2/-/-/ (P Bowen), P Bowen

2451 Agfa Hurdle Class B (5-y-o and up) £10,162 2m 110yds. . . . .(1:20)

DOUBLE SYMPHONY (Ire) 9-10-4 J Osborne, *midfield, hdwy gng wl 3 out, chlgd last, styd on strly to ld flt.* . . . . (13 to 2 op 5 to 1 tchd 7 to 1) 1
2218[5] CHIEF'S SONG 7-11-4 R Dunwoody, *chsd clr ldr, rdn and slight ld 2 out, hdd sn aftr last, unbl to quicken.* . . . . (11 to 10 on op 5 to 4 tchd 11 to 8 and 6 to 4) 2
1508[5] GROUND NUT (Ire) 7-11-0 P Holley, *sn clr, hit 5th, drvn alng and hdd 2 out, ev ch till fdd aftr last.* . . . . (10 to 1 op 6 to 1 tchd 11 to 1) 3
FLORID (USA) 6-10-9 G Bradley, *keen hold in midfield, chsd ldrs frm 3 out, outpcd nxt, sn wknd and eased.* . . . . (7 to 2 op 2 to 1 tchd 9 to 2 and 5 to 1) 4
2333[4] IONIO (USA) 6-11-0 J R Kavanagh, *beh, not fluent, struggling hfwy, sn tld off.* . . . . (11 to 1 op 6 to 1 tchd 12 to 1) 5
2255[7] DAUNT 5-10-9 A Thornton, *hld up, not fluent, rdn and lost tch 3 out, sn wl beh.* . . . .(16 to 1 op 12 to 1 tchd 7 to 1 and 20 to 1) 6
Dist: 5l, 4l, 21l, 6l, dist. 3m 56.80s. a 9.80s (6 Ran).
SR: 44/53/45/19/18/-/ (Anthony Pye-Jeary), C P E Brooks

2452 Agfa Diamond Chase Limited Handicap Class A Grade 2 (5-y-o and up) £19,014 3m 110yds. . . . .(1:50)

2196* DEXTRA DOVE [137] 10-11-2 N Williamson, *in tch, led appr 16th, drvn alng frm 3 out, lft clr 2 out, styd on wl.* . . . .(8 to 1 op 6 to 1 tchd 9 to 1) 1
1878[3] NORTHERN HIDE [127] 11-10-6 P Holley, *sn led, hdd appr 16th, pushed alng and ev ch 3 out, one pace frm nxt.* . . . . (12 to 1 op 8 to 1) 2
1639* COOME HILL (Ire) [147] 8-11-12 J Osborne, *chsd ldrs till f second.* . . . . .(11 to 4 fav op 3 to 1 tchd 100 to 30 and 5 to 2) f
1999* GO BALLISTIC [135] 8-11-0 R Dunwoody, *hld up, mstk 7th, gd hdwy hfwy, blun 6 out, cl second whn f nxt.* . . . .(3 to 1 tchd 100 to 30) f
1757[2] MAJOR SUMMIT (Ire) [134] 8-10-13 P Hide, *hld up, not fluent, mstk tenth, lft second 5 out, pressing wnr whn f 2 out, dead.* . . . . (4 to 1 tchd 9 to 2 and 5 to 1) f
2209[3] AVRO ANSON [143] 9-11-8 P Niven, *keen hold, jnd ldr 5th till blun and uns rdr 11th.* . .(100 to 30 op 5 to 2 tchd 7 to 2) ur
Dist: 2½l. 6m 21.00s. a 22.00s (6 Ran).
(Dextra Lighting Systems), Simon Earle

2453 Tote Bookmakers Sandown Handicap Hurdle Class A Grade 3 (4-y-o and up) £27,700 2¾m. . . . .(2:25)

1467* TULLYMURRY TOFF (Ire) [127] 6-10-12 (3*) E Callaghan, *cl up gng wl, slight ld 2 out, drvn and hng rght flt, styd on strly.* . . . .(7 to 2 op 3 to 1 tchd 4 to 1) 1
1852* YAHMI (Ire) [124] 7-10-12 J Osborne, *al hndy, chlgd gng wl appr 2 out, chasing wnr whn short of room aftr last, kpt on.* . . . . (100 to 30 fav op 3 to 1 tchd 7 to 2) 2
2027[4] OUTSET (Ire) [124] 7-10-9 (3*) Mr C Bonner, *set steady pace, hdd 3rd, led and quickened aftr 5th, headed ag'n 2 out, ran on one pace.* . . . . (16 to 1 op 14 to 1 tchd 20 to 1) 3
2289[2] ERZADJAN (Ire) [128] 7-11-2 P Niven, *hld up in rear, hdwy 4 out, hrd drvn frm 2 out, styd on stdly.* . . . . (5 to 1 op 11 to 2 tchd 6 to 1) 4
1876* TARRS BRIDGE (Ire) [121] (bl) 6-10-9 J Railton, *al hndy, chlgd gng wl appr 2 out, no extr betw last two.* . . . . (13 to 2 op 7 to 1 tchd 15 to 2) 5
1867[2] RUNAWAY PETE (USA) [124] 7-10-12 R Dunwoody, *cl up, led 3rd to 5th, drvn alng wth ldrs appr 2 out, unbl to quicken.* . . . . (9 to 1 op 8 to 1 tchd 10 to 1) 6
2198[4] TIM (Ire) [115] 7-10-3 P Hide, *hld up, hdwy to chase ldrs whn hit 7th, unbl to quicken aftr 3 out, sn no extr.* . . . .(16 to 1 tchd 20 to 1) 7
969* FIRED EARTH (Ire) [130] 9-11-4 N Williamson, *keen in midfield, not fluent 7th, rdn and outpcd 2 out, sn btn.* . . . .(12 to 1 tchd 14 to 1) 8
1628[2] BURNT IMP (USA) [131] 7-11-5 J Callaghan, *hld up in rear, struggling 4 out, styd on to pass btn horses frm 2 out.* . . . . (20 to 1 op 16 to 1) 9
2151[2] LOCHNAGRAIN (Ire) [124] 9-10-9 (3*) G Lee, *hld up on outsd, improved to chase ldrs 8th, drvn and fdd appr 2 out.* . . . . (12 to 1 op 10 to 1 tchd 14 to 1) 10
2128 EXPRESS GIFT [136] 8-11-10 N Smith, *midfield, hit 6th, rallied to chase ldrs aftr 3 out, fdd frm nxt.* (33 to 1 op 25 to 1) 11
1032[6] MR KERMIT [125] 6-10-13 L Harvey, *settled rear, pushed alng and outpcd as ldrs quickened hfwy, sn no dngr.* (25 to 1) 12
2246[8] LANSDOWNE [124] 9-10-7 (5*) O Burrows, *struggling in rear hfwy, sn wl beh.* . . . .(25 to 1) 13
Dist: 1¾l, 3½l, ½l, 1¾l, 2l, ½l, hd, 14l, 2½l, 11l. 5m 20.00s. a 17.00s (13 Ran).
SR: 5/-/-/-/-/-/ (John H Wilson And Mr J H Riley), J M Jefferson

2454 Ripley Juvenile Novices' Hurdle Class C (4-y-o) £3,517 2m 110yds . . . . (3:00)

HAYAAIN 10-10 J Railton, *hld up, took clr order whn pckd 3 out, clr when slight mstk nxt, cmftbly*.... (8 to 1 op 3 to 1) 1

2255⁴ NORTHERN FLEET 11-0 G Bradley, *hld up, hdwy to chase ldrs 3 out, reminders nxt, one pace.*
.... (2 to 1 fav op 5 to 2 tchd 11 to 4 and 3 to 1) 2

1922* NAME OF OUR FATHER (USA) 11-4 D Walsh, *chsd ldrs, led 5th, drvn and hdd appr 2 out, sn no extr.* (12 to 1 op 8 to 1) 3

1854⁶ GO WITH THE WIND 11-0 M Richards, *chsd ldrs, mstk 3 out, fdd frm nxt*............. (33 to 1 op 25 to 1 tchd 50 to 1) 4

1737⁶ BELMARITA (Ire) 10-9 N Williamson, *chsd clr ldr, led 4th to nxt, styd hndy till lost tch 2 out.*
.... (12 to 1 op 10 to 1 tchd 14 to 1) 5

SILVRETTA (Ire) 10-5 P Hide, *not fluent in rear, wl beh 4 out, nvr a factor*................ (7 to 1 op 5 to 1 tchd 8 to 1) 6

1861² SOCIETY MAGIC (USA) 11-0 R Dunwoody, *beh, hdwy to chase ldrs 3 out, wknd quickly nxt.*
..........................(3 to 1 op 9 to 2 tchd 5 to 1) 7

2324 MACMORRIS (USA) (bl) 11-0 P Holley, *pld hrd, clr till jmpd slwly 3rd, veered lft and hdd nxt, wknd quickly, tld off whn f 2 out*...................(14 to 1 op 16 to 1 tchd 12 to 1) f

HEART 10-5 J Osborne, *settled rear, some hdwy 3 out, wknd nxt, beh whn pld up bef last.* (9 to 2 op 9 to 4 tchd 5 to 1) pu

2195 MAGIC ROLE 11-0 W Marston, *in tch, hit 3rd, struggling 3 out, wl beh whn pld up bef last*........ (50 to 1 op 33 to 1) pu

Dist: 9l, 6l, 4l, 5l, 10l, nk. 4m 0.50s. a 13.50s (10 Ran).

SR: 13/8/6/-/-/-/   (Quicksilver Racing Partnership), K C Bailey

2455 Elmbridge Handicap Chase Class B (5-y-o and up) £6,485 2m..... (3:30)

CERTAINLY STRONG (Ire) [135] 7-10-3³ R Dunwoody, *led, blun badly second, jmpd wl aftr, drvn clr 2 out, ran on strly.*
..................(9 to 4 fav op 3 to 1 tchd 5 to 2) 1

2191* WEE RIVER (Ire) [132] 8-10-0 J Callaghan, *hld up, chsd wnr 6th, cl up whn jmpd slwly 3 out, drvn and styd on stdly frm nxt.*
.... (5 to 2 tchd 11 to 4 and 9 to 4) 2

2218² GALES CAVALIER (Ire) [159] 9-11-13 J Osborne, *chsd ldr to 6th, niggled alng and outpcd aftr 4 out, nvr on terms after.*
..................................(3 to 1 op 9 to 4) 3

2194* SUPER TACTICS (Ire) [135] 9-10-0 (3*) P Henley, *chsd ldrs, 3rd whn f third*........... (7 to 2 op 11 to 4 tchd 4 to 1) f

Dist: 3l, 4l. 3m 57.60s. a 8.60s (4 Ran).

SR: 45/39/62/-/   (Nick Skelton), D Nicholson

2456 February Maiden Hurdle Class D (5-y-o and up) £3,087 2¾m...... (4:05)

1938 EL FREDDIE 7-11-7 L Harvey, *hld up, chsd ldrs 6th, drvn to take slight ld 2 out, styd on wl und pres.*
..................................(9 to 2 op 9 to 4 tchd 5 to 1) 1

2277⁸ PHYSICAL FUN 6-11-4 (3*) P Henley, *hit 1st, rcd midfield, hdwy to ld appr 2 out, sn hdd, kpt on und pres till no extr cl hme*......................(13 to 2 op 12 to 1 tchd 6 to 1) 2

1615⁵ RIDING CROP (Ire) 7-11-7 P Niven, *sn led, rdn and hdd appr 2 out, fdd*.....................(2 to 1 fav tchd 11 to 4) 3

CAMERA MAN 7-11-7 J R Kavanagh, *hld up, jmpd slwly 3rd, outpcd and lost tch 7th, sn wl beh.*
.... (7 to 1 op 6 to 1 tchd 9 to 1) 4

1556⁵ ARCTIC TRIUMPH 6-11-7 P Holley, *pld hrd wth ldrs, hit 4th and 6th, wknd und pres appr 2 out.*
.... (10 to 1 tchd 12 to 1 and 14 to 1) 5

1763⁴ RED BRONZE (Ire) 6-11-7 G Bradley, *hld up, hdwy to track ldrs 4 out, outpcd aftr nxt, sn beh.*
.... (12 to 1 op 10 to 1 tchd 14 to 1 and 16 to 1) 6

1555⁴ LORD KHALICE (Ire) 6-11-0 (7*) N Rossiter, *cl up, mstk and wknd 3 out, tld off*...... (16 to 1 op 7 to 1 tchd 20 to 1) 7

2193² BLAZING MIRACLE 5-10-11 (5*) D Salter, *al beh, tld off frm 5*...................(20 to 1 op 10 to 1 tchd 25 to 1) 8

2215⁵ COUNTRY TARQUIN 5-11-7 R Dunwoody, *chsd ldrs, mstk 5th, wknd quickly 3 out, tld off*...........(11 to 2 op 3 to 1) 9

Dist: 1¼l, 23l, 20l, 1l, 15l, ½l, 21l, 3½l. 5m 20.70s. a 20.70s (9 Ran).

(Martin Lovatt), J A B Old

STRATFORD (good)
Saturday February 1st
Going Correction: PLUS 0.60 sec. per fur. (races 1,3,5), PLUS 0.80 (2,4,6)

2457 Merry Hill Shopping Centre Novices' Chase Class E (5-y-o and up) £2,875 2m 1f 110yds................(1:05)

EUDIPE (Fr) 5-11-11 S Wynne, *prmnt, chsd ldr 6th, led appr 2 out, sn clr, eased run in.*
.... (9 to 4 on op 2 to 1 on tchd 7 to 4 on) 1

2278 BLAIR CASTLE (Ire) 6-11-2 B Fenton, *in tch, rdn 4 out, styd on to go second run in, no ch wth wnr*...... (9 to 1 op 7 to 1) 2

1421⁴ CLIFTON GAME 7-11-2 D Gallagher, *chsd ldr till led 4th, sn clr, rdn whn blun 2 out, wkng when hit last.*
..................................(7 to 2 op 5 to 2) 3

2010* STAGE PLAYER 11-11-8 I Lawrence, *al in rear.*
.... (16 to 1 op 12 to 1) 4

1609 THE SECRET GREY 6-11-2 T Jenks, *mstk 4th, al in rear.*
..................................(100 to 1 op 50 to 1) 5

2278⁸ WARSPITE 7-10-11 (5*) S Ryan, *prmnt to 6th, tld off.*
..................................(100 to 1 op 50 to 1) 6

2244 KINO'S CROSS 8-10-13 (3*) G Hogan, *mid-div, rdn whn f 7th.*..................... (33 to 1 op 20 to 1) f

2330³ CURRAGH PETER 10-10-13 (3*) Guy Lewis, *led to 4th, wknd 5 out, beh whn blun and uns rdr 2 out.*
.... (33 to 1 op 20 to 1 tchd 40 to 1) ur

1100 WIN A HAND 7-10-11 R Greene, *blun and uns rdr second.*
.... (33 to 1 op 25 to 1 tchd 50 to 1) ur

2181 WOODLANDS ENERGY 6-10-11 R Bellamy, *al beh, tld off whn pld up bef 4 out*..................(200 to 1 op 100 to 1) pu

Dist: 12l, 4l, 25l, 2l, dist. 4m 18.30s. a 16.30s (10 Ran).

SR: 40/19/15/-/-/-/   (D A Johnson), M C Pipe

2458 European Breeders Fund 'National Hunt' Novices' Hurdle Qualifier Class E (5,6,7-y-o) £2,253 2m 110yds......................(1:35)

1887* KING OF CAMELOT (Ire) 7-10-11 (3*) R Massey, *chsd ldrs, rcd keenly, mstk 4th, led 3 out, mistake nxt, easily.*
.... (5 to 2 on op 4 to 1 on) 1

1000⁸ WINTER ROSE 6-10-7 (7*) K Hibbert, *led to 3 out, no ch wth wnr*..........................(5 to 1 op 8 to 1) 2

1594⁸ FRENO (Ire) 6-11-0 W McFarland, *hld up, mstk 5th, hdwy 4 out, styd on same pace frm 2 out*...... (6 to 1 op 7 to 2) 3

ELGINTORUS (Ire) 7-10-11 (3*) J Magee, *chsd ldrs till wknd appr 2 out*.........................(100 to 1 op 66 to 1) 4

CUMBERLAND YOUTH 6-11-0 I Lawrence, *in rear, hdwy 5th, wknd nxt, tld off whn pld up bef 2 out.* (100 to 1 op 66 to 1) pu

Dist: 4l, 5l, 8l. 4m 12.50s. a 26.50s (5 Ran).

(Jerry Wright), D Nicholson

2459 A.H.P. Trailers Wombourne Handicap Chase Class D (0-125 5-y-o and up) £3,582 2m 5f 110yds......(2:05)

2314 DISTINCTIVE (Ire) [97] 8-10-6 I Lawrence, *chsd ldrs, led 5 out, rdn out*..................(4 to 1 co-fav op 3 to 1) 1

2217 SEOD RIOGA (Ire) [110] 8-11-2 (3*) D Fortt, *led 3rd, hdd 5 out, rdn appr 2 out, mstk last, no extr r-in.*.. (8 to 1 tchd 9 to 1) 2

1730 OVER THE POLE [107] 10-11-2 T Jenks, *al prmnt, rdn appr 2 out, styd on same pace approaching last.*
.... (16 to 1 tchd 20 to 1) 3

2034 CELTINO [97] 9-10-6 S Wynne, *hld up, hdwy 5 out, styd on same pace frm 2 out.*......... (7 to 1 op 5 to 1) 4

1721 MERRY PANTO (Ire) [100] 8-10-9 D Gallagher, *hld up, hdwy 5 out, wknd 3 out.*..............(4 to 1 co-fav op 3 to 1) 5

1920 SCOTONI [95] 11-10-4 D O'Sullivan, *led to 3rd, lost pl 5th, wknd 11th*.........................(12 to 1 op 10 to 1) 6

2252 ROYAL SQUARE (Can) [95] 11-10-4 Mr D Verco, *mid-div, hit 7th, wknd 6 out*.............................(20 to 1) 7

2300⁴ LINDEN'S LOTTO (Ire) [115] (bl) 8-11-5 (5*) S Ryan, *hld up, hdwy 7th, hit nxt, wknd 11th*........(14 to 1 tchd 16 to 1) 8

2314⁶ THE CAUMRUE (Ire) [105] 9-11-0 B Fenton, *prmnt till f 7th.*
.... (7 to 1 op 6 to 1 tchd 8 to 1) f

ARTIC WINGS (Ire) [103] 9-10-12 M Brennan, *hld up, al in rear, tld off whn pld up bef 4 out.* (4 to 1 co-fav tchd 9 to 2) pu

Dist: 1¾l, 5l, 2½l, 10l, 16l, 27l, dist. 5m 23.70s. a 23.70s (10 Ran).

(Jeremy Hancock), M J Wilkinson

2460 Hartshorne Motor Services Ltd. Walsall Handicap Hurdle Class D (0-120 4-y-o and up) £2,920 2¾m 110yds...............................(2:35)

2253³ SILVER STANDARD [104] (bl) 7-11-3 S Wynne, *trkd ldr, led 4 out, mstk last, pushed out*.......(7 to 4 on op 6 to 4 on) 1

2313⁶ SMITH TOO (Ire) [113] 9-11-9 (3*) D Fortt, *led, rdn and hdd 4 out, styd on same pace frm 2 out.*
.... (100 to 30 op 7 to 4 tchd 7 to 2) 2

2253 CAMBO (USA) [89] 11-10-2 D Skyrme, *patiently rdn, mstk 4th, took clr order 6 out, one pace frm 3 out.*
.... (9 to 2 op 5 to 1 tchd 4 to 1) 3

Dist: 2½l, 5l. 5m 42.10s. a 30.10s (3 Ran).

(G W Lugg), Capt T A Forster

2461 Richardson's Merlin Park Novices' Chase Class E (5-y-o and up) £2,927 3m...........................(3:05)

2330 DOMAINE DE PRON (Fr) 6-11-4 R Bellamy, *led 3rd to 6th, remained prmnt, hrd drvn 3 out, led r-in, styd on wl.*
.... (25 to 1 op 14 to 1) 1

1701² PARAHANDY (Ire) 7-11-4 B Fenton, *led, mstk second, hdd nxt, hit 5 out, led 3 out, headed and no extr r-in.*
.... (2 to 1 op 7 to 4) 2

1684* POUCHER (Ire) 7-11-10 S Wynne, *hld up, hdwy 11th, hit 6 out, rdn and ev ch last, unbl to quicken.*
.... (11 to 8 fav op 6 to 4 tchd 13 to 8) 3

2247⁴ TOP JAVALIN (NZ) 10-11-4 R Greene, *chsd ldrs, mstk 4th, rdn 9th, wknd 3 out*.....................(5 to 1 op 9 to 2) 4

1804 BIG ARCHIE 7-11-4 D Leahy, *prmnt, jnd ldrs 9th, jmpd slwly 4 out, sn wknd*.....................(20 to 1 op 16 to 1) 5

1994⁷ GEORGE ASHFORD (Ire) 7-11-10 M Sharratt, *beh, mstk 8th, tld off frm tenth*............(16 to 1 tchd 20 to 1) 6

2176⁷ DARA'S COURSE (Ire) 8-10-6 (7") K Hibbert, *prmnt, led 6th to 3 out, wknd quickly, poor 4th whn f 2 out.*
.................................(25 to 1 op 20 to 1) f
2244⁸ COLETTE'S CHOICE (Ire) 8-10-10 (3") D Fortt, *in tch to 6th, tld off frm tenth, pld up bef 4 out.*
.................................(20 to 1 op 16 to 1 tchd 25 to 1) pu
Dist: 2l, 1½l, 20l, 14l, dist. 6m 9.50s. a 24.50s (8 Ran).

(Mrs L C Taylor), Mrs L C Taylor

2462 Stratford-on-Avon Racecourse Company Ltd. 75th Anniversary Novices' H'cap Hurdle Class E (0-105 4-y-o and up) £2,368 2m 3f... (3:40)

876⁸ RIVER WYE (Ire) [87] 5-11-7 V Slattery, *al prmnt, led 3 out, sn clr, eased r-in.......*(14 to 1 op 10 to 1 tchd 16 to 1) 1
2185* LITTLE SHEFFORD [83] 5-11-3 I Lawrence, *led, rdn and hdd 3 out, sn wknd..........*(7 to 1 op 5 to 1 tchd 15 to 2) 2
2207⁷ LEAP IN THE DARK (Ire) [80] 8-11-0 O Pears, *hld up, styd on frm 3 out, nvr dngrs....*(12 to 1 op 10 to 1 tchd 14 to 1) 3
1574* DRAGONMIST (Ire) [72] 7-10-6 D J Burchell, *chsd ldrs, lost pl 5th, styd on frm 2 out............*(7 to 2 fav tchd 4 to 1) 4
2009⁵ PEDALTOTHEMETAL (Ire) [89] 5-11-9 D Gallagher, *hld up, hdwy 4 out, wknd nxt...*(10 to 1 op 6 to 1 tchd 11 to 1) 5
111³ HIGH POST [81] 8-10-12 (3") D Fortt, *hld up, rdn 4 out, nvr dngrs..............*(12 to 1 op 8 to 1 tchd 14 to 1) 6
2185² SKRAM [90] 4-11-0 D Leahy, *prmnt, chsd ldr 5 out, wknd appr 3 out............*(5 to 1 op 6 to 1 tchd 7 to 1) 7
2279 SAM ROCKETT [85] 4-10-4 (5") S Ryan, *hld up, hdwy 5 out, wknd approaching 3 out...........*(12 to 1 op 10 to 1) 8
2279⁹ MILLENIUM LASS (Ire) [90] 9-11-10 Gary Lyons, *prmnt till wknd 4 out...............*(25 to 1 op 20 to 1) 9
2267⁷ THAT OLD FEELING (Ire) [70] 5-10-4 T J Murphy, *chsd ldr, rdn and appr 3 out...........*(16 to 1 op 20 to 1) 10
1921⁴ FONTAINEROUGE (Ire) [84] 7-11-4 B Fenton, *hld up, effrt and not much room appr 4 out, sn btn....*(6 to 1 tchd 5 to 1) 11
2153 CADES BAY [82] 6-11-2 T Jenks, *hld up, hdwy 5 out, 3rd and rdn whn f 3 out......*(12 to 1 op 10 to 1 tchd 14 to 1) f
Dist: 13l, 1¼l, 2l, 3l, 3l, 18l, 1l, 2½l, 1¼l, 16l. 4m 43.80s. a 23.80s (12 Ran).
SR: 17/-/-/-/-/-/

(S Ho), G H Yardley

WETHERBY (good)
Saturday February 1st
Going Correction: PLUS 0.80 sec. per fur. (races 1,3,5,7), PLUS 1.10 (2,4,6)

2463 Demmy In Wetherby Novices' Hurdle Class D (4-y-o and up) £3,239 2m .... (1:10)

2284² DURANO 6-11-3 Derek Byrne, *trkd ldrs, effrt aftr 2 out, led last, ran on wl..........*(9 to 1 op 6 to 1 tchd 10 to 1) 1
2236³ FOREVER NOBLE (Ire) 4-10-7 R Garritty, *prmnt, led 6th till hdd last, no extr...........*(14 to 1 op 10 to 1) 2
NEW CENTURY (USA) 5-11-0 (3") F Leahy, *hld up, hdwy aftr 6th, ch frm 2 out to nxt, one paced last.*
.................................(11 to 1 op 12 to 1 tchd 16 to 1) 3
1869⁷ MUDLARK 5-11-3 W Dwan, *towards rear, styd on frm 3 out, nrst finish..................*(100 to 1 op 50 to 1) 4+
CHOPWELL DRAPES (Ire) 7-11-3 M Moloney, *hld up in mid-field, styd on frm 2 out, nrst finish..*(100 to 1 op 50 to 1) 4+
2284⁶ BALLYRANTER 8-11-3 D Bentley, *mid-div, kpt on frm 3 out, nvr dngrs................*(50 to 1 op 33 to 1) 6
2002 JOE SHAW 4-10-7 R Hodge, *hld up in midfield, nvr nr to chal.*
.................................(12 to 1 op 10 to 1 tchd 14 to 1) 7
2230⁶ NAMOODAJ 4-10-2 (5") Mr R Thornton, *mstks, chsd ldrs, effrt bef 3 out, fdd.........*(5 to 2 tchd 9 to 4 and 11 to 4) 8
ROYAL YORK 5-10-12 P Carberry, *in tch, effrt bef 3 out, no hdwy...................*(7 to 1 op 4 to 1) 9
1868 DOUGAL 6-10-12 (5") B Grattan, *beh, kpt on frm 3 out, nvr dngrs...............*(100 to 1 op 50 to 1) 10
2207³ TREMENDISTO 7-11-8 Richard Guest, *prmnt, blun second, wknd appr 3 out....*(16 to 1 op 14 to 1 tchd 18 to 1) 11
2236 BOLLIN FRANK 5-11-3 A S Smith, *hld up towards rear, nvr nr to chal..........*(25 to 1 op 20 to 1 tchd 33 to 1) 12
1770⁶ PILKINGTON (Ire) 7-10-12 (5") Michael Brennan, *in tch till wknd aftr 6th......*(25 to 1 op 33 to 1) 13
2250 ANTARCTICA (USA) 5-10-12 D Parker, *nvr nr to chal.*
.................................(100 to 1 op 50 to 1) 14
2145* QUANGO 5-11-8 A Dobbin, *in tch, effrt aftr 6th, sn pushed alng, wknd bef 3 out*
.................................(6 to 4 fav op 7 to 4 tchd 2 to 1 and 11 to 8) 15
2298 RUSHEN RAIDER 5-11-3 M Foster, *chsd ldrs till wknd aftr 6th.*
.................................(33 to 1 op 20 to 1) 16
2063⁵ SOMETHING SPEEDY (Ire) 5-10-5 (7") R Burns, *beh most of way.............*(50 to 1 op 33 to 1 tchd 66 to 1) 17
1818⁰ IRISH BUZZ (Ire) 5-11-3 J Supple, *sn beh, tld off.*
.................................(66 to 1 op 50 to 1) 18
THE ROAD WEST (Ire) 8-11-3 B Storey, *in tch till wknd aftr 6th, tld off.......*(33 to 1 op 25 to 1 tchd 50 to 1) 19
2284 BONNY RIGG 5-10-12 T Reed, *sn beh, tld off.*
.................................(66 to 1 op 50 to 1) 20
2357 ON THE OFF CHANCE 5-11-3 N Bentley, *w/ tld off.*
.................................(100 to 1 op 50 to 1) 21

SHADOWS OF SILVER 9-10-12 G Cahill, *keen early, sn led, hdd 6th, wknd bef 3 out, f last........*(33 to 1 op 25 to 1) f
1252 MUBARIZ (Ire) 5-11-3 M Ranger, *sn beh, tld off whn pld up bef 3 out....................*(100 to 1 op 50 to 1) pu
Dist: 2l, 1¼l, 14l, dd-ht, ¾l, 2l, 1¼l, ½l, 4l, 2l. 4m 0.00s. a 19.00s (23 Ran).
SR: 27/15/23/9/9/8/

(C H Stevens), T D Easterby

2464 Demmy Bookmaker Novices' Chase Class D (5-y-o and up) £3,585 2½m 110yds. (1:40)

2286³ CATTLY HANG (Ire) 7-11-3 A Dobbin, *made all, hrd pressed frm 4 out, mstk nxt, styd on wl und pres.*
.................................(11 to 1 op 10 to 1 tchd 12 to 1) 1
2240² CHIEF MINISTER (Ire) 8-11-3 R Garritty, *trkd ldrs, rdn bef 4 out, no hdwy till styd on und pres frm 2 out, ch last, no extr.*
.................................(4 to 1 on tchd 11 to 8 on) 2
1636 COLONEL IN CHIEF (Ire) 7-11-3 P Carberry, *trkd ldrs, chalg whn blun badly 4 out, ev ch frm 2 out till no extr und pres frm last..............*(3 to 1 op 5 to 2 tchd 100 to 30) 3
2297² GOLDEN HELLO 6-11-13 A S Smith, *in tch, mstks 8th and 9th (water), lost touch appr 4 out, tld off...*(5 to 1 tchd 11 to 2) 4
2330 JUST SUPPOSEN (Ire) 6-11-3 B Storey, *beh, lost tch frm 7th, tld off whn pld up bef 11th........*(50 to 1 op 33 to 1) pu
2146 WILD GAME (Ire) 6-10-10 (7") A Todd, *mstks, lost tch frm 7th, tld off whn pld up bef 11th...........*(100 to 1 op 50 to 1) pu
Dist: 1½l, nk, dist. 5m 22.60s. a 29.60s (6 Ran).
SR: 18/16/16/

(W G N Morgan), J P Leigh

2465 Demmy Credit Handicap Hurdle Class C (0-135 4-y-o and up) £2,861 2m 7f........................ (2:10)

2332⁴ PUREVALUE (Ire) [109] 6-10-5 Richard Guest, *led second, made rst, mstk 3 out, rdn, styd on.....*(7 to 1 op 5 to 1) 1
2200* SHARE OPTIONS (Ire) [104] 6-10-0 A S Smith, *trkd ldrs, effrt aftr 3 out, sn chasing wnr, kpt on und pres, no imprsn.*
.................................(9 to 2 op 9 to 4) 2
CAMPAIGN [111] 6-10-7 R Garritty, *in tch, effrt aftr 3 out, kpt on und pres, no extr frm last.........*(10 to 1 op 7 to 1) 3
2001⁴ TIBETAN [132] 5-11-9 (5") Mr R Thornton, *hld up, hdwy bef 3 out, kpt on same pace frm nxt.*
.................................(2 to 1 fav op 5 to 2 tchd 11 to 4) 4
2289⁶ DISCO DES MOTTES (Fr) [132] 6-12-0 P Carberry, *in tch, effrt bef 3 out, sn btn, tld off.......*(20 to 1 op 14 to 1) 5
2209⁴ SCOTTON BANKS (Ire) [130] 8-11-12 B Storey, *beh, lost tch frm 7th, tld off, fnshd lme.......*(16 to 1 op 12 to 1) 6
2289⁴ JOCKS CROSS (Ire) [115] 6-10-11 A Dobbin, *led to second, dsptd ld, hit 8th, sn pushed alng, wknd aftr nxt, tld off.*
.................................(4 to 1 op 3 to 1) 7
Dist: 1½l, ½l, 8l, 21l, 5l, 6l. 5m 51.00s. a 33.00s (7 Ran).

(A D Simmons), M W Easterby

2466 Marston Moor Handicap Chase Class B (5-y-o and up) £8,183 2½m 110yds........................ (2:40)

2212* KONVEKTA KING (Ire) [132] 9-11-4 A Dobbin, *hld up in tch, led 4 out, styd on wl...*(5 to 2 fav op 3 to 1 tchd 9 to 4) 1
2233⁵ KADI (Ger) [138] 8-11-5 (5") Mr R Thornton, *in tch, effrt aftr tenth, rdn bef 4 out, ch frm nxt till no extr appr last.*
.................................(9 to 2 op 4 to 1 tchd 5 to 1) 2
2214⁴ DOWN THE FELL [123] 8-10-9 P Carberry, *led, mstk 7th, hdd 4 out, fdd frm nxt..............*(4 to 1 op 3 to 1) 3
2300³ IN TRUTH [119] 9-10-5 K Gaule, *chsd ldr, outpcd whn mstk 11th, sn lost tch, no dngr aftr.......*(33 to 1 op 25 to 1) 4
2007² VALIANT WARRIOR [133] 9-11-5 R Garritty, *in tch, mstks 7th and 8th, sn lost touch, no dngr aftr......*(7 to 2 op 3 to 1) 5
1891³ THE LAST FLING (Ire) [124] 7-10-10 Richard Guest, *hld up, hdwy to track ldrs 6th, chalg whn f tenth.* (4 to 1 op 7 to 2) f
Dist: 5l, 7l, 2l, 1¾l. 5m 19.90s. a 26.90s (6 Ran).
SR: 46/47/25/19/31/-/

(Konvekta Ltd), O Sherwood

2467 Demmy Switch Handicap Hurdle Class B (0-145 5-y-o and up) £5,585 2m........................ (3:15)

1612 EDELWEIS DU MOULIN (Fr) [127] 5-11-9 P Carberry, *hld up, hdwy on bit to ld 2 out, drw clr aftr last, very easily.*
.................................(11 to 4 op 3 to 1 tchd 7 to 2) 1
2218⁴ TOM BRODIE [128] 7-11-10 A Dobbin, *hld up, smooth hdwy to ld aftr 3 out, hdd nxt and sn rdn, kpt on, no ch wth wnr.*
.................................(7 to 1 op 5 to 1) 2
2331 CELESTIAL CHOIR [114] 7-10-10 B Storey, *hld up, hdwy bef 6th, niggled alng aftr 3 out, styd on und pres frm betw last 2.*
.................................(5 to 2 fav tchd 9 to 4) 3
476² HAM N'EGGS [110] 6-10-6 D Bentley, *in tch, effrt bef 3 out, rdn frm nxt...............*(16 to 1 op 14 to 1) 4
2331⁵ DESERT FIGHTER [112] 6-10-2¹ (7") M Herrington, *trkd ldrs, led appr 3 out, sn hdd, no extr.*(14 to 1 op 12 to 1) 5
2190³ THORNTON GATE [124] 8-11-6 A S Smith, *hld up, hdwy bef 3 out, wknd nxt.....*(7 to 1 op 6 to 1) 6
2217⁷ ELPIDOS [117] 5-10-13 R Garritty, *led to second, cl up till wknd aftr 3 out........*(10 to 1 op 8 to 1) 7
1465 HOLDERS HILL (Ire) [108] 5-10-4 Derek Byrne, *al beh.*
.................................(20 to 1 op 14 to 1) 8

2190² UNCLE DOUG [127] 6-11-9 G Cahill, *led second till hdd appr 3 out, sn wknd, beh whn pld up bef last.*
.... (9 to 1 op 6 to 1 tchd 10 to 1) pu
Dist: 5l, nk, 2l, 4l, 5l, 10l, sht-hd. 3m 59.40s. a 18.40s (9 Ran).

SR: 39/35/21/15/13/20/3/-/-/ (Robert Ogden), G Richards

2468 Harold Charlton Memorial Hunters' Chase Class H (6-y-o and up) £1,192 3m 1f...................... (3:45)

CAB ON TARGET 11-11-10 Mr S Swiers, *hld up, took clr order tenth, trkd ldr frm 4 out, rdn to ld fnl 100 yards.*
...... (13 to 8 on op 6 to 4 on tchd 11 to 8 on and 7 to 4 on) 1
TEAPLANTER 14-11-13 (5*) Mr B Pollock, *led to 5th, mstk 8th, led tenth, mistake 4 out, hdd fnl 100 yards, no extr.*
.... (7 to 2 op 9 to 4) 2
MATT REID 13-11-11 (7*) Mr W Morgan, *in tch, trkd ldr frm tenth, ev ch 4 out, fdd.*............. (20 to 1 tchd 25 to 1) 3
FORDSTOWN (Ire) 8-11-11 (7*) Mr Jamie Alexander, *sn beh, kpt on frm 13th, nvr dngrs.*...................... (33 to 1) 4
SOUTHERN MINSTREL 14-11-7 (7*) Miss C Metcalfe, *in tch till grad wknd frm 12th.*............. (14 to 1 op 12 to 1) 5
PEAJADE 13-11-3 (7*) Miss J Wormall, *sn beh.*...... (20 to 1) 6
HIGHLANDMAN 11-11-3 (7*) Mr M Bradburne, *in tch till outpcd hfwy, no ch aftr.*...................... (50 to 1) 7
TOM LOG 10-11-3 (7*) Mr W Burnell, *mstk 6th, sn beh, tld off.*
.... (50 to 1) 8
1037⁴ KUSHBALOO 12-11-11 (7*) Mr A Parker, *chsd ldrs to hfwy, sn beh, tld off.*............. (6 to 1 op 5 to 1 tchd 13 to 2) 9
NO WORD 10-11-3 (7*) Mr I Baker, *pld hrd, led 5th to tenth, wknd quickly, tld off whn blun 4 out, pulled up bef nxt.*
.... (100 to 1 op 50 to 1) pu
Dist: 2l, 22l, 14l, 2l, sht-hd, 2l, dist, nk. 6m 43.70s. a 35.70s (10 Ran).

SR: 14/20/-/-/-/-/ (N Hurst), Mrs M Reveley

2469 Weatherbys 'Stars Of Tomorrow' Open National Hunt Flat Standard Class H (4,5,6-y-o) £1,413 2m (4:20)

2206³ PHAR SMOOTHER (Ire) 5-11-2 W Dwan, *in tch, effrt o'r 3 fs out, led appr fnl furlong, ran on.*...... (10 to 1 op 7 to 1) 1
WYNYARD KNIGHT 5-11-2 R Hodge, *hld up, hdwy hfwy, led 4 fs out, rdn 2 out, hdd appr fnl furlong, no extr.*
.... (7 to 4 fav tchd 9 to 4) 2
GENEROUS STREAK (Fr) 4-10-1 (5*) Mr R Thornton, *hld up, hdwy 5 fs out, ch o'r 2 out, kpt on same pace.*
.... (6 to 1 op 4 to 1) 3
1989³ ROMAN OUTLAW 5-11-2 R Garritty, *prmnt, drvn alng o'r 3 fs out, kpt on same pace.*..... (9 to 2 op 7 to 2 tchd 5 to 1) 4
SPRIGHTLEY PIP (Ire) 6-10-11 (5*) Michael Brennan, *mid-div, hdwy o'r 4 fs out, ch 3 out, sn rdn, no extr.*
.... (33 to 1 op 20 to 1) 5
1887⁶ BANKER COUNT 5-11-2 A Dobbin, *mid-div, effrt 4 fs out, no hdwy.*...................... (7 to 1 op 8 to 1 tchd 10 to 1) 6
THUNDERPOINT 5-11-2 A S Smith, *prmnt, slight ld 5 fs out, hdd 4 out, sn wknd.*............. (9 to 1 op 6 to 1) 7
STRONG MAGIC (Ire) 5-11-2 Derek Byrne, *nvr dngrs.*
.... (25 to 1 op 20 to 1) 8
2199⁷ OUR CAROL (Ire) 5-10-11 V Smith, *led till hdd 5 fs out, sn wknd.*...................... (50 to 1 op 33 to 1) 9
2262³ NOBLE TOM (Ire) 5-11-2 P Carberry, *keen early, hld up, some hdwy 4 fs out, sn drvn alng and btn.*..... (13 to 2 op 4 to 1) 10
SHANNON SHOON (Ire) 5-10-11 (5*) G F Ryan, *prmnt till wknd o'r 4 fs out.*...................... (20 to 1 op 12 to 1) 11
LADY'S PET 6-10-9 (7*) A Todd, *beh fnl 6 fs.*
.... (33 to 1 op 25 to 1) 12
2262⁷ BLASTER WATSON 6-11-2 M Ranger, *chsd ldrs hrd early, al beh.*...................... (50 to 1 op 33 to 1) 13
STAN'S PRIDE 5-11-2 B Storey, *beh most of way, tld off.*
.... (33 to 1 op 25 to 1) 14
COQUETTISH 4-10-1 D Parker, *beh most of way, tld off.*
.... (33 to 1) 15
CEEJAYELL 4-9-8 (7*) Miss C Metcalfe, *keen, hld up, hdwy and prmnt aftr 5 fs, wknd five out, tld off.*...... (50 to 1) 16
Dist: 1½l, 6l, nk, 2l, 9l, 1½l, 6l, 7l, 4l, 4l. 4m 0.00s. (16 Ran).

(John Smith's Ltd), J G FitzGerald

LEOPARDSTOWN (IRE) (good to yielding) Sunday February 2nd
Going Correction: PLUS 0.25 sec. per fur. (races 1,3,4,7), PLUS 0.10 (2,5,6)

2470 Spring Juvenile Hurdle (Grade 3) (4-y-o) £6,850 2m................. (1:35)

COMMANCHE COURT (Ire) 10-11 N Williamson, *mid-div, hdwy 3 out, wnt second bef nxt, styd on wl to ld aftr last.*
.... (6 to 1) 1
2050⁷ HARD NEWS (USA) 10-11 P Carberry, *led till hdd r-in, no extr.*...................... (14 to 1) 2
2337³ STRATEGIC PLOY 10-6 T J Mitchell, *beh early, hdwy 3rd, wn 4th 2 out, third appr last, styd on.*................. (5 to 2) 3
2230⁵ MARLONETTE (Ire) 10-6 D J Casey, *mid-div, lost pl 4th, prog to go fourth bef last, styd on.*...................... (14 to 1) 4

2230 EVRIZA (Ire) (bl) 10-12 T Horgan, *mid-div, hdwy aftr 2 out, not rch wnr.*...................... (20 to 1) 5
2161⁶ KEAL RYAN (Ire) 10-4 (7*) P J Dobbs, *second early, drpd back aftr 3 out, sn no dngr.*...................... (25 to 1) 6
2105* MISS PENNYHILL (Ire) (bl) 9-13 (7*) J M Maguire, *beh early, hdwy 4 out, chasing ldr 2 out, wknd, sn no dngr.*... (14 to 1) 7
2050* GRIMES 11-3 C O'Dwyer, *beh early, some hdwy 3 out, nvr a factor.*...................... (9 to 4 fav) 8
2050⁶ MISS ROBERTO (Ire) 10-12 J Shortt, *prmnt early, wknd aftr 3 out, sn btn.*...................... (10 to 1) 9
BAVARIO (USA) 10-11 R Dunwoody, *prmnt early, wknd bef 4 out, sn no dngr.*...................... (5 to 1) 10
2230⁷ HIGHLY MOTIVATED 10-6 C F Swan, *mid-div, wknd bef 4 out, nvr a factor.*...................... (8 to 1) 11
2337 NASCIMENTO (USA) 10-11 F J Flood, *al beh, tld off.* (33 to 1) 12
MARCHAWAY (Ire) 10-4 (7*) R P Hogan, *al beh, tld off.*
.... (20 to 1) 13
Dist: 2l, 5½l, 7l, 5l. 3m 52.90s. a 8.90s (13 Ran).
SR: 34/32/21/14/15/-/ (D F Desmond), T M Walsh

2471 Scalp Novice Chase (Grade 2) (5-y-o and up) £9,750 2m 5f......... (2:05)

2083* DORANS PRIDE (Ire) 8-12-0 J P Broderick, *made all, styd on wl.*...................... (11 to 8 on) 1
1652² SEE MORE BUSINESS (Ire) 7-12-0 R Dunwoody, *beh early, wnt second at 3rd, mstks 6 out and 3 out, rdn and not rch wnr.*
.... (11 to 8) 2
2273⁴ DUN BELLE (Ire) 8-11-9 T J Mitchell, *second early, drpd back bef second, 3rd at 4th, wl beh aftr nxt, sn no dngr..*(11 to 1) 3
2224⁵ KALDAN KHAN 6-11-7 C F Swan, *3rd early, wnt second at second, drpd back nxt, no dngr aftr 5th.*........... (40 to 1) 4
Dist: 6l, dist, dist. 5m 33.00s. a 24.00s (4 Ran).
(T J Doran), Michael Hourigan

2472 Deloitte And Touche Novice Hurdle (Grade 2) (5-y-o and up) £13,000 2 ¼m.................. (2:35)

2070* ISTABRAQ (Ire) 5-11-10 C F Swan, *mid-div early, hdwy 3 out, led nxt, jst hld on.*...................... (11 to 4 on) 1
2342² FINNEGAN'S HOLLOW (Ire) 7-11-7 C O'Dwyer, *beh early, hdwy bef 2 out, second at last, styd on wl.*........ (14 to 1) 2
2070² PALETTE (Ire) 5-10-13 D J Casey, *mid-div, wnt 3rd aftr last, kpt on.*...................... (13 to 2) 3
2107* THREE SCHOLARS 6-11-7 R Dunwoody, *beh early, hdwy to go second 2 out, wknd r-in.*...................... (20 to 1) 4
2054³ DUDLEY DO RIGHT (Ire) 5-11-4 N Williamson, *second early, lost grnd bef 2 out, sn btn.*...................... (33 to 1) 5
2082 TARTHOOTH (Ire) 6-11-13 F Woods, *led to 2 out, sn no dngr.*
.... (13 to 2) 6
2113* LISS DE PAOR (Ire) 6-11-8 T Horgan, *prmnt early, wknd bef 3 out, sn no dngr.*...................... (8 to 1) 7
Dist: Hd, 10l, 5l, 3½l. 4m 22.20s. a 10.20s (7 Ran).
SR: 39/36/18/21/14/-/-/ (John P McManus), A P O'Brien

2473 Stepaside Handicap Hurdle (4-y-o and up) £4,110 2m........... (3:05)

2132* TOAST THE SPREECE (Ire) [-] 5-11-2 C F Swan, *(5 to 2 fav)* 1
2272* TOUREEN GALE (Ire) [-] 8-9-9 D J Casey,........ (9 to 1) 2
1761⁹ EMBELLISHED (Ire) [-] 5-11-6 P Carberry,.......... (4 to 1) 3
2124² MR BAXTER BASICS [-] 6-10-6 N Williamson,.... (13 to 2) 4
2170⁸ POWER PACK (Ire) [-] 9-10-6 (3*) Mr B R Hamilton, (14 to 1) 5
2232⁶ NOTCOMPLAININGBUT (Ire) [-] 6-12-0 T P Treacy, (8 to 1) 6
2095⁵ MAYASTA (Ire) [-] 7-10-13 (7*) R P Hogan,........ (12 to 1) 7
2369³ JUSTAWAY (Ire) [-] 7-9-10¹ T Horgan,........... (10 to 1) 8
2076⁷ HOME PORT (Ire) [-] 5-10-10 J Shortt,........... (20 to 1) 9
1761³ TIDJANI (Ire) [-] 5-10-0 C O'Dwyer,............(4 to 1) 10
Dist: 1½l, 1l, 6l, 2l. 3m 54.40s. a 10.40s (10 Ran).
SR: 24/1/25/5/6/-/ (Golden Step Racing Syndicate), A P O'Brien

2474 Hennessy Cognac Gold Cup (Grade 1) (5-y-o and up) £59,000 3m.. (3:40)

2231 DANOLI (Ire) 9-12-0 T P Treacy, *led early, hdd 3rd, led or dsptd frm nxt, lft in ld 6 out, styd on wl.*............(6 to 1) 1
2209* JODAMI 12-12-0 N Williamson, *hld up, hdwy bef 6 out, 3rd 4 out, second aftr last, no extr.*...................... (5 to 1) 2
1753⁴ IMPERIAL CALL (Ire) 8-12-0 C O'Dwyer, *mid-div, hdwy, lft chasing ldr 6 out, wknd aftr 2 out, sn btn.*......(Evens fav) 3
2069* MERRY GALE (Ire) 9-12-0 R Dunwoody, *dsptd ld, wknd bef 4 out, sn no dngr.*...................... (7 to 1) 4
2127³ KING OF THE GALES 10-12-0 C O'Brien, *al beh, tld off.*
.... (50 to 1) 5
1639² THE GREY MONK (Ire) 9-12-0 A Dobbin, *dsptd ld till l 6 out.*
.... f
2123 IDIOTS VENTURE 10-12-0 C F Swan, *al beh, pld up 3 out.*
.... (50 to 1) pu
1746⁶ BELMONT KING (Ire) 9-12-0 D Bridgwater, *mid-div early, wknd bef 11th, beh whn pld up 3 out.*......... (20 to 1) pu
Dist: 1½l, 20l, 25l, dist. 6m 10.20s. a 3.20s (8 Ran).
SR: 92/90/70/45/-/ (D J O'Neill), Thomas Foley

2475 Leopardstown Hunters Chase (5-y-o and up) £6,850 3m........... (4:10)

WHAT A HAND 9-11-13 Mr P Fenton,............. (7 to 2) 1

AIGUILLE (Ire) 8-11-8 Mr B M Cash, ... (9 to 1)   2
MR K'S WINTERBLUES (Ire) 7-10-6 (7*) Mr W Ewing,
....(20 to 1)   3
LIFE OF A KING (Ire) 9-11-9 Mr J A Nash, ...(7 to 4 fav)   4
STAY IN TOUCH (Ire) 7-11-10 (3*) Mr D P Costello, (9 to 4)   5
CADDY MAN (Ire) 8-11-2 (7*) Mr P Cashman, ...(7 to 1)   6
NO MISTAKE VI (Ire) 9-11-6 (3*) Mr R Walsh, ...(14 to 1)   7
LINEKER 10-11-9 Mr A J Martin, ...(20 to 1)   8
Dist: 5l, 3½l, 8l, 6l. 6m 22.90s. a 15.90s (8 Ran).

(Mrs L J Roberts), E J O'Grady

2476 York Racecourse I.N.H. Flat Race (5-y-o and up) £3,082 2m. . . . . (4:40)

2270² TEMPO (Ire) 5-11-8 (7*) Mr D P Daly, ...(5 to 4 fav)   1D
2087¹ CAILIN SUPREME (Ire) 6-12-2 Mr T Mullins, ...(6 to 4)   1
2081³ STORM GEM (Ire) 6-11-13 (3*) Mr R Walsh, ...(8 to 1)   3
IMPULSIVE DREAM (Ire) 6-12-4 Mr P Fenton, ...(7 to 2)   4
MANISSA (Ire) 6-10-13 (7*) Mr P J Crowley, ...(14 to 1)   5
Dist: ½l, 13l, 12l, dist. 3m 54.70s. (5 Ran).

(E Morrissey), P Mullins

FONTWELL (good to firm)
Monday February 3rd
Going Correction: PLUS 0.30 sec. per fur.

2477 Pagham Selling Handicap Hurdle Class G (0-95 4-y-o and up) £2,160 2 ¾m 110yds. . . . . (1:40)

2295⁷ QUELQUE CHOSE [90] 7-11-10 R Hughes, hld up, steady
hdwy frm 7th, led appr last, cmftbly. (2 to 1 fav op 5 to 2)   1
2351¹ DO BE BRAVE [76] 7-10-10 (7ex) B Fenton, rar far away, lft in
ld 6th, hdd nxt, hit 3 out, sn led, rdn and headed appr last, no
extr...........................(10 to 1 op 6 to 1 tchd 11 to 1)   2
MULL HOUSE [85] (v) 10-11-5 A Maguire, hld up, hdwy 5th,
rdn and wknd appr last. (10 to 1 op 7 to 1 tchd 12 to 1)   3
2396 RAAHIN (USA) [70] 12-10-4 S McNeill, chsd ldrs frm 6th, one
pace frm 3 out........................(16 to 1 tchd 20 to 1)   4
2177⁵ CRAVATE (Fr) [66] 7-9-7 (7*) M Moran, hld up in mid-div, hdwy
7th, one pace appr last. (16 to 1 op 14 to 1 tchd 20 to 1)   5
1747 KESANTA [83] 7-10-10 (7*) J Power, mid-div, nvr nr to chal.
.................................(7 to 1 op 5 to 1 tchd 9 to 1)   6
1568 SCORPION BAY [66] 9-10-0³ (3*) J Magee, chsd ldrs, led 7th
till hdd sn aftr 3 out, wknd quickly, tld off.
.................................(33 to 1 tchd 50 to 1)   7
1700⁵ ROGER'S PAL [73] 10-10-7 D Gallagher, beh frm 7th, tld off.
.................................(10 to 1 op 8 to 1 tchd 12 to 1)   8
2351 HIGHLY DECORATED [80] (bl) 12-10-7 (7*) J K McCarthy, in
tch till wknd 6th, tld off. (50 to 1 op 33 to 1 tchd 66 to 1)   9
2267 MASTER GOODENOUGH (Ire) [66] 6-9-13⁶ (7*) D Creech, led
second till hit 3 out..................(33 to 1 op 25 to 1)   f
2030 TUG YOUR FORELOCK [66] 6-9-7 (7*) D Finnegan, in tch whn
hmpd and uns rdr 6th. (12 to 1 op 10 to 1 tchd 14 to 1)   ur
1811² KAYFAAT (USA) [84] (v) 9-11-4 C Maude, rdn frm strt, chsd
ldrs till wknd 4th, tld off whn pld up aftr 7th.
.................................(11 to 2 op 4 to 1)   pu
1700 PROFESSION [66] 6-10-9 R Farrant, in tch till wknd 7th, pld
up bef nxt..............................(33 to 1)   pu
2256 SHAAGNI ANA (USA) [67] 6-10-1 W Marston, led to second,
jmpd slwly 4th, wknd 6th, tld off whn pld up bef last.
.................................(25 to 1 op 14 to 1 tchd 33 to 1)   pu
1939⁹ CAREY'S COTTAGE (Ire) [66] (bl) 7-10-0 D Bridgwater, al beh,
tld off whn pld up bef 6th.
.................................(33 to 1 op 25 to 1 tchd 50 to 1)   pu
2251⁴ REMEMBER STAR [77] 4-10-0 B Powell, al beh, tld off whn
pld up bef 3 out....................(14 to 1 op 10 to 1)   pu
Dist: 11l, 4l, hd, nk, 3l, 18l, 14l, dist. 5m 35.70s. a 21.70s (16 Ran).

(Nigel Stafford), B J Meehan

2478 Sidlesham Handicap Chase Class E (0-110 6-y-o and up) £2,943 2¼m . . . . (2:10)

2355⁶ SHREWD JOHN [91] 10-11-12 D Gallagher, jmpd wl, trkd ldr
frm 5th, led tenth, made rst, rdn out.
.................................(16 to 1 op 10 to 1 tchd 20 to 1)   1
2194⁴ DEAR DO [103] 10-11-10 J R Kavanagh, al prmnt, trkd wnr
frm tenth, rdn appr last, no imprsn r-in.
.................................(11 to 10 fav op 5 to 4 tchd 11 to 8)   2
2355¹ WHIPPERS DELIGHT (Ire) [94] 9-11-1 (7ex) Mr A Charles-
Jones, led till hit and hdd tenth, no ch aftr.
.................................(11 to 4 op 2 to 1 tchd 3 to 1)   3
2010 CASTLECONNER (Ire) [85] (bl) 6-10-6³ J Frost, trkd ldr to 5th,
rdn aftr 8th, btn whn mstk 11th..........(11 to 2 op 5 to 1)   4
1889⁶ RED BEAN [96] 9-11-3 D Bridgwater, al last, not fluent, lost
tch 8th..........................(13 to 2 op 5 to 1 tchd 7 to 1)   5
Dist: 1¾l, 16l, 15l. 4m 35.40s. a 15.40s (5 Ran).

(Geo Taylor), Miss K M George

2479 Chichester Novices' Claiming Hurdle Class F (5-y-o and up) £2,249 2 ¼m 110yds. . . . . (2:40)

1716⁷ JOVIE KING (Ire) 5-11-0 B Powell, al prmnt, led appr 3 out,
rdn out....(11 to 2 op 9 to 2 tchd 6 to 1 and 13 to 2)   1
2264 MULLINTOR (Ire) 6-11-3 D O'Sullivan, hld up, hdwy 3 out, kpt
on und pres r-in........(11 to 2 op 6 to 1 tchd 8 to 1)   2
1813² FAIRELAINE 5-10-2 (7*) Mr R Wakley, hld up, hdwy appr 2 out,
ran on, nvr nrr.....................(11 to 2 op 5 to 2)   3
1230⁵ NIGHT IN A MILLION 6-11-6 J Osborne, not fluent, trkd ldr till
4 out, kpt on one pace.................(16 to 1 op 14 to 1)   4
2353 ADILOV 5-11-3 A Maguire, al in tch, second whn mstk last, not
reco'r................................(7 to 2 fav op 5 to 2)   5
2307⁷ ZESTI 5-10-8 N Mann, in rear, hdwy 4th, one pace appr 2 out.
.................................(10 to 1 op 9 to 2 tchd 11 to 2)   6
1543 OLIVPET 8-9-9 (5*) Mr R Thornton, hld up, effrt 5th, one pace
frm 3 out..........................(50 to 1 tchd 66 to 1)   7
2315⁹ NODDADANTE 7-10-6 (5*) Sophie Mitchell, in rear whn
hit 4th, nvr on terms.................(25 to 1 op 33 to 1)   8
582⁵ JUST-MANA-MOU (Ire) 5-9-12 (7*) N Willmington, mid-div,
wknd appr 3 out....................(7 to 1 op 6 to 1)   9
2263 ZADOK 5-11-0 (3*) P Henley, prmnt early, beh frm 5th.
.................................(20 to 1 op 12 to 1)   10
1927 SPECIAL TOPIC 7-10-3 S Curran, al beh, tld off.
.................................(66 to 1 op 50 to 1 tchd 100 to 1)   11
1843 JUST A BEAU 6-10-8 D Leahy, al beh, tld off.
.................................(66 to 1 op 50 to 1 tchd 100 to 1)   12
2181⁹ BABA SAM (Ire) 6-10-11 D Gallagher, al beh, tld off.
.................................(50 to 1 op 33 to 1 and 66 to 1)   13
1727 FAIR HAUL 6-11-0 J Frost, tld off frm 4th.
.................................(50 to 1 tchd 100 to 1)   14
2315⁹ DECEIT THE SECOND (bl) 5-10-1 (7*) M Griffiths, led till hdd
appr 3 out, wknd quickly, pld up bef nxt.
.................................(66 to 1 op 40 to 1)   pu
2291 JACK OF DIAMONDS 9-10-5 P Holley, al in rear, tld off whn
pld up bef 2 out.................(50 to 1 tchd 66 to 1)   pu
Dist: 3l, nk, 2½l, 1¼l, 4l, 2½l, 4l, 8l, 14l, 26l. 4m 33.40s. a 16.40s (16 Ran).

(M H M Reid), R H Buckler

2480 Bet With The Tote Novices' Chase Qualifier Class D (6-y-o and up) £3,770 3¼m 110yds. . . . . (3:10)

VOL PAR NUIT (USA) 6-10-7² (5*) Mr T Doumen, trkd ldr, led
8th, made rst, styd on wl to go clr r-in.
.................................(3 to 1 op 7 to 4 on tchd 15 to 8 on and 11 to 10)   1
1946 KEEP IT ZIPPED (Ire) (bl) 7-11-3 J Osborne, led to 8th, trkd
wnr for most of race aftr, no imprsn frm 2 out.
.................................(3 to 1 op 5 to 2 tchd 7 to 2)   2
2280 STROKESAVER (Ire) 7-10-8 D Gallagher, chsd ldrs, wnt
second briefly appr 3 out, 3rd and hld whn blun and uns rdr
last, rmntd...........(12 to 1 op 10 to 1 tchd 14 to 1)   3
2312⁵ DUNLIR 7-10-3 (7*) M Griffiths, al beh, tld off whn f 17th.
.................................(50 to 1 op 33 to 1 tchd 100 to 1)   f
2388⁶ THUNDER ROAD (Ire) 10-10 J Culloty, hld up, hdwy 12th,
wkng whn f 17th.................(33 to 1 op 25 to 1 tchd 50 to 1)   f
2308⁵ PAVLOVA (Ire) 7-10-5 D O'Sullivan, jmpd badly, tld off whn
blun and uns rdr 3 out................(10 to 1 op 7 to 1)   ur
2291¹⁶ WITHYCOMBE HILL 7-10-3 (7*) Mr S Durack, jmpd badly in
rear, tld off whn refused 3 out.........(14 to 1 op 10 to 1)   ref
2268 LITTLE ROWLEY 8-10-10 M Richards, al beh, tld off 12th, pld
up bef 17th.......(50 to 1 op 33 to 1 tchd 100 to 1)   pu
Dist: 7l, dist. 6m 50.50s. a 20.50s (8 Ran).

(D O McIntyre), F Doumen

2481 Strebel Boilers And Radiators Handicap Hurdle Series Qualifier Class E (0-115 4-y-o and up) £2,301 2¼m 110yds. . . . . (3:40)

2011⁵ LESSONS LASS (Ire) [100] 5-11-8 J Osborne, al prmnt, led
aftr 4th, drw clr frm 2 out, eased r-in.
.................................(100 to 30 op 3 to 1 tchd 7 to 2)   1
1849⁵ NEAT FEET (Ire) [94] 6-11-2 P Holley, hld up, hdwy appr 4 out,
wnt second aftr 3 out, ev ch nxt, rdn and no ex.
.................................(2 to 1 fav op 5 to 2)   2
FLOW BACK [78] 5-10-0 R Johnson, hld up in tch, chsd wnr 4
out till aftr nxt, wknd appr 2 out, wl btn whn mstk last.
.................................(16 to 1 op 20 to 1 tchd 14 to 1)   3
2004⁵ WATCH MY LIPS [98] 5-11-6 A Maguire, not fluent, hdwy early,
made most till hdd aftr 4th, wknd quickly appr 3 out.
.................................(11 to 2 op 4 to 1 tchd 6 to 1)   4
1925⁴ DOMINION'S DREAM [102] (v) 5-11-3 (7*) G Supple, hld prd,
chsd ldr 3rd, rdn and wknd aftr nxt.....(7 to 2 op 5 to 2)   5
1917² MUHTASHIM (Ire) [90] 7-10-12 B Fenton, al in rear, rdn and
struggling frm 5th, tld off...(9 to 2 op 7 to 2 tchd 5 to 1)   6
Dist: 12l, 20l, 6l, 14l, dist. 4m 29.20s. a 12.20s (6 Ran).

SR: 27/9/-/   (V McCalla), Lady Herries

2482 Bognor Regis Handicap Chase Class F (0-100 5-y-o and up) £2,929 3¼m 110yds. . . . . (4:10)

2268³ BLACK CHURCH [90] 11-11-9 B Fenton, hit 3rd, wl in rear till
hdwy 18th, led 2 out, styd on well......(11 to 2 op 4 to 1)   1
1559⁴ MASTER COMEDY [72] (bl) 13-10-5 A Maguire, hld up in tch,
hdwy 15th, led 4 out, hdd 2 out, sn btn.
.................................(6 to 1 op 5 to 1 tchd 13 to 2)   2

2304³ POLICEMANS PRIDE (Fr) [67] 8-10-0 D Morris, led to tenth, led 13th, hit 15th, hdd 4 out, wknd nxt.
.... (10 to 1 op 6 to 1 tchd 12 to 1) 3
2266 VICTORY GATE (USA) [67] 12-10-0 D Leahy, hld up, nvr on terms.............. (9 to 1 op 33 to 1 tchd 100 to 1) 4
2196³ ROSE KING [95] 10-12-0 Mr T Hills, mid-div, lost tch 4 out.
.... (15 to 8 fav op 7 to 4 tchd 2 to 1) 5
2308 PRIZE MATCH [75] 8-10-8 S McNeill, beh till hdwy 15th, wknd 4 out........................... (16 to 1 op 12 to 1) 6
1593⁴ MINGUS (USA) [76] 10-10-9 B Powell, jmpd slwly 5th, in tch till 117th........................(9 to 1 op 7 to 1) f
2281 ICANTELYA (Ire) [85] (v) 8-11-4 S Curran, prmnt, led tenth to 13th, wknd aftr 15th, tld off whn refused 3 out.
.... (20 to 1 op 14 to 1 tchd 25 to 1) ref
1698⁴ ALBURY GREY [67] 10-10-0 G Crone, beh aftr blun 11th, tld off whn pld up bef last.............. (16 to 1 op 12 to 1) pu
2247 SILVERINO [86] (bl) 11-11-5 C Maude, sn beh and rdn, tld off whn pld up appr 18th...(16 to 1 op 12 to 1 tchd 20 to 1) pu
1859 ROYAL SAXON [95] 11-12-0 R Johnson, prmnt till mstk 18th, sn beh, tld off whn pld up bef last.... (12 to 1 op 10 to 1) pu
1981⁶ RAINBOW FOUNTAIN [72] 10-10-5 Mr A Kinane, blun second, al beh, tld off whn pld up bef 4 out.
.............................(33 to 1 tchd 50 to 1) pu
Dist: 7l, 14l, 9l, 11l, dist. 6m 56.70s. a 26.70s (12 Ran).

(Dr B Alexander), R Rowe

2483 Levy Board Standard National Hunt Flat Class H (4,5,6-y-o) £1,213 2¼m
.... (4:40)

MACY (Ire) 4-10-1 (7*) X Aizpuru, hld up in rear, outpcd 6 fs out, plenty to do 2 out, ran on to ld wl ins last.
...................(7 to 1 op 7 to 2 tchd 8 to 1) 1
1949⁴ GOWER-SLAVE 5-10-13 (5*) Mr R Thornton, led till hdd o'r 4 fs out, rallied and swtchd rght entering fnl furlong, ran on ins.
...................(2 to 1 op 6 to 4 tchd 5 to 2 and 11 to 4) 2
KINGSWOOD IMPERIAL 4-10-1 (7*) N Wilmington, joined ldr, trkd ldr aftr 6 fs, led o'r 4 out, hdd over one out, kpt on one pace....................(10 to 1 op 5 to 1 tchd 12 to 1) 3
2269 CALDEBROOK (Ire) 6-10-11 (7*) S Laird, hld up, hdwy 6 fs out, led o'r one out till wl ins, one pace...(7 to 4 fav op 6 to 1) 4
HULALEA (NZ) 5-11-6² Mr T Hills, chsd ldr for 6 fs, one pace fnl 2........................(8 to 1 op 4 to 1 tchd 10 to 1) 5
CLAREGARY (Ire) 4-9-10 (7*) A Garrity, hld up, effrt hfwy, sn beh..........(5 to 1 op 4 to 1 tchd 11 to 2 and 6 to 1) 6
2269 TEDROSS 6-11-1 (3*) P Henley, hld up, effrt 6 fs out, rdn and sn beh, tld off...................(33 to 1 op 20 to 1) 7
SEE MINNOW 4-9-12 (5*) D Salter, al beh, lost tch hfwy, tld off.
.............................(33 to 1 op 12 to 1) 8
Dist: 1l, 1½l, 1½l, 4l, 11l, dist, dist. 4m 52.70s. (8 Ran).

(Mrs M Payne), R Dickin

NEWCASTLE (good)
Monday February 3rd
Going Correction: PLUS 0.15 sec. per fur.

2484 Kenton Novices' Chase Class E (5-y-o and up) £2,901 3m....... (1:50)

2146³ FOR CATHAL (Ire) 6-11-4 P Niven, sn aftr ldr, led aftr 3 out, hrd pressed whn mstk last, styd on und pres, all out.
.................(7 to 4 fav op 11 to 8 tchd 15 to 8) 1
2146 PANTARA PRINCE (Ire) 8-11-4 A Dobbin, trkd ldrs, chlgd 3 out, ev ch till no extr und pres last 100 yards.
........................(33 to 1 op 20 to 1) 2
2003⁴ BLACK BROOK (Ire) 8-11-4 R Garritty, made most till aftr 3 out, ev ch till wknd appr last.........(16 to 1 op 10 to 1) 3
1658 STRONGALONG (Ire) 7-11-4 A S Smith, chsd ldrs, outpcd bef 14th, sn beh........................(100 to 1 op 66 to 1) 4
1985² CELTIC GIANT 7-11-4 R Supple, keen, hld up, cld 8th, mstk nxt, wknd bef 15th, no ch whn blun 2 out.
.........................(9 to 4 op 5 to 2 tchd 11 to 4) 5
2241⁹ POCAIRE GAOITHE (Ire) 7-11-4 M Moloney, reminders aftr 3rd, lost tch frm 8th, tld off..........(50 to 1 op 33 to 1) 6
1467³ TURNPOLE (Ire) 6-11-4 N Smith, hld up, mstk second, mistake and uns rdr 7th..................(2 to 1 op 13 to 8) ur
1658 ARISTODEMUS 8-11-4 K Johnson, mstks, in tch till wknd aftr 13th, tld off whn pld up bef last...(33 to 1 op 25 to 1) pu
Dist: 1¼l, 14l, 4l, 27l, 30l. 6m 13.50s. a 27.50s (8 Ran).

(D S Hall), Mrs M Reveley

2485 Advent Catering At Pavilion Conditional Jockeys' Selling Handicap Hurdle Class G (0-95 4-y-o and up) £1,983 2m.................(2:20)

2288 PALACE OF GOLD [73] 7-10-1 (10*) W Dowling, dsptd ld, led 5th till aftr nxt, led 2 out, hrd rdn, styd on.
.........................(25 to 1 op 16 to 1) 1
BRACKENTHWAITE [88] 7-11-4 (8*) C Elliott, hld up, steady hdwy frm 5th, chsd wnr appr last, rdn and no imprsn.
........................(14 to 1 op 10 to 1) 2
1869³ OAKBURY (Ire) [68] 5-9-12 (8*) T Siddall, towards rear, styd on frm 2 out, nvr able to chal........(14 to 1 op 10 to 1) 3

2296⁹ NORTHERN FALCON [82] (bl) 4-10-10 F Leahy, chsd ldrs, outpcd bef 3 out, kpt on frm nxt...... (20 to 1 op 16 to 1) 4
2202ᵗ KIERCHEM (Ire) [71] 6-10-9 Michael Brennan, trkd ldrs, led aftr 8th to 2 out, fdd..................(7 to 1 op 5 to 1) 5
2359⁸ DOUBLING DICE [68] 6-10-3 (3*) S Melrose, mid-div, hdwy and prmnt aftr 6th, fdd 3 out.......(12 to 1 op 10 to 1) 6
2320⁶ CHARLVIC [62] 7-9-6 (8*) L McGrath, beh, styd on frm 2 out, nvr dngrs...................................(66 to 1) 7
1953⁵ COOL STEEL (Ire) [67] (bl) 5-10-5 E Callaghan, led to 5th, wknd aftr nxt.......(14 to 1 op 12 to 1 tchd 16 to 1) 8
NOSMO KING (Ire) [67] 6-10-5 E Husband, in tch, effrt bef 6th, sn beh.................................(50 to 1) 9
2320⁴ MEADOWLECK [65] 8-10-3 G Lee, chsd ldrs till wknd aftr 6th.
.....................................(50 to 1) 10
1691⁷ DOOLAR (USA) [78] (bl) 10-11-2 M Newton, chsd ldrs till wknd aftr 6th..............(9 to 1 op 7 to 1 tchd 10 to 1) 11
2344⁸ HENRY HOOLET [77] 8-11-1 G Cahill, settled midfield, drvn alng bef 6th, no hdwy. (11 to 1 op 14 to 1 tchd 7 to 2) 12
1826³ OVER STATED (Ire) [76] 7-11-0 G F Ryan, nvr on terms.
.....................(14 to 1 op 12 to 1 tchd 16 to 1) 13
1331 STORMING LORNA (Ire) [63] 7-9-12² (5*) C McCormack, hld up, gd hdwy to go prmnt 6th, wknd quickly bef 3 out.
.....................(50 to 1 op 33 to 1) 14
2147⁸ COQUET GOLD [62] 6-10-0 S Taylor, chsd ldrs, wknd quickly bef 6th, tld off.......................(100 to 1) 15
FANADIYR (Ire) [66] 5-10-4 R McGrath, sn beh, tld off.
.....................(10 to 1 op 6 to 1) 16
1676⁵ SKIDDAW SAMBA [84] 8-10-12 (10*) D Webb, mstk and uns rdr 1st......................(6 to 1 op 5 to 1) ur
2118² TIOTAO (Ire) [69] 7-9-11 (10*) Tristan Davidson, chsd ldrs, outpcd aftr 6th, mid-div whn ran out 3 out.
.....................(11 to 1 op 10 to 1 tchd 12 to 1) ro
2118⁶ TROY'S DREAM [67] 6-9-12¹ (8*) R Burns, sn beh, tld off whn pld up bef last......................(14 to 1 op 12 to 1) pu
Dist: 1¼l, 6l, ½l, 3l, 6l, 7l, 2½l, 5l, 2½l, sht-hd. 4m 0.70s. a 23.70s (19 Ran).

(Mrs Barbara Lungo), L Lungo

2486 Fenham Novices' Chase Class E (5-y-o and up) £2,771 2m 110yds (2:50)

2345* BOLD BOSS 8-11-9 B Storey, lft in ld 4th, clr 9th, cmftbly.
.......................(5 to 4 on op Evens tchd 11 to 10) 1
2345⁸ FRIENDLY KNIGHT 7-11-2 A S Smith, chsd wnr frm 4th, kpt on from 3 out, no imprsn.......... (25 to 1 tchd 33 to 1) 2
1881⁴ GLAMANGLITZ 7-11-2 R Supple, in tch, outpcd aftr 9th, kpt on frm 3 out..................(16 to 1 op 12 to 1) 3
2201 DARING PAST 7-11-9 R Garritty, in tch, wkng whn mstk 3 out, tld off.................(6 to 4 op 11 to 10 tchd 13 to 8) 4
1983⁹ ROBARA 7-11-2 N Leach, sn lost tch, tld off.
.....................(20 to 1 op 16 to 1) 5
2201 DANDY DES PLAUTS (Fr) 6-10-9 (7*) R Wilkinson, sn lost tch, tried to run out 5th, tld off.
.....................(50 to 1 op 66 to 1 tchd 100 to 1) 6
2345 MOSS PAGEANT 7-11-2 K Johnson, led till f 4th. (100 to 1) f
1965 MONAUGHTY MAN 11-11-6 M Moloney, in tch, wknd aftr 8th, tld off whn pld up bef 3 out........(33 to 1 tchd 50 to 1) pu
Dist: 5l, 4l, dist, dist, 3l. 4m 8.10s. a 9.10s (8 Ran).

SR: 29/17/13/-/-/ (John Robson), G M Moore

2487 Melton Handicap Hurdle Class F (0-105 4-y-o and up) £2,144 3m
.... (3:20)

1824⁴ SCARBA [95] 9-11-3 (3*) E Callaghan, settled midfield, hdwy to ld bef 3 out, lft clr nxt, styd on.
.....................(8 to 1 op 6 to 1 tchd 15 to 8) 1
2241 KINGS LANE [85] 8-10-10 D Parker, chsd ldrs, outpcd bef 3 out, styd on wl frm betw last 2......... (20 to 1 op 16 to 1) 2
2025 JIGGINSTOWN [77] 10-9-9 (7*) L Cooper, hld up beh, steady hdwy frm 9th, styd on frm 3 out, nvr able to chal.
.....................(20 to 1 op 16 to 1) 3
1911² AIDE MEMOIRE (Ire) [76] 8-10-1 K Johnson, in tch, hdwy to ld aftr tenth, hdd bef 3 out, kpt on same pace.
.....................(16 to 1 op 12 to 1) 4
1824* HUDSON BAY TRADER (USA) [84] 10-10-9 Miss P Robson, chsd ldrs, outpcd aftr tenth, styd on frm 3 out.
.....................(7 to 1 op 6 to 1) 5
2207⁹ GALEN (Ire) [89] 6-11-0 P Niven, mid-div, hdwy to track ldrs tenth, rdn bef 3 out, 4th and btn whn mstk last.
.....................(5 to 1 fav tchd 6 to 1) 6
2288 THE OTHER MAN (Ire) [75] 7-10-0 O Pears, in tch, kpt on frm 3 out, nvr dngrs......................(16 to 1 op 14 to 1) 7
2238⁵ DOCKMASTER [83] 6-10-8 A Dobbin, nvr dngrs.
.....................(15 to 2 op 6 to 1 tchd 8 to 1) 8
2387² EXEMPLAR (Ire) [90] 9-11-1 Richard Guest, mid-div, hdwy aftr 9th, wknd bef 3 out..............(12 to 1 op 10 to 1) 9
1824 MARDOOD [75] 12-10-0 J Supple, chsd ldrs, sn drvn alng, wknd aftr 9th...................................(50 to 1) 10
2025 HOTSPUR STREET [78] (bl) 5-10-0 (3*) F Leahy, prmnt, led briefly tenth, wknd quickly bef 3 out. (12 to 1 op 10 to 1) 11
1971³ QUIET MISTRESS [81] (bl) 7-10-6 A S Smith, made most to tenth, sn wknd..................................(14 to 1) 12
SUVLA BAY (Ire) [82] 9-10-7 M Brennan, chsd ldrs till wknd aftr tenth..................................(25 to 1) 13
2204 GRANDMAN (Ire) [85] 6-10-10 D J Moffatt, sn beh.
.....................(16 to 1 op 14 to 1) 14

1825[6] SHALLOW RIVER (Ire) [93] 6-11-4 A Thornton, *prmnt till wknd bef 9th, tld off* ....(14 to 1 op 12 to 1 tchd 16 to 1) 15
2149[4] DUKE OF PERTH [91] 6-11-2 P Carberry, *settled midfield, hdwy bef tenth, chasing wnr and rdn whn f 2 out.* ....(7 to 1 op 6 to 1 tchd 8 to 1) f
MOONSHINE DANCER [100] 7-11-8 (3*) P Midgley, *mid-div, wknd aftr 9th, tld off whn pld up bef 2 out* .... (33 to 1) pu
1952 DORLIN CASTLE [94] 9-11-5 R Supple, *nvr gng wl, tld off whn pld up bef 2 out* ....(8 to 1) pu
2241[3] HAUGHTON LAD (Ire) [75] 8-10-0 V Smith, *prmnt, wknd quickly aftr 9th, tld off whn pld up bef 2 out.* ....(16 to 1 op 12 to 1) pu
2284[4] PRINCE BALTASAR [75] 8-10-0 G Cahill, *sn wl beh, tld off whn pld up bef 9th.* ....(500 to 1) pu
2241 FARMERS SUBSIDY [79] 5-10-4[4] N Bentley, *nvr better than mid-div, tld off whn pld up bef 3 out* .... (50 to 1) pu
Dist: 3l, 3l, 2l, 5l, 3½l, sht-hd, 9l, ½l, 2½l, 6l. 6m 3.80s. a 32.80s (21 Ran).

(Yorkshire Racing Club Owners Group), J M Jefferson

2488 Gosforth Decorating And Building Services Handicap Chase Class D (0-120 5-y-o and up) £3,420 3m
.................................(3:50)

1889[5] CELTIC SILVER [95] 9-10-3[3] Richard Guest, *made all, clr 2 out, mstk last, styd on und pres.* ....(1 to 1 tchd 9 to 2) 1
2203[9] GALE AHEAD (Ire) [97] 7-10-5 B Storey, *chasing wnr whn slpd 12th, mstk and lost pl nxt, styd on wl und pres frm 3 out.* ....(11 to 2 op 5 to 1 tchd 6 to 1) 2
2239[3] SLOTAMATIQUE (Ire) [102] 8-10-10 A Dobbin, *in tch, chsd wnr frm 12th, no imprsn, wknd befd last 2.* ....(7 to 2 fav op 3 to 1 tchd 4 to 1) 3
1660 KILCOLGAN [104] 10-10-12 G Cahill, *ran in snatches, mstk tenth, outpcd aftr 13th, no dngr after* ..... (4 to 1 op 7 to 2) 4
2150[4] ROAD BY THE RIVER (Ire) [96] 9-10-4 A S Smith, *chsd ldrs, wkng whn mstk 15th, tld off* ....(9 to 2 op 4 to 1) 5
OVER THE STREAM [120] 11-12-0 A Thornton, *lost tch frm 11th, tld off* ....(9 to 1 op 16 to 1) 6
2203[3] SNOOK POINT [96] 10-10-4[4] J Burke, *losing tch whn blun tenth, tld off whn pld up bef nxt* ..... (25 to 1 op 20 to 1) pu
2005[4] URANUS COLLONGES (Fr) [111] (bl) 11-11-5 R Garritty, *tld off whn pld up bef 9th* ....(8 to 1 tchd 9 to 1) pu
Dist: 4l, 10l, 10l, dist, dist. 6m 7.10s. a 21.10s (8 Ran).

(Mrs S Smith), Mrs S J Smith

2489 Northern Racing 'National Hunt' Novices' Hurdle Class E (4-y-o and up) £2,368 2m.................(4:20)

2284* WHIP HAND (Ire) 6-11-10 P Carberry, *hld up, hdwy aftr 6th, swtchd lft appr 2 out, sn led, pushed out.* ....(7 to 2 op 5 to 2 on tchd 9 to 4 on) 1
2296[5] DARK PHOENIX (Ire) (v) 7-10-13 M Brennan, *towards rear, pushed alng bef 5th, hdwy to chase ldrs nxt, ev ch 3 out, kpt on frm next, no imprsn on wnr* ....(25 to 1 op 14 to 1) 2
2260 MENALDI (Ire) 7-11-4 A S Smith, *prmnt, ev ch 3 out, kpt on same pace frm nxt* ....(33 to 1 op 20 to 1) 3
2145[4] CLAVERING (Ire) 7-11-4 J F Titley, *prmnt, led 5th till aftr 2 out, fdd.* ....(7 to 1 op 5 to 2 on tchd 9 to 4 on) 4
2008[7] NO FINER MAN 6-11-4 A Dobbin, *in tch, effrt aftr 6th, kpt on same pace.* ....(25 to 1 op 12 to 1) 5
2145[9] ALAN'S PRIDE (Ire) 6-10-13 G Cahill, *chsd ldrs, ev ch 3 out, sn wknd.* ....(50 to 1) 6
1662 LA RIVIERA (Ire) 5-11-4 K Johnson, *chsd ldrs till wknd aftr 6th.* ....(200 to 1) 7
2200 PRINCE OF SAINTS (Ire) 6-11-4 R Garritty, *nvr on terms.* ....(25 to 1 op 16 to 1) 8
DROMORE DREAM (Ire) 8-11-4 Mr S Swiers, *beh, some late hdwy, nvr dngrs* ....(25 to 1 op 20 to 1) 9
2145[3] BUTTERWICK KING (Ire) 5-11-4 Derek Byrne, *prmnt till wknd aftr 6th* ....(200 to 1) 10
2344 SIOUX WARRIOR (bl) 5-11-1 (3*) E Husband, *in tch, hdwy to chase ldrs aftr 5th, wknd aftr nxt.* ....(100 to 1) 11
MASTER FLASHMAN 8-11-4 P Niven, *beh most of way.* ....(50 to 1 op 33 to 1) 12
2006[6] DAN DE MAN 6-11-4 A Thornton, *in tch till wknd aftr 6th.* ....(50 to 1) 13
GRAMPSAWINNA 9-10-10 (3*) E Callaghan, *sn beh.* ....(200 to 1) 14
1968 HENBRIG 7-10-13 B Storey, *al beh.* ....(200 to 1) 15
1962[6] SILVER MINX 5-11-4 R Hodge, *hld to 5th, sn wknd.* (50 to 1) 16
2179[7] ITSAHARDLIFE (Ire) 6-10-11 (7*) R Burns, *beh most of way.* ....(66 to 1 op 50 to 1) 17
RAMBLING LANE 8-10-11 (7*) S Melrose, *beh hfwy.* ....(200 to 1) 18
1280 UN POCO LOCO 5-11-1 (3*) G Lee, *in tch till wknd quickly aftr 6th.* ....(200 to 1) 19
2147[9] MONTEIN 6-11-4 N Leach, *sn beh.* ....(200 to 1) 20
Dist: 3½l, 7l, ½l, 1½l, 10l, 1½l, 1¾l, 2l, 1¾l, ½l. 4m 2.40s. a 25.40s (20 Ran).

(Lady Lloyd Webber), J G FitzGerald

CARLISLE (soft (races 1,3,5,7), good to soft (2,4,6))
Tuesday February 4th

Going Correction: PLUS 1.25 sec. per fur. (races 1,3,5,7), PLUS 1.05 (2,4,6)

2490 Wetheral Novices' Hurdle Class E (4-y-o and up) £2,738 2½m 110yds
.................................(1:40)

2318[2] PAPERISING 5-12-1 A Dobbin, *al prmnt, effrt to ld 2 out, hit last, kpt on.* ....(7 to 4 on tchd 9 to 4 on) 1
2236[4] CATHERINE'S CHOICE 4-10-7 R Garritty, *chsd ldr till led 5th, rdn and hit 3 out, hdd nxt, kpt on und pres.* ....(20 to 1 op 14 to 1 tchd 25 to 1) 2
2241* BARDAROS 8-11-9 M Foster, *chsd ldrs, effrt 4 out, rdn nxt, kpt on same pace.* ....(8 to 1 tchd 10 to 1) 3
1224[8] PENTLANDS FLYER (Ire) 6-11-3 A S Smith, *pld hrd in mid-div, hdwy to join ldrs 5th, rdn 3 out, mstk nxt, sn one pace.* ....(20 to 1 op 14 to 1) 4
COOL GAME 7-11-3 P Niven, *hld up, hit second, hdwy appr 2 out, kpt on nxt rdn ldrs.* ....(66 to 1 op 33 to 1) 5
2117[3] NUTTY SOLERA 7-11-3 B Storey, *trkd ldrs, effrt 4 out, rdn nxt, sn btn.* ....(11 to 2 op 8 to 1 tchd 9 to 1) 6
PAPARAZZO 6-11-3 J Callaghan, *mid-div, hdwy 4 out, rdn alng nxt, no imprsn.* ...(16 to 1 op 14 to 1) 7
2344 TRIONA'S HOPE (Ire) 8-10-10 (7*) Tristan Davidson, *prmnt till rdn and lost pl appr 6th, sn beh.* ....(1000 to 1) 8
1882[8] KILDRUMMY CASTLE 5-11-3 P Carberry, *mid-div, effrt and some hdwy 4 out, rdn bef nxt, sn btn*..(20 to 1 op 14 to 1) 9
1662 LYFORD CAY (Ire) 7-11-3 D Bentley, *led, blun 1st, hdd and wknd quickly 5th, tld off whn pld up bef 2 out.* ....(200 to 1 op 100 to 1) pu
1962 MATACHON 7-11-3 G Harker, *in tch till lost pl and beh frm hfwy, tld off whn pld up bef 3 out.* ....(500 to 1) pu
2236 NEEDLE MATCH 4-10-2 (5*) R McGrath, *al beh, tld off whn pld up aftr 4 out.* ....(100 to 1 op 50 to 1) pu
2344 KIRTLE MONSTAR 6-11-3 R Supple, *mstks, sn beh, tld off whn pld up bef 2 out.* ....(200 to 1 op 100 to 1) pu
2066[4] DANTES AMOUR (Ire) 6-11-0 (3*) Mr C Bonner, *beh frm hfwy, tld off whn pld up bef 2 out.* ....(9 to 1 op 33 to 1) pu
BUNNY BUCK (Ire) 7-11-3 G Cahill, *mstks, al rear, tld off whn pld up bef 2 out.* ....(33 to 1 op 20 to 1) pu
Dist: 4l, 18l, hd, 13l, 1¼l, ½l, dist, 11l. 5m 19.50s. a 37.50s (15 Ran).

(The Jockeys Whips), G Richards

2491 Bet With The Tote Novices' Chase Qualifier Class D (6-y-o and up) £3,861 3m.....................(2:10)

2319 CROWN EQUERRY (Ire) 7-11-3 P Carberry, *made all, hit 3rd, stumbled 11th, clr 2 out, driven out.* ....(7 to 1 op 5 to 1 tchd 8 to 1) 1
2319* SANTA CONCERTO 8-11-3 R Supple, *al chasing wnr, jmpd slwly 4 out, sn rdn, kpt on.* ....(9 to 4 on op 2 to 1 on tchd 5 to 2 on) 2
2362[3] TRUMP 8-10-10 D Parker, *hld up, hdwy to chase ldg pair frm 11th, rdn and 3 out, no imprsn.* ....(7 to 1 op 5 to 1 tchd 14 to 1) 3
2187[3] CALL ME BLACK (Ire) 8-10-7[2] R Garritty, *hld up, hdwy 11th, rdn alng nxt and no imprsn.* ....(12 to 1 op 10 to 1 tchd 14 to 1) 4
2157[2] FINAL BEAT (Ire) 8-10-10 Derek Byrne, *in tch, pushed alng and wknd 11th, sn beh.* ......(20 to 1 op 16 to 1) 5
1630[6] SELDOM BUT SEVERE (Ire) 7-10-5 (5*) G F Ryan, *chsd ldg pair, rdn tenth, sn wknd.* ....(33 to 1 op 20 to 1) 6
2187 ESTABLISH (Ire) 9-10-5 K Johnson, *mstks in rear, beh whn blun 11th, pld up aftr.* ....(100 to 1 op 33 to 1) pu
2347 MAMICA 7-10-10 N Smith, *hld up, effrt and some hdwy 11th, sn rdn and wl beh whn pld up bef 2 out.* ....(16 to 1) pu
Dist: 2l, dist, 12l, 7l, 3½l. 6m 24.90s. a 32.90s (8 Ran).

SR: 12/10/-/-/-/-/ (Robert Ogden), G Richards

2492 Hoechst Roussel Panacur European Breeders Fund Mares' 'National Hunt' Novices' Hurdle Qualifier (5-y-o and up) £2,626 2½m 110yds
.................................(2:40)

1824 DAISY DAYS (Ire) 7-11-5 A S Smith, *chsd ldr, led 5th, quickened clr appr 3 out, styd on strly.* ....(9 to 2 op 5 to 1 tchd 11 to 2) 1
1631 LIPPY LOUISE 5-10-12 P Niven, *hld up and beh, steady hdwy appr 4 out, rdn and kpt on wl approaching last.* ....(14 to 1 op 10 to 1 tchd 16 to 1) 2
1775 AUNTIE ALICE 7-10-12 P Carberry, *trkd ldrs, hdwy to chase wnr frm 5th, rdn 2 out, no imprsn.* ....(3 to 1 op 4 to 1) 3
2344[3] PARSON'S LODGE (Ire) 9-10-12 R Supple, *hld up and beh, steady hdwy 5th, chsd ldrs nxt, rdn and wknd 2 out.* ....(5 to 2 fav op 6 to 4 tchd 11 to 4) 4
1034 CLAIRABELL (Ire) 6-10-12 B Storey, *in tch till rdn alng and beh frm halfway.* ....(10 to 1 op 20 to 1) 5
1989[7] LOVELY RASCAL 5-10-12 A Roche, *hld up, hit second and sn beh, hdwy to chase ldrs 6th, rdn and wknd 3 out.* ....(8 to 1 tchd 14 to 1) 6
2173[6] BEST FRIEND 5-10-12 Derek Byrne, *beh frm hfwy, tld off from 4 out.* ....(16 to 1 op 14 to 1) 7

NATIONAL HUNT RESULTS 1996-97

SANDRIFT 8-10-12 D Parker, *hld up, hdwy hfwy, effrt and hit 4 out, sn wknd, beh whn pld up bef 2 out.*
.... (11 to 1 op 7 to 1 tchd 14 to 1) pu
GOOD VENTURE 6-10-9 (3*) E Callaghan, *led, rdn and hdd 5th, sn wknd, tld off whn pld up bef 2 out.*.......... (50 to 1) pu
1682 WHATYERONABOUT (Ire) 5-10-12 J Callaghan, *sn beh and rdn alng, tld off frm hfwy, pld up bef last.*
.... (50 to 1 op 20 to 1) pu
2200 OTTADINI (Ire) 5-10-12 J Burke, *chsd ldrs till lost pl and beh 5th, tld off whn pld up bef 4 out....* (200 to 1 op 100 to 1) pu
Dist: 10l, 1¼l, 18l, ½l, 16l, dist. 5m 23.80s. a 41.80s (11 Ran).
(The Sun Punters Club), J Howard Johnson

2493 John Brock Memorial Handicap Chase Class D (0-125 5-y-o and up) £3,747 2m.................... (3:10)

2261² MARBLE MAN (Ire) [92] 7-10-0 D Bentley, *led to 5th, cl up till rdn and outpcd appr 2 out, rallied last and drvn to ld nr finish.*
.... (5 to 1 op 4 to 1) 1
2191² REGAL ROMPER (Ire) [112] 9-11-6 Richard Guest, *chsd ldr till led 5th, rdn clr 2 out, drvn flt, hdd and no extr nr finish.*
.... (13 to 8 fav op 7 to 4 tchd 2 to 1) 2
2360⁵ TIMBUCKTOO [117] 10-11-11 B Storey, *chsd ldrs, effrt 5 out, rdn nxt, wknd bef 3 out.*.............. (9 to 4 op 5 to 2) 3
1965³ POSITIVE ACTION [92] (bl) 11-9-9 (5*) S Taylor, *not fluent, blun 5th, sn beh.*.................. (25 to 1 op 16 to 1) 4
2205* MONNAIE FORTE (Ire) [92] 7-10-0 M Moloney, *trkd ldrs, hdwy hfwy, ev ch whn tried to duck out and t 3 out.*
.... (100 to 30 op 9 to 4 tchd 7 to 2) f
Dist: ¾l, 27l, dist. 4m 17.60s. a 23.60s (5 Ran).
SR: 4/23/1/-/-/ (D J Lever), M D Hammond

2494 Hethersgill Conditional Jockeys' Handicap Hurdle Class E (0-115 4-y-o and up) £2,293 3m 110yds.. (3:40)

NORTHERN SQUIRE [97] 9-11-10 E Callaghan, *beh second, rdn 3 out, hdd nxt and sn hrd drvn, rallied last, styd on to ld last 100 yards.*.............. (11 to 4 jt-fav op 3 to 1) 1
HOBKIRK [83] 8-10-10 S Taylor, *trkd ldrs, effrt appr 3 out, rdn nxt, styd on to ld briefly aftr last, no extr last 100 yards.*
.... (3 to 1 tchd 5 to 2) 2
1819² MANETTIA (Ire) [89] 8-11-2 G Cahill, *led to second, cl up till led 2 out, 3 ls clr whn blun badly last, sn hdd, no extr.*
.... (11 to 4 jt-fav op 5 to 2 tchd 4 to 1) 3
FIVE FLAGS (Ire) [88] 9-11-1 R Wilkinson, *hld up, hdwy hfwy, chsd ldrs and rdn 4 out, wknd bef nxt.* (10 to 1 op 12 to 1) 4
LINKSIDE [90] 12-11-3 Michael Brennan, *hld up, effrt and rdn 6th, nvr dngrs.*........ (10 to 1 op 6 to 1 tchd 11 to 1) 5
2151 FARNEY GLEN [88] 10-11-1 R McGrath, *prmnt, rdn alng 4 out, wknd.*.................. (12 to 1 tchd 10 to 1) 6
2359⁶ LITTLE REDWING [73] (bl) 5-9-9 (5*) R Burns, *in tch till rdn alng and wknd 4 out....* (10 to 1 op 12 to 1 tchd 8 to 1) 7
723⁴ BLOOMING SPRING (Ire) [77] 8-10-1 (3*) N Horrocks, *chsd ldrs till rdn and wknd bef 4 out........* (16 to 1 op 10 to 1) 8
Dist: Hd, 12l, 5l, 2½l, 18l, 13l, 19l. 6m 29.00s. a 38.00s (8 Ran).
SR: 22/8/2/-/-/ (Mrs M E Dixon), J M Jefferson

2495 Libra Gravure Cylinders Handicap Chase Class E (0-110 5-y-o and up) £3,230 2½m 110yds.......... (4:10)

2239* SON OF IRIS [105] 9-11-10 P Niven, *chsd ldrs, rdn alng and outpcd 5 out, hdwy 3 out, drvn last, led last 100 yards.*
.... (7 to 1 op 5 to 1 tchd 8 to 1) 1
2362* CUSH SUPREME (Ire) [84] 8-10-3 (7ex) P Carberry, *led, pushed alng 3 out, rdn last, wknd and hdd last 100 yards.*
.... (100 to 30 op 11 to 4 tchd 7 to 2) 2
2237² BOLD ACCOUNT (Ire) [86] (bl) 7-10-5 A Dobbin, *al chasing ldr, rdn 2 out, kpt on same pace appr last.*
.... (11 to 2 op 6 to 1 tchd 7 to 1) 3
2360 GRAND SCENERY (Ire) [88] 9-10-7 A S Smith, *hld up and beh, hdwy hfwy, rdn 4 out, no imprsn frm nxt.*
.... (10 to 1 tchd 12 to 1) 4
2360* WAYUPHILL [105] 10-11-10 (7ex) B Storey, *hld up in mid-div, hdwy hfwy, chsd ldrs 4 out, rdn nxt, wknd 2 out.*
.... (3 to 1 fav op 5 to 2) 5
2121⁶ REBEL KING [88] 7-10-2 (5*) S Taylor, *hdwy to chase ldrs hfwy, rdn and blun 4 out, no imprsn aftr.*
.... (12 to 1 op 14 to 1 tchd 10 to 1) 6
1822* DAWN LAD (Ire) [81] 8-10-0 J Supple, *hld up, effrt 9th, rdn nxt, sn lost pl and beh.*.......... (7 to 2 tchd 4 to 1) 7
2065 BISHOPDALE [82] 16-10-11 F Perratt, *in tch till rdn alng and blun tenth, sn beh.*................ (10 to 1 op 25 to 1) 8
556 KELPIE THE CELT [81] 10-10-0 L O'Hara, *hit 1st, chsd ldrs till wknd quickly 7th, pld up bef nxt.....* (100 to 1 op 50 to 1) pu
2252 CALL ME EARLY [89] 12-10-8 I Lawrence, *chsd ldrs, blun 7th and 8th, sn wknd, beh whn pld up bef last.*
.... (25 to 1 op 33 to 1 tchd 20 to 1) pu
Dist: 1¾l, 1¾l, 13l, ½l, 11l, 22l, 1¾l. 5m 27.60s. a 32.60s (10 Ran).
(M H G Systems Ltd), Mrs M Reveley

2496 Durdar Intermediate National Hunt Flat Class H (4,5,6-y-o) £1,035 2m 1f
.... (4:40)

TOM'S RIVER (Ire) 5-11-1 (3*) G Lee, *hld up, gd hdwy o'r 5 fs out, led over one out, sn rdn and styd on, cmftbly.*
.... (10 to 1 tchd 12 to 1) 1
ONE STOP 4-9-12 (5*) S Taylor, *chsd ldrs, effrt o'r 3 fs out, sn ev ch, rdn appr last, kpt on wl........* (12 to 1 op 10 to 1) 2
1949⁹ WATER FONT (Ire) 5-10-13 (5*) R McGrath, *led, rdn 3 fs out, hdd o'r one out, sn wknd....* (20 to 1 op 16 to 1) 3
2206⁷ EASTCLIFFE (Ire) 5-10-11 (7*) C McCormack, *hld up pulling hrd, sn chasing ldrs, effrt 3 fs out, soon rdn, wknd fnl 2.*
.... (20 to 1 op 14 to 1) 4
1317 JESSOLLE 5-10-13 Mr R Hale, *trkd ldrs, effrt 4 fs out, sn rdn alng, wknd appr fnl 2.*............ (10 to 1 op 8 to 1) 5
WHAT A TALE 5-11-4 G Cahill, *beh, drvn alng hfwy, hdwy o'r 5 fs out, hrd rdn 3 out, no imprsn.*
.... (Evens op 5 to 4 tchd 6 to 4) 6
SUPEREXALT 5-11-1 (3*) F Leahy, *hld up, hdwy o'r 5 fs out, sn chasing ldrs, rdn 3 out, soon one pace.*
.... (100 to 30 op 7 to 2 tchd 4 to 1) 7
SABU 5-11-1 (3*) E Callaghan, *chsd ldr to hfwy, sn lost pl.*
.... (50 to 1) 8
JUMBO'S DREAM 6-11-4 Miss P Robson, *beh frm hfwy.*
.... (50 to 1) 9
BORDER IMAGE 6-10-11 (7*) N Horrocks, *beh frm hfwy*
.... (50 to 1) 10
2363⁵ CASTLE BAY 6-10-13 (5*) B Grattan, *pld hrd, hld up and beh, effrt 6 fs out, no hdwy............* (9 to 2 op 5 to 1) 11
FERRINO FRUITS (Ire) 6-10-13 (5*) Michael Brennan, *in tch till lost pl and beh frm hfwy.....* (33 to 1 op 25 to 1) 12
Dist: 2½l, 13l, 1½l, 1l, 2½l, 9l, 22l, 4l, 3½l, 3½l. 4m 32.60s. (12 Ran).
(Jemm Partnership), Mrs M Reveley

WARWICK (good to firm)
Tuesday February 4th
Going Correction: PLUS 0.30 sec. per fur.

2497 Ryton Juvenile Novices' Hurdle Class E (4-y-o) £2,670 2m..... (1:30)

2173² FITZWILLIAM (USA) 10-12 G Bradley, *made most, quickened clr aftr 3 out, readily.* (11 to 4 fav op 7 to 2 tchd 4 to 1) 1
EXALTED (Ire) 10-12 T Jenks, *nvr far away, hit 4th, chsd wnr frm betw last 2, no imprsn........* (14 to 1 op 12 to 1) 2
712⁵ TAKEAMEMO (Ire) 10-7 J Osborne, *patiently rdn, improved frm off the pace aftr 3 out, styd on one pace frm betw last 2.*
.... (8 to 1 op 6 to 1 tchd 9 to 1) 3
TIUTCHEV 10-12 T Titley, *frnt rnk, ev ch appr 3 out, rdn and no extr frm betw last 2....* (6 to 1 op 4 to 1 tchd 13 to 2) 4
2371⁸ PALAMON (USA) 10-12 B Clifford, *settle wth chasing grp, effrt hfwy, no imprsn on ldrs frm 3 out.*
.... (16 to 1 op 14 to 1 tchd 20 to 1) 5
2195 BRECON 10-12 M Richards, *patiently rdn, steady hdwy frm 3 out, nvr plcd to chal..................* (50 to 1) 6
2256² TOBY BROWN 10-12 A Maguire, *settled wth chasing grp, feeling pace bef 3 out, fdd.* (3 to 1 op 11 to 4 tchd 7 to 2) 7
1188 GULF OF SIAM 10-12 T Eley, *drvn alng wth chasing grp hfwy, struggling bef 3 out, sn lost tch..................* (50 to 1) 8
767⁶ STILL HERE (Ire) 10-12 R Johnson, *settled midfield, feeling pace bef 3 out, no imprsn on ldrs....* (50 to 1 op 33 to 1) 9
2336⁶ MIGHTY KEEN 10-12 D Skyrme, *settled off the pace, effrt hfwy, lost tch bef 3 out......* (33 to 1 op 25 to 1) 10
2012 INDUNA MKUBWA 10-12 K Gaule, *pressed ldrs, wknd appr 3 out, sn lost tch....................* (33 to 1 op 20 to 1) 11
GREEN BOPPER (USA) 10-12 C Maude, *dsptd ld to hfwy, lost tch bef 3 out, tld off..................* (33 to 1 op 25 to 1) 12
2195⁵ SULAWESI (Ire) 10-7 C Llewellyn, *in tch hfwy, lost touch bef 3 out, no ch whn t 2 out.............* (5 to 1 op 11 to 4) f
2255⁵ IMPENDING DANGER 10-12 D Bridgwater, *wth ldrs to hfwy, tld off whn pld up bef 2 out........* (14 to 1 tchd 16 to 1) pu
2255⁶ APACHE PARK (USA) 10-12 D Gallagher, *al wl beh, tld off whn pld up bef last..................* (25 to 1 tchd 33 to 1) pu
ALANA'S BALLAD (Ire) 10-7 Gary Lyons, *lost tch hfwy, tld off whren pld up bef 2 out....................* (100 to 1) pu
Dist: 6l, 4l, 5l, 1¼l, 2l, 6l, 1½l, 10l, 3l, hd. 3m 49.50s. a 10.50s (16 Ran).
SR: 27/21/12/12/10/8/2/-/-/ (Paul Mellon), I A Balding

2498 Princethorpe Novices' Chase Class D (5-y-o and up) £3,777 2½m 110yds
.... (2:00)

2154* GARNWIN (Ire) 7-11-9 J R Kavanagh, *settled midfield, improved frm 6 out, led bef 2 out, styd on wl.*
.... (9 to 4 fav op 6 to 4) 1
2328⁶ FLIGHT LIEUTENANT (USA) 8-11-9 A Thornton, *nvr far away, str chal frm 3 out, kpt on same pace 2 out.*
.... (4 to 1 op 9 to 4 tchd 9 to 2) 2
2176³ LOBSTER COTTAGE 9-11-9 S McNeill, *led early, styd upsides, led 8th till bef 2 out, sn rdn, wknd quickly before last.*
.... (11 to 1 op 8 to 1 tchd 12 to 1) 3
1804 SWISS TACTIC (Ire) 8-11-3 V Smith, *chsd ldrs, effrt aftr 6 out, und pres nxt, wknd quickly, tld off...........* (66 to 1) 4
2201⁶ WEEHEBY (USA) 8-11-3 T J Murphy, *nvr far away, ev ch aftr 4 out, wknd quickly nxt, tld off.......* (25 to 1 tchd 33 to 1) 5
2352³ FURRY FOX (Ire) 9-11-3 D Morris, *settled in tch, feeling pace and drvn alng bef 4 out, tld off.....* (25 to 1 op 20 to 1) 6

335

2266⁸ MOVING OUT 9-11-3 G Bradley, *wth ldrs, ev ch till blun 6 out, sn wknd, tld off* . . . . (3 to 1 tchd 4 to 1) 7

2254⁵ WOT NO GIN 8-11-3 R Johnson, *struggling bef hfwy, tld off.* . . . .(7 to 1 op 6 to 1 tchd 8 to 1) 8

1870 ELITE GOVERNOR (Ire) 8-10-10 (7*) Mr L Baker, *settled to chase ldrs, hit 4 out, 5th and wkng whn f nxt.* . . . . (25 to 1 op 16 to 1) f

CONVAMORE QUEEN (Ire) 8-10-12 V Slattery, *midfield whn blun and uns rdr 4th* . . . .(50 to 1 op 33 to 1) ur

DANDIE IMP 9-11-3 B Powell, *settled midfield, struggling hfwy, tld off whn pld up bef 4 out* . . (14 to 1 tchd 20 to 1) pu

2278 MHEANMETOO 6-11-3 P Holley, *sn led, hdd 8th, wknd quickly hit circuit, tld off whn pld up bef 7 out.* . . . . (100 to 1 op 66 to 1) pu

2156 BROWNSCROFT 9-10-5 (7*) Mr R Wakley, *hit 4th, sn lost tch, tld off whn pld up bef 3 out* . . . . . .(100 to 1 op 50 to 1) pu

2178³ AEOLIAN 6-10-10 (7*) K Hibbert, *lost tch hfwy, tld off whn pld up bef 7 out* . . . .(50 to 1 op 20 to 1) pu

1271 EVENTSINTERNASHNAL (bl) 8-11-3 Mr J M Pritchard, *lost tch bef hfwy, tld off whn pld up before 11th.* . . . . (100 to 1 op 66 to 1) pu

2373⁵ TYPHOON (Ire) 7-11-3 M Sharratt, *refused to race, took no part* . . . .(100 to 1) I

Dist: 1¾l, 22l, 18l, 1¾l, 18l, sht-hd, 3l. 5m 7.50s. a 12.50s (16 Ran).

SR: 30/28/6/-/-/-/   (Pioneer Heat-Treatment), N J Henderson

2499 European Breeders Fund 'National Hunt' Novices' Hurdle Qualifier Class D (5,6,7-y-o) £3,377 2½m 110yds. . . . . (2:30)

1893² MARCHING MARQUIS (Ire) 6-11-0 R Johnson, *al wl plcd, led bef 7th, quickened clr last 3, eased considerably before finish.* . . . . (6 to 5 on op 5 to 4 on tchd 11 to 10 on) 1

2263 RYDER CUP (Ire) 5-11-0 J R Kavanagh, *patiently rdn, improved appr 4 out, styd on frm betw last 2, no ch wth wnr.* . . . . (14 to 1 op 8 to 1) 2

2260 JAYFCEE 5-11-0 B Powell, *nvr far away, ev ch hfwy, rdn bef 5 out, sn struggling, lost tch 3 out* . . . . (33 to 1) 3

2032* MAID FOR ADVENTURE (Ire) 6-11-5 J Culloty, *wth wth, improved hfwy, chsd wnr 4 out till wknd quickly betw last 2.* . . . .(3 to 1 op 7 to 4) 4

TIDEBROOK 7-11-0 C O'Dwyer, *chsd ldrs, effrt hfwy, und pres aftr 3 out, btn whn blun nxt.* . . . .(9 to 2 op 7 to 1 tchd 8 to 1) 5

COMMUTER COUNTRY 6-11-0 B Fenton, *pressed ldrs, struggling whn pace lifted appr 4 out, lost tch, tld off.* . . . . (33 to 1 op 14 to 1) 6

1940⁸ DINGLE WOOD (Ire) 7-11-0 Mr A Kinane, *pressed ldrs, rdn and lost tch quickly aftr 4 out, tld off.* . (33 to 1 op 20 to 1) 7

2035³ MANVULANE (Ire) (v) 7-11-0 J Railton, *led till appr 7th, wknd quickly, lost tch and pld up bef 2 out.* . . (12 to 1 op 6 to 1) pu

Dist: 15l, 3l, 1¾l, 3l, 21l, 5l. 5m 1.60s. a 16.60s (8 Ran).

(Michael and Gerry Worcester), Noel T Chance

2500 George Coney Challenge Cup Handicap Chase Class C (0-130 5-y-o and up) £5,824 3m 5f. . . . . (3:00)

2310⁴ MUSTHAVEASWIG [121] 11-11-10 A Maguire, *patiently rdn, improved fnl circuit, chalg whn crowded by loose horse aftr 3 out, led bef last, styd on to go clr.* . . . .(9 to 2 op 4 to 1 tchd 5 to 1) 1

2252* BENDOR MARK [98] 8-10-11¹ J F Titley, *nvr far away, dsptd ld aftr one circuit, 4 ls adrift whn lft in lead 3 out, hdd bef last, one pace r-in* . . . . (4 to 1 tchd 9 to 2) 2

2293³ TUG OF PEACE [113] 10-11-2 B Fenton, *settled in tch, improved aftr one circuit, feeling pace 7 out, lost touch aftr nxt, tld off.* . . . . (6 to 1 tchd 13 to 2) 3

LIMONAIRE (Fr) [125] (bl) 11-12-0 A Vieira, *led to 5th, struggling and reminders fnl circuit, last and tailing off whn f 6 out.* . . . . (12 to 1 op 10 to 1 tchd 14 to 1) f

2005 CHRISTMAS GORSE [120] 11-11-9 C Llewellyn, *wl plcd, led 5th, jnd aftr one circuit, 4 ls clr and gng well whn blun and uns 3 out, unlucky.* (3 to 1 fav op 5 to 2 tchd 100 to 30) ur

2310⁵ BIG BEN DUN [105] 11-10-1 (7*) M Berry, *tracking ldr whn blun and uns rdr second* . . . .(10 to 1 op 7 to 1) ur

2393⁴ DANGER BABY [105] 7-10-8 P Holley, *chasing ldrs whn mstk and uns rdr 8th* . . . . (100 to 30 op 3 to 1 tchd 7 to 2) ur

Dist: 5l, 28l. 7m 45.40s. a 36.40s (7 Ran).

(P R D Fasteners Ltd), D Nicholson

2501 Ebrington Handicap Hurdle Class C (0-130 4-y-o and up) £3,454 2½m 110yds. . . . . (3:30)

2253⁶ REAGANESQUE (USA) [111] 5-10-11 R Farrant, *wtd wth, improved to ld aftr 6th, clr frm 2 out, styd on strly r-in.* . . . . (9 to 4 op 2 to 1 tchd 5 to 2) 1

2217⁴ BARFORD SOVEREIGN [109] 5-10-9 A Maguire, *led, jnd 3rd, hdd aftr 6th, drvn alng 3 out, kpt on same pace frm betw last 2.* . . . . (7 to 4 fav op 11 to 8 tchd 2 to 1) 2

2331⁹ ALBEMINE (USA) 8-11-10 T Kent, *wth ldr, feeling pace and bustled alng aftr 4 out, struggling nxt, sn btn.* . . . . (9 to 2 op 7 to 2) 3

AMILLIONMEMORIES [100] 7-10-0 R Greene, *settled off the pace, styd on frm 4 out, nvr rch chalg pos.* . . . . (14 to 1 op 20 to 1 tchd 25 to 1) 4

1864³ SOVEREIGNS PARADE [110] 5-10-10 J R Kavanagh, *sn wl beh, steady hdwy 4 out, feeling pace nxt, lost tch, tld off.* . . . .(7 to 1 op 6 to 1) 5

2180⁵ VISION OF FREEDOM (Ire) [100] 9-10-0 N Williamson, *trkd ldg trio, blun 5 out, struggling aftr nxt, tiring whn f 3 out.* . . . . (11 to 1 op 10 to 1 tchd 12 to 1) f

Dist: 4l, 15l, 1l, 30l. 4m 59.20s. a 14.20s (6 Ran).

SR: 2/-/-/   (Mrs John Spielman), P G Murphy

2502 Air Wedding Trophy Hunters' Chase Class H (5-y-o and up) £1,114 3¼m . . . . (4:00)

THE MALAKARMA 11-12-3 (5*) Mr B Pollock, *chsd ldr, nig-gled alng aftr one circuit, jnd lder 6 out, outpcd and rdn 4 out, styd on gmely to lead r-in.* . . . .(6 to 4 on op 7 to 4 on tchd 11 to 8 on) 1

OUT FOR FUN 11-11-9 (7*) Mr N R Mitchell, *led, given breather 6 out, quickened nxt, blun last, hdd and one pace r-in.* . . . . (6 to 4 tchd 7 to 4) 2

SIRISAT 13-11-10¹ (7*) Miss T Blazey, *chsd ldg pair, feeling pace whn hit 8 out, one pace last 4, no imprsn.* . . . . (9 to 1 op 8 to 1) 3

CORN EXCHANGE 9-11-9 (7*) Mr M FitzGerald, *chasing ldg trio whn blun and uns rdr 3rd.* . . . . (25 to 1 op 33 to 1 tchd 50 to 1) ur

Dist: 2l, 15l. 6m 47.20s. a 33.20s (4 Ran).

(Charles Dixey), Miss C Saunders

2503 February Mares' Only Maiden National Hunt Flat Class H (4,5,6-y-o) £1,028 2m. . . . . (4:30)

ERINTANTE (Ire) 4-10-9 (5*) Mr T Doumen, *al gng wl, quick-ened through to ld well o'r one furlong out, sprinted clr, imprsv.* . . . . (6 to 4 fav tchd 2 to 1) 1

MELODY MAID 5-11-3 (7*) T Hagger, *settled to track ldrs, improved to ld o'r 3 fs out, hdd wl over one out, no ch wth wnr.* . . . .(9 to 1 op 6 to 1 tchd 10 to 1) 2

CASTLE MEWS (Ire) 6-11-5 (5*) S Ryan, *wl plcd, effrt and drvn alng o'r 2 fs out, one pace ins last.* . . . .(16 to 1 op 10 to 1) 3

GOOD JOB 5-11-3 (7*) D Kiernan, *swly away, reco'red hfwy, dsptd ld over 3 fs out, rdn and not quicken ins last.* . . . .(9 to 1 op 5 to 1) 4

WISE GUNNER 4-11-0 D Walsh, *nvr far away, drvn alng whn pace quickened o'r 3 fs out, one pace.* . . . .(9 to 1 op 5 to 1 tchd 10 to 1) 5

MISS MATCH 6-11-5 (5*) O Burrows, *wnt hndy hfwy, feeling pace approaching strt, wknd.* . . . . . .(33 to 1 op 25 to 1) 6

SUILVEN 5-11-3 (7*) Mr R Wakley, *chsd ldg bunch, reminders o'r 6 fs out, no imprsn entering staraight.* . . . .(7 to 1 tchd 8 to 1) 7

FRUITATION 6-11-7 (3*) L Aspell, *settled midfield, effrt hfwy, kpt on same pace last 2 fs.* . . . .(7 to 1 op 4 to 1) 8

NEARLY A SCORE 5-11-5 (5*) A Bates, *hmpd strt, beh, improved hfwy, styd on, nvr nr.* . . . . .(14 to 1 op 10 to 1) 9

1514⁸ NIGHT ESCAPADE (Ire) 5-11-3 (7*) L Suthern, *patiently rdn, improved hfwy, ridden and wknd bef strt.* . . . .(9 to 1 op 14 to 1 tchd 10 to 1) 10

2309² WHERE'S MIRANDA 5-11-3 (7*) R Studholme, *wl plcd for o'r one m, tld bef strt.* . . . .(8 to 1 op 7 to 1) 11

GEMS LASS 6-11-3 (7*) Miss J Wormall, *wth ldrs for o'r one m, wknd quickly bef strt.* . . . .(66 to 1) 12

GEISHA 5-11-10 Mr P Scott, *wth ldrs, led bef hfwy till o'r 3 fs out, wknd quickly.* . . . .(100 to 1 op 66 to 1) 13

ARTIC MEADOW 6-11-5 (5*) Mr R Thornton, *slwly away, al wl beh, tld off.* . . . .(100 to 1 op 66 to 1) 14

STORM QUEEN (Ire) 6-11-3 (7*) C Davies, *settled midfield, feeling pace hfwy, lost tch, tld off.* . . . .(14 to 1 op 12 to 1) 15

1874⁹ FINE SPIRIT 5-11-10 Mr A Kinane, *led till bef hfwy, lost tch before strt, tld off.* . . . . (33 to 1) 16

SUNSWORD 6-11-3 (7*) Mr A Wintle, *struggling hfwy, tld off.* . . . .(66 to 1) 17

WELSH DAISY 5-11-3 (7*) X Aizpuru, *slwly away, al beh, tld off.* . . . .(66 to 1) 18

POLLYS SISTER 5-11-10 Mr A Phillips, *wl beh hfwy, tld off.* . . . .(66 to 1) 19

1949 GLENDRONACH 5-11-10 G Tormey, *chsd ldrs to hfwy, tld off.* . . . .(100 to 1) 20

PAPER TIGRESS (Ire) 6-11-7 (3*) R Massey, *pld up bef hfwy, lme.* . . . . (14 to 1 op 12 to 1) pu

GRAND FIASCO 4-11-0 Mr J Grassick, *tld off whn pld up bef strt.* . . . .(50 to 1) pu

Dist: 3l, 11l, hd, 3l, 4l, 1½l, 4l, sht-hd, 5l, 8l. 3m 42.70s. (22 Ran).

(Haras d'Ecouves), F Doumen

ASCOT (good to firm)
Wednesday February 5th
Going Correction: PLUS 0.40 sec. per fur. (races 1,3,6,7), PLUS 0.20 (2,4,5)

2504 Kilfane Conditional Jockeys' Handicap Hurdle Class E (0-120 5-y-o and up) £3,533 2½m.............(1:30)

1700[4] FLYING FIDDLER (Ire) [89] (bl) 6-10-2 P Henley, *hld up, al gng nicely, hdwy 6th, led 3 out, pushed clr frm nxt, easily.*
..................(16 to 1 op 14 to 1 tchd 20 to 1) 1
CAN CAN CHARLIE [100] 7-10-13 L Aspell, *hld up beh ldrs, steady hdwy frm 4 out, kpt on one pace from 2 out.*
..................(9 to 2 op 7 to 2) 2
2396[2] HANDSON [90] 5-10-3 D Salter, *hld up, cld 6th, chsd wnr appr 2 out, sn no imprsn.*...............(5 to 1 op 7 to 2) 3
2356[5] SMUGGLER'S POINT (USA) [105] 7-11-4 Sophie Mitchell, *chsd ldr, led 5th to 7th, outpcd frm 3 out.*
..................(16 to 1 op 12 to 1) 4
1927 ROSEHALL [87] 6-9-11 (3*) L Suthern, *sn detached in rear, styd on appr 2 out, nvr a factor.*........(66 to 1 op 50 to 1) 5
2290[2] MORSTOCK [115] 7-12-0 T Dascombe, *hld up beh ldrs, effrt 3 out, hit nxt and sn wknd.* (8 to 1 op 7 to 1 tchd 9 to 1) 6
2389[8] KIPPANOUR (USA) [109] (bl) 5-11-8 J Magee, *hld up, effrt aftr 7th, btn 3 out, tld off....* (14 to 1 op 12 to 1 tchd 16 to 1) 7
1443[6] SHAHRANI [110] 5-11-9 G Supple, *led, sn clr, reminder and looked reluctant aftr 4th, hdd nxt, led ag'n 7th to 3 out, soon btn, tld off..........*(12 to 1 op 10 to 1 tchd 14 to 1) 8
2204[4] AUBURN BOY [103] 10-11-2 P Midgley, *hld up towards rear, pushed alng aftr 6th, sn struggling, no ch whn pld up bef 2 out.*
..................(11 to 2 tchd 6 to 1 and 5 to 1) pu
1644[4] HOODED HAWK (Ire) [109] 6-11-8 T C Murphy, *chsd ldr, not fluent 4th, mstk 7th, wknd appr four out, pld up bef 2 out.*
..................(100 to 30 fav op 5 to 2 tchd 7 to 2) pu
Dist: 14l, 6l, 2½l, 2½l, ½l, 12l, 11l. 4m 57.50s. a 16.50s (10 Ran).
(Mike Roberts), M J Roberts

2505 Stanlake Novices' Chase Class B (5-y-o and up) £10,215 2m......(2:00)

2352* AMANCIO (USA) 6-11-4 R Dunwoody, *made all, blun 8th, ran on wl, unchigd.*..................(11 to 10 tchd 5 to 4) 1
2297* JATHIB (Can) 6-11-4 Derek Byrne, *al chasing wnr, not fluent 4th and 7th, pckd four out, rdn aftr 2 out, no imprsn whn blun last.*..................(11 to 8 on op 13 to 8 on tchd 5 to 4 on) 2
Won by 5l. 3m 58.40s. a 10.40s (2 Ran).
SR: 18/17/ (Lady Harrison), Mrs A J Perrett

2506 Shenley Enterprises Hurdle Limited Handicap Class B (4-y-o and up) £8,083 3m...................(2:30)

2313* HAILE DERRING [117] 7-10-7 T Jenks, *made all, shaken up and drw clr aftr 2 out, not fluent last, pushed out, unchigd.*
..................(9 to 4 fav tchd 2 to 1 and 5 to 2) 1
1744[2] SPARKLING YASMIN [125] 5-11-1 R Dunwoody, *chsd wnr thrght, hrd rdn aftr 3 out, no imprsn nxt.* (7 to 2 op 3 to 1) 2
2198* COKENNY BOY [114] 12-10-4 N Williamson, *hld up in tch, drvn appr 2 out, sn btn.*...............(4 to 1 tchd 9 to 1) 3
2210[3] TOP SPIN [134] 8-11-10 A Maguire, *hld up in last pl, niggled alng aftr 9th, sn btn.*
..........(8 to 1 op 7 to 1 tchd 9 to 1 and 10 to 1) 4
2047[2] PEATSWOOD [119] 9-10-9 R Hughes, *hld up in tch, drvn appr 4 out, sn btn*..........(11 to 4 tchd 5 to 2 and 3 to 1) 5
Dist: 9l, 8l, 2½l, 10l. 6m 0.10s. a 24.10s (5 Ran).
(Mrs V Stockdale), N A Twiston-Davies

2507 Comet Chase A Grade 1 (5-y-o and up) £37,032 2m 3f 110yds (3:05)

2045[4] STRONG PROMISE (Ire) 6-11-7 N Williamson, *trkd ldr, led 4 out, drvn appr last, not fluent, all out.* (10 to 1 tchd 12 to 1) 1
2327* ONE MAN (Ire) 9-11-7 R Dunwoody, *led, jmpd slwly and hdd 4 out, hrd rdn and ev ch last, one pace und pres.*
..................(7 to 4 on op 13 to 8 on tchd 6 to 4 on) 2
1760* SOUND MAN (Ire) 9-11-7 C F Swan, *trkd ldg pair, hit 4th, not fluent 6th, blun badly 8th, blunded 5 out, no imprsn under pres appr 2 out.*..................(9 to 4 op 7 to 4 tchd 5 to 2) 3
2219[3] BIG MATT (Ire) 9-11-7 J Osborne, *hld up in last pl, lost tch appr 11th, tld off.*..........(25 to 1 op 16 to 1) 4
Dist: 1l, 10l. dist. 4m 47.20s. a 6.20s (4 Ran).
SR: 70/69/59/-/ (G A Hubbard), G A Hubbard

2508 HSBC James Capel Reynoldstown Novices' Chase Class A Grade 2 (5-y-o and up) £15,875 3m 110yds ....(3:35)

2043* DJEDDAH (Fr) 6-11-12 A Kondrat, *trkd ldrs, led 3 out, not extended.*..........(13 to 8 fav op 11 to 8 tchd 7 to 4) 1
2293[2] DROMHANA (Ire) 7-11-5 R Dunwoody, *trkd ldr, mstk 12th, reminders nxt, ev ch 3 out, sn outpcd, swshd tail und pres appr last.*.........(9 to 1 op 8 to 1 tchd 10 to 1) 2
2328[2] POTTER'S BAY 8-11-9 A Maguire, *hld up in last pl, shrtlvd effrt 15th, sn struggling, tld off in 3rd whn f last.*
..................(7 to 2 op 11 to 4 tchd 4 to 1) f
2189[2] MONY-SKIP 8-11-9 Richard Guest, *trkd ldrs, f heavily 6th.*..................(3 to 1 op 9 to 4) f
2146[2] BRANDY CROSS (Ire) 8-11-5 P Carberry, *led, blun 15th, hdd whn f 3 out.*...........(13 to 2 op 6 to 1 tchd 7 to 1) f

Dist: 24l. 6m 16.50s. a 15.50s (5 Ran).
(Mrs Stella Elkaim), F Doumen

2509 Fernbank Novices' Hurdle Class C (4-y-o and up) £3,501 2m 110yds ....(4:05)

2215[3] COURBARIL (bl) 5-11-7 C F Swan, *led to 3rd, led aftr 5th to 3 out, sn hrd rdn, rallied und pres to ld r-in, gmely.*
..................(6 to 1 op 4 to 1 tchd 13 to 2) 1
2249[6] EAGLES REST (Ire) 6-11-4 N Williamson, *hld up, gng wl, hdwy to ld 2 out, hrd rdn and hdd r-in, ran on.* (11 to 2 op 5 to 1) 2
2042[5] LEADING SPIRIT (Ire) 5-11-4 K Gaule, *hld up in tch, cld 4 out, led aftr nxt, hdd but ev ch 2 out, btn whn mstk last.*
..................(8 to 1 op 12 to 1 tchd 14 to 1) 3
2042[3] PROTON 7-11-4 R Dunwoody, *trkd ldrs, hrd rdn 3 out, wknd appr nxt.*..................(5 to 1 op 7 to 2 tchd 11 to 2) 4
2236* MISTER ROSS (Ire) 7-11-4 P Carberry, *trkd ldr, led 3rd till aftr 5th, led 3 out, sn hdd, hrd rdn and slightly hmpd on bend, btn whn mstks last 2.........* (5 to 1 op 7 to 2 tchd 11 to 2) 5
BLAZE OF SONG 5-11-4 W Marston, *hld up in tch till wknd und pres 4 out, tld off.* (20 to 1 op 14 to 1 tchd 25 to 1) 6
2173* PERCY BRAITHWAITE (Ire) 5-10-11 (7*) K Hibbert, *hld up, hdwy aftr 5th, wknd after 3 out, tld off.*
..................(14 to 1 op 12 to 1 tchd 16 to 1) 7
2197[7] BLOMBERG (Ire) 5-11-4 A Maguire, *nvr gng wl in rear, tld off frm 5th, pulling up whn collapsed appr 2 out, dead.*
..................(10 to 1 op 8 to 1 tchd 14 to 1) pu
2277[3] SIERRA BAY (Ire) 7-11-4 J Osborne, *hld up, blun badly 4th, cld four out, sn btn and eased, tld off whn pld up bef 2 out.*
..................(7 to 4 fav op 9 to 4 tchd 5 to 2) pu
2324[5] LEAR JET (USA) 4-10-11 R Garritty, *chsd ldrs to 4 out, sn btn, tld off............*(12 to 1 op 11 to 1 tchd 20 to 1) pu
Dist: ½l, 12l, 7l, ½l, dist, sht-hd. 3m 58.10s. a 12.10s (10 Ran).
SR: 36/32/20/13/12/-/ (Richard Green (Fine Paintings)), M C Pipe

2510 Ascot Standard Open National Hunt Flat Class H (4,5,6-y-o) £2,274 2m 110yds......................(4:35)

2269[3] MISTER ERMYN 4-10-7 R Hughes, *led to o'r 12 fs out, cl up, led 2 out, rdn and ran on wl.*..................(2 to 1 jt-fav tchd 6 to 4 and 9 to 4) 1
1306 BORODINO 5-11-0 (3*) L Aspell, *al hndy, drvn and kpt on wl ins fnl furlong.......*(10 to 1 op 7 to 1 tchd 14 to 1) 2
TUCKERS TOWN 5-11-3 J Osborne, *al hndy, led o'r 3 fs out to 2 out, wknd ins last.*..................(9 to 1 jt-fav op 5 to 4 tchd 9 to 4) 3
2221* CLINKING 6-11-10 Mrs A Perrett, *hld up in last pl, hdwy ovcer 4 fs out, ev ch 2 out, sn rdn and wknd ins last.*
..................(7 to 2 op 3 to 1 tchd 4 to 1 and 11 to 4) 4
ENIGMA BELL 4-10-7 K Gaule, *hld up, keen early, hrd rdn 4 fs out, wknd o'r 2 out, tld off.*
..................(16 to 1 op 8 to 1 tchd 33 to 1) 5
1735[7] JACK (Ire) 5-11-3 S McNeill, *chsd ldrs to o'r 12 fs out to over 3 out, sn wknd, tld off.........*(33 to 1 op 14 to 1 tchd 50 to 1) 6
EVENING DANCER 4-10-4 (3*) T Dascombe, *hld up in cl tch, wknd quickly o'r 3 fs out, tld off.*
..................(25 to 1 op 12 to 1 tchd 33 to 1) 7
YONDER STAR 5-10-10 (7*) C Hynes, *pld hrd, in tch, hard rdn o'r 4 fs out, sn btn, tld off.*
..................(33 to 1 op 14 to 1 tchd 50 to 1) 8
Dist: 2½l, 10l, 2l, 18l, 8l, 6l, dist. 4m 1.80s. (8 Ran).
(J Daniels), L Montague Hall

LUDLOW (good)
Wednesday February 5th
Going Correction: MINUS 0.05 sec. per fur. (races 1,3,5,7), NIL (2,4,6)

2511 Bull Ring Maiden Hurdle Class E (4-y-o and up) £2,542 2m.......(1:40)

2255[2] HIGH IN THE CLOUDS (Ire) 5-11-8 S Wynne, *al gng wl, quickened up to draw level 3 out, led bef nxt, readily.*
..................(11 to 8 on op 6 to 4 on tchd 5 to 4 on) 1
1882[3] TALATHATH (Fr) 5-11-8 R Johnson, *tucked away in midfield, improved to chal 3 out, rdn and not pace of wnr r-in.*
..................(5 to 2 tchd 3 to 1 and 9 to 4) 2
RORY 6-11-8 T Kent, *al hndy, led 5th, jnd 3 out, hdd bef nxt, rdn and one pace frm betw last 2.....*(7 to 1 tchd 8 to 1) 3
2371[5] MUSIC PLEASE 5-11-8 C O'Dwyer, *wtd wth, took clr order aftr 4 out, rdn and kpt on same pace frm nxt.*
..................(20 to 1 op 16 to 1) 4
PINKERTON'S PAL 6-11-8 C Maude, *al wl plcd, led 3rd to nxt, styd hndy till no extr und pres frm 2 out.* (14 to 1 op 6 to 1) 5
1731 GLEN GARNOCK (Ire) 5-11-8 Gary Lyons, *wth ldrs, feeling pace whn ldrs quickened frm 3 out, fdd und pres.*
..................(100 to 1 op 50 to 1) 6
2336[7] SOCIETY GIRL 4-10-2 (5*) Michael Brennan, *settled in tch, feeling pace whn ldrs quickened aftr 4 out, no imprsn.*
..................(66 to 1 op 50 to 1) 7
1922 BRIGHT ECLIPSE (USA) 4-10-6[1] (7*) J T Nolan, *chsd ldg bunch, feeling pace aftr 4 out, nvr rchd chalg pos.*
..................(66 to 1 op 50 to 1) 8

1604 RIVERBANK RED 6-11-3 T Eley, *wth ldrs, led 4th to nxt, wknd*
und pres aftr four out........................(100 to 1) 9
1866 APOLLONO 5-11-8 L Harvey, *sn struggling to keep up, lost*
tch frm hfwy, tld off..................(33 to 1 tchd 50 to 1) 10
MELLOW MASTER 4-10-5 (7*) D Finnegan, *struggling and*
beh frm hfwy, tld off.................(66 to 1 op 50 to 1) 11
JULIAN OLIVER 5-11-1 (7*) N Willmington, *not jump wl, al*
beh, tld off..............................(100 to 1 op 50 to 1) 12
2029 GEM'S PRECIOUS 6-11-5 (3*) R Massey, *sn wl beh, tld off*
whn pld up bef 3 out.......................(100 to 1) pu
Dist: 2l, 4l, 8l, 3l, 4l, 5l, 1½l, ½l, 9l, 12l. 3m 39.10s. a 7.10s (13 Ran).
SR: 15/13/9/1/-/-/ (Mrs J G Griffith & Lady Barlow), Capt T A Forster

2512 Bridgnorth Novices' Chase Class E (5-y-o and up) £2,932 3m..... (2:10)

1996 LUCKY DOLLAR (Ire) 9-11-8 C O'Dwyer, *settled gng wl, wnt*
hndy fnl circuit, led aftr 3 out, drw clr, easily.
..................................(100 to 30 op 7 to 2) 1
1732 KING'S SHILLING (USA) 10-11-2 Jacqui Oliver, *nvr far away,*
led aftr 5 out till after 3 out, kpt on, no ch wth wnr.
....(25 to 1 op 14 to 1) 2
2178* INCH EMPEROR (Ire) 7-11-8 T J Murphy, *tried to make all,*
hdd aftr 5 out, styd hndy till rdn and outpcd frm 3 out.
....(8 to 1 op 14 to 1) 3
2388⁸ BOLSHIE BARON 8-11-2 Mr M Harris, *jmpd rght, tld off till*
some late hdwy frm 3 out, nvr a factor. (20 to 1 op 14 to 1) 4
2328⁵ LA MEZERAY 9-11-3 D Walsh, *nrly f 1st, lost tch aftr one*
circuit, tld off frm 4 out.............(14 to 1 op 10 to 1) 5
2280⁸ DUKES MEADOW (Ire) 7-11-2 A Thornton, *al hndy, 3rd and*
pushed alng whn f 5 out................(16 to 1 op 14 to 1) f
2254 THREE PHILOSOPHERS (Ire) 8-11-2 S Wynne, *pressed ldr,*
cl second whn blun badly and uns rdr 8 out, broke pelvis,
destroyed... (5 to 4 on op 11 to 8 on tchd 11 to 10 on) ur
2391 LORD ANTRIM (Ire) 8-11-2 S Curran, *chasing ldrs whn mstk*
and uns rdr 8th........................(66 to 1 op 50 to 1) ur
Dist: 9l, 19l, 2l, 24l. 5m 53.60s. a 6.60s (8 Ran).
SR: 28/13/-/-/-/ (G P D Milne), K C Bailey

2513 Ashford Mares' Only Handicap Hurdle Class E (0-110 4-y-o and up) £2,304 2m 5f 110yds........ (2:40)

2440* SCOTTISH WEDDING [81] 7-10-10 (3*,6ex) R Massey, *nvr far*
away, nosed ahead frm 4 out, hdd briefly bef nxt, gd jump to
go clr last, rdn and kpt on wl r-in..... (7 to 1 op 6 to 1) 1
2177³ FIRST CRACK [86] 12-11-4 S Wynne, *sn handily plcd, str chal*
3 out to nxt, kpt on same pace r-in..... (7 to 2 op 3 to 1) 2
2180³ FLEUR DE TAL [92] 6-11-3 (7*) J Power, *patiently rdn, steady*
hdwy to ld briefly bef 3 out, ridden and one pace frm betw last
2...................................... (9 to 1 op 8 to 1) 3
2281* MADAME PRESIDENT (Ire) [90] 6-11-5 (3*) D Fortt, *al wl plcd,*
ev ch aftr 4 out, rdn frm nxt, outpcd last 2. (9 to 2 op 7 to 2) 4
2295³ STAC-POLLAIDH [87] 7-11-5 C O'Dwyer, *reminders aftr 3 out,*
niggled alng thrght, no imprsn on ldrs frm 3 out.
........................(11 to 4 fav op 3 to 1 tchd 7 to 2) 5
1847² SCAMALLACH (Ire) [89] (bl) 7-11-7 G Bradley, *settled off the*
pace, effrt hfwy, struggling bef 4 out, nvr a factor.
....(8 to 1 tchd 10 to 1) 6
2281⁹ JOY FOR LIFE (Ire) [69] 6-10-1 R Johnson, *led to 4 out, wknd*
quickly and lost tch....................(20 to 1 op 16 to 1) 7
GO FROLIC [77] 9-10-9 B Powell, *pressed ldrs, lost grnd*
quickly hfwy, tld off....................(11 to 1 op 10 to 1) 8
Dist: 2½l, 3½l, 7l, 5l, 7l, 1¼l, 28l. 5m 1.40s. a 6.40s (8 Ran).
SR: 11/13/15/6/-/ (G A Weetman, Reynolds & Dean), T Wall

2514 Attwood Memorial Trophy Handicap Chase Class D (0-120 5-y-o and up) £3,387 2½m................(3:15)

2175⁵ COOLREE (Ire) [109] 9-11-3 D Bridgwater, *chsd ldr, improved*
und pres to jump ahead 2 out, drvn out.
..........................(11 to 4 op 5 to 2 tchd 3 to 1) 1
1607⁴ SPANISH LIGHT (Ire) [120] 8-12-0 C Maude, *tried to make all,*
not fluent 3 out, blun and hdd nxt, no extr r-in.
....(14 to 1 op 12 to 1) 2
NORSE RAIDER [112] 7-11-6 D Walsh, *trkd ldg pair, hit 3rd*
and nxt, effrt und pres appr 4 out, wknd quickly frm next.
........................(11 to 8 fav op 6 to 4 tchd 13 to 8) 3
2196² PHILIP'S WOODY [112] (bl) 9-11-6 J R Kavanagh, *last and*
hld up, niggled alng frm hfwy, not fluent 7 out, 3rd and no
imprsn whn f 2 out.............. (2 to 1 op 6 to 4) f
Dist: 2½l, 21l. 4m 55.50s. a 6.50s (4 Ran).
SR: 24/32/3/-/ (B T R Weston), P F Nicholls

2515 Church Stretton Selling Handicap Hurdle Class G (0-95 4-y-o and up) £2,038 2m................(3:45)

2385⁴ TANGO MAN (Ire) [61] 5-10-5 C Maude, *settled off the pace,*
gd hdwy appr 3 out, str run to ld bef last, forged clr.
....(10 to 1 op 8 to 1) 1
2351⁹ RUTH'S GAMBLE [56] (v) 9-10-0 D Leahy, *settled to track*
ldrs, improved to ld bef 3 out, hdd and rdn before last, one
pace...(50 to 1) 2

2265 DR DAVE (Ire) [67] 6-10-11 A Thornton, *nvr far away, chlgd 3*
out, ev ch and rdn whn hmpd by faller nxt, kpt on same pace.
........................(20 to 1 op 16 to 1 tchd 25 to 1) 3
1798⁴ JUST FOR A REASON [73] 5-11-0 (3*) E Husband, *settled beh*
ldg grp, improved frm 3 out, styd on from betw last 2, nrst
finish.......................................(6 to 1) 4
2255 SPITFIRE BRIDGE (Ire) [65] 5-10-9 D Bridgwater, *ran in*
snatches, lost grnd hfwy, styd on frm 3 out, no imprsn on ldrs.
....(5 to 2 fav op 3 to 1) 5
2251² INDIAN TEMPLE [69] 6-10-13 R Greene, *al chasing ldrs, effrt*
and drvn alng bef 3 out, one pace frm betw last 2.
......................................(12 to 1 op 10 to 1 tchd 14 to 1) 6
2390 FOLLOW DE CALL [68] 7-10-12 D Walsh, *nvr far away, ev ch*
and rdn 3 out, no extr frm betw last 2. (50 to 1 op 33 to 1) 7
SPANISH ARCH (Ire) [70] 8-11-0 J Culloty, *pressed ldrs till*
rdn and lost grnd bef 3 out............(33 to 1) 8
1596 KALZARI (USA) [78] 12-11-3 (5*) Michael Brennan, *patiently*
rdn, steady hdwy to go hndy bef 3 out, ridden and no extr frm
nxt.. (10 to 1 tchd 12 to 1) 9
2174⁴ THEM TIMES (Ire) [62] 8-10-6 S Wynne, *led till aftr 3rd, styd*
hndy till wknd quickly frm 3 out....... (12 to 1 op 8 to 1) 10
2403 KILLING TIME [75] 6-11-5 D J Burchell, *chsd alng to keep up*
hfwy, lost tch bef 3 out.................. (10 to 1 op 8 to 1) 11
2390⁴ PERSIAN BUTTERFLY [56] 5-10-0 D Gallagher, *wth ldr, led*
aftr 3rd till hdd bef 3 out, wknd quickly.
....(6 to 1 op 5 to 1 tchd 7 to 1) 12
2174² ASTRAL INVASION (USA) [83] (v) 6-11-10 (3*) R Massey, *wth*
ldrs till wknd quickly bef 3 out, sn lost tch. (8 to 1 op 6 to 1) 13
2390⁵ JOBBER'S FIDDLE [69] (bl) 5-10-13 R Johnson, *wl plcd to*
hfwy, wknd quickly bef 3 out......... (14 to 1 tchd 16 to 1) 14
1976 WOODLANDS LAD TOO [56] 5-10-0 R Bellamy, *al beh, nvr a*
factor, tld off................................(66 to 1) 15
1943⁹ NIGHT BOAT [71] 6-11-11 T Eley, *patiently rdn, smooth hdwy*
to chal whn blun and uns rdr 2 out.... (16 to 1 op 14 to 1) ur
Dist: 3½l, ½l, 5l, 6l, sht-hd, 3½l, 2l, sht-hd, 2½l, 1½l. 3m 38.30s. a 6.30s (16 Ran).
SR: 6/-/7/8/-/-/ (My Left Foot Racing Syndicate), R J Price

2516 Pontrilas Hunters' Chase Class H (6-y-o and up) £1,171 2½m...... (4:15)

BEAU DANDY 10-11-7 (7*) Mr T Marks, *al hndy, hmpd by*
faller 8th, reco'red to ld aftr nxt, made rst, kpt on grimly frm 2
out............................. (6 to 5 on op 11 to 8 on tchd Evens) 1
HENNERWOOD OAK 7-11-2 (7*) Mr M Munrowd, *patiently*
rdn, smooth hdwy to chal frm 4 out, ev ch till hit 2 out, kpt on
same pace r-in..(33 to 1) 2
BILLY BATHGATE 11-11-7 (7*) Mr D S Jones, *nvr far away, lft*
in narrow ld aftr 8th, hdd aftr nxt, one pace whn made 4 out, sn lost
tch... (7 to 1 op 6 to 1) 3
HICKELTON LAD 13-11-11 (3*) Mr M Rimell, *chsd ldrs, hrd at*
work to keep up 5 out, sn lost tch, tld off.
....(9 to 1 op 8 to 1 tchd 10 to 1) 4
AL HASHIMI 13-11-7 (7*) Mr N Ridout, *wl plcd whn f 8th.*
....(10 to 1 op 8 to 1) f
PASTORAL PRIDE (USA) 13-11-9 (5*) Miss P Curling, *led, clr*
4th, pld up aftr 8th, broke blood vessel. (11 to 4 op 2 to 1) pu
Dist: ½l, dist, 30l. 5m 2.40s. a 13.40s (6 Ran).
(C C Shand Kydd), Miss C Saunders

2517 Winstanstow Novices' Hurdle Class E (5-y-o and up) £2,444 2m 5f 110yds........................(4:45)

2263⁶ DRUM BATTLE 5-10-12 A Thornton, *nvr far away, led aftr 4*
out, hld briefly after nxt, rdn frm betw last, lft clr last.
....(6 to 1 tchd 7 to 1) 1
2315⁶ TANTARA LODGE (Ire) 6-10-12 C O'Dwyer, *settled to track*
ldrs, effrt and drvn alng frm 3 out, one pace from betw last 2.
....(12 to 1 op 10 to 1) 2
2207 BENFLEET 6-10-12 D Walsh, *settled off the pace, improved*
frm 3 out, styd on r-in, too much to do.
....(7 to 2 op 3 to 1 tchd 4 to 1) 3
2394⁶ CAPTAIN NAVAR (Ire) 7-10-7 (5*) Michael Brennan, *wtd wth,*
effrt and hng lft appr 3 out, hit nxt, left second and blun last,
not reco'r.......................... (25 to 1 op 16 to 1 tchd 33 to 1) 4
2394 DANZANTE (Ire) 5-10-12 D Gallagher, *ran in snatches, short*
lived effrt hfwy, rdn frm 3 out, no imprsn.
....(25 to 1 op 16 to 1) 5
2035⁸ LOUGHDOO (Ire) 9-10-12 O Pears, *chsd ldrs till rdn appr 3*
out, sn outpcd..................................(14 to 1 op 10 to 1) 6
2298 DODGY DANCER (bl) 7-10-12 L O'Hara, *led till hdd and*
reminders aftr 4 out, quickly lost tch...(50 to 1 op 33 to 1) 7
2263⁷ MINELLA DERBY 7-11-5 R Johnson, *co'red up, steady*
hdwy and hng lft bend bef 3 out, wkd whn tried to run out 2
out, succeeded last.
..................(6 to 5 on op 11 to 10 on tchd 6 to 4 on) ro
Dist: 7l, hd, 1¼l, 7l, hd, 11l. 5m 6.70s. a 11.70s (8 Ran).
(David Chown), W G M Turner

CLONMEL (IRE) (yielding to soft) Thursday February 6th

2518 Cashel Maiden Hurdle (4-y-o and up) £2,740 2½m................(1:15)

2368⁵ CASTLE COIN (Ire) 5-11-2 C F Swan, ... (6 to 1)   1
2165⁹ MAGS SUPER TOI (Ire) 8-10-13 (7") M D Murphy, (16 to 1)   2
2414⁶ MALADANTE (Ire) 5-10-11 F Woods, ... (10 to 1)   3
2476 TEMPO (Ire) 5-11-10 C O'Dwyer, ...(5 to 2 on)   4
2368⁷ SHALOM (Ire) 5-10-9 (7") P G Hourigan, ... (16 to 1)   5
2161 RAINBOW TIMES (Ire) 4-10-2 M P Hourigan, ...(20 to 1)   6
2160⁹ ATLANTA FLAME (Ire) 6-11-1 W Slattery, ... (20 to 1)   7
2230⁹ THE SWAN 4-10-7 R Hughes, ... (11 to 2)   8
2276⁸ ACTIVE LADY (Ire) 5-10-4 (7") Mr B Walsh, ... (33 to 1)   9
2079 CLONCANNON BELL (Ire) 7-10-10 (5") J M Donnelly,
. . . . (25 to 1) 10
1904 BOWES LADY (Ire) 6-10-8 (7") R P Hogan, ...(25 to 1) 11
MEGA HUNTER (Ire) 5-11-2 M Moran, ... (14 to 1) 12
SKY LEADER (Ire) 7-11-6 J Shortt, ... (16 to 1) 13
MOSTA (Ire) 4-9-9 (7") M J Collins, ... (20 to 1) 14
2343 CARRAIGMACLEIR (Ire) 6-11-1 T P Treacy, ...(25 to 1) 15
ANSWER THAT (Ire) 6-11-1 C O'Brien, ... (16 to 1) 16
2443 EXPERT ADVICE (Ire) 6-11-6 D J Casey, ... (20 to 1)   f
2416⁷ SINGERS CORNER 5-10-5↓ (7") Mr A J Dempsey, (30 to 1) bd
2079 TAR AN CARRAIG (Ire) 5-10-11 J R Barry, ...(50 to 1) pu
THE KERRY REBEL (Ire) 4-10-7 T J Mitchell, ...(25 to 1) pu
Dist: 3l, ¾l, 4l, 10l. 5m 14.20s. (20 Ran).

(Mrs Geraldine Farrell), A P O'Brien

2519 Redmonstown Maiden Hurdle (Div I) (6-y-o and up) £2,740 2½m... (1:45)

2271² BE HOME EARLY (Ire) 7-12-0 C F Swan, ... (13 to 8 on)   1
2339⁴ MOUNT DRUID (Ire) 7-11-6 J Shortt, ...(10 to 1)   2
2225⁶ BLUE IRISH (Ire) (bl) 6-11-3 (3") K Whelan, ... (14 to 1)   3
2075⁶ SUNSHINE BAY (Ire) 6-11-6 G M O'Neill, ... (6 to 1)   4
2160⁶ LORD OGAN (Ire) 6-11-6 J P Broderick, ... (25 to 1)   5
2228⁸ TORMOND PERK (Ire) 6-11-6 T Horgan, ... (16 to 1)   6
2271 ATHA BEITHE (Ire) (bl) 6-12-0 R Hughes, ... (7 to 1)   7
2107 RING HARRY (Ire) 7-11-1 W Slattery, ... (25 to 1)   8
2088 XANTHOS 7-11-6 L P Cusack, ...(33 to 1)   9
2165 CHOCOLATE GIRL (Ire) 6-11-1 D H O'Connor, ...(50 to 1) 10
NAN'S PET (Ire) 7-11-1 S H O'Donovan, ... (20 to 1) 11
ANDY BURNETT (Ire) 8-11-6 F J Flood, ... (16 to 1) 12
2271 BATTLE AIR (NZ) 9-11-11 (3") J Butler, ... (25 to 1) 13
2443 HAZY WALK (Ire) 6-11-9 T P Treacy, ...(33 to 1) 14
1895⁵ PAPO KHARISMA 7-11-6 F Woods, ... (10 to 1) pu
2093² BUSH TELEGRAPH (Ire) 8-11-6 A Powell, ... (10 to 1) pu
IN LINE FOR DALUS (Ire) 8-10-8 (7") Miss C Gould, (33 to 1) pu
Dist: 1½l, 2l, 6l, 3l. 5m 15.80s. (17 Ran).

(D R Killian), Anthony Mullins

2520 Redmonstown Maiden Hurdle (Div II) (6-y-o and up) £2,740 2½m... (2:15)

2131⁷ PINKPINKFIZZ (Ire) 6-10-13 (7") R P Hogan, ... (7 to 2)   1
2162 COMMITTED SCHEDULE (Ire) 6-11-6 M P Hourigan,
. . . . (20 to 1)   2
2166⁷ RAHEEN RIVER (Ire) 6-11-1 C O'Dwyer, ... (6 to 1)   3
2222² BAWNROCK (Ire) 8-12-0 C F Swan, ... (6 to 4 fav)   4
1090⁸ MILLSOFBALLYSODARE (Ire) 6-10-13 (7") S P McCann,
. . . . (16 to 1)   5
1359⁹ KYLOGUE KING (Ire) 6-11-6 T Horgan, ...(20 to 1)   6
1710⁸ TRUCKINABOUT (Ire) 7-11-6 F Woods, ...(14 to 1)   7
1536³ SARADANTE (Ire) 7-11-6 J P Broderick, ... (7 to 1)   8
536 LIOS NA MAOL (Ire) 6-10-8 (7") M D Murphy, ...(33 to 1)   9
2378 BOLD CAVALIER (Ire) 8-10-13 (7") Mr A Ross, ...(25 to 1) 10
2271⁸ PREMIER WALK 8-11-7 (7") S O'Donnell, ...(10 to 1) 11
2271 WHOSE YER WAN (Ire) 7-11-9 A Powell, ... (14 to 1) 12
2339 ST CAROL (Ire) 6-11-1 T P Treacy, ... (9 to 1) 13
2137 BORLEAGH PILOT (Ire) 6-11-3 (3") K Whelan, ... (25 to 1) 14
BAD BERTRICH (Ire) 6-12-0 L P Cusack, ... (20 to 1) 15
1539⁹ VESPER LADY (Ire) 6-11-1 J Shortt, ... (10 to 1) 16
2413 NOBLE TUNE (Ire) 8-11-6 S H O'Donovan, ... (14 to 1) 17
2222 CLONEE PRIDE (Ire) 6-11-1 P L Malone, ... (33 to 1) 18
2131⁹ ALICE BRENNAN (Ire) 6-11-1 J R Barry, ...(14 to 1)   f
Dist: 2l, 3½l, ¾l, 15l. 5m 22.20s. (19 Ran).

(Mrs T R Quinn), T J Taaffe

2521 White Sands Catering Hurdle (5-y-o) £3,082 2m................(2:45)

2270⁴ WHAT'S THE VERDICT (Ire) 11-9 C F Swan, ... (7 to 4)   1
2106⁴ BOSS DOYLE (Ire) 11-9 C O'Dwyer, ... (Evens fav)   2
2414⁺ MIRACLE ME (Ire) 11-9 F Woods, ...(12 to 1)   3
2075³ PAS POSSIBLE (Ire) 11-9 G M O'Neill, ... (25 to 1)   4
2369⁸ CELTIC LORE 11-9 D T Evans, ... (10 to 1)   5
2049⁶ INCHACOOLEY (Ire) 10-12 A Powell, ...(11 to 2)   6
2413⁹ POISON IVY (Ire) 10-5 (7") J A Robinson, ... (20 to 1)   7
Dist: 1l, 10l, 15l, 8l. 4m 19.10s. (7 Ran).

(Seamus O'Farrell), A P O'Brien

2522 Murphys Irish Stout Chase (5-y-o and up) £3,425 2½m.........(3:15)

2341⁶ FERRYCARRIGCRYSTAL (Ire) 9-11-8 J P Broderick,
. . . . (5 to 4 fav)   1
2410² THE NOBLE ROUGE (Ire) 8-11-4 T Horgan, ... (3 to 1)   2
1618 ANOTHER DEADLY 10-11-4 J Shortt, ...(12 to 1)   3
2078⁷ OVER AGAIN (Ire) 9-11-8 C F Swan, ... (4 to 1)   4
2164⁷ THE BOYLERMAN (Ire) 8-10-11 (7") Mr K O'Sullivan,
. . . . (10 to 1)   5
2143⁶ MONALEE STATEMENT (Ire) 7-11-4 D H O'Connor, (10 to 1)   6

BALLYMACODA LADY (Ire) 8-10-13 F Woods, ... (16 to 1)   7
2143⁵ TOBY'S FRIEND (Ire) 8-10-13 W Slattery, ... (8 to 1)   8
2096⁹ KNOCKMUIRA (Ire) 7-11-4 D J Casey, ... (16 to 1)   f
2048 CRISTYS PICNIC (Ire) 7-11-4 C O'Dwyer, ... (14 to 1) pu
Dist: 5l, 7l, 2l, 20l. 5m 25.30s. (10 Ran).

(Mrs Mary Lambert), S J Lambert

2523 Sportsmans Hunters Chase (5-y-o and up) £2,226 3m...........(3:45)

BOB TREACY (Ire) 8-11-7 (7") Mr A G Costello, ...(7 to 1)   1
INNISCEIN (Ire) 9-11-9 (5") Mr J T McNamara, ...(14 to 1)   2
WEJEM (Ire) 8-11-7 (7") Mr John P Moloney, ...(10 to 1)   3
1119⁷ SHAWS CROSS (Ire) 6-12-0 Mr P Fenton, ... (14 to 1)   4
ITSAJUNGLEOUTTHERE (Ire) 7-11-7 (7") Mr W Ewing,
. . . . (12 to 1)   5
UP AND UNDER (Ire) 8-11-7 (7") Mr T N Geraghty, . . (20 to 1)   6
1092⁸ MAYPOLE FOUNTAIN (Ire) 7-11-9 (5") Mr W M O'Sullivan,
. . . . (12 to 1)   7
PANCHO'S TANGO (Ire) 7-11-7 (7") Mr D P Daly, ... (8 to 1)   8
TEA BOX (Ire) 6-12-0 Mr B M Cash, ...(12 to 1)   9
CROI 7-11-7 (7") Mr M D Scanlon, ...(20 to 1) 10
MCFEPEND (Ire) 7-11-2 (7") Mr N D Fehily, ... (20 to 1) 11
HARRY'S SECRET (Ire) 7-11-7 (7") Mr D Breen, ... (16 to 1) 12
SHIRGALE (Ire) 8-11-2 (7") Mr E Gallagher, ...(16 to 1)   f
1080⁹ JUST A BREEZE (Ire) 9-11-2 (7") Mr T N Cloke, ...(6 to 1)   f
DIXON VARNER (Ire) 7-12-0 Mr E Bolger, ... (10 to 9 on)   f
OUL LARRY ANDY (Ire) 7-11-7 (7") Mr A Ross, ...(14 to 1)   f
SUMMERHILL EXPRESS (Ire) (bl) 7-11-6 (3") Mr T Lombard,
. . . . (10 to 1) ur
MALTESE CROSS (Ire) 8-11-7 (7") Mr T J Nagle Jnr, (33 to 1) pu
Dist: 3l, sht-hd, 15l, 2½l. 6m 36.70s. (18 Ran).

(M W Hickey), M W Hickey

2524 Gerry Chawke Handicap Hurdle (0-116 4-y-o and up) £3,082 2½m ....(4:15)

1361² LETTERLEE (Ire) [-] 7-10-9 (7") Mr M A Cahill, ...(8 to 1)   1
2104² LAURENS FANCY (Ire) [-] 7-10-5 J R Barry, ... (7 to 2)   2
2229⁸ SIR JOHN (Ire) [-] 8-10-11 C F Swan, ... (9 to 4 fav)   3
2415 GARLAND ROSE (Ire) [-] 7-9-9 D J Casey, ...(20 to 1)   4
1778⁹ KERCORLI (Ire) [-] 6-9-1 (7") M D Murphy, ...(10 to 1)   5
2134 PTARMIGAN LODGE [-] 6-10-11 (3") G Kilfeather, . .(8 to 1)   6
1753 LOVE THE LORD (Ire) [-] 7-11-12 T P Treacy, ...(10 to 1)   7
2162⁶ ROSIE LIL (Ire) [-] (bl) 6-9-8 (7") L A Hurley, ...(10 to 1)   8
2272⁹ GLENHAVEN ARTIST (Ire) [-] 7-11-3 F J Flood, ... (7 to 1)   9
2273⁹ BART OWEN [-] (bl) 12-12-0 T Horgan, ...(20 to 1) 10
2104⁹ MAJESTIC JOHN (Ire) [-] 7-9-9 (7") A T Kelly, ...(25 to 1) 11
2164 SIOBHAILIN DUBH (Ire) [-] 8-10-8 P A Roche, ...(14 to 1) 12
2366 TAR AND CEMENT (Ire) [-] (bl) 9-9-7 C O'Brien, . . . (10 to 1) 13
2378⁴ CRANNON BEAUTY (Ire) [-] 9-12-2 (3") J Butler, . . . (20 to 1) 14
Dist: 11l, 2½l, 1l, 5½l. 5m 14.40s. (14 Ran).

(T Cahill), T Cahill

2525 Templemore I.N.H. Flat Race (5-y-o and up) £2,740 2m...........(4:45)

2222⁸ WEST LEADER (Ire) 6-12-0 Mr D Marnane, ...(6 to 4 fav)   1
1907⁷ SOPHIE VICTORIA (Ire) 5-11-5 Mr B M Cash, ... (10 to 1)   2
2343⁷ LADY ELISE (Ire) 6-11-2 (7") Mr J M Roche, ...(16 to 1)   3
SPLEODRACH (Ire) 7-11-6 (3") Mr R Walsh, ... (14 to 1)   4
2343⁵ JENSALEE (Ire) 6-11-9 Mr T Mullins, ... (2 to 1)   5
2343⁶ CLARA ROCK (Ire) 5-10-12 (7") Mr C J Radley, ... (12 to 1)   6
2228 LADY RICHENDA (Ire) 9-11-4 (5") Mr J T McNamara,
. . . . (14 to 1)   7
BE THE ONE (Ire) 6-11-9 Mr P Fenton, ... (28 to 1)   8
2144⁴ MISS PECKSNIFF (Ire) 7-11-2 (7") Mr John P Moloney,
. . . . (16 to 1)   9
2343 ROMANCEINTHEDARK (Ire) 7-11-9 Mr H F Cleary, (25 to 1) 10
DOCKLINE (Ire) 5-11-3 (7") Mr R M Walsh, ... (8 to 1) 11
SUZANN'S GIRL (Ire) 6-11-9 Mr J A Berry, ...(14 to 1) 12
STILLBYHERSELF (Ire) 7-11-6 (3") Mr P English, ...(14 to 1) 13
2093⁸ CALL BOB (Ire) 7-11-7 (7") Mr T J Nagle Jnr, ... (20 to 1) 14
LACKEN RIVER (Ire) 5-10-12 (7") Mr P A Farrell, . . . (14 to 1) 15
2176 TISNOTMYTURN (Ire) 5-10-12 (7") Miss C O'Neill, (33 to 1) 16
2165⁴ PANTOBEACH (Ire) 7-11-2 (7") Mr Mark Walsh, ... (20 to 1) 17
BALLINAMONA LASS (Ire) 5-10-12 (7") Mr B N Doyle,
. . . . (25 to 1) 18
MASTER BOUNCE (Ire) 6-12-0 Mr A R Coonan, . . . (20 to 1) 19
HARVEST STORM (Ire) 5-10-12 (7") Mr T N Cloke, . . (20 to 1) 20
Dist: 7l, ½l, 3½l, 15l. 4m 15.80s. (20 Ran).

(Mrs H O'Toole), J R Bryce-Smith

HUNTINGDON (good)
Thursday February 6th
Going Correction: PLUS 0.30 sec. per fur.

2526 Glatton Claiming Hurdle Class F (4-y-o and up) £2,230 2m 110yds (1:30)

2296⁸ WILLY STAR (Bel) 7-10-11 (7") R Wilkinson, *trkd ldrs, led appr 2 out, mstk last, drvn out*. . (8 to 1 op 6 to 1 tchd 9 to 1)   1
2149⁵ ONCE MORE FOR LUCK (Ire) 6-11-12 J Osborne, *hld up, not fluent 4th, rdn and hdwy aftr 3 out, chlgd last, unbl to quicken r-in*. . . . .(5 to 2 fav op 7 to 2)   2

2257⁹ EUROTWIST 8-11-2 R Supple, *hld up, hdwy aftr 5th, rdn and styd on one pace betw last 2.*
.................................(6 to 1 op 5 to 1 tchd 7 to 1) 3
1956² PETER MOMAMY (bl) 5-11-6 D Walsh, *trkd ldr, pushed alng aftr 5th, lft second and hmpd 3 out, rdn and kpt on one pace betw last 2.*.......................(5 to 1 op 11 to 4) 4
1349 HIGH LOW (USA) 9-11-8 T Jenks, *led, rdn aftr 3 out, hdd appr nxt, sn wknd.*...................(16 to 1 op 12 to 1) 5
3387² BLUNTSWOOD HALL 4-10-5 Gary Lyons, *trkd ldr, rdn alng 3 out, kpt on one pace.*..........(9 to 1 op 7 to 1 tchd 10 to 1) 6
2307⁶ CIRCUS COLOURS 7-11-6 A Maguire, *hld up mid-div, reminder and pushed alng aftr 5th, no imprsn frm 3 out.*
......................................(12 to 1 op 8 to 1) 7
2387 FIRST GOLD 8-11-6 R Johnson, *chsd ldr, drvn alng aftr 5th, sn wknd.*..................(33 to 1 op 20 to 1) 8
2387⁶ OUR TOM 5-11-3 (5*) Mr R Thornton, *trkd ldr frm 3rd, rdn and wknd aftr 5th.*...............(33 to 1 op 20 to 1) 9
1365⁷ AUTUMN FLAME (Ire) 6-10-11 M Brennan, *beh 4th, nvr rch ldrs.*.......................(33 to 1 op 20 to 1) 10
DOLLIVER (USA) 5-11-2 I Lawrence, *hld up, beh 3rd, al rear.*
......................................(33 to 1 op 14 to 1) 11
1811⁴ AL HAAL (USA) 4-10-2 J Culloty, *prmnt whn blun 3rd, beh 5th, btn whn hit last.*.......(14 to 1 op 16 to 1 tchd 25 to 1) 12
BROUGHTONS RELISH 4-10-4 P Hide, *al beh.*
......................................(33 to 1 op 25 to 1) 13
2390⁷ CLASSIC DELIGHT (USA) 4-10-0 K Gaule, *chsd ldr to 3 out, wknd quickly.*............(33 to 1 op 20 to 1) 14
2390 JUST FLAMENCO 6-11-4 J Ryan, *hld up, beh 3rd, sn lost tch.*
......................................(33 to 1 op 16 to 1) 15
FRIENDLY COAST 11-11-0 B Fenton, *hld up, beh 3rd, sn lost tch, tld off 3 out.*..............(33 to 1 op 20 to 1) 16
1990⁷ EUROLINK THE LAD 10-11-0 D J Burchell, *hld up, steady hdwy aftr 4th, cl second whn f 3 out.*
....................................(9 to 1 op 6 to 1 tchd 10 to 1) f
1599⁴ HAYLING-BILLY 4-10-0 (7*) M Clinton, *hld up, hdwy to chase ldr aftr 5th, sn ev ch, 6th and wknd whn blun and uns rdr 2 out.*
.....................................(16 to 1 op 12 to 1) ur
Dist: 2l, 7l, 8l, 2l, ¾l, 10l, 7l, 18l, nk, 15l. 3m 59.20s. a 18.20s (18 Ran).
(Mrs S Smith), Mrs S J Smith

2527 Whittlesey Novices' Handicap Chase Class D (0-110 5-y-o and up) £4,313 3m.....................................(2:00)

2330² CARIBOO GOLD (USA) [92] (bl) 8-11-1 J Osborne, *hld up, hdwy to track ldrs aftr tenth, led 2 out, styd on wl.* (4 to 1 jt-fav op 7 to 2 tchd 9 to 2) 1
1765⁵ GOLDENSWIFT (Ire) [94] 7-11-3 B Fenton, *hld up, steady hdwy aftr 6 out, ev ch after 2 out, rdn and unbl to quicken.*
......................................(5 to 1 op 6 to 1 tchd 7 to 1) 2
2245 FOXTROT ROMEO [104] 7-11-13 G Bradley, *al prmnt, led tenth to 2 out, unbl to quicken.*
......................................(12 to 1 op 8 to 1 tchd 14 to 1) 3
2280⁵ CLAYMORE LAD [77] 7-10-0 T J Murphy, *led to 7th, led ag'n nxt to tenth, wknd aftr 5 out.*...........(9 to 2 op 3 to 1) 4
1944² BAYLINE STAR (Ire) [96] 7-11-5 J Culloty, *hld up, hdwy aftr 4 out, kpt on one pace.*..........(4 to 1 jt-fav tchd 9 to 2) 5
2216² PAVI'S BROTHER [95] 9-11-4 M Richards, *hld up, hdwy 7 out, styd on one pace.*...................(14 to 1 op 10 to 1) 6
2266⁴ BONNIFER (Ire) [77] 8-10-0 I Lawrence, *hld up, hdwy 8th, blun 12th, sn wknd.*...................(33 to 1 op 16 to 1) 7
2382 RECORD LOVER (Ire) [77] 7-10-0 W Worthington, *lost tch 12th, hit off 4 out.*..............(33 to 1 op 25 to 1) 8
2388⁵ THE MILLMASTER (Ire) [77] 6-10-0 R Supple, *chsd ldrs, wknd aftr 14th, btn whn blun 3 out.*......(33 to 1 op 25 to 1) 9
2291⁴ JAC DEL PRINCE [81] 7-10-4⁴ P Hide, *trkd ldrs to 12th, sn wknd, tld off 4 out.*...........(33 to 1 op 16 to 1) 10
2252⁵ JUST ONE CANALETTO [78] 9-10-11 D Walsh, *chsd ldrs, mstk 4th, blun 11th and nxt, pld up...* (25 to 1 op 16 to 1) pu
2254² UNCLE ALGY [85] 8-10-8 J F Titley, *not fluent, beh tenth, tld off whn pld up bef 2 out.*..........(8 to 1 tchd 10 to 1) pu
2373 STARLIGHT FOOL [79] (bl) 8-10-2² W McFarland, *hld up, lost tch aftr 11th, tld off whn pld up bef 14th.*(33 to 1 op 25 to 1) pu
2266 BASSENHALLY [83] 7-10-6 M Brennan, *lost tch 11th, tld off whn pld up bef 15th....* (20 to 1 op 16 to 1 tchd 25 to 1) pu
1339⁴ THE GO AHEAD (Ire) [90] 7-10-13 A Thornton, *prmnt, wknd quickly aftr 9th, pld up aftr nxt.*
......................................(9 to 1 op 8 to 1 tchd 10 to 1) pu
Dist: 3½l, 1¼l, 15l, 4l, 18l, 6l, 24l, nk, 5l. 6m 17.10s. a 37.10s (15 Ran).
(Mrs Sharon C Nelson), K C Bailey

2528 Sidney Banks Memorial Novices' Hurdle Class B (4-y-o and up) £7,181 2½m 110yds...................(2:30)

1995* AGISTMENT 6-11-4 R Dunwoody, *trkd ldrs, mstk 6th, led 3 out, drvn out nr finish.*
......................................(6 to 5 fav op 11 to 8 tchd 11 to 10) 1
1673⁴ FOREST IVORY (NZ) 6-11-4 A Maguire, *trkd ldr, rdn alng aftr 3 out, mstk and jnd lder nxt, ev ch last, swtchd r-in, kpt on wl nr finish.*....................(11 to 4 op 5 to 2 tchd 3 to 1) 2
2263² EMERALD STATEMENT (Ire) 7-11-4 B Fenton, *hld up, in tch aftr 6th, rdn and outpcd after 3 out, kpt on wl betw last 2, ran on nr finish.*......(9 to 1 op 5 to 1 tchd 13 to 2) 3
2371⁷ CARLITO BRIGANTE 5-11-4 A Thornton, *hld up, hdwy to track ldrs aftr 6th, rdn alng 3 out, sn wknd.*
......................................(9 to 1 op 7 to 1 tchd 10 to 1) 4

2183* SPRING GALE (Ire) 6-11-4 J Osborne, *pressed ldr till rdn and wknd quickly aftr 4 out, tld off.*.......(11 to 2 op 5 to 1) 5
MONKS SOHAM (Ire) 9-11-4 R Johnson, *hld up, effrt and drvn alng 4 out, sn wknd, tld off....*(33 to 1 op 20 to 1) 6
2264 THIRTY BELOW (Ire) 8-11-4 G Upton, *sn last and struggling, tld off aftr 6th.*..............(50 to 1 op 20 to 1) 7
2250² EDREDON BLEU (Fr) 5-11-4 J Culloty, *led to 3 out, wknd quickly aftr 4 out.*.......(14 to 1 op 12 to 1) 8
Dist: Nk, ½l, 20l, dist, 11l, 8l, dist. 4m 49.60s. a 14.60s (8 Ran).
SR: 6/6/5/-/-/   (Marquesa de Moratalla), J G FitzGerald

2529 Farcet Fen Handicap Chase Class D (0-120 5-y-o and up) £3,582 2½m 110yds.....................(3:00)

2459⁴ DISTINCTIVE (Ire) [103] 8-11-3 (6ex) R Dunwoody, *made all, styd on wl frm 3 out.*...........(100 to 30 op 5 to 2) 1
2355² KINGS CHERRY (Ire) [104] 9-11-4 G Upton, *hld up, steady hdwy aftr 5 out, wnt second appr 2 out, no imprsn approaching last.*....................(4 to 1 op 11 to 4) 2
2244⁵ THE LANCER (Ire) [95] 8-10-6 (3*) D Fortt, *hld up and beh, hdwy aftr 6 out, chsd ldr frm 4 out, wknd after nxt.*
......................................(4 to 1 op 7 to 2) 3
2314² FLAPJACK LAD [95] 8-10-9 D Walsh, *pressed ldr, ev ch 5 out, rdn and wknd appr 2 out.*.........(5 to 2 fav tchd 3 to 1) 4
1981 RAMSTOWN LAD (Ire) [86] 8-9-12⁵ (7*) Mr R Wakley, *hld up, lost tch aftr 11th.*........(10 to 1 op 7 to 1 tchd 12 to 1) 5
2308* OXFORD QUILL [86] 10-10-0 D Morris, *trkd ldr, ev ch frm 9th, wknd aftr 12th, 6th and btn whn blun and uns rdr 3 out.*
......................................(14 to 1) ur
PHARSILK (Ire) [110] 8-11-10 P McLoughlin, *in tch till wknd aftr 8th, blun tenth, sn tld off, pld up after 3 out.*
......................................(10 to 1 op 12 to 1 tchd 9 to 1) pu
Dist: 5l, 11l, 8l, 13l. 5m 13.10s. a 26.10s (7 Ran).
(Jeremy Hancock), M J Wilkinson

2530 Huntingdon Gold Card Handicap Hurdle Qualifier Class B (4-y-o and up) £4,799 2m 5f 110yds.....(3:30)

2253* HENRIETTA HOWARD (Ire) [115] 7-10-2 J F Titley, *chsd ldr, pair frm 3rd, ev ch 5 out, led 4 out, styd on wl.*
......................................(5 to 2 fav op 3 to 1) 1
2438² KORBELL (Ire) [113] 8-10-0 R Johnson, *pressed ldr till led aftr 4 out, hdd after 3 out, rdn and styd on, no imprsn betw last 2.*..................(3 to 1 op 5 to 2) 2
2453⁷ TIM (Ire) [115] 7-10-2 J Osborne, *hld up and beh, hdwy aftr 6th, chsd ldrs frm 4 out, wknd appr 2 out.* (9 to 2 op 7 to 1) 3
URON V (Fr) [119] 11-10-6 K Gaule, *chsd ldrs aftr 5th, ev ch 4 out, sn wknd, btn whn hit 2 out.*
......................................(16 to 1 op 12 to 1 tchd 20 to 1) 4
2331⁸ NIJMEGEN [130] 9-11-3 R Dunwoody, *hld up, some hdwy aftr 6th, sn no imprsn.*..........(6 to 1 tchd 11 to 2) 5
1700* MIRADOR [113] 6-10-0 D Morris, *hld up, hdwy aftr 5th, sn wknd.*.........(10 to 1 op 11 to 1 tchd 8 to 1) 6
2329 NON VINTAGE (Ire) [125] 6-10-12 W Worthington, *nvr rch ldrs.*...............(14 to 1 op 12 to 1 tchd 16 to 1) 7
2217 LUCKY BLUE [128] 10-11-1 A Maguire, *led till aftr 4 out, wknd rpdly.*....................(14 to 1 op 12 to 1) 8
2217⁹ DJAIS (Fr) [115] 8-10-2 R Supple, *hld up, rdn alng aftr 6th, sn beh.*......................(16 to 1 tchd 20 to 1) 9
SWEET GLOW (Fr) [137] 10-11-10 D Walsh, *hld up, pushed alng aftr 5th, tld off after 4 out, pld up bef 2 out.*
......................................(14 to 1 op 10 to 1) pu
Dist: 4l, 9l, 1½l, 11l, 8l, 3½l, 7l, 12l. 5m 11.10s. a 22.10s (10 Ran).
(Mrs Solna Thomson Jones), Mrs D Haine

2531 Duck's Cross Novices' Hunters' Chase Class H (5-y-o and up) £1,044 3m.....................................(4:00)

ORCHESTRAL SUITE (Ire) 9-11-7 (7*) Mr F Hutsby, *al hndy, led 5 out, styd on wl frm 2 out....*(2 to 1 fav op 6 to 4) 1
LURRIGA GLITTER (Ire) 9-11-7 (7*) Mr R Wakley, *hld up, hdwy 11th, led 13th to 6 out, rdn and rallied 2 out, not quicken.*
......................................(16 to 1 op 14 to 1 tchd 20 to 1) 2
SYMBOL OF SUCCESS (Ire) (v) 6-11-11 (3*) Mr M Rimell, *hld up, wnt 3rd aftr 4 out, rdn after nxt, styd on one pace.*
......................................(14 to 1 op 12 to 1) 3
STEDE QUARTER 10-11-11 (7*) Mr P Bull, *chsd ldrs, led aftr 12th to nxt, hdwy quickly after 5 out. tld off.*
......................................(10 to 1 op 14 to 1) 4
NO JOKER (Ire) 9-11-7 (7*) Capt R Hall, *mstk 1st, led 3rd to nxt, wkng whn uns rdr 11th.*............(6 to 1 op 4 to 1) ur
AMAZON LILY 10-11-2 (7*) Mr M Gorman, *led 4th to 9th, wkng whn mstk, swrvd and uns rdr 11th.*
......................................(9 to 2 op 4 to 1 tchd 5 to 1) ur
GREEN'S VAN GOYEN (Ire) 9-11-9 (5*) Mr T McCarthy, *led to 3rd, chsd ldrs till wknd aftr 11th, beh whn pld up bef 5 out.*
......................................(3 to 1 tchd 7 to 2) pu
MEDIANE (USA) 12-11-11 (3*) Mr Simon Andrews, *prmnt whn mstk 8th, sn wknd, tld off aftr 12th, pld up 4 out.*
......................................(33 to 1 op 25 to 1) pu
NOT MY LINE (Ire) 8-11-9 (5*) Mr A Sansome, *hdwy 7th, led 9th to 11th, sn wknd, beh whn pld up bef 13th.*
......................................(16 to 1 op 12 to 1) pu

RISING SAP 7-11-7 (7*) Mr A Dalton, *hld up, hdwy 9th, led 11th till aftr 12th, mstk 4 out, wkng whn pld up bef nxt.* .... (10 to 1 op 8 to 1) pu
Dist: 3½l, hd, dist. 6m 27.50s. a 47.50s (10 Ran).
(Exors Of The Late Mr G Pidgeon), Miss Jennifer Pidgeon

2532 Long Stanton Handicap Hurdle Class D (0-120 5-y-o and up) £2,863 2m 110yds........................ (4:30)

1894^{3} MORE DASH THANCASH (Ire) [92] 7-10-5 Derek Byrne, *al prmnt, led 3 out, jmpd rght last, ran on strly.* ....(5 to 1 op 7 to 2) 1
2257^{7} GLANMERIN (Ire) [115] 6-12-0 G Bradley, *in tch, chsd ldrs frm 5th, ev ch 2 out, not quicken appr last.* .... (11 to 1 op 10 to 1 tchd 12 to 1) 2
932^{3} PRIZEFIGHTER [114] 6-11-13 A Maguire, *hld up, hdwy 5th, ev ch 3 out, not quicken betw last 2*.... (9 to 4 fav op 11 to 4) 3
2281^{7} BIGWHEEL BILL (Ire) [87] 8-9-7 (7*) D Yellowlees, *hld up, some hdwy aftr 5th, kpt on one pace*...(14 to 1 op 12 to 1) 4
2149 ANABRANCH [110] 6-11-2 (7*) M Newton, *hld up, rapid hdwy to ld 5th, mstk and hdd 3 out, sn wknd*....(5 to 1 op 9 to 2) 5
241^{5} CHIEFTAIN'S CROWN (USA) [90] 6-10-3 P McLoughlin, *chsd ldrs till rdn and wknd aftr 5th*......... (20 to 1 op 12 to 1) 6
LUCAYAN CAY (Ire) [88] 6-10-1 D Leahy, *chsd ldrs, rdn alng aftr 5th, sn no imprsn*..............(16 to 1 op 14 to 1) 7
STORM FALCON (USA) [95] 7-10-8 J Osborne, *led aftr 1st till after 3rd, wknd after 5th*...(11 to 2 op 5 to 1 tchd 6 to 1) 8
265^{3} GREEN LANE (USA) [110] 9-11-9 J Culloty, *lost pl aftr 3rd, sn tld off*.............................(20 to 1 op 12 to 1) 9
2387^{5} RE ROI (Ire) [99] 5-10-12 R Dunwoody, *hld up, tld off aftr 5th.* .... (10 to 1 op 12 to 1) 10
2331^{3} SEVERN GALE [102] 7-10-8 (7*) X Aizpuru, *led to 1st, led aftr 3rd to 5th, drvn alng 3 out, 6th and btn whn f 2 out.* ....(5 to 1 op 6 to 1 tchd 7 to 1) f
Dist: 4l, 3l, 3l, 2l, 2l, 19l, 1¾l, dist, 15l. 3m 52.00s. a 11.00s (11 Ran).
SR: 16/35/31/1/22/-/ (F J Sainsbury), Mrs Merrita Jones

KELSO (good)
Thursday February 6th
Going Correction: PLUS 0.85 sec. per fur.

2533 Weatherbys Bulletin Magazine Maiden Hurdle Class D (4-y-o and up) £3,022 2m 110yds........ (1:50)

SECRET SERVICE (Ire) 5-11-5 M Foster, *trkd ldrs, hdwy 3 out, effrt nxt, hmpd last, styd on to ld last 100 yards.* ....(6 to 1 op 4 to 1) 1
2236^{5} LUMBACK LADY 7-11-0 B Storey, *cl up, chlgd 2 out, sn rdn, lft in ld last, hdd and no extr last 100 yards.* .... (16 to 1 op 14 to 1) 2
BILLY BUSHWACKER 6-11-5 P Niven, *hld up and not fluent, hdwy to chase ldrs appr 3 out, rdn nxt and kpt on same pace.* .... (11 to 8 fav op 11 to 10 tchd Evens) 3
SWIFT RIPOSTE (Ire) 6-11-5 A Dobbin, *hmpd 1st and beh, smooth hdwy 4th, chsd ldrs nxt, rdn and wknd 2 out, fourth and btn whn hampered last.* .... (11 to 2 op 4 to 1 tchd 6 to 1) 4
2296 JARROW 6-11-0 (5*) Michael Brennan, *prmnt, mstk 4th, rdn alng 3 out and grad wknd*...................... (100 to 1) 5
2346^{9} OBVIOUS RISK 6-10-12 (7*) Tristan Davidson, *nvr rch ldrs.* ....(500 to 1) 6
WESTERN GENERAL 6-11-5 A S Smith, *hld up and beh, nvr rch ldrs*..................(16 to 1 op 14 to 1) 7
2206^{8} SUNSTRIKE 5-11-5 K Jones, *nvr rch ldrs*........ (100 to 1) 8
CHAIN LINE 7-11-2 (3*) Mr C Bonner, *beh till some heaadway frm 2 out, nvr a factor*......................... (300 to 1) 9
POINT DUTY 7-11-5 D Bentley, *chsd ldrs, rdn alng and blun 3 out, sn wknd*.......................................(100 to 1) 10
PEARLS OF THOUGHT (Ire) 4-10-4 K Johnson, *al beh, tld off frm hfwy*.. (100 to 1) 11
1935* CARLISLE BANDITO'S (Ire) 5-11-5 M Moloney, *prmnt, led 5th, rdn alng 2 out, f last*....(3 to 1 op 4 to 1 tchd 9 to 2) f
SOLWAY KING 7-11-0 (5*) S Taylor, *pld hrd, in tch whn f 1st.* ....(100 to 1) f
BROCKVILLE BAIRN 4-10-9 J Supple, *pld hrd, prmnt till rdn and wknd 4th, beh whn pulled up bef 2 out*.........(66 to 1) pu
2344 BLOOD BROTHER 5-10-12 (7*) N Horrocks, *led, hdd 5th and grad wknd, beh whn pld up bef 2 out*............(100 to 1) pu
EVENING DUSK (Ire) 5-11-0 R Garritty, *tld off frm hfwy, pld up bef 2 out*.......................... (50 to 1 op 33 to 1) pu
Dist: 3l, 7l, 19l, 2l, 3½l, 6l, 1¼l, 1¾l, nk, dist. 4m 7.00s. a 24.00s (16 Ran).
(Guy Reed), C W Thornton

2534 Bet With The Tote Novices' Handicap Chase Qualifier Class D (0-110 6-y-o and up) £3,663 3m 1f......... (2:20)

2362 D'ARBLAY STREET (Ire) [72] 8-10-3 P Carberry, *wth ldr, led 14th, clr 3 out, eased flt*.... (8 to 1 op 7 to 1 tchd 9 to 1) 1
2319^{4} ASK ME LATER (Ire) [79] 8-10-10 M Foster, *chsd ldrs, rdn alng 5 out, plugged on one pace*..........(12 to 1 op 10 to 1) 2
2362^{2} TOUGH TEST (Ire) [84] 7-11-1 G Cahill, *led, hdd 14th and sn rdn alng, one pace frm 3 out.* .... (6 to 1 tchd 7 to 1 and 11 to 2) 3
2347 MISTER TRICK (Ire) [78] 7-10-9 R Garritty, *beh, pushed alng and hdwy 13th, chsd ldrs and hit 15th, kpt on one pace frm nxt.* ....(9 to 2 jt-fav op 6 to 1) 4
2258^{6} COOL WEATHER (Ire) [78] (bl) 9-10-9 A S Smith, *chsd leaders, rdn alng 14th, no imprsn*........(12 to 1 op 8 to 1) 5
1681* MAJORITY MAJOR (Ire) [84] 8-10-10 (5*) G F Ryan, *mid-div, hit 4th, pushed alng and beh frm 13th*...(10 to 1 op 8 to 1) 6
2203^{2} KENMARE RIVER (Ire) [72] (bl) 7-10-3 B Storey, *led, rdn alng and hdd 14th, grad wknd frm nxt.* ....(9 to 2 jt-fav op 4 to 1 tchd 5 to 1) 7
1930^{3} MISS LAMPLIGHT [72] 7-10-3 A Dobbin, *al beh, tld off hfwy.* .... (33 to 1 op 25 to 1) 8
2347 MR SLOAN [69] 7-9-11 (3*) G Lee, *rear whn f 11th.* ....(100 to 1 op 200 to 1) 0
2146^{5} NAUGHTY FUTURE [93] 8-11-10 A Roche, *mstks, in tch whn f 12th*.................... (7 to 1 op 8 to 1 tchd 6 to 1) f
2347^{7} QUIXALL CROSSETT [69] 12-9-8^{1} (7*) Tristan Davidson, *al rear, tld off whn blun and uns rdr 14th*..............(200 to 1) ur
1930 CORPORAL KIRKWOOD (Ire) [76] 7-10-7 J Callaghan, *in tch till lost palce and beh frm hfwy, tld off whn pld up bef 3 out.* .... (12 to 1 op 10 to 1) pu
2362 CLASSIC CREST (Ire) [69] (v) 6-10-0^{5} (5*) Michael Brennan, *prmnt till lost pl and beh frm hfwy, tld off whn pld up bef 4 out.* ....(33 to 1) pu
2347 ANSURO AGAIN [78] 8-10-9 P Niven, *not jump wl, al beh, pld up aftr 12th*...................... (12 to 1 tchd 14 to 1) pu
Dist: 11l, 5l, 3l, dist, 3½l, 7l, dist. 6m 28.30s. a 31.30s (14 Ran).
(Green For Luck), W T Kemp

2535 Forresters Handicap Hurdle Class D (0-125 4-y-o and up) £2,745 2¾m 110yds...................... (2:50)

1125* TRIBUNE [94] 6-10-13 M Foster, *made all, hit second, rdn 2 out, ran on wl*................. (5 to 4 fav tchd 11 to 8) 1
TURKISH TOWER [86] 6-10-5 A Dobbin, *trkd wnr frm 3rd, hdwy to chal and hit 2 out, sn rdn and no extr from last.* ....(9 to 4 op 5 to 2 tchd 3 to 1) 2
2321^{6} WILLIE SPARKLE [87] (v) 11-10-6 G Cahill, *lost tch frm 7th, sn tld off*................................ (12 to 1 op 8 to 1) 3
2332 RALITSA (Ire) [105] 5-11-10 R Garritty, *prmnt till pld up aftr 3rd*.................................. (3 to 1 op 2 to 1) pu
Dist: 12l, dist. 5m 40.20s. a 31.20s (4 Ran).
(Hexagon Racing), C W Thornton

2536 Isle Of Skye Blended Scotch Whisky Handicap Chase Class E (0-115 5-y-o and up) £3,241 3m 1f....... (3:20)

DAVY BLAKE [105] 10-11-6 A Dobbin, *made all, lft clr 3 out, styd on wl*.......................(16 to 1 op 14 to 1) 1
1988* OFF THE BRU [87] 12-10-1^{6} (7*) Mr M Bradburne, *chsd ldrs, rdn alng and outpcd 14th, styd on frm 2 out.* ....(6 to 1 op 5 to 1 tchd 7 to 1) 2
2319^{2} SEEKING GOLD (Ire) [92] 8-10-7 B Storey, *al chasing ldrs, rdn alng and outpcd 14th, lft second and no imprsn 3 out.* ....(11 to 4 op 5 to 2) 3
2488* CELTIC SILVER [98] 9-10-13 (6ex) Richard Guest, *hld up, hdwy 12th, pushed alng to chase ldrs 14th, hmpd 3 out, no ch aftr*................. (9 to 4 fav op 2 to 1 tchd 5 to 2) 4
2203 JENDEE (Ire) [85] 9-10-0 K Johnson, *chsd ldrs, hit 3rd, outpcd frm 14th*..................................(16 to 1) 5
ACAJOU III (Fr) [110] 9-11-11 P Carberry, *chsd ldrs, wth wnr frm 4th, gng wl whn f 3 out.* (9 to 2 op 6 to 1 tchd 7 to 1) f
2189 SIDE OF HILL [91] 12-10-3 (3*) G Lee, *in tch, blun 11th, outpcd and lost touch 14th, tld off whn pld up bef 3 out.* .... (33 to 1 op 25 to 1) pu
2203 THE TOASTER [95] 10-10-10 A S Smith, *al rear, rdn alng 12th, tld off whn pld up bef 3 out*...............(33 to 1) pu
STONEY BURKE (Ire) [100] 8-11-1 M Foster, *sn beh, tld off whn pld up 13th*.......(14 to 1 op 12 to 1 tchd 16 to 1) pu
Dist: 11l, sht-hd, 12l, 16l. 6m 30.50s. a 33.50s (9 Ran).
(T N Dalgetty), T N Dalgetty

2537 Beltane Partners Handicap Hurdle Class E (0-115 4-y-o and up) £2,316 2m 110yds................... (3:50)

2190^{4} INGLETONIAN [105] 8-11-7 B Storey, *made all, rdn appr last, styd on gmely*.....................(6 to 1 op 5 to 1) 1
2122^{2} FLYAWAY BLUES [93] 5-10-9 P Niven, *hld up. steady hdwy 3 out, rdn last and ev ch, kpt on nr finish*...........(4 to 1 jt-fav tchd 9 to 2) 2
SUMMERHILL SPECIAL (Ire) [112] 6-12-0 Richard Guest, *hld up in rear, gd hdwy 3 out, ev ch last, rdn and no extr last 100 yards*.. (50 to 1) 3
2332* DUAL IMAGE [110] 10-11-12 P Carberry, *hld up in tch, hdwy 3 out, rdn nxt and sn one pace*.... (4 to 1 jt-fav tchd 9 to 2) 4
1635^{8} COOL LUKE (Ire) [100] 8-10-11 (5*) Michael Brennan, *in tch, hdwy to chase wnr 3 out, rdn nxt and sn wknd.* ....(6 to 1 tchd 7 to 1) 5
2316^{3} ADAMATIC (Ire) [98] 6-10-7 (7*) S Melrose, *hld up, hdwy appr 3 out, ev ch nxt, sn rdn and btn*.........(6 to 1 op 5 to 1) 6

2357* MAPLE BAY (Ire) [91] 8-10-7 (7ex) K Johnson, *hld up in rear, effrt appr 3 out and no hdwy.*
..........................(11 to 2 op 5 to 1 tchd 6 to 1) 7
1786⁴ HEE'S A DANCER [98] 5-11-0 M Foster, *chsd ldrs till rdn appr 3 out and sn wknd*...............................(12 to 1) 8
1823 VINTAGE RED [97] 7-10-3 A Dobbin, *in tch on inner till rdn and wknd appr 3 out*..........................(25 to 1) 9
GOING PUBLIC [95] 10-10-11 A S Smith, *chsd ldrs till rdn and wknd bef 3 out*...................(40 to 1 op 33 to 1) 10
2359 RUBISLAW [84] (v) 5-9-7 (7*) Miss S Lamb, *prmnt till rdn and wknd appr 3 out*...................(200 to 1) 11
Dist: Nk, 1¼l, 7l, 1¼l, 21l, 4l, 4l, 3l, 1½l, 17l. 4m 3.90s. a 20.90s (11 Ran).
SR: 24/12/29/20/8/-/   (Mrs Hilary Mactaggart), B Mactaggart

2538 Moet & Chandon Novices' Hurdle Class D (4-y-o and up) £2,996 2¾m 110yds.......................... (4:20)

2123³ MEADOW HYMN (Ire) 6-11-4 P Niven, *chsd ldrs, pushed alng and outpcd appr 3 out, styd on to chal and hit nxt, sn led, drvn flt and ran on wl*.........................(7 to 1 op 5 to 1) 1
1591⁵ GROSVENOR (Ire) 6-11-4 P Carberry, *hld up and beh, steady hdwy 7th, hit 3 out and pushed alng, headway to chal nxt and ev ch till drvn and no extr flt.*
...................................(9 to 4 fav op 11 to 4 tchd 3 to 1) 2
2346² SMIDDY LAD 6-11-4 D Bentley, *in tch, hdwy 7th, effrt 2 out and ev ch last, sn drvn and wknd nr finish.*
.........................(9 to 2 op 4 to 1 tchd 5 to 1) 3
2316² SUPREME SOVIET 7-11-4 A Dobbin, *trkd ldrs, hdwy to ld 7th, rdn alng and hdd 3 out, wknd nxt.*
.........................(4 to 1 op 3 to 1 tchd 9 to 2) 4
2192⁴ MALTA MAN (Ire) 7-11-4 A S Smith, *cl up, led 3 out till blun nxt and sn hdd, wknd und pres last*...........(7 to 2 op 11 to 4) 5
2200 LIAM'S LOSS (Ire) 8-11-4 V Smith, *nvr rch ldrs*...(200 to 1) 6
2260⁸ BOYZONTOOWA (Ire) 5-11-4 Richard Guest, *pld hrd, prmnt till rdn alng and wknd 7th*........................(100 to 1) 7
STEPDAUGHTER 11-10-13 L O'Hara, *prmnt till pushed alng and lost pl hfwy*.................................(100 to 1) 8
ROYAL RANK (USA) 7-11-4 K Johnson, *beh frm hfwy.*
....(100 to 1) 9
2187 WEEJUMPAWUD 7-10-13 Mr C Storey, *made most to 7th, sn lost pl and beh*...........................(200 to 1) 10
2288 PERSIAN GRANGE (Ire) 7-11-4 J Burke, *in tch till rdn alng and f 7th*...........................(100 to 1 op 50 to 1) f
1677⁴ PAPPA CHARLIE (USA) 6-11-4 B Storey, *f second.*
.........................(12 to 1 tchd 14 to 1) f
RYE RUM (Ire) 6-11-4 M Moloney, *al rear, tld off whn pld up bef 7th*.............................(200 to 1) pu
Dist: 4l, 9l, ½l, 3½l, dist, nk, 11l, dist, 17l. 5m 49.70s. a 40.70s (13 Ran).
SR: -/-/-/-/-/-/   (Mrs M Nowell), J G FitzGerald

WINCANTON (good to firm)
Thursday February 6th
Going Correction: PLUS 0.45 sec. per fur.

2539 Hoechst Roussel Panacur European Breeders Fund Mares' 'National Hunt' Novices' Hurdle Qualifier (5-y-o and up) £2,784 2¾m...... (1:40)

2032² GALATASORI JANE (Ire) 7-10-10 (7*) L Cummins, *trkd ldrs, led 7th, clr aftr 3 out, rdn nxt, drvn out*...........(2 to 1 jt-fav op 3 to 1) 1
1479⁷ TREMPLIN (Ire) 6-10-10 J R Kavanagh, *in tch, hdwy 7th, chsd ldr 3 out, effrt und pres frm nxt, no extr r-in*......(2 to 1 jt-fav op 6 to 4 tchd 9 to 4) 2
2242 WIN I DID (Ire) 7-10-7 (3*) P Henley, *beh whn hit 6th, not fluent aftr, hdwy 3 out, one pace and not a danger aftr.*
.........................(11 to 1 op 8 to 1 tchd 12 to 1) 3
1369⁹ BEL-DE-MOOR 5-10-10 W Marston, *chsd ldrs till rdn and wknd 3 out*.........................(33 to 1 op 25 to 1) 4
1670 DUNNICKS COUNTRY 7-10-3 (7*) M Griffiths, *led second to 5th, wknd 7th, tld off*...............(50 to 1 op 33 to 1) 5
2394⁸ DAYDREAM BELIEVER 5-10-10 P Holley, *in tch, rdn appr 7th, sn wknd, tld off*..................(33 to 1 op 25 to 1) 6
2288⁸ SPARKLING BUCK 5-10-10 J A McCarthy, *led to second, led 5th to 7th, wknd quickly 3 out, tld off.*
.........................(100 to 30 op 5 tchd 7 to 2) 7
1560⁹ CASTLE LYNCH (Ire) 5-10-10 S McNeill, *beh 5th, tld off.*
.........................(25 to 1 op 14 to 1) 8
2248 JOYFUL PABS 6-10-10 R Greene, *tld off 5th.*
.........................(50 to 1 op 33 to 1) 9
GAY TIME 5-10-3 (7*) Mr S Durack, *tld off 5th.*
.........................(20 to 1 op 16 to 1) 10
2263 FORTUNES GLEAM (Ire) 6-10-10 C Maude, *tld off 5th, pld up bef 7th*...........................(33 to 1 op 20 to 1) pu
1810 QUEEN OF THE SUIR (Ire) 8-10-5 (5*) Sophie Mitchell, *beh 3rd, tld off whn pld up bef 3 out*......(50 to 1 op 33 to 1) pu
2243 CAMILLAS LEGACY 6-10-10 D Gallagher, *mstk 4th, lost tch nxt, tld off whn pld up bef 2 out*........(33 to 1 op 25 to 1) pu
WESTWOOD TREAT 5-10-5 (5*) D Salter, *tld off 5th, pld up bef 7th*...........................(33 to 1 op 25 to 1) pu
Dist: 1¼l, dist, 3½l, 1¼l, 29l, 1¾l, 14l, 3l. 5m 24.00s. a 18.00s (14 Ran).
SR: 8/6/-/-/-/-/   (B L Blinman), P F Nicholls

2540 Bet With The Tote Novices' Chase Qualifier Class D (6-y-o and up) £3,680 2m 5f................. (2:10)

2354⁷ KOO'S PROMISE 6-10-9 (3*) T Dascombe, *outpcd 9th, cld on ldrs 11th, drvn to ld 3 out, ran on wl.*
.........................(9 to 1 op 7 to 1 tchd 10 to 1) 1
2328 AFTER THE FOX 10-10-10 B Powell, *chlgd 4th, in clr second pl at 7th, chald tenth, led nxt, rdn and hdd 3 out, sn btn.*
.........................(15 to 8 op 5 to 2) 2
2391² PALOSANTO (Ire) 7-11-3 C Maude, *led hit 7th, rdn tenth, hdd nxt, blun and drpd 3rd 12th, f next.* (2 to 1 on op 5 to 2 on) f
Dist: 4l. 5m 30.90s. a 26.90s (3 Ran).
(G A Warren Limited), C L Popham

2541 Premiere 'National Hunt' Auction Novices' Hurdle Class B Guaranteed minimum value £17,500 (5,6,7-y-o) £12,200 2¾m................. (2:40)

2315⁴ LUCIA FORTE 6-10-11 J Railton, *hld up and wl beh, smooth hdwy aftr 3 out, quickened to chal nxt, sn led, drvn out.*
.........................(4 to 1 jt-fav op 3 to 1 tchd 9 to 2) 1
1759⁵ LADY PETA (Ire) 7-11-11 J R Kavanagh, *hld up, hdwy 7th, chlgd on bit frm 2 out, rdn nxt, no extr and wnt flt und pres r-in*...........................(13 to 2 op 9 to 2) 2
2350⁶ BARBARY FALCON 7-10-9 C Maude, *keen hold, chsd ldrs till rdn and outpcd aftr 3 out, styd on und pres appr last.*
.........................(33 to 1 op 16 to 1) 3
1505³ DACELO (Fr) 6-10-12 J A McCarthy, *in tch, chsd ldrs 3 out, ev ch appr nxt, sn outpcd...(11 to 1 op 7 to 1 tchd 12 to 1) 4
1592⁴ MILLERSFORD 6-11-4 D Gallagher, *in tch, chlgd and mstk 3 out, slight ld nxt, sn hdd and wknd......(5 to 1 op 7 to 2) 5
2277 SUPREME CHARM (Ire) 5-10-6 S McNeill, *chsd ldr to 3 out, rdn and rallied appr nxt, sn wknd.*
.........................(5 to 1 op 8 to 1 tchd 10 to 1) 6
2153⁵ SILVER THYNE (Ire) 5-11-4 N Williamson, *jmpd slwly and rear 1st, hdwy 5th, rdn 7th, sn wknd...(4 to 1 jt-fav tchd 5 to 1) 7
2374³ THE BREWMASTER (Ire) 5-10-12 B Powell, *led till hdd and wknd appr 2 out*...................(12 to 1 tchd 14 to 1) 8
2264⁹ CYPHRATIS (Ire) 6-11-1 W Marston, *mstk 3rd, hdwy nxt, rdn and wknd 7th*.....................(14 to 1 op 8 to 1) 9
800⁸ REGAL GEM (Ire) 6-10-4 R Farrant, *hdwy 6th, wknd quickly aftr 3 out*...................(50 to 1 op 20 to 1) 10
2243 ONE FOR NAVIGATION (Ire) 5-10-6 D Bridgwater, *trkd ldrs, str chal 3 out till wknd appr nxt, pld up bef last.*
.........................(14 to 1 op 8 to 1 tchd 16 to 1) pu
Dist: 1¼l, 6l, 6l, 1l, 5l, 5l, 2l, dist, 18l. 5m 23.60s. a 17.60s (11 Ran).
SR: 6/18/-/-/-/-/   (Mrs Lucia Farmer), K C Bailey

2542 Racing In Wessex Chase Class B (5-y-o and up) £6,612 2m 5f..... (3:10)

2325⁶ CHALLENGER DU LUC (Fr) (bl) 7-12-0 C Maude, *hld up and confidently rdn, hdwy on bit to cl with ldrs frm 4 out, chlgd 2 out, led last, very easily*........ (3 to 1 on op 4 to 1 on) 1
2204³ BEATSON (Ire) 8-11-6 B Powell, *trkd ldr, jmpd slwly 3rd, chlgd frm 6th, led 8th to last, sn btn.*
.........................(11 to 4 op 7 to 2 tchd 3 to 1) 2
2308⁴ CHANNEL PASTIME 13-11-6 Guy Lewis, *led to 8th, styd pressing ldr to 3 out, one pace nxt.....(25 to 1 op 14 to 1) 3
2244 FENWICK 10-11-6 T Dascombe, *in 3rd pl to 11th, sn lost tch.*
.........................(25 to 1 op 14 to 1) 4
Dist: 5l, 2l, 26l. 5m 30.90s. a 26.90s (4 Ran).
(D A Johnson), M C Pipe

2543 Gillingham Handicap Hurdle Class D (0-125 4-y-o and up) £2,826 2m................................. (3:40)

NORTHERN STARLIGHT [99] 6-10-3 C Maude, *made all, sn clr, unchlgd*...........................(9 to 2 op 7 to 2) 1
GOLDINGO [104] 10-10-8 J R Kavanagh, *rcd in 3rd, hdwy to chase ldr appr 2 out, no imprsn*..........(7 to 1 op 5 to 1) 2
2323⁵ HAY DANCE [109] 6-10-13 N Williamson, *hld up chasing clr ldr, lost second appr 2 out, sn btn.*
.........................(13 to 8 on op 5 to 4 on) 3
KEEP ME IN MIND (Ire) [108] 8-10-12 D Skyrme, *rcd in 4th, no ch whn rdn and hng badly lft appr 2 out.* (6 to 1 op 4 to 1) 4
2442⁸ ROS CASTLE [124] 6-11-7 (7*) J Harris, *reluctant to race, sn tld off*...........................(25 to 1 op 8 to 1) 5
Dist: 9l, 7l, 20l, dist. 3m 46.00s. a 12.00s (5 Ran).
SR: 27/23/21/-/-/   (Arthur Souch), M C Pipe

2544 Somerset Hunters' Chase Class H (6-y-o and up) £1,119 3m 1f 110yds................................. (4:10)

DOUBLE SILK 13-12-10 (3*) Mr R Treloggen, *led second, made nxt, drew readily clr frm 4 out.*
.........................(5 to 1 on op 15 to 8 on) 1
VISAGA 11-12-6 (7*) Mr S Lloyd, *led to second, chlgd 8th, hit 12th, chald nxt, chsd wnr till appr 3 out, wnt second at last, one pace*.........................(5 to 1 op 4 to 1) 2
SONOFAGIPSY 13-12-6 (7*) Mr R Nuttall, *in 3rd most of way, rdn frm 14th, no ch*....................(6 to 1 op 5 to 1) 3

FURRY KNOWE 12-12-6 (7") Mr D Pritchard, *mstks 3rd and 4th, hit 8th, hdwy and hit nxt, fourth and in tch whn f 11th.*
.......................(66 to 1 op 25 to 1 tchd 100 to 1)   f
UPHAM CLOSE 11-11-7 (7") Mrs A Hand, *wl beh 12th, hdwy 16th, chsd wnr 3 out to nxt, 3rd and wkng whn f last.*
.......................(11 to 1 op 8 to 1 tchd 12 to 1)   f
JUPITER MOON 8-12-3 (7") Mr R Hicks, *un beh, tld off 9th, pld up bef 12th.*.......................(20 to 1 tchd 25 to 1)   pu
Dist: 16l, 2l. 6m 56.00s. a 40.00s (6 Ran).

(R C Wilkins), R C Wilkins

2545 Wincanton Standard Open Claiming National Hunt Flat Class H (4,5,6-y-o) £1,150 2m.............. (4:40)

2179[8] SOCIETY TIMES (USA) 4-10-6 C Maude, *keen hold, wth ldr frm 5 fs out, slight ld on bit from 3 out, very easily.*
.......................(11 to 4 op 2 to 1)   1
1802[7] KYLAMI (NZ) 5-11-7 R Greene, *led to 3 fs out, kpt on und pres but no ch wth wnr.*......(11 to 4 op 5 to 2 tchd 7 to 2)   2
GOLDEN LILY 4-10-2 (7") L Reynolds, *hdwy to chase ldrs aftr 7 fs, one pace und pres frm 3 out.*.......(9 to 2 op 9 to 4)   3
COUNTRY COUSIN 5-11-4 D Bridgwater, *beh, hdwy 5 fs out, hrd rdn and one pace frm 3 out.*
.........(5 to 2 fav op 2 to 1 tchd 7 to 4 and 11 to 4)   4
1357[7] BOOZYS DREAM 6-10-12 (3") Guy Lewis, *hdwy hfwy, wknd 5 fs out, tld off.*.......................(33 to 1 op 16 to 1)   5
2248 SPLASH OF BLAKENEY 6-10-5 (5") D Salter, *chsd ldrs ten fs, sn wknd, tld off.*.......(40 to 1 op 20 to 1 tchd 50 to 1)   6
1809 THAT MAN CARTER (Ire) 6-11-3 (5") S Ryan, *chsd ldrs to hfwy, wknd 5 fs out, tld off.* (8 to 1 op 7 to 1 tchd 12 to 1)   7
Dist: 4l, 2l, 6l, dist, 6l, 7l. 3m 49.90s. (7 Ran).

(M C Pipe), M C Pipe

BANGOR (good)
Friday February 7th
Going Correction: PLUS 0.45 sec. per fur.

2546 European Breeders Fund 'National Hunt' Novices' Hurdle Qualifier Class E (5,6,7-y-o) £2,836 2m 1f .... (1:45)

2260[3] DARAKSHAN (Ire) 5-11-0 J Culloty, *trkd ldrs gng wl, led betw last 2, ran on und pres.*.......................(7 to 4 op 2 to 1)   1
GODS SQUAD 5-11-0 R Supple, *prmnt, led appr 2 out, hdd betw last two, ev ch till no extr aftr last.*
.......................(7 to 1 op 6 to 1 tchd 8 to 1)   2
2243[5] ST MELLION DRIVE 7-11-0 D Walsh, *mstks, led bit hdd appr 2 out, rdn and grad wknd.*......(5 to 4 fav tchd 6 to 4)   3
ALTHREY PLOT (Ire) 6-11-0 S McNeill, *hld up, hdwy hfwy, chasing ldrs 3 out, sn wknd.*.........(20 to 1 op 10 to 1)   4
1893 MARKET MAYHEM 7-10-9 (5") Michael Brennan, *in tch, drvn alng aftr 3 out, fdd.*......(12 to 1 op 7 to 1 tchd 14 to 1)   5
2255 SLEAZEY (bl) 6-11-0 S Curran, *in tch, hdwy to chase ldrs hfwy, wknd quickly aftr 3 out, tld off.*.............(50 to 1)   6
1949[5] THE EENS 5-11-0 R Garritty, *in tch till wknd bef 3 out, tld off.*.......................(33 to 1 op 25 to 1)   7
FRED FUGGLES 5-10-9 (5") O Burrows, *beh most of way, tld off.*.......................(50 to 1)   8
2116[5] GAZANALI (Ire) 6-11-0 N Bentley, *hld up, lost tch frm bef 3 out, tld off.*.......................(16 to 1 op 14 to 1)   9
1642 COUNTESS MILLIE 5-10-9 S Wynne, *f 1st.*.......(100 to 1)   f
2008 JUST ONE QUESTION (Ire) 7-11-0 P Niven, *prmnt till wknd quickly aftr 6th, beh whn pld up bef 2 out.*
.......................(16 to 1 op 14 to 1)   pu
1729 ALTHREY GALE (Ire) 6-11-0 T Eley, *al beh, lost tch frm 6th, tld off whn pld up bef 2 out.*.......(100 to 1)   pu
Dist: 2l, 14l, ½l, 3½l, 27l, 1½l, 8l, 14l. 4m 3.80s. a 13.80s (12 Ran).
SR: 25/23/9/8/4/-/   (Michael H Watt), Miss H C Knight

2547 Edward Symmons Hotel & Leisure Novices' Handicap Chase Class D (0-110 5-y-o and up) £3,745 2m 1f 110yds...................... (2:20)

2420[3] SAYMORE [76] 11-10-0 S Wynne, *in tch, blun 9th, sn chasing ldrs, ch whn hmpd and swtchd r-in, jst fld, fnshd second, awarded race.*.......................(33 to 1 op 20 to 1)   1
1741 JACK DOYLE (Ire) [94] 6-11-4 P Niven, *hld up, hdwy to ld aftr 3 out, rdn and edgd rght r-in, jst held on, fnshd 1st, plcd second.*.......................(14 to 1 op 10 to 1)   2
1805 LATEST THYNE (Ire) [90] 7-11-0 A Thornton, *chsd ldrs, disputing ld whn blun 2 out, rallied appr last, kpt on wl.*
.......................(16 to 1 op 12 to 1)   3
1605[2] WHIRLY (Ire) [95] 8-11-5 S McNeill, *trkd ldrs, ev ch 3 out, fdd.*.......................(11 to 2 op 9 to 2 tchd 6 to 1)   4
2311[8] BURNTWOOD MELODY [76] 6-10-0 P McLoughlin, *beh, some late hdwy, nvr dngrs.*.......................(50 to 1)   5
1577[5] GLENDOE (Ire) [84] 6-10-8 L Harvey, *mid-div, mstk 7th, wknd aftr 3 out.*.......(14 to 1 op 8 to 1)   6
2244* INDIAN ARROW (NZ) [100] 9-11-10 D Walsh, *made most till hdd aftr 3 out, sn wknd.*
.......................(9 to 4 fav op 11 to 4 tchd 3 to 1)   7

2253 CAWARRA BOY [98] 9-11-8 Mr E James, *nvr dngrs.*
.......................(20 to 1 op 16 to 1)   8
2304[2] MR BEAN [92] 7-11-2 A Larnach, *nvr better than mid-div.*
.......................(16 to 1 op 12 to 1)   9
2204[5] SHAHGRAM (Ire) [86] 9-10-10 R Supple, *nvr dngrs.*
.......................(14 to 1 op 12 to 1 tchd 16 to 1)   10
2119[2] DEVILRY [93] 7-11-3 T Eley, *blun 6th, sn lost tch, tld off.*
.......................(20 to 1 op 16 to 1)   11
2304 BOLD ACRE [80] 7-10-4 J Culloty, *in tch to 7th, wl beh whn pld up bef 3 out.*.......................(9 to 1 op 7 to 1)   pu
1722[2] RACHAEL'S OWEN [80] 7-10-4 M Richards, *beh frm hfwy, tld off whn pld up bef 2 out.*.......(14 to 1 op 14 to 1)   pu
2297 SIGMA RUN (Ire) [81] (v) 8-10-0 (5") Michael Brennan, *chsd ldrs, blun 7th, wknd aftr 9th, beh whn pld up bef 2 out.*
.......................(9 to 1 op 8 to 1)   pu
2352[2] ROBINS PRIDE (Ire) [100] 7-11-7 (3") T Dascombe, *dsptd ld till wknd quickly aftr 3 out, pld up bef nxt.*
.......................(16 to 1 op 14 to 1 tchd 20 to 1)   pu
Dist: Sht-hd, 1¼l, 19l, 7l, nk, 2l, 2½l, 2½l, 1½l, dist. 4m 30.60s. a 28.60s (15 Ran).

(P Morris & G Evans), W Clay

2548 Bermans Handicap Hurdle Class E (0-110 4-y-o and up) £3,517 2m 1f .... (2:50)

2329 NASHVILLE STAR (USA) [92] (v) 6-11-4 A Thornton, *made most, styd on wl und pres frm 2 out.*
.......................(7 to 1 op 6 to 1 tchd 15 to 2 and 8 to 1)   1
2403[4] KADARI [88] (v) 8-10-11 (3") Guy Lewis, *in tch, effrt aftr 3 out, ch nxt, styd on frm last.*...(15 to 2 op 6 to 1 tchd 8 to 1)   2
2417* RUSSIAN RASCAL (Ire) [102] 4-11-4 (3ex) R Garritty, *hld up, hdwy bef 3 out, rdn aftr nxt, kpt on same pace.*
.......................(7 to 4 on op 13 to 8 on)   3
2204 SHIFTING MOON [79] (bl) 5-10-5 S Wynne, *prmnt till wknd aftr 2 out.*.......................(8 to 1 op 7 to 1 tchd 9 to 1)   4
2407 ALASKAN HEIR [84] 6-10-10 T Eley, *beh and drvn alng aftr 4th, kpt on frm 2 out, nvr able to chal.* (25 to 1 op 16 to 1)   5
NIPPER REED [98] 7-11-10 P McLoughlin, *prmnt, led 5th, sn hdd, wknd quickly bef 3 out, tld off.*
.......................(15 to 2 op 8 to 1 tchd 10 to 1)   6
2252 HOUGHTON [95] 11-11-0 (7") Mr R Burton, *beh frm hfwy, tld off.*.......................(33 to 1 op 25 to 1)   7
Dist: 2½l, 1¼l, 6l, 3½l, dist, 9l. 4m 4.60s. a 14.60s (7 Ran).
SR: 21/14/16/-/   (Robin Mathew), R Mathew

2549 Old Hall Estates Handicap Chase Class E (0-115 6-y-o and up) £4,630 3¾m.................................. (3:20)

1734* CERIDWEN [80] 7-10-0 N Mann, *hld up, hdwy to join ldrs 16th, led 2 out, styd on wl.*
.......................(9 to 2 op 5 to 1 tchd 11 to 2 and 6 to 1)   1
2388[4] LOCH GARMAN HOTEL (Ire) [81] 8-10-1 R Supple, *nvr far away, slight ld 18th till hdd 2 out, no extr und pres.*
.......................(7 to 1 op 5 to 1)   2
2245 ANYTHINGYOULIKE [87] 8-10-7 M Richards, *hld up, took clr order 16th, sn chasing ldrs, kpt on same pace frm 2 out.*
.......................(20 to 1)   3
2427 THREE SAINTS (Ire) [96] 8-11-2 S Wynne, *trkd ldrs, rdn aftr 16th, sn wknd.*.......(8 to 1 op 7 to 1 tchd 9 to 1)   4
2434* BANNTOWN BILL (Ire) [99] (v) 8-11-5 (4ex) D Walsh, *prmnt, led 17th, mstk and hdd nxt, sn wknd.* (9 to 4 fav op 6 to 4)   5
2268[8] KEANO (Ire) [93] 8-10-13 G Tormey, *made most till hdd 17th, wkng whn blun nxt, tld off.*.......(6 to 1 op 5 to 1)   6
2393[7] CLAXTON GREENE [97] 13-11-3 D Gallagher, *in tch, mstk 13th, sn drvn alng and lost touch, tld off whn pld up bef 16th.*.......................(25 to 1 op 14 to 1)   pu
2306[4] CELTIC TOWN [104] (bl) 9-11-10 J A McCarthy, *mstk 3rd, beh frm 13th, tld off whn pld up bef 18th.*...(14 to 1 op 10 to 1)   pu
2254 PENNANT COTTAGE (Ire) [84] 9-10-4* Mr A Mitchell, *blun 6th and 7th, lost tch and pld up bef 9th.*...(66 to 1 op 50 to 1)   pu
Dist: 5l, 5l, 23l, 6l, 25l. 8m 10.40s. a 60.40s (9 Ran).

(Mrs S Greathead), T R Greathead

2550 TBR Construction Novices' Handicap Hurdle Class E (0-105 4-y-o and up) £3,004 2½m............. (3:50)

2372[6] MILLING BROOK [76] 5-10-0 S Wynne, *trkd ldrs, led quickened aftr 8th, clr 2 out, rdn r-in, jst hld on.*
.......................(16 to 1 op 12 to 1)   1
874[3] VALLINGALE (Ire) [85] 6-10-9 J Culloty, *in tch, hdwy aftr 3 out, styd on wl und pres frm last, jst fld.*
.......................(7 to 1 op 6 to 1 tchd 8 to 1)   2
60[5] MRS ROBINSON (Ire) [76] 6-9-11 (3") E Husband, *in tch, drvn alng and hdwy aftr 3 out, styd on wl und pres frm nxt.*
.......................(20 to 1 op 16 to 1)   3
2372[7] LOTHIAN COMMANDER [78] 5-10-2 D Walsh, *al prmnt, drvn alng bef 7th, chsd wnr frm aftr 8th, kpt on wl from last.*
.......................(16 to 1 op 14 to 1 tchd 20 to 1)   4
2249[4] DONT FORGET CURTIS (Ire) [88] 5-10-12 J Callaghan, *beh, hdwy aftr 7th, no headway frm nxt.*...(15 to 2 op 10 to 1)   5
2315[8] SCALLY HICKS [76] 6-10-0 T Eley, *beh, some late hdwy, nvr dngrs.*.......................(66 to 1 op 33 to 1)   6

1521* ANGLESEY SEA VIEW [104] 8-12-0 T Kent, *beh, hdwy into midfield aftr 5th, effrt aftr 8th, sn btn* . . . .(9 to 2 jt-fav op 5 to 1 tchd 11 to 2)   7

2296³ RARE OCCURANCE [80] 7-9-13 (5*) Michael Brennan, *mid-div till wknd aftr 8th* . . . .(7 to 1 op 6 to 1)   8

1995⁶ AUT EVEN (Ire) [96] 7-11-6 A Thornton, *in tch till wknd bef 8th.* . . . .(9 to 2 jt-fav op 4 to 1 tchd 5 to 1)   9

2263 BAYERD (Ire) [97] (bl) 6-11-7 J A McCarthy, *led till hdd aftr 8th, wknd quickly, tld off* . . . .(20 to 1 op 14 to 1)   10

2252 CONEY ROAD [76] (v) 8-10-0 D Gallagher, *not jump wl, chsd ldrs till wknd aftr 7th, tld off whn pld up bef 2 out.* . . . . (16 to 1 op 12 to 1)   pu

2236⁸ CRABBIE'S PRIDE [87] (bl) 4-9-11 (3*) F Leahy, *in tch, drvn alng aftr 7th, sn wknd, tld off whn pld up bef 2 out.* . . . . (16 to 1 op 12 to 1)   pu

2277 LIBERTARIAN (Ire) [90] 7-11-0 M Richards, *hld up, steady hdwy frm hfwy, mid-div whn pld up bef 2 out.* . . . . (11 to 1 op 8 to 1 tchd 12 to 1)   pu

1922 CROWN AND CUSHION [87] 4-10-0 N Mann, *al beh, tld off whn pld up bef 3 out.* . . . .(20 to 1 op 14 to 1)   pu

1260 LASTOFTHEIDIOTS [76] 8-9-11 (3*) R Massey, *chsd ldr to 5th, wknd quickly, tld off whn pld up bef 7th.* . . . . (100 to 1 op 50 to 1)   pu

Dist: Hd, nk, ¾l, 25l, 1l, hd, 8l, 24l, dist. 4m 54.90s. a 24.90s (15 Ran).
(Martyn James), J M Bradley

2551 Gilbert Cotton Memorial Hunters' Chase Class H (6-y-o and up) £1,530 2½m 110yds. . . . . (4:20)

INCH MAID 11-11-9 (7*) Miss H Brookshaw, *hld up, hdwy aftr 6th, led 3 out, styd on wl.* (10 to 1 op 8 to 1 tchd 12 to 1)   1

LORD RELIC (NZ) 11-12-0 (7*) Mr R Ford, *trkd ldrs, led 8th till hdd 3 out, chsd wnr aftr, no imprsn.* . . . .(7 to 2 op 3 to 1 tchd 4 to 1)   2

MY NOMINEE (bl) 9-12-0 (7*) Mr R Burton, *prmnt, led 7th to 8th, wknd aftr 12th, tld off* . . . . (5 to 2 jt-fav op 3 to 1)   3

DRIVING FORCE (bl) 11-12-4 (3*) Mr M Rimell, *led 6th to 7th, drvn alng aftr tenth, sn wknd, tld off.* . . . . (8 to 1 tchd 9 to 1 and 10 to 1)   4

1009⁴ NATIVE RAMBLER (Ire) 7-11-7 (7*) Miss E James, *towards rear whn f 5th* . . . .(50 to 1)   f

SPY'S DELIGHT 11-11-7 (7*) Mr E Woolley, *blun and uns rdr second* . . . .(33 to 1 op 25 to 1)   ur

KING OF SHADOWS 10-11-7 (7*) Mr S Prior, *beh whn brght dwn 5th* . . . .(20 to 1 op 14 to 1)   bd

PALM READER 13-12-0 (7*) Mr C J B Barlow, *sn wl beh, tld off whn pld up bef tenth.* . . . .(33 to 1)   pu

KINO 10-12-0 (7*) Mr Andrew Martin, *led to 4th, wknd aftr 7th, lost tch and pld up bef 9th* . . . . (33 to 1)   pu

MY YOUNG MAN 12-12-0 (7*) Mr E James, *led 4th to 6th, lost tch bef tenth, tld off whn pld up before 3 out.* . . . . . . (5 to 2 jt-fav op 2 to 1)   pu

BARKISLAND 12-12-0 (7*) Mr J M Pritchard, *sn wl beh, tld off whn pld up bef 11th.* . . . .(33 to 1 tchd 50 to 1)   pu

Dist: 3l, dist, 25l. 5m 32.20s. a 46.20s (11 Ran).
(S A Brookshaw), S A Brookshaw

2552 Denbigh Mares' Only Intermediate National Hunt Flat Class H (4,5,6-y-o) £1,371 2m 1f. . . . . (4:50)

2302² POTTER AGAIN (Ire) 5-11-0 (3*) R Massey, *settled midfield, hdwy to ld 2 fs out, ran on wl, eased towards finish.* . . . . (7 to 4 on op 5 to 4 on tchd 11 to 10 on)   1

ALL DONE 4-10-7 Mr P Scott, *hld up, hdwy 4 fs out, chsd wnr frm o'r one out, ran on wl towards finish.* (14 to 1 op 8 to 1)   2

2248⁴ HOT 'N SAUCY 5-11-3 Mr S Bush, *cl up, slight ld 5 fs out till hdd 2 out, no extr* . . . . (9 to 1 op 4 to 1 tchd 11 to 1)   3

CRYSTAL JEWEL 5-11-3 G Tormey, *settled midfield, effrt 5 fs out, sn drvn alng, kpt on fnl 2 furlongs.* . . . .(8 to 1 op 5 to 1 tchd 9 to 1)   4

SIDE BY SIDE (Ire) 4-10-0 (7*) N Horrocks, *hld up and beh, hdwy into midfield 4 fs out, kpt on same pace fnl 3 furlongs.* . . . . (14 to 1 op 8 to 1)   5

2309⁹ MISTRESS TUDOR 6-11-0 (3*) E Husband, *made most till hdd 5 fs out, wknd o'r 2 out.* . . . .(33 to 1 op 16 to 1)   6

2206⁴ SUPREME TARGET (Ire) 5-11-0 (3*) G Lee, *hld up, hdwy 6 fs out, ev ch o'r 2 out, sn wknd.* . . . .(6 to 1 op 3 to 1)   7

2302 PEARL SILK 4-10-2 (5*) O Burrows, *hld up, hdwy to chase ldrs 4 fs out, wknd o'r 2 out* . . . .(16 to 1 op 10 to 1)   8

1292⁶ SAUCY NUN (Ire) 5-10-10 (7*) F Bogle, *chsd ldrs, rdn and ev ch 4 fs out, wknd o'r 2 out.* . . . . (10 to 1 op 14 to 1 tchd 8 to 1)   9

TA-RA-ABIT (Ire) 4-10-4 (3*) L Aspell, *dsptd ld till wknd 5 fs out* . . . .(33 to 1 op 16 to 1)   10

BE IN SPACE 6-10-10 (7*) K Hibbert, *mid-div till wknd 5 fs out.* . . . .(50 to 1 op 33 to 1)   11

DIAMOND TIME 6-10-12 (5*) A Bates, *keen early, hld up, wknd 5 fs out.* . . . .(20 to 1 op 8 to 1)   12

TAFZALETTE 5-10-10 (7*) S Fowler, *chsd ldrs till wknd o'r 5 fs out.* . . . .(50 to 1 op 33 to 1)   13

Dist: Nk, 2½l, 6l, 5l, 7l, 1¾l, 1¾l, 1l, 8l, 4l. 4m 7.00s. (13 Ran).
(J E Potter), D Nicholson

NEWBURY (good)

Friday February 7th
Going Correction: PLUS 0.50 sec. per fur. (races 1,5,6,7), PLUS 0.65 (2,3,4)

2553 Stroud Green Juvenile Novices' Hurdle Class C (4-y-o) £3,980 2m 110yds. . . . . (1:30)

1890 KERAWI 11-5 C Llewellyn, *chsd ldrs, drvn alng frm 4th, hrd rdn and no imprsn 3 out, styd on und pres to ld r-in, all out.* . . . . (12 to 1 op 10 to 1 tchd 14 to 1)   1

1610* WHITE SEA (Ire) 11-0 C F Swan, *led, clr 4th, in command 3 out, eased frm nxt, hdd r-in, rdn and rallied, not quicken nr finish.* . . . . (2 to 1 fav op 9 to 4 tchd 5 to 2)   2

2324² NOBLE LORD 11-0 B Powell, *chsd ldrs, rdn and kpt on same pace frm 3 out* . . . . (14 to 1 op 10 to 1 tchd 16 to 1)   3

2188² SOLDAT (USA) 11-5 D Bridgwater, *hld up, rapid hdwy to chase ldrs aftr, hrd rdn 3 out, no response.* . . . . (13 to 2 op 9 to 1 tchd 14 to 1)   4

2195* SUMMER SPELL (USA) 11-5 R Dunwoody, *prmnt, trkd ldr 5th to 2 out, sn wknd* . . . .(100 to 30 op 5 to 2 tchd 7 to 2)   5

FLY FISHING (USA) 11-5 A Kondrat, *chsd ldr to 5th, sn wknd.* . . . . (5 to 1 op 4 to 1 tchd 11 to 2)   6

2303* DESERT MOUNTAIN (Ire) 11-0 R Hughes, *hdwy to chase ldrs 5th, sn rdn, wknd nxt...* (11 to 1 op 10 to 1 tchd 12 to 1)   7

FULL THROTTLE 11-0 Richard Guest, *beh 4th.* . . . . (33 to 1 op 16 to 1 tchd 50 to 1)   8

MUHTADI (Ire) 11-0 P Hide, *chsd ldrs to 5th, sn rdn and wknd.* . . . . (33 to 1 op 16 to 1 tchd 50 to 1)   9

2333⁵ SQUIRE'S OCCASION (Can) 10-12 (7*) X Aizpuru, *al wl beh.* . . . . (50 to 1 op 25 to 1 tchd 66 to 1)   10

KUTMAN (USA) 11-0 B Fenton, *beh 3rd.* . . . . (33 to 1 op 16 to 1 tchd 50 to 1)   11

BOLD BUSTER 11-0 J F Titley, *hit second and beh, tld off whn pld up bef 2 out* . . . .(50 to 1 op 20 to 1 tchd 66 to 1)   pu

SASSY STREET (Ire) 11-0 N Williamson, *jmpd hesitantly in rear, al beh, tld off whn pld up bef 2 out.* . . . . (66 to 1 op 33 to 1 tchd 100 to 1)   pu

Dist: 1¾l, 16l, 13l, 1l, 5l, 4l, sht-hd, 7l, 8l, 1l. 4m 3.30s. a 14.30s (13 Ran).
SR: 30/23/7/-/-/-/ (Matt Archer & Miss Jean Broadhurst), N A Twiston-Davies

2554 Aldermaston Novices' Chase Class D (5-y-o and up) £3,543 2m 1f (2:00)

1725⁷ SQUIRE SILK 8-11-2 P Carberry, *settled in 3rd, quickened to track ldr 9th, led 2 out, imprsv* . . . .(11 to 8 tchd 6 to 4)   1

2457* EUDIPE (Fr) 5-11-1 C F Swan, *led to 3 out, styd on gmely, no ch wth wnr* . . . .(11 to 8 on op 7 to 4)   2

2329 INTERMAGIC 7-11-2 S Fox, *chsd ldr, blun 8th, mstk nxt and lost second, sn wl beh, no ch whn blunded last.* . . . . (14 to 1 op 10 to 1 tchd 16 to 1)   3

Dist: 1½l, dist. 4m 15.90s. a 15.90s (3 Ran).
SR: 40/37/-/ (Robert Ogden), Andrew Turnell

2555 Arkell Brewery Handicap Chase Class C (0-135 5-y-o and up) £4,532 2m 1f. . . . . (2:30)

1993² MISTER ODDY [128] 11-11-4 (3*) D Fortt, *wth ldr, lft in ld second, drvn and ran on frm 2 out, rdn out nr finish.* . . . . (11 to 4 fav op 5 to 2)   1

1342 HIGH ALLTITUDE (Ire) [107] 9-10-0 B Powell, *in tch, hdwy 9th, styd on frm 2 out, kpt on wl r-in, not quite get up.* . . . .(7 to 1 tchd 8 to 1)   2

2335² NATIVE MISSION [135] 10-12-0 P Carberry, *hld up, hdwy and hit 9th, chsd wnr frm 3 out, not fluent last, sn wknd.* . . . .(3 to 1 op 5 to 2)   3

2294² THUMBS UP [127] 11-11-6 R Dunwoody, *lft chasing wnr second, ev ch 3 out, no peace* . . . . . (13 to 2 op 5 to 1 tchd 7 to 1)   4

2287* EASTERN MAGIC [107] 9-10-0 R Farrant, *hdwy 8th, in tch whn blun 9th, not reco'r...* (9 to 2 op 7 to 2 tchd 5 to 1)   5

2355⁷ CHURCHTOWN PORT (Ire) [107] 7-10-0 N Williamson, *disputing ld whn f second.* (16 to 1 op 20 to 1 tchd 25 to 1)   f

1918* JAMES THE FIRST [121] (bl) 9-11-0 P Hide, *dsptd ld till blun second, effrt to stay in tch whn blunded 6th, sn beh, tld off whn pld up bef last...*(12 to 1 op 10 to 1 tchd 14 to 1)   pu

Dist: 1¼l, 5l, 2½l, dist. 4m 16.40s. a 16.40s (7 Ran).
SR: 39/16/39/28/ (Mrs R M Hill), J S King

2556 Charles Higgins Memorial Foxhunters' Cup Hunters' Chase Class H (5-y-o and up) £1,604 2½m. . . . . . . (3:00)

SLIEVENAMON MIST 11-12-2 (5*) Mr J Jukes, *hdwy and hit 9th, trkd ldr 12th, chlgd 4 out, slight ld frm nxt, drvn out r-in.* . . . . (5 to 2 op 2 to 1 tchd 11 to 4)   1

PRINCIPLE MUSIC (USA) 9-11-5 (7*) Mr A Phillips, *hdwy 8th, led tenth, clr appr 12th, hdd 3 out, styd on one pace r-in.* . . . . (25 to 1 op 16 to 1 tchd 33 to 1)   2

BOBENBOB 10-11-5 (7*) Mr J Docker, *some hdwy frm 3 out, not trble ldrs*. . . . . (14 to 1 op 10 to 1 tchd 16 to 1)   3

FLOWING RIVER (USA) 11-11-5 (7*) Mr N R Mitchell, *in tch, staying on in 4th whn hmpd 12th, sn btn.* . . . . (33 to 1 op 20 to 1 tchd 40 to 1)   4

TEA CEE KAY 7-11-7 (5*) Mr A Sansome, *beh 6th.* . . . . (16 to 1 op 10 to 1 tchd 20 to 1)   5

FLAME O'FRENSI 11-11-9 (7*) Miss J Cumings, *led to 6th, wknd tenth*............. (12 to 1 op 8 to 1 tchd 14 to 1) 6
ORUJO (Ire) 9-11-5 (7*) Mr P T Young, *prmnt, led 6th to tenth, wkng whn hmpd 12th*...(33 to 1 op 20 to 1 tchd 50 to 1) 7
195[9] CHARLIES DELIGHT (Ire) 9-11-11[7] (7*) Mr R Hicks, *mstks, sn beh, tld off*............. (50 to 1 op 33 to 1 tchd 66 to 1) 8
IDIOTIC 9-11-12 (5*) Mr C Vigors, *f second.*
....(2 to 1 fav op 5 to 2) f
PRO BONO (Ire) 7-11-10 (7*) Mr A Dalton, *with ldrs 6th, chlgd tenth to 11th, 3rd and othn f nxt.*
........................(12 to 1 op 8 to 1 tchd 14 to 1) f
111[43] RAMSTAR 9-12-5 (5*) Miss P Curling, *hdwy tenth, wknd aftr 12th, tld off whn pld up bef last*.........(10 to 1 op 6 to 1) pu
BIRCHALL BOY 9-11-5 (7*) Miss W Southcombe, *hit 4th, sn beh, tld off whn pld up bef 2 out.*
.... (33 to 1 op 20 to 1 tchd 50 to 1) pu
Dist: 6l, 26l, 3½l, sht-hd, 26l, 4l. 5m 19.70s. a 31.70s (12 Ran).
(Nick Viney), Victor Dartnall

2557 Mayor Of Boston Handicap Hurdle Class B (5-y-o and up) £4,858 2m 5f
.... (3:30)

1597* COPPER BOY [119] 8-10-3 B Powell, *led, rdn and blun 2 out, all out r-in*..........(11 to 4 fav op 5 to 2 tchd 9 to 4) 1
174[46] KINGDOM OF SHADES (USA) [124] 7-10-8 P Carberry, *hld up in tch, hdwy to track wnr 3 out, rdn and styd on frm 2 out, no extr und str pres r-in*.....(13 to 2 op 6 to 1 tchd 7 to 1) 2
1880* KARSHI [142] 7-11-12 J F Titley, *wth wnr till aftr 4th, in second to 3 out, sn rdn and wknd*...(7 to 2 op 3 to 1 tchd 4 to 1) 3
176[16] BARNA BOY (Ire) [132] 9-11-2 R Dunwoody, *hld up rear, lost tch 8th*.........................(10 to 1 op 7 to 1) 4
220[85] RIGHT WIN (Ire) [144] 7-12-0 N Williamson, *in tch, rdn 5th, hdwy nxt, sn ridden ag'n, wknd 8th, no ch whn mstk 3 out.*
..............................(9 to 1 op 14 to 1 tchd 16 to 1) 5
23[292] BOLIVAR (Ire) [118] 5-9-11 (5*) S Ryan, *chsd ldrs, mstk 3rd, rdn 7th, hdwy 8th, wknd nxt.* (7 to 2 op 3 to 1 tchd 4 to 1) 6
23[892] MOMENT OF GLORY (Ire) [116] (v) 6-10-0 R Hughes, *hld up rear, rdn and wknd 8th.*........(8 to 1 op 6 to 1) 7
Dist: 1l, 17l, 9l, 6l, 4l, dist. 5m 12.30s. a 18.30s (7 Ran).
SR: -/1/2/-/
(C Raymond), R H Buckler

2558 February Novices' Handicap Hurdle Class D (0-115 4-y-o and up) £3,054 2m 110yds.................... (4:00)

23[234] RANGITIKEI (NZ) [104] 6-11-10 R Dunwoody, *trkd ldrs, led 4th, shaken up whn chlgd 3 out, drw clr frm nxt, cmftbly.*
.......................(2 to 1 fav op 7 to 4 tchd 9 to 4) 1
248[12] NEAT FEAT (Ire) [94] 6-11-0 P Holley, *hdwy to chase ldrs 5th, rdn 2 out, styd on to go second r-in, no ch wth wnr.*
....(5 to 1 op 6 to 1) 2
2279[7] BIETSCHHORN BARD [90] (b) 7-10-7 (3*) D Fortt, *hld up, steady hdwy 5th, chsd wnr 2 out, sn rdn, wknd r-in.*
.........................(11 to 2 op 5 to 1 tchd 6 to 1) 3
164[19] I RECALL (Ire) [80] 6-10-0 B Fenton, *wth ldr to 4th, lost pos appr 3 out, styd on und pres r-in*......(33 to 1 op 25 to 1) 4
2277 REVERSE THRUST [84] 6-9-11 (7*) M Clinton, *hdwy 5th, chlgd 3 out, sn rdn, wknd aftr nxt.*
.......................(16 to 1 op 12 to 1 tchd 20 to 1) 5
2277[6] HENRYS PORT [98] 7-11-4 N Williamson, *in tch, hdwy to chase wnr 5th, chlgd nxt, wknd 2 out*.....(4 to 1 op 5 to 2) 6
251[2] ZAHID (USA) [96] 6-11-2 R Hughes, *steady hdwy to track ldrs 4th, rdn 3 out, sn wknd*..........(10 to 1 op 8 to 1) 7
2153 MAZIRAH [83] 6-10-3 D Morris, *beh, lost tch 5th.*
.......................(11 to 1 op 9 to 1 tchd 11 to 1) 8
LAGHAM LAD [84] 8-10-4 P Carberry, *made most to 4th, wknd appr nxt, tld off*...........(16 to 1 op 12 to 1) 9
Dist: 8l, 2½l, 2½l, 11l, 3l, 18l, 16l, dist. 4m 8.60s. a 19.60s (9 Ran).
(Mrs J M Mayo), C J Mann

2559 Levy Board Handicap Hurdle Class C (0-130 4-y-o and up) £3,727 3m 110yds........................... (4:30)

2245 BANKHEAD (Ire) [116] 8-11-3 (7*) Miss C Spearing, *trkd ldrs, led appr 9th, rdn alng 2 out, hld on wl r-in.*
.................................(33 to 1 tchd 40 to 1) 1
238[94] ALLOW (Ire) [93] 6-9-10 (5*) D J Kavanagh, *hld hdwy frm 9th, chsd wnr from 3 out, hld on no imprsn r-in.*
.......................(7 to 1 op 8 to 1 tchd 9 to 1) 2
224[62] EALING COURT [99] 8-10-7 N Williamson, *rcd wide, hdwy 6th, chsd ldrs 9th, one pace frm 2 out.*
.......................(4 to 1 fav op 5 to 1 tchd 11 to 2) 3
229[54] GENERAL MOUKTAR [105] 7-10-13 C F Swan, *hld up, hdwy 9th, styd on one pace frm 2 out.*
.......................(9 to 1 op 8 to 1 tchd 10 to 1) 4
221[72] ROYAL PIPER (NZ) [108] 10-11-2 R Greene, *hld up, hdwy 9th, one pace frm 3 out*............(10 to 1 op 7 to 1) 5
231[34] FAST THOUGHTS [101] (bl) 10-10-9 R Dunwoody, *led till appr 9th, rdn 3 out, sn wknd*........(12 to 1 op 14 to 1) 6
231[33] DERRING BRIDGE [92] 7-10-0 B Fenton, *beh and rdn alng 5th, no imprsn aftr.*................(25 to 1 tchd 33 to 1) 7
221[75] KALASADI (USA) [103] (bl) 6-10-11 J F Titley, *beh and rdn 7th, no dngr aftr.*................(16 to 1 op 12 to 1) 8
21[985] SORBIERE [95] 10-10-3 J R Kavanagh, *al rear.*
.................................(33 to 1 op 25 to 1 tchd 40 to 1) 9

228[93] THE TOISEACH (Ire) [112] 6-11-6 P Hide, *hdwy 5th, wknd 3 out*...........................(8 to 1 op 6 to 1) 10
150[25] HUNTERS ROCK (Ire) [115] 8-11-2 (7*) Mr R Wakley, *chsd ldrs to 9th*.........................(14 to 1 op 8 to 1) 11
145[46] BETTER BYTHE GLASS (Ire) [97] 8-10-5 T Jenks, *prssed ldrs to 9th, sn wknd*.......(12 to 1 op 10 to 1 tchd 14 to 1) 12
231[32] RIMOUSKI [97] 9-10-5 Gary Lyons, *chsd ldrs to 9th.*
.................(10 to 1 tchd 11 to 1 and 9 to 1) 13
204[75] ULURU (Ire) [111] 9-11-2 (3*) D Fortt, *prmnt, rdn 6th, sn wknd, tld off whn pld up bef 2 out.*
.......................(20 to 1 op 14 to 1 tchd 25 to 1) pu
187[68] QUEEN'S AWARD (Ire) [92] 8-10-0 B Powell, *hdwy 6th, wknd 9th, tld off whn pld up bef 3 out*.........(8 to 1 op 5 to 1) pu
Dist: 3l, 7l, 4l, 5l, 6l, 11l, 6l, nk, 2l, 4l. 6m 8.00s. a 22.00s (15 Ran).
(Mrs Liz Brazier), J L Spearing

TOWCESTER (soft (races 1,3,4,6,8), good to soft (2,5,7))
Friday February 7th
Going Correction: PLUS 0.75 sec. per fur. (races 1,3,4,6,8), PLUS 0.65 (2,5,7)

2560 Woodcock Novices' Hurdle Class E (Div I) (4-y-o and up) £1,976 2m
.... (1:10)

2260* SPENDID (Ire) 5-11-9 A Maguire, *hld up, took clr order 4th, chlgd 2 out, led last, all out.*
..............................(5 to 4 fav tchd 11 to 8 and 11 to 10) 1
221[54] READY MONEY CREEK (Ire) 6-11-9 J Osborne, *chsd ldr, led appr 3 out, hrd pressed frm 2 out, hdd last, ran on und pres.*
.........................(13 to 8 op 6 to 4 tchd 9 to 4) 2
127[06] LOGICAL STEP (Ire) 7-11-3 D Leahy, *hld up, clr order 4th, rdn and one pace frm 3 out.*.........(14 to 1 op 10 to 1) 3
125[22] SHARED RISK 5-11-0 (3*) E Callaghan, *hdwy 4th, rdn and one pace 3 out.*....................(16 to 1 op 10 to 1) 4
227[79] HARLEQUIN CHORUS 7-11-3 G Upton, *beh till styd on frm 3 out, nvr nrr*....(12 to 1 op 10 to 1 tchd 14 to 1) 5
FIRE ON ICE (Ire) 5-11-3 T J Murphy, *hdwy 4th, rdn 3 out, fourth and btn whn mstk nxt.*........(14 to 1 op 8 to 1) 6
2152 HILLS GAMBLE 7-11-3 W Worthington, *led till appr 3 out, wknd bef nxt.*...................(50 to 1 op 33 to 1) 7
2264 CALM DOWN (Ire) 6-11-3 R Johnson, *hdwy 4th, wknd 3 out.*
....................................(33 to 1 op 20 to 1) 8
228[43] KHALIKHOUM (Ire) 4-10-7 C Maude, *hdwy 4th, rdn appr 3 out, sn wknd, tld off whn pld up bef last*
.................................(10 to 1 tchd 12 to 1) pu
RED RIVER (Ire) 6-10-7 (5*) Mr R Thornton, *al beh, tld off 3rd, pld up bef 2 out*........(50 to 1 op 33 to 1 tchd 66 to 1) pu
GENTLEMAN JAMES (Ire) 7-11-3 Derek Byrne, *reminders aftr 1st, al beh, tld off 3rd, pld up bef 5th.*
.................(25 to 1 op 20 to 1 tchd 33 to 1) pu
Dist: Hd, 11l, hd, 10l, 3l, ½l, dist. 4m 1.40s. a 18.40s (11 Ran).
SR: 31/31/14/14/4/-/
(Mrs Stewart Catherwood), D Nicholson

2561 Partridge Novices' Chase Class E (5-y-o and up) £2,875 2m 110yds (1:40)

2278* LIGHTENING LAD 9-11-8 C Maude, *jmpd wl, led 1st, made rst, edgd lft whn drvn out r-in, ran on well.*
.......................(11 to 8 fav op 5 to 4 tchd 6 to 4) 1
2033* SUPER COIN 9-11-8 R Johnson, *nvr far away, rdn and effrt 2 out, ran on.*..................(5 to 2 op 7 to 2) 2
154[62] DOMINOS RING (Ire) 8-11-2 Mr A Walton, *wtd wth, blun 4th, hdwy 5th, rdn appr 3 out, styd on r-in.*
.......................(14 to 1 op 12 to 1 tchd 16 to 1) 3
2373* DREAM RIDE (Ire) 7-11-8 A Maguire, *in tch, rdn frm 3 out, 3rd whn hit nxt, one pace.*........(5 to 1 op 4 to 1) 4
1970 BUCKET OF GOLD 7-11-2 M Brennan, *trkd ldrs, blun 6th, rdn and wknd appr 2 out*.............(20 to 1 tchd 25 to 1) 5
1881 OLD REDWOOD 10-11-2 L O'Hara, *trkd ldrs and wknd frm 3 out*....................(50 to 1 op 33 to 1 tchd 66 to 1) 6
2425 HAWKER HUNTER (USA) (bl) 6-11-2 J Railton, *not fluent, led till jmpd slwly 1st, jumped slowly and lost pl 5th, rallied 7th, wknd frm 3 out.*....(50 to 1 op 20 to 1 tchd 33 to 1) 7
2259 SAKBAH (USA) 8-10-11 W Marston, *hld up, blun 4th, reminders and hdwy aftr nxt, wknd whn blunded 3 out.*
.................(50 to 1 op 33 to 1 tchd 66 to 1) 8
2288 KENTUCKY GOLD (Ire) 8-11-2 A S Smith, *al beh, tld off whn pld up bef 3 out*.....(50 to 1 op 33 to 1 tchd 66 to 1) pu
1957[5] DODGY DEALER (Ire) 7-11-2 Derek Byrne, *al beh, tld off whn pld up bef 5th*..........(40 to 1 op 20 to 1) pu
Dist: 1¼l, 2l, 3l, 14l, 2l, 3l, dist. 4m 19.20s. a 22.20s (10 Ran).
(Richard Peterson), J S King

2562 Teal Handicap Hurdle Class E (0-115 4-y-o and up) £2,410 3m...... (2:10)

224[63] GRUNGE (Ire) [94] 9-10-7 A Maguire, *confidently rdn, prog appr 7th, led 3 out, ridden out, ran on wl.*
.................................(5 to 1 tchd 6 to 1) 1
224[64] EHTERAAL (USA) [92] 6-10-5 T J Murphy, *hld up, hdwy frm 6th, rdn appr 3 out, ran on und pres r-in.*
.......................(11 to 2 op 5 to 1 tchd 6 to 1) 2

2120² SNOW BOARD [92] 8-10-5 Derek Byrne, *hld up, steady hdwy frm 7th, in tch whn hit 3 out, kpt on r-in*.
..................................(9 to 4 fav op 7 to 4)   3
2177 MISTER BLAKE [90] 7-10-3 R Johnson, *hdwy 4th, hit 3 out, sn rdn and btn*........... (16 to 1 op 20 to 1 tchd 25 to 1)   4
2403² WHITEBONNET (Ire) [87] (bl) 7-9-9 (5*) Sophie Mitchell, *prmnt, led 8th to 3 out, sn wknd*.......... (9 to 1 op 10 to 1)   5
2246 MOUNTAIN REACH [92] 7-10-5 J Osborne, *trkd ldrs, ev ch appr 3 out, sn wknd*.... (14 to 1 op 12 to 1 tchd 16 to 1)   6
2246 ST VILLE [91] 11-10-4 P Holley, *made most till 6th, wknd appr 3 out*.................................(14 to 1 op 10 to 1)   7
2422 JOHNNY'S TURN [109] 12-11-8 Mr N Kent, *beh frm 8th, tld off pld up bef 2 out*......................(33 to 1 op 16 to 1)   pu
CUNNINGHAMS FORD (Ire) [112] 9-11-11 A S Smith, *beh frm 5th, tld off whn pld up bef 8th*.
..................................(33 to 1 op 12 to 1 tchd 40 to 1)   pu
2268 CHIEF RAGER [104] 8-11-3 T Jenks, *prmnt, led 6th to 8th, wknd 3 out, beh whn pld up bef 2 out*.. (14 to 1 op 8 to 1)   pu
2245 HUGE MISTAKE [96] 8-10-9 C Maude, *mid-div, reminders aftr second, beh frm 6th, tld off whn pld up bef 3 out*.
..................................(10 to 1 op 8 to 1 tchd 12 to 1)   pu
2156⁶ MENDIP PRINCE (Ire) [93] 7-10-6 C O'Dwyer, *prmnt, rdn 7th, sn wknd, tld off whn pld up bef 3 out*.
..................................(13 to 2 op 5 to 1 tchd 10 to 1)   pu
Dist: 1½l, 2l, 15l, 9l, nk, sht-hd. 6m 16.80s. a 34.80s (12 Ran).
(Mrs R D Cowell), D J G Murray Smith

2563 Sporting Life Champion Hurdle Trial Hurdle Class B (5-y-o and up) £4,556 2m..........................(2:40)

COLLIER BAY 7-11-8 J Osborne, *pressed wnr, led briefly appr 2 out, rgned ld r-in, ran on wl*.
..................................(11 to 8 on op 2 to 1 on tchd 5 to 4 on)   1
RELKEEL 8-11-0 A Maguire, *keen hold early, hld up in cl tch, took narrow advantage 2 out, shaken up betw fnl two, hdd r-in, unbl to quicken*......................(11 to 8 op 6 to 4)   2
2232⁵ ESCARTEFIGUE (Fr) 5-11-0 D Bridgwater, *led, jmpd slwly 3rd, hdd appr 2 out, sn btn*.
..................................(11 to 2 op 9 to 1 tchd 10 to 1)   3
Dist: ¾l, 15l. 3m 56.60s. a 13.60s (3 Ran).
SR: 78/69/54/   (W E Sturt), J A B Old

2564 Duck Handicap Chase Class C (0-135 5-y-o and up) £4,401 3m 1f ....(3:10)

2268* BRAVE BUCCANEER [110] 10-10-3 D Bridgwater, *hld up, hdwy 9th, not fluent and lost pl nxt 2, rallied 13th, led appr two out, ran on wl*.
..................................(9 to 4 op 3 to 1 tchd 100 to 30 and 7 to 2)   1
CAMELOT KNIGHT [117] 11-10-10 C Maude, *prmnt, hit 11th, lost pl and ran on betw fnl 2*.
..................................(16 to 1 op 10 to 1 tchd 20 to 1)   2
2314* MELY MOSS (Fr) [126] 6-12-0 J Osborne, *hld up, led 3 out, hdd appr nxt, one pace*.
..................................(6 to 4 fav op 11 to 10 tchd 13 to 8 and 7 to 4)   3
2306⁵ BEAUREPAIRE (Ire) [107] 9-10-0 R Johnson, *nvr far away, rdn alng 14th, lost pl 3 out, styd on frm nxt*.
..................................(14 to 1 op 10 to 1)   4
2310⁶ BALLYEA BOY [113] 7-10-6 A Maguire, *prmnt, led 4 out to 3 out, one pace*......................(4 to 1 tchd 9 to 2)   5
2182 WOODLANDS BOY (Ire) [107] 9-9-12¹ (3*) P Henley, *hld up, rdn and styd on one pace frm 3 out, nvr nrr*.
..................................(12 to 1 tchd 14 to 1)   6
1948 DOLIKOS [107] 10-10-0 T J Murphy, *hld up, hdwy and effrt 4 out, wknd nxt, tld off*... (40 to 1 op 33 to 1 tchd 50 to 1)   7
INVASION [107] (bl) 13-10-0 M Brennan, *al beh, tld off whn pld up bef 2 out*....(14 to 1 op 12 to 1 tchd 16 to 1)   pu
1892⁷ LUCKY LANE [110] (bl) 13-10-3 I Lawrence, *hld up beh ldrs, hit and reminder 8th, behind frm 11th, tld off whn pld up bef 4 out*.................................(50 to 1 op 33 to 1)   pu
2156 SO FAR BOLD (Ire) [110] (bl) 7-10-3 C O'Dwyer, *made most till jmpd slwly and hdd 4 out, sn wknd, tld off whn pld up bef 2 out*.................(16 to 1 op 14 to 1 tchd 20 to 1)   pu
Dist: 1½l, 1¾l, 2l, 2l, sht-hd, dist. 6m 34.30s. a 22.30s (10 Ran).
SR: 14/19/35/5/9/3/   (R C Watts), Andrew Turnell

2565 Woodcock Novices' Hurdle Class E (Div II) (4-y-o and up) £1,976 2m ....(3:40)

MY CHEEKY MAN 6-11-3 R Johnson, *hld up, steady hdwy frm 5th, led 2 out, drvn out*.
..................................(12 to 1 op 10 to 1 tchd 14 to 1)   1
1893* THE PROMS (Ire) 6-11-9 C Llewellyn, *led till aftr second, remained prmnt, ev ch 2 out, one pace*.
..................................(11 to 8 fav op 5 to 4 tchd 13 to 8 and 7 to 4)   2
TONKA 5-11-3 D Leahy, *not fluent 1st and nxt, sn led, hdd 2 out, btn whn hit last*..... (14 to 1 op 12 to 1 tchd 16 to 1)   3
2267 COOL GUNNER 7-11-9 C Maude, *hld up, prog 4th, rdn and one pace 3 out*.........(9 to 2 op 4 to 1 tchd 5 to 1)   4
1973⁷ CAPTAIN WALTER (Ire) 7-11-3 J Osborne, *hld up, hdwy 3 out, wknd whn hit last*...... (6 to 1 tchd 7 to 1 and 5 to 1)   5
2311⁷ BLAZING STORM (Ire) 5-10-12 (5*) Mr R Thornton, *nvr nr to chal*..................(11 to 2 op 6 to 1 tchd 4 to 1)   6

2353⁵ WORTHY MEMORIES 8-10-12 Derek Byrne, *nvr on terms*.
..................................(25 to 1 tchd 33 to 1)   7
2384 WELSH SILK 5-10-12 (5*) Sophie Mitchell, *nvr nr to chal*.
..................................(10 to 1 op 8 to 1 tchd 12 to 1)   8
MUSIC CLASS (Ire) 6-11-3 A Maguire, *hld up, hdwy 4th, wknd frm 3 out*..........(12 to 1 op 6 to 1 tchd 14 to 1)   9
ORCHARD KING 7-11-3 M Brennan, *in tch till rdn and wknd frm 3 out*.........(14 to 1 op 12 to 1 tchd 16 to 1)   10
TUDOR FALCON 4-10-7 T J Murphy, *prmnt, hit 3 out sn wknd*.
..................................(25 to 1 tchd 33 to 1)   11
2419⁷ FERRERS 4-11-3 W Marston, *hld up, hdwy 4th, effrt 2 out, second and held whn f last*.
..................................(14 to 1 op 12 to 1 tchd 16 to 1)   f
A BADGE TOO FAR (Ire) 7-10-12 L O'Hara, *mstk second, beh frm nxt, tld off whn pld up bef 3 out*..........(33 to 1)   pu
2264 BENJI 6-11-3 C O'Dwyer, *chsd ldrs, wknd 3 out, tld off whn pld up bef last*...........(25 to 1 op 20 to 1)   pu
Dist: 4l, 5l, 3l, 8l, 3l, 4l, 3l, 6l, 13l, 15l. 4m 6.10s. a 23.10s (14 Ran).
(Mrs A A Shutes), D Nicholson

2566 Pheasant Novices' Chase Class E (5-y-o and up) £3,044 3m 1f......(4:10)

1268⁹ JET RULES (Ire) 7-11-4 R Farrant, *in tch, hit 4 out, ran on und pres to ld cl hme*.....................(3 to 1 op 6 to 4)   1
2406⁴ ROBSAND (Ire) 8-11-4 B Clifford, *led 5th, hdd and no extr cl hme*.................................(20 to 1 op 14 to 1)   2
2157 WISLEY WONDER (Ire) (bl) 7-11-4 C Llewellyn, *wtd wth, hdwy 14th, ev ch appr 2 out, wknd run- in*.
..................................(7 to 2 op 4 to 1 tchd 5 to 1)   3
2259* KAMIKAZE (bl) 7-11-10 C O'Dwyer, *blun badly 1st, wl beh till hdwy 9th, mstk 12th, 4th and no ch whn mistake last*.
..................................(6 to 4 fav op 7 to 4 tchd 15 to 8 and 11 to 8)   4
2406³ ARDENT LOVE (Ire) 8-10-13 A Maguire, *hld up, mstk 6th, effrt 4 out, wekened frm 3 out*.
..................................(10 to 1 op 12 to 1 tchd 14 to 1)   5
2406 FORTYTWO DEE (Ire) 7-10-13 T J Murphy, *in tch till wknd 3 out*..............................(50 to 1 op 33 to 1)   6
1347 COOL RUNNER 7-11-4 Derek Byrne, *hld up, rdn alng 12th, beh whn hit 14th, no dngr aftr*.........(20 to 1 op 14 to 1)   7
2354 RING CORBITTS 9-11-1 (3*) P Henley, *prmnt, struggling 13th, no danged aftr*......................(25 to 1 op 20 to 1)   8
1232² MYSTIC ISLE (Ire) 7-11-4 W Marston, *not fluent, hld up beh ldrs, rdn and wknde frm 3 out*.
..................................(11 to 1 op 8 to 1 tchd 12 to 1)   9
2441 MAJOR NOVA 8-11-4 J Ryan, *hld up, hmpd 8th, sn beh*.
..................................(40 to 1 op 33 to 1 tchd 50 to 1)   10
2404³ RED PARADE (NZ) 9-11-4 C Maude, *led to 5th, hit 13th, fifth and btn whn blun and uns rdr 2 out*.
..................................(16 to 1 op 14 to 1 tchd 20 to 1)   ur
2291³ GLENDINE (Ire) (bl) 7-11-4 J Railton, *chsd ldrs, hit and rdn 9th, sn wknd tld off whn pld up bef 13th*.
..................................(33 to 1 tchd 40 to 1 and 50 to 1)   pu
2375³ MUSICAL HIT 6-11-4 R Bellamy, *nvr on terms, tld off whn pld up bef 2 out*............(40 to 1 op 33 to 1 tchd 50 to 1)   pu
2388⁷ ROYAL HAND 7-11-4 Mr R Armson, *hld up, blun badly 11th, sn beh, tld off whn blunded badly 3 out, pld up bef nxt*.
..................................(50 to 1 op 33 to 1)   pu
PRINCE CANUTE 7-10-13 (5*) D Salter, *not fluent, beh whn jmpd badly rght 8th, tld off whn pld up aftr nxt*.
..................................(33 to 1 tchd 50 to 1)   pu
Dist: ¾l, 13l, 7l, 5l, ¾l, 1¼l, 10l, 10l, 26l. 6m 38.20s. a 26.20s (15 Ran).
(The Jet Stationery Company Limited), Mrs J Pitman

2567 Snipe Standard Open National Hunt Flat Class H (4,5,6-y-o) £1,276 2m ....(4:40)

1769³ ENDEAVOUR (Fr) 5-11-4 J Railton, *al hndy, led 3 fs out, ran on wl*....................(9 to 1 op 7 to 1 tchd 10 to 1)   1
2283* KING MOLE 6-11-11 G Upton, *hld up, hdwy aftr 7 fs, ev ch frm 3 out, no extr ins last. OR 13*
..................................(6 to 4 on op 5 to 4 on tchd 11 to 10 on and 6 to 5 on)   2
SIR PRIZE (Ire) 4-10-8 B Clifford, *in tch, rdn 3 fs out, styd on und pres ins last*.........(7 to 1 op 4 to 1 tchd 8 to 1)   3
PRUSSIAN STEEL (Ire) 6-11-4 C O'Dwyer, *hld up, hdwy hfwy, rdn 3 fs out, ran on one pace fnl 2*.
..................................(16 to 1 op 14 to 1 tchd 20 to 1)   4
2377³ COBLE LANE 5-11-4 J Osborne, *pld hrd, hld up, hdwy aftr 6 fs, led six out, hdd 3 out, eased whn btn o'r one out*.
..................................(8 to 1 tchd 9 to 1)   5
2206² BILLY BUCKSKIN 5-10-13 (5*) Mr R Thornton, *prmnt, led aftr 7 fs, hdd 6 out, wknd o'r 2 out*.
..................................(11 to 2 op 7 to 2 tchd 6 to 1)   6
REGENCY LEISURE 5-11-4 V Slattery, *prmnt till wknd o'r 4 fs out*......................(20 to 1 op 16 to 1 tchd 25 to 1)   7
2409 LUDO'S ORCHESTRA (Ire) 6-11-4 D Bridgwater, *led 7 fs, wknd o'r 3 out*.........(16 to 1 op 14 to 1 tchd 20 to 1)   8
WILMA'S CHOICE 6-10-13 J Supple, *beh frm hfwy*.
..................................(25 to 1 op 20 to 1)   9
DENSTAR (Ire) 4-10-8 T J Murphy, *al beh*.
..................................(12 to 1 op 7 to 1 tchd 16 to 1)   10
CARACTACUS POTTS 5-11-4 A Maguire, *al beh*.
..................................(12 to 1 op 6 to 1 tchd 16 to 1)   11
2302 SEVEN FOUR SEVEN 6-10-13 L O'Hara, *beh fnl 5 fs*.
..................................(25 to 1 op 20 to 1)   12

COOLEST BY PHAR (Ire) 5-11-4 R Johnson, *trkd ldrs, wknd o'r 5 fs out, beh whn swrvd and uns rdr ins last.
...............................(14 to 1 op 14 to 1 tchd 16 to 1)　ur
Dist: 1¼l, ½l, 1l, 21l, 3l, 5l, 2l, 11l, 9l, ½l. 4m 8.50s. (13 Ran).
(Mike Roberts), M J Roberts

AYR (soft)
Saturday February 8th
Going Correction: PLUS 1.20 sec. per fur. (races 1,3,5,7), PLUS 1.60 (2,4,6)

# 2568 Galloway Gazette Juvenile Novices' Hurdle Class E (4-y-o) £2,290 2m
...............................(1:00)

2188[8] CRY BABY 10-7 (5*) S Taylor, *nvr far away, rdn to ld bef last, ran on strly*...........................(7 to 1 op 6 to 1)　1
CLASH OF SWORDS 10-12 T Reed, *jmpd lft thrght, hndy, effrt whn blun 2 out, kpt on frm last.*
.....................(6 to 1 op 5 to 1 tchd 13 to 2)　2
930[3] PHANTOM HAZE 10-12 D Parker, *led till hdd appr 3 out, rallied to ld 2 out till approaching last, not quicken.*
..................(7 to 4 op 11 to 8 tchd 15 to 8)　3
2336[4] PARROT'S HILL (Ire) 10-12 B Storey, *pressed ldr, led appr 3 out till nxt, one pace last*...........(6 to 4 fav tchd 7 to 4)　4
KNOWN SECRET (USA) 10-12 A Dobbin, *mstks, beh, struggling 5th, sn tld off*....(20 to 1 op 12 to 1 tchd 25 to 1)　5
Dist: 2½l, ¾l, ½l, dist. 4m 1.80s. (5 Ran).
SR: 18/15/14/13/-/-　(Allan Gilchrist), A C Whillans

2569 Evening Times Novices' Chase Class D (6-y-o and up) £3,808 2½m (1:30)

2240* SPARKY GAYLE (Ire) 7-11-8 B Storey, *jmpd wl, nvr far away, led 4 out, clr 2 out, cmftbly.....* (5 to 2 on tchd 9 to 4)　1
2348[2] LANSBOROUGH 12-12 A Dobbin, *chsd clr ldr till mstk 11th, rdn alng 4 out, chased wnr fnl 2, no imprsn.*
......................(3 to 1 op 5 to 2 tchd 7 to 2)　2
2319 COQUI LANE 10-10-12 T Reed, *led and clr to eigth, hdd 4 out, no extr fnl 2*...........(14 to 1 op 12 to 1 tchd 16 to 1)　3
1630[5] LE DENSTAN 10-11-3 D Parker, *beh, outpcd 9th, sn no dngr.*
.....................(25 to 1 op 20 to 1)　4
2486 MONAUGHTY MAN 11-10-12 M Moloney, *in tch chasing grp, struggling 9th, sn btn.*
.................(100 to 1 op 200 to 1 tchd 500 to 1)　5
2347 VALLEY GARDEN (bl) 7-10-12 G Cahill, *mstks, sn beh, pushed alng 8th, soon struggling, pld up bef 11th..*(33 to 1)　6
Dist: 11l, 8l, dist, 1¾l. 5m 24.20s. a 37.20s (6 Ran).
SR: 42/21/3/　(Mr & Mrs Raymond Anderson Green), C Parker

2570 D. M. Hall 'National Hunt' Novices' Hurdle Class E (5-y-o and up) £2,696 2½m (2:00)

1962[2] LAGEN BRIDGE (Ire) 8-11-4 D J Moffatt, *al wl plcd, led 4 out, clr nxt, rdn out*...........(7 to 2 op 11 to 4 tchd 4 to 1)　1
1989[4] SIR BOB (Ire) 5-10-12 G Cahill, *nvr far away, rdn alng aftr 4 out, kpt on wl frm last*.......(9 to 2 op 4 to 1 tchd 5 to 1)　2
1989[6] DERANNIE (Ire) 5-10-12 A Dobbin, *hld up, effrt 5 out, rdn 3 out, one pace frm last*..................(7 to 2 op 5 to 2)　3
1893[4] CUTHILL HOPE (Ire) 6-10-12 B Storey, *hld up, improved to chase wnr bef 3 out, sn rdn, outpcd before last.*
....................(2 to 1 fav op 6 to 4 tchd 9 to 4)　4
2213[4] MONSIEUR DARCY (Ire) 6-10-12 Mr C Storey, *in tch, outpcd bef 4 out, no dngr aftr*...............(40 to 1 op 25 to 1)　5
2344[9] STORM CALL 6-10-7 D Bentley, *handily plcd, outpcd bef 4 out, sn struggling*..............(25 to 1 op 16 to 1)　6
2485 MEADOWLECK 8-10-2 (5*) S Taylor, *led and clr, hdd 4 out, struggling nxt......*(100 to 1 op 250 to 1 tchd 500 to 1)　7
2490[8] TRIONA'S HOPE (Ire) 8-10-5 (7*) Tristan Davidson, *beh, struggling bef 4 out, tld off*...........................(500 to 1)　8
THROMEDOWNSOMETING 7-10-10[3] T Reed, *beh, hit second, tld off whn pld up bef 6th........*(50 to 1 op 33 to 1)　pu
2344 SHARP SAND 7-10-12 M Moloney, *chsd clr ldr, struggling bef 5 out, tld off whn pld up before 3 out.*
...................................(40 to 1 op 25 to 1)　pu
ASHGROVE DANCER (Ire) 7-10-5 (7*) I Jardine, *hld up, struggling aftr 5 out, tld off whn pld up bef 3 out........*(100 to 1)　pu
CREAM OF THE BORDER 5-10-7 F Perratt, *mid-div, struggling aftr 5th, tld off whn pld up bef 3 out........*(100 to 1)　pu
Dist: 1½l, 7l, 5l, 14l, 4l, 19l, dist. 5m 7.90s. a 29.90s (12 Ran).
SR: 31/23/16/11/-/-/　(Mrs Eileen M Milligan), D Moffatt

2571 Strachan Kerr Handicap Chase Class B (0-140 5-y-o and up) £6,490 3m 1f...............(2:30)

2317[2] WHISPERING STEEL [128] 11-11-2 B Storey, *keen hold, prmnt, led 6 out, clr 2 out, kpt on wl.*
..................(11 to 8 fav op 5 to 4 tchd 6 to 4)　1
2488[4] KILCOLGAN [117] (bl) 10-10-5[5] N Bentley, *led till hdd 6 out, sn outpcd, rallied 2 out, no ch wth wnr.* (16 to 1 op 10 to 1)　2
NORTHANTS [124] 11-10-12 M Moloney, *hld up in tch, pushed alng 12th, chlgd 5 out, outpcd 3 out, sn no dngr.*
......................................(3 to 1 tchd 7 to 2)　3

2027[6] BEACHY HEAD [128] 9-11-2 G Cahill, *prmnt, pushed alng 11th, effrt bef 4 out, no imprsn whn blun badly nxt.*
..................................(20 to 1 op 10 to 1)　4
1637 BETTER TIMES AHEAD [140] 11-12-0 A Dobbin, *pressed ldr, outpcd 6 out, struggling last 3*....................(5 to 2)　5
Dist: 3l, 8l, ¾l, 11l. 6m 51.90s. a 51.90s (5 Ran).
(J Michael Gillow), G Richards

2572 Martnaham Novice Hurdle Class E (5-y-o and up) £2,430 2m..... (3:00)

FORESWORN (USA) 5-10-12 D Bentley, *nvr far away, led 2 out, ran on strly.........*(16 to 1 op 5 to 1 tchd 20 to 1)　1
2344* JERVAULX (Ire) 6-11-4 A Dobbin, *hld up, improved to chal 3 out, one pace frm last.*.........(5 to 4 fav tchd 11 to 8)　2
2236[2] NORTHERN UNION (Ire) 6-10-12 D Parker, *wl plcd, improved 5th, led bef 3 out to nxt, fdg whn blun last.*
.....................................(6 to 4 tchd 13 to 8)　3
2206[9] THE STUFFED PUFFIN (Ire) 5-10-12 N Bentley, *mstk 1st, made most till hdd bef 3 out, sn struggling.*
.....................(14 to 1 op 10 to 1 tchd 16 to 1)　4
2533[6] OBVIOUS RISK 6-10-5 (7*) Tristan Davidson, *hld up, effrt hfwy, outpcd last 4...*(33 to 1 op 100 to 1 tchd 200 to 1)　5
NORDISK LEGEND 5-10-12 T Reed, *pld hrd in rear, nvr on terms...*...............(200 to 1 op 100 to 1)　6
DE-VEERS CURRIE (Ire) 5-10-7 D J Moffatt, *beh, struggling hfwy, nvr on terms...*...........(25 to 1 op 20 to 1)　7
OPERATIC DANCER 6-10-12 M Moloney, *jmpd badly, mid-div, struggling hfwy, pld up bef 3 out.*
......................................(200 to 1 op 100 to 1)　pu
MR MEDLEY 5-10-12 B Storey, *chsd ldrs, struggling hfwy, pld up bef 3 out........*(16 to 1 op 12 to 1 tchd 20 to 1)　pu
2489[6] ALAN'S PRIDE (Ire) 6-10-7 G Cahill, *chsd ldr, struggling bef 4 out, sn btn, pld up nxt.............*(14 to 1 op 16 to 1)　pu
Dist: 7l, 9l, 15l, 1½l, 26l, 18l. 4m 2.40s. a 26.40s (10 Ran).
SR: 12/11/-/-/-/　(D W Whillans), D W Whillans

2573 Field And Lawn Handicap Chase Class D for the Mellerays Belle Challenge Cup (0-125 5-y-o and up) £3,522 2½m..................(3:30)

2321 NICHOLAS PLANT [97] 8-10-0 G Cahill, *made all, rdn and ran on strly fnl 3............*(8 to 1 op 10 to 1 tchd 12 to 1)　1
2321[2] JUDICIAL FIELD (Ire) [97] (bl) 8-9-12[1] (3*) E Husband, *trkd wnr gng wl, rdn out, effrt 4 out, hit 2 out, not quicken.*
..............................(9 to 2 op 9 to 2)　2
1628 VILLAGE REINDEER (NZ) [107] 10-10-10 T Reed, *hld up, improved 9th, chsd ldrs 11th, rdn whn hit and hmpd 2 out, fdd.*
.....................................(5 to 1 op 4 to 1)　3
2317[6] SOLBA (USA) [100] 8-10-3 D Parker, *chsd ldrs, outpcd tenth, rallied to chase ldrs appr 4 out, blun nxt, fdd.*
..................(4 to 1 op 7 to 2 tchd 5 to 1)　4
2321[3] GOLDEN FIDDLE (Ire) [97] 9-10-0 B Storey, *in tch, outpcd 11th, no dngr frm nxt..........*(3 to 1 fav tchd 7 to 2)　5
2534 QUIXALL CROSSETT [97] 12-9-8[1] (7*) Tristan Davidson, *beh, lost tch fnl circuit, tld off.........*(300 to 1 op 200 to 1)　6
PETER [97] 9-10-0 D Bentley, *chasing ldrs whn blun badly and uns rdr 8th.................*(12 to 1 op 10 to 1)　ur
2189[9] WHAAT FETTLE [125] 12-12-0 A Dobbin, *chsd ldrs, outpcd aftr 8th, rallied nxt, tdd 11th, pld up bef 4 out.*
.......................(10 to 1 op 8 to 1 tchd 12 to 1)　pu
ISLAND GALE [98] 12-10-11 F Perratt, *beh, struggling fnl circuit, tld off whn pld up bef 4 out....*(50 to 1 op 33 to 1)　pu
Dist: 8l, 13l, 19l, 7l, dist. 5m 27.50s. a 40.50s (9 Ran).
(Mrs M F Paterson), J S Goldie

2574 Gaiety Theatre Handicap Hurdle Class D (0-120 4-y-o and up) £3,057 2½m..........................(4:00)

2348[4] OAT COUTURE [115] 9-11-9 A Dobbin, *nvr far away, led 3 out, hdd briefly aftr last, gmely.......*(8 to 1 tchd 10 to 1)　1
2349[3] PARIAH (Ire) [92] 8-10-0 G Cahill, *hld up, improved aftr 4 out, styd on und pres to ld briefly after last, rallied. ..*(7 to 2 co-fav op 4 to 1 tchd 9 to 2)　2
2128 PALACEGATE KING [116] 8-11-5 (5*) S Taylor, *in tch, rdn to chal bef 2 out, no extr aftr last....*(7 to 2 co-fav op 3 to 1)　3
2389* CITTADINO [106] 7-10-7 (7*) N Horrocks, *hndy on outer, improved to chal 3 out, one pace appr last. .....*(7 to 2 co-fav tchd 4 to 1)　4
2238[2] KEMO SABO [92] 5-10-0 D Parker, *led till hdd 3 out, fdd.*
....................................(5 to 1 op 4 to 1)　5
NEW CHARGES [97] 10-10-0 (5*) B Grattan, *prmnt till rdn and fdd bef 3 out........*.................(20 to 1 op 14 to 1)　6
BANG IN TROUBLE (Ire) [106] 6-10-7 (7*) D Jewett, *cl up till fdd 4 out.........*.........................(12 to 1)　7
2238[3] GLENUGIE [99] (v) 6-10-7 N Bentley, *towards rear, drvn alng frm 5th, sn struggling.......*(5 to 1 op 4 to 1)　8
KIRSTENBOSCH [92] 10-9-8[1] (7*) W Dowling, *beh, struggling 4 out, pld up nxt..................*(66 to 1 tchd 100 to 1)　9
Dist: ½l, 2l, 20l, hd, 7l, dist. 5m 15.90s. a 37.90s (9 Ran).
(Mackinnon Mills), L Lungo

CATTERICK (good)

347

Saturday February 8th
Going Correction: PLUS 0.50 sec. per fur.

2575 Levy Board Mares' Only Novices' Hurdle Class E (4-y-o and up) £2,458 2m. . . . . (1:30)

2173[5] MEG'S MEMORY (Ire) 4-10-4 T Eley, *chsd ldrs, rdn alng 2 out, styd on appr last, led nr finish.* . . . . (8 to 1 op 5 to 1) 1
2419* SPRITZER (Ire) 5-11-7 P Niven, *hld up, steady hdwy hfwy, cl up 3 out, led nxt and sn rdn, hdd and no extr nr finish.* . . . . (7 to 4 op 6 to 4 tchd 15 to 8) 2
880[2] NISHAMIRA (Ire) 5-11-0 D Gallagher, *hld up in tch, smooth hdwy 5th, led 3 out to nxt, ev ch till no extr und pres last.* . . . . (6 to 4 fav tchd 13 to 8) 3
2260[6] DERRING FLOSS 7-10-7 (7*) Miss J Wormall, *mid-div, hdwy aftr 3 out, chsd ldrs nxt, kpt on same pace.* . . . . (20 to 1 op 14 to 1) 4
1943[5] ANALOGICAL 4-10-4 R Supple, *pld hrd, chsd ldrs till wknd appr 2 out.* . . . . (50 to 1 op 33 to 1) 5
1909[5] FRO 4-9-13 (5*) R McGrath, *pld hrd, made most till hdd 5th, grad wknd frm nxt.* . . . . (6 to 1 op 10 to 1) 6
2153 GAUTBY HENPECKED (bl) 4-10-4 J Callaghan, *al rear.* . . . . (50 to 1 op 33 to 1) 7
2158 CARLY-J 6-11-0 Mr N Kent, *chsd ldrs till wknd aftr 3 out.* . . . . (50 to 1 op 33 to 1) 8
MARJIMEL 6-11-0 M Foster, *beh frm hfwy* . . . . (50 to 1 op 33 to 1 tchd 66 to 1) 9
2387[9] KAYE'S SECRET 4-10-4 J Supple, *chsd ldrs, blun second, drvn alng 4th, sn lost pl and beh.* . . . . . (50 to 1 op 33 to 1) 10
2256 SKIP TO SOMERFIELD 5-11-0 A S Smith, *chsd ldrs, led 5th to nxt, sn wknd.* . . . . (20 to 1 tchd 25 to 1) 11
ALLERBECK 7-11-0 L O'Hara, *not jump wl, sn beh, tld off frm 3rd.* . . . . (50 to 1 op 33 to 1) 12
1669 PERSIAN SUNSET (Ire) 5-11-0 K Gaule, *beh frm hfwy, tld off aftr 3 out.* . . . . (50 to 1 tchd 66 to 1) 13
1783[7] FAIRY-LAND (Ire) 5-10-9 (5*) G F Ryan, *pld hrd, cl up till wknd 4th, tld off aftr 3 out.* . . . . (25 to 1 op 20 to 1) 14
2008[8] PRIMITIVE LIGHT 7-10-7 (7*) M Newton, *mid-div, effrt and hdwy to chase ldg grp 3 out, rdn and btn nxt, f last.* . . . . (20 to 1 op 16 to 1) f
REGAL JEST 7-10-11 (3*) E Callaghan, *beh frm 3rd, tld off whn pld up bef last.* . . . . (50 to 1 op 33 to 1 tchd 66 to 1) pu

Dist: ¾l, 1¾l, 10l, 14l, 9l, 13l, 3l, nk, 10l, 4l. 3m 57.20s. a 17.20s (16 Ran).
(Centaur Racing), A Streeter

2576 Whitby Novices' Chase Class E (5-y-o and up) £2,989 2m. . . . . (2:05)

2289 ROBERTY LEA 9-11-2 P Niven, *jmpd slow early and beh, steady hdwy 7th, effrt aftr 3 out, rdn last and styd on to ld last 100 yards.* . . . . (7 to 2 op 6 to 4) 1
2201[5] ROYAL CRIMSON 6-11-2 R Garritty, *in tch, hdwy 4 out, led 2 out, rdn last, hdd and no extr last 100 yards.* . . . . (7 to 2 op 9 to 2) 2
2286[5] MARLINGFORD 10-11-2 (7*) L McGrath, *led to 4th, hit 5th, lft in ld 3 out, hdd nxt and btn whn hit last.* . . (8 to 1 op 7 to 1) 3
1912 COOLRENY (Ire) 8-11-2 Mr M Thompson, *sn beh, tld off frm hfwy.* . . . . (100 to 1 op 33 to 1) 4
1797[4] THE FENCE SHRINKER 6-11-2 J Supple, *chsd ldrs, rdn alng 7th, wknd nxt and sn tld off.* . . . . (33 to 1 op 25 to 1) 5
2201[8] CHILDSWAY 9-10-11 (5*) D J Kavanagh, *prmnt, led 4th till f 8th.* . . . . (20 to 1 op 25 to 1 tchd 16 to 1) f
2358 CHORUS LINE (Ire) 8-10-11 R Supple, *chsd ldrs till f 5th.* . . . . (9 to 4 fav op 2 to 1 tchd 5 to 2) f
1263[9] DASH TO THE PHONE (USA) 5-10-7 A S Smith, *prmnt, hdwy 7th, led nxt till f 3 out.* . . . . (14 to 1 op 10 to 1) f
2192 GREAT GABLE (Ire) 6-11-2 L O'Hara, *f second.* . . . . (50 to 1 op 33 to 1) f
2205 MOST RICH (Ire) 9-11-2 K Johnson, *beh, some hdwy whn blun and uns rdr 3 out.* . . . . (33 to 1 op 20 to 1) ur
2259 LEPTON (Ire) (bl) 6-11-2 Derek Byrne, *brght dwn second.* . . . . (50 to 1 op 33 to 1) bd
2407[6] RAIN-N-SUN 11-11-2 D Gallagher, *al rear, tld off whn pld up bef 3 out.* . . . . (16 to 1 op 10 to 1) pu

Dist: 2½l, 9l, dist, dist. 4m 5.00s. a 18.00s (12 Ran).
(Wentdale Const Ltd), Mrs M Reveley

2577 Bridge Selling Hurdle Class G (4-y-o and up) £2,066 2m. . . . . (2:35)

2417 LUCKY BEA 4-10-7 P Niven, *hld up, steady hdwy 5th, effrt 2 out, rdn appr last, styd on to ld flt.* . . . . . . (6 to 1 op 4 to 1) 1
1909 AMAZING SAIL (Ire) 4-10-7 A S Smith, *cl up, led aftr 3rd, rdn 2 out, hdd last, no extr und pres flt.* . . . . . (33 to 1 op 20 to 1) 2
2492[3] AUNTIE ALICE 7-10-12 W Dwan, *beh, steady hdwy 5th, chsd ldrs aftr 3 out, ev ch nxt, sn drvn and no extr flt.* . . . . (7 to 2 fav tchd 4 to 1) 3
2204[8] ROBSERA (Ire) 6-11-10 R Garritty, *hld up, gd hdwy appr 6th, chal 2 out, rdn to ld last, hdd and no extr flt.* . . . . (4 to 1 op 11 to 2) 4
2417 RADMORE BRANDY 4-9-13 (3*) G Lee, *al prmnt, chal 2 out and ev ch till drvn last and no extr.* . . . . (15 to 2 op 6 to 1 tchd 8 to 1) 5
2440 NEVER SO BLUE (Ire) 6-11-3 (7*) R Wilkinson, *in tch, effrt and ev ch whn hmpd appr 2 out, one pace.* (14 to 1 op 16 to 1) 6
2485[8] COOL STEEL (Ire) 5-11-0 (3*) E Callaghan, *beh till styd on frm 2 out, nvr dngrs.* . . . . (20 to 1 op 16 to 1) 7
BEAUMAN 7-11-3 K Gaule, *led till aftr 3rd, rdn alng 3 out and weakenend appr nxt.* . . . . (6 to 1 tchd 7 to 1) 8
2420[7] ANORAK (USA) 7-11-3 (7*) N Hannity, *prmnt till rdn and wknd bef 3 out.* . . . . (12 to 1 op 10 to 1) 9
2123 PORT VALENSKA (Ire) 4-10-7 D Gallagher, *nvr rch ldrs.* . . . . (50 to 1 op 33 to 1) 10
2201 SOUTH COAST STAR (Ire) 7-11-3 M Foster, *chsd ldrs till rdn and wknd bef 3 out.* . . . . (50 to 1 op 25 to 1) 11
2417 BEACON HILL LADY 4-9-11 (5*) R McGrath, *beh frm hfwy.* . . . . (50 to 1 op 33 to 1) 12
1689[9] LOMOND LASSIE (USA) 4-9-9 (7*) M Newton, *sn beh, tld off frm 3rd.* . . . . (50 to 1 op 33 to 1) 13
2236 MILETRIAN CITY 4-10-7 D Byrne, *in tch till wknd 5th and sn beh.* . . . . (20 to 1 op 14 to 1 tchd 25 to 1) 14
SUN MARK (Ire) 6-11-3 J Supple, *beh frm hfwy.* . . . . (8 to 1 op 10 to 1 tchd 14 to 1) 15
2390[8] SHARMOOR 5-10-12 R Supple, *in tch till wknd and beh frm 5th.* . . . . (14 to 1 op 16 to 1) 16
2464 JUST SUPPOSEN (Ire) (bl) 6-11-10 J Callaghan, *in tch, rdn alng whn f 3 out.* . . . . (20 to 1 op 16 to 1) f
BADGER HILL 4-10-0 (7*) A Todd, *mid-div whn f 5th.* . . . . (50 to 1 op 25 to 1) f

Dist: Nk, ¾l, sht-hd, 2l, ¾l, 2½l, 23l, hd, 28l, ½l. 3m 59.70s. a 19.70s (18 Ran).
(Bee Health Ltd), M W Easterby

2578 Ian Hutchinson Memorial Challenge Cup An Amateur Riders' Novices' Handicap Hurdle Class F (0-105 4-y-o and up) £2,202 3m 1f 110yds (3:05)

2241[4] RUBER [75] 10-9-13 (5*) Miss P Robson, *al prmnt, led 3 out, rdn aftr nxt and ran on wl.* . . . . (8 to 1 op 10 to 1) 1
2256[8] INDICATOR [96] 5-11-4 (7*) Mr A Balding, *hld up and beh, steady hdwy 8, hit 3 out, callenged nxt and ev ch till no extr und pres flt.* . . . . . . (13 to 2 op 6 to 1 tchd 7 to 1) 2
2256 PONTEVEDRA (Ire) [83] 4-9-12[5] (7*) Mr R Wakley, *hld up and beh, gd hdwy 9th, effrt 2 out, sn rdn and one pace.* . . . . (14 to 1 op 20 to 1) 3
1822 LAST REFUGE (Ire) [86] 8-10-8 (7*) Mr C Mulhall, *in tch, rdn alng 3 out and one pace frm nxt.* . . . . (25 to 1 tchd 33 to 1) 4
2236[9] BLACK ICE (Ire) [72] 6-9-8 (7*) Mr W Burnell, *prmnt, rdn alng aftr 3 out, grad wknd.* . . . . (10 to 1) 5
1951[7] SKI PATH [71] 8-9-9[2] (7*) Miss R Clark, *not fluent, chsd ldrs till rdn alng and wknd 8th.* . . . . (33 to 1 tchd 50 to 1) 6
2392 GUTTERIDGE (Ire) [71] 7-9-12[5] (7*) Mr W McLaughlin, *chsd ldrs, rdn alng 8 and wknd bef 3 out.* . . . (12 to 1 op 10 to 1) 7
STRONG CHARACTER [71] 11-9-7 (7*) Miss S Lamb, *beh frm hfwy, tld off whn pld up bef 2 out.* . . . . (50 to 1 op 33 to 1) pu
2320[2] BELLE ROSE (Ire) [88] 7-10-12 (5*) Mr R Hale, *prmnt till wknd 7th, tld off whn pld up bef 2 out.* . . . . (4 to 1 op 3 to 1) pu
2418 DRY HILL LAD [87] 6-10-9 (7*) Mr P Scott, *beh frm hfwy, tld off whn pld up bef 2 out.* . . . (16 to 1 op 14 to 1 tchd 20 to 1) pu
2463 IRISH BUZZ (Ire) [74] 5-10-3[10] (7*) Mr Chris Wilson, *prmnt till rdn alng and wknd bef 3 out, beh whn pld up before nxt.* . . . . (25 to 1) pu
2349[2] LIFEBUOY (Ire) [86] 6-11-1 Mr S Swiers, *al rear, beh whn pld up bef last.* . . . . (3 to 1 fav op 7 to 2 tchd 4 to 1) pu
2288[5] GLENBOWER [85] 5-10-11 (3*) Mr C Bonner, *made most to 3 out, sn wknd and beh whn pld up bef 2 out.* . . . . (7 to 2 op 5 to 2) pu

Dist: 1½l, 8l, 8l, 4l, 24l, ½l. 6m 40.20s. a 39.20s (13 Ran).
(R W Thomson), R W Thomson

2579 Red Onion Grand National Trial Handicap Chase Class C (0-130 5-y-o and up) £7,302 3¾m. . . . . (3:35)

1819[3] ACT THE WAG (Ire) [108] 8-11-8 P Niven, *trkd ldrs, hdwy 6 out, lft in ld 4 out, rdn appr last and ran on.* . . . . (13 to 2 op 6 to 1 tchd 7 to 1) 1
2203[5] HEAVENLY CITIZEN (Ire) [93] 9-10-7 K Johnson, *prmnt, hit 14th, rdn and lft second 4 out, ridden nxt and one pace.* . . . . (9 to 1 op 7 to 1) 2
2334[9] PIMS GUNNER (Ire) [102] 9-11-2 R Garritty, *hld up in tch, effrt and hdwy whn hmpd 4 out, drvn 2 out, one pace last.* . . . . (11 to 2 op 7 to 2 tchd 6 to 1) 3
2175[3] DARK OAK [110] 11-11-10 Derek Byrne, *not fluent, al rear, tld off frm 17th.* . . . . (7 to 1 tchd 8 to 1) 4
2239[2] WESTWELL BOY [105] 11-11-5 R Supple, *cl up, led 8th, rdn and hit 5 out, f nxt.* . . . . (100 to 30 op 5 to 2) f
2285* CHOISTY (Ire) [108] 7-11-8 J Supple, *not fluent, made most to 8th, rdn alng and hit 16th, wkng whn blun and uns rdr 6 out.* . . . . (7 to 4 fav op 6 to 4 tchd 15 to 8) ur

Dist: 6l, 1l, dist. 8m 7.80s. (6 Ran).
(Robert Ogden), Martin Todhunter

2580 Aske Handicap Hurdle Class C (0-130 4-y-o and up) £3,413 2m . . . . (4:05)

2329[3] STAR RAGE (Ire) [127] 7-12-0 D Gallagher, *in tch, sddl slpd and pushed alng 4th, hdwy nxt, led bef 2 out, sn rdn, ran on gmely flt.* . . . . (9 to 4 fav op 2 to 1 tchd 5 to 2) 1

2467⁵ DESERT FIGHTER [111] 6-10-12 P Niven, *trkd ldrs, pushed alng and outpcd bef 3 out, gd hdwy to chal nxt and ev ch till no extr nr finish*............(5 to 1 op 9 to 2 tchd 11 to 2) 2
2128 CENTAUR EXPRESS [118] 5-11-5 T Eley, *led, rdn alng 3 out, hdd bef nxt, drvn and ch last, no extr nr finish.* ....(3 to 1 tchd 100 to 30) 3
2358 TAPATCH [Ire] [99] (bl) 9-9-11 (3*) G Lee, *prmnt, chsd ldr 4th till rdn and wknd aftr 3 out.* ....(16 to 1 op 12 to 1 tchd 20 to 1) 4
2256* NIGHT DANCE [104] 5-10-5 A S Smith, *cl up, rdn alng 5th and grad wknd, beh 2 out.* ....(5 to 2 op 9 to 4) 5
2467⁷ ELPIDOS [115] 5-11-2 R Garritty, *al rear, lost tch hfwy, tld off whn pld up bef 2 out.* ....(10 to 1 op 8 to 1) pu
Dist: 2½l, ¾l, dist, 28l. 3m 53.70s. a 13.70s (6 Ran).
SR: 43/24/30/ (J David Abell), J L Harris

2581 Brough Handicap Hurdle Class F (0-105 4-y-o and up) £2,132 2m 3f
.........................(4:35)

2359³ HERE COMES HERBIE [82] 5-10-4 (5*) R McGrath, *hld up, steady hdwy 7th, led 2 out, sn rdn and styd on wl.* ....(11 to 2 op 7 to 2) 1
TOPSAWYER [93] 9-11-6 K Gaule, *hld up, steady hdwy 7th, chlgd 2 out and ev ch till no extr und pres flt.* ....(7 to 1 op 10 to 1) 2
2122 FRYUP SATELLITE [82] 6-10-9 Miss P Robson, *al prmnt, led 3 out, rdn and hdd nxt, one pace appr last.* ....(14 to 1 op 10 to 1) 3
1740⁴ INNOCENT GEORGE [87] 8-11-0 R Supple, *mid-div, efrt and hdwy 3 out, rdn nxt and kpt on same pace.* ....(14 to 1 op 12 to 1 tchd 16 to 1) 4
2296² SILLY MONEY [91] 6-11-4 R Garritty, *cl up, ev ch 3 out, rdn and wknd appr nxt.*........(11 to 2 op 5 to 1 tchd 13 to 2) 5
2288⁶ DON'T TELL TOM [Ire] [86] 7-10-10 (3*) E Callaghan, *beh, efrt and some hdwy appr 3 out, sn rdn and no imprsn.* ....(16 to 1 tchd 20 to 1) 6
2204² OPERA FAN [Ire] [86] 5-10-13 A S Smith, *led, rdn alng, hdd and hit 6th, wknd quickly, beh frm 3 out.* ....(4 to 1 fav op 7 to 2) 7
1691* TIP IT IN [90] 8-10-10 (7*) M Newton, *trkd ldrs, pushed alng and hit 7th, sn wknd.....*(6 to 1 op 5 to 1 tchd 13 to 2) 8
1259* APOLLO'S DAUGHTER [73] 9-10-0 J Supple, *al rear, beh hfwy, tld off....*..................(20 to 1 op 12 to 1) 9
BIRTHPLACE [Ire] [73] 7-10-0 K Johnson, *prmnt till f 4th.* ....(33 to 1 op 20 to 1) f
2204³ JEMIMA PUDDLEDUCK [95] (v) 6-11-8 T Eley, *in tch, rdn alng 7th, f 3 out.*..................(6 to 1 op 5 to 1) f
2122⁴ COURT JOKER [Ire] [82] 5-10-9 P Niven, *mid-divison till brght dwn 4th.*..................(12 to 1 op 10 to 1) bd
QUEEN BUZZARD [88] 9-11-1 Mr J Weymes, *beh frm hfwy, pld up bef 2 out.*..................(25 to 1 op 20 to 1) pu
Dist: 3l, 6l, sht-hd, 6l, 8l, 26l, 1¼l, 20l. 4m 50.40s. a 30.40s (13 Ran).
(H S Hutchinson), W Storey

NAVAN (IRE) (yielding to soft)
Saturday February 8th

2582 Dunboyne E.B.F. Mares Hurdle (4-y-o and up) £4,110 2m.............(1:30)

2275* BORO BOW [Ire] 6-11-13 T P Treacy, ...(5 to 1) 1
2413² BORN TO WIN [Ire] 7-11-6 T P Rudd, ...(10 to 1) 2
2088² BAI-BRUN KATE [Ire] 6-11-6 C O'Dwyer, ...(9 to 1) 3
2088⁸ MARYOBEE [Ire] 7-10-13 (7*) Mr P M Cloke, ...(14 to 1) 4
2166* WINDY BEE [Ire] 6-11-6 (7*) A Nolan, ...(3 to 1 jt-fav) 5
2225² MONTELISA [Ire] 5-11-10 C F Swan, ...(3 to 1 jt-fav) 6
1536 SUPREME ALLIANCE [Ire] 7-11-6 T J Mitchell, ...(14 to 1) 7
VALENTINE GALE [Ire] 7-11-6 D J Casey, ...(7 to 1) 8
2449 RATHCOLMAN GALE [Ire] 7-11-3 (3*) K Whelan, (100 to 1) 9
TINY'S CARMEL [Ire] 6-11-3 (3*) U Smyth, ...(25 to 1) 10
269⁴ PARSEE [Ire] 5-11-3 F Woods, ...(12 to 1) 11
ANNAELAINE [Ire] 6-10-13 (7*) B J Geraghty, ...(12 to 1) 12
2339 FLOWERS OF MAY [Ire] 6-10-13 (7*) R P Hogan, ..(66 to 1) 13
2270 LADY OF GRANGE [Ire] 5-11-3 F J Flood, ...(20 to 1) 14
2270 NIL FAIC [Ire] 5-11-3 M P Hourigan, ...(66 to 1) 15
SCOBIE GIRL [Ire] 7-11-6 P A Roche, ...(16 to 1) 16
2449 BARNA GIRL [Ire] 7-11-6 J R Barry, ...(25 to 1) 17
1908 MAY BLOOM [Ire] 6-11-6 J Shortt, ...(25 to 1) 18
2380⁶ POLITICAL TROUBLES [Ire] 7-11-6 A Powell, ...(25 to 1) 19
2276 MAGS DWYER [Ire] (bl) 7-11-1 (5*) T Martin, ...(25 to 1) 20
CASTLEHUME [Ire] 5-11-3 H Rogers, ...(33 to 1) 21
GOLDWERN [Ire] 8-11-6 L P Cusack, ...(50 to 1) 22
2443 DIVINE LILY [Ire] 6-11-6 K F O'Brien, ...(100 to 1) pu
Dist: 1l, 2½l, 2½l, 4l. 4m 6.30s. (23 Ran).
(J P Hill), P Mullins

2583 Boyerstown Maiden Hurdle (5 & 6-y-o) £3,082 2¼m.............(2:00)

COQ HARDI VENTURE [Ire] 6-10-13 (7*) B J Geraghty, ...(20 to 1) 1
2049³ SILVIAN BLISS [USA] 5-11-10 C O'Dwyer, ...(5 to 1) 2
2081¹⁴ HEAVY HUSTLER [Ire] 6-11-6 F Woods, ...(15 to 2) 3
2368² IRIDAL (bl) 5-11-10 K F O'Brien, ...(11 to 4 fav) 4
EVENKEEL [Ire] 5-10-9 (7*) P J Dobbs, ...(20 to 1) 5

1457⁶ KAISER SOSA [Ire] 6-10-13 (7*) R P Hogan, ...(12 to 1) 6
POLLTRIC [Ire] 6-11-6 P L Malone, ...(33 to 1) 7
2368⁴ FANE PATH [Ire] 5-11-10 J Shortt, ...(8 to 1) 8
2443 HEART 'N SOUL-ON [Ire] 6-10-13 (7*) D K Budds, (33 to 1) 9
928 STAR CLUB [Ire] 5-11-5 H Rogers, ...(20 to 1) 10
2037 KILCAR [Ire] 6-11-6 D T Evans, ...(25 to 1) 11
2168³ FILL THE BILL [Ire] 5-11-10 C F Swan, ...(9 to 2) 12
2414 ZACOPANI [Ire] 5-11-2 D J Casey, ...(25 to 1) 13
2160⁷ SUIR FIND [Ire] 5-11-2 L P Cusack, ...(16 to 1) 14
1548 MAIRTINS BUCK [Ire] 6-10-13 (7*) R M Murphy, ..(33 to 1) 15
CNOCAN GLAS [Ire] 5-11-2 A Powell, ...(25 to 1) 16
NORMINS HUSSAR [Ire] 5-11-2 T J Mitchell, ...(14 to 1) 17
2443 JACKPOT JOHNNY [Ire] 6-10-13 (7*) M D Murphy, (33 to 1) 18
2129⁸ HI-LO PICCOLO [Ire] 5-10-11 T P Treacy, ...(33 to 1) 19
MANISTER ABBEY [Ire] 5-11-2 J P Broderick, ...(33 to 1) 20
2443 YASHGANS VISION [Ire] 6-11-2 (7*) S FitzGerald, (14 to 1) 21
1364⁶ PORT NA SON [Ire] 6-11-6 T Horgan, ...(33 to 1) 22
BITOFRAZZ [Ire] 6-10-13 (7*) M J D Moore, ...(20 to 1) 23
2380⁸ BARORA GALE [Ire] 6-10-10 (5*) T Martin, ...(50 to 1) 24
2108⁴ TRUVARO [Ire] 6-11-6 F J Flood, ...(10 to 1) f
183 DUNMORE DOM [Ire] 5-10-9 (7*) D M Bean, ...(50 to 1) pu
2107 IFIELD COURT HOTEL [Ire] 6-11-1 P A Roche, ...(33 to 1) pu
Dist: 5½l, 2½l, 2½l, ¾l. 4m 45.50s. (27 Ran).
(Mrs Catherine Howard), Noel Meade

2584 Boyne E.B.F. Hurdle (Grade 2) (5-y-o and up) £9,675 3m.............(2:30)

2084* WHAT A QUESTION [Ire] 9-11-9 C O'Dwyer, *wl plcd, prog to ld 3 out, rdn aftr nxt, styd on well r-in.*...........(4 to 1) 1
2364 ANTAPOURA [Ire] 5-10-10 C F Swan, *trkd ldr, mstk 6th, prog to ld appr 4 out, hdd nxt, sn rdn to dispute lead 2 out, headed last.*............................(2 to 1 fav) 2
2364² DERRYMOYLE [Ire] 8-11-5 J P Broderick, *wtd wth, prog bef 4 out to track ldrs 2 out, kpt on wl.*..................(5 to 1) 3
2473⁶ NOTCOMPLAININGBUT [Ire] 6-11-0 T P Treacy, *mid-div, prog 4 out, rdn aftr nxt, kpt on.*..................(8 to 1) 4
2342⁶ BLUSHING SAND [Ire] 7-10-9 (7*) Mr T J Beattie, *rear till rdn and prog bef 2 out.*..................(33 to 1) 5
2134⁷ DIFFICULT TIMES [Ire] 5-10-12 S C Lyons, *wl plcd, rdn aftr 3 out, sn wknd.*..................(20 to 1) 6
2340 CHANCE COFFEY 12-11-5 G M O'Neill, *rear, slow 4th, rdn bef 2 out, no extr.*..................(33 to 1) 7
2232⁴ URUBANDE [Ire] 7-11-9 T Horgan, *hld up till some prog bef 3 out, no extr.*..................(4 to 1) 8
2170 LOVE AND PORTER [Ire] 9-11-0 D H O'Connor, *led till hdd bef 4 out, wknd.*..................(33 to 1) 9
Dist: 2½l, 3½l, 10l, 3l. 6m 5.70s. (9 Ran).
(Mrs Miles Valentine), M F Morris

2585 Boardsmill Handicap Hurdle (0-109 4-y-o and up) £3,082 3m......(3:00)

2366⁸ HI KNIGHT [Ire] [-] 7-11-8 K F O'Brien, ...(10 to 1) 1
2366 JIMMY THE WEED [Ire] [-] 8-9-12 J R Barry, ...(25 to 1) 2
2366² COOLREE LORD [Ire] [-] 6-9-8 M P Hourigan, ...(9 to 1) 3
2366³ TREANAREE [Ire] [-] 8-9-13 (7*) S Kelly, ...(14 to 1) 4
2229³ LISCAHILL FORT [Ire] [-] 8-10-11 (7*) Mr D M Loughnane, ...(10 to 1) 5
2340⁴ APPELLATE COURT [Ire] [-] (bl) 9-10-12 (7*) B J Geraghty, ...(20 to 1) 6
2366⁶ MONDEO ROSE [Ire] [-] 5-11-2 C F Swan, ...(8 to 1) 7
2229³ GRANGE COURT [Ire] [-] 7-11-7 (7*) R P Hogan, (20 to 1) 8
2339⁶ EBONY KING [Ire] [-] 7-11-7 (3*) U Smyth, ...(14 to 1) 9
2379 GLENFIELDS CASTLE [Ire] [-] 7-11-0 L P Cusack, (14 to 1) 10
2272 MISS BERTAINE [Ire] [-] (bl) 8-9-7 (7*) J Casey, (16 to 1) 11
2339 DROICHEAD LAPEEN [Ire] [-] 10-10-6 (7*) Mr T J Beattie, ...(25 to 1) 12
2135³ LEAMHOG [Ire] [-] (bl) 7-11-12 T P Treacy, ...(8 to 1) 13
2068 TOTAL CONFUSION [-] 10-11-1 (7*) M P Horan, (20 to 1) 14
2379⁸ HANNAH'S PET [Ire] [-] 7-9-2 (5*) T Martin, ...(50 to 1) 15
2366 THE PARSON'S FILLY [Ire] [-] 7-10-7 D H O'Connor, ...(14 to 1) 16
2272⁴ VEREDARIUS [Fr] [-] 6-11-2 F Woods, ...(10 to 1) 17
2271 NATIVE FLECK [Ire] [-] 7-11-10 A Powell, ...(33 to 1) 18
2379⁷ THE THIRD MAN [Ire] [-] (bl) 8-9-7 P McWilliams, (20 to 1) 19
2381⁶ LAURA'S BEAU [-] 13-10-9 (7*) F M Berry, ...(33 to 1) 20
2366 DOUBLE STRIKE [Ire] [-] (bl) 6-10-11 H Rogers, (25 to 1) 21
2379 FOREST STAR [USA] [-] (bl) 8-9-0 (7*) J M Maguire, (66 to 1) 22
2378⁵ MICK MAN [Ire] [-] 6-9-6 (7*) P G Hourigan, ...(10 to 1) 23
2366⁹ CELTIC SUNRISE [-] 9-10-13 C O'Brien, ...(20 to 1) 24
2446 YOUR CALL [Ire] [-] 8-11-2 J Shortt, ...(16 to 1) 25
1904³ ICED HONEY [-] 10-10-13 T J Mitchell, ...(12 to 1) 26
2366 DEESIDE DOINGS [Ire] [-] (bl) 9-9-7 P L Malone, (66 to 1) pu
PATTISE TIM [Ire] [-] 8-11-9 J P Broderick, ...(12 to 1) pu
1460² DIAMOND DOUBLE [Ire] [-] 6-11-2 T Horgan, ...(20 to 1) pu
2366* VASILIKI [Ire] [-] 5-11-1 C O'Dwyer, ...(9 to 1) pu
Dist: Hd, 3l, 3l, 6l. 6m 3.90s. (30 Ran).
(M D McGrath), J R H Fowler

2586 Nobber Handicap Chase (5-y-o and up) £5,480 2m 1f.............(3:30)

2069² KLAIRON DAVIS [Fr] [-] 8-12-0 F Woods, ...(9 to 4 on) 1
2474 IDIOTS VENTURE [-] 10-10-7 C F Swan, ...(4 to 1) 2
2273 SHANAGARRY [Ire] [-] 8-10-7 C O'Dwyer, ...(9 to 1) 3
MONALEE RIVER [Ire] [-] 9-10-7 T P Treacy, ...(5 to 1) 4

349

Dist: 8l, 15l, 7l. 4m 19.70s. (4 Ran).

(C Jones), A L T Moore

2587 Navan E.B.F. Novice Chase (5-y-o and up) £4,110 2½m. . . . . (4:00)

2133*	CORKET (Ire) 7-11-9 C F Swan, ...(10 to 9 on)	1
1618⁵	CURRENCY BASKET (Ire) 8-11-4 J Shortt, ... (6 to 1)	2
2382²	MIROSWAKI (USA) 7-11-4 T J Mitchell, ... (12 to 1)	3
2231⁶	HEADBANGER 10-11-9 D H O'Connor, ... (5 to 2)	4
2135	MOORE'S MELODIES (Ire) 6-11-4 J P Broderick, . .(20 to 1)	5
2367	JOHNNY'S DREAM (Ire) 7-10-11 (7*) Mr A J Dempsey,	
	. . . .(14 to 1)	6
	HILLHEAD (Ire) 8-11-4 L P Cusack, ... (33 to 1)	7
2382⁴	OVER THE MAINE (Ire) 7-11-9 H Rogers, ...(14 to 1)	8
1837	FIELD OF DESTINY (Ire) 8-10-10 (3*) K Whelan, . . . (40 to 1)	9
	PARADISE ROAD 8-11-4 C O'Brien, ... (16 to 1)	10
2446	CHESLOCK (Ire (bl) 8-11-11 (3*) F Woods, ...(66 to 1)	ur
2446	CLERICAL COUSIN (Ire) 8-11-4 F Woods, ... (12 to 1)	ur

Dist: 11l, hd, 1½l, 15l. 5m 27.90s. (12 Ran).

(S J O'Sullivan), A P O'Brien

2588 Kilmessan I.N.H. Flat Race (5-y-o) £3,082 2m. . . . . (4:30)

	ROCKFIELD LEADER (Ire) 11-7 (7*) Mr A C Coyle,	
	. . . . (7 to 4 fav)	1
2022⁹	TOTAL SUCCESS (Ire) 11-7 (7*) Mr D Broad, ...(14 to 1)	2
2168⁷	THINKERS CORNER (Ire) 11-7 (7*) Mr A J Dempsey, (5 to 2)	3
	MINELLA HOTEL (Ire) 12-0 Mr B M Cash, ... (8 to 1)	4
	MONAVALE (Ire) 11-2 (7*) Mr M P Madden, ...(10 to 1)	5
	JONS GALE (Ire) 11-7 (7*) Mr I Buchanan, ... (25 to 1)	6
2092²	KINGMAN (Ire) 11-7 (7*) Miss A M Kent, ... (12 to 1)	7
1409⁴	AUBURN ROILELET (Ire) 11-9 Mr A R Coonan, ...(10 to 1)	8
2222	THE TICK-TACK MAN (Ire) 11-9 (5*) Mr J T McNamara,	
	. . . .(14 to 1)	9
	NEARLY A LINE 11-7 (7*) Mr A Fitzgerald, ...(10 to 1)	10
	DYRALLAGH (Ire) 11-2 (7*) Miss A McDonogh, . . .(20 to 1)	11
	MOUNT HALL (Ire) 11-2 (7*) Mr A G Cash, ... (16 to 1)	12
2172	SHOW UP (Ire) 11-7 (7*) Mr R Geraghty, ... (16 to 1)	13
	LANCASTER STREET (Ire) 12-0 Mr J P Dempsey, (12 to 1)	14

Dist: 1l, hd, 2l. 4m 15.30s. (14 Ran).

(M C Syndicate), P Mullins

NEWBURY (good)
Saturday February 8th
Going Correction: PLUS 0.70 sec. per fur. (races 1,2,4,5), PLUS 0.45 (3,6,7)

2589 Cathay Pacific Airways Handicap Chase Class B (0-145 6-y-o and up) £7,196 3¼m 110yds. . . . . (1:15)

2233³	CALL IT A DAY (Ire) [138] 7-11-12 A Maguire, hld up, smooth prog appr 17th, shaken up betw fnl 2, led last, ran on wl	
	. . . . (11 to 4 op 9 to 4 tchd 3 to 1)	1
2404²	RIVER MANDATE [125] (bl) 10-10-13 A Thornton, chsd ldr, lft in ld appr 17th, hdd 2 out, swtchd rght r-in, styd on.	
	. . . .(100 to 30 op 7 to 2 tchd 4 to 1)	2
2196⁴	LE MEILLE (Ire) [112] 8-10-0 N Williamson, wtd wth, smooth hdwy appr 17th, led 2 out to last, wknd r-in.	
	. . . . (10 to 1 op 12 to 1 tchd 14 to 1)	3
2325⁷	BRADBURY STAR [135] 12-11-9 P Hide, trkd ldrs, hit 3rd, lost pl 6th, beh whn hit 16th, tld off when pld up bef 2 out.	
	. . . . (20 to 1 op 12 to 1 tchd 25 to 1)	pu
2439²	SUNLEY BAY [120] 11-10-8 D Bridgwater, hld up, rdn alng tenth, jmpd slwly 12th, sn beh, hit 14th, tld off whn pld up bef 17th. . . . . (6 to 1 op 5 to 1 tchd 13 to 2)	pu
2247²	MONTEBEL (Ire) [118] 9-10-6 C Llewellyn, led till pld up and dismounted bef 17th, lme. . . . . . . (2 to 1 fav op 7 to 4)	pu

Dist: 1¼l, 5l. 6m 55.20s. a 27.20s (6 Ran).
SR: 11/-/-/

(Mrs Jane Lane), D Nicholson

2590 Mitsubishi Shogun Game Spirit Chase Class A Grade 2 (5-y-o and up) £18,690 2m 1f. . . . . (1:45)

2451*	DOUBLE SYMPHONY (Ire) 9-10-12 J Osborne, wtd wth, chlgd 2 out, led on bit last, shaken up and ran on wl r-in.	
	. . . .(5 to 4 on op 6 to 4 tchd 5 to 5 on)	1
2219	DANCING PADDY 9-11-3 D Walsh, mstk second, pressed ldr, lft in ld 5th, hit nxt, mistake 4 out, hdd last, one pace.	
	. . . .(100 to 30 op 9 to 2 tchd 3 to 1)	2
	ARCTIC KINSMAN 9-11-10 C Llewellyn, led till blun and uns rdr 5th. (9 to 4 op 7 to 4)	ur

Dist: 3½l. 4m 14.80s. a 14.80s (3 Ran).
SR: 55/56/-/

(Anthony Pye-Jeary), C P E Brooks

2591 Tote Gold Trophy Handicap Hurdle Class A (4-y-o and up) £58,796 2m 110yds. . . . . (2:20)

2218*	MAKE A STAND [136] 6-11-7 (4ex) C Maude, made all, clr frm 3rd, rdn alng appr 3 out, unchlgd.	
	. . . . (6 to 1 op 5 to 1 tchd 13 to 2)	1

Dist: 8l, 15l, 7l. 4m 19.70s. (4 Ran).

(C Jones), A L T Moore

Dist: 11l, hd, 1½l, 15l. 5m 27.90s. (12 Ran).

1500³	HAMILTON SILK [126] 5-10-11 Jamie Evans, hld up and beh, styd on wl frm 3 out, ran on to take second r-in, no imprsn on wnr. . . . .(40 to 1 op 33 to 1 tchd 50 to 1)	2
2190*	DIRECT ROUTE (Ire) [133] 6-11-4 N Williamson, wtd wth, cld 3rd, kpt on one pace und pres frm 2 out. (7 to 1 op 6 to 1)	3
2208*	MISTINGUETT (Ire) [138] 5-11-9 (4ex) J Osborne, hld up beh ldrs, rdn and styd on frm 2 out.	
	. . . . (7 to 1 tchd 13 to 2 and 15 to 2)	4
2218³	SILVER GROOM (Ire) [137] 7-11-3 (5*) S Ryan, hld up, chsd wnr 3 out till wknd r-in. . . . .(33 to 1 op 20 to 1)	5
2467*	EDELWEIS DU MOULIN (Fr) [127] 5-10-12 P Carberry, hld up, prog hfwy, wknd und pres appr last.	
	. . . . (5 to 2 fav tchd 3 to 1)	6
1612*	MISTER MOROSE (Ire) [138] 7-11-9 D Walsh, trkd ldrs, chsd wnr 5th to 3 out, sn wknd. . . . .(12 to 1)	7
2218³	KISSAIR (Ire) [134] 6-11-5 J F Titley, hld up beh ldrs, rdn appr 2 out, wknd r-in. . . . . . .(50 to 1 op 33 to 1 tchd 100 to 1)	8
2190	HATTA BREEZE [129] 5-10-11 (3*) R Massey, nvr nr to chal.	
	. . . . (20 to 1 op 25 to 1)	9
2329⁶	DR LEUNT (Ire) [134] 6-11-5 G Tormey, rdn alng 3rd, nvr better than mid-div. . . . .(50 to 1 op 66 to 1)	10
2001	PADDY'S RETURN (Ire) [141] (bl) 5-11-12 R Dunwoody, hld up beh ldrs, wknd 3 out.(11 to 1 op 12 to 1 tchd 14 to 1)	11
2208⁶	ESKIMO NEL (Ire) [135] 6-11-3 (3*) L Aspell, wtd wth, improved 3rd, wknd 3 out. . . . .(25 to 1 op 33 to 1)	12
2329⁷	ROLL A DOLLAR [127] 11-10-12 P Holley, al beh.	
	. . . .(66 to 1 tchd 50 to 1)	13
2451²	CHIEF'S SONG [136] 7-11-7 A Dicken, rdn 3rd, no imprsn on ldrs. . . . .(33 to 1 tchd 50 to 1)	14
2327²	ZABADI (Ire) [143] 5-12-0 A Maguire, rear, brief effrt 5th, sn beh. . . . .(20 to 1 tchd 25 to 1)	15
	ROMANCER (Ire) [139] (bl) 6-11-10 M Richards, chsd wnr to 5th, wknd 3 out. . . . .(100 to 1 op 8 to 1 tchd 11 to 1)	16
	STORM DAMAGE (Ire) [136] 5-11-7 D Bridgwater, hld up, rdn 4th, no dngr. . . . .(14 to 1 op 20 to 1)	17
	CLIFTON BEAT (USA) [141] 6-11-12 R Hughes, al beh, tld off whn pld up bef last. . . . .(33 to 1 tchd 40 to 1)	pu

Dist: 9l, 1l, nk, 2½l, 6l, 5l, 3½l, 1¾l, 2½l, 10l. 3m 58.40s. a 9.40s (18 Ran).
SR: 73/54/60/65/61/45/51/43/36/

(P A Deal), M C Pipe

2592 Harwell Chase Limited Handicap Class B (0-145 5-y-o and up) £6,807 2½m. . . . . (2:50)

2334³	GOLDEN SPINNER [128] 10-10-11 R Dunwoody, al in tch, led 8th, drvn clr r-in. . . . .(6 to 4 fav op 7 to 4 tchd 15 to 8)	1
2212²	EASTHORPE [138] (bl) 9-11-7 J F Titley, led to 8th, chlgd 3 out, wknd r-in. . . . .(11 to 2 op 4 to 1 tchd 5 to 1)	2
2314³	RIVER BOUNTY [124] 11-10-7 N Williamson, hld up beh ldrs, hit second, rdn appr 12th, sn behind, lft moderate 3rd 3 out.	
	. . . .(9 to 1 op 7 to 1 tchd 11 to 1)	3
1878⁷	ALL FOR LUCK [130] 12-10-13 C Maude, blun second, wl beh 6th. . . . .(10 to 1 op 7 to 1)	4
	FOREST SUN [125] 12-10-8 B Clifford, beh 5th.	
	. . . .(25 to 1 op 16 to 1)	5
1878⁸	OLD BRIDGE (Ire) [132] 9-11-1 S McNeill, hld up, hdwy 12th, cl 3rd whn f nxt. . . . . (6 to 1 op 5 to 1 tchd 13 to 2)	f
1640	FRONT STREET [135] 10-11-4 J Osborne, beh tenth, pld up bef 4 out. . . . .(14 to 1 op 8 to 1)	pu
2335⁴	AROUND THE HORN [129] 10-10-12 P Hide, chsd ldrs to 12th, lft 3rd and slightly hmpd 4 out, pld up bef nxt.	
	. . . .(6 to 1 op 5 to 1)	pu

Dist: 10l, 13l, 3l, nk. 5m 11.80s. a 23.80s (8 Ran).

(Mrs Hugh Maitland-Jones), N J Henderson

2593 Year Of The Ox Novices' Chase Class C (5-y-o and up) £5,085 3m. . . (3:20)

2245*	CYBORGO (Fr) 7-11-8 R Dunwoody, led to second, led aftr 13th, ran on wl. . . .(11 to 10 on op 6 to 4 on tchd Evens)	1
2043	BUCKHOUSE BOY 7-11-12 C Maude, prmnt, blun 4th, rdn appr 2 out, chsd wnr approaching last, one pace.	
	. . . .(8 to 1 op 7 to 1 tchd 9 to 1)	2
1850³	TRIPLE WITCHING 11-11-2 N Williamson, hld up beh ldrs, eveery ch 3 out, sn rdn, not fluent nxt, wkng whn jmpd lft last.	
	. . . .(8 to 1 op 9 to 1)	3
1448	JUST 'N ACE (Ire) 6-11-2 P Hide, beh 13th.	
	. . . .(50 to 1 op 33 to 1 tchd 66 to 1)	4
2187	TELLICHERRY 8-10-11 J F Titley, mstk 3rd, al beh.	
	. . . .(50 to 1 op 33 to 1 tchd 66 to 1)	5
2043³	AARDWOLF 6-11-12 J Osborne, led second till aftr 13th, wknd appr 4 out, tld off whn pld up bef last.	
	. . . .(9 to 4 op 3 to 1 tchd 100 to 30)	pu
2527	UNCLE ALGY 8-11-2 B Fenton, al beh, hit 11th, sn tld off, pld up bef 3 out. . . . . .(66 to 1 op 33 to 1 tchd 100 to 1)	pu

Dist: 6l, 11l, 18l, 2l. 6m 9.60s. a 24.60s (7 Ran).
SR: 16/14/-/-/

(County Stores (Somerset) Holdings Ltd), M C Pipe

2594 Kung Hei Fat Choy Novices' Hurdle Class C (4-y-o and up) £4,019 2m 110yds. . . . . (3:50)

2397*	SHADOW LEADER 6-11-9 N Williamson, hld up beh, hdwy on bit appr 5th, led approaching last, readily.	
	. . . .(5 to 1 tchd 11 to 2)	1
2001³	MR PERCY (Ire) 6-11-12 P Hide, led to 3rd, led 2 out till appr last, one pace. . . . .(5 to 1 tchd 9 to 2 and 11 to 2)	2

POLYDAMAS 5-11-4 R Hughes, *prmnt, rdn and ev ch 3 out,*
btn appr last.............(15 to 2 op 5 to 1 tchd 8 to 1) 3
ANDANITO (Ire) 6-11-4 R Dunwoody, *trkd ldrs, led appr 3 out*
to nxt, wknd bef last.............(7 to 2 jt-fav op 3 to 1) 4
2315* DONNINGTON (Ire) 7-11-9 J Osborne, *keen hold early, hld*
up in tch, effrt 3 out, wknd betw fnl 2, eased......(7 to 2 jt-
fav op 9 to 4) 5
GET REAL (Ire) 6-10-13 (5*) Mr C Vigors, *pld hrd, prmnt, led*
3rd till appr 3 out, sn wknd .
.................(16 to 1 op 12 to 1 tchd 20 to 1) 6
1997³ BOWCLIFFE COURT (Ire) 5-11-4 (5*) S Ryan, *hld up, hdwy*
4th, effrt 3 out, wknd nxt.
.................(14 to 1 op 10 to 1 tchd 16 to 1) 7
THE FLYING DOCTOR (Ire) 7-11-4 B Fenton, *keen hold early,*
nvr nr to chal...............(33 to 1 tchd 40 to 1) 8
UMBERSTON (Ire) 4-10-8 M Richards, *nvr on terms.*
.................(33 to 1 op 25 to 1) 9
2153⁷ MORPHEUS 8-11-4 A Maguire, *hld up rear, some prog 3 out,*
wknd nxt.................(20 to 1 op 16 to 1) 10
2350 PERFECT PAL (Ire) 6-10-11 (7*) L Reynolds, *al beh, tld off.*
.................(66 to 1 op 33 to 1 tchd 100 to 1) 11
MISTER GOODGUY (Ire) 8-11-4 D Morris, *al beh, tld off.*
.................(50 to 1 tchd 66 to 1) 12
2430 QU'APPELLE 4-10-8 I Lawrence, *al beh, tld off.*
.................(200 to 1 op 66 to 1 tchd 250 to 1) 13
IMMENSE (Ire) 7-11-4 C Maude, *nvr a factor, tld off.*
.................(14 to 1 op 33 to 1) 14
1749⁶ SNOWSHILL HARVEST (Ire) 6-11-4 S McNeill, *pld hrd early,*
hld up rear, hmpd and f 5th.
.................(50 to 1 op 33 to 1 tchd 66 to 1) f
Dist: 4l, 7l, 4l, 8l, nk, 2l, 10l, 3½l, 8l, 13l. 4m 5.30s. a 16.30s (15 Ran).
SR: 6/5/-/-/-/-/ (James Blackshaw), C R Egerton

2595 Weatherbys Stars Of Tomorrow N H Flat Series Final Class H (4 - 7-y-o) £7,006 2m 110yds............(4:20)

1292* MR MARKHAM (Ire) 5-11-9 P Hide, *hld up, hdwy ten fs out,*
short of room and swtchd lft 3 out, led 2 out, ran on wl.
.................(7 to 2 fav op 4 to 1 tchd 5 to 1) 1
2248² DOM BELTRANO (Fr) 5-11-9 C Maude, *chsd ldr, led o'r 3 fs*
out to 2 out, one pace...(11 to 2 op 7 to 2 tchd 6 to 1) 2
2269* ARKLEY ROYAL 6-12-0 G Upton, *hld up rear, hdwy o'r 4 fs*
out, ev ch 2 out, one pace...............(6 to 1 op 7 to 1) 3
1975² BILLINGSGATE 5-11-2 (7*) N Willmington, *hld up, prog hfwy,*
ev ch 2 fs out, outpcd o'r one out, kpt on ins last.
.................(9 to 1 op 8 to 1 tchd 10 to 1) 4
2248⁷ IRANOS (Fr) 5-12-0 R Hughes, *led till o'r 3 fs out, btn over 2*
out.................(11 to 2 op 7 to 2 tchd 6 to 1) 5
2283² NEW LEAF (Ire) 5-11-4 R Dunwoody, *hld up, hdwy ten fs out,*
ev ch 2 out, wknd entering last.........(4 to 1 op 5 to 1) 6
2123² IN THE VAN 5-11-4 J F Titley, *hld up, rdn 7 fs out, wknd and*
eased o'r 4 out, tld off.
.................(6 to 1 op 8 to 1 tchd 10 to 1 and 5 to 1) 7
2123 MOON DEVIL (Ire) 7-11-4 J Osborne, *wtd wth, wknd and*
eased o'r 4 fs out, tld off............(33 to 1 op 25 to 1) 8
1648⁶ BELLIDIUM 5-10-13 G Tormey, *al beh, tld off hfwy.*
.................(50 to 1 op 33 to 1 tchd 66 to 1) 9
2469⁵ SPRIGHTLEY PIP (Ire) 6-11-4 B Fenton, *trkd ldrs, rdn o'r 9 fs*
out, sn beh, tld off.................(33 to 1 op 25 to 1) 10
2363⁹ MIDAS 6-11-9 N Williamson, *in tch till wknd 7 fs out.*
.................(33 to 1 op 20 to 1 tchd 40 to 1) 11
Dist: 6l, nk, 1¼l, 1½l, ½l, dist, 17l, 17l, 9l, 6l. 4m 3.60s. (11 Ran).
(Felix Rosenstiel's Widow & Son), J T Gifford

UTTOXETER (good)
Saturday February 8th
Going Correction: NIL (races 1,2,4,5), PLUS 0.30 (3,6,7)

2596 European Breeders Fund Tattersalls Ireland Mares' Only Novices' Chase Qualifier Class D (6-y-o and up) £3,631 2½m................(1:40)

HARVEST VIEW 7-10-7 (7*) M Berry, *hld up, hdwy 6 out,*
led appr 4 out, rdn out.....(8 to 1 op 6 to 1 tchd 9 to 1) 1
2278² GUINDA (Ire) 7-11-6 T J Murphy, *al prmnt, chsd wnr 4 out, no*
extr run in....(11 to 8 on op 5 to 4 on tchd 6 to 5 on) 2
2245 JASILU (bl) 7-11-12 J Railton, *led, hdd appr 4 out, wknd 2 out.*
.................(10 to 1 op 7 to 1) 3
2308³ PEARL'S CHOICE (Ire) 9-11-0 B Powell, *chsd ldr, mstk 8th, hit*
5 out, wknd nxt.................(10 to 1 op 7 to 1) 4
2244⁶ WONDERFULL POLLY (Ire) 9-10-9 (5*) O Burrows, *hld up,*
hdwy 6 out, wknd 3 out..(10 to 1 op 5 to 1 tchd 11 to 1) 5
1801⁵ CAPTIVA BAY 8-11-0 S Wynne, *chsd ldrs, lost pl 5 out, styd*
on frm 2 out.................(66 to 1 op 33 to 1) 6
2247 MAMMY'S CHOICE (Ire) 7-11-9 (3*) P Henley, *prmnt, hit 6 out,*
sn rdn and wknd.........(7 to 1 op 6 to 1 tchd 15 to 2) 7
LAMBRINI (Ire) 7-11-0 T Jenks, *mid-div, rdn 9th sn beh.*
.................(66 to 1 op 33 to 1) 8
1916⁷ BOURNEL (v) 9-11-0 Richard Guest, *beh and rdn 6th, tld off.*
.................(66 to 1 op 33 to 1) 9
2152 BECKY'S GIRL 7-11-0 L Harvey, *hld up, al in rear, tld off.*
.................(66 to 1 op 33 to 1 tchd 100 to 1) 10

2251 MINI FETE (Fr) 8-11-0 A Larnach, *al beh, tld off.*
.................(66 to 1 op 33 to 1) 11
Dist: 2½l, 13l, 1½l, 6l, 18l, 12l, 5l, 17l, hd, 8l. 5m 2.70s. a 18.70s (11 Ran).
(Dr P P Brown), C P E Brooks

2597 Pertemps Cream Novices' Handicap Chase Class C (5-y-o and up) £8,793 2m 5f..........................(2:10)

2300* BELL STAFFBOY (Ire) [117] 8-11-5 (5*) Michael Brennan, *hld*
up in tch, led appr 4 out, clr 2 out, pushed out.....(2 to 1 jt-
fav tchd 9 to 4) 1
2201* NOYAN [110] 7-10-12 (5*) Mr R Thornton, *prmnt, rdn to chase*
wnr 3 out, no imprsn...........(2 to 1 jt-fav tchd 9 to 4) 2
2278⁴ WHO IS EQUINAME (Ire) [105] 7-10-12 J R Kavanagh,
patiently rdn, outpcd tenth, nvr dngrs aftr. (8 to 1 op 6 to 1) 3
2282* KHALIDI (Ire) [107] 8-11-0 R Johnson, *prmnt, jnd ldr 6th, rdn 5*
out, sn btn.................(6 to 1 op 5 to 1 tchd 13 to 2) 4
1920⁵ BIT OF A TOUCH [93] 11-10-0 B Powell, *chsd ldrs til hit and*
lost pl 8th, sn beh, tld off.
.................(14 to 1 op 12 to 1 tchd 16 to 1) 5
2425⁴ EXTERIOR PROFILES (Ire) [110] 7-11-3 T J Murphy, *led, hdd*
appr 4 out, rdn and hld whn stumbled and uns rdr 3 out.
.................(6 to 1 tchd 7 to 1) ur
Dist: 9l, 11l, 1½l, dist. 5m 12.60s. a 14.60s (6 Ran).
(K W Bell & Son Ltd), J G M O'Shea

2598 Ladbroke Handicap Hurdle Class B (0-145 4-y-o and up) £10,679 2¾m 110yds......................(2:40)

1699* SUPREME LADY (Ire) [119] 6-11-0 J Culloty, *hld up, hdwy 3*
out, led appr last, rdn out. (5 to 1 op 9 to 2 tchd 11 to 2) 1
2004³ HOUSE CAPTAIN [120] 8-10-12 (3*) F Leahy, *hld up, hdwy 4*
out, outpcd nxt, styd on und pres run in.
.................(7 to 2 fav tchd 4 to 1) 2
1945* FREDDIE MUCK [129] 7-11-10 T Jenks, *chsd ldrs, led 3 out,*
hdd appr last, wknd towards finish.
.................(13 to 2 op 5 to 1 tchd 7 to 1) 3
155⁶ ALL ON [109] 6-10-4 T J Murphy, *chsd ldrs, lost pl 3rd, beh*
6th, hdwy 3 out, no imprsn...........(33 to 1 op 25 to 1) 4
1928* LETS BE FRANK [105] 6-10-0 R Johnson, *chsd ldrs, ev ch 3*
out, wknd appr last.................(6 to 1 tchd 13 to 2) 5
LINTON ROCKS [120] 8-11-1 B Powell, *prmnt till wknd appr 3*
out.................(20 to 1) 6
2027* ARITHMETIC [117] 7-10-12 W Marston, *led, hdd appr 3 out,*
sn btn.................(9 to 2 op 4 to 1 tchd 5 to 1) 7
2217⁸ CALL MY GUEST (Ire) [119] (bl) 7-11-0 Richard Guest, *prmnt*
till wknd 4 out.................(33 to 1 op 20 to 1) 8
2289* NICK THE BEAK (Ire) [111] 8-9-13 (7*) G Supple, *chsd ldr till*
wknd 4 out.................(13 to 2 op 6 to 1) 9
2210⁵ RULING (USA) [127] 11-11-3 (5*) Mr R Thornton, *al in rear,*
drvn alng 6th, beh whn pld up and dismounted run in, lme.
.................(33 to 1 op 25 to 1) pu
241* GIMME (Ire) [105] (v) 7-9-9 (5*) Michael Brennan, *prmnt to 5th,*
tld off and pld up bef 4 out..........(33 to 1 op 20 to 1) pu
Dist: 1½l, hd, 6l, 5l, 4l, 28l, 12l, sht-hd. 5m 17.70s. a 10.70s (11 Ran).
SR: 46/43/52/26/17/28/ (The Supreme Lady Partnership), Miss H C Knight

2599 Singer & Friedlander National Trial Handicap Chase Class B (6-y-o and up) £24,136 4¼m............(3:10)

2310* LORD GYLLENE (NZ) [132] 9-11-9 R Johnson, *jmpd wl, made*
all, rdn out..................(11 to 8 fav) 1
2210⁴ MUDAHIM [125] 11-11-2 W Marston, *chsd wnr frm 5th,*
reminder 16th, no imprsn from 4 out.. (6 to 1 tchd 7 to 1) 2
2306* COURT MELODY (Ire) [120] (bl) 9-10-11 J Culloty, *hld up,*
hdwy 7th, chsd wnr 4 out, one pace frm nxt.
.................(10 to 1 op 8 to 1) 3
2310² SAMLEE (Ire) [115] 8-10-6 J R Kavanagh, *prmnt, drvn alng 5*
out, wknd nxt.................(11 to 2 op 5 to 1) 4
2334⁵ BETTY'S BOY (Ire) [119] 11-11-1 J Railton, *hld up, hdwy 17th,*
hit 5 out, sn wknd.......(9 to 1 op 8 to 1 tchd 10 to 1) 5
1529 ANDROS PRINCE [109] 12-9-9 (5*) Mr R Thornton, *chsd wnr*
to 5th, drvn alng 16th, wknd 5 out, tld off.
.................(66 to 1 op 50 to 1) 6
2182* WOODLANDS GENHIRE [109] (bl) 12-10-0 R Bellamy, *prmnt,*
lost pl 4th, sn wknd, tld off, pld up aftr 16th.
.................(33 to 1 op 50 to 1) pu
2310⁹ CHURCH LAW [109] 10-9-9 (5*) Sophie Mitchell, *al in rear, tld*
off frm 12th, pld up bef 5 out.......(25 to 1 op 20 to 1) pu
2439* FLYER'S NAP [137] 11-12-0 B Powell, *patiently rdn, effrt 16th,*
sn beh, tld off whn pld up bef 5 out.
.................(9 to 2 op 4 to 1 tchd 5 to 1) pu
Dist: 8l, 1½l, 17l, 15l, dist. 8m 34.40s. a 4.40s (9 Ran).
SR: 51/36/29/7/1/-/ (Stanley W Clarke), S A Brookshaw

2600 Doncaster Bloodstock Sales Breeders' Trophy Novices' Handicap Chase Class C (6-y-o and up) £14,720 3¼m............(3:40)

1879² GENERAL PONGO [100] 8-10-0 R Farrant, *al prmnt, led 6 out,*
rdn out.................(8 to 1 tchd 9 to 1) 1

2319 LORD OF THE WEST (Ire) [107] 8-10-7 A Thornton, *hld up, hdwy 14th, ev ch 2 out, hrd rdn run in, no extr.*
.... (25 to 1 op 20 to 1) 2

2245 WHAT'S YOUR STORY (Ire) [111] 8-10-11 R Johnson, *mid-div, hdwy 12th, rdn 3 out, styd on same pace.*
.... (14 to 1 op 10 to 1) 3

2375* FLIMSY TRUTH [104] 11-9-13 (5*) Mr R Thornton, *chsd ldrs, led 4th to nxt, wknd 3 out.* ....(10 to 1 op 10 to 1) 4

2254⁴ KARAR (Ire) [101] 7-10-1¹ D O'Sullivan, *beh, styd on frm 2 out, nvr nrr.* ....(11 to 1 op 10 to 1) 5

2312² FEEL THE POWER (Ire) [128] 9-12-0 J Railton, *hld up, hdwy 5 out, rdn and hit nxt, wknd 3 out.* ....(16 to 1) 6

2280* SIR LEONARD (Ire) [117] 7-11-3 J A McCarthy, *sn wl beh, hdwy 12th, wknd 4 out.* ....(11 to 2 op 9 to 2) 7

2306² LITTLE MARTINA (Ire) [109] 9-10-9 J R Kavanagh, *prmnt, mstk 6th (water), sn lost pl, beh whn pld up bef tenth.*
.... (5 to 1 fav tchd 11 to 2) pu

2301* GOD SPEED YOU (Ire) [108] (bl) 8-10-5 (3*) D Fortt, *led to 4th, led ag'n nxt, hdd 6 out, sn wknd, pld up bef 2 out.*
.... (7 to 1 op 8 to 1 tchd 10 to 1) pu

2247* ORSWELL LAD [112] 8-10-12 L Harvey, *prmnt to 12th, beh whn pld up bef 4 out.* ....(8 to 1 op 6 to 1) pu

2252² WELL TIMED [100] 7-10-0 B Powell, *chsd ldrs, rdn 4 out, pld up bef nxt.* ....(14 to 1 op 12 to 1) pu

2259⁴ MAJOR LOOK (NZ) [107] 9-10-7 Richard Guest, *prmnt, rdn 5 out, wknd nxt, pld up bef 2 out.* ....(16 to 1 op 14 to 1) pu

2282² HATCHAM BOY (Ire) [114] 7-11-0 W Marston, *prmnt, drvn along 12th, hit 5 out, pld up bef nxt.*.....(10 to 1 op 9 to 1) pu

Dist: 1½l, 6l, 6l, 11l, 28l, 12l. 6m 41.20s. a 29.20s (13 Ran).

(Mrs J K Powell), T R George

2601 BBC Radio Stoke Novices' Hurdle Class C (5-y-o and up) £3,891 3m 110yds...................... (4:10)

2249² MENTMORE TOWERS (Ire) 5-10-12 R Farrant, *chsd ldrs, led 5 out, styd on wl......*(9 to 4 fav op 11 to 4 tchd 3 to 1) 1

2311* BARTON WARD 6-11-3 Richard Guest, *hld up, hdwy 5 out, chsd wnr 3 out, rdn appr last no extr..*(3 to 1 tchd 7 to 2) 2

2250⁴ BANNY HILL LAD 7-10-9 (3*) D Fortt, *hld up, hdwy 6th, ev ch 3 out and wknd nxt.*............(25 to 1 op 16 to 1) 3

STORMY SESSION 7-10-12 T J Murphy, *hld up, mstk 1st, hdwy 6 out, rdn and wknd nxt.*......(20 to 1 op 25 to 1) 4

1815* COPPER COIL 7-10-10 (7*) J Power, *prmnt, drvn along 4 out, wknd nxt.*..................(14 to 1 op 12 to 1) 5

2288² LOVE THE BLUES 5-10-7 R Johnson, *hld up, hdwy 5 out, mstk nxt, wknd 3 out......*....(7 to 2 op 3 to 1) 6

2243 CLASSIC CHAT 5-10-7 (5*) Michael Brennan, *prmnt to 7th, sn lost pl..................*(66 to 1 op 50 to 1) 7

2152⁸ JOBSAGOODUN 6-10-12 J R Kavanagh, *prmnt till wknd 5 out.*..........(11 to 2 op 5 to 1 tchd 6 to 1) 8

1984⁶ OLD CAVALIER 6-10-12 A Thornton, *made most to 5 out, grad wknd...................*....(20 to 1 op 10 to 1) 9

2249⁸ WESTCOTE LAD 12-10-12 T Jenks, *chsd ldrs, drvn alng and wknd 4 out..................*....(66 to 1 op 33 to 1) 10

2394⁴ COOLE CHERRY 7-10-12 B Powell, *wth ldrs till wknd 5 out.*....................(33 to 1 op 20 to 1) 11

GRANHAM PRIDE (Ire) 7-10-12 J Railton, *hld up, beh whn pld up bef 3 out.*.........(10 to 1 op 6 to 1) pu

1545 SOUTHSEA SCANDALS (Ire) 6-10-12 R Greene, *beh frm hfwy, pld up bef 3 out.*....(40 to 1 op 33 to 1) pu

1979 THE WAYWARD BISHOP (Ire) (bl) 8-10-12 D Leahy, *in tch wknd 6 out, beh whn pld up bef 3 out.* (66 to 1 op 33 to 1) pu

Dist: 12l, 20l, 6l, 1¾l, 9l, 19l, sht-hd, 3l, 30l, 8l. 5m 53.70s. a 16.70s (14 Ran).

(Philip Matton), Mrs J Pitman

2602 Wellman PLC Novices' Handicap Hurdle Class E (0-105 4-y-o and up) £2,347 2m.................... (4:40)

1384 GLOBE RUNNER [91] 4-10-6 A Roche, *al prmnt, led appr last, rdn out..........*(6 to 1 tchd 7 to 1 and 8 to 1) 1

2323⁸ SAMANID (Ire) [99] 5-11-10 O Pears, *hld up, hdwy 6th ev ch frm 3 out, styd on same pace run in.*
.... (14 to 1 op 12 to 1 tchd 16 to 1) 2

2419² TAKE COVER (Ire) [92] 6-11-3 Richard Guest, *chsd ldr, led appr 3 out, hdd last, wknd run in..........*(4 to 1 op 5 to 1) 3

2417³ ARABIAN HEIGHTS [89] 4-10-4 W Marston, *rcd keenly, hmpd 1st, in tch, drvn along 3 out, styd on same pace.*
.... (9 to 4 op 9 to 4 tchd 2 to 1) 4

2372⁸ ALPHA LEATHER [75] 6-10-0 Mr J Grassick, *hld up, mstk 4th, nvr plcd to chal.................*(33 to 1 tchd 50 to 1) 5

2432⁷ NAGARA SOUND [80] 6-9-12 (7*) J Mogford, *hld up, drvn alng 3 out, nvr dngrs.............*(12 to 1 op 8 to 1) 6

2311⁹ PRUSSIA [98] 6-11-9 R Johnson, *led till hdd and wknd appr 3 out..................*(13 to 2 op 6 to 1) 7

2428⁶ SNOWSHILL SHAKER [85] 8-10-10 T Jenks, *prmnt till wknd 4 out..................*(12 to 1 op 10 to 1) 8

2407⁸ BOWLES PATROL (Ire) [75] 5-9-7 (7*) G Supple, *prmnt, jnd ldrs 4 out, sn rdn and wknd...........*(20 to 1 op 25 to 1) 9

1869* TOULSTON LADY (Ire) [75] (bl) 5-9-9 (5*) Mr R Thornton, *prmnt, rdn 3 out, 3rd and hld whn f last............*(8 to 1) f

1798 OUT OF THE BLUE [75] 5-10-0 P McLoughlin, *blun and uns rdr 1st..........................*(33 to 1) ur

Dist: 2½l, 7l, 7l, 7l, 2½l, nk, 9l, 4l. 3m 51.60s. a 14.60s (11 Ran).

(G & P Barker Ltd/Globe Engineering), J J O'Neill

HEREFORD (good to soft)
Monday February 10th
Going Correction: PLUS 1.00 sec. per fur. (races 1,3,5,7), PLUS 0.85 (2,4,6)

2603 Ewyas Harold Novices' Handicap Hurdle Class F (0-90 4-y-o and up) £2,570 2m 1f.................... (2:00)

1955⁶ RANGER SLOANE [74] 5-10-13 R Farrant, *hdwy 5th, trkd ldrs 3 out, chlgd nxt, sn led, clr last, pushed out.*
.... (25 to 1 op 20 to 1) 1

1592⁶ OPERETTO (Ire) [76] 7-11-1 G Bradley, *prmnt, chlgd 5th to 4 out, rdn and ev ch nxt, styd on same pace appr last.*
.... (8 to 1 op 10 to 1) 2

1348 SYLVESTER (Ire) [73] 7-10-12 Michael Brennan, *hdwy 4th, chlgd 3 out, one pace nxt........*(40 to 1 op 33 to 1) 3

2267⁶ O MY LOVE [78] 6-11-3 J Osborne, *in tch, led 5th, rdn 3 out, hdd sn aftr nxt, wknd appr last........*(8 to 1 op 6 to 1) 4

2372² FASTINI GOLD [77] 5-11-2 R Johnson, *hdwy 4th, rdn to chal 3 out, styd on till wknd r-in.* (13 to 2 op 6 to 1 tchd 7 to 1) 5

2432² ALMAPA [83] 5-11-5 (3*) T Dascombe, *in tch, lost pos 4th, hdwy four out, wknd aftr nxt.*...........(10 to 1 op 8 to 1) 6

1428³ THE CARROT MAN [85] 9-11-3 (7*) X Aizpuru, *pressed ldrs, rdn and wknd aftr 4 out.................*(8 to 1 op 7 to 1) 7

2385³ FLEET CADET [87] (v) 6-11-12 Jamie Evans, *in tch, pressed ldrs 4 out, wknd appr nxt..........*(6 to 1 op 5 to 1) 8

HAPPY BRAVE [78] 5-11-3 L Harvey, *prmnt early, lost pos 4th, aftr four out, wknd nxt.*............(10 to 1 op 10 to 1) 9

1452 SAAFI (Ire) [75] 6-11-0 V Slattery, *sn beh.............*(33 to 1 op 10 to 1) 10

2185³ ATH CHEANNAITHE (Fr) [82] 5-11-7 N Williamson, *led till aftr 4th, sn rdn and wknd..................*(10 to 1) 11

FLASHMAN [80] 7-11-5 Mr J L Llewellyn, *al beh.*
.... (14 to 1 op 12 to 1) 12

2426⁶ HIGH POST [80] 8-11-2 (3*) R Massey, *beh till f 4 out.*
.... (12 to 1 tchd 14 to 1) f

2277 GLENMAVIS [80] 10-11-5 Dr P Pritchard, *pressed ldr to 3rd, led aftr 4th till appr nxt, wknd four out, tld off whn pld up bef last.*..................(40 to 1 op 33 to 1) pu

2279² STORM TIGER (Ire) [75] (v) 6-10-11 (3*) E Husband, *chsd ldrs to 5th, sn wknd, tld off whn pld up bef 2 out. ....*(5 to 1 jt-fav op 9 to 2) pu

2292* LADY MAGNUM (Ire) [93] 4-11-8 N Mann, *sn wl beh, tld off whn pld up bef 4 out.* (5 to 1 jt-fav op 4 to 1) pu

Dist: 5l, 1l, 1¼l, 4l, 3l, 9l, 12l, 7l, 11l, 1¼l. 4m 9.10s. a 24.10s (16 Ran).

SR: 14/11/7/10/5/8/1/-/ (G Fierro), G Fierro

2604 Wormelow Novices' Handicap Chase Class E (0-100 5-y-o and up) £3,100 2m 3f........................(2:30)

2354* CARDINAL RULE (Ire) [73] 8-10-7 N Williamson, *jmpd wl, made all, pckd last, styd on well..* (4 to 1 fav tchd 9 to 2) 1

2280⁹ BOOTS N ALL (Ire) [70] 7-10-4 W Marston, *chsd wnr, rdn 3 out, no imprsn frm nxt..............*(16 to 1 op 14 to 1) 2

2184⁴ CHRIS'S GLEN [75] (v) 8-10-9 R Johnson, *chsd ldrs, drvn alng and wknd 4 out, lft poor 3rd at last.*(14 to 1 op 12 to 1) 3

2353³ OLLIVER DUCKETT [84] 8-11-4 G Tormey, *prmnt, drvn alng 7th, wknd 4 out.......*(11 to 2 op 5 to 1 tchd 6 to 1) 4

2442 MANOLETE [87] 6-11-7 Derek Byrne, *hld up, hrd rdn 6 out, nvr nr ldrs..................*(9 to 1 op 12 to 1 tchd 8 to 1) 5

2033² EULOGY (Fr) [82] 10-11-2 A Larnach, *mid-div, effrt 7th, wknd nxt..........................*(10 to 1 op 8 to 1) 6

2406⁹ JOLLY BOAT [90] 10-11-10 S Wynne, *hld up, hdwy 6th, wknd nxt..................*(14 to 1 op 12 to 1) 7

2478⁴ CASTLECONNER (Ire) [82] 6-11-2 J Frost, *al beh.*
.... (10 to 1 op 8 to 1) 8

2395⁷ BATHWICK BOBBIE [78] 10-10-12 S McNeill, *prmnt till wknd 9th..................................*(20 to 1) 9

1939⁷ NIGHT FANCY [69] 9-10-3 J R Kavanagh, *al wl beh.* (25 to 1) 10

2512² KING'S SHILLING (USA) [79] 10-10-13 Jacqui Oliver, *chsd ldrs, wknd 4 out, 3rd and no ch whn f last.*
.... (7 to 1 tchd 8 to 1) f

2428 HELLO ME MAN (Ire) [74] 9-10-8 Mr J L Llewellyn, *beh and rdn 6th, tld off whn pld up bef 4 out........*(20 to 1) pu

COLONEL COLT [75] 6-10-9 J Culloty, *al rear, hit 6th, tld off whn pld up bef 4 out.............*(16 to 1 op 14 to 1) pu

2025⁷ QUITE A MAN [83] 9-11-3 T Eley, *hld up, hdwy 5th, wknd 7th, tld off whn pld up bef 4 out..........*(9 to 1 op 8 to 1) pu

2184⁶ GORDON [87] 6-11-7 J Osborne, *al rear, rdn 6th, tld off whn pld up bef 4 out..............*(14 to 1 op 12 to 1) pu

2354⁸ MEL (Ire) [71] 7-10-5 B Powell, *al rear, tld off whn pld up bef 4 out......................*(20 to 1) pu

Dist: 4l, dist, 1¾l, 2½l, 7l, 5l, 2½l, 20l, 2½l. 4m 49.60s. a 24.60s (16 Ran).

(Peter J Burch), Miss Venetia Williams

2605 Hoechst Roussel Panacur European Breeders Fund Mares' 'National Hunt' Novices' Hurdle Qualifier Class E (5-y-o and up) £2,598 2m 3f 110yds...................... (3:00)

2405³ HALONA 7-10-12 G Bradley, *led aftr second, sn clr, hit 2 out, ran on wl..................*(11 to 10 fav op 6 to 4 on) 1

1961³ MOONLIGHTER 7-10-7 (5") O Burrows, *steady hdwy frm 6th, chsd wnr aftr 4 out, no imprsn* .... (10 to 1 op 7 to 1) 2
1675⁶ KOSHEEN (Ire) 6-10-12 J Culloty, *chsd ldrs, one pace frm 3 out* .... (6 to 1 op 5 to 1 tchd 7 to 1) 3
2428⁵ QUICK QUOTE 7-10-12 L Harvey, *hdwy 6th, wknd 4 out.* .... (5 to 1 tchd 9 to 2) 4
1476⁷ FUN WHILE IT LASTS 6-10-12 S Wynne, *mid-div, lost tch 4 out.* .... (20 to 1) 5
ARCTIC MUSE 6-10-12 G Tormey, *lost pos 6th, effrt nxt, sn wknd* .... (33 to 1) 6
2243 MADAM POLLY 5-10-5 (7") K Hibbert, *prmnt to 6th.* (33 to 1) 7
2207⁸ CLUB CARIBBEAN 5-10-12 N Williamson, *chsd ldr 6th till aftr 4 out, sn btn*...................... (14 to 1 op 12 to 1) 8
2243 LADY OF MINE 7-10-12 R Johnson, *led to second, wkng whn blun 4 out*.. (33 to 1) 9
FAITHLEGG (Ire) 6-10-12 J R Kavanagh, *chsd ldrs, wknd 4 out, pld up bef last*...... (13 to 2 op 6 to 1 tchd 7 to 1) pu
2248 ELLY'S DREAM 6-10-12 S Fox, *mstks in rear, tld off whn pld up bef 7th*.. (33 to 1) pu
1476⁸ LADY ROSEBURY 7-10-9 (3") T Dascombe, *wl beh and tld off whn pld up bef 7th. £*.............................. (33 to 1) pu
1214 MISS STARTEAM 7-10-12 J Frost, *beh 5th, tld off whn pld up bef 3 out*.. (50 to 1) pu
1961 PHARMOREFUN (Ire) 5-10-12 B Clifford, *beh 5th, tld off whn pld up bef 2 out*.................. (33 to 1 op 20 to 1) pu
2433⁸ SULA'S DREAM 8-10-9 (3") R Massey, *beh 5th, tld off whn pld up bef 3 out*.............................. (50 to 1) pu
PENNYAHEI 6-10-12 T Eley, *beh 5th, tld off whn pld up bef 2 out*.............................. (33 to 1 op 20 to 1) pu
Dist: 2l, 17l, 3l, 26l, 30l, 12l, 2½l, ½l. 4m 58.10s. a 40.10s (16 Ran).
(Mrs Z S Clark), C P E Brooks

2606 Weatherbys Leasing Directory Handicap Chase Class F (0-100 5-y-o and up) £2,840 2m........ (3:30)

1686 THATS THE LIFE [75] 12-10-3 R Johnson, *made all, blun 3 out, hit nxt, rdn out*....................... (14 to 1 op 12 to 1) 1
2261⁵ DR ROCKET [82] (bl) 12-10-3 (7") X Aizpuru, *chsd wnr, rdn appr 2 out, styd on same pace frm 3 out*..... (6 to 1 op 5 to 1) 2
2444⁷ BLAZER MORINIERE (Fr) [84] 8-10-12 S Fox, *mid-div, hdwy 6 out, styd on same pace frm 3 out..* (16 to 1 tchd 20 to 1) 3
2542⁴ FENWICK [85] 10-10-10 (3") T Dascombe, *prmnt till wknd 4 out*............................... (8 to 1 op 7 to 1) 4
2355⁹ PEGMARINE (USA) [79] 14-10-7 N Williamson, *nvr nr to chal.* .... (14 to 1 tchd 16 to 1) f
2031⁶ FAIRY PARK [84] (v) 12-10-5 (7") Mr H J Oliver, *hld up, rear whn blun and uns rdr 3 out*................ (12 to 1) ur
1686⁶ PRUDENT PEGGY [72] 10-10-0 Mr A Holdsworth, *mid-div, hdwy 6th, wknd 4 out, blun and uns rdr 2 out*...... (14 to 1 op 12 to 1) ur
2355⁴ WINSPIT (Ire) [86] 7-11-0 J R Kavanagh, *in tch to 4th, beh whn blun and uns rdr four out*........... (6 to 1 op 9 to 2) ur
1946 LEINTHALL PRINCESS [77] 11-10-5 Miss P Jones, *al wl beh, tld off whn pld up bef last*......... (16 to 1 op 14 to 1) pu
2355 HALHAM TARN (Ire) [90] 7-10-11 (7") A Dowling, *al rear, tld off whn pld up bef last*................ (20 to 1 tchd 25 to 1) pu
2355⁸ RUSTIC GENT (Ire) [72] (v) 9-10-0 D Leahy, *prmnt, wknd 4 out, blun 3 out, pld up bef nxt*..................... (33 to 1) pu
2431 NORTHERN SINGER [81] 7-10-9 B Powell, *hld up, hit 4th, hdwy 6th, wknd four out, beh whn pld up bef last.* ...... (5 to 2 fav op 11 to 4 tchd 3 to 1) pu
1730⁴ MONKS JAY (Ire) [88] 8-11-2 I Lawrence, *mid-div, wkng whn hit 6 out, pld up bef 3 out*................... (8 to 1 op 7 to 1) pu
Dist: 3½l, 4l, 14l, dist. 4m 7.80s. a 20.80s (14 Ran).
SR: 3/6/4/-/-/-/ (Ms Liz Kilfeather), T R George

2607 Arrow Maiden Claiming Hurdle Class F (4-y-o and up) £2,178 2m 3f 110yds .... (4:00)

2304 CARACOL 8-11-3 (3") T Dascombe, *led to 3rd, led 6th, rdn and edgd lft und pres r-in, all out*...... (6 to 1 tchd 7 to 1) 1
1474⁴ ARIOSO 9-10-6 (5") Michael Brennan, *hdwy 6th, chsd wnr frm nxt, staying on und pres whn not much room nr finish.* .... (10 to 1 op 7 to 1) 2
2371 NICKY WILDE 7-11-10 G Bradley, *hdwy 6th, hit nxt, staying on whn mstk 4 out, chlgd next, sn outpcd.* .... (10 to 1 op 7 to 1) 3
2405⁶ COME ON IN 4-10-11 J Culloty, *hit 5th, hdwy 7th, one pace whn hit 2 out*.......................... (7 to 1 op 6 to 1) 4
2479³ FAIRELAINE 5-10-12 (7") Mr R Wakley, *wl beh till moderate hdwy frm 4 out, not rch ldrs.* .... (11 to 4 fav op 9 to 4 tchd 3 to 1) 5
2243 ALPINE SONG 12-10-13 Miss V Stephens, *chsd 4th, hit 4th, wknd 3 out*....................... (33 to 1 op 25 to 1) 6
2390³ TREAD THE BOARDS (bl) 6-10-11 Jamie Evans, *hdwy 6th, rdn and wkng whn hit 4 out*............ (7 to 2 op 5 to 2) 7
2242⁶ BLADE OF FORTUNE 9-11-8 B Powell, *hdwy 5th, wknd nxt, tld off.* .... (14 to 1 op 10 to 1) 8
2498 BROWNSCROFT 9-10-10 (7") K Hibbert, *beh hdwy, tld off.* .... (33 to 1) 9
1861⁹ NOBLE COLOURS 4-11-5 Mr J Jukes, *chsd ldrs to 6th, tld off.* .... (11 to 1 op 10 to 1 tchd 12 to 1) 10

2292³ ESKIMO KISS (Ire) 4-10-6 N Williamson, *rdn alng and wknd aftr 5th, tld off*............... (11 to 1 op 4 to 1) 11
2152 BURFORDS FOR SCRAP 5-11-6 W Marston, *chsd ldrs to 5th, sn wknd, tld off*........................ (20 to 1 tchd 25 to 1) 12
2387 A MILLION WATTS (bl) 6-11-2 B Clifford, *led 3rd to 6th, sn wknd, tld off*............... (14 to 1 op 12 to 1 tchd 16 to 1) 13
2405 PART LADY (Ire) (v) 8-10-13 L Harvey, *tld off 5th, pld up bef 3 out*......................... (33 to 1 op 25 to 1) pu
1350 ARKLOW KING (Ire) 5-12-0 Gary Lyons, *tld off 5th, pld up bef 4 out*................................. (50 to 1 op 33 to 1) pu
2265 TOMORROWS HARVEST 5-10-11 I Lawrence, *beh hdwy, tld off whn pld up bef 3 out*................. (33 to 1 op 20 to 1) pu
Dist: 1¼l, 9l, 3½l, 14l, 6l, sht-hd, 6l, dist, 5l, dist. 5m 3.40s. a 45.40s (16 Ran).
(C G Bolton), J Neville

2608 Golden Valley Hunters' Chase Class H (6-y-o and up) £1,339 3m 1f 110yds...................... (4:30)

MISS MILLBROOK 9-11-2 (7") Mr E Williams, *hld up, hdwy 7th, led 12th, clr 3 out, blun last.* .... (4 to 1 op 5 to 1 tchd 11 to 2) 1
CAPE COTTAGE 13-11-7 (7") Mr A Phillips, *in tch, rdn 6 out, chsd wnr 4 out, wknd nxt.* .... (12 to 1) 2
RUSTY BRIDGE 10-12-5 (5") Mr R Burton, *led, hit 6th and hdd, wknd six out*....................................... (20 to 1) 3
2531 NOT MY LINE (Ire) 8-11-2 (5") Mr A Sansome, *prmnt, led aftr 6th to 12th, wknd 4 out*.......................... (33 to 1) 4
CATCHAPENNY (b) 12-12-3 (7") Mr W Tellwright, *prmnt to 12th, sn beh*.......................... (12 to 1 op 10 to 1) 5
SOME-TOY 11-11-7 (7") Miss L Blackford, *nvr trble ldrs.* .... (8 to 1 op 7 to 1) 6
KETTLES 10-10-9 (7") Mr S Wakley, *nvr better than mid-div, rear whn blun and uns rdr 3 out*.......... (10 to 1 op 7 to 1) ur
FIDDLERS PIKE 16-12-3 (7") Mrs R Henderson, *prmnt to 9th, tld off whn pld up bef 3 out*.......... (20 to 1 op 14 to 1) pu
ROSS VENTURE 12-12-3 (7") Mr C Stockton, *chsd ldrs, prmnt and wknd 6 out*............................. (33 to 1 tchd 25 to 1) pu
J B LAD 11-11-0 (7") Miss P Gundry, *beh 9th, pld up bef 3 out.* .... (25 to 1) pu
LIGHTEN THE LOAD 10-11-0 (7") Mr A Wintle, *al rear, pld up bef 3 out*........................ (11 to 1 op 10 to 1 tchd 12 to 1) pu
2502 CORN EXCHANGE 9-11-4 (3") Mr M Rimell, *al rear, pld up bef 3 out*................................... (33 to 1) pu
BODDINGTON HILL 9-10-11 (5") Mr C Vigors, *tld off whn pld up bef 11th*... (25 to 1) pu
THE RUM MARINER 10-11-2 (5") Mr J Jukes, *prmnt till wknd 6 out, pld up bef 3 out*...................... (8 to 1 op 7 to 1) pu
CELTIC ABBEY 9-12-0 (7") Mr D S Jones, *mid-div, hit 9th, mstk 11th, sn beh, pld up bef 5 out.* .... (9 to 4 fav op 2 to 1 tchd 5 to 2) pu
JUDY LINE 8-10-9 (7") Miss V Roberts, *beh hfwy, pld up bef 3 out*.. (33 to 1) pu
PHARRAGO (Ire) 8-11-0 (7") Miss E J Jones, *beh whn pld up bef 8th*.. (33 to 1) pu
FOREST FOUNTAIN (Ire) 6-11-0 (7") Mr A Dalton, *hld up, effrt 9th, sn beh, pld up bef 3 out*........ (7 to 2 op 5 to 2) pu
Dist: 25l, 22l, 2½l, 5l, dist. 6m 43.90s. a 37.90s (18 Ran).
(D T Goldsworthy), D T Goldsworthy

2609 Ledbury Handicap Hurdle Class F (0-105 4-y-o and up) £2,318 2m 1f .... (5:00)

2307* ADDED DIMENSION (Ire) [93] 6-11-3 (7") X Aizpuru, *keen hold, trkd ldr, led 3 out, in command whn blun last, drvn out.* .... (5 to 1 op 7 to 1) 1
2396⁶ DONTDRESSFORDINNER [89] 7-11-3 (3") T Dascombe, *chsd ldrs to 4th, lost pos, rallied und pres 3 out, chased wnr frm nxt, no imprsn*................................. (7 to 1 op 5 to 1) 2
2440² FONTANAYS (Ire) [91] 9-11-1 (7") R Hobson, *chsd ldrs, lost pos 5th, styd on frm 2 out, not a dngr.* .... (2 to 1 fav op 9 to 4 tchd 5 to 2) 3
2396³ SUPERMICK [88] 6-11-5 N Williamson, *led to 3 out, wknd aftr nxt, no ch whn hit last..*.......... (11 to 4 op 9 to 4 tchd 3 to 1) 4
2407 MRS JAWLEYFORD (USA) [80] 9-10-11 M Ranger, *keen hold, chsd ldrs frm 3rd, rdn and wknd 4 out*......... (33 to 1) 5
2429³ DAILY SPORT GIRL [85] 8-11-2 Mr J L Llewellyn, *in tch till r-in and wknd 5th..*.............. (11 to 2 op 7 to 1 tchd 8 to 1) 6
2396⁸ ERLKING (Ire) [90] (v) 7-11-7 J Osborne, *beh, lost tch 5th.* .... (12 to 1 op 10 to 1 tchd 14 to 1) 7
2407 KARLINE KA (Fr) [90] 6-11-7 J Culloty, *beh whn f 3rd.* .... (20 to 1 op 14 to 1) f
Dist: 4l, 2l, 7l, nk, 10l. 4m 11.10s. a 26.10s (8 Ran).
SR: 3/-/-/-/-/ (N A Dunger), P Winkworth

PLUMPTON (good to soft)
Monday February 10th
Going Correction: PLUS 1.65 sec. per fur.

2610 Cowfold Conditional Jockeys' Selling Handicap Hurdle Class G (0-95 4-y-o and up) £1,924 2m 1f... (1:50)

2424³ KENTAVRUS WAY (Ire) [61] 6-9-9 (5*) M Batchelor, hld up, rdn alng 4th, prog appr 2 out, led bef last, styd on.
....(14 to 1 op 12 to 1) 1

2351³ SUMMER VILLA [67] (bl) 5-10-6 L Aspell, hdwy 5th, rdn appr 2 out, chsd wnr bef nxt, one pace. ....(9 to 2 jt-fav op 4 to 1 tchd 5 to 1) 2

2424⁴ DERISBAY (Ire) [74] (bl) 9-10-13 Sophie Mitchell, hdwy 3rd, lost pl 6th, styd on one pace frm 3 out. (25 to 1 op 20 to 1) 3

2479 ZADOK [66] (bl) 5-10-5 P Henley, hld up, hdwy 5th, led nxt, hdd and wknd appr last..................(12 to 1 op 10 to 1) 4

1425 PRECIOUS WONDER [63] 8-10-2 A Bates, nvr nr to chal.
....(14 to 1 op 12 to 1 tchd 16 to 1) 5

990⁶ DEPTFORD BELLE [68] 7-10-7 D Walsh, chsd ldrs, wknd frm 3 out..(14 to 1 op 16 to 1) 6

2424² SLIGHTLY SPECIAL (Ire) [64] 5-10-3 S Ryan, led sn clr, not fluent second, hdd 6th, wknd 3 out......(6 to 1 op 5 to 1) 7

2351⁶ MINSTER'S MADAM [88] (v) 6-11-13 J Harris, nvr gng wl, al beh.................(9 to 2 jt-fav tchd 5 to 1 and 3 to 1) 8

2012⁷ EMBROIDERED [71] 4-9-13⁶ (7*) J K McCarthy, al beh, tld off.
....(33 to 1 tchd 50 to 1) 9

2265 ANOTHER FIDDLE (Ire) [69] 7-10-4³ (7*) Gordon Gallagher, nvr on terms, tld off whn pld up, bef 2 out.
....(33 to 1 op 25 to 1) pu

1846⁷ NATIONAL FLAG (Fr) [70] (v) 7-10-4 (5*) A Watt, pld hrd, chsd ldrs, 6th whn pulled up and dismounted bef 3 out. Dead.
....(12 to 1 op 10 to 1) pu

2305 MEMORY'S MUSIC [68] 5-10-2 (5*) J Power, beh frm 7th, pld up bef last.................(14 to 1 op 12 to 1) pu

2390 BATTLESHIP BRUCE [89] (bl) 5-12-0 D Fortt, in tch, chsd ldr appr 3 out till bef nxt, wknd rpdly, beh whn pld up before last.
....(9 to 1 op 5 to 1 tchd 10 to 1) pu

2479 DECEIT THE SECOND [61] (v) 5-10-0 M Griffiths, hit 4th, chsd ldr to 5th, sn wknd, beh whn pld up bef last.
.... pu

2350⁸ BELLE PERK (Ire) [61] 6-10-0 C Rae, beh frm 7th, pld up bef last.................(5 to 1 tchd 6 to 1 and 9 to 2) pu

Dist: 13l, 4l, 6l, 1¼l, 5l, 1½l, 11l, dist. 4m 44.80s. a 47.80s (15 Ran).

(F L Hill), G L Moore

2611 Dyke Juvenile Novices' Claiming Hurdle Class F (4-y-o) £2,176 2m 1f ....(2:20)

SUPREME ILLUSION (Aus) 10-0 V Smith, beh till hdwy appoaching 2 out, led bef last out...(50 to 1 op 25 to 1) 1

2440⁴ HAWANAFA (bl) 10-2² W McFarland, in tch, led 6th, sn clr, blun 2 out, wkng whn blundered and hdd last.
....(4 to 1 op 3 to 1) 2

1702 PETROS GEM 9-13 (7*) J Harris, hld up, hit 6th, took second appr 3 out till approaching last, fdd....(50 to 1 op 25 to 1) 3

2387³ WHISPERING DAWN 11-1 D Gallagher, led to 6th, wknd frm 3 out, tld off.................(2 to 1 op 5 to 1) 4

2336⁸ CLASSIC COLOURS (USA) 11-3 K Gaule, beh frm 6th, tld off.
....(12 to 1 op 8 to 1 tchd 16 to 1) 5

1610 PETROS PRIDE 10-3 (3*) L Aspell, al beh, tld off whn pld up bef 2 out.................(50 to 1 op 25 to 1) pu

1702⁶ EMBER 10-6 D Bridgwater, al beh, tld off whn pld up bef 4 out.
....(8 to 1 op 6 to 1 tchd 9 to 1) pu

SIMPLY SEVEN 10-5 P Holley, al beh, tld off whn pld up bef 4 out.................(50 to 1 op 25 to 1) pu

NOBLESSE OBLIGE 11-3 A Thornton, hld up, wkng whn blun 6th, tld off whn pld up bef nxt.
....(15 to 8 fav op 7 to 4 tchd 13 to 8) pu

Dist: 3½l, 3l, dist, dist. 4m 55.30s. a 58.30s (9 Ran).

(John Berry), John Berry

2612 Hassocks Novices' Chase Class E (5-y-o and up) £3,183 2m.......(2:50)

2376 COOLTEEN HERO (Ire) 7-11-7 W McFarland, made all, not fluent 3 out, blun nxt, rdn out.
....(13 to 2 op 5 to 1 tchd 7 to 1) 1

2352 PURBECK CAVALIER 8-11-0 A Thornton, in tch, wnt second appr 2 out, styd on one pace...............(7 to 2 jt-fav op 5 to 1 tchd 7 to 1 and 3 to 1) 2

BUCKLAND LAD (Ire) 6-11-0 B Fenton, hld up, rdn alng frm 4 out, styd on from 2 out, nvr nrr.....(4 to 1 op 9 to 4) 3

1698⁶ DRESS DANCE (Ire) 7-10-9 (5*) Sophie Mitchell, trkd ldrs, lost pl 6th, rallied 9th, one pace 3 out. 4

2290³ SHOW FAITH (Ire) 7-11-0 J A McCarthy, prmnt, chsd wnr frm 4th till appr 2 out, wknd nxt......(7 to 2 jt-fav op 5 to 2) 5

REGAL AURA (Ire) 7-11-0 P Hide, beh frm 8th.
....(25 to 1 op 20 to 1) 6

2290⁵ WINDWARD ARIOM 11-11-0 J F Titley, hld up, rdn and wknd 4 out.................(13 to 2 op 6 to 1 tchd 12 to 1) 7

2352⁴ BRIGADIER SUPREME (Ire) 8-11-0 T J Murphy, reluctant to race, al beh, tld off frm 7th............(33 to 1 op 12 to 1) 8

2263 EAU SO SLOE 6-11-0 A Dicken, beh frm 7th, f 4 out.
....(50 to 1 op 16 to 1) f

Dist: 6l, 7l, 1¾l, 14l, 6l, 25l, dist. 4m 26.20s. a 34.20s (9 Ran).

SR: 15/2/-/-/-/-/ (J P M & J W Cook), R H Alner

2613 Bet With The Tote Novices' Chase Qualifier Class E (6-y-o and up)

£3,290 3m 1f 110yds........(3:20)

HIGH LEARIE 7-10-10 J A McCarthy, jmpd wl, made virtually all, drvn out betw fnl 2...(14 to 1 op 6 to 1 tchd 16 to 1) 1

2312⁴ EASY BREEZY 7-10-10 J Railton, sn in tch, chlgd 3 out, no extr r-in.................(16 to 1 op 12 to 1 tchd 20 to 1) 2

1981⁴ APATURA HATI 8-10-5 A Thornton, hld up, hdwy 13th, effrt 4 out, wknd last.................(10 to 1 tchd 12 to 1) 3

2480 DUNLIR 7-10-3 (7*) M Griffiths, mstks 3rd and 14th, al wl beh, tld off.................(33 to 1 op 20 to 1 tchd 50 to 1) 4

2354⁴ THERMAL WARRIOR 9-10-10 G Upton, wtd wth, hdwy 14th, 4th and rdn whn blun and uns rdr 2 out.
....(5 to 2 op 9 to 4 tchd 2 to 1) ur

1698 PINOCCIO 10-10-10 P Hide, trkd ldrs, hit 5th, lost pl 9th, tld off whn pld up bef 14th...............(50 to 1 op 25 to 1) pu

2280 MELNIK 6-11-3 C Maude, chsd ldrs to tenth, tld off whn pld up bef 2 out.................(6 to 4 fav op 5 to 4 tchd 7 to 4) pu

NIKKIS PET 10-10-5 D Walsh, in tch, mstk 13th, wknd 15th, tld off whn pld up bef 2 out. (14 to 1 op 10 to 1 tchd 16 to 1) pu

2391 GIVUS A CALL (Ire) 7-10-7 (3*) L Aspell, mstks 3rd and 12th, al beh, tld off whn pld up bef 15th.
....(5 to 2 op 5 to 1 tchd 6 to 1) pu

Dist: 2l, 9l, dist. 7m 14.80s. a 60.80s (9 Ran).

(Edward Harvey), A H Harvey

2614 Sheffield Park Mares' Only Novices' Hurdle Class E (4-y-o and up) £2,679 2m 1f........................(3:50)

2353³ BULA VOGUE (Ire) 7-11-0 D O'Sullivan, led second, made 1st, rdn out, ran on wl.
...(11 to 10 on op 6 to 4 on tchd Evens and 11 to 10) 1

2215 MAYLIN MAGIC 6-11-0 D Bridgwater, hld up, hdwy appr 3 out, wnt second betw fnl 2, hit last, no extr r-in.
....(14 to 1 op 6 to 1) 2

1942⁹ KILSHEY 6-11-0 P Hide, led to second, ev ch appr 2 out, btn bef last.................(14 to 1 op 8 to 1) 3

FINLANA 4-10-4 J F Titley, hld up, hdwy frm 4 out, wknd appr 2 out.................(5 to 1 op 4 to 1 tchd 11 to 2) 4

1716⁵ ILANDRA (Ire) 5-11-0 A Maguire, hld up, hdwy appr 3 out, wknd bef nxt.................(6 to 1 op 5 to 1) 5

1802⁴ FLOOSY 6-11-0 T Jenks, al beh, tld off. (16 to 1 op 8 to 1) 6

2267 ILEWIN JANINE (Ire) 6-11-0 D Gallagher, hld up, f 3rd.
....(8 to 1 op 12 to 1 tchd 7 to 1) f

ORCHID HOUSE 5-11-0 G Upton, whipped round and uns rdr strt.................(33 to 1 op 20 to 1) ur

5243³ KNOT TRUE 7-11-0 P Holley, hld up, brght dwn 3rd.
....(40 to 1 op 25 to 1 tchd 50 to 1) bd

OUR EMMA 8-11-0 D Skyrme, prmnt, mstk second, beh frm 7th, tld off whn pld up bef 2 out.
....(66 to 1 op 33 to 1 tchd 100 to 1) pu

TAPESTRY ROSE 6-11-0 A Dicken, in tch to 6th, tld off whn pld up bef 2 out...(66 to 1 op 25 to 1 tchd 100 to 1) pu

Dist: 5l, 4l, 18l, 9l, 25l. 4m 45.30s. a 48.30s (11 Ran).

(The In Vogue Partnership), R Rowe

2615 Flyaway Challenge Cup Hunters' Chase Class H (5-y-o and up) £1,590 3m 1f 110yds.................(4:20)

LOYAL NOTE 9-12-2 (3*) Mr Simon Andrews, dsptd ld, not fluent 15th, hit nxt, led appr last, ran on wl.
....(7 to 1 op 9 to 2) 1

TRIFAST LAD 12-11-11 (3*) Mr P Hacking, made most, hit 16th, hdd appr last, one pace......(7 to 2 op 6 to 1) 2

SUNNY MOUNT 11-11-7 (7*) Mr S Morris, hld up, prog 13th, ev ch 2 out, one pace.
....(13 to 8 on op 5 to 2 on tchd 6 to 4 on) 3

ANNIO CHILONE 11-11-7 (7*) Mr P O'Keeffe, hld up, rdn frm 4 out, wknd appr 2 out... (11 to 2 op 4 to 1 tchd 6 to 1) 4

COLONEL KENSON 11-11-7 (7*) Mr M Gingell, led to 3rd, lost pl 6th, beh whn blun badly and uns rdr 8th.
....(33 to 1 op 14 to 1) ur

Dist: 2½l, ¾l, 22l. 7m 30.00s. a 76.00s (5 Ran).

(R Andrews), S R Andrews

2616 Firle Place Handicap Hurdle Class F (0–105 4-y-o and up) £2,194 2½m ....(4:50)

955⁵ MAYB-MAYB [68] 7-10-1 D Walsh, led to 5th, rgned ld appr 4 out, drvn clr bef 2 out, ran on wl.......(6 to 1 op 4 to 1) 1

2351⁷ LAJADHAL (Fr) [69] 8-10-2² W McFarland, hld up beh ldrs, lost pl 4 out, rallied 2 out, wnt second last, one pace.
....(20 to 1 op 12 to 1 tchd 25 to 1) 2

2356⁹ MILLMOUNT (Ire) [89] 7-11-1 (7*) C Rae, in tch, led appr 6th till approaching 4 out, rdn bef 2 out, btn whn hit last.
....(4 to 1 op 5 to 1 tchd 6 to 1) 3

2532⁶ CHIEFTAIN'S CROWN (USA) [90] 6-11-9 D Bridgwater, hdwy 7th, led briefly aftr 3 out, wknd bef nxt...(8 to 1 op 6 to 1) 4

2356⁷ KILCORAN BAY [95] (v) 5-11-7 (7*) Mr A Balding, nvr on terms.................(12 to 1 op 8 to 1 tchd 14 to 1) 5

2277 KYBO'S REVENGE (Ire) [68] 6-10-1¹ D O'Sullivan, hit second, beh frm 7th.................(100 to 30 op 5 to 1) 6

2429 YELLOW DRAGON (Ire) [95] 4-11-3 K Gaule, hld up beh ldrs, rdn appr 3 out, sn wknd.
....(5 to 2 fav op 3 to 1 tchd 3 to 1) 7

1110[5] CAVO GRECO (USA) [70] 8-10-3 D Skyrme, *prmnt, led 5th till bef nxt, wknd 4 out, tld off whn pld up before 2 out.
.... (33 to 1 op 14 to 1)   pu

Dist: 9l, 4l, 17l, 3l, 6l, 2½l. 5m 35.60s. a 58.60s (8 Ran).

(J Neville), J Neville

AYR (soft)
Tuesday February 11th
Going Correction: PLUS 1.40 sec. per fur. (races 1,2,3,7), PLUS 1.55 (4,5,6)

2617 Levy Board Novices' Handicap Hurdle Class E (0-100 4-y-o and up) £2,626 2m.................(1:40)

2192 SOLSGIRTH [69] 6-10-8 A Thornton, *midfield, chlgd 6th, drvn to ld 2 out, kpt on gmely und pres.....* (20 to 1 op 14 to 1)   1
2463[7] JOE SHAW [85] 4-11-0 P Niven, *hld up, improved hfwy, ev ch appr 2 out, styd on till no extr cl nme..* (11 to 4 op 12 to 1)   2
3335[5] POLITICAL TOWER [85] 10-11-10 B Storey, *hld up, hdwy to ld 6th, rdn and hdd 2 out, fdd frm last.*
.... (5 to 2 fav tchd 11 to 4)   3
2357[6] NANCYS CHOICE [75] 7-11-0 J Burke, *led second, mstk and hdd 6th, wknd quickly appr nxt.....* (20 to 1 tchd 25 to 1)   4
1986[4] SEGALA (Ire) [79] 6-11-4 P Carberry, *led to second, cl up, reminders 5th, blun and lost tch nxt, tld off.*
.... (14 to 1 op 10 to 1)   5
2284[5] BOWCLIFFE [78] 6-11-3 M Foster, *hld up, lost tch 4 out, tld off whn pld up bef nxt.......* (14 to 1 op 10 to 1)   pu
2349[6] TEEJAY 'N'AITCH (Ire) [78] 5-11-3 G Cahill, *chsd ldrs, lost pl 4th, tld off whn pld up bef 3 out....* (14 to 1 op 12 to 1)   pu
RUNNING GREEN [64] 6-10-3[2] D J Moffatt, *beh, improved to chase ldrs 4 out, wknd nxt, behind whn pld up betw last 2.*
.... (25 to 1 op 14 to 1)   pu
2444[4] FILS DE CRESSON (Ire) [85] 7-11-10 M Moloney, *in tch, effrt whn hit 6th, wknd quickly and pld up bef nxt.*
.......................(4 to 1 op 7 to 2 tchd 9 to 2)   pu
1656[5] BILL'S PRIDE [78] 6-11-3 A Dobbin, *in tch, fdg whn hit 4 out, tld off whn pld up bef nxt.......* (20 to 1 op 14 to 1)   pu

Dist: 1¼l, 8l, dist, 26l. 4m 8.50s. a 32.50s (10 Ran).

(Kinneston Farmers), J Barclay

2618 River Doon Handicap Hurdle Class D (0-125 4-y-o and up) £2,777 2m .... (2:10)

2204[9] STAR SELECTION [97] 6-10-4 (3°) E Husband, *dsptd ld, led o'rall 4 out, clr whn hit 2 out, easily.*
.... (11 to 4 op 5 to 2 tchd 3 to 1)   1
MERRY MERMAID [96] 7-10-6 B Storey, *dsptd ld to 4 out, outpcd aftr nxt, sn no extr.............* (7 to 2 op 5 to 2)   2
2159° MONICA'S CHOICE (Ire) [116] 6-11-12 P Niven, *steadied rear, pushed alng whn hit 6th, lost tch bef nxt.*
.......................(5 to 2 fav op 2 to 1 tchd 11 to 4)   3
OUR PROBER [95] 5-10-5 P Carberry, *hld up, hdwy to chase ldrs 5th, outpcd appr 3 out, sn wknd.*
.... (9 to 1 op 8 to 1 tchd 10 to 1)   4
2316[4] COMMON SOUND (Ire) [110] 6-11-6 A Thornton, *chsd ldrs, outpcd appr 3 out, sn wl beh.*
.... (9 to 2 op 4 to 1 tchd 5 to 1)   5

Dist: 21l, 4l, 6l, 30l. 4m 3.50s. a 27.50s (5 Ran).

SR: 28/6/22/-/-/

(R M Mitchell), J Mackie

2619 River Cree Novices' Hurdle Class E (4-y-o and up) £2,582 2¾m... (2:40)

1631[3] MILITARY ACADEMY 8-12-0 P Carberry, *cl up, led on bit aftr 4 out, eased considerably frm last, cmftbly.*
.... (11 to 8 on 6 to 4 on tchd 5 to 4 on)   1
2349[4] SUNNY LEITH 6-11-7 A Dobbin, *keen hold, chsd ldrs, drvn alng 3 out, styd on one pace.............* (33 to 1)   2
2320* ADIB (USA) 7-12-0 N Bentley, *midfield, chsd ldrs 4 out, outpcd frm nxt..........................* (11 to 2 op 4 to 1)   3
1657[5] DRAKEWRATH (Ire) 7-11-7 D Parker, *not fluent 4th, led 7th till mstk and hdd four out, fdd...........* (16 to 1 op 10 to 1)   4
2288° CHERRY DEE 6-10-11 (5°) B Grattan, *not fluent rear, struggling 4 out, some late hdwy, nvr a factor.*
.... (10 to 1 op 6 to 1 tchd 12 to 1)   5
2346[4] ALLERBANK 6-11-7 Mr C Storey, *hld up, not fluent 7th, lost tch aftr nxt...........* (14 to 1 op 12 to 1 tchd 16 to 1)   6
2188° DOUBLE DASH (Ire) 4-11-3 D J Moffatt, *in tch, struggling whn mstk 8th, sn no dngr...........* (20 to 1 op 14 to 1)   7
FAYETTE COUNTY (Ire) 6-11-7 A Thornton, *beh, hdwy fnl circuit, midfield whn hit 4 out, sn lost tch.*
.... (10 to 1 op 7 to 1 tchd 8 to 1)   8
1987[7] NAWTINOOKEY (Ire) 7-10-13 (3°) G Lee, *in tch, drvn and wknd aftr 4 out, tld off.............* (100 to 1 op 200 to 1)   9
2570[7] MEADOWLECK 8-11-2 G Cahill, *hld up to 7th, btn whn f 4 out.*
.... (100 to 1 op 500 to 1)   f
JUST EVE 10-11-2 T Reed, *struggling 7th, tld off whn pld up 4 out.......................* (500 to 1)   pu
2260° HARFDECENT 6-11-7 P Niven, *midfield, hdwy and chasing ldrs whn mstk 4 out, wknd quickly and pld up bef nxt.*
.... (16 to 1 op 14 to 1 tchd 20 to 1)   pu

---

2322[7] ROYAL SPRUCE (Ire) 6-11-7 J Callaghan, *jmpd poorly, nvr gng wl in rear, tld off and pld up 8th...* (50 to 1 op 33 to 1)   pu
2496 BORDER IMAGE 6-11-7 A Roche, *pushed alng to join ldrs 6th, lost tch 8th, tld off whn pld up 4 out.* (66 to 1 op 50 to 1)   pu

Dist: 7l, 12l, 8l, nk, 5l, 6l, 2½l, 16l. 6m 7.00s. a 60.00s (14 Ran).

(Robert Ogden), G Richards

2620 River Girvan Novices' Chase Class D (6-y-o and up) £3,704 3m 3f 110yds .... (3:10)

2348[3] JUDICIOUS CAPTAIN 10-10-10 Mr C Storey, *midfield, blun 11th, drvn to ld 3 out, styd on wl......* (4 to 1 tchd 5 to 1)   1
2534 NAUGHTY FUTURE 8-11-3 R Supple, *hld up, not fluent, steady hdwy fnl circuit, ev ch 2 out, kpt on.*
.... (100 to 30 op 3 to 1 tchd 7 to 2)   2
2534* D'ARBLAY STREET (Ire) 8-11-3 P Carberry, *led 4th, hit 15th, hdd 3 out, pckd nxt, wknd and eased whn btn.*
.... (7 to 2 op 5 to 2)   3
2285[3] CLONROCHE LUCKY (Ire) 7-10-10 K Jones, *in tch, mstk tenth, outpcd 6 out, no dngr aftr.............* (100 to 1)   4
2347[6] ABBEY LAMP (Ire) 8-10-10 A Thornton, *cl up, mstk and drvn alng 13th, wl beh 5 out.................* (33 to 1)   5
2573[6] QUIXALL CROSSETT 12-10-3 (7°) Tristan Davidson, *led to 4th, in tch till blun 14th, f nxt......* (300 to 1 op 200 to 1)   f
2347[2] NOOSA SOUND (Ire) 7-10-10 B Storey, *hdwy to chase ldrs 12th, fdg whn hit 4 out, fourth and btn when f nxt.*
.... (3 to 1 fav op 5 to 2)   f
1963 SPRINGHILL QUAY (Ire) 8-10-10 A Dobbin, *blun 3rd, chsd ldrs, wknd quickly and pld up 13th.*
.... (11 to 1 op 10 to 1 tchd 12 to 1)   pu
2491[6] SELDOM BUT SEVERE (Ire) 7-10-5 (5°) G F Ryan, *not fluent rear, beh whn hmpd 15th, tld off and pld up 3 out..* (50 to 1)   pu
2347[5] BRIGHT DESTINY (v) 6-10-10 G Cahill, *al rear, tld off whn pld up 4 out.................* (66 to 1 op 50 to 1)   pu
2484[6] POCAINE GAOITHE (Ire) 7-10-5 (5°) R McGrath, *reminders in rear 8th, tld off whn pld up 6 out...........* (50 to 1)   pu

Dist: 1¾l, 21l, dist, dist. 7m 51.10s. a 69.10s (11 Ran).

(James R Adam), Mrs J Storey

2621 River Tig Novices' Chase Class E (5-y-o and up) £3,068 2m 5f 110yds .... (3:40)

2464[3] COLONEL IN CHIEF (Ire) 7-11-4 P Carberry, *jmpd wl, led 9th, clr 5 out, mstk 2 out, unchlgd.....* (5 to 4 fav op 11 to 8)   1
2348* MR KNITWIT 10-11-11 A Dobbin, *chsd ldr, pressed wnr fnl circuit, jmpd slwly and lost tch 5 out, fnshd tired.*
.... (11 to 8 op 5 to 4)   2
2259[6] DESPERATE DAYS (Ire) 8-11-4 W Dwan, *beh, mstk 5th, tld off hfwy.......................* (100 to 1 op 200 to 1)   3
2205[7] LIEN DE FAMILLE (Ire) 7-11-11 B Storey, *hld up, not fluent, chasing ldrs whn blun tenth, sn beh, tld off when pld up 3 out.*
.... (12 to 1 op 8 to 1)   pu
2319[3] BALLYLINE (Ire) 6-11-11 A S Smith, *made most to 9th, lost tch quickly 11th, tld off whn pld up 4 out.....* (7 to 1 op 6 to 1)   pu

Dist: Dist, dist. 6m 5.20s. a 59.20s (5 Ran).

(Robert Ogden), G Richards

2622 Loch Enoch Handicap Chase Class E (0-110 5-y-o and up) £3,163 2m .... (4:10)

2345[3] RALLEGIO [90] 8-11-0 A Dobbin, *hld up, steady hdwy 5 out, slight ld 3 out, ran on strly.......* (7 to 2 co-fav op 5 to 2)   1
2573* NICHOLAS PLANT [94] 8-11-4 (Tex) G Cahill, *chsd ldrs, lost ld 4th, beh whn blun 7th, ran on frm 3 out, nrst finish.*
.... (7 to 2 co-fav op 5 to 2)   2
2261* NETHERBY SAID [104] 7-12-0 R Supple, *str hold, made most frm 3rd, lft in ld 4 out, hdd nxt, sn drvn and one pace.*
.... (7 to 2 co-fav op 3 to 1)   3
2321[4] FUNNY OLD GAME [76] 10-9-11 (3°) Michael Brennan, *hld up, niggled alng 6 out, no imprsn aftr nxt.*
.... (25 to 1 op 20 to 1)   4
2191[4] ONE FOR THE POT [100] 12-11-10 M Foster, *in tch, mstk 7th, outpcd 4 out, btn whn blun 2 out........* (9 to 2 op 4 to 1)   5
2569[5] MONAUGHTY MAN [76] 11-10-0 M Moloney, *in tch, reminders 6th, beh 4 out.............* (100 to 1 op 50 to 1)   6
2150[6] SUPER SANDY [78] 10-10-2 K Johnson, *led to 3rd, chsd ldrs till drvn and mstk 5 out, sn wknd, tld off.* (7 to 1 op 6 to 1)   7
2349[5] BLAZING TRAIL (Ire) [103] 9-11-13 A Thornton, *al hndy, chlgd 5 out, slight ld whn f nxt.* (10 to 1 op 8 to 1 tchd 11 to 1)   f
2345 EMERALD SEA (USA) [82] 10-10-6 B Storey, *not fluent rear, tld off whn pld up 6 out.............* (50 to 1 op 33 to 1)   pu

Dist: 5l, 1½l, 8l, 13l, 17l, 5l. 4m 16.40s. a 31.40s (9 Ran).

SR: 20/19/27/-/-/-/

(Guthrie Robertson), P Monteith

2623 River Ayr Maiden National Hunt Flat Class H (4,5,6-y-o) £1,380 2m (4:40)

2283[4] MERRY MASQUERADE (Ire) 6-11-5 (3°) G Lee, *midfield, pushed alng 3 fs out, styd on wl to ld o'r one out, drvn clr.*
.... (11 to 8 fav op 6 to 4 tchd 2 to 1)   1
PRIME EXAMPLE (Ire) 6-11-5 (3°) Michael Brennan, *hld up, hdwy gng wl to ld o'r 2 fs out, hdd over one out, kpt on.*
.......................(4 to 1 op 3 to 1 tchd 9 to 2)   2

NO GIMMICKS (Ire) 5-11-5 (3*) F Leahy, settled rear, hdwy and ev ch 3 fs out, styd on same pace.
.............................(9 to 2 op 3 to 1 tchd 5 to 1)   3
LINWOOD 6-11-3 Mr R Hale, hld up, pushed alng and outpcd entering strt, styd on ag'n fnl 2 fs.
.............................(12 to 1 op 8 to 1 tchd 14 to 1)   4
EASBY BLUE 5-11-5 (3*) M C Bonner, al hndy, chlgd entering strt, one pace whn slightly hmpd 2 out.
....   5
COOL KEVIN 4-10-12 Mrs M Kendall, chsd ldrs, slight ld o'r 3 fs out, hdd over 2 out, fdd ....(100 to 1)   6
2363⁴ JUST NED 6-11-1 (7*) N Horrocks, str hold, slight ld till o'r 3 fs out, fdd..................(20 to 1 tchd 25 to 1)   7
YOUNG SEMELE 5-11-3 Mr G Storey, in tch, chlgd entering strt, wndrd and wknd o'r 2 out.........(10 to 1 op 8 to 1)   8
2363³ DELIGHTFOOL 6-11-3 G Cahill, pld hrd, drpd rear aftr 3 fs, no dngr after....................................(14 to 1)   9
2363   CHIEF CHIPPIE 4-10-5 (7*) S Haworth, hld up, pushed alng hfwy, sn lost tch..............................(100 to 1)   10
2213⁶ CHAMPS-GIRL (Ire) 4-10-4 (3*) E Callaghan, chsd ldrs till wknd sn aftr hfwy, tld off.......................(100 to 1)   11
CHAN MOVE 5-11-3 (5*) S Taylor, tld off fnl 4 fs ..(100 to 1)   12
Dist: 3l, 3½l, 3l, 4l, 11l, 5l, 7l, 29l, 2l, dist. 4m 6.40s. (12 Ran).
(G S Brown), Mrs M Reveley

LEICESTER (good to firm (races 1,3,4), good to soft (2,5,6))
Tuesday February 11th
Going Correction: PLUS 0.15 sec. per fur. (races 1,3,4), PLUS 0.40 (2,5,6)

2624 Wren Handicap Chase Class E (0-115 5-y-o and up) £3,179 2½m 110yds..............................(2:00)

2286* MACGEORGE (Ire) [107] 7-11-6 A Maguire, jmpd wl, made virtually all, clr last, easily.........(7 to 4 fav op 6 to 4)   1
2314⁴ SAILOR JIM [105] 10-11-4 N Williamson, hld up, cld 7th, jmpd slwly nxt, chsd wnr 4 out, hrd rdn appr 2 out, no imprsn whn jumped lft last two.......................(4 to 1 tchd 5 to 1)   2
2386⁶ HOWGILL [94] (bl) 11-10-7 S Wynne, trkd ldrs, not fluent 3 out, sn one pace.........................(12 to 1 op 8 to 1)   3
1974⁵ EVEN BLUE [115] 9-12-0 J Railton, trkd ldrs, wkng whn blun 4 out...(7 to 2 op 5 to 2)   4
2386⁵ CROPREDY LAD [92] 10-10-5 J Osborne, hld up, struggling and lost tch 10th, styd on one pace, nvr a factor.
.............................(11 to 2 op 6 to 1 tchd 7 to 1 and 8 to 1)   5
2026   SPEARHEAD AGAIN (Ire) [87] 8-10-0 B Powell, hld up, mstk 7th, struggling in rear 11th.
.............................(25 to 1 op 20 to 1 tchd 33 to 1)   6
2408⁴ COUNT BARACHOIS (USA) [87] 9-10-0 K Gaule, wth wnr, led briefly 5th, lost pl appr 4 out, sn btn, tld off.
....(33 to 1 op 20 to 1)   7
2395⁸ TRIBAL RULER [87] 12-10-0 D Walsh, hld up in tch, mstk 7th, blun 9th, pld def nxt.(25 to 1 op 20 to 1 tchd 33 to 1)   pu
Dist: 18l, 5l, 1l, 1¼l, 4l, 30l. 5m 10.80s. a 8.80s (8 Ran).
SR: 35/15/-/19/-/   (J H Watson), R Lee

2625 Vicarage Claiming Hurdle Class F (4-y-o and up) £2,595 2m.......(2:30)

2497   APACHE PARK (USA) (bl) 4-10-5 D Gallagher, trkd ldrs, led aftr 5th, jmpd rght 2 out and ag'n whn hit last, kpt on wl.
.............................(14 to 1 op 10 to 1)   1
THREESOCKS 4-10-3 I Lawrence, hld up in mid-div, hdwy appr 5th, chsd wnr frm 4 out, hrd rdn approaching last, kpt on.
....(12 to 1)   2
TULU 6-11-9 R Garritty, hld up, hdwy 5th, hrd rdn appr 2 out, one pace......................(2 to 1 fav op Evens)   3
2442   WHITE WILLOW (v) 8-11-8 (3*) R Massey, beh, styd on frm 2 out, nvr nr to chal............(4 to 1 op 5 to 1 tchd 6 to 1)   4
2526⁵ HIGH LOW (USA) (bl) 9-11-8 T Jenks, cl up, led aftr 4th till aftr nxt, hrd rdn and btn appr 2 out.....(5 to 1 op 4 to 1)   5
2387⁷ GI MOSS (bl) 10-10-11 W Marston, hld up, effrt 5th, no imprsn on ldrs whn hit 4 out...........(20 to 1 op 33 to 1)   6
2425   ERNEST ARAGORN (v) 8-11-5 R Farrant, mid-div, pushed alng 4th, hdwy nxt, btn whn badly hmpd 3 out......(50 to 1)   7
225   KHAZARI (USA) 9-11-5 L Harvey, struggling in rear frm 4th.
.............................(25 to 1 op 20 to 1 tchd 33 to 1)   8
2387   BITES 4-10-0 T Eley, al beh..........(66 to 1 op 50 to 1)   9
1731⁹ MONTY 5-11-5 V Slattery, al beh.........................(50 to 1)   10
1800⁷ MILL DANCER (Ire) 5-10-8 S Wynne, led, hit second, hdd aftr 4th, mstk nxt, sn btn.......................(33 to 1)   11
1943⁶ ADMIRAL'S GUEST (Ire) (v) 5-11-5 R Johnson, trkd ldrs, hrd rdn and btn aftr 5th, tld off........................(33 to 1)   12
2390⁹ ESPLA 6-11-8 W McFarland, f second.(14 to 1 op 10 to 1)   f
2385² SHEECKY 6-11-3 (5*) S Ryan, chsd ldrs, hrd rdn aftr 4 out, btn whn f nxt..................(9 to 1 op 8 to 1 tchd 10 to 1)   f
MANABAR 5-11-5 V Smith, beh whn blun and uns rdr 3 out.
.............................(33 to 1 op 20 to 1)   ur
BRICK COURT (Ire) 6-11-8 N Williamson, bright dwn second.
.............................(10 to 1 op 8 to 1 tchd 11 to 1)   bd
2431   ASHLEY HOUSE (bl) 8-10-11 (5*) D Salter, chsd ldrs, hrd rdn appr 5th, sn btn, tld off whn pld up bef 4 out.
.............................(66 to 1 op 50 to 1)   pu

960   BACKHANDER (Ire) 5-11-2 J Railton, al beh, tld off whn pld up bef 2 out..................(20 to 1 op 14 to 1)   pu
ARABIAN DESIGN 5-11-5 B Powell, al beh, tld off whn pld up bef 4 out....................................(33 to 1)   pu
Dist: 1¼l, 13l, 23l, 4l, 1¼l, 1¾l, 6l, ½l, 6l, ¾l. 3m 55.80s. a 12.80s (19 Ran).
SR: 13/9/16/-/-/-/   (M G Hynes), M Sheppard

2626 Thurnby Maiden Chase Class F (5-y-o and up) £2,626 2m 1f.......(3:00)

2278⁵ JUST BRUCE 8-11-5 K Gaule, wth ldr till outpcd and rdn alng appr 4 out, wl hld whn lft in ld 2 out, ridden out.
.............................(7 to 1 tchd 8 to 1 and 9 to 1)   1
FRANK KNOWS 7-11-5 R Johnson, trkd ldrs, lost pl 6th, lft modest 3rd 3 out, rallied, kpt on......(100 to 1 op 50 to 1)   2
2433³ CHARLIE PARROT (Ire) 7-11-5 Jamie Evans, chsd ldrs, lft second 2 out, one pace............(9 to 2 op 7 to 2)   3
2395   FULL SHILLING (USA) (bl) 8-11-2 (3*) Guy Lewis, trkd ldrs till wknd 6th.........................(25 to 1 op 20 to 1)   4
1673   ALTHREY ARISTOCRAT (Ire) 7-11-5 S McNeill, in tch to 6th, sn wl beh, tld off...................(100 to 1 op 50 to 1)   5
2304⁵ VIRBAZAR (Fr) 10-11-5 G Upton, beh whn f 7th, dead.
.............................(25 to 1 op 20 to 1)   f
PLEASURE CRUISE 7-10-12 (7*) N T Egan, f 1st.
.............................(66 to 1 op 50 to 1)   f
2269   WHOD OF THOUGHT IT (Ire) 6-11-0 (5*) Mr C Vigors, beh whn f 6th.......................................(50 to 1 op 33 to 1)   f
2457⁵ THE SECRET GREY 6-11-5 D Walsh, f 1st..........(50 to 1)   f
ELZOBA (Fr) 5-10-10 C Maude, led, mstk 4th, wnt clr aproaching four out, wl clear whn f 2 out. OR 13
.............................(6 to 4 on op 2 to 1 on tchd 11 to 8 on and 5 to 4 on)   f
2298   DANNICUS 6-11-5 V Slattery, badly hmpd 1st, beh whn pld up bef 6th.....................(11 to 1 op 8 to 1 tchd 12 to 1)   pu
Dist: 2½l, 17l, 10l, dist. 4m 23.40s. a 15.40s (11 Ran).
(A M Heath), Mrs E H Heath

2627 Trial Handicap Chase Class D (0-125 5-y-o and up) £5,481 3m......(3:30)

1064* MERLINS DREAM (Ire) [108] 8-11-3 J Osborne, trkd ldr, led 3 out, drvn out................(11 to 2 op 9 to 2 tchd 6 to 1)   1
2334   ROMANY CREEK (Ire) [116] (v) 8-11-11 N Williamson, hld up, keen hold, mstks 12th, 14th and nxt, rallied appr 2 out, ev ch last, kpt on und pres............(7 to 1 op 5 to 1 tchd 10 to 1)   2
2293* ACT OF PARLIAMENT (Ire) [119] (bl) 9-11-7 (7*) Mr R Wakley, hld up, cld aftr 8th, pushed alng 13th and sn lost pl, styd on wl frm 2 out...........(9 to 2 op 4 to 1 tchd 5 to 1)   3
2386⁷ MUGONI BEACH [117] 12-11-12 Jamie Evans, hld up, hit 10th and mstk 12th, hrd rdn aftr 3 out, one pace.
.............................(16 to 1 op 8 to 1 tchd 20 to 1)   4
2386* SHINING LIGHT (Ire) [114] 8-11-9 A Maguire, wth in tch, hit 10th, pushed alng aftr 14th, rdn along and no imprsn whn mstk 2 out.......................(9 to 4 fav tchd 5 to 2)   5
2389⁹ THE GLOW (Ire) [113] (bl) 9-11-8 R Farrant, hld up in cl tch, gng wl, ev ch 3 out, hrd rdn and no extr appr nxt.
....   6
2310   DONT TELL THE WIFE [116] 11-11-4 (7*) M Berry, hld up, mstk 13th, sn struggling, nvr on terms.
.............................(16 to 1 op 12 to 1 tchd 20 to 1)   7
2175   WELL BRIEFED [110] 10-11-5 B Powell, hld to 3 out, sn btn, tld off...........................(20 to 1 op 16 to 1)   8
2426⁶ MAKES ME GOOSEY (Ire) [96] (bl) 9-10-5 L Harvey, trkd ldrs, lost pl and blun 9th, pld up, dead.....(10 to 1 op 8 to 1)   pu
Dist: ¾l, 8l, 1¼l, 5l, 8l, 4l, dist. 6m 7.00s. a 22.00s (9 Ran).
(W S Watt), O Sherwood

2628 Somerby Juvenile Novices' Hurdle Class E (4-y-o) £2,721 2m......(4:00)

FONT ROMEU (Fr) 10-12 Jamie Evans, chsd ldrs, reminders aftr 5th, led appr 2 out, drvn alng, ran on wl.
.............................(25 to 1 op 20 to 1 tchd 33 to 1)   1
2284   CIRCUS STAR 10-12 A Maguire, hld up, smooth hdwy aftr 5th, led 3 out to appr nxt, no extr...........(6 to 1 tchd 8 to 1)   2
2311   TOPAGLOW (Ire) 10-12 B Fenton, hld up, steady hdwy appr 4 out, kpt on wl und pres frm last.......(50 to 1 op 33 to 1)   3
2454² NORTHERN FLEET 10-12 C Maude, rdn aing to lie hndy, led aftr 5th, hdd 3 out, one pace..........(8 to 1 op 4 to 1)   4
1702² SIBERIAN HENRY 10-12 I Lawrence, hld up beh ldrs, hdwy to chase lder appr 4 out, rdn and one pace approaching 2 out.
.............................(25 to 1 op 20 to 1)   5
2454³ NAME OF OUR FATHER (USA) 11-5 R Johnson, chsd ldrs, hrd rdn appr 3 out, one pace und pres. (25 to 1 op 14 to 1)   6
2303⁶ DAYDREAMER (USA) 10-12 B Powell, hld up in mid-div, nvr nr to chal.......................(66 to 1 op 50 to 1)   7
1398⁵ PRECIOUS ISLAND 10-7 J Supple, hld up, hdwy appr 4 out, sn rdn alng and no extr.............(50 to 1 op 33 to 1)   8
EZANAK (Ire) 10-12 J Culloty, reminders in rear aftr 3rd, drvn aftr 5th, nvr on terms...................(14 to 1 op 12 to 1)   9
2497   MIGHTY KEEN 10-12 D Skyrme, trkd ldrs, hrd rdn and btn appr 3 out...................(25 to 1 op 20 to 1 tchd 33 to 1)   10
2426³ MAGIC COMBINATION (Ire) 10-9 (3*) L Aspell, hld up, nvr plcd to chal.........................(10 to 1 op 3 to 1)   11
2392   STERLING FELLOW (v) 10-12 M Clarke, sn wl beh.
.............................(66 to 1 op 33 to 1)   12
2242⁵ FENCER'S QUEST (Ire) 10-12 N Williamson, al beh.
.............................(25 to 1 op 20 to 1)   13

2387 THE ODDFELLOW 10-12 O Pears, *al beh, tld off.*
.... (66 to 1 op 50 to 1)   14
2350* POMME SECRET (Fr) 11-3 J Osborne, *not fluent, cl up,*
   reminders aftr 4th and after nxt, btn after four out, tld off.
.... (11 to 10 fav op Evens tchd 5 to 4)   15
   CIRCLED (USA) 10-7 D Gallagher, *mid-div, mstk 5th, sn beh,*
   tld off..................................(25 to 1 op 33 to 1)   16
2303³ ANNA SOLEIL (Ire) 10-12 J A McCarthy, *f second.*
.... (8 to 1 tchd 10 to 1 and 7 to 1)   f
2397 COURTING DANGER (bl) 10-9 (3") D Fortt, *led till aftr 5th,*
   wknd quickly, tld off whn pld up bef 2 out.
.... (66 to 1 op 50 to 1)   pu
1844⁶ POETRY (Ire) 10-7 J Railton, *pld hrd, hld up in mid-div, effrt*
   5th, btn whn pulled up bef 2 out.......(33 to 1 op 20 to 1)   pu
   GEMINI DREAM 10-12 R Bellamy, *pld hrd, sn beh, tld off whn*
   pulled up bef 4 out..............................(50 to 1)   pu
Dist: 5l, ½l, 1¾l, 3l, 3l, 1l, 5l, ¾l, 16l, 5l. 3m 58.50s. a 15.50s (20 Ran).
(Pond House Gold), M C Pipe

2629 Oadby Handicap Hurdle Class E (0-110 4-y-o and up) £2,406 2m .... (4:30)

1939⁶ SHERIFFMUIR [105] 8-12-0 J F Titley, *al hndy, led appr 2 out,*
   drvn alng and ran on wl.............(16 to 1 op 10 to 1)   1
1947¹ KINTAVI [90] 7-10-13 T Eley, *hld up in cl tch, hdwy to hold ev*
   ch frm 2 out to last, no extr r-in...........(3 to 1 op 5 to 2)   2
2385* BEECHFIELD FLYER [85] 6-10-8 G Tormey, *trkd ldrs, pushed*
   alng 5th, outpcd appr 3 out, kpt on.
.... (11 to 2 op 7 to 2 tchd 6 to 1)   3
2389 CHILL WIND [86] 8-10-9 R Johnson, *hld up in cl tch, led 3 out*
   to appr nxt, one pace.................(33 to 1 op 25 to 1)   4
2204* MR MORIARTY (Ire) [97] 6-11-6 A Maguire, *made most, hdd*
   and hit 3 out, sn btn................. (7 to 2 op 11 to 4)   5
2296⁷ PAST MASTER (USA) [81] 9-10-4 K Gaule, *hld up beh,*
   pushed alng aftr 3rd, mstk 4 out, sn btn, tld off.
.... (10 to 1 tchd 12 to 1 and 14 to 1)   6
2407⁴ BOB'S PLOY [81] (v) 5-10-4 N Williamson, *wth ldr, led briefly*
   second, wknd quickly aftr 3 out, tld off.
.... (13 to 2 fav op 5 to 2 tchd 3 to 1)   7
2400⁴ RIVER ISLAND (USA) [92] 9-11-1 G Upton, *hld up, lost tch 5th,*
   tld off whn pld up bef 2 out...........(16 to 1 op 10 to 1)   pu
Dist: 2l, 6l, ¾l, 3½l, 21l, 6l. 3m 58.10s. a 15.10s (8 Ran).
SR: 13/-/-/-/-/   (J J W Wadham), Mrs L Wadham

MUSSELBURGH (good to firm (races 1,2,3,4), good to soft (5,6)) Wednesday February 12th
Going Correction: PLUS 0.10 sec. per fur.

2630 Musselburgh Conditional Jockeys' Selling Handicap Hurdle Class E (0-95 4-y-o and up) £2,427 2m (2:10)

2485* PALACE OF GOLD [80] 7-10-9 (8",7ex) W Dowling, *made all,*
   ran on wl and pres frm last........(9 to 2 jt-fav op 5 to 2)   1
2485³ OAKBURY (Ire) [68] 5-9-11 (8") T Siddall, *prmnt early, outpcd*
   and beh fifth, styd on wl and pres frm 2 out, no imprsn on wnr
   clsg stages.....................(9 to 2 jt-fav op 7 to 2)   2
2485⁶ DOUBLING DICE [66] 6-10-0 (3") S Melrose, *hld up, hdwy to*
   chase ldrs 5th, kpt on same pace frm 3 out.
.... (11 to 10 to 1 tchd 12 to 1)   3
2485 HENRY HOOLET [77] 8-10-9 (5") C McCormack, *sn tracking*
   ldrs, ev ch appr 2 out, no extr.(7 to 1 tchd 8 to 1)   4
2420⁹ KISMETIM [63] 7-10-0 B Grattan, *hld up, effrt bef 2 out, no*
   real hdwy..........................(16 to 1 op 25 to 1)   5
2485 TIOTAO (Ire) [69] 7-9-10 (10") Tristan Davidson, *cl up, outpcd*
   bef 2 out, no dngr aftr..............(6 to 1 tchd 7 to 1)   6
2533⁵ JARROW [65] 6-10-2 Michael Brennan, *prmnt, ev ch 2 out, sn*
   rdn and wknd............(9 to 1 op 8 to 1 tchd 10 to 1)   7
2537⁹ VINTAGE RED [87] 7-11-10 E Callaghan, *in tch till wknd bef 2*
   out............................(11 to 2 op 6 to 1)   8
2202⁷ BUD'S BET (Ire) [74] 9-10-11 M Newton, *al beh....* (12 to 1)   9
2359 SECONDS AWAY [63] 6-10-0 G Cahill, *al beh.*
.... (25 to 1 op 20 to 1)   10
Dist: 1¼l, 9l, 2½l, 2½l, 1¾l, 2l, 3l, 5l, 7l. 3m 49.80s. a 12.80s (10 Ran).
(Mrs Barbara Lungo), L Lungo

2631 Anderson Strathern Novices' Handicap Chase Class E (0-100 5-y-o and up) £2,976 2m .... (2:40)

2348 SINGING SAND [74] 7-10-11 R Supple, *led second, styd on*
   wl frm 3 out.......................(6 to 4 fav op 7 to 4)   1
2537⁸ HEE'S A DANCER [100] 5-12-0 A Thornton, *led to second, cl*
   up, ev ch whn mstk 4 out, sn drvn alng, kpt on same pace.
.... (11 to 8 op 5 to 4)   2
2345⁶ KNOW-NO-NO (Ire) [80] 8-11-3 B Storey, *in tch, cld hfwy,*
   chlgd 4 out, fdd aftr nxt..................(7 to 1 op 5 to 1)   3
   SPECTRE BROWN [72] 7-10-9⁵ T Reed, *in tch, outpcd bef*
   8th, sn beh, tld off...................(33 to 1 op 50 to 1)   4
1693 SHUT UP [63] 8-10-0 F Perratt, *in tch, effrt aftr 8th, 4th and no*
   imprsn whn f 3 out...............................(50 to 1)   f

---

2358² APPEARANCE MONEY (Ire) [87] 6-11-10 P Carberry, *hld up,*
   hdwy bef 4 out, fourth and no imprsn on ldrs whn f 2 out.
.... (5 to 2 op 2 to 1)   f
2576 MOST RICH (Ire) [73] 9-10-10 K Johnson, *in tch whn blun and*
   uns rdr 8th.........................(9 to 1 op 10 to 1)   ur
2118 MISS MONT [63] 8-10-0 D Bentley, *beh, blun 7th, sn lost tch,*
   tld off whn pld up bef 4 out......................(50 to 1)   pu
1912⁴ ISLANDREAGH (Ire) [72] 6-10-9 A Dobbin, *chsd ldrs, blun 8th,*
   sn lost tch, tld off whn pld up bef 4 out.
.... (16 to 1 op 10 to 1 tchd 20 to 1)   pu
Dist: 9l, 2l, 20l. 3m 57.30s. a 8.30s (9 Ran).
SR: 16/24/11/-/-/-/   (Hamilton House Limited), P Monteith

2632 Tom McConnell Memorial Juvenile Novices' Hurdle Class E (4-y-o) £2,399 2m................... (3:10)

2188⁶ DOUBLE AGENT 10-12 P Carberry, *made all, hrd pressed*
   frm 3 out, rdn appr last, ran on wl.
.... (15 to 8 op 7 to 4 tchd 2 to 1)   1
2185⁵ MELTEMISON 10-9 (3") Mr C Bonner, *hld up in tch, hdwy and*
   cl up 3 out, dsptd ld frm nxt till rdn and no extr aftr last.
.... (7 to 4 fav op 6 to 4 tchd 15 to 8)   2
2417⁶ FORMIDABLE PARTNER (v) 10-12 B Storey, *trkd ldrs, ev ch 2*
   out, sn rdn and btn....................(4 to 1 tchd 7 to 2)   3
2357³ FALCON'S FLAME (USA) 10-12 Mr M Thompson, *keen early,*
   sn cl up, wknd appr 2 out. (6 to 1 op 8 to 1 tchd 10 to 1)   4
2357⁸ KNAVE 10-12 A Dobbin, *beh, lost tch aftr 3 out.*
.... (25 to 1 op 20 to 1)   5
2344 SOUNDS DEVIOUS 10-7 D Parker, *prmnt till wknd quickly aftr*
   3 out, tld off whn pld up bef last......(100 to 1 op 50 to 1)   pu
Dist: 1¼l, 8l, 18l, 8l. 3m 55.90s. a 18.90s (6 Ran).
(Hertford Offset Limited), J Howard Johnson

2633 J. R. McNair Handicap Chase Class F (0-105 5-y-o and up) £2,950 3m .... (3:40)

2495² CUSH SUPREME (Ire) [84] 8-11-2 P Carberry, *jmpd lft, made*
   all, left clr 14th, eased finish........(11 to 10 on op Evens)   1
1863² BUYERS DREAM (Ire) [89] (v) 7-11-7 T Reed, *in tch, effrt aftr*
   12th, chsd wnr frm 3 out, no imprsn......(6 to 1 op 5 to 1)   2
2065⁴ RISKY DEE [74] 8-10-6 D Bentley, *chsd ldrs, chased wnr frm*
   14th, no imprsn, wknd 3 out.......................(16 to 1)   3
2362 TACTIX [68] 7-10-0 B Storey, *beh, blun 11th, lost tch bef 14th,*
   nvr dngrs..........................(25 to 1)   4
2239 FORWARD GLEN [76] (bl) 10-10-8 A S Smith, *beh, blun 12th,*
   lost tch bef 14th......................(7 to 1 op 5 to 1)   5
   OAKLEY [88] 8-11-6 A Thornton, *sn chasing wnr, 3 ls beh*
   whn f 14th...........................(10 to 1 op 7 to 1)   f
2258 HURRICANE ANDREW (Ire) [88] 9-11-6 N Smith, *chsd ldrs,*
   no imprsn whn hmpd 14th, sn wknd, wl beh whn pld up bef 2
   out............................(9 to 1 op 6 to 1 tchd 10 to 1)   pu
   RUSTY BLADE [92] 8-11-10 A Dobbin, *beh hfwy, tld off whn*
   pld up bef 3 out.....................(16 to 1 op 20 to 1)   pu
Dist: 7l, 5l, 8l, 15l. 6m 14.40s. a 25.40s (8 Ran).
(Robert Ogden), Martin Todhunter

2634 Fife Hunt Club Cup Class H Hunters' Chase (5-y-o and up) £1,576 3m .... (4:10)

   HOWAYMAN 7-11-7 (7") Mr A Parker, *trkd ldrs, led 4 out, styd*
   on und pres.................(7 to 2 op 3 to 1 tchd 4 to 1)   1
   MURDER MOSS (Ire) 7-11-7 (7") Mr M J Ruddy, *hld up, cld*
   hfwy, led aftr 14th to 4 out, chsd wnr after, no imprsn.
.... (7 to 1 op 8 to 1)   2
   FREE TRANSFER (Ire) 8-11-9 (5") Mr C Storey, *in tch, blun*
   12th, sn outpcd, rallied bef 4 out, mstk 2 out, no ch aftr.
.... (8 to 1 op 7 to 1 tchd 9 to 1)   3
   FISH QUAY 14-11-7 (7") Miss S Lamb, *led second to 4th, mstk*
   tenth, sn lost tch, tld off......................(100 to 1)   4
   MASTER KIT (Ire) 8-12-0 (7") Mr J Billinge, *keen, led 7th till*
   aftr 14th, chsd 1st 2 after, mstk 3 out, rdn after nxt, no imprsn
   whn f last.......(11 to 10 on op 5 to 4 on tchd Evens)   f
   KILMINFOYLE 10-11-7 (7") Mr T Scott, *beh whn mstk 4th,*
   mistake and uns rdr nxt...................(14 to 1)   ur
   POLITICAL ISSUE 13-11-9 (5") Mr P Johnson, *led to second,*
   led 4th to 7th, lost tch 11th, tld off whn pld up bef four out.
.... (12 to 1 op 10 to 1)   pu
   LITTLE WENLOCK 11-12-2 (5") Mrs V Jackson, *beh hfwy, tld*
   off whn pld up bef 2 out.........(16 to 1 tchd 20 to 1)   pu
Dist: 7l, 12l, dist. 6m 26.30s. a 37.30s (8 Ran).
(Dennis Waggott), K Anderson

2635 Goosegreen Novices' Handicap Hurdle Class E (0-100 4-y-o and up) £2,807 3m.....................(4:40)

2392⁵ MR CHRISTIE [83] 5-11-5 A Thornton, *hld up in tch, effrt appr*
   2 out, styd on wl to ld nr finish........(7 to 2 op 11 to 4)   1
1962⁹ ETERNAL CITY [84] 6-11-6 A Dobbin, *trkd ldrs, rdn to ld aftr*
   last, hdd and no extr nr finish........(12 to 1 op 5 to 1)   2
2359* HEAVENS ABOVE [70] 5-10-6 P Carberry, *led 4th till aftr last,*
   no extr und pres.......................(7 to 1 op 8 to 1)   3
2320⁵ CROFTON LAKE [64] 9-10-0 B Storey, *mid-div, rdn aftr 8th,*
   kpt on frm 2 out, nvr dngrs..................(20 to 1)   4

2494⁷ LITTLE REDWING [68] (v) 5-10-1 (3*) Mr C Bonner, chsd ldrs,
no imprsn whn hmpd 2 out, sn wknd.....(8 to 1 op 6 to 1) 5
2494⁸ BLOOMING SPRING (Ire) [77] 8-10-13 D Parker, led to 4th,
chsd ldrs till outpcd aftr tenth, no dngr after.
...................................(16 to 1 op 12 to 1) 6
1034⁹ DALUSMAN (Ire) [75] 9-10-11 R Supple, nvr better than mid-
div...........................(12 to 1 op 10 to 1 tchd 14 to 1) 7
1550 FRISKY THYNE (Ire) [88] 8-11-10 D Bentley, beh most of way.
..............................(1 to 2 op 5 to 4) 8
2192⁹ PERSUASIVE TALENT (Ire) [67] 6-10-3 J Burke, beh most of
way, tld off.........................(10 to 1 op 12 to 1) 9
1662² CASH BOX (Ire) [78] 9-11-0 N Smith, keen early, in tch, mstk
4th, hdwy and ev ch whn f 2 out...........(4 to 1 op 7 to 2) f
1826⁹ CANONBIEBOTHERED [64] 6-10-0 F Perratt, beh, hdwy to
dispute ld 5th, pld up aftr 7th, sddl slpd.(33 to 1 op 20 to 1) pu
Dist: 1l, 1¼l, 14l, 3½l, 15l, 12l, 1¾l, dist. 6m 2.70s. a 25.70s (11 Ran).
(David Mann Partnership), Miss L C Siddall

LINGFIELD (heavy)
Wednesday February 12th
**Going Correction: PLUS 1.50 sec. per fur. (races
1,2,4,5,7), PLUS 2.15 (3,6)**

# 2636 Orpington Novices' Hurdle Class D (4-y-o and up) £3,224 2m 110yds
...................................(2:00)

2423 HARBET HOUSE (Fr) 4-10-7 N Williamson, al prmnt, led appr
2 out, ran on wl.........(6 to 1 tchd 8 to 1 and 5 to 1) 1
2350³ EAU DE COLOGNE 5-11-3 M Richards, hdwy 3 out, ev ch
appr 2 out, no imprsn...............(12 to 1 op 6 to 1) 2
2350⁴ IVORY COASTER (NZ) 6-11-3 J Osborne, gd hdwy 3 out, ev
ch appr 2 out, not quicken...........(33 to 1 op 20 to 1) 3
798⁶ RISING DOUGH (Ire) 5-11-3 D Gallagher, hdwy 3rd, led 3 out
till appr 2 out, wknd last...(3 to 1 op 4 to 1 tchd 5 to 2) 4
FRYS NO FOOL 7-11-3 G Upton, gd hdwy and ev ch appr 2
out, wknd approaching last.
..............................(8 to 1 op 6 to 1 tchd 10 to 1) 5
2372² TROUVAILLE (Ire) 6-11-9 L Harvey, in tch till wknd 3 out, tld
off.............................(14 to 1 op 8 to 1) 6
1729³ BALLESWHIDDEN 5-11-3 C Llewellyn, hdwy 3rd, wknd appr
3 out, tld off...........(8 to 1 op 12 to 1 tchd 14 to 1) 7
2426² MUTANASSIB (Ire) 4-10-7 R Dunwoody, wth ldr, led 4th till
wknd quickly 3 out, tld off........(7 to 4 fav op Evens) 8
CHEEKY CHARLIE 5-11-3 B Fenton, al beh, tld off.
..............................(66 to 1 op 33 to 1 tchd 100 to 1) 9
OTTO E MEZZO 5-11-3 V Smith, prmnt to 3rd, tld off.
..............................(25 to 1 op 20 to 1 tchd 33 to 1) 10
ANIF (USA) 6-11-3 D Skyrme, tld off whn pld up bef 3 out.
..............................(66 to 1 op 50 to 1 tchd 100 to 1) pu
DIA GEORGY 6-11-3 I Lawrence, tld off frm 3rd, pld up bef 2
out....................................(50 to 1 op 33 to 1) pu
BARBARA'S JEWEL 5-11-3 T Kent, led till wknd quickly 4th,
tld off whn pld up bef 3 out..........(50 to 1 op 20 to 1) pu
2350⁵ CLOCK WATCHERS 9-11-3 D Morris, prmnt till wknd quickly
3rd, tld off whn pld up bef 2 out.
..............................(66 to 1 op 50 to 1 tchd 100 to 1) pu
1805 BALLYQUINTET (Ire) 6-10-12 K Gaule, prmnt till wknd quickly
3rd, pld up bef nxt....(66 to 1 op 50 to 1 tchd 100 to 1) pu
Dist: 7l, 1½l, 7l, 9l, 28l, 3l, 6l, 17l, 10l. 4m 22.40s. a 31.40s (15 Ran).
SR: 12/15/13/6/-/-/-/   (C A Washbourn), R J O'Sullivan

2637 Sanderstead Maiden Hurdle Class E (4-y-o and up) £2,729 2m 7f... (2:30)

2438⁵ WARNER FOR PLAYERS 6-11-8 N Williamson, al prmnt,
led 6th, clr appr last, eased flt.
.(11 to 10 on op 11 to 8 on tchd Evens and 11 to 10) 1
1673⁵ DANCETILLYOUDROP (Ire) 6-11-8 D Bridgwater, hdwy 6th,
ev ch appr 2 out, ran on one pace.
..............................(9 to 4 op 7 to 2 tchd 3 to 1) 2
1344 CREDO BOY 8-11-8 B Powell, mstk 1st, wl beh till hdwy 3 out,
nvr nr first 2...................(25 to 1 op 50 to 1) 3
1975⁸ WILLOWS ROULETTE 5-11-8 R Greene, hdwy 6th, ev ch 3
out, wknd appr 2 out...............(50 to 1 op 33 to 1) 4
GREG'S PROFILES 6-11-8 T J Murphy, al beh, tld off.
..............................(12 to 1 tchd 14 to 1) 5
2248⁹ BRAVE EDWIN (Ire) 7-11-8 J Osborne, al hdwy 6th, ev ch 3
out, wknd quickly, tld off.
..............................(15 to 2 op 10 to 1 tchd 14 to 1 and 7 to 1) 6
FOREST MILL 5-11-3 R Johnson, wl beh frm 6th, tld off.
..............................(50 to 1 op 33 to 1 tchd 33 to 1) 7
1540⁷ HIGH MOOD 7-11-8 R Farrant, wl beh frm 6th, tld off.
..............................(50 to 1 tchd 66 to 1) 8
PAPRIKA (Ire) 8-11-3 D Gallagher, hdwy 6th, wknd 3 out, pld
up bef nxt...........(14 to 1 op 10 to 1 tchd 16 to 1) pu
2398 GENTLE TUNE (Ire) 7-11-1 (7*) Mr P O'Keeffe, led till wknd
quickly 6th, tld off whn pld up bef 3 out.
..............................(50 to 1 op 33 to 1 tchd 66 to 1) pu
KING'S AFFAIR 7-11-1 (7*) M Clinton, wth ldr, hrd rdn and
wknd aftr 6th, pld up bef 2 out........(50 to 1 tchd 33 to 1) pu
1981 MR LOVELY (Ire) 6-11-8 W Marston, prmnt till wknd frm 5th, tld off
whn pld up bef 3 out........(9 to 1 op 12 to 1 tchd 8 to 1) pu
1669⁸ DERRYBELLE 6-11-3 M Clarke, tld off frm 5th.
..............................(50 to 1 op 33 to 1 tchd 66 to 1) pu

2264⁶ CHARLIE'S FOLLY 6-11-8 C Llewellyn, hdwy 6th, rdn and
wknd nxt, tld off whn pld up bef 2 out.
..............................(20 to 1 op 16 to 1 tchd 25 to 1) pu
1115 FASHION LEADER (Ire) 6-11-8 B Powell, prmnt till mstk and
wknd 4th, tld off whn pld up bef 6th.
..............................(50 to 1 op 33 to 1 tchd 66 to 1) pu
2199⁹ ROLL AGAIN 6-11-8 C Maude, prmnt till wknd 5th, tld off whn
pld up bef 2 out...............(20 to 1 op 16 to 1) pu
Dist: 5l, dist, 2l, dist, 12l, dist, 1¾l. 6m 31.40s. a 65.40s (16 Ran).
(Terry Warner Sports), P J Hobbs

2638 Oxted Novices' Chase Class D (5-y-o and up) £3,996 2½m 110yds.. (3:00)

2425* GLITTER ISLE (Ire) 7-11-10 P Hide, al prmnt, led 2 out, ran on
wl..................(13 to 8 fav op 5 to 4 tchd 7 to 4) 1
ANGELO'S DOUBLE (Ire) 9-11-4 B Powell, led, mstk 9th, hdd
2 out, wknd last...........(5 to 2 op 9 to 4 tchd 7 to 2) 2
INDIAN DELIGHT 7-11-4 C Maude, chsd ldrs till wknd appr 3
out...................(25 to 1 op 14 to 1 tchd 33 to 1) 3
PLUMBRIDGE 9-11-4 B Fenton, al beh, mstk 9th, tld off.
..............................(25 to 1 op 16 to 1) 4
2266⁷ REESHLOCH (bl) 8-11-4 N Williamson, mstks, prmnt till blun
and wknd 4 out, tld off...(12 to 1 op 8 to 1 tchd 14 to 1) 5
WITH IMPUNITY 8-11-4 D Bridgwater, chsd ldrs, mstk 5th,
fifth whn f 8th
..............................(9 to 2 op 5 to 1 tchd 11 to 2 and 6 to 1) f
1991 SLIPMATIC 8-10-13 L Harvey, last whn jmpd slwly 7th, tld off
when f 8th..................(16 to 1 op 12 to 1) f
2244⁴ COUNTRY KEEPER 9-11-4 G Upton, beh whn blun 7th, tld off
when f 2 out...............(20 to 1 tchd 25 to 1) f
2278⁶ ALTHREY BLUE (Ire) 8-11-4 S McNeill, tld off whn f 2 out.
..............................(50 to 1 op 33 to 1) f
1573 LUCKY CALL (NZ) 6-11-4 R Greene, in rear whn blun and uns
rdr 6th.........................(50 to 1) ur
2308 SPY DESSA 9-11-4 D Gallagher, beh fron 6th, tld off whn pld
up bef 3 out...............(50 to 1 tchd 66 to 1) pu
SOUND STATEMENT (Ire) 8-11-4 Mr T Hills, prmnt to 6th, tld
off whn pld up bef 3 out.(20 to 1 op 14 to 1 tchd 25 to 1) pu
2354 MINOR KEY (Ire) 7-11-4 J Osborne, beh whn blun 7th and 8th,
tld off whn pld up bef 9th...........(33 to 1 op 20 to 1) pu
Dist: 12l, dist, 22l, 29l. 5m 50.90s. a 49.90s (13 Ran).
SR: 37/19/-/-/-/-/   (Mrs Timothy Pilkington), J T Gifford

2639 Three Counties Handicap Hurdle Class E (0-110 4-y-o and up) £2,201 2m 110yds.................. (3:30)

2548⁶ NIPPER REED [98] 7-11-2 R Dunwoody, strted slwly, sn led,
ran on wl..................(7 to 1 op 5 to 1) 1
2400² AUGUST TWELFTH [85] 9-10-3² P Hide, hld up, hdwy and ev
ch last, not quicken........(11 to 4 op 3 to 1 tchd 7 to 2) 2
2429⁷ TICKERTY'S GIFT [110] 7-11-7 (7*) M Attwater, al prmnt, ev
ch 2 out, wknd last.....(6 to 4 fav op Evens tchd 13 to 8) 3
587 EL GRANDO [83] 7-10-1 D Gallagher, chsd wnr to 5th, wknd 2
out, tld off.....................(5 to 1 op 15 to 1) 4
2407⁵ WINSFORD HILL [89] 6-10-7 G Tormey, strted slwly, al last,
tld off frm 3 out...........(9 to 2 op 3 to 1 tchd 5 to 1) 5
Dist: 3½l, 9l, 22l, 19l. 4m 27.60s. a 36.60s (5 Ran).
(G Piper), T Hind

2640 Warlingham Handicap Hurdle Class F (0-100 4-y-o and up) £2,250 2m 3f 110yds..................... (4:00)

2356³ TOTAL JOY (Ire) [92] 6-11-13 R Dunwoody, hdwy 5th, led 3
out, ran on wl..............(5 to 1 co-fav op 7 to 2) 1
2281⁵ LORD ROOBLE [93] 6-11-7 (7*) S Laird, hdwy 3 out, rdn
appr last, no imprsn..................(6 to 1) 2
1938³ ROSKEEN BRIDGE (Ire) [69] 6-10-4 N Williamson, jnd ldr 5th,
rdn 6th, wknd appr last...........(5 to 1 co-fav op 4 to 1) 3
2243⁶ SHANAGORE WARRIOR (Ire) [86] 5-11-0 (7*) S Hearn, prmnt
to 3 out, one pace.(5 to 1 co-fav op 4 to 1 tchd 11 to 2) 4
RED LIGHTER [70] 8-10-5 G Upton, wth ldrs till wknd appr 3
out.............................(20 to 1 op 16 to 1) 5
2390⁶ EWAR BOLD [75] 4-10-0 D Gallagher, al wl beh....(20 to 1) 6
1673 MISS MYLETTE (Ire) [65] 6-10-0 W Marston, led till wknd 3
out, tld off.........................(33 to 1) 7
2265⁷ CELTIC LILLEY [65] 6b) 7-9-11 (3*) P Henley, beh frm 6th, tld
off.............................(16 to 1) 8
2392⁸ KAREN'S TYPHOON (Ire) [72] 6-10-7 R Johnson, wth ldr whn
slpd up bend aftr 4th.........(16 to 1 tchd 20 to 1) su
1068⁶ DANCING DANCER [73] 8-10-8 J Supple, beh frm 6th, tld off
whn pld up bef 2 out...(14 to 1 op 16 to 1 tchd 20 to 1) pu
2462 FONTAINEROUGE (Ire) [80] 7-11-1 B Fenton, mstk 4th, wknd
6th, beh whn pld up bef 2 out.
..............................(15 to 2 op 6 to 1 tchd 8 to 1) pu
2428⁷ EQUITY'S DARLING [82] (bl) 5-11-3 P Hide, strted slwly,
tld off whn pld up bef 2 out.(16 to 1 op 12 to 1 tchd 14 to 1) pu
1154² AMBER RING [75] 4-10-0 J R Kavanagh, beh frm 6th, tld off
whn pld up bef 2 out...............(14 to 1) pu
Dist: 11l, 3½l, 8l, 10l, 11l, dist. 5m 36.00s. a 63.00s (13 Ran).
(P M Warren), C J Mann

2641 R. E. Sassoon Memorial Hunters' Chase Class H (5-y-o and up) £1,110

3m......................... (4:30)

VICOMPT DE VALMONT 12-12-2 (5*) Mr T Mitchell, *hdwy 8th,
led last, ran on wl*........(3 to 1 op 9 to 4 tchd 4 to 1)   1
AVOSTAR 10-12-2 (5*) Mr B Pollock, *led, jmpd rght frm 12th,
hdd last*... (8 to 1 op 4 to 1 tchd 10 to 1 and 12 to 1)   2
FIFTH AMENDMENT (bd) 12-12-0 (7*) Mr A Hales, *chsd ldrs,
5th whn blun 12th, no ch aftr.*
..................................(12 to 1 op 10 to 1 tchd 20 to 1)   3
CENTRE STAGE 11-11-7 (7*) Mr A Warr, *tld off frm 5th.*
...................................(33 to 1 op 25 to 1)   4
ELL GEE 7-11-2 (7*) Miss C Townsley, *3rd whn f 7th.*
...................................(50 to 1 op 33 to 1)   f
HOLLAND HOUSE 11-12-2 (5*) Mr C Vigors, *chsd ldrs, 3rd
whn stumbled and uns rdr appr 3 out.*
..................................(11 to 8 fav op Evens)   ur
CASTLEBAY LAD 14-11-7 (7*) Mr M Appleby, *8th whn refused
11th*..................................(50 to 1 op 33 to 1)   ref
GAMBLING ROYAL 14-12-0 (7*) Dr P Pritchard, *second whn
blun 9th, 4th whn blunded 12th, tld off whn pld up bef 3 out.*
...................................(33 to 1 op 25 to 1)   pu
FARINGO 12-12-0 (7*) Mr W Gowlett, *tld off frm 5th, pld up bef
4 out*.................................(20 to 1 tchd 25 to 1)   pu
OVER THE EDGE 11-12-0 (7*) Mr S Sporborg, *beh frm 9th, tld
off whn pld up bef 3 out.*...............(8 to 1 op 5 to 1)   pu
AMADEUS (Fr) 9-11-7 (7*) Mr C Ward, *tld off whn pld up bef
12th*.....................(12 to 1 op 14 to 1 tchd 25 to 1)   pu
COLONIAL KELLY 9-11-11 (3*) Mr P Hacking, *blun tenth, beh
whn pld up bef 11th*.......(9 to 2 op 7 to 2 tchd 11 to 2)   pu
MAJOR MAC 10-11-7 (7*) Mr S Durack, *tld off whn pld up bef
4 out*.................................(50 to 1 op 33 to 1)   pu
Dist: 12l, dist, dist. 7m 12.00s. a 78.00s (13 Ran).

(Mrs Bridget Nicholls), P F Nicholls

2642 Levy Board Intermediate Open
National Hunt Flat Class H (4,5,6-
y-o) £1,318 2m 110yds.......(5:00)

2269⁴ RASAK 5-11-4 R Dunwoody, *hdwy one m out, led o'r one
furlong out, all out nr finish*..................(2 to 1 op Evens)   1
1214* CURRADUFF MOLL (Ire) 6-11-6 C Llewellyn, *led till o'r one
furlong out, rallied ins fnl furlong.*
..................(6 to 4 fav op 5 to 2 tchd 3 to 1)   2
FIN BEC (Fr) 4-10-8 S Curran, *hdwy aftr 4 fs, ev ch 2 furlongs
out, one pace.*................................(20 to 1)   3
2409² ROYAL POT BLACK (Ire) 6-11-4 G Tormey, *hdwy 7 fs out, one
pace fnl 3 furlongs.*....................(6 to 1 op 5 to 2)   4
2269 FRED MOTH 4-10-8 D Skyrme, *al prmnt, one pace fnl 3 fs.*
...................................(33 to 1 op 25 to 1)   5
BROOK BEE 5-11-4 W Marston, *same pl fnl 4 fs.*
..................(12 to 1 op 10 to 1 tchd 14 to 1)   6
2409³ CRACKON JAKE (Ire) 4-10-8 W McFarland, *nvr nr to chal.*
..................................(6 to 1 op 7 to 2)   7
2309⁶ BEBE GREY 6-10-6 (7*) M Clinton, *prmnt till wknd 7 fs out.*
...................................(25 to 1)   8
MONMOUTH WAY (Ire) 5-11-4 B Fenton, *prmnt till wknd one
m out.*.................................(33 to 1 op 25 to 1)   9
OVERRUNNING 5-10-13 M Richards, *al beh, tld off.* (25 to 1)   10
PAPERPRINCE (NZ) 5-10-11 (7*) Mr G Shenkin, *al beh, tld off.*
..................(14 to 1 op 12 to 1 tchd 20 to 1)   11
2402⁸ DON'TCALLMEGEORGE 6-10-11 (7*) Mr P O'Keeffe, *al beh,
tld off*.................................(33 to 1 op 25 to 1)   12
HOLD MY HAND 6-11-4 N Williamson, *al beh, tld off.*
..................(12 to 1 tchd 14 to 1)   13
MUALLAF (Ire) 5-11-4 J A McCarthy, *hdwy aftr 4 fs, wknd 6
furlongs out, tld off.*...................(33 to 1 op 25 to 1)   14
Dist: Nk, 12l, 17l, nk, 1¼l, 16l, 9l, 2½l, dist, 20l. 4m 20.40s. (14 Ran).

(Lady Herries), Lady Herries

NAAS (IRE) (soft)
Wednesday February 12th

2643 Bishopscourt Maiden Hurdle (4-y-o)
£3,082 2m...................(2:00)

2337⁸ WELCOME PARADE 11-2 C O'Dwyer, ...(8 to 1)   1
2337⁴ PEGUS JUNIOR (Ire) 10-4 (7*) S M McGovern, ...(7 to 1)   2
2337² CORN ABBEY (Ire) 10-11 P Woods, ...(11 to 8 fav)   3
ATHLEAGUE GUEST (Ire) (bl) 10-11 T P Rudd, ...(14 to 1)   4
2050 APACHE TWIST (Ire) 11-2 C F Swan, ...(7 to 1)   5
2161⁴ DUNEMER (Ire) 10-8 (3*) Mr R Walsh, ...(10 to 1)   6
2112 WOODEN DANCE (Ire) 10-11 J Mitchell, ...(20 to 1)   7
2337 GOLD GLIDER (Ire) 10-11 H Rogers, ...(20 to 1)   8
1709 SPIONAN (Ire) 10-4 (7*) P J Dobbs, ...(14 to 1)   9
2337⁷ RIVER VALLEY LADY (Ire) 10-6 T P Treacy, ...(6 to 1)   10
1547 MIND ME BRODIE (Ire) 10-11 A Powell, ...(10 to 1)   11
620 GALICI (Ire) 10-4 (7*) J M Maguire, ...(14 to 1)   12
BAILENAGUN (Ire) 10-4 (7*) B J Geraghty, ...(14 to 1)   13
MOUNTAIN ROCKET 10-4 (7*) D M Bean, ...(16 to 1)   14
2337 LOVELY PROSPECT 10-11 S H O'Donovan, ...(25 to 1)   15
2112⁸ SIGMA COMMS (Ire) (bl) 10-11 K F O'Brien, ...(10 to 1)   16
882 PLAYPRINT 10-4 (7*) D K Budds, ...(20 to 1)   17
MONKS ERROR (Ire) 10-11 (7*) P Hogan, ...(25 to 1)   18
2234⁹ CAJUN ROSE (Ire) 10-6 J P Broderick, ...(33 to 1)   19
OH SO RECKLESS (Ire) 10-6 C N Bowens, ...(20 to 1)   20
2112⁶ SLIGHTLY SPEEDY (Ire) 11-2 J Shortt, ...(10 to 1)   f

Dist: 1½l, 2½l, 1½l, 3½l. 4m 10.20s. (21 Ran).

(Mrs M O'Callaghan), T J Taaffe

2644 Leinster Beginners Chase (5-y-o and
up) £3,082 2m...............(2:30)

YANKIE LORD (Ire) 5-10-12 F Woods, ...(12 to 1)   1
2367⁴ ARDSHUIL 8-12-0 J P Broderick, ...(8 to 1)   2
2587³ MIROSWAKI (USA) 7-12-0 C O'Dwyer, ...(8 to 1)   3
2446 LUCKY BUST (Ire) 7-11-9 T Horgan, ...(12 to 1)   4
2224³ BANGABUNNY 7-11-11 (3*) K Whelan, ...(4 to 1)   5
2052 CROSSFARNOGUE (Ire) 8-12-0 Mr B M Cash, (6 to 4 fav)   6
2143 EASTERN FOX (Ire) 8-11-9 D T Evans, ...(33 to 1)   7
2367⁵ FONTAINE FABLES (Ire) 7-12-0 D H O'Connor, ...(8 to 1)   8
1146 NO TAG (Ire) 9-12-0 T J Mitchell, ...(8 to 1)   9
2089 NATIVE CHAMPION (Ire) 8-11-2 (7*) Mr P P O'Brien,
...................................(33 to 1)   10
2041⁵ ROCHE MENTOR (Ire) 7-11-9 T P Rudd, ...(20 to 1)   11
2367⁶ LINDA'S BOY (Ire) 7-12-0 K F O'Brien, ...(12 to 1)   f
2382 BUCKAMERE (Ire) 6-11-4 P L Malone, ...(33 to 1)   f
Dist: 3l, 2l, 2½l, 1l. 4m 34.40s. (13 Ran).

(John Halliday), A L T Moore

2645 Kildare Maiden Hurdle (5-y-o)
£3,082 2m 3f.................(3:00)

1907⁴ SUPER DEALER (Ire) 11-3 C F Swan, ...(9 to 4 fav)   1
GAZALANI (Ire) 11-11 F Woods, ...(4 to 1)   2
2414⁵ GENTLE MOSSY (Ire) 11-3 D H O'Connor, ...(6 to 1)   3
2416 THE HOLY PARSON (Ire) 10-10 (7*) M P Cooney, ..(16 to 1)   4
2343 ANDREA COVA (Ire) 10-9 (3*) B Bowens, ...(16 to 1)   5
1777 BOULABALLY (Ire) 11-3 K F O'Brien, ...(16 to 1)   6
2419⁹ ROYAL SANTAL (Ire) 10-12 M P Hourigan, ...(33 to 1)   7
2414² MR MAGGET (Ire) 11-3 T P Rudd, ...(5 to 1)   8
2168 ARE YOU SAILING (Ire) 11-3 C O'Brien, ...(12 to 1)   9
2445⁷ CORYROSE (Ire) 11-1 (5*) T Martin, ...(10 to 1)   f
2414⁴ ROSEY ELLEN (Ire) 10-5 (7*) M D Murphy, ...(8 to 1)   f
2054 SWIFT PICK (Ire) 10-12 (7*) B J Geraghty, ...(10 to 1)   bd
2270⁵ ORMOND JENNY (Ire) 11-6 J P Broderick, ...(16 to 1)   pu
2055 TAZ (Ire) 10-12 J Flood, ...(50 to 1)   pu
2443 CAHERMURPHY (Ire) 11-3 T P Treacy, ...(33 to 1)   pu
2172 TEACH NA FINIUNA (Ire) 10-12 H Rogers, ...(50 to 1)   pu
2443 KEITHS CHOICE (Ire) 10-7 (5*) J M Donnelly, ...(20 to 1)   pu
2054 ETAT MAJOR (Fr) 11-0 (3*) K Whelan, ...(33 to 1)   pu
2270⁸ IT'S HIMSELF 11-3 C O'Dwyer, ...(14 to 1)   pu
2378 SAMBAGUIRE (Ire) 11-0 (3*) U Smyth, ...(25 to 1)   pu
Dist: 7l, 2l, 2l, 2½l. 5m 3.70s. (20 Ran).

(S Mulryan), D T Hughes

2646 Kill Handicap Chase (0-109 4-y-o
and up) £3,082 2½m.........(3:30)

2274⁴ MASTER MCCARTAN (Ire) [-] 8-11-5 (7*) Mr Brian Moran,
...................................(5 to 2 fav)   1
2411 BEAUCHAMP GRACE [-] 8-10-8 (3*) K Whelan, ..(10 to 1)   2
2412⁴ ANOTHER COURSE (Ire) [-] 9-10-9 D H O'Connor, (14 to 1)   3
2365⁶ PERSPEX GALE (Ire) [-] 9-11-0 F Woods, ...(10 to 1)   4
2657 DAMODAR [-] 8-10-13 F J Flood, ...(10 to 1)   5
2415⁷ ZVORNIK [-] 10-11-8 P A Roche, ...(14 to 1)   6
2099 TOP RUN (Ire) [-] 9-10-1 T P Rudd, ...(20 to 1)   7
2365⁵ BOB DEVANI [-] 11-11-11 C O'Dwyer, ...(12 to 1)   8
GRAPHIC IMAGE (Ire) [-] 7-11-1 A Powell, ...(16 to 1)   9
2448 AMME ENAEK (Ire) [-] (bl) 8-11-8 H Rogers, ...(10 to 1)   10
NORTHERN ACE [-] 11-9-7 T Horgan, ...(25 to 1)   11
2411⁹ RICH TRADITION (Ire) [-] 9-10-13 (3*) U Smyth, ..(14 to 1)   12
2382 PILS INVADER (Ire) [-] 9-9-13 P L Malone, ...(25 to 1)   f
2448 MARGUERITA SONG [-] 7-10-6 J P Broderick, ...(12 to 1)   f
1711⁹ PROGRAMMED TO WIN [-] 10-10-8 D T Evans, ..(16 to 1)   bd
2379⁵ NOELS DANCER (Ire) [-] 7-10-5 T P Treacy, ...(10 to 1)   bd
1434 TWIN RAINBOW [-] 10-12-0 L P Cusack, ...(10 to 1)   pu
2411⁶ STRADDALLEY (Ire) [-] 7-10-5 T J Mitchell, ...(14 to 1)   pu
Dist: 15l, 2l, 1½l, 3l. 5m 52.00s. (18 Ran).

(A Lillingston), A Lillingston

2647 Kilwarden Handicap Hurdle (0-102
4-y-o and up) £3,082 2m 3f... (4:00)

2524² LAURENS FANCY (Ire) [-] 7-11-0 J R Barry, ...(6 to 1 fav)   1
1492² VALMAR (Ire) [-] 9-10-6 F Woods, ...(8 to 1)   2
2413⁵ WOODBORO LASS (Ire) [-] 7-9-7 (7*) Miss A Sloane,
...................................(14 to 1)   3
2103⁴ ECLIPTIC MOON (Ire) [-] 7-10-0 M Duffy, ...(13 to 2)   4
2380³ PINTPLEASE PAT (Ire) [-] 6-10-4² L P Cusack, ...(20 to 1)   5
2103⁹ CLONMEL COMMERCIAL (Ire) [-] 6-9-6 (7*) D McCullagh,
...................................(20 to 1)   6
1836 BYPHARBEANNT (Ire) [-] 6-10-8 T P Rudd, ...(16 to 1)   7
2089 RUN ROSE RUN (Ire) [-] (bl) 7-9-3 (7*) J M Maguire, (16 to 1)   8
2520⁹ LIOS NA MAOL (Ire) [-] 6-9-9 (7*) M D Murphy, ..(25 to 1)   9
2379 WADABLAST (Ire) [-] 7-10-8 D J Casey, ...(16 to 1)   10
2170⁶ MERCHANTS QUAY (Ire) [-] 6-11-6 (7*) Mr A J Dempsey,
...................................(8 to 1)   11
2272⁵ IADA (Ire) [-] 6-11-0 D T Evans, ...(14 to 1)   12
2447* COLLIERS HILL (Ire) [-] 6-10-9 (7*) P Hogan, ...(13 to 2)   13
1078⁸ ALLARACKET (Ire) [-] 8-10-7⁴ (7*) Mr D M Fogarty, (20 to 1)   14
2413⁸ SHIR ROSE (Ire) [-] 7-10-8 T Horgan, ...(14 to 1)   15
2524 SIOBHAILIN DUBH (Ire) [-] 8-11-2 P A Roche, ...(14 to 1)   16
2162³ ARTIC PEARL (Ire) [-] 7-10-1 (3*) K Whelan, ...(14 to 1)   17
2339⁹ VERYWELL (Ire) [-] 6-10-5 (7*) Mr R Geraghty, ..(14 to 1)   18

578⁶ RONETTE (Ire) [-] 6-9-4 (5*) T Martin, ... (33 to 1) 19
2379³ VINTNERS VENTURE (Ire) [-] 5-11-5 C F Swan, ... (7 to 1) 20
       HOLLYBROOK LADY (Ire) [-] 6-11-0 (7*) D Fisher, ..(12 to 1) 21
1273 ASTRID (Ire) [-] 6-9-7 C O'Brien, ... (33 to 1) 22
2339⁷ BRASS BAND (Ire) [-] 6-10-11 (7*) Mr R H Fowler, (10 to 1) f
2366 ADARAMANN (Ire) [-] 5-10-8 (3*) Mr R Walsh, ...(14 to 1) bd
Dist: 1½l, 2l, 4½l, 1l. 5m 4.90s. (24 Ran).

(Noel Delahunty), Patrick Joseph Flynn

2648 Saggart Novice Chase (5-y-o and up) £3,082 3m................(4:30)

2523⁵ ITSAJUNGLEOUTTHERE (Ire) 7-11-5 D J Casey, ... (14 to 1) 1
2274* ROYAL ROSY (Ire) 6-11-6 C F Swan, ... (2 to 1 fav) 2
2341 CESAR DU MANOIR (Fr) 7-11-2 (3*) K Whelan, ...(25 to 1) 3
2143 J J JACKSON 8-11-8 A Powell, ... (33 to 1) 4
1092 CORRIBLOUGH (Ire) 9-11-5 T Horgan, ... (33 to 1) 5
2341⁸ BAILEYS BRIDGE (Ire) 6-10-12 (7*) M D Murphy, ..(33 to 1) 6
2224* BUCKMINSTER 10-11-1 (7*) Mr Brian Moran, ...(4 to 1) f
2163* MATTS DILEMMA (Ire) 9-11-11 D H O'Connor, ... (7 to 1) f
       MAID FOR DANCING (Ire) 8-10-7 (7*) Mr R H Fowler, (8 to 1) f
2143 CAVALLO (Fr) 7-11-5 T P Rudd, ... (50 to 1) f
2410 PENNY POT 5-9-12 (7*) Mr J L Cullen, ...(66 to 1) f
2341³ LE GINNO (Fr) 10-11-8 C O'Dwyer, ... (6 to 1) bd
2141* BOBBYJO (Ire) 7-11-11 P L Malone, ...(11 to 2) bd
       PHARALLEY (Ire) 7-11-0 D T Evans, ... (33 to 1) bd
Dist: 12l, sht-hd, 25l, 4½l. 7m 14.30s. (14 Ran).

(M F Morris), M F Morris

2649 Go Racing In Kildare I.N.H. Flat Race (5-y-o and up) £3,082 2m 3f...(5:00)

2519² MOUNT DRUID (Ire) 7-12-0 Mr D Marnane, .. (5 to 1 jt-fav) 1
       LADY MOSKVA (Ire) 5-10-13 (7*) Mr P J Scanlon, .(16 to 1) 2
2343⁴ BACK TO THE NEST (Ire) 6-11-6 (3*) Mr R Walsh, .(10 to 1) 3
2087⁴ BELLS BRIDGE (Ire) 7-12-0 Mr B M Cash, ... (5 to 1 jt-fav) 4
2137⁴ BRIAN'S DELIGHT (Ire) 6-11-9 Mr A J Martin, ...(11 to 2) 5
       GOLDEN PERK (Ire) 6-11-11 (3*) Mrs M Mullins, ...(8 to 1) 6
       FINE GRAIN (Ire) 7-11-11 (3*) Mr P English, ...(12 to 1) 7
2140⁵ PHAREIGN (Ire) 6-12-0 Mr P Fenton, ... (14 to 1) 8
       LIMESTONE LAD (Ire) 5-11-4 (7*) Mr M J Bowe, ...(20 to 1) 9
       ROYAL OASIS (Ire) 6-11-9 (5*) Mr J T McNamara, .(16 to 1) 10
2228 ROSE ANA (Ire) 7-11-2 (7*) Mr J P McNamara, ...(25 to 1) 11
2443⁵ EQUIVOCATOR (Ire) 6-11-11 (3*) Mr D Valentine, ...(6 to 1) 12
2115⁷ MINSTRELS PRIDE (Ire) 6-12-0 Mr A R Coonan, ...(25 to 1) 13
2144² KNOCKAULIN (Ire) 6-12-0 Mr H F Cleary, ...(11 to 2) 14
2093 CHANCERY RIVER (Ire) 8-11-2 (7*) Mr R P O'Gorman,
       ....(14 to 1) 15
       CJAY BLEU (Ire) 6-11-7 (7*) Mr D Breen, ...(25 to 1) 16
2276 DRUMCLIFFE (Ire) 6-11-7 (7*) Mr J Cullen, ...(20 to 1) 17
       CHOC MAINE 10-11-2 (7*) Mr R F Coonan, ...(33 to 1) 18
1782⁶ FORTY SECRETS (Ire) 6-11-4 (5*) Mr J P Berry, ...(25 to 1) 19
2017 CROSSEROADS (Ire) 7-11-7 (7*) Mr J Cash, ...(25 to 1) 20
1147 MAJESTIC LORD (Ire) 7-11-7 (7*) Mr P J Gilligan, ..(20 to 1) 21
2048⁷ DIAMANTINO (Fr) 6-11-7 (7*) Mr G Donnelly, ...(8 to 1) su
2228⁵ CHOICE JENNY (Ire) 5-10-13 (7*) Mr A C Coyle, ...(10 to 1) su
       SADIE LADY (Ire) 6-11-2 (7*) Mr A G Cash, ...(20 to 1) su
Dist: 4l, 5l, 2l, 7l. 4m 57.70s. (24 Ran).

(Jerome Foley), Mrs John Harrington

CATTERICK (good)
Thursday February 13th
Going Correction: PLUS 1.10 sec. per fur.

2650 West Of Yore Novices' Chase Class E (5-y-o and up) £2,823 2m (1:50)

2376⁴ COVER POINT (Ire) 6-11-2 P Carberry, sn chasing ldr, took clr
       order fnl circuit, led and lft clr 2 out, eased finish.
       ....(7 to 4 on tchd 6 to 4 on and 2 to 1 on) 1
114⁶ STEALING HOME (Ire) 7-10-11 P Niven, wtd wh, improved to
       chase ldg pair fnl circuit, rdn alng frm 4 out, styd on, not rch
       wnr..(9 to 2 op 3 to 1) 2
2155³ ALICAT (Ire) 6-11-2 Derek Byrne, chsd ldrs, mstk 6th, feeling
       pace and lost grnd quickly fnl circuit, tld off 4 out.
       ....(50 to 1 op 33 to 1) 3
       DON'T TELL JUDY (Ire) 9-11-2 A S Smith, beh whn blun and
       uns rdr second.....................(12 to 1 op 10 to 1) ur
2205⁴ KARENASTINO 6-11-2 T Reed, led and sn clr, jnd 3 out, hdd
       and wkng whn blun and uns rdr nxt.
       ....(11 to 2 op 5 to 1 tchd 6 to 1) ur
2464 WILD GAME (Ire) 6-11-2 B Storey, sn toiling in rear, shrtlvd
       effrt hfwy, tld off whn pld up bef 5 out. (50 to 1 op 20 to 1) pu
1989 BANNER YEAR (Ire) 6-11-2 N Smith, in tch for a circuit, effrt
       hfwy, lost touch quickly bef 6 out, tld off whn pld up before 3
       out....................................(50 to 1 op 25 to 1) pu
Dist: 5l, dist. 5m 4.80s. a 34.80s (7 Ran).

(Mrs Anne Henson), J G FitzGerald

2651 Sinnington Maiden Hurdle Class F (4-y-o and up) £2,029 2m...(2:20)

1737² SIX CLERKS (Ire) 4-10-9 P Carberry, patiently rdn, steady
       hdwy 3 out, led nxt, jnd last, kpt on wl to ld r-in.
       ....(9 to 4 on op 2 to 1 tchd 7 to 4 on) 1

728⁴ TAWAFIJ (USA) 8-11-2 (3*) Mr C Bonner, settled to track ldrs,
       improved 3 out, str chal to draw level nxt, rdn and one pace
       r-in...(7 to 1 op 6 to 1) 2
2403 DIDDY RYMER 7-11-0 T Reed, nvr far away, ev ch aftr 3 out,
       rdn and no extr betw last 2..................(12 to 1) 3
2489 SILVER MINX 5-11-5 P Niven, led, hit 4th, hdd and rdn 2 out,
       fdd betw last two.........(16 to 1 op 10 to 1 tchd 20 to 1) 4
1682 MILENBERG JOYS 5-11-2 (3*) P Midgley, settled in tch, blun
       4th, feeling pace and lost grnd 3 out, no imprsn frm nxt.
       ....(66 to 1 op 25 to 1 tchd 100 to 1) 5
2206 HELPERBY (Ire) 5-11-0 (5*) G F Ryan, chsd ldrs, feeling pace
       and lost grnd aftr 3 out, sn struggling.
       ....(33 to 1 op 16 to 1 tchd 50 to 1) 6
2419 TSANGA 5-11-5 N Bentley, settled midfield, struggling whn
       pace quickened hfwy, lost tch 3 out, tld off.
       ....(50 to 1 op 20 to 1) 7
2063⁷ PENNY PEPPERMINT 5-11-0 G Cahill, in tch to hfwy, sn
       struggling, tld off........................(100 to 1 op 50 to 1) 8
2066³ SALEM BEACH 5-11-0 A Dobbin, not jump wl, pressed ldrs to
       hfwy, sn lost tch, tld off...............(12 to 1 op 8 to 1) 9
1677 PARRY 5-11-0 B Storey, beh whn f 1st.(50 to 1 op 25 to 1) f
2533 POINT DUTY 7-11-5 D Bentley, lost tch quickly hfwy, tld off
       whn pld up bef 2 out....(14 to 1 op 12 to 1 tchd 16 to 1) pu
       RED-STOAT (Ire) 8-11-0 K Johnson, sn tld off, pld up bef 3 out.
       ....(50 to 1 op 25 to 1) pu
1783 NORTH END LADY 6-11-0 N Smith, reminders 3rd, tld off bef
       hfwy, pld up aftr 3 out..............(14 to 1 tchd 16 to 1) pu
Dist: 1¾l, 7l, 4l, 13l, 7l, 10l, 6l, 12l. 4m 4.60s. a 24.60s (13 Ran).
SR: 11/19/7/8/-/-/   (Marquesa de Moratalla), J G FitzGerald

2652 Zetland Handicap Chase Class E (0-115 5-y-o and up) £2,771 3m 1f 110yds.......................(2:55)

1825 GOLD PIGEON (Ire) [75] 8-10-0 B Storey, made all, styd on
       strly frm 4 out, drvn out r-in...........(14 to 1 op 16 to 1) 1
2418* TICO GOLD [84] (bl) 9-10-9 A S Smith, nvr far away, drvn alng
       frm 4 out, rallied last 2, one pace r-in...........(6 to 4 jt-
       ....fav op 11 to 8) 2
2258⁴ SPARROW HALL [87] 10-10-12 P Carberry, al wl plcd,
       reminders hfwy, rallied fnl circuit, rdn and wknd quickly last 2,
       eased r-in......................(6 to 4 jt-fav op 11 to 8) 3
2488 SNOOK POINT [77] 10-10-2² J Burke, settled off the pace,
       improved hfwy, lost pl quickly bef twelfth (water), tld off whn
       pld up before 7 out.........(9 to 2 op 5 to 1 tchd 11 to 2) pu
2151 JOHNNY KELLY [99] 10-11-7 (3*) F Leahy, improved to join
       ldrs hfwy, losing pl quickly whn blun twelfth (water), tld off
       whn pld up bef 7 out....(12 to 1 op 6 to 1 tchd 16 to 1) pu
Dist: 5l, 18l. 7m 0.50s. a 45.50s (5 Ran).

(Contrac Promotions Ltd), B S Rothwell

2653 Cleveland Novices' Hurdle Class E (5-y-o and up) £2,232 3m 1f 110yds ....(3:30)

2538* MEADOW HYMN (Ire) 6-11-4 P Carberry, al wl plcd, drw level
       3 out, led bef nxt, styd on well r-in. (Evens fav op 7 to 4 on) 1
2298⁶ CLEVER BOY (Ire) 6-11-4 Derek Byrne, al frnt rnk, led briefly
       3rd, led 7th, jnd 3 out, hdd nxt, kpt on same pace r-in.
       ....(7 to 1 op 5 to 1) 2
2119⁴ ELLIOTT'S WISH (Ire) 6-10-12 A Dobbin, al chasing ldrs, chsd
       clr ldg pair frm 3 out, no imprsn.....(20 to 1 tchd 25 to 1) 3
2200³ CHILL FACTOR 7-10-12 P Niven, sluggish strt, took clr order
       aftr one circuit, struggling 4 out, tld off.
       ....(85 to 40 op 11 to 4 tchd 2 to 1) 4
1989⁹ HOUSELOPE SPRING 5-10-7 (5*) G F Ryan, pressed ldrs for
       o'r a circuit, lost tch quickly, tld off 4 out.
       ....(20 to 1 op 16 to 1) 5
1543 LA CHANCE 7-10-12 Mr A Walton, lost tch bef hfwy, sn wl tld
       off..(66 to 1 op 50 to 1) 6
2566 ROYAL HAND 7-10-12 Mr R Armson, sn struggling to keep
       up, poor 4th and tld off whn f last................(100 to 1) f
2298 KICKCASHTAL 8-10-12 M Sharratt, tkd ldrs for a circuit, tld
       off whn pld up aftr 7th.........(100 to 1 tchd 200 to 1) pu
       AL JINN 6-10-12 A S Smith, chsd ldrs for o'r a circuit, sn lost
       tch, tld off bef 4 out.....................(100 to 1 op 50 to 1) pu
2538 PERSIAN GRANGE (Ire) 7-10-12 J Burke, sn wl beh, tld whn
       pld up aftr 7th...(100 to 1) pu
       BELTINO 6-10-12 K Johnson, tld off hfwy, pld up aftr 7th.
       ....(100 to 1 op 50 to 1) pu
2200 BASINCROFT 7-10-5 (7*) A Todd, lost tch bef 4 out, tld off,
       headed 7th, lost tch bef 4 out, tld off whn pld up before 2 out.
       MONNEDELL 5-10-12 D Bentley, struggling midfield aftr
       a circuit, tld off whn pld bef 4 out................(100 to 1) pu
2496³ WATER FONT 5-10-7 (5*) R McGrath, sn beh, tld off whn
       pld up bef 2 out..........................(20 to 1 op 14 to 1) pu
2200 KAMBLETREE (Ire) 6-10-12 D Parker, wl plcd for nrly a circuit,
       sn lost tch, tld off whn pld up bef 2 out.
       ....(200 to 1 op 100 to 1) pu
Dist: 2l, dist, dist, 18l, 8l. 6m 47.00s. a 46.00s (15 Ran).

(M S Nowell), J G FitzGerald

2654 Bedale Handicap Chase Class E (0-110 5-y-o and up) £2,706 2m 3f ....(4:05)

2421* WEAVER GEORGE (Ire) [104] 7-11-8 M Moloney, wth ldr, led
5th till aftr 7th, led seven out, quickened, styd on strly betw
last 2 . . . . (11 to 8 fav op 11 to 10 tchd 6 to 4)   1
22613 ALJADEER (USA) [110] (bl) 8-12-0 P Carberry, nvr far away,
mstk 8th (water), ev ch and rdn 3 out, styd on one pace und
pres r-in . . . . (13 to 8 op 6 to 4 tchd 7 to 4)   2
2622 BLAZING TRAIL (Ire) [103] 9-11-7 M Foster, set modest pace,
jmpd slow early, hdd 5th, led aftr 7th till seven out, mstks and
wknd last 3 . . . .(11 to 4 op 5 to 2 tchd 3 to 1)   3
Dist: 2l, 23l. 5m 10.60s. a 40.60s (3 Ran).

(Regent Decorators Ltd), W Storey

2655 Goathland Novices' Handicap Hurdle Class E (0-105 4-y-o and up) £2,211 2m 3f. . . . . (4:35)

ENCHANTED COTTAGE [75] 5-10-13 (3*) E Callaghan,
patiently rdn, improved 3 out, led nxt, hit last, kpt on grimly.
. . . .(5 to 1 op 4 to 1)   1
2463 PILKINGTON (Ire) [82] 7-11-6 (3*) Michael Brennan, nvr far
away, str chal appr 2 out, faltered and hit rng rail aftr last,
rallied gmely und pres . . . .(8 to 1)   2
25813 FRYUP SATELLITE [82] 6-11-9 Miss P Robson, jmpd wl, al
frnt rnk, slight ld 6th till appr 2 out, kpt on well r-in.
. . . . (4 to 1 fav op 9 to 2)   3
2487 HOTSPUR STREET [78] (bl) 5-11-5 P Niven, al hdwy, led aftr
3rd to 6th, styd handy, rdn and kpt on und pres frm last.
. . . .(6 to 1 op 5 to 1)   4
2256 HIGHLY CHARMING (Ire) [80] 5-11-7 R Supple, settled midfield, took clr order aftr 3 out, ev ch nxt, one pace r-in.
. . . .(8 to 1 tchd 10 to 1)   5
22794 BAASM [80] 4-10-11 Derek Byrne, tucked away midfield,
improved aftr 3 out, rdn and not quicken betw last 2.
. . . .(6 to 1 op 9 to 2)   6
24909 KILDRUMMY CASTLE [83] 5-11-10 P Carberry, led till aftr
3rd, styd hndy, short of room bend aftr 5th, lost pl 3 out, tld
off . . . .(10 to 1 op 6 to 1)   7
5516 AHBEJAYBUS (Ire) [59] 8-10-0 K Johnson, lost pl quickly
hfwy, tld off whn pld up bef 2 out . . . . .(100 to 1 op 66 to 1) pu
2288 TEN PAST SIX [74] 5-11-1 A S Smith, settled travelling wl, ev
ch 3 out, wknd rpdly and pld up bef nxt.
. . . . (15 to 2 op 7 to 1 tchd 8 to 1) pu
2463 DOUGAL [76] 6-10-12 (5*) B Grattan, sn beh, took clr order
hfwy, lost tch quickly aftr 3 out, tld off whn pld up bef nxt.
. . . . (7 to 1 tchd 7 to 1) pu
Dist: Hd, ½l, nk, 3l, 1½l, dist. 4m 57.10s. a 37.10s (10 Ran).

(Mrs J M Davenport), J M Jefferson

SANDOWN (good to soft (races 1,3,6), good (2,4,5))
Thursday February 13th
Going Correction: PLUS 1.10 sec. per fur. (races 1,3,6), PLUS 1.00 (2,4,5)

2656 Village Novices' Hurdle Class D (4-y-o and up) £2,905 2m 110yds (2:00)

2405* JUYUSH (USA) 5-11-12 J Osborne, trkd ldrs, rstrained appr 3
out, hdwy to ld approaching nxt, clr whn blun last.
. . . . (6 to 1 on op 5 to 1 on)   1
GLIDE PATH (USA) 8-11-4 A Maguire, hld up, smooth hdwy
appr 2 out, sn chsd wnr, no imprsn approaching last, fnshd
tired . . . . (14 to 1 op 6 to 1)   2
KEEN BID (Ire) 6-11-4 M Richards, made most till appr 4th,
wknd approaching 2 out.
. . . . (33 to 1 op 20 to 1 tchd 40 to 1)   3
24054 ABSOLUTE LIMIT 5-11-4 P Hide, cl up, led appr 4th till
approaching 2 out, wknd.
. . . . (14 to 1 op 10 to 1 tchd 16 to 1)   4
HE KNOWS THE RULES 5-11-4 B Powell, hld up beh ldrs,
hdwy appr out, ch approaching nxt, sn rdn alng and wknd.
. . . . (33 to 1 op 20 to 1 tchd 50 to 1)   5
2250 KILCARNE BAY (Ire) 7-11-4 J A McCarthy, trkd ldrs, wknd aftr
4th, tld off . . . . (16 to 1 op 5 to 1)   6
MODAJJAJ 5-11-4 L Harvey, hld up beh, struggling aftr 3rd,
tld off. . . . .(66 to 1 op 25 to 1 tchd 100 to 1)   7
24544 GO WITH THE WIND 4-10-8 D O'Sullivan, not fluent second,
beh, struggling 4th, tld off, fnshd lme.
. . . . (14 to 1 op 8 to 1 tchd 16 to 1)   8
ZIPALONG 6-11-4 W McFarland, beh, lost tch aftr 3rd, tld off.
. . . . (33 to 1 op 33 to 1 tchd 100 to 1)   9
1922 DECISION MAKER (Ire) 4-10-8 N Williamson, awkward 1st, al
beh, tld off aftr 3rd . . . .(66 to 1 op 33 to 1) 10
17687 PEALINGS (Ire) 5-10-11 (7*) N Rossiter, awkward 1st, hld up
beh ldrs, not fluent and uns rdr 3rd.
. . . . (66 to 1 op 33 to 1 tchd 100 to 1) ur
Dist: 21l, 2l, 5l, 5l, 10l, ½l, 29l, 26l, 4l. 4m 12.20s. a 25.20s (11 Ran).
SR: 27/-/-/-/-/-/   (W E Sturt), J A B Old

2657 First Half Club Novices' Handicap Chase Class D (0-120 5-y-o and up) £3,437 3m 110yds. . . . . (2:35)

23912 HAWAIIAN SAM (Ire) [98] 7-11-2 G Crone, led 5th, mstk 16th,
ran on wl . . . .(2 to 1 fav op 7 to 4 tchd 13 to 8)   1

19914 TAKE THE BUCKSKIN [98] 10-11-2 R Dunwoody, hld up in cl
tch, lft second tenth, jmpd slwly and lost grnd 15th, shaken up
and ev ch 3 out, btn whn awkward last.
. . . .(15 to 8 op 6 to 4 tchd 2 to 1)   2
22803 WEE WINDY (Ire) [110] 8-12-0 P Hide, led till blun and uns rdr
4th . . . .(7 to 4 fav op 6 to 4 tchd 2 to 1) ur
2266 ONEOFUS [82] 8-10-0 M Richards, lft in ld 4th, hdd nxt, cl
second whn blun and uns rdr tenth.
. . . . (25 to 1 op 20 to 1 tchd 33 to 1) ur
Dist: 18l. 6m 43.00s. a 44.00s (4 Ran).

(Robert K Russell), Andrew Turnell

2658 Fairmile Conditional Jockeys' Handicap Hurdle Class E (0-120 4-y-o and up) £2,640 2m 110yds. . . . . . . (3:10)

24423 DOCTOOR (USA) [113] 7-11-9 D Walsh, not fluent 1st and 4th,
in cl tch, chlgd 2 out, shaken up to ld r-in, cmftbly.
. . . . (11 to 8 fav op Evens tchd 6 to 4)   1
2396* ROYAL EVENT [102] 6-10-12 D Fortt, led, hrd rdn appr last,
hdd r-in, no extr. . . . . . . (100 to 30 op 5 to 2 tchd 7 to 2)   2
25042 CAN CAN CHARLIE [100] 7-10-10 S Ryan, in cl tch, pushed
alng 5th, wknd appr 2 out, tld off.
. . . . (11 to 4 op 3 to 1 tchd 100 to 30)   3
23073 MAZZINI (Ire) [96] 6-10-6 L Aspell, in cl tch, hrd rdn appr 2 out,
no response, tld off . . . .(13 to 2 op 5 to 1 tchd 7 to 1)   4
2442 COURT NAP (Ire) [108] 5-10-11 (7*) S Hearn, in cl tch, wknd
aftr 3 out, tld off whn hit nxt and uns rdr.
. . . . (20 to 1 op 12 to 1 tchd 25 to 1) ur
Dist: 5l, 30l, 22l. 4m 11.20s. a 24.20s (5 Ran).
SR: 36/20/   (Alfred Walls), M C Pipe

2659 Londesborough Handicap Chase Class C (0-130 5-y-o and up) £4,880 2½m 110yds. . . . . (3:45)

1666* TOO PLUSH [109] 8-10-13 L Harvey, keen early, cl up, lft in ld
5 out, all out . . . . (6 to 1 op 3 to 1 tchd 13 to 2)   1
18925 NO PAIN NO GAIN (Ire) [120] 9-11-10 P Hide, in cl tch, chsd
wnr frm 5 out, ev ch appr 2 out, no extr.
. . . . (3 to 1 op 5 to 2 tchd 100 to 30)   2
2220* GARRYLOUGH (Ire) [118] (bl) 8-11-8 R Dunwoody, led, f 5 out.
. . . .(5 to 4 on tchd 5 to 4 on and 13 to 8 on)   f
25527 SOLO GENT [96] 8-10-0 N Williamson, hld up in last pl,
pushed alng appr 7th, losing tch whn pld up bef tenth.
. . . . (8 to 1 op 7 to 1 tchd 9 to 1) pu
Dist: 2½l. 5m 28.00s. a 28.00s (4 Ran).
SR: 10/18/-/-/   (Mrs C C Williams), Andrew Turnell

2660 Wilfred Johnstone Hunters' Chase Class H (6-y-o and up) £1,604 2½m 110yds. . . . . (4:15)

MR BOSTON 12-12-1 Mr S Swiers, hld up in cl tch, shaken up
appr 2 out, led sn aftr last, pushed out, ran on wl. (13 to 8 jt-
fav op 6 to 4 tchd 7 to 4)   1
HOWARYASUN (Ire) (v) 9-11-11 (7*) Mr D S Jones, led to 4th,
cl up, led 3 out till sn aftr last, no extr.
. . . . (9 to 2 op 5 to 1 tchd 11 to 2)   2
WILD ILLUSION 13-11-11 (7*) Mr R Lawther, cl up, rdn aftr 3
out, styd on appr last, one pace . . . .(13 to 8 jt-
fav op 11 to 8 tchd 5 to 4)   3
POORS WOOD 10-11-3 (7*) Mr P O'Keeffe, led 4th to 3 out,
hrd rdn appr last, wknd. (12 to 1 op 16 to 1 tchd 20 to 1)   4
AMARI KING 13-11-8 (7*) Mr C Ward Thomas, hld up in cl tch,
wknd appr 3 out, tld off . . . . .(15 to 2 op 6 to 1 tchd 8 to 1)   5
ROYAL IRISH 13-10-13 (7*) Miss C Townsley, mstk second,
lost tch 7th, pld up bef tenth.
. . . . (40 to 1 op 33 to 1 tchd 50 to 1) pu
Dist: 5l, ½l, 12l, dist. 5m 36.60s. a 36.60s (6 Ran).
(M K Oldham), Mrs M Reveley

2661 Spring Novices' Handicap Hurdle Class D (0-110 4-y-o and up) £3,035 2¾m. . . . . (4:50)

21583 LOUGH TULLY (Ire) [80] 7-10-3 J Osborne, led second, clr 2
out, rdn out . . . . (6 to 1 tchd 7 to 1 and 11 to 2)   1
24567 LORD KHALICE (Ire) [79] 5-10-2 N Williamson, al hndy, drvn
appr 2 out, kpt on same pace und pres.
. . . . (14 to 1 op 12 to 1 tchd 16 to 1)   2
24562 PHYSICAL FUN [89] 6-10-12 D Skyrme, hld up beh, hit 5th,
hrd rdn and hdwy appr 2 out, one pace und pres frm last.
. . . . (9 to 2 op 7 to 2 tchd 5 to 1)   3
22635 MAHLER [94] 7-11-3 D Walsh, trkd ldrs, ev ch 3 out, wknd
appr nxt . . . .(14 to 1 op 10 to 1 tchd 16 to 1)   4
25592 ALLOW (Ire) [93] 6-11-2 A Maguire, led to second, trkd ldrs,
pushed alng 7th, hrd rdn aftr 3 out, sn btn.
. . . . (2 to 1 fav op 5 to 2 tchd 9 to 4)   5
VINTAGE CLARET [101] 8-11-7 (3*) L Aspell, hld up rear, effrt
aftr 3 out, sn no imprsn, eased appr nxt.
. . . . (25 to 1 op 14 to 1 tchd 33 to 1)   6
18765 SPACEAGE GOLD [99] 8-11-5 A G Upton, hld up, not fluent,
reminders 4th and nxt, nvr on terms . . . .(10 to 1 op 6 to 1)   7
21569 RATHKEAL (Ire) [83] (v) 6-10-6 B Powell, hld up, cld appr 6th,
struggling sn aftr. . . . . (9 to 1 op 14 to 1 tchd 33 to 1)   8

361

2392 FARLEYER ROSE (Ire) [77] 8-10-0 M Richards, *hld up, rdn alng and hdwy aftr 3 out, btn appr nxt, eased.* ....(25 to 1 op 12 to 1 tchd 33 to 1) 9
2250* SPECIAL BEAT [96] 5-11-0 (5*) Mr C Vigors, *hndy, mstk 4 out, hrd rdn aftr nxt, sn btn*.....(7 to 1 op 4 to 1 tchd 8 to 1) 10
2398^{2} ROYAL RAVEN (Ire) [97] 6-11-6 P Hide, *trkd ldrs, wknd quickly aftr 3 out, pld up bef nxt*...(13 to 2 op 5 to 1 tchd 7 to 1) pu
Dist: 8l, 1l, 18l, ¾l, 4l, 11l, 3½l. 5m 32.70s. a 29.70s (11 Ran).
SR: 20/11/20/7/5/9/ (R A Hancocks), F Jordan

TAUNTON (good)
Thursday February 13th

Going Correction: PLUS 1.10 sec. per fur. (races 1,2,4,6,7), PLUS 1.25 (3,5)

2662 Blackdown Maiden Hurdle Class F (Div I) (4-y-o and up) £1,707 2m 1f .... (1:40)

2430^{2} BREAK THE RULES 5-10-12 (7*) G Supple, *hld up, steady hdwy 3 out, led appr nxt, cmftbly*... (13 to 8 fav op 5 to 4) 1
1749^{4} DEVON PEASANT 5-11-0 Mr L Jefford, *in tch, chlgd 3 out, sn led, hdd appr 2 out, soon one pace.* .... (5 to 2 op 9 to 4 tchd 11 to 4) 2
KINNESCASH (Ire) 4-10-9 R Johnson, *hdwy to track ldrs 5th, ev ch appr 2 out, sn one pace*.........(14 to 1 op 12 to 1) 3
2430^{9} MYSTIC HILL 6-11-5 J Frost, *trkd ldrs till outpcd aftr 3 out.* .... (11 to 1 op 7 to 1) 4
1452^{7} WALTER'S DESTINY 5-11-5 S McNeill, *chsd ldrs to 3 out, sn rdn and wknd*.........(33 to 1 tchd 50 to 1) 5
RUMPELSTILTSKIN 5-11-5 R Farrant, *beh 4th, hdwy and mstk 3 out, sn wknd*................. (66 to 1 op 33 to 1) 6
2242^{7} ALPINE JOKER 4-10-9 G Tormey, *prmnt, ev ch aftr 3 out, sn wknd*.......................................(14 to 1) 7
SOLDIER COVE (USA) 7-11-5 C Maude, *mstk 1st, al beh.* .... (25 to 1 op 20 to 1) 8
VANBOROUGH LAD 8-11-2 (3*) T Dascombe, *prmnt, chlgd 3 out till wknd nxt*.....................(33 to 1 op 20 to 1) 9
2035^{5} SOUTH WEST EXPRESS (Ire) 5-11-5 W Marston, *led till hdd and wknd quickly aftr 2 out*..........(20 to 1 op 16 to 1) 10
VENICE BEACH 5-11-5 G Bradley, *hld up, mstk 5th and nxt, sn wknd*..................(9 to 2 op 4 to 1 tchd 5 to 1) 11
MASTER-H 4-10-9 A Thornton, *pushed alng and hdwy 6th, pressed ldrs 3 out, wknd rpdly, tld off.* (20 to 1 op 12 to 1) 12
JOBIE 7-11-5 J Railton, *hld up, effrt 5th, wl beh whn mstk and pld up aftr 2 out*.................... (33 to 1 op 20 to 1) pu
Dist: 3½l, 1¼l, 11l, 4l, 2½l, 2l, 5l, 2½l, 4l, 10l. 4m 13.50s. a 30.50s (13 Ran).
(A J Lomas), M C Pipe

2663 Porlock Selling Handicap Hurdle Class G (0-95 4-y-o and up) £2,004 2m 1f..........................(2:10)

1614 DISSOLVE [71] 5-10-1 (7*) Mr L Baker, *trkd ldrs, chlgd aftr 2 out till led sn after last, rdn out*........(33 to 1 op 25 to 1) 1
2432* D'NAAN (Ire) [93] (bl) 4-11-6 C Maude, *led aftr 1st, rdn alng frm 5th, stumbled after 3 out, hdd after last, rallied und pres, no extr nr finish*...... (3 to 1 fav op 7 to 2 tchd 4 to 1) 2
2390* PROUD IMAGE [84] 5-11-7 D Bridgwater, *led till aftr 1st, styd chasing ldrs, chlgd and hit 2 out, sn one pace.* ....(5 to 1 op 7 to 2) 3
1211^{7} STEER POINT [72] 6-10-9 J Frost, *beh till hdwy 6th, styd on same pace appr 2 out*............. (20 to 1 op 16 to 1) 4
1969^{5} KASHAN (Ire) [63] 9-10-0 B Fenton, *beh, rdn alng aftr 3 out, rapid hdwy appr last, fnshd wl.* .... (6 to 1 op 5 to 1 tchd 13 to 2) 5
2424^{5} GLOWING PATH [87] 7-11-3 (7*) J Harris, *chsd ldrs till wknd aftr 3 out*...................(10 to 1 op 7 to 1) 6
SHANAKEE [73] 10-10-10 Mr J L Llewellyn, *chsd ldrs, chlgd 5th to 3 out, wknd appr nxt*......................(20 to 1) 7
2440^{6} LIME STREET BLUES (Ire) [76] (bl) 6-10-13 G Bradley, *hdwy 5th, mstk nxt, sn wknd*.....(9 to 1 op 8 to 1 tchd 10 to 1) 8
2424^{7} NORD LYS (Ire) [67] 6-10-4 I Lawrence, *al beh.* .... (16 to 1 op 12 to 1) 9
2266 GENERAL SHIRLEY (Ire) [80] 6-10-10 (7*) M Clinton, *beh till hdwy to track ldrs 6th, wknd aftr 3 out*...(10 to 1 op 8 to 1) 10
2390 MARROWFAT LADY (Ire) [68] 6-10-5 J Railton, *in tch to 4th, sn beh*..(25 to 1) 11
2440 MICK THE YANK (Ire) [68] 7-10-5 Jacqui Oliver, *prmnt to 4th, sn beh*.. (12 to 1) 12
2351 ALDWICK COLONNADE [70] 10-10-7 W Marston, *prominet to 5th, sn wknd*..................(25 to 1 op 20 to 1) 13
2440^{8} LITTLE HOOLIGAN [76] (bl) 6-10-10 (3*) T Dascombe, *beh frm 4th*.............................(14 to 1 op 8 to 1) 14
COURAGE-MON-BRAVE [63] 9-10-0 R Johnson, *chsd ldrs to 5th, sn wknd, tld off whn pld up bef 2 out* .... (12 to 1 op 33 to 1) pu
BOLD REINE (Fr) [63] 8-10-0 A Procter, *sn beh, tld off whn pld up bef 2 out*....................... (33 to 1 op 25 to 1) pu
Dist: Nk, 4l, 10l, 4l, 1¼l, 2l, 3½l, 15l, ¾l, 1½l. 4m 9.80s. a 26.80s (16 Ran).
SR: -/11/8/-/-/-/ (Western Solvents Ltd), N M Lampard

2664 Henlade Novices' Chase Class D (5-y-o and up) £3,517 2m 3f......(2:45)

2450 MISTER DRUM (Ire) 8-12-0 W Marston, *led 3rd, made rst, cmftbly*........................(11 to 10 fav op 5 to 4) 1
2425^{2} GAROLO (Fr) (bl) 7-11-8 G Bradley, *in tch, chsd wnr frm 4 out, rdn 3 out, hld whn hit last*..............(5 to 4 op Evens) 2
2376^{6} LUCKY EDDIE (Ire) (bl) 6-11-2 C Maude, *chsd wnr frm 4th, hit tenth, wknd from four out*..............(10 to 1 op 8 to 1) 3
1979 DUNNICKS VIEW 8-10-9 (7*) M Griffiths, *led to second, stumbled bend aftr 8th, sn lost tch, tld off.* .... (40 to 1 op 20 to 1) 4
2515 ASTRAL INVASION (USA) (v) 6-10-13 (3*) R Massey, *sn beh and tld off*.........................(33 to 1 op 20 to 1) 5
2263 LUCKY TANNER 6-11-2 J Culloty, *f 1st.* .... (20 to 1 op 12 to 1) f
2457 WIN A HAND 7-10-8 (3*) T Dascombe, *refused and uns second*.......................... (40 to 1 op 33 to 1) ref
RUSTIC FLIGHT 10-11-2 D Leahy, *tld off frm 4th, blun 5th, pld up bef 3 out*.......................... (66 to 1 op 50 to 1) pu
1893 GEMINI MIST 6-10-11 Mr L Jefford, *hit 1st, sn wl beh, tld off whn pld up bef 9th*.................. (40 to 1 op 33 to 1) pu
SYDNEY BOON 6-11-2 P Holley, *led second to 3rd, tld off 7th, pld up bef tenth*.....................(33 to 1 op 20 to 1) pu
Dist: 6l, 2½l, dist, 12l. 5m 1.40s. a 30.40s (10 Ran).
SR: 34/22/13/-/-/-/ (Malcolm Batchelor), M J Wilkinson

2665 Cranmore Mares' Only Handicap Hurdle Class F (0-100 4-y-o and up) £2,400 3m 110yds............(3:20)

2435* MAID EQUAL [100] 6-11-7 (7*) G Supple, *hld up, rapid hdwy to ld 8th, in command whn lft clr last.* ....(9 to 4 fav op 3 to 1 tchd 7 to 2) 1
1558^{8} APACHEE FLOWER [74] 7-10-2 R Johnson, *hdwy 4th, drvn alng frm 8th, styd on to take second r-in.* .... (16 to 1 op 14 to 1) 2
2513^{3} FLEUR DE TAL [92] 6-10-13 (7*) J Power, *chsd ldrs, rdn 3 out, btn appr 2 out*..................... (16 to 1 op 12 to 1) 3
2513* SCOTTISH WEDDING [85] 7-10-10 (3*,7ex) R Massey, *chsd ldrs to 3 out, sn wknd*.....(8 to 1 op 7 to 1 tchd 9 to 1) 4
1815^{3} MISS SECRET [76] 7-10-4 D Bridgwater, *beh till some hdwy frm 3 out but not a dngr*...............(10 to 1 op 8 to 1) 5
2403 ALICE'S MIRROR [72] (bl) 8-9-7 (7*) M Griffiths, *chsd ldrs till wknd 9th*... (33 to 1) 6
2461 COLETTE'S CHOICE (Ire) [85] 8-10-13 A Thornton, *wth ldr to second, wknd 8th*................. (25 to 1 op 16 to 1) 7
STRAY HARMONY [73] 7-10-1^{1} C Maude, *nvr rchd ldrs.* .... (50 to 1 op 33 to 1) 8
2440^{3} STRIKE-A-POSE [74] 7-10-2 I Lawrence, *hld up in tch, chsd ldrs 8th, wknd nxt*................... (20 to 1 op 14 to 1) 9
2433^{4} BROWN WREN [72] 6-10-0 G Tormey, *hdwy 5th, wknd 8th.* .... (10 to 1 op 7 to 1) 10
1938^{4} SUMMER HAVEN [72] 8-10-0 Mr A Kinane, *led, sn clr, hdd 8th, wkng whn f 3 out*.................(33 to 1 op 20 to 1) f
2396^{4} MISS MARIGOLD [92] (bl) 8-11-3 (3*) T Dascombe, *hdwy 7th, chlgd 3 out to nxt, hld whn mstk and uns rdr last.* .... (16 to 1 op 14 to 1 tchd 20 to 1) ur
2462^{4} DRAGONMIST (Ire) [72] (h) 7-10-0 D J Burchell, *tld off frm 7th, pld up bef 2 out*.......... (4 to 1 op 9 to 2 tchd 5 to 1) pu
800^{3} MYBLACKTHORN (Ire) [92] 7-11-1 (5*) O Burrows, *hdwy 7th, chlgd 9th, hld in 3rd whn lft second last, pld up r-in and dismounted*.......................................(12 to 1) pu
2403 KONGIES MELODY [72] 6-10-0 R Greene, *mstks and al rear, tld off whn pld up bef 2 out*........... (50 to 1 op 25 to 1) pu
Dist: 12l, 1½l, 1½l, 29l, 3l, 1½l, 2½l, ½l, dist. 6m 3.60s. a 35.60s (15 Ran).
SR: 14/-/-/-/-/-/ (Heeru Kirpalani), M C Pipe

2666 Cheddar Handicap Chase Class E (0-115 5-y-o and up) £3,712 3m .... (3:55)

2280^{4} MR PICKPOCKET (Ire) [106] 9-11-7 J F Titley, *made virtually all, came clr frm 3 out, readily*..... (11 to 4 fav op 4 to 1) 1
2334^{8} DUHALLOW LODGE [110] 10-11-11 B Fenton, *hit 7th, lost pos 13th, sn reco'red, styd on to chase wnr frm 3 out, no imprsn*...............................(12 to 1 op 6 to 1) 2
2395^{4} JAILBREAKER [85] 10-9-10^{1} (5*) D Salter, *prmnt, chsd wnr frm 4 out to nxt, sn wknd*.............. (12 to 1 op 8 to 1) 3
2252^{3} CALL ME RIVER (Ire) [85] 9-10-0 I Lawrence, *sn prmnt, chsd ldrs 4 out, soon hrd rdn and wknd*... (11 to 2 tchd 13 to 2) 4
JASON'S BOY [85] 7-10-0 R Johnson, *prmnt, chsd wnr 14th to 4 out, sn wknd*........................(11 to 1 op 9 to 1) 5
2459^{4} CELTINO [94] 9-10-9 S Wynne, *chsd ldrs, hit 6th, wknd 4 out.* .... (13 to 2 op 4 to 1) 6
2393^{6} REALLY A RASCAL [105] 10-11-6 M A Fitzgerald, *hdwy 11th, wknd 13th, f 15th*......... (6 to 1 op 4 to 1 tchd 13 to 2) f
2482 MINGUS (USA) [85] 10-10-0 S McNeill, *hdwy 12th, wknd, blun and uns rdr 14th*.................... (16 to 1 op 14 to 1) ur
2437^{7} BENJAMIN LANCASTER [97] 13-10-5 (7*) M Griffiths, *wth wnr 5th to 8th, wknd 14th, tld of whn pld up bef 3 out.* .... (16 to 1 op 12 to 1) pu
SPRING TO IT [95] 11-10-10 Jamie Evans, *hdwy 11th, wknd 13th, tld off whn pld up bef 3 out*.......(10 to 1 op 6 to 1) pu
ASWAMEDH [85] 9-10-0 G Tormey, *hit 6th, wknd 12th, hmpd 15th, tld off whn pld up bef 3 out*......(20 to 1 op 14 to 1) pu
2439 DISTILLATION [85] 12-9-12^{1} (3*) T Dascombe, *beh frm 4th, tld off whn pld up bef 3 out*............. (66 to 1 op 25 to 1) pu
Dist: 4l, 6l, 7l, 8l, 5l. 6m 20.50s. a 37.50s (12 Ran).
SR: 18/18/-/-/-/-/ (John Holmes), Miss H C Knight

2667 February Handicap Hurdle Class D (0-120 4-y-o and up) £2,814 2m 3f 110yds. .... (4:25)

2389⁶	JEFFERIES [101] 8-11-5 C Llewellyn, lost pos 3rd, sn reco'red, led 3 out, rdn nxt, styd on gmely. .... (5 to 2 op 9 to 4 tchd 11 to 4)	1
2186²	NINE O THREE [105] 8-11-9 A Thornton, hld up, trkd ldrs gng wl 3 out, str chal frm 2 out, rdn and ev ch whn blun last, rallied and ran on. .... (7 to 4 fav op 2 to 1)	2
2356²	FAWLEY FLYER [94] 7-10-5 (7*) J Power, chsd ldrs, led aftr 6th, hdd 3 out, styd pressing ldrs till wknd 2 out.	3
2296⁸	MOOR HALL LADY [85] (v) 6-10-3 W Marston, led second till aftr 6th, wknd quickly 3 out, tld off.... (13 to 2 op 11 to 2)	4
1056⁸	SPRING TO GLORY [102] 10-11-6 B Fenton, led to second, styd chasing ldrs, 3rd and rdn whn f 6th. .... (14 to 1 op 12 to 1 tchd 16 to 1)	f
2389	SPRING SAINT [106] 8-11-10 C Maude, beh and rdn 5th, tld off whn pld up bef 2 out. .... (8 to 1 op 6 to 1)	pu
2356	SAUSALITO BOY [82] (bl) 9-10-0 D Bridgwater, tld off frm 5th, pld up bef nxt. .... (66 to 1 op 33 to 1)	pu

Dist: ¾l, 4l, dist. 4m 46.30s. a 28.30s (7 Ran).

SR: 22/25/10/-/ (Miss S Blumberg), J A B Old

2668 Blackdown Maiden Hurdle Class F (Div II) (4-y-o and up) £1,696 2m 1f .... (4:55)

2153	TRISTRAM'S IMAGE (NZ) 6-11-5 M A Fitzgerald, al tracking ldrs, outpcd and jmpd slwly 3 out, chlgd 2 out, sn led, drvn out. .... (2 to 1 fav tchd 9 to 4)	1
	WELTON ARSENAL 5-11-5 R Greene, hdwy to track ldrs 6th, styd on to chase wnr aproaching last, one pace. .... (6 to 1 op 4 to 1 tchd 13 to 2)	2
	GIVE AND TAKE 4-10-9 James Evans, led second, mstk, rdr lost iron and hdd aftr 2 out, unbalanced r-in, reco'red and ran on cl hme, unlucky. .... (9 to 4 op 7 to 4 tchd 5 to 2)	3
	DORMY THREE 7-11-2 (3*) T Dascombe, al in tch, one pace frm 3 out. .... (16 to 1 op 12 to 1)	4
2207	GIVRY (Ire) 7-11-0 (5*) Sophie Mitchell, chsd ldrs till wknd appr 2 out. .... (25 to 1 op 16 to 1)	5
126²	CUBAN NIGHTS (USA) 5-11-5 R Johnson, keen hold, chsd ldrs till wknd 3 out. .... (7 to 1 op 6 to 1 tchd 15 to 2)	6
1696⁶	PRINCELY AFFAIR 4-10-9 S Wynne, led to second, wknd 3 out. .... (16 to 1 op 14 to 1 tchd 20 to 1)	7
	PEARL HART 5-10-7 (7*) Martin Smith, beh, some hdwy 3 out, not a dngr. .... (20 to 1 op 12 to 1)	8
	LANGTONIAN 8-11-5 B Fenton, al in rear. ...... (33 to 1)	9
	SONG OF KENDA 5-10-9 (5*) D Salter, al in rear. .... (33 to 1 op 20 to 1)	10
545⁶	ABBEYDORRAN 6 11 0 W Marston, al in rear. .... (66 to 1 op 50 to 1)	11
614	RAPID LINER 4-10-9 V Slattery, not fluent, al beh. (50 to 1)	12
775	FIERY FOOTSTEPS 5-10-7 (7*) T O'Connor, effrt 4th, wknd 6th. .... (66 to 1 op 50 to 1)	13
	MOOR DUTCH 6-11-5 Mr A Holdsworth, prmnt till wknd 5th, beh whn pld up bef 2 out. .... (50 to 1 op 33 to 1)	pu

Dist: ¾l, 2l, 5l, 3½l, 11l, ½l, 5l, 6l, 1l, 28l. 4m 12.60s. a 29.60s (14 Ran).

(S Keeling), J N Henderson

THURLES (IRE) (soft)
Thursday February 13th

2669 Golden Hurdle (4-y-o) £2,740 2m .... (2:00)

2470⁴	MARLONETTE (Ire) 11-2 D J Casey, ... (5 to 2 fav)	1
2225³	GO SASHA (Ire) (bl) 11-2 (5*) T Martin, ... (3 to 1)	2
2270	COULTHARD (Ire) 10-7 (7*) Miss S J Leahy, ...(16 to 1)	3
	PERSIAN DREAM (Ire) 10-4 C F Swan, ... (5 to 1)	4
	PEPPANOORA (Ire) 10-4 C O'Dwyer, ...(20 to 1)	5
2337	COMRADE CHINNERY (Ire) 11-0 J P Broderick, ..(12 to 1)	6
	SUBLIME POLLY (Ire) 10-4 F Woods, ...(16 to 1)	7
2470⁷	MISS PENNYHILL (Ire) (bl) 10-9 (7*) J M Maguire, ..(11 to 2)	ur
	FAATEQ 10-9 S H O'Donovan, ... (7 to 1)	pu
	CREWMAN (Ire) 10-2 (7*) S FitzGerald, ...(20 to 1)	pu
	DIGITAL SIGNAL (Ire) 10-9 G M O'Neill, ...(20 to 1)	l

Dist: 4l, 9l, 11l, 11l. 4m 8.40s. (11 Ran).

(J Doran), W P Mullins

2670 I.N.H. Stallion Owners E.B.F. Novice Hurdle (5-y-o and up) £3,767 2¾m .... (2:30)

2445⁵	KINGS RETURN (Ire) 6-12-0 D J Casey, ...(4 to 1)	1
2518*	CASTLE COIN (Ire) 5-11-6 C F Swan, ... (6 to 1)	2
2135²	TONI'S TIP (Ire) 5-11-3 (3*) K Whelan, ... (11 to 4 fav)	3
2445⁴	DUKY RIVER (Ire) 6-11-9 F Woods, ... (7 to 2)	4
2135⁸	MISS ORCHESTRA (Ire) 6-11-4 J Shortt, ...(10 to 1)	5
1404⁵	HOLLYBANK BUCK (Ire) 7-11-9 A Powell, ...(10 to 1)	6
2275⁴	MORAL SUPPORT (Ire) 5-11-1 C O'Dwyer, ...(10 to 1)	7
1432	DUN CARRAIG (Ire) 9-11-1 (3*) D Bromley, ...(25 to 1)	8
2445⁸	YELAPA PRINCE (Ire) 6-12-0 A J O'Brien, ...(12 to 1)	9
2525	SUZANN'S GIRL (Ire) 6-10-13 T Horgan, ...(33 to 1)	10

2671 Kinloch Brae Chase (Grade 2) (6-y-o and up) £9,675 2½m .... (3:00)

2474⁴	MERRY GALE (Ire) 9-12-0 C O'Dwyer, wl plcd, mstk 8th, rdn aftr 3 out, dsptd ld last, led r-in. .... (9 to 4)	1
2233⁸	ROYAL MOUNTBROWNE 9-12-0 C F Swan, led, jmpd 3rd, hdd 7th, mstk nxt, rdn aftr 3 out, lft clr after next, headed and no extr r-in. .... (7 to 1)	2
2365²	THE REAL ARTICLE (Ire) 8-11-4 L P Cusack, al rear, mstk 1st, lost tch aftr 4 out. .... (33 to 1)	3
2169⁷	CORSTON DANCER (Ire) (bl) 9-10-13 T Horgan, al rear, lost tch aftr 8th. .... (100 to 1)	4
2471*	DORANS PRIDE 8-12-0 J P Broderick, trkd ldr, prog to dispute ld 3rd, led and quickened 7th, clr whn f 2 out. .... (2 to 1 on)	f

Dist: ¾l, dist, dist. 5m 30.90s. (5 Ran).

(Herb M Stanley), J T R Dreaper

2672 Executive Perk Hunters Chase (5-y-o and up) £3,425 3m .... (3:30)

2523	DIXON VARNER (Ire) 7-11-4 Mr F Fenton, ...(6 to 4 fav)	1
2475⁵	STAY IN TOUCH (Ire) 7-11-11 (3*) Mr D P Costello, (5 to 1)	2
1092⁵	TWO IN TUNE (Ire) 9-10-11 (7*) Mr D Keane, ...(14 to 1)	3
2523⁸	PANCHO'S TANGO (Ire) 7-11-0 (7*) Mr D P Daly, ..(20 to 1)	4
2475⁶	CADDY MAN 8-11-2 (7*) Mr P Cashman, ...(14 to 1)	5
2475²	AIGUILLE (Ire) 8-11-9 Mr B M Cash, ... (7 to 1)	6
2475³	MR K'S WINTERBLUES (Ire) 7-10-6 (7*) Mr J G Sheehan, ... (10 to 1)	7
2523	JUST A BREEZE (Ire) 9-10-6 (7*) Mr E Gallagher, ..(12 to 1)	8
2523²	INNISCEIN (Ire) 9-10-13 (5*) Mr J T McNamara, ...(14 to 1)	9
2457	NO MISTAKE VI (Ire) 9-11-6 (3*) Mr R Walsh, ...(25 to 1)	f
	CREDIT TRANSFER (Ire) 9-11-13 Mr H F Cleary, ...(3 to 1)	bd

Dist: 2l, 16, 15l, 4½l. 6m 38.60s. (11 Ran).

(Mrs John Magnier), E Bolger

2673 Tattersalls Ireland E.B.F. Mares Novice Chase (6-y-o and up) £3,425 2¼m. .... (4:00)

2410³	BLAZE OF HONOUR (Ire) 6-11-2 C F Swan, ...(2 to 1 fav)	1
2171	CREHELP EXPRESS (Ire) 7-10-13 (3*) B Bowens, (13 to 2)	2
2448²	COOLAFINKA (Ire) 8-11-2 C O'Dwyer, ...(6 to 1)	3
	VALERIE OWENS (Ire) 8-10-9 (7*) D K Budds, ...(12 to 1)	4
2103	YOUNG MRS KELLY (Ire) 7-11-2 J Jones, ...(10 to 1)	5
2139³	ARTISTIC QUAY (Ire) 8-10-9 (7*) M D Murphy, ...(20 to 1)	6
2410	CREATIVE BLAZE 8-11-2 J P Broderick, ...(9 to 2)	7
2587⁹	FIELD OF DESTINY (Ire) 8-10-13 (3*) K Whelan, ...(20 to 1)	8
2410⁵	V'OSSKE GALE (Ire) 7-11-2 A Powell, ...(12 to 1)	f
2276	RATHCUHE LADY (Ire) 6-11-2 T P Treacy, ...(25 to 1)	f
2411⁴	MARIES POLLY 7-11-2 F Woods, ...(10 to 1)	bd
2410	CASTLELAKE LADY (Ire) 8-11-2 D T Evans, ...(33 to 1)	bd
1714	MARLAST (Ire) 6-11-2 J Shortt, ...(14 to 1)	pu

Dist: 5½l, 1l, 2l, ½l. 4m 57.90s. (13 Ran).

(Mrs Anne Leahy), A P O'Brien

2674 Littleton Handicap Hurdle (0-116 4-y-o and up) £2,740 2m...... (4:30)

2413*	BALLYRIHY BOY (Ire) [-] 6-11-7 C F Swan, ...(9 to 4 fav)	1
2159⁴	HEIGHT OF LUXURY (Ire) [-] 9-9-0 (7*) M D Murphy, (14 to 1)	2
2413⁶	ZIGGY THE GREAT (Ire) [-] (bl) 5-10-4 D J Casey, ..(14 to 1)	3
564	MUSKERRY KING (Ire) [-] 6-10-13 W Slattery, ...(14 to 1)	4
1426⁶	WEST ON BRIDGE ST (Ire) [-] 7-11-5 C O'Dwyer, ..(12 to 1)	5
2124⁴	REGENCY RAKE (Ire) [-] 5-11-4 F Woods, ...(6 to 1)	6
	DONICKMORE (Ire) [-] 6-11-5 K F O'Brien, ...(12 to 1)	7
2275³	MIDNIGHT JAZZ (Ire) [-] 7-11-1 J P Broderick, ...(13 to 2)	8
2272	THEPRINCESS MANHAR (Ire) [-] 5-9-12 (7*) D M Bean, ... (12 to 1)	9
	CLANCY NOSSEL (Ire) [-] 6-10-6 (7*) R P Hogan, ..(20 to 1)	10
2271	GORRANA (Ire) [-] 7-10-1 (5*) T Martin, ...(20 to 1)	11
	MAGNUM STAR (Ire) [-] 8-9-12 J Jones, ...(33 to 1)	12
2159³	BEAU CYRANO (Ire) [-] 5-10-8 (7*) M J Collins, ...(12 to 1)	pu
2415²	WITHOUT EQUAL (USA) [-] 10-11-4 (7*) Mr R J Curran, ... (7 to 1)	pu
2447⁴	MULKEY PRINCE (Ire) [-] 6-12-0 J Shortt, ...(8 to 1)	pu

Dist: 1l, 2½l, 2l, 3l. 4m 8.50s. (15 Ran).

(M J Collison), Capt D G Swan

2675 Horse And Jockey I.N.H. Flat Race (6-y-o and up) £2,740 2m..... (5:00)

2525⁵	JENSALEE (Ire) 6-11-2 (7*) Mr A C Coyle, ...(7 to 1)	1
2098³	TIME TO LEAD (Ire) 7-12-0 Mr P Fenton, ...(7 to 4 fav)	2
2079⁵	KAITHEY CHOICE (Ire) 6-11-2 (7*) Mr J Boland, ...(12 to 1)	3
	TENDER SITUATION 6-11-7 (7*) Mr G Donnelly, ..(5 to 2)	4
2416²	PRIZE OF PEACE (Ire) 7-11-2 (7*) Mr M T Hartrey, (10 to 1)	5
	COSTS SO MUCH (Ire) 6-11-2 (7*) Mr M A Cahill, ..(25 to 1)	6
2048	YOUNG CAL (Ire) 8-12-0 Mr A J Martin, ... (7 to 1)	7
	SUTTREE (Ire) 6-11-7 (7*) Mr M A Flood, ...(14 to 1)	8
2519⁸	RING HARRY (Ire) 7-11-9 Mr B M Cash, ...(20 to 1)	9
2525⁴	SPLEODRACH (Ire) 7-11-6 (3*) Mr R Walsh, ...(10 to 1)	10
2449	CONAGHER LEADER (Ire) 6-11-7 (7*) Mr A J Dempsey, ... (20 to 1)	11

PIYALA (Ire) 7-11-2 (7*) Mr P G Murphy, ... (12 to 1) 12
2276[9] MARIA-NOELLE (Ire) 7-11-2 (7*) Mr J P McNamara, (25 to 1) 13
2416[6] LISKILNEWABBEY (Ire) 6-11-9 Mr D Marnane, ... (16 to 1) 14
ROISIN BEAG (Ire) 6-11-9 Mr H F Cleary, ... (20 to 1) 15
2172 WOOLPACKER (Ire) 6-11-7 (7*) Mr E Sheehy, ... (14 to 1) 16
2383[2] COUNCILLOR (Ire) 6-11-7 (7*) Mr M P Horan, ... (12 to 1) 17
1463 ASFREEASTHEWIND (Ire) 6-11-9 Mr J P Dempsey, (16 to 1) 18
Dist: 9l, hd, 5½l, 5l. 4m 4.60s. (18 Ran).
(P M Kiely), P Mullins

FAKENHAM (good)
Friday February 14th
Going Correction: PLUS 0.05 sec. per fur.

2676 Sheringham Selling Handicap Hurdle Class G (0-90 4-y-o and up) £2,739 2m.....................(1:45)

2515[2] RUTH'S GAMBLE [54] (v) 9-10-2 D Leahy, *hdwy aftr 4th, ev ch four out, led appr last, drvn out*........(6 to 1 tchd 7 to 1) 1
1848[7] NAGOBELIA [76] 9-11-10 N Mann, *led till aftr 3rd, led ag'n after 3 out till hdd appr last, not quicken.* .... (14 to 1 op 12 to 1 tchd 16 to 1) 2
CAPTAIN MARMALADE [73] 8-11-7 K Gaule, *chsd ldrs, drvn alng aftr 5th, ev ch after 3 out, not quicken after nxt.* ....(9 to 1 op 5 to 1) 3
2188[7] SOUSSE [80] 4-11-4 P Niven, *hld up, hdwy aftr 5th, ev ch after 3 out, sn rdn, wknd*................ (7 to 4 fav op 6 to 4) 4
EMERALD VENTURE [68] 10-11-2 J F Titley, *hld up, pushed alng aftr 6th, styd on one pace frm 3 out.* .... (12 to 1 op 6 to 1 tchd 14 to 1) 5
2255 STONE ISLAND [80] 4-10-11 (7*) Mr R Wakley, *chsd ldrs, pushed alng aftr 4 out, sn wknd*....... (16 to 1 op 14 to 1) 6
2515[3] DR DAVE (Ire) [67] 6-11-1 B Fenton, *hld up, rapid hdwy to ld aftr 3rd, hdd after 3 out, wknd quickly.* ....(9 to 2 op 6 to 1 tchd 7 to 2) 7
389 WORDY'S WIND [67] 8-10-8 (7*) C Rae, *hld up, drvn alng and lost tch aftr 6th*..................... (20 to 1 op 14 to 1) 8
2610[2] SUMMER VILLA [67] (bl) 5-11-1 J Ryan, *hld up, chsd ldrs frm 5th, wknd aftr 3 out*...... (11 to 2 op 6 to 1 tchd 7 to 1) 9
891 POCONO KNIGHT [64] 7-10-12 J A McCarthy, *chsd ldrs to 4th, pushed alng aftr nxt, mstks four out, btn whn f 2 out.* ....(20 to 1 op 16 to 1 tchd 25 to 1) f
Dist: 3l, 3l, 11l, 6l, 4l, 1½l, 1¾l, 5l. 3m 56.30s. a 12.30s (10 Ran).
(Mrs A Emanuel), Mrs L C Jewell

2677 Prince Carlton Handicap Chase Class F (0-100 5-y-o and up) £4,036 3m 110yds.................... (2:20)

2459 ARTIC WINGS (Ire) [100] 9-12-0 M Brennan, *hld up, hdwy aftr 12th, ev ch after 6 out, led 3 out, sn clr.* .... (11 to 2 op 9 to 2 tchd 6 to 1) 1
2478[3] WHIPPERS DELIGHT (Ire) [92] 9-10-13 (7*) X Aizpuru, *led to 5th, led ag'n nxt til 5 out, rdn and styd on one pace frm 3 out.* ....(7 to 1 op 5 to 1) 2
2268[5] DARREN THE BRAVE [100] 9-12-0 G Bradley, *trkd ldrs, lost pl aftr 12th, rdn and styd on after 4 out, not trble 1st 2.* .... (100 to 30 fav op 9 to 4 tchd 7 to 2) 3
1734[2] WIXOE WONDER (Ire) [79] 7-10-7 P Holley, *hld up, hdwy 11th, led 5 out to 3 out, sn rdn and wknd.* .... (6 to 1 tchd 13 to 2 and 11 to 2) 4
2395[2] GOOD FOR A LAUGH [82] 13-10-3 (7*) Mr G Shenkin, *hld up in tch, wknd and pushed alng aftr 13th, no ch whn mstk 4 out.* ....(9 to 2 op 4 to 1 tchd 5 to 1) 5
2434 GLEN MIRAGE [90] 12-11-4 Miss M Coombe, *hld up, lost tch aftr 11th, tld off after nxt.* (11 to 1 op 8 to 1 tchd 12 to 1) 6
2495 CALL ME EARLY [89] 12-11-3 I Lawrence, *hld up, hdwy 11th, lost tch aftr 13th, tld off.* (33 to 1 op 20 to 1 tchd 40 to 1) 7
2482[4] VICTORY GATE (USA) [72] 12-10-0 D Leahy, *hld up, tld off aftr tenth*................ (40 to 1 op 33 to 1 tchd 50 to 1) 8
2393[5] MR INVADER [90] (bl) 10-11-4 W Marston, *trkd ldr, led 5th to nxt, tracked ldr, jmpd slwly 9th, drvn alng aftr 11th, sn lost tch, tld off 4 out*..................(5 to 1 tchd 6 to 1) 9
Dist: 7l, 19l, 12l, 1½l, 1½l, 10l, 11l, 17l. 6m 20.10s. a 23.10s (9 Ran).
(Lady Anne Bentinck), O Brennan

2678 European Breeders Fund 'National Hunt' Novices' Hurdle Qualifier Class D (5,6,7-y-o) £2,700 2½m .... (2:55)

2260[2] PEACE LORD (Ire) 7-11-0 J F Titley, *dsptd ld til definite advantage 4 out, styd on wl*.......... (7 to 4 tchd 2 to 1) 1
2277[2] CLINTON (Ire) 6-11-0 C O'Dwyer, *hld up, hdwy aftr 7th, chsd ldr frm nxt, ev ch 3 out, rdn and not quicken appr last.* .... (6 to 4 fav op Evens) 2
1556[6] SUPER RAPIER (Ire) 5-11-0 B Fenton, *chsd ldg pair, drvn alng aftr 6th, kpt on one pace frm 3 out.* (14 to 1 op 8 to 1) 3
2456[5] ARCTIC TRIUMPH 6-11-0 P Holley, *chsd ldg pair, pushed alng frm 5 out, styd on one pace from nxt.* .... (14 to 1 op 8 to 1) 4
2199 HOLKHAM BAY 5-11-0 J Ryan, *hld up, tld off aftr 4th.* .... (33 to 1 op 20 to 1 tchd 40 to 1) 5
2192[8] APRIL SEVENTH (Ire) 6-11-0 W Marston, *tld off, dsptd ld till 4 out, sn rdn and wknd quickly.* ....(9 to 2 op 8 to 1 tchd 4 to 1) 6
73 CLASHAWAN (Ire) 7-10-9 M Brennan, *hld up, tld off aftr 5th, pld up after 7th,*....... (25 to 1 op 16 to 1 tchd 33 to 1) pu
2409[5] THE LADY CAPTAIN 5-10-9 K Gaule, *hld up, hdwy 5th, wknd aftr 7th, tld off whn pld up bef last.* ....(14 to 1 op 12 to 1 tchd 20 to 1 and 25 to 1) pu
Dist: 5l, 23l, 2½l, 23l, 5l. 4m 55.90s. a 14.90s (8 Ran).
(Sir Peter & Lady Gibbings), Mrs D Haine

2679 Bet With The Tote Novices' Chase Qualifier Class D (6-y-o and up) £3,378 3m 110yds............(3:30)

2399[4] FLIPPANCE 7-10-10 W Marston, *trkd ldrs, lft in ld 12th, sn hdd, chsd leader frm nxt, second whn mstks 3 out and next, led appr last, soon clr.* ....(5 to 4 on op 2 to 1 on tchd Evens) 1
2354[9] ROLLESTON BLADE 10-10-3 (7*) Mr P O'Keeffe, *blun badly and rdr lost irons 1st, hdwy tenth, led aftr 12th, til hdd appr last, one pace.* ....(8 to 1 op 10 to 1 tchd 12 to 1 and 7 to 1) 2
2399[8] CHARTER LANE (Ire) 7-10-10 D Leahy, *hld up, hdwy tenth, chsd ldg pair frm 4 out, kpt on one pace.* .... (40 to 1 op 25 to 1 tchd 50 to 1) 3
2406 MILWAUKEE (Ire) 8-10-5 M Brennan, *hld up beh, hdwy aftr 14th, sn wknd*.......................(12 to 1 op 8 to 1) 4
1937 JOKER JACK 12-10-7 (3*) T Dascombe, *led til hdd 8th, sn pushed alng, no ch whn mstk 13th, tld off.* ....(25 to 1 op 16 to 1) 5
SHARROW BAY (NZ) 10-10-10 R Greene, *in tch whn f 3rd.* ....(11 to 1 op 16 to 1 tchd 20 to 1 and 10 to 1) f
1740[5] MERILENA (Ire) 7-10-5 B Fenton, *al prmnt, led 8th til f 12th.* ....(3 to 1 tchd 5 to 2 and 10 to 3) f
Dist: 8l, 15l, 1¼l, 3l. 6m 27.70s. a 30.70s (7 Ran).
(Exors Of The Late Mr C L Rykens), N A Gaselee

2680 Walter Wales Memorial Cup Hunters' Chase Class H (5-y-o and up) £2,566 2m 5f 110yds.................(4:05)

2468* CAB ON TARGET 11-11-10 Mr S Swiers, *hld up, mstk 6th, hdwy 8th, wnt 3rd tenth, trkd ldr 4 out, rdn to ld nr finish.* ....(6 to 4 on op 5 to 2 on tchd 11 to 8 on) 1
ARISE (Ire) 8-11-3 (7*) Mr E James, *hld up, chsd ldrs 11th, led 4 out, rdn 2 out, hdd nr finish* .... (40 to 1 op 25 to 1 tchd 50 to 1) 2
2556 PRO BONO (Ire) 7-11-3 (7*) Mr A Dalton, *lft in ld 8th, hdd 4 out, styd on one pace*.........(8 to 1 op 7 to 1 tchd 9 to 1) 3
JUST JACK 11-11-3 (7*) Mr R Wakley, *chsd ldrs frm tenth til wknd aftr 5 out*........(16 to 1 op 20 to 1 tchd 25 to 1) 4
2556 IDIOTIC 9-11-5 (5*) Mr C Vigors, *lost tch aftr 11th, sn beh.* .... (3 to 1 op 5 to 1 tchd 11 to 4) 5
EMSEE-H 12-11-5 (5*) Mr A Sansome, *hld up, tld off aftr 12th.* .... (25 to 1 op 16 to 1 tchd 40 to 1) 6
ICARUS (USA) (bl) 11-11-3 (7*) Mr A Rebori, *chsd clr ldr, lft second tenth, f nxt, dead.* .... (33 to 1 op 25 to 1 tchd 40 to 1) f
NO MORE TRIX 11-11-3 (7*) Mr W Burnell, *in tch whn blun and uns rdr 4th*........ (25 to 1 op 20 to 1 tchd 33 to 1) ur
1264[4] PRINZAL 10-11-3 (7*) Mr M Emmanuel, *mstks, led, clr aftr 4th, blun and uns rdr 8th*............... (9 to 1 op 8 to 1) ur
SPARTAN SILVER 11-11-5[2] (7*) Mr N Bloom, *prmnt to 5th, tld off 8th, pld up bef tenth*............. (20 to 1 op 25 to 1) pu
Dist: 1¼l, 11l, 18l, ½l, dist. 5m 30.20s. a 18.20s (10 Ran).
(N Hurst), Mrs M Reveley

2681 Cromer Handicap Hurdle Class E (0-115 4-y-o and up) £2,988 2m .... (4:40)

2629[2] KINTAVI [90] 7-10-7 P Niven, *hld up, trkd ldrs aftr 5th, led 3 out, sn wl clr, hit last, eased finish.* .... (13 to 8 fav op 7 to 4 tchd 2 to 1 and 6 to 4) 1
2407[9] AJDAR [83] 6-10-0 M Brennan, *hld up in last pl, hdwy aftr 4 out, styd on to take second place after 2 out, no ch wth wnr.* ....(16 to 1 tchd 20 to 1) 2
1925[2] LORD MCMURROUGH (Ire) [111] 7-11-11 (3*) T Dascombe, *chsd clr ldr, drvn alng aftr 4 out, sn no imprsn.* ....(7 to 2 op 2 to 1 tchd 4 to 1) 3
IRISH EMERALD [87] 10-10-4 K Gaule, *chsd clr ldr, led 4 out to nxt, sn rdn, wknd quickly.* (5 to 1 op 6 to 1 tchd 9 to 2) 4
1807[3] MENELAVE (Ire) [107] 7-11-10 J A McCarthy, *chsd clr ldr to 5th, sn lost pl*............ (9 to 2 op 3 to 1 tchd 5 to 1) 5
2400[5] THEFIELDSOFATHENRY (Ire) [105] 7-11-1 (7*) M Berry, *led, sn wl clr, hdd 6th, rdn and wknd rpdly, tld off aftr 3 out.* ....(5 to 1 op 4 to 1 tchd 6 to 1) 6
Dist: 10l, 2l, 24l, 2½l, 30l. 3m 51.30s. a 7.30s (6 Ran).
SR: 14/-/23/ (S Taberner), T W Donnelly

NEWCASTLE (good)
Friday February 14th
Going Correction: PLUS 1.00 sec. per fur. (races 1,3,6), PLUS 0.70 (2,4,5)

2682 Northern Racing Handicap Hurdle Class E (0-115 4-y-o and up) £2,284

2602[2] SAMANID (Ire) [99] 5-11-3 O Pears, *hld up in tch, steady hdwy aftr 4 out, led on bit appr 2 out, quickened clr last.* .... (100 to 30 op 7 to 2 tchd 4 to 1) 1
2407[2] DANBYS GORSE [90] 5-10-5 (3*) E Callaghan, *hld up, gd hdwy to join ldrs 4 out, led nxt, hdd and one pace appr 2 out.* .... (5 to 2 fav) 2
2204 BEND SABLE (Ire) [109] 7-11-13 B Storey, *trkd ldrs till hit 3rd and lost pl, hdwy aftr 4 out, pushed alng nxt and sn no imprsn.* .... (3 to 1 op 5 to 2 tchd 100 to 30) 3
1983[2] ELASTIC [93] 11-10-11 L O'Hara, *led, rdn alng 4 out, hdd nxt, sn one pace*.................... (8 to 1 op 7 to 1) 4
2238[6] ELATION [110] 5-12-0 A Dobbin, *chsd ldrs till pushed alng and lost pl bef 4 out, styd on frm 2 out, nvr dngrs.* .... (16 to 1 op 14 to 1 tchd 20 to 1) 5
2485 SKIDDAW SAMBA [84] 8-9-13 (3*) G Lee, *in tch, hdwy 4th, rdn alng four out and wknd aftr nxt.* .... (14 to 1 op 12 to 1 tchd 16 to 1) 6
2316[7] FOX SPARROW [105] 7-11-9 A S Smith, *chsd ldr, rdn 4 out, sn wknd*.................... (20 to 1 tchd 25 to 1) 7
2316[6] ALL CLEAR (Ire) [86] 6-10-4 P Carberry, *hld up, hdwy to join ldrs 4th, rdn and wknd four out, beh whn blun nxt.* .... (14 to 1 op 12 to 1 tchd 16 to 1) 8

Dist: 9l, 3½l, 6l, 1½l, 13l, 2l, dist. 4m 2.70s. a 25.70s (8 Ran).

(Magnum Construction Ltd), Miss L C Siddall

2683 Border Minstrel Sunday Lunch Novices' Chase Class D (5-y-o and up) £3,533 2½m..................(2:40)

2495[3] BOLD ACCOUNT (Ire) (bl) 7-11-3 A Dobbin, *chsd ldr, led 7th, rdn appr last, hld on gmely nr finish*..... (3 to 1 op 7 to 1) 1
2569[3] COQUI LANE 10-11-3 T Reed, *mstks, led till jmpd badly rght 7th, cl up, rdn alng 4 out, drvn last, styd on wl flt, jst fld.* .... (7 to 4 jt-fav op 5 to 4) 2
2205[3] KILTULLA (Ire) 7-11-3 Richard Guest, *al prmnt, chsd wnr frm 11th, rdn alng 3 out, kpt on one pace from nxt.* .... (16 to 1 op 20 to 1 tchd 25 to 1) 3
2569[4] LE DENSTAN 10-11-8 D Parker, *in tch, effrt and rdn alng 5 out, no imprsn*.................... (33 to 1 op 20 to 1) 4
2486[5] ROBARA 7-11-3 N Leach, *hit 1st, sn chasing ldrs, hit 11th and soon rdn alng, wknd aftr 4 out*.................... (100 to 1) 5
2484 ARISTODEMUS 8-11-3 K Johnson, *prmnt till hit 7th and nxt, blun badly 9th and sn beh*.................... (150 to 1 op 100 to 1) 6
2237 DARK BUOY 8-11-3 B Storey, *hld up, effrt and some hdwy 8th, rdn alng and beh frm 11th pld up bef 3 out.* .... (33 to 1 op 16 to 1) 0
REAL TONIC 7-11-3 P Carberry, *pld hrd, prmnt whn f 5th.* .... (7 to 4 jt-fav op 11 to 8) f
2576[4] COOLRENY (Ire) 8-11-3 Mr M Thompson, *al rear, pld up bef 8th, broke leg, dead*.................... (150 to 1 op 100 to 1) pu

Dist: Nk, 6l, 11l, 5l, 14l. 5m 17.00s. a 30.00s (9 Ran).

(John Robson), G M Moore

2684 Hennessy Cognac Special Series Novices' Hurdle Class B (4-y-o and up) £6,148 2m................(3:15)

2192* ALZULU (Ire) 6-11-7 A Dobbin, *cl up, led 3rd, quickened clr aftr 3 out, pushed out.* (13 to 8 fav op 6 to 4 tchd 7 to 4) 1
2405[2] DANA POINT (Ire) 5-11-3 Richard Guest, *trkd ldrs, effrt appr 3 out, rdn bef nxt, kpt on wl und pres flt.* .... (9 to 4 op 2 to 1 tchd 5 to 2) 2
2006[2] GOOD VIBES 5-11-7 R Garritty, *trkd ldrs, chsd wnr frm 5th, rdn alng 3 out and sn one pace*.................... (7 to 4 op 6 to 4) 3
2490[2] CATHERINE'S CHOICE 4-10-7 Mr C Bonner, *in tch, effrt 4 out, sn rdn and no imprsn*.................... (33 to 1 op 25 to 1) 4
2489[3] MENALDI (Ire) 7-11-3 A S Smith, *led to 3rd, cl up till mstk and wknd 4 out*.................... (50 to 1 op 33 to 1) 5
JUNGLE FRESH 4-10-7 T Reed, *al beh, tld off whn pld up bef 3 out*.................... (200 to 1) pu

Dist: 5l, 14l, 7l, dist. 3m 57.90s. a 20.90s (6 Ran).

SR: 44/35/25/4/-/-/ (D Buckle), J G FitzGerald

2685 New Champagne & Seafood Restaurant Handicap Chase Class D (0-125 5-y-o and up) £3,412 2m 110yds ....(3:50)

2537[4] DUAL IMAGE [103] 10-11-5 R Garritty, *trkd ldrs, hit 6th, slow nxt and not fluent 8th, hdwy 3 out, led last, rdn out.* (6 to 4 jt-fav op 5 to 4 tchd 13 to 8 and 7 to 4) 1
2495[6] REBEL KING [88] 7-10-4 B Storey, *led to 3rd, cl up till led 8th, rdn alng 3 out, hdd last, kpt on und pres.* .... (11 to 2 op 7 to 2 tchd 7 to 1) 2
2203 POTATO MAN [95] (v) 11-10-11 A Dobbin, *cl up, led 3rd to 8th, sn rdn and wknd 2 out.* .... (9 to 1 op 6 to 1 tchd 10 to 1 and 11 to 1) 3
2493 MONNAIE FORTE (Ire) [90] 7-10-6 M Moloney, *trkd ldrs, hdwy 7th, chalg whn f 4 out*.................... (6 to 4 jt-fav op 5 to 4) f

Dist: 2l, 18l. 4m 17.60s. a 18.60s (4 Ran).

SR: 20/3/-/-/ (Datum Building Supplies Limited), J G FitzGerald

2686 St Modwen Novices' Chase Class D (5-y-o and up) £3,680 3m..... (4:20)

2534[2] ASK ME LATER (Ire) 8-11-4 M Foster, *trkd ldrs, hdwy tenth, led 2 out, sn rdn, ran on wl.* .... (11 to 2 op 5 to 1 tchd 6 to 1) 1
1771[3] RIVER UNSHION (Ire) 7-11-4 Richard Guest, *al prmnt, effrt 4 out and ev ch till cl second, rdn and blun last, not reco'r.* .... (11 to 10 on op 6 to 4) 2
2534[6] MAJORITY MAJOR (Ire) 8-11-9 A S Smith, *hld up and beh, steady hdwy whn hit 11th, rdn alng 4 out, kpt on same pace.* .... (16 to 1 op 7 to 1 tchd 20 to 1) 3
2187[4] CULLANE LAKE (Ire) 7-10-13 R Supple, *led, rdn alng and blun 12th, hdd and wknd 2 out.* .... (8 to 1 op 6 to 1 tchd 10 to 1) 4
2484[2] PANTARA PRINCE (Ire) 8-11-4 A Dobbin, *hld up, hdwy and hit tenth, mstk nxt, effrt to join ldrs 5 out, rdn appr 3 out and sn btn*.................... (9 to 2 op 7 to 2 tchd 5 to 1) 5
2347[4] GARBO'S BOY 7-11-9 K Johnson, *prmnt, blun 7th, pushed alng and outpcd 12th, staying on whn blunded 3 out, sn wknd.* .... (10 to 1 op 7 to 1) 6
2362[4] KALAJO 7-11-4 B Storey, *hld up, hdwy 11th, chsd ldrs whn blun badly 13th, beh aftr*.................... (33 to 1 op 12 to 1) 7
OYKEL RIVER (Ire) 9-11-4 J Supple, *prmnt till reminders 7th, beh frm nxt and sn tld off*.................... (100 to 1 op 25 to 1) 8
1913[6] DISTILLERY HILL (Ire) 9-11-4 Mr M Thompson, *al rear, tld off whn pld up bef 3 out*.. (66 to 1 op 33 to 1 tchd 100 to 1) pu
2406[7] ROYAL PARIS (Ire) 9-11-4 T Reed, *chsd leaders, rdn alng and wknd 12th, tld off whn pld up bef 3 out*........ (25 to 1) pu

Dist: 12l, 9l, ¾l, 8l, 3l, 9l, dist. 6m 9.30s. a 23.30s (10 Ran).

SR: 25/13/9/-/-/-/ (Timothy Hardie), Mrs S C Bradburne

2687 Be My Valentine Standard Open National Hunt Flat Class H (4,5,6-y-o) £1,402 2m............... (4:55)

1514[5] MAC'S SUPREME (Ire) 5-11-1 (3*) Michael Brennan, *trkd ldrs, hdwy o'r 5 fs out, led 3 out, rdn appr last and styd on wl.* .... (3 to 1 fav op 4 to 1 tchd 9 to 2) 1
2213[3] INTO THE BLACK (Ire) 6-11-4 G Cahill, *hld up and beh, steady hdwy o'r 6 fs out, effrt 4 out, rdn to chase wnr appr last, kpt on.* .... (8 to 1 op 6 to 1) 2
2469[7] THUNDERPOINT (Ire) 5-11-4 R Garritty, *hld up in mid-div, hdwy o'r 6 fs out, chsd wnr 3 out, sn rdn and kpt on one pace.* .... (9 to 1 op 8 to 1 tchd 10 to 1) 3
2469[3] GENEROUS STREAK (Fr) 4-10-5 (3*) E Callaghan, *hld up in mid-div, hdwy 6 fs out, rdn fnl 2 and staying on in 3rd whn rdr drpd hands nr finish*...... (6 to 1 op 4 to 1 tchd 7 to 1) 4
MAJOR HAGE (Ire) 6-11-4 Richard Guest, *chsd ldrs, hdwy o'r 6 fs out, ev ch over 3 out, sn rdn and wknd fnl 2.* .... (11 to 2 op 10 to 1) 5
MISS MONEYPENNY 5-10-6 (7*) R Burns, *hld up and beh, steady hdwy hfwy, chsd ldrs o'r 4 fs out, sn rdn and btn 3 out.* .... (100 to 1) 6
LORD KNOWS (Ire) 6-11-4 K Johnson, *prmnt on outer, effrt and ev ch 4 fs out, rdn and btn 3 out*... (16 to 1 op 20 to 1) 7
2363[7] SUNRISE SENSATION 4-10-8 K Jones, *hld up, steady hdwy hfwy, chsd ldrs 4 fs out, rdn 3 out and sn wknd*..... (20 to 1) 8
2302[4] JACK ROBBO (Ire) 5-11-1 (3*) G Lee, *trkd ldrs, pushed alng hfwy, sn lost pl and beh fnl 4 fs*.......... (5 to 1 op 5 to 2) 9
2496[2] ONE STOP 4-10-3 B Storey, *prmnt, led 7 fs out, rdn 4 out, sn hdd and wknd*.......... (6 to 1 op 4 to 1 tchd 13 to 2) 10
LORD OF THE RINGS 5-10-11 (7*) Mr T J Barry, *mid-div, rdn alng hfwy and grad wknd*.................... (33 to 1) 11
HOLLOW PALM (Ire) 6-11-4 R Supple, *hld up in rear, beh frm hfwy*.................... (33 to 1 op 25 to 1) 12
ALLFORUS (Ire) 5-10-13 T Reed, *in tch till rdn alng hfwy and grad wknd*.................... (100 to 1 op 33 to 1) 13
2469 SHANNON SHOON (Ire) 5-10-13 (5*) G F Ryan, *led and clr, hdd and wknd 7 fs out, sn beh*.................... (33 to 1) 14
2206 JO LIGHTNING (Ire) 4-10-8 Mr R Hale, *prmnt till rdn alng 6 fs out and sn wknd*.................... (200 to 1 op 100 to 1) 15
POLITICAL MANDATE 4-10-3 A Dobbin, *beh frm hfwy.* .... (20 to 1 tchd 25 to 1) 16
ROMALDKIRK 5-11-4 Mr M Thompson, *mid-div till lost pl and beh frm hfwy*.................... (200 to 1 op 100 to 1) 17
MICHANDRA BOY 4-10-8 A S Smith, *al beh.* .... (20 to 1 op 14 to 1) 18

Dist: 2l, 3½l, hd, 14l, ½l, 2½l, ½l, 3½l, nk, 2l. 3m 58.10s. (18 Ran).

(B McEntaggart), F Murphy

SANDOWN (good)
Friday February 14th
Going Correction: PLUS 0.80 sec. per fur.

2688 Fox 'National Hunt' Novices' Hurdle Class D (5-y-o and up) £3,035 2m 110yds........................(1:30)

1641[2] QUEEN OF SPADES (Ire) 7-11-4 C Llewellyn, *made all, clr 3rd, unchlgd*...... (15 to 8 fav op 11 to 10 tchd 2 to 1) 1
2264[5] LIVELY ENCOUNTER (Ire) 6-11-0 Derek Byrne, *jmpd slwly 1st, mstk and beh 3rd, styd on frm 2 out, took second r-in, no ch wth wnr*.......... (20 to 1 op 14 to 1 tchd 25 to 1) 2
2264* SPLENDID THYNE 5-11-4 R Dunwoody, *hdwy 3 out, styd on frm nxt, one pace r-in.* .... (100 to 30 op 3 to 1 tchd 7 to 2 and 5 to 2) 3

STAR MYSTERY 6-11-0 J Osborne, *chsd wnr till rdn and no extr r-in*...............(13 to 2 op 6 to 1 tchd 7 to 1) 4
FATHER HENRY (Ire) 6-11-0 M A Fitzgerald, *chsd ldrs till blun 4th, styd on to dispute second frm 2 out till blunded and wknd last*...............(12 to 1 op 8 to 1 tchd 14 to 1) 5
2528⁷ THIRTY BELOW (Ire) 8-11-0 S McNeill, *al rear.*
....(50 to 1 op 33 to 1) 6
1483⁷ CHARLIE BANKER (Ire) 5-11-0 A Larnach, *mstk second, nvr better than mid-div, tld off*...........(33 to 1 tchd 50 to 1) 7
2264⁴ DARK ORCHARD (Ire) 6-11-0 M Richards, *sn in tch, rdn appr 2 out, soon wknd, tld off.* (14 to 1 op 12 to 1 tchd 16 to 1) 8
1975⁹ BELVENTO (Ire) 5-10-11 (3*) L Aspell, *prmnt, hit 4th, wknd nxt, tld off.*.......................(33 to 1 op 16 to 1) 9
MAENAD 6-10-9 B Powell, *sn beh, tld off whn pld up bef 2 out.*
.......................(50 to 1 op 33 to 1 tchd 66 to 1) pu
1338² TOWER STREET 6-11-0 P Hide, *prmnt, rdn to stay 3rd whn pld up bend appr 2 out, lme.*.........(4 to 1 op 7 to 2) pu
Dist: 6l, 3l, 3l, 5l, 18l, dist, 7l, 8l. 4m 5.90s. a 18.90s (11 Ran).
SR: 33/23/24/17/12/-/   (Mrs R Vaughan), N A Twiston-Davies

2689 Sabrina Goodwill 'I Love You Always' Handicap Chase Class B (0-145 5-y-o and up) £6,350 2m.........(2:00)

2555* MISTER ODDY [133] 11-11-8 (3*,5ex) D Fortt, *pressed ldr, lft ld in 4th, pushed clr frm 3 out*...........(7 to 2 op 11 to 4) 1
2335* LORD DORCET (Ire) [136] 7-12-0 R Johnson, *lft second 4th, pressed wnr 8th to tenth, one pace frm 3 out.*
.........................(8 to 1 op 11 to 4 tchd 7 to 2) 2
2555⁴ THUMBS UP [127] 11-11-5 R Dunwoody, *rcd in 3rd, lost tch 5th, rallied to chase ldrs 9th, sn outpcd.*
.........................(16 to 1 op 12 to 1 tchd 20 to 1) 3
2455* CERTAINLY STRONG (Ire) [134] 7-11-12 A Maguire, *led till f 4th.*.........................(11 to 8 on tchd 11 to 10 on) f
Dist: 13l, 4l. 4m 6.70s. a 17.70s (4 Ran).
SR: 48/38/25/-/   (Mrs R M Hill), J S King

2690 Badger Novices' Chase Class D (5-y-o and up) £3,420 2½m 110yds
....(2:35)

2408² ARFER MOLE (Ire) 9-11-7 J Osborne, *hld up, drvn and hdwy appr 3 out, sn chalg, led 2 out, ran on wl.*
....(Evens fav tchd 11 to 10) 1
2438⁷ EULOGY (Ire) 7-11-3 R Dunwoody, *in tch, lost poo 9th, ran on appr 3 out, chlgd last, one pace.*
.........................(8 to 1 op 7 to 1 tchd 10 to 1) 2
2311⁴ THE CAPTAIN'S WISH 6-11-3 A Maguire, *in tch, hit second 12th, rdn and not much room bend aftr 3 out, ev ch last, sn one pace.*.........................(4 to 1 tchd 5 to 1) 3
2266⁶ JULEIT JONES (Ire) 8-10-9 (3*) L Aspell, *led, clr 5th, rdn 3 out, hdd nxt, wknd last.*.....(33 to 1 op 14 to 1 tchd 40 to 1) 4
2406⁵ SAFEGLIDE (Ire) 7-11-3 P Hide, *not fluent, al beh, lost tch frm tenth.*.................(12 to 1 op 8 to 1 tchd 14 to 1) 5
2254* SLINGSBY 7-11-10 A Thornton, *chsd ldrs till f 6th, destroyed.*.................(9 to 2 op 3 to 1 tchd 5 to 1) f
2373² RED BRANCH 8-11-3 T J Murphy, *chsd ldr till rdn, blun and uns rdr 12th.*.......(25 to 1 op 16 to 1 tchd 33 to 1) ur
Dist: 2l, hd, 12l, 12l. 5m 24.40s. a 24.40s (7 Ran).
SR: 12/6/6/-/   (W E Sturt), J A B Old

2691 Scottish Equitable/Jockeys Association Series Handicap Hurdle Qualifier Class D (0-120 4-y-o and up) £3,615 2¾m.........(3:10)

2246⁷ OATIS ROSE [96] 7-10-7 A Maguire, *led 3rd, styd wth ldr, led 3 out, rdn in, rallied gmely und pres to ld last strd.*
.........................(10 to 1 op 8 to 1) 1
2013⁴ DANTES CAVALIER (Ire) [105] 7-11-2 R Dunwoody, *hld up, steady hdwy appr 2 out, sn chalg, led r-in, hrd rdn, ct last strd.*
.........................(2 to 1 fav op 7 to 4 tchd 9 to 4) 2
1795² JACKSON FLINT [90] 9-10-1 J Culloty, *hld up, hdwy 7th, outpcd 3 out, gd headway nxt, styd on same pace r-in.*
.........................(10 to 1 op 7 to 1 tchd 11 to 1) 3
1858* ROSIE-B [89] 7-10-0 N Williamson, *led to 3rd, styd wth wnr, led 8th to 3 out, wknd aftr nxt.*
....(3 to 1 op 7 to 2 tchd 4 to 1) 4
1663⁶ KILMINGTON (Ire) [106] 8-11-3 P Hide, *chsd ldrs, rdn and one pace frm 2 out.*.........(7 to 1 op 5 to 1 tchd 15 to 2) 5
2389 DARK HONEY [104] 12-11-1 A Dicken, *in tch, drpd rear 6th, no dngr aftr.*.................(12 to 1 tchd 14 to 1) 6
2253⁴ CASSIO'S BOY [90] 6-10-1 R Johnson, *in tch 4th, pressed ldrs aftr 3 out, wknd quickly nxt.*
.........................(13 to 2 op 8 to 1 tchd 9 to 1) 7
2427 BRAES OF MAR [113] 7-11-10 M A Fitzgerald, *hdwy to track ldrs 6th, wknd aftr nxt.*.........(20 to 1 op 12 to 1) 8
Dist: Sht-hd, 14l, hd, ½l, 16l, ½l, 5l. 5m 31.90s. a 28.90s (8 Ran).
(Mrs John Redvers), M Sheppard

2692 Stag Handicap Chase Class B (0-145 5-y-o and up) £6,469 3m 110yds
....(3:45)

2437⁵ DENVER BAY [115] 10-10-0 (3*) L Aspell, *in tch, quickened to track ldr 14th, led nxt, rdn and hld on gmely r-in.*
.........................(100 to 30 op 4 to 1 tchd 9 to 2) 1

2325³ HILL OF TULLOW (Ire) [134] (bl) 8-11-8 A Maguire, *hld up, hdwy to cl on ldrs 11th, not fluent 18th, styd on to chal r-in, rdn and not go by.........* (2 to 1 fav op 9 to 4 tchd 5 to 2) 2
SUPERIOR FINISH [140] 11-12-0 R Farrant, *pressed ldrs 8th, led 9th to nxt, lost pl 16th, styd on und pres r-in.*
.........................(10 to 1 op 6 to 1 tchd 11 to 1) 3
2452* DEXTRA DOVE [140] 10-12-0 C Maude, *slight ld to 4th, led tenth to 15th, wknd aftr 3 out.*
.........................(9 to 4 op 6 to 4 tchd 5 to 2) 4
SIBTON ABBEY [138] (v) 12-11-12 A Thornton, *chlgd 6th to nxt, rdn 11th, rallied to chal next, wknd appr 3 out.*
.........................(7 to 1 op 5 to 1) 5
JAMES PIGG [130] 10-11-4 D Bridgwater, *wth ldr, led 4th to 9th, hit 12th, wknd nxt, tld off.*...........(10 to 1 op 7 to 1) 6
Dist: Hd, 23l, 1½l, 8l, dist. 6m 32.50s. a 33.50s (6 Ran).
(Bill Naylor), J T Gifford

2693 Cat & Mouse Claiming Hurdle Class F (5-y-o and up) £2,262 2m 110yds
....(4:15)

2453 EXPRESS GIFT 8-11-10 R Dunwoody, *hld up in tch, trkd ldr 5th, led 2 out, easily.*
.........................(11 to 4 on op 3 to 1 on tchd 5 to 2 on) 1
DANCE KING 5-11-2 V Smith, *hdwy 3 out, styd on to take second and hld last, one pace.*
.........................(12 to 1 op 10 to 1 tchd 14 to 1) 2
2462⁵ PEDALTOTHEMETAL (Ire) 5-10-7 G Tormey, *chsd ldr to 5th, hrd rdn 2 out, styd on und pres.*
.........................(12 to 1 op 12 to 1 tchd 16 to 1) 3
2509⁶ BLAZE OF SONG 5-11-7 C Llewellyn, *led, sn clr, hdd 2 out, wknd last.*.................(25 to 1 op 16 to 1 tchd 33 to 1) 4
1894² STONEY VALLEY 7-10-9 N Williamson, *al beh, rdn and lost tch 2 out.*.........(7 to 2 op 3 to 1 tchd 4 to 1) 5
MICKY BROWN 6-10-12 W McFarland, *al beh, tld off whn mstk 4th.*.........................(66 to 1 op 50 to 1) 6
Dist: 6l, hd, 1½l, 19l, dist. 4m 12.50s. 45m 12.70s. a 25.70s (6 Ran).
(M W Horner, H Young, And D S Arnold), Mrs M Reveley

2694 Otter Standard Open National Hunt Flat Class H (4,5,6-y-o) £1,448 2m 110yds.........(4:50)

DAWN LEADER (Ire) 6-11-10 G Upton, *hld up rear, keen hold, steady hdwy to track ldrs 5 fs out, led o'r 3 out, sn clr, sn very easily.*.........(7 to 4 fav op 5 to 1 tchd 6 to 4) 1
740³ DAMIEN'S CHOICE (Ire) 5-11-3 Derek Byrne, *beh, steady hdwy frm 4 fs out, chsd wnr from 2 out, no imprsn.*
.........................(14 to 1 op 12 to 1 tchd 33 to 1) 2
2179² SHEBANG (Ire) 5-10-10 (7*) Mr H Dunlop, *in tch, outpcd hfwy, hdwy 4 fs out, styd on frm 2 out.*
.........................(9 to 1 op 7 to 1 tchd 12 to 1) 3
1109² COUNTRYMAN (Ire) 6-11-3 R Dunwoody, *prmnt, pushed alng 7t fs out, styd on same pace frm 3 out...* (10 to 1 op 5 to 1) 4
1073⁸ LITTLE CRUMPLIN 5-11-3 J Osborne, *led aftr 4 fs till o'r 3 out, sn btn.*.........................(6 to 1 op 5 to 2) 5
ZEPHYRELLE (Ire) 5-10-12 N Williamson, *beh, drvn alng 3 fs out, styd on same pace.* (14 to 1 op 10 to 1 tchd 16 to 1) 6
1975⁵ SHORE PARTY 5-11-3 C Llewellyn, *chsd ldrs, outpcd aftr 6 fs, sn drvn to chase ldrs, wknd o'r 2 out.*
.........................(9 to 2 op 4 to 1 tchd 7 to 1 and 7 to 2) 7
2377⁸ STANMORE (Ire) 5-11-3 D Gallagher, *beh, hmpd 5 fs out, not a dngr.*.........(16 to 1 op 10 to 1 tchd 20 to 1) 8
CINNAMON CLUB 5-10-12 A Thornton, *nvr better than mid-div.*.........(20 to 1 op 12 to 1 tchd 25 to 1) 9
2483² GOWER-SLAVE 5-11-3 R Johnson, *prmnt 11 fs.*
.........................(25 to 1 op 10 to 1 tchd 33 to 1) 10
EDITORIAL 5-10-12 (3*) L Aspell, *nvr better than mid-div.*
....(33 to 1 op 20 to 1) 11
THE PHANTOM FARMER (Ire) 6-11-3 M A Fitzgerald, *beh whn hmpd 5 fs out, nvr dngrs.*.........(14 to 1 op 5 to 1) 12
THUNDERBIRD 5-10-12 M Richards, *al rear.*
.........................(50 to 1 op 20 to 1) 13
2377⁹ SHEET LIGHTNING 5-10-10 (7*) L Suthern, *led 4 fs, styd chasing ldr till wknd four out...*(66 to 1 op 25 to 1) 14
FIRE OPAL 5-11-3 J R Kavanagh, *beh hfwy.*
.........................(20 to 1 op 10 to 1 tchd 33 to 1) 15
2377⁵ MASTER PIP 5-11-3 S McNeill, *prmnt, chsd wnr 3 fs out till broke off-hind and pld up 2 out, destroyed.*
.........................(25 to 1 op 20 to 1 tchd 33 to 1) pu
Dist: 13l, 7l, 3l, 3½l, 1l, 4l, hd, 12l, 4l, 1½l. 4m 5.80s. (16 Ran).
(Bonusprint), J A B Old

CHEPSTOW (soft)
Saturday February 15th
Going Correction: PLUS 0.80 sec. per fur. (races 1,3,5,7), PLUS 1.10 (2,4,6)

2695 M & N Group Hurdle Class B Limited Handicap (4-y-o and up) £7,022 2½m 110yds.................(1:15)

2442⁵ BRAVE TORNADO [125] 6-10-12 B Fenton, *tracker ldrs, led appr 4 out, hrd drivven frm nxt, styd on gmely.*
.........................(8 to 1 op 7 to 1 tchd 10 to 1) 1

18777 MOORISH [135] 7-11-8 C Llewellyn, *hld up, rapid hdwy 4 out, pressed wnr frm 2 out, no extr und pres r-in.*
..............................(11 to 1 op 12 to 1 tchd 10 to 1) 2
1628* ANZUM [137] 6-11-10 R Johnson, *pushed alng to chase ldrs frm 4th, styd on und pres appr last, not pace to rch 1st 2 nr finish*.................(15 to 2 op 5 to 1 tchd 8 to 1) 3
1744* CADOUGOLD (Fr) [130] 6-11-3 R Dunwoody, *hld up, smooth hdwy 6th, pressed wnr frm 3 out, rdn appr last, sn one pace.*
..............................(11 to 10 fav op 6 to 4 tchd 13 to 8) 4
2591 DR LEUNT (Ire) [127] 6-11-0 G Tormey, *chsd ldrs, wknd frm 2 out*........................(12 to 1 op 10 to 1) 5
LYING EYES [123] 6-10-3 (7*) J Power, *chsd ldrs, offrd 3 out, wknd nxt*.......(20 to 1 op 33 to 1 tchd 40 to 1) 6
2442* KADASTROF (Fr) [134] 7-11-0 (7*) X Aizpuru, *led, sn clr, hdd appr 4 out, wknd nxt*...............(10 to 1 op 7 to 1) 7
21905 HOME COUNTIES (Ire) [139] 8-11-12 D J Moffatt, *al beh, lost tch frm 4 out*....................(16 to 1 op 12 to 1) 8
2329 THINKING TWICE (USA) [133] 8-11-6 R Farrant, *beh, lost tch and tld off frm 4 out*...............(12 to 1 op 8 to 1) 9
2591 STORM DAMAGE (Ire) [136] 5-11-9 D Bridgwater, *chsd ldrs till jmpd slwly and wknd 5th, tld off frm 4 out.*
..............................(12 to 1 tchd 14 to 1) 10
23135 SPARKLING CONE [118] 8-10-5 C Maude, *al beh, lost tch 4 out, tld off whn pld up bef 2 out.*
..............................(40 to 1 op 33 to 1 tchd 50 to 1) pu
2329 ABBEY STREET (Ire) [122] 5-10-9 J Osborne, *some hdwy appr 4 out, sn wknd, tld off whn pld up bef last, lme.*
..............................(16 to 1 op 12 to 1) pu
Dist: 1l, ¾l, 2l, nk, 8l, dist, 5l, 4l. 4m 58.40s. a 20.40s (12 Ran).
SR: 44/53/54/45/30/25/28/-/-/ (Miss B Swire), G B Balding

2696 Fledgling Chase Class B (6-y-o and up) £6,775 2m 3f 110yds......(1:45)

AIR SHOT 7-11-0 R Johnson, *trkd ldrs, quickened to ld 2 out, readily*....................(5 to 2 op 3 to 1) 1
2209 NAHTHEN LAD (Ire) 8-11-12 R Farrant, *led till hdd 12th, rallied gmely to ld ag'n 3 out, headed nxt, styd on und pres.*
..............................(100 to 30 op 5 to 2 tchd 4 to 1) 2
2437* BELLS LIFE (Ire) 8-11-3 G Tormey, *trkd ldrs, led 12th, hdd 3 out, chlgd and hit nxt,sn btn.*
..............................(13 to 8 fav op 11 to 8 tchd 7 to 4) 3
23116 MONTECOT (Fr) 8-11-3 B Fenton, *jmpd big 1st, wknd quickly 7th and sn tld off*......(7 to 1 op 6 to 1 tchd 8 to 1) 4
2514* COOLREE (Ire) (bl) 9-11-0 D Bridgwater, *wth ldr, reminder appr 5th, jmpd slwly and wknd nxt, tld off whn pld up bef 11th.*
..............................(14 to 1 op 12 to 1 tchd 16 to 1) pu
Dist: 6l, 9l, dist. 5m 8.70s. a 25.70s (5 Ran).
SR: 44/50/32/-/-/ (Mrs Peter Prowting), D Nicholson

2697 Colin Davies Persian War Premier Novices' Hurdle Class A Grade 2 (4-y-o and up) £9,735 2½m 110yds ....(2:15)

2323* BOARDROOM SHUFFLE (Ire) 6-11-6 P Hide, *hld up and confidently rdn, steady hdwy frm 3 out, quickened to chal last, sn led, pushed out*...(5 to 4 fav op 5 to 4 tchd 13 to 8) 1
23332 MIGHTY MOSS (Ire) 6-11-6 Mr F Hutsby, *trkd ldrs till led 5th, rdn frm 2 out, sprawled last and sn hdd, kpt on.*
..............................(9 to 2 op 4 to 1) 2
2499* MARCHING MARQUIS (Ire) 6-11-6 R Johnson, *prmnt, trkd leder frm 7th, chlgd 3 out, one pace from nxt.*
..............................(8 to 1 tchd 9 to 1 and 10 to 1) 3
2398* FIDDLING THE FACTS (Ire) 6-11-1 J Osborne, *hld up, hdwy 6th, chsd ldrs 4 out to nxt, wknd 2 out.* (11 to 1 op 10 to 1) 4
2570* LAGEN BRIDGE (Ire) 8-11-6 D J Moffatt, *hdwy 8th, styd on one pace frm 3 out*.......(20 to 1 tchd 25 to 1) 5
2374 HARBOUR ISLAND 5-11-6 R Dunwoody, *wth ldr till sn aftr 4th, jmpd slwly and hdd nxt, reminder, rdn 8th, wknd 3 out, tld off*..............(7 to 2 op 3 to 1 tchd 4 to 1) 6
21565 PARIS FASHION (Fr) 6-11-1 T Jenks, *led till aftr 4th, wknd 6th, tld off whn pld up aftr 7th*..........(25 to 1) pu
25534 SOLDAT (USA) 4-11-1 D Bridgwater, *al beh, tld off whn pld up bef 6th*..............(11 to 1 op 9 to 1) pu
Dist: 2½l, 5l, 3½l, 1l, dist. 5m 0.00s. a 22.00s (8 Ran).
SR: 36/33/28/19/23/ (A D Weller), J T Gifford

2698 Ashfields Farm Handicap Chase Class D (0-125 5-y-o and up) £3,715 3¼m 110yds ....(2:45)

2427* GIVENTIME [111] 9-11-0 L Harvey, *prmnt, hdwy 12th, hit 19th, chsd ldr appr 18th, chlgd last sn led, rdn out.*
..............................(4 to 1 fav tchd 7 to 2 and 9 to 2) 1
24012 ROCKY PARK [97] 11-10-0 B Fenton, *led till rdn and hit 2 out, hdd r-in, rallied but no extr nr finish...*(14 to 1 op 12 to 1) 2
2439 SPUFFINGTON [113] 9-11-2 P Hide, *prominet, chsd ldr 16th to 18th, styd same pace und pres frm 3 out.*
..............................(9 to 1 tchd 8 to 1) 3
19744 SPECIAL ACCOUNT [97] 11-10-12† (3*) P Henley, *hdwy 12th, styd on und pres frm 4 out*...............(20 to 1) 4
24277 DOM SAMOURAI (Fr) [113] (v) 6-11-2 B Powell, *chsd ldrs, drvn alng frm 11th, effrt ag'n appr 18th, wknd 4 out.*
..............................(20 to 1 op 14 to 1) 5
24273 PLASTIC SPACEAGE [115] 14-11-4 G Upton, *al beh.*
..............................(11 to 1 op 7 to 1 tchd 8 to 1) 6

22585 HOLY STING (Ire) [97] (bl) 8-10-0 C Maude, *al beh.*
..............................(16 to 1 op 14 to 1) 7
24272 A N C EXPRESS [114] 9-11-3 T J Murphy, *mstks, hdwy 9th, rdn alng frm 12th, mistake 13th, wknd quickly 3 out.*
..............................(9 to 2 op 7 to 2) 8
1946* SHAMARPHIL [97] 11-10-0 Miss S Barraclough, *mstks, al beh.*........................(50 to 1) 9
SPACE CAPPA [97] 9-10-0 Miss V Stephens, *al beh.*
..............................(33 to 1 op 25 to 1) 10
24394 DAKYNS BOY [122] 12-11-11 C Llewellyn, *al beh.*
..............................(8 to 1 op 7 to 1) 11
SCRIBBLER [121] 11-11-10 D Bridgwater, *al beh.*
..............................(25 to 1 op 20 to 1) 12
23067 SHEER ABILITY [120] (bl) 11-11-5 J Magee, *miin tch till mstk tenth, not fluent aftr and sn wknd, tld off whn pld up bef 3 out*.......................(25 to 1 op 20 to 1) pu
2182 HAVE TO THINK [125] 9-12-0 R Johnson, *chsd ldr to 12th, wknd 16th, tld off whn pld up bef 18th.*.........pu
2306 TOP BRASS (Ire) [103] 9-10-6 J Osborne, *chsd ldrs to 12th, tld of whn pld up bef 14th.*.............(20 to 1) pu
21897 NAZZARO [125] (bl) 8-12-0 R Dunwoody, *chsd ldrs to tenth, wknd quickly nxt, tld off whn pld up bef 18th.*
..............................(14 to 1 tchd 16 to 1) pu
Dist: 1¼l, 14l, nk, 8l, 2½l, 24l, 2½l, 10l, hd, 2l. 7m 13.30s. a 38.30s (16 Ran).
(L G Kimber), Andrew Turnell

2699 European Breeders Fund 'National Hunt' Novices' Hurdle Qualifier Class E (5,6,7-y-o) £2,514 2m 110yds......................(3:15)

23845 PRINCEFUL (Ire) 6-11-0 R Farrant, *trkd ldr till led aftr 4th, rdn 2 out, styd on gmely whn strly chlgd r-in.* (7 to 2 op 3 to 1) 1
20135 JOHN DRUMM 6-11-0 J Osborne, *hld up appr second, hdd aftr 4th and drvn alng, chlgd frm four out,ev ch und pres r-in, no extr cl hme.*..............................(8 to 1) 2
BELMOREBRUNO 7-11-0 C Maude, *chsd ldrs, ev ch 3 out, hit nxt and sn btn.*................(8 to 1 op 9 to 1) 3
21536 TOMPETOO (Ire) 6-11-10 C Llewellyn, *led till appr second, mstk and lost palce 4th, ran on ag'n frm 2 out.*
..............................(6 to 1 op 9 to 1) 4
12087 RHYTHM AND BLUES 7-11-0 B Powell, *chsd ldrs, outpcd appr 5th, styd on ag'n frm 2 out...*(25 to 1 op 20 to 1) 5
CLOSE HARMONY 5-10-9 R Dunwoody, *hdwy aftr 4th, eased whn btn frm 3 out.*...(4 to 1 op 7 to 2 tchd 9 to 2) 6
HIGHTECH TOUCH 7-11-0 Mr J Grassick, *hdwy aftr 4th, sn wknd*....................(50 to 1 op 33 to 1) 7
13572 LITTLE JAKE (Ire) 7-11-0 R Johnson, *jmpd slwly 3rd, sn beh.*..............................(10 to 1 op 8 to 1) 8
1355 DUKES CASTLE (Ire) 6-11-0 J Frost, *wth ldrs 1st, sn steadied and beh frm 4th.*...........(50 to 1 op 33 to 1) 9
LIZZYS FIRST 5-10-9 (5*) D Salter, *hdwy 4th, sn wknd.*
..............................(50 to 1 op 33 to 1) 10
23973 WISE KING 7-11-0 G Upton, *hld up, steady hdwy aftr 4th, rdn 2 out, fourth and btn whn f last.*.......(2 to 1 op 5 to 2) f
Dist: ¾l, 7l, 3l, 2½l, 27l, ¾l, ¾l, 2½l, 28l. 4m 11.40s. a 24.40s (11 Ran).
(Robert & Elizabeth Hitchins), Mrs J Pitman

2700 Clive Graham Novices' Chase Class E (5-y-o and up) £3,512 3m....(3:50)

2593* CYBORGO (Fr) 7-12-0 R Dunwoody, *pressed ldr till led 12th, forged clr frm 2 out but not fluent last, readily.*
..............................(7 to 4 on tchd 13 to 8 on and 6 to 4 on) 1
2593* BUCKHOUSE BOY 7-11-8 C Maude, *trkd ldrs, chsd wnr frm 14th, one pace from 2 out*.............(4 to 1 op 7 to 2) 2
23129 HIM OF PRAISE (Ire) 7-11-2 J Osborne, *made most to 12th, hit 13th, styd 3rd but lost tch frm 4 out.*
..............................(8 to 1 op 7 to 1 tchd 10 to 1) 3
24612 PARAHANDY (Ire) 7-11-0 (7*) M A Balding, *hdwy 7th, styd on same pace frm 14th...*.......(16 to 1 tchd 14 to 1) 4
2245 GOLDEN DROPS (NZ) 9-11-2 R Greene, *beh frm 11th.*
..............................(66 to 1 op 50 to 1 tchd 100 to 1) 5
24416 FOODBROKER STAR (Ire) 7-11-8 P Hide, *chsd ldrs till blun tenth, sn btn...*..........(20 to 1 op 16 to 1) 6
18295 CLONTOURA (Ire) 9-11-2 B Powell, *hdwy 11th, wknd aftr nxt.*....................(50 to 1 op 33 to 1) 7
24069 BALLYDOUGAN (Ire) (v) 9-11-2 T J Murphy, *hit 6th, sn beh.*
..............................(100 to 1) 8
BETTER FUTURE (Ire) 8-11-2 R Johnson, *al beh.*
..............................(50 to 1 op 33 to 1) 9
19818 WANDERING LIGHT (Ire) 8-11-2 C Llewellyn, *al beh.*
..............................(25 to 1 op 20 to 1) 10
2591 MYSTIC MANNA 11-11-2 G Crone, *sn beh, tld off whn pld up bef 14th*...................(50 to 1 op 33 to 1) pu
SOUND CARRIER (USA) 9-11-2 G Tormey, *in tch to tenth, tld off whn pld up bef 14th...*..........(66 to 1 op 50 to 1) pu
19817 GREENFIELD GEORGE (Ire) 6-11-2 L Harvey, *in tch 5th, hdwy tenth, chsd ldrs 12th, wknd 14th, tld off whn pld up bef 17th.*pu
24419 CREDO IS KING (Ire) 7-11-8 D Bridgwater, *chsd ldrs, mstk 8th, sn wknd, tld off whn pld up bef 14th.*.....................pu
Dist: 9l, 21l, 10l, 7l, 8l, 24l, 28l, 28l, sht-hd. 6m 25.30s. a 35.30s (14 Ran).
SR: 11/-/-/-/-/-/ (County Stores (Somerset) Holdings Ltd), M C Pipe

2701 Flyover Handicap Hurdle Class C (0-135 4-y-o and up) £3,715 3m
.... (4:25)

2559*	BANKHEAD (Ire) [122] 8-10-8 (7*) Miss C Spearing, *chlgd second led appr 4 out, ran on wl r-in.*	
	.... (15 to 2 op 5 to 1 tchd 8 to 1)	1
2438*	SCOTBY (Bel) [107] 7-10-0 B Powell, *chlgd 5th, chald ag'n frm 4 out, hrd rdn and mstk last, one pace.*	
	..........................(12 to 1 tchd 14 to 1)	2
1867*	GLENGARRIF GIRL (Ire) [107] v 7-10-0 G Tormey, *al chasing ldrs, one pace frm 3 out...*(8 to 1 op 7 to 1 tchd 13 to 2)	3
	MY ROSSINI [116] 8-10-6 (3*) J Magee, *prmnt, chlgd 7th, led 8th to appr 4 out, wknd 2 out.*	
	........................(12 to 1 op 8 to 1 tchd 14 to 1)	4
2438*	MENESONIC (Ire) [112] 7-10-5 J Culloty, *made most to 8th, one pace frm 3 out...* (7 to 2 op 3 to 1 tchd 4 to 1)	5
2442*	PENNYMOOR PRINCE [112] 8-10-5* J Frost, *outpcd 6th, hdwy 8th, wknd 3 out...*......(14 to 1 op 25 to 1)	6
2427*	VERYVEL (Cze) [112] 6-10-5 T J Murphy, *effrt 6th, mstk and wknd 8th...*..................(14 to 1 op 12 to 1)	7
1637*	HEBRIDEAN [135] 10-12-0 J Osborne, *effrt 6th, wknd 8th.*	
	...............................(20 to 1 op 14 to 1)	8
2246*	TEXAN BABY (Bel) [112] 8-10-5 C Llewellyn, *hmpd 3rd, al beh...*..............................(14 to 1 op 10 to 1)	9
1919*	SPIRIT LEVEL [107] 9-9-7 (7*) Mr S Durack, *sn beh and tld off.*	
	...................................(100 to 1)	10
2530*	KORBELL (Ire) [111] 8-10-4 R Johnson, *pressed ldrs till 13rd, dead...*..................(2 to 1 fav op 5 to 2)	f
	THE MEXICANS GONE [107] 9-10-0 V Slattery, *al beh, tld off whn pld up bef 2 out...*(14 to 1 op 16 to 1 tchd 20 to 1)	pu

Dist: 2l, 6l, 4l, 1l, 26l, 14l, 15l, 12l, dist. 6m 12.20s. a 37.20s (12 Ran).

(Mrs L Jaz Brazier), J L Spearing

GOWRAN PARK (IRE) (yielding)
Saturday February 15th

2702 Red Mills Premier Maiden Hurdle (4-y-o) £3,082 2m .... (1:30)

2470*	KEAL RYAN (Ire) 10-9 R Hughes, ...(7 to 1)	1
2230	VICTORY BOUND (USA) 10-9 D J Casey, ...(5 to 1)	2
2337*	RED TONIC (USA) 10-9 L P Cusack, ...(7 to 1)	3
2337*	ALAMBAR (Ire) 10-7 (7*) B J Geraghty, ...(9 to 4 fav)	4
2643*	DUNEMER (Ire) 10-6 (3*) Mr M Walsh, ...(10 to 1)	5
	SHARP OUTLOOK (Ire) 10-4 T P Rudd, ...(16 to 1)	6
2337	NATIVE ECLIPSE (Ire) 10-9 C F Swan, ...(3 to 1)	7
2337	FAMILY PROJECT (Ire) 10-9 S H O'Donovan, .(6 to 1)	8
2337	BLUE BIT (Ire) bl 10-4 K F O'Brien, ...(16 to 1)	9
2067	UNASSISTED (Ire) 10-4 C N Bowens, ...(16 to 1)	10
2470	MARCHAWAY (Ire) 11-0 C O'Dwyer, ...(20 to 1)	f

Dist: ½l, 9l, 3l, 7l. 3m 55.80s. (11 Ran).

(Cloverway Racing Club), D T Hughes

2703 Red Mills Quality Feed Maiden Hurdle (Div I) (5-y-o and up) £3,082 2m .... (2:00)

2443*	PHARDANA (Ire) 6-11-6 J P Broderick, ...(4 to 1)	1
2443*	AS ROYAL (Ire) 6-12-0 T P Treacy, ...(100 to 30 fav)	2
2583	TRUVARO (Ire) 6-11-6 F J Flood, ...(7 to 1)	3
2222	CAVALIER D'OR (USA) 6-12-0 F Woods, ...(10 to 1)	4
2378*	BAHAO (Ire) 6-11-6 D J Casey, ...(10 to 1)	5
2270*	IMPERIAL PLAICE (Ire) 5-10-10 (7*) D M Bean, ..(12 to 1)	6
2413*	RYTHM ROCK 8-10-13 (7*) J T Nolan, ...(10 to 1)	7
2520	PREMIER WALK 8-11-7 (7*) S O'Donnell, ...(12 to 1)	8
2416*	BOPTWOPHAR (Ire) 5-11-3 J R Barry, ...(14 to 1)	9
2160	BOCCACHERA (Ire) 5-10-12 C O'Dwyer, ...(25 to 1)	10
2049	COLONEL GEORGE 5-11-8 (3*) K Whelan, ...(14 to 1)	11
1195	LAS ALMANDAS (Ire) 6-11-1 D H O'Connor, .(25 to 1)	12
1782*	GALE JOHNSTON (Ire) 6-11-1 T P Rudd, ...(25 to 1)	13
2110	GRAIGNAMANAGH (Ire) 6-11-6 J Shortt, ...(14 to 1)	14
2271	CASEY JUNIOR (Ire) 9-11-7 (7*) R P Hogan, ..(25 to 1)	15
	CONNA BRIDE LADY (Ire) 5-10-5 (7*) F J Keniry, .(33 to 1)	16
2276*	BRIDGES DAUGHTER (Ire) 6-11-9 P A Roche, ..(12 to 1)	17
2416*	STRICT TEMPO 8-11-6 R Hughes, ...(25 to 1)	18
	BOBROSS (Ire) 7-11-7 (7*) M P Cooney, ...(33 to 1)	19
172*	DRAMATIST (Ire) 6-12-0 C F Swan, ...(11 to 2)	f

Dist: 2l, ¾l, 1l, 7l. 4m 0.60s. (20 Ran).

(Banner View Syndicate), S J Treacy

2704 Red Mills Quality Feed Maiden Hurdle (Div II) (5-y-o and up) £3,082 2m .... (2:30)

2080*	CEOIL AGUS CRAIC (Ire) 6-12-0 F Woods, ..(8 to 1)	1
2519*	TORMOND PERK (Ire) 6-11-6 C F Swan, ...(14 to 1)	2
2168*	SAVING BOND (Ire) 5-11-11 K F O'Brien, ...(10 to 9 on)	3
2270*	PRAGUE SPRING 5-11-6 R Hughes, ...(7 to 2)	4
	SHE'LL BE GOOD (Ire) 5-10-12 J R Barry, ...(33 to 1)	5
2443	BRACKENVALE (Ire) 6-11-1 D H O'Connor, ..(16 to 1)	6
2520	BAD BERTRICH (Ire) 6-12-0 L P Cusack, ...(33 to 1)	7
2413	RAMDON ROCKS 10-12-0 P McWilliams, ...(20 to 1)	8
1908*	GALLIC HONEY (Ire) 6-10-8 (7*) Mrs C Harrison, ..(14 to 1)	9
2520	ST CAROL (Ire) 5-11-1 T P Treacy, ...(10 to 1)	10

2705 Red Mills Stable Feed Beginners Chase (5-y-o and up) £3,082 2¼m .... (3:00)

2166	CLOSING THYNE (Ire) 6-11-1 F J Flood, ...(20 to 1)	11
2271*	FRIARSTOWN DUKE 7-11-11 (3*) U Smyth, ..(9 to 1)	12
	MILITATION (Ire) 7-11-3 (3*) K Whelan, ...(33 to 1)	13
2476*	MANISSA (Ire) 6-11-1 J P Broderick, ...(16 to 1)	14
	THATSWHATITHOUGHT (Ire) 5-11-3 C O'Dwyer, ..(20 to 1)	15
883*	BALMY NATIVE (Ire) 5-11-3 A Powell, ...(16 to 1)	16
	DUEONE (Ire) 9-12-0 M Duffy, ...(14 to 1)	17
2094*	SAFRANNE 9-11-6 Mr A R Coonan, ...(50 to 1)	18
	FAHY'S FIELD (Ire) 5-11-3 M P Hourigan, ...(20 to 1)	19
208*	BEASTY MAXX (Ger) 5-11-6 D T Evans, ...(33 to 1)	20

Dist: ½l, 6l, 4½l, 4½l. 4m 1.10s. (20 Ran).

(S Bolger), Michael G Holden

2705 Red Mills Stable Feed Beginners Chase (5-y-o and up) £3,082 2¼m .... (3:00)

	KEELSON (Ire) 6-11-7 (7*) Mr B Moran, ...(33 to 1)	1
2224*	ARCTIC BUCK (Ire) 7-12-0 A Powell, ...(20 to 1)	2
1172*	GENTLE BUCK (Ire) 8-12-0 C O'Dwyer, ...(6 to 4 fav)	3
2224*	LIVIN IT UP (Ire) 7-12-0 F Woods, ...(4 to 1)	4
2410	HAVE A BRANDY (Ire) 8-12-0 C O'Brien, ...(25 to 1)	5
874	HELLO MONKEY 10-12-0 T P Treacy, ...(12 to 1)	6
2410*	SAM VAUGHAN (Ire) 8-11-9 (5*) Mr W M O'Sullivan, (12 to 1)	f
2133	GREAT SVENGALI (Ire) 8-12-0 J R Barry, ...(10 to 1)	f
2367*	SCENIC ROUTE (Ire) 8-11-9 (5*) Mr T P Hyde, ...(7 to 2)	f
2673	V'SOSKE GALE (Ire) 7-11-9 C F Swan, ...(20 to 1)	f
2143*	SHISOMA (Ire) 7-12-0 J P Broderick, ...(8 to 1)	f
2519	ANDY BURNETT (Ire) 8-12-0 F J Flood, ...(20 to 1)	f
1714	GEALLAINNBAN (Ire) 7-11-7 (7*) R P Hogan, ..(14 to 1)	bd

Dist: Nk, 20l, 1l, dist. 4m 56.50s. (13 Ran).

(Patrick Heffernan), Patrick Heffernan

2706 Red Mills Trial Hurdle (Grade 3) (4-y-o and up) £6,850 2m .... (3:30)

2232*	THEATREWORLD (Ire) 5-11-9 C F Swan, *jmpd slwly 1st, wl plcd, rdn aftr 3 out, led last, styd on strly....*(9 to 4 jt-fav)	1
2364*	GUEST PERFORMANCE (Ire) 5-11-9 R Hughes, *trkd ldr, rdn to ld bef 3 out, hdd last, no extr.....*........(7 to 2)	2
2227*	LADY DAISY (Ire) 8-10-5 (7*) A O'Shea, *wl plcd, rdn aftr 4 out, kpt on well.....*...........................(7 to 1)	3
2232*	DARDJINI (USA) 7-11-6 K F O'Brien, *wl plcd, rdn aftr 3 out, not quicken...*....................(9 to 4 jt-fav)	4
2340*	MAGICAL LADY 5-11-1 F Woods, *led till hdd and wknd bef 3 out...*.............................(10 to 1)	5
1900*	BOLINO STAR (Ire) 6-11-7 T P Treacy, *rear, prog bef 3 out, kpt on...*.........................(10 to 1)	6
2273*	NEW CO (Ire) 9-11-3 C O'Dwyer, *mid-div, rdn aftr 3 out, not quicken...*..................(11 to 1)	7
2364*	ANUSHA 7-10-12 D T Evans, *mid-div, rdn and wknd bef 4 out.*	
	...................................(33 to 1)	8
2473*	MAYASTA (Ire) 5-10-5 (7*) R P Hogan, *rear, wknd 4 out.*	
	...................................(33 to 1)	9
2521*	PAS POSSIBLE 5-11-3 G M O'Neill, *al rear...*..(100 to 1)	10

Dist: 1½l, 8l, 12l, 6l. 3m 51.40s. (10 Ran).

(Mrs John Magnier), A P O'Brien

2707 Red Mills Trial Chase (5-y-o and up) £4,200 3m .... (4:00)

2273	NUAFFE (Ire) 11-11-6 T J Mitchell, ...(9 to 2)	1
2648	LE GINNO (Fr) 10-11-3 T P Treacy, ...(5 to 1)	2
2587	CHESLOCK (Ire) bl 8-11-0 P A Roche, ...(50 to 1)	3
	HARCON (Ire) 9-11-12 C F Swan, ...(9 to 4 on)	f

Dist: 1l, dist. 6m 28.00s. (4 Ran).

(John G Doyle), P A Fahy

2708 Red Mills Hi-Pro Handicap Hurdle (0-130 4-y-o and up) £3,425 2½m .... (4:30)

2340*	CLIFDON FOG (Ire) [-] 6-11-3 (3*) Mr R Walsh, ..(11 to 2)	1
2585*	APPELLATE COURT [-] (bl) 9-9-10 (7*) B J Geraghty,	
	....(9 to 1)	2
2271*	KILCOO BOY (Ire) [-] 6-11-4 C F Swan, ...(10 to 9 on)	3
2229*	FALLOW TRIX (Ire) [-] 5-10-1 J P Broderick, ..(14 to 1)	4
2340	TRYFIRION (Ire) [-] 8-11-11 (3*) B Bowens, ..(20 to 1)	5
2056*	CIARA'S PRINCE (Ire) [-] 6-10-13 F J Flood, ..(12 to 1)	6
2048*	DUISKE ABBEY (Ire) [-] 7-10-4 T P Treacy, ...(12 to 1)	7
2366	DARK SWAN (Ire) [-] 7-10-6 (3*) K Whelan, ..(14 to 1)	8
2584*	CHANCE COFFEY [-] 12-11-9 G M O'Neill, ...(16 to 1)	9
2447*	KASELECTRIC (Ire) [-] (bl) 6-10-4 T Horgan, ..(8 to 1)	10
2272*	LADY ARPEL (Ire) [-] 5-11-9 K F O'Brien, ...(7 to 1)	11
2340*	REASILVIA (Ire) [-] 7-11-6 J Shortt, ...(10 to 1)	12
1118*	TOMMY PAUD (Ire) [-] 8-11-1 M Duffy, ...(10 to 1)	13
2410*	COCK COCKBURN [-] 11-11-8 T P Rudd, ...(20 to 1)	14
	STRALDI (Ire) [-] 9-11-8 T J Mitchell, ...(20 to 1)	15
2340	KARABAKH (Ire) [-] 8-11-6 D J Casey, ...(10 to 1)	pu

Dist: 7l, 4½l, 6l, hd. 5m 7.40s. (16 Ran).

(J P Hill), J S Bolger

2709 Valmet Tractor I.N.H. Flat Race (5-y-o) £3,425 2m 1f............(5:00)

2588*	THINKERS CORNER (Ire) 11-4 (7*) Mr A J Dempsey,	
	....(2 to 1 fav)	1

RASH REFLECTION (Ire) 11-11 Mr J P Dempsey, . .(12 to 1) 2D
MOVIE MAID (Ire) 10-13 (7*) Mr P J Crowley, ... (5 to 1) 2
DONAGHMORE LADY (Ire) 11-1 (5*) Mr D McGoona, ...(33 to 1) 4
MEGA GALE (Ire) 11-11 Mr B M Cash, ... (7 to 2) 5
2416[4] THE RED SIDE (Ire) 11-6 Mr P Fenton, ... (5 to 1) 6
LITTLE CANTER (Ire) 11-6 Mr J A Nash, ...(14 to 1) 7
FINCHOGUE (Ire) 11-6 Mr D Marnane, ...(12 to 1) 8
WHITE SMOKE (Ire) 11-4 (7*) Mrs W O'Leary, ... (20 to 1) 9
BLACKHALL BAY (Ire) 10-13 (7*) Mr M Kavanagh, . (33 to 1) 10
2054 TULLIBARDS FLYER (Ire) 11-6 (5*) Mr A C Coyle, . .(33 to 1) 11
SEVEN AIRS (Ire) 10-13 (7*) Mr F J Crowley, ... (20 to 1) 12
DANTE'S BATTLE (Ire) 11-4 (7*) Mr P Fahey, ... (10 to 1) 13
LORD PENNY (Ire) 11-11 Mr H F Cleary, ...(12 to 1) 14
2270 LISARDBOULA (Ire) 11-4 (7*) Mr R M Collins, ... (33 to 1) 15
2144 BEATRICE ALLEGRO (Ire) 10-13 (7*) Mr J P McNamara, ...(33 to 1) 16
PADDY DOG (Ire) 11-4 (7*) Mr C J Swords, ... (20 to 1) 17
2518[3] MALADANTE (Ire) 10-13 (7*) Mr A K Wyse, ... (14 to 1) pu

Dist: ½l, 1l, 4½l, nk. 4m 18.00s. (18 Ran).

(B P MacMahon), D T Hughes

NEWCASTLE (good)
Saturday February 15th
Going Correction: PLUS 0.90 sec. per fur. (races 1,2,3,7), PLUS 0.10 (4,5,6)

2710 Northern Racing Conditional Jockeys' Handicap Hurdle Class F (0-105 4-y-o and up) £2,267 3m . . . . (1:25)

2487[8] DOCKMASTER [81] 6-9-13 (5*) N Horrocks, *hndy, led 7th, clr 3 out, styd on strly*. . . . . (14 to 1 op 12 to 1 tchd 16 to 1) 1
1951[4] FLAT TOP [95] 6-11-4 P Midgley, *hld up, improved 5 out, badly hmpd 3 out, sn chasing wnr, kpt on wl.* . . . . (10 to 1 op 8 to 1) 2
1628[9] GIVE BEST [100] 6-11-9 R McGrath, *patiently rdn, hdwy to chase ldrs 3 out, styd on, nrst finish.* . . . . (9 to 1 op 8 to 1 tchd 10 to 1) 3
2241 WHAT JIM WANTS (Ire) [89] 4-9-7 (7*) D Jewett, *cl up till outpcd 4 out, styd on ag'n betw last 2, unbl to chal.* . . . . (33 to 1 op 25 to 1) 4
2535[2] TURKISH TOWER [86] 6-10-9 F Leahy, *midfield, hdwy and in tch aftr 4 out, one pace whn hit last*. . . .(12 to 1 op 10 to 1) 5
2487[5] HUDSON BAY TRADER (USA) [84] 10-10-7 G Supple, *wth ldrs, sn pushed alng, drvn and outpcd aftr 4 out.* . . . .(12 to 1 tchd 14 to 1) 6
2534 ANSURO AGAIN [82] 8-10-0 (5*) M Herrington, *hdwy to press ldrs hfwy, drvn alng 5 out, btn whn hmpd 3 out.* . . . . (25 to 1 op 20 to 1) 7
2487[3] JIGGINSTOWN [77] 10-9-7 (7*) L Cooper, *hld up, some hdwy 4 out, sn no extr, btn whn hit last*. . . . (12 to 1 tchd 14 to 1) 8
2359[5] ARIAN SPIRIT (Ire) [80] 6-10-0[2] (5*) C Elliott, *not fluent towards rear, moderate hdwy 8th, sn lost tch.* . . . . (7 to 1 op 6 to 1 tchd 15 to 2) 9
2487[2] KINGS LANE [86] 8-10-4 (5*) C McCormack, *pressed ldr hfwy till wknd quickly 3 out*. . . . .(8 to 1 op 7 to 1) 10
2578[6] SKI PATH [77] 8-9-9 (5*) A Scholes, *chsd ldrs, wknd 5 out, tld off*. . . . . (200 to 1) 11
2487* SCARBA [100] 9-11-9 E Callaghan, *midfield, hdwy hfwy, second and staying on whn f 3 out.* . . . .(8 to 1 op 7 to 1 tchd 9 to 1) f
2574[6] NEW CHARGES [95] 10-11-4 B Grattan, *al beh, btn whn brght dwn 3 out*. . . . . (16 to 1 op 14 to 1) bd
1966[6] DENTICULATA [77] 9-9-9 (5*) S Haworth, *wth ldr, struggling 5 out, tld off whn pld up 3 out*. . . . . (100 to 1) pu
MURPHAIDEEZ [77] 10-10-0 M Newton, *al rear, tld off whn pld up 3 out*. . . . .(100 to 1) pu
1661[4] DIG DEEPER [95] 10-11-4 S Melrose, *led to 7th, sn wknd, tld off whn pld up 4 out*. . . . (14 to 1 op 12 to 1 tchd 16 to 1) pu
2494[3] MANETTIA (Ire) [91] 8-11-0 G Cahill, *cl up, lost pl 5th, beh whn pld up 3 out*. . . . .(5 to 1 fav op 9 to 2 tchd 11 to 2) pu
1764[8] BARK'N'BITE [87] 5-10-10 G Lee, *chsd ldrs hfwy, lost tch 4 out, beh whn pld up aftr nxt*. (25 to 1) pu
2534 MR SLOAN [77] 7-9-7 (7*) N Hannity, *beh, struggling hfwy, tld off whn pld up 3 out*. . . . .(200 to 1) pu
2392* MONTEL EXPRESS (Ire) [105] 5-11-9 (5*) W Walsh, *midfield whn broke dwn and pld up hfwy, dead.* (9 to 1 op 10 to 1) pu

Dist: 1½l, 1½l, 8l, nk, 6l, 1½l, ½l, 2½l, 1¾l, dist. 6m 2.50s. a 31.50s (20 Ran).

(J D Gordon), Miss M K Milligan

2711 Newsham Novices' Hurdle Class E (4-y-o and up) £2,484 2m. . . . . (1:55)

1464* MARELLO 6-11-5 P Niven, *hld up, smooth hdwy to chal whn slight mstk 2 out, led and quickened last, readily.* . . . . (2 to 1 on tchd 7 to 4 on) 1
NIGEL'S LAD (Ire) 5-11-4 M Foster, *chsd clr ldr, lft clear 3rd, rdn and hdd last, kpt on, no ch wth wnr.* (12 to 1 op 7 to 1) 2
2463* DURANO 6-11-10 R Garritty, *chsd ldrs, drvn and not quicken 3 out, one pace*. . . . . (6 to 1 op 5 to 1 tchd 13 to 2) 3
FAR AHEAD 5-11-4 B Storey, *hld up, pushed alng aftr 4 out, styd on, unbl to chal*. . . . .(16 to 1 op 14 to 1) 4
2463 QUANGO 5-11-10 D Gallagher, *in tch, drvn alng aftr 4 out, fdd stdly*. . . . .(6 to 1 op 5 to 1 tchd 7 to 1) 5
2256[6] BARTON SCAMP 5-11-4 T Eley, *hld up, some hdwy 4 out, sn lost tch*. . . . .(20 to 1 tchd 25 to 1) 6
GOSPEL SONG 5-11-4 A S Smith, *in tch, shaken up and lost touch 3 out, eased whn btn*. . . . . (9 to 1 op 6 to 1) 7
2417 DIAMOND BEACH 4-10-8 N Bentley, *beh, lost tch 4 out, nvr a dngr*. . . . .(66 to 1 op 50 to 1) 8
2496[5] JESSOLLE 5-10-13 A Dobbin, *hld up, pushed alng and outpcd aftr 4 out, sn btn*. . . . . (33 to 1 tchd 50 to 1) 9
1882 TOSHIBA TALK (Ire) 5-11-4 T Reed, *hld up, moderate hdwy 4 out, sn wknd*. . . . .(25 to 1 op 16 to 1) 10
2489 SIOUX WARRIOR (bl) 5-11-1 (3*) E Husband, *in tch, rdn alng 4 out, wknd*. . . . . (50 to 1) 11
GREENFINCH (Can) (v) 6-11-4 J Supple, *struggling hfwy, wl beh aftr*. . . . . (200 to 1) 12
2302[8] CHASING DREAMS 6-11-4 J Callaghan, *chsd ldrs to 5th, sn lost tch*. . . . .(100 to 1) 13
CRAIGIE BOY 7-11-4 O Pears, *nvr a factor*. . . . . . .(200 to 1) 14
2463 ON THE OFF CHANCE 5-10-11 (7*) I Jardine, *al rear.* . . . .(200 to 1) 15
AFRICAN SUN (Ire) 4-10-8 K Gaule, *struggling rear 5th, sn tld off*. . . . .(50 to 1 op 33 to 1) 16
JAMAICAN FLIGHT (USA) 4-10-8 J A McCarthy, *sn clr, attempted to refuse and uns rdr 3rd*. . . (33 to 1 op 25 to 1) ur
1953[8] ROBERT THE BRAVE 5-11-1 (3*) E Callaghan, *beh, reminders 3rd, tld off whn pld up bef last*. . . . . (200 to 1) pu
2256 SHIRLEY'S TIME 6-11-4 G Cahill, *rear, wl beh whn pld up bef 2 out*. . . . . (66 to 1) pu

Dist: 2½l, 17l, 1¼l, 1l, nk, 16l, 2l, 5l, 11l, 3l. 3m 56.70s. a 19.70s (19 Ran).

SR: 38/34/23/15/20/14/ (Mrs M Williams), Mrs M Reveley

2712 Levy Board Novices' Hurdle Class E (4-y-o and up) £2,473 2½m. . . (2:25)

2288* BOBBY GRANT 6-11-10 P Niven, *hdwy hfwy, led aftr 4 out, blun 2 out, styd on strly*. . . . .(3 to 1 fav op 9 to 4) 1
2570 ASHGROVE DANCER (Ire) 7-10-11 (7*) I Jardine, *hld up, pushed alng and plenty to do 4 out, ran on wl frm nxt, nrst finish*. . . . . (200 to 1) 2
2560[4] SHARED RISK 5-11-1 (3*) E Callaghan, *hdwy 6th, chalg 2 out, blun badly nxt, not reco'r*. . . . .(8 to 1 op 6 to 1) 3
2384 CHARLEY LAMBERT (Ire) 6-11-1 (3*) E Husband, *settled rear, pushed alng and styd on frm 2 out, nvr nrr.* . . . . (16 to 1 op 12 to 1) 4
2489[5] NO FINER MAN (Ire) 6-11-4 A Dobbin, *keen hold, chsd ldrs gng wl hfwy, rdn and one pace frm 3 out.* (7 to 2 op 5 to 2) 5
2260 BOLD ACTION (Ire) 6-11-1 (3*) G Lee, *midfield, effrt 7th, rdn and outpcd aftr 3 out*. . . . . (20 to 1) 6
2538 PAPPA CHARLIE (USA) 6-11-4 B Storey, *hld up, some hdwy 4 out, outpcd nxt, btn whn hit 2 out.* . . . . (20 to 1 op 16 to 1 tchd 25 to 1) 7
2538[5] MALTA MAN (Ire) 7-11-4 A S Smith, *midfield, hdwy hfwy, struggling 3 out, sn no dngr.* . . . .(7 to 2 op 9 to 2 tchd 5 to 1) 8
2581[6] DON'T TELL TOM (Ire) 7-11-4 G Cahill, *in tch, niggled alng hfwy, sn no imprsn*. . . . . (33 to 1) 9
2152 SUTHERLAND MOSS 6-11-10 R Garritty, *cl up, slight ld 5 out till aftr nxt, wknd appr 2 out, eased whn btn.* . . . . (12 to 1 op 8 to 1 tchd 14 to 1) 10
3014 WELL ARMED (Ire) 6-10-13 (5*) R McGrath, *in tch till wknd aftr 4 out*. . . . .(10 to 1 op 6 to 1) 11
2490[4] PENTLANDS FLYER (Ire) 6-11-4 Richard Guest, *midfield, drvn alng 4 out, beh whn blun nxt*. . . . . (16 to 1 op 14 to 1) 12
2490[7] PAPARAZZO 6-11-4 J Callaghan, *wth ldr till wknd 7th, sn beh.* . . . . (20 to 1 op 25 to 1) 13
2463 BONNY RIGG (Ire) 5-10-13 T Reed, *al rear*. . . . . . .(100 to 1) 14
1818 WHITEGATES WILLIE 5-11-4 D Parker, *wth ldrs to hfwy, tld off frm 3 out*. . . . .(200 to 1 op 100 to 1) 15
2490 LYFORD CAY (Ire) 7-11-4 D Bentley, *sn beh, tld off whn pld up 3 out*. . . . .(500 to 1) pu
RACHAEL'S DAWN 7-10-13 M Moloney, *wl beh whn pld up 6th*. . . . .(50 to 1) pu
694[5] WAR WHOOP 5-11-10 L O'Hara, *cl up till lost pl 5 out, beh whn pld up 3 out*. (33 to 1 op 25 to 1) pu
2200[9] KING FLY 7-11-4 M Foster, *led till hdd 5 out, wknd quickly and tld off whn pld up 3 out*. . . . .(66 to 1 op 50 to 1) pu

Dist: 4l, 2½l, ½l, 3l, 2l, 4l, 2½l, 6l, 15l, 3l. 5m 6.40s. a 28.40s (19 Ran).

(John J Thompson), C Grant

2713 BBC Radio Newcastle Breakfast Show Handicap Chase Class B (0-140 5-y-o and up) £8,557 2½m . . . . (3:00)

1974 ALL THE ACES [120] 10-10-13 S McNeill, *settled rear, plenty to do whn mstk 5 out, steady hdwy frm nxt, shaken up and ran on strly to ld r-in*. . . . . . (14 to 1 op 20 to 1 tchd 25 to 1) 1
2317* FIVELEIGH BUILDS [124] 10-11-3 M Foster, *pressed ldr, not fluent 11th, drvn and slight ld last, hdd and no extr r-in.* . . . .(3 to 1 tchd 100 to 30) 2
2466 THE LAST FLING (Ire) [124] 7-11-3 Richard Guest, *midfield, not jump wl, 3rd whn blun tenth, chsd ldrs 2 out, kpt on same pace*. . . . . (5 to 2 jt-fav op 9 to 4) 3
1932[5] CROSS CANNON [107] 11-10-0 B Storey, *made most str pace, rdn and hdd last, no extr*. . . . .(14 to 1 tchd 16 to 1) 4

2466[5] VALIANT WARRIOR [133] 9-11-12 R Garritty, *midfield struggling 4 out, sn beh*.................(7 to 1 op 5 to 1)   5
2571[5] BETTER TIMES AHEAD [133] 11-11-12 A Dobbin, *drpd rear
6th, tld off frm 9th*..................(14 to 1 op 8 to 1)   6
2334 EASBY JOKER [129] 9-11-8 P Niven, *hld up, mstk 5th, blun
8th, tld off whn pld up bef tenth, lme* ....(5 to 2 jt-
fav op 11 to 4 tchd 3 to 1)   pu
Dist: 2½l, 1½l, 3½l, dist, dist. 5m 4.80s. a 17.80s (7 Ran).
(J P McManus), J J O'Neill

2714 Gordon Armstrong Wines Novices' Chase Class C (5-y-o and up) £5,044 2m 110yds. (3:35)

2464[2] CHIEF MINISTER (Ire) 8-11-3 R Garritty, *jmpd wl, al hndy, led
3 out, drw clr und pres frm last*.
.................(11 to 10 fav tchd 11 to 8 and Evens)   1
2486[*] BOLD BOSS 8-11-13 B Storey, *wth ldr, mstk 5th, ev ch frm 3
out, one pace*..........(11 to 4 op 3 to 1 tchd 5 to 2)   2
2345[2] NOORAN 6-11-3 A S Smith, *made most till jmpd slwly and
hdd 3 out, sn wknd, eased whn btn*....(5 to 1 tchd 6 to 1)   3
2345[4] CROSSHOT 10-11-9 K Jones, *hld up, mstk second, blun
badly 5th, wl beh frm 4 out*.
.....................(16 to 1 op 12 to 1 tchd 25 to 1)   4
2331[7] MR BUREAUCRAT (NZ) 8-11-3 A Dobbin, *hld up, jmpd
poorly, blun badly 5 out, tld off whn pld up 3 out*.
......................(11 to 2 op 4 to 1 tchd 6 to 1)   pu
Dist: 16l, 30l, 28l. 4m 5.90s. a 6.90s (5 Ran).
SR: 36/30/
(G Shiel), M D Hammond

2715 Tote Eider Handicap Chase Class B (0-140 5-y-o and up) £22,053 4m 1f (4:10)

2189[*] SEVEN TOWERS (Ire) [127] 8-11-8 P Niven, *hld up, pushed
alng to improve fnl circuit, led gng wl aftr 3 out, pushed clr,
readily*................(2 to 1 fav op 5 to 2 tchd 11 to 4)   1
1739[1] IVY HOUSE (Ire) [106] 9-9-10 (5*) R McGrath, *settled rear,
steady hdwy fnl circuit, chsd ldrs 3 out, kpt on till no extr cl
hme*...........................(5 to 1 op 9 to 2)   2
2439[5] KILLESHIN [130] 11-11-11 S Curran, *hld up, jnd ldrs 15th, led
5 out till blun and outpcd aftr 3 out, rallied flt*.
.......................(25 to 1 op 20 to 1 tchd 33 to 1)   3
2406[*] DRUID'S BROOK [105] 8-10-0 J A McCarthy, *in tch, jnd ldrs
14th, rdn and one pace appr 3 out*......(8 to 1 op 5 to 1)   4
2571[2] KILCOLGAN [105] (bl) 10-10-0 N Bentley, *cl up, lft in ld 14th,
blun and hdd 16th, sn outpcd*.........(6 to 1 op 10 to 1)   5
2468[3] MATT REID [110] 13-10-5 K Gaule, *al hndy, led 16th till mstk
and hdd 5 out, fdd frm 3 out*.....(40 to 1 op 33 to 1)   6
2148 PENNINE PRIDE [105] 10-10-0 D Bentley, *midfield, struggling aftr 6 out, sn lost tch*.
....................(25 to 1 tchd 33 to 1)   7
2439 SEE ENOUGH [110] 9-10-5 S McNeill, *cl up, str hold, drvn
and lost tg 6 out, wl wknd*.............(10 to 1 op 8 to 1)   8
1626[*] PARSONS BOY [127] 8-11-8 A Dobbin, *midfield, niggled alng
frm 15th, struggling whn blun 5 out, tld off*.
.......................(9 to 2 op 3 to 1 tchd 5 to 1)   9
1946 FRONT LINE [112] (bl) 10-10-7 Richard Guest, *settled rear,
blun tenth, drvn alng 16th, sn no dngr*.
.....................(20 to 1 tchd 25 to 1)   10
2317[4] CEILIDH BOY [117] (v) 11-10-12 A S Smith, *led till blun and
uns rdr 14th*............(20 to 1 op 16 to 1 tchd 25 to 1)   ur
2189 PINK GIN [113] 10-10-8 B Storey, *in tch, pushed alng and
outpcd 15th, wl beh whn pld up bef 3 out*.
.......................(25 to 1 op 20 to 1)   pu
Dist: 8l, nk, 7l, 12l, 11l, 15l, 5l, 1¾l, 3l. 8m 32.00s. a 21.00s (12 Ran).
(Mrs E A Murray), Mrs M Reveley

2716 Gosforth Handicap Hurdle Class B (0-140 4-y-o and up) £6,937 2½m (4:45)

2467[3] CELESTIAL CHOIR [114] 7-10-12 B Storey, *hld up, led and
quickened 3 out, drvn and styd on strly betw last 2*.
.........................(9 to 2 op 4 to 1 tchd 7 to 2)   1
2484 TURNPOLE (Ire) [128] 6-11-12 P Niven, *settled rear, steady
hdwy 4 out, chasing wnr whn hit last, kpt on*.
.......................(5 to 1 tchd 11 to 2)   2
2467[2] TOM BRODIE [128] 7-11-12 A S Smith, *hld up in rear, hdwy 4
out, staying on in 3rd whn hit last, kpt on*.
.......................(7 to 1 op 5 to 1 tchd 15 to 2)   3
2331[4] KAITAK (Ire) [119] 6-11-0 (3*) F Leahy, *chsd ldrs, rdn and
outpcd appr 3 out, no imprsn aftr*.
.......................(12 to 1 tchd 14 to 1 and 16 to 1)   4
2289[5] DALLY BOY [114] 5-10-12 J Callaghan, *set steady pace, drvn
and hdd 4 out, fdd frm nxt*..........(10 to 1 tchd 12 to 1)   5
2361[5] OLD HABITS (Ire) [106] 8-10-4 T Eley, *nvr better than midfield*.
.......................(25 to 1 op 20 to 1)   6
2530[5] NIJMEGEN [128] 9-11-12 W Dwan, *midfield, shaken up and
outpcd 3 out, no dngr aftr*.
.......................(14 to 1 op 7 to 1 tchd 16 to 1)   7
2190[6] MARCHANT MING (Ire) [128] 5-11-12 A Dobbin, *pckd 1st, wth
ldr till led briefly 4 out, lost tch quickly nxt*.
.......................(33 to 1 op 20 to 1)   8
2215[*] SEA VICTOR [118] 5-11-2 D Gallagher, *keen hold, chsd ldrs,
lost pl quickly 3 out, sn wl beh*.
.......................(10 to 8 fav op 6 to 4 tchd 7 to 4)   9

417[*] VIARDOT (Ire) [107] 8-10-0 (5*) R McGrath, *str hold in rear,
lost tch 4 out, sn tld off*...............(20 to 1 op 25 to 1)   10
Dist: 2½l, 4l, 7l, 1l, 5l, 1¼l, nk, 23l, 14l. 5m 4.50s. a 26.50s (10 Ran).
SR: -/10/6/-/-/-/
(Mrs Carole Sykes), J L Eyre

WARWICK (good)
Saturday February 15th
Going Correction: PLUS 0.25 sec. per fur. (races 1,3,5,7), MINUS 0.25 (2,4,6)

2717 Michael Page Group Handicap Hurdle Class C (0-135 4-y-o and up) £4,150 2m (1:50)

2543[2] GOLDINGO [106] 10-10-0 J R Kavanagh, *hld up, hdwy appr 2
out, ran on to ld towards finish*......(9 to 2 op 5 to 1)   1
2467[6] THORNTON GATE [122] 8-11-2 P Carberry, *chsd ldr, led appr
2 out, hdd nr finish*.......(9 to 2 op 5 to 1 tchd 11 to 2)   2
2329[4] CHICODARI [127] (bl) 5-11-7 A Maguire, *trkd ldrs, rdn appr 2
out, styd on*...........(100 to 30 fav op 3 to 1 tchd 7 to 2)   3
2331[2] NEW INN [122] 6-10-13 (3*) Michael Brennan, *led, hdd appr 2
out, styd on same pace*..........(4 to 1 op 3 to 1)   4
1238[5] FROGMARCH (USA) [130] 7-11-10 N Williamson, *hld up, effrt
3 out, nvr rchd ldrs*.................(8 to 1 op 5 to 1)   5
2457 KINO'S CROSS [114] 8-10-8 J Culloty, *mid-division, effrt 5th,
wknd 3 out*............................(7 to 1 op 9 to 1)   6
2331 SAINT CIEL (USA) [106] 9-10-0 R Supple, *hld up, al in rear*.
.......................(12 to 1 op 8 to 1)   7
1959 DECIDE YOURSELF (Ire) [110] 7-10-4[3] A Thornton, *prmnt,
rdn 5th, wknd 3 out, irons broke*......(20 to 1 op 14 to 1)   8
Dist: 1½l, ¾l, nk, 5l, 9l, 8l, dist. 3m 48.50s. a 9.50s (8 Ran).
SR: 17/31/35/30/33/8/-/-/
(G M Price), G M Price

2718 Michael Page Legal Novices' Chase Class B (5-y-o and up) £7,197 3¼m (2:20)

1876[3] CAROLE'S CRUSADER 6-10-11 A Maguire, *led second to
4th, lost pl 6th, hdwy 12th, chsd ldr 14th, pckd six out, styd on
und pres to ld nr finish*..............(3 to 1 tchd 10 to 3)   1
2437[3] MARINERS MIRROR 10-11-5 Mr M Rimell, *hld up, hdwy to ld
8th, clr 4 out, hdd and no extr nr finish*.
.......................(3 to 1 op 11 to 4 tchd 10 to 3)   2
2566[*] JET RULES (Ire) 7-11-6 N Williamson, *hld up, hdwy to ld 5th,
hdd 8th, rdn and hit 13th, pckd nxt, wknd appr 2 out*.
.......................(Evens fav op 5 to 4 on tchd 11 to 10)   3
2301[3] THE BOOLEY HOUSE (Ire) 7-11-2 P Carberry, *led to second,
led 4th to nxt, wknd appr 3 out*.......(25 to 1 op 20 to 1)   4
1106[2] CAPO CASTANUM 8-11-6 J Culloty, *hld up, blun and uns rdr
13th*................(12 to 1 op 10 to 1 tchd 16 to 1)   ur
TOP IT ALL 9-11-2 D Walsh, *prmnt, rdn and wknd tenth, beh
whn pld up bef 13th*............(100 to 1 op 50 to 1)   pu
Dist: ¾l, dist, 27l. 6m 39.30s. a 25.30s (6 Ran).
(Mrs C Skipworth), D R Gandolfo

2719 Michael Page Sales And Marketing Handicap Hurdle Class E (0-115 4-y-o and up) £2,433 2½m 110yds (2:50)

2598[5] LETS BE FRANK [104] 6-11-6 N Williamson, *hld up, hdwy 5
out, led 3 out, rdn out*...........(3 to 1 jt-fav op 7 to 2)   1
2372[3] BEAUMONT (Ire) [98] 7-11-0 P Carberry, *hld up, hdwy 5 out,
led 3 out, rdn and hdd nxt, styd on same pace*....(3 to 1 jt-
fav op 7 to 2)   2
2295[5] FIRST CLASS [84] 7-9-9 (5*) A Bates, *chsd ldr, led 5 out, hdd 3
out, styd on same pace*.............(10 to 1 tchd 11 to 1)   3
2249[3] PENROSE LAD (NZ) [100] 7-11-2 A Maguire, *prmnt, rdn 4 out,
wknd appr 3 out*..............(11 to 2 op 5 to 1)   4
2504 HOODED HAWK (Ire) [103] 6-11-5 J R Kavanagh, *hld up, effrt
4 out, eased whn btn nxt*...........(13 to 2 op 6 to 1)   5
2562 CHIEF RAGER [99] 8-11-1 D Walsh, *led till aftr 3rd, rdn and
wknd 3 out*...........................(20 to 1 op 16 to 1)   6
NO FIDDLING (Ire) [93] 6-10-2 (7*) R Studholme, *blun second,
nvr nr ldrs*............(14 to 1 op 12 to 1 tchd 16 to 1)   7
DOUALAGO (Fr) [110] (bl) 7-11-12 Jamie Evans, *prmnt to 5
out, sn wknd*................(5 to 1 tchd 11 to 2)   8
NEEDWOOD POPPY [94] 9-10-10 B Clifford, *prmnt till wknd 5
out*.......................(33 to 1 op 25 to 1 tchd 40 to 1)   9
2198[6] LITTLE GUNNER [108] 7-11-10 R Bellamy, *mid-div, rdn and
wknd 5 out*..........................(16 to 1 op 10 to 1)   10
FINNIGAN FREE [86] 7-10-2[9] (7*) Mr M Frith, *led aftr 3rd, sn
clr, hdd and wknd 5 out*..................(66 to 1)   11
1691 MILL THYME [90] 5-10-6 R Supple, *beh frm 5 out*.
.......................(33 to 1 op 25 to 1 tchd 40 to 1)   12
1683[4] CELTIC EMERALD [84] 9-9-11 (3*) Michael Brennan, *al in
rear, tld off whn pld up bef 3 out*.....(100 to 1 op 50 to 1)   pu
Dist: 5l, 1¾l, 7l, 12l, ¾l, ½l, 3l, ¾l, 3½l, 23l. 4m 59.70s. a 14.70s (13 Ran).
(Mrs M M Stobart), Noel T Chance

2720 Michael Page Group Kingmaker Novices' Chase Class A Grade 2 (5-y-o and up) £11,540 2m (3:20)

2231* MULLIGAN (Ire) 7-11-12 A Maguire, jmpd wl, made all, styd
on strly.
.....(6 to 5 on op Evens tchd 11 to 10 and 5 to 4 on) 1
2554* SQUIRE SILK 8-11-5 P Carberry, hld up, hit 4th, blun badly
nxt, hdwy 5 out, chsd wnr 2 out, rdn and wknd run in.
....................(Evens op 5 to 4 on tchd 11 to 10) 2
1761 FLYING INSTRUCTOR 7-11-5 R Bellamy, chsd wnr, mstk 5
out, rdn appr 2 out, styd on same pace.
.......................(25 to 1 op 20 to 1 tchd 33 to 1) 3
2457² BLAIR CASTLE (Ire) 6-11-5 B Clifford, trkd ldrs, rdn 3 out, sn
btn...... (16 to 1 op 20 to 1 tchd 25 to 1 and 28 to 1) 4
Dist: 6l, 1l, 11l. 3m 53.30s. a 1.30s (4 Ran).
SR: 45/32/31/20/ (Lady Harris), D Nicholson

2721 Questor International Novices' Trial Hurdle Class B (4-y-o and up) £7,100 2½m 110yds.................. (3:55)

1861⁶ INFLUENCE PEDLAR 4-10-6 N Williamson, prmnt, jnd ldr 5th,
lft in ld appr 5 out, clr last, styd on wl. (16 to 1 tchd 25 to 1) 1
2323² POTTER'S GALE (Ire) 6-11-7 A Maguire, hld up in tch, chsd
wnr 3 out, sn rdn, styd on same pace.
...................(13 to 8 op 6 to 4 tchd 15 to 8) 2
2318* KING PIN 5-11-12 R Supple, hld up, not fluent 3rd, took clr
order 5 out, mstk 3 out, sn rdn and btn.
.......(5 to 4 fav op 11 to 8 tchd 13 to 8 and 6 to 5) 3
2458³ KING OF CAMELOT (Ire) 7-11-8 R Massey, chsd ldrs, rcd
keenly, rdn and wknd appr 2 out.
.................(7 to 1 op 3 to 1 tchd 15 to 2) 4
2243⁷ ROCKCLIFFE LAD 8-11-8 D Walsh, led, blun 6th, pld up bef
nxt, lme.......................(9 to 1 op 6 to 1 tchd 10 to 1) pu
Dist: 7l, 7l, 8l. 5m 3.30s. a 18.30s (5 Ran).
(Miss S Blumbery), J A B Old

2722 Michael Page Finance Handicap Chase Class B (5-y-o and up) £6,498 2½m 110yds.................. (4:30)

2437⁶ SENOR EL BETRUTTI (Ire) [129] 8-10-12 N Williamson, chsd
ldr, led 11th, clr 3 out, eased r-in.
...............(9 to 4 op 5 to 2 tchd 11 to 4) 1
1518³ SOUTHAMPTON [123] (v) 7-10-6 B Clifford, hld up, took clr
order aftr tenth, outpcd frm nxt, wnt second r-in.
.................(11 to 10 on op 6 to 4 on tchd Evens) 2
2437⁸ GENERAL PERSHING [135] 11-11-4 A Maguire, led and sn wl
clr, hdd 11th, wknd 3 out.
.............(100 to 30 op 5 to 2 tchd 7 to 2) 3
Dist: 10l. 5m 8.20s. a 13.20s (3 Ran).
(Gerard Nock), Mrs Susan Nock

2723 Michael Page Technology Standard National Hunt Flat Class H (4,5,6-y-o) £1,028 2m.............. (5:00)

SAMUEL WILDERSPIN 5-11-0 (3*) R Massey, hld up, hdwy
hfwy, led wl o'r one furlong out, pushed clr.
.......................(Evens fav op 2 to 1) 1
LIGHT THE FUSE (Ire) 5-10-10 (7*) C Scudder, sn in rear and
pushed alng, hdwy o'r one furlong out, ran on, not rch wnr.
..................(12 to 1 op 5 to 1 tchd 14 to 1) 2
2269² BOLD LEAP 5-11-3 Mr A Sansome, prmnt, drvn alng 3 fs out,
styd on...............(33 to 1 op 25 to 1 tchd 50 to 1) 3
WAR PAINT (Ire) 5-10-10 (7*) Mr G Baines, mid-div, hdwy
hfwy, rdn and wknd o'r one furlong out.
.................(15 to 2 op 7 to 2 tchd 8 to 1) 4
2377² LORD FOLEY (NZ) 5-11-7 (3*) Michael Brennan, hld up, hdwy
hfwy, rdn 2 fs out, sn btn.. (6 to 1 op 5 to 1 tchd 7 to 1) 5
RIVER DAWN (Ire) 5-10-10 (7*) M Berry, chsd ldrs, led o'r 2
out, hdd and wknd wl over one furlong out.
.................(15 to 2 op 5 to 1 tchd 8 to 1) 6
1142 JEMARO (Ire) 6-11-3 Mr A Mitchell, made most til hdd and
wknd o'r 2 fs out.................(50 to 1 op 33 to 1) 7
WEAPONS FREE 6-10-10 (7*) R McCarthy, prmnt, rdn and ev
ch o'r 2 fs out, sn wknd. (12 to 1 op 6 to 1 tchd 14 to 1) 8
PROPER PRIMITIVE 4-9-9 (7*) C Rae, strted slwly, beh til styd
on fnl 2 fs..................(20 to 1 op 33 to 1) 9
2269 GOOD TIME DANCER 5-10-5 (7*) D Thomas, prmnt, rcd
keenly, wknd o'r 4 fs out...........(33 to 1 op 25 to 1) 10
2377⁶ SILENT CRACKER 5-10-10 (7*) X Aizpuru, prmnt till wknd 5 fs
out......................(8 to 1 op 7 to 1 tchd 10 to 1) 11
CAPTAIN CULPEPPER (Ire) 6-10-10 (7*) N T Egan, prmnt to
hfwy.......................(100 to 1 op 50 to 1) 12
2409⁸ HIJACK 6-10-10 (7*) Mr A Wintle, hld up, hdwy hfwy, wknd o'r
5 fs out..............(16 to 1 op 12 to 1 tchd 20 to 1) 13
PAYPNUTSGETMONKEYS (Ire) 4-10-2 Mrs D Smith, sn beh
and pushed alng, nvr dngrs.........(66 to 1 op 33 to 1) 14
CELTIC CARROT 5-11-0 (3*) Guy Lewis, mid-div, hdwy ten fs
out, wknd o'r 6 out..... (33 to 1 op 20 to 1 tchd 50 to 1) 15
MISS FOLEY 4-9-10¹ (7*) L Suthern, hld up, beh frm hfwy.
....................(100 to 1 op 33 to 1) 16
HABERDASHER 6-10-10 (7*) K Hibbert, hld up, al in rear
.................(50 to 1 op 33 to 1 tchd 66 to 1) 17
1560 TABBITS HILL 5-10-12 Mr P Scott, al in rear.
.......................(33 to 1 op 20 to 1) 18
NEWSKI LASS 5-10-5 (7*) J Power, in tch to hfwy, sn lost pl.
....................(66 to 1 op 50 to 1) 19

SWEET PERRY 6-11-3 D Walsh, prmnt 6 fs, sn wl beh.
....................(50 to 1 op 33 to 1 tchd 66 to 1) 20
GINGER WATT (Ire) 5-11-0 (3*) T Dascombe, chsd ldrs, sddl
slpd aftr 4 fs, sn lost pl...............(33 to 1 op 25 to 1) 21
1181⁷ HONEST GEORGE 6-10-10 (7*) M Griffiths, strted slwly, hld
up, al beh...............(25 to 1 op 14 to 1 tchd 33 to 1) 22
Dist: 11l, 3l, nk, 5l, 2½l, 3½l, 1¾l, nk, 8l, 13l. 3m 43.40s. (22 Ran).
(County Graphix Colour Limited), D Nicholson

WINDSOR (good)
Saturday February 15th
Going Correction: PLUS 0.30 sec. per fur. (races 1,2,4,7), PLUS 0.40 (3,5,6)

2724 King John Novices' Hurdle Class D (Div I) (5-y-o and up) £2,679 2¾m 110yds.................. (1:30)

2384⁴ FRIENDSHIP (Ire) 5-11-0 M A Fitzgerald, hld up, not fluent 6th
and 8th, led on bit appr 2 out, easily.
...............(15 to 8 on op 6 to 4 on) 1
RIOT LEADER (Ire) 7-10-7 (7*) C Hynes, trkd ldrs, led 7th to
appr 2 out, one pace und pres.
................(66 to 1 op 33 to 1 tchd 100 to 1) 2
2397² SALAMAN (Fr) 5-11-0 G Bradley, led second to 7th, ev ch 3
out, one pace.........(10 to 1 op 5 to 1 tchd 11 to 1) 3
873³ BOMBADIL 5-11-0 J Railton, drvn alng in rear aftr 4th, hdwy
four out, sn no imprsn. (10 to 1 op 12 to 1 tchd 16 to 1) 4
2243⁴ SHARIAKANNDI (Fr) 5-11-0 W Marston, prmnt till rdn and
wknd appr 4 out..........(7 to 1 op 7 to 2 tchd 8 to 1) 5
2250 CHAPILLIERE (Fr) 5-11-0 M Richards, hld up, hdwy 3rd, rdn
appr 3 out, 5th and btn whn blun last. (50 to 1 op 25 to 1) 6
2255 MAN OF THE MATCH 7-11-0 D Leahy, hld up in rear, hdwy
7th, wknd aftr 4 out....(16 to 1 op 12 to 1 tchd 20 to 1) 7
2436* MILLCROFT RIVIERA (Ire) 6-11-6 J F Titley, cl up, mstk 7th,
hrd rdn and wknd aftr 4 out. (8 to 1 op 5 to 1 tchd 9 to 1) 8
2243⁶ FULL OF BOUNCE (Ire) 6-10-11 (3*) T Dascombe, led to
second, wknd 6th, tld off.............(66 to 1 op 33 to 1) 9
GRIZZLY BEAR (Ire) 7-11-0 S Wynne, chsd ldrs, wknd aftr 6th,
tld off................(16 to 1 op 5 to 1 tchd 20 to 1) 10
UCKERBY LAD 6-10-11 (3*) D Forth, lost tch 4th, mstk nxt, tld
off whn pld up bef 3 out.............(66 to 1 op 33 to 1) pu
2264 ILEWINIT (Ire) 8-11-0 S Fox, not fluent in rear second, lost tch
4th, pld up bef 3 out..............(66 to 1 op 33 to 1) pu
Dist: 11l, 6l, 5l, 13l, 3l, 1½l, ¾l, 7l, 38l. 3m 60.50s. a 21.50s (12 Ran).
(T Benfield and Mr W Brown), N J Henderson

2725 King John Novices' Hurdle Class D (Div II) (5-y-o and up) £2,658 2¾m 110yds.................. (2:00)

2384⁶ JAZZMAN (Ire) 5-11-0 J F Titley, hld up in rear, hdwy to track
ldrs 4th, pushed alng 3 out, led approaching nxt, ran on
gmely und pres....................(4 to 1 op 5 to 1) 1
2311² SPARKLING SPRING 6-11-6 J Railton, al hndy, str chal
frm 2 out, bumped appr last, ev ch r-in, kpt on.
...................(13 to 8 fav op 5 to 4 tchd 7 to 4) 2
HIGH PATRIARCH (Ire) 5-11-0 I Lawrence, hld up beh, keen
early, hdwy appr 4 out, ev ch nxt, outpcd approaching 2 out.
....................(16 to 1 op 7 to 1 tchd 20 to 1) 3
2264⁸ BROOKHAMPTON LANE (Ire) 6-11-0 D Leahy, hld up, hdwy
aftr 4 out, one pace frm nxt.
..................(33 to 1 op 20 to 1 tchd 50 to 1) 4
PROFESSOR PAGE (Ire) 7-11-0 Derek Byrne, beh, reminders
aftr 6th, nvr nrr.........(16 to 1 op 10 to 1 tchd 20 to 1) 5
2433² OVER THE WATER (Ire) 5-11-0 W Marston, trkd ldrs, led 4 out
to appr 2 out, hrd rdn and sn wknd.
....................(20 to 1 op 10 to 1 tchd 25 to 1) 6
2374² STORMYFAIRWEATHER (Ire) 5-11-0 M A Fitzgerald, hld up
beh ldrs, wknd 3 out. (13 to 2 op 3 to 1 tchd 7 to 1) 7
2430 GALE SPRING (Ire) 5-10-6 (3*) T Dascombe, al beh, tld off.
....................(66 to 1 op 50 to 1) 8
1995 BLACK STATEMENT (Ire) 7-10-11 (3*) L Aspell, keen early,
trkd ldrs, wknd aproaching 3 out, tld off.
....................(50 to 1 op 20 to 1) 9
2636 ANIF (USA) 6-11-0 D Skyrme, cl up till wknd appr 6th, pld up
aftr nxt.................(16 to 1 op 50 to 1 tchd 100 to 1) pu
MRS BARTY (Ire) 7-10-9 M Richards, chsd ldrs, wknd 7th, pld
up bef 3 out...........(20 to 1 op 16 to 1 tchd 25 to 1) pu
1570² MARLOUSION (Ire) 5-10-9 G Bradley, led to 4 out, wknd
quickly, pld up bef 2 out....(6 to 1 op 5 to 1 tchd 7 to 1) pu
2567⁴ PRUSSIAN STEEL (Ire) 6-11-0 P Holley, in tch, pushed alng
5th, wknd 7th, pld up bef 3 out......(20 to 1 op 12 to 1) pu
Dist: ½l, 15l, 5l, 2½l, 9l, 10l, dist, dist. 5m 35.80s. a 20.80s (13 Ran).
(L Fust), A P Jarvis

2726 Magna Carta Novices' Chase Class E (5-y-o and up) £3,340 2m 5f... (2:30)

2011* SAIL BY THE STARS 8-10-12 S Wynne, trkd ldrs, pckd 3 out,
led 2 out, mstk last, ran on wl.
....................(5 to 2 tand op 4 to 1 tchd 11 to 4) 1
2480³ STROKESAVER (Ire) (bl) 7-11-3 G Bradley, trkd ldr, lft in ld
3rd, hrd rdn appr 3 out, hdd 2 out, no extr und pres.
...................(16 to 1 op 10 to 1 tchd 20 to 1) 2

1883[2] MONICASMAN (Ire) 7-11-3 J F Titley, *blun second, wth ldr frm 3rd, ev ch 2 out, one pace und pres.* ....(9 to 2 op 3 to 1 tchd 5 to 1) 3

2388[3] CALLEVA STAR (Ire) 6-11-3 M A Fitzgerald, *chsd ldrs, pushed alng aftr 5 out, no extr frm 3 out.* ....(8 to 1 op 7 to 1 tchd 10 to 1) 4

1961 COUNTRY TOWN 7-10-12 P Holley, *beh, moderate prog frm 4 out, nvr nr to chal.*..........(33 to 1 tchd 50 to 1) 5

2308 CRUISE CONTROL 11-11-3 D O'Sullivan, *beh frm 9th, nvr nr to chal.*..........(33 to 1 op 20 to 1 tchd 40 to 1) 6

2391[5] VOLLEYBALL (Ire) 8-11-3 M Richards, *hld up, btn appr tenth, tld off.*..........(33 to 1 op 20 to 1 tchd 50 to 1) 7

1939[4] SLEETMORE GALE (Ire) 7-10-9 (3*) T Dascombe, *trkd ldrs, rdn and wknd appr tenth, tld off.* ....(13 to 2 op 10 to 1 tchd 12 to 1 and 6 to 1) 8

MULTI LINE 7-10-12 Derek Byrne, *al beh, tld off.* ....(66 to 1 op 50 to 1) 9

2498 CONVAMORE QUEEN (Ire) 8-10-12 W Marston, *beh frm 6th, tld off.*..........(66 to 1 op 50 to 1) 10

1448 THE WEATHERMAN 9-11-3 T Kent, *f 6th.* ....(66 to 1 op 50 to 1 tchd 100 to 1) f

2247[6] BROGEEN LADY (Ire) 7-10-9 (3*) D Fortt, *led, f 3rd.* ....(4 to 1 op 11 to 4) f

1568[8] MY WARRIOR 9-11-3 J Railton, *blun and uns rdr second.* ....(50 to 1 op 33 to 1 tchd 66 to 1) ur

1577[6] MYSTIC COURT (Ire) 6-11-3 I Lawrence, *beh whn blun and uns rdr 3rd.*..........(25 to 1 tchd 33 to 1) ur

1442[2] JOLIS ABSENT 7-10-12 J Ryan, *mstk 5th, al beh, pld up aftr 11th.*..........(10 to 1 op 6 to 1 tchd 12 to 1) pu

2403[9] DERRYS PREROGATIVE 7-11-3 D Leahy, *al beh, tld off whn pld up bef 4 out.*..........(50 to 1) pu

Dist: 7l, 4l, 5l, 17l, 8l, 18l, 2½l, 6l, 25l. 5m 23.10s. a 14.10s (16 Ran).
SR: 27/25/21/16/-/-/ (T F F Nixon), Capt T A Forster

2727 Hatch Bridge Juvenile Novices' Hurdle Class B (4-y-o) £7,546 2m (3:05)

2423[5] RED RAJA 11-0 M Richards, *made all, rdn clr appr 2 out, not fluent last, eased nr finish.* ....(13 to 2 op 7 to 1 tchd 10 to 1) 1

2195[4] FAR DAWN (USA) 11-0 Derek Byrne, *jmpd rght second, cl up, outpcd and drvn 4th, hdwy aftr four out, hit nxt, one pace und pres.*..........(11 to 4 fav op 3 to 1 tchd 7 to 2) 2

INFAMOUS (USA) 11-0 D O'Sullivan, *keen early, cl up, hng lft and no imprsn appr 2 out, one pace*... (16 to 1 op 12 to 1) 3

2454* HAYAAIN 11-4 J Railton, *trkd ldrs, pushed alng appr 3 out, sn one pace.*..........(3 to 1 tchd 7 to 2) 4

2423[2] ELA AGAPI MOU (USA) 11-0 P Holley, *trkd ldrs, pushed alng appr 5th, wknd aftr 4 out.* ....(14 to 1 op 10 to 1 tchd 16 to 1) 5

SALTY GIRL (Ire) 10-9 W McFarland, *not fluent in rear, reminders second, pushed alng and hdwy appr 3 out, sn btn.* ....(33 to 1 op 20 to 1) 6

2303[4] MR WILD (USA) 11-0 W Marston, *awkward 1st, hld up beh ldrs, rdn and struggling 5th, sn btn.* ....(11 to 2 op 7 to 2 tchd 6 to 1) 7

FASIL (Ire) 11-0 I Lawrence, *hld up, hdwy 4th and reminders, wknd four out*..........(12 to 1 op 8 to 1 tchd 14 to 1) 8

HISAR (Ire) 11-0 G Bradley, *hld up, pld hrd, hdwy 4th, wknd 3 out.*..........(9 to 1 op 6 to 1 tchd 10 to 1) 9

2497[5] PALAMON (USA) 11-0 S Ryan, *beh, lost tch 5th, tld off.* ....(33 to 1 op 20 to 1 tchd 50 to 1) 10

1890* SERENUS (USA) 11-7 M A Fitzgerald, *tracking ldrs whn hmpd and f second.*..........(15 to 2 op 4 to 1 tchd 8 to 1) f

Dist: 6l, 2l, 3½l, 6l, 5l, 12l, 1½l, 9l, 21l. 3m 54.90s. a 9.90s (11 Ran).
SR: 35/29/27/27/17/7/ (J R Ali), P Mitchell

2728 Fairlawne Handicap Chase Class D (0-125 5-y-o and up) £3,848 3m (3:40)

EQUITY PLAYER [102] 12-10-13 D Morris, *hld up, pushed alng tenth, drvn and hdwy appr 4 out, led 3 out, styd on wl.* ....(4 to 1 op 5 to 1 tchd 11 to 2) 1

2500 BIG BEN DUN [105] 11-11-2 G Bradley, *cl up, led 4 out to 3 out, no extr.* (5 to 1 op 4 to 1 tchd 11 to 2 and 6 to 1) 2

2482 ROYAL SAXON [94] 11-10-5 W Marston, *wth ldr, reminder 4th, led 11th to four out, no extr und pres frm nxt.* ....(25 to 1 op 16 to 1) 3

2559[6] FAST THOUGHTS [107] (bl) 10-11-1 (3*) D Fortt, *led, mstk 6th, hdd 11th, sn btn.*..........(13 to 2 op 5 to 1 tchd 7 to 1) 4

2386[4] PLUNDER BAY (USA) [113] 6-11-10 M A Fitzgerald, *blun 1st and uns rdr.*..........(4 to 1 op 3 to 1 tchd 9 to 2) ur

2393* ZAMBEZI SPIRIT (Ire) [98] 8-10-9 Derek Byrne, *hld up, hdwy 9th, ev ch 13th, sn wknd, pld up bef 2 out.* ....(7 to 4 fav op 5 to 4 tchd 15 to 8 and 2 to 1) pu

Dist: 12l, 4l, 26l. 6m 13.00s. a 20.00s (6 Ran).
(The Mrs S Partnership), R Curtis

2729 Staines Handicap Chase Class E (0-110 5-y-o and up) £3,028 2m 5f (4:15)

2395* HAWAIIAN YOUTH (Ire) [104] 9-11-9 (3*) D Fortt, *hld up, pushed alng 7th, outpcd and hrd rdn tenth, hdwy to chase ldr 2 out, styd on to ld r-in, all out.* ......(9 to 4 fav op 3 to 1 tchd 100 to 30 and 2 to 1) 1

2425[6] JOVIAL MAN (Ire) [94] 8-11-2 P Holley, *led 3rd, clr 11th, hdd r-in, rallied.*..........(7 to 1 op 5 to 1 tchd 15 to 2) 2

2304* KEY PLAYER (Ire) [79] 8-10-1[1] D O'Sullivan, *hdwy to track ldrs aftr 6th, mstk 3 out, styd on same pace.* ....(8 to 1 op 5 to 1) 3

2395[5] BE SURPRISED [78] 11-9-7 (7*) M Batchelor, *led to 3rd, cl up, outpcd tenth, styd on frm 3 out, wknd r-in, fnshd tired.* ....(16 to 1 op 14 to 1 tchd 20 to 1) 4

2314[5] TOO SHARP [102] 9-11-10 J F Titley, *chsd ldrs, rdn appr 9th, one pace frm 3 out, wknd approaching last.* ....(5 to 1 tchd 6 to 1 and 13 to 2) 5

2401[5] RUBINS BOY [78] 11-9-7 (7*) D Finnegan, *trkd ldrs, pushed alng and lost pl aftr 6th, rdn 8th, beh after.* ....(33 to 1 tchd 40 to 1) 6

2266* SOPHIE MAY [89] (bl) 6-10-11 W Marston, *hld up, f 5th.* ....(7 to 2 op 3 to 1 tchd 4 to 1) f

2555 CHURCHTOWN PORT (Ire) [99] 7-11-4 (3*) L Aspell, *wth ldr frm 6th, ev ch whn mstk 11th, sn rdn and btn, no chance when f 2 out.*..........(10 to 1 op 8 to 1) f

2308 DEEPENDABLE [88] (v) 10-10-10 M Richards, *al beh, tld off whn pld up bef 4 out.*...(20 to 1 op 16 to 1 tchd 25 to 1) pu

2459 THE CAUMRUE (Ire) [105] 9-11-13 G Bradley, *in tch, lost pl 7th, mstk nxt (water), pld up bef tenth.* ....(11 to 1 op 8 to 1 tchd 12 to 1 and 14 to 1) pu

2392 KING'S COURTIER (Ire) [78] (v) 8-10-0 N Mann, *al beh, tld off whn pld up bef 4 out.*..........(50 to 1 tchd 66 to 1) pu

Dist: Nk, 3l, 11l, 3l, 10l. 5m 27.20s. a 18.20s (11 Ran).
(G Redford), G M McCourt

2730 Runnymede Handicap Hurdle Class D (0-125 4-y-o and up) £2,819 2m (4:50)

2532* MORE DASH THANCASH (Ire) [101] 7-10-5 Derek Byrne, *trkd ldrs, led appr 2 out, shaken up and quickened r-in, readily.* ....(11 to 10 fav op 6 to 4 tchd 13 to 8) 1

2429[2] SHEPHERDS REST (Ire) [101] 5-10-5 N Mann, *trkd ldrs, chlgd 2 out, ev ch r-in, not quicken.* ....(5 to 1 op 3 to 1 tchd 11 to 2 and 6 to 1) 2

COLOSSUS OF ROADS [100] 8-10-4 M Richards, *got loose bef strt, hld up beh ldrs, shaken up and outpcd appr 2 out, no extr, better for race*......(11 to 2 op 8 to 1 tchd 5 to 1) 3

2396[5] KELLY MAC [96] 7-10-0 W Marston, *trkd ldr, ev ch 3 out, outpcd appr nxt, kpt on.*..........(10 to 1 tchd 14 to 1) 4

2543[5] ROS CASTLE [120] (bl) 6-11-10 J Railton, *hld up, drvn 4 out, sn rallied, outpcd appr 2 out.*..........(25 to 1 op 14 to 1) 5

2501[3] ALBEMINE (USA) [124] 8-12-0 T Kent, *led to appr 2 out, hrd rdn, wknd r-in.* ....(9 to 2 op 7 to 2 tchd 11 to 2 and 6 to 1) 6

1517[5] HEVER GOLF DIAMOND [106] 4-9-13[6] (7*) Mr P O'Keeffe, *beh frm 5th, tld off.*..........(10 to 1 tchd 14 to 1) 7

2459[8] LINDEN'S LOTTO (Ire) [103] 8-10-0 (7*) S Parker, *al beh, tld off.*..........(33 to 1 op 14 to 1) 8

2532[9] GREEN LANE (USA) [105] 9-10-9 D Skyrme, *al beh, tld off.* ....(25 to 1 op 16 to 1 tchd 33 to 1) 9

Dist: 3½l, 7l, 1½l, ½l, 1¾l, 17l, ¾l, 19l. 3m 54.90s. a 9.90s (9 Ran).
SR: 26/22/14/8/31/33/ (F J Sainsbury), Mrs Merrita Jones

PUNCHESTOWN (IRE) (soft)
Sunday February 16th
Going Correction: PLUS 1.70 sec. per fur.

2731 Juvenile Hurdle (Grade 3) (4-y-o) £6,850 2m..........(2:10)

2470* COMMANCHE COURT (Ire) 11-0 N Williamson, *trkd ldr, prog to ld 4 out, rdn aftr 2 out, kpt on.*..........(6 to 4 on) 1

2470[8] GRIMES 11-3 C O'Dwyer, *wl plcd, jmpd slwly 5th, prog to track ldr 3 out, sn rdn, jumped slowly last.*..........(13 to 2) 2

2470[9] MISS ROBERTO (Ire) 10-2 (7*) R P Hogan, *led to 4 out, sn rdn, kpt on one pace.*..........(16 to 1) 3

2230[3] SPIRIT DANCER (Ire) 11-0 S C Lyons, *wtd wth, prog bef 4 out, rdn aftr nxt, kpt on.*..........(9 to 1) 4

2369[4] RESCUE TIME (Ire) 11-0 J Shortt, *mid-div, jmpd slwly second, wknd bef 5th, rdn aftr 3 out, not quicken.*..........(10 to 1) 5

2470 HIGHLY MOTIVATED 10-9 C F Swan, *wl plcd till rdn and wknd aftr 2 out.*..........(14 to 1) 6

2669 MISS PENNYHILL (Ire) 10-4 (5*) T Martin, *wtd wth, some prog bef 5th, rdn and wknd before 2 out.*..........(33 to 1) 7

2230* DR BONES (Ire) 11-0 T P Rudd, *rear, some prog 5th, rdn and wknd aftr 3 out.*..........(5 to 1) 8

Dist: 5l, 1l, 9l, 10l. 4m 20.10s. a 35.10s (8 Ran).
SR: 7/5/-/-/-/ (D F Desmond), T M Walsh

2732 Emerald Bloodstock INH Novice Hurdle Series (Grade 3) (5-y-o and up) £8,220 2m..........(2:40)

1189[2] PRIVATE PEACE (Ire) 7-11-8 R Hughes, *trkd ldrs, prog to ld 3 out, rdn bef last, styd on wl.*..........(14 to 1) 1

2072* BUKHARI (Ire) 5-11-1 C O'Dwyer, *wl plcd, prog to track ldrs 3 out, rdn aftr nxt, kpt on.*..........(5 to 2) 2

2472[4] THREE SCHOLARS 6-11-8 T P Treacy, *mid-div, prog bef 3 out, kpt on.*..........(14 to 1) 3

2582⁵ WINDY BEE (Ire) 6-10-6 (7*) A Nolan, *wtd wth, prog 5th to track ldr 3 out, sn rdn, kpt on* . . . .(16 to 1) 4

2472³ PALETTE (Ire) 5-11-0 D J Casey, *trkd ldrs till rdn and wknd aftr 2 out* . . . .(11 to 2) 5

291³ COLM'S ROCK (Ire) 6-11-4 T Horgan, *mid-div, rdn aftr 2 out, kpt on* . . . .(25 to 1) 6

2222* FISHIN JOELLA (Ire) 5-10-10 P Carberry, *wl plcd, prog to dispute ld 5th to 6th, rdn and wknd aftr nxt* . . . .(100 to 30) 7

552* DROMINEER (Ire) 6-11-4 N Williamson, *rear, some prog bef 3 out, sn rdn, kpt on* . . . .(12 to 1) 8

718² IDEAL PLAN (Ire) 7-11-4 R Dunwoody, *rear, some prog aftr 3 out, no ext* . . . .(10 to 1) 9

2473* TOAST THE SPREECE (Ire) 5-11-8 C F Swan, *rear, prog aftr 4 out, rdn after nxt, sn wknd* . . . .(9 to 4 fav) 10

APPLEFORT (Ire) 7-10-11 (7*) D K Budds, *dsptd ld till bef 4 out, sn wknd* 11

2583⁴ IRIDAL 5-11-1 K F O'Brien, *dsptd ld till bef 5th, led 4 out to nxt, sn wknd* . . . .(16 to 1) 12

Dist: 2½l, 10l, sht-hd, 1½l. 4m 16.00s. a 31.00s (12 Ran).

SR: 56/46/43/34/33/-/   (Mrs A M Daly), A P O'Brien

2733 I.A.W.S. Novice Chase (Grade 2) (5-y-o and up) £13,200 2m . . . . . . (3:10)

2052⁶ JEFFELL 7-11-7 F Woods, *made all, jmpd wl, rdn bef last, styd on strly* . . . .(5 to 2 jt-fav) 1

1898³ PAPILLON (Ire) 6-11-4 N Williamson, *wtd wth, prog bef 3 out, sn rdn, mstk last* . . . .(10 to 1) 2

2231⁴ KHARASAR (Ire) 7-11-4 C O'Dwyer, *wtd wth, prog 5 out, jmpd slwly nxt, rdn bef 3 out, not quicken* . . . .(7 to 2) 3

2587² CURRENCY BASKET (Ire) 8-11-0 J Shortt, *rear till f second.* . . . . .f

2367* PENNDARA (Ire) 8-11-4 C F Swan, *trkd ldr, rdn whn f 2 out.* . . . . .f

2442² BEAKSTOWN (Ire) 8-11-10 T P Treacy, *wl plcd, jmpd slwly 3rd and 5th, rdn bef 4 out, pld up before nxt* . . . .(9 to 2) pu

2367 ROCKETTS CASTLE (Ire) 7-11-0 P Carberry, *wl plcd, jmpd slwly 5th, lost tch bef 4 out, pld up before nxt* . . . . . .(16 to 1) pu

Dist: 15l, ¾l. 4m 31.70s. a 32.70s (7 Ran).

SR: 38/20/19/-/   (Thomas Bailey), A L T Moore

2734 Ericsson G.S.M. Grand National Trial Handicap Chase (5-y-o and up) £19,800 3¼m . . . . (3:40)

2071⁵ ANTONIN (Fr) [-] 9-10-0 C O'Dwyer, *wl plcd, prog to ld aftr 7th, drw away bef 4 out, easily* . . . .(6 to 1) 1

2474⁵ KING OF THE GALES [-] 10-10-6 C F Swan, *wtd wth, prog bef 11th, trkd ldr 4 out, sn rdn, no ext* . . . .(9 to 2) 2

2365⁴ CARRIGEEN KERRIA (Ire) [-] 9-9-7 D J Casey, *mid-div, mstk 3rd, prog 5th, wknd aftr 8th, jmpd slwly 7 out, rdn after 4 out, kpt on* . . . .(20 to 1) 3

2273⁸ FISSURE SEAL [-] 11-9-8 F Woods, *rear, mstk 8th, f tenth.* . . . .(12 to 1) f

2085⁵ SON OF WAR [-] 10-10-7 R Dunwoody, *trkd ldr, jmpd slwly 4th and 6th, mstk 9th, sn wknd, uns rdr 2 out* . . . . . .(5 to 1) ur

2446⁵ EXECUTIVE OPTIONS (Ire) [-] 8-9-10³ P Carberry, *mid-div till uns rdr 4th* . . . .(20 to 1) ur

2071 SECOND SCHEDUAL [-] 12-9-8¹ T P Treacy, *wl plcd, wknd bef 5th, pld up aftr 7th* . . . .(9 to 1) pu

MASTER OATS [-] 11-12-0 N Williamson, *wtd wth, prog 9th, rdn aftr 11th, trkd ldr 7 out, wknd after 5 out, pld up 4 out* . . . .(7 to 4 fav) pu

2273² CORYMANDEL (Ire) [-] 8-9-7 T P Rudd, *led, blun and hdd 7th, trkd ldr till wknd seven out, pld up bef 4 out* . . . . .(10 to 1) pu

Dist: Dist, 5l. 7m 27.20s. a 56.20s (9 Ran).

(G R Bailey Ltd), Mrs S A Bramall

2735 Dennis Coe Fencing Handicap Hurdle (0-109 4-y-o and up) £3,767 2m . . . . (4:10)

2369* VALLEY ERNE (Ire) [-] 6-11-4 J P Broderick, ...(3 to 1) 1
2447 MARINERS REEF (Ire) [-] 6-9-13 (7*) D McCullagh, (14 to 1) 2
2369² GOOD GLOW [-] 7-11-10 F Woods, ...(5 to 2 fav) 3
2369⁵ UPPER MOUNT STREET (Ire) [-] 7-10-9 T Horgan, (13 to 2) 4
2168 MIDDLEOFTHENIGHT (Ire) [-] 5-9-12 P Carberry, . .(16 to 1) 5
2518⁷ ATLANTA FLAME (Ire) [-] 6-9-9 W Slattery, ...(33 to 1) 6
1895 EUROTHATCH (Ire) [-] 9-9-11 (5*) T Martin, ...(25 to 1) 7
2415* CHOOSEY'S TREASURE (Ire) [-] 4-11-12 C F Swan, ...(12 to 1) 8
2378⁶ FOYLE WANDERER (Ire) [-] 6-13 T P Treacy, ...(20 to 1) 9
2366 JIHAAD (USA) [-] 7-9-2 (7*) J M Maguire, ...(25 to 1) 10
2473 TIDJANI (Ire) [-] 5-11-10 C O'Dwyer, ...(11 to 1) 11
2369⁹ SOFT SPOT (Ire) [-] 5-10-0 H Rogers, ...(20 to 1) 12
2378³ US FOUR (Ire) [-] 7-9-13 (7*) K A Kelly, ...(25 to 1) 13
2222⁷ NA HUIBHEACHU (Ire) [-] 6-10-2 R Hughes, ...(16 to 1) 14
2037 QUENNIE MO GHRA (Ire) [-] 6-9-0 (7*) L J Fleming, (33 to 1) 15
2415³ BE MY FOLLY (Ire) [-] 5-10-13 G M O'Neill, ...(16 to 1) 16
292* KEPHREN (USA) [-] 8-12-0 J Shortt, ...(16 to 1) 17
2272 SUPER FLAME (Ire) [-] 10-11-8 A Powell, ...(16 to 1) 18
2342⁸ AFGHANI (Ire) [-] 8-10-11 (5*) P Morris, ...(20 to 1) f
FANE'S TREASURE (Ire) [-] 8-11-2 R Dunwoody, . . (16 to 1) pu

Dist: 7l, 1l, 9l, 1l. 4m 20.40s. a 35.40s (20 Ran).

SR: 8/-/6/-/-/-/   (S A M Syndicate), Michael Cunningham

2736 Rathcoole Handicap Chase (0-133 5-y-o and up) £3,425 2m . . . . . . (4:40)

2412* THE CRAZY BISHOP (Ire) [-] (bl) 9-11-10 C O'Dwyer, (7 to 1) 1
2444⁴ SORRY ABOUT THAT [-] 11-9-0 (7*) L J Fleming, . .(14 to 1) 2
2167² BARNAGEERA BOY (Ire) [-] 8-11-1 K F O'Brien, ...(5 to 2 fav) 3
2444 ARCTIC WEATHER (Ire) [-] 8-11-11 T P Rudd, . .(7 to 2 fav) 4
2071⁶ DANCING VISION (Ire) [-] 7-10-8 J Jones, ...(10 to 1) 5
2136⁴ DOONANDORAS (Ire) [-] 9-11-7 F Woods, ...(4 to 1) 6
2019⁴ PERSIAN HALO (Ire) [-] 9-11-11 R Dunwoody, ...(8 to 1) f
2053² PERKNAPP [-] 10-10-12 G Bradley, ...(9 to 2) pu
2586⁴ MONALEE RIVER (Ire) [-] 9-12-0 T P Treacy, ...(14 to 1) pu
CABLE BEACH [-] 8-11-12 J P Broderick, ...(12 to 1) pu
2444* FIFTYSEVENCHANNELS (Ire) [-] 8-11-13 C F Swan, (6 to 1) pu

Dist: 6l, 6l, 15l, 20l. 4m 36.50s. a 37.50s (11 Ran).

(John J Hanlon), Anthony Mullins

2737 Ardenode I.N.H. Flat Race (4-y-o and up) £3,082 2m . . . . (5:10)

2235* PROMALEE (Ire) 5-11-11 (7*) Miss A L Crowley, (100 to 30) 1+
FINE DE CLAIRE 4-10-1 (7*) Mr R Geraghty, ...(10 to 1) 1+
2370³ DIVINE DANCER (Ire) 4-10-1 (7*) Mr M P Horan, . .(12 to 1) 3
2476³ STORM GEM (Ire) 6-11-13 (3*) Mr M Walsh, ...(12 to 1) 4
2276* RAINBOW VICTOR (Ire) 4-11-2 (7*) Mr R M Walsh, . .(7 to 1) 5
304 ONE WORD (Ire) 5-11-1 (7*) Mr A Stafford, ...(20 to 1) 6
FOREST RUN FOREST 5-11-8 Mr B M Cash, . . (2 to 1 fav) 7
CAPTAIN CHAOS (Ire) 6-11-4 (7*) Mr K R O'Ryan, (16 to 1) 8
KILLBALDONRUSH (Ire) 4-10-1 (7*) Mr J P Brennan, ...(25 to 1) 9
2449 PRINCE WOT A MESS (Ire) 6-11-4 (7*) Mr S McGonagle, ...(50 to 1) 10
MUSIC CITY BEAT (Ire) 7-11-4 (7*) Mr L J Fagan, . .(50 to 1) 11
2025⁵ MISS HOT TAMALLI (Ire) 6-11-3 (3*) Mr P M Kelly, (12 to 1) 12
2588 MOUNT HALL (Ire) 5-10-10 (7*) Mr A G Cash, ...(25 to 1) 13
DARSARAK (Ire) 4-10-13 Mr J P Dempsey, ...(7 to 1) 14
2129³ CLAY AND WATTLES (Ire) 6-12-0 (7*) Mr A K Wyse, (10 to 1) 15
2022 NIANTIC BAY (Ire) 5-11-1 (7*) Mr J P McNamara, . .(20 to 1) 16
HAZEL ROCK (Ire) 5-10-10 (7*) Mr A J Dempsey, . .(25 to 1) pu

Dist: Dd-ht, 5½l, 11l, 40l. 4m 20.30s. (17 Ran).

(Seamus O'Farrell & S P Tindall), A P O'Brien & J R H Fowler

FONTWELL (good to soft (race 1), good (2), soft (3,4,5,6))

Monday February 17th

Going Correction: PLUS 1.60 sec. per fur. (races 1,3,6), PLUS 1.50 (2,4,5)

2738 February Novices' Hurdle Class E (4-y-o and up) £3,099 2¾m 110yds . . . . (2:20)

2384² DENHAM HILL (Ire) 6-11-4 J Railton, *made all, drw clr appr 2 out, cmftbly.* . . . .(6 to 5 on op Evens tchd 11 to 10 and 11 to 8 on) 1
1447⁷ BRACKENHEATH (Ire) 6-11-4 B Fenton, *chsd ldrs, rdn 6th, outpcd appr 2 out, second and btn whn blun last.* . . . .(33 to 1 op 20 to 1 tchd 50 to 1) 2
2353⁴ PERSIAN ELITE (Ire) 6-11-4 J A McCarthy, *chsd wnr to 7th, rdn and wknd 3 out* . . . .(5 to 1 op 3 to 1) 3
2517* DRUM BATTLE 5-11-3 J Power, *prmnt, mstk second, chsd wnr 7th till wknd appr 2 out.* . . . .(7 to 1 op 5 to 1 tchd 14 to 1) 4
1893 TIN PAN ALLEY 8-11-4 M Richards, *mid-div, rdn 7th, sn lost tch* . . . .(50 to 1 op 33 to 1) 5
2607⁶ ALPINE SONG 12-10-13 Miss V Stephens, *chsd ldrs to 5th, beh frm 7th* . . . .(50 to 1 op 33 to 1) 6
1961⁶ COUNTRY STYLE 8-10-13 A Maguire, *chsd ldrs to 3rd, sn lost pl, tld off whn pld up bef 3 out* . . . .(50 to 1 op 16 to 1) pu
CHARLIE BEE 8-11-4 B Powell, *al rear, tld off whn pld up bef 2 out* . . . .(50 to 1 op 25 to 1 tchd 66 to 1) pu
2392⁷ NORDIC SPREE 5-11-4 P Holley, *beh whn pld up aftr 3rd* . . . .(14 to 1 op 12 to 1) pu
1971⁵ FRANK NAYLAR (bl) 6-11-4 D Bridgwater, *sn drvn alng, hdwy to chase ldrs second, wknd 8th* . . . . . .(50 to 1 op 33 to 1) pu
LORD LOVE (Ire) 5-11-4 S McNeill, *rear, mstk 4th, tld off whn pld up bef 8th* . . . .(50 to 1 op 25 to 1) pu
1338 MILLCROFT REGATTA (Ire) 9-11-4 J Culloty, *rear, some hdwy 5th, wknd 7th, tld off whn pld off bef last.* . . . .(50 to 1 op 25 to 1 tchd 66 to 1) pu
2263⁴ CLARKES GORSE 6-11-4 P Hide, *nvr dngrs, lost tch 7th, tld off whn pld up bef 2 out* . . . .(50 to 1 op 16 to 1) pu

Dist: 14l, 8l, 2l, dist, dist. 5m 55.60s. a 41.60s (13 Ran).

SR: 34/20/12/16/-/-/   (J E Brown), C J Mann

2739 Wittering Selling Handicap Chase Class G (0-95 5-y-o and up) £2,553 2m 3f . . . . (2:50)

2308⁶ OPAL'S TENSPOT [69] 10-10-5 B Fenton, *chsd ldrs, led 3 out, sn rdn* . . . .(10 to 1) 1
2247 GOLDEN OPAL [84] 12-11-6 D Bridgwater, *mid-div, blun tenth, hdwy to chase ldrs appr 3 out, sn btn.* . . . .(25 to 1 tchd 33 to 1) 2

2355⁵ WHISTLING BUCK (Ire) [81] 9-11-3 D O'Sullivan, *led to 3rd, led 6th, mstk twelfth, hdd 3 out, not quicken.*
.... (13 to 2 op 6 to 1 tchd 7 to 1) 3

2482² MASTER COMEDY [72] (bl) 13-10-8 A Maguire, *prmnt, cl 4th whn mstk 13th, sn outpcd.*
.... (11 to 4 fav tchd 3 to 1 and 7 to 2) 4

1559² RHOMAN FUN (Ire) [69] 8-10-5 B Powell, *mid-div, no hdwy frm 12th.*.................. (5 to 1 op 9 to 2) 5

2626⁴ FULL SHILLING (USA) [64] (bl) 8-9-13² (3*) Guy Lewis, *hdwy 5th, rdn 11th, wknd appr 3 out.*
.... (9 to 1 op 14 to 1 tchd 20 to 1) 6

1471 SALCOMBE HARBOUR (NZ) [64] 13-10-0 Dr P Pritchard, *al rear, tld off.*.................. (33 to 1 tchd 50 to 1) 7

2385⁵ SPRING LOADED [77] (v) 6-10-10 (3*) Michael Brennan, *prmnt till f 11th.*
.... (9 to 1 op 6 to 1 tchd 14 to 1) f

2547⁹ MR BEAN [92] 7-11-7 (7*) A Watt, *mid-div, mstk 4th, effrt 12th, 5th and hld whn blun and uns rdr 3 out.*
.... (9 to 1 op 5 to 1 tchd 10 to 1) ur

2477 TUG YOUR FORELOCK [64] 6-10-0 J Culloty, *slwly away, al beh, blun and uns rdr 12th.*
.... (11 to 1 op 12 to 1 tchd 14 to 1 and 10 to 1) ur

2247 TAPAGEUR [91] 12-11-13 D Walsh, *beh whn mstk 7th, tld off when pld up bef tenth.* (10 to 1 op 14 to 1) pu

1794 FIGHTING DAYS (USA) [86] (v) 11-11-8 P Holley, *hdwy to ld 3rd, hdd 6th, mstk and wknd 8th, tld off whn pld up bef 3 out.*
.... (20 to 1 op 14 to 1 tchd 25 to 1) pu

2482 ALBURY GREY [64] 10-10-0 G Crone, *slwly away, al tld off, pld up bef 7th.*.................. (25 to 1 op 16 to 1) pu

2457⁶ WARSPITE [67] (bl) 7-9-12 (5*) R Ryan, *prmnt till mstk 6th, tld off whn pld up bef tenth.*.................. (15 to 2 op 6 to 1) pu

Dist: 8l, 3l, 2½l, nk, 1½l, 8l. 5m 10.40s. a 35.40s (14 Ran).
SR: 8/15/9/-/-/-/ (Miss Joy Mailes), J M Bradley

2740 British Equestrian Insurance Brokers Handicap Hurdle Class E (0-115 4-y-o and up) £2,929 2¾m (3:20)

1858² PADDYSWAY [92] 10-10-6 D Bridgwater, *pressed ldr, led 5th to 3 out, rallied gmely to ld nr finish...*(9 to 2 tchd 5 to 1) 1

2392⁹ RELUCKINO [86] (v) 7-9-13² (3*) Michael Brennan, *rdn 4th, hdwy nxt, led 3 out, wknd r-in, ct nr finish.*
.... (25 to 1 op 16 to 1 tchd 33 to 1) 2

2562⁷ ST VILLE [88] (bl) 11-10-2 B Powell, *prmnt till rdn and lost pl 7th, rallied r-in, fnshd strly.*
.... (14 to 1 op 12 to 1 tchd 16 to 1) 3

2530⁶ MIRADOR [94] 6-10-3 D Morris, *hld up, hdwy 6th, trkd wnr 8th, rdn and btn aftr nxt.*
.... (2 to 1 fav op 7 to 4 tchd 9 to 4) 4

1628 ARABIAN SULTAN [107] 10-11-7 D Walsh, *led to 5th, tld off whn pld up bef 8th.*....... (5 to 1 op 9 to 2) pu

833⁸ PUNCH'S HOTEL [97] (bl) 12-10-11 D O'Sullivan, *hrd rdn and lost tch 7th, pld up bef 2 out.*......(10 to 1 tchd 11 to 1) pu

1700² DARING KING [87] 7-9-12 (3*) L Aspell, *beh frm 7th, pld up bef 2 out.*.................. (7 to 1 op 9 to 1 tchd 10 to 1) pu

2562 CUNNINGHAMS FORD (Ire) [105] 9-11-5 J A McCarthy, *chsd ldrs to 5th, sn hrd rdn and lost pl, pld up bef 8th.*
.... (33 to 1 op 25 to 1) pu

2389³ ROSENCRANTZ (Ire) [110] 5-11-10 A Maguire, *hld up and beh, mstk 4th, some hdwy 8th, sn wknd, poor 5th whn pld up bef 2 out.*.................. (7 to 2 op 9 to 4 tchd 4 to 1) pu

Dist: ½l, ½l, 6l. 6m 1.90s. a 47.90s (9 Ran).
(R T C Searle), R H Buckler

2741 Amberley Novices' Handicap Chase Class E (0-100 5-y-o and up) £3,183 3¼m 110yds (3:50)

2498⁶ FURRY FOX (Ire) [72] 9-11-6 D Morris, *hdwy 12th, jnd ldr 16th, led last, styd on wl....*(7 to 2 fav op 4 to 1 tchd 5 to 1) 1

2527 JAC DEL PRINCE [60] 7-10-8 P Hide, *led to second, mstk 12th, hdwy to chal appr 3 out, kpt on same pace.*
.... (4 to 1 op 3 to 1 tchd 9 to 2) 2

2291⁵ PLASSY BOY (Ire) [70] 8-11-4 A Maguire, *prmnt, slight ld 16th, hdd and blun last, no extr.......* (12 to 1 op 7 to 1) 3

2596⁹ BOURNEL [76] 9-11-10 B Fenton, *lft in ld 7th, hdd 13th, wknd 3 out.*.................. (9 to 1 op 10 to 1 tchd 12 to 1) 4

1236 BELLS WOOD [60] 8-10-8 S McNeill, *prmnt, led 13th to 16th, wknd and btn 3 out.*.................. (16 to 1 op 33 to 1) 5

2391⁶ MILLFRONE (Ire) [60] 7-10-8 D O'Sullivan, *led second till f 17th.*.................. (16 to 1 op 33 to 1) f

2657 ONEOFUS [69] 8-11-3 M Richards, *chsd ldrs till slpd up bend aftr 12th.*.................. (14 to 1 op 8 to 1) su

QUAKER BOB [60] 12-10-8 K Gaule, *lost tch 7th, sn tld off, pld up bef 13th.* (9 to 1 op 12 to 1 tchd 14 to 1 and 8 to 1) pu

23014 RONANS GLEN [72] 10-11-6 T J O'Sullivan, *mstk 5th, losing tch whn blun tenth, sn tld off, pld up bef 15th.*
.... (8 to 1 op 6 to 1) pu

24344 COOL CHARACTER (Ire) [72] 9-11-6 B Powell, *al rear, pld up bef 17th.*.................. (9 to 2 op 6 to 1 tchd 5 to 1) pu

1724⁷ AKIYMANN (USA) [68] 7-11-3 D Walsh, *hdwy 11th, chasing ldrs whn pld up appr 16th.*
.... pu

2527² THE MILLMASTER (Ire) [69] 6-11-0 (3*) Michael Brennan, *tld off frm 12th, pld up bef 16th.*....(16 to 1 op 25 to 1) pu

2354 GERRY'S PRIDE (Ire) [65] 6-10-13 S Curran, *beh whn mstk 18th, pld up bef 3 out.*..........(16 to 1 op 10 to 1) pu

---

Dist: 4l, 5l, 8l, 2l. 7m 28.30s. a 58.30s (13 Ran).
(Four Play Racing), R Curtis

2742 John Rogerson Memorial Challenge Trophy Handicap Chase Class D (0-120 5-y-o and up) £3,770 3¼m 110yds (4:20)

2245 FLAKED OATS [101] 8-11-8 D Bridgwater, *hdwy and mstk 12th, led and hit 17th, styd on gmely.*
.... (Evens fav op 5 to 4 tchd 11 to 8) 1

2564⁶ WOODLANDS BOY (Ire) [102] 9-11-9 D Morris, *led, mstk 16th, hdd nxt, rdn 4 out, kpt on gmely.*
.... (9 to 2 op 5 to 1 tchd 4 to 1) 2

1937⁴ CREDON [100] 9-11-7 S McNeill, *chsd ldrs to 16th, second and hld whn pckd 2 out, wknd last, virtually pld up r-in.*
.... (20 to 1 op 7 to 1) 3

1916⁵ LORNA-GAIL [95] 11-11-2 A Maguire, *al beh, tld off whn f 14th.*...... (5 to 1 op 9 to 2 tchd 4 to 1) f

2482* BLACK CHURCH [97] 11-11-4 D O'Sullivan, *beh, some hdwy 15th, sn wknd, poor 4th whn tld off bef last.*
.... (13 to 2 op 7 to 2 tchd 7 to 1) pu

2500 DANGER BABY [103] 7-11-10 B Powell, *hdwy 12th, wknd appr 16th, losing tch whn pld up bef nxt.*(11 to 2 op 3 to 1) pu

Dist: 1¼l, 30l. 7m 25.30s. a 55.30s (6 Ran).
(E B Swaffield), P F Nicholls

2743 Strebel Boilers And Radiators Handicap Hurdle Series Qualifier Class D (0-125 5-y-o and up) £3,172 2¼m 110yds (4:50)

1493³ GROUSEMAN [113] (bl) 11-11-7 J Culloty, *cl up, led aftr 3 out, styd on wl.*.................. (3 to 1 op 9 to 2) 1

2400* MARIUS (Ire) [118] 7-11-9 (3*) L Aspell, *in tch, hit 3rd, ev ch 3 out, kpt on same pace.*........(13 to 8 op 11 to 10) 2

WALKING TALL (Ire) [106] 6-11-0 D Bridgwater, *hld up, outpcd 6th, hrd rdn and some hdwy 2 out, not trble ldrs.*
.... (14 to 1 op 3 to 1 tchd 20 to 1) 3

2351 NEVER FORGOTTEN [92] 12-10-0 P Holley, *hld up rear, lost tch 3 out.*.................. (40 to 1 op 25 to 1 tchd 50 to 1) 4

2257² ISAIAH [109] 8-11-3 T Kent, *led till appr 2 out, sn btn.*
.... (11 to 8 fav op 7 to 4) 5

Dist: 11l, 10l, 19l, 14l. 4m 58.90s. a 41.90s (5 Ran).
(Aquarius), Miss H C Knight

HEREFORD (soft)
Monday February 17th
Going Correction: PLUS 1.25 sec. per fur.

2744 Primrose Novices' Hurdle Class E (4-y-o and up) £2,347 2m 1f (2:10)

2350² AVANTI EXPRESS (Ire) 7-11-3 J Osborne, *made all, clr frm 3 out, very easily.*.................. (5 to 4 on op 5 to 4) 1

INTO THE WEB (Ire) 6-11-3 Derek Byrne, *hld up, steady hdwy frm 3 out, styd on to take second r-in, no ch wth wnr.*
.... (16 to 1 op 8 to 1) 2

2430³ MERAWANG (Ire) 4-10-7 R Johnson, *sn prmnt, chsd wnr aftr 4 out till wknd r-in.*.................. (7 to 2 op 5 to 2) 3

2517³ BENFLEET 6-11-3 C Maude, *keen hold, chlgd and jmpd slwly second, wknd aftr 4 out....* (7 to 1 op 9 to 2) 4

1949² CALLINDOE (Ire) 7-10-12 N Williamson, *hdwy 5th, sn wknd.*
.... (16 to 1 op 14 to 1) 5

226⁵ BACKVIEW 5-11-3 Mr J L Llewellyn, *prmnt, chsd wnr 5th to 4 out, wknd nxt....*.................. (50 to 1) 6

1514⁹ LOOK IN THE MIRROR 6-11-3 C Llewellyn, *prmnt to 5th.*
.... (33 to 1 op 16 to 1) 7

2405 ALISTOVER 4-9-9 (7*) A Aizpuru, *al beh, tld off.....*(33 to 1) 8

1735 COOL HARRY (USA) 6-10-10 (7*) Mr S Durack, *sn beh, tld off.*.................. (100 to 1) 9

LUCKY ESCAPE 6-11-3 S Wynne, *sn beh, tld off.*
.... (33 to 1 op 16 to 1) 10

2250 BELGRAN (USA) 8-11-3 T Jenks, *rdn and beh frm 4th, tld off whn pld up bef 3 out.*.................. (100 to 1) pu

T'NIEL 6-10-5 (7*) S Lycett, *slwly away, tld off whn pld up bef 2 out.*.................. (100 to 1) pu

2430⁶ CHIEF MOUSE 4-11-5 G Bradley, *chsd ldrs, wknd and mstk 4 out, tld off whn pld up bef 2 out......*(8 to 1 op 5 to 1) pu

2550 CROWN AND CUSHION (bl) 4-10-13 N Mann, *al beh, tld off whn pld up bef 2 out.*.................. (25 to 1 op 16 to 1) pu

1977⁷ NANJIZAL 5-11-0 (3*) R Massey, *al beh, tld off whn pld up bef 2 out.*.................. (16 to 1 op 10 to 1) pu

Dist: 22l, 2½l, ½l, 10l, ¾l, 9l, 6l. 4m 12.50s. a 27.50s (15 Ran).
SR: 26/4/-/-/-/-/ (Mrs Sarah Stevens), C R Egerton

2745 Daffodil Handicap Chase Class E (0-115 5-y-o and up) £2,875 3m 1f 110yds (2:40)

2461³ POUCHER (Ire) [100] 7-11-5 S Wynne, *hld up, steady hdwy 12th, tracking ldrs whn hit 15th, led 2 out, clr when not fluent last.*.................. (9 to 4 fav op 5 to 2) 1

ALICE SMITH [85] 10-10-4 R Johnson, *pressed ldr, led 7th to 9th, led 3 out to nxt, one pace.*........(12 to 1 op 10 to 1) 2

1231⁵ NEVADA GOLD [98] 11-11-3 W Marston, *made most to 7th, led 9th, jmpd slwly 12th, rdn 4 out, hdd nxt, sn one pace.*
.... (12 to 1 op 10 to 1) 3
2252 PANT LLIN [81] 11-10-0 R Supple, *some hdwy 14th, wknd aftr 4 out.*.................................... (20 to 1) 4
1920⁶ BRAMBLEHILL BUCK (Ire) [109] 8-11-7 (7*) Mr J Tizzard, *chsd ldrs, hit 6th, wknd 14th.*............. (8 to 1 op 6 to 1) 5
2306 DIAMOND FORT [100] 12-11-5 N Williamson, *lost tch tenth, tld off whn pld up bef 15th.* (5 to 1 op 4 to 1 tchd 11 to 2) pu
2401⁷ MASTER JOLSON [102] 9-11-7 J R Kavanagh, *beh hfwy, tld off whn pld up bef 3 out.*............... (20 to 1 op 14 to 1) pu
TIRLEY MISSILE [81] 11-10-0 T J Murphy, *al beh, tld off whn pld up bef 15th.*.................... (33 to 1 op 25 to 1) pu
2480² KEEP IT ZIPPED (Ire) [99] 7-11-4 J Osborne, *jmpd slwly 3rd, lost tch tenth, tld off whn pld up bef 15th.*
.... (9 to 2 op 7 to 2 tchd 5 to 1) pu
2549² LOCH GARMAN HOTEL (Ire) [82] 8-10-11 C Maude, *chsd ldrs to 11th, tld off whn pld up bef 3 out.*
.... (100 to 30 op 3 to 1) pu
Dist: 14l, hd, 30l, 5l. 6m 55.80s. a 49.80s (10 Ran).

(Mrs A L Wood), Capt T A Forster

2746 Cowslip Novices' Handicap Hurdle Class E (0-105 4-y-o and up) £2,337 2m 3f 110yds................ (3:10)

2249⁵ SPRING DOUBLE (Ire) [91] 6-11-6 C Llewellyn, *hdwy 6th, chlgd and hit 4 out, led appr nxt, hdd last, sn led ag'n, ran on wl.*.................................. (12 to 1 op 10 to 1) 1
2207⁵ KONVEKTA QUEEN (Ire) [90] 6-11-5 J Osborne, *hdwy 6th, trkd ldrs 3 out, led last, sn rdn and hdd, no extr......* (6 to 1) 2
2158⁵ MELSTOCK MEGGIE [90] 7-11-5 N Williamson, *chsd ldrs, led appr 7th to 3 out, btn nxt.*............... (4 to 1 op 3 to 1) 3
2458² WINTER ROSE [76] 6-9-12 (7*) K Hibbert, *beh, some hdwy 3 out, nt a dngr.*......................... (16 to 1 op 14 to 1) 4
2603⁵ FASTINI GOLD [77] 5-10-6 C Maude, *nvr rch ldrs.* (16 to 1) 5
2462² LITTLE SHEFFORD [83] 5-10-12 I Lawrence, *led till appr 7th, sn wknd.*............... (12 to 1 op 10 to 1 tchd 14 to 1) 6
2428 HANGING GROVE (Ire) [85] 7-11-0 N Mann, *al rear.*
.... (25 to 1 op 16 to 1) 7
2603* RANGER SLOANE [81] 5-10-10 (7ex) R Farrant, *mid-div till f 5th.*............................... (8 to 1 op 7 to 1) f
2603 HIGH POST [80] 8-10-6 (3*) R Massey, *beh whn pld up and dismounted aftr 4th, dead.*......... (33 to 1 op 20 to 1) pu
2603³ SYLVESTER (Ire) [73] 7-9-13 (3*) P Henley, *sn beh, tld off whn pld up bef 3 out.*..................... (16 to 1) pu
2462* RIVER WYE (Ire) [95] 5-11-10 V Slattery, *chsd ldrs 5th, sn wknd, tld off whn pld up bef 2 out....* (7 to 2 fav op 5 to 1) pu
2423⁹ DARK TRUFFLE [82] 4-10-1 S Wynne, *chsd ldrs to 6th, sn wknd, tld off whn pld up bef 3 out......* (16 to 1 op 33 to 1) pu
2546⁵ MARKET MAYHEM [88] 7-11-3 T J Murphy, *beh 5th, tld off whn pld up bef 3 out.*.................. (14 to 1 op 10 to 1) pu
2323 COUNTRY MINSTREL (Ire) [74] 6-9-10 (7*) C Rae, *hdwy 6th, wknd 4 out, tld off whn pld up bef last.* (14 to 1 op 12 to 1) pu
2436 SIOUX TO SPEAK [89] 5-11-4 G Bradley, *chsd ldrs to 6th, sn wknd, tld off whn pld up bef 2 out.*
.... (11 to 2 op 6 to 1) pu
2550* MILLING BROOK [82] 5-10-11 R Johnson, *hmpd 5th and beh, tld off whn pld up bef 3 out..........* (12 to 1 op 10 to 1) pu
Dist: 1¾l, 9l, 24l, 14l, 16l. 5m 1.90s. a 43.90s (16 Ran).

(Mrs Lorna Berryman), N A Twiston-Davies

2747 Snowdrop Novices' Chase Class E (5-y-o and up) £2,791 2m..... (3:40)

2626 ELZOBA (Fr) 5-10-7 C Maude, *made all, in command whn lft clr 4 out, very easily.*
.... (Evens op 11 to 10 on tchd 11 to 10) 1
2376⁵ HEATHYARDS BOY (bl) 7-11-2 T Jenks, *chsd ldrs, hit 5th, blun 7th, lft poor second 2 out......* (66 to 1 op 33 to 1) 2
RELAXED LAD 8-11-2 R Bellamy, *mstk 3rd, lost tch frm 6th.*
.... (200 to 1 op 50 to 1) 3
2612² PURBECK CAVALIER (bl) 8-11-2 R Johnson, *dsptd ld second, styd chasing wnr till blun 4 out, second and no ch whn f 2 out.*
.... (10 to 1 op 8 to 1) f
2208 MASTER TRIBE (Ire) 7-11-2 N Williamson, *in tch, chlgd 5th, mstk nxt, rdn 7th, tld off whn pld up bef 4 out.*
.... (11 to 10 on tchd Evens) pu
Dist: Dist, 21l. 4m 12.10s. a 25.10s (5 Ran).
SR: 28/-/ (M C Pipe), M C Pipe

2748 Bluebell Novices' Handicap Chase Class E (0-105 5-y-o and up) £2,875 2m 3f......................... (4:10)

2604* CARDINAL RULE (Ire) [80] 8-10-13 (7ex) N Williamson, *made virtually all, drw readily clr frm 3 out.*
.... (6 to 4 fav op 7 to 4 tchd 9 to 4) 1
2391³ SUPER RITCHART [84] 9-11-3 T Jenks, *prmnt, chsd wnr frm 4 out, no imprsn...................* (10 to 1 tchd 12 to 1) 2
2604³ CHRIS'S GLEN [75] (v) 8-10-8 R Johnson, *chlgd second, chsd wnr to 4 out, wknd nxt......................* (16 to 1) 3
2354² WINNOW [71] 7-9-11 (7*) C Rae, *hdwy to chase ldrs 6th, wknd tenth....................* (11 to 2 op 5 to 1 tchd 6 to 1) 4
2547⁵ BURNTWOOD MELODY [67] 6-10-0 R Supple, *beh 5th, tld off..................................* (25 to 1 op 20 to 1) pu

2431⁶ MADAM ROSE (Ire) [67] 7-9-8¹ (7*) David Turner, *hdwy 5th, wknd 8th, tld off whn mstk and uns rdr 2 out, rmntd.* (50 to 1) 6
MINDYEROWNBUSINESS (Ire) [67] 8-10-0 S Wynne, *hmpd 4th, f nxt...........................* (20 to 1 tchd 25 to 1) f
2354 SAXON MEAD [67] (bl) 7-10-0 G Tormey, *f 4th.*
.... (10 to 1 op 6 to 1) f
2434² MOYNOO [84] 10-11-3 C Maude, *chsd ldrs till mstk and uns rdr 6th.....................* (13 to 2 op 7 to 2 tchd 7 to 1) ur
2154⁴ GIPSY RAMBLER [67] 12-10-0 W Worthington, *tld off 7th, pld up bef 3 out..........................* (16 to 1 tchd 20 to 1) pu
2604 COLONEL COLT [75] 6-10-8 W Marston, *al beh, tld off whn pld up bef 3 out............................* (20 to 1) pu
2461 DARA'S COURSE (Ire) [74] 8-10-7 Mr A Phillips, *beh 5th, tld off whn pld up bef 3 out.............* (20 to 1 op 25 to 1) pu
2547³ LATEST THYNE (Ire) [95] 7-12-0 C Llewellyn, *al beh, tld off whn pld up bef 3 out......* (7 to 2 tchd 3 to 1 and 4 to 1) pu
LITTLE GAINS [67] 8-9-13² (3*) P Henley, *sn beh, tld off whn pld up bef 3 out....................* (33 to 1) pu
2373³ EKEUS (Ire) [67] 7-10-0 T J Murphy, *chsd ldrs to 7th, tld off whn pld up bef 3 out............* (20 to 1 op 16 to 1) pu
Dist: 13l, 13l, 16l, dist, dist. 5m 2.20s. a 37.20s (15 Ran).

(Peter J Burch), Miss Venetia Williams

2749 Crocus Novices' Hurdle Class E (Div I) (5-y-o and up) £1,882 3¼m..(4:40)

2249⁷ FANCY NANCY (Ire) 6-10-7 C Maude, *hit 5th, hdwy 7th, led 9th, drw clr frm 2 out.....................* (7 to 1 op 6 to 1) 1
2392 CARDINAL GAYLE (Ire) 7-10-9 (3*) P Henley, *in tch, styd on und pres frm 3 out, not rch wnr.....* (3 to 1 fav op 4 to 1) 2
2625⁶ GI MOSS (bl) 10-10-7 W Marston, *prmnt, lost pl 7th, rallied und pres 4 out, one pace 2 out.*
.... (15 to 2 op 8 to 1 tchd 7 to 1) 3
1318³ ONE MORE DIME (Ire) 7-10-7 N Williamson, *made most to 9th, wknd 2 out..........................* (7 to 2 op 11 to 4) 4
1969⁸ WICKENS ONE 7-10-7 R Supple, *drpd rear 4th, rdn and hdwy sventh, wknd appr 3 out.*................ (16 to 1) 5
1456⁹ ZAGGY LANE 5-10-7 (5*) D Salter, *with ldr to 7th, wknd aftr 4 out................* (33 to 1 op 20 to 1) 6
1958⁴ TUDOR TOWN 9-10-12 L Harvey, *gd hdwy to chase ldrs 8th, chlgd nxt, sn wknd.*................ (11 to 1 op 6 to 1) 7
1567⁸ MILLY LE MOSS (Ire) (v) 8-10-7 V Slattery, *prmnt early, beh 6th, tld off nxt, pld up bef 3 out.....* (9 to 1 op 10 to 1) pu
2152 KYLE DAVID (Ire) 5-10-12 R Johnson, *prmnt, rdn 7th, sn wknd, tld off whn pld up aftr nxt.......* (20 to 1 op 16 to 1) pu
WOLDSMAN 7-10-12 C Llewellyn, *gd hdwy to chase ldrs 6th, pld up bef nxt.....................* (4 to 1 op 5 to 1) pu
Dist: 13l, 10l, 16l, 11l, 14l, 18l. 7m 11.60s. a 69.60s (10 Ran).

(T A Johnsey), Miss C Johnsey

2750 Crocus Novices' Hurdle Class E (Div II) (5-y-o and up) £1,871 3¼m (5:10)

2298⁹ SAMMORELLO (Ire) 6-10-12 C Llewellyn, *beh, drvn and hdwy 9th, second and no ch whn lft in ld 2 out, pushed out.*
.... (11 to 4 op 7 to 2 tchd 5 to 2) 1
2477⁵ CRAVATE (Fr) 7-10-0 (7*) M Moran, *led second to 4 out, 3rd and no ch whn lft second 2 out, styd on r-in.*
.... (9 to 2 op 7 to 2 tchd 5 to 1) 2
2428⁸ OTTER PRINCE 8-10-12 R Johnson, *prmnt, chlgd 4 out, sn wknd, tld off...........................* (7 to 1 tchd 8 to 1) 3
2456⁸ BLAZING MIRACLE 5-10-2 (5*) D Salter, *pressed ldrs, led 4 out, wl clr whn f 2 out...............* (2 to 1 fav op Evens) f
2030 BETHS WISH 8-10-7 J R Kavanagh, *led to second, beh 6th, tld off whn pld up bef 3 out.....* (16 to 1 op 10 to 1) pu
2436⁶ MINGAY 6-10-5 (7*) J Prior, *pld hrd, steadied rear aftr 4th, tld off whn pulled up bef 9th........* (25 to 1 op 20 to 1) pu
1727⁸ SHRIMP 6-10-7 N Williamson, *beh 5th, tld off whn pld up bef 3 out.........................* (9 to 1 op 10 to 1 tchd 10 to 1) pu
2029⁶ LEDBURIAN 7-10-5 (7*) K Hibbert, *effrt 8th, sn wknd, tld off whn pld up bef 3 out.......* (6 to 1 op 7 to 1 tchd 8 to 1) pu
Dist: 5l, dist. 7m 20.80s. a 78.80s (8 Ran).

(Mrs S A MacEchern), N A Twiston-Davies

CLONMEL (IRE) (heavy) Tuesday February 18th

2751 Vee Hurdle (4-y-o) £2,226 2m (2:15)

2669* MARLONETTE (Ire) 11-6 D J Casey, ... (15 to 8 on) 1
2161* NO AVAIL (Ire) 11-1 T P Treacy,....................(5 to 1) 2
2643⁵ APACHE TWIST (Ire) 11-0 C F Swan,................(5 to 2) 3
2669 CREWMAN (Ire) 10-7 (7*) S FitzGerald,..........(33 to 1) 4
Dist: 1l, 5l, dist. 4m 28.60s. (4 Ran).

(J Doran), W P Mullins

2752 Templemore Maiden Hurdle (6-y-o and up) £2,226 3m........... (2:45)

2582⁴ MARYOBEE (Ire) 7-11-1 T P Treacy,................(4 to 1) 1
2519⁴ SUNSHINE BAY (Ire) 6-11-6 G M O'Neill, ... (2 to 1 fav) 2
2520⁴ BAWNROCK (Ire) 8-12-0 C F Swan,................ (6 to 1) 3
2520³ RAHEEN RIVER (Ire) 6-11-3 (3*) Mr J A Berry,..... (7 to 1) 4
2519³ BLUE IRISH (Ire) (bl) 6-11-3 (3*) K Whelan,........ (7 to 1) 5
2585 MISS BERTAINE (Ire) (bl) 8-10-8 (7*) J E Casey, ... (16 to 1) 6

2582⁸ VALENTINE GALE (Ire) 7-11-9 D J Casey, ... (7 to 1) 7
2411 ROSEEN (Ire) 8-11-1 W Slattery, ... (16 to 1) 8
2520⁵ MILLSOFBALLYSODARE (Ire) 6-11-6 M P Hourigan,
. . . . (12 to 1) 9
2520 ALICE BRENNAN (Ire) 6-11-1 K F O'Brien, ... (20 to 1) 10
2520⁶ KYLOGUE KING (Ire) 6-11-6 T Horgan, ... (25 to 1) 11
2339³ JORIDI LE FORIGE (Ire) 6-11-6 T P Rudd, ... (8 to 1) 12
2520⁷ TRUCKINABOUT (Ire) 7-11-6 F Woods, ... (12 to 1) 13
2518 CARRAIGMACLEIR (Ire) 6-11-1 (7*) D McCullagh, . (25 to 1) 14
2276⁵ MICKS MAN (Ire) 6-12-0 M Duffy, ... (12 to 1) 15
2519 BATTLE AIR (NZ) 9-11-11 (3*) J Butler, ... (25 to 1) 16
2081 PUNTERS DREAM 7-11-6 J P Broderick, ... (25 to 1) pu
2520 VESPER LADY (Ire) 6-11-1 J Shortt, ... (20 to 1) pu
2704 CLOSING THYNE (Ire) 6-11-1 F J Flood, ... (25 to 1) pu
BROE'S CROSS (Ire) 7-10-13 (7*) A O'Shea, ... (50 to 1) pu
Dist: 12l, 2l, 8l, 6l. 6m 31.30s. (20 Ran).

(Gerard Halley) J A Berry

2753 Kilkenny Handicap Hurdle (0-109 5-y-o and up) £2,226 2½m. . . . (3:15)

2524⁵ KERCORLI (Ire) [-] 6-9-1 (7*) M D Murphy, ... (10 to 1) 1
2524* LETTERLEE (Ire) [-] 7-11-3 (7*) Mr M A Cahill, . . (2 to 1 fav) 2
2647⁶ CLONMEL COMMERCIAL (Ire) [-] 6-9-0 (7*) D McCullagh,
. . . . (10 to 1) 3
2520² COMMITTED SCHEDULE (Ire) [-] 6-10-1 M P Hourigan,
. . . . (7 to 1) 4
2585³ COOLREE LORD (Ire) [-] 6-9-0 (7*) P G Hourigan, . (3 to 1) 5
2519⁵ LORD OGAN (Ire) [-] 6-10-7 J P Broderick, ... (20 to 1) 6
2585 DIAMOND DOUBLE (Ire) [-] 6-11-0 C F Swan, ... (10 to 1) 7
2524⁴ GARLAND ROSE (Ire) [-] 7-9-11 D J Casey, ... (10 to 1) 8
2524 MAJESTIC JOHN (Ire) [-] 7-9-11 (7*) A T Kelly, . . . (20 to 1) 9
2647⁹ LIOS NA MAOL (Ire) [-] 6-9-0 (7*) J M Maguire, . . (20 to 1) 10
1460 REGIT (Ire) [-] 7-9-9 (7*) M J Collins, ... (20 to 1) 11
1752⁶ CNOCADRUM VI (Ire) [-] 6-9-7 W Slattery, ... (33 to 1) 12
1899 NATIVE GALE (Ire) [-] 5-11-1 (5*) T Martin, ... (10 to 1) 13
1899 TULLOLOUGH [-] 14-10-4 T Horgan, ... (25 to 1) 14
Dist: 1l, 4l, nk, 13l. 5m 29.80s. (14 Ran).

(Brendan Moriarty), A J McNamara

2754 Tipperary Maiden Hurdle (5-y-o) £2,226 2½m. . . . . (3:45)

2270 COMKILRED (Ire) 11-6 T P Treacy, ... (9 to 2) 1
2583 MANISTER ABBEY (Ire) 11-11 J P Broderick, ... (20 to 1) 2
2518⁹ ACTIVE LADY (Ire) 10-13 (7*) Mr B Walsh, ... (20 to 1) 3
2144³ ASHTALE (Ire) 11-6 D J Casey, ... (3 to 1) 4
2583 FILL THE BILL (Ire) 11-11 C F Swan, ... (9 to 4 fav) 5
2416³ AHINDUCLINT (Ire) 11-6 G M O'Neill, ... (100 to 30) ro
2525 TISNOTMYTURN (Ire) 10-13 (7*) Miss C O'Neill, . (20 to 1) ro
2583 ZACOPANI (Ire) 11-6 (5*) P Morris, ... (20 to 1) pu
2443 THE SIDHE (Ire) 11-3 (3*) J Butler, ... (20 to 1) pu
Dist: 4l, 25l, 1½l, 15l. 5m 39.20s. (9 Ran).

(Cull Island Syndicate), F M Somers

2755 Clonmel Novice Chase (5-y-o and up) £2,226 2¼m. . . . . (4:15)

2522³ ANOTHER DEADLY 10-11-5 T P Treacy, ... (9 to 4 fav) 1
2165³ CARROLLS ROCK (Ire) 6-11-5 P A Roche, ... (8 to 1) 2
2143 COLLON (Ire) 8-11-5 T J Mitchell, ... (8 to 1) 3
85⁴ PUNTERS BAR 10-11-5 J Shortt, ... (6 to 1) 4
2705 ANDY BURNETT (Ire) 8-11-5 F J Flood, ... (7 to 2) 5
2674⁸ MIDNIGHT JAZZ (Ire) 7-11-2 J P Broderick, ... (7 to 1) 6
2411 LAKE TOUR (Ire) 7-11-4 (3*) K Whelan, ... (10 to 1) 7
2413 LISHILLAUN (Ire) 7-10-7 (7*) Mr J A Collins, ... (100 to 1) 8
ROSEL WALK 8-11-5 A J O'Brien, ... (20 to 1) 9
2222 WHINNEY HILL (Ire) 7-11-0 A Powell, ... (20 to 1) 10
2093 THE YELLOW BOG (Ire) 7-10-12 (7*) D Flood, ... (20 to 1) ur
Dist: 11l, 2l, 3½l, 1½l. 4m 55.70s. (11 Ran).

(Peter O'Connor), Patrick G Kelly

2756 Ballyvaughan Q.R. Handicap Chase (0-109 5-y-o and up) £2,226 3m
. . . . (4:45)

COMING ON STRONG (Ire) [-] 8-10-8 (7*) Mr D P Daly,
. . . . (11 to 1) 1
2411² INDESTRUCTIBLE (Ire) [-] 9-11-5 (3*) Mr R Walsh, . (7 to 1) 2
2448⁶ ALL IN THE GAME (Ire) [-] 9-9-11 (7*) Mr J P Moloney,
. . . . (7 to 1) 3
2274⁷ STRONG HICKS (Ire) [-] 9-11-8 (7*) Mr A J Dempsey,
. . . . (10 to 1) 4
2274⁹ TOUT VA BIEN (Ire) [-] 9-10-10 (3*) Mr B R Hamilton, (12 to 1) 5
1553² FINAL TUB (Ire) [-] 14-11-4 (7*) Mr B Moran, ... (14 to 1) 6
2411⁵ DOONEGA (Ire) [-] 9-10-4⁷ (7*) Mr E Gallagher, . . . (12 to 1) 7
2410* SIDCUP HILL (Ire) [-] 8-11-3 (3*) Mr T Lombard, . . . (10 to 1) 8
2169⁸ VELEDA II (Fr) [-] 10-10-11 (7*) Mr J L Cullen, ... (20 to 1) 9
2163⁶ CANAILLOU II (Fr) [-] 7-10-13 Mr B M Cash, ... (6 to 1) 10
2338³ OLYMPIC D'OR (Ire) [-] 9-10-10 (7*) Mr W Ewing, . . (10 to 1) f
2338* IRISH LIGHT (Ire) [-] 9-11-7 (5*) Mr J T McNamara,
. . . . (4 to 1 fav) ur
2673⁸ FIELD OF DESTINY (Ire) [-] (bl) 8-9-13 (7*) Mr A Ross,
. . . . (20 to 1) ur
2021⁶ SHARONS PRIDE (Ire) [-] 7-10-5⁴ (5*) Mr A C Coyle, (5 to 1) ur
2671⁴ CORSTON DANCER (Ire) [-] 9-10-5 (7*) Mr P M Cloke,
. . . . (20 to 1) pu

Dist: Sht-hd, 3l, ¾l, 2l. 6m 48.80s. (15 Ran).

(Lisselan Farms Ltd), Fergus Sutherland

2757 Kilsheelan I.N.H. Flat Race (5-y-o and up) £2,226 2m. . . . . (5:15)

SEE JUST THERE (Ire) 7-11-11 (3*) Mr R Walsh, (6 to 4 fav) 1
SLAVICA 6-11-2 (7*) Mr J P Shaw, ... (10 to 1) 2
2449⁵ LAFONTO'OR (Ire) 6-11-7 (7*) Mr B Moran, ... (3 to 1) 3
COLLON DIAMONDS (Ire) 9-11-2 (7*) Mr C P McGivern,
. . . . (8 to 1) 4
2449 TOUGH TERMS (Ire) 5-11-6 (5*) Mr A C Coyle, . . . (10 to 1) 5
TONGUE-IN-CHEEK (Ire) 6-12-0 Mr B M Cash, ... (7 to 1) 6
IN YOUR EYES 6-11-9 Mr D Marnane, ... (20 to 1) 7
2675 SPLEODRACH (Ire) 7-11-9 Mr J A Berry, ... (14 to 1) 8
2525⁶ CLARA ROCK (Ire) 5-10-13 (7*) Mr C J Radley, ... (8 to 1) 9
SWEET STEP (Ire) 6-11-7 (7*) Mr M J Bowe, ... (20 to 1) 10
INCHIQUIN CASTLE (Ire) 5-11-4 (7*) Mr R J Curran, (14 to 1) 11
2588 NEARLY A LINE 5-11-4 (7*) Mr A FitzGerald, ... (14 to 1) 12
2343 TULIP (Ire) 6-11-6 (3*) Mr D Valentine, ... (16 to 1) 13
LADY MEARGAN (Ire) 6-11-2 (7*) Mr J A Smith, . . (20 to 1) 14
BURN AGAIN 7-11-2 (7*) Mr J Boland, ... (20 to 1) 15
CORVARO FLYER (Ire) 6-11-7 (7*) Mr S P Hennessy,
. . . . (10 to 1) 16
FARVELLA (Ire) 6-11-7 (7*) Mr A J Costello, ... (20 to 1) 17
2675 MARIA-NOELLE (Ire) 7-11-9 Mr J A Nash, ... (25 to 1) 18
GOOD LEADER (Ire) 6-11-2 (7*) Mr B N Doyle, ... (25 to 1) 19
THEATRE SISTER (Ire) 6-11-2 (7*) Mr K Hadnett, . (16 to 1) pu
Dist: 13l, 8l, 9l, 9l. 4m 22.00s. (20 Ran).

(Olde Crowbars Syndicate), W P Mullins

MARKET RASEN (good)
Tuesday February 18th
Going Correction: PLUS 0.65 sec. per fur. (races 1,3,5,7), PLUS 1.10 (2,4,6)

2758 Louth Novices' Hurdle Class D (4-y-o and up) £3,300 2m 1f 110yds (2:00)

2565* MY CHEEKY MAN 6-11-9 R Johnson, settled with chasing
grp, improved frm hfwy, chlgd and hit 2 out, rallied gmely to ld
on line. . . . . (15 to 2 op 9 to 2 tchd 8 to 1) 1
2489* WHIP HAND (Ire) 6-12-1 J Osborne, settled travelling wl,
smooth hdwy frm off the pace bef 3 out, led on bit appr nxt, wnt
clr, ct on line. . . . . (6 to 5 fav op 7 to 4 tchd 15 to 8) 2
2594 MORPHEUS 8-11-3 A Maguire, settled off the pace,
improved frm 3 out, styd on, nvr plcd to chal.
. . . . (11 to 1 op 14 to 1 tchd 10 to 1) 3
2371³ COUNTRY LOVER (bl) 6-11-3 C Maude, wth ldr, led 3 out till
bef nxt, fdd und prs betw last 2.
. . . . (11 to 1 op 8 to 1 tchd 12 to 1) 4
2353² COTTEIR CHIEF (Ire) 6-11-3 R Dunwoody, patiently rdn, cld
appr 3 out, reminders aftr nxt, no extr.
. . . . (9 to 2 op 4 to 1 tchd 6 to 1) 5
2533³ BILLY BUSHWACKER 5-11-3 N Smith, settled with chasing
grp, effrt hfwy, rdn, nvr rch chalg pos. . (10 to 1 op 6 to 1) 6
TONTO 4-10-7 Derek Byrne, sn beh, drvn alng hfwy, nvr able
to rch chalg pos. . . . . (50 to 1 op 33 to 1) 7
2417 NEXSIS STAR 4-10-7 R Guest, chsd clr ldg pair, rdn bef 3 out,
sn lost tch. (50 to 1 op 20 to 1) 8
2526⁸ FIRST GOLD 8-11-3 J R Kavanagh, struggling to keep in tch
hfwy, tld off 3 out. . . . . (50 to 1) 9
O K KEALY 7-11-3 W Worthington, lost tch hfwy, tld off whn
pld up betw last 2. . . . . (50 to 1) pu
MARIGLIANO (USA) 4-10-7 A S Smith, set str pace, hdd 3 out,
wknd quickly, tld off whn pld up betw last 2.
. . . . (17 to 2 op 5 to 1) pu
2199² SLIDE ON 7-11-3 N Williamson, blun 4th, sn lost tch, tld off
whn pld up betw last 2, lme. . . . . (14 to 1 op 12 to 1) pu
2419 FLORRIE GUNNER 7-10-12 J Callaghan, tld off till pld up
betw last 2. . . . . (50 to 1 op up) pu
Dist: Sht-hd, 19l, ¾l, 24l, ½l, 6l, 7l, dist. 4m 18.50s. a 17.50s (13 Ran).
SR: 34/40/9/8/-/-/ (Mrs A A Shutes), D Nicholson

2759 Queens Royal Lancers Handicap Chase Class D For the 17th/21st Lancers Challenge Cup (0-120 5-y-o and up) £3,522 2½m. . . . . (2:30)

2654² ALJADEER (USA) [110] 8-11-10 N Williamson, patiently rdn,
steady hdwy 6 out, led bef 2 out, styd on to go clr frm last.
. . . . (7 to 1 tchd 6 to 1) 1
2386³ RUSTIC AIR [104] 10-11-4 P Carberry, led second, lft clr 5 out,
blun 4 out, jnd nxt, sn hdd, rdn and one pace frm last.
. . . . (6 to 1 tchd 7 to 1) 2
2622³ NETHERBY SAID [104] 7-11-4 R Supple, settled with ldrs,
blun 6th, hit nxt, nrly f six out, rallied, wknd betw last 2.
. . . . (4 to 1 op 7 to 2) 3
2247 JACOB'S WIFE [106] 7-11-6 J Osborne, patiently rdn, steady
hdwy frm hfwy, kpt on, no imprsn on ldrs. . . . . (14 to 1) 4
2494⁶ FARNEY GLEN [87] 10-9-10 (5*) R McGrath, last hfwy, chsd
alng frm 6 out, nvr rch chalg pos. . . . (7 to 1 tchd 25 to 1) 5
2564⁷ DOLIKOS [97] 10-10-11 T J Murphy, lost tch hfwy, tld off.
. . . . (25 to 1 op 33 to 1) 6

2464* CATTLY HANG (Ire) [105] 7-11-5 A Dobbin, *struggling to keep in tch hfwy, tld off 6 out*.......... (2 to 1 fav tchd 6 to 4) 7
2282 THE FLYING FOOTMAN [90] 11-10-4 J Culloty, *beh whn pld up bef 8th*........................ (33 to 1 op 25 to 1) pu
2529* DISTINCTIVE (Ire) [109] 8-11-9 R Dunwoody, *led to second, lost tch 6 out, tld off whn pld up bef 3 out*.
..................................(3 to 1 tchd 7 to 2) pu
Dist: 17l, hd, 6l, 5l, 10l, 1l. 5m 17.10s. a 28.10s (9 Ran).
SR: 35/12/12/8/-/-/ (Miss V Foster), M W Easterby

2760 Sherwood Rangers Yeomanry Handicap Hurdle Class D (0-120 4-y-o and up) £2,796 2m 1f 110yds.....(3:00)

2530⁷ NON VINTAGE (Ire) [120] 6-12-0 W Worthington, *niggled alng beh ldrs, improved frm 3 out, styd on to ld betw last 2, drw clr r-in*....................... (4 to 1 tchd 9 to 2) 1
2581⁸ TIP IT IN [92] 8-9-7 (7*) N Horrocks, *chsd ldrs, effrt hfwy, feeling pace 3 out, styd on betw last 2, no imprsn on wnr*.
..................................(4 to 1 op 5 to 1) 2
2332⁵ OUR KRIS [116] (bl) 5-11-10 J R Kavanagh, *chsd ldr, effrt hfwy, led appr 2 out till betw last two, no extr*.
.................................(12 to 1 op 14 to 1) 3
2580⁴ TAPATCH (Ire) [95] 9-10-3 N Williamson, *settled in tch, effrt hfwy, reminders to hold pl 3 out, struggling bef nxt, sn btn*.
.................................(7 to 1) 4
2537³ SUMMERHILL SPECIAL (Ire) [113] 6-11-7 R Guest, *settled to track ldrs, pckd and lost grnd 3rd, struggling bef 3 out, sn lost tch*....................(5 to 2 fav op 2 to 1) 5
1982⁸ ROBERT'S TOY (Ire) [115] (bl) 6-11-9 C Maude, *led, clr hfwy, rdn and hdd appr 2 out, wknd quickly*.
.................................(3 to 1 op 2 to 1) 6
Dist: 7l, 2½l, 2l, 2l, 1l. 4m 22.50s. a 21.50s (6 Ran).
(Alan Mann), M C Chapman

2761 European Breeders Fund Tattersalls Ireland Mares' Only Novices' Chase Qualifier Class E (6-y-o and up) £3,094 2m 1f 110yds........(3:30)

1331⁴ CHADWICK'S GINGER 9-10-12 Derek Byrne, *made most, hesitated 6th and nxt, quickened clr 3 out, styd on strly r-in*.
...................(2 to 1 fav op 3 to 1 tchd 7 to 2) 1
2419 HUTCEL LOCH 6-10-12 A S Smith, *settled midfield, cld 5 out, drvn alng and not fluent last 3, one pace r-in*.
..................................(8 to 1 tchd 10 to 1) 2
2679 MERILENA (Ire) 7-10-12 B Fenton, *in tch, lost pl quickly aftr 5th, styd on strly frm 3 out, fnshd wl*.
.................(9 to 2 op 7 to 2 tchd 5 to 1) 3
2577³ AUNTIE ALICE 7-10-12 J Osborne, *settled to track ldrs, not fluent and lost pl 5 out, reminders nxt, no imprsn*.
..................................(9 to 2 tchd 5 to 1) 4
2576 CHORUS LINE (Ire) 8-10-12 R Supple, *with ldrs, led briefly second, hndy till wknd betw last 2*.... (4 to 1 op 7 to 2) 5
KNOCKREIGH CROSS (Ire) 8-10-12 J Supple, *last and drvn alng hfwy, tld off 4 out*.............. (50 to 1 op 33 to 1) 6
2422⁹ HIGH PENHOWE 9-10-12 W Marston, *settled in tch, lost pl quickly hfwy, tld off 4 out*.............. (50 to 1 op 33 to 1) 6 7
123² MORCAT 8-10-12 Mr C Mulhall, *settled off the pace, some hdwy 4 out, no ch whn pld up appr 2 out*.
..................................(12 to 1 op 10 to 1) pu
2511⁹ RIVERBANK RED 6-10-9 (3*) Guy Lewis, *pressed ldrs, lost grnd quickly fnl circuit, tld off whn pld up appr 2 out*.
..................................(33 to 1 op 25 to 1) pu
Dist: 6l, 7l, 12l, 21l, 8l, dist. 4m 47.20s. a 33.20s (9 Ran).
(W H Tinning), W H Tinning

2762 Levy Board Handicap Hurdle Class F (0-105 4-y-o and up) £2,442 2m 5f 110yds...................(4:00)

2241 BOSTON MAN [84] 6-10-11 P Carberry, *chsd ldr, led 6th, rdn aftr last, styd on gmely finish*...... (16 to 1 tchd 20 to 1) 1
1568 HANCOCK [73] 5-10-0 W Marston, *settled with chasing grp, improved to chase wnr aftr 3 out, effrt and rdn frm last, kpt on*.
..................................(50 to 1) 2
2487⁶ GALEN (Ire) [89] 6-11-2 R Dunwoody, *patiently rdn, improved aftr 3 out, styd on frm betw last 2, not rch ldrs*.
.................(13 to 2 op 6 to 1 tchd 7 to 1) 3
2289 WASSL STREET (Ire) [101] 5-12-0 A S Smith, *nvr far away, chsd alng whn pace quickened aftr 3 out, no imprsn*.
..................................(9 to 1 op 8 to 1) 4
2548⁵ ALASKAN HEIR [79] 6-10-6 T Eley, *nvr far away, chsd alng whn ldrs quickened 3 out, one pace*... (20 to 1 op 14 to 1) 5
2548² KADARI [87] (v) 8-10-11 (3*) Guy Lewis, *settled with chasing grp, effrt fnl circuit, kpt on, no imprsn frm 3 out*.
..................................(8 to 1 op 7 to 1 tchd 9 to 1) 6
2487⁹ EXEMPLAR (Ire) [88] 9-11-1 R Guest, *chsd ldg bunch, effrt fnl circuit, one pace 3 out*......... (16 to 1 op 12 to 1) 7
2550³ MRS ROBINSON (Ire) [78] 6-10-2 (3*) E Husband, *co'red up wth chasing grp, effrt fnl circuit, no imprsn on ldrs frm 3 out*.
..................................(8 to 1 op 7 to 1) 8
2407⁷ MAJOR YAASI (USA) [85] (bl) 7-10-12 J Osborne, *wnt hndy hfwy, feeling pace last 3 out, no imprsn*....(16 to 1) 9
2400³ SASSIVER (USA) [88] 7-11-1 K Gaule, *hmpd 5th, drvn alng fnl circuit, no imprsn frm 3 out*..........(10 to 1 op 8 to 1) 10

SHOOFE (USA) [75] 9-10-2 R Johnson, *sn beh, nvr rch chalg pos*...........................(20 to 1 op 14 to 1) 11
2440 BILL AND WIN [73] (v) 6-9-11 (3*) R Massey, *sn struggling, nvr a factor*.................(66 to 1 op 50 to 1) 12
2158 GRAND CRU [89] 6-10-13 (3*) G Lee, *hampered 5th, nvr able to rch chalg pos*............(14 to 1 op 12 to 1) 13
2577 JUST SUPPOSEN (Ire) [83] 6-10-10 J Supple, *wl beh hfwy, tld off*..................................(50 to 1) 14
2491⁵ FINAL BEAT (Ire) [76] 8-10-3 B Fenton, *lost tch hfwy, tld off*..................................(33 to 1) 15
GRACE CARD [95] 11-11-8 N Williamson, *reminders 3rd, sn tld off*..................................(20 to 1) 16
2435 PASSED PAWN [101] 10-11-7 (7*) G Supple, *led, sn clr, wknd and hdd 6th, lost tch, tld off*.........(20 to 1) 17
2616* MAYB-MAYB [75] 7-10-2 (7ex) T J Murphy, *chasing ldrs whn f 5th*.............(11 to 4 fav op 3 to 1 tchd 7 to 2) f
2257⁶ GYMCRAK TIGER (Ire) [87] 7-11-0 A Maguire, *chasing ldrs whn brght dwn 5th*................(9 to 1 op 8 to 1) bd
Dist: 1l, 27l, 4l, 2l, ¾l, 3l, nk, 9l, 5l, 5l. 5m 33.10s. a 30.10s (19 Ran).
(M K Oldham), R D E Woodhouse

2763 Alford Novices' Chase Class E (5-y-o and up) £3,068 3m 1f.........(4:30)

2286² RANDOM HARVEST 8-11-10 R Dunwoody, *wth ldr, led 9th, clr 3 out, styd on strly, easily.* (11 to 10 fav op 6 to 4) 1
1970⁶ SLIDEOFHILL (Ire) 8-11-4 Mr P Fenton, *chsd ldrs, effrt hfwy, styd on frm betw last 2, no ch wth wnr*.
..................................(9 to 1 op 6 to 1 tchd 10 to 1) 2
2406 WHATBADS (Ire) 8-11-10 N Williamson, *sn handily plcd, wnt second fnl circuit, hit 5 out, rdn aftr 4 out, fdd nxt*.
..................................(2 to 1 op 7 to 4) 3
2348⁵ HIGHBEATH 6-11-4 N Smith, *in tch to hfwy, lost pl quickly, tld off 4 out*..........(20 to 1 op 16 to 1 tchd 25 to 1) 4
2347⁷ KINGS SERMON (Ire) 8-11-10 R Supple, *led to 9th, blun and lost grnd 6 out, poor 4th whn f 2 out*.
..................................(11 to 1 op 8 to 1 tchd 12 to 1) f
1797⁷ PANDORA'S PRIZE (bl) 11-10-6 (7*) Mr S Joynes, *pressed ldrs for o'r one circuit, lost 4 out, tld off whn pld up betw last 2*.............(50 to 1 op 33 to 1 tchd 66 to 1) pu
2203 I'M IN CLOVER (Ire) (v) 8-11-4 W Marston, *struggling and lost grnd quickly 7th, tld off whn pld up aftr 11th*.
..................................(50 to 1 tchd 66 to 1) pu
CLAVERHOUSE (Ire) 8-11-4 J Osborne, *chsd alng to keep up hfwy, hit tenth, tld off whn pld up bef 4 out*.
..................................(10 to 1 op 8 to 1) pu
Dist: 23l, 28l, dist. 6m 51.50s. a 51.50s (8 Ran).
(C C Buckley), Mrs M Reveley

2764 Market Rasen Intermediate Open National Hunt Flat Class H (4,5,6-y-o) £1,339 1m 5f 110yds.....(5:00)

2206* AUTUMN LORD 4-10-10 (5*) B Grattan, *made all, hrd pressed frm o'r one furlong out, ran green, hld on gmely nr finish*............... (6 to 4 fav op 2 to 1 tchd 5 to 4) 1
1942* GUIDO (Ire) 6-11-11 N Williamson, *settled travelling wl, smooth hdwy to chal frm o'r one furlong out, ran on, jst hld*.
..................................(5 to 1 op 7 to 2 tchd 11 to 2) 2
2262³ ALISANDE (Ire) 5-10-10 (3*) Mr C Bonner, *wtd wth, improved frm off the pace last 3 fs, styd on finish.* (8 to 1 tchd 9 to 1) 3
2483* MACY (Ire) 4-10-8 (7*) X Aizpuru, *nvr far away, chsd alng whn pace quickened entering strt, one pace last 2 fs*.
..................................(12 to 1 op 8 to 1) 4
BROTHER HARRY 5-11-1 (3*) R Massey, *patiently rdn, steady hdwy frm midfield appr strt, not trble ldrs*.
..................................(40 to 1 op 20 to 1) 5
2503⁸ FRUITATION 6-10-13 R Dunwoody, *settled wth chasing grp, styd on in strt, nvr nr to chal*.
..................................(12 to 1 op 8 to 1 tchd 14 to 1) 6
PAUSE FOR THOUGHT 4-10-8 R Hodge, *sn beh, styd on last half-m, nvr able to chal...* (11 to 2 op 7 to 1 tchd 9 to 1) 7
THE COUNTRY DON 5-11-4 W Marston, *settled off the pace, styd on strt, nvr trble ldrs*...........(33 to 1 op 25 to 1) 8
2199 RED OASSIS 6-11-4 Jacqui Oliver, *wtd wth, effrt aftr one m, no imprsn strt*.............(33 to 1 op 25 to 1) 9
PHONE THE PIPELINE 4-10-1 (7*) G Supple, *shwd up wl for o'r one m, hld bef strt*.............(16 to 1 op 8 to 1) 10
SISTER JANE 4-10-3 Mr W McLaughlin, *pressed ldrs for o'r one m, wknd bef strt*................(33 to 1) 11
2262 MY VANTAGE 4-10-8 L Wyer, *steadied strt, keen hold, nvr rch chalg pos*...................(40 to 1 op 25 to 1) 12
2322⁸ SIR BOSTON 4-10-8 A S Smith, *wth wnr, wknd quickly back strt, tld off*..................(20 to 1 op 16 to 1) 13
2262 FARM TALK 5-11-4 J R Kavanagh, *al beh, nvr a factor*.
..................................(50 to 1 tchd 66 to 1) 14
WITHY CLOSE (Ire) 4-10-8 R Johnson, *settled midfield, nvr a factor, tld off*.......(11 to 1 op 8 to 1 tchd 12 to 1) 15
LANDLER 4-10-5 (3*) G Lee, *al beh, tld off strt*.
..................................(16 to 1 op 14 to 1 tchd 20 to 1) 16
2469 STAN'S PRIDE 5-11-4 B Fenton, *sn beh, tld off strt.* (33 to 1) 17
FRUGAL 4-10-8 W Dwan, *lost tch hfwy, tld off*.....(33 to 1) 18
1887 CAHERLOW (Ire) 6-11-4 M Brennan, *al beh, tld off, virtually pld up*........(40 to 1 op 25 to 1 tchd 50 to 1) 19
Dist: Nk, 11l, 1½l, 18l, 3½l, 4l, 1¾l, 10l, hd. 3m 19.80s. (19 Ran).
(A R Boocock), P Beaumont

FOLKESTONE (heavy (races 1,2,4,6), soft (3,5))
Wednesday February 19th
Going Correction: PLUS 1.85 sec. per fur. (races 1,2,4,6), PLUS 1.30 (3,5)

2765 David Benge Novices' Handicap Hurdle Class F (0-95 4-y-o and up) £1,777 2m 1f 110yds.........(2:10)

2267[8] MUSEUM (Ire) [82] 6-11-1 (7*) X Aizpuru, *al prmnt, led 6th, rdn out*..................................(8 to 1 op 6 to 1) 1
2663* DISSOLVE [78] 5-10-11 (7*,7ex) Mr L Baker, *al in tch, chsd wnr aftr 2 out, no imprsn.* (9 to 1 op 9 to 2 tchd 10 to 1) 2
2292[5] TATHMIN [70] (v) 4-10-0 I Lawrence, *wl in rear till styd on and passed btn horses aftr 2 out.*
.........................(11 to 1 op 12 to 1 tchd 10 to 1) 3
1922[2] THEME ARENA [93] 4-11-9 A P McCoy, *al prmnt, mstk 3rd, ev ch 6th, rdn and wknd aftr 2 out.*
...............(3 to 1 fav op 5 to 2 tchd 9 to 2) 4
SWINGING SIXTIES (Ire) [79] 6-11-5 D Gallagher, *hld up, mstk 5th, hdwy 3 out, wknd aftr nxt.*
.............................(5 to 1 op 7 to 1 tchd 9 to 2) 5
1922[5] WARNING REEF [76] (bl) 4-10-6 G Tormey, *al towards rear.*
....(10 to 1 op 6 to 1) 6
2481[3] FLOW BACK [75] 5-11-1 R Johnson, *led to 3rd, wknd 6th.*
.........................(16 to 1 op 14 to 1 tchd 20 to 1) 7
867 DANNY GALE (Ire) [88] (bl) 6-12-0 S McNeill, *led 3rd to 6th, sn btn*..................(10 to 1 op 8 to 1 tchd 14 to 1) 8
2610* KENTAVRUS WAY (Ire) [60] 6-9-7 (7*) M Batchelor, *unruly bef strt, slwly away, hdwy 3rd, wknd quickly 2 out, tld off.*
.........................(9 to 2 op 4 to 1 tchd 5 to 1) 9
1866[6] DOCKLANDS COURIER [84] 5-11-10 C Llewellyn, *prmnt to 4th, tld off*..............................(8 to 1 op 5 to 1) 10
PATONG BEACH [64] 7-10-4 S Fox, *al beh, tld off whn pld up bef last*...........................(33 to 1 op 20 to 1) pu
1977[5] ROYRACE [65] 5-10-2 (3*) R Massey, *prmnt to hfwy, tld off whn pld up bef last*...............(12 to 1 op 12 to 1) pu

Dist: 11l, ¾l, 24l, 9l, 9l, ½l, 5l, ½l, dist. 4m 37.40s. a 40.40s (12 Ran).
SR: 14/-/-/-/-/-/ (R D Barber & R J B Blake), P Winkworth

2766 Lympne Novices' Claiming Hurdle Class F (4-y-o and up) £2,232 2¾m 110yds......................(2:40)

2177[7] RARE SPREAD (Ire) 7-11-12 A P McCoy, *hld up, hdwy 5th, trkd ldr nxt, led and edgd lft, appr last, clr r-in, fnshd tired.*
.........................(9 to 4 fav op 2 to 1 tchd 5 to 2) 1
2477[7] SCORPION BAY 9-10-11 (3*) J Magee, *mid-div, hdwy 7th, rdn whn hit last, wnt second r-in.*
.........................(16 to 1 op 20 to 1 tchd 25 to 1) 2
1742[2] SPRIG MUSLIN (v) 5-10-12 (5*) Sophie Mitchell, *led and pckd 1st, hit 2 out, hdd appr last, no extr.*
.........................(11 to 4 op 2 to 1 tchd 3 to 1) 3
TEOROMA 7-11-8 Mr M Gingell, *prmnt till wknd 2 out.*
....(16 to 1 op 12 to 1) 4
2640[6] EWAR BOLD 4-10-9 B Fenton, *led to 1st, beh frm 7th.*
....(8 to 1 op 14 to 1) 5
2351 ECU DE FRANCE (Ire) 7-11-2 S Fox, *prmnt till wknd appr 2 out, tld off*............................(10 to 1 op 6 to 1) 6
1927[6] WISE 'N' SHINE 6-10-4 (7*) Mr L Baker, *al beh, tld off 4 out.*
....(14 to 1 op 14 to 1) 7
157[7] DOUBLE TROUBLE 6-11-1 (3*) D Fortt, *mid-div, lost tch 7th, tld off*.............................(16 to 1 op 10 to 1) 8
2153 SERIOUS OPTION (Ire) 6-11-4 D Morris, *tld off whn pld up bef 7th*..................(16 to 1 op 12 to 1 tchd 20 to 1) pu
2292 SEVEN CROWNS (USA) 4-10-7 G Tormey, *beh frm 4th, tld off whn pld up bef 7th*...................(25 to 1 op 20 to 1) pu
2526 DOLLIVER (USA) 5-11-0 I Lawrence, *prmnt to 5th, wknd quickly, tld off whn pld up bef 7th*......(33 to 1 op 25 to 1) pu
2242[9] PIPER'S ROCK (Ire) 6-11-12 R Greene, *tld off 6th, pld up bef nxt*...................................(8 to 1 op 6 to 1) pu
2479 BABA SAM (Ire) 6-11-2 D Gallagher, *tld off 5th, pld up bef 7th.*
.........................(16 to 1 op 12 to 1 tchd 20 to 1) pu
2260 ST MELLION LEISURE (Ire) 5-10-9 (7*) G Supple, *beh whn pld up bef 7th*..................(14 to 1 op 12 to 1 tchd 16 to 1) pu

Dist: 16l, 1l, 20l, 1½l, dist, 19l, 28l. 6m 25.60s. a 75.60s (14 Ran).
(Malcolm B Jones), M C Pipe

2767 'Gay Record' Challenge Trophy Handicap Chase Class F (0-100 5-y-o and up) £2,612 2m.........(3:10)

2612[3] BUCKLAND LAD (Ire) [78] 6-11-2 B Fenton, *al prmnt, led 7th, clr whn slight mstk last, styd on.*
.........................(15 to 8 fav op 6 to 4 tchd 2 to 1) 1
2606[4] FENWICK [85] 10-11-6 (3*) T Dascombe, *hld up, hdwy to go second aftr 3 out, one pace.*
.........................(13 to 2 op 9 to 2 tchd 7 to 1) 2
2308 RETAIL RUNNER [90] 12-12-0 Mr T Hills, *trkd ldr to 6th, rallied appr 2 out, one pace*..........(4 to 1 op 7 to 2) 3
2478[5] RED BEAN [90] (v) 9-12-0 A Maguire, *led to 7th, chsd wnr till wknd appr 2 out*.........(15 to 2 op 5 to 1 tchd 8 to 1) 4
2606 RUSTIC GENT (Ire) [72] (v) 9-10-10 D Leahy, *al beh, tld off.*
.........................(25 to 1 op 14 to 1 tchd 33 to 1) 5
DREWITTS DANCER [67] 10-10-5 D Bridgwater, *blun and uns rdr 3rd*..................................(7 to 1 op 7 to 1) ur
2529 OXFORD QUILL [77] 10-11-1 D Morris, *al beh, lost tch 5 out, tld off whn pld up bef last*...............(5 to 1 op 7 to 2) pu

Dist: 1¾l, 2½l, 15l, 24l. 4m 19.80s. a 28.80s (7 Ran).
SR: 8/13/15/-/ (Mrs R M Hepburn), D M Grissell

2768 Stanford Selling Handicap Hurdle Class G (0-90 5-y-o and up) £1,639 2m 1f 110yds..................(3:40)

2515 KILLING TIME [72] 6-10-10 D J Burchell, *hld up in tch, hdwy 4th, led appr last, rdn out.*
.........................(14 to 1 op 10 to 1 tchd 16 to 1) 1
1567 PARISIAN [62] 12-9-7 (7*) A Lucas, *hld up, hdwy and plenty to do aftr 2 out, ran on to go second r-in.* (16 to 1 op 12 to 1) 2
2610[5] PRECIOUS WONDER [63] 8-10-1 T J Murphy, *hld up, hdwy 6th, ev ch whn hit last, one pace r-in*.....(7 to 1 op 5 to 1) 3
2614 ILEWIN JANINE (Ire) [78] 6-11-2 D Gallagher, *chsd ldrs, ev ch appr last, one pace*....................(6 to 1 op 8 to 1) 4
2610[3] DERISBAY (Ire) [74] (bl) 9-10-12 A Maguire, *chsd ldrs till wknd 2 out*..................................(5 to 1 op 4 to 1) 5
2640[8] CELTIC LILLEY [65] (bl) 7-10-3 B Fenton, *prmnt till wknd 3 out*..(14 to 1) 6
2526 AL HAAL (USA) [66] 8-10-4 D Skyrme, *pld hrd, dsptd ld, led 4 out, hdd and wknd appr last*.........(16 to 1 op 10 to 1) 7
VALIANTHE (USA) [90] (bl) 9-11-7 (7*) G Supple, *chsd ldrs till wknd aftr 2 out*..............................(7 to 1 op 4 to 1) 8
2663 ALDWICK COLONNADE [70] 10-10-8 W McFarland, *al beh, tld off*..............................(16 to 1 op 10 to 1) 9
2424* SCRIPT [74] 6-10-12 J Osborne, *al beh, tld off.*
.........................(9 to 4 fav op 5 to 2 tchd 3 to 1) 10
100 SIDE BAR [62] (bl) 7-10-0 J R Kavanagh, *made most to 4 out, wknd quickly, tld off*...................................(20 to 1) 11
2610[6] DEPTFORD BELLE [68] 7-10-6 D Morris, *al beh, tld off.*
....(16 to 1 op 12 to 1) 12
1917[6] TILT TECH FLYER [82] 12-11-6 Miss E J Jones, *prmnt till wknd appr 5th, tld off whn pld up approaching last.*
.........................(9 to 1 op 6 to 1 tchd 10 to 1) pu

Dist: ¾l, 3l, 1l, 21l, 1l, 3½l, 1½l, 10l, 14l, 13l. 4m 41.50s. a 44.50s (13 Ran).
(Simon T Lewis), D Burchell

2769 Flisher Foods Maiden Hunters' Chase Class H (5-y-o and up) £1,067 2m 5f......................(4:10)

2615[2] TRIFAST LAD 12-12-5 (3*) Mr P Hacking, *trkd ldr, chlgd 4 out, led 2 out, styd on.*
.......(11 to 10 fav op 5 to 4 tchd 11 to 8 and Evens) 1
SANDS OF GOLD (Ire) 9-12-1 (7*) Mr L Lay, *led till rdn and hdd 2 out, kpt on one pace.*
.........................(12 to 1 op 5 to 1 tchd 14 to 1) 2
KING HIGH 10-12-1 (7*) Mr C Ward, *chsd ldrs, one pace frm 3 out*..................................(33 to 1 op 25 to 1) 3
ASTOUND (Ire) 6-12-1 (7*) Lt-Col R Webb-Bowen, *beh till hdwy frm 3 out, nvr nr to chal.*
.........................(16 to 1 op 8 to 1 tchd 20 to 1) 4
GYPSY KING (Ire) 9-12-1 (7*) Mr A Coe, *chsd ldrs till wknd 3 out*.....................(9 to 2 op 4 to 1 tchd 5 to 1) 5
2641 ELL GEE 7-11-10 (7*) Miss C Townsley, *chsd ldrs till hit 9th, sn beh, tld off*........................(33 to 1 op 20 to 1) 6
2641[4] CENTRE STAGE 11-12-1 (7*) Mr A Warr, *tld off frm 8th.*
.........................(10 to 1 op 12 to 1 tchd 20 to 1) 7
JOCTOR DON (Ire) 5-11-5 (7*) Mr E Babington, *f 1st.*
....(20 to 1 op 16 to 1) f
GREYBURY LANE (Ire) 9-12-1 (7*) Mr P Bull, *blun and uns rdr second*............................(11 to 2 op 5 to 2) ur
DASHBOARD LIGHT 7-12-5 (3*) Mr Simon Andrews, *chsd ldrs till wknd 5 out, tld off whn pld up bef 2 out.*
...........(8 to 1 op 5 to 1 tchd 10 to 1 and 12 to 1) pu

Dist: 2½l, 8l, 4l, 1l, dist, 16l. 5m 48.60s. a 37.60s (10 Ran).
SR: 5/2/-/-/-/-/ (Mike Roberts), M J Roberts

2770 Folkestone Handicap Hurdle Class E (0-115 4-y-o and up) £2,363 2¾m 110yds......................(4:40)

2616[3] MILLMOUNT (Ire) [89] (bl) 7-10-13 D Bridgwater, *hld up, trkd ldr 6th, led appr last, kpt on*..........(5 to 1 tchd 6 to 1) 1
2246 AINSI SOIT IL (Fr) [99] (bl) 6-11-6 (3*) D Fortt, *led till hdd appr last, no extr*............(3 to 1 op 7 to 2 tchd 11 to 4) 2
2477[8] ROGER'S PAL [76] 10-10-0 D Gallagher, *al prmnt, ev ch 4 out till wknd aftr 2 out*.....(20 to 1 op 12 to 1 tchd 25 to 1) 3
2639[2] AUGUST TWELFTH [84] 9-10-8 C Llewellyn, *hld up, nvr on terms, tld off*......................(11 to 4 fav op 2 to 1) 4
2528[6] MONKS SOHAM (Ire) [100] 9-11-10 N Williamson, *al beh, tld off*..................(5 to 1 op 7 to 2 tchd 11 to 2) 5
2616[2] LAJADHAL (Fr) [76] 8-10-0 L Harvey, *trkd ldr till wknd 6th, tld off*..................................(8 to 1 tchd 6 to 1) 6
541[3] CELTIC LAIRD [85] 9-10-9 D J Burchell, *prmnt till wknd aftr 6th, tld off whn pld up bef 3 out*.......(25 to 1 op 20 to 1) pu
2479[2] MULLINTOR (Ire) [85] 6-10-9 D O'Sullivan, *hld up, lost tch 7th, tld off whn pld up bef last*...............(5 to 1 op 6 to 1) pu

Dist: 4l, 18l, dist, 10l, 5l. 6m 16.10s. a 66.10s (8 Ran).
(Tommy Breen), T P McGovern

HUNTINGDON (good to soft)
Thursday February 20th
Going Correction: PLUS 0.85 sec. per fur. (races 1,3,5,7), PLUS 1.45 (2,4,6)

2771 Unique Consultants Novices' Handicap Hurdle Class E (0-105 4-y-o and up) £3,176 2½m 110yds...... (1:50)

2428²	LADY HIGH SHERIFF (Ire) [78] 7-11-1 S Wynne, hld up beh ldrs, led 4 out, clr appr 2 out, rdn out. ....(9 to 2 op 5 to 1 tchd 11 to 2 and 6 to 1)	1
2384⁷	SEABROOK LAD [79] 6-11-2 W Marston, keen early, hld up in cl tch, hdwy to ld 6th, hdd nxt, ev ch 3 out, sn drvn alng and one pace.........................(11 to 8 fav op 7 to 4)	2
2462	CADES BAY [82] 6-11-5 T Jenks, hld up, hdwy to track ldrs aftr 6th, hrd rdn after 3 out, one pace. (16 to 1 op 12 to 1)	3
1843⁷	KATBALLOU [63] 8-9-7 (7⁴) Mr O McPhail, hld up, cld 6th, one pace frm 3 out.....................(33 to 1)	4
2497⁷	TOBY BROWN [98] 4-11-10 R Johnson, hld up, pushed alng appr 6th, sn hdwy to track ldrs, ev ch whn not fluent 3 out, soon no extr..........................(9 to 1 op 5 to 1)	5
2607⁴	COME ON IN [76] 4-9-9 (7⁴) X Aizpuru, trkd ldrs, wknd appr 3 out.........................(16 to 1 op 14 to 1)	6
2428	TORCH VERT (Ire) [87] 5-11-10 I Lawrence, hld up, hdwy 5th, ch whn not fluent and drvn 3 out, btn when edgd lft r-in.	7
2550⁶	SCALLY HICKS [65] 6-10-22 Gary Lyons, mid-div, lost tch and rdn alng 7th, tld off....................(50 to 1 op 33 to 1)	8
2371	FRED JEFFREY [79] 6-11-2 L Harvey, trkd ldrs, mstk second, wknd 6th, tld off...........(25 to 1 op 16 to 1)	9
1567	OUR RAINBOW [81] 5-11-4 M Brennan, cl up, drvn alng appr 6th, sn lost pl, tld off...............(33 to 1 op 16 to 1)	10
2565⁹	MUSIC CLASS (Ire) [85] 6-11-8 D Gallagher, al beh, effrt 4 out, no response, tld off......(16 to 1 op 8 to 1 tchd 20 to 1)	11
2279⁵	RED LIGHT [76] (bl) 5-10-13 P Carberry, nvr far away, wknd quickly und pres appr 3 out, tld off...............(20 to 1)	12
2637⁷	FOREST MILL [80] 5-11-3 D Bridgwater, chsd ldrs, drvn alng aftr 5th, wknd nxt, pld up bef 7th......(33 to 1)	pu
2371	TODD (USA) [77] 6-11-0 J A McCarthy, hld up, hdwy 6th, wknd aftr 4 out, tld off whn pld up bef 2 out. (25 to 1 op 16 to 1)	pu
2153	BROWN AND MILD [67] 6-10-4 K Gaule, hdwy to track ldrs aftr second, hmpd and mstk 6th, wknd quickly and pld up nxt. ....(14 to 1 op 12 to 1)	pu
2267⁹	SIR DANTE (Ire) [84] 6-11-7 D O'Sullivan, led to 6th, sn lost pl, tld off whn pld up bef 2 out...........(14 to 1 op 12 to 1)	pu

Dist: 10l, nk, 1¼l, ½l, 17l, ½l, 29l, 9l, 2½l, 11l. 5m 4.90s. a. 29.90s (16 Ran).
(Mrs Michael Ward-Thomas), Capt T A Forster

2772 Horseley Fen Handicap Chase Class E (0-110 5-y-o and up) £3,228 3m ...... (2:20)

2306⁶	CELTIC BARLE [-] 13-11-4 S McNeill, chsd ldrs, mstk 11th, cld 15th, chased lder aftr 3 out, kpt on und pres to lead hr finish. ....(10 to 1 op 7 to 1)	1
2268⁷	EASTERN RIVER [-] 11-10-4 S Wynne, chsd ldrs, led 13th, clr 2 out, idled r-in, hdd nr finish. ....(13 to 8 fav op 6 to 4 tchd 7 to 4)	2
2659	SOLO GENT [-] 8-10-12 S Curran, trkd ldrs, pushed alng 4 out, kpt on same pace......................(9 to 1 op 10 to 1)	3
2421²	TIM SOLDIER (Fr) [-] 10-10-7 R Supple, mstk 1st, in tch, one pace whn mistake 2 out...(4 to 1 op 5 to 2 tchd 9 to 2)	4
2252	GRIFFINS BAR [-] 9-10-3 J Culloty, made most to 13th, pushed alng nxt, hrd rdn aftr 4 out, eased whn hld after 2 out, tld off.......................(16 to 1 op 12 to 1)	5
2268	SHEELIN LAD (Ire) [-] 9-10-4³ (3⁴) D Fortt, cl up, led briefly 5th, outpcd frm 4 out, tld off.............(33 to 1 op 20 to 1)	6
2401⁶	YEOMAN WARRIOR [-] 10-11-10 D O'Sullivan, trkd ldrs, blun 3rd, lost pl 11th, rallied briefly 3 out, btn whn jmpd very slwly last, virtually pld up..............(10 to 1 op 6 to 1)	7
2393⁸	KNOCKARNEY (Ire) [-] 9-11-1 W Marston, mid-div, not fluent 8th, btn whn blun and uns rdr 4 out....(20 to 1 op 14 to 1)	ur
2564	INVASION [-] 13-11-7 M Brennan, sn struggling in rear, tld off whn pld up bef 9th...............(25 to 1 op 14 to 1)	pu
2268	MIGHTY FROLIC [-] 10-10-13 P Hide, hld up, mstk 1st, outpcd 13th, tld off whn pld up 3 out...................(25 to 1 op 20 to 1 tchd 33 to 1)	pu
2239⁴	SUPPOSIN [-] 9-10-9 Richard Guest, lost tch 8th, tld off whn pld up 5 out...........(14 to 1 op 12 to 1 tchd 16 to 1)	pu
2566⁷	COOL RUNNER [-] 7-10-10 Derek Byrne, not fluent, pushed alng in rear 8th, sn tld off, pld up bef 4 out. ....(8 to 1 tchd 10 to 1)	pu

Dist: ½l, 4l, 1½l, dist, 18l, 8l. 6m 35.20s. a. 55.20s (12 Ran).
(Mrs Irene Hodge), H B Hodge

2773 Equitable House Juvenile Novices' Hurdle Class C (4-y-o) £3,601 2m 110yds...................... (2:50)

2397⁴	KINGS WITNESS (USA) 10-12 D Bridgwater, hld up, smooth hdwy to chal 3 out, led nxt, sn clr, hrd held. ....(6 to 4 fav tchd 15 to 8)	1

2774 Longwood Fen Handicap Chase Class D (0-125 5-y-o and up) £4,442 2m 110yds. (3:20)

2689³	THUMBS UP [125] 11-11-7 (7⁴) R Hobson, trkd ldr, led 6th, hdd briefly 9th, made rst, lft clr last...(5 to 1 tchd 11 to 2)	1
2493²	REGAL ROMPER (Ire) [111] 9-11-0 Richard Guest, chsd ldrs, no imprsn frm 4 out, 3rd and wl hld whn lft second at last. ....(9 to 4 op 7 to 4 tchd 5 to 2)	2
2287⁴	RANDOM ASSAULT (NZ) [125] 8-12-0 R Johnson, led to 6th, led briefly 9th, chsd wnr, hrd rdn and hld whn f last. ....(50 to 1 op 33 to 1)	f
2555⁵	EASTERN MAGIC [103] 9-10-6 D Bridgwater, hld up beh, niggled alng 7th, sn struggling, wl held whn hmpd by faller and uns rdr last....................(2 to 1 fav op 7 to 4)	ur
1104⁴	LOWAWATHA [99] 9-10-2 K Gaule, mstks 1st and 3rd, sn struggling, tld off whn pld up aftr 3 out. (12 to 1 op 6 to 1)	pu

Dist: 15l. 4m 26.30s. a. 32.30s (5 Ran).
SR: 17/-/
(Mrs B Taylor), G M McCourt

2775 Pidley Fen Mares' Only Maiden Hurdle Class E (4-y-o and up) £2,810 2m 110yds..................... (3:50)

2575³	NISHAMIRA 5-11-5 D Gallagher, trkd ldrs, led appr 3 out to approaching nxt, lft in ld last, ran on wl. ....(3 to 1 fav tchd 7 to 2)	1
2419⁶	ARDRINA 6-11-5 P Carberry, trkd ldrs, drvn alng frm 3 out, ev ch r-in, kpt on wl...................(5 to 1 op 8 to 1)	2
2497³	TAKEAMEMO (Ire) 4-10-9 J A McCarthy, hld up, hdwy to track ldrs 4th, ev ch whn hmpd by faller at last, kpt on. ....(7 to 2 op 3 to 1 tchd 4 to 1)	3
2436	MRS EM 5-11-5 R Johnson, hdwy to track ldrs 4th, chsd lder nxt, shaken up appr 2 out, kpt on one pace. ....(9 to 2 op 3 to 1 tchd 5 to 1)	4
2264	SUPREME TROGLODYTE (Ire) 5-11-2 (3⁴) D Fortt, hld up, hdwy to track ldrs 5th, outpcd aftr 3 out. (16 to 1 op 12 to 1)	5
2264	RING FOR ROSIE 6-11-5 J Culloty, beh, hdwy 4th, no imprsn frm 3 out............(33 to 1 op 14 to 1 tchd 50 to 1)	6
2264	SUMMER PRINCESS 4-10-9 Gary Lyons, hld up beh, steady hdwy frm 5th, mstk 3 out, sn no extr, better for race. ....(40 to 1 op 33 to 1)	7
2454⁵	BELMARITA (Ire) 4-10-9 Richard Guest, led to appr 3 out, wknd quickly......(10 to 1 op 7 to 1 tchd 11 to 1)	8
2575⁴	DERRING FLOSS 7-10-12 (7⁴) Miss J Wormall, mid-div, no hdwy frm 5th..................(20 to 1 op 14 to 1)	9
	CALLERMINE 8-11-5 M Foster, trkd ldrs till wknd aftr 5th, tld off.........................(66 to 1 op 25 to 1)	10
2377	LUCRATIVE PERK (Ire) 5-11-5 D Leahy, hld up, hdwy 4th, wknd aftr nxt, tld off..............(50 to 1 op 25 to 1)	11
2248	SLACK ALICE 6-11-5 T J Murphy, stumbled strt, hld up beh, struggling 5th, tld off.............(50 to 1 op 33 to 1)	12
2552	DIAMOND TIME 6-11-5 S Wynne, hld up, al beh, tld off. ....(20 to 1 op 14 to 1 tchd 25 to 1)	13
2552⁶	MISTRESS TUDOR 6-11-5 N Mann, in tch to 4th, tld off. ....(40 to 1 op 25 to 1)	14
2371	MOLLIE SILVERS (v) 5-10-12 (7⁴) N T Egan, chsd ldrs till wknd quickly 4th, tld off................(50 to 1 op 33 to 1)	15
2433⁵	ANNIE RUTH (Ire) 6-11-5 R Farrant, wth ldrs till drpd out quickly aftr 4th, tld off..............(25 to 1 op 20 to 1)	16
2625²	THREESOCKS 4-10-9 I Lawrence, hld up, cld on ldrs 4th, led appr 2 out, gng wl whn f last. ....(7 to 1 op 8 to 1 tchd 9 to 1)	f
2614	OUR EMMA 8-11-5 L Harvey, in tch, pushed alng appr 4th, sn lost touch, tld off whn pld up bef 2 out. ....(66 to 1 op 33 to 1 tchd 100 to 1)	pu
2405	BALLY WONDER 5-11-5 K Gaule, keen early, cl up till wknd quickly appr 4th, tld off whn pld up bef 2 out. ....(66 to 1 op 25 to 1)	pu
2575	SKIP TO SOMERFIELD 5-11-5 A S Smith, in tch to 4th, tld off whn pld up bef 3 out..........(40 to 1 op 33 to 1)	pu
2179⁰	SWEET MOUNT (Ire) 5-11-5 C Maude, trkd ldrs to second, tld off whn pld up bef 2 out.........(25 to 1 op 14 to 1)	pu
2264	SHOULDHAVESAIDNO (Ire) 6-11-5 D O'Sullivan, trkd ldrs, wknd 4th, pld up bef 3 out.........(50 to 1 op 33 to 1)	pu

Dist: 2l, 1½l, 4l, 13l, 14l, 1½l, 7l, 1¼l, 14l, 6l. 4m 4.20s. a 23.20s (22 Ran).
(M P Burke Developments Limited), T D Barron

2497	SULAWESI (Ire) 10-7 C Maude, hld up beh, effrt 5th, styd on und pres, no ch wth wnr.............(10 to 1 op 7 to 1)	2
2568⁴	PARROT'S WELL (Ire) 10-12 Richard Guest, trkd ldr, led appr 4th, not fluent 3 out, hdd nxt, no extr. ....(6 to 1 op 8 to 1 tchd 10 to 1)	3
2497²	EXALTED (Ire) 10-12 T Jenks, in tch, ev ch 3 out, wknd appr nxt.........................(11 to 4 op 5 to 2)	4
2454⁶	SILVRETTA (Ire) 10-7 P Hide, hld up beh, not fluent, effrt 5th, sn btn.........................(10 to 1 op 7 to 1)	5
2454	MAGIC ROLE (v) 10-12 P Carberry, keen early, in tch till outpcd frm 5th, tld off............(33 to 1 op 14 to 1)	6
	CABALLUS (USA) 10-12 R Farrant, keen early, trkd ldrs, wknd aftr 4th, tld off. ....(8 to 1 op 6 to 1 tchd 9 to 1 and 10 to 1)	7
2423	GULLIVER (bl) 10-12 I Lawrence, led, looked reluctant and hdd appr 4th, hrd rdn and no response, pld up bef 3 out. ....(25 to 1 op 14 to 1 tchd 33 to 1)	pu

Dist: 14l, 1l, 17l, 18l, dist, dist. 4m 4.90s. a 23.90s (8 Ran).
(Jeffrey Hordle), P F Nicholls

2776 Euximoor Fen Novices' Chase Class E (5-y-o and up) £3,023 2½m 110yds
.... (4:25)

2399² FRAZER ISLAND (Ire) 8-11-3 D O'Sullivan, *made virtually all, hit 2 out, all out*...................... (14 to 1 op 8 to 1) 1
2214³ MANDYS MANTINO 7-11-3 P Hide, *hld up beh ldg pair, chsd wnr appr 12th, led briefly approaching 2 out, ev ch last, rdn and found little r-in.*
...... (5 to 2 on op 2 to 1 on tchd 7 to 4 on and 11 to 4 on) 2
2408² SECOND CALL 8-11-10 S Wynne, *hld up, mstk 10th, effrt 3 out, sn no imprsn.*
.... (7 to 2 op 3 to 1 tchd 11 to 4 and 4 to 1) 3
2391 DREAM LEADER (Ire) 7-11-3 J Railton, *trkd ldrs, blun 9th, wkng whn mstk 3 out, tld off.*
.... (33 to 1 op 20 to 1 tchd 50 to 1) 4
2763 PANDORA'S PRIZE 11-10-12 T J Murphy, *trkd wnr till jmpd slwly 11th and sn lost pl, tld off.*
....................(150 to 1 op 100 to 1 tchd 200 to 1) 5
THE ELOPER 9-10-10 (7*) N T Egan, *beh, mstk 3rd, losing tch whn blun 8th, pld up bef nxt.*
....................(150 to 1 op 100 to 1 tchd 200 to 1) pu
2561⁵ BUCKET OF GOLD 7-11-3 M Brennan, *not jump wl, losing tch whn blun 8th, pld up bef nxt.*...... (20 to 1 op 12 to 1) pu
Dist: 2l, 20l, dist, dist. 5m 23.40s. a 36.40s (7 Ran).
SR: 22/20/-/-/ (Dr B Alexander), R Rowe

2777 Wimblington Fen Amateur Riders' Handicap Hurdle Class E (0-115 4-y-o and up) £2,337 2m 110yds.. (4:55)

2629* SHERIFFMUIR [112] 8-11-10 (7*,7ex) Mr P Scott, *in cl tch, led aftr 3 out, drw clr r-in, cmftbly.*
....................(13 to 8 fav op 6 to 4 tchd 7 to 4) 1
ALKA INTERNATIONAL [81] 5-9-7 (7*) Miss C Townsley, *in cl tch, keen early, ev ch appr 2 out, kpt on.*
.... (50 to 1 op 10 to 1 tchd 66 to 1) 2
2532⁴ BIGWHEEL BILL (Ire) [85] 8-10-1 (3*) Mr C Bonner, *led 4th, hdd aftr 3 out, ev ch nxt, one pace appr last.*
.... (2 to 1 op 9 to 4) 3
1947⁵ BIYA (Ire) [81] 5-9-7 (7*) Mr G Lake, *led second to 4th, cl up, outpcd aftr 2 out.*...... (12 to 1 op 8 to 1 tchd 14 to 1) 4
2606 HALHAM TARN (Ire) [81] 7-9-7 (7*) Miss A Dudley, *hld up, cld 3 out, outpcd appr last.*.. (16 to 1 op 12 to 1 tchd 20 to 1) 5
2526* WILLY STAR (Bel) [103] 7-11-1 (7*) Mr E Babington, *hld up, cld 4th, wknd appr 3 out, btn quickly, tld off.* (3 to 1 op 9 to 4) 6
PAULA'S BOY [81] 7-9-10³ (7*) Miss K Di Marte, *cl up till drpd rear 4th, tld off...*(66 to 1 op 25 to 1 tchd 100 to 1) 7
SILENT SOVEREIGN [89] (bl) 8-10-8¹⁵ (7*) Mr P Clarke, *pld hrd, rcd wide and ran out appr second.*
....................................(150 to 1 op 33 to 1) ref
Dist: 9l, ¾l, 7l, 1l, 19l, dist. 4m 2.30s. a 21.30s (8 Ran).
SR: 30/-/-/-/-/ (J J W Wadham), Mrs L Wadham

WINCANTON (good (races 1,7), yielding (2,3,4,5,6))
Thursday February 20th
Going Correction: PLUS 0.55 sec. per fur. (races 1,2,4), PLUS 0.50 (3,5,6,7)

2778 Georgie Newall Novices' Chase Class D (5-y-o and up) £3,614 2m
.... (2:05)

2431* INDIAN JOCKEY 5-10-13 N Williamson, *led aftr 1st to 9th, drvn into slight ld 4 out, clr nxt, pushed out.*
.... (11 to 8 op 5 to 4 tchd 13 to 8) 1
2540² AFTER THE FOX 10-11-2 G Upton, *led till aftr 1st, styd wth wnr, jmpd slwly 5th, hit nxt, chlgd 8th, led 9th to 4 out, btn next.*
.... (11 to 1 op 8 to 1 tchd 12 to 1) 2
2547 ROBINS PRIDE (Ire) 7-10-13 (3*) T Dascombe, *hmpd whn lft poor 3rd at 4th, effrt 8th, no ch frm 3 out.* (16 to 1 op 7 to 1) 3
2606 SWAHILI RUN 9-10-13 (3*) Michael Brennan, *hit 3rd, f nxt.*
.... (100 to 1 op 25 to 1) f
SHANKAR (Ire) 6-11-2 A Maguire, *f 4th.*
.... (5 to 4 fav tchd 11 to 10) f
2384 MR GOONHILLY 7-11-2 A Thornton, *f second.*
.... (100 to 1 op 20 to 1) f
HOLD YOUR RANKS 10-11-2 J Frost, *sn wl beh, no ch whn blun and uns rdr 7th.*...................(20 to 1 op 8 to 1) ur
Dist: 7l, 11l. 4m 5.40s. a 17.40s (7 Ran).
(Stuart M Mercer), M C Pipe

2779 Jim Ford Challenge Cup Chase Class B (5-y-o and up) £12,055 3m 1f 110yds...................... (2:35)

2452 COOME HILL (Ire) 8-11-2 J Osborne, *led to 4 out, sn drvn to ld ag'n, styd on wl frm nxt, pushed out.*
.... (7 to 4 op 6 to 4 tchd 15 to 8) 1
2209² UNGUIDED MISSILE 9-11-8 R Dunwoody, *hld up tracking wnr, chlgd 8th, hit 16th, led briefly 4 out, chald 3 out, mstk nxt, sn one pace.*..................(11 to 8 fav op 6 to 4) 2

1565 HANAKHAM (Ire) 8-11-2 B Powell, *hdwy 13th, styd on wl to take 3rd r-in, no ch wth 1st 2*........(33 to 1 op 20 to 1) 3
MAAMUR (USA) 9-11-2 A Thornton, *chsd ldg pair, jmpd slwly 5th, mstk 15th, hit 17th, wknd 4 out.*
.... (9 to 2 tchd 5 to 1 and 4 to 1) 4
2466² KADI (Ger) 8-11-2 A Maguire, *hld up, hdwy 12th, staying on in 3rd whn blun 3 out, not reco'r.*
.... (10 to 1 op 8 to 1 tchd 11 to 1) 5
2592⁴ ALL FOR LUCK 12-11-2 B Fenton, *beh 5th, no dngr aftr.*
.... (50 to 1 op 20 to 1) 6
1345* CHERRYNUT 8-11-2 N Williamson, *hld up, hdwy whn jmpd slwly 13th, blun 16th and wknd, no ch whn f 4 out.*
.... (16 to 1 op 8 to 1) f
Dist: 1¼l, 10l, 5l, 7l, 26l. 6m 33.70s. a 17.70s (7 Ran).
SR: 50/54/38/33/26/-/-/ (Mrs Jill Dennis), W W Dennis

2780 K. J. Pike & Sons Kingwell Hurdle Class A Grade 2 (4-y-o and up) £15,625 2m.................. (3:05)

2442⁶ DREAMS END 9-11-10 R Dunwoody, *trkd ldrs, chsd lder aftr 3 out, led appr nxt, drvn clr r-in........*(16 to 1 op 10 to 1) 1
2591 ROMANCER (Ire) (bl) 6-11-2 C Llewellyn, *beh, hdwy 3 out, wide appr nxt, styd on und pres, no imprsn on wnr r-in.*
.... (11 to 4 fav op 3 to 1 tchd 100 to 30) 2
2332 BLAST FREEZE (Ire) 8-10-11 J R Kavanagh, *in tch, mstk and lost pl 3 out, ran on appr last, kpt on r-in.*
.... (4 to 1 op 3 to 1 tchd 9 to 2) 3
2442² AMBLESIDE (Ire) 6-11-2 N Williamson, *hmpd strt and wl beh, some hdwy 3 out, styd on und pres appr last.*
.... (20 to 1 op 16 to 1) 4
2591 ZABADI (Ire) 5-11-10 A Maguire, *beh, steady hdwy 3 out, chsd wnr nxt, sn rdn, appr last..........*(4 to 1 tchd 9 to 2) 5
2451³ GROUND NUT (Ire) 7-11-2 B Powell, *made most to 5th, wknd quickly aftr 3 out..........*(7 to 1 op 8 to 1 tchd 9 to 1) 6
1888³ POTENTATE (USA) 6-11-2 A P McCoy, *wth ldr, rdn to chal 4th, led nxt till appr 2 out, wknd rpdly..........*(5 to 1 op 6 to 1) 7
2451⁴ FLORID (USA) 6-11-2 G Bradley, *refused to race.*
.... (9 to 1 op 6 to 1) l
Dist: 8l, 7l, ½l, sht-hd, 14l, 5l. 3m 45.50s. a 11.50s (8 Ran).
SR: 61/45/33/37/45/23/18/-/ (T G Price), P Bowen

2781 Ladbroke Handicap Chase Class D (0-125 5-y-o and up) £6,840 2m 5f
.... (3:35)

2401⁴ MAESTRO PAUL [96] 11-10-0 (3*) L Aspell, *rdn to stay in tch 9th, drvn alng 11th, styd on to chase ldr 2 out, sn led, stayed on wl...........*(13 to 2 op 5 to 1) 1
2459⁶ SCOTONI [93] 11-10-N Williamson, *made most to 6th, chalg whn lft clr nxt, hdd 2 out, styd on und pres r-in.*
.... (16 to 1 op 10 to 1) 2
2596* HARVEST VIEW (Ire) [100] 7-10-7 G Bradley, *not fluent, hdwy 9th, chsd ldr nxt, hit 14th, led 2 out, sn hdd and one pace.*
.... (13 to 8 fav op 6 to 4) 3
2542³ CHANNEL PASTIME [93] 13-9-13² (3*) Guy Lewis, *hit 3rd, chsd ldrs, jmpd big 8th, styd on one pace frm 3 out.* (25 to 1) 4
2603⁷ THE CARROT MAN [107] 9-11-0 J R Kavanagh, *mstk 5th and beh, hmpd 7th, rdn alng tenth, styd on frm 3 out.*
.... (14 to 1 op 10 to 1) 5
CHIEF JOSEPH [102] 10-10-9 C Llewellyn, *mstk 4th, beh whn f 6th, broke leg, destroyed.*...........(6 to 1 op 5 to 1) f
2393² FIVE TO SEVEN (USA) [117] (bl) 8-11-10 R Dunwoody, *pressed ldr, led 6th, narrowly hdd whn f nxt, destroyed.*
.... (2 to 1) f
Dist: 2l, hd, 3l, 2½l. 5m 34.80s. a 30.80s (7 Ran).
(H T Pelham), J T Gifford

2782 Mere Maiden Hurdle Class E (4-y-o and up) £2,862 2m........... (4:05)

THE FLYING PHANTOM 6-11-5 R Dunwoody, *keen hold, trkd ldr, led 2 out, edgd rght last, drvn out.*
.... (5 to 1 op 3 to 1 tchd 11 to 2) 1
2668³ GIVE AND TAKE 4-10-9 A P McCoy, *led, drvn alng frm 5th, hdd 2 out, rallied und pres and kpt on r-in.*
.... (6 to 4 fav op 5 to 2 tchd 3 to 1) 2
CRANDON BOULEVARD 4-10-9 J Osborne, *in tch, hdwy 4th, styd on frm 2 out, not pace to trble ldrs.* (20 to 1 op 12 to 1) 3
EMBANKMENT (Ire) 7-11-0 (5*) Mr C Vigors, *beh, hdwy 3 out, one pace appr last...*(12 to 1 op 10 to 1 tchd 14 to 1) 4
SPREAD THE WORD 5-10-9 (5*) D Salter, *beh 4th, styd on frm 2 out..........*(33 to 1 op 25 to 1) 5
1716³ FAIRY KNIGHT 5-11-5 N Williamson, *hdwy 3rd, effrt 3 out, wknd nxt..........*(11 to 2 op 7 to 2 tchd 6 to 1) 6
ZIDAC 5-11-5 B Fenton, *pld hrd in tch, wknd appr 2 out.*
.... (25 to 1 op 20 to 1 tchd 33 to 1) 7
2662³ KINNESCASH (Ire) 4-10-9 A Maguire, *chsd ldrs till wknd aftr 3 out..........*(12 to 1 op 10 to 1) 8
1849⁷ LOCH NA KEAL 5-11-0 C Llewellyn, *beh, hdwy 5th, wknd 2 out..........*(20 to 1 op 33 to 1 tchd 16 to 1) 9
2668³ LANGTONIAN 8-11-2 (3*) Michael Brennan, *prmnt to 3 out.*
.... (100 to 1 op 66 to 1) 10
ARTISTIC PLAN (Ire) 5-11-5 B Powell, *chsd ldrs to 3 out.*
.... (12 to 1 op 10 to 1 tchd 10 to 1) 11
2302 PROTOTYPE 6-11-5 A Thornton, *al beh.*
.... (16 to 1 op 12 to 1) 12

2668[4] DORMY THREE 7-11-2 (3*) T Dascombe, *prmnt to 5th.* .... (33 to 1 op 20 to 1) 13
FREELINE FONTAINE (Ire) 5-11-5 J R Kavanagh, *al beh.* .... (33 to 1 op 16 to 1) 14
2668 MOOR DUTCH 6-11-5 J Frost, *al beh.* .... (100 to 1 op 66 to 1) 15
ELRAAS (USA) 5-10-12 (7*) N Willmington, *sn beh.* .... (50 to 1 op 33 to 1 tchd 66 to 1) 16
2668[2] WELTON ARSENAL 5-11-5 R Greene, *mstk 1st, sn beh, tld off whn pld up bef 2 out*........... (7 to 1 op 5 to 1 tchd 8 to 1) pu
2545[5] BOOZYS DREAM 6-11-2 (3*) Guy Lewis, *sn beh, tld off whn pld up bef 2 out*................. (100 to 1 op 50 to 1) pu
Dist: 1½l, 5l, 3l, 1¼l, 11l, 3l, 2½l, 1¼l, 8l, ½l. 3m 49.60s. a 15.60s (18 Ran).
SR: 15/3/-/5/-/-/ (P H Betts (Holdings) Ltd), M H Tompkins

2783 Ilchester Handicap Hurdle Class F (0-105 4-y-o and up) £2,250 2m .... (4:35)

2307[4] ALWAYS HAPPY [93] 4-10-11 A Maguire, *hld up, steady hdwy 3 out, chlgd last, sn drvn to ld, ran on wl.*........ (7 to 2 jt-fav op 5 to 1 tchd 13 to 2) 1
2307[2] CLASSIC PAL (USA) [74] 6-10-2 D Skyrme, *steady hdwy 3 out, led appr nxt, rdn last, hdd and one pace r-in.* (7 to 2 jt-fav op 5 to 1 tchd 6 to 1) 2
2279 THE BREWER [72] 5-10-0 R Bellamy, *chsd ldrs, chlgd frm 2 out till one pace r-in.*. (66 to 1 op 33 to 1 tchd 100 to 1) 3
2532[7] LUCAYAN CAY (Ire) [88] 6-11-2 B Powell, *sn chasing ldrs, ev ch 2 out, stayee on one pace.* .... (14 to 1 op 10 to 1 tchd 16 to 1) 4
2609[5] MRS JAWLEYFORD (USA) [80] 9-10-8 M Ranger, *hld up, steady hdwy frm 3 out, staying on whn mstk nxt, sn one pace.* .... (33 to 1 op 25 to 1 tchd 50 to 1) 5
TISSISAT (USA) [92] 8-11-6 G Upton, *hld up and beh, steady hdwy appr 3 out, not rch ldrs.* .... (16 to 1 op 12 to 1 tchd 20 to 1) 6
2558[4] I RECALL (Ire) [78] 6-10-6 B Fenton, *chsd ldrs till aftr 3 out.* .... (7 to 1 op 5 to 1) 7
2609[2] DONTDRESSFORDINNER [89] 7-11-3 R Dunwoody, *chsd ldrs, ev ch 3 out, wknd nxt.* (11 to 2 op 9 to 2 tchd 6 to 1) 8
2548* NASHVILLE STAR (USA) [96] (v) 6-11-10 A Thornton, *led till appr 2 out, sn wknd*........ (8 to 1 op 5 to 1 tchd 9 to 1) 9
1452 IMALIGHT [82] 8-10-10 J Frost, *beh till some hdwy frm 2 out.* .... (20 to 1) 10
2603 SAAFI (Ire) [75] (bl) 6-10-0 (3*) T Dascombe, *hdwy to chase ldrs 3 out, wknd nxt*.... (50 to 1 op 25 to 1 tchd 66 to 1) 11
GLADYS EMMANUEL [78] 10-10-3 (3*) P Henley, *pressed ldr to 3rd, prmnt till wknd aftr 3 out.* .... (25 to 1 op 16 to 1 tchd 33 to 1) 12
2639[4] EL GRANDO [83] 7-10-11 N Williamson, *mid-div, mstk 4th, wknd 3 out.* (10 to 1 op 8 to 1 tchd 7 to 1 and 12 to 1) 13
2295 FANE PARK (Ire) [82] 9-10-10 G Tormey, *chsd ldrs to 3 out* .... (33 to 1 op 16 to 1) 14
2577[6] NEVER SO BLUE (Ire) [87] 6-10-10 (5*) Sophie Mitchell, *sn beh.*.............. (16 to 1 op 12 to 1 tchd 20 to 1) 15
2609[6] DAILY SPORT GIRL [85] 8-10-13 Mr J L Llewellyn, *chsd ldrs to 3 out*.............. (16 to 1 op 10 to 1 tchd 20 to 1) 16
1982[7] ETHBAAT (USA) [87] 6-11-1 M Richards, *al beh.* .... (33 to 1 op 25 to 1) 17
2432[8] CONCINNITY (USA) [72] 8-10-0 Mr A Holdsworth, *chsd ldrs to 4th, tld off whn pld up bef 2 out.* .... (66 to 1 op 33 to 1 tchd 100 to 1) pu
1668[5] MU-TADIL [72] 5-10-0 V Slattery, *al beh, tld off whn pld up bef 2 out*.............. (66 to 1 op 20 to 1 tchd 100 to 1) pu
1599[7] IN CAHOOTS [82] 4-9-12[1] (3*) Michael Brennan, *sn beh, tld off whn pld up bef 2 out*............. (50 to 1 op 20 to 1) pu
Dist: 1½l, 2½l, 1¼l, 2½l, 4l, 5l, ½l, 5l, 1¼l, nk. 3m 49.30s. a 15.30s (20 Ran).
SR: 10/-/-/8/-/5/ (C R Fleet), Miss Gay Kelleway

2784 Golf Course Standard National Hunt Flat Class H (4,5,6-y-o) £1,264 2m .... (5:05)

NOISY MINER (Ire) 5-11-1 (3*) R Massey, *steady hdwy hfwy, chsd ldrs 3 fs out, led o'r 2 out, clr fnl furlong.* ....(15 to 8 fav op 5 to 2 tchd 7 to 4) 1
FILSCOT 5-10-11 (7*) J Power, *prmnt, led o'r 3 fs out till over 2 out, styd on same pace*............(33 to 1 op 20 to 1) 2
REDGRAVE WOLF 4-9-10 (7*) G Supple, *prmnt, pushed alng hfwy, styd on fnl 2 fs*................(33 to 1 op 16 to 1) 3
RACKETBALL 4-10-1 (7*) L Suthern, *chsd ldrs, styd on one pace fnl 2 fs*........................ (10 to 1 op 6 to 1) 4
GORMAN (Ire) 5-11-1 (3*) P Henley, *prmnt, chsd ldrs 5 fs out, wknd frm 2 out*......................... (5 to 1 tchd 6 to 1) 5
MOONRAKER'S MIRAGE 6-10-11 (7*) Mr N Moran, *beh, hdwy 5 fs out, came wide and wknd frm 2 out.* .... (12 to 1 op 10 to 1) 6
WILD NATIVE (Ire) 5-10-11 (7*) L Cummins, *slwly away, hdwy into midfield hfwy, weakeened 3 fs out.* ....(4 to 1 op 3 to 1 tchd 9 to 2) 7
SPRUCE LODGE 4-10-3 (5*) Sophie Mitchell, *some hdwy 6 fs out, wknd 3 out*....... (16 to 1 op 10 to 1 tchd 20 to 1) 8
ACT IN TIME (Ire) 5-10-11 (7*) C Hynes, *led till hdd and wknd o'r 3 fs out*......... (12 to 1 op 20 to 1 tchd 25 to 1) 9
TWO LORDS 5-11-4 G Tormey, *slwly away, al rear.* .... (33 to 1 op 20 to 1) 10
129[2] ARRANGE 5-10-11 (7*) Mr S Walker, *chsd ldrs 11 fs.* .... (20 to 1 op 10 to 1) 11
SALIX 5-10-13 (5*) O Burrows, *beh most of way.* .... (50 to 1 op 33 to 1) 12
CATHAY (Ire) 5-10-11 (7*) Mr G Baines, *slwly away, al beh.* ....(6 to 1 op 3 to 1) 13
GENERAL KILLINEY (Ire) 5-11-4 Mr A Phillips, *nvr better than mid-div*.......................... (50 to 1 op 25 to 1) 14
TOM DIAMOND 5-11-1 (3*) Michael Brennan, *in tch ten fs.* ....(33 to 1 tchd 50 to 1) 15
MAC'SMYUNCLE (bl) 6-11-4 Mr A Holdsworth, *chsd ldrs 11 fs*.......................... (50 to 1 op 25 to 1) 16
CHARLIE PIP 5-11-4 Mr M Appleby, *sn beh.* .... (33 to 1 op 25 to 1) 17
Dist: 12l, sht-hd, 2l, 8l, 3½l, 13l, 3½l, 3l, 6l, 1½l. 3m 45.30s. (17 Ran).
(Mrs R J Skan), D Nicholson

HAYDOCK (good to soft (races 1,2,3), good (4,5,6,7)) Friday February 21st

Going Correction: PLUS 0.65 sec. per fur. (races 1,3,5,7), PLUS 0.40 (2,4,6)

2785 Tweedle Dum 'National Hunt' Novices' Handicap Hurdle Class C (4-y-o and up) £3,533 2m............(2:00)

2565[2] THE PROMS (Ire) [109] 6-11-10 C Llewellyn, *in tch, lost pl 5th, hdwy 3 out, slight ld last, hld on wl und pres.* ....(7 to 2 op 3 to 1) 1
2581[5] SILLY MONEY [90] 6-10-5 R Garritty, *hld up, not fluent second, effrt to chase ldrs 2 out, styd on strly und pres.* ....(8 to 1 op 7 to 1) 2
2349* PHAR ECHO (Ire) [94] 6-10-9 R Supple, *nvr far away, slight ld betw last 2, hdd last, fdd*................ (8 to 1 op 6 to 1) 3
2560[3] LOGICAL STEP (Ire) [97] 7-10-12 R Dunwoody, *settled rear, hdwy and in tch 5th, ev ch 2 out, no extr frm last.* ....(7 to 2 op 3 to 1 tchd 4 to 1) 4
2489[8] PRINCE OF SAINTS (Ire) [85] 6-10-0 D Bentley, *hld up, pushed alng and outpcd 3 out, no dngr aftr.* .... (10 to 1 op 12 to 1 tchd 14 to 1) 5
2344[6] MAPLETON [95] 4-9-7 (7*) R Wilkinson, *chsd ldrs, led appr 5th, rdn and hdd betw last 2, fdd*...... (12 to 1 op 10 to 1) 6
2572[2] JERVAULX (Ire) [96] 6-10-11 P Carberry, *wth ldr, not fluent 4th, rdn and lost tch appr 2 out, sn beh.* ....(15 to 8 fav op 2 to 1 tchd 9 to 4) 7
WHITER MORN [85] 7-9-7 (7*) N Horrocks, *sn led, hdd and outpcd appr 5th, wl beh 2 out*.................. (100 to 1) 8
Dist: ¾l, 6l, ¾l, 6l, 2½l, 16l, ½l. 3m 55.00s. a 17.00s (8 Ran).
SR: 30/10/8/10/-/ (Mrs J Mould), N A Twiston-Davies

2786 White Rabbit Handicap Chase Class C (0-135 5-y-o and up) £4,531 3m .... (2:30)

GENERAL WOLFE [135] 8-12-0 R Dunwoody, *settled midfield, smooth hdwy to press ldr 6 out, hrd rdn frm last, ran on strly to get up cl hme*...... (7 to 2 op 3 to 1 tchd 4 to 1) 1
1420* MCGREGOR THE THIRD [125] 11-11-4 A Dobbin, *jmpd wl, wth ldr till led 11th, strly pressed frm 3 out, kpt on gmely, hdd last strds*.................... (4 to 1 tchd 9 to 2) 2
2438[4] DESTIN D'ESTRUVAL (Fr) [123] 6-11-2 D Bridgwater, *in tch, pckd 13th, pressed ldrs 4 out, drvn alng nxt, fdd frm last, eased whn btn*....(11 to 4 fav op 3 to 1 tchd 100 to 30) 3
2564[2] CAMELOT KNIGHT [119] 11-10-12 C Llewellyn, *pckd 1st, rear and reminders 7th, jmpd slwly 9th and nxt, lost tch 4 out, sn beh*.................(13 to 2 op 5 to 1 tchd 7 to 1) 4
CAMITROV (Fr) [133] 7-11-12 P Carberry, *set gd pace till hdd 11th, wknd quickly 5 out, tld off*........(16 to 1 op 12 to 1) 5
2571[3] NORTHANTS [121] 11-10-9 (5*) R McGrath, *beh, blun 3rd, mstk 5th, wl behind 14th, tld off whn pld up r-in, lme.* ....(4 to 1 op 7 to 2) pu
2592[3] RIVER BOUNTY [119] (bl) 11-10-12 G Bradley, *cl up, chlgd tenth, wknd and pld up 12th, lme*...... (14 to 1 op 10 to 1) pu
Dist: Nk, 16l, dist, dist. 6m 19.30s. a 14.30s (7 Ran).
SR: 53/43/25/-/ (Winning Line Racing Limited), Capt T A Forster

2787 Queen Of Hearts Handicap Hurdle Class B (0-145 4-y-o and up) £4,815 2½m........................ (3:00)

1628[6] ALLEGATION [132] (v) 7-11-1 Jamie Evans, *led chasing grp, pushed alng 3 out, str run to ld appr last, drvn clr.* .... (25 to 1 op 14 to 1) 1
2716[4] KAITAK (Ire) [119] 6-9-13 (3*) F Leahy, *cl up in chasing grp, led and pushed clr appr 3 out, blun nxt, hdd and one pace bef last.* ....(14 to 1 tchd 16 to 1) 2
2557[2] KINGDOM OF SHADES (USA) [127] 7-10-10 P Carberry, *hld up, effrt and in tch 4 our, outpcd nxt, kpt on frm last.* ....(7 to 4 fav op 9 to 4) 3
2453[3] OUTSET (Ire) [127] 7-10-7 (3*) Mr C Bonner, *hld up, hdwy and in tch whn mstk 4 out, not quicken nxt, sn no extr.* .... (11 to 2 op 5 to 1 tchd 6 to 1) 4

2453^{9} BURNT IMP (USA) [130] 7-10-13 J Callaghan, *hld up, niggled alng in rear whn hit 5th, lost tch 5 out, moderate late hdwy.* ....(9 to 1 op 8 to 1) 5
2591^{7} MISTER MOROSE (Ire) [135] 7-11-4 C Llewellyn, *midfield, reminders and outpcd aftr 4 out, btn whn not fluent 2 out.* ....(3 to 1 tchd 100 to 30) 6
2465^{4} TIBETAN [131] 5-11-0 R Dunwoody, *hld up, hdwy to chase ldrs 4 out, outpcd nxt, sn fdd*..........(5 to 1 op 4 to 1) 7
2389^{7} DIWALI DANCER [117] 7-9-7 (7*) G Supple, *sn clr, mstk 6th, hdd and wknd appr 3 out, tld off*.......(16 to 1 op 14 to 1) 8
2713^{6} BETTER TIMES AHEAD [145] 11-12-0 A Dobbin, *sn niggled alng in rear, tld off 4th, pld up bef 3 out.* (25 to 1 op 16 to 1) pu
Dist: 10l, 2½l, 5l, 1½l, 6l, 22l, 11l. 4m 52.20s. a 16.20s (9 Ran).
SR: 55/32/37/32/33/32/6/-/-/ (Martin Pipe Racing Club), M C Pipe

2788 Glengoyne Highland Malt Novices' Chase Class D Tamerosia Series Qualifier (5-y-o and up) £3,631 2½m .... (3:30)

2554^{2} EUDIPE (Fr) 5-11-4 R Dunwoody, *settled 3rd, not fluent 7th, niggled alng 4 out, chsd ldr bef nxt, styd on strly und pres to ld r-in*..........(11 to 10 jt-fav op 11 to 10 on) 1
2450 SIMPLY DASHING (Ire) 6-12-0 R Garritty, *mstk second, cl up, led 11th, drw clr 3 out, mistake last, hdd and no extr last 100 yards*..........(11 to 10 jt-fav op Evens tchd 6 to 5) 2
2406^{2} GARETHSON (Ire) 6-11-4 D Bridgwater, *led to 11th, rdn and lost tch appr 3 out, sn no dngr*.......(10 to 1 op 12 to 1) 3
2600 MAJOR LOOK (NZ) 9-11-8 A Dobbin, *sn beh, tld off 6th.* ....(33 to 1 op 25 to 1) 4
2237^{4} GONE AWAY (Ire) 8-11-1 (3*) Mr C Bonner, *sn tld off.* ....(100 to 1 op 66 to 1) 5
Dist: 2½l, dist, 9l, 28l. 5m 18.10s. a 21.10s (5 Ran).
(D A Johnson), M C Pipe

2789 Scottish Equitable/Jockeys Association Series Handicap Hurdle Qualifier Class D (0-120 4-y-o and up) £2,853 2½m.............. (4:00)

1921^{2} BIG STRAND (Ire) [115] 8-11-10 Jamie Evans, *settled rear, steady hdwy frm 3 out, swtchd rght and str run to ld last 100 yards*..........(11 to 2 op 5 to 1) 1
2601^{2} BARTON WARD [105] 6-11-0 A Dobbin, *hld up, reminders 4 out, rallied to ld 2 out, kpt on till hdd and no extr r-in.* ....(11 to 4 fav op 3 to 1 tchd 5 to 2) 2
2253^{7} SELATAN (Ire) [110] 5-11-5 R Dunwoody, *made most, pushed alng and hdd appr 2 out, styd on same pace.* ....(10 to 1 op 8 to 1) 3
2581^{2} TOPSAWYER [95] 9-10-4 K Gaule, *midfield, hdwy to chal 2 out, sn rdn alng, no extr appr last*.......(7 to 1 op 6 to 1) 4
2691^{7} CASSIO'S BOY [91] 6-10-0 P Carberry, *hld up, hdwy and in tch aftr 4 out, btn whn hit last*....... (12 to 1 tchd 14 to 1) 5
2465* PUREVALUE (Ire) [112] 6-11-7 Richard Guest, *cl up, ev ch whn slight mstk 2 out, fdd*..........(6 to 1) 6
2374^{6} SWEET TRENTINO (Ire) [91] 6-10-0 C Llewellyn, *al rear, nvr a factor*..........(50 to 1) 7
2574* OAT COUTURE [119] 9-12-0 R Supple, *hld up, hrd rdn hfwy, nvr able to chal*..........(9 to 1 op 7 to 1) 8
2501^{4} AMILLIONMEMORIES [93] 7-10-2 P Holley, *beh, drvn alng 4 out, sn struggling*..........(16 to 1) 9
2253 HOODWINKER (Ire) [109] 8-11-4 D Bridgwater, *reminders second, wth ldr frm nxt till wknd 3 out, sn beh*...... (14 to 1) 10
1671 NUNS CONE [91] 9-9-11 (3*) R Massey, *beh hfwy.* (33 to 1) 11
2574^{7} BANG IN TROUBLE (Ire) [104] 6-10-8 (5*) R McGrath, *pld up and dismounted bef 4th*..........(14 to 1) pu
2580 ELPIDOS [115] 5-11-7 (3*) Mr C Bonner, *hld up, drpd rear 4 out, wl beh whn pld up 2 out*.........(25 to 1 op 20 to 1) pu
Dist: 1¼l, 8l, 1¾l, 7l, 6l, 1¼l, ½l, 6l, 10l, 3l. 4m 57.80s. a 21.80s (13 Ran).
SR: 8/-/-/-/-/-/ (E C Jones), M C Pipe

2790 Walrus Hunters' Chase Class H (5-y-o and up) £1,544 3m........ (4:30)

2551^{2} LORD RELIC (NZ) 11-12-0 (7*) Mr R Ford, *cl up, led 2 out, pushed clr aftr last*..........(9 to 4 fav tchd 2 to 1) 1
COUNTRY TARROGEN 8-12-2 (5*) Mr N Wilson, *hld up, improved hfwy, chasing ldrs whn pckd 3 out, kpt on appr last.* ....(7 to 2 op 3 to 1) 2
GLEN OAK 12-11-7 (7*) Mr M P FitzGerald, *not jump wl, hdwy and in tch 4 out, fdd 2 out*.......... (33 to 1 op 25 to 1) 3
2551^{3} MY NOMINEE (bl) 9-12-0 (7*) Mr R Burton, *led 4th, pushed alng and hdd 2 out, sn wndrd, fdd appr last.* ....(5 to 1 op 9 to 2) 4
TRAVEL BOUND (bl) 12-11-9² (7*) Mr D Barlow, *chsd ldrs, lost pl hfwy, wl beh 5 out*..........(50 to 1 op 20 to 1) 5
1113 MOBILE MESSENGER (NZ) 9-11-7 (7*) Miss S Samworth, *led to 4th, 5th and in tch whn f 9th*........ (20 to 1 op 16 to 1) f
2556^{8} CHARLIES DELIGHT (Ire) 9-11-13 (5*) Mr A Sansome, *midfield, hdwy tenth, 6th and drvn alng whn f 14th.* ....(66 to 1 op 50 to 1) f
2634 MASTER KIT (Ire) 8-11-11 (7*) Mr J Billinge, *str hold, chsd ldrs frm 5th, 6th and struggling whn uns rdr 4 out.* .... (9 to 2 op 5 to 1 tchd 11 to 2) ur
WILL IT LAST 11-11-2 (7*) Mr L Brown, *sn wl beh, tld off whn pld up 11th*..........(100 to 1 op 50 to 1) pu
MHEMEANLES 7-11-7 (7*) Mr N R Mitchell, *jmpd poorly, al wl beh, tld off whn pld up 5 out*......... (50 to 1 op 33 to 1) pu
THE MAJOR GENERAL 10-12-0 (7*) Capt A Ogden, *hld up, hdwy and in tch 9th, blun 13th and nxt, wl beh whn pld up 3 out*..........(9 to 2 tchd 5 to 1) pu
Dist: 6l, 13l, 5l, dist. 6m 32.00s. a 27.00s (11 Ran).
(Mrs H J Clarke), S A Brookshaw

2791 Levy Board Novices' Hurdle Class D (4-y-o and up) £3,039 2m..... (5:00)

2662* BREAK THE RULES 5-11-2 (7*) G Supple, *hld up, steady hdwy aftr 4 out, led betw last 2, styd on strly und pres.* (5 to 1) 1
ROYAL SCIMITAR (USA) 5-11-4 R Dunwoody, *keen hold, al hndy, ev ch 2 out, wndrd und pres, styd on wl cl hme.* ....(11 to 8 fav op 5 to 4 tchd 6 to 4) 2
2636^{8} MUTANASSIB (Ire) 4-10-8 Jamie Evans, *set gd pace, rdn and hdd betw last 2, unbl to quicken*...... (6 to 1 tchd 7 to 1) 3
2283^{3} MR MOONLIGHT (Ire) 5-11-4 G Bradley, *chsd ldrs, ev ch appr 2 out, fdd betw last two*..........(7 to 1 op 6 to 1) 4
2315^{7} EUROFAST PET (Ire) 7-11-4 C Llewellyn, *in tch, mstks 3rd and 5th, drvn and outpcd appr 2 out*..........(50 to 1) 5
2489 BUTTERWICK KING (Ire) 5-11-4 P Niven, *hld up in rear, pushed alng and lost tch aftr 3 out, sn no dngr.* ....(14 to 1 op 12 to 1 tchd 16 to 1) 6
RIVEAUX (Ire) 7-11-4 P Carberry, *hld up, shaken up and lost tch 3 out, sn beh*.......... (16 to 1 op 14 to 1) 7
2409^{6} COOL AS A CUCUMBER (Ire) 6-11-4 M Richards, *hld up in rear, some hdwy appr 3 out, beh frm nxt.* ....(9 to 2 op 7 to 1 tchd 4 to 1) 8
2711^{9} JESSOLLE 5-10-13 A Dobbin, *hld up, outpcd appr 3 out, tld off*..........(33 to 1 op 50 to 1) 9
PRAISE BE (Fr) 7-11-4 R Garritty, *beh frm 3rd, tld off.* ....(33 to 1 op 20 to 1) 10
Dist: 1½l, 2½l, 16l, 8l, 3l, 9l, 1¾l, 16l, hd. 3m 55.70s. a 17.70s (10 Ran).
SR: 22/15/2/-/-/-/ (A J Lomas), M C Pipe

KEMPTON (good)
Friday February 21st
Going Correction: PLUS 0.80 sec. per fur.

2792 Bedfont Novices' Hurdle Class D (5-y-o and up) £2,969 2m 5f.....(2:10)

ROYALTINO (Ire) 5-11-5 A Kondrat, *trkd ldrs and rcd on rls thrght, quickened into slight ld 2 out, drvn and hld on wl r-in.* ....(5 to 2 op 2 to 1 tchd 11 to 4) 1
2250 AWARD (Ire) 6-10-10 N Williamson, *hld up in rear, hdwy frm 3 fs out, chlgd 2 out, ran on und pres r-in, not quite get up.* ....(6 to 4 fav op 2 to 1) 2
2560^{2} READY MONEY CREEK (Ire) 6-11-0 J Osborne, *led aftr 1st to 5th, ld ag'n after nxt, hdd 2 out, styd on same pace.* ....(7 to 2 op 3 to 1 tchd 4 to 1) 3
2250^{5} LATAHAAB (USA) 6-10-10 P Hide, *led till aftr 1st, slight ld ag'n 5th till after 6th, styd pressing ldrs till one pace frm 2 out.* .... (33 to 1 op 25 to 1 tchd 50 to 1) 4
2541^{5} MILLERSFORD 6-11-0 J Culloty, *in tch, outpcd aftr 3 out, styd on und pres frm nxt*.......... (10 to 1 op 12 to 1) 5
2250^{3} SYMPHONY'S SON (Ire) 6-10-10 A Maguire, *beh till hdwy 6th, chsd ldrs appr 2 out, sn wknd.* .... (16 to 1 op 12 to 1 tchd 20 to 1) 6
2504^{5} ROSEHALL 6-10-2 (7*) L Suthern, *chsd ldrs till rdn and wknd appr 2 out*..........(66 to 1 op 50 to 1) 7
2405^{7} TIME TO PARLEZ 6-10-10 S Curran, *beh frm hfwy.* .... (66 to 1 op 50 to 1) 8
2323 IRON N GOLD 5-11-0 D Gallagher, *trkd ldrs frm 3rd till came wide and wknd appr 2 out.* .... (40 to 1 op 33 to 1 tchd 50 to 1) 9
250^{4} MISTER GENEROSITY (Ire) 6-10-10 B Powell, *in tch 4th, wknd aftr 6th, tld off*.......... (100 to 1 op 50 to 1) 10
SMART ROOKIE (Ire) 7-10-10 J R Kavanagh, *mid-div, wknd and f 2 out*.......... (14 to 1 op 10 to 1 tchd 16 to 1) f
2637^{5} GREG'S PROFILES 6-10-10 C Maude, *prominet till wknd aftr 6th, tld off whn pld up bef 2 out*.......(50 to 1 op 25 to 1) pu
Dist: ¾l, 7l, 3l, nk, 7l, 8l, 23l, 3l, dist. 5m 18.50s. a 32.50s (12 Ran).
(Henri de Pracomtal), F Doumen

2793 Corinthian Hunters' Chase Class H (5-y-o and up) £1,548 3m..... (2:40)

THE JOGGER 12-12-0 (7*) Mr J Tizzard, *wth ldr till led 3rd, came clr frm 4 out, readily*..........(9 to 2 op 3 to 1) 1
2531 MEDIANE (USA) 12-11-11 (3*) Mr Simon Andrews, *reluctant to line up, chsd ldrs 6th, chlgd tenth to 14th, outpcd aftr 4 out, styd on ag'n to take second r-in.* ....(150 to 1 op 50 to 1 tchd 200 to 1) 2
2660^{4} POORS WOOD 10-11-7 (7*) Mr P O'Keeffe, *hld up, hdwy and hit 12th, chsd wnr frm 4 out till wknd r-in.* ....(11 to 1 op 7 to 1 tchd 12 to 1) 3
2468^{2} TEAPLANTER 14-12-2 (5*) Mr B Pollock, *led to 3rd, in trble and rdn tenth, hit 12th and wknd.* ....(5 to 2 on op 7 to 4 on tchd 11 to 4 on) 4
2641^{3} FIFTH AMENDMENT (bl) 12-12-0 (7*) Mr A Hales, *pressed ldrs 3rd and rcd wide, wknd tenth, jmpd poorly and tried to refuse in rear till blun and uns rdr 12th.* ....(25 to 1 op 10 to 1 tchd 33 to 1) ur

2660⁵ AMARI KING 13-12-0 (7*) Mr C Ward Thomas, *chsd ldrs 6th, lost pl 8th, wknd 12th, tld off whn pld up bef 2 out.*
.................................(33 to 1 op 10 to 1 tchd 40 to 1) pu
Dist: 13l, 14l, 14l. 6m 23.60s. a 34.60s (6 Ran).

(Mrs P Tizzard), C L Tizzard

2794 Manor Novices' Chase Class D (5-y-o and up) £3,485 3m............(3:10)

2441⁴ BERUDE NOT TO (Ire) (bl) 8-11-12 J Osborne, *jmpd wl, wth ldr till slight ld 5th to 9th, led 11th to 13th, slight lead 3 out, clr nxt, ran on well.*........(13 to 2 op 6 to 1 tchd 8 to 1) 1
1991* OBAN 7-11-12 J Culloty, *dsptd 3rd most of way, styd on frm 3 out, wnt second r-in but no imprsn on wnr.*
...............................(6 to 1 tchd 13 to 2) 2
2593 AARDWOLF 6-11-12 D Gallagher, *led to 5th, styd wth wnr till led 9th to 11th, led ag'n 13th, hdd 3 out, wknd nxt, ct for second r-in.*...........................(9 to 2 op 3 to 1) 3
2593³ TRIPLE WITCHING 11-11-5 N Williamson, *dsptd ld most of way till jmpd slwly and wknd 4 out, tld off.*
.....................(7 to 2 op 3 to 1 tchd 4 to 1) 4
2210² PLEASURE SHARED (Ire) 9-11-12 C Maude, *hit 1st, blun second, f 5th.*........(6 to 4 fav op 7 to 4 tchd 15 to 8) f
2498⁴ SWISS TACTIC (Ire) 8-11-5 T Kent, *hit 5th, sn lost tch and tld off, pld up bef 11th.*...........(100 to 1 op 50 to 1) pu
Dist: 13l, ¾l, dist. 6m 14.00s. a 25.00s (6 Ran).

SR: 40/33/32/

(G Addiscott), O Sherwood

2795 Kempton Park 'National Hunt' Novices' Hurdle Class D (5-y-o and up) £2,843 2m...................(3:40)

2315² WADE ROAD (Ire) 6-11-8 J Culloty, *trkd ldrs, drvn to chal frm 2 out, styd on wl und pres to ld r-in, rdn out.*
.....................(15 to 8 op 6 to 4 tchd 2 to 1) 1
2042⁴ KAILASH (USA) 6-11-8 C Maude, *steady hdwy to track ldrs 3 out, slight ld 2 out, hdd r-in, styd on und pres.*
.............................(11 to 10 fav op 7 to 3) 2
2371⁴ TREE CREEPER (Ire) 5-11-0 L Harvey, *chsd ldrs, chlgd 3 out to 2 out, one pace appr last.*
...................(12 to 1 op 8 to 1 tchd 14 to 1) 3
IN THE ROUGH (Ire) 6-11-0 A Maguire, *hld up, hdwy aftr 3 out, kpt on one pace.*.........(13 to 2 op 4 to 1 tchd 7 to 1) 4
2302⁵ WENTWORTH (USA) 5-11-0 B Powell, *wth ldr till led 4th, styd on wl whn chlgd frm 3 out, one pace nxt.*
.............................(33 to 1 op 20 to 1) 5
2560⁰ CALM DOWN (Ire) 6-11-0 J Osborne, *beh till steady hdwy to track ldrs 4 out, wknd nxt.*
...................(66 to 1 op 50 to 1 tchd 100 to 1) 6
FLEETING MANDATE (Ire) 5-11-0 J R Kavanagh, *in tch till mstk 3rd, drpd rear aftr 4th, some hdwy 2 out but not a dngr.*
...................(20 to 1 op 14 to 1 tchd 25 to 1) 7
2199 HUISH (Ire) 6-11-0 Mr A Charles-Jones, *nvr better than mid-div.*.................................(100 to 1) 8
2405⁹ SMART REMARK 5-11-0 D Skyrme, *made most to 4th, sn pushed alng, styd wth ldr till wknd appr 2 out.*...(100 to 1) 9
2277 BLUE HAVANA 5-10-9 W Marston, *al beh, lost tch frm 5th, tld off.*.............................(100 to 1) 10
Dist: 1l, 4l, 2½l, 2½l, 7l, 8l, 1½l, 28l, dist. 3m 58.90s. a 18.90s (10 Ran).

SR: 33/32/20/17/14/7/

(Lord Chelsea), Miss H C Knight

2796 Portlane Handicap Chase Class C (0-135 5-y-o and up) £4,746 2½m 110yds....................(4:10)

2722³ GENERAL PERSHING [135] 11-12-0 A Maguire, *made all and al gng wl, hit last, easily.*
.............(11 to 10 op Evens tchd 6 to 5 and 5 to 4) 1
2220³ LACKENDARA [115] 10-10-8 B Fenton, *chsd wnr, hit 5th, rdn, effrt and mstk 4 out, ran on ag'n 3 out, sn one pace.*
.............(11 to 8 on op 6 to 4 on tchd 5 to 4 on) 2
Won by 4l. 5m 20.40s. a 27.40s (2 Ran).

SR: -/-/

(J E Potter), D Nicholson

2797 Littleton Handicap Hurdle Class D (0-125 5-y-o and up) £2,866 2m 5f ....(4:40)

2481* LESSONS LASS (Ire) [110] 5-11-2 J Osborne, *made all, rdn and styd on wl r-in.....*(100 to 30 op 7 to 2 tchd 4 to 1) 1
1481² HIGH GRADE [114] 9-11-6 N Williamson, *trkd ldrs, rdn, effrt and swshd tail appr last, not run on.*
.....................(10 to 1 tchd 9 to 1 and 11 to 1) 2
2559⁵ ROYAL PIPER (NZ) [107] 10-10-13 R Greene, *hld up, hdwy 3 out, styd on frm 2 out.*...............(10 to 1 op 8 to 1) 3
2667 SPRING TO GLORY [102] 10-10-8 B Fenton, *chsd wnr to 2 out, sn one pace und pres.*...........(33 to 1 op 20 to 1) 4
2530³ TIM (Ire) [113] 7-11-5 A Maguire, *hld up, some hdwy frm 2 out, not a dngr.*.................(5 to 1 tchd 6 to 1) 5
2667² NINE CO THREE (Ire) 5-8-10-11 D Gallagher, *led ldrs, rdn aftr 3 out, wknd nxt.*.....(5 to 2 fav tchd 11 to 4) 6
PURPLE SPLASH [117] (v) 7-11-9 J R Kavanagh, *beh, rapid hdwy to chase ldrs aftr 3 out, wknd 2 out.*
.....................(9 to 1 op 6 to 1 tchd 10 to 1) 7
2389⁵ WINGS COVE [118] 7-11-7 (3*) A Aspell, *hld up, jmpd slwly 7th, nvr nr ldrs.*.....................(11 to 2 op 7 to 2) 8

2442 BELL ONE (USA) [102] 8-10-8 S McNeill, *chsd ldrs to 3 out, sn wknd.*...........................(25 to 1 op 16 to 1) 9
Dist: 1½l, 4l, 4l, 1½l, 1l, 8l, 24l, 9l. 5m 17.70s. a 31.70s (9 Ran).

(V McCalla), Lady Herries

SOUTHWELL (good)
Friday February 21st
Going Correction: PLUS 0.30 sec. per fur.

2798 Nightingale Novices' Handicap Chase Class D (0-110 5-y-o and up) £3,452 2m....................(2:20)

2498⁵ WEEHEBY (USA) [81] 8-11-2 G Tormey, *cl up, hit 9th, staying on whn lft in ld 2 out, drvn out.*
...................(6 to 1 op 5 to 1 tchd 7 to 1) 1
2527⁸ RECORD LOVER (Ire) [69] 7-10-4 W Worthington, *chsd ldg grp, effrt 4 out, styd on frm 2 out, not rch wnr.*
.............................(16 to 1 op 12 to 1) 2
2604 GORDON [87] 6-11-5 (3*) E Husband, *in tch, hmpd 3rd, drvn alng thrght, styd on frm 2 out, no imprsn.*
.............................(20 to 1 op 12 to 1) 3
2376³ SNOWY PETREL (Ire) [89] (bl) 5-11-1 A Thornton, *hld up, rdn alng 4 out, nvr able to chal.*.....(7 to 2 jt-fav tchd 4 to 1) 4
2547² SAYMORE [83] 11-11-4 S Wynne, *hld up, pushed alng 4 out, no imprsn frm nxt.*.................(11 to 2 op 4 to 1) 5
2561⁶ OLD REDWOOD [67] 10-10-2 R Bellamy, *lft in ld 3rd, hdd aftr 4 out, grad fdd.*...........(11 to 1 op 10 to 1 tchd 12 to 1) 6
2739 MR BEAN [92] 7-11-13 A Larnach, *cl up, blun second, chlgd 7th, led briefly aftr 4 out, wknd alng whn hmpd 2 out.*
.............................(20 to 1 op 12 to 1) 7
2376⁴ FLAMING MIRACLE (Ire) [78] (bl) 7-10-13 R Farrant, *trkd ldrs, improved to ld aftr 4 out, 2 ls in frnt and gng wl whn f two out.*
.....................(7 to 2 jt-fav op 3 to 1) f
RINUS MAJOR (Ire) [67] 6-10-2² T Jenks, *led till f 3rd.*
.............................(33 to 1 op 20 to 1) f
2498 DANDIE IMP [78] 9-10-13 T J Murphy, *tracking ldr whn brght dwn 3rd.*.....................(10 to 1 op 12 to 1) bd
Dist: 2½l, 3l, 10l, ½l, 2l, ½l. 4m 5.90s. a 11.90s (10 Ran).

SR: 17/2/17/-/2/-/

(The Dana Partnership), M F Barraclough

2799 Phoenix Novices' Chase Class D (5-y-o and up) £3,485 3m 110yds (2:50)

2425³ AS DU TREFLE (Fr) 9-11-4 A P McCoy, *jmpd wl, made all, ran on strly frm 3 out, readily.....*(2 to 1 on tchd 13 to 8 on) 1
2596⁴ PEARL'S CHOICE (Ire) 9-10-13 A Thornton, *chsd wnr, blun badly 6th, kpt on frm 3 out, no imprsn.*
.............(12 to 1 op 8 to 1 tchd 14 to 1) 2
2280 PEARL EPEE 8-10-13 R Johnson, *chsd ldrs, hit 12th, sn rdn alng, fdg whn hit 4 out.*.................(16 to 1 op 10 to 1) 3
2613² EASY BREEZY 7-11-4 J Railton, *in tch, outpcd eigth, nvr dngrs aftr.*...................(10 to 1 op 14 to 1) 4
1339² LOTTERY TICKET (Ire) 8-11-4 J A McCarthy, *beh whn blun and uns rdr second.*.............(5 to 1 op 5 to 2) ur
1593 DAMCADA (Ire) 9-11-4 S Wynne, *hld up, struggling hfwy, tld off whn pld up bef 4 out.*.............(33 to 1 op 20 to 1) pu
LISNAVARAGH 11-11-4 V Smith, *strted slwly, tld off thrght, pld up bef 3 out.*...................(66 to 1 op 50 to 1) pu
2561 KENTUCKY GOLD (Ire) 8-11-4 R Bellamy, *beh, struggling hfwy, tld off whn pld up 4 out.*....(66 to 1 op 50 to 1) pu
2566⁶ FORTYTWO DEE (Ire) 7-10-13 J Ryan, *beh, drvn and outpcd frm hfwy, tld off whn pld up bef 2 out.*(33 to 1 tchd 40 to 1) pu
Dist: 8l, dist, 1¾l. 6m 17.40s. a 23.40s (9 Ran).

(D A Johnson), M C Pipe

2800 Adelphi For CNC Machining Handicap Chase Class D (0-120 5-y-o and up) £3,355 3m 110yds........(3:20)

2301² FATHER SKY [110] (bl) 6-11-7 J A McCarthy, *al prmnt, improved to ld aftr 4 out, ran on wl frm 2 out.*
...................(100 to 30 op 5 to 2 tchd 7 to 2) 1
YOUNG MINER [94] 11-10-5 G Upton, *chsd ldr, led briefly 4 out, kpt on frm nxt, one pace last.*(20 to 1 op 16 to 1) 2
2434³ CHILDHAY CHOCOLATE [99] 9-10-10 R Johnson, *led to 4 out, outpcd bef nxt, kpt on betw last 2, no imprsn.*
...................(6 to 1 op 11 to 2 tchd 7 to 1) 3
2666 REALLY A RASCAL [105] 10-10-13 (3*) D Fortt, *hld up, improved to chase ldrs 4 out, blun nxt, sn outpcd.*
.............................(4 to 1 op 3 to 1) 4
2627⁴ MUGONI BEACH [117] 12-12-0 A P McCoy, *chsd ldrs, blun 6th, struggling appr 5 out, sn lost tch, fnshd lme.*
.....................(5 to 2 fav op 6 to 4) 5
2624⁵ CROPREDY LAD [92] 10-10-3 A Thornton, *chsd ldrs till wknd 4 out, tld off.*...................(5 to 1 op 7 to 1) 6
Dist: 5l, 1¾l, 10l, dist, 4l. 6m 24.40s. a 30.40s (6 Ran).

(Kenneth Kornfeld), O Sherwood

2801 East Midlands Electricity Lincoln Handicap Hurdle Class D (0-120 4-y-o and up) £2,745 3m 110yds.. (3:50)

2435² MR STRONG GALE (Ire) [95] 6-10-3 R Johnson, *al in tch, effrt 4 out, led betw last 2, kpt on wl.*
.............................(11 to 4 fav op 5 to 2 tchd 3 to 1)   1

2598⁶ LINTON ROCKS [120] 8-11-7 (7*) X Aizpuru, *al hndy, improved aftr 5 out, led bef 2 out till betw last two, kpt on wl.*
.............................(4 to 1 tchd 9 to 2)   2

2762⁶ KADARI [92] (v) 8-9-12¹ Guy Lewis, *cl up, led bef 4 out, hdd before 2 out, rallied last.*.........(14 to 1 op 12 to 1)   3

2289⁷ PHARARE (Ire) [102] 7-10-10 A S Smith, *sn led, hdd bef 4 out, outpcd aftr nxt.*...................................(12 to 1)   4

2504⁷ KIPPANOUR (USA) [103] (bl) 5-10-4 (7*) D Kiernan, *wl beh till styd on frm 2 out, nvr dngrs.*.......................(12 to 1)   5

2559 RIMOUSKI [94] 9-10-2¹ Gary Lyons, *sn beh, nvr on terms.*
.............................(12 to 1)   6

2598⁸ NICK THE BEAK [120] 8-11-4 J Supple, *mid-div, struggling fnl circuit, btn frm 3 out.*
.............................(11 to 2 op 5 to 1 tchd 6 to 1)   7

2175² FORTUNES COURSE (Ire) [110] 8-11-4 A P McCoy, *wth ldr, reminders 7th, outpcd frm 9th.*........(4 to 1 op 5 to 2)   8

2487 SUVLA BAY [92] 9-10-0 M Brennan, *midfield till fdd frm 4 out.*...................................(20 to 1)   9

2281 WE'RE IN THE MONEY [92] 13-9-7 (7*) Claudine Froggitt, *sn beh, tld off frm hfwy.*...........(100 to 1 tchd 200 to 1)   10

2562 JOHNNY'S TURN [94] 12-10-2 Mr N Kent, *hld up, struggling fnl circuit, tld off whn pld up bef 2 out.* (33 to 1 op 20 to 1)   pu

Dist: 1l, 1¾l, 13l, 9l, 9l, 1½l, 1½l, 24l, 17l. 6m 14.50s. a 32.50s (11 Ran).

(T G A Chappell), P F Nicholls

2802 Albatros Novices' Hurdle Class D (4-y-o and up) £2,829 2m....... (4:20)

2636 OTTO E MEZZO 5-11-2 V Smith, *nvr far away, chsd ldr frm 4th, drvn to ld bef last, all out.*..........(9 to 1 op 6 to 1)   1

2511⁵ PINKERTON'S PAL 6-11-2 A P McCoy, *led, drvn bef 2 out, hdd before last, no extr und pres.*
.............................(13 to 8 op 5 to 4 tchd 7 to 4)   2

2533 CARLISLE BANDITO'S (Ire) 5-11-2 M Moloney, *prmnt, effrt and rdn aftr 3 out, fdd nxt.*
.............................(6 to 5 fav op Evens tchd 11 to 8)   3

NEBAAL (USA) 7-11-2 S Wynne, *beh, struggling 4th, nvr on terms.*..........................(50 to 1 tchd 66 to 1)   4

2517⁷ DODGY DANCER (bl) 7-11-2 R Bellamy, *chsd ldr to 4th, sn lost tch.*..........................(50 to 1 tchd 66 to 1)   5

2636 DIA GEORGY 6-10-13 (3*) M Brennan, *beh, struggling 4th, pld up aftr 3 out.*...................(33 to 1 op 25 to 1)   pu

RISKY TU 6-10-11 R Johnson, *chsd ldrs, rdn 4th, struggling and pld up aftr four out.* (11 to 1 op 7 to 1 tchd 12 to 1)   pu

GREENACRES STAR 7-10-8 (3*) Guy Lewis, *beh, blun 3rd, sn struggling, tld off whn pld up bef 5th.*.............(33 to 1)   pu

Dist: 2½l, 13l, dist, 2l. 4m 3.30s. a 17.30s (8 Ran).

(J P M & J W Cook), M J Polglase

2803 Vulture Novices' Hurdle Class D (4-y-o and up) £2,997 2½m 110yds
.............................(4:50)

2640* TOTAL JOY (Ire) 6-11-10 J Railton, *made al, clr 5th, unchlgd.*
.............................(2 to 1 fav)   1

2629³ BEECHFIELD FLYER 6-11-4 G Tormey, *al prmnt, chsd wnr 7th, no imprsn frm 2 out.*..(9 to 1 op 6 to 1 tchd 10 to 1)   2

2063* SMOLENSK (Ire) 5-11-10 M Moloney, *settled midfield, effrt 4 out, outpcd bef 2 out.*.........(9 to 4 op 5 to 2 tchd 3 to 1)   3

2397⁶ GEISWAY (Can) 7-11-4 R Johnson, *midfield, effrt bef 4 out, fdd before 2 out.*.........(11 to 1 op 8 to 1 tchd 12 to 1)   4

2578 DRY HILL LAD (bl) 6-11-1 (3*) E Husband, *in tch, outpcd 4 out, sn btn.*............................(20 to 1 tchd 25 to 1)   5

2463 ANTARCTICA (USA) 5-10-13 D Parker, *beh, nvr on terms.*
.............................(33 to 1 tchd 66 to 1)   6

2405⁸ OVER ZEALOUS 5-11-4 J Supple, *mid-div, struggling 5th, sn btn.*...................(9 to 1 op 8 to 1 tchd 12 to 1)   7

1322³ WELSH LOOT (Ire) 6-11-4 J A McCarthy, *hld up, effrt 7th, 4th and wkng whn f last.*....(11 to 1 op 8 to 1 tchd 12 to 1)   f

1968 PUSH ON POLLY 7-10-13 V Smith, *uns rdr 1st.*
.............................(25 to 1 op 20 to 1)   ur

FRADICANT 8-11-4 S Wynne, *pld hrd, sn chasing wnr, struggling 7th, pulled up bef 3 out.*..............(50 to 1)   pu

2423 JELALI 4-10-13 A P McCoy, *not fluent in rear, hdwy aftr 6th, fdd 3 out, pld up aftr nxt.*
.............................(15 to 2 op 5 to 1 tchd 8 to 1)   pu

2458 CUMBERLAND YOUTH (bl) 6-11-4 D Leahy, *prmnt to 4th, sn struggling, pld up bef 4 out.*.............(50 to 1)   pu

2517⁴ CAPTAIN NAVAR (Ire) 7-11-1 (3*) Michael Brennan, *chsd ldrs, blun 6th, sn struggling, pld up bef 4 out.* (10 to 1 op 8 to 1)   pu

Dist: 7l, 15l, 16l, 18l, 5l, 23l. 5m 14.50s. a 28.50s (13 Ran).

(P M Warren), C J Mann

DONCASTER (good)
Saturday February 22nd

Going Correction: PLUS 0.15 sec. per fur. (races 1,3,4,7), PLUS 0.05 (2,5,6)

2804 'Open Morning' Selling Hurdle Class G (4,5,6-y-o) £1,639 2m 110yds
.............................(2:00)

2676⁴ SOUSSE 4-9-13 (3*) G Lee, *settled wth chasing grp, improved to ld 2 out, drvn out r-in.*............(4 to 1 jt-fav op 4 to 1 tchd 5 to 1 and 11 to 2)   1

2663³ PROUD IMAGE 5-11-6 (3*) D Fortt, *patiently rdn, took clr order aftr 4 out, led nxt, hdd 2 out, ridden and kpt on same pace r-in.*..........(4 to 1 jt-fav op 7 to 2 tchd 9 to 2)   2

2025 RIVERBANK ROSE (v) 6-10-9 (3*) Guy Lewis, *chsd clr ldr, led aftr 4th till hdd 3 out, rdn and one pace frm betw last 2.*
.............................(14 to 1 op 16 to 1)   3

2265³ ARCH ANGEL (Ire) 4-9-9 (7*) X Aizpuru, *settled off the pace, gd hdwy appr 3 out, styd on wl frm betw last 2, nrst finish.*
.............................(12 to 1)   4

2202 BOY BLAKENEY 4-10-7 Richard Guest, *settled wth chasing grp, improved und pres 3 out, kpt on same pace frm betw last 2.*...................(9 to 1 op 8 to 1)   5

2283 DAME PROSPECT 6-11-1 (3*) P Midgley, *settled off the pace, improved frm 3 out, styd on same pace last 2.*
.............................(20 to 1 op 33 to 1)   6

2630² GREEN KING 5-11-3 S McNeill, *chsd alng wth main grp, effrt appr 3 out, no imprsn frm nxt.*.......(33 to 1 op 20 to 1)   7

2526 OAKBURY (Ire) 5-10-10 (7*) T Siddall, *wtd wth, some hdwy 3 out, no imprsn frm nxt.*..............(9 to 1 op 6 to 1)   8

2611² AUTUMN FLAME (Ire) 6-10-12 M Brennan, *drvn alng to go pace hfwy, nvr able to rch chalg pos..*(50 to 1 op 33 to 1)   9

2526⁶ HAWANAFA (bl) 4-10-2 W McFarland, *wtd wth, improved to go hndy appr 3 out, wknd quickly frm nxt.*(8 to 1 op 7 to 1)   10

BLUNTSWOOD HALL 4-10-7 Gary Lyons, *chsd alng hfwy, nvr a factor.*........................(8 to 1 op 7 to 1)   11

2577 SHARMOOR 5-10-12 O Pears, *struggling hfwy, nvr a factor.*
.............................(20 to 1 tchd 25 to 1)   12

1330⁵ CULRAIN 6-11-6 (3*) Michael Brennan, *chsd ldrs to hfwy, sn lost tch.*..............(16 to 1 op 14 to 1 tchd 20 to 1)   13

2625 MILL DANCER (Ire) 5-10-9 (3*) E Husband, *led, jmpd rght, clr till hdd aftr 4th, lost tch, tld off.*...................(33 to 1)   14

QUIXOTRY 6-11-3 T Eley, *settled off the pace, nvr able to rch chalg pos, tld off.*........................(50 to 1)   15

2387 RIVIANNA 4-10-2 L Harvey, *al beh, tld off.*
.............................(50 to 1 op 33 to 1)   16

RENO'S TREASURE (USA) 4-10-2 D Gallagher, *al wl beh, tld off.*....................(50 to 1 op 33 to 1)   17

MAGICAL BLUES (Ire) 5-11-3 J Ryan, *patiently rdn, gd hdwy to chal aftr 4 out, 5th and staying on whn f 3 out.*
.............................(11 to 1 op 5 to 1 tchd 12 to 1)   f

2265⁸ CODE RED 4-10-2 (5*) A Bates, *wtd wth, gd hdwy aftr 4 out, fourth and staying on whn blun and uns rdr nxt.*
.............................(12 to 1 op 10 to 1)   ur

Dist: 2l, 1½l, 4l, 6l, sht-hd, ¾l, 15l, 2½l, 2½l, 1l. 4m 1.30s. a 11.30s (19 Ran).

SR: -/5/-/-/-/-/   (Wentdale Racing Partnership), Mrs M Reveley

2805 'Come Behind The Scenes' Novices' Chase Class E (6-y-o and up) £3,052 3m...................(2:30)

2597* BELL STAFFBOY 8-11-7 (3*) Michael Brennan, *jmpd rght, led aftr 3rd, clr hfwy, not fluent 4 out, drvn out.*
.............................(9 to 4 on op 5 to 2 on tchd 2 to 1 on)   1

2259² MONYMOSS (Ire) 8-11-4 Richard Guest, *chsd wnr frm hfwy, effrt and hit 7 out, rdn last 3, one pace..* (5 to 2 op 9 to 4)   2

2787 MR MOTIVATOR 7-10-12 S McNeill, *chsd ldrs, struggling to keep up fnl circuit, disputing 3rd and no imprsn whn blun and uns rdr 6 out.*.................(50 to 1 op 33 to 1)   ur

1055⁸ SEYMOUR SPY 8-10-12 S Wynne, *led till aftr 3rd, styd hndy, feeling pace and lost grnd fnl circuit, third and no imprsn whn pld up bef 4 out, lme.*..........(14 to 1 tchd 16 to 1)   pu

Dist: 9l. 6m 8.50s. a 14.50s (4 Ran).

(K W Bell & Son Ltd), J G M O'Shea

2806 Doncaster Racecourse Sponsorship Club Handicap Hurdle Class B (0-140 6-y-o and up) £4,896 2m 110yds....................(3:05)

2331* SHINING EDGE [121] 5-11-3 B Fenton, *patiently rdn, steady hdwy aftr 4 out, drw level last, sn led, ran on gmely und pres.*
.............................(7 to 2 op 3 to 1)   1

2580² STAR RAGE (Ire) [130] 7-11-12 D Gallagher, *settled travelling wl, improved to ld appr 3 out, jnd last, sn hdd, rdn and kpt on same pace.*..........(11 to 4 fav op 5 to 2 tchd 3 to 1)   2

2580² DESERT FIGHTER [111] 6-10-7 P Niven, *nvr far away, dsptd ld appr 3 out, rdn betw last 2, one pace r-in.*
.............................(11 to 2 op 9 to 2)   3

2501² BARFORD SOVEREIGN [109] 5-10-5 Richard Guest, *set modest pace, hdd appr 3 out, sn drvn alng, no extr frm betw last 2.*..................(6 to 1 tchd 13 to 2)   4

SESAME SEED (Ire) [119] 9-11-1 W McFarland, *al thabts, effrt and bustled alng aftr 3 out, one pace frm nxt.*
.............................(14 to 1 tchd 16 to 1)   5

2717⁸ DECIDE YOURSELF (Ire) [107] 7-10-3 J Culloty, *settled midfield, effrt hfwy, rdn frm 3 out, fdd....*(33 to 1 op 25 to 1)   6

FRICKLEY [130] 11-11-9 (3*) Michael Brennan, *slwly into strd, improved to go hndy bef hfwy, fdd und pres aftr 3 out.*
.............................(16 to 1 op 12 to 1)   7

2335³ CALLISOE BAY (Ire) [132] 8-12-0 J A McCarthy, *settled in tch, effrt hfwy, feeling pace 3 out, fdd und pres.*
.............................(11 to 1 op 10 to 1 tchd 12 to 1)   8

1627⁴ SPEEDWELL PRINCE (Ire) [129] 7-11-11 T Jenks, *pressed ldrs, ev ch hfwy, feeling pace and lost grnd bef 3 out, sn lost pl* ....(8 to 1 op 7 to 1) 9
Dist: 1¼l, 6l, hd, ¾l, 6l, 6l, 4l, 19l. 3m 56.70s. a 6.70s (9 Ran).
SR: 47/54/29/27/36/18/35/33/11/ (G Graham), T D Easterby

2807 'Racing Is Fun' Juvenile Novices' Hurdle Class E (4-y-o) £2,485 2½m
................................(3:40)

2371² DISALLOWED (Ire) 10-13 J Culloty, *nvr far away, jnd ldg pair 3 out, styd on wl to ld appr finish, edgd lft, drvn out.* ....(2 to 1 tchd 9 to 4) 1
2628⁵ TOPAGLOW (Ire) 10-12 B Fenton, *patiently rdn, improved to draw level 3 out, led r-in, hdd and not quicken appr finish.* ....(9 to 1 op 8 to 1) 2
2497⁴ FITZWILLIAM (Ire) 10-12¹ (7*) Mr A Balding, *made most till hdd aftr 3rd, rgned ld bef 3 out, sn hrd pressed, headed and not quicken r-in.*...............(6 to 4 fav tchd 13 to 8) 3
2628⁸ PRECIOUS ISLAND 10-7 J Supple, *settled in tch, effrt hfwy, feeling pace bef 3 out, rallied, kpt on one pace frm 2 out.* ....(25 to 1 op 20 to 1) 4
2628 ANNA SOLEIL (Ire) 10-12 J A McCarthy, *nvr far away, bustled alng whn pace quickened 3 out, no imprsn frm nxt.* ....(11 to 2 op 5 to 1) 5
2417⁷ NOIR ESPRIT 10-9 (3*) F Leahy, *pressed ldrs, rdn whn lders quickened bef 3 out fdd und pres*......(20 to 1 op 16 to 1) 6
2236⁷ RECRUITMENT 10-12 M Brennan, *settled off the pace, nvr able to rch chalg pos, tld off*.....................(50 to 1) 7
2577² AMAZING SAIL (Ire) 10-9 (3*) Michael Brennan, *wl plcd to hfwy, lost tch quickly appr 4 out, tld off.* (50 to 1 op 33 to 1) 8
2497⁸ GULF OF SIAM 10-12 T Eley, *chsd ldrs, feeling pace and lost grnd appr 3 out, tld off frm three out...* (50 to 1 op 33 to 1) 9
2417⁸ TAGATAY 10-12 Richard Guest, *with ldrs, led aftr 3rd, clr hfwy, hdd and wknd quickly appr 3 out, tld off.* ....(20 to 1 op 16 to 1) 10
2577 PORT VALENSKA (Ire) (bl) 10-12 D Gallagher, *led briefly to 1st, rcd freely, reminders and lost pl 4th, tld off whn pld up appr 3 out*..............(66 to 1 op 50 to 1) pu
Dist: 1½l, 2l, 5l, 3l, 6l, 18l, 1¼l, 1l, 16l. 4m 51.20s. a 16.20s (11 Ran).
(Million In Mind Partnership (6)), Miss H C Knight

2808 Bawtry Novices' Handicap Chase Class D (0-115 5-y-o and up) £3,600 2m 3f 110yds...............(4:15)

2597² NOYAN [110] 7-12-0 P Niven, *wtd wth, improved gng wl hfwy, led 5 out, clr whn not fluent 2 out, very easily.* ....(6 to 4 fav tchd 13 to 8) 1
1967² KENMORE-SPEED [100] 10-11-4 Richard Guest, *al hndy, led 4th till hdd 5 out, chsd wnr frm nxt, no imprsn.* ....(4 to 1 op 7 to 2) 2
2486³ GLAMANGLITZ [82] 7-10-0 B Fenton, *dsptd ld to 4th, styd hndy, rdn whn pace quickened frm four out, kpt on same pace last 2*...........................(10 to 1 op 5 to 1) 3
2157³ KEY TO MOYADE (Ire) [95] 7-10-13 S McNeill, *nvr far away, und pres frm 4 out, one pace aftr....*(10 to 1 op 14 to 1) 4
2540* KOO'S PROMISE [83] 6-9-12 (3*) T Dascombe, *dsptd ld to 4th, styd hndy till rdn and lost grnd 6 out, no imprsn frm nxt.* ....(12 to 1 op 10 to 1) 5
2650* COVER POINT (Ire) [95] 6-10-13 R Garritty, *settled in tch, hit 7th, struggling whn pace lifted 5 out, nvr able to chal.* ....(4 to 1 op 7 to 2) 6
2457⁴ STAGE PLAYER [89] 11-10-7 D Leahy, *lost pl quickly 6th, blun and reminders nxt, tld off aftr*........(20 to 1 op 16 to 1) 7
Dist: 14l, ¾l, 1¾l, 3l, 15l, dist. 4m 53.40s. a 8.40s (7 Ran).
SR: 26/5/-/-/ (C H McGhie), R A Fahey

2809 Finningley Handicap Chase Class E (0-110 5-y-o and up) £2,885 2m 3f 110yds......................(4:45)

2459³ OVER THE POLE [105] 10-11-11 (3*) Mr C Bonner, *settled to track ldrs, chlgd 4 out, rdn nxt, rallied to ld betw last 2, styd on wl*....................................(7 to 2 tchd 4 to 1) 1
2666⁵ JASON'S BOY [82] 7-10-5 B Fenton, *led or dsptd ld till definite advantage 6 out, jnd 3 out, hdd nxt, kpt on same pace r-in.*....................................(2 to 1 op 7 to 2) 2
2685* DUAL IMAGE [103] 10-11-12 R Garritty, *ran in snatches, niggled alng hfwy, improved to chal 4 out, led 2 out, sn hdd, found nothing r-in.*.............(11 to 8 fav op 11 to 10) 3
2650 KARENASTINO [77] 6-9-7 (7*) R Wilkinson, *led or dsptd ld till blun and hdd 6 out, wknd quickly aftr nxt, tld off last 4.* ....(11 to 1 op 10 to 1) 4
Dist: 9l, 1¾l, dist. 4m 54.10s. a 9.10s (4 Ran).
SR: 20/-/8/-/ (Pell-Mell Partners), P R Chamings

2810 Doncaster Mares' Only Intermediate Open National Hunt Flat (4,5,6-y-o) £1,035 2m 110yds...........(5:15)

MEMSAHIB OFESTEEM 6-11-2 K Gaule, *set slow pace for 2 fs, rgned ld hfwy, drvn clr o'r two furlongs out, styd on und pres*....................................(50 to 1) 1
2552* ALL DONE 4-10-6 N Mann, *settled gng wl, improved to chase wnr frm o'r 2 fs out, rdn and one pace ins last.* ....(6 to 4 fav tchd 7 to 4 and 5 to 4) 2

2283 RACHEL LOUISE 5-11-2 S McNeill, *trkd ldrs, ev ch o'r 2 fs out, rdn and not quicken appr last...* (5 to 1 tchd 11 to 2) 3
2363* COUNTRY ORCHID 6-11-9 P Niven, *settled wth chasing grp, improved entering strt, rdn and hng lft o'r 2 fs out, sn btn.* ....(7 to 4 tchd 2 to 1) 4
2552⁵ SIDE BY SIDE (Ire) 4-9-13 (7*) N Horrocks, *chsd ldrs, badly outpcd and drvn alng appr strt, styd on fnl furlong, no imprsn.* ....(13 to 2 op 6 to 1 tchd 7 to 1) 5
WHAT THE DEVIL 4-10-6 W Worthington, *settled wth chasing pack, effrt hfwy, feeling pace bef strt, fdd und pres.* ....(66 to 1 op 50 to 1) 6
ISLAWEN LADY 4-10-6 B Fenton, *in tch wth chasing grp, effrt hfwy, wknd bef strt*....(40 to 1 op 50 to 1 tchd 33 to 1) 7
LADY BOCO 4-9-13 (7*) C Rae, *unruly and uns rdr in paddock, in tch, effrt hfwy, wknd quickly bef strt, tld off.* ....(66 to 1 op 50 to 1) 8
2469 CEEJAYELL 4-9-13 (7*) Miss C Metcalfe, *led and quickened pace aftr 2 fs, sn clr, hdd hfwy, wknd rpdly, tld off.* ....(66 to 1 op 50 to 1) 9
Dist: 3½l, 5l, 7l, 8l, 2½l, nk, 12l, dist. 4m 2.00s. (9 Ran).
(Mrs R H Coole), S Gollings

MUSSELBURGH (good)
Saturday February 22nd
Going Correction: PLUS 0.25 sec. per fur.

2811 Royal Bank Of Scotland Maiden Hurdle Class E (Div I) (4-y-o and up) £1,720 2m....................(2:10)

2533⁴ SWIFT RIPOSTE (Ire) 6-11-7 R Supple, *trkd ldrs, lft second frm 3rd, effrt and led 3 out, clr whn blun last.* ....(11 to 10 on 6 to 4 on tchd Evens) 1
1677⁸ LAUGHING FONTAINE (Ire) 7-11-7 M Foster, *prmnt, lft in ld 3rd, hdd 3 out and sn one pace, btn whn blun last.* ....(9 to 2 op 5 to 2) 2
2533 PEARLS OF THOUGHT (Ire) 4-10-1 (5*) S Taylor, *prmnt, rdn alng 3 out, sn one pace.*...........(33 to 1 op 25 to 1) 3
1887 RASIN STANDARDS 7-11-7 G Cahill, *chsd ldrs, pushed alng and some hdwy bef 3 out, sn rdn and no imprsn.* ....(50 to 1 op 33 to 1) 4
2687 ROMALDKIRK 5-11-7 Mr M Thompson, *al rear, tld off frm hfwy*.............................(66 to 1 op 50 to 1) 5
ANASTASIA WINDSOR (v) 6-11-2 D J Moffatt, *dsptd ld till crrd out 3rd*....................(14 to 1 op 10 to 1) co
2711 JAMAICAN FLIGHT (USA) 4-10-8 (3*) E Callaghan, *dsptd ld, hit second, ran out nxt...*...........(5 to 1 op 5 to 1) ro
2533 BLOOD BROTHER 5-11-7 D Parker, *al rear, tld off frm hfwy, pld up bef 2 out*........................(33 to 1) pu
Dist: 9l, 5l, 23l, 28l. 3m 51.50s. a 14.50s (8 Ran).
(T P Finch), P Monteith

2812 Fiona P. Craig Novices' Handicap Chase Class E (0-105 5-y-o and up) £2,688 3m......................(2:40)

2534⁴ MISTER TRICK (Ire) [78] (bl) 7-11-2 R Supple, *al prmnt, pushed alng hfwy, led 13th, rdn 2 out, hdd appr last, rallied und pres to ld nr finish............* (5 to 2 tchd 11 to 4) 1
2484⁴ STRONGALONG (Ire) [68] 7-10-6 A S Smith, *al prmnt, effrt to join wnr 5 out, led appr last, sn rdn, hdd and no extr nr finish.* ....(9 to 1 op 6 to 1) 2
2620 SELDOM BUT SEVERE (Ire) [65] 7-9-12 (5*) G F Ryan, *prmnt, hit 11th and lost pl, sn drvn alng, hdwy appr 4 out, styd on und pres frm nxt.*....................(33 to 1 op 20 to 1) 3
2286⁶ MASTER OF TROY [79] 9-11-3 D Parker, *chsd ldrs, hit 3rd, rdn alng 12th, kpt on und pres frm 4 out.* ....(10 to 1 op 9 to 1) 4
2348 FINE TUNE (Ire) [62] 7-10-0 M Foster, *hld up, hdwy 11th, hit nxt, no imprsn frm 4 out*.................(10 to 1 op 7 to 1) 5
2631 MOST RICH (Ire) [68] (v) 9-10-6¹ T Reed, *chsd ldrs, blun 5th, hdwy 7th, led appr 11th till hdd 13th, one pace frm 4 out.* ....(10 to 1 op 7 to 1) 6
2633⁴ TACTIX [65] 7-10-3 B Storey, *mstk 1st and beh, hdwy 6th, hit 9th and sn rdn alng, no imprsn.* ....(8 to 1 op 7 to 1 tchd 9 to 1) 7
2686 DISTILLERY HILL (Ire) [71] 9-10-9⁴ Mr M Thompson, *led till hdd appr 11th, wknd approaching 4 out...........*(33 to 1) 8
2620 BRIGHT DESTINY [62] 6-10-0 K Johnson, *not fluent, al beh.* ....(33 to 1 op 20 to 1) 9
2358⁴ MOVAC (Ire) [86] 8-11-10 M Moloney, *prmnt, rdn alng 12th, grad wknd frm nxt.....* (12 to 1 op 10 to 1 tchd 14 to 1) 10
2489 MASTER FLASHAM [73] 8-10-11 G Cahill, *chsd ldrs, blun 4th, lost pl 8, beh whn pld up bef 12th...* (7 to 1 op 9 to 2) pu
Dist: Nk, 6l, 6l, 5l, 7l, 10l, 1½l, 7l, 2½l. 6m 8.80s. a 19.80s (11 Ran).
(Edward Birkbeck), L Lungo

2813 Royal Bank Of Scotland European Breeders Fund 'National Hunt' Novices' Hurdle Qualifier Class D (5,6,7-y-o) £3,105 2½m.............(3:10)

2318⁴ SHANAVOGH 6-11-10 J Callaghan, *led to 5th, cl up, led appr 3 out, clr nxt........* (6 to 4 on op 5 to 4 on tchd Evens) 1

2489^{4} CLAVERING (Ire) 7-11-0 A S Smith, *cl up, led 5th, rdn and hdd appr 3 out, sn drvn and one pace*......(5 to 2 tchd 3 to 1) 2
2419^{9} CAUGHT AT LAST (Ire) 6-11-0 G Cahill, *hld up, pushed alng and hdwy appr 3 out, rdn nxt, kpt on same pace.* .... (33 to 1 op 12 to 1) 3
2288^{7} ANTARCTIC WIND (Ire) 7-11-7 (3*) E Callaghan, *chsd ldrs, hit 4th, rdn alng and hit four out, drvn nxt, one pace.* ....(6 to 1 op 4 to 1) 4
2357^{7} THE SHARROW LEGEND (Ire) 5-10-9 (5*) S Taylor, *hld up, effrt 4 out, sn rdn and no hdwy*........(33 to 1 op 25 to 1) 5
2346 BORIS BROOK 6-10-7 (7*) S Melrose, *cl up, hit 5th, rdn alng 7th, wknd 4 out*........ (40 to 1 op 33 to 1 tchd 50 to 1) 6
2619^{4} DRAKEWRATH (Ire) 7-11-0 D Parker, *hld up, blun and uns rdr 5th*.................... (20 to 1 op 16 to 1 tchd 25 to 1) ur
Dist: 8l, ¾l, 4l, 24l, 13l. 4m 52.00s. a 14.00s (7 Ran).
SR: 6/-/-/-/ (Sean Graham), G M Moore

2814 Scottish Life Handicap Chase Class E (0-115 5-y-o and up) £3,200 2½m .... (3:45)

2573^{2} JUDICIAL FIELD (Ire) [93] (bl) 8-11-1 B Storey, *trkd ldrs till blun 9th and sn outpcd, hdwy appr 4 out, led nxt, drvn out.* ....(7 to 2 op 3 to 1 tchd 4 to 1) 1
2317^{5} ALY DALEY (Ire) [97] 9-11-5 A S Smith, *led to 7th, cl up till led 12th, hdd 3 out, close up and rdn whn blun nxt, kpt on.* .... (8 to 1 op 6 to 1 tchd 10 to 1) 2
2633^{3} RISKY DEE [78] 8-10-0 D Bentley, *cl up, led 7th till blun and hdd 12th, wknd 3 out*............................(20 to 1) 3
2633^{2} BUYERS DREAM (Ire) [89] (v) 7-10-11 T Reed, *blun 3rd, al rear*.................................. (3 to 1 op 5 to 2) 4
2321* MONTRAVE [105] 8-11-13 R Supple, *chsd ldrs, mstk 7th, hit 4 out, rdn nxt, sn btn and beh whn blun last.* ....(Evens fav op 5 to 4) 5
Dist: 1¼l, 6l, 12l, 3l. 5m 6.60s. a 19.60s (5 Ran).
(Mrs E E Newbould), N Tinkler

2815 Scotmid Handicap Hurdle Class E (0-115 4-y-o and up) £2,560 2½m .... (4:20)

2581* HERE COMES HERBIE [87] 5-10-0 (5*) R McGrath, *hld up, smooth hdwy bef 4 out, chlgd on bit last, sn led, cheekily.* ....(2 to 1 fav op 9 to 4 tchd 5 to 2) 1
2598^{4} ALL ON [110] 6-11-11 (3*) E Callaghan, *hld up in tch, hdwy to track ldrs 4 out, led nxt, rdn 2 out, hdd and hrd drvn flt, no ch wth wnr*...............................(9 to 2 op 4 to 1) 2
2716^{6} OLD HABITS (Ire) [102] 8-10-13 (7*) C Elliott, *chsd ldrs, hit 6th, effrt appr 3 out, sn rdn and styd on frm nxt.* ....(9 to 2 op 5 to 1) 3
2574^{8} GLENUGIE [94] 6-10-12 N Bentley, *chsd ldrs, hdwy to dispute ld 7th, hit nxt, effrt and ev ch 3 out, sn rdn and wknd.* .... (16 to 1 op 8 to 1) 4
1786^{3} PEGGY GORDON [82] 6-9-7 (7*) C McCormack, *chsd ldrs, hdwy to chal 4 out, rdn nxt and wkng whn hit 2 out.* .... (14 to 1 op 12 to 1 tchd 16 to 1) 5
2361* CHEATER (Ire) [92] (bl) 6-10-10 A S Smith, *led, rdn alng 8th, hdd 3 out and sn wknd*...................(9 to 2 op 3 to 1) 6
2711 TOSHIBA TALK (Ire) [90] 5-10-8 T Reed, *prmnt, rdn alng and hit 7th, wknd aftr 4 out.* (20 to 1 op 16 to 1 tchd 25 to 1) 7
STINGRAY CITY (USA) [91] 8-10-9 D Parker, *prmnt till lost pl 6th, tld off whn pld up bef 4 out.* .... (33 to 1 op 20 to 1 tchd 50 to 1) pu
817^{5} JABAROOT (Ire) [82] 6-10-0 G Cahill, *al rear, tld off whn pld up bef 4 out*........... (25 to 1 op 12 to 1 tchd 33 to 1) pu
Dist: ¾l, 6l, 5l, 8l, 6l, 7l. 4m 50.00s. a 12.00s (9 Ran).
SR: 7/29/15/-/-/-/ (H S Hutchinson), W Storey

2816 Edinburgh University Turf Club 'Hole In The Wall' Juvenile Novices' Handicap Hurdle Class E (0-105 4-y-o) £2,560 2m....................(4:50)

2632* DOUBLE AGENT [98] 12-0 A S Smith, *trkd ldr, led appr 3 out and sn clr, rdn aftr nxt, hdd whn lft clear last.* ....(11 to 8 fav op 5 to 4 tchd 6 to 4) 1
2619^{7} DOUBLE DASH (Ire) [84] (v) 11-0 D J Moffatt, *hld up in tch, effrt and rdn alng 4 out, hit nxt, sn drvn and wl held whn lft second at last*.......... (10 to 1 op 12 to 1 tchd 14 to 1) 2
2188 PERPETUAL LIGHT [80] 10-7 (3*) E Callaghan, *hld up in tch, effrt and hdwy 4 out, rdn and hit nxt, sn btn.* .... (100 to 30 op 7 to 2 tchd 4 to 1) 3
2417 BRIDLINGTON BAY [70] 9-7 (7*) C McCormack, *led, rdn and hdd bef 3 out, sn wknd*...............(25 to 1 op 20 to 1) 4
2617^{2} JOE SHAW [89] 11-5 G Cahill, *chsd ldrs, hit 5th, rdn alng, outpcd and hit 3 out, hdwy nxt, ridden to ld and f last.* ....(2 to 1 tchd 7 to 4) f
Dist: 10l, 6l, 6l. 3m 50.80s. a 13.80s (5 Ran).
SR: 2/-/ (Hertford Offset Limited), J Howard Johnson

2817 Royal Bank Of Scotland Maiden Hurdle Class E (Div II) (4-y-o and up) £1,720 2m....................(5:20)

2711^{4} FAR AHEAD 5-11-7 B Storey, *trkd ldrs, led appr 3 out, sn clr, blun last, pushed out.* ....(13 to 8 on op 2 to 1 on tchd 6 to 4 on) 1
2372^{4} TILAAL (USA) 5-11-7 D Bentley, *hld up, steady hdwy aftr 4 out, chsd wnr after nxt, drvn appr last, kpt on same pace.* ....(2 to 1 tchd 9 to 4) 2
2363 COTTSTOWN BOY (Ire) 6-11-7 M Foster, *in tch, hit 4th, hdwy four out, rdn nxt, no imprsn*...................... (50 to 1) 3
2568^{5} KNOWN SECRET (USA) 4-10-11 M Moloney, *beh, hdwy 4 out, styd on frm nxt, nvr a factor*........ (25 to 1 op 33 to 1) 4
2651^{6} HELPERBY (Ire) 5-11-7 A S Smith, *prmnt, rdn alng 5th, wknd bef 3 out*.......................... (16 to 1 tchd 20 to 1) 5
2572^{6} NORDISK LEGEND 5-11-7 T Reed, *in tch, rdn alng 4 out, sn wknd*.. (100 to 1) 6
2537 RUBISLAW (v) 5-11-0 (7*) Miss S Lamb, *led, rdn alng 4 out, sn hdd, blun 3 out and wknd quickly*................ (100 to 1) 7
2236 COEUR FRANCAIS (Fr) 5-11-0 (7*) S Haworth, *prmnt to 4th, sn lost pl and tld off aftr four out.* .... (25 to 1 op 20 to 1 tchd 33 to 1) 8
Dist: 3l, 11l, 10l, 1¾l, 12l, 1½l, 16l. 3m 52.80s. a 15.80s (8 Ran).
(Sunpak Potatoes), J L Eyre

HAYDOCK (good)
Saturday February 22nd

Going Correction: PLUS 0.35 sec. per fur. (races 1,3,5), PLUS 0.15 (2,4,6,7)

2818 Schlitz Victor Ludorum Novices' Hurdle Limited Handicap Class C (4-y-o) £5,015 2m............... (1:15)

2407* NO MORE HASSLE (Ire) [101] 10-11 P Niven, *cl up gng wl, led or dsptd ld frm 5th, rdn aftr last, ran on well.* ....(9 to 2 tchd 5 to 1) 1
2602* GLOBE RUNNER [101] 10-11 A Roche, *hld up, smooth hdwy to dispute ld 2 out, ev ch till no extr und pres fnl 100 yards.* ....(9 to 1 op 7 to 1) 2
2628* FONT ROMEU (Fr) [114] 11-10 C F Swan, *sn wl beh and pushed alng, rdn aftr 5th, hdwy bef 3 out, styd on same pace frm nxt*............(4 to 1 co-fav op 7 to 2 tchd 9 to 2) 3
2311 SHU GAA (Ire) [101] 10-11 J Osborne, *led to 5th, rallied to dispute ld 3 out, wknd aftr nxt*...............(4 to 1 co-fav) 4
2632^{2} MELTEMISON [97] 10-7 R Garritty, *hld up, effrt bef 3 out, sn btn*.............(4 to 1 op 7 to 1 tchd 11 to 2) 5
2336* JACKSON PARK [108] 11-4 G Bradley, *prmnt, drvn alng aftr 4th, sn outpcd, lost tch after 3 out*........(8 to 1 op 6 to 1) 6
2188* ROSSEL (USA) [114] 11-10 A Dobbin, *cl up, dsptd ld 5th till wknd aftr 3 out*................(4 to 1 co-fav tchd 7 to 2) 7
Dist: 1¾l, 4l, 5l, 10l, 14l, 1¼l. 3m 49.00s. a 11.00s (7 Ran).
SR: 29/27/36/18/4/1/5/ (The No Hassle Partnership), Mrs M Reveley

2819 Black Death Vodka Handicap Chase Class B (0-145 6-y-o and up) £14,332 2½m................ (1:45)

2474 THE GREY MONK (Ire) [145] 9-12-0 A Dobbin, *ade all, styd on strly frm 2 out, eased finish.* ....(13 to 8 on op 7 to 4 on tchd 6 to 4 on) 1
2437^{9} TERAO [121] 11-10-4 C F Swan, *trkd ldrs, ch whn hit 2 out, sn rdn, styd on wl clsg stages, no chance wth wnr.* .... (11 to 1 op 12 to 1 tchd 10 to 1) 2
1999^{3} MAJOR BELL [135] 9-11-4 J Osborne, *hld up in rear, hdwy aftr 12th, ch 2 out, sn rdn, kpt on same pace*.........(7 to 2) 3
1640^{3} UNCLE ERNIE [139] 12-11-8 P Carberry, *hld up, cld 9th, rdn aftr 2 out, fdd*........... (10 to 1 op 8 to 1 tchd 11 to 1) 4
2514^{2} SPANISH LIGHT (Ire) [120] 8-10-3 C Maude, *prmnt, wknd bef 12th, sn lost tch*.......................... (8 to 1 tchd 10 to 1) 5
2466^{4} IN TRUTH [117] 9-10-0 K Gaule, *blun and uns rdr 1st.* .... (16 to 1 op 14 to 1 tchd 20 to 1) ur
Dist: 1l, ¾l, 10l, 15l. 5m 12.50s. a 15.50s (6 Ran).
(Alistair Duff), G Richards

2820 Stretton Leisure Select Hurdle Class B (5-y-o and up) £10,065 2m.. (2:15)

2656* JUYUSH (USA) 5-11-4 J Osborne, *led to 3rd, cl up, led 2 out, styd on wl und pres*..... (5 to 2 tchd 11 to 4 and 9 to 4) 1
2591^{4} MISTINGUETT (Ire) 5-11-7 C Maude, *sn clr wth wnr, led 3rd to 2 out, styd on und pres.* ....(11 to 8 fav op 6 to 4 tchd 13 to 8) 2
2591^{8} KISSAIR (Ire) 6-11-4 J R Kavanagh, *beh and rdn hfwy, kpt on frm 3 out, nvr dngrs*.......................... (10 to 1 op 8 to 1) 3
2695^{2} MOORISH 7-11-0 D Walsh, *beh, hdwy to chase 1st 2 5th, wknd aftr 3 out*..................................(4 to 1 op 7 to 2) 4
2208^{8} TRAGIC HERO (bl) 5-11-12 C F Swan, *sn beh.* .... (16 to 1 op 14 to 1) 5
1612^{7} KINGSFOLD PET 8-11-4 D Skyrme, *beh, some hdwy aftr 5th, sn wknd, virtually pld up clsg stages.* (20 to 1 op 16 to 1) 6
2716^{8} MARCHANT MING (Ire) 5-11-4 R Garritty, *chsd clr ldrs, wknd aftr 5th, wl beh whn pld up bef last*.... (33 to 1 op 25 to 1) pu
Dist: 1¾l, 22l, 6l, 3½l, 18l. 3m 46.60s. a 8.60s (7 Ran).
SR: 60/61/36/26/34/8/-/ (W E Sturt), J A B Old

2821 Greenalls Grand National Trial Handicap Chase Class A Grade 3 (5-y-o and up) £48,984 3½m 110yds (2:45)

1480⁵ SUNY BAY (Ire) [144] 8-10-8 J Osborne, *made all, jmpd slwly
4th, clr 2 out, styd on wl*..............(7 to 2 op 11 to 4) 1
2189⁴ INTO THE RED [136] 13-10-0 A Dobbin, *al chasing ldrs, styd
on same pace frm 3 out, no imprsn on wnr.*
....(7 to 1 op 6 to 1) 2
2189⁵ ST MELLION FAIRWAY (Ire) [136] 8-10-0 A Thornton, *mstk
1st, sn prmnt, rdn aftr 3 out, fdd*..........(12 to 1 op 8 to 1) 3
2273* COULDNT BE BETTER [160] 10-11-10 G Bradley, *in tch, drpd
rear and mstk 17th, drvn alng and hdwy bef 3 out, sn wknd.*
....(4 to 1 op 7 to 2) 4
2189³ LO STREGONE [145] (bl) 11-10-9 C F Swan, *in tch, drpd rear
and reminders aftr 13th, lost touch after 19th, tld off.*
....(5 to 4 on op 5 to 4) 5
Dist: 19l, 2½l, 10l, 18l. 7m 20.80s. a 8.80s (5 Ran).
SR: 35/8/5/19/-/ (Uplands Bloodstock), C P E Brooks

2822 Sporting Life Maiden Hurdle Class D (4-y-o and up) £3,165 2¾m... (3:20)

2298² ABSOLUTELY EQUINAME (Ire) 6-11-7 B Powell, *prmnt, led bef
7th, styd on wl frm 3 out.*.......(3 to 1 jt-fav tchd 7 to 2) 1
2541³ BARBARY FALCON 7-11-7 G Upton, *keen, prmnt, ch 3 out,
kpt on, no imprsn on wnr.*............(16 to 1 op 12 to 1) 2
2539² TREMPLIN (Ire) 6-11-2 J R Kavanagh, *al chasing ldrs, kpt on
same pace frm 3 out.*..............................(7 to 1) 3
2601⁶ LOVE THE BLUES (bl) 5-10-13 (3*) R Massey, *in tch, sn
pushed alng, hdwy to chase ldrs hfwy, fdd 3 out.*
....(9 to 1 op 8 to 1) 4
2538² GROSVENOR (Ire) 6-11-7 P Carberry, *in tch till wknd appr 3
out.*..........................(3 to 1 jt-fav tchd 100 to 30) 5
2288 SOVEREIGN PASS 5-11-7 C F Swan, *nvr dngrs.*
....(50 to 1 op 33 to 1) 6
BATTLE CREEK (Ire) 7-11-7 W Dwan, *nvr on terms.* (50 to 1) 7
2570² SIR BOB (Ire) 5-11-7 A Dobbin, *mid-div, reminder bef 5th, beh
8th.*.........................(7 to 2 op 4 to 1 tchd 9 to 2) 8
DOCS BOY 7-11-7 J Osborne, *nvr nr to chal.*
....(12 to 1 tchd 14 to 1) 9
2619⁸ FAYETTE COUNTY (Ire) 6-11-7 A Thornton, *chsd ldrs, wknd
bef 9th, tld off.*............................(20 to 1 op 12 to 1) 10
2250⁶ SUPREMO (Ire) 8-11-7 T J O'Sullivan, *beh hfwy, tld off.*
....(25 to 1 op 20 to 1) 11
2601⁴ STORMY SESSION 7-11-7 D Walsh, *chsd ldrs, wknd bef 9th,
tld off.*......................(20 to 1 op 16 to 1) 12
SWARF (Ire) 7-11-7 G Bradley, *led till bef 7th, wknd quickly,
tld off whn pld up before 9th.*.......(16 to 1 op 14 to 1) pu
1623 SILVER GROVE 7-11-0 (7*) D Jewett, *sn tld off, pld up aftr 6th.*
....(50 to 1) pu
THIS TIME LUCKY 7-11-7 C Maude, *sn beh, tld off whn pld up
bef 3 out.*....................(12 to 1 op 8 to 1) pu
PALAFICO 7-11-7 R Bellamy, *tld off whn pld up bef 8th.*
....(33 to 1 op 25 to 1) pu
Dist. 8l, 5l, 13l, 21l, 3½l, 12l, 4l, 9l, dist, 8l. 5m 32.90s. a 25.90s (16 Ran).
(F J Sainsbury), M J Heaton-Ellis

2823 Bellcharm Renault Novices' Chase Class C (5-y-o and up) £4,485 2m (3:50)

2720³ FLYING INSTRUCTOR 7-11-5 R Bellamy, *hld up, hdwy to ld 3
out, drvn out frm last.*..................(6 to 4 op 5 to 4) 1
1421* CELIBATE (Ire) 6-11-12 J Railton, *hld up, hdwy bef 3 out, ch
whn hit last, no extr.*
..............................(13 to 8 on op 6 to 4 on tchd 11 to 8 on) 2
2747² HEATHYARDS BOY (bl) 7-11-5 D Walsh, *led second to 6th,
led 9th to 3 out, rdn and wknd nxt, tld off.*
....(50 to 1 op 40 to 1) 3
2626² FRANK KNOWS 7-11-5 P Carberry, *led to second, led 6th till
mstk and hdd 9th, lost tch 3 out, tld off.*
..............................(11 to 1 op 16 to 1 tchd 10 to 1) 4
Dist: 4l, 28l, 12l. 4m 3.50s. a 7.50s (4 Ran).
SR: 40/43/8/-/ (Lady Lyell), P R Webber

2824 Tarvin Standard National Hunt Flat Class H (4,5,6-y-o) £1,556 2m (4:25)

HARRIS CROFT STAR (Ire) 6-11-4 (3*) R Massey, *towards
rear, hdwy 4 fs out, sn drvn alng, styd on wl und pres to ld ins
last.*..............................(3 to 1 op 2 to 1) 1
SHROPSHIRE GALE (Ire) 6-11-0 (7*) X Aizpuru, *keen early, in
tch, effrt o'r 3 fs out, led over one out till ins last, no extr.*
....(12 to 1) 2
2503⁵ WISE GUNNER 4-9-13 (7*) G Supple, *led till o'r one furlong
out, no extr.*..........(13 to 8 fav op 9 to 4 tchd 5 to 2) 3
ARCTIC FOX (Ire) 5-11-0 (7*) Mr A Wintle, *hmpd strt, hld up,
effrt o'r 3 fs out, edgd lft, no prog frm 2 out.*
....(5 to 1 op 9 to 1) 4
3322⁴ PORTMAN 5-11-4 (3*) P Midgley, *prmnt till rdn and wknd o'r 2
fs out.*..(9 to 1) 5
POLITICAL POWER 6-11-7 Mr A Mitchell, *nvr nr to chal.*
....(33 to 1 op 25 to 1) 6
2623⁴ LINWOOD 6-11-2 Mr R Hale, *hmpd strt, nvr dngrs.*
....(4 to 1 tchd 7 to 2) 7
DONNYBROOK (Ire) 4-10-6 (5*) B Grattan, *in tch till wknd 4 fs
out.*..(16 to 1) 8
LAST ACTION 4-10-3 (3*) G Lee, *trkd ldrs till wknd o'r 3 fs out.*
....(25 to 1 op 16 to 1) 9

SHAWKEY (Ire) 4-10-11 D Walsh, *mid-div, rdn o'r 3 fs out, sn
wknd.*..............................(33 to 1 op 25 to 1) 10
2377 BUCKS REEF 5-11-4 (3*) D Fortt, *whipped round strt, al beh,
tld off.*..............................(33 to 1) 11
2496 FERRINO FRUITS (Ire) 6-11-7 G Tormey, *beh and rdn hfwy, sn
lost tch, wl tld off.*................(50 to 1 op 33 to 1) 12
Dist: 2½l, 5l, 1¾l, 4l, 3½l, ½l, 3½l, 12l, 8l, 21l. 3m 53.90s. (12 Ran).
(R F Nutland), D Nicholson

KEMPTON (good)
Saturday February 22nd
Going Correction: PLUS 0.45 sec. per fur. (races
1,4,6,7), PLUS 0.50 (2,3,5)

2825 Dovecote Novices' Hurdle Class A Grade 2 (4-y-o and up) £8,792 2m (1:55)

2255* SANMARTINO (Ire) 5-11-10 A Maguire, *hld up gng wl, led and
hit 2 out, rdn out, readily.*....(5 to 2 on tchd 9 to 4 on) 1
2299⁴ MISTER RM 5-11-3 C Llewellyn, *hld up, rdn aftr 3 out, chlgd
frm 2 out, ev ch r-in, unbl to quicken.*
..............................(20 to 1 op 14 to 1 tchd 25 to 1) 2
2353* NO PATTERN 5-11-3 A P McCoy, *wtd wth, prog 5th, ev ch 3
out, btn appr last.*......(11 to 1 op 10 to 1 tchd 12 to 1) 3
2594³ POLYDAMAS 5-11-3 D Bridgwater, *dsptd ld to 4th, ev ch 3
out, wknd appr last.*................(11 to 2 op 4 to 1) 4
CLASSY LAD (NZ) 7-11-3 R Dunwoody, *hld up, hdwy appr 2
out, sn rdn, wknd approaching last....(20 to 1 op 14 to 1) 5
2727 SERENUS (USA) 4-11-0 R Johnson, *made most to 2 out,
wknd appr last.*..........................(14 to 1 op 8 to 1) 6
2656² GLIDE PATH (USA) 8-11-3 N Williamson, *hld up, rdn appr 2
out, sn btn, eased.*..............(40 to 1 op 20 to 1) 7
Dist: 2l, 7l, 1l, 3l, 1l, 23l. 3m 54.90s. a 14.90s (7 Ran).
SR: 19/10/3/2/ (K Abdulla), D Nicholson

2826 Emblem Chase Class B (5-y-o and up) £6,695 2m... (2:25)

2219⁴ VIKING FLAGSHIP 10-12-0 A Maguire, *chsd ldr, hit 5th, led
7th, shaken up appr last, cmftbly.*
..............................(13 to 8 on op 2 to 1 on tchd 6 to 4 on) 1
2590 ARCTIC KINSMAN 9-12-0 C Llewellyn, *led to 7th, rdn and ev
ch 2 out, one pace appr last.*
..............................(4 to 1 op 7 to 2 tchd 9 to 2) 2
2576³ MARLINGFORD 10-11-0 L McGrath, *mstk and beh frm 3rd,
tld off 7th, blun last.*................(100 to 1 op 66 to 1) 3
MARTHA'S SON 10-12-0 N Williamson, *f second.*
....(5 to 2 tchd 11 to 4) f
Dist: 3l, dist. 3m 57.30s. a 11.30s (4 Ran).
SR: 67/64/-/-/ (Roach Foods Limited), D Nicholson

2827 Pendil Novices' Chase Class A Grade 2 (5-y-o and up) £12,159 2½m 110yds... (3:00)

2450² LAND AFAR 10-11-7 A Maguire, *patiently rdn, prog appr 11th,
wnt second 4 out, led approaching 2 out, ran on wl.*
....(4 to 1 op 3 to 1) 1
1944* AROUND THE GALE (Ire) 6-11-3 R Dunwoody, *dsptd ld, led
6th, hdd appr 2 out, unbl to quicken r-in.*
..............................(5 to 2 fav op 2 to 1 tchd 11 to 4) 2
2046* GREENBACK (Bel) 6-11-10 J Frost, *hld up beh ldrs, hit 6th,
btn appr 3 out.*..............(9 to 1 op 10 to 1 tchd 7 to 1) 3
2216* FINE THYNE (Ire) 8-11-7 N Williamson, *hld up, hdwy 13th, rdn
and wknd bef 3 out.*....................(3 to 1 tchd 4 to 1) 4
2596² GUINDA (Ire) 7-11-2 C Llewellyn, *hld up beh ldrs, jmpd lft 7th,
hdwy appr 13th, wknd bef 3 out.*....(20 to 1 tchd 25 to 1) 5
2450* STATELY HOME (Ire) 6-11-10 R Johnson, *blun badly second,
made most till 8th, rdn 12th, wknd 4 out, beh whn pld up bef
nxt.*..............................(4 to 1 op 3 to 1) pu
Dist: 2l, 16l, 6l, 5l. 5m 12.20s. a 19.20s (6 Ran).
SR: 3/-/-/ (T J Ford), P R Webber

2828 Voice Newspaper Adonis Juvenile Novices' Hurdle Class A Grade 2 (4-y-o) £8,750 2m... (3:35)

L'OPERA (Fr) 10-12 A Maguire, *wtd wth, steady hdwy frm 5th,
led appr last, rdn out......* (7 to 2 op 5 to 2 tchd 4 to 1) 1
2553* KERAWI 11-2 C Llewellyn, *in tch, led aftr 3 out, hdd briefly nxt,
headed by wnr appr last, one pace r-in.*
..............................(6 to 4 fav tchd 2 to 1) 2
2553⁸ SUMMER SPELL (USA) 11-2 R Dunwoody, *hld up, hdwy 3
out, led briefly and hit nxt, ev ch last, fdd r-in.*
....(6 to 1 tchd 7 to 1) 3
2423⁴ CHABROL (Can) 10-12 R Johnson, *prmnt, rdn 3 out, sn btn.*
..............................(25 to 1 op 20 to 1 tchd 33 to 1) 4
2727⁵ RED RAJA 11-6 M Richards, *led till aftr 3 out, wknd bef nxt.*
....(8 to 1 op 6 to 1) 5
1309⁸ FAIRLY SHARP (Ire) 10-7 N Williamson, *prmnt, rdn 3 out,
wknd appr nxt.*..........................(33 to 1 op 20 to 1) 6
1890⁴ BEN BOWDEN 10-12 D Bridgwater, *hld up, rdn and lost tch
frm 3 out.*..............................(66 to 1 op 33 to 1) 7

1890[5] PROVINCE 10-12 J Magee, *nvr on terms.*
.................................(66 to 1 op 33 to 1) 8
2397[2] GRIEF (Ire) 10-12 P Holley, *hld up, wknd 3 out.*
.................................(5 o 1 op 6 to 1) 9
ALLSTARS EXPRESS 10-12 P Hide, *al beh.*
.................................(33 to 1 op 10 to 1 tchd 50 to 1) 10
Dist: 2½l, 8l, 6l, 2½l, ½l, 26l, 3l, ½l, 13l. 3m 52.40s. a 12.40s (10 Ran).
SR: 32/33/25/15/20/6/ (Sheikh Ahmed Al Maktoum), D Nicholson

2829 Racing Post Chase Handicap Class A Guaranteed minimum value £50000 Grade 3 (5-y-o and up) £30,380 3m.................(4:10)

2599[2] MUDAHIM [125] 11-10-2 R Farrant, *prmnt, led 3rd, made most aftr till hdd appr last, rgned ld and ran on wl und pres r-in.*........(14 to 1 op 10 to 1 tchd 16 to 1) 1
2334[2] KING LUCIFER (Ire) [130] 8-10-7 R Johnson, *in tch, chsd wnr frm 12th, led appr last to r-in, kpt on.* (6 to 1 tchd 3 to 2) 2
PERCY SMOLLETT [147] 9-11-10 N Williamson, *hld up, hit tenth, hdwy 13th, wknd 15th, tld off.*
.................................(6 to 1 op 5 to 1 tchd 7 to 1) 3
2589* CALL IT A DAY (Ire) [138] 7-11-1 A Maguire, *hld up, hdwy 13th, rdn bef 15th, wknd 4 out, tld off.*
.................................(9 to 4 fav op 2 to 1 tchd 7 to 4) 4
ENCORE UN PEU (Ire) [141] 10-11-4 A McCoy, *trkd ldrs, mstk and wknd 15th, tld off, fnshd lme.*
.................................(8 to 1 op 6 to 1 tchd 9 to 1) 5
2471[2] SEE MORE BUSINESS (Ire) [144] 7-11-7 R Dunwoody, *not fluent, hld up, hdwy tenth, mid-div whn f nxt.*........(5 to 2) f
2592[5] FOREST SUN [125] 12-10-2 B Clifford, *led to 3rd, beh whn badly hmpd 11th, tld off whn pld up and dismounted bef 3 out.*........(66 to 1 op 50 to 1) pu
2692[6] SIBTON ABBEY [138] (v) 12-10-12 (3*) P Henley, *prmnt, hit 5th, beh whn badly hmpd 11th, tld off whn pld up bef 15th.*
.................................(33 to 1 op 25 to 1 tchd 40 to 1) pu
2692[4] DEXTRA DOVE [140] 10-11-3 (3ex) D Bridgwater, *hit 5th, prmnt to 11th, tld off whn pld up bef 15th.*
.................................(16 to 1 op 12 to 1 tchd 20 to 1) pu
Dist: Nk, dist, 5l, 3l. 6m 3.30s. a 14.30s (9 Ran).
SR: 51/56/-/-/-/-/ (In Touch Racing Club), Mrs J Pitman

2830 Rendlesham Hurdle Limited Handicap Class A Grade 2 (4-y-o and up) £12,034 3m 110yds.........(4:40)

1891 PHARANEAR (Ire) [140] 7-10-9 A Maguire, *not fluent, hld up, prog frm 3 out, led r-in, drvn out.*
.................................(6 to 1 op 9 to 2 tchd 13 to 2) 1
2399 CONQUERING LEADER (Ire) [139] 8-10-8 R Johnson, *prmnt, led appr 2 out to r-in, unbl to quicken.*
.................................(11 to 2 op 5 to 1 tchd 6 to 1) 2
2563[3] ESCARTEFIGUE (Fr) [148] 5-11-3 D Bridgwater, *wtd wth, effrt whn not clr run and lost pl aftr 3 out, rallied betw fnl 2, ran on strly r-in.*........(6 to 1 op 5 to 1) 3
1957 CASTLEKELLYLEADER (Ire) [142] 6-10-11 P Hide, *prmnt, led 3rd till appr 2 out, ev ch whn stumbled two out, one pace.*
.................................(16 to 1 op 12 to 1 tchd 20 to 1) 4
2453[5] TARRS BRIDGE (Ire) [138] (bl) 6-10-4 (3*) J Magee, *hld up in tch, rdn aftr 3 out, kpt on one pace...*(8 to 1 tchd 10 to 1) 5
2506[4] TOP SPIN [138] 8-10-7 N Williamson, *beh, rdn and effrt appr 2 out, sn wknd.*........(12 to 1 op 16 to 1) 6
2657 WEE WINDY (Ire) [138] 8-10-4 (3*) L Aspell, *hld up beh ldrs, rdn 4 out, wknd frm nxt.* (25 to 1 op 14 to 1 tchd 33 to 1) 7
2210* OCEAN HAWK (USA) [152] 5-11-7 C Llewellyn, *made most to 4 out, wknd frm nxt.*........(6 to 4 fav tchd 7 to 4) 8
GILLAN COVE (Ire) [140] 8-10-9 A McCoy, *prmnt, led 4 out to 3 out, sn wknd.*....(12 to 1 op 10 to 1 tchd 14 to 1) 9
FATACK [138] 8-10-7 S Curran, *in tch till lost pl 4th, beh frm 3 out, tld off.*........(33 to 1 tchd 40 to 1) 10
Dist: 2l, hd, 3l, 3l, 19l, 21l, 13l, 13l, dist. 6m 7.30s. a 22.30s (10 Ran).
(Stainless Threaded Fasteners Ltd), D Nicholson

2831 Kempton Standard Open National Hunt Flat Class H (4,5,6-y-o) £1,413 2m..........................(5:10)

2248[6] COUNTRY BEAU 5-11-3 M Richards, *wtd wth, rdn and hdwy o'r 3 fs out, led over 4 out, ran on wl.* (50 to 1 op 20 to 1) 1
2172* ARCTIC CAMPER 5-11-10 A Maguire, *patiently rdn, hdwy frm 7 fs out, wnt second o'r 4 out, led over 2 out till appr last, one pace.*
.........(11 to 10 on op Evens tchd 11 to 8 on and 11 to 10) 2
1949* SCORING PEDIGREE (Ire) 5-11-10 S Curran, *keen hold early, hdwy frm hfwy, led 6 fs out till o'r 2 out, wknd fnl furlong.*
.................................(13 to 2 op 8 to 1 tchd 10 to 1) 3
THE LIGHTMAKER (Ire) 4-10-7 D Bridgwater, *pld hrd early, hdwy o'r 4 fs out, sn rdn, one pace fnl 3.*
.................................(9 to 1 op 33 to 1 tchd 66 to 1) 4
MONTROE (Ire) 5-11-3 D O'Sullivan, *wl beh till styd on fnl 2 fs, nrst finish.*.................(33 to 1 op 16 to 1) 5
2269[6] WISLEY WARRIOR 6-11-3 C Llewellyn, *hld up beh ldrs, rdn and wknd o'r 3 fs out.*..........(12 to 1 tchd 16 to 1) 6
2567[3] SIR PRIZE (Ire) 4-10-7 B Clifford, *chsd ldr till o'r 7 fs out, wknd over 4 out.*..................(10 to 1 op 5 to 1) 7
2510* MISTER ERMYN 4-11-0 A P McCoy, *pld hrd, hld up, hdwy 7 fs out, wknd 4 out.*..........(9 to 2 op 4 to 1 tchd 5 to 1) 8

2309 AINTGOTWON 6-10-12 P Hide, *pld hrd, led till 6 fs out, sn wknd.*................(66 to 1 op 33 to 1 tchd 100 to 1) 9
JET SPECIALS (Ire) 4-10-7 R Farrant, *mid-div, effrt o'r 5 fs out, wknd 4 out.*................(9 to 2 op 8 to 1) 10
2008[5] BEN EIGER (Ire) 5-10-10 (7*) M Keighley, *prmnt till wknd appr hfwy.*................(33 to 1 op 14 to 1) 11
2483[4] CALDEBROOK (Ire) 6-10-10 (7*) S Laird, *hld up, prog o'r 6 fs out, wknd over 4 out.*........(33 to 1 op 16 to 1) 12
GRACIOUS IMP (USA) 4-10-2 N T Egan, *beh frm 13th.*
.................................(66 to 1 op 33 to 1 tchd 100 to 1) 13
HOUR HORSE 6-11-3 R Greene, *trkd ldrs till wknd o'r 6 fs out.*
.................................(50 to 1 op 20 to 1) 14
2483[3] KINGSWOOD IMPERIAL 4-10-7 N Williamson, *pld hrd early, nvr trbld ldrs, tld off....* (20 to 1 op 14 to 1 tchd 25 to 1) 15
2283 TUPENNY SMOKE 5-10-9 (3*) P Henley, *nvr on terms, tld off.*
.................................(66 to 1 op 33 to 1 tchd 100 to 1) 16
942[2] WOODSTOCK WANDERER (Ire) 5-11-3 R Johnson, *in tch till wknd 6 fs out, tld off....*(20 to 1 op 12 to 1) 17
Dist: 2½l, 4l, 5l, 8l, 1¼l, 3l, 4l, 10l, 1l, 2l. 3m 49.70s. (17 Ran).
(Mrs J J Peppiatt), J S King

NAAS (IRE) (yielding to soft)
Saturday February 22nd

2832 Saggart Maiden Hurdle (4-y-o) £3,082 2m.......................(2:00)

2643[3] CORN ABBEY (Ire) 11-2 F Woods, ...(5 to 2) 1
2643[2] PEGUS JUNIOR (Ire) 11-2 C O'Dwyer, ...(6 to 4 fav) 2
2705[5] DUNEMER (Ire) 10-13 (3*) Mr R Walsh, ...(8 to 1) 3
2643 RIVER VALLEY LADY (Ire) 10-11 T P Treacy, ...(7 to 1) 4
2643[7] WOODEN DANCE (Ire) 10-11 J T Mitchell, ...(12 to 1) 5
GIVEUPTHEFAGS (Ire) 10-9 (7*) A O'Shea, ...(14 to 1) 6
KEEP RUNNING (Ire) 10-9 (7*) D M O'Sullivan, ...(14 to 1) 7
2643 PLAYPRINCE 10-9 (7*) D K Budds, ...(33 to 1) 8
1173 MOSCOW'S FLAME (Ire) 11-2 S N O'Donovan, ...(50 to 1) 9
COOL SCOTCH (Ire) 10-8 (3*) D Bromley, ...(20 to 1) 10
2643 SLIGHTLY SPEEDY (Ire) 11-7 J Shortt, ...(10 to 1) f
2518[8] THE SWAN 11-2 R Hughes, ...(8 to 1) bd
2643 GALICI (Ire) 10-9 (7*) J M Maguire, ...(16 to 1) pu
POINT LUCK (Ire) 10-4 (7*) Mr S P Hennessy, ...(16 to 1) pu
Dist: ¾l, 20l, 20l, ¾l. 4m 5.90s. (14 Ran).
(Mrs C Collins), Miss S Collins

2833 Nas Na Riogh E.B.F. Novice Chase (Grade 3) (5-y-o and up) £6,850 2½m
...................................(2:30)

2587* CORKET (Ire) 7-11-9 T Horgan, *made all, jmpd wl, hng rght aftr 5th, quickened bef last, cmftbly.*.........(10 to 1) 1
2707[2] LE GINNO (Fr) 10-11-6 T P Treacy, *wl plcd, jmpd slwly 1st, 4 out and 3 out, rdn and chlgd nxt, sn no extr.*.........(5 to 1) 2
2648 MAID FOR DANCING (Ire) 8-10-4 (7*) Mr R H Fowler, *wd wth, rear 7th, jmpd slwly nxt, rdn bef 2 out, kpt on r-in...*(9 to 1) 3
2705 SHISOMA (Ire) 7-11-2 J P Broderick, *wtd wth, jmpd slwly 6th, prog to track ldr 8th, rdn bef 2 out, sn wknd..........*(9 to 1) 4
Dist: 15l, 3l, nk. 5m 52.10s. (4 Ran).
(S J O'Sullivan), A P O'Brien

2834 Naas Supporters Handicap Hurdle (5-y-o and up) £3,425 2m.....(3:00)

2708[6] CIARA'S PRINCE (Ire) [-] (bl) 6-10-7 F J Flood, ...(10 to 1) 1
2706[3] LADY DAISY (Ire) [-] 8-11-7 (7*) A O'Shea, ...(7 to 4 fav) 2
2227[3] OWENDUFF (USA) [-] 7-10-10 F Woods, ...(15 to 8) 3
2340[7] TALINA'S LAW (Ire) [-] (bl) 5-10-12 T P Treacy, ...(7 to 1) 4
1905[3] RANDOM RING (Ire) [-] 6-9-11 (7*) M D Murphy, ...(12 to 1) 5
2521[5] CELTIC LORE (-] 5-11-0 D T Evans, ...(10 to 1) 6
2585 LAURA'S BEAU [-] 13-9-0 (7*) F M Berry, ...(50 to 1) 7
2647 ALLARACKET (Ire) [-] 8-9-0 (7*) L J Fleming, ...(20 to 1) 8
2674[7] DONICKMORE (Ire) [-] 6-10-3 K F O'Brien, ...(12 to 1) 9
2128 SHANES HERO (Ire) [-] 7-11-6 J P Broderick, ...(10 to 1) pu
Dist: 2½l, 5½l, sht-hd, 12l. 3m 59.70s. (10 Ran).
(Raymond McConn), F Flood

2835 Johnstown E.B.F. Novice Hurdle (Grade 3) (5-y-o and up) £9,675 2½m
...................................(3:30)

2342[5] DELPHI LODGE (Ire) 7-11-3 C O'Dwyer, *wtd wth, prog bef 4 out, trkd ldrs 2 out, chlgd before last, styd on wl to ld ins fnl 100 yards..........................*(8 to 1) 1
2472[6] TARTHOOTH (Ire) 6-11-9 F Woods, *led, rdn bef 2 out, sn jnd, hdd last 100 yards.........................*(3 to 1 fav) 2
2584[6] DIFFICULT TIMES (Ire) 5-11-6 S C Lyons, *wl plcd, lost pos bef 4 out, mstk nxt, sn rdn, ran on wel.*.............(10 to 1) 3
2670* KINGS RETURN (Ire) 6-11-9 D J Casey, *wl plcd, prog to track ldrs 4th, dsptd ld 2 out, hdd and wknd r-in.........*(9 to 2) 4
2379* CAIRNCROSS (Ire) 6-11-3 J P Broderick, *rear, gd prog aftr 4 out, rdn after nxt, no extr after 2 out..........*(11 to 1) 5
2645[2] GAZALANI (Ire) 5-10-11 T P Treacy, *wl plcd, rdn bef 2 out, sn wknd................................*(7 to 1) 6
COG HARDI VENTURE (Ire) 6-11-3 R Hughes, *wtd wth, improved 4 out, rdn and wknd aftr 2 out........*(7 to 1) 7
2225[5] JODESI (Ire) 7-10-12 (5*) P Morris, *wl plcd, prog to dispute ld 4th, hdd bef 5 out, mstk nxt, wknd aftr 3 out........*(11 to 1) 8

2378* CLADY BOY (Ire) 6-10-10 (7*) R P Hogan, trkd ldr, lost pl and
wknd bef 5 out................................(16 to 1) 9
2342⁴ BUGGY (Ire) 8-11-3 T J Mitchell, rear, lost tch 3 out, pld up bef
last...(7 to 1) pu
Dist: Nk, 2l, 1l, 2l. 5m 6.70s. (10 Ran).

(Mark Ferran), T J Taaffe

2836 Q.K. Cold Stores Newlands Chase (Listed) (5-y-o and up) £12,900 2m
....(4:00)

2233⁶ OPERA HAT (Ire) 9-11-4 A Powell, led till aftr second, wl plcd,
led after 3 out, quickened frm last................(2 to 1 fav) 1
2671* MERRY GALE (Ire) 9-11-9 C O'Dwyer, wl plcd, prog to ld 5 out,
hdd aftr 3 out, sn rdn, no extr....................(5 to 2) 2
2671² ROYAL MOUNTBROWNE 9-11-9 T Horgan, wl plcd, prog to
ld briefly bef 5 out, rdn aftr 3 out, no extr..........(8 to 1) 3
2127* TIME FOR A RUN 10-11-2 Mr P Fenton, rear, rdn bef 2 out,
kpt on...(10 to 1) 4
2736* THE CRAZY BISHOP (Ire) (bl) 9-11-5 T P Treacy, wl plcd, prog
to ld aftr second, hdd bef 5 out, wknd before 3 out..(6 to 1) 5
2586² IDIOTS VENTURE 10-11-5 Mr B M Cash, wtd wth, gd prog bef
5 out, f nxt.....................................(7 to 1) f
2141⁷ WACKO JACKO (Ire) 8-11-2 J P Broderick, rear, jmpd slwly
3rd and 4th, lost tch aftr nxt, pld up bef 5 out......(100 to 1) pu
Dist: 4½l, 3l, 8l, 4l. 4m 29.40s. (7 Ran).

(Mrs T K Cooper), J R H Fowler

2837 Paddy Power Handicap Hurdle (4-y-o and up) £6,850 3m...........(4:30)

2585⁵ LISCAHILL FORT (Ire) [-] 8-9-9 (7*) M D Murphy, ...(10 to 1) 1
2126* ROSIN THE BOW (Ire) [-] 8-11-11 (3*) J Butler, ...(8 to 1) 2
2585⁴ TREANAREE (Ire) [-] 8-9-0 (7*) R P Hogan, ...(12 to 1) 3
2519* BE HOME EARLY (Ire) [-] 7-10-9 (7*) A O'Shea, ...(7 to 1) 4
1076* GO NOW (Ire) [-] 7-11-2 C O'Dwyer, ...(8 to 1) 5
2752* MARYOBEE (Ire) [-] 7-10-0 (5ex) T P Treacy, ...(7 to 2 fav) 6
2673⁷ CREATIVE BLAZE (Ire) [-] 8-11-2 J P Broderick, ..(14 to 1) 7
2757³ DIAMOND DOUBLE (Ire) [-] 6-10-1 R Hughes, ...(20 to 1) 8
2410⁴ DEARBORN TEC (Ire) [-] 8-10-2 C O'Brien, ...(16 to 1) 9
2585² JIMMY THE WEED (Ire) [-] 8-9-0 (7*) P G Hourigan, (14 to 1) 10
2343² BAR FLUTE (Ire) [-] 6-9-8 F Woods, ...(8 to 1) 11
2670² CASTLE COIN (Ire) [-] 5-10-8 T Horgan, ...(5 to 1) 12
2134⁴ ANNADOT (Ire) [-] 7-10-7 (7*) L J Fleming, ...(9 to 1) f
2585* HI KNIGHT (Ire) [-] 7-10-11 K F O'Brien, ...(7 to 1) pu
Dist: 2½l, nk, 7l, 9l. 6m 10.30s. (14 Ran).

(Mrs G McLoughney), James McLoughney

2838 Rathcoole I.N.H. Flat Race (5-y-o and up) £3,082 2m 3f............(5:00)

2222 GARRYS LOCK (Ire) 8-12-1 (3*) Mr P English, ...(8 to 1) 1
2339 THE GREY MARE (Ire) 8-11-6 (7*) Mr J P Fahey, ...(11 to 1) 2
CLASH OF THE GALES (Ire) 5-11-0 (3*) Mr R Walsh, (8 to 1) 3
1121* CLOONE BRIDGE 5-12-1 Mr B M Cash, ...(6 to 4 fav) 4
2518 CLONCANNON BELL (Ire) 7-11-6 Miss M Olivefalk, (25 to 1) 5
2132⁸ WINDGAP HILL (Ire) 6-11-4 (7*) Mr G Donnelly, ...(10 to 1) 6
2093* HOLLOW GOLD (Ire) 8-11-6 (7*) Mr D W Cullen, ...(5 to 1) 7
OONAGH'S STAR (Ire) 5-11-8 Mr T Mullins, ...(5 to 1) 8
2416* OUR-DANTE (Ire) 5-11-3 (7*) Mr Sean O O'Brien, ..(7 to 1) 9
2645 SWIFT PICK (Ire) 5-11-8 Mr G J Harford, ...(10 to 1) 10
2737 MUSIC CITY BEAT (Ire) 7-11-4 (7*) Mr L J Fagan, ..(33 to 1) 11
FOLK HERO (Ire) 5-11-3 (5*) Mr A C Coyle, ...(12 to 1) 12
701⁷ BALLYHAYS LODGE (Ire) 8-10-13 (7*) Mr A J Dempsey,
....(25 to 1) 13
GLENPATRICK PEACH (Ire) 8-10-13 (7*) Mr Peter Fahy,
....(16 to 1) 14
2709 LORD PENNY 5-11-8 Mr H F Cleary, ...(20 to 1) pu
Dist: 10l, sht-hd, sht-hd, 8l. 4m 48.30s. (15 Ran).

(Mrs Dorothy Weld), Thomas Foley

FAIRYHOUSE (IRE) (yielding to soft)
Sunday February 23rd
Going Correction: PLUS 0.70 sec. per fur. (races 1,3,7), PLUS 0.95 (2,4,5,6)

2839 Tolka River Maiden Hurdle (5-y-o and up) £3,425 2½m............(2:15)

2649⁴ BELLS BRIDGE (Ire) 7-11-6 C F Swan, ...(10 to 1) 1
2583⁸ FANE PATH (Ire) 5-11-11 P Carberry, ...(12 to 1) 2
2584⁵ BLUSHING SAND (Ire) 7-11-7 (7*) Mr T J Beattie, ..(5 to 1) 3
2166⁴ LADY ARGYLE (Ire) 6-11-1 F J Flood, ...(12 to 1) 4
2647 BRASS BAND (Ire) 6-10-8 (7*) Mr R H Fowler, ...(14 to 1) 5
PRIVATE SECTOR (Ire) 6-11-6 C O'Brien, ...(12 to 1) 6
2583 STAR CLUB (Ire) 5-11-6 R Hughes, ...(20 to 1) 7
2081 ISLE OF IONA (Ire) 6-11-6 T P Rudd, ...(50 to 1) 8
2443² DIGIN FOR GOLD (Ire) 6-11-6 F Woods, ...(Evens fav) 9
2222⁹ CONAGHER BOY (Ire) 7-12-0 A Powell, ...(20 to 1) 10
2525⁹ MISS PECKSNIFF (Ire) 7-11-1 S H O'Donovan, ...(33 to 1) 11
2704⁴ PRAGUE SPRING 5-11-6 R Hughes, ...(8 to 1) 12
2582⁹ RATHCOLMAN GALE (Ire) 7-11-1 T P Treacy, ...(33 to 1) 13
2583 KILCAR (Ire) 6-11-6 D T Evans, ...(33 to 1) 14
2520 BOLD CAVALIER (Ire) 8-10-13 (7*) Mr A Ross, ...(33 to 1) 15
2378⁷ JUST 'R JAKE (Ire) 8-11-1 (5*) M D Murphy, ...(66 to 1) 16
2443 GLEN CAMDEN (Ire) 5-11-3 N Williamson, ...(20 to 1) 17

2704⁷ BAD BERTRICH (Ire) 6-11-11 (3*) K Whelan, ...(50 to 1) 18
647⁴ KARA'S DREAM (Ire) 9-10-12 (3*) B Bowens, ...(25 to 1) 19
2582⁷ SUPREME ALLIANCE (Ire) 7-11-6 (3*) J Butler, ...(14 to 1) 20
1013 JUST SUPREME (Ire) 6-10-13 (7*) D K Budds, ...(33 to 1) 21
2675 PIYALA (Ire) 7-10-8 (7*) A O'Shea, ...(16 to 1) 22
2339 HEAD CHAPLAIN (Ire) 6-11-6 K F O'Brien, ...(25 to 1) 23
2343⁹ DROMARA BREEZE (Ire) 9-11-6 T Horgan, ...(14 to 1) 24
2582 MAY BLOOM (Ire) 6-11-1 J Shortt, ...(66 to 1) 25
1712⁷ NORE GLEN (Ire) 6-11-6 J R Barry, ...(25 to 1) 26
2132⁵ WELCOME DEAL (Ire) 9-11-6 L P Cusack, ...(25 to 1) f
2518 EXPERT ADVICE (Ire) 6-11-1 (5*) P Morris, ...(25 to 1) f
Dist: 4l, 2½l, 3l, ¾l. 5m 4.30s. a 20.30s (28 Ran).
SR: 29/30/30/14/13/-/

(Patrick G J Murphy), A P O'Brien

2840 Ballyduag Beginners Chase (4-y-o and up) £3,425 2¼m..........(2:45)

2445⁹ FLASHY LAD (Ire) 6-12-0 J P Broderick, ...(20 to 1) 1
1898⁵ NATIVE STATUS (Ire) 7-12-0 P Carberry, ...(5 to 2 jt-fav) 2
2446² BRAVE FOUNTAIN (Ire) 9-12-0 C F Swan, ...(5 to 2 jt-fav) 3
2644⁹ NO TAG (Ire) 9-12-0 T J Mitchell, ...(14 to 1) 4
2649 ROYAL OASIS (Ire) 6-11-7 (7*) Mr Brian Moran, ..(14 to 1) 5
LORD MUFF (Ire) 8-12-0 J K Kinane, ...(25 to 1) 6
2644³ MIROSWAKI (USA) 7-12-0 C O'Dwyer, ...(5 to 1) 7
2587 PARADISE ROAD 8-12-0 C O'Brien, ...(20 to 1) 8
2587⁶ JOHNNY'S DREAM (Ire) 7-11-7 (7*) Mr A J Dempsey,
....(12 to 1) 9
2585 VEREDARIUS (Fr) 6-12-0 F Woods, ...(7 to 1) 10
2644 ROCHE MENTOR (Ire) 7-12-0 T P Rudd, ...(25 to 1) 11
2446⁴ MYSTICAL AIR (Ire) 7-12-0 D T Evans, ...(16 to 1) 12
2644⁸ FONTAINE FABLES (Ire) (bl) 7-12-0 J Shortt, ...(10 to 1) 13
2705 GEALLAINNBAN (Ire) 7-12-0 N Williamson, ...(7 to 1) f
Dist: 4l, 1½l, 9l, 6l. 4m 54.80s. a 29.80s (14 Ran).

(Mrs Denise Reddan), T J Taaffe

2841 Sutherland River Handicap Hurdle (0-140 5-y-o and up) £4,110 2½m
....(3:15)

2708⁵ TRYFIRION (Ire) [-] 8-10-9 (3*) B Bowens, ...(9 to 1) 1
2051⁴ TARAJAN (USA) [-] (bl) 5-10-2 T Hazlett, ...(10 to 1) 2
2708² APPELLATE COURT [-] (bl) 9-9-0 (7*) B J Geraghty, (14 to 1) 3
2134* GRAVITY GATE (Ire) [-] 8-9-9 (5*) T Martin, ...(4 to 1) 4
2340* METASTASIO [-] (bl) 5-10-10 H Rogers, ...(5 to 1) 5
2128² BLACK QUEEN (Ire) [-] 6-10-4 C F Swan, ...(9 to 4 fav) 6
2584³ DERRYMOYLE (Ire) [-] 8-11-7 (7*) D K Budds, ...(9 to 1) 7
2447² SLANEY GLOW (Ire) [-] 6-10-1 C O'Dwyer, ...(7 to 1) 8
2708 REASILVIA (Ire) [-] 7-10-2 N Williamson, ...(14 to 1) 9
2379 NORDIC SENSATION (Ire) [-] 8-9-11 (7*) R P Hogan, (66 to 1) 10
2340 MAJESTIC MAN [-] 6-9-9 R Hughes, ...(20 to 1) 11
2708 STRALDI (Ire) [-] 9-10-3 T J Mitchell, ...(20 to 1) 12
Dist: 1½l, sht-hd, 9l, 4½l. 5m 3.50s. a 19.50s (12 Ran).
SR: 29/17/8/6/11/-/

(Mrs M T Quinn), Victor Bowens

2842 European Breeders Fund Novices Handicap Chase (Grade 3) (5-y-o and up) £9,675 3m 1f............(3:45)

2733² PAPILLON (Ire) [-] 6-11-13 N Williamson, wtd wth, prog bef 5
out to ld aftr nxt, quickened after 2 out, styd on strly.
....(7 to 4 fav) 1
2673² COOLAFINKA (Ire) [-] 8-10-7 T Horgan, led 1st 3, prmnt, led
12th till aftr 4 out, kpt on wl......................(9 to 1) 2
2734 EXECUTIVE OPTIONS (Ire) [-] 8-11-5 P Carberry, wtd wth, gd
prog bef 4 out, trkd ldr aftr nxt, rdn before 2 out, no extr.
....(14 to 1) 3
2648² ROYAL ROSY (Ire) [-] 6-11-3 C F Swan, wl plcd, prog aftr 5
out, rdn after 3 out, wknd after nxt.................(9 to 1) 4
2341² AMBLE SPEEDY (Ire) [-] 7-12-0 F Woods, rear, mstk second,
kpt on aftr 2 out.................................(10 to 30) 5
2171* SHINING WILLOW [-] 7-11-1 C O'Dwyer, wl plcd, prog to ld
bef 8th, hdd 12th, dsptd lead nxt till mstk 6 out, rdn aftr 3 out,
sn wknd.......................................(9 to 2) 6
2223² BAILE NA GCLOCH (Ire) [-] 8-10-9 (3*) D P Murphy, wl plcd,
jmpd slwly 1st 2, led 4th till bef 8th, rdn aftr 3 out, sn wknd.
....(10 to 1) 7
2673² CREHELP EXPRESS (Ire) [-] 7-10-6 (3*) B Bowens, mid-div,
lost pl aftr 6 out, pld up bef 2 out, broke blood vessel. (12 to 1) pu
Dist: 6l, 9l, 4l, ½l. 6m 54.20s. a 39.20s (8 Ran).

(Mrs J Maxwell Moran), T M Walsh

2843 Tom Dreaper Handicap Chase (5-y-o and up) £5,480 3m 1f........(4:15)

2648 BOBBYJO (Ire) [-] 7-9-12 P Carberry, ...(7 to 1) 1
2524⁷ LOVE THE LORD (Ire) [-] 7-10-10 T P Treacy, ...(12 to 1) 2
COQ HARDI AFFAIR (Ire) [-] 9-10-11 N Williamson, (16 to 1) 3
2338⁶ CASTALINO [-] 11-9-11 (7*) R P Hogan, ...(16 to 1) 4
2226 UNA'S CHOICE (Ire) [-] 9-9-0 (7*) L J Fleming, ...(14 to 1) 5
2646* MASTER MCCARTAN [-] 8-10-1 C O'Dwyer,
....(15 to 8 fav) 6
2646⁸ BOB DEVANI [-] (bl) 11-9-0 (7*) B J Geraghty, ...(20 to 1) 7
2223 LA-GREINE [-] 10-9-4 (3*) J Butler, ...(20 to 1) 8
2273⁷ BACK BAR (Ire) [-] 9-10-4 J P Broderick, ...(13 to 2) 9
2734 SON OF WAR [-] (bl) 10-12-0 F Woods, ...(10 to 1) 10
2586³ SHANAGARRY (Ire) [-] 8-10-11 (7*) Mr Brian Moran, (9 to 1) 11
2734³ CARRIGEEN KERRIA (Ire) [-] 9-9-11 D J Casey, ...(10 to 1) ur

2524 BART OWEN [-] 12-10-2 T J Mitchell, ...(33 to 1) pu
2273 JASSU [-] 11-10-10 C F Swan, ...(16 to 1) pu
Dist: 3½l, 3l, 1½l, 20l. 6m 42.20s. a 27.20s (14 Ran).
SR: 36/44/42/23/2/-/ (Robert Burke), Thomas Carberry

2844 Hurley River Hunters Chase (5-y-o and up) £3,425 3m 1f......... (4:45)

2672^{2} STAY IN TOUCH (Ire) 7-11-11 (3*) Mr D P Costello, (7 to 4) 1
IRISH STOUT (Ire) 6-11-1 (3*) Mr R Walsh, ...(33 to 1) 2
2523* BOB TREACY (Ire) 8-11-2 (7*) Mr A G Costello, ...(7 to 1) 3
1042 ONLY ONE (Ire) 7-10-11 (7*) Mr M O'Connor, ...(40 to 1) 4
UPSHEPOPS (Ire) 9-10-7^{1} (7*) Mr A J Costello, ...(50 to 1) f
2475^{4} LIFE OF A KING (Ire) 9-11-9 Mr J A Nash, ...(11 to 2) f
2672* DIXON VARNER (Ire) 7-11-9 Mr P Fenton, ...(5 to 4 fav) f
KILLMURRAY BUCK (Ire) 9-10-13 Mr G J Harford, (50 to 1) pu
Dist: ½l, dist, dist. 6m 55.60s. a 40.60s (8 Ran).
(Barry Brazier), John J Costello

2845 St.Margarets (Pro-Am) I.N.H. Flat Race (5-y-o and up) £3,425 2m (5:15)

2449^{3} LANCASTRIAN PRIDE (Ire) 7-11-11 (3*) Mr R Walsh, ...(Evens fav) 1
2368^{6} ROYAL MARINE (Ire) 5-11-4 (7*) Mr G Donnelly, ... (10 to 1) 2
2588^{4} MINELLA HOTEL (Ire) 5-11-8 (3*) K Whelan, ... (5 to 1) 3
2072^{6} TIDAL PRINCESS (Ire) 5-10-13 (7*) Mr E G FitzGerald, ...(14 to 1) 4
KILCALM KING (Ire) 5-11-11 Mr G J Harford, ... (12 to 1) 5
2449^{3} TALKALOT (Ire) 6-12-0 Mr P Fenton, ...(10 to 1) 6
EMERALD LORD (Ire) 5-11-4 (7*) K A Kelly, ...(14 to 1) 7
2583^{5} EVENKEEL (Ire) 5-11-4 (7*) Mr A J Dempsey, ...(8 to 1) 8
2649 CHOICE JENNY (Ire) 5-11-1 (5*) Mr A C Coyle, ...(12 to 1) 9
2704 BALMY NATIVE (Ire) 5-11-6 (5*) M D Murphy, ... (33 to 1) 10
ARDENTIUM 6-11-9 (5*) J M Donnelly, ... (25 to 1) 11
KING MOLINEUX (Ire) 6-12-0 Mr A R Coonan, ... (16 to 1) 12
2443 GETTING CLOSER (Ire) 6-11-7 (7*) Mr R J Barnwell, ...(14 to 1) 13
2649 CHANCERY RIVER (Ire) 8-11-2 (7*) Mr R F O'Gorman, ...(20 to 1) 14
SILVER RIVER (Ire) 5-10-13 (7*) Ms W Fox, ... (20 to 1) 15
MISSILE GLEN (Ire) 5-11-8 (3*) B Bowens, ...(16 to 1) 16
QUIETLY (Ire) 5-11-11 Mr D Marnane, ...(16 to 1) 17
CORNCAP (Ire) 5-11-4 (7*) Mr S J Mahon, ...(33 to 1) 18
ELECTRICAL STORM 5-11-1 (5*) T Martin, ...(14 to 1) 19
983 KILLALOONTY ROSE (Ire) 6-11-2 (7*) Mr A J Costello, ...(33 to 1) 20
ORCHESTRAL WIND (Ire) 6-11-6 (3*) Mr P J Casey, (25 to 1) 21
TRAVIS (Ire) 7-11-7 (7*) Mr L J Gracey, ...(50 to 1) 22
Dist: Hd, 3l, 2½l, ¾l. 3m 59.10s. (22 Ran).
(Kilcarn Bridge Syndicate), W P Mullins

NEWCASTLE (good)
Monday February 24th
Going Correction: PLUS 0.50 sec. per fur. (races 1,3,5), PLUS 1.10 (2,4,6)

2846 John J. Straker Challenge Trophy Handicap Chase Class D (0-125 5-y-o and up) £3,501 2½m........ (2:10)

2573^{4} SOLBA (USA) [96] (bl) 8-10-10 D Parker, *hld up, took clr order 8th, led 3 out, rdn aftr last, styd on wl.* ....(11 to 1 op 10 to 1 tchd 12 to 1) 1
2622^{2} NICHOLAS PLANT [96] 8-10-10 G Cahill, *led to 5th, led 8th till hdd 3 out, ev ch whn hit last, no extr und pres.* ....(11 to 8 fav op 5 to 4 tchd 6 to 4) 2
FORBIDDEN TIME (Ire) [110] 9-11-10 R Supple, *trkd ldrs, rdn bef 3 out, fdd, fnshd lme.*...............(9 to 2 op 3 to 1) 3
2573^{3} VILLAGE REINDEER (NZ) [103] 10-11-3 L Wyer, *mstks, beh, kpt on frm 3 out, nvr dngrs*..........(5 to 1 tchd 11 to 2) 4
39* GROUSE-N-HEATHER [94] 8-10-8 A Dobbin, *in tch, hit 7th, wknd aftr 11th, tld off*...............(9 to 2 op 5 to 1) 5
2685^{3} POTATO MAN [90] (v) 11-10-4 B Storey, *cl up, led 5th till hdd 8th, wknd aftr 11th, tld off*....................... (20 to 1) 6
Dist: 7l, 7l, 6l, 27l, 8l. 5m 11.60s. a 24.60s (6 Ran).
(Mr & Mrs Raymond Anderson Green), C Parker

2847 Great North Road Selling Handicap Hurdle Class G (0-95 4-y-o and up) £2,057 2m.................... (2:40)

1933^{4} LATIN LEADER [83] (bl) 7-11-8 D Parker, *sn tracking ldrs, led 3 out, styd on wl*......................(6 to 1 op 5 to 1) 1
2420^{4} IN A MOMENT (USA) [70] 6-10-9 R Garritty, *beh, effrt bef 3 out, styd on strly frm nxt, not rch wnr*.... (5 to 1 op 7 to 1) 2
2572^{5} OBVIOUS RISK [61] 6-9-7 (7*) Tristan Davidson, *towards rear, blun 3rd, hdwy bef 3 out, mstks last 2, styd on.* .... (16 to 1 op 14 to 1) 3
2630* PALACE OF GOLD [85] 7-11-3 (7*) W Dowling, *led, hit second, jmpd slwly 4th, hit 3 out and hdd, kpt on same pace.* ....(4 to 1 fav op 3 to 1) 4
2617 BILL'S PRIDE [75] 6-11-0 M Moloney, *chsd ldrs, ev ch frm 3 out till wknd und pres r-in*............(14 to 1 op 12 to 1) 5
2710 DENTICULATA [70] 9-10-9 B Storey, *towards rear, styd on frm 2 out, nvr dngrs*....................(25 to 1 op 20 to 1) 6
2577 BEACON HILL LADY [71] 4-9-7 (7*) N Horrocks, *beh, hdwy into midfield hfwy, no further prog frm 3 out*..... (100 to 1) 7
2710 BARK'N'BITE [81] 5-11-6 P Niven, *in tch, drvn alng and lost pl hfwy, no dngr aftr*..................... (7 to 1 op 5 to 1) 8
2236 THE FINAL SPARK [75] 6-11-0 A Dobbin, *nvr dngrs.* ....(14 to 1 op 12 to 1) 9
2485^{7} CHARLVIC [61] 7-9-7 (7*) L McGrath, *mid-div till outpcd aftr 6th, no dngr after*....................(12 to 1 op 8 to 1) 10
2538^{6} LIAM'S LOSS (Ire) [61] (v) 8-9-9 (5*) B Grattan, *in tch till wknd aftr 6th*.................................(100 to 1) 11
2118^{4} BLUE DOMAIN [70] 6-10-6 (3*) Michael Brennan, *prmnt, rdn aftr 3 out, wknd quickly after nxt*........(9 to 1 op 7 to 1) 12
THE GREY TEXAN [67] 8-10-6 D Bentley, *al beh.* ....(50 to 1 op 33 to 1) 13
2804 SHARMOOR [68] 5-10-7 A Thornton, *mid-div till wknd bef 3 out, tld off*.................................. (16 to 1) 14
2145^{6} GAELIC CHARM (Ire) [78] 9-11-3 K Johnson, *prmnt till rdn and wknd quickly aftr 6th, pld up lme bef 3 out.* ....(8 to 1 tchd 9 to 1) pu
2619^{9} NAWTINOOKEY [61] (bl) 7-9-7 (7*) C McCormack, *chsd ldrs to 5th, sn wknd, wl beh whn pld up bef 2 out.* .... (16 to 1 op 10 to 1) pu
2485 COQUET GOLD [61] 6-10-0 G Cahill, *beh most of way, pld up bef last*....................(100 to 1 op 50 to 1) pu
1464^{9} PROMISE TO TRY (Ire) [68] 5-10-2 (5*) S Taylor, *mid-div, mstk 4th, wknd quickly bef 6th, tld off whn pld up before 3 out.* ....(100 to 1) pu
Dist: ½l, 5l, hd, ½l, 1¼l, 3½l, 3½l, 1¼l, 2½l, ½l. 4m 5.00s. a 28.00s (18 Ran).
(Mr & Mrs Raymond Anderson Green), C Parker

2848 Gosforth Park Novices' Chase Class E (5-y-o and up) £2,862 2½m..(3:10)

1317^{6} BRIGHTER SHADE (Ire) 7-11-4 P Niven, *hld up, hdwy to track ldrs 7th, chlgd 3 out, led nxt, shaken up and drw clr aftr last.* ....(11 to 1 op 8 to 1 tchd 12 to 1) 1
2621* COLONEL IN CHIEF (Ire) 7-11-10 P Carberry, *led, blun tenth, jnd 3 out, hdd nxt, kpt on same pace, broke blood vessel.* ....(2 to 1 on op 6 to 4 on) 2
1952^{3} SHAWWELL 10-11-4 B Storey, *beh, hdwy to chase ldrs tenth, drvn alng bef 3 out, fdd*............ (25 to 1 op 50 to 1) 3
1930^{4} OVERWHELM (Ire) 9-11-8 Mr M Thompson, *mstks, beh, lost tch frm 11th, tld off*........................(200 to 1) 4
2576 CHILDSWAY 9-11-1 (3*) Michael Brennan, *mstks, prmnt till blun 6th, sn lost pl, lost tch aftr 11th, tld off*........(100 to 1) 5
2240^{4} NIJWAY 7-10-13 (5*) S Taylor, *beh and drvn alng whn f 9th.* ....(66 to 1 op 50 to 1) f
2508 BRANDY CROSS (Ire) 8-11-4 A Dobbin, *chsd ldr, reminder aftr 7th, hit 11th, sn wknd, lost tch and pld up bef 3 out.* ....(2 to 1 op 6 to 4) pu
Dist: 9l, 16l, 30l, 9l. 5m 15.00s. a 28.00s (7 Ran).
(D S Hall), Mrs M Reveley

2849 Brandling House Maiden Hurdle Class E (4-y-o and up) £2,494 2m .... (3:40)

2711^{2} NIGEL'S LAD (Ire) 5-11-8 M Foster, *made all, quickened clr aftr 3 out, easily*................ (5 to 2 on op 7 to 4 on) 1
2538^{4} SUPREME SOVIET 7-11-8 A Dobbin, *prmnt, rdn bef 3 out, sn outpcd by wnr, kpt on same pace*........(6 to 1 tchd 7 to 1) 2
2489^{2} DARK PHOENIX (Ire) (v) 7-11-3 M Brennan, *in tch, hdwy aftr 5th, sn drvn alng, kpt on same pace frm 3 out.* ....(7 to 1 op 6 to 1 tchd 8 to 1) 3
2344 BOLD STATEMENT 5-11-8 N Bentley, *trkd ldrs, pushed alng aftr 6th, btn whn hmpd 3 out*............ (8 to 1 op 7 to 1) 4
MIKE STAN (Ire) 6-11-8 R Supple, *beh, some late hdwy, nvr dngrs*......................(33 to 1 op 14 to 1) 5
2490^{6} NUTTY SOLERA 7-11-8 B Storey, *mid-div, effrt bef 6th, sn btn*................................(14 to 1 op 12 to 1) 6
2632^{4} FALCON'S FLAME (USA) 4-10-12 Mr M Thompson, *hld up, effrt aftr 5th, sn btn*..................(33 to 1 op 16 to 1) 7
2492 OTTADINI (Ire) 5-11-3 T Reed, *sn beh, tld off*.......(200 to 1) 8
2419 ONLY A SIOUX 5-11-8 D Parker, *in tch to hfwy, sn beh, tld off.* ....(100 to 1) 9
2533 EVENING DUSK (Ire) 5-10-10 (7*) S Melrose, *in tch to hfwy, sn beh, tld off*.................................(200 to 1) 10
1682 FLY EXECUTIVE 6-11-8 Mr Chris Wilson, *in tch to hfwy, sn beh, tld off*.................(200 to 1 op 100 to 1) 11
2463^{9} ROYAL YORK 5-11-3 P Carberry, *prmnt, ev ch 6th, sn drvn alng, 4th and wkng whn f 3 out.* .... (10 to 1 op 6 to 1 tchd 12 to 1) f
THORNWOOD (Ire) 5-11-8 A Thornton, *sn beh, f 2 out.* .... (33 to 1 op 50 to 1) f
2533 SOLWAY KING 7-11-3 (5*) S Taylor, *keen, mstk 1st, tld off whn pld up bef 5th*................................(100 to 1) pu
Dist: 10l, 4l, 18l, 8l, ¾l, 3l, dist, 10l, 10l, 9l. 4m 1.00s. a 24.00s (14 Ran).
SR: 30/20/11/-/-/-/ (N C Dunnington), P C Haslam

2850 Northern Racing Handicap Chase Class C (0-130 5-y-o and up) £4,279 3m........................ (4:10)

2579* ACT THE WAG (Ire) [113] 8-10-11 P Carberry, *prmnt, led on bit appr 3 out, quickened r-in, cmftbly*....(7 to 2 op 5 to 2) 1

2536 STONEY BURKE (Ire) [107] 8-10-5⁵ A Thornton, *in tch, ch frm 3 out till no extr und pres from last*... (50 to 1 op 33 to 1) 2
2148* STORMY CORAL (Ire) [106] 7-10-4 B Storey, *trkd ldrs, pushed alng aftr 13th, hit 15th, fdd frm 2 out.*
.................................(5 to 4 fav tchd 11 to 8) 3
2536* DAVY BLAKE [111] 10-10-9 A Dobbin, *led till hdd appr 3 out, fdd*...................(100 to 30 op 7 to 2 tchd 4 to 1) 4
STRATH ROYAL [130] 11-12-0 M Brennan, *beh, lost tch frm tenth, tld off*.......................(9 to 2 op 5 to 1) 5
2652 JOHNNY KELLY [102] 10-9-11 (3*) F Leahy, *beh, lost tch frm 9th, tld off whn pld bef 15th*......(100 to 1 op 66 to 1) pu
Dist: 2½l, 10l, 2l, dist. 6m 3.90s. a 17.90s (6 Ran).
SR: 24/15/4/7/-/-/   (Robert Ogden), Martin Todhunter

2851 St. Modwen Handicap Hurdle Class C (0-130 4-y-o and up) £3,485 3m .... (4:40)

2535* TRIBUNE [98] 6-10-10 M Foster, *cl up, led tenth, stumbled badly last, styd on wl, eased towards finish.*
.................(11 to 4 fav op 4 to 1 tchd 5 to 2) 1
2494* NORTHERN SQUIRE [99] 9-10-11 A Dobbin, *made most till hdd tenth, outpcd aftr 3 out, styd on wl ag'n appr last.*
.................(7 to 2 tchd 4 to 1) 2
2716⁵ DALLY BOY [112] 5-11-10 L Wyer, *prmnt, ev ch 2 out, kpt on same pace und pres*..............(9 to 2 tchd 5 to 1) 3
2346* SWANBISTER (Ire) [105] 7-11-3 R Supple, *hld up, hdwy bef tenth, styd on same pace frm 2 out*...(7 to 2 tchd 4 to 1) 4
2538³ SMIDDY LAD [95] 6-10-7 D Bentley, *in tch, effrt bef 3 out, wkng whn mstk 2 out*...........(9 to 1 op 9 to 2) 5
2789 BANG IN TROUBLE (Ire) [104] 6-10-11 (5*) R McGrath, *in tch till grad wknd frm 3 out.* (12 to 1 op 10 to 1 tchd 14 to 1) 6
THIS NETTLE DANGER [88] 13-10-0 M Brennan, *hld up, smooth hdwy bef tenth, wknd quickly frm 2 out, tld off.*
.................(100 to 1 op 50 to 1) 7
2285 MANOR COURT (Ire) [101] 9-10-13 J Burke, *in tch till wknd aftr 9th, tld off whn pld up bef 3 out*...(100 to 1 op 50 to 1) pu
2710² FLAT TOP [100] 6-10-12 R Garritty, *hld up, wknd quickly aftr tenth, tld off whn pld up bef 3 out.*
.................(9 to 2 op 3 to 1 tchd 5 to 1) pu
Dist: 1½l, 3l, nk, 10l, 5l, 17l. 6m 6.00s. a 35.00s (9 Ran).
(Hexagon Racing), C W Thornton

CATTERICK (good to soft)
Tuesday February 25th
Going Correction: PLUS 0.95 sec. per fur.

2852 Middleham Novices' Hurdle Class E (4-y-o and up) £2,505 2m..... (1:50)

2145² CUMBRIAN MAESTRO 4-10-7 L Wyer, *chsd ldrs, led and blun 2 out, styd on strly und pres*..............(6 to 1) 1
2711² GOSPEL SONG 5-11-3 A S Smith, *led, rdn and hdd 2 out, kpt on same pace und pres.*
.................(11 to 4 fav op 3 to 1 tchd 5 to 2) 2
2560⁶ FIRE ON ICE (Ire) 5-11-3 N Williamson, *chsd ldrs, drvn alng appr 2 out, wn one pace*.........(4 to 1 tchd 7 to 2) 3
2619 HARFDECENT 6-11-3 G Cahill, *hld up, pushed alng and outpcd 3 out, styd on wl betw last 2, nrst finish.*
.................(40 to 1 op 25 to 1) 4
2372 KING RAT (Ire) (v) 6-11-0 (3*) Michael Brennan, *midfield, chsd ldrs hfwy till wknd appr 2 out.*
.................(16 to 1 op 12 to 1 tchd 20 to 1) 5
NASAYER (Ire) 7-10-10 (7*) S Haworth, *beh, rdn and lost tch 3 out, sn no dngr*................(66 to 1 op 33 to 1) 6
1983⁵ CALDER KING 6-11-3 P Niven, *midfield, mstk 3rd, outpcd 3 out, sn lost tch*.................(6 to 1 tchd 13 to 2) 7
2712 KING FLY 7-11-3 A Thornton, *wth ldr, drvn alng appr 2 out, sn wknd*.......................(100 to 1 op 50 to 1) 8
SNIPER 5-11-3 A Dobbin, *hmpd 1st, al beh, tld off appr 2 out.*
.................(33 to 1) 9
2489 UN POCO LOCO 5-11-3 G Lee, *al beh, tld off.* (100 to 1) 10
2575 ALLERBECK 7-10-12 J Supple, *reminders in rear 3rd, tld off frm hfwy*...................(200 to 1 op 100 to 1) 11
2553⁸ FULL THROTTLE 4-10-7 D Gallagher, *cl up whn f 1st.*
.................(100 to 30 op 9 to 4 tchd 7 to 2) f
2651² TAWAFIJ (USA) 8-11-3 R Garritty, *in tch, hdwy and chasing ldrs and cl up whn blun and uns rdr 5th.*
.................(7 to 1 op 8 to 1 tchd 10 to 1) ur
2492 GOOD VENTURE 6-10-12 B Storey, *sn beh, tld off whn pld up 4 out*............................(100 to 1) pu
Dist: 8l, 7l, 1¼l, 2½l, 11l, 1¼l, 2½l, 14l, dist. 3l. 4m 5.00s. a 25.00s (14 Ran).
(Cumbrian Industrials Ltd), T D Easterby

2853 Wensley Mares' Only Novices' Handicap Hurdle Class F (0-95 4-y-o and up) £2,145 2m............... (2:20)

1826 FIRST IN THE FIELD [68] 6-9-8 (7*) S Haworth, *al gng wl, chlgd 2 out, sliight ld last, ran on well.*
.................(25 to 1 tchd 33 to 1) 1
2533² LUMBACK LADY [88] 7-11-7 B Storey, *in tch, slight ld 3 out till wndrd and fdd last, kpt on same pace*...(6 to 1 op 4 to 1) 2
2346⁷ DECENT PENNY (Ire) [68] 8-10-1 T Eley, *cl up, mstk and drvn alng 3 out, kpt on stdly frm nxt*.......(33 to 1 op 25 to 1) 3

1800³ CLIBURNEL NEWS (Ire) [78] 7-10-11 Gary Lyons, *in tch, pushed alng and outpcd aftr 3 out, styd on same pace.*
.................(12 to 1 tchd 14 to 1) 4
2572 ALAN'S PRIDE (Ire) [68] 6-10-1 G Cahill, *led to 3 out, sn pushed alng, btn whn mstk last*.....(20 to 1 tchd 8 to 1) 5
2357² BEST OF ALL (Ire) [95] 5-11-7 (7*) N Horrocks, *chsd ldrs till lost pl 3 out, sn no dngr*.........(5 to 1 fav tchd 6 to 1) 6
2631 APPEARANCE MONEY (Ire) [72] 6-10-5 P Carberry, *hld up, gd hdwy to chase ldrs 3 out, fdd frm nxt.*
.................(11 to 2 op 5 to 1 tchd 6 to 1) 7
2492⁴ PARSON'S LODGE (Ire) [77] 9-10-10 R Supple, *hld up, reminders and outpcd aftr 3 out, sn btn.* (6 to 1 op 4 to 1) 8
2651³ DIDDY RYMER [75] 7-10-8 N Williamson, *hld up, lost tch appr 2 out, sn fdd*.....................(6 to 1 tchd 7 to 1) 9
2575⁸ CARLY-J [69] 6-10-2 Mr N Kent, *wth ldr, led briefly 3 out, wknd quickly appr nxt*..............(50 to 1 op 33 to 1) 10
2398⁷ QUINAG [89] 6-11-8 A Thornton, *struggling in rear whn hit 4th, sn beh*....................(14 to 1 op 12 to 1) 11
2372 URSHI-JADE [67] 9-10-0³ (3*) Michael Brennan, *sn tld off, pld up 3 out*....................(50 to 1 op 33 to 1) pu
2463 SOMETHING SPEEDY (Ire) [70] 5-10-3 A Dobbin, *chsd ldrs, wknd quickly 3 out, tld off whn pld up nxt.*
.................(8 to 1 op 10 to 1) pu
2349⁷ BAREFOOT LANDING (USA) [75] 6-10-8 D Parker, *hld up, lost tch 3 out, beh whn pld up nxt.*
.................(9 to 1 op 10 to 1 tchd 12 to 1) pu
1164³ KASHANA (Ire) [70] (v) 5-10-3 M Moloney, *midfield, lost pl and blun 5th, sn pld up*...........(14 to 1 tchd 16 to 1) pu
Dist: 2l, 2l, 2½l, 2½l, 6l, 1½l, ½l, 9l, 17l, 3l. 4m 7.70s. a 27.70s (15 Ran).
(N B Mason), N B Mason

2854 Malton Novices' Chase Class E (5-y-o and up) £2,894 2m 3f..... (2:50)

2421³ TWIN FALLS (Ire) 6-12-0 J Callaghan, *jmpd wl, made most frm 5th, clr appr 3 out, readily*..........(8 to 1 op 9 to 2) 1
2576* ROBERTY LEA 9-11-8 P Niven, *chsd ldrs, mstk 4th, rdn and lost tch 9th, styd on 2 out, nvr nrr.*
.................(Evens fav op 11 to 10 on tchd 11 to 10) 2
2240 KILLBALLY BOY (Ire) 7-11-2 A Thornton, *led to 5th, pressed wnr till outpcd appr 3 out, sn no extr...* (8 to 1 tchd 7 to 1) 3
2486⁶ DANDY DES PLAUTS (Fr) 6-11-2 T Reed, *hld up, struggling whn hit 9th, sn wl beh*...............(66 to 1 op 50 to 1) 4
2575⁵ COOL LUKE (Ire) 8-11-2 P Carberry, *chsd ldrs, not fluent 6th, drvn and outpcd 4 out, btn whn pckd nxt.* (4 to 1 op 3 to 1) 5
2486² FRIENDLY KNIGHT 7-11-2 A S Smith, *refused to race.*
.................(7 to 1 op 8 to 1 tchd 10 to 1) ref
2534⁸ MISS LAMPLIGHT 7-10-11 A Dobbin, *mstk 3rd, pushed alng in rear 7th, wl beh whn pld up tenth...* (50 to 1 op 25 to 1) pu
Dist: 5l, 13l, 2½l, 8l. 5m 9.30s. a 39.30s (7 Ran).
(Mrs Susan Moore), G M Moore

2855 Ripon Selling Handicap Hurdle Class G (0-90 4-y-o and up) £2,009 2m .... (3:20)

2651⁴ SILVER MINX [78] 5-11-2 P Niven, *led, mstk 5th, rdn and hdd 2 out, rallied to ld last, drvn clr.*
.................(9 to 2 tchd 5 to 1 and 6 to 1) 1
2202⁵ CHUMMY'S SAGA [73] (bl) 7-10-11 R Supple, *chsd ldrs, led gng wl appr 2 out, mstk and hdd last, no extr.*
.................(7 to 1 op 5 to 1) 2
2420⁶ ARTHUR BEE [62] 10-10-0 B Storey, *gd hdwy to press ldrs 4th, ev ch frm 3 out, one pace frm nxt.*
.................(9 to 1 op 8 to 1 tchd 10 to 1) 3
2485 STORMING LORNA (Ire) [62] 7-10-0 G Cahill, *not fluent in rear, rdn and outpcd 3 out, styd on frm nxt, unbl to chal.*
.................(20 to 1 frm tchd 25 to 1) 4
2577⁴ ROBSERA (Ire) [90] 6-11-9 (5*) R McGrath, *hld up, some hdwy 3 out, outpcd bef nxt*..............(8 to 1 op 7 to 1) 5
2577⁷ COOL STEEL (Ire) [70] 5-10-8 P Carberry, *midfield, short of room on same aftr 3 out, one pace in 4th whn blun nxt, sn btn.*
.................(11 to 1 op 8 to 1 tchd 12 to 1) 6
2485⁹ NOSMO KING (Ire) [64] 6-10-2 Mrs M Kendall, *blun 1st, cl up till 3 out, sn wknd*..................(20 to 1) 7
2630⁶ TIOTAO (Ire) [66] 7-10-4 D Parker, *in tch, drvn and outpcd aftr 3 out, sn wknd*..............(8 to 1 op 6 to 1) 8
2485⁵ KIERCHEM (Ire) [71] 6-10-6 (3*) Michael Brennan, *hld up, mstk 4th, drvn and wknd frm 3 out.*
.................(9 to 1 op 5 to 1 tchd 4 to 1) 9
2629⁶ PAST MASTER (USA) [77] 9-11-1 N Williamson, *reminders 3rd, towards rear whn blun badly 5th, sn wl beh.*
.................(11 to 2 op 7 to 1 tchd 4 to 1) 10
2570⁸ TRIONA'S HOPE (Ire) [62] 8-9-9² (7*) Tristan Davidson, *chsd ldrs till wknd quickly aftr 4 out, tld off*.........(100 to 1) 11
2581 BIRTHPLACE (Ire) [72] 7-10-3 (7*) N Horrocks, *pld hrd, cl up till wknd quickly 3 out, beh whn pulled up nxt.*
.... pu
2238 EUROLINK THE REBEL (USA) [89] 5-11-13 R Garritty, *hld up, effrt to chase ldrs 4 out, lost tch frm nxt, beh whn pld up 2 out.*
.................(25 to 1 op 16 to 1) pu
Dist: 4l, 10l, 1¼l, nk, 2l, 10l, 9l, 20l, 7l. 4m 2.90s. a 22.90s (13 Ran).
SR: 11/2/-/-/4/-/   (Mrs E A Kettlewell), Mrs M Reveley

2856 Barton Novices' Handicap Hurdle Class E (0-100 4-y-o and up) £2,668

3m 1f 110yds................. (3:50)

2655²	PILKINGTON (Ire) [84] 7-11-5 P Carberry, *led 5th, hit 7th, clr whn blun last, cmftbly*.......... (11 to 4 fav tchd 3 to 1)	1
2578*	RUBER [80] 10-11-1 D Parker, *al hndy, drvn alng frm 4 out, styd on stdly, no ch wth wnr*........ (6 to 1 op 5 to 1)	2
2152⁹	CYPRESS AVENUE (Ire) [89] 5-11-10 N Williamson, *beh, struggling frm 4 out, nvr a factor*...... (20 to 1 op 16 to 1)	3
2635*	MR CHRISTIE [88] 5-11-9 A Thornton, *chsd ldrs, drvn and lost tch 4 out, sn no dngr...* (9 to 2 op 4 to 1 tchd 5 to 1)	4
1987³	CORBLEU (Ire) [72] 7-10-7 K Johnson, *led to 5th, chsd ldr till outpcd aftr 3 out, wknd*.............(14 to 1 op 12 to 1)	5
2635	CASH BOX (Ire) [78] 9-10-13 N Smith, *settled rear, mstk 6th, struggling 4 out, sn wl beh*........... (11 to 2 op 6 to 1)	6
2359	GREENFIELD MANOR [68] 10-9-12 (5*) S Taylor, *hld up, pushed alng in midfield whn blun 5 out, sn fdd, tld off*........................... (25 to 1 op 16 to 1)	7
2575⁶	FRO [83] 4-10-6 B Storey, *hld up, improved to chase ldrs fnl circuit, wknd quickly aftr 3 out, tld off*....................... (11 to 2 op 5 to 1 tchd 6 to 1)	8
2650	DON'T TELL JUDY (Ire) [72] 9-10-0 (7*) N Horrocks, *hld up, struggling fnl circuit, sn tld off*....... (25 to 1 op 20 to 1)	9
2635	CANONBIEBOTHERED [65] 6-10-0 F Perratt, *al rear, tld off frm 3 out*..........................(50 to 1 op 33 to 1)	10
2346	BUSY BOY [68] 10-10-3 J Burke, *midfield, wknd quickly fnl circuit, sn tld off*.........................(50 to 1 op 33 to 1)	11
1971	ESCADARO (USA) [70] (v) 8-10-5¹² (7*) M Berry, *cl up, wkng whn f 6th, dead*....................(150 to 1 op 100 to 1)	f
2740²	RELUCKINO [78] (v) 7-10-10 (3*) Michael Brennan, *wth ldrs, struggling fnl circuit, wl tld off whn pld up aftr 3 out*.............................(9 to 2 op 3 to 1 tchd 5 to 1)	pu

Dist: 11l, 17l, 17l, nk, 5l, ½l, 6l, dist, 19l, dist. 6m 44.50s. a 43.50s (13 Ran).

(Mrs Alurie O'Sullivan), J Howard Johnson

2857 Greta Bridge Handicap Chase Class E (0-115 5-y-o and up) £2,842 2m
.... (4:20)

2654*	WEAVER GEORGE (Ire) [105] 7-11-9 M Moloney, *hld up, gd hdwy to ld aftr 4 out, clr nxt, mstk last, readily.*........................(15 to 8 fav op 11 to 8 tchd 2 to 1)	1
2486	MOSS PAGEANT [82] 7-10-0 B Storey, *str hold, led till hdd aftr 4 out, kpt on same pace, no ch wth wnr.*............................(100 to 1 op 50 to 1)	2
1873²	NEWHALL PRINCE [110] (v) 9-12-0 T Eley, *chsd ldrs, hit 6th, drvn and no imprsn appr 3 out.*....... (5 to 1 tchd 6 to 1)	3
2826³	MARLINGFORD [82] 10-9-7 (7*) L McGrath, *chsd ldr, losing pl whn blun 5 out, sn beh.*................(6 to 1 op 8 to 1)	4
2685²	REBEL KING [84] 7-9-11 (5*) S Taylor, *not fluent in rear, wl beh whn pld up aftr 4 out...*(8 to 1 op 5 to 1 tchd 9 to 1)	pu
2547²	JACK DOYLE (Ire) [100] 6-11-4 N Williamson, *hld up, niggled alng and lost tch 4 out, beh whn pld up aftr nxt.*........................(9 to 4 op 2 to 1)	pu

Dist: 7l, 6l, 11l. 4m 9.10s. a 22.10s (6 Ran).

SR: 26/-/18/   (Regent Decorators Ltd), W Storey

2858 Aysgarth Intermediate National Hunt Flat Class H (4,5,6-y-o) £1,255 2m
.... (4:50)

	SPIRIT OF STEEL 4-10-1 (7*) R McCarthy, *cl up, led on bit 6 fs out, clr entering strt, drvn out.*........................(7 to 1 op 6 to 1 tchd 8 to 1)	1
1989⁵	FIRST LIGHT 5-11-4 G Tormey, *in tch, drvn to chase wnr appr strt, styd on wl.*...........(11 to 4 op 3 to 1 tchd 7 to 2)	2
1887⁸	JENNIE'S PROSPECT 6-10-13 (5*) R McGrath, *chsd ldrs frm hfwy, rdn and outpcd entering strt.*........................(11 to 2 op 3 to 1 tchd 6 to 1)	3
	THE GNOME 5-11-1 (3*) Michael Brennan, *hld up, pushed alng 5 fs out, sn no imprsn.*........................(11 to 1 op 7 to 2 tchd 8 to 1)	4
2687³	THUNDERPOINT 5-11-4 G Cahill, *midfield, lost tch 5 fs out, no dngr aftr.*.................. (5 to 2 fav tchd 3 to 1)	5
2623⁶	COOL KEVIN 4-10-8 Mrs M Kendall, *sn niggled alng in rear, wl beh 5 fs out, moderate late hdwy.*...............(33 to 1)	6
2687	SHANNON SHOON (Ire) 5-10-13 (5*) G F Ryan, *midfield, struggling 4 fs out, sn beh, eased whn btn.*........ (33 to 1)	7
1742⁶	AIR BRIDGE 5-11-1 (3*) E Husband, *led till hdd 6 fs out, wknd quickly appr strt.*........................(20 to 1)	8
2623	CHAN MOVE 5-10-13 (5*) S Taylor, *wl beh frm hfwy.*........................(200 to 1)	9
	DASH ON BY 4-10-5 (3*) G Lee, *in tch, struggling 4 fs out, sn wknd.*....................... (33 to 1 op 20 to 1)	10
2402²	DANTE'S GOLD (Ire) 6-10-13 (5*) Sophie Mitchell, *pld hrd, wth ldrs till wknd quickly 4 fs out.*....... (5 to 1 tchd 4 fs)	11
1968⁷	BROOK HOUSE 6-10-6 (7*) C McCormack, *tld off fnl 4 fs.*..............................(20 to 1 op 16 to 1)	12

Dist: 4l, 16l, 16l, 5l, 1¼l, 1¼l, sht-hd, dist, ½l, 1¼l. 3m 59.20s. (12 Ran).

(T P Tate), T P Tate

LEICESTER (good)
Tuesday February 25th
Going Correction: PLUS 0.55 sec. per fur.

2859 Pickwell Novices' Handicap Chase Class E (0-100 5-y-o and up) £3,315 2½m 110yds................. (2:10)

2690	RED BRANCH (Ire) [71] 8-10-0 J Culloty, *made all, jmpd lft last 3, rallied whn chlgd r-in, all out.*.......................(4 to 1 op 5 to 2 tchd 9 to 2)	1
2266²	SCORESHEET (Ire) [95] 7-11-10 P Hide, *blun second, hld up, hdwy 4 out, rdn appr 2 out, pressed wnr r-in.*........................(3 to 1 fav tchd 100 to 30 and 9 to 4)	2
2354⁵	HANGOVER [72] 11-10-1 A Maguire, *trkd wnr most of way, rdn and wknd appr last.*.................. (9 to 1 op 7 to 1)	3
2683³	KILTULLA (Ire) [71] 7-9-7 (7*) R Wilkinson, *al prmnt, ev ch 3 out, wknd aftr nxt.*..................(6 to 1 op 5 to 1)	4
2761⁶	KNOCKREIGH CROSS [71] 8-10-0 B Powell, *mstk 1st, al beh, tld off whn hmpd 4 out.*.................... (100 to 1)	5
2596	MINI FETE (Fr) [71] (bl) 8-10-0 S Fox, *prmnt to 7th, sn beh, tld off.*..............................(66 to 1 op 50 to 1)	6
2304	SMART CASANOVA [71] 8-10-0 T J O'Sullivan, *al beh, tld off.*......................... (25 to 1 op 16 to 1)	7
2604⁹	BATHWICK BOBBIE [72] 10-9-12 (3*) Guy Lewis, *sn rdn, al beh, tld off.*.............(20 to 1 op 16 to 1 tchd 25 to 1)	8
2604⁶	EULOGY (Fr) [79] 10-10-8 A Larnach, *al beh, tld off.*.......................(14 to 1 op 12 to 1 tchd 16 to 1)	9
2487	PRINCE BALTASAR [71] 8-9-7 (7*) A Scholes, *prmnt, wkng in 5th whn f 4 out.*............................(100 to 1)	f
2547⁶	GLENDOE (Ire) [79] 6-10-8 G Upton, *hld up, rear whn f 8th.*.............................(6 to 1 op 5 to 1 tchd 7 to 1)	f
2748²	SUPER RITCHART [84] 9-10-13 R Farrant, *blun and uns rdr second.*.............(9 to 2 op 4 to 1 tchd 5 to 1)	ur
2626⁵	ALTHREY ARISTOCRAT (Ire) [71] 7-10-0 S McNeill, *badly hmpd second, pld up bef nxt.*....................(100 to 1)	pu

Dist: Sht-hd, 11l, 3l, dist, 1¼l, 9l, 8l, 9l. 5m 22.60s. a 20.60s (13 Ran).

(E J Mangan), J S King

2860 Dragon Handicap Chase Class E (0-110 6-y-o and up) £3,315 3m
.... (2:40)

2759⁵	FARNEY GLEN [87] 10-10-6 A Maguire, *hld up, hdwy 14th, led appr last, sn clr, fnshd lme.*........... (3 to 1 op 5 to 1)	1
	REAPERS ROCK [81] 10-10-0 R Wilkinson, *hld up, hdwy 5th, led 13th, rdn and hdd appr last, one pace.*......................(10 to 1 op 6 to 1)	2
2401*	SIMPSON [91] 12-10-10 G Upton, *not jump wl in rear, styd on frm 3 out, nvr nrr.*.............. (5 to 4 fav op 11 to 10 on tchd 11 to 8)	3
2604	NIGHT FANCY [81] 9-10-0 J A McCarthy, *prmnt, led tenth to 13th, wknd appr 3 out.*..........(40 to 1 op 25 to 1)	4
2389	FAR SENIOR [105] 11-11-10 S Wynne, *beh 5th, tld off whn pld up bef tenth.*................. (33 to 1 op 20 to 1)	pu
2395	COASTING [81] 11-10-0 B Clifford, *led to second, wknd 9th, pld up bef 2 out.*..............(14 to 1 op 10 to 1)	pu
2247	CANTORIS FRATER [101] 10-11-6 B Powell, *made most frm second to tenth, wknd 13th, tld off whn pld up bef 3 out.*.............(7 to 2 op 3 to 1 tchd 4 to 1)	pu
2392	LODESTONE LAD (Ire) [85] 7-10-4 J Culloty, *in tch, mstk tenth, sn beh, tld off whn pld up bef 4 out.*.........................(12 to 1 op 8 to 1)	pu

Dist: 5l, 15l, 6l. 6m 17.90s. a 32.90s (8 Ran).

(Mrs A Meller), J J O'Neill

2861 Syston Handicap Chase Class B (0-110 5-y-o and up) £2,906 2½m 110yds...................... (3:10)

2318³	LANCE ARMSTRONG (Ire) [103] 7-11-11 (3*) D Fortt, *trkd ldr to 5th, hit 7th, wnt second 4 out, led nxt, styd on.*..............(11 to 8 fav op Evens tchd 6 to 4)	1
2690*	JULEIT JONES (Ire) [87] 8-10-9 (3*) L Aspell, *led till appr 3 out, rdn and no imprsn nxt.*..............(3 to 1 tchd 7 to 2)	2
2759⁶	DOLIKOS [97] 10-11-8 D Walsh, *beh 6th, tld off.*..............................(16 to 1 tchd 20 to 1)	3
2686	ROYAL PARIS (Ire) [75] 9-9-7 (7*) R Wilkinson, *al beh, tld off whn blun and uns rdr 2 out, rmntd.*....(20 to 1 op 16 to 1)	4
2666³	JAILBREAKER [81] 10-10-1 (5*) D Salter, *trkd ldr 5th to 4 out, rdn and chalg whn f nxt.*............. (7 to 2 tchd 4 to 1)	f
593³	BALLAD RULER [75] 11-10-0 R Bellamy, *al beh, tld off whn pld up bef tenth.*........(100 to 1 op 66 to 1)	pu
2268⁷	LITTLE-NIPPER [95] 12-11-6 C Maude, *al beh, tld off whn pld up bef 11th.*..............(5 to 1 op 7 to 1)	pu

Dist: 8l, dist, dist. 5m 22.50s. a 20.50s (7 Ran).

SR: 8/-/-/-/   (G L Porter), G M McCourt

2862 Rutland Water Novices' Chase Class D (6-y-o and up) £4,207 3m... (3:40)

	MASTER TOBY 7-10-12 C Llewellyn, *al prominent, chlgd frm 3 out, rdn to ld r-in, cleverly.*............ (11 to 4 op 6 to 1)	1
2328³	LIVELY KNIGHT (Ire) 8-11-4 P Hide, *al prmnt, led tenth, rdn and hdd r-in.*..................(11 to 4 jt-fav op 5 to 2)	2
2597³	WHO IS EQUINAME (Ire) 7-10-12 J R Kavanagh, *prmnt, ev ch whn mstk 4 out, rdn and wknd 2 out.*.............(11 to 4 jt-fav op 7 to 2)	3
2748	LITTLE GAINS 8-10-12 J Railton, *led, hit tenth and hdd, ev ch 3 out, wknd quickly, tld off.*....................... (100 to 1)	4

2566 MAJOR NOVA 8-10-12 J Culloty, *hmpd second, al beh, tld off.*
.... (25 to 1 op 66 to 1) 5
2700⁹ BETTER FUTURE (Ire) 8-10-12 R Johnson, *jmpd slwly 1st, sn beh, tld off* .... (25 to 1 op 20 to 1 tchd 33 to 1) 6
2566 MUSICAL HIT (bl) 6-10-12 R Bellamy, *hld up, hdwy 7th, wknd 9th, tld off.* .... (100 to 1) 7
2403⁷ NORDIC FLIGHT 9-10-12 V Slattery, *hmpd second, al beh, tld off* .... (100 to 1) 8
      BEAR CLAW (bl) 8-10-12 J Osborne, *f 1st.*
.... (3 to 1 op 7 to 4) f
      FOXWOODS VALLEY (Ire) 8-10-12 A Maguire, *f second.*
.... (11 to 2 op 5 to 1 tchd 6 to 1) f
2441 SWIFT POKEY 7-10-12 M Clarke, *prmnt, wknd 9th, tld off whn refused 11th.* .... (100 to 1) ref
2418⁴ DEAR JEAN 7-10-4 (3*) F Leahy, *beh, tld off whn pld up bef tenth.* .... (100 to 1) pu
      STRONG GLEN 9-10-12 S Wynne, *al beh, tld off whn pld up bef 11th.* .... (100 to 1) pu
Dist: 1l, 13l, dist, 10l, 11l, 25l, 15l. 6m 16.80s. a 31.80s (13 Ran).
(R D Russell), N A Twiston-Davies

2863 Great Glen Novices' Chase Class E (5-y-o and up) £3,124 2½m 110yds
.... (4:10)

2312* WILD WEST WIND (Ire) 7-11-8 J Culloty, *blun second, led 8th to 11th, chlgd frm 3 out, lft in ld last, all out.*
.... (11 to 8 op 5 to 4 tchd 6 to 4) 1
2624⁴ MACGEORGE (Ire) 7-12-0 R Johnson, *led, blun and hdd second, led 7th, hit nxt and headed, led 11th, hit last and headed, rallied.* .... (6 to 4 on op 7 to 4 on) 2
2406⁶ GEMMA'S WAGER (Ire) 7-10-11 L Harvey, *hld up, hdwy 5th, wknd 7th, tld off tenth.* (25 to 1 op 50 to 1 tchd 100 to 1) 3
      DEEP SONG 9-11-2 R Bellamy, *pld hrd, lft in ld second, hdd 7th, wknd quickly, tld off....* (150 to 1 op 50 to 1) 4
      CRAIGHILL (Ire) 8-11-2 J R Kavanagh, *beh, blun 4th, remote 3rd whn hit 3 out, pld up bef nxt.....* (20 to 1 op 8 to 1) pu
Dist: ¾l, dist, dist. 5m 22.60s. a 20.60s (5 Ran).
(Lord Vestey), Miss H C Knight

2864 Oakham Handicap Chase Class E (0-110 5-y-o and up) £2,933 2m 1f
.... (4:40)

2176 SCOTTISH BAMBI [105] 9-12-0 J Osborne, *hld up, lost pl 7th, hdwy to go second 3 out, led last, rdn out.* (5 to 1 op 9 to 2) 1
2629⁴ CHILL WIND [87] 8-10-10 M Foster, *hld up rear, hdwy 6th, rdn appr 3 out, styd on to go second r-in........* (100 to 30 jt-fav op 7 to 2) 2
2606* THATS THE LIFE [77] 12-10-0 R Johnson, *hdwy to 5th, led 4 out till rdn and hdd last, one pace.* .... (100 to 30 jt-fav op 7 to 2 tchd 3 to 1) 3
2470² DEAR DO [103] 10-11-12 J R Kavanagh, *hld up in tch, rdn appr 3 out, one pace aftr...* (7 to 2 op 4 to 1 tchd 9 to 2) 4
2547⁸ CAWARRA BOY [93] 9-11-2 Mr E James, *hld up, rdn 7th, no hdwy frm 4 out........* (9 to 1 op 8 to 1 tchd 10 to 1) 5
2606⁵ PEGMARINE (USA) [77] 14-10-0 J A McCarthy, *chsd ldrs till wknd 7th.* .... (12 to 1) 6
2606² DR ROCKET [82] (bl) 12-9-12 (7*) A Aizpuru, *trkd ldr, led 5th to 4 out, rdn and wknd quickly aftr nxt.....* (6 to 1 op 14 to 1) 7
2729 CHURCHTOWN PORT (Ire) [99] 7-11-5 (3*) L Aspell, *beh, blun 5th, sn tld off, pld up bef 3 out.......* (16 to 1 op 14 to 1) pu
Dist: 4l, 3l, 4l, 5l, 1¼l, 23l. 4m 24.80s. a 16.80s (8 Ran).
SR: 26/4/-/13/-/ (William J Kelly), P R Webber

DOWNPATRICK (IRE) (heavy)
Wednesday February 26th

2865 Morning Star Belfast Opportunity Maiden Hurdle (6-y-o and up) £1,712 2m 1f 172yds
.... (2:30)

2735⁷ EUROTHATCH (Ire) 9-11-4 (2*) T Martin, ...(9 to 4 fav) 1
2703⁷ RYTHM ROCK (Ire) 8-11-2 (4*) A O'Shea, ...(3 to 1) 2
2583⁸ HEART 'N SOUL-ON (Ire) 6-11-2 (4*) D K Budds, ..(10 to 1) 3
2520 BORLEAGH PILOT (Ire) 6-11-6 K Whelan, ...(20 to 1) 4
2839 JUST 'R JAKE (Ire) 8-11-2 (4*) M D Murphy, ...(33 to 1) 5
2382 SPECTACLE (Ire) (bl) 7-11-6 J Butler, ...(16 to 1) 6
2704⁶ BRACKENVALE (Ire) 6-10-11 (4*) D A McLoughlin, ..(7 to 1) 7
1649 CARNANEE (Ire) 7-11-2 (4*) S FitzGerald, ...(33 to 1) 8
2585 HANNAH'S PET (Ire) 7-11-1 D Bromley, ...(25 to 1) 9
2039 STAR OF FERMANAGH (Ire) 8-11-2 (4*) S M McGovern,
.... (33 to 1) 10
2582 GOLDWREN (Ire) 8-10-11 (4*) N Hannity, ...(33 to 1) 11
2041⁹ LORD NOAN (Ire) 7-11-2 (4*) K A Kelly, ...(33 to 1) 12
2649⁸ PHAREIGN (Ire) 6-11-2 (4*) J M Maguire, ...(7 to 1) f
2582 ANNAELAINE (Ire) 6-11-5 (4*) B J Geraghty, ...(7 to 1) bd
2752 CLOSING THYNE (Ire) 6-10-11 (4*) L J Fleming, ..(14 to 1) pu
Dist: 7l, 4½l, sht-hd, 14l. 4m 41.10s. (15 Ran).
(Ballymac Racing Syndicate), George Stewart

2866 Potter Cowan Electrical Maiden Hurdle (4 & 5-y-o) £1,712 2m 1f 172yds
.... (3:00)

2735⁵ MIDDLEOFTHENIGHT (Ire) 5-10-5 (7*) L J Fleming,
.... (5 to 2 fav) 1
2343 LOVELY LYNSEY (Ire) 5-10-5 (7*) Mr A J Dempsey,
.... (25 to 1) 2
2703 COLONEL GEORGE 5-11-8 (3*) K Whelan, ...(8 to 1) 3
2379⁸ SCATHACH (Ire) 5-10-5 (7*) R J Gordon, ...(14 to 1) 4
2447 AUTOBABBLE (Ire) 4-10-11 T P Rudd, ...(16 to 1) 5
2669⁶ COMRADE CHINNERY (Ire) 4-11-2 J P Broderick, ..(8 to 1) 6
2583 DUNMORE DOM (Ire) 5-11-3 A Powell, ...(33 to 1) 7
2643 BAILENAGUN (Ire) 4-10-4 (7*) B J Geraghty, ...(20 to 1) 8
      THE MALL (Ire) 5-11-8 (3*) Mr B R Hamilton, ...(4 to 1) 9
      TAP PRACTICE (Ire) 5-10-10 (7*) J M Maguire, ..(16 to 1) 10
2645⁶ BOULABALLY (Ire) 5-11-3 K F O'Brien, ...(9 to 2) 11
2379 ABIGAIL ROSE (Bel) 5-10-12 H Rogers, ...(14 to 1) 12
2383⁹ CARA GAIL (Ire) 5-10-12 C O'Dwyer, ...(12 to 1) 13
2582 LADY OF GRANGE (Ire) (bl) 5-11-6 F J Flood, ..(12 to 1) f
2588⁶ JONS GALE (Ire) 5-10-12 (5*) T Martin, ...(12 to 1) f
Dist: 11l, 7l, 8l, 5l. 4m 35.90s. (15 Ran).
(P F Toole), Thomas Carberry

2867 Jameson Ulster National EBF Handicap Chase (5-y-o and up) £7,021 3 ½m
.... (3:30)

2448* TEAL BRIDGE [-] 12-10-4 C O'Dwyer, ...(6 to 1) 1
2756⁵ TOUT VA BIEN [-] 9-9-0 (7*) L J Fleming, ...(10 to 1) 2
2169⁵ FAIRY MIST (Ire) [-] 9-9-2² (7*) R P Hogan, ..(33 to 1) 3
2381⁵ CABBERY ROSE (Ire) [-] 9-9-11 (7*) A O'Shea, ..(25 to 1) 4
2734 FISSURE SEAL [-] 11-11-7 (7*) Mr W Ewing, ...(14 to 1) 5
2381⁴ PENNYBRIDGE (Ire) [-] 8-10-4 L P Cusack, ...(10 to 1) 6
2756 OLYMPIC D'OR (Ire) [-] 9-9-10 D J Casey, ...(14 to 1) 7
2587⁸ OVER THE MAINE (Ire) [-] 7-9-8 P McWilliams, ..(25 to 1) 8
2273⁶ MONKEY AGO [-] 10-10-5 (3*) K Whelan, ...(16 to 1) 9
2448⁴ DIORRAING (Ire) [-] 12-10-9 (7*) J M Maguire, ..(25 to 1) 10
2756⁹ FINAL TUB [-] 14-10-5 T P Treacy, ...(14 to 1) pu
2338² DEE ELL [-] 11-10-3 F Woods, ...(4 to 1 fav) pu
2707* NUAFFE [-] 12-11-13 T J Mitchell, ...(9 to 1) pu
2734 CORYMANDEL (Ire) [-] 8-11-1 T P Rudd, ...(6 to 1) pu
2381² TRENCH HILL LASS (Ire) [-] 8-10-8 J Shortt, ...(6 to 1) pu
Dist: 6l, 9l, 2½l, 4½l. 7m 42.00s. (15 Ran).
(Mrs M Heffernan), Andrew Heffernan

2868 Downpatrick On Course Bookmakers Beginners' Chase (5-y-o and up) £1,712 2¼m
.... (4:00)

2840 GEALLAINNBAN (Ire) (bl) 7-12-0 C O'Dwyer, ...(5 to 1) 1
2162⁹ HERSILIA (Ire) 6-11-9 F J Flood, ...(8 to 1) 2
2224 SPIRE HILL (Ire) 8-11-9 Mr K Ross, ...(25 to 1) 3
2755³ COLLON (Ire) 8-11-9 J P Broderick, ...(5 to 4 fav) 4
2644⁷ EASTERN FOX (Ire) 8-11-9 D T Evans, ...(14 to 1) 5
      PEDE GALE (Ire) 9-10-11 (7*) J M Maguire, ...(33 to 1) 6
2673 MARIOS POLLY 7-11-9 D O'Connor, ...(7 to 1) 7
1360 CASTLE TIGER BAY (Ire) 6-11-9 T P Treacy, ...(33 to 1) 8
2735 FANE'S TREASURE (Ire) 8-11-7 (7*) B J Geraghty, ..(8 to 1) 9
2648 PENNY POT 5-10-4 (3*) K Whelan, ...(25 to 1) 10
2646 NOELS DANCER (Ire) (bl) 7-11-7 (7*) D K Budds, ..(8 to 1) 11
2587 CLERICAL COUSIN (Ire) 8-11-9 F Woods, ...(12 to 1) pu
2383 TOBYS PAL (Ire) 7-11-9 A Powell, ...(12 to 1) pu
2382⁵ SHUIL DAINGEAN (Ire) 7-11-9 T P Rudd, ...(8 to 1) pu
Dist: 7l, 5½l, 12l, 10l. 4m 58.10s. (14 Ran).
(Kerr Technology Ltd), T J Taaffe

2869 Heart Of Down Hunters' Chase (5-y-o and up) £1,712 3m
.... (4:30)

      YES BOSS (Ire) 7-10-11 (7*) Mr R P McNalley, ..(6 to 4 fav) 1
196⁶ GALE GRIFFIN (Ire) 8-10-13 (5*) Mr L Lennon, ..(2 to 1) 2
623³ ROYAL STAR (Ire) 8-10-11 (7*) Mr T Gibney, ...(16 to 1) 3
      HILTON MILL (Ire) 9-11-4 (5*) Mr R J Patton, ..(8 to 1) 4
      VINTAGE CLASSIC (Ire) 6-11-4 Mr G J Harford, ..(4 to 1) 5
2523⁴ SHAWS CROSS (Ire) 6-11-9 Mr P Fenton, ...(9 to 4) f
      RIAS RASCAL 10-11-2 (7*) Mr A Fleming, ...(16 to 1) pu
      CHENE ROSE (Ire) 9-10-11 (7*) Mr K Ross, ...(12 to 1) pu
      HILTONSTOWN LASS (Ire) 7-10-11 (7*) Mr Richard J Walker,
.... (12 to 1) pu
      PAULS POINT 10-11-2 (7*) Mr A Tate, ...(16 to 1) pu
Dist: 15l, 2½l, 9l, dist. 6m 50.10s. (10 Ran).
(Getting Grey Syndicate), A J Martin

2870 Sean Graham Bookmakers INH Flat Race (4 & 5-y-o) £3,425 2m 1f 172yds
.... (5:00)

2645⁵ ANDREA COVA (Ire) 5-11-2 (7*) Mr A J Dempsey, ..(6 to 1) 1
2383³ RUN SPARKY (Ire) 5-11-5³ (7*) Mr M McNeilly, ..(15 to 1) 2
      WILLYELKRA 5-12-0 Mr P Fenton, ...(3 to 1) 3
2588⁹ THE TICK-TACK MAN (Ire) 5-11-9 (5*) Mr A C Coyle,
.... (10 to 1) 4D
      MRS DOYLE (Ire) 5-11-9 Mr D Marnane, ...(14 to 1) 4
2709 SEVEN AIRS (Ire) 5-11-2 (7*) Mr M T Hartrey, ..(14 to 1) 5
2588⁵ MONAVALE (Ire) 5-11-9 Mr G J Harford, ...(5 to 4 fav) 6
      SPRING CABBAGE (Ire) 5-11-7 (7*) Mr L Madine, ..(10 to 1) 7
      ZAFFRIDGE (Ire) 5-11-2 (7*) Mr G T Cuthbert, ..(20 to 1) 8
      SHEQUANAH (Ire) 5-11-2 (7*) Mr G T Morrow, ..(16 to 1) 9
1279 VALLEY PLAYER (Ire) 5-11-7 (7*) Mr M O'Connor, ..(20 to 1) pu
Dist: 7l, 14l, dist, sht-hd. 4m 34.40s. (11 Ran).

(Basil Brindley), Victor Bowens

TAUNTON (good to soft (races 1,2,3,4,5,6), good (7,8))
Wednesday February 26th
Going Correction: PLUS 1.35 sec. per fur.

2871 Taunton 'National Hunt' Novices' Hurdle Class D (Div I) (4-y-o and up) £2,567 2m 3f 110yds........ (1:50)

1893[7] STRONG PALADIN (Ire) 6-11-1 (3*) L Aspell, mstk second, hdwy 7th, styd on appr 2 out, chlgd last, led r-in, all out.
.................(7 to 2 op 3 to 1 tchd 4 to 1) 1
2426[5] MASTER PILGRIM 5-11-4 A P McCoy, rapid hdwy to track ldrs 6th, rdn and ev ch last, styd on und pres r-in, no extr nr finish........................(5 to 2 fav op 9 to 4 tchd 11 to 4) 2
2243[2] DEFENDTHEREALM 6-11-4 J Frost, led 3rd to 3 out, rallied to ld ag'n appr last, hdd and one pace r-in. (6 to 1 op 9 to 2) 3
1476[5] JUST JASMINE 5-10-13 R Greene, chsd ldrs till led 3 out, hdd appr last, sn one pace...............(12 to 1 op 7 to 1) 4
1685[5] MOONLIGHT ESCAPADE (Ire) 6-11-1 (3*) T Dascombe, mstk 1st, hdwy 6th, no headway frm 2 out.
.................(25 to 1 op 12 to 1 tchd 33 to 1) 5
2311 CONNAUGHT'S PRIDE 6-10-13 N Williamson, al in rear.
.................(15 to 1 op 16 to 1 tchd 33 to 1) 6
2662[5] WALTER'S DESTINY 5-11-4 S McNeill, pressed ldrs to 3 out, sn wknd........................(20 to 1 op 16 to 1) 7
2546[8] FRED FUGGLES 5-10-13 (5*) O Burrows, in tch, rdn 5th, wknd aftr nxt.......................(50 to 1 op 20 to 1) 8
2430[8] SOUTHERNHAY BOY (bl) 6-11-4 Mr I Dowrick, with ldrs to 5th, tld off pld up aftr 3 out.
.................(25 to 1 op 12 to 1 tchd 33 to 1) pu
2264 DOUBLE ACHIEVEMENT (Ire) 7-11-4 C Maude, beh frm 5th, tld off whn pld up aftr 3 out...........(33 to 1 op 12 to 1) pu
1012[4] STRIKE A LIGHT (Ire) 5-11-4 J Culloty, chsd ldrs to 7th, wknd aftr 3 out, pld up bef last...........(7 to 2 op 9 to 2) pu
COOL CAT (Ire) 6-11-4 R Bellamy, prmnt to 4th, mstk 5th and sn beh, tld off whn pld up bef 2 out.
.................(50 to 1 op 33 to 1 tchd 66 to 1) pu
2614 ORCHID HOUSE 5-10-13 D Skyrme, sn beh, tld off whn pld up bef 3 out.....................(100 to 1 op 33 to 1) pu
2377 GREMATIC 6-11-4 J Railton, beh frm 6th, mstk and pld up 3 out....................(50 to 1 op 20 to 1 tchd 66 to 1) pu
Dist: Hd, 1¼l, nk, 16l, 2½l, 1¼l, 15l. 4m 59.40s. a 41.40s (14 Ran).

(Mrs Angela Brodie), J T Gifford

2872 Pitminster Selling Handicap Hurdle Class G (0-95 4-y-o and up) £1,931 2m 1f.......................(2:20)

2607[8] BLADE OF FORTUNE [68] 9-10-6[6] (7*) Mr J Tizzard, made all, wnt clr appr 5th, unchlgd................(10 to 1 op 12 to 1) 1
2783 SAAFI (Ire) [70] (bl) 6-10-9 V Slattery, hdwy 5th, mstk and chsd wnr 3 out, no imprsn..............(14 to 1 op 33 to 1) 2
2603[6] ALMAPA [82] 5-11-4 (3*) T Dascombe, hdwy 5th, styd on same pace frm 3 out.
.................(7 to 1 op 6 to 1 tchd 15 to 2 and 8 to 1) 3
2663[7] SHANAKEE [73] 10-10-12 Mr J L Llewellyn, some hdwy frm 5th, no prog from 3 out.
.................(12 to 1 tchd 14 to 1 and 16 to 1) 4
POOH STICK [68] 7-10-7[3] J Frost, some hdwy 6th, wknd aftr 3 out......................(14 to 1 tchd 16 to 1) 5
2663 MICK THE YANK (Ire) [63] (v) 7-10-2 Jacqui Oliver, al in rear.
.................(20 to 1 tchd 25 to 1) 6
2515 THEM TIMES (Ire) [61] 8-10-0 S Wynne, chsd wnr, hit 3rd, lost second 5th, wknd nxt.. (16 to 1 op 12 to 1 tchd 20 to 1) 7
2387[8] DENOMINATION (USA) [84] 5-11-2 (7*) B Moore, in tch, rdn and wknd 6th.........(25 to 1 op 16 to 1 tchd 33 to 1) 8
2610[8] MINSTER'S MADAM [86] (v) 6-11-6 (5*) A Bates, nvr better than mid-div......................(10 to 1 op 6 to 1) 9
VA UTU [82] 9-11-0 (7*) J Prior, prmnt, chsd wnr 5th to 3 out, sn wknd.................(25 to 1 op 16 to 1 tchd 33 to 1) 10
2390 RED PHANTOM (Ire) [70] (v) 5-10-9 N Mann, al beh, lost tch frm 5th.......................(14 to 1 op 20 to 1) 11
2665[6] ALICE'S MIRROR [68] (bl) 8-10-7 R Greene, blun and uns rdr 1st.....................(9 to 1 op 5 to 1 tchd 10 to 1) ur
2768[*] KILLING TIME [79] 6-11-4 (7ex) D J Burchell, blun and uns rdr second. (4 to 1 fav op 9 to 2 tchd 4 to 1 and 11 to 2) ur
2767 DREWITT'S DANCER [69] 10-10-8 D Bridgwater, beh frm 5th, tld off whn pld up bef 2 out.
.................(12 to 1 tchd 14 to 1 tchd 11 to 1) pu
2431[4] OCTOBER BREW (USA) [89] (bl) 7-12-0 A P McCoy, lost tch 5th, sn tld off, pld up aftr 3 out.
.................(8 to 1 op 7 to 1 tchd 9 to 1) pu
Dist: 20l, 6l, 1l, 19l, 5l, 1½l, 8l, 3l, 7l, 16l. 4m 15.50s. a 32.50s (15 Ran).

(V G Greenway), V G Greenway

2873 Bet With The Tote Novices' Chase Qualifier Class D (6-y-o and up) £3,712 3m.......................(2:50)

2527[3] FOXTROT ROMEO 7-10-10 G Bradley, led 6th to 14th, led ag'n 4 out, sn clr, mstk last, cmftbly. (6 to 4 fav op 5 to 4)

2244[2] MR PLAYFULL 7-11-3 J Frost, led 5th to nxt, styd chasing ldrs, chlgd 13th, stayed on one pace frm 3 out.
.................(9 to 1 op 6 to 1 tchd 11 to 1) 2
2638[3] INDIAN DELIGHT 7-10-10 C Maude, hit 8th and wl beh, moderate hdwy frm 3 out.
.................(13 to 2 op 10 to 1 tchd 11 to 1) 3
2748 EKEUS (Ire) 7-10-10 J Culloty, led second to 5th, chlgd 13th, led nxt, hdd 4 out, sn wknd.
.................(13 to 1 op 25 to 1 tchd 50 to 1) 4
2741[5] BELLS WOOD 8-10-10 S McNeill, effrt 12th, wknd aftr nxt, tld off.......................(50 to 1 op 20 to 1) 5
2612[4] DRESS DANCE (Ire) 7-10-5 (5*) Sophie Mitchell, hit 3rd, chsd ldrs, hit 6th, chlgd 9th, second and hld whn 13 out.
.................(33 to 1 op 14 to 1) f
2726 BROGEEN LADY (Ire) 7-10-5 A P McCoy, led to second, chalg whn f 4th.......................(9 to 1 op 7 to 1 tchd 11 to 2) f
SILVER HILL 7-10-4[2] (3*) P Henley, beh whn f 7th.
.................(13 to 1 op 14 to 1 tchd 100 to 1) f
1957 BULLANGUERO (Ire) 8-10-10 G Tormey, hit 3rd, rdn and rear 7th, tld off whn pld up bef 13th......(100 to 1 op 50 to 1) pu
2030[5] ITS GRAND 8-10-10 S Fox, chsd ldrs early, beh 11th, mstk nxt, tld off whn pld up bef 3 out.
.................(50 to 1 op 20 to 1 tchd 66 to 1) pu
2406 BROWN ROBBER 9-10-10 C Llewellyn, hit 11th, hdwy nxt, wknd 14th, tld off whn pld up bef 3 out.
.................(14 to 1 op 10 to 1 tchd 40 to 1) pu
1451[6] STRONG TARQUIN 7-11-3 D Bridgwater, beh frm tenth, tld off whn pld up bef 2 out. (15 to 2 op 5 to 1 tchd 8 to 1) pu
REBEL PRIEST (Ire) 7-10-10 N Williamson, some hdwy 13th, staying on but not a dngr whn blun 4 out, tld off when pld up bef 3 out......(20 to 1 op 14 to 1 tchd 25 to 1) pu
CORALETTE (Ire) 7-10-10 J R Kavanagh, hdwy 11th, wknd 14th, tld off whn pld up bef 3 out.
.................(6 to 1 op 3 to 1 tchd 13 to 2) pu
Dist: 17l, 10l, 3l, dist. 6m 31.20s. a 48.20s (14 Ran).

(Lady Cobham), C P E Brooks

2874 Crocombe Novices' Hurdle Class E (4-y-o and up) £2,638 3m 110yds.......................(3:20)

1228[3] MOUNTAIN PATH 7-11-5 J R Kavanagh, in tch, chlgd 3 out, sn led, ran on wl r-in.
.......(Evens fav op 6 to 4 on tchd 11 to 8 and 6 to 4) 1
2766[*] RARE SPREAD (Ire) 7-11-11 A P McCoy, hdwy 8th, staying on in second whn hit 2 out, one pace und pres r-in.
.................(7 to 2 op 4 to 1 tchd 9 to 2 and 3 to 1) 2
1856[4] TE AMO 5-11-5 Jamie Evans, hdwy 5th, lost pos 8th, ran on ag'n frm 2 out, not rch ldrs.
.................(14 to 1 op 8 to 1 tchd 16 to 1) 3
2699[8] LITTLE JAKE (Ire) 7-11-5 D Leahy, al chasing ldrs, rdn 3 out, sn one pace........(12 to 1 op 10 to 1 tchd 14 to 1) 4
2637[3] CREDO BOY 8-11-5 R Greene, prmnt, led 6th to 7th, led aftr 8th till after 3 out, sn wknd.
.................(20 to 1 op 10 to 1 tchd 25 to 1) 5
2747 LOOK IN THE MIRROR 6-11-5 C Llewellyn, hld up, hdwy 8th, wknd 3 out.
.................(15 to 2 op 14 to 1 tchd 16 to 1 and 7 to 1) 6
2637 MR LOVELY (Ire) 6-11-2 (3*) T Dascombe, beh till hdwy aftr 7th, wknd 3 out....(25 to 1 op 20 to 1 tchd 33 to 1) 7
2353[7] TANGLEFOOT TIPPLE 6-11-5 D Bridgwater, beh till brief effrt 8th, sn weakend...................(8 to 1 op 4 to 1) 8
2436 RORY'M (Ire) (bl) 8-10-12 (7*) M Griffiths, mstks, chlgd 4th, hit 5th, sn wknd, tld off whn pld up bef 3 out.
.................(100 to 1 op 50 to 1) pu
2437[*] ALICE SHORELARK 6-11-0 Mr T Greed, led to 6th, led ag'n 7th, hdd aftr nxt, sn wknd, tld off whn pld up bef last.
.................(100 to 1 op 50 to 1) pu
2668 ABBEYDORAN 6-11-0 R Bellamy, chsd ldrs to 8th, sn wknd, tld off whn pld up bef 2 out......(100 to 1 op 50 to 1) pu
MISS GEE-ELL 5-10-11 (3*) Guy Lewis, tld off frm 5th, pld up bef 6th.......................(100 to 1 op 50 to 1) pu
Dist: 2½l, 5l, 1¼l, 8l, 5l, 13l, 29l. 6m 24.00s. a 56.00s (12 Ran).

(Anthony Speelman), N J Henderson

2875 Mitford Slade Challenge Trophy Hunters' Chase Class H (6-y-o and up) £3,631 4¼m 110yds.......(3:50)

2608[3] RUSTY BRIDGE 10-12-8 (7*) Mr R Burton, made all, clr frm 9th, hit 3 out, styd on wl. (20 to 1 op 14 to 1 tchd 25 to 1) 1
2641[*] VICOMPT DE VALMONT 12-12-8 (7*) Mr J Tizzard, sn wl beh, rdn alng frm 7th, hit 22nd, styd on to go second aftr 2 out, not rch wnr...........(Evens fav op 5 to 4 on tchd 11 to 10) 2
2608 KETTLES 10-11-0 (7*) Mr A Phillips, al in tch, effrt to cl on ldrs 16th, styd on same pace frm 3 out.
.................(11 to 2 op 5 to 1 tchd 6 to 1) 3
SIRISAT 13-11-12 (7*) Miss T Blazey, chsd ldrs, blun 11th, styd on ag'n frm 14th, one pace from 3 out.
.................(10 to 1 op 16 to 1 tchd 33 to 1) 4
EXPRESSMENT 13-11-12 (7*) Mr G Penfold, hit 6th, beh frm 12th, tld off........(13 to 2 op 7 to 1 tchd 9 to 1) 5
FINAL EXPRESS 9-11-0 (7*) Miss S Vickery, beh frm 6th, tld off.......................(33 to 1) 6
GOLDEN MAC 10-11-5 (7*) Major O Ellwood, prmnt, wknd 17th, tld off and virtually pld up r-in....(50 to 1 op 33 to 1) 7

NOISY WELCOME 11-11-7² (7*) Mr M P Jones, f 4th.
.... (50 to 1 op 33 to 1 tchd 66 to 1)   f
CONNA MOSS (Ire) 8-11-7 (5*) Mr J Jukes, mid-div till blun
and uns rdr tenth.................(16 to 1 tchd 20 to 1)   ur
NEARLY SPLENDID 12-12-8 (7*) Mr T Greed, hit 6th, blun 8th,
hdwy 17th, tld off whn pld up bef 2 out.
.... (11 to 1 op 8 to 1 tchd 12 to 1)   pu
MISTY (NZ) 10-11-5 (7*) Mr J M Pritchard, chsd ldrs to 11th,
tld off whn pld up bef 3 out........ (50 to 1 op 25 to 1)   pu
AFTERKELLY 12-11-12 (7*) Mr I Dowrick, beh frm 12th, tld off
whn pld up bef 21st..................(10 to 1 op 5 to 1)   pu
PRINCESS WENLLYAN 12-11-0 (7*) Mr A Holdsworth, hdwy
14th, wknd 18th, tld off whn pld up bef 3 out.
.... (66 to 1 op 50 to 1)   pu
LAZZARETTO 9-11-5 (7*) Mr I Johnson, tld off frm 5th, pld up
bef 23rd..........................(66 to 1 op 33 to 1)   pu
2641 MAJOR MAC 10-11-5 (7*) Mr S Durack, chsd ldrs to 11th, lost
tch 15th, tld off whn pld up bef 3 out.
.... (50 to 1 op 33 to 1 tchd 66 to 1)   pu
2531 RISING SAP 7-11-5 (7*) Mr A Dalton, hit 6th, hdwy 13th, wknd
18th, tld off whn pld up bef 3 out.........(25 to 1 op 16 to 1)   pu
Dist: 7l, 3l, ½l, dist, dist. 9m 55.50s. a 94.50s (16 Ran).
(I K Johnson), Mrs S M Johnson

2876 Taunton 'National Hunt' Novices' Hurdle Class D (Div II) (4-y-o and up) £2,567 2m 3f 110yds......... (4:20)

1995⁷ COLONEL BLAZER 5-11-4 J Culloty, sn tracking ldrs, chlgd 3
out, slight ld and in control whn lft clr last.
.... (11 to 2 op 4 to 1 tchd 6 to 1)   1
2668² TRISTRAM'S IMAGE (NZ) 6-11-6 (5*) Mr C Vigors, chsd ldrs,
chlgd 3 out, one pace and hld whn lft second at last.
.... (7 to 1 op 5 to 1)   2
2433² ATAVISTIC (Ire) 5-11-8 (3*) T Dascombe, chsd ldrs, drvn alng
frm 6th, one pace whn lft 3rd at last.
.... (11 to 2 op 9 to 2 tchd 6 to 1)   3
2637 ROLL AGAIN 6-11-4 Jamie Evans, chlgd 4th to nxt, outpcd
6th, nvr dngrs aftr.................(25 to 1 op 16 to 1)   4
2688⁴ STAR MYSTERY 6-11-4 N Williamson, hld up tracking ldrs,
chlgd 5th, led nxt, hdd 3 out, wknd quickly appr next, no ch
whn hmpd last...........................(6 to 4 fav)   5
2269 NORLANDIC (NZ) 5-11-4 G Tormey, al beh.
.... (33 to 1 op 16 to 1 tchd 40 to 1)   6
2539 CAMILLAS LEGACY 6-10-13 D Gallagher, al in rear.
.... (100 to 1 op 50 to 1)   7
2668⁵ GIVRY 7-11-4 D Bridgwater, led, hit 4th and 5th, hdd appr
nxt, wknd 7th.......(16 to 1 op 12 to 1 tchd 20 to 1)   8
CLIFTON MATCH 5-10-8 (5*) D Salter, some hdwy 5th, wknd
aftr nxt............ (66 to 1 op 33 to 1 tchd 100 to 1)   9
2405 OUT FOR A DUCK 6-10-11 (7*) Mr S Durack, chsd ldrs, keen
hold, chased ldrs to 6th.
.... (66 to 1 op 50 to 1 tchd 100 to 1)   10
2503 FINE SPIRIT 5-10-6 (7*) Mr L Baker, al in rear.
.... (66 to 1 op 33 to 1)   11
2782 BOOZYS DREAM 6-11-4 S Burrough, pld hrd, mstk 3rd and
sn beh, tld off...............(50 to 1 op 33 to 1)   12
585* STORM RUN (Ire) 7-11-11 A P McCoy, prmnt, chlgd 4th, led
aftr 5th to nxt, led ag'n 3 out, narrowly hdd and rdn whn f last.
.... (11 to 2 op 9 to 2 tchd 6 to 1)   f
1976 AQUA AMBER 5-11-1 (3*) L Aspell, sn beh, no ch whn hmpd
and uns rdr last..................(100 to 1 op 50 to 1)   ur
Dist: 13l, 3l, hd, 3l, 3l, 1¼l, 9l, 2l, 10l, 13l. 4m 58.30s. a 40.30s (14 Ran).
(Exors Of The Late Mr T H Shrimpton), Miss H C Knight

2877 Sannacott Novices' Handicap Chase Class E (0-100 5-y-o and up) £2,913 2m 110yds.................. (4:50)

2606 NORTHERN SINGER [81] 7-11-5 (3*) T Dascombe, trkd ldrs,
chlgd 4 out, sn led, clr frm nxt..........(9 to 1 op 8 to 1)   1
SPEEDY SNAPS IMAGE [72] 6-10-13 S Burrough, pressed
ldrs till led appr 7th, hdd aftr 4 out, sn one pace.
.... (33 to 1 op 25 to 1 tchd 40 to 1)   2
2428⁷ ROVESTAR [81] 6-11-8 C Maude, hdwy and hmpd 8th, mstk 4
out, sn one pace..........(9 to 1 op 7 to 1 tchd 10 to 1)   3
2778² AFTER THE FOX [84] 10-11-4 (7*) Mr J Tizzard, beh, drvn alng
frm 7th, moderate hdwy und pres from 4 out.
.... (5 to 1 fav op 7 to 2 tchd 4 to 1 and 9 to 2)   4
2739⁶ FULL SHILLING (USA) [64] 8-10-13 (3*) Guy Lewis, chsd
ldrs to 8th, sn wknd.............(33 to 1 op 25 to 1)   5
2547 BOLD ACRE [80] (bl) 7-11-7 S Wynne, hdwy 7th, wknd 4 out.
.... (8 to 1 op 6 to 1 tchd 9 to 1)   6
2304 MASTER PANGLOSS (Ire) [62] 7-9-10 (7*) C Rae, mstk 3rd,
effrt 7th, sn wknd.....(33 to 1 op 16 to 1 tchd 40 to 1)   7
2431³ NORDIC VALLEY (Ire) [86] 6-11-13 A P McCoy, beh and nvr
dngrs frm 6th...........(11 to 2 op 5 to 1 tchd 6 to 1)   8
2604⁴ OLLIVER DUCKETT [82] 8-11-9 G Tormey, wth ldr to 3rd, hit
8th and sn wknd................(9 to 1 op 5 to 1)   9
2626 DANNICUS [76] 6-11-3 V Slattery, wl beh frm 5th.
.... (16 to 1 tchd 20 to 1)   10
2556⁴ FLOWING RIVER (USA) [72] 11-10-8 (5*) Sophie Mitchell, beh
frm 8th, tld off whn f 3 out.
.... (14 to 1 op 12 to 1 tchd 16 to 1)   f
2498³ LOBSTER COTTAGE [87] 9-12-0 S McNeill, led, hdd aftr 6th,
mstk nxt, wknd, tld off whn pld up bef 3 out.
.... (9 to 1 op 5 to 1 tchd 20 to 1)   pu

KETCHICAN [76] 5-10-8 S Curran, hit 6th and beh, tld off whn
pld up bef 3 out.......(33 to 1 op 25 to 1 tchd 40 to 1)   pu
2304 RELKOWEN [80] 7-11-7 M Richards, hdwy 6th, wknd 8th, tld
off whn pld up bef 4 out.
.... (15 to 2 op 7 to 1 tchd 5 to 1 and 6 to 1)   pu
Dist: 8l, 3½l, 19l, 4l, nk, 5l, 8l, 3½l, 3l. 4m 25.40s. a 33.40s (14 Ran).
(Joe Panes), R J Hodges

2878 Blackdown Hills Handicap Hurdle Class F (0-105 4-y-o and up) £1,962 2m 1f.........................(5:20)

2609* ADDED DIMENSION (Ire) [99] 6-11-4 (7*) X Aizpuru, trkd ldr till
led 5th, drvn clr aftr 2 out.......(3 to 1 jt-fav tchd 7 to 2)   1
2504³ HANDSON [90] 5-10-11 (5*) D Salter, hdwy to track ldrs 5th,
chsd wnr aftr 3 out, chlgd nxt, sn one pace. ......(3 to 1 jt-
fav tchd 100 to 30 and 11 to 4)   2
2663² D'NAAN (Ire) [98] (bl) 4-11-0 A P McCoy, led, reminder aftr
second, rdn and hdd 5th, chlgd nxt, one pace frm 2 out.
.... (100 to 30 op 9 to 4)   3
RUNIC SYMBOL [74] 6-10-0 D Gallagher, chsd ldrs rdn 3 out,
styd on one pace und pres r-in.
.... (16 to 1 op 12 to 1 tchd 20 to 1)   4
2783 CONCINNITY (USA) [74] 8-9-7 (7*) Mr O McPhail, hdwy 4th,
one pace und pres frm 2 out.......(100 to 1 op 33 to 1)   5
SEVSO [89] 8-11-1 V Slattery, chsd ldrs to 3 out, sn one pace.
.... (10 to 1 op 16 to 1)   6
2089 PERSIAN MYSTIC (Ire) [98] 5-11-10 W Marston, beh, riden
and no response 3 out...(12 to 1 op 6 to 1 tchd 14 to 1)   7
2428³ STEEL GEM (Ire) [74] 8-9-7 (7*) M Griffiths, slwly into strd, sn
wl beh, fnshd lme...................(4 to 1 op 3 to 1)   8
900 DANTE'S RUBICON (Ire) [75] 6-10-1¹ C Maude, tld off frm 4th,
pld up bef 3 out......(66 to 1 op 33 to 1 tchd 100 to 1)   pu
Dist: 8l, 5l, ½l, sht-hd, 1½l, 13l, 8l. 4m 13.40s. a 30.40s (9 Ran).
SR: 23/6/-/-/-/-/   (N A Dunger), P Winkworth

WETHERBY (soft)
Wednesday February 26th
Going Correction: PLUS 1.60 sec. per fur. (races
1,2,4,7), PLUS 1.80 (3,5,6)

2879 Hogarth Novices' Hurdle Class E (4-y-o and up) £2,670 2m....... (2:00)

2528⁴ CARLITO BRIGANTE 5-11-9 J Osborne, dsptd ld to 3rd, trkd
ldrs, led 3 out, styd on wl. (5 to 1 op 4 to 1 tchd 11 to 2)   1
2257⁸ FASSAN (Ire) 5-11-4 R Garritty, made most to 3 out, chsd wnr
aftr, no imprsn...........(5 to 1 op 4 to 1 tchd 11 to 2)   2
2204 MITHRAIC (Ire) 5-11-9 R Johnson, prmnt, ev ch 3 out, one
pace nxt...........................(20 to 1 op 14 to 1)   3
OLD HUSH WING (Ire) 4-10-8 J Callaghan, hld up in tch,
outpcd 3 out, styd on frm betw last 2.............(33 to 1)   4
CHINA CASTLE 4-10-8 M Foster, mid-div, rdn to chal 3 out,
wkng whn mstk nxt...............(10 to 1 op 7 to 1)   5
2618³ MONICA'S CHOICE (Ire) 6-11-9 P Niven, hld up rear, hmpd
4th, some late hdwy, nvr dngrs.
.... (100 to 30 op 9 to 4 tchd 7 to 2)   6
2712 WELL ARMED (Ire) 6-10-13 (5*) R McGrath, trkd ldrs till wknd
bef 3 out...........................(20 to 1 op 14 to 1)   7
1882⁹ ROTHARI 5-11-4 B Storey, beh most of way.
.... (20 to 1 tchd 25 to 1)   8
1629⁵ BOLD CLASSIC (Ire) 4-10-9¹ T Reed, prmnt till wknd quickly
bef 3 out..........(12 to 1 op 16 to 1 tchd 20 to 1)   9
WINDYEDGE (USA) 4-10-8 J Supple, keen early, al beh.
.... (40 to 1 op 33 to 1)   10
2284⁹ PETRICO 5-11-4 R Supple, in tch till wknd aftr 5th, tld off.
.... (50 to 1 op 25 to 1)   11
2489 DAN DE MAN (Ire) 6-11-4 A Thornton, mid-div whn f 4th.
.... (50 to 1 op 33 to 1)   f
2572* FORESWORN (Ire) 5-11-9 D Bentley, in tch whn hmpd and
broke leg 4th, pld up, destroyed.
.... (7 to 2 op 7 to 2 tchd 4 to 1)   pu
Dist: 4l, 3l, ½l, 14l, 2l, 4l, 7l, 14l, 22l, dist. 4m 13.80s. a 32.80s (13 Ran).
SR: 23/14/16/-/-/-/   (Lady Bamford), P R Webber

2880 Askham Bryan Handicap Hurdle Class E (0-110 4-y-o and up) £2,460 2m........................ (2:30)

2711³ DURANO [100] 6-11-4 L Wyer, prmnt, led gng wl bef 3 out, rdn
betw last 2, styd on well. ....(100 to 30 jt-
fav op 5 to 2 tchd 7 to 2)   1
2467⁴ HAM N'EGGS [110] 6-12-0 R Garritty, settled midfield, hdwy
bef 3 out, ch nxt, no extr und pres r-in.
.... (9 to 1 op 7 to 1 tchd 10 to 1)   2
2581 COURT JOKER (Ire) [82] 5-10-0 R Johnson, in tch, hdwy bef 3
out, kpt on same pace frm nxt.......(20 to 1 op 16 to 1)   3
2618⁴ OUR ROBERT [92] 5-10-7 (3*) F Leahy, rear, hdwy bef 3 out,
chalg whn blun last, not reco'r........(10 to 1 op 8 to 1)   4
2581⁴ INNOCENT GEORGE [87] 8-10-5 A Thornton, in tch, kpt on
frm 3 out, nvr dngrs....................(16 to 1 op 14 to 1)   5
2625³ TULU [104] 6-11-1 (7*) Mr A Balding, hld up rear, styd on frm 3
out, nvr dngrs..................(13 to 2 op 6 to 1)   6
2526³ EUROTWIST [99] 8-11-0 (3*) G Lee, nvr better than mid-div.
.... (14 to 1)   7

1141 MUIZENBERG [82] 10-9-12[1] (3*) Michael Brennan, *led 3rd to 4th, prmnt till wknd appr 3 out*....... (100 to 1 op 50 to 1) 8
2682[7] FOX SPARROW [100] 7-11-4 A S Smith, *chsd ldrs till wknd aftr 3 out*.............(14 to 1 op 12 to 1 tchd 16 to 1) 9
2618[2] MERRY MERMAID [96] 7-11-0 A Dobbin, *made most till bef 3 out, sn wknd*...............(100 to 30 jt-fav op 7 to 2) 10
1044[4] SEA GOD [83] 6-10-1 W Worthington, *nvr better than mid-div.* ....(20 to 1) 11
2681[2] AJDAR [82] 6-10-0 M Brennan, *beh most of way.* .... (16 to 1 op 14 to 1) 12
2682[3] BEND SABLE (Ire) [106] 7-11-10 B Storey, *chsd ldrs till wknd bef 3 out*.................................(5 to 1 tchd 6 to 1) 13

Dist: 1¾l, 4l, 5l, 5l, 1¾l, ¾l, 4l, 3½l, 5l, 1l. 4m 13.10s. a 32.10s (13 Ran).
SR: 25/33/1/6/-/11/5/-/-/ (C H Stevens), T D Easterby

2881 Sicklinghall Novices' Chase Class D (5-y-o and up) £3,574 3m 1f...(3:00)

2700 CREDO IS KING (Ire) 7-11-10 J Osborne, *al prmnt, rdn bef 4 out, led appr last, styd on und pres.* ....(9 to 2 op 7 to 2 tchd 5 to 1) 1
2491* CROWN EQUERRY (Ire) 7-11-13 P Carberry, *led till rdn and hdd appr last, no extr*........... (7 to 4 jt-fav op 11 to 8) 2
2487 DORLIN CASTLE 9-11-4 R Supple, *hld up, smooth hdwy aftr 4 out, ev ch whn mstk 2 out, sn drvn alng, no extr frm last.* .... (9 to 1 op 8 to 1 tchd 10 to 1) 3
2600[3] WHAT'S YOUR STORY (Ire) 8-11-4 R Johnson, *several mstks, blun second, in tch, rdn whn blunded 4 out, wknd nxt.* .... (7 to 4 jt-fav tchd 15 to 8) 4
DEE LIGHT 8-10-13 A Dobbin, *in tch, wknd quickly aftr 11th, tld off whn pld up bef 4 out.* .... (20 to 1 op 16 to 1 tchd 25 to 1) pu
2620[4] CLONROCHE LUCKY (Ire) (bl) 7-11-4 K Jones, *lost tch hfwy, tld off whn pld up bef 4 out*.......... (100 to 1 op 50 to 1) pu
2484[3] BLACK BROOK (Ire) 8-11-4 R Garritty, *prmnt, wkng whn pld up bef 4 out*.............................(9 to 1 op 7 to 1) pu

Dist: 1l, ¾l, 15l. 7m 2.50s. a 54.50s (7 Ran).
SR: 1/3/-/-/ (G L Porter), P R Webber

2882 Hoechst Roussel Panacur European Breeders Fund Mares' 'National Hunt' Novices' Hurdle Qualifier (5-y-o and up) £2,985 2½m 110yds .... (3:30)

2428[4] FANTASY LINE 6-10-7 J Osborne, *trkd ldrs, led gng wl bef 3 out, sn clr, cmftbly*.....................(6 to 1 op 5 to 1) 1
2492[2] LIPPY LOUISE 5-10-7 P Niven, *chsd ldrs, chased wnr frm 3 out, no imprsn*.............(4 to 1 op 7 to 2 tchd 9 to 2) 2
2619[5] CHERRY DEE 6-10-2 (5*) B Grattan, *in tch, pushed alng and outpcd aftr 5th, kpt on frm 3 out*....... (12 to 1 op 10 to 1) 3
RAISE A DOLLAR 7-10-7 Mr S Swiers, *prmnt, dsptd ld aftr 5th, wknd appr 3 out, tld off*......... (20 to 1 tchd 25 to 1) 4
2575[2] SPRITZER (Ire) 5-11-0 P Carberry, *hld up, drvn alng and outpcd aftr 5th, some hdwy bef 3 out, sn rdn and btn, tld off.* ....(6 to 5 on op Evens) 5
1770 PHARRAMBLING (Ire) 6-10-4 (3*) G Lee, *al beh, tld off.* .... (33 to 1 op 20 to 1) 6
2492* DAISY DAYS (Ire) 7-11-7 A S Smith, *made most till bef 3 out, wknd quickly, tld off*.......................(9 to 2 op 3 to 1) 7

Dist: 7l, ½l, 29l, 9l, 12l, 10l. 5m 33.70s. a 51.70s (7 Ran).
(Mrs P Starkey), P R Webber

2883 East Keswick Handicap Chase Class C (0-135 5-y-o and up) £4,402 2½m 110yds........................ (4:00)

2571[4] BEACHY HEAD [115] 9-10-4 (5*) R McGrath, *hld up, hdwy to ld 4 out, hrd pressed last, pushed out.* (3 to 1 tchd 5 to 2) 1
2759* ALJADEER (USA) [114] 8-10-8 (5ex) R Garritty, *beh, cld 7th, rdn to chal last, no extr und pres.* .... (11 to 4 op 5 to 4 tchd 3 to 1) 2
2659[2] NO PAIN NO GAIN (Ire) [120] 9-11-0 P Hide, *cl up, led tenth to 4 out, ch 2 out, sn rdn and btn.* ....(2 to 1 fav op 5 to 2 tchd 7 to 4) 3
2624[2] SAILOR JIM [106] 10-10-0 J Osborne, *led to 3rd, in tch, hdwy on bit to dispute ld aftr tenth, lost pl rpdly bef 4 out, tld off.* ....(9 to 2) 4
974 MASTER BOSTON (Ire) [130] 9-11-10 P Carberry, *led 3rd, blun 8th, hdd tenth, wknd quickly, tld off whn pld up bef 4 out.* .... (12 to 1 op 8 to 1) pu

Dist: ¾l, 13l, dist. 5m 35.00s. a 42.00s (5 Ran).
SR: 30/28/21/-/-/ (M Tabor), J J O'Neill

2884 Helmsley Novices' Handicap Chase Class C (5-y-o and up) £4,355 2m .... (4:30)

2714[4] CROSSHOT [85] 10-10-0 R Johnson, *hld up, mstk 5th, led on bit 3 out, clr whn jinked last, rdr lost iron and sddl slpd, drvn out*......................(7 to 2 op 3 to 1 tchd 4 to 1) 1
2714[2] BOLD BOSS [109] 8-11-10 B Storey, *chsd ldr, slightly hmpd 4 out, lost pl and sn drvn alng, rallied aftr 2 out, no imprsn on wnr*.......... (11 to 10 fav op 11 to 10 on tchd 6 to 5) 2
2493* MARBLE MAN (Ire) [92] 7-10-7 R Garritty, *led to 3 out, sn wknd, tld off*.................................. (13 to 8 op 6 to 4) 3

Dist: 7l, 23l. 4m 26.20s. a 39.20s (3 Ran).
(R McDonald), R McDonald

2885 Micklethwaite Handicap Hurdle Class D (0-125 4-y-o and up) £2,792 2½m 110yds................ (5:00)

2682[2] DANBYS GORSE [90] 5-10-0 L Wyer, *hld up beh, steady hdwy to ld appr last, edgd lft, styd on und pres, all out.* ....(9 to 4 fav op 5 to 2 tchd 11 to 4) 1
2487 DUKE OF PERTH [91] 6-10-1 A S Smith, *hld up, hdwy to chal 3 out, slight ld nxt, hdd appr last, kpt on.* (11 to 2 op 9 to 2) 2
2815[2] ALL ON [110] 6-11-6 Derek Byrne, *cl up, led 4th till aftr 5th, outpcd after 2 out, styd on frm last.* ....(4 to 1 op 9 to 2 tchd 5 to 1) 3
2356[4] CLAIRESWAN (Ire) [97] 5-10-7 K Gaule, *chsd ldrs, slight ld 3 out, hdd nxt, kpt on same pace.* ....(7 to 1 op 5 to 1 tchd 8 to 1) 4
2762* BOSTON MAN [90] 6-10-0 (6ex) P Carberry, *led, jmpd slwly and hdd 4th, led aftr 5th to 3 out, wknd after nxt.* ....(7 to 2 op 9 to 4) 5
2487 MOONSHINE DANCER [95] 7-10-5 J Callaghan, *in tch till wknd bef 2 out*..................................... (20 to 1) 6
2760[5] SUMMERHILL SPECIAL (Ire) [113] 6-11-9 R Johnson, *in tch till wknd bef 3 out*...... (11 to 1 op 8 to 1 tchd 12 to 1) 7
2716 VIARDOT (Ire) [102] 8-10-7 (5*) R McGrath, *sn wl beh.* .... (16 to 1 op 14 to 1) 8

Dist: ½l, 1½l, 1¼l, 20l, 2l, 9l, 4l. 5m 34.10s. a 52.10s (8 Ran).
(D T Todd), J M Jefferson

HUNTINGDON (good to soft) Thursday February 27th

Going Correction: PLUS 0.95 sec. per fur. (races 1,4,7), PLUS 1.40 (2,3,5,6)

2886 Colesden Selling Hurdle Class G (4-y-o and up) £2,075 2m 110yds (2:00)

2511 MELLOW MASTER 4-10-7 R Farrant, *nvr far away, effrt and drvn alng frm 2 out, styd on to ld appr finish.* .... (20 to 1 op 14 to 1 tchd 25 to 1) 1
2777[5] HALHAM TARN (Ire) 7-11-1 (7*) A Dowling, *chsd clr ldr, led bend aftr 3rd, sn clear, rdn betw last 2, hdd and no extr appr finish*..................(12 to 1 op 8 to 1 tchd 14 to 1) 2
2610 BATTLESHIP BRUCE (bl) 5-11-2 D Gallagher, *settled wth chasing grp, improved bef 3 out, styd on one pace frm betw last 2*..................(11 to 2 op 5 to 1 tchd 8 to 1) 3
1475[5] TENAYESTELIGN 9-11-3 J A McCarthy, *wtd wth, took clr order aftr 3 out, effrt and rdn betw last 2, one pace r-in.* .... (6 to 1 op 5 to 1 tchd 13 to 2) 4
2351 LUCY TUFTY 6-11-3 N Mann, *al wl in tch, improved frm 3 out, effrt and rdn betw last 2, one pace r-in.* ....(14 to 1 op 10 to 1 tchd 16 to 1) 5
2292[6] SONG FOR JESS (Ire) 4-9-13 (3*) L Aspell, *trkd ldrs, effrt aftr 3 out, rdn and not quicken frm betw last 2.* ....(16 to 1 op 10 to 1 tchd 20 to 1) 6
2681[6] THEFIELDSOFATHENRY (Ire) 7-12-0 N Williamson, *settled off the pace, chsd alng hfwy, rdn and no imprsn frm 3 out.* ....(5 to 1 tchd 4 to 1) 7
2765 PATONG BEACH 7-10-11 S Fox, *settled in rear, chsd alng frm hfwy, nvr able to rch chalg pos.* ....(50 to 1 op 25 to 1 tchd 66 to 1) 8
JONBEL 9-11-2 C Maude, *chsd alng to keep up hfwy, nvr able to rch chalg pos*................ (50 to 1 op 20 to 1) 9
RAFTER-J 6-11-2 J Railton, *bustled alng in midfield hfwy, nvr a serious threat*.......(33 to 1 op 20 to 1 tchd 50 to 1) 10
TIGANA 5-10-11 D Leahy, *struggling frm hfwy, tld off.* .... (25 to 1 op 16 to 1 tchd 33 to 1) 11
2726 CONVAMORE QUEEN (Ire) 8-10-11 V Slattery, *in tch to hfwy, sn beh, tld off*.........(33 to 1 op 25 to 1 tchd 50 to 1) 12
2269 X-RAY (Ire) 4-10-0 (7*) N T Egan, *bolted and uns rdr gng to post, led and sn clr, hdd bend aftr 3rd, soon tld off.* .... (66 to 1 op 25 to 1 tchd 100 to 1) 13
FOREIGN JUDGEMENT (USA) 4-10-7 D Fuhrmann, *beh whn blun and uns rdr second.* ....(40 to 1 op 16 to 1 tchd 66 to 1) ur
2265* BELLA SEDONA 5-11-3 J Osborne, *nvr gng wl, tld off till pld up bef 4 out*........(13 to 8 fav op 7 to 4 tchd 11 to 8) pu

Dist: 1¼l, 1¼l, 1¼l, 3l, 22l, 4l, 2½l, 17l, 10l, ½l. 4m 4.10s. a 23.10s (15 Ran).
SR: 4/17/9/8/5/-/ (Paul Green), N J H Walker

2887 Colmworth Hunters' Chase Class H (5-y-o and up) £1,213 3m.... (2:30)

2660* MR BOSTON 12-12-5 Mr S Swiers, *patiently rdn, steady hdwy to chase ldr fnl circuit, led bef 2 out, styd on strly r-in.* .... (11 to 8 on op Evens tchd 6 to 4 on) 1
GRANVILLE GUEST 11-11-7 (7*) Mr J Tizzard, *settled wth chasing grp, gd hdwy to join ldg pair aftr 3 out, effrt and wndrd r-in, no extr*.................(11 to 1 op 5 to 1 tchd 14 to 1) 2
2641 COLONIAL KELLY 9-12-4 (3*) Mr P Hacking, *settled in tch, wnt second hfwy, feeling pace fnl circuit, no imprsn frm 3 out.* .... (12 to 1 op 8 to 1 tchd 14 to 1) 3
2615* LOYAL NOTE 9-12-4 (3*) Mr Simon Andrews, *not fluent, in tch, wnt hndy aftr one circuit, struggling 6 out, no imprsn after.* ....(14 to 1 op 8 to 1 tchd 16 to 1) 4

GAY RUFFIAN 11-11-7 (7*) Miss C Dyson, *al chasing ldrs, wnt hndy aftr one circuit, struggling 6 out, sn lost tch, tld off.*
.... (40 to 1 op 25 to 1 tchd 50 to 1) 5
FIRE AND REIGN (Ire) 9-11-7 (7*) Mr N King, *not jump wl, feeling pace whn f 4th.*.................. (100 to 1 op 50 to 1) f
RICHARD HUNT 13-11-7 (7*) Miss L Rowe, *struggling to keep up aftr one circuit, tld off whn pld up appr 3 out.*
.... (9 to 1 op 8 to 1 tchd 10 to 1) pu
ITSGONEOFF 8-11-9 (5*) Mr B Pollock, *led and sn clr, not fluent fnl circuit, hdd aftr 3 out, 3rd whn pld up bef nxt, broke dwn, destroyed......*(3 to 1 tchd 11 to 4 and 100 to 30) pu
Dist: 5l, 12l, 1½l, 27l. 6m 27.20s. a 47.20s (8 Ran).

(M K Oldham), Mrs M Reveley

2888 Chawston Handicap Chase Class F (0-100 5-y-o and up) £3,116 3m
.... (3:00)

2527* CARIBOO GOLD (USA) [99] (bl) 8-12-0 J Osborne, *patiently rdn, improved fnl circuit, led betw last 2, eased bef line.*
.... (11 to 10 on op 11 to 8 on) 1
2512⁴ BOLSHIE BARON [72] 8-10-1 D Gallagher, *chsd ldg bunch, feeling pace aftr one circuit, plenty to do 3 out, styd on wl r-in.*
.... (14 to 1 op 8 to 1 tchd 16 to 1) 2
2606³ BLAZER MORINIERE (Fr) [78] 8-10-7 S Fox, *settled midfield, improved to ld aftr 3 out, hdd betw last 2, wndrd r-in, no extr.*
.... (7 to 1 op 5 to 1 tchd 8 to 1) 3
2698 SPACE CAPPA [92] 9-11-7 Miss V Stephens, *wth ldrs, ev ch fnl circuit, feeling pace bef 3 out, sn tld off.*
.... (16 to 1 op 14 to 1 tchd 20 to 1) 4
2741* FURRY FOX (Ire) [78] 9-10-7 (6ex) D Walsh, *wth ldrs, hit 7 out, struggling bef 3 out, lost tch, tld off......* (2 to 1 op 7 to 1) 5
2745⁴ PANT LLIN [80] (bl) 11-10-6 (3*) L Aspell, *not fluent, struggling aftr one circuit, tld off after.*
.... (25 to 1 op 12 to 1 tchd 33 to 1) 6
2729 KING'S COURTIER (Ire) [71] (v) 8-10-0 N Mann, *led, jmpd slwly 4th, hdd and wknd quickly aftr 3 out, pld up bef nxt.*
.... (50 to 1 op 20 to 1 tchd 66 to 1) pu
Dist: 3l, 1¼l, dist, hd, dist. 6m 29.20s. a 49.20s (7 Ran).

(Mrs Sharon C Nelson), K C Bailey

2889 Levy Board 'National Hunt' Novices' Hurdle Class E (4-y-o and up) £2,600 3¼m
.... (3:30)

2152² FLYING GUNNER 6-11-7 (3*) R Massey, *al hndy, led 2 out, all out.*................... (Evens fav tchd 6 to 4) 1
2601³ BANNY HILL LAD 7-11-1 (3*) D Fortt, *wtd wth, hdwy 5 out, led 3 out, hdd nxt, rallied und pres.*
.... (25 to 1 op 12 to 1 tchd 33 to 1) 2
2298³ SATCOTINO (Ire) 6-10-13 N Williamson, *al wl plcd, led 4 out to nxt, rdn and kpt on r-in......*(7 to 1 op 9 to 1 tchd 10 to 1) 3
2398⁴ MUSIC MASTER (Ire) (bl) 7-11-4 J A McCarthy, *patiently rdn, improved 4 out, feeling pace nxt, wknd quickly appr 2 out.*
.... (16 to 1 op 12 to 1 tchd 20 to 1) 4
2419⁴ SEPTEMBER BREEZE (Ire) 6-10-13 A S Smith, *chsd ldrs, ev ch 4 out, struggling aftr nxt, fdd......*(16 to 1 op 12 to 1) 5
1893⁶ WRISTBURN 7-11-4 J Railton, *wtd wth, improved 8th, feeling pace 4 out, sn btn.........*(9 to 2 tchd 4 to 1 and 5 to 1) 6
2398⁶ HARDY BREEZE (Ire) 6-11-4 D Gallagher, *chsd alng to keep in tch hfwy, nvr rchd chalg pos.........*(50 to 1 op 33 to 1) 7
2637⁶ BRAVE EDWIN (Ire) 7-10-13 (5*) Sophie Mitchell, *hmpd strt, given time to reco'r, nvr rchd chalg pos.*
.... (12 to 1 tchd 16 to 1 and 25 to 1) 8
2311 MADAM'S WALK 7-10-13 D Walsh, *whipped round strt, sn reco'red, lost tch frm 3 out.........*(50 to 1 op 33 to 1) 9
1026⁸ COUNTER ATTACK (Ire) 6-10-13 K Gaule, *pld hrd in midfield, nvr a threat.........*(50 to 1 op 33 to 1 tchd 100 to 1) 10
2678⁵ HOLKHAM BAY 5-10-11 (7*) C Rae, *al wl beh, tld off.*
.... (50 to 1 op 33 to 1 tchd 66 to 1) 11
2750* SAMMORELLO (Ire) 6-11-10 C Maude, *led to 4th, led ag'n 8th, hdd 3 out, wknd quickly, pld up bef last.*
.... (25 to 1 op 12 to 1 tchd 33 to 1) pu
2311 JET FILES (Ire) 6-11-4 R Farrant, *chsd ldrs, wknd appr 3 out, pld up bef nxt.........*(9 to 1 op 12 to 1 tchd 16 to 1) pu
2384⁹ ELY'S HARBOUR (Ire) 6-11-4 J Osborne, *wth ldrs, led 4th to 8th, tld off whn pld up bef 2 out.*
.... (16 to 1 op 8 to 1 tchd 20 to 1) pu
2803 PUSH ON POLLY (Ire) 7-10-13 G Cahill, *hmpd strt, nvr a threat, pld up bef 2 out.*
.... (50 to 1 op 33 to 1 tchd 100 to 1) pu
Dist: Hd, 3½l, 19l, 8l, 5l, ½l, nk, 16l, dist, 4l. 6m 43.50s. a 51.50s (15 Ran).

(Mrs R J Skan), D Nicholson

2890 Wyboston Novices' Chase Class E (5-y-o and up) £3,023 2½m 110yds
.... (4:00)

2425 TEINEIN (Fr) 6-11-2 N Williamson, *patiently rdn, hdwy 9th, hit 11th, chsd ldr 3 out, jmpd lft nxt, led r-in, easily.*
.... (6 to 5 op 11 to 10 tchd 11 to 8) 1
2613* HIGH LEARIE 7-11-8 J A McCarthy, *led, hdd r-in, no ch wth wnr.*...................... (7 to 1 tchd 8 to 1) 2
2690* ARFER MOLE (Ire) 9-12-0 J Osborne, *chsd ldr, pckd 5 out, blun nxt, wknd appr 2 out, virtually pld up r-in.*
.... (11 to 10 fav tchd 6 to 5 and Evens) 3

CORRIB SONG 8-10-13 (3*) L Aspell, *wl plcd to 8th, lost tch frm nxt, tld off......*...................(33 to 1 op 20 to 1) 4
2726 JOLIS ABSENT 7-10-11 D Gallagher, *not jump wl, sn well beh, tld off.........*.........(20 to 1 op 14 to 1) 5
2565 BENJI 6-10-13 (3*) D Fortt, *patiently rdn, blun and uns rdr 8th.*
.... (100 to 1 op 50 to 1) ur
Dist: 1¼l, dist, 6l, 1¾l. 5m 22.10s. a 35.10s (6 Ran).
SR: 24/28/-/ (Simon Sainsbury), Capt T A Forster

2891 Langford End Novices' Hunters' Chase Class H (6-y-o and up) £1,262 3m
.... (4:30)

BITOFAMIXUP (Ire) 6-12-2 (3*) Mr P Hacking, *chsd ldrs, lost pl 11th, rallied nxt, led 5 out, drvn out.........*(7 to 2 co-fav op 9 to 4) 1
ASK ANTONY (Ire) 7-12-0 (5*) Mr N Wilson, *patiently rdn, hdwy hfwy, chsd wnr frm 2 out, kpt on. ....*(7 to 2 co-fav tchd 4 to 1) 2
BROAD STEANE 8-12-0 (5*) Mr A Sansome, *chsd ldrs, led 13th, hdd 5 out, wknd appr 2 out.........*(7 to 2 co-fav tchd 9 to 2 and 3 to 1) 3
IDEAL PARTNER (Ire) 8-11-12 (7*) Mr J Tizzard, *wtd wth, improved 9th, wknd 3 out, tld off.*
.... (11 to 1 op 6 to 1 tchd 12 to 1) 4
2769² SANDS OF GOLD (Ire) 9-11-12 (7*) Mr L Lay, *led to 13th, wknd appr 3 out, tld off......*(11 to 1 op 8 to 1 tchd 12 to 1) 5
2531² LURRIGA GLITTER (Ire) 9-11-12 (7*) Mr S Joynes, *wtd wth, improved 11th, wknd appr 4 out, tld off.* (10 to 1 op 7 to 1) 6
COOLVAWN LADY (Ire) 8-11-7 (7*) Mr S Walker, *wl plcd, hit 13th, wknd aftr 4 out, tld off.*
.... (20 to 1 op 14 to 1 tchd 25 to 1) 7
2726⁹ MULTI LINE 7-11-7 (7*) Miss C Townsley, *sluggish strt, reco'red to race in tch to 13th, lost pl, tld off.*
.... (40 to 1 op 25 to 1 tchd 50 to 1) 8
TAURA'S RASCAL 8-11-12 (7*) Mr F Brennan, *chasing ldrs whn f 7th.........*...................(40 to 1 op 20 to 1) f
DAD'S PIPE 7-11-12 (7*) Mr T E G Smith, *beh whn f 3rd.*
.... (40 to 1 op 20 to 1) f
TRUE STEEL 11-12-0 (5*) Mr J Trice-Rolph, *al beh, tld off whn pld up bef 5 out.........*(14 to 1 op 12 to 1 tchd 16 to 1) pu
LA FONTAINBLEAU (Ire) 9-11-12 (7*) Mr A Rebori, *al in rear, tld off whn pld up bef 5 out.........*(50 to 1 op 25 to 1) pu
2641 AMADEUS (Fr) 9-11-12 (7*) Mr C Ward, *settled midfield, feeling pace 8th, tld off whn pld up bef 13th.*
.... (40 to 1 op 20 to 1) pu
Dist: 1¼l, 15l, dist, 1l, 3l, dist, 1¼l. 6m 30.60s. a 50.60s (13 Ran).

(Mike Roberts), M J Roberts

2892 Wilden Handicap Hurdle Class E (0-110 4-y-o and up) £2,635 3¼m
.... (5:00)

2640⁵ RED LIGHTER [77] 8-10-0 J Osborne, *chsd ldr, led appr 3 out, drvn clr.........*...................(12 to 1 tchd 14 to 1) 1
2562² EHTEFAAL (USA) [95] 6-11-4 T J Murphy, *patiently rdn, improved 7th, ridden 2 out, styd on.*
.... (9 to 2 op 5 to 1 tchd 11 to 2) 2
2422* TILTY (USA) [101] (v) 7-11-10 T Eley, *led to 3rd, led ag'n 7th, hit 4 out, sn hdd, kpt on same pace frm 2 out.*
.... (9 to 1 op 7 to 1) 3
2710* DOCKMASTER [89] 6-10-12 N Williamson, *wtd wth, improved 7th, wknd quickly appr last.*
.... (4 to 1 fav tchd 9 to 2) 4
2710⁶ HUDSON BAY TRADER (USA) [84] 10-10-7 Miss P Robson, *improved 5th, lost pl 7th, styd on ag'n frm 2 out.*
.... (8 to 1 op 12 to 1 tchd 14 to 1) 5
2487 QUIET MISTRESS [79] (bl) 7-10-2 A S Smith, *wl plcd till wknd appr 3 out.........*(14 to 1 op 8 to 1 tchd 16 to 1) 6
2513⁴ MADAME PRESIDENT (Ire) [85] 6-10-5 (3*) D Fortt, *wnt hndy 6th, feeling pace 4 out, sn lost tch......* (5 to 1 op 4 to 1) 7
2761³ MERILENA (Ire) [87] 7-10-3 (7*) N Rossiter, *chsd ldrs, feeling pace 4 out, lost tch, tld off......*(10 to 1 op 10 to 1) 8
2691⁴ ROSIE-B [89] 7-10-9 (3*) L Aspell, *struggling to keep up aftr one circuit, tld off......* (6 to 1 op 9 to 2 tchd 13 to 2) 9
2740 CUNNINGHAMS FORD (Ire) [94] (bl) 9-11-3 J A McCarthy, *led 3rd to 7th, sn wknd, tld off whn pld up bef 9th.*
.... (33 to 1 op 20 to 1) pu
2749 MILLY LE MOSS (Ire) [77] (v) 8-10-0 V Slattery, *al beh, tld off whn pld up bef 2 out...*(33 to 1 op 20 to 1 tchd 40 to 1) pu
2710⁷ ANSURO AGAIN [81] 8-10-4 G Cahill, *al in rear, tld off whn pld up bef 2 out.........*...................(12 to 1 tchd 14 to 1) pu
Dist: 6l, 3½l, 22l, 1½l, 10l, 5l, dist, 8l. 6m 31.30s. a 39.30s (12 Ran).

(Mrs C H Antrobus), J A B Old

LUDLOW (good)
Thursday February 27th
Going Correction: PLUS 0.10 sec. per fur. (races 1,4,6,7), PLUS 0.20 (2,3,5)

2893 Corvedale Novices' Hurdle Class E (4-y-o and up) £2,654 2m..... (2:10)

2299³ GREEN GREEN DESERT (Fr) 6-11-9 D Bridgwater, hld up in rear, steady hdwy 4 out, led on bit last, very easily.
..............(9 to 1 op 7 to 1 tchd 10 to 1 and 12 to 1) 1

2511* HIGH IN THE CLOUDS (Ire) 5-11-9 S Wynne, hld up in mid-div, hdwy 5th, led 3 out to last, outpcd.
..................................(6 to 5 fav op 11 to 10) 2

2727⁸ FASIL (Ire) 4-10-7 T Jenks, hld up in rear, hdwy 4 out, styd on frm 2 out..............(33 to 1 op 25 to 1 tchd 40 to 1) 3

MIDNIGHT LEGEND 5-10-7 R Johnson, al prmnt, chsd ldr appr 4th, led aftr four out, hdd nxt, btn whn mstk last.
..............................(5 to 1 op 2 to 1) 4

2632³ FORMIDABLE PARTNER (v) 4-10-7 J R Kavanagh, mid-div, rdn appr 3 out, sn btn...............(50 to 1 op 33 to 1) 5

2255³ MOONAX (Ire) 6-11-3 B Powell, hld up in rear, styd on frm 3 out, nvr dngrs.
.............(3 to 1 op 5 to 2 tchd 100 to 30) 6

2002 SHARP COMMAND 4-10-7 P Holley, in tch till no hdwy frm 4 out..........................(100 to 1 op 50 to 1) 7

2780 FLORID (USA) 6-11-3 G Bradley, rcd keenly, led till hdd aftr 4 out, rdn and wknd bef nxt..........(16 to 1 op 10 to 1) 8

2803⁴ GEISWAY (Can) 7-11-3 M Richards, wl in rear, nvr nr to chal.
.............................(100 to 1 op 50 to 1) 9

2693⁴ BLAZE OF SONG (bl) 5-11-3 L Harvey, trkd ldr till wknd appr 4th......................(50 to 1 tchd 66 to 1) 10

1669³ SLIPPERY FIN 5-10-5 (7*) N Willmington, mid-div, nvr on terms....................(66 to 1 op 33 to 1) 11

TORAJA 5-11-3 S Curran, al beh..... (50 to 1 op 25 to 1) 12

2511⁶ GLEN GARNOCK (Ire) 5-11-3 Gary Lyons, mstks, hit 4th, wl beh frm 6th...................(100 to 1 op 50 to 1) 13

2628 FENCER'S QUEST (Ire) 4-10-7 A Thornton, prmnt till wknd 5th.......................(66 to 1 op 33 to 1) 14

2611 NOBLESSE OBLIGE 4-10-7 S McNeill, al towards rear.
.................................(100 to 1 op 50 to 1) 15

SAFECRACKER 4-10-7 W McFarland, al beh, blun 4 out, tld off..............................(100 to 1 op 50 to 1) 16

CHURCHWORTH 6-11-3 J Culloty, blun 1st, al beh, tld off.
...............................(50 to 1 op 20 to 1) 17

1300⁷ ADMIRAL BRUNY (Ire) 6-11-3 C Llewellyn, slwly away, al beh, tld off.................(100 to 1 op 50 to 1) 18
Dist: 3½l, sht-hd, 5l, 7l, 3l, 10l, 3½l, 3l, ½l, 6l. 3m 39.10s. a 7.10s (18 Ran).
SR: 40/36/20/25/8/15/   (Darren C Mercer), O Sherwood

2894 European Breeders Fund Tattersalls Ireland Mares' Only Novices' Chase Qualifier Class D (6-y-o and up) £3,501 2½m..................(2:40)

2593⁵ TELLICHERRY 8-10-10 J Culloty, al prmnt, led 2 out, rdn out.
..............(11 to 8 fav op 6 to 4 tchd 13 to 8 and 7 to 4) 1

2298⁴ COOLE HILL (Ire) 6-10-10 R Johnson, hld up, hit 5th, hdwy tenth, led 3 out, hdd nxt, rallied und pres r-in.
...................(7 to 4 op 11 to 8 tchd 2 to 1) 2

2596³ JASILU (bl) 7-11-8 S McNeill, led till hdd 3 out, wknd quickly.
.........(3 to 1 op 5 to 2 tchd 100 to 30 and 7 to 2) 3

2726⁵ COUNTRY TOWN 7-10-10 P Holley, prmnt whn mstk 9th, no hdwy frm 3 out.............(33 to 1 op 25 to 1) 4

2596⁸ LAMBRINI (Ire) 7-10-10 T Jenks, al beh, lost tch 5 out.
.................................(66 to 1 op 50 to 1) 5

2388⁹ RENT DAY 8-10-10 S Curran, hld up, lost tch 11th, tld off.
.................(33 to 1 op 25 to 1 tchd 40 to 1) 6

2665 SUMMER HAVEN 8-10-10 Mr A Kinane, beh whn hit 7th, sn tld off.............(25 to 1 op 20 to 1 tchd 33 to 1) 7

2183⁵ ELEANORA MUSE 7-10-7 (3*) Guy Lewis, chsd ldrs till wknd 5 out, btn 5th whn f 2 out............(25 to 1 tchd 33 to 1) f

2403 DARING HEN (Ire) 7-10-10 Gary Lyons, jmpd badly in rear, tld off whn pld up bef 12th..........................(66 to 1) pu

2183 TINKER'S CUSS 6-10-10 L Harvey, jmpd slwly in rear, tld off 4th, pld up bef 12th..................(66 to 1) pu
Dist: Nk, 13l, 15l, hd, dist, 1¾l. 5m 4.40s. a 15.40s (10 Ran).
(Mrs C Clatworthy), Miss H C Knight

2895 Forbra Gold Challenge Cup Handicap Chase Class D (0-125 5-y-o and up) £3,777 3m..................(3:10)

2310³ RECTORY GARDEN (Ire) [110] 8-11-2 A Thornton, wth ldrs, mstk 8th, wnt second 12th till appr 4 out, rallied to ld last, rdn out...............(11 to 8 fav op 6 to 4 tchd 13 to 8) 1

2627⁷ ROMANY CREEK (Ire) [117] (v) 8-11-9 A P McCoy, led till pckd and mstk last, one pace r-in..........(5 to 2 op 2 to 1) 2

2627⁷ DONT TELL THE WIFE [112] 11-11-4 J Culloty, hld up, hdwy to chal 4 out, wknd appr last.............(16 to 1 op 14 to 1) 3

2728³ ROYAL SAXON [94] 11-10-0 R Johnson, trkd ldr to 12th, hit nxt, sn btn........................(7 to 1 op 5 to 1) 4

2627³ ACT OF PARLIAMENT (Ire) [118] (bl) 9-11-10 S McNeill, al struggling in rear, tld off whn blun 9th.............(4 to 1) 5

2745² ALICE SMITH [95] 10-10-1* W McFarland, al beh, tld off 6th.
...............(9 to 1 op 8 to 1 tchd 10 to 1) 6
Dist: 1½l, 7l, 12l, 21l, 3l. 5m 58.44s. a 11.40s (6 Ran).
SR: 22/27/15/   (Lord Cadogan), Capt T A Forster

2896 Henley Hall Gold Challenge Cup Handicap Hurdle Class E (0-110 4-y-o and up) £2,682 2m 5f 110yds (3:40)

2691³ JACKSON FLINT [90] 9-10-7 (7*) X Aizpuru, in tch, hdwy 7th, led 2 out, edgd lft und pres r-in.
...............(13 to 2 op 11 to 2 tchd 7 to 1) 1

2603² OPERETTO (Ire) [78] 7-10-2 J R Kavanagh, al prmnt, led appr 2 out, sn hdd, one pace r-in.
..............(13 to 2 op 6 to 1 tchd 7 to 1) 2

2513² FIRST CRACK [84] 12-10-8 S Wynne, hld up, hdwy whn mstk 3 out, one pace aftr..........(7 to 1 tchd 8 to 1) 3

2667³ FAWLEY FLYER [94] 8-10-11 (7*) J Power, al prmnt, ev ch 3 out, one pace aftr............(13 to 2 op 7 to 1) 4

BLATANT OUTBURST [82] 7-10-4 (3*) Michael Brennan, pld hrd, wnt second 6th, led aftr 4 out till hdd appr 2 out, no extr.
.................(20 to 1 op 16 to 1 tchd 25 to 1) 5

1915² STAR PERFORMER (Ire) [100] 6-11-3 (7*) Mr G Shenkin, hld up in tch, rdn 7th, hdwy nxt, wknd appr 3 out......(14 to 1) 6

2403³ VISCOUNT TULLY [77] 12-10-1 Miss S Jackson, hld up in rear, hdwy 4 out, wknd bef nxt......(14 to 1 tchd 16 to 1) 7

2559⁷ DERRING BRIDGE [85] 7-10-9 R Johnson, in tch till wknd appr 3 out......................(20 to 1 op 16 to 1) 8

1708² DESERT FORCE (Ire) [92] 8-11-2 G Bradley, hld up, hdwy appr 4th, wknd approaching 3 out. (5 to 1 jt-fav op 9 to 2) 9

2205 BOSSYMOSS (Ire) [78] 8-10-2² Gary Lyons, al beh, tld off.
.................(25 to 1 op 20 to 1) 10

2665 MISS MARIGOLD [96] (bl) 8-11-6 B Powell, very slwly away, hdwy aftr second, wknd 7th, tld off..........(5 to 1 jt-fav op 6 to 1 tchd 13 to 2) 11

2559 BETTER BYTHE GLASS (Ire) [93] 8-11-3 C Llewellyn, al beh, tld off.................(16 to 1 op 11 to 1) 12

2440 DEEP ISLE [76] 11-10-0 P Holley, led till hdd appr 3rd, weak-end quickly, tld off whn pld up aftr 5th...........(50 to 1) pu

2789 HOODWINKER (Ire) [104] (bl) 8-12-0 T Jenks, led appr 3rd, hdd and weakend quickly aftr 4 out, pld up bef nxt.
.........(16 to 1 op 12 to 1 tchd 20 to 1) pu

2606 MONKS JAY (Ire) [81] 8-10-5 J Culloty, prmnt to 6th, rdn 4 out, pld up bef nxt............(9 to 1 op 14 to 1) pu
Dist: 2½l, 3l, 2½l, 1¾l, 1½l, 1¼l, ½l, nk, 25l, ½l. 5m 7.90s. a 12.90s (15 Ran).
(Mrs L G Turner), T Thomson Jones

2897 Weatherbys Hunter Chase Planner Hunters' Chase Class H (6-y-o and up) £1,563 3m...............(4:10)

2608² CAPE COTTAGE 13-11-7 (7*) Mr A Phillips, hld up, hdwy 12th, led 3 out, styd on........(7 to 2 op 3 to 1 tchd 4 to 1) 1

FOX POINTER 12-11-9 (5*) Mr J Jukes, al beh, led appr 5 out, hdd 2 out, one pace.........(5 to 2 op 2 to 1) 2

2551* INCH MAID 11-11-9 (7*) Miss H Brookshaw, prmnt till lost pl 5 out, styd on frm 2 out..........(11 to 10 on tchd 11 to 10) 3

2608 J B LAD 11-11-7 (7*) Miss P Gundry, prmnt to 6th, beh whn mstk 9th, tld off..................(66 to 1 op 50 to 1) 4

WELSH LIGHTNING 9-11-7 (7*) Capt R Inglesant, mstks in rear, tld off frm 12th.............(66 to 1 op 50 to 1) 5

KINGFISHER BAY 12-11-7 (7*) Mr G Shenkin, beh whn blun 11th, sn tld off...............(66 to 1 op 50 to 1) 6

STAR OATS 11-11-7 (7*) Mr A Kinane, hit 3rd, led 5th, sn clr, hit 9th, hdd appr 5 out, wknd quickly, pld up bef nxt, lme.
.........(14 to 1 op 10 to 1) pu

2551 KING OF SHADOWS 10-12-0 (7*) Mr S Prior, led to 5th, mstk 11th, sn beh, tld off whn pld up bef 2 out.
.................(25 to 1 op 16 to 1) pu
Dist: 3l, ¾l, dist, dist, sht-hd. 6m 9.00s. a 22.00s (8 Ran).
(D J Caro), D J Caro

2898 Clee Hill Novices' Hurdle Class E (4-y-o and up) £2,556 2m 5f 110yds ....(4:40)

2451⁵ IONIO (USA) 6-11-10 J R Kavanagh, al prmnt, wnt second 6th, hit nxt, rdn appr 3 out, led r-in, ran on.
.................(5 to 2 op 3 to 1 tchd 4 to 1) 1

2288³ CHEROKEE CHIEF 6-11-4 M Richards, hld up, hdwy 7th, led aftr 4 out, rdn appr 2 out, hdd r-in...(2 to 1 fav op 5 to 4) 2

2628⁹ EZANAK (Ire) 4-10-7 J Culloty, hld up in rear, styd on frm 3 out, nvr dngrs................(7 to 2 op 3 to 1) 3

2725⁴ BROOKHAMPTON LANE (Ire) 6-11-4 B Powell, in tch till outpcd 7th, nvr dngrs aftr. (8 to 1 op 6 to 1 tchd 10 to 1) 4

880 CARLINGFORD GALE (Ire) 6-10-13 S Wynne, led appr 3rd, hdd aftr 4 out, sn wknd...(12 to 1 op 7 to 1 tchd 14 to 1) 5

1881 HIGH HANDED (Ire) 6-11-4 Gary Lyons, al towards rear.
.................................(50 to 1) 6

2605⁹ LADY OF MINE 7-10-13 R Johnson, prmnt to 5th, rallied 7th, wknd aftr nxt...................(100 to 1 op 50 to 1) 7

2607⁹ BROWNSCROFT 9-10-6 (7*) K Hibbert, mid-div, lost tch 7th, tld off........................(100 to 1 op 50 to 1) 8

2662 SOUTH WEST EXPRESS (Ire) 5-10-11 (7*) Mr A Wintle, al beh, tld off...........................(25 to 1) 9

1598⁷ ROC AGE 6-11-0⁸ (7*) J T Nolan, beh frm 5th, tld off.
.................(16 to 1 tchd 20 to 1) 10

2594 MISTER GOODGUY (Ire) 8-10-13 (5*) A Bates, led till hdd appr 3rd, wknd aftr 4 out, tld off.....(33 to 1 op 20 to 1) 11

2607² ARIOSO 9-10-10 (3*) Michael Brennan, hld up, effrt 7th, sn tld off.............(10 to 1 op 16 to 1 tchd 20 to 1) 12

2173⁹ RED LANE 7-11-4 Mr A Dalton, al beh, tld off.
.................................(100 to 1 op 50 to 1) 13

2567 SEVEN FOUR SEVEN 6-10-13 S McNeill, al beh, tld off.
.................(100 to 1 op 50 to 1) 14

2545^{2} KYLAMI (NZ) 5-11-4 R Greene, *f second.* ....(25 to 1 op 20 to 1) f
2565 A BADGE TOO FAR (Ire) 7-10-13 R Bellamy, *pld hrd, prmnt to 5th, tld off whn pulled up aftr 4 out*.. (100 to 1 op 50 to 1) pu
2298 ONE MORE RUPEE 6-11-4 A Thornton, *reminders aftr 3rd, sn tld off, pld up bef 3 out*.......... (100 to 1 op 50 to 1) pu
Dist: 1¾l, 24l, 1¼l, 19l, ¾l, ¾l, 18l, 2l, 3l, ¾l. 5m 8.40s. a 13.40s (17 Ran).
(Mrs R F Key & Mrs V C Ward), Mrs V C Ward

2899 Border Intermediate Open National Hunt Flat Class H (4,5,6-y-o) £1,266 2m........................... (5:10)

1809^{6} BENVENUTO 6-11-4 S McNeill, *al prmnt, led o'r 2 fs out, ran on strly*.......... (9 to 2 op 7 to 2) 1
GOOD LORD MURPHY (Ire) 5-11-4 L Harvey, *hld up, hdwy o'r 4 fs out, styd on to go second cl hme.* .... (8 to 1 op 4 to 1 tchd 10 to 1) 2
2363^{2} ES GO 4-10-5 (3*) H Bastiman, *led aftr 4 fs, hdd o'r 2 out, eased wl ins last and lost second cl hme.* ....(100 to 30 op 5 to 2 tchd 7 to 2) 3
COUNT KARMUSKI 5-11-4 T Jenks, *beh till hdwy o'r 4 fs out, nvr nr to chal*......................(33 to 1 op 20 to 1) 4
2503^{6} MISS MATCH 6-10-8 (5*) O Burrows, *in tch till rdn and wknd o'r 2 fs out*..........................(10 to 1 op 7 to 1) 5
2784^{2} FILSCOT 5-10-11 (7*) J Power, *prmnt till wknd o'r 3 fs out.* ....(6 to 1 op 3 to 1) 6
2409 BOUNDTOHONOUR (Ire) 5-11-4 Jacqui Oliver, *beind till styd on ins fnl 4 fs, nvr dngrs*............ (20 to 1 op 11 to 1) 7
2552 TA-RA-ABIT (Ire) 4-10-3 B Powell, *al mid-div.* ....(66 to 1 op 50 to 1) 8
2784 TWO LORDS 5-11-4 S Burrough, *prmnt till wknd o'r 5 fs out.* .... (50 to 1 op 33 to 1) 9
GALLANT TAFFY 5-11-4 C Llewellyn, *al beh.* .... (50 to 1 op 33 to 1) 10
CARIBOO (Ire) 5-10-11 (7*) J Mogford, *hld up in tch, wknd sn aftr hfwy*.......................(50 to 1 op 33 to 1) 11
2469^{8} STRONG MAGIC (Ire) 5-11-1 (3*) Michael Brennan, *al beh.* .... (20 to 1 op 14 to 1) 12
2723 CELTIC CARROT 5-11-4 J R Kavanagh, *prmnt till wknd 5 fs out*..............................(50 to 1 op 25 to 1) 13
2723 HABERDASHER 6-10-11 (7*) K Hibbert, *al beh.* .... (50 to 1 op 33 to 1) 14
2409 ORIENTAL BOY (Ire) 5-11-4 R Johnson, *beh frm hfwy.* .... (50 to 1 op 20 to 1) 15
ASK IN TIME (Ire) 5-11-4 D Bridgwater, *prmnt till wknd quickly 4 fs out, eased whn btn.* ....(11 to 8 fav op 3 to 1 tchd 7 to 2) 16
2723 GINGER WATT (Ire) 5-11-1 (3*) T Dascombe, *al beh, tld off.* .... (33 to 1 op 25 to 1) 17
2377 MISS MIGHTY 4-10-3 R Bellamy, *led for 4 fs, wknd hfwy, tld off*.............................(100 to 1 op 50 to 1) 18
Dist: 10l, ½l, 6l, 4l, 9l, ½l, 9l, 10l, 10l, nk. 3m 38.50s. (18 Ran).
(Mrs Lucia Farmer), K C Bailey

THURLES (IRE) (heavy)
Thursday February 27th

2900 Horse And Jockey Novice Hurdle (5 & 6-y-o) £2,226 2m........... (2:00)

2732^{6} COLM'S ROCK (Ire) 6-11-9 C F Swan,.......(7 to 2 jt-fav) 1
2525* WEST LEADER (Ire) 6-11-2 C O'Dwyer,.......(7 to 2 jt-fav) 2
2675* JENSALEE (Ire) 6-10-11 T P Treacy,...............(6 to 1) 3
2415^{4} HEN HANSEL (Ire) 6-11-2 T Horgan,.............(10 to 1) 4
2670^{5} MISS ORCHESTRA (Ire) 6-11-4 J Shortt,..........(12 to 1) 5
2704^{5} SHE'LL BE GOOD (Ire) 5-10-8 J R Barry,..........(16 to 1) 6
2704 ST CAROL (Ire) 6-10-11 T J Mitchell,.............(16 to 1) 7
AKTEON (Ire) 5-10-13 L P Cusack,.................(20 to 1) 8
MR CAVALLO (Ire) 5-10-6 (7*) A O'Shea,..........(20 to 1) 9
2645 ORMOND JENNY (Ire) 5-10-8 J P Broderick,......(16 to 1) 10
2583 PORT NA SON (Ire) 6-11-2 A Powell,...............(20 to 1) 11
HI-WAY TONIGHT (Ire) 6-10-6 (5*) P Morris,........(20 to 1) 12
CAPTAIN WALLACE (Ire) 5-10-13 F Woods,.......(14 to 1) 13
278* MIDNIGHT CYCLONE (Ire) 6-10-11 D J Casey,....(12 to 1) f
2732^{4} WINDY BEE (Ire) 6-10-11 (7*) A Nolan,............(4 to 1) f
TOM THISTLE (Ire) 5-10-13 K F O'Brien,..........(20 to 1) f
2582^{3} BAI-BRUN KATE (Ire) 6-10-4 (7*) L J Fleming,......(4 to 1) bd
COTTAGE LORD (Ire) 5-10-8 M Duffy,.............(20 to 1) l
Dist: 10l, 15l, 3½l, 2l. 4m 15.90s. (18 Ran).
(R Finnegan), A P O'Brien

2901 Devils Bit Handicap Hurdle (0-116 4-y-o and up) £2,226 2m...... (2:30)

2735 JIHAAD (USA) [-] (bl) 7-9-0 (7*) J M Maguire,.......(14 to 1) 1
2674^{3} ZIGGY THE GREAT (Ire) [-] (bl) 5-10-7 P A Roche,.. (7 to 1) 2
2735^{2} MARINERS REEF (Ire) [-] 6-9-11 (7*) D McCullagh, (7 to 2 jt-fav) 3
2708^{7} DUISKE ABBEY (Ire) [-] 7-11-1 T P Treacy,............(6 to 1) 4
2753 REGIT (Ire) [-] 7-10-1 T Hazlett,....................(16 to 1) 5
2227^{5} IODER WAN (Ire) [-] 5-11-0 M P Hourigan,..........(6 to 1) 6
2674^{4} MUSKERRY KING (Ire) [-] 6-11-0 W Slattery,........(5 to 1) 7
2647^{7} BYPHARBEANRI (Ire) [-] 6-9-12 T Horgan,.... (7 to 2 jt-fav) 8
2703^{6} IMPERIAL PLAICE (Ire) [-] 5-10-13 C O'Dwyer,...... (5 to 1) 9
2704^{8} RAMDON ROCKS [-] 10-10-10 P McWilliams,..... (14 to 1) 10
2708 COCK COCKBURN [-] 11-12-0 T P Rudd,.........(20 to 1) f
Dist: ½l, 2½l, 1l, 12l. 4m 22.30s. (11 Ran).
(Mattie O'Toole), Michael A Kelly

2902 Cashel Maiden Hurdle (4-y-o and up) £2,226 2¾m.................. (3:00)

2583^{6} KAISER SOSA (Ire) 6-11-6 C O'Dwyer,............. (4 to 1) 1
2838^{2} THE GREY MARE (Ire) 8-11-2 (7*) Mr P Fahey,..... (12 to 1) 2
2649* MOUNT DRUID (Ire) 7-12-0 J Shortt,............(5 to 4 on) 3
2752^{3} BAWNROCK (Ire) 8-12-0 C F Swan,................(6 to 1) 4
BOBBIT BACK ON (Ire) 7-11-6 D J Casey,.........(12 to 1) 5
2753^{4} COMMITTED SCHEDULE (Ire) 6-11-6 M P Hourigan, ...(12 to 1) 6
2752 TRUCKINABOUT (Ire) 7-11-6 F Woods,...........(20 to 1) 7
2703 BRIDGES DAUGHTER (Ire) 6-11-9 P A Roche,......(14 to 1) 8
2518^{2} MAGS SUPER TOI (Ire) 8-10-13 (7*) M D Murphy, (14 to 1) 9
2524 TAR AND CEMENT (Ire) (bl) 9-10-13 (7*) A O'Shea, (20 to 1) 10
2704 DUEONE (Ire) 9-12-0 M Duffy,.....................(20 to 1) 11
MERCHANTS ROAD 10-10-13 (7*) R M Murphy,.. (33 to 1) 12
2703 CASEY JUNIOR (Ire) 9-11-7 (7*) R P Hogan,......(25 to 1) 13
2649 ROSE ANA (Ire) 7-10-8 (7*) D McCullagh,..........(33 to 1) 14
2368^{9} AROUND THE STUMP (Ire) 5-10-12 T P Treacy,.... (33 to 1) 15
2518 MOSTA (Ire) 4-9-11 (7*) M J Collins,..............(33 to 1) 16
2449 MAJESTIC RED (Ire) 6-11-6 J R Barry,............(14 to 1) f
RYEV (Ire) 5-10-12 A J O'Brien,..................(20 to 1) f
Dist: Nk, 1½l, nk, 15l. 6m 8.30s. (18 Ran).
(Mrs Peaches Taaffe), T J Taaffe

2903 Golden Novice Chase (5-y-o and up) £2,740 2m................... (3:30)

2058^{3} WOODVILLE STAR (Ire) 8-11-9 C O'Dwyer,......(5 to 4 fav) 1
2705* KEELSON (Ire) 6-11-7 (7*) Mr Brian Moran,........(8 to 1) 2
2673* BLAZE OF HONOUR (Ire) 6-11-9 C F Swan,.......(13 to 8) 3
2164^{5} TEMPLEROAN PRINCE 10-11-7 J R Barry,........(10 to 1) 4
2673^{5} YOUNG MRS KELLY (Ire) 7-11-2 J Jones,..........(9 to 1) 5
2644 LINDA'S BOY (Ire) 7-11-4 (3*) K Whelan,..........(14 to 1) 6
2755 WHINNEY HILL (Ire) 7-11-2 D T Evans,............(33 to 1) 7
29^{4} NOBULL (Ire) 7-11-2 A Powell,...................(12 to 1) f
Dist: 6l, 2l, 20l, 2l. 4m 37.80s. (8 Ran).
(Sean Donnelly), W J Burke

2904 Thurles Beginners Chase (5-y-o and up) £2,226 3m................ (4:00)

2522^{2} THE NOBLE ROUGE (Ire) 8-12-0 T Horgan,.. (3 to 1 jt-fav) 1
2705^{2} ARCTIC BUCK (Ire) 7-11-9 Mr P Fenton,............(7 to 1) 2
2143^{7} RYHANE (Ire) 8-11-9 F Woods,...................(10 to 1) 3
2673^{4} VALERIE OWENS (Ire) 8-10-11 (7*) D K Budds,......(8 to 1) 4
2522^{5} THE BOYLERMAN (Ire) 8-11-7 (7*) Mr K O'Sullivan, (10 to 1) 5
2648 PHARALLEY (Ire) 7-11-4 D T Evans,...............(25 to 1) 6
2648^{3} CESAR DU MANOIR (Fr) 7-11-6 (3*) K Whelan,.....(10 to 1) 7
2088 CELTIC WHO (Ire) 6-11-9 D J Casey,...............(20 to 1) 8
2585 LEAMHOG (Ire) 7-11-11 (3*) J Butler,..............(10 to 1) 9
2755^{9} ROSEL WALK (Ire) 8-11-9 A J O'Brien,............(25 to 1) 10
2705^{5} HAVE A BRANDY (Ire) 8-12-0 C O'Brien,...........(14 to 1) 11
2756^{7} DOONEGA (Ire) 9-12-0 J P Broderick,.............(10 to 1) 12
2648 CAVALLO (Fr) 7-11-9 T P Rudd,....................(16 to 1) f
2705^{3} GENTLE BUCK (Ire) 8-12-0 C O'Dwyer,.......(3 to 1 jt-fav) pu
2587^{7} HILLHEAD (Ire) 8-11-9 L P Cusack,................(14 to 1) pu
2755^{5} ANDY BURNETT (Ire) 8-11-9 F J Flood,.............(8 to 1) pu
Dist: 9l, 5l, 7l, 2l. 6m 52.80s. (16 Ran).
(Mrs M Nolan), David Fenton

2905 Tipperary I.N.H. Flat Race (4-y-o) £2,226 2m.................... (4:30)

2234^{7} BILL BISHOP (Ire) 11-5 Mr D Marnane,.............(4 to 1) 1
MAGGIE MACCLOONE (Ire) 10-7 (7*) Mr Sean O O'Brien, ...(3 to 1) 2
2737^{3} DIVINE DANCER (Ire) 10-7 (7*) Mr M P Horan,.. (9 to 4 fav) 3
GREATWESTERN LADY (Ire) 10-7 (7*) Mr J Keville, (10 to 1) 4
2370^{9} COULDN'T SAY (Ire) 11-5 Mr T Mullins,.............(5 to 1) 5
COCHIS RUN (Ire) 11-2 (3*) Mr E Norris,.............(8 to 1) 6
FIDALUS (Ire) 10-12 (7*) Mr M T Hartrey,...........(14 to 1) 7
2370 TONIBEROLI (Ire) 10-7 (7*) Mr J P McNamara,..... (16 to 1) 8
DERRAVARAGH SECRET (Ire) 10-7 (7*) Mr A Ross, (14 to 1) 9
2737^{9} KILLBALDONRUSH (Ire) 10-7 (7*) Mr J P Brennan, (16 to 1) 10
BALLERIN FLYER (Ire) 10-11 (3*) Mr R Walsh,.....(14 to 1) 11
Dist: 15l, nk, 25l, 1l. 4m 15.50s. (11 Ran).
(R Lucidi), John Roche

2906 Clonoulty I.N.H. Flat Race (Div I) (6-y-o and up) £2,226 2m........ (5:00)

2757^{3} LAFONTD'OR (Ire) 6-11-7 (7*) Mr B Moran,.........(7 to 2) 1
2704^{2} TORMOND PERK (Ire) 6-11-7 (7*) Mr C A Murphy, ...(13 to 8 fav) 2
DOOLAN'S STAND (Ire) 6-11-7 (7*) Mr M T Hartrey, (20 to 1) 3
BUCK THE WEST (Ire) 7-12-0 Mr P Fenton,........(12 to 1) 4
2092^{8} MR MAGNETIC (Ire) 6-11-7 (7*) Mrs C Doyle,....... (7 to 1) 5
AS AN SLI (Ire) 6-11-9 Mr M Phillips,..............(20 to 1) 6
BALLINREE (Ire) 6-11-4 (5*) Mr A C Coyle,..........(6 to 1) 7
2704 MANISSA (Ire) 6-11-4 (5*) Mr J T McNamara,..... (12 to 1) 8
GREY HORIZON (Ire) 6-12-0 Mr D M O'Brien,.......(20 to 1) 9
2582 SCOBIE GIRL (Ire) 7-11-9 Mr D Marnane,.........(10 to 1) 10
SWINFORD BOY (Ire) 9-11-7 (7*) Mr P A Rattigan, (20 to 1) 11

```
           MICKSCOTT (Ire) 7-11-11 (3*) Mr R Walsh, ....... (20 to 1)    12
           PRINCE PINE (Ire) 6-11-7 (7*) Mr E Gallagher, .....(12 to 1)  13
2757  THEATRE SISTER (Ire) 6-11-2 (7*) Mr K Hadnett, ..(20 to 1)         14
      CAROLKATE (Ire) 7-11-2 (7*) Mr A J Dempsey, .....(14 to 1)         15
1364  EVE'S DAUGHTER (Ire) 6-11-2 (7*) Mr John P Moloney,
                                                 .........(20 to 1)      pu
Dist: 8l, 15l, nk, 1½l. 4m 24.50s. (16 Ran).
```

(W J Austin), W J Austin

2907 Clonoulty I.N.H. Flat Race (Div II) (6-y-o and up) £2,226 2m........ (5:30)

```
2649³  BACK TO THE NEST (Ire) 6-11-6 (3*) Mr R Walsh,
                                          ..............(11 to 10 fav)    1
       DUSKY LAMP (Ire) 7-12-0 Mr J A Berry, ...........(12 to 1)        2
2649   KNOCKAULIN (Ire) 6-12-0 Mr H F Cleary, ...........(4 to 1)        3
2737⁸  CAPTAIN CHAOS (Ire) 6-11-7 (7*) Mr K R O'Ryan, ..(8 to 1)         4
2446¹⁹ THE VENDOR (Ire) 7-11-9 Mr P Fenton, ...........(11 to 2)         5
2416   THE MILLMAN (Ire) 6-11-7 (7*) Mr D Deacon, ......(14 to 1)        6
2703   LAS ALMANDAS (Ire) 6-11-2 (7*) Mr E Gallagher, ..(12 to 1)        7
       OAKLAND BRIDGE (Ire) 6-11-7 (7*) Mr J P McNamara,
                                              ..........(10 to 1)        8
2343   CALLELLA PARSONS (Ire) 7-11-2 (7*) Mr A J Dempsey,
                                              ..........(20 to 1)        9
2845   CHANCERY RIVER (Ire) 8-11-2 (7*) Mr R F O'Gorman,
                                              ..........(14 to 1)        10
2838   GLENPATRICK PEACH (Ire) 8-11-2 (7*) Mr P Fahey, (12 to 1)        11
2752⁹  MILLSOFBALLYSODARE (Ire) 6-11-7 (7*) Mr A FitzGerald,
                                              ..........(8 to 1)         12
       MERRY CHIEFTAIN (Ire) 8-11-7 (7*) Mr B Hassett, ..(8 to 1)        pu
Dist: 8l, dist, nk, 8l. 4m 18.40s. (13 Ran).
```

(J P M O'Connor), W P Mullins

WETHERBY (heavy (races 1,2,3,4), soft (5,6))
Thursday February 27th
Going Correction: PLUS 2.00 sec. per fur. (races 1,3,6), PLUS 1.90 (2,4,5)

2908 Replacement 'National Hunt' Novices' Hurdle Class E (4-y-o and up) £2,389 2m..................... (2:20)

```
2546²  GODS SQUAD 5-11-2 R Supple, nvr far away, effrt and ev ch
       2 out, led aftr last, drvn out. (4 to 1 op 3 to 1 tchd 5 to 1)    1
2684³  GOOD VIBES 5-11-7 L Wyer, set steady pace, hdd aftr last, no
       extr....................................(5 to 4 on op 5 to 4)     2
2469⁶  BANKER COUNT 5-10-13 (3*) P Midgley, hld up, shaken up
       whn hit 3 out, styd on, nvr dngrs......(33 to 1 op 25 to 1)       3
       LORD FORTUNE (Ire) 7-11-2 R Garritty, hld up beh ldg grp,
       effrt bef 3 out, outpcd nxt.
                                 ....(16 to 1 op 14 to 1 tchd 20 to 1)   4
2344²  ARDARROCH PRINCE 6-11-2 P Niven, trkd ldrs, rdn 3 out,
       struggling nxt........................(5 to 1 op 4 to 1)          5
2565   FERRERS 6-11-2 W Marston, hld up, rdn alng 3 out, nvr able
       to chal................................(10 to 1 op 8 to 1)        6
2200   EDSTONE (Ire) 5-11-2 Derek Byrne, dsptd ld to 4th, struggling
       bef 3 out, sn outpcd......................(100 to 1 op 33 to 1)   7
2008   STRONG MINT (Ire) 6-10-13 (3*) G Lee, chsd ldg grp, rdn appr
       3 out, sn btn.....................(9 to 1 op 6 to 1 tchd 10 to 1) 8
       SECOND FIDDLE (Ire) 7-10-11 M Brennan, cl up, struggling
       aftr 4th, sn btn.......................(16 to 1 op 33 to 1)       9
1390⁷  SKIDDAW KNIGHT (Ire) 6-11-2 N Smith, hld up, struggling
       bef 3 out, sn btn.........................(33 to 1)               10
       PERKY TOO (Ire) 5-11-2 P Carberry, beh, mstk 5th, sn lost tch,
       pld up 2 out.....................(20 to 1 op 16 to 1)             pu
Dist: 1¾l, 9l, 7l, sht-hd, 1¼l, 11l, 12l, 14l, 3½l. 4m 19.00s. a 38.00s (11 Ran).
SR: 28/31/17/10/10/8/
```

(R M Kirkland), J Mackie

2909 Understudy Novices' Chase Class E (5-y-o and up) £3,317 2½m 110yds .... (2:50)

```
2686²  RIVER UNSHION (Ire) 7-11-3 P Carberry, keen hold, trkd ldrs,
       led bef 7th, kpt on stcly frm 3 out, hit last, easily.
                                ....(11 to 4 on op 5 to 2 on tchd 9 to 4 on)  1
2652²  TICO GOLD 9-11-8 R Supple, dsptd ld till blun 4 out, sn drvn
       alng, no imprsn whn hit last............(5 to 2 op 2 to 1)        2
2650³  ALICAT (Ire) 6-11-3 Derek Byrne, dsptd ld till blun 6th, sn
       struggling, tld off.....................(6 to 1 op 5 to 1)        3
Dist: 13l, dist. 5m 51.80s. a 58.80s (3 Ran).
```

(R J Crake), J Howard Johnson

2910 Proxy Novices' Hurdle Class E (5-y-o and up) £2,337 3m 1f......... (3:20)

```
2438*  YOUNG KENNY 6-11-7 R Supple, nvr far away, led on bit bef
       3 out, clr whn hit nxt, easily.
                               .....(13 to 8 op 2 to 1 tchd 9 to 4)      1
2200²  SMART APPROACH 7-10-12 P Niven, chsd ldrs, outpcd
       aftr 6th, styd on betw last 2, no ch whn wnr.
                               ........(8 to 1 op 7 to 1 tchd 9 to 1)    2
2619*  MILITARY ACADEMY (Ire) 6-11-7 P Carberry, settled in tch,
       improved and ev ch 6th, mstk nxt, sn outpcd.
       .... (11 to 10 fav op Evens tchd 5 to 4 on and 5 to 4)           3
```

```
2465²  SHARE OPTIONS (Ire) 6-11-3 L Wyer, led till bef 3 out, sn
       struggling...........................(7 to 1 op 5 to 1)          4
2487⁷  THE OTHER MAN (Ire) 7-10-12 O Pears, hld up, reminders
       bef 6th, struggling nxt, tld off......... (50 to 1 op 33 to 1)   5
2653⁶  LA CHANCE (v) 7-10-12 Mr A Walton, chsd ldrs, hit 4th,
       struggling aftr nxt, tld off...........(100 to 1 op 33 to 1)     6
2489⁹  DROMORE DREAM (Ire) 8-10-12 A Dobbin, hndy, pushed
       alng whn mstk 6th, sn struggling, pld up bef 3 out.
                                           .....(5 to 1 op 20 to 1)     pu
Dist: 16l, nk, 26l, 13l, dist. 6m 55.20s. a 69.20s (7 Ran).
```

(J G Read), P Beaumont

2911 Weatherbys Insurance Services Handicap Chase Class C (0-135 5-y-o and up) £4,571 2m......... (3:50)

```
2617³  POLITICAL TOWER [128] 10-11-10 A Dobbin, trkd ldrs, out-
       pcd whn hit 4 out, rallied to ld aftr 2 out, hit last, pushed out.
                              ........(6 to 5 fav op Evens tchd 5 to 4)  1
2774²  REGAL ROMPER (Ire) [111] 9-10-7 Richard Guest, jmpd wl,
       led till aftr 2 out, hit last, one pace.
                              ..........(2 to 1 op 7 to 4 tchd 9 to 4)   2
2713⁴  CROSS CANNON [105] 11-10-1 B Storey, trkd ldr, ev ch 4
       out, outpcd nxt........(11 to 4 op 5 to 2 tchd 3 to 1)           3
Dist: 6l, 13l. 4m 23.40s. a 36.40s (3 Ran).
SR: 36/13/-/
```

(G R S Nixon), R Nixon

2912 Substitute Novices' Handicap Chase Class D (0-115 5-y-o and up) £3,566 3m 1f.............................(4:20)

```
2347³  COVERDALE LANE [90] 10-11-10 Richard Guest, jmpd wl,
       made most, clr fnl circuit, all out. (3 to 1 tchd 7 to 2)        1
2652*  GOLD PIGEON (Ire) [75] 8-10-9 B Storey, nvr far away, chsd
       wnr 5 out, kpt on fnl 2......(8 to 1 op 6 to 1 tchd 9 to 1)       2
2686⁶  GARBO'S BOY [79] 7-10-13 D Parker, hld up, improved 6th,
       blun tenth, sn outpcd..................(12 to 1 tchd 14 to 1)     3
2620³  D'ARBLAY STREET (Ire) [80] 8-11-0 P Carberry, al prmnt,
       struggling 5 out, tld off nxt.............(3 to 1 p
                            fav op 5 to 2 tchd 100 to 30)                4
2286⁴  BE BRAVE [78] 7-10-12 R Rourke, mstks, in tch whn 19th.
                                  .....(16 to 1 op 14 to 1)              f
       KING OF STEEL [86] 11-11-6 R Garritty, dsptd ld, cl second
       whn blun and uns 6th..........(16 to 1 op 14 to 1)               ur
2620   QUIXALL CROSSETT [66] 12-9-7 (7*) Tristan Davidson, sn tld
       off, pld up bef 4 out....................(50 to 1 op 33 to 1)     pu
2741³  PLASSY BOY (Ire) [70] 8-10-4 A Dobbin, chsd ldrs, lost pl aftr
       5th, tld off whn pld up bef 9th..........(8 to 1 op 7 to 1)       pu
2620   NOOSA SOUND (Ire) [79] 7-10-13 R Supple, settled in tch,
       struggling bef 9th, tld off whn pld up before 4 out.
                                  ........(6 to 1 op 7 to 2)             pu
Dist: 2½l, dist, dist. 7m 9.30s. a 61.30s (9 Ran).
```

(Jim Pilkington), Mrs S J Smith

2913 Surrogate Novices' Handicap Hurdle Class D (0-115 4-y-o and up) £2,871 2½m 110yds............... (4:50)

```
       INTO THE WEST (Ire) [96] 8-11-10 Richard Guest, wide, hld
       up in tch, smooth hdwy aftr 4 out, led bef last, ran on wl.
                               .....(11 to 2 op 5 to 1 tchd 8 to 1)      1
2655*  ENCHANTED COTTAGE [78] 5-10-3 (3*) E Callaghan, al
       prmnt, improved to ld bef 3 out, jst hdd whn mstk last, no extr.
                               .....(11 to 8 fav op 11 to 10)            2
2527   BASSENHALLY [89] 7-11-3 W Marston, led till bef 3 out, sn
       outpcd.................................(9 to 1 tchd 10 to 1)      3
2550⁵  DONT FORGET CURTIS (Ire) [87] 5-11-1 J Callaghan, prmnt
       in chasing grp, struggling 3 out, fdd....(4 to 1 tchd 5 to 1)     4
2847³  OBVIOUS RISK [72] 6-9-7 (7*) Tristan Davidson, chsd ldrs,
       struggling aftr 4 out, virtually pld up r-in.
                               .....(14 to 1 op 16 to 1 tchd 16 to 1)    5
2463⁴  MUDLARK [90] 5-11-4 W Dwan, settled in chasing grp,
       imprvg whn hit 4th, wknd 3 out, virtually pld up r-in.
                               .....(5 to 1 op 4 to 1 tchd 11 to 2)      6
2711   GREENFINCH (Can) [72] (v) 6-10-0 M Foster, chsd ldrs,
       reminders aftr 3rd, sn lost pl, tld off whn pld up bef last.
                               .....(14 to 1 op 10 to 1)                 pu
Dist: 4l, dist, 2l, dist, 10l. 5m 34.70s. a 52.70s (7 Ran).
```

(J Mason), Mrs S J Smith

KELSO (good to soft)
Friday February 28th
Going Correction: PLUS 1.25 sec. per fur. (races 1,3,5), PLUS 1.10 (2,4,6)

2914 Cyril Alexander Memorial Maiden Chase Class D (6-y-o and up) £3,598 3m 1f.........................(2:20)

```
2686⁷  KALAJO 7-11-5 B Storey, chsd ldrs, led 6 out, lft clr last, drvn
       out...................................(10 to 1 op 5 to 1 tchd 7 to 1)  1
2621³  DESPERATE DAYS (Ire) 8-11-5 W Dwan, in tch, chlgd 4 out, ev
       ch whn blun last, not reco'r..........(12 to 1 op 10 to 1)        2
```

TWO FOR ONE (Ire) 8-11-5 T Reed, *chsd ldrs, outpcd and jmpd slwly 13th, sn lost tch.*
.......................(5 to 1 tchd 6 to 1 and 9 to 2) 3

2812⁵ FINE TUNE (Ire) 7-11-5 M Foster, *jmpd slwly, made most to 6 out, btn whn veered lft aftr last.*..........(8 to 1 op 6 to 1) 4

1820⁸ MISS COLETTE 9-11-0 D Parker, *chsd ldrs, lost pl hfwy, struggling whn mstk 5 out, sn no dngr.* (50 to 1 op 20 to 1) 5

2418³ MILLIES IMAGE 6-11-0 A Dobbin, *hld up, hdwy whn mstk 12th, btn when blun 4 out, tld off.*....(25 to 1 op 12 to 1) 6

2683⁶ ARISTODEMUS 8-11-5 K Johnson, *beh, hit 8th, blun 11th, sn tld off.*..........................(25 to 1 op 20 to 1) 7

2712 LYFORD CAY (Ire) 7-10-12 (7*) S Melrose, *in tch, hit 8th, drvn alng and hit 5 out, 5th and btn whn f 3 out.*

SAFETY FACTOR (Ire) 9-11-5 A S Smith, *led till f 3rd.*
.......................(100 to 1 op 33 to 1) f

.......................(16 to 1 op 5 to 1) f

2619 JUST EVE 10-11-0 G Cahill, *hld up, blun 9th, pld up 12th.*
.......................(100 to 1 op 33 to 1) pu

2491⁴ CALL ME BLACK (Ire) 8-11-0 R Garritty, *cl up, drvn alng 4 out, outpcd in 3rd whn broke dwn aftr 2 out, dead.*
.......................(Evens fav op 5 to 4 tchd 11 to 8) pu

Dist: 15l, 8l, nk, 1½l, dist, dist. 6m 41.40s. a 44.40s (11 Ran).
(Kelso Members Lowflyers Club), B Mactaggart

2915 Penny Farthing Restaurant Juvenile Novices' Hurdle Class D (4-y-o) £2,749 2m 110yds...........(2:50)

2568² CLASH OF SWORDS 10-12 L Wyer, *chsd clr ldr, hdwy to ld last, sn clear, easily.*........(11 to 8 on op 11 to 10 on) 1

ANIKA'S GEM (Ire) 10-7 M Foster, *hld up, pushed alng 5th, hdwy whn not fluent 2 out, kpt on same pace und pres.*
.......................(33 to 1 op 20 to 1) 2

2568⁷ CRY BABY 10-13 (5*) S Taylor, *cl up in chasing grp, niggled alng 2 out, unbl to quicken.*..........(6 to 4 op 5 to 4) 3

2417 PRINCIPAL BOY 10-12 R Rourke, *pld hrd, sn clr, hit 3rd, mstk 2 out, hdd last, soon btn.*
.......................(16 to 1 op 10 to 1 tchd 25 to 1) 4

2632⁵ KNAVE 10-12 A Dobbin, *hld up, struggling 5th, sn wl beh.*
.......................(10 to 1 op 8 to 1) 5

2687 POLITICAL MANDATE 10-7 B Storey, *beh, wl tld off 5th.*
.......................(50 to 1 op 16 to 1) 6

Dist: 8l, hd, 15l, 25l, 5l. 4m 16.00s. a 33.00s (6 Ran).
(Mrs Janis MacPherson), P Calver

2916 M. & J. Ballantyne Amateur Riders' Handicap Chase Class E for the Hamilton Memorial Trophy (0-125 5-y-o and up) £3,117 3½m.... (3:20)

2536² OFF THE BRU [93] 12-10-1⁸ (7*) Mr M Bradburne, *made most to 7th, led 11th to 17th, chlgd 2 out, led and drvn clr aftr last.*
.......................(4 to 1) 1

2715 CEILIDH BOY [117] 11-11-6 (5*) Mr R Hale, *wth ldrs, mstks, rdn and outpcd 4 out, styd on frm last.* (5 to 1 tchd 11 to 2) 2

2573 WHAAT FETTLE [120] 12-11-7 (7*) Capt A Ogden, *keen hold, al hndy, led 17th till aftr last, styd on one pace.*
.......................(16 to 1 op 14 to 1) 3

2536³ SEEKING GOLD (Ire) [92] 8-9-9 (5*) Miss P Robson, *hld up, pushed alng hfwy, lost tch 5 out, styd on frm 2 out, nvr dngrs.*
.......................(12 to 1 op 7 to 2) 4

2178⁶ WHITE DIAMOND [92] 9-9-10³ (7*) Mr D Reid, *cl up, led 7th to 11th, chsd ldrs till outpcd 2 out, no ex.* (66 to 1 op 33 to 1) 5

2715 PINK GIN [108] 10-10-13 (3*) Mr C Bonner, *niggled alng in rear frm tenth, beh 4 out.*.........(14 to 1 tchd 12 to 1) 6

2579² HEAVENLY CITIZEN [93] 9-10-1¹ Mr P Craggs, *hld up, in tch whn hit 15th, struggling nxt, tld off 3 out.*
.......................(9 to 2 op 4 to 1) 7

2620* JUDICIOUS CAPTAIN [92] 10-9-11² (5*) Mr C Storey, *in tch till f 13th.*......................(7 to 2 fav tchd 4 to 1) f

Dist: 9l, hd, 4l, ½l, 15l, dist. 7m 27.80s. a 41.80s (8 Ran).
SR: 5/20/23/-/-/ (The Fife Steeplechasing Partnership), Mrs S C Bradburne

2917 Hennessy Cognac Special Series Final Class B Novices' Hurdle (4-y-o and up) £13,745 2¼m........(3:50)

2711* MARELLO 6-10-12 P Niven, *settled rear, hdwy whn not fluent 6th, led on bit 2 out, quickened clr last, imprsv.*
.......................(2 to 1 on tchd 7 to 4 on) 1

2618* STAR SELECTION 6-11-3 E Husband, *keen hold, led and clr 5th, drvn and hdd 2 out, kpt on, no ch wth wnr.*
.......................(14 to 1 op 10 to 1) 2

2684² DANA POINT (Ire) 5-11-3 Richard Guest, *cl up, drvn to chase ldr 3 out, outpcd whn slight mstk nxt, styd on.*
.......................(4 to 1 op 7 to 2) 3

2509⁵ MISTER ROSS (Ire) 7-11-3 P Carberry, *wth ldr, mstks 1st and 3rd, drvn and lost pl 4 out, sn no dngr.*
.......................(20 to 1 op 16 to 1 tchd 25 to 1) 4

2113 ASK THE BUTLER (Ire) 6-11-10 R Hughes, *hld up, cld hfwy, drvn alng 3 out, sn outpcd, eased and lost 4th close hme.*
.......................(7 to 1 op 5 to 1) 5

2387³ BRAMBLES WAY (bl) 8-11-10 Mr S Swiers, *hld up, drvn and lost tch 4 out, sn wl beh.*.................(33 to 1) 6

2537⁷ MAPLE BAY (Ire) 8-11-3 A Dobbin, *beh, not fluent second, struggling 5 out, sn tld off.*..........(100 to 1 op 66 to 1) 7

1657³ NICK ROSS 6-11-3 B Storey, *midfield, drpd rear and pushed alng 5th, tld off 7th.*....................(100 to 1) 8

Dist: 8l, 7l, dist, 2l, 6l, dist, 2l. 4m 31.50s. a 24.50s (8 Ran).
SR: 37/34/27/-/-/ (Mrs M Williams), Mrs M Reveley

2918 Alba Country Foods Hunters' Chase Class H (6-y-o and up) £1,982 3m 1f .... (4:20)

JIGTIME 8-11-7 (7*) Mr M Bradburne, *cl up, led 12th, strly pressed frm 2 out, drvn clr aftr last.*
.......................(5 to 2 fav op 9 to 4 tchd 11 to 4) 1

ROYAL JESTER 13-12-7 (5*) Mr C Storey, *al hndy, chlgd tenth, pushed alng frm 3 out, styd on same pace.*
.......................(4 to 1 op 7 to 2) 2

2634* HOWAYMAN 7-11-12 (7*) Mr A Parker, *hld up, hdwy hfwy, second whn hit 2 out, hmpd last, no extr.*
.......................(100 to 30 op 7 to 2 tchd 4 to 1) 3

2634 LITTLE WENLOCK 13-12-3 (3*) Mr S Jackson, *hld up in tch, pushed alng to chase ldg grp 3 out, one pace betw last 2.*
.......................(40 to 1 op 25 to 1) 4

FORDSTOWN (Ire) 8-12-1 (7*) Mr Jamie Alexander, *led to 6th, jmpd slwly and lost pl 9th, rallied to chal 14th, drvn and no extr betw last 2.*.......................(20 to 1 op 14 to 1) 5

LITTLE GENERAL 14-12-5 (7*) Mr T Scott, *in tch, drpd rear 13th, struggling appr 2 out, sn no dngr.*
.......................(66 to 1 op 50 to 1 tchd 100 to 1) 6

SAVOY 10-11-7 (7*) Capt A Ogden, *hld up, hit 6th, cld hfwy, pressing wnr whn f last.*...........(11 to 4 op 5 to 2) f

BUCK'S DELIGHT (Ire) 9-11-9 (3*) Mr C Bonner, *led 6th to 12th, wknd quickly 4 out, pld up bef nxt.* (14 to 1 op 10 to 1) pu

Dist: 12l, 6l, ¾l, 14l, 14l. 6m 43.70s. a 46.70s (8 Ran).
(J W Hughes), J W Hughes

2919 Ship Hotel, Eyemouth Handicap Hurdle Class D (0-120 4-y-o and up) £2,892 2¼m..................(4:50)

2537* INGLETONIAN [110] 8-11-6 B Storey, *led, quickened hfwy, strly pressed frm 2 out, kpt on gmely.*
.......................(9 to 2 op 4 to 1 tchd 5 to 1) 1

2682⁵ ELATION [107] 5-11-3 A Dobbin, *chsd ldr, chlgd 3 out, drvn alng aftr nxt, kpt on till no imprsn cl hme.* (4 to 1 op 3 to 1) 2

2064³ IFALLELSEFAILS [90] 9-10-0 R Supple, *settled rear, plenty to do aftr 3 out, shaken up and styd on after nxt, nrst finish.*
.......................(12 to 1 op 10 to 1 tchd 14 to 1) 3

1335³ FIELD OF VISION (Ire) [104] 7-11-0 J Supple, *midfield, effrt to chase ldrs 3 out, rdn and one pace betw last 2.*
.......................(25 to 1 op 20 to 1) 4

2574² PARIAH (Ire) [93] 8-10-3 P Carberry, *hld up, hdwy whn pckd 7th, chasing ldrs when hit 3 out, wknd appr nxt.*
.......................(5 to 2 fav op 3 to 1 tchd 7 to 2) 5

FESTIVAL FANCY [93] 10-10-0 (3*) G Lee, *cl up, pushed alng frm 6th, outpcd 3 out, sn btn.*
.......................(66 to 1 op 50 to 1 tchd 100 to 1) 6

2574³ PALACEGATE KING [116] 8-11-7 (5*) S Taylor, *chsd ldrs, drpd rear 6th, lost tch 3 out, no dngr aftr.*....(4 to 1 op 3 to 1) 7

2190⁷ ARAGON AYR [118] 9-11-7 (7*) C McCormack, *hld up rear, outpcd 3 out, sn lost tch...*(6 to 1 op 7 to 1 tchd 8 to 1) 8

2618⁵ COMMON SOUND (Ire) [103] 6-10-13 P Niven, *midfield, mstk 7th, lost tch quickly aftr 3 out, tld off.* (14 to 1 op 20 to 1) 9

Dist: 5l, 2½l, 1¾l, nk, 10l, ½l, 30l. 4m 39.60s. a 32.60s (9 Ran).
(Mrs Hilary Mactaggart), B Mactaggart

NEWBURY (good to soft)
Friday February 28th
Going Correction: PLUS 0.95 sec. per fur. (races 1,4,6,7), PLUS 0.80 (2,3,5)

2920 Ardington 'National Hunt' Novices' Hurdle Class C (5-y-o and up) £4,068 2m 110yds.................. (2:00)

2688³ SPLENDID THYNE 5-11-4 J Osborne, *al prmnt gng wl, led 3 out, pushed clr r-in...* (9 to 4 fav op 5 to 2 tchd 3 to 1) 1

2678² CLINTON (Ire) 6-11-0 C O'Dwyer, *hld up in rear, hdwy 4th, ev ch 2 out, not pace of wnr.*...........(4 to 1 tchd 7 to 2) 2

1578³ STRONG TEL (Ire) 7-11-0 D Walsh, *hld up, hdwy 4th, rdn and ev ch 3 out, wknd appr last.*..........(14 to 1 op 10 to 1) 3

2595⁸ MOON DEVIL (Ire) 7-11-0 J Railton, *pld hrd, hdwy to ld aftr 5th, hdd 3 out, rdn and wknd appr last.*...........(33 to 1) 4

2594⁶ GET REAL (Ire) 6-11-0 N Williamson, *hld up, hdwy second, hdwy 4th, ev ch 3 out, wknd aftr nxt.*
.......................(9 to 1 op 9 to 4 tchd 100 to 30) 5

1483⁴ MILITARY LAW 6-11-0 J Culloty, *trkd ldrs till wknd appr 2 out.*
.......................(7 to 1 op 8 to 1 tchd 12 to 1) 6

NEWS FLASH (Ire) 5-11-0 S McNeill, *hld up, nvr on terms.*
.......................(12 to 1 op 8 to 1 tchd 14 to 1) 7

CATHERINE'S WAY (Ire) 5-11-0 L Harvey, *al beh.*
.......................(12 to 1 op 8 to 1) 8

MARCHIES MAGIC 7-10-11 (3*) L Aspell, *hld off hdd aftr 5th, sn wknd, tld off.*.........(50 to 1 op 33 to 1) 9

2483⁵ HULALEA (NZ) 5-11-0 G Tormey, *tld off frm 4th.*
.......................(50 to 1 op 33 to 1) 10

RELKANDER 7-11-0 R Farrant, *mid-div, lost tch 4th, tld off.*
.... (16 to 1 op 14 to 1 tchd 20 to 1) 11

2353 CRAMPSCASTLE (Ire) 7-10-7 (7*) P Ryan, *trkd ldr, pckd 3rd,*
wknd 5th, tld off......................(33 to 1 op 16 to 1) 12

GEORGETOWN 6-11-0 P Hide, *al beh, tld off.*
.... (12 to 1 op 7 to 1) 13

PRESTIGIOUS MAN (Ire) 6-10-7 (7*) N T Egan, *al beh, tld off.*
.... (20 to 1 op 10 to 1 tchd 25 to 1) 14

1673 WEST BAY BREEZE 5-10-9 P Holley, *beh wkn 15th.*
.... (50 to 1 op 33 to 1) f

2636⁵ FRYS NO FOOL 7-11-0 C Llewellyn, *blun and uns rdr 3rd.*
.... (8 to 1 op 7 to 1 tchd 10 to 1) ur

Dist: 9l, 5l, 4l, 6l, 19l, 9l, 3½l, 19l, 3½l, 5l. 4m 9.90s. a 20.90s (16 Ran).
SR: 38/25/20/16/10/-/   (John Galvanoni), T Casey

2921 Hampshire Novices' Handicap Chase Class D (0-115 5-y-o and up) £3,852 3m ....(2:30)

2461⁴ TOP JAVALIN (NZ) [88] 10-10-11 R Greene, *hld up, hdwy appr 5 out, rdn 2 out, styd on to ld r-in.*
.... (6 to 1 op 5 to 1 tchd 13 to 2) 1

1994² MAJORS LEGACY (Ire) [83] 8-10-6 A Thornton, *chsd ldr, ev ch r-in, one pace.*....................(6 to 1 op 7 to 1) 2

2441⁸ PENNCALER (Ire) [86] (bl) 7-10-9 C Llewellyn, *led, blun 2 out, rdn and hdd r-in.*...... (16 to 1 op 14 to 1 tchd 20 to 1) 3

2441⁷ KENDAL CAVALIER [92] 7-11-1 B Fenton, *hld up, rdn and effrt appr 5 out, wknd bef nxt.*
.... (9 to 2 op 5 to 2 tchd 5 to 1) 4

2748* CARDINAL RULE (Ire) [89] 8-10-12 (6ex) N Williamson, *trkd ldr, mstk 7th, hdwy nxt, blun badly 11th, hit 5 out, rdn and wknd 3 out.*
.... (9 to 4 fav op 2 to 1 tchd 7 to 4 and 5 to 2) 5

2638 COUNTRY KEEPER [77] 9-10-0 S McNeill, *mstks 1st and 3rd, pld up bef nxt.*........(16 to 1 op 14 to 1 tchd 20 to 1) pu

2729 SOME MAY [89] (bl) 6-10-12 J F Titley, *al beh, tld off whn pld up bef 2 out.*......... (11 to 2 op 9 to 2 tchd 6 to 1) pu

2799 LOTTERY TICKET (Ire) [101] 8-11-10 C O'Dwyer, *beh frm 9th, jmpd slwly nxt, tld off 13th, pld up bef 4 out.*
.... (13 to 2 op 5 to 1 tchd 15 to 2) pu

2354⁶ PURBECK RAMBLER [77] 6-10-0 J R Kavanagh, *al beh, tld off whn pld up bef 4 out.*..........(33 to 1 tchd 40 to 1) pu

Dist: 2½l, 2l, 14l, 20l. 6m 18.60s. a 33.60s (9 Ran).
                    (Mrs Valerie Thum), N J Hawke

2922 Geoffrey Gilbey Handicap Chase Class C (0-135 5-y-o and up) £4,429 2m 1f ....(3:00)

2529² KINGS CHERRY (Ire) [106] 9-10-0 C Llewellyn, *made all, wnt clr last, rdn on.*........(11 to 2 op 5 to 1 tchd 6 to 1) 1

2555² HIGH ALLTITUDE (Ire) [106] 9-10-0 D Gallagher, *hld up, hdwy appr 4 out, ran on to go second r-in.*...... (9 to 4 op 6 to 2) 2

2689* MISTER ODDY [133] 11-11-10 (3*) D Fortt, *trkd wnr till rdn and wknd r-in.*........(5 to 4 on op Evens tchd 11 to 10) 3

2555 JAMES THE FIRST [121] 9-11-1 P Hide, *hld up, effrt appr 4 out, wkng whn hng lft 2 out, tld off.*
.... (12 to 1 op 6 to 1 tchd 14 to 1) 4

Dist: 1½l, 11l, dist. 4m 18.60s. a 18.60s (4 Ran).
SR: 22/20/36/-/   (T J Swaffield), J A B Old

2923 Scottish Equitable / Jockeys Association Series Handicap Hurdle Qualifier Class D (0-125 5-y-o and up) £3,288 2m 5f ....(3:30)

2681³ LORD MCMURROUGH (Ire) [109] 7-11-2 R Farrant, *hld up in rear, hdwy on ins aftr 7th, led appr 2 out, clr last, rdn out r-in.*
.... (6 to 1 op 7 to 2 tchd 13 to 2) 1

2691* OATIS ROSE [107] 7-10-10 N Williamson, *mid-div, rdn hfwy, mstk 6th, hdwy appr 3 out, styd on wl r-in.*
.... (11 to 4 fav op 5 to 2 tchd 3 to 1) 2

2719⁵ HOODED HAWK (Ire) [99] 6-10-6 J R Kavanagh, *hld up in rear, hdwy 7th, rdn and ev ch 2 out, wknd appr last.*
.... (11 to 2 op 3 to 1 tchd 6 to 1) 3

2559 THE TOISEACH (Ire) [110] 6-11-3 J Osborne, *led till mstk second, led appr 3 out, hdd bef nxt, wknd approaching last.*
.... (8 to 1 tchd 7 to 1) 4

1919² LAKE KARIBA [120] 6-11-6 (7*) L Cummins, *slwly away, hdwy appr 5th, wknd 3 out.*...... (7 to 1 op 6 to 1 tchd 8 to 1) 5

1916⁸ CARMEL'S JOY (Ire) [102] 8-10-9 R Johnson, *led second to 3rd, wknd appr 4 out.*......... (13 to 2 op 7 to 1 tchd 8 to 1) 6

2530⁴ URON V (Fr) [115] 11-11-8 K Gaule, *led 3rd till hdd and wknd appr 3 out.*..........(10 to 1 tchd 8 to 1) 7

2701 THE MEXICANS GONE [104] 9-10-11 V Slattery, *in tch till tld off.*.................. (20 to 1 op 16 to 1) 8

2717⁶ KINO'S CROSS [110] 8-11-3 A Thornton, *mstk 3rd, hld up in tch, wknd 4 out, tld off.*..............(16 to 1 op 14 to 1) 9

2740 ARABIAN SULTAN [107] 10-11-0 Jamie Evans, *beh, lost tch 5th, tld off whn pld up bef 4 out.*
.... (9 to 1 op 16 to 1 tchd 20 to 1 and 8 to 1) pu

2770⁵ MONKS SOHAM (Ire) [100] (bl) 9-10-7 B Fenton, *pld hrd, lost tch 6th, pulled up bef nxt.*...... (20 to 1 tchd 25 to 1) pu

Dist: 1¼l, 8l, 2½l, 14l, 10l, 6l, 18l, 7l. 5m 22.40s. a 28.40s (11 Ran).
SR: 4/-/-/-/-/-/   (J Neville), J Neville

2924 Peter Hamer Memorial Hunters' Chase Class H (6-y-o and up) £1,576 3m ....(4:00)

2641 HOLLAND HOUSE 11-12-0 (5*) Mr C Vigors, *made all, hit 5 out and nxt, clr whn mstk 3 out, unchlgd.*
.... (5 to 4 on op 6 to 4 on tchd 11 to 10) 1

2608* MISS MILLBROOK 9-11-7 (7*) Mr E Williams, *hld up, mstk 3rd, blun and lost pl 11th, lft third 3 out, styd on to go second r-in.*.................. (7 to 4 op 2 to 1 tchd 6 to 4) 2

CLOBRACKEN LAD 9-11-2 (7*) Mr G Baines, *chsd wnr to tenth and ag'n 5 out till wknd r-in.*
.... (20 to 1 op 8 to 1 tchd 33 to 1) 3

2556² PRINCIPLE MUSIC (USA) 9-11-2 (7*) Mr A Phillips, *hld up, hdwy whn hit 9th, chsd wnr nxt to 5 out, btn 3rd when blun and uns rdr 3 out.*..........(10 to 1 op 8 to 1 tchd 14 to 1) ur

OTTER RIVER 8-11-2 (7*) Mr E James, *al beh, lost tch aftr hit 7th, blun 12th, tld off whn pld up bef last.*
.... (66 to 1 op 33 to 1) pu

2793² MEDIANE (USA) (v) 12-11-7* (3*) Mr Simon Andrews, *unruly strt, refused to race....* (25 to 1 op 14 to 1 tchd 33 to 1) l

Dist: 12l, 28l. 6m 25.70s. a 40.70s (6 Ran).
                    (E Knight), P R Chamings

2925 Highclere Juvenile Novices' Hurdle Class C (4-y-o) £3,652 2m 110yds ....(4:30)

2775³ TAKEAMEMO (Ire) 10-9 J Osborne, *made all, sn clr, came back to field 4 out, shaken up 2 out, cmftbly.*
.... (9 to 2 op 5 to 1) 1

2628² CIRCUS STAR 11-0 R Johnson, *hld up in tch, lft second last, no imprsn r-in.*.............. (5 to 1 op 4 to 1) 2

2727⁶ SALTY GIRL (Ire) 10-9 D Gallagher, *al prmnt, one pace frm 3 out.*.................. (20 to 1) 3

GINGER FOX (USA) 11-0 R Farrant, *hld up, hdwy whn mstk 5th, wknd aftr 2 out.*...... (7 to 2 op 3 to 1 tchd 4 to 1) 4

2662⁷ ALPINE JOKER 11-0 G Tormey, *hld up, nvr on terms.*
.... (33 to 1 op 20 to 1) 5

TIMIDJAR (Ire) 10-11 (3*) D Fortt, *hld up, hdwy 3 out, wkng and btn whn hmpd last...*(10 to 1 op 8 to 1 tchd 12 to 1) 6

2727⁹ HISAR (Ire) 11-0 G Bradley, *pld hrd, hld up in rear, hdwy appr 3 out, wkng whn mstk nxt...*(8 to 1 op 7 to 1 tchd 9 to 1) 7

WITHERKAY 10-9 (5*) O Burrows, *al beh, tld off.*
.... (20 to 1 op 16 to 1) 8

2264 ZAISAN (Ire) 11-0 P Hide, *trkd wnr to 3rd, wknd aftr nxt, tld off.*.................. (20 to 1) 9

CLASSIC VICTORY 11-0 K Gaule, *in rear till hdwy 3rd, wknd aftr nxt, mstk 3 out, tld off.*..........(33 to 1 op 25 to 1) 10

2497⁴ TIUTCHEV 11-0 J F Titley, *hld up, hdwy and mstk 5th, wknd 2 out, f last.*.................(11 to 2 op 5 to 1 tchd 6 to 1) f

2727³ INFAMOUS (USA) 11-0 N Williamson, *chsd wnr frm 3rd, rdn and hld whn f last.* (3 to 1 fav op 5 to 2 tchd 100 to 30) f

BARON HRABOVSKY 11-0 J Culloty, *beh, rdn 4th, tld off whn pld up bef 2 out.*..........(33 to 1 op 25 to 1) pu

Dist: 5l, 4l, 1¼l, 20l, 10l, 12l, 5l, 20l, 10l. 4m 12.50s. a 23.50s (14 Ran).
SR: 3/3/-/-/-/-/   (Sherwood Partnership Owners Club), O Sherwood

2926 Whatcombe Conditional Jockeys' Novices' Handicap Hurdle Class E (0-115 4-y-o and up) £2,978 2m 5f ....(5:00)

2023² STORMY PASSAGE (Ire) [103] 7-11-11 (3*) G Tormey, *hld up in tch, al gng wl, led appr 2 out, clr whn mstk last, kpt on.*
.... (5 to 2 op 5 to 1 tchd 4 to 1) 1

2661² LORD KHALICE (Ire) [79] 6-10-4 Michael Brennan, *led to 3rd, lft in ld 3 out, sn hdd, outpcd.*................(7 to 2 jt-fav op 4 to 1 tchd 9 to 2) 2

2398³ UNSINKABLE BOXER (Ire) [96] 8-10-13 (8*) D Finnegan, *hld up, hdwy 4 out, nvr nr to chal.*
.... (11 to 2 op 4 to 1 tchd 6 to 1) 3

2193* CAPTAIN JACK [103] 7-12-0 D Walsh, *chsd ldrs till rdn and wknd appr 3 out, tld off....*(6 to 1 op 9 to 2 tchd 7 to 1) 4

2436⁴ LAUREN'S TREASURE (Ire) [80] 6-10-5 L Aspell, *al in rear, tld off whn pld up bef 3 out.*(33 to 1 op 16 to 1 tchd 20 to 1) pu

2605² MOONLIGHTER [78] 7-10-0 (3*) O Burrows, *al beh, tld off 7th, pld up bef 2 out.*..........(7 to 2 jt-fav tchd 4 to 1) pu

2356⁷ FLAXLEY WOOD [88] 6-10-10 (3*) G Supple, *rcd keenly, led 3rd till rdn and blun badly 3 out, not reco'r, pld up bef nxt.*
.... (4 to 1 op 7 to 2 tchd 9 to 2) pu

Dist: 9l, 8l, dist. 5m 23.20s. a 29.20s (7 Ran).
SR: 8/-/-/-/   (Peter Luff), P J Hobbs

PLUMPTON (soft)
Friday February 28th
Going Correction: PLUS 2.00 sec. per fur. (races 1,3,6), PLUS 1.35 (2,4,5)

2927 Crowborough Novices' Hurdle Class E (4-y-o and up) £2,284 2m 1f (2:10)

402

2699⁵ RHYTHM AND BLUES 7-11-2 B Powell, *chsd ldrs, outpcd 7th, rallied to ld appr last, styd on wl.*
............................(7 to 2 op 9 to 4 tchd 4 to 1) 1
2565³ TONKA 5-11-2 A P McCoy, *led, mstk 3 out, hdd appr last, no extr r-in.* (7 to 4 fav op 6 to 4 tchd 15 to 8 and 2 to 1) 2
2744² INTO THE WEB (Ire) 6-11-2 Derek Byrne, *chsd ldr most of way, rdn 3 out, ev ch appr nxt, sn wknd.*
............................(9 to 4 op 2 to 1 tchd 5 to 2) 3
WELSH WIZZARD 5-10-9 (7*) Mr P O'Keeffe, *prmnt, jmpd slwly 3rd, mstk and wknd 3 out.*
............................(50 to 1 op 20 to 1 tchd 66 to 1) 4
MAY SUNSET (Ire) 7-11-2 J A McCarthy, *not fluent, hdwy 4th, mstk and outpcd nxt, lost tch 7th.*
............................(7 to 1 op 6 to 1 tchd 8 to 1) 5
2405 CONTRACT BRIDGE (Ire) 4-10-3 W McFarland, *rear, mstk 1st, pushed alng 5th, tld off whn hit 7th.*
............................(16 to 1 op 12 to 1 tchd 20 to 1) 6
2511 APOLLONO 5-11-2 W Marston, *in tch till rdn and wknd 7th.*
............................(20 to 1 op 10 to 1 tchd 25 to 1) 7
MY NAD KNOWS 4-10-8 T J Murphy, *rear 3rd, hrd rdn 6th, sn tld off, f 3 out.*............(50 to 1 op 20 to 1) f
Dist: 6l, 12l, 7l, 12l, 10l, sht-hd. 4m 38.30s. a 41.30s (8 Ran).
SR: 15/9/-/-/-/   (Mrs Peter Gregson), R H Buckler

2928 Plumpton Novices' Chase Class E (5-y-o and up) £2,753 2m........ (2:40)

2547³ INDIAN ARROW (NZ) 9-11-8 C Maude, *jmpd wl, led second, clr 2 out, easily.*........................(11 to 8 op Evens) 1
2399⁵ COURT MASTER (Ire) 9-11-2 B Powell, *blun 3rd, chsd wnr 5th, mstk 9th, no imprsn frm 3 out.* (11 to 10 fav op 6 to 4) 2
2747 PURBECK CAVALIER 8-11-2 W McFarland, *al prmnt, one pace frm 4 out, 3rd and btn whn mstk 2 out.*
............................(11 to 2 op 7 to 2 tchd 5 to 1) 3
2612 EAU SO SLOE 6-11-2 A Dicken, *al beh, tld off frm 5th.*
............................(50 to 1 op 25 to 1) 4
FINNEGAIS 10-11-2 T J Murphy, *beh, mstk 1st, wl tld off frm 7th.*........................(50 to 1 op 33 to 1) 5
ROADRUNNER 7-11-2 M Richards, *led, jmpd slwly 1st, jumped slowly and hdd second, chasing ldrs whn f 5th.*
............................(50 to 1 op 33 to 1) f
Dist: 15l, 2l, dist, dist. 4m 20.00s. a 28.00s (6 Ran).
SR: 30/9/7/   (Joe & Joanne Bickley), M C Pipe

2929 Wivelsfield Novices' Handicap Hurdle Class E (0-105 4-y-o and up) £2,200 3m 110yds............ (3:10)

2640³ ROSKEEN BRIDGE (Ire) [71] 6-10-0 M Richards, *chsd ldr, led 3 out to last, led r-in, styd on wl.*
............................(6 to 1 op 5 to 1 tchd 13 to 2) 1
2637² DANCETILLYOUDROP (Ire) [96] 6-11-11 A P McCoy, *hld up, motko oooond, 6th and 11th, offrt 3 out, led and blun last, sn hdd, kpt on.*
........(5 to 2 fav op 9 to 4 tchd 11 to 4 and 3 to 1) 2
2562⁴ MISTER BLAKE [89] 7-10-11 (7*) X Aizpuru, *in tch, outpcd tenth, rallied 3 out, one pace appr nxt...*(7 to 1 op 5 to 1) 3
2565⁶ BLAZING STORM (Ire) [89] 5-11-4 J A McCarthy, *prmnt, hrd rdn 11th, wknd quickly 3 out, tld off.*
............................(100 to 30 op 7 to 2 tchd 3 to 1) 4
2638 MINOR KEY (Ire) [92] 7-11-7 B Powell, *hld up rear, lost tch 7th, hrd rdn nxt, pld up bef tenth......*(20 to 1 op 10 to 1) pu
2770² AINSI SOIT IL (Fr) [99] (bl) 6-12-0 D Bridgwater, *led, rdn alng 11th, hdd 3 out, sn btn, 4th and wkng whn pld up bef last.*
............................(7 to 2 op 3 to 1 tchd 4 to 1) pu
2616⁶ KYBO'S REVENGE (Ire) [73] 6-10-2² D O'Sullivan, *beh, tld off 8th, pld up bef 11th.*............(20 to 1 op 10 to 1) pu
Dist: ½l, 8l, dist. 6m 38.70s. (7 Ran).
                              (Tony Rooth), C Weedon

2930 Cooksbridge Maiden Chase Class F (5-y-o and up) £2,541 3m 1f 110yds............................ (3:40)

2613³ APATURA HATI 8-11-0 W McFarland, *hdwy to track ldr tenth, led 16th, lft clr last.*................(7 to 1 op 5 to 1) 1
2399³ NORMARANGE (Ire) 7-11-5 M Richards, *prmnt to 7th, rear 9th, hdwy 13th, rdn 15th, wknd nxt.*
............................(11 to 8 fav op 5 to 4 on tchd 6 to 4) 2
2799 FORTYTWO DEE (Ire) 7-11-0 T J Murphy, *hdwy 16th, hrd rdn aftr 2 out, chalg whn f last, rmntd.*
............................(20 to 1 op 14 to 1 tchd 25 to 1) 3
2613 NIKKIS PET 10-11-0 W Marston, *cl up to 12th, lost tch 14th, poor 4th whn refused last, continued.* (20 to 1 op 12 to 1) 4
2679² ROLLESTON BLADE 10-10-12 (7*) Mr P O'Keeffe, *led to 16th, chasing wnr whn f nxt.*................(8 to 1 op 5 to 1) f
2441 DEXTRA 7-11-5 C Maude, *rear till f 8th.*
............................(33 to 1 op 20 to 1) f
2741² JAC DEL PRINCE 7-11-5 A P McCoy, *prmnt to 6th, beh frm 9th, f 12th.*........................(6 to 1 op 5 to 1) f
2700⁷ CLONTOURA (Ire) 9-11-5 B Powell, *mstk 1st and 5th, some hdwy 12th, wknd 14th, poor fifth whn f 16th.*
............................(13 to 2 op 10 to 1) f
2638⁴ PLUMBRIDGE 9-11-5 T Jenks, *prmnt to 14th, tld off whn pld up bef 2 out.*........(10 to 1 op 11 to 2) pu
Dist: Dist, dist, 26l. 7m 7.40s. a 53.40s (9 Ran).
                              (Mrs R O Hutchings), R H Alner

2931 Chailey Handicap Chase Class E (0-115 5-y-o and up) £2,778 2m 5f .... (4:10)

2480 PAVLOVA (Ire) [87] 7-10-2² D O'Sullivan, *beh tenth, styd on frm 4 out, rdn to ld r-in.*........(16 to 1 op 12 to 1) 1
2606 WINSPIT (Ire) [87] 7-10-2¹ W McFarland, *led, mstks 7th, 8th and 2 out, hdd and no extr r-in.*
............................(4 to 1 op 7 to 2 tchd 9 to 2) 2
2395⁹ BEAU BABILLARD [113] (bl) 10-12-0 A P McCoy, *lft second 8th, hrd rdn and effrt 2 out, wknd last...* (2 to 1 op 7 to 4) 3
2739² GOLDEN OPAL [85] 12-10-0 B Powell, *in tch, 4th whn brght dwn 8th.*........(6 to 1 op 9 to 2 tchd 13 to 2) bd
2596⁷ MAMMY'S CHOICE (Ire) [95] 7-10-10 D Bridgwater, *prmnt, second whn jmpd into back of ldr and brght dwn 8th.*
............................(15 to 8 fav op 6 to 4 tchd 9 to 4) bd
Dist: 3l, 11l. 5m 54.10s. a 48.10s (5 Ran).
                              (Mrs Margaret McGlone), R Rowe

2932 Portslade Handicap Hurdle Class F (0-100 4-y-o and up) £1,941 2½m .... (4:40)

2762 MAYB-MAYB [76] 7-10-4 A P McCoy, *pressed ldr, led 6th, rdn and styd on wl frm 2 out.*
........(2 to 1 fav op 7 to 4 tchd 9 to 4 and 5 to 2) 1
2740³ ST VILLE [88] 11-11-2 B Powell, *in tch till hrd rdn and outpcd 8th, rallied appr 2 out, styd on r-in.....*(7 to 1 op 4 to 1) 2
2614* BULA VOGUE (Ire) [95] 7-11-9 D O'Sullivan, *cl up, pressed wnr 3 out till wknd appr last.*........(5 to 2 op 7 to 4) 3
2768 SCRIPT [74] 6-10-2 T J Murphy, *in tch, rdn 9th, no hdwy frm 3 out.*................(12 to 1 op 10 to 1 tchd 14 to 1) 4
2267⁵ KING'S GOLD [77] 7-10-5 M Richards, *hdwy 9th, wknd appr 2 out.*........(7 to 1 op 6 to 1 tchd 8 to 1) 5
TONYS GIFT [100] 5-12-0 C Maude, *al rear, lost tch 8th, tld off.*........................(6 to 1 op 4 to 1) 6
2374⁵ QUIET MOMENTS (Ire) [83] 4-10-0 W Marston, *led to 6th, hrd rdn 8th, wknd nxt, tld off...*(16 to 1 tchd 20 to 1) 7
Dist: 6l, 5l, 7l, 4l, dist, 9l. 5m 28.80s. a 51.80s (7 Ran).
                              (J Neville), J Neville

DONCASTER (good)
Saturday March 1st
Going Correction: PLUS 0.30 sec. per fur.

2933 Light Infantry Plate Class C Handicap Hurdle (0-135 4-y-o and up) £3,678 2m 110yds.......... (12:50)

2730* MORE DASH THANCASH (Ire) [108] 7-10-8 Derek Byrne, *set steady pace, jmpd rght thrght, quickened 3 out, lft clr last, easily.*................(15 to 8 fav op 7 to 4 tchd 2 to 1) 1
2467⁸ HOLDERS HILL (Ire) [103] 5-10-3 P Carberry, *in tch, effrt 3 out, reminders nxt, styd on same pace.*
............................(20 to 1 op 16 to 1 tchd 25 to 1) 2
2716⁹ SEA VICTOR [118] 5-11-4 D Gallagher, *wth ldr, reminders appr 3 out, one pace whn hit nxt, sn no imprsn.*
............................(5 to 1 op 7 to 2) 3
2532² GLANMERIN (Ire) [118] 6-11-4 A Dobbin, *cl up, drvn and outpcd appr 3 out, btn frm nxt.*
............................(11 to 4 op 9 to 4) 4
2331⁶ CHARMING GIRL (USA) [127] 6-11-13 J Osborne, *steadied rear, plenty to do 4 out, outpcd appr 2 out, sn no dngr.*
............................(16 to 1 op 14 to 1) 5
2467 UNCLE DOUG [125] 6-11-8 (3*) G Lee, *hld up, rdn and lost tch appr 3 out, tld off.*................(16 to 1 op 12 to 1) 6
2717² THORNTON GATE [110] 6-10-10 P Niven, *midfield, hdwy 4 out, 5 is second but hld whn f last....*(7 to 1 tchd 15 to 2) f
2806⁵ DESERT FIGHTER [110] 6-10-10 B Clifford, *lsped and died aftr race.*............(5 to 1 tchd 11 to 2) f
Dist: 5l, 5l, 5l, 6l, 28l. 3m 59.90s. a 9.90s (8 Ran).
SR: 30/20/30/25/28/   (F J Sainsbury), Mrs Merrita Jones

2934 Mitsubishi Shogun Trophy Handicap Chase Class C (0-130 5-y-o and up) £6,840 2m 3f 110yds........ (1:25)

2806⁷ FRICKLEY [98] 11-10-10 P Carberry, *hld up, steady hdwy 3 out, led betw last 2, ran on stnly.*
............................(9 to 1 op 7 to 1 tchd 10 to 1) 1
DESTINY CALLS [123] 7-11-9 P Niven, *nvr far away, slight ld appr 4 out to nxt, ev ch last, styd on.*
............................(2 to 1 fav op 5 to 2 tchd 7 to 4) 2
2437⁴ CONTI D'ESTRUVAL (Fr) [112] 7-10-12 B Clifford, *in tch, cl up hfwy till slight ld 3 out, hdd betw last 2, styd on stdly.*
............................(9 to 2 tchd 11 to 2) 3
2455² WEE RIVER (Ire) [128] 8-12-0 J Callaghan, *hld up, some hdwy whn hit 6 out, outpcd frm 3 out, sn no dngr.*
............................(9 to 2 op 7 to 2 tchd 5 to 1) 4
2819 IN TRUTH [114] 9-11-0 K Gaule, *chsd ldrs till lost pl hfwy, struggling 5 out, sn beh.*
............................(16 to 1 op 12 to 1 tchd 20 to 1) 5
2677* ARTIC WINGS (Ire) [105] 9-10-5 M Brennan, *hld up, mstk 6th, blun six out, sn beh.*............(4 to 1 op 3 to 1) 6

2261[4] REAL GLEE (Ire) [106] 8-10-6 A Thornton, *jmpd badly, made most till appr 5 out, sn wknd, wl beh whn blun last.* ....(16 to 1 op 12 to 1 tchd 20 to 1) 7
2685 MONNAIE FORTE (Ire) [100] 7-10-0 M Moloney, *hld up in rear, reminders 4th, hdwy gng wl and in tch whn f 5 out.* ....(20 to 1 op 16 to 1 tchd 25 to 1) f
Dist: 2½l, sht-hd, 18l, hd, 12l, 15l. 4m 56.50s. a 11.50s (8 Ran).
SR: 26/36/25/23/9/ (Robert Ogden), G Richards

2935 Velka Pardubicka Grimthorpe Handicap Chase Class B (0-145 5-y-o and up) £10,191 3¼m.............(2:00)

2800* FATHER SKY [115] (bl) 6-10-11 J Osborne, *cl up, not fluent 6 out, chlgd gng wl 4 out, jmpd ahead 2 out, clr last, readily.* ....(9 to 2 op 4 to 1) 1
2258[3] CHANGE THE REIGN [107] 10-10-3 P Carberry, *sn led, quickened 9th, rdn and hdd 2 out, no extr..* (12 to 1 op 10 to 1) 2
2571* WHISPERING STEEL [128] 11-11-10 A Dobbin, *hndy, drvn and unbl to quicken aftr 4 out, wknd after nxt.* ....(4 to 1 jt-fav op 7 to 2 tchd 9 to 2) 3
2500* MUSTHAVEASWIG [123] 11-11-5 A Thornton, *chsd ldr, mstk 9th (water), sn lost pl, drvn to chase lders 6 out, fdd appr 3 out.* ....(4 to 1 jt-fav op 7 to 2) 4
2589[3] LE MEILLE (Ire) [109] 8-10-5 A Larnach, *keen hold in rear, drvn alng 4 out, sn lost tch, broke blood vessel.* ....(9 to 2 op 7 to 2) 5
2579[3] PIMS GUNNER (Ire) [104] 9-10-0 D Bentley, *chsd ldrs till outpcd 12th, wl beh frm 5 out, tld off..* (16 to 1 op 14 to 1) 6
2334 MERRY MASTER [111] (bl) 13-10-7[1] J Callaghan, *hld up, not fluent, tld off frm 5 out, pld up bef 3 out..* ....(33 to 1) pu
2317[3] ALI'S ALIBI [113] 10-10-9 P Niven, *pld up bef second.* ....(9 to 2 tchd 5 to 1 and 4 to 1) pu
Dist: 14l, 15l, 13l, 1½l, 13l. 6m 34.10s. a 13.10s (8 Ran).
SR: 30/8/14/-/-/ (Kenneth Kornfeld), O Sherwood

2936 Air Power Products Handicap Hurdle Class B (4-y-o and up) £4,711 3m 110yds.......................(2:30)

2559[3] EALING COURT [101] 8-10-0 J Osborne, *prmnt frm 4th, chlgd and mstk 3 out, ran on strly und pres to ld cl hme.* ....(9 to 2 op 4 to 1 tchd 5 to 1) 1
2460[2] SMITH TOO (Ire) [109] 9-10-8 A Thornton, *led, hit 5th, not fluent nxt, strly pressed frm 3 out, kpt on wl, ct cl hme.* ....(7 to 2 fav tchd 4 to 1) 2
2453 LOCHNAGRAIN (Ire) [122] 9-11-7 P Niven, *settled rear, clr order 7th, drvn and unbl to quicken aftr 3 out, styd on ag'n flt.* ....(4 to 1 op 7 to 2) 3
2701* BANKHEAD (Ire) [128] 8-11-6 (7*) Miss C Spearing, *pressed ldr, not fluent 6th, chlgd appr 3 out, one pace frm nxt.* ....(4 to 1 op 3 to 1 tchd 9 to 2) 4
2453[8] FIRED EARTH (Ire) [129] 9-12-0 P Carberry, *settled rear, pushed alng and outpcd 3 out, no dngr aftr.* ....(5 to 1 op 9 to 2) 5
2789[9] AMILLIONMEMORIES [101] 7-10-0 R Greene, *hld up, clr order 7th, drvn and effrt 3 out, fdg whn hit nxt, eased flt.* ....(20 to 1 tchd 25 to 1) 6
2465[7] JOCKS CROSS (Ire) [114] 6-10-13 A Dobbin, *chsd ldrs, struggling whn hit 3 out, sn tld off..* ....(7 to 1) 7
Dist: Sht-hd, 6l, ½l, 10l, 30l, ½l. 5m 57.00s. a 15.00s (7 Ran).
SR: -/4/11/16/7/-/-/ (R S Brookhouse), N M Babbage

2937 Pardubice Novices' Hurdle Class E (4-y-o and up) £2,547 2½m... (3:05)

2849* NIGEL'S LAD (Ire) 5-11-8 M Foster, *rcd keenly, led to 4th, led ag'n 6th, shaken up to go clr aftr 2 out, drvn out and ran on strly..* ....(5 to 2 on op 2 to 1 on) 1
2533* SECRET SERVICE (Ire) 5-11-8 P Carberry, *cl up, not fluent 5th, outpcd by wnr aftr 2 out, btn whn slight mstk last, eased close hme..* ....(11 to 4 op 9 to 4 tchd 3 to 1) 2
2462[3] LEAP IN THE DARK (Ire) 8-11-2 A Thornton, *hld up, hdwy to go 3rd appr strt, no ch wth 1st 2..* .....(20 to 1 op 12 to 1) 3
2550[8] RARE OCCURANCE 7-11-2 K Gaule, *hld up, not fluent 6th, some hdwy 4 out, wknd frm nxt..* ..... (33 to 1 op 25 to 1) 4
2811[2] LAUGHING FONTAINE (Ire) 7-11-2 D Bentley, *hld up, plenty to do hfwy, lost tch 4 out, nvr plcd to chal.* ....(25 to 1 op 16 to 1 tchd 33 to 1) 5
2811 ANASTASIA WINDSOR (v) 6-10-11 D J Moffatt, *led 4th till mstk and hdd 6th, hit four out, sn btn, tld off.* ....(66 to 1 op 50 to 1) 6
880 MISS NONNIE 5-10-4 (7*) M Moloney, *chsd ldrs till lost tch appr 4 out, tld off..* ....(100 to 1) 7
THE WASP (Ire) 5-11-2 A S Smith, *sn pushed alng in rear, tld off frm 6th..* ....(25 to 1 op 20 to 1 tchd 33 to 1) 8
2298 BOOK OF DREAMS (Ire) 9-11-2 D Gallagher, *midfield, pushed alng hfwy, sn wl beh, pld up 3 out.* ....(100 to 1 op 66 to 1) pu
2775 BALLY WONDER 5-10-11 J Supple, *pld hrd in rear, tld off 6th, pulled up 3 out..* ....(100 to 1) pu
Dist: 22l, 10l, 17l, 1½l, 15l, ½l, dist. 4m 48.50s. a 13.50s (10 Ran).
SR: 19/-/-/-/-/-/ (N C Dunnington), P C Haslam

2938 HMS Andromeda Novices' Chase Class D (5-y-o and up) £3,526 2m 110yds......................(3:40)

2335[6] SUBLIME FELLOW (Ire) 7-11-12 J Osborne, *cl up, jmpd ahead 5 out, clr nxt, drvn out close hme.* ....(2 to 1 op 7 to 4 tchd 9 to 4) 1
2626* JUST BRUCE 8-11-7 D Gallagher, *led, mstk 4th, hdd and outpcd 5 out, drvn and styd on betw last 2.* ....(16 to 1 op 12 to 1) 2
2598 GIMME (Ire) (v) 7-11-2 K Gaule, *cl up, mstks, drvn and outpcd appr strt, styd on stdly frm 2 out..* .....(16 to 1 op 12 to 1) 3
2547 SIGMA RUN (Ire) 8-11-7 M Foster, *hld up, pushed alng and lost tch 5 out, sn beh..* ....(16 to 1 op 12 to 1) 4
2576 GREAT GABLE (Ire) 6-11-2 D J Moffatt, *jmpd slwly in rear, tld off frm 6th..* ....(66 to 1 op 50 to 1) 5
2720[4] BLAIR CASTLE (Ire) 6-11-2 B Clifford, *cl up, mstk 4th, pckd and uns rdr nxt..* .. (5 to 4 fav op 11 to 10 tchd 11 to 8) ur
2576[2] ROYAL CRIMSON 6-11-2 R Garritty, *hld up, struggling 5 out, tld off whn pld up bef 2 out.* (13 to 2 op 7 to 1 tchd 8 to 1) pu
Dist: 3l, 1¼l, 30l, 25l. 4m 5.20s. a 11.20s (7 Ran).
SR: 35/27/20/-/ (Rory McGrath), N J Henderson

2939 Town Moor Standard National Hunt Flat Class H (4,5,6-y-o) £1,035 2m 110yds.......................(4:10)

2764 LANDLER 4-10-6 (3*) E Callaghan, *hld up, steady hdwy to ld 2 fs out, edgd lft und pres..* .... (33 to 1 op 20 to 1) 1
CARLINGFORD TYKE (Ire) 5-11-3 G Cahill, *al hndy, ev ch o'r 2 fs out, styd on wl..* ....(33 to 1 op 20 to 1) 2
2687[4] GENEROUS STREAK (Fr) 4-10-4 (5*) B Grattan, *chsd ldrs, slight ld entering strt till o'r 3 fs out, styd on stdly.* ....(13 to 2 op 6 to 1 tchd 8 to 1) 3
2262[9] DIG FOR GOLD 4-10-6 (3*) F Leahy, *settled midfield, improved gng wl 6 fs out, slight ld o'r 3 out till 2 out, fdd entering last..* ....(12 to 1 op 7 to 1) 4
2283 PEDLAR'S CROSS (Ire) 5-11-0 (3*) D Fortt, *pressed ldr, ev ch entering strt till fdd fnl 2 fs..* ....(20 to 1 op 16 to 1) 5
2687 LORD OF THE RINGS 5-10-10 (7*) Mr T J Barry, *hld up, pushed alng towards rear antering strt, styd on entering fnl furlong, unbl to chal..* ....(14 to 1 op 10 to 1) 6
2723[8] WEAPONS FREE 6-10-10 (7*) R McCarthy, *keen hold, effrt to chase ldrs 5 fs out, rdn and outpcd o'r 3 out.* ....(7 to 1 tchd 6 to 1) 7
NOTHING TO IT 6-11-0 (3*) Mr C Bonner, *hld up, pld hrd, effrt hfwy, fdd o'r 2 fs out..* ....(33 to 1 op 20 to 1) 8
2595 SPRIGHTLEY PIP (Ire) 6-10-10 (7*) J Power, *led till hdd 5 fs out, lost tch o'r 3 out, sn btn..* ....(20 to 1 op 16 to 1) 9
JUDICIOUS CHARLIE (Ire) 5-10-12 (5*) R McGrath, *str hold, hdwy and in tch 6 fs out, wknd 3 out, eased whn btn, tld off.* ....(9 to 2 op 2 to 1 tchd 6 to 1) 10
AEOLUS 4-10-2 (7*) N Horrocks, *tld off frm hfwy.* ....(33 to 1 op 20 to 1) 11
MILL BAY SAM 6-10-10 (7*) M Lane, *unruly strt, refused to race..* ....(16 to 1 op 20 to 1) ref
2469[2] WYNYARD KNIGHT 5-11-0 (3*) G Lee, *midfield, short of room and ran out hfwy.* ....(11 to 8 on op Evens tchd 5 to 4 and 11 to 8) ro
Dist: 1l, 1l, 7l, 4l, 6l, 1½l, 6l, 1½l, 29l, 5l. 4m 3.10s. (13 Ran).
(Bradlor Developments Limited), J Norton

LISTOWEL (IRE) (soft)
Saturday March 1st

2940 Kingdom Maiden Hurdle (4-y-o) £2,740 2m....................(2:30)

2702[3] RED TONIC (USA) 11-4 L P Cusack, ...(7 to 1) 1
SHAHRUR (USA) 11-4 D T Evans, ...(6 to 4) 2
2702[6] SHARP OUTLOOK (Ire) 10-13 T P Rudd, ...(25 to 1) 3
2669[4] PERSIAN DREAM (Ire) 10-13 C F Swan, ...(7 to 1) 4
2832[2] PEGUS JUNIOR (Ire) 11-4 C O'Dwyer, ...(Evens fav) 5
MULTEEN JET (Ire) 11-4 T P Treacy, ...(25 to 1) 6
2832 POINT LUCK (Ire) 10-13 M P Hourigan, ...(12 to 1) pu
TONY IMPORT (Ire) 11-4 T Horgan, ...(14 to 1) pu
MONEYCLEAR (Ire) 11-1 (3*) J Butler, ...(20 to 1) I
Dist: 2l, 4½l, 4l, 1l. 4m 41.90s. (9 Ran).
(Yoshiki Akazawa), John Muldoon

2941 Ballybunion E.B.F. Beginners Chase (4-y-o and up) £3,425 2¼m... (3:00)

2705 V'SOSKE GALE (Ire) 7-11-9 C O'Dwyer, ...(6 to 1) 1
2840[4] NO TAG (Ire) 9-12-0 T J Mitchell, ...(3 to 1) 2
2648[5] CORRIBLOUGH (Ire) 9-11-9 T Horgan, ...(12 to 1) 3
2142[7] SCEAL SIOG (Ire) 8-11-4 L P Cusack, ...(20 to 1) 4
2674 ORANGE JUICE (Ire) 7-11-6 (3*) K Whelan, ...(20 to 1) f
2705 SCENIC ROUTE (Ire) 8-11-9 (5*) Mr T P Hyde, (11 to 10 fav) ur
2868[7] MARIES POLLY (bl) 7-11-9 D H O'Connor, ...(8 to 1) ur
2755[6] MIDNIGHT JAZZ (Ire) 7-12-0 J P Broderick, ...(7 to 1) pu
Dist: ½l, 25l, dist. 5m 18.40s. (8 Ran).
(Michael Dixon), James Joseph Mangan

2942 Ring Of Kerry Maiden Hurdle (5-y-o) £2,740 2m....................(3:30)

2413 LOCKBEG LASS (Ire) 10-6 (7*) M D Murphy, ... (20 to 1) 1

2518⁵ SHALOM (Ire) 11-4 M P Hourigan, ... (5 to 2 jt-fav) 2
2414⁷ THE BOY KING (Ire) 10-11 (7⁷) J M Maguire, ... (9 to 2) 3
2754⁴ ASHTALE (Ire) 10-13 D J Casey, ... (5 to 2 jt-fav) 4
2443⁹ WINTER MELODY (Ire) 10-11 (7⁷) M W Martin, ... (7 to 1) 5
2757 NEARLY A LINE 10-11 (7⁷) P G Hourigan, ...(20 to 1) 6
1193 OVER ALICE (Ire) 10-13 F J Flood, ...(14 to 1) 7
2414 NEWBERRY ROSE (Ire) 10-5 S H O'Donovan, ... (33 to 1) 8
2518 MEGA HUNTER (Ire) 11-4 M Moran, ... (16 to 1) 9
2704 FAHY'S FIELD (Ire) 11-4 K F O'Brien, ... (20 to 1) 10
2582 NIL FAIC (Ire) 10-6 (7⁷) S P McCann, ... (20 to 1) 11
2414⁸ SEXTON'S MIRROR (Ire) 11-4 C F Swan, ...(6 to 1) 12
2703 CONNA BRIDE LADY (Ire) 10-6 (7⁷) F J Keniry, ... (20 to 1) 13
560⁸ HONEY TRADER 11-4 J P Broderick, ... (14 to 1) 14
QUEEN OFTHE ISLAND (Ire) 10-8 (5⁷) Susan A Finn,
. . . .(14 to 1) 15
Dist: 2l, 3½l, 3l, 7l. 4m 46.40s. (15 Ran).

(Ringaskiddy Racing Club), Eugene M O'Sullivan

2943 Tarbert Handicap Hurdle (0-102 4-y-o and up) £2,740 2m . . . . (4:00)

2647⁴ ECLIPTIC MOON (Ire) [-] 7-10-0 T P Treacy, ... (3 to 1 fav) 1
685⁶ HELORHIWATER (Ire) [-] 6-11-5 J P Broderick, ...(7 to 1) 2
2106⁵ BLITZER (Ire) [-] 5-11-4 (3⁷) M R Walsh, ...(10 to 1) 3
2275⁶ ROSDEMON (Ire) [-] 9-11-12 P A Roche, ... (12 to 1) 4
DISTRICT JUSTICE [-] 10-10-13 M Duffy, ...(6 to 1) 5
2707 NATIVE ECLIPSE (Ire) [-] 4-11-11 C F Swan, ... (10 to 1) 6
2369⁶ ILLBETHEREFORYOU (Ire) [-] 6-10-8 (7⁷) P G Hourigan,
. . . .(7 to 1) 7
2901* JIHAAD (USA) [-] (bl) 7-10-4 (7⁷,6ex) J M Maguire, . . .(7 to 1) 8
2753 CNOCADRUM VI (Ire) [-] 6-10-2 F Woods, ...(33 to 1) 9
2735⁶ ATLANTA FLAME (Ire) [-] 6-10-6 W Slattery, ...(6 to 1) 10
2755 THE YELLOW BOG (Ire) [-] 7-11-1 P L Malone, ...(20 to 1) 11
2704⁹ GALLIC HONEY (Ire) [-] 6-9-11 (7⁷) Mrs C Harrison, . (14 to 1) 12
2901⁵ REGIT (Ire) [-] 7-11-1 T Hazlett, ...(10 to 1) 13
2089 PERMIT ME (Ire) [-] 5-10-7 (7⁷) A O'Shea, ...(14 to 1) 14
2647 ASTRID (Ire) [-] 6-9-7 T Horgan, ... (33 to 1) 15
1579⁷ HARRY WELSH (Ire) [-] (bl) 5-10-9 C O'Dwyer, ...(12 to 1) 16
2735 BE MY FOLLY (Ire) [-] 5-11-0 M O'Neill, ...(8 to 1) 17
2647 RONETTE (Ire) [-] 6-9-9 (5⁷) T Martin, ... (33 to 1) pu
Dist: 6l, 1½l, 2½l, 5½l. 4m 38.50s. (18 Ran).

(Michael J Daly), P Mullins

2944 Kerry Handicap Hurdle (0-116 4-y-o and up) £3,425 2½m . . . . (4:30)

563* ANOTHER GROUSE [-] 10-10-4 T P Treacy, ... (12 to 1) 1
2585⁷ MONDEO ROSE (Ire) [-] 5-10-13 C F Swan, ...(5 to 1) 2
2585 PATTIE TIM (Ire) [-] 8-11-4 (3⁷) K Whelan, ... (8 to 1) 3
2837* LISCAHILL FORT (Ire) [-] 8-10-13 (7⁷) Mr D M Loughnane,
. . . .(5 to 1) 4
2753⁸ GARLAND ROSE (Ire) [-] 7-9-7 D J Casey, ... (10 to 1) 5
2229⁶ TELL THE NIPPER (Ire) [-] (bl) 6-11-11 J P Broderick, .(5 to 1) 6
2647 HOLLYBROOK LADY (Ire) [-] 6-10-5 (7⁷) D Fisher, . .(10 to 1) 7
2753 TULLOLOUGH [-] 14-9-12 T Horgan, ... (25 to 1) 8
2366 ROSEAUSTIN (Ire) [-] 7-9-2 (7⁷) D McCullagh, ...(11 to 2) 9
2647² VALMAR (Ire) [-] 9-9-13 F Woods, ... (7 to 4 fav) pu
WINTRY DAWN (Ire) [-] 7-10-1 W Slattery, ... (20 to 1) pu
Dist: 2l, 1l, 1l, hd. 6m 18.50s. (11 Ran).

(M Kelly), Edward P Mitchell

2945 Spring Handicap Chase (0-102 4-y-o and up) £2,740 2½m . . . . (5:00)

2411* MACAUNTA (Ire) [-] 7-10-2 (7⁷) M D Murphy, ... (4 to 1) 1
2646 NORTHERN ACE [-] 11-9-8 T Horgan, ... (20 to 1) 2
2647 SIOBHAILIN DUBH (Ire) [-] (bl) 8-10-11 D J Casey, (14 to 1) 3
2274⁸ YOUNG WOLF [-] 9-10-0 (7⁷) R P Hogan, ... (14 to 1) 4
2448⁵ FAIR GO [-] 11-9-0 (7⁷) Mrs C Harrison, ... (10 to 1) 5
2756³ ALL IN THE GAME (Ire) [-] 9-10-8 P A Roche, ... (4 to 1) 6
2755* ANOTHER DEADLY [-] 10-11-3 T P Treacy, ... (3 to 1 fav) f
2756 SHARONS PRIDE (Ire) [-] 7-10-12 J R Barry, ... (7 to 1) f
2646⁶ ZVORNIK [-] 10-11-7 (7⁷) L A Hurley, ...(12 to 1) ur
2646³ ANOTHER COURSE (Ire) [-] 9-11-0 D H O'Connor, . .(5 to 1) pu
2410 BALLYBRIT BOY [-] 11-10-0⁷ D T Evans, ... (16 to 1) pu
2646⁵ DAMODAR [-] 8-11-4 F J Flood, ... (11 to 2) pu
Dist: 6l, sht-hd, 11l, 1l. 5m 59.20s. (12 Ran).

(Mrs F Whelan), A J McNamara

2946 Listowel I.N.H. Flat Race (5-y-o) £2,740 2m . . . . (5:30)

VITAL ISSUE (Ire) 11-12 Mr P Fenton, ... (5 to 2) 1
GARRYDUFF SUPREME (Ire) 11-0 (7⁷) Mr Mark Walsh,
. . . .(12 to 1) 2
2449⁷ RING ABLAZE (Ire) 11-9 (3⁷) Mr R Walsh, ... (5 to 4 fav) 3
2709⁵ MEGA GALE (Ire) 11-5 (7⁷) Mr C A Murphy, ... (5 to 2) 4
1907 LAURAS ELECTRIC (Ire) 11-0 (7⁷) Mr Sean O O'Brien,
. . . .(9 to 1) 5
2055 TOUGHERTHANTHEREST (Ire) 11-7 Mr D Marnane,
. . . . (20 to 1) 6
Dist: 2½l, ½l, 15l, 10l. 4m 37.90s. (6 Ran).

(Paul Shanahan), David Wachman

NEWBURY (good to soft)
Saturday March 1st

Going Correction: PLUS 0.75 sec. per fur.

2947 North Sydmonton Handicap Chase Class C (0-135 5-y-o and up) £4,497 2½m . . . . (1:15)

2659* TOO PLUSH [113] 8-10-6 L Harvey, hld up, hdwy 12th, led and
blun last, all out.
. . . .(9 to 2 op 11 to 4 tchd 5 to 1 and 11 to 2) 1
2564³ MELY MOSS (Fr) [135] 6-12-0 G Bradley, led to second, led
5th to last, hrd rdn, ran on.
. . . . (11 to 8 fav op 11 to 10 tchd 6 to 4) 2
2294* NEWLANDS-GENERAL [118] 11-10-11 A P McCoy, prmnt till
wknd appr 3 out. . . . .(4 to 1 tchd 5 to 1) 3
THE FROG PRINCE (Ire) [125] 9-11-4 C Llewellyn, led second
to 5th, ev ch 12th, wknd quickly appr 4 out, tld off.
. . . . (100 to 30 op 4 to 1) 4
2846⁶ POTATO MAN [107] (v) 11-9-9 (5⁷) D J Kavanagh, tld off frm
8th. . . . .(66 to 1 op 50 to 1) 5
Dist: Hd, 26l, dist, 27l. 5m 15.30s. a 27.30s (5 Ran).

(Mrs C C Williams), Andrew Turnell

2948 Berkshire Handicap Chase Class C (0-135 5-y-o and up) £4,627 3m . . . . (1:45)

2334⁴ TURNING TRIX [125] 10-11-4 J R Kavanagh, hdwy 14th, led
aftr last, sn hdd, led last strds. . . . .(11 to 4 op 5 to 2) 1
2404* SISTER STEPHANIE (Ire) [123] 8-11-2 D Bridgwater, led to
second, remained cl up, mstk 3 out, led appr last, hdd r-in, sn
led ag'n, headed fnl strds.
. . . .(9 to 4 fav tchd 5 to 2 and 11 to 4) 2
2589² RIVER MANDATE [123] (bl) 10-11-2 A P McCoy, led second,
reminders 11th and 13th, hdd appr last, swtchd rght and
rallied r-in. . . . .(5 to 2 op 9 to 4) 3
HILL TRIX [119] 11-10-12 B Powell, jmpd stickily, tld off frm
tenth. . . . .(40 to 1 op 25 to 1) 4
SMITH'S BAND (Ire) [135] 9-12-0 R Farrant, prmnt till wknd
appr 4 out, pld up bef 3 out. (7 to 2 op 5 to 2 tchd 4 to 1) pu
Dist: Hd, 1l, dist. 6m 12.10s. a 27.10s (5 Ran).

(Mel Davies), D Nicholson

2949 Eastleigh Handicap Hurdle Class C (0-130 4-y-o and up) £3,785 2m 110yds. . . . . (2:15)

2777* SHERIFFMUIR [117] 8-11-7 J F Titley, hdwy 5th, led appr last,
ran on wl.
. . . . (4 to 1 fav op 9 to 2 tchd 5 to 1 and 11 to 2) 1
2558* RANGITIKEI (NZ) [112] 6-11-2 J Railton, led 4th till appr last,
ran on. . . . .(9 to 2 op 7 to 2 tchd 5 to 1) 2
2639* NIPPER REED [103] 7-10-7 D Bridgwater, led to 4th, ran on
one pace frm 3 out. . . . . .(10 to 1 op 8 to 1 tchd 11 to 1) 3
2442⁹ SLEW MAN (Fr) [117] 6-11-7 A P McCoy, al prmnt, one pace
frm 3 out. . . . . (8 to 1 tchd 7 to 1 and 9 to 1) 4
2498⁷ MOVING OUT [120] 9-11-3 (7⁷) Mr A Wintle, prmnt to 5th.
. . . . (40 to 1 op 25 to 1) 5
2717* GOLDING [108] 10-10-12 J R Kavanagh, hdwy 3 out, one
pace frm nxt. . . . .(10 to 1 op 8 to 1 tchd 11 to 1) 6
2730⁵ ROS CASTLE [115] (bl) 6-10-12 (7⁷) J Harris, beh till hdwy 5th,
wknd appr last. . . . .(16 to 1 op 14 to 1 tchd 20 to 1) 7
2730² SHEPHERDS REST (Ire) [101] 5-10-5 N Mann, nvr nr to chal.
. . . .(7 to 1 op 8 to 1) 8
'IGGINS (Ire) [110] 7-11-0 R Dunwoody, nvr trbld ldrs.
. . . . (12 to 1 op 10 to 1 tchd 14 to 1) 9
2580³ CENTAUR EXPRESS [117] 5-11-7 T Eley, nvr trbld ldrs.
. . . .(8 to 1 op 7 to 1 tchd 10 to 1) 10
2554³ INTERMAGIC [110] 7-11-0 S Fox, beh frm 5th.
. . . . (25 to 1 tchd 33 to 1) 11
2717⁷ SAINT CIEL (USA) [105] 9-10-9 R Farrant, wl beh frm 5th, tld
off. . . . .(33 to 1 op 25 to 1) 12
1572³ CHEF COMEDIEN (Ire) [120] 7-11-10 W Marston, tld off whn
pld up bef 5th. . . . .(25 to 1 op 16 to 1 tchd 33 to 1) pu
Dist: 3½l, 7l, 7l, 3l, 5l, ¾l, 12l, 2l, 9l, 8l. 4m 7.00s. a 18.00s (13 Ran).
SR: 37/28/12/19/19/2/8/-/-/ (J J W Wadham), Mrs L Wadham

2950 Jack O'Newbury Novices' Chase Class E (5-y-o and up) £2,927 2½m . . . . (2:45)

2498² FLIGHT LIEUTENANT (USA) 8-11-9 D Bridgwater, hdwy 11th,
lft in ld 3 out, unchlgd. . . . . .(4 to 1 op 5 to 2 tchd 9 to 2) 1
2247 MADISON COUNTY (Ire) (v) 7-11-4 C Llewellyn, prmnt till
outpcd 12th, styd on ag'n frm 2 out.
. . . . (6 to 1 op 9 to 2 tchd 13 to 2) 2
2793³ GORDON (bl) 6-11-1 (3⁷) E Husband, led 4th to four out, wknd
quickly appr last. . . . .(14 to 1 op 20 to 1 tchd 25 to 1) 3
SPIN ECHO (Ire) 8-11-4 W Marston, mstks, wl beh frm 8th.
. . . . (50 to 1 op 33 to 1 tchd 66 to 1) 4
2638² ANGELO'S DOUBLE (Ire) 9-11-4 B Powell, led to 4th, led four
out, gng wl whn l 3 out.
. . . . (Evens fav op 5 to 4 on tchd 5 to 4) f
Dist: 20l, 5l, 8l. 5m 23.80s. a 35.80s (5 Ran).

(Mrs Laura Pegg), T Casey

2951 Scudamore Clothing 0800 301 301 'National Hunt' Novices' Hurdle Class D (4-y-o and up) £3,467 2m 5f
.... (3:15)

2746* SPRING DOUBLE (Ire) 6-11-7 C Llewellyn, al prmnt, hrd rdn 3 out, styd on to ld r-in................(9 to 1 op 6 to 1) 1

26974 FIDDLING THE FACTS (Ire) 6-11-2 J R Kavanagh, al prmnt, led appr 2 out, hdd and not quicken r-in.
...............(6 to 5 on op 5 to 4 tchd 11 to 8 and 6 to 4) 2

2678* PEACE LORD (Ire) 7-11-7 J F Titley, al prmnt, ev ch 2 out, wknd last......(7 to 2 op 5 to 2 tchd 4 to 1 and 9 to 2) 3

26615 ALLOW (Ire) (bl) 6-11-2 (5*) D J Kavanagh, al prmnt, led 6th to 8th, hrd rdn 3 out, one pace.
.........(14 to 1 op 8 to 1 tchd 16 to 1 and 20 to 1) 4

15433 FASHION MAKER (Ire) 7-11-2 L Harvey, some hdwy 7th, nvr nr to chal..................(33 to 1 op 20 to 1) 5

27255 PROFESSOR PAGE (Ire) 7-11-2 J Railton, beh frm 5th.
..............................(33 to 1 op 20 to 1) 6

26616 VINTAGE CLARET 8-11-2 P Hide, led to second, led 8th till appr 2 out, 4th and btn whn f last.........(9 to 1 op 8 to 1) f

24097 JUPITER PROBE (Ire) 6-11-2 W Marston, prmnt to 7th, beh whn f last.........................(66 to 1 op 33 to 1) f

2605* HALONA 7-11-2 G Bradley, led second, mstk 5th, hdd 6th, wkng whn pld up bef 8th......(9 to 1 op 5 to 1) pu
MODEL TEE (Ire) 8-11-2 D Bridgwater, tld off whn pld up bef 3 out..............................(33 to 1 op 12 to 1) pu
GRATOMI (Ire) 7-11-2 S Fox, tld off whn pld up bef 7th.
.................................(66 to 1 op 50 to 1) pu

1984 TOSHIBA HOUSE (Ire) 6-10-11 K Johnson, tld off whn pld up bef last...........................(66 to 1 op 33 to 1) pu

2775 MISTRESS TUDOR 6-10-11 N Mann, tld off whn pld up bef 3 out..............................(66 to 1 op 33 to 1) pu

Dist: 2½l, 27l, 21l, 5l, 1¾l. 5m 17.70s. a 23.70s (13 Ran).

SR: 14/6/-/-/-/-/ (Mrs Lorna Berryman), N A Twiston-Davies

2952 Levy Board Novices' Handicap Hurdle Class D (0-110 4-y-o and up) £3,566 2m 110yds........... (3:50)

25418 THE BREWMASTER (Ire) [85] 5-10-9 P Hide, made all, lft clr 2 out, ran on wl..................(7 to 1 op 5 to 1) 1

16463 MR POPPLETON [76] 8-11-0 L Harvey, chsd wnr to 3 out, lft second 2 out, no imprsn.
.........(12 to 1 op 10 to 1 tchd 14 to 1) 2

2607 NOBLE COLOURS [84] 4-9-9 (5*) D J Kavanagh, hdwy appr 3 out, one pace frm 2 out...(100 to 30 op 5 to 1 tchd 40 to 1) 3

27837 I RECALL (Ire) [76] (v) 6-10-0 R Farrant, hdwy 3 out, no pace frm 2 out.....................(12 to 1 op 10 to 1) 4

26364 RISING DOUGH (Ire) [100] 5-11-10 A P McCoy, effrt and rdn appr 3 out, sn wknd....(100 to 30 op 5 to 2 tchd 7 to 2) 5

23236 PALLADIUM BOY [82] 7-10-6 G Bradley, beh frm 5th.
.....................................(6 to 1 tchd 8 to 1) 6

24516 DAUNT [88] 5-10-12 D Bridgwater, wl beh frm 5th.
.....................................(6 to 1 op 5 to 1) 7

28157 TOSHIBA TALK (Ire) [84] 5-10-8 W Marston, chsd ldrs, mstk and rdn 4th, wknd nxt...(20 to 1 op 14 to 1 tchd 25 to 1) 8

21589 SUPREME GENOTIN (Ire) [95] 8-11-5 C Llewellyn, hld up gng wl, wth wnr and ev ch whn blun and uns 2nd out.
............(11 to 4 fav op 7 to 2 tchd 4 to 1) ur

1938 SWEETLY DISPOSED (Ire) [88] 9-10-12 J R Kavanagh, tld off whn pld up bef 2 out...............(33 to 1 op 20 to 1) pu

Dist: 8l, hd, 7l, 21l, 12l, 1l, 13l. 4m 8.80s. a 19.80s (10 Ran).

SR: 7/-/-/-/-/-/ (John Poynton & Mr Jim Brewer), I P Williams

2953 Thatcham Standard Open National Hunt Flat Class H (4,5,6-y-o) £1,323 2m 110yds............ (4:20)

RED CURATE (Ire) 6-11-2 D Bridgwater, hdwy aftr 6 fs, led o'r 2 out, ran on wl..........(16 to 1 op 7 to 1 tchd 20 to 1) 1

27233 BOLD LEAP 5-11-2 Mr A Sansome, led till 6 fs out, ev ch 2 out, ran on one pace..............(11 to 2 op 10 to 1) 2

28102 ALL DONE 4-10-3 N Mann, al prmnt, led 6 fs out till o'r 2 out, not quicken...................(6 to 1 op 4 to 1) 3

25524 CRYSTAL JEWEL 5-10-11 A P McCoy, middle div, rdn and hdwy 3 fs out, nvr nr to chal.
...............(11 to 2 op 4 to 1 tchd 6 to 1) 4

2409 EMBARGO (Ire) 5-10-9 (7*) Mr H Dunlop, hdwy and rdn 3 fs out, nvr on terms.................(12 to 1 op 16 to 1) 5
CELTIC SEASON 5-10-9 (7*) Mr A Wintle, nvr better than mid-div....................................(14 to 1) 6

26423 FIN BEC (Fr) 4-10-8 S McNeill, prmnt till wknd o'r 2 fs out.
...............(10 to 1 op 6 to 1 tchd 12 to 1) 7
PURPLE ACE (Ire) 5-11-2 C Llewellyn, hdwy on ins 3 fs out, not rch ldrs........(16 to 1 op 7 to 1 tchd 20 to 1) 8
CONQUER THE KILT 6-11-2 S Curran, hdwy 5 fs out, rdn and wknd o'r 2 out........(33 to 1 op 25 to 1 tchd 50 to 1) 9
SWEEP CLEAN 5-11-2 P Hide, chsd ldrs, rdn and wknd 3 fs out............(4 to 1 fav op 3 to 1 tchd 11 to 2) 10
CARAS ROSE 5-11-2 R Farrant, beh fnl 3 fs.
...................(7 to 1 op 5 to 1 tchd 10 to 1) 11
MILLERS ACTION 4-10-3 Miss M Coombe, al beh, tld off.
.................................(33 to 1 op 20 to 1 tchd 50 to 1) 12

CHAMPAGNE FRIEND 6-10-11 L Harvey, prmnt till wknd quickly one m out, sn tld off.
.........(14 to 1 op 16 to 1 tchd 33 to 1) 13

26429 MONMOUTH WAY 5-11-2 J R Kavanagh, chsd ldr 4 fs, wknd one m out, tld off fnl four furlongs.
.........(33 to 1 op 25 to 1 tchd 50 to 1) 14

27236 RIVER DAWN (Ire) 5-11-2 G Bradley, prmnt for a m, wknd quickly, tld off...(16 to 1 op 7 to 1 tchd 20 to 1) 15

25108 YONDER STAR 5-10-9 (7*) C Hynes, rdn and wknd one m out, tld off fnl 6 fs.........(33 to 1 op 10 to 1 tchd 50 to 1) 16

Dist: 9l, 3l, 2l, ½l, ½l, 6l, 4l, nk, 3½l, 10l. 4m 9.70s. (16 Ran).

(Mrs M Turner & Mr C White), G M McCourt

WARWICK (good)
Saturday March 1st
Going Correction: PLUS 0.35 sec. per fur. (races 1,4,5,6,8), PLUS 0.45 (2,3,7)

2954 Watergall Novices' Hurdle Class E (Div I) (4-y-o and up) £2,197 2½m 110yds...................... (1:30)

25417 SILVER THYNE (Ire) 5-11-2 D Leahy, made all, sn wl clr, styd on strly frm betw last 2............(7 to 1 op 4 to 1) 1

2423* CHEERFUL ASPECT (Ire) 4-10-13 N Williamson, nvr far away, chsd clr ldr frm hfwy, improved 3 out, rdn and no imprsn whn nrly f last.........(7 to 4 on tchd 6 to 4 on) 2
VADLAWYS (Fr) 6-11-2 R Johnson, patiently rdn, steady hdwy to chase clr ldg pair frm 4 out, styd on, prmsg.
............(13 to 2 op 3 to 1 tchd 7 to 1) 3

27717 TORCH VERT (Ire) 5-11-2 C Maude, wtd wth, improved in midfield hfwy, styd on frm 3 out, nvr nr to chal.
.........(12 to 1 op 16 to 1 tchd 10 to 1) 4

19193 RAFFLES ROOSTER 5-11-2 P Holley, patiently rdn, effrt hfwy, lost pl, steady hdwy ag'n frm 3 out, nvr plcd to chal.
.....................................(14 to 1 tchd 16 to 1) 5

9943 KIROV ROYALE 6-10-11 W McFarland, sn beh, nvr able to rch chalg pos...........(66 to 1 op 50 to 1) 6
TURSAL (Ire) 8-11-2 Mr R Armson, slwly away, al wl beh.
.....................................(100 to 1) 7

2575 KAYE'S SECRET 4-10-2 R Supple, drvn alng to keep up, wl beh frm hfwy, tld off.........(66 to 1 op 50 to 1) 8
GLAISNOCK LAD (Ire) 5-11-2 Richard Guest, sn wl beh, tld off frm hfwy.........(100 to 1 op 50 to 1) 9

2724 GRIZZLY BEAR (Ire) 7-11-2 S Wynne, wl plcd wth chasing grp to hfwy, lost tch, tld off...........(50 to 1 op 33 to 1) 10

2311 GOATSFUT (Ire) 7-11-2 T Jenks, settled wth chasing bunch, sn lost tch, tld off..........(100 to 1 op 50 to 1) 11

24584 ELGINTORUS (Ire) 7-10-13 (3*) J Magee, settled midfield, lost grnd hfwy, tld off...........(50 to 1 op 33 to 1) 12

2664 LUCKY TANNER 6-11-2 J Culloty, chsd ldrs, effrt hfwy, sn lost tch, tld off...........(40 to 1 op 25 to 1) 13

1955 MY SHENANDOAH 6-11-2 Jacqui Oliver, wl beh whn blun and uns rdr 3 out..................(50 to 1 op 33 to 1) ur
GILDORAN PALACE 6-11-2 D Walsh, al wl beh, tld off whn pld up bef 5 out.............(100 to 1 op 50 to 1) pu

Dist: 18l, 10l, 12l, hd, 5l, 8l, 2½l, 4l, 1l, 26l. 5m 3.10s. a 18.10s (15 Ran).

(Robert & Elizabeth Hitchins), Mrs J Pitman

2955 Exterior Profiles Ltd. Novices' Handicap Chase Class C (5-y-o and up) £7,165 2½m 110yds......... (2:05)

2498* GARNWIN (Ire) [106] 7-11-5 N Williamson, jmpd wl, nvr far away, jumped ahead 4 out, hrd pressed r-in, ran on strly.
.........(3 to 1 fav op 7 to 2 tchd 4 to 1) 1

25474 WHIRLY (Ire) [95] 8-10-8 S McNeill, settled midfield, hit second, improved to chal 4 out, rdn and ran on r-in.
.........(10 to 1 op 8 to 1) 2

2597 EXTERIOR PROFILES (Ire) [110] 7-11-9 T J Murphy, trkd ldrs, lost grnd whn pace quickened 7 out, rallied last 3, kpt on same pace frm betw last 2.....(9 to 2 op 7 to 2 tchd 5 to 1) 3

24503 AMBER VALLEY (USA) [97] 6-11-2 (3*) Guy Lewis, patiently rdn, improved frm off the pace fnl circuit, effrt 6 out, drvn alng from nxt, sn btn..............(33 to 1 op 20 to 1) 4

27262 STROKESAVER (Ire) [88] (bl) 7-10-1 J Culloty, led to 3rd, rgned ld tenth, blun and hdd 6 out, struggling aftr nxt, lost tch frm 4 out...............(7 to 1 tchd 8 to 1) 5

2728 PLUNDER BAY (USA) [113] 6-11-7 (5*) Mr C Vigors, wth ldrs, led 3rd till blun and hdd tenth, feeling pace 6 out, sn lost tch.
.....................(20 to 1 op 12 to 1) 6

2399* THE REVEREND BERT (Ire) [110] 9-11-9 B Fenton, sn wl beh, f tenth....................(4 to 1 op 9 to 2 tchd 7 to 1) ur

27292 JOVIAL MAN (Ire) [95] 8-10-8 P Holley, wth ldrs thrght, jmpd ahead 6 out, hdd 4 out, 3rd and drvn alng whn blun and uns rdr nxt...............(7 to 1 op 5 to 1 tchd 8 to 1) ur

25614 DREAM RIDE (Ire) [115] 7-12-0 R Johnson, midfield whn blun and uns rdr 5th.................(9 to 1 op 6 to 1) ur

Dist: 1¾l, ¾l, 20l, 29l, 8l. 5m 10.70s. a 15.70s (9 Ran).

SR: 26/13/27/-/-/-/ (Pioneer Heat-Treatment), N J Henderson

2956 Crudwell Cup Handicap Chase Class C (0-135 5-y-o and up) £7,262 3m 5f
.... (2:35)

2427⁵ JURASSIC CLASSIC [112] 10-10-6 M Richards, *led till aftr second, led ag'n 5th till after tenth, led 13th, hit 3 out and last, very gmely*................................(14 to 1 op 10 to 1) 1

2564⁴ BEAUREPAIRE (Ire) [106] 9-10-0 S McNeill, *nvr far away, not fluent 13th and nxt, rallied frm 6 out, str run and pres r-in, ran on*.......................................(7 to 1 tchd 8 to 1) 2

2439³ FULL OF OATS [119] 11-10-13 J Culloty, *settled to track ldrs, took clr order frm 6 out, effrt und pres frm betw last 2, styd on under pressure r-in*........................(100 to 30 jt-fav op 4 to 1 tchd 5 to 1) 3

2715³ KILLESHIN [130] 11-11-10 S Curran, *sn beh, drvn alng to fnl circuit, feeling pace 6 out, fdd frm nxt*.
....(11 to 2 op 4 to 1) 4

2698² ROCKY PARK [106] 7-9-11-0 B Fenton, *settled midfield, effrt whn blun 13th, rallied fnl circuit, lost grnd 6 out, sn btn*.
....(10 to 1 op 6 to 1) 5

2742 DANGER BABY [106] 7-9-11 (3⁵) Guy Lewis, *chsd ldrs, blun and nrly uns rdr 8th, rallied and blunded 14th, feeling pace 6 out, no imprsn aftr*..............(16 to 1 op 10 to 1) 6

2599 WOODLANDS GENHIRE [106] (bl) 12-10-0 R Bellamy, *reminders 4th, tld off frm hfwy, pld up aftr 3 out*.
....(50 to 1 op 25 to 1) pu

2698 NAZZARO [121] (bl) 8-11-1 N Williamson, *led aftr second to 5th, led ag'n tenth, hdd 13th, struggling 7 out, wknd quickly and pld up bef 5 out*....................(10 to 1 op 8 to 1) pu

2334⁶ SOUNDS STRONG (Ire) [126] 8-11-6 R Johnson, *losing grnd whn hit 5th, not reco'r, pld up bef 11th, dismounted*.
....(100 to 30 jt-fav op 7 to 2) pu

Dist: ¾l, ¾l, 7l, 9l, 3½l. 7m 29.10s. a 20.10s (9 Ran).

SR: 7/-/12/16/-/-/ (Brian Seal & Roger Rees), Mrs L Richards

2957 Emscott Conditional Jockeys' Handicap Hurdle Class F (0-100 4-y-o and up) £2,390 2m............... (3:10)

2371⁹ GALWAY BOSS (Ire) [68] 5-10-1 T Dascombe, *settled off the pace, steady hdwy frm 3 out, str run und pres to ld nr finish*.
....(10 to 1 op 7 to 1) 1

2746 SYLVESTER (Ire) [74] 7-10-2 (5⁵) M Griffiths, *al wl plcd, led 4th, rdn betw last 2, hdd and no extr nr finish*.
....(16 to 1 op 14 to 1) 2

2676² NAGOBELIA [79] 9-10-7 (5⁵) J O'Shaughnessy, *settled midfield, took clr order aftr 3 out, effrt and rdn betw last 2, kpt on same pace*..........................(13 to 2 op 5 to 1) 3

2460³ CAMBO (USA) [83] 11-10-11 (5⁵) R Hobson, *co'red up in midfield, improved frm 5 out, rdn and kpt on one pace from betw last 2*........................(10 to 1 op 7 to 1) 4

2407³ AMBIDEXTROUS (Ire) [86] 5-11-0 (5⁵) L Cummins, *settled wth chasing grp, drvn alng to improve frm 3 out, rdn and one pace appr last*.........................(13 to 2 op 5 to 2) 5

2440 ANOTHERONE TO NOTE [67] 6-9-9 (5⁵) A Dowling, *settled midfield, bustled alng to improve aftr 4 out, rdn and one pace frm betw last*..................(50 to 1 op 33 to 1) 6

2548⁴ SHIFTING MOON [77] (bl) 5-10-10 L Aspell, *led to 4th, styd hndy till rdn and no extr frm betw last 2.* (5 to 1 op 10 to 1) 7

2602 OUT OF THE BLUE [67] 5-9-9 (5⁵) X Aizpuru, *chsd ldrs, feeling pace and drvn alng aftr 3 out, no imprsn after*.
....(14 to 1 op 20 to 1 tchd 25 to 1) 8

2432⁶ ROYAL GLINT [67] 10-10-0 Sophie Mitchell, *settled off the pace, not rch chalg pos*..............(25 to 1 op 20 to 1) 9

2576 RAIN-N-SUN [76] 11-10-9 Chris Webb, *in tch to hfwy, feeling pace aftr 4 out, wknd quickly und pres.* (16 to 1 op 12 to 1) 10

2515⁺ TANGO MAN (Ire) [72] 5-10-5 Michael Brennan, *wtd wth, improved to go hndy hfwy, 3rd and drvn alng whn hit 3 out, not reco'r, tld off*.............(9 to 2 op 4 to 1 tchd 5 to 1) 11

2609⁷ ERLKING (Ire) [85] (v) 7-10-13 (5⁵) S Hearn, *wl plcd to hfwy, lost tch, tld off aftr 4 out*.............(20 to 1 op 16 to 1) 12

505 DAYS OF THUNDER [79] 9-10-12 D Walsh, *settled in midfield, lost pl quickly hfwy, tld off*......(25 to 1 op 16 to 1) 13

STEVE FORD [91] 8-11-3 (7⁵) M Handley, *mstk and uns rdr 1st*.................................(25 to 1 op 12 to 1) ur

2462⁹ MILLENIUM LASS (Ire) [84] 9-11-3 P Midgley, *settle midfield, lost tch frm hfwy, tld off whn pld up bef 2 out*....(33 to 1) pu

KANO WARRIOR [86] 10-11-0 (5⁵) J Mogford, *lost tch quickly frm hfwy, tld off whn pld up aftr 4 out.* (50 to 1 op 33 to 1) pu

Dist: ½l, 3½l, 6l, ½l, 1¼l, nk, 6l, 13l, ½l, ¾l. 3m 50.30s. a 11.30s (16 Ran).

SR: 16/21/22/20/22/1/ (Mr & Mrs John Poynton), I P Williams

2958 Blackdown Handicap Hurdle Class C (0-135 4-y-o and up) £3,649 2½m 110yds...................... (3:45)

2438⁹ EDGEMOOR PRINCE [104] 6-10-2 G Tormey, *al wl plcd, led 7th, hrd pressed last 2, kpt on grimly r-in*.
....(14 to 1 op 12 to 1) 1

2719⁺ LETS BE FRANK [108] 6-10-6 R Johnson, *chsd ldg trio, improved to chal aftr 3 out, ev ch nxt, rdn and swtchd r-in, kpt on*....................(15 to 8 fav op 7 to 4 tchd 2 to 1) 2

2257 MIM-LOU-AND [113] 5-10-11 J Culloty, *beh, plenty to do hfwy, styd on last 3, nrst finish*......(12 to 1 op 10 to 1) 3

2501⁺ REAGANESQUE (USA) [115] 5-10-10 (3⁵) L Aspell, *wtd wth, improved to go hndy hfwy, ev ch till rdn alng aftr 3 out, no imprsn aftr*.....................(4 to 1 op 11 to 2) 4

2658³ CAN CAN CHARLIE [102] 7-9-7 (7⁵) J O'Shaughnessy, *slightly hmpd by fallers 4th, struggling frm hfwy, nvr nr to chal*..........................(16 to 1 op 12 to 1) 5

2332³ ALLTIME DANCER (Ire) [117] (bl) 5-11-1 J A McCarthy, *wth ldrs, led 3rd to 5th, feeling pace aftr 4 out, lost tch, tld off*.
....(7 to 1 tchd 9 to 1) 6

2695⁹ THINKING TWICE (USA) [128] 8-11-12 B Fenton, *led to 3rd, rgned ld 5th, hdd 7th, wknd quickly frm 3 out, tld off*.
....(20 to 1 op 12 to 1) 7

2730⁸ LINDEN'S LOTTO (Ire) [102] 8-9-12⁵ (7⁵) S Parker, *wl beh frm hfwy, tld off*........................(66 to 1 op 50 to 1) 8

2460⁺ SILVER STANDARD [108] (bl) 7-10-6 S Wynne, *chasing ldrs whn f 4th*................(13 to 2 op 6 to 1 tchd 7 to 1) f

SO PROUD [121] 12-11-5 C Maude, *in tch, effrt whn mstk, hmpd and brght dwn 4th*............(33 to 1 op 25 to 1) bd

2011⁴ SILVER SHRED [130] 6-12-0 N Williamson, *chasing ldrs whn hmpd and brght dwn 4th*.(11 to 1 op 8 to 1 tchd 16 to 1) bd

Dist: Nk, 20l, 1¼l, 8l, 6l, 14l, 22l. 5m 2.70s. a 17.70s (11 Ran).

(The Racing Hares), P J Hobbs

2959 Watergall Novices' Hurdle Class E (Div II) (4-y-o and up) £2,197 2½m 110yds...................... (4:15)

2023 MANASIS (NZ) 6-11-2 R Johnson, *nvr far away, led aftr 4 out, lft clr nxt, styd on und pres*..........(16 to 1 op 12 to 1) 1

2456⁺ EL FREDDIE 7-11-8 N Williamson, *led, clr 4th, hdd aand drvn alng aftr four out, hmpd by faller nxt, rallied last 2, kpt on same pace r-in*........(11 to 8 op 6 to 4 tchd 5 to 4) 2

2640 AMBER RING 4-10-2 B Fenton, *wtd wh, improved hfwy, feeling pace and drvn alng 3 out, no imprsn aftr*.
....(20 to 1 op 10 to 1) 3

2744⁹ COOL HARRY (USA) 6-10-9 (7⁵) Mr S Durack, *settled in rear, drvn alng hfwy, not rch chalg pos*.....(66 to 1 op 50 to 1) 4

2602⁵ ALPHA LEATHER 6-11-2 Mr J Grassick, *struggling frm hfwy, lost tch, tld off from 3 out*.........(66 to 1 op 33 to 1) 5

SILLE ME (Ire) 5-11-2 Richard Guest, *struggling and lost tch frm hfwy, tld off from 3 out*.
....(25 to 1 op 20 to 1 tchd 33 to 1) 6

RI NA MARA (Ire) 6-10-11 (5⁵) S Ryan, *chsd ldrs to hfwy, sn lost tch, tld off*....................(66 to 1 op 50 to 1) 7

2426⁴ MR DARCY 5-11-2 C Maude, *nvr far away, feeling pace and lost grnd 4 out, rallied to go second whn f 3 out*.
....(6 to 5 fav op 11 to 10 tchd 6 to 4) f

1129 KIRBY MOORSIDE 6-11-2 V Slattery, *sluggish strt, reco'ring whn f 1st*............................(100 to 1) f

CLERIC ON BROADWAY (Ire) 9-10-4 (7⁵) J O'Shaughnessy, *wl plcd, feeling pace and lost grnd 7th, 4th and tiring whn blun and uns rdr four out*...............(66 to 1 op 50 to 1) ur

557 POT BLACKBIRD 8-10-11 R Supple, *struck into and brght dwn 1st*........................(33 to 1 op 25 to 1) bd

CHARLIE BIGTIME 7-11-2 J Culloty, *sn wl beh, tld off whn pld up bef 5 out*...................(25 to 1 op 14 to 1) pu

1763 LUMO (Ire) 6-10-13 (3⁵) R Massey, *broke nr hind and pld up aftr 1st, destroyed*.............(50 to 1 op 33 to 1) pu

2243 SUMMIT ELSE 6-10-11 T Jenks, *tld off whn pld up bef 5 out*.
....(25 to 1 op 14 to 1) pu

Dist: 3l, 25l, dist, 2½l, 5l, dist. 5m 8.00s. a 23.00s (14 Ran).

(Stanley W Clarke), S A Brookshaw

2960 Town Of Warwick Foxhunters' Trophy Hunters' Chase Class H (5-y-o and up) £1,095 3¼m.......... (4:45)

2502⁺ THE MALAKARMA 11-12-5 (5⁵) Mr B Pollock, *patiently rdn, steady hdwy fnl circuit, jmpd ahead 4 out, styd on strly frm betw last 2*.......................(9 to 2 op 3 to 1) 1

2790⁺ LORD RELIC (NZ) 11-12-2 (5⁵) Mr R Ford, *chsd clr ldr, improved to ld appr 7 out, jmpd slwly nxt, hdd 4 out, rallied frm last, fnshd lme*..............(2 to 1 on tchd 7 to 4 on) 2

ARDESEE 17-11-10 (7⁵) Mr J Goldstein, *sn wl beh, prog fnl circuit, effrt 6 out, struggling nxt, soon btn*.
....(66 to 1 op 50 to 1) 3

2790 WILL IT LAST (v) 11-11-5 (7⁵) Mr L Brown, *jmpd slwly, sn tld off and 2 fences beh, jumped slowly and uns rdr 6 out*.
....(150 to 1 op 100 to 1) ur

CAPPAJUNE (Ire) 9-11-9 (3⁵) Mr M Rimell, *chasing ldrs whn blun and uns rdr 3rd*...............(33 to 1 op 20 to 1) ur

2551 MY YOUNG MAN 12-11-10 (7⁵) Mr E James, *led and sn wl clr, slowed and hdd appr 7 out, wknd rpdly 5 out, tld off whn pld up bef 2 out*................(16 to 1 op 10 to 1) pu

Dist: 1¾l, 28l, 6m 50.40s. a 36.40s (6 Ran).

(Charles Dixey), Miss C Saunders

2961 Edstone Mares' Only Intermediate Open National Hunt Flat Class H (4,5,6-y-o) £1,028 2m......... (5:15)

2503² MELODY MAID 5-11-4 N Williamson, *al gng best, led on bit o'r one furlong out, imprsv*.
....(5 to 4 fav op 6 to 4 tchd 11 to 10) 1

2824³ WISE GUNNER 4-10-10 Jamie Evans, *led till hdd o'r one furlong out, no ch wth wnr*.(11 to 2 op 6 to 1 tchd 8 to 1) 2

CAPSOFF (Ire) 4-10-10 Richard Guest, *patiently rdn, steady hdwy on ins last half m, kpt on last furlong, better for race*.
....(33 to 1 op 20 to 1) 3

2552⁺ POTTER AGAIN (Ire) 5-11-8 (3⁵) R Massey, *nvr far away, ev ch and rdn 2 fs out, ridden and no extr ins last*.
....(3 to 1 op 5 to 1 tchd 7 to 2) 4

2694⁹ CINNAMON CLUB 5-11-4 A Thornton, *settled gng wl, smooth hdwy frm hfwy, effrt and rdn 2 fs out, one pace, improve.*
.... (33 to 1 op 20 to 1) 5
DRESSED IN STYLE (Ire) 5-11-4 P Holley, *wtd wth, improved frm nfwy, feeling pace o'r 3 fs out, grad wknd.*
.... (33 to 1 op 16 to 1) 6
2545³ GOLDEN LILY 4-10-7 (3*) T Dascombe, *settled midfield, effrt hfwy, lost grnd bef strt, no imprsn.*
.... (16 to 1 op 10 to 1 tchd 20 to 1) 7
CURTIS THE SECOND 4-10-10 R Johnson, *settled off the pace, improved frm o'r 3 fs out, no imprsn.*
.... (50 to 1 op 25 to 1) 8
PHOEBE THE FREEBEE (Ire) 6-11-4 J Culloty, *beh till improved hfwy, feeling pace o'r 3 fs out, fdd.* ..... (33 to 1) 9
2483⁸ SEE MINNOW 4-10-3 (7*) N Willmington, *beh till styd on fnl 3 fs, nrst finish.* .... (66 to 1 op 50 to 1) 10
2642 OVERRUNNING 5-11-4 M Richards, *pressed ldrs till fdd und pres frm o'r 4 fs out.* .... (100 to 1 op 50 to 1) 11
2831 GRACIOUS IMP (USA) 4-10-3 (7*) N T Egan, *wth ldrs for o'r a m, wknd bef strt.* .... (33 to 1) 12
1648⁵ OXBRIDGE LADY 6-11-4 T Jenks, *drvn alng hfwy, nvr a factor.* .... (20 to 1 op 10 to 1) 13
2503⁹ NEARLY A SCORE 5-11-4 B Fenton, *beh and drvn alng hfwy, nvr a factor.* .... (16 to 1 op 10 to 1) 14
HILL SPRITE 6-11-4 D Leahy, *sn beh, nvr a factor.*
.... (100 to 1 op 50 to 1) 15
2309⁶ FOLESCLAVE (Ire) 5-11-4 T J Murphy, *al wl beh, nvr dngrs.*
.... (33 to 1 op 25 to 1) 16
2723⁹ PROPER PRIMITIVE 4-10-3 (7*) C Rae, *al beh, nvr on terms.*
.... (33 to 1 op 20 to 1) 17
2302⁹ COROMANDEL 5-11-4 J A McCarthy, *al in rear, nvr a factor.*
.... (33 to 1 op 20 to 1) 18
GLOWING MOON 4-10-5 (5*) A Bates, *chsd clr ldr to hfwy, grad wknd.* .... (50 to 1 op tchd 14 to 1) 19
MISS KILWORTH (Ire) 6-11-4 R Supple, *al beh.*
.... (66 to 1 op 50 to 1) 20
NEWGATE PIXIE (Ire) 4-10-5 (5*) S Ryan, *in tch to hfwy, tld off.*
.... (50 to 1 op 33 to 1) 21
1802 HANDS OFF MILLIE 6-10-13 (5*) O Burrows, *al wl beh, tld off whn slpd up appr strt.* .... (50 to 1 op 25 to 1) su
Dist: 2l, 5l, 3½l, 2½l, 7l, 2l, 1½l, sht-hd, 11l, 2½l. 3m 48.00s. (22 Ran).
(R J Parish), N J Henderson

LEOPARDSTOWN (IRE) (soft)
Sunday March 2nd
Going Correction: PLUS 0.85 sec. per fur.

2962 Stepaside Novice Chase (5-y-o and up) £3,082 2m 5f............ (2:30)

2644⁴ LUCKY BUST (Ire) 7-11-8 T Horgan, ... (5 to 2) 1
2840⁶ LORD MUFF (Ire) 8-11-8 J K Kinane, ... (10 to 1) 2
2840 MYSTICAL AIR (Ire) 7-11-8 P Carberry, ... (10 to 1) 3
1408⁶ FRIDAY THIRTEENTH (Ire) 8-12-0 J P Broderick, . (10 to 1) 4
2341⁵ FOLLY ROAD (Ire) 7-12-0 P L Malone, ... (5 to 1) f
Dist: 5½l, ½l, dist. 5m 58.20s. a 49.20s (5 Ran).
(Mrs W Harney), W Harney

2963 Brannockstown Handicap Hurdle (0-144 4-y-o and up) £4,110 2m
.... (3:00)

1633¹ SPACE TRUCKER (Ire) [-] 6-12-0 J Shortt, ... (9 to 2) 1
2056¹ SENTOSA STAR (Ire) [-] 6-10-1 M P Hourigan, ... (7 to 1) 2
2834¹ CIARA'S PRINCE (Ire) [-] (bl) 6-9-0 (7*) L J Fleming, (11 to 2) 3
2068¹ MILTONFIELD [-] 8-10-3 T Horgan, ... (9 to 2) 4
2706⁶ BOLINO STAR (Ire) [-] 6-10-12 T P Treacy, ... (7 to 2 fav) 5
2473⁵ POWER PACK (Ire) [-] 9-9-2 (7*) R P Hogan, ... (8 to 1) 6
2706⁹ MAYASTA (Ire) [-] 7-10-6 C F Swan, ... (7 to 1) 7
2097¹ COLLON LEADER (Ire) [-] 8-9-7 J R Barry, ... (7 to 1) 8
2708 LADY ARPEL (Ire) [-] 5-10-2² K F O'Brien, ... (8 to 1) 9
2835 BUGGY (Ire) [-] 8-9-12 (7*) Mr A J Dempsey, ... (12 to 1) 10
2706⁸ ANUSHA [-] 7-10-12 L P Cusack, ... (14 to 1) 11
Dist: 2l, 4l, 12l, sht-hd. 4m 0.20s. a 16.20s (11 Ran).
SR: 74/45/33/31/38/-/ (Mrs E Queally), Mrs John Harrington

2964 Lansdowne Maiden Hurdle (5-y-o and up) £3,082 2½m.......... (3:30)

PAT HARTIGAN 7-11-6 F Woods, ... (2 to 1 fav) 1
2752⁷ VALENTINE GALE (Ire) 7-11-9 D J Casey, ... (8 to 1) 2
2583⁷ POLLTRIC (Ire) 6-11-6 P L Malone, ... (14 to 1) 3
2839² FANE PATH (Ire) 5-11-12 P Carberry, ... (11 to 2) 4
2443⁴ CORRACHOILL (Ire) 6-11-11 (3*) U Smyth, ... (11 to 2) 5
2835⁶ GAZALANI (Ire) 5-11-12 T P Treacy, ... (3 to 1) 6
WOLSELEY LORD (Ire) 5-10-11 (7*) Mr A J Dempsey,
.... (14 to 1) 7
2081⁷ BIT O'SPEED (Ire) 6-11-6 C O'Dwyer, ... (8 to 1) 8
BITOFA DIVIL (Ire) 6-11-6 K F O'Brien, ... (14 to 1) 9
2757⁴ COLLON DIAMONDS (Ire) 9-11-1 J P Broderick, .. (10 to 1) 10
1782⁷ HANDSOME ANTHONY (Ire) 6-11-3 (3*) Mr B R Hamilton,
.... (16 to 1) 11
1908 SAIL AWAY SAILOR (Ire) 7-11-1 Mr M Quinlan, .. (25 to 1) 12
2140⁶ TULLABAWN (Ire) 5-11-4 J Shortt, ... (14 to 1) 13
THEODANTE (Ire) 5-10-13 D T Evans, ... (10 to 1) 14
2838⁵ CLONCANNON BELL (Ire) 7-11-1 C F Swan, ... (12 to 1) 15

CHATTERBUCK (Ire) 8-10-13 (7*) D A McLoughlin, (20 to 1) 16
VINTAGE IRLANDE (Ire) 5-10-11 (7*) B J Geraghty, (14 to 1) 17
1275⁸ CLASSPERFORMER (Ire) 5-11-4 L P Cusack, ...(10 to 1) 18
JIMMY MAGEE (Ire) 6-10-13 (7*) R P Hogan, ...(16 to 1) 19
DAWN TO DUSK (Ire) 6-10-13 (7*) D McCullagh, .. (20 to 1) 20
1710⁹ ANOTHER GALLOP (Ire) 9-11-6 S H O'Donovan, .. (25 to 1) 21
KATIES FOUNTAIN (Ire) 5-10-11 (7*) Mr D Broad, .. (20 to 1) 22
2449 AMAZING ALL (Ire) 8-11-6 T P Rudd, ... (50 to 1) 23
2583 NORMINS HUSSAR (Ire) 5-11-4 T J Mitchell, ... (50 to 1) 24
COCO (Ire) 6-11-1 (5*) T Martin, ... (50 to 1) 25
1536 MAVISANDPEDS (Ire) 8-10-13 (7*) J P Deegan, .. (100 to 1) 26
CATEMPO (Ire) 7-11-6 T Horgan, ... (50 to 1) f
EMMSONS PRIDE (Ire) 5-10-10 (3*) K Whelan, ... (50 to 1) pu
Dist: 1½l, 3½l, 1½l, 2l. 5m 26.80s. a 46.80s (28 Ran).
(John P McManus), A L T Moore

2965 Ballsbridge Hurdle (4 & 5-y-o) £3,082 2m.................. (4:00)

STYLISH ALLURE (USA) 4-10-13 D T Evans, ...(6 to 1) 1
2732⁷ FISHIN JOELLA (Ire) 5-11-2 (7*) A O'Shea, ... (9 to 2) 2
2168¹ GREY GUY (Ire) 5-12-0 F Woods, ... (9 to 4 fav) 3
2470³ STRATEGIC PLOY 4-11-1 T J Mitchell, ... (5 to 1) 4
2339 DOUBLE COLOUR 5-11-0 (7*) A P Sweeney, .. (50 to 1) 5
2643* WELCOME PARADE 4-11-6 C O'Dwyer, ...(7 to 1) 6
2737⁵ RAINBOW VICTOR 4-10-13 T Horgan, ... (12 to 1) 7
1641⁶ MURPHY'S MALT (Ire) 5-12-0 C F Swan, ... (11 to 2) 8
2832⁵ WOODEN DANCE (Ire) (bl) 4-10-1 (7*) M P Cooney, (10 to 1) 9
1173 DOUBLEBACK (Ire) 4-10-1 (7*) K A Kelly, ... (33 to 1) 10
2645⁷ ROYAL SANTAL 5-11-2 M P Hourigan, ... (50 to 1) 11
Dist: 3l, 6l, sht-hd, sht-hd. 4m 7.30s. a 23.30s (11 Ran).
(P A Byrnes), D K Weld

2966 Kilternan Handicap Chase (5-y-o and up) £6,850 2m 5f........ (4:30)

2071² WYLDE HIDE [-] 10-11-9 P Carberry, ...(11 to 8 fav) 1
2736 MONALEE RIVER (Ire) [-] 9-10-12 T P Treacy, ... (14 to 1) 2
2736³ BARNAGEERA BOY (Ire) [-] 8-10-0 T J Mitchell, ... (5 to 1) 3
2234⁴ BELVEDERIAN (Ire) [-] 10-11-7 C O'Dwyer, ... (5 to 2) 4
2071⁷ FEATHERED GALE [-] 10-12-0 F Woods, ... (5 to 1) 5
Dist: 4½l, 7l, 15l, 4l. 5m 47.10s. a 38.10s (5 Ran).
(John P McManus), A L T Moore

2967 Firmount I.N.H. Flat Race (4-y-o) £3,082 2m.............. (5:00)

2370² ALL THE COLOURS (Ire) 11-5 Mrs C Barker, .. (10 to 9 on) 1
2370 KOHOUTEK 11-2 (3*) Mr R Walsh, ... (10 to 1) 2
2737* FINE DE CLAIRE 11-0 (7*) Mr R Geraghty, ... (10 to 1) 3
2370⁷ ALOTAWANNA (Ire) 10-12 (7*) Mr J Cash, ... (10 to 1) 4
BENEFICENT (F) 11-5 Mr P Fenton, ... (8 to 1) 5
HARBIMONT (Ire) 11-2 (3*) Mr P M Kelly, ... (8 to 1) 6
CAREFREE LEGEND (Ire) 10-12 (7*) Mr D P Coakley,
.... (33 to 1) 7
DETROIT FLYER (Ire) 10-12 (7*) Mr A J Dempsey, . (25 to 1) 8
Dist: 11l, 1l, 3l, 3l. 4m 10.40s. (8 Ran).
(P A Byrnes), J E Mulhern

2968 Rockbrook I.N.H. Flat Race (5-y-o and up) £3,082 2m............ (5:30)

OLLIMAR (Ire) 5-11-12 Mr P Fenton, ... (8 to 1) 1
2100² CELEBRITY STATUS (Ire) 6-11-7 (7*) Mr D Delaney, (7 to 2) 2
AIR FORCE ONE (Ire) 5-11-9 (3*) Mr R Walsh, .. (5 to 4 fav) 3
2757² SLAVICA 6-11-2 (7*) Mr J P Shaw, ... (8 to 1) 4
2588² TOTAL SUCCESS (Ire) 5-11-5 (7*) Mr D Broad, ... (3 to 1) 5
2222 MONALEA (Ire) 6-12-0 Mr A R Coonan, ... (20 to 1) 6
2525 DOCKLINE (Ire) 5-11-5 (7*) Mr R M Walsh, ... (10 to 1) 7
Dist: Sht-hd, 4l, ¾l, 1l. 4m 7.30s. (7 Ran).
(Triplex Syndicate), J T R Dreaper

DONCASTER (good to firm)
Monday March 3rd
Going Correction: MINUS 0.05 sec. per fur.

2969 Sprotbrough Claiming Hurdle Class G (4-y-o and up) £1,639 2½m (2:00)

2789⁷ SWEET TRENTINO (Ire) 6-11-2 W Marston, *trkd ldrs, hdwy 4 out, led 2 out, rdn and edgd lft last, ran on wl.*
.... (16 to 1 op 10 to 1 tchd 20 to 1) 1
2762 JUST SUPPOSEN (Ire) 6-10-12 B Storey, *in tch, hdwy appr 4 out, led approaching 3 out, rdn and hdd nxt, kpt on und pres r-in.* .... (33 to 1) 2
CUTTHROAT KID (v) 7-11-12 P Niven, *hld up, hdwy to chase ldrs 6th, rdn alng 3 out, ev ch till drvn and one pace frm last.* .... (13 to 8 on op 11 to 8 on) 3
2177⁹ WESTERLY GALE (Ire) 7-11-8 J R Kavanagh, *chsd ldr, rdn 4 out, sn wknd.* .... (11 to 1 op 8 to 1 tchd 12 to 1) 4
2625⁴ WHITE WILLOW (bl) 8-11-1 (3*) R Massey, *led, rdn and hdd appr 3 out, sn wknd.* .... (11 to 2 op 4 to 1) 5
2804⁶ DAME PROSPECT (v) 6-10-9 Gary Lyons, *chsd ldrs, rdn alng 4 out, sn wknd.* .... (9 to 1 op 8 to 1 tchd 10 to 1) 6
1259⁶ MARSH'S LAW 10-11-1 (3*) P Midgley, *al beh, tld off 4th.*
.... (25 to 1 op 16 to 1) 7

COUP DE VENT 7-10-9 (3*) Michael Brennan, *al rear, tld off hfwy*.................................(50 to 1)   8
2315⁶ TARRY 4-10-8 T Eley, *chsd ldrs, rdn alng 6th, sn wknd, beh whn pld up bef 2 out*...............(10 to 1 op 7 to 1)   pu
1975 THETWOKAYS 6-11-2 M Brennan, *in tch 5th, sn beh, tld off whn pld up bef 3 out*.................(33 to 1 op 25 to 1)   pu
Dist: 2½l, hd, 10l, 2l, 7l, 27l, 1¾l. 4m 49.60s. a 14.60s (10 Ran).
(R C Smith), M Tate

2970 Wadworth Novices' Chase Class E (5-y-o and up) £3,029 3m..... (2:30)

2801⁹ SUVLA BAY 9-11-3 M Brennan, *trkd ldr, hit 3rd and tenth, rdn to ld last, styd on*....(13 to 2 op 6 to 1 tchd 7 to 1)   1
2762 FINAL BEAT (Ire) (bl) 8-11-3 P Niven, *cl up, effrt to chal 3 out, led nxt, rdn and hdd last, not quicken*...(5 to 1 op 4 to 1)   2
2726³ MONICASMAN (Ire) 7-11-3 J F Titley, *led, rdn alng 4 out, hdd 2 out, sn drvn and btn*........(3 to 1 on op 11 to 4 on)   3
Dist: 2l, 7l. 6m 16.90s. a 22.90s (3 Ran).
(Lady Anne Bentinck), O Brennan

2971 John Bootle Memorial Novices' Handicap Chase Class D (0-110 5-y-o and up) £4,305 2m 3f 110yds (3:05)

2763⁴ HIGHBEATH [79] 6-11-5 P Niven, *trkd ldrs, hdwy 7th, led 5 out, lft clr 3 out*...............(7 to 2 op 9 to 2 tchd 5 to 1)   1
2604⁷ JOLLY BOAT [82] 10-11-8 P Carberry, *chsd ldrs, effrt 5 out, hit nxt, sn rdn, no imprsn whn lft second 3 out*.
.................................(7 to 1 op 5 to 1)   2
2358³ ARCTIC SANDY (Ire) [85] 7-11-11 B Storey, *hld up, hdwy 9th, rdn alng appr 4 out, no imprsn*.....(9 to 4 fav op 7 to 4)   3
2762 SHOOFE (USA) [83] 9-11-9 R Johnson, *cl up, rdn alng 5 out, sn wknd*..........................(10 to 1 op 8 to 1)   4
2547 DEVILRY [88] 7-12-0 T Eley, *hld up, mstks 5th and nxt, sn beh*.
..................................(12 to 1)   5
2259 FAIR ALLY [77] 7-11-3 D Parker, *cl up, led 6th to 9th, rdn nxt, wknd bef 4 out*...............(20 to 1 tchd 25 to 1)   6
2808³ GLAMANGLITZ [80] 7-11-6 R Supple, *led to 6th, led 9th to 5 out, cl second whn f 3 out*..................(5 to 1)   f
2748 GIPSY RAMBLER [67] 12-10-7 W Worthington, *rear whn pld up bef 6th*......................(16 to 1 op 14 to 1)   pu
2435⁴ BATTY'S ISLAND [72] 8-10-12 T Jenks, *prmnt, hit 8th, sn lost pl, tld off whn pld up bef 3 out*......(16 to 1 tchd 20 to 1)   pu
Dist: 11l, 7l, 6l, 21l, 1¼l. 4m 55.10s. a 10.10s (9 Ran).
(A Sharratt), Mrs M Reveley

2972 European Breeders Fund 'National Hunt' Novices' Hurdle Qualifier Class E (5,6,7-y-o) £2,679 2½m .... (3:35)

2528⁵ SPRING GALE (Ire) 6-11-10 J Osborne, *trkd ldrs, effrt 3 out, shaken up nxt, drvn and awkward last, styd on to ld last 100 yards*.........(Evens fav op 11 to 10 on tchd 11 to 10)   1
2712⁴ CHARLEY LAMBERT (Ire) 6-10-11 (3*) E Husband, *al prmnt, led aftr 4 out, pushed alng and hit 2 out, rdn and hit last, hdd and no extr last 100 yards*...........(11 to 2 op 9 to 2)   2
2463⁴ CHOPWELL DRAPES (Ire) 7-11-0 P Carberry, *trkd ldrs, effrt 4 out, rdn and outpcd nxt, styd on appr last*.
..................................(7 to 2 tchd 3 to 1)   3
2503³ CASTLE MEWS (Ire) 6-10-9 K Gaule, *hld up, hdwy 4 out, rdn nxt, styd on appr last, nvr a factor*.......(7 to 1 op 6 to 1)   4
1928⁴ SMART LORD 6-11-0 S McNeill, *chsd ldrs, rdn alng 4 out, sn wknd*..........................(10 to 1 op 7 to 1)   5
2758 FLORRIE GUNNER 7-10-6 (3*) E Callaghan, *chsd ldrs, rdn alng and lost pl 6th, sn beh*...........(50 to 1 op 33 to 1)   6
BELLE BARONESS 7-10-9 J R Kavanagh, *chsd ldrs pulling hrd, led 4th till aftr four out, sn wknd*...(50 to 1 op 33 to 1)   7
2655 DOUGAL 6-11-0 B Storey, *led to 4th, lost pl hfwy, tld off whn pld up bef 3 out*........................(33 to 1)   pu
BARNABE LAD 7-11-0 Gary Lyons, *al rear, tld off 6th, pld up bef 4 out*.........................(50 to 1)   pu
Dist: 1¼l, 10l, 8l, 15l, 9l, 5l. 4m 47.80s. a 12.80s (9 Ran).
(M Crabb, B Ead, P May, M Moore), O Sherwood

2973 South Yorkshire Novices' Handicap Hurdle Class E (0-105 4-y-o and up) £2,616 2m 110yds............ (4:05)

2785² SILLY MONEY [93] 6-11-4 R Garritty, *mid-div, hdwy 4 out, pushed alng nxt, rdn to chal last, hrd drvn, led last 100 yards*.
.................................(11 to 2 op 5 to 1 tchd 6 to 1)   1
1958⁶ ABOVE THE CUT (USA) [85] 5-10-8 R Johnson, *hld up, hdwy appr 4 out, chlgd nxt, led 2 out, sn rdn, hdd and no extr last 100 yards*.........................(16 to 1 op 14 to 1)   2
2719² BEAUMONT (Ire) [98] 7-11-9 J R Kavanagh, *chsd ldrs, hdwy 4 out, chlgd nxt, ev ch till drvn and no extr last 100 yards*.
.................................(11 to 4 fav op 3 to 1 tchd 7 to 2)   3
2533⁷ WESTERN GENERAL [75] 6-9-7 (7*) N Horrocks, *chsd clr ldr, led aftr 4 out till rdn and hdd 2 out, kpt on und pres*.
.................................(10 to 1 op 8 to 1)   4
2602⁴ ARABIAN HEIGHTS [89] 4-10-6 T Eley, *hld up, hdwy 4 out, chsd ldrs aftr nxt, sn rdn, kpt on same pce*.
.................................(11 to 2 op 7 to 2 tchd 6 to 1)   5
DARU (USA) [87] 8-10-12 J Railton, *beh, hdwy appr 3 out, rdn nxt, kpt on, not rch ldrs*....................(33 to 1)   6

2813⁵ THE SHARROW LEGEND (Ire) [75] 5-10-0 P Carberry, *prmnt, rdn alng 3 out, wknd nxt*.......................(14 to 1)   7
1442⁶ CHILDREN'S CHOICE (Ire) [75] 6-10-0 W Marston, *mid-div, hdwy appr 3 out, rdn nxt, no imprsn*...(10 to 1 op 8 to 1)   8
2296* I'M A DREAMER (Ire) [99] 7-11-10 Gary Lyons, *chsd ldrs, effrt and hdwy aftr 4 out, ev ch nxt, sn rdn and wknd*.
.................................(10 to 1 op 7 to 1)   9
2602⁶ NAGARA SOUND [77] 6-9-9 (7*) J Mogford, *nvr rch ldrs*.
.................................(20 to 1)   10
2511⁸ BRIGHT ECLIPSE (USA) [83] 4-9-11 (3*) Michael Brennan, *hld up, effrt and some hdwy appr 3 out, sn rdn and btn*.
.................................(25 to 1 op 20 to 1)   11
2765⁸ DANNY GALE (Ire) [85] 6-10-10 S McNeill, *chsd ldrs, rdn alng aftr 4 out, wknd bef 2 out*..................(14 to 1)   12
2565 ORCHARD KING [90] 7-11-1 M Brennan, *in tch, hdwy aftr 4 out, ch nxt, sn rdn and wknd*.........(16 to 1 op 14 to 1)   13
2602 TOULSTON LADY (Ire) [75] (bl) 5-9-9 (5*) Mr R Thornton, *al rear*.......................(14 to 1 op 8 to 1)   14
2711 SIOUX WARRIOR [75] (bl) 5-10-0 B Storey, *beh, effrt and some hdwy aftr 4 out, sn rdn and btn*. (20 to 1 op 16 to 1)   15
BLOTOFT [75] (v) 5-10-0 K Gaule, *sn wl clr, hit 3rd and nxt, hdd aftr 4 out, wknd quickly, tld off*....(33 to 1 op 25 to 1)   16
Dist: Nk, 1¼l, 1l, 1¾l, 5l, 1¼l, 3l, 1¾l, 4l, sht-hd. 3m 55.30s. a 5.30s (16 Ran).
SR: 29/19/32/8/12/13/-/-/16/   (Mrs Jean P Connew), T D Easterby

2974 Hambleton Hills Hunters' Chase Class H (5-y-o and up) £1,177 2m 3f 110yds...................... (4:40)

2556* SLIEVENAMON MIST 11-11-13 (5*) Mr J Jukes, *in tch, hdwy to chase ldr 6th, led 9th, clr 2 out, styd on wl*.
.................................(11 to 8 op 5 to 4)   1
DRIVING FORCE (bl) 11-12-1 (7*) Mr A Charles-Jones, *mid-div, hdwy to chase ldrs tenth, rdn 4 out, lft second nxt, no ch wth wnr*............................(20 to 1 op 16 to 1)   2
DOUBLE COLLECT 11-11-11 (7*) Mr A Rebori, *al prmnt, hit 3rd, rdn alng 4 out, sn one pace nxt*....(12 to 1 tchd 14 to 1)   3
TOMMYS WEBB (Ire) 9-11-7 (7*) Mr L Lay, *hld up, hdwy to chase ldrs 5 out, sn rdn and no imprsn*.(66 to 1 op 50 to 1)   4
2516 AL HASHIMI 13-11-7 (7*) Mr N Ridout, *in tch, rdn alng 5 out, sn one pace*......................(20 to 1 op 14 to 1)   5
NO WORD 10-11-7 (7*) Mr I Baker, *cl up, led 3rd and sn clr, hdd 9th, wknd aftr nxt*................(66 to 1 op 50 to 1)   6
TIPP DOWN 14-11-7 (7*) Mr R Thomas, *chsd ldrs till f 8th, dead*...............(50 to 1 op 33 to 1 tchd 66 to 1)   f
2634³ FREE TRANSFER (Ire) 8-11-11 (3*) Mr C Bonner, *in tch, rdn alng to chase ldrs whn blun and uns rdr 11th*.
.................................(12 to 1 op 10 to 1)   ur
SHEER JEST 12-12-5 (3*) Mr A Hill, *hld up, smooth hdwy 5 out, cl 3rd whn pld up lme aftr 3 out*.
.................................(5 to 4 fav tchd 11 to 8)   pu
THE COMMUNICATOR (bl) 11-11-7 (7*) Mr M Munrowd, *led to 3rd, lost pl 8th, tld off whn pld up bef 3 out*......(33 to 1)   pu
885⁵ DEAH EMILY 9-11-9 Mr S Swiers, *mstks, al beh, tld off whn pld up bef 4 out*......................(33 to 1)   pu
Dist: 20l, 11l, 6l, 20l, dist. 4m 55.40s. a 10.40s (11 Ran).
(Nick Viney), Victor Dartnall

2975 Doncaster Mares' Only Standard Open National Hunt Flat Class H (4,5,6-y-o) £1,070 2m 110yds (5:10)

2309⁷ ARDROM 5-11-4 J Osborne, *al prmnt, rdn alng 3 fs out, styd on to ld ins last, ran on strly*..........(6 to 1 op 5 to 1)   1
2262⁴ JESSICA ONE (Ire) 6-11-4 P Niven, *hld up beh, smooth hdwy hfwy, jnd ldr on bit o'r 3 fs out, shaken up entering last, not quicken*.......................(6 to 1 op 5 to 1)   2
2810* MEMSAHIB OFESTEEM 6-11-11 K Gaule, *led, rdn alng 3 fs out, hdd entering last, kpt on*.........(6 to 1 op 5 to 1)   3
2764³ ALISANDE (Ire) 5-11-1 (3*) Mr C Bonner, *hld up, steady hdwy 6 fs out, chsd ldrs and outpcd o'r 3 out, kpt on fnl furlong*.
.................................(11 to 2 op 6 to 1 tchd 7 to 1)   4
2623⁹ DELIGHTFOOL 6-11-4 A Dobbin, *chsd ldrs, rdn alng 5 fs out, one pace 3 out*........................(20 to 1)   5
COMMUNITY SERVICE (Ire) 6-11-1 (3*) E Callaghan, *hld up beh, styd on fnl 4 fs, nvr rch ldrs*.
.................................(11 to 1 op 10 to 1 tchd 12 to 1)   6
ASKED TO LEAVE 5-10-13 (5*) B Grattan, *in tch, rdn alng o'r 6 fs out, sn wknd*....................(20 to 1 op 16 to 1)   7
2503⁷ SUILVEN 5-11-4 C O'Dwyer, *mid-div, hdwy hfwy, rdn alng 6 fs out, sn btn*.........(2 to 1 fav op 9 to 4 tchd 11 to 4)   8
2687⁶ MISS MONEYPENNY 5-10-11 (7*) R Burns, *in tch, rdn alng o'r 5 fs out, sn wknd*...................(20 to 1)   9
2694⁶ ZEPHYRELLE (Ire) 5-11-4 J R Kavanagh, *al rear*.
.................................(6 to 1 op 4 to 1)   10
2824⁹ LAST ACTION 4-10-7 (3*) G Lee, *prmnt, rdn alng 6 fs out, sn wknd*.........................(25 to 1 op 20 to 1)   11
CONNIE LEATHART 6-11-4 D Bentley, *al rear*.
.................................(33 to 1 op 25 to 1)   12
NANGEO BRAE (Ire) 6-11-4 O Pears, *chsd ldrs, rdn alng aftr 6 fs, beh frm hfwy*.......(12 to 1 op 10 to 1)   13
Dist: 3l, 1¼l, 4l, 11l, 1¾l, 5l, 3½l, ½l, 1¼l, 11l. 3m 54.30s. (13 Ran).
(F J Haggas), P R Webber

WINDSOR (good (races 1,2,5,7), good to

firm (3,4,6))

Monday March 3rd

Going Correction: PLUS 0.30 sec. per fur.

2976 Bonusprint Novices' Hurdle Class E (Div I) (4-y-o and up) £2,022 2½m .... (1:50)

2423^{3} PLEASURELAND (Ire) 4-10-7 D Morris, *hld up in tch and al gng wl, rdn clr appr 3 out, cmftbly.* (13 to 8 fav op 5 to 4) 1
758^{3} GARRYNISK (Ire) 7-10-13 (3*) D Fortt, *led to 7th, outpcd, rallied to go second r-in.* ....(100 to 30 op 3 to 1 tchd 4 to 1) 2
1942^{7} CHRISTCHURCH (Fr) 7-11-2 C Maude, *hld up, hdwy 6th, lft second 2 out, awkward last, no extr r-in.* ....(16 to 1 op 14 to 1 tchd 20 to 1) 3
2546^{6} SLEAZEY (bl) 6-11-2 S Curran, *hld up in rear, hdwy frm 2 out, nvr nrr, tld off..*..............................(33 to 1) 4
2661^{9} FARLEYER ROSE (Ire) 8-10-11 M Richards, *prmnt till wknd appr 3 out, tld off*.......(25 to 1 op 20 to 1 tchd 33 to 1) 5
2394^{7} MAETERLINCK (Ire) 5-10-9 (7*) Clare Thorner, *trkd ldr, led briefly 7th, wknd quickly, tld off..* (50 to 1 op 33 to 1) 6
2656^{7} MODAJJAJ 5-11-2 L Harvey, *hld up in rear, making hdwy whn blun 7th, not reco'r, tld off.* ....(50 to 1 op 33 to 1 tchd 66 to 1) 7
2402^{4} MIKE'S MUSIC (Ire) 6-11-2 D Gallagher, *al beh, tld off.* ....(9 to 1 op 6 to 1) 8
1447^{6} DICTUM (Ire) 6-11-2 J Culloty, *al prmnt, rdn and hld in second whn f 2 out..*......................... (11 to 2 op 3 to 1) f
DELOS (NZ) 7-11-2 Derek Byrne, *jinked lft and uns rdr appr 3rd*.................................(7 to 1 op 3 to 1) ur

Dist: 4l, ¾l, dist, 2l, 1¾l, 25l, 11l. 4m 57.20s. a 17.20s (10 Ran).
(Mrs Sylvia E M McGarvie), R Curtis

2977 Final Selling Handicap Hurdle Class G (0-95 4-y-o and up) £2,300 2¾m 110yds....................... (2:20)

2479^{8} NODDADANTE (Ire) [60] 7-9-7 (7*) M Griffiths, *hld up in rear, rdn and hdwy 2 out, plenty to do last, str brst to ld nr finish.* ....(16 to 1 op 14 to 1 tchd 20 to 1) 1
2625^{8} KHAZARI (USA) [64] 9-10-4 S Curran, *hld up, hdwy 8th, led appr 2 out, rdn and hdd nr finish*...... (20 to 1 op 16 to 1) 2
2604 HELLO ME MAN (Ire) [79] 9-11-5 Mr J L Llewellyn, *al prmnt, led 6th till hdd appr 2 out, no extr r-in.* ....(25 to 1 tchd 33 to 1) 3
2392^{6} JAY EM ESS (NZ) [83] 8-11-2 (7*) Mr G Shenkin, *hld up, gd hdwy appr 3 out, rdn and one pace aftr nxt.* ....(6 to 1 jt-fav op 8 to 1 tchd 9 to 1 and 11 to 2) 4
2766^{5} EWAR BOLD [69] 4-10-0 C Llewellyn, *mstks, hdwy appr 3rd, no ch frm 3 out*......................(16 to 1 tchd 20 to 1) 5
756 FOX CHAPEL [83] 10-11-9 G Tormey, *mid-div, nvr rchd ldrs.* ....(20 to 1 op 14 to 1) 6
2770^{6} LAJADHAL (Fr) [71] 8-10-11 L Harvey, *nvr on terms.* ....(14 to 1 op 8 to 1) 7
1971 SEMINOLE WIND [60] (v) 6-9-12^{1} (3*) P Henley, *hld up, gd hdwy appr 8th, wknd bef nxt (3 out)*............... (33 to 1) 8
2663^{5} KASHAN (Ire) [63] 9-10-3 N Williamson, *al mid-div, mstk 8th.* ....(6 to 1 jt-fav op 9 to 2) 9
2770^{3} ROGER'S PAL [72] (bl) 10-10-12 D Gallagher, *al mid-div, lost tch 8th*............................(14 to 1 op 12 to 1) 10
2771^{4} KATBALLOU [61] 8-9-8 (7*) Mr O McPhail, *in tch till wknd appr 3 out*.................. (12 to 1 op 14 to 1 tchd 16 to 1) 11
2267 MURPHY'S RUN (Ire) [60] 7-9-9 (5*) D J Kavanagh, *beh frm 6th*...(33 to 1) 12
2515 JOBBER'S FIDDLE [60] (v) 5-10-0 M Clarke, *prmnt till wknd 7th*.......................................(20 to 1 op 14 to 1) 13
2562^{5} WHITEBONNET (Ire) [84] (bl) 7-11-5 (5*) Sophie Mitchell, *prmnt, wkng whn mstk 8th.* ....(11 to 1 op 10 to 1 tchd 12 to 1) 14
2403^{5} FORTUNES ROSE (Ire) [61] 5-10-1 T J Murphy, *led to 5th, wknd 8th*...........................(16 to 1 op 14 to 1) 15
2392 SCALP 'EM (Ire) [60] 9-10-0 Dr P Pritchard, *prmnt, led 5th to 6th, wknd nxt*.......................................(33 to 1) 16
2783 FANE PARK (Ire) [78] 9-10-11 (7*) X Aizpuru, *beh frm 7th.* ....(14 to 1 op 12 to 1 tchd 16 to 1) 17
2477^{4} RAAHIN (USA) [69] 12-10-9 M Richards, *al beh.* ....(14 to 1 op 12 to 1) 18
2392 TREHANE [70] (bl) 5-10-10 P Hide, *al beh, tld off.* ....(33 to 1 op 20 to 1) 19
1919 LEES PLEASE (Ire) [60] 5-10-0 J Culloty, *al beh, tld off.* ....(33 to 1) 20
2440^{9} JONJAS CHUDLEIGH [74] 10-11-0 J Frost, *mid-div to 8th, beh whn pld up bef last.* (11 to 1 op 10 to 1 tchd 12 to 1) pu
2477 KAYFAAT (USA) [82] (v) 9-11-8 A P McCoy, *pld up aftr second.* ....(11 to 1 op 8 to 1 tchd 12 to 1) pu
2766^{2} SCORPION BAY [61] 9-9-12 (3*) J Magee, *mid-div, wknd 6th, pld up aftr 8th*.........................(12 to 1 op 10 to 1) pu
2766 SEVEN CROWNS (USA) [69] (bl) 4-10-0^{3} (3*) T Dascombe, *prmnt to 7th, tld off whn pld up bef 3 out*.............. (33 to 1) pu

Dist: 1¼l, 5l, 2l, 6l, hd, 1¼l, 2l, 6l, 2l, ¾l. 5m 38.10s. a 23.10s (24 Ran).
(N R Mitchell), N R Mitchell

2978 Storacall Novices' Chase Class E (5-y-o and up) £3,114 2m........ (2:50)

2605^{4} QUICK QUOTE 7-10-10 L Harvey, *whipped round strt, remote 3rd whn lft in ld last*.........(9 to 2 op 4 to 1 tchd 5 to 1) 1
2725^{9} BLACK STATEMENT (Ire) 7-10-12 (3*) L Aspell, *al beh, tld off whn lft 3rd last, wnt second r-in*........(12 to 1 op 8 to 1) 2
2498 MHEANMETOO 6-11-1 P Holley, *led till hdd aftr 8th, wkng whn blun 2 out, lft poor second last.* (33 to 1 tchd 40 to 1) 3
1917^{7} QUEENS CURATE 10-10-10 D Leahy, *al beh, tld off.* ....(40 to 1 op 33 to 1 tchd 50 to 1) 4
MALWOOD CASTLE (Ire) 7-11-1 A Thornton, *f 1st.* ....(11 to 2 op 5 to 1 tchd 6 to 1) f
1478^{4} MARKSMAN SPARKS 7-11-1 S Burrough, *hld up, hdwy to second 5th, led aftr 8th, rdn and f last.* ....(5 to 1 op 9 to 2 tchd 11 to 2) f
2778^{3} ROBINS PRIDE (Ire) 7-10-12 (3*) T Dascombe, *al prmnt, wnt second 8th, und pres and one l dwn whn badly hmpd and uns rdr last*.......................(11 to 4 jt-fav op 9 to 4) ur
2714 MR BUREAUCRAT (NZ) 8-11-1 C Llewellyn, *hit 3rd, blun and uns rdr 6th*.........(11 to 4 jt-fav op 9 to 4 tchd 3 to 1) ur

Dist: 19l, ¾l, dist. 4m 10.50s. a 16.50s (8 Ran).
(M H D Barlow), Mrs I McKie

2979 Robert Walters Handicap Chase Class D (0-120 5-y-o and up) £3,933 3¼m 110yds................. (3:25)

2677^{9} MR INVADER [88] 10-10-4 C Llewellyn, *al prmnt, led 14th, clr 3 out, cmftbly, fnshd lme.* (11 to 2 op 9 to 2 tchd 6 to 1) 1
2728^{4} FAST THOUGHTS [99] 10-11-1 G Bradley, *ran in snatches, styd on to go second appr last, ran on.* ....(13 to 2 op 5 to 1 tchd 7 to 1) 2
1418^{4} VICOSA (Ire) [108] 8-11-10 A Thornton, *al prmnt, hit 15th, second and hld whn mstk 3 out, one pace.* ....(9 to 2 tchd 5 to 1 and 4 to 1) 3
2742^{3} CREDON [100] 9-11-2 M Richards, *al beh, lost tch 13th.* ....(11 to 2 op 9 to 2 tchd 6 to 1) 4
2549^{5} BANNTOWN BILL (Ire) [99] (v) 8-11-1 A P McCoy, *dsptd ld, led 13th, hdd nxt, wknd appr 4 out.* ....(5 to 2 fav op 2 to 1 tchd 11 to 4) 5
RIO HAINA [95] (v) 12-10-11 D Gallagher, *jmpd wl, made most till wknd 13th, tld off whn pld up bef 4 out.* ....(25 to 1 op 20 to 1 tchd 33 to 1) pu
2726^{6} CRUISE CONTROL [86] 11-10-2^{2} D O'Sullivan, *in tch till wknd 5 out, tld off whn pld up bef 2 out.* (14 to 1 op 20 to 1) pu
2549 CELTIC TOWN [104] 9-11-6 J A McCarthy, *struggling frm 9th, tld off whn pld up bef 17th*.......... (8 to 1 tchd 10 to 1) pu

Dist: 3l, 9l, 11l, 16l. 7m 27.00s. a 28.00s (8 Ran).
(M A Boddington), N A Gaselee

2980 Bonusprint Novices' Hurdle Class E (Div II) (4-y-o and up) £2,022 2½m .... (3:55)

2640^{2} LORD ROOBLE (Ire) 6-11-2 P Hide, *trkd ldr, led 4 out, rdn out r-in*.......... (5 to 4 on op 7 to 4 on tchd 6 to 5 on) 1
2636^{9} CHEEKY CHARLIE 5-10-13 (3*) P Henley, *hld up, hdwy 4 out, chsd wnr 2 out, kpt on r-in*............(50 to 1 op 33 to 1) 2
2263 LETMO WARRIOR (Ire) 5-11-2 C Maude, *hld up, styd on frm 3 out, nvr nr to chal*............... (33 to 1 tchd 40 to 1) 3
2678^{3} SUPER RAPIER (Ire) 5-11-2 N Williamson, *al prmnt, chsd wnr appr 3 out till hit nxt, sn btn*............ (4 to 1 tchd 9 to 2) 4
TAARISH (Ire) 4-10-7 N Mann, *in tch till wknd appr 2 out.* ....(7 to 2 op 3 to 1 tchd 4 to 1) 5
2802 RISKY TU 6-10-11 A P McCoy, *chsd ldrs, chlgd 3 out, wknd quickly bef nxt*................................(12 to 1 op 8 to 1) 6
641 BATH TIMES 5-10-11 A Thornton, *in tch till wknd 6th, tld off.* ....(33 to 1) 7
2637 KING'S AFFAIR 7-11-2 M Richards, *led till hdd 4 out, wknd quickly, pld up bef nxt*.........(33 to 1 tchd 40 to 1) pu
EXECUTIVE (Ire) 5-10-13 (3*) J Magee, *mstks 1st 2, pld up aftr 3rd*..........................(20 to 1 op 5 to 1 tchd 25 to 1) pu

Dist: 3l, 6l, 1½l, 15l, 3½l, dist. 5m 1.90s. a 21.90s (9 Ran).
(The Findon Partnership), J T Gifford

2981 Thames Valley Hunters' Chase Class H (5-y-o and up) £1,287 3m... (4:25)

2718 CAPO CASTANUM 8-11-7 (7*) Mr A Wintle, *al prmnt, lft second 13th, led aftr 4 out, ran on wl.* ....(9 to 2 op 4 to 1 tchd 5 to 1) 1
2544 JUPITER MOON 8-11-7 (7*) Mr J M Pritchard, *nvr far away, hdwy to chase wnr frm 2 out*..........(25 to 1 op 20 to 1) 2
2641 GAMBLING ROYAL 14-11-7 (7*) Dr P Pritchard, *chsd ldr, lft in ld 13th, hdd aftr 4 out, wknd nxt*....... (33 to 1 op 20 to 1) 3
BOLLINGER 11-11-7 (7*) Mr P O'Keeffe, *in rear, styd on frm 4 out, nvr nr to chal*....... (13 to 2 op 5 to 1 tchd 7 to 1) 4
2544^{3} SONOFAGIPSY 13-11-7 (7*) Mr R Nuttall, *in tch till wknd appr 4 out*..................................(5 to 1 op 3 to 1) 5
ANNIO CHILONE 11-11-9 (5*) Mr T McCarthy, *beh frm hfwy, tld off*..................(12 to 1 op 8 to 1 tchd 14 to 1) 6
FARINGO 12-11-11^{4} (7*) Mr W Gowlett, *al beh, sn tld off.* ....(25 to 1 op 20 to 1 tchd 33 to 1) 7
513^{8} EMERALD MOON 10-11-7 (7*) Mr D Maitland, *in tch till wknd 13th, tld off whn blun and uns rdr 3 out.* (33 to 1 op 25 to 1) ur
2680 PRINZAL 10-11-7 (7*) Mr M Emmanuel, *slwly away, blun and uns rdr 1st*...............(5 to 1 op 4 to 1 tchd 6 to 1) ur
QUIET CONFIDENCE (Ire) 7-11-2 (7*) Miss D Stafford, *led, clr tenth, hit 13th, uns rdr*..........(5 to 2 fav tchd 11 to 4) ur

GREAT SIMPLICITY (bl) 10-11-9 (5*) Mr A Sansome, *al in rear, pld up bef 9th* . . . . (50 to 1 op 33 to 1 tchd 66 to 1)   pu
Dist: 8l, 14l, ¾l, 12l, dist, dist. 6m 12.70s. a 19.70s (11 Ran).

(D C G Gyle-Thompson), Miss H C Knight

2982 March Conditional Jockeys' Handicap Hurdle Class F (0-105 4-y-o and up) £2,104 2m. . . . . (5:00)

2603	STORM TIGER (Ire) [75] (v) 6-10-7 Chris Webb, *hld up, hdwy 4th, led nxt, drvn out* . . . . (14 to 1 op 8 to 1)	1
2609³	FONTANAYS (Ire) [91] 9-11-9 D Fortt, *al prmnt, kpt on und pres frm 2 out* . . . . (7 to 2 op 3 to 1)	2
2768⁵	DERISBAY (Ire) [71] (bl) 9-10-0 (3*) M Batchelor, *chsd ldrs, rdn frm 5th, hit 2 out, kpt on one pace* . . . . . (20 to 1 op 12 to 1)	3
2253	BOYFRIEND [88] 7-11-6 L Aspell, *mid-div, rdn and hdwy appr 3 out, wknd aoproaching last* . . . . . . (12 to 1 tchd 14 to 1)	4
2783⁶	TISSISAT (USA) [92] 8-11-10 Sophie Mitchell, *mid-div, rdn frm 5th, one pace from 2 out.*	
	. . . . (6 to 1 op 8 to 1 tchd 5 to 1)	5
2693³	PEDALTOTHEMETAL (Ire) [88] 5-11-6 G Tormey, *rdn frm hfwy, kpt on one pace from 3 out.*	
	. . . . (10 to 1 op 7 to 1 tchd 11 to 1)	6
2479⁴	NIGHT IN A MILLION [80] 6-10-9 (3*) X Aizpuru, *al prmnt, rdn and wknd appr 2 out* . . (11 to 1 op 10 to 1 tchd 12 to 1)	7
2663	GENERAL SHIRLEY (Ire) [79] 6-10-8 (3*) M Clinton, *hld up, hdwy 5th, wknd appr 2 out.*	
	. . . . (16 to 1 op 12 to 1 tchd 20 to 1)	8
2400	PLAY GAMES (USA) [88] 9-11-6 D J Kavanagh, *mid-div, wknd appr 2 out* . . . . (20 to 1 op 14 to 1 tchd 25 to 1)	9
2350	THE BIZZO [68] 6-10-0 P Henley, *al towards rear.*	
	. . . . (66 to 1 op 33 to 1 tchd 100 to 1)	10
2765⁴	THEME ARENA [90] 4-11-0 D Walsh, *trkd ldr, led 4th, till jmpd slwly nxt, sn btn* . . . . (5 to 1 fav op 9 to 4)	11
848⁴	BATH KNIGHT [76] (bl) 4-10-0 J Magee, *in tch till wknd appr 3 out.* . . . . (16 to 1 op 12 to 1)	12
1729	ACHILL PRINCE (Ire) [68] 6-10-0 Guy Lewis, *al beh.* . . . . (33 to 1 tchd 40 to 1)	13
2428	BRAYDON FOREST [68] (bl) 5-10-0 C Rae, *mid-div till wknd appr 3 out* . . . . (33 to 1)	14
2610⁷	SLIGHTLY SPECIAL (Ire) [68] 5-10-0 S Ryan, *led to 4th, rdn and sn wknd* . . . . (20 to 1 op 14 to 1)	15
2768³	PRECIOUS WONDER [68] 8-10-0 A Bates, *al beh.* . . . . (20 to 1 op 14 to 1)	16
1251⁷	CHAPEL OF BARRAS (Ire) [78] 8-10-10 T Dascombe, *pld hrd, beh frm 3rd.* . . . . (33 to 1)	17

Dist: 1¼l, sht-hd, 7l, nk, nk, 7l, hd, 8l, 5l, 2½l. 3m 57.10s. a 12.10s (17 Ran).
SR: 6/20/-/10/14/10/   (W R Partnership), S Mellor

KELSO (good to soft (races 1,2,6,7), good (3,4,5)) Tuesday March 4th
Going Correction: PLUS 0.90 sec. per fur.

2983 Tweed Conditional Jockeys' Selling Handicap Hurdle Class G (0-90 4-y-o and up) £1,866 2m 110yds. . . . (2:00)

2241	CUILLIN CAPER [61] (bl) 5-10-4 E Callaghan, *made all, rdn alng 2 out, drvn out* . . . . . . (15 to 2 op 10 to 1 tchd 7 to 1)	1
2855³	ARTHUR BEE [62] 10-10-0 (5*) C McCormack, *al prmnt, chsd wnr 3 out, sn rdn, one pace last* . . . . (5 to 1 op 4 to 1)	2
2422⁴	BARTON HEIGHTS [81] 5-11-5 (5*) M Herrington, *in tch, pushed alng and outpcd bef 3 out, styd on appr last.*	
	. . . . (3 to 1 fav op 5 to 2 tchd 100 to 30)	3
2913⁵	OBVIOUS RISK [68] 6-9-10 (7*) Tristan Davidson, *chsd ldrs, rdn alng 3 out, sn one pace* . . . . (9 to 2 op 4 to 1)	4
2855⁴	STORMING LORNA (Ire) [62] 7-10-5 Michael Brennan, *hld up, gd hdwy 5th, effrt appr last, sn rdn and wknd.*	
	. . . . (9 to 2 op 4 to 1)	5
2577⁹	ANORAK (USA) [85] 7-11-9 (5*) T Hogg, *prmnt till outpcd 4th, sn beh.* . . . . (7 to 1 op 6 to 1)	6
2811	BLOOD BROTHER [57] (bl) 5-9-11 (3*) N Horrocks, *prmnt, rdn alng appr 3 out, sn wknd.* . . . . . . (25 to 1 op 12 to 1)	7
2855	BIRTHPLACE (Ire) [72] 7-11-1 D J Kavanagh, *sn rear, outpcd and beh frm 3rd, tld off whn pld up bef 2 out.*	
	. . . . (50 to 1 op 16 to 1)	pu

Dist: 3½l, 5l, ½l, 2½l, 24l, 1¾l. 4m 7.50s. a 24.50s (8 Ran).

(R T Watson), T R Watson

2984 Levy Board 'National Hunt' Maiden Hurdle Class F (5-y-o and up) £2,090 3m 3f. (2:30)

2491	ESTABLISH (Ire) 9-11-0 A Thornton, *dsptd ld till led 9th, rdn and hdd appr last, rallied und pres to lead last 100 yards.*	
	. . . . (50 to 1 op 33 to 1)	1
2712²	ASHGROVE DANCER (Ire) 7-11-5 R Supple, *not fluent, hld up, hdwy nxt, chlgd to lead last, ev ch till drvn flt, no extr last 100 yards.* (2 to 1 on op 7 to 4 on tchd 13 to 8 on)	2
2791⁷	RIVEAUX (Ire) 7-11-5 P Carberry, *hld up, steady hdwy 4 out, chlgd 2 out, led last, sn rdn, hdd and found nil last 100 yards.*	
	. . . . (5 to 1 op 11 to 4)	3

2862	DEAR JEAN 7-11-0 D Parker, *dsptd ld till hdd 9th and sn rdn alng, wknd and hmpd 3 out.*	
	. . . . (100 to 1 op 33 to 1 tchd 200 to 1)	4
1695⁶	HADAWAY LAD 5-11-5 A Dobbin, *prmnt, rdn alng 4 out, sn wknd.* . . . . (11 to 1 op 7 to 1 tchd 12 to 1)	5
2856	BUSY BOY 10-11-5 J Burke, *chsd ldrs, rdn appr 4 out, sn wknd.* . . . . (100 to 1 op 33 to 1)	6
2619⁶	ALLERBANK 6-11-5 Mr C Storey, *in tch till pushed alng and outpcd appr 4 out, rdn and staying on whn f 3 out.*	
	. . . . (10 to 1 op 8 to 1)	f
2822⁶	SOVEREIGN PASS 5-11-5 R Garritty, *blun 1st, pld up aftr 3rd, lme* . . . . (8 to 1 op 16 to 1 tchd 20 to 1)	pu
2489	GRAMPSAWINNA 9-11-0 G Cahill, *in tch till wknd 7th, beh whn pld up bef 9th, broke blood vessel.*	
2764	FARM TALK 5-11-5 B Storey, *al rear, tld off whn pld up aftr 8th.* . . . . (25 to 1 op 33 to 1 tchd 200 to 1)	pu

Dist: ½l, 2l, dist, 5l, dist. 6m 56.00s. a 42.00s (10 Ran).
(William Harvey), J P Dodds

2985 Teviot Novices' Chase Class D (5-y-o and up) £3,600 2m 1f. . . . . (3:00)

2683	REAL TONIC 7-11-1 P Carberry, *al prmnt, led 8th, very easily.* . . . . (11 to 10 fav op 11 to 10 on)	1
2857²	MOSS PAGEANT 7-11-1 B Storey, *led, blun 6th, hdd 8th, rdn alng nxt, no ch whn mstk.* . (9 to 1 op 7 to 1 tchd 10 to 1)	2
2201	CARDINAL SINNER (Ire) (bl) 8-11-1 K Jones, *sn beh, tld off frm 6th.* . . . . (66 to 1 op 33 to 1)	3
2848⁵	CHILDSWAY 9-10-12 (3*) Michael Brennan, *beh, hdwy 6th, rdn alng whn f 8th.* . . . . (66 to 1 op 33 to 1)	f
2631²	HE'S A DANCER 5-10-7 A Thornton, *prmnt, chsd ldr whn f 7th.* . . . . (5 to 4 tchd 6 to 5)	f
2848	NUWAY 7-10-10 (5*) S Taylor, *chsd ldrs, hit 3 out, blun and uns rdr nxt.* . . . . (33 to 1 op 14 to 1)	ur

Dist: 11l, dist. 4m 26.30s. a 21.30s (6 Ran).
SR: 27/16/-/   (Robert Ogden), G Richards

2986 Ettrick Handicap Chase Class C (0-130 5-y-o and up) £6,775 3½m . . . . (3:30)

2258²	CALL THE SHOTS (Ire) [100] 8-10-0 R Johnson, *cl up, led 4th to 7th, 2nd 2 out, styd on und pres r-in to ld nr finish.*	
	. . . . (10 to 1 op 8 to 1)	1
2713²	FIVELEIGH BUILDS [124] 10-11-10 A Thornton, *led to 4th, led 7th to 15th, cl up four out, lft in ld 2 out drvn r-in, hdd and no extr nr finish.* . . . . (9 to 2 op 9 to 4)	2
2715⁹	PARSONS BOY [125] 8-11-11 A Dobbin, *trkd ldrs, pushed alng 14th, hit 17th, rdn and one pace frm bef 3 out.*	
	. . . . (7 to 2 op 2 to 1)	3
2883	MASTER BOSTON (Ire) [128] 9-12-0 P Niven, *hld up in tch, hdwy and blun 12th, beh frm 14th* . . . (25 to 1 op 12 to 1)	4
2599⁹	COURT MELODY (Ire) [119] (bl) 11-11-5 A P McCoy, *cl up, led 15th, blun 4 out, rdn and hit nxt, blunded badly and uns rdr 2 out.* . . . . (11 to 8 fav op 7 to 4)	ur

Dist: Hd, 24l, dist. 7m 24.10s. a 38.10s (5 Ran).

(John Wade), J Wade

2987 Yarrow Handicap Chase Class E (0-110 5-y-o and up) £3,418 2¾m 110yds. (4:00)

2465⁵	DISCO DES MOTTES (Fr) [102] 6-12-0 P Carberry, *trkd ldr, led 6th, clr aftr 2 out, easily.* . . . . . (6 to 4 fav op Evens)	1
2578⁴	LAST REFUGE (Ire) [94] 8-11-6 N Smith, *made most to 6th, hit tenth, sn chsd wnr, no ch whn wnr.* . . . . (25 to 1 op 8 to 1)	2
1910⁵	BLAZING DAWN [88] 10-11-0 B Storey, *hld up, hdwy 10th, dsptd ld nxt till hit 13th, wknd 3 out* . . . (25 to 1 op 12 to 1)	3
2809²	JASON'S BOY [82] 7-10-8 R Johnson, *chsd ldrs, hit 9th, rdn alng to chase wnr 14th, second and wkng whn blun last.*	
	. . . . (9 to 4 op 5 to 2 tchd 2 to 1)	4
2495⁴	GRAND SCENERY (Ire) [85] 9-10-11 A Dobbin, *in tch till f 8th.* . . . . (9 to 2 op 7 to 2 tchd 5 to 1)	5

Dist: 3½l, 3l, dist. 5m 55.00s. a 31.00s (5 Ran).

(Robert Ogden), G Richards

2988 Glen Novices' Hurdle Class E (4-y-o and up) £2,320 2¾m 110yds. . (4:30)

2697⁵	LAGEN BRIDGE (Ire) 8-12-0 D J Moffatt, *made most frm second, clr aftr 2 out, kpt on.*	
	. . . . (7 to 2 on op 3 to 1 on tchd 5 to 2 on)	1
1198⁸	CASTLE RED (Ire) 6-11-2 K Jones, *hld up, hdwy to chase ldrs hfwy, rdn 2 out, styd on und pres frm last.*	
	. . . . (14 to 1 op 10 to 1)	2
2653	PERSIAN GRANGE (Ire) 7-11-2 J Burke, *cl up, rdn alng 3 out, wknd aftr nxt.* . . . . (100 to 1)	3
2419	DONNEGALE (Ire) 5-11-2 R Garritty, *chsd ldrs, rdn alng appr 2 out, sn one pace* . . . . . . (20 to 1 tchd 25 to 1)	4
2813³	CAUGHT AT LAST (Ire) 6-11-2 P Niven, *hld up, effrt and some hdwy appr 3 out, sn wknd and btn nxt.*	
	. . . . (5 to 1 tchd 4 to 1)	5
	ABSOLUTELY JOHN (Ire) 9-10-9 (7*) C McCormack, *chsd ldrs, rdn and wknd 4 out, tld off whn pld up bef last.* (50 to 1)	pu

2538 RYE RUM (Ire) 6-11-2 B Storey, *led to second, prmnt till lost pl and beh frm 5th, tld off whn pld up aftr 7th.*
....(150 to 1 op 100 to 1) pu
2653⁵ HOUSELOPE SPRING 5-10-11 (5") S Taylor, *prmnt to second, sn lost pl and beh, tld off whn pld up bef 7th.*
....(25 to 1 op 14 to 1) pu
Dist: 9l, 5l, 18l, 15l. 5m 46.10s. a 37.10s (8 Ran).
(Mrs Eileen M Milligan), D Moffatt

2989 Till Handicap Hurdle Class D (0-120 4-y-o and up) £2,763 3m 3f... (5:00)

2910² SMART APPROACH (Ire) [98] 7-11-4 P Niven, *trkd ldrs, hdwy 8th, led appr 3 out, sn clr, rdn out.* (5 to 4 fav tchd 11 to 8) 1
2422² SOLOMAN SPRINGS (USA) [80] 7-10-0 R Johnson, *chsd ldrs, pushed alng frm 5th, chased wnr appr 3 out, drvn last, styd on.*.............................(8 to 1 op 7 to 1) 2
1443⁷ MASTER OF THE ROCK [104] (v) 8-11-7 (3") E Husband, *dsptd ld to 9th, rdn alng 4 out, wknd nxt.* (5 to 1 op 9 to 2) 3
2801⁴ PHARARE (Ire) [97] 7-11-3 P Carberry, *dsptd ld till led 9th, rdn alng 4 out and sn hdd, wknd quickly aftr nxt, eased.*
....(7 to 4 op 6 to 4) 4
KIR (Ire) [82] 9-10-2 D Bentley, *tld off frm 5th, pld up aftr 8th.*
....(50 to 1 op 33 to 1) pu
Dist: 3½l, 22l, dist. 6m 46.00s. a 32.00s (5 Ran).
SR: 13/-/   (Mrs M B Thwaites), Mrs M Reveley

LEICESTER (good)
Tuesday March 4th
Going Correction: PLUS 0.40 sec. per fur.

2990 Squire Osbaldeston Maiden Hunters' Chase Class H (6-y-o and up) £2,087 2½m 110yds..... (2:20)

TEETON MILL 8-12-2 (5") Mr B Pollock, *hld up, hdwy 6th, led 9th, drvn out.*
.......(11 to 10 fav op Evens tchd 5 to 4 and 11 to 8) 1
CHERRY ISLAND (Ire) 9-12-2 (5") Mr J Jukes, *hld up, hdwy 8th, ev ch appr last, styd on same pace.*
....(10 to 1 op 6 to 1 tchd 11 to 1) 2
1127⁴ UP FOR RANSOME (Ire) 8-12-0 (7") Mr G Shenkin, *prmnt, rdn appr 2 out, ran on one pace.*.........(50 to 1 op 33 to 1) 3
ARCTIC CHILL (Ire) 7-12-0 (7") Miss S Vickery, *prmnt till wknd 4 out.*.........................(33 to 1 op 25 to 1) 4
COUNT BALIOS (Ire) 8-12-0 (7") Mr P Howse, *prmnt, mstk 7th, sn beh.*.........................(20 to 1 op 16 to 1) 5
DARK RHYTHAM 8-12-0 (7") Mr S Morris, *hdwy 6th, wknd 3 out.*.........................(20 to 1 op 16 to 1) 6
2769 DASHBOARD LIGHT 7-12-4 (3") Mr Simon Andrews, *chsd ldrs till wknd appr 3 out.*.........(66 to 1 op 50 to 1) 7
DIAMOND WIND (USA) 9-11-9 (7") Mr A Beedles, *in tch, chsd ldrs 5 out, wknd 3 out.*.........(16 to 1 op 10 to 1) 8
PAMELA'S LAD 11-12-0 (7") Mr G Hanmer, *al in rear.*
....(16 to 1 op 10 to 1) 9
POKEY GRANGE 9-12-0 (7") Major S J Robinson, *beh frm 9th.*.........................(40 to 1 op 25 to 1 tchd 50 to 1) 10
NOBLE ANGEL (Ire) 9-12-0 (7") Mr A Dalton, *pld hrd, led 4th to appr 6th, wkng whn I 9th.*
....(66 to 1 op 50 to 1 tchd 100 to 1) f
CRAFTSMAN 11-12-0 (7") Miss A Embiricos, *blun and uns rdr 3rd.*.........................(10 to 1 op 8 to 1) ur
JUDGEROGER 11-12-0 (7") Mr G Lewis, *beh frm 5th, pld up bef 3 out.*.........................(20 to 1 op 10 to 1) pu
COOLGREEN (Ire) 9-12-0 (7") Mr N Bradley, *led to 4th, beh appr 6th, hdd 9th, sn lost pl, beh whn pld up bef four out.*
....(66 to 1 tchd 100 to 1) pu
SAMSWORD 8-12-0 (7") Mr J I Pritchard, *al in rear, pld up bef 2 out.*.........................(40 to 1 op 25 to 1 tchd 50 to 1) pu
Dist: 3l, 3½l, dist, 3½l, 2l, 21l, ¾l, 5l, dist. 5m 19.40s. a 17.40s (15 Ran).
SR: 15/12/8/-/-/-/   (C R Saunders), Miss C Saunders

2991 Leicestershire And Derbyshire Yeomanry Handicap Chase Amateur Riders' Class F (0-105 5-y-o and up) £2,846 2½m 110yds......... (2:50)

2772⁴ EASTERN RIVER [87] 11-11-5 (5") Mr R Thornton, *chsd ldrs, hit 7th, led 6 out, all out.*.........(7 to 4 on op 6 to 4 on) 1
2861³ DOLIKOS [87] 10-11-5 (5") Mr R Ford, *beh, styd on appr last, not much room r-in, nvr nrr.*.........(25 to 1 op 20 to 1) 2
2482⁶ PRIZE MATCH [72] 8-10-2 (7") Mr O McPhail, *chsd ldrs till appr 4 out, wknd nxt.*.........................(14 to 1 op 10 to 1) 3
2739⁷ SALCOMBE HARBOUR (NZ) [63] 13-9-10³ (7") Dr P Pritchard, *made most to 6 out, wknd 3 out.*
....(9 to 1 op 33 to 1 tchd 66 to 1) 4
STRATTON FLYER [65] 7-9-9 (7") Mr R Widger, *in rear whn hmpd 3rd, nvr nr to chal.*
....(50 to 1 op 33 to 1 tchd 66 to 1) 5
1471 ENNISTYMON (Ire) [64] 6-9-10² (7") Mr G Weatherley, *al in rear.*.........................(25 to 1 op 16 to 1) 6
2606 PRUDENT PEGGY [69] (bl) 10-9-13 (7") Mr A Holdsworth, *prmnt to 7th.*.........................(11 to 2 op 6 to 1) 7
2739* OPAL'S TENSPOT [72] 10-10-2 (7") Miss V Roberts, *f 3rd.*
....(8 to 1 op 6 to 1) f

2677⁶ GLEN MIRAGE [82] 12-10-12 (7") Miss M Coombe, *al in rear, f 9th.*.........................(12 to 1 op 8 to 1) f
Dist: 5l, nd, 3l, 12l, 15l, 3½l. 5m 29.10s. a 27.10s (9 Ran).
(Gamston Equine), Capt T A Forster

2992 Melton Hunt Club Hunters' Chase Class H (6-y-o and up) £2,005 2½m 110yds..................... (3:20)

2769* TRIFAST LAD 12-11-12 (3") Mr P Hacking, *chsd ldrs, lost pl 3rd, took clr order 9th, led 2 out, mstk last, styd on wl.*
....(5 to 1 op 4 to 1 tchd 11 to 2 and 6 to 1) 1
MINELLA EXPRESS (Ire) 8-11-12 (7") Miss C Spearing, *led, jmpd lft, hdd 6 out, ev ch 2 out, styd on same pace r-in.*
....(15 to 8 fav op 5 to 2 tchd 11 to 4) 2
BUSMAN (Ire) 8-11-8 (7") Mr D S Jones, *prmnt, chsd ldr 6th, led six out, mstk 3 out, hdd and hit 2 out, styd on same pace.*
....(9 to 2 op 3 to 1 tchd 5 to 2) 3
KAMBALDA RAMBLER 13-11-3 (7") Mr R Armson, *rcd keenly, sn chasing ldrs, ev ch 2 out, wknd last.*
....(7 to 2 op 3 to 1) 4
YOUNG NIMROD 10-11-3 (7") Mr G Wragg, *hld up, effrt appr 3 out, sn wknd.*.........(12 to 1 op 5 to 1 tchd 19 to 1) 5
2680³ PRO BONO (Ire) 7-11-10 (5") Mr A Sansome, *chsd ldrs, mstk 8th, wknd 6 out, pld up bef 2 out.*
....(7 to 1 op 7 to 2 tchd 8 to 1) pu
Dist: 2l, 3½l, 5l, 21l. 5m 24.00s. a 22.00s (6 Ran).
(Mike Roberts), M J Roberts

2993 Arthur Clerke-Brown & Graham Pidgeon Memorial Hunters' Chase Class H (6-y-o and up) £3,590 3m .... (3:50)

2468⁷ HIGHLANDMAN 11-11-0 (7") Mr Chris Wilson, *al prmnt, led tenth to 6 out, lft in ld aftr 3 out, sn hdd, led r-in, drvn out.*
....(66 to 1 op 33 to 1) 1
2468⁸ PEAJADE 13-11-0 (7") Miss J Wormall, *led to tenth, led appr 2 out, hdd r-in, styd on und pres.*
....(25 to 1 op 20 to 1 tchd 33 to 1) 2
2790³ GLEN OAK 12-11-0 (7") Mr M FitzGerald, *al prmnt, reminder tenth, cl up whn hmpd 3 out, styd on same pace appr last.*
....(20 to 1 op 12 to 1) 3
CORNER BOY 10-11-0 (7") Mrs J Dawson, *hld up, hdwy 6th, led and jmpd rght 3 out, sn hdd, still ev ch whn blundd nxt, soon btn.*.........(4 to 4 fav op 2 to 1 tchd 9 to 4) 4
GREEN ARCHER 14-11-0 (7") Mrs T Hill, *al in rear.*
....(20 to 1 op 12 to 1) 5
2790² COUNTRY TARROGEN 8-11-2 (5") Mr N Wilson, *hld up, hdwy 7th, led 6 out, hdd whn brght dwn 3 out.*
....(9 to 4 op 7 to 4 tchd 5 to 2) bd
2641² AVOSTAR 13-11-0 (5") Mr B Pollock, *prmnt, lost pl 7th, beh whn pld up bef 3 out.*.......(9 to 4 op 2 to 1 tchd 5 to 2) pu
Dist: ½l, 2½l, 10l, 1¼l. 6m 16.90s. a 31.90s (7 Ran).
(Mrs Hugh Fraser), J S Haldane

2994 Garthorpe Maiden Hunters' Chase Class H (6-y-o and up) £2,152 3m .... (4:20)

COPPER THISTLE (Ire) 9-11-12 (7") Mr R Hunnisett, *al prmnt, lft in ld 12th, hdd 4 out, led ag'n nxt, ran on wl.*
....(13 to 2 op 3 to 1 tchd 7 to 1) 1
ELMORE 10-12-2 (3") Mr P Hacking, *led to 4th, led four out, hdd nxt, outpcd frm last.*.........................(9 to 4 jt-fav op 7 to 4 tchd 5 to 2) 2
MITCHELLS BEST 11-12-0 (5") Mr J Jukes, *prmnt, rdn appr 3 out, styd on same pace.*...........(6 to 1 op 8 to 1) 3
GARRYLUCAS 11-11-12 (7") Mr G Hanmer, *hld up, hrd rdn 3 out, nvr able to chal.*....(10 to 1 op 6 to 1 tchd 12 to 1) 4
PENLET 9-11-12 (7") Mr J I Pritchard, *hld up, mstk 6th, hdwy tenth, rdn and btn whn pckd 3 out.* ....(9 to 4 jt-fav op 2 to 1 tchd 11 to 4) 5
THE DIFFERENCE 10-11-12 (7") Mr M Chatterton, *al in rear.*
....(10 to 1 op 8 to 1) 6
SCALE DOWN (Ire) 8-12-0 (5") Mr A Sansome, *led 4th till f 12th.*.........................(20 to 1 op 14 to 1) f
MOON MONKEY (Ire) 9-11-12 (7") Mr O McPhail, *chsd ldrs, rdn 9th, wknd 11th, beh whn mstk and uns rdr 2 out.*
....(50 to 1 op 33 to 1) ur
OLLARDALE (Ire) 9-11-12 (7") Mr A Dalton, *prmnt, hit second, sn lost pl, pushed alng 8th, lost tch tenth, tld off whn pld up bef 5 out.*.........................(20 to 1 op 16 to 1) pu
Dist: 11l, 11l, 5l, 1¾l, 6l. 6m 21.00s. a 36.00s (9 Ran).
(R S Hunnisett), N J Pomfret

2995 Thrusters Hunters' Chase Class H (6-y-o and up) £2,057 2m 1f... (4:50)

A WINDY CITIZEN (Ire) 8-11-4 (5") Mr A Sansome, *hld up, mstk 5th, hdwy 5 out, led 2 out, rdn out.*.........(5 to 2 jt-fav tchd 3 to 1 and 100 to 30) 1
NOWHISKI 9-11-3 (7") Miss C Tarratt, *chsd ldrs, led appr 2 out, no extr r-in.*.....................(8 to 1 op 9 to 2) 2
CORLY SPECIAL 10-11-3 (7") Mr E James, *in rear, effrt 4 out, not rch ldrs.*.........(9 to 2 op 7 to 2 tchd 5 to 1) 3

2516* BEAU DANDY 10-12-1 (7*) Mr T Marks, chsd ldrs, rdn 3 out, one pace appr last. (5 to 2 jt-fav op 2 to 1 tchd 11 to 4) 4
TUMLIN OOT (Ire) 8-11-3 (7*) Mr Chris Wilson, hld up, hdwy 5 out, wkng whn hmpd 2 out.
.... (40 to 1 op 33 to 1 tchd 50 to 1) 5
QUARTER MARKER (Ire) 9-11-3 (7*) Mr J M Pritchard, in tch till wknd 3 out. ....(50 to 1 tchd 66 to 1) 6
HAPPY PADDY (bl) 14-11-3 (7*) Mr M Cowley, beh frm 5 out.
.... (50 to 1 op 33 to 1) 7
HOW FRIENDLY 7-11-3 (7*) Mr M FitzGerald, chsd ldrs till f 5 out. ....(20 to 1 op 14 to 1) f
JACK THE TD (Ire) 8-11-3 (7*) Mr J Cornwall, led, hdd whn unsighted and uns rdr 2 out. ....(14 to 1 tchd 20 to 1) ur
MICHELLES CRYSTAL 6-11-0² (7*) Mr L Brown, blun and uns rdr second. ....(100 to 1) ur
TBILISI 10-11-3 (7*) Mr R Munrowd, reluctant to race, al wl beh, pld up bef 4 out. ....(100 to 1) pu
MASTER CROZINA 9-11-3 (7*) Mr P Cornforth, mstk 3rd, al in rear, beh whn pld up bef 2 out. ....(25 to 1 op 16 to 1) pu
2960 CAPPAJUNE (Ire) 9-11-2 (3*) Mr M Rimell, in tch, mstk 4 out, sn beh, pld up bef last. ....(7 to 1 op 4 to 1 tchd 8 to 1) pu
Dist: 2l, 4l, nk, 11l, dist, dist. 4m 30.70s. a 22.70s (13 Ran).
(Mrs J A Thomson), Mrs C Hicks

BANGOR (good to soft)
Wednesday March 5th
Going Correction: PLUS 0.90 sec. per fur. (races 1,4,6), PLUS 2.40 (2,3,5)

2996 Chirk 'National Hunt' Novices' Hurdle Class E (4-y-o and up) £2,379 2m 1f............................ (2:10)

2546* DARAKSHAN (Ire) 5-11-8 J Culloty, hndy in chasing grp, chsd clr ldr 4 out, chlgd 2 out, ran on to ld cl hme.
............(11 to 8 on op 6 to 4 on tchd 5 to 4 on) 1
2264 ZANDER 5-11-2 C Llewellyn, midfield, hdwy frm 4 out, led appr 2 out to last, led briefly r-in, kpt on.
............(7 to 1 op 8 to 1 tchd 10 to 1) 2
2758³ MORPHEUS 8-11-2 R Johnson, hld up rear, hdwy 4 out, chlgd 2 out, led last, sn hdd, no extr cl hme.
............(15 to 8 op 13 to 8 tchd 2 to 1) 3
2560⁷ HILLS GAMBLE 7-11-2 W Worthington, not fluent, led and sn clr, wknd and hdd appr 2 out. ....(10 to 1 op 16 to 1) 4
FLUTTERBUD 5-10-11 J R Kavanagh, rear, effrt whn blun 4 out, not trble ldrs.............................(100 to 1) 5
1648⁹ GAF 5-11-2 Gary Lyons, midfield, niggled alng appr 4th, wknd 3 out, no ch whn blun last.................(100 to 1) 6
2822 PALAFICO 7-11-2 A Thornton, midfield, struggling hfwy, sn beh. ....(40 to 1 op 33 to 1) 7
2195 SAUCY DANCER 4-10-3 S McNeill, hld up, jmpd slwly 4th, sn lost pl, rdn and beh 3 out. ....(100 to 1) 8
2179 VITA NUOVA 6-10-11 R Bellamy, strted slwly, al beh, tld off. ....(66 to 1 op 40 to 1) 9
A BOY CALLED ROSIE 6-10-13 (3*) Michael Brennan, al beh, tld off whn f last. ....(66 to 1) f
GUNNY'S GIRL 6-10-11 R Farrant, hndy in chasing grp, chsd clr ldr 5th to nxt, sn wknd, tld off whn hmpd and uns rdr last.
2255 WORTH THE BILL 4-10-8 Derek Byrne, chsd clr ldr early, wknd appr 5th, tld off whn pld up bef 2 out.
............................(100 to 1 op 66 to 1) pu
ALTHREY MIST (Ire) 5-11-2 T J Murphy, in tch in chasing grp, mstk 5th, sn beh, tld off whn pld up bef 2 out.
............................(100 to 1 op 66 to 1) pu
MICKLEOVER 7-11-2 D Walsh, not fluent, in tch, tld off 5th, pld up bef 2 out. ....(100 to 1) pu
Dist: ½l, hd, 18l, 22l, 1½l, 10l, 16l, 25l. 4m 14.00s. a 24.00s (14 Ran).
SR: 7/-/-/-/-/-/ (Michael H Watt), Miss H C Knight

2997 Hugh Peel Challenge Trophy Hunters' Chase Class H (5-y-o and up) £1,474 3m 110yds........ (2:40)

HIGHWAY FIVE (Ire) 9-12-0 (7*) Miss E James, beh and niggled alng 5th, cl up 9th, led 4 out to nxt, pressed ldr, styd on to ld close hme......................(20 to 1 op 14 to 1) 1
TEATRADER 11-11-7 (7*) Miss T Blazey, led to 9th, remained prmnt, led ag'n 3 out, hrd pressed, slightly hmpd r-in by loose horse, hdd cl hme..................(7 to 1 tchd hme) 2
2897* CAPE COTTAGE 13-12-0 (7*) Mr R Lawther, hld up, niggled alng 9th, hmpd 4 out, ev ch frm 2 out, no extr r-in.
............(5 to 4 fav op 11 to 10 tchd 11 to 8) 3
ORTON HOUSE 10-11-7 (7*) Mr R Burton, prmnt, led 9th to 4 out, pushed alng and wknd appr 2 out. (14 to 1 op 8 to 1) 4
TRUE FORTUNE 7-11-9 (5*) Mr J Jukes, hndy till f 9th.
............(13 to 8 op 6 to 4 tchd 7 to 4) f
2608 CORN EXCHANGE 9-11-11 (3*) Mr M Rimell, cl up whn blun and uns rdr 4th. ....(33 to 1 op 25 to 1) ur
Dist: Sht-hd, 1l, 12l. 7m 0.10s. a 75.10s (6 Ran).
(Lady Susan Brooke), Lady Susan Brooke

2998 Croxton Novices' Chase Class D (5-y-o and up) £3,387 2m 1f 110yds

.... (3:10)

2778¹ INDIAN JOCKEY 5-11-5 A P McCoy, made all, clr frm 4 out, eased r-in......(9 to 4 on op 4 to 1 on tchd 2 to 1 on) 1
2626 THE SECRET GREY 6-11-1 D Walsh, hld up, mstk 6th, chsd clr ldr frm 4 out, no imprsn...............(20 to 1) 2
SANTARAY 11-11-1 Mr R Armson, hndy, und pres and btn frm 4 out..................(5 to 1 op 12 to 1 tchd 14 to 1) 3
507 ANOTHER COMEDY 7-11-1 R Johnson, cl up, drvn aftr 7th, wknd 4 out..............(17 to 2 op 7 to 1 tchd 10 to 1) 4
2747³ RELAXED LAD 11-11-8 Bellamy, hld up whn blun and uns rdr second.............(33 to 1 op 50 to 1) ur
JASONS FARM 7-10-12 (3*) Guy Lewis, cl up, wkng whn blun 4 out, tld off whn pld up bef 3 out.
............................(50 to 1 op 33 to 1 tchd 66 to 1) ur
2859 ALTHREY ARISTOCRAT (Ire) 7-11-1 S McNeill, al beh, tld off whn pld up bef 7th...............(66 to 1 op 33 to 1) pu
ALTHREY LORD (Ire) 7-11-1 T J Murphy, beh frm 3rd, tld off whn pld up bef 7th............(66 to 1 op 50 to 1) pu
Dist: 9l, hd, 28l. 4m 50.90s. a 48.90s (8 Ran).
SR: 22/9/9/-/-/ (Stuart M Mercer), M C Pipe

2999 Holywell Selling Hurdle Class G (4-y-o and up) £2,337 2m 1f......(3:40)

801⁵ KNIGHT IN SIDE 11-12-0 C Maude, led to second, led 5th, clr frm 3 out, styd on wl.....(10 to 1 op 7 to 1 tchd 12 to 1) 1
EDWARD SEYMOUR (USA) 10-11-1 (7*) Mr R Burton, midfield, hdwy 4th, chsd wnr appr 2 out, no imprsn.
............................(16 to 1 tchd 20 to 1) 2
1642⁸ A S JIM 6-11-2 V Slattery, midfield, hdwy und pres 4 out, nvr nrr.............................(20 to 1) 3
2432⁴ LAUGHING BUCCANEER 4-10-8 B Powell, hld up, niggled alng 4 out, kpt on, nvr dngrs..........(20 to 1 op 14 to 1) 4
2804 QUIXOTRY 6-11-2 W Marston, rear, late hdwy past btn horses.............................(50 to 1) 5
2886² HALHAM TARN (Ire) 7-11-1 (7*) A Dowling, led second to 5th, not fluent 3 out, sn wknd..........(13 to 2 op 6 to 1) 6
VERRO (Ire) 10-11-2 L Harvey, prmnt till wknd 5th. (50 to 1) 7
2372 KINGS VISION 5-11-2 T Jenks, al beh, no ch frm 4 out.
............................(50 to 1 op 33 to 1) 8
2575⁵ ANALOGICAL 4-10-3 D Walsh, chsd ldrs till wknd 4 out.
............................(20 to 1 op 16 to 1) 9
2253 RAMSDENS (Ire) 5-11-8 C Llewellyn, al rear div, nvr dngrs.
............(11 to 4 fav op 7 to 2 tchd 3 to 1) 10
1604² ELA MAN HOWA 6-11-2 D Gallagher, chsd ldrs to 5th, sn wl beh................(11 to 2 op 5 to 1 tchd 6 to 1) 11
BIT OF ROUGH (Ire) 7-11-2 R Johnson, in tch to 3rd, sn beh, tld off hfwy.....................(50 to 1 op 33 to 1) 12
2852⁵ KING RAT (Ire) (bl) 6-11-2 A P McCoy, midfield early, wl beh whn f 2 out....................(5 to 1 tchd 11 to 2) f
2292⁴ EL BARDADOR (Ire) (bl) 4-10-5 (3*) T Dascombe, in tch early, wl beh whn f 2 out..................(10 to 1 op 7 to 1) f
2676⁵ EMERALD VENTURE 10-11-7 (7*) C Rae, al rear, drvn 4th, wl beh whn hmpd and uns rdr 2 out. ....(33 to 1 op 20 to 1) ur
2625 BACKHANDER (Ire) 5-11-2 D Bridgwater, al beh, tld off whn pld up bef 2 out. ....(33 to 1 op 25 to 1) pu
1800* FIRST BEE 6-11-3 J Osborne, hld up rear, pld up bef second, dismounted, lme. ....(10 to 1 op 12 to 1) pu
Dist: 11l, 13l, ½l, 7l, 7l, 29l, 2¼l, 10l, 12l, 4l. 4m 13.50s. a 23.50s (17 Ran).
SR: 18/1/-/-/-/ (Joe & Joanne Richards), M C Pipe

3000 Cloy Novices' Handicap Chase Class E (0-105 5-y-o and up) £3,712 3m 110yds.................. (4:10)

2888* CARIBOO GOLD (USA) [105] (bl) 8-12-2 (6ex) J Osborne, hld up in tch, hdwy 11th, led on bit 2 out, rdn out frm last.
............(5 to 4 on op 11 to 8 on tchd 11 to 10 on) 1
2726⁴ CALLEVA STAR (Ire) [82] 6-10-7 A Thornton, hndy, led 8th, blun 12th, had 2 out, und pres and hld whn mstk last, one pace...........................(9 to 2 op 4 to 1) 2
2729⁶ RUBINS BOY [75] 11-10-0 R Farrant, prmnt, und pres and btn frm 3 out............................(33 to 1) 3
2748⁵ BURNTWOOD MELODY [75] (bl) 6-10-0 B Fenton, cl up, lost pl 15th, sn beh. ....(50 to 1) 4
2596⁶ CAPTIVA BAY [75] 8-10-0 J R Kavanagh, al beh, eased whn no ch frm 13th, tld off. ....(25 to 1 op 20 to 1) 5
2664⁵ ASTRAL INVASION (USA) [78] (bl) 6-10-0 (3*) R Massey, trkd ldrs, f 7th...........................(25 to 1 op 20 to 1) f
CANAVER [80] 11-10-5 R Bellamy, led to 8th, led 6th to nxt, mstk 9th, wknd 13th, tld off whn pld up bef 3 out.. (10 to 1) pu
2527⁷ BONNIFER (Ire) [75] 8-10-0 W Marston, cl up, led 4th to 6th, led 7th to nxt, wknd four out, tld off whn pld up bef 2 out.
............................(25 to 1) pu
2258 OCEAN LEADER [92] 10-11-3 J F Titley, hld up, hdwy to chase ldrs 13th, wknd quickly 3 out, tld off whn pld up bef nxt.
............(17 to 2 op 6 to 1 tchd 9 to 1) pu
2862⁸ NORDIC FLIGHT [75] 9-10-0 V Slattery, beh, reminders appr 5th, blun nxt, tld off 9th, pld up bef 12th. ...(50 to 1) pu
1608 OVER THE WREKIN [78] 10-10-3³ D Gallagher, al beh, tld off whn pld up bef 14th.............(66 to 1 op 33 to 1) pu
2912 PLASSY BOY (Ire) [75] (v) 8-10-0 J Culloty, cl up, wknd 4 out, tld off whn pld up bef 2 out....(16 to 1 op 14 to 1) pu
2391⁹ NAPOLEON'S GOLD (Ire) [80] 7-10-5² (7*) D Creech, al tld off, pld up bef 3 out............(100 to 1) pu

2679⁴ MILWAUKEE (Ire) [75] 8-10-0 M Brennan, *beh, struggling 9th, tld off whn pld up bef 14th.* .... (20 to 1) pu
Dist: 3l, 25l, 14l, 25l. 6m 51.20s. a 66.20s (14 Ran).

SR: 28/2/-/-/-/-/ (Mrs Sharon C Nelson), K C Bailey

3001 Sandy Lane Novices' Handicap Hurdle Class E (0-105 4-y-o and up) £2,442 2½m................(4:40)

2661* LOUGH TULLY (Ire) [87] 7-10-10 J Osborne, *made all, clr frm 3 out, not fluent last, easily.* ....(6 to 4 fav op 2 to 1) 1
2602⁶ SNOWSHILL SHAKER [80] 8-10-3 C Llewellyn, *midfield, hdwy 7th, chsd wnr appr 3 out, no imprsn.*
.... (12 to 1 op 8 to 1 tchd 14 to 1) 2
2281³ LUKE WARM [77] 7-9-9 (5*) Sophie Mitchell, *beh, gd hdwy 7th, drvn appr 3 out, sn one pace.*
.... (15 to 1 2 op 6 to 1 tchd 8 to 1) 3
2550⁴ LOTHIAN COMMANDER [83] 5-10-6⁵ D Walsh, *prmnt, rdn alng appr 6th, fdd 4 out.* .... (10 to 1 op 7 to 1) 4
2957⁸ OUT OF THE BLUE [77] 5-9-12¹ (3*) Michael Brennan, *beh, niggled alng 7th, nvr dngrs.* .... (50 to 1) 5
1922⁶ BALMORAL PRINCESS [86] (bl) 4-10-0 R Bellamy, *midfield early, struggling frm 6th, sn beh.* ....(25 to 1) 6
779³ ORDOG MOR (Ire) [103] 8-11-12 Derek Byrne, *beh, nvr plcd to chal.* ....(16 to 1 op 12 to 1) 7
2428⁹ KENNETT SQUARE (Ire) [77] 8-10-0 J A McCarthy, *trkd ldrs, beh whn pld up bef 2 out.* ....(33 to 1) pu
MONTEZUMAS REVENGE (Ire) [84] 9-10-7 W Marston, *cl up, losing pl whn mstk 4th, tld off whn pld up bef 6th.* (33 to 1) pu
2023⁸ ROOD MUSIC [79] 6-10-2 B Powell, *midfield early, wl beh 7th, tld off whn pld up bef 2 out.*
.... (14 to 1 op 10 to 1 tchd 16 to 1) pu
1220⁵ ALPINE MIST (Ire) [92] 5-10-11³ (7*) J T Nolan, *al beh, tld off whn pld up bef 2 out.* ....(25 to 1 op 14 to 1) pu
2878³ D'NAAN (Ire) [98] (bl) 4-10-12 A P McCoy, *hndy, reminders aftr 5th, wl beh 7th, tld off whn pld up bef 2 out.*
.... (7 to 1 op 6 to 1) pu
2550² VALLINGALE (Ire) [89] 6-10-12 J Culloty, *sn niggled alng and beh, tld off whn pld up bef 6th.* ....(9 to 2 op 3 to 1) pu
Dist: 10l, 3½l, 29l, 6l, 1½l, 20l, 22l. 5m 1.20s. a 31.20s (13 Ran).
(R A Hancocks), F Jordan

CATTERICK (good) Wednesday March 5th
Going Correction: PLUS 0.40 sec. per fur.

3002 Askew Design And Print Selling Hurdle Class G (4-y-o and up) £1,952 2m ....(1:55)

2577⁵ RADMORE BRANDY 4-9-12 (3*) G Lee, *chsd ldrs, pushed alng and outpcd 3 out, gd hdwy to chal nxt, sn led, rdn clr flt.*
.... (7 to 1 op 6 to 1) 1
2807⁶ NOIR ESPRIT 4-10-3 (3*) F Leahy, *trkd ldrs, gd hdwy to ld 5th, rdn 2 out and sn hdd, one pace last.*
.... (15 to 8 fav op 2 to 1 tchd 9 to 4 and 7 to 4) 2
1524⁸ FIASCO 4-10-0² (3*) E Callaghan, *prmnt till outpcd and beh 4th, styd on frm 2 out, nvr dngrs.* ....(14 to 1 op 12 to 1) 3
2811⁴ RASIN STANDARDS 7-11-0 A Dobbin, *mid-div, hdwy 3 out, rdn nxt and kpt on same pace.* .... (25 to 1 op 33 to 1) 4
2855⁹ KIERCHEM (Ire) 6-11-0 P Niven, *chsd ldrs, effrt 3 out, sn rdn and one pace.* .... (6 to 1 tchd 11 to 2) 5
I'M TYSON (NZ) 9-11-0 M Moloney, *prmnt, chsd ldr 3 out, rdn bef nxt and sn btn.* ......(7 to 1 op 12 to 1 tchd 14 to 1) 6
2622 EMERALD SEA (USA) 10-11-7 B Storey, *beh, steady hdwy appr 3 out, nvr rdn and wknd 2 out.*
.... (10 to 1 op 14 to 1 tchd 8 to 1) 7
LIXOS 6-11-2 (5*) R McGrath, *not fluent, pushed alng and beh 4th, tld off bef 3 out.* .... (3 to 1 op 5 to 2) 8
2357⁹ PRIMITIVE HEART (bl) 5-11-0 A Larnach, *trkd to 5th, sn wknd and tld off bef 2 out.* .... (100 to 1) 9
2847 THE GREY TEXAN 8-11-0 Mr M Thompson, *in tch till lost pl and beh frm hfwy.* ....(100 to 1) 10
MR TITCH 4-10-6 G Cahill, *f 1st.* .... (50 to 1) f
2817⁶ COEUR FRANCAIS (Fr) (bl) 5-10-7 (7*) S Haworth, *prmnt, mstk 4th and wkng whn blun and uns rdr nmext...* (200 to 1) ur
Dist: 7l, 18l, 2½l, 5l, 3l, dist, 19l, 1½l, 3½l. 3m 52.60s. a 12.60s (12 Ran).

SR: 11/9/-/-/-/-/ (J R Salter), G Richards

3003 Beauford Plc Novices' Hurdle Class E (4-y-o and up) £2,469 2m....(2:25)

2852* CUMBRIAN MAESTRO 4-10-13 R Garritty, *al prmnt, led 5th, rdn appr last, styd on strly.*
.... (9 to 4 on op 2 to 1 on tchd 15 to 8 on and 7 to 4 on) 1
1629 OVERSMAN 4-10-6 P Carberry, *chsd ldrs, hdwy 3 out, chlgd nxt, rdn appr last, one pace of wnr flt.* ....(7 to 1 op 5 to 1) 2
UNDAWATERSCUBADIVA 5-11-0 A Dobbin, *trkd ldrs, hdwy 5th, chsd wnr 3 out, rdn nxt and one pace.*
.... (10 to 1 op 7 to 1) 3
1955² LAST TRY (Ire) 6-11-11 (3*) E Callaghan, *hld up, hdwy appr 3 out, rdn and one pace bef nxt.* ......(6 to 1 op 9 to 2) 4
2651⁸ PENNY PEPPERMINT 5-10-9 D Parker, *prmnt till rdn and wknd bef 3 out.* .... (200 to 1) 5

2651⁵ MILENBERG JOYS 5-11-0 T Reed, *hld up and beh, hdwy appr 2 out, kpt on approaching last, not rch ldrs...* (33 to 1) 6
2791 PRAISE BE (Fr) 7-11-0 J Callaghan, *hld up, hdwy 3 out, sn rdn and no imprsn.* ....(33 to 1 op 25 to 1) 7
QUEEN'S COUNSEL (Ire) 4-10-1 B Storey, *mid-div, hdwy 4th, hit nxt, sn rdn and wknd 3 out, blun 2 out.*
.... (12 to 1 op 10 to 1) 8
ALLERBY 9-11-0 J Supple, *al rear...*(25 to 1 op 20 to 1) 9
2061⁸ RESPECTING 4-10-6 N Smith, *al beh, tld off 3 out.*(100 to 1) 10
TWABLADE (Ire) 9-10-9 M Foster, *al rear, tld off 2 out.*
.... (50 to 1) 11
2206 HUNTING SLANE (Ire) 4-10-6 P Niven, *cl up pulling hrd, led second to 5th, wknd 3 out, hng badly rght 2 out, tld off.*
.... (25 to 1) 12
2811⁸ ROMALDKIRK 5-11-0 Mr M Thompson, *pld hrd, led to 3rd, blun 5th, sn lost pl and tld off 2 out.* ....(500 to 1) 13
Dist: 9l, 3l, 7l, 5l, ½l, 16l, ½l, 8l, 7l, 23l. 3m 56.80s. a 16.80s (13 Ran).
(Cumbrian Industrials Ltd), T D Easterby

3004 Pytchley Echo Novices' Hunters' Chase Class H (5-y-o and up) £1,116 3m 1f 110yds....................(3:00)

SAYIN NOWT 9-11-2 (7*) Mr A Parker, *not fluent, hld up and beh, steady hdwy 14th, blun 3 out, chlgd nxt, rdn to ld aftr last, styd on strly.* ....(5 to 2 fav op 2 to 1) 1
GREENMOUNT LAD (Ire) 9-11-7 (7*) Mr P Cornforth, *al cl up, dsptd ld 13th, blun 4 out, led nxt, rdn 2 out, hdd and not quicken aftr last.* .... (20 to 1 op 16 to 1 tchd 25 to 1) 2
ADMISSION (Ire) 7-11-7 (7*) Miss L Horner, *slwly away, hdwy 6th, chsd ldrs whn blun 11th, rdn appr 3 out, kpt on same pace.*
.... (8 to 1) 3
EASTLANDS HI-LIGHT 8-11-7 (7*) Mr T Morrison, *chsd ldrs, rdn alng 4 out, sn one pace, blun 2 out.*
.... (12 to 1 tchd 14 to 1) 4
POLITICAL SAM 8-11-7 (7*) Mr N F Smith, *cl up, hit 9th, led 12th till rdn and hdd appr 3 out, grad wknd.*
.... (9 to 2 op 7 to 2 tchd 5 to 1) 5
2790 MOBILE MESSENGER (Ire) 9-11-7 (7*) Miss S Samworth, *prmnt till outpcd and beh frm hfwy.* ....(8 to 1) 6
BERVIE HOUSE (Ire) 9-11-9 (5*) Mr R Ford, *prmnt, rdn alng 12th, wknd frm 4 out.* ....(20 to 1 op 16 to 1) 7
BOULEVARD BAY (Ire) 6-11-9 (5*) Mr N Wilson, *trkd ldrs, mstk 3rd, cl up whn blun 5 out, ev ch whn blunded 2 out, sn wknd and virtually pld up flt.* ....(3 to 1 tchd 7 to 2) 8
GALZIG 9-11-7 (7*) Mr W Tellwright, *led to 12th, wknd bef 4 out, beh whn pld up before 2 out...* (12 to 1 tchd 14 to 1) pu
SIR HARRY RINUS 11-11-9 (5*) Mr R Hale, *chsd ldrs, blun tenth and sn lost pl, beh whn blunded 12th and pld up aftr.*
.... (33 to 1 op 25 to 1) pu
Dist: 3½l, 2l, 9l, 14l, 3l, 12l, dist. 6m 52.50s. a 37.50s (10 Ran).
(Dennis Waggott), K Anderson

3005 Robert Fleming Novices' Handicap Chase Class E (0-100 5-y-o and up) £3,102 3m 1f 110yds........(3:30)

2809⁴ KARENASTINO [65] 6-9-9 (7*) R Wilkinson, *chsd ldr, hit 4th, lft in second 13th, rdn appr last, styd on to ld r-in, ran on.*
.... (8 to 1 op 7 to 1) 1
2763 KINGS SERMON (Ire) [85] 8-11-8 R Supple, *hld up, mstks, outpcd and rdn alng 12th, hdwy and blun 4 out and nxt, ev ch last, drvn and no extr r-in finish.*
.... (3 to 1 op 9 to 4 tchd 100 to 30) 2
2909² TICO GOLD [84] 9-11-7 T Reed, *in tch, hit 6th, hdwy and blun 5 out, rdn nxt, one pace 2 out.* ......(9 to 2 op 7 to 1) 3
2855 TRIONA'S HOPE (Ire) [63] 8-9-9 (5*) S Taylor, *chsd ldrs, hit tenth, blun and outpcd 5 out, styd on und press frm 2 out.*
.... (200 to 1 op 100 to 1) 4
2683* BOLD ACCOUNT (Ire) [87] (bl) 7-11-10 A Dobbin, *al prmnt, lft in ld 13th, clr 2 out, rdn appr last, hdd and wknd quickly flt.*
.... (13 to 8 fav op 9 to 4 tchd 5 to 2) 5
2859⁵ KNOCKREIGH CROSS (Ire) [63] 8-10-0 B Storey, *led till f 13th...* ....(50 to 1 op 33 to 1) f
2146⁹ RATHFARDON (Ire) [72] 9-10-9 P Carberry, *not fluent, chsd ldrs till outpcd and rdn alng 7th, beh whn pld up aftr 11th, broke blood vessel.* ....(6 to 1 op 5 to 1) pu
2653⁸ ELLIOTT'S WISH (Ire) [81] 6-11-4 M Moloney, *hld up, some hdwy 12th, wl beh 14th, wknd 4 out, beh whn blun 3 out and pld up aftr.* ....(11 to 1 op 8 to 1 tchd 12 to 1) pu
Dist: Nk, 6l, 4l, nk. 6m 51.20s. a 36.20s (8 Ran).
(Miss J Wood), Mrs S J Smith

3006 Coniston Hall Restaurant Handicap Hurdle Class F (0-100 4-y-o and up) £2,110 2m 3f................(4:00)

2762⁹ MAJOR YAASI (USA) [82] (bl) 7-10-13 A Dobbin, *al prmnt, led 9th, clr 2 out, styd on wl.* ....(14 to 1 op 12 to 1) 1
2655³ FRYUP SATELLITE [83] 6-11-0 Miss P Robson, *al prmnt, chsd wnr 3 out and ev ch till rdn and one pace frm 2 out.*
.... (7 to 1 op 8 to 1) 2
2783⁵ MRS JAWLEYFORD (USA) [78] 9-10-9 M Ranger, *hld up, steady hdwy 4 out, chsd ldrs nxt, sn rdn and one pace frm 2 out.* .... (7 to 1 op 6 to 1) 3

2853* FIRST IN THE FIELD [74] 6-9-12 (7*,6ex) S Haworth, mid-div,
hdwy and blun 6th, styd on und pres frm 3 out.
....(9 to 1 op 8 to 1)   4
24874 AIDE MEMOIRE (Ire) [76] 8-10-7 K Johnson, hld up and beh,
hdwy 7th, rdn alng 3 out, lost pl 2 out, kpt on frm last.
....(9 to 1 op 10 to 1)   5
2420* YACHT CLUB [72] 15-9-13³ (7*) C Elliott, mid-div, rdn alng 4
out, styd on frm nxt, nvr rch ldrs........ (10 to 1 op 9 to 1)   6
2760² TIP IT IN [90] 8-11-0 (7*) N Horrocks, chsd ldrs till rdn alng 4
out and sn one pace..................................... (7 to 1)   7
9113 SHELTON ABBEY [69] (bl) 11-10-0 B Storey, in tch till rdn
alng and one pace 4 out..............(20 to 1 op 25 to 1)   8
1953* TIRMIZI (USA) [97] 6-12-0 J Supple, in tch till rdn alng and
lost pl 4th, styd on appr 2 out, nvr rch ldrs.
....(20 to 1 op 16 to 1)   9
2064⁴ HELENS BAY [78] 7-10-9³ Mr M Thompson, al rear.
....(25 to 1 tchd 20 to 1)   10
2885⁶ MOONSHINE DANCER [95] 7-11-9 (3*) P Midgley, cl up till
rdn appr 3 out and grad wknd........(16 to 1 tchd 20 to 1)   11
2761⁴ AUNTIE ALICE [79] 7-10-10 P Carberry, chsd ldrs, rdn 3 out
and sn wknd....................................(14 to 1 op 12 to 1)   12
2853⁵ ALAN'S PRIDE (Ire) [72] 6-10-3³ N Smith, made most to 6th,
prmnt till rdn 3 out and sn wknd....................(20 to 1)   13
2853³ DECENT PENNY (Ire) [69] 8-10-0 T Eley, in tch to hfwy, sn lost
pl and beh...(12 to 1 op 10 to 1)   14
2880³ COURT JOKER (Ire) [82] 5-10-8 (5*) R McGrath, hld up and
beh, effrt and some hdwy 4 out, wknd and pld up bre bef 2 out.
....(6 to 1 fav op 5 to 1)   pu
2682⁸ ALL CLEAR (Ire) [81] 6-10-12 D Parker, in tch to 5th, tld off whn
pld up bef 2 out....................................(25 to 1 op 20 to 1)   pu
Dist: 5l, 8l, nk, ½l, ¾l, 5l, ½l, ½l, 2l, 1½l. 4m 47.30s. a 27.30s (16 Ran).
(P And S Partnership), J A Glover

3007 Peter Vaux Memorial Trophy Novices' Chase Class D (5-y-o and up)
£3,557 2m 3f................(4:30)

2854² ROBERTY LEA 9-11-9 P Niven, in tch, rdn alng 5 out, hdwy to
chal 3 out, ridden last, styd on to ld last 50 yards.
................................(5 to 4 on op 11 to 8 on tchd 11 to 10 on)   1
2760⁴ TAPATCH (Ire) 9-11-2 P Carberry, trkd ldrs, hdwy 7th, led 3
out, drvn last, hdd and no extr last 50 yards.
................................(4 to 1 op 7 to 2 tchd 9 to 2)   2
MONKEY WENCH (Ire) 6-10-11 B Storey, hld up in tch, hdwy
7th, ev ch 3 out, sn rdn and wknd appr last.
....(6 to 1 op 5 to 1)   3
2637⁸ HIGH MOOD 7-11-2 K Johnson, pld hrd, cl up, led 7th, hit nxt,
hdd aftr 4 out, wknd bef 2 out........(33 to 1 op 25 to 1)   4
2812⁶ MOST RICH (Ire) (v) 9-11-2 T Reed, cl up, led 3rd to 7th, wknd
3 out..............................(9 to 1 op 8 to 1 tchd 10 to 1)   5
2812⁸ DISTILLERY HILL (Ire) 9-11-2 Mr M Thompson, led to 3rd, rdn
alng 7th, sn beh, tld off 5 out............(33 to 1 op 25 to 1)   6
1962 FORT ZEDDAAN (Ire) 7-10-9 (7*) R Wilkinson, in tch till f 6th.
....(16 to 1 tchd 20 to 1)   f
OAKLANDS BILLY 8-11-2 N Smith, cl up, hit 3rd, wkng whn
pld up 4 out, tld off 4 out, pld up bef last.. (20 to 1 op 14 to 1)   pu
Dist: ¾l, 13l, 6l, 5l, dist. 4m 57.70s. a 27.70s (8 Ran).
(Wentdale Const Ltd), Mrs M Reveley

3008 Lane, Clark & Peacock Intermediate
Open National Hunt Flat Class H
(4,5,6-y-o) £1,175 2m........(5:00)

2623⁵ EASBY BLUE 5-11-2 P Niven, hld up, smooth hdwy o'r 4 fs
out, chal over 2 furlongs out, sn led, rdn clr fnl furlong.
................................(Evens fav tchd 11 to 10)   1
GOING PRIMITIVE 6-11-2 A Dobbin, trkd ldrs, hdwy 6 fs out,
led o'r 2 furlongs out, sn rdn, edgd lft and hdd, kpt on.
................................(15 to 2 op 6 to 1 tchd 8 to 1)   2
2496⁴ EASTCLIFFE (Ire) 5-11-2 N Smith, led, pushed alng 4 fs out,
hdd o'r 2 furlongs out and kpt on same pace.
................................(9 to 2 op 4 to 1 tchd 4 to 1)   3
KERIALI (USA) 4-10-8 R Garritty, hld up, hdwy hfwy, rdn alng
6 fs out, one pace fnl 4 furlongs.
................................(7 to 1 op 5 to 1 tchd 8 to 1)   4
ROYAL CHIP 5-10-9 (7*) N Horrocks, chsd ldr, rdn alng 5 fs
out and sn wknd........(12 to 1 op 6 to 1 tchd 14 to 1)   5
STANWICK HALL 5-11-2 J Supple, chsd ldrs till rdn alng 6 fs
out and sn wknd....................................(20 to 1 op 14 to 1)   6
OH BROTHER 4-10-8 J Callaghan, chsd ldrs, rdn o'r 5 fs out,
sn wknd..(16 to 1 op 14 to 1)   7
BOSTON BOMBER 6-11-2 P Carberry, chsd ldrs, rdn o'r 5 fs
out, sn wknd....................................(8 to 1 op 6 to 1)   8
WHINHOLME LASS (Ire) 5-10-11 W Dwan, in tch till outpcd
and beh hfwy, sn tld off......................................(33 to 1)   9
Dist: 7l, 10l, 11l, 18l, ½l, dist, dist. 3m 54.70s. (9 Ran).
(G R Orchard), S E Kettlewell

CARLISLE (soft)
Thursday March 6th
Going Correction: PLUS 1.00 sec. per fur. (races
1,3,5,7), PLUS 1.05 (2,4,6)

3009 Border Esk 'National Hunt' Novices'
Handicap Hurdle Class E (0-100 4-y-

o and up) £2,416 3m 110yds.. (2:00)

2892 ANSURO AGAIN [81] 8-11-2 P Niven, hld up, hdwy to chase
ldrs 9th, hng rght aftr 2 out, styd on wl und pres to ld fnl 50
yards...............................(11 to 1 op 8 to 1 tchd 14 to 1)   1
2762⁸ MRS ROBINSON (Ire) [76] 6-10-8 (3*) E Husband, chsd ldrs,
led last, hdd fnl 50 yards, no extr und pres.
................................(6 to 1 op 5 to 1 tchd 13 to 2)   2
2882⁶ PHARRAMBLING (Ire) [78] 6-10-10 (3*) G Lee, hld up, hdwy to
track ldrs 9th, swtchd lft aftr 2 out, styd on und pres towards
finish.............................(14 to 1 op 16 to 1 tchd 25 to 1)   3
2853⁹ DIDDY RYMER [75] 7-10-10 Richard Guest, prmnt, led 8th,
hdd last, sn beh....................................(11 to 1 op 7 to 1)   4
2403* PARADE RACER [78] 6-10-13 W McFarland, in tch gng wl,
effrt aftr 3 out, sn rdn, kpt on same pace.
................................(2 to 1 fav op 5 to 2 tchd 7 to 1)   5
2492 SANDRIFT [80] 8-11-1 D Parker, in tch, hdwy aftr 7th, outpcd
after 9th, no dngr after........................(14 to 1 op 8 to 1)   6
1955 JONAEM (Ire) [77] 7-10-12 K Johnson, beh, hdwy bef 7th,
wknd before 3 out................................(20 to 1 op 10 to 1)   7
2578 STRONG CHARACTER [70] 11-10-5⁵ J Burke, chsd ldr to 4th,
towards rear whn blun 7th, sn lost tch.
....(100 to 1 op 66 to 1)   8
2578⁵ BLACK ICE (Ire) [67] 6-10-2 J Callaghan, chsd ldrs till wknd
aftr 8th......................................(6 to 1 tchd 5 to 1)   9
2241⁵ DASHMAR [68] (v) 10-10-3 D Bentley, lost tch frm hfwy.
................................(8 to 1 op 7 to 1 tchd 9 to 1)   10
2710 SKI PATH [65] 8-10-0 M Foster, prmnt, led 6th till hdd 8th,
wknd aftr nxt, wl beh whn pld up bef 2 out.
....(100 to 1 op 33 to 1)   pu
1631 WILLIE WANNABE (Ire) [65] 7-10-0 B Storey, led till hdd 6th,
wknd quickly aftr 8th, tld off whn pld up bef 3 out.
................................(16 to 1 op 33 to 1 tchd 40 to 1 and 14 to 1)   pu
Dist: Nk, ½l, 7l, 3½l, 16l, 12l, 19l, ½l, 7l. 6m 21.90s. a 30.90s (12 Ran).
SR: 24/19/20/10/9/-/   (Frickley Holdings Ltd), Mrs M Reveley

3010 Derwent Handicap Chase Class F
(0-100 5-y-o and up) £2,696 2m
........................(2:30)

2864² CHILL WIND [87] 8-11-2 M Foster, dsptd ld frm 5th, led 4 out,
hrd pressed from nxt, styd on wl und pres.
................................(5 to 2 op 2 to 1 tchd 11 to 4)   1
2919⁵ PARIAH (Ire) [91] 8-11-6 P Carberry, hld up, hdwy on bit to
chal aftr 3 out, jmpd lft last, sn drvn alng, ev ch till no extr clsg
stages.............................(2 to 1 fav tchd 9 to 4)   2
2846⁵ GROUSE-N-HEATHER [94] 8-11-9 A Dobbin, in tch, rdn and
outpcd aftr 4 out, no dngr after.
................................(6 to 1 op 7 to 1 tchd 5 to 1)   3
2622⁷ SUPER SANDY [72] 10-10-1 K Johnson, made most till hdd 4
out, wknd aftr 2 out................(6 to 1 op 11 to 2)   4
2857 REBEL KING [84] 7-10-8 (5*) S Taylor, in tch, rdn aftr 8th, sn
wknd....................................(10 to 1 op 8 to 1)   5
2654³ QUIXALL CROSSETT [71] (bl) 12-10-0 M Moloney, dsptd ld to
4th, wknd aftr 8th..................................(50 to 1)   6
2654³ BLAZING TRAIL (Ire) [99] 9-12-0 T Reed, tld off whn pld up bef
4 out.............................(7 to 1 op 13 to 2 tchd 8 to 1)   pu
Dist: Nk, 14l, 1¾l, 20l, 3½l. 4m 17.70s. a 23.70s (7 Ran).
SR: 19/23/12/-/   (E H Daley), N Bycroft

3011 Golden Pheasant, Youngers Novices' Hurdle Class E (4-y-o and up)
£2,584 2½m 110yds.........(3:00)

2775² ARDRINA 6-10-11 A Dobbin, prmnt chasing grp, led aftr 3
out, styd on strly...............................(4 to 1 op 3 to 1)   1
2913* INTO THE WEST (Ire) 8-11-8 Richard Guest, prmnt chasing
grp, chlgd 3 out, sn chasing wnr, no imprsn.
................................(2 to 1 fav tchd 9 to 4 and 7 to 4)   2
2852⁶ NASAYER (Ire) 7-10-9 (7*) S Haworth, in tch, pushed alng
hfwy, styd on wl frm 2 out, nvr able to chal.
....(33 to 1 op 25 to 1)   3
2849⁵ MIKE STAN (Ire) 6-11-2 R Supple, hld up, hdwy to chase ldrs
8th, 4th and btn whn blun last........(14 to 1 tchd 16 to 1)   4
2849⁴ BOLD STATEMENT 5-11-2 N Bentley, hld up, took clr order
5th, led gng wl aftr 8th, hdd after 3 out, fdd.
................................(12 to 1 op 7 to 1)   5
2623² PRIME EXAMPLE (Ire) 6-11-2 P Carberry, in tch till wknd bef 3
out....................................(6 to 1 op 5 to 1)   6
2857 NOSMO KING (Ire) 6-11-2 Mrs M Kendall, nvr better than
mid-div......................................(100 to 1 op 66 to 1)   7
2346⁵ THE KHOINOA (Ire) 7-11-2 J Supple, hit 4th, in tch till wknd
aftr 8th........................(14 to 1 op 7 to 1 tchd 20 to 1)   8
2858³ JENNIE'S PROSPECT 6-10-11 (5*) R McGrath, beh frm 8th.
....(33 to 1, op 16 to 1)   9
PEAK A BOO 6-10-11 D Bentley, chsd ldrs till wknd aftr 8th.
....(100 to 1 op 33 to 1)   10
2822⁸ SIR BOB (Ire) 5-11-2 G Cahill, prmnt early, beh frm 5th.
................................(9 to 2 op 5 to 1 tchd 4 to 1)   11
2499³ JAYFCEE 5-11-2 T Reed, led and sn clr, hdd aftr 8th, wknd
quickly.........................(16 to 1 op 10 to 1)   12
2619 BORDER IMAGE 6-10-13 (3*) E Callaghan, beh frm 8th.
....(200 to 1 op 50 to 1)   13
2489 MONTEIN 6-11-2 N Leach, lost tch frm hfwy, tld off.
................................(500 to 1 op 100 to 1)   14
2570 THROMEDOWNSOMETING 7-10-11 B Storey, lost tch and
pld up bef 8th..................................(100 to 1 op 33 to 1)   pu

415

Dist: 11l, 6l, ½l, sht-hd, 20l, 7l, 1¾l, 1l, 9l, 9l. 5m 19.40s. a 37.40s (15 Ran).
(L G M Racing), F Murphy

3012 Edinburgh Woollen Mill Novices' Chase Class C (5-y-o and up) £4,442 2½m 110yds............... (3:30)

2808²	KENMORE-SPEED 10-11-3 Richard Guest, *made all, styd on wl frm 4 out*...................(7 to 4 op 2 to 1)	1
2043²	SOLOMON'S DANCER (USA) 7-11-13 A Dobbin, *hld up in tch, chsd wnr frm 12th, rdn aftr 4 out, no imprsn*..............(7 to 4 on op 5 to 2 on)	2
2985	NIJWAY 7-10-12 (5*) Taylor, *in tch, hit 4th and 9th, drvn alng whn blun 12th, sn lost touch*................(33 to 1 op 25 to 1 tchd 50 to 1)	3
2812⁴	MASTER OF TROY (bl) 9-11-3 D Parker, *in tch, wkng whn blun 3 out*.................(20 to 1 op 14 to 1)	4

Dist: 13l, 12l, 5l. 5m 29.80s. a 34.80s (4 Ran).
(K M Dacker), Mrs S J Smith

3013 Waver Conditional Jockeys' Handicap Hurdle Class E (0-110 4-y-o and up) £2,374 2m 1f........... (4:00)

2919³	IFALLELSEFAILS [90] 9-10-6 (8*) I Jardine, *dwlt, sn chasing ldrs, led bef 2 out, styd on wl.*.............(8 to 1 op 6 to 1 tchd 9 to 1)	1
2913²	ENCHANTED COTTAGE [78] 5-10-0¹ (3*) E Callaghan, *hld up, hdwy aftr 3 out, rdn to chase wnr last, kpt on wl, no imprsn.*.................(9 to 4 fav op 5 to 2)	2
2712⁷	PAPPA CHARLIE (USA) [82] 6-10-6 G Lee, *prmnt, led aftr 6th, hdd bef 2 out, kpt on same pace.*...............(9 to 1 op 7 to 1 tchd 10 to 1)	3
2574⁹	KIRSTENBOSCH [80] 10-9-10 (8*) W Dowling, *hld up and beh, styd on wl frm 3 out, nvr nr to chal.* (33 to 1 op 12 to 1)	4
2815⁴	GLENUGIE [92] 6-10-6 (10*) N Hannity, *chsd ldrs, rdn aftr 5th, kpt on same pace frm 3 out.*...........(16 to 1 op 12 to 1)	5
2581⁹	APOLLO'S DAUGHTER [76] 9-10-0 B Grattan, *hld up, effrt aftr 6th, styd on frm 3 out, nvr dngrs..* (50 to 1 op 20 to 1)	6
1986⁵	HIGHLAND WAY (Ire) [90] 9-10-6 (8*) C McCormack, *hld up, smooth hdwy aftr 6th, ev ch 2 out, sn wknd.*...........(20 to 1)	7
2880⁴	OUR ROBERT [92] 5-10-13 (3*) F Leahy, *towards rear, some hdwy bef 3 out, sn btn.*.................(7 to 1 op 6 to 1)	8
2849²	SUPREME SOVIET [94] 7-11-4 S Taylor, *nvr better than mid-div.*..................(7 to 1 op 6 to 1)	9
2635²	ETERNAL CITY [88] 6-10-4 (8*) R Burns, *chsd ldrs, rdn bef 3 out, sn wknd, tld off.*.............(10 to 1 op 8 to 1)	10
2880⁹	FOX SPARROW [100] 7-11-7 (3*) E Husband, *in tch till wknd bef 3 out, tld off.*.................(25 to 1 op 20 to 1)	11
2880	MERRY MERMAID [96] 7-11-6 S Melrose, *led till hdd aftr 6th, sn wknd, tld off.*...............(8 to 1 op 6 to 1)	12
2345⁹	SEE YOU ALWAYS (Ire) [76] 7-9-7³ (10*) I Pike, *lost tch frm 5th, tld off..*..............(100 to 1 op 33 to 1)	13

Dist: 2l, 5l, 3½l, 1l, 2l, ½l, nk, 5l, 28l, 5l. 4m 32.20s. a 29.20s (13 Ran).
(Mrs Barbara Lungo), L Lungo

3014 Eden Handicap Chase Class D (0-120 5-y-o and up) £3,623 3¼m .... (4:30)

2851²	NORTHERN SQUIRE [105] 9-10-12 (3*) E Callaghan, *in tch, mstk 13th, rdn to ld betw last 2, styd on wl.*..................(7 to 4 fav tchd 2 to 1)	1
2916²	CEILIDH BOY [117] (v) 11-11-13 Mr R Hale, *led or dsptd ld, mstk 5th, pckd 4 out, hdd betw last 2, styd on und pres.*.................(7 to 2 tchd 4 to 1)	2
2536	ACAJOU III (Fr) [110] 9-11-6 P Carberry, *keen, hld up in tch, hdwy to dispute ld 14th, rdn aftr 3 out, wknd quickly, tld off.*.................(9 to 1 op 4 to 1)	3
2148⁴	UBU VAL (Fr) [118] 11-12-0 B Storey, *with ldr till hit 12th, rdn aftr 4 out, sn lost tch, tld off.* (9 to 2 op 4 to 1 tchd 5 to 1)	4

Dist: 1¾l, 26l, 17l. 7m 13.00s. a 45.00s (4 Ran).
(Mrs M E Dixon), J M Jefferson

3015 Liddel Water Intermediate Open National Hunt Flat Class H (4,5,6-y-o) £1,213 2m 1f..........(5:00)

2824⁷	LINWOOD 6-10-13 A Dobbin, *settled midfield, hdwy on bit 5 fs out, led o'r 2 out, ran on wl.....* (11 to 10 fav op 6 to 4)	1
2496*	TOM'S RIVER 5-11-8 (3*) G Lee, *mid-div, hdwy 5 fs out, ch o'r 2 out, sn chasing wnr, no imprsn.* (2 to 1 op 5 to 4)	2
2810⁵	SIDE BY SIDE (Ire) 4-9-12 (7*) N Horrocks, *chsd ldr, led 4 fs out, hdd o'r 2 out, sn btn.* (11 to 4 op 6 to 4)	3
2858⁶	COOL KEVIN 4-10-10 Mrs M Kendall, *chsd ldrs, outpcd 4 fs out, no dngr aftr.*.................(25 to 1 tchd 33 to 1)	4
2206	SNOOTY ESKIMO (Ire) 5-11-1 (3*) E Callaghan, *hld up, gd hdwy 4 fs out, swrvd rght o'r 2 out, sn wknd.*..........(25 to 1 op 16 to 1)	5
	SMILE PLEEZE (Ire) 5-11-4 M Foster, *nvr dngrs*.................(16 to 1 tchd 20 to 1)	6
2623⁷	JUST NED 6-11-4 B Storey, *nvr dngrs*.................(12 to 1 op 10 to 1 tchd 14 to 1)	7
2496⁹	JUMBO'S DREAM 6-11-4 F Perratt, *led till hdd 4 fs out, sn wknd.*..........(66 to 1 op 50 to 1)	8
2496⁷	SUPEREXALT 5-11-4 W Dwan, *mid-div, hng lft bend aftr 5 fs, wknd 4 out, tld off.*.................(10 to 1 op 11 to 2)	9

2302	WOODHOUSE LANE 5-10-11 (7*) Miss C Metcalfe, *al beh, tld off.*..................(100 to 1 op 50 to 1)	10
2858⁹	CHAN MOVE (bl) 5-10-13 (5*) S Taylor, *chsd ldrs till wknd o'r 4 fs out, wl tld off.....*(100 to 1 op 50 to 1 tchd 200 to 1)	11
2262	GYMCRAK-GYPSY 5-10-13 R Garritty, *beh most of way, lost tch fnl 5 fs, virtually pld up final furlong, wl tld off.*.................(9 to 1 op 10 to 1 tchd 12 to 1)	12

Dist: 9l, 3l, 17l, 2l, 2l, 6l, 1¼l, 24l, 13l, 48l. 4m 28.30s. (12 Ran).
(Emral Lakes Partnership), G Richards

TOWCESTER (soft (races 1,4,6), good to soft (2,3,5))
Thursday March 6th
Going Correction: PLUS 1.30 sec. per fur. (races 1,4,6), PLUS 1.00 (2,3,5)

3016 Banque Arjil Espana Conditional Jockeys' Novices' Handicap Hurdle Class E (0-100 4-y-o and up) £2,547 3m........................... (2:20)

2746⁴	WINTER ROSE [72] 6-10-5 (7*) K Hibbert, *hld up, gd hdwy aftr 6th, led 2 out, rdn out...*(10 to 1 op 14 to 1 tchd 20 to 1)	1
2566⁵	ARDENT LOVE (Ire) [68] 8-10-7 R Massey, *hld up, rdn and hdwy appr 2 out, ev ch last, no imprsn r-in..*.................(11 to 4 fav tchd 9 to 4 and 3 to 1)	2
2762²	HANCOCK [76] 5-10-12 (3*) J Power, *hld up, hdwy hfwy, led appr 3 out, hdd nxt, one pace aftr.......*(6 to 1 op 9 to 1)	3
2640	KAREN'S TYPHOON (Ire) [72] 6-10-6 (5*) M Batchelor, *al prmnt, led 4 out, hdd appr nxt, hit and one pace aftr..*...........(16 to 1 op 20 to 1 tchd 25 to 1)	4
2392	ROSS DANGER (Ire) [85] 5-11-10 J Magee, *led till hdd aftr 6th, wknd 3 out....*(25 to 1 op 16 to 1 tchd 33 to 1)	5
2792⁷	ROSEHALL [82] 6-11-4 (3*) L Suthern, *al in rear.*.................(9 to 1 op 5 to 1 tchd 10 to 1)	6
2872	KILLING TIME [76] 6-10-10 (5*) J Prior, *beh aftr hmpd 6th, tld off.*...............(14 to 1 op 10 to 1 tchd 16 to 1)	7
2749²	CARDINAL GAYLE (Ire) [75] 7-11-0 D Walsh, *in tch, rdn and wknd, wknd quickly appr 2 out, eased, tld off.*.................(14 to 1 tchd 16 to 1)	8
2403⁶	LOVELARK [61] 8-9-11 (3*) X Aizpuru, *beh frm hfwy, pld up bef 2 out.*.................(16 to 1 tchd 20 to 1)	pu
2177	EVEZIO RUFO [84] (v) 5-11-9 D J Kavanagh, *in tch to 7th, beh whn pld up bef 2 out....*(16 to 1 op 8 to 1 tchd 20 to 1)	pu
2750³	OTTER PRINCE [61] (bl) 8-9-7 (7*) C Hynes, *prmnt, led aftr 6th, mstk nxt, hdd 4 out, wknd and beh whn pld up bef 2 out.*.................(33 to 1 op 20 to 1)	pu
2749⁴	ONE MORE DIME (Ire) [70] 7-10-9 A Bates, *prmnt to 7th, wknd appr 3 out, pld up bef nxt.*...........(25 to 1 op 20 to 1 tchd 33 to 1)	pu
2749⁵	WICKENS ONE [65] (bl) 7-10-4 G Supple, *in tch to 8th, beh whn pld up bef 2 out..*.................(33 to 1 op 20 to 1)	pu
2726	MYSTIC COURT (Ire) [68] 6-10-7 C Rae, *hld up, hdwy 7th, hit nxt, weakend 4 out, pld up bef 2 out. (10 to 1 tchd 12 to 1)	pu
2749*	FANCY NANCY (Ire) [79] 6-11-4 Michael Brennan, *whipped round strt, hdwy hfwy, wknd 8th, beh whn pld up bef 2 out..*.................(6 to 1 tchd 7 to 1)	pu

Dist: 1½l, 7l, 16l, 3l, 7l, 16l, 21l. 6m 31.00s. a 49.00s (15 Ran).
(Glass Pig Racing Syndicate), Miss P M Whittle

3017 John Webber Memorial Novices' Chase Class E (5-y-o and up) £3,483 2¾m.......................... (2:50)

2700³	HIM OF PRAISE (Ire) 7-11-3 J Osborne, *jmpd lft, led to 8th, chlgd 2 out, hng left appr last, rallied to ld cl hme.*.................(5 to 4 on op 7 to 4 on)	1
2862⁵	MAJOR NOVA 8-11-3 J Culloty, *hld up, hdwy 11th, rdn to ld 2 out, ran on und pres, hdd cl hme.*.................(20 to 1 op 14 to 1 tchd 25 to 1)	2
2700⁸	BALLYDOUGAN (Ire) (v) 5-11-3 D Walsh, *al prmnt, rdn 4 out, ev ch 2 out, one pace aftr.*.................(50 to 1 op 25 to 1 tchd 66 to 1)	3
2613	THERMAL WARRIOR 9-11-3 G Upton, *mstks in rear, some hdwy 4 out, nvr dngrs.* (12 to 1 op 10 to 1 tchd 14 to 1)	4
2873	BROGEEN LADY (Ire) 7-10-12 J F Titley, *trkd ldrs, led 11th, hdd 2 out, wknd quickly...*(11 to 2 op 4 to 1 tchd 6 to 1)	5
2718⁴	THE BOOLEY HOUSE (Ire) 7-11-3 Derek Byrne, *in tch, ev ch whn blun 4 out, not reco'r......*(10 to 1 tchd 11 to 1)	6
	SENNA BLUE 12-11-3 M Sharratt, *in rear frm 12th, tld off.*.................(40 to 1 op 25 to 1 tchd 50 to 1)	7
	ARDSCUD 10-11-3 W Marston, *mstk 8th, al beh, tld off.*.................(33 to 1 op 25 to 1)	8
2700	MYSTIC MANNA 11-11-3 G Crone, *in rear whn blun and uns rdr 7th.*.................(33 to 1 op 25 to 1)	ur
2596	BECKY'S GIRL 7-10-9 (3*) Guy Lewis, *in tch till blun and uns rdr 4th.*.................(66 to 1 op 50 to 1 tchd 100 to 1)	ur
2862	SWIFT POKEY 7-11-3 M Clarke, *blun 1st and 5th, in rear whn refused 6th.*.................(66 to 1 op 50 to 1)	ref
1916²	COUNTRY STORE 8-10-12 S McNeill, *trkd ldr, led 8th to 11th, mstk nxt, wknd 4 out, tld off whn pld up bef last.*.................(7 to 2 op 4 to 1 tchd 9 to 2)	pu

Dist: ½l, 12l, 12l, 7l, 17l, dist, 1½l. 5m 54.40s. a 38.40s. (12 Ran).
SR: 25/24/12/-/-/-/ (M G St Quinton), O Sherwood

3018 Banque Arjil Italia Hunters' Chase Class H (6-y-o and up) £1,563 3m 1f
.... (3:20)

2793⁴ TEAPLANTER 14-12-1 (5*) Mr B Pollock, *made most, kpt on gmely frm 2 out.*
............(13 to 8 on op 6 to 4 on tchd 5 to 4 on) 1
FIDDLERS PIKE 16-11-5 (7*) Mrs R Henderson, *pld hrd, trkd wnr frm hfwy, ev ch 2 out, one pace aftr.* (7 to 1 op 5 to 1) 2
2891⁶ LURRIGA GLITTER (Ire) 9-11-5 (7*) Mr S Joynes, *prmnt, chsd ldrs, wknd 4 out, tld off....* (7 to 1 op 5 to 1 tchd 8 to 1) 3
DIRECT 14-11-11² (7*) Mr T Edwards, *beh frm tenth, tld off.*
...................(8 to 1 op 4 to 1) 4
2875 MAJOR MAC 10-11-5 (7*) Mr S Durack, *beh, effrt 11th, wknd nxt, tld off........*(33 to 1 op 20 to 1) 5
WHAT A TO DO 13-11-13 (7*) Miss L Sweeting, *prmnt to tenth, btn 4th whn blun and uns rdr last.* (8 to 1 op 5 to 1) ur
SOLAR GEM 10-11-5 (7*) Mr S McCarthy, *jmpd poorly in rear, blun tenth, tld off whn hit 3 out, uns rdr.*
...................(33 to 1 op 25 to 1) ur
Dist: 3l, dist, 21l, 9l. 6m 59.00s. a 47.00s (7 Ran).
(R G Russell), Miss C Saunders

3019 Hoechst Roussel Panacur EBF Mares' 'National Hunt' Novices' Hurdle Qualifier Class D (5-y-o and up) £3,247 2m 5f............... (3:50)

2746² KONVEKTA QUEEN (Ire) 6-11-0 J Osborne, *hld up in tch, hdwy 7th, led 2 out, pushed out.*
...............(5 to 4 op 5 to 4 on tchd 11 to 8) 1
2771* LADY HIGH SHERIFF (Ire) 7-11-0 N Williamson, *hld up in tch, led appr 3 out, hdd nxt, one pace.*
...............(6 to 5 fav op 6 to 4 tchd 11 to 10) 2
2605³ KOSHEEN (Ire) 6-10-7 J Culloty, *hld up, hdwy 7th, rdn and wkng whn hit 2 out......* (7 to 1 op 5 to 1 tchd 8 to 1) 3
2605⁵ FUN WHILE IT LASTS 6-10-7 C Llewellyn, *mid-div, outpcd 6th, styd on past btn horses frm 3 out.* (33 to 1 op 20 to 1) 4
KING'S RAINBOW (Ire) 8-10-7 J F Titley, *dsptd ld, led 6th, hdd appr 3 out, sn wknd.............*(20 to 1 op 10 to 1) 5
2560 RED RIVER (Ire) 6-10-2 (5*) Mr R Thornton, *trkd ldrs till wknd 3 out.................*(50 to 1 op 25 to 1 tchd 66 to 1) 6
FINAL ROSE 7-10-7 D Walsh, *in tch to 6th, tld off whn pld up bef 2 out......*(25 to 1 op 20 to 1 tchd 33 to 1) pu
2640⁷ MISS MYLETTE (Ire) 6-10-7 W Marston, *made most to 6th, wknd quickly, tld off whn pld up bef 2 out.*
...............(50 to 1 op 20 to 1 tchd 66 to 1) pu
PINXTON PENNY 5-10-7 T Eley, *al beh, tld off whn pld up bef 7th....................*(50 to 1 op 20 to 1) pu
Dist: 5l, 8l, 14l, 1½l, 7l. 5m 46.40s. a 47.00s (9 Ran).
(Konvekta Ltd), O Sherwood

3020 Banque Arjil & Compagnie Handicap Chase Class D (0-120 5-y-o and up) £3,643 3m 1f............... (4:20)

2268⁴ CARLINGFORD LAKES (Ire) [89] 9-10-0 J Culloty, *led to 11th, dsptd ld 3 out, led bef nxt, all out.*
...............(3 to 1 fav op 11 to 4 tchd 7 to 2) 1
2860³ SIMPSON [91] 12-10-2 G Upton, *nvr far away, pressed wnr frm 2 out, kpt on r-in, jst fld.* (7 to 2 op 3 to 1 tchd 4 to 1) 2
2698⁷ HOLY STING (Ire) [92] (bl) 8-10-3 C Llewellyn, *prmnt till outpcd 4 out, styd on frm 2 out.........* (7 to 1 tchd 8 to 1) 3
2698⁹ SHAMARPHIL [89] 11-10-0 Miss S Barraclough, *wl in rear till styd on strly frm 2 out, nvr nrr........* (33 to 1 op 20 to 1) 4
2698 SCRIBBLER [117] (bl) 11-12-0 J F Titley, *al prmnt, led 11th till rdn and hdd appr 2 out, wknd r-in.*
...............(14 to 1 op 10 to 1 tchd 16 to 1) 5
2772³ SOLO GENT [93] 8-10-4 Derek Byrne, *hld up, hdwy 13th, wknd 4 out, tld off........* (6 to 1 op 9 to 2 tchd 13 to 2) 6
2772* CELTIC BARLE [102] 13-10-13 S McNeill, *mstk 5th, in tch till hit and uns rdr 11th.................*(7 to 2 op 5 to 2) ur
PRIMITIVE SINGER [89] 9-10-0 W Marston, *al beh, tld off whn pld up bef 2 out.......*(33 to 1 op 20 to 1 tchd 50 to 1) pu
TARAMOSS [114] 10-11-11 N Williamson, *in tch till pld up bef 14th.................*(10 to 1 tchd 11 to 1) pu
Dist: Sht-hd, 1½l, 1½l, 5l, dist. 6m 51.00s. a 39.00s (9 Ran).
(Mrs L G Turner), T Thomson Jones

3021 Banque Arjil Polska Handicap Hurdle Class D (0-120 4-y-o and up) £2,714 2m............................ (4:50)

2762⁴ WASSL STREET (Ire) [100] 5-11-10 N Williamson, *rcd 3rd till wnt second 3 out, mstk nxt, rdn to take narrow ld appr last, all out...................*(11 to 8 fav op Evens tchd 6 to 4) 1
2560⁵ HARLEQUIN CHORUS [91] 7-11-1 G Upton, *trkd ldr, led 4th, hdd appr last, kpt on, jst fld.*
...............(11 to 8 fav op Evens tchd 6 to 4) 2
513³ SIMPLY (Ire) [100] 8-11-10 J Osborne, *led to 4th, ev ch 3 out, wknd bef nxt...................*(4 to 1 op 3 to 1) 3
2609 KARLINE KA (Fr) [90] 6-10-7 (7*) X Aizpuru, *al last, lost tch appr 4th, tld off........* (11 to 1 op 6 to 1 tchd 12 to 1) 4
Dist: Sht-hd, 18l, dist. 4m 10.90s. a 27.90s (4 Ran).
SR: 25/16/7/-/ (Rex Norton), K A Morgan

WINCANTON (good)
Thursday March 6th
Going Correction: PLUS 0.45 sec. per fur. (races 1,4,6,7), PLUS 0.55 (2,3,5)

3022 Seavington Maiden Hurdle Class F (Div I) (4-y-o and up) £1,917 2m
.... (2:10)

2511² TALATHATH (Fr) 5-11-5 R Johnson, *hld up, hdwy aftr 4th, chlgd aftr 3 out, slight ld last, drvn out.........*(2 to 1 jt-fav tchd 9 to 4) 1
SAMUEL SCOTT 4-10-11 A P McCoy, *hld up, hdwy aftr 4th, led after 3 out, mstk nxt, hdd last, rallied r-in, not quite get up.......................*(2 op 4 to 1 tchd 6 to 1) 2
2405⁵ NORDANCE PRINCE (Ire) 6-11-5 D Bridgwater, *chsd ldrs, ev ch aftr 3 out, one pace nxt.* (13 to 2 op 4 to 1 tchd 7 to 1) 3
2195³ QUALITY (Ire) 4-10-11 G Tormey, *wnl prmnt aftr 3rd, rdn aftr 3 out, sn one pace...* (2 to 1 jt-fav op 6 to 4 tchd 5 to 2) 4
2572⁴ THE STUFFED PUFFIN (Ire) 5-11-5 J Railton, *hld up, hdwy aftr 5th, one pace frm 3 out.*
...................(50 to 1 op 33 to 1 tchd 66 to 1) 5
REGAL SPLENDOUR (Can) 4-10-11 D O'Sullivan, *chsd ldrs 4th till no hdwy frm 3 out.............*(25 to 1 op 10 to 1) 6
ISIS DAWN 5-11-0 A Thornton, *chsd ldrs 4th, weakened aftr 3 out.......................*(6 to 1 op 33 to 1) 7
2497 GREEN BOPPER (USA) 4-10-11 C Maude, *wl beh second, some hdwy aftr 3 out............*(50 to 1 op 20 to 1) 8
2371 CLASSIC MODEL 6-11-5 R Bellamy, *chsd ldrs till wknd 3 out.*
...................(66 to 1 op 25 to 1) 9
ALSAHIB (USA) 4-10-11 B Powell, *al rear.* (15 to 2 op 5 to 1) 10
2782⁷ ZIDAC 5-11-5 J R Kavanagh, *sn wl beh.*
...................(25 to 1 op 16 to 1) 11
2283 STONEHENGE SAM (Ire) 5-11-5 S Curran, *f 1st.*
...................(66 to 1 op 20 to 1) f
2871 ORCHID HOUSE 5-11-0 D Skyrme, *hmpd and uns rdr 1st.*
...................(100 to 1 op 25 to 1) ur
2668⁸ PEARL HART 5-10-11 (3*) D Fortt, *jmpd slwly, tld off aftr 3rd, pld up bef 2 out.................*(50 to 1 op 20 to 1) pu
2558⁵ REVERSE THRUST 6-11-5 M Richards, *led till aftr 3 out, wknd quickly, pld up bef nxt.........*(50 to 1 op 20 to 1) pu
STELLAR LINE (USA) 4-10-11 P Holley, *pressed ldr, wknd quickly aftr 5th, tld off whn pld up bef 2 out.* pu
HONEYSHAN 5-11-0 G Bradley, *wl beh aftr second, tld off whn pld up bef 3 out.........*(66 to 1 op 33 to 1) pu
Dist: ¾l, 7l, 3½l, 3l, 17l, 6l, 12l, 12l, dist, 8l. 3m 47.80s. a 13.80s (17 Ran).
SR: 25/16/17/5/10/-/ (Million In Mind Partnership (6)), D Nicholson

3023 Broadstone Novices' Chase Class D (5-y-o and up) £3,704 2m 5f... (2:40)

2724⁹ FULL OF BOUNCE (Ire) 6-11-1 (3*) T Dascombe, *in tch, chsd ldr appr 4 out, hld in second whn lft clr last.*
...................(33 to 1 op 16 to 1 tchd 50 to 1) 1
2776* FRAZER ISLAND (Ire) 8-11-10 D O'Sullivan, *hit second, hit 5th and beh, hit 11th, 4th and wl behind whn lft poor second at last.................*(11 to 8 fav op 5 to 4) 2
188⁹ TRUST DEED (USA) (bl) 9-11-4 M Richards, *al wl beh, lft distant 3rd at last.........* (11 to 8 fav op 5 to 4) 3
2638⁵ REESHLOCH (Ire) 8-11-4 L Harvey, *pressed ldrs, led 6th to nxt, hit 11th, sn wknd.................*(8 to 1 op 6 to 1) 4
RAINCHECK 6-11-4 J Railton, *in tch, hit 5th, wknd aftr tenth.*
...................(33 to 1 op 20 to 1 tchd 50 to 1) 5
2873 DRESS DANCE (Ire) 7-10-13 (5*) Sophie Mitchell, *al beh, hit 14th, no ch whn f 2 out............*(12 to 1 tchd 14 to 1) f
CAMPECHE BAY 8-11-4 A P McCoy, *chsd ldrs, led second, led 3rd to nxt, led 8th to 9th, led nxt, clr frm 3 out till f last, unlucky.......................*(6 to 4 tchd 7 to 4) f
2921 PURBECK RAMBLER (v) 6-11-4 B Fenton, *led second to 3rd, led nxt to 6th, led 7th to 8th, led 9th to nxt, wknd 3 out, third and no ch whn f last.........*(33 to 1 op 20 to 1) f
LE GRAND LOUP 8-11-4 A Thornton, *tld off 9th, pld up bef 11th.................*(100 to 1 op 50 to 1) pu
2699⁹ DUKES CASTLE (Ire) 9-11-4 J Frost, *in tch, blun tenth, tld off whn pld up bef 13th.........*(25 to 1 op 20 to 1) pu
Dist: 21l, 3½l, 9l, 20l. 5m 29.70s. a 25.70s (10 Ran).
(Fieldspring Racing), R J Hodges

3024 'Wincanton Logistics' Handicap Chase Class C (0-135 5-y-o and up) £5,410 2m 5f.................. (3:10)

2722* SENOR EL BETRUTTI (Ire) [135] 8-12-0 G Bradley, *jmpd slwly 3rd, chsd ldr 5th, led 12th to nxt, led 3 out, rdn and hld on wl frm next.........*(15 to 8 op 2 to 1 tchd 9 to 4) 1
2729* HAWAIIAN YOUTH (Ire) [107] 9-10-0 D Bridgwater, *chsd ldrs, led 11th to 12th, led nxt to 3 out, rallied and ev ch frm next till no extr nr finish.................*(7 to 4 fav op 6 to 4) 2
2393 FOOLS ERRAND (Ire) [115] 7-10-8 A P McCoy, *mstk second, jmpd slwly nxt, rdn aftr 9th, hit next, mistake 4 out, sn btn.*
...................(6 to 1 op 5 to 1 tchd 13 to 2) 3

2742 BLACK CHURCH [107] 11-10-0 D O'Sullivan, *led till mstk and hdd 11th, wknd 4 out*.................(20 to 1 op 14 to 1) 4
2781* MAESTRO PAUL [107] 11-9-13² (3*) L Aspell, *jmpd slwly 5th and beh, hit 8th, sn lost tch* (9 to 2 op 7 to 2 tchd 5 to 1) 5
Dist: 1¼l, 13l, 14l, dist. 5m 21.80s. a 17.80s (5 Ran).
SR: 37/7/2/-/-/   (Gerard Nock), Mrs Susan Nock

3025 Tommy Wallis Handicap Hurdle Class C (0-130 4-y-o and up) £3,415 2m................... (3:40)

2543* NORTHERN STARLIGHT [108] 6-11-6 A P McCoy, *made all, pushed alng frm 3rd, rdn 2 out, not fluent last, hrd ridden and hld on wl*........(11 to 10 fav op 5 to 4 on tchd 6 to 5) 1
2504² FLYING FIDDLER (Ire) [99] (bl) 6-10-8 (3*) P Henley, *in 4th till steady hdwy and pushed alng aftr 3 out, styd on und pres to take second r-in, not rch wnr*.
...........................(9 to 4 op 2 to 1 tchd 5 to 2) 2
2504⁶ MORSTOCK [112] 7-11-7 (3*) T Dascombe, *chsd wnr, rdn 2 out, chlgd last, one pace*..............(5 to 1 op 7 to 2) 3
12655 MUTAZZ (USA) [102] 5-11-0 R Farrant, *dsptd second till aftr 4th, lost tch aftr 3 out*...............(13 to 2 op 6 to 1) 4
Dist: 1¾l, 2½l, dist. 3m 47.10s. a 13.10s (4 Ran).
SR: 33/22/32/-/   (Arthur Souch), M C Pipe

3026 Dick Woodhouse Hunters' Chase Class H (5-y-o and up) £1,492 3m 1f 110yds........................ (4:10)

RYMING CUPLET 12-12-0 (7*) Mr L Jefford, *dsptd ld, led and mstk 6th, hdd 9th, led nxt, hrd pressed and rdn whn lft clr 3 out, drvn and hld on wl r-in*...............(6 to 1 op 7 to 2) 1
2660³ WILD ILLUSION 13-12-0 (7*) Mr R Lawther, *dsptd ld to 6th, jmpd slwly 8th, led 9th to nxt, jumped slowly 12th, rallied and ev ch last, styd on*...................(20 to 1 op 16 to 1) 2
YOUNG BRAVE 11-12-0 (7*) Mr M G Miller, *in tch, hdwy 13th, chsd ldrs and mstk 17th, wkng whn blun 2 out*.
.....................(5 to 2 op 1 to 1 tchd 11 to 4) 3
153 TOM'S GEMINI STAR 9-11-7 (7*) Mr E James, *pressing ldrs whn f 9th*.................(50 to 1 tchd 100 to 1) f
PANDA SHANDY 11-12-0 (7*) Mr R Nuttall, *hmpd 9th and lost pos, hdwy 13th, chsd wnr 15th, chlgd 4 out till f nxt*.
.........................(7 to 2 tchd 4 to 1) f
2924 MEDIANE (USA) (v) 12-11-11 (3*) Mr Simon Andrews, *refused to race*...............(25 to 1 op 12 to 1) l
Dist: 1¾l, 3½l. 7m 0.30s. a 44.30s (6 Ran).
                                    (Gerald Tanner), M J Trickey

3027 Sparkford Handicap Hurdle Class F (0-100 4-y-o and up) £2,425 2¾m....................... (4:40)

2456⁹ COUNTRY TARQUIN [71] 5-9-11 (3*) T Dascombe, *in tch, hdwy to track ldrs 7th, slight ld aftr 3 out, rdn nxt, hld on wl*.......................(16 to 1 op 14 to 1) 1
1576 SPRING HEBE [90] 7-11-0 (5*) Sophie Mitchell, *wl beh, plenty to do aftr 3 out, styd on well frm nxt, str run appr last to take second r-in, no ch wth wnr*....................(20 to 1) 2
2892² EHTEFAAL (USA) [95] 6-11-10 T J Murphy, *al prmnt, drvn to chase ldrs 2 out, one pace r-in*.
........................(11 to 2 op 6 to 1 tchd 7 to 1) 3
2740 DARING KING [83] 7-10-9 (3*) L Aspell, *hdwy 6th, rdn and chsd ldrs king 3 out, one pace r-in*...(20 to 1 op 16 to 1) 4
2665² APACHEE FLOWER [74] 7-10-3 R Johnson, *prmnt, chlgd 4th, led 6th till aftr 3 out, wknd appr last*...(14 to 1 op 12 to 1) 5
2477* QUELQUE CHOSE [97] 7-11-12 D Gallagher, *hld up, steady hdwy 3 out, chlgd nxt, ev ch last, wknd r-in*.
....(5 to 2 fav) 6
2539* GALATASORI JANE [98] 7-11-6 (7*) L Cummins, *prmnt, chlgd 7th to 3 out, wknd nxt*.
..........................(13 to 2 op 11 to 2 tchd 7 to 1) 7
2783 IMALIGHT [80] 8-10-9 J Frost, *mid-div, hdwy 6th, wknd aftr 3 out*....................(16 to 1 op 14 to 1) 8
800⁴ CROHANE QUAY (Ire) [90] 8-10-12 (7*) Mr A Balding, *chsd ldrs, lost pos 5th, no dngr aftr*.......(10 to 1 op 8 to 1) 9
2562⁶ MOUNTAIN REACH [89] 7-11-4 A Thornton, *in tch till rdn and wknd 7th*.........(11 to 1 op 10 to 1 tchd 12 to 1) 10
2878⁵ CONCINNITY (USA) [71] 8-9-7 (7*) Mr O McPhail, *in tch beh*.
...................(50 to 1 op 33 to 1 tchd 66 to 1) 11
2746⁷ HANGING GROVE (Ire) [81] 7-10-10 N Mann, *sn beh*.
.......................(20 to 1 op 16 to 1) 12
AN SPAILPIN FANACH (Ire) [90] 8-11-2 (3*) D Fortt, *nvr better than mid-div*.........................(20 to 1) 13
2740⁵ PADDYSWAY [94] 10-11-9 B Powell, *nvr dngrs*.......(8 to 1) 14
2789 NUNS CONE [84] 9-10-13 J R Kavanagh, *al rear*.
.......................(33 to 1 op 25 to 1) 15
2539⁵ DUNNICKS COUNTRY [71] 7-9-10³ (7*) M Griffiths, *led 3rd to 6th, wknd nxt, tld off whn hld up bef 2 out*.....(50 to 1 op 33 to 1) 16
2783⁴ LUCAYAN CAY (Ire) [88] 6-11-3 D Leahy, *brief effrt 7th, sn wknd, tld off whn pld up bef 2 out*....(10 to 1 op 8 to 1) pu
2562 HUGE MISTAKE [89] (bl) 8-11-4 D Bridgwater, *jmpd poorly, drvn to press ldrs 1st to 3rd, sn wl beh, tld off whn pld up bef 7th*.......................(20 to 1 op 16 to 1) pu
2616⁵ KILCORAN BAY [88] (v) 5-11-3 R Greene, *sn tld off and jumping poorly, tld off aftr 5th*........(33 to 1 op 25 to 1) pu

---

1665 PROVE THE POINT (Ire) [80] 4-10-0 P Holley, *led to 3rd, wknd 6th, tld off whn pld up bef 2 out*.....(50 to 1 op 33 to 1) pu
Dist: 3l, ½l, ¾l, 1¼l, 4l, 16l, 12l, 10l, ¾l, 1¾l. 5m 24.60s. a 18.60s (20 Ran).
SR: -/1/5/-/-/-/   (Miss C A James), R J Hodges

3028 Seavington Maiden Hurdle Class F (Div II) (4-y-o and up) £1,900 2m................................. (5:10)

2553⁹ MUHTADI (Ire) 4-10-11 R Johnson, *in tch, hdwy to track ldrs 3 out, led aftr nxt, drvn out*.........(9 to 1 op 7 to 1) 1
RING OF VISION (Ire) 5-11-5 J Railton, *trkd ldrs, rdn aftr 3 out, ev ch nxt till one pace und pres r-in*...(16 to 1 op 7 to 1) 2
KEDWICK (Ire) 5-11-5 G Bradley, *hld up, steady hdwy 3 out, chlgd on bit 2 out, ev ch last, one pace und pres*.
..........................(14 to 1 op 16 to 1) 3
2782⁴ EMBANKMENT (Ire) 7-11-0 (5*) Mr C Vigors, *trkd ldrs, str chal frm 2 out till hit last and one pace*.
...............(5 to 2 fav tchd 9 to 4 and 11 to 4) 4
2766 PIPER'S ROCK (Ire) 6-10-12 (7*) Mr A Balding, *led to 3rd, styd frnt rnk, slight ld 2 out, sn hdd and wknd*.
.........................(33 to 1 op 20 to 1) 5
2256⁹ WHITE PLAINS (Ire) 4-10-11 B Fenton, *chsd ldrs, rdn and ev ch 2 out, one pace last*..............(7 to 2 tchd 5 to 1) 6
LITTLE ELLIOT (Ire) 9-11-5 C Maude, *beh and drive alng 5th, styd on frm 2 out*......(20 to 1 op 16 to 1 tchd 25 to 1) 7
2782 PROTOTYPE 6-11-5 D Gallagher, *keen hold, led 3rd, hit 3 out, hdd appr 2 out, sn wknd*.......(25 to 1 op 20 to 1) 8
2662⁹ VANBOROUGH LAD 8-11-2 (3*) T Dascombe, *hdwy to chase ldrs 3 out, wknd nxt*..................(50 to 1 op 20 to 1) 9
2546⁴ ALTHREY PILOT (Ire) 6-11-5 L Harvey, *in tch, hdwy to press ldrs 3 out, wknd nxt*......(7 to 1 op 5 to 1 tchd 8 to 1) 10
VIKING DREAM (Ire) 5-11-0 S Fox, *al rear*.
.........................(50 to 1 op 20 to 1) 11
2920 WEST BAY BREEZE 5-11-0 B Powell, *chsd ldrs to 3 out*.
.........................(33 to 1 op 20 to 1) 12
QUIET ARCH (Ire) 4-10-11 M Richards, *not fluent, al rear, tld off*......................(8 to 1 op 5 to 1) 13
2662 JOBIE 7-11-5 D Bridgwater, *al beh, tld off*.
.........................(50 to 1 op 33 to 1) 14
1306 BEWELDERED 5-11-5 J Frost, *al beh, tld off*.
.........................(50 to 1 op 25 to 1) 15
COOL VIRTUE (Ire) 6-11-0 A Thornton, *mstk second, in tch whn stumbled and uns rdr 5th*.
.................(11 to 2 op 4 to 1 tchd 6 to 1) ur
GENEREUX 4-10-11 N Mann, *al beh, tld off whn pld up bef 3 out*.........................(50 to 1 op 25 to 1) pu
Dist: 2½l, 1¼l, 1¾l, 4l, sht-hd, 15l, 2l, 5l, 10l, 3l. 3m 50.30s. a 16.30s (17 Ran).
                              The C I G S Partnership), Lady Herries

AYR (soft)
Friday March 7th
Going Correction: PLUS 1.20 sec. per fur.

3029 Loch Doon 'National Hunt' Maiden Hurdle Class F (4-y-o and up) £2,335 2m........................... (1:50)

2570³ DERANNIE (Ire) 5-11-8 A Dobbin, *hld up, hdwy hfwy, led 3 out, quickened clr aftr nxt, easily*....(6 to 5 on op Evens) 1
2802³ CARLISLE BANDITO'S (Ire) 5-11-8 M Moloney, *hld up, effrt whn not clr run aftr 5th and after nxt, hdwy to chase wnr 2 out, kpt on, no imprsn*...................(9 to 2 op 3 to 1) 2
2489⁷ LA RIVIERA (Ire) 5-11-8 K Johnson, *in tch, hdwy to track ldrs 3 out, kpt on same pace*...(25 to 1 op 16 to 1) 3
2853² LUMBACK LADY 7-11-3 B Storey, *in tch, outpcd aftr 6th, no dngr after*..............(3 to 1 op 5 to 2 tchd 7 to 2) 4
2570 CREAM O THE BORDER 5-11-3 F Perratt, *mid-div, effrt aftr 3 out*...................(100 to 1 op 50 to 1) 5
1377⁵ ALNBROOK 6-11-8 D Parker, *in tch till outpcd bef 6th, no dngr after*.....................(25 to 1 op 16 to 1) 6
2817³ COTTSTOWN BOY (Ire) 6-11-8 M Foster, *prmnt, led 5th till hdd 3 out, wknd quickly aftr nxt*.......(20 to 1 op 12 to 1) 7
2619 MEADOWLECK 8-11-3 P Carberry, *led till hdd 5th, sn wknd, tld off*....................(66 to 1 op 33 to 1) 8
CRAIGIE RAMBLER (Ire) 8-11-3 J Burke, *f 1st*.
.........................(100 to 1 op 50 to 1) f
2687 ONE STOP 4-10-4 (5*) S Taylor, *chsd ldrs till wknd aftr 5th, beh whn f last*....................(25 to 1 op 14 to 1) f
PRINCE OF THYNE (Ire) 8-11-8 G Cahill, *beh, lost tch aftr 6th, pld up bef 3 out*..................(50 to 1 op 20 to 1) pu
Dist: 14l, 3l, 7l, 7l, ½l, ½l, dist. 4m 2.60s. a 26.60s (11 Ran).
SR: 20/6/3/-/-/-/   (Mrs Stewart Catherwood), G Richards

3030 John Brown Memorial Novices' Chase Class E (5-y-o and up) £3,119 2m........................... (2:20)

2631* SINGING SAND 7-11-10 A Dobbin, *led till aftr 3rd, led 8th, styd 4 out, drw wl clr, eased r-in*.....(8 to 1 op 5 to 1) 1
2985* REAL TONIC 7-11-10 (6ex) P Carberry, *prmnt, mstk 5th, rdn aftr 8th, sn wknd, lft poor second 2 out*.
.................(2 to 1 op 7 to 4 on tchd 9 to 4 on) 2
2345⁷ CORSTON JOKER 7-11-4 J Callaghan, *mstks, beh, lost tch frm 7th, tld off whn blun last*.........(9 to 1 op 12 to 1) 3

2631 SHUT UP 8-10-13 K Johnson, lost tch frm 4th, sn tld off.
.... (200 to 1 op 50 to 1) 4
2714³ NOORAN 6-11-4 B Storey, led aftr 3rd till hdd 8th, outpcd bef 4 out, poor second whn blun and uns rdr 2 out.
..........................(4 to 1 op 9 to 4 tchd 9 to 2) ur
2919⁸ ARAGON AYR 9-11-4 M Moloney, not jump wl and early reminders, well beh whn pld up bef 7th.
.... (12 to 1 op 6 to 1 tchd 14 to 1) pu
Dist: 27l, 28l, 25l. 4m 11.70s. a 26.70s (6 Ran).
SR: 21/-/-/-/ (Hamilton House Limited), P Monteith

3031 James Barclay Memorial Handicap Hurdle Class D (0-125 4-y-o and up) £2,815 3m 110yds........... (2:55)

2851* TRIBUNE [104] 6-11-6 (6ex) M Foster, made most, styd on strly frm 3 out................... (2 to 1 fav tchd 9 to 4) 1
2361⁷ LEADING PROSPECT [97] 10-10-6 (7°) N Horrocks, cl up, ev ch 3 out, kpt on und pres............(20 to 1 op 14 to 1) 2
2851⁶ BANG IN TROUBLE (Ire) [104] 6-11-1 (5°) R McGrath, hld up, steady hdwy to chase 1st 2 appr 3 out, sn rdn and btn.
.... (9 to 1 op 6 to 1) 3
2619² SUNNY LEITH [84] 6-10-0 A Dobbin, trkd ldrs, drvn alng aftr 9th, hld.......................... (7 to 2 tchd 4 to 1) 4
2892⁵ HUDSON BAY TRADER (USA) [84] 10-10-0 Miss P Robson, cl up till drvn alng and outpcd aftr 7th, no dngr after.
.... (7 to 1 tchd 8 to 1) 5
2910³ MILITARY ACADEMY [112] 8-12-0 P Carberry, hld up, took clr order hfwy, rdn aftr 9th, sn wknd........ (6 to 1 op 7 to 2) 6
2919⁶ FESTIVAL FANCY [93] 10-10-6 (3°) G Lee, in tch, pushed alng hfwy, beh frm 8th................... (20 to 1 op 14 to 1) 7
2851⁵ SMIDDY LAD [95] 6-10-11 D Bentley, hld up in tch, effrt bef 9th, sn wknd, tld off.........(8 to 1 op 6 to 1 tchd 9 to 1) 8
Dist: 6l, 22l, 4l, 1¼l, 10l, 6l, dist. 6m 26.20s. a 45.20s (8 Ran).
(Hexagon Racing), C W Thornton

3032 Arthur Challenge Cup Handicap Chase Class D (0-120 5-y-o and up) £3,557 2½m................. (3:30)

2987* DISCO DES MOTTES (Fr) [107] 6-11-12 (5ex) P Carberry, jmpd wl, made most, clr 3 out, easily.
.... (13 to 8 on op 6 to 4 on) 1
2846¹ SOLBA (USA) [101] (bl) 8-11-6 (5ex) D Parker, hld up, mstk 9th, lost tch frm 11th, styd on und pres to take second cl hme.
.... (5 to 1 tchd 100 to 30) 2
2854¹ TWIN FALLS (Ire) [99] 6-11-4 (5ex) J Callaghan, cl up to 9th, chsd ldrs aftr, outpcd whn blun 4 out, no dngr after.
..........................(9 to 1 op 6 to 1) 3
2814⁵ MONTRAVE [105] 8-11-10 A Dobbin, in tch, chsd wnr frm 9th, outpcd from 4 out........ (7 to 1 op 6 to 1 tchd 9 to 1) 4
2573 PETER [91] 9-10-10 D Bentley, in tch whn f 5th.
.... (20 to 1 op 16 to 1) f
Dist: 23l, 1l, ½l. 5m 31.20s. a 44.20s (5 Ran).
(Robert Ogden), G Richards

3033 Ayrshire Agricultural Association Hunters' Challenge Cup Novices' Hunters' Chase Class H (5-y-o and up) £1,339 2m 5f 110yds..... (4:00)

DENIM BLUE 8-11-5 (5°) Miss P Robson, chsd ldr, led 12th, clr 2 out, easily....................(9 to 4 fav op 7 to 4) 1
WOODY DARE 7-11-3 (7°) Mr Chris Wilson, led, blun and hdd 12th, chasing wnr whn blunded badly 4 out, no ch aftr.
.... (11 to 2 op 6 to 1 tchd 13 to 2) 2
FROZEN STIFF (Ire) 9-11-5 (5°) Mr N Wilson, chsd ldrs, mstks 5th and 14th, tdd frm 4 out............... (9 to 2 op 6 to 4) 3
CANNY CHRONICLE 9-11-3 (7°) Mr A Parker, chsd ldrs till f 12th................... (14 to 1 op 12 to 1) f
PLANNING GAIN 6-11-3 (7°) Mr M Bradburne, strted slwly, sn in tch, rcd wide, not jump wl, lost touch aftr 14th, 4th and staying on whn f 3 out....................(6 to 1 op 4 to 1) f
MOLLY GREY (Ire) 6-11-0 (5°) Mr R Hale, blun 3rd, beh, mstks, tld off whn pld up bef 4 out.
.... (10 to 1 op 7 to 1 tchd 10 to 1) pu
ELI PECKANPAH (Ire) 7-11-3 (7°) Mr A Robson, very unruly strt and dismounted, deemed to have refused to race.
.... (10 to 1 op 8 to 1) f
Dist: 21l, 8l. 6m 17.30s. a 71.30s (7 Ran).
(Mrs L Walby), Miss P Robson

3034 Doon Novices' Handicap Hurdle Class D (0-110 4-y-o and up) £2,933 2m........................ (4:35)

2785³ PHAR ECHO (Ire) [93] 6-11-9 M Foster, dsptd ld, led 3rd, hrd pressed frm 3 out, styd on wl und pres.
.... (5 to 2 fav op 3 to 1 tchd 7 to 2) 1
2785⁷ JERVAULX (Ire) [95] 6-11-11 P Carberry, trkd ldrs, rdn to dispute ld aftr last, no extr clsg stages... (9 to 1 op 4 to 1) 2
2617* SOLSGIRTH [77] 6-10-7 B Storey, trkd ldrs, chlgd 3 out, no extr appr last................... (7 to 2 tchd 4 to 1) 3
2574⁶ KEMO SABO [89] (bl) 5-11-5 D Parker, led to 3rd, cl up, rdn and outpcd bef 3 out, styd on frm nxt.
.... (9 to 2 op 4 to 1 tchd 5 to 1) 4

2684⁵ MENALDI (Ire) [73] 7-10-3 G Cahill, hld up, pushed alng bef 6th, sn lost tch............... (7 to 2 op 3 to 1 tchd 4 to 1) 5
2847⁵ BILL'S PRIDE [75] 6-9-12 (7°) C McCormack, hld up, effrt bef 3 out, sn rdn and wknd..............(14 to 1 op 12 to 1) 6
1372⁴ SKANE RIVER (Ire) [71] 6-10-1 A Dobbin, bolted circuit bef strt, beh, lost tch frm 6th, tld off....... (10 to 1 op 6 to 1) 7
2711 ON THE OFF CHANCE [70] 5-9-7 (7°) I Jardine, hld up, in tch whn f 6th...........(50 to 1 op 25 to 1 tchd 100 to 1) f
Dist: ½l, 2l, 3l, 22l, ¾l, 21l. 4m 6.20s. a 30.20s (8 Ran).
(S H C Racing), L Lungo

EXETER (good to soft)
Friday March 7th
Going Correction: PLUS 1.55 sec. per fur.

3035 HMS Exeter Novices' Hurdle Class E (Div I) (5-y-o and up) £2,008 2m 3f 110yds....................... (1:45)

2818³ FONT ROMEU (Fr) 4-11-0 A P McCoy, trkd ldrs, led 2 out, readily.....(6 to 4 on op 7 to 4 on tchd 11 to 10 on) 1
1973 FOXIES LAD 6-11-2 R Johnson, hdwy 5th, chsd ldrs 3 out, rdn 2 out, styd on to take second r-in but no ch wth wnr.
.... (10 to 1 op 8 to 1 tchd 12 to 1) 2
2782³ CRANDON BOULEVARD 4-10-8 J Osborne, chsd ldrs, led 4th, hdd 2 out, one pace appr last.
.... (7 to 2 tchd 3 to 1 and 4 to 1) 3
2664⁴ MYSTIC HILL 6-11-2 J Frost, chsd ldrs till stdly lost pl appr 2 out....................(12 to 1 op 5 to 1 tchd 14 to 1) 4
2782⁵ SPREAD THE WORD (v) 5-10-11 Mr L Jefford, hdwy 4th, chlgd nxt till wknd appr 2 out, tld off.
.... (10 to 1 op 5 to 1 tchd 12 to 1) 5
2499⁶ COMMUTER COUNTRY 6-10-13 (3°) P Henley, in tch till hmpd and lost pl 4th, tld off.........(100 to 1 op 50 to 1) 6
2738 MILLCROFT REGATTA (Ire) 5-11-2 A Thornton, chsd ldrs to 4th, tld off...........(50 to 1 op 20 to 1 tchd 100 to 1) 7
2782 LANGTONIAN 8-10-9 (7°) Mr T Dennis, hdwy 4th, sn wknd, tld off....................(100 to 1 op 50 to 1) 8
DUNNICKS WELL 8-10-9 (7°) M Griffiths, led to 4th, wknd rpdly, tld off....................(100 to 1 op 50 to 1) 9
NEARLY ALL RIGHT 8-11-2 C Maude, chsd ldrs till mstk and uns rdr 4th....................(100 to 1 op 50 to 1) ur
1675 SUPREME CRUSADER (Ire) 6-11-2 E Byrne, chsd ldrs to 4th, tld off whn pld up bef 2 out........ (100 to 1 op 50 to 1) pu
Dist: 7l, nk, dist, 2l, dist, 7l, 18l, dist. 4m 56.70s. a 35.70s (11 Ran).
SR: 31/26/18/-/-/-/ (Pond House Gold), M C Pipe

3036 HMS Exeter Novices' Hurdle Class E (Div II) (4-y-o and up) £2,008 2m 3f 110yds....................... (2:15)

2782² GIVE AND TAKE 4-10-8 A P McCoy, made all, sn clr, reminders 2 out, drvn out r-in.
.... (11 to 10 fav op 6 to 4 tchd 7 to 4) 1
SOLAZZI (Fr) 5-10-6 (5°) O Burrows, hdwy 4th, chsd wnr frm 3 out, no imprsn approching last..... (100 to 1 op 50 to 1) 2
2663⁴ STEER POINT 6-11-2 J Frost, in tch, chsd ldrs till wknd appr 2 out....................(33 to 1 op 25 to 1) 3
2701 SPIRIT LEVEL 9-11-3⁶ Mr R Payne, al wl beh.
.... (100 to 1 op 50 to 1) 4
2874 RORY'M (Ire) (bl) 8-10-9 (7°) M Griffiths, sn rdn and wl beh.
.... (100 to 1 op 50 to 1) 5
2898 KYLAMI (NZ) 5-11-2 R Greene, mstks, al wl beh.
.... (20 to 1 op 12 to 1) 6
2874⁷ MR LOVELY (Ire) 6-10-13 (3°) T Dascombe, uns rdr strt.
.... (40 to 1 op 20 to 1 tchd 50 to 1) ur
1805 TALK BACK (Ire) 5-11-2 (7°) T Filley, blun second, in tch till wknd 3 out, tld off whn pld up bef nxt.
.... (7 to 1 op 6 to 1 tchd 8 to 1) pu
2371 CUILLIN 5-10-11 S McNeill, keen hold in rear, lost tch 4th, tld off whn pld up bef 3 out............(100 to 1 op 66 to 1) pu
2668 RAPID LINER 4-10-8 V Slattery, chsd ldrs to 5th, tld off whn pld up bef 2 out....................(100 to 1 op 66 to 1) pu
2744* AVANTI EXPRESS (Ire) 7-11-8 J Osborne, in tch, chsd wnr 4th to 3 out, wknd rpdly and pld up bef nxt.
.... (5 to 4 op 5 to 4 on tchd 6 to 4) pu
Dist: 14l, 16l, 28l, 23l, ½l. 4m 57.60s. a 36.60s (11 Ran).
SR: 15/4/-/-/-/-/ (Nelson, Newman And Moran), M C Pipe

3037 Diamond Edge Novices' Chase Class E (6-y-o and up) £3,440 2m 7f 110yds....................... (2:50)

2862 BEAR CLAW (bl) 8-11-2 J Osborne, made virtually all, jmpd lft 9th, clr frm 4 out................... (5 to 2 op 2 to 1) 1
2718* CAROLE'S CRUSADER 6-11-3 G Bradley, drpd rear 7th, hdwy 12th, chasing wnr whn took wrong course aftr 4 out, fnshd second, disqualified...... (9 to 4 fav tchd 2 to 1) 2D
2978 MALWOOD CASTLE (Ire) 7-11-2 A Thornton, hdwy to chase wnr 12th, one pace frm 4 out, fnshd 3rd, plcd second.
.... (20 to 1 op 16 to 1) 2
2873³ INDIAN DELIGHT 7-11-2 C Maude, in tch till wknd 13th, fnshd 4th, plcd 3rd.................... (8 to 1 op 6 to 1) 3
2794 PLEASURE SHARED (Ire) 9-11-8 G Tormey, f 3rd.
.... (5 to 2 op 2 to 1 tchd 11 to 4) f

2391[7] SECRET BID (Ire) 7-11-2 W McFarland, *wth wnr to 3rd, styd prmnt till wknd, blun and uns rdr 11th.* ....(10 to 1 tchd 11 to 1) ur

2291* STORMY SUNSET 10-10-10 (7*) Mr T Dennis, *wth wnr to 3rd, styd prmnt till wknd quickly 11th, tld off whn pld up bef 4 out.* ....(20 to 1) pu

2441 OATS N BARLEY 8-11-2 S Burrough, *in tch, chsd wnr 10th, hit nxt, and 12th, wknd 3 out, tld off whn pld up bef last.* ....(33 to 1 op 50 to 1) pu

2930 DEXTRA (Ire) 7-11-2 S McNeill, *sn wl beh, tld off whn pld up bef 12th.* ....(66 to 1) pu

2661[8] RATHKEAL (Ire) 6-11-2 B Powell, *chsd ldrs, wknd 4 out, blun nxt and pld up.* ....(100 to 1 op 66 to 1) pu

2873 SILVER HILL 7-10-11 R Greene, *sn tld off, pld up bef 9th.* ....(100 to 1 op 66 to 1) pu

Dist: 15l, 13l, 1¾l. 6m 18.10s. a 44.10s (11 Ran).
SR: 11/-/-/-/-/-/ (Roach Foods Limited), O Sherwood

3038 Sitwell Arms Novices' Handicap Chase Class E (0-105 5-y-o and up) £2,981 2¼m.................(3:25)

2431[5] BISHOPS CASTLE (Ire) [87] 9-11-4 J Frost, *in tch, steady hdwy appr 4 out, chlgd 2 out, sn led, rdn and hld on wl r-in.* ....(6 to 1 op 5 to 1) 1

2738[6] ALPINE SONG [69] 12-10-0 Miss V Stephens, *sn led, clr 4th, hdd four out, lost pos aftr 2 out, rallied r-in, jst fld.* ....(33 to 1 op 25 to 1) 2

2877[4] AFTER THE FOX [80] 10-10-11[7] (7*) Mr J Tizzard, *chsd ldr frm 4th till led four out, hdd aftr 2 out, one pace appr last.* ....(3 to 1 jt-fav op 5 to 2 tchd 7 to 2) 3

2515[6] INDIAN TEMPLE [69] 6-10-0 R Greene, *wth ldrs to 3rd, chsd lders 7th, lost tch appr 4 out.* ....(20 to 1 op 16 to 1 tchd 25 to 1) 4

2664 GEMINI MIST [69] 6-10-0 A Procter, *beh frm 3rd, tld off.* ....(50 to 1 op 33 to 1) 5

2864[5] CAWARRA BOY [93] 9-11-10 Mr E James, *hmpd and uns rdr 3rd.* ....(13 to 2 op 6 to 1) ur

2185 CHILI HEIGHTS [69] (bl) 7-9-11[4] (7*) M Griffiths, *wth ldrs, wnt badly lft, hmpd and uns rdr 3rd.* ......(33 to 1 op 16 to 1) ur

2665[7] COLETTE'S CHOICE (Ire) [72] 8-10-3[2] S Burrough, *hmpd and uns rdr 3rd.* ....(25 to 1 op 16 to 1) ur

2266[3] AMBER SPARK (Ire) [88] 8-11-5 G Bradley, *hmpd and uns rdr 3rd.* ....(3 to 1 jt-fav op 5 to 2) ur

1291[9] TRAIL BOSS (Ire) [88] 6-11-5 J F Titley, *in tch to 6th, wknd and pld up bef 8th, broke blood vessel.* ....(5 to 1 op 4 to 1 tchd 11 to 2 and 6 to 1) pu

Dist: ½l, 9l, 16l, 30l. 4m 45.40s. a 35.40s (10 Ran).
SR: 15/-/-/-/-/-/ (A E C Electric Fencing Ltd (Hotline)), R G Frost

3039 British Racing Centre Handicap Hurdle Class D (0-120 4-y-o and up) £2,775 2m 3f 110yds......... (3:55)

2565[4] COOL GUNNER [84] 7-10-4 C Maude, *hld up, steady hdwy to ld appr 2 out, readily.* (13 to 8 fav op 7 to 4 tchd 2 to 1) 1

2662[2] DEVON PEASANT [95] 5-11-1 Mr L Jefford, *chsd ldrs, chlgd appr 2 out, sn rdn and one pace.* .....(5 to 1 tchd 11 to 2) 2

2429[5] FRIENDLY HOUSE (Ire) [94] 8-11-0 A P McCoy, *al chasing ldrs, chlgd appr 2 out, sn outpcd.* .... (6 to 1 op 7 to 1) 3

2636[6] TROUVAILLE (Ire) [96] 6-11-2 L Harvey, *pressed ldr till wknd appr 2 out.* ....(7 to 1 op 6 to 1 tchd 8 to 1) 4

2311[5] THE BARGEMAN (NZ) [95] 9-10-12 (3*) D Fortt, *made most till hdd and wknd appr 2 out.* ..(7 to 2 op 3 to 1 tchd 9 to 2) 5

2701[6] PENNYMOOR PRINCE [104] 8-11-10 J Frost, *chsd ldrs till lost pos 4th, nvr dngrs aftr.* ....(13 to 2 op 6 to 1 tchd 7 to 1 and 8 to 1) 6

Dist: 3l, 12l, 6l, 7l, dist. 4m 57.10s. a 36.10s (6 Ran).
SR: 17/25/12/8/-/-/ (Richard Peterson), J S King

3040 Weatherbys Bulletin Magazine Handicap Chase Class E (0-115 5-y-o and up) £2,860 2m 3f 110yds (4:30)

2861* LANCE ARMSTRONG (Ire) [109] 7-11-6 (3*,6ex) D Fortt, *outpcd 8th, hdwy and rdn 11th, lft disputing ld 4 out, hmpd appr last, led r-in, all out.* ....(2 to 1 fav op 7 to 4) 1

2931 MAMMY'S CHOICE (Ire) [95] 7-10-9 A Thornton, *led till hdd but lft in ld ag'n 4 out, headed r-in, styd on und pres.* ....(7 to 1 op 5 to 1) 2

2627[5] SHINING LIGHT (Ire) [114] 8-12-0 R Johnson, *blun 7th, hit 8th, staying on whn hmpd 4 out, kpt on r-in.* (9 to 4 op 15 to 8) 3

2873[2] MR PLAYFULL [91] 7-10-5 J Frost, *chsd ldr, hit tenth, quickened to ld, blun and uns rdr 4 out.* ....(9 to 4 op 2 to 1 tchd 5 to 2) ur

Dist: 1¼l, nk. 5m 16.40s. a 43.40s (4 Ran).
(G L Porter), G M McCourt

3041 Enjoyment Of Being An Owner Novices' Hurdle Class E (5-y-o and up) £2,452 3¼m.................(5:00)

2701[5] MENESONIC (Ire) 7-10-7 (3*) P Henley, *in tch, hdwy to chsd ldrs 8th, rdn alng 2 out, chlgd last, sn led and styd on wl.* ....(9 to 4 op 3 to 1 tchd 100 to 30) 1

2701[2] SCOTBY (Bel) 7-11-8 B Powell, *al in tch, drvn to ld appr 2 out, hdd r-in, sn outpcd.* .... (6 to 1 op 5 to 1 tchd 7 to 1) 2

2661[7] SPACEAGE GOLD 8-11-2 G Upton, *led till hdd appr 2 out, styd on same pace.* .....(10 to 1 op 6 to 1 tchd 12 to 1) 3

2601 COOLE CHERRY 7-10-10 R Johnson, *sn in tch, effrt 8th, wknd 3 out.* ....(33 to 1 op 20 to 1 tchd 50 to 1) 4

2750 BLAZING MIRACLE 5-10-0 (5*) D Salter, *chsd ldrs to 3 out, sn wknd.* ....(20 to 1 tchd 25 to 1) 5

2783 MU-TADIL 5-10-10 V Slattery, *tld off frm 4th.* ....(66 to 1 op 25 to 1) 6

2610 DECEIT THE SECOND 5-10-10 S Burrough, *beh frm 5th, tld off.* ....(100 to 1 op 50 to 1) 7

2156 BANK AVENUE 6-10-10 R Farrant, *chsd ldrs till wknd 3 out, wl beh whn blun and uns rdr 2 out.* .....(10 to 1 tchd 8 to 1) ur

2603 FLASHMAN 7-10-10 Mr J L Llewellyn, *beh frm 6th, tld off whn pld up bef 9th.* ....(50 to 1 op 25 to 1) pu

HAN LINE 9-10-10 Mr L Jefford, *mstk 1st, in tch 7th, tld off whn pld up bef 3 out.* ....(66 to 1 op 50 to 1) pu

1961[7] GINGER MAID 9-10-0 (5*) G Supple, *beh frm 6th, tld off whn pld up bef 3 out.* ....(25 to 1 op 14 to 1) pu

2785[4] LOGICAL STEP (Ire) 7-10-10 G Bradley, *beh till hdwy 8th, wknd 3 out, tld of whn pld up bef last...* (10 to 1 op 6 to 1) pu

2741 AKIYMANN (USA) (bl) 7-10-9 (7*) B Moore, *sn tld off, pld up bef 4 out.* ....(33 to 1 op 16 to 1) pu

2263* KIND CLERIC 6-11-2 A P McCoy, *rdn alng 6th, hdwy 8th, wknd aftr 3 out, tld off whn pld up bef 2 out.* ....(7 to 4 fav op 5 to 4 tchd 15 to 8) pu

2605 SULA'S DREAM 8-10-5 R Greene, *sn beh, tld off whn pld up bef 4 out.* ....(100 to 1 op 50 to 1) pu

POLLERMAN 7-10-10 C Maude, *chsd ldrs till rdn and wknd 7th, tld off whn pld up bef 2 out.* ....(33 to 1 op 20 to 1 tchd 50 to 1) pu

Dist: 5l, 2½l, dist, 2½l, dist, 23l. 6m 42.30s. a 46.30s (16 Ran).
SR: 22/29/20/-/-/-/ (Mrs W H Walter), R H Alner

MARKET RASEN (good)
Friday March 7th

Going Correction: PLUS 0.25 sec. per fur. (races 1,3,4,7), PLUS 0.75 (2,5,6)

3042 'Farmers Day' Selling Handicap Hurdle Class G (0-95 4 & 5-y-o) £1,864 2m 1f 110yds................(1:40)

2515[5] SPITFIRE BRIDGE (Ire) [65] 5-10-8 D Bridgwater, *settled in chasing grp, improved bef 4th, outpcd and reminders aftr nxt, styd on frm 2 out to ld last 75 yards, ran on.* ....(7 to 4 fav op 3 to 1) 1

2676[9] SUMMER VILLA [67] (bl) 5-10-10 K Gaule, *keen hold, nvr far away, led second, hit nxt, sn clr, jnd 3 out, hdd last 75 yards, no extr.* ....(9 to 2 op 3 to 1) 2

2804[8] OAKBURY (Ire) [70] 5-10-6 (7*) T Siddall, *cl up to 3rd, struggling nxt, styd on wl frm 2 out, not rch 1st two.* ....(5 to 1 op 4 to 1) 3

2855 EUROLINK THE REBEL (USA) [85] 5-11-7 (7*) Miss R Clark, *prmnt chasing grp, effrt aftr 3 out, hit nxt, no imprsn.* ....(33 to 1 op 20 to 1) 4

2611* SUPREME ILLUSION (Aus) [72] 4-10-7 P Holley, *set steady pace to second, styd cl up, outpcd bef 3 out.* ....(5 to 1 op 4 to 1) 5

2973 BLOTOFT [72] 5-11-1 R Garritty, *nvr far away, chlgd 3 out, wknd nxt, btn whn blun last.* ....(12 to 1 op 7 to 1) 6

2515 WOODLANDS LAD TOO [57] 5-10-0 R Bellamy, *beh, struggling hfwy, nvr on terms.* ....(50 to 1) 7

2855[6] COOL STEEL (Ire) [70] 5-10-10 (3*) E Callaghan, *beh, struggling hfwy, btn whn f 2 out, dead.* ...... (13 to 2 op 5 to 1) f

Dist: 1½l, 3½l, ½l, 22l, sht-hd, 30l. 4m 20.50s. a 19.50s (8 Ran).
(Mercaston Consultants Ltd), G M McCourt

3043 Beaumontcote Hunters' Chase Class H (6-y-o and up) £1,329 3m 1f .... (2:10)

2887* MR BOSTON 12-12-12 Mr S Swiers, *nvr far away, improved and ev ch fnl circuit, edgd rght and led bef 3 out, drw clr.* ....(11 to 4 on op 5 to 2 on) 1

CARLY BRRIN 12-11-12 (7*) Mr C Mulhall, *led 3rd, hdd bef 3 out, sn outpcd, no imprsn whn hit last.* ....(7 to 1 op 6 to 1 tchd 8 to 1) 2

2715[6] MATT REID 13-12-5 (7*) Mr W Morgan, *beh, effrt aftr 12th, outpcd bef 4 out, no dngr after.* .... (4 to 1 op 5 to 2) 3

R N COMMANDER 11-11-12 (7*) Mr J R Cornwall, *led to 3rd, cl up till lost pl 11th, struggling last 5.* (33 to 1 op 20 to 1) 4

2634[4] FISH QUAY 14-11-12 (7*) Miss S Lamb, *improved to chase wnr aftr 4th, blun and lost pl tenth, sn tld off, refused 2 out.* ....(66 to 1 op 33 to 1) ref

Dist: 20l, 7l, dist. 6m 44.20s. a 44.20s (5 Ran).
(M K Oldham), Mrs M Reveley

3044 Wheatley Packaging Juvenile Novices' Hurdle Class D (4-y-o) £2,997 2m 1f 110yds................(2:45)

2775[8] BELMARITA (Ire) 10-6 (3*) Michael Brennan, *al wl plcd, effrt bef 2 out, led aftr last, kpt on strly.* ..... (11 to 1 op 7 to 1) 1

2828⁶ FAIRLY SHARP (Ire) 11-1 Richard Guest, *nvr far away, led 5th, blun 2 out, hdd aftr last, rallied.*
.................................(6 to 4 fav tchd 7 to 4 and 11 to 8) 2
2651¹ SIX CLERKS (Ire) 11-3 (3*) F Leahy, *mid-div, effrt and rdn alng bef 3 out, no imprsn frm nxt*.................(7 to 2 op 3 to 1) 3
2893⁷ SHARP COMMAND 11-0 P Holley, *made most till hdd 5th, drvn alng nxt, outpcd fnl 2*.................(9 to 1 op 6 to 1) 4
2811 JAMAICAN FLIGHT (USA) 11-0 J Railton, *beh till styd on fnl 2. nvr able to chal*....................(16 to 1 op 10 to 1) 5
614³ DOWN THE YARD 10-9 W Worthington, *in tch on ins, rdn 5th, outpcd nxt*.........................(20 to 1 op 14 to 1) 6
2915⁴ PRINCIPAL BOY (Ire) 11-0 R Rourke, *chsd ldrs till rdn and wknd 3 out*.........................(25 to 1 op 20 to 1) 7
2758 MARIGLIANO (USA) 11-0 R Garritty, *pld hrd, hld up towards rear, nvr dngrs*........(11 to 1 op 8 to 1 tchd 12 to 1) 8
2711 AFRICAN SUN (Ire) 11-0 K Gaule, *beh, nvr dngrs whn hmpd by faller 2 out*.........................(50 to 1) 9
2560 KHALIKHOUM (USA) 11-0 R Supple, *in tch till rdn and outpcd appr 3 out*........................(16 to 1 op 12 to 1) 10
2879 WINDYEDGE (Ire) 11-0 J Supple, *keen hold in rear, nvr able to chal*......................(33 to 1 op 25 to 1) 11
SPENCER STALLONE 10-11 (3*) R Massey, *beh and detatched, nvr on terms*............(50 to 1 op 25 to 1) 12
2711 SATURIBA (USA) 11-0 P Niven, *al beh, nvr a factor.* (33 to 1) 13
GOLD OF ARABIA (USA) 10-11 (3*) E Callaghan, *hld up towards rear, no imprsn whn f 2 out.* (20 to 1 tchd 25 to 1) f
ALPHETON PRINCE 11-0 D Bridgwater, *beh, struggling hfwy, pld up bef 2 out*......................(33 to 1) pu
2758⁷ TONTO 11-0 Derek Byrne, *beh whn broke leg and pld up aftr 3rd, dead*.........................(25 to 1 op 20 to 1) pu
2775⁷ SUMMER PRINCESS 10-9 Gary Lyons, *beh and struggling, tld off whn pld up bef 2 out*..........(16 to 1 op 14 to 1) pu
Dist: ¾l, 4l, 2l, 1l, 10l, 3l, 10l, 12l, 2l, 14l. 4m 11.70s. a 10.70s (17 Ran).
SR: 17/22/19/11/4/-/   (G A Hubbard), G A Hubbard

3045 Lincolnshire Agricultural Society Handicap Hurdle Class E (0-110 4-y-o and up) £2,477 2m 5f 110yds (3:20)

2762 SASSIVER (USA) [85] 7-10-5 K Gaule, *nvr far away, drvn alng 3 out, rallied to ld appr last, kpt on gmely.*
.................................(11 to 2 op 5 to 1) 1
2151³ THURSDAY NIGHT (Ire) [108] 6-12-0 P Niven, *prmnt on ins, improved and ev ch whn blun 2 out, rallied last, kpt on.*
.................................(4 to 1 op 7 to 2) 2
2891 LA FONTAINBLEAU (Ire) [85] 9-10-5 P Holley, *made most till hdd appr last, sn one pace*............(33 to 1 op 25 to 1) 3
2281 MOOBAKKR (USA) [82] 6-10-2² Derek Byrne, *hld up, effrt bef 2 out, styd on from 2 out, nrst finish.*
.................................(9 to 1 op 6 to 1) 4
2719⁹ NEEDWOOD POPPY [91] 9-10-11 B Clifford, *beh till styd on frm 2 out, nrst finish*................(16 to 1 op 10 to 1) 5
2719⁷ NO FIDDLING (Ire) [90] (bl) 6-10-10 D Bridgwater, *hndy on outer, improved and ev ch aftr 3 out, outpcd after nxt.*
.................................(5 to 2 fav tchd 11 to 4 and 9 to 4) 6
DOCTOR DUNKLIN (USA) [80] 8-9-13² (3*) Michael Brennan, *dsptd ld, outpcd 3 out, btn nxt*.........(50 to 1) 7
1883³ DAWN MISSION [101] 5-11-7 R Garritty, *hld up in rear, pushed alng aftr 3 out, nvr dngrs.*
.................................(6 to 1 op 5 to 1 tchd 13 to 2) 8
606⁴ CRAZY HORSE DANCER (USA) [81] 9-10-1 R Supple, *beh, rdn aftr 4 out, no dngr*.........(14 to 1 op 12 to 1) 9
2761⁷ HIGH PENHOWE [80] 9-9-9 (5*) Mr T Thornton, *chsd ldrs. struggling bef 4 out, tld off*............(20 to 1 op 12 to 1) 10
660¹ WHAT'S SECRETO (USA) [88] (v) 5-10-8 J Railton, *cl up, blun 4th, hit nxt, wknd and pld up bef 7th...* (12 to 1 op 10 to 1) 11
Dist: 2½l, 3l, nk, 2½l, 1¼l, 15l, 12l, 6l, 13l. 5m 27.60s. a 24.60s (11 Ran).
                               (P A Kelleway), P A Kelleway

3046 Wheatley Packaging Novices' Chase Class D (6-y-o and up) £3,678 2½m ....(3:50)

2286 GAELIC BLUE 7-10-10 Richard Guest, *chsd ldr, rdn to ld last, ran on strly*.....................(6 to 1 op 8 to 1) 1
2464⁴ GOLDEN HELLO 6-11-8 R Garritty, *nvr far away, not fluent 9th, led 3 out, blun nxt, hdd last, no extr.*
.................................(11 to 10 fav op Evens tchd 5 to 4) 2
82⁴ GORBY'S MYTH 7-10-10 K Gaule, *settled in tch, improved to chal 3 out, blun nxt, no extr aftr last*....(10 to 1 op 9 to 1) 3
2763 CLAVERHOUSE (Ire) 8-10-10 P Niven, *hit 1st, cl up, mstk 8th, outpcd last 4*....................(7 to 2 op 5 to 1) 4
2776⁴ DREAM LEADER (Ire) 7-10-10 J Railton, *led till hdd 3 out, blun nxt, sn btn*....................(9 to 1 op 10 to 1) 5
2739 TUG YOUR FORELOCK 6-10-7 (3*) Michael Brennan, *beh, struggling frm 8th, no imprsn fnl 3*....(50 to 1 op 25 to 1) 6
1834 CAPTAIN MY CAPTAIN (Ire) 9-10-10 S Curran, *beh, rdn fnl circuit, nvr able to chal*..........(50 to 1 op 33 to 1) 7
PARSONS BELLE (Ire) 9-10-5 M Sharratt, *prmnt, hit 6th and 10th, fdd last 4*................(33 to 1 op 25 to 1) 8
2626 PLEASURE CRUISE 7-10-3 (7*) N T Egan, *mstks in rear, tld off fnl circuit, pld up bef 3 out*.........(50 to 1 tchd 66 to 1) pu
SEABRIGHT SAGA 7-10-10 W Worthington, *beh, struggling fnl circuit, tld off whn pld up bef 3 out*.....(50 to 1) pu
Dist: 3l, sht-hd, 13l, 1¼l, 1l, 3l, 14l. 5m 16.70s. a 27.70s (10 Ran).
                               (Trevor Hemmings), Mrs S J Smith

3047 Linpac Garages Group Handicap Chase Class E (0-110 5-y-o and up) £2,808 2m 1f 110yds........(4:25)

2759³ NETHERBY SAID [105] 7-12-0 R Supple, *keen hold, pressed ldr, chlgd 7th, led 4 out, jnd nxt, ran on gmely und pres last 2.*
.................................(5 to 4 fav op 6 to 4 tchd 11 to 10) 1
2809² DUAL IMAGE [103] 10-11-12 R Garritty, *hld up in tch, improved aftr 6th, chlgd 3 out, hit nxt, rdn and found little after last*.........................(9 to 4 op 7 to 4) 2
2798² RECORD LOVER (Ire) [77] 7-10-0 W Worthington, *prmnt, struggling 5 out, no dngr aftr*.....(12 to 1 tchd 14 to 1) 3
1176¹ SUPER SHARP [90] 9-10-13 Jacqui Oliver, *made most till hdd 4 out, sn btn*.............(3 to 1 op 5 to 2) 4
2767⁵ RUSTIC GENT [77] 10-10-0 D Leahy, *in tch, drvn 7th, struggling last 5, tld off*.............(50 to 1 op 33 to 1) 5
Dist: 4l, 30l, 28l, 3l. 4m 34.10s. a 20.10s (5 Ran).
SR: 30/24/   (Mrs S Sunter), P Beaumont

3048 Farmers Standard Open National Hunt Flat Class H (4,5,6-y-o) £1,308 1m 5f 110yds............(4:55)

1809³ BESSIE BROWNE (Ire) 5-10-13 Richard Guest, *nvr far away, led o'r one furlong out, pushed clr*.......(8 to 1 op 5 to 1) 1
CLASSIC JENNY (Ire) 4-10-5 T G McLaughlin, *hld up, gd hdwy to ld 3 fs out, hdd o'r one out, no extr.*
.................................(12 to 1 op 7 to 1 tchd 14 to 1) 2
2206 STONESBY (Ire) 5-11-4 N Bentley, *prmnt on ins, chlgd and hng rght o'r one 2 fs out, no extr over one out.*
.................................(8 to 1 op 16 to 1 tchd 20 to 1) 3
HAPPY DAYS BILL 5-11-4 Gary Lyons, *led till hdd 3 fs out, kpt on same pace*.........................(25 to 1) 4
2323³ WOODFIELD VISION (Ire) 5-11-4 P Niven, *hld up, steady hdwy last 2 fs, nvr nr to chal*......(7 to 2 jt-fav op 3 to 1) 5
KOTA 4-10-7 (3*) R Massey, *hld up, improved and in tch o'r 4 fs out, outpcd 2 out*.................(7 to 1 op 10 to 1) 6
DINKY DORA 4-9-12 (7*) N T Egan, *beh till styd on last 2 fs, nrst finish*........................(33 to 1 op 25 to 1) 7
2262⁵ JUNIPER HILL 5-10-13 (5*) Mr R Thornton, *cl up, rdn appr strt, btn o'r 2 out*.......(10 to 1 op 8 to 1 tchd 12 to 1) 8
2469 NOBLE TOM (Ire) 5-11-4 J Supple, *keen hold, chsd ldrs, lost pl hfwy, no dngr aftr*.............(12 to 1 op 10 to 1) 9
PERCY'S JOY 5-11-4 R Garritty, *mid-div, struggling o'r 4 fs out, sn btn*.....................(10 to 1 op 7 to 1) 10
BRANDON BRIDGE 6-11-4 R Supple, *beh, struggling hfwy, nvr on terms*.......................(14 to 1 op 12 to 1) 11
2269⁸ WELSH ASSET 6-10-11 (7*) Mr A Wintle, *beh and drvn hfwy, sn btn*......................(14 to 1 op 12 to 1) 12
2858⁴ THE GNOME (Ire) 5-11-1 (3*) Michael Brennan, *cl up, drvn 5 fs out, btn and eased entering strt*..........(7 to 2 jt-fav op 3 to 1 tchd 4 to 1) 13
1735 SURPRISE CITY 6-11-4 D Leahy, *chsd ldrs to hfwy, sn btn.*
.................................(20 to 1) 14
1648 TORO LOCO (Ire) 5-10-11 (7*) F Bogle, *hld up, improved hfwy, struggling last half m*.................(20 to 1) 15
DELLEN WALKER (Ire) 4-10-10 Derek Byrne, *midfield to hfwy, sn btn*........................(20 to 1 op 16 to 1) 16
THE CHASE 6-10-11 (7*) M Newton, *al beh*........(33 to 1) 17
SWEEPAWAY (Ire) 4-10-5 J Railton, *chsd ldg bunch, struggling appr strt, sn btn, pld up ins fnl furlong.*
.................................(14 to 1 op 12 to 1) pu
Dist: 6l, 2l, sht-hd, 1¼l, 2½l, 3l, ¾l, 9l, 3½l, 8l. 3m 15.50s. (18 Ran).
                               (G A Hubbard), G A Hubbard

SANDOWN (good)
Friday March 7th
Going Correction: PLUS 0.70 sec. per fur.

3049 Worcester Park Novices' Handicap Hurdle Class D (0-110 4-y-o and up) £2,885 2m 110yds..............(2:00)

2771 SIR DANTE (Ire) [78] 6-10-0 D O'Sullivan, *mstk 1st, sn beh, rapid hdwy aftr 3 out, chlgd last, led r-in, drvn clr.*
.................................(11 to 2 op 6 to 1 tchd 7 to 1) 1
2765¹ MUSEUM (Ire) [88] 6-10-3 (7*) X Aizpuru, *chsd ldrs, led 2 out till aftr last, not quicken*.......(9 to 2 op 7 to 2 tchd 5 to 1) 2
2504⁸ SHAHRANI [105] 5-11-13 Jamie Evans, *trkd ldr, led 5th to 2 out, rdn and styd on one pace.*
.................................(7 to 1 op 10 to 1 tchd 11 to 1) 3
PREMIER LEAGUE (Ire) [78] 7-10-0 Leesa Long, *led, jmpd slwly 3rd, hdd nxt, chsd ldrs, kpt on one pace frm 3 out.*
.................................(33 to 1 op 25 to 1 tchd 40 to 1) 4
2802¹ OTTO E MEZZO [100] 5-11-8 R Dunwoody, *chsd ldrs frm 3rd, rdn aftr 3 out, kpt on one pace*....(4 to 1 jt-fav op 5 to 1) 5
1503² REGAL PURSUIT (Ire) [103] 6-11-4 (7*) P Maher, *hld up, rdn and hdwy aftr 5th, no imprsn after 3 out.* (9 to 2 op 9 to 4) 6
2264³ JAKES JUSTICE (Ire) [92] 6-11-1 P Hide, *hld up beh, rdn and effrt aftr 5th, sn wl behind.* ....(4 to 1 jt-fav op 7 to 2 tchd 9 to 2) 7
2611⁴ WHISPERING DAWN [88] 4-10-2 D Gallagher, *f second.*
.................................(12 to 1 op 8 to 1) f
Dist: 6l, 2½l, 2l, 1½l, 18l, 3l. 4m 4.40s. a 17.40s (8 Ran).

SR: 14/18/32/3/23/8/-/-/ (Peter R Wilby), R Rowe

3050 Anite Systems Novices' Handicap Chase Class D (0-110 5-y-o and up) £3,567 3m 110yds............(2:35)

2266 PARLIAMENTARIAN (Ire) [82] 8-10-0 J A McCarthy, *trkd ldr, led to 6 out, struggling 4 out, second and btn whn lft in ld 2 out, all out*..........(16 to 1 op 8 to 1 tchd 20 to 1) 1
2873⁴ EKEUS (Ire) [82] 7-10-0 J Culloty, *trkd ldr, rdn 6 out, struggling frm 4 out, 3rd and btn whn lft second 2 out.*
....................................(9 to 2 op 8 to 1) 2
2690² EULOGY (Ire) [108] 7-11-9 (3*) L Aspell, *trkd ldr, led 6 out, sn drw clr, f 2 out*...(11 to 10 on op 11 to 8 on tchd Evens) f
2677⁸ VICTORY GATE (USA) [82] (v) 12-9-10¹ (5*) Chris Webb, *sn beh, tld off 12th, pld up bef 6 out.*
....................(66 to 1 op 25 to 1 tchd 100 to 1) pu
1559* FUNCHEON GALE [95] 10-10-13 D Morris, *trkd ldr, 4th whn pckd 6 out, pld up bef nxt*...(9 to 4 op 6 to 4 tchd 5 to 2) pu
Dist: 16l. 6m 44.40s. a 45.40s (5 Ran).
(J G M Wates), T Casey

3051 Horse And Hound Grand Military Gold Cup Class E Chase For Amateur Riders (5-y-o and up) £4,879 3m 110yds......................(3:10)

2850* ACT THE WAG (Ire) 8-12-1 (7*) Captain A Ogden, *hld up, hdwy tenth, ev ch 6 out, led 2 out, eased nr finish, shaken up cl hme*..........(11 to 10 on op 5 to 4 on tchd Evens) 1
2375² JULTARA (Ire) 8-11-5 (7*) Major G Wheeler, *led 5th, mstk 12th, hdd 2 out, rallied last, rdn and ran on nr finish.*
.........................(8 to 1 op 6 to 1 tchd 9 to 1) 2
1859⁵ MAXXUM EXPRESS (Ire) 9-11-5 (7*) Major O Ellwood, *chsd ldr frm tenth, ev ch 6 out, unbl to quicken from 4 out, kpt on one pace*..........................(33 to 1 op 16 to 1) 3
CARDINAL RICHELIEU 10-11-5 (7*) Mr S Sporborg, *led to 5th, chsd ldr, blun 6 out, wknd aftr nxt, tld off after 4 out.*
.........................(9 to 2 op 4 to 1 tchd 5 to 1) 4
2666² DUHALLOW LODGE 10-11-10 (7*) Captain D Alers-Hankey, *hld up, wl beh till hdwy 12th, in tch whn blun 6 out and nxt, sn wknd, tld off aftr 4 out*.....(9 to 2 op 4 to 1 tchd 5 to 1) 5
GUNNER STREAM 13-11-5 (7*) Captain A Wood, *f 1st.*
....................(66 to 1 op 33 to 1 tchd 100 to 1) f
2921⁴ KENDAL CAVALIER (v) 7-11-5 (7*) Captain C Ward Thomas, *hld up, rdn and hdwy aftr 13th, pushed alng frm nxt, 5th and ridden whn f 5 out*.....(10 to 1 tchd 12 to 1 and 9 to 1) f
2482 ICANTELYA (Ire) (v) 8-11-5 (7*) Lt-Col R Webb-Bowen, *prmnt, jmpd slwly 12th, wknd nxt, tld off whn pld up bef 4 out.*
....................(50 to 1 op 25 to 1 tchd 66 to 1) pu
2243 VANCOUVER LAD (Ire) 8-11-5 (7*) Gunner S Greany, *mstks, sn wl beh, tld off 11th, pld up bef 3 out.*
....................(66 to 1 op 50 to 1 tchd 100 to 1) pu
TODDLING INN 10-11-3³ (7*) Captain C Farr, *al beh, tld off 11th, pld up bef 4 out*...(50 to 1 op 33 to 1 tchd 66 to 1) pu
Dist: ½l, 18l, dist, 22l. 6m 34.80s. a 35.80s (10 Ran).
(Robert Ogden), Martin Todhunter

3052 Racal Novices' Hurdle Class D (4-y-o and up) £3,022 2¾m..........(3:45)

2724* FRIENDSHIP (Ire) 5-11-7 R Dunwoody, *hld up, hdwy 6th, ev ch 3 out, swtchd appr last, rdn to ld r-in, all out.*
..............................(11 to 4 tchd 7 to 2) 1
2792⁵ MILLERSFORD 6-11-7 W Marston, *led, rdn aftr 3 out, hng lft appr last, hdd r-in, not quicken nr finish.*
....................(14 to 1 op 10 to 1 tchd 16 to 1) 2
2528³ EMERALD STATEMENT (Ire) 7-11-7 B Fenton, *trkd ldrs, blun 3rd, drvn alng aftr 5 out, rallied betw last 2, not quicken r-in.*
................(11 to 10 on op Evens tchd 5 to 4 on) 3
2725* JAZZMAN (Ire) 5-11-7 N Williamson, *hld up, hdwy aftr 5th, ev ch 3 out, not quicken betw last 2.*
.........................(9 to 1 op 7 to 1 tchd 10 to 1) 4
SCENIC WATERS 5-10-11 C Llewellyn, *hld up, pushed alng aftr 5th, chsd ldrs till wknd after 3 out.* (16 to 1 op 12 to 1) 5
2771 MUSIC CLASS (Ire) 6-11-2 D Gallagher, *hld up, hdwy aftr 6th, chsd ldrs, rdn 3 out, sn wknd*.........(66 to 1 op 25 to 1) 6
2456⁴ CAMERA MAN 7-11-2 J R Kavanagh, *trkd ldr, wknd 7th, sn beh*..........(25 to 1 op 20 to 1 tchd 33 to 1) 7
2394² JACK GALLAGHER 6-11-2 M Richards, *trkd ldr, ev ch 3 out, sn wknd*..................(8 to 1 op 7 to 1 tchd 9 to 1) 8
2792 MISTER GENEROSITY (Ire) 6-11-2 D O'Sullivan, *chsd ldr, wknd quickly 6th, tld off 4 out, pld up bef 2 out.*
....(66 to 1 op 33 to 1) pu
Dist: ¾l, 2½l, 7l, 12l, 18l, 1l, ¾l. 5m 27.50s. a 24.50s (9 Ran).
SR: 2/1/-/-/-/-/ (T Benfield And Mr W Brown), N J Henderson

3053 Duke Of Gloucester Memorial Hunters' Chase Past And Present Class H (5-y-o and up) £1,348 3m 110yds......................(4:15)

BRACKENFIELD (bl) 11-11-11 (7*) Captain D Alers-Hankey, *mstk 1st, led 4th to 12th, mistake nxt, led 7 out, drw clr four out, unchlgd*........(5 to 4 on tchd 11 to 10 on and Evens) 1
ACROSS THE CARD 9-12-4 (7*) Capt W Ramsay, *sn wl beh, tld off 13th, styd on aftr 3 out, wnt second r-in, no ch wth wnr.*
..........................(14 to 1 op 10 to 1) 2
OVER THE EDGE 11-12-4 (7*) Mr S Sporborg, *chsd ldrs, lost pl aftr 12th, styd on one pace after 4 out*..........(3 to 1) 3
2891 TRUE STEEL 11-11-13 (5*) Mr J Trice-Rolph, *hld up, hdwy whn mstk 9th, led 12th, mistake nxt, hdd 16th, wknd aftr 2 out, lost second pl r-in, fnshd tired*..........(7 to 1 op 5 to 1) 4
2531 NO JOKER (Ire) 9-11-11 (7*) Capt R Hall, *led to 4th, wknd aftr 12th, sn tld off, no ch whn blun four out.*
....................(16 to 1 op 12 to 1 tchd 20 to 1) 5
2875⁷ GOLDEN MAC 10-11-11 (7*) Major O Ellwood, *chsd ldrs to 12th, sn beh, tld off whn blun and uns rdr 6 out.*
..........................(33 to 1 op 25 to 1) ur
AMERICAN EYRE 12-12-3⁶ (7*) Mr R Gladders, *beh tenth, tld off whn pld up bef 12th.* (16 to 1 op 10 to 1 tchd 20 to 1) pu
Dist: 26l, 13l, 6l, 4l. 6m 42.40s. a 43.40s (7 Ran).
(Mrs Susan Humphreys), R Barber

3054 Raynes Park Handicap Hurdle Class D (0-125 4-y-o and up) £3,550 2¾m ....(4:45)

2281 SWING QUARTET (Ire) [92] 7-10-2 C Llewellyn, *chsd ldg pair, ev ch 3 out, chlgd nxt, wth ldr last, rdn to ld last strd.*
..................................(14 to 1 op 12 to 1) 1
2667* JEFFERIES [103] 8-10-13 N Williamson, *hld up, reminder aftr 4th, mstk nxt, sn reco'red, second and gng wl 3 out, led next, rdn and hdd last strd.*
.........(2 to 1 fav op 9 to 4 tchd 5 to 2 and 7 to 4) 2
2356⁶ INDIAN QUEST [101] 8-10-11 W Marston, *led, rdn aftr 4 out, hdd 2 out, sn wknd*........(8 to 1 op 7 to 1 tchd 9 to 1) 3
2504⁴ SMUGGLER'S POINT (USA) [102] 7-10-7 (5*) Sophie Mitchell, *pressed ldr till aftr 4 out, wknd after 2 out.*
....................(12 to 1 op 10 to 1 tchd 14 to 1) 4
2801⁸ FORTUNES COURSE (Ire) [107] 8-11-3 T J Murphy, *beh and pushed alng aftr 4th, hdwy after four out, kpt on one pace.*
....................(13 to 2 op 11 to 2 tchd 7 to 1) 5
2658 COURT NAP (Ire) [104] 5-11-0 Mr P Scott, *hld up, hdwy aftr 7th, no imprsn after 3 out*............(33 to 1 op 25 to 1) 6
2740⁴ MIRADOR [92] 6-10-2 D Morris, *hld up, wl beh till rdn and some hdwy aftr 3 out, kpt on one pace.*
....................(11 to 4 op 2 to 1 tchd 3 to 1) 7
2797⁸ WINGS COVE [114] 7-11-10 R Dunwoody, *chsd ldg pair, wknd quickly aftr 4 out, eased whn btn appr 2 out.*
....................(6 to 1 op 11 to 2 tchd 13 to 2) 8
Dist: Nk, 15l, 1¼l, 10l, ½l, 8l, 16l. 5m 25.40s. a 22.40s (8 Ran).
SR: 4/15/-/-/-/ (T Gold Blyth), N A Twiston-Davies

AYR (soft)
Saturday March 8th
Going Correction: PLUS 1.50 sec. per fur.

3055 Craigie Juvenile Novices' Hurdle Class E (4-y-o) £2,134 2m.....(1:50)

2147 SON OF ANSHAN 11-4 J Supple, *cl up, led aftr 4th, drw clr frm 6th, unchlgd.*
..............(6 to 4 on op 13 to 8 on tchd 7 to 4 on) 1
2550 CRABBIE'S PRIDE 10-12 Richard Guest, *prmnt, chsd wnr frm 5th, kpt on, no imprsn*..........(20 to 1 op 14 to 1) 2
BOURBON DYNASTY (Fr) 10-12 A Dobbin, *hld up, effrt aftr 4 out, kpt on same pace, nvr dngrs*.......(10 to 1 op 7 to 1) 3
2568³ PHANTOM HAZE 10-12 D Parker, *in tch, effrt aftr 6th, fdd.*
....................(3 to 1 op 5 to 2 tchd 100 to 30) 4
2816² DOUBLE DASH (Ire) (v) 11-4 D J Moffatt, *chsd ldrs, outpcd whn mstk 6th, sn beh*................(14 to 1 op 12 to 1) 5
2817⁴ KNOWN SECRET (USA) 10-12 M Moloney, *beh, outpcd frm 6th, tld off*..............................(33 to 1 op 16 to 1) 6
2684 JUNGLE FRESH 10-12 B Storey, *led till hdd aftr 4th, sn wknd, tld off whn pld up bef 3 out*.......................(50 to 1) pu
Dist: 19l, 3½l, 1l, 9l, dist. 4m 6.00s. a 30.00s (7 Ran).
SR: 30/5/1/-/ (F J Sainsbury), Mrs A Swinbank

3056 Mad March Hare Novices' Chase Class D (5-y-o and up) £2,924 3m 1f ....(2:20)

2914* KALAJO 7-11-9 B Storey, *hld up, hdwy hfwy, led 12th, styd on wl frm 3 out*..........................(9 to 1 op 8 to 1) 1
2846² NICHOLAS PLANT 8-11-9 G Cahill, *mstks, trkd ldrs, chsd wnr frm 14th, kpt on from 3 out, no imprsn.*
...................................(2 to 1 fav op 6 to 4) 2
2484⁵ CELTIC GIANT 7-11-3 R Supple, *led to 5th, led 9th till hdd 12th, ch 4 out, sn outpcd, kpt on frm last.* (3 to 1 op 9 to 4) 3
ROYAL BANKER (Ire) 7-11-3 P Niven, *led 5th to 9th, blun nxt, losing tch whn f 13th*..................(6 to 1 tchd 7 to 1) f
2686³ MAJORITY MAJOR (Ire) 8-11-9 A Dobbin, *trkd ldrs, pushed alng bef 11th, lost tch and pld up before 13th.*
..................................(11 to 2 op 9 to 2) pu
STRATHMORE LODGE 8-10-12 M Foster, *mstks, blun tenth, lost tch frm 12th, tld off whn pld up bef 15th.*
..................................(12 to 1 op 8 to 1) pu
Dist: 3½l, 1¾l. 7m 3.10s. a 63.10s (6 Ran).
(Kelso Members Lowflyers Club), B Mactaggart

3057 Mason Organisation Novices' Handicap Hurdle Class D (0-110 4-y-o and up) £3,652 3m 110yds....... (2:50)

2882³ CHERRY DEE [78] 6-9-12 (5*) B Grattan, *made all, hrd pressed appr last, styd on wl* .... (5 to 2 op 3 to 1) 1
2851⁴ SWANBISTER (Ire) [103] 7-12-0 R Supple, *cl up, drvn alng and outpcd aftr 7th, rallied aftr nxt, chsd wnr frm bef 3 out, rdn to chal last, no extr*.(9 to 4 fav op 2 to 1 tchd 5 to 2) 2
2710 KINGS LANE [85] 8-10-10 D Parker, *in tch, outpcd aftr 7th, styd on frm 3 out*.......(10 to 1 op 8 to 1 tchd 11 to 1) 3
2538⁸ STEPDAUGHTER [75] 11-10-0 L O'Hara, *mid-div, outpcd aftr 7th, no dngr after* .... (100 to 1) 4
2653² CLEVER BOY (Ire) [82] 6-10-7 Richard Guest, *prmnt till wknd quickly appr 3 out*........(4 to 1 op 7 to 2 tchd 9 to 2) 5
2619³ ADIB (USA) [92] (bl) 7-11-3 N Bentley, *settled midfield, took clr order 7th, rdn and wknd aftr nxt, tld off, fnshd lme.* .... (10 to 1 op 8 to 1) 6
2578 BELLE ROSE (Ire) [87] 7-10-12 A Dobbin, *in tch, reminder aftr 5th, wknd after 7th, tld off whn pld up bef 3 out.* .... (12 to 1 op 8 to 1 tchd 14 to 1) pu
1984 CRASHBALLOO (Ire) [77] 6-10-2 G Cahill, *al beh, tld off whn pld up bef 3 out.*................... (25 to 1 op 33 to 1) pu
Dist: 1½l, 16l, 13l, 2l, dist. 6m 35.90s. a 54.90s (8 Ran).

(George Dilger), P Beaumont

3058 Hugh Barclay Challenge Cup Handicap Chase Class E (0-115 5-y-o and up) £3,492 2m............... (3:25)

2683² COQUI LANE [86] 10-10-4 D Parker, *made all, styd on wl frm 4 out*...................(7 to 4 op 6 to 4 tchd 15 to 8) 1
2621² MR KNITWIT [110] 10-12-0 A Dobbin, *hld up, effrt bef 4 out, wnt second nxt, ch 2 out, no extr appr last.* ....(9 to 4 op 7 to 4 tchd 5 to 2) 2
2884² BOLD BOSS [109] 8-11-13 B Storey, *sn chasing wnr, drvn alng bef 4 out, fdd, btn whn mstk last.* ....(13 to 8 fav op 7 to 4 tchd 2 to 1) 3
2617 TEEJAY'N'AITCH (Ire) [90] 5-10-0 G Cahill, *mstks, lost tch frm 7th.*.....................(25 to 1 op 20 to 1 tchd 33 to 1) 4
Dist: 11l, 10l, 6l. 4m 15.80s. a 30.80s (4 Ran).
SR: 8/21/10/-/

(J M Dun), J M Dun

3059 Ayrshire Yeomanry Cup Handicap Hurdle Class D (0-125 4-y-o and up) £2,924 2½m...............(4:00)

2919* INGLETONIAN [116] 8-11-13 B Storey, *led, jnd 2 out, hdd last, styd on wl und pres to ld fnl 50 yards.* .... (100 to 30 op 5 to 2 tchd 7 to 2) 1
2789⁸ OAT COUTURE [117] 9-12-0 R Supple, *trkd ldrs, pushed alng to draw clr wth wnr aftr 8th, rdn to ld last, hdd fnl 50 yards, no extr*...................(9 to 2 op 7 to 2 tchd 5 to 1) 2
2919⁴ FIELD OF VISION (Ire) [104] 7-11-1 J Supple, *hld up, outpcd bef 7th, styd on frm 3 out, nvr dngrs....* (11 to 2 op 9 to 2) 3
1986* BRUMON (Ire) [92] (v) 6-10-3 D J Moffatt, *settled midfield, effrt aftr 7th, fdd.*..........(11 to 2 op 8 to 1 tchd 5 to 1) 4
LINNGATE [108] 8-11-5 M Foster, *nvr nr to chal.* .... (33 to 1 op 12 to 1) 5
723³ JUBRAN (USA) [95] 11-10-6 Richard Guest, *chsd ldrs till outpcd bef 7th, sn beh.* (20 to 1 op 14 to 1 tchd 25 to 1) 6
2919² ELATION [108] 5-11-5 A Dobbin, *chsd wnr, reminders aftr 6th, wknd quickly aftr 8th.* ....(3 to 1 fav op 5 to 2 tchd 100 to 30) 7
2815 STINGRAY CITY (USA) [89] 8-10-0 D Parker, *beh, lost tch aftr 7th.*.....................(100 to 1 op 33 to 1) 8
Dist: Nk, 24l, 14l, 8l, 10l, 8l, 13l. 5m 17.50s. a 39.50s (8 Ran).
SR: 4/5/-/-/-/

(Mrs Hilary Mactaggart), B Mactaggart

3060 Polyflor Handicap Chase Class E (0-115 5-y-o and up) £3,548 3m 1f .... (4:30)

2715⁵ KILCOLGAN [104] 10-11-8 N Bentley, *in tch, pushed alng bef 11th, led 13th, hrd pressed frm 4 out, styd on strly.* .... (16 to 1 op 10 to 1) 1
2686* ASK ME LATER (Ire) [86] 8-10-4 M Foster, *nvr far away, chlgd bef 4 out, ev ch till no extr betw last 2.* ....(5 to 4 fav op 6 to 4 tchd 11 to 10) 2
2860* FARNEY GLEN [104] 10-10-8 A Dobbin, *in tch till rdn and wknd aftr 13th, tld off*........................(7 to 2 op 9 to 4) 3
2846⁴ VILLAGE REINDEER (NZ) [100] 10-11-4 T Reed, *hld up, hdwy aftr 12th, ev ch frm 4 out till f 2 out, broke leg, destroyed.* ....(10 to 1 tchd 12 to 1) f
2579⁴ DARK OAK [110] 11-12-0 Richard Guest, *beh, lost tch frm 11th, tld off whn pld up bef 15th.* ....(12 to 1 op 14 to 1 tchd 16 to 1) pu
1984 BARNEY RUBBLE [92] 12-10-10 D Bentley, *led, mstk 1st, hdd 13th, sn wknd, tld off whn pld up bef 3 out.* ....(25 to 1 op 16 to 1) pu
2622⁴ FUNNY OLD GAME [82] 10-9-13² (3*) Michael Brennan, *chsd ldrs till blun and lost pl 12th, sn lost tch, tld off whn pld up bef 3 out.*.................................. (20 to 1) pu
Dist: 5l, dist. 6m 57.50s. a 57.50s (7 Ran).

(J D Goodfellow), Mrs J D Goodfellow

3061 Ayr Standard Open National Hunt Flat Class H (4,5,6-y-o) £1,035 2m .... (5:00)

CASTLE CLEAR (Ire) 4-10-10 P Niven, *trkd ldrs, led on bit 2 fs out, shaken up and sn clr*.........(7 to 4 fav op 11 to 8) 1
MINISIOUX 4-10-3 (7*) N Horrocks, *prmnt, led 5 fs out till rdn and hdd 2 out, kpt on, no ch wth wnr.* ....(15 to 2 op 8 to 1 tchd 6 to 1) 2
2322* LORD PODGSKI (Ire) 6-11-11 A Dobbin, *prmnt, drvn alng o'r 3 fs out, kpt on fnl furlong.* (2 to 1 op 5 to 2 tchd 3 to 1) 3
AMLWCH 4-10-10 M Moloney, *hld up, hdwy 5 fs out, chlgd 3 out, fdd fnl 2 furlongs....*(12 to 1 op 8 to 1 tchd 14 to 1) 4
2687* MAC'S SUPREME (Ire) 5-11-8 (3*) Michael Brennan, *prmnt till outpcd o'r 3 fs out, no dngr aftr..........*(4 to 1 op 2 to 1) 5
2687⁷ LORD KNOWS (Ire) 6-11-4 K Johnson, *in tch till wknd o'r 3 fs out.*...................(20 to 1 op 16 to 1) 6
ABOVE THE GRASS (Ire) 6-10-13 F Perratt, *in tch till wknd 4 fs out.*...............(250 to 1 op 200 to 1) 7
HIGH CELLESTE (Ire) 6-10-6 (7*) C McCormack, *in tch till wknd 4 fs out.* ....(50 to 1 op 25 to 1) 8
MEGGIE SCOTT 4-10-6¹ Richard Guest, *made most till hdd 5 fs out, sn wknd.*.............(150 to 1 op 100 to 1) 9
Dist: 8l, 4l, hd, 2½l, 6l, 15l, 1½l, 4l. 4m 16.20s. (9 Ran).

(R Hilley), Mrs M Reveley

CHEPSTOW (soft)
Saturday March 8th
Going Correction: PLUS 1.35 sec. per fur. (races 1,3,5), PLUS 1.90 (2,4,6)

3062 'The Racing Post For Cheltenham' Handicap Hurdle Class C (0-130 4-y-o and up) £5,637 2½m 110yds (1:15)

2807⁷ POTENTATE (USA) [128] 6-11-12 A P McCoy, *made all, clr 7th, hit 4 out, ran on wl frm 2 out.* ....(4 to 1 op 7 to 2 tchd 9 to 2) 1
2787³ KINGDOM OF SHADES (USA) [127] 7-11-11 P Carberry, *rdn alng to stay chasing ldrs 6th, drvn along frm 4 out, styd on to go second aftr 2 out, no imprsn r-in....*(4 to 1 op 3 to 1) 2
2789³ SELATAN (Ire) [111] 5-10-9 R Dunwoody, *prmnt, chsd wnr frm 6th, rdn 3 out, wknd aftr 2 out........*(7 to 2 op 4 to 1) 3
2743² MARIUS (Ire) [118] 7-11-2 P Hide, *hld up, effrt appr 4 out, btn nxt.*....................(9 to 1 op 6 to 1 tchd 10 to 1) 4
2598⁴ CALL MY GUEST (Ire) [112] 7-10-10 N Williamson, *chsd wnr to 6th, wknd 3 out........*...........(9 to 1 op 25 to 1) 5
2923* LAKE KARIBA [119] 6-11-3 R Johnson, *beh frm 6th.* ....(12 to 1 op 6 to 1) 6
2977⁷ PURPLE SPLASH [117] 9-7-11-1 J R Kavanagh, *al beh, lost tch frm 7th, tld off whn pld up bef last* ....(4 to 1 op 7 to 2 tchd 9 to 2) pu
2949 INTERMAGIC [107] 7-10-5 S Fox, *chsd ldrs till hit 5th and wknd, tld off whn pld up bef 4 out......*(33 to 1 op 20 to 1) pu
Dist: 3l, 9l, 5l, 1½l, 17l. 5m 10.90s. a 32.90s (8 Ran).
SR: 45/41/16/18/10/

(Jim Weeden), M C Pipe

3063 Tote Ten To Follow Handicap Chase Class B (5-y-o and up) £8,431 3¼m 110yds...................... (1:45)

2698* GIVENTIME [115] 9-10-1 L Harvey, *chsd ldrs till led 13th, drvn alng frm 4 out, styd on wl.........*(11 to 4 tchd 5 to 2) 1
2474 BELMONT KING (Ire) [142] 9-12-0 A P McCoy, *beh till hdwy to chal 14th, styd pressing wnr till one pace frm 3 out.* ....(11 to 2 op 9 to 2 tchd 6 to 1) 2
2698³ SPUFFINGTON [116] 9-10-2² P Hide, *hld up, hdwy 18th, chsd ldrs frm 3 out, no imprsn........*(20 to 1 tchd 25 to 1) 3
2786* GENERAL WOLFE [140] 8-11-12 R Dunwoody, *led to second, chlgd frm 9th till led 12th, blun and hdd nxt, some hdwy 18th, sn wknd.........*(5 to 4 fav tchd 6 to 4) 4
719* BISHOPS HALL [142] 11-12-0 N Williamson, *led second to 12th, wknd 15th, tld off whn pld up bef 3 out.* ....(16 to 1 op 10 to 1) pu
BUCKBOARD BOUNCE [142] 11-12-0 P Carberry, *in tch, hit 14th, effrt aftr 17th, sn wknd, tld of whn pld up bef 4 out.* ....(9 to 1 op 5 to 1 tchd 10 to 1) pu
2715* SEE ENOUGH [114] 9-10-0 S McNeill, *pressed ldrs till wknd 12th, mstk nxt, tld off whn pld up bef 15th, broke blood vessel.* ....(20 to 1 op 33 to 1) pu
Dist: 7l, 6l, dist. 7m 30.00s. a 55.00s (7 Ran).
SR: 26/46/14/-/

(L G Kimber), Andrew Turnell

3064 Peter O'Sullevan Novices' Hurdle Class B (5-y-o) £13,875 2m 110yds .... (2:15)

2521* WHAT'S THE VERDICT (Ire) 11-5 C F Swan, *hld up, steady hdwy appr 4 out, quickened to ld last, gng clr whn lft clear r-in.* ....(13 to 8 fav op 7 to 4 tchd 2 to 1) 1
2374* MOTOQUA 11-0 R Johnson, *al chasing ldrs, hit 2 out, styd on one pace and hld in 3rd whn lft second r-in.* ....(8 to 1 op 6 to 1) 2

423

2791* BREAK THE RULES 11-5 A P McCoy, *hld up, hit 4th, rdn 3 out, styd on one pace*.....(11 to 2 op 4 to 1 tchd 6 to 1) 3

2350⁷ BURN OUT 11-5 P Carberry, *hld up, rdn 4 out, sn no imprsn.*
....(16 to 1 op 10 to 1) 4

2791² ROYAL SCIMITAR (USA) 11-5 R Dunwoody, *made most till hdd 4 out, sn wknd*.......(5 to 1 op 4 to 1 tchd 11 to 2) 5

2825³ NO PATTERN 11-5 D Gallagher, *al in rear.*
....(9 to 1 op 10 to 1 tchd 8 to 1) 6

2509⁷ PERCY BRAITHWAITE (Ire) 11-5 C Llewellyn, *not fluent and al beh*.......................(50 to 1 tchd 100 to 1) 7

2656⁴ ABSOLUTE LIMIT 11-5 P Hide, *al beh, pld up bef 4 out.*
....(33 to 1 op 25 to 1) pu

2908* GODS SQUAD 11-5 N Williamson, *chsd ldrs, chlgd 4th, led four out, rdn and hdd last, hld whn faltered and dismounted r-in, destroyed*.......................(11 to 2 op 9 to 1) pu
Dist: 8l, ¾l, 17l, 8l, 12l, 3½l. 4m 18.00s. a 31.00s (9 Ran).
SR: 4/-/-/-/-/-/   (Seamus O'Farrell), A P O'Brien

3065 Llangibby Novices' Chase Class E (5 - 8-y-o) £2,908 2m 3f 110yds..(2:45)

2638 WITH IMPUNITY 8-11-2 R Johnson, *led, hit 7th, hdd nxt, led ag'n tenth, ran on wl frm 3 out*...........(2 to 1 op 11 to 8) 1

2566⁹ MYSTIC ISLE (Ire) 7-11-2 C Llewellyn, *hit 1st, hdwy to chase ldrs 11th, 3rd and staying on whn mstk and lft second 2 out, one pace*................(5 to 1 op 6 to 1 tchd 7 to 1) 2

2664⁴ DUNNICKS VIEW 8-10-9 (7*) M Griffiths, *hit second, chsd ldr 6th till led 8th, hdd and hit tenth, sn wknd.*
....(20 to 1 tchd 25 to 1) 3

2859² SCORESHEET (Ire) 7-11-9 P Hide, *in tch, hdwy 11th, chsd ldrs nxt, second and rdn whn f 2 out.*
....(11 to 10 fav op 5 to 4 on tchd 6 to 5) f

1981 SAUCY'S WOLF 7-11-2 M Sharratt, *sn tld off and jmpd poorly, pld up bef 11th*...............(100 to 1 op 33 to 1) pu

2428 FELLOO (Ire) 8-11-2 P Carberry, *pressed ldr to 6th, mstk nxt, tld off whn pld up bef 9th*...........(14 to 1 op 12 to 1) pu
Dist: 9l, dist. 5m 24.90s. a 41.90s (6 Ran).
(Guest Leasing & Bloodstock Co Ltd), P F Nicholls

3066 Tote Quadpot Juvenile Novices' Handicap Hurdle Class C (4-y-o) £3,488 2m 110yds.............(3:20)

2818⁴ SHU GAA (Ire) [100] 11-0 A McCarthy, *lost pos 4th, hdwy to chal four out, led nxt, rdn and hld on gmely r-in.*
....(2 to 1 fav op 9 to 4) 1

2721* INFLUENCE PEDLER [113] 11-3 C Llewellyn, *hdwy to track ldrs 3rd, rdn and ev ch last, str chal r-in, jst fld.*
....(9 to 4 op 2 to 1) 2

2336³ SEATTLE ALLEY (USA) [97] 10-11 P Carberry, *hld up, steady hdwy on bit 3 out, riden to chal last, sn no extr.*
....(11 to 4 op 5 to 2 tchd 3 to 1) 3

2430⁵ DOCTOR GREEN (Fr) [114] (v) 12-0 Jamie Evans, *led, clr aftr 4th, rdn four out, hdd nxt, one pace and pres appr last.*
....(4 to 1 tchd 9 to 2) 4

2771⁶ COME ON IN [86] 9-9 (5*) Mr R Thornton, *chsd ldrs to 4th, wknd four out*.................(33 to 1 tchd 40 to 1) 5
Dist: Sht-hd, 3½l, 1½l, 30l. 4m 23.10s. a 36.10s (5 Ran).
(Ali K Al Jafleh), O Sherwood

3067 Cotswold Vale Chase Handicap Class D (0-125 5-y-o and up) £3,488 2m 110yds................(3:50)

DONJUAN COLLONGES (Fr) [103] 6-11-4 P Carberry, *al gng wl, hit 7th, chlgd 8th, led tenth, clr 4 out, easily.*
....(6 to 1 op 3 to 1) 1

2928² COURT MASTER (Ire) [90] 9-10-5 B Powell, *beh, hdwy 12th, jmpd lft 4 out, chsd wnr frm nxt, no imprsn.*
....(13 to 2 op 5 to 1 tchd 7 to 1) 2

2666 BENJAMIN LANCASTER [95] 13-10-3 (7*) M Griffiths, *beh till styd on frm 12th, one pace from 3 out.* (25 to 1 op 16 to 1) 3

2928* INDIAN ARROW (NZ) [105] 9-11-6 C Maude, *wth ldrs, rdn appr 12th, wknd 4 out.*
....(11 to 8 fav op 13 to 8 tchd 7 to 4) 4

2922* KINGS CHERRY (Ire) [109] 9-11-10 C Llewellyn, *led to tenth, wknd quickly 4 out*.................(7 to 2 tchd 4 to 1) 5

2759⁴ JACOB'S WIFE [103] 7-11-4 R Bellamy, *al beh, tld off whn f 4 out*...................(7 to 1 op 6 to 1) f

PERSIAN SWORD [92] 11-10-4 (3*) R Massey, *al beh, tld off whn hmpd and rdn 4 out*...........(14 to 1 op 8 to 1) ur
Dist: 9l, 6l, 14l, 16l. 5m 26.70s. a 43.70s (7 Ran).
SR: 23/1/-/-/   (Robert Ogden), Capt T A Forster

NAVAN (IRE) (soft)
Saturday March 8th

3068 Ballivor Maiden Hurdle (Div I) (5-y-o and up) £3,082 2m.............(2:00)

2704³ SAVING BOND (Ire) 5-11-5 (7*) B J Geraghty, ...(100 to 30) 1
2222⁴ NATIVE-DARRIG (Ire) 6-12-0 D J Casey, ...(5 to 2 fav) 2
2703³ TRUVARO (Ire) 6-11-6 F J Flood, ...(6 to 1) 3
2271⁴ PAULS RUN (Ire) 8-12-0 L P Cusack, ...(4 to 1) 4
2703 DRAMATIST (Ire) 6-12-0 T Horgan, ...(8 to 1) 5
2054⁸ PRINCE DANTE (Ire) 5-11-4 F Woods, ...(12 to 1) 6

2343 PRIDE OF TIPPERARY (Ire) 6-10-8 (7*) R Burke, ...(20 to 1) 7
2732 APPLEFORT (Ire) 7-10-13 (7*) D K Budds, ...(14 to 1) 8
     KAMACTAY (Ire) 5-10-11 (7*) P J Dobbs, ...(20 to 1) 9
2865⁷ BRACKENVALE (Ire) 6-11-1 D H O'Connor, ...(16 to 1) 10
     SCENT ON (Ire) 5-10-11 (7*) D W O'Sullivan, ...(14 to 1) 11
2839 KILCAR (Ire) 6-11-6 P L Malone, ...(25 to 1) 12
2964 CLASSPERFORMER (Ire) 5-11-4 D T Evans, ...(14 to 1) 13
     DRISHOGUE LAD 10-11-6 A J O'Brien, ...(20 to 1) 14
2839 NORE GLEN (Ire) 6-11-6 J R Barry, ...(66 to 1) 15
2906 PRINCE PINE (Ire) 6-11-3 (3*) K Whelan, ...(20 to 1) 16
     CUTE AGREEMENT (Ire) 5-10-13 M Duffy, ...(20 to 1) 17
2839 MAY BLOOM (Ire) 6-11-1 J Shortt, ...(33 to 1) 18
2383⁶ SHINORA (Ire) 11-11-1 K F O'Brien, ...(20 to 1) 19
2604⁴ CROMWELLS KEEP (Ire) 6-10-13 (7*) Mr P M Cloke,
     ....(20 to 1) pu
Dist: 1l, 15l, 3l, 3½l. 4m 3.60s. (20 Ran).
(Mrs F Towey), Noel Meade

3069 Ballivor Maiden Hurdle (Div II) (5-y-o and up) £3,082 2m.............(2:30)

2649 DIAMANTINO (Fr) 6-11-6 F Woods, ...(11 to 10 fav) 1
2368⁸ HEATHER VILLE (Ire) 5-10-6 (7*) B J Geraghty, ...(8 to 1) 2
2965⁵ DOUBLE COLOUR (Ire) 5-11-5 (7*) A P Sweeney, ...(7 to 2) 3
2583 JACKPOT JOHNNY (Ire) 6-10-13 (7*) D A McLoughlin,
     ....(25 to 1) 4
2093 POWER CORE (Ire) 7-11-6 T Horgan, ...(14 to 1) 5
2907⁵ LAS ALMANDAS (Ire) 6-10-8 (7*) Mr E Gallagher, ...(14 to 1) 6
2041⁷ LYNX MARINE (Ire) 6-11-6 D T Evans, ...(33 to 1) 7
2866⁷ DUNMORE DOM (Ire) 5-11-4 K F O'Brien, ...(25 to 1) 8
2079 KITTYGALE (Ire) 6-10-12 (3*) K Whelan, ...(20 to 1) 9
2172 PLATIN GALE (Ire) 5-11-4 P Leech, ...(25 to 1) 10
2443 BALLYBANE LASSIE (Ire) 6-11-1 L P Cusack, ...(25 to 1) 11
     JERMYN STREET (USA) 6-11-9 (5*) T Martin, ...(12 to 1) 12
2129⁹ GROWTOWN LAD (Ire) 6-10-13 (7*) Mr P M Cloke, (16 to 1) 13
     CALL DIRECT (Ire) 7-10-13 (7*) R M Murphy, ...(20 to 1) 14
     KNOCKMOYLAN CASTLE (Ire) 7-11-1 (5*) P Morris,
     ....(20 to 1) 15
1409⁶ STRONG MARTINA (Ire) 5-10-13 J P Broderick, ...(14 to 1) 16
2094 STRONG AUCTION (Ire) 6-10-8 (7*) Mr D P Coakley,
     ....(40 to 1) 17
     MYRA PLUCK (Ire) 9-10-8 (7*) J P Deegan, ...(20 to 1) 18
     MR MARK (Ire) 5-11-4 F J Flood, ...(20 to 1) 19
2845⁶ TALKALOT (Ire) 6-10-13 A O'Shea, ...(13 to 2) f
Dist: 9l, 1l, 15l, sht-hd. 4m 7.70s. (20 Ran).
(C Jones), A L T Moore

3070 Castletown Handicap Hurdle (0-116 4-y-o and up) £3,082 2m......(3:00)

2735³ GOOD GLOW [-] 7-11-8 F Woods, ...(2 to 1 fav) 1
2369⁷ PRE ORDAINED (Ire) [-] 5-11-0 F J Flood, ...(8 to 1) 2
1535⁹ DIGADUST (Ire) [-] 5-11-8 M Duffy, ...(7 to 1) 3
2866 ABIGAIL ROSE (Bel) [-] 5-9-3 (7*) S FitzGerald, ..(33 to 1) 4
2142⁶ MATTORIA (Ire) [-] 6-9-12 (7*) A O'Shea, ...(14 to 1) 5
2142* CAITRIONA'S CHOICE (Ire) [-] 6-12-0 J P Broderick, (5 to 2) 6
2647 WADABLAST (Ire) [-] 7-9-12 D J Casey, ...(7 to 1) 7
2943⁸ JIHAAD (USA) [-] (bl) 7-9-6 (5*) T Martin, ...(11 to 1) 8
2865 STAR OF FERMANAGH (Ire) [-] 8-9-11 (7*) M D Murphy,
     ....(66 to 1) 9
Dist: 1l, 6l, 7l, 2l. 4m 8.10s. (9 Ran).
(Miss Elaine Lawlor), A L T Moore

3071 I.N.H. Stallion Owners EBF Nov.Hcap Hdle (Grade 3) (5-y-o and up) £9,675 3m................(3:30)

2839³ BLUSHING SAND (Ire) [-] 7-10-1 (7*) Mr T J Beattie, (11 to 2) 1
2964* PAT HARTIGAN (Ire) [-] 7-10-0 F Woods, ...(9 to 2 fav) 2
2670⁶ HOLLYBANK BUCK (Ire) [-] 7-10-8 J Shortt, ...(7 to 1) 3
2839* BELLS BRIDGE (Ire) [-] 7-10-9 T Horgan, ...(7 to 1) 4
2837⁵ GO INSTEAD (Ire) [-] 7-11-2 T P Treacy, ...(7 to 1) 5
2837⁷ COQ HARDI VENTURE (Ire) [-] 8-10-8 (7*) B J Geraghty,
     ....(12 to 1) 6
2837⁴ BE HOME EARLY (Ire) [-] 7-10-9 (7*) A O'Shea, ...(8 to 1) 7
2837⁸ DIAMOND DOUBLE (Ire) [-] 6-10-4 (3*) J Butler, ..(33 to 1) 8
2583³ HEAVY HUSTLER (Ire) [-] 6-10-7 J P Broderick, ...(12 to 1) 9
2473² TOUREEN GALE (Ire) [-] 8-10-2 (5*) P Morris, ...(7 to 1) 10
2839⁵ BRASS BAND (Ire) [-] 6-10-0 (7*) Mr R H Fowler, .(14 to 1) 11
2520* PINKPINKFIZZ (Ire) [-] 6-10-0 (7*) P G Hourigan, ..(10 to 1) 12
2835⁴ KINGS RETURN (Ire) [-] 6-12-0 D J Casey, ...(8 to 1) 13
Dist: ½l, 1l, sht-hd, sht-hd. 6m 5.00s. (13 Ran).
(Miss D Leonard), P T Leonard

3072 Long Distance Handicap Hurdle (4-y-o and up) £5,480 3m...........(4:00)

2229* THE QUADS [-] 5-9-11 F Woods, ...(7 to 2 fav) 1
2837³ TREANAREE (Ire) [-] 8-9-5 (7*) A O'Shea, ...(6 to 1) 2
2865* EUROTHATCH (Ire) [-] 6-9-4 (5*) T Martin, ...(5 to 1) 3
2837 HI KNIGHT (Ire) [-] 7-10-11 (7*) R Burke, ...(8 to 1) 4
2837 JIMMY THE WEED (Ire) [-] 8-9-7 J R Barry, ...(10 to 1) 5
2524⁹ GLENHAVEN ARTIST (Ire) [-] 7-10-11 F J Flood, ...(9 to 1) 6
2585 TOTAL CONFUSION [-] 10-10-5 (7*) Mr D Broad, ..(14 to 1) 7
2753² LETTERLEE (Ire) [-] 7-11-5 M Duffy, ...(6 to 1) 8
2944* ANOTHER GROUSE [-] 10-10-4 T P Treacy, ...(7 to 1) 9
2839 RATHCOLMAN GALE (Ire) [-] 7-9-4 (3*) J Butler, ...(40 to 1) 10

1619⁷ SPANKERS HILL (Ire) [-] 8-12-0 J Shortt, ... (14 to 1) 11
2901 COCK COCKBURN [-] 11-11-4 T P Rudd, ...(25 to 1) pu
Dist: Nk, 9l, 5l, sht-hd. 6m 10.10s. (12 Ran).

(I Told You So Syndicate), A L T Moore

3073 Baltinglass Beginners Chase (5-y-o and up) £3,082 2m 1f. . . . . (4:30)

2705⁴ LIVIN IT UP (Ire) 7-11-10 F Woods, ... (6 to 1) 1
2706⁵ MAGICAL LADY (Ire) 5-10-11 T J Mitchell, ... (7 to 2 jt-fav) 2
2833⁴ SHISOMA (Ire) 7-11-10 J P Broderick, ... (10 to 1) 3
2644⁵ BANGABUNNY 7-11-7 (3*) K Whelan, ...(8 to 1) 4
FIRE DUSTER (Ire) 7-10-12 (7*) Mr J P McNamara, (14 to 1) 5
2840³ BRAVE FOUNTAIN 9-11-10 T Horgan, . . . (7 to 2 jt-fav) 6
CASEY'S TROUBLE 12-11-7 (3*) Mr P J Casey, . . . (20 to 1) 7
2840⁸ PARADISE ROAD 8-11-5 C O'Brien, ... (20 to 1) 8
2941⁴ SCEAL SIOG (Ire) 8-11-0 L P Cusack, ... (33 to 1) 9
2903 NOBULL (Ire) 7-10-12 (7*) M D Murphy, ... (12 to 1) 10
2644⁶ CROSSFARNOGUE (Ire) 8-11-7 (3*) J Butler, ...(8 to 1) 11
2840⁹ JOHNNY'S DREAM (Ire) 7-11-3 (7*) Mr A J Dempsey,
. . . . (12 to 1) 12
NIGHTMAN 8-11-7 (3*) U Smyth, ...(20 to 1) 13
2077⁶ LABAN LADY (Ire) 8-11-0 T P Rudd, ... (33 to 1) 14
2675² TIME TO LEAD (Ire) 7-11-5 K F O'Brien, ...(6 to 1) 15
2868⁹ FANE'S TREASURE (Ire) 8-11-3 (7*) B J Geraghty, (20 to 1) 16
2673 RATHCORE LADY (Ire) 6-11-0 D H O'Connor, ... (20 to 1) ro
980⁸ PINGO HILL (Ire) 5-11-2 P L Malone, ... (20 to 1) pu
Dist: 3½l, 13l, 15l, 3l. 4m 25.00s. (18 Ran).

(H R C Catherwood), A L T Moore

3074 Trim Handicap Chase (0-109 4-y-o and up) £3,082 2½m. . . . . (5:00)

2941³ CORRIBLOUGH (Ire) [-] 9-9-10 T Horgan, ...(9 to 1) 1
2945⁴ YOUNG WOLF [-] 9-10-3 P L Malone, ...(8 to 1) 2
2843⁸ LA-GREINE [-] 10-10-12 (7*) Mr K Ross, ...(12 to 1) 3
2837⁹ DEARBORN TEC (Ire) [-] 8-10-12 (7*) M D Murphy, (12 to 1) 4
2843⁷ BOB DEVANI [-] 11-11-7 (7*) B J Geraghty, ...(14 to 1) 5
2646⁴ PERSPEX GALE (Ire) [-] (bl) 9-11-5 F Woods, . . . (4 to 1 fav) 6
2646² BEAUCHAMP GRACE [-] 8-11-0 (3*) K Whelan, ... (9 to 2) 7
2962³ MYSTICAL AIR (Ire) [-] 7-11-2 D T Evans, ...(8 to 1) 8
2868 NOELS DANCER (Ire) [-] 7-10-9 J P Broderick, ... (14 to 1) 9
2842⁷ BAILE NA GCLOCH (Ire) [-] 8-11-10 (3*) D P Murphy,
. . . . (11 to 2) 10
2053 MUSICAL DUKE (Ire) [-] (bl) 8-11-1 D H O'Connor, (12 to 1) 11
2448 WHY AILBHE (Ire) [-] 7-9-8† P Leech, ... (50 to 1) 12
2646 PILS INVADER (Ire) [-] 9-9-11† (7*) D K Budds, ... (33 to 1) ur
Dist: 4l, 7l, 3l, nk. 5m 32.50s. (13 Ran).

(Patrick Molloy), V T O'Brien

3075 Bective I.N.H. Flat Race (5-y-o and up) £3,082 2m. . . . . (5:30)

2757* SEE JUST THERE (Ire) 7-12-1 (3*) Mr R Walsh, . .(5 to 4 on) 1
2380² SARAH BLUE (Ire) /-10-13 (7*) Mr K O'Ryan, . . . (8 to 1) 2
2525³ LADY ELISE (Ire) 6-10-13 (7*) Mr J M Roche, ...(8 to 1) 3
2868 CLERICAL COUSIN (Ire) 8-11-4 (7*) Mr G Donnelly, (14 to 1) 4
2838⁷ HOLLOW GOLD (Ire) 6-11-6 (7*) Mr D W Cullen, ...(8 to 1) 5
2144⁶ KATOUCHE (Ire) 6-11-4 (7*) Mr A J Dempsey, ... (14 to 1) 6
2378 HARBOUR BLAZE (Ire) 7-11-4 (7*) Mr J P McNamara,
. . . . (20 to 1) 7
1895 SECTION SEVEN (Ire) 7-12-4 Mr P Fenton, ... (5 to 1) 8
2737 MISS HOT TAMALLI (Ire) 6-11-3 (3*) Mr P M Kelly, (14 to 1) 9
1655 BELMONT DUKE (Ire) 6-11-8 (3*) Mr P English, ...(20 to 1) 10
2839 JUST SUPREME (Ire) 6-11-11 Mr G J Harford, ... (20 to 1) 11
2906 SWINFORD BOY (Ire) 9-11-4 (7*) Mr P A Rattigan, (25 to 1) 12
NIPPY CHERRY (Ire) 6-11-4 (7*) Mr M O'Connor, . . (16 to 1) 13
2582 MAGS DWYER (Ire) 7-11-6 (7*) Mr J J Lennon, ...(20 to 1) ur
Dist: 11l, 1½l, nk, 3l. 4m 4.80s. (14 Ran).

(Olde Crowbars Syndicate), W P Mullins

SANDOWN (good)
Saturday March 8th
Going Correction: PLUS 0.35 sec. per fur.

3076 Dick McCreery Hunters' Chase Class H (5-y-o and up) £2,684 2½m 110yds. (1:55)

ARCHIES OATS 8-11-9 (5*) Mr J Trice-Rolph, hld up, hdwy
12th, led last, rdn out and styd on wl.
. . . . (11 to 2 op 4 to 1 tchd 6 to 1) 1
MISTER MAIN MAN (Ire) 9-11-7 (7*) Mr S Sporborg, blun 4th,
hdwy 12th, ev ch whn hit last, kpt on same pace r-in.
. . . .(11 to 10 on op 5evens 5 to 4 to 5 to 4) 2
BERRINGS DASHER 10-11-7 (7*) Major M Watson, wtd wth,
chsd clr ldr frm 6th, clr order tenth, led appr 2 out, hdd and hit
last, fdd r-in. . . . . (5 to 1 op 3 to 1 tchd 11 to 2) 3
ELECTRIC COMMITTEE (Ire) 7-11-7 (7*) Capt A Wood, led,
clr frm 3rd, hdd appr 2 out, wknd approaching last.
. . . . (16 to 1 op 12 to 1) 4
2516⁴ HICKELTON LAD 13-11-13 (7*) Major S J Robinson, blun 1st,
hdwy tenth, wknd appr 3 out.
. . . . (12 to 1 op 7 to 1 tchd 14 to 1) 5
TAUREAN TYCOON 13-11-7 (7*) Major O Ellwood, not fluent,
beh frm 7th. . . . . (12 to 1 op 14 to 1 tchd 10 to 1) 6

3077 Bushy Park 'National Hunt' Novices' Hurdle Class D (4-y-o and up) £2,957 2m 110yds. . . . . (2:25)

2323 SOUNDS LIKE FUN 6-11-7 J F Titley, chsd ldr, rdn aft 2 out,
lft in ld last, hdd r-in, kpt on to lead cl hme.
. . . .(20 to 1 op 14 to 1 tchd 25 to 1) 1
2699 WISE KING 7-11-2 G Upton, led to 2 out, led r-in, hdd cl hme.
. . . . (13 to 2 op 5 to 1 tchd 7 to 1) 2
2558² NEAT FEAT (Ire) 6-11-2 P Holley, hld up beh ldrs, rdn appr 2
out, sn btn. . . . .(16 to 1 op 12 to 1 tchd 20 to 1) 3
2594⁵ DONNINGTON (Ire) 7-11-7 J Osborne, wtd wth in rear, hit
second, steady hdwy 4th, ridden whn hmpd 3 out, nvr
nr to chal. . . . .(4 to 1 op 5 to 2 tchd 5 to 1) 4
2795⁶ CALM DOWN (Ire) 6-11-2 D Bridgwater, nvr nr to chal.
. . . .(20 to 1 op 14 to 1 tchd 33 to 1) 5
2795⁸ HUISH (Ire) 6-11-2 Mr A Charles-Jones, nvr on terms.
. . . . (100 to 1 op 50 to 1) 6
2594⁸ THE FLYING DOCTOR (Ire) 7-11-2 B Fenton, mid-div, wknd
appr 2 out. . . . . (12 to 1 tchd 14 to 1) 7
2699⁶ CLOSE HARMONY 5-10-11 M A Fitzgerald, mid-div, wknd 3
out, tld off. . . . . (10 to 1 op 7 to 1 tchd 11 to 1) 8
TOM PINCH (Ire) 8-11-2 R Greene, al beh, tld off.
. . . . (20 to 1 op 16 to 1 tchd 25 to 1) 9
2299² HURRICANE LAMP 6-11-12 A Thornton, hld up beh ldrs, led
2 out till f last. . . . . (2 to 1 fav op 6 to 4) f
2688² LIVELY ENCOUNTER (Ire) 6-11-2 Derek Byrne, hld up, prog
5th, 4th and in tch whn bright dwn last. (6 to 1 tchd 7 to 1) bd
2527 STARLIGHT FOOL (bl) 8-11-2 W McFarland, hit 3rd, beh 5th,
tld off whn pld up bef last. . . . . (66 to 1 op 33 to 1) pu
KNOCK STAR (Ire) 6-11-2 J Railton, trkd ldrs, wknd 5th, tld off
whn pld up bef last. . . . . . (33 to 1 op 16 to 1 tchd 66 to 1) pu
Dist: Sht-hd, 17l, 2l, 1l, 9l, ½l, dist, 2l. 4m 4.40s. a 17.40s (13 Ran).

(Mrs H Brown), Miss H C Knight

3078 Barclays Bank Handicap Hurdle For Amateur Riders Class E (0-120 4-y-o and up) £4,065 2m 110yds. . . . (2:55)

2479* JOVIE KING (Ire) [89] 5-11-3 (7*) Capt D Alers-Hankey, made
all, ran on wl. . . . . (7 to 2 op 3 to 1 tchd 4 to 1) 1
2730⁴ KELLY MAC [89] 7-11-3 (7*) Major O Ellwood, chsd wnr, rdn
appr 2 out, one pace. . . . . . .(9 to 2 op 7 to 2 tchd 5 to 1) 2
2792⁹ IRON N GOLD [90] 5-11-4 (7*) Major G Wheeler, hld up, some
prog frm 2 out, no imprsn. (11 to 2 op 5 to 1 tchd 6 to 1) 3
1087³ DESERT CALM (Ire) [85] 8-11-1² (7*) Capt J Fuller, hld up, rdn
appr 2 out, sn wknd. . . . . (10 to 1 op 7 to 1 tchd 12 to 1) 4
2777³ BIGWHEEL BILL (Ire) [84] 8-10-12 (7*) Miss V Haigh, hld up
beh ldrs, rdn appr 2 out, sn btn.
. . . . (11 to 2 op 6 to 1 tchd 5 to 1) 5
2730³ COLOSSUS OF ROADS [100] 8-12-1⁴ Mr T Thomson Jones,
wtd wth, hit 3rd, impd lft 3 out, sn rdn and wknd, beh whn pld
up bef 2 out. . . . . . .(15 to 8 fav op 6 to 4 tchd 2 to 1) pu
Dist: 3½l, 10l, 2½l, 15l. 4m 6.00s. a 19.00s (6 Ran).

(R H Buckler), R H Buckler

3079 Burnt Oak & Special Cargo Novices' Chase Class C (5-y-o and up) £4,463 2m. . . . . (3:30)

2938* SUBLIME FELLOW (Ire) 7-11-6 M A Fitzgerald, chsd ldr frm
4th, led appr 2 out, ran on wl.
. . . . (3 to 1 op 5 to 2 tchd 100 to 30) 1
2861² JULEIT JONES (Ire) 8-10-8 (3*) L Aspell, led till appr 2 out, sn
one pace. . . . .(7 to 2 tchd 4 to 1) 2
2864* SCOTTISH BAMBI 9-11-6 J Osborne, hld up, hdwy frm 4 out,
rdn and effrt appr 2 out, one pace. . . .(2 to 1 fav op 7 to 4) 3
2938 BLAIR CASTLE (Ire) 6-11-2 B Fenton, chsd ldr to 3rd, mstk
and lost pl nxt, effrt appr 3 out, wknd bef next.
. . . . (3 to 1 op 9 to 4 tchd 100 to 30) 4
1704⁵ CHEEKA 8-11-2 M Ranger, al beh, tld off.
. . . . (66 to 1 op 33 to 1) 5
2823³ HEATHYARDS BOY (bl) 7-11-2 D Walsh, beh 8th, tld off.
. . . . (40 to 1 op 20 to 1 tchd 50 to 1) 6
Dist: 8l, 2½l, 5l, dist, 1¾l. 4m 1.60s. a 12.60s (6 Ran).
SR: 22/5/11/2/-/-/

(Rory McGrath), N J Henderson

3080 Sunderlands Imperial Cup Handicap Hurdle Class B (0-150 4-y-o and up) £21,456 2m 110yds. . . . .(4:05)

2879* CARLITO BRIGANTE [112] 5-10-0 J Osborne, hld up beh
ldrs, rdn appr 2 out, led r-in, styd on strly.
. . . . (10 to 1 tchd 11 to 1) 1
2658* DOCTOOR (USA) [122] 7-10-10 A P McCoy, hld up in tch, led
2 out, hdd r-in, no extr. (13 to 2 op 7 to 2 tchd 4 to 1) 2
2693* EXPRESS GIFT [130] 8-11-4 N Williamson, mid-div, hdwy 3
out, str chal frm nxt, no extr r-in. . . . . (9 to 1 op 8 to 1) 3
2834² LADY DAISY (Ire) [133] 8-11-7 C F Swan, wtd wth, prog 5th,
rdn alng appr 2 out, styd on one pace. . . . . . . (14 to 1) 4
2329* FORESTAL [117] 5-10-5 T J Murphy, prmnt, pckd 3rd, rdn
appr 2 out, one pace. . . . .(10 to 1 op 8 to 1) 5

425

2695⁷ KADASTROF (Fr) [134] 7-11-1 (7*) X Aizpuru, *led to second,
led briefly appr 2 out, wkng whn not fluent last.*
..................................(40 to 1 op 33 to 1)   6
2933* MORE DASH THANCASH (Ire) [118] 7-10-6 Derek Byrne, *hld
up, hdwy 3 out, wknd appr nxt.*
.....................(13 to 2 op 6 to 1 tchd 7 to 1)   7
2591¹⁵ SILVER GROOM (Ire) [138] 7-11-7 (5*) S Ryan, *nvr better than
mid-div.*............................(20 to 1 op 16 to 1)   8
2591 CHIEF'S SONG [134] 7-11-8 R Dunwoody, *prmnt, lost pl
hfwy, rallied appr 2 out, wknd bef last.* (25 to 1 op 33 to 1)   9
2682* SAMANID (Ire) [112] 5-10-0 O Pears, *nvr better than mid-div.*
....(25 to 1 tchd 33 to 1)   10
2820⁶ KINGSFOLD PET [100] 8-11-4 D Skyrme, *mid-div, lost pl 3
out, some prog appr nxt, fdd.*
..................................(50 to 1 op 33 to 1 tchd 66 to 1)   11
2594² MR PERCY (Ire) [124] 6-10-12 S McNeill, *mid-div, wknd appr
2 out.*...................(12 to 1 op 10 to 1 tchd 14 to 1)   12
2806* SHINING EDGE [126] 5-11-0 G Bradley, *prmnt till wknd appr
2 out.*...................(12 to 1 op 10 to 1 tchd 14 to 1)   13
2780⁶ GROUND NUT (Ire) [123] 7-10-6 (5*) G Supple, *led second till
appr 2 out, sn wknd.*.......................(33 to 1 op 25 to 1)   14
2323³ DANEGOLD (Ire) [112] (v) 5-10-0 R Hughes, *midfield, lost pl 3
out, no dngr aftr.*.......................(14 to 1 tchd 16 to 1)   15
2778 SHANKAR (Ire) [131] 6-11-5 W Marston, *nvr dngrs, tld off.*
....(20 to 1 op 16 to 1 tchd 22 to 1)   16
2044² CHAI-YO [126] 7-11-0 G Upton, *hld up, str hdwy frm 3 out, ev
ch on bit whn f nxt.*......(14 to 1 op 12 to 1 tchd 16 to 1)   f
2806² STAR RAGE (Ire) [133] 7-11-7 D Gallagher, *hld up beh ldrs, hit
4th, not fluent and behind nxt, tld off whn pld up bef last.*
....(8 to 1 op 7 to 1 tchd 10 to 1)   pu
Dist: 2l, 1l, 1¾l, 3l, ½l, 4l, ½l, 2½l, 3½l, 3l. 3m 55.80s. a 8.80s (18 Ran).
SR: 42/50/57/58/39/55/35/54/47/   (Lady Bamford), P R Webber

3081 Hambro Countrywide Handicap Chase Class C (0-135 5-y-o and up) £6,872 3m 110yds........... (4:40)

2599⁴ SAMLEE (Ire) [115] 8-10-11 D Bridgwater, *wtd wth, prog frm
16th, led appr 3 out, drvn out and hld on flat.*
....(4 to 1 tchd 5 to 1)   1
1960* FULL OF FIRE [119] 10-11-1 A Thornton, *hld up, steady hdwy
11th, blun 13th, chsd wnr frm 2 out, ev ch r-in, kpt on same
pace.*......................(4 to 1 op 7 to 2 tchd 9 to 2)   2
2794³ AARDWOLF [128] 6-11-10 G Bradley, *led to 18th, lost pl and
out, rallied betw fnl 2, one pace r-in.*
....(3 to 1 fav op 11 to 4 tchd 100 to 30)   3
2692* DENVER BAY [119] 10-10-12 (3*) L Aspell, *hld up, led 18th till
appr 3 out, wknd bef last.*....(4 to 1 op 9 to 2 tchd 5 to 1)   4
2698 TOP BRASS (Ire) [104] 9-10-0 S McNeill, *mstk 16th, chsd ldr to
18th, wknd appr 3 out.*..(33 to 1 op 25 to 1 tchd 40 to 1)   5
2728² EQUITY PLAYER [107] 12-10-3 D Morris, *hld up, not fluent
16th, sn wknd, tld off whn pld up bef 3 out.*
....(9 to 2 tchd 6 to 1)   pu
2696⁴ MONTECOT (Fr) [120] 8-11-2 D Gallagher, *hld up, blun 8th, tld
off 12th, pld up bef nxt, broke blood vessel.*
....(10 to 1 op 8 to 1 tchd 14 to 1)   pu
Dist: ½l, 1l, 16l, 5l. 6m 28.80s. a 29.80s (7 Ran).
(White Lion Partnership), P J Hobbs

3082 H.M.S. Sandown Standard Open National Hunt Flat Class H (4,5,6-y-o) £1,406 2m 110yds....... (5:15)

BILLY BOX 5-11-4 D Bridgwater, *wtd wth, improved hfwy, led
o'r 2 fs out, styd on strly.*
....(11 to 4 fav op 4 to 1 tchd 9 to 2)   1
FORTUNES FLIGHT (Ire) 4-10-10 T J Murphy, *prmnt, chsd
wnr frm 2 fs out, no imprsn.*
....(25 to 1 op 20 to 1 tchd 33 to 1)   2
TIMELY MAGIC 5-11-4 A P McCoy, *hld up beh ldrs, ev ch
o'r 2 fs out, one pace.*....(9 to 1 op 6 to 1 tchd 10 to 1)   3
GOLDEN EAGLE 5-11-4 M A Fitzgerald, *hld up, hdwy o'r 2 fs
out, styd on frm over one out.*
....(4 to 1 op 3 to 1 tchd 5 to 1)   4
DESERT WAY (Ire) 4-10-10 J Culloty, *hld up, hdwy o'r 3 fs out,
one pace frm 2 out.*......(9 to 1 op 5 to 1 tchd 7 to 1)   5
HOMME DE FER 5-10-11 (7*) C Scudder, *wtd wth, improved
o'r 3 fs out, wknd appr last.*
....(14 to 1 op 16 to 1 tchd 20 to 1)   6
KABYLIE OUEST (Fr) 4-9-12 (7*) X Aizpuru, *styd on fnl 2 fs,
nrst finish.*.......................(33 to 1 op 20 to 1)   7
SATELLITE EXPRESS (Ire) 4-10-10 W Marston, *hld up, prog
o'r 6 fs out, wkng whn veered lft over one out.*
....(20 to 1 op 14 to 1 tchd 20 to 1)   8
KAPCO 5-11-4 G Bradley, *hld up, rapid hdwy aftr 4 fs, led
hfwy till o'r 2 out, sn wknd.*..........(16 to 1 op 8 to 1)   9
EAGLE DANCER 5-11-4 R Dunwoody, *wtd wth, hdwy o'r 6 fs
out, wknd over 2 out.*........(14 to 1 op 8 to 1 tchd 16 to 1)   10
2831⁷ SIR PRIZE 4-10-10 B Clifford, *led to hfwy, wknd o'r 2 fs
out.*......................(14 to 1 op 8 to 1)   11
2784⁶ MOONRAKER'S MIRAGE 6-11-4 P Holley, *nvr better than
mid-div.*......................(20 to 1 op 16 to 1 tchd 33 to 1)   12
EXPRESS AGAIN 5-11-4 J Railton, *trkd ldrs, wknd o'r 5 fs out.*
....(33 to 1)   13
SECURON GALE (Ire) 5-11-4 J R Kavanagh, *nvr better than
mid-div.*......................(20 to 1 op 10 to 1)   14

2939 MILL BAY SAM 6-11-4 Derek Byrne, *in tch till wknd o'r 2 fs
out.*......................(33 to 1 op 25 to 1)   15
CLARE'S SPRING (Ire) 4-10-7 (3*) T Dascombe, *al beh.*
....(16 to 1 op 10 to 1)   16
1648 TATIBAG 5-10-11 (7*) L Suthern, *midfield, lost pl o'r 4 fs out,
tld off.*......................(33 to 1 op 20 to 1)   17
PLUMPTON WOOD (Ire) 5-10-13 N Williamson, *beh fnl 5 fs,
tld off.*......(25 to 1 op 10 to 1 tchd 33 to 1)   18
LIFT THE LATCH (Ire) 5-11-4 L Harvey, *al beh, tld off.*
....(33 to 1 op 14 to 1)   19
LOVELY OUTLOOK 5-11-4 D Morris, *prmnt, wknd o'r 6 fs out,
tld off whn pld up ins last.*
....(25 to 1 op 20 to 1 tchd 33 to 1)   pu
Dist: 5l, 2½l, hd, 3½l, 2l, 3l, 3l, 2l, 2l, hd. 4m 5.70s. (20 Ran).
(Alec Tuckerman), G M McCourt

NAAS (IRE) (yielding to soft) Sunday March 9th

3083 Lakelands Maiden Hurdle (Div I) (5-y-o and up) £3,082 2m....... (2:00)

2703⁵ BAHAO (Ire) 6-11-6 D J Casey,............(7 to 1)   1
2901⁴ DUISKE ABBEY (Ire) 7-11-9 T P Treacy,.....(4 to 1 co-fav)   2
2647 VERYWELL (Ire) (bl) 6-10-13 (7*) B J Geraghty,.....(16 to 1)   3
538⁷ APPLAUSE (Ire) 6-11-6 M Moran,..............(8 to 1)   4
1554⁶ PROUDANDAMBITIOUS (Ire) 6-12-0 M Duffy,.....(7 to 1)   5
2649⁵ BRIAN'S DELIGHT (Ire) 6-11-7 (7*) D K Budds,.....(5 to 1)   6
2942⁶ NEARLY A LINE 5-10-11 (7*) P G Hourigan,.....(10 to 1)   7
2443 QUIPTECH (Ire) 6-11-6 T J Mitchell,...........(10 to 1)   8
2649⁶ GOLDEN PERK (Ire) 6-10-13 (7*) A O'Shea,.....(8 to 1)   9
2072⁸ CHATEAU MARTIN (Ire) 5-11-4 F Woods,.....(4 to 1 co-fav)   10
2649 MINSTRELS PRIDE (Ire) 6-10-13 (7*) M P Cooney, (20 to 1)   11
NOMINEE (Ire) 5-10-13 L P Cusack,...........(14 to 1)   12
2839 KARA'S DREAM (Ire) 9-11-1 C N Bowens,.....(16 to 1)   13
2866 TAP PRACTICE (Ire) 5-11-4 J P Broderick,.....(25 to 1)   14
1838 WARLOCKFOE (Ire) 6-10-8 (7*) Mr P J Crowley,.....(25 to 1)   15
LADY DE HATTON (Ire) 5-10-13 (7*) P Morris,.....(16 to 1)   16
2865 GOLDWREN (Ire) 8-10-8 (7*) R J Gordon,.....(100 to 1)   17
2839 PRAGUE SPRING 5-11-0 (7*) Mr A J Dempsey,.....(6 to 1)   18
2519⁷ ATHA BEITHE (Ire) (bl) 6-12-0 P Carberry,.....(4 to 1 co-fav)   f
Dist: ½l, 12l, 5½l, 2l. 3m 59.20s. (20 Ran).
(Michael Johnson), Gerard Stack

3084 Moat Handicap Chase (0-109 4-y-o and up) £3,082 2m 40yds...... (2:30)

2448³ PRATE BOX [-] 7-11-7 (7*) M D Murphy,.....(4 to 1)   1
2644* YANKIE LORD (Ire) [-] 5-11-9 F Woods,.....(9 to 4 fav)   2
2945² NORTHERN ACE [-] 11-9-7 T Horgan,.........(13 to 2)   3
2736² SORRY ABOUT THAT [-] 11-11-3 P Carberry,.....(5 to 2)   4
2868⁶ PEDE GALE (Ire) [-] 9-9-3 (7*) L J Fleming,.....(25 to 1)   5
2903⁴ TEMPLEROAN PRINCE [-] 10-11-9 J R Barry,.....(13 to 2)   6
1906⁸ TREENS FOLLY [-] 8-9-12 (3*) K Whelan,.....(16 to 1)   7
Dist: 3l, 6l, 10l, 20l. 4m 23.60s. (7 Ran).
(Miss Heather Scully), P Hughes

3085 Lakelands Maiden Hurdle (Div II) (5-y-o and up) £3,082 2m....... (3:00)

2737⁶ ONE WORD (Ire) 5-11-4 J Shortt,............(3 to 1 fav)   1
2865² RYTHM ROCK (Ire) 8-10-13 (7*) M W Martin,.....(7 to 1)   2
MOTION CARRIED (Ire) 5-10-11 (7*) Mr J Cash,.....(5 to 1)   3
2703⁹ BOPTWOPHAR (Ire) 5-11-4 J R Barry,.........(12 to 1)   4
2588⁵ AUBURN ROILELET (Ire) 5-10-10 (3*) U Smyth,.....(12 to 1)   5
977 COMAN'S JET (Ire) 7-11-7 (7*) M D Murphy,.....(4 to 1)   6
2383⁷ AISLING ALAINN (Ire) 5-11-4 P Carberry,.....(12 to 1)   7
LA GAZELLE (Ire) 5-10-13 D J Casey,.........(14 to 1)   8
2703 GALE JOHNSTON (Ire) 6-11-1 J P Broderick,.....(25 to 1)   9
2839⁷ STAR CLUB (Ire) 5-11-7 H Rogers,...........(8 to 1)   10
2900⁹ MR CAVALLO (Ire) 5-10-11 (7*) A O'Shea,.....(14 to 1)   11
2906⁹ GREY HORIZON (Ire) 6-11-6 P McWilliams,.....(20 to 1)   12
2757⁸ SPLEODRACH (Ire) 7-11-1 T P Treacy,.........(9 to 1)   13
SOCIETY BRIEF (Ire) 5-11-4 F Woods,.........(8 to 1)   14
GLENMULLEN ROSE (Ire) 5-10-8 (5*) P Morris,.....(14 to 1)   15
STORMY MISS (Ire) 5-10-13 T J Mitchell,.........(20 to 1)   16
BURTON BLACK (Ire) 6-10-10 (5*) T Martin,.....(20 to 1)   17
2866 LADY OF GRANGE (Ire) (bl) 5-11-7 F J Flood,.....(14 to 1)   18
OYSTON PRINCESS (Ire) 5-10-13 T Horgan,.....(14 to 1)   19
BOLD LILLIAN (Ire) 8-11-2 (7*) S McGovern,.....(14 to 1)   20
Dist: ¾l, 3l, 6l, 1½l. 4m 2.60s. (20 Ran).
(Reginald Roberts), Reginald Roberts

3086 Naas Handicap Hurdle (4-y-o and up) £6,850 2m 3f................ (3:30)

2841* TRYFIRION (Ire) [-] 8-11-4 K F O'Brien,.....(13 to 2)   1
2841³ APPELLATE COURT [-] (bl) 9-9-0 (7*) B J Geraghty, (10 to 1)   2
2836* OPERA HAT (Ire) [-] 5-9-10-3 P Carberry,.....(2 to 1 fav)   3
2170⁷ OWENBWEE (Ire) [-] 6-10-0 F Woods,.........(8 to 1)   4
2841² TARAJAN (USA) [-] (bl) 5-10-6 J Shortt,.........(8 to 1)   5
3072⁷ TOTAL CONFUSION [-] 10-9-8¹ D Bentley,.....(16 to 1)   6
2835* DELPHI LODGE (Ire) [-] 7-11-2 C F Swan,.....(13 to 2)   7
2733³ KHARASAR (Ire) [-] 7-11-7 (7*) A O'Shea,.....(10 to 1)   8
2837 ANNADOT (Ire) [-] 7-10-1 F J Flood,...........(14 to 1)   9

2835⁸ JODESI (Ire) [-] 7-10-8 D J Casey, ... (14 to 1) 10
2944³ PATTIE TIM (Ire) [-] 8-9-3 (7*) M D Murphy, ... (10 to 1) 11
    EMPEROR GLEN (Ire) [-] 9-9-7 T Horgan, ...(20 to 1) 12
2963⁷ MAYASTA (Ire) [-] 7-11-0 T J Mitchell, ... (10 to 1) 13
Dist: 2l, hd, ½l. 4m 41.40s. (13 Ran).

(Mrs M T Quinn), Victor Bowens

3087 Fishery Novice Hurdle (4-y-o and up) £3,082 2m. . . . .(4:00)

2708³ KILCOO BOY (Ire) 6-12-0 C F Swan. . . . .(Evens fav) 1
    GO ROGER GO (Ire) 5-11-3 (3*) K Whelan, ... (20 to 1) 2
2965⁷ RAINBOW VICTOR (Ire) 4-10-12 T Horgan, ... (12 to 1) 3
2732⁹ IDEAL PLAN (Ire) 7-12-0 D T Evans, ...(7 to 1) 4
2965⁴ STRATEGIC PLOY 4-10-13 T J Mitchell, ...(7 to 2) 5
2702* KEAL RYAN (Ire) 4-10-11 (7*) P J Dobbs, ... (10 to 1) 6
2965⁶ WELCOME PARADE 4-11-4 K F O'Brien, ...(8 to 1) 7
2643 MIND ME BRODY (Ire) 4-10-7 (5*) P Morris, ...(16 to 1) 8
2050 TAX REFORM (USA) 4-11-4 H Rogers, ... (10 to 1) 9
    MYSTERY LADY (Ire) 4-10-7 P Carberry, ... (50 to 1) 10
2832⁶ GIVEUPTHEFAGS (Ire) 4-10-5 (7*) A O'Shea, ...(33 to 1) 11
1709 DISPOSEN (Ire) 4-10-7 T P Treacy, ... (50 to 1) 12
2900 TOM THISTLE (Ire) 5-11-6 J R Barry, ... (33 to 1) 13
2669 FAATEQ 4-10-12 J Shortt, ...(16 to 1) 14
Dist: 2l, 3½l, 2l, nk. 3m 3.90s. (14 Ran).

(Patrick G J Murphy), A P O'Brien

3088 Monread Novice Chase (5-y-o and up) £3,082 3m. . . . . (4:30)

2904⁹ LEAMHOG (Ire) 7-11-8 T Horgan, ... (10 to 1) 1
2833² LE GINNO (Fr) 10-12-0 T P Treacy, ...(3 to 1) 2
2708⁹ CHANCE COFFEY 12-11-8 P F O'Donnell, ...(8 to 1) 3
2868³ SPIRE HILL (Ire) 8-11-1 (7*) Mr K Ross, ... (14 to 1) 4
2945⁷ ANOTHER DEADLY 10-12-0 P L Malone, ...(8 to 1) 5
    NEWTOWN ROAD (Ire) 6-11-8 P Leech, ... (50 to 1) 6
2904 CAVALLO (Fr) 7-11-5 (3*) K Whelan, ... (16 to 1) 7
2833³ MAID FOR DANCING (Ire) 8-10-10 (7*) Mr R H Fowler,
    . . . .(6 to 1) f
2840² NATIVE STATUS (Ire) 7-11-8 P Carberry, ...(7 to 4 fav) f
2868 SHUIL DAINGEAN (Ire) (bl) 7-11-8 T P Rudd, ... (16 to 1) f
2904 HILLHEAD (Ire) 8-11-8 L P Cusack, ... (12 to 1) f
2868⁶ BAILEYS BRIDGE (Ire) (bl) 6-11-1 (7*) M D Murphy, (25 to 1) f
2904⁸ CELTIC WHO (Ire) 6-11-8 T J Mitchell, ... (14 to 1) bd
2755⁷ LAKE TOUR (Ire) 7-11-9 J R Barry, ... (14 to 1) pu
2868⁵ CASTLE TIGER BAY (Ire) 6-11-8 K F O'Brien, ... (33 to 1) pu
Dist: 3½l, 12l, 7l, 5½l. 7m 2.30s. (15 Ran).

(Walter James Purcell), A P O'Brien

3089 Johnstown Handicap Hurdle (0-102 4-y-o and up) £3,082 2m. . . . . . (5:00)

1125 QUEEN'S FLAGSHIP (Ire) [-] 5-11-1 C N Bowens, (10 to 1) 1
2943³ BLITZER (Ire) [-] 5-11-3 (3*) Mr R Walsh, ...(8 to 1) 2
2943* ECLIPTIC MOON (Ire) [-] 7-10-5 T P Treacy, ... (4 to 1 fav) 3
2841 NORDIC SENSATION (Ire) [-] 8-11-0 (7*) Mr K Ross, (14 to 1) 4
21597 JOHNNY HANDSOME (Ire) [-] 7-10-13 C F Swan, . .(8 to 1) 5
1076⁹ SECRET PRINCE (Ire) [-] 6-9-11 C O'Brien, ...(20 to 1) 6
2585 DROICHEAD LAPEEN [-] 10-11-0 (7*) Mr T J Beattie,
    . . . .(14 to 1) 7
2366 HOME I'LL BE (Ire) [-] 7-9-1¹ (7*) M D Murphy, ... (16 to 1) 8
2445 KAVANAGHS DREAM (Ire) [-] 8-10-11 H Rogers, . . (20 to 1) 9
1839⁶ CLASHBEG (Ire) [-] 6-11-9 (3*) K Whelan, ... (10 to 1) 10
2834⁷ LAURA'S BEAU [-] 13-10-12 (7*) F M Berry, ... (33 to 1) 11
2866* MIDDLEOFTHENIGHT (Ire) [-] 5-10-7 (7*) L J Fleming,
    . . . . (6 to 1) 12
2834⁸ ALLARACKET (Ire) [-] (bl) 8-10-6 (7*) A O'Shea, . . .(25 to 1) 13
2753 LIOS NA MAOL (Ire) [-] 6-9-8 (5*) T Martin, ... (20 to 1) 14
2942⁷ OVER ALICE (Ire) [-] 5-10-6 F J Flood, ... (20 to 1) 15
2380⁴ COOKSGROVE ROSIE (Ire) [-] 5-10-5 P Leech, . . . (25 to 1) 16
2943⁵ DISTRICT JUSTICE [-] 10-10-11 M Duffy, ...(7 to 1) 17
1361 VALLEY OF KINGS (Ire) [-] 7-10-4 T Horgan, ... (10 to 1) 18
2865 ANNAELAINE (Ire) [-] 6-10-9 J Shortt, ... (10 to 1) 19
2415⁹ RUTABAGA (Ire) [-] 8-10-6 P L Malone, ... (20 to 1) 20
2865³ HEART 'N SOUL-ON (Ire) [-] 6-10-11 (7*) S M McGovern,
    . . . .(14 to 1) 21
2832⁸ PLAYPRINT [-] 4-9-12 (7*) D K Budds, ...(16 to 1) 22
Dist: ½l, 1l, 1½l, nk. 4m 0.70s. (22 Ran).

(A P Brady), Victor Bowens

3090 Maudlins I.N.H. Flat Race (5-y-o) £3,082 2m. . . . .(5:30)

    VERRAZANO BRIDGE (Ire) 11-9 (3*) Mr R Walsh, (4 to 1 co-
    . . . . fav) 1
2845⁸ EVENKEEL (Ire) (bl) 11-5 (7*) Mr A J Dempsey, ... (10 to 1) 2
2838³ CLASH OF THE GALES (Ire) 11-0 (7*) Mr J P McNamara,
    . . . . (13 to 2) 3
2845⁹ CHOICE JENNY (Ire) 11-7 Mr J A Nash, ... (10 to 1) 4
    BE MY MOT (Ire) 11-7 Mr A J Martin, ... (10 to 1) 5
2900 COTTAGE LORD (Ire) 11-0 (7*) Mr S P McCarthy, . . (25 to 1) 6
2845 CORNCAP (Ire) 11-5 (7*) Mr S J Mahon, ... (20 to 1) 7
1121⁸ NATIVE SHORE (Ire) 11-0 (7*) Mr K R O'Ryan, ... (12 to 1) 8
2946² GARRYDUFF SUPREME (Ire) 11-0 (7*) Mr Mark Walsh,
    . . . . (7 to 1) 9
2709 RASH REFLECTION (Ire) 11-12 Mr J P Dempsey, . . . (6 to 1) 10
    INAGH BROWNE (Ire) 11-7 Mr A R Coonan, ... (14 to 1) 11
    ASHWELL APRIL (Ire) 11-0 (7*) Miss M McKee, . . . (20 to 1) 12

    CALDRY LAD (Ire) 11-5 (7*) Mr A Fleming, . . (4 to 1 co-fav) 13
    PHARBRIG (Ire) 11-12 Mr D Marnane, ... (10 to 1) 14
    PAY THE MAN (Ire) 11-12 Mr P Fenton, ...(4 to 1 co-fav) 15
782 KARMAJO (Ire) 11-9 (3*) Mr E Norris, ... (25 to 1) 16
2525 LACKEN RIVER (Ire) 11-0 (7*) Mr R C Foster, ...(20 to 1) 17
2709⁹ WHITE SMOKE (Ire) 11-5 (7*) Mrs W O'Leary, ...(20 to 1) 18
    BUSHEY BOY (Ire) 11-12 Mr B M Cash, ... (14 to 1) 19
    BOYNE ROYALE (Ire) 11-5 (7*) Mr T J Beattie, ... (14 to 1) 20
Dist: 3l, 2½l, 20l, 8l. 3m 57.30s. (20 Ran).

(Mrs Peaches Taaffe), T J Taaffe

PLUMPTON (good to soft)
Monday March 10th
Going Correction: PLUS 1.40 sec. per fur. (races
1,3,5,7), PLUS 1.25 (2,4,6)

3091 Ardingly Novices' Hurdle Class E (4-y-o and up) £2,553 2m 1f. . . . . .(2:10)

2570⁴ CUTHILL HOPE (Ire) 6-11-2 Richard Guest, prmnt, trkd ldr 3
    out, rdn and led appr last, styd on wl.
    . . . . (13 to 8 fav op 6 to 4 tchd 2 to 1) 1
2256 SURANOM (Ire) 5-11-2 J F Titley, not fluent early, led till hrd
    rdn and hdd appr last, not quicken.
    . . . .(7 to 2 op 4 to 1 tchd 9 to 2) 2
2628⁷ DAYDREAMER (USA) 4-10-8 B Powell, mid-div, mstk second,
    hdwy 4th, one pace frm 3 out.
    . . . . (9 to 4 op 6 to 4 tchd 5 to 2) 3
2610⁴ ZADOK (bl) 5-11-2 B Fenton, styd on frm 3 out, nvr dngrs.
    . . . . (33 to 1 op 20 to 1) 4
2614³ KILSHEY 6-10-8 (3*) L Aspell, hdwy 3rd, jnd ldr nxt, wknd 3
    out. . . . . (7 to 1 op 5 to 1 tchd 8 to 1) 5
2927⁴ WELSH WIZZARD 5-10-9 (7*) Mr P O'Keeffe, mid-div, rdn 4th,
    wknd 6th. . . . .(25 to 1 op 20 to 1 tchd 33 to 1) 6
2614 KNOT TRUE 7-10-11 P Holley, nvr dngrs, lost tch 6th.
    . . . . (50 to 1 op 25 to 1) 7
2927 MY NAD KNOWS 4-10-8 T J O'Sullivan, prmnt, hrd rdn 6th,
    wkng whn blun nxt. . . . . (66 to 1 op 33 to 1) 8
    ARCUS (Ire) 4-10-3 (5*) A Bates, not fluent, al rear.
    . . . .(33 to 1 op 16 to 1 tchd 50 to 1) 9
2614 MEGAS 5-11-2 A Dicken, mid-div till wknd 6th.
    . . . . (33 to 1 op 14 to 1) 10
    CIVIL LANE (Ire) 5-11-2 D Morris, in tch till jmpd slwly and rear
    5th, pld up bef nxt. . . . . (50 to 1 op 20 to 1) pu
Dist: 5l, 12l, 8l, 26l, 2l, 2l, sht-hd, 12l, 12l. 4m 27.80s. a 30.80s (11 Ran).
SR: 18/13/-/-/-/-/

(Mrs Emma Gilchrist), M H Tompkins

3092 Corinthian-Casuals Novices' Chase Class E (5-y-o and up) £3,099 2m 5f . . . .(2:40)

2862² LIVELY KNIGHT 8-11-6 (3*) L Aspell, jmpd wl, led 5th, clr
    3 out, easily. . . . . (13 to 8 op 7 to 4 tchd 2 to 1) 1
2950 ANGELO'S DOUBLE (Ire) 9-11-2 B Powell, led to 5th, blun
    nxt, outpcd 4 out, no ch wth wnr.
    . . . . (15 to 8 on op 9 to 4 on tchd 7 to 4 on) 2
2928⁴ EAU SO SLOE 6-11-2 A Dicken, chsd ldrs, reminder 9th, sn
    lost tch, f 11th. . . . . (50 to 1 op 14 to 1) f
Dist: 23l. 5m 38.80s. a 32.80s (3 Ran).
SR: 29/-/-/

(A D Weller), J T Gifford

3093 Don Butchers Challenge Trophy Handicap Hurdle Class F (0-100 4-y-o and up) £2,012 2½m. . . . .(3:10)

2932* MAYB-MAYB [82] 7-11-4 J P McCoy, led to second,
    reminders 4th, mstk nxt, led 9th, clr 2 out, eased r-in.
    . . . . (Evens fav op 11 to 8) 1
2477² DO BE WARE [77] 7-11-5 B Fenton, hdwy hfwy, outpcd 9th,
    styd on to chase wnr appr last, no imprsn.
    . . . . (11 to 1 op 8 to 1 tchd 12 to 1) 2
2932⁴ SCRIPT [71] 6-10-13 W Marston, led second to 4th, mstk nxt,
    rdn and lost tch hfwy, ran on frm 2 out.
    . . . . (11 to 2 op 5 to 1 tchd 12 to 1) 3
2977³ HELLO ME MAN (Ire) [79] 9-11-7 Mr J L Llewellyn, led 4th,
    mstk and rdn 7th, hdd and pckd 9th, wknd appr 2 out.
    . . . .(6 to 1 op 5 to 1 tchd 13 to 2) 4
2770⁴ AUGUST TWELFTH [81] 9-11-9 D J Kavanagh, chsd ldrs till
    hrd rdn and wknd 8th, fnshd lme.
    . . . . (100 to 30 op 3 to 1 tchd 9 to 2) 5
2765⁹ KENTAVRUS WAY (Ire) [69] 6-10-4 (7*) M Batchelor, unruly
    bef strt, refused to race, took no part.
    . . . . (12 to 1 op 8 to 1 tchd 14 to 1) I
Dist: 12l, 7l, 2½l, 14l. 5m 23.20s. a 46.20s (6 Ran).

(J Neville), J Neville

3094 Philip Hall Memorial Handicap Chase Class E (0-110 5-y-o and up) £2,878 2m 5f. . . . .(3:40)

2612⁶ REGAL AURA [64] 7-10-2 W Marston, led to 3rd, led 8th,
    clr whn jmpd lft 2 out. . . (16 to 1 op 12 to 1 tchd 20 to 1) 1
2931² WINSPIT (Ire) [86] 7-11-10 W McFarland, led 7th to 8th, hrd
    rdn and outpcd appr 3 out, second and btn whn blun nxt.
    . . . . (11 to 4 op 5 to 2 tchd 3 to 1) 2

2729³ KEY PLAYER (Ire) [77] 8-11-1 D O'Sullivan, *led 3rd to 7th, jmpd slwly and lost tch 11th.*
............................(11 to 10 on op 11 to 8 on tchd Evens) 3
2931 GOLDEN OPAL [79] 12-11-3 B Powell, *rear till blun and uns rdr 4th.*............................(3 to 1 op 5 to 2 tchd 100 to 30) ur
Dist: Dist, 28l. 5m 50.90s. a 44.90s (4 Ran).

(Mrs V O'Brien), D C O'Brien

3095 Uckfield Handicap Hurdle Class E
(0-110 4-y-o and up) £2,217 2m 1f ....(4:10)

2982³ DERISBAY (Ire) [79] (bl) 9-9-7 (7*) M Batchelor, *chsd ldrs, plxn and outpcd 7th, hrd ridden appr last, styd on to ld r-in.*
............................(13 to 2 op 9 to 2 tchd 7 to 1) 1
2949³ NIPPER REED [103] 7-11-10 A P McCoy, *led to 7th, rdn 3 out, rallied to ld 2 out, hdd and not quicken r-in.*
............................(11 to 10 on op 5 to 4 tchd 6 to 5 on) 2
3078² KELLY MAC [89] 7-10-10 L Aspell, *cl up, led 7th to 2 out, no extr r-in.*............................(5 to 2 op 7 to 4) 3
2878⁷ PERSIAN MYSTIC (Ire) [90] 5-10-11 W Marston, *chsd ldr to hfwy, outpcd 6th, beh frm 3 out.*
............................(12 to 1 op 9 to 2 tchd 14 to 1) 4
DOCTOR DEATH (Ire) [88] (v) 6-10-9 A Dicken, *rear, jmpd slwly second and 3rd, hrd rdn and lost tch 4th, pld up bef 2 out.*
............................(9 to 1 op 12 to 1 tchd 14 to 1) pu
Dist: 3l, hd, 21l. 4m 27.70s. a 30.70s (5 Ran).
SR: 3/24/10/-/-/ (Miss Julie Self), J J Bridger

3096 'Clapper' Challenge Cup Hunters'
Chase Class H (5-y-o and up) £1,492
3m 1f 110yds. ....(4:40)

2981² JUPITER MOON 8-11-7 (7*) Mr J M Pritchard, *chsd ldrs, led 16th, hng lft r-in, hld on wl.* (8 to 1 op 5 to 1 tchd 9 to 1) 1
2887⁴ LOYAL NOTE 9-12-5 (3*) Mr Simon Andrews, *hdwy 8th, str chal frm 2 out, kpt on wl.*............................(5 to 2 tchd 3 to 1) 2
2875² VICOMPT DE VALMONT (bl) 12-12-0 (5*) Mr T Mitchell, *beh, rdn 7th, prmsg hdwy 14th, chsd ldrs nxt, one pace frm 4 out.*
............................(6 to 5 on op 6 to 4 on tchd 11 to 10 on) 3
NORTHERN VILLAGE 10-11-7 (7*) Capt D Alers-Hankey, *chsd ldrs, wknd 14th, wknd nxt.*
............................(14 to 1 op 16 to 1 tchd 12 to 1) 4
2793 FIFTH AMENDMENT (bl) 12-11-11⁴ (7*) Mr A Hales, *led 7th to 16th, wknd quickly, 5th and no ch whn refused nxt.*
............................(20 to 1 op 14 to 1) ref
ROYAL IRISH 13-11-7 (7*) Miss C Townsley, *in tch till rdn and outpcd 13th, sn beh, pld up bef 4 out.*
............................(40 to 1 op 20 to 1 tchd 50 to 1) pu
BALLYANDREW 12-11-7 (7*) Miss S Gritton, *led to 7th, lost tch and rdn 13th, pld up aftr nxt.*
............................(25 to 1 op 20 to 1 tchd 33 to 1) pu
Dist: 1½l, 6l, dist. 7m 6.50s. a 52.50s (7 Ran).

(The Stanton Seven), Mrs C Hicks

3097 European Breeders Fund 'National
Hunt' Novices' Hurdle Qualifier
Class E (5,6,7-y-o) £2,343 2½m ....(5:10)

2926* STORMY PASSAGE (Ire) 7-11-3 A P McCoy, *trkd ldr 5th, led nxt, clr 9th, easily.*............................(10 to 1 on op 7 to 1 on) 1
2775⁵ SUPREME TROGLODYTE (Ire) 5-10-2 (5*) Sophie Mitchell, *hdwy to chase ldrs 6th, outpcd 9th, sn btn, wnt second r-in.*
............................(12 to 1 op 5 to 1 tchd 14 to 1) 2
2642⁶ BROOK BEE 5-10-12 W Marston, *led to 6th, outpcd 9th, sn btn, lost second pl r-in.*............................(25 to 1 op 5 to 1) 3
2015⁸ PITARRY 7-10-12 B Fenton, *chsd ldrs till mstk 5th, sn lost tch, f 7th.*............................(25 to 1 op 12 to 1) f
Dist: 21l, 3½l. 5m 18.30s. a 41.30s (4 Ran).

(Peter Luff), P J Hobbs

STRATFORD (good)
Monday March 10th
Going Correction: PLUS 0.60 sec. per fur.

3098 'Tip-top Timeform Ratings' Novices'
Chase Class D (5-y-o and up) £4,354
2½m. ....(2:20)

2890* TEINEIN (Fr) 6-11-7 N Williamson, *hld up, hdwy 5 out, led r-in, cmftbly.*............................(11 to 8 on op 5 to 4 on tchd 6 to 4 on) 1
2690³ THE CAPTAIN'S WISH 6-11-2 R Johnson, *chsd ldrs, led 2 out, hdd r-in, no ch whn wnr.* (3 to 1 op 9 to 4 tchd 100 to 30) 2
2798 DANDIE IMP 9-11-2 D Walsh, *led, hdd 2 out, styd on same pace.*............................(66 to 1 op 33 to 1) 3
1805⁵ TOTAL ASSET 7-11-2 Gary Lyons, *mid-div, effrt 5 out, sn lost tch.*............................(66 to 1 op 33 to 1) 4
2724⁶ CHAPILLIERE (Fr) 7-11-2 S McNeill, *prmnt till wknd 4 out.*
............................(33 to 1 op 25 to 1 tchd 50 to 1) 5
GO MARY 11-10-11 J R Kavanagh, *in tch, rdn 6 out, sn wknd.*
............................(33 to 1 op 25 to 1 tchd 50 to 1) 6
1671³ MR SNAGGLE (Ire) 8-11-2 S Curran, *f 1st.*
............................(16 to 1 op 10 to 1) f

2890 BENJI 6-11-2 J A McCarthy, *in rear till f 6th.*
............................(100 to 1 op 33 to 1) f
2726 MY WARRIOR 9-11-2 L Harvey, *sn beh, pld up bef 4th.*
............................(100 to 1 op 33 to 1) pu
2438 BEST OF FRIENDS (Ire) 7-11-2 J Culloty, *chsd ldrs till pld up bef 3 out, lme.*............................(6 to 1 op 9 to 2) pu
2750 LEDBURIAN 7-10-13 (3*) P Henley, *al in rear, beh whn pld up bef tenth.*............................(100 to 1 op 50 to 1) pu
Dist: 2l, 6l, 21l, 24l, 13l. 5m 6.60s. a 26.60s (11 Ran).

(Simon Sainsbury), Capt T A Forster

3099 Richardson Parkway Selling Hurdle
Class G (4,5,6-y-o) £2,999 2m 3f ....(2:50)

2804³ RIVERBANK ROSE (v) 6-10-7 (3*) Guy Lewis, *made all, mstk last, rdn out.*............................(13 to 2 op 6 to 1) 1
1928³ ALWAYS GREENER (Ire) 6-11-8 S Curran, *chsd ldrs, rdn 2 out, styd on same pace appr last.*
............................(9 to 2 op 4 to 1 tchd 7 to 1) 2
2896⁶ STAR PERFORMER (Ire) 6-11-2 (5*) O Burrows, *prmnt, rdn appr 2 out, styd on same pace.*
............................(5 to 2 fav op 4 to 1 tchd 11 to 4) 3
2973 DANNY GALE (Ire) 6-11-7 S McNeill, *chsd ldrs till lost pl 5th, styd on appr last.*............................(10 to 1 op 5 to 1 tchd 11 to 1) 4
2886³ BATTLESHIP BRUCE (bl) 5-11-1 R Dunwoody, *trkd ldrs till wknd appr 3 out.*............................(4 to 1 op 7 to 2 tchd 9 to 2) 5
2616⁷ YELLOW DRAGON (Ire) 4-10-13 K Gaule, *mid-div, effrt 5 out, wknd nxt.*............................(11 to 2 op 4 to 1 tchd 13 to 2) 6
2898 ROC AGE 6-10-10 D Leahy, *in tch to 6th.*............................(20 to 1) 7
2387 STIPPLE 6-10-10 J Culloty, *al in rear.* (50 to 1 op 33 to 1) 8
2387 IRISH KINSMAN 4-10-2 (5*) Mr R Thornton, *mid-div, rdn 6th, sn beh.*............................(50 to 1 op 33 to 1) 9
ERIC THE KING 6-11-7 P McLoughlin, *mid-div, mstk 6th, sn beh.*............................(20 to 1 op 50 to 1) 10
BOLD TIME MONKEY 6-10-10 C Llewellyn, *al in rear.*
............................(50 to 1 op 33 to 1) 11
NEW REGIME (Ire) 4-10-2 J Supple, *beh frm 5th, tld off whn pld up bef 2 out.*............................(66 to 1 op 33 to 1) pu
401 KERRIER (Ire) 5-10-8 (7*) A Dowling, *al in rear, tld off whn pld up bef 3 out.*............................(50 to 1 op 33 to 1) pu
MS JONES (Ire) 4-9-10¹ (7*) L Suthern, *blundd 3rd sn wl beh, tld off.*............................(100 to 1 op 50 to 1) pu
Dist: 10l, 1l, 16l, 4l, dist, 2½l, 9l, 8l, 24l, 30l. 4m 38.30s. a 18.30s (14 Ran).
SR: 13/15/13/-/-/-/ (Don Walker, Mr F E & Mrs J J Brindley), W Clay

3100 'Make Your Racing Pay With
Timeform' Handicap Hurdle Class C
(0-130 4-y-o and up) £4,328 2m
110yds. ....(3:20)

2553⁷ DESERT MOUNTAIN (Ire) [109] 4-10-7 D Gallagher, *al prmnt, led last, rdn out.*............................(5 to 1 tchd 11 to 2) 1
2880* DURANO [107] 6-10-13 R Garritty, *with ldr, led 5th, rdn and hdd last, not quicken.*......(7 to 2 op 3 to 1 tchd 4 to 1) 2
2681* KINTAVI [99] 7-10-5 P Niven, *trkd ldrs, ev ch frm 3 out, mstk last, no extr.*............................(9 to 4 fav tchd 5 to 2) 3
2716* CELESTIAL CHOIR [120] 7-11-12 B Storey, *hld up, hdwy 5th, ran on one pace frm 2 out.* (7 to 2 op 3 to 1 tchd 4 to 1) 4
2949⁶ GOLDINGO [107] 10-10-13 J R Kavanagh, *hld up, outpcd 5th, no dngr aftr.*............................(10 to 1 op 7 to 1) 5
2923⁹ KINO'S CROSS [105] 8-10-11 R Johnson, *chsd ldrs till wknd appr 3 out.*............................(16 to 1 op 5 to 1 tchd 33 to 1) 6
2933² HOLDERS HILL (Ire) [103] 5-10-9 R Dunwoody, *made most to 5th, sn rdn and wknd.*....(15 to 2 op 7 to 1 tchd 8 to 1) 7
BALLET ROYAL (USA) [115] 8-11-0 (7*) A Dowling, *sn beh, tld off whn pld up bef 3 out.*...(25 to 1 op 20 to 1) pu
Dist: 2½l, 3l, 3l, 13l, 5l, 8l. 4m 2.20s. a 16.20s (8 Ran).
SR: 16/19/8/26/-/ (Easy Monk Partnership), N A Callaghan

3101 '50 Years Of Timeform' Handicap
Chase Class C (0-130 5-y-o and up)
£5,312 3m. ....(3:50)

2599 CHURCH LAW [102] 10-10-1 R Supple, *hld up, hdwy to chase ldr 5th, led 2 out, styd on strly.*......(6 to 1 tchd 7 to 1) 1
2627* MERLINS DREAM (Ire) [113] 8-10-12 J Osborne, *led till hdd 2 out, mstk last, styd on same pace.*... (5 to 4 fav op Evens) 2
2069⁵ PYR FOUR [125] 10-11-10 D Bridgwater, *chsd ldr, mstk 4th, lost pl nxt, rallied 9th, rdn appr last, styd on same pace.*
............................(14 to 1 op 10 to 1 tchd 16 to 1) 3
2883³ NO PAIN NO GAIN (Ire) [117] 9-11-2 P Hide, *hld up in tch, effrt 4 out, wknd nxt.*............................(3 to 1 op 7 to 2 tchd 4 to 1) 4
2314 POSTMAN'S PATH [103] 11-10-2 N Williamson, *prmnt till wknd 3 out.*............................(25 to 1 op 20 to 1) 5
LIGHT VENEER [120] 12-11-5 Derek Byrne, *prmnt till lost pl 5th, sn beh, tld off.*......(11 to 1 op 7 to 1 tchd 12 to 1) 6
2592 AROUND THE HORN [129] 10-12-0 S McNeill, *hld up, blundd and uns rdr 12th.*....(10 to 1 op 8 to 1 tchd 11 to 1) ur
Dist: 6l, 4l, 4l, 8l, dist. 6m 9.40s. a 24.40s (7 Ran).

(Mrs L C Taylor), Mrs L C Taylor

3102 Credit Call Cup Novices' Hunters'
Chase Class H (5-y-o and up) £1,943
3m. ....(4:20)

2531* ORCHESTRAL SUITE (Ire) 9-11-13 (7*) Mr F Hutsby, *chsd ldrs, led 3 out, styd on strly*............ (5 to 2 tchd 3 to 1) 1
KING'S TREASURE (USA) 8-12-3 (7*) Mr A Balding, *chsd ldrs, led 5th, hdd 3 out, outpcd appr last.*
.... (Evens fav op 11 to 10 tchd 6 to 5) 2
2891⁴ IDEAL PARTNER (Ire) 8-11-12 (5*) Mr R Thornton, *prmnt, drvn alng 4 out, wknd appr 2 out*...... (12 to 1 op 8 to 1) 3
ROYAL SEGOS 10-11-11¹ (7*) Mr C Stockton, *led till 5th, rdn and wknd 4 out.*.................. (16 to 1 op 14 to 1) 4
TANGLE BARON 9-11-10 (7*) Miss J Cumings, *prmnt, mstk 11th, wknd 5 out.*.......................... (20 to 1) 5
2608⁴ NOT MY LINE (Ire) 8-11-12 (5*) Mr A Sansome, *mid-div, rdn appr 5 out, sn lost tch*............... (50 to 1 op 33 to 1) 6
RAMBLING LORD (Ire) 9-11-10 (7*) Mr G J Smith, *hld up, nvr dngrs.*........................ (25 to 1 op 20 to 1) 7
2875 RISING SAP 7-11-10 (7*) Mr A Dalton, *hld up, hdwy tenth, wknd 4 out.*.................... (33 to 1 op 25 to 1) 8
FANTASTIC FLEET (Ire) 5-11-0 (7*) Mr R Wakley, *hld up, hdwy whn blundd and uns rdr 11th..* (25 to 1 op 16 to 1) ur
TELLAPORKY 8-11-10 (7*) Mr A Middleton, *hld up, mstk 3rd, hdwy 7th, blundd and uns rdr 11th..* (66 to 1 op 100 to 1) ur
BABIL 12-11-12 (5*) Mr J Trice-Rolph, *prmnt to tenth, beh whn pld up bef 4 out.*............. (16 to 1 tchd 20 to 1) pu
FREDDIE FOX 11-11-13 (7*) Mr T Garton, *beh frm 6th, pld up bef 12th.*..................... (16 to 1 op 14 to 1) pu
Dist: 14l, 3l, 2l, 1l, 20l, 3l, 3l. 6m 12.00s. a 27.00s (12 Ran).
(Exors Of The Late Mr G Pidgeon), Miss Jennifer Pidgeon

3103 'Bet-Compelling Timeform Commentaries' Novices' Hurdle Class D (4-y-o and up) £3,421 2¾m 110yds
.... (4:50)

2666¹ MAHLER 7-11-2 D Walsh, *al prmnt, led appr 4 out, rdn out.*
.... (5 to 1 tchd 9 to 2) 1
2248⁵ DUBLIN FREDDY 6-11-9 N Williamson, *hld up, hdwy 5 out, pckd 2 out, rdn appr last, ran on.*
.... (9 to 2 op 3 to 1 tchd 5 to 1) 2
2771⁵ TOBY BROWN 4-10-7 R Dunwoody, *al prmnt, chsd wnr 4 out, mstk nxt, rdn and hit last, not quicken.*
.... (5 to 4 fav op 11 to 8 tchd 13 to 8) 3
1866¹ SUN OF SPRING 7-11-2 J Culloty, *chsd ldrs, lost pl appr 4 out, kpt on frm 2 out.*............ (33 to 1 op 20 to 1) 4
2785⁸ WHITER MORN 7-10-4 (7*) Mr O McPhail, *nvr trbld ldrs.*
.... (66 to 1 op 33 to 1 tchd 100 to 1) 5
2384 HIT THE BID (Ire) 6-11-2 J R Kavanagh, *hld up, hdwy hfwy, wkng whn blundd badly 3 out.*...... (66 to 1 op 50 to 1) 6
2874⁴ LITTLE JAKE (Ire) 7-11-2 R Johnson, *prmnt till wknd appr 4 out.*.................... (5 to 1 op 4 to 1 tchd 11 to 2) 7
2283 JUSTJIM 5-11-2 C Llewellyn, *chsd ldrs, drvn alng 5 out, sn wknd.*..................... (20 to 1 op 16 to 1) 8
2498 TYPHOON (Ire) 7-11-2 L Harvey, *strted slwly, al towards rear, beh whn pld up bef 2 out.*.......... (66 to 1 op 50 to 1) pu
1928⁹ BLUE AND ROYAL (Ire) (bl) 5-11-2 Derek Byrne, *in tch till wknd appr 4 out, beh whn pld up bef 2 out.*
.... (25 to 1 op 16 to 1) pu
2605⁷ MADAM POLLY 5-10-8 (3*) P Henley, *prmnt till wknd 6th, beh whn pld up bef 3 out.*............... (50 to 1 op 33 to 1) pu
1792 STELLAR FORCE (Ire) 6-11-2 J A McCarthy, *rcd keenly, led appr 3rd, hdd 4 out, wknd quickly, pld up bef 2 out.*
.... (25 to 1 op 10 to 1) pu
2784⁹ ACT IN TIME (Ire) 5-11-2 P Niven, *led till appr 3rd, wknd aftr 5 out, pld up bef 2 out*.... (20 to 1 op 16 to 1 tchd 25 to 1) pu
Dist: 1½l, 1½l, 14l, 20l, 2l, 22l, 6l. 5m 40.30s. a 28.30s (13 Ran).
(English Badminton Partnership), N A Twiston-Davies

TAUNTON (good)
Monday March 10th
Going Correction: PLUS 0.50 sec. per fur.

3104 Shepton Mallet Conditional Jockeys' Handicap Chase Class F (0-105 4-y-o and up) £2,556 2m 110yds
.... (2:00)

2864⁷ DR ROCKET [77] (v) 12-9-9 (8*) X Aizpuru, *in tch, chsd ldr frm 5th, led 3 out, drvn out and ran on wl r-in.*
.... (10 to 30 op 5 to 2) 1
2261⁸ LASATA [102] 12-11-9 (5*) J Power, *hld up beh ldrs, hit 3rd, chlgd frm 3 out, hit last, unbl to quicken r-in.*
.... (9 to 1 op 5 to 1) 2
2748³ CHRIS'S GLEN [75] (v) 8-10-11 Michael Brennan, *chsd ldr, hit 4th, lft in ld nxt, hdd 3 out, wn tire.*
.... (11 to 4 op 3 to 1 tchd 7 to 2) 3
2876⁸ GIVRY (Ire) [80] 7-9-10 (10*) R Hobson, *led till f 5th.*
.... (6 to 1 op 4 to 1) f
2767² FENWICK [82] 10-10-5 (3*) T Dascombe, *hld up beh ldrs, cl appr 7th, wknd and uns rdr 9th*..... (9 to 4 fav tchd 11 to 4) ur
Dist: 2l, 14l. 4m 12.40s. a 20.40s (5 Ran).
(The Rocketeers), R Dickin

3105 Melody Man Challenge Cup Handicap Hurdle Class E (0-110 4-y-o and up) £2,242 2m 3f 110yds......(2:30)

2982² FONTANAYS (Ire) [91] (v) 9-10-3 (7*) R Hobson, *chsd ldr frm second, led 7th, clr from nxt, rdn out betw fnl 2..* (11 to 4 jt-fav op 3 to 1 tchd 100 to 30 and 7 to 2) 1
2896⁹ DESERT FORCE (Ire) [92] 8-10-11 R Farrant, *hld up, hdwy 7th, chsd wnr frm nxt, rdn and no imprsn...* (11 to 2 op 9 to 2) 2
2896 MISS MARIGOLD [92] (bl) 8-10-8 (3*) T Dascombe, *hld up, rdn alng appr 7th, hdwy 3 out, wknd bef nxt.*
.... (5 to 1 op 4 to 1) 3
3049³ SHAHRANI [105] (bl) 5-11-10 Jamie Evans, *prmnt, hit 7th, sn rdn and btn*...... (11 to 4 jt-fav op 5 to 2 tchd 3 to 1) 4
FROWN [97] 7-11-2 M A Fitzgerald, *hld up, hdwy 7th, wknd nxt.*..................... (11 to 2 op 9 to 2 tchd 6 to 1) 5
3027 CONCINNITY (USA) [81] 8-9-8¹ (7*) M Griffiths, *not fluent, nvr dngrs.*................. (25 to 1 tchd 33 to 1 and 20 to 1) 6
1947¹ SHEEP STEALER [86] 9-10-5 (7*) Chris Webb, *led, jmpd slwly second, hdd and mstk second, fdd.....* (11 to 1 op 8 to 1) 7
Dist: 9l, 7l, 13l, 5l, 1½l, 18l. 4m 36.40s. a 18.40s (7 Ran).
(M A Dore), G M McCourt

3106 March Selling Hurdle Class G (4,5,6-y-o) £1,889 2m 1f............(3:00)

2804 HAWANAFA 4-10-3 C Maude, *al hndy, led appr 2 out, drvn out.*...................... (4 to 1 op 5 to 2) 1
2999³ A S JIM 6-11-2 V Slattery, *led till appr 2 out, still ev ch und pres last, unbl to quicken r-in....* (7 to 2 fav op 4 to 1) 2
2872⁸ DENOMINATION (USA) 5-12-2 B Moore, *took keen hold, prmnt, rdn and outpcd frm 3 out.*....... (7 to 1 op 4 to 1) 3
2385⁸ PAULTON 4-10-8 R Greene, *towards rear, styd on one pace frm 3 out, nvr nrr..*................ (7 to 1 op 4 to 1) 4
2668 SONG OF KENDA 5-10-6 (5*) D Salter, *trkd ldrs to 6th, sn btn.*
.... (10 to 1 op 14 to 1 tchd 16 to 1) 5
2390 ROSE OF GLENN 6-10-11 T Jenks, *prmnt, hit 1st, jmpd slwly 5th, wknd frm 3 out.*.................. (20 to 1) 6
2784 MAC'SMYUNCLE 6-11-2 Mr A Holdsworth, *rdn appr 6th, no imprsn.*.................. (25 to 1 op 16 to 1) 7
2242 MISS NIGHT OWL 6-10-11 J Frost, *hld up, hdwy frm 3 out, jmpd lft nxt, sn wknd.*............ (20 to 1 op 12 to 1) 8
NDABA 6-10-13 (3*) T Dascombe, *mid-div, effrt 6th, wknd 3 out.*...................... (25 to 1 op 16 to 1) 9
2668 FIERY FOOTSTEPS 5-10-4 (7*) T O'Connor, *al beh, tld off.*
.... (25 to 1 op 16 to 1) 10
2430 CHALCUCHIMA 4-10-8 J Railton, *al beh, tld off whn pld up bef 2 out.*................. (33 to 1 tchd 50 to 1) pu
2959 KIRBY MOORSIDE 6-11-2 S Burrough, *prmnt, wknd 5th, tld off whn pld up bef 3 out.*......... (33 to 1 tchd 50 to 1) pu
Dist: 2½l, 15l, 2½l, ½l, 5l, 2½l, 8l, 5l, dist. 4m 2.60s. a 19.60s (12 Ran).
(Geo Taylor), Miss K M George

3107 Royal Bath & West Novices' Chase Class D (5-y-o and up) £3,355 2m 3f
.... (3:30)

3038³ AFTER THE FOX 10-10-9 (7*) Mr J Tizzard, *hld up, jnd issue 8th, led sn aftr 4 out, clr whn hit last.....* (4 to 1 op 3 to 1) 1
2748 MOZEMO 10-11-2 Jamie Evans, *chsd ldr, hit 6th, led 8th, hdd sn aftr 4 out, one pace aftr 3 out.*
.... (15 to 8 op 2 to 1 tchd 9 to 4) 2
2664³ LUCKY EDDIE (Ire) (bl) 6-11-2 C Maude, *led to 8th, wkng whn hit 3 out.....*........ (11 to 10 on op Evens tchd 6 to 5 on) 3
2664 RUSTIC FLIGHT 10-10-9 (7*) M Griffiths, *not fluent, sn beh, tld off.*...................... (50 to 1 op 20 to 1) 4
Dist: 9l, 29l, 24l. 4m 58.80s. a 27.80s (4 Ran).
(Mrs Robert Blackburn), N J Hawke

3108 Bath & West Members Maiden Hurdle Class F (4-y-o and up) £2,249 2m 3f 110yds....................(4:00)

2893³ FASIL (Ire) 4-10-10 T Jenks, *hld up beh ldrs, hdwy appr 7th, led bef 2 out, drvn out.* (7 to 4 fav op Evens tchd 15 to 8) 1
2782⁸ KINNESCASH (Ire) 4-10-10 M A Fitzgerald, *hld up in tch, ev ch 2 out, one pace r-in.* (12 to 1 op 10 to 1 tchd 14 to 1) 2
LORD MILLS (Ire) 6-11-5 T J Murphy, *hld up towards rear, prog appr 6th, ev ch 2 out, no extr r-in.*
.... (10 to 1 op 8 to 1 tchd 12 to 1) 3
2758⁴ COUNTRY LOVER (bl) 6-11-5 Jamie Evans, *prmnt, rdn and ev ch 3 out, wknd bef nxt..* (7 to 1 op 5 to 1) 4
2656³ KEEN BID (Ire) 6-11-5 M Richards, *trkd ldrs, led 6th till appr 2 out, sn wknd.*............... (10 to 1 op 6 to 1) 5
THE PARSONS FOX 5-11-5 S Wynne, *nvr on terms.*
.... (33 to 1 op 14 to 1) 6
2959³ AMBER RING 4-10-5 C Maude, *beh frm 7th.*
.... (40 to 1 op 20 to 1) 7
2899⁵ MISS MATCH 6-10-9 (5*) D Salter, *beh frm 7th.*
.... (33 to 1 op 20 to 1) 8
3028 COOL VIRTUE (Ire) 6-11-0 A Thornton, *hld up beh ldrs, wknd appr 7th.*................. (9 to 2 op 5 to 1 tchd 4 to 1) 9
2876⁴ ROLL AGAIN 6-11-5 G Supple, *nvr on terms.*
.... (25 to 1 op 16 to 1) 10
2893 CHURCHWORTH 6-11-5 J Railton, *led to second, wknd quickly 6th, tld off whn pld up bef nxt.* (33 to 1 op 12 to 1) pu
MILESTONE 5-11-5 T Dascombe, *al beh, tld off whn pld up bef 7th.*.................. (150 to 1 op 33 to 1 tchd 200 to 1) pu
2898⁵ CARLINGFORD GALE (Ire) 6-11-0 R Farrant, *keen hold, led second, hit 5th, hdd nxt, sn wknd, tld off whn pld up bef 2 out.*
.... (10 to 1 op 12 to 1 tchd 16 to 1) pu

2248 ST MABYN INN BOY 5-11-5 S Burrough, *al beh, tld off whn pld up bef 2 out*......(100 to 1 op 50 to 1 tchd 150 to 1) pu
Dist: 2½l, 1¼l, 12l, 6l, 8l, 5l, 2l, ½l, 10l. 4m 36.70s. a 18.70s (14 Ran).

(Tony Usher), N J H Walker

3109 Somerset Hunters' Chase Class H
(6-y-o and up) £1,040 3m..... (4:30)

FULL ALIRT 9-11-7 (7*) Miss S Young, *led 5th, made rst, hrd pressed last, ran on wl*................(11 to 2 op 7 to 2) 1
2887² GRANVILLE GUEST 11-12-5 (7*) Mr J Tizzard, *al hndy, chsd wnr frm 12th, str chal whn hit last, edgd lft and wknd r-in.*
.....................(11 to 8 fav op 5 to 4 tchd 6 to 4) 2
RAGTIME BOY 9-12-0 (5*) Mr A Farrant, *hld up, hdwy 13th, wknd frm 4 out*..............(3 to 1 tchd 100 to 30) 3
1101 ARTFUL ARTHUR 11-11-12 (7*) Mr J Grassick, *hld up, rdn aftr 12th, sn tld off*..................(20 to 1 op 16 to 1) 4
PRINCE NEPAL 13-12-5 (7*) Mr G Barfoot-Saunt, *lft in ld 1st, hit nxt, hdd 3rd, mstks 6th and nxt, wknd 13th.*
.....................(40 to 1 op 33 to 1 tchd 50 to 1) 5
MO'S CHORISTER 11-11-12 (7*) Miss F Wilson, *led till f 1st.*
.....................(33 to 1 op 25 to 1 tchd 40 to 1) f
DOUBTING DONNA 11-12-2 (5*) Mr J Jukes, *hld up, reminders appr 11th, prog 13th, cl 4th whn blun and uns rdr 15th.*......................(9 to 1 op 10 to 1) ur
GREAT POKEY 12-12-5 (7*) Miss N Courtenay, *led 3rd to 5th, remained prmnt till wknd frm 12th, tld off whn pld up bef 3 out.*
.....................(9 to 1 op 7 to 1 tchd 10 to 1) pu
Dist: 7l, 17l, 21l, 5l. 6m 19.40s. a 36.40s (8 Ran).

(B R J Young), Miss Susan Young

3110 Widcombe Novices' Handicap Hurdle Class F (0-95 4-y-o and up) £2,123 2m 1f................ (5:00)

1665⁴ SIBERIAN MYSTIC [79] 4-10-12 W McFarland, *hld up, hdwy appr 3 out, led bef last, quickened clr r-in.*
.....................(11 to 2 fav tchd 6 to 1 and 13 to 2) 1
2893⁹ GEISWAY (Can) [78] 7-11-5 T Jenks, *nvr far away, led 3 out, hdd appr last, one pace*...(15 to 2 op 8 to 1 tchd 7 to 1) 2
DOVETTO [76] 8-11-3 S Wynne, *hld up, hdwy appr 3 out, one pace nxt*......................(25 to 1 op 20 to 1) 3
2765² DISSOLVE [77] 5-10-11 (7*) Mr L Baker, *al prmnt, led 6th to 3 out, ev ch whn hit 2 out, one pace*..............(10 to 1) 4
2746⁵ FASTINI GOLD [75] 5-11-2 M A Fitzgerald, *hld up, shaken up and improved appr 2 out, sn one pace.* (10 to 1 op 7 to 1) 5
2893 BLAZE OF SONG [82] 5-11-9 M Richards, *towards rear, hdwy appr 2 out, nvr nr to chal*...........(7 to 1 op 5 to 1) 6
2872² SAAFI (Ire) [70] (bl) 6-10-11 V Slattery, *in tch, led 5th to nxt, wknd appr 2 out*........(16 to 1 op 12 to 1 tchd 20 to 1) 7
2746 RANGER SLOANE [81] 5-11-8 R Farrant, *mid-div, not fluent 4th, wknd 3 out*...................(6 to 1 op 7 to 1) 8
2871⁵ MOONLIGHT ESCAPADE (Ire) [77] 6-10-11 (7*) J Harris, *blun 1st, al beh*...............(11 to 1 op 8 to 1 tchd 14 to 1) 9
2497⁹ STILL HERE (Ire) [76] 4-10-9 Michael Brennan, *beh frm 5th.*
.....................(14 to 1 op 12 to 1) 10
2872¹ BLADE OF FORTUNE [86] 9-11-6 (7*) Mr J Tizzard, *led till aftr second, wknd 5th*...................(7 to 1 tchd 9 to 1) 11
2952⁷ DOUNT [84] 5-11-11 A Thornton, *led aftr second to 5th, wknd nxt*.....................(12 to 1 op 7 to 1) 12
2782 DORMY THREE [84] (bl) 7-11-8 (3*) T Dascombe, *al beh, tld off whn pld up bef 2 out*..............(16 to 1 op 12 to 1) pu
Dist: 7l, 1¾l, nk, ¾l, 4l, 2l, 2½l, 10l, 11l, 2½l. 3m 58.40s. a 15.40s (13 Ran).
SR: 15/15/11/11/8/11/-/5/-/   (Glenferry And Partners), P G Murphy

CHELTENHAM (good)
Tuesday March 11th
Going Correction: MINUS 0.15 sec. per fur. (races 1,3,6), MINUS 0.10 (2,4,5)

3111 Citroen Supreme Novices' Hurdle Class A Grade 1 (4-y-o and up) £45,884 2m 110yds...........(2:00)

2594⁴ SHADOW LEADER 6-11-8 J Osborne, *confidently rdn, gd hdwy 3 out, led bef nxt, quickened clr last.*
.....................(5 to 1 op 9 to 2 tchd 6 to 1) 1
2699¹ PRINCEFUL (Ire) 6-11-8 R Farrant, *settled off the pace, improved frm 3 out, feeling pace aftr nxt, styd on strly r-in, no ch wth wnr*...................(25 to 1 op 20 to 1) 2
2180 NORDIC BREEZE (Ire) 5-11-8 D Walsh, *settled in tch, improved 3 out, ev ch nxt, rdn and hit last, one pace r-in.*
.....................(100 to 1 op 66 to 1) 3
2795⁴ WADE ROAD (Ire) 5-11-8 J Culloty, *wtd wth, hdwy on outsd to join ldrs 3 out, rdn betw last 2, no imprsn whn hit last.*
.....................(12 to 1 op 10 to 1 tchd 14 to 1) 4
2342³ GRAPHIC EQUALISER (Ire) 5-11-8 D T Evans, *patiently rdn, styd on, sn ev ch, one pace betw last 2.*
.....................(12 to 1 op 10 to 1) 5
2732³ THREE SCHOLARS 6-11-8 D J Casey, *settled midfield, hdwy and lft in ld 3 out, sn hdd, fdd betw last 2.*
.....................(20 to 1 op 25 to 1) 6
1919⁴ DEANO'S BEENO 5-11-8 C Maude, *pressed ldrs, feeling pace and lost grnd 3 out, rdn and btn nxt.*
.....................(14 to 1 op 11 to 1 tchd 16 to 1) 7

2825⁴ POLYDAMAS 5-11-8 C O'Dwyer, *not fluent in midfield, struggling bef 3 out, sn lost tch.*
.....................(33 to 1 op 20 to 1 tchd 40 to 1) 8
2688⁵ QUEEN OF SPADES (Ire) 7-11-3 C Llewellyn, *made most, blun 4th, hdd bef 3 out, fdg und pres whn badly hmpd nxt.*
.....................(15 to 2 op 6 to 1 tchd 8 to 1) 9
2758² WHIP HAND (Ire) 6-11-8 G Bradley, *chsd ldg pair, not fluent second, almost f nxt, losing tch whn blun and badly hmpd 2 out*......................(14 to 1 op 16 to 1) 10
2782⁴ THE FLYING PHANTOM 6-11-8 P Niven, *tracking ldrs whn f second*............(20 to 1 op 14 to 1 tchd 25 to 1) f
2825² MISTER RM 5-11-8 D Bridgwater, *patiently rdn, gd hdwy to go hndy whn f 2 out*..............(25 to 1 tchd 33 to 1) f
2472² FINNEGAN'S HOLLOW (Ire) 7-11-8 C F Swan, *settled gng wl, gd hdwy and slight ld whn f 3 out.*
.....................(2 to 1 fav op 3 to 1 tchd 100 to 30) f
2795² KAILASH (USA) 6-11-8 A P McCoy, *lost tch hfwy, wl beh whn f last*...................(20 to 1 tchd 16 to 1) f
2803³ SMOLENSK (Ire) 5-11-8 M A Fitzgerald, *hmpd second, lost tch bef 3 out, pld up appr nxt*...(200 to 1 op 100 to 1) pu
2443⁷ HUMBEL (USA) (bl) 5-11-8 R Dunwoody, *wth ldr, hit 3rd, reminders hfwy, lost tch and pld up bef nxt.*
.....................(7 to 1 op 6 to 1 tchd 15 to 2) pu
Dist: 10l, ½l, 4l, 3½l, 1¼l, 2l, 5l, sht-hd, dist. 3m 49.90s. a 0.90s (16 Ran).
SR: 61/51/50/46/42/40/38/33/28/   (James Blackshaw), C R Egerton

3112 Guinness Arkle Challenge Trophy Chase Class A Grade 1 (5-y-o and up) £53,762 2m................ (2:35)

1996² OR ROYAL (Fr) (bl) 6-11-8 A P McCoy, *chsd ldrs, mstk 8th, hmpd 4 out, chalg whn not fluent 2 out, ran on strly und pres to ld cl hme.*.................(11 to 2 op 4 to 1 tchd 6 to 1) 1
2720² SQUIRE SILK 8-11-8 J Osborne, *hld up, hdwy 5th, not fluent 7th, slight ld 2 out, clr appr last, ran on wl, ct cl hme.*
.....................(11 to 2 op 9 to 2) 2
2823² CELIBATE (Ire) 6-11-8 J Railton, *al hndy, chalg whn hit 2 out, sn drvn alng, styd on*....(13 to 2 op 7 to 1 tchd 8 to 1) 3
2823¹ FLYING INSTRUCTOR 7-11-8 R Bellamy, *hld up, hdwy to chase ldrs 3 out, outpcd nxt, no imprsn aftr.*
.....................(8 to 1 op 7 to 1 tchd 9 to 1) 4
2561⁵ LIGHTENING LAD 9-11-8 C Maude, *wth ldr, lft in ld 4 out, blun and hdd 2 out, sn no extr*........(11 to 1 op 9 to 1) 5
2733 PENNDARA (Ire) 8-11-8 C F Swan, *hld up, struggling 4 out, sn no dngr*......................(33 to 1 op 25 to 1) 6
2733 BEAKSTOWN (Ire) 8-11-8 T P Treacy, *not fluent in rear, lost tch 3 out*............(33 to 1 op 25 to 1 tchd 40 to 1) 7
2720¹ MULLIGAN (Ire) 7-11-8 R Dunwoody, *sn led, jmpd wl, slight ld whn f 4 out*.........(11 to 10 fav op Evens tchd 6 to 5) f
2827⁵ GUINDA (Ire) 7-11-3 C Llewellyn, *hld up, outpcd 6th and btn when f last*....................(66 to 1 op 50 to 1) f
Dist: ½l, 6l, 11¼l, 10¼l, 18l, nk. 3m 52.50s. a 0.50s (9 Ran).
SR: 73/72/66/64/62/44/43/-/-/   (D A Johnson), M C Pipe

3113 Smurfit Champion Hurdle Challenge Trophy Class A Grade 1 (4-y-o and up) £124,138 2m 110yds......(3:15)

2591⁵ MAKE A STAND 6-12-0 A P McCoy, *made al, clr frm 3rd, styd on strly from betw last 2*...(7 to 1 op 5 to 1 tchd 8 to 1) 1
2706⁴ THEATREWORLD (Ire) 5-12-0 N Williamson, *patiently rdn, improved frm 3 out, styd on strly from betw last 2, not rch wnr.*...................(33 to 1 tchd 40 to 1) 2
2963² SPACE TRUCKER (Ire) 6-12-0 J Shortt, *wtd wth, improved gng wl hfwy, chsd wnr 3 out, rdn and one pace betw last 2.*
.....................(20 to 1 op 7 to 2 tchd 5 to 1) 3
2342⁴ I'M SUPPOSIN (Ire) 6-12-0 C F Swan, *str hold, improved frm 3 out, rdn and not quicken betw last 2.*
.....................(13 to 2 op 11 to 2 tchd 7 to 1) 4
2128 HILL SOCIETY (Ire) 5-12-0 J F Titley, *al chasing ldrs, effrt and drvn alng 3 out, no imprsn nxt*.................(100 to 1) 5
2825⁴ SANMARTINO (Ire) 5-12-0 R Dunwoody, *wtd wth, gd hdwy hfwy, effrt 3 out, no extr nxt.*
.....................(9 to 1 op 8 to 1 tchd 10 to 1) 6
2326² PRIDWELL 7-12-0 C Maude, *sn beh, styd on und pres frm 3 out, nvr nr to chal*...........(25 to 1 tchd 33 to 1) 7
2820⁴ MOORISH 7-12-0 D Bridgwater, *sn beh, rdn and some hdwy frm 3 out, nvr on terms*.................(100 to 1) 8
2232⁴ COCKNEY LAD (Ire) 8-12-0 J Culloty, *wtd wth, effrt and bustled alng hfwy, nvr rch chalg pos..*(33 to 1 op 25 to 1) 9
2820² MISTINGUETT (Ire) 5-11-9 C Llewellyn, *chsd wnr to 3 out, wknd quickly betw last 2*...........(33 to 1 tchd 40 to 1) 10
2780⁵ ZABADI (Ire) 5-12-0 R Johnson, *hld up midfield, drvn alng hfwy, nvr trble ldrs*.........(100 to 1 op 66 to 1) 11
2706⁴ DARDJINI (USA) 7-12-0 C O'Dwyer, *co'red up in midfield, feeling pace hfwy, nvr dngrs.........*(50 to 1 tchd 66 to 1) 12
2208³ BIMSEY (Ire) 7-12-0 M A Fitzgerald, *settled midfield, struggling to go pace hfwy, lost tch 3 out...* (33 to 1 op 25 to 1) 13
2780¹ DREAMS END 9-12-0 R Farrant, *settled midfield, struggling to go pace hfwy, lost tch 3 out........*(100 to 1) 14
2706² GUEST PERFORMANCE (Ire) (v) 5-12-0 R Hughes, *in tch, chsd alng hfwy, hit 4 out, wknd quickly, no ch whn hit 2 out.*......................(100 to 1) 15
2563⁴ COLLIER BAY 7-12-0 G Bradley, *chsd ldrs, not fluent 3rd, lost tch quickly, tld off whn pld up bef 3 out.*
.....................(4 to 1 op 7 to 2 tchd 9 to 2) pu

NATIONAL HUNT RESULTS 1996-97

2326* LARGE ACTION (Ire) 9-12-0 J Osborne, *pld up aftr second,*
dismounted . . . . (7 to 2 fav op 4 to 1 tchd 9 to 2) pu
Dist: 5l, ¾l, 2l, 3½l, sht-hd, ¾l, 2l, 4l, 3l, 3l. 3m 48.40s. b 0.60s (17 Ran).
SR: 82/77/76/74/70/70/69/67/63/ (P A Deal), M C Pipe

3114 Astec Buzz Shop National Hunt Handicap Chase Class B (5-y-o and up) £34,414 3m 1f . . . . (3:55)

2599 FLYER'S NAP [137] 11-11-2 D Bridgwater, *settled rear, mstk
4 out, steady prog frm nxt, str run to ld aftr last, drvn clr.*
. . . . (20 to 1 op 16 to 1) 1
1382* STORMTRACKER (Ire) [121] 8-10-0 M Richards, *led to 6th,
pressed ldr, led 3 out till aftr last, kpt on wl.*
. . . . (25 to 1 op 33 to 1) 2
2334* GENERAL COMMAND (Ire) [137] 9-11-2 J Osborne, *mstk 5th,
led nxt till pckd and hdd 3 out, rallied wl frm last, fnshd lme.*
. . . . (9 to 4 fav op 2 to 1 tchd 5 to 2) 3
2895² ROMANY CREEK (Ire) [121] (v) 8-10-0 J Culloty, *hld up,
steady hdwy to chase ldrs 4 out, drvn to ld briefly betw last 2,
styd on* . . . . (25 to 1 op 20 to 1) 4
2829⁴ CALL IT A DAY (Ire) [138] 7-11-3 R Johnson, *midfield, not
fluent 13th (water), drvn to chase ldrs 3 out, one pace appr
last* . . . . (9 to 1 op 8 to 1 tchd 10 to 1) 5
2829¹ MUDAHIM [129] 11-10-8 R Farrant, *trkd ldrs till mstk 12th,
pushed alng and outpcd 4 out, one pace frm last, gng on
finish* . . . . (5 to 1 op 6 to 1 tchd 13 to 2) 6
3227³ YORKSHIRE GALE [137] 11-11-2 N Williamson, *in tch,
pressed ldrs frm 14th, drvn and no extr betw last 2.*
. . . . (11 to 1 op 10 to 1 tchd 12 to 1) 7
2779⁵ KADI (Ger) [138] 8-11-3 R Dunwoody, *hld up, hdwy 13th,
midfield whn hit 15th, drvn and one pace 2 out.*
. . . . (8 to 1 op 6 to 1) 8
2829 SIBTON ABBEY [132] 12-10-8 (3") Michael Brennan, *hld up,
pushed alng 5 out, lost tch nxt* . . . . . . (66 to 1 op 50 to 1) 9
2209 GRANGE BRAKE [125] (bl) 11-10-4 D Walsh, *pressed ldrs,
drvn alng 14th, wl beh appr 3 out* . . . (33 to 1 tchd 50 to 1) 10
1394⁸ BAVARD DIEU (Ire) [135] 9-11-0 C Llewellyn, *jmpd poorly in
rear, blun 11th, sn wl beh* . . . . (33 to 1 op 25 to 1) 11
2779⁴ MAAMUR (USA) [145] 9-11-10 A Thornton, *cl up till f 5th,
broke leg, destroyed* . . . . . . (9 to 1 op 6 to 1 tchd 10 to 1) f
2948³ RIVER MANDATE [123] 10-10-2 A P McCoy, *chsd ldrs till f
5th* . . . . (8 to 1 op 6 to 1 tchd 10 to 1) f
2692⁶ JAMES PIGG [130] 10-10-9 M A Fitzgerald, *sn struggling, wl
beh whn pld up 8th* . . . (25 to 1 op 20 to 1 tchd 33 to 1) pu
Dist: 1½l, 1¾l, ½l, nk, 4l, 1l, ½l, 22l, 14l, 1l. 6m 13.80s. a 5.80s (14 Ran).
SR: 5/-/1/-/1/-/ (R J Tory), R H Alner

3115 Fulke Walwyn Kim Muir Challenge Cup Handicap Chase Amateur Riders Class B (5-y-o and up) £21,362 3m 1f . . . . (4:30)

2829² KING LUCIFER (Ire) [132] 8-11-5 (5") Mr R Thornton, *patiently
rdn, improved fnl circuit, led aftr 4 out, pld up on gmely
nr finish* . . . . . (7 to 2 op 3 to 1 tchd 5 to 2 and 4 to 1) 1
2836⁴ TIME FOR A RUN [130] 10-11-8 Mr P Fenton, *wtd wth,
smooth hdwy 7 out, rdn to draw level last, hld nr finish.*
. . . . (15 to 8 fav op 6 to 4 tchd 2 to 1) 2
2512* LUCKY DOLLAR (Ire) [108] 9-9-7 (7") Mr O McPhail, *settle wth
chasing grp, feeling pace fnl circuit, styd on frm 3 out, no
imprsn on 1st 2.* . . . . (20 to 1 tchd 25 to 1) 3
2779⁶ ALL FOR LUCK [126] 12-11-1 (3") Mr B R Hamilton, *settled in
tch, feeling pace fnl circuit, styd on frm 3 out, no imprsn.*
. . . . (16 to 1 op 14 to 1 tchd 20 to 1) 4
2956⁶ DANGER BABY [108] (v) 7-9-7 (7") Mr S Durack, *nvr far away,
ev ch till rdn alng appr 3 out, fdd nxt.*
. . . . (40 to 1 op 33 to 1 tchd 50 to 1) 5
2786⁴ CAMELOT KNIGHT [117] 11-10-6 (3") Mr M Rimell, *led to 6th,
reminders 7 out, rallied 3 out, fdd nxt.* (12 to 1 op 8 to 1) 6
2589 BRADBURY STAR [129] 12-11-0 (7") Mr P O'Keeffe, *trkd ldrs,
feeling pace aftr one circuit, lost tch 6 out, tld off.*
. . . . (25 to 1 tchd 33 to 1) 7
2564 SO FAR BOLD (Ire) [110] (bl) 7-10-2⁶ (5") Mr T Doumen, *wth
ldrs, pckd 3rd, led 6th, sn clr, hdd aftr 4 out, btn whn hit nxt, tld
off* . . . . (20 to 1 op 33 to 1) 8
2500 CHRISTMAS GORSE [120] 11-10-5 (7") Mr P Scott, *sn beh,
struggling hfwy, tld off* . . . . (8 to 1 op 6 to 1) 9
2600² LORD OF THE WEST (Ire) [110] 8-9-13 (3") Mr C Bonner, *not
fluent, last whn f 12th* . . . . (15 to 2 op 8 to 1 tchd 9 to 1) f
2779 CHERRYNUT [130] 8-11-1 (7") Mr J Tizzard, *nvr gng wl, hit
8th, niggled alng aftr nxt, sn lost tch, jmpd slwly and pld up
after 6 out* . . . . (8 to 1 op 6 to 1) pu
Dist: Nk, 15l, 5l, 2l, 7l, 24l, 8l, 6l. 6m 9.80s. a 1.80s (11 Ran).
SR: 53/51/14/27/7/9/ (A J Davies), D Nicholson

3116 Hamlet Extra Mild Cigars Gold Card Handicap Hurdle Final Class B (4-y-o and up) £27,910 3¼m . . . . (5:05)

2830* PHARANEAR (Ire) [145] 7-11-9 (5") Mr R Thornton, *in tch, drvn
to ld betw last 2, strly pressed and edgd lft aftr last, ran on
gmely.* . . . . (14 to 1 op 10 to 1) 1
2453² YAHMI (Ire) [130] 7-10-13 J Osborne, *chsd ldrs, chlgd gng wl
2 out, ev ch whn slightly hmpd r-in, styd on well.*
. . . . (7 to 2 fav op 9 to 2 tchd 5 to 1) 2

1381 DANJING (Ire) [128] (bl) 5-10-11 A P McCoy, *hld up, effrt appr
2 out, sn rdn alng, styd on same pace.* (33 to 1 op 25 to 1) 3
2506* HAILE DERRING [123] 7-10-6 T Jenks, *hndy, led appr 8th,
drvn and hdd betw last 2, hit last, no extr.*
. . . . (9 to 1 op 7 to 1 tchd 10 to 1) 4
2963⁴ MILTONFIELD [128] 8-10-11 R Dunwoody, *settled rear,
smooth hdwy and in tch 4 out, slight mstk and drvn alng 2 out,
unbl to quicken* . . . . (9 to 2 op 7 to 2 tchd 5 to 1) 5
2598³ FREDDIE MUCK [132] 7-11-1 C Llewellyn, *al chasing ldrs,
niggled alng frm 3 out, styd on from nxt.* (10 to 1 op 7 to 1) 6
2530* HENRIETTA HOWARD (Ire) [121] 7-10-4 J F Titley, *hld up,
hdwy and in tch tenth, drvn and one pace aftr 2 out.*
. . . . (8 to 1 op 7 to 1 tchd 9 to 1) 7
2801² LINTON ROCKS [123] 8-9-13 (7") X Aizpuru, *hndy, second
whn hit 9th, pressed ldrs till no extr appr last.*
. . . . (11 to 1 op 20 to 1) 8
2559⁴ GENERAL MOUKTAR [117] 7-10-0 R Hughes, *hld up in rear,
steady hdwy 4 out till outpcd 2 out, no imprsn aftr.* (50 to 1) 9
2787⁸ DIWALI DANCER [117] 7-9-9 (5") G Supple, *hld up, hdwy
hfwy, outpcd aftr 4 out.* (40 to 1 op 33 to 1 tchd 50 to 1) 10
2929³ MISTER BLAKE [117] 7-10-0 R Johnson, *midfield, pushed
alng whn hmpd appr 2 out, sn no dngr.*
. . . . (66 to 1 op 200 to 1) 11
2710³ GIVE BEST [117] 6-10-0 C F Swan, *patiently rdn, improved to
chase ldrs aftr 3 out, fdd betw last 2.* (14 to 1 tchd 16 to 1) 12
2797⁵ TIM (Ire) [121] 7-10-4⁴ M A Fitzgerald, *hld up, niggled alng 3
out, lost tch.* . . . . (50 to 1 op 33 to 1) 13
2540 PALOSANTO (Ire) [119] 7-9-11 (5") Sophie Mitchell, *not fluent
in rear, hrd drvn frm hfwy, nvr a factor.*
. . . . (33 to 1 tchd 40 to 1) 14
3051⁵ DUHALLOW LODGE [117] 10-10-0 J R Kavanagh, *hld up,
struggling appr 3 out, sn btn.* . . . . (100 to 1) 15
2605⁵ KARAR (Ire) [117] 7-9-9 (5") D J Kavanagh, *in tch, chsd ldrs
hfwy till fdd 3 out.* . . . . (50 to 1 op 33 to 1) 16
2923⁷ URON V (Fr) [117] 11-10-0 K Gaule, *pushed alng in rear hfwy,
nvr able to chal* . . . . (50 to 1 tchd 66 to 1) 17
2562³ SNOW BOARD [117] 8-10-0 Derek Byrne, *beh, struggling 5
out, sn lost tch.* . . . . (66 to 1 op 100 to 1) 18
2453⁶ RUNAWAY PETE (USA) [123] 7-10-6 D Walsh, *cl up, mstk 3rd,
reminders to chase ldrs tenth, wkng whn short of room appr 2
out.* . . . . (25 to 1 op 20 to 1) 19
2851³ DALLY BOY [117] 5-9-11 (3") Michael Brennan, *pressed ldr,
lost pl 9th, wknd quickly.* . . . . . . (33 to 1 tchd 40 to 1) 20
2198² OLYMPIAN [121] (bl) 10-10-4 N Williamson, *sn led, blun 4th,
hdd and wknd appr 8th, wl beh whn blunded 3 out.*
. . . . (20 to 1 tchd 25 to 1) 21
2453⁴ ERZADJAN (Ire) [131] 7-11-0 P Niven, *beh, niggled alng frm
hfwy, improved from 4 out, drvn in 5th and staying on whn
mstk and uns rdr last.* . . . . (10 to 1 op 8 to 1) ur
1876² SOUTHERN NIGHTS [117] 7-10-0 C O'Dwyer, *midfield, drvn
alng 5 out, wknd and pld up aftr 3 out, lme.*
. . . . (10 to 1 tchd 11 to 1) pu
2598⁷ ARITHMETIC [117] 7-10-0 R Farrant, *midfield, not fluent 6th,
wknd and pld up bef 8th* . . . . (25 to 1 op 20 to 1) pu
Dist: 2l, 5l, 1l, 5l, nk, 3½l, 1l, 12l, 3½l, 1l. 6m 24.40s. a 8.40s (24 Ran).
(Stainless Threaded Fasteners Ltd), D Nicholson

FONTWELL (good)
Tuesday March 11th
Going Correction: PLUS 0.40 sec. per fur.

3117 Brighton Juvenile Novices' Hurdle Class D (4-y-o) £2,906 2¼m 110yds
. . . . (2:10)

2727⁵ ELA AGAPI MOU (USA) 10-10 D Gallagher, *hld up, smooth
hdwy 5th, led appr 3 out, hrd rdn approaching last, drvn out.*
. . . . (7 to 1 op 12 to 1) 1
2925 INFAMOUS (USA) 10-10 D O'Sullivan, *hld up beh, hdwy 4 out,
chlgd gng wl and ev ch 2 out, one pace appr last.*
. . . . (6 to 4 fav op 5 to 4 tchd 13 to 8) 2
2807² TOPAGLOW (Ire) 10-10 B Fenton, *trkd ldrs, ev ch 3 out, hrd
rdn nxt and sn one pace.* . . . . . . (4 to 1 op 7 to 1) 3
584³ SPRING CAMPAIGN (Ire) 10-10 Jamie Evans, *led till aftr 5th,
cl up till wknd und pres appr 2 out.* . . . (12 to 1 op 7 to 1) 4
2925³ SALTY GIRL (Ire) 10-5 W McFarland, *hld up in mid-div,
shaken up aftr 3 out, sn btn.* . . . (7 to 1 tchd 8 to 1) 5
DUBAI DOLLY (Ire) 10-5 S Curran, *hld up beh, hdwy and mstk
4 out, wknd aftr nxt.* . . . . (100 to 1 op 50 to 1) 6
2730⁷ HEVER GOLF DIAMOND 10-13 (3") P Henley, *trkd ldrs till one
pace and wknd appr 3 out.* . . . . (20 to 1 op 14 to 1) 7
2773⁵ SILVRETTA (Ire) (bl) 10-5 P Hide, *trkd ldr, led aftr 5th, hdd appr
3 out, sn wknd.* . . . . (14 to 1 op 8 to 1) 8
2925⁶ TIMIDJAR (Ire) 10-7 (3") D Fortt, *hld up, al beh, virtually pld up
r-in.* . . . . (7 to 1 op 6 to 1) 9
2893 SAFECRACKER (bl) 10-10 B Powell, *trkd ldrs, not fluent,
wknd 4 out, tld off whn pld up bef 2 out.* (33 to 1 op 20 to 1) pu
2611³ PETROS GEM 9-12 (7") J Harris, *hld up in mid-div, rdn alng
aftr 5th, sn btn, tld off whn pld up bef 2 out.*
. . . . (66 to 1 op 33 to 1) pu
Dist: 3l, 6l, 17l, nk, 22l, 8l, 8l, dist. 4m 36.40s. a 19.40s (11 Ran).
(Ballard (1834) Limited), G L Moore

3118 Houghton Novices' Handicap Chase Class E (0-100 5-y-o and up) £2,916

431

2m 3f........................(2:45)

2859* RED BRANCH (Ire) [73] 8-10-11 T J Murphy, *made all, clr frm 3 out, eased nr finish*.............(6 to 4 on op 5 to 4)
2873 BROWN ROBBER [69] 9-10-7 B Fenton, *trkd wnr, hit 9th, blunds nxt 2, not fluent 4 out (water), outpcd frm next*.
..............................(6 to 1 op 4 to 1) 2
2748 COLONEL COLT [75] 6-10-13 D Leahy, *al same pl, no imprsn frm 4 out*...............(14 to 1 op 10 to 1 tchd 16 to 1) 3
2877B NORDIC VALLEY (Ire) [86] 6-11-10 Jamie Evans, *hld up in last pl, mstk 11th and sn struggling, tld off*...(11 to 4 op 9 to 4) 4
Dist: 4l, 7l, 24l. 5m 0.70s. a 25.70s (4 Ran).

(E J Mangan), J S King

3119 Storrington Maiden Hurdle Class E (5-y-o and up) £2,274 3m 3f... (3:20)

2738² BRACKENHEATH (Ire) 6-10-10 B Fenton, *led chasing grp, o'rall ldr 9th, mstk last, edgd rght und pres r-in, all out, fnshd 1st, plcd second*.....................(4 to 1 op 5 to 2) 1D
2889³ SATCOTINO (Ire) 6-10-2 (3*) P Henley, *cl up in chasing grp, chsd ldr frm 4 out, ev ch last, swtchd lft and kpt on, fnshd second, plcd 1st*.
.............(13 to 8 on op 7 to 4 on tchd 6 to 4 on) 1
2539³ WIN I DID (Ire) 7-10-5 B Powell, *hld up beh, cld 9th, chsd ldg pair frm 3 out, sn no imprsn and one pace*.
.........................(14 to 1 op 10 to 1) 3
2982⁷ NIGHT IN A MILLION 6-10-10 D Morris, *wth ldrs in chasing grp, wknd 4 out, tld off*............(16 to 1 op 12 to 1) 4
HIGH BURNSHOT 10-10-10 D Leahy, *led, sn wl clr, hdd 9th and soon wknd, tld off whn pld up aftr 3 out*.
...........................(33 to 1 op 25 to 1) pu
2954⁴ TORCH VERT (Ire) 5-10-10 D Gallagher, *hld up, mstk 5th, hdwy 8th, wknd appr 3 out, pld up bef nxt*.
.................(11 to 1 op 6 to 1 tchd 13 to 2) pu
2937⁷ MISS NONNIE 5-9-12 (7*) M Lane, *al beh, tld off whn pld up bef 8th*............(66 to 1 op 50 to 1 tchd 100 to 1) pu
2874 MISS GEE-ELL 5-9-12 (7*) Mr E Babington, *nvr on terms, tld off whn pld up bef 9th*...........(100 to 1 op 50 to 1) pu
2954⁹ GLAISNOCK LAD (Ire) 5-10-10 R Greene, *beh, hrd rdn 5th, mstks nxt 2, tld off whn pld up bef 8th*.
.........................(40 to 1 op 33 to 1 tchd 50 to 1) pu
Dist: Hd, 23l, dist. 6m 55.50s. a 31.50s (9 Ran).

(Grangewood (Sales & Marketing) Ltd), M H Tompkins

3120 National Spirit Handicap Hurdle Class E (0-110 4-y-o and up) £2,200 2¾m 110yds....................(3:50)

2932² ST VILLE [88] 11-11-8 B Powell, *al hndy, drvn alng 4 out, led aftr nxt, clr whn idled und pres r-in, jst hld on*.
.........................(3 to 1 op 9 to 4 tchd 7 to 2) 1
2977 ROGER'S PAL [70] 10-10-4 D Gallagher, *hld up, cld 7th, mstk 4 out, staying on whn hit 2 out, rallied aftr last, jst held*.
.........................(10 to 1 op 8 to 1 tchd 12 to 1) 2
2977 RAAHIN (USA) [66] 12-10-0 D Morris, *led aftr 3rd, drvn alng 4 out, hdd after nxt, one pace*.........(12 to 1 tchd 14 to 1) 3
2740 PUNCH'S HOTEL [90] (bl) 12-11-3 (7*) A Garrity, *led till aftr 3rd, reminders 6th, sn drpd out, tld off. (7 to 2 tchd 4 to 1)* 4
2281⁴ SWAN STREET (NZ) [83] 6-11-0 (3*) J Magee, *trkd ldrs, wknd aftr 4 out, tld off*.....(11 to 4 fav op 9 to 4 tchd 3 to 1) 5
2936⁶ AMILLIONMEMORIES [69] 7-11-9 R Greene, *hld up, pushed alng 5th, lost tch 7th, tld off whn pld up bef 2 out*.... (4 to 1) pu
Dist: Sht-hd, 9l, 24l, 11l. 5m 51.40s. a 37.40s (6 Ran).

(Melplash Racing), R H Buckler

3121 Fontwell Handicap Chase Class D (0-120 5-y-o and up) £3,403 3¼m 110yds.........................(4:20)

2979⁴ CREDON [100] 9-10-8 B Fenton, *led 3rd till appr 6th, led 8th, hdd briefly 12th, made rst, lft clr 5 out, eased r-in*.
.........................(7 to 1 op 5 to 1) 1
2310⁷ HARRISTOWN LADY [105] (bl) 10-10-13 B Clifford, *nvr far away, pushed alng 15th, lft second 5 out, no ch wth wnr*.
.........................(6 to 1 op 5 to 1 tchd 8 to 1) 2
2739⁴ MASTER COMEDY [92] (bl) 13-10-0 D Gallagher, *beh, not fluent, styd on frm 2 out, nvr able to chal*.
.........................(14 to 1 op 12 to 1 tchd 16 to 1) 3
2956 NAZZARO [120] 8-12-0 T J Murphy, *led to 3rd, drvn alng thrght, led appr 6th to 8th, struggling 13th, tld off*.
.........................(6 to 1 op 5 to 1 tchd 7 to 1) 4
2979³ VICOSA (Ire) [108] 8-10-13 (3*) P Henley, *in tch, not fluent 6th, f 14th*...........................(9 to 4 op 2 to 1 tchd 5 to 2) f
2800¹ CHILDHAY CHOCOLATE [98] 9-10-6 R Greene, *wth ldr frm 11th, led briefly nxt, not fluent 17th, pld up lme bef next*.
.........................(9 to 4 op 2 to 1 tchd 5 to 2) pu
Dist: 2½l, 2l, 18l. 7m 11.00s. a 41.00s (6 Ran).

(Fusilier Racing), S Woodman

3122 Tortington Intermediate Open National Hunt Flat Class H (4,5,6-y-o) £1,255 2¼m............. (4:55)

2377² SPUNKIE 4-10-10 D Gallagher, *hld up in cl tch, led on bit wl o'r one furlong out, shaken up and quickened clr, readily*.
......(15 to 8 jt-fav op 5 to 2 tchd 1 and 7 to 4) 1

2179⁴ CERTAIN SHOT 6-11-1 (3*) D Fortt, *al hndy, led o'r 2 fs out till wl over one out, hrd rdn and not quicken*........(15 to 8 jt-fav op 6 to 4) 2
2552³ HOT 'N SAUCY 5-10-13 Mr S Bush, *hld up, hdwy o'r 4 fs out, kpt on one pace frm 2 out.* (6 to 1 op 5 to 1 tchd 7 to 1) 3
2644⁴ MACY (Ire) 4-11-3 T J Murphy, *chsd ldrs, led o'r 6 fs out, hdd over 2 out, one pace*................(10 to 1 op 6 to 1) 4
BLAZING BATMAN 4-10-10 Mr W Henderson, *trkd ldrs till drpd rear aftr 3 fs, styd on and hng rght ins last*.
.........................(40 to 1 op 33 to 1) 5
2377 TINGRITH LAD 5-11-4 W McFarland, *hld up beh ldrs, hrd rdn o'r 4 fs out, sn no extr*...............(50 to 1 op 33 to 1) 6
1942 YOUNG MANNY 6-11-1 (3*) R Massey, *hld up in mid-div, hdwy 5 fs out, sn wknd.* (40 to 1 op 33 to 1 tchd 50 to 1) 7
2784 ARRANGE 5-11-4 V Slattery, *trkd ldr, led hfwy till o'r 6 fs out, sn wknd*.....................(20 to 1 op 12 to 1) 8
MINNIE 4-10-5 S Curran, *hld up, al beh*.
.........................(16 to 1 op 12 to 1) 9
2831 KINGSWOOD IMPERIAL 4-10-10 A McCabe, *trkd ldrs till wknd o'r 4 fs out*.............(16 to 1 op 12 to 1) 10
ROYAL MEMBER 4-10-5 R Greene, *al beh, tld off*.
.........................(14 to 1 op 20 to 1) 11
2642 HOLD MY HAND 6-11-4 B Fenton, *led to hfwy, sn drpd out, tld off*................(33 to 1 tchd 50 to 1) 12
SISSINGHURST FLYER (Ire) 5-10-13 D Leahy, *hld up beh ldrs, lost pl quickly o'r 7 fs out, tld off, virtually pld up*.
.........................(20 to 1 op 16 to 1) 13
Dist: 6l, 12l, 3l, 17l, 22l, 17l, 10l, 2½l, 1½l, 9l. 4m 34.00s. (13 Ran).

(Jim Short), R F Johnson Houghton

SEDGEFIELD (good to firm (race 1), good (2,3,4,5,6)) Tuesday March 11th
Going Correction: NIL

3123 Monkey Puzzle Selling Handicap Hurdle Class G (0-90 4-y-o and up) £2,080 3m 3f 110yds........ (2:20)

2856⁷ GREENFIELD MANOR [64] 10-10-3 (5*) S Taylor, *wth ldrs, led 5th, made rst, ran on wl fnl 2*......(33 to 1 tchd 50 to 1) 1
3006⁸ SHELTON ABBEY [67] (bl) 11-10-8 (3*) E Callaghan, *beh, struggling aftr 4 out, styd on strly fnl 2, no ch wth wnr*.
.........................(8 to 1 op 10 to 1) 2
2812⁹ BRIGHT DESTINY [56] (v) 6-10-0 G Cahill, *keen hold, led 5th, hit nxt, outpcd 3 out, rallied last*.. (50 to 1 op 25 to 1) 3
2487 HAUGHTON LAD (Ire) [68] 8-10-12 V Smith, *hld up, improved and ev ch 3 out, wknd und pres aftr nxt*.... (7 to 1 op 6 to 1) 4
3006 HELENS BAY (Ire) [72] 7-11-2 Mr M Thompson, *chsd ldg grp, outpcd appr 3 out*......(16 to 1 op 20 to 1) 5
2847⁶ DENTICULATA [70] 9-11-0 B Storey, *hld up, improved 6th, ev ch 3 out, one pace frm nxt*.................(16 to 1 op 8 to 1) 6
2202 WEATHER ALERT (Ire) [73] 6-10-10 (7*) N Horrocks, *nvr far away, pushed alng aftr 4 out, outpcd nxt*.
.........................(9 to 1 op 7 to 1 tchd 10 to 1) 7
2487 MARDOOD [69] 12-10-6 (7*) Miss R Clark, *mid-div, pushed alng 4 out, no imprsn fnl 2*............(25 to 1 op 20 to 1) 8
2856² RUBER [80] 10-11-10 D Parker, *mstks in rear, nvr able to chal*.........................(5 to 2 fav op 11 to 4) 9
2710 MURPHAIDEEZ [60] 10-10-4 R Hodge, *beh, struggling strting fnl circuit, nvr dngrs*...........(33 to 1 op 20 to 1) 10
2856⁹ DON'T TELL JUDY (Ire) [69] 9-10-13 A Dobbin, *hld up, improved 8th, outpcd 3 out*......(20 to 1 op 16 to 1) 11
2989 KIR (Ire) [74] 9-11-4 K Jones, *beh, struggling fnl circuit, nvr on terms*.....................(50 to 1 op 33 to 1) 12
2771 OUR RAINBOW [75] (v) 5-11-5 M Brennan, *wl plcd, struggling aftr 4 out, eased 2, virtually pld up r-in.* (6 to 1 op 5 to 1) 13
2538⁷ BOYZONTOOWA (Ire) [62] 5-10-6 W Marston, *pld hrd in rear, beh, outpcd bef 3 out*................(25 to 1) 14
2420⁵ LIAB (Can) [78] 7-11-8 M Moloney, *beh, struggling fnl circuit, tld off*...........................(20 to 1 op 14 to 1) 15
550* PLAYFUL JULIET (Can) [82] (bl) 9-11-12 Mr C Stockton, *prmnt, outpcd aftr 4 out, pld up after 2 out*.
.........................(11 to 1 op 10 to 1 tchd 12 to 1) pu
Dist: 3l, ½l, 1l, 2½l, ¾l, 6l, 3½l, 5l, 16l, ½l. 6m 36.20s. a 14.20s (16 Ran).

(J Sisterson), J Sisterson

3124 Bet With The Tote Novices' Chase Class E (5-y-o and up) £3,023 2m 5f..............................(2:55)

3012³ NIJWAY 7-10-11 (5*) S Taylor, *hld to 9th, led 3 out, jnd 2 out, hit last, gmely*................(5 to 1 op 6 to 1 tchd 7 to 1) 1
2812 MASTER FLASHMAN 8-10-13 (3*) K Gaule, *nvr far away, led 4 out to nxt, str chal fnl 2, jst hld*......... (8 to 1 op 9 to 2) 2
2123⁶ FERN LEADER (Ire) 7-11-2 J Supple, *blun and nrly uns rdr 1st, beh, chsd ldrs 9th, rdn and one pace fnl 2*.
.........................(11 to 8 on op 6 to 4 on) 3
3007 FORT ZEDDAAN (Ire) 7-10-9 (7*) R Wilkinson, *nvr far away, mstk tenth, rdn and pushed 3 out*..(16 to 1 op 14 to 1) 4
2205⁸ CAMPTOSAURUS (Ire) 8-11-2 B Storey, *al prmnt, outpcd 4 out, no dngr nxt*...........(16 to 1 op 14 to 1) 5
ARCTIC BLOOM 11-10-11 Mr C Mulhall, *strred slwly, hld up in tch, hit 8th, rdn and outpcd whn blun 3 out, tld off*.
.........................(25 to 1 op 20 to 1) 6

432

3005⁴ TRIONA'S HOPE (Ire) 8-11-2 M Moloney, *cl up, led 9th to 4 out, sn struggling, btn whn nrly uns rdr last.*
................................(20 to 1 op 16 to 1) 7
1678 NOBODYS FLAME (Ire) 9-11-2 K Johnson, *beh, tld off fnl circuit*...........................(16 to 1 op 14 to 1) 8
2985 CHILDSWAY 9-11-2 K Jones, *sn tld off, f 3 out.*
................................(20 to 1 op 16 to 1) f
2914 SAFETY FACTOR (Ire) 9-10-11 (5*) G F Ryan, *chsd ldrs whn f heavily 7th*............(11 to 1 op 7 to 1 tchd 12 to 1) f
2848⁴ OVERWHELM (Ire) 9-11-6 Mr M Thompson, *chsd ldg grp, hmpd 7th, struggling 11th, pld up bef 2 out.*
................................(10 to 1 op 8 to 1) pu
2063⁸ RINGRONE (Ire) 8-10-11 N Bentley, *beh and sn struggling, tld off whn pld up bef 9th*...........(100 to 1 op 33 to 1) pu
Dist: Sht-hd, 8l, 6l, 3l, 7l, 12l, 14l. 5m 11.10s. a 15.10s (12 Ran).

(T A Barnes), M A Barnes

3125 Win With The Tote Hunters' Chase
Class H (6-y-o and up) £1,140 3m 3f
.....................................(3:30)

2993³ GLEN OAK 12-11-7 (7*) Mr J M Pritchard, *nvr far away, hit 5 out, styd on bef last to ld nr finish.*
................................(2 to 1 op 7 to 4 tchd 9 to 4) 1
2468⁹ KUSHBALOO 12-12-3 (7*) Mr A Parker, *slight ld to 8th, led ag'n 15th, clr 3 out, shaken up and hdd nr finish.*
................................(11 to 10 fav op Evens tchd 5 to 4) 2
2918⁵ FORDSTOWN (Ire) 8-12-0 (7*) Mr Jamie Alexander, *dsptd ld, led 8th to 15th, outpcd 4 out, styd on frm last.*
................................(7 to 2 op 4 to 1 tchd 9 to 2) 3
TARTAN TORNADO 11-12-2 (5*) Mr P Johnson, *prmnt, out-pcd 4 out, no imprsn fnl 2*...........(16 to 1 op 14 to 1) 4
FAST STUDY 12-12-3 (7*) Mr Simon Robinson, *jmpd badly, hld up, improved 8th, struggling 13th, tld off.*
................................(16 to 1 op 14 to 1) 5
SIDE BRACE (NZ) 13-11-7 (7*) Miss S Swirdells, *not jump wl, beh, tld off fnl circuit*.........................(25 to 1) 6
POLYNTH 8-11-7 (7*) Mr G Markham, *jmpd badly in tch, mstk and lost pl 6th, tld off fnl circuit, pld up bef last*
................................(20 to 1 op 16 to 1) pu
Dist: 1l, nk, 4l, dist, 9l. 6m 51.30s. a 18.30s (7 Ran).

(R J Mansell), D G Duggan

3126 Screenco Jumbotron Handicap
Chase Class D (0-120 5-y-o and up)
£3,366 2m 110yds...........(4:10)

2911³ CROSS CANNON [103] 11-11-7 B Storey, *made all, clr last 3, unchlgd*................(4 to 1 op 9 to 4 tchd 7 to 2) 1
2857⁷ WEAVER GEORGE (Ire) [109] 7-11-13 M Moloney, *chsd wnr thrght, rdn whn hit 3 out, no imprsn nxt.*
................................(6 to 5 fav op 11 to 10) 2
2261¹⁰ REVE DE VALSE (USA) [91] 10-10-9 K Johnson, *in tch, struggling 8th, no imprsn fnl 2*............(8 to 1 op 7 to 1) 3
2911² REGAL ROMPER (Ire) [110] 9-12-0 Richard Guest, *chsd ldrs, hit 8th and nxt, sn outpcd, btn last 2.*
................................(13 to 8 op 11 to 8 tchd 7 to 4) 4
Dist: 7l, 10l, 20l. 3m 59.30s. a 7.30s (4 Ran).
SR: 20/19/-/-/

(John Wade), J Wade

3127 Stanley Racing Golden Numbers
Series Mares Only Novices Hdle (4-y-o and up) £2,845 2m 5f 110yds
.....................................(4:45)

2578³ PONTEVEDRA (Ire) 4-9-10 (7*) N Horrocks, *nvr far away, led 3 out, hld on wl frm last*.............(10 to 1 op 5 to 1) 1
2810⁴ COUNTRY ORCHID 6-10-9 (3*) G Lee, *hld up, improved bef 3 out, rdn to challlenge betw last 2, kpt on r-in.*
................................(11 to 4 op 7 to 2 tchd 9 to 4) 2
2495⁵ WAYUPHILL 10-10-12 B Storey, *hld up, improved bef 3 out, chasing ldrs before nxt, kpt on same pace frm last.*
................................(5 to 2 fav op 2 to 1 tchd 11 to 4) 3
2552⁷ SUPREME TARGET (Ire) 5-10-12 G Cahill, *al hndy, blun 3 out, eased nxt*...(8 to 1 op 7 to 1 tchd 9 to 1 and 10 to 1) 4
2550⁷ ANGLESEY SEA VIEW 8-11-4 T Kent, *nvr far away, led 5th, hdd 3 out, outpcd appr nxt*........(3 to 1 tchd 7 to 2) 5
2492⁷ BEST FRIEND 5-10-12 J Callaghan, *swrvd rght strt, sn cl up, rdn and outpcd bef 2 out*.............(25 to 1 op 20 to 1) 6
2849⁸ OTTADINI (Ire) 5-10-12 T Reed, *beh, struggling fnl circuit, nvr on terms*..................(66 to 1 op 50 to 1) 7
2572⁷ DE-VEERS CURRIE (Ire) 5-10-12 D J Moffatt, *pld hrd in rear, nvr on terms*...................(25 to 1 op 16 to 1) 8
2957⁷ ASKED TO LEAVE 5-10-9 (3*) E Callaghan, *mstks in rear, nvr on terms*.....................(16 to 1 tchd 20 to 1) 9
2489 HENBRIG 7-10-5 (7*) C McCormack, *led to 5th, struggling 3 out, pld up bef 6th*..................(50 to 1) pu
SHULTAN (Ire) 8-10-12 K Johnson, *in tch, struggling aftr 4 out, pld up bef last*...............(33 to 1 op 25 to 1) pu
2653 KAMBLETREE (Ire) (bl) 6-10-12 D Parker, *cl up till wknd quickly 4th, pld up bef 6th*.........(66 to 1 op 50 to 1) pu
Dist: ¾l, 1½l, 1½l, 15l, 9l, 2½l, hd, 21l. 5m 4.10s. a 16.10s (12 Ran).

(Mrs P A L Butler), K A Morgan

3128 Tote Placepot Novices' Handicap
Hurdle Class E (0-105 4-y-o and up)

£2,442 2m 1f.................(5:20)

2879⁸ ROTHARI [82] 5-10-12 R Supple, *pressed ldr, led 3 out to nxt, rallied last to ld on line*...........(7 to 1 op 6 to 1) 1
2711⁸ DIAMOND BEACH [83] 4-10-5 N Bentley, *hld up, improved 3 out, hit nxt, led last, hdd line*.........(14 to 1 op 12 to 1) 2
JENDORCET [70] 7-10-0 J Callaghan, *hld up rear, hdwy bef 3 out, chlgd betw last 2, kpt on*...............(16 to 1) 3
2908⁶ FERRERS [85] 6-11-1 W Marston, *mid-div, pushed alng 3 out, styd on last, no imprsn*.....(7 to 2 op 3 to 1 tchd 4 to 1) 4
2359⁹ PANGERAN (USA) [85] 5-11-1 J Supple, *chsd ldg bunch, hit 3rd, drvn 3 out, kpt on last.*(11 to 2 op 5 to 1 tchd 6 to 1) 5
2204 BEAU MATELOT [80] 5-10-3 (7*) N Horrocks, *hld up, improved and ev ch 3 out, one pace betw last 2.*
................................(16 to 1 tchd 20 to 1) 6
2537⁶ ADAMATIC (Ire) [98] 6-12-0 B Storey, *hld up and beh, hdwy to chal 3 out, outpcd aftr nxt*...............(8 to 1) 7
2849⁷ FALCON'S FLAME (USA) [88] 4-10-10 Mr M Thompson, *chsd ldrs till nxt and outpcd aftr 3 out*......(16 to 1 op 10 to 1) 8
2655 TEN PAST SIX [70] 5-10-0 L O'Hara, *chsd ldg bunch, strug-gling 3 out, eased whn btn nxt.*
................................(13 to 2 op 14 to 1 tchd 6 to 1) 9
2817⁷ RUBISLAW [70] (v) 5-9-7 (7*) Miss S Lamb, *in tch to 3rd, sn beh, no dngr aftr*.....................(33 to 1 op 25 to 1) 10
2913⁹ BASSENHALLY [89] 7-11-5 R Brennan, *led till 3 out, sn btn.*
................................(11 to 1 op 10 to 1) 11
2785⁶ MAPLETON [87] 4-10-9 Richard Guest, *chsd ldg bunch, struggling bef 3 out, sn btn.*
................................(11 to 1 op 10 to 1 tchd 12 to 1) 12
2847 PROMISE TO TRY (Ire) [70] 5-9-9 (5*) S Taylor, *beh and sn detatched, tld off*..................(33 to 1 op 25 to 1) 13
2813² CLAVERING (Ire) [88] 7-11-4 A Dobbin, *cl up, drvn alng aftr 4 out, struggling nxt, pld up after 2 out.*
................................(9 to 4 fav op 3 to 1 tchd 7 to 2) pu
Dist: Sht-hd, sht-hd, 2l, 2l, 3l, 1¾l, 5l, 3l, 3½l, 11l. 3m 55.00s. a 9.00s (14 Ran).

(Michael Saunders), B S Rothwell

CHELTENHAM (good to firm (races 1,4,6), good (2,3,5,7))
Wednesday March 12th
Going Correction: MINUS 0.10 sec. per fur. (races 1,3,7), MINUS 0.20 (2,4,5,6)

3129 Royal Sunalliance Novices' Hurdle
Class A Grade 1 (4-y-o and up)
£49,585 2m 5f.................(2:00)

2472* ISTABRAQ (Ire) 5-11-7 C F Swan, *confidently rdn in rear, smooth hdwy frm 4 out, bumped 2 out, drvn to ld appr last, styd on out.*.........(6 to 5 fav op 11 to 10 tchd 11 to 8) 1
2697¹² MIGHTY MOGG (Ire) 6-11-7 Mr M F Hutsby, *led aftr 4th, strly pressed frm 3 out, hdd appr last, rallied and ran on gmely.*
................................(11 to 1 op 10 to 1 tchd 12 to 1) 2
2323⁷ DARAYDAN (Ire) 5-11-7 R Hughes, *al hndy, chlgd 3 out, drvn alng nxt, styd on wl*...(16 to 1 op 25 to 1 tchd 33 to 1) 3
2528² FOREST IVORY (NZ) 6-11-7 R Johnson, *in tch, chalg whn bumped 2 out, not fluent last, styd on same pace.*
................................(14 to 1 op 10 to 1) 4
2697 SOLDAT (USA) 4-10-12 D Bridgwater, *slightly hmpd 1st, set-tled rear, drvn and some hdwy appr 3 out, unbl to chal.*
................................(33 to 1 tchd 40 to 1) 5
2697⁶ HARBOUR ISLAND (bl) 5-11-7 N Williamson, *midfield, effrt whn blun 5th, hit nxt, no imprsn aftr.*
................................(25 to 1 op 33 to 1 tchd 40 to 1 and 20 to 1) 6
2835³ DIFFICULT TIMES (Ire) 5-11-7 S C Lyons, *cl up, drvn and outpcd 7th, no dngr aftr*.......(33 to 1 tchd 25 to 1) 7
2697³ MARCHING MARQUIS (Ire) 6-11-7 A P McCoy, *midfield, blun 7th, drvn and outpcd appr 3 out, sn btn.*(20 to 1 op 33 to 1) 8
2792* ROYALTINO (Ire) 5-11-7 A Kondrat, *midfield, gd hdwy to track ldrs whn hit 7th, struggling when hit 2 out, wknd.*
................................(9 to 1 op 6 to 1 tchd 10 to 1) 9
2298⁸ HAND WOVEN 5-11-7 C Maude, *in tch till wknd quickly appr 3 out*....................(66 to 1 op 33 to 1) 10
2521² BOSS DOYLE (Ire) 5-11-7 C O'Dwyer, *chsd ldrs till outpcd 7th, sn wknd*...................(20 to 1 op 16 to 1) 11
2785* THE PROMS (Ire) 6-11-7 C Llewellyn, *hld up, struggling 4 out, sn wl beh*.........(20 to 1 op 25 to 1 tchd 33 to 1) 12
2775 NASONE (Ire) 6-11-7 P Hide, *keen hold, pressed ldrs to 3 out, sn wknd, eased whn btn*............(100 to 1 op 66 to 1) 13
2607² PRUSSIA 6-11-7 Guy Lewis, *al rear, tld off aftr 7th.*(200 to 1) 14
2438⁶ HURDANTE (Ire) 7-11-7 B Fenton, *pld hrd, cl up till wknd quickly aftr 7th, tld off*............(50 to 1 op 33 to 1) 15
2792⁴ AGISTMENT 6-11-7 R Dunwoody, *f 1st, broke neck, dead.*
................................(9 to 1 op 5 to 1 tchd 13 to 2) f
Dist: 1l, ¾l, 3l, 7l, 14l, dist, 7l, 7l, 1½l, 14l. 4m 58.30s. a 23.30s (17 Ran).
SR: 49/48/47/44/28/27/27/26/19/

(J P McManus), A P O'Brien

3130 Queen Mother Champion Chase
Class A Grade 1 (5-y-o and up)
£81,650 2m.................(2:35)

2826 MARTHA'S SON 10-12-0 R Farrant, settled in tch, niggled alng hfwy, improved gng wl 3 out, led last, drvn clr r-in.
...................................(9 to 1 op 10 to 1 tchd 11 to 1) 1
2219* ASK TOM (Ire) 8-12-0 R Garritty, jmpd boldly, led second to 6th (water), styd upsides, lft in ld 3 out till aftr nxt, ev ch last, kpt on.......................................(5 to 1 op 9 to 1) 2
2826* VIKING FLAGSHIP 10-12-0 N Dunwoody, trkd ldrs, improved bef 3 out, led aftr nxt, stumbled bend betw last 2, hdd last, kpt on....................(3 to 1 op 5 to 2 tchd 100 to 30) 3
2586* KLAIRON DAVIS (Fr) 8-12-0 F Woods, not fluent 3rd and 7th, improved hfwy, feeling pace aftr 3 out, styd on r-in.
....(3 to 1 op 9 to 4) 4
2507* STRONG PROMISE (Ire) 6-12-0 N Williamson, pld hrd, led to second, led 6th (water), blun and hdd 3 out, fdd bef last.
...........................(5 to 2 fav op 11 to 4 tchd 3 to 1) 5
2689² LORD DORCET (Ire) 7-12-0 J Osborne, wth ldrs, feeling pace and hit 8th, rallied 3 out, wknd betw last 2.
.....................................(50 to 1 tchd 33 to 1) 6
Dist: 2½l, ½l, 1l, 5l, 8l. 3m 50.20s. b 1.80s (6 Ran).
SR: 86/83/82/81/76/68/   (P J Hartigan), Capt T A Forster

3131 Coral Cup Handicap Hurdle Class B (5-y-o and up) £41,486 2m 5f. .(3:15)

2789* BIG STRAND (Ire) [122] 8-10-0 Jamie Evans, settled off the pace, drvn alng and plenty to do 7th, tenth appr last, str run und pres to ld on line..(16 to 1 op 14 to 1 tchd 18 to 1) 1
2787* ALLEGATION [142] (v) 7-11-6 A P McCoy, wth ldr, led aftr 4 out to last, sn led ag'n, ran on, ct on line.
....(20 to 1 op 16 to 1) 2
2326³ CASTLE SWEEP (Ire) [126] 6-12-0 R Johnson, nvr far away, chlgd gng wl 3 out, led and hit last, sn hdd, rallied finish.
....(14 to 1) 3
2453* TULLYMURRY TOFF (Ire) [135] 6-10-10 (3") E Callaghan, settled midfield, niggled alng frm hfwy, styd on wl from betw last 2, nrst finish.....(9 to 2 fav tchd 5 to 1 and 4 to 1) 4
TAMARPOUR (USA) [122] (bl) 10-9-7 (7*) B Moore, sn beh, improved aftr 3 out, styd on betw last 2, nvr nrr... (100 to 1) 5
2695⁵ DR LEUNT (Ire) [125] 6-10-3 G Tormey, nvr far away, ev ch 3 out, styd on same pace r-in.
...........................(40 to 1 op 33 to 1 tchd 50 to 1) 6
2674* BALLYRIHY BOY [122] 6-10-0 C F Swan, sn beh, styd on strly betw last 2, fnshd wl.
...........................(33 to 1 op 25 to 1 tchd 40 to 1) 7
2445³ ETON GALE (Ire) [122] 8-10-0 R Hughes, settled off the pace, gd hdwy aftr 4 out, styd on one pace betw last 2.
......................................(100 to 1 op 66 to 1) 8
1761⁷ MYSTICAL CITY (Ire) [137] 7-10-12 (3*) D J Casey, hld up gng wl, plenty to do 3 out, styd on well betw last 2, nrst finish.
...........................(25 to 1 op 14 to 1 tchd 33 to 1) 9
2776² MANDYS MANTINO (Ire) [144] 7-11-8 P Hide, trkd ldrs, feeling pace aftr 3 out, kpt on same pace frm nxt.
....(20 to 1 op 25 to 1) 10
2841⁵ METASTASIO [125] (bl) 5-10-3 H Rogers, wtd wth, gd hdwy to chase ldrs hfwy, kpt on same pace frm 2 out.
...........................(33 to 1 op 20 to 1 tchd 40 to 1) 11
2598² SUPREME LADY (Ire) [128] 6-10-6 J Culloty, settled rear, plenty to do hfwy, drvn alng 2 out, no imprsn.
.......................(10 to 1 op 6 to 1 tchd 11 to 1) 12
2238* ELA MATA [124] 5-10-2 J Railton, tucked away on ins, feeling pace aftr 4 out, fdg whn blun 2 out....(10 to 1 op 12 to 1) 13
2124* RAWY (USA) [126] (bl) 5-10-4 C O'Dwyer, pressed ldrs, drvn alng whn pace quickened betw last 2, eased whn btn r-in.
...........................(12 to 1 op 10 to 1 tchd 14 to 1) 14
2780³ BLAST FREEZE (Ire) [126] 8-10-4 M A Fitzgerald, settled midfield, feeling pace 3 out, fdd und pres.
...........................(12 to 1 tchd 14 to 1) 15
2760² NON VINTAGE (Ire) [126] 6-10-4 W Worthington, midfield whn mstk 4th, struggling aftr.
...........................(40 to 1 op 33 to 1 tchd 50 to 1) 16
2128⁷ EXECUTIVE DESIGN [132] 5-10-10 P Niven, sn beh, nvr able to rch chalg pos......................(16 to 1 tchd 20 to 1) 17
2716⁷ NIJMEGEN [125] (bl) 9-10-3 Derek Byrne, settled in tch, effrt and drvn alng 4 out, bumped nxt, nvr a threat.
...........................(33 to 1 op 25 to 1 tchd 50 to 1) 18
2695⁶ LYING EYES [122] 6-9-7 (7*) J Power, al beh.
....(50 to 1 op 33 to 1) 19
2820³ KISSAIR (Ire) [130] 6-10-8 R Dunwoody, in tch, feeling pace aftr 4 out, fdd nxt.............(33 to 1 tchd 50 to 1) 20
2157 GYSART (Ire) [122] (bl) 8-10-0 C Maude, wl plcd till wknd 3 out.......................................(33 to 1 tchd 50 to 1) 21
2830 FATACK [122] 8-10-0 S Curran, chsd ldrs, struggling and short of room appr 3 out, fdd.......(50 to 1 tchd 66 to 1) 22
2806⁶ SESAME SEED (Ire) [122] 9-10-0 J Osborne, wl plcd, feeling pace whn hit 3 out, sn btn.......(33 to 1 op 50 to 1) 23
2557⁷ COPPER BOY [126] 8-10-4 B Powell, pld hrd, not fluent, led aftr 4 out, fdg whn blun nxt, sn lost tch.
...........................(10 to 1 op 6 to 1 tchd 11 to 1) 24
2665⁴ SCOTTISH WEDDING [122] 7-9-11 (3*) R Massey, al wl beh, tld off......................................(200 to 1) 25
2933³ SEA VICTOR [122] 5-10-0 D Gallagher, settled in tch, lost pl quickly aftr 4 out, tld off. (12 to 1 op 14 to 1 tchd 16 to 1) 26
2128⁴ FAMILY WAY [127] 10-10-5 F Woods, struggling in rear hfwy, lost tch and pld up bef 3 out.......(16 to 1 tchd 20 to 1) pu
2591³ DIRECT ROUTE (Ire) [126] 6-11-2 N Williamson, settled in tch, hit 6th, hmpd bend aftr 4 out and nxt, pld up 2 out, lme.
...........................(16 to 1 op 14 to 1 tchd 20 to 1) pu

Dist: Sht-hd, hd, 1l, 1l, 1l, ½l, hd, ¾l, 2½l, 5l. 4m 57.00s. a 1.00s (28 Ran).
SR: 41/61/69/53/39/41/37/37/51/   (E C Jones), M C Pipe

3132 Royal Sunalliance Chase Class A Grade 1 (5-y-o and up) £57,282 3m 1f...........................(3:55)

2779³ HANAKHAM (Ire) 8-11-4 R Dunwoody, midfield, mstk front 3rd, chasing ldrs whn slight mstk 4 out, led 2 out, four ls clr when blun last, kpt on gmely.
.......................(13 to 2 op 6 to 1 tchd 7 to 1) 1
2788* EUDIPE (Fr) 5-10-8 A P McCoy, hld up, jmpd wl, gd hdwy 5 out, chsd wnr frm 2 out, styd on well, no imprsn cl hme.
...........................(9 to 2 op 5 to 2 tchd 7 to 2) 2
2508* DJEDDAH (Fr) 6-11-4 A Kondrat, hld up, hdwy 7th, pressed ldrs frm 12th, drvn alng bef 2 out, kpt on same pace.
.......................(100 to 30 fav op 5 to 2 tchd 7 to 2) 3
2794* BERUDE NOT TO (Ire) 8-11-4 J Osborne, jmpd wl, al hndy, led 5 out to 2 out, no extr appr last.
.......................(15 to 2 op 8 to 1 tchd 9 to 1) 4
2833* CORKET (Ire) 7-11-4 C F Swan, midfield, some hdwy 9th, tch 13th, rallied and styd on aftr 2 out, unbl to chal.
.......................(9 to 1 op 8 to 1 tchd 10 to 1) 5
2638⁵ GLITTER ISLE (Ire) 7-11-4 P Hide, midfield, not fluent 6th, in tch whn mstk 5 out, fdd nxt.........(16 to 1 op 12 to 1) 6
2657⁵ HAWAIIAN SAM (Ire) 7-11-4 G Crone, keen hold, led 6th, jmpd wl till fdd 5 out, sn lost tch, tld off....(66 to 1 op 33 to 1) 7
2443³ BARONET (Ire) 7-11-4 R Johnson, hld up rear, struggling frm 5 out, sn tld off.................(25 to 1 tchd 33 to 1) 8
2962² LORD MUFF (Ire) 8-11-4 J K Kinane, beh, blun 8th and 12th, sn tld off....................(100 to 1 op 66 to 1) 9
2805* BELL STAFFBOY (Ire) 8-11-4 Michael Brennan, beh, mstk 11th, tld off 4 out..(14 to 1 op 10 to 1 tchd 16 to 1) 10
2441² INDIAN TRACKER 7-11-4 C Maude, sn led, blun and hdd 5th, cl up till wknd quickly appr 2 out, eased considerably whn btn.
.......................(10 to 1 op 8 to 1 tchd 11 to 1) 11
2713³ THE LAST FLING (Ire) 7-11-4 Richard Guest, patiently rdn, hit 11th, gd hdwy 14th, chasing ldrs and cl up whn pld up 2 out.
.......................(33 to 1 op 25 to 1 tchd 40 to 1) ur
2700² BUCKHOUSE BOY 7-11-4 D Bridgwater, al rear, hit 7th, struggling tenth, tld off whn pld up 13th.
.......................(11 to 1 op 10 to 1 tchd 12 to 1) pu
2621 BALLYLINE (Ire) 6-11-4 J Railton, chsd ldrs, hit second, beh 9th, tld off whn pld up 10th.
.......................(150 to 1 op 100 to 1 tchd 200 to 1) pu

Dist: 2½l, 5l, 2l, 9l, 6l, 16l, 1½l, 1l, ½l, 3l. 6m 9.00s. a 1.00s (14 Ran).
SR: 30/17/22/20/11/5/   (M Brereton), R J Hodges

3133 127th Year Of The National Hunt Chase Challenge Cup Amateur Riders Class B (5-y-o and up) £21,525 4m...............(4:30)

2600⁴ FLIMSY TRUTH 11-12-7 Mr M Harris, jmpd wl, led frm second, clr appr 3 out, styd on gmely und pres r-in.
.......................(33 to 1 op 25 to 1 tchd 40 to 1) 1
2480* VOL PAR NUIT (USA) 6-12-4 Mr T Doumen, al hndy, chsd wnr most of way, rdn to improve 2 out, ridden last, kpt on und pres.
.......................(13 to 2 op 6 to 1 tchd 7 to 1) 2
2566² ROBSAND (Ire) 8-12-0 Mr A Balding, nvr far away, drvn alng fnl circuit, one pace frm 3 out.
.......................(9 to 1 op 7 to 1 tchd 10 to 1) 3
2756 IRISH LIGHT (Ire) 9-12-7 Mr Anthony Martin, beh, gd hdwy fnl circuit, effrt 4 out, one pace........(16 to 1 op 14 to 1) 4
2508² DROMHANA (Ire) 7-12-7 Mr J Tizzard, nvr far away, hit 4th 19th, feeling pace 3 out, wknd.
.......................(10 to 1 op 10 to 1 tchd 8 to 1) 5
2700⁴ PARAHANDY (Ire) 7-12-0 Mr D O'Brien, wtd wth, hit 7th, drvn alng fnl circuit, struggling whn blun 2 out, sn lost tch.
.......................(16 to 1 op 14 to 1 tchd 20 to 1) 6
2842² COOLAFINKA (Ire) 8-11-9 Mr J Berry, patiently rdn, improved fnl circuit, drvn alng 3 out, fdd.....(12 to 1 op 14 to 1) 7
2564⁵ BALLYEA BOY (Ire) (bl) 7-12-7 Mr R Thornton, chsd ldrs, effrt whn hit 4 out, fdd und pres nxt.....(14 to 1 op 12 to 1) 8
2745 LOCH GARMAN HOTEL (Ire) 8-12-0 Mr B Pollock, chsd ldrs, drvn alng whn pace quickened 3 out, sn lost tch.
.......................(100 to 1 op 50 to 1) 9
2903⁵ YOUNG MRS KELLY (Ire) 7-11-9 Mr G J Harford, early reminders, al beh, t 14th.
.......................(33 to 1 op 25 to 1 tchd 50 to 1) f
2790 MASTER KIT (Ire) 8-12-4 Mr J Billinge, struggling aftr one circuit, hit tenth, f 16th.....(50 to 1 op 40 to 1) f
2600 LITTLE MARTINA (Ire) 9-11-13 Mr C Bonner, led to second, wl plcd till blun and uns rdr 12th.....(14 to 1 op 16 to 1) ur
2981* CAPO CASTANUM 8-12-7 Mr A Wintle, midfield whn blun and uns rdr 12th......(33 to 1 op 25 to 1 tchd 50 to 1) ur
2894³ JASILU (Ire) 7-12-2 Mr O McPhail, midfield whn hit 14th, lost tch and pld up bef 3 out.........(50 to 1 op 33 to 1) pu
3000 PLASSY BOY (Ire) 9-12-0 Mr N Wilson, hit 13th, hmpd by faller nxt, lost tch and pld up bef 17th.
.......................(100 to 1 tchd 150 to 1) pu
2600* GENERAL PONGO 8-12-7 Mr C Vigors, hit 1st, settled midfield, losing tch whn nrly uns rdr 4 out, not reco'r, pld up bef nxt...........................(25 to 1 tchd 33 to 1) pu
2945* MACAUNTA (Ire) 7-12-7 Mr J T McNamara, tld off whn pld up bef 3 out.........................(25 to 1 tchd 33 to 1) pu

2648* ITSAJUNGLEOUTTHERE (Ire) 7-12-4 Mr W Ewing, *midfield whn hit 7th, lost tch fnl circuit, pld up bef 2 out.*
.................................(16 to 1 op 14 to 1) pu

2763* RANDOM HARVEST (Ire) 8-12-7 Mr S Swiers, *settled midfield, jmpd rght 5th, effrt fnl circuit, btn whn hit 3 out, pld up bef nxt*........................(6 to 1 fav tchd 13 to 2) pu

2677⁴ WIXOE WONDER (Ire) 7-12-0 Mr E James, *beh, effrt fnl circuit, lost tch quickly and pld up bef 3 out.*
.................................(66 to 1 op 50 to 1 tchd 100 to 1) pu

2626³ CHARLIE PARROT (Ire) 7-12-0 Mr A Farrant, *jmpd poorly, tld off whn pld up bef 16th.*..........(50 to 1 tchd 66 to 1) pu

2921⁵ CARDINAL RULE (Ire) 8-12-7 Mr R Burton, *chsd ldrs for o'r a circuit, lost tch quickly and pld up bef 2 out.*
.................................(50 to 1 op 25 to 1 tchd 66 to 1) pu

2763² SLIDEOFHILL (Ire) (bl) 8-12-0 Mr P Fenton, *nvr gng wl, blun 5th, tld off whn pld up bef 3 out.*
.................................(7 to 1 op 6 to 1 tchd 10 to 1) pu

Dist: 1¼l, 27l, 3l, 1¼l, 7l, 12l, 6l, 8l. 8m 11.90s. a 6.90s (23 Ran).

(M H Weston), M H Weston

3134 47th Year Of The Mildmay Of Flete Challenge Cup Handicap Chase Class B (5-y-o and up) £30,044 2½m 110yds......................(5:05)

2819² TERAO [121] 11-10-7 T J Murphy, *led 6th to 4 out, rallied to ld appr last, styd on strly.*..............(20 to 1 op 16 to 1) 1

2713* ALL THE ACES [125] 10-10-11 C F Swan, *settled mid-field, pushed alng to improve 5 out, short of room entering strt, staying on wl whn hit last, nrst finish.*
.................................(14 to 1 tchd 16 to 1 and 12 to 1) 2

2696⁴ AIR SHOT [135] 7-11-7 R Johnson, *hld up, midfield whn blun 4 out, slight mstk nxt, rallied frm 2 out, kpt on wl from last.*
.................................(15 to 2 op 8 to 1 tchd 9 to 1 and 7 to 1) 3

2808* NOYAN [115] 7-10-1 A Dobbin, *midfield, pushed alng tenth, chsd ldrs frm 3 out, hit last, kpt on same pace.*
.................................(11 to 2 op 5 to 1 tchd 6 to 1) 4

2934² DESTINY CALLS [123] 7-10-9 P Niven, *al hndy, wnt second aftr 4 out, slight ld 2 out, hdd and no extr appr last.*
.................................(6 to 1 tchd 13 to 2) 5

2799² AS DU TREFLE (Fr) [114] 9-10-0 A P McCoy, *str hold, sn led, hdd 6th, not fluent 8th, led 4 out to 2 out, fdd appr last.*
.................................(100 to 30 fav op 5 to 2 tchd 7 to 2) 6

2722² SOUTHAMPTON [120] (v) 7-10-6 B Fenton, *hld up, pushed alng and outpcd 4 out, some hdwy nxt, sn no imprsn.*
.................................(16 to 1 op 20 to 1) 7

2696³ BELLS LIFE [132] 8-11-4 G Tormey, *hld up, mstk 3rd, struggling 4 out, sn beh.*
.................................(25 to 1 op 20 to 1) 8

2452² NORTHERN HIDE [127] 11-10-13 P Holley, *in tch, niggled alng nfwy, struggling whn blun 4 out, sn lost touch.*
.................................(16 to 1 tchd 20 to 1) 9

2706⁷ NEW CO (Ire) [136] 9-11-8 C O'Dwyer, *settled rear, mstks, hdwy whn hit 4 out and nxt, sn fdd, eased when btn.*
.................................(14 to 1 op 12 to 1) 10

2325⁵ PASHTO [130] 10-11-2 R Dunwoody, *keen hold, chsd ldrs, losing tch whn blun 4 out, tld off .*
.................................(16 to 1 op 14 to 1 tchd 20 to 1) 11

2466* KONVEKTA KING (Ire) [138] 9-11-10 J Osborne, *al rear, beh whn pld up 4 out, lme...*(11 to 1 op 10 to 1 tchd 12 to 1) pu

2592² GOLDEN SPINNER [133] 10-11-5 M A Fitzgerald, *blun 1st, midfield till lost tch 5 out, beh whn pld up 3 out.*
.................................(7 to 1 op 8 to 1 tchd 6 to 1) pu

Dist: 1¼l, hd, 1¾l, 1½l, 8l, 2½l, 5l, 3½l, 9l, dist. 5m 1.10s. a 4.10s (13 Ran).

SR: -/-/10/-/-/-/ (B A Kilpatrick), M C Pipe

3135 Weatherbys Champion Bumper Standard Open National Hunt Flat Class A Grade 1 (4,5,6-y-o) £18,760 2m 110yds......................(5:40)

2054* FLORIDA PEARL (Ire) 5-11-6 R Dunwoody, *al gng wl, led o'r 3 fs out, imprsv*............(6 to 1 op 4 to 1 tchd 7 to 1) 1

2831¹² ARCTIC CAMPER 5-11-6 R Johnson, *patiently rdn, steady hdwy frm hfwy, ran on strly, no ch wth wnr.*
.................................(16 to 1 op 1 op 14 to 1 tchd 20 to 1) 2

2967* ALL THE COLOURS (Ire) 4-10-12 J Osborne, *al wl plcd, bustled alng entering strt, styd on one pace.*
.................................(10 to 1 op 8 to 1 tchd 12 to 1) 3

2831¹³ SCORING PEDIGREE (Ire) 5-11-6 S Curran, *settled in tch, improved to press ldrs appr strt, kpt on same pace ins fnl furlong.*.............(66 to 1 op 50 to 1 tchd 100 to 1) 4

2595* MR MARKHAM (Ire) 5-11-6 P Hide, *wtd wth, improved o'r 3 fs out, rdn and one pace ins last.*
.................................(9 to 1 tchd 10 to 1 and 8 to 1) 5

FRENCH HOLLY (USA) 6-11-6 R Hughes, *settle midfield, improved o'r 3 fs out, not quicken appr last.*
.................................(10 to 1 op 8 to 1) 6

2723* SAMUEL WILDERSPIN 5-11-3 (3*) R Massey, *patiently rdn, improved on outsd to go hndy o'r 3 fs out, no extr fnl furlong.*
.................................(7 to 1 tchd 6 to 1 and 8 to 1) 7

1942² BROWNES HILL LAD (Ire) 5-11-6 D Bridgwater, *nvr far away, drvn alng whn pace quickened entering strt, no extr fnl furlong.*.................................(33 to 1) 8

2449* MUSICAL MAYHEM (Ire) 4-10-12 C O'Dwyer, *settled to track ldrs, feeling pace and drvn alng appr strt, no extr approaching fnl furlong*........(16 to 1 op 12 to 1 tchd 20 to 1) 9

2503* ERINTANTE (Ire) 4-10-2 (5*) Mr T Doumen, *settled in midfield, effrt o'r 3 fs out, one pace.* (8 to 1 op 6 to 1 tchd 9 to 1) 10

1735³ BOZO (Ire) 4-11-6 B Fenton, *wtd wth, improved o'r 3 fs out, not quicken appr last.*........................(100 to 1) 11

2642² CURRADUFF MOLL (Ire) 6-11-1 C Llewellyn, *settled midfield, effrt aftr one m, fdd entering strt.*
.................................(33 to 1 op 20 to 1 tchd 40 to 1) 12

2694* DAWN LEADER (Ire) 6-11-6 G Upton, *chsd ldrs till fdd o'r 3 fs out*.........................(4 to 1 fav tchd 5 to 1) 13

2595⁵ IRANOS (Fr) 5-11-6 A P McCoy, *led till hdd and wknd o'r 3 fs out.*........................(33 to 1 tchd 40 to 1) 14

2567² KING MOLE 6-11-6 M A Fitzgerald, *sn beh, effrt hfwy, no imprsn appr strt.*........(40 to 1 op 33 to 1 tchd 50 to 1) 15

2595² DOM BELTRANO (Fr) 5-11-6 C Maude, *wl plcd till wknd o'r 3 fs out.*.................(50 to 1 op 33 to 1 tchd 66 to 1) 16

2100* FURNITUREVILLE (Ire) 7-11-6 Mr D McGoona, *settled in tch, feeling pace appr strt, fdd.*.........(16 to 1 tchd 20 to 1) 17

2129* OUR BID (Ire) 6-11-6 S Craine, *chsd ldrs till wknd appr strt.*
.................................(20 to 1 tchd 25 to 1) 18

2302* MR LURPAK 5-11-6 P Niven, *beh and drvn alng hfwy, no imprsn on ldrs*.........(10 to 1 op 8 to 1 tchd 12 to 1) 19

2567⁷ ENDEAVOUR (Fr) 5-11-6 J Railton, *wl plcd for o'r one m, fdd appr strt.*........................(100 to 1) 20

2402* TOP NOTE (Ire) 5-11-3 (3*) L Aspell, *in tch, drvn alng hfwy, sn btn.*...............(50 to 1 tchd 66 to 1) 21

2213² BALLAD MINSTREL (Ire) 5-11-6 N Williamson, *settled midfield, struggling aftr one m, fdd.*
.................................(40 to 1 op 33 to 1 tchd 50 to 1) 22

2383* FRANKIE WILLOW (Ire) 4-10-12 Mr P Graffin, *lost tch hfwy, tld off*.........................(50 to 1) 23

2234* FAWN PRINCE (Ire) 4-10-12 C F Swan, *al beh, tld off.*
.................................(12 to 1 op 10 to 1 tchd 14 to 1) 24

2975³ MEMSAHIB OFESTEEM 6-11-1 J Culloty, *settled midfield, struggling hfwy, tld off.*...............(100 to 1) 25

Dist: 5l, 2l, ¾l, 1½l, sht-hd, ¾l, ¾l, 1¾l, 1¾l, nk. 3m 45.10s. (25 Ran).

(Mrs V O'Leary), W P Mullins

HUNTINGDON (good to firm) Wednesday March 12th
Going Correction: MINUS 0.20 sec. per fur.

3136 Keysoe Selling Handicap Hurdle Class G (0-90 4-y-o and up) £1,978 2m 5f 110yds......................(1:50)

2999² EDWARD SEYMOUR (USA) [74] 10-11-4 T Jenks, *hld up, al gng wl, cld 3 out, led bit aftr last, shaken up and quickened nr finish, cleverly.*.................(3 to 1 fav op 5 to 2) 1

2804 CODE RED [75] 4-10-10 M Richards, *mstk 1st, hld up beh, hdwy appr 3 out, lft in ld aftr nxt, hdd r-in, no ch wth wnr.*
.................................(6 to 1 op 5 to 1 tchd 13 to 2 and 7 to 1) 2

2847⁸ BARK'N'BITE [80] 5-11-7 (3*) G Lee, *hld up, mstk 4 out, rallied and jmpd slwly nxt, kpt on.*(6 to 1 op 7 to 1 tchd 13 to 2) 3

2886⁶ SONG FOR JESS (Ire) [70] 4-10-5 S Wynne, *trkd ldr, led aftr 6th, mstk, swrvd lft and hdd after 2 out, one pace...*(16 to 1) 4

2872⁶ MICK THE YANK (Ire) [59] (bl) 7-10-3 Jacqui Oliver, *trkd ldrs, chlgd 3 out, still ev ch nxt, sn hmpd and btn.*
.................................(5 to 1 op 10 to 1) 5

2896⁷ VISCOUNT TULLY [74] 12-10-13 (5*) O Burrows, *hld up beh, hdwy aftr 4 out, ev ch nxt, wknd appr 2 out.*
.................................(6 to 1 op 5 to 1 tchd 13 to 2) 6

2804⁹ AUTUMN FLAME (Ire) [62] 6-10-6 M Brennan, *beh, pushed alng aftr 5th, lost tch 3 out, tld off.....*(14 to 1 op 12 to 1) 7

2982 SLIGHTLY SPECIAL (Ire) [58] 5-10-2 K Gaule, *cl up, hit 3rd and 6th, outpcd aftr 4 out, tld off......*(14 to 1 op 10 to 1) 8

2957 KANO WARRIOR [80] 10-11-3 (7*) J Mogford, *led till aftr 6th, sn drpd out, tld off....................*(33 to 1 op 25 to 1) 9

2872⁴ SHANAKEE [73] 10-11-3 Mr J L Llewellyn, *chsd ldrs till wknd 4 out, tld off whn pld up bef 2 out.*
.................................(6 to 1 op 4 to 1 tchd 7 to 1) pu

Dist: 1½l, 3l, 1½l, 2l, 3l, dist, 2l, 5l. 5m 5.80s. a 16.80s (10 Ran).

(W Jenks), W Jenks

3137 Melchbourne Maiden Hurdle Class E (4-y-o and up) £2,635 2m 5f 110yds ....(2:25)

1768⁸ NORTHERN STAR 6-10-12 (7*) Miss J Wormall, *beh, not fluent 1st 2, pushed alng aftr 5th, rapid hdwy after 4 out, led after nxt, ran on wl...*(16 to 1 op 12 to 1 tchd 20 to 1) 1

2782⁹ LOCH NA KEAL 5-10-11 (3*) D Fortt, *al hndy, chsd wnr frm 2 out, ev ch last, no extr und press.*
.................................(9 to 1 op 9 to 2 tchd 10 to 1) 2

2954⁷ TURSAL (Ire) 8-11-5 Mr R Armson, *keen hold, nvr far away, drvn appr 2 out, kpt on same pace.*
.................................(66 to 1 op 33 to 1 tchd 100 to 1) 3

2359⁷ NOT TO PANIC (Ire) 7-11-0 R Supple, *chsd ldrs, lost pl appr 3 out, rallied approaching nxt, hrd rdn and no extr approaching last.*... 4

2937³ LEAP IN THE DARK (Ire) 8-10-12 (7*) T Siddall, *prmnt till rdn and wknd aftr 3 out.*...............(10 to 1 tchd 12 to 1) 5

435

28997 BOUNDTOHONOUR (Ire) 5-11-5 Jacqui Oliver, chsd ldrs till
wknd 3 out............(20 to 1 op 14 to 1 tchd 25 to 1) 6
29724 CASTLE MEWS (Ire) 6-11-0 K Gaule, hld up in mid-div,
pushed alng aftr 5th, sn cld on ldrs, hrd rdn appr 2 out, soon
btn.............................(6 to 1 op 4 to 1) 7
25414 DACELO (Fr) 6-11-5 J A McCarthy, hld up mid-div, cld 4
out, pushed alng and btn quickly appr 2 out.
.............................(4 to 1 op 5 to 1 tchd 9 to 2) 8
28965 BLATANT OUTBURST 7-11-5 Gary Lyons, hld up beh, hdwy
aftr 5th, mstk and wknd 3 out.
.............................(16 to 1 op 6 to 1 tchd 20 to 1) 9
28493 DARK PHOENIX (Ire) (v) 7-11-0 M Brennan, prmnt, led 4 out to
aftr nxt, sn drvn and wknd, fnshd sore, tld off.
.............................(3 to 1 fav op 7 to 2 tchd 4 to 1) 10
BRIGHT FLAME (Ire) 5-11-5 Mr T Hills, al beh, tld off.
.............................(66 to 1 op 16 to 1 tchd 100 to 1) 11
27664 TEOROMA 7-11-5 Mr M Gingell, led 4 out, sn btn, tld off.
.............................(25 to 1 op 14 to 1 tchd 33 to 1) 12
2371 NUNS LUCY 6-11-0 S Wynne, prmnt till wknd appr 3 out, tld
off..............................(50 to 1 op 33 to 1) 13
BUSTER 9-11-5 E Byrne, pld hrd, al beh, tld off.
.............................(33 to 1 op 10 to 1) 14
LILLY THE FILLY 6-11-0 R Bellamy, al beh, tld off.
.............................(66 to 1 op 33 to 1 tchd 100 to 1) 15
BANDIT BOY 4-10-10 T Jenks, beh, hrd rdn aftr 5th, tld off
whn pld up bef 3 out...(16 to 1 op 25 to 1 tchd 33 to 1) pu
19736 STRATHMINSTER 6-11-5 T J O'Sullivan, tracking ldrs and ev
ch whn broke dwn and pld up appr 2 out, dead.
.............................(100 to 30 op 11 to 4 tchd 7 to 2) pu
Dist: 2l, 3l, 2l, 4l, nk, sht-hd, 1½l, 20l, 18l, 2½l. 5m 2.50s. a 13.50s (17 Ran).
(Mrs R Wormall), J A Pickering

3138 Bletsoe Handicap Chase Class F (0-105 5-y-o and up) £2,822 3m
.... (3:00)

27726 SHEELIN LAD (Ire) [81] 9-10-13 T Reed, beh, mstk 9th, hdwy
to track late 14th, led 4 out, sn rdn alng, all out.
.............................(33 to 1 op 16 to 1) 1
27724 TIM SOLDIER (Fr) [89] 10-11-7 R Supple, hld up beh ldrs,
outpcd 5 out, rallied nxt, chsd wnr aftr 3 out, str chal frm last,
jst held.............................(11 to 4 op 2 to 1) 2
28604 NIGHT FANCY [68] 9-10-0 J A McCarthy, al hndy, drw level 5
out, outpcd aftr 3 out, hld whn mstk nxt.
.............................(20 to 1 op 25 to 1 tchd 33 to 1) 3
2860 COASTING [76] 11-10-3 (5*) A Bates, trkd ldrs, rdn alng aftr
8th, outpcd 14th, no imprsn.............(20 to 1 op 16 to 1) 4
2604 KING'S SHILLING (USA) [79] 10-10-11 Jacqui Oliver, chsd
ldrs to 6th, beh whn mstk 12th, tld off....(7 to 1 op 6 to 1) 5
24597 ROYAL SQUARE (Can) [91] 11-11-9 K Gaule, hld up, mstk 4th,
hdwy to track ldrs 6th, pushed alng 12th, wknd quickly four
out.............................(5 to 2 fav op 11 to 4 tchd 3 to 1) 6
2861 BALLAD RULER [68] 11-10-0 R Bellamy, beh frm 6th, pld up
bef 14th.............................(40 to 1 op 33 to 1 tchd 50 to 1) pu
27673 RETAIL RUNNER [87] 12-11-5 Mr T Hills, al beh, tld off whn
pld up bef 3 out.............(5 to 1 op 4 to 1 tchd 11 to 2) pu
2770 CELTIC LAIRD [80] 9-10-12 D J Burchell, sn led, hdd but ev ch
4 out, wknd quickly, pld up aftr 3 out...(25 to 1 op 20 to 1) pu
26666 CELTINO [92] 9-11-10 S Wynne, hld up, pld up lme bef 10th,
dead.............................(5 to 1 op 7 to 2) pu
Dist: Nk, 15l, 4l, 16l, 10l. 5m 56.40s. a 16.40s (11 Ran).
(Mrs T J McInnes Skinner), Mrs T J McInnes Skinner

3139 Lady Riders' Champion Hurdle Handicap Hurdle Class E (0-110 4-y-o and up) £2,267 2m 110yds.. (3:35)

30783 IRON N GOLD [90] 5-11-4 (5*) Sophie Mitchell, hld up beh
ldrs, hdwy to chase ldr appr 2 out, hrd rdn to lead r-in, ran
on.............................(2 to 1 fav op 7 to 2) 1
26555 HIGHLY CHARMING (Ire) [78] 5-10-11 Ann Stokell, hld up, pld
hrd early, hdwy 4th, led aftr nxt, hdd r-in, kpt on.
.............................(9 to 2 op 5 to 2) 2
29577 SHIFTING MOON [75] (bl) 5-10-8 Jacqui Oliver, led aftr 1st till
after 5th, chsd ldr to appr 2 out, one pace.
.............................(11 to 2 op 6 to 1 tchd 7 to 1) 3
27772 ALKA INTERNATIONAL [80] 5-11-6 (7*) Miss C Townsley, led
till aftr 1st, cl up, reminders after 5th, one pace after 3 out.
.............................(4 to 1 op 5 to 2) 4
2012 VERONICA FRANCO [75] 4-10-0 Leesa Long, hld up, effrt 4th,
not pace to chal.............................(14 to 1 op 10 to 1) 5
2957 STEVE FORD [91] 8-11-10 Miss P Jones, trkd ldrs, lost pl 5th,
mstk 3 out, sn btn......(25 to 1 op 16 to 1 tchd 33 to 1) 6
2606 FAIRY PARK [95] (bl) 12-11-7 (7*) Miss C Spearing, hld up,
pushed alng and lost tch aftr 4th, tld off.
.............................(12 to 1 op 8 to 1 tchd 14 to 1) 7
2783 DAILY SPORT GIRL [80] 8-10-13 Miss E J Jones, hld up a
tch, outpcd 5th, tld off whn pld up bef last.........(10 to 1) pu
HIGHLAND FLAME [67] 8-10-0 Mrs F Needham, cl up till
wknd quickly aftr 4th, tld off whn pld up bef 2 out.
Dist: ½l, 11l, sht-hd, 3½l, sht-hd, dist. 3m 45.20s. a 4.20s (9 Ran).
SR: 20/7/-/-/-/5/   (D C T Partnership), T Casey

3140 Thurleigh Handicap Hurdle Class E (0-110 4-y-o and up) £2,285 3¼m
.... (4:05)

28923 TILTY (USA) [101] (v) 7-11-6 T Eley, led, rdn alng on bit 8th,
2 out, hrd ridden to ld ag'n r-in, ran on wl.
.............................(7 to 4 fav op Evens tchd 15 to 8 and 2 to 1) 1
28517 THIS NETTLE DANGER [81] 13-10-0 M Brennan, settled to
track ldg pair, took keen hold early, chlgd 3 out, led nxt, hrd
rdn and hdd r-in.............................(11 to 2 op 4 to 1) 2
24353 TIGER CLAW (USA) [81] 11-9-9 (5*) O Burrows, trkd wnr, rdn
alng 8th, drvn and no extr frm 3 out.
.............................(8 to 1 op 6 to 1 tchd 9 to 1) 3
25136 STAC-POLLAIDH [82] 7-9-8 (7*) W Walsh, hld up, outpcd appr
2 out, nvr plcd to chal.
.............................(10 to 1 tchd 100 to 30 and 7 to 2) 4
JOHNSTONS BUCK (Ire) [81] 8-10-0 E Murphy, hld up in last
pl, took keen hold early, outpcd aftr 3 out, nvr plcd to chal.
.............................(9 to 4 op 6 to 4 tchd 5 to 2) 5
Dist: 2½l, ½l, 4l, 26l. 6m 8.70s. a 16.70s (5 Ran).
(Cheadle Racing), A Streeter

3141 Bolnhurst Novices' Chase Class E (5-y-o and up) £2,864 2½m 110yds
.... (4:40)

23953 MR CONDUCTOR (Ire) 6-11-8 J R Kavanagh, made all, clr
appr 2 out, eased r-in.
.............................(6 to 1 on op 10 to 1 on tchd 11 to 2 on and 5 to 1 on) 1
2977 KATBALLOU 8-11-2 K Gaule, in last pl, chsd wnr appr 2 out,
no imprsn.............................(6 to 1 tchd 5 to 1) 2
28634 DEEP SONG 7-11-2 R Bellamy, chsd wnr, mstk 11th (water),
pckd 4 out, lost pl aftr 3 out, btn whn mistake nxt.
.............................(11 to 1 op 10 to 1 tchd 12 to 1 and 14 to 1) 3
Dist: 21l, 14l. 5m 8.60s. a 21.60s (3 Ran).
(P M de Wilde), R H Alner

3142 Swineshead Standard Open National Hunt Flat Class H (4,5,6-y-o) £1,329 2m 110yds................. (5:15)

2066* LORD LAMB 5-11-11 (3*) G Lee, trkd ldrs, shaken up 2 fs out,
led o'r one out, hng rght, ran on wl.
.............................(5 to 4 on op 6 to 4 on tchd 5 to 4 on) 1
DAD'S ARMY TWO (Ire) 4-10-10 E Murphy, hld up beh ldrs,
shaken up 2 fs out, no extr ins last.
.............................(7 to 2 op 5 to 2 tchd 6 to 1 and 7 to 1) 2
KANDYSON 4-11-4 R Supple, trkd ldrs, led o'r 2 fs out to over
one out, one pace.............(12 to 1 op 10 to 1 tchd 14 to 1) 3
2409 QUERY LINE 6-10-6 (7*) Miss C Spearing, set slow pace for 6
fs, led ag'n o'r 4 out to over 2 out, one pace.
.............................(33 to 1 op 20 to 1) 4
29536 EMBARGO (Ire) 5-10-11 (7*) Mr H Dunlop, prmnt, not quicken
o'r 2 fs out, kpt on same pace.............(12 to 1 op 9 to 2) 5
TEEJAY'S FUTURE (Ire) 6-10-6 (7*) W Walsh, hld up beh, effrt
o'r 2 fs out, kpt on........(14 to 1 op 10 to 1 tchd 16 to 1) 6
20294 MR MONTAGUE (Ire) 5-11-4 T Eley, hld up beh, hdwy o'r 5 fs
out, outpcd, one pace 2 out, outpcd.
.............................(6 to 1 op 5 to 1 tchd 3 to 1 and 7 to 1) 7
NIRVANA PRINCESS 5-10-6 (7*) J Mogford, unruly to post,
hld up beh, pld hrd, hmpd and almost uns rdr hfwy, nvr on
terms.............................(20 to 1 op 10 to 1) 8
2567 DENSTAR (Ire) 4-10-10 K Gaule, hld up, effrt o'r 2 fs out, nvr
on terms.............................(14 to 1 op 16 to 1 tchd 20 to 1) 9
2642 MUALLAF (Ire) 4-11-4 J A McCarthy, pld hrd, led aftr 6 fs to o'r
4 out, sn wknd........(25 to 1 op 16 to 1 tchd 33 to 1) 10
PERFECT ANSWER 4-10-2 (3*) T Dascombe, pld hrd, hit
rail 9 fs out, hdwy to track ldrs 7 out, wknd rpdly o'r 4 out, tld
off.............................(6 to 1 op 7 to 2 tchd 8 to 1) 11
Dist: 4l, 2l, 2½l, nk, nk, 8l, 14l, 8l, hd, dist. 3m 51.10s. (11 Ran).
(A Sharratt & Mr J Renton), Mrs M Reveley

NEWTON ABBOT (heavy)
Wednesday March 12th
Going Correction: PLUS 1.65 sec. per fur.

3143 East Ogwell Maiden Chase Class F (5-y-o and up) £2,346 2m 110yds
.... (2:10)

30672 COURT MASTER (Ire) 9-11-5 P Holley, made all, jmpd slwly
7th, rdn clr.............................(11 to 8 on tchd 5 to 4) 1
2719 FINNIGAN FREE 7-10-12 (7*) Mr M Frith, hld up, hdwy 6th,
wnt second six out, no imprsn und pres frm 2 out.
.............................(10 to 1 op 8 to 1) 2
30278 IMALIGHT 8-11-0 J Frost, trkd wnr to 6 out, wknd 3 out.
.............................(5 to 1 op 7 to 2) 3
2746 MARKET MAYHEM 7-11-5 A Tory, hmpd 1st, in rear, mstk 6 out,
tld off.............................(5 to 1 op 4 to 1 tchd 6 to 1) 4
WALK IN THE WOODS 10-11-0 Mr A Holdsworth, prmnt till
wknd quickly aftr 6th, tld off...........(16 to 1 op 10 to 1) 5
28735 BELLS WOOD 8-11-0 (5*) D J Kavanagh, in tch till mstk 4th,
tld off 7th, pld up bef 5 out...........(10 to 1 op 7 to 1) pu

2998² THE SECRET GREY 6-11-5 D Walsh, jmpd badly in rear, tld
off whn pld up bef 5 out.................(6 to 1 op 4 to 1)   pu
Dist: 1l, 11l, dist, dist. 4m 32.70s. a 34.70s (7 Ran).
SR: 17/16/-/-/   (Vice Admiral Sir Fitzroy Talbot), R H Buckler

3144 Teaboy Maiden Hurdle Class E (4-y-o and up) £2,284 2¾m..........(2:40)

2871³ DEFENDTHEREALM 6-11-5 J Frost, hld up, hdwy 6th, led
appr 2 out, clr last...(11 to 8 fav op 6 to 4 tchd 13 to 8)   1
ARMATEUR (Fr) 9-11-5 D Leahy, chsd ldrs till lost pl 4 out,
styd on und pres to go second last.... (25 to 1 op 20 to 1)   2
RICH TYCOON (Ire) 8-11-5 W Marston, rcd wide, led appr
5th, hdd and wknd approaching 2 out............ (33 to 1)   3
2324⁶ SALLY'S TWINS 4-10-4 W McFarland, hld up, hdwy appr 5th,
wknd aftr 3 out....................... (3 to 1 tchd 11 to 4)   4
2959⁴ COOL HARRY (USA) 6-10-12 (7ʳ) Mr S Durack, led till hdd
appr 3rd, wknd 3 out....................(33 to 1 op 25 to 1)   5
3036⁴ SPIRIT LEVEL 9-11-1¹ Mr R Payne, beh frm 3rd, some late
hdwy, nvr on terms.....................(50 to 1 op 33 to 1)   6
3001⁴ LOTHIAN COMMANDER 5-11-5 V Slattery, led appr 3rd, hdd
bef 5th, rdn approaching 4 out, sn wknd, tld off.
..............................(9 to 1 op 6 to 1)   7
2744⁴ BENFLEET 6-11-5 D Walsh, hld up, hdwy aftr 5th, wnt second
4 out, wknd rpdly after nxt, pld up bef 2 out.
.........................(11 to 2 op 3 to 1 tchd 6 to 1)   pu
BRIDIE'S PRIDE 6-11-2 (3ʳ) P Henley, prmnt to 5th, tld off whn
pld up aftr 3 out........................(25 to 1)   pu
2637 PAPRIKA (Ire) 8-11-0 A Thornton, in tch till weakend 4 out, tld
off whn pld up bef last................(7 to 1 op 12 to 1)   pu
2871⁶ CONNAUGHT'S PRIDE 6-10-9 (5ʳ) D J Kavanagh, al beh, tld
off whn pld up aftr 3 out.............(14 to 1 tchd 16 to 1)   pu
2876 BOOZYS DREAM 6-11-5 S Burrough, sn beh, tld off whn pld
up aftr 6th..........................(100 to 1 op 50 to 1)   pu
1919 JACKAMUS (Ire) 6-10-12 (7ʳ) Mr M Frith, al beh, tld off whn
pld up appr 4 out.....................(50 to 1)   pu
Dist: 7l, 6l, 7l, 2½l, 22l, 23l. 6m 1.30s. a 60.30s (13 Ran).
(George Standing), R G Frost

3145 Horses For Courses Handicap Chase Class E (0-115 5-y-o and up) £2,764 2m 5f 110yds.................(3:10)

2600 ORSWELL LAD [112] 8-11-6 (7ʳ) Mr S Durack, made all, drw
clr appr 3 out, unchlgd.
....................(6 to 4 fav op 2 to 1 tchd 11 to 8)   1
2861 JAILBREAKER [85] 10-9-11² (5ʳ) D Salter, in tch till mstks
tenth and nxt, lost pl, rallied to go second appr 2 out.
......................(11 to 4 op 3 to 1 tchd 5 to 2)   2
2597⁵ BIT OF A TOUCH [90] 11-10-5¹ J Frost, hld up, beh frm 5th,
hdwy whn hit 4 out, wknd sn aftr.
...........................(4 to 1 op 3 to 1 tchd 9 to 2)   3
1918⁴ ALLO GEORGE [113] 11-12-0 A Thornton, trkd wnr till wknd
quickly 4 out, virtually pld up r-in........(3 to 1 op 7 to 4)   4
Dist: 12l, 15l, dist. 5m 56.80s. a 54.80s (4 Ran).
(R M E Wright), P J Hobbs

3146 Little Close Handicap Hurdle Class D (0-120 4-y-o and up) £2,695 2¾m ....(3:45)

2778 HOLD YOUR RANKS [112] 10-12-0 J Frost, hld up, smooth
hdwy to ld 2 out, all out...............(5 to 1 op 3 to 1)   1
2789⁵ CASSIO'S BOY [88] 6-9-11 (7ʳ) X Aizpuru, hld up, hdwy to
track ldr 6th, led briefly appr 2 out, rallied r-in. ...(2 to 1 jt-
fav op 5 to 2)   2
1370⁵ LA MENORQUINA (USA) [95] 7-10-6 (5ʳ) D J Kavanagh, trkd
ldr till mstk 6th, rallied and ev ch appr 2 out, wknd bef last.
.............................(9 to 2 op 3 to 1)   3
2768⁸ VALIANTHE (USA) [90] (bl) 9-10-6 D Walsh, hld up, mstks,
hdwy appr 4 out, wknd bef nxt, tld off whn pld up before 2 out.
.........................(7 to 1 op 9 to 2)   pu
1449¹ RITTO [95] 7-10-11 W Marston, led, clr second, rdn and hdd
aftr 3 out, pld up bef nxt, lme......(2 to 1 jt-fav op 6 to 4)   pu
Dist: ¾l, 5l. 5m 59.50s. a 58.50s (5 Ran).
(Mrs C Loze), R G Frost

3147 Little Town Novices' Hunters' Chase Class H (5-y-o and up) £978 2m 5f 110yds.....................(4:20)

HERHORSE 10-11-5 (7ʳ) Mr L Jefford, chsd ldrs, hit 9th, sn
reco'red led 2 out, lft wl clr last.
.....................(16 to 1 op 10 to 1 tchd 20 to 1)   1
KALOORE 8-11-10 (7ʳ) Mr R Nuttall, in rear, rdn and hdwy 6
out, wkng whn lft second last...(7 to 4 jt-fav op 6 to 4)   2
GOOD KING HENRY 11-11-10 (7ʳ) Mr I Widdicombe, in tch
till wknd tenth, tld off....................(9 to 1 op 8 to 1)   3
CEDAR SQUARE (Ire) 6-11-12 (5ʳ) Mr J Jukes, led till blun 2
out, btn whn f last.................(7 to 4 jt-fav op 6 to 4)   f
3026 TOM'S GEMINI STAR 9-11-10 (7ʳ) Mr G Penfold, beh whn
blun and uns rdr 6th.................(8 to 1 op 12 to 1)   ur
MECADO (v) 10-11-10 (7ʳ) Mr M Munrowd, hld up, hdwy 8th,
wknd 6 out, tld off whn refused 2 out...(20 to 1 op 12 to 1)   ref
ABSENT MINDS 11-11-5 (7ʳ) Miss S Young, mid-div till wknd
9th, tld off whn pld up bef last..................(33 to 1)   pu

SEVENTH LOCK 11-11-10 (7ʳ) Miss L Blackford, trkd ldr, blun
6th, wknd nxt, tld off whn pld up bef 4 out.
......................(10 to 1 op 7 to 1)   pu
TOM'S APACHE 8-11-10 (7ʳ) Mr I Dowrick, mstk 1st, tld off
whn pld up bef tenth..................(25 to 1 op 20 to 1)   pu
BRYN'S STORY 10-11-10 (7ʳ) Major G Wheeler, tld off 3rd, pld
up bef tenth........................(50 to 1 op 33 to 1)   pu
BALDHU CHANCE 9-11-10 (7ʳ) Mr James Young, in tch to
9th, tld off whn pld up bef 4 out........(12 to 1 op 8 to 1)   pu
Dist: 12l, dist. 6m 5.70s. a 63.70s (11 Ran).
(Miss A Howard-Chappell), Miss A Howard-Chappell

3148 Jokers Handicap Hurdle Class F (0-100 4-y-o and up) £1,871 2m 1f ....(4:55)

2872 ALICE'S MIRROR [68] (bl) 8-10-2 R Greene, hld up in rear,
hdwy 3 out, led appr last, quickened clr. (12 to 1 op 7 to 1)   1
2925⁵ ALPINE JOKER [82] 4-10-3 (5ʳ) D J Kavanagh, hld up, hdwy to
track ldrs 4 out, led aftr nxt, hdd appr last, one pace.
......................(5 to 2 jt-fav op 5 to 1 tchd 9 to 1)   2
3039³ FRIENDLY HOUSE (Ire) [94] 8-12-0 D Walsh, hld up, hdwy 4
out, rdn appr 2 out, kpt on one pace..........(5 to 2 jt-
fav op 2 to 1 tchd 7 to 4)   3
2440⁵ URBAN LILY [75] (bl) 7-10-2 (7ʳ) J Harris, al prmnt, led 4 out,
hdd aftr nxt, rdn and wknd 2 out.
.......................(9 to 2 op 4 to 1 tchd 5 to 1)   4
2768⁹ ALDWICK COLONNADE [67] 10-10-11 W McFarland, hld up
in tch, wknd 4 out....................(25 to 1 op 12 to 1)   5
2872⁵ POOH STICK [66] 7-10-0 Mr A Holdsworth, hld up, hdwy 4th,
wknd 3 out..........................(16 to 1 op 10 to 1)   6
2768 TILT TECH FLYER [78] 12-10-5 (7ʳ) J Prior, led till hdd 4 out,
wknd quickly aftr nxt... (16 to 1 op 12 to 1 tchd 20 to 1)   7
2878⁴ RUNIC SYMBOL [70] 6-10-4 A Thornton, hld up in tch, wknd
bef 3 out, tld off.............(13 to 2 op 6 to 1 tchd 8 to 1)   8
2957⁹ ROYAL GLINT [66] 8-9-7 (7ʳ) Mr L Baker, prmnt till wknd 4 out,
tld off whn pld up bef 2 out...........(20 to 1 op 12 to 1)   pu
Dist: 3l, 5l, 16l, 16l, nk, 1l, 16l. 4m 34.00s. a 45.00s (9 Ran).
(A M Partnership), K Bishop

3149 Templers Road Handicap Chase Class F (0-105 5-y-o and up) £2,527 3¼m 110yds.................(5:30)

2482 SILVERINO [81] 11-10-12 S Burrough, al in tch, wnt second
12th, led 14th, clr 4 out, unchlgd........(14 to 1 op 12 to 1)   1
2921* TOP JAVALIN (NZ) [93] 10-11-3 (7ʳ) Mr G Shenkin, hld up,
jmpd slwly tenth, trkd ldrs 14th, hdwy to go second 5 out, sn
rdn and outpcd..................(5 to 4 fav tchd 11 to 10)   2
2741⁴ BOURNEL [76] 9-10-4 (3ʳ) P Henley, trkd ldr to 12th, wkng
whn hit 6 out.....................(7 to 1 op 5 to 1 tchd 7 to 1)   3
2549⁶ KEANO (Ire) [92] 8-11-9 W Marston, led till hdd 14th, wknd
quickly.............................(2 to 1 tchd 7 to 4)   4
BOTTLE BLACK [81] 10-10-12 P McLoughlin, in tch till wknd
13th, tld off whn pld up bef 5 out........(25 to 1 op 16 to 1)   pu
2888⁴ SPACE CAPPA [89] 9-11-6 Miss V Stephens, mstks in rear,
tld off 11th, pld up bef last..............(8 to 1 op 6 to 1)   pu
Dist: Dist, 1¼l, 3l. 7m 30.70s. a 70.70s (6 Ran).
(S N Burfield), P R Rodford

CHELTENHAM (good)
Thursday March 13th
Going Correction: PLUS 0.10 sec. per fur. (races 1,2,7), MINUS 0.05 (3,4,5,6)

3150 Elite Racing Club Triumph Hurdle Class A Grade 1 (4-y-o) £44,289 2m 1f............................(2:00)

2731* COMMANCHE COURT (Ire) 11-0 N Williamson, settled gng
wl, improved 3 out, led jst aftr last, drvn out.
.......................(9 to 1 op 8 to 1 tchd 10 to 1)   1
2925² CIRCUS STAR 11-0 R Johnson, nvr far away, chlgd and not
fluent 2 out, drw level last, kpt on und pres r-in.
.......................(40 to 1 op 33 to 1 tchd 50 to 1)   2
2324* SHOOTING LIGHT (Ire) 11-0 R Dunwoody, al wl plcd, ev ch
frm 3 out, rdn and kpt on same pace r-in.(7 to 1 op 11 to 2)   3
2828* L'OPERA (Fr) 11-0 J Osborne, led till aftr 1st, styd hndy, led
betw last 2 till jst after last, not quicken.
.......................(11 to 2 tchd 13 to 2)   4
2727⁴ HAYAAIN 11-0 J Railton, hit second, settled midfield, effrt to
chase ldrs 2 out, no extr betw last two.
.......................(33 to 1 tchd 40 to 1)   5
2751* MARLONETTE (Ire) 10-9 D J Casey, beh, styd on frm 3 out, nvr
nrr............................(33 to 1 tchd 40 to 1)   6
3066³ SEATTLE ALLEY (USA) 11-0 J A McCarthy, wtd wth, improved
and in tch 3 out, not quicken betw last 2.
.......................(66 to 1 tchd 100 to 1)   7
2727⁷ MR WILD (USA) 11-0 J Culloty, settled midfield, effrt and drvn
alng 3 out, no imprsn...(50 to 1 op 40 to 1 tchd 66 to 1)   8
2553² WHITE SEA (Ire) 10-9 C F Swan, led aftr 1st till betw last 2, fdd,
finshd lme....................(9 to 2 fav op 7 to 2)   9
2818* NO MORE HASSLE (Ire) 11-0 P Niven, sn hndy, ev ch 3 out,
fdd aftr nxt, hit last........(16 to 1 op 14 to 1 tchd 20 to 1)   10

437

2976* PLEASURELAND (Ire) 11-0 D Morris, *settled rear, nvr rch chalg pos*...(100 to 1) 11

2791³ MUTANASSIB (Ire) 11-0 C Maude, *str hold, midfield whn hit 6th, rdn and no imprsn 3 out*........(50 to 1 tchd 66 to 1) 12

2828² KERAWI 11-0 C Llewellyn, *chsd ldrs, effrt and drvn alng hfwy, hit 2 out, sn btn*.......................(10 to 1 op 7 to 1) 13

2825⁶ SERENUS (USA) 11-0 M A Fitzgerald, *settled midfield, effrt 3 out, fdd*................................(50 to 1 op 40 to 1) 14

2965* STYLISH ALLURE (USA) 11-0 C O'Dwyer, *wtd wth, effrt 3 out, fdd nxt*.............................(12 to 1 tchd 14 to 1) 15

2783* ALWAYS HAPPY 10-9 T Dascombe, *settled midfield, rdn hfwy, nvr dngrs*....................................(66 to 1) 16

2628 POMME SECRET (Fr) (bl) 11-0 A P McCoy, *wth ldrs, hit 3rd, lost tch 3 out*..............................(25 to 1) 17

2470⁵ EVRIZA (Ire) (bl) 10-9 T Horgan, *sn beh, nvr a factor*. ....(50 to 1 op 40 to 1 tchd 100 to 1) 18

2727 PALAMON (USA) 11-0 T J Murphy, *wth ldrs, hit 3rd, wknd 3 out*...(200 to 1) 19

2773⁴ EXALTED (Ire) 11-0 T Jenks, *lost tch hfwy, tld off*. ....(100 to 1 op 66 to 1) 20

2511⁷ SOCIETY GIRL 10-9 J R Kavanagh, *sn beh, tld off*. (200 to 1) 21

2731³ MISS ROBERTO (Ire) 10-9 K F O'Brien, *beh hfwy, tld off*. ....(33 to 1) 22

2744³ MERAWANG (Ire) 11-0 P Hide, *hld up, struggling hfwy, tld off*........................(100 to 1 tchd 200 to 1) 23

2765⁶ WARNING REEF (bl) 11-0 W Marston, *slwly away, blun 1st, tld off hfwy*..(200 to 1) 24

3044* BELMARITA (Ire) 10-9 Michael Brennan, *sn wl beh, tld off*. ....(50 to 1 op 66 to 1) 25

2816* DOUBLE AGENT 11-0 A Dobbin, *beh whn 1 3rd*. ....(50 to 1 op 40 to 1 tchd 66 to 1) f

2636* HARBET HOUSE (Fr) 11-0 D O'Sullivan, *f second*. ....(40 to 1 op 33 to 1 tchd 50 to 1) f

2773* KINGS WITNESS (USA) 11-0 D Bridgwater, *not jump wl, hit 4th, tld off whn pld up bef last*......(14 to 1 tchd 16 to 1) pu

Dist: 1l, 1¼l, 1¾l, 4l, 1l, 3l, 4l, ½l, 1½l, ¾l. 4m 0.20s. a 6.20s (28 Ran).

SR: 41/40/38/36/32/26/28/24/18/   (D F Desmond), T M Walsh

3151 Bonusprint Stayers' Hurdle Class A Grade 1 (4-y-o and up) £53,440 3m 110yds..............................(2:35)

2557³ KARSHI 7-11-10 J Osborne, *cl up, led 5th to 7th, outpcd 3 out, str run to ld last, hld on gmely*. ....(20 to 1 op 16 to 1 tchd 25 to 1) 1

2695³ ANZUM 6-11-10 R Johnson, *chsd ldrs, niggled alng frm hfwy, lost tch 3 out, plenty to do appr last, fnshd wl*. ....(25 to 1 op 20 to 1 tchd 28 to 1) 2

2591 PADDY'S RETURN (bl) 5-11-10 R Hughes, *hld up, gd hdwy hfwy, led 8th till aftr 3 out, led betw last 2, hdd last, sn one pace*.....................................(20 to 1) 3

SOHRAB (Ire) 9-11-10 C Maude, *settled rear, hit 9th, drvn and outpcd bef 3 out, styd on frm nxt, unbl to chal*. (33 to 1) 4

2830³ ESCARTEFIGUE (Fr) 5-11-10 D Bridgwater, *hld up, jnd ldrs 8th, led and quickened aftr 3 out, hdd betw last 2, fnshd tired*. ....(9 to 2 fav op 3 to 1 tchd 5 to 1) 5

2584² WHAT A QUESTION (Ire) 9-11-5 C O'Dwyer, *midfield, in tch and drvn alng 9th, outpcd appr 3 out, styd on frm nxt*. ....(6 to 1 op 11 to 2 tchd 13 to 2) 6

1998² TRAINGLOT 10-11-10 R Dunwoody, *rear, drvn alng and struggling 4 out, no response, sn btn*.....(7 to 1 op 5 to 1 tchd 8 to 1) 7

3113⁷ PRIDWELL 7-11-10 A P McCoy, *settled rear, drvn alng 4 out, no response, sn btn*....................................(25 to 1) 8

2830⁵ TARRS BRIDGE (bl) 6-11-10 J Magee, *cl up, led 7th to nxt, drvn and lost pl 3 out, tld off*......(40 to 1 op 50 to 1) 9

2841⁷ DERRYMOYLE (Ire) 8-11-10 J P Broderick, *hld up, struggling aftr 4 out, sn wl beh, tld off*. ....(25 to 1 op 20 to 1 tchd 33 to 1) 10

2830⁵ OCEAN HAWK (USA) (bl) 5-11-10 C Llewellyn, *led to 5th, cl up till lost pl 7th, sn beh, tld off*..........(7 to 1 op 9 to 1) 11

2936⁷ EALING COURT 8-11-10 B Fenton, *pushed alng in rear frm hfwy, wl beh 3 out, tld off*....(100 to 1 tchd 150 to 1) 12

2830⁵ TOP SPIN 8-11-10 T J Murphy, *beh, mstk 4th, tld off 5 out*. ....(100 to 1) 13

2566³ WISLEY WONDER (Ire) 7-11-10 D Walsh, *in tch, niggled alng hfwy, wknd quickly 4 out, tld off*.........(66 to 1 op 50 to 1) 14

2830⁵ CONQUERING LEADER (Ire) 8-11-5 M A Fitzgerald, *midfield, f 7th*.......................(15 to 2 op 7 to 1 tchd 8 to 1) f

2584⁸ URUBANDE (Ire) 7-11-10 C F Swan, *f second*. ....(6 to 1 op 11 to 2 tchd 13 to 2) f

2820⁵ TRAGIC HERO (bl) 5-11-10 N Williamson, *hld up, jinked lft and ran out 6th*..................(50 to 1 op 33 to 1) ro

Dist: 2½l, 2l, 1½l, sht-hd, 1¾l, 10l, ¾l, 20l, 13l, hd. 5m 44.00s. a 5.00s (17 Ran).

SR: 70/67/65/63/63/61/51/50/30/   (Lord Vestey), Miss H C Knight

---

3152 Tote Cheltenham Gold Cup Chase Class A Grade 1 (5-y-o and up) £134,810 3¼m 110yds............(3:15)

2045 MR MULLIGAN (Ire) 9-12-0 A P McCoy, *jmpd boldly, wth ldr, led 13th, blun 4 out, wnt clr 2 out, edgd rght r-in, styd on gmely*................(20 to 1 op 12 to 1 tchd 25 to 1) 1

2327² BARTON BANK 11-12-0 D Walsh, *al wl plcd, hit 9th and 13th, drvn alng frm 16th, hit 5 out, styd on frm betw last 2, no imprsn r-in*........................(33 to 1 tchd 50 to 1) 2

2671 DORANS PRIDE (Ire) 8-12-0 J P Broderick, *tucked away in midfield, rdn to improve frm 3 out, styd on same pace from betw last 2*.....................(10 to 1 op 7 to 1 tchd 11 to 1) 3

2452 GO BALLISTIC 8-12-0 A Dobbin, *wtd wth, effrt aftr one circuit, struggling whn pace lifted 5 out, styd on after nxt, no imprsn*........................(50 to 1 tchd 66 to 1) 4

2542* CHALLENGER DU LUC (Fr) (bl) 7-12-0 C Maude, *hit 3rd, settled rear, effrt aftr one circuit, drvn alng after 3 out, no imprsn*......................(16 to 1 op 14 to 1 tchd 20 to 1) 5

2507² ONE MAN (Ire) 9-12-0 R Dunwoody, *patiently rdn, blun 7th, steady hdwy fnl circuit, chsd wnr aftr 2 out, wknd last, fnshd tired*...................(7 to 1 op 11 to 2 tchd 15 to 2) 6

2779* COOME HILL (Ire) 8-12-0 J Osborne, *settled to track ldrs, feeling pace and lost tch 5 out, eased whn btn, tld off*. ....(15 to 2 op 9 to 2 tchd 8 to 1) 7

2700* CYBORGO (Fr) 7-12-0 C F Swan, *wtd wth, effrt and pushed alng 12th, struggling bef 3 out, lost tch, tld off*. ....(12 to 1 op 10 to 1) 8

2474* DANOLI (Ire) 9-12-0 T P Treacy, *settled to track ldrs, pckd 9th and nxt, struggling 6 out, no chn whn f 2 out*. f

2779² UNGUIDED MISSILE (Ire) 9-12-0 N Williamson, *wtd wth, hit 7th, struggling and losing tch whn f 13th*. ....(16 to 1 op 12 to 1 tchd 20 to 1) f

2325* DUBLIN FLYER 11-12-0 B Powell, *led to 13th, rdn and wknd quickly nxt, tld off whn pld up bef 2 out*. ....(8 to 1 op 5 to 1 tchd 10 to 1) pu

2474³ IMPERIAL CALL (Ire) 8-12-0 C O'Dwyer, *rcd wide thrght, hit 9th, effrt hfwy, struggling frm 14th, tld off whn pld up bef 5 out*. ....(4 to 1 fav tchd 9 to 2) pu

2696² NAHTHEN LAD (Ire) 8-12-0 R Farrant, *reminders in midfield hfwy, struggling frm 12th, tld off whn pld up bef 2 out*. ....(20 to 1 op 16 to 1) pu

BANJO (Fr) 7-12-0 D Bridgwater, *al beh, slightly hmpd 13th, tld off whn pld up bef 2 out*. pu

Dist: 9l, ½l, 6l, 3l, 16l, 16l, 7l. 6m 35.50s. a 3.50s (14 Ran).

SR: 52/43/42/36/33/17/1/-/-/   (Michael And Gerry Worcester), Noel T Chance

---

3153 Christies Foxhunter Chase Challenge Cup Class B (5-y-o and up) £19,867 3¼m 110yds............(3:55)

FANTUS 10-12-0 Mr T Mitchell, *in tch, pressing ldrs whn hit 16th, led aftr nxt, strly pressed last, kpt on gmely*. ....(10 to 1 op 6 to 1) 1

2680* CAB ON TARGET 11-12-0 Mr S Swiers, *hld up, steady hdwy fnl circuit, chlgd last, kpt on till no extr cl hme*. ....(4 to 1 fav op 3 to 1 tchd 9 to 2) 2

2475* WHAT A HAND 9-12-0 Mr P Fenton, *hld up, pushed alng to improve fnl circuit, hit 4 out, chsd ldrs aftr nxt, sn one pace*. ....(6 to 1 op 5 to 1) 3

2608 CELTIC ABBEY 9-12-0 Mr D S Jones, *midfield, hdwy 14th, chsd ldrs 3 out, fdd nxt*..................(16 to 1 op 10 to 1) 4

2544² DOUBLE SILK 13-12-0 Mr R Treloggen, *cl up, led 9th till aftr 17th, wknd 3 out*.........................(7 to 1 tchd 8 to 1) 5

FINAL PRIDE 11-11-9 Miss P Jones, *set str pace, blun and hdd 9th, lost tch aftr 4 out, sn btn*.....(33 to 1 tchd 40 to 1) 6

2793* THE JOGGER 12-12-0 Mr J Tizzard, *chsd ldrs, chlgd hfwy, drvn alng 5 out, sn btn*....................(10 to 1 op 8 to 1) 7

CLONROSH SLAVE 10-12-0 Mr S H Hadden, *wl beh hfwy, tld off*..................................(100 to 1 tchd 66 to 1) 8

2994* COPPER THISTLE (Ire) 9-12-0 Mr R Hunnisett, *jmpd rght 5th, wl beh tenth, sn tld off*..........................(33 to 1 op 25 to 1) 9

STILL IN BUSINESS 9-12-0 Miss P Curling, *uns rdr 1st*. ....(9 to 1 op 8 to 1 tchd 10 to 1) ur

2924* HOLLAND HOUSE 11-12-0 Mr C Vigors, *hld up, pushed alng tenth, beh whn pld up 6 out*...........(10 to 1 op 7 to 1) pu

MY NOMINEE (bl) 9-12-0 Mr R Burton, *cl up, rdn and outpcd 6 out, beh whn pld up 2 out*............(33 to 1 op 25 to 1) pu

2960² LORD RELIC (NZ) 11-12-0 Mr R Ford, *hld up, struggling 14th, beh whn pld up 6 out*...(12 to 1 op 10 to 1 tchd 14 to 1) pu

MR GOLIGHTLY 10-12-0 Mrs S Godfrey, *jmpd poorly in rear, tld off whn pld up tenth*. (20 to 1 op 16 to 1 tchd 25 to 1) pu

2924³ CLOBRACKEN LAD 9-12-0 Mr G Baines, *hit 4th, al rear, tld off whn pld up 15th*.................(100 to 1 op 50 to 1) pu

2887³ COLONIAL KELLY 9-12-0 Mr P Hacking, *rear whn mstk 12th, blun nxt, tld off whn pld up 6 out*. ..(33 to 1 tchd 50 to 1) pu

2924² MISS MILLBROOK 9-11-9 Mr E Williams, *in tch, pushed alng whn hit 15th and nxt, sn btn, beh when pld up 2 out*. pu

1754³ TEARAWAY KING (Ire) 7-12-0 Mr E Bolger, *beh, jmpd rght, hdwy and in tch 13th, hit 17th, lost touch nxt, pld up 2 out*. ....(13 to 2 op 6 to 1 tchd 7 to 1) pu

Dist: 1¾l, 11l, 7l, 9l, 15l, 18l, 2l, dist. 6m 44.70s. a 12.70s (18 Ran).

SR: 1¾l, ½l, 6l, 3l, 16l, 16l, 7l. 6m 35.50s. a 3.50s (14 Ran).

          (J A Keighley), R Barber

3154 125th Year Of The Cheltenham Grand Annual Chase Challenge Cup Handicap Class B (5-y-o and up) £28,679 2m 110yds............(4:30)

2819⁴ UNCLE ERNIE [137] 12-11-4 G Bradley, *patiently rdn, hdwy on outsd 4 out, led bef last, ran on wl*. ....(20 to 1 op 16 to 1 tchd 25 to 1) 1

438

2747* ELZOBA (Fr) [135] (bl) 5-10-8 A P McCoy, *al frnt rnk, led 8th, rdn and hdd bef last, kpt on same pace.* ....(13 to 2 op 5 to 1 tchd 7 to 1) 2
2736 PERKNAPP [119] 10-10-0 C F Swan, *wtd wth, drvn alng to improve frm 3 out, styd on same pace from betw last 2.* ....(25 to 1 op 20 to 1) 3
2335³ TIME WON'T WAIT (Ire) [134] 8-11-1 J Railton, *settled in tch, improved 5 out, rdn alng last 2, kpt on same pace.* ....(8 to 1 tchd 7 to 1) 4
2412² SCOBIE BOY (Ire) [120] 9-10-1 J P Broderick, *hit second, improved frm hfwy, effrt and drvn alng 2 out, one pace.* ....(25 to 1 op 20 to 1) 5
2911* POLITICAL TOWER [130] 10-10-11 (3ex) A Dobbin, *sn beh, styd on frm off the pace betw last 2, not pace of ldrs.* ....(16 to 1 op 14 to 1 tchd 20 to 1) 6
2442⁴ KIBREET [142] 10-11-9 N Williamson, *led till aftr 1st, styd hndy, feeling pace after 3 out, wknd betw last 2.* ....(14 to 1 op 10 to 1) 7
2689 CERTAINLY STRONG (Ire) [134] 7-11-1 R Dunwoody, *led aftr 1st to 7th, styd hndy, rdn and lost grnd bef 2 out, fdd.* ....(7 to 2 fav op 3 to 1 tchd 4 to 1) 8
2736 CABLE BEACH (Ire) [130] 8-10-11 C O'Dwyer, *al hndy, led 7th to nxt, cl up till fdd und pres 2 out.....* (25 to 1 op 20 to 1) 9
2590² DANCING PADDY [147] 9-12-0 D Walsh, *settled in tch, effrt whn blun 4 out, fdd und pres nxt.....*(16 to 1 tchd 20 to 1) 10
2561² SUPER COIN [120] 9-10-1 R Johnson, *chsd ldrs, feeling pace aftr 4 out, fdd nxt, sn btn.* (9 to 1 op 8 to 1 tchd 10 to 1) 11
2532⁸ STORM FALCON (USA) [121] 7-9-11 (5*) Chris Webb, *settled midfield, und pres aftr 4 out, sn struggling.* ....(20 to 1 op 33 to 1 tchd 50 to 1) 12
2514³ NORSE RAIDER [119] 7-10-0 C Maude, *chsd alng whn f 4th.* ....(33 to 1 op 25 to 1) f
2922³ MISTER ODDY [133] 11-11-0 J Culloty, *tracking ldrs whn blun and uns rdr 5 out...............* (16 to 1 op 14 to 1) ur
2592² EASTHORPE [136] 9-11-3 J F Titley, *struggling to keep up hfwy, pld up bef tenth...............* (8 to 1 tchd 9 to 1) pu
2664² GAROLO (Fr) [119] (bl) 7-10-0 J Osborne, *al wl beh, tld off whn pld up bef last......*(10 to 1 op 7 to 1 tchd 11 to 1) pu

Dist: 2l, 1l, 2½l, 3l, nk, 7l, 1¼l, 5l, 4l, 3l. 4m 0.40s. a 7.40s (16 Ran).
SR: 8/-/-/-/-/-/ (Lady Lloyd Webber), J G FitzGerald

3155 Cathcart Challenge Cup Chase Class B (6-y-o and up) £32,850 2m 5f .... (5:05)

2569* SPARKY GAYLE (Ire) 7-11-3 B Storey, *hld up, jmpd wl, hdwy on bit 11th, led and pckd slightly 3 out, quickened clr aftr nxt, styd on strly.........* (3 to 1 fav op 4 to 1 tchd 9 to 2) 1
2819³ MAJOR BELL 9-11-3 A Dobbin, *chsd clr ldr to 6th, hdwy and slight ld 4 out, hdd nxt, sn drvn alng, styd on wl.* ....(5 to 1 tchd 13 to 2) 2
3112* OR ROYAL (Fr) (bl) 6-11-3 A P McCoy, *hld up, hdwy and not fluent 8th, pushed alng 3 out, outpcd nxt, kpt on.* ....(4 to 1 op 7 to 4 tchd 9 to 2) 3
2863* WILD WEST WIND (Ire) 7-11-0 J F Titley, *chsd ldrs, pushed alng and outpcd appr 3 out, sn lost tch.* ....(10 to 1 tchd 9 to 1 and 12 to 1) 4
2786³ DESTIN D'ESTRUVAL (Fr) 6-11-7 D Bridgwater, *hld up rear, struggling 5 out, moderate late hdwy, nvr a factor.* (20 to 1) 5
2827 STATELY HOME (Ire) 6-11-3 N Williamson, *sn clr, hit 12th, mstk and hdd 4 out, wknd nxt.* ....(11 to 1 op 10 to 1 tchd 12 to 1) 6
1518⁶ PIMBERLEY PLACE (Ire) 9-11-3 C Llewellyn, *hdwy to chase clr ldr 6th, mstk 8th, wknd 11th, sn wl beh..........*(66 to 1) 7
2955 THE REVEREND BERT (Ire) 9-11-0 B Fenton, *beh, struggling 6 out, sn wl behind.....*(40 to 1 op 33 to 1 tchd 50 to 1) 8
2590* DOUBLE SYMPHONY (Ire) 9-11-7 G Bradley, *midfield, pushed alng tenth, struggling whn blun 5 out, pld up nxt.* ....(4 to 1 tchd 9 to 2) pu
2233* MANHATTAN CASTLE (Ire) 8-11-7 F Woods, *beh, pld up bef 8th.....................* (15 to 2 op 6 to 1 tchd 8 to 1) pu

Dist: 4l, 2½l, 13l, 8l, 2½l, nk, 12l. 5m 5.70s. a 1.70s (10 Ran).
SR: 62/58/55/39/38/31/31/16/-/ (Mr & Mrs Raymond Anderson Green), C Parker

3156 Vincent O'Brien County Handicap Hurdle Class A Grade 3 (5-y-o and up) £26,614 2m 1f............ (5:40)

2557⁴ BARNA BOY (Ire) [130] 9-10-12 R Dunwoody, *beh, hdwy 4th, str run appr last, led r-in, ran on strongly.* ....(14 to 1 tchd 16 to 1) 1
3080* CARLITO BRIGANTE [118] 5-10-0 (7ex) J Osborne, *in tch, smooth hdwy frm 2 out, chlgd last, kpt on strly.* ....(13 to 2 op 5 to 1 tchd 7 to 1) 2
2128³ PENNY A DAY (Ire) [140] 7-11-8 P Niven, *in tch, mstk and niggled alng 5th, sn lost pl, rallied wl appr last, nrst finish.* ....(15 to 2 op 6 to 1 tchd 8 to 1) 3
2841⁶ BLACK QUEEN (Ire) [122] 6-10-4 A J O'Brien, *settled rear, plenty to do whn slight mstk 2 out, ran on wl frm last, unbl to chal.......................* (12 to 1 tchd 14 to 1) 4
2735 TIDJANI (Ire) [118] 5-10-0 C O'Dwyer, *nvr far away, drvn to take slight ld betw last 2, hdd and no extr aftr last.* ....(11 to 2 fav op 10 to 1 tchd 12 to 1) 5
3025³ MORSTOCK [118] 7-9-11 (3*) T Dascombe, *hld up, pushed alng and outpcd 2 out, styd on appr last, gng on finish.* ....(50 to 1 tchd 66 to 1) 6
2716³ TOM BRODIE [128] 7-10-10 A Dobbin, *hld up, hdwy to press ldrs 2 out, drvn and not quicken frm last.* ....(14 to 1 tchd 16 to 1) 7
3080 GROUND NUT (Ire) [124] 7-10-6 B Powell, *pld hrd in rear, plenty to do 3 out, shaken up and ran on wl appr last, nvr plcd to chal...............*(40 to 1 op 33 to 1 tchd 50 to 1) 8
2218⁶ MYTTON'S CHOICE (Ire) [127] 6-10-4 (5*) Mr R Thornton, *midfield, drvn alng 2 out, unbl to quicken.* ....(33 to 1 op 25 to 1) 9
2780⁴ AMBLESIDE (Ire) [118] 6-10-0 D Bridgwater, *midfield, effrt appr 2 out, sn one pace.* (16 to 1 op 12 to 1 tchd 20 to 1) 10
1996⁴ CHERYL'S LAD (Ire) [136] 7-11-4 M A Fitzgerald, *hld up, some hdwy 3 out, rdn and one pace aftr nxt.* (14 to 1 op 12 to 1) 11
3080⁴ LADY DAISY (Ire) [133] 8-11-1 G Bradley, *led 3rd, tried to run out and hdd 2 out, fdd.* (14 to 1 op 12 to 1 tchd 16 to 1) 12
2949⁴ SLEW MAN (Fr) [118] (bl) 6-10-0 D Walsh, *cl up, chlgd aftr 2 out, sn drvn and no extr.* ....(16 to 1 op 14 to 1 tchd 20 to 1) 13
2591² HAMILTON SILK [132] 5-11-0 A P McCoy, *hld up rear, some hdwy whn mstk 2 out, nvr on terms.....* (7 to 1 op 6 to 1) 14
2732 TOAST THE SPREECE (Ire) [133] 5-11-1 C F Swan, *patiently rdn, smooth hdwy frm 3 out, chalg gng wl whn blun last, not reco'r........................*(12 to 1 tchd 14 to 1) 15
2780² ROMANCER (Ire) [138] (bl) 6-11-6 C Llewellyn, *in tch, struggling whn hit 2 out, sn no dngr.......*(12 to 1 op 10 to 1) 16
3080 STAR RAGE (Ire) [133] 7-11-1 D Gallagher, *chsd ldrs till drvn and outpcd aftr 2 out, fdd............*(16 to 1 op 14 to 1) 17
STOMPIN [142] 6-11-10 J Culloty, *led to 3rd, styd hndy, slightly hmpd 2 out, fdd..............* (33 to 1 op 25 to 1) 18
2834⁶ CELTIC LORE [118] (bl) 5-10-0 N Williamson, *al hndy, lft in slight ld 2 out, sn hdd and wknd.......* (8 to 1 tchd 9 to 1) 19
798⁹ FAUSTINO [118] 5-10-0 R Johnson, *beh, some hdwy 4 out, struggling whn hit nxt, sn behind......*(50 to 1 op 33 to 1) 20

Dist: 1l, 3l, 1l, hd, nk, 1l, 1l, 1l, nk, 1¼l. 3m 58.70s. a 4.70s (20 Ran).
SR: 54/41/60/41/37/37/46/41/43/ (Lynn Wilson), N J Henderson

HEXHAM (good)
Thursday March 13th
Going Correction: PLUS 0.50 sec. per fur. (races 1,4,6), PLUS 0.55 (2,3,5)

3157 Medallion Lager Conditional Jockeys' Mares' Only Handicap Hurdle Class E (0-110 4-y-o and up) £2,322 2m.................. (2:25)

3013⁶ APOLLO'S DAUGHTER [68] 9-10-6 F Leahy, *nvr far away, chlgd 4th, led bef 2 out, clr betw last two.* (5 to 1 op 3 to 1) 1
3009 SKI PATH [64] 8-10-2 G Lee, *chsd ldg grp, rdn alng aftr 4th, styd on to chase wnr appr last, no imprsn.........* (25 to 1) 2
2815⁵ PEGGY GORDON [76] 6-10-11 (3*) N Horrocks, *sn led, jnd aftr 4th, hdd bef 2 out, soon outpcd.* ....(4 to 1 op 9 to 4 tchd 9 to 2 and 5 to 1) 3
2405 MILLERS GOLDENGIRL (Ire) [65] 6-10-3 G F Ryan, *nvr far away, ev ch aftr 3 out, outpcd nxt.* ....(12 to 1 op 10 to 1 tchd 14 to 1) 4
1830⁸ QUALITAIR PRIDE [88] 5-11-12 E Callaghan, *hld up, struggling aftr 3 out, no dngr after........*(3 to 1 fav op 6 to 1) 5
2719 MILL THYME [84] 5-11-8 B Grattan, *sn beh and pushed alng, nvr on terms.........* (11 to 1 op 10 to 1 tchd 12 to 1) 6
1828 AMBER HOLLY [75] 8-10-8 (5*) I Jardine, *cl up, hit 4th, struggling bef 3 out, sn btn....*(11 to 1 op 8 to 1 tchd 12 to 1) 7
CATCH THE PIGEON [78] 8-11-2 R McGrath, *f 1st.* ....(10 to 1 op 7 to 1) f
3034⁶ BILL'S PRIDE [75] 6-10-8 (5*) C McCormack, *hld up, steady hdwy and in tch whn uns rdr 2 out......* (8 to 1 op 5 to 1) ur
3029⁸ MEADOWLECK [62] 8-10-0 S Taylor, *brght dwn 1st.* (25 to 1) bd
1784⁶ TANCRED MISCHIEF [78] 6-11-2 P Midgley, *brght dwn 1st.* ....(15 to 2 op 6 to 1 tchd 8 to 1) bd

Dist: 13l, 11l, 4l, 2½l, 17l, 19l. 4m 6.50s. a 17.50s (11 Ran).
(Mrs M Goulding), J L Goulding

3158 Ann Lebon Novices' Chase Class E (5-y-o and up) £2,961 2m 110yds .... (3:00)

2622* RALLEGIO 8-11-10 G Cahill, *nvr far away, lft cl second 5 out, rdn to ld 2 out, kpt on strly last.* ....(11 to 10 on op 7 to 4 on tchd Evens) 1
2762⁷ EXEMPLAR (Ire) 9-10-12 (5*) G F Ryan, *chsd clr ldr, hit 4th, lft in ld 5 out, hdd 2 out, one pace last......* (6 to 1 op 5 to 1) 2
3007² TAPATCH (Ire) 9-11-3 R Garritty, *settled in chasing grp, outpcd aftr 3 out, staying on whn rdr lost iron and mstk last, no imprsn..................*(7 to 4 op 9 to 4 tchd 13 to 8) 3
2847 NAWTINOOKEY 7-10-5 (7*) C McCormack, *hld up in chasing grp, blun 3 out, sn outpcd.* (25 to 1 op 20 to 1) 4
2859 PRINCE BALTASAR 8-11-3 M Foster, *cl up to 5 out, sn outpcd and beh...........................*(33 to 1 op 20 to 1) 5
2983⁴ OBVIOUS RISK 6-10-12 (5*) S Taylor, *beh whn blun and uns rdr 6th...* (7 to 1 op 16 to 1) ur
3007⁶ DISTILLERY HILL (Ire) 9-11-3 Mr M Thompson, *led and clr till blun and uns rdr 5 out...............* (40 to 1 op 33 to 1) ur
2988 ABSOLUTELY JOHN (Ire) 9-11-3 M Moloney, *prmnt in chasing grp, lost pl whn blun 5 out, sn btn, pld up bef last.* ....(40 to 1 op 33 to 1) pu

Dist: 1¾l, 3l, 27l, 24l. 4m 14.10s. a 16.10s (8 Ran).

SR: 26/17/14/-/-/ (Guthrie Robertson), P Monteith

3159 Win With The Tote Handicap Chase Class D (0-120 5-y-o and up) £4,056
4m............................. (3:35)

3031⁵ HUDSON BAY TRADER (USA) [87] 10-10-3 (5*) B Grattan, chsd ldg grp, pckpd 12th, rallied 16th, led bef 3 out, ran on strly betw last 2................... (10 to 1 op 12 to 1) 1

2916* OFF THE BRU [92] 12-10-6 (7*) Mr M Bradburne, nvr far away, outpcd aftr 3 out, rallied to chase wnr, kpt on.
.... (2 to 1 fav op 9 to 4 tchd 5 to 2) 2

2912² GOLD PIGEON (Ire) [79] 8-10-0 R Supple, pressed ldr, dsptd ld bef 3 out, one pace betw last 2....... (5 to 1 op 6 to 1) 3

2916⁷ HEAVENLY CITIZEN (Ire) [91] 9-10-12 K Johnson, led till bef 3 out, sn drvn alng. outpcd aftr nxt........ (9 to 1 op 6 to 1) 4

3005³ TICO GOLD [84] 9-10-5 G Cahill, settled in tch, improved 16th, hit 6 out, outpcd bef 3 out, tld off... (8 to 1 op 7 to 1) 5

3010⁶ QUIXALL CROSSETT [79] 12-9-10¹ (5*) S Taylor, hld up, struggling 18th, jmpd slwly 5 out, pld up bef nxt.... (50 to 1) pu

2715⁷ PENNINE PRIDE [96] (bl) 10-11-3 R Garritty, mstks, in tch, reminders 9th, blun 17th, pld up bef nxt.
.... (9 to 2 op 7 to 2) pu

2850² STONEY BURKE (Ire) [103] 8-11-10 A Thornton, blun 1st, beh, blunded 19th, sn struggling, pld up bef 4 out.
.... (9 to 2 op 7 to 2) pu

Dist: 1½l, 3l, 11l, dist. 8m 42.90s. a 39.90s (8 Ran).

(P C N Curtis), P Beaumont

3160 Keoghans Novices' Hurdle Class E (4-y-o and up) £2,490 3m..... (4:05)

2322² MAGPIE MELODY (Ire) 6-11-3 R Supple, al pld, led bef last, ran on well.................... (11 to 4 op 5 to 2) 1

2346 PEBBLE BEACH 7-11-9 J Callaghan, led till hld bef last, kpt on run in.............................. (8 to 1) 2

2260⁴ SOUTHERN CROSS 5-11-0 (3*) P Midgley, not fluent, hld up, improved bef 4 out, outpcd nxt, styd on bsde last, not rch ldrs................................. (9 to 4 fav tchd 5 to 2) 3

2241⁷ FENLOE RAMBLER (Ire) 6-11-3 K Johnson, nvr far away, ridn alng 2 out, one pace whn hit last..... (10 to 1 op 14 to 1) 4

2984 ALLERBANK 6-11-3 Mr C Storey, settled in tch, hit 4th, outpcd aftr 3 out............. (12 to 1 op 10 to 1 tchd 14 to 1) 5

2856⁴ MR CHRISTIE 5-11-9 A Thornton, beh, struggling last 4, nvr on terms............................ (8 to 1 tchd 10 to 1) 6

2346³ CELTIC DUKE 5-11-3 R Garritty, jmpd badly in rear, nvr a factor......................... (6 to 1 op 5 to 1 tchd 7 to 1) 7

3009⁴ DIDDY RYMER 7-10-12 Richard Guest, chsd ldrs struggling aftr 3 out, tld off............. (9 to 1 op 8 to 1 tchd 10 to 1) 8

2712 SUTHERLAND MOSS 6-11-9 M Foster, beh whn f 7th, dead.
.... (7 to 1 op 6 to 1) f

2984⁵ HADAWAY LAD 5-11-3 M Moloney, chsd ldrs to 7th, struggling nxt, pld up bef 2 out.
.... (12 to 1 op 10 to 1) pu

3009 WILLIE WANNABE (Ire) 7-11-3 D Parker, beh, hit second, struggling bef 4 out, pld up before 2 out.......... (33 to 1) pu

1887⁹ TARTAN JOY 6-11-3 N Smith, jmpd badly, al beh, tld off whn pld up bef 3 out............... (33 to 1) pu

Dist: 2l, 3½l, 3½l, 11l, 1l, 2½l, 23l. 6m 7.30s. a 19.30s (12 Ran).

SR: 16/20/10/6/-/-/ (R J Gilbert), L Lungo

3161 Federation Brewery Handicap Chase Class F (0-100 5-y-o and up) £3,013 2½m 110yds..... (4:40)

2686⁴ CULLANE LAKE (Ire) [73] 7-10-1 R Supple, al wl pld, led bef 5 out, drw clr fnl 2................... (6 to 1 tchd 7 to 1) 1

2535³ WILLIE SPARKLE [72] 11-10-0 G Cahill, nvr far away, outpcd bef 2 out, styd on to chase wnr before last, no imprsn.
.... (12 to 1) 2

2652 SNOOK POINT [77] 10-10-5¹ J Burke, al hndy, mstk 5 out, chsd wnr 3 out, sn ridn, outpcd fnl 2......... (20 to 1) 3

2814³ RISKY DEE [78] 8-10-0 K Johnson, beh, hit 7th and 6 out, effrt 3 out, no imprsn................. (14 to 1 op 12 to 1) 4

2987² LAST REFUGE (Ire) [94] 8-11-8 N Smith, chsd ldg bunch, hmpd 9th, no dngr aftr................. (8 to 1 tchd 10 to 1) 5

1785⁴ TIGHTER BUDGET (USA) [100] 10-12-0 M Moloney, cl up, led 5th to bef 5 out, sn lost pl, rallied 3 out, fdd nxt.
.... (6 to 1 tchd 7 to 1) 6

2987 GRAND SCENERY (Ire) [85] 9-10-13 A Thornton, blun second, sn chasing ldrs, drvn 3 out, outpcd nxt.
.... (7 to 1 op 6 to 1 tchd 8 to 1) 7

2772 SUPPOSIN [91] 9-11-5 Richard Guest, chsd ldg bunch, struggling 7th, sn beh....................... (16 to 1) 8

2633 RUSTY BLADE [90] 8-11-4 Mr R Hale, blun 5th, al struggling.
.... (25 to 1 op 20 to 1) 9

3010* CHILL WIND [94] 9-11-8 M Foster, hld up, chsd ldrs, sn chasing ldrs whn f 9th. (4 to 1 op 3 to 1 tchd 9 to 2) f

3010² PARIAH (Ire) [91] 8-11-5 J Callaghan, beh whn blun and uns rdr 5th............ (13 to 8 fav op 6 to 4 tchd 2 to 1) ur

MOSS BEE [80] 10-10-8² T Reed, led to 5th, hit 7th, wknd and pld up aftr 9th.................. (33 to 1) pu

Dist: 8l, 11l, 6l, 1l, 12l, 1¼l, 16l, 1¾l. 5m 16.90s. a 18.90s (12 Ran).

(Mrs J M L Milligan), Miss M K Milligan

3162 Buchanan Ale Handicap Hurdle Class F (0-100 4-y-o and up) £2,284
3m........................... (5:15)

2856⁵ CORBLEU (Ire) [72] 7-10-0 K Johnson, hld up, improved 4 out, rdn to ld bef last, held on wl..... (12 to 1 op 10 to 1) 1

2494⁴ FIVE FLAGS (Ire) [88] 9-11-2 Richard Guest, prmnt on ins, swtchd to outsd aftr 6th, outpcd aftr 3 out, styd on wl last.
.... (6 to 1 op 5 to 1 tchd 7 to 1) 2

2910⁵ THE OTHER MAN (Ire) [72] 7-10-0 O Pears, chsd ldg grp, improved 7th, ev ch bef 2 out, kpt on frm last.
.... (10 to 1 op 5 to 1) 3

3057³ KINGS LANE [85] 8-10-13 D Parker, chsd ldrs, reminders aftr 5 out, outpcd bef 2 out, kpt on last.
.... (4 to 1 op 7 to 2 tchd 9 to 2) 4

2801⁶ RIMOUSKI [91] 9-11-5 Gary Lyons, hld up and beh, steady hdwy aftr 2 out, kpt on, nvr nr to chal.... (8 to 1 op 5 to 1) 5

2320³ MENSHAAR (USA) [100] 5-12-0 R Supple, mstks, prmnt, rdn to chal bef last, one pace run in.
.... (3 to 1 fav op 4 to 1 tchd 5 to 2) 6

2892⁴ DOCKMASTER [87] 6-10-8 (7*) N Horrocks, prmnt on ins, outpcd bef 2 out, kpt on frm last, no dngr.
.... (7 to 2 op 5 to 2 tchd 4 to 1) 7

2710 NEW CHARGES [92] 10-11-1 (5*) B Grattan, hld up and beh, hdwy to ld bef 2 out, hdd before last, fdd. (8 to 1 op 7 to 1) 8

2762 GRACE CARD [90] (bl) 11-11-4 Miss P Robson, pressed ldr till wknd 9th......................... (25 to 1) 9

2349 KINGS MINSTRAL (Ire) [76] 7-10-4¹ J Burke, led till hdd bef 3 out, sn struggling................ (14 to 1) 10

KENILWORTH LAD [93] 9-11-0 (7*) L McGrath, chsd ldrs, blun 4th, struggling 5 out, tld off whn pld up bef 2 out.
.... (25 to 1 op 14 to 1) pu

Dist: 1¼l, nk, 1½l, ¾l, nk, sht-hd, 12l, dist, 10l. 6m 10.70s. a 22.70s (11 Ran).

(David Woodcock), S B Bell

FAKENHAM (good)
Friday March 14th
Going Correction: MINUS 0.15 sec. per fur.

3163 Wymondham Selling Handicap Hurdle Class G (0-90 4-y-o and up) £2,785 2m.....................(2:10)

1969 ANTIGUAN FLYER [65] (v) 8-10-2 (3*) Michael Brennan, led, clr aftr 3rd, mstk 2 out, drvn out and styd on wl.
.... (20 to 1 op 14 to 1 tchd 25 to 1) 1

2982⁸ GENERAL SHIRLEY (Ire) [76] 6-10-12 (7*) M Clinton, hld up, rdn and hdwy aftr 5th, chsd clr ldr after 3 out, no imprsn appr last........................... (9 to 1 op 8 to 1) 2

2804⁴ ARCH ANGEL (Ire) [76] 4-10-1 (7*) X Aizpuru, beh, hdwy aftr 3 out, styd on after nxt, not quicken appr last.
.... (7 to 1 op 5 to 1 tchd 8 to 1) 3

2603⁹ HAPPY BRAVE [78] 5-11-4 L Harvey, chsd clr ldr frm 5th, sn drvn alng, kpt on one pace aftr 2 out..(16 to 1 op 12 to 1) 4

1800² CADDY'S FIRST [84] 5-11-5 (5*) Chris Webb, chsd clr ldr in second pl till wknd aftr 2 out.......... (5 to 1 op 4 to 1) 5

2847 BLUE DOMAIN [68] 6-10-8 A Dobbin, hld up, hdwy aftr 5th, wnt second after 3 out, wknd appr last. (12 to 1 op 8 to 1) 6

2957³ NAGOBELIA [80] 9-10-13 (7*) J O'Shaughnessy, chsd clr ldr till wknd aftr 3 out............ (4 to 1 tchd 7 to 2) 7

1044⁹ WORDSMITH (Ire) [79] 7-11-2 (3*) R Massey, hld up, beh frm 5th, tld off.................. (12 to 1 op 7 to 1) 8

2676* RUTH'S GAMBLE [62] (v) 9-10-2 D Leahy, hld up, rdn alng aftr 5th, sn lost pl, tld off.......... (3 to 1 fav op 4 to 1) 9

2174³ COSMIC STAR [64] (bl) 7-9-13 (5*) Mr R Thornton, chsd clr ldr to 5th, sn drvn alng and lost pl, tld off aftr 3 out.
.... (7 to 1 op 5 to 1) 10

2886 RAFTER-J [66] 6-10-6 M Brennan, hld up, pushed alng aftr 5th, sn lost tch, tld off after 3 out.... (33 to 1 op 20 to 1) 11

2044⁴ PYRRHIC DANCE [75] 7-11-1 J Railton, chsd clr ldr to 5th, sn lost pl, tld off whn pld up aftr 5th....(10 to 1 op 6 to 1) pu

Dist: 11l, 2l, 3l, 2½l, 1l, 2½l, 25l, 10l, 3½l, 7l. 3m 55.50s. a 11.50s (12 Ran).

(George Prodromou), G Prodromou

3164 William Bulwer-Long Memorial Novices' Hunters' Chase Class H (5-y-o and up) £2,382 2m 5f 110yds (2:40)

WHAT CHANCE (Ire) 9-10-11 (7*) Mr A Charles-Jones, hld up, hdwy to track ldrs aftr 9th, cld up after 3 out, led nxt, styd on wl............................ (7 to 2 op 5 to 1 tchd 6 to 1) 1

3004 GUSSIE 9-11-4² (7*) Mr W Tellwright, pressed ldr, led 9th to 11th, ev ch 4 out, rdn and kpt on one pace aftr 2 out.
.... (5 to 1 op 4 to 1) 2

2769⁵ GYPSY KING (Ire) 9-11-2 (7*) Mr A Coe, al chasing ldrs, ev ch 4 out, jmpd slwly nxt, kpt on one pace...(5 to 1 op 4 to 1) 3

3102 TELLAPORKY 8-11-2 (7*) Mr A Middleton, led to 9th, pressed ldr, led 11th to 2 out, sn wknd..... (10 to 1 op 33 to 1) 4

ARISE (Ire) 8-11-2 (7*) Mr N R Mitchell, hmpd strt and slwly away, hdwy to track ldrs aftr 9th, ev ch 3 out, sn rdn, wknd after nxt............. (11 to 10 fav op Evens tchd 6 to 5) 5

TRY GOD 10-11-2 (7*) Miss L Allan, trkd ldrs, ev ch 5 out, rdn and wknd aftr nxt................ (14 to 1 op 20 to 1) 6

RAYMAN (Ire) 9-11-2 (7") Mr R Lawther, *beh 8th, brief effrt aftr tenth, sn behind*..................(50 to 1 op 20 to 1)   7
FOXBOW (Ire) 7-11-4 (5") Mr A Sansome, *f 3rd*.
.............................(14 to 1 op 8 to 1)   f
OLD DUNDALK (bl) 13-11-2 (7") Mr N King, *mstk 7th, sn wl beh, tld off whn pld up bef last*........(50 to 1 op 20 to 1)   pu
GONE FOR LUNCH 6-11-2 (7") Mr M Gingell, *whipped round strt, very slwly away, tld off whn jmpd slowly 5th and pld up*.
.............................(14 to 1 op 12 to 1)   pu
Dist: 3½l, 2l, 8l, 9l, 11l, 8l. 5m 38.50s. a 26.50s (10 Ran).
(C W Booth), Mrs H Mobley

3165
Jewson Handicap Chase Class D (0-120 5-y-o and up) £4,335 2m 5f 110yds....................(3:10)

1988[5] PATS MINSTREL [100] 12-11-4 A Dobbin, *made all, rallied whn chlgd 2 out, drvn out r-in.*
.............................(9 to 1 op 8 to 1 tchd 10 to 1)   1
2934[6] ARTIC WINGS (Ire) [105] 9-11-9 M Brennan, *hld up, wnt 3rd 9th, went second 3 out, wth wnr nxt, rdn and not quicken appr last*...........................(9 to 4 op 5 to 2)   2
2677[2] WHIPPERS DELIGHT (Ire) [92] 9-10-3 (7") X Aizpuru, *trkd ldg pair, mstk 8th, drvn alng aftr 11th, sn beh.*
..........................(100 to 30 op 7 to 2 tchd 4 to 1)   3
3024[2] HAWAIIAN YOUTH (Ire) [106] 9-11-7 (3") D Fortt, *trkd ldr, second whn blun 11th, drvn alng aftr 4 out, btn when jmpd slwly nxt*.................(Evens fav tchd 11 to 10)   4
2860 LODESTONE LAD (Ire) [82] (v) 7-10-0 D Leahy, *sn last, mstks, tld off whn pld up aftr 11th.*
.............................(25 to 1 op 20 to 1 tchd 33 to 1)   pu
Dist: 2l, 20l, 1¾l. 5m 29.20s. a 17.20s (5 Ran).
(K J Hunt), R Champion

3166
Downham Market Handicap Hurdle Class E (0-115 4-y-o and up) £3,696 2m.........................(3:40)

2806[4] BARFORD SOVEREIGN [109] 5-12-0 A Dobbin, *led aftr 3rd till after 5th, led nxt to 3 out, wth ldr next, ev ch last, hrd rdn to ld last strd*....................(3 to 1 op 7 to 2)   1
3100[3] KINTAVI [99] 7-11-4 P Niven, *trkd ldrs 4th, led aftr nxt to four out, led next, hit last, hrd rdn and hdd last strd.*
.............................(6 to 4 fav op 7 to 4 tchd 5 to 4)   2
2880 AJDAR [81] 6-10-0 M Brennan, *hld up, hrd rdn and hdwy aftr 4 out, no imprsn after 2 out*............(8 to 1 tchd 10 to 1)   3
SALMAN (USA) [93] 11-10-7 (5") Mr R Thornton, *led till aftr 1st, prmnt whn hit 5th, sn drvn alng, lost tch after 4 out.*
.............................(20 to 1 tchd 16 to 1)   4
2743[6] ISAIAH [108] 8-11-13 T Kent, *led aftr 1st till after 3rd, chsd ldrs till lost pl after 4 out, sn beh*......(9 to 2 tchd 11 to 2)   5
2886[5] LUCY TUFTY [81] 6 9-7 (7") J O'Shaughnessy, *beh, rdn and some hdwy aftr 5th, kpt on one pace frm 3 out.*
.............................(7 to 1 op 8 to 1 tchd 10 to 1)   6
127 ERINY (USA) [93] 8-10-9 (3") E Callaghan, *chsd ldrs, mstk 6th, sn beh*.....................(16 to 1 tchd 20 to 1)   7
2676[8] STONE ISLAND [89] 4-9-7 (7") Miss C Townsley, *sn beh, tld off aftr 3rd, blun and sns tbr 2 out*.....(50 to 1 op 20 to 1)   ur
Dist: Hd, 16l, 7l, 1l, 5l, 17l. 3m 53.40s. a 9.40s (8 Ran).
(Barford Bloodstock), J R Fanshawe

3167
Castleacre Maiden Chase Class D (5-y-o and up) £3,417 3m 110yds ....(4:10)

3017[5] BROGEEN LADY (Ire) 7-11-0 P Niven, *led 5th to 3 out, rallied appr last, led r-in, drvn out.*
.............................(6 to 4 fav op 11 to 8 tchd 15 to 8)   1
2971[2] JOLLY BOAT 10-11-5 S Wynne, *hld up, hdwy aftr 11th, hmpd nxt, led 3 out, sn clr, wknd appr last, hdd and not quicken r-in.*
.............................(4 to 1 op 3 to 2)   2
2679[3] CHARTER LANE (Ire) 7-11-3 D Leahy, *chsd ldrs, ev ch 5 out, wknd aftr nxt, kpt on one pace frm 3 out.*(12 to 1 op 8 to 1)   3
2914[2] DESPERATE DAYS (Ire) 8-11-5 W Dwan, *sn beh, pushed alng aftr 13th, one pace frm 5 out*.........(11 to 2 op 5 to 1)   4
2769[6] ELL GEE 7-10-7 (7") Miss C Townsley, *hld up, hdwy tenth, chsd ldrs to 6 out, wknd quickly, tld off.* (50 to 1 op 33 to 1)   5
2566 GLENDINE (Ire) 7-11-5 J Railton, *led to 5th, pressed ldr, mstk 9th, second whn f 6 out*...(8 to 1 op 7 to 1 tchd 9 to 1)   f
3046 SEABRIGHT SAGA 7-11-5 W Worthington, *in tch whn f 7th.*
.............................(50 to 1 op 25 to 1)   f
2889[4] MUSIC MASTER (Ire) (bl) 7-11-5 A Dobbin, *trkd ldrs, mstk 7th, wknd 11th, lost tch aftr 13th, sn tld off, pld up bef 2 out.*
.............................(7 to 2 op 5 to 1)   pu
Dist: 2½l, 18l, 13l, dist. 6m 28.10s. a 31.10s (8 Ran).
(Starlight Racing), D R Gandolfo

3168
Holkham Conditional Jockeys' Maiden Hurdle Class E (Div I) (4-y-o and up) £1,838 2m...........(4:40)

2893[8] FLORID (USA) 6-11-8 M Berry, *led till aftr 1st, led 4th, drw clr frm 3 out, hit nxt, unchlgd*..........(3 to 1 op 9 to 4)   1
2980[5] TAARISH (Ire) 4-11-0 Chris Webb, *trkd ldrs, outpcd and drvn alng aftr 4 out, ran on to take second pl r-in, not trble wnr.*
.............................(9 to 2 op 6 to 1)   2

2893[5] FORMIDABLE PARTNER (v) 4-11-0 Michael Brennan, *chsd ldr frm 4th, wnt poor second appr 2 out, rdn and lost second pl r-in*.......(9 to 4 fav op 7 to 4 tchd 5 to 2)   3
3022[5] THE STUFFED PUFFIN (Ire) 5-11-8 J Magee, *hld up, drvn alng and outpcd aftr 4 out, no ch frm nxt.* (3 to 1 op 4 to 1)   4
MAJRA (USA) 5-11-8 D Fortt, *led aftr 1st to 4th, pressed ldr, wknd after four out, sn beh*...........(5 to 1 tchd 6 to 1)   5
COVEN MOON 7-11-3 E Callaghan, *al rear, drvn alng aftr 5th, sn tld off*.................(33 to 1 op 20 to 1)   6
666 SHEDANSAR (Ire) 5-11-8 C Rae, *slwly away, sn beh, pushed alng aftr 5th, soon tld off*.........(33 to 1 op 20 to 1)   7
Dist: 22l, ¾l, 7l, 19l, dist, 12l. 3m 46.90s. a 2.90s (7 Ran).
SR: 41/11/10/11/   (Lord Howard de Walden), C P E Brooks

3169
Holkham Conditional Jockeys' Maiden Hurdle Class E (Div II) (4-y-o and up) £1,831 2m...........(5:10)

MUHANDAM (Ire) 4-11-0 P Henley, *trkd ldrs, ev ch 4 out, chalg whn blun 2 out, sn reco'red, led appr last, drvn out.*
.............................(6 to 1 op 4 to 1)   1
2795[4] WENTWORTH (USA) 5-11-8 Clare Thorner, *hld up, hdwy 5th, led aftr nxt till appr last, rdn and not quicken.*
.............................(2 to 1 op 6 to 4)   2
AIR COMMODORE (Ire) 4-11-8 D J Kavanagh, *trkd ldrs, ev ch 4 out, rdn aftr 2 out, not quicken appr last, fnshd tme.*
.............................(5 to 4 fav op 6 to 4 tchd 7 to 4)   3
3028 GENEREUX 4-11-0 Chris Webb, *hld up, hdwy aftr 6th, kpt on one pace aftr nxt*....................(20 to 1 op 16 to 1)   4
2889 HOLKHAM BAY 5-11-8 D Fortt, *hld up, pushed alng aftr 5th, no ch frm 4 out*....................(8 to 1 op 20 to 1)   5
RESERVATION ROCK (Ire) 6-11-8 A Bates, *led till aftr 4 out, rdn and wknd after nxt*............(20 to 1 tchd 25 to 1)   6
CREDITE RISQUE 4-10-9 R Massey, *slwly away, beh 5th, sn lost tch, no ch whn f 3 out*...........(14 to 1 op 10 to 1)   f
ACERBUS DULCIS 6-11-8 F Leahy, *pressed ldr to 5th, wknd quickly aftr nxt, sn beh, pld up bef last.* (20 to 1 op 10 to 1)   pu
Dist: 6l, 3l, 7l, 17l, 1½l. 4m 3.50s. a 19.50s (8 Ran).
(Mrs Diana Haine), Mrs D Haine

FOLKESTONE (good)
Friday March 14th
Going Correction: PLUS 0.85 sec. per fur. (races 1,3,5,7), NIL (2,4,6)

3170
Sandgate Mares' Only Claiming Hurdle Class F (4-y-o and up) £2,092 2m 1f 110yds............(2:00)

2265 FLASH IN THE PAN (Ire) 4-10-3 W McFarland, *trkd ldrs, wnt second 2 out, mstk last, styd on to ld r-in.*
.............................(5 to 1 op 5 to 1 tchd 6 to 1)   1
2265[4] LAURA LYE (Ire) 7-11-0 J Osborne, *al prmnt, led 5th, rdn appr last, wknd and hdd r-in*...........(6 to 1 op 8 to 1)   2
2982[6] PEDALTOTHEMETAL (Ire) 5-11-3 G Tormey, *hld up, rdn and hdwy appr 5th, wknd bef last.*
.............................(9 to 4 fav op 2 to 1 tchd 7 to 4)   3
3049 WHISPERING DAWN 4-10-12 G Bradley, *hld up, hdwy 5th, rdn and wknd aftr 2 out*...(9 to 2 op 4 to 1 tchd 5 to 1)   4
UONI 4-10-0 T J Murphy, *chsd ldrs, rdn and wknd aftr 2 out.*........(12 to 1 op 14 to 1 tchd 16 to 1 and 25 to 1)   5
2479[7] OLIVIPET 8-10-5 R Farrant, *in rear, nvr on terms.*
.............................(25 to 1 op 12 to 1 tchd 33 to 1)   6
2479 SPECIAL TOPIC 7-9-12 (7") D Carey, *chsd ldrs till wknd 5th, tld off*......................(33 to 1 op 14 to 1)   7
2872[9] MINSTER'S MADAM (v) 6-10-11 A P McCoy, *led aftr 4th, hit and hdd nxt, sn wknd, tld off.*
.............................(9 to 2 op 7 to 2 tchd 5 to 1)   8
2526 CLASSIC DELIGHT (USA) 4-10-0 Mr R Barrett, *jmpd poorly in rear, tld off*....................(25 to 1 op 14 to 1)   9
2886 TIGANA 5-10-5 J R Kavanagh, *beh hfwy, tld off whn pld up bef last*.....................(33 to 1 tchd 50 to 1)   pu
1663 PRUSSIAN EAGLE (Ire) (bl) 5-11-12 P Holley, *led till hdd aftr 4th, wknd rpdly, pld up bef 2 out.*
.............................(25 to 1 op 16 to 1 tchd 33 to 1)   pu
Dist: 8l, 7l, 5l, nk, 22l, 16l, 3l, 3l. 4m 22.50s. a 25.50s (11 Ran).
(Mrs Victoria Goodman), J S Moore

3171
Whitelaw Gold Cup Novices' Chase Class D (5-y-o and up) £3,773 3¼m.....................(2:30)

2679* FLIPPANCE 7-11-11 C Llewellyn, *hld up, hdwy wth circuit to go, wnt second 2 out, led appr last, styd on.*
.............................(6 to 1 op 7 to 1)   1
2890[2] HIGH LEARIE 7-11-11 J A McCarthy, *made all till tired and hdd appr last*.............(9 to 4 op 2 to 1 tchd 5 to 2)   2
1745 BOND JNR (Ire) 8-11-11 R Johnson, *trkd ldr, mstks second, 9th and 13th, rdn and wknd appr 2 out.*
.............................(100 to 30 op 9 to 4)   3
2890[4] CORRIB SONG 8-11-1 (3") L Aspell, *al beh, tld off.*
.............................(5 to 1 op 20 to 1)   4
2894[7] SUMMER HAVEN 8-10-13 Mr A Kinane, *hld up beh wth circuit to go, tld off whn blun 3 out.*
.............................(66 to 1 op 50 to 1 tchd 100 to 1)   5

2928[5] FINNEGAIS 10-11-4 T J Murphy, *tld off 5th, pld up bef 11th.*
.... (100 to 1 op 66 to 1 tchd 150 to 1) pu
2600[7] SIR LEONARD (Ire) 7-11-11 J Osborne, *chsd ldrs, nvr gng wl aftr reminders 4th, wknd 11th, pld up bef 13th.*
.... (13 to 8 fav op Evens tchd 7 to 4) pu
Dist: 8l, 16l, dist, 30l. 6m 43.10s. a 28.10s (7 Ran).

(Exors Of The Late Mr C L Rykens), N A Gaselee

3172 Somerfield Court Novices' Hurdle Class E (4-y-o and up) £2,566 2m 1f 110yds. .... (3:00)

2197[2] SHARPICAL 5-11-9 M A Fitzgerald, *hld up in rear, hdwy whn slight mstk 6th, led on bit sn aftr last, hrd held.*
.... (12 to 1 op 6 to 1 on) 1
2852[3] FIRE ON ICE (Ire) 5-11-2 (7") F Titley, *led to 5th, led ag'n nxt, rdn and hdd sn aftr last, no ch wth wnr.*
.... (14 to 1 op 6 to 1 tchd 16 to 1) 2
1727[4] LEAP FROG 6-11-2 W Marston, *hld up, hdwy to track ldrs 5th, rdn appr 2 out, styd on r-in.*
.... (14 to 1 op 7 to 1 tchd 16 to 1) 3
2012[8] HANBITOOH (USA) 4-10-8 C Maude, *hld up, outpcd 2 out, styd on.* .... (50 to 1 op 10 to 1) 4
1893   HI MARBLE (Ire) 6-10-11 Derek Byrne, *trkd ldr to 4th, wknd 2 out.* .... (50 to 1 op 16 to 1) 5
1882[7] RISING MAN 6-10-13 (3") L Aspell, *trkd ldrs, led 5th, hdd nxt, wknd aftr 2 out.* .... (50 to 1 op 16 to 1) 6
2886[9] JONBEL 9-11-2 N Mann, *pld hrd, in tch to 6th, sn wknd, tld off.*
.... (100 to 1 op 33 to 1 tchd 150 to 1) 7
2954[6] KIROV ROYALE 6-10-11 W McFarland, *al beh, wknd 6th, pld up bef last.* .... (50 to 1 op 25 to 1 tchd 66 to 1) pu
Dist: 3l, nk, 4l, 11l, 13l, 30l. 4m 23.80s. a 26.80s (8 Ran).

(Thurloe Thoroughbreds II), N J Henderson

3173 Cliftonville Handicap Chase Class D (0-125 5-y-o and up) £3,536 2m .... (3:30)

2781[5] THE CARROT MAN (Ire) 9-10-9 P Hide, *trkd ldr frm 4th, led 5 out,gng wl whn lft well clr 3 out, unchlgd.*
.... (7 to 4 fav op 9 to 4 tchd 5 to 2 and 11 to 4) 1
2612[*] COOLTEEN HERO (Ire) [93] 7-10-2[3] W McFarland, *trkd ldr to 4th, impd slwly 6th, dsptd 3rd 3 out, sn wnt second, no ch wth wnr.* .... (3 to 1 tchd 7 to 2) 2
3104[2] LASATA [102] 12-10-11 D Morris, *hld up, effrt appr 6th, blun nxt, lft second whn hmpd by faller 3 out, not reco'r, tld off.*
.... (13 to 2 op 7 to 2 tchd 7 to 1) 3
2947[3] NEWLANDS-GENERAL [115] 11-11-10 A P McCoy, *led till hdd 5 out, wknd whn l 3 out.* .... (2 to 1 op 6 to 4) f
Dist: 24l, dist. 3m 56.70s. a 5.70s (4 Ran).

SR: 24/   (Mrs Jill Winkworth), P Winkworth

3174 Peasmarsh Selling Handicap Hurdle Class G (0-90 4-y-o and up) £1,961 2m 1f 110yds. .... (4:00)

2607[*] CARACOL [68] 8-10-10 (3") T Dascombe, *al in tch, led aftr 2 out, rdn out.* .... (6 to 1 op 11 to 1) 1
2770   MULLINTOR (Ire) [80] 6-11-11 D O'Sullivan, *led to 4th, led 3 out, hdd aftr nxt, one pace.*
.... (8 to 1 op 4 to 1 tchd 10 to 1 and 11 to 1) 2
2765[5] SWINGING SIXTIES (Ire) [75] 6-11-6 A P McCoy, *hld up, hdwy 3 out, styd on one pace.* .... (7 to 2 tchd 9 to 2) 3
2768[2] PARISIAN [63] 12-10-1 (7") A Lucas, *hld up, hdwy 6th, rdn and fdd appr last.* .... (14 to 1 op 8 to 1 tchd 16 to 1) 4
2725   ANIF (USA) [55] 6-10-0 D Skyrme, *hld up in rear, hdwy 5th, wknd aftr 2 out.* .... (40 to 1 op 25 to 1 tchd 50 to 1) 5
2479[6] ZESTI [75] 5-11-6 R Johnson, *al prmnt, trkd ldr 6th, 3rd and struggling whn blun last, not reco'r.*
.... (10 to 1 op 5 to 1 tchd 12 to 1) 6
3047[5] RUSTIC GENT (Ire) [60] (bl) 9-10-0 (5") Sophie Mitchell, *beh frm 5th, nvr on terms...* (40 to 1 op 33 to 1 tchd 50 to 1) 7
2403   ANNABEL'S BABY (Ire) [64] 8-10-9 W Marston, *prmnt, led 4th till hdd aftr 2 out, wknd quickly, tld off.*
.... (9 to 2 tchd 6 to 1 and 7 to 1) 8
1693   VINTAGE TAITTINGER (Ire) [63] 5-10-8 M Richards, *prmnt till wknd 2 out, eased, tld off.* (9 to 1 op 12 to 1 tchd 14 to 1) 9
2982   PRECIOUS WONDER [62] 8-10-7 T J Murphy, *beh whn pld up aftr 4th, broke blood vessel.*
.... (20 to 1 op 10 to 1 tchd 25 to 1) pu
       MOYNSHA HOUSE (Ire) [83] 9-12-0 B Fenton, *tld off 4th, pld up bef nxt.* .... (5 to 1 tchd 8 to 1 and 4 to 1) pu
       MIRAGE OF WINDSOR (Ire) [60] 9-10-5 E Murphy, *in tch till wknd aftr 3 out, tld off whn pld bef last.*
.... (3 to 1 fav op 8 to 1) pu
Dist: 3l, 3½l, 3l, nk, 1½l, 26l, dist, 2½l. 4m 20.10s. a 23.10s (12 Ran).

SR: 3/12/3/-/-/-/   (C G Bolton), J Neville

3175 Fair Rosamund Handicap Chase Class F (0-105 5-y-o and up) £2,779 3¼m. .... (4:30)

2895[4] ROYAL SAXON [85] 11-10-8 R Johnson, *sn trkd ldr, led 13th, rallied and pres appr 2 out, styd on.*
.... (5 to 1 tchd 11 to 2 and 6 to 1) 1

3020[4] SHAMARPHIL [83] 11-10-6 Miss S Barraclough, *wl in rear till hdwy appr 2 out, styd on to go second nr finish.*
.... (13 to 2 op 5 to 1 tchd 7 to 1 and 8 to 1) 2
2772[7] YEOMAN WARRIOR [102] 10-11-11 D O'Sullivan, *led to 13th, pressed wnr 3 out till no extr frm last.*
.... (11 to 2 op 4 to 1 tchd 6 to 1) 3
3000[3] RUBINS BOY [77] 11-10-0 R Farrant, *hld up, hdwy tenth, rdn thre out, one pace aftr.* (16 to 1 op 12 to 1 tchd 20 to 1) 4
2930[*] APATURA HATI [87] 8-10-10 W McFarland, *beh frm 12th, nvr on terms...* .... (5 to 1 op 4 to 1 tchd 11 to 2) 5
2729[4] BE SURPRISED [77] 11-10-0 B Powell, *in tch to 11th, wkng whn blun 13th, pld up bef nxt.*
.... (14 to 1 op 10 to 1 tchd 16 to 1) pu
2679[5] JOKER JACK [77] 12-9-12[1] (3") T Dascombe, *lost tch 7th, tld off whn pld up bef 13th.* .... (33 to 1 op 20 to 1) pu
2930[4] NIKKIS PET [77] 10-10-0 W Marston, *al beh, tld off whn pld up bef 9th.* .... (16 to 1 tchd 20 to 1) pu
2480   LITTLE ROWLEY [77] 8-10-0 M Richards, *chsd ldrs till wknd aftr 12th, tld off whn pld up bef 2 out...* (50 to 1 op 40 to 1) pu
2268[6] SUGAR HILL (Ire) [90] 7-10-13 P Hide, *prmnt till hit tenth, struggling aftr, tld off whn pld up bef 2 out.*
.... (5 to 2 fav op 9 to 4 tchd 2 to 1) pu
Dist: 2½l, ½l, 3l, 13l. 6m 39.70s. a 24.70s (10 Ran).

(G Morris), P Bowen

3176 H.B.L.B. Folkestone Maiden Open National Hunt Flat Class H (4,5,6-y-o) £1,329 2m 1f 110yds. ..... (5:00)

1735[2] SUNDAY VENTURE (NZ) 5-11-8 M A Fitzgerald, *mid-div, smooth hdwy o'r 2 fs out, led entering fnl furlong.*
.... (15 to 8 fav op 2 to 1 tchd 9 to 4) 1
2694[3] SHEBANG 5-11-1 (7") Mr H Dunlop, *trkd ldrs, ev ch entering fnl furlong, kpt on.* (8 to 1 op 12 to 1 tchd 9 to 4) 2
       SILVER SIROCCO (Ire) 5-11-8 Derek Byrne, *made most till rdn and hdd entering fnl furlong, no extr ins.*
.... (14 to 1 op 12 to 1 tchd 20 to 1) 3
       CUE CALL (Ire) 4-10-9 J F Titley, *hld up, gd hdwy o'r 2 fs out, ev ch till wknd ins last.* .... (10 to 1 op 5 to 1) 4
2953   SWEEP CLEAN 5-11-8 P Hide, *al prmnt, ev ch o'r 2 fs out, wknd appr last.* .... (6 to 1 op 4 to 1) 5
       MAINE MARIE 5-11-3 J R Kavanagh, *mid-div, styd on ins fnl 2 fs.* .... (25 to 1) 6
2302[6] POLO RIDGE (Ire) 5-11-8 J Osborne, *prmnt till wknd o'r 2 fs out.* .... (4 to 1 tchd 5 to 1) 7
       CEEYOU AT MIDNIGHT 4-11-1 (7") J Power, *in rear till hdwy 7 fs out, wknd o'r 2 out.* (25 to 1 op 20 to 1 tchd 33 to 1) 8
2694   GOWER-SLAVE 5-11-8 R Johnson, *prmnt till wknd o'r 2 fs out.* .... (25 to 1 op 20 to 1) 9
       LEGGIES LEGACY 6-11-8 R Farrant, *hld up, rdn and wknd o'r 2 fs out.* .... (25 to 1 op 20 to 1 tchd 33 to 1) 10
1948[8] THE CROPPY BOY 5-11-5 (3") T Dascombe, *al beh.*
.... (20 to 1 op 16 to 1 tchd 25 to 1) 11
2961[7] GOLDEN LILY 4-10-9 A P McCoy, *trkd ldr, dsptd ld 7 fs out, wknd quickly o'r 2 out.* .... (16 to 1 tchd 20 to 1) 12
       PURE SWING 4-11-0 N Mann, *al beh, tld off.*
.... (12 to 1 op 8 to 1) 13
       KING OF SWING (Ire) 5-11-8 J Culloty, *mid-div, lost tch hfwy, tld off.* .... (25 to 1 op 20 to 1) 14
       SMART GUY 5-11-8 A Thornton, *al beh, tld off.*
.... (25 to 1 tchd 33 to 1) 15
       LAST PENNY (bl) 5-11-3 B Powell, *al beh, tld off whn pld up lme ins fnl furlong, dismounted.* .... (25 to 1) pu
Dist: ¾l, 3½l, 3l, 6l, 1½l, 3½l, 2½l, ½l, ½l, 33l. 4m 17.10s. (16 Ran).

(F J Sainsbury), N J Henderson

GOWRAN PARK (IRE) (good to yielding) Saturday March 15th

3177 Lukeswell Novice Hurdle (5-y-o and up) £2,740 2m. .... (2:30)

2704[*] CEOIL AGUS CRAIC (Ire) 6-11-11 F Woods, ... (2 to 1) 1
2900[*] COLM'S ROCK (Ire) 6-12-0 T Horgan, ... (9 to 4 on) 2
       FIDDLERS TUNE 7-11-0 (7") D K Budds, ... (10 to 1) 3
1485[9] NICOLA MARIE (Ire) 8-10-13 (3") K Whelan, ...(20 to 1) 4
Dist: ½l, 1l, dist. 3m 53.60s. (4 Ran).

(S Bolger), Michael G Holden

3178 Ballyhale Maiden Hurdle (5-y-o and up) £2,740 2½m. .... (3:00)

2845[*] LANCASTRIAN PRIDE (Ire) 7-12-0 D J Casey, .. (5 to 4 on) 1
       DAN'S YOUR MAN (Ire) 5-11-5 (7") Mr P Cashman, (7 to 1) 2
3069[2] HEATHER VILLE (Ire) 5-10-6 (7") B J Geraghty, ... (6 to 1) 3
2645[4] THE HOLY PARSON (Ire) 5-10-11 (7") M P Cooney, (14 to 1) 4
2585[9] EBONY KING (Ire) 7-12-0 Mr B M Cash, ... (11 to 2) 5
2839   MISS PECKSNIFF (Ire) 7-11-1 L P Cusack, ... (20 to 1) 6
2942   CONNA BRIDE LADY (Ire) 5-10-6 (7") F J Keniry, .. (50 to 1) 7
2839   PIYALA (Ire) 7-11-1 T J Mitchell, ... (20 to 1) 8
       KERKY (Ire) 7-11-6 J Shortt, ... (33 to 1) 9
2588[7] KINGMAN (Ire) 5-11-4 P A Roche, ... (20 to 1) 10
2839[6] ISLE OF IONA (Ire) 6-11-6 T P Rudd, ... (20 to 1) 11
       MENDELUCI (Ire) 5-11-12 S H O'Donovan, ... (14 to 1) 12
3085   MR CAVALLO (Ire) 5-10-11 (7") A O'Shea, ... (33 to 1) 13
1907   SOME ORCHESTRA (Ire) 5-10-13 F Woods, ... (20 to 1) 14

2443 OCTOBER SEVENTH 6-11-6 K F O'Brien, ...(20 to 1) 15
3069 KNOCKMOYLAN CASTLE (Ire) 7-11-1 (5*) P Morris, ...(33 to 1) 16
2670 ACCOUNTANCY NATIVE (Ire) 5-11-7 T P Treacy, .. (14 to 1) 17
3085 OYSTON PRINCESS (Ire) 5-10-13 T Horgan, ...(50 to 1) 18
2520 NOBLE TUNE (Ire) 8-11-6 J P Broderick, ... (25 to 1) 19
MINNY DOZER (Ire) 8-10-13 (7*) J P Deegan, ... (50 to 1) 20
Dist: 2l, 2½l, 4½l, 1l. 5m 8.20s. (20 Ran).
(Kilcarn Bridge Syndicate), W P Mullins

3179 Kilkenny Hunters Chase (5-y-o and up) £2,740 3m................ (3:30)

2844[3] BOB TREACY (Ire) 8-11-4 (7*) Mr A G Costello, ...(7 to 2) 1
TULLIBARDNICENEASY (Ire) 6-10-10 (5*) Mr A C Coyle, ...(12 to 1) 2
BEATIN SIDE (Ire) 6-11-6 Mr B M Cash, ... (5 to 1) 3
2844 LIFE OF A KING (Ire) 9-11-11 Mr J A Nash, ...(5 to 2 jt-fav) 4
2672[6] AIGUILLE (Ire) 8-11-2 (7*) Mr A Fleming, ... (5 to 2 jt-fav) f
2672[7] MR K'S WINTERBLUES (Ire) 7-10-8 (7*) Mr E Gallagher, ...(6 to 1) f
PARISH RANGER (Ire) (bl) 6-10-13 (7*) Mr J G Sheehan, ...(12 to 1) ur
979 COURT AMBER (Ire) 6-11-1 (5*) Mr J T McNamara, (10 to 1) pu
Dist: 3½l, 11l, 12l. 6m 30.60s. (8 Ran).
(M W Hickey), M W Hickey

3180 Kilkenny Handicap Hurdle (0-102 4-y-o and up) £2,740 2½m.... (4:00)

2380* STAGALIER (Ire) [-] 5-10-12 (7*) B J Geraghty, ...(7 to 1) 1
2366 EXPEDIENT EXPRESS (Ire) [-] 7-10-2[1] L P Cusack, (20 to 1) 2
3089 LIOS NA MAOL (Ire) [-] 6-9-2[2] (7*) M D Murphy, ... (25 to 1) 3
3089[3] ECLIPTIC MOON (Ire) [-] 7-9-13 T P Treacy, ... (3 to 1 fav) 4
2647* LAURENS FANCY (Ire) [-] 7-11-4 J R Barry, ... (5 to 1) 5
2647[3] WOODBORO LASS (Ire) [-] 7-9-6 (7*) Miss A Sloane, (8 to 1) 6
2585 DOUBLE STRIKE (Ire) [-] (bl) 6-11-0 T P Rudd, ... (25 to 1) 7
2585 THE PARSON'S FILLY (Ire) [-] (bl) 7-10-10 D H O'Connor, ...(12 to 1) 8
2902[7] TRUCKINABOUT (Ire) [-] 7-10-7 F Woods, ...(14 to 1) 9
2753[9] MAJESTIC JOHN (Ire) [-] 7-10-1 (7*) A T Kelly, ...(25 to 1) 10
3089 COOKSGROVE ROSIE (Ire) [-] (bl) 5-9-10 P Leech, (33 to 1) 11
2521[3] MIRACLE ME (Ire) [-] 5-10-13 (7*) Mr J G Sheehan, (7 to 1) 12
2054[7] SUPREME CHANTER (Ire) [-] 5-11-1 S H O'Donovan, ...(12 to 1) 13
2114[4] HILL OF HOPE (Ire) [-] 6-11-10 W Slattery, ...(14 to 1) 14
2902 CASEY JUNIOR (Ire) [-] 9-10-2 (7*) A O'Shea, ... (33 to 1) 15
2944[7] HOLLYBROOK LADY (Ire) [-] 6-11-3 J P Broderick, (10 to 1) 16
2647 COLLIERS HILL (Ire) [-] (bl) 9-11-1 P L Malone, ...(10 to 1) 17
3089 HEART 'N SOUL-ON (Ire) [-] (bl) 6-10-3 (7*) D K Budds, ...(25 to 1) 18
2070[4] DUKY RIVER (Ire) [-] 6-12-0 J Shortt, ...(10 to 1) 19
3086 EMPEROR GLEN (Ire) [-] 9-11-8 (3*) K Whelan, ...(25 to 1) 20
Dist: 1½l, ½l, nk, ¾l. 5m 4.20s. (20 Ran).
(Gerard Callaghan), Noel Meade

3181 Bargaincity Carpets Handicap Chase (0-132 5-y-o and up) £5,480 3m............................ (4:30)

2843[4] CASTALINO [-] 11-9-8 (7*) M D Murphy, ... (9 to 1) 1
1194[2] GO GO GALLANT (Ire) [-] 8-11-12 T Horgan, ... (5 to 2) 2
2843[5] UNA'S CHOICE (Ire) [-] 9-10-7 F J Flood, ... (7 to 1) 3
2966[2] MONALEE RIVER (Ire) [-] 9-12-0 T P Treacy, ...(2 to 1 fav) 4
2867[2] TOUT VA BIEN [-] 9-9-1 (7*) L J Fleming, ... (6 to 1) 5
636[7] VISIBLE DIFFERENCE [-] 11-11-4 K F O'Brien, ...(10 to 1) 6
3072 SPANKERS HILL (Ire) [-] 8-11-10 J P Broderick, ...(10 to 1) 7
Dist: 3l, 2l, 20l, 11l. 6m 17.30s. (7 Ran).
(Stephen Ryan), Stephen Ryan

3182 Freshford Mares I.N.H. Flat Race (5-y-o and up) £2,740 2½m...... (5:00)

GOLDEN GOLD (Ire) 5-11-0 (7*) Miss C O'Neill, ... (16 to 1) 1
3090[3] CLASH OF THE GALES (Ire) 5-11-0 (7*) Mr J P McNamara, ...(3 to 1) 2
DON'T WASTE IT (Ire) 7-11-2 (7*) Mr A FitzGerald, (10 to 1) 3
2752[4] RAHEEN RIVER (Ire) 6-11-9 Mr J A Berry, ... (10 to 1) 4
253[4] FRESHFIELD GALE (Ire) 7-11-6 (3*) Mr P English, (10 to 1) 5
3075[2] SARAH BLUE (Ire) 7-11-2 (7*) Mr K R O'Ryan, ...(8 to 1) 6
FAIR FONTAINE (Ire) 5-11-0 (7*) Mr J P Moloney, ... (9 to 1) 7
2649[2] LADY MOSKVA (Ire) 5-11-7 Mr B M Cash, ... (7 to 4 fav) 8
2906[6] AS AN SLI (Ire) 6-11-2 (7*) Mr D J Barry, ...(16 to 1) 9
1278[2] CHRISTINES RUN (Ire) 7-11-2 (7*) Miss A O'Brien, ..(7 to 1) 10
ALOTINALITTLE (Ire) 5-11-0 (7*) Mr M G Coleman, (20 to 1) 11
RILMOUNT (Ire) 5-11-0 (7*) Mr A J Dempsey, ... (10 to 1) 12
3090 LACKEN RIVER (Ire) 5-11-0 (7*) Mr R C Foster, ...(33 to 1) 13
2525 HARVEST STORM (Ire) 5-11-2 (5*) Mr A C Coyle, ...(20 to 1) 14
1077[8] ASHLEY'S PRINCESS (Ire) 5-11-0 (7*) Mr A Fleming, ...(12 to 1) 15
CASTLE-ETTA (Ire) 7-11-2 (7*) Miss K Rudd, ...(33 to 1) pu
LA CIGALE (Ire) 6-11-2 (7*) Mr M Kavanagh, ... (25 to 1) pu
LITTLE LANE (Ire) 7-11-2 (7*) Mr M Nakauchida, .. (25 to 1) pu
Dist: 1½l, 4½l, 4l, 1½l. 5m 2.40s. (18 Ran).
(R P Cody), Redmond Cody

3183 Urlingford (Pro-Am) I.N.H. Flat Race (4-y-o) £2,740 2m............. (5:30)

KAZARAN (Ire) 10-13 (7*) Mr D Breen, ... (8 to 1) 1
2449[9] LOST ALPHABET (Ire) 10-13 (7*) Mr Peter Fahy, (5 to 4 on) 2
2940 MONEYCLEAR (Ire) 11-6 Mr B M Cash, ... (8 to 1) 3
SMILING ALWAYS (Ire) 11-1 Mr P Fenton, ... (6 to 1) 4
2905[7] FIDALUS (Ire) 10-13 (7*) Mr M T Hartrey, ...(20 to 1) 5
2905[8] TONIBEROLI (Ire) 10-8 (7*) Mr J P McNamara, ... (12 to 1) 6
PRINCE OF ERIN (Ire) 10-13 (7*) Mr P Whelan, ...(12 to 1) 7
BALLYROE FLASH (Ire) 11-1 Mr J A Berry, ...(7 to 1) 8
2967[7] CAREFREE LEGEND (Ire) 11-6 Mr A R Coonan, ... (10 to 1) 9
TIMMYS CHOICE (Ire) 10-13 (7*) T Leech, ... (33 to 1) 10
KNOCKONTIME (Ire) 10-13 (7*) Mr J P Moloney, .. (10 to 1) 11
ROSES NIECE (Ire) 10-8 (7*) M D Murphy, ... (8 to 1) 12
SCHWARTZ STORY (Ire) 10-8 (7*) Mr A J Dempsey, (12 to 1) 13
INTERIM STATEMENT (Ire) 10-12 (3*) Mr E Norris, (12 to 1) pu
Dist: 1½l, 2l, 5l, nk. 3m 57.60s. (14 Ran).
(Thomas Curran), Martin Michael Lynch

HEREFORD (good to firm)
Saturday March 15th
Going Correction: PLUS 0.40 sec. per fur.

3184 March Novices' Selling Hurdle Class G (4-y-o and up) £2,122 2m 1f (2:20)

3027 HANGING GROVE (Ire) 7-11-1 W McFarland, *chsd ldrs till lft in ld 5th, mstk nxt, rdn 2 out, styd on und pres.* .... (15 to 2 op 6 to 1 tchd 8 to 1) 1
2804[2] PROUD IMAGE 5-11-7 J Osborne, *in tch, chsd wnr frm 3 out, chlgd nxt, no extr und pres from last.* (11 to 8 on op Evens) 2
1425[3] SHARP THRILL 6-11-1 C Llewellyn, *mid-div till hdwy 5th, chsd ldrs 3 out, sn one pace.*.......(8 to 1 tchd 10 to 1) 3
2999 EL BARDADOR (Ire) 4-10-4 (3*) T Dascombe, *wl beh till hdwy aftr 3 out, kpt on, no dngr.* .... (10 to 1 op 7 to 1 tchd 11 to 1) 4
3110 STILL HERE (Ire) (bl) 4-10-2 (5*) Mr R Thornton, *chsd laders till led and blun 5th, not reco'r.* .... (10 to 1 op 5 to 1 tchd 11 to 1) 5
2996[9] VITA NUOVA (Ire) 6-10-10 V Slattery, *chsd ldrs till wknd and mstk 6th.*.......................... (33 to 1 op 20 to 1) 6
VITAL WONDER 9-10-8 (7*) M Griffiths, *nvr rchd ldrs.* .... (66 to 1 op 50 to 1) 7
CORPORATE IMAGE 7-11-1 P McLoughlin, *prmnt, rdn alng 6th, 4th and one pace whn blun 3 out, not reco'r.* .... (100 to 1 op 50 to 1) 8
1940 NOQUITA (NZ) 10-10-8 (7*) X Aizpuru, *al beh, hit 6th.* .... (66 to 1 op 50 to 1) 9
2898 A BADGE TOO FAR (Ire) 7-10-10 R Bellamy, *sn beh.* .... (66 to 1 op 50 to 1) 10
140[5] SLANEY RASHER 10-11-1 Mr J L Llewellyn, *beh frm 4th.* .... (10 to 1 op 7 to 1 tchd 12 to 1) 11
KARIBU (Ger) 6-11-1 L Harvey, *led till hdd and f 5th, dead.* .... (100 to 1 op 33 to 1) f
2625[7] ERNEST ARAGORN (v) 8-10-12 (3*) R Massey, *jmpd poorly in rear till pld up bef 3 out.* (50 to 1 op 25 to 1 tchd 66 to 1) pu
AMANY (Ire) 5-10-10 D J Burchell, *sn wl beh, tld off whn pld up bef 5th.*.......................(16 to 1 op 14 to 1) pu
BOOT JACK (Ire) 8-11-1 W Marston, *bolted bef strt, sn tld off, pld up before 5th.*......(50 to 1 op 33 to 1 tchd 66 to 1) pu
Dist: 3½l, 5l, 21l, hd, 1½l, ¾l, 10l, 2½l, 8l, 2l. 4m 7.80s. a 22.80s (15 Ran).
(J H Forbes), P G Murphy

3185 Newent Handicap Chase Class D (0-120 5-y-o and up) £3,387 2m .... (2:55)

3079[3] SCOTTISH BAMBI [110] 9-11-10 J Osborne, *trkd ldrs till led 6th, shaken up whn chlgd frm 2 out, ran on wl r-in.* ....(11 to 8 on op Evens) 1
1643[5] MONDAY CLUB [100] 13-11-0 R Bellamy, *in tch, keen hold, pushed alng 9th, chsd wnr 3 out, chlgd nxt, one pace r-in.* .... (9 to 1 op 6 to 1 tchd 10 to 1) 2
3104* DR ROCKET [86] (v) 12-9-7 (7*) X Aizpuru, *chsd ldrs, hit 4th, rdn 3 out, sn wknd*......................(4 to 1 op 3 to 1) 3
CORPUS [86] 8-9-13[2] (3*) T Dascombe, *led to 6th, fdd.* .... (25 to 1 op 8 to 1) 4
1471[6] NORTHERN OPTIMIST [87] 9-9-10 (5*) Mr R Thornton, *in tch whn blun badly 6th, not reco'r.*........ (11 to 2 op 4 to 1) 5
Dist: 5l, 8l, 28l, nk. 4m 2.60s. a 15.60s (5 Ran).
SR: 4/-/ (William J Kelly), P R Webber

3186 Bosbury Handicap Hurdle Class D (0-120 4-y-o and up) £2,717 2m 1f .... (3:25)

2872 VA UTU [83] 9-9-11 (3*) Sophie Mitchell, *made virtually all, rdn and hld on wl aproaching last*.. (16 to 1 tchd 20 to 1) 1
2878* ADDED DIMENSION (Ire) [107] 6-11-3 (7*) X Aizpuru, *pld hrd, chlgd second, styd pressing wnr till rdn and mstk 2 out, rallied r-in, no extr nr finish.*........... (5 to 4 on op 6 to 4 on) 2
1947[6] SCHNOZZLE (Ire) [89] 6-10-3 (3*) R Massey, *hdwy to go 3rd 3 out, effrt nxt, sn outpcd.*.............(4 to 1 tchd 5 to 1) 3

2681⁵ MENELAVE (Ire) [103] (bl) 7-11-6 J Osborne, *chsd ldrs till lost tch 3 out*...................... (5 to 2 op 2 to 1) 4

Dist: 1¼l, 9l, 20l. 4m 4.60s. a 19.60s (4 Ran).

(D M Lloyd), D M Lloyd

3187 Charlie Knipe Hunters' Chase Class H (6-y-o and up) £1,492 3m 1f 110yds...................... (4:00)

PENLEA LADY 10-11-2 (7*) Mr S Lloyd, *in tch, mstk tenth, bumped and nrly uns rdr 12th, styd on to chase ldr 15th, shaken up and quickened to ld cl hme*.
.... (7 to 1 op 9 to 1 tchd 12 to 1) 1
THE RUM MARINER 10-11-9 (5*) Mr R Thornton, *led, rdn 3 out, hdd and no error cl hme.* (5 to 1 op 7 to 1 tchd 8 to 1) 2
CHIP'N'RUN 11-11-7 (7*) Mr J Cornes, *chsd ldr to 15th, wknd 3 out*.................... (4 to 1 op 3 to 1 tchd 5 to 2) 3
2887⁵ GAY RUFFIAN 11-11-7 (7*) Miss C Dyson, *hdwy 8th, wknd 13th*.................... (20 to 1 op 16 to 1) 4
FIRST HARVEST 10-11-7 (7*) Mr P Hanly, *hdwy 7th, chsd ldrs whn blun 14th, sn wknd*... (6 to 1 op 5 to 1) 5
KINGFISHER BAY 12-11-7 (7*) Mr G Shenkin, *beh frm 11th, lld off whn pld up bef 13th*...... (50 to 1 op 33 to 1) pu
2997⁴ ORTON HOUSE 10-11-7 (7*) Mr R Burton, *beh frm 9th, tld off whn pld up bef 15th*.............. (20 to 1 op 16 to 1) pu
2997² TEATRADER 11-11-7 (7*) Miss T Blazey, *hit 6th and beh, tld off whn pld up bef 4 out*.....(15 to 2 op 5 to 1 tchd 8 to 1) pu
PRINCE OF VERONA 10-11-7 (7*) Mr Rupert Sweeting, *sn outpcd and beh, effrt tenth, soon wknd, tld off whn pld up bef 15th*.................... (7 to 2 fav op 2 to 1) pu
2997* HIGHWAY FIVE (Ire) 9-12-0 (7*) Miss E James, *sn beh, tld off whn pld up bef 15th*..... (11 to 1 op 6 to 1 tchd 12 to 1) pu

Dist: 1¼l, 17l, 16l, 23l. 6m 39.00s. a 33.00s (10 Ran).

(Mrs S G Addinsell), Mrs S G Addinsell

3188 Teme Mares' Only Handicap Hurdle Class D (0-120 4-y-o and up) £2,703 2m 3f 110yds.................... (4:30)

2801³ KADARI [93] (v) 8-10-1 (3*) Guy Lewis, *in tch, shaken up and hdwy to ld 7th, hdd 3 out, led ag'n nxt, ran on wl*.
.... (7 to 2 op 5 to 2 tchd 4 to 1) 1
3054* SWING QUARTET (Ire) [98] 7-10-9 C Llewellyn, *not fluent 5th and beh, steady hdwy whn mstk 4 out, rallied frm 2 out, styd on r-in, nt rch wnr*.................... (11 to 10 fav tchd 6 to 5) 2
2878⁶ SEVSO [89] 8-10-0 V Slattery, *mstk second, chsd ldrs, rdn to ld 3 out, heaaded nxt, sn one pace*.... (7 to 1 op 5 to 1) 3
1957⁷ JOSIFINA [115] 6-11-7 (5*) Mr R Thornton, *al beh, rdn alng 6th, sn tld off*.................... (13 to 2 op 4 to 1) 4
2807⁴ PRECIOUS ISLAND [97] 4-10-0 W Marston, *led to 7th, sn wknd*.................... (9 to 2 op 7 to 1) 5

Dist: 1½l, 8l, 24l, 16l. 4m 49.90s. a 31.90s (5 Ran).

(H Clewlow), W Clay

3189 Malvern Novices' Chase Class E (5-y-o and up) £2,867 2m....... (5:00)

2978* QUICK QUOTE 7-11-3 L Harvey, *prmnt, chlgd 4th till led 6th, jmpd lft aftr, clr frm 2 out, easily*.......... (7 to 4 op 2 to 1) 1
2886⁴ TENAYESTELIGN 9-10-12 (5*) Mr R Thornton, *hdwy to chase ldrs 6th, disputing second but no ch whn lft chasing wnr last*.
.... (7 to 2 tchd 4 to 1) 2
2998 RELAXED LAD 8-11-2 R Bellamy, *jmpd poorly in rear, nvr dngrs, lft 3rd last*.................... (20 to 1 op 16 to 1) 3
2626 WHOD OF THOUGHT IT (Ire) 6-11-2 V Slattery, *hdwy to chase ldrs 8th, mstk and wknd 3 out*.......... (25 to 1) 4
2373⁴ QUICK DECISION (Ire) 6-10-9 (7*) N T Egan, *prmnt till hit 5th, no dngr aftr, tld off*.......... (25 to 1 op 14 to 1) 5
2877* NORTHERN SINGER 7-11-11 (3*) T Dascombe, *led to 6th, styd chasing wnr but no ch and chlgd for second whn f last*.
.... (6 to 5 fav op 5 to 4 tchd 5 to 4) f
2998 JASONS PARTNER 7-10-13 (3*) Guy Lewis, *f 1st*.
.... (6 to 1 op 50 to 1) f
2978⁴ QUEENS CURATE 10-10-11 B Powell, *prmnt till wknd 6th, tld off frm 8th, pld up bef last, lme*.......(16 to 1 op 33 to 1) pu

Dist: 6l, 18l, 11l, dist. 4m 8.30s. a 21.30s (8 Ran).

(M H D Barlow), Mrs I McKie

3190 Levy Board Novices' Handicap Hurdle Class F (0-95 4-y-o and up) £2,528 3¼m.................... (5:30)

1474 YOUNG TESS [72] 7-10-0 (5*) Mr R Thornton, *in tch ldrs till rdn and lost pl 8th, hdwy nxt, chlgd 3 out, led aftr next, styd on wl*.
.... (5 to 1 jt-fav op 6 to 1) 1
2889 SAMMORELLO (Ire) [73] 6-10-6 C Llewellyn, *led to 6th, styd prmnt, led 3 out, hdd aftr nxt, one pace.* (7 to 1 tchd 8 to 1) 2
2601⁵ COPPER COIL [94] 7-11-6 (7*) J Power, *chsd ldrs till outpcd 8th, styd on ag'n frm 3 out*.......... (13 to 2 op 5 to 1) 3
2665 BROWN WREN [67] 6-10-0 G Tormey, *in tch 4th, hdwy 9th, no prog und press frm 3 out*. (11 to 1 op 8 to 1 tchd 4 to 1) 4
3042* SPITFIRE BRIDGE (Ire) [71] 5-9-11 (7*) R Hobson, *rapid hdwy to press ldrs 8th, led 9th, hdd and hit 3 out, sn wknd*.
.... (6 to 1 op 4 to 1) 5
2898⁷ LADY OF MINE [67] 7-10-0 W Marston, *trkd ldrs, rdn and wknd appr 3 out*.................... (20 to 1 op 12 to 1) 6

2750² CRAVATE (Fr) [67] 7-9-7 (7*) M Moran, *hit 6th and beh, some hdwy frm 3 out*.......... (7 to 2 op 10 to 1 tchd 14 to 1) 7
2951⁶ PROFESSOR PAGE (Ire) [84] 7-10-10 (7*) X Aizpuru, *in tch to 7th, wknd*.................... (6 to 1 op 5 to 1) 8
1981 LORD NITROGEN (USA) [88] 7-11-7 Mr J L Llewellyn, *chsd ldr till led 6th, mstk and hdd 9th, sn wknd*.
.... (25 to 1 op 20 to 1) 9
986⁴ MANOR BOUND [67] 7-9-11 (3*) R Massey, *al in rear*.
.... (16 to 1 op 14 to 1) 10
2549 PENNANT COTTAGE (Ire) [67] 9-10-0 R Bellamy, *prmnt till wknd 8th*.................... (50 to 1 op 33 to 1) 11
3041⁴ COOLE CHERRY [78] 7-10-11 L Harvey, *al in rear*.
.... (10 to 1 op 7 to 1 tchd 20 to 1) 12
2799 KENTUCKY GOLD (Ire) [67] (bl) 8-10-0 L O'Hara, *mstk 5th, al beh*.................... (25 to 1 op 14 to 1 tchd 33 to 1) 13
2977⁸ SEMINOLE WIND [67] (v) 6-10-0 B Powell, *al beh, tld off*.... 14
2977* NODDADANTE (Ire) [69] 7-9-13 (3*) Sophie Mitchell, *hdwy 7th, hit 4 out and sn wknd, no ch whn blun and uns rdr last*.
.... (5 to 1 jt-fav tchd 9 to 1 and 9 to 2) ur
3000 NORDIC FLIGHT [67] (h,bl) 9-10-0 V Slattery, *mstk second, tld off 7th, pld up bef 9th*.................... (50 to 1) pu

Dist: 7l, 8l, 7l, 3l, 3½l, 8l, 5l, 2½l, 14l, 6l. 6m 29.00s. a 27.00s (16 Ran).

(G Morris), P Bowen

LINGFIELD (good to soft)
Saturday March 15th
Going Correction: PLUS 1.00 sec. per fur. (races 1,3,5), PLUS 1.10 (2,4,6,7)

3191 Ruby Conditional Jockeys' Selling Handicap Chase Class G (0-95 5-y-o and up) £2,244 2½m 110yds.. (2:10)

2859³ HANGOVER [68] 11-11-6 P Henley, *lft in ld 3rd, hdd 5th, led aftr 4 out, sn clr, jnd 3 out, clear nxt, eased r-in, dismounted*.
.... (5 to 4 fav op 11 to 10 tchd 11 to 8 and 6 to 4) 1
2748⁶ MADAM ROSE (Ire) [60] 7-10-5 (7*) David Turner, *pld hrd, led 5th, hdd and outpcd aftr 4 out, rallied and ev ch nxt, btn whn hmpd by loose horse 2 out, tld off*.... (50 to 1 op 20 to 1) 2
499⁵ FATTASH (USA) [69] (b) 5-10-12 S Ryan, *in tch, wknd 9th, tld off, very tired whn scrambled o'r last*... (14 to 1 op 8 to 1) 3
RISEUPWILLIEREILLY [60] 11-10-5 (7*) W Greatrex, *led, clr second, f nxt.* (13 to 2 op 7 to 1 tchd 8 to 1 and 9 to 1) f
2877⁵ FULL SHILLING (USA) [60] (bl) 8-10-12 D J Kavanagh, *in cl tch whn hmpd and uns rdr 4th*.
.... (10 to 1 tchd 8 to 1) ur
2991 OPAL'S TENSPOT [72] 10-11-10 L Aspell, *in cl tch, wth ldr whn blun and pld up 6th, dead*........ (2 to 1 op 6 to 4) pu

Dist: Dist, dist. 5m 40.10s. a 39.10s (6 Ran).

(Richard Edwards), R Lee

3192 Guild Venture Diamond Novices' Hurdle Class D (4-y-o and up) £3,400 2m 3f 110yds.................... (2:40)

3117* ELA AGAPI MOU (USA) 4-10-13 (6ex) P Holley, *pld hrd, cl up, lft in ld 6th, wndrd appr 2 out, hard rdn and hit last, ran on gmely*.................... (9 to 2 op 5 to 1 tchd 11 to 1) 1
2954² CHEERFUL ASPECT (Ire) 4-10-13 N Williamson, *cl up in chasing grp, wth wnr frm 6th, drvn appr last, drw level r-in, no extr nr finish*.................... (7 to 4 op 5 to 4) 2
2920* SPLENDID THYNE 5-12-0 M A Fitzgerald, *hld up beh ldrs in chasing grp, not fluent 4 out and sn pushed alng, mstk nxt, btn quickly, tld off*.................... (7 to 4 jt-fav op 2 to 1) 3
2980² CHEEKY CHARLIE 5-10-13 (3*) P Henley, *hld up in tch, reminder aftr 6th, hrd rdn and outpcd after 3 out, tld off*.
.... (14 to 1 op 10 to 1 tchd 16 to 1) 4
2893 TORAJA 5-11-2 D Leahy, *hld up beh ldrs in chasing grp, pushed alng aftr 5th, outpcd 7th (4 out), tld off*.
.... (20 to 1 tchd 25 to 1 and 33 to 1) 5
2637 CHARLIE'S FOLLY 6-11-2 G Upton, *hld up, hrd rdn and struggling 6th, tld off*.............(50 to 1 op 20 to 1) 6
2953³ ALL DONE 4-10-2 N Mann, *hld up, beh frm 7th, tld off*.
.... (10 to 1 op 6 to 1 tchd 12 to 1) 7
3035 SUPREME CRUSADER (Ire) 6-11-2 E Byrne, *al last, lost tch 3rd, tld off*.................(100 to 1 op 33 to 1) 8
COOL SPOT (Ire) 9-11-2 J R Kavanagh, *jmpd rght, led till jumped badly right and hdd 6th, sn beh, tld off whn pld up bef 2 out*.................... (50 to 1 op 20 to 1) pu

Dist: ½l, dist, 14l, 22l, 8l, 1l, 28l. 5m 1.30s. a 28.30s (9 Ran).
SR: 16/15/-/-/-/-/ (Ballard (1834) Limited), G L Moore

3193 Northern Trust Sapphire Handicap Chase Class E (0-110 5-y-o and up) £3,052 2m....................(3:10)

2767⁴ RED BEAN [86] 9-11-5 M A Fitzgerald, *led 3rd to nxt, cl up, led 2 out, drvn out*.
.... (6 to 1 op 5 to 1 tchd 13 to 2 and 7 to 1) 1
2767* BUCKLAND LAD (Ire) [81] 6-11-0 J R Kavanagh, *in cl tch, gd jump to join ldr 4 out, led nxt, blun badly and hdd 2 out, hrd rdn and not reco'r*.................... (5 to 4 on fav Evens) 2
2304³ RIVER LEVEN [91] (bl) 8-11-10 N Williamson, *reluctant and reminders to race, led 4th, jnd four out, hdd nxt, hrd rdn and btn appr last*............... (7 to 2 op 7 to 4 tchd 4 to 1) 3

1941³ FICHU (USA) [78] 9-10-11 M Richards, *led to 3rd, cl up till lost pl 7th, closed 3 out, btn appr last.*
.........................(9 to 2 op 4 to 1 tchd 5 to 1) 4
Dist: 4l, 3l, 12l. 4m 17.20s. a 23.20s (4 Ran).
SR: 19/10/17/-/   (Kage Vincent), K Vincent

3194 **T.J.H. Group Lingfield Gold Cup Handicap Hurdle Class C (0-130 4-y-o and up) £4,441 2m 3f 110yds (3:45)**

2639³ TICKERY'S GIFT [109] 7-11-6 (7*) M Batchelor, *keen early, in cl tch, led 4 out, rdn clr appr 2 out, ran on wl.*
.........(11 to 4 op 5 to 2 tchd 3 to 1 and 9 to 4) 1
2797⁴ SPRING TO GLORY [100] 10-11-4 M A Fitzgerald, *cl up, hrd rdn aftr 3 out, chsd wnr appr nxt, no extr. (9 to 2 op 5 to 1)* 2
2547 RACHAEL'S OWEN [85] 7-10-3 M Richards, *hld up, outpcd aftr 6th, cld after 3 out, btn nxt.*
.... (11 to 4 op 9 to 4 tchd 3 to 1) 3
2640 EQUITY'S DARLING (Ire) [82] (bl) 5-10-0 N Williamson, *hld up, reminders appr 6th, sn hrd rdn and btn.* (10 to 1 op 7 to 1) 4
1973² SPRINTFAYRE [98] 9-10-9 (7*) A Irvine, *jmpd rght, led to 4 out, ev ch whn mstk nxt, sn btn.*
...................(5 to 2 fav op 9 to 4 tchd 11 to 4) 5
Dist: 5l, 16l, 7l, 11l. 5m 5.50s. a 22.50s (5 Ran).
                                       (K Higson), G L Moore

3195 **Opal Maiden Chase Class E (5-y-o and up) £2,946 2½m 110yds.. (4:15)**

3038 AMBER SPARK (Ire) 8-11-10 N Williamson, *hld up, cld 10th, led 3 out, hdd out.........(3 to 1 op 2 to 1 tchd 4 to 1)* 1
2930² NORMARANGE (Ire) 7-11-7 (3*) P Henley, *led till aftr second, cl up, outpcd appr 4 out, rallied nxt, ev ch 2 out, one pace and pres whn mstk last......* (11 to 4 op 2 to 1 tchd 3 to 1) 2
DEBONAIR DUDE (Ire) 7-11-10 M A Fitzgerald, *led 4th to nxt, not fluent 7th, wth ldr, blun 3 out, ev ch next, sn btn.*
......................(6 to 4 fav op 7 to 4 tchd 5 to 4) 3
2741 ONEOFUS 8-11-10 M Richards, *led aftr second to 4th, led and hit 6th, mstk 10th, hdd 3 out, btn whn mistake nxt, very tired when scrambled o'r last.*
.................(16 to 1 op 20 to 1 tchd 25 to 1 and 33 to 1) 4
2930 PLUMBRIDGE 9-11-10 J R Kavanagh, *hld up, struggling in rear frm 9th, tld off....* (25 to 1 op 14 to 1 tchd 33 to 1) 5
2601 THE WAYWARD BISHOP (Ire) 8-11-10 J A McCarthy, *hld up, f 4th.........(8 to 1 op 10 to 1 tchd 12 to 1 and 14 to 1)* f
Dist: 3½l, 18l, dist, 11l. 5m 30.20s. a 29.20s (6 Ran).
SR: 9/5/-/   (R E Brinkworth), D R Gandolfo

3196 **HBLB Bull Information Systems Ltd. Novices' Handicap Hurdle Class E (0-100 4-y-o and up) £2,442 2m 7f .... (4:45)**

WORKINGFORPEANUTS (Ire) [64] 7-10-0 Mrs D Smith, *hld up in rear, mstk 5th, steady hdwy 8th, trkd ldr appr 2 out, led approaching last, ran on strly.*
.....................(5 to 1 op 6 to 1 tchd 7 to 1) 1
2892* RED LIGHTER [86] 8-11-8 G Upton, *trkd ldrs, led 7th, hdd appr last, no extr....* (9 to 4 fav op 5 to 2 tchd 11 to 4) 2
2640⁴ SHANAGORE WARRIOR (Ire) [85] 5-11-7 N Mann, *hld up in mid-div, cld appr 7th, hit nxt, wth ldr frm 4 out till wknd approaching 2 out.....*(13 to 2 op 9 to 2 tchd 7 to 1) 3
2929¹ ROSKEEN BRIDGE (Ire) [76] 6-10-12 M Richards, *hld up, niggled alng 8th, sn drvn and btn.*
.....................(3 to 1 op 5 to 2 tchd 100 to 30) 4
2738 NORDIC SPREE (Ire) [83] 5-11-5 P Holley, *cl up, hrd rdn 8th, sn btn, tld off.*
.........(7 to 1 op 10 to 1 tchd 12 to 1 and 14 to 1) 5
2822 STORMY SESSION [85] 7-11-7 C Maude, *trkd ldrs, rdn alng and lost pl aftr 6th, tld off whn pld up bef 3 out.*
.................(13 to 2 op 6 to 1 tchd 7 to 1) pu
2462 THAT OLD FEELING (Ire) [65] (bl) 5-10-1 D Gallagher, *hit second, led to 7th, wknd quickly aftr nxt, tld off whn pld up bef 2 out...............* (20 to 1 op 16 to 1 tchd 25 to 1) pu
2977⁵ EWAR BOLD [73] (bl) 4-10-0 J R Kavanagh, *mstk 1st, al beh, lost tch 6th, tld off whn hit 8th, pld up bef nxt (4 out).*
........................(14 to 1 op 20 to 1) pu
2372⁹ UPHAM RASCAL [64] 6-10-0 D Leahy, *trkd ldrs, hrd rdn 8th, sn btn, tld off whn pld up bef 2 out.*
.................(25 to 1 op 20 to 1 tchd 33 to 1) pu
3042⁵ SUPREME ILLUSION (Aus) [73] 4-10-0 N Williamson, *hld up, hrd rdn 8th, sn btn, tld off whn pld up bef 2 out.*
.................(12 to 1 op 8 to 1 tchd 14 to 1) pu
Dist: 8l, 17l, 3l, 22l. 5m 57.40s. a 31.40s (10 Ran).
SR: 11/25/7/-/-/-/   (Mrs D A Smith & Nick Shutts), C A Smith

3197 **Emerald Intermediate Open National Hunt Flat Class H (4,5,6-y-o) £1,203 2m 110yds.................... (5:15)**

2309³ QUISTAQUAY 5-10-8 (3*) P Henley, *pld hrd, cl up till lost pl o'r 7 fs out, rdn and hdwy over 2 out, brst through to ld ins last, drvn out...............*(7 to 2 op 3 to 1 tchd 4 to 1) 1
COUNTRY HOUSE 6-10-11 G Upton, *hld up in tch, shaken up o'r 2 fs out, led over one out, hdd ins last, ran on.*
.................(2 to 1 fav op 5 to 4 tchd 5 to 2) 2

2015⁵ PEACE INITIATIVE 5-11-2 M A Fitzgerald, *cl up, led 11 fs out to 7 out, drvn and ev ch ins last, no extr fnl 100 yards.*
.................(11 to 2 op 6 to 1 tchd 5 to 1) 3
DUNSFOLD DOLLY 4-10-0 (3*) L Aspell, *trkd ldrs, led 7 fs out to o'r one out, one pace...(7 to 2 op 5 to 1 tchd 6 to 1)* 4
1769⁵ BIG STAN'S BOY 6-11-2 D Gallagher, *pld hrd, hld up, cld o'r 7 fs out, pushed alng over 4 out, wknd over 3 out, tld off.*
.................(9 to 2 op 5 to 2 tchd 5 to 1) 5
1975 MR ROBSTEE 6-10-11 (5*) O Burrows, *led to 11 fs out, reminders 7 out, sn wknd, tld off.*
.................(33 to 1 op 20 to 1 tchd 50 to 1) 6
3082 EXPRESS AGAIN 5-11-2 N Williamson, *pld hrd, trkd ldrs till wknd 6 fs out, tld off...............*(6 to 1 tchd 7 to 1) 7
WHISKY WILMA 5-10-11 D Morris, *al beh, struggling o'r 6 fs out, tld off...............*(15 to 2 op 7 to 1) 8
Dist: 1½l, 1¾l, 1¾l, 27l, 14l, 23l, 13l. 4m 15.00s. (8 Ran).
                                       (Mrs Heather Bare), J W Mullins

NEWCASTLE (good)
Saturday March 15th
Going Correction: PLUS 0.30 sec. per fur. (races 1,3,6), MINUS 0.15 (2,4,5)

3198 **'Welcome To Gosforth Park' Novices' Hurdle Class E (4-y-o and up) £2,452 2m.....................(2:15)**

2817* FAR AHEAD 5-11-8 B Storey, *nvr far away, led aftr 3 out, styd on wl r-in.....................*(3 to 1 op 3 to 1 tchd 9 to 2) 1
2908³ BANKER COUNT 5-10-13 (3*) P Midgley, *settled to track ldrs, rdn to join wnr appr 2 out, kpt on und pres r-in.*
.................(5 to 1 op 4 to 1 tchd 11 to 2) 2
2852² GOSPEL SONG 5-10-13 (3*) G Lee, *al hndy, led 4 out till aftr 2 out, one and one pace after.*
.................(7 to 2 fav op 4 to 1 tchd 11 to 2) 3
2879³ MITHRAIC (Ire) 5-11-8 M Foster, *al tracking ldrs, ev ch aftr 4 out, feeling pace frm nxt............*(4 to 1 op 7 to 2) 4
BATTERY FIRED 8-10-9 (7*) S Haworth, *sn tracking ldrs, ev ch appr 4 out, drvn alng aftr nxt, no extr.........*(100 to 1) 5
2712 PAPARAZZO 6-11-2 J Callaghan, *nvr far away, ev ch 4 out, und pres aftr nxt, btn whn blun 2 out. (33 to 1 tchd 50 to 1)* 6
1882⁵ ADVANCE EAST 5-11-8 R Supple, *took keen hold in midfield, improved 4 out, lost grnd frm nxt, fdd....* (7 to 1 op 9 to 2) 7
2882⁴ RAISE A DOLLAR 7-10-11 Mr S Swiers, *wl plcd to 4 out, lost grnd frm nxt, fdd last 2.........................*(50 to 1) 8
2854³ KILLBALLY BOY (Ire) 7-11-8 M Moloney, *al hndy, led 4th to four out, wknd frm nxt, sn lost tch....(20 to 1 tchd 25 to 1)* 9
1690⁵ ONYOUROWN (Ire) 4-10-3 D Parker, *in tch to hfwy, lost grnd quickly 4 out, sn beh...* (16 to 1 op 10 to 1 tchd 20 to 1) 10
3003⁷ PRAISE BE (Fr) 7-11-2 R Garritty, *patiently rdn, effrt bef 4 out, grad wknd frm nxt.............*(50 to 1 op 33 to 1) 11
RAMBLING RAJAH 5-10-9 (7*) R Burn, *settled midfield, effrt frm 4 out, wknd frm nxt, sn beh.............*(100 to 1) 12
2975⁵ DELIGHTFOOL 6-10-11 G Cahill, *struggling and lost grnd quickly hfwy, tld off............(100 to 1 op 200 to 1)* 13
3044 KHALIKHOUM (Ire) 4-10-8 J Supple, *al wl beh, tld off.*
.................(33 to 1 tchd 50 to 1) 14
SHARLEY COP 5-10-11 L Wyer, *settled off the pace, nvr a factor, tld off.........................*(100 to 1 op 200 to 1) 15
2852⁹ SNIPER 5-11-2 A Roche, *settled in tch, struggling frm hfwy, tld off..........................*(200 to 1) 16
2849 EVENING DUSK (Ire) 5-10-4 (7*) S Melrose, *settled midfield, lost tch hfwy, tld off..................*(200 to 1) 17
2879 PETRICO 5-10-11 (5*) B Grattan, *wl plcd till aproaching 4 out, tld off..........................*(100 to 1) 18
377 SOCCER BALL 7-10-13 (3*) E Callaghan, *led to 4th, lost tch four out, tld off.....................*(200 to 1) 19
2849 SOLWAY KING 7-10-11 (5*) S Taylor, *lost tch frm hfwy, tld off whn pld up bef 3 out...................*(200 to 1) pu
INYOUGOBLUE (Ire) 5-10-9 (7*) Mr T J Barry, *struggling frm hfwy, tld off whn pld up bef 3 out...............*(100 to 1) pu
Dist: ¾l, 10l, 5l, hd, 9l, 3l, 7l, 1¼l, 2l, hd. 3m 49.10s. a 12.10s (21 Ran).
SR: 21/14/4/5/-/-/   (Sunpak Potatoes), J L Eyre

3199 **Grainger Town Handicap Chase Class E (0-115 5-y-o and up) £2,784 2m 110yds.................... (2:50)**

2884* CROSSHOT [-] 10-10-5 R Supple, *nvr far away, nosed ahead last, ran on strly to go clr r-in.................*(5 to 2 jt-fav op 9 to 4 tchd 11 to 4) 1
2987³ BLAZING DAWN [-] 10-9-11 (3*) G Lee, *tried to make all, hdd and bustled alng aftr 3 out, rallied and ran on to take second r-in......................*(4 to 1 op 7 to 1) 2
3010³ GROUSE-N-HEATHER [-] 8-10-3 G Cahill, *al wl plcd, led aftr 3 out, hdd and rdn last, one pace r-in.........*(5 to 2 jt-fav tchd 11 to 4 and 9 to 4) 3
3047² DUAL IMAGE [-] 10-11-1 R Garritty, *patiently rdn, jmpd slwly 6 out, improved aftr nxt, hng fire betw last 2, styd on finish.*
.................(3 to 1 op 9 to 1) 4
2493³ TIMBUCKTOO [-] 10-12-0 B Storey, *nvr far away, niggled alng to hold pl 5 out, lost tch nxt, tld off.*
.................(14 to 1 op 7 to 1 tchd 16 to 1) 5
Dist: 1¼l, 1¼l, 1¾l, dist. 4m 2.50s. a 3.50s (5 Ran).
SR: 17/10/11/21/-/   (R McDonald), R McDonald

3200 Tyne Bridge Handicap Hurdle Class C (0-130 4-y-o and up) £3,403 3m .... (3:20)

2789[6] PUREVALUE (Ire) [-] 6-11-10 R Garritty, *dictated pace, quickened bef 9th, hdd 2 out, rallied gmely to rgn ld r-in, ran on wl.* ....(5 to 2 tchd 3 to 1) 1
LINLATHEN [-] 7-11-5 (3*) G Lee, *patiently rdn, improved to chase ldr 4 out, swtchd lft to ld 2 out, hdd and ridden r-in, no extr.*..........(2 to 1 fav op 9 to 4 tchd 7 to 4) 2
2151[9] SUDDEN SPIN [-] 7-10-8 (3*) E Callaghan, *nvr far away, effrt and bustled alng appr 3 out, not quicken frm nxt.* ....(10 to 1 op 7 to 1) 3
3031[2] LEADING PROSPECT [-] 10-10-3 (7*) N Horrocks, *pressed ldr, mstks 3rd and 6th, ev ch 3 out, rdn and fdd frm nxt.* ....(11 to 4 op 9 to 4 tchd 3 to 1) 4
2854[5] COOL LUKE (Ire) [-] 8-10-10 (3*) Michael Brennan, *settled in tch, effrt 8th, struggling bef 3 out, lost touch, tld off frm nxt.* ....(20 to 1 op 12 to 1) 5
KINDA GROOVY [-] 8-10-12 N Smith, *trkd ldrs, effrt 8th, rdn and lost grnd 4 out, tld off*..........(20 to 1 op 16 to 1) 6

Dist: 1¾l, 9l, 9l, 14l, dist. 5m 52.70s. a 21.70s (6 Ran).
(A D Simmons), M W Easterby

3201 Newcastle Handicap Chase Class C (0-135 5-y-o and up) £4,279 3m .... (3:55)

2883[2] ALJADEER (USA) [-] 8-10-12 R Garritty, *patiently rdn, steady hdwy to chal aftr 4 out, str run und pres to ld nring finish.* ....(7 to 4 fav op 6 to 4 tchd 15 to 8) 1
2317[7] DEEP DECISION [-] 11-10-0 K Johnson, *nvr far away, chlgd gng wl frm 4 out, nosed ahead last, ran on und pres, worn dwn nring finish*..........(7 to 2 op 4 to 1) 2
2579 WESTWELL BOY [-] 11-10-3 R Supple, *led, not fluent 4 out, rdn and quickened nxt, hdd last, one pace.* ....(3 to 1 op 5 to 2 tchd 100 to 30) 3
3014[2] CEILIDH BOY [-] 11-10-10 Mr R Hale, *pressed ldrs, reminders 6 out, almost f nxt, continued tld off.* ....(11 to 4 op 9 to 4 tchd 3 to 1) 4

Dist: ½l, 11l, dist. 5m 58.30s. a 12.30s (4 Ran).
(Miss V Foster), M W Easterby

3202 Northumberland Novices' Chase Class E (5-y-o and up) £2,849 2½m .... (4:25)

3030[3] CORSTON JOKER 7-11-2 R Supple, *made most, hrd pressed frm 3 out, gd jump last, styd on strly to go clr r-in.* ....(20 to 1 op 12 to 1 tchd 25 to 1) 1
2848* BRIGHTER SHADE (Ire) 7-11-8 R Garritty, *patiently rdn, improved gng wl 6 out, chlgd and not fluent last, one pace und pres r-in*..........(2 to 1 on op 9 to 4 on tchd 5 to 2 on) 2
3005[5] BOLD ACCOUNT (Ire) 7-11-8 B Storey, *nvr far away, drw level 3 out, not fluent last 2, outpcd r-in.* ....(100 to 30 op 3 to 1 tchd 7 to 2) 3
2914[4] FINE TUNE (Ire) 7-11-2 M Foster, *blun 1st, struggling to keep up frm 7 out, tld off from nxt.* ....(14 to 1 op 16 to 1 tchd 25 to 1) 4
3030[4] SHUT UP 8-10-11 K Johnson, *chsd ldrs, und pres and lost pl quickly 7 out, tld off*..........(50 to 1 op 33 to 1) 5
3124* NIJWAY 7-11-3 (5*,6ex) S Taylor, *not jump wl, struggling whn blun 8 out, blunded badly and uns rdr nxt.* ....(10 to 1 op 8 to 1 tchd 12 to 1) ur

Dist: 2½l, 9l, dist, 5l. 5m 6.00s. a 19.00s (6 Ran).
(A S Lyburn), L Lungo

3203 Student City Novices' Handicap Hurdle Class C (4-y-o and up) £3,550 2 ½m........................... (4:55)

1679[4] STAN'S YOUR MAN [-] 7-11-4 N Bentley, *al wl plcd, led 5th to nxt, rgned ld 4 out, hdd betw last 2, rdn and lft clr last.* ....(8 to 1 op 6 to 1) 1
2158* MOCK TRIAL (Ire) [-] 4-10-7 R Garritty, *wtd wth, effrt whn hmpd by faller 5th, rallied und pres last 3, not quicken frm betw last 2*..........(7 to 2 op 3 to 1 tchd 9 to 2) 2
2813* SHANAVOGH [-] 6-11-10 J Callaghan, *nvr far away, effrt and bustled alng 4 out, und pres aftr nxt, fdd.* ....(4 to 1 op 3 to 1 tchd 9 to 2) 3
2346[8] LOSTRIS (Ire) [-] 6-10-3 N Smith, *pressed ldrs to hfwy, struggling bef 4 out, lost tch, tld off*..........(20 to 1 op 12 to 1) 4
3059[6] JUBRAN (USA) [-] 11-10-9 B Storey, *trkd ldrs, hit 6th, struggling bef 4 out, tld off*..........(20 to 1 op 12 to 1) 5
2815* HERE COMES HERBIE [-] 5-10-10 (5*) R McGrath, *settled gng wl, improved on bit 3 out, led betw last 2, f last, unlucky.* ....(2 to 1 fav op 5 to 2 tchd 7 to 4) f
1868[3] TWEEDSWOOD (Ire) [-] 7-10-10 R Supple, *led till hdd and f 5th*..........(9 to 2 op 7 to 2 tchd 5 to 1) f

Dist: 21l, 5l, dist, 1½l. 4m 50.60s. a 12.60s (7 Ran).
SR: 24/-/4/-/ (Mrs J D Goodfellow), Mrs J D Goodfellow

UTTOXETER (good)
Saturday March 15th

Going Correction: NIL (races 1,3,4,5), PLUS 0.40 (2,6,7)

3204 European Breeders Fund Tattersalls Ireland Mares' Novices' Chase Final Handicap Class C (6-y-o and up) £10,796 2m 5f.............. (12:45)

2894* TELLICHERRY [90] 8-10-7 J Culloty, *al prmnt, led 3 out, hrd rdn r-in, ran on*..........(6 to 1 op 5 to 1) 1
2527[2] GOLDENSWIFT (Ire) [94] 7-10-11 B Fenton, *mid-div, hdwy tenth, ev ch last, ran on und pres.* ....(3 to 1 fav op 5 to 2 tchd 100 to 30) 2
2808[5] KOO'S PROMISE [83] 6-10-0 R Farrant, *chsd ldrs, ev ch 4 out, styd on same pace*..........(25 to 1) 3
2781[3] HARVEST VIEW (Ire) [99] 7-10-9 (7*) M Berry, *hld up, hdwy 8th, led appr 4 out, hdd and mstk nxt, styd on same pace.* ....(9 to 1 op 7 to 1) 4
2776[3] SECOND CALL [110] 8-11-13 R Dunwoody, *patiently rdn, pushed alng tenth, nvr nr ldrs*..........(10 to 1) 5
2245[5] MISS DISKIN (Ire) [100] 8-11-3 B Powell, *chsd ldrs, rdn appr 4 out, sn btn*..........(12 to 1 op 8 to 1) 6
2903[3] BLAZE OF HONOUR (Ire) [111] 6-12-0 C F Swan, *hld up, nvr nr ldrs*..........(15 to 2 op 6 to 1 tchd 8 to 1) 7
2912* COVERDALE LANE [95] 10-10-12 Richard Guest, *prmnt, led aftr 4th, hdd 6th, wknd four out*..........(16 to 1 op 10 to 1) 8
920[3] DUBELLE [83] 7-10-0 T J Murphy, *rcd keenly, led to second, led 6th, mstk tenth, hdd aftr 4 out, sn wknd.* ....(14 to 1 op 12 to 1) 9
3017 COUNTRY STORE [89] 8-10-6 D Bridgwater, *led second till aftr 4th, f 9th*..........(20 to 1 op 14 to 1) f
2726* SAIL BY THE STARS [107] 8-11-10 S Wynne, *hld up, hdwy 5 out, 5th and btn whn blun and uns rdr 2 out.* ....(9 to 2 op 7 to 2) ur

Dist: Nk, 15l, ½l, 1l, 1¼l, 12l, dist, 10l. 5m 14.20s. a 16.20s (11 Ran).
(Mrs C Clatworthy), Miss H C Knight

3205 Scottish Equitable / Jockeys Association Series Final Handicap Hurdle Class B (4-y-o and up) £10,065 2½m 110yds..................... (1:15)

2332[2] DOMAPPEL [111] 5-11-7 T Kent, *hld up, hdwy 4 out, led appr 2 out, mstk last, rdn out*..........(7 to 2 op 3 to 1) 1
3045[2] THURSDAY NIGHT (Ire) [109] 6-11-5 P Niven, *trkd ldr, led 5 out, hdd appr 2 out, styd on same pace.* ....(4 to 1 op 7 to 2 tchd 9 to 2) 2
2923* LORD MCMURROUGH (Ire) [115] 7-11-11 R Farrant, *chsd ldrs, drvn alng 4 out, wknd nxt*..........(11 to 2 op 9 to 2) 3
2958* EDGEMOOR PRINCE [110] 6-11-6 G Tormey, *prmnt, drvn alng 5 out, wknd 3 out*..........(3 to 1 fav op 5 to 2) 4
2743* GROUSEMAN [118] (bl) 11-12-0 J Culloty, *made most to 5 out, wknd quickly and pld up bef 3 out*..........(7 to 1) pu
2789[4] TOPSAWYER [95] 9-10-5 A P McCoy, *chsd ldrs, chlgd 4 out, sn rdn and wknd nxt, pld up bef 2 out.* ....(9 to 2 op 4 to 1 tchd 5 to 1) pu

Dist: 3½l, 15l, 2½l. 4m 58.20s. a 19.20s (6 Ran).
(M C Banks), Mrs J Cecil

3206 Marstons Pedigree Midlands Grand National Handicap Chase Class A (6-y-o and up) £30,867 4¼m..... (1:50)

2715* SEVEN TOWERS (Ire) [134] 8-11-4 P Niven, *hld up, hdwy 6th, led aftr 3 out, rdn out*..........(4 to 1 op 3 to 1) 1
2599* LORD GYLLENE (NZ) [140] 9-11-10 A Dobbin, *led till 16th, led ag'n nxt, rdn and hdd aftr 3 out, styd on same pace.* ....(5 to 2 fav op 7 to 4) 2
2948[2] SISTER STEPHANIE (Ire) [124] 8-10-8 D Bridgwater, *hld up, mstk 9th, hdwy 6 out, styd on und pres.* ....(8 to 1 op 6 to 1 tchd 10 to 1) 3
2956[4] KILLESHIN [129] 11-10-13 S Curran, *patiently rdn, styd on frm 4 out, nvr nrr*..........(16 to 1 op 14 to 1) 4
2786[2] MCGREGOR THE THIRD [125] 11-10-9 R Dunwoody, *chsd ldr, led 16th, hdd nxt, wknd 4 out*..........(9 to 2 op 5 to 1) 5
2698[4] SPECIAL ACCOUNT [116] 11-10-0 B Fenton, *prmnt, lost pl 6th, no dngr aftr*..........(100 to 1 op 50 to 1) 6
2956[2] BEAUREPAIRE (Ire) [118] 9-10-2[2] A Thornton, *prmnt till wknd 6 out*..........(25 to 1) 7
3051* ACT THE WAG (Ire) [119] 8-10-3 A P McCoy, *hld up, rdn 17th, sn beh*..........(11 to 2 op 5 to 1 tchd 6 to 1) 8
3020[5] SCRIBBLER [116] (bl) 11-10-0 C F Swan, *prmnt till wknd 5 out, beh whn f 3 out*..........(25 to 1 op 33 to 1) f
2935[4] MUSTHAVEASWIG [121] 11-10-5 R Johnson, *prmnt, lost pl 14th, wknd 17th, pld up bef 3 out*..........(14 to 1) pu

Dist: 7l, sht-hd, 12l, 23l, 17l, 12l, 6l. 8m 33.70s. a 3.70s (10 Ran).
SR: 53/52/36/29/-/-/ (Mrs E A Murray), Mrs M Reveley

3207 Bet With The Tote Novices' Chase Final Handicap Class C for the Tom Wragg Trophy (6-y-o and up) £14,070 3¼m........................ (2:25)

2916 JUDICIOUS CAPTAIN [92] 10-10-0 Mr C Storey, *hld up, hdwy 8th, ev ch 4 out, second and held whn lft clr last, rdn out.* ....(12 to 1 op 9 to 1) 1

2873* FOXTROT ROMEO [100] 7-10-8 G Bradley, *hld up, hdwy 6th, chsd ldr 12th, wknd appr 2 out, lft second last.*
.................................(9 to 4 fav op 2 to 1) 2
2666* MR PICKPOCKET (Ire) [112] 9-11-6 J F Titley, *led, rdn and hdd appr 2 out, sn wknd, lft 3rd last.*
.................................(7 to 2 op 3 to 1 tchd 4 to 1) 3
2931* PAVLOVA (Ire) [93] 7-10-11 D O'Sullivan, *chsd ldrs, mstk 6 out, sn wknd.*...........................(25 to 1 op 16 to 1) 4
2564⁴ KAMIKAZE [116] (bl) 7-11-10 C O'Dwyer, *hld up, hit 5th, hdwy 12th, led appr 2 out, clr whn f last.*
.................................(9 to 2 op 4 to 1 tchd 5 to 1) f
3017³ BALLYDOUGAN (Ire) [92] (v) 9-10-0 D Walsh, *strted very slwly, al in rear, wl beh whn pld up bef 5 out.*
.................................(50 to 1 op 33 to 1) pu
2805² MONYMOSS (Ire) [105] 8-10-13 Richard Guest, *chsd ldrs, lost jd 13th, rallied appr 4 out, sn rdn and wknd, pld up bef 2 out.*.......................(11 to 2 op 9 to 2) pu
2280⁷ THE SHY PADRE (Ire) [92] 8-10-0 R Farrant, *patiently rdn, hdwy 12th, wknd 14th, beh whn pld up bef 5 out.*
.................................(10 to 1 op 7 to 1) pu
Dist: 12l, 5l, 11l. 6m 45.60s. a 33.60s (8 Ran).

(James A Adam), Mrs J Storey

3208 DHL Worldwide Express Handicap Chase Class C (0-135 5-y-o and up) £4,508 2m 5f................(3:00)

3032* DISCO DES MOTTES (Fr) [115] 6-11-7 R Dunwoody, *chsd ldrs, led 5 out, clr nxt, eased r-in.*
.................................(11 to 8 fav op 11 to 10 tchd 6 to 4) 1
3012* KENMORE-SPEED (Ire) [100] 10-10-6 Richard Guest, *led, blun 4th, hdd 5 out, wknd nxt.*............(13 to 2 op 11 to 2) 2
2809* OVER THE POLE [110] 10-11-2 A Thornton, *hld up, mstk 5th, hdwy 9th, wknd 5 out.*...........(9 to 1 op 7 to 1) 3
2659 GARRYLOUGH (Ire) [118] (v) 8-11-7 (3*) D Fortt, *chsd ldr to 7th, lost pl 10th, no dngr aftr.*...........(9 to 1 op 7 to 1) 4
2934³ CONTI D'ESTRUVAL (Fr) [112] (v) 7-11-4 A P McCoy, *hld up, hdwy 9th, rdn appr 4 out, sn wknd.*......(9 to 2 op 4 to 1) 5
1687 FLORIDA SKY [105] 10-10-11 G Bradley, *al in rear, tld off frm 8th, pld up bef 5 out.*......................(33 to 1) pu
2529⁴ FLAPJACK LAD [95] 8-10-1 D Walsh, *prmnt, chsd ldr 7th till wknd 9th, tld off whn pld up bef 3 out.* (20 to 1 op 14 to 1) pu
Dist: 12l, 5l, 5l, 5l. 5m 17.30s. a 19.30s (7 Ran).

(Robert Ogden), G Richards

3209 Weatherbys Insurance Handicap Hurdle Class C (0-135 5-y-o and up) £3,501 2¾m 110yds.........(3:30)

WINN'S PRIDE (Ire) [101] 6-10-8 S Wynne, *hld up, hdwy 4 out, led nxt, rdn out.*.........................(25 to 1) 1
752⁴ SANTELI A BOY (USA) [105] (bl) 5-10-12 J Railton, *hld up, hdwy 4 out, chsd wnr 2 out, ev ch last, no extr r-in.*
.................................(9 to 2 op 4 to 1 tchd 5 to 1) 2
2797³ ROYAL PIPER (NZ) [107] 10-11-0 R Greene, *chsd ldrs, mstk second, rdn and ev ch last, not quicken.* (9 to 2 tchd 5 to 1) 3
2949⁵ MOVING OUT [117] 9-11-10 R Dunwoody, *led to 6 out, wknd appr 3 out.*................(5 to 2 op 9 to 4 tchd 11 to 4) 4
2712* BOBBY GRANT [108] 6-11-1 P Niven, *prmnt, pld ldr 6th, led six out, hdd and mstk 3 out, sn wknd.*
.................................(11 to 8 fav op 5 to 4 tchd 6 to 4) 5
Dist: 3l, 1¾l, 24l, 1½l. 5m 22.40s. a 15.40s (5 Ran).
SR: 16/17/17/3/-/

(Mrs W L Bailey), R Hollinshead

3210 Prue Farmer 17th Birthday 'National Hunt' Novices' Hurdle Class E (4-y-o and up) £2,389 2m........(4:05)

2277⁴ SHEKELS (Ire) 6-11-1 G Bradley, *made all, rdn appr last, styd on wl.*................(4 to 1 op 3 to 1 tchd 5 to 1) 1
2949² RANGITIKEI (NZ) 6-11-8 R Dunwoody, *chsd wnr 4th, chlgd 3 out, sn rdn and styd on same pace.*
.................................(13 to 8 on op 2 to 1 on tchd 6 to 4 on) 2
2617 FILS DE CRESSON (Fr) 7-11-1 J Railton, *prmnt, drvn alng 4 out, no imprsn.*......................(20 to 1 op 14 to 1) 3
2344⁵ MAITRE DE MUSIQUE (Fr) 6-11-1 A P McCoy, *chsd wnr to 4th, wknd appr 3 out.*...............(10 to 1 op 7 to 1) 4
2791⁵ EUROFAST PET (Ire) 7-11-1 A Dobbin, *prmnt till rdn and wknd appr 3 out.*...............(25 to 1 op 20 to 1) 5
2546⁷ THE EENS 5-11-1 T Jenks, *nvr plcd to chal.*.....(50 to 1) 6
EAGER BEAVER 5-11-1 J F Titley, *nvr nr to chal.*
.................................(8 to 1 op 9 to 1) 7
2764⁹ RED OASSIS 6-11-1 Jacqui Oliver, *al in rear.*
.................................(66 to 1 op 50 to 1) 8
BARTY BOY 5-11-1 T Eley, *al beh.* (16 to 1 op 20 to 1) 9
2824 SHAWKEY (Ire) 4-10-7 D Walsh, *hld up, hdwy whn f 5th.*
.................................(100 to 1 op 33 to 1) f
2738 LORD LOVE 5-11-1 A Thornton, *f aftr 1st.*
.................................(100 to 1 op 50 to 1) f
2503 SUNSWORD 6-10-10 T J Murphy, *al beh, tld off and pld up bef 3 out.*......................(50 to 1) pu
Dist: 10l, 5l, 4l, 15l, 1½l, 7l, dist, 5l. 3m 48.50s. a 11.50s (12 Ran).
SR: 36/33/21/17/2/-/

(Uplands Bloodstock), C P E Brooks

LEOPARDSTOWN (IRE) (good)

Sunday March 16th
Going Correction: MINUS 0.05 sec. per fur. (races 1,3,4,6,7), PLUS 0.15 (2,5)

3211 Careysfort Hurdle (4-y-o and up) £3,082 2½m.................(2:30)

2445¹ MOSCOW EXPRESS (Ire) 5-11-13 C F Swan, ...(7 to 4 on) 1
2473⁴ MR BAXTER BASICS 6-11-9 N Williamson, ...(2 to 1) 2
427⁵ SIBERIAN TALE (Ire) 7-11-6 (3*) Mr P J Casey, ... (20 to 1) 3
2843⁹ BACK BAR (Ire) 9-11-3 R Dunwoody, ...(8 to 1) 4
Dist: ½l, dist, 4½l. 4m 59.30s. a 19.30s (4 Ran).

(T Conroy), A P O'Brien

3212 Silchester Handicap Chase (0-130 4-y-o and up) £3,082 2m 5f... (3:00)

2836⁵ THE CRAZY BISHOP (Ire) [-] (bl) 9-12-0 C F Swan, (3 to 1) 1
2843² LOVE THE LORD (Ire) [-] 7-11-10 T P Treacy, ...(6 to 4 fav) 2
2840* FLASHY LAD (Ire) [-] 6-11-0 N Williamson, ...(5 to 1) 3
2671³ THE REAL ARTICLE (Ire) [-] 8-11-9 L P Cusack, ...(5 to 1) 4
Dist: 5½l, ¾l, dist. 5m 28.90s. a 19.90s (4 Ran).

(John J Hanlon), Anthony Mullins

3213 Cabinteely Maiden Hurdle (4-y-o and up) £3,082 2¾m........... (3:30)

2964 CHATTERBUCK (Ire) 8-10-13 (7*) D A McLoughlin, (14 to 1) 1
2902⁴ BAWNROCK (Ire) 8-12-0 C F Swan, ...(5 to 2 fav) 2
2902² THE GREY MARE (Ire) 8-11-2 (7*) Mr P Fahey, ...(11 to 4) 3
2964 SAIL AWAY SAILOR (Ire) 6-10-13 (7*) Mr M Quinlan, (20 to 1) 4
2520⁶ SARADANTE (Ire) 7-11-6 K F O'Brien, ...(15 to 2) 5
2378 L'AMI DE LARME (Ire) 6-11-1 N Williamson, ...(10 to 1) 6
2587⁵ MOORE'S MELODIES (Ire) 6-11-6 F Woods, ...(7 to 1) 7
2964⁹ BITOFA DIVIL (Ire) 6-11-6 L P Cusack, ...(8 to 1) 8
2643⁹ SPIONAN (USA) 4-10-4 (7*) P J Dobbs, ...(14 to 1) 9
1275⁴ JACK CHAUCER 5-11-4 R Dunwoody, ...(6 to 1) 10
3069⁷ LYNX MARINE (Ire) 6-11-6 T P Treacy, ...(20 to 1) 11
2964 THEODANTE (Ire) 5-10-13 D T Evans, ...(25 to 1) 12
DOYAWANAGIVEUP (Ire) 4-10-1 (5*) T Martin, ...(25 to 1) 13
2703 GRAIGNAMANAGH (Ire) 6-11-6 J R Barry, ...(20 to 1) 14
2343 DESMARFRAN (Ire) 8-11-6 W Slattery, ...(20 to 1) 15
Dist: 1½l, 1l, 8l, 1l. 5m 29.20s. a 23.20s (15 Ran).

(Mountrose Syndicate), J T R Dreaper

3214 Harcourt Handicap Hurdle (4-y-o and up) £6,850 2½m.............(4:00)

2708* CLIFDON FOG [-] 6-11-1 A P McCoy, ...(7 to 4 fav) 1
3087* KILCOO BOY (Ire) [-] 6-11-0 C F Swan, ...(6 to 1) 2
2841⁴ GRAVITY GATE (Ire) [-] 8-10-0 (5*) T Martin, ...(7 to 1) 3
2841 STRALDI (Ire) [-] 9-10-5 N Williamson, ...(33 to 1) 4
3086* TRYFIRION (Ire) [-] 8-12-0 K F O'Brien, ...(9 to 2) 5
3086² APPELLATE COURT [-] 9-9-3 (7*) B Geraghty, ...(10 to 1) 6
3086⁴ OWENBWEE (Ire) [-] 6-10-2 F Woods, ...(/ to 1) 7
3071 TOUREEN GALE (Ire) [-] 8-9-11² T P Treacy, ...(10 to 1) 8
3087⁴ IDEAL PLAN (Ire) [-] 7-10-12 R Dunwoody, ...(7 to 1) pu
Dist: 2l, 6l, nk, 8l. 4m 52.70s. a 12.70s (9 Ran).

(J P Hill), J S Bolger

3215 Kilgobbin Beginners Chase (4-y-o and up) £3,082 3m...........(4:30)

3073³ SHISOMA (Ire) 7-12-0 R Dunwoody, ...(9 to 2) 1
3073⁶ BRAVE FOUNTAIN (Ire) 9-12-0 C F Swan, ...(100 to 30) 2
2868⁴ COLLON (Ire) 8-12-0 D H O'Connor, ...(6 to 1) 3
2907⁵ THE VENDOR (Ire) 7-11-9 T P Treacy, ...(10 to 1) 4
2840 VEREDARIUS (Fr) 6-12-0 F Woods, ...(8 to 1) 5
3088 HILLHEAD (Ire) 8-12-0 L P Cusack, ...(12 to 1) 6
2904² ARCTIC BUCK (Ire) 7-12-0 N Williamson, ...(7 to 4 fav) f
2522⁶ MONALEE STATEMENT (Ire) (bl) 7-12-0 K F O'Brien,
.................................(10 to 1) pu
Dist: 9l, 20l, 14l, 25l. 6m 17.60s. a 10.60s (8 Ran).
SR: 30/21/1/-/-/

(J B O'Connor), Patrick Day

3216 Hudson Handicap Hurdle (0-109 4-y-o and up) £3,082 2m............(5:00)

3068* SAVING BOND [-] 5-11-2 (7*) B Geraghty, (11 to 4 fav) 1
2901³ MARINERS REEF (Ire) [-] 6-9-12 (7*) D McCullagh, ..(8 to 1) 2
2674⁶ REGENCY RAKE (Ire) [-] 5-11-6 F Woods, ...(9 to 1) 3
3089* QUEEN'S FLAGSHIP (Ire) [-] 5-10-8 C N Bowens, ..(5 to 1) 4
3089⁵ JOHNNY HANDSOME (Ire) [-] 7-10-1 T P Treacy, ...(8 to 1) 5
683² INNOVATIVE (Ire) [-] 6-10-7 D T Evans, ...(12 to 1) 6
2735 SOFT SPOT (Ire) [-] (bl) 5-9-11 H Rogers, ...(13 to 2) 7
2735 US FOUR (Ire) [-] 7-9-10 (7*) K A Kelly, ...(20 to 1) 8
303 RUPERT BELLE (Ire) [-] 6-11-10 K F O'Brien, ...(16 to 1) 9
2735 NA HUIBHEACHU (Ire) [-] 6-9-6 (7*) P J Dobbs, ...(16 to 1) 10
2943⁶ NATIVE ECLIPSE (Ire) [-] 4-10-11 C F Swan, ...(20 to 1) 11
2669² GO SASHA (Ire) [-] (bl) 4-11-1 (5*) T Martin, ...(10 to 1) 12
3087⁸ MIND ME BRODY (Ire) [-] 4-10-11 (7*) A O'Shea, ..(20 to 1) 13
908⁵ ACES AND EIGHTS (Ire) [-] 7-11-10 R Dunwoody, ...(8 to 1) f
Dist: Hd, 5l, 3½l, 2l. 3m 49.30s. a 5.30s (14 Ran).
SR: 34/16/26/10/1/-/

(Mrs F Towey), Noel Meade

3217 Glasthule I.N.H. Flat Race (4-y-o and up) £3,082 2m..............(5:30)

NATIONAL HUNT RESULTS 1996-97

2838⁴	CLOONE BRIDGE (Ire) 5-12-2 Mr B M Cash, ... (3 to 1)	1
782⁵	MEN OF NINETYEIGHT (Ire) 5-11-9 Mr D Marnane, (8 to 1)	2
	CAKE BAKER (Ire) 7-11-11 Mr J P Dempsey, ... (12 to 1)	3
	IN THE RUNNING (Ire) 9-11-8 (3") Mr P J Casey, . . (10 to 1)	4
2588*	ROCKFIELD LEADER (Ire) 5-11-11 (5") Mr A C Coyle,	
	. . . . (11 to 10 fav)	5
2709	DANTE'S BATTLE (Ire) 5-11-9 Mr P F Graffin, ... (20 to 1)	6
	GLOBAL LEGEND 7-11-4 (7") Mr M O'Connor, ... (12 to 1)	7
2906*	LAFONTD'OR (Ire) 6-11-13 (5") Mr Brian Moran, ...(8 to 1)	8
	KING'S FAYRE (Ire) 6-11-11 Mr A J Martin, ... (20 to 1)	9
	COLRAYASH (Ire) 5-11-2 (7") Mr R J Curran, . . . (14 to 1)	10

Dist: 4l, ¾l, 7l, ½l. 3m 51.10s. (10 Ran).

(Mrs K Gillane), A P O'Brien

LIMERICK (IRE) (yielding to soft)
Sunday March 16th

3218 St. Patrick Handicap Chase (0-116 5-y-o and up) £2,740 2m. . . . . (2:25)

2943⁴	ROSDEMON (Ire) [-] 9-10-4 P A Roche, ... (11 to 1)	1
2903*	WOODVILLE STAR (Ire) [-] 8-12-0 C O'Dwyer, . . . (Evens fav)	2
2966³	BARNAGEERA BOY (Ire) [-] 8-11-9 T J Mitchell, ... (7 to 4)	3
2412³	HANNIES GIRL (Ire) [-] 8-9-7 (7") L J Fleming, ... (14 to 1)	4

Dist: 1½l, 2½l, 20l. 3m 58.90s. (4 Ran).

(Mrs O E Matthews), John Roche

3219 J.J.O'Toole (Packaging) Novice Handicap Hurdle (0-116 4-y-o and up) £3,425 2½m. . . . . (2:55)

2837	BAR FLUTE (Ire) [-] 6-10-13 T Horgan, ... (9 to 1)	1
3070²	PRE ORDAINED (Ire) [-] 5-11-8 F J Flood, ...(6 to 4 fav)	2
2902⁶	COMMITTED SCHEDULE (Ire) [-] 6-10-7 M P Hourigan,	
	. . . .(10 to 1)	3
2834⁵	RANDOM RING (Ire) [-] 6-11-0 J P Broderick, ... (4 to 1)	4
2415⁸	TIP YOUR WAITRESS (Ire) [-] 4-10-10 T Hazlett, . . .(10 to 1)	5
2703	BOCCACHERA (Ire) [-] 5-10-6 A J O'Brien, ... (16 to 1)	6
	PARKS PRIDE (Ire) [-] 6-9-0 (7") Mr M P Madden, . .(20 to 1)	7
2477	AMERICAN CONKER (Ire) [-] 6-10-5 C O'Brien, . . (20 to 1)	ur
2942	NIL FAIC (Ire) [-] 5-9-2 (7") P G Hourigan, ... (16 to 1)	ur
2447⁶	SORCERER'S DRUM (Ire) [-] 6-11-3 (3") W Slattery,	pu

Dist: Sht-hd, 2l, 5½l, 2½l. 5m 33.70s. (10 Ran).

(Roderick McGahon), A P O'Brien

3220 Dawn Milk Beginners Chase (5-y-o and up) £3,767 2m. . . . . (3:25)

2644²	ARDSHUIL 8-12-0 C O'Dwyer, ... (5 to 2)	1
2941	MIDNIGHT JAZZ (Ire) 7-12-0 J P Broderick, ... (12 to 1)	2
2755⁸	LISHILLAUN (Ire) 7-11-4 (5") Susan A Finn, ... (25 to 1)	3
2755²	CARROLLS ROCK (Ire) 6-12-0 P A Roche, ... (13 to 2)	f
2941	SCENIC ROUTE (Ire) 8-11-9 (5") Mr T P Hyde, . .(7 to 4 fav)	ur
2943	REGIT (Ire) 7-12-0 T Hazlett, ... (12 to 1)	ro
	AUTUMN GORSE (Ire) 8-12-0 T Horgan, ... (100 to 30)	pu

Dist: 25l, 7l. 4m 5.50s. (7 Ran).

(N McCarthy), A L T Moore

3221 Birdhill Hurdle (4-y-o and up) £2,740 2m. . . . . (3:55)

2731⁸	DR BONES (Ire) 4-11-6 T P Rudd, ... (5 to 1)	1
2703⁴	CAVALIER D'OR (USA) 6-11-7 C O'Dwyer, ...(7 to 2)	2
2106²	IRVINE (Ire) 5-11-0 (7") Miss S J Leahy, ... (10 to 1)	3
2705	GREAT SVENGALI (Ire) 8-12-0 M Duffy, ... (10 to 1)	4
	DANTES BANK (Ire) 7-11-7 M P Hourigan, ... (20 to 1)	5
3086	JODESI (Ire) 7-12-0 D J Casey, ... (5 to 2 fav)	6
2901	RAMDON ROCKS 10-11-7 P McWilliams, ... (20 to 1)	7
	TOMORROW'S STORY (Ire) 5-11-7 J P Broderick, (20 to 1)	8
2942	QUEEN OFTHE ISLAND (Ire) 5-10-11 (5") Susan A Finn,	
	. . . .(20 to 1)	9
2942	HAPSY'S FIELD (Ire) 5-11-7 (7") S P McCann, . . . (20 to 1)	10
1246	FINCHLEY LEADER (Ire) 5-11-0 (7") S FitzGerald, . (20 to 1)	11
2709⁸	FINCHOGUE (Ire) 5-11-2 G M O'Neill, ... (14 to 1)	12
1173	SOVIET DREAMER 4-10-6 (7") Mr M P Madden, . . (20 to 1)	13
3069	MR MARK (Ire) 5-11-7 F J Flood, ... (20 to 1)	14

Dist: ¾l, 13l, 6l, 13l. 4m 12.40s. (14 Ran).

(Mrs Denis Fortune), M J P O'Brien

3222 Co. Limerick Hunt Hunters Chase (5-y-o and up) £3,425 2¾m. . . . . . (4:25)

	AN OON ISS AN OWL (Ire) 7-11-7 (7") Mr R Flavin, (11 to 2)	1
2672⁴	PANCHO'S TANGO (Ire) 7-11-7 (7") Mr D P Daly, . . (5 to 1)	2
2672³	TWO IN TUNE (Ire) 9-11-7 (7") Mr D Keane, ... (2 to 1 fav)	3
	CHELSEA KING (Ire) 6-11-7 (7") Mr T J Nagle, . . . (12 to 1)	4
1118⁷	DANGER FLYNN (Ire) 7-11-7 (7") Mr K O'Sullivan, (12 to 1)	5
2672⁹	INNISCEIN (Ire) 9-12-0 Mr J A Nash, ... (12 to 1)	6
2523	SHIRGALE (Ire) 8-11-4 (5") Mr W M O'Sullivan, . . (12 to 1)	7
114	OKDO 10-11-7 (7") Mr M J Walsh, ... (20 to 1)	8
	TOMMY THE DUKE (Ire) 9-11-7 (7") Mr E Fehily, . . .(9 to 1)	9
2523	SUMMERHILL EXPRESS (Ire) (bl) 7-11-2 (7") Mr P R Crowley,	
	. . . .(8 to 1)	10
2844	UPSHEPOPS (Ire) 9-11-2 (7") Mr J Keville, ... (14 to 1)	pu
	EDDIE (Ire) 5-11-6 Mr H F Cleary, ... (11 to 2)	pu

Dist: 1l, 15l, ¾l, 11l. 5m 37.70s. (12 Ran).

(Frank Brady), William Flavin

3223 Limerick E.B.F. Mares Novice Hurdle (4-y-o and up) £3,767 2½m. . . (4:55)

2900	WINDY BEE (Ire) 6-11-7 (7") A Nolan, ... (3 to 1)	1
2964²	VALENTINE GALE (Ire) 7-11-10 D J Casey, ... (9 to 4 fav)	2
2900	BAI-BRUN KATE (Ire) 6-11-7 (7") L J Fleming, ... (7 to 1)	3
2942*	LOCKBEG LASS (Ire) 5-11-5 (7") M D Murphy, . . . (14 to 1)	4
2754*	COMKILRED (Ire) 5-11-12 C O'Dwyer, ... (8 to 1)	5
2942⁴	ASHTALE (Ire) 5-11-3 (5") P Morris, ... (16 to 1)	6
2837⁶	MARYOBEE (Ire) 7-11-7 (7") Mr P M Cloke, ... (10 to 1)	7
2944²	MONDEO ROSE (Ire) 5-11-12 T Horgan, ... (10 to 1)	8
2519	NAN'S PET (Ire) 7-11-10 S H O'Donovan, ... (25 to 1)	9
132⁶	SNUGVILLE SALLY 5-11-7 (7") S P McCann, ... (33 to 1)	10
2900⁵	MISS ORCHESTRA (Ire) 6-12-0 J Short, ... (33 to 1)	11
2942⁸	NEWBERRY ROSE (Ire) 5-11-3 (5") Mr W M O'Sullivan,	
	. . . .(33 to 1)	12
	LIZES BIRTHDAY (Ire) 5-11-8 J P Broderick, ... (20 to 1)	13
2902⁸	BRIDGES DAUGHTER (Ire) 6-11-10 P A Roche, . . (14 to 1)	14
2518⁶	RAINBOW TIMES (Ire) 4-10-12 M P Hourigan, . . . (33 to 1)	15
	PYTHON WOLF (Ire) 6-11-10 G M O'Neill, ... (12 to 1)	16
3073	LABAN LADY (Ire) (bl) 8-11-7 (3") K Whelan, . . . (25 to 1)	17

Dist: 5l, 11l, 2½l, 15l. 5m 30.30s. (17 Ran).

(Brian Nolan), Brian Nolan

3224 Rathkeale I.N.H. Flat Race (4-y-o and up) £2,740 2m. . . . . (5:25)

2901²	ZIGGY THE GREAT (Ire) (bl) 5-11-5 (7") Mr John P Moloney,	
	. . . .(6 to 1)	1
	THE OOZLER (Ire) 4-10-11 (7") Mr A K Wyse, . . . (10 to 1)	2
	CASTLE ANGEL (Ire) 4-10-6 (7") Mr J C Kelly, . . . (12 to 1)	3
	HOW RAN ON (Ire) 6-12-0 Mr J A Nash, ... (5 to 4 fav)	4
1487²	LORD EDENBURY (Ire) 6-12-0 Mr P Fenton, ... (10 to 1)	5
	BODAWN BRADACH (Ire) 7-11-7 (7") Mr P J Burke, (7 to 1)	6
2675⁸	SUTTREE (Ire) 6-12-0 Mr J A Berry, ... (10 to 1)	7
2416	CHELSEA BELLE (Ire) 5-11-0 (7") Mr P A Murphy, (20 to 1)	8
	RED BANNER (Ire) 6-11-2 (7") Mr P M Cloke, . . . (14 to 1)	9
2583	BITOFABUZZ (Ire) 6-11-7 (7") Mr J D Moore, ... (10 to 1)	10
2757	FARVELLA (Ire) 6-11-7 (7") Mr J Keville, ... (20 to 1)	11
2649	SADIE LADY (Ire) 6-11-2 (7") Miss F Loughran, . . (25 to 1)	12
	ANY MANS FANCY (Ire) 6-11-6 (3") Mr E Norris, . . (10 to 1)	13
	COOLTEEN LAD (Ire) 8-11-11 (3") Mr P English, . (20 to 1)	14

Dist: 7l, 4l, 1½l, 7l. 4m 14.20s. (14 Ran).

(Mrs Padraig Nolan), David Wachman

DOWN ROYAL (IRE) (good to yielding)
Monday March 17th

3225 Alf Scott Memorial Maiden Hurdle (Div I) (4-y-o and up) £1,712 2m . . . . (2:20)

2074⁴	VINCITORE (Ire) 4-11-4 L P Cusack, ... (5 to 1)	1
3083	ATHA BEITHE (Ire) (bl) 6-11-7 (7") B Geraghty, (13 to 8 fav)	2
	FABRIANO (USA) 6-11-6 K F O'Brien, ... (3 to 1)	3
3069⁸	DUNMORE DOM (Ire) 5-10-11 (7") Mr L J Gracey, (9 to 1)	4
3085	BOLD LILLIAN (Ire) 8-11-2 (7") S M McGovern, . . (16 to 1)	5
2870⁴	MRS DOYLE (Ire) 5-10-6 (7") R Burke, ... (33 to 1)	6
2866⁵	AUTOBABBLE (Ire) 4-10-6 (7") Mr K Ross, ... (16 to 1)	7
3069	JERMYN STREET (USA) 6-11-9 (5") T Martin, . . . (16 to 1)	8
1655	RED ISLAND GIRL (Ire) 6-10-9 (7") D A McLoughlin, (25 to 1)	9
2449	DUE TO YOU (Ire) 4-10-13 P Leech, ... (33 to 1)	10
2022	STRATEGIC AFFAIR (Ire) 6-11-6 T J Mitchell, . . . (50 to 1)	11
2383	CAROLANNS CHOICE (Ire) 8-11-1 P L Malone, . . (50 to 1)	12
	BALLINEVA (Ire) 8-12-0 H Rogers, ... (33 to 1)	13
	MYSTIC ROSE (Ire) 6-10-8 (7") D Fisher, ... (66 to 1)	14

Dist: 3l, 5l, 13l, 2½l. 3m 50.80s. (14 Ran).

(Mrs Lucia Farmer), G A Cusack

3226 Alf Scott Memorial Maiden Hurdle (Div II) (4-y-o and up) £1,712 2m . . . . (2:50)

2964⁴	FANE PATH (Ire) 5-11-5 (7") B Geraghty, ... (5 to 4 fav)	1
2378⁹	PRAY FOR PEACE (Ire) 6-10-9³ (7") Mr P Fahey, . .(12 to 1)	2
2337³	CENTO (Ire) (bl) 4-10-13 D T Evans, ... (9 to 4)	3
2968⁶	MONALEA (Ire) 6-10-13 (7") A P Sweeney, ... (14 to 1)	4
2866⁹	THE MALL (Ire) 5-11-9 (3") Mr B R Hamilton, ... (7 to 1)	5
2669⁷	SUBLIME POLLY (Ire) 4-10-3 (5") T Martin, ... (16 to 1)	6
3068	SHINORA (Ire) 6-10-13 Mr G T Morrow, ... (33 to 1)	7
1580	EIRE (Ire) 8-12-0 K F O'Brien, ... (20 to 1)	8
2137	DR DOLITTLE (Ire) 6-11-6 L P Cusack, ... (10 to 1)	9
2866	JONS GALE (Ire) 5-10-11 (7") Mr N W Toal, ... (20 to 1)	10
2845	ELECTRICAL STORM 5-10-13 T J Mitchell, ... (25 to 1)	11
	CALDRY LASS (Ire) 6-11-1 C N Bowens, ... (10 to 1)	12
	XAVIER (Ire) (bl) 4-10-13 P McWilliams, ... (25 to 1)	13
	KILLCHRIS DREAM (Ire) 6-10-8 (7") D A McLoughlin,	
	. . . .(25 to 1)	14

Dist: 11l, 3½l, 2l, sht-hd. 3m 54.70s. (14 Ran).

(N Coburn), Noel Meade

3227 Bet With The Tote Handicap Hurdle (0-109 4-y-o and up) £1,712 2m

448

. . . . . (3:20)

3089⁴ NORDIC SENSATION (Ire) [-] 8-10-12 (7") B Geraghty,	
. . . . (11 to 4)	1
2865⁶ SPECTACLE (Ire) [-] 7-9-5 (7") R Burke, ... (16 to 1)	2
3216⁴ QUEEN'S FLAGSHIP (Ire) [-] 5-11-4 C N Bowens,	
. . . . (5 to 2 fav)	3
3089⁸ HOME I'LL BE (Ire) [-] 7-9-0 (7") N P Mulholland, . . (12 to 1)	4
2585 GLENFIELDS CASTLE (Ire) [-] 7-11-2 (7") Mr A Stronge,	
. . . . (7 to 1)	5
2585 THE THIRD MAN (Ire) [-] 8-9-13 P McWilliams, ... (9 to 1)	6
3070⁴ ABIGAIL ROSE (Bel) [-] 5-10-2 (3") D Bromley, ... (10 to 1)	7
2415⁵ SLEWMORE (Ire) [-] 6-10-8 T J Mitchell, ... (14 to 1)	8
1581 CORALDA (Ire) [-] 6-9-8⁷ (7") S M McGovern, ... (40 to 1)	9
ANOTHER BONNY [-] 11-9-2 (7") L J Fleming, . . . (33 to 1)	10
2835⁹ CLADY BOY (Ire) [-] 6-11-7 (7") Mr K Ross, ... (7 to 1)	11
2866⁴ SCATHACH (Ire) [-] 5-9-5 (7") R J Gordon, ... (20 to 1)	12
2865⁵ JUST 'R JAKE (Ire) [-] 8-10-3 (3") Mr P J Casey, . . (25 to 1)	13
3089⁹ KAVANAGHS DREAM (Ire) [-] 8-10-6 H Rogers, . . (10 to 1)	14
2379 JOSHUA TREE (Ire) [-] 12-11-2 J K Kinane, ... (33 to 1)	15
2378 SINGLE OR BUST (Ire) [-] 7-9-10 P L Malone, . . (25 to 1)	16
2964 CATEMPO (Ire) [-] 7-9-7 P Leech, ... (40 to 1)	17
2379 JIMMY JANE (Ire) [-] (bl) 5-9-7⁷ (7") Mr J J Canavan,	
. . . . (100 to 1)	18

Dist: ½l, 3½l, 5l, 2l. 3m 48.30s. (18 Ran).

(D & L Syndicate), I A Duncan

3228 Mount Top Stud W E Rooney Memorial Hunter Chase (5-y-o and up) £1,712 3m 1f. . . . . (3:50)

HIGH STAR (Ire) 9-11-7 (7") Mr I Buchanan, ... (5 to 4 on)	1
FIND OUT MORE (Ire) 9-11-7 (7") Mr B Potts, ... (20 to 1)	2
2869² GALE GRIFFIN (Ire) 8-11-9 L P Cusack, ... (11 to 2)	3
MITCHELSTOWN RIVER 10-11-7 (7") Mr R P McNalley,	
. . . . (5 to 1)	4
1042 WILLY WEE (Ire) 6-11-7 (7") Mr W Ewing, ... (11 to 1)	5
2869³ ROYAL STAR (Ire) 8-11-9 Mr G J Harford, ... (10 to 1)	6
FLORIDA OR BUST (Ire) 7-11-7 (7") Mr G J McKeever,	
. . . . (16 to 1)	7
RAT RACE (Ire) 7-11-7 (7") Mr M O'Connor, ... (8 to 1)	8
RIVER MAGNET (Ire) 8-12-0 Mr P F Graffin, ... (14 to 1)	f
122 ROCK ON BUD (Ire) 6-11-7 (7") Mr A J Dempsey, . (12 to 1)	f

Dist: 9l, 5l, 10l, 8l. 6m 37.80s. (10 Ran).

(Victor Wilson), George Stewart

3229 Gilbeys Handicap Chase (0-109 5-y-o and up) £3,425 2½m. . . . . (4:20)

2867 TRENCH HILL LASS (Ire) [-] 8-11-7 (7") Mr I Buchanan,	
. . . . (8 to 1)	1
3074⁵ BOB DEVANI [-] 11-11-1 (7") B Geraghty, ... (4 to 1)	2
2867⁶ PENNYRRIDGE (Ire) 8-11-9 L P Cusack, (100 to 30 fav)	3
3074³ LA-GREINE [-] 10-10-6 (7") Mr K Ross, ... (11 to 2)	4
2962⁴ FRIDAY THIRTEENTH (Ire) [-] 8-11-2 (3") Mr B R Hamilton,	
. . . . (20 to 1)	5
2646 AMME ENAEK (Ire) [-] (bl) 8-11-8 H Rogers, ... (7 to 1)	6
2169⁹ EDENAKILL LAD [-] 10-10-3 (3") D Bromley, . . . (12 to 1)	7
2842 CREHELP EXPRESS (Ire) [-] 7-11-5 C N Bowens, . . (7 to 1)	8
721⁵ CARAGH BRIDGE [-] 10-10-12 T J Mitchell, ... (10 to 1)	9
3074⁹ NOELS DANCER (Ire) [-] 7-10-1 P L Malone, . . . (20 to 1)	10
3085⁴ PEDE GALE (Ire) [-] 9-9-0 (7") L J Fleming, . . . (25 to 1)	ro
2646 RICH TRADITION (Ire) [-] 9-11-1 P McWilliams, . . (33 to 1)	pu

Dist: 4l, 4l, 4l, 6l. 5m 10.90s. (12 Ran).

(Mrs Sharon Metcalfe), George Stewart

3230 Martell Beginners Chase (5-y-o and up) £2,397 2m. . . . . (4:50)

2868² HERSILIA (Ire) 6-11-2 (7") L J Fleming, ... (7 to 4)	1
3073⁹ SCEAL SIOG (Ire) (bl) 8-11-4 L P Cusack, ... (14 to 1)	2
3073 JOHNNY'S DREAM (Ire) 7-11-7 (7") Mr A J Dempsey,	
. . . . (6 to 4 fav)	3
2704 FRIARSTOWN DUKE 7-11-9 T J Mitchell, ... (7 to 1)	4
3073 FANE'S TREASURE (Ire) 8-11-7 (7") B Geraghty, . (14 to 1)	5
3088 SHUIL DAINGEAN (Ire) (bl) 7-11-4 (5") T Martin, . . (9 to 1)	f
3073 PINGO HILL (Ire) 5-11-6 P L Malone, ... (25 to 1)	f

Dist: 1½l, ½l, 2½l, 15l. 4m 10.40s. (7 Ran).

(Mrs F J O'Reilly), F Flood

3231 Dunygartin INH Flat Race (5-y-o and up) £1,712 2m. . . . . (5:20)

2845⁴ TIDAL PRINCESS (Ire) 5-11-4 (3") Mr B R Hamilton, (7 to 2)	1
2709⁶ THE RED SIDE (Ire) 5-11-7 Mr G J Harford, ... (8 to 1)	2
1584 DJENNE (Ire) 5-11-0 (7") Mr K Ross, ... (14 to 1)	3
2968² CELEBRITY STATUS (Ire) 6-11-7 (7") Mr D Delaney,	
. . . . (6 to 4 fav)	4
GET EVEN (Ire) 5-11-12 Mr B M Cash, ... (7 to 1)	5
2870² RUN SPARKY (Ire) 5-11-2 (5") Mr P J Patton, . . . (8 to 1)	6
2845 QUIETLY (Ire) 5-11-12 Mr D Marnane, ... (16 to 1)	7
BELLE O' THE BAY (Ire) 8-11-2 (7") Mr S M Cox, . (50 to 1)	8
2870³ WILLYELKRA 5-11-5 (7") Mr M P Madden, ... (12 to 1)	9
3075 SWINFORD BOY (Ire) 9-11-7 (7") Mr P A Rattigan, . (50 to 1)	10
IRISH TEEDEE (Ire) 5-11-5 (7") Mr J Bright, ... (50 to 1)	11
LORD ESKER (Ire) 5-11-5 (7") Mr A J Dempsey, . . (6 to 1)	12
2582 POLITICAL TROUBLES (Ire) 7-11-6 (3") Mr P J Casey,	
. . . . (20 to 1)	13

HOLLYMEAD (Ire) 6-11-2 (7") Mr A Stronge, ... (50 to 1)	14
FISHER KING BOB (Ire) 5-11-5 (7") Mr B Potts, . . (33 to 1)	15
DERRING LINE (Ire) 5-11-5 (7") Mr G Martin, ... (33 to 1)	16
2870⁸ ZAFFRIDGE (Ire) 5-11-0 (7") Mr G T Cuthbert, . . (40 to 1)	17
2845 TRAVIS (Ire) 7-11-7 (7") Mr L J Gracey, ... (50 to 1)	18
637⁶ ROSE'S PERK (Ire) 5-11-0 (7") Miss A Reilly, . . . (33 to 1)	19

Dist: 10l, 4l, 8l, 3l. 3m 46.00s. (19 Ran).

(W M Roper), W M Roper

LIMERICK (IRE) (yielding to soft)
Monday March 17th

3232 Shannon Maiden Hurdle (4-y-o) £2,740 2m 1f. . . . . (2:30)

2230² AFARKA (Ire) 10-13 T P Treacy, ... (11 to 8 on)	1
CELTIC PROJECT (Ire) 10-13 P A Roche, ... (10 to 1)	2
2669³ COULTHARD (Ire) 10-6 (7") Miss S J Leahy, ... (9 to 2)	3
CINNIBAR 10-8 J Shortt, ... (11 to 2)	4
2965 DOUBLEBACK (Ire) 10-1 (7") K A Kelly, ... (16 to 1)	5
ARTIQUE FISH (Ire) 10-13 C O'Dwyer, ... (12 to 1)	6
NORTH OF KALA (Ire) 10-1 (7") Mr J P McNamara, (25 to 1)	7
2902 MOSTA (Ire) 10-8 T Hazlett, ... (20 to 1)	8
2940 POINT LUCK (Ire) 10-8 M P Hourigan, ... (20 to 1)	9
WILLOWMOUNT (Ire) 10-10 (3") K Whelan, ... (14 to 1)	10
2832⁷ KEEP RUNNING (Ire) 10-6 (7") D W O'Sullivan, . . (10 to 1)	11
MAGICAL MIST (Ire) 10-7 (7") Mr P P O'Brien, . . (33 to 1)	12
2832⁹ MOSCOW'S FLAME (Ire) 10-13 S H O'Donovan, . (25 to 1)	13
KNOCKDOO (Ire) 10-13 F J Flood, ... (16 to 1)	14
1709 ARCTIC ZIPPER (USA) 10-6 (7") M D Murphy, . . (25 to 1)	pu
2161 CALM BEAUTY (Ire) 10-8 T P Rudd, ... (33 to 1)	pu

Dist: 2½l, 6l, sht-hd, 6l. 4m 29.10s. (16 Ran).

(D Brennan Accountants Synd), S J Treacy

3233 Newcastle West Maiden Hurdle (6-y-o and up) £2,740 2m 1f. . . . . (3:00)

3068² NATIVE-DARRIG (Ire) 6-12-0 D J Casey, ... (5 to 4 on)	1
3085² RYTHM ROCK (Ire) 8-10-13 (7") A O'Shea, ... (8 to 1)	2
GOOLDS DIAMOND (Ire) 6-11-6 T P Rudd, ... (25 to 1)	3
2943 THE YELLOW BOG (Ire) 7-11-6 G M O'Neill, . . . (20 to 1)	4
3085 SPLEODRACH (Ire) 7-11-1 T P Treacy, ... (20 to 1)	5
2675 CONAGHER LEADER (Ire) 6-11-6 A J O'Brien, . . (20 to 1)	6
3085⁶ COMAN'S JET (Ire) 7-11-7 (7") M D Murphy, ... (8 to 1)	7
3083⁶ PROUDANDAMBITIOUS (Ire) 6-12-0 M Duffy, . . . (5 to 1)	8
2703⁸ PREMIER WALK 8-12-0 J Shortt, ... (12 to 1)	9
CRUISIN ON CREDIT (Ire) (bl) 6-11-6 J P Broderick, (25 to 1)	10
2900 MIDNIGHT CYCLONE (Ire) 6-11-4 (5") P Morris, . (14 to 1)	11
2906⁸ MANISSA (Ire) 6-11-1 C F Swan, ... (12 to 1)	12
2964 ANOTHER GALLOP (Ire) 9-11-6 S H O'Donovan, . (25 to 1)	13
3069⁵ POWER CORE (Ire) 7-10-13 (7") J A Robinson, . . (16 to 1)	14
3069 BALLYBANE LASSIE (Ire) 6-10-12 (3") K Whelan, . (33 to 1)	15
2900⁴ HEN HANSEL (Ire) 6-12-0 T Horgan, ... (14 to 1)	16
2865 PHAREIGN (Ire) 6-11-6 C O'Dwyer, ... (16 to 1)	17
GROVE GALE (Ire) 6-11-1 C O'Brien, ... (33 to 1)	18
ENTITLED LADY (Ire) 6-11-1 W Slattery, ... (33 to 1)	19
3069 CALL DIRECT (Ire) 7-10-13 (7") R M Murphy, . . (25 to 1)	20

Dist: 3l, ½l, 6l, 3½l. 4m 31.10s. (20 Ran).

(W P Kerwin), W P Mullins

3234 Corbally Handicap Hurdle (0-116 4-y-o and up) £2,740 3m. . . . . . (3:30)

2708 KASELECTRIC (Ire) [-] 6-11-4 T Horgan, ... (8 to 1)	1
2585 VASILIKI (Ire) [-] 5-11-3 C O'Dwyer, ... (33 to 1)	2
2944⁸ TULLOLOUGH [-] 14-9-3 (7") M D Murphy, ... (33 to 1)	3
2524³ SIR JOHN (Ire) [-] 8-11-1 C F Swan, ... (9 to 2 fav)	4
3072⁵ JIMMY THE WEED (Ire) [-] 8-10-0 J R Barry, . . . (10 to 1)	5
2753⁶ COOLREE LORD (Ire) [-] (bl) 6-9-0 (7") P G Hourigan, (16 to 1)	6
2902 TAR AND CEMENT (Ire) [-] 9-9-0 (7") A O'Shea, (20 to 1)	7
3072⁸ LETTERLEE (Ire) [-] 7-11-7 (7") Mr M A Cahill, . . (33 to 1)	8
2944⁸ GARLAND ROSE (Ire) [-] 7-9-9 D J Casey, ... (8 to 1)	9
2366 BERNESTIC WONDER (Ire) [-] 8-9-7 J Jones, . . (33 to 1)	10
2943 PERMIT ME (Ire) [-] 5-10-0 J P Broderick, ... (25 to 1)	11
1550 CLASHWILLIAM GIRL (Ire) [-] 9-11-3 (7") Mr R M Walsh,	
. . . . (20 to 1)	12
1836 COOLSHAMROCK (Ire) [-] 5-9-1 (7") S FitzGerald, (12 to 1)	13
2944 WINTRY DAWN (Ire) [-] 7-10-3 W Slattery, ... (20 to 1)	f
3086⁶ TOTAL CONFUSION [-] 10-11-2 J Shortt, ... (10 to 1)	pu
2839 SUPREME ALLIANCE (Ire) [-] 7-9-11 (3") J Butler, (14 to 1)	pu

Dist: 5½l, hd, hd, 1½l. 6m 40.30s. (16 Ran).

(J J Canty), E McNamara

3235 Thomond Handicap Hurdle (0-123 4-y-o and up) £2,740 2m. . . . . . (4:00)

2473⁹ HOME PORT (Ire) [-] 5-11-9 C O'Dwyer, ... (16 to 1)	1
2963³ CIARA'S PRINCE (Ire) [-] (bl) 6-11-6 F J Flood, . . (5 to 2 fav)	2
2901⁷ MUSKERRY KING (Ire) [-] 6-10-6 W Slattery, . . . (14 to 1)	3
2706 PAS POSSIBLE (Ire) [-] 5-11-0 G M O'Neill, ... (10 to 1)	4
1904⁹ WELSH GRIT (Ire) [-] 8-10-13 D J Casey, ... (10 to 1)	5
2837⁷ CREATIVE BLAZE (Ire) [-] 8-11-2 (5") Mr Brian Moran,	
. . . . (16 to 1)	6
3089 CLASHBEG (Ire) [-] 6-10-2 (3") K Whelan, ... (10 to 1)	7
1095² I REMEMBER IT WELL (Ire) [-] 5-10-11 J P Broderick,	
. . . . (10 to 1)	8

2943[7]	ILLBETHEREFORYOU (Ire) [-] 6-9-0 (7*) P G Hourigan,		
	.... (12 to 1)	9
2582[2]	BORN TO WIN (Ire) [-] 7-10-7 T P Rudd, ...(9 to 2)	10
2674[5]	WEST ON BRIDGE ST (Ire) [-] 7-10-13 T Horgan, ...(7 to 1)	11
2834[9]	DONICKMORE (Ire) [-] 6-10-4 (7*) M D Murphy, ...(14 to 1)	12
2674	BEAU CYRANO (Ire) [-] 5-10-3 (7*) M J Collins, ...(20 to 1)	13
2708	TOMMY PAUD (Ire) [-] 8-11-5 M Duffy, ...(14 to 1)	14
1095[5]	BRONICA (Ire) [-] 5-10-9 C F Swan, ...(10 to 1)	15

Dist: 1½l, 1½l, 4½l, ½l. 4m 10.50s. (15 Ran).

(Lisselan Farms Ltd), Andrew Lee

3236 W B Fitt & Co Ltd Handicap Chase (0-116 5-y-o and up) £3,425 2¾m
.... (4:30)

2945[6]	ALL IN THE GAME (Ire) [-] 9-9-2 (7*) M D Murphy, (10 to 1)	1
2962*	LUCKY BUST (Ire) [-] 7-10-10 C F Swan, ...(7 to 1)	2
2756*	COMING ON STRONG (Ire) [-] 8-10-13 C O'Dwyer,	
	.... (9 to 4 fav)	3
2904*	VALERIE OWENS (Ire) [-] 8-9-12[3] (7*) D K Budds, ..(14 to 1)	4
2756[2]	INDESTRUCTIBLE (Ire) [-] 9-11-2 G M O'Neill, ...(5 to 1)	5
2756*	STRONG HICKS (Ire) [-] 9-11-7 F J Flood, ...(7 to 1)	6
	WATERLOO KING (Ire) [-] 10-9-10 (7*) J E Casey, ..(25 to 1)	7
3074*	CORRIBLOUGH (Ire) [-] 9-9-7 T Horgan, ...(8 to 1)	8
2646	MARGUERITA SONG (Ire) [-] 7-10-0 J P Broderick, ..(12 to 1)	9
2338	IF YOU SAY YES (Ire) [-] (bl) 9-9-7 D J Casey, ...(14 to 1)	10
2648	MATTS DILEMMA (Ire) [-] 9-11-6 D H O'Connor, ...(7 to 1)	f
2648[4]	J J JACKSON (Ire) [-] 8-9-0 (7*) A O'Shea, ...(9 to 1)	f
2904	HAVE A BRANDY (Ire) [-] 8-9-7 C O'Brien, ...(20 to 1)	pu

Dist: 1l, 7l, 2l, ¾l. 5m 35.20s. (13 Ran).

(Fiacra J Hensey), John Brassil

3237 Limerick Racing Club Novice Chase (5-y-o and up) £3,425 2¾m... (5:00)

2944[6]	TELL THE NIPPER (Ire) 6-11-8 J P Broderick, ...(4 to 1)	1
2756[8]	SIDCUP HILL (Ire) 8-11-9 T P Rudd, ...(8 to 1)	2
3088[2]	LE GINNO (Fr) 10-12-0 T P Treacy, ...(5 to 2 fav)	3
3088*	LEAMHOG (Ire) 7-12-0 T Horgan, ...(8 to 1)	4
2945	SHARONS PRIDE (Ire) 7-11-3 J H Barry, ...(8 to 1)	5D
2941	V'SOSKE GALE (Ire) 7-11-9 C O'Dwyer, ...(9 to 2)	5
2904	ROSEL WALK (Ire) 8-11-8 A O'Brien, ...(20 to 1)	6
2904[6]	PHARALLEY (Ire) 7-11-3 B M Clifford, ...(14 to 1)	7
2446	FINGAL BOY (Ire) 9-11-5 (3*) J Butler, ...(25 to 1)	8
2524[8]	ROSIE LIL (Ire) 6-10-10 (7*) L A Hurley, ...(12 to 1)	f
2518	ANSWER THAT (Ire) 6-10-10 (7*) M D Murphy, ...(25 to 1)	pu

Dist: Nk, 4l, 1l, 25l. 5m 40.40s. (11 Ran).

(Mrs S McCloy), Michael Hourigan

3238 Limerick INH Flat Race (5-y-o and up) £2,740 2m 1f.
.... (5:30)

2838[6]	WINDGAP HILL (Ire) 6-12-0 Mr J A Berry, ...(5 to 1)	1
2907[2]	DUSKY LAMP (Ire) 7-12-0 Mr H F Cleary, ...(7 to 1)	2
	PRETTY MIMOSA (Ire) 7-11-6 (3*) Mr E Norris, ...(14 to 1)	3
2968[3]	AIR FORCE ONE (Ire) 5-11-12 Mr J A Nash, ...(11 to 8 fav)	4
1907[6]	MISTER AUDI (Ire) 5-11-7 (5*) Mr J T McNamara, ..(8 to 1)	5
3083[9]	QUIPTECH (Ire) 6-11-7 (7*) Mr J P McNamara, ...(8 to 1)	6
121[2]	MASTER CHUZZLEWIT (Ire) 6-11-7 (7*) Mr M J Daly,	
	.... (14 to 1)	7
2845	ARDENTIUM 6-11-7 (7*) Mr B Hassett, ...(20 to 1)	8
2902	MERCHANTS ROAD 10-11-7 (7*) Mr D A Harney, ...(25 to 1)	9
	LUCKY ROSS (Ire) 6-12-0 Miss M Olivefalk, ...(14 to 1)	10
2675[3]	KAITHEY CHOICE (Ire) 6-11-2 (7*) Mr J Boland, ...(14 to 1)	11
2906[4]	BUCK THE WEST (Ire) 7-12-0 Mr P Fenton, ...(12 to 1)	12
2060	EARL OF NAAS (Ire) 6-11-11 (3*) Mr T Lombard, ..(25 to 1)	13
2757	SWEET STEP (Ire) 9-11-2 (7*) Mr K O'Sullivan, ...(20 to 1)	14
829	TOTALLY FRANK (Ire) 9-11-7 (7*) Mr P J Colville, ..(25 to 1)	15
	ECOLOGIC (Ire) 6-12-0 Mr R Hurley, ...(8 to 1)	pu

Dist: 5½l, 3l, 3l, ½l. 4m 28.80s. (16 Ran).

(Sunny South Syndicate), A L T Moore

MARKET RASEN (good)
Monday March 17th
Going Correction: PLUS 0.35 sec. per fur. (races 1,3,6), PLUS 0.20 (2,4,5)

3239 Bonus Day Claiming Hurdle Class F (4-y-o and up) £1,994 2m 3f 110yds
.... (2:10)

2969[3]	CUTTHROAT KID (Ire) (v) 7-11-3 M A Fitzgerald, hld up, mstk 4 out, hdwy nxt, led and pckd 2 out, pushed out.	
	...........(13 to 8 on 6 to 4 on tchd 11 to 8 on)	1
2607	ESKIMO KISS (Ire) 4-10-4 D Gallagher, hld up, hdwy 4 out, ev ch 2 out, no extr r-in............(12 to 1 op 8 to 1)	2
2969[2]	JUST SUPPOSEN (Ire) 6-10-11 R Johnson, chsd ldr 3rd, ev ch appr 2 out, sn rdn, styd on same pace, fnshd lme.	
	...........(11 to 2 op 6 to 1)	3
2855[2]	CHUMMY'S SAGA (bl) 7-11-1 R Supple, prmnt, drvn alng appr 2 out, styd on same pace...........(1 to 1 op 9 to 2)	4
2420	WORLD WITHOUT END (USA) (bl) 8-10-13 D Parker, chsd ldrs, led 4 out till appr 2 out, sn btn.....(25 to 1 op 20 to 1)	5
3108	CHURCHWORTH (bl) 6-10-13 J Culloty, led to second, f nxt.	
	...........(12 to 1 op 14 to 1)	f

	MAN OF WISLEY (Ire) 7-10-13 Gary Lyons, led second, sn clr, mstk 4th, hdd and wknd four out, tld off whn pld up bef last.	
	...........(50 to 1 op 33 to 1)	pu
1742[5]	GAME DRIVE (Ire) 5-11-1 W Fry, al rear, tld off whn pld up bef last.............(20 to 1 op 16 to 1)	pu
2575	PRIMITIVE LIGHT 7-11-3 (3*) P Midgley, hld up, hdwy 6th, wknd 3 out, tld off whn pld up bef last. (25 to 1 op 16 to 1)	pu

Dist: 2½l, 7l, nk, 2½l. 4m 43.10s. a 13.10s (9 Ran).
SR: 26/10/10/14/9/-/

(P D Savill), Mrs M Reveley

3240 Additional Meeting Novices' Chase Class D (5-y-o and up) £3,445 2¾m 110yds. (2:40)

3046[4]	CLAVERHOUSE (Ire) 8-11-2 R Garritty, hld up, hdwy 6th, mstk 4 out, outpcd nxt, rallied appr last, led r-in, rdn out.	
	...........(11 to 2 op 7 to 2 tchd 6 to 1)	1
2848	BRANDY CROSS (Ire) 8-11-2 J Osborne, led, rdn and hdd r-in, no extr............(9 to 4 op 6 to 4 tchd 5 to 2)	2
2788[3]	GARETHSON (Ire) 6-11-2 D Bridgwater, trkd wnr, mstk 7th, hmpd aftr 4 out, ev ch nxt, blun 2 out, no extr.	
	...........(5 to 4 fav op 6 to 4 tchd 7 to 4)	3
3046[3]	GORBY'S MYTH 7-11-2 K Gaule, hld up, cld 6th, rdn appr 3 out, 4th and btn whn f nxt...........(5 to 1 op 9 to 1)	f

Dist: 3l, 7l. 5m 43.10s. a 16.10s (4 Ran).

(Mrs Peter Corbett), J G FitzGerald

3241 More Opportunities Novices' Hurdle Class E (5-y-o and up) £2,305 3m
.... (3:10)

2311[3]	SUPREME FLYER (Ire) 7-10-10 J Osborne, hld up, hdwy to chase ldr 4 out, led appr 2 out, hit last, rdn out.	
	...........(11 to 8 on op 13 to 8 on tchd 5 to 4 on)	1
2288	LARKSHILL (Ire) 6-10-10 W Dwan, hld up, rcd keenly, hdwy 6th, ev ch frm 2 out, ran on...........(7 to 2 op 7 to 2)	2
2889[5]	SEPTEMBER BREEZE (Ire) 6-9-12 (7*) X Aizpuru, led to 4th, ev ch 2 out, ran on und pres...........(9 to 2 op 6 to 1)	3
3110[8]	RANGER SLOANE 5-11-2 R Farrant, prmnt, effrt appr 2 out, styd on same pace...........(11 to 1 op 10 to 1)	4
2803[5]	DRY HILL LAD (Ire) 6-10-10 Derek Byrne, chsd ldrs, lost tch 5 out, styd on, wknd...........(20 to 1 op 14 to 1)	5
2889	COUNTER ATTACK (Ire) 6-10-5 R Johnson, chsd ldr, led 4th to 5 out, wknd appr 2 out...........(33 to 1 op 20 to 1)	6
	EDGE OF NIGHT 8-10-10 K Gaule, hld up, hdwy 3 out, wknd quickly nxt...........(50 to 1 op 33 to 1)	7
	OUR LAUGHTER 7-10-5 M Brennan, prmnt to 6th, sn wl beh.	
	...........(50 to 1 op 33 to 1)	8

Dist: ¾l, ½l, 4l, 24l, 1½l, 3½l, dist. 6m 3.20s. a 24.20s (8 Ran).

(Mrs E A Kellar), K C Bailey

3242 Two Enclosure Day Handicap Chase Class E (0-115 5-y-o and up) £3,078 2½m. (3:45)

3047*	NETHERBY SAID [108] 7-11-8 R Supple, made all, sn wl clr, pckd 3 out, jmpd rght last, eased r-in, unchlgd.	
	...........(15 to 8 fav op 5 to 4 tchd 2 to 1)	1
2936[3]	LOCHNAGRAIN (Ire) [110] 9-11-10 M A Fitzgerald, hld up and wl beh, hdwy 8th, nvr nr to challenge.	
	...........(2 to 1 op 7 to 4 tchd 9 to 4)	2
2987[4]	JASON'S BOY [86] 7-10-0 R Johnson, chsd wnr, drvn alng 4 out, no imprsn...........(9 to 2 op 5 to 1)	3
2321[5]	JUKE BOX BILLY (Ire) [86] 9-10-0 J Culloty, chsd ldrs, rdn and btn whn blun 2 out...........(5 to 1 tchd 11 to 2)	4

SR: 34/30/6/-/

(Mrs S Sunter), P Beaumont

3243 Annual Box Holders Novices' Handicap Chase Class E (0-105 5-y-o and up) £3,168 3m 1f. (4:15)

3046[3]	GAELIC BLUE [79] 7-11-5 Richard Guest, led to 4 out, led nxt, sn clr, eased r-in...........(15 to 8 fav op 7 to 4 tchd 2 to 1)	1
3000	MILWAUKEE (Ire) [60] (v) 8-10-4 M Brennan, prmnt, chsd wnr 13th, led 4 out to nxt, sn wknd, jmpd slwly last.	
	...........(20 to 1 op 16 to 1)	2
3047[3]	RECORD LOVER (Ire) [69] 7-10-9 W Worthington, hld up in tch, outpcd 14th, sn wl beh, tld off whn hit 2 out, fnshd lme.	
	...........(11 to 2 op 4 to 1 tchd 6 to 1)	3
2812*	MISTER TRICK (Ire) [84] (bl) 7-11-10 R Garritty, trkd ldrs, lost pl 8th, blun 11th, tld off whn pld up aftr nxt.	
	...........(9 to 4 op 5 to 2 tchd 100 to 30)	pu
2388*	PRIMITIVE PENNY [82] 6-11-8 J F Titley, chsd wnr, mstk 5th, wknd quickly 13th, pld up bef nxt.	
	...........(3 to 1 op 5 to 2 tchd 100 to 30)	pu

Dist: 19l, dist. 6m 34.00s. a 34.00s (5 Ran).

(Trevor Hemmings), Mrs S J Smith

3244 Easter Monday Comes Next Handicap Hurdle Class E (0-110 4-y-o and up) £2,263 2m 5f 110yds.....(4:45)

| 2957[4] | CAMBO (USA) [83] 11-10-4 D Skyrme, chsd ldrs, outpcd 6th, rallied 3 out, chalg whn lft in ld last, rdn out. | |
| | ....(11 to 2 op 5 to 1 tchd 6 to 1) | 1 |

3105² DESERT FORCE (Ire) [92] 8-10-13 R Farrant, *mid-div, hdwy 6th, rdn appr last, styd on*.............. (7 to 1 op 6 to 1) 2

3045* SASSIVER (USA) [90] 7-10-11 K Gaule, *hld up, mstk 4th, hdwy 6th, styd on same pace appr last*........ (7 to 1 op 9 to 2) 3

694¹ SUJUD (Ire) [92] 5-10-13 R Garritty, *chsd ldrs, rdn 2 out, btn whn hmpd last*........(9 to 1 op 8 to 1 tchd 10 to 1) 4

3006* MAJOR YAASI (USA) [91] (bl) 7-10-12 J Osborne, *led, blun and hdd 2 out, btn whn hmpd last*....... (5 to 1 op 5 to 2) 5

2281⁶ BRANCHER [90] 6-10-6 (5*) B Grattan, *hld up, hdwy 4 out, led aftr 2 out till f last*...................(11 to 2 op 6 to 1) f

3045⁴ MOOBAKKR (USA) [80] 6-9-8 (7*) X Aizpuru, *chsd ldrs, cl up whn sddl slpd and uns rdr appr 2 out.* (7 to 2 fav op 4 to 1) ur

CASTLEBAY LAD [92] 14-10-13¹³ Mr M Appleby, *slwly into strd, beh and rdn 5th, tld off whn pld up bef 2 out.*

3001⁷ ORDOG MOR (Ire) [103] 8-11-10 Derek Byrne, *al beh, tld off whn pld up bef 2 out*..................(10 to 1 op 5 to 1) pu

Dist: 1¾l, 3l, 6l, 1½l. 5m 19.20s. a 16.20s (9 Ran).

(M C Banks), M C Banks

NEWCASTLE (good to firm)
Monday March 17th
Going Correction: PLUS 0.20 sec. per fur.

3245 Great North Road Handicap Chase Class E (0-115 5-y-o and up) £2,862 3m........................... (2:00)

2573⁵ GOLDEN FIDDLE (Ire) [93] (v) 9-10-6 A Thornton, *prmnt, led aftr 8th till hdd tenth, led 12th, drw clr after 2 out, styd on wl.* .... (10 to 1 op 5 to 1) 1

3014* NORTHERN SQUIRE [105] 9-11-1 (3*) E Callaghan, *hld up, mstks, hdwy aftr 3 out, styd on wl frm last, not rch wnr.* .... (11 to 4 op 2 to 1 tchd 3 to 1) 2

165⁵ STRONG SOUND [100] 10-10-8 (5*) G F Ryan, *hld up, hdwy whn hit 14th, chasing wnr 3 out, kpt on same pace.* .... (14 to 1 op 10 to 1) 3

2759² RUSTIC AIR [104] 10-11-3 P Niven, *in tch, hdwy to dispute ld 13th, wknd aftr 3 out, 4th and btn whn mstk last.* ....(9 to 2 op 3 to 1 tchd 5 to 1) 4

2488² GALE AHEAD (Ire) [97] 7-10-10 B Storey, *prmnt, led tenth till hdd 12th, drvn alng aftr 15th, staying on whn blun 2 out, no ch after*....................... (9 to 4 fav op 5 to 2) 5

2360² VICARIDGE [93] 10-10-6 A Dobbin, *chsd ldrs, wknd bef 3 out, tld off*.................. (6 to 1 tchd 7 to 1 and 8 to 1) 6

2488⁶ OVER THE STREAM [115] 11-12-0 T J Murphy, *led till hdd aftr 8th, sn lost pl, wl tld off*........... (25 to 1 op 16 to 1) 7

Dist: 3l, 7l, 3l, 6l, dist, dist. 5m 57.50s. a 11.50s (7 Ran).

SR: 11/20/8/9/ (W Stuart Wilson), J K M Oliver

3246 Town Moor Selling Handicap Hurdle Class G (0-95 4-y-o and up) £2,025 2 ½m........................... (2:30)

2420² JALMAID [67] 5-9-13 (5*) R McGrath, *trkd ldrs, led 3 out, hrd pressed and rdn aftr last, styd on wl.*...........(6 to 1 op 4 to 1 jt-fav tchd 13 to 2 and 11 to 2) 1

2712⁹ DON'T TELL TOM (Ire) [80] 7-10-12 (5*) S Taylor, *al chasing ldrs, rdn to chal aftr last, no extr clsg stages.* .... (10 to 1 op 7 to 1 tchd 14 to 1) 2

3013⁴ KIRSTENBOSCH [80] 10-10-10 (7*) W Dowling, *mid-div, gd hdwy to chase ldrs 3 out, kpt on frm nxt, no imprsn on 1st 2.* .... (6 to 1 jt-fav tchd 7 to 1) 3

3002³ FIASCO [75] 4-10-0 (3*) F Leahy, *chsd ldrs, pushed alng aftr 7th, styd on same pace frm 3 out.*................. (16 to 1) 4

2913 GREENFINCH (Can) [65] (v) 6-10-2 J Supple, *mid-div, rdn aftr 8th, kpt on same pace frm 3 out.*.................. (20 to 1) 5

2635⁷ DALUSMAN (Ire) [68] 9-10-2 (3*) E Callaghan, *beh till styd on frm 3 out, nvr dngrs.*....(16 to 1 op 12 to 1 tchd 20 to 1) 6

3006⁶ YACHT CLUB [72] 15-10-9 B Storey, *mid-div, gd hdwy to ld 6th, hdd 3 out, fdd.*....................(10 to 1 op 8 to 1) 7

2847² IN A MOMENT (USA) [73] 6-10-10 A Thornton, *beh, pushed alng aftr 4th, some late hdwy, nvr dngrs.* (7 to 1 op 6 to 1) 8

2913⁴ DONT FORGET CURTIS (Ire) [87] 5-11-10 J Callaghan, *nvr on terms*..............................(16 to 1 op 10 to 1) 9

3009 DASHMAR [63] 10-10-0 M Moloney, *in tch, reminders aftr 4th, wknd after 8th*.............. (16 to 1 op 14 to 1) 10

3042³ OAKBURY (Ire) [70] 5-10-0 (7*) T Siddall, *towards rear and sn pushed alng, nvr on terms*....... (8 to 1 op 7 to 1) 11

2485 OVER STATED (Ire) [73] 7-10-5 (5*) G F Ryan, *hld up in tch, effrt bef 8th, sn btn*...................... (20 to 1) 12

3011⁷ NOSMO KING (Ire) [63] 6-10-10 Mrs M Kendall, *led till hdd 5th, wknd aftr 8th*............... (33 to 1 op 20 to 1) 13

2983² ARTHUR BEE [63] 10-9-7 (7*) C McCormack, *mid-div, hdwy and prmnt 8th, rdn bef 3 out, wknd.*.......(14 to 1 op 10 to 1) 14

RHYMING THOMAS [77] 9-11-0 T Reed, *prmnt, led 5th, hdd nxt, cl up till wknd quickly bef 3 out.*...(25 to 1 op 20 to 1) 15

2361² HIGHLAND PARK [89] 11-11-12 A Dobbin, *chsd ldrs, pushed alng frm hfwy, wknd aftr 8th.* ....(7 to 1 op 5 to 1 tchd 8 to 1) 16

NO TAKERS [73] 10-10-7 (3*) G Lee, *al beh, tld off whn pld up bef 3 out.*....................(20 to 1 op 14 to 1) pu

1786⁷ DOON RIDGE [63] 6-10-0 O Pears, *prmnt to 5th, sn wknd, beh whn pld up bef 7th*..................(50 to 1 op 25 to 1) pu

3136³ BARK'N'BITE [80] (bl) 5-11-3 P Niven, *al beh, pld up bef 3 out.* ....(8 to 1 op 7 to 1) pu

2988³ PERSIAN GRANGE (Ire) [69] 7-10-6³ J Burke, *in tch till wknd aftr 7th, tld off whn pld up bef 3 out.* (14 to 1 tchd 16 to 1) pu

Dist: ¾l, 2l, 12l, 1¼l, hd, ½l, ¾l, 1½l, 1½l, 1¾l. 4m 56.20s. a 18.20s (20 Ran).

(R V Jackson), H Alexander

3247 Northumberland Hussars Hunters' Chase Class H (6-y-o and up) £1,108 3m........................... (3:00)

FINAL HOPE (Ire) 9-11-3 (7*) Mrs F Needham, *chsd ldrs, led 13th, styd on wl und pres frm last*...... (10 to 1 op 8 to 1) 1

2918⁴ LITTLE WENLOCK 13-11-10 (5*) Mrs V Jackson, *beh, hdwy bef 3 out, chlgd last, no extr und pres clsg stages.* ....(9 to 2 op 5 to 1 tchd 4 to 1) 2+

2993* HIGHLANDMAN 11-11-6 (7*) Mr Chris Wilson, *led, hdd 13th, dsptd ld till outpcd appr last, styd on wl und pres towards finish*...................... (5 to 1 op 7 to 2) 2+

PIPER O'DRUMMOND 10-11-5 (5*) Miss P Robson, *in tch, effrt bef 3 out, kpt on same pace frm nxt.* (9 to 2 op 7 to 2) 4

2974 FREE TRANSFER (Ire) 8-11-5 (5*) Mr C Storey, *in tch, outpcd whn hmpd 14th, some hdwy aftr 3 out, wknd after nxt, fnshd lme*.....................(9 to 1 op 8 to 1 tchd 10 to 1) 5

WASHAKIE 12-11-5 (5*) Mr P Johnson, *lost tch frm 8th, tld off.* .... (2 to 1 fav tchd 9 to 4) 6

GATHERING TIME 11-11-3 (7*) Mr A Birch, *sn lost tch, tld off.* ....(33 to 1) 7

2974³ DOUBLE COLLECT 11-11-3 (7*) Mr A Rebori, *chsd ldr, wkng whn f 14th*.....................(9 to 1 op 17 to 1) f

Dist: ½l, dd-ht, 3l, 21l, 21l, 17l. 6m 0.20s. a 14.20s (8 Ran).

SR: 2/4/4/-/-/ (R Tate), R Tate

3248 Town & Country Novices' Hunters' Chase Class H (5-y-o and up) £1,047 2½m........................... (3:35)

3033² WOODY DARE 7-12-2 (5*) Mr R Thornton, *trkd ldrs, led 4 out, styd on wl frm 2 out.*...............(7 to 1 op 4 to 1) 1

GENERAL DELIGHT 10-12-0 (7*) Mr D Wood, *beh early, took clr order hfwy, effrt bef 3 out, chsd wnr frm nxt, no imprsn.* ....(12 to 1 op 8 to 1) 2

PENNINE VIEW 10-12-2 (5*) Mr R Ford, *cl up, dsptd ld 4 out, ch 2 out, kpt on same pace*................ (7 to 1 op 6 to 1) 3

BELLS WILL RING (Ire) 7-12-0 (7*) Mr T Scott, *keen, mstks, led till hdd 4 out, sn wknd, tld off*......(4 to 1 tchd 5 to 1) 4

2995 MASTER CROZINA 9-12-0 (7*) Mr P Cornforth, *in tch till wknd bef 4 out, tld off*................. (33 to 1 op 20 to 1) 5

2995⁵ TUMLIN OOT (Ire) 8-12-0 (7*) Mr Chris Wilson, *beh, hdwy whn blun tenth, wknd bef 4 out, tld off.* ....(10 to 1 op 8 to 1 tchd 12 to 1) 6

EILID ANOIR 8-12-2 (5*) Mr R Shiels, *in tch till wknd bef 4 out, tld off*...................... (14 to 1 op 7 to 1) 7

DRUMCAIRN (Ire) 9 12 2 (5*) Mr P Johnson, *blun 1st, sn tld off*.........................(20 to 1 op 14 to 1) 8

2990³ UP FOR RANSOME (Ire) 8-12-0 (7*) Mr G Shenkin, *f 1st.* ....(7 to 4 fav op 2 to 1 tchd 5 to 2) f

LINDON RUN 8-12-0 (7*) Mr R Morgan, *in tch whn blun and uns rdr 9th*.....................(10 to 1 op 7 to 1) ur

COUNT SURVEYOR 10-12-0 (7*) Mr A Parker, *pld up lme aftr 1st*.........................(20 to 1 op 14 to 1) pu

Dist: 2l, ½l, 29l, 20l, 19l, 7l, 5l. 5m 5.40s. a 18.40s (11 Ran).

(P Needham), P Needham

3249 Newcastle City Novices' Claiming Hurdle Class F (4-y-o and up) £2,039 2m........................... (4:05)

2917⁶ BRAMBLES WAY (bl) 8-11-8 P Niven, *hld up, jnd ldr 6th, led on bit bef 3 out, shaken up betw last 2, ran on wl.* ....(11 to 4 on op 5 to 1) 1

934¹ PARKLIFE (Ire) 5-11-4 M Foster, *nvr far away, chlgd 3 out, ch nxt, sn rdn and no extr*....(11 to 4 op 9 to 4 tchd 3 to 1) 2

LUCKER 10-11-0 K Johnson, *led till hdd bef 3 out, sn rdn and wknd, tld off*........(16 to 1 op 20 to 1 tchd 14 to 1) 3

NINE PIPES (Ire) 6-11-2 L O'Hara, *sn chasing ldr, wknd aftr 6th, tailing off whn f 2 out*............(33 to 1 op 20 to 1) f

Dist: 4l, dist. 4m 0.90s. a 23.90s (4 Ran).

(Nigel E M Jones), Mrs M Reveley

3250 Glengoyne Highland Malt Novices' Chase Tamerosia Series Qualifier Class E (5-y-o and up) £2,966 3m .... (4:35)

3056¹ KALAJO 7-12-2 B Storey, *beh whn stumbled second, hdwy to track ldr 9th, hit 12th, led 14th, styd on wl.* ....(7 to 4 fav op 5 to 4) 1

3124³ FERN LEADER (Ire) 7-11-4 J Supple, *led, mstk 7th, hdd 14th, chsd wnr aftr, kpt on wl frm last.* ....(15 to 8 op 2 to 1 tchd 9 to 4) 2

2812² STRONGALONG (Ire) 7-11-4 A Dobbin, *trkd ldrs, effrt bef 14th, disputing second and no imprsn on wnr whn blun last, no ch aftr*.......................(3 to 1 op 4 ^) 3

2620⁵ ABBEY LAMP (Ire) 8-11-4 A Thornton, *in tch wknd before 3 out, tld off*...............

2812³ SELDOM BUT SEVERE (Ire) 7-10-13 (5*) G F Ryan, *in tch, rdn aftr 6th, wknd frm 13th, sn tld off*...... (20 to 1 op 16 to 1) 5
Dist: 2½l, 9l, 26l, 11l. 6m 0.50s. a 14.50s (5 Ran).
SR: 5/-/-   (Kelso Members Lowflyers Club), B Mactaggart

3251 Northumberland Intermediate National Hunt Flat Class H (4,5,6-y-o) £1,215 2m.............. (5:05)

GO NATIVE (Ire) 5-10-11 (7*) R Wilkinson, *trkd ldrs, led one furlong out, ran on wl*..(12 to 1 op 10 to 1 tchd 14 to 1) 1
2939 WYNYARD KNIGHT 5-11-1 (3*) G Lee, *hld up, steady hdwy to chal one furlong out, rdn and no extr.*
.....................................(6 to 4 on op 5 to 4 on) 2
2939* LANDLER 4-10-12 (5*) Mr T Thornton, *cl up, slight ld o'r 2 fs out, hdd one out, kpt on*.................. (7 to 1 op 4 to 1) 3
POLAR KING (Ire) 4-10-3 (7*) N Horrocks, *led till hdd o'r 2 fs out, ev ch till no extr fnl furlong*........ (8 to 1 op 6 to 1) 4
SALMON CELLAR (Ire) 4-10-7 (3*) E Callaghan, *keen, mid-div, pushed alng 3 fs out, no hdwy till styd on fnl furlong.*
.....................................(9 to 2 op 4 to 1 tchd 3 to 1) 5
KIT SMARTIE (Ire) 5-10-13 (5*) G F Ryan, *hld up, hdwy o'r 3 fs out, kpt on same pace fnl 2 furlongs*. (14 to 1 tchd 33 to 1) 6
MERRY MAJOR 4-10-5 (5*) R McGrath, *hld up, outpcd o'r 3 fs out, nvr dngrs*........................(50 to 1 op 20 to 1) 7
RUNHIM 5-10-11 (7*) S Melrose, *trkd ldrs till wknd 4 fs out.*
.....................................(50 to 1 op 20 to 1) 8
MILLSTONE HILL 5-10-13 (5*) S Taylor, *in tch, pushed alng 5 fs out, sn wknd.*...............(100 to 1 op 25 to 1) 9
RISING MILL 6-11-4 Mr A Robson, *prmnt till wknd quickly o'r 4 fs out, tld off*...................(50 to 1 op 66 to 1) 10
Dist: 1½l, 2l, ½l, ¾l, nk, 9l, 13l, 18l, 20l. 3m 57.40s. (10 Ran).
                                (Trevor Hemmings), Mrs S J Smith

FONTWELL (good to firm)
Tuesday March 18th
Going Correction: PLUS 0.30 sec. per fur.

3252 'Certain Justice' Challenge Cup Novices' Handicap Chase Class E (0-100 5-y-o and up) £2,961 2¼m
.... (2:00)

3118* RED BRANCH (Ire) [79] 8-11-4 (6ex) T J Murphy, *jmpd wl, made all, clr appr 3 out, eased to walk r-in.*
....(6 to 5 on op 5 to 4 on tchd Evens and 11 to 8 on) 1
2877² SPEEDY SNAPS IMAGE [73] 6-10-12 S Burrough, *al prmnt, wnt second appr 6th, hld whn jmpd badly rght last 2.*
.....................................(5 to 1 op 4 to 1 tchd 7 to 2) 2
3104³ CHRIS'S GLEN [70] (v) 8-10-9 B Fenton, *chsd wnr till aftr 5th, blun badly nxt, no ch frm 4 out.*
.....................................(11 to 2 op 4 to 1) 3
3050 VICTORY GATE (USA) [61] 12-9-11 (3*) Sophie Mitchell, *al beh*.................. (40 to 1 op 25 to 1 tchd 20 to 1) 4
2877 KETCHICAN [76] 5-10-7 S Anderson, *pld hrd, not jump wl, lost tch 9th*.............(50 to 1 op 33 to 1 tchd 66 to 1) 5
2955³ STROKESAVER [88] (bl) 7-11-13 D Gallagher, *al beh, lost tch 9th, tld off*............(5 to 1 op 5 to 2 tchd 11 to 4) 6
Dist: 12l, 4l, nk, 8l, 20l. 4m 37.70s. a 17.70s (6 Ran).
                                      (E J Mangan), J S King

3253 European Breeders Fund National Hunt' Novices' Hurdle Qualifier Class E (5,6,7-y-o) £2,385 2¼m 110yds.................... (2:30)

2871* STRONG PALADIN (Ire) 6-11-7 (3*) L Aspell, *made all, ran on wl whn chlgd frm 2 out.*
.....................................(100 to 30 op 11 to 4 tchd 4 to 1) 1
3077³ NEAT FEAT (Ire) 6-11-10 P Holley, *hld up in tch, hdwy to go second 4 out, chlgd and ev ch 2 out, swtchd lft r-in, no imprsn.*
.....................................(15 to 8 fav op 6 to 4 tchd 11 to 8) 2
2927² RHYTHM AND BLUES 7-11-5 B Powell, *in tch, trkd wnr 4th to four out, wknd appr 2 out.*
.....................................(3 to 1 op 5 to 2 tchd 100 to 30) 3
2353⁸ YARSLEY JESTER 5-10-9 J R Kavanagh, *pld hrd, prmnt till wknd appr 3 out*.......(66 to 1 op 33 to 1 tchd 100 to 1) 4
3077³ THE FLYING DOCTOR (Ire) 7-11-0 B Fenton, *hld up, hdwy 4 out, wknd nxt, eased r-in.*.............(7 to 2 tchd 9 to 2) 5
WOMAN FROM HELL 7-10-9 M Richards, *trkd wnr to 4th, wknd appr four out, tld off whn pld up bef 2 out.*
.....................................(66 to 1 op 33 to 1) pu
Dist: ....9l, 4m 34.30s. a 17.30s (6 Ran).
                                    (Mrs Angela Brodie), J T Gifford

Simpson Memorial Challenge ... Maiden Chase Class E (5-y-o ... 006 3¼m 110yds.. (3:00)

...nton, *patiently rdn, wnt*
.....................................ns tchd 2 to 1) 1
...ht, led 4th till   11 to 10) 2

2979 CRUISE CONTROL 11-11-8 D O'Sullivan, *led to 4th, outpcd 16th, tld off*............(9 to 2 op 5 to 1 tchd 6 to 1) 3
2391⁸ BONITA BLAKENEY 7-11-3 B Fenton, *jmpd slwly second, hdwy 8th, trkd ldr 12th to 17th, f nxt.*
.....................................(16 to 1 op 10 to 1 tchd 20 to 1) f
Dist: 3½l, dist. 7m 3.10s. a 33.10s (4 Ran).
                                    (Mrs Sharon C Nelson), K C Bailey

3255 Grand Splendour Handicap Hurdle Class E (0-115 4-y-o and up) £2,807 2¾m 110yds................ (3:30)

3054² SMUGGLER'S POINT (USA) [101] 7-11-6 (3*) Sophie Mitchell, *led second till hdd 4 out, rallied and led appr last, styd on*......................(5 to 1 op 4 to 1 tchd 11 to 2) 1
2951 VINTAGE CLARET [98] 8-11-6 P Hide, *prmnt till lost pl 4 out, rallied last to go second cl hme.* (7 to 2 jt-fav tchd 4 to 1) 2
2559⁹ SORBIERE [90] (bl) 10-11-12 M A Fitzgerald, *led to second, led ag'n 4 out, rdn and hdd appr last, no extr and lost second cl hme*.....................(7 to 1 op 6 to 1 tchd 8 to 1) 3
GENTLEMAN SID [78] 7-10-0³ (3*) L Aspell, *hld up, effrt 4 out, wknd nxt*........................(9 to 2 op 5 to 1) 4
3120³ RAAHIN (USA) [78] 12-10-0 D Morris, *struggling frm 6th, tld off whn pld up bef 4 out.* (20 to 1 op 14 to 1 tchd 25 to 1) pu
2743⁴ NEVER FORGOTTEN [80] 12-10-2 P Holley, *sddl slpd, pld up bef second*................(20 to 1 tchd 25 to 1) pu
3027 PADDYSWAY [92] 10-11-0 B Powell, *beh whn pld up bef 3rd, dismounted, lme*....................(11 to 2 op 4 to 1) pu
2743³ WALKING TALL (Ire) [104] 6-11-12 D Bridgwater, *jmpd rght, hit 5th, wknd 4 out, tld off whn pld up bef 2 out.* ...(7 to 2 jt-fav op 4 to 1 tchd 9 to 2) pu
Dist: 5l, hd, 19l. 5m 30.40s. a 16.40s (8 Ran).
                                    (Mrs V R Hoare), J J Bridger

3256 Horse And Hound Charlton Hunt Challenge Cup Hunters' Chase Class H (5-y-o and up) £1,562 2m 3f
.... (4:00)

2992³ BUSMAN (Ire) 8-11-13 (7*) Mr D S Jones, *al in tch, chalg whn hit 12th, led nxt, clr 3 out, unchlgd.*
.....................................(11 to 4 op 5 to 2 tchd 3 to 1) 1
TEA CEE KAY 7-11-9 (5*) Mr A Sansome, *al prmnt, led 4th to 13th, kpt on one pace frm 2 out.*
.....................................(12 to 1 op 8 to 1 tchd 14 to 1) 2
SPITFIRE JUBILEE 11-11-7 (7*) Mr R Nuttall, *led to 4th, lost pl 9th, styd on frm 2 out.*...........(2 to 1 fav op Evens) 3
EAGLE BID (h) 9-11-9 (5*) Mr T McCarthy, *hld up in tch, hdwy 9th, wknd 2 out.*........(7 to 2 op 3 to 1 tchd 4 to 1) 4
2995³ CORLY SPECIAL 10-11-7 (7*) Mr E James, *prmnt early, beh frm 7th*.........................(4 to 1 op 7 to 2) 5
MISS MAGIC 12-11-2 (7*) Mr F Brennan, *trkd ldr, hit 6th, mstk tenth, sn beh*............(50 to 1 op 20 to 1 tchd 66 to 1) 6
FELTHAM MISTRESS 7-11-2 (7*) Mr E Babington, *beh till hdwy tenth, wknd appr 3 out, pld up bef last.*
.....................................(66 to 1 op 20 to 1 tchd 100 to 1) pu
Dist: 10l, 9l, 1l, 1¾l, ¾l. 4m 49.70s. a 14.70s (7 Ran).
SR: 16/-/-/-/-/   (Keith R Pearce), Keith R Pearce

3257 R.N.L.I. Handicap Hurdle Class E (0-110 4-y-o and up) £2,280 2¼m 110yds.................... (4:30)

2885⁴ CLAIRESWAN (Ire) [97] 5-11-1 Richard Guest, *trkd ldrs, mstk 5th, led sn aftr 3 out, hdd nxt, rallied und pres to ld cl hme.*
.....................................(7 to 4 fav tchd 2 to 1) 1
2806⁶ DECIDE YOURSELF (Ire) [100] 7-11-4 M A Fitzgerald, *hld up, hdwy 3 out, slight ld nxt, hrd rdn and hdd nr finish.*
.....................................(9 to 2 op 4 to 1 tchd 6 to 1) 2
2267 TOPANGA [83] (bl) 10-11-5 C Llewellyn, *led till aftr 3rd, ev ch 3 out, one pace after*......(7 to 1 op 11 to 2 tchd 8 to 1) 3
FROZEN SEA (USA) [110] 6-11-9 (5*) Mr R Thornton, *hld up in tch, wnt second 3 out, ev ch nxt, rdn and wknd appr last.*
.....................................(3 to 1 op 7 to 2 tchd 4 to 1) 4
2479⁵ ADILOV [88] 5-10-3 (3*) Sophie Mitchell, *hld up, hdwy 5th, wknd appr 3 out*..........(13 to 2 op 4 to 1 tchd 7 to 1) 5
SEA BARN [82] 14-9-9 (5*) G Supple, *trkd ldr, led aftr 3rd, hdd second out, wknd*....(25 to 1 tchd 20 to 1) 6
1425 MATAMOROS [83] 5-10-11 D O'Sullivan, *al beh, tld off whn pld up bef 2 out.*....(12 to 1 op 5 to 1 tchd 16 to 1) pu
Dist: Hd, 6l, 1¾l, 7l, 2½l. 4m 29.30s. a 12.30s (7 Ran).
SR: 20/23/-/25/   (Claire And Beryl), M H Tompkins

SEDGEFIELD (good to firm)
Tuesday March 18th
Going Correction: PLUS 0.20 sec. per fur.

3258 Stanley Racing Series Novices' Hurdle Class E (4-y-o and up) £2,253 2m 1f.................... (2:10)

2122 STYLISH INTERVAL 5-11-8 R Supple, *cl up, led 4th, hrd pressed frm 2 out, hit last, styd on und pres.*
.....................................(5 to 1 op 9 to 2 tchd 11 to 2) 1

NATIONAL HUNT RESULTS 1996-97

7757 SUVALU (USA) 5-11-2 Derek Byrne, *trkd ldrs till lost pl aftr 4th, hdwy bef 3 out, chlgd last, no extr...* (6 to 1 op 8 to 1) 2

30033 UNDAWATERSCUBADIVA 5-11-2 A Dobbin, *hld up, hdwy to track ldrs 5th, ev ch appr last, no extr.*
.................(13 to 8 fav op 6 to 4 tchd 11 to 8) 3

26517 TSANGA 5-11-2 J Callaghan, *led till hdd 4th, cl up till wknd betw last 2...........*.(33 to 1 op 25 to 1 tchd 20 to 1) 4

30026 I'M TYSON (NZ) 9-11-2 M Moloney, *hld up, rdn aftr 3 out, styd on frm nxt, nvr dngrs.................* (12 to 1 op 6 to 1) 5

2651 POINT DUTY 7-11-2 D Bentley, *chsd ldrs, rdn bef 2 out, fdd.*
.................(25 to 1 op 20 to 1 tchd 33 to 1) 6

2712 WHITEGATES WILLIE 5-11-2 D Parker, *in tch till outpcd aftr 3 out, no dngr after..................* (100 to 1 op 66 to 1) 7

25469 GAZANALI (Ire) 6-11-2 N Bentley, *hld up, some hdwy aftr 3 out, sn btn.............*(13 to 1 op 5 to 1 tchd 7 to 1) 8

3002 THE GREY TEXAN 8-11-2 Mr M Thompson, *in tch till wknd aftr 5th, tld off.....................*(66 to 1 op 40 to 1) 9

2988 RYE RUM (bl) 6-11-2 B Storey, *sn beh, tld off whn pld up bef 2 out.....................*(100 to 1 op 50 to 1) pu

29397 WEAPONS FREE 6-11-2 R Garritty, *hld up, lost tch aftr 3 out, pld up bef last......*...........(7 to 1 op 5 to 1) pu

Dist: 1l, 3l, 3½l, 1½l, 7l, 1¾l, 1l, dist. 4m 1.50s. a 15.50s (11 Ran).
(Mrs J Waggott), N Waggott

3259 Stanley Casinos Novices' Chase Class E (5-y-o and up) £2,770 3m 3f
.... (2:40)

29145 MISS COLETTE 9-10-11 M Foster, *in tch, outpcd and reminders aftr 12th, rallied bef 16th, led aftr 3 out, styd on wl.*
.....................(9 to 1 op 7 to 1) 1

25345 COOL WEATHER (Ire) (bl) 9-11-2 R Supple, *in tch, drvn alng aftr 18th, chlgd 2 out, no extr.........*(6 to 1 tchd 7 to 1) 2

28127 TACTIX 7-10-11 B Storey, *mstks, hld up, hdwy to track ldrs 11th, outpcd bef 18th, no dngr after.....*(8 to 1 op 5 to 1) 3

29716 FAIR ALLY 7-11-2 D Parker, *beh, jmpd badly rght thrght, took clr order hfwy, ev ch 17th, sn btn......* (6 to 1 op 5 to 1) 4

3007 OAKLANDS BILLY 8-11-2 P Niven, *led, hit 3 out, sn hdd and wknd............................*(9 to 1 op 7 to 1) 5

3158 DISTILLERY HILL (Ire) 9-11-2 Mr M Thompson, *in tch, reminders aftr 13th, wknd after 18th...*(20 to 1 op 14 to 1) 6

29124 D'ARBLAY STREET (Ire) 8-11-8 R Garritty, *chsd ldr, hit 17th, sn lost pl, tld off whn pld up and dismounted bef 3 out. Broke blood vessel............*(6 to 5 fav op 5 to 4 tchd Evens) pu

Dist: 6l, 4l, 4l, 18l, ½l. 6m 55.30s. a 22.30s (7 Ran).
(Robert Drysdale), Mrs D Thomson

3260 Robin And John Simpson Memorial Handicap Chase Class E (0-110 5-y-o and up) 2m 5f....... (3:10)

2536 THE TOASTER [95] 10-10-13 (3*) E Callaghan, *in tch, chsd ldr frm 12th, rdn aftr nxt, led last, styd on.*
.................(9 to 2 op 11 to 2 tchd 13 to 2) 1

3126* CROSS CANNON [109] 11-12-2 (6ex) B Storey, *led, rdn aftr 2 out, hdd last, no extr...........*(5 to 4 on op 11 to 8 on) 2

30323 TWIN FALLS (Ire) [99] 6-11-6 J Callaghan, *chsd ldr till outpcd aftr 11th, no dngr after......*(9 to 4 op 7 to 4 tchd 5 to 2) 3

Dist: 2l, 12l. 5m 11.80s. a 15.80s (3 Ran).
(The Aunts), Miss M K Milligan

3261 Mary Reveley Racing Club Novices' Chase Class E (5-y-o and up) £2,753 2m 5f.......................(3:40)

2909* RIVER UNSHION (Ire) 7-11-8 A Dobbin, *hld up, gd hdwy to ld aftr 9th, blun 12th, styd on und pres frm 2 out.*
.....................(2 to 1 fav op 6 to 4) 1

30075 MOST RICH (v) 9-10-13 (3*) E Callaghan, *led to 5th, led 7th till aftr 9th, remained prmnt, chsd wnr frm last, no imprsn.*
.....................(14 to 1 op 12 to 1) 2

24957 DAWN LAD 8-11-8 J Supple, *in tch, dsptd ld 13th, ev ch 2 out, no extr...............*(4 to 1 op 5 to 1 tchd 11 to 2) 3

26834 LE DENISTAN 10-11-8 D Parker, *hld up, reminders hfwy, mstk 11th, sn outpcd, no dngr aftr..........* (4 to 1 op 7 to 2) 4

31243 MASTER FLASHMAN 8-11-2 P Niven, *prmnt, mstks 4th and tenth, wknd aftr nxt, tld off...............*(11 to 4 op 5 to 2) 5

30468 PARSONS BELLE 9-10-11 W Fry, *beh frm 6th, tld off whn pld up bef 2 out....................*(33 to 1 op 25 to 1) pu

3124 RINGRONE (Ire) 8-10-11 Mr M Thompson, *led 5th to 7th, wknd bef 9th, tld off whn pld up before 13th.*
.....................(100 to 1 op 50 to 1) pu

Dist: 2½l, 4l, 5l, dist. 5m 12.90s. a 16.90s (7 Ran).
(R J Crake), J Howard Johnson

3262 Stanley Racing Golden Numbers Series Novices' Hurdle Class E (4-y-o and up) £2,253 2m 5f 110yds
.... (4:10)

28524 HARFDECENT 6-11-2 P Niven, *prmnt, led 5th, rdn and hdd appr last, sn led ag'n, all out............*(5 to 4 fav op 9 to 4) 1

28528 KING FLY 7-11-2 M Foster, *al prmnt, drw clr with wnr frm 3 out, mstk nxt, slight ld appr last, sn hdd and no extr.*
.....................(33 to 1 op 20 to 1) 2

22006 ERNI (Fr) 5-10-9 (7*) R McCarthy, *chsd ldrs, one-paced frm 3 out...................*(9 to 2 op 7 to 2 tchd 5 to 1) 3

26875 MAJOR HAGE (Ire) 6-11-2 A Dobbin, *settled midfield, gd hdwy to track ldrs 3 out, sn wknd.*
.................(4 to 1 op 3 to 1 tchd 9 to 2) 4

29846 BUSY BOY 10-10-9 (7*) Miss S Lamb, *wl beh hfwy, some late hdwy, nvr dngrs..............*(100 to 1 op 50 to 1) 5

3162 KINGS MINSTRAL (Ire) 7-11-8 J Burke, *chsd ldrs till wknd aftr 7th...........................*(10 to 1) 6

2490 BUNNY BUCK (Ire) 7-11-2 M Moloney, *sn wl beh, tld off.*
.....................(50 to 1) 7

2653 AL JINN 6-11-2 B Storey, *sn wl beh, tld off whn pld up bef 7th.*
.....................(33 to 1) pu

2116[9] OUR WILMA 8-10-11 O Pears, *in tch to hfwy, tld off whn pld up bef 2 out...................*(50 to 1) pu

29737 THE SHARROW LEGEND (Ire) 5-10-11 (5*) S Taylor, *made most till hdd 5th, chsd ldrs aftr till wknd bef 3 out, tld off whn pld up before last.............* (9 to 2 op 4 to 1) pu

3003 ROMALDKIRK 5-11-2 Mr M Thompson, *in tch, drvn alng and outpcd hfwy, tld off whn pld up bef last.*
.....................(100 to 1 op 50 to 1) pu

Dist: ¾l, 23l, 7l, 2½l, 6l, dist. 5m 8.80s. a 20.80s (11 Ran).
(A G Knowles), Mrs M Reveley

3263 Stanley Racing Handicap Hurdle Class E (0-115 4-y-o and up) £2,169 2m 1f...........................(4:40)

30135 GLENUGIE [90] 6-10-4 N Bentley, *beh, lost tch aftr 5th, gd hdwy frm 3 out, led r-in, ran on wl...* (2 to 1 fav op 5 to 2) 1

30062 FRYUP SATELLITE [88] 6-10-2 Miss P Robson, *trkd ldr gng wl, led 3 out, sn clr, hdd r-in, no extr.....* (3 to 1 op 5 to 2) 2

27603 OUR KRIS (bl) 5-12-0 D Parker, *led, drvn alng frm hfwy, hdd 3 out, sn wknd...................* (9 to 2 op 4 to 1) 3

28857 SUMMERHILL SPECIAL (Ire) [110] 6-11-10 J Callaghan, *trkd ldrs till wknd bef 3 out........* (8 to 1 op 6 to 1) 4

2880 BEND SABLE (Ire) [105] 7-11-5 B Storey, *beh, lost tch aftr 5th, tld off........................*(7 to 1 op 11 to 4) 5

Dist: 2½l, 27l, ¾l, 21. 3m 54.80s. a 8.80s (5 Ran).
SR: 22/17/16/11/-/
(Frazer Hines), G M Moore

UTTOXETER (good to firm)
Tuesday March 18th
Going Correction: PLUS 0.30 sec. per fur.

3264 King Sturge Handicap Chase Class E (0-110 5-y-o and up) £2,888 3¼m
.... (2:20)

3138* SHEELIN LAD (Ire) [87] 9-10-7 (6ex) T Reed, *midfield, not fluent 9th, second whn pckd 4 out, led nxt, hld on wl cl hme.*
.....................(5 to 1 op 7 to 2) 1

28834 SAILOR JIM [100] 10-11-6 C Maude, *sn led, jmpd wl, hdd 3 out, rallied well last, no extr cl hme.....*(11 to 2 op 4 to 1) 2

22526 LAY IT OFF (Ire) [82] 8-10-2 S Curran, *wl dtr, drvn alng frm 4 out, one pace from nxt...*(11 to 1 op 8 to 1 tchd 12 to 1) 3

2488 URANUS COLLONGES (Fr) [105] 11-11-11 K Gaule, *sn nig-gled alng, hdwy to chase ldrs hfwy, drvn along 5 out, fdd frm nxt.......................*(16 to 1 op 10 to 1) 4

SHEEPHAVEN [90] 13-10-10 R Johnson, *cl up, drvn alng frm 5 out, wknd from nxt, beh whn pld up betw last 2.*
.....................(7 to 2 op 3 to 1) pu

28953 DONT TELL THE WIFE [108] 11-11-7 (7*) M Berry, *beh, hit tenth, outpcd 14th, behind whn pld up 2 out.*
.....................(3 to 1 fav tchd 7 to 2) pu

30815 TOP BRASS (Ire) [99] 9-11-5 C O'Dwyer, *hld up, lost tch 12th, tld off and pld up nxt................*(5 to 1 op 4 to 1) pu

2794 SWISS TACTIC (Ire) [80] 8-10-0 V Smith, *in tch till drpd rear 9th, sn struggling, tld off whn pld up 2 out.*
.....................(50 to 1 op 25 to 1) pu

Dist: 1l, 13l, 18l. 6m 39.40s. a 27.40s (8 Ran).
(Mrs T J McInnes Skinner), Mrs T J McInnes Skinner

3265 Geo. Hodges & Son Novices' Selling Hurdle Class G (4,5,6-y-o) £1,899 2m
.... (2:50)

3002* RADMORE BRANDY 4-10-5 (3*) G Lee, *in tch, hit 6th, led gng wl 3 out, strly pressed nxt, ran on well.*
.....................(7 to 4 fav tchd 2 to 1) 1

DISTANT STORM 4-10-7 V Slattery, *in tch, chalg whn not fluent 2 out and last, kpt on..........*(25 to 1 op 16 to 1) 2

29999 ANALOGICAL 4-10-2 D Walsh, *hld up, midfield whn pckd aftr 4 out, hdwy gng wl nxt, chlgd 2 out, styd on stdly.*
.....................(25 to 1 op 16 to 1) 3

3099* RIVERBANK ROSE (v) 6-10-13 (3*) Guy Lewis, *cl up, led briefly 6th, drvn appr 2 out, no extr whn hit nxt.*
.....................(4 to 1 tchd 9 to 2) 4

30422 SUMMER VILLA (bl) 5-10-10 K Gaule, *hld up, pushed alng 3 out, nvr a factor...................*(11 to 4 op 7 to 2) 5

31844 EL BARDADOR (Ire) 4-10-7 W McFarland, *hld up, struggling appr 7th, no dngr frm 2 out.............*(11 to 1 op 7 to 1) 6

19923 HOW COULD-I (Ire) 4-10-2 W Marston, *made most till hd── and hit 3 out, sn drvn and wknd...........*(9 to 2 o──

3048 WELSH ASSET 6-10-11³ (7*) Mr A Wintle, *──── outpcd 3 out, btn whn hit nxt.*
.....................(16 to ──

2925⁸ WITHERKAY 4-10-2 (5°) O Burrows, *hld up, some hdwy on outsd appr 4 out, fdd nxt*.................(7 to 1 op 5 to 1) 9

2886 FOREIGN JUDGEMENT (USA) 4-10-7 C Maude, *jmpd slwly in rear, tld off frm 4 out*............(25 to 1 op 20 to 1) 10

2565 TUDOR FALCON (bl) 4-10-7 S Wynne, *hld up, not fluent 3rd, struggling 6th, tld off frm 3 out*........(14 to 1 op 12 to 1) 11

3099⁸ STIPPLE 6-10-10 J Culloty, *str hold, in tch till wknd quickly appr 3 out, eased, tld off*..........(50 to 1 op 33 to 1) 12

TOAT CHIEFTAIN 5-11-1 R Johnson, *chsd ldrs to hfwy, sn wknd, tld off*..........................(33 to 1 op 14 to 1) 13

Dist: 1l, 4l, 4l, 7l, 3½l, 1½l, 2½l, 1½l, 20l, 6l. 3m 49.80s. a 12.80s (13 Ran).

(J R Salter), G Richards

3266 Montracon Handicap Hurdle Class B (0-140 4-y-o and up) £4,621 3m 110yds....................(3:20)

2936² SMITH TOO (Ire) [112] 9-10-8 R Farrant, *led, quickened appr 3 out, drvn clr last, styd on strly*....................(11 to 10 on op Evens tchd 11 to 10) 1

2936⁴ BANKHEAD (Ire) [128] 8-11-3 (7°) Miss C Spearing, *chsd ldr, not fluent and niggled alng 9th, styd on same pace frm 2 out*....................(3 to 1 op 9 to 4 tchd 100 to 30 and 7 to 2) 2

2453 LANSDOWNE [120] 9-11-2 A P McCoy, *settled in tch, pressed ldrs frm hfwy, not fluent 3 out and nxt, no extr*....................(5 to 2 tchd 11 to 4) 3

2977⁶ FOX CHAPEL [104] 10-10-0 W Marston, *hld up, pushed alng in rear 8th, wl beh frm 4 out, tld off...* (33 to 1 op 16 to 1) 4

Dist: 2½l, 3½l, dist. 5m 50.00s. a 13.00s (4 Ran).

SR: 23/36/24/-/ (Smith Mansfield Meat Co Ltd), Mrs J Pitman

3267 Exterior Profiles Novices' Handicap Chase Class E (0-100 5-y-o and up) £3,018 2½m....................(3:50)

2604 QUITE A MAN [83] 9-11-10 C Maude, *nvr far away, chlgd tenth, led aftr 2 out, pushed clr whn runner-up blun last*....................(7 to 1 tchd 11 to 1) 1

3079⁶ HEATHYARDS BOY [67] (bl) 7-10-8 D Walsh, *pld hrd, al hndy, blun 5th, led 8th, hdd betw last 2, blunded last, one pace*....................(7 to 1 op 10 to 1 tchd 14 to 1) 2

2998⁴ ANOTHER COMEDY [67] 7-10-8 R Johnson, *not fluent, mid-field till hdwy 6 out, blun nxt, lost tch frm 4 out*....................(12 to 1 op 8 to 1) 3

3000 ASTRAL INVASION (USA) [78] 6-11-2 (3°) R Massey, *chsd ldrs, reminders tenth, lost tch aftr 5 out, sn beh*....................(16 to 1 op 12 to 1) 4

2929 AINSI SOIT IL (Fr) [73] (bl) 6-10-11 (3°) D Fortt, *sn led, jmpd slwly and hdd 8th, lost pl nxt, wl beh frm 4 out*....................(9 to 2 op 4 to 1 tchd 5 to 1) 5

2762⁵ ALASKAN HEIR [72] 6-10-13 T Eley, *mstks in rear 4th and 7th, reminders 9th, wl beh frm 5 out*.......(10 to 1 op 8 to 1) 6

3098⁴ TOTAL ASSET [72] (v) 7-10-13 Gary Lyons, *mstk in rear 3rd, improved fnl circuit, disputing 4th but one pace whn f four out*....................(11 to 2 op 5 to 1) f

3107° AFTER THE FOX [87] 10-11-7 (7°,7ex) Mr J Tizzard, *in tch, chlgd tenth, level wth ldr and gng strly whn f 3 out*....................(3 to 1 fav op 2 to 1) f

1498⁷ SWEET BUCK [61] 8-10-21 M Sharratt, *mstk and hmpd 1st, uns rdr nxt*..........................(50 to 1 op 20 to 1) ur

2457 CURRAGH PETER [72] 10-10-10 (3°) Guy Lewis, *mstk 1st, pld up bef nxt*....................(11 to 1 op 8 to 1) pu

Dist: 5l, 22l, 1¼l, 2½l, 2½l. 5m 0.50s. a 16.50s (10 Ran).

(W R J Everall), S A Brookshaw

3268 Strebel Boilers & Radiators Conditional Jockeys' Novices' Handicap Hurdle Class E (0-100 4-y-o and up) £2,316 2m....................(4:20)

2655⁷ KILDRUMMY CASTLE [74] 5-10-5 F Leahy, *chsd ldrs, led 3 out, strly pressed frm nxt, hld on wl*. (20 to 1 tchd 25 to 1) 1

2746 COUNTRY MINSTREL (Ire) [70] 6-10-1 C Rae, *midfield, effrt 3 out, sn pushed alng, ran on strly to go second cl hme*....................(16 to 1 tchd 20 to 1) 2

2957° GALWAY BOSS (Ire) [75] 5-10-6 T Dascombe, *hld up, clr order appr 3 out, pressed ldrs nxt, styd on till no extr close hme*..........................(5 to 1 op 4 to 1) 3

2853⁴ CLIBURNEL NEWS (Ire) [78] 7-10-9 P Henley, *sn pushed alng to cl ▢se ldrs, drvn alng appr 2 out, styd on till one pace aftr la*..........................(12 to 1 op 10 to 1) 4

2927⁷ ▢ [70] 5-10-1 G Lee, *hld up, pushed alng frm 6th, ▢ out, unbl to chal*..........................(9 to 1 op 8 to 1 tchd 10 to 1) 5

2▢ ▢R [85] 6-11-2 Guy Lewis, *sn led, ▢3 out, slight mstk nxt, fdd*....................(9 to 2 op 6 to 1) 6

8 ▢X Aizpuru, *pckd 1st, chsd ldrs ▢tr..*(4 to 1 fav op 5 to 2) 7

▢ l Kavanagh, *in tch, effrt ▢..*..........................(33 to 1) 8

°) J Harris, hld up,

▢p 8 to 1) 9

▢d, cl up ▢o 2) 10

3269 SQ Magazine 'National Hunt' Novices' Hurdle Class D (4-y-o and up) £3,044 2½m 110yds..........(4:50)

2976 DICTUM (Ire) 6-11-2 J Culloty, *chsd ldrs, chlgd last, sn led, ran on strly und pres*..................(9 to 1 op 5 to 1) 1

2954° SILVER THYNE (Ire) 5-11-9 D Leahy, *pld hrd, led and wndrd appr 1st, clr aftr nxt, blun last, sn hdd, rallied wl cl hme*....................(7 to 4 fav op 5 to 4) 2

2724⁷ MAN OF THE MATCH 7-11-2 R Farrant, *nvr far away, chsd ldr 4 out, not fluent nxt, fdd stdly*........(16 to 1 op 12 to 1) 3

2371⁶ POT BLACK UK 6-11-2 J Frost, *hld up, hdwy hfwy, pushed alng and wknd aftr 3 out*..............(12 to 1 op 8 to 1) 4

2879 DAN DE MAN (Ire) 6-11-2 C Maude, *beh, moderate hdwy aftr 4 out, sn lost tch*..................(50 to 1 op 33 to 1) 5

2595⁹ BELLIDIUM 5-10-11 T Kent, *hld up, outpcd 4 out, sn beh*....................(100 to 1 op 50 to 1) 6

SIDNEY 8-11-2 S Wynne, *struggling hfwy, sn wl beh*....................(100 to 1 op 50 to 1) 7

2951 MISTRESS TUDOR 6-10-11 N Mann, *al rear, tld off*....................(100 to 1 op 50 to 1) 8

2972² CHARLEY LAMBERT (Ire) 6-10-13 (3°) E Husband, *hmpd and brght dwn 1st*..................(7 to 2 op 9 to 2) bd

2920³ STRONG TEL (Ire) 7-11-2 A P McCoy, *jinked rght and ran out 1st*..........................(3 to 1 op 5 to 2 tchd 4 to 1) ro

2215⁸ GWITHIAN 5-11-2 J Railton, *hld up, pld up bef 5th*....................(100 to 1 op 50 to 1) pu

2749 KYLE DAVID (Ire) 5-10-13 (3°) Guy Lewis, *chsd ldr to 4th, tld off whn pld up bef 6th*............(100 to 1 op 50 to 1) pu

Dist: Nk, 21l, 4l, 6l, 10l, 12l, 8l. 4m 51.90s. a 12.90s (12 Ran).

SR: 21/28/-/-/-/-/ (Mrs R A Humphries), Miss H C Knight

EXETER (good to firm)
Wednesday March 19th
Going Correction: PLUS 0.40 sec. per fur.

3270 Robert Webb Travel Novices' Selling Hurdle Class G (4 - 7-y-o) £1,940 2¼m....................(2:20)

2603⁸ FLEET CADET (v) 6-10-11 (5°) G Supple, *hld up, wl beh aftr 3rd, steady hdwy after 4 out, led on bit after 2 out, easily*....................(13 to 8 on op 2 to 1 on) 1

3106⁶ ROSE OF GLENN 6-10-11 T Jenks, *hld up, hdwy aftr second, trkd ldr til led after 3 out, sn rdn and unbl to quicken*....................(6 to 1 op 9 to 2) 2

3190 SEMINOLE WIND (v) 6-11-2 B Powell, *led, hdd aftr 3 out, rdn and kpt on one pace...*(16 to 1 op 14 to 1 tchd 20 to 1) 3

3027 PROVE THE POINT (v) 4-10-3 P Holley, *chsd ldrs frm 4th, drvn alng aftr 2 out, kpt on one pace....*(10 to 1 op 7 to 1) 4

ACROSS THE BOW (USA) 7-11-2 G Tormey, *mid-div, chsd ldrs frm 4th, rdn and kpt on one pace frm 2 out*....................(14 to 1 op 7 to 1) 5

3036 RAPID LINER 4-10-8 V Slattery, *hld up, beh 3rd, hdwy aftr 4 out, kpt on one pace*..................(33 to 1 op 16 to 1) 6

3041⁷ DECEIT THE SECOND 5-11-2 S Burrough, *chsd ldrs frm 4th til rdn and wknd aftr 3 out*............(50 to 1) 7

2977 SEVEN CROWNS (USA) (v) 4-10-5 (3°) T Dascombe, *chsd ldrs frm second til wknd aftr 3 out*....................(13 to 1 op 25 to 1 tchd 50 to 1) 8

TALES OF HEARSAY (Ger) 7-10-11 (5°) O Burrows, *hld up, beh second, rdn and wknd aftr 4 out...*(11 to 2 op 9 to 2) 9

3106 CHALCUCHIMA (bl) 4-10-8 J Railton, *chsd ldr to 5th, sn wknd, no ch whn blun and uns rdr last.* (50 to 1 op 25 to 1) ur

3028 BEWELDERED 5-11-2 J Frost, *chsd ldr till wknd quickly aftr 5th, sn tld off, pld up bef 2 out*....................(25 to 1 op 20 to 1 tchd 33 to 1) pu

Dist: 8l, 6l, 7l, ¾l, 2l, 5l, 3½l, 12l. 4m 31.60s. a 32.60s (11 Ran).

(Sir John Swaine), M C Pipe

3271 Axworthys' Ltd. Novices' Handicap Chase Class E (0-100 5-y-o and up) £4,337 2m 7f 110yds..........(2:50)

3023⁸ TRUST DEED (USA) [74] (bl) 9-10-2 (5°) D Salter, *trkd ldr frm 6th, ev ch 7 out, led 3 out, sn clr....*(14 to 1 op 10 to 1) 1

3016⁸ CARDINAL GAYLE (Ire) [67] 7-10-0 R Kavanagh, *hld up, beh 7th, hdwy aftr seven out, chsd ldr frm 3 out, no imprsn*....................(14 to 1 op 12 to 1) 2

2527⁴ CLAYMORE LAD [70] 7-10-3 T J Murphy, *led aftr second, hdd 11th, rdn and rallied after 5 out, styd on one pace*....................(4 to 1 fav tchd 9 to 2) 3

2562 MENDIP PRINCE (Ire) [82] 7-11-1 G Tormey, *hld up, beh 7th, hdwy aftr tenth, kpt on one pace frm 4 out.* (6 to 1 op 9 to 2) 4

2807⁹ GULF OF SIAM [78] 4-10-1 E Husband, *str hold, not fluent, pld rear 6th, sn no dngr*..........(11 to 1 op 8 to 1) 11

3001⁵ OUT OF THE BLUE [69] (v) 5-9-10 (4°) J Mogford, *struggling frm 3 out*..........................(40 to 1 op 33 to 1) 12

2872⁷ THEM TIMES (Ire) [69] 8-9-7 (7°) R Hodges, *wl beh frm 3 out*....................(40 to 1 op 33 to 1) 13

3077 STARLIGHT FOOL [73] (bl) 8-10-0 (4°) W Walsh, *al rear, wl beh frm 3 out, tld off*..............(33 to 1 op 16 to 1) 14

Dist: ½l, ¾l, nk, 1¾l, ¾l, 1½l, 2½l, 2l, 3½l, 12l. 3m 48.30s. a 11.30s (14 Ran).

SR: 12/7/11/13/3/17/23/4/2/ (The Kildrummy Partnership), J G FitzGerald

2748⁴ WINNOW [69] 7-10-2 C Rae, *chsd ldrs til rdn and one pace frm 6 out.*
..................................(9 to 1 op 6 to 1) 5
3023 PURBECK RAMBLER [67] (v) 6-10-0 B Fenton, *chsd ldrs, in tch 7 out, wknd aftr 4 out.* (15 to 2 op 7 to 1 tchd 8 to 1) 6
2738 CHARLIE BEE [67] 8-10-0 B Powell, *beh 7th, sn lost tch, tld off aftr tenth.*......................(33 to 1 op 25 to 1) 7
2726⁷ VOLLEYBALL (Ire) [72] (bl) 8-10-5 M Richards, *hld up, hdwy 9th, led 11th to 3 out, wknd quickly....* (14 to 1 op 25 to 1) 8
2613⁴ DUNLIR [70] 7-10-3¹ S Burrough, *hld up, beh 7th, hdwy tenth, chasing ldrs whn blun and uns rdr 6 out.*
..................................(33 to 1 op 25 to 1) ur
3023⁷ FULL OF BOUNCE (Ire) [94] 6-11-10 (3⁷) T Dascombe, *chsd ldrs frm 7th, 3rd and ev ch whn blun and uns rdr 6 out.*
..................................(7 to 1 op 5 to 1 tchd 15 to 2) ur
3107² MOZEMO [84] 10-11-3 C Maude, *hld up, chsd ldrs frm tenth, sn wknd, beh whn pld up bef 4 out.*
..................................(9 to 2 op 5 to 1 tchd 11 to 2 and 6 to 1) pu
2888 KING'S COURTIER (Ire) [67] 8-10-0 N Mann, *chsd ldrs, wknd aftr 6 out, beh whn pld up bef 4 out....* (33 to 1 op 25 to 1) pu
PHILATELIC (Ire) [85] 6-11-4 J Railton, *hld up, hdwy aftr tenth, chsd ldrs til wknd 4 out, beh whn pld up bef 2 out.*
..................................(14 to 1 op 10 to 1) pu
787 RIVER GALA (Ire) [68] 7-10-1 P Holley, *prmnt, chsd ldrs til wknd quickly aftr 6 out, beh whn pld up bef 4 out.*
..................................(9 to 1 op 7 to 1) pu
Dist: 10l, 2½l, 12l, 1l, ½l, 23l, 15l. 6m 7.70s. a 33.70s (14 Ran).

(Malcolm Enticott), S G Knight

3272 Axworthys' Computer Supplies Handicap Hurdle Class D (0-125 4-y-o and up) £3,034 3¼m....... (3:20)

3116 SNOW BOARD [93] 8-10-9 Derek Byrne, *hld up, steady hdwy aftr 5 out, led 2 out, drvn out and jst held on.*
..................................(9 to 2 op 5 to 1 tchd 6 to 1 and 3 to 2) 1
3120⁴ ST VILLE [93] 11-10-9 (5ex) B Powell, *chsd ldg pair, drvn aftr 5 out, rallied after 3 out, chlgd last, jst hld nr finish.*
..................................(12 to 1 op 10 to 1) 2
3027³ EHTEFAAL (USA) [95] 6-10-11 T J Murphy, *hld up, hdwy aftr 8th, chsd ldrs frm 3 out, rdn and unbl to quicken...* (3 to 1 jt-fav tchd 7 to 2 and 11 to 4) 3
3027⁵ APACHEE FLOWER [84] 7-10-0 G Tormey, *chsd ldg pair, drvn alng 5 out, kpt on one pace frm 3 out.* (16 to 1 tchd 20 to 1) 4
2665⁴ MAID EQUAL [108] 6-11-5 (5⁷) G Supple, *hld up, rdn and hdwy aftr 5 out, sn btn 3 out.* ....(3 to 1 jt-fav op 9 to 4) 5
2896⁸ DERRING BRIDGE [84] 7-9-9 (5⁷) Mr R Thornton, *led 2nd, hdd 5 out, rdn and rallied to ld ag'n aftr 3 out, headed nxt, sn wknd.*
..................................(14 to 1 op 16 to 1) 6
3051 KENDAL CAVALIER [102] (v) 7-11-4 B Fenton, *hld up, beh 7th, no ch frm 4 out.* ....(33 to 1 op 25 to 1) 7
SAME DIFFERENCE (Ire) [97] 9-10-10 (3⁷) D Fortt, *nvr gng wl, struggling frm 6th, tld off whn pld up bef 5 out.*
..................................(25 to 1 op 10 to 1) pu
3037 SECRET BID (Ire) [96] 7-10-12 J R Kavanagh, *hld up, hdwy to chase ldrs aftr 8th, wknd after 3 out, beh whn pld up r-in.*
..................................(14 to 1 op 10 to 1) pu
3066⁴ DOCTOR GREEN (Fr) [113] (v) 4-11-5 M Richards, *led to 3rd, pressed ldr til led ag'n 5 out, hdd aftr 3 out, wknd quickly, pld up r-in...*.....................(8 to 1 op 5 to 1) pu
Dist: Hd, 2½l, 11l, 2½l, 4l, 3½l. 6m 27.10s. a 31.10s (10 Ran).

(F J Sainsbury), Mrs Merrita Jones

3273 Heavitree Brewery Challenge Cup Handicap Chase Class C (0-130 5-y-o and up) £4,919 2¼m....... (3:50)

2774* THUMBS UP [127] 11-11-4 (7⁷) R Hobson, *trkd ldg pair, wnt second 5 out, led 3 out, clr last, rdn out nr finish.*
..................................(9 to 4 op 7 to 4) 1
48² POLDEN PRIDE [113] 9-10-11 B Fenton, *hld up, wnt 3rd and gng wl aftr 4 out, rdn appr last, fnshd strly, too much to do.*
..................................(5 to 2 op 2 to 1 tchd 11 to 4) 2
3038² ALPINE SONG [102] 12-10-0 Miss V Stephens, *pressed ldr, led aftr 4th to 5 out, kpt on one pace frm 3 out.*
..................................(33 to 1 op 20 to 1) 3
2194² FINE HARVEST [122] 11-11-6 T J Murphy, *led til aftr 4th, pressed ldr, led ag'n 5 out to 3 out, sn btn and eased.*
..................................(5 to 4 fav op 6 to 4) 4
Dist: 1¼l, 5l, 18l. 4m 37.30s. a 27.30s (4 Ran).

(Mrs B Taylor), G M McCourt

3274 Robert Webb Travel Hunters' Chase Class H (5-y-o and up) £1,568 3¼m .... (4:20)

TINOTOPS 7-11-10 (7⁷) Miss S Vickery, *trkd ldrs, wnt second 12th, led 6 out to nxt, led ag'n 4 out, mstk 2 out, sn clr, drvn out.*
..................................(5 to 2 op 5 to 2 fav op 5 to 2) 1
2875⁴ SIRISAT 13-11-10 (7⁷) Miss T Blazey, *hld up, hdwy tenth, chsd ldrs frm 6 out, kpt on one pace.* ....(12 to 1 op 10 to 1) 2
2960* THE MALAKARMA 11-12-5 (5⁷) Mr B Pollock, *trkd ldr, led 12th to 6 out, led ag'n 5 out to nxt, sn rdn and unbl to quicken.*
..................................(100 to 30 op 9 to 4) 3
2875⁵ RUSTY BRIDGE 10-12-3 (7⁷) Mr R Burton, *led to 12th, lost pl, rdn and rallied aftr 6 out, kpt on one pace.* (9 to 1 op 6 to 1) 4

BRABAZON (USA) 12-11-10 (7⁷) Mr J Scott, *tld off aftr 5th, styd on one pace after 5 out...*.....(50 to 1 op 25 to 1) 5
BARON'S HEIR 10-11-10 (7⁷) Mr S Lloyd, *hld up, chsd ldrs frm 12th til wknd 4 out....* ....(20 to 1 op 25 to 1) 6
2875⁴ FLY ME (USA) 11-11-10 (7⁷) Miss P Cooper, *blun and uns rdr 1st....*......................(100 to 1 op 66 to 1) ur
3018² FIDDLERS PIKE 16-11-10 (7⁷) Mrs R Henderson, *bright dwn 1st...*....................(14 to 1 op 8 to 1 tchd 16 to 1) bd
MORE MANNERS 12-11-10 (7⁷) Mr J Creighton, *chsd ldrs, mstk 7 out, sn wknd, beh whn pld up aftr 5 out.*
..................................(50 to 1 op 25 to 1 tchd 66 to 1) pu
KNIFEBOARD 11-11-12 (5⁷) Mr A Farrant, *trkd ldrs til wknd aftr 4 out, pld up bef 2 out...........*(25 to 1 op 20 to 1) pu
3109* FULL ALIRT 9-11-12 (7⁷) Miss S Young, *chsd ldrs to 6 out, sn wknd, beh whn pld up bef 4 out.....*(6 to 1 op 5 to 1) pu
MILES MORE FUN 8-11-5 (7⁷) Mr L Jefford, *hld up, pushed alng aftr 7 out, sn wknd, beh whn pld up bef 4 out.*
..................................(4 to 1 op 9 to 2) pu
Dist: 12l, 1l, 14l, 21l, 5l. 6m 52.30s. a 56.30s (12 Ran).

(R H H Targett), Mrs R A Vickery

3275 Robert Webb Travel Handicap Hurdle Class E (0-115 4-y-o and up) £2,444 2¼m................. (4:50)

3039* COOL GUNNER [92] 7-11-10 C Maude, *hld up, cld up aftr 4 out, led on bit appr last, easily.......*(7 to 4 fav op Evens) 1
2878² HANDSON [95] 5-11-3 (5⁷) D Salter, *hld up, cld up aftr 4th, ev ch 3 out, slight ld nxt, sn hdd and unbl to quicken.*
..................................(3 to 1 op 5 to 2 tchd 100 to 30) 2
328⁵ COMMANCHE CREEK [80] 7-10-9 (3⁷) Sophie Mitchell, *led to 2 out, rdn and kpt on one pace.*
..................................(8 to 1 op 7 to 1 tchd 9 to 1) 3
3036⁵ RORY'M (Ire) [68] (bl) 8-9-7 (7⁷) M Griffiths, *chsd ldr, mstk 4th, sn drvn alng and lost pl, tld off aftr nxt.* (66 to 1 op 50 to 1) 4
2558³ BIETSCHHORN BARD [90] (bl) 7-11-5 (3⁷) D Fortt, *trkd ldr, cl second whn f 3 out................*(11 to 4 op 4 to 1) f
3105⁶ CONCINNITY (USA) [68] 8-9-9 (5⁷) G Supple, *blun and uns rdr 1st......................*(33 to 1 op 20 to 1) ur
1956⁵ BORJITO (Spa) [80] 6-10-12 B Fenton, *blun and pld up second.....................*(10 to 1 tchd 8 to 1) pu
Dist: 3l, 4l, dist. 4m 30.00s. a 31.00s (7 Ran).

(Richard Peterson), J S King

LUDLOW (good to firm)
Wednesday March 19th
Going Correction: PLUS 0.05 sec. per fur. (races 1,3,5,7), MINUS 0.20 (2,4,6)

3276 Seifton Claiming Hurdle Class F (4-y-o and up) £2,094 2m....... (2:00)

2744 CHIEF MOUSE 4-11-3 J F Titley, *trkd ldr, led 4 out, rdn out frm last..................*(5 to 4 on op 11 to 10 on tchd Evens) 1
2515 NIGHT BOAT 6-10-13 (3⁷) Guy Lewis, *mid-div, hdwy 4 out, chlgd 2 out, rdn and no imprsn r-in.....* (5 to 1 op 4 to 1) 2
1857 ANLACE 8-10-10 (5⁷) Chris Webb, *mid-div, hdwy 4th, ev ch whn mstk 3 out, rdn and one pace aftr.*
..................................(8 to 1 op 7 to 1 tchd 9 to 1) 3
2676⁷ DR DAVE (Ire) 6-11-8 A Thornton, *pld hrd, chsd ldrs till wknd appr 3 out....................*(12 to 1 op 6 to 1) 4
2532 RE ROI (Ire) 5-10-11 (7⁷) N Willmington, *hld up rear, hdwy 4 out, wknd bef nxt...................*(7 to 1 op 4 to 1) 5
2999⁸ KINGS VISION 5-11-0 D Walsh, *beh whn blun 4th, tld off.*
..................................(50 to 1 op 33 to 1) 6
3099 BOLD TIME MONKEY 6-10-9 C Llewellyn, *al beh, tld off.*
..................................(50 to 1 op 33 to 1) 7
DOUBLE VINTAGE (Ire) 4-10-9 W Worthington, *al beh, tld off 5th......................*(66 to 1 op 33 to 1) 8
3184⁷ VITAL WONDER 9-10-5 (7⁷) X Aizpuru, *pld hrd, led till mstk and hdd 4 out, wknd bef nxt, tld off whn blun and uns rdr last.*
..................................(50 to 1 op 33 to 1) ur
Dist: 2½l, 3l, 10l, 6l, dist, 8l, 20l. 3m 43.60s. a 11.60s (9 Ran).

(Lady Vestey), Miss H C Knight

3277 Banks's Business Builder Handicap Chase Class E (0-115 5-y-o and up) £3,387 3m................. (2:30)

2031⁴ FOXGROVE [-] 11-9-7 (7⁷) X Aizpuru, *al prmnt, led sn aftr 5 out, rdn and wnt clr appr last.*
..................................(16 to 1 op 14 to 1 tchd 20 to 1) 1
1569⁴ TRUMPET [-] 8-11-5 R Johnson, *trkd ldr, led 3rd to 11th, pressed wnr 4 out till wknd appr last.*
..................................(3 to 1 tchd 100 to 30) 2
2781² SCOTONI [-] 11-11-2 A Thornton, *led to 3rd, prmnt till wknd 5 out....................*(9 to 4 tchd 5 to 2) 3
2888⁶ PANT LLIN [-] 11-10-0 R Supple, *hld up, hdwy to ld 11th, rdn and hdd aftr 5 out, sn wknd.*
..................................(10 to 14 to 1 tchd 16 to 1) 4
2729⁵ TOO SHARP [-] 9-11-10 J F Titley, *not jump wl 3rd to 6th, effrt fnl circuit, wknd bef 12th, pld up before nxt.*
..................................(7 to 4 fav op 5 to 4) pu
Dist: 4l, 13l, 5l. 5m 56.10s. a 9.10s (5 Ran).

(Mrs C W Middleton), R J Price

455

3278 Racing Channel Handicap Hurdle Class E (0-115 4-y-o and up) £2,584 2m............................ (3:00)

2973[2]	ABOVE THE CUT (USA) [87] 5-10-12 C Llewellyn, hld up, wnt second appr 3 out, led sn aftr last, readily. ....(15 to 8 fav op 7 to 4 tchd 2 to 1)	
2880[6]	MUIZENBERG [79] 10-10-4 A Thornton, nvr far away, led sn aftr 5th, hit last, soon hdd, one pace. ....(11 to 1 op 10 to 1 tchd 14 to 1)	1
		2
3078[4]	DESERT CALM (Ire) [85] 8-10-8 D Walsh, hld up rear, hdwy 3 out, nvr nr to chal......................... (7 to 1 op 6 to 1)	3
1572[7]	ZINE LANE [100] 5-11-11 R Johnson, hld up, hdwy to go second 4 out, wknd bef nxt. (9 to 2 op 4 to 1 tchd 5 to 1)	4
1798	BRITANNIA MILLS [75] 6-10-0 W Worthington, al beh. .... (33 to 1 op 20 to 1)	5
	LIVE ACTION [99] 10-11-10 J Culloty, mstk second, led 3rd to 5th, wknd quickly nxt, sn tld off........(15 to 2 op 9 to 2)	6
2501	VISION OF FREEDOM (Ire) [92] 9-11-3 R Farrant, pld hrd, led to 3rd, f nxt............................ (6 to 1 op 4 to 1)	f
2778	SWAHILI RUN [80] 9-10-0 (5[*]) D J Kavanagh, prmnt, led briefly 5th, wknd quickly aftr nxt, pld up bef 3 out. ....(25 to 1 op 20 to 1 tchd 33 to 1)	pu

Dist: 1¾l, 18l, ½l, 10l, dist. 3m 39.40s. a 7.40s (8 Ran).
SR: 18/8/-/10/-/ (J P M & J W Cook), C P Morlock

3279 Magnus-Allcroft Memorial Trophy Hunters' Chase Class H (6-y-o and up) £1,642 2½m.............. (3:30)

	BLUE CHEEK 11-11-11 (7[*]) Mr N Bradley, made virtually all, drw clr frm 2 out......... (9 to 2 op 5 to 1 tchd 6 to 1)	1
	LANDSKER MISSILE 8-11-9 (7[*]) Mr E Williams, chsd wnr thrght, hld whn blun 2 out, not reco'r. (12 to 1 tchd 14 to 1)	2
2992[2]	MINELLA EXPRESS (Ire) 8-12-0 (7[*]) Miss C Spearing, al prmnt, one pace appr 4 out........(9 to 4 fav tchd 5 to 2)	3
41[*]	TUFFNUT GEORGE 10-12-0 (7[*]) Mr A Phillips, in tch, hdwy 8th, mstk 11th, no ch frm 5 out.......... (13 to 2 op 6 to 1)	4
	GREAT GUSTO 11-11-11 (7[*]) Miss L Blackford, hld up rear, hdwy 11th, one pace appr 4 out. ....(9 to 1 op 10 to 1 tchd 8 to 1)	5
	SIMPLY PERFECT 11-11-7 (7[*]) Mr K Swindells, beh, nvr on terms.......................... (16 to 1 op 14 to 1)	6
2556	RAMSTAR 9-12-2 (5[*]) Miss P Curling, chsd ldrs, mstk 5th, wknd 11th............................... (10 to 1 tchd 11 to 1)	7
2897	KING OF SHADOWS 10-11-11 (7[*]) Mr S Prior, chsd ldrs till wknd 12th............................. (33 to 1 op 25 to 1)	8
	KINO 10-11-7 (7[*]) Mr Andrew Martin, al beh. ....(9 to 1 op 10 to 1 tchd 8 to 1)	9
2974[5]	AL HASHIMI 13-11-7 (7[*]) Mr N Ridout, mid-div till wknd 12th. .... (33 to 1)	10
	FAMILIAR FRIEND (bl) 11-12-0 (7[*]) Mr L Lay, mid-div, wknd 5 out, tld off................ (16 to 1 op 14 to 1 tchd 20 to 1)	11
3109	GREAT POKEY 12-11-7 (7[*]) Miss N Courtenay, slwly away, tld off 3rd............................. (25 to 1 op 20 to 1)	12
	MAJIC BELLE (bl) 9-11-2 (7[*]) Mr A Wintle, f second. .... (66 to 1 tchd 100 to 1)	f
	STYLISH GENT 10-11-7 (7[*]) Mr A Dalton, blun and uns rdr 4th................................... (66 to 1 op 50 to 1)	ur
2790	MHEMEANLES 7-11-7 (7[*]) Mr A Gribbin, chsd ldrs to 9th, wkng whn blun and uns rdr 11th..... (66 to 1 op 50 to 1)	ur
	WINTER'S LANE 13-11-7 (7[*]) Capt D Alers-Hankey, beh, hit and pld up bef 12th................ (33 to 1 op 50 to 1)	pu
2974	THE COMMUNICATOR (bl) 11-11-9 (5[*]) Mr C Vigors, rear whn pld up aftr 9th....................... (50 to 1)	pu
	HENNERWOOD OAK 7-11-2 (7[*]) Mr M Munrowd, mstk 4th, al beh, tld off whn pld up 8th.....(16 to 1 op 14 to 1)	pu

Dist: 16l, 4l, 10l, hd, 8l, ½l, 3l, 2½l, 1¾l, 6l. 4m 53.60s. a 4.60s (18 Ran).
SR: 18/-/1/-/-/-/ (Mrs B Graham), J Mahon

3280 Banks's Leases And Tenancies Juvenile Novices' Hurdle Class F (4-y-o) £2,696 2m............... (4:00)

3035[3]	CRANDON BOULEVARD 10-12 J Culloty, trkd ldr, led appr 3 out, rdn out................... (3 to 1 jt-fav op 2 to 1)	1
2773[2]	SULAWESI (Ire) 10-7 C Llewellyn, trkd ldrs, mstk 4 out, wnt second sn aftr 3 out, hit nxt, one pace. ....(100 to 30 op 5 to 2 tchd 4 to 1)	2
2952[3]	NOBLE COLOURS 10-7 (5[*]) D J Kavanagh, hld up rear, hdwy 4 out, styd on......................... (10 to 1)	3
2575[*]	MEG'S MEMORY (Ire) 11-0 T Eley, in tch till wknd appr 3 out. ....(3 to 1 jt-fav tchd 100 to 30)	4
3044[6]	DOWN THE YARD 10-7 W Worthington, beh, nvr on terms. ....(16 to 1 op 10 to 1)	5
3022[8]	GREEN BOPPER (USA) 10-12 R Johnson, al beh....(25 to 1)	6
3028[6]	WHITE PLAINS (Ire) 10-12 D Walsh, led till appr 3 out, wknd rpdly, eased, tld off........... (7 to 2 op 5 to 2)	7
3044[9]	AFRICAN SUN (Ire) 10-12 R Supple, al beh, tld off. ....(66 to 1 op 33 to 1)	8

Dist: 3l, 4l, 13l, 8l, 3l, 21l, 1l. 3m 41.40s. a 9.40s (8 Ran).
(Ms S Morris), Mrs J Pitman

3281 Aston Munslow Novices' Chase Class D (5-y-o and up) £3,371 2½m

---

.... (4:30)

3098	MR SNAGGLE (Ire) 8-11-2 R Johnson, hld up rear, hdwy 8th, cl 3rd 5 out, wnt second nxt, lft clr and mstk 2 out, rdn out. ....(4 to 1 op 7 to 2 tchd 5 to 1)	1
2896[4]	FAWLEY FLYER 8-11-2 A Thornton, al prmnt, led tenth to 5 out, hit nxt, btn whn lft second 2 out. ....(4 to 6 fav op 2 to 1 tchd 3 to 1)	2
2991[3]	PRIZE MATCH 8-10-11 S McNeill, chsd ldrs till wknd aftr 5 out......................... (8 to 1 op 6 to 1)	3
1555[8]	SPORTING FIXTURE (Ire) 6-10-13 (3[*]) R Massey, blun 4th, sn beh.................... (40 to 1 op 33 to 1 tchd 50 to 1)	4
2761	RIVERBANK RED (v) 6-10-8 (3[*]) Guy Lewis, not fluent, lost tch 5 out, tld off........................ (33 to 1)	f
2578[7]	GUTTERIDGE (Ire) 7-11-2 D Walsh, mstk second, sn prmnt, led 5 out, 2 ls clr whn f two out.........(5 to 1 op 6 to 1)	f
1916	KNOWING 10-10-11 Miss E James, al beh, tld off whn pld up bef 2 out............... (50 to 1 op 33 to 1)	pu
2601	WESTCOTE LAD 8-11-2 C Llewellyn, prmnt whn mstk 4th, blun 12th, sn wknd, pld up bef 2 out.... (6 to 1 tchd 7 to 1)	pu
3038	TRAIL BOSS (Ire) 6-11-2 J F Titley, led to tenth, wknd quickly, pld up bef 12th, broke blood vessel. ....(11 to 2 op 4 to 1 tchd 6 to 1)	pu

Dist: 6l, 24l, 5l. 4m 56.00s. a 7.00s (9 Ran).
(The Plum Merchants), Simon Earle

3282 Ludlow Standard Open National Hunt Flat Class H (4,5,6-y-o) £1,329 2m............................ (5:00)

	MAYDAY LAUREN 5-10-13 S Wynne, al prmnt, led o'r 2 fs out, drw clr................ (5 to 1 op 7 to 2 tchd 6 to 1)	1
2377	SANDVILLE LAD 5-11-1 (3[*]) Guy Lewis, led till o'r 2 fs out, one pace..........................(50 to 1 op 33 to 1)	2
	RAJADORA 5-10-13 A Thornton, hld up in tch, hdwy 6 fs out, ev ch 3 out, kpt on one pace. ....(10 to 1 op 6 to 1 tchd 12 to 1)	3
	MAZILEO 4-10-3 (7[*]) F Bogle, hld up in tch, hdwy hfwy, ev ch whn came wide into hme strt, styd on. ....(10 to 1 op 6 to 1 tchd 12 to 1)	4
	DIAMOND HALL 4-10-10 R Johnson, hld up, hdwy 5 fs out, wknd 2 out..................(3 to 1 op 6 to 1 tchd 8 to 1)	5
3082[6]	HOMME DE FER 5-10-11 (7[*]) C Scudder, prmnt till wknd 5 fs out.............(11 to 8 fav op 11 to 10 on tchd 6 to 4)	6
	TEAL BAY 5-10-6 (7[*]) X Aizpuru, hld up rear, hdwy hfwy, wknd 4 fs out.......................(9 to 1 op 5 to 1 tchd 10 to 1)	7
2810[6]	WHAT THE DEVIL 4-10-5 W Worthington, chsd ldrs, lost tch hfwy.............................(20 to 1 op 33 to 1)	8
	COMMANCHE CUP (Ire) 4-10-10 D Walsh, unruly and uns rdr bef strt, al beh, tld off............. (20 to 1 op 12 to 1)	9
2961	MISS KILWORTH (Ire) 6-10-10 (3[*]) R Massey, al rear, tld off. ....(50 to 1 op 33 to 1)	10
	PECAN PRINCESS (Ire) 4-10-5 Mrs D Smith, al beh, tld off. ....(33 to 1 op 16 to 1)	11

Dist: 4l, hd, hd, 1¼l, 12l, 3l, ¾l, 7l, 14l, 6l. 3m 36.50s. (11 Ran).
(B K Racing), A Bailey

TOWCESTER (good to firm)
Wednesday March 19th
Going Correction: PLUS 0.10 sec. per fur. (races 1,3,5,7), PLUS 0.25 (2,4,6)

3283 Grafton Amateur Riders' Selling Hurdle Class G (4 - 7-y-o) £1,824 2m .... (2:10)

2637	DERRYBELLE 6-10-13 (7[*]) Mr S Durack, patiently rdn, improved hfwy, led 2 out, ridden clr. (33 to 1 tchd 40 to 1)	1
3184[*]	HANGING GROVE (Ire) 7-11-10 (7[*],6ex) Mr Matthew Wells, prmnt, hit 4th, pckd 2 out, chsd wnr last, no imprsn. ....(11 to 4 op 9 to 4)	2
2804[5]	BOY BLAKENEY 4-10-10 (7[*]) Mr C Mulhall, beh, hdwy appr 2 out, styd on approaching last, nvr nrr. ....(9 to 4 fav op 2 to 1 tchd 5 to 2)	3
2777[7]	PAULA'S BOY (Ire) 7-11-4 (7[*]) Miss K Di Marte, trkd ldrs, rdn frm 5th, wknd betw frnl 2............ (40 to 1 op 20 to 1)	4
2653	ROYAL HAND (v) 7-11-4 (7[*]) Mr R Armson, in tch, chsd ldr frm 3rd, led nxt, sn clr, hdd and wknd 2 out.	5
2766[3]	SPRIG MUSLIN (v) 5-11-1 (5[*]) Miss P Jones, led to 4th, wknd frm 3 out....................(3 to 1 op 5 to 2)	6
	CURRA MINSTRAL (Ire) 7-10-13 (7[*]) Mr J Ryan, beh frm 5th. ....(33 to 1 tchd 40 to 1)	7
3137	TEOROMA 7-11-4 (7[*]) Mr M Gingell, nvr trbld ldrs. ....(16 to 1 tchd 25 to 1 and 14 to 1)	8
1921[9]	WEB OF STEEL (bl) 7-11-4 (7[*]) Miss A Dudley, mid-div, effrt 3 out, 6th and no ch whn f last. Dead. ....(33 to 1 op 25 to 1 tchd 40 to 1)	f
2263	RAKAPOSHI IMP 7-10-13 (7[*]) Miss B Small, veered lft and uns rdr 1st.............. (40 to 1 op 33 to 1 tchd 50 to 1)	ur
2999[6]	HALLAM TARN (Ire) 7-11-10 (7[*]) Mr A Charles-Jones, hld up, improved hfwy, wknd 3 out, tld off whn pld up bef 2 out. ....(11 to 2 op 4 to 1 tchd 6 to 1)	pu

Dist: 6l, 1½l, 4l, 1½l, 15l, 12l, 30l. 3m 58.30s. a 15.30s (11 Ran).
(Miss B W Palmer), D L Williams

3284 Alex Lawrie Novices' Chase Class D (5-y-o and up) £3,465 2m 110yds
.... (2:40)

2450 GROOVING (Ire) 8-11-9 R Dunwoody, hld up, blun 4th, hdwy 7th, not fluent nxt, led and hit 2 out, sn clr, easily.
.... (11 to 10 on op 5 to 4 on tchd Evens) 1
2976⁴ SLEAZEY 6-11-2 S Curran, hit 4th, chsd ldr, led 9th, hdd 2 out, no extr................ (20 to 1 op 16 to 1 tchd 25 to 1) 2
2938² JUST BRUCE 8-11-9 D Gallagher, sn led, hdd 9th, wknd appr 2 out................... (5 to 2 op 2 to 1 tchd 11 to 4) 3
2955⁴ AMBER VALLEY (USA) 6-10-9 (7*) Mr S Durack, strted slwly, hld up, in tch 4th whn f 3 out, rmntd, tld off. (7 to 2 op 5 to 2) 4
Dist: 12l, 4l, dist. 4m 8.30s. a 11.30s (4 Ran).
SR: 22/3/6/-/ (Mrs T Brown), J T Gifford

3285 British Bakels Handicap Hurdle Class D (0-120 4-y-o and up) £2,945 2m 5f...................(3:10)

2923⁴ THE TOISEACH (Ire) [109] (v) 6-11-11 J Osborne, made all, hit 4th, rdn and ran on wl frm 2 out................(11 to 4 jt-fav op 5 to 2 tchd 3 to 1) 1
3021* WASSL STREET (Ire) [102] 5-11-4 R Dunwoody, chsd wnr, effrt appr 2 out, sn one pace..(11 to 4 jt-fav tchd 5 to 2) 2
2629⁷ BOB'S PLOY [84] 5-9-13² (3*) P Henley, hld up, hdwy 6th, rdn and one pace appr 2 out.. (7 to 1 op 5 to 1 tchd 8 to 1) 3
3045⁶ NO FIDDLING (Ire) [87] (v) 6-10-3 D Bridgwater, hld up, not fluent and reminder 3rd, hit 8th, moderate prog frm 3 out, no imprsn..................(3 to 1 op 9 to 4) 4
822⁴ CABOCHON [90] 10-10-6 D Skyrme, hld up, hdwy 5th, beh frm 8th, no ch whn mstk 2 out.
.... (20 to 1 op 14 to 1 tchd 25 to 1) 5
3140² THIS NETTLE DANGER [84] 13-10-0 M Brennan, hld up, hdwy 8th, wknd appr 3 out. (7 to 1 op 6 to 1 tchd 8 to 1) 6
Dist: 7l, 2½l, 9l, 18l, 20l. 5m 9.80s. a 10.80s (6 Ran).
SR: 10/-/-/ (T & J Vestey), J R Fanshawe

3286 Julian Belfrage Memorial Handicap Chase Class C (0-130 5-y-o and up) £4,435 3m 1f.................. (3:40)

3121² HARRISTOWN LADY [105] (bl) 10-10-3 B Clifford, nvr far away, jmpd slwly second, led 11th, made rst, clr frm 4 out, unchlgd................(100 to 30 op 7 to 1 tchd 7 to 2) 1
2979² FAST THOUGHTS [102] 10-10-0 J Osborne, led, jmpd slwly 3rd, not fluent nxt and tenth, hdd 11th, outpcd appr 4 out, took moderate second last.
.... (11 to 8 fav op 6 to 4 tchd 13 to 8) 2
3138 REAPERS ROCK [102] 10-9-7 (7*) R Wilkinson, prmnt, outpcd by wnr 4 out, lost second pl last, fdd.... (10 to 1 op 7 to 1) 3
2850⁵ STRATH HOYAL [130] 11-12-0 M Brennan, hld up, reminders aftr 9th, mstks 12th and nxt, sn wknd, tld off.
.... (2 to 1 tchd 9 to 4 and 7 to 4) 4
Dist: 15l, 4l, 25l. 6m 23.10s. a 11.10s (4 Ran).
SR: 26/8/4/7/ (Roger J Spencer), G B Balding

3287 Hartwell Land Rover Novices' Handicap Hurdle Class E (0-100 4-y-o and up) £2,495 2m.................. (4:10)

3110⁴ DISSOLVE [77] 5-10-6 (7*) Mr L Baker, chsd clr ldr, led 2 out, rdn out and ran on wl................... (7 to 1 op 5 to 1) 1
1928 POSITIVO [72] 6-10-8 D Leahy, hld up, hdwy appr 2 out, chsd wnr last, kpt on................... (10 to 1 op 7 to 1) 2
2952² MR POPPLETON [72] 8-10-8 L Harvey, led to 2 out, no extr.
..................(6 to 1 op 5 to 1) 3
2625* APACHE PARK (USA) [96] 4-11-10 D J Burchell, hld up beh ldrs, effrt frm 3 out, one pace 2 out.
.... (5 to 1 op 3 to 2 tchd 6 to 1) 4
3128⁴ FERRERS [85] 6-11-7 W Marston, hld up beh ldrs, clr order appr 4th, effrt approaching 3 out, wknd frm nxt.
.... (5 to 2 fav op 9 to 4 tchd 3 to 1) 5
3157⁴ MILLERS GOLDENGIRL (Ire) [65] 6-9-8 (7*) R Wilkinson, dsptd second till appr 3 out, sn wknd.
.... (12 to 1 op 10 to 1 tchd 14 to 1) 6
2395 ROMANY BLUES [66] 8-10-2 D Gallagher, hld up, rdn alng frm 4th, btn aftr nxt.............(16 to 1 op 14 to 1) 7
2607⁵ FAIRELAINE [78] 5-11-0 C O'Dwyer, hld up, rdn alng 4th, no dngr..................(11 to 2 op 9 to 2 tchd 6 to 1) 8
2937 BALLY WONDER [64] 5-10-0 J Supple, nvr on terms.
.... (33 to 1 op 20 to 1) 9
Dist: 1½l, 1¾l, ¾l, 9l, 11l, 5l, 21l, 14l. 3m 52.00s. a 9.00s (9 Ran).
SR: 11/4/2/17/5/- (Western Solvents Ltd), N M Lampard

3288 Empress Elizabeth Of Austria Open Hunters' Chase Class H (5-y-o and up) £1,605 2¾m............. (4:40)

2897 STAR OATS 11-11-7 (7*) Mr A Kinane, hld up, hdwy to ld 2 out, rdn out and styd on wl.... (7 to 1 op 10 to 1 tchd 4 to 1) 1
3076⁵ HICKELTON LAD 13-11-11 (7*) Mr S Durack, led aftr 1st to 5th, ev ch appr 2 out, kpt on same pace r-in.
.... (7 to 2 op 4 to 1 tchd 4 to 1) 2

2981⁴ BOLLINGER 11-11-7 (7*) Mr P O'Keeffe, hld up, hdwy to chase ldr frm 9th till hit nxt, sn outpcd, rallied 3 out, one pace next......................... (7 to 4 on op 5 to 2 on) 3
2790 CHARLIES DELIGHT (Ire) 9-11-9 (5*) Mr A Sansome, led till aftr 1st, rgned ld 5th, hdd 2 out, sn btn.
.... (8 to 1 op 10 to 1 tchd 14 to 1) 4
Dist: 4l, 1½l, 4l. 5m 48.50s. a 22.50s (4 Ran).
(Hayden Phillips), Mrs R M Lampard

3289 Letheby & Christopher 'National Hunt' Novices' Hurdle Class E (4-y-o and up) £2,722 2m 5f........ (5:10)

2725⁷ STORMYFAIRWEATHER (Ire) 5-11-2 M A Fitzgerald, confidently rdn beh ldrs, led betw fnl 2, ridden out and edgd lft r-in.
.... (2 to 1 op 9 to 4 tchd 5 to 2) 1
2980* LORD ROOBLE (Ire) 6-11-8 P Hide, led, hdd betw fnl 2, unbl to quicken r-in................ (5 to 4 fav op 7 to 4 on) 2
2951⁵ FASHION MAKER (Ire) 7-11-2 L Harvey, hld up in tch, hdwy to chase ldr appr 7th to 3 out, sn wknd, tld off.
.... (5 to 2 op 3 to 1 tchd 7 to 2) 3
2288 CORRIMULZIE (Ire) (v) 6-11-2 W Fry, dsptd second to 7th, sn rdn, wknd appr 3 out, tld off......(33 to 1 op 14 to 1) 4
2920 PRESTIGIOUS MAN (Ire) 6-11-2 W Marston, chsd ldr till appr 7th, sn wknd, tld off......(33 to 1 op 20 to 1) 5
SILVER SPINNEY 6-10-11 D Gallagher, sn tld off, pld up bef 3 out................ (33 to 1 tchd 50 to 1) pu
Dist: 1¼l, dist, dist, dist. 5m 13.70s. a 14.70s (6 Ran).
(Mrs Christopher Hanbury), N J Henderson

PLUMPTON (good to firm)
Thursday March 20th
Going Correction: NIL

3290 Pease Pottage Novices' Hurdle Class E (4-y-o and up) £2,826 2½m
.... (2:25)

2636² EAU DE COLOGNE 5-11-2 M Richards, chsd clr ldr, led 3 out, rdn alng and styd on wl... (2 to 1 op 6 to 4 tchd 9 to 4) 1
3108³ LORD MILLS (Ire) 6-11-2 T J Murphy, hld up in tch, cld 7th, chsd wnr frm 3 out and sn shaken up, ev ch nxt, one pace whn hit last..........(Evens fav op 6 to 4 tchd 7 to 4) 2
3028⁸ PROTOTYPE 6-11-2 D Gallagher, hld up, hdwy aftr 8th, one pace appr 2 out......(16 to 1 op 8 to 1 tchd 20 to 1) 3
2614² MAYLIN MAGIC 6-10-11 D Bridgwater, chsd ldrs, pushed alng 8th, no imprsn appr 3 out.
.... (7 to 1 op 5 to 1 tchd 15 to 2) 4
2929 KYBO'S REVENGE (Ire) 6-11-2 D O'Sullivan, trkd ldrs to 7th, lost pl, kpt on frm last............(20 to 1 op 12 to 1) 5
2636 CLOCK WATCHERS 9-11-2 D Morris, led, clr 5th, blun badly and hdd 3 out, sn btn..(66 to 1 op 33 to 1 tchd 100 to 1) 6
3098 BENJI 6-11-2 J A McCarthy, trkd ldrs till outpcd frm 4 out.
.... (66 to 1 op 25 to 1 tchd 100 to 1) 7
PHILISITATE 8-10-8 (3*) P Henley, hld up, al rear.
.... (66 to 1 op 33 to 1) 8
2303 JAMIES FIRST (Ire) 4-10-0 (7*) B Dove, pld hrd rear, al beh, tld off...............(66 to 1 op 33 to 1 tchd 100 to 1) 9
3091⁷ KNOT TRUE 7-10-11 A McCabe, not fluent rear, nvr on terms, tld off........(50 to 1 op 25 to 1 tchd 66 to 1) 10
3035 NEARLY ALL RIGHT 8-11-2 S Curran, trkd ldrs, pushed alng and wknd aftr 8th, tld off.
.... (66 to 1 op 50 to 1 tchd 100 to 1) 11
2980 KING'S AFFAIR 7-10-9 (7*) M Clinton, hld up, stumbled aftr 1st, pushed alng aftr 5th, tld off whn pld up bef 4 out.
.... (50 to 1 op 33 to 1) pu
Dist: 3½l, 7l, 8l, 16l, 3½l, 9l, 1¼l, 12l, 3½l, 22l. 4m 48.80s. a 11.80s (12 Ran).
(D And M Evans), Mrs L Richards

3291 Cuckfield Handicap Chase Class F (0-105 5-y-o and up) £2,887 2m 5f
.... (2:55)

3094* REGAL AURA (Ire) [76] 7-10-0 (6ex) W Marston, led to 3rd, led 9th to nxt, led 11th, drvn alng aftr 4 out, kpt on und pres.
.... (5 to 1 op 7 to 2 tchd 11 to 2) 1
SUFFOLK ROAD [102] 10-11-12 D O'Sullivan, trkd ldrs till lost pl tenth, styd on aftr 3 out, chsd wnr appr last, no extr.
.... (9 to 1 op 5 to 1 tchd 13 to 2) 2
2955 JOVIAL MAN (Ire) [95] 8-11-5 J Osborne, trkd ldrs, pushed alng and lost pl aftr 11th, styd on appr last.
.... (8 to 8 fav op 6 to 4 tchd 13 to 8) 3
2767 OXFORD QUILL [77] 10-10-1 D Morris, hld up beh, mstk tenth, hdwy 12th, chsd wnr 3 out till aftr nxt, wknd.
.... (12 to 1 op 8 to 1 tchd 14 to 1) 4
3050* PARLIAMENTARIAN (Ire) [82] (bl) 8-10-6 J A McCarthy, led 3rd, blun 8th, hdd nxt, led briefly 10th, mstk next, lost pl 3 out, wknd..................(10 to 1 op 7 to 1) 5
2991⁴ SALCOMBE HARBOUR (NZ) [76] 13-10-0 Dr P Pritchard, in tch, struggling whn mstk in rear 12th, pld up bef last.
.... (50 to 1 op 33 to 1) pu
2355 YOUNG ALFIE [77] (bl) 12-9-13¹ (3*) P Henley, al beh, lost tch 6th, pld up bef last.......(100 to 1 op 33 to 1) pu
3021³ SIMPLY (Ire) [99] 8-11-9 D Bridgwater, hld up, pushed alng in rear 9th, pld up aftr nxt..........(6 to 1 op 5 to 1) pu

Dist: 6l, 4l, 5l, 10l. 5m 18.20s. a 12.20s (8 Ran).

(Mrs V Costello & Mrs V O'Brien), D C O'Brien

3292 March Selling Handicap Hurdle
Class G (0-90 4-y-o and up) £2,111
2m 1f............................(3:25)

3163[2] GENERAL SHIRLEY (Ire) [75] 6-10-11 (7*) M Clinton, hld up
rear, keen hold early, hdwy 4 out, led aftr nxt, ran on wl.
.......................(11 to 4 jt-fav op 7 to 4) 1
2977 SCALP 'EM (Ire) [57] 9-10-0 Dr P Pritchard, al hndy chasing
grp, ev ch appr 2 out, one pace approaching last.
.......................(25 to 1 op 20 to 1 tchd 50 to 1) 2
3028[3] VANBOROUGH LAD [68] 8-10-11 J Osborne, hld up rear, gd
hdwy aftr 3 out, no imprsn frm nxt.
.......................(9 to 1 op 6 to 1 tchd 10 to 1) 3
3174[5] ANIF (USA) [57] 6-10-0 D Skyrme, hld up, cld 4 out, hrd rdn
appr 2 out, one pace und press......(11 to 2 tchd 14 to 1) 4
3099[5] BATTLESHIP BRUCE [81] 5-11-5 (5*) S Ryan, hld up, hdwy
appr 3 out, sn drvn alng, btn nxt.
.......................(7 to 1 op 4 to 1 tchd 8 to 1) 5
3091[4] ZADOK [65] (bl) 5-10-5 (3*) P Henley, hld up beh, pushed alng
aftr 5th, drpd rear 4 out, styd on frm last.
.......................(5 to 1 op 9 to 2 tchd 6 to 1) 6
3119 HIGH BURNSHOT [59] 10-10-2 D Leahy, led, clr second,
mstk 3 out and hdd, sn btn..........(14 to 1 op 20 to 1) 7
2424 TOMAL [70] 5-10-13 D Gallagher, hld up rear, not jump wl,
mstk and drvn 6th, no response, tld off, fnshd lme (11 to 4 jt-
fav op 11 to 4) 8
2426[8] NISHAMAN [67] 6-10-10 P McLoughlin, chsd ldrs till wknd
appr 3 out, tld off......(16 to 1 op 12 to 1 tchd 20 to 1) 9
3170 TIGANA [57] 5-10-0 S Curran, cl up chasing grp, mstk 4th,
pushed alng and wknd aftr 6th, tld off.
.......................(50 to 1 op 33 to 1 tchd 66 to 1) 10
Dist: 5l, 6l, 2½l, 4l, 2½l, 3l, 22l, 4l, 1¾l. 4m 6.70s. a 9.70s (10 Ran).

(P R Hedger), P R Hedger

3293 Weatherbys Data Services Novices'
Chase Class E (5-y-o and up) £2,906
2m............................(4:00)

2950* FLIGHT LIEUTENANT (USA) 8-12-0 D Bridgwater, chsd clr
ldr, reminder 7th, cld nxt, blun 4 out, pushed alng and
checked bend into strt, led aftr 2 out, drvn out.
(4 to 1 on op 5 to 1 on tchd 6 to 1 on and 7 to 2 on) 1
2978 ROBINS PRIDE (Ire) 7-10-11 (5*) Mr R Thornton, mstk 3rd,
chsd clr ldr, cld 8th, led 4 out to aftr 2 out, no extr.
.......................(7 to 2 op 4 to 1 tchd 5 to 1) 2
2978[3] MHEANMETOO 6-10-9 (7*) Mr S Durack, led, clr to 8th, hdd 4
out, sn wknd.......................(50 to 1 op 20 to 1) 3
1811[6] FRUIT TOWN (Ire) 8-11-2 T J Murphy, tld off 4th.
.......................(33 to 1 op 16 to 1 tchd 40 to 1) 4
2738* TIN PAN ALLEY 8-10-13 (3*) P Henley, blun and uns rdr 3rd.
.......................(33 to 1 op 20 to 1 tchd 40 to 1) ur
Dist: 4l, 25l, dist. 3m 59.10s. a 7.10s (5 Ran).

SR: 29/13/ (Mrs Laura Pegg), T Casey

3294 Hailsham Handicap Chase Class F
(0-100 5-y-o and up) £2,937 3m 1f
110yds............................(4:30)

3024[4] BLACK CHURCH [97] 11-11-12 D O'Sullivan, hld up, jmpd
into ld 5 out, very easily........(5 to 2 on op 5 to 1 on) 1
3175 JOKER JACK [71] 12-10-0 D Leahy, trkd ldr, led 8th to 5 out,
kpt on, no ch wth wnr...(14 to 1 op 12 to 1 tchd 16 to 1) 2
2613 PINOCCIO [72] 10-10-1 W Marston, led to 8th, reminders
14th, sn wknd, tld off......................(7 to 1 op 10 to 1) 3
2679 SHARROW BAY (NZ) [71] 10-10-0 R Greene, drpd rear 7th, tld
off whn blun 15th, pld up bef 4 out......(7 to 1 op 10 to 1) pu
Dist: 4l. dist. 6m 33.50s. a 19.50s (4 Ran).

(Dr B Alexander), R Rowe

3295 Lewes Amateur Riders' Handicap
Hurdle Class F (0-105 4-y-o and up)
£2,193 2½m............................(5:00)

3095[3] KELLY MAC [89] 7-11-5 (5*) Mr R Thornton, cl up, led 4 out,
drvn alng appr 2 out, kpt on wl.
.......................(11 to 4 op 5 to 2 tchd 7 to 2) 1
3099[2] ALWAYS GREENER (Ire) [82] 6-10-10 (7*) Mr P O'Keeffe, led
aftr 3rd till 5th, cl up, ev ch 2 out till appr last, no extr.
.......................(2 to 1 fav op 11 to 10 tchd 9 to 4) 2
2932[5] KING'S GOLD [73] 7-10-1 (7*) Miss S Vickery, pld hrd, led till
aftr 3rd, led 5th to 4 out, one pace after nxt.
.......................(5 to 1 op 6 to 1 tchd 9 to 2) 3
3036 MR LOVELY (Ire) [68] (bl) 6-9-10 (7*) Mr O McPhail, hld up in
tch, pushed alng 7th, drvn and outpcd aftr 4 out, not pace to
chal.......................(16 to 1 op 10 to 1 tchd 25 to 1) 4
251[6] PRINCE OF SPADES [66] 5-10-0[6] (7*) Mr G Shenkin, hld up,
cld 7th, hrd rdn and ev ch appr 2 out, sn wknd.
.......................(9 to 2 op 6 to 1 tchd 10 to 1) 5
BAYLORD PRINCE (Ire) [65] 9-9-7 (7*) Mr J Goldstein, beh,
cld 7th, sn struggling...(33 to 1 op 25 to 1 tchd 40 to 1) 6
2558[8] MAZIRAH [80] 6-10-10[2] (7*) Mr M Appleby, pld hrd, in tch till
wknd appr 3 out.......................(7 to 1 op 8 to 1 tchd 10 to 1) 7

3164 GONE FOR LUNCH [85] 6-11-2[3] (7*) Mr M Gingell, trkd ldrs
till drpd rear 8th, tld off whn pld up bef 2 out.
.......................(25 to 1 op 10 to 1 tchd 33 to 1) pu
Dist: 2½l, 6l, 7l, 1½l, 10l, 1¼l. 4m 52.50s. a 15.50s (8 Ran).

(Mrs V O'Brien), D C O'Brien

WINCANTON (good to firm)
Thursday March 20th
Going Correction: MINUS 0.25 sec. per fur.

3296 British Field Sports Society Maiden
Hurdle Class F (4-y-o and up) £2,477
2m............................(2:15)

2893[4] MIDNIGHT LEGEND 6-11-3 R Johnson, pressed ldr, led appr
2 out, jmpd lft last, rdn out......(7 to 4 on tchd 6 to 4 on) 1
3028[4] EMBANKMENT (Ire) 7-11-2 M A Fitzgerald, hld up mid-div,
smooth hdwy 3 out, jnd wnr nxt, not quicken r-in.
.......................(10 to 1 op 7 to 1) 2
3028[2] RING OF VISION (Ire) 5-11-2 R Dunwoody, al prmnt, rdn and
one pace frm 2 out......(13 to 2 op 5 to 1 tchd 7 to 1) 3
3022[3] NORDANCE PRINCE (Ire) 6-10-11 (5*) A Bates, hdwy to
chase ldrs 5th, one pace frm 2 out.
.......................(7 to 1 op 5 to 1 tchd 8 to 1) 4
3028[5] PIPER'S ROCK (Ire) 6-10-10[1] (7*) Mr A Balding, led till appr 2
out, sn btn.......................(33 to 1 op 14 to 1) 5
2656[5] HE KNOWS THE RULES 5-11-2 B Powell, hld up, effrt appr 2
out, sn btn whn blun last..........(20 to 1 op 7 to 1) 6
2725[6] OVER THE WATER (Ire) 5-11-2 A Thornton, cl up till wknd
appr 2 out.......................(33 to 1 op 16 to 1) 7
1673 DERRING JACK 6-10-13 (3*) R Massey, mid-div, mstk 3rd,
effrt 6th, wknd appr nxt. (40 to 1 op 20 to 1 tchd 50 to 1) 8
2775 CALLERMINE 8-10-11 M Foster, prmnt to 5th.
.......................(100 to 1 op 50 to 1) 9
2920 HULALEA (NZ) 5-10-13 (3*) L Aspell, al beh.
.......................(100 to 1 op 33 to 1) 10
3035[6] COMMUTER COUNTRY 6-11-2 J R Kavanagh, al rear.
.......................(66 to 1 op 33 to 1 tchd 100 to 1) 11
3022[9] CLASSIC MODEL 6-11-2 S McNeill, towards rear whn blun
badly 4th, sn lost tch.......(100 to 1 op 25 to 1) 12
2920 GEORGETOWN 6-11-2 P Hide, prmnt till wknd appr 2 out.
.......................(33 to 1 op 20 to 1) 13
OSCILIGHTS GIFT 5-10-11 L Harvey, swrvd lft strt, slwly
away, al tld off, pld up bef 2 out....(100 to 1 op 33 to 1) pu
Dist: 3½l, nk, 5l, 11l, 6l, 6l, 1½l, 10l, 1½l, 3l. 3m 36.70s. a 2.70s (14 Ran).
SR: 21/17/17/12/2/-/ (Mrs H J Clarke), D Nicholson

3297 Corton Denham Novices' Chase
Class E (5-y-o and up) £3,246 2m 5f
............................(2:45)

3037[2] MALWOOD CASTLE (Ire) 7-11-3 A Thornton, hld up rear,
hdwy tenth, led 12th to 4 out, drvn to get back up on line.
.......................(5 to 2 op 7 to 4) 1
3023[5] RAINCHECK 6-11-3 J Railton, led 3rd to 12th, led 4 out, mstk
nxt, hrd rdn r-in, hdd on line..........(33 to 1 op 25 to 1) 2
2955 DREAM RIDE (Ire) 7-11-10 R Johnson, in tch, ev ch 3 out, 3rd
and btn whn blun last.........(11 to 8 on op 11 to 10 on) 3
2620 POCAIRE GAOITHE (Ire) 7-11-0 (3*) T Dascombe, not fluent,
cl up, rdn 9th, wknd 11th..........(40 to 1 op 33 to 1) 4
1979[5] SAN DIEGO CHARGER (Ire) 6-11-3 P Holley, hld up, hdwy
8th, outpcd 12th, 4th and held whn f four out, dead.
.......................(20 to 1 tchd 25 to 1) f
2613 GIVUS A CALL (Ire) 7-11-0 (3*) L Aspell, led to 3rd, bumped
6th, wknd 11th, 5th and no ch whn hmpd and uns rdr 4 out.
.......................(11 to 2 op 4 to 1) ur
Dist: Hd, 7l. dist. 5m 22.50s. a 18.50s (6 Ran).

(Mrs U Wainwright), R H Alner

3298 Stewart Tory Memorial Trophy
Chase Class D Handicap Chase For
Amateur Riders (0-120 5-y-o and up)
£4,160 3m 1f 110yds........(3:15)

3024[3] FOOLS ERRAND (Ire) [112] (v) 7-10-13 (7*) Mr A Balding, led
to 4th, led tenth to 13th, hit 15th, led four out, rdn clr r-in,
dismounted aftr line, twisted shoe.
.......................(7 to 4 op 11 to 8 tchd 15 to 8) 1
2589 SUNLEY BAY [120] 11-11-9 (5*) Miss P Curling, led 4th to 6th,
hit 11th, led 13th, mstk and hdd 16th, jmpd slwly four out, kpt
on same pace.......................(6 to 1 fav op 11 to 10 on) 2
2666 SPRING TO IT [95] 11-9-12[2] (7*) Mr M Frith, keen hold, led 6th
to tenth, led 15th to 4 out, wknd appr nxt.(5 to 2 op 9 to 4) 3
Dist: 4l, 10l. 6m 39.20s. a 23.20s (3 Ran).

(Mrs David Russell), G B Balding

3299 Motcombe Mares' Only Novices'
Hurdle Class E (4-y-o and up) £2,635
2¾m............................(3:50)

3064[2] MOTOQUA 5-11-6 R Johnson, trkd ldrs, led appr 2 out,
cmftbly.......................(2 to 1 on op 7 to 4 on) 1
2541 REGAL GEM (Ire) 6-11-0 J R Kavanagh, mid-div, effrt 8th,
chsd wnr frm 2 out, no imprsn......(20 to 1 op 14 to 1) 2

3052^{5} SCENIC WATERS 5-11-0 C Llewellyn, *hdwy 7th, rdn 3 out, styd on same pace frm nxt.* (9 to 2 op 7 to 2 tchd 5 to 1) 3
2783 GLADYS EMMANUEL 10-10-9 (5*) D J Kavanagh, *hdwy 6th, ev ch 3 out, wknd nxt..* (16 to 1 op 12 to 1 tchd 20 to 1) 4
2853 QUINAG 6-11-0 S McNeill, *prmnt, led aftr 6th till appr 2 out, sn btn..* (10 to 1 op 8 to 1 tchd 11 to 1) 5
2539^{8} CASTLE LYNCH (Ire) 5-11-0 J Culloty, *chsd ldrs till wknd appr 2 out..* (25 to 1 op 20 to 1 tchd 33 to 1) 6
873^{9} GOBALINO GIRL (Ire) 5-10-11 (3*) D Fortt, *mid-div, no prog frm 3 out..* (25 to 1 op 33 to 1 tchd 20 to 1) 7
2927^{6} CONTRACT BRIDGE (Ire) 4-10-5 W McFarland, *prmnt to hfwy, lost tch 3 out..* (33 to 1) 8
AREAL (Ire) 8-11-0 T Jenks, *hld up rear, hdwy 7th, wknd and eased appr 2 out.* (66 to 1 op 50 to 1 tchd 100 to 1) 9
LADY CALLERNISH 7-11-0 M Foster, *rear, mstk 1st, blun and uns rdr second..* (100 to 1 op 50 to 1) ur
2663 BOLD REINE (Fr) 8-11-0 P Holley, *in tch till blun badly 5th, sn lost touch, pld up bef 7th..* (100 to 1 op 50 to 1) pu
2539 QUEEN OF THE SUIR (Ire) 8-10-11 (3*) Sophie Mitchell, *chsd ldr, mstks 3rd and 4th, wknd 7th, beh whn pld up bef 2 out.* (100 to 1 op 50 to 1) pu
936^{7} LUNAR GRIS 4-10-5 B Powell, *hmpd strt, al beh, mstk 7th, tld off whn pld up bef 2 out..* (100 to 1 op 50 to 1) pu
2874 ABBEYDORAN 6-11-0 D Walsh, *led till aftr 6th, 3rd whn blun nxt, sn wknd, tld off when pld up bef 2 out.* (100 to 1 op 50 to 1) pu
BUCKBEE FLYER 5-11-0 A Thornton, *mstk 1st, nvr dngrs, tld off whn pld up bef 2 out.* (16 to 1 op 10 to 1 tchd 20 to 1) pu

Dist: 8l, 2½l, 3l, 7l, 15l, 3l, 22l, 2½l. 5m 18.30s. a 12.30s (15 Ran).
(Mrs Claire Smith), D Nicholson

3300 Somerton Novices' Hunters' Chase Class H (6-y-o and up) £1,174 2m 5f (4:20)

3147 TOM'S GEMINI STAR 9-11-7 (7*) Mr E James, *hdwy 12th, in tch whn lft cl second and hmpd 4 out, led nxt, pushed clr frm 2 out..* (33 to 1 op 20 to 1 tchd 66 to 1) 1
VITAL SONG 11-11-7 (7*) Mr G Matthews, *prmnt, slightly outpcd 13th, lft in ld 4 out, btn whn mstk last.* (7 to 2 op 5 to 2) 2
3096^{4} NORTHERN VILLAGE 10-11-7 (7*) Capt D Alers-Hankey, *rear, hrd rdn 8th, styd on frm 4 out, nvr nr ldrs.* (33 to 1 op 12 to 1) 3
SOME-TOY 11-11-13 (7*) Miss L Blackford, *in tch whn mstk 11th, sn rdn and lost pl.* (14 to 1 op 10 to 1 tchd 16 to 1) 4
MASTER DONNINGTON 9-11-7 (7*) Mr J M Pritchard, *in tch till wknd 13th..* (33 to 1 op 20 to 1) 5
3102^{2} KING'S TREASURE (USA) 8-11-13 (7*) Mr A Balding, *prmnt, 3rd whn f 6th..* (5 to 4 fav op 11 to 8 tchd 13 to 8) f
SALVO 6-11-8^{1} (7*) Mr I Dowrick, *keen hold, led 3rd to 13th, cl up whn lft in ld, mstk and uns rdr 4 out.* (12 to 1 op 10 to 1) ur
WEST QUAY 11-11-7 (7*) Mr J Creighton, *led to 3rd, led 13th till pld up lme appr 4 out..* (4 to 1 op 3 to 1) pu
3143^{2} FINNIGAN FREE 7-11-7 (7*) Mr M Frith, *rear whn pld up bef 7th..* (16 to 1 op 10 to 1) pu

Dist: 5l, 10l, 5l, 3l. 5m 19.50s. a 15.50s (9 Ran).
(O J Carter), O J Carter

3301 Quantock Handicap Hurdle Class D (0-120 4-y-o and up) £2,805 2m (4:50)

3025* NORTHERN STARLIGHT [112] 6-11-11 C Maude, *made all, hrd rdn appr 2 out, ran on gmely.* (13 to 8 op Evens tchd 7 to 4) 1
2430* EASY LISTENING (USA) [104] 5-11-3 J Railton, *trkd wnr, ev ch 2 out, hrd rdn and blun last, eased whn btn r-in.* (11 to 8 fav op 6 to 4 tchd 5 to 4) 2
3100^{6} KINO'S CROSS [105] 8-11-4 A Thornton, *in tch, jmpd slwly and pushed alng 4th, sn btn..* (12 to 1 op 7 to 1) 3
2783^{8} DONTDRESSFORDINNER [89] 7-9-13 (3*) T Dascombe, *beh, rdn 3 out, tld off..* (7 to 2 op 4 to 1 tchd 9 to 2) 4

Dist: 12l, 18l, dist. 3m 36.00s. a 2.00s (4 Ran).
SR: 37/17/-/-/ (Arthur Souch), M C Pipe

3302 Levy Board Standard Open National Hunt Flat Class H (4,5,6-y-o) £1,490 2m. (5:20)

2784* NOISY MINER (Ire) 5-11-8 (3*) R Massey, *hdwy to track ldrs 6 fs out, hrd rdn to ld ins last, edgd lft, drvn out.* (3 to 1 on op 5 to 2 on tchd 9 to 4 on) 1
NORMANIA (NZ) 5-11-4 Mr T Hills, *prmnt, ran wide bend into strt, ev ch fnl 2 fs, slightly hmpd ins last, kpt on wl.* (33 to 1 op 20 to 1) 2
SALLY SCALLY 5-10-13 Mr L Jefford, *prmnt, led 3 fs out till ins last, ran on..* (14 to 1 op 25 to 1 tchd 33 to 1) 3
TOMMY TICKLE 5-11-4 J R Kavanagh, *chsd ldrs, outpcd hfwy, rdn and rallied 4 fs out, one pace fnl 3.* (20 to 1 op 10 to 1 tchd 25 to 1) 4
MISTER RIVER (Ire) 6-11-4 P Holley, *keen hold, mid-div, effrt 5 fs out, one pace fnl 3..* (9 to 1 op 4 to 1) 5
LONGSTONE LAD 5-10-11 (7*) Mr J Tizzard, *hdwy hfwy, ev ch o'r 3 fs out, wknd over 2 out.* (16 to 1 op 20 to 1 tchd 33 to 1) 6
SEE PROSPERITY 5-10-11 (7*) N Willmington, *chsd ldrs till wknd 4 fs out..* (50 to 1 op 33 to 1) 7
FESTIVAL (Fr) 4-10-10 S McNeill, *led till 3 fs out, sn wknd.* (14 to 1 op 7 to 1) 8
FIVE BOYS (Ire) 5-11-1 (3*) T Dascombe, *nvr dngrs.* (16 to 1 op 10 to 1) 9
TECHNICAL MOVE (Ire) 6-10-13 S Burrough, *pressed ldr 12 fs, wknd 3 out..* (66 to 1 op 20 to 1) 10
LITTLE BEAU 6-11-4 Mr A Charles-Jones, *nvr trbld ldrs.* (50 to 1 op 33 to 1 tchd 66 to 1) 11
2545^{6} SPLASH OF BLAKENEY 6-10-13 S Anderson, *keen hold rear, hdwy hfwy..* (66 to 1 op 50 to 1) 12
DUNNICKS DOLITTLE 4-10-4^{1} (7*) M Griffiths, *slwly away, rear till rapid hdwy aftr 6 fs, wknd quickly six out, sn tld off.* (66 to 1 op 20 to 1) 13
KELLSBORO QUEEN 6-10-13 B Powell, *keen hold rear, hdwy appr hfwy, wknd 6 fs out, tld off whn pld up 3 furlongs out..* (14 to 1 op 8 to 1 tchd 16 to 1) pu

Dist: 1¼l, 1l, 11l, ¾l, 1½l, 6l, 4l, 1¼l, 12l, 14l. 3m 37.80s. (14 Ran).
(Mrs R J Skan), D Nicholson

KELSO (good)
Friday March 21st
Going Correction: PLUS 0.05 sec. per fur.

3303 Percy Arms Juvenile Novices' Hurdle Class D (4-y-o) £2,815 2¼m (1:40)

3055* SON OF ANSHAN 11-10 J Supple, *made all, sn clr, rdn alng 3 out, eased nr finish..* (5 to 4 fav tchd 6 to 4) 1
2879^{9} BOLD CLASSIC (Ire) 10-12 T Reed, *mid-div, hdwy and pushed alng 5th, rdn along 3 out, kpt on appr last, no ch wth wnr..* (5 to 1 op 6 to 1) 2
2915* CLASH OF SWORDS 11-4 L Wyer, *chsd ldrs, rdn alng and mstk 3 out, drvn last, kpt on one pace..* (5 to 1) 3
3055^{3} BOURBON DYNASTY (Fr) 10-12 A Dobbin, *hld up beh, hdwy whn hit 3 out, styd on appr last..* (20 to 1 op 14 to 1) 4
3003^{2} OVERSMAN 10-12 P Niven, *prmnt, chsd wnr frm 5th, drvn 2 out, wknd last..* (7 to 1 tchd 8 to 1) 5
3055^{6} KNOWN SECRET (USA) 10-12 M Moloney, *pld hrd, hld up rear, hdwy appr 3 out, kpt on frm last, not much room nr finish.* (50 to 1 op 33 to 1) 6
2256 HONEYSCHOICE (Ire) 10-12 R Garritty, *hld up, hdwy 4 out, rdn nxt, wknd 2 out..* (10 to 1 op 7 to 1) 7
3003^{8} QUEEN'S COUNSEL (Ire) 10-7 B Storey, *al rear..* (33 to 1) 8
2915^{2} ANIKA'S GEM (Ire) 10-7 M Foster, *chsd ldrs till wknd 4 out, sn beh..* (33 to 1) 9
CAULKER 10-7 (5*) S Taylor, *mstks, chsd ldrs till wknd 5th, sn beh..* (200 to 1 op 100 to 1) 10
MYSTICAL MIND 10-12 A S Smith, *al beh, hit 4th, tld off whn pld up bef four out..* (200 to 1 op 100 to 1) pu
2623 CHIEF CHIPPIE 10-12 S McDougall, *beh hfwy, tld off whn pld up bef last..* (200 to 1 op 100 to 1) pu

Dist: 22l, ½l, hd, 1l, 1¼l, 30l, 7l, hd. 4m 26.60s. a 19.60s (12 Ran).
(F J Sainsbury), Mrs A Swinbank

3304 Tweeddale Press Novices' Chase Class D (5-y-o and up) £3,947 2m 1f (2:15)

AMERICAN HERO 9-11-2 B Storey, *jmpd wl, made all, rdn 2 out, styd on well..* (9 to 1 op 8 to 1) 1
3058^{2} MR KNITWIT 10-11-8 A Dobbin, *chsd ldrs, effrt and rdn 3 out, hit nxt, kpt on und pres last, not rch wnr.* (2 to 1 op 9 to 4 tchd 7 to 4) 2
3030^{2} REAL TONIC 7-11-8 R Dunwoody, *not fluent, chsd ldrs, blun 3rd, rdn alng 8th, drvn and mstk 2 out, sn btn.* (7 to 4 fav op 6 to 4 tchd 15 to 8) 3
2985^{2} MOSS PAGEANT 7-11-2 K Johnson, *chsd wnr, rdn alng 4 out, wkng whn blun nxt..* (50 to 1 op 33 to 1) 4
2712^{8} MALTA MAN (Ire) 7-11-2 A S Smith, *beh, styd on frm 2 out, nvr a factor..* (25 to 1 op 20 to 1) 5
2150^{5} JYMJAM JOHNNY (Ire) 8-10-11 (5*) R McGrath, *hit 1st, hld up beh, nvr a factor..* (16 to 1 op 20 to 1) 6
1822^{4} MUSIC BLITZ 6-11-2 T Reed, *beh, rdn alng whn mstk 6th, sn wl outpcd..* (16 to 1 op 12 to 1) 7
3007^{3} MONKEY WENCH (Ire) 6-10-11 A Thornton, *chsd ldrs, hit 7th, sn rdn alng, lost pl 4 out and beh.* (8 to 1 op 10 to 1 tchd 12 to 1) 8

Dist: 5l, 2l, 17l, 9l, 4l, 8l, 18l. 4m 11.80s. a 6.80s (8 Ran).
SR: 28/29/27/4/-/ (Mrs R P Aggio), R Allan

3305 Lothian Plumbing Handicap Hurdle Class D (0-120 4-y-o and up) £2,827 2¼m. (2:45)

2934 MONNAIE FORTE (Ire) [94] 7-10-2^{2} J Railton, *dsptd ld to 7th, cl up, effrt and led last, sn rdn, kpt on wl.* (7 to 1 op 10 to 1) 1
3059* INGLETONIAN [120] 8-12-0 B Storey, *dsptd ld till led 7th, rdn 2 out, hdd last, rallied flt, no extr nr finish.* (4 to 1 fav op 5 to 2) 2
3013^{8} OUR ROBERT [92] 5-9-11 (3*) F Leahy, *chsd ldrs, rdn alng and outpcd 2 out, styd on und pres frm last.* (10 to 1 op 8 to 1) 3

3013[9] SUPREME SOVIET [94] 7-10-2 A Dobbin, *chsd ldrs, effrt 3 out, drvn nxt, sn one pace*.............(8 to 1 op 6 to 1) 4

2933[6] UNCLE DOUG [120] 6-12-0 P Niven, *chsd ldrs, rdn alng bef 3 out, drvn nxt, one pace.* (10 to 1 op 7 to 1 tchd 12 to 1) 5

2880[2] HAM N'EGGS [114] 6-11-8 R Garritty, *trkd ldrs, hdwy 7th, rdn appr 2 out, sn btn*....................(5 to 1 tchd 11 to 2) 6

3059[5] LINNGATE [105] 8-10-13 R Supple, *help up beh, effrt and hdwy 4 out, rdn alng nxt, one pace frm 2 out, blun last.* ....(5 to 1 op 7 to 1) 7

3030 ARAGON AYR [114] 9-11-1 (7*) C McCormack, *hld up, rdn alng 4 out, sn outpcd and beh*........ (33 to 1 op 12 to 1) 8

3128[7] ADAMATIC (Ire) [98] 6-10-6 L Wyer, *hld up, hit 6th, sn rdn alng, outpcd and wl beh*.................(6 to 1 tchd 13 to 2) 9

Dist: ½l, 5l, hd, ½l, 12l, 12l, 30l, 13l. 4m 26.30s. a 19.30s (9 Ran).

(James R Adam), J R Adam

3306 King's Own Scottish Borderers Challenge Cup Class D Handicap Chase (0-125 5-y-o and up) £4,143 3m 1f .... (3:15)

2495* SON OF IRIS [109] 9-11-5 P Niven, *hld up, pushed alng 13th, hdwy 4 out, led 2 out, rdn last, ran on*...........(2 to 1 jt-fav tchd 9 to 4) 1

3058* COQUI LANE [93] 10-10-3 D Parker, *chsd ldr, rdn alng 3 out, ev ch last, hrd drvn and one pace flt*.............. (4 to 1) 2

3161[6] TIGHTER BUDGET (USA) [100] 10-10-10 M Moloney, *led, rdn 3 out, hdd 2 out, drvn and wknd last.* ....(12 to 1 op 14 to 1 tchd 16 to 1) 3

2916[3] WHAAT FETTLE [114] 12-11-10 A Dobbin, *cl up, pushed alng 14th, rdn and hit 4 out, sn btn*...................(2 to 1 jt-fav op 7 to 4 tchd 9 to 4) 4

3060* KILCOLGAN [106] 10-11-2 N Bentley, *hit 1st, cl up, not fluent, blun and uns rdr 11th*..................(11 to 2 op 9 to 2) ur

Dist: 1l, 13l, dist. 6m 17.00s. a 20.00s (5 Ran).

(M H G Systems Ltd), Mrs M Reveley

3307 J. Rutherford Earlston Hunters' Chase Class H For Stewart Wight Memorial Trophy (5-y-o and up) £2,211 3½m..................(3:50)

2918* JIGTIME 8-11-4 (7*) Mr M Bradburne, *trkd ldg pair, hdwy 16th, led 3 out, rdn last, ran on strly.* ....(2 to 1 on op 6 to 4 on tchd 11 to 8 on) 1

2918[2] ROYAL JESTER 13-11-11 (5*) Mr C Storey, *cl up, rdn alng and outpcd appr 4 out, styd on frm last, not rch wnr.* ....(3 to 1 tchd 5 to 2) 2

ORANGE RAGUSA 11-11-5 (5*) Miss P Robson, *led, rdn alng 4 out, hdd nxt, drvn and one pace last.* (11 to 2 op 9 to 2) 3

SOUTHERN MINSTREL 14-11-9 (7*) Miss C Metcalfe, *in tch, effrt and rdn alng 5 out, sn outpcd.* ....(25 to 1 op 20 to 1 tchd 33 to 1) 4

3125[4] TARTAN TORNADO 11-11-11 (5*) Mr P Johnson, *mstks, al rear, beh 16th*...................... (33 to 1 op 20 to 1) 5

Dist: 7l, 1¼l, 2½l, dist. 7m 13.30s. a 27.30s (5 Ran).

(J W Hughes), J W Hughes

3308 Kelso Annual Members 'National Hunt' Novices' Hurdle Class D (Div I) (5-y-o and up) £2,409 2¾m 110yds .... (4:20)

2856[6] CASH BOX (Ire) 9-10-12 N Smith, *hld up, hdwy 8th, chlgd last, rdn to ld flt, kpt on*.....(14 to 1 op 20 to 1 tchd 25 to 1) 1

2344[7] MAJOR HARRIS (Ire) 5-10-12 R Garritty, *hld up, hdwy to chase ldrs hfwy, effrt 2 out, led last, sn rdn and hdd, kpt on.* .... (12 to 1 op 8 to 1) 2

2623[3] NO GIMMICKS (Ire) 5-10-12 R Dunwoody, *al prmnt, rdn alng aftr 4 out, drvn appr last, kpt on*......... (9 to 2 op 5 to 1) 3

2972[3] CHOPWELL DRAPES (Ire) 7-10-12 M Moloney, *cl up, led 4 out, rdn 2 out, wndrd and hdd last, wknd flt.* ....(7 to 1 op 6 to 1) 4

2145[5] POLITICAL MILLSTAR 5-10-12 B Storey, *hld up, gd hdwy bef 4 out, chsd ldrs 2 out, sn rdn, no imprsn.* ....(8 to 1 op 7 to 1 tchd 9 to 1) 5

2570[5] MONSIEUR DARCY (Ire) 6-10-12 J Railton, *led, rdn alng and hdd 4 out, wknd 2 out*................(12 to 1 op 10 to 1) 6

DOWSHI 6-10-7 R Supple, *al beh*.............. (33 to 1) 7

3246 PERSIAN GRANGE (Ire) 7-10-12 J Burke, *hld up, hdwy on outer to chase ldrs hfwy, rdn and wknd bef 3 out.* (100 to 1) 8

3034[5] MENALDI (Ire) 7-10-12 A S Smith, *prmnt, rdn alng 7th, sn wknd*.............................. (20 to 1 op 16 to 1) 9

3029* DERANNIE (Ire) 5-11-5 A Dobbin, *trkd ldrs, pushed alng appr 4 out, sn lost pl*......(6 to 5 fav op 5 to 4 tchd 11 to 10) 10

LORD PAT (Ire) 6-10-9 (3*) E Callaghan, *chsd ldrs, rdn 4 out, sn wknd*...(33 to 1) 11

2984* ESTABLISH (Ire) 9-11-0 A Thornton, *prmnt, lost pl 7th, sn beh.* ....(25 to 1 op 16 to 1) 12

2200 JUST POLLY 5-10-2 (5*) R McGrath, *chhased ldrs to hfwy, sn lost pl and beh*...............................(100 to 1) 13

2489 RAMBLING LANE 8-10-5 (7*) S Melrose, *beh 5th, tld off whn pld up bef 3 out*.............................. (100 to 1) pu

MOREFLASH 5-10-4 (3*) F Leahy, *slwly away, tld off 4th, pld up aftr 6th*...............(250 to 1 tchd 500 to 1) pu

Dist: 1¼l, 3l, 6l, hd, 8l, 7l, 5l, 8l, 7l, 5l. 5m 32.00s. a 23.00s (15 Ran).

(Dr T A Wadrop), T J Carr

3309 Kelso Annual Members 'National Hunt' Novices' Hurdle Class D (Div II) (5-y-o and up) £2,395 2¾m 110yds .... (4:50)

2917[4] MISTER ROSS (Ire) 7-11-12 A Dobbin, *al prmnt, hdwy to chase ldr 7th, led 2 out, sn clr, rdn out.* ....(7 to 4 fav op 6 to 4 tchd 2 to 1) 1

2546 JUST ONE QUESTION (Ire) 7-10-12 P Niven, *led, rdn alng 4 out, hdd and hit 2 out, kpt on*..........(6 to 1 tchd 7 to 1) 2

2822[5] GROSVENOR (Ire) 6-10-12 R Dunwoody, *in tch, effrt 4 out, drvn 2 out, kpt on, no imprsn.* ....(7 to 2 op 3 to 1 tchd 4 to 1) 3

2344 MY MAVOURNEEN 5-10-7 M Foster, *in tch, hit 7th and outpcd, styd on frm 2 out, nvr dngrs*......(20 to 1 op 16 to 1) 4

2711 CHASING DREAMS 6-10-12 R Garritty, *al chasing ldrs, rdn alng 4 out, sn one pace*.............(25 to 1 op 33 to 1) 5

3015[6] SMILE PLEEZE (Ire) 5-10-12 Mr S Swiers, *jmpd slwly 4th, sn beh, some hdwy 2 out, nvr a factor*................(20 to 1) 6

3029 PRINCE OF THYNE (Ire) 8-10-12 N Bentley, *hld up, hdwy to chase ldrs 7th, rdn 3 out, wknd nxt*.... (33 to 1 op 20 to 1) 7

3011[4] MIKE STAN (Ire) 6-10-12 R Supple, *prmnt, drvn alng and outpcd 4 out, nvr dngrs aftr.* ....(100 to 30 op 3 to 1 tchd 7 to 2) 8

1162[8] FASTER RON (Ire) 6-10-5 (7*) S Melrose, *mid-div, hdwy 7th, chsd ldg pair 3 out, sn drvn alng and wknd nxt*.... (100 to 1) 9

3009[7] JONAEM (Ire) 7-11-5 K Johnson, *hld up, effrt and some hdwy 4 out, sn wknd*.................................(33 to 1) 10

3057[4] STEPDAUGHTER 11-10-7 L O'Hara, *chsd ldrs, lost tch and beh hfwy, sn tld off*.............................(33 to 1) 11

2538 WEEJUMPAWUD 7-10-7 Mr C Storey, *beh hfwy, sn tld off.* ....(200 to 1) 12

3262[5] BUSY BOY 10-10-12 J Burke, *prmnt, lost pl hfwy, sn beh, tld off*...(100 to 1) 13

3015 WOODHOUSE LANE 5-10-5 (7*) Miss C Metcalfe, *al beh, tld off hfwy*.. (200 to 1) 14

Dist: 6l, 5l, 4l, 4l, 8l, 3½l, 1¼l, 1½l, 1½l, 17l. 5m 35.20s. a 26.20s (14 Ran).

(Gordon Brown), J Howard Johnson

NEWBURY (good (races 1,3,6), good to firm (2,4,5))
Friday March 21st
Going Correction: NIL

3310 Wantage Novices' Hurdle Class D (4-y-o and up) £3,176 3m 110yds (1:50)

2792[3] READY MONEY CREEK (Ire) 6-11-12 J Osborne, *hld up beh, steady hdwy frm 4 out, led last, styd on wl.* ....(11 to 2 op 5 to 1 tchd 6 to 1) 1

2822* ABSOLUTLY EQUINAME (Ire) 6-11-12 B Powell, *dsptd ld thrght, led briefly appr last, edgd rght, kpt on und pres.* ....(11 to 4 fav op 3 to 1) 2

3041* MENESONIC (Ire) 7-11-5 (3*) P Henley, *hld up beh, steady hdwy appr 4 out, hrd rdn aftr nxt, kpt on und pres.* ....(7 to 2 op 3 to 1) 3

2738 CLARKES GORSE (Ire) 6-11-4 P Hide, *dsptd ld thrght, ev ch 2 out, hdd and one pace appr last*..... (20 to 1 op 14 to 1) 4

2822[3] TREMPLIN (Ire) 6-10-13 M A Fitzgerald, *nvr far away, ev ch whn blun badly 2 out, not reco'r*........(7 to 1 op 10 to 1) 5

3144[5] COOL HARRY (USA) 6-10-11 (7*) Mr S Durack, *trkd ldrs, pushed alng 7th, hrd rdn and outpcd appr 3 out.* .... (66 to 1 op 50 to 1) 6

2898* IONIO (USA) 6-11-12 J R Kavanagh, *in cl tch, blun 4th, reminder nxt and sn lost pl, hrd rdn aftr 8th, no response.* ....(4 to 1 op 3 to 1) 7

2976[3] CHRISTCHURCH (Fr) 7-11-4 C Maude, *hld up in cl tch, mstk 7th, wknd appr 4 out, tld off*.......(14 to 1 op 12 to 1) 8

SUPREME RAMBLER (Ire) 8-11-4 W Marston, *al beh, tld off frm 8th*..................................(33 to 1 op 25 to 1) 9

2928[6] ROADRUNNER 7-11-4 M Richards, *not fluent in rear, tld off whn pld up bef 9th*................. (66 to 1 op 50 to 1) pu

2782 ARTISTIC PLAN (Ire) 5-10-13 (5*) Mr R Thornton, *in tch, pushed alng appr 3 out, sn wknd, pld up bef last.* ....(50 to 1 tchd 66 to 1) pu

1942 SPIRIT OF SUCCESS 7-11-4 Mr A Kinane, *al beh, tld off whn pld up aftr 5th*.......................(66 to 1 op 50 to 1) pu

2874[6] LOOK IN THE MIRROR 6-11-4 C Llewellyn, *hld up, al beh, tld off whn pld up bef 6th*...................(66 to 1 op 50 to 1) pu

JOHNYMOSS (Ire) 8-11-4 W McFarland, *keen hold, trkd ldrs till pld up lme aftr 6th*................(40 to 1 op 33 to 1) pu

Dist: 1½l, ½l, 2l, 26l, 4l, 1¼l, 18l, 12l. 6m 0.60s. a 14.60s (14 Ran).

(Roach Foods Limited), O Sherwood

3311 Betterton Novices' Chase Class D (5-y-o and up) £3,574 3m..... (2:25)

3116[8] LINTON ROCKS 8-11-4 B Powell, *jmpd wl, led second, made rst, shaken up r-in, not extended.* ....(6 to 5 fav op 5 to 4 on tchd 5 to 4) 1

2600 HATCHAM BOY (Ire) 7-11-12 R Johnson, *hld up in cl tch, blun 11th, shaken up appr 3 out, no imprsn on wnr.* ....(11 to 8 op 5 to 4 tchd 13 to 8 and 7 to 4) 2

3284[4] AMBER VALLEY (USA) 6-10-11 (7*) Mr S Durack, *hld up in last pl, hdwy appr 4 out, kpt on same pace approaching last.*
..................(17 to 2 op 5 to 1 tchd 9 to 1) 3
2498 ELITE GOVERNOR (Ire) 8-10-11 (7*) Mr L Baker, *in cl tch, reminder aftr 5 out, sn outpcd.......* (16 to 1 op 12 to 1) 4
3037 DEXTRA (Ire) (bl) 7-11-4 C Maude, *led to second, in tch, struggling whn mstk 12th, blun nxt, losing touch when pld up bef 5 out...........................* (50 to 1 op 33 to 1) pu
Dist: 2l, 2½l, 18l. 6m 6.00s. a 21.00s (5 Ran).

(The Hon Mrs Townshend), T Thomson Jones

3312 Sabin du Loir Maiden Hurdle Class D (4-y-o and up) £4,102 2m 5f... (2:55)

2263[3] QUINI EAGLE (Fr) 5-11-9 Jamie Evans, *trkd ldrs, led 3 out, mstk nxt, rdn alng and ran on wl.*
..................(8 to 1 op 7 to 1 tchd 10 to 1) 1
3077 LIVELY ENCOUNTER (Ire) 6-11-9 Derek Byrne, *settled beh ldrs, ev ch 2 out, hrd rdn and one pace appr last.*
..................(15 to 8 fav op 7 to 4 tchd 2 to 1) 2
3035[2] FOXIES LAD 6-11-9 R Johnson, *hld up beh ldrs gng wl, shaken up appr 2 out, hrd rdn and ev ch r-in, no extr fnl 100 yards...........................* (9 to 1 op 5 to 1) 3
2889[9] MADAM'S WALK 7-11-4 C Llewellyn, *trkd ldrs, pushed alng appr 3 out, kpt on same pace........* (4 to 1 op 11 to 2) 4
HIGH SUMMER 7-11-9 J Culloty, *trkd ldrs till wknd appr 2 out.................* (16 to 1 op 12 to 1 tchd 20 to 1) 5
3064[4] BURN OUT 5-11-2 (7*) J O'Shaughnessy, *hld up beh, effrt 7th, not fluent 4 out, styd on, nvr able to chal.* (7 to 1 op 5 to 1) 6
3077[9] TOM PINCH (Ire) 8-11-9 R Greene, *hmpd 1st, hld up, outpcd by ldg grp 7th, no imprsn..........* (33 to 1 op 20 to 1) 7
2688[5] FATHER HENRY 6-11-9 M A Fitzgerald, *hld up beh ldg grp, shaken up aftr 4 out, stdly outpcd.*
..................(8 to 1 op 6 to 1 tchd 10 to 1) 8
2008[6] BREATH OF SCANDAL (Ire) 6-11-9 D Osborne, *led aftr 1st, sn clr, hdd 3 out, btn whn hit nxt, eased....* (7 to 1 op 6 to 1) 9
1765 PROUD TOBY (Ire) 7-11-9 J R Kavanagh, *al beh.*
..................(50 to 1 tchd 66 to 1) 10
185[6] COCKPIT (Ire) 6-11-9 B Clifford, *al beh.*
..................(50 to 1 op 25 to 1) 11
HAPPY HENRY 7-11-9 T J Murphy, *taken dwn slwly, hmpd 1st, hld up in mid-div, outpcd 7th, tld off.*
..................(66 to 1 op 50 to 1) 12
1971 IMPERIAL HONORS (Ire) 6-11-4 (5*) Chris Webb, *al beh, tld off.............................* (66 to 1 op 50 to 1) 13
1663[8] WARRIO 7-11-9 L Harvey, *hmpd 1st, al beh, tld off.*
..................(66 to 1 op 50 to 1) 14
2953[9] CONQUER THE KILT 6-11-9 S Curran, *f 1st.*
..................(66 to 1 op 50 to 1) f
ARCTIC CHARMER (USA) 5-11-9 T J O'Sullivan, *hld up, al beh, tld off whn pld up bef 8th........* (66 to 1 op 33 to 1) pu
3144[3] RICH TYCOON (Ire) 8-11-9 W Marston, *led briefly 1st, prmnt whn pld up bef 6th................* (33 to 1 op 50 to 1) pu
BLAZING DOVE 6-11-9 S Wynne, *in tch, jmpd rght 4th, jumped deliberately nxt and lost pl, pld up bef 7th, broke blood vessel....................* (50 to 1 op 33 to 1) pu
2831 HOUR HORSE 6-11-9 C Maude, *in rear whn mstk second, tld off when pld up bef 3 out..........* (66 to 1 op 50 to 1) pu
Dist: 2l, hd, 8l, 15l, 12l, ¾l, 17l, 4l, 8l, hd. 5m 3.20s. a 9.20s (19 Ran).
SR: 3/1/1/-/-/-/

(B A Kilpatrick), M C Pipe

3313 Alison Associates Hunters' Chase Class H (5-y-o and up) £2,775 3m .... (3:25)

2897[2] FOX POINTER 12-12-13 (5*) Mr R Thornton, *jmpd wl, made all, shaken up appr last, quickened clr.*
..................(7 to 4 fav op 2 to 1 tchd 9 to 4) 1
ARDBRENNAN 10-11-11 (7*) Mr E James, *cl up, pressed wnr strt, outpcd frm 2 out..........* (100 to 30 op 4 to 1) 2
3026* RYMING CUPLET 12-12-3 (7*) Mr L Jefford, *al beh, unbl to chal fnl circuit....................* (2 to 1 op 11 to 8) 3
3187 TEATRADER 11-11-11 (7*) Miss T Blazey, *in tch, beh fnl circuit.....................................* (16 to 1) 4
2875[5] EXPRESSMENT 13-12-3 (7*) Mr G Penfold, *al beh, tld off.*
..................(12 to 1 op 8 to 1) 5
THE BODHRAN (Ire) 7-11-11 (7*) Mr S Durack, *f 4th.* (33 to 1) f
ALAPA 10-11-11 (7*) Mr V Coogan, *in cl tch, blun 4 out, 3rd and hld whn mstk and uns rdr 3 out...* (50 to 1 op 33 to 1) ur
Dist: 18l, 21l, sht-hd, 12l. 5m 58.10s. a 13.10s (7 Ran).

(Mrs L T J Evans), Mrs L T J Evans

3314 Paul Croucher Memorial Trophy Handicap Chase Class C (0-135 5-y-o and up) £4,727 2½m......... (4:00)

3134* TERAO [127] 11-11-10 (6ex) T J Murphy, *blun 1st, led 3rd, made rst, hit 11th, ran on wl whn pressed frm 2 out.*
..................(9 to 4 op 7 to 4 tchd 5 to 2) 1
CHANGE THE ACT [110] 12-10-7 R Johnson, *al hndy, drvn to chal 2 out, ev ch appr last, sn no extr...*(9 to 1 op 7 to 1) 2
2922* HIGH ALLTITUDE (Ire) [105] 9-10-12 B Powell, *hld up, cld 11th, effrt to chal appr 4 out, one pace approaching 2 out.*
..................(3 to 1 op 7 to 2) 3
2696 COOLREE (Ire) [112] 9-10-9 M A Fitzgerald, *hld up, mstk 9th, shaken up appr 4 out, btn aftr nxt, tld off.*
..................(9 to 1 op 2 tchd 5 to 1) 4

MR JAMBOREE [127] 11-11-7 (3*) D Fortt, *led to 3rd, in tch till 11th, tld off........................* (8 to 1 tchd 10 to 1) 5
Dist: 2½l, 12l, 20l, 26l. 4m 53.50s. a 5.50s (5 Ran).
SR: 41/21/4/-/-/

(B A Kilpatrick), M C Pipe

3315 Newbury Racecourse Station Handicap Hurdle Class D (0-125 4-y-o) £3,317 2m 110yds........... (4:35)

2828[5] RED RAJA [118] 12-0 J Osborne, *led to 3rd, trkd ldr, hit 4 out, shaken up to ld last, ran on wl.*
..................(2 to 1 op 6 to 4 tchd 9 to 4) 1
3044[2] FAIRLY SHARP (Ire) [100] 10-10 Richard Guest, *trkd ldr, led 3rd, jmpd rght 4 out, hdd last, no extr.*
..................(13 to 8 fav op 6 to 4) 2
2828[8] PROVINCE [90] 9-11 (3*) J Magee, *hld up in tch, effrt 3 out, sn btn.......................* (10 to 1 tchd 8 to 1) 3
2628[4] NORTHERN FLEET [106] 11-2 M A Fitzgerald, *hld up, not fluent second, sn struggling aftr, reminders and no response after 3 out, tld off....* (5 to 2 tchd 3 to 1) 4
Dist: 3½l, 16l, 18l. 3m 55.20s. a 6.20s (4 Ran).
SR: 38/16/-/-/

(J R Ali), P Mitchell

BANGOR (good)
Saturday March 22nd
Going Correction: PLUS 0.05 sec. per fur. (races 1,2,6,7), PLUS 0.40 (3,4,5)

3316 Stan Clarke Novices' Hurdle Class E (4-y-o and up) £3,186 2m 1f... (2:10)

3168* FLORID (USA) 6-10-9 (7*) M Berry, *led to 1st, led ag'n nxt, made rst, drvn clr r-in............* (6 to 4 fav op 2 to 1) 1
3108[2] KINNESCASH (Ire) 4-10-1 (7*) L Cummins, *led 1st to nxt, continued to press wnr, not fluent 3 out and last, one pace r-in.............................* (14 to 1 op 10 to 1) 2
2791[9] JESSOLLE 5-10-4 (7*) R Burns, *midfield, stdly imprvg whn slightly hmpd 3 out, kpt on, not trble ldrs.*
..................(66 to 1 op 33 to 1) 3
3022* TALATHATH (Fr) 5-11-8 R Johnson, *midfield, hdwy 4 out, rdn to chase ldrs nxt, no imprsn frm 2 out, fourth and btn whn blun last.............* (100 to 30 op 3 to 1 tchd 7 to 2) 4
3028* MUHTADI (Ire) 4-11-0 P Niven, *midfield, hdwy to go cl up 5th, mstk nxt, btn..............* (5 to 1 op 4 to 1 tchd 11 to 2) 5
2959 POT BLACKBIRD 8-10-11 W Marston, *midfield, brief effrt 3 out, nvr dngrs.............* (100 to 1 op 50 to 1) 6
TABRIZ 4-10-3 O Pears, *hld up and beh, nvr nr to chal.*
..................(66 to 1 op 33 to 1) 7
MR LOWRY 5-11-2 S Wynne, *handily plcd till wknd 4 out.*
..................(66 to 1 op 33 to 1) 8
3028 ALTHREY PILOT (Ire) 6-11-2 C Rae, *hld up, effrt appr 5th, wknd nxt......................* (33 to 1) 9
2798 RINUS MAJOR (Ire) 6-11-2 D Walsh, *trkd ldrs till wknd 4 out, eased whn btn bef 2 out........* (100 to 1 op 50 to 1) 10
2954[3] VADLAWYS (Fr) 6-11-2 A Dobbin, *in tch, improved into cl 5th whn f 3 out...............* (13 to 2 op 11 to 2) f
2405 REACH THE CLOUDS (Ire) 5-11-2 R Supple, *towards rear, reminders bef 4 out, no ch whn f 2 out.* (66 to 1 op 50 to 1) f
3048 BRANDON BRIDGE 6-11-2 V Slattery, *al beh, niggled alng aftr 3rd, tld off whn pld up bef last....* (66 to 1 op 50 to 1) pu
2996[6] GAF 5-11-2 T Eley, *beh frm 3rd, lost tch nxt, tld off whn pld up.................* (100 to 1 op 66 to 1) pu
2201[3] EL CRANK SENOR 5-11-2 R Dunwoody, *in tch, improved to chase ldrs 5th, drvn but cl 3rd whn pld up appr 2 out, dismounted, lme...................* (14 to 1 op 12 to 1) pu
Dist: 3½l, 5l, 10l, 4l, 1¾l, 3l, 12l, 2½l, 12l. 3m 56.40s. a 6.40s (15 Ran).
SR: 32/20/18/19/7/2/

(Lord Howard de Walden), C P E Brooks

3317 Cross Lanes Hotel Conditional Jockeys' Selling Handicap Hurdle Class G (0-95 4-y-o and up) £2,358 2m 1f.........................(2:45)

3276[2] NIGHT BOAT [71] 6-10-10 Guy Lewis, *midfield, gd hdwy appr 5th, led 2 out, drvn out r-in..........* (7 to 2 jt-fav) 1
2663[9] NORD LYS (Ire) [64] 6-10-3 Michael Brennan, *in tch, hdwy 5th, lft in ld 4 out, hdd 2 out, one pace.*
..................(20 to 1 op 14 to 1 tchd 25 to 1) 2
2783 NEVER SO BLUE (Ire) [83] 6-11-5 (3*) R Wilkinson, *midfield, hdwy to chase ldrs 3 out, kpt on same pace.*
..................(9 to 1 op 10 to 1) 3
2847[4] PALACE OF GOLD [85] 7-11-5 (5*) W Dowling, *nvr far away, effrt 4 out, one pace frm 2 out.*
..................(9 to 1 op 10 to 1) 4
3013 ETERNAL CITY [85] 6-11-5 (5*) R Burns, *trkd ldrs, pushed alng 3 out, no imprsn frm nxt............* (8 to 1 op 6 to 1) 5
2665[9] STRIKE-A-POSE [68] 7-10-7 G Lee, *hld up, hdwy to chase ldrs appr 5th, outpcd bef 3 out.*
..................(8 to 1 op 7 to 1 tchd 9 to 1) 6
2630[5] KISMETIM [61] 7-9-9 (5*) T Hogg, *beh, lost tch 4th, late hdwy, not trble ldrs..............* (25 to 1 op 16 to 1) 7
2999[5] QUIXOTRY [69] 6-10-8 E Husband, *hld up, mstk 5th, sn drvn alng, nvr on terms..* (25 to 1 op 20 to 1 tchd 33 to 1) 8
2630[7] JARROW [61] 6-10-0 G F Ryan, *chsd ldrs till wknd appr 4 out, tld off........................* (25 to 1 op 16 to 1) 9

3184⁵ STILL HERE (Ire) [70] (bl) 4-9-10 (5*) L Cummins, *led to second, remained cl up, drvn aftr 4th, sn wknd, tld off.*
.... (11 to 1 op 8 to 1) 10
2630⁹ BUD'S BET (Ire) [68] 9-10-4 (3*) M Newton, *beh, lost tch 4th, tld off...* (25 to 1 op 16 to 1) 11
3184 A BADGE TOO FAR (Ire) [61] 7-9-11 (3*) S Taylor, *al beh, tld off.....................* (66 to 1 op 33 to 1) 12
CLASSIC ACCOUNT [70] 9-10-4 (3*) C Elliott, *led second, clr 4th, four ls ahead whn f four out...* (7 to 2 jt-fav op 5 to 1) f
762³ RED MARCH HARE [72] 6-10-6 (5*) C McCormack, *in tch, blun 4th, wknd nxt, tld off whn pld up bef 3 out.*
.... (16 to 1 op 14 to 1 tchd 25 to 1) pu
2575 REGAL JEST [61] 7-9-9 (5*) N Horrocks, *midfield early, beh frm 4th, tld off whn pld up bef 2 out...* (50 to 1 op 33 to 1) pu
2999 BIT OF ROUGH (Ire) [61] 7-10-0 D J Kavanagh, *beh, reminders appr 3rd, lost tch nxt, tld off whn pld up bef 3 out.*
.... (50 to 1 op 33 to 1) pu
Dist: 3l, 1½l, 1¼l, 2l, sht-hd, 2l, 7l, 26l, 3l, ¾l. 4m 1.90s. a 11.90s (16 Ran).

(M Bray-Cotton, V Lockley & J Davies), W Clay

3318 Althrey Woodhouse Handicap Chase
Class C (0-130 5-y-o and up) £4,879
2½m 110yds................ (3:15)

2934* FRICKLEY [112] 11-10-10 R Dunwoody, *in tch, lft in ld 5th, mstk 2 out, drvn clr appr last, eased cl hme.*
.... (13 to 8 fav op 11 to 8) 1
1871³ CUMBRIAN CHALLENGE (Ire) [128] 8-11-12 L Wyer, *hld up, hdwy to chase ldrs tenth, chlgd 2 out, no extr betw last two.*
.... (4 to 1 op 7 to 2 tchd 9 to 2) 2
3134⁷ SOUTHAMPTON [115] (v) 7-10-13 Richard Guest, *hld up in rear, hdwy und pres 4 out to chase ldrs, drvn appr 2 out, sn no imprsn.....................* (5 to 2 op 7 to 2) 3
2991² DOLIKOS [102] 10-10-0³ (3*) Michael Brennan, *chsd ldrs, lost pl tenth, no dngr aftrwards......* (33 to 1 op 25 to 1) 4
2786⁵ CAMITROV (Fr) [130] 7-12-0 P Niven, *chsd clr ldr to 5th, cl up till wknd aftr 3 out, eased whn btn frm nxt, broke blood vessel.*
.... (14 to 1 tchd 16 to 1 and 20 to 1) 5
ANDERMATT [117] 10-11-1 W Marston, *hld up in rear, struggling whn mstk 11th, sn no dngr.....* (16 to 1 op 12 to 1) 6
2796³ GENERAL PERSHING [130] 11-12-0 R Johnson, *led, clr 4th, f nxt........................* (5 to 1 tchd 6 to 1) f
Dist: 5l, 7l, 17l, 16l, 12l. 5m 14.80s. a 28.80s (7 Ran).

(Robert Ogden), G Richards

3319 Miles MacAdam Novices' Chase
Class D (5-y-o and up) £4,357 3m
110yds................ (3:50)

1585* CHOPWELL CURTAINS 7-11-11 L Wyer, *trkd ldrs, improved to ld 2 out, blun last, all out............* (11 to 2 op 4 to 1) 1
3065² MYSTIC ISLE (Ire) 7-11-5 W Marston, *hld up, hdwy und pres 5 out, chlgd last, staying on whn edgd lft cl hme.*
.... (16 to 1 op 10 to 1) 2
2827² AROUND THE GALE (Ire) 6-12-0 R Dunwoody, *led, mstks 3rd and 12th, hdd 2 out, rallied aftr last, no extr cl hme.*
.... (2 to 1 on op 13 to 8 on tchd 6 to 4) 3
3207 MONYMOSS (Ire) 8-11-11 Richard Guest, *pressed ldr, mstk 3 out, wknd appr nxt, sn eased.......* (9 to 1 op 5 to 1) 4
3155⁸ THE REVEREND BERT 9-11-11 B Clifford, *in rear, brief effrt 13th, sn no dngr.............* (10 to 1 op 8 to 1) 5
2954 GRIZZLY BEAR (Ire) 7-11-5 S Wynne, *trkd ldrs till lost pl and beh 13th, tld off........* (150 to 1 op 50 to 1) 6
2862 FOXWOODS VALLEY (Ire) 8-11-5 R Johnson, *hld up, imprvg whn blun badly 13th, sn beh, jmpd rght 3 out, 6th and no ch when blunded and uns rdr last......* (14 to 1 op 10 to 1) ur
Dist: 1l, 1¼l, 18l, 10l, 28l. 6m 16.40s. a 31.40s (7 Ran).

(Durham Drapes Ltd), T D Easterby

3320 North West Racing Club Maiden
Chase Class D (5-y-o and up) £3,696
2½m 110yds................ (4:25)

2799³ PEARL EPEE 8-11-2 R Johnson, *prmnt, lft in ld appr second, drw clr approaching last, easily......* (14 to 1 op 8 to 1) 1
3023 CAMPECHE BAY (Ire) 8-11-7 R Dunwoody, *prmnt, drvn aftr 3 out, sn btn...........* (7 to 4 on op 6 to 4 on tchd 5 to 4 on) 2
2881 DEE LIGHT 8-11-2 P Niven, *hld up, hdwy 8th, chlgd 3 out, btn frm nxt.......................* (25 to 1 op 10 to 1) 3
2246⁶ CRANE HILL (bl) 7-11-7 W Marston, *in rear, und pres tenth, struggling whn mstk 3 out, sn no ch.*
.... (12 to 1 op 2 to 2 tchd 6 to 1) 4
3124⁴ FORT ZEDDAAN (Ire) 7-11-0 (7*) R Wilkinson, *hld up in tch, hdwy appr tenth, 4th and und pres whn f four out.*
.... (25 to 1 op 16 to 1) f
1543² LITTLE NOTICE (Ire) 6-11-7 S Wynne, *hld up in tch till f 6th.*
.... (11 to 1 op 8 to 1 tchd 12 to 1) f
3098³ DANDIE IMP 9-11-7 D Walsh, *led till rein broke and ran out appr second.*
.... (7 to 1 op 8 to 1 tchd 10 to 1 and 12 to 1) ro
3046⁶ TUG YOUR FORELOCK 6-11-4 (3*) Michael Brennan, *sn tld off, mstk 4th, pld up bef 9th.*
.... (66 to 1 op 50 to 1 tchd 100 to 1) pu
2605 LADY ROSEBURY 7-11-2 T Jenks, *sn tld off, mstk 3rd, pld up bef 6th.........................* (66 to 1 op 50 to 1) pu

3098 LEDBURIAN 7-11-4 (3*) Guy Lewis, *trkd ldrs, drvn alng frm 6th, lost pl tenth, sn beh, tld off whn pld up bef 2 out.*
.... (100 to 1 op 66 to 1) pu
Dist: 21l, ½l, 2l. 5m 11.90s. a 25.90s (10 Ran).

(Mrs A A Shutes), D Nicholson

3321 Lightwood Green Handicap Hurdle
Class E (0-115 5-y-o and up) £2,957
3m........................ (4:55)

3062³ SELATAN (Ire) [109] 5-12-0 R Dunwoody, *chsd clr ldr early, cld to chal 3 out, ran on to ld close hme.* (4 to 1 tchd 5 to 1) 1
3129 PRUSSIA [95] 6-10-11 (3*) Guy Lewis, *chsd ldrs, led appr 2 out, hdd and no extr cl hme.........* (10 to 1 op 8 to 1) 2
3209* WINN'S PRIDE (Ire) [105] 6-11-10 S Wynne, *hld up in rear, hdwy aftr 6th, sn in tch, ev ch frm 2 out till one pace r-in.*
.... (4 to 1 tchd 9 to 2) 3
2851 FLAT TOP [98] 6-11-0 (3*) P Midgley, *hld up in rear, effrt and hdwy 4 out, swrvd to avoid faller nxt, chsd ldrs 2 out, unbl to quicken appr last...............* (11 to 1 op 10 to 1) 4
2710⁸ JIGGINSTOWN [81] 10-9-7 (7*) L Cooper, *hld up, hdwy 4 out, chasing ldg bunch aftr nxt, no imprsn.* (20 to 1 op 14 to 1) 5
3045⁵ NEEDWOOD POPPY [88] 9-10-7 B Clifford, *beh 4th, late hdwy, nvr nrr......................* (11 to 2 op 5 to 1) 6
3034² JERVAULX (Ire) [99] 6-11-4 P Niven, *midfield, hdwy appr 5 out, lft in ld 3 out, hdd approaching nxt, eased whn btn betw last 2.....................* (7 to 2 fav op 5 to 1 tchd 11 to 2) 7
2977 WHITEBONNET (Ire) [82] (bl) 7-9-12 (3*) Sophie Mitchell, *midfield early, beh frm 5 out.........* (25 to 1 op 14 to 1) 8
2969⁵ WHITE WILLOW [95] (bl) 8-11-0 T Jenks, *sn led and clr, hdd 5 out, wknd, tld off..........* (16 to 1 op 12 to 1) 9
2485 DOOLAR (USA) [81] 10-9-13² (3*) Michael Brennan, *midfield early, beh 5th, collapsed aftr nxt, dead.*
.... (33 to 1 op 20 to 1 tchd 50 to 1) f
3054³ INDIAN QUEST [101] 8-11-6 W Marston, *chsd clr ldr frm 3rd, improved to ld 5 out, one l in frnt whn f 3 out.*
.... (11 to 1 op 10 to 1) f
3146² CASSIO'S BOY [91] 6-10-10 R Johnson, *hld up, hdwy into second, sn beh, lost tch 7th, tld off whn pld up bef nxt.*
.... (8 to 1 op 7 to 1 tchd 12 to 1) f
2860 FAR SENIOR [81] 11-9-9 (5*) D J Kavanagh, *prmnt, lost pl second, sn beh, lost tch 7th, tld off whn pld up bef nxt.*
.... (50 to 1 op 33 to 1) pu
Dist: Nk, 2½l, sht-hd, 5l, ½l, 3½l, 6l, dist. 5m 39.00s. a 10.00s (13 Ran).
SR: 12/-/5/-/-/-/ (Starlight Racing), D R Gandolfo

3322 Bangor-on-Dee Maiden National
Hunt Flat Class H (4,5,6-y-o) £1,549
2m 1f................ (5:25)

GO CAHOOTS (USA) 4-11-2 C Rae, *al prmnt, led 6 fs out, hdd entering fnl 2, rallied to rgn ld cl hme.* (12 to 1 op 7 to 1) 1
3048⁷ DINKY DORA 4-10-4 (7*) N T Egan, *in tch, improved 4 fs out, led gng wl entering fnl 2, hdd cl hme.* (16 to 1 tchd 20 to 1) 2
GALESHAN (Ire) 5-11-3 (7*) R Burns, *hld up, hdwy on ins o'r 4 fs out, tracking ldrs whn not clr run over 3 out, ran on inside last.......................* (12 to 1 op 7 to 1) 3
PENNYBRYN 4-10-4 (7*) C Elliott, *midfield, hdwy o'r 4 fs out, wndrd und pres over one out, styd on.* (10 to 1 op 16 to 1) 4
MAZZELMO 4-10-4 (7*) S Melrose, *midfield, effrt and hdwy o'r 3 fs out, sn chasing ldrs, unbl to quicken ins last.*
.... (9 to 1 tchd 14 to 1) 5
STAR ADVENTURE 5-11-10 Miss E James, *strted slwly, in rear, hdwy 4 fs out, kpt on.........* (50 to 1 op 33 to 1) 6
2552 BE IN SPACE 6-11-2 (3*) Sophie Mitchell, *strted slwly, sn reco'red and prmnt, rdn and one pace fnl 2 fs.*
.... (50 to 1 op 33 to 1) 7
DAKOTA III (Fr) 6-11-3 (7*) Mr O McPhail, *towards rear, hdwy 6 fs out, pushed alng o'r 4 out, fdd over 3 out.*
.... (6 to 1 op 4 to 1) 8
2824² SHROPSHIRE GALE (Ire) 6-11-5 (5*) O Burrows, *hld up, hdwy 6 fs out, sn cl up, rdn 3 furlongs out, soon wknd...* (9 to 4 jt-fav op 7 to 2) 9
2824⁴ ARCTIC FOX (Ire) 5-11-3 (7*) Mr A Wintle, *whipped round strt, reco'red to race in midfield, hdwy over 5 fs out, chsd ldrs til wknd over 3 out.............* (9 to 4 jt-fav op 3 to 1) 10
MICHIGAN BLUE 5-11-10 Mr A Mitchell, *pld hrd, sn led, hdd 6 fs out, wknd o'r 3 out.............* (33 to 1 op 25 to 1) 11
SEE MORE ANGELS 6-11-2 (3*) E Husband, *hmpd strt, in rear, pushed alng 5 fs out, nvr a factor.* (50 to 1 op 33 to 1) 12
ROCKY BALBOA 5-11-7 (3*) Guy Lewis, *cl up till rdn and wknd o'r 4 fs out.................* (50 to 1 op 33 to 1) 13
OUTRAGEOUS AFFAIR 5-11-2 (3*) G Lee, *pld hrd, in tch, hdwy and rcd wide hlwy, sn prmnt, wknd 4 fs out, tld off.*
.... (33 to 1 op 25 to 1) 14
RAMILLION 5-11-5 Mr A Brown, *strted slwly, towards rear, hdwy hlwy, in tch till wknd 5 fs out, tld off.*
.... (50 to 1 op 33 to 1) 15
3082 EAGLE DANCER 5-11-7 (3*) Michael Brennan, *whipped round and uns rdr strt.............* (14 to 1 op 9 to 2) ur
3142⁸ NIRVANA PRINCESS 5-10-12 (7*) J Mogford, *refused to race, took no part...........* (10 to 1 op 33 to 1 tchd 50 to 1) 1
Dist: Hd, 1¾l, 1¼l, 1¼l, nk, 3l, 7l, 8l, 5l, nk. 4m 5.30s. (17 Ran).
(Marisa Bartoli & John Moreton), Andrew Turnell

LINGFIELD (good to firm)

Saturday March 22nd
Going Correction: MINUS 0.40 sec. per fur.

3323 Newleaf Juvenile Maiden Hurdle Class E (4-y-o) £2,360 2m 110yds
.... (1:30)

3150[7] SEATTLE ALLEY (USA) 11-0 J A McCarthy, *confidently rdn, prog 4th, led appr 2 out, ridden out.*
.... (13 to 8 op 5 to 4 tchd 7 to 4) 1
QUAKERS FIELD 11-0 D Gallagher, *hld up, str chal whn not fluent 2 out and last, ran on wl r-in.*
.... (11 to 8 on tchd 6 to 4 on and 5 to 4 on) 2
3139[5] VERONICA FRANCO 10-6 (3*) P Henley, *wth ldr, led 3 out till appr nxt, 4th and btn whn hit 2 out.*
.... (66 to 1 op 25 to 1 tchd 100 to 1) 3
3117[8] SILVRETTA (Ire) 10-6 (3*) L Aspell, *hld up beh ldrs, reminders aftr second, ev ch appr 2 out, wknd approaching last.*
.... (25 to 1 op 14 to 1 tchd 33 to 1) 4
2925[9] ZAISAN (Ire) 11-0 P Hide, *made most to 3 out, wknd appr nxt.*
.... (14 to 1 tchd 12 to 1) 5
2303[5] ILLUMINATE 11-0 J R Kavanagh, *pld hrd, prmnt till wknd 3 out, tld off whn pulled up bef last.*
.... (14 to 1 op 10 to 1 tchd 16 to 1) pu
3091[8] MY NAD KNOWS 11-0 T J O'Sullivan, *hld up in rear, hit and rdn 5th, sn wknd, beh whn mstk nxt, tld off when pld up bef 2 out.*
.... (100 to 1) pu
Dist: ¾l, 11l, ½l, 12l. 3m 57.80s. a 6.80s (7 Ran).

(L & P Partnership), P R Webber

3324 Malcolm And Sue Have Said I Do Novices' Handicap Chase Class F (0-95 5-y-o and up) £2,467 2m (2:05)

3193[2] BUCKLAND LAD (Ire) [81] 6-11-10 J R Kavanagh, *wth wdh, hdwy to track ldr 4th, led four out, lft clr 2 out, eased r-in.*
.... (11 to 4 on op 3 to 1 on tchd 5 to 2 on) 1
2877[7] MASTER PANGLOSS (Ire) [60] 7-10-3 W McFarland, *wth ldr, led 3rd, jmpd slwly 4th, mstk and hdd four out, wknd nxt, lft moderate second and blun 2 out.*
.... (11 to 1 op 7 to 1 tchd 12 to 1) 2
1857[6] NAUTICAL GEORGE (Ire) [80] 7-11-9 Gary Lyons, *led to 3rd, outpcd frm 8th.*
.... (6 to 1 op 4 to 1 tchd 13 to 2) 3
3092 EAU SO SLOE [60] 6-10-3 A Dicken, *beh frm 5th, no ch whn mstk last.*
.... (40 to 1 op 25 to 1 tchd 50 to 1) 4
2977 FANE PARK (Ire) [70] 9-10-10 (3*) P Henley, *hld up, hdwy 4 out, chlgd nxt, second and held whn f 2 out, dead.*
.... (10 to 1 op 12 to 1 tchd 16 to 1) f
BRIGHT SEASON [61] 9-10-4 T J O'Sullivan, *beh frm 7th, tld off whn pld up bef 3 out.* (40 to 1 op 33 to 1 tchd 50 to 1) pu
Dist: 4l, 3½l, nk. 4m 9.30s. a 15.30s (6 Ran).

(Mrs R M Hepburn), D M Grissell

3325 Chelsham Selling Handicap Hurdle Class G (0-95 4-y-o and up) £2,024 2m 110yds. (2:40)

3163[9] RUTH'S GAMBLE [60] (v) 9-10-3 J A McCarthy, *hld up in tch, led last, rdn out.*
.... (5 to 1 op 6 to 1) 1
3099[6] YELLOW DRAGON (Ire) [80] 4-10-12 (3*) P Henley, *hld up, hdwy 4th, led betw fnl 2, mstk and hdd last, no extr.*
.... (13 to 2 op 5 to 1 tchd 7 to 1) 2
3095[*] DERISBAY (Ire) [81] (bl) 9-11-3 (7*) M Batchelor, *prmnt, led appr 2 out, hdd approaching last, one pace.*
.... (9 to 2 op 3 to 1 tchd 5 to 1) 3
3174[3] SWINGING SIXTIES (Ire) [75] 6-11-4 J R Kavanagh, *hdwy 5th, one pace appr 2 out.*
.... (7 to 4 fav op 7 to 4 tchd 13 to 8) 4
3093[3] SCRIPT [70] 6-10-13 D Morris, *led till appr 2 out, sn wknd.*
.... (10 to 1 op 7 to 1) 5
3148[5] ALDWICK COLONNADE [62] 10-10-5 W McFarland, *beh frm 5th.* .... (25 to 1 op 20 to 1) 6
2614 TAPESTRY ROSE [57] 6-10-0 A Dicken, *hld up beh ldrs, wknd 5th.* .... (50 to 1 op 33 to 1) 7
1343[6] COOLEGALE [65] 11-10-8 P Hide, *prmnt, pckd second, wknd 5th.* .... (25 to 1 op 20 to 1 tchd 33 to 1) 8
2616 CAVO GRECO (USA) [64] 8-10-7 D Skyrme, *beh till pld up bef 5th.* .... (20 to 1 tchd 25 to 1) pu
3292 TIGANA [57] (v) 5-10-0 K Gaule, *hld up beh ldrs, wknd appr 5th, tld off whn pld up aftr 3 out.* .... (50 to 1 op 33 to 1) pu
Dist: 1¾l, ½l, 6l, 5l, 6l, 10l, 20l. 3m 55.00s. a 13.00s (10 Ran).

(Mrs A Emanuel), Mrs L C Jewell

3326 Chris Pye 50th Birthday Novices' Chase Class E (5-y-o and up) £3,316 3m. (3:10)

2830[7] WEE WINDY (Ire) 8-11-4 P Hide, *al hndy, dsptd ld frm 11th, led 3 out, all out.* .... (11 to 4 op 6 to 5 on tchd Evens) 1
3133 LITTLE MARTINA (Ire) 9-11-5 J R Kavanagh, *made most to 3 out, hrd rdn, ran on.*
.... (11 to 10 on op 6 to 5 on tchd Evens) 2
3000 NAPOLEON'S GOLD (Ire) (bl) 7-11-4 D Morris, *hit second, dsptd ld to 11th, sn wknd, tld off frm 4 out.*
.... (20 to 1 op 25 to 1 tchd 16 to 1) 3
Dist: Sht-hd, dist. 6m 5.00s. a 11.00s (3 Ran).

(W E Gale), J T Gifford

3327 Eden Hunters' Chase Class H (6-y-o and up) £1,122 3m. .... (3:45)

3153 COLONIAL KELLY 9-12-7 (5*) Mr C Vigors, *in tch, led 8th, made rst, lft wl clr 2 out.* .... (5 to 2) 1
RUN FOR FREE 13-12-2 (3*) Mr A Hill, *hld up, jmpd slwly tenth, sn beh, lft frm 13th, lft poor second 2 out.*
.... (7 to 2 op 9 to 4) 2
PRINCE BUCK (Ire) 7-12-2 (3*) Mr P Hacking, *led till aftr 4th, led 7th to nxt, one l second and rdn whn f 2 out.*
.... (Evens fav op 6 to 4 tchd 7 to 4) f
2992 PRO BONO (Ire) 7-12-5 (7*) Mr A Dalton, *hld up beh ldrs, 4th whn blun and uns rdr 8th.*
.... (11 to 4 op 5 to 2) ur
LOYAL GAIT (NZ) 9-11-12 (7*) Mr Andrew Martin, *prmnt, led aftr 4th to 7th, wknd frm 11th, tld off whn pld up bef 3 out.*
.... (20 to 1 op 10 to 1 tchd 25 to 1) pu
Dist: Dist. 6m 17.30s. a 23.30s (5 Ran).

(Alan Cowing), Mrs D M Grissell

3328 Gummer Handicap Hurdle Class E (0-115 4-y-o and up) £2,343 2m 110yds. .... (4:20)

3194[*] TICKERTY'S GIFT [114] 7-11-6 (7*) M Batchelor, *made all, clr appr 2 out, pushed out.* (11 to 8 op 11 to 10 tchd 7 to 4) 1
3062[4] MARIUS (Ire) [115] 7-11-7 (7*) W Greatrex, *chsd wnr frm second, rdn appr 2 out, one pace.*
.... (5 to 4 fav op 11 to 10 on tchd 11 to 8) 2
3344[2] COURAGEOUS KNIGHT [87] 8-9-12[1] (3*) P Henley, *chsd wnr to second, rdn aftr 4th, wknd frm 3 out.* .... (3 to 1) 3
Dist: 2½l, 18l. 3m 51.30s. a 0.30s (3 Ran).
SR: 30/28/-/

(K Higson), G L Moore

NEWBURY (good to firm (races 1,5), good (2,3,4,6,7))
Saturday March 22nd
Going Correction: NIL (races 1,5), PLUS 0.15 (2,3,4,6,7)

3329 Brown Chamberlin Handicap Chase Class B (6-y-o and up) £6,853 3m
.... (1:15)

3024[*] SENOR EL BETRUTTI (Ire) [138] 8-11-13 J Osborne, *made all, quickened wl whn chlgd frm 2 out, readily.*
.... (Evens fav op 11 to 10 tchd 6 to 5) 1
3101[3] PYR FOUR [125] 10-11-0 D Bridgwater, *hld up in 4th, hdwy to dispute 3rd frm 12th, styd on to take second r-in, no imprsn.*
.... (4 to 1 tchd 11 to 2) 2
2713[6] VALIANT WARRIOR [129] 9-11-4 R Garritty, *rcd in 3rd till hdwy to track wnr aftr 8th, rdn to chlgd frm 2 out, outpcd r-in.*
.... (3 to 1 op 7 to 2) 3
2677[3] DARREN THE BRAVE [111] 9-10-0 C Llewellyn, *chsd wnr till rdn and wknd frm 4 out.* .. (9 to 1 op 6 to 1 tchd 10 to 1) 4
Dist: 2½l, 1½l, 12l. 5m 53.60s. a 8.60s (4 Ran).
SR: 13/

(Gerard Nock), Mrs Susan Nock

3330 Lambourn Handicap Hurdle Class B (4-y-o and up) £4,883 2m 110yds
.... (1:45)

3080[6] KADASTROF (Fr) [133] 7-11-4 (7*) X Aizpuru, *made all, sn clr, rdn whn lft clear ag'n 2 out, all out.*
.... (6 to 1 tchd 8 to 1 and 11 to 2) 1
2218 ASHWELL BOY (Ire) [132] 6-11-10 D Bridgwater, *in tch, hdwy to chase ldrs whn hmpd 2 out, hrd rdn and rallied run in, not quite get up.* .... (8 to 1 op 10 to 1) 2
3080 SHANKAR (Ire) [128] 6-11-1 (5*) Mr R Thornton, *sn in tch, lft chasing wnr 2 out, rdn, crrd head to one side and found little r-in.* .... (11 to 1 op 8 to 1 tchd 12 to 1) 3
2958[3] MIM-LOU-AND [112] 5-10-4 J Culloty, *hdwy to chase ldrs aftr 4th, wknd 2 out.* .. (7 to 2 op 5 to 2 tchd 4 to 1) 4
2113[3] RADANPOUR [112] 5-10-4 A S Smith, *hld up, hdwy to chase ldrs 3 out, sn one pace.* .... (5 to 1 op 4 to 1) 5
3079[4] BLAIR CASTLE (Ire) [114] 6-10-6 M A Fitzgerald, *chsd ldrs till wknd 3 out.* .... (7 to 1 op 6 to 1) 6
3156 HAMILTON SILK [132] 5-11-10 J Osborne, *sn tracking wnr, gng wl whn f 2 out.* .... (9 to 4 fav op 5 to 2 tchd 11 to 4) f
Dist: ¾l, nk, 12l, sht-hd, 3l. 4m 0.20s. a 11.20s (7 Ran).
SR: 10/8/4/-/

(A P Paton), R Dickin

3331 Hoechst Roussel Vet Panacur EBF Mares' 'National Hunt' Novices' Hurdle Final Handicap Class C (5-y-o and up) £10,502 2m 5f. .... (2:15)

2541[*] LUCIA FORTE [102] 6-11-8 C O'Dwyer, *hld up, steady hdwy aftr 7th, chsd ldr aftr 2 out, chlgd last, hrd rdn to ld r-in, all out.* .... (7 to 2 fav op 4 to 1 tchd 3 to 1) 1

2882* FANTASY LINE [96] 6-11-2 A Thornton, *chsd ldrs, chlgd 2 out, sn led, rdn last, hdd r-in, no extr cl hme.*
.......................(12 to 1 op 10 to 1 tchd 14 to 1) 2

2951² FIDDLING THE FACTS (Ire) [104] 6-11-10 M A Fitzgerald, *sn tracking ldrs, slight ld 3 out, hdd aftr 2 out, soon one pace.*
.......................(9 to 2 op 4 to 1 tchd 5 to 1) 3

2721² POTTER'S GALE (Ire) [108] 6-11-9 (5*) Mr R Thornton, *trkd ldrs till chlgd 8th to nxt, wknd 2 out.*
.......................(9 to 2 op 7 to 2 tchd 5 to 1) 4

2932³ BULA VOGUE (Ire) 7-11-0 D O'Sullivan, *led to 4th, styd chasing ldrs till wknd aftr 3 out.......* (20 to 1 op 16 to 1) 5

2513⁷ JOY FOR LIFE (Ire) [80] 6-9-7 (7*) X Aizpuru, *al in rear.*
.......................(50 to 1 tchd 66 to 1) 6

2882* DAISY DAYS (Ire) [92] 7-10-12 A S Smith, *pressed ldr till led 4th, hdd 3 out, sn btn.....................* (20 to 1 op 16 to 1) 7

3019* KONVEKTA QUEEN (Ire) [102] 6-11-8 M Richards, *mid-divison, rdn 7th, sn btn...................*(11 to 2 op 5 to 1) 8

2298⁵ GAYE FAME [92] 6-10-12 S McNeill, *al in rear, sn tld off.*
.......................(12 to 1 op 10 to 1) 9

3137⁷ LOCH NA KEAL [80] 5-10-0 C Llewellyn, *chsd ldrs, chlgd 6th, wknd nxt, tld off.........*(8 to 1 op 14 to 1 tchd 16 to 1) 10

2394³ RIVER BAY (Ire) [99] 6-11-5 J Culloty, *beh 4th, rdn 7th, sn wknd, tld off whn pld up bef 3 out.*
.......................(12 to 1 op 10 to 1 tchd 14 to 1) pu

Dist: Hd, 5l, 26l, 4l, 8l, 4l, ¾l, dist, 15l. 5m 2.80s. a 8.80s (11 Ran).
SR: 38/32/25/13/-/-/ (Mrs Lucia Farmer), K C Bailey

3332 Final Novices' Hurdle Class D (Div I) (4-y-o and up) £3,169 2m 110yds .... (2:50)

3022⁴ QUALITY (Ire) 4-10-13 G Tormey, *trkd ldrs, chsd wnr frm 5th, rdn to ld r-in, kpt on wl.*
.......................(9 to 4 fav op 5 to 2 tchd 11 to 4) 1

2925¹ HISAR (Ire) 4-10-13 C O'Dwyer, *led, clr second, rdn appr last, hdd and no extr r-in.............*(7 to 1 tchd 6 to 1) 2

RIPARIUS (USA) 6-11-7 R Bellamy, *hdwy 5th, styd on und pres frm 2 out, not pace to rch ldrs.....* (6 to 1 op 4 to 1) 3

2920⁶ GET REAL (Ire) 6-11-7 M A Fitzgerald, *hld up, hdwy 5th, one pace frm 3 out.....................*(7 to 2 op 4 to 1) 4

2952⁴ I RECALL (Ire) (v) 6-11-7 S McNeill, *chsd ldr to 5th, wknd aftr 3 out.........................*(33 to 1 op 20 to 1) 5

2656 PEALINGS 5-11-2 (5*) Mr R Thornton, *nvr rchd ldrs.*
.......................(33 to 1 op 20 to 1) 6

2255 NO MATTER (Ire) 6-11-7 D Bridgwater, *beh, some hdwy frm 3 out, not a dngr...........*(33 to 1 op 20 to 1 tchd 40 to 1) 7

PEERS FOLLY (Ire) 7-11-7 J F Titley, *nvr rchd ldrs.*
.......................(14 to 1 op 12 to 1) 8

2250 DON'T MIND IF I DO (Ire) (bl) 6-11-7 A Thornton, *chsd ldrs to 5th, wknd rpdly...................*(50 to 1 op 20 to 1) 9

3120⁵ SWAN STREET (NZ) 6-11-7 J Railton, *chsd ldrs till wknd quickly appr 3 out...............*(14 to 1 tchd 16 to 1) 10

3022⁶ REGAL SPLENDOUR (Can) 4-10-13 D O'Sullivan, *in tch, hdwy to chase ldrs 5th, sn wknd.*
.......................(16 to 1 op 14 to 1 tchd 20 to 1) 11

2463⁹ BALLYRANTER 8-11-7 R Garritty, *mstks second and 3rd, sn beh...................................*(14 to 1) 12

2426⁹ BON LUCK (Ire) 5-11-7 L Harvey, *mstk 1st, blun second, sn wl beh...........................*(33 to 1 op 20 to 1) 13

LAS ANIMAS (USA) (bl) 6-11-2 B Powell, *al beh, tld off.*
.......................(33 to 1 op 14 to 1) 14

3036 CUILLIN 5-11-2 T J Murphy, *hit 1st and beh, tld off whn pld up bef 5th.......................*(66 to 1 op 33 to 1) pu

1641 LIZIUM 5-11-2 S Fox, *sn beh, tld off whn pld up bef 3 out.*
.......................(33 to 1) pu

Dist: 1½l, 9l, 1l, 20l, 2½l, 7l, 1l, 9l, 5l, 14l. 3m 57.80s. a 8.80s (16 Ran).
SR: 22/20/19/18/-/-/ (D B O'Connor), P J Hobbs

3333 March Novices' Handicap Chase Class D (0-110 5-y-o and up) £3,493 2½m..................... (3:20)

3252⁴ RED BRANCH (Ire) [85] 8-11-0 (5ex) T J Murphy, *jmpd wl, made all, wnt rght last, came clr r-in.*
.......................(6 to 5 on op Evens tchd 11 to 10) 1

2604² BOOTS N ALL (Ire) [72] 7-10-1 R Greene, *chsd ldrs till lost pos and mstk 12th, rallied to track wnr 4 out, sn ev ch, wnt rght last, soon outpcd........*(5 to 1 op 7 to 2 tchd 11 to 2) 2

3040² MAMMY'S CHOICE (Ire) [95] 7-11-5 (5*) Mr R Thornton, *chsd wnr, chlgd 12th till one pace frm 3 out.*
.......................(8 to 1 op 6 to 1 tchd 9 to 2) 3

3194² SPRING TO GLORY [95] 10-11-10 B Powell, *hld up, hdwy 12th, rdn aftr 4 out, wknd 2 out.*
.......................(8 to 1 op 6 to 1 tchd 9 to 1) 4

3204³ KOO'S PROMISE [82] 6-10-8 (3*) T Dascombe, *hdwy to chase ldrs 12th, wknd 3 out.(7 to 1 op 6 to 1 tchd 8 to 1)* 5

2558⁹ LAGHAM LAD [77] 8-10-6 S McNeill, *hdwy and hit 12th, wknd quickly 3 out, tld off............*(33 to 1 op 12 to 1) 6

3052⁶ MUSIC CLASS (Ire) [80] 6-10-9 D Gallagher, *sn tld off.*
.......................(20 to 1 op 10 to 1) 7

Dist: 3½l, 10l, 4l, 1¼l, dist, 2l. 4m 53.60s. a 5.60s (7 Ran).
SR: 30/13/26/22/7/-/ (E J Mangan), J S King

3334 Final Novices' Hurdle Class D (Div II) (4-y-o and up) £3,148 2m 110yds .... (3:55)

2699⁶ JOHN DRUMM 6-11-7 R Garritty, *led till appr second, chsd ldr till led aftr 3 out, rdn and hld on wl frm approaching last.*
.......................(2 to 1 op 6 to 4 tchd 9 to 4) 1

2825⁵ CLASSY LAD (NZ) 7-11-7 M A Fitzgerald, *hld up, hdwy 5th, chsd wnr frm 2 out, hrd rdn and one pace appr last.*
.......................(7 to 4 fav op 6 to 4 tchd 15 to 8) 2

2976⁶ MAETERLINCK (Ire) 5-11-0 (7*) Clare Thorner, *chsd ldrs, hit 5th and lost pl, ran on und pres frm 2 out, no dngr.*
.......................(50 to 1 op 20 to 1) 3

LUCKY ARCHER 4-10-13 D Bridgwater, *mstk second, gd hdwy to chase ldrs 3 out, wknd quickly aftr nxt.*
.......................(12 to 1 op 6 to 1) 4

REAL MADRID 6-11-2 (5*) Mr R Thornton, *nvr better than mid-div...........................*(66 to 1 op 25 to 1) 5

3022 HONEYSHAN 5-11-2 S McNeill, *hdwy 5th, wknd 3 out.*
.......................(66 to 1 op 25 to 1) 6

SADLER'S REALM 4-10-13 G Tormey, *effrt appr 5th, sn wknd.*
.......................(20 to 1 op 7 to 1) 7

2996⁷ PALAFICO 7-11-7 R Bellamy, *al beh, tld off.*
.......................(66 to 1 op 20 to 1) 8

SPECTACLE JIM 8-11-0 (7*) Gordon Gallagher, *chsd ldrs till wknd quickly 5th, tld off............*(66 to 1 op 20 to 1) 9

3064 ABSOLUTE LIMIT 5-11-4 (3*) L Aspell, *led appr second, clr nxt, hdd aftr 3 out, 4th and wkng whn blun and uns ridder next.*
.......................(14 to 1 op 12 to 1 tchd 16 to 1) ur

2996² ZANDER 5-11-7 C Llewellyn, *chsd ldrs, rdn and 3rd whn stumbled and uns rdr 3 out...........*(4 to 1 tchd 5 to 1) ur

2283⁹ ROYAL TEAM 5-11-7 D Gallagher, *keen hold, beh frm 3rd, slpd up bend aftr nxt, destroyed.*
.......................(50 to 1 op 20 to 1 tchd 66 to 1) su

2876 OUT FOR A DUCK 6-11-7 C Maude, *al beh, tld off whn pld up bef 3 out.......................*(66 to 1 op 25 to 1) pu

Dist: 4l, 14l, ½l, 11l, 2l, 6l, dist, 30l. 4m 1.90s. a 12.90s (13 Ran).
(Andrew Jenkins), P R Webber

3335 Spring Standard Open National Hunt Flat Class H (4,5,6-y-o) £1,320 2m 110yds........................ (4:30)

2831* COUNTRY BEAU 5-11-11 M Richards, *hld up, gd hdwy 5 fs out, led 2 furlongs out, drvn and ran on wl fnl furlong.*
.......................(11 to 4 fav op 3 to 1 tchd 9 to 4) 1

3082⁴ GOLDEN EAGLE 5-11-4 M A Fitzgerald, *in tch, hdwy to chal 3 fs out, rdn 2 out, styd on und pres ins last.*
.......................(7 to 2 tchd 9 to 2) 2

2953² BOLD LEAP 5-11-4 Mr A Sansome, *chsd ldrs, rdn to ld 3 fs out, hdd 2 out, one pace.......* (16 to 1 op 12 to 1) 3

3048* BESSIE BROWNE (Ire) 5-11-1 (5*) Mr R Thornton, *chsd ldrs, one pace fnl 3 fs..................* (16 to 1 op 8 to 1) 4

BROWJOSHY (Ire) 4-10-10 J F Titley, *hdwy hfwy, lost pl 6 fs out, ran on ag'n fnl 2 furlongs........*(20 to 1 op 16 to 1) 5

2694² DAMIEN'S CHOICE (Ire) 5-11-4 Derek Byrne, *bumped ris aftr 3 fs, steady hdwy frm 5 furlongs out, one pace fnl 2 furlongs.*
.......................(10 to 1 tchd 12 to 1) 6

2179³ JIM'S QUEST 4-10-10 D Bridgwater, *led till hdd 3 fs out, sn wknd...................*(12 to 1 op 14 to 1 tchd 14 to 1) 7

ANOTHER RUMPUS 5-11-1 (3*) D Fortt, *hdwy to chase ldrs 7 fs out, wknd o'r 2 out...........*(66 to 1 op 33 to 1) 8

GLEVUM 5-10-13 C Llewellyn, *some hdwy 3 fs out, no dngr.*
.......................(16 to 1 op 14 to 1 tchd 20 to 1) 9

ICKFORD OKEY 5-11-4 D Gallagher, *beh till some hdwy fnl 3 fs.......................*(50 to 1 op 25 to 1) 10

WHISTLING RUFUS (Ire) 5-11-4 C Maude, *hdwy 7 fs out, wknd 3 out..........................*(25 to 1 op 14 to 1) 11

2723⁴ WAR PAINT (Ire) 5-10-11 (7*) Mr G Baines, *prmnt 12 fs.*
.......................(8 to 1 op 14 to 1 tchd 12 to 1) 12

KEYNOTE 5-11-4 R Greene, *nvr rchd ldrs.*
.......................(16 to 1 op 10 to 1 tchd 20 to 1) 13

3082⁷ KABYLIE OUEST (Fr) 4-9-12 (7*) X Aizpuru, *prmnt 12 fs.*
.......................(25 to 1 op 16 to 1 tchd 33 to 1) 14

ZABARI (Ire) 4-10-10 B Powell, *hdwy 7 fs out, wknd o'r 4 out.*
.......................(33 to 1 op 25 to 1) 15

CLAN ROSS (Ire) 6-10-13 P Holley, *al beh.*
.......................(33 to 1 op 20 to 1) 16

2784 CATHAY (Ire) 5-11-4 D Leahy, *promenent ten fs.*
.......................(33 to 1 op 25 to 1) 17

2824* HARRIS CROFT STAR (Ire) 6-11-8 (3*) R Massey, *mid-divsion till wknd quickly o'r 5 fs out.*
.......................(11 to 2 op 4 to 1 tchd 6 to 1) 18

SILVER TREASURE (Ire) 6-10-11 (7*) M Lane, *chsd ldrs 11 fs.*
.......................(33 to 1 op 20 to 1) 19

PHAR BETTER OFF (Ire) 6-10-13 S Curran, *al beh.* (33 to 1) 20

JUST NORMAN 6-11-4 J Culloty, *al beh.*
.......................(33 to 1) 21

Dist: 1l, 3l, 13l, sht-hd, 2l, 1¾l, 6l, 1¾l, 1l, 2l. 3m 56.50s. (21 Ran).
(Mrs J J Peppiatt), J S King

TRAMORE (IRE) (good) Saturday March 22nd

3336 Nore Maiden Hurdle (6-y-o and up) £2,226 2m..................... (2:30)

3226² PRAY FOR PEACE 6-10-8 (7*) Mr P Fahey, ...(10 to 1) 1
3235⁵ WELSH GRIT 8-12-0 D J Casey, ...(6 to 4 fav) 2
3233 PHAREIGN (Ire) 6-10-13 (7*) J M Maguire, ...(14 to 1) 3

2675⁴ TENDER SITUATION 6-10-13 (7") D W O'Sullivan, . . (4 to 1) 4
TULLY'S BALL (Ire) 7-11-6 J P Broderick, ... (12 to 1) 5
3177⁴ NICOLA MARIE (Ire) 8-11-6 (3") K Whelan, ...(10 to 1) 6
3235 BORN TO WIN (Ire) 7-11-1 T P Rudd, ... (5 to 1) 7
1710 SHOWBOAT MELODY (Ire) 7-10-8 (7") M D Murphy,
. . . .(14 to 1) 8
CAME AWAY (Ire) 6-10-8 (7") L A Hurley, ... (20 to 1) 9
2840⁵ ROYAL OASIS (Ire) 6-11-6 T P Treacy, ...(12 to 1) 10
3220 CARROLLS ROCK 6-11-6 J Shortt, ...(9 to 1) 11
RAY LORD (Ire) 6-10-13 (7") R M Murphy, ...(20 to 1) 12
2228⁹ HOLLOW FINGER (Ire) 6-11-6 D H O'Connor, ... (14 to 1) 13
2752 MICKS MAN (Ire) 6-12-0 M Duffy, ...(8 to 1) 14
PAT BARRY 6-11-1 P A Roche, ...(16 to 1) 15
Dist: 4½l, 3l, 3l, 3l. 3m 56.40s. (15 Ran).

(Seamus Fahey), Seamus Fahey

3337 Annstown Handicap Hurdle (0-102 4-y-o and up) £2,226 2m. . . . (3:00)

2943⁹ CNOCADRUM VI (Ire) [-] 6-9-10 W Slattery, ...(16 to 1) 1
3068 NORE GLEN (Ire) [-] (bl) 6-9-13 J R Barry, ...(14 to 1) 2
2943² HELORHIWATER (Ire) [-] 6-11-2 J P Broderick, (9 to 4 fav) 3
2674² HEIGHT OF LUXURY (Ire) [-] 5-9-7 (7") M D Murphy, (6 to 1) 4
3233 MANISSA (Ire) [-] 6-10-6 C F Swan, ...(12 to 1) 5
3089 ALLARACKET (Ire) [-] (bl) 8-10-1 (7") A O'Shea, ...(14 to 1) 6
2735⁴ UPPER MOUNT STREET (Ire) [-] 7-11-2 T Horgan, . .(7 to 2) 7
2520 CLONEE PRIDE (Ire) [-] 6-9-3 (7") L J Fleming, ... (25 to 1) 8
2518 SINGERS CORNER [-] (bl) 5-10-0 D J Casey, ... (20 to 1) 9
3227 ANOTHER BONNY [-] 11-9-4 (3") J Butler, ...(25 to 1) 10
2943 BE MY FOLLY (Ire) [-] 5-10-11 (7") P G Hourigan, . .(10 to 1) 11
3070⁸ JIHAAD (USA) [-] (bl) 7-9-13 (7") J M Maguire, ...(10 to 1) 12
1059³ STROLL HOME (Ire) [-] 7-10-4 T P Treacy, ...(15 to 2) 13
2162 KUDOS (Ire) [-] 6-10-8 K F O'Brien, ...(20 to 1) 14
1904² BEHY BRIDGE (Ire) [-] 5-10-1 (7") S P Kelly, ...(16 to 1) 15
Dist: ½l, 1½l, ¾l, nk. 3m 54.90s. (15 Ran).

(Mrs A Cooney), V T O'Brien

3338 Suir Mares Maiden Hurdle (5-y-o and up) £2,226 2½m. . . . . (3:30)

2737⁴ STORM GEM (Ire) 6-12-0 T J Mitchell, ... (5 to 4 on) 1
3182⁴ RAHEEN RIVER (Ire) 6-12-0 J Shortt, ... (100 to 30) 2
3178⁸ PIYALA 7-11-7 (7") A O'Shea, ...(10 to 1) 3
2645 ROSEY ELLEN (Ire) 5-11-5 (7") M D Murphy, ...(8 to 1) 4
2525 STILLBYHERSELF (Ire) 7-12-0 T P Treacy, ...(8 to 1) 5
2582 TINY'S CARMEL (Ire) 6-11-11 (3") U Smyth, ... (16 to 1) 6
3085⁸ LA GAZELLE (Ire) 5-11-12 D J Casey, ...(8 to 1) 7
2902 RYEV (Ire) 5-11-12 A J O'Brien, ...(14 to 1) 8
2275 TEA-VINE (Ire) 8-12-0 J P Broderick, ...(14 to 1) 9
Dist: 1½l, 1½l, 15l, 4l. 4m 33.90s. (9 Ran).

(Town And Country Racing Club), P A Fahy

3339 Dungarvan Chase (4-y-o and up) £2,226 2m. . . . . (4:00)

3236⁴ VALERIE OWENS (Ire) 8-10-10 (7") D K Budds, (100 to 30) 1
2674 WITHOUT EQUAL (USA) 10-11-1 (7") A O'Shea,
. . . .(11 to 4 fav) 2
MASTER BRIN (NZ) 12-12-0 D H O'Connor, ... (13 to 2) 3
2522 CRISTYS PICNIC (Ire) 7-11-8 D J Casey, ... (8 to 1) 4
2094 JUMPING FOR JOY (Ire) 8-11-1 (7") K A Kelly, ...(6 to 1) 5
2410² MAJOR GALE (Ire) 8-11-1 (7") M D Murphy, ...(10 to 1) 6
3088 CASTLE TIGER BAY (Ire) 6-11-8 K F O'Brien, ... (12 to 1) 7
2159⁸ EVER SO BOLD 10-12-0 T P Treacy, ...(10 to 1) 8
1904 AISEIRI 10-11-1 (7") V T Keane, ...(20 to 1) 9
3220 REGIT (Ire) 7-11-8 G M O'Neill, ...(12 to 1) 10
Dist: ½l, 7l, 1l, ¾l. 4m 5.10s. (10 Ran).

(Michael J Long), P Budds

3340 Waterford Opportunity Handicap Chase (0-102 5-y-o and up) £2,637 2m. . . . . (4:30)

3218⁴ HANNIES GIRL (Ire) [-] 6-10-10 (4") L J Fleming, ...(4 to 1) 1
2941 MARIES POLLY [-] 7-10-10 (2") J M Donnelly, ...(8 to 1) 2
2411⁸ SILENTBROOK [-] 12-9-4 (4") A O'Shea, ... (8 to 1) 3
1780 KILLERK LADY [-] 6-9-6 (4") B Geraghty, ... (8 to 1) 4
3229 RICH TRADITION (Ire) [-] (bl) 9-11-3 (3") U Smyth, (12 to 1) 5
3084³ NORTHERN ACE [-] (bl) 11-9-4 (4") M D Murphy,
. . . .(11 to 4 fav) 6
3084⁷ TREENS FOLLY [-] 8-9-11 (3") K Whelan, ... (12 to 1) 7
3237⁵ V'SOSKE GALE (Ire) [-] 7-11-12 (2") T Martin, ...(7 to 2) 8
Dist: 9l, 1l, 7l, 1½l. 4m 2.90s. (8 Ran).

(Michael L Flynn), F Flood

3341 Dunmore East Hunters Chase (4-y-o and up) £2,226 2¾m. . . . .(5:00)

2869 SHAWS CROSS (Ire) 6-11-7 (7") Mr John P Moloney,
. . . .(100 to 30) 1
CORRIGEEN RAMBLER (Ire) 8-11-7 (7") Mr P P Curran,
. . . .(20 to 1) 2
713 VIKING BUOY (Ire) 5-10-3 (7") Mr E Gallagher, ...(6 to 1) 3
3222⁴ CHELSEA KING (Ire) 6-11-7 (7") Mr T J Nagle-Jnr, . .(4 to 1) 4
3179 PARISH RANGER (Ire) (bl) 6-11-7 (7") Mr J G Sheehan,
. . . .(13 to 2) 5
FOOLS WITH HORSES (Ire) 6-11-7 (7") Mr A McNamara,
. . . .(10 to 1) 6

CATHAIR NEIDIN (Ire) 7-11-9 (5") Mr J T McNamara,
. . . .(5 to 2 fav) f
170⁵ DROMOD POINT (Ire) 8-12-0 Mr H F Cleary, ...(6 to 1) pu
Dist: 3l, 6l, ½l, dist. 5m 42.00s. (8 Ran).

(Mrs M Slattery), Andrew Slattery

3342 Barrow I.N.H. Flat Race (4 & 5-y-o) £2,226 2½m. . . . .(5:30)

ZAFFARAN RUN (Ire) 5-11-1 (7") Mr A FitzGerald, . . (3 to 1) 1
3090⁴ CHOICE JENNY (Ire) 5-11-3 (5") Mr A C Coyle, (5 to 2 fav) 2
3090⁶ COTTAGE LORD (Ire) 5-11-7 (7") Mr S P McCarthy, (7 to 1) 3
ENTOUR (Ire) 5-11-1 (7") Mr A J Dempsey, ... (12 to 1) 4
2645⁸ MR MAGGET (Ire) 5-11-10 (3") Mr D Valentine, ... (6 to 1) 5
3183⁸ BALLYROE FLASH (Ire) 4-11-0 Mr J A Berry, ...(7 to 1) 6
LOFTUS BELLE (Ire) 5-11-8 Mr J A Nash, ...(7 to 1) 7
CAPALL DUBH (Ire) 5-11-8 Mr J P Dempsey, ...(16 to 1) 8
FORTLAWN BAY 4-10-7 (7") Mr K M Nolan, ...(10 to 1) 9
2380⁵ KILCOGY CROSS (Ire) 5-11-8 Mr B M Cash, ...(6 to 1) pu
Dist: 6l, 2½l, ¾l, 2l. 5m 36.80s. (10 Ran).

(Michael Hourigan), Michael Hourigan

NAAS (IRE) (good to yielding)
Sunday March 23rd

3343 Dawn Farms Distribution Transport Maiden Hurdle (5-y-o and up) £3,425 3m. . . . . (2:30)

3178³ HEATHER VILLE (Ire) 5-10-6 (7") B Geraghty, (4 to 1 jt-fav) 1
2839⁴ LADY ARGYLE (Ire) 6-11-1 F J Flood, ...(6 to 1) 2
2752⁵ BLUE IRISH (Ire) (bl) 6-11-3 (3") K Whelan, ...(10 to 1) 3
3072² TREANAREE (Ire) 8-10-13 (7") A O'Shea, ... (5 to 1) 4
2752 JORIDI LE FORIGE (Ire) (bl) 6-11-6 T P Rudd, ...(10 to 1) 5
3075⁴ CLERICAL COUSIN (Ire) 8-11-6 J P Broderick, ...(10 to 1) 6
3083⁹ VERYWELL (Ire) (bl) 6-10-13 (7") N Geraghty, ...(14 to 1) 7
3182³ DON'T WASTE IT (Ire) 7-11-1 M P Hourigan, ...(20 to 1) 8
3089⁶ SECRET PRINCE (Ire) 6-11-3 (3") D P Murphy, ...(20 to 1) 9
3182 ALOTINALITTLE (Ire) 5-10-6 (7") M W Martin, ... (33 to 1) 10
2339 DAN PATCH 11-11-7 (7") L J Fleming, ... (20 to 1) 11
2675 ROISIN BEAG (Ire) 6-10-8 (7") M D Murphy, ...(20 to 1) 12
TIRADE (Ire) 5-10-11 (7") S P McCann, ...(25 to 1) 13
2339 CAN'T BE STOPPED (Ire) 5-10-11 (7") J P Deegan, (66 to 1) 14
3083⁷ BRIAN'S DELIGHT (Ire) (bl) 6-10-8 (7") D K Budds, (4 to 1 jt-
fav) 15
3085 GREY HORIZON (Ire) 6-11-6 P McWilliams, ...(20 to 1) f
3075⁷ HARBOUR BLAZE (Ire) 7-11-6 H Rogers, ...(33 to 1) f
2583 MAIRTINS BUCK (Ire) 6-10-13 (7") R M Murphy, ...(33 to 1) bd
3075⁸ SECTION SEVEN (Ire) 7-12-0 C O'Dwyer, ...(10 to 1) pu
2845 MISSILE GLEN (Ire) 5-11-4 K F O'Brien, ...(20 to 1) pu
Dist: Hd, 2l, 2½l, 9l. 5m 48.50s. (20 Ran).

(Denis Hannon), Noel Meade

3344 Karl Hannan Beginners Chase (5-y-o and up) £3,425 2m. . . . . (3:00)

2963⁶ POWER PACK (Ire) 9-11-11 (3") Mr B R Hamilton,
. . . .(100 to 30) 1
3068⁸ APPLEFORT (Ire) 7-11-2 (7") D K Budds, ...(7 to 1) 2
2733 ROCKETTS CASTLE (Ire) 7-11-6 (3") K Whelan, (100 to 30) 3
3073 NIGHTMAN 8-12-0 T J Mitchell, ...(12 to 1) 4
1581 JESSIE'S BOY (Ire) 8-12-0 J K Kinane, ...(12 to 1) 5
2645⁹ ARE YOU SAILING (Ire) 5-10-12 J P Broderick, ...(10 to 1) f
FLIP YOUR LID 8-11-11 (3") U Smyth, ...(10 to 1) f
3073 TIME TO LEAD (Ire) 7-11-9 K F O'Brien, ... (10 to 1) f
3073⁵ FIRE DUSTER (Ire) 7-11-9 C F Swan, ...(5 to 2 fav) pu
1649 MASTER VALENTINE (Ire) 6-11-9 T P Rudd, ... (20 to 1) pu
Dist: 10l, 20l, 20l, dist. 4m 8.50s. (10 Ran).

(P A D Scouller), J F C Maxwell

3345 Naas Hurdle (4-y-o) £3,082 2m (3:30)

3087⁶ KEAL RYAN 11-13 J Shortt, ...(4 to 1) 1
DOVALY 11-7 K F O'Brien, ...(7 to 4 fav) 2
2832* CORN ABBEY (Ire) 11-13 C O'Dwyer, ...(6 to 1) 3
2751³ APACHE TWIST (Ire) 11-7 C F Swan, ... (11 to 2) 4
2940* RED TONIC (USA) 11-6 (7") M W Martin, ...(10 to 1) 5
1750 MOFASA 11-4 (3") K Whelan, ...(14 to 1) 6
3087 GIVEUPTHEFAGS (Ire) 11-0 (7") A O'Shea, ... (33 to 1) 7
HARDYCOMESTOHARDY (Ire) 11-0 D J Casey, ... (20 to 1) 8
2332⁶ ARTIQUE FISH (Ire) 10-7 (7") M D Murphy, ...(14 to 1) 9
2702 MARCHAWAY (Ire) 11-7 F J Flood, ... (20 to 1) 10
TROSKIE (USA) 11-7 D T Evans, ...(10 to 1) 11
2327 NORTH OF KALA (Ire) 11-0 (7") D McCullagh, ...(25 to 1) 12
3087 FAATEQ 11-7 T P Treacy, ... (20 to 1) 13
2337 MAGICAL IMPACT (Ire) 11-7 P L Malone, ... (33 to 1) 14
Dist: 1½l, 1½l, ½l, 2l. 3m 47.60s. (14 Ran).

(Coverway Racing Club), D T Hughes

3346 Foran Equine Products Handicap Hurdle (0-137 4-y-o and up) £3,767 2m. . . . . (4:00)

3235² CIARA'S PRINCE (Ire) [-] (bl) 6-11-3 F J Flood, ...(4 to 1) 1
3070* GOOD GLOW [-] 7-11-1 C F Swan, ...(5 to 2) 2

2841⁹ REASILVIA (Ire) [-] 7-10-11 (7*) M D Murphy, ... (8 to 1) 3
2735* VALLEY ERNE (Ire) [-] 6-11-4 J P Broderick, ... (Evens fav) 4
3180 HILL OF HOPE (Ire) [-] 6-10-5 W Slattery, ... (16 to 1) 5
Dist: Sht-hd, 10l, hd, 1l. 3m 47.20s. (5 Ran).

(R McConn), F Flood

3347 Abbey Bridge Handicap Chase (5-y-o and up) £6,850 3m . . . . (4:30)

3236⁵ INDESTRUCTIBLE (Ire) [-] 9-9-0 (7*) A O'Shea, ... (8 to 1) 1
2842⁶ SHINING WILLOW [-] 7-9-0 (7*) R Burke, ... (5 to 1) 2
3181³ UNA'S CHOICE (Ire) [-] 11-10-2 (7*) L J Fleming, ... (5 to 1) 3
3181* CASTALINO [-] 11-9-0 (7*) M D Murphy, ... (5 to 1) 4
2843* BOBBY JO (Ire) [-] 7-9-13 C F Swan, ... (11 to 8 fav) 5
1903⁵ STEEL DAWN [-] 10-9-7 J R Barry, ... (12 to 1) 6
3132⁹ LORD MUFF (Ire) [-] 8-9-9² T P Treacy, ... (14 to 1) ur
Dist: 2l, 7l, 7l, 3l. 6m 22.50s. (7 Ran).

(John Quane), Augustine Leahy

3348 Dawn Farms Distribution Suppliers Hurdle (5-y-o and up) £3,425 2m 3f . . . . (5:00)

2339* LIVER BIRD (Ire) 7-11-10 C O'Dwyer, ... (7 to 2) 1
2645* SUPER DEALER (Ire) 5-11-8 C F Swan, ... (5 to 4 fav) 2
3085² ONE WORD (Ire) 5-11-1 (7*) B Geraghty, ... (10 to 1) 3
2965² FISHIN JOELLA (Ire) 5-10-10 (7*) A O'Shea, ... (5 to 1) 4
3086⁵ TARAJAN (USA) (bl) 5-11-12 J Shortt, ... (7 to 2) 5
3083⁸ NEARLY A LINE 5-10-12 (7*) P G Hourigan, ... (20 to 1) 6
TYNDARIUS (Ire) 6-11-7 J P Broderick, ... (33 to 1) 7
3069 MYRA PLUCK (Ire) 9-10-9 (7*) J P Deegan, ... (100 to 1) 8
STRONG IMAGE (Ire) 5-10-7 (7*) D Flood, ... (50 to 1) 9
Dist: 5½l, 1l, 5l, 5½l. 4m 31.20s. (9 Ran).

(G B F Clarke), J A Berry

3349 Sallins I.N.H. Flat Race (4 & 5-y-o) £3,082 2m. . . . . (5:30)

TWIN GALE 5-11-1 (7*) Mr J P McNamara, ... (7 to 1) 1
3183² LOST ALPHABET (Ire) 4-10-12 (7*) Mr P Fahey, (7 to 4 fav) 2
HAZY BUCK (Ire) 5-11-6 (7*) Mr P J Prendergast, . .(12 to 1) 3
LELARI (Ire) 4-10-12 (7*) Miss A Foley, ... (10 to 1) 4
TEMPLEMARY LAD (Ire) 5-11-13 Mr J P Dempsey, (12 to 1) 5
2737 MOUNT HALL (Ire) 5-11-8 Mr J A Nash, ... (50 to 1) 6
3090² EVENKEEL (bl) 5-11-6 (7*) Mr A J Dempsey, . . (3 to 1) 7
2968⁷ DOCKLINE (Ire) 5-11-6 (7*) Mr Mark Walsh, ... (16 to 1) 8
3083⁴ BALMY NATIVE (Ire) 5-11-10 (3*) Mr E Norris, ... (12 to 1) 9
1364 THE TOLLAH (Ire) 5-11-13 Mr P J Faulkner, . . . (16 to 1) 10
2449 NOBLE GESTURE (Ire) 5-11-13 Mr G J Harford, . . . (12 to 1) 11
EBONY PRINCE (Ire) 5-11-13 Mr A R Coonan, . . . (10 to 1) 12
GLENDING BOY (Ire) 5-11-10 (3*) Mr D Valentine, (12 to 1) 13
KEPPOLS PRINCESS (Ire) 4-10-8³ (7*) Mr B Valentine,
. . . . (16 to 1) 14
MERCANTILE MAN 4-11-5 Mr D Marnane, . . (12 to 1) 15
2838 FOLK HERO 5-11-8 (5*) Mr A C Coyle, ... (12 to 1) 16
LADYSWELL CROSS (Ire) 4-10-8³ (7*) Mr R F Coonan,
. . . . (20 to 1) 17
DREAM ON SONNY (Ire) 5-11-1 (7*) Mr R J Barnwell,
. . . . (20 to 1) 18
2940 TONY IMPORT (Ire) 4-11-5 Mr B M Cash, ... (12 to 1) 19
BALLINTEMPLE TRAMP (Ire) 4-10-7 (7*) Mr D P Coakley,
. . . . (16 to 1) 20
BELON BREEZE (Ire) 5-11-1 (7*) Mr R Geraghty, . . (10 to 1) su
Dist: 1½l, ½l, nk. 3m 44.90s. (21 Ran).

(CKC Syndicate), S J Treacy

HEXHAM (soft)
Monday March 24th
Going Correction: PLUS 0.90 sec. per fur. (races 1,2,4,6,7), PLUS 1.30 (3,5)

3350 Buchanan Ales Conditional Jockeys' Handicap Hurdle Class E (0-110 4-y-o and up) £2,311 2m . . . . (2:00)

3128² DIAMOND BEACH [86] 4-10-6 E Callaghan, hld up beh, hdwy
on bit to ld last, shaken up and ran on. . . (7 to 1 op 3 to 1) 1
3013⁷ HIGHLAND WAY (Ire) [87] 9-10-10 (5*) C McCormack, hld up
beh, hdwy appr last, sn rdn, not pace of wnr flt.
. . . . (2 to 1 op 7 to 1 tchd 9 to 4) 2
3006 COURT JOKER (Ire) [83] 5-10-11 R McGrath, hld up in tch,
hdwy 2 out, rdn and outpcd last, styd on und pres towards
finish. . . . . (13 to 2 op 5 to 1 tchd 7 to 1) 3
3013* IFALLELSEFAILS [96] 9-11-5 (5*) I Jardine, set steady pace,
pushed alng aftr 2 out, hdd last, sn wknd.
. . . . (11 to 4 op 3 to 1 tchd 7 to 2) 4
1676⁶ MISS GREENYARDS [83] 6-10-11 S Taylor, hld up, hdwy 2
out, chlgd and hit last, sn rdn and wknd. (6 to 1 op 9 to 2) 5
2204 GALLARDINI (Ire) [82] 8-10-3 (7*) A Currie, cl up, rdn aftr 2 out,
wknd appr last. . . . . (20 to 1 op 16 to 1 tchd 33 to 1) 6
3157* APOLLO'S DAUGHTER [76] 9-10-4 F Leahy, chsd ldg pair,
effrt and hdwy aftr 2 out, rdn and wknd bef last.
. . . . (4 to 1 op 3 to 1 tchd 9 to 2) 7
FIERY SUN [86] 12-10-11 (3*) N Horrocks, chsd ldrs, rdn alng
appr 2 out, sn lost pl. . . . (25 to 1 op 14 to 1 tchd 33 to 1) 8

Dist: 4l, 4l, sht-hd, 4l, 7l, 2½l, 10l. 4m 12.80s. a 23.80s (8 Ran).

(Valueplace Ltd), G M Moore

3351 European Breeders Fund 'National Hunt' Novices' Hurdle Qualifier Class E (5,6,7-y-o) £2,917 2m (2:30)

3011⁵ BOLD STATEMENT 5-11-0 N Bentley, trkd ldrs, hdwy to ld
4th, rdn last, styd on wl. . . . . (5 to 1 op 7 to 2) 1
3160³ SOUTHERN CROSS 5-11-0 R Garritty, hld up mid-div, hdwy
appr 2 out, chsd wnr and mstk last, hrd drvn, kpt on.
. . . . (4 to 1 op 3 to 1 tchd 9 to 2) 2
3008⁸ EASTCLIFFE (Ire) 5-10-11 (3*) Michael Brennan, beh, pld hrd,
rapid hdwy second, chsd ldrs nxt, effrt to chal aftr 2 out, sn rdn
and one pace. . . . . (12 to 1 op 10 to 1) 3
3011⁶ PRIME EXAMPLE (Ire) 6-11-0 P Niven, hld up beh, hdwy appr
2 out, sn rdn, nvr dngrs. . . (13 to 2 op 5 to 1 tchd 7 to 1) 4
2006³ PENTLAND SQUIRE 6-11-0 Richard Guest, hld up beh, hdwy
hfwy, effrt to chase ldrs aftr 2 out, sn no imprsn.
. . . . (3 to 1 fav tchd 4 to 1) 5
3316 REACH THE CLOUDS (Ire) 5-11-0 J Supple, mid-divsion,
some hdwy 2 out, nvr a factor. . . . . (33 to 1 op 25 to 1) 6
3029⁵ CREAM O THE BORDER 5-10-9 F Perratt, led, pushed alng
and hdd 4th, cl up till wknd und pres aftr 2 out.
. . . . (25 to 1 op 14 to 1 tchd 33 to 1) 7
2803⁷ OVER ZEALOUS (Ire) 5-11-0 R Supple, al mid-div.
. . . . (20 to 1 op 16 to 1) 8
3015⁷ JUST NED 6-10-11 (3*) E Husband, beh hfwy. . . . . . (25 to 1) 9
2988⁴ DONNEGALE (Ire) 5-11-0 J Callaghan, chsd ldrs to hfwy, sn
lost pl and beh. . . . . (20 to 1 op 16 to 1) 10
2917⁸ NICK ROSS 6-11-0 B Storey, beh hfwy. . . . . (50 to 1 op 25 to 1) 11
1182 HOPEFUL LORD (Ire) 5-11-0 A S Smith, chsd ldrs, rdn alng
appr 2 out, wknd bef last. . . . . (25 to 1 op 33 to 1) 12
2975 CONNIE LEATHART 6-10-9 D Bentley, cl up, rdn alng 5th,
wknd aftr 2 out. . . . . (50 to 1) 13
2972⁶ FLORRIE GUNNER 7-10-9 L Wyer, al beh.
. . . . (20 to 1 op 33 to 1) 14
2817⁵ HELPERBY (Ire) 5-11-0 M Moloney, mid-div, lost pl hfwy, sn
tld off. . . . . (25 to 1 op 20 to 1 tchd 33 to 1) 15
3198 SOCCER BALL 7-10-11 (3*) E Callaghan, tld off hfwy.
. . . . (50 to 1) 16
2650 BANNER YEAR (Ire) 6-11-0 N Smith, cl up, lost pl quickly
hfwy, sn wl beh. . . . . (50 to 1) 17
2653 BELTINO 6-11-0 Mr C Storey, tld off hfwy. . . . . . . (50 to 1) 18
3029³ LA RIVIERA (Ire) 5-11-0 K Johnson, beh hfwy, tld off whn pld
up bef last. . . . . (15 to 2 op 7 to 1 tchd 8 to 1) pu
2908 PERKY TOO (Ire) 5-10-7 (7*) Mr S Durack, mstks, tld off hfwy,
pld up aftr 3 out. (50 to 1) pu
Dist: 1¼l, dist, 5l, 1¼l, 7l, 2½l, 1¾l, hd, hd, 10l. 4m 9.70s. a 20.70s (20 Ran).
SR: 23/21/-/-/-/-/

(R I Graham), G M Moore

3352 Federation Brewery Amateur Riders' Selling Handicap Chase Class G (0-90 5-y-o and up) £2,357 3m 1f . . . . (3:00)

3123³ BRIGHT DESTINY [60] (v) 6-9-10 (7*) Mr O McPhail, cl up, led
9th, wl clr 4 out. . . . . (7 to 1 op 5 to 1) 1
JUST FOR ME (Ire) [60] 8-9-12 (5*) Mr C Storey, beh, hdwy
11th, rdn alng 4 out, styd on frm 2 out, no ch wth wnr.
. . . . (100 to 1 op 50 to 1) 2
3161⁹ RUSTY BLADE [85] 8-11-0 (5*) Mr R Hale, led to 9th, chsd wnr
to 5 out, sn drvn and wknd.
. . . . (12 to 1 op 8 to 1 tchd 14 to 1) 3
915⁶ UPWELL [67] 13-10-5 (5*) Mr M H Naughton, al chasing ldrs,
drvn alng 13th, sn beh. (25 to 1 op 20 to 1 tchd 33 to 1) 4
2536³ JENDEE (Ire) [82] 9-11-6 (5*) Miss P Robson, beh, blun tenth,
nvr a factor aftr. . . . . (5 to 1 tchd 7 to 1) 5
2881 CLONROCHE LUCKY (Ire) [67] 7-10-6³ (7*) Mrs S Grant, al
beh, tld off 9th. . . . . (33 to 1 op 20 to 1 tchd 50 to 1) 6
3159 QUIXALL CROSSETT [57] 12-9-7 (7*) Mr C Russell, in tch whn
blun and uns rdr 11th. . . . . (50 to 1 op 33 to 1) ur
3247⁷ GATHERING TIME [63] 11-10-6⁸ (7*) Mr A Birch, mid-div, beh
hfwy, tld off whn hmpd and uns rdr 11th.
. . . . (16 to 1 op 12 to 1) ur
3139⁷ FAIRY PARK [84] (v) 12-11-6 (7*) Mr N H Oliver, in tch, effrt to
chase ldrs 11th, rdn and wknd aftr 5 out, tld off whn pld up bef
last. . . . . (7 to 1 op 5 to 1 tchd 8 to 1) pu
3124 OVERWHELM (Ire) [77] 9-11-3 (3*) Mr M Thompson, tld off
hfwy, jmpd very slwly 2 out and pld up.
. . . . (16 to 1 op 10 to 1 tchd 20 to 1) pu
1161³ DONOVANS REEF [61] 11-9-11 (7*) Mr S Durack, prmnt, chsd
wnr frm 13th, rdn and wkng whn blun 3 out and nxt, lost pl
rpdly, pld up bef last. . . (14 to 1 op 10 to 1 tchd 16 to 1) pu
1630⁹ MORE JOY [72] 9-10-11 (5*) Mr N Wilson, al beh, tld off whn
pld up bef 13th. . . . . (9 to 1 op 7 to 1 tchd 10 to 1) pu
2914³ TWO FOR ONE (Ire) [67] 8-10-10 Mr S Swiers, in tch, lost pl
and beh 9th, tld off whn pld up bef 13th.
. . . . (11 to 4 fav op 5 to 2 tchd 3 to 1) pu
Dist: 22l, 14l, 1l, 10l, dist. 6m 47.20s. a 42.20s (13 Ran).

(J S Goldie), J S Goldie

3353 LCL Pils Novices' Handicap Hurdle Class E (0-100 4-y-o and up) £2,794 2½m 110yds. . . . . (3:30)

3013² ENCHANTED COTTAGE [85] 5-11-4 (3*) E Callaghan, *hld up, steady hdwy 6th, rdn to ld appr last, kpt on gmely und pres.*
..................(7 to 2 fav op 5 to 2 tchd 4 to 1) 1

3210⁴ MAITRE DE MUSIQUE (Fr) [92] 6-11-7 (7*) C McCormack, *trkd ldrs, hdwy 5th, led aftr 2 out, rdn and hdd appr last, drvn and kpt on flt.*.....................(10 to 1 op 7 to 1) 2

3013³ PAPPA CHARLIE (USA) [82] 6-11-4 B Storey, *hld up beh, steady hdwy 6th, chsd ldrs 2 out, sn rdn and one pace.*
..................(8 to 1 op 5 to 1) 3

1984⁸ MY MISSILE [65] 7-10-1 L O'Hara, *hld up beh, hdwy 6th, rdn aftr 2 out, sn one pace*...............(20 to 1 op 16 to 1) 4

3157 MEADOWLECK [64] 8-9-9 (5*) S Taylor, *chsd ldrs, hdwy 5th, ev ch aftr 2 out, sn drvn, wknd bef last*............(33 to 1) 5

3162* CORBLEU (Ire) [74] 7-10-10 K Johnson, *hld up beh, gd hdwy 6th, chsd ldrs aftr 2 out, sn rdn, no imprsn*..........(7 to 1) 6

2885⁵ BOSTON MAN [89] (bl) 6-11-11 Richard Guest, *chsd ldrs, led 5th, rdn alng 6th, hdd aftr 2 out, grad wknd.*
..................(7 to 1 op 5 to 1 tchd 8 to 1) 7

3011³ NASAYER (Ire) [84] 7-10-13 (7*) S Haworth, *chsd ldrs, rdn alng 6th, wknd aftr 2 out...(15 to 2 op 6 to 1 tchd 8 to 1)* 8

3034⁷ SKANE RIVER (Ire) [71] 6-10-0 (7*) R Burns, *al beh.*
..................(14 to 1 op 10 to 1) 9

3124⁷ TRIONA'S HOPE (Ire) [64] 8-9-9 (5*) Mr M H Naughton, *chsd ldrs to 4th, sn lost pl and beh*........(33 to 1 op 20 to 1) 10

3161⁵ LAST REFUGE (Ire) [81] 8-11-3 N Smith, *beh hfwy.* (12 to 1) 11

3128³ JENDORCET [73] 7-10-9 J Callaghan, *al rear.*
..................(7 to 1 op 6 to 1) 12

1737⁵ KINGFISHER BRAVE [83] 4-10-10 L Wyer, *led to 3rd, cl up to 5th, wknd and wl beh appr 2 out*........(12 to 1 op 8 to 1) 13

2710 MR SLOAN [64] 7-9-11 (3*) G Lee, *cl up, led 3rd to 5th, rdn nxt, wknd aftr 2 out*.....................(33 to 1 op 20 to 1) 14

3157² SKI PATH [67] 8-10-3 M Foster, *chsd ldrs to 4th, sn lost pl and beh*.................(14 to 1 op 10 to 1) 15

3198 ONYOUROWN (Ire) [80] 4-10-7 A S Smith, *al beh, tld off 2 out.*
..................(14 to 1 op 10 to 1) 16

2712 WAR WHOOP [89] 5-11-11 T Reed, *in tch, lost pl and beh hfwy, tld off bef last*...(20 to 1 op 16 to 1 tchd 25 to 1) pu
Dist: 1¼l, 6l, 7l, 3l, 7l, nk, 10l, 15l, 2½l, 3l. 5m 23.60s. a 32.60s (17 Ran).
(Mrs J M Davenport), J M Jefferson

3354 Federation Brewery Novices' Chase Class E (5-y-o and up) £3,140 2m 110yds......................(4:00)

2854 FRIENDLY KNIGHT 7-11-3 A S Smith, *in tch, outpcd and beh 5 out, gd hdwy aftr 2 out, styd on to ld flt, ran on strly.*
..................(5 to 1 op 7 to 2 tchd 11 to 2) 1

3158⁴ NAWTINOOKEY 7-10-5 (7*) C McCormack, *hld up beh, steady hdwy 5 out, chlgd 3 out, ev ch and drvn last, kpt on one pace*..................(12 to 1 tchd 14 to 1) 2

3158² EXEMPLAR (Ire) 9-10-12 (5*) G F Ryan, *mid-div, hit 1st, hdwy to chase ldrs 7th, rdn alng and outpcd whn blun 3 out, kpt on appr last*...........(9 to 4 fav op 2 to 1 tchd 11 to 4) 3

3030 NOORAN 6-11-3 K Johnson, *hld up, gd hdwy aftr 4 out, rdn to ld appr last, hdd and wknd flt.*
..................(100 to 30 op 2 to 1 tchd 7 to 2) 4

3124⁵ CAMPTOSAURUS (Ire) 8-11-3 B Storey, *led to 5th, cl up, rdn alng 4 out, one pace frm nxt*.........(10 to 1 tchd 12 to 1) 5

2798⁶ OLD REDWOOD 9-11-3 L O'Hara, *prmnt, led 5th, rdn 3 out, hdd and wknd appr last*.................(12 to 1 op 10 to 1) 6

2683⁵ ROBARA 7-11-3 N Leach, *outpcd, hit 6th, sn beh*..(20 to 1) 7

3058⁴ TEEJAY'N'AITCH (Ire) 5-10-6 (3*) G Lee, *chsd ldrs till blun and uns rdr 7th*........(15 to 2 op 12 to 1 tchd 14 to 1) ur

3202⁵ SHUT UP [8-10-9 (3*) E Husband, *prmnt, rdn alng 3 out, blun badly nxt, pld up aftr*..................(33 to 1) pu

3158⁵ PRINCE BALTASAR 8-11-3 M Foster, *hld up, hdwy 7th, cl up nxt till rdn and wknd 3 out, beh whn pld up bef last.*
..................(25 to 1 op 20 to 1) pu

2914⁷ ARISTODEMUS 8-10-10 (7*) Mr S Durack, *chsd ldrs, hit 3rd, blun nxt, sn beh, tld off whn pld up bef last.*
..................(25 to 1 op 20 to 1) pu
Dist: 5l, ½l, nk, 1¾l, 5l, dist. 4m 26.80s. a 28.80s (11 Ran).
SR: 16/6/10/10/8/3/ (G J Johnston), J S Haldane

3355 Keoghan Handicap Hurdle Class D (0-120 4-y-o and up) £2,802 2½m 110yds......................(4:30)

3161 PARIAH (Ire) [92] 8-10-13 P Niven, *trkd ldrs, hdwy 2 out, led last, hng lft flt, rdn out*.................(4 to 1 op 7 to 2) 1

2885² DUKE OF PERTH [94] 6-11-1 A S Smith, *hld up, smooth hdwy to ld appr 2 out, rdn and hdd last, drvn and ran on flt.*
..................(7 to 2 op 3 to 1 tchd 4 to 1) 2

3161 CHILL WIND [83] 8-10-4 M Foster, *hit second, al prmnt, hdwy to ld 5th, rdn alng and hdd appr 2 out, drvn and one pace approaching last*.........(9 to 2 op 4 to 1 tchd 5 to 1) 3

RASCALLY [88] 7-10-9 R Supple, *al chasing ldrs, rdn alng aftr 2 out, wknd appr last*.........(14 to 1 op 12 to 1) 4

2885* DANBYS GORSE [96] 5-11-0 (3*) E Callaghan, *hld up, hdwy aftr 5th, rdn alng after 2 out, wknd appr last.*
..................(5 to 2 fav op 4 to 1 tchd 11 to 4) 5

2204 MASTER HYDE [55] 8-10-0 B Storey, *hld up, hdwy appr 2 out, rdn and btn approaching last.*
..................(16 to 1 tchd 25 to 1) 6

3162 KENILWORTH LAD [87] 9-10-8¹ Richard Guest, *led to 3rd, rdn alng 5th, one pace frm aftr 2 out.*
..................(20 to 1 op 20 to 1 tchd 33 to 1) 7

3056 STRATHMORE LODGE [90] 8-10-11⁵ T Reed, *cl up, led 3rd to 5th, sn lost pl and beh, tld off whn pld up bef last.*
..................(14 to 1 op 8 to 1) pu
Dist: 1l, 23l, nk, hd, 18l, 28l. 5m 25.00s. a 34.00s (8 Ran).
(Mrs D Miller), Martin Todhunter

3356 Levy Board Maiden National Hunt Flat Class H (4,5,6-y-o) £1,350 2m ....(5:00)

2687² INTO THE BLACK (Ire) 6-11-5 (3*) G Lee, *chsd ldrs, pushed alng 4 fs out, rdn to ld appr last, styd on.*
..................(6 to 4 fav op 5 to 2 tchd 11 to 4) 1

3061⁶ LORD KNOWS (Ire) 6-11-1 (7*) D Thomas, *cl up, led hfwy, rdn and hdd o'r one furlong out, kpt on one pace.*
..................(12 to 1 op 8 to 1) 2

2302³ THE SNOW BURN 4-10-7 (7*) R McCarthy, *al prmnt, effrt and ev ch o'r 2 fs out, sn rdn, one pace appr last.*
..................(6 to 1 op 3 to 1) 3

3008² GOING PRIMITIVE 6-11-8 Mr S Swiers, *in tch, hdwy hfwy, rdn alng 3 fs out, kpt on same pace.*
..................(5 to 1 op 5 to 1 tchd 10 to 1) 4

PEPPER POT BOY (Ire) 5-11-1 (7*) M Herrington, *hld up beh, hdwy 3 fs out, styd on wl appr last, nrst finish.*
..................(8 to 1 op 7 to 1) 5

TIME WARRIOR (Ire) 6-11-1 (7*) N Hannity, *beh, styd on wl fnl 2 fs, nrst finish*........(12 to 1 op 8 to 1 tchd 14 to 1) 6

OPEN FAIRWAY 4-10-9 (5*) R McGrath, *chsd ldrs, effrt and hdwy to chal 3 fs out, ev ch till rdn and wknd appr last, eased.*
..................(7 to 1 op 8 to 1 tchd 10 to 1) 7

MADEMIST SAM 5-11-3 (5*) B Grattan, *hld up beh, gd hdwy on outer o'r 4 fs out, rdn 2 out, one pace appr last.*
..................(20 to 1 op 14 to 1) 8

2764 SIR BOSTON 4-10-9 (5*) D J Kavanagh, *led to hfwy, rdn alng o'r 4 fs out, wknd over 2 out.*
..................(16 to 1 op 14 to 1 tchd 20 to 1) 9

2363 BUDDLEIA 4-10-2 (7*) N Horrocks, *hld up beh, hdwy to chase ldrs 7 fs out, rdn alng and wknd o'r 3 out.*
..................(50 to 1 op 20 to 1) 10

1989 JOHNNEYS SPIRIT 5-11-8 Mr R Hale, *nvr rch ldrs.*
..................(20 to 1 op 12 to 1) 11

3015⁵ SNOOTY ESKIMO (Ire) 5-11-5 (3*) E Husband, *beh hfwy.*
..................(20 to 1 op 12 to 1) 12

LIAM'S RIVER (Ire) 5-11-3 (5*) S Taylor, *in tch, lost pl o'r 6 fs out, sn beh*..................(12 to 1 op 10 to 1) 13

2899 GALLANT TAFFY 5-11-1 (7*) R Burns, *in tch to hfwy, sn lost pl and beh*..................(33 to 1) 14

3061⁸ HIGH CELLESTE (Ire) 6-10-10 (7*) C McCormack, *al beh, tld off fnl 6 fs*.................(50 to 1 op 25 to 1) 15

HEY SAM (Ire) 4-11-0 Mr N Wilson, *al beh, tld off fnl 6 fs.*
..................(33 to 1 op 20 to 1) 16

NICKYS PERIL 5-10-10 (7*) S Haworth, *chsd ldrs, rdn and wknd fi fs out, sn beh*........(33 to 1 op 20 to 1) 17

THE TRUE MILLER 6-11-5 (3*) E Callaghan, *al beh, tld off fnl 6 fs*..................(50 to 1 op 20 to 1) 18

3061⁹ MEGGIE SCOTT 4-10-2 (7*) S Melrose, *chsd ldrs, wknd quickly o'r 5 fs out, tld off*..........(50 to 1 op 33 to 1) 19
Dist: 4l, sht-hd, hd, hd, 2½l, 2l, 10l, ½l, 4l, 1l. 4m 20.70s. (19 Ran).
(J Huckle), Mrs M Reveley

LUDLOW (good to firm)
Monday March 24th
Going Correction: PLUS 0.15 sec. per fur.

3357 Officials Novices' Hurdle Class E (5-y-o and up) £2,158 2m......(2:10)

3091² SURANOM (Ire) 5-10-12 J F Titley, *trkd ldr, led appr 3 out, rdn out r-in*..................(15 to 8 on op 13 to 8 on) 1

2746⁶ LITTLE SHEFFORD 5-11-4 S Curran, *led till hdd appr 3 three out, ev ch till no extr und pres r-in*......(3 to 1 op 7 to 4) 2

2565⁷ WORTHY MEMORIES 8-10-7 Derek Byrne, *al same pl, one pace frm 3 out*............(9 to 1 op 4 to 1 tchd 10 to 1) 3

3110⁷ SAAFI (Ire) (bl) 6-10-12 V Slattery, *al toward rear, lost tch aftr 4 out*..................(14 to 1 op 8 to 1) 4

1977⁹ EUROLINK SHADOW 5-10-12 D Walsh, *in tch till rdn aftr 4 out, sn btn*.................(50 to 1 op 14 to 1) 5

2744 LUCKY ESCAPE 6-10-12 S Wynne, *al beh, lost tch 4 out, tld off*..................(25 to 1 op 10 to 1) 6

2744 NANJIZAL (bl) 5-10-9 (3*) R Massey, *al last, tld off 4th.*
..................(66 to 1 op 33 to 1) 7
Dist: 3l, 6l, 16l, 14l, dist, 7l. 3m 41.00s. a 9.00s (7 Ran).
SR: 18/21/4/-/ (Mrs Ann Leat), Mrs D Haine

3358 National Riding Week Novices' Chase Class E (5-y-o and up) £2,771 3m..........................(2:40)

3000⁵ CAPTIVA BAY 8-10-11 S Wynne, *jmpd wl, made all, kpt on well whn chlgd frm 4 out, rdn.*
..................(11 to 4 op 5 to 2 tchd 3 to 1) 1

3271 PHILATELIC (Ire) 6-11-2 J Railton, *trkd wnr frm 4th, ev ch from four out, rdn and no extr r-in.*
..................(11 to 4 op 5 to 2 tchd 3 to 1) 2

3281² FAWLEY FLYER 8-11-2 A Thornton, *trkd wnr to 4th, dsptd second till outpcd 5 out, rallied 3 out, one pace.*
.... (6 to 4 on op 13 to 8 on tchd 11 to 8 on) 3

2894⁵ LAMBRINI (Ire) 7-10-11 D Walsh, *in tch till wknd 11th, tld off whn refused 2 out, continued.*
.... (16 to 1 op 8 to 1 tchd 20 to 1) 4

STORMHILL WARRIOR 6-11-2 V Slattery, *outpcd frm strt, sn tld off, pld up bef 12th.*.(25 to 1 op 10 to 1 tchd 33 to 1) pu

Dist: 1l, 6l, dist. 6m 1.40s. a 14.40s (5 Ran).

(Miss M A de Quincey), Mrs A R Hewitt

3359 Clive Pavilion Handicap Hurdle Class E (0-115 4-y-o and up) £2,158 2m 5f 110yds.................(3:10)

2896³ FIRST CRACK [84] 12-11-1 S Wynne, *hld up, al gng wl, wnt second aftr 4 out, led appr 2 out, sn clr.*
.... (6 to 4 fav op 5 to 2) 1

2738⁴ DRUM BATTLE [93] 5-11-10 A Thornton, *al prmnt, led 4 out, hdd appr 2 out, no extr.*.............(7 to 2 op 2 to 1) 2

3016 ONE MORE DIME (Ire) [69] 7-9-9 (5*) A Bates, *hld up in rear, gd hdwy aftr 5th, outpcd 4 out, kpt on frm nxt.*
.... (8 to 1 tchd 10 to 1) 3

3137⁹ BLATANT OUTBURST [80] 7-10-11 R Johnson, *led till aftr second, prmnt till wknd quickly after 4 out, tld off.*
.... (5 to 1 op 7 to 2) 4

2392³ COLWALL [89] 6-11-1 (5*) Mr R Thornton, *led aftr second, hdd 4 out, wknd quickly, tld off.*...(7 to 2 op 3 to 1) 5

Dist: 9l, 4l, dist, 5l. 5m 10.80s. a 15.80s (5 Ran).

(D Pugh), F Jordan

3360 Annual Members Handicap Chase Class E (0-115 5-y-o and up) £2,745 2m.........................(3:40)

3193⁴ FICHU (USA) [78] 9-10-2 M Richards, *hld up, hdwy hfwy, chalg whn bad mstk 3 out, rallied und pres to ld r-in.*
.... (7 to 2 tchd 4 to 1) 1

3173² COOLTEEN HERO (Ire) [89] 7-10-13 W McFarland, *trkd ldr, led 3 out, blun last, rdn and hdd r-in.*.(11 to 2 op 7 to 2) 2

3104 FENWICK [82] 10-10-3 (3*) T Dascombe, *in tch whn hit 9th, rallied 3 out, one pace.*.....(7 to 2 op 5 to 2 tchd 3 to 1) 3

3047⁴ SUPER SHARP (NZ) [88] 9-10-12 Jacqui Oliver, *set str pace till hdd and wknd 3 out.*
.... (11 to 4 fav op 5 to 2 tchd 3 to 1) 4

3185² MONDAY CLUB [100] 13-11-10 S McNeill, *mstk second, in rear till hdwy 9th, weakend 4 out, sn btn.*
.... (7 to 2 op 100 to 30 tchd 4 to 1) 5

2995⁶ QUARTER MARKER (Ire) [76] 9-10-0 Mrs C Ford, *outpcd frm strt, tld off 8th.*...............(50 to 1 op 33 to 1) 6

2576⁵ THE FENCE SHRINKER [76] 6-10-0 S Wynne, *chsd ldrs till wknd aftr 5 out, tld off.*..........(33 to 1 tchd 50 to 1) 7

Dist: 1¼l, 5l, 9l, 1½l, 24l, 6l. 3m 59.70s. a 9.70s (7 Ran).

SR: 1/10/-/-/5/-/-/

(B Seal), Mrs L Richards

3361 Hughes Caterers Novices' Handicap Chase Class E (0-105 5-y-o and up) £2,758 2½m....................(4:10)

3267* QUITE A MAN [89] 9-12-2 (6ex) C Maude, *hld up, hdwy and 3rd whn hit 12th, slight ld 4 out, ran on four out, ran on strly frm 2 out.*...............(6 to 4 op 5 to 4) 1

1111⁷ RYTON RUN [81] 12-11-8 T J O'Sullivan, *led 3rd till hdd 4 out, wkng whn blun 2 out.*............(16 to 1 op 8 to 1) 2

3175 LITTLE ROWLEY [60] 8-10-1 M Richards, *chsd ldrs. outpcd tenth, styd on frm 3 out.*.(25 to 1 op 20 to 1 tchd 33 to 1) 3

3281³ PRIZE MATCH [68] 8-10-9 S McNeill, *led to 3rd, in tch till wknd appr 4 out.*..........(8 to 1 op 5 to 1 tchd 9 to 1) 4

3167² JOLLY BOAT [82] 10-11-9 S Wynne, *beh whn pld up aftr 4th, lme.*...............(5 to 4 fav op 11 to 8 tchd 6 to 4) pu

2498 AEOLIAN [68] 6-10-4 (5*) Mr R Thornton, *beh till hdwy appr tenth, wknd bef 4 out, blun nxt, pld up before 2 out.*
.... (12 to 1 op 10 to 1) pu

Dist: 16l, 2½l, 1½l. 4m 59.80s. a 10.80s (6 Ran).

SR: 24/-/-/

(W R J Everall), S A Brookshaw

3362 Raceday Staff Novices' Handicap Hurdle Class E (0-105 4-y-o and up) £2,190 3¼m 110yds..........(4:40)

3190² SAMMORELLO (Ire) [75] 6-10-9 C Llewellyn, *made all, styd on best whn chlgd 3 out.*
.... (11 to 10 on op Evens tchd 5 to 4 on) 1

3110⁵ FASTINI GOLD [75] 5-10-2 (7*) X Aizpuru, *hld up, hdwy 5th, wnt second 4 out, chlgd nxt, rdn and wknd appr 2 out.*
.... (6 to 1 op 8 to 1) 2

3190³ COPPER COIL [94] 7-11-7 (7*) J Power, *trkd wnr 6th till wknd appr 3 out.*.............(11 to 4 op 7 to 4) 3

2177⁶ AWESTRUCK [66] (bl) 7-9-7 (7*) J Mogford, *wl in rear till styd on frm 3 out.*...............(12 to 1 tchd 20 to 1) 4

3119³ WIN I DID (Ire) [81] 7-11-2 (5*) Mr R Thornton, *rcd wide, prmnt till wknd appr 8th, tld off.*..(8 to 1 op 6 to 1 tchd 10 to 1) 5

Dist: 3½l, 12l, nk, dist. 6m 21.60s. a 16.60s (5 Ran).

(Mrs S A MacEchern), N A Twiston-Davies

SANDOWN (good to firm)

Tuesday March 25th
Going Correction: PLUS 0.15 sec. per fur.

3363 Gunner Heritage Campaign Novices' Chase Class D (5-y-o and up) £4,030 2m.........................(2:15)

3284³ JUST BRUCE 8-11-6 D Gallagher, *chsd ldr, slight ld 2 out, hrd rdn and hld on wl r-in.*.(20 to 1 op 12 to 1 tchd 25 to 1) 1

2664* MISTER DRUM (Ire) 8-11-6 (4ex) W Marston, *led to 2 out, hrd rdn appr last, kpt on r-in.*.(13 to 8 op 6 to 4 tchd 11 to 8) 2

3112⁴ FLYING INSTRUCTOR 7-11-10 R Bellamy, *hld up rear, effrt 3 out, ev ch whn blun and hrd rdn 2 out, rallied and ran on r-in.*
.... (7 to 4 on op 2 to 1 on tchd 11 to 8 on) 3

Dist: 1¼l, 1l. 4m 0.30s. a 11.30s (3 Ran).

SR: 3/1/4/

(A M Heath), Mrs E H Heath

3364 Mousetrap Challenge Cup Novices' Chase Class D (5-y-o and up) £3,839 2½m 110yds.................(2:50)

190² PONTOON BRIDGE 10-11-4 R Dunwoody, *led second, lft wl clr 12th, eased to a trot r-in.*
.... (9 to 4 on op 5 to 2 on tchd 2 to 1 on) 1

1970⁹ CHIAPPUCCI (Ire) 7-11-0 D Gallagher, *hld up in 3rd, hit 8th, blun and lost tch tenth, mstk nxt, lft poor second 12th, no ch wth wnr.*...............(6 to 1 op 10 to 1) 2

3167⁵ ELL GEE 7-10-2 (7*) Miss C Townsley, *rear, blun 3rd, f 5th.*
.... (40 to 1 op 25 to 1 tchd 50 to 1) f

3094³ KEY PLAYER (Ire) 8-11-4 D O'Sullivan, *led to second, jnd wnr and f 12th.*.....(7 to 2 op 2 to 1 tchd 4 to 1) f

Dist: 3l. 5m 28.70s. a 28.70s (4 Ran).

(Sir Eric Parker), Mrs A J Perrett

3365 Royal Artillery Gold Cup Chase Class E (5-y-o and up) £3,468 3m 110yds ....(3:20)

3115³ LUCKY DOLLAR (Ire) 9-11-12 (7*) Major S J Robinson, *hmpd 6th, sn prmnt, led 16th, mstk last, rdn out.*
.... (2 to 1 op 9 to 4 tchd 5 to 2) 1

3053⁵ NO JOKER (Ire) 9-11-3 (7*) Capt R Hall, *in tch to 14th, outpcd 16th, mstk last, rallied and ran on wl r-in.*
.... (25 to 1 op 20 to 1) 2

2981⁵ SONOFAGIPSY 13-11-12 (7*) Mr A Wood, *mstks, reminders 5th, sn prmnt, led 14th to 16th, ev ch whn blun last, hmpd r-in, not quicken.*...............(6 to 1 op 10 to 1) 3

3051³ MAXXUM EXPRESS (Ire) 9-11-12 Mr J Thatcher, *prmnt, jmpd slwly 12th, sn outpcd.*
.... (16 to 1 op 12 to 1 tchd 20 to 1) 4

3076* ARCHIES OATS 8-12-0 (5*) Mr J Trice-Rolph, *shrtlvd effrt 11th, nvr trbld ldrs.*.........(8 to 1 tchd 10 to 1) 5

2991⁶ ENNISTYMON (Ire) 6-10-12 (7*) Mr G Weatherley, *in tch to 11th, poor 6th whn blun nxt, no ch whn mstk 2 out.*
.... (66 to 1 op 16 to 1 tchd 100 to 1) 6

3053* BRACKENFIELD (bl) 11-12-3 (7*) Mr D Alers-Hankey, *prmnt, disputing 3rd whn f 6th.*...........(5 to 5 fav op 6 to 5 on) f

NEW GHOST (v) 12-11-7 (7*) Major O Ellwood, *prmnt, disputing ld whn f 6th.*......(16 to 1 op 20 to 1 tchd 25 to 1) f

3051 ICANTELYA (Ire) (v) 8-11-3 (7*) Mr S Greany, *not fluent, tld off 11th, f 18th.*...............(100 to 1 tchd 100 to 1) f

TAUREAN TYCOON 13-11-12 (7*) Mr B Logan, *mid-div, pckd 5th, blun and uns rdr 7th.*
.... (66 to 1 op 10 to 1 tchd 100 to 1) ur

3018⁶ MAJOR MAG 10-11-3 (7*) Capt E Andrews, *prmnt to 5th, lost tch 11th, tld off whn pld up bef 2 out.*
.... (66 to 1 op 50 to 1 tchd 100 to 1) pu

3051 TODDLING INN 10-11-13 (7*) Mr C Farr, *lost tch 11th, tld off whn pld up bef last.*.(66 to 1 op 50 to 1 tchd 100 to 1) pu

Dist: 2l, nk, 17l, 3l, 15l. 6m 32.90s. a 33.90s (12 Ran).

(Major-Gen R L T Burges), K C Bailey

3366 Alanbrooke Memorial Handicap Chase Class C (0-135 5-y-o and up) £5,169 3m 110yds..........(3:55)

3081⁴ DENVER BAY [116] 10-11-7 (3*) L Aspell, *cl up, led 14th, rdn clr appr 2 out.*...........(7 to 4 jt-fav op 6 to 4) 1

3121* CREDON [103] 9-10-11 R Dunwoody, *led to 14th, jmpd slwly 17th and nxt, hrd rdn 3 out, sn btn.*......(2 to 1 tchd 9 to 4) 2

3286* HARRISTOWN LADY [102] (bl) 10-10-10 (4ex) B Clifford, *wth ldr whn uns rdr 3rd.*.(7 to 4 jt-fav op 6 to 4 tchd 15 to 8) ur

Dist: 19l. 6m 33.80s. a 34.80s (3 Ran).

(Bill Naylor), J T Gifford

3367 Royal Star And Garter Home Handicap Chase Class D (0-125 5-y-o and up) £4,045 2m...................(4:30)

3193³ RED BEAN [90] 9-10-2 R Johnson, *in tch, jnd ldrs and mstk 7th, led 3 out, rdn out.*.....(5 to 2 op 9 to 4 tchd 11 to 4) 1

3173* THE CARROT MAN [107] 9-11-5 P Hide, *cl up, led 8th to 3 out, not quicken r-in.*.....(10 to 1 op 5 to 4 tchd 11 to 8) 2

2624⁷ COUNT BARACHOIS (USA) [88] 9-10-2 D Gallagher, *led till pckd 8th, sn btn.*.....(16 to 1 op 14 to 1 tchd 20 to 1) 3

3154 NORSE RAIDER [112] 7-11-10 Jamie Evans, *rear, lost tch 8th, hrd rdn and no hdwy appr 3 out*.........(4 to 1 op 2 to 1) 4

3291 YOUNG ALFIE [88] (bl) 12-10-0 W Marston, *cl up till jmpd slwly 5th, beh and rdn 7th, tld off tenth.* ....(66 to 1 op 33 to 1 tchd 100 to 1) 5

Dist: 1¾l, 24l, 7l, 21l. 3m 58.40s. a 9.40s (5 Ran).

SR: 4/19/ (Kage Vincent), K Vincent

3368 'Ubique' Hunters' Chase Class H (5-y-o and up) £1,576 2½m 110yds
.... (5:00)

3076[4] ELECTRIC COMMITTEE (Ire) 7-11-5 (7") Mr A Wood, *led 3rd, slight mstks 6th and 14th, rdn and styd on wl r-in.* ....(9 to 1 op 10 to 1 tchd 12 to 1) 1

3279 GREAT POKEY 12-11-5 (7") Miss N Courtenay, *led to 3rd, outpcd 14th, rallied and ran on r-in.* (20 to 1 tchd 16 to 1) 2

2974[2] DRIVING FORCE (bl) 11-11-13 (7") Mr A Charles-Jones, *cl up, chsd wnr 13th till wknd r-in.* ....(7 to 2 tchd 4 to 1 and 3 to 1) 3

3053[4] TRUE STEEL 11-11-3 (5") Mr J Trice-Rolph, *hdwy 7th, mstk nxt, jmpd slwly and lost pl 9th, btn 13th.* ....(7 to 4 fav op Evens tchd 2 to 1) 4

3164[2] GALZIG 9-11-1 (7") Mr W Tellwright, *rear, hdwy and hit 6th, mstk nxt, blun and wknd 13th, 5th and no ch whn pld up appr 3 out.*...................(11 to 4 op 5 to 2 tchd 3 to 1) pu

THE MILL HEIGHT (Ire) 7-11-1 (7") Mr C Ward Thomas, *in tch to 6th, tld off 8th, pld up bef 12th.* ....(9 to 1 op 10 to 1 tchd 12 to 1 and 8 to 1) pu

Dist: 3l, 16l, 9l. 5m 24.10s. a 24.10s (6 Ran).

(James R Kearsley), A W Wood

SOUTHWELL (good)
Tuesday March 25th
Going Correction: PLUS 0.35 sec. per fur.

3369 Newcastle Handicap Chase Class D (0-120 5-y-o and up) £3,692 3m 110yds................ (2:25)

2935* FATHER SKY [120] (bl) 6-12-0 J Osborne, *trkd ldr, lft in ld 5 out, drw clr appr last 3, easily.* (5 to 4 on tchd 6 to 5 on) 1

2728 ZAMBEZI SPIRIT (Ire) [98] 8-10-6 Derek Byrne, *strained, improved to go hndy 7 out, hit nxt, wknd quickly appr last 3, tld off.*......................(5 to 2) 2

3277[2] TRUMPET [95] (v) 8-10-0 (3") Michael Brennan, *dictated pace till 15 out, broke shoulder, destroyed.* (100 to 30 op 3 to 1) f

Dist: Dist. 6m 26.90s. a 32.90s (3 Ran).

(Kenneth Kornfeld), O Sherwood

3370 Birmingham Novices' Chase Class E (5-y-o and up) £3,095 2m..... (3:00)

2761[5] CHORUS LINE (Ire) 8-10-11 R Supple, *led to second, led ag'n 5th, lft wl clr bef 3 out, unchlgd.* ....(3 to 1 op 7 to 2 tchd 4 to 1) 1

3189[2] TENAYESTELIGN 9-10-12 (5") Mr R Thornton, *settled wth chasing grp, chasing grp pace quickened 6 out, styd on to take second, no ch with wnr.*.........(7 to 1 op 5 to 1) 2

2998[3] SANTARAY 11-11-2 Mr R Armson, *settled to track ldrs, bustled alng whn hit 7th, struggling bef 4 out, one pace last 3.* ....(6 to 1 op 4 to 1) 3

2261 COPPER CABLE 10-11-2 M Ranger, *settled in tch, drvn alng whn hit 7th, no imprsn frm 3 out*......(20 to 1 op 16 to 1) 4

2977 JONJAS CHUDLEIGH 10-11-2 J Frost, *al struggling in rear, tld off frm hfwy.*........(14 to 1 op 12 to 1 tchd 16 to 1) 5

3139 HIGHLAND FLAME 8-10-13 (3") P Henley, *led second to 5th, styd hndy, 4th and beginning to tire whn f four out.* ....(40 to 1 op 33 to 1 tchd 50 to 1) f

2576 DASH TO THE PHONE (USA) 5-10-8 A S Smith, *pressing ldrs whn blun and uns rdr second.* ....(5 to 1 op 4 to 1 tchd 11 to 2) ur

2938[3] GIMME (Ire) (v) 7-11-2 A Thornton, *wl plcd whn blun and uns rdr 1st*...............(2 to 1 fav op 7 to 4 tchd 9 to 4) ur

3268[8] MILLENIUM LASS (Ire) 9-10-11 Gary Lyons, *patiently rdn, gd hdwy to go second 6 out, no imprsn on wnr whn broke leg and pld up bef 3 out, destroyed.*...........(25 to 1 op 20 to 1) pu

Dist: 25l, ½l, 1l, 20l. 4m 6.20s. a 12.20s (9 Ran).

SR: 17/-/-/-/-/-/ (Mrs A P Stead), P Beaumont

3371 London Handicap Chase Class E (0-115 5-y-o and up) £3,046 2½m 110yds................ (3:30)

57[3] COUNTERBALANCE [93] 10-11-5 M McNeill, *al wl plcd, lft in ld 5 out, styd on well to go clr frm 3 out.* (11 to 2 op 5 to 1) 1

3267 CURRAGH PETER [74] 10-9-12[1] (3") Guy Lewis, *led till jmpd slwly and hdd second, styd in tch, stayed on frm 3 out, no imprsn on wnr.*......................(4 to 1 op 7 to 2) 2

3145[3] BIT OF A TOUCH [86] 11-10-12 J Frost, *settled wth chasing grp, feeling pace and drvn alng aftr one circuit, tld off bef 4 out, nvr able to chal.*................(4 to 1 op 7 to 2) 3

1926[2] LAKE OF LOUGHREA (Ire) [102] 7-12-0 C O'Dwyer, *nvr gng wl, reminders 5th, tld off fnl circuit.*......(5 to 1 op 4 to 1) 4

3277 TOO SHARP [100] (bl) 9-11-12 J Culloty, *led second, jmpd rght 6th, hdd six out, lost tch quickly 4 out, tld off.* ....(5 to 1 op 4 to 1) 5

2888[3] BLAZER MORINIERE (Fr) [78] 8-10-4 S Fox, *al hndy, led 6 out, f nxt.*......................(7 to 2 fav) f

3185[5] NORTHERN OPTIMIST [87] 9-10-13 Mr J L Llewellyn, *midfield whn blun and uns rdr 4th*........(8 to 1 tchd 9 to 1) ur

PEACE OFFICER [95] 11-11-7 M A Fitzgerald, *struggling to keep in tch bef hfwy, tld off whn pld up before 7 out.* ....(8 to 1 op 14 to 1) pu

Dist: 21l, 11l, 12l, 6l. 5m 15.30s. a 15.30s (8 Ran).

SR: 10/-/-/-/-/ (Derwent Dene Farm), J C McConnochie

3372 Manchester 'National Hunt' Novices' Hurdle Class E (4-y-o and up) £2,295 2½m 110yds................ (4:05)

2951[3] PEACE LORD (Ire) 7-11-8 J F Titley, *al travelling wl, smooth hdwy to nose ahead 2 out, drw clr, very easily.* (9 to 4 on op 2 to 1 on tchd 7 to 4 on and 5 to 2 on) 1

2746 SIOUX TO SPEAK 5-11-2 J Culloty, *settled in tch, wnt hndy hfwy, drvn alng to chase wnr frm 2 out, kpt on, no imprsn.* ....(11 to 2 op 7 to 2) 2

2981 PRINZAL 10-10-9 (7") R Hobson, *pld hrd, al frnt rnk, led aftr 3 out till hdd nxt, one pace after.*.........(9 to 1 op 14 to 1) 3

2853 CARLY-J 6-10-11 Mr N Kent, *held till aftr 1st, styd hndy till lost grnd 6th, rallied, one pace und pres frm 2 out.* ....(40 to 1 op 33 to 1 tchd 50 to 1) 4

3241[5] DRY HILL LAD (bl) 6-11-2 Derek Byrne, *wth wdr, improved quickly to ld 3rd, hdd aftr 3 out, fdd und pres frm nxt.* ....(25 to 1 tchd 33 to 1) 5

3137[3] TURSAL (Ire) 8-11-2 Mr R Armson, *ran in snatches, wnt hndy 6th, und pres aftr 3 out, wknd quickly.* ....(9 to 1 op 8 to 1 tchd 12 to 1) 6

3036[3] STEER POINT 6-11-2 J Frost, *trkd ldrs, ev ch hfwy, lost grnd quickly 3 out, sn lost tch.*......................(20 to 1) 7

MORE TO LIFE 8-10-4 (7") Mr O McPhail, *chsd ldrs, wnt hndy hfwy, struggling frm 3 out, beh whn blun and uns rdr nxt.* ....(66 to 1 op 50 to 1) ur

Dist: 7l, 2l, 2½l, 1¾l, 6l, 18l. 5m 14.10s. a 28.10s (8 Ran).

(Sir Peter & Lady Gibbings), Mrs D Haine

3373 Glasgow Maiden Hurdle Class F (5-y-o and up) £2,025 3m 110yds (4:40)

2738[3] PERSIAN ELITE (Ire) 6-11-5 J Osborne, *led aftr 1st, hit 7th and nxt 2, hrd pressed 3 out, styd on to go clr frm betw last two.* ....(9 to 1 op 7 to 1) 1

2499[2] RYDER CUP (Ire) 5-11-5 M A Fitzgerald, *led till aftr 1st, styd hndy, drvn up to join wnr 3 out, sn struggling, outpcd frm betw last 2.*.................(9 to 4 tchd 2 to 1) 2

1545[5] JET BOYS (Ire) (bl) 7-11-5 D Leahy, *struggling and reminders 6th, nvr gng wl aftr, moderate late prog to take poor 3rd r-in.* ....(13 to 8 fav op 6 to 4 tchd 7 to 4) 3

3137[5] LEAP IN THE DARK (Ire) 8-11-5 R Supple, *hit 4th, trkd ldrs till lost grnd und pres bef four out, struggling frm nxt.* ....(9 to 1 op 8 to 1 tchd 10 to 1) 4

Dist: 12l, 14l, 8l. 6m 16.60s. a 34.60s (4 Ran).

(Elite Racing Club), C R Egerton

SOUTHWELL (A.W) (std)
Tuesday March 25th
Going Correction: NIL

3374 Dublin Standard Open National Hunt Flat Class H (4,5,6-y-o) £1,131 2m
.... (5:10)

3282* MAYDAY LAUREN 5-11-6 S Wynne, *made all, hrd pressed entering strt, styd on srtly to clr fnl furlong.* ....(9 to 4 op 3 to 1) 1

MIRY LEADER 4-10-5 T Kent, *keen hold, tucked away on ins, jnd wnr entering strt, one pace fnl furlong.* ....(13 to 8 fav op 11 to 10 tchd 2 to 1) 2

BALLYMACOOL 5-11-4 J Osborne, *settled gng wl, improved to join ldes bef strt, lost action and eased o'r 2 fs out, fnshd lme.*.............(13 to 2 op 4 to 1 tchd 7 to 1) 3

2764[5] BROTHER HARRY 5-10-13 (5") Mr R Thornton, *nvr far away, ev ch appr strt, fdd und pres last 2 fs.* ....(9 to 1 op 14 to 1 tchd 16 to 1) 4

CHARLIE KEAY (Ire) 5-11-1 (3") D Fortt, *pressed ldrs, ran in snatches frm hfwy, struggling in strt, lost tch.* ....(9 to 2 op 2 to 1) 5

3176[6] CEEYOU AT MIDNIGHT 6-10-11 (7") J Power, *wth ldrs one m, sn struggling, tld off in strt.*.........(20 to 1 op 12 to 1) 6

ONE BOY 5-11-1 (7") Mr R J Barrett, *trkd ldrs, lost grnd quickly aftr one m, tld off in strt.*......(20 to 1 op 14 to 1) 7

2975[6] COMMUNITY SERVICE (Ire) 6-10-10 (3") E Callaghan, *sn struggling to keep up, tld off hfwy.*......(10 to 1 op 8 to 1) 8

Dist: 3l, 21l, 4l, 5l, 28l, 3½l, 26l. 3m 58.70s. (8 Ran).

(B K Racing), A Bailey

WEXFORD (IRE) (good)
Tuesday March 25th

3375 Rosslare Novice Hurdle (6-y-o up) £2,226 3m............(2:30)

3178* LANCASTRIAN PRIDE (Ire) 7-11-9 D J Casey, (11 to 8 on)	1
3223² VALENTINE GALE (Ire) 7-10-8 (5*) P Morris, ...(9 to 4)	2
3213* CHATTERBUCK (Ire) 8-11-2 (7*) D A McLoughlin, ...(9 to 2)	3
3178⁹ KERKY (Ire) 7-11-4 J Shortt, ...(50 to 1)	4
Dist: 1l, 20l, 1½l. 6m 17.60s. (4 Ran).

(Kilcarn Bridge Syndicate), W P Mullins

3376 Wexford Mares Maiden Hurdle (4-y-o and up) £2,226 2m...........(3:00)

2900³ JENSALEE (Ire) 6-12-0 T P Treacy, ...(2 to 1 fav)	1
3233 MIDNIGHT CYCLONE (Ire) 6-12-0 D J Casey, ...(5 to 1)	2
3337³ HELORHIWATER (Ire) 6-12-0 J P Broderick, ...(5 to 2)	3
2900⁶ SHE'LL BE GOOD (Ire) 5-11-4 J R Barry, ...(10 to 1)	4
3178 SOME ORCHESTRA (Ire) 5-10-11 (7*) M D Murphy, (14 to 1)	5
3223 PYTHON WOLF (Ire) 6-12-0 C F Swan, ...(6 to 1)	6
3226⁶ SUBLIME POLLY (Ire) 4-10-8 (5*) T Martin, ...(14 to 1)	7
ELM TREE (Ire) 8-11-6 T J Mitchell, ...(20 to 1)	8
3069⁶ LAS ALMANDAS (Ire) 6-10-13 (7*) M E Gallagher, (10 to 1)	9
JOHNS TOUGH LADY (Ire) 5-11-4 K F O'Brien, ..(16 to 1)	10
3225⁹ RED ISLAND GIRL (Ire) 6-10-13 (7*) D A McLoughlin,	
....(25 to 1)	11
2337 MY NIECE (Ire) 4-10-13 P L Malone, ...(25 to 1)	12
BALLINAHAUN (Ire) 5-11-4 C N Bowens, ...(25 to 1)	13
2964 EMMSONS PRIDE (Ire) 5-11-4 F Woods, ...(20 to 1)	ur
3069⁹ KITTYGALE (Ire) 6-11-3 (3*) K Whelan, ...(16 to 1)	ur
Dist: 3½l, 3l, 8l, 11l. 3m 49.10s. (15 Ran).

(P M Kiely), P Mullins

3377 Gorey Handicap Hurdle (0-116 5-y-o and up) £2,226 2½m.........(3:30)

2645³ GENTLE MOSSY (Ire) [-] 5-10-4 D H O'Connor, ...(5 to 1)	1
3216² MARINERS REEF (Ire) [-] 6-9-9 (7*) D McCullagh,	
....(3 to 1 fav)	2
3224⁸ CHELSEA BELLE (Ire) [-] 5-9-4 (5*) A O'Shea, ...(33 to 1)	3
311⁶ THE BOULD VIC (Ire) [-] 5-10-7 J B Geraghty, ...(14 to 1)	4
3180⁷ DOUBLE STRIKE (Ire) [-] (bl) 6-10-3 T P Rudd, ...(14 to 1)	5
2647 VINTNERS VENTURE (Ire) [-] 5-10-8 C F Swan, ...(5 to 1)	6
2160² JAY MAN (Ire) [-] 7-11-6 J R Barry, ...(6 to 1)	7
3234⁹ GARLAND ROSE (Ire) [-] 7-9-7 D J Casey, ...(10 to 1)	8
2272 THE ROAD TO MOSCOW (Ire) [-] 9-9-9 M Duffy, ..(14 to 1)	9
3180 MAJESTIC JOHN (Ire) [-] 7-9-4 (7*) A T Kelly, ...(20 to 1)	10
2900⁷ ST CAROL (Ire) [-] 6-9-10¹ T P Treacy, ...(14 to 1)	11
3234 WINTRY DAWN (Ire) [-] (bl) 7-9-11 W Slattery, ...(25 to 1)	12
3235⁶ CREATIVE BLAZE (Ire) [-] 8-11-10 F Woods, ...(8 to 1)	pu
2841 MAJESTIC MAN (Ire) [-] 6-11-4 T J Mitchell, ...(16 to 1)	pu
Dist: ½l, 3½l, nk, sht-hd. 4m 52.00s. (14 Ran).

(Purple And Gold Syndicate), James Joseph O'Connor

3378 Oilgate Hunters Chase (5-y-o and up) £2,226 3m............(4:00)

DENFIELD (Ire) 6-11-7 (7*) Mr I Buchanan, ...(9 to 2)	1
943 LOTTOVER (Ire) 8-11-2 (7*) Mr B Hassett, ...(6 to 1)	2
3222 SUMMERHILL EXPRESS (Ire) 7-11-6 (3*) Mr T Lombard,	
....(10 to 1)	3
3222 EDDIE (Ire) 5-11-6 Mr H F Cleary, ...(8 to 1)	4
HENLEYDOWN (Ire) 8-11-7 (7*) Mr D Keane, ...(10 to 1)	5
BELLA BROWNIE (Ire) 6-11-2 (7*) Mr E Gallagher, ..(8 to 1)	ur
405⁵ EVEN CALL 11-11-7 (7*) Mr M J Kavanagh, ...(14 to 1)	pu
3179² TULLIBARDNICENEASY (Ire) 6-11-4 (5*) Mr A C Coyle,	
....(9 to 4 fav)	pu
IMPECCABLE BEAU (Ire) 6-12-0 Mr G J Harford, ...(6 to 1)	pu
Dist: 1½l, 20l, dist, 5l. 6m 28.90s. (9 Ran).

(Ian McDonald), C A McBratney

3379 Enniscorthy Handicap Chase (0-109 5-y-o and up) £2,226 2m......(4:30)

3218* ROSDEMON (Ire) [-] 9-11-5 P A Roche, ...(11 to 8 fav)	1
3340* HANNIES GIRL (Ire) [-] 8-10-8 (7*) Mrs(es) L J Fleming, (9 to 4)	2
3074² YOUNG WOLF (Ire) [-] 9-9-7 (7*) B J Geraghty, ...(9 to 2)	3
2410⁹ LET BUNNY RUN (Ire) [-] 7-9-5 (5*) A O'Shea, ...(25 to 1)	4
2945 ANOTHER COURSE (Ire) [-] 9-10-8 D H O'Connor, ..(8 to 1)	5
3230² SCEAL SIOG (Ire) [-] (bl) 8-10-7 L F Cusack, ...(8 to 1)	6
Dist: 1½l, 15l, hd, 3½l. 4m 3.90s. (6 Ran).

(Mrs O E Matthews), John Roche

3380 Bunclody Mares I.N.H. Flat Race (4-y-o and up) £2,226 2½m......(5:00)

3075³ LADY ELISE (Ire) 6-11-7 (7*) Mr J M Roche, ...(9 to 2)	1
3221 FINCHOGUE (Ire) 5-11-12 Mr P Fenton, ...(10 to 1)	2
2968⁴ SLAVICA 6-11-7 (7*) Mr J P Shaw, ...(7 to 2)	3
2139⁴ ALAMILLO (Ire) 8-12-0 Mr J P Dempsey, ...(10 to 1)	4
SISTER ROSE (Ire) 6-11-7 (7*) Mr Peter Fahy, ...(9 to 1)	5
FIERY FINCH 5-11-5 (7*) Mr E Gallagher, ...(20 to 1)	6
2709⁴ DONAGHMORE LADY (Ire) 5-11-7 (5*) Mr D McGoona,	
....(100 to 30 fav)	7
BORREEVA (Ire) 7-11-7 (7*) Mr J P Fahey, ...(20 to 1)	8
2343 CULRUA ROSIE (Ire) (bl) 6-11-7 (7*) Mr P Barcoe, .(14 to 1)	9
MOLL'S CHOICE (Ire) 6-11-7 (7*) Mr O O'Connor, (20 to 1)	10
NORTHCHA LADY (Ire) 5-11-5 (7*) Mr M T Hartrey, (7 to 1)	11

2754 TISNOTMYTURN (Ire) 5-11-5 (7*) Miss D O'Neill, ..(20 to 1)	12
APPLE RIVER (Ire) 4-10-11 (7*) Mr M T Hogan, ...(12 to 1)	13
2906 SCOBIE GIRL (Ire) 7-12-0 Mr D Marnane, ...(12 to 1)	14
Dist: 4l, nk, 15l, 5l. 4m 48.20s. (14 Ran).

(Mrs Mary Devereux), R O'Connor

3381 Arklow (Pro-Am) I.N.H. Flat Race (5-y-o and up) £2,226 2¼m......(5:30)

MESA VERDE (Ire) 6-12-0 Mr J A Berry, ...(10 to 9 on)	1
410⁶ LIMIT THE DAMAGE (USA) (bl) 5-11-5 (7*) G T Hourigan,	
....(12 to 1)	2
3182⁵ FRESHFIELD GALE (Ire) 7-11-6 (3*) Mr P English, ..(8 to 1)	3
1895 THE ZAFFRING (Ire) 6-11-7 (7*) K A Kelly, ...(20 to 1)	4
3238⁷ MASTER CHUZZLEWIT (Ire) 6-11-7 (7*) Mr M J Daly, (8 to 1)	5
2906² TORMOND PERK (Ire) 6-12-0 Mr B M Cash, ...(4 to 1)	6
2907⁸ OAKLAND BRIDGE (Ire) 6-11-9 (5*) Mr A C Coyle, (20 to 1)	7
2449 SUPREME GAZETTE (Ire) 5-11-5 (7*) Mr S P Hennessy,	
....(12 to 1)	8
2838 LORD PENNY (Ire) 5-11-5 (7*) Mr T P Walsh, ...(20 to 1)	9
2518 SKY LEADER (Ire) 7-11-7 (7*) Mr Peter Fahy, ...(16 to 1)	10
2907⁶ THE MILLMAN (Ire) 6-11-7 (7*) Mr D Deacon, ...(25 to 1)	11
3090 PAY THE MAN (Ire) 5-11-12 Mr P Fenton, ...(10 to 1)	12
BLASE (Ire) 5-11-5 (7*) D McCullagh, ...(14 to 1)	su
Dist: 7l, 7l, 4½l, 3½l. 4m 15.90s. (13 Ran).

(P M Berry), J A Berry

ASCOT (good)
Wednesday March 26th
Going Correction: PLUS 0.25 sec. per fur.

3382 City Index Spread Betting Novices' Hurdle Class C (4-y-o and up) £3,745 2½m........................(2:00)

2792⁶ SYMPHONY'S SON (Ire) 6-11-2 R Johnson, hld up beh ldrs, cld aftr 7th, led appr 2 out, clr last, styd on wl.	
..........................(12 to 1 op 8 to 1 tchd 14 to 1)	1
2636³ IVORY COASTER (NZ) 6-11-2 C Llewellyn, hld up towards rear, pushed along aftr 7th, styd on appr 2 out, nvr able to chal.	
..........................(16 to 1 op 10 to 1 tchd 20 to 1)	2
2807⁴ DISALLOWED (Ire) 4-10-12 M A Fitzgerald, trkd ldr, led aftr 3 out to appr nxt, sn wknd, fnshd tired.	
..........................(100 to 30 op 3 to 1 tchd 7 to 2)	3
3129 LATAHAAB (USA) 6-11-2 P Hide, trkd ldrs, mstk 7th, sn pushed alng, drvn and btn 3 out.	
..........................(8 to 1 op 6 to 1 tchd 9 to 1)	4
2871⁷ WALTER'S DESTINY 5-11-2 S McNeill, hld up towards rear, effrt 6th, nvr on terms...............(50 to 1 op 33 to 1)	5
3025² FLYING FIDDLER (Ire) (bl) 6-10-13 (3*) P Henley, mid-div, hrd rdn aftr 3 out, sn btn....(100 to 30 op 5 to 2 tchd 7 to 2)	6
3111 THE FLYING PHANTOM 6-11-7 Richard Guest, led till aftr 3 out, sn rdn and btn..................(5 to 2 fav op 6 to 4)	7
3210 LORD LOVE (Ire) 5-11-2 J Culloty, trkd ldrs, hit 3rd, wknd appr 4 out, tld off.......................(100 to 1 op 50 to 1)	8
2825⁷ GLIDE PATH (USA) 8-11-2 J Osborne, hld up beh, shrtlvd effrt 7th, wl behind whn hit 2 out, pld up bef last.	
..........................(14 to 1 op 10 to 1 tchd 16 to 1)	pu
2656⁹ ZIPALONG 6-11-2 D Byrne, al beh, trkd second, lost tch 5th, tld off whn pld up bef 4 out........(66 to 1 op 33 to 1)	pu
Dist: 11l, 7l, 7l, 13l, 3l, 5l, 10l. 4m 57.10s. a 16.10s (10 Ran).

(Mrs J Mould), D Nicholson

3383 Fairview New Homes Novices' Chase Class B (5-y-o and up) £10,892 3m 110yds..........(2:30)

3051² JULTARA (Ire) 8-11-9 B Powell, trkd ldr, led 7th, lft clr tenth, chlgd frm 2 out, drvn alng and ran on gmely r-in. (11 to 4 jt-fav op 3 to 1 tchd 100 to 30)	1
2862³ WHO IS EQUINAME (Ire) (bl) 7-11-9 M A Fitzgerald, trkd ldrs, lft second at tenth, not fluent nxt, chalg whn outjmpd 2 out, drvn and ev ch r-in, ran on..........(4 to 1 op 7 to 2)	2
3207 BALLYDOUGAN (Ire) (v) 9-11-9 D Walsh, mstk 3rd, chsd ldrs till outpcd 11th, tld off whn not fluent 16th.	
..........................(50 to 1 op 25 to 1)	3
3017² MAJOR NOVA 8-11-9 J Culloty, in tch till outpcd frm 11th, struggling whn mstks 13th and nxt (water), tld off.	
..........................(13 to 2 op 5 to 1 tchd 7 to 1)	4
3167 GLENDINE (Ire) 7-11-9 J Railton, chsd ldrs till outpcd frm 11th, tld off whn hit 2 out.	
..........................(20 to 1 op 14 to 1 tchd 25 to 1)	5
2955³ EXTERIOR PROFILES (Ire) 7-11-9 T J Murphy, led to 7th, wth wnr whn f 10th......(11 to 4 jt-fav op 7 to 4 tchd 3 to 1)	f
3118² BROWN ROBBER 9-11-9 B Fenton, mstk second, beh whn blun and uns rdr 7th....(40 to 1 op 33 to 1 tchd 50 to 1)	ur
2921³ PENNCALER (Ire) (bl) 7-11-9 R Dunwoody, al beh, lost tch 8th, pld up bef 11th.........(11 to 2 op 5 to 1 tchd 6 to 1)	pu
Dist: ¾l, dist, 10l, 25l. 6m 12.90s. a 11.90s (8 Ran).
SR: 36/35/-/-/-/

(Alan C Elliot), I P Williams

3384 Daily Telegraph Novices' Chase Handicap Class C (5-y-o and up) £14,070 2m 3f 110yds........(3:05)

2955* GARNWIN (Ire) [112] 7-10-10 M A Fitzgerald, *in cl tch, trkd ldr frm tenth gng wl, led last, hrd rdn, all out.*
.................(11 to 8 fav op 6 to 4 tchd 13 to 8)   1
3023² FRAZER ISLAND (Ire) [110] 8-10-8 D O'Sullivan, *cl up, led 8th, mstk 2 out, hdd and not fluent last, hrd rdn, rallied.*
.................(9 to 1 op 8 to 1 tchd 10 to 1)   2
2827³ GREENBACK (Bel) [126] 6-11-10 R Dunwoody, *hld up, mstks 4th and 8th, in cl tch whn mistake 3 out, sn btn.*
.................(7 to 2 op 9 to 4 tchd 75 to 20)   3
2862* MASTER TOBY (Ire) [114] 7-10-12 C Llewellyn, *hld up, drpd to last pl 6th, mstks nxt 2, rdn alng 11th, sn struggling.*
.................(4 to 1 op 3 to 1 tchd 9 to 2)   4
1478² WILDE MUSIC (Ire) [115] 7-10-13 D Gallagher, *led to 8th, in tch, rdn alng 11th, outpcd..............(8 to 1 op 6 to 1)*   5
Dist: ½l, 26l, 3½l, 1l. 4m 53.30s. a 12.30s (5 Ran).
SR: 8/5/   (Pioneer Heat-Treatment), N J Henderson

3385 City Index Spread Betting Handicap Hurdle Class C (0-135 4-y-o and up) £4,856 2m 110yds............ (3:35)

2740 ROSENCRANTZ (Ire) [108] 5-10-8 R Johnson, *hld up in cl tch, led on bit 2 out, pushed clr r-in, cmftbly.*
.................(100 to 30 op 4 to 1)   1
3111 MISTER RM [111] 5-10-11 D Bridgwater, *hld up in cl tch, rdn alng 4 out, squeezed through to ld aftr 3 out, hdd nxt, one pace whn not fluent last.*
.................(6 to 4 fav op 5 to 4 on tchd 13 to 8)   2
2329⁵ FOURTH IN LINE (Ire) [124] 9-11-10 W Marston, *lft in ld 3rd, hdd nxt, led 3 out, sn headed, one pace.*
.................(14 to 1 op 12 to 1 tchd 16 to 1)   3
3156⁸ GROUND NUT (Ire) [122] 7-11-8 B Powell, *hld up, hdwy to ld 4th, hdd 3 out, sn rdn and btn.*
.................(9 to 2 op 5 to 1 tchd 4 to 1)   4
2543⁴ KEEP ME IN MIND (Ire) [108] 8-10-8 D Skyrme, *hld up in cl tch, keen early, wknd appr 2 out.*
.................(16 to 1 op 12 to 1 tchd 25 to 1)   5
1496⁵ CHICKAWICKA (Ire) [100] 6-9-9 (5*) Mr R Thornton, *led, not fluent 1st 2, clr whn refused nxt........ (11 to 2 tchd 5 to 1)*   ref
Dist: 7l, 3l, 3½l, 5l. 4m 0.70s. a 14.70s (6 Ran).
(L J Fulford), Miss Venetia Williams

3386 Alpine Meadow Handicap Hurdle Class C (0-135 4-y-o and up) £4,924 3m........................ (4:10)

3031* TRIBUNE [111] 6-10-10 M Foster, *al hndy, led 7th, made rst, wndrd appr last, drvn out.*
.................(100 to 30 op 3 to 1 tchd 7 to 2)   1
3116 RUNAWAY PETE (USA) [121] 7-11-6 R Dunwoody, *led to 5th, cl up, hrd rdn aftr 9th, wh wnr frm 3 out, ev ch r-in, no extr und pres........................*   2
3131⁵ TAMARPOUR (USA) [125] (bl) 10-11-10 C Maude, *hld up beh, steady hdwy frm 4 out, drvn appr 2 out, no extr und pres.*
.................(4 to 1 op 11 to 4 tchd 9 to 2)   3
3116⁴ HAILE DERRING [124] 7-11-9 C Llewellyn, *hld up beh ldrs, cld aftr 9th, not fluent nxt, outpcd 3 out, hrd rdn, one pace.*
.................(11 to 4 fav tchd 3 to 1 and 5 to 2)   4
3041³ SPACEAGE GOLD [108] 8-10-8 C G Upton, *hld up beh, niggled alng appr 7th, nvr nr to chal........ (10 to 1 op 8 to 1)*   5
3255* SMUGGLER'S POINT (USA) [105] 7-10-1 (3*,4ex) Sophie Mitchell, *cl up, led 5th to 7th, hrd rdn aftr 4 out, sn wknd.*
.................(14 to 1 op 10 to 1)   6
3116 MISTER BLAKE [101] 7-9-7 (7*) X Aizpuru, *trkd ldrs, outpcd appr 7th, pushed alng approaching 9th, sn btn, tld off.*
.................(9 to 1 op 10 to 1 tchd 12 to 1)   7
Dist: 1¼l, 2½l, 7l, 5l, 8l, 24l. 5m 54.80s. a 18.80s (7 Ran).
(Hexagon Racing), C W Thornton

3387 Mahonia Hunters' Chase Class H (5-y-o and up) £2,762 2m 3f 110yds
.... (4:45)

2793³ POORS WOOD 10-11-9 (5*) Mr T McCarthy, *hld up beh, hdwy tenth, led 4 out, clr 2 out, ran on..........(5 to 1)*   1
2981 QUIET CONFIDENCE (Ire) 7-11-2 (7*) Miss D Stafford, *led 3rd till hdd 4 out, one pace.*
.................(15 to 8 fav op 6 to 4 tchd 2 to 1)   2
2981³ GAMBLING ROYAL 14-11-7 (7*) Dr P Pritchard, *trkd ldrs, mstk 11th, one pace appr 4 out.........(33 to 1 op 20 to 1)*   3
2877 FLOWING RIVER (USA) 11-11-7 (7*) Mr N R Mitchell, *hld up, blun 8th, beh frm tenth, tld off.*
.................(20 to 1 op 14 to 1 tchd 25 to 1)   4
TOM FURZE 10-11-11 (7*) Mr M Batters, *led to 3rd, wth ldr to 11th, sn wknd, tld off whn blun last..(12 to 1 tchd 14 to 1)*   5
3164⁴ TELLAPORKY 8-11-7 (7*) Mr A Middleton, *hld up, mstks 6th and nxt, hrd rdn aftr 9th, beh next, tld off.*   6
2995* A WINDY CITIZEN (Ire) 8-11-12 (5*) Mr A Sansome, *tracking ldrs whn 19th, dead.........(9 to 4 tchd 2 to 1 and 5 to 2)*   f
3288* STAR OATS 11-12-1 (7*) Mr A Kinane, *strted slwly, hld up in last pl, not jump wl, tld of whn pld up.*   pu
3279 FAMILIAR FRIEND (bl) 11-12-1 (7*) Mr L Lay, *trkd ldrs, wknd tenth, tld off whn mstk 3 out, pld up bef nxt.*
.................(20 to 1 op 10 to 1)   pu
Dist: 2½l, 5l, 26l, 19l, 2l. 4m 59.90s. a 18.90s (9 Ran).

3388 Fairview New Homes Standard National Hunt Flat Class H (4,5,6-y-o) £1,955 2m 110yds........(5:15)

GATFLAX (Ire) 5-11-1 (7*) M Keighley, *hld up beh ldrs, lost pl 7 fs out, shaken up and hdwy o'r 4 out, led over 2 out, rdn clr.*
.................(15 to 2 op 10 to 1 tchd 12 to 1 and 7 to 1)   1
DRAGON KING 5-11-5 (3*) P Henley, *hld up in mid-div, cld on ldrs hfwy, styd on wl fnl 2 fs.*
.................(16 to 1 op 14 to 1 tchd 25 to 1)   2
2642⁴ ROYAL POT BLACK (Ire) 6-11-1 (7*) M Moran, *pld hrd beh ldrs, rdn 3 fs out, kpt on same pace.....(8 to 1 op 9 to 1)*   3
3082⁹ KAPCO (Ire) 5-11-1 (7*) G Brace, *sn led, hdd o'r 2 fs out, wknd ins last.................(16 to 1 op 12 to 1 tchd 9 to 1)*   4
COLD FEET 6-10-10 (7*) J Power, *beh, hdwy o'r 4 fs out, kpt on same pace frm 2 out..........(50 to 1 op 25 to 1)*   5
3082 MOONRAKER'S MIRAGE 6-11-1 (7*) M Batchelor, *hld up beh, hdwy aftr 3 fs, drvn alng o'r three out, sn outpcd.*
.................(12 to 1 op 6 to 1 tchd 14 to 1)   6
2377 BULKO BOY (NZ) 5-11-3 (5*) D J Kavanagh, *hld up beh, cld hfwy, hrd rdn o'r 3 fs out, sn btn.*
.................(14 to 1 op 8 to 1 tchd 16 to 1)   7
MR BOJANGLES (Ire) 6-11-3 (5*) Mr R Thornton, *trkd ldrs till wknd o'r 3 fs out.................(7 to 1 op 8 to 1)*   8
1675 NICANJON 6-11-1 (7*) X Aizpuru, *nvr nr to chal.*
.................(33 to 1 op 25 to 1)   9
3122⁵ BLAZING BATMAN 4-11-0 Mr W Henderson, *cl up till wknd o'r 7 fs out.................(50 to 1 op 25 to 1)*   10
BORN AT KINGS 4-10-11 (3*) Michael Brennan, *keen early, beh frm hfwy..................(25 to 1 op 12 to 1)*   11
SEYMOUR WHO 4-10-9 (5*) G Supple, *effrt o'r 3 fs out, al beh.................(25 to 1 op 12 to 1 tchd 33 to 1)*   12
2858* SPIRIT OF STEEL 4-11-0 (7*) R McCarthy, *pld hrd, trkd ldrs, wknd quickly 4 fs out, tld off........(7 to 4 fav tchd 9 to 4)*   13
2784⁴ RACKETBALL 4-10-7 (7*) L Suthern, *trkd ldrs till wknd quickly o'r 4 fs out, tld off.....(25 to 1 op 12 to 1)*   14
Dist: 12l, 7l, 4l, nk, 3l, 1¼l, 1¾l, 4l, ½l, 8l. 3m 55.50s. (14 Ran).
(Giles Clarke), N A Twiston-Davies

DOWNPATRICK (IRE) (good to yielding)
Wednesday March 26th

3389 Downpatrick On Course Book-makers EBF Mares Hurdle (4-y-o and up) £2,397 2½m............. (2:30)

2964 COLLON DIAMONDS (Ire) 9-11-10 J P Broderick,
.................(5 to 2 co-fav)   1
3074 PILS INVADER (Ire) 9-11-10 D T Evans, ...(33 to 1)   2
3213⁶ L'AMI DE ADAM (Ire) 6-11-10 C O'Dwyer, ..(5 to 2 co-fav)   3
3073 RATHCORE LADY (Ire) 6-11-7 (3*) K Whelan, ...(33 to 1)   4
2054 DANNKALIA (Ire) 5-11-8 H Rogers, ...(10 to 1)   5
3083 KARA'S DREAM (Ire) 9-11-7 (3*) B Bowens, ...(12 to 1)   6
1584 WINTER PRINCESS 6-11-10 P McWilliams, ...(20 to 1)   7
3226⁷ SHINORA (Ire) 6-11-3 (7*) Mr G T Murrow, ...(5 to 2 co-fav)   8
2055 RACHEL'S SWALLOW (Ire) 5-11-8 L P Cusack, (5 to 2 co-fav)   9
3231 ZAFFRIDGE (Ire) 5-11-5 (3*) D Bromley, ...(33 to 1)   10
3068 CUTE AGREEMENT (Ire) 5-11-8 M Duffy, ...(16 to 1)   11
3225 MYSTIC ROSE (Ire) 6-11-3 (7*) M D Murphy, ...(50 to 1)   pu
Dist: 1½l, 20l, 3½l, 10l. 5m 10.70s. (12 Ran).
(Mrs I M Murphy), A J Martin

3390 John Turley Building Contractor Handicap Hurdle (0-102 4-y-o and up) £1,712 2½m............. (3:00)

3227⁴ HOME I'LL BE (Ire) [-] 7-9-6 (3*) B Bowens, ...(10 to 1)   1
2036⁵ STAR TRIX (Ire) [-] 6-10-2 (3*) D Bromley, ...(14 to 1)   2
2585 MICK MAN (Ire) [-] 6-10-11 K F O'Brien, ...(6 to 1)   3
3227² SPECTACLE (Ire) [-] 7-9-11 (7*) R Burke, ...(7 to 1)   4
3072³ EUROTHATCH (Ire) [-] 9-10-12 (7*) Mr N W Toal, (4 to 1 jt-fav)   5
3227⁵ GLENEAGLES CASTLE (Ire) [-] 7-11-6 (7*) Mr A Stronge, ...(10 to 1)   6
3180³ LIOS NA MAOL (Ire) [-] 6-9-10 (7*) M D Murphy, ...(7 to 1)   7
3180⁵ LAURENS FANCY (Ire) [-] 7-11-13 J R Barry, (4 to 1 jt-fav)   8
495² PETITE MEWS (Ire) [-] 6-10-2 (7*) Mr R P McNalley, (14 to 1)   9
3227 JUST 'R JAKE (Ire) [-] 8-10-4 (5*) A O'Shea, ...(25 to 1)   10
3225⁷ AUTOBABBLE (Ire) [-] 4-11-1 T P Rudd, ...(20 to 1)   11
3069⁴ JACKPOT JOHNNY (Ire) [-] 6-10-7 (7*) D A McLoughlin, ...(11 to 1)   12
2582 FLOWERS OF MAY (Ire) [-] 6-10-8 D J Casey, ...(20 to 1)   13
2379 QUEEN OF ALL GALES (Ire) [-] 6-10-10 C O'Dwyer, (14 to 1)   14
3227 SCATHACH (Ire) [-] 5-10-1 P McWilliams, ...(25 to 1)   f
Dist: 4½l, 11l, 1l, hd. 5m 6.70s. (15 Ran).
(H Smyth), H Smyth

3391 Breeders Supporting Downpatrick Hunters Chase (5-y-o and up) £1,712 3m........................ (3:30)

3228² FIND OUT MORE (Ire) 9-11-7 (7*) Mr B Potts, ...(11 to 2)   1

2869 HILTONSTOWN LASS (Ire) 7-11-2 (7*) Mr Richard J Walker, ...(20 to 1) 2
CHRISTIMATT (Ire) 6-11-7 (7*) Mr L D McBratney, (16 to 1) 3
2844 KILLMURRAY BUCK (Ire) 9-11-2 (7*) Mr R J Barnwell, ...(20 to 1) 4
3228⁴ MITCHELSTOWN RIVER 10-11-7 (7*) Mr R P McNalley, ...(8 to 1) 5
SISTER NORA (Ire) 9-11-2 (7*) Mr L J Gracey, ...(20 to 1) 6
LISTRAKELT (Ire) 7-11-7 (7*) Mr J O McGurgan, ...(20 to 1) 7
MISCHIEVOUS ANDY (Ire) 8-11-7 (7*) Mr A Ross, (20 to 1) 8
FUNNY YE KNOW (Ire) 8-12-0 Mr P F Graffin, ..(5 to 1 co-fav) f
THE BOOLYA (Ire) 9-11-7 (7*) Mr N W Toal, ..(5 to 1 co-fav) ur
HAVEAFEWMANNERS (Ire) 7-11-9 Mr A J Martin, ...(5 to 1 co-fav) bd
702³ PALMURA 10-11-7 (7*) Mr J G O'Connell, ...(25 to 1) pu
3228⁶ ROYAL STAR (Ire) 8-11-9 Mr G J Harford, ...(20 to 1) pu
2523⁶ UP AND UNDER (Ire) 8-11-7 (7*) Mr N Geraghty, ...(7 to 1) pu
Dist: 1l, 6l, 3½l, 2l. 6m 26.60s. (14 Ran).

(Peter Mulligan), S A Kirk

3392 New Weighroom Handicap Chase (0-109 4-y-o and up) £2,055 3m
....(4:00)

2382* BALLYMACREVAN (Ire) [-] 7-12-0 T P Treacy, ...(7 to 4 fav) 1
3230* HERSILIA (Ire) [-] 6-11-3 F J Flood, ...(3 to 1) 2
2867⁴ CABBERY ROSE (Ire) [-] 9-10-6 (5*) A O'Shea, ...(9 to 2) 3
2868⁵ EASTERN FOX (Ire) [-] 8-10-2² D T Evans, ...(14 to 1) 4
3229⁷ EDENAKILL LAD [-] 10-10-5 (3*) D Bromley, ...(12 to 1) 5
2020 JOHNEEN [-] (bl) 11-11-13 C O'Dwyer, ...(13 to 2) pu
2867⁸ OVER THE MAINE (Ire) [-] (bl) 7-11-1 H Rogers, ...(10 to 1) pu
Dist: Nk, dist, 4½l, 11l. 6m 13.90s. (7 Ran).

(Good Time Managers Syndicate), I A Duncan

3393 Frank Magee Memorial EBF Beginners Chase (5-y-o and up) £1,712 2½m
....(4:30)

MR FIVE WOOD (9-12-0 D T Evans, ...(2 to 1) 1
3227⁶ THE THIRD MAN (Ire) 8-11-7 (7*) Mr K Ross, ...(6 to 1) 2
2085⁶ MACALLISTER (Ire) 7-12-0 K F O'Brien, ...(Evens fav) 3
3229 PEDE GALE (Ire) 9-11-4 F Woods, ...(14 to 1) 4
3230 PINGO HILL (Ire) 5-11-6 P L Malone, ...(33 to 1) 5
HALL'S MILL (Ire) 6-11-6 (3*) K Whelan, ...(16 to 1) 6
3083 GOLDWREN (Ire) 8-10-11 (7*) Mr N W Toal, ...(33 to 1) f
Dist: Nk, dist, 15l, 8l. 5m 30.80s. (7 Ran).

(Mrs T Doherty), J F C Maxwell

3394 Breeders Supporting Downpatrick INH Flat Race (4-y-o and up) £1,712 2m 1f 172yds.................(5:00)

2870* ANDREA COVA (Ire) 5-11-6 (5*) Mr A C Coyle, ...(7 to 1) 1
3182² GOLDEN GOLD (Ire) 5-11-4 (7*) Miss C O'Neill, ...(8 to 1) 2
2709⁴ THINKERS CORNER (Ire) 5-11-9 (7*) Mr A J Dempsey, ...(9 to 4 fav) 3
3135 FRANKIE WILLOW (Ire) 4-11-8 Mr P F Graffin, ...(3 to 1) 4
3075⁶ KATOUCHE (Ire) 6-11-8 (3*) Mr B R Hamilton, ...(16 to 1) 5
3231⁶ RUN SPARKY (Ire) 5-10-13 (5*) Mr R J Patton, ...(12 to 1) 6
3231³ DJENNE (Ire) 5-10-11 (7*) Mr K Ross, ...(33 to 1) 7
3231⁸ BELLE O' THE BAY (Ire) 8-10-13 (7*) Mr E Durnan, (33 to 1) 8
IT'SNOTSIMPLE (Ire) 5-10-11 (7*) Mr Richard J Walker, ...(33 to 1) 9
MANHATTAN RAINBOW (Ire) 6-11-8 (3*) Mr D Valentine, ...(7 to 1) 10
YOU'RE IN LUCK (Ire) 6-11-2 (7*) Mr Edgar Byrne, (33 to 1) 11
GAYE CHATELAINE (Ire) 4-10-3 (7*) Miss F Martin, (20 to 1) 12
JIMMYJOE (Ire) 4-10-8 (7*) Mr J J Canavan, ...(66 to 1) 13
Dist: 1½l, 7l, 4l, 2½l. 4m 17.80s. (13 Ran).

(Basil Brindley), Victor Bowens

CARLISLE (good to soft)
Saturday March 29th
Going Correction: PLUS 0.70 sec. per fur.

3395 Border Garden Centre Novices' Chase Class E (5-y-o and up) £3,077 3m.......................(2:05)

2848² COLONEL IN CHIEF (Ire) 7-11-8 R Dunwoody, led till aftr 1st, cl up, hit 12th, led nxt, rdn appr last, styd on wl. ....(5 to 2 op 2 to 1) 1
3037 CAROLE'S CRUSADER 6-11-3 G Bradley, trkd ldrs, pushed alng 12th, hdwy 5 out, ev ch last, sn drvn and kpt on. ....(2 to 1 fav op 7 to 4) 2
3017⁴ THERMAL WARRIOR 7-11-3 C Llewellyn, al prmnt, rdn 3 out, ev ch last, no extr r-in..................(20 to 1 op 16 to 1) 3
2881³ DORLIN CASTLE (Ire) 8-11-7 R Supple, hld up in rear, hdwy 11th, chsd ldrs and hit 4 out, rdn nxt and sn one pace. ....(4 to 1 op 9 to 2) 4
3056 MAJORITY MAJOR (Ire) 8-11-8 A S Smith, chsd ldrs, rdn alng 4 out, wkng whn hit 2 out...................(50 to 1) 5

HARRISTOWN (Ire) 9-11-2 P Niven, hld up in rear, steady hdwy 12th, jnd ldrs 4 out, rdn and one pace frm 2 out. ....(50 to 1 op 33 to 1 tchd 66 to 1) 6
3031⁷ FESTIVAL FANCY 10-10-8 (3*) G Lee, hld up in rear, hdwy 12th, hit nxt, rdn alng and wknd frm 4 out. ....(100 to 1 op 50 to 1) 7
2620² NAUGHTY FUTURE 8-11-8 S McNeill, hld up, hdwy and hit 12th, chsd ldrs 5 out, rdn 3 out, sn wknd. ....(10 to 1 tchd 12 to 1) 8
3250² FERN LEADER (Ire) 7-11-2 J Supple, led aftr 1st, blun 6th, blunded and hdd six out, sn wknd, blundered badly and uns rdr 3 out...................(6 to 1 op 10 to 1 tchd 12 to 1) ur
SUPERMARINE 11-11-2 B Storey, al rear, beh whn pld up 4 out...(500 to 1 op 100 to 1) pu
2912 KING OF STEEL 11-11-2 R Garritty, chsd ldrs till pld up bef 11th...(50 to 1 tchd 100 to 1) pu
3190 KENTUCKY GOLD (Ire) 8-11-2 L O'Hara, hld up, hdwy and hit 9th, hit nxt and sn rdn alng, beh whn pld up 3 out. ....(100 to 1) pu
3056 ROYAL BANKER (Ire) 7-11-2 L Wyer, not fluent, al rear, beh whn pld up 4 out...................(66 to 1 op 33 to 1) pu
Dist: 2l, 5l, 12l, 6l, 1l, 14l, 3l. 6m 28.30s. a 36.30s (13 Ran).

(Robert Ogden), G Richards

3396 B.B.C. Radio Cumbria Novices' Hurdle Class E (Div I) (4-y-o and up) £2,136 2m 1f................(2:35)

2917² STAR SELECTION 6-11-9 (3*) E Husband, prmnt, led 3rd, clr appr 3 out, unchlgd. ....(11 to 8 on op 5 to 4 on tchd 11 to 10 on) 1
1390³ ARDRONAN (Ire) 7-11-0 S McNeill, mid-div whn hit 4th and lost pl, beh till gd hdwy 3 out, styd on appr last, no ch wth wnr. ....(14 to 1 op 12 to 1 tchd 16 to 1) 2
3303⁴ BOURBON DYNASTY (Ire) 4-11-0 A Dobbin, chsd ldrs, hit 5th, rdn alng 3 out, kpt on one pace.......(16 to 1 op 14 to 1) 3
2879² FASSAN (Ire) 5-11-0 R Garritty, led to 3rd, chsd wnr, rdn alng 4 out, drvn nxt, sn wknd....................(4 to 1) 4
2849 THORNWOOD (Ire) 5-10-7 (7*) S Melrose, chsd ldrs, rdn alng 4 out, sn one pace...................(100 to 1 op 50 to 1) 5
2811⁵ SWIFT RIPOSTE (Ire) 6-11-6 R Dunwoody, mid-div, hdwy 5th, rdn alng aftr 4 out, sn btn...(7 to 1 op 6 to 1 tchd 8 to 1) 6
3003⁹ ALLERBY 9-10-9 (5*) B Grattan, beh frm hfwy. ....(66 to 1 op 33 to 1) 7
3128* ROTHARI 5-11-6 R Supple, cl up, rdn alng 4 out, blun nxt, sn wknd...................(10 to 1 op 7 to 1 tchd 12 to 1) 8
3249 NINE PIPES (Ire) 6-11-0 L O'Hara, beh frm hfwy. ....(100 to 1 op 66 to 1) 9
3029 ONE STOP 4-9-12 (5*) S Taylor, mid-div, effrt and hdwy 6th, sn rdn and btn nxt...................(100 to 1 op 33 to 1) 10
HEADS OR TAILS (Ire) 6-10-9 B Storey, beh frm hfwy. ....(100 to 1 op 50 to 1) 11
3011 PEAK A BOO 6-10-9 D Bentley, in tch till lost pl and beh frm hfwy...(66 to 1 op 50 to 1) 12
3127 SHULTAN (Ire) 8-10-9 K Jones, cl up to 4th, sn lost pl and beh, tld off 3 out...................(66 to 1 op 50 to 1) 13
3011⁸ THE KHOINOA (Ire) 7-11-0 J Supple, in tch, effrt and rdn 5th, wknd nxt, pld up bef 3 out...........(25 to 1 op 20 to 1) pu
3198 SNIPER 5-11-0 A Roche, beh frm hfwy, pld up bef 3 out. ....(100 to 1 op 66 to 1) pu
Dist: 12l, ½l, 7l, 4l, 4l, 12l, 4l, 13l, 1¼l, ½l. 4m 20.50s. a 17.50s (15 Ran).
SR: 42/18/11/10/6/8/

(R M Mitchell), J Mackie

3397 Quilter Handicap Chase Class D (0-125 5-y-o and up) £3,485 3m
....(3:05)

3204⁶ COVERDALE LANE [95] 10-9-7 (7*) R Wilkinson, chsd ldr, led tenth, rdn alng 3 out, styd on strly........(9 to 1 op 6 to 1) 1
3245² NORTHERN SQUIRE [105] 9-10-7 (3*) E Callaghan, hld up in tch, hdwy to chase wnr 12th, rdn 3 out, one pace. ....(6 to 4 fav tchd 2 to 1) 2
3306 KILCOLGAN [106] (bl) 10-10-11 N Bentley, led to tenth, cl up till rdn alng 5 out, grad wknd frm nxt.......(6 to 1 op 5 to 1) 3
3206⁶ ACT THE WAG (Ire) [119] 8-11-10 R Dunwoody, hld up in tch, hdwy to chase ldrs 12th, rdn alng 4 out, wknd frm nxt. ....(9 to 2 op 4 to 1) 4
3020² SIMPSON [95] 12-10-0 C Llewellyn, chsd ldrs, hit 11th, rdn alng nxt, sn wknd..........(9 to 2 op 4 to 1 tchd 5 to 1) 5
2800⁴ REALLY A RASCAL [100] 10-10-5 G Bradley, al rear, beh whn pld up bef 2 out...................(15 to 2 op 6 to 1) pu
Dist: 11l, 1¼l, dist, 16l. 6m 25.30s. a 33.30s (6 Ran).

(Jim Pilkington), Mrs S J Smith

3398 Cummersdale Handicap Hurdle Class D (0-125 4-y-o and up) £2,885 2½m 110yds................(3:35)

3057² SWANBISTER (Ire) [106] 7-10-9 R Supple, al prmnt, pushed alng 3 out, led nxt, drvn last, styd on strly. (7 to 1 op 6 to 1) 1
TRUE SCOT (Ire) [97] 7-10-0 A S Smith, hld up and beh, steady hdwy aftr 4 out, rdn and ch last, kpt on same pace. ....(20 to 1 op 16 to 1) 2
2919⁷ PALACEGATE KING [113] 8-10-9 (7*) I Jardine, trkd ldrs, smooth hdwy 4 out, chlgd nxt, ev ch chance till rdn and one pace r-in...................(16 to 1 op 14 to 1) 3

19445 CHIPPED OUT [107] 7-10-3 (7*) C McCormack, *in tch, smooth hdwy 4 out, hit nxt, ev ch whn blun 2 out, sn wknd.*
.... (14 to 1 op 12 to 1) 4

2490* PAPERISING [112] 5-11-1 A Dobbin, *prmnt, effrt and led 3 out, rdn and hdd nxt, grad wknd.*
..................................(11 to 8 fav op 7 to 4 tchd 2 to 1) 5

28153 OLD HABITS (Ire) [101] 8-10-4 B Storey, *led, rdn aing and hdd 3 out, grad wknd frm nxt.* (10 to 1 op 8 to 1 tchd 11 to 1) 6

3045* DAWN MISSION [98] 5-10-1 L Wyer, *in tch, rdn aing 4 out, sn wknd.*.................................. (16 to 1 op 10 to 1) 7

3063 BUCKBOARD BOUNCE [125] 11-12-0 R Dunwoody, *beh frm hfwy.*...................(16 to 1 op 14 to 1 tchd 20 to 1) 8

30069 TIRMIZI (USA) [97] 6-10-0 J Supple, *al rear, beh frm hfwy.*
.... (14 to 1 tchd 16 to 1) 9

32442 DESERT FORCE (Ire) [97] 8-10-0 K Gaule, *al rear, beh frm hfwy.*..............................(20 to 1 op 12 to 1) 10

30313 BANG IN TROUBLE (Ire) [100] 6-10-3 S McNeill, *prmnt till rdn aing and lost pl 6th, sn beh and tld off whn pld up ime aftr 2 out, dead.*.......................(12 to 1 op 10 to 1) pu

2574* CITTADINO [104] 7-10-7 M Foster, *chsd ldrs, rdn aing 6th, lost pl and beh frm 4 out, pld up bef last.*..... (8 to 1 op 7 to 1) pu
Dist: 5l, 2½l, 1½l, ¾l, 5l, 5l, 13l, 1¼l, 16l. 5m 11.60s. a 29.60s (12 Ran).

(Colonel D C Greig), L Lungo

3399 Sunday Car Boot Handicap Chase Class F (0-105 5-y-o and up) £3,046 2½m 110yds................ (4:05)

32614 LE DENSTAN [77] 10-10-0 G Cahill, *hld up and beh, gd hdwy 12th, effrt to chal last, sn led, rdn and ran on strly*
.... (12 to 1 op 10 to 1) 1

33046 JYMJAM JOHNNY (Ire) [97] 8-11-6 S McNeill, *led second, mstks 11th and 12th, rdn aing and hit 3 out, drvn last, sn hdd and not quicken.*....................(8 to 1 op 7 to 1) 2

3355* PARIAH (Ire) [91] 8-11-0 P Niven, *hld up, steady hdwy 11th, jnd ldrs 4 out, rdn 2 out, ev ch till drvn and one pace last.*
.... (4 to 1 jt-fav op 5 to 1) 3

30143 ACAJOU III (Fr) [105] 9-12-0 R Dunwoody, *cl up, chsd ldr and ev ch whn blun 3 out, sn btn.*
.... (9 to 1 op 8 to 1 tchd 10 to 1) 4

3032 PETER [91] 9-11-0 K Johnson, *hld up and beh, some hdwy 4 out, not rch ldrs.*.................(20 to 1 op 16 to 1) 5

30322 SOLBA (USA) [101] (bl) 8-11-10 D Parker, *in tch, hit 11th and sn drvn aing, beh frm 5 out.*........... (7 to 1 op 6 to 1) 6

31618 SUPPOSIN [86] 9-10-9 Richard Guest, *beh frm hfwy.*
.... (16 to 1 op 25 to 1 tchd 33 to 1) 7

28574 MARLINGFORD [77] 10-9-7 (7*) L McGrath, *blun 3rd and beh, hit 11th, nvr a factor.*................(16 to 1 op 14 to 1) 8
JAUNTY GIG [79] (bl) 11-10-2 L O'Hara, *in tch till lost pl and beh frm 9th.*..............................(66 to 1 op 50 to 1) 9

3161* CULLANE LAKE (Ire) [79] 7-10-2 R Supple, *not fluent, in tch, hdwy to chase ldrs 8th, rdn aing 11th, grad lost pl 4 out, sn fav tchd 9 to 2) 10

31992 BLAZING DAWN [87] 10-10-10 B Storey, *led to second, prmnt till lost pl appr 9th, sn beh.*........(10 to 1 op 8 to 1) 11

1987* PRECIPICE RUN [89] 12-10-12 M Moloney, *in tch, mstk 7th, f 9th.*..............................(33 to 1 op 25 to 1) f

33553 CHILL WIND [88] 8-10-11 M Foster, *al prmnt, effrt 3 out and sn ev ch, rdn 2 out, cl 3rd whn f last.*......(8 to 1 op 7 to 1) f

33184 DOLIKOS [83] 10-10-6 A Dobbin, *mid-div, blun 6th and lost pl, pld up bef 9th.*..................(14 to 1 op 12 to 1) pu

32466 DALUSMAN (Ire) [77] 9-10-0 A Roche, *prmnt, blun 6th, rdn aing and lost pl 11th, beh whn pld up bef 3 out.*
.... (66 to 1 op 50 to 1) pu
OVERFLOWING RIVER (Ire) [89] 8-10-12 K Jones, *beh frm 8th, pld up bef tenth.*.............(33 to 1 op 25 to 1) pu
Dist: 5l, 12l, sht-hd, 4l, 15l, 1l, ½l, 5l, 2l, dist. 5m 16.20s. a 21.20s (16 Ran).
SR: 4/19/1/15/-/-/ (L Wright), Mrs D Thomson

3400 Carlisle Club Members Novices' Handicap Hurdle Class E (0-105 4-y-o and up) £3,081 2½m 110yds (4:35)

3057* CHERRY DEE [84] 6-10-6 (5*) B Grattan, *led to 6th, cl up, rdn last, led r-in, styd on wl.*.............. (6 to 1 op 5 to 1) 1

25658 WELSH SILK [73] 5-10-0 C Llewellyn, *hld up and beh, steady hdwy 3 out, effrt appoaching last, rdn and styd on r-in.*
.... (10 to 1 op 8 to 1) 2

33032 BOLD CLASSIC (Ire) [88] 4-10-6 P Niven, *cl up, led 6th, rdn 2 out, hdd and no extr r-in...* (5 to 1 op 4 to 1 tchd 6 to 1) 3

3196* WORKINGFORPEANUTS (Ire) [75] 7-10-7 Mrs D Smith, *in tch till lost pl hfwy, rdn aing and styd on frm 3 out, no dngr.*
.... (11 to 2 op 6 to 1 tchd 5 to 1) 4

24925 CLAIRABELL (Ire) [75] 6-10-2 K Johnson, *al chasing ldrs, drvn aing 2 out, plugged on same pace.*
.... (25 to 1 op 20 to 1) 5

31985 BATTERY FIRED [73] 8-9-7 (7*) S Haworth, *hld up and beh, steady hdwy 7th, chsd ldrs 3 out, sn one pace.*
.... (25 to 1 op 20 to 1) 6

31624 KINGS LANE [83] 8-10-10 D Parker, *mid-div and drvn aing hfwy, nvr a factor.*...........(16 to 1 op 14 to 1) 7

1784* BARNSTORMER [73] (bl) 11-9-9 (5*) G F Ryan, *prmnt, rdn aing 7th, hit nxt, wknd frm next.*............(50 to 1) 8

32414 RANGER SLOANE [81] 5-10-8 K Gaule, *midfield, steady hdwy 6th, dsptd ld 4 out, rdn nxt, wknd 2 out.*
.... (20 to 1 tchd 25 to 1) 9

3034* PHAR ECHO (Ire) [98] 6-11-11 R Supple, *chsd ldrs, rdn appr 3 out, sn btn.*....................(8 to 1 tchd 9 to 1) 10

29153 CRY BABY [88] 4-10-6 G Bradley, *beh frm hfwy.*
.... (25 to 1 op 20 to 1) 11

28496 NUTTY SOLERA [81] 7-10-8 B Storey, *in tch, rdn aing and hit 7th, wknd 4 out.*....................(25 to 1 op 16 to 1) 12

2856* PILKINGTON (Ire) [93] 7-11-6 R Dunwoody, *chsd ldrs, reminders 6th and sn lost pl, tld off 4 out.*
.... (3 to 1 fav tchd 10 to 3 and 11 to 4) 13

32035 JUBRAN (USA) [85] 11-10-12 Richard Guest, *hld up and beh, hdwy to join ldrs 6th, rdn aftr nxt and sn wknd, behind whn pld up bef 3 out.*..................(50 to 1 op 25 to 1) pu

2463 TREMENDISTO [96] 7-11-9 A Dobbin, *chsd ldrs till lost pl and pld up bef 6th.*.............(33 to 1 op 25 to 1) pu

30343 SOLSGIRTH [79] 6-10-6 G Cahill, *al beh, tld off whn pld up bef 3 out.*..............................(14 to 1 op 12 to 1) pu

26886 THIRTY BELOW (Ire) [77] 8-10-4 S McNeill, *al rear, beh whn pld up bef last.*............(14 to 1 op 12 to 1) pu

3057 CRASHBALLOO (Ire) [73] 6-10-0 A S Smith, *sn beh, tld off whn pld up bef 6th...*.........(100 to 1 op 50 to 1) pu
Dist: 1¾l, hd, 4l, nk, 16l, 3l, 14l, 4l, nk, 20l. 5m 10.70s. a 28.70s (18 Ran).

(George Dilger), P Beaumont

3401 B.B.C. Radio Cumbria Novices' Hurdle Class E (Div II) (4-y-o and up) £2,122 2m 1f............... (5:05)

25956 NEW LEAF (Ire) 5-11-0 G Bradley, *hld up in rear, smooth hdwy 3 out, led aftr last, quickened clr.*
.... (5 to 2 fav op 3 to 1 tchd 100 to 30) 1

30594 BRUMON (Ire) (v) 6-11-6 D J Moffatt, *in tch, gd hdwy 6th, led aftr 2 out, rdn and hit last, sn hdd and not quicken und pres...*..................(10 to 1 op 8 to 1) 2

30552 CRABBIE'S PRIDE 4-10-8 Richard Guest, *chsd ldrs, rdn aing 3 out, styd on appr last...*......(10 to 1 tchd 12 to 1) 3
SWANDALE FLYER 5-10-9 (5*) B Grattan, *hld up, hdwy 3 out, chsd ldrs nxt, rdn and one pace appr last.*
.... (100 to 1 op 50 to 1) 4

3128 MAPLETON 4-10-1 (7*) R Wilkinson, *al prmnt, hdwy to ld appr 3 out, rdn and hit nxt, sn hdd and wknd last.*
.... (20 to 1 op 16 to 1) 5

30024 RASIN STANDARDS 7-11-0 B Storey, *beh till styd on appr last, nrst finish.*................(50 to 1 op 33 to 1) 6

29843 RIVEAUX (Ire) 7-11-0 R Dunwoody, *al prmnt, effrt and ev ch 3 out, rdn nxt and sn wknd.*...........(7 to 2 tchd 3 to 1) 7

2712 BONNY RIGG (Ire) 5-10-9 T Reed, *led, rdn and hdd appr 3 out, grad wknd nxt...*...........(100 to 1 tchd 200 to 1) 8

30153 SIDE BY SIDE (Ire) 4-9-10 (7*) N Horrocks, *al rear.*
.... (25 to 1 op 20 to 1) 9

30064 FIRST IN THE FIELD 6-10-8 (7*) S Haworth, *beh frm hfwy.*
.... (20 to 1 op 16 to 1) 10

3034* KEMO SABO (bl) 5-11-0 D Parker, *cl up, rdn aing appr 3 out, sn wknd...*.............(9 to 2 op 4 to 1 tchd 5 to 1) 11

33036 KNOWN SECRET (USA) 4-10-8 A Dobbin, *chsd ldrs, rdn aing and wknd 6th...*......(10 to 1 op 8 to 1 tchd 12 to 1) 12
JUST WHISTLE 5-10-9 A S Smith, *al beh, f 3 out...*(50 to 1) f
JUNGLE PATROL (Ire) 5-11-0 M Foster, *chsd ldrs to 5th, sn wknd.*....................(25 to 1 op 16 to 1) pu

25339 CHAIN LINE 7-11-0 P Niven, *al rear, beh whn pld up bef 3 out.*
.... (100 to 1 op 33 to 1) pu
Dist: 3½l, 3l, 2½l, 2l, sht-hd, 24l, 1¾l, nk, 16l, 2½l. 4m 27.10s. a 24.10s (15 Ran).

(Mrs D J Hues), D R Gandolfo

NEWTON ABBOT (good to firm)
Saturday March 29th
Going Correction: PLUS 0.10 sec. per fur. (races 1,2,4,6,7), PLUS 0.20 (3,5)

3402 Mile End Mares' Only Maiden Hurdle Class E (4-y-o and up) £2,400 2m 1f .... (1:30)

1470 SECRET GIFT (bl) 4-10-8 D Leahy, *al prmnt, led aftr 4th, clr appr 2 out, unchlgd...*.............(5 to 1 op 7 to 2) 1
POWDER MONKEY 7-11-0 G Tormey, *hld up beh ldrs, rdn aing 3 out, sn one pace, lft second betw fnl 2.*
.... (14 to 1 op 12 to 1) 2

31065 SONG OF KENDA 5-10-9 (5*) D Salter, *hld up beh ldrs, rdn 3 out, one pace...*..................(11 to 1 op 10 to 1) 3

3299 LADY CALLERNISH 7-10-7 (7*) Mr S Durack, *hld up, some hdwy frm 3 out, nvr nr to chal...*....(100 to 1 op 50 to 1) 4

18326 SCOTTISH PARK 8-11-0 Jamie Evans, *blun 2 out, nvr nr to chal...*................(15 to 2 op 5 to 1 tchd 8 to 1) 5

31068 MISS NIGHT OWL 6-11-0 J Frost, *mstks 3 out and nxt, nvr nrr...*................(20 to 1 op 14 to 1 tchd 25 to 1) 6

1830 NEPTUNES MISS 5-11-0 W Marston, *chsd ldrs to 5th, sn wknd...*................(25 to 1 op 33 to 1) 7
OYSTER DELIGHT (Ire) 6-10-7 (7*) P Ryan, *mid-div, rdn 3 out, no imprsn...*................(4 to 1 op 3 to 1) 8

2961 FOLESCLAVE (Ire) 5-11-0 D Walsh, *trkd ldrs, wknd frm 3 out.*
.... (20 to 1 op 14 to 1) 9

31229 MINNIE (Ire) 4-10-8 S Curran, *mid-div, rdn and wknd appr 3 out...*..................(16 to 1 op 10 to 1) 10

473

3122 ROYAL MEMBER 4-10-8 E Byrne, al beh, tld off whn veered
rght and uns rdr last.. (50 to 1 op 20 to 1 tchd 66 to 1) ur
1134 LADY NOSO 6-11-0 B Powell, led till aftr 4th, chsd wnr after,
second and hld whn pld up 3me betw fnl 2.
.... (5 to 2 fav op 3 to 1 tchd 100 to 30) pu
231 FINAL SCORE (Ire) 7-10-11 (3*) T Dascombe, hld up, effrt 5th,
wknd quickly frm 3 out, beh whn pld up bef last.
3299 ABBEYDORAN 6-10-9 (5*) D J Kavanagh, chsd ldrs, wknd frm
6 out. .... (50 to 1) pu
Dist: 9l, 10l, 3l, 6l, 2½l, 3l, 1¼l, 10l, 25l. 4m 5.40s. a 16.40s (14 Ran).
(Regal Racing), Mrs J Pitman

3403 South West Racing Club Challenge Trophy Class D Handicap Hurdle (0-125 4-y-o and up) £2,849 2m 1f
.... (2:00)

3301* NORTHERN STARLIGHT [118] 6-11-10 C Maude, made virtually all, awkward last, rdn out.
.... (9 to 4 on op 2 to 1 on tchd 7 to 4 on) 1
3110 BLADE OF FORTUNE [94] 9-9-7 (7*) X Aizpuru, dsptd ld to
3rd, chsd wnr aftr, rdn and ev ch 2 out, unbl to quicken r-in.
.... (10 to 1 op 8 to 1 tchd 12 to 1) 2
3186* VA UTU [94] 9-9-11 (3*) Sophie Mitchell, hld up, prog 4th, rdn
4 out, one pace bef nxt. ....(5 to 1 op 4 to 1) 3
839 VERDE LUNA 5-9-9 (5*) D J Kavanagh, hed up, hdwy 4th,
wknd appr 2 out. ....(6 to 1 op 5 to 1) 4
3035⁸ LANGTONIAN [94] 8-9-12³ (5*) D Salter, hld up, clr order 4th,
wknd frm 3 out, tld off.............(50 to 1 op 33 to 1) 5
Dist: ¾l, 4l, 13l, dist. 3m 56.20s. a 7.20s (5 Ran).
SR: 41/16/12/-/-/ (Arthur Souch), M C Pipe

3404 Haccombe Selling Handicap Chase Class G (0-95 5-y-o and up) £2,390 2m 5f 110yds
.... (2:30)

JAY JAY'S VOYAGE [74] 14-10-4 (3*) T Dascombe, in tch, led
tenth, made rst, drvn out.
.... (25 to 1 op 20 to 1 tchd 33 to 1) 1
3094 GOLDEN OPAL [79] 12-10-12 B Powell, trkd ldrs, outpcd 12th,
rallied to chase wnr appr 2 out, ran on one pace.
.... (9 to 1 op 7 to 1) 2
3298³ SPRING TO IT [92] 11-11-11 Jamie Evans, led second to 5th,
remained hndy, 3rd and rdn whn not fluent 3 out, sn btn.
.... (5 to 2 fav op 2 to 1 tchd 3 to 1) 3
2677⁵ GOOD FOR A LAUGH [80] 13-10-8 (5*) O Burrows, chsd ldrs,
rdn alng 12th, sn one pace.........(4 to 1 op 3 to 1) 4
2700 SOUND CARRIER (USA) [85] 9-11-4 S Wynne, led to second,
rgned ld 5th, hdd tenth, chsd wnr aftr till wknd appr 2 out.
.... (12 to 1 op 8 to 1) 5
2268 VALNAU (Fr) [81] (bl) 10-10-7 (7*) B Moore, chsd ldrs till pckd
and lost pl 4th, jmpd slwly nxt, no dngr aftr, tld off.
.... (10 to 1 op 6 to 1) 6
1956 ALLAHRAKHA [67] 6-10-0 S Fox, mid-div whn blun and uns
rdr 6th.................(16 to 1 op 10 to 1 tchd 20 to 1) ur
3065 SAUCY'S WOLF [68] 7-10-1¹ M Sharratt, al beh, tld off whn
ran out appr tenth.............(66 to 1 op 25 to 1) ref
3352 FAIRY PARK [84] (v) 12-11-3 Jacqui Oliver, nvr on terms, tld
off whn pld up bef tenth.............(10 to 1 op 8 to 1) pu
2291 MIRAMARE [67] 7-9-7 (7*) X Aizpuru, al beh, tld off whn pld up
bef 11th. ....(20 to 1 op 16 to 1) pu
Dist: 1½l, 7l, nk, 3½l, dist. 5m 18.90s. a 16.90s (10 Ran).
(Mrs J Scrivens), Mrs J Scrivens

3405 St Austell Claiming Hurdle Class F (4-y-o and up) £2,071 3m 3f... (3:00)

3116 PALOSANTO (Ire) (bl) 7-12-0 Jamie Evans, chsd ldr, led appr
9th, clr nxt, rdn out.............(5 to 2 jt-fav op 7 to 4) 1
3272⁴ ST VILLE 11-11-8 B Powell, nvr far away, chsd wnr appr 2
out, kpt on one pace. ....(5 to 2 jt-
fav op 3 to 1 tchd 7 to 2 and 4 to 1) 2
3140³ TIGER CLAW (USA) 11-10-12 R Greene, hld up, hdwy 3 out,
effrt appr nxt, one pace.............(5 to 1 op 4 to 1) 3
3099³ STAR PERFORMER (Ire) 6-10-13 (5*) O Burrows, hld up,
some progs frm 3 out, no imprsn on ldrs. (8 to 1 op 6 to 1) 4
2873 ITS GRAND 8-11-6 S Fox, in tch till rdn and wknd frm 9th.
.... (33 to 1 op 25 to 1) 5
1971⁴ SNOWY LANE (Ire) (bl) 9-11-2 D Walsh, led till appr 9th,
wknd approaching 2 out.............(14 to 1 op 8 to 1) 6
3041⁶ MU-TADIL (bl) 5-11-4 V Slattery, al beh.
.... (66 to 1 op 25 to 1) 7
3271 DUNLIR 7-11-4 S Burrough, beh whn blun badly and uns rdr
5th.................(20 to 1 op 25 to 1 tchd 33 to 1) ur
612⁶ BRAVO STAR (USA) 12-11-6 W Marston, al beh, tld off whn
pld up bef 2 out. ....(25 to 1 op 20 to 1) pu
3244 CASTLEBAY LAD 14-10-13¹ Mr M Appleby, nvr dngrs, tld off
whn pld up bef 2 out.............(100 to 1 op 33 to 1) pu
1526⁴ NICK THE DREAMER 12-10-7 (7*) N Willmington, beh frm 8th,
tld off whn pld up bef 2 out.............(8 to 1 op 6 to 1) pu
3286² FAST THOUGHTS (bl) 10-11-3 (3*) Sophie Mitchell, trkd ldrs,
wknd 3 out, beh whn pld up bef 2 out. (7 to 1 op 5 to 1) pu
3290 NEARLY ALL RIGHT 8-11-2 C Maude, hld up, lost tch 9th, tld
off whn pld up bef 2 out.............(50 to 1 op 33 to 1) pu
2295⁹ TOP SKIPPER (Ire) 5-10-13 (7*) Mr J Tizzard, nvr dngrs, tld off
whn pld up bef 2 out.............(12 to 1 op 10 to 1) pu

2724 ILEWINIT (Ire) (v) 8-11-4 G Upton, beh frm 7th, tld off whn pld
up bef 2 out. ....(50 to 1 op 25 to 1) pu
Dist: 2l, 3l, 16l, 1¼l, 4l, 23l. 6m 28.20s. a 12.20s (15 Ran).
SR: 3/-/-/-/-/-/ (B A Kilpatrick), M C Pipe

3406 'Touch Of Spring' Handicap Chase Class D (0-120 5-y-o and up) £3,680 3¼m 110yds
.... (3:35)

3054⁵ FORTUNES COURSE (Ire) [95] 8-11-0 D Walsh, led to 8th,
rgned ld tenth, hrd pressed frm 2 out, kpt on gmely und pres
r-in.................(Evens fav op 11 to 10 tchd 5 to 4) 1
2745 DIAMOND FORT [97] 12-11-2 S Wynne, in tch, chsd wnr appr
14th, str chal fnl 2, no extr r-in.
.... (11 to 2 op 4 to 1 tchd 6 to 1) 2
3149* SILVERINO [89] 11-10-8 S Burrough, hld up, wl beh 11th, tld
off.................(5 to 2 op 2 to 1 tchd 11 to 4) 3
3208 FLORIDA SKY [100] 10-10-12 (7*) M Berry, prmnt, led 8th to
tenth, hit 14th, wknd 16th, tld off.
.... (6 to 1 op 4 to 1 tchd 13 to 2) 4
Dist: ½l, dist, dist. 6m 31.70s. a 11.70s (4 Ran).
SR: 22/23/-/-/ (Mrs A J Garrett), J S King

3407 Dartmoor Conditional Jockeys' Novices' Handicap Hurdle Class E (0-100 4-y-o and up) £2,379 2¾m
.... (4:05)

3144 CONNAUGHT'S PRIDE [64] 6-10-1 D J Kavanagh, wtd wth,
hdwy to chase ldr aftr 3 out, sn led, wndrd fnl 2, ran on.
.... (4 to 1 tchd 5 to 1) 1
3028⁷ LITTLE ELLIOT (Ire) [72] 9-10-10 P Henley, prmnt, led 6th till
tld off. ....(5 to 2 jt-fav op 2 to 1) 2
3190⁹ LORD NITROGEN (USA) [83] 7-11-7 Michael Brennan, hld up,
hdwy 6th, effrt 3 out, outpcd appr nxt....(7 to 1 op 5 to 1) 3
RISING'S LASS (Ire) [75] 7-10-10 (3*) N Willmington, hld up,
hdwy to chase ldrs frm 3 out, one pace frm nxt.
.... (14 to 1 op 7 to 1) 4
3287⁷ ROMANY BLUES [62] 8-9-7 (7*) C Rafter, prmnt, blun and uns
rdr 3rd.................(9 to 1 op 6 to 1) ur
IRISH DOMINION [62] 7-10-0 O Burrows, pld hrd, sn led, hdd
6th, soon wknd, tld off whn pulled up bef nxt.
.... (20 to 1 op 12 to 1) pu
2972⁵ SMART LORD [86] 6-11-10 X Aizpuru, hld up, wknd frm 3 out,
tld off whn pld up bef nxt. ....(5 to 2 jt-
fav op 11 to 4) pu
Dist: 2l, 8l, 4l. 5m 17.60s. a 16.60s (7 Ran).
(Mrs Angela Tincknell), P J Hobbs

3408 Dartmoor Maiden Open National Hunt Flat Class H (4,5,6-y-o) £1,299 2m 1f
.... (4:35)

3282⁴ MAZILEO 4-10-7 (7*) F Bogle, wtd wth, smooth prog to track
ldrs o'r 5 fs out, led one out, rdn out.
.... (9 to 2 op 3 to 1 tchd 5 to 1) 1
ABIGAILS STAR 5-11-6 B Powell, hld up beh ldrs, led o'r 2 fs
out, hdd one out, no extr.
.... (12 to 1 op 20 to 1 tchd 25 to 1) 2
RUN FOR COVER (Ire) 5-11-1 A Procter, hld up, hdwy 4 fs out,
effrt 2 out, kpt on one pace. ....(20 to 1 op 12 to 1) 3
1578 COUNTRY KRIS 5-11-6 G Upton, hld up beh ldrs, led o'r 6 fs
out till over 2 out, sn btn................(5 to 1 op 4 to 1) 4
3302⁶ LONGSTONE LAD 5-10-13 (7*) Mr J Tizzard, hld up, hdwy 6 fs
out, btn 3 out.................(12 to 1 op 10 to 1) 5
2409 BOMBA CHARGER 5-11-6 R Greene, nvr nr to chal.
.... (5 to 1 op 10 to 1) 6
2248 BABY LANCASTER 6-10-13 (7*) M Griffiths, chsd ldrs, wknd 4
fs out.................(10 to 1 op 33 to 1) 7
3335⁷ JIM'S QUEST 4-11-0 G Tormey, sn prmnt, wknd 5 fs out.
.... (3 to 1 fav op 2 to 1) 8
3082⁸ SATELLITE EXPRESS (Ire) 4-11-0 W Marston, beh hlf 6 fs, tld
off.................(5 to 1 op 4 to 1 tchd 6 to 1) 9
2961 SEE MINNOW 4-10-2 (7*) N Willmington, al beh, tld off.
.... (50 to 1 op 33 to 1) 10
2764 PHONE THE PIPELINE 4-10-7 (7*) B Moore, led till o'r 6 fs
out, wknd 5 furlongs out, tld off........(10 to 1 op 7 to 1) 11
ETTA DOVE 6-10-8 (7*) Mr S Durack, trkd ldrs, wknd 6 fs out,
tld off.................(50 to 1 op 33 to 1) 12
2784 SALIX 5-11-6 J Railton, chsd ldrs till wknd quickly hfwy, tld
off.................(50 to 1 op 33 to 1) 13
3302⁹ FIVE BOYS 5-11-3 (3*) T Dascombe, al beh, tld off whn
pld up o'r 7 fs out.................(50 to 1 op 33 to 1) pu
VEXFORD LUCY 4-10-2 (7*) X Aizpuru, al beh, tld off whn pld
up 4 fs out.................(50 to 1 op 33 to 1) pu
Dist: 2l, ¾l, 6l, 3½l, sht-hd, 7l, 18l, 21l, 8l, 1l. 3m 54.50s. (15 Ran).
(Mrs H Parrott), I P Williams

PLUMPTON (good to firm)
Saturday March 29th
Going Correction: NIL

3409 American Express Foreign Exchange Conditional Jockeys' Selling Handicap Hurdle Class G (0-95

4-y-o and up) £2,111 2m 1f... (2:25)

33253 DERISBAY (Ire) [82] (bl) 9-11-6 L Aspell, hld up in tch, hdwy
6th, led 3 out, sn clr, pushed out.
..................................(2 to 1 fav op 9 to 4 tchd 5 to 2) 1
31742 MULLINTOR (Ire) [82] 6-11-1 (5*) A Garrity, al prmnt, ev ch 3
out, rdn and outpcd appr nxt..........(9 to 4 tchd 5 to 2) 2
26636 GLOWING PATH [86] 7-11-7 (3*) J Harris, hld up, hdwy appr 3
out, rdn and one pace nxt. (3 to 1 op 9 to 4 tchd 4 to 1) 3
31706 OLIVIPET [62] 8-9-9 (5*) N T Egan, al rear.
..................................(25 to 1 op 10 to 1 tchd 33 to 1) 4
3255 NEVER FORGOTTEN [80] 12-11-1 (3*) M Batchelor, led, hit
4th, hdd 3 out, wknd quickly.
..................................(7 to 1 op 8 to 1 tchd 10 to 1) 5
21749 AGAINST THE CLOCK [63] 5-10-11 Guy Lewis, prmnt, wknd
quickly 3 out, tld off......(11 to 1 op 8 to 1 tchd 12 to 1) 6
33257 TAPESTRY ROSE [62] 6-9-9 (5*) M Clinton, al beh, tld off.
..................................(66 to 1 op 25 to 1 tchd 100 to 1) 7
2305 SABOTEUSE [63] (bl) 5-10-18 (7*) Gordon Gallagher, pld hrd,
in tch, rdn hfwy, sn beh, tld off.
..................................(50 to 1 op 16 to 1 tchd 66 to 1) 8
Dist: 6l, 2½l, 15l, 11l, 15l, 20l, 8l. 4m 4.10s. a 7.10s (8 Ran).
SR: 21/15/16/-/-/ (Miss Julie Self), J J Bridger

3410 Ashdown Hospital Handicap Chase Class E (0-110 5-y-o and up) £3,124 2¼m........................ (2:55)

33603 FENWICK [82] 10-11-6 P Holley, al prmnt, led appr 6 out, clr
whn hit nxt, ran on....(11 to 8 fav op 5 to 4 tchd 6 to 4) 1
30942 WINSPIT (Ire) [86] 7-11-10 J R Kavanagh, al prmnt, wnt
second appr 3 out, no imprsn aftr.
..................................(13 to 8 op 6 to 4 tchd 7 to 4) 2
24257 FULL OF TRICKS [63] 9-10-11 P Hide, led till appr 6 out, mstk
nxt, wknd aftr 3 out....(25 to 1 op 20 to 1 tchd 40 to 1) 3
2957 DAYS OF THUNDER [85] 9-11-9 T J O'Sullivan, prmnt till
wknd 6 out................(8 to 1 op 5 to 1 tchd 9 to 1) 4
UPWARD SURGE (Ire) [62] 7-10-0 Mrs N Ledger, in tch till
wknd 4 out, btn whn hit 2 out............(5 to 1 tchd 7 to 1) 5
Dist: 5l, 14l, 6l, 5l. 4m 31.60s. a 10.60s (5 Ran).
(Major A W C Pearn), R J Hodges

3411 Mella Hopkins Juvenile Novices' Hurdle Class E (4-y-o) £2,490 2m 1f .... (3:30)

33162 KINNESCASH (Ire) 10-12 M A Fitzgerald, led to second, led
appr 4 out, gng clr whn hit nxt, easily.
..................................(5 to 4 on op Evens tchd 11 to 10) 1
2982 BATH KNIGHT 10-5 (7*) Mr J Goldstein, pld hrd, led second
till appr 4 out, no ch frm nxt.
..................................(33 to 1 op 16 to 1 tchd 40 to 1) 2
3169* MIJHANDAM (Ire) 10-12 J F Titley, al same pl, wknd appr 3
out....................(2 to 1 op 7 to 4 tchd 9 to 4) 3
3323 ILLUMINATE 10-12 P Hide, al abt same pl, lost tch 4 out.
..................................(14 to 1 op 8 to 1 tchd 16 to 1) 4
2662 MASTER-H 10-12 A Thornton, al beh, lost tch hfwy.
..................................(50 to 1 op 14 to 1 tchd 66 to 1) 5
HEVER GOLF EAGLE 10-12 R Johnson, mstk second, al beh,
reminders 4 out, sn lost tch. (6 to 1 op 5 to 1 tchd 8 to 1) 6
Dist: 26l, 24l, 1¾l, 4l, 4l. 4m 4.00s. a 7.00s (6 Ran).
SR: 14/-/-/ (D R James), P Bowen

3412 Singer & Friedlander Handicap Chase Class F (0-105 5-y-o and up) £3,038 3m 1f 110yds..... (4:00)

3294* BLACK CHURCH [97] 11-11-10 D O'Sullivan, hld up, hdwy
whn lft second 13th, led 4 out, sn clr, easily.
..................................(11 to 10 fav tchd 6 to 5) 1
3175 BE SURPRISED [73] 11-10-0 P Holley, led to 4 out, sn btn.
..................................(5 to 1 op 6 to 1 tchd 12 to 1 and 9 to 2) 2
3175* ROYAL SAXON [87] 11-11-0 R Johnson, nvr gng wl, chsd ldr
to 7th, wknd appr 6 out. (11 to 8 op 11 to 10 tchd 6 to 4) 3
32942 JOKER JACK [73] 12-9-7 (7*) N T Egan, chsd ldr 7th till blun
badly 13th, lost tch aftr 6 out.
..................................(16 to 1 op 8 to 1 tchd 20 to 1) 4
Dist: 12l, 2½l, 3l. 6m 25.60s. a 11.60s (4 Ran).
(Dr B Alexander), R Rowe

3413 Seeboard Novices' Chase Class E (5-y-o and up) £3,368 2m 5f......(4:30)

14985 STORMHILL PILGRIM 8-11-2 P Hide, led aftr second, rdn clr
frm 2 out..................(9 to 1 op 5 to 1 tchd 10 to 1) 1
30922 LIVELY KNIGHT (Ire) 8-11-11 (3*) L Aspell, hld up, not race
freely, hdwy 6 out, wnt second 4 out, rdn and no imprsn frm 2
out..................(1 to 2 op 8 to 1 op 8 to 1 on tchd 6 to 1 on) 2
32543 CRUISE CONTROL 11-11-2 D O'Sullivan, led till aftr second,
trkd wnr to 4 out, wknd after nxt.
..................................(6 to 1 op 8 to 1 tchd 12 to 1) 3
Dist: 7l, 12l. 5m 16.00s. a 10.00s (3 Ran).
(Mike Roberts), M J Roberts

3414 Europ Assistance Novices' Hurdle Class E (4-y-o and up) £2,826 2½m

27252 SPARKLING SPRING (Ire) 6-11-9 A Thornton, trkd ldrs, led
appr 3 out, rdn out............(5 to 4 on op 7 to 4 on) 1
32903 PROTOTYPE 6-11-2 M A Fitzgerald, hld up, hdwy 4 out, wnt
second aftr nxt, rdn and one pace.
..................................(7 to 2 op 5 to 1 tchd 6 to 1 and 3 to 1) 2
31965 NORDIC SPREE (Ire) (v) 5-11-2 P Holley, al prmnt, led appr
5th till approaching 3 out, one pace aftr.
..................................(7 to 1 op 10 to 1 tchd 25 to 1) 3
32892 LORD ROOBLE (Ire) 6-11-9 P Hide, led till appr 5th, wknd aftr
3 out..................(4 to 1 op 5 to 1 tchd 9 to 1) 4
32575 ADILOV 5-11-2 D O'Sullivan, pld hrd, in cl tch till wknd 3 out.
..................................(20 to 1 op 10 to 1 tchd 25 to 1) 5
2804 MAGICAL BLUES (Ire) 5-11-2 R Johnson, virtually refused to
race, tld off whn pld up aftr 3rd.
..................................(12 to 1 op 5 to 1 tchd 14 to 1) pu
3103 TYPHOON (Ire) 7-11-2 W McFarland, unruly bef strt, virtually
refused to race, tld off whn pld up aftr 7th.
..................................(50 to 1 op 25 to 1 tchd 100 to 1) pu
SILLY POINT 5-10-4 (7*) Mr J Goldstein, beh 5th, pld up aftr
7th....................(50 to 1 op 25 to 1 tchd 100 to 1) pu
Dist: 1¾l, 9l, 11l, 11l. 4m 48.10s. a 11.10s (8 Ran).
(E Benfield), K C Bailey

THURLES (IRE) (good)
Saturday March 29th

3415 Templemore Maiden Hurdle (4-y-o) £2,740 2m...................(2:30)

29404 PERSIAN DREAM (Ire) 10-3 (5*) J M Donnelly, ...(12 to 1) 1
33454 APACHE TWIST (Ire) 11-4 C F Swan, ...(7 to 4 jt-fav) 2
29403 SHARP OUTLOOK (Ire) 10-8 T P Rudd, ...(8 to 1) 3
33456 MOFASA 10-13 (3*) K Whelan, ...(14 to 1) 4
27028 FAMILY PROJECT (Ire) 10-13 S H O'Donovan, ...(10 to 1) 5
28668 BAILENAGUN (Ire) 10-6 (7*) B J Geraghty, ...(20 to 1) 6
2702 UNASSISTED (Ire) 10-5 (3*) B Bowens, ...(14 to 1) 7
29406 MULTEEN JET (Ire) 10-13 T P Treacy, ...(25 to 1) 8
3232 KEEP RUNNING (Ire) 10-6 (7*) D W O'Sullivan, ...(12 to 1) 9
WESTERN SEAS (Ire) 11-4 K F O'Brien, ...(10 to 1) 10
32325 DOUBLEBACK (Ire) 10-1 (7*) K A Kelly, ...(14 to 1) 11
GAELIC ROYALE (Ire) 10-5 (3*) R P O'Brien, ...(25 to 1) 12
3232 WILLOWMOUNT (Ire) 10-13 F Woods, ...(20 to 1) 13
GAYEPHAR 10-8 T Horgan, ...(14 to 1) 14
LISDOONAN TESSA (Ire) 10-8 J Shortt, ...(14 to 1) 15
32329 POINT LUCK (Ire) 10-8 M P Hourigan, ...(14 to 1) 16
29402 SHAHRUR (USA) 10-13 D T Evans, ...(7 to 4 jt-fav) f
3232 MOSCOW'S FLAME (Ire) 10-6 (7*) M D Murphy, ..(25 to 1) f
Dist: ¾l, 2l, hd, ½l. 3m 49.60s. (18 Ran).
(C H Pettigrew), Capt D G Swan

3416 Tipperary Maiden Hurdle (6-y-o and up) £2,740 2m............... (3:00)

2839 CONAGHER BOY (Ire) 7-12-0 C F Swan, ...(14 to 1) 1
33762 MIDNIGHT CYCLONE (Ire) 6-11-9 D J Casey, ...(7 to 1) 2
7817 PHARADISO (Ire) 6-11-6 T Horgan, ...(14 to 1) 3
183* STAR DEFECTOR (Ire) 6-11-7 (7*) M W Martin, ...(100 to 30) 4
33364 TENDER SITUATION 6-11-6 F Woods, ...(8 to 1) 5
21665 ARABIAN SPRITE (Ire) 9-11-9 Mr P J Healy, ...(8 to 1) 6
33368 SHOWBOAT MELODY (Ire) 7-10-8 (7*) M D Murphy,
..................................(20 to 1) 7
14317 WHO IS (Ire) 6-11-6 J P Broderick, ...(20 to 1) 8
2563 RUSHEEN BAY (Ire) 8-11-1 (5*) A O'Shea, ...(16 to 1) 9
28654 BORLEAGH PILOT (Ire) 6-11-3 (3*) K Whelan, ...(14 to 1) 10
2943 RONETTE (Ire) 6-10-13 (7*) J M Maguire, ...(50 to 1) 11
29002 WEST LEADER (Ire) 6-12-0 C O'Dwyer, ...(2 to 1 fav) 12
3238 EARL OF NAAS (Ire) (bl) 6-11-6 W Slattery, ...(33 to 1) 13
32178 LAFONTO'OR (Ire) 6-11-6 J O Shortt, ...(8 to 1) 14
CASHEL GREEN (Ire) 6-10-13 (7*) D A McLoughlin, (20 to 1) 15
33385 STILLBYHERSELF (Ire) 7-11-1 T P Treacy, ...(33 to 1) 16
3225 BALLINEVA (Ire) 8-12-0 H Rogers, ...(14 to 1) 17
3336 MICKS MAN (Ire) 6-12-0 M Duffy, ...(14 to 1) 18
Dist: 4½l, ½l, 4½l, 1l. 3m 48.40s. (18 Ran).
(Fergal O'Toole), Michael Flynn

3417 W.T.O'Grady Memorial Hurdle (5-y-o and up) £2,740 3m............(3:30)

3129 BOSS DOYLE (Ire) 5-11-11 D J Casey, ...(7 to 4 on) 1
2837 CASTLE COIN (Ire) 5-11-11 C F Swan, ...(5 to 2) 2
32374 LEAMHOG (Ire) 7-12-0 T Horgan, ...(6 to 1) 3
2645 IT'S HIMSELF 5-11-6 J Shortt, ...(33 to 1) 4
2900 PORT NA SON (Ire) 6-11-9 K F O'Brien, ...(33 to 1) 5
3083 TAP PRACTICE (Ire) 5-10-13 (7*) J M Maguire, ...(50 to 1) 6
27526 MISS BERTAINE (Ire) 8-11-2 J E Casey, ..(14 to 1) ur
21046 OVER THE WALL (Ire) 8-11-4 P A Roche, ...(33 to 1) pu
Dist: 1l, 3l, dist, 20l. 5m 37.20s. (8 Ran).
(Mrs A M Daly), M F Morris

3418 Phil Sweeney Memorial Novice Chase (5-y-o and up) £2,740 2¾m .... (4:00)

8979 FATHER RECTOR (Ire) 8-11-1 T Horgan, ...(8 to 1) 1

3230[4]	FRIARSTOWN DUKE 7-11-1 T J Mitchell, ... (8 to 1)	2
3088	CELTIC WHO (Ire) 6-11-1 D J Casey, ... (14 to 1)	3
3074[4]	DEARBORN TEC (Ire) 8-11-1 C O'Dwyer, ... (11 to 2)	4
3339[9]	AISEIRI 10-10-8 (7") V T Keane, ... (25 to 1)	5
3088[7]	CAVALLO (Fr) 7-10-12 (3") K Whelan, ... (16 to 1)	6
3339[6]	MAJOR GALE (Ire) 8-10-8 (7") M D Murphy, ... (10 to 1)	7
3220[3]	LISHILLAUN (Ire) 7-10-5 (5") Susan A Finn, ... (12 to 1)	8
3236[2]	LUCKY BUST (Ire) 7-11-7 C F Swan, ... (6 to 4 fav)	f
702*	BLACKIE CONNORS (Ire) 6-11-7 P L Malone, ... (10 to 1)	f
2903[7]	WHINNEY HILL (Ire) 7-10-10 D T Evans, ... (33 to 1)	f
3234[7]	TAR AND CEMENT (Ire) 9-11-1 A J R Barry, ... (14 to 1)	bd
3237[6]	ROSEL WALK (Ire) (bl) 8-11-1 A J O'Brien, ... (25 to 1)	pu

Dist: ¾l, 15l, sht-hd, 20l. 5m 34.10s. (13 Ran).

(Paddy Fennelly, Paddy Fennelly)

3419 Easter Festival Handicap Hurdle (0-116 5-y-o and up) £2,740 2m
. . . . (4:30)

3227[8]	SLEWMORE (Ire) [-] 6-9-0 (7") J M Maguire, ... (25 to 1)	1
3235[7]	CLASHBEG (Ire) [-] 6-10-1 (3") K Whelan, ... (11 to 1)	2
3224*	ZIGGY THE GREAT (Ire) [-] (bl) 5-9-9 (7") Mr John P Moloney,	
	. . . . (7 to 1)	3
3337[4]	HEIGHT OF LUXURY (Ire) [-] 9-9-11 (7") M D Murphy,	
	. . . . (10 to 1)	4
3226*	FANE PATH (Ire) [-] 5-10-5 (7") B J Geraghty, . . . (3 to 1 fav)	5
3223[6]	ASHTALE (Ire) [-] 5-9-7 D J Casey, ... (6 to 1)	6
3337	JIHAAD (USA) [-] 7-9-2 (5") T Martin, ... (12 to 1)	7
	CLUB COUPE (Ire) [-] 5-9-12 P McWilliams, ... (10 to 1)	8
3216	ACES AND EIGHTS (Ire) [-] 7-11-3 F Woods, ... (9 to 2)	9
3235[3]	MUSKERRY KING (Ire) [-] 6-10-7 W Slattery, ... (7 to 1)	10
3337[9]	SINGERS CORNER [-] (bl) 5-9-11 (7") L J Fleming, . (20 to 1)	11
1078[9]	BOBSTAR DANCER (Ire) [-] 6-11-2 J Shortt, ... (10 to 1)	12
553*	AN MAINEACH (Ire) [-] 8-11-13 C F Swan, ... (8 to 1)	13

Dist: 4l, 4l, 4l, 2l. 3m 43.00s. (13 Ran).

(Mrs S Gilmore), Peter McCreery

3420 Molony Cup Handicap Chase (0-102 5-y-o and up) £2,740 3m
. . . . . . (5:00)

2867[3]	FAIRY MIST (Ire) [-] 9-9-12 T Horgan, ... (8 to 1)	1
2903[6]	LINDA'S BOY (Ire) [-] 7-10-10 (7") P G Hourigan, . . (10 to 1)	2
1191	TRIPTODICKS (Ire) [-] 7-10-5 C F Swan, ... (7 to 1)	3
3236[3]	COMING ON STRONG (Ire) [-] 8-12-0 C O'Dwyer,	
	. . . . (9 to 2 fav)	4
2904[5]	THE BOYLERMAN (Ire) [-] 8-11-3 T J Mitchell, ... (12 to 1)	5
3222[6]	INNISCEIN (Ire) [-] 9-10-12 J P Broderick, ... (12 to 1)	6
3236[7]	WATERLOO KING [-] 10-10-9 (7") J E Casey, ... (14 to 1)	7
2163[3]	THE DASHER DOYLE (Ire) [-] 9-11-6 Mr P J Healy, . (10 to 1)	8
3347[6]	STEEL DAWN [-] 10-11-7 J R Barry, ... (8 to 1)	9
3340[4]	KILLER LADY (Ire) [-] 6-9-3 (7") B J Geraghty, ... (7 to 1)	10
2338[8]	HOTEL SALTEES (Ire) [-] 9-10-6 A O'Shea, ... (14 to 1)	11
2867[7]	OLYMPIC D'OR (Ire) [-] 9-11-7 D J Casey, ... (12 to 1)	12
2223[6]	BALLYBODEN [-] 10-10-12 M P Hourigan, ... (12 to 1)	13
2756	CANAILLOU II (Fr) [-] 7-11-3 (3") K Whelan, ... (14 to 1)	14
2945[5]	FAIR GO [-] 11-9-0 (7") Mrs C Harrison, ... (10 to 1)	pu
3236	IF YOU SAY YES (Ire) [-] (bl) 9-10-2 (3") B Bowens, (14 to 1)	pu

Dist: Nk, 2½l, 2l, hd. 6m 9.20s. (16 Ran).

(John Patrick Ryan), John Patrick Ryan

3421 Munster I.N.H. Flat Race (5-y-o and up) £2,740 2¼m
. . . . (5:30)

	RITH DUBH (Ire) 5-11-5 (7") R Flavin, ... (4 to 1)	1
2449[8]	DINES (Ire) 5-11-12 Mr P Fenton, ... (6 to 4 fav)	2
	KINNEGAD GIRL (Ire) 5-11-7 Mr J P Dempsey, ... (12 to 1)	3
681[7]	JOSH'S FANCY (Ire) 6-11-2 (7") Mr A J Dempsey, . . (12 to 1)	4
3238	KAITHEY CHOICE (Ire) 6-11-2 (7") Mr J Butler, . . . (100 to 1)	5
2447[7]	PADDY'S PET (Ire) 8-11-7 (7") Mr M A O'Dwyer, . . . (12 to 1)	6
	LORD KILTOOM (Ire) 6-11-7 (7") Mr D W Cullen, . . . (10 to 1)	7
2943	GALLIC HONEY (Ire) 6-11-2 (7") Mrs C Harrison, . . . (12 to 1)	8
2845	KILLALOONTY ROSE (Ire) 6-11-2 (7") Mr J P McNamara,	
	. . . . (20 to 1)	9
3178	KINGMAN (Ire) 5-11-7 (5") Mr A C Coyle, ... (10 to 1)	10
177	GERRY O MALLEY (Ire) 7-11-9 (5") Mr P A Deegan, . (14 to 1)	11
3182[6]	SARAH BLUE (Ire) (bl) 7-11-2 (7") Mr K R O'Ryan, . . (7 to 1)	12
2839	GLEN CAMDEN (Ire) 5-11-5 (7") Mr J Cash, ... (10 to 1)	13
	DE CLARE DE MARE (Ire) 6-11-3[1] (7") Mr J S Cullen,	
	. . . . (12 to 1)	14
2275[8]	SISTER WEST (Ire) 5-11-0 (7") Mr K N McDonagh, . . (20 to 1)	15
	TIN CUP 5-11-5 (7") Mr N Nevin, ... (12 to 1)	16
	TURBINE (Ire) 5-11-9[4] (7") Mr G Monroe, ... (20 to 1)	pu
	BLACK TROUT (Ire) 8-11-2 (7") Mr M Kavanagh, . . . (20 to 1)	pu

Dist: 6l, 4½l, 1½l, 4l. 4m 4.70s. (18 Ran).

(Beyts Livestock Ltd), William Flavin

TOWCESTER (good to firm)
Saturday March 29th
Going Correction: PLUS 0.05 sec. per fur. (races 1,3,6), PLUS 0.20 (2,4,5)

3422 Grace Novices' Hurdle Class E (4-y-o and up) £2,652 3m
. . . . (2:20)

3150	PLEASURELAND (Ire) 4-11-0 D Morris, trkd ldrs, mstk 5th, led appr 8th, sn wl clr, rdn out.	
	. . . . (5 to 4 on op Evens tchd 11 to 10)	1
3290[4]	MAYLIN MAGIC 6-10-11 D Bridgwater, hld up in tch, wnt second and outpcd 8th, styd on frm 2 out, not rch wnr.	
	. . . . (7 to 2 op 9 to 4 tchd 4 to 1)	2
2398[5]	KINGSWOOD MANOR 5-10-11 (5") Mr R Thornton, chsd ldr, mstk and lost pl 7th, no dngr aftr.	
	. . . . (12 to 1 op 6 to 1 tchd 14 to 1)	3
3019[5]	KING'S RAINBOW (Ire) 8-10-11 J Osborne, led to appr 8th, sn wknd. . . . . (11 to 4 op 9 to 4 tchd 3 to 1)	4
3312	IMPERIAL HONORS (Ire) 6-11-2 Mr A Kinane, hld up in tch, jnd ldrs 6th, wknd appr 8th. . . . . (66 to 1 op 20 to 1)	5

Dist: 1¼l, 10l, 11l, dist. 6m 8.90s. a 26.90s (5 Ran).

(Mrs Sylvia E M McGarvie), R Curtis

3423 32nd Year Of The Schilizzi 1906 Commemorative Challenge Cup Handicap Chase Class C (0-130 5-y-o and up) £4,647 2¾m
. . . . (2:50)

3050	FUNCHEON GALE [95] 10-11-0 D Morris, hld up in tch, chsd ldr 9th to 12th, outpcd 3 out, hit 2 out, rallied appr last, styd on wl to ld nr finish. . . . . (3 to 1 op 11 to 4 tchd 7 to 2)	1
3101[5]	POSTMAN'S PATH [98] 11-11-3 J Osborne, led, jmpd lft, rdn appr 2 out, hdd nr finish.	
	. . . . (3 to 1 op 5 to 2 tchd 100 to 30)	2
3165[2]	ARTIC WINGS [105] 9-11-10 M Brennan, chsd ldr to 9th, wnt second 12th, ev ch appr 2 out, styd on same pace.	
	. . . . (11 to 10 op on 11 to 8)	3
2393	STAUNCH RIVAL (USA) [105] (bl) 10-11-3 (7") Clare Thorner, patiently rdn, reminder and hit 6th, wknd tenth.	
	. . . . (9 to 1 op 4 to 1)	4

Dist: 1l, 5l, 21l. 5m 37.00s. a 11.00s (4 Ran).

SR: 20/22/24/3/   *(Kings Of The Road Partnership), R Curtis*

3424 Turf Club Handicap Hurdle Class F (0-105 4-y-o and up) £2,160 2m
. . . . (3:25)

2180[4]	EURO SINGER [92] 5-11-2 (5") S Ryan, chsd ldrs, led appr 2 out, mstk last, drvn out. (14 to 1 op 10 to 1 tchd 16 to 1)	1
725[5]	BOURDONNER [89] 5-11-1 (3") Mr C Bonner, led second to 5th, chsd wnr 2 out, ran on.	
	. . . . (9 to 1 op 8 to 1 tchd 10 to 1)	2
3139[6]	STEVE FORD [88] 8-11-3 J A McCarthy, prmnt, rdn and pckd 3 out, styd on same pace. . . . . (10 to 1 tchd 12 to 1)	3
3139*	IRON N GOLD [91] 5-11-6 D Bridgwater, mstk 1st, sn pushed alng, styd on frm 2 out, nvr nr ldrs.	
	. . . . (100 to 30 fav op 7 to 2 tchd 4 to 1)	4
	NORTHERN CHARMER [89] 5-10-11 (7") L Cummins, hld up, hdwy 5th, wknd 2 out. . . . (7 to 1 op 8 to 1 tchd 6 to 1)	5
2783[9]	NASHVILLE STAR (USA) [95] (v) 6-11-10 J Osborne, led to second, led 5th to appr 2 out, mstk last, wknd r-in.	
	. . . . (10 to 1 tchd 7 to 1)	6
3287[2]	POSITIVO [73] 6-10-12 (3") D Fortt, mid-div, sn pushed alng, nvr nr ldrs. . . . . (9 to 2 op 4 to 1 tchd 5 to 1)	7
3276[3]	ANLACE [80] 8-10-4 (5") Chris Webb, nvr nr to chal.	
	. . . . (14 to 1 op 12 to 1 tchd 20 to 1)	8
3166[3]	AJDAR [77] 6-10-6 M Brennan, al beh, tld off.	
	. . . . (9 to 1 op 12 to 1 tchd 20 to 1)	9
3328[3]	COURAGEOUS KNIGHT [82] 8-10-11 D Gallagher, beh frm 3rd, tld off from nxt. . . . . (12 to 1 tchd 14 to 1)	10
3006[3]	MRS JAWLEYFORD (USA) [78] 9-10-7 M Ranger, sn prmnt, wknd 5th, beh whn pld up bef 2 out. . (16 to 1 op 12 to 1)	pu
3287*	DISSOLVE [80] 5-10-2 (7") Mr L Baker, chsd ldrs, rdn and wknd 5th, beh whn pld up bef 2 out. . . (5 to 1 tchd 9 to 1)	pu

Dist: ½l, 9l, nk, 2l, ¾l, hd, 5l, 19l, 3½l. 3m 51.10s. a 8.10s (12 Ran).

SR: 20/16/6/9/5/9/   *(Bcd Steels Ltd), T Keddy*

3425 36th Year Of The Schilizzi Challenge Bowl Handicap Chase Class D (0-125 5-y-o and up) £3,435 2m 110yds.
. . . . (3:55)

3281*	MR SNAGGLE (Ire) [89] 8-10-5 J Osborne, hld up, mstk 5th, hdwy 7th, chlgd last, led r-in, drvn out.	
	. . . . (11 to 8 op 6 to 5 tchd 6 to 4)	1
3291[5]	PARLIAMENTARIAN (Ire) [84] (bl) 8-10-0 D Bridgwater, led, rdn 2 out, mstk last, hdd and not quicken r-in.	
	. . . . (13 to 2 op 8 to 1)	2
2796[2]	LACKENDARA [105] 10-11-7 J Culloty, chsd ldr, rdn and ev ch appr 2 out, wknd r-in.	
	. . . . (11 to 10 fav op 6 to 5 tchd 5 to 4)	3
2958[6]	LINDEN'S LOTTO (Ire) [108] 8-11-5 (5") Mr R Thornton, prmnt lost pl 6th, rdn and wknd 3 out.	
	. . . . (9 to 1 op 7 to 1 tchd 10 to 1)	4

Dist: ½l, 7l, 5l. 4m 6.80s. a 9.80s (4 Ran).

SR: 12/6/20/18/   *(The Plum Merchants), Simon Earle*

3426 Larry Connell Memorial Hunters' Chase Class H (5-y-o and up) £1,150 3m 1f.
. . . . (4:25)

3300³ NORTHERN VILLAGE 10-11-7 (7*) Mr D Alers-Hankey, *hld up, mstk second, hdwy 11th, chsd ldr 2 out, styd on to ld nr finish.* . . . .(10 to 1 tchd 14 to 1) 1
2993 AVOSTAR 10-11-9 (5*) Mr B Pollock, *led to 7th, led 9th to 11th, mstk 4 out, led approching 2 out, hrd rdn r-in, hdd nr finish.*
. . . .(100 to 30 op 5 to 2 tchd 7 to 2) 2
2993² PEAJADE 13-11-7 (7*) Miss J Wormall, *chsd ldrs, led 7th to 9th, led 11th to appr 2 out, styd on same pace.*
. . . .(4 to 1 op 3 to 1 tchd 9 to 2) 3
BROAD STEANE 8-11-9 (5*) Mr A Sansome, *hld up in tch, hit 6th, rdn appr 2 out, no imprsn.*
. . . .(5 to 2 fav op 9 to 4 tchd 3 to 1) 4
3125⁴ GLEN OAK 12-11-13 (5*) Mr R Thornton, *chsd ldrs, rdn appr 2 out, styd on same pace.* . . . .(11 to 4 op 7 to 2) 5
3109⁴ ARTFUL ARTHUR 11-11-7 (7*) Mr J Grassick, *patiently rdn, hit 7th, lost tch 6 out, tld off.* . . . .(33 to 1 op 25 to 1) 6
3313⁴ TEATRADER 11-11-7 (7*) Miss T Blazey, *prmnt to 11th, sn lost pl, tld off.* . . . .(14 to 1 op 10 to 1) 7
SOLAR GEM (bl) 10-11-7 (7*) Mrs C McCarthy, *mstk 1st, in rear whn hit 8th, tld off and pld up bef 6 out.*
. . . .(33 to 1 op 25 to 1) pu

Dist: ¾l, 5l, 1¼l, 1½l, 17l, ½l. 6m 28.50s. a 16.50s (8 Ran).

(L P Dace), Luke Dace

3427 Hoile Intermediate Open National Hunt Flat Class H (4,5,6-y-o) £1,413 2m. . . . . (4:55)

SIR LUNCHALOT (Ire) 4-10-12 J Osborne, *hld up, hdwy 4 fs out, shaken up to ld wl ins last.* . . . . . (9 to 4 fav tchd 7 to 2) 1
MURCHAN TYNE (Ire) 4-10-7 (7*) L Cummins, *al prmnt, led o'r 2 fs out, hdd wl ins last.* . . . .(10 to 1 op 6 to 1) 2
3176³ SILVER SIROCCO (Ire) 5-11-4 Derek Byrne, *led, rdn and hdd o'r 2 fs out, styd on.* . . . . . (5 to 2 op 9 to 4 tchd 3 to 1) 3
MISTY CLASS (Ire) 5-11-4 D Gallagher, *hld up, pld hrd, hdwy hfwy, ev ch o'r 2 fs out, styd on same pace.*
. . . . (13 to 2 op 5 to 1 tchd 7 to 1) 4
3142⁶ TEEJAY'S FUTURE (Ire) 6-10-6 (7*) W Walsh, *hld up, hrd rdn frm 2 fs out, no imprsn.*
. . . .(15 to 2 op 8 to 1 tchd 9 to 1) 5
2939³ GENEROUS STREAK (Fr) 4-10-7 (5*) Mr R Thornton, *chsd ldrs, rdn and wknd o'r 2 fs out.*
. . . .(5 to 1 op 4 to 1 tchd 6 to 1) 6
FRESH ROSE MARY (Ire) 5-10-6 (7*) J Keenan, *strted slwly, sn prmnt, ev ch 3 fs out, soon rdn and btn.*
. . . .(25 to 1 tchd 33 to 1) 7
WISHING WILLIAM (Ire) 5-11-4 J Culloty, *rcd keenly, chsd ldrs, wknd o'r 2 fs out.* . . . .(33 to 1 op 20 to 1) 8
THE MILLSTONE 6-10-11 (7*) M Keighley, *chsd ldrs, drvn alng o'r 3 fs out, wknd over 2 out.*
. . . .(25 to 1 op 20 to 1 tchd 33 to 1) 9
HIGHLAND PRINCE 5-10-13 (5*) S Ryan, *trkd ldrs, lost pl o'r 5 fs out, wknd 3 out.* . . . .(25 to 1 tchd 33 to 1) 10

Dist: 1l, 2½l, 4l, 2½l, 3½l, ¾l, ¾l, 29l, 29l. 3m 57.50s. (10 Ran).

(The Random Partnership), P R Webber

TIPPERARY (IRE) (good to yielding)
Sunday March 30th

3428 Kevin McManus Novice Chase (5-y-o and up) £6,850 3m. . . . . (4:00)

3218² WOODVILLE STAR (Ire) 8-11-6 C O'Dwyer, ...(6 to 4 fav) 1
3237* TELL THE NIPPER (Ire) 6-11-8 J P Broderick, ...(4 to 1) 2
3133 ITSAJUNGLEOUTTHERE (Ire) 7-11-8 D J Casey, . . (16 to 1) 3
VERY ADAPTABLE (Ire) 8-11-4 C F Swan, ... (12 to 1) 4
3237³ LE GINNO (Fr) 10-11-8 T P Treacy, ...(6 to 1) 5
2585 CELTIC SUNRISE 9-11-4 F Woods, ...(20 to 1) 6
2648 BUCKMINSTON 10-11-8 G Bradley, ...(6 to 1) f
3237 ROSIE LIL (Ire) 6-10-13 A J O'Brien, ...(33 to 1) f
3086 PATTIE TIM (Ire) 8-11-1 (3*) K Whelan, ... (12 to 1) f
3237² SIDCUP HILL (Ire) 8-11-3 T P Rudd, ...(8 to 1) pu

Dist: 9l, 10l, 25l, 20l. 6m 8.70s. (10 Ran).

(Sean Donnelly), W J Burke

3429 Easter Maiden Hurdle (Div I) (5-y-o and up) £3,425 2½m. . . . . (4:30)

2670⁷ MORAL SUPPORT (Ire) 5-11-4 G Bradley, ... (7 to 1) 1
BELHABOUR (Ire) 6-11-3 (3*) K Whelan, ...(12 to 1) 2
3237 CONAN'S JET (Ire) 7-12-0 C O'Dwyer, ...(3 to 1) 3
3178 MENDELUCI (Ire) 5-11-12 S H O'Donovan, ... (14 to 1) 4
3238 LUCKY ROSS (Ire) 5-11-6 C F Swan, ...(16 to 1) 5
3085⁵ AUBURN ROILELET (Ire) 5-10-13 T J Mitchell, ... (9 to 1) 6
BURREN VALLEY (Ire) 6-11-4 I K F O'Brien, ... (33 to 1) 7
CEASERS REIGN (Ire) 5-11-4 T P Treacy, ...(33 to 1) 8
3238* WINDGAP HILL (Ire) 6-12-0 F Woods, ... (6 to 4 fav) 9
1487⁴ ROSENWALD (Ire) 7-11-3 (3*) J Butler, ... (12 to 1) 10
3226⁹ DR DOLITTLE (Ire) 6-11-6 D T Evans, ... (33 to 1) 11
3221⁹ QUEEN OFTHE ISLAND (Ire) 5-10-8 (5*) Susan A Finn,
. . . .(33 to 1) 12
3182 LACKEN RIVER (Ire) 5-10-13 P McWilliams, ... (25 to 1) 13
2055⁹ PENNY POET (Ire) 5-10-11 (7*) M D Murphy, ...(33 to 1) 14
WINDTEKIN (Ire) 7-11-1 (5*) A O'Shea, ...(14 to 1) 15
3226⁴ MONALEA (Ire) 6-10-13 (7*) A P Sweeney, ... (10 to 1) ur

Dist: 3½l, 3½l, ¾l, 15l. 4m 50.00s. (16 Ran).

(Mrs T Hyde), M F Morris

3430 Easter Maiden Hurdle (Div II) (5-y-o and up) £3,425 2½m. . . . . (5:00)

3068⁴ PAULS RUN (Ire) 8-12-0 L P Cusack, ...(5 to 1) 1
3085 STORMY MISS (Ire) 5-10-8 (5*) A O'Shea, ... (20 to 1) 2
3085⁴ BOPTWOPHAR (Ire) 5-11-4 J R Barry, ...(8 to 1) 3
2964³ POLLTRIC (Ire) 6-11-6 P L Malone, ...(7 to 1) 4
3068⁶ PRINCE DANTE (Ire) 5-11-4 F Woods, ...(9 to 1) 5
2645 CORYROSE (Ire) 5-11-0 (7*) J M Maguire, ...(14 to 1) 6
3180⁶ WOODBORO LASS (Ire) 7-10-8 (7*) Miss A Sloane, (16 to 1) 7
3343 GREY HORIZON (Ire) 6-11-6 P McWilliams, ... (20 to 1) 8
3178² DAN'S YOUR MAN (Ire) 5-11-12 C O'Dwyer, . . . (5 to 4 on) 9
2704 THATSWHATITHOUGHT (Ire) 5-11-4 D J Casey, . . (33 to 1) 10
3238 BUCK THE WEST (Ire) 7-11-6 J Shortt, ...(20 to 1) 11
2343 TINVACOOSH (Ire) (bl) 6-11-6 T Horgan, ... (20 to 1) 12
3233 BALLYBANE LASSIE (Ire) 6-10-8 (7*) R M Murphy, (33 to 1) 13
3182⁷ FAIR FONTAINE (Ire) 5-10-13 T P Treacy, ... (14 to 1) 14
3221 MR MARK (Ire) 5-11-4 F J Flood, ...(14 to 1) 15
3178 OYSTON PRINCESS (Ire) 5-10-10 (3*) K Whelan, . . (66 to 1) 16
2709 LISARDBOULA (Ire) 5-11-4 K F O'Brien, ...(33 to 1) pu

Dist: 3½l, hd, 5½l, ½l. 4m 52.00s. (17 Ran).

(Diamond Syndicate), W J Lanigan

3431 Homecoming Handicap Hurdle (0-123 4-y-o and up) £4,110 2½m . . . . (5:30)

2340⁸ SLEEPY RIVER (Ire) [-] 6-11-0 C O'Dwyer, ...(13 to 2) 1
3071⁷ BE HOME EARLY (Ire) [-] 7-11-6 (5*) A O'Shea, (5 to 2 fav) 2
3336² WELSH GRIT (Ire) [-] 8-11-3 D J Casey, ...(7 to 1) 3
2731⁴ SPIRIT DANCER (Ire) [-] 4-11-7 S C Lyons, ...(7 to 1) 4
3214⁷ OWENBWEE (Ire) [-] 6-11-5 F Woods, ...(6 to 1) 5
3234⁴ SIR JOHN (Ire) [-] 8-10-8 C F Swan, ...(8 to 1) 6
3219² PRE ORDAINED (Ire) [-] 5-11-0 F J Flood, ...(3 to 1) 7
3377 MAJESTIC JOHN (Ire) [-] 7-9-3 (7*) A T Kelly, ... (16 to 1) 8
2168⁸ TOURING-TURTLE (Ire) [-] 5-9-4 (7*) F J Keniry, . . . (16 to 1) 9
3180 EMPEROR GLEN (Ire) [-] 9-10-9 (3*) K Whelan, . . . (16 to 1) 10
FOURTH OF JULY [-] 13-11-8 J P Broderick, ... (16 to 1) 11
2674 MAGNUM STAR (Ire) [-] (bl) 8-9-8¹ T P Treacy, ...(25 to 1) 12

Dist: ½l, 3l, 1½l, 1l. 4m 48.20s. (12 Ran).

(John P McManus), A L T Moore

3432 Jimmy Moloumby Memorial I.N.H. Flat Race (4-y-o) £3,425 2m. . . (6:00)

2967⁵ BENEFICENT (Fr) 11-6 Mr D Marnane, ...(9 to 2) 1D
JOHANN STRAUSS (Ire) 11-6 Mr J P Dempsey, (6 to 4 on) 1
RAINBOW TOUR (Ire) 11-6 Mr B M Cash, ...(11 to 2) 3
COILLTE AN CEOIL (Ire) 10-13 (7*) Mr A K Wyse, . .(10 to 1) 4
FRANKLINS BEST (Ire) 10-13 (7*) Mr G Finlay, ... (16 to 1) 5
3183⁶ TONIBEROLI (Ire) 10-13 (7*) Mr P McNamara, ... (14 to 1) 6
3232⁸ MOSTA (Ire) 10-8 (7*) Miss S J Leahy, ...(33 to 1) 7
LINEN HILL (Ire) 11-6 Mr P J Healy, ...(14 to 1) 8
2643 MONKS ERROR (Ire) 10-13 (7*) Mr A J Dempsey, . .(25 to 1) 9
CICERO'S LAW (Ire) 11-1 (5*) Mr G Elliott, ... (16 to 1) 10
STRADBALLY KATE (Ire) 10-9¹ (7*) Mr Mark Walsh, (20 to 1) 11
3183 KNOCKONTIME (Ire) 10-13 (7*) Mr J P Shaw, ...(33 to 1) pu

Dist: Hd, 1½l, nk, 20l. 3m 46.50s. (12 Ran).

(Oliver Lehane), Kevin Prendergast

CARLISLE (good)
Monday March 31st
Going Correction: PLUS 0.60 sec. per fur.

3433 Solway Mares' Only Novices' Claiming Hurdle Class G (4-y-o and up) £1,828 2m 1f. . . . . (2:20)

2804* SOUSSE 4-10-12 (3*) G Lee, *nvr far away, led 5th, blun 3 out, jnd bef last, ran on wl.* (6 to 4 fav op 9 to 4 tchd 3 to 1) 1
3316⁷ TABRIZ 4-10-9 O Pears, *hld up, improved 4 out, chlgd bef last, kpt on run in.* . . . . .(7 to 1 op 6 to 1 tchd 9 to 1) 2
2811³ PEARLS OF THOUGHT (Ire) 4-10-2⁵ (3*) E Callaghan, *hld up, steady hdwy bef 3 out, rdn and kpt on r-in.*
. . . .(12 to 1 op 8 to 1) 3
2118 SIMAND 5-10-6 N Bentley, *chsd ldrs, rdn alng aftr 3 out, not quicken last.* . . . . (8 to 1 op 7 to 1) 4
3009⁶ SANDRIFT 8-11-1 D Parker, *in tch, drvn alng bef 3 out, no imprsn frm next.* . . . . (12 to 1 op 8 to 1) 5
3351 CONNIE LEATHART 6-10-9 M Moloney, *chsd ldrs, drvn bef 3 out, btn nxt.* . . . .(16 to 1) 6
3006 ALAN'S PRIDE (Ire) 6-10-12 G Cahill, *taken early to post, led to 3rd, cl up, struggling 3 out, btn nxt.* (12 to 1 op 10 to 1) 7
2853 SOMETHING SPEEDY (Ire) 5-10-6 D Bentley, *prmnt on ins, drvn and struggling aftr 5th, sn no dngr.*
. . . .(33 to 1 op 16 to 1) 8
2187 GAME POINT 8-11-7 J Burke, *cl up, struggling 4 out, sn btn.* . . . .(100 to 1) 9
3157 BILL'S PRIDE 6-9-13 (7*) C McCormack, *hld up, blun 3rd, nvr able to chal and btn last 3.* (9 to 2 op 3 to 1 tchd 5 to 1) 10
2847⁷ BEACON HILL LADY 4-9-7 (7*) N Horrocks, *jmpd badly in rear, nvr on terms.* . . . . (20 to 1 op 16 to 1) 11
3127⁸ DE-VEERS CURRIE (Ire) 5-11-4 B Storey, *cl up, led 3rd to 5th, sn lost pl.* . . . . (25 to 1 op 12 to 1) 12

477

1953 MEESONETTE 5-10-6 K Johnson, *beh, struggling bef 4th, sn
btn*..........................(33 to 1)   13
Dist: 2½l, 1l, 4l, 3l, 15l, 29l, 1¼l, 1¾l, 2l. 4m 20.60s. a 17.60s (13 Ran).
SR: 13/4/-/-/2/-/   (Wentdale Racing Partnership), Mrs M Reveley

3434 Barclays Corporate Banking Novices' Handicap Chase Class E (0-100 5-y-o and up) £2,957 2½m 110yds
.... (2:50)

2534³ TOUGH TEST (Ire) [80] 7-10-8 B Storey, *jmpd slwly 1st, al cl
up, drvn to ld 2 out, styd on strly*.........(33 to 1)   1
2859⁴ KILTULLA (Ire) [72] 7-9-9 (5*) G F Ryan, *al wl plcd, led 4 out till
2 out, one pace r-in*.......(11 to 2 op 6 to 1 tchd 5 to 1)   2
3202* CORSTON JOKER [82] 7-10-10 J Supple, *led till hdd 4 out,
rallied and ev ch 2 out, one pace last.
.... (11 to 4 fav op 3 to 1 tchd 100 to 30)   3
2491³ TRUMP [88] 8-11-2 D Parker, *handily plcd, outpcd aftr tenth,
no imprsn frm 3 out*...........(7 to 1 tchd 8 to 1)   4
3007* ROBERTY LEA [99] 9-11-10 (3*) G Lee, *hld up, mstk 4th,
improved 8th, outpcd aftr 5 out, no imprsn whn hit last.
.....................(4 to 1 op 7 to 2 tchd 9 to 2)   5
3309 JONAEM (Ire) [72] 7-10-0 K Johnson, *beh, nvr on terms.
.......................(25 to 1 op 20 to 1 tchd 33 to 1)   6
3304⁷ MUSIC BLITZ [73] 6-10-1 M Foster, *chsd ldrs, struggling 4
out, sn btn*.........................(5 to 1 op 4 to 1)   7
887⁶ GERMAN LEGEND [80] 7-10-8 J Burke, *prmnt on outer, hit
7th, chlgd 9th to nxt, hit 11th, sn btn*...(20 to 1 op 16 to 1)   8
2854⁴ DANDY DES PLAUTS (Fr) [72] 6-10-0 D Bentley, *beh, struggling fnl circuit, nvr on terms*.........(16 to 1 tchd 20 to 1)   9
3261² MOST RICH (Ire) [72] (v) 9-9-11 (3*) E Callaghan, *wth ldrs to
tenth, sn wknd, pld up bef 4 out*..........(10 to 1 op 7 to 1)   pu
3246 DASHMAR [72] 10-10-0 M Moloney, *in tch on ins, struggling
bef 9th, sn beh, pld up before 2 out*.....(66 to 1 op 50 to 1)   pu
2748 MINDYEROWNBUSINESS (Ire) [72] 8-10-0 O Pears, *beh,
struggling whn hit 9th, pld up bef nxt.* (25 to 1 op 16 to 1)   pu
2854 MISS LAMPLIGHT [72] 7-10-0 G Cahill, *beh, struggling 11th,
tld off whn pld up bef 4 out*..........(66 to 1 op 50 to 1)   pu
Dist: 9l, sht-hd, 3l, 3l, 18l, 4l, 12l, 12l. 5m 14.10s. a 19.10s (13 Ran).
SR: 12/-/5/8/16/-/   (J D Goodfellow), Mrs J D Goodfellow

3435 Border Television Novices' Hurdle Class E (4-y-o and up) £2,444 2½m 110yds
.... (3:20)

3011⁵ ARDRINA 6-11-1 M Foster, *nvr far away, led 7th till bef 3 out,
rallied to ld appr last, gmely.
.....................(2 to 1 fav op 9 to 4 tchd 5 to 2)   1
2653⁴ MEADOW HYMN (Ire) 6-11-12 W Dwan, *chsd ldrs, led bef 3
out till hdd appr last, kpt on*.............(6 to 1 op 4 to 1)   2
3160⁴ MAGPIE MELODY (Ire) 6-11-1 (5*) B Grattan, *cl up, led aftr
5th, hdd 7th, outpcd bef 2 out.*.........(9 to 2 op 4 to 1)   3
3011² INTO THE WEST (Ire) 8-11-1 G F Ryan, *prmnt, chlgd 6th,
outpcd fnl 2.*........(100 to 30 op 5 to 2 tchd 7 to 2)   4
2910 DROMORE DREAM (Ire) 8-10-11 (3*) M C Bonner, *midfield,
rdn 6th, nvr able to chal*...........(33 to 1 tchd 50 to 1)   5
3262³ KING FLY 7-10-7 (7*) C McCormack, *trkd ldrs, ev ch 3 out,
outpcd bef nxt*.....................(5 to 1 tchd 16 to 1)   6
THORNTOUN HOUSE (Ire) 4-10-7 D Parker, *chsd ldrs, outpcd
6th, no dngr aftr*....................(100 to 1)   7
2619 ROYAL SPRUCE 6-11-0 N Bentley, *mid-div, drvn alng
6th, sn outpcd*....................(50 to 1 op 33 to 1)   8
3015² TOM'S RIVER (Ire) 5-10-11 (3*) G Lee, *hld up, improved to
chase ldg grp bef 3 out, fdd before nxt.
.......................(5 to 1 op 8 to 1 tchd 9 to 2)   9
2889 PUSH ON POLLY (Ire) 7-10-6 (3*) E Callaghan, *beh thrght, nvr
on terms.*....................(100 to 1)   10
3316⁶ POT BLACKBIRD 8-10-9 O Pears, *beh, some hdwy aftr 6th,
sn btn*........................(50 to 1 op 25 to 1)   11
3160 HADAWAY LAD 5-11-0 M Moloney, *prmnt on ins, struggling
aftr 6th, sn btn*....................(100 to 1 op 66 to 1)   12
ANOTHER GEORGE 7-11-0 B Storey, *chsd ldg grp, struggling 5 out, sn btn*....................(33 to 1 op 20 to 1)   13
3309 BUSY BOY 10-11-0 J Burke, *hit 1st in rear, struggling 5th, sn
btn*........................(66 to 1 op 100 to 1)   14
2489 ITSAHARDLIFE (Ire) 6-11-0 D Bentley, *al beh, struggling frm
6th*..........................(100 to 1 op 66 to 1)   15
3011 MONTEIN (bl) 6-11-0 N Leach, *led till hdd aftr 5th, wknd
quickly, pld up bef 7th*.............(250 to 1 tchd 500 to 1)   pu
PITSBURGH 6-11-0 G Cahill, *hit 1st, sn struggling, tld off whn
pld up bef 6th*................(100 to 1 op 66 to 1)   pu
Dist: 2l, 11l, 1¼l, 3l, 18l, 12l, 1¼l, 1¾l, ½l, 22l. 5m 7.50s. a 25.50s (17 Ran).
                    (L G M Racing), F Murphy

3436 John Dixon Handicap Chase Class F (0-105 5-y-o and up) £3,355 3m
.... (3:50)

3202 NIJWAY [77] 7-10-0 B Storey, *hld up, improved 11th, led 3 out,
kpt on wl frm last*.........(20 to 1 op 16 to 1 tchd 25 to 1)   1
3245⁵ GALE AHEAD (Ire) [95] 7-11-4 M Foster, *settled beh ldg grp,
hdwy 8th, pckd 4 out, ran on wl fnl 2*......(3 to 1 tchd 4 to 1)   2
3286³ REAPERS ROCK [81] 10-9-13 (5*) G F Ryan, *nvr far away, led
8th to 11th, rgned ld 13th to 3 out, sn outpcd.
.......................(11 to 2 op 5 to 1 tchd 6 to 1)   3

3399⁶ SOLBA (USA) [101] (bl) 8-11-10 D Parker, *settled beh ldg grp,
rdn to ld 11th, hdd 13th, sn ridden, outpcd whn blun badly 3
out*......................(14 to 1 op 12 to 1)   4
3352 MORE JOY [77] 9-9-7 (7*) C McCormack, *al prmnt, improved
12th, ev ch bef 4 out, outpcd nxt*.....(50 to 1 op 33 to 1)   5
3159⁴ HEAVENLY CITIZEN (Ire) [91] 9-11-0 K Johnson, *led to 3rd,
lost pl bef 7th, lost tch frm 11th.
.........................(11 to 1 op 10 to 1 tchd 12 to 1)   6
3060³ FARNEY GLEN [88] 10-10-11 G Cahill, *hit second, sn beh,
blun and uns rdr 9th*..........(5 to 1 op 5 to 1 tchd 7 to 1)   ur
3159¹ HUDSON BAY TRADER (USA) [90] 10-10-8 (5*) B Grattan,
beh and sn outpcd, tld off whn pld up 4 out........(6 to 1)   pu
3306³ TIGHTER BUDGET (USA) [99] 10-11-8 M Moloney, *led 3rd till
hdd 8th, hit 11th and nxt, pld up bef 13th.* (7 to 1 op 5 to 1)   pu
3397² NORTHERN SQUIRE [105] 9-11-11 (3*) E Callaghan, *in tch on
ins, lost pl whn hit 9th, sn struggling, pld up bef 4 out*
....................(2 to 1 fav op 5 to 2 tchd 11 to 4)   pu
Dist: 2½l, 14l, 15l, 15l, 15l. 6m 21.50s. a 29.50s (10 Ran).
                    (T A Barnes), M A Barnes

3437 Barclays Premier Banking Handicap Hurdle Class E (0-115 4-y-o and up) £2,213 2m 1f
.... (4:20)

3305* MONNAIE FORTE (Ire) [99] 7-11-10 B Storey, *led second,
made rst, clr 4 out, hld on wl frm last.
.......................(11 to 4 op 9 to 4 tchd 3 to 1)   1
1588⁸ WELL APPOINTED (Ire) [94] 8-11-2 (3*) G Lee, *hld up,
improved to chase ldrs aftr 3 out, kpt on frm last.
.......................(10 to 1 op 8 to 1)   2
3355³ DANBYS GORSE [96] 5-11-4 (3*) E Callaghan, *hld up in rear,
improved bef 3 out, rdn nxt, not quicken frm last.
.......................(9 to 1 op 8 to 1 tchd 10 to 1)   3
3157³ PEGGY GORDON [75] 6-9-7 (7*) N Horrocks, *cl up, struggling
3 out, sn btn*........................(7 to 1 tchd 9 to 1)   4
2937² SECRET SERVICE (Ire) [98] 5-11-9 M Foster, *in tch, effrt 4 out,
outpcd aftr nxt*............(9 to 4 fav tchd 5 to 2)   5
2847¹ LATIN LEADER [89] (bl) 7-11-0 D Parker, *nvr far away, outpcd
aftr 3 out, sn struggling*.............(12 to 1 tchd 14 to 1)   6
3246⁸ IN A MOMENT (USA) [75] 6-10-0 G Cahill, *led to second, lost
pl nxt, no dngr aftr*........(16 to 1 op 14 to 1 tchd 20 to 1)   7
3150 DOUBLE AGENT [102] 4-11-5 M Moloney, *pressed ldr, struggling 4 out, sn btn*.........(3 to 1 op 4 to 1 tchd 9 to 2)   8
Dist: 4l, hd, 19l, 12l, 5l, 29l, 1l. 4m 20.80s. a 17.80s (8 Ran).
SR: 20/11/13/-/-/   (James R Adam), J R Adam

3438 John Mckie Maiden Hunters' Chase Class H (5-y-o and up) £1,272 3¼m
.... (4:50)

BUCK'S DELIGHT (Ire) 9-12-0 (7*) Mr M Bradburne, *al prmnt,
led 5 out, hrd pressed frm last, ran on wl.
....................(33 to 1 op 25 to 1)   1
2891² ASK ANTONY (Ire) 7-12-0 (5*) Mr R Ford, *improved to ld aftr
3rd, jnd fnl circuit, hdd 5 out, rallied gmely frm last.
....................(5 to 4 on op 5 to 4 tchd 6 to 4)   2
ADMISSION (Ire) 7-12-0 (7*) Miss L Horner, *strted slwly, sn in
tch, effrt 13th, no imprsn fnl 3*..........(8 to 1 op 9 to 2)   3
ROLY PRIOR 8-11-9 (5*) Mrs V Jackson, *beh and rdn alng,
improved 5 out, no imprsn fnl 4.
....................(9 to 2 op 5 to 2 tchd 6 to 1)   4
ALL OR NOTHING 9-11-2 (7*) Mr J Ewart, *mstks in rear, nvr
on terms*......................(33 to 1 op 20 to 1)   5
3248² GENERAL DELIGHT 10-12-0 (7*) Mr D Wood, *mid-div, rdn
11th, outpcd bef 5 out*..............(10 to 1 op 8 to 1)   6
3352² JUST FOR ME (Ire) 8-12-2 (5*) Mr M H Naughton, *chsd ldrs,
hit 8th, outpcd last 5...* (20 to 1 op 33 to 1 tchd 50 to 1)   7
RUSHING BURN 11-11-9 (7*) Miss N C Snowden, *blun 1st,
improved to chase ldrs 8th, fdd 5 out, tld off.
....................(33 to 1 op 20 to 1)   8
3004 SIR HARRY RINUS 11-12-0 (7*) Miss T Barnes, *jmpd badly in
rear, tld off whn pld up bef 2 out*....(33 to 1 tchd 66 to 1)   pu
GREEN SHEEN (Ire) 9-12-0 (7*) Mr Chris Wilson, *prmnt till
outpcd 12th, pld up 3 out.
....................(10 to 1 op 12 to 1 tchd 14 to 1)   pu
3033³ FROZEN STIFF (Ire) 9-12-2 (5*) Mr R Shiels, *chsd ldrs, struggling whn hit tenth, sn btn, pld up 5 out.
....................(10 to 1 op 8 to 1 tchd 12 to 1)   pu
MADAME BECK 8-11-10¹ (7*) Mr R M Smith, *hld up,
improved to chase ldrs 12th, struggling 5 out, pld up last.
....................(33 to 1 op 20 to 1 tchd 50 to 1)   pu
EOSTRE 8-12-0 Mr P Craggs, *led to 3rd, lost pl 11th, pld up
bef 4 out*..............(11 to 1 op 14 to 1 tchd 20 to 1)   pu
SOLWAYSANDS 7-11-7 (7*) Mr B Gibson, *chsd ldrs, struggling fnl circuit, pld up 4 out*..................(33 to 1)   pu
Dist: ½l, 14l, 8l, 1½l, 13l, 29l, dist. 7m 4.20s. a 36.20s (14 Ran).
                (Mrs Richard Arthur), Mrs Richard Arthur

3439 Finale Intermediate National Hunt Flat Class H (4,5,6-y-o) £1,035 2m 1f
.... (5:20)

BROTHER OF IRIS (Ire) 4-10-9 (3*) G Lee, *hld up, smooth
hdwy to chal o'r 2 fs out, led one out, quickened readily.
.......................(9 to 4 fav op 5 to 4 tchd 5 to 2)   1
WHAT A FIDDLER (Ire) 4-10-5 (7*) L Cooper, *chsd ldg grp, ev
ch o'r 3 fs out, kpt on, no chance wth wnr*...........(33 to 1)   2

3251⁶ KIT SMARTIE (Ire) 5-11-6² R Ford, *midfield, improved to ld hfwy, hdd one furlong out, no extr.*
.................................(14 to 1 op 12 to 1 tchd 16 to 1) 3
2469⁴ ROMAN OUTLAW 5-11-1 (3*) Mr C Bonner, *al prmnt, rdn 3 fs out, no extr o'r one out*..................(8 to 1 tchd 10 to 1) 4
CHINA KING (Ire) 6-11-4 (7*) M Bradburne, *chsd ldrs, rdn and no extr last 2 fs*....................(4 to 1 tchd 5 to 1) 5
BEN DOULA 5-10-13 (5*) Mr M H Naughton, *hld up, steady hdwy 6 fs out, no imprsn last 2 furlongs.*
.................................(25 to 1 op 14 to 1) 6
3251⁵ SALMON CELLAR (Ire) 4-10-9 (3*) E Callaghan, *led to hfwy, hng lft and wknd last 3 fs...*(5 to 2 op 3 to 1 tchd 4 to 1) 7
3015⁴ COOL KEVIN 4-10-5 (7*) I Jardine, *chsd ldrs, outpcd hfwy, no dngr aftr.*......................(33 to 1 op 25 to 1) 8
2687 HOLLOW PALM (Ire) 6-10-11 (7*) W Dowling, *hld up, nvr plcd to chal*............(50 to 1 op 33 to 1 tchd 66 to 1) 9
MILL-DOT 5-10-11 (7*) C McCormack, *hld up, steady hdwy hfwy, rdn and outpcd o'r 2 fs out.*...(33 to 1 op 25 to 1) 10
FLOSS THE BOSS 4-10-0 (7*) N Hannity, *beh and nvr on terms.*....................................(33 to 1) 11
2824⁶ POLITICAL POWER 6-11-4 Mr A Mitchell, *chsd ldrs till wknd o'r 4 fs*........................(20 to 1 op 16 to 1) 12
2723 PAYPNUTSGETMONKEYS (Ire) 4-10-7 Mrs D Smith, *chsd ldrs to 6 fs out, fdd.*....................(50 to 1) 13
2469⁹ OUR CAROL (Ire) 5-10-6 (7*) T Siddall, *midfield, struggling hfwy, fdd.*........................(66 to 1 op 50 to 1) 14
3322⁵ MAZZELMO 4-10-0 (7*) S Melrose, *in tch, struggling 6 fs out, btn and eased entering strt.*
.................................(9 to 1 op 8 to 1 tchd 10 to 1) 15
3356⁸ MADEMIST SAM 5-10-13 (5*) B Grattan, *settled on outer, improved to chal aftr 6 fs, struggling six out.*
.................................(12 to 1 op 7 to 1) 16
GRACELAND 5-10-6 (7*) N Horrocks, *beh and sn tld off, nvr a factor.*............(25 to 1 op 20 to 1 tchd 33 to 1) 17
3251⁸ RUNHIM 5-10-11 (7*) S Haworth, *al beh, struggling frm hfwy.*
.................................(100 to 1) 18
ELLIOTT THE BUTLER 5-10-13 (5*) G F Ryan, *in tch to hfwy, sn struggling.*...............(50 to 1 op 33 to 1) 19
RAG DOLL 5-10-8 (5*) S Taylor, *chsd ldr 6 fs, sn struggling.*
.................................(16 to 1 op 14 to 1) 20
Dist: 5l, 4l, 2½l, 1¾l, 3½l, 13l, 20l, ¾l, 10l, 2½l. 4m 12.50s. (20 Ran).
(M H G Systems Ltd), Mrs M Reveley

CHEPSTOW (good)
Monday March 31st
Going Correction: MINUS 0.15 sec. per fur.

# 3440 Springtime Claiming Hurdle Class F (4-y-o and up) £2,094 2½m 110yds
.................................(2:00)

2253⁸ OUT RANKING (Fr) 5-11-9 Jamie Evans, *jmpd rght, made all, drw clr frm 4 out, eased r-in.*
.................................(15 to 8 fav op 7 to 4 tchd 2 to 1) 1
844* HOLY JOE 15-11-0 D J Burchell, *chsd ldrs, kpt on same pace frm 8th, no ch wth wnr*............(15 to 2 op 6 to 1) 2
3188* KADARI (v) 8-10-13 J Osborne, *al prmnt, hrd rdn and one pace frm 8th*............(6 to 1 op 5 to 1 tchd 13 to 2) 3
3239* CUTTHROAT KID (Ire) (v) 7-11-6 M A Fitzgerald, *hld up mid-div, effrt appr 8th, not pace to chal.*
.................................(100 to 30 op 3 to 1 tchd 7 to 1) 4
3105* FONTANAYS (Ire) (v) 9-11-1 (3*) D Fortt, *cl up till wknd 3 out.*
.................................(11 to 2 op 9 to 2 tchd 6 to 1) 5
2999 RAMSDENS (Ire) 5-11-6 C Llewellyn, *chsd ldrs till wkng 9th, mstk 7th, wknd nxt*...........(10 to 1 tchd 14 to 1) 6
FATHER O'BRIEN 10-11-6 A Thornton, *ticked, lost tch 7th, tld off.*..................(33 to 1 op 16 to 1) 7
3148⁷ TILT TECH FLYER 12-10-7 (7*) J Prior, *al rear, tld off 6th, pld up appr nxt*..........(50 to 1 op 25 to 1) pu
2957 ERLKING (v) 7-11-4 N Mann, *al rear, tld off 6th, pld up bef 8th*........................(33 to 1 op 20 to 1) pu
2999⁴ LAUGHING BUCCANEER 4-10-12 B Powell, *rear, rdn 5th, tld off nxt, pld up bef 8th, lme*........(25 to 1 op 16 to 1) pu
Dist: 3l, ½l, 4l, 9l, 7l, dist. 4m 45.90s. a 7.10s (10 Ran).
(Knight Hawks Partnership), M C Pipe

# 3441 Fulke Walwyn Handicap Chase Class C (0-135 5-y-o and up) £4,783 3m
.................................(2:30)

2459² SEOD RIOGA (Ire) [110] 8-10-6 N Mann, *trkd ldrs gng wl, slight ld 2 out, rdn and ran on strly r-in.*........(3 to 1 co-fav op 7 to 2) 1
1767¹ HARWELL LAD (Ire) [125] 8-11-7 Mr R Nuttall, *led to second, led 4th to 2 out, outpcd r-in.*........................(7 to 2) 2
2592 OLD BRIDGE (Ire) [130] 9-11-12 J Osborne, *pressed ldrs till wknd 3 out, eased whn btn.* (3 to 1 co-fav tchd 100 to 30) 3
3298¹ FOOLS ERRAND (Ire) [115] (v) 7-10-11 M A Fitzgerald, *bad mstk 1st, hdwy 7th, wknd 11th, beh whn blun 2 out.*
.................................(3 to 1 co-fav) 4
3114 BAVARD DIEU (Ire) [132] (bl) 9-12-0 C Llewellyn, *led second to 4th, jmpd slwly and rear 9th, shrtlvd effrt appr 14th, sn beh.*
.................................(13 to 2 op 6 to 1 tchd 4 to 1) 5
3204⁶ MISS DISKIN (Ire) [104] 8-10-0 B Powell, *last but in tch whn pld up bef 8th*..................(14 to 1 op 12 to 1) pu

Dist: 6l, 26l, 3½l, 2l. 5m 59.90s. a 9.90s (6 Ran).
(S P Tindall), S Mellor

3442 Welsh Champion Hurdle Class B (4-y-o and up) £6,947 2m 110yds (3:00)

3062* POTENTATE (USA) 6-11-6 Jamie Evans, *made all, drvn alng frm 8th, ran on gmely...*(100 to 30 op 3 to 1 tchd 7 to 2) 1
3129³ DARAYDAN (Ire) 5-11-6 M A Fitzgerald, *cl up, rdn appr 5th, one pace frm 2 out*..............(9 to 4 op 6 to 4) 2
3113 MISTINGUETT (Ire) 5-11-9 C Llewellyn, *prmnt to 4th, hrd rdn and outpcd appr nxt, styd on same pace frm 2 out.*
.................................(11 to 8 fav op 6 to 4) 3
2553³ NOBLE LORD 4-11-0 B Powell, *prmnt till wknd 5th.*
.................................(9 to 1 op 7 to 1 tchd 11 to 1) 4
CASTLE SECRET 11-11-6 D J Burchell, *sn tld off, styd on frm 3 out, nvr nr ldrs*..................(20 to 1 op 12 to 1) 5
Dist: 3½l, 1¼l, 15l, 1¼l. 3m 48.10s. a 1.10s (5 Ran).
SR: 57/53/54/30/34/ (Jim Weeden), M C Pipe

3443 Castle Novices' Hurdle Class E (4-y-o and up) £2,654 2m 110yds (3:30)

3334 ZANDER 5-11-0 C Llewellyn, *cl up, chsd ldr 5th, hrd rdn to ld nr finish*....................(9 to 4 op 2 to 1 tchd 5 to 2) 1
2423⁶ MAJOR DUNDEE (Ire) 4-10-7 Jamie Evans, *led, clr 5th, rdn appr last, hng lft r-in, hdd nr finish*........(9 to 4 op 5 to 2) 2
2662⁶ RUMPELSTILTSKIN 5-10-11 (3*) D Fortt, *rear, hdwy to dispute second pl 5th, wknd nxt, 3rd and btn whn mstk 2 out.*
.................................(25 to 1 op 33 to 1 tchd 20 to 1) 3
2876 AQUA AMBER 5-10-7 (7*) J Power, *prmnt to hfwy, beh frm 5th..............(40 to 1 op 25 to 1 tchd 50 to 1) 4
2795⁹ SMART REMARK 5-11-0 P McLoughlin, *lost tch hfwy.*
.................................(33 to 1 op 25 to 1) 5
2925 BARON HRABOVSKY (bl) 4-10-7 B Powell, *hdwy to chase ldr 4th, wknd nxt*......(66 to 1 op 50 to 1 tchd 100 to 1) 6
FOREST ROSE 7-10-2 (7*) M Moran, *mstk and lost tch 3rd, tld off whn blun last*.....(66 to 1 op 50 to 1 tchd 100 to 1) 7
3077⁴ DONNINGTON (Ire) 7-11-5 J Osborne, *chsd ldr second to 3rd, prmnt whn pld up bef nxt*..........(6 to 4 fav op Evens) pu
3099 KERRIER 5-10-7 (7*) A Dowling, *cl up till blun second, sn beh, tld off whn pld up bef 5th.*
.................................(66 to 1 op 50 to 1 tchd 100 to 1) pu
Dist: 1¼l, 13l, 15l, 2½l, 23l, dist. 3m 52.30s. a 5.30s (9 Ran).
SR: 6/-/-/-/-/-/ (Mrs Karen Duggan), N A Twiston-Davies

3444 Easter Bonnet Handicap Chase Class D (0-120 5-y-o and up) £3,670 2m 3f 110yds. (4:00)

2922⁴ JAMES THE FIRST [117] 9-12-0 M A Fitzgerald, *cld on ldg pair 6th, led 11th, sn quickened clr, easily.*
.................................(4 to 1 tchd 9 to 2) 1
2529 PHARSILK (Ire) [104] 8-11-1 P McLoughlin, *led 4th to 9th, led tenth till blun nxt, rdn and no imprsn frm four out.*
.................................(10 to 1 op 6 to 1 tchd 12 to 1) 2
3297* MALWOOD CASTLE (Ire) [89] 7-10-0 N Mann, *sn outpcd and wl beh, mstk 4 out, styd on, nvr nr ldrs.*
.................................(5 to 4 fav op 11 to 10) 3
2759 DISTINCTIVE (Ire) [109] 8-11-6 C Llewellyn, *set fst pace to 4th, led 9th to nxt, sn outpcd and lost tch.*
.................................(9 to 4 tchd 5 to 2 op 2 to 1) 4
2991 GLEN MIRAGE [89] 12-10-0 B Powell, *jmpd slwly, sn outpcd and beh, tld off frm 5th*............(9 to 1 op 7 to 1) 5
Dist: 5l, 16l, 22l, 1¼l. 4m 59.20s. a 16.20s (5 Ran).
(B L Blinman), P F Nicholls

3445 Easter Surprise Handicap Hurdle Class D (0-125 4-y-o and up) £3,160 2½m 110yds. (4:30)

3321 CASSIO'S BOY [95] 6-10-11 N Mann, *beh, smooth hdwy 7th, led aftr 3 out, rdn clr r-in*............(20 to 1 op 10 to 1) 1
2958⁴ REAGANESQUE (USA) [114] 5-11-6 M A Fitzgerald, *prmnt, jnd ldrs 7th, ev ch last, not quicken r-in.*
.................................(11 to 2 op 4 to 1 tchd 6 to 1) 2
3078* JOVIE KING [94] 5-10-0 B Powell, *led to 3rd, led 5th till aftr 3 out, third and btn whn mstk nxt....*(5 to 1 op 4 to 1) 3
3131 LYING EYES [118] 6-11-3 (7*) J Power, *hld up, hdwy 8th, styd on same pace*....................(11 to 4 op 9 to 4) 4
3385⁵ KEEP ME IN MIND (Ire) [108] 8-11-0 Mr R Nuttall, *hld up and beh, hdwy 8th, rdn 2 out, nvr able to chal.*
.................................(10 to 1 op 12 to 1) 5
HENRY CONE [109] 8-11-1 D J Burchell, *rear, pushed alng 4th, hdwy 7th, wknd nxt.*................(14 to 1 op 10 to 1) 6
PROPAGANDA [94] 9-10-0 P McLoughlin, *in tch, mstk 6th, sn rdn and btn, lost touch 8th.*.........(25 to 1 op 20 to 1) 7
3188² SWING QUARTET (Ire) [99] 7-10-5 C Llewellyn, *mid-div till outpcd 4th, lost tch 6th.* (9 to 2 fav op 4 to 1 tchd 5 to 1) 8
3131 SLEW MAN (Fr) [112] (bl) 6-11-4 Jamie Evans, *cl up to hfwy, lost tch 8th*..............(11 to 2 op 5 to 1 tchd 6 to 1) 9
3062⁵ CALL MY GUEST (Ire) [107] 7-10-6 (7*) M Moran, *chsd ldrs, wknd aftr 7th*.........................(20 to 1 op 14 to 1) f
2876³ ATAVISTIC (Ire) [96] 5-9-9 (7*) T O'Connor, *cl up, rdn and wknd aftr 7th, seventh and btn whn f nxt*................(9 to 1) f
3131 FATACK [115] 8-11-7 J Osborne, *led 3rd to 5th, lost pl 7th, sn beh, pld up bef nxt.*......(6 to 1 op 10 to 1 tchd 12 to 1) pu

Dist: 1¾l, 11l, 2½l, 1½l, 15l, dist. 4m 42.80s. a 4.80s (12 Ran).
SR: -/12/-/2/-/-/   (Lyonshall Racing), R J Eckley

CLONMEL (IRE) (good)
Monday March 31st

3446 Bank Of Ireland Finance Handicap Chase (0-116 4-y-o and up) £4,110 2m .... (4:10)

1059[6]	LOUGH ATALIA [-] 10-9-10 S H O'Donovan, ... (10 to 1)	1
3339[5]	JUMPING FOR JOY (Ire) [-] 8-9-5 (5*) A O'Shea, ..(10 to 1)	2
3133	MACAUNTA (Ire) [-] 7-9-10 (7*) M Morris, ...(5 to 1)	3
3379[2]	HANNIES GIRL (Ire) [-] 8-9-13 (7*) L J Fleming, (2 to 1 fav)	4
3340[2]	MARIES POLLY [-] 7-10-1[2] D H O'Connor, ...(7 to 1)	5
3339[8]	EVER SO BOLD [-] 10-10-5 (3*) J Butler, ...(9 to 1)	6
2444[3]	MINSTREL FIRE (Ire) [-] 9-10-10 (7*) Mr B Hassett, ..(3 to 1)	7
2868*	GEALLAINNBAN (Ire) [-] (bl) 7-11-3 P L Malone, ...(9 to 2)	ur

Dist: 1½l, nk, 2½l, 3l. 3m 50.50s. (8 Ran).

(P J O'Brien), V T O'Brien

3447 Bank Of Ireland Hunters Chase (5-y-o and up) £3,082 3m .... (4:40)

	RIVER OF DREAMS (Ire) 7-11-7 (7*) Mr B Hassett, ..(8 to 1)	1
	KILARA 10-11-7 (7*) Mr K O'Sullivan, ...(11 to 1)	2
	SANDFAIR (Ire) 7-11-2 (7*) Mr C A Murphy, ...(11 to 1)	3
3222[2]	PANCHO'S TANGO (Ire) 7-11-7 (7*) Mr D P Daly,	
	....(11 to 10 fav)	4
3341[3]	VIKING BUOY (Ire) 5-11-4 (7*) Mr E Gallagher, ...(7 to 1)	5
3378	EVEN CALL 11-11-7 (7*) Mr M Kavanagh, ...(14 to 1)	6
3222[3]	TWO IN TUNE (Ire) 9-11-7 (7*) Mr R Keane, ...(4 to 1)	7
3341[6]	FOOLS WITH HORSES (Ire) 6-11-9 (5*) Mr J T McNamara,	
	....(11 to 1)	8
	BARNA LAD (Ire) 7-11-7 (7*) Mr A J Dempsey, ...(12 to 1)	f
	TEADS BORREEN 8-11-7 (7*) Mr M Budds, ...(12 to 1)	f
	KILLENAGH MOSS 10-12-0 Mr D M O'Brien, ...(13 to 1)	pu
829	RING MAM 6-11-2 (7*) Mr D M Loughnane, ...(20 to 1)	pu

Dist: 5½l, 1l, 1l, 6l. 6m 3.60s. (12 Ran).

(Joseph Quinn), Joseph Quinn

3448 Surehaul Mercedes Handicap Hurdle (0-102 4-y-o and up) £3,425 3m .... (5:10)

3234[6]	COOLREE LORD (Ire) [-] (bl) 6-9-3 (7*) P G Hourigan, (6 to 1)	1
3180[4]	ECLIPTIC MOON (Ire) [-] 7-9-9 (5*) P Morris, ..(4 to 1 jt-fav)	2
3219[3]	COMMITTED SCHEDULE (Ire) [-] 6-10-8 M P Hourigan,	
	....(7 to 1)	3
3216[5]	JOHNNY HANDSOME (Ire) [-] 7-10-8 A J O'Brien, ...(10 to 1)	4
3180	CASEY JUNIOR (Ire) [-] (bl) 9-10-0 (7*) D W O'Sullivan,	
	....(14 to 1)	5
3337[6]	ALLARACKET (Ire) [-] (bl) 8-9-12 (5*) A O'Shea, ..(11 to 1)	6
3377[8]	GARLAND ROSE (Ire) [-] (bl) 7-9-3 (7*) F J Keniry, ..(12 to 1)	7
3338[4]	ROSEY ELLEN (Ire) [-] 5-9-12 (7*) M D Murphy, ...(11 to 1)	8
2944[9]	ROSEAUSTIN (Ire) [-] 7-9-8 (7*) D McCullagh, ...(12 to 1)	9
3219[4]	RANDOM RING (Ire) [-] 6-10-8 (5*) Mr J T McNamara,	
	....(11 to 1)	f
3390[7]	LIOS NA MAOL (Ire) [-] 6-9-4 (5*) T Martin, ...(14 to 1)	f
3390[4]	SPECTACLE (Ire) [-] 7-9-7 (3*) J Butler, ...(12 to 1)	f
3180[2]	EXPEDIENT EXPRESS (Ire) [-] 7-10-3 S H O'Donovan,	
	....(4 to 1 jt-fav)	pu

Dist: 9l, 2l, 7l. 5m 44.70s. (13 Ran).

(Miss Ann Johnson), Michael Hourigan

3449 Bank Of Ireland Finance (Pro-Am) Flat Race (4-y-o and up) £3,425 2m .... (5:40)

	DYNAMIC DESIGN (Ire) 5-11-7 (7*) Mr T P Hyde, ...(4 to 1)	1
2060[5]	SARAH SUPREME (Ire) 6-11-2 (7*) G T Hourigan, ..(12 to 1)	2
3182[9]	AS AN SLI (Ire) 6-11-2 (7*) Mr D F Barry, ...(25 to 1)	3
2092[3]	BERE HAVEN (Ire) 5-11-7 (5*) Mr J T McNamara, ...(4 to 1)	4
3183[3]	MONEYCLEAR (Ire) 4-10-11 (7*) Mr C A Murphy, ...(7 to 1)	5
1247[6]	LETTIR LAD (Ire) 5-11-5 (7*) M D Murphy, ...(12 to 1)	6
2709[2]	MOVIE MAID (Ire) 5-11-0 (7*) Mr P J Crowley, ...(9 to 2)	7
3069	TALKALOT (Ire) 6-11-11 (3*) Mrs M Mullins, ...(12 to 2 fav)	8
2965	ROYAL SANTAL (Ire) 5-11-0 (7*) Mr A FitzGerald, ..(12 to 1)	9
	OLYMPIC LADY (Ire) 5-11-0 (7*) Mr M A Cahill, ...(8 to 1)	10
3069	GROWTOWN LAD (Ire) 6-12-0 Mr J A Berry, ...(16 to 1)	11
2942[5]	WINTER MELODY (Ire) 5-11-5 (7*) M W Martin, ...(10 to 1)	12
2583	SUIR FIND (Ire) 5-11-5 (7*) Mr M Scanlon, ...(20 to 1)	13
	MR GRIMSDALE (Ire) 5-11-5 (7*) Mr A J Dempsey, (16 to 1)	14
	SMILING MINSTREL (Ire) 6-12-0 Mr D Marnane, ...(16 to 1)	15
	DAME SUS (Ire) 7-11-9 Mr D M O'Brien, ...(20 to 1)	16
3182	CASTLE-ETTA (Ire) 7-11-2 (7*) Miss K Rudd, ...(25 to 1)	17
	NORTHERN CRUSADE (Ire) 6-11-2 (7*) Mr F Barry, (25 to 1)	18
199	HAND CARE (Ire) 6-11-2 (7*) Mr K M Roche, ...(25 to 1)	pu

Dist: 1l, 8l, 4l, hd. 3m 47.00s. (19 Ran).

(T E Hyde), David Wachman

FAIRYHOUSE (IRE) (good)
Monday March 31st
Going Correction: MINUS 0.25 sec. per fur. (races

3450 Sam Dennigan & Co. Hurdle (4-y-o) £4,795 2m .... (2:05)

1,2,3,7), PLUS 0.15 (4,5,6)

3150	STYLISH ALLURE (USA) 11-7 R Dunwoody, ...(6 to 4 fav)	1
3087[5]	STRATEGIC PLOY 11-2 C O'Dwyer, ...(7 to 1)	2
2067	ROYAL MIDYAN 11-0 D T Evans, ...(20 to 1)	3
3345[2]	DOVALY 11-0 K F O'Brien, ...(7 to 2)	4
2940[5]	PEGUS JUNIOR (Ire) 10-7 (7*) M McGovern, ...(12 to 1)	5
	LUNA FLEUR 10-2 (7*) B J Geraghty, ...(10 to 1)	6
	QUINZE 11-0 C F Swan, ...(14 to 1)	7
3087[9]	TAX REFORM (USA) 11-7 H Rogers, ...(16 to 1)	8
3225	DUE TO YOU (Ire) 11-0 P Leech, ...(66 to 1)	9
3225*	VINCITORE (Ire) 11-4 L P Cusack, ...(10 to 1)	10
3232[2]	CELTIC PROJECT (Ire) 11-0 P A Roche, ...(12 to 1)	11
2832	COOL SCOTCH (Ire) 10-6 (3*) D Bromley, ...(50 to 1)	12
3087	MYSTERY LADY (Ire) 10-9 S C Lyons, ...(50 to 1)	13
	LADY PATRICE (Ire) 10-9 M Duffy, ...(14 to 1)	14
	MAID TO MOVE (Ire) 10-4 (5*) Mr G Elliott, ...(14 to 1)	15
3232	KNOCKDOO (Ire) 11-0 F J Flood, ...(66 to 1)	16
3221	SOVIET DREAMER 10-7 (7*) J M Maguire, ...(33 to 1)	f

Dist: 2½l, 4l, 2½l, 2l. 3m 59.20s. a 15.20s (17 Ran).

(P A Byrnes), D K Weld

3451 Dunshaughlin Leinster Petroleum Handicap Hurdle (Listed) (4-y-o and up) £6,850 2¾m .... (2:40)

3214[3]	GRAVITY GATE (Ire) [-] 8-10-13 R Dunwoody, beh early, hdwy bef 7th, trkd ldrs, ran on wl to ld cl hme ....(11 to 2)	1
3234*	KASELECTRIC (Ire) [-] 6-10-6 T Horgan, beh early, hdwy 4 out, second 2 out, styd on aftr last ....(10 to 1)	2
3072*	THE QUADS [-] 5-9-7 F Woods, beh early, prog to go 4th 3 out, led bef last, hdd and wknd cl hme..........(5 to 1)	3
2170*	FIDDLERS BOW VI (Ire) [-] 9-10-11 J F Titley, beh early, prog to go second 3 out, led 2 out, hdd and wknd bef last (10 to 1)	4
3086[9]	ANNADOT (Ire) [-] 7-10-10 F J Flood, led early, drpd back bef 3rd, styd on frm 4 out ....(14 to 1)	5
3234[2]	VASILIKI (Ire) [-] 5-9-13 D J Casey, mid-div, drpd back bef tenth, styd on aftr 3 out ....(10 to 1)	6
3071[6]	COQ HARDI VENTURE (Ire) [-] 6-10-6 (7*) B J Geraghty, mid-div, hdwy to go 3rd at 6th, no extr frm 4 out ....(10 to 1)	7
3214[4]	STRALDI (Ire) [-] 9-10-13 J Shortt, chsd ldrs, led bef 3rd to 7th, led 3 out to nxt, wknd quickly ....(7 to 1)	8
3131	METASTASIO [-] (bl) 5-11-7 H Rogers, mid-div, hdwy to go 3rd 4 out, wknd bef 2 out, sn no dngr............(8 to 1)	9
1297[7]	DIFFICULT TIMES (Ire) [-] 5-11-11 S C Lyons, chsd ldrs, led 7th, wknd quickly and hdd aftr 4 out, sn btn.........(8 to 1)	10
2164[6]	ALWAYS IN TROUBLE [-] (bl) 10-10-2 T P Rudd, mid-div, wknd bef 4 out, sn no dngr...................(12 to 1)	11
2837[6]	ROSIN THE BOW (Ire) [-] 8-12-0 C F Swan, trkd ldr, wknd bef 6th, beh and pld up before 3 out ....(13 to 2)	pu
2902*	KAISER SOSA (Ire) [-] 6-10-0 C O'Dwyer, al beh, pld up 4 out. ....(8 to 1)	pu

Dist: ½l, 1½l, 10l, 4l. 5m 17.40s. a 6.40s (13 Ran).

(Donald King), R H MacNabb

3452 Jameson Gold Cup Novice Chase (Grade 2) (5-y-o and up) £13,000 2m .... (3:15)

2964[6]	GAZALANI (Ire) 5-11-3 T P Treacy, trkd ldrs, hdwy bef 2 out, styd on aftr last to ld cl hme............(33 to 1)	1
3111	HUMBEL (USA) (bl) 5-11-6 R Dunwoody, led till ct cl hme. ....(6 to 1)	2
2965[3]	GREY GUY (Ire) 5-11-6 F Woods, trkd ldr till rdn and no extr bef 2 out ....(14 to 1)	3
2963[2]	SENTOSA STAR (Ire) 6-11-11 J P Broderick, beh early, hdwy 4 out, kpt on same pace ....(7 to 1)	4
3111	FINNEGAN'S HOLLOW (Ire) 7-11-8 C F Swan, beh early, hdwy into 3rd 4 out, ev ch till wknd quickly 2 out. (7 to 4 on)	5
3233*	NATIVE-DARRIG (Ire) 6-11-8 D J Casey, mid-div, wknd bef 4 out, sn no dngr...................(14 to 1)	6
3111[2]	PRINCEFUL (Ire) 6-11-8 J F Titley, mid-div, mstk 4th, pld up aftr 4 out.	pu

Dist: 1½l, 14l, 6l, sht-hd. 3m 43.80s. b 0.20s (7 Ran).
SR: 51/52/38/37/34/-/-/   (Miss Rita Shah), Patrick O Brady

3453 Jameson Irish Grand National Chase Handicap (Grade 1) (4-y-o and up) £62,700 3m 5f .... (3:55)

3114[6]	MUDAHIM [-] 11-10-3 J F Titley, beh early, hdwy bef tenth, second nxt, led 2 out till aftr last, styd on to ld cl hme. (13 to 2)	1
2842[5]	AMBLE SPEEDY (Ire) [-] 10-10-0 F Woods, beh early, hdwy 7 out, second 2 out, led aftr last, hdd cl hme............(14 to 1)	2
2819*	THE GREY MONK (Ire) [-] 7-12-0 A Dobbin, mid-div, hdwy 11th, 4th at 14th, 3rd 3 out, rdn and no extr.......(9 to 2 fav)	3
2842*	PAPILLON (Ire) [-] 6-10-4 C F Swan, beh early, hdwy 14th, trkd ldrs, rdn and no extr bef 2 out ....(6 to 1)	4
2821[3]	ST MELLION FAIRWAY (Ire) [-] 8-10-4[1] A Thornton, trkd ldrs, wknd aftr 3 out, sn btn..................(20 to 1)	5
2071	LORD SINGAPORE (Ire) [-] 9-10-10 D J Casey, beh early, hdwy 11th, rdn bef 3 out, styd on..................(8 to 1)	6
2071[8]	HEIST [-] 8-10-0 K F O'Brien, beh early, ran on wl frm 4 out. ....(20 to 1)	7

2867⁵ FISSURE SEAL [-] 11-10-3 T P Treacy, *beh early, styd on frm 4 out*..(20 to 1) 8
2867 CORYMANDEL (Ire) [-] 8-10-0 T P Rudd, *led till wknd quickly and hdd 2 out*.................................(33 to 1) 9
3101* CHURCH LAW [-] 10-10-0 R Bellamy, *al beh, tld off*. (50 to 1) 10
3212³ FLASHY LAD (Ire) [-] 6-10-0 J P Broderick, *trkd ldrs, wknd aftr 6 out, sn no dngr*.........................(33 to 1) 11
2867* TEAL BRIDGE [-] 12-10-0 T J Mitchell, *beh till f 13th*. (20 to 1) f
3081³ AARDWOLF [-] (bl) 6-10-3² G Bradley, *trkd ldrs till f second*.
....(20 to 1) f
2843³ COQ HARDI AFFAIR (Ire) [-] 9-10-1 Mr B M Cash, *mid-div till f 9th*...(20 to 1) f
2446* THE LATVIAN LARK (Ire) [-] 9-10-0 C O'Dwyer, *mid-div till f tenth*...(14 to 1) f
3063* GIVENTIME [-] 9-10-01 Harvey, *trkd ldrs, wknd aftr 5th, pld up bef 12th*...................................(10 to 1) pu
2829³ PERCY SMOLLETT [-] 9-11-5 R Dunwoody, *mid-div till pld up 6 out*...(14 to 1) pu
1146² CONSHARON (Ire) [-] 9-10-3 T Horgan, *al beh, pld up bef 14th*..(33 to 1) pu
3229* TRENCH HILL LASS (Ire) [-] 8-10-1¹ (3ex) L P Cusack, *mid-div, wknd aftr 12th, pld up bef 6 out*........(50 to 1) pu
3206³ SISTER STEPHANIE (Ire) [-] 8-10-0 D Bridgwater, *refused to strt, took no part*............................(10 to 1) l
Dist: Sht-hd, 11l, 2l, 25l, 3l. 7m 28.60s. a 8.60s (20 Ran).
SR: 27/24/41/15/-/-/ (In Touch Racing Club), Mrs J Pitman

3454 **Saltan Properties Beginners Chase (5-y-o and up) £6,850 2¼m... (4:35)**

3336 ROYAL OASIS (Ire) 6-11-9 J P Broderick, ...(14 to 1) 1
3144² APPLEFORT (Ire) 7-11-9 C O'Dwyer, ...(6 to 1) 2
3215² BRAVE FOUNTAIN (Ire) 9-12-0 C F Swan, ...(4 to 1) 3
2096 MOON-FROG 10-11-9 J K Kinane, ...(25 to 1) 4
2834³ OWENDUFF (USA) 7-12-0 F Woods, ...(7 to 2) 5
2755⁴ PUNTERS BAR 10-11-2 J Shortt, ...(9 to 1) f
3073⁴ BANGABUNNY 7-11-11 (3*) K Whelan, ...(8 to 1) f
3088⁶ NEWTOWN ROAD (Ire) 6-11-9 P Leech, ...(20 to 1) f
2941² NO TAG (Ire) 9-12-0 T J Mitchell, ...(2 to 1 fav) ur
3393² THE THIRD MAN (Ire) 8-12-0 T P Treacy, ...(10 to 1) ur
Dist: 1½l, dist, 13l, 15l. 4m 34.40s. a 9.40s (10 Ran).
SR: 28/26/-/-/-/-/ (Patrick Heffernan), Patrick Heffernan

3455 **Nuzum Handicap Chase (0-109 5-y-o and up) £4,795 2½m... (5:05)**

3084* PRATE BOX (Ire) [-] 7-11-12 R Dunwoody, ...(9 to 4 fav) 1
FAMOUS STOUT [-] 12-9-11 (7*) B J Geraghty, ...(20 to 1) 2
3229³ CARAGH BRIDGE [-] 10-10-9 C F Swan, ...(9 to 2) 3
3229⁶ AMENE ENAEK (Ire) [-] (bl) 8-11-4 H Rogers, ...(8 to 1) 4
3074⁷ BEAUCHAMP GRACE [-] 8-10-5 (3*) K Whelan, ...(6 to 1) 5
3088⁵ ANOTHER DEADLY [-] 10-10-8 J P Broderick, ...(8 to 1) f
3073* LIVIN IT UP (Ire) [-] 7-12-0 F Woods, ...(5 to 2) f
3084⁸ TEMPLEROAN PRINCE [-] 10-10-12 J R Barry, ...(11 to 1) pu
Dist: 2l, 15l, 9l, dist. 5m 3.90s. a 8.90s (8 Ran).
SR: 39/15/5/5/-/ (Miss Heather Scully), P Hughes

3456 **Kelly Timber Merchants I.N.H. Flat Race (5 & 6-y-o) £4,795 2m... (5:35)**

FEATHERED LEADER (Ire) 5-11-12 Mr A J Martin, (12 to 1) 1
2845⁵ KILCALM KING (Ire) 5-11-5 (7*) Mr M P Madden, ...(6 to 1) 2
2054⁴ FIRMOUNT CROSS (Ire) 5-11-5 (7*) Mr P J Prendergast,
....(11 to 2) 3
3083⁵ APPLAUSE (Ire) 6-11-7 (7*) Mr R M Walsh, ...(14 to 1) 4
2946³ RING ALBERT (Ire) 5-11-7 (5*) Mr A C Coyle, ...(10 to 1) 5
CHINA TEALEAF (Ire) 5-11-7 Mr P F Graffin, ...(25 to 1) 6
3090⁸ NATIVE SHORE (Ire) 5-11-0 (7*) Mr K O'Ryan, ...(16 to 1) 7
3231² THE RED SIDE (Ire) 5-11-0 (7*) Mr M Phillips, ...(9 to 1) 8
DRY HIGHLINE (Ire) 5-11-12 Mr J A Nash, ...(5 to 1) 9
805 J-R ASHFORD (Ire) 6-11-7 (7*) Mr P J Colville, ...(33 to 1) 10
3087² GO ROGER GO (Ire) 5-11-12 Mr P Fenton, ...(9 to 4 fav) 11
AMBERLEIGH HOUSE (Ire) 5-11-9 (3*) Mr D P Costello,
....(11 to 2) 12
3090⁵ BE MY MOT (Ire) 5-11-2 (5*) Mr G Elliott, ...(10 to 1) 13
2870⁷ SPRING CABBAGE (Ire) 5-11-5 (7*) Mr M O'Connor,
....(20 to 1) 14
2319¹ WILLYELKRA 5-11-12 Mr J P Dempsey, ...(16 to 1) 15
3221¹⁸ TOMORROW'S STORY (Ire) 5-11-9 (3*) Mr E Norris, (5 to 1) 16
THE BELFRY BID (Ire) 5-11-5 (7*) Mr D Coakley, (33 to 1) 17
AVRO EXPRESS (Ire) 6-11-7 (7*) Mr P J Scallan, ...(7 to 1) 18
WHAT A BARGAIN (Ire) 5-11-0 (7*) Mr A G Cash, ..(25 to 1) 19
3090⁷ CORNCAP (Ire) 5-11-6¹ (7*) Mr S J Mahon, ...(50 to 1) 20
NEW STOCK (Ire) 5-11-0 (7*) Mr J J Canavan, ...(20 to 1) 21
SPENCER HOUSE (Ire) 5-11-5 (7*) Mr J J O'Sullivan,
....(33 to 1) 22
Dist: 2½l, 1½l, 2½l, 5l. 3m 41.70s. (22 Ran).
  (M D O'Connor), Michael J O'Connor

FAKENHAM (good)
Monday March 31st
Going Correction: PLUS 0.45 sec. per fur.

3457 **Raynham Selling Handicap Hurdle Class G (0-90 4-y-o and up) £3,071**

2m........................... (2:30)

3042⁶ BLOTOFT [67] 5-11-2 D O'Sullivan, *wl plcd, led 2 out, drvn out*..(16 to 1) 1
3325* RUTH'S GAMBLE [66] (v) 9-11-1¹ Mr A Sansome, *in tch frm 4th, str chal r-in, jst fld*.............(7 to 2 jt-fav op 4 to 1) 2
3163³ ARCH ANGEL (Ire) [76] 4-10-10 (7*) X Aizpuru, *hld up in rear, hdwy 6th, styd on frm 2 out*..........(9 to 2 jt-fav op 4 to 1) 3
1992 LEBEDINSKI (Ire) [74] 4-11-1 V Smith, *chsd ldrs 5th, ev ch 2 out, no extr then*......................(25 to 1 op 20 to 1) 4
3292² SCALP 'EM (Ire) [59] 8-10-8 Dr P Pritchard, *mid-div, kpt on one pace frm 3 out*..........................(6 to 1 op 11 to 2) 5
1353² BLURRED IMAGE (Ire) [65] 6-11-0 Leesa Long, *hdwy frm rear 6th, no extr from 2 out*...................(9 to 2 op 4 to 1) 6
1843⁶ ALOSAILI [70] 10-11-5 Mr A Charles-Jones, *made most till hdd 2 out, sn wknd*........................(20 to 1 op 16 to 1) 7
WICKLOW BOY (Ire) [54] 6-10-3¹ W Fry, *nvr rchd ldrs*.
....(33 to 1 op 25 to 1) 8
2999 EMERALD VENTURE [66] 10-11-1 C Rae, *beh most of way*.
....(20 to 1 op 16 to 1) 9
3169⁵ HOLKHAM BAY [65] 5-11-0 R Rourke, *nvr dngrs*.
....(12 to 1 op 10 to 1) 10
3292⁹ NISHAMAN [60] 6-10-2 (7*) A Garrity, *wth ldr, ev ch 3 out, btn nxt*..(50 to 1 op 25 to 1) 11
3168⁷ SHEDANSAR (Ire) [61] (v) 5-10-10 M Sharratt, *prmnt till drpd rear 5th*....................................(20 to 1 op 33 to 1) 12
3292³ ZESTI [75] 5-11-3 (7*) Mr R Wakley, *hdwy 5th, chasing ldrs whn blun and uns rdr 2 out*..................(14 to 1 op 12 to 1) ur
3292⁴ VANBOROUGH LAD [68] 8-11-3 M Richards, *nvr on terms, pld up bef last*...................................(50 to 1 op 11 to 2) pu
STRIFFOLINO [65] 5-11-0 T Kent, *wl plcd till wknd 6th, pld up bef 2 out*...................................(14 to 1) pu
Dist: Nk, 5l, 1½l, 2½l, 6l, ¾l, 2½l, ½l, 19l, 10l. 3m 59.30s. a 15.30s (15 Ran).
SR: 7/6/3/-/-/-/ (R N Forman), S Gollings

3458 **Robert Hoare Memorial Novices' Hunters' Chase Class H (5-y-o and up) £2,388 2m 5f 110yds.....(3:05)**

3102⁶ NOT MY LINE (Ire) 8-11-9 (5*) Mr W Wales, *hld up, jnd ldr 13th, led aftr 2 out, all out*..................(20 to 1 op 16 to 1) 1
3248 UP FOR RANSOME (Ire) 8-11-7 (7*) Mr T J Barry, *in tch, hit 3rd, led 12th till aftr 2 out, rallied r-in*...(10 to 4 op 3 to 1) 2
3368 GALZIG 9-11-7 (7*) Mr W Tellwright, *chsd ldrs, rdn and one pace frm 3 out*...............................(10 to 1 op 9 to 2) 3
REVEREND BROWN (Ire) 7-11-9 (5*) Mr A Sansome, *not fluent early, kpt on one pace frm 3 out*.
....(5 to 2 fav op 2 to 1) 4
SPERRIN VIEW 11-11-2 (7*) Mr A Charles-Jones, *rear most of way*...(5 to 1 op 7 to 2) 5
3256² TEA CEE KAY 7-11-7 (7*) Mr Rupert Sweeting, *wl plcd till rear 8th, sn lost tch*......................(4 to 1 op 5 to 1) 6
SCRAPTASTIC 6-11-7 (7*) Mr N M Bell, *led 3rd to 7th, rear whn f tenth*.....................................(20 to 1 op 33 to 1) f
CARDINAL BLACK 11-11-7 (7*) Mr R Wakley, *led to 3rd, led 7th to 12th, rear whn pld up aftr 2 out*.
....(8 to 1 op 8 to 1 tchd 10 to 1) pu
SUNSET RUN (bl) 11-11-7 (7*) Miss C Tuke, *beh till pld up bef 7th*.......................................(40 to 1 op 33 to 1) pu
Dist: ½l, 5l, 7l, 4l, 20l. 5m 37.90s. a 25.90s (9 Ran).
  (P C Caudwell), Andy Morgan

3459 **Event Caterers Handicap Hurdle Class F (0-100 4-y-o and up) £3,755 2½m........................... (3:40)**

3049* SIR DANTE (Ire) [86] 6-11-6 D O'Sullivan, *chsd ldr, led 2 out, clr last, not extended*.....................(9 to 4 fav) 1
3163* ANTIGUAN FLYER [78] (v) 8-10-5 (7*) X Aizpuru, *set str pace, clr 3rd, hdd 2 out, kpt on wl*..........(6 to 1 op 11 to 2) 2
3172² FINE ON ICE (Ire) [90] 5-11-3 (7*) Mr R Wakley, *hld up in rear, hdwy 7th, not quicken frm 2 out*.....(5 to 1 op 9 to 2) 3
3247* CAMBO (USA) [85] 11-11-5 T Kent, *hld up early, outpcd frm 3 out*....................................(7 to 2 op 4 to 1 tchd 9 to 2) 4
3287⁴ APACHE PARK (USA) [96] 4-11-7 C Rae, *not pace to chal frm hfwy*.......................................(16 to 1 op 10 to 1) 5
3128 BASSENHALLY [84] 7-11-4 V Smith, *chsd ldrs to 5th, sn beh*.
....(16 to 1 op 14 to 1) 6
3027⁴ DARING KING [83] 7-11-3 M Richards, *sn rdn and wl beh, tld off whn pld up bef 7th*..................(7 to 1 op 6 to 1) pu
Dist: 9l, 2½l, 8l, 21l, 18l. 4m 57.60s. a 16.60s (7 Ran).
SR: 16/-/8/-/ (Peter R Wilby), R Rowe

3460 **Queen's Cup, An Eastern Counties Hunters' Chase Class H (5-y-o and up) £2,510 3m 110yds.........(4:15)**

DROMIN LEADER 12-11-7 (5*) Mr W Wales, *chsd ldr, lft in ld 4 out, drvn out, hld on wl*.................(7 to 4 fav op 6 to 4) 1
CHERRY CHAP 12-11-5 (7*) Capt D R Parker, *hld up, jnd ldrs 14th, ev ch last, rallied nr line*........(20 to 1 op 12 to 1) 2
SAINT BENET (Ire) (bl) 9-11-5 (7*) Mr J G Townson, *drpd rear 5th, lost tch 14th, styd on wl frm 2 out*..(8 to 1 op 10 to 1) 3
ROMANY ARK 11-11-1 (7*) Mr N M Bell, *drpd rear 4th, hdwy whn mstk 13th, no extr frm 3 out*......(4 to 1 op 5 to 1) 4
JUST JACK 11-11-5 (7*) Mr N Bloom, *in tch, rdn and one pace frm 3 out*....................................(6 to 1 op 7 to 1) 5

TAMMY'S FRIEND (bl) 10-11-5 (7*) Mr J Ferguson, *led, mstk 6th, blun and uns rdr 4 out*..................(7 to 1 op 5 to 1) ur
LYME GOLD (Ire) 8-11-5 (7*) Mr D Keane, *not fluent early, mstk 9th, wknd 14th, pld up bef 2 out*......(9 to 2 op 4 to 1) pu
Dist: Hd, 10l, 1l, 10l. 6m 34.40s. a 37.40s (7 Ran).

(J M Turner), J M Turner

3461 4th Year Of The Betty And Herbert Cassell Memorial Handicap Chase Class F (0-100 5-y-o and up) £4,712 2m 5f 110yds................(4:50)

3138[2] TIM SOLDIER (Fr) [91] 10-11-3 (7*) Mr R Wakley, *hld up in tch, hdwy 13th, led last, rdn out*...........(2 to 1 op 5 to 4) 1
3165[3] WHIPPERS DELIGHT (Ire) [90] 9-11-2 (7*) X Aizpuru, *dsptd ld to 5th, led 14th, hdd last, ran on*..........(3 to 1 op 5 to 2) 2
1321[4] CALL ME ALBI (Ire) [78] 6-10-11 M Richards, *trkd ldrs, led 13th to nxt, ev ch last, not quicken*.......(6 to 1 op 5 to 1) 3
2979 RIO HAINA [95] (v) 12-12-0 T Kent, *hld up, rdn and outpcd frm 13th, tld off*...............................(25 to 1 op 16 to 1) 4
3372[3] PRINZAL [92] 10-11-11 V Smith, *mstks, led and clr 6th, hdd and wknd 13th, pld up bef 2 out*.....(7 to 2 op 4 to 1) pu
3149 BOTTLE BLACK [81] 10-11-0 C Rae, *mstks, tld off whn pld up bef 7th*.......................................(25 to 1 op 20 to 1) pu
3364 KEY PLAYER (Ire) [77] 8-10-10 D O'Sullivan, *second whn pld up aftr 11th, dismounted*...............(7 to 2 op 3 to 1) pu
Dist: 2l, nk, 18l. 5m 34.10s. a 22.10s (7 Ran).

(Ken Dale), Miss A Stokell

3462 St John Ambulance Novices' Handicap Hurdle Class E (0-100 4-y-o and up) £2,885 2m................(5:25)

3110[2] GEISWAY (Can) [81] 7-10-5 (7*) X Aizpuru, *pld hrd early, str run appr last, led nr finish.*
.................................(6 to 5 fav op Evens tchd 5 to 4) 1
2511[4] MUSIC PLEASE [92] 5-11-2 (7*) Mr R Wakley, *hld up, cld frm 5th, led appr last, hdd nr line*.......(11 to 4 op 5 to 2) 2
3049[5] OTTO E MEZZO [97] 5-12-0 V Smith, *led, mstk 3 out, hdd appr last, no extr r-in*.........(3 to 1 op 5 to 1 tchd 10 to 30) 3
3044[7] PRINCIPAL BOY (Ire) [77] 4-10-0 R Rourke, *chsd ldrs, rdn and not quicken 2 out*.................(6 to 1 op 7 to 1) 4
3166 STONE ISLAND [77] 4-10-0 C Rae, *in tch till wknd 2 out, tld off*.......................(20 to 1 op 16 to 1) 5
Dist: Nk, 4l, nk, 18l. 4m 1.50s. a 17.50s (5 Ran).

(Paul Green), N J H Walker

HEREFORD (good to firm)
Monday March 31st
Going Correction: PLUS 0.10 sec. per fur.

3463 Ross-on-Wye Juvenile Novices' Hurdle Class E (4-y-o) £2,402 2m 1f
..................................(2:30)

3280[3] NOBLE COLOURS 10-7 (7*) Mr A Wintle, *made all, rcd keenly, sn wl clr, rdn out r-in.*
................................(7 to 2 op 9 to 2 tchd 5 to 1) 1
3323* SEATTLE ALLEY (USA) 11-3 (3*) E Husband, *hld up, hdwy to chase wnr appr 3 out, drvn bef last, no imprsn.*
.................................(7 to 4 on op 9 to 4 on) 2
3117 SAFECRACKER 11-0 S Wynne, *chsd clr ldr early, struggling frm 5th, tld off*.............(5 to 1 tchd 40 to 1) 3
3044 SPENCER STALLONE 10-9 (5*) D Salter, *hld up, chsd clr ldr 5th till appr 3 out, wknd quickly, tld off.*
.....................................(100 to 1 op 25 to 1) 4
1102 STARTINGO 10-7 (7*) N T Egan, *pld hrd, hld up, chasing clr ldr whn blun 4th, lost pl nxt, struggling in 5th whn f four out.*...................(40 to 1 op 25 to 1) f
2553 KUTMAN (USA) 11-0 G Tormey, *beh, mstk second, struggling 4th, tld off whn pld up bef 2 out, dismounted.*
.................................(7 to 2 tchd 4 to 1) pu
2996 WORTH THE BILL 11-0 Jacqui Oliver, *al beh, tld off whn pld up bef 3 out*.............(100 to 1 op 50 to 1) pu
Dist: 4l, dist, 3l. 3m 52.90s. a 7.90s (7 Ran).
SR: 23/25/-/-/-/

(S G Griffiths), S G Griffiths

3464 James Daly Hunters' Chase Class H (5-y-o and up) £1,537 2m 3f...(3:05)

3279[2] LANDSKER MISSILE 8-11-2 (7*) Mr N Bradley, *prmnt, led 7th, hrd pressed frm 3 out till drvn clr from last.*
.............................(Evens fav op 5 to 4 tchd 6 to 4) 1
3387 FAMILIAR FRIEND (bl) 11-12-3 (7*) Mr P Scott, *in tch, pressed wnr frm 3 out, no extr from last.*
.....................(5 to 2 tchd 9 to 4) 2
BOWL OF OATS (bl) 11-11-7 (7*) Mr A R Price, *sn beh, moderate hdwy 3 out, nvr dngrs*.........(5 to 1 op 4 to 1) 3
LEESWOOD (v) 9-11-7 (7*) Mrs C Ford, *al beh, struggling frm hfwy, nvr a factor*.....................(14 to 1 op 10 to 1) 4
ENCHANTED MAN 13-11-7 (7*) Mr A Wintle, *beh 6th, tld off whn pld up bef 3 out*..................(8 to 1 op 6 to 1) pu
EMRYS 14-11-7 (7*) Miss E J Jones, *chsd ldrs, wknd 8th, tld off whn pld up bef 2 out*........(8 to 1 op 9 to 2) pu

2516 PASTORAL PRIDE (USA) 13-11-9 (5*) Miss P Curling, *led to 7th, lost pl quickly 9th, beh whn pld up bef nxt.*
..................................(7 to 1 op 5 to 1) pu
SHAREEF STAR (bl) 9-11-7 (7*) Mr S Joynes, *not jump wl, al well beh, tld off whn pld up bef 4 out*...(66 to 1 op 50 to 1) pu
DOUBLE THE STAKES (USA) 8-11-7 (7*) Mr J Creighton, *in tch, blun 5th, hdwy to go prmnt 7th, wknd nxt, beh whn pld up bef tenth*..................(12 to 1 tchd 14 to 1) pu
Dist: 15l, 30l, 15l. 4m 39.00s. a 14.00s (9 Ran).

(W J Evans), Mrs Mary Evans

3465 Newtown Handicap Chase Class F (0-100 5-y-o and up) £3,130 3m 1f 110yds.......................(3:40)

2527 JUST ONE CANALETTO [71] (bl) 9-10 (7*) Mr J Goldstein, *al prmnt, outpcd by ldr 4 out, ran on frm 2 out, led cl hme.*
.................................(9 to 1 op 4 to 1) 1
2624[3] HOWGILL [88] (bl) 11-11-6 S Wynne, *trkd ldrs, pckd tenth, led 12th, quickened 4 out, drvn r-in, hdd and no extr cl hme.*
.............(9 to 2 op 3 to 1 tchd 5 to 1) 2
3271* TRUST DEED (USA) [82] (bl) 9-10-9 (5*) D Salter, *hndy, hit 14th, outpcd, styd on und pres frm 2 out, not rch ldrs.*
...................................(5 to 2 op 3 to 1) 3
3277[4] PANT LLIN [72] (bl) 11-10-4 D Walsh, *hld up, feeling pace frm 12th, hdwy and pld up bef 5 out*......(16 to 1 op 10 to 1) pu
3020[6] SOLO GENT [92] 8-11-10 S Burrough, *hld up, mstk 11th, lost tch 14th, pld up bef 2 out.* (13 to 2 op 7 to 1 tchd 9 to 1) pu
3242[3] JASON'S BOY [79] 7-10-4 (7*) M Keighley, *hld up, mstk 6th, niggled alng tenth, pld up bef 2 out.*
.................................(7 to 1 op 12 to 1 tchd 7 to 1) pu
657[*] WARNER'S SPORTS [80] 8-10-12 G Tormey, *led to 12th, sn pushed alng and outpcd, beh whn pld up bef 2 out.*
................................(15 to 8 fav op 7 to 4 tchd 9 to 4) pu
Dist: ½l, 6l. 6m 18.80s. a 12.80s (7 Ran).

(Farmers Racing Partnership), N A Twiston-Davies

3466 Holiday Novices' Selling Chase Class G (4-y-o and up) £2,080 3¼m
...............................(4:15)

2030[4] LE BARON (b) 6-11-2 G Tormey, *made all, mstk 5th, clr to 9th, drvn 3 out, all out*............(5 to 2 op 3 to 1) 1
3136[4] SONG FOR JESS (Ire) 4-10-3 S Wynne, *hld up, chsd wnr 8th, styd on und pres r-in, not rch winner.*
..................(100 to 30 op 3 to 1 tchd 7 to 2) 2
3041 AKIYMANN (USA) (b) 7-11-8 D Walsh, *chsd wnr to 8th, sn beh, kpt on frm 2 out, no imprsn*......(7 to 4 on op 5 to 2) 3
2893 SLIPPERY FIN 5-10-11 S Burrough, *keen hold, hld up, effrt 9th, wknd appr 3 out, tld off.*
..................(7 to 4 fav op 6 to 4 tchd 15 to 8) 4
Dist: 2½l, 3½l, dist. 6m 24.70s. a 22.70s (4 Ran).

(Charles Egerton), C R Egerton

3467 Marlbrook Novices' Chase Class E (5-y-o and up) £2,866 2m......(4:50)

3370[2] TENAYESTELIGN 9-11-2 S Wynne, *hld up in tch, hdwy 8th, led nxt, drw clr 2 out, mstk last, cmftbly.*
.................(6 to 4 op 7 to 4 tchd 11 to 8) 1
3107[3] LUCKY EDDIE (Ire) 6-11-0 G Tormey, *chsd ldr, jmpd slwly 6th, no imprsn frm 2 out*........(5 to 4 on op 2 to 1 tchd 10 to 10 on) 2
3360[6] QUARTER MARKER (Ire) 9-11-0 S Burrough, *led to 9th, sn beh*..............(7 to 1 op 10 to 1 tchd 12 to 1) 3
3281 KNOWING 10-10-9 Miss E J Jones, *cl up, drpd to rear 8th, no dngr aftrwards*...(14 to 1 op 16 to 1 tchd 20 to 1) 4
Dist: 6l, 7l, 5l. 4m 0.30s. a 13.30s (4 Ran).

(G J King), D Marks

3468 Peterstow Novices' Handicap Hurdle Class F (0-95 4-y-o and up) £2,486 2m 3f 110yds................(5:25)

854* KYMIN (Ire) [84] 5-10-11 (7*) Mr A Wintle, *al hndy, led 4 out, drw clr 2 out, drvn out frm last.*
.................................(4 to 1 op 7 to 2 tchd 9 to 2) 1
2748 SAXON MEAD [66] (bl) 7-10-0 G Tormey, *led to 4 out, sn drvn alng and one pace*............(8 to 1 op 7 to 1 tchd 5 to 1) 2
2180[2] BURLINGTON SAM (NZ) [90] 9-11-5 (5*) O Burrows, *prmnt, pushed alng 4 out, sn outpcd, 3rd and hld whn blun 2 out.*
.................................(5 to 2 tchd 7 to 2) 3
2513[8] GO FROLIC [68] 9-9-12[1] (5*) D Salter, *in tch, niggled alng 4 out, sn wknd*................(9 to 1 op 5 to 1) 4
2765 ROYRACE [66] 5-9-7 (7*) Mr J Goldstein, *hld up in rear, nvr nr to chal*.......................(33 to 1 op 20 to 1) 5
2973[5] ARABIAN HEIGHTS [89] 4-11-1 D Walsh, *hld up, hmpd by faller 6th, hdwy to chase ldrs nxt, wknd appr 3 out.*
.................(2 to 1 fav op 9 to 4 tchd 5 to 2) 6
2746 MILLING BROOK [81] 5-11-1 S Wynne, *trkd ldrs till f 6th.*
....f
3267[3] ANOTHER COMEDY [66] 7-9-9[2] (7*) M Keighley, *in rear, tried to refuse and hmpd by faller 6th, sn lost tch, tld off whn pld up bef 2 out*...(10 to 1 op 10 to 1 tchd 12 to 1) pu
WHATASHOT [69] 7-10-3[2] S Burrough, *prmnt, mstk 4th, wknd appr 7th, blun nxt, wl beh whn pld up bef 3 out.*
.................................(33 to 1 op 16 to 1) pu

Dist: 14l, 3½l, 4l, 12l, 7l. 4m 34.60s. a 16.60s (9 Ran).

(Martyn James), J M Bradley

HUNTINGDON (good to firm)
Monday March 31st
Going Correction: NIL

3469 Addenbrookes Dialysis Selling Handicap Hurdle Class G (0-95 4-y-o and up) £2,090 2m 110yds.... (2:00)

3016	EVEZIO RUFO [80] (bl) 5-11-10 K Gaule, *led 1st, trkd ldr till ld ag'n aftr 3 out, pushed clr, cmftbly.*	
	..............(12 to 1 op 8 to 1 tchd 16 to 1)	1
3184³	SHARP THRILL [72] 6-11-2 W Marston, *hdwy frm hfwy, wnt second aftr 2 out, no imprsn on wnr.*	
	.............(11 to 4 fav op 9 to 2 tchd 5 to 1)	2
3265⁵	SUMMER VILLA [67] (bl) 5-10-4 (7*) D Yellowlees, *trkd ldr, al prmnt, one pace aftr 2 out.*	
	..............(10 to 1 op 12 to 1 tchd 14 to 1)	3
3163⁷	NAGOBELIA [79] 9-11-2 (7*) J O'Shaughnessy, *led aftr 1st till hdd aftr 3 out, kpt on one pace clsg stages.*	
	..............(6 to 1 op 9 to 2)	4
3170²	LAURA LYE (Ire) [76] 7-11-6 S McNeill, *cl up till wknd aftr 3 out....................* (7 to 2 op 5 to 2 tchd 4 to 1)	5
2515⁴	JUST FOR A REASON [73] 5-11-3 L O'Hara, *chsd ldrs till wknd aftr 3 out........................* (13 to 2 op 9 to 2)	6
	OUR EDDIE [71] 8-11-1 T Jenks, *chsd ldrs till aftr 6th, sn wknd...............* (14 to 1 op 12 to 1 tchd 16 to 1)	7
	FRET (USA) [64] 7-10-1 (7*) W Walsh, *beh frm 5th, sn tld off.*	
	..............(20 to 1 op 25 to 1 tchd 16 to 1)	8
3295⁷	MAZIRAH [76] 6-11-6 D Morris, *sn beh, tld off aftr 5th.*	
	..............(6 to 1 tchd 7 to 1)	9

Dist: 8l, 2l, ¾l, 6l, 3½l, 8l, 6l, 23l. (Time not taken) (9 Ran).

(T Clarke), N P Littmoden

3470 Sidney Kidney Novices' Chase Class E (5-y-o and up) £3,046 3m.... (2:30)

3133	JASILU (bl) 7-11-9 S McNeill, *led till 4th, led ag'n 8th to 12th, led again r-in, drvn out.*	
	..............(Evens fav op 5 to 4 on tchd 11 to 10)	1
3274⁶	BARON'S HEIR 10-11-2 W Marston, *led 4th to 8th, led ag'n 12th to last, ran on und pres........* (10 to 1 op 8 to 1)	2
2686⁵	PANTARA PRINCE (Ire) 8-11-2 L O'Hara, *chsd ldrs, al in same pos, wknd 2 out.........* (9 to 4 op 2 to 1 tchd 5 to 2)	3
3138³	NIGHT FANCY 9-10-9 (7*) W Walsh, *chsd ldr till lost tch aftr 11th, sn beh, tld off........* (8 to 1 op 5 to 1 tchd 9 to 1)	4
3141²	KATBALLOU 8-11-2 K Gaule, *mstk 5th, sn beh, refused and uns rdr 15th......................* (8 to 1 tchd 10 to 1)	ref

Dist: 1¼l, 20l, 11l. (Time not taken) (5 Ran).

(A G Lay), K C Bailey

3471 Sherriffs Grain Handicap Hurdle Class E (0-110 4-y-o and up) £2,419 2m 5f 110yds................... (3:00)

3244³	SASSIVER (USA) [89] 7-11-4 K Gaule, *chsd ldr till led 7th, rdn last, ran on......* (15 to 8 fav op 6 to 4 tchd 2 to 1)	1
1251⁵	SCUD MISSILE (Ire) [91] 6-11-6 Mr M Armytage, *hld up, hdwy 3 out, ev ch last, no extr r-in.......* (4 to 1 op 3 to 1)	2
3146³	LA MENORQUINA (USA) [95] 7-11-10 S McNeill, *pushed alng appr 2 out..................* (3 to 1 tchd 7 to 2)	3
2193⁵	WANSTEAD (Ire) [82] (bl) 5-10-11 T Jenks, *chsd ldrs till wknd appr 2 out.........* (7 to 2 op 4 to 1 tchd 9 to 2)	4
2741	RONANS GLEN [75] (bl) 10-10-4 W Marston, *led till wknd quickly aftr 7th, pld up bef last.........* (6 to 1 op 8 to 1)	pu

Dist: 1l, 20l, 2½l. (Time not taken) (5 Ran).

(P A Kelleway), P A Kelleway

3472 Sherriffs Grain Handicap Chase Class D (0-125 5-y-o and up) £3,987 2½m 110yds.................... (3:30)

	RABA RIBA [122] 12-11-11 T Jenks, *made all, lft in clr ld 5th, came und pres aftr 2 out, hld on under pressure, all out.*	
	..............(9 to 2 op 7 to 2 tchd 5 to 1)	1
3141*	MR CONDUCTOR (Ire) [108] 6-10-11 S McNeill, *lft in second 5th, hdwy frm 2 out, kpt on strly r-in.*	
	..............(11 to 8 op 6 to 4 tchd 5 to 4)	2
3363²	MISTER DRUM (Ire) [125] 8-12-0 W Marston, *cl second whn blun and uns rdr 5th.*	
	..............(Evens fav op 5 to 4 on tchd 11 to 10)	f

Dist: Hd. (Time not taken) (3 Ran).

(J Spearing), J L Spearing

3473 Huntingdon Association Of Tourism Maiden Hurdle Class E (4-y-o and up) £2,867 2m 5f 110yds....... (4:05)

2771²	SEABROOK LAD 6-11-3 W Marston, *gd prog to ld aftr 3 out, sn clr aftr 2 out, styd on strly....* (2 to 1 fav op 11 to 8)	1
3312⁶	BURN OUT 5-11-3 L O'Hara, *trkd ldrs in 5th, wnt second aftr 3 out, came und pres bef 2 out, no extr r-in.*	
	..............(9 to 4 op 5 to 2 tchd 11 to 4)	2

3299³	SCENIC WATERS (bl) 5-10-12 T Jenks, *led or dsptd ld till clr advantage 4th, hdd aftr 3 out, sn wknd, no extr.*	
	..............(100 to 30 op 5 to 2 tchd 7 to 2)	3
3137⁷	CASTLE MEWS (Ire) 6-10-12 Mr M Armytage, *led or dsptd ld till 4th, one pace frm 3 out.*	
	..............(12 to 1 op 10 to 1 tchd 14 to 1)	4
2775⁹	DERRING FLOSS 7-10-5 (7*) Miss J Wormall, *led or dsptd ld till 4th, wknd frm 3 out........* (10 to 1 op 16 to 1)	5
3241⁶	COUNTER ATTACK (Ire) 6-10-5 (7*) J O'Shaughnessy, *al beh.*	
	..............(25 to 1 op 20 to 1 tchd 33 to 1)	6
2529⁵	RAMSTOWN LAD (Ire) 8-11-3 S McNeill, *chsd ldrs till beh frm hfwy........................* (8 to 1)	7
3265	TOAT CHIEFTAIN 5-11-3 K Gaule, *chsd ldrs to hfwy, sn beh, tld off..................* (33 to 1)	8
2377	ROYAL MIST (Ire) 6-11-3 D Morris, *sn beh tld off frm hfwy, pld up bef 2 out...* (7 to 1 op 8 to 1 tchd 10 to 1)	pu

Dist: 7l, 6l, 12l, 12l, 16l, 12l, dist. (Time not taken) (9 Ran).

(Seabrook Partners), M J Wilkinson

3474 Kidney Foundation Novices' Chase Class E (5-y-o and up) £3,258 2m 110yds.................... (4:35)

1647⁶	ODELL (Ire) 7-11-0 S McNeill, *made all, sn clr, given breather aftr 3 out, pull clear ag'n after 2 out, cmftbly.*	
	..............(11 to 4 op 5 to 2 tchd 3 to 1)	1
3189⁷	QUICK QUOTE 7-11-9 W Marston, *chsd ldr, cld up aftr 3 out, outpcd ag'n after 2 out.....* (Evens fav tchd 11 to 10 on)	2
2853⁷	APPEARANCE MONEY (Ire) 6-10-9 K Gaule, *chsd ldr in 3rd, cld up aftr 3 out, outpcd ag'n after 2 out, sn beh.*	
	..............(9 to 4 tchd 5 to 2 and 2 to 1)	3

Dist: 4l, 30l. (Time not taken) (3 Ran).

(Mrs Christine Davies), K C Bailey

3475 Eastertide Maiden Open National Hunt Flat Class H (4,5,6-y-o) £1,539 2m 110yds.................... (5:05)

	MAD HARRY 5-11-6 S McNeill, *al gng wl, led 3 fs out, pushed clr, ran on well..................* (7 to 4 fav tchd 2 to 1)	1
3176⁴	CUE CALL (Ire) 4-10-9 Miss A Embiricos, *trkd ldrs, gng wl 3 fs out, came und pres one and a half out, one pace ins last.*	
	..............(9 to 4 op 7 to 4)	2
	FRENCH COUNTY (Ire) 5-10-13 (7*) D Yellowlees, *beh till styd on wl fnl 2 fs................* (12 to 1 tchd 14 to 1)	3
2939⁶	LORD OF THE RINGS 5-11-6 K Gaule, *al prmnt, ev ch 3 fs out, fdd fnl 2.................* (4 to 1 tchd 9 to 2)	4
2496⁸	SABU 5-11-6 L O'Hara, *chsd ldrs, led 5 fs out, hdd 3 out, sn wknd...................* (11 to 1 op 14 to 1)	5
2961	COROMANDEL 5-11-1 T Jenks, *cld up 5 fs out, fdd fnl 3.*	
	..............(20 to 1 op 12 to 1)	6
	PIRATE MINSTREL (Ire) 5-11-6 Mr M Armytage, *led one furlong, prmnt till wknd 5 out........* (33 to 1 op 14 to 1)	7
	TROYSTAR 6-11-6 D Morris, *led aftr one furlong till hdd after 5 out, sn wknd........* (25 to 1 op 20 to 1 tchd 33 to 1)	8
2377	SUPER NOVA 6-10-13 (7*) Miss A Dudley, *beh frm hfwy, sn tld off....................* (25 to 1 tchd 33 to 1)	9
3176	KING OF SWING (Ire) 5-11-6 W Marston, *sn beh, wknd quickly fnl 6 fs..................* (20 to 1 tchd 25 to 1)	10

Dist: 4l, 3l, 8l, 3½l, 3l, 19l, 3l, dist, 12l. (Time not taken) (10 Ran).

(W J Ives), K C Bailey

MARKET RASEN (good to firm)
Monday March 31st
Going Correction: MINUS 0.05 sec. per fur.

3476 'Pay And Play Golf' Selling Hurdle Class G (4,5,6-y-o) £1,716 2m 1f 110yds....................... (2:15)

3305³	OUR ROBERT 5-11-4 (3*) F Leahy, *trkd ldrs, hdwy to chase lder 5th, chlgd and hit 2 out, led and blun last, sn hdd, rallied to lead nr finish........................* (5 to 2 op 2 to 1)	1
2982	THEME ARENA 4-10-10 R Johnson, *made most, hit 2 out, sn rdn, hdd briefly last, drvn and headed nr finish.*	
	..............(7 to 4 fav op 11 to 4)	2
2490	DANTES AMOUR (Ire) 6-11-0 R Garritty, *trkd ldrs, hdwy appr 3 out, effrt and ch nxt, sn rdn, edgd lft last and one pace.*	
	..............(25 to 1 op 20 to 1)	3
3317³	NEVER SO BLUE (Ire) 6-11-0 (7*) R Wilkinson, *in tch, hdwy 3 out, rdn alng aftr nxt, one pace last....* (5 to 1 op 9 to 2)	4
3166⁶	LUCY TUFTY 6-11-2 M Brennan, *hld up, hdwy 5th, chsd ldrs 3 out, effrt nxt, sn rdn and one pace.........* (12 to 1)	5
2487	GRANDMAN (Ire) 6-11-7 D J Moffatt, *chsd ldrs, rdn alng bef 3 out, sn wknd.............* (14 to 1 op 12 to 1)	6
3265³	ANALOGICAL 4-10-3 R Supple, *in tch pulling hrd, pushed alng 5th, wknd nxt.................* (8 to 1)	7
2913⁶	MUDLARK (v) 5-10-7 (7*) M Newton, *beh hfwy.*	
	..............(10 to 1 op 9 to 1)	8
2651	PARRY 5-11-0 N Smith, *al rear, lost tch hfwy.......* (33 to 1)	9
3048⁴	HAPPY DAYS BILL 5-11-0 A S Smith, *chsd ldr, rdn alng 4th, sn wknd, tld off 3 out.................* (11 to 1 op 12 to 1)	10
3276⁸	DOUBLE VINTAGE (Ire) (bl) 4-10-8 W Worthington, *al rear, tld off hfwy.....................* (66 to 1)	11

Dist: Hd, 4l, 2l, ½l, 4l, 16l, 2l, dist, 4l. 4m 7.60s. a 6.60s (11 Ran).

SR: 19/8/8/13/7/8/   (Tony Fawcett), J G FitzGerald

3477 Geoffrey Booth Memorial Novices' Chase Class D (5-y-o and up) £3,773 2½m.................... (2:45)

1704² FORMAL INVITATION (Ire) 8-11-2 R Johnson, hld up midfield, smooth hdwy 11th, jnd ldr 3 out, rdn to lft clr.
.............(7 to 4 on op 6 to 4 on tchd 2 to 1 on)   1
2602⁹ BOWLES PATROL (Ire) 5-10-8 R Supple, hld up beh, hit 8th, steady hdwy 4 out, lft second at last.. (33 to 1 op 25 to 1)   2
1692 DESERT BRAVE (Ire) 7-10-9 (7*) R Wilkinson, chsd ldrs, pushed alng 11th, wknd appr 4 out, lft 3rd at last.
.............................(6 to 1 op 4 to 1)   3
3267² HEATHYARDS BOY (bl) 7-11-2 A S Smith, prmnt, rdn alng 9th, wknd appr 4 out, sn beh.......(10 to 1 op 7 to 1)   4
2923 MONKS SOHAM (Ire) 9-10-13 (3*) Michael Brennan, led, jnd and rdn alng 3 out, hdd and f last......(10 to 1 op 7 to 1)   f
2581 QUEEN BUZZARD 9-10-8 (3*) F Leahy, at rear, jmpd slwly 3rd, sn tld off, pld up aftr 4 out.......(33 to 1 tchd 50 to 1)   pu
2776 BUCKET OF GOLD 7-11-2 M Brennan, hit 1st, prmnt, wkng aftr 11th, beh when pld up aftr 4 out. (8 to 1 op 5 to 1)   pu
Dist: Dist, 4l, 13l. 5m 1.00s. a 12.00s (7 Ran).

(The Plough Partnership), D Nicholson

3478 Caravan & Camping Site Handicap Hurdle Class D (0-120 4-y-o and up) £3,043 2m 3f 110yds......... (3:20)

2758⁴ MY CHEEKY MAN [110] 6-11-12 R Johnson, hld up in tch, rdn alng and outpcd aftr 6th, hdwy to chase ldrs 2 out, drvn and styd on to ld last, ran on strly.... (11 to 10 fav op 5 to 4)   1
2238⁴ KEEN TO THE LAST (Fr) [97] (v) 5-10-13 R Garritty, trkd ldrs, hdwy 3 out, chlgd nxt and ev ch, drvn and not quicken last.
...........................(9 to 1 op 7 to 1)   2
3263³ OUR KRIS [110] (bl) 5-11-12 A S Smith, chsd ldrs, hdwy to ld 3 out, hdd last, no extr................(10 to 1)   3
3244⁵ MAJOR YAASI (USA) [92] 7-10-8 R Supple, led, rdn 7th, hdd 3 out, wknd nxt....................(9 to 2 tchd 5 to 1)   4
2656⁸ GO WITH THE WIND [95] 4-10-3 D J Moffatt, chsd ldrs, hdwy 7th, ev ch 2 out, sn rdn, wknd bef last.
.................(5 to 1 op 9 to 2 tchd 14 to 1)   5
3116 DIWALI DANCER [112] 7-12-0 M Brennan, chsd ldr, pushed alng and hit 7th, sn wknd, beh 2 out.
...................(5 to 1 op 12 to 1 tchd 14 to 1)   6
606 RUDI'S PRIDE (Ire) [97] 6-10-13 N Smith, rear, reminders 4th, rdn alng bef 6th, sn wl beh.
.................(16 to 1 op 12 to 1 tchd 20 to 1)   7
Dist: 6l, 2½l, 3l, 10l, 15l, dist. 4m 57.40s. a 7.40s (7 Ran).

SR: 14/-/5/-/   (Mrs A A Shutes), D Nicholson

3479 Victor Lucas Memorial Handicap Chase Class D (0-120 5-y-o and up) £3,878 2m 1f 110yds......... (3:55)

3242⁴ NETHERBY SAID [114] 7-12-0 R Supple, made all, sn clr, jmpd rght and blun 3 out, unchlgd. (2 to 1 on op 9 to 4 on)   1
2486⁴ DARING PAST [100] 7-11-0 R Garritty, chsd wnr frm 5th, rdn alng and blun 4 out, no imprsn aftr.
...........................(7 to 2 op 3 to 1 tchd 4 to 1)   2
2857³ NEWHALL PRINCE [108] (v) 9-11-8 T Eley, chsd wnr to 5th, rdn alng 7th, sn beh, tld off...(3 to 1 tchd 4 to 1)   3
Dist: 22l, 26l. 4m 28.80s. a 14.80s (3 Ran).

(Mrs S Sunter), P Beaumont

3480 Easter Monday 'National Hunt' Novices' Hurdle Class D (5-y-o and up) £3,260 2m 3f 110yds......... (4:30)

2469⁴ PHAR SMOOTHER (Ire) 5-10-11 (3*) F Leahy, trkd ldr, hdwy to ld 3 out, drvn alng aftr nxt, hit last, styd on wl.
...............................(11 to 10 tchd 5 to 4)   1
2996³ MORPHEUS 8-11-0 R Johnson, pld hrd, hld up in tch, hdwy 6th, chlgd 2 out, rdn and edgd rght appr last, not quicken.
.............(11 to 10 op Evens tchd 5 to 4 on)   2
3198⁸ RAISE A DOLLAR 7-11-0 R Supple, led, rdn alng and hdd 3 out, one pace appr nxt...............(12 to 1 op 14 to 1)   3
3332⁶ PEALINGS (Ire) 5-11-0 A S Smith, hld up, hdwy 3 out, rdn bef nxt, no imprsn............(10 to 1 op 8 to 1 tchd 11 to 1)   4
3167 SEABRIGHT SAGA (Ire) 7-11-0 W Worthington, chsd ldg pair, hit 3rd, rdn 3 out, sn wknd............(50 to 1)   5
Dist: 7l, 3l, 1½l, dist. 4m 41.40s. a 11.40s (5 Ran).

(John Smith's Ltd), J G FitzGerald

3481 West Lindsey Easter Cup Class E Novices' Handicap Chase (0-100 5-y-o and up) £3,103 3m 1f... (5:00)

3000 OCEAN LEADER [92] 10-11-10 R Johnson, hld up beh, steady hdwy hfwy, chasing ldrs whn hit 5 out, chlgd 3 out, sn rdn, drvn r-in, led nr finish.
.......................(15 to 2 op 5 to 1 tchd 8 to 1)   1
3005⁴ KARENASTINO [70] 6-9-9 (7*) R Wilkinson, al prmnt, led 9th, rdn alng 3 out, drvn r-in, edgd rght and hdd nr finish.
.......................(3 to 1 op 11 to 4 tchd 10 to 30)   2

3267⁶ ALASKAN HEIR [68] (v) 6-10-10 T Eley, made most to 9th, cl up, rdn alng 5 out, wknd nxt.
.......................(14 to 1 op 12 to 1 tchd 16 to 1)   3
2970⁴ SUVLA BAY (Ire) [80] 9-10-12 M Brennan, trkd ldrs, hdwy 13th, cl up till rdn and wknd appr 3 out.
.......................(3 to 1 op 9 to 2 tchd 5 to 1)   4
2971⁴ SHOOFE (USA) [77] 9-10-9 A S Smith, cl up, rdn alng 5 out, sn wknd.......................(10 to 1 op 9 to 2 tchd 12 to 1)   5
915² THE GALLOPIN'MAJOR (Ire) [90] (bl) 7-11-8 N Smith, hld up in tch, hdwy 14th, cl 4th whn f four out, dead.
.......................(5 to 4 fav op 7 to 4)   f
3259⁴ FAIR ALLY [70] 7-10-0¹ (3*) F Leahy, in tch, rdn alng and lost pl tenth, beh whn pld up bef 13th........(12 to 1 op 10 to 1)   pu
2741 THE MILLMASTER (Ire) [69] 6-10-1 R Supple, beh 6th, pld up bef 13th......................(33 to 1 op 25 to 1)   pu
Dist: ½l, dist, 18l, nk. 6m 25.40s. a 25.40s (8 Ran).

(Sir Peter Gibbings), Mrs D Haine

3482 Market Rasen Standard National Hunt Flat Class H (4,5,6-y-o) £1,318 1m 5f 110yds................(5:30)

LAREDO (Ire) 4-10-5 (7*) C Scudder, hld up midfield, hdwy 5 fs out, led and edgd rght 2 out, drvn clr.....(8 to 1 op 5 to 1)   1
SAWAAB (USA) 5-10-11 (7*) M Newton, chsd ldrs, hdwy 5 fs out, led 3 out, rdn and hdd 2 out, not quicken.
.......................(10 to 1 op 8 to 1)   2
DOUBLE STAR 6-11-4 Mr C Watson, beh, hdwy 3 fs out, styd on wl appr last, nrst finish.........(20 to 1 op 14 to 1)   3
3048⁸ JUNIPER HILL 5-10-11 (7*) L Suthern, pld hrd, made most till rdn and hdd 3 fs out, kpt on one pace...(10 to 1 op 8 to 1)   4
A DAY ON THE DUB 4-10-5 (7*) R McCarthy, hld up in tch, hdwy 3 fs out, 3rd and ev ch whn rdn and took wrong course o'r one out, fnshd 5th, disqualified.
.......................(15 to 2 op 5 to 1 tchd 8 to 1)   5D
TOTEM FOLE 4-10-5 (7*) M Herrington, beh, styd on fnl 3 fs, nvr rch ldrs, fnshd 6th, plcd 5th.
.......................(9 to 2 op 7 to 2 tchd 5 to 1)   5
2503 NIGHT ESCAPADE (Ire) 5-10-6 (7*) R Wilkinson, in tch, rdn o'r 3 fs out, sn wknd................(10 to 1 op 8 to 1)   7
WESTERLY (Ire) 6-11-1 (3*) F Leahy, pld hrd, cl up till rdn and wknd 3 fs out................(4 to 1 op 9 to 4)   8
MOLONYS DRAM 6-10-11 (7*) D Webb, pld hrd early, in tch till rdn and wknd 4 fs out.........(10 to 1 op 12 to 1)   9
2939⁴ DIG FOR GOLD 4-10-5 (7*) R Burns, pld hrd, cl up, effrt and rdn 3 fs out, wknd over 2 out....(Evens fav op 4 to 1)   10
LISLAUGHTIN ABBEY 5-10-11 (7*) W Walsh, chsd ldrs, hdwy on outsd o'r 3 fs out, sn rdn and wknd. (10 to 1 op 8 to 1)   11
2961³ CAPSOFF (Ire) 4-10-10³ Mr J Weymes, keen hold, chsd ldrs, effrt on outsd 4 fs out, rdn and wknd 3 out. (4 to 1 op 9 to 2)   12
WEST LUTTON 5-11-1 (3*) P Midgley, outpcd and beh frm hfwy.......................(10 to 1 op 12 to 1)   13
3082 PLUMPTON WOOD (Ire) 5-10-13 Mr A Brown, al rear, lost tch hfwy, sn tld off.................(10 to 1 op 12 to 1)   14
Dist: 5l, 2½l, ¾l, hd, hd, 2l, ½l, 3½l, 2½l, 3½l. 3m 6.80s. (14 Ran).

(Michael And Gerry Worcester), Noel T Chance

NEWTON ABBOT (firm)
Monday March 31st
Going Correction: MINUS 0.25 sec. per fur.

3483 French Connection Four Years Old Novices' Hurdle Class D £2,871 2m 1f...........................(2:15)

2430⁷ MELT THE CLOUDS (Can) (bl) 10-12 C Maude, trkd ldr frm second, cld 3 out, led nxt, sn clr.
.......................(7 to 4 on tchd 13 to 8 on)   1
3280⁷ WHITE PLAINS (Ire) 10-5 (7*) B Moore, led to 2 out, one pace aftr.......................(9 to 4 op 2 to 1 tchd 5 to 2)   2
3169⁴ GENEREUX 10-7 (5*) Chris Webb, trkd ldr to second, stdly lost tch frm hfwy..........(9 to 4 on tchd 4 to 1)   3
Dist: 7l, 20l. 4m 1.00s. a 12.00s (3 Ran).

(Promo-Sherring Ltd), M C Pipe

3484 Hill Breeze Novices' Chase Class E (5-y-o and up) £3,182 2m 5f 110yds ....(2:50)

2436² DECYBORG (Fr) 6-11-8 C Maude, made all, jmpd wl, clr frm second, unchlgd.
.......................(5 to 2 on op 2 to 1 on tchd 3 to 1 on)   1
2921 COUNTRY KEEPER 9-11-2 J Frost, jmpd slwly second, wnt second wth circuit to go, no ch with wnr.
.......................(9 to 4 op 6 to 4 tchd 5 to 2)   2
3107⁴ RUSTIC FLIGHT 10-10-9 A S Smith, jmpd rght and slwly, chsd wnr till circuit to go, tld off, broke blood vessel.
.......................(9 to 1 op 8 to 1 tchd 14 to 1)   3
Dist: Dist, dist. 5m 21.60s. a 19.60s (3 Ran).

(Terry Neill), M C Pipe

3485 Terrace Restaurant Selling Handicap Hurdle Class G (0-95 4-y-o and up) £1,932 2¾m.............(3:25)

1915 BOWDEN SURPRISE [60] 7-10-0 V Slattery, *hld up in tch, rdn to go second 3 out, led nxt, drvn out*... (16 to 1 op 10 to 1) 1

451^{4} SUKAAB [75] 12-10-10 (5*) Chris Webb, *hld up, hdwy 3 out, ev ch nxt, no extr r-in*.................... (4 to 1 op 8 to 1) 2

2977^{4} JAY EM ESS (NZ) [83] 8-11-9 R Greene, *hld up, hdwy 4 out, wknd appr 2 out*..... (11 to 8 fav op 5 to 2 tchd 11 to 4) 3

2872 OCTOBER BREW (USA) [84] (bl) 7-11-3 (7*) B Moore, *hld up in tch, led 4 out, drvn clr, wknd and hdd 2 out.* .... (15 to 2 op 5 to 1 tchd 8 to 1) 4

3405 CASTLEBAY LAD [60] 14-9-7 (7*) J Parkhouse, *led till appr 3rd, led nxt to 4 out, wknd next*........ (33 to 1 op 20 to 1) 5

3257^{6} SEA BARN [70] 14-10-10 Miss M Coombe, *rcd wide, trkd ldr, led appr 3rd, hdd nxt, wknd 3 out.* .... (100 to 30 op 5 to 2 tchd 7 to 2) 6

3275 CONCINNITY (USA) [66] (bl) 8-10-0^{1} (7*) C R Weaver, *trkd ldrs till wknd appr 4 out*...................... (14 to 1 op 9 to 1) 7

3110 DORMY THREE [81] 7-11-7 C Maude, *prmnt till wknd 4 out.* ....(5 to 1 op 4 to 1 tchd 7 to 1) 8

3275^{4} RORY'M (Ire) [60] (bl) 8-9-7 (7*) M Griffiths, *tld off 4th.* .... (25 to 1 op 20 to 1) 9

Dist: 2l, 6l, 2l, 7l, ½l, 6l, 1½l, 23l. 5m 15.90s. a 14.90s (9 Ran).

(R J Baker), R J Baker

3486 Manicou Restaurant Mares' Only Handicap Chase Class F (0-105 5-y-o and up) £2,566 2m 110yds.. (4:00)

2244 MISTRESS ROSIE [69] 10-10-7 (5*) C Webb, *al in tch, led 6th, drw clr frm 3 out*.......... (9 to 2 op 6 to 1 tchd 9 to 1) 1

3143^{5} WALK IN THE WOODS [72] 10-11-1 R Greene, *led to 6th, lost tch appr 3 out*............(9 to 4 op 11 to 4 tchd 2 to 1) 2

3204^{9} DUBELLE [81] 7-11-10 C Maude, *trkd ldr to 6th, losing tch whn hit six out, pld up bef nxt*.... (9 to 4 on op 3 to 1 on) pu

Dist: 14l. 4m 1.20s. a 3.20s (3 Ran).

SR: 11/-/-/ (Martin Hill), M Hill

3487 Bank Holiday Monday Novices' Handicap Hurdle Class E (0-100 4-y-o and up) £2,431 2m 1f....... (4:35)

2886* MELLOW MASTER [85] 4-11-10 C Maude, *al prmnt, led 3 out, jmpd lft last 2, eased r-in.* (15 to 8 op 2 to 1 tchd 9 to 4) 1

3268 THE BREWER [72] 5-11-0 (5*) Chris Webb, *hld up in tch, hdwy to ld appr 5th, hdd 3 out, no imprsn frm 2 out.* ....(5 to 1 op 3 to 1) 2

3268^{9} MOONLIGHT ESCAPADE (Ire) [73] 6-11-6 V Slattery, *hld up, rdn 5th, no hdwy appr 2 out*.............(4 to 1 tchd 6 to 1) 3

3295^{5} PRINCE OF SPADES [66] 5-10-13 R Greene, *in tch till wknd appr 2 out*............ (6 to 4 fav op 7 to 2 tchd 4 to 1) 4

2982 ACHILL PRINCE (Ire) [62] 6-10-2 (7*) M Griffiths, *pld hrd, led till wknd quickly and hdd appr 5th, pulled up bef nxt.* .... (12 to 1 op 16 to 1 tchd 20 to 1) pu

3280^{6} GREEN BOPPER (USA) [75] 4-11-0 J Frost, *hld up in tch, wknd 3 out, pld up bef nxt*............. (13 to 2 op 3 to 1) pu

Dist: 2½l, 4l, 3½l. 4m 2.70s. a 13.70s (6 Ran).

(Paul Green), N J H Walker

3488 Teign Suite Handicap Hurdle Class D (0-125 4-y-o and up) £3,346 2¾m .... (5:10)

2373 HOLDIMCLOSE [115] 7-11-11 J Frost,.................... 1

Walked over. (Time not taken) (1 Ran).

SR: -/ (Mrs C Loze), R G Frost

PLUMPTON (good to firm)
Monday March 31st
Going Correction: PLUS 0.10 sec. per fur.

3489 Jevington Juvenile Novices' Handicap Hurdle Class E (0-100 4-y-o) £2,364 2½m.................. (2:30)

2807^{5} ANNA SOLEIL (Ire) [100] 11-7 (7*) D Thomas, *al cl up, led appr 3 out, rdn out*............(9 to 2 op 7 to 2 tchd 11 to 2) 1

3150 PALAMON (USA) [85] 10-13 J R Kavanagh, *hld up, hdwy 4 out, sn chsd wnr, ev ch r-in, no extr nr finish*........ (4 to 1) 2

2828^{7} BEN BOWDEN [92] 11-3 (3*) L Aspell, *led, hdd briefly 7th, headed appr 3 out, sn rdn and one pace.* ....(4 to 1 op 3 to 1 tchd 9 to 2) 3

2423^{8} BIGWIG (Ire) [73] (v) 9-8 (7*) M Batchelor, *in tch, hrd rdn 4 out, ch nxt, sn outpcd*.................... (20 to 1 tchd 33 to 1) 4

3323^{3} VERONICA FRANCO [75] 10-0 (3*) Sophie Mitchell, *cl up, led briefly 7th, wknd aftr 4 out, btn whn blun nxt, tld off.* .... (20 to 1 op 14 to 1 tchd 25 to 1) 5

3265^{6} EL BARDADOR (Ire) [72] (bl) 10-0 P Holley, *hld up in tch, btn whn blun 4 out, tld off*.. (16 to 1 op 12 to 1 tchd 20 to 1) 6

3239^{2} ESKIMO KISS (Ire) [79] (v) 10-7 D Gallagher, *jmpd rght, hld up beh, not fluent drvn aftr 8th, sn btn, tld off whn pld up bef 2 out.* ....(11 to 4 fav op 7 to 2 tchd 5 to 2) pu

3325^{2} YELLOW DRAGON (Ire) [82] 10-10 A Larnach, *refused to race*.................................... (4 to 1 op 11 to 2) r

Dist: ½l, 13l, 20l, 11l, 6l. 4m 54.10s. a 17.10s (8 Ran).

(M G St Quinton), O Sherwood

3490 Easter Selling Handicap Chase Class G (0-90 5-y-o and up) £2,385 2m.......................... (3:00)

3174^{7} RUSTIC GENT (Ire) [65] 9-10-6 J R Kavanagh, *cl up, led aftr 3 out, mstk and lft clr nxt, easily*......(10 to 1 tchd 12 to 1) 1

2798^{7} MR BEAN [87] 7-12-0 A Larnach, *in tch, rdn and outpcd 4 out, no imprsn whn lft modest second 2 out.* ....(7 to 4 op 6 to 4 tchd 2 to 1) 2

1941^{6} DAWN CHANCE [77] 11-11-4 P Holley, *cl up, mstks 6th and 9th, wknd appr 3 out*............(6 to 4 fav tchd 9 to 8) 3

3324 BRIGHT SEASON [61] (bl) 9-10-1^{6} (7*) Gordon Gallagher, *f 1st*.............................. (50 to 1 op 20 to 1) f

3191 RISEUPWILLIEREILLY [60] 11-9-8 (7*) C Rafter, *led, hdd aftr 3 out, cl second whn mstk and uns rdr nxt.* (7 to 2 op 3 to 1) ur

3191^{3} FATTASH (USA) [68] (bl) 5-10-1^{3} (3*) L Aspell, *al beh, tld off whn pld up bef 9th*........(8 to 1 op 6 to 1 tchd 9 to 1) pu

Dist: 12l, 4l. 4m 0.90s. a 8.90s (6 Ran).

SR: 5/15/1/ (Mrs A Emanuel), Mrs L C Jewell

3491 Alfriston Novices' Hurdle Class E (5-y-o and up) £2,742 2m 1f.....(3:30)

3022 REVERSE THRUST 6-10-7 (7*) M Clinton, *hld up, rapid hdwy 7th, led and hit last, all out.* ....(14 to 1 op 12 to 1 tchd 16 to 1) 1

3139^{4} ALKA INTERNATIONAL 5-10-11 (3*) L Aspell, *trkd ldrs, led 7th, hdd last, ev ch r-in, jst hld*.......... (7 to 2 op 2 to 1) 2

3334^{5} REAL MADRID 6-10-7 (7*) M Batchelor, *hld up beh ldrs, chlgd aftr 7th, mstk 3 out, ev ch nxt, one pace appr last.* ....(6 to 1 tchd 7 to 1) 3

3290^{6} CLOCK WATCHERS 9-10-11 (3*) Sophie Mitchell, *led briefly second, led aftr 5th till 7th, sn outpcd, styd on frm last.* ....(16 to 1 op 20 to 1 tchd 25 to 1) 4

3103^{4} SUN OF SPRING 7-11-0 J R Kavanagh, *trkd ldrs, pushed alng aftr 7th, sn outpcd*...........(7 to 4 fav op 11 to 4) 5

2614^{5} ILANDRA (Ire) 5-10-9 D Gallagher, *cl up till wknd aftr 4 out.* ....(9 to 2 op 6 to 1 tchd 7 to 1) 6

3022 PEARL HART 5-10-2 (7*) Martin Smith, *trkd ldrs to 7th, tld off.* .... (33 to 1 op 14 to 1) 7

BLASTED 5-11-0 P Holley, *hld up beh, effrt 6th, sn no imprsn, tld off*................................(10 to 1 op 6 to 1) 8

3091^{6} WELSH WIZZARD 5-10-7 (7*) Mr P O'Keeffe, *led briefly 1st, in tch till reminders 6th, sn btn, tld off.* (33 to 1 op 16 to 1) 9

3334^{9} SPECTACLE JIM 8-10-7 (7*) Gordon Gallagher, *hld up, mstk 3rd, lost tch 6th, tld off*.............. (33 to 1 op 20 to 1) 10

GLOBAL DANCER 6-10-7 (7*) W Greatrex, *pld hrd, led aftr second, clr nxt, wknd and hdd after 5th, lost tch and pulled up after next.* ....(14 to 1 op 10 to 1 tchd 16 to 1 and 20 to 1) pu

Dist: Sht-hd, 5l, ¾l, 7l, 15l, 16l, 14l, 1½l, 20l. 4m 9.40s. a 12.40s (11 Ran).

(Mrs M N Tufnell), P R Hedger

3492 Abergavenny Challenge Cup Novices' Handicap Chase Class F (0-95 5-y-o and up) £2,959 3m 1f 110yds .... (4:00)

3046^{5} DREAM LEADER (Ire) [72] 7-11-3 D Gallagher, *hld up, not fluent 12th, led 16th (5 out), drw clr frm 3 out, easily.* ....(9 to 4 op 2 to 1 tchd 5 to 2) 1

2768 SIDE BAR [60] (v) 7-10-2 (3*) L Aspell, *led 3rd till hdd 5 out, ev ch nxt, outpcd frm 3 out.* ....(14 to 1 op 20 to 1 tchd 33 to 1 and 40 to 1) 2

3294^{3} PINOCCIO [62] 10-10-4 (3*) Sophie Mitchell, *led to 3rd, cl up till wknd 15th, tld off*.................. (7 to 1 op 12 to 1) 3

2666^{4} CALL ME RIVER (Ire) [79] 9-11-10 J R Kavanagh, *hld up in cl tch whn f 9th*...................... (5 to 4 on op 11 to 10) f

3324^{3} NAUTICAL GEORGE (Ire) [77] 7-11-8 P Holley, *hld up in tch, btn whn blun and uns rdr 4 out*........(6 to 1 op 11 to 4) ur

Dist: 28l, 16l. (Time not taken) (5 Ran).

(Mike Roberts), M J Roberts

3493 Holiday Maiden Chase Class F (5-y-o and up) £2,678 2¼m..........(4:30)

3195^{2} NORMARANGE (Ire) 7-11-7 J R Kavanagh, *led briefly 1st, in cl tch, lft in ld 5 out, drvn out*....(2 to 1 on tchd 6 to 4 on) 1

3271 RIVER GALA (Ire) 7-11-7 P Holley, *in cl tch, lft close second 5 out, drvn and ch appr 2 out, kpt on.* ....(7 to 2 op 4 to 1 tchd 5 to 1) 2

3293^{4} FRUIT TOWN (Ire) 8-11-4 (3*) L Aspell, *in tch whn f 8th.* .... (14 to 1 op 12 to 1 tchd 20 to 1) f

SHANAGORE HILL (Ire) 7-11-7 A Larnach, *led aftr 1st, f 5 out, dead*...............................(9 to 2 op 3 to 1) f

Dist: 4l. 4m 33.50s. a 12.50s (4 Ran).

(D Curtis), D M Grissell

3494 'Manhattan Boy' Handicap Hurdle Class E (0-110 5-y-o and up) £2,637 2½m........................ (5:00)

3119^{4} NIGHT IN A MILLION [79] 6-9-13^{2} (3*) L Aspell, *trkd ldr, led 7th, jnd 2 out, ran on gmely*............(7 to 1 op 8 to 1) 1

2356[8] BON VOYAGE (USA) [92] (bl) 5-10-13 J R Kavanagh, *hld up in tch, smooth hdwy 3 out, chlgd ldr nxt, ev nr extr nr finish*................................. (4 to 1 tchd 6 to 1) 2
3386[6] SMUGGLER'S POINT (USA) [107] 7-12-0 P Holley, *led to 7th, sn drvn alng, one pace frm 3 out.*
.........................(7 to 2 op 3 to 1 tchd 9 to 1) 3
3027 AN SPAILPIN FANACH (Ire) [86] (bl) 8-10-4 (3*) Sophie Mitchell, *trkd ldrs, pushed alng and outpcd frm 3 out.*
.... (9 to 1 op 7 to 1 tchd 10 to 1) 4
3016[4] KAREN'S TYPHOON (Ire) [86] 7-11-9 (7*) M Batchelor, *hld up in cl tch, drvn alng appr 8th, sn outpcd*............ (7 to 1) 5
3295[4] KELLY MAC [93] 7-11-0 D Gallagher, *hld up beh ldrs, niggled alng appr 8th, stuggling to get on terms aftr, btn after 3 out.*
.................................(11 to 8 fav op 6 to 4 tchd 15 to 8) 6
3295[6] BAYLORD PRINCE (Ire) [79] 9-10-0 Mr K Goble, *al beh, drvn alng 8th, nvr on terms.*.............. (50 to 1 op 20 to 1) 7
Dist: 2½l, 10l, 4l, 9l, ¾l, 6l. 4m 53.70s. a 16.70s (7 Ran).

(Leith Hill Chasers), S Woodman

TOWCESTER (good to firm)
Monday March 31st
Going Correction: MINUS 0.10 sec. per fur.

3495 Lisa Holman 18th Birthday Selling Handicap Hurdle Class G (0-95 4-y-o and up) £2,034 2m............(2:15)

3292[4] ANIF (USA) [58] 6-10-11 D Skyrme, *chsd ldrs, swtchd rght to chal last, ran on to take ld cl hme whn leader hng badly lft.*
.... (5 to 1 op 9 to 2 tchd 11 to 2) 1
3106[4] PAULTON [65] (bl) 4-9-9 (5*) S Ryan, *trkd ldrs till led appr 2 out, hng badly lft r-in and hdd nr finish.*
.... (9 to 2 op 6 to 1 tchd 13 to 2) 2
1969 CAPTAIN TANDY (Ire) [70] 8-10-13 T Reed, *trkd ldr till led appr 3 out, hdd approaching 2 out and sn btn.*
.... (10 to 1 op 8 to 1 tchd 11 to 1) 3
3283* DERRYBELLE [81] 6-11-3 (7*) Mr S Durack, *hld up, hdwy 5th, mstk 3 out, sn no extr....* (3 to 1 op 11 to 4 tchd 7 to 2) 4
971[7] TIMELY EXAMPLE (USA) [68] 6-10-11 Gary Lyons, *al beh.*
.... (10 to 1 op 7 to 1 tchd 11 to 1) 5
3170[*] FLASH IN THE PAN (Ire) [87] 4-11-8 W McFarland, *beh, rdn alng aftr 3rd, nvr a factor after.*
.... (9 to 4 fav op 2 to 1 tchd 5 to 2 and 2 to 1) 6
2030[8] CATWALKER (Ire) [57] 6-10-0 S Curran, *beh and rdn 4th, sn btn*.............................. (8 to 1 op 8 to 1 tchd 9 to 1) 7
3184 ERNEST ARAGORN [57] (v) 8-10-0 M Ranger, *led, mstk 1st, pld hrd and sn wl clr, hit 5th, hdd and wknd quickly appr 3 out, pld up bef nxt.*...... (25 to 1 op 14 to 1 tchd 33 to 1) pu
Dist: Sht-hd, 8l, 20l, 6l, 3l, 20l. 3m 50.90s. a 7.90s (8 Ran).

(Jack Joseph), J Joseph

3496 Hartwell Landrover Novices' Handicap Chase Class E (0-100 5-y-o and up) £3,137 2m 110yds....... (2:45)

3284[2] SLEAZEY [72] 6-11-10 S Curran, *led to second, led ag'n 5th, hdd 2 out, rallied und pres to ld again r-in, all out.*
.... (5 to 4 on Evens tchd 11 to 10) 1
3191 FULL SHILLING (USA) [60] (bl) 8-10-5 (7*) Mr S Durack, *led second to 5th, styd chasing wnr till led ag'n und pres 2 out, hdd r-in, one pace.*.....................(5 to 2 op 4 to 1) 2
3370[4] COPPER CABLE [70] 10-11-8 M Ranger, *al in 3rd and jumping hesitently, lost tch frm 4 out.*..... (4 to 1 op 9 to 4) 3
3370 HIGHLAND FLAME [60] 8-10-12 B Clifford, *tld off frm 4th.*
.... (9 to 1 op 5 to 1 tchd 10 to 1) 4
Dist: 1l, dist, dist. 4m 4.50s. a 7.50s (4 Ran).
SR: 5/

(J G O'Neill), J G O'Neill

3497 Philip Brangwyn Memorial Handicap Chase Class E (0-115 5-y-o and up) £3,455 3m 1f................ (3:15)

3101[2] MERLINS DREAM (Ire) [114] 8-12-0 J A McCarthy, *trkd ldr, chlgd 4 out, led nxt, drvn out...........* (7 to 2 tchd 4 to 1) 1
3264[3] LAY IT OFF (Ire) [86] 8-10-3 S Curran, *led to 3 out, lost second appr 2 out, rallied to chase wnr ag'n r-in, no extr.*
.... (6 to 1 op 14 to 1) 2
3115[5] DANGER BABY [98] (v) 7-10-5 (7*) Mr S Durack, *chsd ldrs frm 6th, styd on same pace from 3 out.....* (5 to 1 op 7 to 2) 3
3264* SHEELIN LAD (Ire) [92] 9-10-6 T Reed, *hld up, hit 3rd, hdwy 12th, chsd wnr appr 2 out till wknd approaching last.*
.... (3 to 1 fav op 9 to 4 tchd 7 to 2) 4
2434[5] STEEPLE JACK [86] (bl) 10-9-9 (5*) S Ryan, *hit second, chsd ldrs 5th, lost pl 12th, styd on ag'n frm 2 out.*
.... (33 to 1 op 20 to 1) 5
3132[7] HAWAIIAN SAM (Ire) [105] 7-11-5 G Crone, *hit 5th, blun nxt, hdwy 9th, hit next, wknd 4 out.......* (7 to 2 tchd 3 to 1) 6
2956 WOODLANDS GENHIRE [89] (v) 12-10-3 W McFarland, *beh and rdn alng frm 8th.......*(33 to 1 op 20 to 1) 7
3366 HARRISTOWN LADY [103] (bl) 10-11-3 B Clifford, *chsd ldrs till wknd tenth, sn tld off........* (7 to 2 tchd 4 to 1) 8
Dist: 3l, 1½l, 4l, 9l, 15l, 14l, 30l. 6m 16.60s. a 4.60s (8 Ran).
SR: 29/-/8/-/-/

(W S Watt), O Sherwood

3498 Penrhyn Handicap Hurdle Class F (0-105 4-y-o and up) £2,372 3m
.... (3:50)

3016[5] ROSS DANCER (Ire) [85] 5-11-3 (3*) J Magee, *led till appr second, led ag'n 5th, rdn 2 out, hld on wl.*
.... (7 to 1 op 8 to 1 tchd 9 to 1) 1
3140[4] STAC-POLLAIDH [77] 7-10-12 W McFarland, *sn in tch, chsd wnr appr 2 out, ev ch last, styd on but not quite get up.*
.... (9 to 4 fav op 2 to 1 tchd 5 to 2) 2
3285[5] CABOCHON [85] 10-11-6 D Skyrme, *chsd ldrs till outpcd 4 out, ran on ag'n frm nxt, chlgd and hit 2 out, one pace.*
.... (8 to 1 op 4 to 1 tchd 10 to 1) 3
3272[6] DERRING BRIDGE [80] 7-11-1 J A McCarthy, *chsd ldrs, chlgd 8th to 4 out, wknd appr 2 out.........* (9 to 2 op 5 to 2) 4
2628 STERLING FELLOW [80] (v) 4-9-12 (7*) Mr S Durack, *jmpd slwly 1st, mstk 7th, hdwy appr 8th, one pace frm 2 out.*
.... (6 to 1 op 7 to 1 tchd 9 to 1) 5
1801 CROWN IVORY (NZ) [74] 9-10-9 S Fox, *hdwy 7th, no headway frm 3 out.......................* (12 to 1 tchd 14 to 1) 6
3162[5] RIMOUSKI [89] 9-11-10 Gary Lyons, *hdwy 7th, chsd ldrs aftr 4 out, wknd 2 out.................* (100 to 30 op 7 to 1) 7
3171[5] SUMMER HAVEN [69] 8-9-11 (7*) Mr L Baker, *led appr second, hdd 5th, wknd 8th, tld off whn pld up bef 3 out.*
.... (16 to 1 op 25 to 1) pu
Dist: Nk, 1¼l, 2l, ½l, 5l, 22l. 6m 0.50s. a 18.50s (8 Ran).

(Gerard P O'Loughlin), J S Moore

3499 23rd Year Of The Schilizzi 1906 Sixty Years Commemorative Challenge Cup Hunters' Chase Class H (5-y-o and up) £1,059 2¾m.........(4:25)

3018* TEAPLANTER 14-12-0 (5*) Mr B Pollock, *led to 7th, styd tracking ldr, chlgd 4 out, led, blun and hdd nxt, led ag'n appr last, stayed on gmely...........*(9 to 4 on op 2 to 1 on) 1
3279[4] TUFFNUT GEORGE 10-11-7 (7*) Mr A Phillips, *trkd wnr, chlgd 6th, led nxt, hdd 3 out but sn lft in frnt ag'n, headed 2 out, soon btn.......................* (5 to 2 op 3 to 1) 2
3288[2] HICKELTON LAD 13-11-7 (7*) Mr S Durack, *al 3rd, lost tch 8th, mstk nxt, tld off.......*(7 to 1 op 4 to 1 tchd 5 to 1) 3
Dist: 19l, dist. 5m 37.70s. a 11.70s (3 Ran).

(R G Russell), Miss C Saunders

3500 Duncote Maiden Hurdle Class F (4-y-o and up) £2,706 2m........ (4:55)

3296[3] RING OF VISION 11-3-2 (3*) J Magee, *hdwy to track ldrs 5th, chlgd 2 out, sn led, drvn out.......*(9 to 4 tchd 11 to 4) 1
3044[5] JAMAICAN FLIGHT (USA) 4-10-13 M Ranger, *steady hdwy 3 out, chsd wnr r-in, no extr............*(25 to 1 op 20 to 1) 2
2952[5] RISING DOUGH (Ire) 5-11-5 W McFarland, *steady hdwy 3 out, chlgd last, one pace.....*(3 to 1 op 7 to 2 tchd 11 to 4) 3
GIPSY GEOF (Ire) 6-11-5 T Reed, *steady hdwy on bit to track ldrs aftr 3 out, led appr nxt, hdd approaching last, sn btn.*
.... (16 to 1 op 12 to 1) 4
1521[2] ARADIA'S DIAMOND 6-10-9 (5*) S Ryan, *chsd ldrs till wknd aproaching 2 out.........*(9 to 1 op 7 to 1 tchd 8 to 1) 5
2959 MR DARCY 5-11-5 J A McCarthy, *wth ldr, led 3rd, hdd 5th, rdn 3 out, sn wknd...............*(2 to 1 fav op 7 to 4) 6
2553 SASSY STREET (Ire) 4-10-13 B Clifford, *pld hrd, led second to nxt, styd with ldr till wknd 3 out......*(12 to 1 op 14 to 1) 7
RED VIPER 5-11-5 Mr A Kinane, *prmnt, led 5th till hdd appr 2 out, wknd rpdly.....................*(25 to 1 op 16 to 1) 8
3017 SWIFT POKEY 7-10-12 (7*) Mr S Durack, *beh frm 4th.*
.... (50 to 1 op 33 to 1 tchd 66 to 1) 9
2807 PORT VALENSKA (Ire) (bl) 4-10-13 Miss L Allan, *chsd ldrs 4th, sn wknd, tld off...* (66 to 1 op 50 to 1 tchd 100 to 1) 10
Dist: 1¾l, 4l, hd, 18l, 1¾l, 8l, 6l, 6l, dist. 3m 51.50s. a 8.50s (10 Ran).

(Harold Bray), C J Mann

UTTOXETER (good to firm)
Monday March 31st
Going Correction: PLUS 0.40 sec. per fur.

3501 Jenkinsons Caterers Juvenile Novices' Hurdle Class E (4-y-o) £2,200 2½m 110yds..................(2:15)

3150[5] HAYAAIN 11-4 T J O'Sullivan, *settled 3rd, cl up frm hfwy, led 3 out, strly pressed last, styd on strongly und pres.*
.... (5 to 2 on op 3 to 1 on) 1
1861[8] ARROGANT HEIR 10-12 Derek Byrne, *hld up in rear, hdwy 4 out, chlgd appr last, ran on strly......* (16 to 1 op 14 to 1) 2
2898[3] EZANAK (Ire) 10-12 J Culloty, *pressed ldr, pushed alng and outpcd aftr 4 out, rallied 2 out, styd on stdly.*
.... (7 to 2 op 11 to 4) 3
3168[3] FORMIDABLE PARTNER (v) 10-7 (5*) Mr R Thornton, *pld hrd, sn led, drvn and hdd 3 out, lost tch frm nxt.*
.... (5 to 1 op 5 to 1 tchd 11 to 2) 4
Dist: Nk, 2½l, 20l. 4m 54.70s. a 15.70s (4 Ran).
SR: 15/9/6/-/

(Quicksilver Racing Partnership), K C Bailey

486

3502 1152 XTRA AM Selling Handicap Chase Class G (0-90 5-y-o and up) £2,358 2m 5f................ (2:50)

3404[4] GOOD FOR A LAUGH [80] 13-11-2 (5*) O Burrows, *chsd ldrs, mstk 9th, led 3 out, clr betw last 2, ran on wl.* ....(7 to 2 op 5 to 2) 1
3267[4] ASTRAL INVASION (USA) [71] 6-10-7 (5*) Mr R Thornton, *hndy, led hfwy till mstk and hdd 3 out, hit nxt, sn one pace.* ....(12 to 1 op 10 to 1) 2
3404 FAIRY PARK [84] (v) 12-11-11 Mr M Munrowd, *in tch, chsd ldrs frm 5 out, no extr from 3 out*......(11 to 1 op 6 to 1) 3
2798[5] SAYMORE [83] 11-11-7 (3*) Guy Lewis, *midfield, pushed alng aftr 5 out, outpcd frm nxt*............ (4 to 1 op 5 to 2) 4
3000[4] BURNTWOOD MELODY [60] (bl) 6-9-8 (7*) T Hagger, *hld up, beh whn mstk tenth (water), nvr a factor.* (6 to 1 op 5 to 1) 5
3138[6] ROYAL SQUARE (Can) [84] 11-11-11 D Leahy, *trkd ldrs till drvn alng 5 out, fdd*.................(20 to 1 op 14 to 1) 6
855[2] TURPIN'S GREEN [71] 14-10-12 J Culloty, *slight ld to hfwy, lost tch aftr 5 out, sn btn*..........(11 to 4 fav op 5 to 1) 7
3358[4] LAMBRINI (Ire) [67] (bl) 7-10-8 F Perratt, *midfield, hit 4th, struggling 6 out, tld off*..............(16 to 1 op 14 to 1) 8
2776[5] PANDORA'S PRIZE [65] 11-10-6[12] (7*) S Lycett, *sn wl beh, tld off*......(14 to 1 op 12 to 1 tchd 10 to 1 and 16 to 1) 9
3361[2] RYTON RUN [81] 12-11-8 T J O'Sullivan, *cl up till lost pl hfwy, beh whn pld up 5 out*..... (7 to 1 op 8 to 1 tchd 10 to 1) pu
1980[9] APPLIANCEOFSCIENCE [74] 10-11-1 Derek Byrne, *pckd second, beh whn pld up 4th*..................(20 to 1) pu
2873 REBEL PRIEST (Ire) [60] 7-10-1 G Upton, *beh frm 4th, tld off whn pld up tenth*.................(9 to 1 op 6 to 1) pu

Dist: 15l, 5l, nk, 1½l, 7l, 9l, 27l, 2½l. 5m 15.30s. a 17.30s (12 Ran).
SR: 4/-/-/-/-/-/ (Derek Walker), A G Hobbs

3503 John Partridge English Clothing Novices' Handicap Hurdle Class E (0-100 5-y-o and up) £2,568 3m 110yds...................... (3:25)

2959[2] EL FREDDIE [93] 7-11-10 G Upton, *set steady pace, quickened 5 out, strly pressed frm 2 out, hld on gmely.* ....(5 to 2 fav op 9 to 4 tchd 11 to 4) 1
3268[6] BEECHFIELD FLYER [85] 6-10-13 (3*) Guy Lewis, *hld up, clr order hfwy, pressed wnr frm 3 out, ev ch last, styd on strly.* .... (12 to 1 op 10 to 1) 2
3268[4] CLIBURNEL NEWS (Ire) [79] 7-10-3 (7*) E Greehy, *hld up, hdwy fnl circuit, chsd ldrs 3 out, one pace frm nxt, fdd flt.* ....(8 to 1 op 6 to 1) 3
3016[3] HANCOCK [77] 5-10-8 F Perratt, *not fluent in rear, some hdwy appr 3 out, sn no extr*............(7 to 2 op 5 to 1) 4
3160[6] MR CHRISTIE [86] 5-10-10 (7*) S Lycett, *hld up, drpd rear hfwy, outpcd 4 out, struggling whn hit 2 out, unbl to chal.* .... (12 to 1 op 6 to 1) 5
3144[7] LOTHIAN COMMANDER [75] (v) 5-10-6 J Culloty, *hld up, reminders hfwy, lost tch appr 4 out, sn beh.* .... (20 to 1 op 16 to 1) 6
3001 ROOD MUSIC [71] 6-9-9 (7*) J Mogford, *cl up, pushed alng 4 out, wknd quickly frm nxt*............(25 to 1 op 20 to 1) 7
3011 JAYFCEE [84] 5-11-1 D Leahy, *chsd ldrs till lost pl aftr 5 out, sn beh*..................(14 to 1 op 10 to 1) 8
2856[3] CYPRESS AVENUE (Ire) [89] (bl) 5-11-1 (5*) Mr R Thornton, *midfield, struggling whn hit 5 out, sn wl beh.* .... (10 to 1 op 6 to 1) 9
3359[3] ONE MORE DIME (Ire) [69] 7-9-7 (7*) T Hagger, *chsd ldrs till lost tch quickly 5 out, sn no dngr*......(25 to 1 op 16 to 1) 10
3057[5] CLEVER BOY (Ire) [81] 6-10-12 Derek Byrne, *beh, reminders and no response aftr 5 out, tld off whn pld up 3 out, lme.* ....(7 to 1 op 6 to 1) pu
2517[2] TANTARA LODGE (Ire) [77] 6-10-8 T J O'Sullivan, *cl up, struggling 5 out, tld off whn pld up 3 out.* £....(9 to 2 op 7 to 2) pu

Dist: Nk, 8l, nk, sht-hd, dist, 4l, 6l, 4l, sht-hd. 5m 55.70s. a 18.70s (12 Ran).
SR: 7/-/-/-/-/-/ (Martin Lovatt), J A B Old

3504 Wellman Plc Novices' Chase Class E (5-y-o and up) £2,918 3¼m... (4:00)

3319[6] GRIZZLY BEAR (Ire) 7-11-2 J Culloty, *cl up, chalg whn pckd 3 out, drvn ahead flt, styd on strly.* .... (14 to 1 op 14 to 1 tchd 16 to 1) 1
3133[9] LOCH GARMAN HOTEL (Ire) 8-10-11 (5*) Mr R Thornton, *led till hdd appr 9th, led ag'n 14th, drvn and headed sn aftr last, kpt on same pace*..................(7 to 4 op 5 to 4) 2
2970[2] FINAL BEAT (Ire) (bl) 8-11-2 F Perratt, *hld up, hdwy and in tch appr 4 out, wknd nxt*............ (13 to 8 fav op 2 to 1) 3
3266[4] FOX CHAPEL 10-10-13 (3*) Guy Lewis, *hld up, mstk 7th, lost tch 12th, beh whn pld up nxt*........... (4 to 1 op 5 to 2) pu
3098[5] CHAPILLIERE (Fr) 7-11-2 G Upton, *cl up, led appr 9th till 14th, mstk and lost tch 5 out, beh whn pld up 3 out.* ....(7 to 1 op 6 to 1) pu
3267 SWEET BUCK 8-11-2 D Leahy, *beh, not fluent 9th, struggling nxt, tld off whn pld up 6 out*.........(33 to 1 op 25 to 1) pu
2862[7] MUSICAL HIT (bl) 6-11-2 T J O'Sullivan, *hld up, drvn in rear 12th, sn wl beh, tld off whn pld up 2 out.* (20 to 1 op 14 to 1) pu

Dist: 2l, 22l. 6m 48.00s. a 36.00s (7 Ran).
(G B Barlow), R M Stronge

3505 Houghton Vaughan Handicap Chase Class D (0-125 5-y-o and up) £3,517 3m.......................... (4:35)

3020* CARLINGFORD LAKES (Ire) [96] 9-10-2[2] G Upton, *chsd ldr, reminder tenth, lost tch aftr 5 out, remote 3rd whn lft clr 3 out.* ....(3 to 1 op 2 to 1) 1
3133[8] BALLYEA BOY (Ire) [110] 7-10-11 (5*) Mr R Thornton, *sn pushed alng to chase ldrs, mstk 6 out, soon lost tch, hmpd and lft second 3 out, no imprsn.* ....(11 to 4 op 5 to 2 tchd 3 to 1) 2
3060 DARK OAK [110] 11-10-13 (3*) Guy Lewis, *hld up, not fluent 8th and 9th, wl beh aftr*.................(5 to 1 op 3 to 1) 3
2860 CANTORIS FRATER [101] 10-10-7 D Leahy, *hld up, gd hdwy 11th, sn pressing ldr, 3 ls second whn blun and uns rdr three out*..........................(6 to 1 op 4 to 1) ur
2328[4] IMPERIAL VINTAGE (Ire) [118] 7-11-10 J Culloty, *keen hold, led, quickened 6 out, 3 ls clr whn blun and uns rdr three out.* ....(7 to 4 fav op 7 to 4 tchd 9 to 4) ur

Dist: 16l, 8l. 6m 17.30s. (5 Ran).
(Mrs Solna Thomson Jones), T Thomson Jones

3506 Lloyd Hopkinson Mares' Only Novices' Hurdle Class E (5-y-o and up) £2,473 2½m 110yds.......... (5:10)

3299* MOTOQUA 5-11-1 (5*) Mr R Thornton, *chsd ldrs, drvn alng 3 out, ten ls second and hld whn lft clr last, rdn out.* .... (6 to 4 op 5 to 4 tchd 13 to 8) 1
KAYTU'S CAROUSEL 8-10-10 G Upton, *beh, clr order hfwy, rdn and outpcd 4 out, lft moderate second last, styd on same pace*...... (16 to 1 op 10 to 1 tchd 20 to 1) 2
3265[4] RIVERBANK ROSE (v) 6-10-13 (3*) Guy Lewis, *led, mstk 3rd, hdd appr 4 out, sn outpcd, lft moderate third last.* .... (10 to 1 op 8 to 1) 3
3019[3] KOSHEEN (Ire) 6-10-10 J Culloty, *midfield, drvn and outpcd 4 out, sn no extr*...................... (4 to 1 op 3 to 1) 4
2996[5] FLUTTERBUD 5-10-3 (7*) T Hagger, *mstk 1st, beh till moderate hdwy hfwy, lost tch appr 4 out, tld off.* .... (33 to 1 op 20 to 1) 5
3372 MORE TO LIFE 8-10-10 D Leahy, *hld up, struggling 5 out, tld off nxt*........................ (33 to 1 op 20 to 1) 6
3331[2] FANTASY LINE 6-10-13 (3*) E Husband, *cl up, led appr 4 out, clr 2 out, ten ls ahead whn f last.* ....(11 to 8 fav op 6 to 4 tchd 13 to 8) f
3019 FINAL ROSE 7-10-6[3] (7*) S Lycett, *pld hrd, wth ldrs till wknd quickly 5 out, tld off and pulled up nxt.* (25 to 1 op 14 to 1) pu
SHABO SHABO 5-10-10 T J O'Sullivan, *sn tld off, pld up 4 out*..................(40 to 1 op 25 to 1 tchd 50 to 1) pu

Dist: 6l, 1¼l, 5l, 24l, dist. 4m 56.40s. a 17.40s (9 Ran).
(Mrs Claire Smith), D Nicholson

WETHERBY (good)
Monday March 31st
Going Correction: PLUS 0.30 sec. per fur.

3507 Wharfedale Selling Handicap Hurdle Class G (0-100 4-y-o and up) £2,250 2m 7f........................(2:15)

2983[3] BARTON HEIGHTS [80] 5-11-5 P Niven, *al prmnt, pressed ldr frm 4 out, slight ld last, rdn out*.... (5 to 2 jt-fav op 2 to 1) 1
3246* JALMAID [71] 5-10-5 (5*) R McGrath, *trkd ldr, led 8th till hdd last, kpt on und pres*.....(11 to 4 op 3 to 1 tchd 7 to 2) 2
3123[8] MARDOOD [65] 12-9-11 (7*) Miss R Clark, *settled in rear, prog to track ldrs 8th, kpt on one pace frm 3 out.* .... (33 to 1 op 25 to 1) 3
3162[2] FIVE FLAGS (Ire) [88] 9-11-13 Richard Guest, *trkd ldrs, rdn 4 out, no imprsn frm nxt*........................(5 to 2 jt-fav op 9 to 4 tchd 11 to 4) 4
817 VALIANT DASH [86] 11-11-11 J Callaghan, *led to 8th, wknd frm nxt*..........................(5 to 1 tchd 6 to 1) 5
2847 CHARLVIC [61] (bl) 7-9-7 (7*) L McGrath, *gd prog to track ldrs hme turn, sn rdn and wknd quickly.* ....(33 to 1 op 25 to 1 tchd 50 to 1) 6
3353 MR SLOAN [61] 7-9-7 (7*) Mr O McPhail, *prmnt till wknd appr 3 out*........................(50 to 1 op 33 to 1) 7
OWES THE TILL [61] 7-10-0 Miss P Robson, *in rear whn mstk 6th, lost tch frm nxt, tld off when pld up 3 out*......(33 to 1) pu
3246[4] FIASCO [74] 4-10-4 L Wyer, *trkd ldrs till wknd 4 out, tld off whn pld up bef nxt*.........(8 to 1 op 10 to 1 tchd 12 to 1) pu

Dist: ¾l, 7l, 5l, 22l, 1¼l, 6l. 5m 41.30s. (9 Ran).
(Miss C J Raines), Mrs M Reveley

3508 Huddersfield Novices' Chase Class D (5-y-o and up) £3,652 2½m 110yds .... (2:45)

3202[2] BRIGHTER SHADE (Ire) 7-11-8 P Niven, *pressed ldr till blun 7th, led briefly tenth, dsptd ld 2 out, slight lead last, drvn out.* ....(11 to 10 on op Evens tchd 11 to 10) 1
3132 BALLYLINE (Ire) 6-11-8 J Callaghan, *led, hdd tenth led ag'n 11th till headed last, no extr*........... (5 to 1 op 9 to 2) 2

3046² GOLDEN HELLO 6-12-0 L Wyer, *prog to press ldrs fnl circuit, cl 3rd whn blun 3 out, no ch aftr.* ....(13 to 8 op 5 to 4 tchd 7 to 4) 3
EVENING RUSH 11-11-6 Richard Guest, *lost tch frm tenth, tld off from 5 out*..........(12 to 1 op 25 to 1 tchd 33 to 1) 4
Dist: 3l, 12l, dist. 5m 13.70s. a 20.70s (4 Ran).
(D S Hall), Mrs M Reveley

3509 Malton Racing Association Novices' Hurdle Class D (5-y-o and up) £2,985 2m......................... (3:15)

2908² GOOD VIBES 5-11-2 L Wyer, *made all, drw clr frm 2 out, pushed out*.................. (11 to 4 on op 2 to 1 on) 1
2908⁵ ARDARROCH PRINCE 6-10-10 P Niven, *pressed ldr till one pace frm 2 out*............ (3 to 1 op 5 to 2 tchd 7 to 2) 2
STARLIN SAM 8-10-3 (7*) Mr O McPhail, *prog to track ldrs hfwy, wknd appr 3 out*..............................(33 to 1) 3
M-I-FIVE (Ire) 6-10-10 Richard Guest, *trkd ldrs to 4 out, wknd appr nxt*................(15 to 2 op 7 to 1 tchd 8 to 1) 4
THOMAS RAND 8-10-5 (5*) R McGrath, *rear till some prog hfwy, no imprsn frm 4 out*..............................(33 to 1) 5
3015⁹ SUPEREXALT 5-10-10 Miss P Robson, *al rear.* ....(33 to 1 tchd 50 to 1) 6
RED HOT PRINCE 6-10-3 (7*) L McGrath, *mstks, al beh, tld off frm hfwy*.................................(50 to 1 op 33 to 1) 7
3003 HUNTING SLANE 5-10-10 J Callaghan, *lost tch frm 5th, pld up 3 out*.............................(33 to 1 op 25 to 1) pu
Dist: 3l, 25l, 5l, 13l, 4l, dist. 3m 51.10s. a 10.10s (8 Ran).
SR: 35/26/1/-/-/ (G E Shouler), T D Easterby

3510 Wetherby Handicap Chase Class B (0-140 5-y-o and up) £6,694 3m 1f .... (3:45)

3208² KENMORE-SPEED [107] 10-10-3³ Richard Guest, *jmpd wl, made all, lft clr 4 out, eased r-in.* ....(5 to 1 tchd 11 to 2 and 6 to 1) 1
3201² DEEP DECISION [104] 11-9-9 (5*) R McGrath, *rear, styd on frm 4 out, nvr plcd to chal*..............................(7 to 1) 2
1283² ROYAL VACATION [114] 8-10-10 J Callaghan, *trkd ldrs till lost tch frm 14th, hit 3 out, blun last*... (4 to 1 tchd 9 to 2) 3
3133 RANDOM HARVEST (Ire) [112] 8-10-8 P Niven, *trkd ldr, dsptd ld whn pckd 5 out, 3 ls second when blun and uns rdr nxt.* ....(5 to 4 fav tchd Evens) ur
1069⁶ TOOGOOD TO BE TRUE [128] 9-11-10 L Wyer, *lost tch tenth, pld up 5 out*..................(3 to 1 tchd 100 to 30) pu
Dist: 17l, 4l. 6m 23.70s. a 15.70s (5 Ran).
(K M Dacker), Mrs S J Smith

3511 Leeds Novices' Handicap Chase Class D (0-110 5-y-o and up) £3,718 3m 1f.........................(4:15)

3005² KINGS SERMON (Ire) [89] 8-11-10 L Wyer, *led, hit tenth, hdd nxt, rdn 5 out, blun 3 out, hld in second whn lft in ld last.* ....(9 to 2 op 7 to 2) 1
3159⁵ TICO GOLD [82] 9-10-12 (5*) R McGrath, *trkd ldrs, rdn alng frm 4 out, not get on terms*........... (7 to 1 op 11 to 2) 2
3259² COOL WEATHER (Ire) [72] (bl) 9-10-7 Miss P Robson, *settled in rear, chsd ldr frm 4 out, not get on terms.* ....(11 to 2 op 6 to 1) 3
3352* BRIGHT DESTINY [66] (v) 6-9-8 (7*,6ex) Mr O McPhail, *pressed ldr, dsptd ld tenth till led 13th, slight lead whn f 4 out.* ....(11 to 2 op 7 to 1) f
3243* GAELIC BLUE [85] 7-11-6 Richard Guest, *trkd ldrs, prog and slight ld 4 out, drw clr frm nxt, 6 ls clear whn f last.* ....(Evens fav tchd 5 to 4) f
3259 D'ARBLAY STREET (Ire) [80] 8-11-1 J Callaghan, *beh whn broke blood vessel, pld up aftr 9th*......(10 to 1 op 8 to 1) pu
Dist: 11l, 1½l. 6m 29.70s. a 21.70s (6 Ran).
(Mrs P A H Hartley), P Beaumont

3512 Wilstrop Amateur Riders' Handicap Hurdle Class F (0-100 4-y-o and up) £2,477 2m....................(4:45)

3002⁵ KIERCHEM (Ire) [71] 6-9-13 (7*) Mrs S Grant, *chsd ldrs, styd on wl frm 2 out to ld cl hme*............(8 to 1 op 6 to 1) 1
3354 TEEJAY'N'AITCH (Ire) [77] 5-10-5 (7*) Mr O McPhail, *led, pushed alng frm 3 out, rdn r-in, hdd cl hme.* ....(7 to 1 tchd 8 to 1) 2
1872² FAITHFUL HAND [89] 7-11-3 (7*) Captain A Ogden, *pressed ldr til one pace frm 2 out*............ (3 to 1 op 9 to 4) 3
3042⁴ EUROLINK THE REBEL (USA) [85] 5-10-13 (7*) Miss R Clark, *al prmnt, one pace frm 3 out*............(7 to 1 op 6 to 1) 4
3263² FRYUP SATELLITE [89] 6-11-5 (5*) Miss P Robson, *trkd ldrs, effrt 3 out, sn rdn and btn*...............(Evens fav op 2 to 1) 5
3198 PETRICO [65] 5-9-7 (7*) Miss A Armitage, *al rear.* ....(20 to 1 tchd 25 to 1) 6
792⁸ SWANK GILBERT [65] 11-9-7 (7*) Miss H Cuthbert, *al rear.* .... (33 to 1 op 25 to 1) 7
2969⁷ MARSH'S LAW [74] (bl) 10-10-2 (7*) Mr A Birch, *prmnt to 5th, wknd frm nxt*.............................. (12 to 1 op 8 to 1) 8
3128 RUBISLAW [65] (v) 5-9-7 (7*) Miss S Lamb, *prmnt, rdn 4 out, sn lost pl*..............................(33 to 1 op 25 to 1) 9

DANCING HOLLY [82] 10-10-10 (7*) Mr M Bennison, *al in rear, tld off frm 3 out, pld up bef last*............. (33 to 1) pu
Dist: 1¼l, 12l, 3½l, 10l, 9l, 10l, hd, 1½l. 3m 52.90s. a 11.90s (10 Ran).
SR: 7/11/11/3/-/-/ (Mrs M Hunter), C Grant

WINCANTON (firm)
Monday March 31st
Going Correction: MINUS 0.55 sec. per fur.

3513 Nine Hole 'National Hunt' Novices' Hurdle Class E (4-y-o and up) £2,232 2m......................... (2:00)

2775⁴ MRS EM 5-10-2 (7*) L Cummins, *al prmnt, chlgd 2 out, slight ld last, quickened und pres r-in.* (2 to 1 jt-fav tchd 9 to 4) 1
2426⁷ ROYAL RULER (Ire) 6-10-9 P Hide, *al prmnt, led 5th, hdd last, no extr r-in*.............................(14 to 1 op 8 to 1) 2
3253² NEAT FEAT (Ire) 6-10-11 (3*) T Dascombe, *hld up, hdwy appr 2 out, one pace approaching last*...................(2 to 1 jt-fav op 9 to 4 tchd 5 to 2) 3
3296⁵ PIPER'S ROCK (Ire) 6-10-9 (5*) A Bates, *led second to 5th, rdn 2 out, styd on ag'n frm last.* (9 to 2 op 4 to 1 tchd 5 to 1) 4
2432⁵ LONICERA 7-10-6 (3*) P Henley, *prmnt to 2 out, rdn and one pace*...........................(8 to 1 op 5 to 1) 5
2277 TIDAL FORCE (Ire) 6-10-9 (5*) D J Kavanagh, *al mid-div.* ....(14 to 1 op 10 to 1) 6
3022 ORCHID HOUSE 5-10-4 (5*) G Supple, *beh frm 6th, tld off.* ....(66 to 1 op 25 to 1) 7
3144 BOOZYS DREAM (bl) 6-10-7 (7*) Mr E Babington, *al rear, no ch frm 6th, tld off*.....................(50 to 1 op 33 to 1) 8
3282² SANDVILLE LAD 5-10-7 (7*) Mr J Tizzard, *led, pckd 1st, blun 3rd, sn beh, tld off whn pld up appr 2 out.* ....(14 to 1 op 10 to 1) pu
Dist: 1½l, 1¾l, ¾l, ¾l, hd, dist, 3l. 3m 33.00s. b 1.00s (9 Ran).
SR: 3/1/-/-/-/-/ (G Z Mizel), P F Nicholls

3514 Gardens Night Club Novices' Chase Class E (5-y-o and up) £3,303 3m 1f 110yds......................(2:30)

3252⁶ STROKESAVER (Ire) (bl) 7-10-9 (7*) M Berry, *lft in ld 13th, drw clr frm 15th, unchlgd*................(5 to 1 op 4 to 1) 1
3133⁵ DROMHANA (Ire) 7-11-7 (7*) Mr J Tizzard, *hld up, chsd ldr frm 13th, rdn appraoching nxt, btn whn blun 4 out and ag'n 3 out.* ....(7 to 4 on op 2 to 1 on tchd 6 to 4 on) 2
3023 LE GRAND LOUP 8-10-11 (5*) A Bates, *led 3rd, wknd frm 4 out, tld off in third pl whn f 3 out*.......(50 to 1 op 33 to 1) f
3271 FULL OF BOUNCE (Ire) 6-11-5 (3*) T Dascombe, *led to second, led ag'n 4th till blun and uns rdr 13th.* ....(3 to 1 op 7 to 2) ur
2738 COUNTRY STYLE 8-10-8 (3*) P Henley, *beh frm 7th, tld off whn pld up bef 12th*................ (20 to 1 op 12 to 1) pu
3190⁷ CRAVATE (Fr) 7-10-6 (5*) D J Kavanagh, *not jump wl, tld off whn pld up bef 12th*................ (12 to 1 op 10 to 1) pu
Dist: 20l. 6m 34.60s. a 18.60s (6 Ran).
(The Bow Lane Partnership), C P E Brooks

3515 Golf Course Conditional Jockeys' Claiming Hurdle Class F (4,5,6-y-o) £1,970 2m....................(3:00)

3184² PROUD IMAGE 5-10-12 (4*) R Hobson, *hld up, smooth hdwy to chase ldr frm 3 out, led appr last, ran on strly*.....(2 to 1) 1
2603 ATH CHEANNAITHE (Fr) (v) 5-11-2 P Henley, *led, pld hrd, sn clr, rdn appr 2 out, hdd approaching last, no extr.* ....(5 to 1 op 4 to 1) 2
2872³ ALMAPA 5-11-4 T Dascombe, *chsd ldr till effrt 3 out, sn rdn and btn*..............................(3 to 1 tchd 7 to 2) 3
3270* FLEET CADET (v) 6-11-8 G Supple, *hld up, rdn 3 out, no response*............(6 to 4 fav op 7 to 4 tchd 2 to 1) 4
3276⁵ RE ROI (Ire) 5-10-8 (4*) N Willmington, *chsd ldr till appr 3 out, wknd quickly*.............................(8 to 1 op 5 to 1) 5
Dist: 5l, 10l, 6l, dist. 3m 32.00s. b 2.00s (5 Ran).
SR: 20/15/7/5/-/ (Town And Country Tyre Services Limited), G M McCourt

3516 Gardens Night Club Handicap Hurdle Class E (0-115 4-y-o and up) £2,385 2¾m.................(3:30)

3188³ SEVSO [86] 8-10-4 (3*) P Henley, *dsptd ld frm 4th till wnt on 8th, drvn clr from last*.................(11 to 2 op 7 to 2) 1
3105³ MISS MARIGOLD [89] (bl) 8-10-7 (3*) T Dascombe, *trkd ldrs, chlgd 2 out, outpcd frm last*...............(4 to 1 op 9 to 2) 2
3255² VINTAGE CLARET [99] 8-11-6 P Hide, *led to 8th, mstk nxt, wknd quickly, tld off*...................(2 to 1 tchd 7 to 4) 3
3209² SANTELLA BOY (USA) [106] (bl) 5-11-13 J Railton, *hld up gng wl in second, whn f 2 out.* ....(6 to 5 fav op 5 to 4 tchd 11 to 8) f
Dist: 2l, dist. 5m 2.00s. b 4.00s (4 Ran).
(G K Hullett), R J Baker

3517 Dick Hunt 80th Birthday Handicap Chase Class D (0-125 5-y-o and up) £3,524 2m....................(4:00)

3185⁴ CORPUS [87] 8-9-9 (5*) D J Kavanagh, *chsd ldr, cld appr 4 out, ev ch nxt, 2 ls dwn whn lft clr two out.*
.... (12 to 1 op 8 to 1 tchd 14 to 1) 1

2877⁹ OLLIVER DUCKETT [87] 8-9-12¹ (3*) P Henley, *beh frm 8th, tld off whn lft second 2 out...* (11 to 2 op 5 to 1 tchd 6 to 1) 2

230⁵ EVENING RAIN [87] 11-9-9² (7*) R Hobson, *strted slwly, al beh, no ch whn uns rdr 9th.]*
.... (11 to 2 op 4 to 1 tchd 20 to 1) ur

3173 NEWLANDS-GENERAL [115] 11-11-7 (7*) Mr J Tizzard, *led, clr 4th, still gng wl whn blun badly and uns rdr 2 out.*
.... (7 to 4 op Evens) ur

3189 NORTHERN SINGER [88] 7-9-12 (3*) T Dascombe, *al towards rear, blun 7th, tld off whn pld up bef 2 out.*
.... (13 to 8 fav op 6 to 4 tchd 7 to 4) pu

Dist: 25l. 3m 52.00s. a 4.00s (5 Ran).

(J Newsome), R J Hodges

3518 Pay And Play 'National Hunt' Novices' Hurdle Class E (4-y-o and up) £2,425 2¾m.................(4:30)

2691⁵ KILMINGTON (Ire) 8-11-7 P Hide, *made virtually all, quickened 3 out, clr whn mstk last, easily.*
.... (9 to 4 op 2 to 1 tchd 5 to 2) 1

2871 SOUTHERNHAY BOY 6-10-9 (5*) D J Kavanagh, *hld up, hdwy to go second appr 2 out, not pace to chal wnr.*
.... (16 to 1 op 12 to 1 tchd 20 to 1) 2

3299² REGAL GEM 6-10-6 (3*) P Henley, *al prmnt, effrt frm 3 out, one pace.* .... (7 to 2 op 3 to 1) 3

2801* MR STRONG GALE 6-11-0 (7*) Mr J Tizzard, *hld up, moderate hdwy frm 7th, nvr rch ldrs. (Evens fav op 7 to 4)* 4

2954 ELGINTORUS 7-11-0 J Railton, *trkd ldrs till outpcd frm 4 out.* .... (25 to 1 op 14 to 1) 5

3312 COCKPIT (Ire) 6-10-9 (5*) A Bates, *prmnt till outpcd frm 3 out.* .... (20 to 1 op 8 to 1) 6

3299⁶ CASTLE LYNCH 5-10-6 (3*) T Dascombe, *reminder 5th, mstk nxt, beh frm 8th, tld off.* ..... (14 to 1 op 7 to 1) 7

3312 HAPPY HENRY 7-10-9 (5*) G Supple, *strted slwly, sn prmnt, lost pl 5th, beh frm nxt, tld off...(12 to 1 op 14 to 1)* 8

Dist: 15l, 3½l, 4l, 1¼l, 2½l, dist, dist. 5m 6.00s. (8 Ran).

(H T Pelham), J T Gifford

LES LANDES (JER) (good) Monday March 31st

3519 Supporters Handicap Hurdle (4-y-o and up) £900 2m.............(2:30)

839³ WOLLBOLL 7-12-0 D Evans, ... (2 to 1 on) 1
3196 SUPREME ILLUSION (Aus) 4-9-7 C McEntee, ...(5 to 4) 2
Won by 4l. (Time not taken) (2 Ran).
SR: -/-/

(Mike Weaver), H J Collingridge

FAIRYHOUSE (IRE) (good to firm) Tuesday April 1st

Going Correction: MINUS 0.30 sec. per fur. (races 1,2,4,5,8), MINUS 0.05 (3,6,7)

3520 Autozero Maiden Hurdle (5-y-o and up) £4,795 2¾m.............(2:10)

3225² ATHA BEITHE (Ire) (bl) 6-11-7 (7*) B J Geraghty, .. (9 to 1) 1
3235⁵ SPLEODRACH (Ire) 7-11-1 J F Titley, ... (16 to 1) 2
1193 ARCTIC GALE (Ire) 6-11-1 C F Swan, ... (14 to 1) 3
3213³ THE GREY MARE (Ire) 8-11-2 (7*) Mr P Fahey, ... (10 to 1) 4
3085 STAR CLUB (Ire) 5-11-8 H Rogers, ... (12 to 1) 5
3131⁸ ETON GALE (Ire) 8-12-0 C O'Dwyer, ...(9 to 4 fav) 6
3182 CHRISTINES RUN (Ire) 7-11-1 T P Rudd, ...(10 to 1) 7
2964⁵ CORRACHOILL (Ire) 6-12-0 R Dunwoody, ... (8 to 1) 8
3071⁹ HEAVY HUSTLER (Ire) 6-11-6 F Woods, ... (7 to 1) 9
3068 CLASSPERFORMER (Ire) 5-11-5 L P Cusack, ...(20 to 1) 10
3226⁶ THE MALL (Ire) 5-11-10 (3*) Mr B R Hamilton, ...(16 to 1) 11
2019² GROUND WAR 10-12-0 T P Treacy, ...(9 to 2) 12
3349 NOBLE GESTURE (Ire) 5-11-5 T Horgan, ...(50 to 1) 13
2900⁸ AKTEON (Ire) 5-11-5 D J Casey, ... (20 to 1) 14
3069 PLATIN GALE (Ire) 5-11-2 (3*) K Whelan, ... (33 to 1) 15
MAC'S LEGEND (Ire) 6-10-13 (7*) M D Murphy, .. (20 to 1) 16
2645 CAHERMURPHY (Ire) 5-11-0 (5*) T Martin, ...(100 to 1) 17
3217⁷ QUIETLY (Ire) 5-11-5 J Shortt, ...(20 to 1) 18
EDEN KING (Fr) 5-10-7 (7*) J M Maguire, ...(33 to 1) 19
2518 TAR AN CARRAIG (Ire) 5-11-0 J R Barry, ... (33 to 1) 20
3238⁶ QUIPTECH (Ire) 6-11-6 T J Mitchell, ...(16 to 1) pu

Dist: 3l, 1l, ½l, ½l. 5m 20.20s. a 9.20s (21 Ran).

(Ballyboy Racing Syndicate), Noel Meade

3521 R.F.L. Steel Hurdle (5-y-o and up) £6,850 2m.................(2:40)

2732⁸ DROMINEER (Ire) 6-11-4 (7*) P G Hourigan, ... (15 to 2) 1
3113⁵ HILL SOCIETY 5-11-13 R Dunwoody, ... (5 to 2 on) 2
3217⁷ GLOBAL LEGEND 7-11-4 J F Titley, ...(25 to 1) 3
3214² KILGOO BOY (Ire) 6-12-0 C F Swan, ...(3 to 1) 4
3225⁸ JERMYN STREET (USA) 6-11-1 (3*) D Bromley, .. (100 to 1) 5

Dist: 4½l, 4l, 20l, 14l. 3m 49.30s. a 5.30s (5 Ran).

(Christopher Cashin), T J Taaffe

3522 Power Gold Cup (Grade 1) (6-y-o and up) £23,100 2½m.............(3:15)

3152³ DORANS PRIDE 8-11-7 R Dunwoody, *trkd ldrs, hdwy frm 4 out, led bef 2 out, styd on wl.................*(7 to 4 on) 1
2733* JEFFELL 7-11-7 F Woods, *led to second, led ag'n 4th, hdd bef 2 out, rdn and no extr.....................* (3 to 1) 2
3453 CONSHARON (Ire) 9-11-2 T Horgan, *trkd ldrs, beh second, wknd bef 9th, sn no dngr......................* (20 to 1) 3
3132 BELL STAFFBOY (Ire) 8-11-7 C O'Dwyer, *beh early, hdwy bef 5th, dsptd ld till wknd aftr 4 out, f nxt..............*(10 to 1) f
3337 STROLL HOME (Ire) 7-11-7 M D Murphy, *al beh, f 8th.* ....(33 to 1) f
3112⁶ PENINDARA (Ire) 8-11-7 C F Swan, *trkd ldrs, led second, hdd 4th, wknd bef 9th, pld up before four out, broke blood vessel.*
.....................(9 to 1) pu

Dist: 5l, dist. 4m 56.10s. a 1.10s (6 Ran).
SR: 72/67/-/

(T J Doran), Michael Hourigan

3523 Bisquit Cognac Handicap Hurdle (Grade 2) (4-y-o and up) £13,000 2m ....(3:50)

2128⁶ KHAYRAWANI (Ire) [-] 5-10-5 C O'Dwyer, *mid-div, hdwy bef 3 out, led aftr nxt, styd on...................* (7 to 4 on) 1
2732⁵ PALETTE (Ire) [-] 5-9-8 D J Casey, *mid-div, hdwy bef 2 out, mstk last, styd on....................* (10 to 1) 2
3131⁹ MYSTICAL CITY (Ire) [-] 7-10-11 R Dunwoody, *trkd ldrs, drpd back bef 3 out, hdwy before nxt, styd on wl............*(13 to 2) 3
3216* SAVING BOND (Ire) [-] 5-9-7 B J Geraghty, *mid-div, lost pl aftr 3 out, styd on frm nxt, nrst finish.............* (9 to 1) 4
3113² THEATREWORLD (Ire) [-] 5-12-0 C F Swan, *beh, hdwy aftr 3 out, styd on.........................* (6 to 1) 5
3330* KADASTROF (Fr) [-] 7-10-1 (7*,2ex) A Aizzuru, *led, hdd 7th, led ag'n nxt, headed and wknd aftr 2 out...........* (9 to 2) 6
3346⁴ VALLEY ERNE (Ire) [-] 6-9-7 F Woods, *trkd ldrs, led 7th till nxt, rdn and wknd frm 3 out.....................*(14 to 1) 7
BANK STATEMENT (Ire) [-] 6-9-7 P G Hourigan, *al beh, wknd bef 4 out, sn no dngr.....................* (25 to 1) 8
3111⁶ THREE SCHOLARS [-] 6-9-11 T P Treacy, *al beh, sn btn.*
.....................(12 to 1) 9

Dist: 1l, ½l, ½l, hd. 3m 41.40s. b 2.60s (9 Ran).
SR: 55/43/59/40/75/-/

(J P McManus), C Roche

3524 Goffs Land Rover Bumper (4 & 5-y-o) £29,500 2m.............(4:25)

3224² THE OOZLER (Ire) 4-11-3 Mr A J Martin, ... (14 to 1) 1
2137³ NATIVE ESTATES (Ire) 5-11-10 Mr G J Harford, ...(7 to 1) 2
1043² DO YE KNOW WHA (Ire) 5-12-6 Mr J P McNamara, (8 to 1) 3
2845³ MINELLA HOTEL (Ire) 5-11-10 Mr A J Martin, ... (8 to 1) 4
3340⁶ TEMPLEARY LAD (Ire) 5 11 10 Mr J P Dompoy, (12 to 1) 5
3238⁴ AIR FORCE ONE (Ire) 5-11-10 Mr A C Coyle, ...(16 to 1) 6
3217² MEN OF NINETYEIGHT (Ire) 5-11-10 Mr D Marnane, (6 to 1) 7
2130² MYKON GOLD (Ire) 4-11-3 Mr R Walsh, ... (4 to 1 fav) 8
HOMEVILLE (Ire) 5-11-7 (3*) Mr P M Kelly, ... (20 to 1) 9
TOSCANINI (Ire) 4-10-12 (5*) Mr G Elliott, ...(20 to 1) 10
2967⁴ ALOTAWANNA (Ire) 4-11-3 Mr J A Berry, ... (12 to 1) 11
3124⁴ MACY (Ire) 4-11-10 Mr F Hutsby, ...(14 to 1) 12
3183* KAZARAN (Ire) 4-11-10 Mr P F Graffin, ...(10 to 1) 13
3231⁵ GET EVEN (Ire) 5-11-7 (3*) Mr B R Hamilton, ...(14 to 1) 14
2968⁵ TOTAL SUCCESS (Ire) 5-11-10 Mr E Bolger, ... (14 to 1) 15
3238⁵ MISTER AUDI (Ire) (bl) 5-11-10 Mr J T McNamara, (20 to 1) 16
3090 ASHWELL APRIL (Ire) 5-11-5 Mr Edgar Byrne, ...(33 to 1) 17
CANDY GALE (Ire) 5-11-2 (3*) Mr P English, ...(50 to 1) 18
2784⁵ GORMAN (Ire) 5-11-10 Mr A R Coonan, ...(20 to 1) 19
2946⁴ MEGA GALE (Ire) 5-11-7 Mr J Hussey, ... (16 to 1) 20
PAULA JANE (Ire) 4-10-12 Mr C A Murphy, ... (33 to 1) 21
3349⁸ DOCKLINE (Ire) 5-11-10 Mr M Phillips, ...(20 to 1) 22
3217⁶ DANTE'S BATTLE (Ire) 5-11-10 Mr J Healy, ...(25 to 1) 23
MICHELLES GOLD (Ire) 5-11-5 Mr M O'Connor, ..(50 to 1) 24
DATEM (Ire) 5-11-10 Mr A J Dempsey, ...(25 to 1) 25
3183 ROSES NIECE (Ire) 4-10-5 (7*) Mr R Flavin, ...(50 to 1) 26
2642⁷ CRACKON JAKE (Ire) 4-11-3 Mr E James, ... (20 to 1) 0
3183⁴ SMILING ALWAYS (Ire) 4-10-12 Mr F Fenton, ... (8 to 1) pu

Dist: Hd, 2½l, 2½l, sht-hd, 1½l. 3m 40.80s. (28 Ran).

(The Birdie Racing Club), M F Morris

3525 Powers Gold Label Point-To-Point Championship Final (5 & 6-y-o) £6,350 2¼m.............(4:55)

SOLVANG (Ire) 5-11-7 (5*) Mr W M O'Sullivan, ...(7 to 1) 1
CIRVIN (Ire) 5-11-12 Mr P Fenton, ...(8 to 1) 2
HYELORD (Ire) 6-11-7 (7*) Mr C A Murphy, ...(12 to 1) 3
NICHOLLS CROSS (Ire) 5-11-5 (7*) Mr K F O'Donnell,
.....................(14 to 1) 4
I'LL SAY NOTHING (Ire) 6-11-7 (7*) Mr R Flavin, (6 to 4 fav) 5
HARBOUR LEADER (Ire) 5-11-5 (7*) Mr E Gallagher,
.....................(10 to 1) 6
HI JAMIE (Ire) 5-11-12 Mr A J Martin, ...(11 to 1) 7
SWAN POINT (Ire) 5-11-7 (5*) Mr G Elliott, ... (14 to 1) 8
MAJOR SPONSOR (Ire) 5-11-9 (3*) Mr B R Hamilton, (6 to 1) 9
BRUSH THE FLAG (Ire) 5-11-5 (7*) Mr A K Wyse, ..(5 to 1) 10
PONDERNOT (Ire) 6-11-7 (7*) Miss A L Crowley, ...(16 to 1) 11

PERKY LAD (Ire) 5-11-9 (3*) Mr R Walsh, ... (14 to 1)   12
ALL BUT (Ire) 5-11-5 (7*) Mr Edgar Byrne, ... (16 to 1)   13
713⁵ JACK DORY (Ire) 5-11-5 (7*) Mr K O'Sullivan, ... (16 to 1)   14
MOUNTNUGENT-JACK (Ire) 6-11-7 (7*) Mr I Buchanan,
....(14 to 1)   15
FREESTYLING (Ire) 5-11-9 (3*) Mr D Valentine, ...(25 to 1)   16
METRO FASHION (Ire) 6-11-7 (7*) Mr M A Cahill, .. (25 to 1)   17
Dist: 3l, sht-hd, sht-hd, ½l, 2l. 5m 10.40s. a 44.60s (17 Ran).

(D L O'Byrne), David A Kiely

3526 'Happy Ring House' Handicap Chase (0-109 5-y-o and up) £4,110 2¾m 110yds. .... (5:25)

2020⁴ THE GOPHER (Ire) [-] 8-11-2 L P Cusack, ... (7 to 2)   1
3133 YOUNG MRS KELLY (Ire) [-] 7-10-6 T Horgan, ...(6 to 1)   2
3074⁶ PERSPEX GALE (Ire) [-] 9-10-9 R Dunwoody, ... (3 to 1)   3
3073⁸ PARADISE ROAD [-] 8-10-8 F Woods, ... (9 to 4 fav)   4
2867 FINAL TUB [-] 14-11-7 C F Swan, ... (9 to 2)   5
Dist: 1l, sht-hd, 3½l, dist. 5m 44.70s. a 11.70s (5 Ran).

(T F Lacy), T F Lacy

3527 Ladbroke-Tote Arena Joseph R. O'Reilly Memorial Cup (5-y-o and up) £6,850 3m 1f. .... (5:55)

2844* STAY IN TOUCH (Ire) 7-12-4 (3*) Mr D P Costello, ...(3 to 1)   1
2844² IRISH STOUT (Ire) 6-11-0 (3*) Mr R Walsh, ... (9 to 4 fav)   2
3179 MR K'S WINTERBLUES (Ire) (bl) 7-10-5 (7*) Mr E Gallagher,
....(12 to 1)   3
2475⁸ LINEKER 10-11-9 Mr G J Harford, ... (14 to 1)   4
3341⁶ SHAWS CROSS (Ire) 6-11-2 (7*) Mr John P Moloney, ... (5 to 1)   5
3228* HIGH STAR (Ire) 9-11-2 (7*) Mr I Buchanan, ...(4 to 1)   f
3378 TULLIBARDNICENEASY (Ire) 6-10-7 (5*) Mr A C Coyle,
....(20 to 1)   ur
BAVARD JET (Ire) 5-10-5 (5*) Mr G Elliott, ...(8 to 1)   ur
LIGHT ARGUMENT (Ire) 8-11-11 (5*) Mr J T McNamara,
....(7 to 1)   pu
Dist: 1l, 15l, 2½l, dist. 6m 24.00s. a 9.00s (9 Ran).

(Barry Brazier), John J Costello

UTTOXETER (good to firm)
Tuesday April 1st
Going Correction: PLUS 0.05 sec. per fur. (races 1,3,5,7), PLUS 0.15 (2,4,6)

3528 Central Telecom/SDX Novices' Handicap Hurdle Class E (0-105 4-y-o and up) £2,536 2m. .... (2:10)

ERIN'S LAD [-] 6-10-0 J Culloty, steady hdwy 5th, quickened
to ld appr 2 out, readily.................... (33 to 1 op 25 to 1)   1
3268* KILDRUMMY CASTLE [-] 5-10-3 (3*) F Leahy, sn chasing ldrs,
rdn alng 3 out, styd on same pace.
.... (11 to 2 fav op 4 to 1 tchd 5 to 1)   2
2893 FENCER'S QUEST (Ire) [-] 4-10-0 S Wynne, mid-div, hdwy
6th, rdn 2 out, styd on and not much room r-in.
....(8 to 1 op 20 to 1)   3
3317* NIGHT BOAT [-] 6-10-3 (3*) Guy Lewis, bet till hdwy 5th, chsd
ldrs 3 out, one pace................... (8 to 1 op 10 to 1)   4
3357³ WORTHY MEMORIES [-] 8-10-0 D Bridgwater, led and jmpd
persistently rght, hdd appr 2 out, wknd last.
....(8 to 1 op 7 to 1)   5
2603⁴ O MY LOVE [-] 6-10-6 J Osborne, beh till some hdwy frm 2
out, not a dngr......................... (6 to 1 op 4 to 1)   6
3258¹ STYLISH INTERVAL [-] 5-10-13 (5*) Mr R Thornton, chsd ldrs,
rdn alng 4 out, wknd appr 2 out......... (12 to 1 op 8 to 1)   7
2973⁹ I'M A DREAMER (Ire) [-] 7-11-13 Gary Lyons, nvr rchd ldrs.
...................................(11 to 1 op 8 to 1 tchd 12 to 1)   8
2147⁵ GOLF LAND (Ire) [-] 5-10-10 M Foster, hld up in rear,nvr rchd
ldrs........................... (16 to 1 op 12 to 1)   9
2541⁹ CYPHRATIS (Ire) [-] 6-11-3 D Leahy, unruly strt and slwly
away, al beh.........................(10 to 1)   10
3278³ DESERT CALM (Ire) [-] (bl) 8-10-8 D Walsh, chsd ldrs till rdn
and wknd 4 out.................. (16 to 1 op 14 to 1)   11
3268² COUNTRY MINSTREL (Ire) [-] 6-10-0 C Rae, nvr better than
mid-div....................... (8 to 1 op 7 to 1 tchd 9 to 1)   12
3001 ALPINE MIST (Ire) [-] (v) 5-11-5 M A Fitzgerald, chsd ldrs till
wknd 3 out.................... (25 to 1 op 16 to 1)   13
3137 DARK PHOENIX (Ire) [-] 7-10-10 M Brennan, beh, rdn 4 out,
no response...................(8 to 1 op 7 to 1 tchd 9 to 1)   14
Dist: 10l, 1l, 11l, 1½l, 8l, 2½l, 7l, ¾l, 2l, 2l. 3m 43.30s. a 6.30s (14 Ran).
SR: 17/13/6/12/4/2/11/13/-/-

(Anthony Smith), R Dickin

3529 Mount Argus Hunters' Chase Class H (5-y-o and up) £1,584 2m 7f (2:40)

2680⁵ IDIOTIC 9-11-12 (5*) Mr C Vigors, hdwy to chase ldrs tenth,
chlgd 3 out, blun nxt, rallied last, rdn to ld nr finish.
....(4 to 1 tchd 9 to 2)   1
MY NOMINEE (Ire) 9-11-10 (7*) Mr R Burton, in tch, rdn to chal
3 out, led nxt, ridden and st r-in—in... (5 to 4 fav op 6 to 4)   2
3327 PRO BONO (Ire) 7-11-12 (5*) Mr A Samsome, sn chasing ldrs,
chlgd frm tenth, hit 11th, ev ch 3 out, wknd nxt.
....(9 to 1 op 8 to 1 tchd 10 to 1)   3

3279⁸ KING OF SHADOWS 10-11-10 (7*) Mr S Prior, made most to
5th, wknd tenth, no ch whn blun 12th, tld off.
....(12 to 1 op 20 to 1)   4
3247 DOUBLE COLLECT 11-11-10 (7*) Mr N F Smith, in tch whn
blun and uns rdr 7th.....(9 to 1 op 10 to 1 tchd 8 to 1)   ur
3102 BABIL 12-11-12 (5*) Mr J Trice-Rolph, prmnt till wknd 7th, tld
off whn pld up bef 9th..........(25 to 1 op 14 to 1)   pu
FRANK BE LUCKY 11-11-12 (5*) Mr R Thornton, chlgd 3rd till
led 5th, hdd appr 2 out, wknd rpdly and pld up bef last.
....(9 to 2 op 7 to 2 tchd 5 to 1)   pu
3102⁸ RISING SAP 7-11-10 (7*) Mr M Munrowd, beh whn blun badly
8th, hdwy 11th, hit 4 out, wknd quickley, tld off when pld up bef
last......................................(40 to 1 op 33 to 1)   pu
IDIOMATIC 8-11-10 (7*) Mr D Sherlock, tld off frm 5th, pld up
bef tenth.............................(66 to 1 tchd 100 to 1)   pu
Dist: Nk, 17l, dist. 5m 40.00s. a 12.00s (9 Ran).
SR: 16/16/-/-/-/-/

(E Knight), P R Chamings

3530 Marston's Free Trade Selling Handicap Hurdle Class G (0-95 4-y-o and up) £1,857 2½m 110yds. ...... (3:10)

2403⁸ POLO PONY (Ire) [-] 5-10-0 J Supple, beh, rdn alng 6th, hdwy
3 out, styd on und pres to ld nr finish.
....(20 to 1 op 14 to 1 tchd 25 to 1)   1
3136⁴ EDWARD SEYMOUR (USA) [-] 10-11-5 T Jenks, hld up,
steady hdwy frm 6th, led appr last, rdn r-in, ct cl hme.
....(5 to 2 fav tchd 3 to 1)   2
2932⁷ QUIET MOMENTS (Ire) [-] 4-10-3 W McFarland, beh till hdwy
frm 6th, kpt on same pace appr last.
....(8 to 1 op 7 to 1 tchd 9 to 1)   3
2625⁹ BITES [-] 4-10-3³ J Railton, trkd ldr, chlgd and hit 4 out, sn
chalg, led 2 out, hdd and wknd last....(50 to 1 op 33 to 1)   4
2625 SHEECKY [-] 6-10-9 D Bridgwater, chsd ldrs, led 3 out, hdd
nxt, sn wknd.................(11 to 1 op 10 to 1 tchd 12 to 1)   5
3045⁹ CRAZY HORSE DANCER (USA) [-] 9-10-12 (3*) L Aspell, in
tch, no hdwy frm 3 out...................(7 to 1 op 10 to 1)   6
2625 ADMIRAL'S GUEST (Ire) [-] 5-9-13¹ (3*) Guy Lewis, chsd ldrs
till wknd appr 3 out........................(25 to 1)   7
3321⁹ WHITE WILLOW [-] (bl) 8-12-0 R Johnson, led, sn clr, hdd 3
out, wknd frm nxt........(12 to 1 op 10 to 1 tchd 14 to 1)   8
2804 BLUNTSWOOD HALL [-] 4-11-3 Gary Lyons, beh frm 5th.
.................................(14 to 1 op 10 to 1 tchd 16 to 1)   9
3246 OAKBURY (Ire) [-] 5-10-4 C Maude, effrt 5th, sn wknd.
....(8 to 1 tchd 9 to 1)   10
1796⁵ SALTIS (Ire) [-] 5-10-9 (3*) P Henley, chsd ldrs till wknd aftr 4
out.......................................(6 to 1 tchd 7 to 1)   11
3163⁸ WORDSMITH (Ire) [-] (bl) 7-11-0 D Gallagher, al beh, tld off
whn pld up bef 3 out.......(14 to 1 op 12 to 1 tchd 16 to 1)   pu
2803 CAPTAIN NAVAR (Ire) [-] 7-10-8 M A Fitzgerald, effrt 5th, sn
wknd, tld off whn pld up bef 2 out.
.................................(6 to 1 op 5 to 1 tchd 13 to 2)   pu
Dist: 1¼l, 1½l, ½l, 3l, ½l, 5l, 10l, 7l, 6l, 26l. 4m 52.90s. a 13.90s (13 Ran).
SR: (T S Palin), John R Upson

3531 CJ Pearce Handicap Chase Class C (0-135 5-y-o and up) £4,856 2½m .... (3:40)

2955⁶ PLUNDER BAY (USA) [-] 6-10-3¹ M A Fitzgerald, trkd ldr frm
5th, slight ld 4 out, rdn last, hld on, all out. (5 to 2 op 9 to 4)   1
2806⁸ CALLISOE BAY [-] 8-11-10 J Osborne, led, sn clr, steadied 4th, hdd four out, rallied last, str chal r-in, no extr cl hme.
....(13 to 8 jt-fav op 6 to 4)   2
2542² BEATSON (Ire) [-] 8-10-6 B Powell, mstk 1st, al beh, hit 7th, tld
off frm 11th..................... (13 to 8 jt-fav op 6 to 4)   3
Dist: Nk, dist. 4m 53.80s. a 9.80s (3 Ran).
SR: 7/28/-/

(W V & Mrs E S Robins), N J Henderson

3532 Mobilefone Group Handicap Hurdle Class B (0-140 4-y-o and up) £4,756 2m .... (4:10)

1806⁷ SERIOUS [-] 7-10-0 S McNeill, hld up, steady hdwy 3 out, led
nxt, ran on wl.........(11 to 4 co-fav tchd 3 to 1)   1
2331 TEJANO GOLD (USA) [-] 7-10-12 S Wynne, led till hdd 2 out,
rallied last, not much room and swtchd rght r-in, one pace.
.................................(11 to 4 co-fav op 2 to 1 tchd 3 to 1)   2
3156 STAR RAGE (Ire) [-] 7-11-11 D Gallagher, chsd ldrs, rdn alng 3
out, styd on same pace und pres...........(11 to 4 co-
fav op 5 to 2 tchd 3 to 1)   3
2978 MR BUREAUCRAT (NZ) [-] 8-10-7 C Maude, chsd ldr, chlgd 3
out, wknd 2 out.....................(12 to 1 op 8 to 1)   4
2933⁵ CHARMING GIRL (USA) [-] 6-11-3 J Osborne, hld up, keen
hold, hdwy to press ldrs and gng wl whn f 3 out.
....(11 to 2 op 4 to 1)   f
TEST MATCH [-] 10-9-13² (3*) Guy Lewis, al beh, wknd and
pld up aftr 4th.....................(16 to 1 op 25 to 1)   pu
Dist: 2l, 11l, 4l. 3m 45.90s. a 8.90s (6 Ran).
SR: -/-/3/

(Tony And Dee Lousada), K C Bailey

3533 CJ Pearce Novices' Chase Class D (5-y-o and up) £3,550 2m 5f. ... (4:40)

3361¹ QUITE A MAN 9-12-0 C Maude, trkd ldrs till blun and lost pos
9th, rallied 4 out, led appr 2 out, ran on wl.
.................................(15 to 8 op 6 to 4 tchd 11 to 8)   1

3320* PEARL EPEE 8-11-3 R Johnson, *led and hit 1st, hdd nxt, led 11th to 4 out, rallied last, ran on*. (11 to 8 fav tchd 13 to 8) 2
2971 GLAMANGLITZ 7-10-11 (5*) Mr R Thornton, *led second, hdd 11th, led ag'n 4 out, headed appr 2 out, sn one pace*.
.................................(9 to 1 op 5 to 1) 3
2937⁴ RARE OCCURANCE 7-10-9 (7*) J T Nolan, *hdwy tenth, wknd 4 out*.................(14 to 1 op 12 to 1 tchd 16 to 1) 4
3370³ SANTARAY 11-11-2 Mr R Armson, *hdwy tenth, wknd 12th*.
.................................(16 to 1 op 10 to 1 tchd 20 to 1) 5
3267 TOTAL ASSET 7-11-2 Gary Lyons, *hdwy 7th, wknd and hit 12th*..................(20 to 1 op 16 to 1 tchd 25 to 1) 6
Dist: 2½l, 6l, 14l, 7l, 12l. 5m 10.80s. a 12.80s (6 Ran).
SR: 3/-/-/ (W R J Everall), S A Brookshaw

3534 Jenkinsons Caterers Maiden Hurdle Class E (4-y-o and up) £2,432 2m
.................................(5:10)

2284 KING OF SPARTA 4-11-0 D Bridgwater, *hld up in tch, quickened to ld last, drvn and ran on wl*.
.................................(5 to 1 op 9 to 2 tchd 11 to 2) 1
3316 VADLAWYS (Fr) 6-11-6 C Maude, *hld up, hdwy 4 out, chlgd last, ev ch r-in, not clr run but held cl hme*.
.................................(11 to 8 fav op 6 to 4 tchd 7 to 4) 2
SICARIAN 5-11-6 Derek Byrne, *hld up in rear, steady hdwy frm 4 out, chlgd last, one pace*.
.................................(25 to 1 op 16 to 1 tchd 33 to 1) 3
2153⁹ LABURNUM GOLD (Ire) 6-11-6 D Leahy, *trkd ldr till led 4 out, rdn 2 out, hdd and blun last, one pace*.
.................................(3 to 1 op 9 to 4 tchd 100 to 30) 4
2959⁵ ALPHA LEATHER 6-11-6 Mr J Grassick, *hdwy 4 out, no prog frm nxt*.............(50 to 1 op 33 to 1 tchd 66 to 1) 5
IF ONLY 7-11-6 Gary Lyons, *mstk 4th, hdwy four out, wknd nxt*....................(50 to 1 op 33 to 1 tchd 66 to 1) 6
3258² SUVALU (USA) 5-11-6 M A Fitzgerald, *chsd ldrs till rdn and wknd 3 out*.............(6 to 1 hld 8 to 1) 7
2458³ FRENO 6-11-6 S McNeill, *in tch till wknd 4 out*.
.................................(11 to 1 op 7 to 1 tchd 12 to 1) 8
POLAR WIND 8-11-6 M Foster, *led to 4 out, wknd quickly*.
.................................(50 to 1 op 33 to 1 tchd 66 to 1) 9
3189 JASONS FARM 7-11-3 (3*) Guy Lewis, *in tch till wknd aftr 5th*.
.................................(100 to 1 op 33 to 1) 10
3077 KNOCK STAR (Ire) 6-11-6 B Powell, *beh and prom 4th*.
.................................(50 to 1 op 33 to 1 tchd 66 to 1) 11
Dist: 1¼l, 1½l, 4l, 6l, 9l, 9l, 13l, 18l, 15l, 18l. 3m 47.90s. a 10.90s (11 Ran).
(Darren C Mercer), O Sherwood

WETHERBY (good to firm)
Tuesday April 1st
Going Correction: MINUS 0.05 sec. per fur.

3535 W. Clifford Watts Ltd. Novices' Hurdle Class D (4-y-o and up) £3,265 2 ½m 110yds..................(2:20)

3308² MAJOR HARRIS (Ire) 5-11-0 R Garritty, *settled midfield, hdwy to chal 3 out, disputing ld whn hit last, edgd lft, found extr und pres cl hme*...........................(11 to 2 op 4 to 1) 1
2463 THE ROAD WEST 8-11-0 B Storey, *chsd ldrs, led 3 out, sn hrd pressed, edgd rght r-in, ct cl hme*.
.................................(2 to 1 op 14 to 1) 2
3351² SOUTHERN CROSS 5-11-0 P Niven, *in tch, effrt and ch 3 out, no extr btwn last 2*.............(7 to 2 op 3 to 1) 3
3127⁴ PONTEVEDRA (Ire) 4-10-1 (7*) N Horrocks, *in tch, effrt aftr 7th, kpt on same pace frm 3 out*.
.................................(14 to 1 op 12 to 1 tchd 16 to 1) 4
2882⁵ SPRITZER (Ire) 5-11-1 W Dwan, *hld up, hdwy to chase ldrs 3 out, sn rdn and btn*.(100 to 30 fav op 3 to 1 tchd 7 to 2) 5
3011 BORDER IMAGE 6-11-0 A Dobbin, *chsd ldrs till wknd aftr 3 out*.................................(50 to 1) 6
3203 TWEEDSWOOD (Ire) 7-11-0 R Supple, *led till hd 5th, cl up till rdn and wknd bef 3 out*...(13 to 2 op 6 to 1 tchd 8 to 1) 7
1125⁴ RULE OUT THE REST 6-11-6 A Thornton, *beh, lost tch aftr 7th, tld off whn f 3 out*.............(10 to 1 op 12 to 1) f
3137⁶ NORTHERN STAR 6-10-13 (7*) Miss J Wormall, *tried to run out and uns rdr 1st*.....(16 to 1 op 12 to 1) ur
3198 PRAISE BE (Fr) 7-11-0 J Callaghan, *chsd ldrs to 6th, sn wknd, tld off whn pld up bef 3 out*.......(33 to 1 op 20 to 1) pu
3269 CHARLEY LAMBERT (Ire) 6-10-11 (3*) E Husband, *prmnt, slight ld 5th till squeezed out and hdd 3 out, stumbled very badly nxt, lost tch and pld up bef last*...(4 to 1 tchd 9 to 2) pu
Dist: Sht-hd, 3l, 8l, 4l, 6l, 12l. 4m 54.60s. a 11.60s (11 Ran).
(H G Owen), M D Hammond

3536 Ferdy Murphy's Owners Handicap Chase Class E (0-115 5-y-o and up) £3,171 2m...................(2:50)

3199³ GROUSE-N-HEATHER [-] 8-10-3 A Dobbin, *nvr far away, led 4 out, styd on wl, cmftbly*.
.................................(6 to 5 fav op 5 to 4 tchd 11 to 8) 1
3010⁵ REBEL KING [-] 7-10-0 B Storey, *sn tracking ldr, led 8th, hdd 4 out, chsd wnr aftr, no imprsn*.........(8 to 1 op 4 to 1) 2
3126⁴ REGAL ROMPER [-] 9-11-4 Richard Guest, *led till hdd 8th, fdd*................(15 to 8 op 7 to 4 tchd 2 to 1) 3

1108 DE JORDAAN [-] 10-12-0 N Smith, *lost tch frm 4th, tld off*.
.................................(4 to 1 op 3 to 1 tchd 9 to 2) 4
Dist: 8l, 10l, dist. 3m 59.50s. a 12.50s (4 Ran).
(D J Fairbairn), P Monteith

3537 Lambson Handicap Hurdle Class C (0-135 4-y-o and up) £3,731 2½m 110yds......................(3:20)

3100⁴ CELESTIAL CHOIR [-] 7-11-4 B Storey, *hld up, hdwy to track ldrs aftr 7th, led 3 out, sn clr*.
.................................(15 to 8 fav op 7 to 4 tchd 2 to 1) 1
2936⁵ FIRED EARTH (Ire) [-] 9-11-11 A Dobbin, *prmnt, led 7th, hdd bef 3 out and outpcd, styd on frm nxt*.
.................................(5 to 1 op 9 to 2 tchd 11 to 2) 2
3205* DOMAPPEL [-] 5-11-2 T Kent, *hld up, smooth hdwy to ld bef 3 out, sn hdd, chsd wnr aftr, no imprsn*.
.................................(11 to 4 op 5 to 2 tchd 3 to 1) 3
3385³ FOURTH IN LINE (Ire) [-] 9-11-4 W Marston, *chsd ldrs, drvn alng bef 3 out, kpt on same pace*......(10 to 1 op 8 to 1) 4
3205² THURSDAY NIGHT (Ire) [-] 6-10-9 A Thornton, *prmnt, hit 7th, sn wknd, tld off*.........(11 to 1 op 12 to 1 tchd 14 to 1) 5
3200⁶ KINDA GROOVY [-] (bl) 8-10-0 N Smith, *led till hdd 7th, sn rdn and wknd, tld off*..............(25 to 1 op 20 to 1) 6
2288⁴ SUAS LEAT (Ire) [-] 7-9-7 (7*) M Newton, *hld up, rdn aftr 7th, sn wknd, tld off*.....(8 to 1 op 8 to 1 tchd 10 to 1) 7
Dist: 6l, ½l, 3½l, 25l, 7l, ¾l. 4m 53.30s. a 11.30s (7 Ran).
(Mrs Carole Sykes), J L Eyre

3538 Sebel House Group Novices' 'National' Handicap Chase Class C (5-y-o and up) £4,771 3m 5f...(3:50)

3243 MISTER TRICK (Ire) [-] (bl) 7-10-0 R Supple, *made most frm second to 9th, nvr far away, rdn to ld appr last, styd on wl*.
.................................(16 to 1 op 10 to 1) 1
3254* THE WHOLE HOG (Ire) [-] 8-10-0 A Thornton, *trkd ldrs, rdn to ld bef 2 out, hdd appr last, no extr*.
.................................(6 to 1 op 12 to 1 tchd 14 to 1) 2
3369* FATHER SKY [-] (bl) 6-12-0 (4ex) J A McCarthy, *led to second, made most frm 9th till hdd bef 2 out, fdd*.........(5 to 4 jt-fav op 11 to 10 tchd 11 to 8) 3
2715² IVY HOUSE (Ire) [-] 9-10-5 (5*) R McGrath, *hld up and beh, pld up and dismounted aftr 17th*...(5 to 4 jt-fav op Evens) pu
Dist: 6l, 10l. 7m 23.10s. a 11.10s (4 Ran).
(Edward Birkbeck), L Lungo

3539 Howard Brown Memorial Novices' Hunters' Chase Class H (5-y-o and up) £1,155 3m 1f.............(4:20)

3033* DENIM BLUE 8-11-7 (5*) Miss P Robson, *hld up, hdwy to track ldr hfwy, rdn to chal 3 out, styd on und pres to ld r-in, all out*.................(11 to 4 on op 9 to 4 on) 1
SOVEREIGNS MATCH 9-11-7 (5*) Mr N Wilson, *led, jmpd slwly 4 out, jnd nxt and rdn, hdd r-in, rallied towards finish*.
.................................(11 to 2 op 5 to 1 tchd 13 to 2) 2
SYRUS P TURNTABLE 11-11-5 (7*) Mr J Saville, *chsd ldrs till wknd aftr 14th, tld off*......(33 to 1 op 20 to 1) 3
TOM LOG 10-11-5 (7*) Mr W Burnell, *mstk 6th, blun nxt, sn lost tch, tld off*..........(13 to 2 op 5 to 1 tchd 7 to 1) 4
3043⁴ R N COMMANDER 11-11-5 (7*) Mr J R Cornwall, *lost tch frm hfwy, wl tld off*.......(12 to 1 op 8 to 1 tchd 14 to 1) 5
Dist: ½l, dist, 18l, dist. 6m 30.10s. a 22.10s (5 Ran).
(Mrs L Walby), Miss Pauline Robson

3540 Henderson Insurance Brokers Ltd. Handicap Hurdle Class D (0-125 4-y-o and up) £2,880 2m..........(4:50)

2933 DESERT FIGHTER [-] 6-11-10 P Niven, *in tch gng wl, led bef 3 out, clr betw last 2, cmftbly*.
.................................(9 to 4 fav op 4 to 1 tchd 9 to 2) 1
2532⁵ ANABRANCH [-] 6-11-6 (3*) E Callaghan, *hld up, hdwy on bit bef 3 out, chsd wnr aftr nxt, no imprsn*.
.................................(11 to 1 op 10 to 1 tchd 12 to 1) 2
3003⁴ LAST TRY (Ire) [-] 6-10-9 A S Smith, *trkd ldrs, effrt bef 3 out, kpt on same pace frm nxt*.............(7 to 1 op 11 to 2) 3
3080 SAMANID (Ire) [-] 5-11-6 O Pears, *ran in snatches, shaken up to track ldrs aftr 6th, sn rdn, wkng whn blun 2 out*.
.................................(3 to 1 op 9 to 4) 4
1200³ BURES (Ire) [-] 6-11-5 (5*) B Grattan, *led till hdd bef 3 out, sn wknd*.................(14 to 1 op 10 to 1) 5
3013 FOX SPARROW [-] (bl) 7-10-9 A Dobbin, *chsd ldr till wknd aftr 6th, tld off*................(25 to 1 op 20 to 1) 6
3100⁷ HOLDERS HILL (Ire) [-] 5-11-2 Richard Guest, *beh most of way, f last*............(14 to 1 op 12 to 1) f
2548³ RUSSIAN RASCAL (Ire) [-] 4-10-10 L Wyer, *mstk 1st, losing tch whn jmpd slwly 4th, tld off whn pld up aftr nxt, broke blood vessel*................(4 to 1 op 7 to 2 tchd 9 to 2) pu
2535 RALITSA (Ire) [-] 5-11-4 R Garritty, *refused to race, took no part*....................(16 to 1 op 14 to 1) pu
Dist: 3l, 8l, 1¼l, 10l, 30l. 3m 46.10s. a 5.10s (9 Ran).
SR: 37/33/11/20/14/-/ (A Frame), Mrs M Reveley

EXETER (firm)

Wednesday April 2nd
Going Correction: NIL

3541 All Wool Axminster 100 Juvenile Novices' Hurdle Class E (4-y-o) £2,248 2¼m.................(2:20)

3280²	SULAWESI (Ire) 10-0 (7*) Mr J Goldstein, *made virtually all, rdn clr appr last, not extended.*	
	......................(9 to 4 op 7 to 4 tchd 5 to 2)	1
3036*	GIVE AND TAKE 11-4 G Maude, *dsptd ld, mstk 3rd, reminders appr 5th, rdn approaching 2 out, no extr aftr.*	
	......................(13 to 8 on op 2 to 1 on tchd 6 to 4 on)	2
3117⁹	TIMIDJAR (Ire) 10-9 (3*) D Fortt, *hld up, effrt 3rd, lost tch appr 3 out.*......(13 to 2 op 7 to 1 tchd 6 to 1)	3
Dist: 5l, 12l. 4m 11.50s. a 12.50s (3 Ran).

(Jack Joseph), N A Twiston-Davies

3542 Moorland Axminster 100 Mares' Only Selling Handicap Hurdle Class G (0-100 4-y-o and up) £1,895 2¼m ....(2:50)

582	ON MY TOES [56] 6-10-6² J Frost, *made all, ran on whn chlgd aftr 6th.*......(14 to 1 op 9 to 2)	1
2305⁴	QUAKER WALTZ [74] 7-11-3 (7*) Mr A Wintle, *al in tch, wnt second aftr 6th, hrd rdn and no imprsn nr finish.*	
	......................(5 to 1 tchd 11 to 2)	2
3270⁴	PROVE THE POINT (Ire) [59] 4-10-3 A Procter, *chsd ldrs, rdn aftr 6th, one pace.*........(6 to 1 op 7 to 1 tchd 8 to 1)	3
3016	LOVELARK [55] 8-10-5 R Johnson, *trkd wnr, reminders aftr 6th, wknd bef nxt.*........(13 to 1 op 9 to 4 tchd 3 to 1)	4
3144⁶	SPIRIT LEVEL [66] 9-11-2 Mr R Payne, *in tch till wknd 6th.*	
	......................(14 to 1 op 10 to 1)	5
3270²	ROSE OF GLENN [70] 6-11-6 T Jenks, *hmpd 1st, hdwy appr 3rd, rdn and wknd on bend aftr 6th.* (5 to 2 fav tchd 7 to 2)	6
2886⁶	PATONG BEACH [59] 7-10-9 C Maude, *al in rear.*	
	......................(12 to 1 op 10 to 1)	7
3268	THEM TIMES (Ire) [57] 8-10-4 (3*) L Aspell, *f 1st.*	
	......................(10 to 1 op 8 to 1 tchd 12 to 1)	f
Dist: ¾l, 11l, 5l, 2½l, 14l. 4m 15.70s. a 16.70s (8 Ran).

(G Chambers), R G Frost

3543 Royal Seaton Axminster 100 Novices' Chase Class D (5-y-o and up) £3,629 2m 3f 110yds.........(3:20)

	SORCIERE 6-10-11 B Clifford, *al prmnt, led 4 out, jmpd lft nxt, rallied and ran on strly r-in.* (3 to 1 op 4 to 1 tchd 5 to 2)	1
3271	MOZEMO 10-11-2 C Maude, *hld up, hdwy 8th, chlgd last, no extr r-in.*........(2 to 1 op 6 to 4 tchd 9 to 4)	2
3370⁵	JONJAS CHUDLEIGH 10-11-2 J Frost, *trkd ldr, lft in ld 5th, hdd 4 out, one pace frm nxt.*........(12 to 1 op 10 to 1)	3
3038⁵	GEMINI MIST 6-10-11 A Procter, *hld up, lost tch aftr 8th, tld off.*........(25 to 1 op 20 to 1 tchd 33 to 1)	4
2719³	FIRST CLASS 7-11-2 R Greene, *led till f 5th.*	
	......................(6 to 4 fav op 11 to 10 tchd 13 to 8)	f
Dist: 3½l, 6l, dist. 4m 54.80s. a 21.80s (5 Ran).

(M Henriques, W M Robarts & J Sacchi), G B Balding

3544 Torbay Axminster 100 Handicap Hurdle Class D (0-120 4-y-o and up) £2,862 2m 3f 110yds.........(3:50)

3425*	MR SNAGGLE (Ire) [90] 8-10-0 C Maude, *hld up in tch, wnt second appr 2 out, led bef last, all out.*	
	......................(2 to 1 op 6 to 4 tchd 9 to 4)	1
	KIWI CRYSTAL (NZ) [94] 9-10-4 R Greene, *wl beh frm 3rd, plenty to do 3 out, styd on from nxt to press wnr r-in.*	
	......................(7 to 1 op 5 to 1)	2
3105⁴	SHAHRANI [104] (bl) 5-10-7 (7*) B Moore, *led to 3rd, reminders to dispute ld 5th, rallied bef last, no extr r-in.*	
	......................(3 to 1 op 5 to 1)	3
2455	SUPER TACTICS [115] 9-11-6 (5*) Mr R Thornton, *led 3rd till hdd appr last, wknd r-in.*	
	......................(7 to 4 fav op 6 to 4 tchd 15 to 8)	4
Dist: Nk, 2l, 2l. 4m 33.60s. a 12.60s (4 Ran).

(The Plum Merchants), Simon Earle

3545 Royal Dartmouth Axminster 100 Handicap Chase Class D (0-125 5-y-o and up) £3,798 2¼m.........(4:20)

2896	MONKS JAY [89] 8-10-0 C Maude, *trkd ldr, led appr 5th, rdn clr r-in.*........(12 to 1 op 8 to 1 tchd 14 to 1)	1
3273²	POLDEN PRIDE [113] 9-11-10 B Clifford, *hld up, hdwy to go second aftr 5 out, not fluent 2 out, no extr aftr.*	
	......................(Evens fav op 11 to 10 on tchd 5 to 4)	2
1602⁴	HERBERT BUCHANAN (Ire) [101] 7-10-12 R Johnson, *hld up, trkd wnr 6th till aftr 5 out, wknd 4th 2 out.*	
	......................(4 to 1 tchd 9 to 2 and 7 to 2)	3
3038*	BISHOPS CASTLE (Ire) [94] 9-10-5⁴ J Frost, *led till hdd appr 5th, no hdwy frm 4 out.*....(9 to 4 op 6 to 4 tchd 5 to 2)	4
Dist: 5l, 4l, 3l. 4m 17.80s. a 7.80s (4 Ran).

SR: -/13/-/-/

(J A Cover), G Thorner

3546 Tamar Axminster 100 Amateur Riders' Novices' Hurdle Class E (5-y-o and up) £2,830 2m 3f 110yds ....(4:50)

3108⁴	COUNTRY LOVER (v) 6-11-3¹ (5*) Mr A Farrant, *hld up in tch, led 3 out, drw clr frm nxt.* (11 to 4 op 3 to 1 tchd 7 to 2)	1
3312³	FOXIES LAD 6-11-2 (5*) Mr R Thornton, *hld up in tch, hdwy to ld 6th, hdd nxt, outpcd frm 2 out.*...(Evens fav op 5 to 4 on)	2
2604⁸	CASTLECONNER (Ire) (bl) 6-11-0 (7*) Mr A Holdsworth, *prmnt to 4th, rallied appr 2 out, one pace aftr.* (25 to 1 op 16 to 1)	3
	MON AMIE 7-11-0 (7*) Mr G Shenkin, *beh till hdwy appr 2 out, nvr nrr.*......................(25 to 1 op 14 to 1)	4
3190	NODDADANTE (Ire) 7-11-6 (7*) Mr N R Mitchell, *in rear, styd on frm 2 out, nvr nr to chal.*......(25 to 1 op 20 to 1)	5
3283⁴	PAULA'S BOY (Ire) 7-11-0 (7*) Miss K Di Marte, *pld hrd, led second, clr nxt, hdd 6th, sn wknd, tld off.*	
	......................(66 to 1 op 50 to 1)	6
	ROGERSON 9-11-0 (7*) Mr L Jefford, *beh, brief effrt aftr 3rd, tld off whn pld up bef 2 out.*......(66 to 1 op 50 to 1)	pu
2934⁷	REAL GLEE 8-11-0 (7*) Mr A Wintle, *trkd ldrs till wknd quickly appr 2 out, pld up bef last.*......(9 to 2 op 4 to 1)	pu
	SHARP THYNE (Ire) 7-11-0 (7*) Mr S Mulcaire, *prmnt early, wkng whn mstk 3rd, tld off when pld up bef 2 out.*	
	......................(25 to 1 op 14 to 1)	pu
2769	JOCTOR DON (Ire) 5-11-0 (7*) Mr E Babington, *led to second, beh frm 4th, tld off whn pld up bef 2 out.* (33 to 1 op 20 to 1)	pu
Dist: 8l, 2½l, 2l, 3l, dist. 4m 33.80s. a 12.80s (10 Ran).

(Pond House Gold), M C Pipe

FAIRYHOUSE (IRE) (good to firm)
Wednesday April 2nd

3547 Seamus Maguire Maiden Hurdle (5-y-o and up) £4,110 2m.........(2:15)

2558³	SILVIAN BLISS (USA) 5-11-13 C O'Dwyer, ...(Evens fav)	1
2732	IRIDAL (Ire) 5-11-13 C F Swan, ...(8 to 1)	2
2585	NATIVE FLECK (Ire) 7-12-0 D H O'Connor, ...(20 to 1)	3
3221²	CAVALIER D'OR (USA) 6-12-0 F Woods, ...(6 to 1)	4
2094⁸	EDUARDO (Ire) 7-11-11 (3*) K Whelan, ...(10 to 1)	5
	PREMIER PROJECT (Ire) 5-11-13 D P Donovan, (8 to 1)	6
3068⁷	PRIDE OF TIPPERARY (Ire) 6-10-8 (7*) R Burke, ..(33 to 1)	7
3083	CHATEAU MARTIN (Ire) 5-11-5 C O'Brien, ...(33 to 1)	8
3233⁶	CONAGHER LEADER (Ire) 6-11-6 A J O'Brien, ..(20 to 1)	9
1649²	ANN'S DESIRE (Ire) 6-11-1 P L Malone, ...(12 to 1)	10
	SEVENTY SEVEN MILL (Ire) 8-11-9 (5*) A O'Shea, ..(20 to 1)	11
2443	FANORE (Ire) 6-10-13 (7*) D A McLoughlin, ...(33 to 1)	12
3083	NOMINEE (Ire) 5-11-0 L P Cusack, ...(25 to 1)	13
3224	BITOFABUZZ (Ire) 6-10-13 (7*) Mr J D Moore, .(16 to 1)	14
2054	ALVINE (Ire) 5-11-5 M Duffy, ...(50 to 1)	15
1463⁹	THE TEXAS KID (Ire) 6-10-13 (7*) D M Bean, ..(66 to 1)	16
2582	PARSEE (Ire) 5-10-7 (7*) D W O'Sullivan, ...(16 to 1)	17
	ZALARA 5-11-8 D J Casey, ...(16 to 1)	18
	HUNYANI (Ire) 5-10-12 (7*) B J Geraghty, ...(16 to 1)	19
3226	ELECTRICAL STORM 5-11-0 J Short, ...(33 to 1)	20
2845	SILVER RIVER (Ire) 5-11-0 T J Mitchell, ...(50 to 1)	21
2582	BARNA GIRL (Ire) 7-11-1 J R Barry, ...(100 to 1)	22
3226	KILLCHRIS DREAM (Ire) 6-11-1 T P Rudd, ...(100 to 1)	23
2443	KNOCKAROO (Ire) 6-12-0 T P Treacy, ...(12 to 1)	24
1195	REGGIE'S HONOUR (Ire) 5-10-11 (3*) J Butler, ..(33 to 1)	25
2901⁹	IMPERIAL PLAICE (Ire) 5-10-12 (7*) P G Hourigan, (16 to 1)	f
2964	COCO (Ire) 6-11-1 (5*) T Martin, ...(100 to 1)	pu
Dist: 9l, 6l, ¾l, 5½l. 3m 45.30s. a 1.30s (27 Ran).

SR: 38/29/24/23/17/-/

(Jack Tierney), D K Weld

3548 Oliver Freaney & Co Dan Moore Handicap Chase (Listed) (4-y-o and up) £13,000 2m.............(2:45)

2836	IDIOTS VENTURE [-] 10-10-11 C F Swan, *mstk 1st and drpd beh, hdwy bef 4 out, second 2 out, led aftr last, styd on wl.*	
	......................(10 to 30)	1
3154⁹	CABLE BEACH (Ire) [-] 8-10-11 R Dunwoody, *led till appr 3 out, led nxt, mstk last, sn hdd, styd on.*.....(2 to 1 fav)	2
	OH SO GRUMPY [-] 9-10-11 J Shortt, *trkd ldrs, led bef 3 out to nxt, rdn and no extr.*......................(6 to 1)	3
3112²	BEAKSTOWN (Ire) [-] 8-10-11 T P Treacy, *beh, 3rd at second, drpd back bef 3 out, styd on.*......(3 to 1)	4
2736⁴	ARCTIC WEATHER (Ire) [-] 8-10-11 T P Rudd, *al beh, wknd bef 3 out, sn btn.*......................(6 to 1)	5
Dist: 1½l, 11l, sht-hd, dist. 3m 52.30s. b 1.70s (5 Ran).

SR: 52/50/39/39/-/

(Blackwater Racing Syndicate), A P O'Brien

3549 O'Dea Crop Flex Nutrition Festival Novice Hurdle (Grade 3) (5-y-o and up) £6,850 2½m.............(3:15)

3211³	MOSCOW EXPRESS 5-11-12 C F Swan, *trkd ldrs, hdwy bef 3 out, second nxt, mstk last, sn led, ran on wl....* (5 to 2)	1
3348¹	LIVER BIRD (Ire) 7-11-10 C O'Dwyer, *trkd ldr, led 5 out, hdd aftr last, styd on.*......................(6 to 4 fav)	2
3071¹	BLUSHING SAND (Ire) 7-11-0 (7*) Mr T J Beattie, *hld up rear, hdwy bef 2 out, 3rd appr last, styd on.*...(9 to 1)	3

3375* LANCASTRIAN PRIDE (Ire) 7-11-10 D J Casey, *led to 5 out, rdn and wknd aftr 3 out*............................(7 to 1) 4
1487* STEP ON EYRE (Ire) 7-11-7 R Dunwoody, *mid-div, wknd bef 2 out, sn no dngr*.................................(13 to 2) 5
3523⁹ THREE SCHOLARS 6-11-10 T P Treacy, *al beh, wknd aftr 4 out, sn no dngr*............................(8 to 1) 6
Dist: ½l, 7l, 1l, 4l. 4m 44.70s. a 0.70s (6 Ran).
SR: 31/28/18/20/13/-/ (T Conroy), A P O'Brien

3550 Aer Rianta Duty Free Handicap Chase (5-y-o and up) £9,675 2½m
..............................(3:45)

3155 MANHATTAN CASTLE (Ire) [-] 8-11-6 F Woods, ..(7 to 2 jt-fav) 1
1650 COMMON POLICY (Ire) [-] 8-10-4 C O'Dwyer, ...(5 to 1) 2
2966⁴ BELVEDERIAN [-] 10-11-2 D J Casey, ...(11 to 2) 3
3419 AN MAINEACH (Ire) [-] 8-10-11 C F Swan, ...(8 to 1) 4
2273 THE OUTBACK WAY (Ire) [-] (bl) 7-10-6 D H O'Connor,
....(8 to 1) f
2736 PERSIAN HALO (Ire) [-] 9-10-10 R Dunwoody, (7 to 2 jt-fav) pu
VITAL TRIX [-] 10-9-7 (7*) B J Geraghty, ...(6 to 1) pu
Dist: 1l, dist. 4m 57.30s. a 2.30s (7 Ran).
SR: 9/-/4/-/ (P Fitzpatrick), A L T Moore

3551 Tattersalls EBF Mares Hurdle Championship Final (Listed) (4-y-o and up) £9,675 2½m..............................(4:15)

3223* WINDY BEE (Ire) 6-11-0 (7*) A Nolan, *hld up rear, hdwy bef 4 out, second at nxt, led appr last, styd on wl*.........(6 to 1) 1
3232* AFARKA (Ire) 4-10-2 (7*) B J Geraghty, *led till aftr 3 out, ran on wl frm nxt, not rch wnr*............................(5 to 1) 2
2582* BORO BOW 6-11-7 T P Treacy, *trkd ldrs, rdn frm 2 out, styd on*.......................................(3 to 1 fav) 3
3375² VALENTINE GALE 7-11-2 D J Casey, *mid-div, hdwy appr 4th, second at 6th, led bef 2 out till approaching last, no extr r-in*.......................................(4 to 1) 4
3214⁸ TOUREEN GALE (Ire) 8-11-5 J Shortt, *mid-div, hdwy bef 5 out, 3rd 4 out, rdn and wknd nxt*.................(14 to 1) 5
3346³ REASILVIA (Ire) 7-11-10 R Dunwoody, *beh, hdwy bef 3 out, rdn and sn no dngr*............................(7 to 1) 6
3389⁵ DANNKALIA (Ire) 5-11-1 H Rogers, *trkd ldrs, wknd bef second, sn beh*..................................(50 to 1) 7
3219* BAR FLUTE (Ire) 6-11-5 T Horgan, *trkd ldr, wknd bef 5 out, sn no dngr*...................................(12 to 1) 8
3223⁸ MONDEO ROSE (Ire) 5-11-4 L P Cusack, *mid-div, wknd bef 6th, tld off*..................................(11 to 1) 9
3178⁷ CONNA BRIDE LADY (Ire) 5-11-1 F Woods, *al beh, tld off*.
....(33 to 1) 10
3223³ COMKILRED (Ire) 5-11-4 C O'Dwyer, *beh, hdwy appr 5 out, wknd bef 2 out, pld up before nxt*.................(20 to 1) pu
Dist: Nk, 2½l, hd, 12l. 4m 49.60s. a 5.60s (11 Ran).
 (Brian Nolan), Brian Nolan

3552 Pat Donnelly & Sons Handicap Chase (0-123 4-y-o and up) £5,480 3m 1f......................................(4:45)

2904³ RYHANE (Ire) [-] 8-10-10 F Woods, ...(6 to 4 jt-fav) 1
3074⁸ MYSTICAL AIR (Ire) [-] 7-10-1 (7*) B J Geraghty, ...(5 to 1) 2
2867⁹ MONKEY AGO [-] 10-11-6 (3*) K Whelan, ...(6 to 1) f
2962 FOLLY ROAD (Ire) [-] 7-11-11 C O'Dwyer, ...(6 to 4 jt-fav) f
Dist: Dist. 6m 34.20s. a 19.20s (4 Ran).
 (Mrs B M McKinney), A L T Moore

3553 Davey Auctioneers Champion Flat Race (4-y-o and up) £4,110 2m (5:15)

2235³ DR KING (Ire) 5-12-0 (3*) Mr R Walsh, ...(3 to 1) 1
2270 NAZMI (Ire) 5-11-13 (7*) Mr A K Wyse, ...(8 to 1) 2
OHIO (Ire) 4-11-3 Mr G J Harford, ...(5 to 2 jt-fav) 3
3068⁵ DRAMATIST (Ire) 6-11-11 (7*) Mr R M Walsh, ...(8 to 1) 4
2703² AS ROYAL (Ire) 6-12-1 (3*) Mr P English, ...(8 to 1) 5
3349* TWIN GALE (Ire) 5-11-5 (7*) Mr J P McNamara, ..(5 to 2 jt-fav) 6
2022 JAPAMA (Ire) 6-11-11 Mr A R Coonan, ...(12 to 1) 7
137² PHARDUBH (Ire) 6-11-11 (7*) Mr C A Murphy, ...(8 to 1) 8
BELCAMP BELLE (Ire) 4-10-5 (7*) Mr S P McCarthy,
....(12 to 1) 9
3226⁸ EIRE (Ire) 8-11-11 (7*) Mr M O'Connor, ...(20 to 1) 10
Dist: ½l, hd, 5½l, 4½l. 3m 44.60s. (10 Ran).
 (Mrs George Donohoe), S Donohoe

WORCESTER (good)
Wednesday April 2nd
Going Correction: PLUS 0.40 sec. per fur.

3554 Roundhead Selling Hurdle Class G (4-y-o and up) £2,048 2m......(2:00)

3106² A S JIM 6-11-0 V Slattery, *hld up, hdwy 4 out, led 2 out, styd on wl*..................................(11 to 4 op 2 to 1) 1
BRAVE SPY 6-11-0 D J Burchell, *hld up, hdwy 4 out, ev ch 2 out, one pace frm last*..............(16 to 1 op 12 to 1) 2

3317⁶ STRIKE-A-POSE 7-11-2 Mr J L Llewellyn, *chsd ldrs, ev ch 3 out, styd on same pace*....................(6 to 1 op 6 to 1) 3
2539⁶ DAYDREAM BELIEVER 5-10-9 P Holley, *patiently rdn, styd on frm 3 out, not rch ldrs.*
.........(14 to 1 op 10 to 1 tchd 16 to 1 and 20 to 1) 4
2603 GLENMAVIS 10-11-0 Dr P Pritchard, *prmnt, led aftr 4 out, hdd and wknd 2 out*......(33 to 1 op 20 to 1 tchd 50 to 1) 5
3184⁸ CORPORATE IMAGE 7-11-0 P McLoughlin, *prmnt till wknd aftr 4 out*.........................(16 to 1 op 14 to 1) 6
3317 A BADGE TOO FAR (Ire) (bl) 7-10-9 R Bellamy, *led to second, led briefly 4 out, wknd nxt.*
.........................(50 to 1 op 33 to 1 tchd 66 to 1) 7
WESTCOAST 6-11-0 W Marston, *led second, hdd 4 out, sn wknd*..................(25 to 1 op 10 to 1 tchd 33 to 1) 8
2277 JUST ANDY (v) 6-10-7 (7*) J Mogford, *patiently rdn, effrt 4 out, bhn whn blun and sn rdr 2 out*...(50 to 1 op 33 to 1) ur
3184⁶ VITA NUOVA (Ire) 6-10-9 Mr A Mitchell, *mstk and uns rdr 1st.*
.........................(20 to 1 op 14 to 1 tchd 25 to 1) ur
2768⁴ ILEWIN JANINE (Ire) 6-10-9 D Gallagher, *mid-div whn blun 4th, pld up bef nxt*....(5 to 2 fav op 9 to 4 tchd 3 to 1) pu
3283⁶ SPRIG MUSLIN 5-10-6 (3*) Sophie Mitchell, *al in rear, tld off frm 3rd, pld up bef 2 out..(11 to 2 op 7 to 1 tchd 6 to 1) pu
3283 RAKAPOSHI IMP 7-10-2 (7*) M Keighley, *pld up aftr second, sddl slpd*.......................(50 to 1 op 20 to 1) pu
Dist: 7l, 7l, 7l, 1½l, 7l, dist, 12l. 3m 55.60s. a 15.60s (13 Ran).
 (Owen O'Neill), O O'Neill

3555 Levy Board Novices' Hurdle Class E (4-y-o and up) £2,880 2m.....(2:30)

3332³ RIPARIUS (USA) 6-11-0 J Osborne, *al prmnt, led 2 out, pushed out.*
........(13 to 8 fav op 6 to 4 tchd 15 to 8 and 2 to 1) 1
MISCHIEF STAR 4-10-3 M A Fitzgerald, *led to 2 out, hrd rdn, ran on one pace*.........(9 to 1 op 7 to 1 tchd 10 to 1) 2
2920⁴ MOON DEVIL (Ire) 7-11-0 J Railton, *al prmnt, chs on appr 3 out, ran on flt*..........................(10 to 1 tchd 12 to 1) 3
3117⁴ SPRING CAMPAIGN (Ire) 4-10-8 Jamie Evans, *al prmnt, ev ch 3 out, wknd last*..........................(9 to 1 op 5 to 1) 4
3172³ LEAP FROG 6-11-0 W Marston, *hdwy 4th, wknd 3 out.*
.........................(7 to 1 op 5 to 1 tchd 15 to 2) 5
2242⁸ KEVASINGO 5-11-0 D Bridgwater, *chsd ldr to 4th, wknd appr 3 out*.......................(14 to 1 op 25 to 1) 6
3108⁵ KEEN BID (Ire) 6-11-0 M Richards, *hdwy 3rd, wknd 5th.*
.........................(6 to 1 tchd 7 to 1 and 5 to 1) 7
3253⁵ THE FLYING DOCTOR (Ire) (v) 7-11-0 J R Kavanagh, *al beh.*
.........................(20 to 1 tchd 25 to 1) 8
FEARLESS HUSSAR 7-11-0 P Holley, *al beh*......(50 to 1) 9
MORDROS 7-10-11 (3*) T Dascombe, *hdwy 5th, wknd appr 3 out*.......................(100 to 1 op 66 to 1 tchd 150 to 1) 10
ROUGH DIAMOND 5-11-0 B Powell, *al beh, tld off frm 3rd*........................(66 to 1 op 33 to 1) 11
2925 TIUTCHEV 4-10-8 J Culloty, *beh whn blun and uns rdr 3rd.*
.........................(11 to 2 op 5 to 1 tchd 6 to 1) ur
2503 ARTIC MEADOW 6-10-9 T Kent, *mstks 1st 2, sddl slpd and pld up bef 3rd*......(100 to 1 op 50 to 1 tchd 200 to 1) pu
Dist: 3l, 4l, 1¼l, 9l, 7l, 2l, sht-hd, 1½l, 13l, 30l. 3m 56.50s. a 16.50s (13 Ran).
 (Mrs David Blackburn), P R Webber

3556 Bromyard Novices' Chase Class D (5-y-o and up) £4,666 2m 7f 110yds...................................(3:00)

2461* DOMAINE DE PRON (Fr) 6-11-8 R Bellamy, *chsd ldr, led 11th, hdd nxt, led briefly 5 out, not clr run appr next, led and lft clear 3 out*.........................(7 to 2 op 3 to 1) 1
3171² HIGH LEARIE 7-11-8 J A McCarthy, *led to 11th, led ag'n nxt, jmpd right and hdd briefly 5 out, headed and wknd 3 out.*
.........................(13 to 8 fav op 6 to 4 tchd 7 to 4) 2
2259 HALKOPOUS 11-11-2 N Williamson, *hld up, hdwy 6th, pld ldr 4 out, gng wl whn f nxt*...(11 to 4 op 2 to 1 tchd 5 to 1) f
2950⁴ SPIN ECHO 8-11-2 W Marston, *chsd ldrs till f 8th.*
.........................(16 to 1 tchd 20 to 1) f
HAZLE WAND 10-11-2 Mr R Armson, *prmnt to hfwy, in rear whn blun and uns rdr 6 out*..........(66 to 1 op 50 to 1) ur
3320 LEDBURIAN (bl) 7-10-13 (3*) Guy Lewis, *prmnt till blun and uns rdr 6th*.......................(66 to 1 op 50 to 1) ur
3271⁷ CHARLIE BEE 8-11-2 B Powell, *not jump wl, sn tld off, pld up bef 12th*...................(50 to 1 op 33 to 1) pu
5277⁶ PAVI'S BROTHER 9-11-8 M Richards, *chsd ldrs, hit 9th, sn lost pl, pld up bef 12th, broke blood vessel.*
.........................(9 to 2 op 6 to 1) pu
Dist: Dist. 6m 8.30s. (8 Ran).
 (Mrs L C Taylor), Mrs L C Taylor

3557 Evesham Handicap Hurdle Class C (0-135 4-y-o and up) £3,955 3m..............................(3:30)

3209³ ROYAL PIPER (NZ) [106] 10-10-4 L Harvey, *hdwy 4 out, led r-in, all out*........................(14 to 1 op 12 to 1) 1
3166* BARFORD SOVEREIGN [112] 5-10-10 A Dobbin, *al prmnt, led 4 out, hdd r-in, ran on.*(13 to 2 op 5 to 1 tchd 7 to 1) 2
2923² OATIS ROSE [105] 7-10-3 N Williamson, *chsd ldrs, hrd rdn 5th, lost pl 7th, rallied appr 3 out, ran on.*
.........................(6 to 1 op 5 to 1 tchd 13 to 2) 3

493

3266² BANKHEAD (Ire) [127] 8-11-4 (7⁰) Miss C Spearing, *lost pl 5th, rallied 7th, outpcd appr 3 out, ran on frm last.*
.................................(9 to 2 fav op 5 to 1 tchd 4 to 1) 4

3041² SCOTBY (Bel) [112] 7-10-10 B Powell, *al prmnt, rdn 3 out, one pace.*...................(9 to 1 op 8 to 1) 5

2559 ULURU (Ire) [104] 9-10-2 J A McCarthy, *prmnt till rdn and outpcd 8th, ran on frm last.*...........(10 to 1 op 8 to 1) 6

3116⁹ GENERAL MOUKTAR [110] 7-10-8 Jamie Evans, *hld up, steady hdwy appr 3 out, wknd approaching last.*
.... 7

3151 WISLEY WONDER (Ire) [125] 7-11-9 C Llewellyn, *jmpd slwly, led, hdd 4th, hdd 4 out, wknd last.*
.................................(6 to 1 op 11 to 2 tchd 13 to 2) 8

JIMBALOU [102] 14-10-0 D Gallagher, *tld off till ran on frm 3 out.*..(100 to 1) 9

2801⁷ NICK THE BEAK (Ire) [107] 8-10-5 R Supple, *prmnt till wknd 2 out.*.............................(14 to 1 op 12 to 1) 10

3119 BRACKENHEATH (Ire) [105] 6-10-3 J R Kavanagh, *wth ldr to 7th, wknd appr 3 out.*.................(9 to 1 op 7 to 1) pu

Dist: ½l, 1½l, 1¼l, 1¼l, 2l, sht-hd, 3½l, nk, 14l, 3½l. 5m 58.60s. a 22.60s (11 Ran).

(A M Darlington), A J Wilson

3558 Commandery Amateur Riders' Handicap Hurdle Class E (0-115 4-y-o and up) £2,635 2¼m....... (4:00)

2356 HANDY LASS [95] 8-10-2 (7⁰) Mr O McPhail, *hld up, hdwy 5th, led appr last, rdn out....* (10 to 1 op 8 to 1 tchd 11 to 1) 1

2526⁴ PETER MONAMY [100] (bl) 5-10-11 (3⁰) Mr M Rimell, *chsd ldrs, rdn and ev ch appr 2 out, styd on same pace.*
.................................(11 to 2 op 5 to 1 tchd 9 to 2) 2

3301³ KING'S CROSS [100] 8-10-9 (5⁰) Mr J Jukes, *patiently rdn, hdwy 4 out, ridden 2 out, styd on same pace.*
.................................(16 to 1 op 14 to 1) 3

3268⁷ BARTON SCAMP [93] 5-10-11 (7⁰) Mr R Wakley, *led, hdd and edgd rght appr last, sn wknd.*
.... 4

3278⁸ ABOVE THE CUT (USA) [89] 5-10-1⁵ (7⁰) Mr P Scott, *hld up, jmp ldd dr 3 out, wknd nxt....* (3 to 1 fav op 7 to 2) 5

3444⁵ GLEN MIRAGE [86] 12-9-7 (7⁰) Miss M Coombe, *chsd ldrs, lost pl 4th, nvr dngrs aftrwards.......*(20 to 1 op 16 to 1) 6

3283 HALHAM TARN (Ire) [88] 7-9-9 (7⁰) Miss A Dudley, *nvr rchd chalg pos.*...............(20 to 1 op 14 to 1 tchd 25 to 1) 7

3139 DAILY SPORT GIRL [86] 8-9-7 (7⁰) Miss E J Jones, *hdwy 4th, rdn and wknd 2 out...........*(33 to 1 op 20 to 1) 8

3283² HANGING GROVE (Ire) [86] 7-9-7 (7⁰) Mr Matthew Wells, *chsd ldrs, mstk 5th, wknd 3 out...........*(12 to 1 op 7 to 1) 9

3100 BALLET ROYAL (USA) [114] 8-11-7 (7⁰) Mr A Charles-Jones, *sn wl beh.*......................................(33 to 1) 10

3252³ CHRIS'S GLEN [88] (v) 8-9-10¹ (7⁰) Miss V Roberts, *prmnt till wknd 4 out.*............(16 to 1 op 14 to 1) 11

3028 WEST BAY BREEZE [86] 5-9-7 (7⁰) Mr S Durack, *beh frm 5th.*...(33 to 1) 12

2877 RELKOWEN [86] 7-9-9² (7⁰) Mr J Rees, *prmnt to 5th, sn wl beh.*......................(14 to 1 op 10 to 1) 13

2783² CLASSIC PAL (USA) [86] 6-9-9 (5⁰) Miss P Jones, *mid-div, hmpd bend aftr 3rd, taking clr order whn f nxt.* f

2729 THE CAUMRUE (Ire) [110] 9-11-3 (7⁰) Mr J Thatcher, *al beh, tld off whn pld up bef 3 out.*..........(20 to 1 op 14 to 1) pu

Dist: 3l, 10l, 2l, 6l, ¾l, 2½l, 8l, 7l, 1½l, 10l. 4m 21.10s. a 14.10s (15 Ran).
SR: 12/14/4/-/-/-/   (G W Hackling), J S Smith

3559 Restoration Novices' Handicap Chase Class E (0-100 5-y-o and up) £3,910 2½m 110yds......... (4:30)

3285⁴ NO FIDDLING (Ire) [79] 6-10-9 D Bridgwater, *hdwy 4 out, str run frm last, led cl hme.* (10 to 1 op 8 to 1 tchd 11 to 1) 1

3271⁵ WINNOW [70] 7-10-0 C Rae, *hdwy 11th, ran on wl frm last.*
.................................(14 to 1 op 10 to 1 tchd 20 to 1) 2

2877 LOBSTER COTTAGE [87] 9-11-3 S McNeill, *chsd ldr, led tenth, clr 4 out, hit 2 out, wknd and hdd nr finish.*
.................................(14 to 1 op 16 to 1) 3

3320 DANDIE IMP [78] 9-10-8 D Walsh, *led to tenth, ev ch appr 4 out, one pace.*..................(8 to 1 op 7 to 1) 4

3333² BOOTS N ALL (Ire) [77] 7-10-7 A Dobbin, *chsd ldrs, 3rd whn hit 2 out, sn wknd.*
.................................(11 to 4 fav op 9 to 4 tchd 3 to 1 and 100 to 30) 5

2889⁷ HARDY BREEZE (Ire) [80] 6-10-7 (3⁰) P Henley, *hdwy 5th, wknd 4 out.*..........................(33 to 1) 6

3333⁴ SPRING TO GLORY [93] 10-11-9 A Thornton, *prmnt till wknd off....*..................(14 to 1 op 12 to 1) 7

3143⁴ COURT MASTER (Ire) [88] 9-11-4 B Powell, *wl beh frm 9th, tld off....*...................(9 to 1 op 10 to 1) 8

3138⁵ KING'S SHILLING (USA) [75] 10-10-5 Jacqui Oliver, *hdwy 7th, sn rdn and wknd, tld off whn pld up bef 4 out.*
.................................(16 to 1 op 14 to 1) pu

2718 TOP IT ALL [70] 9-10-0 C Llewellyn, *beh frm 6th, tld off whn pld up bef 4 out.*....................(50 to 1) pu

3000 BONNIFER (Ire) [70] 8-10-0 W Marston, *al beh, tld off whn blun 11th, pld up bef 4 out.*..............(33 to 1) pu

STAMP DUTY [74] 10-10-4³ M A Fitzgerald, *mstks, beh frm 7th, tld off whn pld up bef 4 out.*...........(14 to 1) pu

3023 DRESS DANCE (Ire) [72] 7-10-2 G Upton, *tld off whn blun 8th, pld up bef 4 out.*......(20 to 1 op 16 to 1 tchd 25 to 1) pu

---

2913³ JOVIAL MAN (Ire) [94] 8-11-10 P Holley, *tld off whn pld up bef 4 out.*...................(11 to 1 op 8 to 1 tchd 12 to 1) pu

3297² RAINCHECK [75] 6-10-5 L Harvey, *middle div whn blun 5th, rdn nxt, sn beh, tld off when pld up bef 4 out.*
.................................(16 to 1 op 14 to 1) pu

3104 GIVRY (Ire) [80] 7-10-7 (3⁰) Sophie Mitchell, *al beh, tld off whn pld up bef 4 out.*..........(20 to 1 op 16 to 1) pu

2456³ RIDING CROP (Ire) [88] 7-11-4 J R Kavanagh, *mstk second, beh frm 5th, tld off whn pld up bef 4 out.* (7 to 1 op 6 to 1) pu

Dist: ½l, 1l, 13l, 2½l, 4l, nk, 17l. 5m 19.80s. a 22.80s (17 Ran).

(Malcolm Batchelor), G M McCourt

3560 Worcester Standard Open National Hunt Flat Class H (Div I) (4,5,6-y-o) £1,399 2m.............(5:00)

RUPERT BLUES 5-11-4 M Richards, *hld up, hdwy 5 fs out, led o'r 2 out, drvn clr.* (12 to 1 op 14 to 1 tchd 20 to 1) 1

3322⁶ STAR ADVENTURE 5-11-4 Miss E James, *hld up, hdwy 5 fs out, crrd rght 3 out, ran on und pres, ins last.*
.................................(12 to 1 op 5 to 1) 2

3122² CERTAIN SHOT 6-11-4 D Bridgwater, *al prmnt, led 3 fs out, sn hdd....*...............(5 to 1 op 5 to 1) 3

3335⁶ DAMIEN'S CHOICE (Ire) 5-11-4 Derek Byrne, *hld up, hdwy 6 fs out, styd on....* (4 to 1 fav op 3 to 1 tchd 9 to 2) 4

DUTY FREE 4-10-12 J A McCarthy, *hld up, hdwy o'r 5 fs out, kpt on.*...........................(50 to 1 op 33 to 1) 5

2831⁵ MONTROE (Ire) 5-11-4 D O'Sullivan, *hld up, hdwy o'r 4 fs out, ran on.*...................(9 to 2 op 5 to 2) 6

WINDLE BROOK 5-11-4 S McNeill, *hld up, nvr plcd to chal.*
.................................(16 to 1 op 8 to 1) 7

JAZZ DUKE 4-10-12 A McCabe, *hld up, hdwy hfwy, rdn and hng rght, 3 fs out, sn btn.......*(20 to 1 op 16 to 1) 8

KNIGHTSBRIDGE GIRL (Ire) 6-10-13 N Williamson, *hdwy hfwy, wknd o'r 3 fs out.*....................(20 to 1 op 16 to 1) 9

EMERALD LAMP 6-11-4 V Slattery, *nvr nr to chal.*
.................................(33 to 1 tchd 20 to 1 and 50 to 1) 10

3322⁹ SHROPSHIRE GALE (Ire) 6-10-11 (7⁰) X Aizpuru, *rcd keenly, chsd ldr, led ten fs out, rdn and hdd 3 out, sn wknd.*
.................................(9 to 1 op 5 to 1 tchd 10 to 1) 11

3335 ICKFORD OKEY 5-11-4 D Gallagher, *chsd ldrs, rdn 7 fs out, sn lost pl.....................*(16 to 1 op 16 to 1) 12

TWELVE CLUB 4-10-12 A Thornton, *hld up, hdwy 5 fs out, wknd 3 out..........................*(10 to 1 op 4 to 1) 13

BERTIE BAVARD 5-11-4 Miss E Johnson Houghton, *mid-div, effrt hfwy, btn 4 fs out....*(16 to 1 op 7 to 1 tchd 20 to 1) 14

JOLSON 6-11-1 (3⁰) P Henley, *hld up, hdwy hfwy, wknd 5 fs out.*.................................(25 to 1 tchd 33 to 1) 15

MINER'S ROSE (Ire) 6-10-13 M A Fitzgerald, *in tch, effrt hfwy, wknd o'r 5 fs out...........*(50 to 1 op 33 to 1) 16

AVONCLIFF 4-10-7 W Marston, *in tch till wknd 6 fs out.*
.................................(14 to 1 op 8 to 1 tchd 16 to 1) 17

1802⁶ BALLINA 5-10-11 (7⁰) J T Nolan, *patiently rdn, hdwy hfwy, wknd 4 out.................*(25 to 1 op 14 to 1) 18

CHATTER BOX 5-10-13 R Supple, *nvr rchd ldrs.*
.................................(33 to 1 op 50 to 1) 19

HOTEL CASINO (NZ) 5-11-4 G Tormey, *hdwy 8 fs out, wknd 6 out......................*(33 to 1 tchd 50 to 1) 20

SO WELCOME 5-10-13 T G McLaughlin, *led, hdd ten fs out, sn lost pl, pld up.*.........(50 to 1 tchd 66 to 1) pu

Dist: ¾l, nk, 2½l, 3½l, nk, nk, 1½l, 10l, 3½l, 3l. 3m 56.20s. (21 Ran).

(Robert Skillen), J S King

3561 Worcester Standard Open National Hunt Flat Class H (Div II) (4,5,6-y-o) £1,399 2m....................(5:30)

2961⁴ MELODY MAID 5-11-6 M A Fitzgerald, *prmnt, chsd clr ldr frm 5 fs out, led o'r 2 out, drvn clear.*
.................................(2 to 1 fav op 5 to 4 on) 1

2567⁵ COBLE LANE 5-11-4 J Osborne, *led, sn clr, hdd o'r 2 fs out, ran on.................*(16 to 1 op 10 to 1) 2

BRUSH WITH FAME (Ire) 5-11-4 G Tormey, *hdwy 6 fs out, ran on wl fnl furlong, not rch 1st 2......*(16 to 1 op 10 to 1) 3

QUABMATIC 4-10-7 (5⁰) G Supple, *chsd ldr till 5 fs out, ran on one pace.*.................(50 to 1 op 33 to 1) 4

REGAL SPRING (Ire) 5-11-4 A Thornton, *hdwy 6 fs out, styd on, nvr nr to chal.....*(9 to 1 op 5 to 1 tchd 10 to 1) 5

1942 SARAS DELIGHT 5-11-1 (3⁰) R Massey, *hdwy fnl 2 fs, nvr nrr.*.................(14 to 1 op 12 to 1 tchd 16 to 1) 6

3082⁴ FORTUNES FLIGHT (Ire) 4-10-12 M Richards, *chsd ldrs, rdn 7 fs, hng lft 3 out, sn wknd...*(9 to 2 tchd 5 to 1 and 4 to 1) 7

MISS BLUES SINGER 4-10-7 B Powell, *beh till styd on fnl 2 fs.*.................(66 to 1 op 50 to 1 tchd 100 to 1) 8

LIGHTENING STEEL 6-11-4 Mr A Phillips, *nvr nr ldrs.*
.................................(50 to 1) 9

OUR MAN FLIN (Ire) 4-10-12 S Burrough, *hdwy 6 fs out, nvr rchd ldrs..................*(25 to 1 op 16 to 1 tchd 33 to 1) 10

DANDE DOVE 6-11-4 S McNeill, *hdwy 6 fs out, wknd 3 out.*
.................................(6 to 1 op 7 to 1) 11

LONGSHORE 4-11-4 M Brennan, *prmnt till wknd 6 fs out.*
.................................(66 to 1 op 33 to 1 tchd 100 to 1) 12

3335 SILVER TREASURE (Ire) 5-11-4 Derek Byrne, *beh fnl 5 fs.*
.................................(16 to 1 op 25 to 1) 13

ROSGLINN (Ire) 5-10-13 Jacqui Oliver, *prmnt 6 fs.*
.................................(66 to 1 op 50 to 1 tchd 100 to 1) 14

ROXY HICKS 5-10-6 (7*) Mr O McPhail, *prmnt till wknd 6 fs out*..................(66 to 1 op 40 to 1 tchd 100 to 1)   15
NATIONAL FIASCO 4-10-12 S Wynne, *tld off fnl ten fs*...............(33 to 1 op 25 to 1 tchd 50 to 1)   16
LUCYS RED SLIPPER 5-10-6 (7*) Mr L Baker, *prmnt 6 fs, tld off*........(66 to 1 op 50 to 1 tchd 100 to 1)   17
2961⁸ CURTIS THE SECOND 4-10-4 (3*) P Henley, *tld off*...........................(50 to 1 op 25 to 1)   18
3082⁵ DESERT WAY (Ire) 4-10-12 N Williamson, *tld off whn pld up o'r 4 fs out*..............................(7 to 1 op 5 to 1)   pu
HEY ZOE 4-10-0 (7*) M Keighley, *sn tld off, pld up o'r one furlong out*.............(66 to 1 op 50 to 1 tchd 100 to 1)   pu
Dist: 10l, 2l, 2½l, 1l, 16l, 3l, 6l, hd, ¾l, 2½l. 3m 51.10s. (20 Ran).
(R J Parish), N J Henderson

AINTREE (good)
Thursday April 3rd
Going Correction: PLUS 0.35 sec. per fur. (races 1,5,6,7), PLUS 0.40 (2,3,4)

3562 Seagram Top Novices' Hurdle Class A Grade 2 (4-y-o and up) £16,730 2m 110yds...................... (2:00)

3296* MIDNIGHT LEGEND 6-11-0 R Johnson, *pressed ldr, led 3 out, not fluent nxt, styd on wl r-in.*..........................(11 to 2 op 7 to 2 tchd 6 to 1)   1
3172* SHARPICAL 5-11-0 M A Fitzgerald, *patiently rdn, smooth hdwy frm 4 out, chsd wnr from betw last 2, hit last, hng lft r-in, no extr.*..........(100 to 30 fav op 5 to 2 tchd 7 to 2)   2
2893² HIGH IN THE CLOUDS (Ire) 5-11-0 S Wynne, *settled midfield, improved gng wl to track ldrs 3 out, ev ch nxt, ran on same pace r-in*..........................(9 to 1 op 6 to 1)   3
3385² MISTER RM 5-11-0 C Llewellyn, *co'red up midfield, not fluent 5th, niggled alng and shrtlvd effrt 3 out, no imprsn frm nxt.*..........................(11 to 1 op 8 to 1 tchd 12 to 1)   4
2937* NIGEL'S LAD (Ire) 5-11-0 M Foster, *led till hdd and rdn 3 out, fdd nxt.*..........................(9 to 2 op 7 to 2 tchd 5 to 1)   5
2893* GREEN GREEN DESERT (Fr) 6-11-0 D Bridgwater, *settled rear, mstk 4th, outpcd and rdn aftr four out, sn lost tch, tld off.*..........................(4 to 1 op 5 to 2)   6
3111³ NORDIC BREEZE (Ire) (bl) 5-11-0 D Walsh, *wtd wth, not fluent second, struggling and lost tch aftr 4 out, tld off.*..........................(9 to 1 op 5 to 1)   7
3064⁶ NO PATTERN (v) 5-11-0 L Wyer, *pld hrd, blun 1st, not jump wl aftr, tld off hfwy, pulled up bef 2 out...*(25 to 1 op 16 to 1)   pu
3280* CRANDON BOULEVARD 4-10-8 J Osborne, *trkd ldrs, mstk 5th and 4 out, sn struggling to hold pl, lost tch and pld up bef 2 out.*..........................(20 to 1 tchd 25 to 1)   pu
Dist: 2l, 3l, 10l, 2l, dist, 25l. 3m 56.30s. a 8.30s (9 Ran).
SR: 60/58/55/45/43/-/   (Mrs H J Clarke), D Nicholson

3563 Martell Cup Chase Class A Grade 2 (5-y-o and up) £37,961 3m 1f..(2:35)

3152² BARTON BANK 11-11-5 D Walsh, *nt 1st, led, not fluent tenth, mstk and hdd 3 out, rallied to ld betw last 2, clr last, styd on strly.*..........(100 to 30 op 5 to 2 tchd 7 to 2)   1
2836² MERRY GALE (Ire) 9-11-5 C O'Dwyer, *trkd ldr, not fluent tenth and nxt, chlgd 4 out, sn led, hdd betw last 2, soon no extr.*..........................(11 to 2 op 5 to 1 tchd 13 to 2)   2
ROUYAN 11-11-5 J F Titley, *chsd ldg pair, not fluent 6th, rdn and styd on appr last, no imprsn.*..........................(20 to 1 op 25 to 1 tchd 33 to 1)   3
3152⁵ CHALLENGER DU LUC (Fr) (bl) 7-11-5 C Maude, *settled rear, blun 5 out, jmpd slwly and outpcd nxt, nvr able to chal.*..........................(7 to 2 op 5 to 2)   4
3152⁶ ONE MAN (Ire) 9-11-13 R Dunwoody, *hld up, hdwy 8th, not fluent tenth, pld up bef nxt, broke blood vessel.*..........................(6 to 4 fav op Evens)   pu
Dist: 9l, 1½l, 2l. 6m 25.90s. a 20.90s (5 Ran).
(Mrs J Mould), D Nicholson

3564 Sandeman Maghull Novices' Chase Class A Grade 1 (5-y-o and up) £28,850 2m................ (3:10)

3112² SQUIRE SILK 8-11-4 J Osborne, *wtd wth, improved frm 4 out, lft second nxt, hmpd and left in ld 2 out, clr whn blun last.*..........................(2 to 1 op 6 to 4 tchd 9 to 4)   1
1996³ OH SO RISKY 10-11-4 P Holley, *chsd ldrs, sn in tch, pushed alng whn slightly hmpd 3 out, rdn and one pace frm nxt.*..........................(11 to 1 op 14 to 1 tchd 16 to 1)   2
3079* SUBLIME FELLOW (Ire) 7-11-4 M A Fitzgerald, *settled in tch, keen, chalg whn hit 7th, feeling pace 4 out, no imprsn aftr.*..........................(16 to 1 op 20 to 1)   3
2505* AMANCIO (USA) 6-11-4 C Maude, *led till hdd and jmpd slwly 6th, rallied 8th, wknd quickly aftr 4 out, beh whn jumped slowly nxt, tld off.*........(15 to 2 op 6 to 1 tchd 8 to 1)   4
3112 MULLIGAN (Ire) 9-11-4 D Gallagher, *chsd ldr, led 6th, quickened 4 out, still gng wl whn f 2 out.* (11 to 8 fav op 5 to 4)   f
3363³ FLYING INSTRUCTOR 7-11-4 N Williamson, *wtd wth, cld 8th, chlgd 4 out, ev ch whn f nxt.* (8 to 1 op 7 to 1 tchd 9 to 1)   f
Dist: 15l, 16l, 12l. 3m 58.70s. a 11.70s (6 Ran).
SR: 37/22/6/   (Robert Ogden), Andrew Turnell

3565 John Hughes Trophy Chase Handicap Class B (0-145 5-y-o and up) £23,577 2¾m............... (3:45)

3134⁸ BELLS LIFE (Ire) [130] 8-11-4 G Tormey, *hld up, steady hdwy hfwy, led 4 out, clr nxt, badly hmpd elbow, rdn and ran on strly cl hme.*..........................(14 to 1 tchd 16 to 1)   1
3175³ YEOMAN WARRIOR [115] 10-10-3³ D O'Sullivan, *hld up in rear, improved frm hfwy, trkd ldrs 3 out, styd on wl r-in, no imprsn cl hme.*..........................(33 to 1 tchd 40 to 1)   2
3114⁸ KADI (Ger) [135] 8-11-9 R Johnson, *in tch, pushed alng and not fluent 4 out, chalg whn mstk 2 out, sn rdn and one pace.*..........................(8 to 1 co-fav op 6 to 1)   3
2814² ALY DALEY (Ire) [112] 9-9-11 (3*) Mr C Bonner, *not fluent towards rear, pckd tenth, hit 13th, outpcd aftr 4 out, styd on betw last 2, unbl to chal.*..........................(33 to 1)   4
3101⁴ NO PAIN NO GAIN (Ire) [116] 9-10-4 P Hide, *hld up, steady hdwy to chase ldrs aftr 4 out, chalg whn slight mstk 2 out, fdd appr last.*..........................(14 to 1 tchd 16 to 1)   5
3329" SENOR EL BETRUTTI (Ire) [140] 8-12-0 G Bradley, *hld up, hmpd 3rd (Chair), pushed alng and outpcd 5 out, no dngr aftr nxt.*..........................(8 to 1 co-fav op 6 to 1)   6
3010⁴ SUPER SANDY [112] 10-10-0 K Johnson, *cl up till lost pl 9th, wl beh 5 out, sn no dngr.*..........................(150 to 1 op 100 to 1 tchd 200 to 1)   7
3264² SAILOR JIM [112] 10-10-0 N Williamson, *keen hold, chsd ldr till lft in ld tenth (Becher's), jmpd slwly and hdd 4 out, wknd quickly aftr nxt.*..........................(20 to 1)   8
3134 GOLDEN SPINNER [133] 10-11-7 M A Fitzgerald, *in tch, not fluent 8th, lost touch 12th (Canal Turn), sn wl beh.* (8 to 1 co-fav op 6 to 1)   9
3067⁵ KINGS CHERRY (Ire) [112] 9-10-0 C Llewellyn, *f 1st.* (20 to 1)   f
3133* FLIMSY TRUTH [121] 11-10-9⁷ Mr M Harris, *hld up towards rear, not fluent 6th, f 9th.*..................(12 to 1 op 8 to 1)   f
2800⁶ CROPREDY LAD [114] 10-10-2² A Thornton, *f 1st.*..........................(50 to 1 op 33 to 1 tchd 100 to 1)   f
2947" TOO PLUSH [115] 8-10-3 L Harvey, *midfield whn f 3rd (Chair).*..........................(10 to 1 op 6 to 1)   f
2772⁵ GRIFFINS BAR [112] 9-10-0 W Marston, *cl up, 3rd whn rdr lost iron and uns rider 12th (Canal Turn)...*(100 to 1)   ur
2986⁴ MASTER BOSTON (Ire) [125] 9-10-13 Richard Guest, *in tch, mstk and uns rdr second.*..........................(20 to 1 op 25 to 1 tchd 33 to 1)   ur
447 POND HOUSE (Ire) [112] 8-10-0 Jamie Evans, *hmpd and uns rdr 1st...*..........................(20 to 1 tchd 25 to 1)   ur
2935² CHANGE THE REIGN [112] 10-9-9 (5*) Mr R Thornton, *hmpd and brght dwn 1st...*..........................(20 to 1)   bd
COONAWARA [137] 11-11-11 R Dunwoody, *keen hold, led and jmpd wl till blun tenth (Becher's), sn pld up, broke leg, destroyed...*..........................(9 to 1 op 13 to 1 tchd 16 to 1)   pu
2947¹⁴ THE FROG PRINCE (Ire) [125] 9-10-13 J Osborne, *hld up, beh whn pld up 7th, lme....* (9 to 1 op 6 to 1 tchd 10 to 1)   pu
3114⁴ ROMANY CREEK [117] (v) 8-10-5 J Culloty, *jmpd poorly in rear, wl beh whn pld up 9th, lme.*..........................(5 to 1 co-fav op 6 to 1)   pu
Dist: 3l, 5l, 1¼l, 4l, 18l, 11l, 3½l, 4l. 5m 38.60s. a 12.60s (20 Ran).
SR: 52/34/49/24/24/30/-/-/   (R Gibbs), P J Hobbs

3566 Glenlivet Anniversary 4-y-o Novices' Hurdle Class A Grade 2 £26,234 2m 110yds...................... (4:20)

3323² QUAKERS FIELD 11-0 D Gallagher, *settled in tch, gd hdwy frm off the pace appr 3 out, led betw last 2, forged clr r-in.*..........................(8 to 1 tchd 9 to 1)   1
2727² FAR DAWN (USA) 11-0 C Maude, *nvr far away, led 3 out, jnd nxt, hdd and rdn betw last 2, not quicken r-in.*..........................(14 to 1 op 10 to 1)   2
3150² CIRCUS STAR 11-0 R Johnson, *wtd wth, improved frm hfwy, effrt appr 3 out, rdn and one pace from betw last 2.*..........................(6 to 1 op 4 to 1 tchd 13 to 2)   3
2828³ SUMMER SPELL (USA) 11-0 M A Fitzgerald, *tucked away on ins, effrt whn squeezed for room appr 3 out, effrt aftr nxt, no imprsn.*..........................(7 to 1 tchd 8 to 1)   4
3150⁸ MR WILD (USA) 11-0 R Dunwoody, *trkd ldrs, effrt appr 3 out, und pres and fdg whn hmpd nxt, sn btn.*..........................(16 to 1 op 14 to 1 tchd 20 to 1)   5
3332" QUALITY (Ire) 11-0 N Williamson, *nvr far away, ev ch whn edgd rght and bumped appr 3 out, fdd bef nxt.*..........................(14 to 1 op 12 to 1)   6
3150⁶ MARLONETTE (Ire) 10-9 D J Casey, *wtd wth, improved appr 3 out, drvn alng bef nxt, wknd quickly and lost tch.*..........................(10 to 1 tchd 12 to 1)   7
2405 BALLADUR (USA) 11-0 J F Titley, *patiently rdn, effrt appr 3 out, wknd bef nxt, lost tch...*(25 to 1 tchd 33 to 1)   8
3442⁴ NOBLE LORD 11-0 B Powell, *led to second, hndy till fdd aftr 3 out, tld off...*..........................(20 to 1)   9
2470² HARD NEWS (USA) 11-0 C O'Dwyer, *led second, clr 4th, hdd 3 out, sn btn, tld off.*..................(13 to 2 op 5 to 1)   10
3150⁴ L'OPERA (Fr) 11-0 J Osborne, *tucked away beh ldrs, imprvg whn short of room and hmpd appr 3 out, 4th and drvn alng when f 2 out........* (5 to 2 fav op 2 to 1 tchd 11 to 4)   f
2925⁴ GINGER FOX (USA) 11-0 J Culloty, *tucked away beh ldrs, effrt pushed alng whn hmpd appr 3 out, not reco'r, pld up bef nxt....*..........................(12 to 1 op 10 to 1 tchd 14 to 1)   pu
Dist: 5l, 5l, 1l, 1l, 4l, 2l, 11l, 2l, 17l, ½l. 3m 58.00s. a 10.00s (12 Ran).

SR: 43/38/33/32/28/26/10/13/-/

(K Higson), G L Moore

3567 Cuvee Napa Novices' Hunters' Chase Class B (5-y-o and up) £7,107 3m 1f...................................(4:50)

2891⁴ BITOFAMIXUP (Ire) 6-12-0 Mr P Hacking, *jmpd wl, hld up, smooth hdwy to chase ldr 6 out, led sn aftr 4 out, soon quickened clr, imprsv*..................(9 to 4 op 7 to 4) 1
HOWAYMAN 7-12-0 Mr A Parker, *in tch, not fluent 4th, trkd ldrs hfwy till outpcd four out, no extr wth wnr.*
....(7 to 1 op 6 to 1) 2
3313² ARDBRENNAN 10-12-0 Mr E James, *sn led, hit tenth, rdn and hdd aftr 4 out, soon outpcd.* (8 to 1 op 6 to 1 tchd 9 to 1) 3
2891⁵ SANDS OF GOLD (Ire) 9-12-0 Mr L Lay, *hld up, niggled alng hfwy, mstk 12th, beh whn jmpd slwly nxt, tld off.*
.....................(20 to 1 op 16 to 1 tchd 25 to 1) 4
3018³ LURRIGA GLITTER (Ire) 9-12-0 Mr R Wakley, *beh, mstk 9th, tld off 11th.*.......................................(20 to 1) 5
3102⁵ TANGLE BARON 9-12-0 Miss J Cumings, *sn chasing ldr, lost pl 6 out, wknd quickly aftr nxt, tld off.*..............(33 to 1) 6
3300⁷ TOM'S GEMINI STAR 9-12-0 Mr M Harris, *hld up, 1 3rd.*
..............................(9 to 1 op 8 to 1 tchd 10 to 1) f
3102⁷ ORCHESTRAL SUITE (Ire) 9-12-0 Mr F Hutsby, *chsd ldrs, f 3rd.*................(7 to 4 fav op 2 to 1 tchd 9 to 4) f
JOHNNY THE FOX (Ire) 9-12-0 Mr R Lawther, *uns rdr 1st.*
.................................(16 to 1 op 12 to 1 tchd 20 to 1) ur
Dist: Dist, 1l, 1l, 3½l, 4l. 6m 33.20s. a 28.20s (9 Ran).

(Mike Roberts), M J Roberts

3568 Barton & Guestier Handicap Hurdle Class B (5-y-o and up) £11,088 3m 110yds......................................(5:20)

3151⁵ ESCARTEFIGUE (Fr) [151] 5-11-10 R Dunwoody, *settled gng wl, smooth hdwy to join ldrs appr 3 out, led last, ran on strly to go clr.*...................(6 to 1 fav op 9 to 2 tchd 13 to 2) 1
3131² BIG STRAND (Ire) [129] 8-10-2 C Maude, *patiently rdn, imprvg whn hit 3 out, rallied and not much room appr last, styd on, not quicken wth wnr.*.........(8 to 1 tchd 7 to 1) 2
3116⁶ FREDDIE MUCK [132] 7-10-5 T Jenks, *al wl plcd, ev ch and rdn approaching last, no extr r-in.*
............................(10 to 1 op 8 to 1 tchd 9 to 1) 3
3151⁶ WHAT A QUESTION (Ire) [143] 9-11-2 C O'Dwyer, *al frnt rnk, ev ch and rdn betw last 2, fdd r-in.*
..........................(15 to 2 op 7 to 1 tchd 8 to 1) 4
3131⁶ DR LEUNT (Ire) [127] 6-10-8 G Tormey, *al tracking ldrs, rdn and ev ch betw last 2, fdd r-in.*.........(14 to 1 op 12 to 1) 5
1391¹ VICTOR BRAVO (NZ) [127] (bl) 10-10-0 W Marston, *made most, hrd pressed and rdn betw last 2, hdd last, wknd r-in.*
...............................(25 to 1) 6
3116 ERZADJAN [130] (bl) 7-10-3 P Niven, *settled midfield, improved 4 out, rdn aftr nxt, wknd quickly 2 out.*
.................................(13 to 2 op 8 to 1) 7
3386³ TAMARPOUR (USA) [127] (bl) 10-9-7 (7*) B Moore, *mstk 1st, reminders in rear 3rd, nvr rch chalg pos.*
...........................(14 to 1 op 12 to 1) 8
3062² KINGDOM OF SHADES (USA) [127] 7-10-0 J Osborne, *settled midfield, struggling whn pace quickened appr last, lost tch, tld off.*........................(14 to 1 op 12 to 1) 9
2695³ BRAVE TORNADO [130] 6-10-3 B Clifford, *in tch for o'r one circuit, struggling 4 out, tld off.*...(12 to 1 tchd 14 to 1) 10
3266⁴ SMITH TOO (Ire) [127] 9-10-0 B Powell, *settled in tch, feeling pace fnl circuit, lost touch 4 out, tld off.*
................(14 to 1 op 12 to 1 tchd 16 to 1) 11
3116³ DANJING (Ire) [127] (bl) 5-10-2 D Walsh, *settled midfield, lost grnd whn pace quickened fnl circuit, tld off appr 3 out.*
..............................(11 to 1 op 10 to 1 tchd 12 to 1) 12
3151 TOP SPIN [130] 8-10-3 R Supple, *nvr gng wl, al beh, tld off.*
.................................(20 to 1) 13
2787 BETTER TIMES AHEAD [138] 11-10-11 A Dobbin, *chsd ldrs, lost tch quickly aftr one circuit, tld off whn pld up bef 9th.*
................................(33 to 1) pu
2482⁵ ROSE KING [130] 10-10-3³ P Hide, *trkd ldrs, lost pl quickly and pld up bef 9th.*.............................(100 to 1) pu
2598² HOUSE CAPTAIN [127] 8-10-0 R Johnson, *pld up bef 5th.*
..................................(12 to 1 tchd 14 to 1) pu
2958 SILVER SHRED [130] 6-10-3 N Williamson, *in tch, lost pl quickly and pld up bef 8th, broke nr-hind pastern, destroyed.*
..................................(14 to 1 op 16 to 1) pu
Dist: 3l, 5l, 1l, 3½l, hd, 12l, 1¼l, 21l, 9l, 2½l. 6m 0.10s. a 12.10s (17 Ran).
SR: 61/36/34/44/24/24/15/10/-/

(Darren C Mercer), D Nicholson

TAUNTON (firm)
Thursday April 3rd
Going Correction: MINUS 0.40 sec. per fur.

3569 Orchard FM Tim Manns Maiden Hurdle Class F (4-y-o and up) £2,039 2m 1f......................................(2:15)

3035⁴ MYSTIC HILL 6-11-5 J Frost, *led, set steady pace till hdd aftr 4th, pressed ldr after, rgned ld last, hrd hld.*
..................................(6 to 1 on tchd 5 to 1 on) 1

1179 KAI'S LADY (Ire) 4-10-5 (3*) T Dascombe, *chsd ldr, led aftr 4th, rdn whn hdd and btn last.*........(5 to 1 tchd 11 to 2) 2
3119 MISS GEE-ELL 5-10-7 (7*) Mr E Babington, *hld up, reminder aftr 4th, rdn frm 3 out, sn wknd.*
.......................(20 to 1 op 14 to 1 tchd 25 to 1) 3
3296 OSCILIGHTS GIFT 5-11-0 W McFarland, *pld very hrd, hld up, beh frm 6th.*.......................(25 to 1 op 10 to 1) 4
Dist: 2½l, 12l, nk. 4m 7.90s. a 24.90s (4 Ran).

(Jack Joseph), R G Frost

3570 March Hare Conditional Jockeys' Selling Handicap Hurdle Class G (0-95 4-y-o and up) £1,880 3m 110yds......................................(2:45)

CO-TACK [66] 12-10-2 Chris Webb, *chsd clr ldr frm 3rd, led appr 4 out, sn clear, unchlgd.*
...................................(5 to 1 tchd 6 to 1) 1
2983⁶ ANORAK (USA) [80] 7-11-3 X Aizpuru, *pld hrd, hld up, outpcd frm 7th, wnt moderate second 4 out, no imprsn...*(6 to 4 jt-fav op 5 to 4) 2
2477 MASTER GOODENOUGH (Ire) [65] 6-10-1⁵ (5*) D Creech, *pld hrd, led, clr frm second, hdd appr 4 out, 3rd and wkng whn mstk 3 out.*..............(13 to 2 op 6 to 1 tchd 7 to 1) 3
PRINCE EQUINAME [92] 5-11-7 (7*) N Rossiter, *keen hold, chsd ldr to 3rd, beh frm 7th, tld off whn blun 3 out.* (6 to 4 jt-fav op Evens) 4
Dist: 20l, dist, 2½l. 5m 47.20s. a 19.20s (4 Ran).

(Mrs J L Livermore), R E Livermore

3571 WSM Mercedes Benz Actros Chase Class D Handicap (0-125 5-y-o and up) £4,155 3m......................................(3:20)

2719⁸ DOUALAGO (Fr) [117] (bl) 7-11-9 (5*) G Supple, *led till aftr 8th, lft in ld nxt, rdn alng 15th, ran on wl frm 3 out.*
.................................(7 to 4 on tchd 13 to 8 on) 1
3545³ HERBERT BUCHANAN (Ire) [101] 7-10-5 (7*) Mr J Tizzard, *keen hold, led aftr 8th till blun and hdd nxt, mstk 12th, btn 3 out.*.......................(6 to 4 op 5 to 4) 2
Won by 11l. 5m 57.60s. a 14.60s (2 Ran).
SR: -/-/

(Martin Pipe Racing Club), M C Pipe

3572 Orchard FM Bob McCreadie Handicap Hurdle Class E (0-115 4-y-o and up) £2,200 2m 1f......................................(3:55)

3139³ SHIFTING MOON [75] 5-10-6 Derek Byrne, *hld up, chsd ldr aftr 4th, led appr 6th, rdn out.*
.................................(7 to 4 op 2 to 1 tchd 9 to 4) 1
810⁴ LAYHAM LOW (Ire) [90] 6-11-10 J A McCarthy, *chsd ldr till aftr 4th, wnt 3rd 3 out, sn rdn, one pace.*
....................(7 to 2 op 3 to 1 tchd 4 to 1) 2
3357² LITTLE SHEFFORD [81] 5-11-1 S Curran, *led, hit 3rd, hdd appr 6th, third whn l 3 out, rmntd.*
.................(10 to 1 fav op 5 to 4 on tchd 6 to 5) 3
Dist: 7l, dist. 3m 44.00s. a 1.00s (3 Ran).
SR: -/11/-/

(Mrs K Roberts-Hindle), F Jordan

3573 WSM Mercedes Benz Sprinter Novices' Chase Class E (5-y-o and up) £3,317 2m 110yds......................................(4:30)

3517 NORTHERN SINGER 7-11-1 (3*) T Dascombe, *keen hold, hld up, chsd ldr frm 3rd, led appr 3 out, ran on wl frm nxt.*
..............................(Evens fav op 7 to 4 on tchd 11 to 10) 1
3252⁵ KETCHICAN 5-10-7 S Anderson, *keen hold, led second, hdd appr 3 out, hld whn hit nxt.*................(4 to 1) 2
3038⁴ INDIAN TEMPLE 6-11-0 R Greene, *led to second, not fluent 9th, sn beh, kpt on ag'n r-in.*
.......................(7 to 4 op 2 to 1 tchd 13 to 8) 3
Dist: 7l, 1¾l. 4m 6.90s. a 14.90s (3 Ran).

(Joe Panes), R J Hodges

3574 WSM Mercedes Benz Vito Hunters' Chase Class H (5-y-o and up) £1,145 3m......................................(5:00)

L'UOMO PIU 13-12-0 (7*) Mr O McPhail, *made all, hit 12th, drvn out.*..............(10 to 1 tchd 12 to 1) 1
3274⁴ RUSTY BRIDGE 10-12-0 (7*) Mr R Button, *chsd wnr, mstk 4th, rdn whn hit 2 out, edgd lft and kpt on r-in.*
.................(2 to 1 fav op 11 to 10 tchd 9 to 4) 2
J B LAD 11-11-7 (7*) Miss P Gundry, *hld up, hdwy 14th, hit nxt, staying on whn crrd lft r-in.*........(25 to 1 op 20 to 1) 3
ARCTIC BARON 12-12-0 (7*) Miss L Blackford, *hld up, prog 9th, 4th and wkng whn blun four out...*(5 to 1 tchd 6 to 1) 4
DEPARTURE 10-11-2 (7*) Mr J Creighton, *sn tld off, pld up bef 14th...*............(11 to 4 op 2 to 1 tchd 3 to 1) pu
CLEASBY HILL 12-11-7 (7*) Mr D Alers-Hankey, *hld up, rdn tenth, beh frm 13th, tld off whn pld up aftr 4 out.*
................................(5 to 1 tchd 16 to 1) pu
3147³ GOOD KING HENRY 11-11-7 (7*) Mr I Widdicombe, *hld up, jmpd slwly 5th, wl beh frm 14th, tld off whn pld up bef 2 out.*
................(100 to 30 op 3 to 1 tchd 7 to 2) pu
Dist: 1¾l, hd, 12l. 5m 53.20s. a 10.20s (7 Ran).

(A Barrow), A Barrow

AINTREE (good)
Friday April 4th
Going Correction: PLUS 0.45 sec. per fur. (races 1,5,6), PLUS 0.50 (2,3,4,7)

3575 Martell Mersey Novices' Hurdle Class A Grade 2 (4-y-o and up) £14,582 2½m................ (2:00)

3113^{6} SANMARTINO (Ire) 5-11-5 R Dunwoody, *confidently rdn, smooth hdwy frm 4 out, chlgd on bit last, led r-in, drvn out.* .... (11 to 8 on op 5 to 4 on tchd Evens) 1
2509* COURBARIL (bl) 5-11-1 N Williamson, *pressed ldrs, reminders bef 4 out, styd on gmely to take second nr finish.* .... (10 to 1 op 8 to 1 tchd 11 to 1) 2
3129 HURDANTE (Ire) 7-11-1 M A Fitzgerald, *wtd wth, hit rail on paddock bend aftr 5th, improved to ld 3 out, jnd last, hdd and one pace r-in*..........(20 to 1 op 12 to 1 tchd 25 to 1) 3
3198* FAR AHEAD 5-11-1 B Storey, *tucked away on ins, swtchd to improve aftr 3 out, rdn and kpt on same pace betw last 2.* ....(12 to 1 op 10 to 1 tchd 14 to 1 and 16 to 1) 4
3111^{7} DEANO'S BEENO 5-11-1 C Maude, *led aftr second to 5th, feeling pace 4 out, rallying whn hit nxt, one pace betw last 2.* .... (7 to 1 op 5 to 1 tchd 15 to 2) 5
2472^{7} LISS DE PAOR (Ire) 6-11-0 C F Swan, *settled gng wl, hit second, improved to ld 4 out, hdd nxt, no extr betw last 2.* .... (9 to 1 op 6 to 1 tchd 10 to 1) 6
3336^{6} NICOLA MARIE (Ire) 8-10-10 W Marston, *wth ldrs, led and hit 7th, hdd 8th, fdd und pres nxt, tld off*... (50 to 1 op 25 to 1) 7
3066^{2} INFLUENCE PEDLER 4-10-12 C Llewellyn, *settled rear, hit second, hmpd bend aftr 5th, sn struggling, tld off.* ....(12 to 1 tchd 14 to 1) 8
3334* JOHN DRUMM 6-11-1 J Osborne, *led till aftr second, steadied into midfield, reminders bef 3 out, wknd quickly, tld off.* .... (11 to 1 op 7 to 1 tchd 12 to 1) 9
3301^{2} EASY LISTENING (USA) 5-11-1 J Railton, *pld hrd, wth ldrs, led 5th to 7th, wknd quickly 4 out, lost tch and pulled up bef nxt*.......... (20 to 1 tchd 33 to 1) pu

Dist: 1¼l, 1½l, sht-hd, 2½l, ½l, dist, 26l, 2½l. 4m 54.70s. a 16.70s (10 Ran).
SR: 14/8/6/6/3/1/ (K Abdulla), D Nicholson

3576 Mumm Melling Chase Class A Grade 1 (5-y-o and up) £47,460 2½m (2:35)

3130* MARTHA'S SON 10-11-10 C Llewellyn, *blun 1st, settled rear, not fluent 8th and 9th, mstk nxt, hdwy aftr 4 out, quickened to ld last, drvn clr*..........(5 to 2 op 7 to 4) 1
3130^{5} STRONG PROMISE (Ire) 6-11-10 N Williamson, *jmpd wl, pressed ldr racing freely, chlgd on bit 3 out, slight ld nxt till hdd last, not quicken.* (9 to 4 fav op 5 to 2 tchd 11 to 4) 2
3130^{3} VIKING FLAGSHIP 10-11-10 R Dunwoody, *settled in 3rd, hdwy 8th, chasing ldrs whn blun nxt, sn rdn and one pace.* .... (11 to 4 op 5 to 2 tchd 3 to 1) 3
3130^{2} ASK TOM (Ire) 8-11-10 R Garritty, *keen, led, dived at 3rd, ran wide bend aftr 8th, drvn alng appr 3 out, hdd nxt, sn fdd, eased*..........(4 to 1 op 3 to 1) 4

Dist: 5l, 3½l, 20l. 4m 58.80s. a 10.80s (4 Ran).
SR: 88/83/79/59/ (P J Hartigan), Capt T A Forster

3577 Mumm Mildmay Novices' Chase Class A Grade 2 (5-y-o and up) £23,604 3m 1f................ (3:10)

3152^{8} CYBORGO (Fr) 7-11-4 R Dunwoody, *chsd ldr, led 9th to nxt, led aftr 11th, hdd 2 out, sn led ag'n, drvn clr.* ....(13 to 8 fav op 5 to 4 tchd 7 to 4) 1
3132 THE LAST FLING (Ire) 7-11-7 Richard Guest, *wtd wth, improved fnl circuit, disputing ld whn pitched 4 out, rallied to lead 2 out, sn hdd, blun last, no extr.* .... (11 to 2 op 5 to 1 tchd 6 to 1) 2
3207* JUDICIOUS CAPTAIN 10-11-7 Mr C Storey, *hit 3rd, mstks 6th and nxt, wknd quickly hfwy, sn tld off.* (33 to 1 op 25 to 1) 3
3132 BUCKHOUSE BOY 7-11-4 C Maude, *settled midfield, jmpd slwly 5th, chasing ldrs whn hit 8th, 3rd when f 12th.* .... (6 to 1 op 5 to 1 tchd 13 to 2) f
3037* BEAR CLAW (bl) 8-11-4 J Osborne, *led, jmpd slwly and hld 9th, blun and reminders 11th, poor 3rd whn blunded and uns rdr 3 out*.......... (9 to 2 op 4 to 1 tchd 5 to 1) ur
3319* CHOPWELL CURTAINS 7-11-4 L Wyer, *jmpd rght 4th, wl beh hfwy, tld off whn pld up bef 5 out.* .... (6 to 1 op 5 to 1 tchd 13 to 2) pu
2881^{2} CROWN EQUERRY (Ire) 7-11-4 P Carberry, *wth ldrs, led tenth till aftr nxt, reminders 12th, 3rd whn blun 6 out, lost tch and pld up bef 3 out*.......... (11 to 1 op 10 to 1 tchd 12 to 1) pu

Dist: 3½l, dist. 6m 23.60s. a 18.60s (7 Ran).
SR: 29/28/-/-/ (County Stores (Somerset) Holdings Ltd), M C Pipe

3578 Martell Fox Hunters' Chase Class B (6-y-o and up) £14,070 2¾m.. (3:45)

3279* BLUE CHEEK 11-12-0 Mr R Thornton, *cl up, mstk 3rd (Chair), jmpd slwly and outpcd 4 out, hdwy frm 3 out, led sn aftr nxt, clr last, easily*.......... (9 to 2 op 4 to 1 tchd 5 to 1) 1
3247^{2} HIGHLANDMAN 11-12-0 Mr Chris Wilson, *midfield, chsd ldrs 8th, outpcd aftr 12th (Canal Turn), styd on appr 2 out, unbl to chal*..........(20 to 1 op 16 to 1 tchd 25 to 1) 2
ABBOTSHAM 12-12-0 Mr E James, *jmpd poorly in rear, blun tenth (Becher's), staying on whn hmpd 2 out, nvr dngrs.* ....(33 to 1) 3
1101^{5} K C'S DANCER 12-12-0 Mr J M Pritchard, *hld up, cld 6th, lost tch 13th (Valentine's), styd on same pace frm 3 out.* .... (66 to 1 op 50 to 1 tchd 100 to 1) 4
YOUNG NIMROD 10-12-0 Mr G Wragg, *in tch, chsd ldr frm hfwy, drw level 3 out, led briefly nxt, drvn and wknd r-in.* .... (14 to 1 op 12 to 1 tchd 16 to 1) 5
2992* TRIFAST LAD 12-12-0 Mr P Hacking, *not fluent in rear, pckd tenth (Becher's), sn lost tch*.......... (6 to 1 tchd 7 to 1) 6
3368^{2} GREAT POKEY 12-12-0 Miss N Courtenay, *sn led, hdd 5th, mstk tenth (Becher's), soon wl beh, tld off.* .... (100 to 1 op 50 to 1) 7
FORDSTOWN (Ire) 8-12-0 Mr Jamie Alexander, *chsd ldrs, struggling hfwy, sn tld off*.......... (100 to 1 op 50 to 1) 8
2981^{7} FARINGO 12-12-0 Mr W Gowlett, *beh, not fluent, tld off hfwy.* .... (100 to 1 op 50 to 1) 9
3043* MR BOSTON 12-12-0 Mr S Swiers, *jmpd rght, led 5th, slight ld and gng wl whn f 2 out.* ....(15 to 8 fav op 5 to 4 tchd 2 to 1) f
3043^{3} MATT REID (bl) 13-12-0 Mr W Morgan, *f 1st.* ....(20 to 1 tchd 25 to 1) f
CHILIPOUR 10-12-0 Mr J Jukes, *f 1st*... (5 to 1 op 6 to 1) f
2993 COUNTRY TARROGEN 8-12-0 Mr N Wilson, *f 1st.* .... (7 to 1 op 6 to 1 tchd 15 to 2) f
3187 HIGHWAY FIVE (Ire) 9-12-0 Mr M P Jones, *f 1st.* .... (40 to 1 op 33 to 1) f

Dist: 17l, 1l, 1¾l, 3½l , 28l, 7l, 1¼l. 5m 48.70s. a 22.70s (14 Ran).
(J Mahon), J Mahon

3579 Belle Epoque Sefton Novices' Hurdle Class A Grade 1 (4-y-o and up) £21,532 3m 110yds...........(4:20)

3129^{4} FOREST IVORY (NZ) 6-11-4 R Johnson, *al in tch, imprvg whn mstk 3 out, led nxt, hrd pressed and edgd rght r-in, hld on gmely*.......... (11 to 2 op 7 to 2) 1
2732* PRIVATE PEACE (Ire) 7-11-4 C F Swan, *settled off the pace, improved appr 3 out, rdn and str run und pres r-in, ran on, jst hld*..........(11 to 2 op 9 to 2) 2
2601* MENTMORE TOWERS (Ire) 5-11-4 B Powell, *nvr far away, led 9th to 2 out, sn drvn alng, one pace whn hit last, no extr.* .... (5 to 1 op 9 to 2 tchd 11 to 2) 3
3116^{2} YAHMI (Ire) 7-11-4 N Williamson, *patiently rdn, steady hdwy to chase ldrs appr 3 out, swtchd rght aftr nxt, no imprsn.* .... (100 to 30 fav op 7 to 2 tchd 3 to 1) 4
2889* FLYING GUNNER 6-11-4 Mr R Thornton, *settled midfield, feeling pace appr 3 out, no imprsn on ldrs.* ....(25 to 1 tchd 33 to 1) 5
2541^{2} LADY PETA (Ire) 7-11-4 J R Kavanagh, *settled off the pace, drvn alng whn ldrs quickened 4 out, lost tch, tld off.* ....(16 to 1 tchd 20 to 1) 6
3129 HAND WOVEN 5-11-4 C Llewellyn, *sn wl plcd, pushed alng 6th, hit 8th, soon lost tch, tld off*..........(33 to 1) 7
3097* STORMY PASSAGE (Ire) 7-11-4 R Dunwoody, *wtd wth, lost tch hfwy, tld off bef 3 out*..........(14 to 1 tchd 16 to 1) 8
3151^{9} TARRS BRIDGE (Ire) (bl) 6-11-4 J Railton, *wth ldrs, not fluent 5th and nxt, led aftr 7th to 9th, hmpd and uns rdr 4 out.* .... (10 to 1 op 8 to 1 tchd 12 to 1) ur
2951* SPRING DOUBLE (Ire) 6-11-4 C Maude, *sn hndy, chalg whn blun 4 out, not reco'r, lost tch and pld up bef 3 out.* ....(14 to 1 tchd 16 to 1) pu
2298* SALMON BREEZE (Ire) 6-11-4 M A Fitzgerald, *wth ldrs, drpd back into midfield hfwy, lost tch bef 4 out, tld off whn pld up before nxt*..........(10 to 1 op 12 to 1 tchd 14 to 1) pu
3269^{2} SILVER THYNE (Ire) 5-11-4 J F Titley, *made most, hit second, jmpd rght nxt, hdd aftr 7th, hit next, wknd quickly and pld up bef 3 out*.......... (16 to 1 tchd 20 to 1) pu

Dist: Sht-hd, 5l, 14l, 28l, 14l, 4l, 11l. 6m 7.50s. a 19.50s (12 Ran).
SR: 5/5/-/-/-/-/ (The Old Foresters Partnership), D Nicholson

3580 Oddbins Handicap Hurdle Class B (4-y-o and up) £12,653 2½m..... (4:50)

2695^{4} CADOUGOLD (Fr) [131] 6-10-4 C F Swan, *steadied rear, smooth hdwy 4 out, led gng strly last, pushed clr.* ....(8 to 1 op 7 to 1) 1
2949* SHERIFFMUIR [127] 8-9-9 (5*) Mr R Thornton, *hld up, drpd rear and not fluent 6th, pushed alng 8th, staying on whn hit 3 out, ran on und pres to go second r-in.* .... (10 to 1 op 8 to 1 tchd 11 to 1) 2
3156 AMBLESIDE (Ire) [127] 6-10-0 D Bridgwater, *beh, pushed alng and hdwy appr 3 out, effrt nxt, styd on.* .... (16 to 1 op 12 to 1 tchd 20 to 1) 3
2787^{4} OUTSET (Ire) [127] 7-9-11 (3*) Mr C Bonner, *chsd ldrs, chlgd 6th, slight ld 3 out to last, not quicken.* .... (9 to 1 op 7 to 1 tchd 10 to 1) 4
3131^{2} ALLEGATION [148] (v) 7-11-7 C Llewellyn, *chsd ldr, led 7th to nxt, reminders appr 3 out, fdd next*..... (8 to 1 op 7 to 1) 5
3330^{2} ASHWELL BOY (Ire) [133] 6-10-6 M A Fitzgerald, *hld up, imprvg whn hmpd 8th, effrt to track ldrs 3 out, hit nxt, sn fdd.* ....(7 to 1 op 5 to 1) 6

3151 TRAGIC HERO [136] (bl) 5-10-9 C Maude, *hld up, not fluent 4th, gd hdwy to ld 8th, hdd 3 out, sn wknd.* ....(33 to 1 op 25 to 1) 7
3318* FRICKLEY [128] 11-10-1 P Carberry, *midfield, hit 5th, wknd quickly appr 4 out, tld off*...............(8 to 1 op 7 to 1) 8
2455³ GALES CAVALIER (Ire) [133] 9-10-6 R Dunwoody, *pressed ldrs, niggled alng 7th, outpcd appr 3 out, sn beh.* ....(5 to 1 op 6 to 1 tchd 7 to 1) 9
2530⁸ LUCKY BLUE [127] 10-10-0 N Williamson, *set gd pace, hdd 7th, wknd quickly 4 out, sn tld off*......(33 to 1 op 25 to 1) 10
3156³ PENNY A DAY (Ire) [141] 7-11-0 P Niven, *midfield, hdwy appr 6th, tracking ldrs gng wl whn f 8th*... (4 to 1 fav op 7 to 2) f
3131³ CASTLE SWEEP (Ire) [155] 6-12-0 R Johnson, *hld up, not fluent 3rd and 6th, hdwy and tracking ldrs whn brght dwn 8th.* ....(6 to 1 op 5 to 1) bd
Dist: 4l, ¾l, 1¼l, 14l, 6l, 17l, 14l, 1½l, 23l. 4m 49.60s. a 11.60s (12 Ran).
SR: 50/42/41/39/46/25/11/-/-/ (D A Johnson), M C Pipe

3581 Perrier Jouet Handicap Chase Class B (5-y-o and up) £10,269 3m 1f (5:20)

3152 UNGUIDED MISSILE (Ire) [157] 9-12-0 R Dunwoody, *jmpd boldly, made all, styd on strly frm 3 out, gmely.* ....(7 to 2 op 5 to 2) 1
3153² CAB ON TARGET [130] 11-10-1 N Williamson, *wl plcd till blun and lost grnd 7th, not fluent and rdn alng 11th, rallied 3 out, kpt on one pace r-in.* ....(100 to 30 fav op 5 to 2 tchd 7 to 2) 2
1878⁴ BERTONE (Ire) [130] 8-10-1 C O'Dwyer, *patiently rdn, improved gng wl 5 out, sn ev ch, ridden and one pace betw last 2*...............(5 to 1 op 9 to 2 tchd 11 to 2) 3
3114⁵ CALL IT A DAY (Ire) [138] 7-10-9 R Johnson, *tucked away beh ldrs, bumped 6th, improved aftr 4 out, drvn alng last 2, one pace appr last*............(7 to 2 op 4 to 1 tchd 9 to 2) 4
2986² FIVELEIGH BUILDS [129] 10-10-0 A Thornton, *trkd ldr, blun 1st, sn reco'red, effrt and drvn alng 4 out, rdn nxt, one pace last 2*..........................(9 to 1 op 8 to 1) 5
3115⁴ ALL FOR LUCK [129] 12-10-0 C F Swan, *settled in tch, blun 8th, drvn alng aftr, no imprsn frm 3 out*...(6 to 1 op 9 to 2) 6
WUDIMP [129] 8-10-0 Mr C Storey, *chsd ldrs, jmpd lft 6th, struggling hfwy, wl beh whn pld up bef last.* ....(33 to 1 op 20 to 1 tchd 50 to 1) pu
Dist: 1¾l, 3l, 1¼l, 3l, 7l. 6m 29.20s. a 24.20s (7 Ran).
(D E Harrison), G Richards

SEDGEFIELD (good to firm)
Friday April 4th
Going Correction: PLUS 0.10 sec. per fur.

3582 Stonegrave Aggregates Novices' Selling Handicap Hurdle Class G (0-95 4-y-o and up) £2,076 2m 5f 110yds........................ (2:10)

2807⁸ AMAZING SAIL (Ire) [83] 4-11-4 A S Smith, *nvr far away, led bef 4 out, lft clr 2 out, ran on strly*........(8 to 1 op 7 to 1) 1
NITE SPRITE [58] 7-9-7 (7*) N Horrocks, *beh till styd on wl fnl 2, no ch wth wnr*.................(50 to 1 tchd 66 to 1) 2
2118³ CATTON LADY [58] 7-9-11 (3*) G Lee, *settled on ins, shaken up 3 out, no imprsn frm nxt*............(6 to 1 op 11 to 2) 3
3283⁵ ROYAL HAND [66] (v) 7-10-8 Mr R Armson, *hld up, improved 4 out, rdn and lft second bef 2 out, one pace.* ....(16 to 1 op 14 to 1) 4
3136⁵ MICK THE YANK (Ire) [59] (bl) 7-10-1 Jacqui Oliver, *settled midfield, improved to chase ldrs 4 out, outpcd fnl 2.* ....(3 to 1 fav op 7 to 2) 5
3246⁵ GREENFINCH (Can) [64] (v) 6-10-6 M Foster, *in tch, drvn 4 out, outpcd bef 2 out*...................(11 to 2 op 4 to 1) 6
2362 BROOMHILL DUKER (Ire) [58] (bl) 7-10-0 A Dobbin, *led till hdd bef 4 out, fdd aftr nxt*............(20 to 1 op 16 to 1) 7
WHITEGATESPRINCESS (Ire) [60] 6-9-9 (7*) C McCormack, *beh, improved bef 3 out, staying on whn badly hmpd by faller 2 out, not reco'r*.................................(20 to 1) 8
3433 BEACON HILL LADY [65] 4-10-0 D Parker, *beh, effrt appr 3 out, struggling nxt*...................(25 to 1 op 20 to 1) 9
3353⁵ MEADOWLECK [58] 8-9-9 (5*) S Taylor, *jmpd badly in rear, nvr on terms*.......................(20 to 1 op 16 to 1) 10
3246⁹ DONT FORGET CURTIS (Ire) [84] 5-11-5 (7*) Miss S Lamb, *beh, struggling fnl circuit, nvr on terms*...........(10 to 1) 11
3246 NOSMO KING (Ire) [58] 6-10-0 K Johnson, *cl up, chlgd bef 4 out, rdn nxt, four ls second whn f 2 out.* (25 to 1 op 20 to 1) f
3246 ARTHUR BEE [61] 10-10-3 M Moloney, *midfield, reminder aftr 4th, struggling 3 out, pld up after nxt.* ....(17 to 2 op 8 to 1 tchd 9 to 1) pu
2403 DUGORT STRAND (Ire) [69] 6-10-4 (7*) X Aizpuru, *keen hold, wth ldr till aftr 4th, sn beh, pld up bef 3 out.* ....(12 to 1 op 6 to 1 tchd 14 to 1) pu
ROSTINO (Ire) [58] 8-10-0 G Cahill, *settled on outer, blun 4 out, sn struggling, pld up bef 2 out*..............(12 to 1) pu
Dist: 9l, 1½l, 4l, 2l, sht-hd, 3l, 2l, hd, 1¾l, 14l. 5m 2.30s. a 14.30s (15 Ran).
(Maritime), Miss M K Milligan

3583 Stanley Racing Golden Numbers Series Novices' Hurdle Class E (4-y-o and up) £2,547 2m 1f......(2:45)

2855* SILVER MINX 5-11-3 (3*) G Lee, *jmpd badly lft thrght, made virtually all, ran on strly fnl 2*...........(6 to 1 op 5 to 1) 1
3350* DIAMOND BEACH 4-10-5 (3*) E Callaghan, *hld up, improved to chase ldrs aftr 3 out, mstk last, kpt on.* ....(2 to 1 fav op 5 to 2 tchd 11 to 4) 2
3044³ SIX CLERKS (Ire) 4-10-11 (3*) F Leahy, *nvr far away, ev ch 3 out, sn rdn, one pace betw last 2*........(5 to 2 op 6 to 4) 3
1818⁸ THE MICKLETONIAN 6-11-0 K Johnson, *hld up beh ldg grp, styd on frm 2 out, nrst finish*..........(66 to 1 op 33 to 1) 4
3003⁶ MILENBERG JOYS 5-11-0 T Reed, *hld up, steady hdwy appr 3 out, outpcd frm nxt*................(20 to 1 op 33 to 1) 5
1196* SILENT GUEST (Ire) 4-11-0 D Bentley, *cl up, ev ch 3 out, fdd nxt*..................................(6 to 1 op 7 to 1) 6
2917⁷ MAPLE BAY (Ire) 8-11-6 A Dobbin, *settled in tch, rdn bef 3 out, sn outpcd*...........................(11 to 2 op 9 to 2) 7
3303⁸ QUEEN'S COUNSEL (Ire) 4-10-3 A S Smith, *keen hold, cl up, chlgd 3 out, wkng whn hit last*.........(33 to 1 op 25 to 1) 8
3246 OVER STATED (Ire) 7-11-0 K Jones, *trkd wnr, lost pl bef 3 out, sn btn*......................................(33 to 1) 9
BELIEVE IT 8-11-0 R Supple, *chsd ldg grp, struggling fnl circuit, tld off whn f 2 out.* ....(100 to 1 op 50 to 1 tchd 200 to 1) f
TOPUP 4-10-3 (5*) S Taylor, *hmpd by wnr and crrd out 1st.* ....(100 to 1 op 33 to 1) co
3003⁵ PENNY PEPPERMINT 5-10-9 D Parker, *hmpd by wnr and crrd out 1st*...................................(33 to 1) co
LUCKY HOOF 4-9-10 (7*) X Aizpuru, *beh, tld off whn tried to refuse 4th, sn pld up*...............(16 to 1 op 14 to 1) pu
Dist: 3l, 1¼l, 3l, 7l, 2l, 14l, 1¼l, 7l. 3m 55.00s. a 9.00s (13 Ran).
SR: 19/4/8/5/-/-/ (Mrs E A Kettlewell), Mrs M Reveley

3584 Washington Hospital Novices' Chase Class D (5-y-o and up) £3,574 2m 110yds........................ (3:20)

3158³ TAPATCH (Ire) 9-11-0 A Dobbin, *sn chasing ldrs, blun 4th, rdn to ld four out, jnd 2 out, hld on wl*.... (9 to 4 fav op 3 to 1) 1
3258⁷ WHITEGATES WILLIE 5-10-7 A S Smith, *chsd ldg grp, improved to chal 2 out, jst hld r-in*...............(33 to 1) 2
3353 TRIONA'S HOPE (Ire) 8-10-9 (5*) Mr M H Naughton, *midfield, effrt bef 4 out, no imprsn fnl 2*......................(50 to 1) 3
3354² NAWTINOOKEY 7-10-2 (7*) C McCormack, *beh till styd on bef 3 out, no imprsn frm nxt*...........(5 to 1 op 9 to 2) 4
2985 HEE'S A DANCER 5-10-7 M Foster, *led till hdd 5 out, btn and eased fnl 2*..........................(5 to 2 op 9 to 4) 5
3260³ TWIN FALLS (Ire) 6-11-12 J Callaghan, *chsd ldrs, struggling 5 out, no dngr aftr*.......................(3 to 1 op 2 to 1) 6
3259⁶ DISTILLERY HILL (Ire) 9-11-0 Mr M Thompson, *cl up, blun and lost pl 5th, sn struggling*......................(25 to 1) 7
3354 ARISTODEMUS 8-11-0 K Johnson, *jmpd badly in rear, nvr on terms*........................(100 to 1 op 66 to 1) 8
3124⁸ NOBODYS FLAME (Ire) 9-10-7 (7*) Mr T J Barry, *pressed ldr, led 5 out till blun and hdd nxt, sn btn*.............(50 to 1) 9
2201 GONE ASHORE (Ire) 6-11-0 J Burke, *settled in tch, struggling fnl circuit, tld off*...................(33 to 1 tchd 50 to 1) 10
ITS A DEAL 11-11-0 G Cahill, *sn tld off, pld up bef 7th.* ....(66 to 1 op 50 to 1 tchd 100 to 1) pu
Dist: Nk, 8l, 10l, 4l, hd, 20l, ¾l, 1l, 2l. 4m 2.90s. a 10.90s (11 Ran).
(Miss V Foster), M W Easterby

3585 Reg And Ridley Lamb Memorial Handicap Chase Class E (0-115 5-y-o and up) £3,496 2m 5f....... (3:55)

3245⁴ RUSTIC AIR [102] 10-11-10 W Dwan, *chsd ldr frm 3rd, led 3 out, kpt on strly from nxt*.............. (9 to 4 op 7 to 4) 1
3260* THE TOASTER [96] 10-11-1 (3*) E Callaghan, *chsd ldrs, effrt 3 out, rdn and no imprsn frm nxt.* ....(2 to 1 fav op 11 to 10 tchd 9 to 4) 2
3126³ REVE DE VALSE (USA) [86] 10-10-8 K Johnson, *led, hit 4 out, hdd nxt, sn outpcd*...................(7 to 2 tchd 4 to 1) 3
3161⁷ GRAND SCENERY (Ire) [80] (bl) 9-10-2 A S Smith, *pld hrd in rear, hit 9th, struggling aftr nxt, nvr on terms.* ....(7 to 2 op 4 to 1 tchd 5 to 1) 4
3352 QUIXALL CROSSETT [78] 12-9-9 (5*) Mr M H Naughton, *chsd ldr, blun second, lost pl nxt, struggling fnl circuit.* ....(50 to 1 op 33 to 1) 5
Dist: 2½l, 7l, 30l, nk. 5m 10.40s. a 14.40s (5 Ran).
(Mrs G M Sturges), J G FitzGerald

3586 Stanley Thompson Memorial Hunters' Chase Class H (5-y-o and up) £1,604 3m 3f............ (4:30)

GREENMOUNT LAD (Ire) 9-11-2 (7*) Mr P Cornforth, *chsd clr ldr, led 6 out, hrd pressed fnl 2, ran on wl.* ....(11 to 10 on op 5 to 4 on tchd Evens) 1
LA MAJA (Ire) 8-10-11 (7*) Mr C Mulhall, *jmpd rght thrght, hld up, improved aftr 13th, chlgd 2 out, hit last, kpt on same pace.* ....(12 to 1 op 14 to 1) 2
3352⁴ UPWELL 13-11-4 (5*) Mr P Johnson, *led till hdd 6 out, outpcd bef 2 out*..........................(3 to 1 op 11 to 4) 3
BOREEN OWEN 13-11-2 (7*) Mr A Parker, *in tch, reminders aftr 13th, outpcd 15th*..... (11 to 4 op 5 to 2 tchd 3 to 1) 4

FISH QUAY 14-11-2 (7*) Miss S Lamb, *in tch, lost pl 13th, sn struggling, grb up aftr 2 out*...................(50 to 1) pu
Dist: 6l, 9l, 7l. 6m 50.70s. a 17.70s (5 Ran).

(J Cornforth), J Cornforth

# 3587 John Joyce Handicap Hurdle Class E (0-115 4-y-o and up) £2,320 2m 1f
..........................(5:00)

3263* GLENUGIE [97] 6-11-8 N Bentley, *nvr far away, led aftr 3 out, hrd pressed nxt, ran on wl*.........(5 to 2 fav op 3 to 1) 1
2682⁶ SKIDDAW SAMBA [80] 8-10-2 (3*) G Lee, *hld up, improved bef 3 out, chlgd nxt, kpt on r-in.*
..................(9 to 1 op 8 to 1 tchd 10 to 1) 2
3350² HIGHLAND WAY (Ire) [87] 9-10-5 (7*) C McCormack, *al prmnt, hrd pressed nxt, one pace betw last two.* (5 to 1 tchd 11 to 2) 3
3166⁷ ERINY (USA) [88] 8-10-10 (3*) E Callaghan, *in tch, no imprsn frm 2 out*.........................(10 to 1) 4
3059³ FIELD OF VISION (Ire) [101] 7-11-12 J Supple, *cl up, outpcd bef 2 out, fdd*.......................(3 to 1 op 9 to 4) 5
3157 CATCH THE PIGEON [78] 8-10-3 N Smith, *chsd ldrs, jmpd lft and lost pl second, no dngr aftr*.......(14 to 1 op 10 to 1) 6
1068⁴ RED JAM JAR [94] 12-11-5 K Johnson, *led till hdd and hmpd aftr 3 out, sn btn*.....................(10 to 1 op 8 to 1) 7
762⁵ STAGS FELL [75] 12-10-0 Carol Cuthbert, *cl up, outpcd aftr 3 out, hit nxt, fdd*..................(25 to 1 tchd 33 to 1) 8
3006⁵ AIDE MEMOIRE (Ire) [76] 8-9-10 (5*) Mr M H Naughton, *sn beh, nvr on terms*.................(12 to 1 tchd 14 to 1) 9
3258⁵ I'M TYSON (NZ) [75] 9-10-0 M Moloney, *beh, not much room 3 out, btn whn blun and uns rdr last.*
...............(11 to 2 op 6 to 1 tchd 10 to 1) ur
Dist: 1¼l, 10l, 3½l, ½l, 1¼l, ¾l, 10l, 2½l. 3m 59.00s. a 13.00s (10 Ran).

(Frazer Hines), G M Moore

HEREFORD (good to firm)
Saturday April 5th
Going Correction: PLUS 0.40 sec. per fur.

3588 Kilpeck Maiden Hurdle Class E (5-y-o and up) £2,332 2m 1f......(1:35)

1541⁶ NAUTICAL JEWEL 5-10-12 (7*) J Power, *hld up, staying on whn lft second 2 out, led last, cmftbly...* (7 to 2 op 11 to 4) 1
456⁸ PRIDEWOOD FUGGLE 7-11-5 W McFarland, *rcd in 3rd but not fluent, chsd ldr 3 out till lft in ld nxt, hdd and blun last, sn btn*................. (Evens fav op 6 to 4 tchd 7 to 4) 2
3276⁷ BOLD TIME MONKEY 6-11-0 W Marston, *keen hold, chsd ldr 3 out, sn btn.*
.................(8 to 1 op 5 to 1 tchd 10 to 1 and 12 to 1) 3
2749 WOLDSMAN 7-10-12 (7*) Mr J Goldstein, *led, sn clr, hng lft 3 out, hung badly left and in command whn ran out nxt.*
..........................(2 to 1 op 5 to 4 tchd 9 to 4) ro
Dist: 6l, 13l. 4m 17.90s. a 32.90s (4 Ran).

(Mrs A Squires), K G Wingrove

3589 Cusop Handicap Chase Class E (0-110 5-y-o and up) £3,186 3m 1f 110yds..................(2:10)

3412³ ROYAL SAXON [86] (bl) 11-11-10 W Marston, *walked o'r....* 1
Walked over. (Time not taken) (1 Ran).
SR: -/

(G Morris), P Bowen

# 3590 Bredwardine Novices' Selling Hurdle Class G (4-y-o and up) £2,010 2m 1f
..........................(2:40)

3299⁸ CONTRACT BRIDGE (Ire) 4-10-3 W McFarland, *hld up in tch, steady hdwy to chal 3 out, sn led, drvn and held on wl r-in.*
..........................(2 to 1 jt-fav op 5 to 4) 1
3414 MAGICAL BLUES (Ire) 5-11-0 K Gaule, *hld up, steady hdwy 3 out, still on bit aftr 2 out, drvn to chase wnr appr last, ran on, too much to do..*.................(8 to 1 op 5 to 1) 2
3515³ ALMAPA 5-11-3 (3*) T Dascombe, *chsd ldrs till steadied aftr 3rd, str chal 3 out, sn outpcd.....*.......(2 to 1 jt-fav op 6 to 4 tchd 9 to 4) 3
2893 GLEN GARNOCK 5-11-0 Gary Lyons, *chsd ldr, led 4th, sn hdd, led ag'n nxt, headed soon aftr 3 out, wknd quickly.*
..........................(7 to 1 op 4 to 1) 4
LADY ECLAT 4-9-12 (5*) S Ryan, *al beh, lost tch frm 4 out, tld off*.........................(16 to 1 op 10 to 1) 5
3082 TATIBAG 5-10-7 (7*) Mr J Goldstein, *sn beh, tld off.*
..........................(40 to 1 op 16 to 1) 6
3270⁶ RAPID LINER (bl) 4-10-8 V Slattery, *led to 4th, sn led ag'n, hdd nxt, wknd quickly 3 out, tld off.*........(20 to 1 op 14 to 1) 7
595⁷ MORE BILLS (Ire) 5-11-0 D J Burchell, *chsd ldrs, str chal 3 out, sn wknd, 4th and no ch whn f last.*
..........................(5 to 1 op 4 to 1) f
MUMMY'S MOLE 6-10-9 (5*) D Salter, *prmnt, hit 5th and beh, tld off whn pld up bef 2 out*..........(50 to 1 op 25 to 1) pu
1690 NORTHERN DIAMOND (Ire) 4-10-5 (3*) P Henley, *chsd ldrs till wknd quickly 4 out.*..............(40 to 1 op 16 to 1) pu
3184 BOOT JACK (Ire) 8-10-7 (7*) M Griffiths, *hit second, sn beh, tld off whn pld up bef 2 out.* (33 to 1 op 20 to 1 tchd 40 to 1) pu
Dist: ½l, 24l, 6l, dist, 4l, 1¾l. 4m 1.70s. a 16.70s (11 Ran).

(LM Racing), P G Murphy

# 3591 Garway Novices' Hunters' Chase Class H (5-y-o and up) £1,095 2m
..........................(3:10)

NECTANEBO (Ire) 9-11-7 (7*) Mr M Frith, *hld up and al gng wl, hdwy 6th, chlgd 3 out till led aftr nxt, sn clr.*
..........................(25 to 1 op 12 to 1) 1
3147 TOM'S APACHE 8-11-7 (7*) Mr E James, *led, sn clr, hdd aftr 2 out, soon outpcd*
.........(13 to 2 op 14 to 1 tchd 16 to 1 and 20 to 1) 2
DALAMETRE 10-11-7 (7*) Mr M Munrowd, *hdwy and rdn alng 6th, effrt 3 out, sn wknd.*
..........................(5 to 1 fav op 5 to 4 tchd 11 to 4 and 11 to 10) 3
1103⁵ CHAN THE MAN 6-11-7 (7*) Mr M Harris, *chsd ldr frm 3rd, hit 8th, ev ch whn mstk 3 out, sn wknd..* (10 to 1 op 7 to 1) 4
ANN'S AMBITION 10-11-7 (7*) Mr C Heard, *mstks, al beh.*
..........................(3 to 1 op 11 to 4) 5
3279 THE COMMUNICATOR 11-11-9 (5*) Mr B Pollock, *chsd ldrs, hit 4 out, sn wknd..*.............(10 to 1 op 8 to 1) 6
OATS FOR NOTES 7-11-2 (7*) Mr R Burton, *al beh, no ch whn mstk 3 out*.....................(7 to 1 op 5 to 1) 7
2995⁷ HAPPY PADDY 14-11-7 (7*) Mr M Cowley, *in tch, mstk and wknd 5th, tld off*........(20 to 1 op 12 to 1 tchd 33 to 1) 8
2995 MICHELLES CRYSTAL 6-11-2 (7*) Mr J Goldstein, *slwly away, f 3rd*.....................(33 to 1 op 25 to 1) f
3256 FELTHAM MISTRESS 7-11-2 (7*) Mr E Babington, *in tch, 4th whn f 7th*.....................(33 to 1 op 20 to 1) f
SPACE MOLLY 8-11-2 (7*) Mr P Cowley, *tld off frm 4th, pld up bef 3 out*.....................(33 to 1 op 25 to 1) pu
Dist: 6l, 16l, 2½l, 12l, 2½l, 14l, dist. 4m 4.20s. a 17.20s (11 Ran).

(Mrs R E Parker), N Parker

3592 Racing Channel Handicap Hurdle Class F (0-105 4-y-o and up) £2,794 2m 1f..........................(4:25)

3424* EURO SINGER [-] 5-11-5 (5*) S Ryan, *pressed ldrs, chlgd 4 out, led drvn, lft in ld 2 out, soon clr.*
..........................(9 to 4 fav op 2 to 1) 1
3403³ VA UTU [-] 9-10-8 (3*) Sophie Mitchell, *led 3rd, hdd aftr 4 out, lft in second 2 out, one pace.* (9 to 4 op 4 to 1) 2
3424 DISSOLVE [-] 5-9-13 (7*) Mr L Baker, *hdwy 5th, pressed ldrs appr 3 out, one pace frm nxt.*
..........................(20 to 1 op 12 to 1) 3
1958⁷ TAP SHOES (Ire) [-] 7-10-0 V Slattery, *hdwy 5th, chsd ldrs 3 out, sn outpcd*.........(14 to 1 tchd 12 to 1) 4
3301⁴ DONTDRESSFORDINNER [-] 7-10-12 (3*) T Dascombe, *hdwy 5th, wknd 3 out*....................(5 to 1 op 9 to 2) 5
1724⁸ JEWEL THIEF [-] 7-10-2 (7*) Mr E Babington, *rdn alng 4th, al beh*.....................(14 to 1 op 10 to 1) 6
243 NOBLE SOCIETY [-] 9-10-11 (7*) J Power, *al beh.*
..........................(10 to 1 op 7 to 1) 7
3424 COURAGEOUS KNIGHT [-] 8-10-4 W Marston, *led to 3rd, styd frnt rnk, drvn to ld aftr 4 out, hrd rdn whn ran out through wing 2 out*.............(7 to 1 op 6 to 1 tchd 8 to 1) ro
Dist: 8l, 2½l, 6l, 13l, 26l, 26l. 4m 2.30s. a 17.30s (8 Ran).

(BCD Steels Ltd), T Keddy

3593 Pandy Novices' Chase Class E (5-y-o and up) £2,918 2m 3f........(4:55)

901 DUKE OF DREAMS 7-11-6 V Slattery, *chsd ldrs, chlgd 8th, led 9th, hit tenth, clr frm nxt.*
..........................(15 to 8 op 11 to 8 tchd 2 to 1) 1
3502⁹ PANDORA'S PRIZE 11-10-9 T Eley, *chsd ldr, hmpd and lft in ld 4th, hdd 9th, hit tenth, no ch whn blun last.*
..........................(10 to 1 op 12 to 1 tchd 14 to 1) 2
SOMETHING CATCHY (Ire) 7-10-9 W Marston, *in tch, hit 7th, chlgd 8th, rdn 4 out, sn btn, blun 2 out.*
..........................(15 to 2 op 12 to 1 tchd 14 to 1 and 16 to 1) 3
DIAMOND LIGHT 10-11-0 Mr S Lloyd, *hit 6th, al beh.*
..........................(5 to 4 on op 7 to 4 on tchd 5 to 4 on) 4
2150 ANOTHER VENTURE (Ire) 7-11-0 M Foster, *led till f 4th.*
..........................(20 to 1 op 12 to 1) f
1211 FREELINE LUSTRE (Ire) 7-11-0 W McFarland, *blun 3rd, tld off 5th, pld up aftr nxt.*...................(20 to 1 op 12 to 1) pu
Dist: 10l, ¾l, dist. 4m 56.80s. a 31.80s (6 Ran).

(Mrs V W Jones), R J Baker

# 3594 Broad Oak Conditional Jockeys' Novices' Handicap Hurdle Class F (0-100 4-y-o and up) £2,248 3¼m
..........................(5:25)

2200⁷ CLONGOUR (Ire) [-] 7-11-1 D J Kavanagh, *hld up, hdwy 8th, led 3 out, drvn out*..........(7 to 2 op 5 to 2 tchd 7 to 1) 1
3422³ KINGSWOOD MANOR [-] 5-11-4 P Henley, *prmnt, chlgd 3rd to 4th, rdn 7th, chald 8th, led nxt, hdd 3 out, styd on same pace*..........................(4 to 1 tchd 5 to 1) 2
3172⁵ HI MARBLE (Ire) [-] 6-10-7 (7*) M Lane, *hdwy 5th, chsd ldrs 3 out, sn outpcd*.............(7 to 4 fav op 5 to 2) 3
3190⁶ LADY OF MINE [-] 7-9-11 (3*) L Cummins, *mstk second, chlgd frm 3rd till led 8th, hdd nxt, sn wknd..............* (5 to 1) 4
3137 NUNS LUCY [-] 6-10-0 Guy Lewis, *led to 7th, sn wknd, tld off whn pld up bef 9th..*.........(50 to 1 op 33 to 1) pu

499

3362³ COPPER COIL [-] 7-11-10 (3*) J Power, *hmpd bend aftr 1st, rdn after 7th, sn beh, tld off whn pld up bef 2 out.* ....(100 to 30 op 2 to 1 tchd 7 to 2 and 4 to 1) pu
3333⁷ MUSIC CLASS (Ire) [-] 6-10-9 (3*) M Berry, *chlgd frm 3rd till led 7th, hdd 8th, wknd quickly appr 3 out, tld off whn pld up bef nxt.*..................... (13 to 2 op 5 to 1 tchd 7 to 1) pu
Dist: 2½l, 23l, ¾l. 6m 31.70s. a 29.70s (7 Ran).
(Liam Mulryan), F Murphy

AINTREE (good)
Saturday April 5th
Going Correction: PLUS 0.50 sec. per fur.

3595 Cordon Bleu Handicap Hurdle Class B (5-y-o and up) £19,870 2m 110yds .... (1:45)

3330³ SHANKAR (Ire) [128] 6-10-7 (5*) Mr R Thornton, *settled gng wl, improved on bit 3 out, led betw last 2, ran on well.* .... (25 to 1 op 20 to 1) 1
3131 DIRECT ROUTE (Ire) [138] 6-11-8 A Dobbin, *settled midfield, improved hfwy, led 2 out till betw last two, kpt on same pace.* .... (16 to 1 op 14 to 1 tchd 20 to 1) 2
3113 DREAMS END [140] 9-11-7 (3*) L Aspell, *tucked away midfield, improved aftr 3 out, kpt on wl betw last 2.* .... (12 to 1 op 10 to 1 tchd 14 to 1) 3
2591 CLIFTON BEAT (USA) [139] 6-11-9 C F Swan, *co'red up midfield, improved 3 out, styd on betw last 2.* .... (16 to 1 op 14 to 1 tchd 20 to 1) 4
3113 ZABADI (Ire) [138] 5-11-8 R Johnson, *wtd wth, improved appr 3 out, rdn and kpt on same pace frm nxt.* .... (14 to 1 op 12 to 1 tchd 16 to 1) 5
2532³ PRIZEFIGHTER [116] 6-10-0 B Storey, *chsd ldr, hit second, drw level hfwy, led 3 out to nxt, no extr.* (20 to 1 op 14 to 1) 6
3080⁵ FORESTAL [117] 5-10-1 T J Murphy, *al wl plcd, effrt and drvn alng 3 out, no extr nxt.*.......................... (14 to 1) 7
3257⁴ FROZEN SEA (USA) [116] 6-10-0 J R Kavanagh, *settled to track ldrs, effrt and pushed alng 3 out, no imprsn nxt.* ....(33 to 1 tchd 40 to 1) 8
479³ AMLAH (USA) [116] (bl) 5-10-0 B Powell, *pld hrd, led and sn clr, jnd hfwy, hdd 3 out, fdd.* .... (40 to 1 op 33 to 1 tchd 50 to 1) 9
3385* ROSENCRANTZ (Ire) [116] 5-10-0 (7ex) N Williamson, *tucked away beh ldrs, effrt appr 3 out, fdd nxt.* (11 to 2 tchd 6 to 1) 10
3532² TEJANO GOLD (USA) [119] 7-10-3 S Wynne, *tucked away midfield, wnt hndy 3 out, wknd nxt.* .... (20 to 1 op 16 to 1 tchd 25 to 1) 11
2197* SECRET SPRING (Fr) [125] 5-10-9 M Richards, *hld up beh, nvr plcd to chal...* (3 to 1 fav op 11 to 4 tchd 100 to 30) 12
3330 HAMILTON SILK [132] 5-11-2 J Osborne, *settled in tch, some hdwy appr 3 out, nvr dngrs.* (8 to 1 op 7 to 1 tchd 9 to 1) 13
2329⁸ MOST EQUAL [116] 7-9-9 (5*) G Supple, *sn rear, nvr a factor.* ....(25 to 1 tchd 33 to 1) 14
3330⁶ BLAIR CASTLE (Ire) [116] 6-10-0 B Fenton, *struggling rear whn blun 5th, nvr a factor*............ (50 to 1 op 33 to 1) 15
3156 STOMPIN [140] 6-11-10 J Culloty, *pressed ldrs, feeling pace 3 out, sn btn*......................... (9 to 1 op 7 to 1) 16
3080 SHINING EDGE [125] 5-10-9 L Wyer, *trkd ldrs, struggling to keep up appr 3 out, sn btn*............(16 to 1 op 14 to 1) 17
2787² KAITAK (Ire) [118] 6-9-13 (3*) F Leahy, *chsd ldrs, struggling aftr 4 out, sn btn*...................(25 to 1 tchd 20 to 1) 18
Dist: 2½l, nk, 3½l, 3½l, 1½l, 8l, hd, sht-hd, 1¾l, sht-hd. 3m 59.90s. a 11.90s (18 Ran).
SR: 48/55/57/52/47/23/16/15/15/ (International Plywood Plc), D Nicholson

3596 Martell Red Rum Chase Limited Handicap Class A Grade 2 (5-y-o and up) £25,780 2m............... (2:20)

2466³ DOWN THE FELL [122] 8-10-7 N Williamson, *al frnt rnk, lft in ld 5th, styd on strly to go clr appr last.* .... (20 to 1 op 16 to 1 tchd 25 to 1) 1
3130⁶ LORD DORCET (Ire) [133] 7-11-4 J Osborne, *settled midfield, swtchd ins to improve frm 3 out, rdn betw last 2, not quicken wth wnr from last*.............................. (13 to 2 op 6 to 1) 2
2934⁴ WEE RIVER (Ire) [125] 8-10-10 J Callaghan, *nvr far away, effrt appr 3 out, sn drvn alng, outpcd betw last 2.* ....(14 to 1 tchd 16 to 1) 3
3154 MISTER ODDY [128] 11-10-13 J Culloty, *chsd ldrs, effrt hfwy, feeling pace appr 3 out, sn btn*........(16 to 1 op 14 to 1) 4
3154⁶ POLITICAL TOWER [127] 10-10-12 A Dobbin, *settled in tch, effrt whn f 6th*....................(12 to 1 tchd 14 to 1) f
2826² ARCTIC KINSMAN [143] 9-12-0 C Llewellyn, *al hndy, chalg ldr and gng wl whn f 2 out.* (5 to 1 op 4 to 1 tchd 11 to 2) f
3112³ CELIBATE (Ire) [132] 6-11-3 R Dunwoody, *tracking ldrs whn f 5th*..................................(7 to 2 fav op 4 to 1) f
3154² ELZOBA (Fr) [138] (bl) 5-11-2 C Maude, *led till f 5th, broke leg, destroyed*.............................(11 to 2 op 4 to 1) f
3154⁴ TIME WON'T WAIT (Ire) [133] 8-11-4 D Bridgwater, *wtd wth, imprvg whn hmpd and uns rdr 5th.* ....(11 to 2 op 5 to 1 tchd 6 to 1) ur
2505² JATHIB (Can) [128] 6-10-13 Derek Byrne, *not fluent, beh and pushed alng hfwy, pld up bef 4 out*...(12 to 1 tchd 14 to 1) pu
Dist: 7l, 6l, 11l. 3m 58.20s. a 11.20s (10 Ran).
SR: 47/51/37/29/-/-/ (Mrs S Johnson), J Howard Johnson

3597 Martell Aintree Hurdle Class A Grade 1 (4-y-o and up) £40,750 2½m .... (2:55)

3113 BIMSEY (Ire) 7-11-7 M A Fitzgerald, *al hndy, led appr 3 out, kpt on wl frm betw last 2, drvn out...* (14 to 1 tchd 16 to 1) 1
3151⁸ PRIDWELL 7-11-7 R Dunwoody, *al wl plcd, effrt on ins appr 3 out, styd on same pace r-in*..........(12 to 1 op 10 to 1) 2
3113* MAKE A STAND 6-11-7 C Maude, *led till appr 3 out, sn drvn alng, no imprsn frm nxt*............(7 to 4 fav op 5 to 4) 3
3113³ SPACE TRUCKER (Ire) 6-11-7 J Shortt, *settled to track ldrs, effrt and hit 7th, feeling pace aftr 3 out, tired whn jmpd slwly last*.....................(5 to 1 op 4 to 1 tchd 11 to 2) 4
3151 URUBANDE (Ire) 7-11-7 C F Swan, *pressed ldrs, feeling pace and drvn alng 3 out, sn struggling*......(13 to 2 op 5 to 1) 5
3113 LARGE ACTION (Ire) 9-11-7 J Osborne, *settled rear, shrtlvd effrt hfwy, lost tch and pld up appr 4 out.* (3 to 1 op 5 to 2) pu
3155 DOUBLE SYMPHONY (Ire) (bl) 9-11-2 G Bradley, *trkd ldrs, lost grnd quickly hfwy, pld up aftr 4 out.* ....(25 to 1 op 33 to 1 tchd 50 to 1) pu
Dist: 1½l, 16l, 2l, dist. 4m 51.10s. a 13.10s (7 Ran).
SR: 62/60/44/42/ (Aidan J Ryan), R Akehurst

KELSO (good to firm)
Monday April 7th
Going Correction: MINUS 0.25 sec. per fur.

3598 Cheviot Rentals Modular Marquees 'National Hunt' Novices' Hurdle Class D (4-y-o and up) £2,871 2m 110yds....................... (2:00)

3316³ JESSOLLE 5-10-2 (7*) R Burns, *hld up in rear, steady hdwy 5th, effrt 2 out, led last, pushed out.* .... (6 to 5 fav op 11 to 10 tchd 11 to 8) 1
3351 NICK ROSS 6-11-0 A S Smith, *keen hold, trkd ldrs gng wl, cl up 3 out, dsptd ld last, sn rdn and not quicken.* .... (11 to 1 op 14 to 1 tchd 25 to 1) 2
2712 PENTLANDS FLYER (Ire) 6-10-7 (7*) C McCormack, *chsd ldrs, effrt and hdwy 2 out, dsptd ld and hit last, rdn and not quicken r-in*..........(16 to 1 op 14 to 1 tchd 20 to 1) 3
3351³ EASTCLIFFE (Ire) 5-11-0 G Cahill, *pld hrd, hld up in rear, gd hdwy 2 out, styd on wl frm last, not rch ldrs.* ....(8 to 1 op 6 to 1 tchd 9 to 1) 4
3351⁵ PENTLAND SQUIRE 6-11-0 N Smith, *hld up in rear, steady hdwy 3 out, chsd ldrs nxt, rdn and one pace appr last.* ....(4 to 1 op 7 to 2) 5
3476³ DANTES AMOUR (Ire) 6-11-0 D Bentley, *hld up midfield, hdwy appr 3 out, rdn 2 out, sn wknd.* (12 to 1 tchd 14 to 1) 6
3157⁷ AMBER HOLLY 8-10-9 F Perratt, *cl up, led 4th, rdn 2 out, hdd and wknd appr last*................(100 to 1 op 33 to 1) 7
2971³ ARCTIC SANDY (Ire) 7-11-0 B Storey, *in tch, rdn alng and hit 3 out, sn outpcd*..........(11 to 2 op 5 to 1 tchd 6 to 1) 8
2915⁶ POLITICAL MANDATE 4-10-0 (3*) F Leahy, *led to 4th, rdn alng nxt, wknd aftr 3 out*....................(100 to 1 op 33 to 1) 9
3303 CAULKER 4-10-3 (5*) S Taylor, *cl up, hit 4th, rdn alng 3 out, hit nxt, sn wknd*.......................... (200 to 1 op 100 to 1) 10
2651⁹ SALEM BEACH 5-10-9 J Callaghan, *mstks, al rear.* .... (50 to 1 op 33 to 1) 11
3401 CHAIN LINE 7-11-0 T Reed, *hld up pulling hrd, hdwy 3rd, rdn alng 5th, sn wknd*.............. (66 to 1 tchd 200 to 1) 12
KINGS ADVENTURE 5-10-11 (3*) G Lee, *chsd ldrs to hfwy, sn lost pl and beh*........ (25 to 1 op 33 to 1 tchd 20 to 1) 13
Dist: 1¾l, 4l, 2½l, 2l, 7l, 8l, 7l, 1l, 1½l, 7l. 3m 49.60s. a 6.60s (13 Ran).
(C R Fleet), G Richards

3599 Holland & Holland Buccleuch Cup Maiden Hunters' Chase Class H (5-y-o and up) £2,081 3m 1f......(2:30)

GALLANTS DELIGHT 7-11-3[1] (7*) Mr A Robson, *chsd ldrs, hit 12th, hdwy 14th, chased lder and blun 3 out, led last, styd on wl*.......................(9 to 2 op 4 to 1 tchd 5 to 1) 1
ENSIGN EWART (Ire) 6-11-9 (5*) Mr C Storey, *hld up, steady hdwy 14th, chsd ldrs 3 out, effrt and rdn nxt, styd on same pace*.. (9 to 4 fav) 2
PENNINE VIEW 10-11-9 (5*) Mr R Ford, *chsd ldr, led 7th, rdn 2 out, hdd and hit last. wknd r-in*...... (10 to 1 tchd 12 to 1) 3
COOL YULE (Ire) 9-11-7 (7*) Mr B Gibson, *hit 1st, al rear, beh frm 8th*....................................(10 to 1 op 12 to 1) 4
LOTHIAN COMMODORE 7-11-7 (7*) Captain A Ogden, *in tch, rdn alng 15th, sn wknd*....(11 to 2 op 9 to 2 tchd 6 to 1) 5
STORM ALIVE (Ire) 6-11-7 (7*) Mr T Scott, *chsd ldrs, hit 9th and sn beh, blun 11th, soon tld off*.....(20 to 1 op 16 to 1) 6
LINDON RUN 8-11-7 (7*) Mr R Morgan, *chsd ldrs, hit 12th, rdn alng and blun 15th, sn wknd and hmpd 3 out, beh whn f last.* .... (9 to 1 op 8 to 1 tchd 10 to 1) f
SEYMOUR FIDDLES 6-11-2 (7*) Mr M Ruddy, *mstks, in rear till f 11th*............................. (66 to 1 op 50 to 1) f
LEANNES MAN (Ire) 8-11-7 (7*) Mr Chris Wilson, *led to 7th, chsd ldr, blun 9th, drvn alng in 3rd whn f 3 out*......(5 to 1) f
HULA 9-11-7 (7*) Mr M Bradburne, *in tch, hdwy 13th, rdn alng and blun 16th, 4th whn brght dwn 3 out*..........(100 to 1) bd

CANISTER CASTLE 9-11-9 (5*) Mr R Shiels, *chsd ldrs, rdn along and blun 15th and nxt, wknd and pld up bef 3 out.*
.................................(16 to 1 tchd 20 to 1)   pu
3248[6] TUMLIN OOT (Ire) 8-11-9 (5*) Mr N Wilson, *hld up, hit 4th, hdwy to chase ldrs and blun 8th, blundered 13th and sn beh, tld off whn pld up 3 out.*...................................(33 to 1)   pu
Dist: 8l, 5l, 19l, 3½l, dist. 6m 14.40s. a 17.40s (12 Ran).

(Mrs C Johnston), Mrs C Johnston

3600 Glengoyne Highland Malt Novices' Chase Class D Tamerosia Series Qualifier (5-y-o and up) £4,111 3m 1f
.................................(3:00)

3304[3] REAL TONIC 7-11-8 Captain A Ogden, *hld up in tch, hdwy 12th, jnd ldr 15th, led 2 out, lft clr last, eased.*
.................................(5 to 2 op 2 to 1 tchd 11 to 4)   1
1951 TALL MEASURE 11-11-2 B Storey, *al chasing ldrs, rdn along 15th, one pace frm nxt, lft second at last.*
.................................(14 to 1 tchd 16 to 1)   2
3434[8] GERMAN LEGEND 7-11-8 J Burke, *in tch, rdn along 13th, outpcd frm nxt.*...................(16 to 1 op 12 to 1)   3
3511[3] COOL WEATHER (Ire) (bl) 9-11-2 A S Smith, *in tch, rdn along and hdwy 14th, drvn nxt, sn outpcd....* (25 to 1 op 20 to 1)   4
3259* MISS COLETTE 9-11-3 M Foster, *cl up, rdn along 14th, sn outpcd, beh frm 3 out...*(14 to 1 op 10 to 1)   5
3202[4] FINE TUNE (Ire) 7-10-9 (7*) Mr M Bradburne, *chsd ldrs, rdn along 13th, sn outpcd, beh whn blun badly 2 out.*
.................................(33 to 1 op 25 to 1)   6
2491 MAMICA 7-11-2 N Smith, *hld up, pushed alng and blun 16th, outpcd and beh aftr....*. (10 to 1 op 8 to 1 tchd 12 to 1)   7
3306[2] COQUI LANE 10-11-8 D Parker, *led, rdn along and jnd 5 out, hdd 2 out, 4 ls second whn f last.*
.................................(11 to 10 on op 5 to 4 on)   f
Dist: 9l, 20l, nk, 1¼l, dist, dist. 6m 15.40s. a 18.40s (8 Ran).

(Robert Ogden), G Richards

3601 Pat De Clermont Handicap Chase Class E for the Scott Briggs Challenge Trophy (0-110 5-y-o and up) £3,217 3m 1f.................................(3:30)

3060[2] ASK ME LATER (Ire) [85] 8-11-3 G Cahill, *chsd ldrs till outpcd and pushed alng 12th, hdwy 4 out, led appr last, ran on strly.*
.................................(3 to 1 fav tchd 7 to 2)   1
3436* NIJWAY [82] 7-10-0 (5ex) B Storey, *chsd ldrs, hit 4th and 11th, pushed alng 14th, rdn appr 3 out, kpt on one pace.*
.................................(9 to 2 op 4 to 1)   2
2633 HURRICANE ANDREW (Ire) [86] 9-10-4 N Smith, *made most till rdn and hdd appr last, wknd r-in...* (20 to 1 op 16 to 1)   3
2633[5] FORWARD GLEN [82] (bl) 10-10-0 A S Smith, *hld up, not fluent, hit 13th and sn outpcd. styd on appr last.*
.................................(14 to 1 op 20 to 1)   4
3436[2] GALE AHEAD (Ire) [95] 7-10-13 M Foster, *chsd ldrs, effrt and ev ch 3 out, rdn nxt, wknd appr last....*(7 to 2 op 4 to 1)   5
2979[5] BANNTOWN BILL (Ire) [99] (v) 8-11-3 T Reed, *chsd ldrs, alng 15th, grad wknd.............*(5 to 1 op 6 to 1)   6
3306[4] WHAAT FETTLE [110] 12-12-0 M Moloney, *cl up, rdn along and beh 3 out.....*. (13 to 2 op 9 to 2 tchd 7 to 1)   7
3395[7] FESTIVAL FANCY [82] 10-11-3 (3*) G Lee, *mstks and al rear, f 4 out.......................*(33 to 1 op 25 to 1)   f
3161[3] SNOOK POINT [86] 10-10-4 J Callaghan, *chsd ldrs till pld up bef 3th, broke blood vessel..........*(33 to 1 op 20 to 1)   pu
Dist: 4l, 1¼l, nk, 6l, 3½l. 6m 18.60s. a 21.60s (9 Ran).

(Timothy Hardie), Mrs S C Bradburne

3602 E. Scarth & Son Handicap Hurdle Class D (0-125 4-y-o and up) £2,788 2m 110yds.................................(4:00)

3437[2] WELL APPOINTED (Ire) [94] 8-9-12 (3*) G Lee, *chsd clr ldr, hdwy 3 out, cl up nxt, rdn to ld r-in, ran on wl.*
.................................(2 to 1 tchd 7 to 4)   1
3198[9] KILLBALLY BOY (Ire) [93] 7-9-7 (7*) C McCormack, *led and sn clr, hit 5th, jnd and hit 2 out, soon rdn, hdd and not quicken r-in...................*(7 to 1 op 5 to 1 tchd 8 to 1)   2
1827[5] DONE WELL (USA) [118] 5-11-11 B Storey, *hld up in tch, hdwy appr 3 out, pushed alng and outpcd approaching nxt, rdn last, no imprsn.............*(11 to 10 fav op 11 to 8)   3
ASTRALEON (Ire) [106] 9-10-6 (7*) S Melrose, *hld up in tch, hdwy 5th, rdn and ev ch 2 out, wknd last, eased.*
.................................(9 to 2 op 3 to 1 tchd 5 to 1)   4
Dist: 2l, 17l, 30l. 3m 44.60s. a 1.60s (4 Ran).
SR: 16/13/21/-/

(Drumlanrig Racing), B Mactaggart

3603 Stefes Champion Hunters' Chase Class H (5-y-o and up) £2,736 3m 1f
.................................(4:30)

NOW YOUNG MAN (Ire) 8-11-7 (7*) Mr Chris Wilson, *in tch till outpcd and rdn along 15th, styd on appr last, ridden r-in to ld nr finish...................*(13 to 2 op 6 to 1 tchd 7 to 1)   1
3307[2] ROYAL JESTER 13-11-9 (5*) Mr C Storey, *chsd ldr, rdn along appr 3 out, styd on approaching last, ridden and ev ch r-in, no extr nr finish........*(13 to 8 fav op 5 to 2 tchd 7 to 4)   2

3125[2] KUSHBALOO 12-12-0 (7*) Mr A Parker, *led, rdn alng and blun 2 out, hdd last 50 yards, no extr........*. (5 to 2 op 3 to 1)   3
DARK DAWN 13-12-0 (7*) Miss Lorna Foxton, *hld up, steady hdwy 12th, chlgd and ev ch 2 out, wknd last.*
.................................(4 to 1 tchd 9 to 2)   4
3247[2] LITTLE WENLOCK 13-11-9 (5*) Mrs V Jackson, *chsd ldrs till pld up lme aftr 9th, dead...* (8 to 1 op 5 to 1 tchd 9 to 1)   pu
Dist: ½l, 2½l, 19l. 6m 22.60s. a 25.60s (5 Ran).

(Grant C Mitchell), Mrs A Swinbank

3604 Croall Bryson Handicap Hurdle Class D (0-120 4-y-o and up) £2,840 2¾m 110yds.................................(5:20)

3355[4] RASCALLY [87] 7-10-10 M Foster, *cl up, led aftr second, rdn 2 out, hld on gmely und pres r-in.........*(8 to 1 op 6 to 1)   1
3162[7] DOCKMASTER [85] 6-10-8 A S Smith, *trkd ldrs on inner, effrt and not much room 2 out, ev ch last, sn drvn and no extr nr finish...................*(7 to 1 op 6 to 1)   2
3308* CASH BOX (Ire) [87] 9-10-10 N Smith, *hld up in tch, hdwy 3 out and sn pushed alng, effrt and ev ch flt, no extr nr finish.
.................................*(3 to 1 fav op 9 to 4 tchd 7 to 2)   3
3398[6] OLD HABITS (Ire) [100] 8-11-2 (7*) C Elliott, *cl up, hit 1st, rdn alng 3 out, ev ch last, drvn r-in, no extr nr finish.*
.................................(9 to 2 op 6 to 1)   4
3012[4] MASTER OF TROY [99] 9-11-8 D Parker, *hld up and beh, hdwy appr 3 out, rdn nxt, kpt on same pace.*
.................................(20 to 1 op 16 to 1 tchd 25 to 1)   5
3396[7] ALLERBY [77] 9-9-9 (5*) B Grattan, *beh frm hfwy.*
.................................(25 to 1 op 16 to 1)   6
1694 MULLINGAR (Ire) [86] 8-10-9 K Johnson, *led till aftr second, prmnt till rdn alng 6th, sn wknd....* (100 to 1 op 66 to 1)   7
3353[2] MAITRE DE MUSIQUE (Fr) [94] 6-10-10 (7*) C McCormack, *trkd ldrs, effrt and ev ch 2 out, sn drvn and wknd bef last.*
.................................(9 to 2 op 3 to 1)   8
3355[6] MASTER HYDE (USA) [101] 8-11-10 B Storey, *hld up and beh, steady hdwy 6th, chsd ldrs whn f 2 out...* (5 to 1 op 7 to 1)   f
Dist: ¾l, ½l, 2l, 2½l, 26l, ¾l, 5l. 5m 17.30s. a 8.30s (9 Ran).

(J Townson), Miss L C Siddall

AINTREE (good)
Monday April 7th
Going Correction: PLUS 0.20 sec. per fur.

3605 Martell Grand National Chase Handicap Class A Grade 3 (110-0 6-y-o and up) £178,146 4½m.......(5:00)

3206[2] LORD GYLLENE (NZ) [141] 9-10-0 A Dobbin, *jmpd boldly, led till hmpd and hdd briefly 16th, pushed clr aftr 3 out, ran on strly, easily.........................*(8 to 1 tchd 10 to 1)   1
2821* SUNY BAY (Ire) [144] 8-10-3 J Osborne, *jmpd wl, pressed ldr, ev ch whn blun badly 4 out, no extr frm nxt.*
.................................(8 to 1 tchd 9 to 1)   2
3115[6] CAMELOT KNIGHT [141] 11-10-0 C Llewellyn, *hld up, hmpd 7th, hdwy frm 24th (Canal Turn), styd on wl from 2 out, nrst finish..........................*(100 to 1)   3
3398[8] BUCKBOARD BOUNCE [142] 11-10-1 P Carberry, *hld up, hdwy gng wl fnl circuit, in tch 22nd (Becher's), rdn and one pace frm 4 out..............*(40 to 1 op 25 to 1)   4
2734 MASTER OATS [165] 11-11-10 N Williamson, *hld up, not fluent 6th (Becher's), slightly hmpd 11th, hdwy gng wl fnl circuit, chsd wnr aftr 3 out, sn no extr.*
.................................(25 to 1 tchd 33 to 1)   5
2452 AVRO ANSON [144] 9-10-3[1] P Niven, *o'rjmpd and almost f 1st, al chasing ldrs, pushed alng and mstk 4 out, sn btn.*
.................................(12 to 1 op 10 to 1)   6
3206[4] KILLESHIN [141] 11-10-0 S Curran, *beh, niggled alng frm hfwy, styd on to pass btn horses from 3 out, nvr a factor.*
.................................(33 to 1)   7
2698 DAKYNS BOY [141] 12-10-0 T J Murphy, *hld up, pushed alng 16th (water), no dngr aftr...............*(100 to 1)   8
3152 NAHTHEN LAD (Ire) [150] 8-10-9 J F Titley, *in tch, chasing ldrs whn hit 22nd (Becher's), outpcd when hit 5 out, tld.*
.................................(14 to 1 tchd 16 to 1)   9
3329[3] VALIANT WARRIOR [144] 9-10-3[1] R Garritty, *hld up, hdwy and in tch 17th, lost pl 6 out (Valentine's), sn btn...* (50 to 1)   10
2734* ANTONIN (Fr) [141] 9-10-0 C D'Wyer, *not fluent, al towards rear, wl beh fnl circuit.................*(14 to 1 op 12 to 1)   11
3134[9] NORTHERN HIDE [142] 11-10-1[1] P Holley, *chsd ldrs, slight mstk 6th (Becher's), struggling whn blun six out (Valentine's), tld off..............*(66 to 1 op 40 to 1)   12
2948* TURNING TRIX [141] 10-10-0 J R Kavanagh, *hld up, badly hmpd 11th, lost tch 22nd (Becher's), sn wl beh......* (25 to 1)   13
2916[6] PINK GIN [141] 10-10-0 Mr C Bonner, *beh, hit 6th (Becher's), struggling fnl circuit, tld off.............*(100 to 1)   14
3134 NEW CO (Ire) [141] 9-10-0 D J Casey, *jmpd very slwly in rear 3rd, badly hmpd 7th, tld off frm 24th (Canal Turn)...* (40 to 1)   15
3063[4] GENERAL WOLFE [141] 8-10-0 L Wyer, *beh, niggled alng 12th, sn no dngr, tld off..........*(16 to 1 tchd 20 to 1)   16
2182[2] EVANGELICA (USA) [141] 7-10-0 R Supple, *hld up, some hdwy 12th, struggling fnl circuit, tld off...........*(33 to 1)   17
2956[3] FULL OF OATS [141] 11-10-0 J Culloty, *f 1st.*
.................................(33 to 1 op 50 to 1)   f

501

DON'T LIGHT UP [141] (bl) 11-10-0 M R Thornton, *beh, blun 4th, in rear whn f 13th*.................................(100 to 1) f
1529 STRAIGHT TALK [144] 10-10-3³ Mr J Tizzard, *hld up, towards rear whn f 14th, broke leg, destroyed*.
....(50 to 1 tchd 66 to 1) f
2867 NUAFFE [141] (bl) 12-10-0 T Mitchell, *mstk second, chsd ldrs till f 11th*.....................................(100 to 1 op 50 to 1) f
3211⁴ BACK BAR (Ire) [141] 9-10-0 T P Treacy, *hld up, badly hmpd and f 7th*..(100 to 1) f
2948 SMITH'S BAND (Ire) [143] 9-10-2² R Dunwoody, *wth ldrs, bad mstk 3rd, jmpd wl aftr, led briefly 16th (water), chasing lder whn f 20th, broke neck, dead*..........(12 to 1 tchd 14 to 1) f
1865² GLEMOT (Ire) [141] 9-10-0 S McNeill, *settled midfield, hmpd, sddl slpd and uns rdr 7th*..ur
3063³ SPUFFINGTON [143] 9-10-2² P Hide, *chsd ldrs, lost tch fnl circuit, mstk 20th, blun and uns rdr 22nd (Becher's)*.
....(100 to 1) ur
2966⁴ WYLDE HIDE [141] 11-10-0 C F Swan, *chsd ldrs till blun and almost f 13th, sn beh, bad mstk 21st, uns rdr nxt*.
....(11 to 1 tchd 12 to 1) ur
3153⁴ CELTIC ABBEY [141] 9-10-0 R Johnson, *cl up, hit 3rd, chasing ldrs whn mstk and uns rdr 15th (Chair)*.
....(66 to 1 tchd 50 to 1) ur
3114 GRANGE BRAKE [145] 11-10-4⁴ D Walsh, *mstks towards rear, wl beh frm 18th, tld off whn refused 4 out*...(100 to 1) ref
2800⁵ MUGONI BEACH [141] (bl) 12-10-0 G Tormey, *midfield whn hit 13th, tld off when pld up 21st*......(100 to 1 op 66 to 1) pu
3063 BISHOPS HALL [142] 11-10-1 M Richards, *midfield, pushed alng and outpcd 20th, remote tenth and tired whn pld up 2 out*.
....(50 to 1 op 33 to 1 tchd 66 to 1) pu
3206 SCRIBBLER [143] 11-10-2² D Fortt, *hld up, mstk 9th (Valentine's), struggling whn blun 17th, wl beh when pld up 21st*.
....(100 to 1) pu
2821⁵ LO STREGONE [145] 11-10-4 G Bradley, *al towards rear, struggling frm hfwy, wl tld off whn pld up 4 out*.
....(14 to 1 tchd 12 to 1) pu
2829 DEXTRA DOVE [141] 10-10-0 C Maude, *hld up, hdwy and in tch 13th, drvn and outpcd 20th, wl beh whn pld up 4 out*.
....(33 to 1) pu
2966⁵ FEATHERED GALE [144] 10-10-3 F Woods, *blun second, jmpd poorly in rear aftr, wl tld off whn pld up 4 out*.
....(16 to 1 op 14 to 1 tchd 18 to 1) pu
3114 RIVER MANDATE [142] (v) 10-10-1¹ A Thornton, *hld up, hmpd 7th, struggling fnl circuit, tld off whn pld up 4 out*.
....(50 to 1 op 40 to 1 tchd 66 to 1) pu
3152⁴ GO BALLISTIC [144] 8-10-3³ M A Fitzgerald, *patiently rdn, moderate hdwy into midfield whn blun badly 6 out (Valentine's), tld off when pld up 2 out, broke blood vessel*.
....(7 to 1 fav op 8 to 1 tchd 9 to 1) pu
Dist: 25l, 2l, 1¾l, 1¾l, 8l, 7l, 9l, 1¼l, 8l, 12l. 9m 5.90s. a 7.90s (36 Ran).
SR: 65/43/38/37/58/29/19/10/17/ (Stanley W Clarke), S A Brookshaw

GOWRAN PARK (IRE) (firm)
Tuesday April 8th

3606 Thomastown Maiden Hurdle (4 & 5-y-o) £2,740 2½m......(4:00)

3415³ SHARP OUTLOOK (Ire) 4-10-8 T P Rudd,......(9 to 4 jt-fav) 1
3216 NATIVE ECLIPSE (Ire) 4-10-13 C F Swan,..........(4 to 1) 2
3547 NOMINEE (Ire) 5-11-5 L P Cusack,...............(12 to 1) 3
3429⁴ MENDELUCI (Ire) 5-11-13 S H O'Donovan,..(9 to 4 jt-fav) 4
CHERGALE (Ire) 5-10-7 (7⁷) B J Geraghty,........(8 to 1) 5
2964 NORMINS HUSSAR (Ire) 5-11-5 J Short,.........(14 to 1) 6
3223 LIZES BIRTHDAY (Ire) 5-11-0 D J Casey,.......(20 to 1) 7
3415 GAYEPHAR 4-10-8 T Horgan,....................(14 to 1) 8
2709 TULLIBARDS FLYER (Ire) 5-11-5 T P Treacy,...(25 to 1) 9
Dist: 4½l, 9l, 2½l, 2l. 4m 55.10s. (9 Ran).

(Paul Hardy), M J P O'Brien

3607 Kilkenny Handicap Hurdle (0-123 4-y-o and up) £2,740 2m 1f... (4:30)

3419⁹ ACES AND EIGHTS (Ire) [-] 7-10-8 (7⁷) P G Hourigan,.(9 to 2) 1
3520⁶ ETON GALE (Ire) [-] 8-10-8 (7⁷) B J Geraghty,.......(9 to 2) 2
1714⁷ TAITS CLOCK (Ire) [-] 8-11-1 T Horgan,.............(8 to 1) 3
3235 BRONICA (Ire) [-] 5-10-10 C F Swan,..............(7 to 1) 4
2447⁹ ANTICS (Ire) [-] 5-9-1 (7⁷) Mrs C Harrison,.......(14 to 1) 5
3216⁶ INNOVATIVE (Ire) [-] 6-10-1 T D T Evans,..........(8 to 1) 6
3235⁴ HOME PORT (USA) [-] 5-12-0 C O'Dwyer,.....(3 to 1 fav) 7
3348⁵ TARAJAN (USA) [-] 6-11-9 J Short,..................(6 to 1) 8
3381⁵ MASTER CHUZZLEWIT (Ire) [-] 6-9-2⁵ (5⁵) A O'Shea,.(12 to 1) 9
2877 MISTER CHIPPY (Ire) [-] 5-11-6 T P Treacy,.........(8 to 1) 10
Dist: 3l, 8l, 3l, 1½l. 3m 59.30s. (10 Ran).

(P Hughes), P Hughes

3608 Mount Leinster (Pro-Am) I.N.H. Flat Race (6-y-o and up) £2,740 2m 1f
....(5:00)

3449² SARAH SUPREME (Ire) 6-11-2 (7⁷) G T Hourigan,
....(9 to 4 fav) 1
3456⁴ APPLAUSE (Ire) 6-11-7 (7⁷) J A Robinson,......(5 to 2) 2
3421 SARAH BLUE (Ire) 7-11-2 (7⁷) Mr R O'Ryan,......(8 to 1) 3
2675 ASFREEASTHEWIND (Ire) 6-11-9 Mr J P Dempsey, (11 to 2) 4
3381⁴ THE ZAFFRING (Ire) 6-11-7 (7⁷) K A Kelly,.......(10 to 1) 5

3421⁸ GALLIC HONEY (Ire) 6-11-2 (7⁷) Mrs C Harrison,..(14 to 1) 6
3083 MINSTRELS PRIDE (Ire) 6-11-7 (7⁷) M P Cooney,..(16 to 1) 7
BLACKWATER CISCO (Ire) 7-11-7 (7⁷) Mr P J Jennings.
....(14 to 1) 8
2941 ORANGE JUICE (Ire) 7-12-0 Mr J A Nash,.........(16 to 1) 9
ZIMMULAINE (Ire) 9-11-7 (7⁷) Mr A J Dempsey,...(20 to 1) 10
RODIRON PRIDE (Ire) 7-11-7 (7⁷) Mr C A Murphy,.(12 to 1) 11
BARRONSTOWN GIRL (Ire) 6-11-6 (3³) Mr E Norris, (14 to 1) 12
3224⁹ RED BANNER (Ire) 6-11-2 (7⁷) Mr A J Costello,....(25 to 1) 13
3336⁹ CAME AWAY (Ire) 6-11-2 (7⁷) L A Hurley,..........(20 to 1) 14
GARRYGLASS ROSE (Ire) 6-11-6 (3³) Mr R Walsh,..(8 to 1) 15
GOLDEN DENEL (Ire) 6-11-7 (7⁷) Mr G Finlay,......(12 to 1) 16
3178 NOBLE TUNE (Ire) 8-11-11 (3³) Mr D Valentine,...(25 to 1) pu
Dist: 3½l, 5l, sht-hd, 1l. 3m 58.50s. (17 Ran).

(Exors Of The Late James F Murphy), G T Hourigan

3609 Bagenalstown Handicap Chase (0-116 4-y-o and up) £2,940 3m
....(5:30)

3420² LINDA'S BOY (Ire) [-] (bl) 7-10-3 (7⁷) P G Hourigan,..(Evens fav) 1
3379⁵ ANOTHER COURSE (Ire) [-] 9-10-4 D H O'Connor, ..(6 to 1) 2
3133⁷ COOLAFINKA (Ire) [-] 8-11-2 T Horgan,...........(5 to 4) 3
Dist: 15l, 14l. 6m 3.40s. (3 Ran).

(Patrick Kearns), E Bolger

CHEPSTOW (firm)
Wednesday April 9th
Going Correction: MINUS 0.55 sec. per fur.

3610 Beagles Novices' Hurdle Class E (4-y-o and up) £2,808 2m 110yds (2:00)

3411* KINNESCASH (Ire) 4-11-0 M A Fitzgerald, *made virtually all, drvn alng whn chlgd frm 3 out, styd on wl appr last*.
....(6 to 4 tchd 13 to 8 and 7 to 4) 1
3064³ BREAK THE RULES 5-11-12 A P McCoy, *hld up, steady hdwy appr 4 out, ev chance whn nr and hit 3 out, soon rdn, one pace approaching last*.............(Evens fav op 6 to 4 on) 2
AMI BLEU (Fr) 5-11-12 J F Titley, *trkd ldrs, keen hold, chsd wnr appr 4 out, rdn and outpcd frm 3 out*.
....(13 to 2 op 5 to 1 tchd 7 to 1) 3
3491 GLOBAL DANCER 6-11-0 M Richards, *some hdwy aftr 4 out, kpt on frm 2 out but not a dngr*.
....(50 to 1 op 33 to 1 tchd 66 to 1 and 100 to 1) 4
3117⁷ HEVER GOLF DIAMOND 4-10-7 (7⁷) Mr P O'Keeffe, *chsd wnr to appr 4 out, sn rdn, wknd 3 out*.
....(20 to 1 op 16 to 1 tchd 25 to 1 and 33 to 1) 5
3463 STARTINGO 4-10-8 Mr A Charles-Jones, *keen hold in rear till pld way to dispute second aftr 1st, wknd appr 4 out, tld off*.
....(100 to 1 op 66 to 1) 6
MARGIER 7-10-9 W Marston, *al beh, tld off frm 4th*.........(100 to 1 op 50 to 1) 7
3443⁷ FOREST ROSE 7-10-2 (7⁷) M Moran, *mstk 1st, al beh, tld off frm 4th*............................(100 to 1 op 50 to 1) 8
BACHE DINGLE 6-11-0 A Thornton, *jmpd poorly, in rear frm 4th, tld off whn pld up aftr 4th*....(100 to 1 op 50 to 1) pu
Dist: 2l, 13l, 12l, 2½l, dist, 22l, dist. 3m 46.30s. b 0.70s (9 Ran).
SR: 3/13/-/-/-/-/ (D R James), P Bowen

3611 Anvil Novices' Handicap Chase Class E (0-100 5-y-o and up) £3,161 2m 3f 110yds..................(2:30)

1724⁵ JHAL FREZI [67] 9-10-10 A Thornton, *made virtually all, drvn and styd on wl frm 2 out*..(7 to 2 op 5 to 2 tchd 4 to 1) 1
3496² FULL SHILLING (USA) [60] 8-9-10 (7⁷) Mr S Durack, *trkd ldr, chlgd 4th to nxt, chald 9th to tenth and ag'n 12th, rdn 3 out, one pace frm next*........(100 to 30 op 4 to 1 tchd 5 to 1) 2
3543² MOZEMO [81] (bl) 10-11-10 A P McCoy, *hld up, hdwy 11th, rdn 3 out, 3rd and no ch wth ldrs whn blun 2 out*.
....(9 to 4 fav op 6 to 4 tchd 5 to 2) 3
3387⁵ FLOWING RIVER (USA) [72] 11-11-1 K Gaule, *in tch, pushed alng frm 6th, effrt 12th, no ch whn hmpd 4 out*.
....(7 to 1 op 6 to 1 tchd 15 to 2) 4
EDEN STREAM [73] 10-11-2 D Leahy, *hit 4th, hdwy tenth, disputing fourth and hld whn f four out*.(20 to 1 op 12 to 1) f
3490 FATTASH (USA) [68] (bl) 5-9-12¹ (7⁷) F Quinlan, *chlgd 7th to 9th, jmpd slwly 11th, rallied nxt, wknd 4 out, no ch whn blun and uns rdr last*.............(25 to 1 op 16 to 1) ur
3470⁴ NIGHT FANCY [66] 9-10-9 J A McCarthy, *in tch, hit 8th, wknd 11th, tld off whn pld up bef 4 out, broke blood vessel*.
....(6 to 1 op 5 to 1) pu
Dist: 8l, 29l, 7l. 4m 49.10s. a 6.10s (7 Ran).

(Mrs R T H Heeley), A Barrow

3612 Farrier Handicap Hurdle Class C (0-135 4-y-o and up) £3,533 2½m 110yds..................(3:00)

2323 EL DON [105] 5-11-8 K Gaule, *keen hold, trkd ldr frm 5th, led aftr 7th, al gng wl after, hit 3 out, very easily*.
....(5 to 2 op 2 to 1) 1

502

2701[3] GLENGARRIF GIRL (Ire) [107] (v) 7-11-10 A P McCoy, *made most till rdn alng 7th and hdd sn aftr, one pace und pres frm from 4 out*............(6 to 5 fav op Evens tchd 6 to 4) 2
3498* ROSS DANCER (Ire) [90] 5-10-4 (3*,5ex) J Magee, *wth ldr to 4th, lost pl and wl beh nxt, rallied appr four out, sn one pace.* ....(4 to 1 op 3 to 1) 3
3445 CALL MY GUEST (Ire) [106] 7-11-9 M A Fitzgerald, *hld up, hdwy 7th, dsptd second 4 out, sn wknd.* ....(11 to 2 op 5 to 1 tchd 9 to 2 and 6 to 1) 4
Dist: 6l, 8l, 7l. 4m 39.80s. a 1.80s (4 Ran).
(Don Morris), M J Ryan

3613 Ostler Handicap Chase Class D (0-120 5-y-o and up) £3,874 3m .... (3:30)

3412* BLACK CHURCH [104] 11-11-10 D O'Sullivan, *hld up and al gng wl, quickened to ld 14th, cmftbly.* ....(6 to 4 fav op 11 to 10 tchd 13 to 8) 1
3497[3] DANGER BABY [98] 7-10-11 (7*) Mr S Durack, *trkd ldr till led 9th, hdd 14th, disputing second whn lft chasing wnr 2 out, no imprsn und pres r-in*.....(7 to 4 op 6 to 4 tchd 15 to 8) 2
3311[4] ELITE GOVERNOR (Ire) [81] 8-9-11[1] (5*) Chris Webb, *led to 9th, sn wknd, tld off 14th, lft poor 3rd 2 out.* ....(11 to 2 op 7 to 1) 3
3425[4] LINDEN'S LOTTO (Ire) [98] 8-11-4 J R Kavanagh, *rcd in 3rd and hit third, rdn alng 14th, disputing second but hld by wnr whn f 2 out*..............(9 to 2 op 7 to 2 tchd 5 to 1) f
Dist: 2l, dist. 6m 2.50s. a 12.50s (4 Ran).
(Dr B Alexander), R Rowe

3614 Court Selling Hurdle Class G (4 - 7-y-o) £2,038 2m 110yds..........(4:00)

3530[5] SHEECKY 6-10-9 (5*) S Ryan, *in tch, trkd ldr frm 4th, led 3 out, rdn and hld on wl appr last.* ....(12 to 1 op 8 to 1 tchd 14 to 1) 1
3476[2] THEME ARENA 4-10-8 A P McCoy, *led to 3 out, hrd rdn and came stands side appr 2 out, wnt lft and str chal last, not fluent, sn no extr*.....(11 to 10 on op Evens tchd 5 to 4) 2
3542[2] QUAKER WALTZ 7-10-9 R Bellamy, *chsd ldrs till rdn and lost pos 4th, ran on ag'n frm 3 out, not trble lders.* ....(5 to 1 op 7 to 2 tchd 11 to 2) 3
3558[7] HALHAM TARN (Ire) 7-11-5 S Curran, *sn prmnt, chsd ldrs appr 4 out, wknd 3 out*..............(16 to 1 op 10 to 1) 4
3469* EVEZIO RUFO (bl) 5-11-5 K Gaule, *beh and rdn alng frm second, moderate effrt und pres 4 out, nvr a dngr.* ....(7 to 2 op 5 to 2 tchd 4 to 1) 5
3495[4] DERRYBELLE 6-10-7 (7*) Mr S Durack, *beh frm 4th, tld off.* ....(7 to 1 op 5 to 1 tchd 8 to 1) 6
3038 CHILI HEIGHTS (v) 7-11-0 G Tormey, *wnt wide bend aftr 1st, sn chasing ldrs, wknd 4th, tld off*......(33 to 1 op 16 to 1) 7
1943 PERSIAN DAWN 4-10-3 A Thornton, *prmnt early, beh and lost tch frm 4th, tld off.* (33 to 1 op 20 to 1 tchd 50 to 1) 8
3332 CUILLIN 5-10-9 C Maude, *beh frm 3rd, tld off whn pld up bef 4 out*..............(33 to 1 op 20 to 1) pu
3402 ABBEYDORAN (bl) 6-10-4 (5*) D J Kavanagh, *chsd ldrs and mstk second, sn wknd, tld off whn pld up aftr 4th.* ....(25 to 1 op 33 to 1 tchd 20 to 1 and 50 to 1) pu
Dist: 1l, 9l, 4l, 3l, dist, 4l, 28l. 3m 45.50s. b 1.50s (10 Ran).
SR: 11/4/-/2/-/-/ (Mrs Angela Beard), B A McMahon

3615 Earthstoppers Hunters' Chase Class H (6-y-o and up) £1,702 3m... (4:30)

SOME-TOY 11-11-8 (7*) Miss L Blackford, *steady hdwy frm 13th, led aftr nxt, shaken up and ran on wl r-in.* ....(5 to 1 op 4 to 1) 1
3574[2] RUSTY BRIDGE 10-11-11 (7*) Mr O McPhail, *led to tenth, sn pushed alng, outpcd appr 14th, rallied and hit 4 out, chsd wnr 2 out, one pace r-in*...(5 to 2 fav op 7 to 4 tchd 11 to 4) 2
3387[3] GAMBLING ROYAL 14-11-5 (7*) Dr P Pritchard, *sn tracking ldr, chlgd 8th till led tenth, hdd aftr 14th, wknd after 3 out.* ....(4 to 1 tchd 9 to 2 and 5 to 1) 3
WHAT A TO DO 13-11-8 (7*) Miss L Sweeting, *in tch till wknd 7th, lost touch frm tenth*..............(13 to 2 op 5 to 1) 4
CATCH THE CROSS (bl) 11-11-12 (7*) Mrs A Hand, *in tch 7th, styd on 14th, sn wknd*...(12 to 1 op 10 to 1 tchd 14 to 1) 5
3365[3] SONOFAGIPSY (bl) 13-11-5 (7*) Mr N R Mitchell, *prmnt till wknd 7th, nvr dngrs aftr.* ....(3 to 1 op 5 to 2 tchd 100 to 30) 6
Dist: 4l, 22l, 9l, ½l, 7l. 6m 0.00s. a 10.00s (6 Ran).
(John Squire), John Squire

3616 Whippers In Standard Open National Hunt Flat Class H (4,5,6-y-o) £1,686 2m 110yds................... (5:00)

3282[5] DIAMOND HALL 4-10-12 A P McCoy, *hld up, steady hdwy 5 fs out, led on bit 2 furlongs out, easily.* ....(100 to 30 op 5 to 2 tchd 7 to 2) 1
3142 MUALLAF (Ire) 5-11-4 J A McCarthy, *pld hrd early and led, hdd 2 fs out, styd on und pres but swshd tail and no ch wth wnr ins last*..............(50 to 1 op 33 to 1 tchd 66 to 1) 2
SHIMMY DANCING 4-10-7 K Gaule, *hdwy 5 fs out, one pace frm o'r 2 furlongs out*................(5 to 1 op 4 to 1) 3
3388 BORN AT KINGS 4-10-12 B Fenton, *sn beh, hdwy o'r 3 fs out, no imprsn*............(20 to 1 op 16 to 1 tchd 25 to 1) 4+
LITTLE TIME 5-10-13 M Sharratt, *ran wide bend aftr 2 fs, sn reco'red, chsd ldrs 4 furlongs out, wknd over two furlongs out.* ....(14 to 1 op 6 to 1) 4+
DANCING IN RIO (Ire) 5-10-6 (7*) L Suthern, *hdwy to chase ldrs ten fs out, wknd o'r 3 out.* ....(40 to 1 op 33 to 1 tchd 50 to 1) 6
1975 BENJAMIN JONES 5-10-11 (7*) Miss A Dudley, *al beh.* ....(33 to 1 op 20 to 1) 7
2784 GENERAL KILLINEY (Ire) 5-11-4 J F Titley, *pld hrd early, chsd ldrs till wknd 4 fs out*...(33 to 1 op 20 to 1 tchd 40 to 1) 8
3302[4] TOMMY TICKLE 5-11-4 J R Kavanagh, *wnt wide bend aftr 2 fs, brief effrt ten furlongs out, wknd 5 furlongs out.* ....(9 to 2 op 5 to 2) 9
OGULLA 5-10-13 D Leahy, *effrt hfwy, wknd 6 fs out.* ....(33 to 1 op 20 to 1 tchd 40 to 1) 10
2858 DASH ON BY (bl) 4-10-12 G Tormey, *chsd ldr till wknd 4 fs out.* ....(50 to 1 op 33 to 1) 11
3322[2] DINKY DORA 4-10-7 M A Fitzgerald, *chsd ldrs, chlgd 3 fs out, 3rd and hld whn wnt lme and virtually pld up ins last.* ....(2 to 1 fav op 6 to 4 tchd 9 to 4 and 5 to 2) 12
Dist: 6l, 6l, ½l, dd-ht, 5l, 11l, ¾l, 8l, 8l, ½l. 3m 47.90s. (12 Ran).
(R D Tudor), K R Burke

LUDLOW (good to firm (races 1,2,3,4), firm (5,6,7)) Wednesday April 9th

Going Correction: MINUS 0.40 sec. per fur.

3617 Caynham Selling Handicap Hurdle Class G (0-90 4-y-o and up) £2,024 2m.......................... (2:20)

2515[9] KALZARI (USA) [75] 12-11-1 (7*) Mr A Wintle, *hld up towards rear, steady prog appr 3 out, led last, rdn out.* ....(12 to 1 op 8 to 1) 1
3495[3] CAPTAIN TANDY (Ire) [70] 8-11-3 P McLoughlin, *hld up, rdn appr 3 out, styd on frm 2 out*..........(12 to 1 op 8 to 1) 2
3409[6] AGAINST THE CLOCK [53] 5-10-0 R Johnson, *led, hit 3 out, hdd last, one pace*.............(20 to 1 tchd 25 to 1) 3
3457* BLOTOFT [74] 5-11-7 (7ex) N Williamson, *trkd ldrs, effrt 3 out, one pace nxt*...........(11 to 2 op 4 to 1 tchd 6 to 1) 4
3530 WORDSMITH (Ire) [77] 7-11-10 R Supple, *al hndy, rdn and one pace appr 3 out*..............(20 to 1 tchd 25 to 1) 5
3278[5] BRITANNIA MILLS [70] 6-11-3 W Worthington, *mid-div, rdn appr 3 out, 6th and no ch whn mstk last.* ....(16 to 1 op 14 to 1) 6
2440 TEE TEE TOO (Ire) [70] 5-11-3 D Walsh, *prmnt, effrt appr 3 out, wknd approaching last.* ....(16 to 1 op 12 to 1 tchd 20 to 1 and 25 to 1) 7
2766[6] ECU DE FRANCE (Ire) [58] (v) 7-10-5 S Fox, *in tch, wknd appr 3 out*................(16 to 1 op 14 to 1 tchd 20 to 1) 8
1832[5] FENIAN COURT (Ire) [75] 6-11-8 T J Murphy, *hld up, hdwy 6th, wknd appr 2 out*.....(3 to 1 jt-fav op 7 to 2 tchd 4 to 1) 9
2251[7] BOLD CHARLIE [53] (bl) 5-10-0 N Mann, *nvr on terms.* ....(33 to 1) 10
3457[2] RUTH'S GAMBLE [71] (v) 9-10-11 (7*) X Aizpuru, *keen hold early, prmnt, wknd 6th*..........(3 to 1 jt-fav tchd 7 to 2) 11
3554[5] GLENMAVIS [75] 10-11-8 Dr P Pritchard, *hld up, hdwy aftr 6th, wknd 3 out*....................(50 to 1 op 33 to 1) 12
3357[4] SAAFI (Ire) [67] (bl) 6-11-0 V Slattery, *nvr dngrs, broke blood vessel*....................(10 to 1 op 8 to 1) 13
Dist: 1½l, ½l, 4l, 2l, 1¼l, 1l, ¾l, 6l, 4l, ½l. 3m 39.10s. a 7.10s (13 Ran).
(Dennis Deacon), A W Carroll

3618 Bundy UK Handicap Chase Class D (0-125 5-y-o and up) £3,387 2½m .... (2:50)

3505 IMPERIAL VINTAGE (Ire) [118] 7-11-10 N Williamson, *chsd ldr, led aftr 13th, came clr appr 2 out.* ....(11 to 10 on op 5 to 4 on tchd Evens) 1
3472* RABA RIBA [128] 12-12-6 (6ex) V Slattery, *hit tenth, made most till hdd aftr 13th,btn after 3 out*...(2 to 1 tchd 9 to 4) 2
3410* FENWICK [94] 10-10-0 T Dascombe, *sn wl beh, tld off.* ....(4 to 1 op 7 to 2 tchd 9 to 2) 3
3593[2] PANDORA'S PRIZE [94] 11-10-0 T Eley, *sn wl beh, tld off.* ....(33 to 1 tchd 50 to 1) 4
Dist: 13l, dist, dist. 4m 48.30s. b 0.70s (4 Ran).
SR: 23/20/-/-/ (David M Williams), Miss Venetia Williams

3619 D.J. Profiles Conditional Jockeys' Novices' Handicap Hurdle Class E (0-100 4-y-o and up) £2,528 2m 5f 110yds...................... (3:20)

3513[4] PIPER'S ROCK (Ire) [76] 6-11-2 A Bates, *chsd ldrs, rdn alng frm 6th, led appr 3 out, hrd pressed whn mstk nxt, ran on wl r-in*..........................(3 to 1 fav tchd 7 to 2) 1
3468* KYMIN (Ire) [91] 5-12-3 (7ex) L Aspell, *hld up, hdwy aftr 4 out, ev ch frm nxt, no extr from last .* ....(4 to 1 op 3 to 1 tchd 9 to 2) 2

3530 SALTIS (Ire) [75] 5-10-8 (7*) E Greehy, wtd wth, prog appr 3
out, one pace bef nxt. . . . . (16 to 1 op 10 to 1)　3
1796[2] SHANNON LAD (Ire) [74] 7-11-0 D Fortt, hld up, improved
appr 3 out, one pace 2 out. . . . . (16 to 1 op 14 to 1)　4
3594[4] LADY OF MINE [61] 7-9-12 (3*) L Cummins, led, not fluent
second, hdd appr 3 out, sn btn.
. . . . (14 to 1 op 12 to 1 tchd 16 to 1)　5
3404 MIRAMARE [60] 7-9-8 (6*) J Harris, chsd ldr frm second till
appr 3 out, sn btn. . . . . (50 to 1 op 33 to 1)　6
3362[2] FASTINI GOLD [75] 5-10-12 (3*) X Aizpuru, nvr dngrs.
. . . . (7 to 1 op 11 to 2)　7
3542[4] LOVELARK [60] 8-9-11 (3*) M Griffiths, hld up beh ldrs, wknd
appr 3 out. . . . . (20 to 1 op 8 to 1)　8
2879[7] WELL ARMED (Ire) [84] 6-11-4 (6*) R McGrath, nvr on terms.
. . . . (11 to 2 op 3 to 1)　9
187 CREDIT CALL (Ire) [60] 9-10-0 R Massey, mid-div, wknd appr
3 out. . . . . (66 to 1 op 50 to 1)　10
3001[6] BALMORAL PRINCESS [80] (bl) 4-10-10 (3*) O Burrows, al
beh, pld up bef 7th. . . . . (33 to 1 op 25 to 1)　pu
Dist: 4l, 6l, 3l, ½l, 5l, 1½l, 3l, 9l, 18l. 4m 59.00s. a 4.00s (11 Ran).

(Mrs G B Balding), G B Balding

3620
**Bundy Europe Novices' Chase Class
E (5-y-o and up) £2,851 2m. . . (3:50)**

2512[3] INCH EMPEROR (Ire) 7-11-7 T J Murphy, led, jmpd lft, clr to
9th, hdd briefly 2 out, drvn out. . . . . .(13 to 8 fav op 5 to 4)　1
2798[4] SNOWY PETREL (Ire) (bl) 5-10-7 S McNeill, patiently rdn,
prog 9th, chlgd 3 out, led briefly nxt, ran on r-in.
. . . .(2 to 1 op 6 to 4)　2
3467* TENAYESTELIGN 9-11-9 S Wynne, hld up, improved 9th, effrt
3 out, one pace nxt. . . . . (4 to 1 op 7 to 2)　3
3189[4] WHOD OF THOUGHT IT (Ire) 6-11-0 V Slattery, hld up, hdwy
9th, rdn appr 4 out, wknd 3 out, tld off.
. . . . (12 to 1 op 33 to 1 tchd 40 to 1)　4
3361 AEOLIAN 6-11-0 D Walsh, mstk 4th, wl beh frm 7th, tld off.
. . . . (40 to 1 op 33 to 1)　5
3467[3] QUARTER MARKER (Ire) 9-11-0 R Johnson, chsd ldr, blun
1st, ev ch 4 out, fourth and hld whn l 2 out.
. . . . (16 to 1 op 14 to 1 tchd 20 to 1)　f
Dist: Hd, 8l, dist, 10l. 3m 57.70s. a 7.70s (6 Ran).

(T V Cullen), A W Carroll

3621
**Sara Hamilton-Russell Memorial
Trophy Handicap Hurdle Class D
(0-120 4-y-o and up) £2,723 2m 5f
110yds. . . . . (4:20)**

3541* SULAWESI (Ire) [101] 4-11-8 (7*,6ex) Mr J Goldstein, made
all, ran on wl. . . . . (3 to 1 op 5 to 2)　1
3359* FIRST CRACK [88] 12-11-9 S Wynne, patiently rdn, prog to
chase wnr appr 3 out, unbl to quicken frm 2 out.
. . . . (5 to 2 fav tchd 3 to 1)　2
3244 MOOBAKKR (USA) [80] 6-11-1 W Fry, hld up beh ldrs, chsd
wnr frm 4 out to appr nxt, one pace 2 out.
. . . . (100 to 30 op 5 to 2 tchd 7 to 2)　3
3516[2] MISS MARIGOLD [89] (bl) 8-11-10 T Dascombe, hld up, hdwy
and effrt appr 3 out, sn btn. . . . .(8 to 1 op 7 to 1)　4
3485[5] CASTLEBAY LAD [65] 14-10-0 D Morris, chsd wnr to 4 out,
rdn and wknd appr 3 out, tld off.
. . . . (66 to 1 op 50 to 1 tchd 100 to 1)　5
3131 SCOTTISH WEDDING [83] 7-11-1 (3*) R Massey, beh frm 3rd,
tld off 7th, tailed off whn pld up bef 3 out.
. . . . (4 to 1 tchd 9 to 2 and 7 to 2)　pu
Dist: 2½l, nk, 15l, dist. 4m 57.50s. a 2.50s (6 Ran).

(Jack Joseph), N A Twiston-Davies

3622
**Chase Meredith Memorial Trophy
Hunters' Chase Class H (5-y-o and
up) £1,481 3m. . . . . (4:50)**

3529[2] MY NOMINEE (bl) 9-11-12 (7*) Mr R Burton, led to second,
rgned ld nxt, made rst, hrd pressed frm 4 out, all out.
. . . . (11 to 4 op 5 to 2 tchd 3 to 1 and 100 to 30)　1
2997[3] CAPE COTTAGE 13-11-12 (7*) Mr A Phillips, hld up in tch,
chsd wnr frm 7th, str chal from 4 out, kpt on.
. . . . (9 to 1 op 7 to 1 tchd 10 to 1)　2
3313* FOX POINTER 12-12-0 (5*) Mr J Jukes, in tch, chsd wnr frm
5th till dived 7th, wknd appr 3 out. . . (7 to 4 fav op 5 to 1)　3
CANDLE GLOW 9-11-7 (7*) Mr S Morris, led second to nxt,
chsd wnr aftr till 5th, rdn 13th, wknd 15th.
. . . . (10 to 1 op 8 to 1)　4
WILD ILLUSION 13-11-12 (7*) Mr H Hutsby, beh, hdwy appr
12th, wknd 14th, tld off whn pld up bef 4 out.
. . . . (11 to 4 op 2 to 1 tchd 3 to 1)　pu
JUDY LINE 8-11-2 (7*) Mr S Shinton, hld up, wl beh frm tenth,
tld off whn pld up bef 4 out.
. . . . (33 to 1 op 25 to 1 tchd 40 to 1)　pu
Dist: Hd, 12l, 5l. 5m 57.80s. a 10.80s (6 Ran).

(D E Nicholls), D E Nicholls

3623
**Burwarton Novices' Hurdle Class E
(4-y-o and up) £2,248 2m. . . (5:20)**

3064[7] PERCY BRAITHWAITE (Ire) 5-10-13 (7*) Mr J Goldstein,
prmnt, led 6th, ran on wl frm 2 out. . . . . (7 to 2 op 5 to 2)　1

2628[6] NAME OF OUR FATHER (USA) 4-11-0 R Johnson, prmnt, wnt
second and ev ch appr 3 out, sn rdn, one pace 2 out.
. . . . (2 to 1 jt-fav tchd 9 to 4)　2
3334* CLASHEM ARCHER 4-10-8 N Williamson, patiently rdn, steady
hdwy frm 6th, ridden 2 out, btn appr last. . . . .(2 to 1 jt-
fav op 5 to 4)　3
3487[3] MOONLIGHT ESCAPADE (Ire) 6-11-0 V Slattery, led to 6th,
wknd appr 3e out. . . . . (14 to 1)　4
1742[3] POPPY'S DREAM 7-10-6 (3*) Mr R Thornton, hld up, lost pl
5th, rallied appr 3 out, sn wknd.
. . . . (9 to 1 op 8 to 1 tchd 10 to 1)　5
3443[6] BARON HRABOVSKY (bl) 4-10-8 B Powell, al beh, tld off frm
5th. . . . . (66 to 1 op 50 to 1)　6
3482[9] MOLONYS DRAM 4-11-0 R Supple, in tch, blun second, hit
4th, sn beh, tld off. . . . . (50 to 1 op 33 to 1)　7
Dist: 3½l, 3½l, 15l, 1l, 20l, 25l. 3m 37.90s. a 5.90s (7 Ran).

(Glass Pig Racing Syndicate), Miss P M Whittle

BALLINROBE (IRE) (yielding)
Thursday April 10th

3624
**Ballinrobe Water Towers Beginners
Chase (5-y-o and up) £2,226 2m 1f
. . . . (4:00)**

3339[2] WITHOUT EQUAL (USA) 10-11-9 (5*) A O'Shea, ... (5 to 1)　1
3454 NO TAG (Ire) 9-12-0 C O'Dwyer, ... (11 to 10 fav)　2
1076 PENNY BRIDE (Ire) 8-11-4 T P Rudd, ... (20 to 1)　3
3344 FLIP YOUR LID 8-11-11 (3*) U Smyth, ...(6 to 1)　4
3339[7] CASTLE TIGER BAY (Ire) (bl) 6-11-9 K F O'Brien, . .(20 to 1)　5
3340[7] TREENS FOLLY 8-11-6 (3*) K Whelan, ... (33 to 1)　6
1581 CORMAC LADY (Ire) 6-11-4 J K Kinane, ...(20 to 1)　7
469[3] LEGITMAN (Ire) 7-12-0 J Shortt, ...(8 to 1)　8
2945 BALLYBRIT BOY 11-12-0 L P Cusack, ... (16 to 1)　9
CASSFINN 11-10-11 (7*) J M Maguire, ... (25 to 1)　10
721[8] SANDY FOREST LADY (Ire) 8-11-9 T P Treacy, . .(12 to 1)　11
2094 GONE ALL DAY (Ire) 7-11-9 J R Barry, ... (25 to 1)　12
3451[6] VASILIKI (Ire) 5-11-7 D J Casey, ... (8 to 1)　f
3416 RONETTE (Ire) 6-11-9 P A Roche, ... (20 to 1)　ur
TAKEITHANDY (Ire) 8-11-2 (7*) M D Murphy, ...(25 to 1)　ur
Dist: 2½l, 1l, 20l, 20l. 4m 42.10s. (15 Ran).

(Michael Mythen), Ronald Curran

3625
**Corrib Maiden Hurdle (4 & 5-y-o)
£2,226 2m. . . . .(4:30)**

2270 ONE MORE SPIN (Ire) 4-10-12 (3*) K Whelan, ... (10 to 1)　1
3223 NEWBERRY ROSE (Ire) 5-11-2[5] (3*) Mr W M O'Sullivan,
. . . . (14 to 1)　2
3450[6] LUNA FLEUR (Ire) 4-10-3 (7*) B J Geraghty, ... (3 to 1 fav)　3
3069[3] DOUBLE COLOUR (Ire) 5-11-13 F Woods, ...(9 to 2)　4
GOOD LAD (Ire) 4-10-8 (7*) P J Dobbs, ...(20 to 1)　5
BELLFAN (Ire) 4-11-6 P L Malone, ... (8 to 1)　6
3429[6] AUBURN ROILELET (Ire) 5-11-0 T J Mitchell, ... (10 to 1)　7
2337 LOUGH SLANIA (Ire) 4-10-8 (7*) I Browne, ...(5 to 1)　8
GENOMIC (Ire) 5-11-5 K F O'Brien, ... (25 to 1)　9
928 TINERANA GLOW (Ire) 5-11-0 D T Evans, ...(12 to 1)　10
1533 PERPETUAL PROSPECT (Ire) 5-10-12 (7*) Mr John P
Moloney, ... (4 to 1)　11
2942[9] MEGA HUNTER (Ire) 5-11-5 C F Swan, ... (10 to 1)　12
3430 MR MARK (Ire) 5-11-5 F J Flood, ...(14 to 1)　13
2870 VALLEY PLAYER (Ire) 5-11-5 W Slattery, ...(33 to 1)　14
3421 SISTER WEST (Ire) 5-11-0 T P Rudd, ... (33 to 1)　15
Dist: 6l, 3l, 4½l, hd. 4m 21.80s. (15 Ran).

(J S Gutkin), E J O'Grady

3626
**Mayo Novice Handicap Hurdle
(0-109 4-y-o and up) £2,226 2m
. . . . (5:00)**

2753[5] CLONMEL COMMERCIAL (Ire) [-] 6-10-0 (7*) D McCullagh,
. . . . (12 to 1)　1
3419[2] CLASHBEG (Ire) [-] 6-11-9 (3*) K Whelan, ...(5 to 2 fav)　2
2366 DOCK'S DELIGHT (Ire) [-] 6-11-6 L P Cusack, ... (10 to 1)　3
2647[6] RUN ROSE RUN (Ire) [-] (bl) 7-9-10 (7*) J M Maguire, (9 to 1)　4
3337 ANOTHER BONNY [-] 11-9-4[2] (7*) M D Murphy, . . . (25 to 1)　5
3337 BEHY BRIDGE (Ire) [-] 5-10-6 (7*) S P Kelly, ... (20 to 1)　6
1152[3] YOUNG DUBLINER (Ire) [-] 8-11-7 (7*) P G Hourigan,
. . . . (12 to 1)　7
3415[6] BAILENASPIG (Ire) [-] 4-10-11 (7*) B J Geraghty, . .(10 to 1)　8
3337[5] MANISSA (Ire) [-] 6-10-11 C F Swan, ...(11 to 2)　9
3379[6] GLENA GALE (Ire) [-] 7-10-4 F Woods, ... (8 to 1)　10
3377 ST CAROL (Ire) [-] 6-10-11 T P Treacy, ... (10 to 1)　11
2943 ASTRID (Ire) [-] 6-9-7 W Slattery, ... (20 to 1)　12
3085 LADY OF GRANGE (Ire) [-] 5-10-10 F J Flood, ... (20 to 1)　ur
3336* PRAY FOR PEACE (Ire) [-] 6-11-6 (7*) Mr P Fahey, (13 to 2)　pu
3089 OVER ALICE (Ire) [-] 5-10-0 (7*) L J Fleming, ... (20 to 1)　pu
Dist: 7l, 8l, nk, 6l. 4m 17.20s. (15 Ran).

(E P Hickey), Michael Donohoe

3627
**River Robe I.N.H. Flat Race (4 & 5-y-
o) £2,226 2m. . . . . (5:30)**

3421 KINGMAN (Ire) 5-11-6 (7*) Mr John P Moloney, ...(14 to 1)　1
MONTEBA (Ire) 5-11-6 (7*) Mr P Cashman, ... (11 to 2)　2
2942[3] THE BOY KING (Ire) 5-11-13 Mr J A Nash, ...(5 to 1)　3

2669 DIGITAL SIGNAL (Ire) 4-11-6 Mr P Fenton, ...(10 to 1) 4
2112[5] RAINBOW ERA (Ire) 4-10-13 (7") Mr R M Walsh, ...(6 to 1) 5
3343 CAN'T BE STOPPED (Ire) 5-11-13 Mr M Phillips, . . .(5 to 1) 6
3349[7] EVENKEEL (Ire) 5-11-6 (7") Mr A J Dempsey, . . .(2 to 1 fav) 7
581 PERFECT (Ire) 5-11-6 (7") Mr M P Madden, ...(10 to 1) 8
3349 BALLINTEMPLE TRAMP (Ire) 4-10-10 (5") Mr G Elliott,
. . . .(20 to 1) 9
2108[5] LADY MINORCA (Ire) 5-11-7 Mr J Curran, . . .(14 to 1) 10
3380[6] FIERY FINCH 5-11-1 (7") Mr E Gallagher, ...(14 to 1) 11
SCREEN LEADER (Ire) 5-11-1 (7") Mr J P Dempsey, . .(14 to 1) 12
CINTARA (Ire) 5-11-1 (7") Mr D A Harney, ...(14 to 1) 13
BALLINSHEEN (Ire) 4-10-9[1] (7") Mr R D Lee, ...(20 to 1) pu
BLACK BIDDY 5-11-8 Mr P F Graffin, ...(14 to 1) pu
Dist: 3½l, 6l, ¾l, 5l. 4m 18.90s. (15 Ran).

(T A Kent), T A Kent

FONTWELL (good to firm)
Thursday April 10th
Going Correction: MINUS 0.05 sec. per fur.

3628 Fontwell Park Selling Handicap Hurdle Class G (0-95 4-y-o and up) £1,941 2¾m 110yds. . . . .(2:10)

3325[6] ALDWICK COLONNADE [60] 10-10-2[2] W McFarland, chsd ldrs, smooth prog to cl aftr 2 out, led appr last, rdn out.
. . . .(14 to 1 op 10 to 1 tchd 16 to 1) 1
3494[7] BAYLORD PRINCE (Ire) [59] 9-9-12 (3") Sophie Mitchell, hld up beh, lost tch 5th, rdn alng 8th, hdwy und pres appr 2 out, ran on wl. . . . .(8 to 1 tchd 10 to 1) 2
3405[5] ITS GRAND [70] 8-10-12 S Fox, led to 3rd, wth ldr, led ag'n 5th to 8th, drvn nxt, kpt on one pace frm last.
. . . .(9 to 2 op 5 to 1 tchd 4 to 1) 3
3405 NICK THE DREAMER [78] 12-11-6 R Dunwoody, wth ldr, led 3rd to 5th, led 8th till appr last, no extr und pres.
. . . .(11 to 1 op 6 to 1 tchd 12 to 1) 4
3320 TUG YOUR FORELOCK [62] 6-10-4 A Thornton, trkd ldrs, ev ch gng wl entering strt, rdn appr last, wknd r-in.
. . . .(9 to 1 op 8 to 1 tchd 7 to 1) 5
3120[2] ROGER'S PAL [75] 10-11-3 D Gallagher, hld up beh, lost tch 5th, effrt aftr 8th, nvr able to chal.
. . . .(5 to 1 op 4 to 1 tchd 11 to 1) 6
INCHYDONEY BOY (Ire) [58] 8-9-7 (7") M Batchelor, tracking ldg pair whn blun and uns rdr second.
. . . .(20 to 1 tchd 25 to 1) ur
3270[5] ACROSS THE BOW (USA) [64] 6-10-6 G Tormey, trkd ldrs, ev ch 8th, wknd and pld up lme appr last.
. . . .(12 to 1 op 14 to 1 tchd 7 to 2) pu
3133 CHARLIE PARROT (Ire) [82] 7-11-10 A P McCoy, steadied strt, tracking ldrs whn broke hind leg appr 6th, dead.
. . . .(100 to 30 fav 16 to 1 tchd 7 to 2) pu
2637 FASHION LEADER (Ire) [58] 6-10-0 M Richards, tld off 5th, pld up bef 7th. . . . .(33 to 1 op 20 to 1) pu
Dist: 1l, 1½l, 3l, 5l. 5m 32.00s. a 18.00s (10 Ran).

(Midweek Racing), M D I Usher

3629 Kybo Maiden Hurdle Class F (Div I) (4-y-o and up) £1,824 2¼m 110yds . . . .(2:40)

3443[2] MAJOR DUNDEE (Ire) 4-11-0 A P McCoy, not fluent, trkd ldr, stumbled on bend aftr 3rd, reminders and led after 5th, clr nxt, eased r-in. . . . .(9 to 4 on op 11 to 8 on) 1
3491[4] CLOCK WATCHERS 9-11-6 D Morris, made most till hdd aftr 5th, outpcd frm nxt, kpt on und pres to hold second from last, no ch wth wnr. . . . .(25 to 1 op 20 to 1 tchd 33 to 1) 2
3382[8] LORD LOVE (Ire) 4-11-0 A Thornton, trkd ldrs, outpcd 6th, kpt on und pres frm last. . . . . . .(50 to 1 op 33 to 1 tchd 66 to 1) 3
129[9] ROBERT SAMUEL 6-11-6 M A Fitzgerald, sn pushed alng in rear, mstk second, soon tld off, late prog.
. . . .(10 to 1 op 7 to 1) 4
3091[5] KILSHEY 6-10-8 (7") S Laird, hld up, outpcd appr 6th, tld off.
. . . .(8 to 1 op 4 to 1 tchd 9 to 1) 5
3491[2] ALKA INTERNATIONAL 5-11-6 Derek Byrne, hld up in rear, shrtlvd effrt and no response whn pld up bef 3 out.
. . . .(6 to 1 op 7 to 1 tchd 8 to 1) pu
2197 ITANI 5-11-6 W Marston, trkd ldrs, pushed alng and lost pl 5th, losing tch whn pld up bef 3 out. . . .(33 to 1 op 16 to 1) pu
DANUCHA 5-11-1 T J Murphy, hld up beh, mstk second, tld off whn pld up bef 6th. . . . .(33 to 1 op 20 to 1) pu
GRANSTOWN LAKE (Ire) 6-11-6 R Dunwoody, hld up, blun 4th, not fluent, losing tch whn pld up bef 6th.
. . . .(9 to 1 op 4 to 1 tchd 10 to 1) pu
Dist: 9l, ½l, dist, 6l. 4m 25.80s. a 8.80s (9 Ran).

(Michael R Jaye), M C Pipe

3630 George Gale & Co. Handicap Chase Class E (0-115 5-y-o and up) £3,343 3¼m 110yds. . . . .(3:10)

3366[2] CREDON [100] 9-11-4 B Fenton, al hndy, jnd ldr 4 out, led 2 out, drvn out. . . . .(4 to 1 op 3 to 1) 1
3175 SUGAR HILL [90] 7-10-8 P Hide, led till hdd and hit 2 out, hrd rdn, no extr. . . . . . .(4 to 1 op 3 to 1 tchd 9 to 2) 2

3121[3] MASTER COMEDY [82] (bl) 13-10-0 N Williamson, hld up, cld 15th, outpcd by 1st 2 4 out, styd on wl. (10 to 1 op 12 to 1) 3
3207[4] PAVLOVA (Ire) [84] 7-10-2[2] D O'Sullivan, hld up beh, struggling 16th, some late prog, nvr on terms. (5 to 1 op 4 to 1) 4
FIDDLERS PIKE [88] 16-10-6 Mrs R Henderson, in tch, jmpd slwly 3rd, mstk 10th, struggling in rear 16th, tld off.
. . . .(14 to 1 op 12 to 1) 5
261[4] NATIVE VENTURE (Ire) [100] 9-11-4 A Thornton, cl up till wknd 16th, tld off. . . . .(12 to 1 op 8 to 1) 6
3565 CHANGE THE REIGN [107] 10-11-8 (3") Mr R Thornton, hld up, not fluent 5th, niggled alng frm 8th, cld nxt, drvn 15th, sn btn, pld up bef 3 out. .(2 to 1 fav op 5 to 2 tchd 11 to 4) pu
Dist: 2l, 2l, 18l, 20l, 25l. 6m 48.70s. a 18.70s (7 Ran).

(Fusilier Racing), S Woodman

3631 Tuscan Novices' Hurdle Class E (4-y-o and up) £2,448 3m 3f . . . . .(3:40)

1815[4] HONEY MOUNT 6-11-6 N Williamson, hld up, al gng wl, led 2 out, not extended . . . .(7 to 4 op 5 to 4 tchd 2 to 1) 1
3290[5] KYBO'S REVENGE (Ire) 6-11-0 D O'Sullivan, hld up gng wl, ev ch 2 out, one pace appr last. . . . .(8 to 1 op 5 to 1) 2
3383[8] GLENDINE (Ire) 7-11-0 J Railton, trkd ldr, blun 7th, made most aftr 9th till hdd 2 out, wknd.
. . . .(12 to 1 op 7 to 1 tchd 14 to 1) 3
3422[2] MAYLIN MAGIC 6-10-9 R Dunwoody, cl up, led briefly 3 out, sn drvn and btn whn hit nxt.
. . . .(11 to 10 fav op 6 to 4 tchd Evens) 4
3473[6] COUNTER ATTACK (Ire) 6-10-9 K Gaule, led, drvn alng and hdd aftr 9th, sn lost tch, tld off.
. . . .(40 to 1 op 14 to 1 tchd 50 to 1) 5
Dist: 3l, 11l, 21l, dist. 6m 34.10s. a 10.10s (5 Ran).

(Paul Green), N J H Walker

3632 Silver Shadow Novices' Chase Class E (5-y-o and up) £3,097 2m 3f (4:10)

3413[3] CRUISE CONTROL 11-11-2 D O'Sullivan, trkd ldrs, lost pl whn mstk 9th, hdwy 4 out, drvn to ld r-in, edgd lft, styd on wl.
. . . .(4 to 1 op 7 to 2 tchd 9 to 2) 1
3383 BROWN ROBBER 9-11-2 B Fenton, in tch, led 11th, hdd r-in, no extr und pres, fnshd lme.
. . . .(7 to 2 fav op 5 to 2 tchd 4 to 1) 2
3143 BELLS WOOD 8-11-2 S McNeill, trkd ldrs, mstk 4th, rallied to hold ev ch 3 out, one pace appr last.
. . . .(11 to 1 op 8 to 1 tchd 12 to 1) 3
2982 CHAPEL OF BARRAS (Ire) 8-11-2 P Hide, hld up in tch, cld 11th, wkng whn mstk 3 out, tld off, broke blood vessel.
. . . .(13 to 2 op 10 to 1 tchd 12 to 1) 4
3410[3] FULL OF TRICKS 9-11-2 D Morris, made most, blun 3rd and 9th, hdd 11th, wknd 4 out, btn whn f nxt. .(7 to 1 op 5 to 1) f
1063 GUNNER JOHN 6-11-2 A Thornton, chasing ldr whn blun and uns i/r 7th. . . . .(8 to 1 op 10 to 1) ur
3365 ICANTELYA (Ire) (v) 8-11-2 S Curran, sn drvn alng in rear, tld off whn refused 11th. . . . .(11 to 2 op 7 to 2 tchd 6 to 1) ref
3490 BRIGHT SEASON (bl) 9-11-2 T J Murphy, mstks, pld up aftr 4th. . . . .(33 to 1 op 20 to 1) pu
3364 ELL GEE 7-10-11 Derek Byrne, sn drvn alng in rear, tld off whn pld up bef 3rd. . . . .(25 to 1 op 20 to 1) pu
Dist: 1¾l, 11l, dist. 4m 50.10s. a 15.10s (9 Ran).

(N Blair), R Rowe

3633 Comedy Of Errors Handicap Hurdle Class E (0-110 4-y-o and up) £2,574 2¼m 110yds. . . . .(4:40)

1872[x] OUT ON A PROMISE (Ire) [100] 5-11-9 N Williamson, hld up, hdwy appr 3 out, led nxt, drvn out.
. . . .(2 to 1 fav op 5 to 2 tchd 3 to 1) 1
3095[4] PERSIAN MYSTIC (Ire) [83] 5-10-6 W Marston, hld up, drpd rear 5th, drvn 2 out, kpt on wl und pres.
. . . .(16 to 1 op 12 to 1 tchd 20 to 1) 2
3494[x] NIGHT IN A MILLION [81] 6-10-1 (3",6ex) L Aspell, led briefly 1st, trkd ldrs, led 4 out to 2 out, one pace.
. . . .(7 to 1 op 5 to 1 tchd 15 to 2) 3
2658[4] MAZZINI (Ire) [96] 6-10-12 (7") Mr P O'Keeffe, hld up, mstk second, rdn aftr 4 out, hmpd by faller 2 out, kpt on.
. . . .(12 to 1 op 8 to 1 tchd 12 to 1) 4
3424[4] IRON N GOLD [91] (v) 5-11-0 R Dunwoody, hld up in tch, hdwy to ld briefly aftr 3 out, wknd und pres nxt.
. . . .(7 to 2 tchd 4 to 1) 5
639[8] STAPLEFORD LADY [86] 9-10-9 W McFarland, hld up, effrt aftr 3 out, sn no imprsn . . .(10 to 1 op 7 to 1 tchd 6 to 1) 6
3409[x] DERISBAY (Ire) [88] (bl) 9-10-8 (3") Sophie Mitchell, led second to nxt, cl up, rdn and wknd appr 3 out, tld off.
. . . .(13 to 2 op 5 to 1 tchd 7 to 1) 7
3498[3] CABOCHON [85] 10-10-8 D Skyrme, led 3rd, hdd 4 out, ev ch whn f 2 out. . . . .(16 to 1 op 12 to 1 tchd 20 to 1) f
3278[6] LIVE ACTION (Ire) 16-10-11-5 J Culloty, led briefly aftr 1st, cl up, hit 5th and struggling, pld up bef nxt.
. . . .(14 to 1 op 12 to 1 tchd 16 to 1) pu
3489 YELLOW DRAGON (Ire) [87] (bl) 4-10-1 (3") P Henley, refused to race. . . . .(20 to 1 op 16 to 1 tchd 14 to 1) l
Dist: 4l, ½l, hd, 6l, 5l, 29l. 4m 23.20s. a 6.20s (10 Ran).
SR: 24/3/-/15/4/-/

(Paul Green), N J H Walker

3634 Kybo Maiden Hurdle Class F (Div II) (4-y-o and up) £1,806 2¼m 110yds
.... (5:10)

3334 ABSOLUTE LIMIT 5-11-6 P Hide, *hld up, took clr order 3rd, led appr 2 out, ran on*............. (2 to 1 fav op 6 to 4) 1
3409² MULLINTOR (Ire) 6-11-6 D O'Sullivan, *led 1st, sn restrained and hld up, steady hdwy appr 2 out, ev ch last, no extr und pres*........................ (4 to 1 tchd 5 to 1) 2
3489⁹ VERONICA FRANCO 4-10-6 (3*) P Henley, *in tch, rdn aftr 3 out, one pace und pres appr last.*
.... (20 to 1 op 12 to 1 tchd 25 to 1) 3
3491³ REAL MADRID 6-11-3 (3*) Mr R Thornton, *hld up, hit 5th, not much room appr 2 out, sn rdn and no imprsn.*
.... (7 to 2 op 4 to 1 tchd 9 to 2) 4
3290⁷ BENJI (bl) 6-11-6 J A McCarthy, *led aftr 1st, hit 5th, hdd appr 2 out, wknd, tld off*.................. (10 to 1 op 20 to 1) 5
3569³ MISS GEE-ELL 5-10-8 (7*) Mr E Babington, *al beh, mstk 4 out, tld off*........................... (50 to 1 op 25 to 1) 6
3322 ARCTIC FOX (Ire) 5-11-6 J F Titley, *chsd ldrs, hit 3rd, wknd 3 out, tld off*............... (3 to 1 op 2 to 1 tchd 7 to 2) 7
3332 LAS ANIMAS (USA) (bl) 6-11-1 B Powell, *reluctant to race, refused 1st*........... (20 to 1 op 25 to 1 tchd 16 to 1) ref
Dist: 2l, 2l, 3l, 20l, 8l, 9l. 4m 26.10s. a 9.10s (8 Ran).

(B M Wootton), J T Gifford

ASCOT (good to firm)
Saturday April 12th
Going Correction: MINUS 0.35 sec. per fur.

3635 Peregrine Handicap Hurdle Class B (4-y-o and up) £5,409 2m 110yds
.... (2:00)

3528⁸ I'M A DREAMER (Ire) [109] 7-9-11 (3*) Mr R Thornton, *hld up beh ldrs, pushed alng to ld appr 2 out, kpt on wl und pres.*
.... (50 to 1 op 33 to 1 tchd 66 to 1) 1
3156 FAUSTINO [110] 5-10-1 N Williamson, *hld up gng wl, smooth hdwy aftr 3 out, chlgd nxt, ev ch last, no extr und pres.*
.... (6 to 1 tchd 7 to 1) 2
2730⁹ ALBEMINE (USA) [122] (bl) 8-10-13 T Kent, *trkd ldg pair, led briefly appr strt, hit 2 out, one pace.*.....(6 to 1 op 9 to 2) 3
3154 DANCING PADDY [137] 9-12-0 R Dunwoody, *hld up beh ldrs, drvn aftr 3 out, sn no imprsn, kpt on und pres r-in.*
.... (10 to 1 op 8 to 1 tchd 12 to 1) 4
2958⁸ ALLTIME DANCER (Ire) [116] (bl) 5-10-7 J Osborne, *dsptd ld till led appr 6th, hdd aftr 3 out, sn no extr.*
.... (9 to 1 op 8 to 1 tchd 10 to 1) 5
3424⁸ NASHVILLE STAR (USA) [109] (v) 6-11-0 C Llewellyn, *dsptd ld till hdd and rdn alng appr 6th, led aftr 3 out to approaching strt, wknd und pres.*...(50 to 1 op 25 to 1 tchd 66 to 1) 6
2278³ CRACK ON [130] 7-11-7 A P McCoy, *hld up, cld 4 out, hrd rdn aftr nxt, no response, sn btn.*
.... (11 to 4 op 3 to 1 tchd 7 to 2) 7
3532⁴ SERIOUS [113] 7-10-4 C O'Dwyer, *hld up, in cl tch and gng wl whn f 3 out*........ (5 to 2 fav op 6 to 4 tchd 11 to 4) f
2176⁶ HOLY WANDERER (USA) [120] 8-10-11 M A Fitzgerald, *sn struggling in rear, tld off whn pld up bef 2 out.*
.... (16 to 1 op 12 to 1 tchd 20 to 1) pu
Dist: 1¾l, 6l, 2l, 1½l, 2½l, 5l. 3m 51.00s. a 5.00s (9 Ran).

(Miss M E Rowland), Miss M E Rowland

3636 Kyle Stewart Handicap Chase Class B (5-y-o and up) £8,122 2m 3f 110yds
.... (2:35)

3581³ BERTONE (Ire) [130] 8-10-4 C O'Dwyer, *confidently rdn, hld up, cld 12th, chlgd 2 out, shaken up and quickened to ld r-in, very easily.*....... (11 to 8 fav tchd 13 to 8 and 5 to 4) 1
3544⁴ SUPER TACTICS (Ire) [135] 9-10-9 R Dunwoody, *hld up in cl tch, led 2 out, hdd r-in, hrd rdn and no ch wth wnr.*
.... (100 to 30 op 7 to 2 tchd 3 to 1) 2
AMTRAK EXPRESS [145] 10-11-5 M A Fitzgerald, *led appr 6th, hdd 2 out, no extr.*....(11 to 2 op 4 to 1 tchd 6 to 1) 3
2219⁶ STORM ALERT [154] 11-12-0 R Johnson, *made most to appr 6th, settled to track ldr, ev ch 4 out, pushed alng and wknd aftr nxt, fnshd tired, tld off.* (3 to 1 op 9 to 4 tchd 100 to 30) 4
3367⁵ YOUNG ALFIE [126] (bl) 12-10-0 C Llewellyn, *led briefly 1st and aftr 4th, drpd rear whn mstk 7th, tld off when not fluent 11th.*.................... (66 to 1 tchd 100 to 1) 5
Dist: 1½l, 9l, dist. dist. 4m 48.70s. a 7.70s (5 Ran).

(Mrs Harry J Duffey), K C Bailey

3637 Letheby & Christopher Long Distance Hurdle Class A Grade 2 (4-y-o and up) £18,750 3m............. (3:10)

3151⁷ TRAINGLOT 10-11-10 R Dunwoody, *hld up in cl tch, chlgd 3 out, reminder appr nxt, led approaching last, sn clr.*
.... (2 to 1 on tchd 13 to 8 on) 1
3422* PLEASURELAND (Ire) 4-10-9 D Morris, *hld up in cl tch, led appr 3 out, hdd approaching last, no extr und pres.*
.... (7 to 1 op 5 to 1 tchd 8 to 1) 2

3471⁷ SASSIVER (USA) 7-11-3 K Gaule, *hld up in cl tch, gng wl, ev ch 3 out, rdn and one pace appr nxt.*
.... (16 to 1 op 20 to 1 tchd 25 to 1) 3
3116 OLYMPIAN (bl) 10-11-3 M A Fitzgerald, *led second, hld second, nt fluent 4th, hdd appr 3 out, kpt on und pres frm last.*
.... (9 to 2 op 4 to 1 tchd 5 to 1) 4
3557³ OATIS ROSE 7-10-12 Sophie Mitchell, *led to second, wth ldr, pushed alng frm 6th, reminders nxt, drpd rear 9th, no imprsn from 2 out.*...........(12 to 1 op 7 to 1 tchd 14 to 1) 5
Dist: 4l, nk, sht-hd, 11l. 5m 33.70s. b 2.30s (5 Ran).
SR: 35/16/24/24/8/ (Marquesa de Moratalla), J G FitzGerald

3638 Kestrel Novices' Chase Class C (5-y-o and up) £5,654 2m 110yds
.... (3:40)

3384³ GREENBACK (Bel) 6-11-12 N Williamson, *hld up in tch, jmpd lft, left in ld 3 out, drvn appr 2 out, ran on gmely und pres r-in.*
.... (11 to 4 op 5 to 2) 1
3384* GARNWIN (Ire) 7-11-12 M A Fitzgerald, *hld up in cl tch, jmpd lft, smooth hdwy to chal 2 out, not fluent last, hrd rdn and not quicken, jst held.*...........(13 to 8 fav op 6 to 4) 2
3363* JUST BRUCE 8-11-12 D Gallagher, *trkd ldr, ev ch whn hit 3 out, outpcd appr nxt.*................. (8 to 1 op 7 to 1) 3
3384² FRAZER ISLAND (Ire) 8-11-9 D O'Sullivan, *led till hit 4 out and uns rdr.*.................. (5 to 2 op 9 to 4 tchd 11 to 4) ur
Dist: Sht-hd, 23l. 4m 52.00s. a 11.00s (4 Ran).

(Jack Joseph), P J Hobbs

3639 'Partnership Parade' Novices' Hurdle Class C (4-y-o and up) £3,728 2 ½m.......................... (4:20)

3442² DARAYDAN (Ire) 5-11-10 A P McCoy, *made all, sn clr, unchlgd.*....................... (4 to 1 op 4 to 1 on) 1
OVER THE WAY (Ire) 7-11-2 M A Fitzgerald, *hld up, hdwy to ld chasing grp 2 out, no ch wth wnr.*
.... (10 to 1 op 6 to 1 tchd 11 to 1) 2
3312⁵ HIGH SUMMER 7-11-2 J Culloty, *not fluent, led chasing grp virtually thrghtt till 2 out, no extr.*
.... (10 to 1 op 7 to 1 tchd 11 to 1) 3
3480⁴ PEALINGS (Ire) 5-11-2 R Johnson, *wth ldr in chasing grp, not fluent 5th, wknd 2 out.*..(33 to 1 op 14 to 1 tchd 40 to 1) 4
3169² WENTWORTH (USA) 5-11-2 B Powell, *hld up, hit 4th, sn beh, tld off.*...................(16 to 1 op 14 to 1 tchd 12 to 1) 5
2898 MISTER GOODGUY (Ire) 5-11-2 D Morris, *hld up in cl tch in chasing grp, struggling aftr 7th, tld off whn pld up bef 2 out.*
.... (66 to 1 op 33 to 1 tchd 100 to 1) pu
3332⁸ PEERS FOLLY (Ire) 7-11-2 J F Titley, *hld up beh, pld up aftr 5th.*................(33 to 1 op 14 to 1 tchd 40 to 1) pu
Dist: 20l, 7l, 1¼l, dist. 4m 49.00s. a 8.00s (7 Ran).

(D A Johnson), M C Pipe

3640 'Merlin' Novices' Hunters' Chase Class H (5-y-o and up) £2,879 3m 110yds.......................... (5:00)

STRUGGLES GLORY (Ire) 6-12-0⁷ (7*) Mr D C Robinson, *cl up, led 10th, made rst, styd on wl.*
.... (3 to 1 fav op 11 to 4 tchd 5 to 2) 1
3567⁵ LURRIGA GLITTER (Ire) (bl) 9-11-7 (7*) Mr R Wakley, *chsd ldrs, blun 12th, lost pl nxt, hdwy 4 out, styd on wl frm 2 out, mstk last, no imprsn.*...(25 to 1 op 14 to 1 tchd 33 to 1) 2
3133 CAPO CASTANUM 8-12-7 (7*) Mr A Wintle, *al hndy, chsd wnr frm 11th till lost pl appr last, one pace.*
.... (8 to 1 op 6 to 1 tchd 10 to 1) 3
BALASANI (Fr) 11-11-9 (5*) Mr A Sansome, *mstk 1st, beh till styd on frm 2 out, nvr nrr.* (10 to 1 op 6 to 1 tchd 12 to 1) 4
BERRINGS DASHER 10-11-7 (7*) Mr M Watson, *al hndy, drvn and wknd frm 3 out.*...(33 to 1 op 20 to 1 tchd 40 to 1) 5
3426* NORTHERN VILLAGE 10-12-0 (7*) Mr D Alers-Hankey, *wth ldrs early, sn hld up in mid-div, mstk 11th, blun 15th, soon wknd.*....................... (9 to 1 op 12 to 1 tchd 14 to 1) 6
APATURA KING 7-12-0⁵ (5*) Mr T Mitchell, *al beh.*
.... (33 to 1 op 20 to 1 tchd 11 to 2) 7
BILBO BAGGINS (Ire) 9-11-7 (7*) Mr M Gorman, *al beh, tld off.*.................... (33 to 1 op 20 to 1) 8
3567 TOM'S GEMINI STAR 9-12-0 (7*) Mr E James, *hld up in tch, hdwy to chase ldrs frm tenth, rdn alng 15th, drvn and held in 4th whn blun and uns rdr 2 out.*
.... (12 to 1 op 6 to 1 tchd 14 to 1) ur
2994² ELMORE 10-11-11 (3*) Mr P Hacking, *mid-div, drpd rear tenth, mstk 12th, pld up bef 3 out.*....... (8 to 1 op 4 to 1) pu
3387⁷ POORS WOOD 10-12-2 (5*) Mr T McCarthy, *pld hrd, hld up, pulled up bef tenth, dismounted.*
.... (10 to 1 op 8 to 1 tchd 12 to 1) pu
AMADEUS (Fr) 9-11-7 (7*) Mr M Gingell, *led to tenth, trkd ldrs, rdn 14th, sn wknd, tld off whn pld up bef last.*
.... (33 to 1 tchd 40 to 1) pu
3327 LOYAL GAIT (NZ) 9-11-9 (5*) Mr J Trice-Rolph, *mid-div whn blun badly 4th (water), beh frm hfwy, tld off when pld up bef 15th.*..............(33 to 1 op 25 to 1 tchd 50 to 1) pu
MAKING TIME 10-11-2 (7*) Mr Andrew Martin, *hld up, hdwy tenth, mstk 12th, sn wknd, pld up bef 3 out.*
.... (25 to 1 op 12 to 1) pu
Dist: 5l, 9l, 11l, 1½l, 2l, 3l, dist. 6m 17.20s. a 16.20s (14 Ran).

(D C Robinson), D C Robinson

3641 **'Royal Ascot Cricket Club' Novices' Handicap Hurdle Class C (4-y-o and up) £5,402 2m 110yds........ (5:35)**

3575[9] JOHN DRUMM [108] 6-11-10 J Osborne, *made virtually all, rdn alng and kpt on wl*..... (9 to 2 op 3 to 1 tchd 5 to 1) 1
3315[2] FAIRLY SHARP (Ire) [100] 4-10-10 N Williamson, *wth wnr, ev ch gng wl appr 2 out, sn rdn and not quicken.* ....(5 to 2 op 3 to 1 tchd 7 to 2 and 9 to 4) 2
2980[4] SUPER RAPIER (Ire) [84] 5-10-0 R Johnson, *hld up in tch, rdn and one pace appr 2 out.* ....(20 to 1 op 12 to 1 tchd 25 to 1) 3
3108* FASIL (Ire) [112] 4-11-8 A P McCoy, *not fluent 1st, hld up, mstk 4 out, sn rdn and no imprsn.* ....(13 to 8 fav op 6 to 4 tchd 7 to 4) 4
3334[3] MAETERLINCK (Ire) [84] 5-9-10[3] (7*) Clare Thorner, *hld up in tch, mstk 3 out, sn no extr*......... (10 to 1 tchd 12 to 1) 5
3049[6] REGAL PURSUIT (Ire) [100] 6-11-2 M A Fitzgerald, *hld up in tch, beh frm 3rd, no imprsn from 3 out.* .... (11 to 1 op 6 to 1 tchd 12 to 1) 6
3414[5] ADILOV [84] 5-9-11 (3*) Sophie Mitchell, *trkd ldrs, rdn aftr 3 out, sn btn*........... (25 to 1 op 14 to 1 tchd 33 to 1) 7
Dist: 2½l, 3½l, 2½l, hd, 3½l, 1l. 3m 52.90s. a 6.90s (7 Ran).
(Andrew Jenkins), P R Webber

DOWN ROYAL (IRE) (good to firm)
Saturday April 12th

3642 **Dumfries Maiden Hurdle (4-y-o and up) £1,712 2m................ (2:30)**

3415[7] UNASSISTED (Ire) 4-10-7 (3*) B Bowens, ...(8 to 1) 1
3626[8] BAILENAGUN (Ire) 4-10-8 (7*) B J Geraghty, ...(14 to 1) 2
3389[2] PILS INVADER (Ire) 9-11-1 D T Evans, ...(10 to 1) 3
3547 ANN'S DESIRE (Ire) 6-11-1 P L Malone, ...(7 to 1) 4
2016 GOLD DEPOSITOR (Ire) 5-11-1 (7*) I Browne, ...(100 to 30) 5
3450[9] DUE TO YOU (Ire) 4-11-1 P Leech, ...(12 to 1) 6
3553 EIRE (Ire) 8-11-7 (7*) Mr M O'Connor, ...(14 to 1) 7
3225[3] FABRIANO (USA) (bl) 6-11-6 J Shortt, ...(15 to 8 fav) 8
3225 STRATEGIC AFFAIR (Ire) 6-11-1 (5*) T Martin, ...(50 to 1) 9
2866 CARA GAIL (Ire) 5-11-0 T P Rudd, ...(25 to 1) 10
3085[7] AISLING ALAINN (Ire) 5-11-5 F Woods, ...(7 to 1) 11
3379[6] SCEAL SIOG (Ire) (bl) 8-11-1 L P Cusack, ...(12 to 1) 12
GRITRICK (Ire) 6-10-8 (7*) D A McLoughlin, ...(40 to 1) 13
CHEEKY HARRY (Ire) 4-10-8 (7*) Mr S McKenna, ..(40 to 1) 14
3415 WESTERN SEAS (Ire) 4-11-6 K F O'Brien, ...(10 to 1) 15
951[7] NEW WEST (Ire) 7-10-13 (7*) S P McCann, ...(25 to 1) 16
3227 CATEMPO (Ire) 7-11-6 P McWilliams, ...(66 to 1) 17
928 RAVEN'S DALE (Ire) 6-10-8 (7*) A David, ...(25 to 1) 18
3231 DERRING LINE (Ire) 5-11-2 (3*) K Whelan, ...(40 to 1) 19
HANDSOME FELLA (Ire) 5-10-12 (7*) Mr J Bright, (33 to 1) 20
Dist: 1½l, 2½l, 2½l, 2½l. 3m 49.40s. (20 Ran).
(M A Begley), Victor Bowens

3643 **Langholm Opportunity Handicap Hurdle (0-116 5-y-o and up) £1,712 2 ½m......................... (3:00)**

3390[6] GLENFIELDS CASTLE (Ire) [-] 7-10-12 J Butler, ...(7 to 1) 1
3089 ANNAELAINE (Ire) [-] 6-9-6 (4*) B J Geraghty, ...(14 to 1) 2
1899 DEIREADH AN SCEAL (Ire) [-] 7-10-3[3] K Whelan, ..(20 to 1) 3
3390* HOME I'LL BE (Ire) [-] 7-9-7 B Bowens, ...(9 to 2) 4
3227[9] CORALDA (Ire) [-] 6-9-3 (4*) R Burke, ...(25 to 1) 5
3068 KILCAR (Ire) [-] 6-9-10 (4*) L J Fleming, ...(16 to 1) 6
3229[3] PENNYBRIDGE (Ire) [-] 8-11-12 (2*) T Martin, ...(8 to 1) 7
3521[5] JERMYN STREET (USA) [-] 6-9-9 (4*) M D Murphy, (12 to 1) 8
3419* SLEWMORE (Ire) [-] 6-10-1 (4*) M P Cooney, ...(7 to 1) 9
3419 BOBSTAR DANCER (Ire) [-] 6-11-4 (4*) D Flood, ...(16 to 1) 10
2835[5] CAIRNCROSS (Ire) [-] 6-11-5 (4*) J M Maguire, (2 to 1 fav) 11
3430[4] POLLTRIC (Ire) [-] 6-10-11 (4*) D A McLoughlin, ... (13 to 2) 12
1535 FERRYCARRIG HOTEL (Ire) [-] 8-11-8 (4*) M W Martin, ...(8 to 1) 13
BALLYCANN [-] 10-11-1 (4*) D Fisher, ...(25 to 1) 14
Dist: ¾l, 7l, 1½l, 9l. 4m 41.20s. (14 Ran).
(T D Stronge), I A Duncan

3644 **Auchtermuchty Maiden Hurdle (5-y-o and up) £1,712 3m....... (3:30)**

3547 SEVENTY SEVEN MILL (Ire) 8-11-9 (5*) A O'Shea, ..(7 to 2) 1
2752[8] ROSEEN (Ire) 8-10-8 (7*) D W O'Sullivan, ...(9 to 1) 2
3389[4] RATHCORE LADY (Ire) 6-10-12 (3*) K Whelan, ...(8 to 1) 3
3342[5] MR MAGGET (Ire) 5-11-4 T P Rudd, ...(5 to 2) 4
3417[6] TAP PRACTICE (Ire) 5-10-11 (7*) J M Maguire, ...(16 to 1) 5
2865[9] HANNAH'S PET (Ire) 7-11-1 F Woods, ...(14 to 1) 6
3421[6] PADDY'S PET (Ire) (bl) 8-10-13 (7*) K A Kelly, ...(9 to 4 fav) f
2865 LORD NOAN (Ire) 7-11-6 J Shortt, ...(40 to 1) pu
3389[7] WINTER PRINCESS 6-11-1 P McWilliams, ...(20 to 1) pu
2583 BARORA GALE (Ire) 6-10-10 (5*) T Martin, ...(33 to 1) pu
Dist: 3½l, 12l, 14l, 11l. 5m 59.80s. (10 Ran).
(J G Cromwell), J G Cromwell

3645 **Bet With The Tote Beginners Chase (4-y-o and up) £1,712 2½m... (4:00)**

3451 ALWAYS IN TROUBLE 10-12-0 T P Rudd, ...(7 to 1) 1
2136 PERSIAN POWER (Ire) 9-11-7 (7*) B J Geraghty, .. (11 to 2) 2
3418[2] FRIARSTOWN DUKE 7-12-0 T J Mitchell, ...(13 to 8 fav) 3
3454 THE THIRD MAN (Ire) 8-11-7 (7*) Mr K Ross, ...(4 to 1) 4
2840 ROCHE MENTOR (Ire) 7-11-11 (3*) K Whelan, ...(16 to 1) 5
680 BORRISMORE FLASH (Ire) 9-11-7 (7*) J M Maguire, ...(16 to 1) f
2039[5] BROWNRATH KING (Ire) 8-11-7 (7*) D M Bean, ... (16 to 1) bd
2519[9] XANTHOS 7-12-0 L P Cusack, ...(25 to 1) co
3344[5] JESSIE'S BOY (Ire) 8-12-0 J K Kinane, ...(16 to 1) pu
3228 ROCK ON BUD (Ire) 6-11-9 (5*) A O'Shea, ...(16 to 1) pu
3454 NEWTOWN ROAD (Ire) 6-12-0 P Leech, ...(14 to 1) pu
Dist: 10l, 8l, 4½l, 12l. 5m 5.80s. (11 Ran).
(Mrs M O'Rourke), M J P O'Brien

3646 **Banbridge Coachworks Hunters Chase (5-y-o and up) £1,712 3m .... (4:30)**

BEST INTEREST (Ire) 9-11-2 (7*) Mr John A Quinn, ...(6 to 4 fav) 1
3391[2] HILTONSTOWN LASS (Ire) 7-10-11 (7*) Mr Richard J Walker, ...(9 to 2) 2
3228[5] WILLY WEE (Ire) 6-11-2 (7*) Mr W Ewing, ...(8 to 1) 3
3391 FUNNY YE KNOW (Ire) 8-11-9 Mr P F Graffin, ...(5 to 2) 4
MYSTERIOUS BEAU (Ire) 9-11-6 (3*) Mr B R Hamilton, ...(14 to 1) pu
Dist: 1l, 15l, 7l. 6m 10.10s. (5 Ran).
(Mrs D McDowell), J Larkin

3647 **Banbridge Coachworks (Mares) Flat Race (4-y-o and up) £1,712 2m (5:00)**

3390[9] PETITE MEWS (Ire) 6-12-0 Mr A J Martin, ...(6 to 1) 1
3456[7] NATIVE SHORE (Ire) 5-11-6 (7*) Mr K R O'Ryan, ...(9 to 2) 2
VILLAGE ROSHEEN (Ire) 5-11-8 (5*) Mr A C Coyle, (9 to 1) 3
OTTER TRACK LADY (Ire) 4-10-13 (7*) Mr Philip Carberry, ...(12 to 1) 4
SOUNDS CONFIDENT (Ire) 5-11-6 (7*) Mr W Ewing, (5 to 1) 5
3608[4] ASFREEASTHEWIND (Ire) 6-12-0 Mr J P Dempsey, (11 to 2) 6
3225[6] MRS DOYLE (Ire) 5-11-6 (7*) Mr John A Quinn, ...(10 to 1) 7
3394 GAYE CHATELAINE (Ire) 4-10-13 (7*) Mr N W Toal, (40 to 1) 8
3349[6] MOUNT HALL (Ire) 5-11-13 Mr J A Nash, ... (2 to 1 fav) 9
3524 CANDY GALE (Ire) 5-11-6 (7*) Mr P Fahey, ...(12 to 1) 10
1096 FELICITY'S PRIDE (Ire) 6-11-7 (7*) Mr D Kirwan, ...(16 to 1) 11
CINDER'S SLIPPER (Ire) 5-11-10 (3*) Mr B R Hamilton, ...(25 to 1) 12
3394[9] IT'SNOTSIMPLE (Ire) 5-11-6 (7*) Mr Richard J Walker, ...(33 to 1) 13
CARNA LADY (Ire) 5-11-13 Mr A R Coonan, ... (14 to 1) 14
2588 DYRALLAGH (Ire) 5-11-6 (7*) Miss A McDonogh, .. (25 to 1) 15
DIVIDED AFFECTION (Ire) 6-11-7 (7*) Mr M O'Connor, ...(25 to 1) 16
Dist: 2l, ½l, 1½l, 2l. 3m 46.30s. (16 Ran).
(J H Lowry), A J Martin

NEWTON ABBOT (firm)
Saturday April 12th

Going Correction: MINUS 0.05 sec. per fur.

3648 **Happy Birthday Partyfare Juvenile Novices' Handicap Hurdle Class E (0-105 4-y-o) £2,169 2m 1f.... (2:10)**

3463[3] SAFECRACKER [72] 10-4 Derek Byrne, *sn chasing ldr, reminder aftr 3rd, not fluent nxt, narrow advantage 2 out, rdn out*.......................... (8 to 1 op 6 to 1) 1
3411[2] BATH KNIGHT [72] 9-11 (7*) Mr J Goldstein, *sn led, hit 1st, hdd 2 out, no extr r-in*.....(9 to 4 op 3 to 1 tchd 2 to 1) 2
3590[7] RAPID LINER [68] 10-0 V Slattery, *hld up, rdn appr 3 out, sn wknd, tld off*..........(20 to 1 op 12 to 1 tchd 25 to 1) 3
2996[8] SAUCY DANCER [68] 10-0 S McNeill, *hld up, rdn alng appr 5th, wknd 3 out, tld off*............... (25 to 1 op 20 to 1) 4
3569[2] KAI'S LADY (Ire) [68] 10-0 T Dascombe, *wtd wth, not fluent 3rd, rdn aftr nxt, wknd 3 out, tld off.* ....(14 to 1 op 12 to 1 tchd 16 to 1) 5
3487* MELLOW MASTER [92] 11-3 (7*) X Aizpuru, *trkd ldg pair, rdn alng aftr 4th, jmpd slwly nxt, 3rd and wkng whn pld up lme bef 2 out*..........(6 to 4 on op 2 to 1 on tchd 11 to 8 on) pu
Dist: ½l, dist, hd, 10l. 3m 59.80s. a 10.80s (6 Ran).
(West Lancs Antiques Export Racing), C P Morlock

3649 **Addisons Quality Meats Novices' Chase Class E (6-y-o and up) £3,507 3¼m 110yds................. (2:45)**

3484[3] RUSTIC FLIGHT 10-10-3 (7*) M Griffiths, *led, took wrong course aftr 3rd, continued, fnshd 1st, disqualified.* .... (16 to 1 op 10 to 1) 1D
3538[2] THE WHOLE HOG (Ire) 8-11-3 S McNeill, *hld up, crrd out by loose horse aftr 3rd, returned to continue, fnshd second, plcd 1st*...........(11 to 4 on op 4 to 1 on tchd 5 to 2 on) 1
3405 DUNLIR 7-10-10 M Sharratt, *hld up, crrd out by loose horse aftr 3rd, returned to continue, tld off, fnshd third, plcd second.* ....(7 to 1 op 5 to 1) 2

3514 CRAVATE (Fr) (bl) 7-10-5 G Tormey, *chsd ldr till blun and uns rdr 3rd.............................*(5 to 1 op 4 to 1) ur
Dist: Dist, dist. 7m 23.60s. a 63.60s (4 Ran).

(Mrs Sharon C Nelson), K C Bailey

3650 Squires Recruitment Conditional Jockeys' Handicap Hurdle Class E (0-125 4-y-o and up) £2,210 2¾m
.... (3:15)

3468³ BURLINGTON SAM (NZ) [89] 9-11-10 O Burrows, *hld up in cl tch, rdn to chase ldr 3 out, led 2 out, ran on wl.*
...............................(11 to 10 fav op Evens) 1
3592³ DISSOLVE [77] 5-10-12 Chris Webb, *led second, hdd 2 out, one pace r-in...........*(11 to 8 op 6 to 5 tchd 6 to 4) 2
3404 ALLAHRAKHA [70] 6-10-5 T Dascombe, *led to second, rdn alng appr 7th, wknd frm 3 out, tld off.....* (9 to 2 op 5 to 1) 3
Dist: 3½l, dist. 5m 21.20s. a 20.20s (3 Ran).

(Mrs Jackie Reip), A G Hobbs

3651 Paignton And Dartmouth Steam Railway Handicap Chase Class B (0-125 5-y-o and up) £3,533 2m 5f 110yds...................... (3:45)

3545² POLDEN PRIDE [113] 9-11-5 B Clifford, *trkd ldg pair, chsd ldr frm tenth, led nxt, drw clr appr 2 out.* (5 to 4 on op 5 to 4) 1
3618³ FENWICK [94] 10-10-0 T Dascombe, *hld up, lost tch frm 6th, styd on from 11th, chsd wnr appr 2 out, no imprsn.*
............................(9 to 1 op 8 to 1 tchd 10 to 1) 2
3571* DOUALAGO (Fr) [122] (bl) 7-11-9 (5*) G Supple, *led to 11th, sn rdn, wknd appr 2 out............*(9 to 4 op 5 to 4) 3
2931³ BEAU BABILLARD [110] (bl) 10-11-2 B Fenton, *chsd ldr to tenth, wknd frm nxt...........*(8 to 1 op 6 to 1) 4
3502 RYTON RUN [94] 12-10-0 T J O'Sullivan, *hld up, lost tch frm 6th, beh whn pld up bef nxt.........*(40 to 1 op 20 to 1) pu
Dist: 8l, 3½l, 16l. 5m 17.60s. a 15.60s (5 Ran).

(D F Lockyer,C A Parry,G B Balding), G B Balding

3652 William Hill Handicap Hurdle Class D (0-125 4-y-o and up) £2,735 2m 1f
.... (4:15)

2543³ HAY DANCE [109] 6-11-3 G Tormey, *hld up, chsd ldr appr 5th, led 2 out, sn clr....................*(7 to 4 tchd 6 to 4) 1
2999¹ KNIGHT IN SIDE [96] 11-10-4 C Maude, *led to 2 out, sn btn.*
............................(7 to 4 fav op 2 to 1) 2
3440² OUT RANKING (Fr) [117] 5-11-4 (7*) X Aizpuru, *hld up, struggling frm hfwy, ran on from 2 out, nrst finish.*
............................(5 to 1 op 5 to 2) 3
3403⁴ VERDE LUNA [92] 10-11-0 S McNeill, *wtd wth, prog 3 out, wknd appr 2 out..................*(14 to 1 op 10 to 1) 4
3409³ GLOWING PATH [92] 7-9-7 (7*) J Harris, *keen hold early, chsd clr ldr till appr 5th, wknd frm 3 out.....*(16 to 1 op 10 to 1) 5
Dist: 7l, 5l, 2½l, 3½l. 3m 53.60s. a 4.60s (5 Ran).
SR: 34/14/30/2/-/ (Wessex Go Racing Partnership), P J Hobbs

3653 Wilf Townsend Memorial Handicap Chase Class F (0-105 5-y-o and up) £2,641 2m 110yds............ (4:45)

3517 EVENING RAIN [80] 11-10-11 T Dascombe, *chsd clr ldr, rdn to cl frm 3 out, led bef nxt, drvn out......* (8 to 1 op 5 to 1) 1
801⁷ TOOMUCH TOOSOON (Ire) [88] 9-11-5 B Fenton, *hld up, prog frm 3 out, chsd wnr and effrt appr 2 out, kpt on same pace..................*(9 to 2 op 4 to 1) 2
3486* MISTRESS ROSIE [72] 10-10-3 S Fox, *hld up, not fluent 3rd, rdn alng 8th, styd on frm 2 out, nvr nrr.* (5 to 1 tchd 6 to 1) 3
3404* JAY JAY'S VOYAGE [76] 14-10-4 (3*) Guy Lewis, *wtd wth, rdn alng 8th, styd on frm 2 out, nvr nrr.*
............................(7 to 1 op 6 to 1 tchd 15 to 2) 4
2034³ SPINNING STEEL [92] 10-11-9 S Burrough, *led, sn clr, wknd and hdd appr 2 out, tired 4th whn hit last.*
............................(5 to 2 fav op 2 to 1) 5
3360⁵ MONDAY CLUB [93] 13-11-10 R Bellamy, *hdwy 8th, wknd appr 2 out..................*(11 to 2 op 5 to 1 tchd 6 to 1) 6
3410⁴ DAYS OF THUNDER [82] 9-10-13 T J O'Sullivan, *nvr nr to chal...........................*(16 to 1 tchd 20 to 1) 7
3490³ DAWN CHANCE [77] 11-10-8 P Holley, *hld up, blun 4th, lost tch frm 6th, tld off whn pld up bef 3 out.* (10 to 1 op 7 to 1) pu
Dist: 2l, 8l, 2½l, 2½l, 7l, 2l. 4m 7.10s. a 9.10s (8 Ran).

(The Gardens Entertainments Ltd), R J Hodges

3654 Sapphire And Diamonds Intermediate Open National Hunt Flat Class H (4,5,6-y-o) £1,278 2m 1f...... (5:15)

2899⁶ FILSCOT 5-10-11 (7*) J Power, *chsd clr ldr, led hfwy, drw clear frm o'r 3 fs out, unchlgd............*(5 to 2 op 2 to 1) 1
3408⁴ COUNTRY KRIS 5-11-4 G Upton, *hld up, hdwy hfwy, outpcd o'r 3 fs out, kpt on to take moderate second one out.*
............................(2 to 1 fav tchd 9 to 4) 2
BROTHER NERO (NZ) 5-11-4 R Greene, *hld up, hdwy to chase wnr frm hfwy, rdn and outpcd o'r 3 fs out, lost moderate second one out...........*(7 to 2 op 9 to 4 tchd 6 to 4) 3

3302⁷ SEE PROSPERITY 5-10-11 (7*) N Willmington, *tld off frm hfwy..........................*(8 to 1 op 6 to 1 tchd 9 to 1) 4
3408 PHONE THE PIPELINE (bl) 4-10-5 (7*) B Moore, *set str pace, clr till hdd and wknd hfwy, tld off........* (7 to 1 op 4 to 1) 5
Dist: 21l, 2l, dist, 1¼l. 3m 53.00s. (5 Ran).

(G F Beazley), W G M Turner

SEDGEFIELD (good to firm)
Saturday April 12th
Going Correction: NIL

3655 J. R. Tiles Maiden Hurdle Class E (4-y-o and up) £2,740 2m 5f 110yds
.... (1:45)

3044⁴ SHARP COMMAND 4-10-12 Richard Guest, *chsd ldrs, smooth hdwy to ld aftr 4 out, drvn out, very easily.*
............................(9 to 4 fav op 2 to 1 tchd 5 to 2) 1
3587⁶ CATCH THE PIGEON 8-11-0 N Smith, *midfield, hdwy 5th, hmpd 3 out, sn chasing wnr, rdn bef 2 out and no imprsn.*
............................(9 to 1 op 7 to 1 tchd 10 to 1) 2
2988⁵ CAUGHT AT LAST (Ire) 6-11-5 G Cahill, *in tch, hdwy 6th, rdn 3 out and sn one pace......*(7 to 2 op 9 to 4 tchd 4 to 1) 3
2361⁶ CARNMONEY (Ire) 9-11-5 B Storey, *prmnt, rdn alng and wknd bef 3 out..................*(20 to 1 tchd 16 to 1) 4
3435⁶ KING FLY 7-11-5 A Thornton, *led, rdn alng and hdd appr 4 out, wknd nxt....................*(7 to 2 tchd 5 to 1) 5
3598 SALEM BEACH 5-11-0 J Callaghan, *beh frm hfwy.*
............................(16 to 1 tchd 20 to 1) 6
3482 WEST LUTTON 5-11-2 (3*) P Midgley, *beh frm hfwy.*
............................(20 to 1 op 16 to 1) 7
3308 MOREFLASH 5-11-0 T Reed, *midfield, drvn alng 4 out and sn beh...........................*(100 to 1 op 50 to 1) 8
3351 BANNER YEAR (Ire) 6-11-5 P Niven, *beh frm hfwy, tld off 3 out...........................*(100 to 1 op 50 to 1) 9
3309⁶ SMILE PLEEZE (Ire) 5-11-5 Mr S Swiers, *not jump wl and al rear, beh whn f last...............*(8 to 1 tchd 7 to 1) f
3317 REGAL JEST 7-11-0 W Dwan, *blun and uns rdr 1st.*
............................(100 to 1 op 50 to 1) ur
2490 MATACHON 7-11-5 R Supple, *chsd ldrs, rdn alng 5th, sn wknd and beh whn slpd up bend bef 2 out.*
............................(100 to 1 op 50 to 1) su
3258⁶ POINT DUTY (bl) 7-11-5 A Dobbin, *chsd ldrs, hdwy 5th, led and blun 4 out, sn hdd, wknd quickly aftr nxt and beh whn pld up bef 2 out.....................*(33 to 1 op 16 to 1) pu
3002⁹ PRIMITIVE HEART 5-11-5 A Smith, *al beh, tld off whn pld up bef 2 out........*(33 to 1 op 20 to 1 tchd 16 to 1) pu
3160 TARTAN JOY (Ire) 6-11-0 (5*) Mr M H Naughton, *beh whn sddl slpd 4th and pld up aftr..........*(50 to 1 op 40 to 1) pu
2939 AEOLUS 4-10-9 (3*) E Callaghan, *sn beh, tld off 5th, pld up bef last...........*(66 to 1 op 50 to 1 tchd 100 to 1) pu
Dist: 15l, 13l, 6l, 6l, 22l, 5l, 6l, dist. 4m 54.60s. a 6.60s (16 Ran).
SR: 18/5/-/-/-/-/ (A P Holland), P Eccles

3656 Trade Windows UK Ltd. Handicap Chase Class E (0-115 5-y-o and up) £3,119 2m 110yds............ (2:15)

3536* GROUSE-N-HEATHER [92] 8-11-10 A Dobbin, *trkd ldrs, hit 7th and shaken up, jnd ldsr 4 out, led bef nxt, clr 2 out.*
............................(11 to 10 on op 5 to 4 on) 1
2176⁴ UK HYGIENE (Ire) [80] 7-10-12 R Garritty, *led, rdn alng and hit 4 out, sn hdd and one pace......*(4 to 1 op 7 to 2) 2
3536² REBEL KING [79] 7-10-6 (5*) S Taylor, *chsd ldr, rdn alng 4 out and sn one pace.........*(4 to 1 tchd 9 to 2) 3
3585³ REVE DE VALSE (USA) [85] 10-11-3 K Johnson, *pushed alng in rear hfwy, some hdwy 3 out, sn one pace.*
............................(11 to 2 op 4 to 1 tchd 6 to 1) 4
Dist: 5l, 2l, 3l. 4m 0.00s. a 8.00s (4 Ran).
SR: 16/ (D J Fairbairn), P Monteith

3657 Stanley Racing Golden Numbers Series Final Novices' Handicap Hurdle Class C (4-y-o and up) £10,503 2m 5f 110yds................ (2:50)

3435² MEADOW HYMN (Ire) [114] 6-12-0 P Carberry, *chsd ldrs, rdn alng bef 2 out, styd on to chal last, drvn flt, led nr finish.*
............................(3 to 1 jt-fav op 5 to 2 tchd 100 to 30) 1
3528⁷ STYLISH INTERVAL [89] 5-10-3 A Dobbin, *al prmnt, led appr 2 out, sn rdn, hdd and no extr nr finish.* (14 to 1 op 12 to 1) 2
3249² BRAMBLES WAY [112] (bl) 8-11-7 N Smith, *hld up, pushed alng 4 out, rdn aftr nxt, chlgd 2 out and ev ch till drvn out flt and no extr nr finish......*(3 to 1 jt-fav op 9 to 4 tchd 100 to 30) 3
3583⁶ SILENT GUEST (Ire) [93] 4-10-0 D Bentley, *chsd ldr, rdn alng aftr 3 out, wknd after nxt...........*(11 to 1 op 8 to 1) 4
3535 RULE OUT THE REST [89] 6-10-3 A Thornton, *chsd ldrs, rdn alng hfwy, lost pl bef 3 out and sn beh.*
............................(10 to 1 tchd 8 to 1 and 12 to 1) 5
569⁷ GOOD HAND (USA) [92] 11-10-6 R Garritty, *hld up, rdn alng 4 out, no imprsn frm nxt..........*(4 to 1 op 6 to 1) 6
473⁵ LONGCROFT [86] 5-9-7 (7*) N Horrocks, *hld up in rear, pushed alng and outpcd hfwy, sn beh...........*(16 to 1) 7
3587 I'M TYSON (NZ) [86] 9-10-0 B Storey, *hld up, steady hdwy to chase ldrs 3 out, rdn and wknd bef nxt.* (25 to 1 op 20 to 1) 8

3583* SILVER MINX [99] 5-10-13 G Lee, led, rdn 3 out, 4th and wkng
whn l nxt..........................(5 to 1 op 9 to 2)   f
3584² WHITEGATES WILLIE [86] 5-9-7 (7*) C McCormack, beh frm
hfwy, tld off whn pld up aftr 2 out......(20 to 1 op 16 to 1)   pu
Dist: Nk, nk, 22l, nk, ¾l, 6l, 2½l. 4m 55.40s. a 7.40s (10 Ran).
SR: 26/1/24/-/-/-/   (Mrs M Nowell), J G FitzGerald

3658 Eden Arms Swallow Hotel Conditional Jockeys' Handicap Chase Class F (0-105 4-y-o and up) £2,547 3m 3f 110yds.................(3:25)

3400⁷ KINGS LANE [82] 8-10-10 E Husband, midfield and pushed
alng hfwy, rdn and outpcd appr 4 out, gd hdwy nxt, led
approaching 2 out and sn clr.
.....................(12 to 1 op 10 to 1 tchd 14 to 1)   1
1819* TROODOS [100] 11-12-0 B Grattan, beh, steady hdwy 4 out,
rdn to chase wnr aftr 2 out, no imprsn.
.............................(7 to 2 fav op 9 to 2)   2
2635⁶ BLOOMING SPRING (Ire) [72] 8-10-0 D Thomas, hld up in
rear, gd hdwy to join ldrs 8th, rdn alng 3 out, kpt on one pace
frm nxt............................(20 to 1 op 16 to 1)   3
2710 SCARBA [100] 9-12-0 E Callaghan, hld up and beh, steady
hdwy 8th, effrt and rdn alng 3 out, kpt on one pace frm nxt.
.....................................(5 to 1 op 4 to 1)   4
2815⁶ CHEATER (Ire) [90] (bl) 6-11-4 C McCormack, cl up, led 8th,
rdn 3 out, hdd bef nxt and btn whn blun 2 out.
.................................(8 to 1 op 7 to 1 tchd 9 to 1)   5
3400⁸ BARNSTORMER [72] (bl) 11-10-0 G F Ryan, al prmnt, ev ch 3
out, sn rdn and wknd 2 out...............(20 to 1)   6
2346 MOVIE MAN [73] 5-10-1 R Burns, in tch, rdn alng 4 out, wknd
aftr nxt..........................(20 to 1 op 16 to 1)   7
2653⁴ CHILL FACTOR [82] 7-10-10 G Lee, midfield, pushed alng
hfwy, some hdwy 4 out, sn rdn and no imprsn.
.................................(11 to 2 op 4 to 1)   8
2989² SOLOMAN SPRINGS (USA) [78] 7-10-6 P Henley, chsd ldrs,
rdn alng hfwy, lost tch aftr 4 out.
.................................(9 to 1 op 7 to 1 tchd 10 to 1)   9
3105⁵ FROWN [95] 7-11-9 L Cummins, chsd ldrs till wknd quickly 4
out and sn beh.........................(16 to 1)   10
3350⁸ FIERY SUN [76] 12-10-4 N Horrocks, led to 8th, cl up till rdn
and f 3 out..........................(33 to 1 op 25 to 1)   f
3594* CLONGOUR (Ire) [85] (bl) 7-10-13 D J Kavanagh, hld up in
midfield, hdwy to chase ldrs whn brght dwn 3 out.
.................................(5 to 1 op 9 to 2)   bd
3309 STEPDAUGHTER [72] 11-10-0 R McGrath, sn beh, tld off whn
pld up 3 out..........................(50 to 1 op 33 to 1)   pu
3009⁸ STRONG CHARACTER [72] 11-9-9 (5*) N Hannity, chsd ldrs,
reminders 6th, hit nxt, beh frm 9th, tld off whn pld up bef 2 out.
.................................(66 to 1 op 50 to 1)   pu
Dist: 6l, 6l, nk, 2l, 3½l, ¾l, 16l, 12l, dist. 6m 29.00s. a 7.00s (14 Ran).
SR: 12/24/-/18/6/-/   (J M Dun), J M Dun

3659 McEwan's Durham National Handicap Chase Class C (0-130 5-y-o and up) £7,132 3½m.................(3:55)

3397⁴ ACT THE WAG (Ire) [117] (bl) 8-11-11 P Carberry, hld up in
tch, smooth hdwy 16th, cl up 4 out, dsptd ld whn lft clr 2 out,
eased nr finish.........................(5 to 1 op 4 to 1 tchd 11 to 2)   1
3589* ROYAL SAXON [92] 11-10-0 W Marston, chsd ldrs, rdn alng
13th, drvn and one pace 3 out, lft second at nxt, styd on frm
last.................................(8 to 1)   2
3201³ WESTWELL BOY [100] 11-10-8 A Dobbin, cl up, reminders
6th, hit 11th, hmpd and lost pl aftr 15th, drvn and styd on one
pace frm 3 out...........(7 to 2 tchd 4 to 1 and 3 to 1)   3
3365* LUCKY DOLLAR (Ire) [99] 9-10-7 A Thornton, hit second, hld
up beh, hdwy 11th, rdn alng nxt, styd on frm 3 out, nvr nr
to chal..........................(11 to 8 fav op 5 to 4 tchd 6 to 4)   4
3264 DONT TELL THE WIFE [108] 11-11-2 J A McCarthy, hld up
and beh, hit 10th, steady hdwy 14th, hit 16th, sn rdn and wknd.
.................................(9 to 1 op 8 to 1)   5
3586³ UPWELL [92] 13-10-0 K Johnson, led to 8, hit nxt and sn lost
pl, beh frm 18th.........................(50 to 1 op 33 to 1)   6
3399⁹ JAUNTY GIG [92] (bl) 11-10-0 L O'Hara, chsd ldrs, effrt and
hdwy 16th, 3rd whn badly hmpd and uns clr 2 out. (33 to 1)   ur
3245⁷ OVER THE STREAM [96] 11-10-4 A S Smith, prmnt, led 14th,
jnd 4 out, dsptd ld whn b lunded and uns rdr 2 out.
.................................(16 to 1 tchd 20 to 1)   ur
3264⁴ URANUS COLLONGES (Fr) [100] (bl) 11-10-8 L Wyer, cl up,
led 10th to 14th, lost pl aftr nxt and beh whn pld up aftr 4 out.
.................................(14 to 1)   pu
3584³ TRIONA'S HOPE (Ire) [92] 8-9-9 (5*) Mr M H Naughton, in tch,
hdwy to chase ldrs 16th, sn rdn and wknd bef 4 out, beh whn
pld up aftr 2 out.........................(66 to 1 op 50 to 1)   pu
Dist: 1½l, 3l, 1¾l, 30l, 2½l. 6m 53.20s. a 6.20s (10 Ran).
SR: 35/8/13/10/-/-/   (Robert Ogden), Martin Todhunter

3660 Keith Thomas Associates Novices' Chase Class E (5-y-o and up) £3,345 3m 3f.................(4:25)

3326² LITTLE MARTINA (Ire) 9-11-4 J R Kavanagh, led to 4th, cl up
till led 13th, rdn 2 out, hdd last, rallied und pres to ld nr finish.
.................................(7 to 4 on op 2 to 1 on)   1

3593 ANOTHER VENTURE (Ire) 7-11-2 P Carberry, hld up in midfield, steady hdwy 14th, challenged on bit 2 out, led last, rdn
flt, hdd nr finish.........................(7 to 1 op 6 to 1)   2
3259³ TACTIX 7-10-11 B Storey, hld up and beh, hdwy 14th, rdn 4
out, sn one pace.........................(16 to 1)   3
2909³ ALICAT (Ire) 6-11-2 M Foster, chsd ldrs, rdn alng and blun 4
out, sn wknd.............................(50 to 1)   4
3352 DONOVANS REEF 11-11-6 K Johnson, midfield, effrt and rdn
alng 14th, no hdwy.......................(50 to 1)   5
3436⁵ MORE JOY 9-10-9 (7*) C McCormack, cl up, led 4th to 13th,
wknd bef 3 out...........(25 to 1 tchd 33 to 1)   6
3005 ELLIOTT'S WISH (Ire) 6-11-2 (7*) Mr T J Barry, chsd ldrs, blun
6th, drvn alng and wknd bef 4 out.........(16 to 1)   7
2914 LYFORD CAY (Ire) 7-10-9 (7*) S Melrose, f 1st....(66 to 1)   f
3600³ GERMAN LEGEND 7-11-9 J Burke, badly hmpd 1st and sn wl
beh, tld off whn pld up bef 11th..........(12 to 1)   pu
3261⁵ MASTER FLASHMAN 8-11-2 G Lee, chsd ldrs, hit 7th and 8th,
wknd 14th, beh whn pld up 4 out....(11 to 2 op 6 to 1)   pu
2788⁵ GONE AWAY (Ire) 8-11-2 D Bentley, in tch, mstks, blun 11th,
hit 13th, blunded nxt, beh and pld up 5 out.
.................................(25 to 1 op 33 to 1)   pu
Dist: Nk, dist, nk, 1¾l, 8l, 1¾l. 6m 39.10s. a 6.10s (11 Ran).
SR: 29/27/-/-/-/-/   (Christopher Newport), D M Grissell

3661 Sedgefield Standard Open National Hunt Flat Class H (4,5,6-y-o) £1,437 2m 1f.................(4:55)

JUST NIP 4-10-1 (7*) R Burns, midfield, hdwy hfwy, led 3 fs
out, rdn appr last and ran on wl........(20 to 1 op 16 to 1)   1
3356⁴ GOING PRIMITIVE 6-11-0 Mr S Swiers, trkd ldrs, hdwy 6 fs
out, effrt 2 out, rdn entering last, edgd lft and no extr nr finish,
fnshd second, plcd 3rd...........(5 to 1 op 4 to 1)   2D
3251³ LANDLER 4-10-12 (3*) E Callaghan, hld up wl beh, hdwy 4 fs
out, rdn appr last, finishing well whn crrd lft nr line, fnshd 3rd,
plcd second...........(9 to 2 op 4 to 1 tchd 5 to 1)   2
OLD BOMBAY (Ire) 5-11-0 A Thornton, in tch, hdwy 5 fs out,
rdn 2 out, no extr und pres ins last.
.................................(13 to 2 op 5 to 1 tchd 7 to 1)   4
3251⁴ POLAR KING (Ire) 4-10-1 (7*) N Horrocks, cl up, led aftr 3 fs to
hfwy, led 5 out till hdd three out and grad wknd.
.................................(6 to 4 favt tchd 2 to 1)   5
HAPPY BLAKE 6-11-0 B Storey, hld up and beh, steady hdwy
6 fs out, chsd ldrs 3 out and sn rdn, wknd appr last. (33 to 1)   6
GIKONGORO 4-10-8 M Foster, hld up and beh, effrt and hdwy
o'r 3 fs out, rdn and one pace fnl 2 furlongs.
.................................(7 to 1 op 4 to 1)   7
2363⁸ CHIEF OF KHORASSAN (Fr) 5-11-0 G Lee, cl up, rdn alng
hfwy, sn lost pl and beh fnl 4 fs........(11 to 1 op 10 to 1)   8
3048 PERCY'S JOY 5-11-0 L Wyer, led 3 fs, cl up till lost pl and beh
frm hfwy...........................(10 to 1 op 8 to 1)   9
SWIFTLY SUPREME (Ire) 4-9-10 (7*) Tristan Davidson, beh
frm hfwy...........................(66 to 1 op 33 to 1)   10
NO TIME TO WAIT 6-11-0 O Pears, in tch, hdwy to ld hfwy,
pushed alng and hdd 5 fs out, sn wknd.
.................................(10 to 1 op 8 to 1 tchd 11 to 1)   11
TOEJAM 4-10-8 N Smith, hld up, gd hdwy hfwy, jnd ldrs o'r 4
fs out, rdn and wknd 3 out..........(25 to 1 op 20 to 1)   12
2687 JO LIGHTNING 4-10-8 K Johnson, al beh.....(50 to 1)   13
2764 FRUGAL 4-10-8 E Husband, beh frm hfwy........(33 to 1)   14
Dist: ½l, nk, 2l, 1½l, 5l, ¾l, 6l, 2l, 3l, 2l. 3m 53.80s. (14 Ran).
                                    (J R Turner), J R Turner

HEXHAM (firm)
Monday April 14th
Going Correction: MINUS 0.30 sec. per fur.

3662 Federation Brewery Novices' Chase Class E (5-y-o and up) £3,206 2m 110yds.................(2:10)

3584 GONE ASHORE (Ire) 6-11-0 A Dobbin, made al, clr 9th, hmpd
by loose horse aftr 2 out, styd on wl.
.................................(13 to 2 op 6 to 1 tchd 7 to 1)   1
3006 ALL CLEAR (Ire) 6-10-11 (3*) Mr C Bonner, sn prmnt, chsd wnr
frm 3 out, no imprsn.....................(7 to 1 op 5 to 1)   2
3434⁶ JONAEM (Ire) 7-11-0 K Johnson, hld up in rear, hdwy 7th, hit
9th, sn rdn alng, no imprsn frm 3 out.
.................................(9 to 4 fav op 11 to 4)   3
3395 SUPERMARINE 11-11-0 B Storey, hit 1st, chsd wnr till rdn
alng and one pace frm 3 out...............(25 to 1)   4
3585⁵ QUIXALL CROSSETT 12-10-7 (7*) Mr T J Barry, chsd ldrs,
reminders 5th, sn lost pl and tld off frm 7th........(33 to 1)   5
3433 MEESONETTE 5-9-9 (7*) C McCormack, chsd ldrs, blun 6th, f
nxt.................................(33 to 1)   f
3481 FAIR ALLY 7-11-0 D Parker, f second...(5 to 1 op 4 to 1)   f
724   SPEAKER'S HOUSE (USA) 8-11-7 T Reed, in tch whn badly
hmpd second and pld up.........(5 to 2 op 6 to 4)   pu
Dist: 6l, 5l, 15l, 18l. 4m 3.30s. a 5.30s (8 Ran).
                                    (Armstrong/Greenwell/Smithson), M A Barnes

3663 Buchanan Ales Novices' Hurdle Class E (4-y-o and up) £2,857 2½m 110yds.................(2:40)

3598^4 EASTCLIFFE (Ire) 5-11-0 G Cahill, *pld hrd, rapid hdwy to ld aftr second, rdn alng 2 out, styd on wl appr last.* .... (7 to 4 fav tchd 9 to 4) 1
3353^3 PAPPA CHARLIE (USA) 6-11-0 B Storey, *trkd ldrs, hdwy to chase wnr 3 out, rdn and one pace whn hit last.* ....(3 to 1 op 7 to 2) 2
3480^3 RAISE A DOLLAR 7-10-9 Mr S Swiers, *prmnt, rdn alng bef 3 out and sn one pace*.......(4 to 1 op 7 to 2 tchd 9 to 2) 3
3582 DONT FORGET CURTIS (Ire) 5-10-7 (7*) Miss S Lamb, *beh till styd on frm 2 out, nvr a factor*.........(20 to 1 op 14 to 1) 4
3262^6 KINGS MINSTRAL (Ire) 7-11-6 J Burke, *not fluent in rear, hdwy to chase ldrs 3 out, rdn and one pace appr nxt.* .... (16 to 1 op 12 to 1) 5
3598^7 AMBER HOLLY 8-10-9 F Perratt, *chsd ldrs, rdn alng 7th and sn one pace*...................... (20 to 1 tchd 25 to 1) 6
3127^7 OTTADINI (Ire) 5-10-11^2 T Reed, *in tch, hit 7th, sn rdn alng and outpcd*...........(40 to 1 op 33 to 1 tchd 50 to 1) 7
3303 CHIEF CHIPPIE 4-10-7 S McDougall, *chsd ldrs to 4th, sn lost pl and tld off frm 7th*.................(50 to 1 op 33 to 1) 8
1983^7 POSTED ABROAD (Ire) 5-10-9 (5*) S Taylor, *hld up, hdwy to chase ldrs 6th, rdn nxt and sn wknd, tld off 2 out.* .... (16 to 1 op 12 to 1) 9
3604^6 ALLERBY 9-11-0 A Dobbin, *led to aftr second, wth ldrs till rdn alng and outpcd whn f 6th*........... (6 to 1 tchd 5 to 1) f
MARGOT'S BOY 6-11-0 K Johnson, *al rear, tld off whn pld up betw last 2*.......................... (66 to 1 op 33 to 1) pu
2117^8 JED ABBEY 5-10-9 D Bentley, *chsd ldrs to 4th, sn outpcd and beh whn pld up aftr 3 out*.............(50 to 1 op 33 to 1) pu
Dist: 5l, 11l, 10l, 13l, nk, 7l, dist, 18l. 4m 51.00s. (12 Ran).
SR: 24/19/3/-/-/-/ (Mrs L E McKeown), W McKeown

3664 LCL Pils Handicap Chase Class F (0-105 5-y-o and up) £3,083 2½m 110yds...................... (3:10)

2495^8 BISHOPDALE [75] 16-10-9 F Perratt, *jmpd wl, made most, rdn 3 out, styd on strly to go clr appr last*........... (6 to 1) 1
2848^3 SHAWWELL [77] 10-10-11 B Storey, *cl up, rdn alng to chal and hit 3 out, hit nxt, sn drvn and one pace.* .... (Evens fav op 5 to 4) 2
3584^8 ARISTODEMUS [66] (bl) 8-10-0 K Johnson, *chsd ldg pair, hdwy to chal and hit 3 out, rdn and hit nxt, sn one pace.* .... (12 to 1 op 10 to 1) 3
3436 HUDSON BAY TRADER (USA) [90] 10-11-10 L Wyer, *outpcd and beh frm 6th, jmpd badly rght 9th and sn tld off.* .... (7 to 4 op 11 to 8) 4
Dist: 18l, 2l, 17l. 5m 4.20s. a 6.20s (4 Ran).
(S Chadwick), S G Chadwick

3665 LCL Lager Handicap Hurdle Class E (0-115 4-y-o and up) £2,395 2m .... (3:40)

3587* GLENUGIE [104] 6-11-10 N Bentley, *cl up, effrt 2 out, rdn to ld appr last, styd on wl.* (Evens fav op 11 to 10 tchd 5 to 4) 1
3587^4 ERINY (USA) [87] 8-10-4 (3*) E Callaghan, *trkd ldg pair, hdwy on inner to ld 2 out, hdd appr last, hit last, kpt on und pres.* .... (15 to 8 op 5 to 4 tchd 2 to 1) 2
3587^3 HIGHLAND WAY (Ire) [89] 9-10-2 (7*) C McCormack, *keen hold, trkd ldg pair, effrt 2 out, rdn and ev ch appr last, kpt on.* ....(7 to 2 op 3 to 1) 3
SON OF TEMPO (Ire) [80] 8-9-7 (7*) Miss S Lamb, *led, rdn and hdd 2 out, wknd quickly.* (40 to 1 op 33 to 1 tchd 50 to 1) 4
Dist: 1¼l, sht-hd, dist. 3m 59.90s. a 10.90s (4 Ran).
(Frazer Hines), G M Moore

3666 Chevy Chase Maiden Hunters' Chase Class H (5-y-o and up) £1,058 3m 1f.......................... (4:10)

SECRET BAY 8-12-7 Mr S Swiers, *led to 4 out, led ag'n 2 out, rdn clr appr last.* .... (5 to 4 on op 6 to 4 on tchd 11 to 10 on) 1
3458^2 UP FOR RANSOME (Ire) 8-12-0 (7*) Mr T J Barry, *cl up, led 4 out, rdn nxt, hdd 2 out and one pace und pres appr last.* ....(9 to 4 tchd 5 to 2) 2
3599^4 COOL YULE (Ire) 9-12-2 (5*) Miss P Robson, *al rear, beh frm 14th*.................. (9 to 1 op 8 to 1 tchd 10 to 1) 3
PARK DRIFT 11-12-0 (7*) Mr R Tate, *trkd ldrs, effrt 4 out, rdn nxt and sn wknd*......................(6 to 1 op 7 to 2) 4
3438^5 ALL OR NOTHING 9-11-9 (7*) Mr J Ewart, *cl up till uns rdr 3rd*.. (20 to 1) ur
Dist: 14l, 19l, 3l. 6m 27.70s. a 22.70s (5 Ran).
(Stuart Dent), C P Dennis

3667 Keoghans Maiden Open National Hunt Flat Class H (4,5,6-y-o) £1,486 2m............................ (4:40)

LUNAR DANCER 5-11-6 K Johnson, *trkd ldrs, smooth hdwy 5 fs out, led 3 furlongs out, sn clr.* .... (11 to 1 op 8 to 1 tchd 14 to 1) 1
2302 CONNEL'S CROFT 5-11-6 T Eley, *hld up in rear, steady hdwy 7 fs out, rdn 2 out and kpt on, no ch wth wnr.* ....(6 to 1 op 3 to 1) 2
MASTER BRADAN 4-11-0 D Bentley, *chsd ldrs, rdn alng and outpcd 4 fs out, styd on fnl 2 furlongs*... (14 to 1 op 8 to 1) 3
BUCKLEY HOUSE 5-11-6 T Reed, *cl up, led 4 fs out, hdd 3 out and one pace*............(5 to 1 op 4 to 1 tchd 6 to 1) 4
2858 BROOK HOUSE 6-11-1 B Storey, *made most till hdd 4 fs out, sn wknd*.......... (12 to 1 op 8 to 1 tchd 14 to 1) 5
GILSAN STAR 4-10-9 L Wyer, *trkd ldrs, hdwy 5 fs out, rdn o'r 3 out and sn wknd*...................... (7 to 2 op 5 to 1) 6
DUNNELLIE 4-10-4 (5*) S Taylor, *sn beh, tld off hfwy, some late hdwy*.............................. (10 to 1 op 5 to 1) 7
3356 NICKYS PERIL 5-10-8 (7*) S Haworth, *in tch till rdn and wknd o'r 5 fs out*........................ (33 to 1 op 20 to 1) 8
SATPURA 5-11-6 G Lee, *prmnt on outer, effrt and rdn alng o'r 4 fs out, sn wknd and eased*........(7 to 4 fav op 6 to 4) 9
Dist: 20l, 1½l, 8l, nk, 2½l, 9l, ¾l, 25l. 3m 50.70s. (9 Ran).
(J W Robson), J I A Charlton

SOUTHWELL (good)
Monday April 14th
Going Correction: MINUS 0.05 sec. per fur.

3668 Norfolk Conditional Jockeys' Handicap Chase Class F (0-100 5-y-o and up) £2,962 2m................ (2:00)

3185^3 DR ROCKET [77] (v) 12-10-10 (3*) X Aizpuru, *chsd ldrs, chlgd 3 out, led last, rdn out*..............(11 to 2 op 9 to 2) 1
3496* SLEAZEY [73] 6-10-9 M Berry, *al prmnt, led 4 out, rdn and hdd last, no extr*.................... (3 to 1 fav tchd 7 to 2) 2
3559* NO FIDDLING (Ire) [82] 6-11-4 D Fortt, *beh, hdwy 7th, nvr rchd ldrs*.....................(7 to 2 op 3 to 1 tchd 4 to 1) 3
3367^3 COUNT BARACHOIS (USA) [78] 9-11-0 J Magee, *led to second, led aftr 3rd, hdd 6 out, wknd 3 out.* .... (12 to 1 op 10 to 1 tchd 14 to 1) 4
3354 SHUT UP [64] (bl) 8-10-0 E Husband, *f 4th.* .... (25 to 1 op 33 to 1 tchd 50 to 1) f
3517* CORPUS [87] 8-11-9 D J Kavanagh, *led second, hdd aftr nxt, led 6 out, headed 4 out, sn rdn and wknd, f next.* ....(8 to 1 op 6 to 1) f
3370* CHORUS LINE (Ire) [90] 8-11-9 (3*) B Grattan, *mid-div, hdwy 6 out, 3rd and btn whn uns rdr 2 out*.......(9 to 2 op 4 to 1) ur
3191^2 MADAM ROSE (Ire) [64] (v) 7-9-4 (10*) David Turner, *beh frm 5th, tld off whn badly hmpd 3 out, mstk and uns rdr nxt.* .... (33 to 1 op 25 to 1 tchd 50 to 1) ur
1686 CHAIN SHOT [68] 12-10-4 O Burrows, *pld up and dismounted bef 3rd*.......................(33 to 1 tchd 40 to 1) pu
3496^4 HIGHLAND FLAME [67] 8-10-3^3 P Henley, *mid-div whn blun badly 4th, pld up bef nxt*.............(33 to 1 op 12 to 1) pu
BALI TENDER [64] 6-10-0 F Leahy, *prmnt to 6th, sn lost pl, tld off whn pld up bef 4 out.* (20 to 1 op 14 to 1 tchd 25 to 1) pu
Dist: 1½l, 9l, 4l. 4m 0.50s. a 6.50s (11 Ran).
SR: 12/6/6/-/-/-/ (The Rocketeers), R Dickin

3669 Daly Novices' Chase Class E (5-y-o and up) £3,050 3m 110yds.... (2:30)

3297^3 DREAM RIDE (Ire) 7-11-8 R Johnson, *al prmnt, chsd ldr 6 out, blun 4 out, led nxt, jmpd lft last 2, rdn out.* .... (13 to 8 fav op Evens) 1
3413* STORMHILL PILGRIM 8-11-8 P Hide, *led, hdd 3 out, no extr appr last*.......................(3 to 1 op 4 to 1) 2
2291 FORTRIA ROSIE DAWN 7-10-11 N Williamson, *hld up, hdwy 12th, blun 6 out, one pace frm 3 out.* .... (16 to 1 op 10 to 1 tchd 20 to 1) 3
3582^5 MICK THE YANK (Ire) (v) 7-11-2 Mr M Munrowd, *mid-div, effrt 12th, wknd 4 out*.................. (20 to 1 op 12 to 1) 4
3507^4 FIVE FLAGS (Ire) 9-10-11 (5*) G F Ryan, *sn wl beh, tld off whn jmpd slwly 13th*......... (8 to 1 tchd 9 to 1 and 12 to 1) 5
3358* CAPTIVA BAY 8-11-3 S Wynne, *chsd ldr to 13th, sn wknd.* .... (11 to 2 op 7 to 2 tchd 6 to 1) 6
3364^2 CHIAPPUCCI (Ire) 7-11-2 D Gallagher, *beh frm 5th, tld off whn pld up bef 6 out*.......... (15 to 2 op 5 to 1 tchd 8 to 1) pu
3045^7 DOCTOR DUNKLIN (USA) 8-11-2 J R Kavanagh, *tld off frm 5th, pld up bef 4 out*..................................(33 to 1) pu
3504 SWEET BUCK 8-11-2 V Slattery, *prmnt, hit 3rd, lost tch 8th, beh whn pld up bef 4 out*..............(50 to 1 op 33 to 1) pu
3556 LEDBURIAN (bl) 7-11-2 D Walsh, *not jump wl, sn well beh, tld off whn pld up bef tenth*..............(50 to 1 op 33 to 1) pu
Dist: 6l, 2½l, dist, 23l, 3½l. 6m 18.90s. a 24.90s (10 Ran).
(C G Clarke And G C Mordaunt), D Nicholson

3670 Harry Bissill Memorial Challenge Trophy Handicap Chase Class E (0-115 5-y-o and up) £4,077 2½m 110yds....................... (3:00)

2761* CHADWICK'S GINGER [95] 9-10-12 Derek Byrne, *al prmnt, jnd ldr 4th, led aftr four out, rdn out*.....(5 to 1 op 4 to 1) 1
3079^5 CHEEKA [83] 8-10-0 M Ranger, *prmnt, chsd wnr 2 out, styd on same pace r-in*..(33 to 1) 2
PERUVIAN GALE (Ire) [91] 8-10-8 Richard Guest, *trkd ldrs, rdn appr last ran on*.................. (8 to 1 op 7 to 1) 3
3533^2 PEARL EPEE [90] 8-10-7 R Johnson, *led, blun 3rd, hit 5 out, blunded nxt, sn hdd, mstk 3 out, styd on same pace.* ....(13 to 8 fav op 2 to 1) 4

3165^{4} HAWAIIAN YOUTH (Ire) [108] 9-11-8 (3*) D Fortt, *chsd ldrs, rdn 3 out, no imprsn frm nxt.* ....(9 to 2 op 7 to 2 tchd 5 to 1) 5
3291^{4} OXFORD QUILL [83] 10-10-0 D Morris, *hld up, hit tenth, nvr nr to chal*..(14 to 1) 6
3502^{3} FAIRY PARK [83] (v) 12-9-9 (5*) G Supple, *in tch, hit 7th, rdn 6 out, wknd 4 out*..(20 to 1) 7
2677^{7} CALL ME EARLY [83] 12-10-0 M Brennan, *hld up, nvr plcd to chal*..............................(50 to 1 op 33 to 1) 8
3536^{4} DE JORDAAN [110] 10-11-13 N Smith, *chsd ldrs till wknd 6 out*.......................................(8 to 1 op 6 to 1) 9
2154^{6} RIVER RED [83] 11-10-0 P McLoughlin, *sn wl beh.* (33 to 1) 10
2761 MORCAT [83] 8-9-11 (3*) F Leahy, *sn wl beh, tld off and pld up bef 6 out*..............................(20 to 1 op 16 to 1) pu

Dist: 3½l, nk, ½l, 1¼l, 24l, ¾l, 1l, 9l, 6l. 5m 15.40s. a 15.40s (11 Ran).

(W H Tinning), W H Tinning

3671 Jack Russell Novices' Hunters' Chase Class H (5-y-o and up) £1,084 3m 110yds.................. (3:30)

MISTER HORATIO 7-11-7 (7*) Mr M Lewis, *chsd ldrs, led appr 3 out, clr nxt*..............................(7 to 2 jt-fav op 5 to 2) 1
3586* GREENMOUNT LAD (Ire) 9-12-0 (7*) Mr P Cornforth, *hld up, hdwy 9th, styd on frm 2 out, not rch wnr.* ....(9 to 2 op 5 to 1 tchd 4 to 1) 2
WOLVER'S PET (Ire) 9-11-7 (7*) Mr D S Jones, *hld up, hit 8th, hdwy nxt, chsd wnr 3 out, styd on same pace.* ....(6 to 1 op 5 to 1 tchd 13 to 2) 3
3458* NOT MY LINE (Ire) 8-12-2 (5*) Mr A Sansome, *prmnt, jnd ldr 12th, led 4 out, sn hdd, one pace frm nxt.* (8 to 1 op 7 to 1) 4
BACK THE ROAD (Ire) 9-11-9^{2} (7*) Mr G Hanmer, *hld up, nvr nr ldrs*..(12 to 1) 5
ANDRETTI'S HEIR 11-11-13^{6} (7*) Mr A Bonson, *strted slwly, hdwy 9th, wkng whn blun and uns rdr 3 out.* ....(25 to 1 op 33 to 1) ur
GUNNER BOON 7-11-9 (5*) Miss P Jones, *prmnt till blun badly and uns rdr 6 out*..............................(7 to 1) ur
THE POINT IS 10-11-7 (7*) Mr P Hewitt, *led, hdd 4 out, sn wknd, pld up bef 2 out*..............................(7 to 2 jt-fav op 5 to 2 tchd 4 to 1) pu
2990 JUDGEROGER 11-11-7 (7*) Mr G Lewis, *beh frm tenth, pld up bef 5 out*..(14 to 1) pu
RYDERS WELLS 10-11-7 (7*) Mr S Walker, *sn in rear, hit 6th, beh whn pld up bef 12th*..............................(14 to 1) pu
GONALSTON PERCY (bl) 9-11-7 (7*) Mr N Kent, *strted slwly, al in rear, tld off and pld up bef tenth*............(100 to 1) pu

Dist: 10l, 1¼l, 2½l, dist. 6m 23.20s. a 29.20s (11 Ran).

(W D Lewis), W D Lewis

3672 Black And Tan 'National Hunt' Novices' Hurdle Class E (4-y-o and up) £2,679 2½m 110yds.......... (4:00)

2409^{9} FORBIDDEN WATERS (Ire) 6-11-0 N Williamson, *hld up, hdwy hfwy, led 2 out, drvn out*....(7 to 2 op 5 to 2 tchd 4 to 1) 1
3534^{6} IF ONLY 7-11-0 Gary Lyons, *chsd ldrs, rdn and ev ch 2 out, kpt on*..........................(3 to 1 fav op 5 to 2 tchd 7 to 2) 2
1679 GENERAL PARKER 6-11-0 A S Smith, *wth ldr, led 4 out, hdd 2 out, unbl to quicken r-in*..............(16 to 1 op 33 to 1) 3
3210^{6} THE EENS 5-11-0 D Walsh, *hld up, hdwy 5th, ev ch 2 out, styd on same pace*..........................(5 to 1 op 4 to 1) 4
SINGH SONG 7-10-9 W Fry, *prmnt, jnd ldrs 5 out, wknd aftr 3 out*..............................(14 to 1 op 20 to 1) 5
BET WILTSHIRE 5-11-0 S Wynne, *hld up, effrt appr 2 out, sn wknd*..............................(10 to 1 op 4 to 1) 6
2029 THE BUG 7-11-0 A Thornton, *made most to 4 out, sn wknd.* ....(8 to 1 op 6 to 1) 7
3022 STONEHENGE SAM (Ire) 5-11-0 S Curran, *prmnt till f 5th.* ....(33 to 1) f
2899 HABERDASHER 6-10-7 (7*) Mr J Goldstein, *f 3rd*...(33 to 1) f
3210^{8} RED OASSIS 6-11-0 Jacqui Oliver, *f 1st.* ....(16 to 1 op 12 to 1 tchd 20 to 1) f
SUTTON BOY 8-10-7 (7*) T Hogg, *chsd ldrs to 5th, pld up bef 5 out*..................(25 to 1 op 20 to 1 tchd 33 to 1) pu
2723 HONEST GEORGE 6-10-7 (7*) M Griffiths, *hld up, effrt 5th, wknd nxt, pld up bef 2 out*..............................(20 to 1) pu
RUNWELL HALL 5-10-9 P McLoughlin, *hmpd 1st, al in rear, tld off and pld up bef 2 out.* ....(20 to 1 op 16 to 1 tchd 25 to 1) pu

Dist: 2l, sht-hd, 1½l, 17l, 1¾l, 17l. 5m 8.50s. a 22.50s (13 Ran).

(Mrs Maureen J Russell), Miss Venetia Williams

3673 Fox Selling Hurdle Class G (4-y-o and up) £2,077 2m................ (4:30)

1783* KILNAMARTYRA GIRL 7-11-1 A Thornton, *chsd ldrs, led 2 out, sn clr*..............(15 to 2 op 4 to 1 tchd 8 to 1) 1
3440^{5} FONTANAYS (Ire) (bl) 9-10-13 (7*) R Hobson, *prmnt, chlgd 3 out, styd on same pace frm nxt.* ....(100 to 30 fav op 5 to 2 tchd 4 to 1) 2
2515^{7} FOLLOW DE CALL 7-11-0 D Walsh, *hld up, hdwy 5th, rdn appr 2 out, styd on same pace*...... (33 to 1 tchd 50 to 1) 3
3166^{4} SALMAN (USA) 11-11-3 (3*) Mr R Thornton, *prmnt, mstk 3rd, rdn appr 2 out, no ch whn hit last.* ....(13 to 2 op 7 to 1 tchd 8 to 1) 4

3512^{3} FAITHFUL HAND 7-11-0 Richard Guest, *trkd ldrs, led aftr 3 out, hdd nxt, sn btn, fnshd lme.* ....(9 to 2 op 7 to 2 tchd 3 to 1) 5
BODANTREE 6-11-6 N Williamson, *hld up, hdwy 3 out, rdn and btn nxt*..............(4 to 1 op 6 to 1 tchd 13 to 2) 6
2749^{3} GI MOSS 10-10-9 W Marston, *al in rear.* ....(33 to 1 op 20 to 1) 7
3002^{2} NOIR ESPRIT 4-10-5 (3*) F Leahy, *mid-div, hdwy 4th, ev ch 3 out, sn wknd*..............(9 to 2 op 5 to 1 tchd 6 to 1) 8
3469^{5} LAURA LYE (Ire) (bl) 7-10-9 C Llewellyn, *rcd keenly, made most frm second till aftr 3 out, wknd quickly.* ....(12 to 1 op 8 to 1 tchd 14 to 1) 9
3554^{6} CORPORATE IMAGE 7-11-0 P McLoughlin, *prmnt, mstk 1st, wknd 5 out*..............................(33 to 1 tchd 50 to 1) 10
3099 NEW REGIME (Ire) 4-10-3 B Fenton, *tld off frm 5th.* ....(50 to 1 op 33 to 1) 11
3457^{9} EMERALD VENTURE 10-11-0 D Gallagher, *sn beh, tld off and pld up bef 2 out*..............................(33 to 1 op 20 to 1) pu
3534^{9} POLAR WIND 8-11-0 M Foster, *slwly into strd, hdwy 4th wknd four out, pld up bef last.* (33 to 1 op 25 to 1 tchd 50 to 1) pu
3249^{3} LUCKER 10-10-11 (3*) E Husband, *led to second, wknd 4th, pld up bef 5 out*..............(33 to 1 op 20 to 1 tchd 50 to 1) pu

Dist: 9l, 3½l, 2½l, 1½l, 1½l, dist, 15l, dist. 3m 53.10s. a 7.10s (14 Ran).

SR: 8/4/-/-/-/-/ (P J Cronin), J Parkes

3674 Border Mares' Only Handicap Hurdle Class F (0-105 4-y-o and up) £2,162 2m.......................... (5:00)

3558^{8} DAILY SPORT GIRL [75] 8-11-10 Mr J L Llewellyn, *trkd ldrs, rdn 2 out, ran on to ld nr finish*..........(8 to 1 op 6 to 1) 1
3794^{4} CROMABOO CROWN [71] 6-11-6 W Worthington, *led, rdn whn lft clr 2 out, hdd nr finish*..........(9 to 1 op 7 to 1) 2
STYLISH ROSE (Ire) [70] 7-11-5 A S Smith, *mid-div, hdwy 5th, rdn 3 out, kpt on*..............................(10 to 1) 3
3124^{6} ARCTIC BLOOM [59] 11-10-5 (3*) F Leahy, *mid-div, hdwy 5th wknd 3 out*..............................(20 to 1 op 16 to 1) 4
3353 JENDORCET [73] 7-11-8 J Callaghan, *hld up, mstks, nvr nr ldrs*..............................(4 to 1 fav op 5 to 2) 5
2392^{2} SAXON MAGIC [70] 7-11-5 L Harvey, *in tch till wknd 4 out.* ....(5 to 1 op 4 to 1) 6
3287^{9} BALLY WONDER [56] 5-10-5 J Supple, *al in rear*...(33 to 1) 7
3582^{3} CATTON LADY [57] 7-10-6 R Johnson, *mid-div, hdwy 5th, sn wknd*..............................(9 to 2 tchd 4 to 1) 8
3287^{6} MILLERS GOLDENGIRL (Ire) [59] 6-10-3 (5*) G F Ryan, *prmnt till lost pl aftr 4th, sn beh*..............................(14 to 1) 9
3424 MRS JAWLEYFORD (USA) [75] 9-11-10 M Ranger, *hld up, hdwy 5th, chalg whn f 2 out*..............(11 to 2 op 9 to 2) f
893^{9} WATER MUSIC MELODY [65] 4-10-3 (5*) A Bates, *chsd ldrs to 5th, beh whn pld up bef 2 out*........(16 to 1 op 33 to 1) pu

Dist: 2l, 3l, 15l, 5l, 8l, 13l, hd, 26l. 3m 58.90s. a 12.90s (11 Ran).

(B J Llewellyn), B J Llewellyn

CHELTENHAM (good to firm)
Tuesday April 15th
Going Correction: NIL (races 1,3,6), MINUS 0.15 (2,4,5)

3675 Mitie Group Hurdle Class B (4-y-o and up) £5,474 2½m.......... (2:20)

3597^{2} PRIDWELL 7-11-8 R Dunwoody, *jmpd wl, made all, easily.* ....(8 to 1 on op 10 to 1 on) 1
3558* HANDY LASS 8-10-9 T J Murphy, *cl up till rdn and wknd appr last*..............................(6 to 1 op 5 to 1) 2

Won by 30l. 4m 53.60s. a 13.60s (2 Ran).

SR: -/-/ (Jones, Berstock And Fleet Partnership), M C Pipe

3676 Faucets For Mira Rada Showers Silver Trophy Chase Class A Grade 2 (5-y-o and up) £18,840 2m 5f.... (2:55)

3576^{2} STRONG PROMISE (Ire) 6-11-7 N Williamson, *chsd ldr, led 12th, easily*..............................(5 to 4 on tchd Evens) 1
3580^{9} GALES CAVALIER (Ire) 9-11-4 R Dunwoody, *led to 12th, ev ch 4 out, btn nxt*..............(5 to 1 op 6 to 1 tchd 9 to 2) 2
3576^{3} VIKING FLAGSHIP 10-11-4 R Johnson, *chsd ldrs, ev ch 4 out, wknd nxt*..............................(2 to 1 op 6 to 4) 3
3138 CELTIC LAIRD 9-11-0 D J Burchell, *al tld off.* ....(100 to 1 op 66 to 1 tchd 150 to 1) 4

Dist: 21l, 17l, dist. 5m 1.90s. b 2.10s (4 Ran).

SR: 83/59/42/-/ (G A Hubbard), G A Hubbard

3677 European Breeders Fund 'National Hunt' Novices' Handicap Hurdle Final Class A Grade 3 (5,6,7-y-o) £16,200 2½m................ (3:30)

3459* SIR DANTE (Ire) [94] 6-10-4 D O'Sullivan, *hdwy 3rd, led aftr 2 out, sn clr, ran on wl*..........(5 to 1 co-fav op 11 to 2) 1
3579 SILVER THYNE (Ire) [105] (bl) 5-11-1 D Leahy, *led till aftr 2 out, ran on, no ch wth wnr*..............(6 to 1 op 9 to 2) 2
3509* GOOD VIBES [115] 5-11-11 L Wyer, *hdwy 3 out, ev ch whn mstk 2 out, not reco'r*.............. (7 to 1 tchd 15 to 2) 3

3473* SEABROOK LAD [90] 6-10-0 W Marston, *hdwy 6th, ev ch 2 out, sn wknd*......................(5 to 1 co-fav) 4
3253[3] RHYTHM AND BLUES [93] 7-10-3 S McNeill, *al beh.* ....(20 to 1 op 16 to 1) 5
3040* LANCE ARMSTRONG (Ire) [106] (v) 7-10-13 (3*) D Fortt, *prmnt till wknd 3 out*....(12 to 1 op 10 to 1 tchd 14 to 1) 6
3052* FRIENDSHIP (Ire) [111] 5-11-7 M A Fitzgerald, *hdwy 3 out, prmnt whn f nxt*................(5 to 1 co-fav op 7 to 2) f
3506 FANTASY LINE [108] 6-11-4 A Thornton, *chsd ldrs, ev ch 2 out, 3rd and btn whn f last*......(5 to 1 co-fav tchd 9 to 2) f
2972* SPRING GALE (Ire) [116] 6-11-12 J Osborne, *prmnt till wknd quickly 7th, tld off whn pld up bef 2 out.* (12 to 1 op 9 to 1) pu
Dist: 14l, 3½l, 1l, 6l, 3½l. 4m 45.00s. a 5.00s (9 Ran).
SR: 26/23/29/3/-/9/ (Peter R Wilby), R Rowe

3678 Larkshill Engineering Golden Miller Handicap Chase Class C (0-135 5-y-o and up) £4,879 3¼m 110yds (4:00)

2935[5] LE MEILLE (Ire) [107] 8-10-9 N Williamson, *hld up in rear till steady hdwy 12th, led 2 out, drvn out*..............(7 to 1) 1
2600 GOD SPEED YOU (Ire) [108] (bl) 8-10-10 J R Kavanagh, *led 3rd to 2 out, mstk last, ran on.* ....(8 to 1 op 9 to 1 tchd 10 to 1) 2
2310 COPPER MINE [117] 11-11-5 J Osborne, *al prmnt, styd on frm 3 out*..............................(9 to 1 op 10 to 1) 3
3206 MUSTHAVEASWIG [121] 11-11-9 R Johnson, *mstk 12th, hdwy whn hit 4 out, ev ch 3 out, wknd appr last.* ....(13 to 2 op 7 to 1 tchd 6 to 1) 4
3114 JAMES PIGG [125] 10-11-13 R Dunwoody, *beh, reminders tenth, hdwy 16th, wknd 3 out.* ....(16 to 1 op 14 to 1 tchd 20 to 1) 5
3277* FOXGROVE [98] 11-9-11 (3*) Mr R Thornton, *al beh.* (50 to 1) 6
3510[3] ROYAL VACATION [114] 8-11-2 J Callaghan, *hdwy 8th, ev ch 4 out, wknd appr 2 out*..........(5 to 1 co-fav op 4 to 1) 7
3291[2] SUFFOLK ROAD [104] 10-10-6 D O'Sullivan, *wth ldrs, losing pl whn hit 13th, beh when pld up bef 3 out.* ....(13 to 2 op 11 to 2 tchd 7 to 1) pu
3565 FLIMSY TRUTH [114] 11-11-2 Mr M Harris, *led to 3rd, prmnt till wknd quickly 17th, tld off whn pld up bef 4 out.* (5 to 1 co-fav op 4 to 1) pu
3366* DENVER BAY [119] 10-11-4 (3*) L Aspell, *wl beh frm 13th, tld off whn pld up bef 4 out*.........(5 to 1 co-fav op 4 to 1) pu
Dist: 1¼l, 3l, 11l, 12l, nk, 18l. 6m 45.00s. a 13.00s (10 Ran).
(N J Mitchell), K R Burke

3679 Cirencester Novices' Handicap Chase Class D (0-115 5-y-o and up) £4,279 2m 5f................ (4:35)

3559[5] BOOTS N ALL (Ire) [76] 7-10-0 B Fenton, *al prmnt, led 3 out, clr whn blun 2 out, ran on*.............. (9 to 2 op 7 to 2) 1
3484* DECYBORG (Fr) [100] 6-11-10 R Dunwoody, *led second to 3 out, no ch wth wnr*..... (100 to 30 op 9 to 4 tchd 7 to 2) 2
2808[4] KEY TO MOYADE (Ire) [93] 7-11-3 W Marston, *mstks, hdwy 8th, outpcd 4 out, no ch aftr*.........(10 to 1 tchd 11 to 1) 3
3291* REGAL AURA (Ire) [80] 7-10-4 P Hide, *led to second, prmnt till rdn and wknd appr 4 out*...........(11 to 4 fav tchd 3 to 1) 4
3493* NORMARANGE (Ire) [86] 7-10-10 J R Kavanagh, *last whn blun and uns rdr tenth*...............(11 to 2 op 9 to 2) ur
3533[3] GLAMANGLITZ [80] 7-10-1 (3*) Mr R Thornton, *uns rdr aftr 1st*...................... (5 to 1 op 6 to 1 tchd 9 to 2) ur
3133 PLASSY BOY (Ire) [76] (v) 8-10-0 N Williamson, *beh and rdn alng, hdwy 11th, 3rd and ev ch whn pld up lme bef 4 out.* ....(25 to 1) pu
Dist: 7l, 3l, dist. 5m 13.40s. a 9.40s (7 Ran).
(Mrs Toni S Tipper), G B Balding

3680 Stoke Orchard Juvenile Novices' Handicap Hurdle Class C (4-y-o) £4,788 2½m..................(5:10)

3276* CHIEF MOUSE [100] 11-4 P Carberry, *hdwy 3 out, hrd rdn aftr 2 out, jnd ldr and lft clr last, eased r-in*... (7 to 2 op 3 to 1) 1
3498[5] STERLING FELLOW [82] 9-7 (7*) Mr S Durack, *hdwy appr 2 out, lft poor second last, ran on*..... (12 to 1 tchd 14 to 1) 2
3501[2] ARROGANT HEIR [87] 10-5 Derek Byrne, *some hdwy 2 out, lft poor 3rd last, nvr on terms*.........(3 to 1 fav op 5 to 1) 3
3541[2] GIVE AND TAKE [106] 11-10 D Walsh, *led to second, chsd ldr till wknd appr 2 out*.....(100 to 30 op 9 to 4 tchd 4 to 1) 4
3463* NOBLE COLOURS [95] 10-6 (7*) Mr A Wintle, *pld hrd, led second, clr 7th, slight ld and staying on whn f last.* ....(7 to 2 op 3 to 1 tchd 4 to 1) f
2553 SQUIRE'S OCCASION (Can) [100] 10-11 (7*) J Parkhouse, *5th and no ch whn blun and uns rdr 2 out*... (7 to 1 op 4 to 1) ur
Dist: 1¼l, 17l, 30l. 4m 50.70s. a 10.70s (6 Ran).
(Bill Gavan), F Jordan

EXETER (firm)
Tuesday April 15th
Going Correction: MINUS 0.20 sec. per fur.

3681 Buzzard Juvenile Novices' Hurdle Class E (4-y-o) £2,332 2¼m...(2:10)

3629* MAJOR DUNDEE (Ire) (v) 11-4 A P McCoy, *made all, not fluent 5th, drvn out.* ....(5 to 4 on tchd 11 to 8 on and 11 to 10 on) 1
3489* ANNA SOLEIL (Ire) 11-4 D Thomas, *chsd wnr, chlgd 3 out, sn rdn, effrt r-in, one pace*............(11 to 10 tchd 5 to 4) 2
3402 ROYAL MEMBER 10-7 E Byrne, *sn tld off.* ....(66 to 1 op 33 to 1 tchd 100 to 1) 3
3463[4] SPENCER STALLONE 10-7 (5*) D Salter, *sn tld off.* (33 to 1) 4
Dist: 2l, dist, 7l. 4m 3.10s. a 4.10s (4 Ran).
SR: 13/11/-/-/ (Michael R Jaye), M C Pipe

3682 Pauline Trundle Novices' Chase Class E (5-y-o and up) £2,948 2m 7f 110yds...................... (2:45)

3404[3] SPRING TO IT 11-11-2 A P McCoy, *made all, hrd pressed frm 3 out, drw clr appr last*..........(Evens fav op 11 to 8) 1
3543[3] JONJAS CHUDLEIGH 10-11-2 J Frost, *hld up, chsd wnr frm 11th, str chal from 3 out, btn appr last*.... (8 to 1 op 9 to 2) 2
3465[3] TRUST DEED (USA) (bl) 9-11-8 G Upton, *hld up, not fluent second, struggling frm 8th, rallied tenth, wknd from 12th.* ....(7 to 4 tchd 2 to 1) 3
3613[3] ELITE GOVERNOR (Ire) 8-10-9 (7*) Mr L Baker, *chsd wnr to 11th, sn rdn and wknd*..... (8 to 1 op 9 to 2 tchd 9 to 1) 4
Dist: 9l, 22l, 12l. 5m 44.30s. a 10.30s (4 Ran).
(M C Pipe), M C Pipe

3683 Tote Credit Handicap Hurdle Class C (0-130 4-y-o and up) £4,448 2m 3f 110yds...................... (3:20)

3403* NORTHERN STARLIGHT [118] 6-12-0 A P McCoy, *made all, not fluent 4th, easily*... (6 to 4 fav op 5 to 4 tchd 7 to 4) 1
3544[2] KIWI CRYSTAL (NZ) [90] 8-10-0 R Greene, *hld up, outpcd appr 4th, styd on frm 2 out, wnt second r-in, no ch wth wnr.* ....(11 to 4 op 9 to 4 tchd 3 to 1) 2
3516* SEVSO [90] 8-10-0 V Slattery, *in tch, chsd wnr frm 5th, rdn and no imprsn appr 2 out, lost second pl r-in.* ....(4 to 1 op 7 to 2 tchd 9 to 2) 3
3546[3] CASTLECONNER (Ire) [90] (bl) 6-10-0 Mr A Holdsworth, *beh frm second, no imprsn aftr*........... (20 to 1 op 25 to 1) 4
957* BORN TO PLEASE (Ire) [98] 5-10-8 G Tormey, *sn rdn alng, chsd wnr to 5th, wknd frm 3 out*.......(7 to 2 tchd 4 to 1) 5
Dist: 5l, ½l, 19l, 1¼l. 4m 23.70s. a 2.70s (5 Ran).
SR: 34/1/ (Arthur Souch), M C Pipe

3684 Peter Owen Farewell Novices' Hurdle Class E (5-y-o and up) £2,521 2m 3f 110yds.....................(3:50)

3546* COUNTRY LOVER (v) 6-11-6 A P McCoy, *al gng wl, hld up in tch, chsd ldr appr 2 out, led on bit r-in, not extended.* ....(10 to 1 on op 8 to 1 on) 1
TOMMY COOPER 6-11-0 E Byrne, *led, rdn alng 3 out, hdd r-in, no ch wth wnr*..................... (9 to 1 op 7 to 1) 2
262[7] CARNIVAL CLOWN 5-11-0 R Greene, *chsd ldr till rdn appr 2 out, wknd bef last*.................. (33 to 1 op 14 to 1) 3
3270[7] DECEIT THE SECOND 5-11-0 S Burrough, *hld up, rdn alng frm 6th, wknd aftr nxt*..............(100 to 1 op 66 to 1) 4
2433 MORECEVA (Ire) 7-11-0 T Dascombe, *hld up, rdn 6th, wknd frm nxt*.............. (40 to 1 op 33 to 1 tchd 50 to 1) 5
Dist: ½l, 13l, 15l, 10l. 4m 35.30s. a 14.30s (5 Ran).
(Pond House Gold), M C Pipe

3685 Tote Bookmakers Handicap Chase Class D (0-125 5-y-o and up) £3,629 2m 3f 110yds................(4:25)

3360[2] COOLTEEN HERO (Ire) [89] 7-11-2 P Holley, *chsd clr ldr, mstk 9th, lost second nxt, effrt whn blun 4 out, rallied frm 2 out, led r-in, all out*.......................... (8 to 1 op 5 to 1) 1
HENLEY REGATTA [93] 9-11-6 S Burrough, *hld up, chsd ldr frm tenth, cld from nxt, led 4 out, hdd and no extr r-in.* ....(9 to 1 op 6 to 1 tchd 12 to 1) 2
3040 MR PLAYFULL [91] 7-11-4 J Frost, *hld up, rdn and lost tch 9th, styd on ag'n frm 2 out.* ....(3 to 1 op 11 to 4 tchd 100 to 30) 3
3565 POND HOUSE (Ire) [97] 8-11-10 A P McCoy, *led, sn clr, hdd 4 out, tired 3rd whn blun last*........(2 to 1 fav tchd 9 to 4) 4
922[5] TANGO'S DELIGHT [73] 9-10-0 V Slattery, *hld up, wknd 9th, beh whn f last*.................... (25 to 1 op 20 to 1) f
3502* GOOD FOR A LAUGH [82] 13-10-2 (7*) Mr G Shenkin, *hld up, wknd frm 8th, tld off whn pld up bef 11th.* ....(9 to 2 op 7 to 2 tchd 5 to 1) pu
1471 MILLIES OWN [93] 10-11-6 G Tormey, *hld up, struggling frm 8th, tld off whn pld up bef tenth*....... (12 to 1 op 14 to 1) pu
3333[3] MAMMY'S CHOICE (Ire) [94] 7-11-7 J Culloty, *beh frm 7th, tld off whn pld up bef nxt*................ (8 to 1 op 5 to 1) pu
Dist: 3l, 12l, 3l. 4m 37.30s. a 4.30s (8 Ran).
SR: 6/7/-/-/-/ (J P M & J W Cook), R H Alner

3686 Kestrel Conditional Jockeys' Handicap Hurdle Class F (0-105 4-y-o and up) £2,031 2¼m............. (5:00)

3513* MRS EM [92] 5-11-5 (5*) L Cummins, *al hndy, chlgd 2 out, sn led, ran on wl*............(9 to 4 op 6 to 4 tchd 5 to 2) 1

2372⁵ TIME LEADER [72] 5-10-1 (3*) X Aizpuru, *keen hold, hld up, prog appr 3rd, led nxt, hrd pressed 2 out, sn hdd, one pace* ....(100 to 30 op 4 to 1 tchd 9 to 2) 2

3275³ COMMANCHE CREEK [75] 7-10-7 Sophie Mitchell, *led till aftr second, remained prmnt till wknd appr 2 out* ....(2 to 1 fav op 11 to 4 tchd 3 to 1) 3

3614⁷ CHILI HEIGHTS [72] (v) 7-9-13 (5*) M Griffiths, *wth ldr, led aftr second to 4th, wknd appr 2 out*............(50 to 1 op 25 to 1) 4

3106³ DENOMINATION (USA) [80] 5-10-7 (5*) B Moore, *trkd ldrs, rdn and wknd frm 3 out*..............(13 to 2 op 5 to 1) 5

1724 UP THE TEMPO [68] 8-10-0 T Dascombe, *trkd ldrs, rdn and wknd frm 3 out*....(20 to 1 op 16 to 1 tchd 25 to 1) 6

STATION EXPRESS (Ire) [68] 9-10-0 Guy Lewis, *nvr trbld ldrs.* ....(50 to 1 op 25 to 1) 7

3546 ROGERSON [68] 9-10-0 D Salter, *nvr dngrs.* ....(66 to 1 op 33 to 1) 8

Dist: 8l, 4l, nk, 16l, 7l, 1¼l, 17l. 4m 6.70s. a 7.70s (8 Ran).
(G Z Mizel), P F Nicholls

CHELTENHAM (good to firm)
Wednesday April 16th
Going Correction: MINUS 0.05 sec. per fur.

3687 New Barn Lane Novices' Hurdle Class D (4-y-o and up) £2,957 2m 1f .... (2:20)

3316⁴ TALATHATH (Fr) 5-11-5 R Johnson, *al hndy, chalg and gng wl whn not much room appr last, led r-in, rdn clr.* ....(5 to 4 op Evens tchd 11 to 8) 1

3534⁴ KING OF SPARTA 4-10-13 J Osborne, *led 5 out, rgned ld appr last, hdd and wknd r-in.* ....(Evens fav op 11 to 10 tchd 6 to 5) 2

3265² DISTANT STORM 4-10-8 V Slattery, *hld up, rdn alng frm 3rd, improved 3 out, wknd 2 out.* ....(9 to 1 op 5 to 1 tchd 10 to 1) 3

3117⁶ DUBAI DOLLY (Ire) 4-10-3 S Curran, *hld up, gd hdwy frm 3 out, led nxt, hdd appr last, sn wknd.* ....(66 to 1 op 25 to 1 tchd 100 to 1) 4

ALLEZ CYRANO (Ire) 6-11-0 D Leahy, *keen hold, chsd ldr frm second till appr 3 out, wknd bef nxt.* ....(33 to 1 op 16 to 1 tchd 40 to 1) 5

Dist: 12l, 4l, 1½l, 22l. 4m 0.00s. a 6.00s (5 Ran).
SR: 23/5/
(Million In Mind Partnership (6)), D Nicholson

3688 Holman Cup Handicap Chase Class C (0-130 5-y-o and up) £5,121 2m 110yds............................. (2:55)

2437² SEEK THE FAITH (USA) [107] 8-11-2 R Dunwoody, *wtd wth, prog 8th, led last, ran on*............(2 to 1 fav op 9 to 4) 1

3517 NEWLANDS GENERAL [115] 11-11-10 P Hide, *led, sn clr, blun and hdd last, kpt on same pace r-in.* ....(9 to 2 op 3 to 1 tchd 5 to 1) 2

3367⁴ RED BEAN [95] 9-10-4 R Johnson, *chsd ldr frm second, chlgd 3 out, rdn and one pace...*(11 to 4 op 9 to 4 tchd 3 to 1) 3

3157⁷ PIMBERLEY PLACE (Ire) [115] 9-11-10 C Llewellyn, *strted slwly, hdwy 4th, outpcd 8th, rdn and rallied tenth, one pace appr 2 out*..............(20 to 1 op 16 to 1 tchd 25 to 1) 4

3490² RUSTIC GENT (Ire) [91] 9-10-0 D J Burchell, *chsd ldr to second, beh frm 8th*..............(25 to 1 op 14 to 1) 5

3371 NORTHERN OPTIMIST [91] 9-10-0 N Williamson, *beh frm 5th.* ....(8 to 1 op 6 to 1) 6

Dist: 1½l, 6l, 1½l, 20l, 10l. 4m 1.00s. a 8.00s (6 Ran).
SR: -/6/-/
(R H F Matthews), M Sheppard

3689 Lynx Express Handicap Hurdle Class B (5-y-o and up) £5,141 2m 5f 110yds........................ (3:30)

3575² COURBARIL [124] (bl) 5-11-10 A P McCoy, *chsd clr ldr till appr 2 out, kpt on und prss to ld r-in, all out.* ....(11 to 4 fav op 2 to 1 r-in) 1

3285* THE TOISEACH (Ire) [114] (v) 6-11-0 J Osborne, *not fluent, led, sn clr, hdd r-in, no extr.* ....(11 to 2 op 9 to 2 tchd 6 to 1) 2

3612* EL DON [110] 5-10-10 (5ex) K Gaule, *hld up, prog frm 5th, chsd ldr appr 2 out, ever cl r-in, unbl to quicken last 50 yards.* ....(3 to 1 op 7 to 2) 3

3516 SANTELLA BOY (USA) [106] (bl) 5-10-6 J Railton, *hld up, hdwy 6th, one pace out, no imprsn.* ....(7 to 1 op 5 to 1 tchd 8 to 1) 4

3440² HOLY JOE [102] 15-10-2 D J Burchell, *beh frm 7th.* ....(14 to 1 op 10 to 1) 5

3445⁸ SWING QUARTET (Ire) [100] 7-10-0 C Llewellyn, *beh frm 6th.* ....(12 to 1 op 8 to 1) 6

1926⁷ NICKLE JOE [100] 11-9-7 (7*) Mr O McPhail, *beh frm 5th, tld off*...................(66 to 1 op 33 to 1) 7

2958 SO PROUD [120] 12-11-6 C Maude, *beh frm 6th, tld off whn pld up and dismounted bef last*.....(20 to 1 op 14 to 1) pu

3116⁷ HENRIETTA HOWARD (Ire) [121] 7-11-7 J F Titley, *beh till pld up bef 5th.*...................(4 to 1 op 11 to 4) pu

Dist: 2l, hd, 8l, 13l, 3l, dist. 5m 2.80s. a 4.80s (9 Ran).
SR: 38/26/22/10/-/-/
(Richard Green (Fine Paintings)), M C Pipe

3690 Howard E. Perry Hunters' Chase Class H (6-y-o and up) £2,801 3¼m 110yds....................... (4:00)

3153⁵ DOUBLE SILK 13-12-0 (7*) Mr E Williams, *chsd ldr, led 3rd, made rst, clr 14th, styd on strly fnl 2.* ....(15 to 8 fav op 2 to 1 tchd 9 to 4) 1

3615* SOME-TOY 11-11-10 (7*) Miss L Blackford, *hld up, hdwy to chase wnr tenth, rdn whn hit 3 out, one pace.* ....(13 to 2 op 5 to 1 tchd 7 to 1) 2

3615² RUSTY BRIDGE 10-11-10 (7*) Mr R Burton, *led to 3rd, rdn and lost pl 11th, kpt on one pace frm 2 out.* ....(14 to 1 op 10 to 1 tchd 16 to 1) 3

3529* IDIOTIC 9-11-12 (5*) Mr C Vigors, *hdwy 7th, mstk and lost pl tenth, rallied 12th, rdn whn hit 3 out, fdd r-in.* ....(7 to 2 op 3 to 1) 4

3026³ YOUNG BRAVE 11-12-0 (7*) Mr M G Miller, *head up, prog 17th, wkng whn hit 3 out..*(13 to 2 op 9 to 1 tchd 7 to 1) 5

3274³ THE MALAKARMA 11-11-12 (5*) Mr B Pollock, *hld up, wknd 11th, tld off.*...................(5 to 1 op 9 to 2) 6

3096* JUPITER MOON 8-11-7 (7*) Mr J M Pritchard, *hld up, blun and one pace fm 5th*......(16 to 1 op 14 to 1 tchd 20 to 1) ro

3574* L'UOMO PIU 13-11-7 (7*) Mr O McPhail, *prmnt, chsd ldr frm 6th to tenth, beh from 12th, tld off whn pld up bef 4 out.* ....(25 to 1 op 20 to 1) pu

Dist: 11l, 11l, 3l, 1¾l, 22l. 6m 45.60s. a 13.60s (8 Ran).
(R C Wilkins), R C Wilkins

3691 Birdlip Novices' Chase Class D (5-y-o and up) £3,397 2m 5f.......(4:35)

3477* FORMAL INVITATION (Ire) 8-11-8 R Johnson, *rcd keenly, in tch, chsd ldr frm 5th, led last, ran on strly r-in.* ....(5 to 2 op 9 to 4 tchd 11 to 4 and 3 to 1) 1

3326* WEE WINDY (Ire) 8-11-8 P Hide, *made most to last, rdn and outpcd by wnr*........(3 to 1 op 9 to 4 tchd 100 to 30) 2

3638* GREENBACK (Bel) 6-11-12 N Williamson, *heald up, hdwy 11th, mstk 4 out, chlgd nxt, sn rdn, wknd frm 2 out.* ....(6 to 5 on op 11 to 8 tchd 6 to 5 on and 11 to 10 on) 3

3492³ PINOCCIO 10-11-2 W Marston, *wth ldr to 3rd, mstk and beh frm 7th, tld off.*........(50 to 1 op 33 to 1 tchd 66 to 1) 4

Dist: 9l, 6l, dist. 5m 14.90s. a 10.90s (4 Ran).
(The Plough Partnership), D Nicholson

3692 Cheltenham Sponsorship Club Novices' Handicap Hurdle Class E (0-105 4-y-o and up) £2,996 2m 5f 110yds........................ (5:10)

3289* STORMYFAIRWEATHER (Ire) [97] 5-11-8 M A Fitzgerald, *hld up in tch, chsd ldr frm 5th, led aftr 2 out, rdn out.* ....(9 to 2 op 7 to 2) 1

3560* MYSTIC HILL [84] 6-10-9 J Frost, *hdwy 4th, challenging whn jumped on bend appr out r-in.* ....(7 to 2 fav op 3 to 1 tchd 4 to 1) 2

1211 PLINTH [79] 6-10-4 N Williamson, *hld up, hdwy 7th, chlgd 2 out, one pace appr last.*..............(14 to 1 op 10 to 1) 3

3544³ SHAHRANI [103] (v) 5-12-0 A P McCoy, *chsd ldr, jmpd slwly second, led 4th, hdd aftr 2 out, wkng whn squeezed up on bend appr last.*..............(7 to 1 op 5 to 1) 4

3016⁷ KILLING TIME [75] 6-10-0 D J Burchell, *nvr nr to chal.* ....(16 to 1 op 14 to 1 tchd 20 to 1) 5

3468⁴ GO FROLIC [75] 9-10-0 R Johnson, *beh frm 6th.* ....(16 to 1 op 33 to 1) 6

3503⁵ MR CHRISTIE [85] 5-10-10 C Maude, *beh frm 6th.* ....(10 to 1 op 8 to 1 tchd 10 to 1) 7

3194⁴ EQUITY'S DARLING (Ire) [82] 5-10-7 P Hide, *al beh.* ....(33 to 1 op 20 to 1) 8

3473³ SCENIC WATERS [75] 5-10-0 C Llewellyn, *beh frm 7th.* ....(5 to 1 tchd 11 to 2 and 6 to 1) 9

1419⁶ HYLTERS CHANCE (Ire) [77] 6-10-2 L Harvey, *led to 4th, beh frm 7th.*...................(9 to 1 op 8 to 1) 10

3359⁵ COLWALL [86] 6-10-4 (7*) Mr J Goldstein, *hld up, hit 5th, sn beh, tld off whn blun and uns rdr last.* (20 to 1 op 14 to 1) ur

2295 GLISTENING DAWN [85] (bl) 7-10-10 S McNeill, *trkd ldrs to 7th, sn wknd, tld off whn pld up bef 2 out.* ....(20 to 1 op 12 to 1) pu

3296 CLASSIC MODEL [75] 6-10-0 R Bellamy, *pld up aftr 3rd, sddl slpd.*...................(50 to 1 op 33 to 1) pu

Dist: 1½l, 3½l, 10l, 11l, 1¼l, 1½l, 12l, 10l, 5l. 5m 4.70s. a 6.70s (13 Ran).
(Mrs Christopher Hanbury), N J Henderson

NAVAN (IRE) (good)
Wednesday April 16th

3693 Webster Beginners Chase (5-y-o and up) £3,082 2½m............. (3:30)

3339⁴ CRISTYS PICNIC (Ire) 7-11-9 C O'Dwyer,..........(5 to 1) 1

3379⁴ LET BUNNY RUN (Ire) 7-11-9 D H O'Connor, ...(14 to 1) 2

3341² CORRIGEEN RAMBLER (Ire) 8-11-4 (5*) A O'Shea, (8 to 1) 3

3454³ BRAVE FOUNTAIN (Ire) 9-12-0 C F Swan, ...(11 to 10 fav) 4

2756 FIELD OF DESTINY (Ire) (bl) 8-11-1 (3*) K Whelan, ..(8 to 1) 5

3645 BORRISMORE FLASH (Ire) 9-12-0 T P Rudd, ...(14 to 1) f

3378 BELLA BROWNIE (Ire) 6-11-4 T Horgan, ...(12 to 1) f

2867 DIORRAING (Ire) 7-11-2 (7*) B J Geraghty, ... (8 to 1)   ur
Dist: 5½l, 2l, 4l, dist. 5m 3.30s. r.30 and nil nil wknd. (8 Ran).

(Ramojo Syndicate), M F Morris

3694 Newgrange Maiden Hurdle (4-y-o and up) £3,082 3m . . . . (4:00)

3380* LADY ELISE (Ire) 6-11-2 (7*) Mr J M Roche, ... (2 to 1)   1
3520³ ARCTIC GALE (Ire) 6-11-1 C F Swan, ... (7 to 4 on)   2
3178 KNOCKMOYLAN CASTLE (Ire) 7-11-1 (5*) P Morris,
. . . . (14 to 1)   3
3429 ROSENWALD (Ire) 7-11-3 (3*) J Butler, ... (8 to 1)   su
Dist: 3l, 2½l. 5m 41.00s. (4 Ran).

(Mrs Mary Devereux), R O'Connor

3695 Dowth Handicap Hurdle (0-116 4-y-o and up) £3,082 3m . . . . (4:30)

3377* GENTLE MOSSY [-] 5-10-10 D H O'Connor, . . . (5 to 1)   1
3520¹ ATHA BEITHE (Ire) [-] (bl) 6-11-0 (5*) B J Geraghty, . .(4 to 1)   2
3448* COOLREE LORD [-] (bl) 6-9-1 (7*) P G Hourigan,
. . . . (3 to 1 fav)   3
3417² CASTLE COIN (Ire) [-] 5-11-7 C F Swan, ... (4 to 1)   4
3417 OVER THE WALL (Ire) [-] 8-9-7 C O'Brien, ... (25 to 1)   5
3227 JOSHUA TREE [-] 12-10-1 J K Kinane, ... (33 to 1)   6
2160⁵ DICK MCCARTHY (Ire) [-] 5-10-2 T P Treacy, ...(10 to 1)   7
3429* MORAL SUPPORT (Ire) [-] 5-10-10 C O'Dwyer, ...(11 to 2)   8
Dist: 1l, sht-hd, ½l, 1½l. 5m 35.90s. (8 Ran).

(Purple And Gold Syndicate), James Joseph O'Connor

3696 Rossnaree Handicap Hurdle (0-116 4-y-o and up) £3,082 2¼m . . . (5:00)

3643² ANNEALAINE (Ire) [-] 6-9-4 (7*) B J Geraghty, . . .(2 to 1 fav)   1
2168⁴ JACK YEATS (Ire) [-] 5-11-8 S C Lyons, ...(9 to 4)   2
3642⁷ EIRE (Ire) [-] 8-9-5 (7*) D A McLoughlin, ... (12 to 1)   3
2227⁶ LOUISES FANCY (Ire) [-] 7-10-4 (7*) L J Fleming, . . (7 to 1)   4
3606⁶ NORMINS HUSSAR (Ire) [-] (bl) 5-9-9 F Woods, . . .(20 to 1)   5
3421 GLEN CAMDEN (Ire) [-] (bl) 5-10-9 C O'Dwyer, ...(8 to 1)   6
252⁴ BOLD FLYER [-] 14-10-13 K F O'Brien, ...(9 to 1)   7
Dist: 6l, ½l, 4l, 6l. 4m 16.80s. (7 Ran).

(N Coburn), Noel Meade

3697 Navan Races Driving Range (Pro-Am) Flat Race (5-y-o and up) £3,082 2¼m . . . . (5:30)

3421³ KINNEGAD GIRL (Ire) 5-11-8 Mr A J Martin, ... (8 to 1)   1
3421² DINES (Ire) 5-11-6 (7*) G T Hourigan, ...(5 to 1)   2
    GENERAL PERK (Ire) 6-11-7 (7*) Mr J Bailey, ... (12 to 1)   3
3380⁵ SISTER ROSE (Ire) 6-11-2 (7*) Mr P Fahey, ...(12 to 1)   4
    CLANAWHILLAN (Ire) 7-12-0 Mr D Marnane, ...(12 to 1)   5
3342³ COTTAGE LORD (Ire) 5-11-5 (3*) Mr R Walsh, ...(10 to 1)   6
3547 THE TEXAS KID (Ire) 6-12-0 Mr P Fenton, ... (14 to 1)   7
3349⁹ BALMY NATIVE (Ire) 5-11-6 (7*) M D Murphy, ...(12 to 1)   8
2737 NIANTIC BAY (Ire) 5-11-6 (7*) Mr J P McNamara, . . (25 to 1)   9
3608 NOBLE TUNE 8-11-11 (3*) Mr D Valentine, ...(33 to 1)   10
3380 MOLL'S CHOICE (Ire) 6-11-2 (7*) Mr J M Roche, . . (20 to 1)   11
    SASSI LAD (Ire) 6-11-7 (7*) Mr D M Bean, ... (25 to 1)   12
    MR FREEMAN (Ire) 6-11-7 (7*) S P McCann, ...(10 to 1)   13
1554⁷ RED OAK (Ire) 6-11-7 (7*) Mr A Fleming, ...(20 to 1)   14
64⁶ BAY FALLOUGH (Ire) 8-11-7 (7*) Mr P J McCrickard,
. . . . (10 to 1)   15
    BYPHARTHEBEST (Ire) 5-11-1 (7*) Mr J Cash, ...(11 to 1)   16
    MSADI MHULU (Ire) 6-11-2 (7*) Mrs S Treacy, ...(25 to 1)   17
2649 CNOC MAINE 10-11-2 (7*) Mr R F Coonan, ...(40 to 1)   18
    BLUME FONTAINE (Ire) 6-11-7 (7*) Mr J D O'Connell,
. . . . (10 to 1)   19
2172⁶ ANTRIM TOWN (Ire) 6-12-0 Mr G J Harford, ... (13 to 2)   20
    FISH AMBLE STREET (Ire) 5-11-13 Mr B M Cash, ...(5 to 1)   21
3394 YOU'RE IN LUCK (Ire) 6-11-6 (7*) Mr A FitzGerald, . .(50 to 1)   22
    COLONEL CRUMP (Ire) 5-11-8 (5*) Mr G Elliott, ...(12 to 1)   23
    BAYTOWNGHOST (Ire) 7-11-7 (7*) Mr V P Devereux,
. . . . (33 to 1)   24
2172 SAN FAIRY ANN (Ire) 6-11-2 (7*) Mr A Ross, ...(14 to 1)   25
3456 SPENCER HOUSE 5-11-6 (7*) Mr J O'Sullivan,
. . . . (25 to 1)   0
3381⁹ LORD PENNY (Ire) 5-11-13 Mr J A Nash, ...(20 to 1)   ur
3217³ CAKE BAKER (Ire) 7-12-0 Mr J P Dempsey, . . .(4 to 1 fav)   pu
2115⁶ ARDCARN PRINCESS (Ire) 5-11-1 (7*) Mr R J Cooper,
. . . . (33 to 1)   pu
3606⁹ TULLIBARDS FLYER (Ire) 5-11-8 (5*) Mr A C Coyle, . (10 to 1)   pu
Dist: 1l, 8l, 4½l, 5l. 4m 5.60s. (30 Ran).

(Lee Bowles), Lee Bowles

AYR (good)
Thursday April 17th
Going Correction: PLUS 0.10 sec. per fur. (races 1,3,6,7), MINUS 0.10 (2,4,5)

3698 'Breath Of Fresh Ayr' 'National Hunt' Novices' Hurdle Class D (Div I) (4-y-o and up) £2,632 3m 110yds . . . . (2:20)

3331³ FIDDLING THE FACTS (Ire) 6-11-2 M A Fitzgerald, al prmnt,
    led aftr 4 out, hit last, rdn and ran on wl
. . . . (11 to 10 fav op 11 to 8 tchd 6 to 4)   1
3579 SPRING DOUBLE (Ire) 6-11-12 C Llewellyn, hld up, hdwy and
    hmpd aftr 4 out, chsd wnr frm nxt, drvn to chal last, kpt on
    same pace . . . . (2 to 1 op 6 to 4)   2
3331 RIVER BAY (Ire) 6-11-2 J Culloty, trkd ldrs, rdn alng bef 3 out
    and sn one pace . . . .(9 to 1 op 7 to 1 tchd 10 to 1)   3
3309⁴ MY MAVOURNEEN 5-10-4 (7*) Mr M Bradburne, chsd ldr, led
    frm 6th to aftr 4 out, sn one pace . . . .(33 to 1)   4
3137 BRIGHT FLAME 5-11-2 Mr T Hills, in tch, effrt 4 out, sn
    rdn and outpcd . . . .(300 to 1 op 200 to 1)   5
3435³ MAGPIE MELODY (Ire) 6-11-2 (5*) B Grattan, led to 6th, rdn 3
    out and sn wknd . . . .(9 to 1 op 7 to 1 tchd 9 to 1)   6
2724⁵ SHARIAKANNDI (Fr) 5-11-2 T J Murphy, in tch till mstk 8 and
    sn wknd . . . .(16 to 1 op 14 to 1)   7
    GENTLEMAN JIM 7-11-2 D Morris, hdwy hfwy, in tch 4 out,,
    sn wknd and f 2 out . . . .(100 to 1)   f
2298 NAUTILUS THE THIRD (Ire) 6-11-2 R Garritty, pld up lme bef
    5th . . . .(100 to 1)   pu
3087 DOWSHI 6-10-4 (7*) I Jardine, mstks, al beh, tld off whn pld up
    bef 3 out . . . .(66 to 1)   pu
    SPRINGLEA TOWER 4-10-8 B Storey, hit 7th and sn tld off,
    pld up bef 3 out . . . .(200 to 1)   pu
Dist: ½l, 12l, 2l, 4l, 1¼l, dist. 6m 2.10s. a 21.10s (11 Ran).

(Mrs E Roberts), N J Henderson

3699 Royal Highland Fusiliers Novices' Chase Class D (5-y-o and up) £3,629 2m . . . . (2:50)

3304* AMERICAN HERO 9-11-6 B Storey, made all, clr frm 3 out,
    blun last, styd on wl . .(11 to 4 fav op 5 to 2 tchd 3 to 1)   1
3030* SINGING SAND 7-11-12 R Dunwoody, al chasing wnr, stay-
    ing on whn blun 3 out, one pace aftr . . . .(5 to 1 op 9 to 2)   2
3344* POWER PACK (Ire) 9-11-6 Mr B R Hamilton, chsd ldrs frm 4th,
    outpcd 8th, kpt on from 3 out, nvr dngrs. (3 to 1 op 11 to 4)   3
3210³ FILS DE CRESSON (Ire) 7-11-0 T Reed, beh, effrt hfwy, nvr
    rch idrs . . . . (20 to 1 op 16 to 1)   4
3479² DARING PAST 7-11-6 R Garritty, beh frm hfwy,
. . . . (14 to 1 op 10 to 1)   5
3477³ DESERT BRAVE 7-11-0 Richard Guest, outpcd and lost
    tch frm 5th . . . .(33 to 1 op 25 to 1)   6
2638 SOUND STATEMENT (Ire) 8-10-11 (3*) L Aspell, al beh, lost
    tch frm hfwy . . . .(100 to 1 op 50 to 1)   7
3154 GAROLO (Fr) 7-11-6 G Bradley, chsd ldrs, hit 6th, 3rd and rdn
    whn blun 4 out, sn btn and f last.
. . . .(3 to 1 op 9 to 4 tchd 100 to 30)   f
    SMART IN SILK 8-10-9 M Foster, al beh, tld off whn pld up 4
    out . . . .   pu
Dist: 2l, 10l, 4l, 18l, 12l, 16l. 3m 48.80s. a 3.80s (9 Ran).
SR: 38/42/26/14/-/-/

(Mrs R P Aggio), R Allan

3700 Friendly Hotels Novices' Hurdle Class D (4-y-o and up) £3,386 2½m . . . . (3:20)

3443³ ZANDER 5-11-7 C Llewellyn, prmnt, led 3 out to nxt, rallied
    und pres last, led nr finish . . . .(8 to 1 op 5 to 1)   1
2384* RED BLAZER 6-11-12 J Osborne, trkd ldrs, hdwy to ld 2 out,
    rdn last, hdd and no extr nr finish.
. . . .(7 to 4 on tchd 13 to 8 on and 6 to 4 on)   2
    SHORTSTAFF (Ire) 8-11-2 P Carberry, prmnt, effrt and evry ch
    2 out, sn rdn and kpt on . . . .(100 to 1 op 33 to 1)   3
2277⁷ CHERRYMORE (Ire) 6-11-2 A P McCoy, hld up, hdwy 7th, in
    tch 4 out and son rdn, fourth and held whn blun last.
. . . .(9 to 1 op 6 to 1 tchd 10 to 1)   4
3509² ARDARROCH PRINCE 4-11-2 P Niven, hld up and beh, hdwy
    hfwy, hit 3 out and sn one pace.
. . . .(12 to 1 op 8 to 1 tchd 14 to 1)   5
3150 HARBET HOUSE (Fr) 4-11-0 N Williamson, chsd ldrs, led 6th
    to 3 out, wkng whn hit nxt . . . .(8 to 1 op 5 to 1)   6
    REGAL EAGLE 4-10-9 R Dunwoody, hld up, effrt and hdwy 4
    out, sn rdn and no imprsn . . . .(66 to 1 op 20 to 1)   7
3401⁶ BONNY RIGG (Ire) 5-10-11 T Reed, led to aftr 1st, prmnt till
    wknd 4 out . . . .(200 to 1 op 66 to 1)   8
3457 THORNTOUN HOUSE 4-10-9 D Parker, beh frm hfwy.
. . . . (200 to 1 op 100 to 1)   9
3560⁹ KNIGHTSBRIDGE GIRL (Ire) 6-10-11 R Johnson, beh frm
    hfwy . . . .(33 to 1 op 25 to 1)   10
2336⁶ APACHE LEN (USA) 4-10-9 R Garritty, prmnt to 6th, sn lost pl.
. . . .(66 to 1 op 33 to 1)   11
1983⁸ STAR MASTER 6-11-2 L Wyer, al rear . . . .(50 to 1)   12
    BOXGROVE MAN (Ire) 7-11-2 M A Fitzgerald, hld up, some
    hdwy 6th, sn wknd and pld up 3 out.
. . . .(14 to 1 op 12 to 1 tchd 16 to 1)   pu
    MINNIES TURN 6-10-11 S McDougall, pulld hrd, led aftr 1st
    till wkng quickly and hdd 6th, sn beh and pld up bef 4 out.
. . . .(100 to 1 tchd 500 to 1 and 1000 to 1)   pu
1371⁹ SMART IN SOCKS 6-11-2 B Storey, tld off frm hfwy, pld up bef
    4 out . . . .(500 to 1 op 100 to 1)   pu
Dist: Hd, 2l, 6l, 6l, 6l, 6l, 13l, 1½l, 13l, 4l. 4m 50.60s. a 12.60s (15 Ran).

(Mrs Karen Duggan), N A Twiston-Davies

3701 George Graham Memorial Handicap Chase Class C (0-135 5-y-o and up)

£5,117 3m 1f.................. (3:50)

3510* KENMORE-SPEED [-] 10-10-4[1] Richard Guest, *prmnt, hdwy to ld 11th, rdn 2 out, hld on wl*........ (7 to 1 tchd 8 to 1) 1
3067* DONJUAN COLLONGES (Fr) [-] 6-10-8 P Carberry, *hdwy to chase ldrs 6th, blun badly 13th, hit nxt and lost pl, headway 4 out, sn rdn, kpt on*.... (7 to 4 fav op 2 to 1 tchd 9 to 4) 2
3000* CARIBOO GOLD (USA) [-] 8-10-13 J Osborne, *hld up, hdwy 13th, rdn and ev ch 2 out, sn one pace.* (13 to 2 op 5 to 1) 3
3329[4] DARREN THE BRAVE [-] 9-10-0 D Gallagher, *hit second and beh, hdwy hfwy, rdn 4 out and kpt on one . pace*....(20 to 1) 4
2850[3] STORMY CORAL (Ire) [-] 7-10-4 B Storey, *beh, hdwy and hit 4 out, kpt on same pace*.............. (12 to 1 op 10 to 1) 5
3397[3] KILCOLGAN [-] 10-10-3 N Bentley, *mstks, outpcd and beh frm hfwy*.............................(20 to 1 op 16 to 1) 6
2935[3] WHISPERING STEEL [-] 11-11-11 R Dunwoody, *hld up, hdwy 10th, ev ch 4 out, sn rdn and wknd*....(14 to 1 op 12 to 1) 7
3581 WUDIMP [-] 8-10-8 Mr C Storey, *midfield, hdwy 10th, rdn and wknd 14th*...................... (25 to 1 tchd 33 to 1) 8
3318[6] ANDERMATT [-] 10-10-11 N Williamson, *al rear, tld off frm 14th*..................................(50 to 1) 9
3441* SEOD RIOGA (Ire) [-] 8-11-0 N Mann, *trkd ldrs, rdn alng and f 4 out*.....................................(8 to 1 tchd 10 to 1) f
2956[5] ROCKY PARK [-] 11-10-0 B Fenton, *led to 6th, prmnt till blun and uns rdr 12th*...........................(20 to 1) ur
3318 GENERAL PERSHING [-] 11-12-0 R Johnson, *cl up, led 6th to 11th, pld up lme aftr 13th.*
...............................(12 to 1 op 14 to 1 tchd 10 to 1) pu
EASTER OATS [-] 10-10-0 G Cahill, *al rear, beh whn pld up bef 12th.*.............................. (100 to 1) pu
3436 NORTHERN SQUIRE [-] 9-10-11 (3*) E Callaghan, *blun 4th and 5th, sn tld off and pld up aftr 10th.* (33 to 1 op 25 to 1) pu
Dist: ½l, 5l, 7l, 2l, 1¼l, 6l, 15l, 26l. 6m 10.50s. a 10.50s (14 Ran).

(K M Dacker), Mrs S J Smith

3702 Eagle Tavern's Novices' Handicap Chase Class D (0-110 5-y-o and up) £4,432 2m 5f 110yds........ (4:25)

3511 GAELIC BLUE [-] 7-10-4[1] Richard Guest, *in tch, effrt 2 out, rdn to chal last, styd on gmely to ld nr finish.*
.................................(9 to 2 op 4 to 1) 1
3056[2] NICHOLAS PLANT [-] 8-10-13 G Cahill, *prmnt, led aftr 4 out, rdn appr last, hdd and no extr nr finish.* (10 to 1 op 8 to 1) 2
3511* KINGS SERMON (Ire) [-] 8-10-7 L Wyer, *midfield, steady hdwy 11th, chsd ldrs 3 out, rdn and one pace.*
.................................(16 to 1 op 12 to 1) 3
3508[2] BALLLINE (Ire) [-] 6-10-6 J Callaghan, *made most till blun 4 out, sn hdd, rdn 3 out, kpt on one pace.*
.................................(11 to 1 op 12 to 1 tchd 14 to 1) 4
3333* RED BRANCH (Ire) [-] 8-10-8 T J Murphy, *cl up, rdn alng 4 out, wknd aftr nxt*....................(3 to 1 fav tchd 4 to 1) 5
3399* LE DENSTAN [-] 10-10-2 R Johnson, *hld up, steady hdwy 12th, rdn 3 out and no imprsn*........(14 to 1 op 12 to 1) 6
3600* REAL TONIC [-] 7-11-7 (6ex) P Carberry, *hld up in midfield, gd hdwy 10th, blun nxt, rdn 4 out, wknd next.*
.................................(9 to 2 op 4 to 1 tchd 5 to 1) 7
3319[5] THE REVEREND BERT (Ire) [-] 9-11-9 (5*) A Bates, *strted slwly, not fluent in rear, blun 7th, al beind.*
.................................(50 to 1 op 14 to 1) 8
2621 LIEN DE FAMILLE (Ire) [-] 7-11-6 P Niven, *al rear.*
.................................(50 to 1 op 33 to 1) 9
2488[3] SLOTAMATIQUE (Ire) [-] 8-11-4 R Dunwoody, *hld up, hit 3rd, hdwy and in tch hfwy, sn rdn and wknd*.........(12 to 1) 10
3600 COQUI LANE [-] 10-11-1 D Parker, *hit 7th and sn beh, tld off whn pld up bef 11th*.............(12 to 1 op 8 to 1) pu
BOB NELSON [-] 10-10-0 C Llewellyn, *chsd ldrs, wknd and blun 13th, beh whn pld up aftr 3 out.* (100 to 1 op 50 to 1) pu
3434[3] CORSTON JOKER [-] 7-10-0 J Supple, *al beh. pld up bef last.*
.................................(16 to 1 op 14 to 1) pu
Dist: Hd, 4l, 1l, 15l, 1l, 7l, 2l, 16l, 3½l. 5m 17.00s. a 11.00s (13 Ran).

(Trevor Hemmings), Mrs S J Smith

3703 Royal Burgh Of Ayr Conditional Jockeys' Handicap Hurdle Class E for the Royal Burgh of Ayr Cup (0-110 4-y-o and up) £3,291 2m
.................................(4:55)

3512[2] TEEJAY'N'AITCH [-] 5-10-0 S Taylor, *made most, clr 3 out, styd on wl*....................(6 to 1 tchd 7 to 1) 1
2853[8] PARSON'S LODGE (Ire) [-] 9-9-9 (5*) W Dowling, *hld up and beh, hdwy 3 out, styd on appr last, no ch wth wnr.*
.................................(14 to 1 tchd 16 to 1) 2
3437[6] LATIN LEADER [-] 7-10-8 F Leahy, *chsd ldrs, effrt 3 out, sn rdn and one pace*..................(14 to 1 op 12 to 1) 3
3194[3] RACHAEL'S OWEN [-] 7-10-7 R McGrath, *al prmnt, rdn alng 3 out, sn one pace*......(6 to 1 op 5 to 1 tchd 13 to 2) 4
3350[6] GALLARDINI (Ire) [-] 8-9-7 (7*) A Currie, *in tch, rdn alng 3 out, sn one pace*.....................(14 to 1 tchd 20 to 1) 5
1964* FEN TERRIER [-] 5-11-11 E Callaghan, *chsd ldrs, rdn appr 3 out, sn rdn and sn btn*......................(7 to 1 tchd 8 to 1) 6
3540[4] SAMANID (Ire) [-] 5-11-13 D J Kavanagh, *nvr better than mid-div*.....................(15 to 2 op 5 to 1 tchd 8 to 1) 7
3587[2] SKIDDAW SAMBA [-] 8-10-6 G Lee, *hld up, gd hdwy 4 out, rdn nxt and sn wknd*.....................(5 to 1 fav) 8

3635[6] NASHVILLE STAR (USA) [-] 6-11-2 R Massey, *prmnt, rdn alng appr 4 out and sn weakened*..........(6 to 1 op 8 to 1) 9
2063 JAUNTY GENERAL [-] 6-9-13 (5*) C McCormack, *in tch till rdn and wknd 4 out*.....................(16 to 1 op 14 to 1) 10
3398 CITTADINO [-] 7-11-7 (3*) N Horrocks, *beh frm hfwy.*
.................................(10 to 1 tchd 12 to 1) 11
2949 SAINT CIEL (USA) [-] 9-11-12 L Aspell, *al rear.*
.................................(20 to 1 op 16 to 1) 12
HIGH MIND (Fr) [-] 8-11-10 E Husband, *beh frm hfwy.*
.................................(5 to 1 op 12 to 1) 13
3424[8] ANLACE [-] 8-10-0 Chris Webb, *al rear.*
.................................(20 to 1 op 16 to 1) 14
Dist: 3½l, 5l, 2l, 1½l, ¾l, 5l, 3l, 8l, sht-hd, 1¾l. 3m 43.10s. a 7.10s (14 Ran).
SR: 17/13/16/13/4/28/25/1/3/   (Andrew Paterson), J S Goldie

3704 'Breath Of Fresh Ayr' 'National Hunt' Novices' Hurdle Class D (Div II) (4-y-o and up) £2,619 3m 110yds.... (5:25)

3400[5] CLAIRABELL [-] 6-10-11 B Storey, *hld up in midfield, hdwy hfwy, effrt 3 out, rdn to chal last, styd on to ld flt.*
.................................(14 to 1 op 10 to 1 tchd 16 to 1) 1
3382[2] IVORY COASTER (NZ) [-] 6-11-2 J Osborne, *trkd ldrs, led aftr 4 out, rdn 2 out, hit last, hdd and no extr flt.*
.................................(2 to 1 fav op 6 to 4) 2
3598[2] NICK ROSS 6-11-2 A S Smith, *hld up, gd hdwy to track ldrs 8th, ev ch and hit 3 out, sn rdn and one pace appr last.*
.................................(7 to 1 op 5 to 1) 3
3353* BOSTON MAN 6-11-7 P Carberry, *cl up, led 8th to aftr 4 out, sn drvn alng and wknd after nxt*........(12 to 1 op 8 to 1) 4
3009[2] MRS ROBINSON [-] 9-11-2 E Husband, *chsd leaders, rdn alng and outpcd hfwy, nvr dngrs aftr.*
.................................(12 to 1 op 10 to 1) 5
2927[5] MAY SUNSET (Ire) 7-11-2 N Williamson, *hld up gng wl, smooth hdwy to join ldrs 4 out, ev ch nxt, rdn 2 out and sn wknd*.....................(20 to 1 op 16 to 1) 6
BIRKDALE (Ire) 6-11-2 J Supple, *al beh.*
.................................(16 to 1 op 14 to 1 tchd 20 to 1) 7
2207 LA MON DERE (Ire) 6-11-7 R Dunwoody, *in tch, pushed alng 6th, sn beh*.....................(12 to 1 op 10 to 1 tchd 14 to 1) 8
3634[7] ARCTIC FOX (Ire) 5-11-2 J F Titley, *chsd ldrs, hit 4th, rdn and wknd bef four out*.................(16 to 1 op 14 to 1) 9
SOLDIER-B 7-10-11 (5*) A Bates, *led and sn clr, hdd 8th and soon wknd, beh whn pld up bef 2 out.* (33 to 1 op 25 to 1) pu
3400* CHERRY DEE 6-11-2 (5*) B Grattan, *prmnt, pushed alng and lost pl 8th, sn beh and pld up bef 2 out.*
.................................(5 to 2 op 7 to 2 tchd 4 to 1) pu
Dist: ½l, 2½l, 16l, 2½l, 1l, 8l, dist. 6m 2.40s. a 21.40s (11 Ran).

(W F Trueman), J I A Charlton

TIPPERARY (IRE) (good)
Thursday April 17th

3705 St.Annes School (Tipp) Trans. Year Maiden Hurdle (4 & 5-y-o) £2,740 2m
.................................(4:30)

3450[5] PEGUS JUNIOR (Ire) 4-11-1 C O'Dwyer, ...(5 to 1) 1
3625[2] NEWBERRY ROSE (Ire) 5-10-7 (7*) M D Murphy, ... (8 to 1) 2
3450 CELTIC PROJECT (Ire) 4-10-8 (7*) B J Geraghty, ... (8 to 1) 3
3607[5] ANTICS (Ire) 5-11-1 (7*) Mrs C Harrison, ...(10 to 1) 4
2368[3] NATIVE FLING (Ire) 5-11-13 F Woods, ...(5 to 1) 5
3389[9] RACHEL'S SWALLOW (Ire) 5-11-5 (3*) Mr R Walsh, (13 to 2) 6
3448[6] NEARLY A LINE 5-11-5 M P Hourigan, ...(14 to 1) 7
3232[4] CINNIBAR 4-10-10 J Shortt, ...(7 to 1) 8
3606[4] MENDELUCI (Ire) (bl) 5-11-13 S H O'Donovan, ...(10 to 1) 9
ASHJAR (USA) 4-11-2 A O'Shea, ...(10 to 1) 10
2100[6] RIPOSTE (Ire) 5-11-0 C F Swan, ...(5 to 2 fav) 11
3520 EDEN KING (Fr) 5-11-0 T P Rudd, ...(40 to 1) 12
2900 ORMOND JENNY (Ire) (bl) 5-11-8 K F O'Brien, ...(16 to 1) 13
3625 TINERANA GLOW (Ire) 5-11-0 D T Evans, ...(16 to 1) 14
1404 CAHONIS (Ire) 5-10-12 (7*) P G Hourigan, ...(33 to 1) 15
3069 STRONG MARTINA (Ire) 5-11-0 P L Malone, ...(33 to 1) 16
HIBBA (Ire) 5-10-7 (7*) V T Keane, ...(40 to 1) 17
DELLSBOY (Ire) 5-11-5 T P Treacy, ...(25 to 1) 18
2946[6] TOUGHERHANTHEREST (Ire) 5-10-11 (3*) K Whelan,
.................................(25 to 1) f
2525 BALLINAMONA LASS (Ire) 5-11-0 J R Barry, ...(50 to 1) pu
Dist: 1½l, 3½l, 1l, 3½l. 3m 49.20s. (20 Ran).

(Patrick O'Leary), Patrick O'Leary

3706 University College Cork Racing Club Handicap Chase (5-y-o and up) £2,740 2½m.................(5:00)

3236[9] MARGUERITA SONG [-] 7-10-11 T P Treacy, ...(5 to 1) 1
3340[5] RICH TRADITION [-] 9-10-12 (3*) U Smyth, ... (12 to 1) 2
563 LOFTUS LAD (Ire) [-] 9-10-10 (7*) M D Murphy, ... (4 to 1) 3
356[6] ROSSBEIGH CREEK [-] 10-11-10 F J Flood, ...(9 to 2) 4
1245[6] SPRINGFORT LADY (Ire) [-] 8-11-0 (7*) J E Casey,
.................................(7 to 2 fav) 5
405[9] RATES RELIEF (Ire) [-] 7-11-12 C F Swan, ...(5 to 1) 6
3624[6] TREENS FOLLY [-] 8-9-2 (5*) T Martin, ...(20 to 1) 7
3420[8] STEEL DAWN [-] 10-11-3 J R Barry, ...(11 to 2) pu
Dist: 3l, 3l, 2½l, hd. 4m 50.80s. (8 Ran).

(Mrs N Mitchell), Edward P Mitchell

3707 Glenstall Abbey Racing Club Flat Race (4-y-o) £2,740 2m...... (5:30)

	BORO SOVEREIGN (Ire) 11-6 Mr P Fenton, ...(7 to 1)	1
2967[2]	KOHOUTEK 11-3 (3*) Mr R Walsh, ...(7 to 2)	2
	KEEP THE PEARL (Ire) 10-8 (7*) Mr N D Fehily, ...(7 to 1)	3
	NATIVE TANGO (Ire) 10-8 (7*) Mr M J Daly, ...(10 to 1)	4
	SWIFT PEARL (Ire) 11-1 (5*) Mr A C Coyle, ...(3 to 1 fav)	5
	MR QUIGLEY (Ire) 11-6 Mr J P Dempsey, ...(12 to 1)	6
	DINGHY (Ire) 10-8 (7*) Mr D P Daly, ...(8 to 1)	7
	BOLTON FOREST (Ire) 11-6 Mr D Marnane, ...(5 to 1)	8
	DISTINCTLY SHARP (Ire) 10-13 (7*) Mr G Kearns, ...(12 to 1)	9
	DUBLIN BOY 11-6 Mr B M Cash, ...(14 to 1)	10
	GOSSIE MADERA 10-13 (7*) Miss A Reilly, ...(14 to 1)	11

Dist: 3l, 2½l, 3l, 3l. 3m 45.80s. (11 Ran.)

(Mrs A F Mee), Anthony Mullins

AYR (good)
Friday April 18th
Going Correction: PLUS 0.10 sec. per fur.

3708 Hamilton Campbell ILPH Novices' Chase Class D for the Hamilton Campbell Challenge Cup (5-y-o and up) £5,478 3m 1f...... (2:00)

3577	CHOPWELL CURTAINS 7-11-12 L Wyer, chsd ldrs, pushed alng 12th, hdwy 5 out, led aftr nxt, rdn and styd on wl fit.	
	............(11 to 2 op 5 to 1 tchd 6 to 1)	1
3012[2]	SOLOMON'S DANCER (USA) 7-11-12 R Dunwoody, trkd ldrs, hdwy 5 out, pushed alng 3 out, rdn bef last, kpt on.	
	...........(Evens 5/2 op 11 to 8 tchd 6 to 4)	2
3577	BEAR CLAW 8-11-7 J Osborne, trkd ldrs, hit 6th, hit 5 out, effrt and rdn whn hit 2 out, sn btn.........(7 to 2 op 3 to 1)	3
1952[4]	GEMS LAD 10-11-12 Richard Guest, chsd ldr, led 12th, rdn 4 out and sn hdd and wknd.........(25 to 1 op 16 to 1)	4
3383[3]	BALLYDOUGAN (Ire) 9-11-2 T J Murphy, al rear, tld off 5 out.	
	.................(100 to 1 op 50 to 1)	5
3511	BRIGHT DESTINY 6-11-7 G Cahill, alwasy beh, tld off 5 out.	
	..................(100 to 1 op 50 to 1)	6
3133	SLIDEOFHILL (Ire) 8-11-2 A P McCoy, not fluent, chsd ldrs to hfwy, grad wknd and beh frm 5 out.	
	.........(16 to 1 op 8 to 1 tchd 20 to 1)	7
2799[4]	EASY BREEZY 7-11-2 J Railton, led, hdd whn blun badly and uns rdr 12th.................(33 to 1 op 16 to 1)	ur
3354*	FRIENDLY KNIGHT 7-11-7 A S Smith, refused to race, took no part.......................(50 to 1)	ref

Dist: 2½l, 4l, 16l, 8l, ½l, 6l. 6m 17.70s. a 17.70s (9 Ran).

(Durham Drapes Ltd), T D Easterby

3709 Evelyn Matthews Memorial Novices' Handicap Hurdle Class C (4-y-o and up) £3,220 2½m.............(2:30)

3103*	MAHLER [-] 7-9-12 (7*) Mr J Goldstein, in tch, hdwy 5th, slight ld nxt, rdn alng 2 out, styd on wl frm last.	
	.................(14 to 1 op 16 to 1)	1
3480[2]	MORPHEUS [-] 8-10-5 R Johnson, mid-div, hdwy on inner hfwy, effrt 3 out, rdn and kpt on appr last.......(16 to 1)	2
3262*	HARFDECENT [-] 6-10-0 J Osborne, strted slwly and beh till gd hdwy 4 out, styd on strly frm 2 out, nvr finish.	
	.................(16 to 1 op 14 to 1)	3
2775*	NISHAMIRA (Ire) [-] 5-9-12 (3*) Mr R Thornton, trkd ldrs, smooth hdwy 8th, cl up frm nxt and ev ch till drvn and no extr from last.........(11 to 2 fav op 6 to 1 tchd 5 to 1)	4
2721[3]	KING PIN [-] 5-11-5 (5*) B Grattan, midfield, hdwy to chase ldrs 6th, effrt and rdn 3 out, sn one pace.	
	.................(12 to 1 op 10 to 1)	5
3575[4]	FAR AHEAD [-] 5-11-10 B Storey, hld up, hdwy 4 out, rdn alng 2 out and kpt on, nvr dngrs.........(6 to 1 tchd 7 to 1)	6
3039[5]	THE BARGEMAN (NZ) [-] 9-9-11 (3*) Sophie Mitchell, nvr rch ldrs.......................(33 to 1 op 20 to 1)	7
3535	CHARLEY LAMBERT (Ire) [-] 9-10-0 N Williamson, midfield, hdwy 4 out, rdn alng whn mstk nxt, sn wknd.	
	.................(16 to 1 op 14 to 1)	8
3275*	COOL GUNNER [-] 7-10-6 G Maude, midfield, effrt and some hdwy appr 3 out, sn rdn and btn.........(8 to 1 op 6 to 1)	9
3321[7]	JERVAULX (Ire) [-] 6-10-4 P Carberry, in tch, rdn alng 4 out and sn wknd.................(14 to 1 op 12 to 1)	10
3537[1]	SUAS LEAT (Ire) [-] 7-9-13 (7*) M Newton, midfield, rdn alng bef 4 out and sn wknd.........(50 to 1 op 33 to 1)	11
2658[2]	ROYAL EVENT [-] 6-10-10 R Dunwoody, led to 6th, cl up till wknd aftr 4 out.........(10 to 1 tchd 14 to 1)	12
3129	NASONE (Ire) [-] 6-10-12 P Hide, cl up, rdn alng 4 out and sn wknd.........(12 to 1 op 10 to 1 tchd 14 to 1)	13
2988*	LAGEN BRIDGE (Ire) [-] 8-11-4 D J Moffatt, midfield till uns rdr 6th.........(16 to 1 op 12 to 1)	ur
2349[8]	KASIRAMA (Ire) [-] 6-9-7 (7*) N Horrocks, prmnt till wknd quickly 6th and sn tld off, pld up bef 3 out.......(100 to 1)	pu
3400	PHAR ECHO (Ire) [-] 6-10-4 M Foster, beh frm hfwy, pld up bef 4 out.................(14 to 1 op 12 to 1)	pu

2876*	COLONEL BLAZER [-] 5-10-8 J F Titley, midfield, hdwy 6th, rdn alng and lost pl 4 out, beh whn pld up bef nxt.	
	.........(13 to 2 op 6 to 1 tchd 7 to 1 and 8 to 1)	pu
2910[4]	SHARE OPTIONS (Ire) [-] 6-10-11 L Wyer, beh frm hfwy, pld up 3 out.................(20 to 1 op 14 to 1)	pu

Dist: 1l, ¾l, 1¾l, 1¼l, ½l, 4l, 9l, 8l, 8l, 5l. 4m 45.90s. a 7.90s (18 Ran).
SR: 18/17/11/10/31/30/2/-/-/ (English Badminton Partnership), N A Twiston-Davies

3710 Royal Bank Of Scotland 'National Hunt' Novices' Hurdle Class C (4-y-o and up) £4,718 2m........(3:00)

2917*	MARELLO 6-11-10 P Niven, trkd ldrs, hdwy 5th, dsptd ld 3 out, shaken up last and sn led, rdn out.	
	.........(8 to 1 on op 6 to 1 on)	1
3443	DONNINGTON (Ire) 7-11-5 J Osborne, hld, hit 4 out, jnd nxt, sn rdn, kpt on wl und pres frm last.........(9 to 1 op 5 to 1)	2
2719[4]	PENROSE LAD (NZ) 7-11-0 R Johnson, chsd ldrs, outpcd appr 3 out.........(10 to 1 tchd 11 to 1)	3
3029[7]	COTTSBOWN BOY 6-11-0 M Foster, chsd ldrs, rdn alng and outpcd bef 4 out.........(50 to 1 tchd 66 to 1)	4
3351	HOPEFUL LORD 5-11-0 A S Smith, hld up, hdwy 5th, rdn 4 out and sn wknd.........(100 to 1 op 66 to 1)	5
	SCALLY BEAU 6-11-0 J Supple, al outpcd and beh, tld off frm hfwy.........(200 to 1 op 100 to 1)	6
1716[8]	SECOND STEP (Ire) 6-11-0 R Dunwoody, in rear whn f 4th.	
	.........(20 to 1 op 14 to 1)	f
	MASTER RUPERT 5-11-0 D Parker, al outpcd and beh, tld off whn pld up bef 4th.........(200 to 1 op 100 to 1)	pu

Dist: 1¼l, 15l, 13l, ½l, dist. 3m 44.20s. a 8.20s (8 Ran).
SR: 30/23/3/-/-/ (Mrs M Williams), Mrs M Reveley

3711 Hillhouse Quarry Handicap Chase Class B (5-y-o and up) £7,390 2½m........(3:30)

3155[5]	DESTIN D'ESTRUVAL (Fr) [-] 6-10-0 R Johnson, hld up, hdwy to chase ldrs 7th, effrt 4 out sn rdn, chsd ldr and 2 ls dwn whn lft clr last.........(7 to 1 tchd 8 to 1)	1
3134[5]	DESTINY CALLS [-] 7-10-2[1] R Dunwoody, hld up, steady hdwy 7th, rdn 4 out and one pace frm nxt.	
	.........(3 to 1 fav op 7 to 2 tchd 4 to 1)	2
	LEOTARD [-] 10-11-0 N Williamson, hld up, steady hdwy 11th, ev ch 3 out, sn rdn and wknd nxt.....(12 to 1 op 10 to 1)	3
3580[8]	FRICKLEY [-] 11-10-0 P Carberry, in tch, rdn alng 5 out, wknd nxt.........(9 to 1 op 8 to 1 tchd 10 to 1)	4
3318[2]	CUMBRIAN CHALLENGE [-] 8-10-7 L Wyer, hld up, hdwy 9th, rdn alng 5 out and sn wknd.........(8 to 1 op 7 to 1)	5
3152	BANJO (Fr) [-] 7-11-7 (3*) Mr R Thornton, prmnt till hit 4th and sn lost pl, beh frm hfwy.........(11 to 1 op 8 to 1)	6
3605	GLEMOT (Ire) [-] 9-10-13 C O'Dwyer, cl up, lft in ld 7th, mstk and hdd 9th, drvn alng 5 out and sn wknd.(8 to 1 op 6 to 1)	7
3441[3]	OLD BRIDGE (Ire) [-] 9-10-9 J Osborne, trkd ldrs, hdwy 7th, led 9th, rdn 2 out, two ls up and staying on whn f last.	
	.........(14 to 1 op 10 to 1)	f
3563[3]	ROUYAN [-] 11-10-13 J F Titley, led till blun badly 7th, pld up bef nxt.........(4 to 1 op 7 to 2)	pu

Dist: 11l, nk, 8l, 1¼l, hd, 16l. 4m 58.20s. a 11.20s (9 Ran).
(Darren C Mercer), D Nicholson

3712 Lickleyhead Castle Handicap Hurdle Class B (0-145 4-y-o and up) £4,500 3¼m 110yds.............(4:00)

2246	MEDITATOR [-] 13-10-0 S Curran, hld up, steady hdwy hfwy, led appr 3 out, rdn and hdd last, rallied und pres to ld nr finish.	
	.........(100 to 1)	1
531*	NIRVANA PRINCE [-] 8-10-12 M A Fitzgerald, hld up, gd hdwy appr 4 out, effrt 2 out, rdn to ld and hit last, hdd and no extr nr finish.........(16 to 1 op 12 to 1)	2
3568[7]	ERZADJAN (Ire) [-] 7-11-7 P Niven, hld up, gd hdwy 4 out, rdn nxt, one pace appr last. (10 to 1 op 8 to 1 tchd 12 to 1)	3
3386*	TRIBUNE [-] 6-10-10 M Foster, cl up, led aftr 9th, rdn alng 4 out, hdd bef nxt, wknd betw last 2.	
	.........(9 to 2 op 4 to 1 tchd 5 to 1)	4
3140*	TILTY (USA) [-] 7-10-0 T Eley, made most till aftr 9th, prmnt till drvn alng and wknd 4 out.........(16 to 1 op 12 to 1)	5
3568[6]	VICTOR BRAVO (NZ) [-] 10-11-0 C Llewellyn, beh, pushed alng hfwy, styd on frm 3 out, nvr a factor.	
	.........(5 to 1 tchd 11 to 2)	6
2881[4]	WHAT'S YOUR STORY (Ire) [-] 6-10-10 R Johnson, in tch, effrt 10th, pushed alng 4 out, wknd nxt.........(14 to 1)	7
2910*	YOUNG KENNY [-] 6-11-2 N Williamson, hld up in midfield, hdwy 9th, rdn alng 4 out and sn btn.	
	.........(7 to 2 fav tchd 4 to 1 and 9 to 2)	8
2465[3]	CAMPAIGN [-] 6-10-5[1] R Garritty, in tch, hit 6th, one pace bef 4 out and sn wknd.........(12 to 1 tchd 14 to 1)	9
3398*	SWANBISTER (Ire) [-] 7-10-6 A P McCoy, cl up, rdn alng 4 out, wknd appr nxt.........(6 to 1 op 5 to 1)	10
3568	BETTER TIMES AHEAD [-] 11-11-10 P Carberry, prmnt to hfwy, sn lost pl and beh 4 out......(50 to 1 op 33 to 1)	11
3050	EULOGY (Ire) [-] 7-10-3[1] R Dunwoody, chsd ldrs, rdn alng 11th, sn lost pl.........(40 to 1 op 25 to 1 tchd 50 to 1)	12
1608	ISLAND JEWEL [-] 9-11-4 C Maude, chsd ldrs to 6th, sn lost pl and tld off whn pld up bef 4 out.....(50 to 1 op 33 to 1)	pu

Dist: ¾l, 5l, nk, 9l, 1¼l, 3½l, 26l, 2½l, ½l, 12l. 6m 26.90s. a 13.90s (13 Ran).

NATIONAL HUNT RESULTS 1996-97

(Miss Jacqueline S Doyle), B de Haan

3713 Royal Scots Dragoon Guards Cup Hunters' Chase Class H (6-y-o and up) £3,688 3m 3f 110yds......(4:30)

3307* JIGTIME 8-11-2 (7*) Mr M Bradburne, *chsd ldr, led 10th, clr 4 out, kpt on*.....(7 to 4 on op 2 to 1 on tchd 13 to 8 on) 1
3603² ROYAL JESTER 13-11-9 (5*) Mr C Storey, *trkd ldrs, hdwy to chase wnr 15th, rdn 3 out, kpt on.*
.... (11 to 2 op 5 to 1 tchd 6 to 1) 2
3307⁴ SOUTHERN MINSTREL 14-11-7 (7*) Miss C Metcalfe, *hld up, hdwy 14th, rdn 5 out, one pace.*......(25 to 1 op 20 to 1) 3
3603* NOW YOUNG MAN (Ire) 8-11-7 (7*) Mr Chris Wilson, *hld up, pushed alng and hdwy whn hit 15th, sn rdn and btn 4 out.*
.... (11 to 4 op 5 to 2 tchd 6 to 1) 4
GREEN TIMES 12-11-7 (7*) Major G Wheeler, *prmnt till lost pl 12th and sn beh, tld off 5 out.*........(50 to 1 op 33 to 1) 5
I'M TOBY 10-11-7 (7*) Mr A Kinane, *al beh, tld off whn 15th.*
.... (100 to 1) f
2960³ ARDESEE 17-11-7 (7*) Mr A Wintle, *made most to 10th, sn wknd and pld up bef 15th.*......................(100 to 1) pu
Dist: 2½l, 12l, 6l, dist. 7m 2.50s. a 20.50s (7 Ran).

(J W Hughes), J W Hughes

AYR (good)
Saturday April 19th
Going Correction: MINUS 0.05 sec. per fur. (races 1,2,4,7,8), MINUS 0.10 (3,5,6)

3714 Albert Bartlett And Sons Juvenile Novices' Handicap Hurdle Class C (4-y-o) £4,402 2m............(1:55)

3066* SHU GAA (Ire) [105] (bl) 11-5 J Osborne, *prmnt till lost pl appr 3 out, hdwy nxt, rdn and hit last, sn led, drvn out.*
.... (3 to 1 fav tchd 7 to 2) 1
2818⁵ MELTEMISON [97] 10-11 R Garritty, *led, rdn clr appr 2 out, hdd aftr last and hng lft, kpt on.*
.... (10 to 1 op 8 to 1 tchd 12 to 1) 2
3303³ CLASH OF SWORDS [94] 10-8 L Wyer, *hld up, hdwy appr 3 out, rdn nxt and hit appr 2 out, one pace.*.....(12 to 1 op 9 to 1) 3
3433* SOUSSE [87] 10-1 G Lee, *prmnt, chsd ldr 4th, rdn 3 out, hit nxt and sn wknd.*..................(7 to 2 op 3 to 1) 4
2818⁷ ROSSEL (USA) [114] 12-0 R Dunwoody, *trkd ldrs, hit 5th, hdwy nxt, rdn 3 out and sn btn.*
.... (5 to 1 op 11 to 2 tchd 6 to 1) 5
3316⁵ MUHTADI (Ire) [100] 11-0 R Johnson, *hld up, hdwy and rdn 4 out, sn btn nxt.*...........(8 to 1 op 5 to 1 tchd 9 to 1) 6
3148² ALPINE JOKER (Ire) [88] 10-0 G Tormey, *hld up, hit 4th, rdn alng and hdwy nxt, wekaned appr 3 out and sn beh.*
.... (11 to 2 op 5 to 1) 7
Dist: 2l, 3l, 3l, 8l, 11l, 5l. 3m 43.50s. a 7.50s (7 Ran).
SR: 8/-/-/-/-/1/-/

(Ali K Al Jafleh), O Sherwood

3715 Hamlet Extra Mild Cigars Gold Card Handicap Hurdle Class B (4-y-o and up) £8,870 2¾m..............(2:25)

3568 HOUSE CAPTAIN [123] 8-10-4 P Carberry, *hld up in midfield, steady hdwy 8th, led appr last, rdn clr flt.*
.... (20 to 1 op 14 to 1) 1
3580² SHERIFFMUIR [128] 8-10-9 J F Titley, *al prmnt, led aftr 7th, rdn 3 out, hdd appr nxt, kpt on.*..............(7 to 1) 2
3131⁴ TULLYMURRY TOFF (Ire) [138] 6-11-2 (3*) E Callaghan, *trkd ldrs, hdwy 7th, led appr 2 out, sn rdn and hdd bef last, one pace.*......................(11 to 4 jt-fav op 7 to 2) 3
3131 SUPREME LADY (Ire) [127] 6-10-8 J Culloty, *hld up, hdwy 7th, rdn aftr 3 out, styd on same pace.*.....(9 to 1 op 7 to 1) 4
3131 EXECUTIVE DESIGN [130] 5-10-11 P Niven, *hld up and beh, hdwy appr 4 out, effrt nxt, sn rdn and no imprsn....*(2 to 1) 5
3580⁴ OUTSET (Ire) [127] 7-10-5 (3*) Mr C Bonner, *cl up, led 5th till aftr nxt, rdn 4 out and sn wknd....*(12 to 1 op 10 to 1) 6
3568⁵ DR LEUNT (Ire) [125] 6-10-6 G Tormey, *cl up, dsptd ld and hit 3 out, sn wknd....*...........(12 to 1 tchd 14 to 1) 7
3537° CELESTIAL CHOIR [126] 7-10-7 B Storey, *hld up in rear, effrt 7th, drvn alng and wknd bef 4 out.* (11 to 4 jt-fav op 5 to 2) 8
3568³ FREDDIE MUCK [132] 10-7-13 C Llewellyn, *chsd ldrs, rdn and lost pl 8th, sn beh.*...............(7 to 1 tchd 8 to 1) 9
3436⁴ SOLBA (USA) [119] (bl) 8-10-0 D Parker, *beh frm 5th, tld off 8th.*....................(66 to 1 op 50 to 1 tchd 100 to 1) 10
2830⁴ CASTLEKELLYLEADER (Ire) [143] 8-11-10 P Hide, *led to 5th, led ag'n and blun badly 7th, sn lost pl and beh whn pld up bef 3 out.*.......................(14 to 1) pu
Dist: 3½l, 3l, ¾l, 17l, ½l, ½l, 20l, 22l, 10l. 5m 17.70s. a 10.70s (11 Ran).

(Mr & Mrs G Middlebrook), J G FitzGerald

3716 Edinburgh Woollen Mill's Future Champion Novices' Chase Class A Grade 2 (5-y-o and up) £14,490 2½m
.... (2:55)

3155* SPARKY GAYLE (Ire) 7-11-10 B Storey, *hld up, hdwy 5 out, led appr 3 out, rdn clr bef last, styd on strly.*
.... (15 to 8 on op 7 to 4 on tchd 2 to 1 on and 6 to 4 on) 1

2863² MACGEORGE (Ire) 7-11-3 R Dunwoody, *chsd ldr, blun and lost pl 11th, hdwy on inner and hmpd hme bend, drvn 3 out, kpt on.*...................(8 to 1 op 7 to 1) 2
3155⁶ STATELY HOME (Ire) 6-11-10 R Johnson, *led, rdn alng and hdd 4 out, drvn nxt and one pace.*.......(8 to 1 op 6 to 1) 3
2714* CHIEF MINISTER (Ire) 8-11-3 R Garritty, *hld up, hdwy 5 out, rdn alng 3 out, one pace appr last.*
.... (7 to 1 op 6 to 1 tchd 8 to 1) 4
3702⁸ THE REVEREND BERT (Ire) 9-11-3 B Fenton, *prmnt, cl up 12th, led and blun badly 4 out, not reco'r.*.......(66 to 1) 5
3577 CROWN EQUERRY (Ire) 7-11-3 P Carberry, *prmnt, reminders and blun 8th, sn lost pl and beh.*...(12 to 1 op 10 to 1) 6
3065* WITH IMPUNITY 8-11-3 A P McCoy, *al rear.*
.... (20 to 1 op 16 to 1) 7
3112 GUINDA (Ire) 7-10-12 C Llewellyn, *whiped round strt and lost many ls, pld up second.*..........(20 to 1 op 14 to 1) 8
Dist: 2½l, ¾l, nk, 30l, 26l, 4l. 4m 58.40s. a 11.40s (8 Ran).

(Mr & Mrs Raymond Anderson Green), C Parker

3717 Samsung Electronics Scottish Champion Hurdle Limited Handicap Class A Grade 2 (4-y-o and up) £16,416 2m.................(3:25)

3111* SHADOW LEADER [136] 6-10-5 J Osborne, *hld up and beh, hdwy on inner 4 out, led on bit 2 out, quickened clr flt, imprsv.*
.... (Evens fav op 6 to 4 tchd 13 to 8) 1
3595⁵ ZABADII (Ire) [137] 5-10-6 R Johnson, *hld up in midfield, hdwy appr 3 out, ev ch nxt, sn rdn and kpt on, no chance wth wnr.*
.... (14 to 1 op 12 to 1) 2
2591⁶ EDELWEIS DU MOULIN (Fr) [135] 5-10-4 P Carberry, *hld up and beh, hdwy appr 3 out, rdn nxt and kpt on same pace.*
.... (10 to 1 tchd 11 to 1) 3
3305² INGLETONIAN [135] 8-10-4 B Storey, *al prmnt, rdn alng and outpcd 3 out, styd on und pres appr last.*
.... (66 to 1 op 50 to 1) 4
3595³ DREAMS END [142] 9-10-11 A P McCoy, *cl up, led appr 3 out, sn rdn, hng rght and hdd nxt, wknd bef last.*
.... (7 to 1 op 8 to 1 tchd 9 to 1) 5
3523⁶ KADASTROF (Fr) [135] 7-9-13 (5*) X Aizpuru, *made most till rdn and hdd appr 3 out, sn wknd.*......(25 to 1) 6
3113⁴ I'M SUPPOSIN (Ire) [152] 5-11-7 R Dunwoody, *chsd ldrs, mstk 4th, rdn bef 3 out and sn wknd....*(7 to 2 op 3 to 1) 7
2695⁸ HOME COUNTIES (Ire) [135] 8-10-4 D J Moffatt, *hld up and beh, effrt appr 3 out, sn rdn and no hdwy.*
.... (33 to 1 op 25 to 1) 8
2218⁷ MASTER BEVELED [139] 7-10-5 (3*) Mr R Thornton, *hld up, effrt and some hdwy on outer 4 out, sn rdn and btn nxt.*
.... (9 to 1) 9
3595⁴ CLIFTON BEAT (USA) [139] 6-10-8 C F Swan, *chsd ldrs, effrt and cl up 4 out, rdn and wknd nxt....*(10 to 1 op 7 to 1) 10
3080³ EXPRESS GIFT [135] 8-10-4 N Williamson, *chsd ldrs, rdn alng and wknd 4 out.*...(14 to 1 op 12 to 1) 11
Dist: 3l, 5l, 2½l, 2l, sht-hd, 1l, 2l, 1¼l, 1l, 3l. 3m 38.30s. a 2.30s (11 Ran).
SR: 46/44/37/34/39/32/48/29/31/

(James Blackshaw), C R Egerton

3718 Stakis Casinos Scottish Grand National Handicap Chase Class A Grade 3 (5-y-o and up) £41,316 4m 1f.................(4:05)

3063² BELMONT KING (Ire) [142] 9-11-10 A P McCoy, *made all, blun 20th, rdn 3 out, blundered last, drvn and styd on gmely.*
.... (16 to 1 op 14 to 1) 1
3081* SAMLEE (Ire) [118] 8-10-0 N Williamson, *midfield, hdwy and blun 12th, sn cl up, blunded badly 21st, chsd wnr frm 5 out, drvn 2 out, kpt on....*..............(3 to 1 tchd 9 to 1) 2
3132⁸ BARONET (Ire) [120] 7-10-2 R Johnson, *hld up, hdwy to chase ldrs hfwy, rdn alng and outpcd 6 out, styd on frm 2 out, fnshd wl.*...........(11 to 1 op 10 to 1 tchd 12 to 1) 3
3659* ACT THE WAG (Ire) [119] (bl) 8-10-1 P Carberry, *hld up, steady hdwy hfwy, chsd ldrs 19th, rdn alng 3 out, kpt on till eased nr line.*.............(15 to 2 op 7 to 1 tchd 8 to 1) 4
2986 COURT MELODY (Ire) [119] (bl) 9-9-12 (3*) Mr R Thornton, *hdwy to join ldrs 8th, cl up and rdn alng 5 out, drvn and kpt on same pace frm 3 out.*..............(14 to 1 tchd 16 to 1) 5
3605⁸ DAKYNS BOY [118] 12-10-0 C Llewellyn, *chsd ldrs, rdn alng same pace....*...............(25 to 1 op 20 to 1) 6
3581⁵ FIVELEIGH BUILDS [123] 10-10-5 A Thornton, *cl up, rdn alng 19th, grad wknd frm 6 out....*....(16 to 1 op 14 to 1) 7
3207 KAMIKAZE [120] (bl) 7-10-2 C O'Dwyer, *hld up, blun 9th, hdwy to chase ldrs 19th, rdn alng 6 out, mstk nxt, 4th whn hit four out, sn wknd....*...........(8 to 1 op 7 to 1 tchd 9 to 1) 8
3577 BUCKHOUSE BOY [132] (bl) 7-11-0 C Maude, *chsd ldrs, effrt 20th, rdn alng and wknd aftr 5 out....*(14 to 1 op 12 to 1) 9
3605⁷ KILLESHIN [127] (v) 11-10-9 S Curran, *al rear, beh 12th, tld off frm 20th.*..................(14 to 1 op 12 to 1) 10
3605⁴ BUCKBOARD BOUNCE [139] 11-11-7 Captain A Ogden, *beh frm 10th, pld up bef 13th.*..............(14 to 1) 11
3453 SISTER STEPHANIE [124] 8-10-6 R Dunwoody, *unruly strt, slwly away and rear whn blun badly and uns rdr 5th.*
.... (4 to 1 fav op 6 to 1 tchd 7 to 1) ur
3581² CAB ON TARGET [130] 11-10-12 P Niven, *hld up, some hdwy hfwy, lost tch and beh whn pld up bef 21st.*
.... (15 to 2 op 8 to 1 tchd 9 to 1 and 7 to 1) pu

517

3578² HIGHLANDMAN [119] 11-10-1¹ Mr Chris Wilson, *chsd ldrs to hfwy, beh whn pld up 5 out*............................. (100 to 1) pu
PARSONS BRIG [118] 11-10-0 A S Smith, *al beh, tld off whn pld up bef 19th*............................. (100 to 1 op 50 to 1) pu
3605 SPUFFINGTON [120] 9-10-2² P Hide, *in tch, chsd ldrs hfwy,, lost pl and beh 4 out, pld up bef 2 out*............ (33 to 1) pu
3114² STORMTRACKER (Ire) [121] 8-10-3 M Richards, *al prmnt, rdn alng 20th, wknd aftr nxt, pld up bef 4 out.* (7 to 1 op 6 to 1) pu
Dist: 1½l, 2l, hd, nk, 5l, 2½l, 4l, 2½l, dist. 8m 24.80s. a 20.80s (17 Ran).

(Mrs Billie Bond), P F Nicholls

3719 Client Entertainment Services Handicap Chase Class C (0-135 5-y-o and up) £5,182 2m......... (4:40)

2287³ MONYMAN (Ire) [105] 7-10-2 N Williamson, *hld up, hdwy 5th, chlgd on bit 3 out, led nxt and sn clr.* (11 to 2 tchd 6 to 1) 1
3596⁴ MISTER ODDY [127] 11-11-10 T J Murphy, *led so soon, chsd ldg pair, led ag'n aftr 5 out, hdd and hit 2 out, kpt on, no ch wth wnr*............................. (7 to 1 op 5 to 1) 2
3126² WEAVER GEORGE (Ire) [109] 7-10-6 M Moloney, *in tch, effrt 5 out, rdn alng nxt, one pace frm 3 out, mstk last.* .... (11 to 2 op 5 to 1 tchd 6 to 1) 3
3508³ GOLDEN HELLO [105] 6-10-2 L Wyer, *in tch, outpcd and beh hfwy, hdwy 4 out, sn rdn and kpt on same pace.* .... (9 to 1 op 7 to 1 tchd 10 to 1) 4
3158* RALLEGIO [103] 8-9-11 (3*) Mr R Thornton, *hld up, hdwy 5 out, rdn nxt and sn btn, broke blood vessel*........... (7 to 1) 5
3596 POLITICAL TOWER [127] 10-11-10 B Storey, *hld up, hdwy 5 out, rdn nxt and sn btn*.................. (11 to 2 op 4 to 1) 6
3154 STORM FALCON (USA) [115] 7-10-7 (5*) Chris Webb, *chsd 4th, hdd aftr 5 out, wkng whn blun nxt, sn beh.* .... (11 to 1 op 8 to 1 tchd 12 to 1) 7
3565⁵ NO PAIN NO GAIN (Ire) [115] (bl) 9-10-12 P Hide, *led second, hdd 4th, cl up and blun 6 out, wknd aftr nxt.* .... (5 to 1 fav tchd 4 to 1) 8
2528⁸ EDREDON BLEU (Fr) [131] 5-11-7 R Dunwoody, *in tch, rdn alng and wknd 5 out, beh whn pld up bef 2 out.* .... (10 to 1 op 8 to 1 tchd 12 to 1) pu
Dist: 8l, 5l, 1½l, 2½l, 3½l, 3½l, 21l. 3m 47.60s. a 2.60s (9 Ran).

SR: 32/46/23/17/12/32/16/-/-/ (Trevor Hemmings), M D Hammond

3720 Glenmuir Future Champion Standard Open National Hunt Flat Class H (Div I) (4,5,6-y-o) £1,710 2m (5:10)

KINGS MEASURE (Ire) 4-10-9 (3*) E Callaghan, *in tch, hdwy 3 fs out, led appr last, rdn, ran green and edgd lft, styd on wl nr finish*........................... (25 to 1 op 14 to 1 tchd 33 to 1) 1
SIREN SONG (Ire) 6-12-0 R Dunwoody, *trkd ldrs gng wl, led on bit o'r 2 fs out, hdd and shaken up appr last, ev ch till not quicken last 100 yards.*.......... (9 to 1 op 7 to 1 tchd 10 to 1) 2
2370² SIMONS CASTLE (Ire) 4-11-5 R Johnson, *in tch, hdwy 6 fs out, rdn o'r 2 furlongs out, kpt on appr last.* .... (7 to 1 tchd 6 to 1) 3
2953⁴ RED CURATE (Ire) 6-11-11 A P McCoy, *cl up, led hfwy, rdn alng 4 fs out, hdd o'r 2 out and grad wknd.* .... (5 to 1 op 4 to 1 tchd 11 to 2 op 6 to 1) 4
LORD OF THE RIVER (Ire) 5-11-4 J Osborne, *midfield, hdwy 5 fs out, rdn alng 3 out, kpt on appr last.* .... (4 to 1 op 7 to 1 tchd 9 to 1) 5
3135⁷ SAMUEL WILDERSPIN 5-11-8 (3*) R Massey, *keen hold, in tch on outer, hdwy 6 fs out, cl up and ev ch o'r 3 out, sn rdn and btn 2 out*............. (6 to 4 fav tchd 5 to 4 and 7 to 4) 6
OH SO COSY (Ire) 4-10-12 B Storey, *beh, hdwy 4 fs out, kpt on fnl 2 furlongs, nvr rch ldrs*............... (20 to 1 op 12 to 1) 7
2824⁸ DONNYBROOK (Ire) 4-10-7 (5*) B Grattan, *beh, hdwy 4 fs out, styd on fnl 2 furlongs, nvr rch ldrs*.....(100 to 1 op 66 to 1) 8
BALA PYJAMA 4-10-12 L Wyer, *beh, hdwy 4 fs out, kpt on fnl 2 furlongs, nvr rch ldrs*.......................(100 to 1) 9
REALLY USEFUL (Ire) 5-11-4 P Carberry, *cl up, rdn 4 fs out, wknd o'r 2 furlongs out*..................(12 to 1 op 7 to 1) 10
THE OPERATOR (Ire) 6-11-4 L O'Hara, *in tch. effrt and hdwy o'r 4 fs out, rdn over 2 out, sn wknd.* (50 to 1 op 33 to 1) 11
RIVER MULLIGAN (Ire) 5-11-4 C F Swan, *hld up, effrt on inner hfwy and sn pushed alng, no hdwy fnl 4 fs.* .... (12 to 1 op 8 to 1) 12
JOWOODY 17-10-7 D Parker, *nvr rch ldrs*.........(200 to 1) 13
2248⁷ HEIDIQUEENOFCLUBS (Ire) 6-10-13 C Maude, *led to hfwy, sn lost pl and beh fnl 4 fs*................. (50 to 1 op 33 to 1) 14
2545* SOCIETY TIMES (USA) 4-11-5 N Williamson, *chsd ldrs, rdn alng 3 fs out, wknd 2 out.* .... (12 to 1 tchd 14 to 1 and 25 to 1) 15
BLAKE'S OEMIN 5-10-11 (7*) R Burns, *al rear.* .... (50 to 1 op 33 to 1) 16
PERRYMAN (Ire) 6-11-4 C O'Dwyer, *beh, effrt and some hdwy 4 fs out, sn rdn and wknd.* .... (50 to 1 op 33 to 1) 17
BUABHALL MOR 4-10-5 (7*) C McCormack, *al rear.* ....(100 to 1) 18
BINGLEY BANK 5-11-4 C Llewellyn, *beh, hdwy on outer hfwy, rdn 6 fs out and sn wknd.* (33 to 1 op 20 to 1) 19
RADICAL STORM (Ire) 6-11-4 K Johnson, *prmnt, rdn alng 6 fs out*........................... (50 to 1 op 100 to 1) 20
Dist: 1½l, 1¼l, 7l, ¾l, 1¼l, 3½l, 1l, 2½l, hd, 1¾l. 3m 39.20s. (20 Ran).

(John H Wilson), J M Jefferson

3721 Glenmuir Future Champion Standard Open National Hunt Flat Class H (Div II) (4,5,6-y-o) £1,710 2m (5:40)

DECOUPAGE 5-11-4 N Williamson, *in tch, hdwy 6 fs out, effrt o'r 2 out, rdn to ld entering last, styd on.* .... (3 to 1 fav tchd 7 to 2) 1
3251* GO NATIVE (Ire) 5-11-6 (5*) R Wilkinson, *cl up, led 3 fs out, rdn 2 out, hdd entering last, kpt on.* .... (6 to 1 op 7 to 1 tchd 8 to 1) 2
VALHALLA (Ire) 4-10-12 A P McCoy, *midfield, hdwy 5 fs out, effrt 3 out, ev ch 2 out, sn rdn and kpt on one pace appr last.* .... (12 to 1) 3
THE VILLAGE WAY (Ire) 6-11-4 R Johnson, *keen hold, chsd ldrs, hdwy 5 fs out, rdn 3 out, kpt on same pace.* .... (10 to 1 op 7 to 1) 4
3048⁵ WOODFIELD VISION (Ire) 6-11-4 P Niven, *hld up and beh, hdwy o'r 5 fs out, rdn over 2 out, styd on.* .... (14 to 1 op 12 to 1 tchd 16 to 1) 5
3335⁹ GLEVUM 5-10-13 C Llewellyn, *cl up, rdn o'r 3 fs out, wknd 2 out.*............................. (33 to 1 op 25 to 1) 6
2939² CARLINGFORD TYKE (Ire) 5-11-4 G Cahill, *in tch, effrt and pushed alng 6 fs out, rdn 3 out and no imprsn.* .... (16 to 1 op 14 to 1) 7
SKILLWISE 5-11-4 L Wyer, *beh till styd on fnl 3 fs, nrst finish.* .... (25 to 1 op 16 to 1) 8
CHOCOLATE DRUM (Ire) 6-11-4 M Moloney, *in rear, pushed alng and hdwy 4 fs out, rdn 3 out and nvr a factor.* .... (100 to 1 op 50 to 1) 9
3302² NORMANIA (NZ) 5-11-4 Mr T Hills, *led, rdn 4 fs out, hdd 3 furlongs out and grad wknd.* (12 to 1 op 14 to 1) 10
3658 OPEN FAIRWAY 4-10-7 (5*) R McGrath, *hld up, effrt and some hdwy 4 fs out, rdn and wknd 3 furlongs out.*........(33 to 1) 11
HACK ON 5-10-13 G Tormey, *in tch, rdn alng and lost pl o'r 6 fs out.*............................. (10 to 1 tchd 14 to 1) 12
WILLIAM OF ORANGE 5-11-4 L O'Hara, *nvr rch ldrs.* .... (33 to 1) 13
KIMDALOO (Ire) 5-11-4 B Storey, *hld up and beh, hdwy o'r 3 fs out, wnt lft and sn wknd*.............(25 to 1 op 16 to 1) 14
TIED FOR TIME (Ire) 5-11-4 J Culloty, *al rear.* .... (33 to 1 tchd 14 to 1) 15
NEEDLE THREAD 5-10-6 (7*) R Burns, *midfield, hdwy to chase ldrs 6 fs out, wknd 4 out.*......(33 to 1 op 20 to 1) 16
STEALS YER THUNDER (Ire) 5-11-4 A Thornton, *chsd ldrs, rdn o'r 6 fs out and sn lost pl, tld off and virtually pld up fnl 2 furlongs*........................... (66 to 1 op 50 to 1) 17
2642* RASAK 5-11-11 R Dunwoody, *hld up in tch, hdwy and prmnt 6 fs out, rdn 4 furlongs out and sn wknd, virtually pld up fnl 2 furlongs*........................... (7 to 2 tchd 4 to 1) 18
GEM OF HOLLY 4-10-4 (3*) Mr R Thornton, *chsd ldrs, rdn alng 6 fs out, wknd and tld off 3 furlongs...*......(100 to 1) 19
2899* BENVENUTO 6-11-11 C O'Dwyer, *chsd ldrs on inner, rdn alng 5 fs out, wknd 3 out and pld up wl o'r one furlong out.* .... (5 to 1 tchd 11 to 2) pu
Dist: 1¼l, 2½l, 3l, 3½l, 7l, sht-hd, ½l, nk, 2½l, 1¼l. 3m 38.50s. (20 Ran).

(J F Dean), C R Egerton

BANGOR (good)
Saturday April 19th
Going Correction: PLUS 0.35 sec. per fur.

3722 Crewe Novices' Hurdle Class E (4-y-o and up) £2,948 2½m...... (2:10)

2661 SPECIAL BEAT 5-10-10 (5*) Mr C Vigors, *in tch, hdwy to chase ldr 5th, led aftr 4 out, gng strly whn lft clr nxt, not fluent last, cmftbly.*...........(11 to 1 op 8 to 1 tchd 12 to 1) 1
2898² CHEROKEE CHIEF 6-11-0 J A McCarthy, *midfield, hdwy aftr 6th, lft chasing wnr 3 out, no imprsn.* .... (11 to 10 fav op 6 to 4) 2
3500* RING OF VISION (Ire) 5-11-6 J Railton, *sn hndy, rdn 3 out, one pace.*............................. (7 to 2 op 3 to 1) 3
3198 KHALIKHOUM (Ire) 4-10-2 (5*) D J Kavanagh, *midfield, hdwy to chase ldrs aftr 6th, rdn 4 out, sn btn.* .... (50 to 1 op 33 to 1 tchd 66 to 1) 4
3176⁹ GOWER-SLAVE 5-11-0 W Marston, *in tch, mstk 1st, chasing ldrs whn mistake 7th, drvn appr 3 out, fdd.* .... (50 to 1 op 33 to 1) 5
THE NAUGHTY VICAR 7-11-0 Richard Guest, *midfield, effrt 7th, no imprsn on ldrs and sn eased.* .... (33 to 1 tchd 40 to 1 and 50 to 1) 6
3535 NORTHERN STAR 6-10-13 (7*) Miss J Wormall, *rear div, und pres 4 out, nvr able to chal.*........ (16 to 1 tchd 20 to 1) 7
WESTERN SUN 7-10-9 (5*) A Bates, *beh, lost tch 5th, tld off.* .... (66 to 1 op 33 to 1 tchd 100 to 1) 8
1776⁵ ASK ME IN (Ire) 6-10-9 M Foster, *chsd clr ldr early, wknd quickly 6th, tld off....*................. (25 to 1 op 16 to 1) 9
PHARMONY (Ire) 7-10-9 (5*) G F Ryan, *hld up and beh, tld off.* .... (50 to 1 op 33 to 1) 10
3373* PERSIAN ELITE (Ire) (bl) 6-11-6 J R Kavanagh, *took keen hold, led and clr early, mstk 4th, hdd aftr four out, cl second whn blun and uns rdr nxt.* (16 to 1 op 10 to 1 tchd 11 to 2) ur

518

ORINOCO VENTURE (Ire) 6-11-0 T Kent, *chsd ldrs till wknd quickly 6th, tld off whn pld up bef nxt.*
.... (50 to 1 op 33 to 1 tchd 66 to 1) pu
2260[7] THE CROOKED OAK 5-11-0 D Walsh, *sn hndy, mstk 6th, wknd 4 out, beh whn pld up bef 2 out.* (20 to 1 op 14 to 1) pu
2871 COOL CAT (Ire) 6-11-0 V Slattery, *beh, lost tch 5th, tld off whn pld up bef 7th........* (66 to 1 op 33 to 1 tchd 100 to 1) pu
DUNSTON KNIGHT 4-10-0 (7") J Mogford, *beh, lost tch 5th, tld off whn pld up bef 3 out.*
.... (66 to 1 op 33 to 1 tchd 100 to 1) pu
2723[7] JEMARO (Ire) 6-11-0 T Jenks, *midfield, struggling 6th, beh whn pld up bef 2 out.*...........(66 to 1 op 33 to 1) pu
1817[7] SOUNDPOST 5-11-0 Mr A Wood, *al beh, lost tch 5th, tld off whn pld up bef 3 out...*(66 to 1 op 33 to 1) pu
3374[7] ONE BOY 5-11-0 P Holley, *beh, mstk second, reminders aftr 4th, sn lost tch, jmpd rght 6th, tld off whn pld up bef nxt.*
.... (66 to 1 op 33 to 1) pu
Dist: 9l, 3½l, 14l, 15l, 2½l, dist, dist, dist. 4m 43.90s. a 13.90s (18 Ran).
SR: 18/8/10/-/-/-/ (C Marner), N J Henderson

3723 Robert Jones 21st Open Hunters' Chase Class H (6-y-o and up) £1,689 2½m 110yds.................. (2:40)

3622[7] MY NOMINEE (bl) 9-12-0 (7") Mr R Burton, *made all, wl clr 4 out, eased dwn r-in.*
.... (13 to 8 on op 7 to 4 on tchd 11 to 8 on) 1
3591[3] DALAMETRE 10-11-7 (7") Mr M Munrowd, *hndy, chsd wnr frm 7th, no imprsn frm 4 out.*............ (8 to 1 op 7 to 1) 2
SAAHI (USA) 8-11-7 (7") Miss S Swindells, *wl beh, styd on frm 3 out, nvr a factor..........* (25 to 1 op 10 to 1) 3
3458[3] GALZIG 9-11-7 (7") Mr W Tellwright, *midfield, mstk 6th, effrt to chase ldrs tenth, btn frm 4 out..........* (9 to 1 op 8 to 1) 4
NADIAD 11-11-7 (7") Mr A Wintle, *beh, hdwy to chase ldrs 6th, reminders appr tenth, wknd nxt, no ch whn blun last, tld off.*
..........................(10 to 1 tchd 12 to 1) 5
3288[4] CHARLIES DELIGHT (Ire) 9-11-9 (5") Mr C Vigors, *in tch till f 5th.....................* (25 to 1 op 16 to 1 tchd 50 to 1) f
3279[6] SIMPLY PERFECT 11-11-7 (7") Miss K Swindells, *blun and uns rdr 1st.............* (14 to 1 op 10 to 1 tchd 16 to 1) ur
3529[4] KING OF SHADOWS 10-12-0 (7") Mr S Prior, *chsd ldrs, lost pl 6th, sn beh, tld off whn pld up bef 2 out..........* (16 to 1) pu
PRESS FOR ACTION 12-11-9 (5") Mr R Ford, *prmnt, jmpd rght 7th, wknd 9th, tld off whn pld up bef 4 out.*
.... (12 to 1 op 10 to 1 tchd 14 to 1) pu
RATHER SHARP 11-12-2 (5") Mr B Pollock, *al beh, lost tch 9th, tld off whn pld up bef nxt........* (50 to 1 op 33 to 1) pu
THORNHILL 7-11-2 (7") Mr A Wood, *beh, reminders 9th and lost tch, tld off whn pld up bef 3 out.*
.... (66 to 1 op 25 to 1 tchd 100 to 1) pu
Dist: 22l, 2l, 8l, 14l. 5m 13.80s. a 27.80s (11 Ran).
(D E Nicholls), D E Nicholls

3724 Halliwell Landau Novices' Chase Class D (5-y-o and up) £4,201 2m 1f 110yds........................ (3:10)

2998* INDIAN JOCKEY 5-11-11 D Walsh, *made all, ran on wl frm 2 out............................*(5 to 2 on op 2 to 1 on) 1
3354[3] EXEMPLAR (Ire) 9-10-9 (5") G F Ryan, *in rear, reminders aftr 7th, mstk 4 out, effrt whn jmpd rght 2 out, styd on to chase wnr r-in, no imprsn..........* (4 to 1 op 7 to 2 tchd 9 to 2) 2
3143 THE SECRET GREY 6-11-0 T Jenks, *chsd wnr, rdn whn mstk last, wknd r-in..................* (20 to 1 op 14 to 1) 3
3357[5] EUROLINK SHADOW 5-10-7 V Slattery, *hld up, effrt whn mstk and hmpd 4 out, wknd appr 2 out....*(33 to 1 op 14 to 1) 4
3320[3] DEE LIGHT 8-10-9 Richard Guest, *chsd ldrs, no imprsn frm 2 out, 4th and tiring whn f heavily last.*
......................(6 to 1 op 5 to 1 tchd 8 to 1) f
Dist: 5l, 2½l, 14l. 4m 24.10s. a 22.10s (5 Ran).
(Stuart M Mercer), M C Pipe

3725 Sotheby's Handicap Hurdle Class D (0-120 4-y-o and up) £3,647 3m .... (3:45)

3621[2] FIRST CRACK [88] 12-10-3 T Eley, *hld up, hdwy 5 out, chlgd 3 out, ran on to ld cl hme.*
.... (6 to 1 op 11 to 2 tchd 7 to 1 and 15 to 2) 1
3498[4] DERRING BRIDGE [85] 7-10-0 W Marston, *midfield, hdwy 7th, led out, al hrd pressed, hdd cl hme.*
.... (25 to 1 op 14 to 1) 2
2923[3] HOODED HAWK (Ire) [99] 6-11-0 J R Kavanagh, *hld up, hdwy 5 out, sn chasing ldrs, no imprsn frm 2 out.*
......................(6 to 1 op 5 to 1) 3
3655* SHARP COMMAND [94] 4-10-4[2] Richard Guest, *hld up, hdwy to track ldrs 5 out, drvn and outpcd frm 3 out.*
......(2 to 1 fav op 3 to 1 tchd 100 to 30 and 7 to 2) 4
2601[9] OLD CAVALIER [85] 6-10-0 J Callaghan, *in tch, effrt 4 out, no imprsn on ldrs............*(25 to 1 op 14 to 1 tchd 33 to 1) 5
2989[4] PHARARE (Ire) [96] 7-10-6 (5") D J Kavanagh, *cl up till wknd 4 out...........................* (14 to 1 op 10 to 1) 6
3572[2] LAYHAM LOW (Ire) [88] 6-10-3 J A McCarthy, *midfield, hdwy to chase ldrs, wknd 4 out.*
.... (14 to 1 op 10 to 1 tchd 16 to 1) 7
3321[2] PRUSSIA [99] 6-10-11 (3") Guy Lewis, *cl up, rdn appr 4 out, sn wknd........*(6 to 1 op 5 to 1 tchd 13 to 2 and 7 to 1) 8

3285[6] THIS NETTLE DANGER [85] 13-10-0 M Brennan, *hld up in rear, struggling frm 5 out, nvr a factor,* (33 to 1 op 16 to 1) 9
3440[4] CUTTHROAT KID (Ire) [103] 7-11-4 P Holley, *midfield, lost pl 4th, sn beh..............* (14 to 1 op 8 to 1) 10
3136[9] KANO WARRIOR [85] 10-9-7 (7") J Mogford, *midfield, beh frm 5 out...................* (50 to 1 op 25 to 1) 11
2896 BETTER BYTHE GLASS (Ire) [89] 8-10-4 D Walsh, *handily plcd till stumbled and uns rdr appr 7th.*
.... (14 to 1 op 12 to 1 tchd 16 to 1) ur
PRIME DISPLAY (USA) [109] 11-11-10 T Jenks, *prmnt to 7th, sn wknd, tld off whn pld up bef 2 out.* (100 to 1 op 20 to 1) pu
3405[3] TIGER CLAW (USA) [85] 11-9-12[5] (7") Mr G Shenkin, *cl up, rdn and lost pl 5th, sn beh, tld off whn pld up bef 4 out.*
.....................(14 to 1 tchd 16 to 1) pu
FED ON OATS [98] 9-10-13 J Railton, *hld up, hdwy 5 out, ev ch and gng wl whn stumbled 2 out, 3rd when pld up appr last.*
.... (33 to 1 op 16 to 1) pu
3157[6] MILL THYME [85] 5-10-0 M Foster, *hld up, wknd quickly, tld off whn pld up bef 2 out.*
.... (33 to 1 op 20 to 1 tchd 50 to 1) pu
Dist: Hd, 19l, 3l, 10l, 7l, 2½l, 6l, 2l, 5l, 6l. 5m 43.40s. a 14.40s (16 Ran).
SR: 15/12/7/-/-/-/ (D Pugh), F Jordan

3726 Brookes Bell Novices' Handicap Chase Class D (0-110 5-y-o and up) £3,598 2½m 110yds.......... (4:15)

3533* QUITE A MAN [104] 9-11-7 (7") Mr R Burton, *midfield, hdwy to go prmnt 9th, led betw last 2 and edgd lft, styd on.* (3 to 1 jt-fav op 9 to 4) 1
3481[3] ALASKAN HEIR [76] (v) 6-10-0 T Eley, *led second to 4th, cl up till lost pl tenth, sn drvn, rallied frm 2 out, mstk last, styd on to take second r-in.................* (11 to 2 tchd 10 to 1) 2
3434[2] KILTULLA (Ire) [76] 7-9-9 (5") G F Ryan, *trkd ldrs, led 11th to 3 out, led ag'n nxt, hdd betw last 2, short of room whn mstk last, lost second and no extr r-in.........* (11 to 2 tchd 6 to 1) 3
3371[2] CURRAGH PETER [76] 10-10-0[3] (3") Guy Lewis, *led to second, led 4th to 11th, led ag'n 3 out to nxt, sn one pace.*
.... (25 to 1 op 16 to 1) 4
1857[1] FRONTIER FLIGHT (USA) [80] 7-10-1 (3") E Husband, *hld up in tch, effrt to chase ldrs appr 2 out, no extr betw last two.*
..........................(10 to 1) 5
2638 ALTHREY BLUE [76] 8-10-0 M Foster, *not jump wl, al beh, nvr a factor.................*(50 to 1 op 33 to 1) 6
3559[2] WINNOW [76] 7-10-0 C Rae, *took keen hold, nvr gng wl and al beh.....................* (11 to 2 tchd 6 to 1) 7
3477[4] HEATHYARDS BOY [78] (bl) 7-10-2[2] D Walsh, *handily plcd till f heavily 9th.............* (9 to 1 op 7 to 1 tchd 10 to 1) f
3204[4] HARVEST VIEW (Ire) [97] 7-11-0 (7") M Berry, *beh, struggling 8th (water), wl behind whn pld up bef tenth........*(3 to 1 jt-fav op 9 to 4) pu
2550 LIBERTARIAN (Ire) [78] 7-10-2 J A McCarthy, *towards rear, hdwy to chase ldrs tenth, pld up appr 3 out, lme.*
.... (25 to 1 op 14 to 1 tchd 33 to 1) pu
Dist: 3½l, nk, 4l, 4l, 12l, 1¾l. 5m 10.90s. a 24.90s (10 Ran).
(W R J Everall), S A Brookshaw

3727 Jane McAlpine Memorial Hunters' Chase Class H (6-y-o and up) £1,616 3m 110yds.................. (4:45)

NODFORM WONDER 10-11-7 (7") Mr R Bevis, *led to 4th, led 7th to 8th, led ag'n tenth, mstk 3 out, clr whn pckd last, cmftbly.*
..........(5 to 2 fav op 11-4 tchd 3 to 1) 1
MR BUSKER (Ire) 8-11-7 (7") Mr C J B Barlow, *hld up, hdwy to chase wnr bef 3 out, no imprsn.*
.... (14 to 1 tchd 12 to 1 and 16 to 1) 2
3690 JUPITER MOON 8-11-13 (5") Mr C Vigors, *in tch, outpcd frm 5 out, no ch ... no dngr........* (8 to 1 tchd 10 to 1 and 9 to 1) 3
3187 ORTON HOUSE 10-11-7 (7") Mr R Burton, *cl up to 4th, outpcd fnl circuit.*
..........(33 to 1 op 25 to 1 tchd 50 to 1 and 66 to 1) 4
3307[3] ORANGE RAGUSA 11-11-9 (5") Mr R Ford, *prmnt, led 4th to 7th, led 8th to tenth, wknd frm 13th.*
..........................(11 to 4 op 5 to 2 tchd 3 to 1) 5
3426[2] AVOSTAR 10-11-13 (5") Mr B Pollock, *nvr gng wl, al beh, no ch whn f last...................*(7 to 2 op 5 to 2) f
FIBREGUIDE TECH 14-11-7 (7") Mr R Thomas, *al in rear, tld off whn pld up bef 2 out.* (14 to 1 op 10 to 1 tchd 16 to 1) pu
FAIR CROSSING 11-12-0 (7") Mr M Emmanuel, *in tch, prmnt 7th, losing grnd whn pckd tenth, tld off when pld up bef 3 out.*
..........(10 to 1 op 7 to 1 tchd 11 to 1 and 12 to 1) pu
3578 HIGHWAY FIVE (Ire) 9-12-0 (7") Miss E James, *al beh, tld off whn pld up bef 13th.................* (33 to 1 op 14 to 1) pu
Dist: 5l, 16l, hd, 2½l. 6m 21.20s. a 36.20s (9 Ran).
(D A Malam), R J Bevis

3728 Emral Handicap Hurdle Class F (0-100 4-y-o and up) £2,853 2m 1f .... (5:15)

3174* CARACOL [76] 8-10-8 T Dascombe, *hndy, led appr 3 out, drvn out frm last.................* (7 to 2 tchd 6 to 1) 1
3487[2] THE BREWER [73] 5-10-5 W Marston, *midfield, hdwy 5th, chsd ldrs 3 out, styd on cl hme, not rch wnr.*
..........(10 to 1 tchd 12 to 1 and 14 to 1) 2

519

3512* KIERCHEM (Ire) [75] 6-10-7 J Callaghan, *midfield, hdwy 5th, ev ch whn not fluent 2 out, und pres when not fluent last, one pace r-in*................................(11 to 1 op 7 to 2) 3
3424⁹ AJDAR [74] 6-10-6 M Brennan, *hld up, effrt and hdwy 5th, no imprsn frm 3 out*.....................(20 to 1 op 10 to 1) 4
3614⁵ EVEZIO RUFO [84] (bl) 5-11-2 V Slattery, *prmnt, led 4th till appr 3 out, sn wknd*.............(12 to 1 op 7 to 1) 5
3476⁴ NEVER SO BLUE (Ire) [84] 6-10-11 (5*) D J Kavanagh, *hndy, effrt 4 out, wknd appr 2 out*........(12 to 1 tchd 14 to 1) 6
1020* HAMADRYAD (Ire) [96] 9-12-2 J R Kavanagh, *hld up in rear, some prog 4 out, nvr dngrs*........(10 to 1 tchd 12 to 1) 7
2185⁴ SHIFT AGAIN (Ire) [83] (bl) 5-10-12 (3*) Sophie Mitchell, *hld up in rear, mstk 4th, nvr a factor*......(8 to 1 op 6 to 1) 8
3479³ NEWHALL PRINCE [88] 9-11-6 T Eley, *led to 4th, cl up till wknd four out*..........................(9 to 1 op 5 to 1) 9
2880⁵ INNOCENT GEORGE [85] 8-11-3 M Foster, *hld up and beh, nvr able to chal*...........(8 to 1 op 7 to 1 tchd 12 to 1) 10
3462⁴ PRINCIPAL BOY (Ire) [72] 4-10-1 R Rourke, *prmnt, lost pl 5th, wkng whn mstk nxt*.............(20 to 1 op 16 to 1) 11
2973 NAGARA SOUND [72] 6-10-4 Gary Lyons, *beh, blun second, some hdwy 4th, sn rdn alng, wknd four out*.
.....................................(25 to 1 op 12 to 1 tchd 33 to 1) 12
3268 OUT OF THE BLUE [68] (bl) 5-9-7 (7*) J Mogford, *took keen hold, cl up, niggled alng appr 4th and lost pl, beh whn pld up bef last*.........................(50 to 1 op 25 to 1) pu
3401⁵ MAPLETON [78] 4-10-4 Richard Guest, *midfield, hdwy to go hndy 4th, wknd four out, beh whn pld up bef 2 out*.
.............................(5 to 1 fav tchd 6 to 1) pu
Dist: 2½l, 1¼l, 5l, 2½l, 19l, 2½l, 5l, 5l, 11l, 1½l. 4m 2.70s. a 12.70s (14 Ran).
(C G Bolton), J Neville

STRATFORD (good)
Saturday April 19th
Going Correction: PLUS 0.40 sec. per fur.

3729 Jenkinsons Novices' Hurdle Class E (Div I) (4-y-o and up) £1,744 2¾m 110yds.....................(2:35)

3022⁷ ISIS DAWN 5-10-4 (3*) P Henley, *hld up, hdwy 5 out, led 2 out, rdn out*........................(16 to 1 op 14 to 1) 1
3210* SHEKELS (Ire) 6-11-4 G Bradley, *led till hdd 2 out, styd on same pace r-in*.
.........(9 to 4 on op 2 to 1 on tchd 7 to 4 on and 13 to 8 on) 2
OCCOLD (Ire) 6-10-12 D Gallagher, *hld up, hdwy 4th, mstk 3 out, ev ch nxt, mistake last no extr r-in*.(16 to 1 op 14 to 1) 3
BECK AND CALL (Ire) 8-10-12 G Upton, *chsd ldr, chlgd 4 out, mstk nxt, sn rdn and btn*...........(11 to 2 op 6 to 1) 4
2015⁴ IRISH DELIGHT 5-10-12 D Morris, *nvr plcd to chal*.
...................................(16 to 1 op 14 to 1) 5
3269⁷ SIDNEY 8-10-12 S Wynne, *prmnt, mstk 4th, wknd 5 out*.
....(66 to 1) 6
2804⁷ GREEN KING 5-10-5 (7*) D Carey, *strted slwly, hdwy 4th, wknd 5 out*.............(20 to 1 op 14 to 1 tchd 25 to 1) 7
3082 MILL BAY SAM 6-10-12 Derek Byrne, *hld up, al in rear*.
....(33 to 1 op 25 to 1) 8
3506 FINAL ROSE 7-10-0 (7*) Mr J Goldstein, *al beh*.
...............................(66 to 1 op 50 to 1) 9
2782 FREELINE FONTAINE (Ire) 5-10-12 M A Fitzgerald, *trkd ldrs, cl up whn hmpd and uns rdr appr 2 out.(16 to 1 op 14 to 1) ur
MARLIES GOHR 5-10-4 (3*) L Aspell, *blun 1st, al in rear, tld off whn pld up bef 5 out*...........(66 to 1 op 50 to 1) pu
Dist: 2l, 1l, 18l, 10l, 1¼l, 25l, dist, 1l. 5m 34.90s. a 22.90s (11 Ran).
(Major Bob Darell), A G Newcombe

3730 Laurent-Perrier Handicap Chase Class C (0-135 5-y-o and up) £4,133 2½m.....................(3:05)

2514 PHILIP'S WOODY [112] 9-10-6 M A Fitzgerald, *beh, hdwy 7th, led 3 out, styd on wl*..............(7 to 1 op 8 to 1) 1
3154 SUPER COIN [117] 9-10-8 (3*) P Henley, *patiently rdn, hdwy 4 out, chsd wnr 2 out, no impresn*.......(8 to 1 op 7 to 1) 2
2459⁵ MERRY PANTO (Ire) [106] 8-9-7 (7*) C Rafter, *wth ldr till led 4th, sn wl clr, blun four out, hdd nxt, soon btn*.
...................................(16 to 1 op 12 to 1) 3
3651* POLDEN PRIDE [115] 9-10-9 B Clifford, *patiently rdn, hdwy 6 out, mstk 9th wknd appr 2 out*.........(4 to 1 op 4) 4
3531² CALLISOE BAY (Ire) [130] 8-11-10 G Bradley, *led till mstk and hdd 4th, wknd 9th*.
.........................(9 to 2 op 4 to 1 tchd 5 to 1 and 11 to 2) 5
1029 BORO VACATION (Ire) [125] 8-11-5 K Gaule, *beh, hdwy 5th, wknd 4 out*..............(14 to 1 op 10 to 1 tchd 16 to 1) 6
3208³ OVER THE POLE [108] 10-10-2⁴ (3*) D Fortt, *mstk 1st, f 4th*.
...............................(7 to 2 fav op 9 to 2) f
3314³ HIGH ALLTITUDE (Ire) [106] 9-10-0 D Gallagher, *al in rear, tld off whn pld up bef 5 out*............(8 to 1 tchd 10 to 1) pu
3101 AROUND THE HORN [129] 10-11-9 S McNeill, *mid-div, hdwy 5th, wkng whn pld up bef 3 out*.
...................................(10 to 1 op 8 to 1 tchd 12 to 1) pu
Dist: 6l, 6l, sht-hd, 18l, 1l. 5m 1.20s. a 21.20s (9 Ran).
(K G Knox), N J Henderson

3731 Richardsons Parkway Novices' Handicap Hurdle Class E (0-100 4-y-

o and up) £2,360 2m 110yds.. (3:35)

3001² SNOWSHILL SHAKER [80] 8-11-0 R Bellamy, *prmnt, led appr 3 out, sn clr, not fluent 2 out, hit last, rdn out*.
...............................(11 to 2 fav op 4 to 1 tchd 6 to 1) 1
3491* REVERSE THRUST [78] 6-10-5 (7*) M Clinton, *hld up, hdwy 5th, chsd wnr 2 out, no imprsn*.
.....................(8 to 1 op 5 to 1 tchd 9 to 1) 2
NAHLA [80] 7-11-0 S McNeill, *led till hdd appr 3 out, styd on same pace*..........................(14 to 1) 3
3528³ FENCER'S QUEST (Ire) [78] 4-10-6 S Wynne, *mid-div, hdwy 5th, one pace frm 2 out*.(13 to 2 op 6 to 1 tchd 7 to 1) 4
3534⁵ ALPHA LEATHER [66] 6-10-0 Mr J Grassick, *hld up, nvr nr to chal*.......................................(16 to 1) 5
2393⁹ BALLY PARSON [82] 11-11-2 D Leahy, *chsd ldrs till wknd 3 out*...(16 to 1) 6
3495¹ ANIF (USA) [66] 6-9-7 (7*) Mr J Goldstein, *hld up, hdwy 4 out, rdn and btn nxt*........(12 to 1 op 10 to 1 tchd 14 to 1) 7
3468 ANOTHER COMEDY [73] 7-10-7² G Upton, *mid-div, rdn 5th, sn beh*.............................(25 to 1 tchd 33 to 1) 8
3573² KETCHIGAN [72] 5-10-6 S Anderson, *beh frm 5th*.
...............................(9 to 1 op 10 to 1) 9
2952⁶ PALLADIUM BOY [79] 7-10-13 M A Fitzgerald, *chsd ldrs till wknd 4 out*....................(10 to 1 op 8 to 1) 10
3146 RITTO [93] 7-11-13 N Mann, *in rear whn f 3rd*.
.............................(9 to 1 op 8 to 1 tchd 10 to 1) f
2766 SERIOUS OPTION (Ire) [66] 6-10-0 D Morris, *beh frm 5th, tld off and pld up bef 2 out*....................(33 to 1) pu
3186³ SCHNOZZLE (Ire) [87] 6-11-7 G Bradley, *beh whn hmpd 3rd, pld up aftr nxt*..........(7 to 1 op 6 to 1 tchd 9 to 1) pu
3457 ZESTI [75] 5-10-6 (3*) L Aspell, *al in rear, tld off and pld up bef 3 out*.....................(14 to 1 tchd 16 to 1) pu
3468 MILLING BROOK [81] 5-11-1 D Gallagher, *al in rear, tld off and pld up bef last*...........(11 to 1 op 8 to 1) pu
3443⁴ AQUA AMBER [66] 5-10-0 W McFarland, *sn beh, tld off and pld up aftr 4th*.........................(33 to 1) pu
3554⁴ DAYDREAM BELIEVER [66] 5-10-0 B Clifford, *al in rear, tld off and pld up bef 3 out*..........(16 to 1 op 33 to 1) pu
Dist: 10l, ½l, ½l, 2l, ¾l, 15l, 1½l, 30l. 4m 2.90s. a 16.90s (17 Ran).
(Austin P Knight), N A Twiston-Davies

3732 Stratford-on-Avon Novices' Chase Class D (6-y-o and up) £4,419 3m.....................(4:05)

2461⁵ BIG ARCHIE 7-10-12 D Leahy, *rcd keenly, led 4th, hdd last, rallied to ld nr finish*..............(33 to 1 tchd 40 to 1) 1
3556⁴ DOMAINE DE PRON (Fr) 6-11-3 R Bellamy, *trkd ldrs, hmpd 5th, chlgd 3 out, led last, hdd nr finish*.(9 to 2 op 5 to 1) 2
2613 MELNIK 6-11-3 G Upton, *led to 4th, lost pl 6 out, styd on appr last*...........................(9 to 2 op 5 to 1) 3
3331⁶ JOY FOR LIFE (Ire) 6-10-7 S Wynne, *nvr rchd chalg pos*.
.............................(33 to 1 op 25 to 1 tchd 50 to 1) 4
3538³ FATHER SKY (bl) 6-11-8 G Bradley, *prmnt, chsd wnr 11th, mstk 5 out, sn wknd*..(2 to 1 fav tchd 9 to 4 and 5 to 2) 5
3384⁴ MASTER TOBY 7-10-10 (7*) Mr J Goldstein, *chsd ldrs till mstk and uns rdr 5th*.
.................(100 to 30 op 7 to 2 tchd 4 to 1 and 3 to 1) ur
3407² LITTLE ELLIOT (Ire) 9-10-9 (3*) L Aspell, *prmnt, lost pl 8th, mstk 11th, effrt nxt, wkng whn blun 4 out, sn pld up.
...................................(20 to 1 op 14 to 1) pu
HI HEDLEY (Ire) 7-10-12 D Gallagher, *al in rear, beh, pld up bef 3 out*.......(10 to 1 tchd 12 to 1 and 9 to 1) pu
3195³ DEBONAIR DUDE (Ire) 7-10-12 M A Fitzgerald, *hld up, effrt whn mstk 8th, wknd 6 out, pld up bef 3 out*.
.........................(13 to 2 op 6 to 1) pu
Dist: Nk, dist, 2l, 10l. 6m 5.50s. a 20.50s (9 Ran).
(Cliff Basson), Mrs A J Bowlby

3733 Richardsons Star Site Hunters' Chase Class H (6-y-o and up) £2,038 2m 5f 110yds.....................(4:35)

MANKIND 6-11-7 (7*) Mr L Baker, *chsd ldrs, led 4th to 9th, led 2 out, rdn out*..................(66 to 1 tchd 100 to 1) 1
3529³ PRO BONO (Ire) 7-11-9 (5*) Mr A Sansome, *al prmnt, led 9th, hdd and mstk 2 out, styd on same pace*.
.............................(9 to 1 op 8 to 1 tchd 12 to 1) 2
EASTERN PLEASURE 10-11-7 (7*) Mr T J Barry, *prmnt till wknd 4 out*...........................(20 to 1 tchd 16 to 1) 3
3622³ FOX POINTER 12-12-0 (7*) Mr O McPhail, *led to 4th, wknd 5 out*...(7 to 4 fav op 9 to 4 tchd 5 to 2) 4
TUDOR FABLE (Ire) 9-12-3 (7*) Mr Rupert Sweeting, *al beh*.
...........................(14 to 1 op 12 to 1 tchd 16 to 1) 5
3387⁶ TELLAPORKY 8-11-7 (7*) Mr A Middleton, *slwly into strd, al beh*......................(33 to 1 tchd 50 to 1) 6
ERLEMO (bl) 8-11-7 (7*) Dr P Pritchard, *strted slwly, al wl beh*.
...............(33 to 1 op 20 to 1 tchd 40 to 1) 7
EMERALD RULER 10-11-10¹ (5*) Mr J Trice-Rolph, *al in rear, tld off and pld up bef 6 out*..........(20 to 1 op 16 to 1) pu
3387 STAR OATS 11-11-7 (7*) Mr A Kinane, *prmnt, hit tenth, blun nxt, sn wknd, pld up bef 4 out*......(14 to 1 op 10 to 1) pu
3499² TUFFNUT GEORGE 10-12-3 (7*) Mr A Phillips, *prmnt till wknd 6 out, pld up bef 3 out*......(6 to 1 op 3 to 1 tchd 7 to 1) pu

3529 FRANK BE LUCKY 11-11-7 (7*) Mr R Wakley, prmnt, mstks, wknd 5 out, pld up bef 2 out.
.... (13 to 2 op 7 to 1 tchd 8 to 1) pu

3622⁴ CANDLE GLOW 9-11-2 (7*) Mr P Hutchinson, chsd ldrs till wknd 7th, pld up bef tenth. (7 to 1 op 6 to 1 tchd 8 to 1) pu

3461 PRINZAL 10-12-0 Mr M Armytage, hld up, hdwy 5 out, wknd nxt, pld up bef 3 out...... (9 to 1 op 6 to 1 tchd 10 to 1) pu

SECRET CASTLE 9-11-7 (7*) Mr L Brown, strted slwly, al beh, pld up bef 9th....................(100 to 1 op 66 to 1) pu

Dist: 1½l, dist, 2½l, 13l, 11l, 5l. 5m 30.80s. a 30.80s (14 Ran).

(J A T de Giles) J A T de Giles

3734 Richardsons Merlin Park Mares' Only Handicap Hurdle Class D (0-120 4-y-o and up) £2,034 2m 110yds...................... (5:05)

3557² BARFORD SOVEREIGN [114] 5-12-0 M A Fitzgerald, led to 3rd, chlgd 3 out, led nxt, hdd last, rallied to ld nr finish.
.... (3 to 1 op 9 to 4 tchd 10 to 30) 1

3675² HANDY LASS [101] 8-10-8 (7*) Mr O McPhail, hld up, hdwy 4 out, led nxt, hdd 2 out, rgned ld last, headed nr finish.
.... (9 to 2 op 5 to 1 tchd 11 to 2) 2

3110* SIBERIAN MYSTIC [92] 4-11-0 W McFarland, hld up, hdwy 3 out, sn ev ch, no extr appr last................... (9 to 4 jt-fav tchd 5 to 2 and 11 to 4) 3

3633⁶ STAPLEFORD LADY [86] 9-10-0 S McNeill, hld up, hdwy to chase ldr 4 out, wknd aftr nxt.
.... (10 to 1 op 12 to 1 tchd 9 to 1) 4

3402* SECRET GIFT [92] (bl) 4-10-0 D Leahy, chsd ldr till led 3rd, hdd 3 out, sn wknd...(9 to 4 jt-fav op 7 to 4 tchd 5 to 2) 5

Dist: Hd, 5l, 16l, 21l. 4m 3.10s. a 17.10s (5 Ran).

(Barford Bloodstock), J R Fanshawe

3735 Jenkinsons Novices' Hurdle Class E (Div II) (4-y-o and up) £1,744 2¾m 110yds.................... (5:35)

3241* SUPREME FLYER (Ire) 7-10-11 (7*) Mr R Wakley, hld up, hdwy 7th, chsd ldr 3 out, led last, ran on wl.
.... (6 to 4 fav tchd 7 to 4 and 11 to 8) 1

2874* MOUNTAIN PATH 7-11-4 M A Fitzgerald, led second, hdd last, unbl to quicken r-in... (7 to 4 op 6 to 4 tchd 2 to 1) 2

PAT BUCKLEY 6-10-5 (7*) Mr J Goldstein, chsd ldrs till lost pl 4th, rallied four out, styd on same pace frm 2 out.
.... (12 to 1 op 9 to 1 tchd 14 to 1) 3

2637⁴ WILLOWS ROULETTE 5-10-12 R Greene, hld up, styd on frm 4 out, nvr plcd to chal..........(20 to 1 op 14 to 1) 4

SKY BURST 7-10-7 G Upton, hld up, hdwy 5th, wknd appr 2 out.................... (8 to 1 op 10 to 1) 5

LORD COOL (Ire) 6-10-12 G Bradley, hld up, hdwy 4th, chsd ldr four out, wknd appr 2 out.........(12 to 1 op 9 to 1) 6

3144² ARMATEUR (Fr) 9-10-12 D Leahy, prmnt till lost pl 4th, nvr dngrs aftrwards....... (11 to 1 op 12 to 1 tchd 10 to 1) 7

FOOLS FUTURE 8-10-12 D Gallagher, rcd keenly, led briefly aftr second, wknd 4 out........ (40 to 1 op 100 to 1) 8

3555⁹ FEARLESS HUSSAR 7-10-12 N Mann, hld up, mstk 5th, wknd 6 out, pld up bef 4 out. (33 to 1 op 25 to 1 tchd 50 to 1) pu

ABOVE THE CLOUDS 6-10-9 (3*) P Henley, pld hrd, led to second, wknd 5 out, pulled up bef nxt. (66 to 1 op 100 to 1) pu

CLOUDY HOUSE 8-10-11 (7*) Mr L Baker, prmnt till wknd 7th, beh whn pld up bef 3 out..........(66 to 1 op 100 to 1) pu

Dist: 2½l, 7l, 9l, 3½l, 19l, 22l, 22l. 5m 36.30s. a 24.30s (11 Ran).

(Mrs E A Kellar), K C Bailey

TOWCESTER (good to firm)
Monday April 21st
Going Correction: MINUS 0.15 sec. per fur. (races 1,3,6), NIL (2,4,5)

3736 Roade Novices' Selling Hurdle Class G (4-y-o and up) £1,950 2m... (2:20)

3588* NAUTICAL JEWEL 5-11-0 (7*) J Power, in tch, hdwy aftr 3 out, drvn to ld after 2 out, driven out........(12 to 1 op 7 to 1) 1

3469⁷ OUR EDDIE (bl) 8-11-0 K Gaule, hdwy and hit 4 out, ran on and sddl slpd frm 2 out, kpt on.................. (20 to 1) 2

3495² PAULTON (bl) 4-10-8 A P McCoy, chsd ldrs, hdwy and hit 3 out, led aftr 2, hdd and outpcd appr last.
.... (3 to 1 op 7 to 2 tchd 4 to 1) 3

3283³ BOY BLAKENEY 4-10-8 Richard Guest, hdwy 3 out, rdn to chase ldrs appr 2 out, styd on same pace.
.... (5 to 2 fav op 2 to 1 tchd 11 to 4) 4

3628 INCHYDONEY BOY (Ire) 8-11-0 J F Titley, chsd ldrs till led 4th, wnt badly lft 2 out and hdd, sn wknd.
.... (33 to 1 op 20 to 1) 5

INISHMANN (Ire) 6-11-0 C Llewellyn, chsd ldrs to 3 out.
.... (20 to 1 op 16 to 1 tchd 25 to 1) 6

3137 BUSTER 9-11-0 E Byrne, hld up, keen hold, rdn and no hdwy 3 out..................(10 to 1 op 7 to 1) 7

3293³ MHEANMETOO 6-10-7 (7*) Mr S Durack, led to 4th, wknd aftr four out..............(12 to 1 op 4 to 1) 8

3628⁵ TUG YOUR FORELOCK 6-11-0 A Thornton, pressed ldr 3rd and ag'n 5th, wknd quickly aftr 3 out.... (7 to 1 op 6 to 1) 9

2607³ NICKY WILDE 7-11-0 G Bradley, hdwy 4th, rdn four out, sn wknd, tld off whn pld up bef last, broke blood vessel.
.... (7 to 2 op 100 to 30 tchd 4 to 1) pu

3468 WHATASHOT 7-11-0 D Walsh, rdn alng and beh frm 3rd, tld off whn pld up bef last............(20 to 1 op 12 to 1) pu

3590⁶ TATIBAG 5-11-0 (7*) Mr J Goldstein, jmpd poorly in rear, sn tld off, pld up bef last........... (33 to 1 op 20 to 1) pu

3184⁹ NOQUITA (NZ) (bl) 10-10-9 (5*) X Aizpuru, chsd ldrs to 4th, sn wknd, tld off whn pld up bef last..(33 to 1 op 25 to 1) pu

Dist: 6l, nk, sht-hd, 9l, 14l, 6l, 3½l, 2½l. 3m 54.20s. a 11.20s (13 Ran).

(Mrs A Squires), K G Wingrove

3737 Milton Novices' Chase Class E (5-y-o and up) £2,560 2¾m.......... (2:50)

3383² WHO IS EQUINAME (Ire) (bl) 7-11-2 M A Fitzgerald, trkd ldr till led 8th, drvn alng aftr 2 out, readily.
.... (11 to 4 on op 5 to 2 on tchd 2 to 1 on) 1

3271⁸ VOLLEYBALL (Ire) 8-11-2 M Richards, hld up, steady hdwy 3 out, chsd wnr appr 2 out, hrd rdn and no imprsn.
.... (16 to 1 op 14 to 1) 2

2726 DERRYS PREROGATIVE 7-11-2 D Walsh, hit 5th, hdwy 7th, chsd ldrs tenth, chased wnr frm nxt and chlgd 4 out, wknd appr 2 out.......... (66 to 1 op 50 to 1 tchd 100 to 1) 3

3669 CHIAPPUCCI (Ire) 7-11-2 D Gallagher, beh 6th, hit 9th, effrt frm 3 out but no a threat.........(20 to 1 op 14 to 1) 4

3543* SORCIERE 6-11-4 B Clifford, led till hdd and hit 8th, wknd 3 out................. (9 to 2 op 7 to 2) 5

2859⁷ SMART CASANOVA 8-11-2 W Marston, chasing ldrs whn hit 4th, rdn 6th, wknd tenth, no ch when blun 3 out.
.... (50 to 1 op 25 to 1) 6

2667 SAUSALITO BOY 9-11-2 C Maude, refused to race.
.... (50 to 1 op 25 to 1) ref

3611² FULL SHILLING (USA) 8-10-9 (7*) Mr S Durack, chsd ldrs, hit 9th, wknd appr 2 out, weakened and pld up bef last.
.... (12 to 1 op 6 to 1) pu

3492² SIDE BAR (v) 7-10-11 (5*) D J Kavanagh, beh and rdn 6th, tld off 7th, pld up bef nxt.
.... (25 to 1 op 20 to 1 tchd 33 to 1 and 40 to 1) pu

Dist: 8l, 11l, 11l, 12l, 20l. 5m 37.50s. a 11.50s (9 Ran).

(Lynn Wilson), N J Henderson

3738 Flore Novices' Handicap Hurdle Class E (0-100 4-y-o and up) £2,132 2m 5f.........................(3:20)

3725⁴ SHARP COMMAND [95] 4-11-9 (5*) X Aizpuru, hdwy 6th, chlgd frm 7th till led appr 3 out, drvn clr from 2 out.
.... (5 to 1 op 5 to 2) 1

3503⁴ HANCOCK [77] 5-11-3 A P McCoy, hld up, hdwy 6th, chsd wnr 3 out, rdn and no imprsn appr 2 out.
.... (5 to 1 fav op 7 to 2 tchd 4 to 1) 2

3617⁸ ECU DE FRANCE (Ire) [60] (v) 7-10-0 S Fox, rear and mstk 3rd, hdwy 5th, lost pl aftr nxt, hrd rdn and styd on frm 3 out to take poor third appr last............. (33 to 1 op 20 to 1) 3

3285³ BOB'S PLOY [82] 5-11-8 Richard Guest, hld up, hdwy to chase ldrs 7tyh, rdn aftr 3 out and wknd quickly.
.... (12 to 1 op 5 to 1 tchd 6 to 1) 4

3485 BOWDEN SURPRISE [65] 7-10-5 V Slattery, slwly away, rdn and mstk 4th, sn lost tch............(10 to 1 op 5 to 1) 5

3674⁹ MILLERS GOLDENGIRL (Ire) [60] 6-9-9 (5*) G F Ryan, effrt to chase ldrs 5th, sn wknd, tld off 4 out.. (33 to 1 op 16 to 1) 6

3528⁵ WORTHY MEMORIES [70] 8-10-10 Derek Byrne, led to 3 out, sn wknd, mstk 2 out, pld up bef last.
.... (10 to 1 op 12 to 1 tchd 8 to 1) pu

3494⁴ AN SPAILPIN FANACH (Ire) [81] (bl) 8-11-7 R Dunwoody, chsd ldrs 5th, wknd quickly nxt,tld off whn pld up bef 7th.
.... (9 to 1 op 6 to 1) pu

3500⁹ SWIFT POKEY [60] 7-9-7 (7*) Mr S Durack, prmnt early, beh frm 6th, tld off whn pld up bef 2 out. (33 to 1 tchd 50 to 1) pu

3372⁴ CARLY-J [67] (bl) 6-10-7 M N Kent, chsd ldr 3rd, wknd 7th, tld off whn pld up bef 2 out. (20 to 1 op 10 to 1 tchd 25 to 1) pu

3530* POLO PONY (Ire) [67] 5-10-7 J Supple, hld up, rdn 5th, tld off whn pld up bef 2 out.....(13 to 2 op 8 to 1 tchd 10 to 1) pu

3634⁵ BENJI [60] (bl) 6-10-0 J A McCarthy, chsd ldrs to 6th, tld off whn pld up bef 2 out....(25 to 1 op 14 to 1 tchd 33 to 1) pu

2822 SUPREMO (Ire) [68] 8-10-8 W Marston, in tch 5th, wknd 7th, sn beh, tld off whn pld up bef 2 out.
.... (25 to 1 op 12 to 1 tchd 20 to 1) pu

Dist: 10l, 30l, 15l, 8l, dist. 5m 12.60s. a 13.60s (13 Ran).

(A P Holland), P Eccles

3739 Tort Handicap Chase Class E (0-115 5-y-o and up) £3,137 3m 1f... (3:50)

3399⁷ SUPPOSIN [85] 9-10-10 Richard Guest, hdwy 9th, styd tracking ldrs till drvn to ld appr last, stayed on wl.
.... (10 to 1 op 8 to 1 tchd 12 to 1) 1

3497² LAY IT OFF (Ire) [82] 8-10-7 S Curran, led, blun 7th, sn reco'red, rdn aftr 3 out, hdd headed 2 out, soon btn.
.... (7 to 2 op 4 to 1) 2

2888⁵ FURRY FOX (Ire) [78] 9-10-3 D Morris, hdwy to chase ldrs 9th, styd on same pace frm 3 out.
.... (6 to 1 op 5 to 1 tchd 13 to 2) 3

3492³ DREAM LEADER (Ire) [79] 7-10-4 J Railton, in tch 5th, chsd ldrs tenth, led 2 out, hdd last, sn wknd... (6 to 1 op 4 to 1) 4

3436³ REAPERS ROCK [79] 10-9-13 (5*) G F Ryan, jmpd poorly in rear, al beh... (13 to 2 op 11 to 2 tchd 7 to 1) 5

MISCHIEVOUS GIRL [75] 9-10-0 Mrs F Needham, *hit second, hdwy 12th, sn wknd, tld off*........... (33 to 1 op 25 to 1) 6
1253³ JIM VALENTINE [99] 11-11-10 W Marston, *hld up, steady hdwy frm 12th, tracking ldrs and staying on in 5th whn blun and uns rdr 2 out*...................(7 to 1 op 6 to 1) ur
3497⁷ WOODLANDS GENHIRE [77] (bl) 12-10-2 C Llewellyn, *chsd ldr to 9th, sn rdn, wknd nxt, tld off whn pld up bef last*. ....(25 to 1 op 16 to 1) pu
3659² ROYAL SAXON [92] 11-11-3 R Johnson, *chsd ldrs to 7th, wknd 9th, tld off whn pld up and dismounted bef nxt*. ....(5 to 1 op 4 to 1) pu
3423² POSTMAN'S PATH [98] 11-11-9 J Osborne, *effrt to chase ldrs 8th, sn wknd, tld off whn pld up bef 3 out*. .... (100 to 30 fav op 3 to 1 tchd 7 to 2) pu
Dist: 8l, 4l, 4l, 25l, dist. 6m 23.30s. a 11.30s (10 Ran).
(J Kemp), Mrs S J Smith

3740 Duston Handicap Chase Class E (0-115 5-y-o and up) £3,000 2m 110yds......................(4:20)

3544* MR SNAGGLE (Ire) [89] 8-10-10 R Johnson, *hld up, hdwy 8th, chlgd on bit aftr 2 out, drvn to ld r-in, ran on*.....(9 to 2 co-fav op 7 to 2) 1
1491 CRACKLING FROST (Ire) [79] 9-9-11⁴ (7*) Mr R Wakley, *chsd ldrs, led 7th, still gng wl whn chlgd last, hdd r-in, no extr*. ....(12 to 1 op 10 to 1) 2
3545* MONKS JAY (Ire) [93] 8-11-0 C Maude, *in tch whn hit 4 out, rdn and one pace frm 2 out*. ....(11 to 2 op 5 to 1 tchd 6 to 1) 3
3367² THE CARROT MAN [107] 9-12-0 P Hide, *chsd ldrs, hit 4th, rdn and one pace appr 2 out*.........(9 to 2 co-fav op 7 to 2) 4
3668⁴ COUNT BARACHOIS (USA) [79] 9-10-0 D Gallagher, *prmnt, led 5th to 7th, styd pressing ldr till outpcd frm 2 out*. ....(14 to 1 op 12 to 1) 5
106* NADJATI (USA) [102] (bl) 8-11-9 R Dunwoody, *al beh, lost tch frm 6th, tld off*...... (9 to 2 co-fav op 7 to 2 tchd 5 to 1) 6
3423³ ARTIC WINGS (Ire) [105] 9-11-12 M Brennan, *beh whn f 4th, broke neck, dead*..............................(6 to 1) f
3492 NAUTICAL GEORGE (Ire) [79] 7-10-0 J Supple, *tld off 5th, blun and uns rdr nxt*................(16 to 1 op 12 to 1) ur
2251 HUGH DANIELS [79] 9-10-0 S Curran, *beh frm 6th, tld off whn pld up bef last*...................(50 to 1 tchd 66 to 1) pu
3636⁵ YOUNG ALFIE [79] (bl) 12-10-0 C Llewellyn, *led to 3rd, tld off 6th, pld up aftr 3 out*................(33 to 1 op 25 to 1) pu
3425² PARLIAMENTARIAN (Ire) [79] (bl) 8-10-0 J Osborne, *in tch, hit second, chsd ldrs frm 5th, hit 3 out and sn wknd, tld off whn pld up 2 out*............................(6 to 1 op 5 to 1) pu
Dist: 2l, 6l, 1¼l, 2½l, dist. 4m 3.50s. a 6.50s (11 Ran).
SR: 17/5/13/25/-/-/ (The Plum Merchants), Simon Earle

3741 Nobottle Handicap Hurdle Class F (0-105 4-y-o and up) £2,034 2m ....(4:50)

3459² ANTIGUAN FLYER [78] (v) 8-10-10 A P McCoy, *led, sn wl clr, steadied aftr 3 out, mstk nxt, pushed out r-in, unchlgd*. ....(3 to 1 fav op 9 to 2) 1
3424³ STEVE FORD [88] 8-11-6 J A McCarthy, *mstk second, hdwy 5th, chsd wnr 3 out, effrt frm 2 out but no imprsn*. ....(7 to 2 op 4 to 1 tchd 9 to 2) 2
3424⁷ POSITIVO [73] 6-10-5 D Leahy, *beh 4th and rdn alng, styd on und pres frm 3 out but not a dngr*.......(7 to 1 op 12 to 1) 3
3592² VA UTU [84] 9-10-13 (3*) Sophie Mitchell, *in tch to 5th*. ....(7 to 1 op 9 to 2) 4
3357* SURANOM (Ire) [92] 5-11-10 J F Titley, *chsd wnr to 4th, wknd quickly*............... (100 to 30 op 5 to 2 tchd 7 to 2) 5
2983 BIRTHPLACE (Ire) [68] 7-9-9 (5*) D J Kavanagh, *effrt 4th, sn wknd*.............................. (25 to 1 op 20 to 1) 6
3512⁴ EUROLINK THE REBEL (USA) [80] 5-10-5 (7*) Miss R Clark, *hdwy 4th, wknd 3 out*................. (12 to 1 op 9 to 2) 7
3674⁷ BALLY WONDER [68] 5-10-0 J Supple, *in tch, hdwy 5th, wknd 3 out*............................ (33 to 1 op 20 to 1) 8
3592⁶ JEWEL THIEF [74] (v) 7-9-13 (7*) Mr E Babington, *beh frm 3rd, tld off*..............................(16 to 1 op 10 to 1) 9
1787 ANTARTICTERN (USA) [71] (v) 7-10-3 G Cahill, *beh whn tried to refuse and uns rdr 4th*. .... (16 to 1 op 12 to 1 tchd 20 to 1) ur
Dist: 7l, 20l, 13l, 20l, 8l, 1½l, ½l, dist. 3m 47.80s. a 4.80s (10 Ran).
SR: 10/13/-/-/-/-/ (George Prodromou), G Prodromou

CHEPSTOW (good to firm)
Tuesday April 22nd
Going Correction: MINUS 0.40 sec. per fur.

3742 Reynard Novices' Chase Class E (5-y-o and up) £3,041 2m 3f 110yds ....(2:40)

PLAN-A (Ire) 7-11-0 P Holley, *al prmnt, mstk last, hrd rdn and led last hundred yards*...(3 to 1 tchd 7 to 2 and 11 to 4) 1
3118⁴ NORDIC VALLEY (Ire) 6-11-12 A P McCoy, *hdwy 6th, ev ch whn blun last, ran on*. .... (13 to 8 fav op 5 to 4 on tchd 7 to 4) 2
2291 GOLDEN DRUM (Ire) (bl) 7-11-0 T J Murphy, *chsd ldr, led 3 out, hdd fnl hundred yards*. ....(12 to 1 op 6 to 1 tchd 14 to 1) 3
3404⁵ SOUND CARRIER (USA) 9-11-0 S Wynne, *led, mstk and hdd 3 out, 4th and btn whn f 2 out*. ....(2 to 1 op 5 to 2 tchd 11 to 4 and 3 to 1) f
3593⁴ DIAMOND LIGHT 10-11-0 Mr S Lloyd, *tld off frm 5th, blun and uns rdr 4 out*............... (40 to 1 op 25 to 1 tchd 50 to 1) ur
Dist: 1l, 1¾l. 4m 51.20s. a 8.20s (5 Ran).
(R J Bullock), R H Alner

3743 Betty's 90th Birthday Mares' Only Novices' Hurdle Class E (4,5,6-y-o) £2,262 2m 110yds............(3:10)

3686* MRS EM 5-10-13 (7*) L Cummins, *chsd clr ldr, led 5th, easily*. ....(7 to 1 on op 6 to 1 on) 1
3554 ILEWIN JANINE (Ire) 6-11-0 C Maude, *hdwy 3rd, ev ch 5th, one pace*..........................(9 to 1 op 7 to 1) 2
NELL VALLEY 6-11-0 G Bradley, *led, sn clr, hdd and wknd 5th*.................... (9 to 1 op 7 to 1 tchd 10 to 1) 3
3299 LUNAR GRIS 4-10-8 Mr J Jukes, *tld off frm 3rd*. ....(50 to 1 op 33 to 1) 4
Dist: 4l, 19l, dist. 3m 50.50s. a 3.50s (4 Ran).
(G Z Mizel), P F Nicholls

3744 Weatherbys Sponsorship In Racing Handicap Chase Class D (0-120 5-y-o and up) £3,533 3¼m 110yds (3:40)

1946² GLENFINN PRINCESS [96] 9-10-4 W Marston, *jmpd wl, led 6th, clr 2 out, eased r-in*..................(5 to 2 op 9 to 4) 1
2293 FROZEN DROP [100] 10-10-8 C Maude, *led to 6th, cl up till outpcd 4 out, rallied last, no ch wth wnr*. .... (100 to 30 op 3 to 1 tchd 7 to 2) 2
3581⁶ ALL FOR LUCK [120] 12-12-0 A P McCoy, *reminders 15th, hdwy 17th, ev ch 4 out, btn 2 out*. ....(2 to 1 fav op 7 to 4 tchd 9 to 4) 3
2698 HAVE TO THINK [119] 9-11-6 (7*) Mr J Tizzard, *in tch till wknd 5 out*......................(7 to 2 tchd 4 to 1 and 3 to 1) 4
Dist: ¾l, ¾l, 11l. 6m 45.30s. a 10.30s (4 Ran).
(Patrick McGinty), P Bowen

3745 Hancocks H.B. Handicap Hurdle Class B (5-y-o and up) £4,674 2m 110yds.......................(4:10)

3580⁶ ASHWELL BOY (Ire) [133] 6-10-7 W Marston, *hdwy 4th, led 2 out, ran on wl*.................(11 to 8 fav op 6 to 4) 1
3675* PRIDWELL [160] 7-12-6 (6ex) A P McCoy, *wth ldr, led 4th to 2 out, ran on wl frm last*.....(6 to 4 op Evens tchd 13 to 8) 2
3595 BLAIR CASTLE (Ire) [126] 6-9-9 (5*) A Bates, *al prmnt, ev ch 2 out, not quicken*....................(16 to 1 op 14 to 1) 3
3595⁷ FORESTAL [126] 5-10-0 T J Murphy, *led to 4th, wknd 3 out*. ....(7 to 2) 4
Dist: 1½l, 2l, 21l. 3m 45.00s. b 2.00s (4 Ran).
SR: 33/58/22/1/ (A B S Racing), P J Hobbs

3746 Dunraven Windows South And West Wales Point-to-Point Championship Hunter Chase Class H (6-y-o and up) £3,649 3m...................(4:40)

FINAL PRIDE 11-11-10 (5*) Miss P Jones, *jmpd wl, made all, sn clr, easily*.................. (2 to 1 fav tchd 9 to 4) 1
MISS MILLBROOK 9-11-12 (7*) Mr E Williams, *hdwy tenth, wnt second and hit 2 out, nvr nr wnr*.....(3 to 1 op 5 to 2) 2
3256* BUSMAN (Ire) 8-12-3 (7*) Mr D S Jones, *chsd wnr 12th to 2 out, one pace*..............(6 to 1 op 5 to 1 tchd 13 to 2) 3
WAKE UP LUV 12-11-13 (7*) Miss P Cooper, *al prmnt, one pace frm 4 out*.........(25 to 1 op 20 to 1 tchd 33 to 1) 4
THE LAST MISTRESS 10-11-5 (7*) Mr S Shinton, *nvr better than middle div*..................... (25 to 1 op 20 to 1) 5
BEINN MOHR 10-11-8 (7*) Mr N R Mitchell, *hit second, sn beh, tld off*........................ (16 to 1 op 14 to 1) 6
KINGFISHER BAY 12-12-1 (7*) Mr J J Price, *al beh, tld off frm 11th*.................(33 to 1 op 20 to 1 tchd 50 to 1) 7
PLAS-HENDY 11-11-10 (7*) Mr G Lewis, *chsd wnr till wknd 12th*....................(9 to 1 op 12 to 1 tchd 8 to 1) 8
ROYAL OATS 12-11-9 (3*) Mr M Rimell, *f 6th*. ....(33 to 1 op 20 to 1) f
DOUBTING DONNA 11-11-7 (5*) Mr J Jukes, *nvr nr ldrs, 6th and no ch whn pld up bef last*.........(10 to 1 op 8 to 1) pu
CULPEPPERS DISH 6-11-5 (7*) Mr A Price, *prmnt to 6th, beh whn tried to refuse 9th, pld up bef nxt*. (33 to 1 op 20 to 1) pu
Dist: 15l, 6l, 1l, ¾l, dist, dist. 5m 56.70s. a 6.70s (11 Ran).
(Grahame Barrett), Mrs C Higgon

3747 Sapling Novices' Hurdle Class E (4,5,6-y-o) £2,234 2½m 110yds ....(5:10)

3684* COUNTRY LOVER (v) 6-11-12 A P McCoy, *al prmnt, wnt second 3 out, quickened to ld last 7ty-5 yards, cleverly*. .... (5 to 4 on tchd 11 to 10 on and Evens) 1
3623² NAME OF OUR FATHER (USA) 4-10-13 D Walsh, *led, hdd and not quicken last 7ty-5 yards*............ (5 to 4 op Evens) 2

3332⁹ DON'T MIND IF I DO (Ire) (bl) 6-11-0 A Thornton, chsd ldr to 3
out, one pace.......................(14 to 1 op 6 to 1) 3
WESTFIELD 5-11-0 D Leahy, hdwy 7th, ev ch 4 out, sn wknd.
......................................(50 to 1 op 16 to 1) 4
3197⁶ MR ROBSTEE 6-11-0 L Harvey, tld off frm 6th.
......................................(66 to 1 op 16 to 1) 5
Dist: ¾l, 11l, 13l, dist. 4m 47.10s. a 9.10s (5 Ran).
(Pond House Gold), M C Pipe

PUNCHESTOWN (IRE) (good)
Tuesday April 22nd

3748 Kildare Chilling Hunters Chase (Bishopscourt Cup) (4-y-o and up) £3,425 2½m.................(2:10)

SALLY WILLOWS (Ire) 8-10-13 (7") Mr J F Robinson,
....(10 to 1) 1
GLENARD LAD (Ire) 9-11-4 (7") Mr W Ewing, ...(20 to 1) 2
3527⁴ LINEKER 10-11-11 Mr G J Harford, ...(5 to 4 fav) 3
PERCUSIONIST 10-11-4 (7") Mr D Broad, ...(12 to 1) 4
BALLYLIME AGAIN (Ire) 8-10-13 (7") Mr J Cash, ..(20 to 1) 5
POLLS GALE 10-10-13 (7") Mr R Flavin, ...(20 to 1) f
SPINANS HILL (Ire) 9-11-4 (7") Mr F L Heffernan, ..(25 to 1) f
POULGILLIE (Ire) 7-11-6 (5") Mr G Elliott, ...(6 to 1) ur
BOUTRUS (Ire) 11-4 (7") Mr J G O'Connell, ...(20 to 1) ur
THE EXECUTRIX (Ire) 5-10-6 (7") Mr B Valentine, ..(20 to 1) bd
THE DANCE (Ire) 11-4 (7") Mr R Kehoe, ...(33 to 1) pu
AREYOUTHEREYET (Ire) 10-13 (7") Mr A Fleming, .(33 to 1) pu
Dist: 2l, ¾l, nk, dist. 5m 28.10s. a 31.10s (12 Ran).
(Peter J Lawler), Peter J Lawler

3749 Ernst & Young Chase (Ladies Perpetual Cup) (4-y-o and up) £8,370 3m
....(2:40)

3153 TEARAWAY KING (Ire) 7-11-11 Mr E Bolger, ..(10 to 9 on) 1
DIGACRE 8-11-11 Mr R Hurley, ...(12 to 1) 2
1754² DENNISTOWNTHRILLER (Ire) 9-11-11 Mr P Fenton, (9 to 4) 3
CARRIGANS LAD (Ire) 9-11-8 (3") Mr B R Hamilton, (25 to 1) 4
TULLY BOY 10-11-4 (7") Mr D McCartan, ...(25 to 1) 5
1754 TAMER'S RUN 11-11-11 Mr A R Coonan, ...(20 to 1) 6
HANDY SALLY (Ire) 10-13 (7") Mr J Meagher, ...(33 to 1) 7
1015 GARRYSPILLANE (Ire) 5-11-4 Mr A J Martin, ...(16 to 1) 8
3527 TULLIBARDNICENEASY (Ire) 6-11-1 (5") Mr A C Coyle,
....(16 to 1) ur
MICKTHECUTAWAY (Ire) 5-10-11 (7") Mr A Fleming, (7 to 1) ur
MAXINE'S FOUNTAIN (Ire) 10-13 (5") Mr J T McNamara,
....(12 to 1) pu
Dist: 4½l, hd, 8l, ½l. 6m 18.10s. a 18.10s (11 Ran).
(Mrs Noreen McManus), E Bolger

3750 Country Pride Champion Novice Hurdle (Grade 2) (5-y-o and up) £24,800 2m............(3:15)

3562* MIDNIGHT LEGEND 6-12-0 R Johnson, dsptd ld, advantage
aftr 3 out, clr last, imprsv.....................(7 to 4 fav) 1
3064* WHAT'S THE VERDICT (Ire) 5-11-13 P Carberry, hld up, prog
aftr 2 out, chlgd appr last, kpt on, no ch wth wnr.....(9 to 1) 2
3452* GAZALANI (Ire) 5-11-13 T P Treacy, mid-div, took clr order 3
out, rdn, styd on frm last......................(14 to 1) 3
3156 TOAST THE SPREECE (Ire) 5-11-13 F Swan, prmnt, rdn aftr
3 out, chlgd 2 out, fdd........................(4 to 1) 4
3177² COLM'S ROCK (Ire) 6-12-0 T Horgan, chsd ldg grp, unbl to
quicken.....................................(25 to 1) 5
3521* DROMINEER (Ire) 6-12-0 N Williamson, hld up, rdn 2 out, no
imprsn......................................(9 to 1) 6
2732² BUKHARI (Ire) 5-11-13 C O'Dwyer, took str hold, wnt second 4
out, fdd aftr 2 out...........................(9 to 2) 7
3523² PALETTE (Ire) 5-11-8 D J Casey, prmnt to hfwy, unbl to chal
frm 2 out....................................(14 to 1) 8
3562² SHARPICAL 5-11-13 M A Fitzgerald, last til improved aftr 4
out, nvr dngr, wknd and spd f 3 out............(7 to 1) f
Dist: 2½l, 4½l, ½l, ½l, 7l. 3m 48.70s. a 3.70s (9 Ran).
SR: 63/59/54/53/53/46/ (Mrs H J Clarke), D Nicholson

3751 B.M.W. Handicap Chase (Grade 1) (4-y-o and up) £31,200 2m......(3:45)

3130⁴ KLAIRON DAVIS (Fr) [-] 8-12-0 F Woods, al prmnt, led 3rd,
wnt clr, easily...............................(11 to 10 fav) 1
2507⁴ BIG MATT (Ire) [-] 9-11-0 M A Fitzgerald, hld up, wnt 4th 3
out, outpcd 2 out, ran on to snatch second cl hme...(7 to 1) 2
3548* IDIOTS VENTURE [-] 10-10-11 C F Swan, reco'red aftr mstk 6
out, wnt second 3 out, chlgd betw last 2, mistake last, lost
second cl hme................................(7 to 2) 3
3596² LORD DORCET (Ire) [-] 7-10-11 J Osborne, rear early, hdwy 3
out, ev ch betw last 2, fdd....................(12 to 1) 4
3086³ OPERA HAT (Ire) [-] 9-10-11 P Carberry, prmnt, early, mstk 4
out, fdd....................................(7 to 1) 5
3596 ARCTIC KINSMAN [-] 9-10-11 C Llewellyn, prmnt, mstk 7 out,
rdn 3 out, no imprsn.........................(7 to 2) 6
3548² CABLE BEACH [-] 8-10-11 C O'Dwyer, wnt second hfwy
til appr 2 out, wknd..........................(14 to 1) 7
Dist: 8l, sht-hd, sht-hd, 12l. 4m 0.10s. a 1.10s (7 Ran).

SR: 89/64/64/64/52/-/-/ (C Jones), A L T Moore

3752 Bradstock Insurance Novice Chase (Listed) (5-y-o and up) £12,900 2½m
....(4:15)

3311* LINTON ROCKS 8-11-8 R Dunwoody, jmpd wl, led 3rd, clr 2
out, kpt on well und pres.....................(7 to 4 fav) 1
2587⁴ HEADBANGER 10-11-8 D H O'Connor, hld up, jmpd wl to go
3rd 2 out, chalg whn mstk last, no extr.........(13 to 2) 2
1891² STAY LUCKY (NZ) (bl) 8-11-8 M A Fitzgerald, gng wl til slight
mstk 3 out, one pace.........................(5 to 1) 3
3559⁸ COURT MASTER (Ire) 9-11-8 B G Powell, wth ldrs, mstk 4 out,
drvn alng, no further prog frm 2................(10 to 1) 4
3454 BANGABUNNY 7-11-3 P Carberry, hld up, took clr order 5
out, 3rd whn mstk 3 out, unbl to reco'r..........(20 to 1) 5
3418* FATHER RECTOR 8-11-8 T Horgan, wtd wth, prog to
chase ldrs 5 out, nvr a dngr frm 3 out..........(13 to 2) 6
3624³ PENNY BRIDE (Ire) 8-11-0 A O'Shea, nvr a factor. (20 to 1) 7
2224⁶ THE SUBBIE (Ire) 8-11-8 T P Treacy, badly hmpd by faller 1st,
reco'red to chase ldrs to hfwy, sn lost tch......(12 to 1) 8
1618⁷ MACNAMARASBAND (Ire) 8-11-3 J Osborne, lost tch frm 5
out...(20 to 1) 9
3645* ALWAYS IN TROUBLE 10-11-8 T P Rudd, f 1st....(10 to 1) f
3454* ROYAL OASIS (Ire) 6-11-8 N Williamson, prmnt til f 6th.
....(14 to 1) f
3343³ ROCKETTS CASTLE (Ire) 7-11-3 C Llewellyn, mid-div whn f
7th...(20 to 1) f
3454⁵ OWENDUFF (USA) 7-11-3 F Woods, hld up, some prog whn
hmpd and brght dwn 6 out....................(8 to 1) bd
3454⁴ MOON-FROG 10-11-3 J K Kinane, tld off whn pld up aftr 6
out...(100 to 1) pu
Dist: 4l, 8l, 11l, 3½l. 5m 10.90s. a 13.90s (14 Ran).
(The Hon Mrs Townshend), T Thomson Jones

3753 Ballymore Properties Handicap Chase (4-y-o and up) £8,220 3m 1f
....(4:45)

3420³ TRIPTODICKS (Ire) [-] 7-9-4 (3") G Cotter, ...(9 to 2 fav) 1
3441 MISS DISKIN (Ire) [-] 8-10-7 B G Powell, ...(12 to 1) 2
3236* ALL IN THE GAME (Ire) [-] 9-9-10 (7") M D Murphy, (9 to 1) 3
3392³ CABBERY ROSE (Ire) [-] 9-9-11 (5") A O'Shea, ..(16 to 1) 4
3418 LUCKY BUST (Ire) [-] 7-11-1 C F Swan, ...(11 to 2) 5
3706³ LOFTUS LAD (Ire) [-] (bl) 9-10-6 N Williamson, ..(13 to 2) 6
3420⁶ INNISCEIN (Ire) [-] 9-9-12 T Horgan, ...(11 to 2) ur
3693 DIORRAING (Ire) [-] (bl) 7-10-2 D J Casey, ...(25 to 1) ur
3552 MONKEY AGO [-] 10-11-4 P Carberry, ...(20 to 1) pu
3236 MATTS DILEMMA (Ire) [-] 9-11-9 D H O'Connor, ..(12 to 1) pu
3526⁴ PARADISE ROAD [-] 8-10-4 F Woods, ...(7 to 1) pu
3393³ MACALLISTER (Ire) [-] 7-11-7 C O'Dwyer, ...(5 to 1) pu
3693⁵ FIELD OF DESTINY (Ire) [-] 8-9-8 (3") K Whelan, ..(33 to 1) pu
Dist: Sht-hd, 15l, 15l, dist. 6m 33.50s. a 18.50s (13 Ran).
(M G O'Huallachain), David A Kiely

3754 Balcas Handicap Hurdle (4-y-o and up) £4,110 2½m..............(5:15)

3523⁷ VALLEY ERNE (Ire) [-] 6-11-1 R Dunwoody, ...(10 to 1) 1
1407⁴ THAI ELECTRIC (Ire) [-] 6-9-13 T J Mitchell, ...(12 to 1) 2
3431² BE HOME EARLY (Ire) [-] 7-11-3 C F Swan, ...(13 to 2) 3
3452⁶ NATIVE-DARRIG (Ire) [-] 6-10-9 D J Casey, ...(5 to 1 fav) 4
3643* GLENFIELDS CASTLE (Ire) [-] 7-9-7 (7") P G Hourigan,
....(16 to 1) 5
3377² MARINERS REEF (Ire) [-] 6-9-0 (7") D McCullagh, ..(10 to 1) 6
3451⁴ FIDDLERS BOW VI (Ire) [-] 9-11-0 P Carberry, ..(6 to 1) 7
2164⁹ MALACCA KING (Ire) [-] 6-10-12 (5") P Morris, ...(25 to 1) 8
2917⁵ ASK THE BUTLER (Ire) [-] 6-11-7 (7") Mr Paul Moloney,
....(8 to 1) 9
3547³ NATIVE FLECK (Ire) [-] 7-10-7 N Williamson, ...(14 to 1) 10
627 THE WISE KNIGHT (Ire) [-] 6-9-6 (7") M D Murphy, (33 to 1) 11
3607⁶ INNOVATIVE (Ire) [-] 6-9-4 (3") G Cotter, ...(25 to 1) 12
3235 WEST ON BRIDGE ST (Ire) [-] 7-10-6 C O'Dwyer, (14 to 1) 13
3451² KASELECTRIC (Ire) [-] 6-10-11 T Horgan, ...(8 to 1) 14
743 MERRY PEOPLE (Ire) [-] 9-11-4 J Short, ...(33 to 1) 15
3213³ SIBERIAN TALE (Ire) [-] 7-10-8 (3") Mr P J Casey, ..(16 to 1) 16
2339 GLENREEF BOY (Ire) [-] 8-9-5 (5") A O'Shea, ...(25 to 1) 17
9447 FRAU DANTE (Ire) [-] 7-9-13¹ P A Roche, ...(20 to 1) 18
3431⁵ SLEEPY RIVER (Ire) [-] 6-10-9 F Woods, ...(7 to 1) 19
3607 MISTER CHIPPY (Ire) [-] 5-10-12 T P Treacy, ...(33 to 1) 20
3385⁴ GROUND NUT (Ire) [-] 7-11-5 B G Powell, ...(10 to 1) 21
3643 FERRYCARRIG HOTEL (Ire) [-] 8-10-9 C N Bowens,
....(33 to 1) 22
Dist: 5l, 2l, sht-hd, 3l. 4m 54.20s. a 12.20s (22 Ran).
(S A M Syndicate), Michael Cunningham

3755 Tom O'Leary Memorial I.N.H. Flat Race (4-y-o) £6,850 2m......(5:45)

2370 THE BONGO MAN (Ire) 11-6 Mr A J Martin, ...(6 to 1) 1
2370⁵ SUPPORT ACT (Ire) 11-6 Mr D Marnane, ...(6 to 1) 2
3524⁸ MYKON GOLD (Ire) 11-6 Mr R M Walsh, ...(6 to 1) 3
3183⁵ FIDALUS (Ire) 10-13 (7") Mr M T Hartrey, ...(20 to 1) 4
3625³ GOOD LAD (Ire) 10-13 (7") Mr A J Dempsey, ...(14 to 1) 5
3432 BENEFICENT (Fr) 11-6 Mr P Dempsey, ...(6 to 1) 6
2737 DARSARAK (Ire) 11-6 Mr J P Dempsey, ...(12 to 1) 7
HARDIMAN (Ire) 10-13 (7") Mr C J Swords, ...(8 to 1) 8

| 3432[6] | TONIBEROLI (Ire) (bl) 10-12 (3*) Mr J Connolly, ...(16 to 1) | 9 |

AN BONNAN BUI (Ire) 10-8 (7*) Mr T J Beattie, ...(20 to 1) 10
3707[6] MR QUIGLEY (Ire) 11-6 Mr A R Coonan, ...(16 to 1) 11
GOOD FOUNDATION (Ire) 10-8 (7*) Mr A Fleming, (25 to 1) 12
3553[3] OHIO (Ire) 11-6 Mr G J Harford, ...(2 to 1 fav) 13
DOUBLE RESOLVE 10-10 (5*) Mr G Elliott, ... (12 to 1) 14
2370 KILCORDION (Ire) 10-8 (7*) Miss G C Feighery, ...(20 to 1) 15
CONNIGAR BAY (Ire) 11-6 Mr B M Cash, ...(25 to 1) 16
3349 KEPPOLS PRINCESS (Ire) 10-8 (7*) Mr B Valentine, (25 to 1) 17
DOC MORRISSEY (Ire) 11-6 Mr R Thornton, ...(20 to 1) 18
3707 DUBLIN BOY (Ire) 11-6 Mr C Vigors, ...(20 to 1) 19
LADY FRANCO (Ire) 10-8 (7*) Mr P Fahey, ...(33 to 1) 20
MR BOSSMAN (Ire) 10-13 (7*) Mr J Cash, ...(12 to 1) 21
2234[8] GERRYS GIFT (Ire) 10-8 (7*) Mr Edgar Byrne, ...(12 to 1) pu
Dist: 2l, 4l, 4½l, 1l. 3m 45.10s. (22 Ran).

(Mrs John Magnier), Anthony Mullins

PERTH (good)
Wednesday April 23rd
Going Correction: PLUS 0.30 sec. per fur.

3756 Party Has Started Moet & Chandon Maiden Hurdle Class E (Div I) (4-y-o and up) £2,080 2½m 110yds. . (2:20)

3598[3] PENTLANDS FLYER (Ire) 6-11-7 P Carberry, wth ldr, led 6th, drw clr frm 2 out, cmftbly.
. . . . (7 to 4 fav op 6 to 4 tchd 15 to 8 and 2 to 1) 1
3308[9] MENALDI (Ire) 7-11-7 A S Smith, in tch, took clr order hfwy, chsd wnr frm 3 out, no imprsn.
. . . . (12 to 1 op 8 to 1 tchd 14 to 1) 2
3468[2] SAXON MEAD (bl) 7-11-7 G Tormey, led till hdd 6th, prmnt till wknd appr 2 out. . . . .(11 to 2 op 6 to 1 tchd 5 to 1) 3
1829[6] RAINING STAIRS (Ire) 6-11-7 L O'Hara, trkd ldrs, rdn bef 3 out, wknd before nxt. . . . . . .(9 to 4 op 2 to 1 tchd 5 to 2) 4
3308 LORD PAT (Ire) 6-11-7 R Garritty, mid-div, lost tch aftr 7th, no dngr after. . . . .(33 to 1 op 20 to 1) 5
3198 RAMBLING RAJAH 5-11-0 (7*) Mr M Bradburne, f 1st.
. . . .(10 to 1 op 12 to 1 tchd 14 to 1) f
3354 PRINCE BALTASAR 8-11-2 (5*) B Grattan, hmpd 1st, al beh, tld off whn pld up bef 2 out. . . . .(100 to 1) pu
2534 CORPORAL KIRKWOOD (Ire) 7-11-0 (7*) C McCormack, mid-div till wknd aftr 7th, lost tch and pld up bef 2 out.
. . . . (20 to 1 op 25 to 1 tchd 33 to 1) pu
3509[7] RED HOT PRINCE 6-11-0 (7*) L McGrath, chsd ldrs to hfwy, sn rdn and wknd, tld off whn pld up bef 2 out. . . . (100 to 1) pu
1983 GUILE POINT 6-11-2 J Burke, sn rear div, wl beh whn pld up bef 2 out. . . . .(50 to 1 tchd 66 to 1) pu
3198 DELIGHTFOOL 6-11-2 N Bentley, rear div frm hfwy, wl beh whn pld up bef 2 out. . . . .(25 to 1 op 20 to 1) pu
ZOOT MONEY 5-11-2 D Parker, sn towards rear, wl beh whn pld up bef 2 out. . . . .(33 to 1) pu
Dist: 5l, 6l, 2½l, 22l. 5m 6.10s. a 26.10s (12 Ran).

(Mrs M W Bird), J Howard Johnson

3757 Winifred Royal Memorial Novices' Hurdle Class E (5-y-o and up) £2,878 2m 110yds. . . . . (2:50)

2852 TAWAFIJ (USA) 8-10-12 R Garritty, settled midfield, steady hdwy to 12 out, sn rdn, tld out. 1
3351* BOLD STATEMENT 5-11-5 N Bentley, made most till hdd 2 out, styd on und pres. . . . .(3 to 1 fav tchd 11 to 4) 2
3401[4] SWANDALE FLYER 5-10-7 (5*) B Grattan, hld up, hdwy bef 3 out, styd on und pres frm nxt. . . . . .(14 to 1 op 10 to 1) 3
2973[4] WESTERN GENERAL 6-10-12 A S Smith, trkd ldrs, jnd ldr 4th, ev ch bef 2 out, kpt on same pace.
. . . .(7 to 1 op 5 to 1 tchd 8 to 1) 4
226[9] HAND OF STRAW (Ire) 5-10-12 K Johnson, beh, styd on frm 3 out, nvr able to chal. . . . .(33 to 1 op 20 to 1) 5
2817[6] NORDIC LEGEND 5-10-12 T Reed, beh, styd on frm 3 out, nvr dngrs. . . . .(100 to 1 op 50 to 1) 6
3168[4] THE STUFFED PUFFIN (Ire) 5-10-12 J Railton, trkd ldrs, till wknd aftr 3 out. . . . .(6 to 1 op 5 to 1) 7
3473[7] RAMSTOWN LAD (Ire) 8-10-12 S McNeill, trkd ldrs, wknd aftr 3 out. . . . .(33 to 1 op 20 to 1) 8
3535[6] BORDER IMAGE 6-10-9 (3*) E Callaghan, mid-div till wknd aftr 3 out. . . . .(25 to 1 op 20 to 1) 9
3583[7] MAPLE BAY 8-10-12 (7*) C McCormack, in tch till wknd aftr 3 out. . . . .(150 to 1 op 50 to 1) 10
3401 JUST WHISTLE 5-10-7 F Perratt, chsd ldrs till wknd aftr 5th, tld off. 11
3396[6] SWIFT RIPOSTE (Ire) 6-11-5 T Jenks, blun second, al beh, tld off. . . . .(13 to 2 op 5 to 1 tchd 7 to 1) 12
3029[4] LUMBACK LADY 7-10-7 B Storey, trkd ldrs till grad lost pl frm hfwy, tld off. . . . .(6 to 1 tchd 7 to 1) 13
3509 HUNTING SLANE (bl) 5-10-12 J Callaghan, sn beh, tld off.
. . . .(100 to 1 op 50 to 1) 14
3700 MINNIES TURN 6-10-7 S McDougall, keen, prmnt till wknd aftr 4th, tld off. . . . .(200 to 1 op 50 to 1) 15
1590 CHINOOK'S DAUGHTER (Ire) 5-10-7 L O'Hara, mid-div to hfwy, lost tch and pld up bef 3 out. . . . .(50 to 1) pu
3356 HIGH CELLESTE (Ire) 6-10-7 M Moloney, beh, lost tch and pld up bef 3 out. . . . .(100 to 1 op 50 to 1) pu
Dist: 1¾l, 1¼l, 3l, 4l, 12l, 3½l, 4l, 3l, 3l, 17l. 3m 53.00s. a 12.00s (17 Ran).

SR: 14/19/10/7/3/-/   (Stephen Laidlaw), M D Hammond

3758 Glengoyne Highland Malt Tamerosia Series Final Class B Novices' Chase (5-y-o and up) £7,064 3m. . . . . (3:20)

3395* COLONEL IN CHIEF (Ire) 7-11-12 P Carberry, trkd ldrs gng wl, led 3 out, rdn appr last, styd on. . . . .(15 to 8 jt-fav op 2 to 1 tchd 7 to 4 and 5 to 2) 1
3601* ASK ME LATER (Ire) 8-11-12 M Foster, mid-div, effrt aftr 15th, sn drvn alng, styd on strly r-in, fnshd wl.
. . . . 2
3261* RIVER UNSHION (Ire) 7-11-12 A S Smith, trkd ldrs, chsd wnr frm aftr 3 out, styd on same pace from nxt.
. . . . (12 to 1 op 10 to 1) 3
3702[3] KINGS SERMON (Ire) 8-11-12 R Supple, mstks, in tch, drvn alng aftr 15th, no hdwy till styd on wl clsg stages
. . . . (14 to 1 op 10 to 1) 4
2930 JAC DEL PRINCE 7-11-5 P Hide, made most till hdd 3 out, fdd. . . . .(66 to 1 op 50 to 1) 5
3708* CHOPWELL CURTAINS (bl) 7-11-12 L Wyer, in tch whn f 12th.
. . . .(15 to 8 jt-fav op 7 to 4 tchd 4 to 1) f
959 KINCARDINE BRIDGE (USA) 8-11-5 Mr M Bradburne, trkd ldrs till wknd quickly aftr 12th, lost tch and pld up bef 14th.
. . . .(100 to 1) pu
3250* KALAJO 7-11-12 B Storey, sn beh, tld off whn pld up bef 3 out.
. . . .(12 to 1 op 10 to 1 tchd 14 to 1) pu
3434* TOUGH TEST (Ire) 7-11-9 G Cahill, wth ldr till wknd aftr 14th, tld off whn pld up bef 3 out. . . . . . .(16 to 1 tchd 20 to 1) pu
3601[2] NIJWAY 7-11-12 P Niven, mid-div, lost tch and pld up bef 3 out. . . . .(25 to 1 op 20 to 1) pu
3352 TWO FOR ONE 8-11-5 T Reed, sn beh, tld off whn pld up bef 2 out. . . . .(100 to 1) pu
Dist: ¾l, 1½l, 1¾l, 13l. 6m 10.20s. a 15.20s (11 Ran).

SR: 18/17/15/13/-/-/   (Robert Ogden), G Richards

3759 Ballathie House Hotel Handicap Hurdle Class D (0-120 4-y-o and up) £3,785 2m 110yds. . . . . (3:50)

3595[9] AMLAH (USA) [110] 5-11-6 B Powell, prmnt, led 3 out, ran on wl. . . . .(5 to 1 tchd 11 to 2) 1
3100[2] DURANO [110] 6-11-6 L Wyer, chsd ldrs, drvn alng aftr 3 out, kpt on wl frm nxt. . . . .(10 to 30 fav op 3 to 1) 2
3703[4] RACHAEL'S OWEN [90] 7-9-9 (5*) R McGrath, beh, hdwy aftr 3 out, styd on wl frm betw last. . . .(25 to 1 op 20 to 1) 3
2316* STASH THE CASH (Ire) [118] 6-12-0 R Garritty, in tch, effrt bef 2 out, kpt on same pace. . . . . .(4 to 1 tchd 9 to 2) 4
3540[2] ANABRANCH [110] 6-11-3 (3*) E Callaghan, trkd ldrs, ev ch 3 out, one-paced frm nxt. . . . .(9 to 2 op 5 to 1) 5
1512[3] SARMATIAN (USA) [112] 6-11-1 (7*) N Horrocks, nvr better than mid-div, tld off. . . . .(16 to 1 op 14 to 1) 6
3540[5] BURES (Ire) [107] 6-11-3 P Carberry, led till hdd 3 out, wknd quickly, tld off. . . . .(11 to 1 op 8 to 1 tchd 12 to 1) 7
3330[5] RADANPOUR (Ire) [111] 5-11-7 A S Smith, al beh, tld off.
. . . . (12 to 1 op 7 to 1) 8
3602[4] ASTRALEON (Ire) [103] 9-10-6 (7*) S Melrose, al beh, tld off whn pld up bef last. . . . .(14 to 1 op 10 to 1) pu
2919[9] COMMON SOUND (Ire) [94] 6-10-4 B Storey, in tch till wknd bef 3 out, tld off whn pld up before nxt. (20 to 1 op 14 to 1) pu
Dist: 2l, hd, 6l, 4l, dist, dist, ½l. 3m 52.10s. a 11.10s (10 Ran).

SR: 31/29/9/31/19/-/   (In Touch Racing Club), P J Hobbs

3760 Shepherd & Wedderburn Handicap Chase Class D (0-125 5-y-o and up) £4,890 2½m 110yds. . . . . (4:20)

3399[4] ACAJOU III (Fr) [105] 9-10-13 P Carberry, made all, clr whn untidy last, easily. . . . .(11 to 2 op 5 to 1) 1
3702[2] NICHOLAS PLANT [95] 8-10-3 G Cahill, hld up, hdwy and prmnt tenth, chasing wnr whn blun 3 out, no imprsn.
. . . .(7 to 4 fav op 13 to 8 tchd 6 to 4) 2
3701 SEOD RIOGA (Ire) [116] 8-11-5 (7*) Chris Webb, hld up, effrt whn hit 11th, sn wknd. . . . .(5 to 2 op 2 to 1 tchd 11 to 4) 3
3510[2] DEEP DECISION [97] 11-10-5 A S Smith, in tch, reminders aftr 7th, rdn and ch 11th, wknd after nxt.
. . . .(6 to 1 tchd 13 to 2) 4
3399 CHILL WIND [92] 8-10-0 M Foster, in tch, wkng whn hit 11th.
. . . .(7 to 1 op 6 to 1 tchd 8 to 1) 5
3656[3] REBEL KING [92] 7-9-9 (5*) S Taylor, in tch till outpcd and drpd rear hfwy, wl beh. . . . .(50 to 1 op 25 to 1) 6
Dist: 5l, 21l, 5l, 18l, 8l. 5m 8.90s. a 16.90s (6 Ran).

(Robert Ogden), G Richards

3761 Newmiln Country Estate Amateur Riders' Handicap Hurdle Class E (0-115 4-y-o and up) £3,408 3m 110yds. . . . . (4:50)

3437[4] PEGGY GORDON [85] 6-9-9 (5*) Miss P Robson, hld up, steady hdwy frm 9th, led last, styd on wl.
. . . .(25 to 1 op 20 to 1) 1
3309[9] GROSVENOR (Ire) [92] 6-10-3[9] (7*) M J Tizzard, nvr far away, ev ch frm 2 out, kpt on same pace. . . .(8 to 1 tchd 9 to 1) 2
3204 COUNTRY STORE [88] 8-10-3[9] (7*) Mr E James, led to 3rd, chsd ldrs, hdd last, no extr. (16 to 1 tchd 14 to 1) 3

3507⁵ VALIANT DASH [85] 11-9-7 (7") Mr O McPhail, *led 3rd to 4th, led 6th to 9th, kpt on same pace frm 2 out.*
................................(12 to 1 tchd 14 to 1) 4

3604² OLD HABITS (Ire) [98] 8-10-8 (5") Mr M H Naughton, *prmnt, led 9th till hdd 3 out, kpt on same pace frm nxt.*
................................(12 to 1 op 8 to 1) 5

3353" ENCHANTED COTTAGE [90] 5-10-1³ (7") Mr M Bradburne, *sn tracking ldrs, ch bef 2 out, kpt on same pace.*
................................(5 to 1 fav tchd 11 to 2) 6

3395⁴ DORLIN CASTLE [88] 9-9-10 (7") Mr B Gibson, *in tch, grad wknd frm 3 out*........(8 to 1 op 10 to 1 tchd 12 to 1) 7

3399³ PARIAH (Ire) [96] 8-10-6 (5") Mr R Hale, *hld up, effrt aftr 9th, no hdwy frm 3 out.*....................(8 to 1 tchd 7 to 1) 8

1848⁴ ABLE PLAYER (USA) [87] 10-10-2⁶ (7") Mr K Drewry, *nvr better than mid-div*...........(16 to 1 tchd 20 to 1) 9

3498² STAC-POLLAIDH [85] 7-9-7 (7") Mr R Forristal, *chsd ldrs till wknd aftr 9th.*........................(10 to 1) 10

3440⁷ FATHER O'BRIEN [90] 10-9-12 (7") Mr J Goldstein, *nvr dngrs.*
................................(16 to 1 tchd 14 to 1) 11

2635⁸ FRISKY THYNE (Ire) [85] 8-9-12¹ (3") Mr C Bonner, *in tch till wknd aftr 9th.*................(33 to 1 op 20 to 1) 12

3205³ LORD MCMURROUGH (Ire) [113] 7-11-7 (7") Mr E Williams, *in tch till wknd aftr 3 out.*..................(20 to 1) 13

3658³ BLOOMING SPRING (Ire) [85] 8-9-8¹ (7") Mrs Jean McGregor, *sn beh.*........................(25 to 1 op 20 to 1) 14

2710 DIG DEEPER [89] 10-9-11 (7") Mr M J Ruddy, *led 4th till hdd 6th, wknd quickly aftr 8th*.................(16 to 1) 15

3601 FESTIVAL FANCY [85] 10-9-7 (7") Mr D R McLeod, *sn beh.*
................................(33 to 1) 16

3435 BUSY BOY [85] 10-9-7 (7") Miss S Lamb, *sn beh.* (100 to 1) 17

2916⁵ WHITE DIAMOND [98] 9-10-13²⁰ (7") Mr T Scott, *sn beh, tld off*..................................(33 to 1) 18

3162⁸ NEW CHARGES [89] 10-10-1⁴ (7") Mr T J Barry, *chsd ldrs to 8th, wknd quickly, tld off whn pld up bef 2 out.*
................................(12 to 1 op 10 to 1) pu
PERSIAN VIEW (Ire) [98] 7-10-6 (7") Mr R Wakley, *refused to race, took no part*...................(10 to 1 op 14 to 1) I

Dist: 3½l, 4l, ¾l, 8l, 3½l, 6l, 12l, 10l, 1¼l, 9l. 6m 4.30s. a 22.30s (20 Ran).

(Frank Flynn And Richard Madden), Mrs D Thomson

3762 Party Has Started Moet & Chandon Maiden Hurdle Class E (Div II) (4-y-o and up) £2,080 2½m 110yds.. (5:20)

2849 ROYAL YORK 5-11-2 P Carberry, *hld up, steady hdwy to ld 2 out, pushed out*.....(11 to 10 fav op 5 to 4 tchd 11 to 8) 1

3704⁷ BIRKDALE 6-11-7 R Supple, *hld up, steady hdwy to ld bef 2 out, sn hdd, chsd wnr aftr, no imprsn.*
................................(10 to 1 tchd 14 to 1) 2

3128⁶ BEAU MATELOT 5-11-7 A S Smith, *towards rear, hdwy aftr 7th, kpt on same pace frm 2 out*......(8 to 1 tchd 9 to 1) 3

2601 GRANHAM PRIDE (Ire) 7-11-7 S McNeill, *in tch, kpt on same pace frm 3 out*..............(7 to 2 op 3 to 1) 4

3704⁵ COTTSTOWN BOY 6-11-7 M Foster, *chsd ldrs, led 7th, rdn and hdd bef 2 out, sn wknd*.........(8 to 1 op 10 to 1) 5

1673 CAREYSVILLE (Ire) 6-11-7 P Niven, *cl up, led aftr 5th, hdd 7th, sn wknd, tld off*.............(16 to 1 op 12 to 1) 6

3309 WEEJUMPAWUD 7-11-2 Mr C Storey, *lost tch frm 6th, tld off*..............................(66 to 1) 7

HYDROPIC 10-11-2 (5") S Taylor, *led till hdd aftr 5th, sn wknd, tld off*...........................(100 to 1) 8

3700 SMART IN SOCKS 6-11-7 T Reed, *beh frm hfwy, tld off.*
................................(66 to 1 tchd 100 to 1) 9

1929⁵ SUPER GUY 5-11-7 G Cahill, *in tch till wknd bef 7th, tld off whn pld up before 2 out*....(25 to 1 tchd 33 to 1) pu
BOLD ECHO 5-11-2 D Bentley, *tld off whn pld up bef 4th.*
................................(100 to 1) pu

Dist: 1¾l, 17l, ½l, 6l, dist, 16l, dist, 2l. 5m 6.30s. a 26.30s (11 Ran).

(Robert Ogden), G Richards

PUNCHESTOWN (IRE) (good)
Wednesday April 23rd

3763 Sean Barrett Bloodstock Insurances Ltd Handicap Chase (Listed) (5-y-o and up) £9,675 2½m....(2:10)

3751³ IDIOTS VENTURE [-] 12-12-0 C F Swan, *hld up, gng wl, smooth prog to join ldr last, ran on*................(9 to 1) 1

3548⁵ ARCTIC WEATHER (Ire) [-] 8-10-8 T P Rudd, *trkd ldr frm hfwy, led appr 2 out, hdd r-in, no extr*.............(4 to 1) 2

3550* MANHATTAN CASTLE (Ire) [-] 8-11-9 F Woods, *hld up, not jump wl, hdwy appr 2 out, no imprsn*.........(11 to 8 fav) 3

3550 AN MAINEACH (Ire) [-] 8-10-7 (5") J M Donnelly, *led till und pres 2 out, fdd*..........................(8 to 1) 4

3548³ OH SO GRUMPY [-] 9-10-10 J Shortt, *hld up, improved 4 out, wknd aftr 2 out*.......................(7 to 1) 5

3455⁵ BEAUCHAMP GRACE [-] 8-9-11 (3") G Cotter, *lost tch frm 4 out*................................(10 to 1) 6
DEEP HERITAGE [-] 11-10-3 A P McCoy, *3rd whn f 5th.*
................................(8 to 1) f

Dist: 1½l, 11l, 20l, 7l. 5m 10.80s. a 13.80s (7 Ran).

(Blackwater Racing Syndicate), A P O'Brien

3764 Stanley Cooker Champion Novice Hurdle (Grade 1) (4-y-o and up) £18,600 2½m...............(2:40)

3129* ISTABRAQ (Ire) 5-11-13 C F Swan, *al prmnt, wnt second and mstk 4 out, jnd ldrs 3 out, led 2 out, ran on strly.* (11 to 4 on) 1

3129⁵ SOLDAT (USA) 4-11-4 R Dunwoody, *al prmnt, wnt second r-in, no ch wth wnr*......................(13 to 2) 2

3551³ BORO BOW (Ire) 6-11-9 T P Treacy, *led to 3 out, ran on one pace*.........................(16 to 1) 3

3435* ARDRINA 6-11-9 N Williamson, *mid-div, und pres and no hdwy frm 4 out.*.......................(20 to 1) 4

3549² LIVER BIRD (Ire) 7-12-0 C O'Dwyer, *prmnt, chsd ldr aftr 5 out, lost tch frm 3 out*.......................(8 to 1) 5

2225* GLEBE LAD (Ire) 5-11-13 T P Rudd, *rdn and wknd frm 4 out.*
................................(20 to 1) 6

781* CLONAGAM (Ire) 8-12-0 J Shortt, *hld up, prog 4 out, mstk 3 out, wknd*....................(25 to 1) 7

3575⁶ LISS DE PAOR (Ire) 6-11-9 T Horgan, *wth ldrs, lost tch aftr 3 out, pld up bef last*...................(10 to 1) pu

Dist: 9l, ½l, 10l, 10l, 20l. 4m 58.70s. a 16.70s (8 Ran).

(J P McManus), A P O'Brien

3765 Heineken Gold Cup (Grade 1) (4-y-o and up) £37,200 3m 1f.......(3:15)

3134⁴ NOYAN [-] 7-11-1 N Williamson, *al gng wl, hdwy 4 out, mstk 2 out, disputing ld whn lft clr last*................(13 to 2) 1

3347⁵ BOBBYJO (Ire) [-] 7-11-2 G Cotter, *hdwy to go 3rd 3 out, lft second last, no ch wth wnr*...................(14 to 1) 2

3428* WOODVILLE STAR (Ire) [-] 8-11-8 C O'Dwyer, *jmpd wl and dsptd ld, slight lead 3 out, wknd quickly frm 2 out*...(7 to 1) 3

3428² TELL THE NIPPER (Ire) [-] (bl) 6-10-9 K F O'Brien, *beh, improved und pres 5 out, rdn alng and one pace frm 3 out.*
................................(12 to 1) 4

3395² CAROLE'S CRUSADER [-] 6-10-8 R Dunwoody, *mid-div, drvn and no hdwy frm 3 out*.................(10 to 1) 5

3453⁴ PAPILLON (Ire) [-] 6-11-12 C F Swan, *badly hmpd second, rdn and no imprsn frm 4 out*..................(4 to 1 fav) 6

3455 LIVIN IT UP (Ire) [-] 7-10-11 A P McCoy, *no prog frm 5 out.*
................................(14 to 1) 7

3550 THE OUTBACK WAY (Ire) [-] (bl) 7-11-5 D H O'Connor, *hld up, some prog 4 out, no imprsn*................(25 to 1) 8

3347² SHINING WILLOW [-] 7-10-7 J Osborne, *wth ldrs, mstks and wknd frm 7 out*..................(14 to 1) 9

3453² AMBLE SPEEDY (Ire) [-] 7-11-12 F Woods, *nvr gng wl.*
................................(8 to 1) 10

3522 STROLL HOME (Ire) [-] 7-10-9 Mr E Gallagher, *lost tch frm 5 out.*...........................(25 to 1) 11

3455* PRATE BOX (Ire) [-] 7-11-0 G Bradley, *f second.*....(14 to 1) f

3132⁵ CORKET (Ire) [-] 7-12-0 T Horgan, *chsd ldrs frm 4 out, wnt second 2 out, disputing ld whn f last*.............(14 to 1) f

3347 LORD MUFF (Ire) [-] 8-10-7 J K Kinane, *f second.* (100 to 1) f

3526" THE GOPHER (Ire) [-] 8-10-7 L P Cusack, *outrd, pld up aftr 6 out*...........................(20 to 1) pu

3133 GENERAL PONGO [-] 8-10-7 M A Fitzgerald, *losing tch whn pld up appr 5 out*.......................(20 to 1) pu

2842⁴ ROYAL ROSY (Ire) [-] 6-10-8 T J Mitchell, *al in rear, pld up bef 6 out*.........................(16 to 1) pu

3392* BALLYMACREVAN (Ire) [-] 7-10-9 T P Treacy, *al beh, pld up appr 5 out*.......................(25 to 1) pu

Dist: 15l, 6l, 3l, nk, 1l. 6m 29.90s. a 14.90s (18 Ran).

(C H McGhie), R A Fahey

# 3766 Paddy Power Handicap Hurdle (Grade 2) (4-y-o and up) £21,700 2m
................................(3:45)

3156 LADY DAISY (Ire) [-] 8-10-6 (5") A O'Shea, *mid-div, hdwy to go second aftr 3 out, chlgd last, drw clr 1nl 100 yards.*.(12 to 1) 1

3595* SHANKAR (Ire) [-] 6-10-8 (3") Mr R Thornton, *hld up, prog 3 out, led aftr 2 out, hdd r-in, no extr.*........(5 to 2 fav) 2

3597⁴ SPACE TRUCKER (Ire) [-] 6-12-0 J Shortt, *improved and chsd ldrs aftr 3 out, styd on one pace.*...............(5 to 1) 3

3523³ MYSTICAL CITY (Ire) [-] 7-10-12 D J Casey, *beh hfwy, drvn alng aftr 2 out, styd on one pace.*...........(7 to 1) 4

3521² HILL SOCIETY (Ire) [-] 5-10-11 R Dunwoody, *rdn alng appr 2 out, not rch ldrs.*.........................(7 to 1) 5

3523" KHAYRAWANI (Ire) [-] (bl) 5-10-11 C O'Dwyer, *hdwy 4 out, no imprsn frm 2 out*.......................(9 to 2) 6

1393 JUST LITTLE [-] 5-10-11 C F Swan, *chsd ldrs and no imprsn frm 2 out*.......................(14 to 1) 7

3073² MAGICAL LADY (Ire) [-] 5-10-11 A P McCoy, *lost tch frm 3 out.*................................(16 to 1) 8

2473³ EMBELLISHED (Ire) [-] 5-10-11 N Williamson, *outpcd aftr 3 out*................................(20 to 1) 9

3156 CHERYL'S LAD (Ire) [-] 7-10-11 M A Fitzgerald, *rdn alng aftr 3 out, lost tch, tld off*................(12 to 1) 10

Dist: 4l, 4l, 1½l, sht-hd, 9l. 3m 45.30s. a 0.30s (10 Ran).
SR: 64/60/73/55/54/45/

(P F Kehoe), Anthony Mullins

3767 Poitin Stil Novice Hurdle (4-y-o and up) £4,795 2m...............(4:15)

3549⁵ STEP ON EYRE (Ire) 7-12-0 D J Casey, ...(8 to 1) 1

3547⁵ EDUARDO (Ire) 7-11-5 (3") K Whelan, ...(12 to 1) 2

3348³	ONE WORD (Ire) 5-11-13 R Dunwoody, ... (8 to 1)	3
430²	ROYAL ZIERO (Ire) 7-11-3 (5°) A O'Shea, ... (16 to 1)	4
3415⁵	FAMILY PROJECT (Ire) 4-10-9 S H O'Donovan, . . . (14 to 1)	5
3575⁷	NICOLA MARIE (Ire) 8-11-3 P A Roche, ... (33 to 1)	6
3551	COMKILRED (Ire) 5-11-8 T P Treacy, ... (33 to 1)	7
3547⁴	SILVIAN BLISS (USA) 5-11-13 C O'Dwyer, ... (13 to 8 on)	8
3430⁷	PAULS RUN (Ire) 8-12-0 L P Cusack, ... (14 to 1)	9
2964	HANDSOME ANTHONY (Ire) 6-11-5 (3°) Mr B R Hamilton,	
	. . . . (50 to 1)	10
3456	AMBERLEIGH HOUSE (Ire) 5-11-2 M McCoy, . . . (16 to 1)	11
2649	DRUMCLIFFE (Ire) 6-11-1 (7°) Capt A Ogden, ... (100 to 1)	12
3524	TOTAL SUCCESS (Ire) 5-11-4 (3°) Mr R Walsh, . . . (16 to 1)	13
3547²	IRIDAL (bl) 5-11-7 N Williamson, ... (8 to 1)	pu
430⁸	GREY HORIZON (Ire) 6-11-8 P McWilliams, ... (50 to 1)	pu
3626⁶	BEHY BRIDGE (Ire) 5-11-2 T J Mitchell, ... (66 to 1)	pu

Dist: 3l, 4½l, 1l, 1½l. 3m 53.20s. a 8.20s (17 Ran).

SR: 2/-/-/-/-/-/

3768 Bank Of Ireland Handicap Hurdle (4 & 5-y-o) £8,220 2¼m. . . . . (4:45)

3451³	THE QUADS [-] 5-9-11 (3°) Mr R Thornton, ...(8 to 1)	1
3419⁵	FANE PATH (Ire) [-] 5-10-1 (7°) B J Geraghty, ... (8 to 1)	2
3695⁴	GENTLE MOSSY (Ire) [-] 5-10-4 D H O'Connor, ...(5 to 1)	3
3216³	REGENCY RAKE (Ire) [-] 5-10-10 F Woods, ... (4 to 1)	4
3235⁸	I REMEMBER IT WELL (Ire) [-] (bl) 5-10-9 M P Hourigan,	
	. . . . (10 to 1)	5
2445⁶	VITUS (USA) [-] 5-11-3 A P McCoy, ... (9 to 4 fav)	6
3566⁷	MARLONETTE (Ire) [-] 4-11-2 D J Casey, ... (6 to 1)	7
3415°	PERSIAN DREAM (Ire) [-] 4-9-10 C F Swan, ... (7 to 1)	8
907	DANCING CLODAGH (Ire) [-] (bl) 5-10-4 C O'Dwyer,	
	. . . . (16 to 1)	9
3696²	JACK YEATS (Ire) [-] 5-10-9 J Shortt, ... (10 to 1)	10

Dist: 3l, 1½l, 1½l, 5l. 4m 10.70s. a 3.70s (10 Ran).

SR: 17/22/16/20/14/-/ (I Told You So Syndicate), A L T Moore

3769 Doncaster Sales Jack White Memorial Flat Race (Grade 1) (4-y-o and up) £12,900 2m. . . . . (5:15)

3135²	ARCTIC CAMPER 5-12-0 Mr R Thornton, ...(11 to 4 fav)	1
3217³	CLOONE BRIDGE (Ire) 5-12-3 Mr J A Berry, ... (16 to 1)	2
3135⁶	FRENCH HOLLY (USA) 6-12-4 Mr P Fenton, ... (3 to 1)	3
3142¹	LORD LAMB 5-12-6 Mr S Swiers, ... (14 to 1)	4
2838⁴	GARRYS LOCK (Ire) 8-12-4 Mr P English, ... (14 to 1)	5
3561¹	MAGIC MEAD 5-11-12 Mr C Vigors, ... (12 to 1)	6
2737⁸	PROMALEE (Ire) 5-12-6 Mr B M Cash, ... (8 to 1)	7
3524³	DO YE KNOW WHA 5-12-3 Mr J P McNamara, (12 to 1)	8
2049	ABORIGINAL (Ire) 5-12-3 Mr A C Coyle, ... (8 to 1)	9
3553°	DR KING 5-12-3 Mr G Elliott, ... (14 to 1)	10
3608¹	SARAH SUPREME (Ire) 6-11-9 Mr D Marnane, ... (20 to 1)	11
3525⁹	SOLVANG 5-12-0 Mr W M O'Sullivan, ... (16 to 1)	12
3394⁷	ANDREA COVA (Ire) 5-11-12 Mr A J Dempsey, . . . (20 to 1)	13
3135⁴	SCORING PEDIGREE 5-12-0 Mr R Walsh, ... (14 to 1)	14
	MR MOYLAN 5-11-10 Mr E Bolger, ... (16 to 1)	15
2967³	FINE DE CLAIRE 4-11-2 Mr A R Coonan, ... (20 to 1)	16
	CINQ FRANK (Ire) 7-11-11 Mr G J Harford, ... (100 to 1)	17
	COTTON EYED JIMMY (Ire) 6-11-11 Mr M J Gilhooly,	
	. . . . (100 to 1)	18
	BARRINGTON (Ire) 4-11-3 Mr Paul Moloney, ... (16 to 1)	19
2737	CLAY AND WATTLES (Ire) 6-12-4 Mr A J Martin, . . (20 to 1)	20
2476°	CAILIN SUPREME (Ire) 6-12-2 Mr T Mullins, ... (14 to 1)	pu

Dist: 5½l, 1½l, ½l, 2l. 3m 41.20s. (21 Ran).

(Lady Harris), D Nicholson

3770 Kevin McManus Champion Hunters Chase (5-y-o and up) £13,000 3m 1f . . . . (5:45)

2844	DIXON VARNER (Ire) 7-12-0 Mr R Walsh, ... (6 to 1)	1
3527²	STAY IN TOUCH (Ire) 7-12-0 Mr D P Costello, . . (100 to 30)	2
	BREE HILL (Ire) 9-12-0 Mr G Elliott, ... (20 to 1)	3
3578	MR BOSTON 12-12-0 Mr S Swiers, ... (7 to 4 fav)	4
602	CAPTAIN BRANDY 12-12-0 Mr D M Christie, ... (20 to 1)	5
	MACK A DAY 10-12-0 Mr K O'Sullivan, ... (25 to 1)	6
10927	CELTIC BUCK 11-12-0 Mr Patrick O'Keeffe, ... (33 to 1)	f
3378²	LOTTOVER (Ire) 8-11-9 Mr B Hassett, ... (20 to 1)	f
3153⁹	WHAT A HAND 9-12-0 Mr P Fenton, ... (7 to 2)	f
3525⁷	HI JAMIE (Ire) 5-11-7 Mr G J Harford, ... (16 to 1)	f
3378°	DENFIELD (Ire) 6-12-0 Mr I Buchanan, ... (16 to 1)	ur
3391⁴	KILLMURRAY BUCK (Ire) 9-11-9 Mr J P McNamara,	
	. . . . (50 to 1)	bd

Dist: 3½l, 9l, 8l, 15l. 6m 44.90s. a 29.90s (12 Ran).

(Mrs John Magnier), E Bolger

FONTWELL (good to firm)
Thursday April 24th
Going Correction: NIL

3771 Rapide Mortgage Services And Finbar Novices' Hurdle Class E (4-y-o and up) £2,363 2¾m 110yds. . (2:20)

3027⁷	GALATASORI JANE (Ire) 7-11-0 (7°) L Cummins, al prmnt, led 6th, drw clr appr 2 out, easily.	
	. . . .(Evens fav tchd 11 to 10 and 11 to 10 on)	1
3359²	DRUM BATTLE 5-10-13 (7°) J Power, led to second, styd prmnt, outpcd appr 2 out. (11 to 4 op 2 to 1 tchd 3 to 1)	2
3414³	NORDIC SPREE (Ire) (v) 5-11-0 P Holley, al prmnt, wknd 3 out. . . . . (100 to 30 op 5 to 2 tchd 7 to 2)	3
3196	EWAR BOLD (bl) 4-10-0 (7°) D Slattery, prmnt till wknd 4 out. . . . . (33 to 1 op 16 to 1)	4
3704	SOLDIER-B 7-11-0 D Morris, pld hrd, led second till hot 6th, wknd 4 out, tld off. . . . . (33 to 1 op 14 to 1)	5
3484²	COUNTRY KEEPER 9-11-0 G Upton, al beh, tld off 5th, pld up aftr jmpd badly lft 2 out.	
	. . . . (25 to 1 op 16 to 1 tchd 33 to 1 and 40 to 1)	pu
2215⁹	HONEST DAVE 7-11-0 K Gaule, al beh, tld off whn pld up aftr 7th. . . . . (50 to 1 op 20 to 1)	pu
3097	PITARRY 7-11-0 J R Kavanagh, tld off 5th, pld up bef 7th. . . . . (50 to 1 op 20 to 1)	pu

Dist: 10l, 8l, 2½l, 30l. 5m 28.10s. a 14.10s (8 Ran).

(B L Blinman), P F Nicholls

3772 Rapide Mortgage Services Novices' Chase Class E (5-y-o and up) £3,058 3¼m 110yds. . . . . (2:50)

3679²	DECYBRIG (Fr) 6-12-0 C Maude, made all, quickened clr 16th, rdn appr 2 out, styd on.	
	. . . . (13 to 8 on op 7 to 4 on tchd 6 to 4 on and 11 to 8 on)	1
2745	KEEP IT ZIPPED (Ire) (bl) 7-11-8 J A McCarthy, trkd wnr, outpcd 16th, rdn to cl 3 out, untidy last, hng lft and no imprsn r-in. . . . . (9 to 4 op 7 to 4 tchd 5 to 2)	2
3271²	CARDINAL GAYLE 7-11-2 J R Kavanagh, al last, tld off frm 5th. . . . . (6 to 1 op 9 to 2 tchd 13 to 2 and 7 to 1)	3

Dist: 2l, dist. 6m 50.20s. a 20.20s (3 Ran).

(Terry Neill), M C Pipe

3773 Strebel Boilers And Radiators Handicap Hurdle Series Qualifier Class E (0-110 4-y-o and up) £2,322 2¾m 110yds. . . . . (3:20)

3471⁸	SCUD MISSILE (Ire) [91] 6-11-5 Richard Guest, hld up in tch, hdwy to track ldr 3 out, rdn to ld r-in.	
	. . . . (5 to 4 fav op 7 to 4 tchd 15 to 8)	1
3641⁷	ADILOV [78] 5-10-3 (3°) L Aspell, hld up, hdwy to ld 3 out, rdn and mstk last, hdd r-in. . . . (13 to 2 op 4 to 1 tchd 7 to 1)	2
3358³	FAWLEY FLYER [92] 8-10-13 (7°) J Power, made most till mstk and hdd 3 out, sn btn, fnshd lme.	
	. . . . (3 to 1 op 5 to 4 tchd 100 to 30)	3
3683⁸	BORN TO PLEASE (Ire) [96] 5-11-10 M A Fitzgerald, wth ldr, led 4th to 5th, reminder aftr 7th, ev ch four out, rdn and sn wknd, eased bef last, tld off. . . . . (11 to 4 op 9 to 4)	4

Dist: 2½l, 17l, dist. 5m 33.00s. a 19.00s (4 Ran).

(J P Power), J W Payne

3774 Rapide Mortgage Services & Cornhill Life Handicap Hurdle Class C (0-130 5-y-o and up) £3,655 3m 3f . . . . (3:50)

3405²	ST VILLE [99] 11-10-0 B Powell, al in tch, led 4 out, drw clr frm 2 out. . . . . (100 to 30 op 3 to 1 tchd 4 to 1)	1
3386²	RUNAWAY PETE (USA) [123] 7-11-10 D Walsh, al prmnt, rdn to ld 9th, ev ch 3 out, wknd und pres frm nxt. . . . . (9 to 2 op 11 to 4 tchd 5 to 1)	2
3297	GIVUS A CALL (Ire) [106] 7-11-0 (3°) L Aspell, hld up, hdwy 9th, mstk 4 out, rdn and outpcd nxt.	
	. . . . (14 to 1 op 12 to 1 tchd 16 to 1)	3
3557⁶	ULURU (Ire) [101] 9-10-2 J R Kavanagh, hld up in tch, reminder 9th, wknd 4 out, tld off.	
	. . . . (3 to 1 op 5 to 2 tchd 100 to 30)	4
3628⁴	NICK THE DREAMER [99] 12-9-9² (7°) N Willmington, led to 9th, wknd 4 out, tld off. (50 to 1 op 33 to 1 tchd 66 to 1)	5
3272°	SNOW BOARD [101] 8-10-2² Derek Byrne, nvr gng wl in rear, effrt 7th, tld off whn pld up bef 4 out. (7 to 1 tchd 5 to 2)	pu
632	MORNING BLUSH (Ire) [100] 7-10-1 B Fenton, prmnt till wknd 4 out, tld off whn pld up aftr 2 out. . . . (10 to 1 tchd 12 to 1)	pu

Dist: 14l, 1½l, dist, 2½l. 6m 30.30s. a 6.30s (7 Ran).

SR: 9/19/-/-/ (Melplash Racing), R H Buckler

3775 George Gale & Co Handicap Chase Class E (0-115 5-y-o and up) £3,042 2¼m. . . . . (4:20)

3371	BLAZER MORINIERE (Fr) [78] 8-10-2 S Fox, nvr far away, led 9th, rdn and kpt on wl frm 2 out.	
	. . . . (9 to 4 fav tchd 3 to 1 and 100 to 30)	1
1562⁵	MILL O'THE RAGS (Ire) [100] 8-11-10 J F Titley, al prmnt, chsd wnr frm 10th, rdn appr 2 out, one pace.	
	. . . . (100 to 30 op 3 to 1 tchd 7 to 2)	2
3360⁴	FICHU (USA) [82] 9-10-6 M Richards, al in rear, lost tch 6th. . . . . (9 to 2 op 5 to 2)	3
3410⁵	UPWARD SURGE (Ire) [76] 7-11-0 Mrs N Ledger, led appr second, mstk and hdd 9th, wknd aftr 4 out.	
	. . . . (50 to 1 op 33 to 1 tchd 66 to 1 and 100 to 1)	4

3653² TOOMUCH TOOSOON (Ire) [91] 9-11-1 B Fenton, *hld up in tch, mstk tenth, pld up bef nxt, lme*..... (11 to 4 op 2 to 1) pu
BEACH BUM [79] 11-10-3 G Upton, *led till hdd appr second, pld up bef 4th, dismounted.*
..........(10 to 1 op 10 to 1 tchd 12 to 1 and 6 to 1) pu
Dist: 10l, 20l, 8l. 4m 30.70s. a 10.70s (6 Ran).

(John Pearl), P C Ritchens

3776 RMS And TCR Maiden Hurdle Class E (4-y-o and up) £2,485 2¼m 110yds .... (4:50)

3634² MULLINTOR (Ire) 6-11-6 D O'Sullivan, *led till aftr 1st, styd prmnt, led appr 3 out, rdn out r-in.*
.................................(5 to 2 tchd 3 to 1 and 100 to 30) 1
3296⁶ HE KNOWS THE RULES 5-11-6 B Powell, *hld up hdwy 4 out, ev ch frm nxt till jmpd path r-in, not reco'r.*
.......(13 to 8 fav op 11 to 10 tchd 7 to 4 and 9 to 5) 2
3610⁴ GLOBAL DANCER 6-11-6 M Richards, *hld up, hdwy appr 4 out, wknd bef 2 out.*........ (6 to 1 op 8 to 1 tchd 9 to 2) 3
3332 SWAN STREET (NZ) 6-11-3 (3") J Magee, *mid-div, hdwy appr 4 out, wknd nxt.*.............(9 to 1 op 6 to 1 tchd 10 to 1) 4
3643³ VERONICA FRANCO 4-10-6 (3") P Henley, *chsd ldrs, wknd appr 2 out, btn whn blun last.*
.... (10 to 1 op 6 to 1 tchd 11 to 1) 5
1423 INDIAN CROWN (bl) 7-11-1 S Burrough, *pld hrd, prmnt till wknd 5th, tld off.*..............(100 to 1 op 33 to 1) 6
3632 FULL OF TRICKS 9-11-6 D Morris, *led aftr 1st till wknd and hdd appr 3 out, tld off...*(50 to 1 op 25 to 1 tchd 66 to 1) 7
2831 CALDEBROOK (Ire) 6-11-3 (3") L Aspell, *hld up, hdwy whn mstk 4 out, rallied nxt, 3rd and held when f 2 out.*
.... (14 to 1 op 7 to 1 tchd 16 to 1) f
3629³ LORD LOVE (Ire) 6-11-2 J Culloty, *al prmnt, ev ch 3 out, wkng and 4th whn brght dwn nxt.*.......... (14 to 1 op 10 to 1) bd
2605 ELLY'S DREAM 6-11-1 S Fox, *tld off 3rd, pld up aftr 5th.*
.... (66 to 1 op 33 to 1) pu
3569⁴ OSCILIGHTS GIFT 5-11-1 W McFarland, *al beh, tld off whn pld up bef 2 out...*(50 to 1 op 20 to 1 tchd 66 to 1) pu
3253 WOMAN FROM HELL 7-11-1 C Maude, *prmnt till wknd aftr 5th, tld off whn pld up bef 2 out.*........(50 to 1 op 33 to 1) pu
Dist: 1½l, 28l, 4l, 4l, dist, 16l. 4m 24.30s. a 7.30s (12 Ran).
SR: 19/17/-/-/-/-/ *(Thomas Thompson), R Rowe*

PERTH (good)
Thursday April 24th
Going Correction: PLUS 0.25 sec. per fur.

3777 Perth Hunt Balnakeilly Challenge Cup Hunters' Chase Class H (5-y-o and up) £2,388 3m ....(2:00)

3599² ENSIGN EWART (Ire) 6-11-9 (5") Mr C Storey, *towards rear, steady hdwy frm 12th, styd on wl to ld fnl 100 yards, all out.*
.... (11 to 2 op 7 to 2 tchd 6 to 1) 1
3567⁴ HOWAYMAN 7-11-12 (7") Mr A Parker, *prmnt, led 13th till hdd fnl 100 yards, kpt on.* (3 to 1 fav tchd 7 to 2 and 4 to 1) 2
ADMISSION (Ire) 7-11-7 (7") Miss L Horner, *prmnt, ev ch 3 out, wknd bef last.*........................ (12 to 1 op 9 to 1) 3
3578⁸ FORDSTOWN 8-11-8¹ (7") Mr Jamie Alexander, *led till hdd 6th, chsd ldrs aftr, one paced frm 15th.*
.... (16 to 1 tchd 20 to 1) 4
3603⁴ DARK DAWN 13-11-12 (7") Miss Lorna Foxton, *nvr on terms.*
.... (8 to 1 tchd 9 to 1) 5
BOW HANDY MAN 15-11-7 (7") Miss S Laidlaw, *nvr dngrs.*
.... (33 to 1 op 20 to 1) 6
ACROSS THE CARD 9-11-12 (7") Mr M Bradburne, *sn beh.*
.... (9 to 1 op 8 to 1 tchd 10 to 1) 7
3133 MASTER KIT (Ire) 8-11-12 (7") Mr J Billinge, *hld up early, gd hdwy to ld 6th, mstk 11th (water), hdd 13th, wknd quickly, tld off, virtually pld up r-in.*...............(7 to 1 op 6 to 1) 8
3539* DENIM BLUE 8-12-3 (5") Miss P Robson, *f second.*
.... (9 to 1 op 5 to 1 tchd 10 to 1) f
THANK U JIM 9-11-7 (7") Miss T Jackson, *blun and uns rdr 1st.*............................ (20 to 1 op 12 to 1) ur
BORDER GLORY 6-11-7 (7") Mr M J Ruddy, *chsd ldrs to hfwy, wkng whn blun and uns rdr 15th.*.... (50 to 1 op 40 to 1) ur
3018⁴ DIRECT 14-11-12 (7") Mr T Edwards, *sn beh, tld off whn pld up bef 15th.*....................... (20 to 1 op 14 to 1) pu
3096 FIFTH AMENDMENT (bl) 12-11-7 (7") Mr A Hales, *hmpd 1st, mstk 5th, lost tch and pld up bef 13th..............*(33 to 1) pu
3352³ RUSTY BLADE 8-11-9 (5") Mr R Hale, *sn beh, tld off whn pld up bef 3 out.*...................(20 to 1 op 16 to 1) pu
Dist: Nk, 18l, 3l, 2½l, 12l, 25l, dist. 6m 21.50s. a 26.50s (14 Ran).

(Major M W Sample), C Storey

3778 Nelson Morrison Underwriting Agency Ltd Future Champions 'National Hunt' Novices' Hurdle Class C (5-y-o and up) £4,695 3m 110yds................................(2:30)

3709 LAGEN BRIDGE (Ire) 8-11-8 D J Moffatt, *settled midfield, effrt aftr 3 out, led bef nxt, hrd pressed last, styd on wl und pres.*
.... (9 to 1 op 8 to 1 tchd 10 to 1) 1

3657* MEADOW HYMN (Ire) 6-11-8 P Carberry, *nvr far away, chlgd 3 out, ev ch last, no extr und pres.*
.... (9 to 4 fav op 2 to 1 tchd 5 to 2) 2
3712⁸ YOUNG KENNY 6-11-8 R Supple, *in tch, ev ch 3 out, sn drvn aing, kpt on same pace...* (7 to 2 op 3 to 1 tchd 4 to 1) 3
3535* MAJOR HARRIS (Ire) 5-11-4 R Garritty, *in tch, ev ch 3 out, wkng rdn and btn...*.................(10 to 1 op 8 to 1) 4
2921 LOTTERY TICKET (Ire) 8-10-12 T J Murphy, *chsd ldrs, ev ch 3 out, sn rdn and btn.*...............(20 to 1 op 14 to 1) 5
3414* SPARKLING SPRING (Ire) 6-11-8 S McNeill, *trkd ldrs, led 8th, hdd 3 out, sn btn....................*(7 to 1 op 5 to 1) 6
3160² PEBBLE BEACH (Ire) 7-11-4 J Callaghan, *chsd ldrs til rdn and wknd 8th, tld off.............*(25 to 1 op 20 to 1) 7
3351⁸ OVER ZEALOUS (Ire) 5-10-12 J Supple, *beh and sn drvn aing, lost tch aftr 8th, tld off...........*(66 to 1 op 33 to 1) 8
3308⁸ PERSIAN GRANGE (Ire) (bl) 7-10-12 J Burke, *beh, reminders aftr 6th, pld up bef 8th..............*(200 to 1 op 100 to 1) pu
3077⁶ HUISH (Ire) 6-10-12 Mr A Charles-Jones, *keen early, led 5th till hdd 8th, wknd quickly, tld off whn pld up bef 2 out.*
.... (33 to 1 tchd 66 to 1) pu
3398⁵ PAPERISING 5-11-8 P Niven, *trkd ldrs, led 3 out, hdd bef nxt, wknd quickly, tld off whn pld up r-in.....*(7 to 1 op 6 to 1) pu
3658⁵ CHEATER (Ire) (bl) 6-11-4 A S Smith, *led to 5th, wknd quickly aftr 8th, tld off whn pld up bef 2 out...* (20 to 1 op 25 to 1) pu
3655⁸ MOREFLASH 5-10-7 T Reed, *sn beh, tld off whn pld up bef 2 out..................*(500 to 1 op 100 to 1) pu
Dist: 1¾l, 22l, ¾l, 1¼l, 1¾l, 15l. 6m 3.60s. a 21.60s (13 Ran).

(Mrs Eileen M Milligan), D Moffatt

3779 R M C Catherwood Ltd 'Little Bay' Handicap Chase Class B (0-145 5-y-o and up) £6,720 2m..........(3:00)

3656* GROUSE-N-HEATHER [100] 8-10-0 P Carberry, *hld up and beh, hdwy und pres aftr 3 out, led after last, ran on wl.*
.... (7 to 2 op 11 to 4) 1
3719² STORM FALCON (USA) [115] 7-10-10 (5") Chris Webb, *beh early, sn tracking ldrs, led 7th, hdd aftr last, no extr und pres.*
.... (14 to 1 op 12 to 1) 2
3719⁶ POLITICAL TOWER [127] 10-11-13 B Storey, *hld up, took clr order 8th, ev ch 3 out, rdn, kpt on frm last.*
.... (9 to 1 op 7 to 1) 3
3719* MONYMAN (Ire) [111] 7-10-11 (6ex) R Garritty, *hld up in tch, hmpd 8th, chlgd 2 out, ev ch last, no extr und pres.*
.... (Evens fav op 5 to 4) 4
3479* NETHERBY SAID [121] 7-11-7 R Supple, *made most till hdd 7th, wknd quickly aftr 9th, tld off........* (9 to 2 op 4 to 1) 5
2321² CARDENDEN (Ire) [100] 9-10-0 G Cahill, *dsptd ld till wknd aftr 7th, tld off.....................*(200 to 1 op 100 to 1) 6
Dist: 3½l, 3l, dist, 8l. 4m 0.60s. a 9.60s (6 Ran).
SR: 16/27/36/20/-/-/ *(D J Fairbairn), P Monteith*

3780 Murrayshall Hotel Selling Hurdle Class G (4-y-o and up) £2,906 2m 110yds................................(3:30)

1828 CHARLISTONA 6-10-2 (7") S Melrose, *in tch, hdwy to ld 2 out, ran on wl......................... (25 to 1) 1
SUSELJA (Ire) 6-10-6 (3") E Callaghan, *beh and drvn aing whn hit 4th, hdwy bef nxt, sn chasing ldrs, kpt on frm 2 out, no imprsn on wrnr.........* (25 to 1 tchd 33 to 1) 2
1807⁸ EDEN DANCER 5-12-0 P Niven, *led second, hdd 2 out, kpt on same pace...................*(7 to 2 jt-fav op 3 to 1) 3
3703 ANLACE (v) 8-10-11 (5") Chris Webb, *in tch, rdn bef 2 out, styd on same pace...................*(12 to 1 op 16 to 1) 4
3304⁸ MONKEY WENCH (Ire) 6-11-2 B Storey, *chsd ldrs, hit 2 out, sn btn.......................*(8 to 1 tchd 10 to 1) 5
3457 VANBOROUGH LAD 8-11-0 P Carberry, *in tch, hdwy to chase ldrs hfwy, wknd aftr 2 out...............* (16 to 1) 6
MEDIA EXPRESS 5-11-0 R Garritty, *chsd ldrs till wknd frm 2 out.......................* (12 to 1 op 8 to 1) 7
MAGGIES LAD 9-11-7 L Wyer, *chsd ldrs, outpcd bef 3 out, no dngr aftr........................*(33 to 1 op 25 to 1) 8
2623⁸ YOUNG SEMELE 5-10-9 J Railton, *nvr on terms.*
.... (16 to 1 op 12 to 1) 9
1911⁶ NONIOS (Ire) 6-11-7 J Callaghan, *prmnt till wknd bef 3 out.*
.... (7 to 2 jt-fav op 3 to 1) 10
3433 DE-VEERS CURRIE (Ire) 5-10-9 D J Moffatt, *al beh.*
.... (100 to 1 op 66 to 1) 11
3396⁰ NINE PIPES (Ire) 6-11-0 L O'Hara, *in tch till wknd aftr 3 out.*
.... (12 to 1 op 33 to 1 tchd 10 to 1) 12
1931⁷ DARK MIDNIGHT (Ire) 8-11-0 J Burke, *sn beh...* (100 to 1) 13
3433 BILL'S PRIDE 8-10-7 T Jenks, *chsd ldrs till wknd aftr 3 out.*
.... (20 to 1 op 14 to 1) 14
3409⁸ SABOTEUSE (bl) 5-10-9 T J Murphy, *sn beh, tld off.*
.... (100 to 1 op 66 to 1) 15
3629 DANUCHA 5-10-9 Leesa Long, *chasing ldrs whn f 5th, broke leg, destroyed.....................*(100 to 1) f
2537 GOING PUBLIC 10-12-0 A S Smith, *sn beh, tld off whn pld up bef 2 out.....................*(12 to 1 op 8 to 1) pu
2630 SECONDS AWAY 6-11-0 G Cahill, *led to second, chsd ldrs to hfwy, sn wknd, tld off whn pld up bef 2 out.*
.... (25 to 1 op 16 to 1 tchd 33 to 1) pu
BALLOCHAN LINN 5-11-0 D Parker, *sn beh, tld off whn pld up bef 2 out........................*(100 to 1) pu
3433⁶ CONNIE LEATHART 6-10-9 D Bentley, *sn beh, tld off whn pld up bef 2 out.....................*(33 to 1 op 25 to 1) pu

1986 TASHREEF (bl) 7-12-0 M Moloney, *refused to race, took no part*............................. (33 to 1 op 25 to 1) I
Dist: 10l, 3½l, 2½l, 6l, ½l, 10l, 8l, 2l, 1¼l, hd. 4m 2.10s. a 21.10s (21 Ran).
(J P Dodds), J P Dodds

3781 Tote Credit Maiden Chase Class D (5-y-o and up) £3,655 2m..... (4:00)

2499[5] TIDEBROOK 7-11-7 S McNeill, *trkd ldrs, blun 4th, led 2 out, 3 ls ahead whn mstk last and lft clr*........(7 to 2 op 9 to 4) 1
3600[4] COOL WEATHER (Ire) (bl) 9-11-7 A S Smith, *several reminders, led 5th to 7th, wknd quickly aftr 9th, lft poor second at last*..........................(10 to 1 op 8 to 1) 2
3354[4] NOORAN 6-11-7 B Storey, *in tch, blun 8th, sn rdn and wknd, tld off*.............. (6 to 4 fav op 5 to 2 tchd 11 to 4) 3
1657 REGAL DOMAIN (Ire) 6-11-7 K Johnson, *badly hmpd 1st, sn tld off*............................(50 to 1 op 33 to 1) 4
3584[4] NAWTINOOKEY 7-10-9 (7*) C McCormack, *nvr far away, led 7th, hdd 2 out, 3 ls beh wnr whn f last, rmntd.*
.........................(9 to 2 op 4 to 1 tchd 5 to 1) 5
3699 SMART IN SILK 8-11-2 T Reed, *f 1st.* (66 to 1 op 33 to 1) f
3007[4] HIGH MOOD 7-11-7 T J Murphy, *blun and uns rdr 3rd.*
.... (12 to 1 op 8 to 1 tchd 14 to 1) ur
3395 ROYAL BANKER (Ire) (bl) 7-11-7 P Carberry, *led to 5th, prmnt, 3rd and rdn whn blun and uns rdr 3 out.*
..................................(14 to 1 op 10 to 1) ur
2318 APOLLO COLOSSO 7-11-7 J Railton, *lost tch and pld up bef 6th*...............................(20 to 1 op 14 to 1) pu
Dist: Dist, dist, 12l, dist. 4m 7.90s. a 16.90s (9 Ran).
(Richard Williams), K C Bailey

3782 Nelson Morrison Handicap Hurdle Class D (0-125 4-y-o and up) £3,647 2½m 110yds................. (4:30)

3424[2] BOURDONNER [93] 5-10-1 (3*) Mr C Bonner, *made all, clr betw last 2, ran on wl*..................(9 to 2 op 7 to 2) 1
3059[7] ELATION [108] 5-11-5 R Garritty, *chsd wnr most of way, kpt on frm 2 out, no imprsn*.................(20 to 1 op 14 to 1) 2
3604[5] MASTER OF TROY [96] 9-10-7 D Parker, *towards rear, styd on frm 3 out, nvr able to chal*......... (16 to 1 op 10 to 1) 3
3200[2] LINLATHEN [113] 7-11-10 P Niven, *trkd ldrs, hit 7th, sn drvn alng, outpcd aftr nxt, no dngr after.*
........(2 to 1 fav op 11 to 4 tchd 3 to 1 and 7 to 4) 4
3703[6] FEN TERRIER [103] 5-11-0 B Storey, *hld up, hdwy hfwy, ch 3 out, wkng whn mstk nxt*..............(20 to 1 op 14 to 1) 5
3537[5] THURSDAY NIGHT (Ire) [109] 6-11-3 (3*) F Leahy, *in tch, drvn alng aftr 7th, sn wknd, tld off*..........(14 to 1 op 12 to 1) 6
3437[3] DANBYS GORSE [96] 5-10-4 (3*) E Callaghan, *sn beh, lost tch bef 7th, tld off*.........(14 to 1 op 10 to 1 tchd 16 to 1) 7
3399[2] JYMJAM JOHNNY (Ire) [105] 8-10-11 (5*) R McGrath, *prmnt till wknd aftr 6th, tld off*..(10 to 1 op 8 to 1 tchd 12 to 1) 8
3309* MISTER ROSS (Ire) [108] 7-11-5 P Carberry, *chsd ldrs till wknd aftr 7th, tld off*.......(4 to 1 op 7 to 2 tchd 9 to 2) 9
FAIR AND FANCY (Fr) [107] 6-11-4 A S Smith, *sn beh, tld off whn pld up bef 3 out*........................... (33 to 1) pu
MOREOF A GUNNER [101] 7-10-12 L Wyer, *al beh, tld off whn pld up bef 2 out*.............. (50 to 1 tchd 66 to 1) pu
3398[4] CHIPPED OUT [106] 7-10-10 (7*) C McCormack, *chsd ldrs, blun second, wknd bef 3 out, lost tch and pld up before nxt.*
..................................(10 to 1 tchd 12 to 1) pu
Dist: 12l, 5l, 5l, ½l, 27l, 3½l, 6l, dist. 5m 1.10s. a 21.10s (12 Ran).
(Cornelius Lysaght), M D Hammond

PUNCHESTOWN (IRE) (good)
Thursday April 24th

3783 Castlemartin Stud Pat Taaffe Handicap Chase (Grade 2) (5-y-o and up) £16,250 3m 1f................(2:10)

3347* INDESTRUCTIBLE (Ire) [-] 9-10-0 C F Swan, *hld up, hdwy to track ldrs 3 out, chlgd and led appr last, rdn out.* (100 to 30) 1
3453[7] HEIST [-] 8-10-10 R Dunwoody, *dsptd ld frm 2 out, no extr und pres flt*...................................(3 to 1 fav) 2
2843 SHANAGARRY (Ire) [-] 8-11-8 N Williamson, *hld up, hdwy to join ldrs 3 out, outpcd and no imprsn frm 2 out*...... (7 to 1) 3
3605 BACK BAR (Ire) [-] 9-10-10 A P McCoy, *led till hdd 2 out, rdn and not pace to chal*............................ (4 to 1) 4
3453 TEAL BRIDGE [-] 12-10-3 C O'Dwyer, *hld up, mstk 7 out, jnd ldrs till mistake 4 out, wknd*.....................(11 to 2) 5
3453[8] FISSURE SEAL [-] 11-11-3 T P Treacy, *prmnt, lost tch bef 5 out*.. (14 to 1) 6
3605 NUAFFE [-] (bl) 12-11-2 T J Mitchell, *mid-div, prog 6 out, mstk 5th, pld up bef 4 out*..........................(16 to 1) pu
Dist: 2l, 7l, 25l, 3½l. 6m 24.20s. a 9.20s (7 Ran).
(John Quane), Augustine Leahy

3784 Quinns Of Baltinglass Chase (La Touche Cup) (5-y-o and up) £8,220 4m 1f.........................(2:40)

1754* RISK OF THUNDER (Ire) 8-12-7 Mr E Bolger, ... (9 to 4 on) 1
3749[2] DIGACRE (Ire) 8-11-7 Mr R Hurley, ... (10 to 1) 2
3391* FIND OUT MORE (Ire) 9-11-5 (7*) Mr B Potts,..... (12 to 1) 3
3749[3] DENNISTOWNTHRILLER (Ire) 9-11-7 Mr P Fenton, (5 to 1) 4
982 WHAT A CHOICE (Ire) 7-10-13 (3*) K Whelan, ... (25 to 1) 5
PRINCE YAZA 10-11-5 (7*) Miss E Hyndman, ... (20 to 1) ref
3215[6] HILLHEAD (Ire) 8-11-0 (7*) Mr W Ewing, ... (25 to 1) ref
3609[2] ANOTHER COURSE (Ire) 9-12-3 D H O'Connor, ... (10 to 1) pu
FOUR ZEROS 10-11-4[4] (7*) Mr D McEvoy, ... (66 to 1) pu
ARD NA GAOITHE (Ire) 5-10-8[1] (7*) Mr B Hassett, (33 to 1) pu
Dist: 15l, 12l, 6l, dist. 8m 53.90s. a 29.90s (10 Ran).
(Sean Connery), E Bolger

3785 Murphys Irish Stout Champion 4-Y-O Hurdle (Grade 1) £31,000 2m..(3:15)

2731[2] GRIMES 11-0 C O'Dwyer, *hld up, trkd ldrs frm hfwy, dsptd ld appr 2 out, clr bef last, easily*.......................(5 to 2) 1
2230[4] SNOW FALCON 11-0 N Williamson, *mid-div, rdn to join ldrs 4 out, led aftr nxt til bef last, unbl to quicken*......... (33 to 1) 2
3566[3] CIRCUS STAR 11-0 R Johnson, *mid-div, jnd ldrs 2 out, rdn and no imprsn on lders bef last, styd on one pace*... (8 to 1) 3
3450* STYLISH ALLURE (USA) 11-0 R Dunwoody, *mid-div, improved to chase ldrs aftr 4 out, wknd and lost pl after 2 out, kpt on one pace*..................................(11 to 2) 4
3566* QUAKERS FIELD 11-0 A P McCoy, *mid-div, chsd ldrs 4 out, mstk and wknd frm 2 out, kpt on one pace*........(5 to 4 fav) 5
3431[4] SPIRIT DANCER (Ire) 11-0 S C Lyons, *wth ldrs, pushed alng frm hfwy, lost tch 2 out*.......................... (33 to 1) 6
3566 HARD NEWS (USA) 11-0 F Woods, *dsptd ld till mstk 5 out, rdn to lead nxt, hdd aftr 3 out*.......................... (16 to 1) 7
3551[2] AFARKA (Ire) 10-9 T P Treacy, *in tch, jmpd wl to ld 5 out till aftr nxt, wknd quickly*.............................(20 to 1) 8
3315* RED RAJA 11-0 J Osborne, *mid-div, pushed alng frm 3 out, sn lost tch and wknd*..............................(12 to 1) 9
3450[2] STRATEGIC PLOY 10-9 C F Swan, *in tch to hfwy, rdn to join ldrs appr 4 out, ev ch til lost pl and wknd aftr 2 out.* (25 to 1) 10
3450[3] ROYAL MIDYAN 11-0 D T Evans, *al in rear, rdn alng 5 out, sn wknd*..(16 to 1) 11
3150 KERAWI 11-0 C Llewellyn, *al in rear*..............(11 to 1) 12
3087[3] RAINBOW VICTOR (Ire) 11-0 K F O'Brien, *mid-div, wknd bef 2 out*.. (25 to 1) 13
Dist: 5l, 4l, 7l, 3l, 15l. 3m 37.40s. b 7.60s (13 Ran).
SR: 50/45/41/34/31/6/ (John P McManus), C Roche

3786 I.A.W.S.Centenary Year Champion Stayers Hurdle (Grade 1) (4-y-o and up) £21,700 3m...............(3:45)

3151[3] PADDY'S RETURN (Ire) (bl) 5-11-12 N Williamson, *hld up, improved to join ldr appr 3 out, led last, rdn out.* (100 to 30) 1
3568* ESCARTEFIGUE (Fr) 5-11-9 R Dunwoody, *hld up, improved to join ldrs appr 3 out, dsptd ld approaching last, no extr und pres flt*..(6 to 4 fav) 2
3151 DERRYMOYLE (Ire) 8-12-0 A P McCoy, *hld up, rdn to join ldrs appr 4 out, outpcd bef 2 out, rallied before last, wnt 3rd flt, nvr nrr*..(16 to 1) 3
3523[5] THEATREWORLD (Ire) 5-11-9 C F Swan, *mid-div, rdn frm 5 out, wnt 3rd bef last, wknd r-in*...................(3 to 1) 4
3568[4] WHAT A QUESTION (Ire) 9-11-6 C O'Dwyer, *in tch, lft in ld appr 7th, jnd approaching 2 out, wknd quickly and lost pl bef last*..(9 to 1) 5
2584[2] ANTAPOURA (Ire) 5-11-4 T P Treacy, *hld up, pushed alng 5 out, sn lost tch, wknd*..........................(16 to 1) 6
3579[2] PRIVATE PEACE (Ire) 7-11-8 J Osborne, *gng wl whn mstk and f 4th*...(7 to 1) f
3551* WINDY BEE (Ire) 6-11-3 A Nolan, *sn clr, mstk and rdr lost irons 5th, pld up bef 7th*..............................(20 to 1) pu
Dist: 2l, 12l, 1½l, 1½l, 20l. 5m 43.40s. b 1.60s (8 Ran).
(P O'Donnell), F Murphy

3787 Tripleprint Novice Chase (Grade 2) (5-y-o and up) £18,600 2m.... (4:15)

3522[2] JEFFELL 7-12-0 F Woods, *dsptd ld till led 3 out, hdd 2 out, rallied and ran on strly to lead flt*............. (11 to 8 fav) 1
3596 CELIBATE (Ire) 6-12-0 R Dunwoody, *wth ldrs, lost tch 5 out, rallied 3 out, styd on und pres to chal r-in*...... (100 to 30) 2
3564 FLYING INSTRUCTOR 7-11-8 N Williamson, *jmpd wl, wth ldrs 4 out, chlgd and dsptd ld appr 2 out, unbl to quicken fnl 100 yards*...(3 to 1) 3
3548[4] BEAKSTOWN (Ire) 8-12-0 T P Treacy, *led to 5 out, mstk last.*
....(16 to 1) 4
3086[8] KHARASAR (Ire) 7-11-8 C F Swan, *hld up, rdn hfwy, nvr on terms, wknd and lost tch aftr 3 out*............... (13 to 2) 5
3446 GEALLAINNBAN (Ire) (bl) 7-11-8 C O'Dwyer, *wth ldrs early, not jump wl, lost pl frm hfwy, tld off from 3 out*.....(50 to 1) 6
Dist: 1½l, 1½l, 15l, 1l, dist. 4m 4.40s. a 5.40s (6 Ran).
(Thomas Bailey), A L T Moore

3788 J.F.Dunne Insurance Handicap Hurdle (4-y-o and up) £6,850 2m..(4:45)

1621[6] MAJOR JAMIE (Ire) [-] 6-10-9 F Woods, ... (7 to 1) 1
3549[6] THREE SCHOLARS [-] 6-11-5 D J Casey, ... (8 to 1) 2
3216[9] RUPERT BELLE (Ire) [-] 6-10-7 K F O'Brien, ...(12 to 1) 3
3523[4] SAVING BOND (Ire) [-] 5-10-7 (7*) B J Geraghty, ...(5 to 1) 4
76[2] SAMBARA (Ire) [-] 6-11-5 (5*) P Morris, ...(9 to 1) 5
3754[8] MALACCA KING (Ire) [-] 6-11-1 R Dunwoody, ...(14 to 1) 6
3523[8] BANK STATEMENT (Ire) [-] 6-10-12 N Williamson, .. (9 to 2) 7
3156[4] BLACK QUEEN (Ire) [-] 6-11-3 C F Swan, ...(3 to 1) ur

3154[5] SCOBIE BOY (Ire) [-] 9-11-2 J Osborne, ... (14 to 1)   pu
3131 RAWY (USA) [-] (bl) 5-11-9 C O'Dwyer, ... (5 to 2 fav)   pu
Dist: 7l, 2l, 2l, 1l. 3m 41.60s. b 3.40s (10 Ran).
SR: 3/6/-/-/-/-/   (C Nolan), A L T Moore

3789 Naas Traders I.N.H. Flat Race (5-y-o) £6,850 2m . . . . (5:15)

10434 RATHBAWN PRINCE (Ire) 11-3 (7") Mr A J Dempsey, (7 to 2)   1
34562 KILCALM KING (Ire) 11-10 Mr G J Harford, ... (8 to 1)   2
20732 STRONTIUM (Ire) 12-3 Mr P Fenton, ... (11 to 2)   3
34563 FIRMOUNT CROSS (Ire) 11-3 (7") Mr P J Prendergast,
. . . . (5 to 1)   4
36273 THE BOY KING (Ire) 11-3 (7") Mr A FitzGerald, ... (25 to 1)   5
DONS DELIGHT (Ire) 11-3 (7") Mr R Walsh, ... (12 to 1)   6
CUSH POINT (Ire) 11-3 (7") Mr M P Madden, ... (20 to 1)   7
FISCAL GALE (Ire) 11-3 (7") Mr A G Donnelly, ... (25 to 1)   8
6865 EXECUTIVE HEIGHTS (Ire) 11-3 (7") Mr P Cody, . . (25 to 1)   9
HIGH GALE (Ire) 11-10 Mr A J Martin, ... (9 to 4 fav) 10
DO IT ONCE (Ire) 11-3 (7") Mr Paul Moloney, ... (8 to 1) 11
EXECUTIVE PEARL (Ire) 10-12 (7") Mr C J Swords, (10 to 1) 12
STRONG CHOICE (Ire) 11-2 (3") Mr R Thornton, . . . (8 to 1) 13
7136 TUAM (USA) 11-3 (7") Mr A Fleming, ... (25 to 1) 14
EASY FEELIN (Ire) 11-10 Mr P F Graffin, ... (25 to 1) 15
TOWNLEYHALL (Ire) 11-3 (7") Mr G A Kingston, . . (14 to 1) 16
34309 DAN'S YOUR MAN (Ire) 11-10 (7") Mr P Cashman, (12 to 1) 17
329" DAFFODIL GLEN (Ire) 11-12 Mr B M Cash, ... (16 to 1) 18
7034 AN SEABHAC (Ire) 11-3 (7") Mr T J Beattie, ... (50 to 1) 19
HORS BORD (Fr) 11-3 (7") Mr J D Moore, ... (20 to 1) 20
33428 CAPALL DUBH (Ire) 11-5 Mr J P Dempsey, ... (33 to 1)   pu
Dist: 4l, 2½l, 8l, 2l. 3m 37.50s. (21 Ran).

(T J Culhane), D T Hughes

ASCOT (good to firm (races 1,2,3,4), good (5,6)) Friday April 25th
Going Correction: PLUS 0.35 sec. per fur. (races 1,3,5), PLUS 0.45 (2,4,6)

3790 Bet With The Tote Amateur Riders' Handicap Chase Class E (0-125 5-y-o and up) £4,279 3m 110yds. . (5:30)

32084 GARRYLOUGH (Ire) [115] 8-11-6 (3") Mr C Bonner, led to
second, rdn to ld ag'n last, styd on wl... (6 to 1 op 5 to 1)   1
13664 DRUMCULLEN (Ire) [99] 8-10-0 (7") Mr R Wakley, led second,
hrd rdn and hdd last, not quicken r-in... (10 to 1 op 7 to 1)   2
34978 HARRISTOWN LADY [103] (bl) 10-10-4 (7") Mr L Jefford, hld
up, steady hdwy frm 15th, one pace from 3 out
. . . . (20 to 1 op 14 to 1)   3
36132 DANGER BABY [93] 7-9-8 (7") Mr S Durack, mstks, roar till
styd on frm 4 out, not rch ldrs. . . . . . . (11 to 2 op 7 to 2)   4
3497" MERLINS DREAM (Ire) [117] 8-11-8 (3") Mr R Thornton,
prmnt, mstk 4 out, one pace.
. . . . (11 to 4 fav op 5 to 2 tchd 3 to 1)   5
34062 DIAMOND FORT [97] 12-10-46 (7") Mr P Scott, beh, hdwy
12th, kpt on same pace frm 4 out.
. . . . (14 to 1 op 16 to 1 tchd 20 to 1 and 25 to 1)   6
AUTO PILOT (NZ) [112] 9-11-1 (5") Mr C Vigors, in tch, mstk
11th, wknd 4 out. . . . . (5 to 1 op 7 to 2 tchd 6 to 1)   7
27282 BIG BEN DUN [105] 11-10-6 (7") Mr E James, beh, blun 6th,
nvr nr ldrs. . . . . (12 to 1 op 8 to 1)   8
FIGHT TO WIN (USA) [92] 9-9-7 (7") Mr J Grassick, chsd ldrs
till wknd 4 out. . . . . (66 to 1 op 50 to 1 tchd 100 to 1)   9
36595 DONT TELL THE WIFE [105] 11-10-6 (7") Mr J Goldstein, f
second. . . . . (16 to 1 op 14 to 1 tchd 100 to 1)   f
3365 NEW GHOST [92] (v) 12-10-07 (7") Major O Ellwood, prmnt till
rdn and wknd 10th, sn rear, tld off whn pld up bef 3 out.
. . . . (66 to 1 op 50 to 1 tchd 100 to 1)   pu
Dist: 2l, 5l, 1¾l, ¾l, 4l, 7l, 11l, 22l. 6m 20.40s. a 19.40s (11 Ran).

(T J Whitley), D R Gandolfo

3791 Woodrow Wyatt Handicap Hurdle Class B (0-140 4-y-o and up) £5,622 2m 110yds. . . . . (6:00)

3437" MONNAIE FORTE (Ire) [107] 7-9-132 (3") L Aspell, prmnt, led
aftr 3 out, jmpd lft nxt, edgd left after last, pushed clr r-in.
. . . . (8 to 1 op 7 to 1)   1
2996" DARRASHAN (Ire) [107] 5-10-0 J Culloty, chsd ldrs, outpcd 3
out, hrd rdn nxt, ran on strly appr last, not rch wnr.
. . . . (4 to 1 op 11 to 2)   2
33282 MARIUS (Ire) [114] 7-10-7 P Hide, chsd ldr, ev ch 3 out,
slightly hmpd nxt, kpt on.
. . . . (12 to 1 op 10 to 1 tchd 14 to 1)   3
36354 DANCING PADDY [135] 9-12-0 B Powell, hld up, hdwy 3 out,
ev ch appr last, one pace.
. . . . (5 to 2 op 20 to 1 tchd 33 to 1)   4
3635" I'M A DREAMER (Ire) [110] 7-10-0 (3") Mr R Thornton, in tch,
no prog frm 3 out.
. . . . (15 to 2 op 7 to 1 tchd 8 to 1 and 9 to 1)   5
3641" JOHN DRUMM [114] 6-10-7 J Osborne, led till aftr 3 out,
wknd frm nxt. . . . . (4 to 1 tchd 9 to 2)   6
36353 ALBEMINE (USA) [120] 8-10-13 T Kent, chsd ldrs till wknd 3
out. . . . . (14 to 1 op 10 to 1 tchd 16 to 1)   7

3635 SERIOUS [113] 7-10-6 N Williamson, rear, lost tch 3 out, sn
rdn and tld off. . . . . (5 to 2 fav op 9 to 1 tchd 100 to 30)   8
669 SUIVEZ [125] 7-11-4 M A Fitzgerald, al rear, hrd rdn and lost
tch 6th, tld off whn pld up bef 2 out. . . (16 to 1 op 14 to 1)   pu
Dist: 1¼l, hd, 2½l, 8l, 7l, 2½l. dist. 3m 58.00s. a 12.00s (9 Ran).
SR: 26/24/31/49/16/13/16/-/-/   (James R Adam), J R Adam

3792 Tote Direct Novices' Handicap Chase Class D (0-110 5-y-o and up) £3,891 2m 3f 110yds. . . . . (6:30)

3679" BOOTS N ALL (Ire) [76] 7-10-1 (4ex) B Fenton, jmpd wl, led
3rd, styd on well frm 3 out, cmftbly.
. . . . (11 to 10 fav op Evens tchd 6 to 5 and 5 to 4)   1
3133 CARDINAL RULE (Ire) [90] 8-11-1 N Williamson, led to 3rd,
effrt and pressed wnr 12th, mstk 3 out, sn btn, wkng whn jmpd
lft last. . . . . (11 to 2 op 4 to 1 tchd 6 to 1)   2
3559" SPRING TO GLORY [88] 10-10-13 M A Fitzgerald, rear, hdwy
tenth, no imprsn on ldg pair frm 4 out. (7 to 1 tchd 8 to 1)   3
36682 SLEAZEY [75] 6-10-0 S Curran, chsd ldrs to 11th, sn outpcd,
4th and no ch whn f 2 out. (11 to 2 op 4 to 1 tchd 6 to 1)   f
3651 RYTON RUN [81] 12-10-6 D Gallagher, mstk 1st, sn tld off, pld
up bef 4th. . . . . (40 to 1 op 33 to 1 tchd 50 to 1)   pu
993" PREROGATIVE [99] 7-11-10 A P McCoy, jmpd slwly, tld off
frm 9th, blun badly 4 out, pld up bef nxt.
. . . . (6 to 1 op 5 to 1 tchd 13 to 2)   pu
32244 EAU SO SLOE [75] 6-10-0 D Morris, chsd ldrs to tenth, beh
frm nxt, tld off whn pld up bef 2 out. (100 to 1 op 66 to 1)   pu
Dist: 7l, 4l. 5m 1.90s. a 20.90s (7 Ran).

(Mrs Toni S Tipper), G B Balding

3793 Tote Mobile Terminal Novices' Hurdle Class C (4-y-o and up) £3,485 2 ½m. . . . . (7:05)

35664 SUMMER SPELL (USA) 4-10-12 M A Fitzgerald, hld up in tch,
smooth hdwy 3 out, led on bit last, easily.
. . . . (Evens fav op 7 to 4 on tchd 11 to 10)   1
3290" EAU DE COLOGNE 5-11-5 M Richards, cl up, led aftr 3 out,
rdn whn mstk and hdd last, no ch wth wnr.
. . . . (4 to 1 tchd 9 to 2)   2
3575" INFLUENCE PEDLER 4-10-12 C Llewellyn, led till aftr 3 out,
sn hrd rdn and wknd... (2 to 1 op 3 to 1 tchd 100 to 30)   3
BAY LOUGH (Ire) 6-10-42 (7") Mr J Luck, sn wl beh, some
hdwy 5th, nvr trbld ldrs. . . . . (50 to 1)   4
1271 JAIME'S JOY 7-10-2 (7") Martin Smith, sn tld off.
. . . . (100 to 1 op 66 to 1)   5
2699" HIGHTECH TOUCH 7-11-0 Mr J Grassick, chsd ldrs to 7th,
wkng whn mstk nxt, sn tld off, remote 5th when f 2 out.
. . . . (66 to 1 op 33 to 1 tchd 100 to 1)   f
MASRUR (USA) 8-11-0 L Harvey, chsd ldrs to 5th, tld off 7th,
pld up bef 2 out. . . . . (100 to 1 op 33 to 1)   pu
Dist: 6l, dist, 16l, dist. 5m 0.70s. a 19.70s (7 Ran).
(W V M W & Mrs E S Robins), N J Henderson

3794 Tote Bookmakers Novices' Chase Class C (5-y-o and up) £5,036 2m . . . . (7:35)

3724" INDIAN JOCKEY 5-11-3 A P McCoy, led, mstk and slightly
hdd last, rallied wl to ld ag'n r-in gmely.
. . . . (11 to 8 op 11 to 10)   1
35643 SUBLIME FELLOW (Ire) 7-11-10 M A Fitzgerald, trkd wnr gng
wl, slight ld aftr last, sn hdd and outpcd.
. . . . (6 to 4 on tchd 11 to 8 on and 5 to 4 on)   2
3737 FULL SHILLING (USA) 8-10-9 (7") Mr S Durack, not fluent, sn
tld off. . . . . (33 to 1 op 20 to 1)   3
Dist: 1¾l, dist. 3m 59.30s. a 11.30s (3 Ran).
SR: 32/37/-/   (Stuart M Mercer), M C Pipe

3795 Tote Credit Novices' Handicap Hurdle Class C (5-y-o and up) £5,061 2m 110yds. . . . . (8:05)

3077" SOUNDS LIKE FUN [112] 6-11-1 J F Titley, cl up, led 2 out,
readily. . . . . (11 to 2 op 5 to 1)   1
34453 JOVIE KING (Ire) [97] 5-10-0 B Powell, led to 5th, led briefly
appr 2 out, one pace. . . . . . . (15 to 2 op 7 to 1 tchd 8 to 1)   2
35462 FOXIES LAD [102] 6-10-5 R Johnson, hld up, effrt 3 out, one
pace appr nxt. . . . . . . (5 to 2 op 7 to 2 tchd 4 to 1)   3
3562 NO PATTERN [102] 5-10-5 D Gallagher, prmnt to 5th.
. . . . (6 to 1 op 4 to 1 tchd 13 to 2)   4
2982 THE BIZZO [97] 6-10-03 (3") P Henley, lost tch 5th, tld off.
. . . . (100 to 1 op 50 to 1 tchd 200 to 1)   5
3595 SECRET SPRING (Fr) [125] 5-11-7 (7") M Clinton, steadied in
rear strt, pld hrd, hdwy to ld 5th, hdd appr 2 out, 4th and btn
whn f heavily last.
. . . . (9 to 4 fav op 2 to 1 tchd 7 to 4 and 5 to 2)   f
3634" ABSOLUTE LIMIT [97] 5-10-22 P Hide, hmpd and slpd up aftr
1st. . . . . (12 to 1 op 10 to 1 tchd 14 to 1)   su
Dist: 6l, 7l, 10l, dist. 4m 7.00s. a 21.00s (7 Ran).
(Mrs H Brown), Miss H C Knight

LUDLOW (good to firm (races 1,5), firm (2,3,4,6))

Friday April 25th
Going Correction: PLUS 0.40 sec. per fur.

3796 Lowe & Oliver Novices' Selling Hurdle Class G (4,5,6-y-o) £1,794 2m
.... (5:45)

3614² THEME ARENA (v) 4-10-9 D Walsh, *made all, clr 3 out, eased r-in*..............(15 to 8 on op 2 to 1 on tchd 13 to 8 on) 1
3731 DAYDREAM BELIEVER 5-10-9 P Holley, *hld up, hdwy to chase wnr 3 out, btn whn mstk last*.... (20 to 1 op 12 to 1) 2
3265⁹ WITHERKAY 4-10-3 (5*) O Burrows, *chsd ldrs, outpcd 4th, rallied appr 3 out, 3rd and btn whn hit 2 out.*
.....................................(7 to 1 op 9 to 2) 3
3617⁷ TEE TEE TOO (Ire) 5-10-8¹ (7*) Mr A Wintle, *hld up, hdwy 3 out, rdn and wknd nxt*................. (7 to 1 op 4 to 1) 4
3590⁴ GLEN GARNOCK (Ire) 5-11-0 Gary Lyons, *chsd wnr, mstk 4 out, wknd nxt*................. (10 to 1 op 6 to 1) 5
3554 VITA NUOVA (Ire) 6-10-9 R Bellamy, *strted slwly, al in rear.*
.............................(40 to 1 op 25 to 1) 6
3495⁵ TIMELY EXAMPLE (USA) (bl) 6-11-0 S Wynne, *beh frm 4th.*
.... (20 to 1 op 14 to 1) 7
3588³ BOLD TIME MONKEY 6-10-9 W Marston, *hld up, pld hrd, al beh*................. (33 to 1 op 20 to 1) 8
3554 JUST ANDY (bl) 6-11-0 T Jenks, *prmnt, stumbled 4th, sn beh, tld off and pld up bef 3 out*.........(100 to 1 op 66 to 1) pu
2431 BAXWORTHY LORD 6-11-0 S McNeill, *mstk 1st, al in rear, tld off and pld up bef 3 out*................. (66 to 1) pu
3561 ROXY HICKS 5-10-9 J R Kavanagh, *hit second, al in rear, tld off and pld up bef 3 out*........ (40 to 1 op 25 to 1) pu
Dist: 6l, 3l, 13l, 3l, 16l, 10l, 17l. 3m 50.50s. a 18.50s (11 Ran).
(Antony Sofroniou), M C Pipe

3797 Bromfield Sand And Gravel Handicap Chase for the Oakly Park Challenge Cup Class D (0-120 5-y-o and up) £3,200 2½m....... (6:15)

3726* QUITE A MAN [110] 9-12-2 (6ex) C Maude, *hld up, hdwy to chase ldr 6 out, led and mstk 3 out, clr nxt, eased r-in.*
.......................(6 to 4 on op 11 to 8 on) 1
3571² HERBERT BUCHANAN (Ire) [99] 7-11-5 W Marston, *with ldr till led 5th, hdd 8th, led ag'n nxt, headed and hit 3 out, sn btn.*........................(6 to 4 op 11 to 8) 2
2548⁷ HOUGHTON [94] 11-10-8¹ (7*) Mr R Burton, *made most to 5th, led 8th to nxt, wknd appr 4 out.*
.............................(9 to 1 op 8 to 1 tchd 11 to 1) 3
3502 APPLIANCEOFSCIENCE [80] 10-10-0 S Wynne, *prmnt, chsd ldr tenth, to 6 out, wknd appr 4 out, tld off whn f 2 out.*
.............................(25 to 1 op 20 to 1 tchd 33 to 1) f
Dist: 16l, 25l. 5m 6.90s. a 17.90s (4 Ran).
SR: 3/ (W R J Everall), S A Brookshaw

3798 Robert Holden Handicap Hurdle Class E (0-115 4-y-o and up) £2,560 2m................. (6:45)

2186⁴ YUBRALEE (USA) [113] 5-12-0 D Walsh, *made all, clr 4 out, eased r-in*...................(7 to 2 op 3 to 1 tchd 4 to 1) 1
3635² FAUSTINO [110] 5-11-11 W Marston, *hld up, drvn alng 4 out, wnt second 2 out, not rch wnr*...... (7 to 4 fav tchd 2 to 1) 2
2429⁴ ZINGIBAR [85] 5-10-0 S Wynne, *prmnt, chsd wnr 3 out, rdn and wknd nxt*...................(8 to 1 op 10 to 1) 3
3572³ LITTLE SHEFFORD [85] 5-10-0 I Lawrence, *chsd wnr till 3 out*................(12 to 1 op 10 to 1 tchd 14 to 1) 4
3652⁴ VERDE LUNA [85] 5-10-0 S McNeill, *hld up, hdwy 4 out, wknd nxt*.......................(11 to 1 op 8 to 1) 5
3665² ERINY (USA) [87] 8-10-2 C Maude, *hld up, hdwy 4 out, rdn and wknd nxt*...........(9 to 2 op 5 to 1 tchd 4 to 1) 6
3617* KALZARI (USA) [85] 12-9-9 (5*) O Burrows, *hld up, al beh, tld off whn pld up bef 3 out*.........(14 to 1 op 12 to 1) pu
Dist: 10l, 6l, 3½l, 3l, 16l. 3m 47.00s. a 15.00s (7 Ran).
SR: 14/1/-/-/ (D A Johnson), M C Pipe

3799 Downton Hall Stables Novices' Handicap Chase Class D (0-110 5-y-o and up) £3,200 3m.......... (7:15)

3470* JASILU [99] 7-11-10 S McNeill, *chsd ldr, led appr 4 out, clr last, pushed out*................. (11 to 8 fav tchd 6 to 4) 1
1611 BLASKET HERO [90] (bl) 9-11-1 W Marston, *beh, hdwy 6th, mstk 11th (water), chsd wnr 4 out, chlgd nxt, jmpd lft and wknd 2 out*.......................(10 to 1 op 5 to 2) 2
3620* INCH EMPEROR (Ire) [92] 7-11-3 T J Murphy, *led till appr 4 out, sn wknd*................... (9 to 4 op 6 to 4) 3
3618⁴ PANDORA'S PRIZE [75] 11-9-11 (3*) R Massey, *prmnt till wknd 9th*..................... (25 to 1 op 16 to 1) 4
Dist: 14l, 30l, sht-hd. 6m 13.50s. a 26.50s (4 Ran).
(A G Lay), K C Bailey

3800 Lane Fox And Balfour & Cooke Hunters' Chase Class H for Ludlow Gold Cup (5-y-o and up) £1,725 2½m................................ (7:45)

GREAT GUSTO 11-12-0 (7*) Miss L Blackford, *chsd ldrs, led appr tenth, clr 5 out, styd on wl....* (6 to 4 on op 11 to 10) 1
3622² CAPE COTTAGE 13-12-0 (7*) Mr A Phillips, *hld up, hdwy tenth, lft second 5 out, effrt 2 out, no extr r-in.*
.............................(2 to 1 op Evens) 2
STYLISH GENT 10-11-7 (7*) Mr A Dalton, *hld up, rcd keenly, outpcd tenth, sn wl beh*.............(25 to 1 op 14 to 1) 3
BALLAD SONG 14-11-7 (7*) Mr M Munrowd, *led to appr tenth, second whn blun badly 5 out, wkng when hit nxt, mstk 3 out, sn pld up*.....................(50 to 1 op 16 to 1) pu
EMERALD CHARM (Ire) 9-11-6 (3*) Mr M Rimell, *chsd ldrs till wknd tenth, tld off whn pld up bef 4 out.*
.............................(11 to 2 op 6 to 1 tchd 7 to 1) pu
Dist: 3l, dist. 5m 15.00s. a 26.00s (5 Ran).
(Eddie Rice), Miss L Blackford

3801 I.T.T. London & Edinburgh Novices' Hurdle Class E (4-y-o and up) £2,070 3¼m 110yds................. (8:15)

3362⁴ AWESTRUCK (bl) 7-10-7 (7*) J Mogford, *trkd ldr, hmpd bend aftr 4th, led appr 3 out, lft wl clr 2 out.* (16 to 1 op 12 to 1) 1
3535⁴ PONTEVEDRA (Ire) 4-10-7 S McNeill, *led till appr 3 out, sn btn, lft second 2 out.*.........(5 to 4 on op 11 to 10 on) 2
3466² SONG FOR JESS (Ire) 4-10-1 S Wynne, *hld up, blun badly 6th, sn wl beh*.............(6 to 1 op 8 to 1 tchd 10 to 1) 3
2874² RARE SPREAD (Ire) 7-11-6 D Walsh, *trkd ldrs, ev ch frm 3 out, broke off fore and f appr nxt, dead*...............(6 to 4) f
Dist: 26l, dist. 6m 42.80s. a 37.80s (4 Ran).
(The Wroxeter Race Club), B Preece

PERTH (good)
Friday April 25th
Going Correction: PLUS 0.40 sec. per fur.

3802 Business Tax Centre Juvenile Novices' Hurdle Class D (4-y-o) £2,804 2m 110yds................. (2:10)

2497⁶ BRECON 10-12 P Niven, *hld up, took clr order hfwy, dsptd ld frm 3 out, found extr und pres aftr last.*
.......................(7 to 4 fav op 3 to 1 tchd 7 to 2) 1
3334⁷ SADLER'S REALM 10-12 G Tormey, *prmnt, slight ld 3 out, sn hrd pressed, hdd aftr last, no extr und pres.*
.............................(4 to 1 op 7 to 2) 2
3437⁸ DOUBLE AGENT 11-7 P Carberry, *trkd ldrs, rdn and outpcd bef 3 out, styd on und pres appr last.*.....(3 to 1 op 2 to 1) 3
2417⁵ PRIDDY FAIR 10-13 Richard Guest, *trkd ldrs, effrt aftr 2 out, wknd appr last*........(15 to 2 op 7 to 1 tchd 8 to 1) 4
3700⁹ THORNTOUN HOUSE (Ire) 10-12 D Parker, *made most till hdd 3 out, sn wknd*..... (50 to 1 op 33 to 1 tchd 100 to 1) 5
3598⁹ POLITICAL MANDATE 10-7 B Storey, *beh, effrt bef 3 out, sn btn*.........................(50 to 1 op 33 to 1) 6
3044 GOLD OF ARABIA (USA) 10-12 R Dunwoody, *hld up, hdwy and prmnt aftr 3rd, ev ch 3 out, sn wknd, tld off.*
.............................(13 to 2 op 6 to 1 tchd 7 to 1) 7
Dist: 4l, sht-hd, 12l, 5l, 5l, dist. 4m 2.00s. a 21.00s (7 Ran).
(The Four Willies Partnership), W R Muir

3803 Scottish News Of The World Conditional Jockeys' Selling Handicap Hurdle Class G (0-95 4-y-o and up) £3,004 2½m 110yds......... (2:45)

3350⁴ IFALLELSEFAILS [95] 9-11-6 (8*) W Dowling, *sn tracking ldrs, led bef 2 out, styd on wl...........*(7 to 2 fav tchd 9 to 2) 1
3435⁵ SANDRIFT [75] 8-10-8 F Leahy, *prmnt, led 7th, hdd bef 2 out, chsd wnr aftr, no imprsn...........*(10 to 1 op 8 to 1) 2
3353⁹ SKANE RIVER (Ire) [85] 4-10-6 (8*) R Burns, *towards rear, hdwy whn not much room aftr 7th, styd on frm 2 out.*
.......................(10 to 1 op 5 to 1 tchd 33 to 1) 3
3317⁵ ETERNAL CITY [84] 6-11-3 G Lee, *al chasing ldrs, kpt on same pace frm 3 out...........*(14 to 1 op 12 to 1) 4
1832³ PARISH WALK (Ire) [78] 6-10-11 B Grattan, *in tch, ch 3 out, kpt on same pace...........*(12 to 1 tchd 14 to 1) 5
2485 FANADIYR (Ire) [67] 5-9-11 (3*) S Melrose, *towards rear, hdwy to chase ldrs 3 out, wknd aftr nxt.*
.............................(12 to 1 op 10 to 1 tchd 6 to 1) 6
3658⁶ BARNSTORMER [70] (bl) 11-10-3 G F Ryan, *mid-div, hdwy to chase ldrs 3 out, wknd bef nxt.*..................(20 to 1) 7
3761 FATHER O'BRIEN [90] 10-11-2 (7*) N Hannity, *nvr dngrs.*
.......................(33 to 1 op 25 to 1) 8
3434 DASHMAR [67] (bl) 10-9-11 (3*) R Wilkinson, *beh and drvn alng hfwy, some late hdwy, nvr dngrs.* (33 to 1 op 25 to 1) 9
3668 SHUT UP [67] 8-10-0 E Husband, *sn beh.*
.......................(40 to 1 op 66 to 1) 10
3399 PRECIPICE RUN [89] 12-11-8 S Taylor, *chsd ldrs to hfwy, sn drvn alng and wknd.*..............(14 to 1 tchd 16 to 1) 11
3582⁸ WHITEGATESPRINCESS (Ire) [67] 6-10-0 R McGrath, *sn beh.*
.......................(10 to 1 op 16 to 1) 12
3582 MEADOWLICK [67] 8-9-9 (5*) I Jardine, *nvr better than mid-div.*......................(100 to 1 op 66 to 1) 13
3123 PLAYFUL JULIET (Can) [82] (bl) 9-11-1 E Callaghan, *sn beh.*
.......................(16 to 1 tchd 20 to 1) 14

1817[8] AKITO RACING (Ire) [67] 6-9-6 (8") C McCormack, *in tch till wknd appr 3 out*................(100 to 1 op 66 to 1) 15
3660 LYFORD CAY (Ire) [67] (v) 7-9-9 (5") T Siddall, *sn beh, tld off.*
..................................(100 to 1 op 66 to 1) 16
3123 DON'T TELL JUDY (Ire) [67] 9-9-9 (5") N Horrocks, *mid-div, drvn alng bef 7th, sn wknd, wl beh whn pld up before 2 out.*
................................(16 to 1 op 14 to 1) pu
3355 STRATHMORE LODGE [82] 8-11-1 P Midgley, *prmnt to hfwy, sn wknd, wl beh whn pld up bef 2 out.*(16 to 1 tchd 20 to 1) pu
3123[7] WEATHER ALERT (Ire) [72] (v) 6-10-2 (3") M Newton, *led till hdd 7th, wknd quickly, wl beh whn pld up bef 2 out.*
..................................(12 to 1 op 8 to 1) pu
Dist: 3l, 1¾l, 10l, ½l, 8l, 14l, 4l, 9l, 1½l, 2l. 5m 2.00s. a 22.00s (19 Ran).
(Mrs Barbara Lungo), L Lungo

3804
Sun Life Of Canada Handicap Chase Class B (5-y-o and up) £8,574 3m
..................................(3:15)

3581* UNGUIDED MISSILE (Ire) [158] 9-12-0 R Dunwoody, *made all, kpt on und pres frm last*..................(5 to 1 on) 1
2895* RECTORY GARDEN (Ire) [130] 8-10-0 P Carberry, *trkd wnr frm hfwy, rdn aftr 2 out, chalg whn mstk last, kpt on.*
..................................(5 to 1 op 4 to 1) 2
1126 TEMPLE GARTH [130] 8-10-0 R Supple, *chsd wnr to hfwy, grad lost tch, tld off*..........(14 to 1 op 11 to 1) 3
3601 SNOOK POINT [133] 10-10-3³ J Burke, *sn lost tch, tld off whn pld up aftr tenth*.................(100 to 1 op 66 to 1) pu
Dist: 1¼l, dist. 6m 8.50s. a 13.50s (4 Ran).
SR: 61/31/-/-/
(D E Harrison), G Richards

3805
Scottish Sun Made In Scotland For Scotland Novices' Handicap Chase Class D (0-110 4-y-o and up) £3,824 2m 110yds..................(3:50)

3703* TEEJAY'N'AITCH (Ire) [78] 5-10-2 (5") S Taylor, *led, hdd fnl 150 yards, ran on wl und pres to ld ag'n last strds.*
..................................(5 to 1 tchd 11 to 2) 1
3287[8] FAIRELAINE [75] (bl) 5-10-4 C O'Dwyer, *hld up, hdwy hfwy, drvn to ld fnl 150 yards, hdd and no extr last strds.*
..................................(25 to 1 tchd 33 to 1) 2
3351[6] REACH THE CLOUDS (Ire) [71] 5-10-0 R Supple, *hld up towards rear, hdwy aftr 5th, kpt on und pres frm 2 out.*
..................................(20 to 1 op 25 to 1) 3
3703² PARSON'S LODGE (Ire) [76] 9-9-12 (7") W Dowling, *towards rear, styd on frm 2 out, nvr able to chal*............(12 to 1) 4
3528² KILDRUMMY CASTLE [78] 5-10-4 (3") F Leahy, *prmnt, mstk 3 out, sn drvn alng, kpt on same pace*....(8 to 1 tchd 9 to 1) 5
3700 STAR MASTER [71] 6-10-0 G Lee, *chsd ldrs, kpt on same pace frm 2 out*..................(10 to 1 op 16 to 1) 6
3401² BRIJMON (Ire) [89] (v) 6-11-4 D J Moffatt, *nvr nr to chal.*
..................................(6 to 1 tchd 7 to 1) 7
3198[6] PAPARAZZO [80] 6-10-9 L Wyer, *beh till some late hdwy, nvr dngrs*...............................(14 to 1 op 12 to 1) 8
3583³ SIX CLERKS [92] 4-11-1 P Carberry, *chsd ldrs, reminder bef 4th, wknd before 2 out*......(9 to 2 fav tchd 5 to 1) 9
2357[5] SHINEROLLA [82] 5-10-11 D Parker, *sn tracking ldrs, rdn and wknd bef 2 out*...........(5 to 1 tchd 11 to 2 op 9 to 2) 10
3540³ LAST TRY (Ire) [93] 6-11-8 A S Smith, *prmnt till wknd aftr 3 out*..................(14 to 1 op 10 to 1 tchd 16 to 1) 11
3757 MAPLE BAY (Ire) [90] (v) 8-11-5 G Cahill, *in tch, outpcd and drvn alng hfwy, beh aftr*..............(9 to 1 op 25 to 1) 12
3598* JESSOLLE [95] 5-11-10 R Dunwoody, *trkd ldrs, wkng whn pld up bef 2 out*..............(9 to 1 op 11 to 2) pu
3757[7] THE STUFFED PUFFIN (Ire) [95] 5-11-10 Richard Guest, *sn tracking ldrs, wknd bef 3 out, lost tch and pld up before nxt.*
..................................(33 to 1 op 25 to 1) pu
Dist: Sht-hd, 1¾l, 1¾l, 3½l, nk, 4l, 6l, 14l, 15l, 8l. 3m 59.10s. a 18.10s (14 Ran).
(Andrew Paterson), J S Goldie

3806
Ernst & Young Novices' Chase Class C (5-y-o and up) £6,235 2½m 110yds
..................................(4:20)

3304[5] MALTA MAN (Ire) 7-11-3 A S Smith, *hld up, took clr order hfwy, dsptd ld frm 11th till led last, styd on und pres.*
..................................(7 to 1 op 6 to 1) 1
3708² SOLOMON'S DANCER (USA) 7-11-11 R Dunwoody, *led, blun 3rd, and 11th, blunded 3 out, hdd last, no extr under pres.*
..................................(9 to 2 on op 5 to 1 on) 2
2026 WALLS COURT 10-11-3 L O'Hara, *great lost tch frm hfwy, tld off*..................(66 to 1 op 50 to 1) 3
3600² TALL MEASURE 11-11-3 B Storey, *mstk 3 out, chsd ldr to hfwy, grad wknd, tld off whn pld up bef 2 out, lme.*
..................................(8 to 1 tchd 9 to 1) pu
Dist: 2½l, dist. 5m 23.40s. a 31.40s (4 Ran).
(J A Stephenson), P Cheesbrough

3807
Party Is Nearly Over Standard Open National Hunt Flat Class H (Div I) (4,5,6-y-o) £2,052 2m 110yds (4:55)

3061³ LORD PODGSKI (Ire) 6-11-11 G Cahill, *led 5 fs, cl up, led 3 out, drw clr, easily*.....(3 to 1 fav op 9 to 2 tchd 5 to 2) 1

3356[6] TIME WARRIOR (Ire) 6-10-11 (7") N Hannity, *prmnt, chsd wnr frm o'r 2 fs out, no imprsn*............(14 to 1 tchd 16 to 1) 2
2322[6] WELLSWOOD (Ire) 4-10-9 (3") E Callaghan, *towards rear, hdwy hfwy, styd on wl fnl 2 fs, nvr nrr.* (16 to 1 op 14 to 1) 3
2309* TARA GALE (Ire) 5-11-6 P Carberry, *hld up towards rear, hdwy hfwy, outpcd 4 fs out, kpt on fnl 2 furlongs.*
..................................(9 to 2 op 6 to 1 tchd 7 to 1) 4
TROUBLE AHEAD (Ire) 6-11-4 C O'Dwyer, *settled midfield, hdwy and ev ch 3 fs out, fdd fnl 2 furlongs.*
..................................(4 to 1 tchd 11 to 2 and 6 to 1) 5
BALLYMANA BOY (Ire) 4-10-12 M Foster, *in tch, kpt on same pace fnl 3 fs*..................(20 to 1 op 16 to 1) 6
2953⁴ CRYSTAL JEWEL 5-10-13 R Dunwoody, *led aftr 5 fs till hdd 3 out, sn wknd*..............(4 to 1 tchd 5 to 1) 7
3482⁴ JUNIPER HILL 5-11-4 W Fry, *mid-div till wknd 4 fs out.*
..................................(25 to 1 op 16 to 1) 8
1809 RUN FOR THE MILL 5-11-4 L Wyer, *chsd ldrs till wknd 6 fs out, tld off*.....................(14 to 1 op 20 to 1) 9
3356 MEGGIE SCOTT 4-10-7 Richard Guest, *chsd ldrs till wknd 5 fs out, tld off*..................(100 to 1) 10
3356 THE TRUE MILLER 6-11-4 B Storey, *beh frm hfwy, tld off.*
..................................(100 to 1 op 66 to 1) 11
NON NON JOESEPHINE 6-10-13 Mr T Morrison, *sn beh, tld off*..................(200 to 1 op 100 to 1) 12
GENERAL MANAGER (USA) 5-11-4 J Supple, *sn beh, tld off.*
..................................(10 to 1) 13
Dist: 3l, 2½l, 3l, 5l, nd, 7l, 23l, dist, 4l, 9l. 3m 57.00s. (13 Ran).
(Mrs G Smyth), P Monteith

3808
Party Is Nearly Over Standard Open National Hunt Flat Class H (Div II) (4,5,6-y-o) £2,052 2m 110yds (5:25)

2723² LIGHT THE FUSE (Ire) 5-11-4 C O'Dwyer, *hld up, hdwy hfwy, led o'r 2 fs out, drw clr, easily*.........(5 to 4 fav op Evens) 1
3439[5] CHINA KING 6-11-11 P Carberry, *cl up, led 7 fs out, rdn and hdd o'r 2 out, chsd wnr aftr, no imprsn.*
..................................(5 to 1 op 4 to 1) 2
3008* EASBY BLUE 5-11-11 P Niven, *settled midfield, hdwy to dispute ld o'r 3 fs out, rdn over 2 out, kpt on same pace.*
..................................(5 to 2 op 7 to 1) 3
TOBY 4-10-5 (7") R Burns, *beh till styd on wl fnl 2 fs, nrst finish*..................................(33 to 1) 4
3475[5] SABU 5-11-4 B Storey, *towards rear, styd on fnl 3 fs, nvr dngrs*..................................(33 to 1 op 25 to 1) 5
CALLING THE TUNE 6-11-4 D Bentley, *chsd ldrs till outpcd and lost pl 5 fs out, no dngr aftr*.............(100 to 1) 6
GEEGEE EMMARR 4-10-2 (5") R McGrath, *in tch till grad wknd fnl 3 fs*..................(10 to 1 tchd 16 to 1) 7
3661 JO LIGHTNING (Ire) 4-10-12 K Johnson, *sn prmnt, wknd 5 fs out*..................................(100 to 1) 8
HANSEL'S STREAK 5-11-4 L O'Hara, *nvr better than mid-div.*
..................................(100 to 1 tchd 200 to 1) 9
3048 TI IC CHASE 6-11-1 (3") E Callaghan, *hld up, hdwy to chase ldrs o'r 3 fs out, sn rdn and wknd*.............(25 to 1) 10
2206 TIDAL RACE (Ire) 5-11-4 A S Smith, *led till hdd 7 fs out, wknd 5 out, tld off*..................(100 to 1 tchd 200 to 1) 11
TOBERLONE 4-10-12 Richard Guest, *lost tch frm hfwy, wl tld off*..................................(33 to 1 tchd 50 to 1) 12
Dist: 7l, 2½l, 3l, 4l, 20l, 2l, ½l, 6l, dist, dist. 3m 59.70s. (12 Ran).
(A F Lousada), K C Bailey

TAUNTON (firm)
Friday April 25th
Going Correction: NIL

3809
Aspen Catering Novices' Handicap Hurdle For Amateur Riders Class G (0-100 4-y-o and up) £1,773 2m 3f 110yds......................(5:35)

3515² ATH CHEANNAITHE (Fr) [83] (v) 5-11-5 (5") Mr J Jukes, *made all, drw clr frm 3 out, cmftbly.*
..................................(6 to 4 on op 7 to 4 on tchd 11 to 8 on) 1
3673[7] GI MOSS [68] (bl) 10-10-2 (7") Mr O McPhail, *chsd wnr, rdn alng frm 7th, outpcd nxt*..........(7 to 1 op 5 to 1) 2
3407 IRISH DOMINION [59] 7-9-12⁵ (7") Mr G Shenkin, *drpd out and pld hrd in rear, moderate hdwy to go 3rd aftr 3 out, no imprsn*..................................(14 to 1 op 12 to 1) 3
3582⁴ ROYAL HAND [68] (v) 7-10-9¹¹ (7") Mr R Armson, *hld up, hit 3rd, lost tch frm 7th...*(3 to 1 tchd 100 to 30 and 7 to 2) 4
3634⁶ MISS GEE-ELL [68] 5-9-8 (7") Mr E Babington, *hld up, reminder 5th, beh frm 7th*..........(25 to 1 op 14 to 1) 5
Dist: 11l, 13l, 21l, 5l. 4m 28.40s. a 10.40s (5 Ran).
(J Neville), J Neville

3810
Taunton Racecourse Conference Centre Selling Handicap Hurdle Class G (0-90 4,5,6-y-o) £1,763 2m 3f 110yds......................(6:05)

3515⁴ FLEET CADET [86] (v) 6-11-9 (5") G Supple, *hld up, smooth prog 7th, led on bit 2 out, sn clr, eased cl hme.*
..................................(3 to 1 fav op 5 to 2 tchd 100 to 30 and 7 to 2) 1

3469[6] JUST FOR A REASON [71] (v) 5-10-13 J Railton, *wtd wth, hdwy appr 7th, sn rdn, styd on to take second pl cl hme, no ch with wnr*..........................(6 to 1 tchd 13 to 2) 2
3617[3] AGAINST THE CLOCK [58] 5-9-7 (7*) L Cummins, *chsd ldr, led 7th, hdd 2 out, one pace*..........(7 to 2 tchd 4 to 1) 3
1697[7] GRIFFIN'S GIRL [68] 5-10-7 (3*) Guy Lewis, *hld up, hdwy 5th, effrt 3 out, wknd nxt*.... (12 to 1 op 10 to 1 tchd 14 to 1) 4
3648[3] RAPID LINER [64] 4-10-0 V Slattery, *hld up, reminders aftr 5th, nvr dngrs*...................... (33 to 1 op 14 to 1) 5
3648[5] KAI'S LADY (Ire) [64] 4-9-7 (7*) Mr O McPhail, *trkd ldrs to 5th, sn wknd, tld off*......................(33 to 1 op 14 to 1) 6
891 NIGHT TIME [71] 5-10-6 (7*) Mr G Shenkin, *al beh, tld off whn pld up aftr 5th, broke blood vessel*.... (6 to 1 tchd 7 to 1) pu
3590 MORE BILLS (Ire) [72] (v) 5-11-0 T Dascombe, *led, mstk and hdd 7th, wknd quickly appr 2 out, tld off whn pld up bef last.*
.................................(5 to 1 op 7 to 2) pu
3570[4] PRINCE EQUINAME [80] (bl) 5-11-8 B Clifford, *mstk second, sn beh, tld off whn pld up bef 6th.*
.... (8 to 1 op 6 to 1 tchd 12 to 1) pu
Dist: 7l, ½l, 4l, 10l, dist. 4m 30.40s. a 12.40s (9 Ran).
(Sir John Swaine), M C Pipe

3811 Peter & Sybil Blackburn Memorial Challenge Trophy Novices' Chase Class D (5-y-o and up) £3,420 2m 3f .... (6:35)

3267 AFTER THE FOX 10-11-0 (7*) Mr J Tizzard, *wtd wth, prog 7th, led appr 9th, in command whn edgd lft r-in, readily.*
................................(5 to 4 fav tchd 11 to 8) 1
3683[4] CASTLECONNER (Ire) (bl) 6-11-7 J Frost, *led till jmpd slwly second, rgned ld 7th, hdd appr 9th, effrt 3 out, styd on same pace r-in*..........................(8 to 1 op 5 to 1) 2
3611[3] MOZEMO (v) 10-10-9 (5*) G Supple, *hld up, lost tch 11th.*
.... (5 to 1 op 7 to 2 tchd 11 to 2) 3
RUN WITH JOY (Ire) 6-11-0 R Greene, *beh frm 9th.*
.... (33 to 1 op 20 to 1) 4
3653[3] MISTRESS ROSIE 10-10-11 (5*) Chris Webb, *led second to 7th, wknd 9th*.......... (10 to 1 op 7 to 1 tchd 11 to 1) 5
3593* DUKE OF DREAMS 7-12-0 V Slattery, *hld up in rear, blun badly and pld up 8th, dead*............ (7 to 2 op 5 to 1) pu
Dist: 2l, 22l, 1¼l, 17l. 4m 41.40s. a 10.40s (6 Ran).
(Mrs Robert Blackburn), N J Hawke

3812 Barnardos Centenary 'National Hunt' Novices' Hurdle Class E (4-y-o and up) £2,169 2m 1f......... (7:10)

3673[9] LAURA LYE (Ire) 7-10-9 G Upton, *patiently rdn, hdwy to chase ldr aftr 4th, led last, readily.*
.... (8 to 1 tchd 10 to 1 and 11 to 1) 1
1703[3] RED TEL (Ire) 5-10-9 (5*) G Supple, *led, rdn and hit 2 out, awkward and hdd last, unbl to quicken r-in.*
...............................(5 to 4 fav op 5 to 4 on) 2
2550 BAYERD (Ire) (bl) 6-11-7 J A McCarthy, *hld up, prog aftr 4th, rdn whn hit 2 out, one pace.*
.... (5 to 2 tchd 2 to 1 and 11 to 4) 3
2183 PICCOLINA 5-10-9 J Railton, *chsd ldr till aftr 4th, beh frm nxt, tld off*..........................(25 to 1 op 12 to 1 tchd 33 to 1) 4
2436[3] MISS FOXY 7-11-2 J Frost, *beh frm 6th, tld off whn pld up cl hme, lme*.... (11 to 4 op 5 to 2 tchd 7 to 2 and 4 to 1) pu
Dist: 1¼l, 1¼l, dist. 3m 51.00s. a 8.00s (5 Ran).
SR: 1/4/9/-/-/ (Charlie Productions), B de Haan

3813 Somerset Nuffield Hospital Chase Class D Handicap (0-120 5-y-o and up) £3,436 3m................ (7:40)

3653[5] SPINNING STEEL [94] 10-10-5[4] S Burrough, *chsd ldr frm 5th, led 13th, clr from 15th, unchlgd.*
.... (15 to 2 op 5 to 1 tchd 8 to 1) 1
3423[4] STAUNCH RIVAL (USA) [97] (bl) 10-10-1 (7*) Clare Thorner, *sn wl beh, styd on frm 3 out, chsd wnr betw fnl 2, no imprsn.*
.... (7 to 2 op 3 to 1 tchd 4 to 1 and 9 to 2) 2
3690 L'UOMO PIU [89] 13-9-7 (7*) Mr O McPhail, *led, sn clr, hit 5th, hdd 13th, outpcd by wnr 15th, lost moderate second betw fnl 2*
........................(5 to 1 op 8 to 1 tchd 9 to 1) 3
3678[6] FOXGROVE [89] 11-9-9 (5*) X Aizpuru, *chsd ldr to 5th, lost pl appraoching 8th, rallied 12th, hit nxt and 15th, sn wknd.*
.................................(5 to 2 fav op 4 to 1) 4
3605 MUGONI BEACH [113] (bl) 12-11-5 (5*) G Supple, *hld up, prog tenth, 3rd whn blun 3 out, not reco'r.*
.... (11 to 4 op 5 to 4 tchd 3 to 1) 5
Dist: 12l, 10l, 3l, 12l. 5m 52.70s. a 9.70s (5 Ran).
(Mrs C A Lewis-Jones), P R Rodford

3814 Red Cross & St John Handicap Hurdle Class F (0-100 4-y-o and up) £1,987 2m 1f................. (8:10)

3590* CONTRACT BRIDGE (Ire) [80] 4-11-3 W McFarland, *hld up, hit 6th and nxt, sn chasing ldr, rdn whn lft in ld 2 out, left clr last*.............................(11 to 8 fav op 7 to 4) 1
3731[9] KETCHICAN [72] 5-11-1 G Upton, *pld hrd, reluctant ldr, hdd 4th, rdn appr 2 out, btn whn lft second last.*
.... (9 to 1 op 10 to 1 tchd 12 to 1) 2

1007[5] GABISH [57] 12-9-9 (5*) G Supple, *chsd ldr to 3 out, rdn and sn btn*............ (25 to 1 tchd 20 to 1 and 33 to 1) 3
3572* SHIFTING MOON [75] 5-11-4 Derek Byrne, *pld hrd, hdwy to ld 4th, in command whn f 2 out.*
.... (13 to 8 op 11 to 8 tchd 7 to 4) f
3485[4] OCTOBER BREW (USA) [81] (bl) 7-11-3 (7*) B Moore, *hld up in rear, heaway 3 out, effrt whn hmpd nxt, second when ran out last*............ (4 to 1 op 2 to 1 tchd 9 to 2) ro
Dist: 5l, 5l. 4m 5.70s. a 22.70s (5 Ran).
(LM Racing), P G Murphy

LISTOWEL (IRE) (good to yielding) Saturday April 26th

3815 Dawn Milk Handicap Chase (0-116 4-y-o and up) £6,850 2½m.... (4:00)

3552* RYHANE (Ire) [-] 8-10-10 F Woods,............... (7 to 1) 1
3693* CRISTYS PICNIC (Ire) [-] 7-10-5 C O'Dwyer,........ (8 to 1) 2
3339* VALERIE OWENS (Ire) [-] 8-9-10 (7*) D K Budds,....(9 to 1) 3
3379* ROSDEMON (Ire) [-] 9-11-2 P A Roche,............... (6 to 1) 4
3753* TRIPTODICKS (Ire) [-] 7-9-8 (3*,6ex) G Cotter,.. (5 to 1 fav) 5
3706[5] SPRINGFORT LADY (Ire) [-] 8-10-1 (7*) J E Casey, (10 to 1) 6
3765 PRATE BOX (Ire) [-] 7-11-13 T P Treacy,........... (7 to 1) 7
3626[7] YOUNG DUBLINER (Ire) [-] 8-11-1 G Bradley,...... (11 to 2) 8
3420 BALLYBODEN [-] 10-9-3 (7*) P G Hourigan,........(25 to 1) 9
3347[4] CASTALINO [-] 11-10-10 (7*) M D Murphy,...........(11 to 1) 10
254[4] MOUNTHENRY STAR (Ire) [-] 9-10-10 (3*) K Whelan,
....(16 to 1) f
3220* ARDSHUIL [-] 8-11-6 J Shortt,....................... (9 to 1) pu
300 IRISH FOUNTAIN (Ire) [-] 9-10-11 (5*) A O'Shea,...(12 to 1) pu
Dist: 6l, 1½l, ½l, 9l. 5m 23.80s. (13 Ran).
(Mrs B M McKinney), A L T Moore

3816 Kerry Spring Water Maiden Hurdle (4-y-o and up) £3,425 2m..... (4:30)

3625[4] DOUBLE COLOUR (Ire) 5-11-13 C O'Dwyer,........ (7 to 1) 1
3547 PARSEE (Ire) 5-11-0 F Woods,......................... (8 to 1) 2
LEGATISSIMO (Ire) 9-12-0 G Bradley,.......... (3 to 1 fav) 3
3705 ASHJAR (USA) 4-11-1 (5*) A O'Shea,................ (6 to 1) 4
3416[2] MIDNIGHT CYCLONE (Ire) 6-11-9 D J Casey, ...(100 to 30) 5
3524 MISTER AUDI (Ire) 5-11-2 (3*) G Cotter,........... (12 to 1) 6
3647[6] ASFREEASTHEWIND (Ire) 6-10-8 (7*) M D Murphy, (12 to 1) 7
3642[4] ANN'S DESIRE (Ire) 6-10-8 (7*) L J Fleming,...... (12 to 1) 8
2964 DAWN TO DUSK (Ire) 6-10-13 (7*) D McCullagh,.. (33 to 1) 9
1193[2] LANTURN (Ire) 7-11-6 T J Mitchell,................. (5 to 1) 10
3547 BARNA GIRL (Ire) 7-11-1 J R Barry,................(50 to 1) 11
3233 HEN HANSEL (Ire) 6-12-0 Mr B M Cash,........... (14 to 1) 12
3705 EDEN KING (Fr) (bl) 5-11-0 T P Rudd,............. (33 to 1) 13
KING'S FLAGSHIP (Ire) 5-11-13 C N Bowens,......(6 to 1) 14
PATIENCE OF ANGELS (Ire) 4-10-10 T P Treacy,.. (14 to 1) 15
2443 PARTLY CLOUDY (Ire) 6-11-6 K F O'Brien,.........(8 to 1) 16
574[8] HENCARLAM (Ire) 4-10-8 (7*) R M Murphy,....... (20 to 1) 17
3233 POWER CORE (Ire) 7-10-13 (7*) J A Robinson,.... (20 to 1) pu
3625 MEGA HUNTER (Ire) 5-11-5 M Moran,............ (20 to 1) pu
Dist: Sht-hd, 3½l, 2l, 3½l. 4m 8.10s. (19 Ran).
(Mrs C Collins), Miss S Collins

3817 Low Low Handicap Hurdle (0-102 4-y-o and up) £3,425 2m...... (5:00)

3551[5] TOUREEN GALE (Ire) [-] 8-11-10 D J Casey,....... (4 to 1) 1
3697 NOBLE TUNE (Ire) [-] 8-9-4[1] (7*) K A Kelly,........ (33 to 1) 2
3642[2] BAILENAGUN (Ire) [-] 4-10-4 (7*) B J Geraghty,..... (8 to 1) 3
3336[3] PHAREIGN (Ire) [-] 6-11-1 F Woods,............. (16 to 1) 4
3223[4] LOCKBEG LASS (Ire) [-] 5-10-10 (7*) M D Murphy,.. (8 to 1) 5
3450 VINCITORE (Ire) [-] 4-11-10 L P Cusack,.......... (10 to 1) 6
3626* CLONMEL COMMERCIAL (Ire) [-] 6-9-10 (7*) D McCullagh,
....(100 to 30 fav) 7
2089[2] CHARLIE-O (Ire) [-] 5-11-5 (3*) G Cotter,............ (7 to 1) 8
3377[3] CHELSEA BELLE (Ire) [-] 5-10-5 M Duffy,.......... (10 to 1) 9
3642* UNASSISTED (Ire) [-] 4-10-7 (3*) B Bowens,........ (8 to 1) 10
3642[3] PILS INVADER (Ire) [-] 9-10-8 D T Evans,......... (20 to 1) 11
494[6] DON'T LOOSE FAITH (Ire) [-] 5-10-13 S C Lyons,.. (16 to 1) 12
2702[2] VICTORY BOUND (USA) [-] 4-11-5 (7*) P G Hourigan,
....(10 to 1) 13
2057[8] RIVER RUMPUS (Ire) [-] 5-10-6 K F O'Brien,....... (20 to 1) 14
3337* CNOCADRUM VI (Ire) [-] 6-9-12 W Slattery,........ (12 to 1) 15
3416[9] RUSHEEN BAY (Ire) [-] (bl) 8-9-10[2] J R Barry,...... (33 to 1) 16
3626 ST CAROL (Ire) [-] 6-10-1 T P Treacy,............. (16 to 1) f
3626[4] RUN ROSE RUN (Ire) [-] (bl) 7-9-2 (5*) T Martin,.... (10 to 1) bd
3178 MR CAVALLO (Ire) [-] (bl) 5-9-12 (5*) A O'Shea,.... (20 to 1) su
1616 BROKEN RITES (Ire) [-] 4-11-12 T P Rudd,........ (16 to 1) pu
Dist: 2l, 2l, 9l, nk. 4m 7.50s. (20 Ran).
(E P Cogan), W P Mullins

3818 Dawn Light Butter I.N.H. Flat Race (4-y-o and up) £3,425 2m..... (5:30)

3381[2] LIMIT THE DAMAGE (USA) (bl) 5-11-10 (3*) Mr R Walsh,
.... (7 to 2 fav) 1
3627[2] MONTEBA (Ire) 5-11-6 (7*) Mr P Cashman,......... (4 to 1) 2
2907 MERRY CHIEFTAIN (Ire) 8-11-7 (7*) Mr B Hassett, (16 to 1) 3
2757 INCHIQUIN CASTLE (Ire) 5-11-13 Mr D Marnane, (10 to 1) 4
3449[3] AS AN SLI (Ire) 6-11-2 (7*) Mr D F Barry,............(8 to 1) 5

36978 BALMY NATIVE (Ire) 5-11-6 (7") Mr A J Dempsey, ...(8 to 1) 6
26757 YOUNG CAL (Ire) 8-11-7 (7") Mr P J Crowley, ...(7 to 1) 7
27577 IN YOUR EYES 6-11-9 Mr P Fenton, ...(9 to 2) 8
33427 LOFTUS BELLE (Ire) 5-11-8 Mr J A Nash, ...(8 to 1) 9
1015 MACCABAEUS (Ire) 5-11-8 (5") Mr J T McNamara, (14 to 1) 10
3336 HOLLOW FINGER (Ire) 6-11-9 (5") Mr G Elliott, ...(16 to 1) 11
36979 NIANTIC BAY (Ire) 5-11-6 (7") Mr P Fahey, ...(20 to 1) 12
29067 BALLINREE (Ire) 6-11-9 Mr T Mullins, ...(8 to 1) 13
36276 CAN'T BE STOPPED (Ire) (bl) 5-11-6 (7") Mr A FitzGerald,
....(20 to 1) 14
2675 WOOLPACKER (Ire) 6-11-7 (7") Mr E Sheehy, ...(14 to 1) 15
ANODFROMALORD (Ire) 5-11-6 (7") Mr N C Kelleher,
....(12 to 1) 16
2754 THE SIDHE (Ire) 5-11-1 (7") Mr Paul Moloney, ...(33 to 1) 17
3456 AVRO EXPRESS (Ire) 6-12-0 Mr B M Cash, ...(10 to 1) bd
3421 TURBINE (Ire) 5-11-13 Miss M Olivefalk, ...(33 to 1) su
ESTHER'S CHOICE (Ire) 5-11-1 (7") Mr E Gallagher, (14 to 1) su
Dist: 7l, 9l, 2l, 1½l. 4m 8.80s. (20 Ran).

(R P M Syndicate), G T Hourigan

MARKET RASEN (good)
Saturday April 26th
Going Correction: PLUS 0.15 sec. per fur. (races 1,2,5,7), PLUS 0.40 (3,4,6)

3819 April Selling Handicap Hurdle Class G (0-95 4 & 5-y-o) £1,936 2m 1f 110yds..................... (2:10)

37417 EUROLINK THE REBEL (USA) [80] 5-10-9 (7") Miss R Clark, cl
up, led drvn 3rd, ran on wl fnl 2........ (20 to 1 op 14 to 1) 1
34693 SUMMER VILLA [66] (bl) 5-10-2 W Marston, chsd ldrs, effrt
aftr 3 out, kpt on wl frm last.............(13 to 1 op 8 to 1) 2
32584 TSANGA [68] 5-10-43 N Bentley, settled midfield, improved
4th, drvn alng fnl 2, no extr............. (8 to 1 op 7 to 1) 3
34574 LEBEDINSKI (Ire) [74] 4-10-4 V Smith, hld up, styd on wl betw
last 2, nvr finish......................(16 to 1 op 10 to 1) 4
TURRILL HOUSE [64] 5-10-0 B Powell, hld up, steady hdwy
fnl 2, nvr plcd to chal..... (11 to 1 op 8 to 1 tchd 12 to 1) 5
21474 MR GOLD (Ire) [78] 4-10-8 K Johnson, beh, effrt aftr 4 out,
drvn and outpcd fnl 2................ (10 to 1 op 8 to 1) 6
34334 SIMAND [71] 5-10-7 J Callaghan, prmnt till rdn and outpcd
aftr 3 out................................ (10 to 1) 7
35838 QUEEN'S COUNSEL (Ire) [70] 4-10-0 A S Smith, hld up,
steady hdwy on ins 4 out, outpcd bef 2 out.
...................................(16 to 1 op 12 to 1) 8
32806 AFRICAN SUN (Ire) [70] 4-10-0 W Worthington, cl up till rdn
and fdd aftr 3 out..................(33 to 1 op 25 to 1) 9
37285 EVEZIO RUFO [84] (bl) 5-11-6 K Gaule, midfield, reminders
aftr second, effrt 3 out, hng rght and fdd appr nxt.
...........................(9 to 1 op 6 to 1 tchd 10 to 1) 10
3500 PORI VALENSKA (Ire) [70] 4-9-9 (5") S Taylor, beh, nvr a
factor............................(50 to 1 op 40 to 1) 11
7754 IRIE MON (Ire) [79] 5-10-8 (7") Mr A Wintle, al beh.
..................................(14 to 1 op 10 to 1) 12
35126 PETRICO [64] 5-9-9 (5") B Grattan, beh, struggling hfwy, nvr
on terms..........................(33 to 1 op 20 to 1) 13
35289 GOLF LAND (Ire) [78] 5-11-0 R Supple, pld hrd, not jump wl,
led till aftr 3rd, struggling whn blun 3 out. (7 to 1 op 6 to 1) 14
3476¹ OUR ROBERT [92] 5-11-11 (3") F Leahy, midfield, struggling
appr 3 out, pld up nxt..............(9 to 4 op 3 to 1) pu
36739 NOIR ESPRIT [79] (vi) 4-10-9 N Smith, prmnt, struggling bef 3
out, pld up nxt.......................(25 to 1 op 16 to 1) pu
Dist: 1l, 7l, 1½l, nk, 2½l, 1½l, hd, ½l, 2½l, 3l. 4m 11.00s. a 10.00s (16 Ran).
SR: 14/-/-/-/-/-/

3820 'Get Away From The Election Campaign' Handicap Hurdle Class F (0-105 4-y-o and up) £2,272 2m 5f 110yds..................... (2:45)

37382 HANCOCK [78] 5-10-9 W Marston, hld up, improved 4 out,
led appr 2 out, rdn out........... (7 to 2 taw to 9 to 1) 1
35827 AMAZING SAIL (Ire) [88] 4-10-12 A S Smith, led, clr 5 out, hdd
appr 2 out, kpt on same pace........ (7 to 1 tchd 8 to 1) 2
37284 AJDAR [74] 6-10-5 M Brennan, pld hrd, in tch, rdn 3 out, fdd
bef nxt........................ (16 to 1 op 14 to 1) 3
35983 DANTES AMOUR (Ire) [81] 6-10-12 R Garritty, mid-div, effrt
6th, outpcd aftr 3 out...............(16 to 1 op 12 to 1) 4
36043 CASH BOX (Ire) [88] 9-11-5 N Smith, hld up, hit 4th, effrt 3 out,
nvr able to chal...................(7 to 1 op 5 to 1) 5
31232 SHELTON ABBEY [70] (bl) 11-10-1 B Storey, hld up, short-
lived effrt aftr 5th, sn no chal......(25 to 1 op 16 to 1) 6
29699 COUP DE VENT [69] 7-10-03 (3") P Henley, in tch till wknd aftr
4 out..........................(50 to 1 op 40 to 1) 7
31103 DOVETTO [79] 8-10-7 (3") Mr R Thornton, keen hold, in tch till
fdd 3 out.................(9 to 1 op 8 to 1 tchd 10 to 1) 8
30067 TIP IT IN [89] 8-11-3 (3") P Midgley, prmnt till fdd bef 3 out.
.............................(11 to 1 op 12 to 1 tchd 10 to 1) 9
35126 MARSH'S LAW [69] (bl) 10-9-7 (7") L McGrath, beh and
struggling, nvr on terms...........(25 to 1 op 20 to 1 tchd 33 to 1) 10
35376 KINDA GROOVY [93] (bl) 8-11-10 J Callaghan, midfield,
struggling fnl circuit..............(25 to 1) 11

2726 THE WEATHERMAN [73] 9-10-44 T Kent, beh, lost tch fnl
circuit..............................(50 to 1 op 33 to 1) 12
35129 RUBISLAW [69] (v) 5-9-7 (7") Miss S Lamb, in tch till wknd bef
3 out................................(66 to 1 op 33 to 1) 13
36213 MOOBAKKR (USA) [79] 6-10-10 B Powell, pressed ldr, 6 ls
second whn blun and uns rdr 3 out...... (9 to 2 tchd 5 to 1) ur
34594 CAMBO (USA) [85] 11-11-2 D Skyrme, chsd ldrs to hfwy, sn
lost pl, pld up bef 2 out...................(33 to 1 op 25 to 1) pu
3398 DESERT FORCE (Ire) [90] 8-11-2 (5") X Aizpuru, beh, struggling fnl circuit, pld up 3 out.
.....................(10 to 1 op 8 to 1 tchd 11 to 1) pu
Dist: 5l, 12l, ¾l, 8l, 22l, ½l, 5l, 3l, 3l, 9l. 5m 15.50s. a 12.50s (16 Ran).
(N Hetherton), J Hetherton

3821 UK Hygiene Novices' Handicap Chase Class E (0-105 5-y-o and up) £3,208 2m 1f 110yds......... (3:15)

36995 DARING PAST [90] 7-11-10 R Garritty, nvr far away, led 3rd
out, ran on strly frm nxt. (3 to 1 op 5 to 2 tchd 100 to 30) 1
3668 BALI TENDER [66] 6-9-11 (3") F Leahy, hld up, improved 4
out, no imprsn fnl 2..................(20 to 1 op 14 to 1) 2
35842 TAPATCH (Ire) [88] (bl) 9-11-5 (3") Mr R Thornton, cl up, led
3rd, hdd bef 3 out, sn outpcd.
...................(9 to 4 fav op 5 to 2 tchd 2 to 1) 3
34963 COPPER CABLE [67] 10-10-1 M Ranger, beh, nvr able to
chal..............................(16 to 1 op 10 to 1) 4
3370 DASH TO THE PHONE (USA) [73] 5-10-0 W Marston, beh, no
imprsn fnl circuit......................(4 to 1 op 3 to 1) 5
36564 REVE DE VALSE (USA) [80] 10-11-0 K Johnson, led to 3rd,
dsptd ld, losing grnd whn hit 4 out, fdd. (4 to 1 tchd 9 to 2) 6
1262 KARLOVAC [70] 11-10-4 F Perratt, beh, tld off whn blun badly
5 out....................(14 to 1 op 12 to 1 tchd 16 to 1) pu
Dist: 4l, 20l, 3l, 5l, 15l, dist. 4m 33.60s. a 19.60s (7 Ran).
(John A Petty), M D Hammond

3822 Eurobale Novices' Chase Class D (5-y-o and up) £3,910 2½m..... (3:50)

3477 MONKS SOHAM (Ire) 9-10-13 (3") P Henley, nvr far away, rdn
alng bef 3 out, rallied to ld last, gmely.
...................(9 to 1 op 5 to 1 tchd 10 to 1) 1
34772 BOWLES PATROL (Ire) 5-10-8 R Supple, settled in tch, steady
hdwy bef 3 out, hit nxt, ev ch last, kpt on.
...................................(25 to 1 op 16 to 1) 2
3618⁴ IMPERIAL VINTAGE (Ire) 7-11-9 (3") Mr R Thornton, led, rdn 3
out, hit and hdd last, no extr.
...................(11 to 8 op 6 to 4 tchd 13 to 8) 3
3472 MISTER DRUM (Ire) 8-11-12 W Marston, not jump wl, cl up till
outpcd bef 3 out..... (11 to 10 fav op Evens tchd 5 to 4) 4
37374 CHIAPPUCCI (Ire) (bl) 7-10-13 (3") J Magee, chsd ldrs, hit 6
out, struggling last 4................(9 to 1 op 8 to 1) 5
29853 CARDINAL SINNER (Ire) 8-11-2 B Storey, sn wl beh, tld off
whn pld up bef 3 out.............(50 to 1 op 33 to 1) pu
Dist: 1¼l, 3l, dist, dist. 5m 4.90s. a 15.90s (6 Ran).
SR: 9/-/15/

3823 Sanderson Teleporters Novices' Hurdle Class D (4-y-o and up) £3,156 2m 3f 110yds..............(4:25)

3687¹ TALATHATH (Fr) 5-11-9 (3") Mr R Thornton, settled on ins,
improved to ld 2 out, rdn out frm last.
.....................(6 to 4 fav op 7 to 4 tchd 2 to 1) 1
32244 MAZAMET (USA) 4-10-7 V Slattery, hld up, improved hfwy,
led briefly bef 2 out, kpt on und pres.
.....................(9 to 4 op 2 to 1 tchd 5 to 2) 2
35004 GIPSY GEOF (Ire) 6-10-11 (3") L Aspell, hld up, steady hdwy 4
out, effrt and rdn 2 out, one pace frm last.
.....................(8 to 1 op 6 to 1 tchd 9 to 1) 3
36235 POPPY'S DREAM 7-10-9 A S Smith, hld up, steady hdwy fnl
2, nvr nr to chal....................(16 to 1 op 14 to 1) 4
36633 RAISE A DOLLAR 7-10-9 R Supple, wth ldr, hit 4th, led nxt,
hdd bef 2 out, fdd............... (16 to 1 op 12 to 1) 5
3351 DONNEGALE (Ire) 5-11-0 J Callaghan, led till hdd 5th, fdd 3
out....................(40 to 1 op 33 to 1 tchd 50 to 1) 6
35094 M-I-FIVE (Ire) 6-11-0 O Pears, hld up, nvr able to chal.
.............................(14 to 1 op 12 to 1) 7
34275 TEEJAY'S FUTURE (Ire) 6-10-9 M Brennan, settled on outer,
effrt hfwy, struggling last 3........ (20 to 1 op 16 to 1) 8
3044 ALPHETON PRINCE 4-10-7 J Supple, cl up till wknd bef 3 out.
.............................(66 to 1 op 33 to 1) 9
32412 LARKSHILL (Ire) 6-10-11 (3") F Leahy, in tch, sn rdn alng,
struggling bef 3 out................(7 to 1 op 14 to 1) 10
CAN SHE CAN CAN 5-10-9 M Ranger, chsd ldrs till fdd appr 4
out.......................(50 to 1 op 33 to 1) 11
2156 MOOR DANCE MAN 7-11-0 D Verco, beh, gd hdwy to chase
ldrs 5th, struggling aftr nxt.......(16 to 1 op 12 to 1) 12
SPRINGFIELD RHYME 6-10-9 K Gaule, mid-div, struggling
fnl circuit, tld off...................(66 to 1 op 50 to 1) 13
28024 NEBAAL (USA) 7-10-9 (5") X Aizpuru, al beh, pld up 3 out.
.............................(66 to 1 op 33 to 1) pu
3700 APACHE LEN (USA) 4-10-7 R Garritty, in tch to hfwy, sn wknd,
pld up 3 out........................(33 to 1 op 25 to 1) pu
32696 BELLIDIUM 5-10-9 T Kent, beh, struggling hfwy, pld up 2 out.
.............................(66 to 1 op 33 to 1) pu
Dist: 1l, 3l, 4l, 6l, 12l, 8l, ¾l, 6l, 5l, 4l. 4m 49.50s. a 19.50s (16 Ran).

(Million In Mind Partnership (6)), D Nicholson

3824 Tony Edwards & Geoff Hunter Handicap Chase Class E (0-115 5-y-o and up) £3,299 2½m............ (5:00)

2971* HIGHBEATH [87] 6-10-0 L Wyer, *settled in tch, steady hdwy fnl circuit, led 3 out, ran on strly.*
................(5 to 2 fav op 9 to 4 tchd 2 to 1) 1
3585* RUSTIC AIR [104] 10-11-3 R Garritty, *chsd ldrs, hit and outpcd tenth, rallied 3 out, no ch wth wnr...*(5 to 1 op 4 to 1) 2
3730³ MERRY PANTO (Ire) [98] 8-10-4 (7") M Berry, *nvr far away, ev ch bef 3 out, one pace betw last 2*........ (8 to 1 op 7 to 1) 3
3670² CHEEKA [87] 8-10-0 M Ranger, *sluggish strt, improved 8th, led 4 out to next, not quicken 2...* (16 to 1 tchd 20 to 1) 4
3731⁶ BALLY PARSON [102] 11-10-10 (5") X Aizpuru, *led till hdd 4 out, one pace frm nxt*................... (9 to 1 op 7 to 1) 5
ALLIMAC NOMIS [88] 8-10-1 D Bentley, *in tch, drvn alng 3 out, sn btn*.................... (20 to 1 op 12 to 1) 6
3260² CROSS CANNON [107] 11-11-6 B Storey, *cl up, lost pl 9th, no dngr aftr*................... (7 to 1 op 6 to 1 tchd 9 to 1) 7
3242⁴ JUKE BOX BILLY (Ire) [87] 9-10-0 A S Smith, *beh, blun second, nvr on terms*................(20 to 1 op 14 to 1) 8
3670⁸ CALL ME EARLY [87] 12-10-0 M Brennan, *jmpd badly in rear, beh, tld off whn pld up bef 3 out.*........ (50 to 1) pu
3040³ SHINING LIGHT (Ire) [114] 8-11-10 (3") Mr R Thornton, *blun 3rd, drpd rear 7th, sn struggling, pld up bef 3 out.*
................(100 to 30 op 4 to 1 tchd 9 to 2) pu
Dist: 4l, ¾l, 4l, ¾l, 4l, 25l. 5m 3.10s. a 14.10s (10 Ran).

SR: 11/24/17/2/16/-/6/-/-/ (A Sharratt), Mrs M Reveley

3825 Spring Standard National Hunt Flat Class H (4,5,6-y-o) £1,402 1m 5f 110yds.............. (5:30)

ROUTE ONE (Ire) 4-10-5 (7") M Berry, *settled midfield, improved 4 fs out, led o'r one out, rdn out.*(8 to 1 op 5 to 1) 1
3482³ DOUBLE STAR 6-11-1 (3") Mr R Thornton, *made most till hdd o'r 2 fs out, rallied and ev ch over one out, not quicken.*
................(6 to 1 op 5 to 1 tchd 7 to 1) 2
3720² SIREN SONG (Ire) 6-11-11 (3") J Magee, *nvr far away, drvn alng o'r 2 fs out, rallied over one out, no imprsn.*
................(5 to 4 fav op Evens tchd 11 to 8) 3
3482 CAPSOFF (Ire) 4-10-4 (3") L Aspell, *mid-div, improved to ld o'r 2 fs out, hdd over one out, not quicken...* (8 to 1 op 5 to 1) 4
ROYAL MINT 4-10-7 (5") X Aizpuru, *midfield, shaken up and styd on last 2 fs, no imprsn.*
................(8 to 1 op 5 to 1 tchd 10 to 1) 5
MISS MOUSE 5-10-3 (3") Mr C Bonner, *cl up, ev ch appr strt, outpcd last 2 fs*.................... (20 to 1 op 16 to 1) 6
MADDIE 5-10-6 (7") M Newton, *hld up, improved 6 fs out, rdn and wknd fnl 2*.................... (25 to 1 op 16 to 1) 7
AILSAE 4-10-4 (3") E Callaghan, *hld up, nvr able to chal.*
................(33 to 1 op 20 to 1) 8
SPANISH SECRET (Ire) 5-10-13 (5") Chris Webb, *chsd ldrs till outpcd appr strt.*................... (10 to 1 op 8 to 1) 9
CAHERMONE LADY (Ire) 6-10-13 Mr N Kent, *prmnt till wknd o'r 4 fs out*................(20 to 1 op 16 to 1 tchd 25 to 1) 10
SWEET LITTLE BRIAR (Ire) 6-10-13 G Lee, *prmnt, drvn o'r 3 fs out, sn outpcd.*.................... (25 to 1 op 12 to 1) 11
BRED FOR PLEASURE 4-10-0 (7") L McGrath, *hld up, nvr dngrs.*.................... (33 to 1 op 20 to 1) 12
DERRING DOVE 5-11-1 (3") F Leahy, *hld up, struggling last half m*.................... (25 to 1 op 20 to 1 tchd 33 to 1) 13
ANGRY NATIVE 5-10-13 (5") S Taylor, *cl up 5 fs, fdd.*
................(33 to 1 op 20 to 1) 14
NEW ROSS (Ire) 5-10-11 (7") L Suthern, *hld up, struggling hfwy, sn btn*.......... (20 to 1 op 16 to 1 tchd 25 to 1) 15
PACKITIN PARKY 4-10-7 (5") O Burrows, *mid-div till outpcd o'r 4 fs out*.................... (33 to 1 op 20 to 1) 16
THE BOMBERS MOON 4-10-7 (5") B Grattan, *hld up on outer, struggling hfwy, fdd*........ (33 to 1 op 20 to 1) 17
LAKE ARIA 4-10-0 (7") Mr T J Barry, *in tch to hfwy, sn btn.*
................(25 to 1 op 16 to 1 tchd 33 to 1) 18
HONEYSUCKLE ROSE 4-10-4 (3") R Massey, *wth ldr till wknd quickly last 5 fs.*.................... (25 to 1 op 20 to 1) 19
Dist: 5l, 2½l, 2½l, 6l, 2l, 1l, 1l, 3l, 2½l, nk. 3m 11.40s. (19 Ran).
(Uplands Bloodstock), C P E Brooks

SANDOWN (good to firm)
Saturday April 26th
Going Correction: PLUS 0.50 sec. per fur.

3826 Brewers Fayre Novices' Handicap Chase Class C (5-y-o and up) £13,705 2½m 110yds........(2:50)

3701* KENMORE-SPEED [110] 10-10-3 Richard Guest, *led to 3rd, styd tracking ldr, chlgd 7th till led 11th, hdd 4 out, led ag'n aftr 3 out, pushed out.*................. (7 to 2 co-fav op 3 to 1) 1
3716³ STATELY HOME (Ire) [135] 6-12-0 R Johnson, *led 3rd to 11th, led ag'n 4 out, hdd aftr nxt, rallied, ev ch and mstk last, no extr*.................... (7 to 1 op 11 to 2 tchd 8 to 1) 2

3514 FULL OF BOUNCE (Ire) [107] 6-10-0 T Dascombe, *mstk second, outpcd 8th, staying on whn mistake 4 out, effrt 3 out, one pace frm nxt*................. (33 to 1 tchd 40 to 1) 3
3204² GOLDENSWIFT (Ire) [107] 7-10-0 B Fenton, *in tch 6th, outpcd 8th, staying on same pace whn hit last.* (6 to 1 tchd 7 to 1) 4
3638² GARNWIN (Ire) [125] 7-11-4 M A Fitzgerald, *nvr gng and al beh*.................... (7 to 2 co-fav op 5 to 2) 5
2827⁴ FINE THYNE (Ire) [120] 8-10-13 R Dunwoody, *in tch whn f 7th.*
................(7 to 2 co-fav op 9 to 2) f
3531¹ PLUNDER BAY (USA) [110] 6-10-3 N Williamson, *hld up, in tch whn f 7th.*.................... (13 to 2 op 5 to 1) f
3591² TOM'S APACHE [107] 8-10-0 D Gallagher, *hit 1st and sn wl beh, tld off whn pld up bef 11th...*(100 to 1 tchd 150 to 1) pu
Dist: 1½l, 8l, sht-hd, 25l. 5m 17.00s. a 17.00s (8 Ran).
SR: 8/31/-/-/-/ (K M Dacker), Mrs S J Smith

3827 41st Whitbread Gold Cup Handicap Chase Class A Grade 3 (5-y-o and up) £57,400 3m 5f 110yds........ (3:30)

3441² HARWELL LAD (Ire) [133] 8-10-0 Mr R Nuttall, *hit 4th, hdwy 13th, chsd ldrs 18th, rdn to chal whn lft in 3 out, drvn out.*
................(14 to 1 tchd 16 to 1) 1
3114* FLYER'S NAP [144] 11-10-7 A P McCoy, *pushed alng 11th, hdwy 13th, chsd ldrs 18th, chlgd 3 out, staying on whn blun last, not reco'r*................. (4 to 1 jt-fav tchd 9 to 2) 2
3206⁵ MCGREGOR THE THIRD [134] 11-10-11 R Dunwoody, *wth ldrs, chlgd 14th, led nxt, hdd 16th, str chal 3 out, wknd next.*
................(13 to 2 op 7 to 1 tchd 15 to 2) 3
3605 FEATHERED GALE [138] 10-10-5 P Carberry, *led to second, jmpd slwly and rear 7th, rdn 13th, lost tch frm 17th, tld off.*
................(9 to 1 op 8 to 1) 4
3605⁶ AVRO ANSON [143] 9-10-10 P Niven, *led second to 9th, led 14th to 15th, wknd 17th, tld off.*
................(5 to 1 op 3 to 1 tchd 11 to 2) 5
3563¹ BARTON BANK [157] 11-11-10 D Walsh, *chsd ldrs, hit 5th, still tracking ldrs whn f 18th*................(4 to 1 jt-fav op 7 to 2 tchd 9 to 2) f
3114⁷ YORKSHIRE GALE [135] 11-10-2 N Williamson, *chsd ldrs till led 9th, hdd 11th, led 13th to to 15th, led ag'n nxt, still slight ld whn rdn and f 3 out.....*(13 to 2 op 8 to 1 tchd 6 to 1) f
3605 BISHOPS HALL [139] 11-10-6 C F Swan, *sn beh, lost tch frm tenth, tld off 13th, pld up bef 17th.*
................(15 to 2 op 11 to 2 tchd 8 to 1) pu
3640 TOM'S GEMINI STAR [133] 9-10-0 D Gallagher, *sn beh, tld off 13th, pld up bef 17th.*
................(150 to 1 op 100 to 1 tchd 200 to 1) pu
Dist: 4l, 4l, dist, 8l. 7m 35.50s. a 22.50s (9 Ran).
(H Wellstead), R H Alner

WORCESTER (soft)
Saturday April 26th
Going Correction: PLUS 1.20 sec. per fur.

3828 Henwick Mares' Only Novices' Hurdle Class E (4-y-o and up) £2,600 2m
.... (5:45)

2775⁶ RING FOR ROSIE 6-10-12 B Fenton, *wtd wth, gd hdwy appr 3 out, chlgd frm nxt, kpt on und pres to ld cl hme.*
................(10 to 1 tchd 11 to 1) 1
2499⁴ MAID FOR ADVENTURE (Ire) 6-11-5 J Culloty, *al hndy, led 3 out, hrd rdn and hdd cl hme.*
................(3 to 1 fav op 7 to 4 tchd 7 to 2) 2
3019⁴ FUN WHILE IT LASTS 6-10-12 S Wynne, *trkd ldrs, rdn and ev ch 2 out, styd on run in*................(12 to 1 op 8 to 1) 3
3641⁶ REGAL PURSUIT (Ire) 6-11-5 M A Fitzgerald, *led till aftr second, styd hndy, ev ch 2 out, one pace last.*
................(7 to 2 op 3 to 1 tchd 9 to 2) 4
3312⁴ MADAM'S WALK 7-10-12 C Llewellyn, *prmnt, led 3rd to nxt, rgned ld 5th, hdd 3 out, wknd appr last.*
................(100 to 30 op 5 to 2 tchd 7 to 2) 5
3108 CARLINGFORD GALE (Ire) 6-10-12 R Johnson, *nvr nr to chal.*
................(20 to 1 op 14 to 1) 6
3299⁴ GLADYS EMMANUEL 10-10-7 (5") D J Kavanagh, *hld up, hdwy 4th, wknd 3 out...*(6 to 1 op 5 to 1 tchd 7 to 1) 7
2775 MOLLIE SILVERS 5-10-12 W McFarland, *beh frm 4th.*
................(100 to 1 op 66 to 1) 8
2775 LUCRATIVE PERK (Ire) 5-10-12 D Leahy, *hld up, hdwy hfwy, wknd frm 5th*................ (50 to 1 op 33 to 1) 9
3554⁷ A BADGE TOO FAR (Ire) (bl) 7-10-12 R Bellamy, *prmnt, lost pl and blun 3rd, no dngr aftr*...(100 to 1 op 66 to 1) 10
2795 BLUE HAVANA 5-10-12 P Hide, *in tch, led to nxt, wknd 3 out*.................... (100 to 1 op 66 to 1) 11
HEATHYARDS JADE 4-10-6 T Eley, *al beh.*
................(50 to 1 op 40 to 1) 12
3122 SISSINGHURST FLYER (Ire) 5-10-12 C Maude, *al beh, f last.*
................(50 to 1 op 40 to 1) f
2744 T'NIEL 6-10-5 (7") S Lycett, *refused to race, took no part.*
................(100 to 1 op 66 to 1) ref
THE FLYING FIDDLE 5-10-12 T Dascombe, *beh whn mstk 3rd, tld off whn pld up bef 3 out...*(100 to 1 op 66 to 1) pu
MADAM CORA 5-10-12 B Powell, *beh, gd prog appr 3 out, lost pl bef nxt, pld up lme approaching last, lame, dead.*
................(50 to 1 op 40 to 1) pu

3735 CLOUDY HOUSE 8-10-5 (7*) Mr L Baker, *led aftr second to nxt, wknd frm 5th, tld off whn pld up bef 2 out.*
.....................(100 to 1 op 66 to 1) pu

3681³ ROYAL MEMBER 4-10-6 E Byrne, *beh frm 4th, tld off whn pld up bef 3 out.*...............(100 to 1 op 66 to 1) pu

3302 TECHNICAL MOVE (Ire) 6-10-12 S Burrough, *trkd ldrs to hfwy, tld off whn pld up bef 3 out.*
.....................(50 to 1 op 40 to 1 tchd 66 to 1) pu
Dist: Hd, ½l, 2½l, 18l, 1¼l, 4l, 6l, 16l, 3½l, 25l. 4m 8.60s. a 28.60s (19 Ran).
(T F F Nixon), Capt T A Forster

3829 West Malvern Novices' Chase Class E (5-y-o and up) £2,841 2m....(6:15)

3467² LUCKY EDDIE (Ire) 6-11-0 C Maude, *in tch, hmpd second, hit 5th, led appr 4 out, clr frm nxt.....*(7 to 4 jt-fav frm nxt) 1

3742 DIAMOND LIGHT 10-11-0 Mr S Lloyd, *hld up, hit 7th, lost tch nxt, styd on appr last, took second r-in, no ch wth wnr.*
.....................(33 to 1 op 25 to 1) 2

3354⁶ OLD REDWOOD (bl) 10-11-0 L O'Hara, *led, pckd 1st, pecked badly and hdd nxt, ev ch 4 out, wknd bef nxt.*
.....................(5 to 2 op 2 to 1 tchd 11 to 4) 3

3320 LADY ROSEBURY 7-10-9 T J Murphy, *hld up, hit 1st, hdwy appr 4th, chlgd frm 8th, blun four out, wkng whn blunded nxt.*
.....................(33 to 1 op 25 to 1 tchd 40 to 1) 4

3620³ TENAYESTELIGN 9-11-9 S Wynne, *hld up, f 4th...*(7 to 4 jt-fav tchd 2 to 1) f

STEEL GOLD 7-10-7 (7*) Mr R Burton, *lft in ld second, hdd and wknd quickly appr 4 out, beh whn blun 3 out, pld up bef nxt.*...........(33 to 1 op 25 to 1 tchd 40 to 1) pu
Dist: 12l, 1½l. 4m 28.60s. a 39.60s (6 Ran).
(I L Shaw), P J Hobbs

3830 Nick Halligan And Peter Higgs Handicap Chase Class C (0-135 5-y-o and up) £4,731 2m 7f 110yds......(6:45)

3670⁵ HAWAIIAN YOUTH (Ire) [107] 9-10-2 R Dunwoody, *led to second, rgned ld 8th, made rst, clr frm 2 out.*
.....................(15 to 8 op 6 to 4 tchd 2 to 1) 1

1937¹ BALLY CLOVER [111] 10-10-6 N Williamson, *hld up, hit 1st and 6th, prog 9th, ev ch whn mstk 3 out, sn beh.*
.....................(7 to 4 fav op 9 to 4) 2

3441⁵ BAVARD DIEU (Ire) [129] 9-11-10 C Llewellyn, *hld up, rdn alng tenth, rallied 13th, wknd bef 3 out.*
.....................(13 to 2 op 5 to 1 tchd 11 to 2) 3

3605 SCRIBBLER [112] (bl) 11-10-4 (3*) D Fortt, *in tch, jmpd slwly second, hdd 4th to 8th, outpcd nxt, wkng whn mstk 12th.*
.....................(100 to 30 op 5 to 1 tchd 7 to 2) 4

3264 TOP BRASS (Ire) [105] 9-10-0 S McNeill, *led second to 4th, wknd tenth, tld off whn pld up bef 2 out.*
.....................(12 to 1 op 10 to 1 tchd 14 to 1) pu
Dist: 10l, 9l. dist. 6m 18.40s. (5 Ran).
(G Redford), G M McCourt

3831 Three Counties Handicap Hurdle Class D (0-125 4-y-o and up) £3,092 2m........................(7:15)

3558³ KINO'S CROSS [99] 8-10-4 L Harvey, *chsd ldrs, hrd rdn to ld r-in, all out.........*(5 to 1 jt-fav op 8 to 1 tchd 9 to 2) 1

3255 WALKING TALL (Ire) [98] (bl) 6-10-3 R Johnson, *led, sn clr, hrd rdn whn hdd r-in, unbl to quicken.*
.....................(16 to 1 op 10 to 1 tchd 20 to 1) 2

3595 TEJANO GOLD (USA) [119] 7-11-10 R Dunwoody, *keen hold, chsd ldr appr 3rd till approaching 2 out, kpt on r-in.* (5 to 1 jt-fav op 4 to 1 tchd 11 to 2) 3

1141³ COOLEY'S VALVE (Ire) [98] 9-10-3 C F Swan, *beh, styd on frm 3 out, nvr nrr................*(9 to 1 op 10 to 1) 4

3592* EURO SINGER [104] 5-10-4 (5*) S Ryan, *hld up, hdwy appr 3 out, one pace bef nxt.....................*(7 to 1 op 5 to 1) 5

328² ROCA MURADA (Ire) [100] 8-10-5 N Williamson, *mid-div, hdwy appr 3 out, wknd bef nxt.*
.....................(14 to 1 op 10 to 1 tchd 16 to 1) 6

3575 EASY LISTENING (USA) [104] 5-10-9 J Railton, *strted slwly, nvr nrr..................*(7 to 1 op 11 to 2 tchd 8 to 1) 7

3445⁵ KEEP ME IN MIND (Ire) [104] 8-10-9 C Maude, *hld up, rdn and wknd appr 3 out.*
.....................(8 to 1 op 6 to 1 tchd 10 to 1 and 12 to 1) 8

3652³ OUT RANKING (Fr) [114] 5-11-5 T Dascombe, *nvr on terms.*
.....................(11 to 1 op 8 to 1 tchd 12 to 1) 9

1647 TIGHT FIST (Ire) [111] 7-11-2 J F Titley, *beh frm 5th.*
.....................(10 to 1 op 5 to 1) 10

3703 SAINT CIEL (USA) [102] 9-10-7 S Wynne, *hld up, heavy frm 5th, effrt whn blun 3 out, not reco'r.....*(12 to 1 op 10 to 1) 11

CARIBBEAN PRINCE [95] (bl) 9-10-0 S McNeill, *beh frm 4th.*
.....................(33 to 1 op 20 to 1) 12

YOUR RISK (Ire) [98] 7-10-3 J A McCarthy, *strted slwly, aways beh.....................*(16 to 1 op 10 to 1 tchd 20 to 1) 13

3623* PERCY BRAITHWAITE (Ire) [103] 5-10-1 (7*) M J Goldstein, *chsd ldr till appr 3rd, remained hndy, chalg whn mstk and uns rdr last.*...........(8 to 1 op 6 to 1 tchd 10 to 1) ur
Dist: 1½l, ½l, 10l, 3½l, 6l, ¾l, 1l, 5l, 18l, 8l. 4m 4.90s. a 24.90s (14 Ran).
SR: 19/16/36/5/7/-/
(N V Harvey), A J Wilson

3832 Upton Upon Severn Novices' Hunters' Chase Class H (5-y-o and

---

up) £1,198 2m 7f 110yds......(7:45)

PHAR TOO TOUCHY 10-11-2 (7*) Mr N Harris, *chsd ldr, led 6th, made rst, clr frm tenth, hit 12th and 2 out, unchlgd.*
.....................(5 to 4 fav tchd 6 to 4) 1

TEA CEE KAY 7-11-7 (7*) Mr Rupert Sweeting, *led to 6th, chsd wnr aftr till outpcd 8th, wnt poor second 3 out, tld off.*
.....................(14 to 1 op 7 to 1) 2

ANN'S AMBITION 10-11-7 (7*) Mr M Frith, *in tch, chsd wnr frm 8th, blun and lost touch tenth, wknd 3 out, lft poor 3rd last, tld off.....................*(10 to 1 op 7 to 1 tchd 12 to 1) 3

BALLYHAMAGE (Ire) 9-11-7 (7*) Mr M Munrowd, *f 1st.*
.....................(20 to 1) f

SULTAN'S SON 11-11-7 (7*) Mr G Lewis, *hld up, lost tch frm 8th, wnt poor 3rd out, blun and uns rdr last.*
.....................(9 to 2 op 3 to 1 tchd 5 to 1) ur

PETE'S SAKE 12-11-9 (5*) Mr C Vigors, *hit 6th, al beh, tld off whn pld up bef 13th......*(9 to 1 op 8 to 1 tchd 12 to 1) pu

CALL-ME-DINKY 14-11-2 (7*) Miss C Thomas, *beh till pld up lme and dismounted bef 4th.*
.....................(25 to 1 op 14 to 1 tchd 33 to 1) pu

3567 JOHNNY THE FOX (Ire) 9-11-7 (7*) Mr R Lawther, *mstk 1st, beh frm 6th, tld off whn pld up bef tenth.*
.....................(7 to 1 op 6 to 1 tchd 8 to 1) pu

3365² NO JOKER (Ire) 9-11-7 (7*) Mr P Scott, *trkd ldrs, hit tenth, sn beh, tld off whn pld up bef 3 out.*
.....................(11 to 2 op 4 to 1 tchd 6 to 1) pu

WHO'S YOUR MAN (Ire) 7-11-7 (7*) Mr R Burton, *beh whn blun 7th, tld off when pld up bef 9th.*
.....................(25 to 1 op 20 to 1 tchd 33 to 1) pu
Dist: Dist, dist. 6m 27.10s. (10 Ran).
(Miss R A Francis), Victor Dartnall

3833 Powick Novices' Handicap Hurdle Class E (0-100 4-y-o and up) £2,775 3m..........................(8:15)

3093* MAYB-MAYB [90] 7-11-10 A P McCoy, *al prmnt, led appr 7th, drvn out.............*(4 to 1 fav op 7 to 2 tchd 9 to 2) 1

3692⁷ MR CHRISTIE [83] 5-11-3 R Dunwoody, *hld up, hdwy 9th, effrt r-in, unbl to quicken ol hme.............*(12 to 1 op 9 to 1) 2

3009⁵ PARADE RACER [78] 6-10-12 W McFarland, *hld up, hdwy 3 out, kpt on frm nxt.....................*(6 to 1 tchd 7 to 1) 3

3093⁴ HELLO ME MAN (Ire) [79] 9-10-11 Mr J L Llewellyn, *wtd wth, gd hdwy appr 7th, effrt 3 out, wknd approaching last.*
.....................(20 to 1 op 16 to 1) 4

3362* SAMMORELLO (Ire) [80] 6-11-0 C Llewellyn, *beh, styd on frm 3 out, nrst finish.............*(7 to 1 op 6 to 1) 5

3196 STORMY SESSION [79] 7-10-13 D Walsh, *hdwy appr 7th, effrt 3 out, sn wknd.............*(25 to 1 op 10 to 1) 6

3001 VALLINGALE (Ire) [87] 6-11-7 J Culloty, *nvr trble ldrs.*
.....................(12 to 1 op 7 to 1 tchd 14 to 1) 7

3099⁴ DANNY GALE (Ire) [80] 6-11-0 S McNeill, *strted slwly, al beh, tld off.............*(11 to 1 op 8 to 1 tchd 12 to 1) 8

3052⁷ CAMERA MAN [89] 7-11-9 M A Fitzgerald, *hld up beh ldrs, rdn and wknd appr 3 out, tld off.*
.....................(11 to 1 op 8 to 1 tchd 10 to 1) 9

2898⁴ BROOKHAMPTON LANE [75] 6-10-9 B Powell, *beh frm 6th, tld off.............*(6 to 1 op 7 to 1) 10

2517⁶ LOUGHDOO (Ire) [76] 9-10-10 B Fenton, *trkd ldrs, wknd appr 3 out, tld off.............*(25 to 1 op 33 to 1) 11

1937 VICAR OF BRAY [79] 10-10-13 M Richards, *beh frm 6th, tld off.....................*(25 to 1 op 20 to 1) 12

3321⁵ JIGGINSTOWN [80] 10-10-7 (7*) L Cooper, *prmnt to 6th, sn beh, tld off.............*(10 to 1 op 12 to 1 tchd 14 to 1) 13

3867 MISTER BLAKE [89] 7-11-9 R Johnson, *beh frm 6th, tld off whn pld up bef 3 out.....*(7 to 1 op 8 to 1 tchd 10 to 1) pu

3684² TOMMY COOPER [80] 6-11-0 E Byrne, *led till appr 7th, wknd quickly nxt, tld off whn pld up bef 9th.* (16 to 1 op 12 to 1) pu

2601⁸ JOBSAGOODUN [88] 6-11-8 J R Kavanagh, *beh frm 6th, tld off whn pld up bef 3 out.* (11 to 1 op 8 to 1 tchd 12 to 1) pu
Dist: 1¼l, 3l, 7l, 8l, 2l, 1¼l, 30l, 17l, dist. 7l. 6m 21.80s. a 45.80s (16 Ran).
(J Neville), J Neville

LISTOWEL (IRE) (good to yielding) Sunday April 27th

3834 Shannon Car Ferry Maiden Hurdle (5-y-o and up) £3,767 3m..... (4:30)

3213² BAWNROCK (Ire) 8-12-0 C F Swan, ...(3 to 1 jt-fav) 1
3520⁴ THE GREY MARE (Ire) 8-11-2 (7*) Mr P Fahey, (3 to 1 jt-fav) 2
3336⁵ TULLY'S BALL (Ire) 7-11-6 F Woods, ...(8 to 1) 3
3430⁷ WOODBORO LASS (Ire) 7-10-8 (7*) Miss A Sloane, (12 to 1) 4
3417 MISS BERTAINE (Ire) 8-10-8 (7*) J E Casey, ...(12 to 1) 5
3223⁹ NAN'S PET (Ire) 7-10-10 (5*) A O'Shea, ...(25 to 1) 6
3429⁵ LUCKY ROSS (Ire) 6-11-1 (5*) J M Donnelly, ...(14 to 1) 7
3429³ COMAN'S JET (Ire) 7-12-0 C O'Dwyer, ...(6 to 1) 8
3178⁶ MISS PECKSNIFF (Ire) 7-11-1 L P Cusack, ...(20 to 1) 9
277⁴ CROHANE PRINCESS (Ire) 8-11-1 S H O'Donovan, (14 to 1) 10
3238⁹ MERCHANTS ROAD 10-10-13 (7*) R M Murphy, .(16 to 1) 11
3343⁷ VERYWELL (Ire) 6-10-13 (7*) B J Geraghty, ...(14 to 1) 12
2525⁸ BE THE ONE (Ire) 6-10-12 (3*) K Whelan, ...(12 to 1) f
1360⁶ JOLLY JOHN (Ire) 6-11-6 D J Casey, ...(10 to 1) ur
3430⁶ CORYROSE (Ire) 5-11-0 (7*) P G Hourigan, ...(12 to 1) su
3695⁵ OVER THE WALL (Ire) 8-11-1 P A Roche, ...(12 to 1) pu

3705	CAHONIS (Ire) 5-11-4 M P Hourigan,	(25 to 1)	pu
2339⁵	DESERTMORE (Ire) 7-11-6 J Shortt,	(9 to 2)	pu
3068	PRINCE PINE (Ire) 6-11-6 D H O'Connor,	(20 to 1)	pu
3697	MSADI MHULU (Ire) 6-11-1 T P Treacy,	(25 to 1)	pu

Dist: 6l, 3½l, 2½l, 2l. 6m 34.80s. (20 Ran).

(New Road Syndicate), A P O'Brien

3835 Triton Showers Handicap Hurdle (0-109 4-y-o and up) £3,425 2½m
.... (5:00)

3068	DRISHOGUE LAD [-] 10-10-0¹ A J O'Brien,	(3 to 1)	1
3180⁷	STAGALIER (Ire) [-] 5-10-11 (7°) B J Geraghty, ..	(4 to 1 fav)	2
3431⁸	WELSH GRIT (Ire) [-] 6-10-6 D J Casey,	(11 to 2)	3
3448²	ECLIPTIC MOON (Ire) [-] 7-9-8¹ T P Treacy,	(9 to 2)	4
2413	THATS MY WIFE (Ire) [-] 6-9-13 (3°) J Butler,	(20 to 1)	5
3705⁷	NEARLY A LINE [-] 5-9-7 (7°) S P McCann,	(12 to 1)	6
679	OFFICIAL PORTRAIT (Ire) [-] 8-11-7 C F Swan,	(12 to 1)	7
3428	PATTIE TIM (Ire) [-] 8-11-3 (3°) K Whelan,	(12 to 1)	8
3551	CONNA BRIDE LADY (Ire) [-] 5-9-4 (7°) F J Keniry,	(25 to 1)	9
1074⁹	THE COBH GALE [-] 10-10-0 H Rogers,	(12 to 1)	10
3233	ANOTHER GALLOP [-] 9-9-7 F Woods,	(20 to 1)	11
3219⁵	TIP YOUR WAITRESS (Ire) [-] 4-9-8 (7°) M J Collins,	(12 to 1)	12
3607⁸	TARAJAN (USA) [-] (bl) 5-12-0 J Shortt,	(10 to 1)	13
3070³	DIGADUST (Ire) [-] 5-11-7 M Duffy,	(8 to 1)	14
3693	BORRISMORE FLASH (Ire) [-] 9-9-7 T P Rudd,	(25 to 1)	pu
525°	VAIN PRINCESS (Ire) [-] 8-10-9 M P Hourigan,	(14 to 1)	pu
3338²	RAHEEN RIVER (Ire) [-] 6-10-6 C O'Dwyer,	(8 to 1)	pu

Dist: 5½l, 2½l, 3½l, 4l. 5m 27.90s. (17 Ran).

(Noel Brett), Noel Brett

3836 Croom House Stud I.N.H. Flat Race (5-y-o and up) £3,425 2½m... (5:30)

3224⁴	HOW RAN ON [-] 6-11-11 (3°) Mr R Walsh,	(3 to 1)	1
2752⁸	SUNSHINE BAY (Ire) 6-11-7 (7°) Mr D P Daly,	(5 to 1)	2
	GAELTEACHT (Ire) 6-11-7 (7°) Mr M Scanlon,	(12 to 1)	3
3380²	FINCHOGUE (Ire) 5-11-8 Mr P Fenton,	(7 to 4 fav)	4
2964⁷	WOLSELEY LORD (Ire) 5-11-6 (7°) Mr A J Dempsey,		
		(7 to 4 fav)	5
3421⁸	JOSH'S FANCY (Ire) 6-11-2 (7°) Mr G A Kingston,	(6 to 1)	6
3381³	FRESHFIELD GALE (Ire) 7-11-6 (3°) Mr P English,	(10 to 1)	7
	FEELING GRAND (Ire) 5-11-6 (7°) Mr M T Hartrey,	(14 to 1)	8
3417⁵	PORT NA SON (Ire) 6-11-7 (7°) Mr D A Harney,	(20 to 1)	9
2523	HARRY'S SECRET (Ire) 7-12-1⁸ (7°) Mr R Sheil,	(33 to 1)	10
3343⁶	CLERICAL COUSIN (Ire) 8-11-7 (7°) Mr G Donnelly,	(12 to 1)	11
3608	RED BANNER (Ire) 6-11-2 (7°) Mr M A Cahill,	(25 to 1)	12
	THE RIGHT ATTITUDE (Ire) 7-12-0 Mr B M Cash,	(14 to 1)	13
3083	WARLOCKFOE (Ire) (bl) 6-11-2 (7°) Mr Sean O O'Brien,		
		(20 to 1)	14
	MOUNTBROWNE (Ire) 5-11-6 (7°) Mr J O'Sullivan,	(14 to 1)	15
3449	NORTHERN CRUSADE (Ire) 6-11-2 (7°) Mr R Barry,	(25 to 1)	16
3697	MR FREEMAN (Ire) (bl) 6-11-7 (7°) Mr A FitzGerald,	(12 to 1)	17
	PRIME THYNE (Ire) 5-11-5 (3°) Mr J Connolly,	(20 to 1)	18

Dist: 4l, 2l, 5½l, 20l. 5m 22.40s. (18 Ran).

(J M Walker), W P Mullins

SLIGO (IRE) (soft (race 1), heavy (2,3,4))
Monday April 28th

3837 Smirnoff Handicap Hurdle (0-109 4-y-o and up) £2,740 3m...... (5:00)

3390³	MICK MAN (Ire) [-] 6-9-3 (7°) P G Hourigan,	(14 to 1)	1
2708⁴	FALLOW TRIX (Ire) [-] 5-10-10 (3°) D Bromley,	(8 to 1)	2
3377⁵	DOUBLE STRIKE (Ire) [-] (bl) 6-10-5 T P Treacy,	(14 to 1)	3
3072⁴	HI KNIGHT (Ire) [-] 7-11-3 (7°) R Burke,	(8 to 1)	4
3071³	HOLLYBANK BUCK (Ire) [-] 7-11-8 R Dunwoody,	(7 to 4 fav)	5
3343³	HEATHER VILLE (Ire) [-] 5-10-1 (7°) B J Geraghty,	(5 to 1)	6
3694*	LADY ELISE (Ire) [-] 6-11-1 F Woods,	(9 to 1)	7
3520⁵	STAR CLUB (Ire) [-] 5-10-8 H Rogers,	(12 to 1)	8
3236⁶	STRONG HICKS (Ire) [-] 9-11-7 (7°) L J Fleming,	(14 to 1)	9
2366⁴	KILCARAMORE (Ire) [-] 6-9-11 (7°) S Fitzgerald,	(12 to 1)	10
3431	EMPEROR GLEN (Ire) [-] (bl) 9-10-10 (3°) K Whelan,	(12 to 1)	11
3643	BOBSTAR DANCER (Ire) [-] 6-10-9 (7°) D Flood,	(20 to 1)	12
3626⁵	ANOTHER BONNY [-] 11-9-2 (5°) A O'Shea,	(25 to 1)	13
3419⁷	JIHAAD (USA) [-] 7-9-10 T P Rudd,	(14 to 1)	pu
1838	COMMERCIAL HOUSE (Ire) [-] 9-10-6 D T Evans,	(20 to 1)	pu
2518	BOWES LADY (Ire) [-] 6-9-9 (3°) G Cotter,	(33 to 1)	pu
3234	COOLSHAMROCK (Ire) [-] 5-9-8¹ J R Barry,	(16 to 1)	pu

Dist: 1l, 5½l, 5½l, 10l. 6m 23.10s. (17 Ran).

(Gabriel Mulholland), Noel Meade

3838 Union Food Distributors Beginners Chase (5-y-o and up) £2,740 2½m
.... (6:30)

3215⁵	VEREDARIUS (Fr) 6-12-0 F Woods,	(6 to 1)	1
3375³	CHATTERBUCK (Ire) 8-11-7 (7°) D A McLoughlin,	(6 to 1)	2
3215²	COLLON (Ire) 8-11-9 D H O'Connor,	(11 to 2)	3
3645⁴	THE THIRD MAN (Ire) 8-11-11 (3°) G Cotter,	(9 to 1)	4
3645	BROWNRATH KING (Ire) 8-12-0 K F O'Brien,	(20 to 1)	5
3448	SPECTACLE (Ire) 7-11-2 (7°) Mr C P McGivern,	(16 to 1)	6
3428⁶	CELTIC SUNRISE (bl) 9-12-0 T P Treacy,	(14 to 1)	7
2136	TIME AND CHARGES (Ire) 7-11-9 C O'Dwyer,	(8 to 1)	8
3624⁴	FLIP YOUR LID 8-11-11 (3°) U Smyth,	(8 to 1)	9

2964	AMAZING ALL (Ire) 8-11-6 (3°) D Bromley,	(25 to 1)	f
3645	XANTHOS 7-11-9 L P Cusack,	(25 to 1)	bd
3706⁷	TREENS FOLLY 8-11-6 (3°) K Whelan,	(33 to 1)	pu
3624⁷	CORMAC LADY (Ire) 6-11-4 J R Barry,	(25 to 1)	pu
3336	CARROLLS ROCK (Ire) 6-11-9 C F Swan,	(4 to 1 fav)	pu

Dist: Sht-hd, 5l, 1½l, 20l. 5m 40.20s. (15 Ran).

(G B F Clarke), A L T Moore

3839 Glencar Handicap Chase (0-102 5-y-o and up) £2,226 2½m... (7:00)

2274⁵	WALLYS RUN [-] 10-10-12 L P Cusack,	(12 to 1)	1
3455³	CARAGH BRIDGE [-] 10-11-3 C F Swan,	(6 to 1)	2
3340³	SILENTBROOK [-] 12-9-3 (5°) A O'Shea,	(16 to 1)	3
3793³	YOUNG WOLF [-] 9-10-5 C O'Dwyer,	(8 to 1)	4
2038³	IF YOU BELIEVE (Ire) [-] 8-11-1 (3°) B Bowens,	(10 to 1)	5
3706²	RICH TRADITION (Ire) [-] 9-11-0 (3°) U Smyth,	(8 to 1)	6
2365³	GREEK MAGIC [-] 10-9-12 (3°) G Cotter,	(14 to 1)	7
3753	FIELD OF DESTINY (Ire) [-] 8-10-4 D H O'Connor,	(25 to 1)	8
2411³	APPALACHEE BAY (Ire) [-] 7-11-5 (3°) J Butler,	(5 to 1)	9
3455²	FAMOUS STOUT [-] 12-11-0 R Dunwoody,	(9 to 2 fav)	ur
3420	KILLERY LADY (Ire) [-] 6-9-2 (7°) B J Geraghty,	(14 to 1)	ur
3526⁵	FINAL TUB [-] 14-12-0 S H O'Donovan,	(16 to 1)	pu
3624⁹	BALLYBRIT BOY [-] 11-9-12 J R Barry,	(33 to 1)	pu
3624⁵	CASTLE TIGER BAY (Ire) [-] 6-10-7 K F O'Brien,	(20 to 1)	pu

Dist: 2½l, 9l, ¾l, dist. 5m 40.90s. (14 Ran).

(Diamond Syndicate), W J Lanigan

3840 Northwest I.N.H. Flat Race (4-y-o and up) £2,226 2m............ (8:00)

	INIS CARA (Ire) 5-11-13 Mr P Fenton,	(15 to 8 fav)	1
3547⁹	CONAGHER LEADER (Ire) 6-11-11 (3°) Mr M Kelly,	(8 to 1)	2
	HEART OF AVONDALE (Ire) 4-11-1 Mr J P Dempsey,		
		(20 to 1)	3
3627⁴	DIGITAL SIGNAL (Ire) 4-10-13 (7°) Mr D P Daly,	(8 to 1)	4
1897	NOT CLEVER (Ire) 5-11-6 (7°) Mr A Ross,	(12 to 1)	5
3349	EBONY PRINCE 5-11-13 Mr B M Cash,	(16 to 1)	6
	BE MY TRUMP (Ire) 5-11-8 Mr D Marnane,	(10 to 1)	7
	AUDACIOUS DANCER (Ire) 5-11-6 (7°) Mr A J Dempsey,		
		(16 to 1)	8
	ANCIENT CHINA 4-11-3 (3°) Mr P J Casey,	(16 to 1)	9
	MODILE (Ire) 6-11-9 Mr G J Harford,	(8 to 1)	10
2022	ELECTRIC LAD (Ire) 6-12-0 Mr A R Coonan,	(20 to 1)	11
3416⁸	WHO IS ED (Ire) 6-11-9 (5°) Mr G Elliott,	(7 to 2)	12
	SOUNDWOMEN (Ire) 5-11-3 (5°) Mr J T McNamara,	(10 to 1)	13
	GOLD CHARIOT (Ire) 6-11-2 (7°) Mr P J Faulkner,	(14 to 1)	14
	KATIE DALY (Ire) 6-11-6 (3°) Mr R Walsh,	(6 to 1)	15
	SECRET TRIX (Ire) 5-11-6 (7°) Mr J Keville,	(16 to 1)	16
	GOLDEN MICHELLE (Ire) 5-11-1 (7°) Mr G A Kingston,		
		(14 to 1)	17

Dist: 5½l, nk, 2½l, 2l. 4m 32.30s. (17 Ran).

(Nancy Hogan Syndicate), Michael Hourigan

ASCOT (good to firm)
Tuesday April 29th
Going Correction: PLUS 0.35 sec. per fur. (races 1,4,6), PLUS 0.10 (2,3,5)

3841 Mitsubishi Diamond Vision Handicap Hurdle Class B (4-y-o and up) £4,756 3m..................................... (5:30)

3503*	EL FREDDIE [102] 7-10-8 G Upton, led to 3rd, led ag'n 5th, made rst, hrd pressed frm 2 out, drvn out, jst hld on.		
		(11 to 4 fav op 5 to 2 tchd 3 to 1)	1
3712*	MEDITATOR [112] (bl) 13-11-4 S Curran, blun second, hld up in tch, cld 9th, str chal frm 2 out, hrd rdn, ran on wl, jst held.		
		(6 to 1 op 5 to 1 tchd 13 to 2 and 7 to 1)	2
3116	KARAR (Ire) [109] 7-11-1 D O'Sullivan, hld up beh, losing tch frm 4 out, styd on wl from last.		
		(6 to 1 op 5 to 1 tchd 7 to 1 and 15 to 2)	3
3445*	CASSIO'S BOY [99] 6-10-5 A P McCoy, hld up in rear, steady hdwy frm 9th, blun 4 out, sn outpcd.		
		(5 to 1 op 9 to 2 tchd 6 to 1)	4
3637⁴	OLYMPIAN [117] (bl) 10-11-9 M A Fitzgerald, dwlt and strted slwly, sn trkd ldrs, blun 7th, struggling frm 4 out.		
		(100 to 30 op 11 to 4 tchd 7 to 2)	5
3272⁴	APACHEE FLOWER [94] 7-10-0 B Powell, cl up, led 3rd to 5th, rdn alng frm 7th, hrd ridden and btn appr 4 out, tld off.		
		(40 to 1 op 25 to 1)	6
	LYPHANTASTIC (USA) [118] 8-11-10 J Railton, hld up towards rear, shrtlvd effrt aftr 3 out, no imprsn, pld up bef 2 out, dismounted.		
		(9 to 1 op 6 to 1 tchd 10 to 1)	pu

Dist: Sht-hd, 27l, 2l, 4l, 10l. 5m 55.90s. a 19.90s (7 Ran).

(Martin Lovatt), J A B Old

3842 Michael Page Group Handicap Chase Class B (5-y-o and up) £10,230 2m.................................. (6:00)

3711⁵	CUMBRIAN CHALLENGE (Ire) [125] 8-10-2 L Wyer, trkd ldrs, shaken up aftr 3 out, chlgd nxt, led r-in, rdn out.		
		(10 to 1 op 8 to 1)	1

3273* THUMBS UP [127] 11-10-4 R Dunwoody, *trkd ldr, led 7th till hdd r-in, no extr*.........................(7 to 1 op 5 to 1) 2

3719² MISTER ODDY [127] 11-10-4 T J Murphy, *led to 7th, rallied and ev ch frm 2 out till appr last kpt on one pace.*
.........................(7 to 1 op 5 to 1 tchd 8 to 1) 3

3596 TIME WON'T WAIT (Ire) [133] 8-10-10 J Railton, *hld up, not fluent 5th, cld nxt, blun 3 out, swtchd lft appr last, one pace and pres*.........................(3 to 1 tchd 7 to 2) 4

2396⁷ SOCIETY GUEST [123] 11-10-0 L Harvey, *jmpd lft, trkd ldrs till lost pl 6th, rallied appr 2 out, no imprsn.*
.........................(25 to 1 op 16 to 1) 5

3636* BERTONE (Ire) [133] 8-10-10 C O'Dwyer, *hld up, blun 4th, smooth hdwy four out, shaken up and wknd appr 2 out.*
.........................(5 to 2 fav op 2 to 1 tchd 11 to 4) 6

3751² BIG MATT (Ire) [144] 9-11-7 M A Fitzgerald, *hld up, not fluent 7th and sn hrd rdn, no response, tld off.*
.........................(4 to 1 op 3 to 1 tchd 9 to 2) 7

Dist: 2½l, nk, hd, 6l, 9l, dist. 3m 52.40s. a 4.40s (7 Ran).
SR: 46/45/45/51/35/36/-/ (Cumbrian Industrials Ltd), T D Easterby

3843 John Mowlem Novices' Handicap Chase Class C (6-y-o and up) £7,230 3m 110yds.................. (6:30)

3383* JULTARA (Ire) [105] 8-11-5 A P McCoy, *jmpd soundly, led to 3rd, led 5th, made rst, drw clr frm 4 out, eased nr finish.*
.............(4 to 1 op 7 to 2 tchd 9 to 2 and 5 to 1) 1

3702² GAELIC BLUE [92] 7-11-6 Richard Guest, *hld up, hdwy 13th, chsd wnr frm 5 out, sn no imprsn.*
.........................(11 to 4 fav op 3 to 1 tchd 9 to 4) 2

3732² DOMAINE DE PRON (Fr) [101] 6-11-1 R Bellamy, *hld up, effrt 14th, hit nxt, styd on wl frm last, nvr on terms.*
.............(13 to 2 op 6 to 1 tchd 7 to 1 and 8 to 1) 3

3207³ MR PICKPOCKET (Ire) [110] 9-11-10 J F Titley, *trkd ldrs frm 3rd, chsd wnr frm 11th to 5 out, sn wknd.*
.........................(14 to 1 op 10 to 1 tchd 16 to 1) 4

3679³ KEY TO MOYADE (Ire) [87] 7-10-1 N Williamson, *hld up, effrt 13th, no imprsn frm 15th.* (8 to 1 tchd 9 to 1 and 10 to 1) 5

3708⁵ BALLYDOUGAN (Ire) [86] (v) 9-10-0 T J Murphy, *hld up, pushed alng 6th, effrt to cl whn hit 11th, hrd rdn and sn struggling aftr, tld off.*.........................(66 to 1 op 33 to 1) 6

3744* GLENFINN PRINCESS [100] 9-11-0 (4ex) W Marston, *led 3rd to 5th, cl up, blun 12th, sn btn, tld off whn pld up bef 2 out.*
.........................(9 to 2 op 7 to 2 tchd 5 to 1) pu

3691² WEE WINDY (Ire) [108] 8-11-8 P Hide, *trkd ldrs till lost pl appr 11th, tld off whn pld up bef 2 out.*
.........................(7 to 1 op 6 to 1 tchd 8 to 1) pu

3504² GRIZZLY BEAR (Ire) [86] 7-10-0 J Culloty, *in tch, mstk 13th sn outpcd, tld off whn pld up bef 2 out.*
.........................(16 to 1 op 12 to 1) pu

Dist: 14l, 2½l, 9l, 9l, 14l. 6m 9.00s. a 8.00s (9 Ran).
SR: 35/8/14/14/-/-/ (Roger Barby), I P Williams

3844 Ernest Ireland Novices' Handicap Hurdle Class D (0-110 4 & 5-y-o) £3,420 2m 110yds...............(7:05)

3680* CHIEF MOUSE [100] 4-11-10 A P McCoy, *hld up beh ldrs, hdwy to ld 2 out, drvn out, jst held on.*
.........................(11 to 4 fav op 9 to 4) 1

3558⁵ ABOVE THE CUT (USA) [90] 5-11-6 C Llewellyn, *hld up beh ldrs, rdn and hdwy appr 2 out, str chal r-in, jst held.*
.............(6 to 1 op 5 to 1 tchd 13 to 2) 2

2957⁵ AMBIDEXTROUS (Ire) [86] 5-10-9 (7*) L Cummins, *hld up, hdwy to hold ev ch 2 out, one pace appr last.*
.........................(9 to 2 op 5 to 1 tchd 6 to 1) 3

1646⁴ COLOUR COUNSELLOR [81] 4-10-5 R Supple, *led, hit 3 out, hdd nxt, one pace.*.......(12 to 1 op 8 to 1 tchd 14 to 1) 4

3515* PROUD IMAGE [88] 5-11-4 R Dunwoody, *hld up beh ldrs, hdwy appr 3 out, btn nxt.*..(9 to 2 op 4 to 1 tchd 5 to 1) 5

2765⁷ FLOW BACK [70] 5-10-0 J R Kavanagh, *trkd ldrs, pushed alng 4 out, outpcd frm nxt.*
.........................(50 to 1 op 25 to 1 tchd 66 to 1) 6

3641⁵ MAETERLINCK (Ire) [83] 5-10-6 (7*) Clare Thorner, *chsd ldrs, hit 3 out, sn btn.*......(14 to 1 op 10 to 1 tchd 16 to 1) 7

3648² BATH KNIGHT [76] 4-10-0 D Morris, *hld up beh, hit 4th, nvr on terms.*.........(12 to 1 op 8 to 1 tchd 14 to 1) 8

3471⁴ WANSTEAD (Ire) [78] (bl) 5-10-8 N Williamson, *cl up, hrd rdn 3 out, wknd appr nxt.*........(12 to 1 op 7 to 1 tchd 14 to 1) 9

3610⁵ HEVER GOLF DIAMOND [90] 4-11-0 M A Fitzgerald, *mstk in rear 5th, pld up bef nxt.* (25 to 1 op 14 to 1 tchd 33 to 1) pu

Dist: Hd, 7l, 3l, 1½l, 10l, 1½l, 2l, 6l. 3m 58.80s. a 12.80s (10 Ran).
SR: 26/22/11/-/8/-/ (Bill Gavan), F Jordan

3845 Michael Page Novices' Chase Class C (6-y-o and up) £4,394 2m 4f 110yds...................(7:35)

SEA PATROL (bl) 10-11-5 M A Fitzgerald, *blun 7th, hdwy 12th, led 3 out, drvn out*......(6 to 1 tchd 5 to 1 and 13 to 2) 1

2593 UNCLE ALGY 8-11-5 J Culloty, *beh, hrd rdn aftr 9th, rapid hdwy frm 2 out, ran on wl, jst fld.*
.........................(100 to 30 op 5 to 2 tchd 7 to 2) 2

2804² BIT OF A DREAM 7-11-5 Richard Guest, *hld up, hdwy to ld 5 out, hdd 3 out, styd on one pace.*
.........................(8 to 1 op 7 to 1 tchd 9 to 1) 3

3195⁴ ONEOFUS 8-11-5 M Richards, *hit 6th and 8th, chlgd frm tenth, hit 3 out, sn wknd.*
.........................(14 to 1 op 25 to 1 tchd 33 to 1) 4

3813³ MOZEMO (bl) 10-11-5 A P McCoy, *led to 5th, led 8th to tenth, wknd rpdly 12th, tld off.*.........................(3 to 1 jt-fav op 11 to 4 tchd 5 to 2 and 100 to 30) 5

3669³ FORTRIA ROSIE DAWN 7-11-0 N Williamson, *not fluent, mstk 6th, beh whn t heavily 9th.*.........................(3 to 1 jt-fav op 5 to 2 tchd 100 to 30) f

3632³ BELLS WOOD 8-11-5 S McNeill, *in tch, hit 8th, beh whn blun and uns rdr 4 out.*......(16 to 1 op 10 to 1 tchd 20 to 1) ur

3668 HIGHLAND FLAME 8-11-2 (3*) P Henley, *led 5th to 6th, led tenth to 5 out, wknd 3 out, pld up bef last.*
.........................(33 to 1 op 25 to 1 tchd 40 to 1) pu

Dist: Nk, 4l, 17l, dist. 5m 2.80s. a 21.80s (8 Ran).
(S G Griffiths), S G Griffiths

3846 Meridian Tonight Novices' Hurdle Class C (5-y-o and up) £3,501 2½m ....(8:05)

3747* COUNTRY LOVER (v) 6-11-0 A P McCoy, *hld up, cld 7th, not fluent 4 out, pushed alng nxt, chlgd 2 out, hrd rdn and styd on wl to ld fnl 50 yards.*
........(5 to 4 on op 11 to 10 tchd 6 to 5 and 5 to 4) 1

3703⁷ SAMANID (Ire) 5-11-5 O Pears, *hld up, shaken up 3 out, smooth hdwy to ld nxt, clr last, jdded r-in, hdd fnl 50 yards, ran on.*.........................(10 to 1 op 8 to 1 tchd 12 to 1) 2

2661³ PHYSICAL FUN 6-11-0 R Dunwoody, *cl up, pushed alng aftr 7th, hrd rdn appr 2 out, one pace approaching last.*
.........................(11 to 2 op 4 to 1 tchd 6 to 1) 3

3555⁵ LEAP FROG 6-11-0 W Marston, *trkd ldrs, led 7th, hdd appr 2 out, sn wknd.*........(16 to 1 op 10 to 1 tchd 20 to 1) 4

3639² OVER THE WAY (Ire) 7-11-0 M A Fitzgerald, *led, hit 3rd, hdd 7th, led ag'n briefly appr 2 out, wknd betw last two.*
.........................(6 to 1 op 4 to 1) 5

3021² HARLEQUIN CHORUS 7-11-0 G Upton, *hld up in mid-div, wknd appr 2 out, eased. Better for run.*
.........................(14 to 1 op 10 to 1 tchd 16 to 1) 6

3735⁵ EDEN ROC 7-11-0 D Gallagher, *keen early, hld up, jmpd slwly 5th and sn pushed alng, rallied 7th, wknd 4 out, tld off.*
.........................(33 to 1 op 25 to 1 tchd 50 to 1) 7

3735² PAT BUCKLEY 6-11-0 C Llewellyn, *awkward 1st, trkd ldrs till lost pl appr 4 out, tld off.*........(12 to 1 op 8 to 1) 8

2694 THE PHANTOM FARMER (Ire) 6-11-0 J R Kavanagh, *hld up, lost tch 7th, tld off.*...............(33 to 1 op 20 to 1) 9

Dist: Nk, 8l, hd, sht-hd, 12l, 25l. 4m 59.10s. a 18.10s (9 Ran).
(Pond House Gold), M C Pipe

HUNTINGDON (good)
Tuesday April 29th
Going Correction: MINUS 0.15 sec. per fur.

3847 Robert Lenton Memorial Hunters' Chase Class H (5-y-o and up) £1,147 3m.........................(5:15)

3603³ KUSHBALOO 12-11-7 (7*) Mr A Parker, *trkd ldr 5th, led aftr 8th, rdn appr last, styd on wl r-in.*................(13 to 8 jt-fav op 6 to 4 tchd 15 to 8 and 2 to 1) 1

3690⁴ IDIOTIC 9-12-2 (5*) Mr C Vigors, *not fluent, hld up, prog 12th, rdn to chase wnr aftr 3 out, ev ch last, veered lft und pres r-in, not quicken.*........(13 to 8 jt-fav op 7 to 4 tchd 9 to 4) 2

3460⁷ DROMIN LEADER 12-12-2 (5*) Mr A Sansome, *keen hold, cl up, chsd wnr 11th, rdn appr 2 out, 3rd and hld whn mstk two out, wknd.*...........(6 to 1 op 4 to 1 tchd 13 to 2) 3

KINO 10-11-7 (7*) Mr Andrew Martin, *wtd wth, hmpd 12th and lost tch, rapid prog and mstk nxt, grad wknd frm 15th.*
.........................(10 to 1 op 5 to 1) 4

WOODY WILL 11-11-7 (7*) Mrs E Coveney, *in tch to 12th, sn wknd, tld off 3 out.*......(20 to 1 op 14 to 1 tchd 25 to 1) 5

TAMMY'S FRIEND (bl) 10-11-7 (7*) Mr J Ferguson, *not fluent, led till aftr 8th, mstk nxt, cl up whn uns rdr 12th.*
.........................(16 to 1 op 8 to 1 tchd 20 to 1) ur

Dist: 2l, 25l, 16l, dist. 6m 6.50s. a 26.50s (6 Ran).
(Mr & Mrs Raymond Anderson Green), C Parker

3848 Geoffrey Bevan Memorial Novices' Hunters' Chase Class H (5-y-o and up) £1,220 3m...............(5:45)

3666⁴ SECRET BAY 8-12-7 Mr S Swiers, *led to 4th, steadied, trkd ldr 8th, led 15th, sn clr, very easily.*
.........................(5 to 2 on op 2 to 1 on) 1

COOL BANDIT (bl) 7-11-7 (7*) Mr T Hills, *jmpd rght, led 6th to 15th, no ch wth wnr aftr, rdn 3 out.* (16 to 1 op 10 to 1 tchd 20 to 1) 2

TAU 12-11-7 (7*) Mr A Wart, *rear, lost tch 11th, kpt on und pres frm 3 out.*..........(40 to 1 op 12 to 1 tchd 50 to 1) 3

NOTARY-NOWELL (bl) 12-11-7 Mr R J Barrett, *mid-div, effrt to chase ldg pair 13th, no imprsn.* (50 to 1 op 14 to 1) 4

SMART PAL 12-11-7 (7*) Mrs F Needham, *chsd ldrs till wknd 12th, sn tld off.*.........................(50 to 1 op 14 to 1) 5

SPACE MOLLY (bl) 8-11-2 (7*) Mr P Cowley, *led 4th to 6th, wknd 8th, wl beh whn f 12th.*.........(25 to 1 op 20 to 1) f

BILLION DOLLARBILL 9-11-7 (7") Mr M Gorman, *sn pushed alng in rear, rdn and struggling tenth, tld off and pld up bef 3 out*.................(4 to 1 op 3 to 1 tchd 25 to 9 on) pu
CARDINAL RED (bl) 10-12-2 (5") Mr A Sansome, *prmnt till reluctant to race and lost pl rpdly frm tenth, tld off and pld up bef 15th*..................(11 to 1 op 10 to 1 tchd 14 to 1) pu
MR PINBALL (bl) 10-11-7 (7") Mr M Cowley, *not jump wl, sn tld off, pld up bef 16th*..(50 to 1 op 25 to 1 tchd 66 to 1) pu
3640 LOYAL GAIT (NZ) 9-11-7 (7") Mr Andrew Martin, *mstk 8th, al rear, tld off and pld up bef 16th.*
.................(25 to 1 op 10 to 1 tchd 33 to 1) pu
Dist: Dist, 3l, dist, dist. 6m 5.00s. a 25.00s (10 Ran).

(Stuart Dent), C P Dennis

3849 SPS Advertising Amateur Riders' Novices' Hurdle Class E (4-y-o and up) £2,250 2m 110yds....... (6:15)

3634⁴ REAL MADRID 6-11-7 (5") Mr J Jukes, *in tch, prog aftr 5th, chsd ldr 3 out, led nxt, ran on wl.*
...................(13 to 2 op 9 to 2 tchd 7 to 1) 1
3795 ABSOLUTE LIMIT 5-11-6 (7") Mr R Wakley, *led and sn wl clr, rdn and hdd 2 out, btn whn mstk last.*
............(11 to 8 fav op 7 to 4 tchd 2 to 1 and 5 to 4) 2
3258³ UNDAWATERSCUBADIVA 5-10-13 (7") Mr A Wintle, *in tch, rdn and one pace frm 3 out*...........(9 to 2 tchd 11 to 2) 3
2792 GREG'S PROFILES 6-11-3 (3") Mr M Rimell, *chsd ldr till aftr 3rd and ag'n frm 5th till mstk 3 out, btn whn mistake nxt.*
.................(16 to 1 op 10 to 1 tchd 20 to 1) 4
2859⁸ BATHWICK BOBBIE 10-11-3⁴ (7") Mr J Naylor, *chsd ldrs till wknd aftr 3rd, sn beh.*..............(50 to 1 op 20 to 1) 5
2959 CLERIC ON BROADWAY (Ire) 9-10-12 (3") Mr C Bonner, *wl beh frm 3rd, nvr dngrs aftr.*.........(20 to 1 op 16 to 1) 6
3809² GI MOSS (bl) 10-10-12⁴ (7") Mr B Harriss, *strted slwly and sn tld off, nvr a factor*.................(33 to 1 op 16 to 1) 7
3743³ NELL VALLEY 6-10-8 (7") Mr E James, *rear, lost tch wth ldrs 4th, no ch aftr*........(16 to 1 op 14 to 1 tchd 20 to 1) 8
3382 GLIDE PATH (USA) 8-10-13 (7") Dr M Mannish, *strted slwly, prog to chase ldr aftr 3rd till 5th, sn wknd.* (7 to 2 op 2 to 1) 9
Dist: 11l, 9l, 4l, 5l, 5l, hd, 4l, 4l, 4l. 3m 45.60s. a 4.60s (9 Ran).
SR: 22/18/2/-/-/-/   (Chris Wall), G P Enright

3850 Huntingdon Restricted Series Novices' Hunters' Chase Final Class H (5-y-o and up) £1,548 3m..... (6:50)

3640¹ STRUGGLES GLORY (Ire) 6-12-0 (7") Mr D C Robinson, *led to second, led 8th, drw clr 2 out, ran on strly.*
.............(13 to 8 on op 5 to 2 on tchd 6 to 4 on) 1
MISTER SPECTATOR (Ire) 8-12-1 (3") Mr Simon Andrews, *led second to 8th, pressed wnr aftr, mstk 12th, ev ch 3 out, wknd nxt, wl btn whn blun last...* (2 to 1 op 3 to 1 tchd 7 to 2) 2
TAURA'S RASCAL 8-11-7 (7") Mr F Brennan, *trkd ldrs, blun 12th, rdn and in tch 15th, wknd 2 out, fnshd tired.*
.................(12 to 1 tchd 14 to 1 and 16 to 1) 3
BALLYALLIA CASTLE (Ire) 8-11-7 (7") Mr N Bloom, *chsd ldrs till blun badly 12th, sn wl beh, styd on frm 3 out, nvr nrr.*
......................(20 to 1 op 8 to 1) 4
GREYBURY STAR (Ire) 9-11-7 (7") Mr P Bull, *chsd ldrs, struggling whn mstk 12th, sn lost tch....* (50 to 1 op 16 to 1) 5
GRASSINGTON (Ire) 8-11-7 (7") Mr Scott Quirk, *al rear, no ch frm 11th.*....................(50 to 1 op 16 to 1) 6
TARRY AWHILE 11-11-10³ (7") Mr J Connell, *sn pushed alng in mid-div, lost tch frm 11th, no ch aftr.*
.....................(25 to 1 tchd 33 to 1) 7
CURRENT ATTRACTION 11-11-2 (7") Miss C Tuke, *al rear, tld off 14th, pld up aftr 3 out*...........(50 to 1 op 25 to 1) pu
GIVE IT A BASH (Ire) 9-11-2 (7") Mr T Moore, *chsd ldrs, jmpd slwly 11th, sn wknd, tld off and pld up bef 2 out.*
.................(50 to 1 op 25 to 1) pu
SOME TOURIST (Ire) 9-11-7 (7") Mr N Benstead, *slwly into strd, al beh, tld off and pld up bef 2 out*..(50 to 1 op 20 to 1) pu
Dist: 20l, 3l, 5l, 9l, 4l, 29l. 6m 5.80s. a 25.80s (10 Ran).

(D C Robinson), D C Robinson

3851 Dr. Wakes-Miller 60th Birthday Hunters' Chase Class H (5-y-o and up) £1,239 2½m 110yds...... (7:20)

2974¹ SLIEVENAMON MIST 11-12-2 (5") Mr J Jukes, *hld up, prog to chase ldg pair 11th, led appr 2 out where mstk, drvn clr.*
.............(11 to 4 on op 9 to 4 on tchd 2 to 1 on) 1
COUNTERBID (bl) 10-11-9 (5") Mr A Sansome, *chsd ldr 5th, rdn and ev ch appr 2 out, unbl to quicken.*
.................(10 to 1 op 14 to 1 tchd 16 to 1) 2
2960 MY YOUNG MAN 12-11-7 (7") Mr E James, *led and set gd pace, mstk 9th, hdd and wknd appr 2 out.*
.................(12 to 1 tchd 14 to 1 and 16 to 1) 3
2992⁴ KAMBALDA RAMBLER 13-11-7 (7") Mr R Armson, *mid-div, lost tch wth ldrs tenth, kpt on one pace frm 3 out, no dngr.*
..................(6 to 1 op 3 to 1) 4
3671⁴ NOT MY LINE (Ire) 8-12-0 (5") Mr W Wales, *chsd ldrs, no prog frm 12th*............(12 to 1 op 14 to 1 tchd 33 to 1) 5
3733 CANDLE GLOW 9-11-7 (7") Mr P Hutchinson, *mstks, chsd ldr to 5th, prmnt till wknd 12th.*
.................(16 to 1 op 14 to 1 tchd 20 to 1) 6

3733⁵ TUDOR FABLE (Ire) 9-11-12 (7") Mr Rupert Sweeting, *mid-div, lost tch whn mstk 9th, no dngr aftr.*
.................(25 to 1 op 14 to 1 tchd 33 to 1) 7
THE LORRYMAN (Ire) 9-11-7 (7") Mr N R Mitchell, *mstks, mid-div, lost tch 9th, tld off.* (33 to 1 op 20 to 1 tchd 50 to 1) 8
KILLIMOR LAD 10-11-7 (7") Miss S Samworth, *al beh, tld off frm 9th*...............(50 to 1 op 20 to 1 tchd 66 to 1) 9
3586 FISH QUAY 14-11-7 (7") Miss S Lamb, *al beh, tld off frm 9th.*
..................(50 to 1 tchd 100 to 1) 10
BASHER BILL 14-11-7 (7") Mrs E Coveney, *al beh, last & tld off whn pld up aftr 11th*..........(50 to 1 op 33 to 1) pu
3775⁴ UPWARD SURGE (Ire) 7-11-7 (7") Mrs N Ledger, *chsd ldrs to tenth, sn wknd, tld off and pld up bef 2 out.*
..................(50 to 1 op 33 to 1) pu
MAKING TIME 10-11-2 (7") Miss T Habgood, *mstks, al beh, tld off and pld up bef 13th*..........(33 to 1 op 14 to 1) pu
LUCKY LANDING (Ire) 8-11-7 (7") Mr Andrew Martin, *mid-div, lost tch 9th, tld off and pld up bef 12th.*
..................(50 to 1 op 40 to 1 tchd 66 to 1) pu
Dist: 9l, 13l, 8l, 12l, 4l, 2l, 17l, ¾l, 5l. 5m 1.90s. a 14.90s (14 Ran).

(Nick Viney), Victor Dartnall

3852 East Anglian Daily Times Amateur Riders' Handicap Hurdle Class E (0-115 4-y-o and up) £2,337 2m 5f 110yds...................... (7:50)

3761⁹ ABLE PLAYER (USA) [86] 10-10-10 (7") Mr K Drewry, *trkd ldr 5th, led aftr 3 out, ran on wl r-in.*
..................(4 to 1 op 3 to 1 tchd 9 to 2) 1
3731* SNOWSHILL SHAKER [91] 8-11-5 (3") Mr M Rimell, *keen hold, trkd ldrs, rdn and mstk 2 out, ev ch last, not quicken.*
..................(6 to 4 on op 2 to 1 on tchd Evens) 2
3761 PERSIAN VIEW (Ire) [97] 7-11-7 (7") Mr R Wakley, *trkd ldr, led 4th till aftr 3 out, ev ch last, unbl to quicken and pres.*
..................(8 to 1 op 5 to 1) 3
3559 KING'S SHILLING (USA) [83] 10-10-7 (7") Mr N H Oliver, *wtd wth, effrt 7th, no imprsn on ldrs aftr 3 out.*
..................(12 to 1 op 7 to 1) 4
3325⁵ SCRIPT [69] 6-9-12¹ (3") Mr C Bonner, *in tch, rdn 7th, sn struggling, no ch whn mstk 2 out.*
..................(9 to 2 op 10 to 1 tchd 12 to 1 and 4 to 1) 5
3725 PRIME DISPLAY (USA) [96] 11-11-6 (7") Mr S Sporborg, *led to 4th, wknd 7th, tld off....*(33 to 1 op 16 to 1 tchd 40 to 1) 6
Dist: 2½l, 3l, 9l, 8l, dist. 5m 0.50s. a 11.50s (6 Ran).

(K J Drewry), K J Drewry

CHELTENHAM (good to firm)
Wednesday April 30th
Going Correction: PLUS 0.20 sec. per fur.

3853 Evesham Maiden Hunters' Chase Class H (5-y-o and up) £1,873 2m 5f .... (5:25)

3300² VITAL SONG 10-11-7 (7") Mr G Matthews, *made all, lft clr 13th, mstk nxt, ran on wl frm 2 out.*
..................(11 to 2 op 9 to 2 tchd 6 to 1) 1
3567³ ARDBRENNAN 10-11-7 (7") Mr E James, *hid up, prog whn mstk 11th, lft second 13th, rdn appr 3 out, unbl to quicken frm nxt.*.........(7 to 1 op 6 to 1 tchd 15 to 2) 2
3153 CLOBRACKEN LAD 9-11-7 (7") Mr G Baines, *not jump wl, in tch, rdn 11th, sn outpcd, styd on well aftr 3 out.*
..................(20 to 1 op 16 to 1) 3
DOUBLE THRILLER 7-11-11 (3") Mr R Treloggen, *sn cl up, chsd wnr 9th, mstk nxt, shaken up and one pace aftr 4 out.*
..................(6 to 5 fav op 6 to 4 tchd 11 to 10) 4
3727⁴ ORTON HOUSE 10-11-7 (7") Mr R Burton, *prmnt to 8th, wkng whn mstk 11th, tld off when hmpd 14th.* (33 to 1 op 20 to 1) 5
VERY DARING 7-11-7 (7") Miss S Sharratt, *beh frm 8th, tld off whn hmpd 14th.*..............(50 to 1 op 33 to 1) 6
WELL BANK 10-11-7 (7") Mr E Walker, *mstks, in tch till rdn and wknd 11th, no ch whn f 14th.*
..................(66 to 1 op 33 to 1 tchd 100 to 1) f
BROAD STEANE 8-11-9 (5") Mr A Sansome, *trkd wnr 5th to 9th and frm 11th, cl second whn f 13th.*
..................(6 to 1 op 5 to 1 tchd 13 to 2) f
TREVVEETHAN (Ire) 8-11-11 (3") Mr M Rimell, *mstk 1st, hld up, prog 8th, sn in tch whn hmpd and uns rdr 13th.*
..................(20 to 1 tchd 33 to 1) bd
3640⁵ BERRINGS DASHER 10-11-7 (7") Mr M Watson, *prog tenth, no imprsn on ldrs aftr 4 out, fith and wl btn whn pld up nr finish, dismounted....* (25 to 1 op 16 to 1 tchd 33 to 1) pu
Dist: 4l, 6l, 2l, dist, dist. 5m 18.70s. a 14.70s (10 Ran).

(G Matthews), M H Dare

3854 Colin Nash Memorial United Hunts' Challenge Cup Hunters' Chase Class H (6-y-o and up) £2,232 3m 1f 110yds...................... (6:00)

3746² MISS MILLBROOK 9-11-5 (7") Mr E Williams, *trkd ldr 7th, led 12th till mstk 15th, rdn and mistake 4 out, rallied to ld 2 out, drvn out.*..................(11 to 10 fav op 5 to 4 on) 1

538

3426[5] GLEN OAK 12-11-10 (7*) Mr J M Pritchard, *wtd wth, pushed alng aftr 11th, prog to chase ldrs 13th, not quicken after 3 out, styd on to chase wnr r-in.* (11 to 2 op 9 to 2 tchd 13 to 2) 2
HILL ISLAND 10-11-10 (7*) Mr Rupert Sweeting, *led 6th to 12th, led ag'n 15th, rdn and hdd 2 out, no extr last*. .... (15 to 8 op 2 to 1 tchd 7 to 4) 3
CAVALERO 8-11-10 (7*) Mr A Charles-Jones, *blun second, in tch, chsd ldrs 12th, cl 4th whn mstk 3 out, sn btn, eased r-in.* .... (20 to 1 op 33 to 1 tchd 40 to 1) 4
J B LAD 11-11-10 (7*) Miss P Gundry, *mstks, led 4th till 6th, wkng whn blun 14th, tld off and pld up bef 17th.* .... (33 to 1 tchd 40 to 1 and 50 to 1) pu
3426[7] TEATRADER 11-11-10 (7*) Miss T Blazey, *led to 4th, wknd 12th, tld off and pld up bef 3 out*....... (25 to 1 op 16 to 1) pu
Dist: 3l, 2½l, 30l. 6m 40.60s. a 25.60s (6 Ran).
(D T Goldsworthy), D T Goldsworthy

3855 Wragge & Co Hunters' Chase Class H (5-y-o and up) £4,260 4m 1f (6:35)

3690[3] RUSTY BRIDGE 10-11-11 (7*) Mr R Burton, *led to 20th, pressed ldr aftr, rdn 4 out, led ag'n last, drvn and hld on gmely*............ (4 to 1 jt-fav tchd 9 to 2 and 5 to 1) 1
3690[6] THE MALAKARMA 11-11-13 (5*) Mr B Pollock, *chsd wnr to 12th, rdn to go second ag'n 18th, led 20th, sn hrd ridden, hdd last, styd on gmely*.................... (5 to 1 op 4 to 1) 2
3690[5] YOUNG BRAVE 11-12-0 (7*) Mr M G Miller, *wtd wth, prog gng easily 18th, trkd ldg pair 22nd, ch 4 out, rdn and one pace aftr.* .... (5 to 1 tchd 11 to 2) 3
3096[2] LOYAL NOTE 9-12-1 (3*) Mr Simon Andrews, *chsd ldrs, pushed alng 18th, blun 22nd, rdn and no imprsn nxt.* .... (6 to 1 op 7 to 2) 4
3426[6] ARTFUL ARTHUR 11-11-7 (7*) Mr J Grassick, *beh, lost tch 14th, rdn and tld off 17th, styd on frm 23rd, no dngr.* .... (50 to 1 op 33 to 1 tchd 66 to 1) 5
3640[2] LURRIGA GLITTER (Ire) (bl) 9-11-7 (7*) Mr R Wakley, *prog to chase ldrs 8th, no imprsn frm 17th, one pace from 22nd.* .... (7 to 1 op 6 to 1) 6
KETTLES 10-11-2 (7*) Mr A Phillips, *not al fluent, wtd wth, effrt aftr 15th, nvr rch ldrs, no ch frm 22nd*............ (4 to 1 jt-fav op 5 to 1) 7
3578[4] K C'S DANCER 12-11-7 (7*) Mr J M Pritchard, *chsd wnr 12th till 20th, wknd 4 out, beh whn pld up bef 2 out.* .... (9 to 1 op 7 to 1 tchd 10 to 1) pu
3460[3] SAINT BENE'T (Ire) (v) 9-11-7 (7*) Mr A Coe, *rdn 8th, al beh, tld off 17th, pld up bef 3 out*.................... (20 to 1) pu
3004[6] MOBILE MESSENGER (NZ) 9-11-7 (7*) Miss S Samworth, *al beh, tld off frm 17th, pld up r-in, lme.* .... (33 to 1 op 12 to 1 tchd 50 to 1) pu
Dist: 1¼l, 13l, 12l, 5l, 2½l, 8l. 8m 37.40s. a 20.40s (10 Ran).
(I K Johnson), Mrs S M Johnson

3856 Cheltenham Champion Hunters' Chase Class H (5-y-o and up) £4,026 3¼m 110yds.................. (7:10)

3605 CELTIC ABBEY 9-11-7 (7*) Mr D S Jones, *trkd ldr, led 15th, drw rght away aftr 3 out, imprsv.* .... (11 to 8 op 11 to 10 tchd 6 to 4) 1
3690* DOUBLE SILK 13-12-3 (3*) Mr R Treloggen, *led to 15th, sn rdn, one pace aftr 3 out, eased whn no ch r-in.* .... (5 to 4 fav tchd 11 to 8) 2
3313[3] RYMING CUPLET 12-11-10 (7*) Mr L Jefford, *chsd ldrs, blun 5th, lost tch ldg pair frm 14th, sn beh*.....(8 to 1 op 7 to 2) 3
3690[2] SOME-TOY 11-11-10 (7*) Miss L Blackford, *chsd ldrs, mstk 9th, struggling frm 12th, sn tld off*.......(15 to 2 op 8 to 1) 4
Dist: 30l, 14l, 2½l. 6m 44.90s. a 12.90s (4 Ran).
SR: 24/ (G J Powell), Miss Venetia Williams

3857 Golden Harvest Hunters' Chase Class H (5-y-o and up) £2,274 2m 5f .... (7:45)

3274* TINOTOPS 7-11-7 (7*) Miss S Vickery, *cl up, trkd ldr 11th, led aftr 3 out, drvn out r-in*.... (7 to 4 op 5 to 4 tchd 15 to 8) 1
3274 KNIFEBOARD 11-11-7 (7*) Mr J M Pritchard, *wtd wth in rear, gd prog frm tenth, mstk 4 out, chsd wnr and mistake last, ran on*.............. (14 to 1 op 12 to 1) 2
3723* MY NOMINEE (bl) 9-12-0 (7*) Mr R Burton, *jmpd rght, made most till aftr 3 out, rdn and unbl to quicken.* .... (11 to 10 on op 5 to 4) 3
GREENWINE (USA) 11-11-7 (7*) Miss L Blackford, *cl up, chsd ldr 9th til jmpd slwly nxt, rdn and not quicken aftr 4 out.* .... (20 to 1 op 16 to 1 tchd 25 to 1) 4
3790[9] FIGHT TO WIN (USA) 9-11-7 (7*) Mr J Grassick, *prmnt, ev ch and gng easily 13th, fdd aftr 4 out.* .... (33 to 1 op 20 to 1 tchd 40 to 1) 5
3733 FRANK BE LUCKY 11-11-11 (3*) Mr R Thornton, *pressed ldr to 9th, cl up aftr til rdn and wknd after 4 out.* .... (14 to 1 tchd 16 to 1) 6
TARA BOY 12-11-7 (7*) Mr R Cambray, *rear, jmpd slwly 5th, rdn 8th, sn wl beh, kpt on und pres frm 3 out.* .... (33 to 1 op 20 to 1) 7
3723 SIMPLY PERFECT 11-11-7 (7*) Miss K Swindells, *mstk 6th, lost pl 8th, nvr on terms aftr.* .... (25 to 1 op 16 to 1 tchd 33 to 1) 8
3611[4] FLOWING RIVER (USA) 11-11-7 (7*) Mr N R Mitchell, *mid-div, lost tch wth ldrs 12th, no prog aftr.* .... (50 to 1 op 33 to 1 tchd 66 to 1) 9
GREAT POKEY 12-11-7 (7*) Miss N Courtenay, *alwys rear, tld off frm 13th*........................(25 to 1 op 12 to 1) 10
LEIGH BOY (USA) 11-11-7 (7*) Mr N H Oliver, *reminder 6th, beh frm tenth, tld off and pld up bef 2 out.* .... (33 to 1 op 25 to 1 tchd 40 to 1) pu
ORUJO (Ire) 9-11-11 (3*) Mr A Hill, *mstks, beh, effrt tenth, sn btn, tld off and pld up bef 2 out*.........(25 to 1 op 14 to 1) pu
Dist: 2l, 1¼l, 9l, 4l, 9l, 2½l, 2½l, sht-hd, 30l. 5m 20.20s. a 16.20s (12 Ran).
(R H H Targett), Mrs R A Vickery

3858 Overbury Hunters' Chase Class H (5-y-o and up) £2,190 2m 110yds (8:20)

3733[2] PRO BONO (Ire) 7-11-13 (5*) Mr A Sansome, *hld up in cl tch, mstk 5th, led 3 out, pushed clr last, hrd rdn and kpt on nr finish*.............. (6 to 4 fav op 7 to 4 tchd 11 to 8) 1
MASTER CRUSADER 11-11-7 (7*) Mr S Durack, *hld up last, gd prog to press wnr 3 out, ev ch nxt, rallied and edgd lft r-in, styd on*.................... (20 to 1 op 10 to 1) 2
FANTASTIC FLEET (Ire) 5-11-5 (3*) Mr R Thornton, *mstks, led 3rd till 7th, mistake 4 out and lost pl, rallied und pres appr 2 out, sn not quicken*.................... (5 to 2 op 3 to 1) 3
3464[2] FAMILIAR FRIEND (bl) 11-12-0 (7*) Mr L Lay, *led to 3rd, led 7th till 3 out, wknd appr last*..(6 to 1 op 7 to 2 tchd 13 to 2) 4
3591* NECTANEBO (Ire) 9-11-11 (7*) Mr M Frith, *keen hold, hld up, in tch whn uns rdr 7th.* (100 to 30 op 2 to 1 tchd 7 to 2) ur
Dist: 1½l, 6l, 2½l. 4m 21.90s. a 28.90s (5 Ran).
(P C Caudwell), Andy Morgan

EXETER (good to firm)
Wednesday April 30th
Going Correction: MINUS 0.10 sec. per fur.

3859 Portman Fixed Interest Bond Novices' Selling Hurdle Class G (4 - 7-y-o) £1,767 2¼m................ (2:20)

3692[5] KILLING TIME 6-12-0 D J Burchell, *trkd ldrs, chsd lder aftr 3 out, slight lead 2 out, drvn out.* .... (11 to 8 fav op 5 to 4 tchd 6 to 4) 1
3619[6] MIRAMARE 7-10-7 (7*) J Harris, *chsd ldr till slight ld 3rd, rdn frm 3 out, hdd nxt, wknd and wndrd appr last.* .... (6 to 1 op 7 to 1) 2
3686[4] CHILI HEIGHTS (v) 7-10-7 (7*) M Griffiths, *led to 3rd, styd wth ldr to 3 out, wknd quickly appr nxt.* .... (100 to 30 op 3 to 1 tchd 7 to 2) 3
2782 MOOR DUTCH 6-11-0 J Frost, *fractious and dived off course and virtually refused to race, continued tld off till f 4th.* .... (14 to 1 op 10 to 1) f
2545[4] COUNTRY COUSIN 5-10-7 (7*) L Cummins, *wnt lft and dived off track strt and virtually refused to race, continued tld off till pld up bef 3 out and dismounted*........ (7 to 2 op 9 to 4) pu
Dist: 7l, 24l. 4m 6.90s. a 7.90s (5 Ran).
SR: 3/-/ (Simon T Lewis), D Burchell

3860 Royal Navy 'National Hunt' Novices' Hurdle Class E (5-y-o and up) £2,367 2¼m........................ (2:55)

3709 COLONEL BLAZER 5-11-7 J F Titley, *trkd ldrs, wnt second aftr 3 out, led nxt, cmftbly.* ....(5 to 2 on tchd 9 to 4 on and 11 to 4 on) 1
2179[6] BLOWING ROCK (Ire) 5-11-0 J Culloty, *trkd ldr till led 3rd, hdd 2 out, sn outpcd*....... (7 to 1 op 5 to 1 tchd 8 to 1) 2
3735[8] FOOLS FUTURE 8-11-0 M A Fitzgerald, *led and veered badly rght 1st till hdd 3rd, continued badly right at each flight and one pace frm 3 out*...... (12 to 1 op 9 to 1 tchd 14 to 1) 3
MR CELEBRATION 6-11-0 C Llewellyn, *beh, lost tch frm 3rd, tld off*.................... (6 to 1 op 3 to 1) 4
2699 LIZZYS FIRST 5-10-9 (5*) D Salter, *sn wl beh, tld off 3rd, pld up bef 5th*............(25 to 1 op 20 to 1 tchd 33 to 1) pu
Dist: 6l, 7l, dist. 4m 11.70s. a 12.70s (5 Ran).
(Exors Of The Late Mr T H Shrimpton), Miss H C Knight

3861 Portman Financial Planners Novices' Chase Class D (5-y-o and up) £4,117 2m 7f 110yds......... (3:30)

2480 THUNDER ROAD (Ire) 6-11-2 J Culloty, *hld up, mstk 8th, hdwy 9th, trkd ldr 3 out, led last, cmftbly.* .... (5 to 2 op 3 to 1 tchd 7 to 2) 1
3016 OTTER PRINCE 8-10-13 (3*) Mr R Thornton, *hdwy 9th, chlgd tenth, lft in ld nxt, hdd last, sn btn*....(14 to 1 tchd 20 to 1) 2
1321[6] SEACHEST 8-10-11 S Burrough, *led, pld hrd, hdd 3rd, styd prmnt, chsd leeader 11th to 3 out, sn outpcd.* .... (16 to 1 op 10 to 1 tchd 20 to 1) 3
3649 RUSTIC FLIGHT 10-10-9 (7*) M Griffiths, *al beh, mstk 7th, tld off nxt*............... (20 to 1 op 10 to 1 tchd 33 to 1) 4
3649[2] DUNLIR 7-11-2 M Sharratt, *f second.* (20 to 1 op 14 to 1) f
3682* SPRING TO IT 11-11-8 D Walsh, *led 3rd, sn drvn alng, blun and uns rdr 11th*............(11 to 10 fav op 11 to 8 on) ur

3593^{3} SOMETHING CATCHY (Ire) 7-10-11 W Marston, *chsd ldrs to 11th, sn wknd, tld off whn pld up bef 4 out.* ....(7 to 1 op 6 to 1 tchd 8 to 1) pu
Dist: 4l, 6l, dist. 5m 45.80s. a 11.80s (7 Ran).
(Mrs Peter Andrews), Miss H C Knight

3862 Portman Instant Access Handicap Chase Class D (0-125 5-y-o and up) £3,844 2m 3f 110yds......... (4:00)

3685^{2} HENLEY REGATTA [94] 9-10-10 S Burrough, *hld up, steady hdwy to ld 4 out, sn clr, blun last, easily.* ....(7 to 2 op 3 to 1 tchd 4 to 1) 1
3545^{4} BISHOPS CASTLE (Ire) [90] 9-10-6 J Frost, *chsd ldrs, chlgd 8 to tenth, outpcd 4 out, styd on ag'n to take second appr last, no ch wth wnr.* ....(3 to 1 op 5 to 2 tchd 100 to 30 and 7 to 2) 2
3472^{2} MR CONDUCTOR (Ire) [108] 6-11-10 M A Fitzgerald, *made most to 5th, jmpd slwly 7th, styd prmnt till lost pos tenth, ran on ag'n frm 2 out*..........(2 to 1 fav tchd 5 to 2) 3
3425^{3} LACKENDARA [100] 10-11-2 J Culloty, *wth ldr till led 5th, hdd 4 out, wknd nxt, broke blood vessel*......(3 to 1 op 2 to 1) 4
[illegible] RUSTIC GENT (Ire) [84] 9-10-0 D J Burchell, *beh and jmpd slwly 6th, chlgd 8th till blun and wknd tenth.* ....(12 to 1 tchd 10 to 1) 5
Dist: 12l, 2l, 7l, dist. 4m 37.30s. (5 Ran).
SR: 19/3/19/4/-/ (E T Wey), P R Rodford

3863 Portman Fixed Rate Mortgage Handicap Hurdle Class E (0-110 4-y-o and up) £2,528 2m 3f 110yds......(4:30)

3692^{2} MYSTIC HILL [90] 6-11-3 J Frost, *trkd ldr till chlgd frm 3 out, rdn appr last, led r-in, drvn out*... (3 to 1 on op 2 to 1 on) 1
3105^{7} SHEEP STEALER [80] 9-10-7 M A Fitzgerald, *led, rdn appr last, hdd r-in, styd on same pace.* ....(6 to 1 op 7 to 1 tchd 8 to 1) 2
582^{2} MISS SOUTER [73] 8-9-11 (3*) Mr R Thornton, *chsd ldrs, jmpd slwly 4th, rdn 3 out, styd on same pace frm nxt.* ....(12 to 1 op 7 to 1) 3
3136^{6} VISCOUNT TULLY [73] 12-10-0 Miss S Jackson, *al in rear.* ....(14 to 1 op 6 to 1) 4
PERSISTENT GUNNER [78] 7-10-5 T Dascombe, *keen hold, chlgd 3 out, wknd nxt*... (14 to 1 op 8 to 1 tchd 16 to 1) 5
Dist: ¾l, 6l, 22l, hd. 4m 28.50s. (5 Ran).
(Jack Joseph), R G Frost

3864 Royal Marines Conditional Jockeys' Novices' Handicap Hurdle Class F (0-100 4-y-o and up) £1,906 2¼m .... (5:00)

3462* GEISWAY (Can) [84] 7-11-7 X Aizpuru, *hld up, al gng wl, chlgd on bit frm 2 out till led last, cmftbly.* ....(9 to 4 op 2 to 1 tchd 11 to 4) 1
3648* SAFECRACKER [75] 4-10-6 P Henley, *chsd ldrs, chlgd frm 5th till led 2 out, rdn and hdd last, sn outpcd.* ....(6 to 1 op 7 to 2) 2
3619* PIPER'S ROCK (Ire) [87] 6-11-10 A Bates, *led, pushed alng frm 3rd, hdd 3 out, sn outpcd.* ...... (13 to 8 fav op 6 to 4 tchd 15 to 8 and 2 to 1) 3
1978^{6} LYPHARD'S FABLE (USA) [64] 6-10-1 T Dascombe, *dsptd ld to second, styd frnt rnk till led 3 out, hdd 2 out, sn btn.* ....(5 to 1 op 8 to 1 tchd 10 to 1) 4
3814* CONTRACT BRIDGE (Ire) [87] 4-11-4 (7ex) Sophie Mitchell, *hld up, hdwy 3rd, outpcd 5th, styd on ag'n frm 2 out.* ....(13 to 2 op 4 to 1 tchd 7 to 1) 5
3485^{9} RORY'M (Ire) [63] (v) 8-10-0 M Griffiths, *sn wl beh, tld off whn pld up bef 3 out*..........(100 to 1 op 25 to 1) pu
Dist: 5l, 4l, 3½l, 1¾l. 4m 8.40s. a 9.40s (6 Ran).
(Paul Green), N J H Walker

KELSO (good to firm)
Wednesday April 30th
Going Correction: MINUS 0.20 sec. per fur. (races 1,3,5), MINUS 0.45 (2,4,6)

3865 Sunlaws Moet & Chandon Novices' Chase Class D (5-y-o and up) £3,420 2m 1f........................(5:45)

3699* AMERICAN HERO 9-11-10 B Storey, *jmpd wl, made all, drw clr frm last*.......... (6 to 4 on tchd 5 to 4 on) 1
3699^{2} SINGING SAND 7-11-10 R Dunwoody, *trkd ldr, mstk 4th, rdn aftr last, no imprsn*...... (11 to 8 op 6 to 4 tchd 7 to 4) 2
3202^{3} BOLD ACCOUNT (Ire) 7-11-5 M Foster, *sn beh, wnt moderate 3rd aftr 8th, soon outpcd by 1st 2.* .... (14 to 1 op 8 to 1 tchd 16 to 1) 3
3584^{9} NOBODYS FLAME (Ire) 9-11-0 G Cahill, *beh and rdn aftr 4th, lost tch frm 7th, tld off*..........(125 to 1 op 50 to 1) 4
3662^{4} SUPERMARINE 11-11-0 G Lee, *chsd ldrs to hfwy, losing tch whn blun and uns rdr 2 out.* ....(100 to 1 op 50 to 1 tchd 150 to 1) ur
3758 KINCARDINE BRIDGE (USA) 8-10-7 (7*) Mr M Bradburne, *chasing ldrs whn blun and uns rdr 8th.* ....(150 to 1 op 50 to 1) ur
Dist: 14l, 25l, dist. 4m 5.90s. a 0.90s (6 Ran).
SR: 53/39/9/ (Mrs R P Aggio), R Allan

3866 Scotsman Maiden Hurdle Class D (4-y-o and up) £2,899 2m 110yds (6:15)

3029^{2} CARLISLE BANDITO'S (Ire) 5-11-5 D Parker, *trkd ldrs, led aftr last, styd on und pres*..........(Evens fav op 11 to 10) 1
3655^{3} CAUGHT AT LAST (Ire) 6-11-5 G Cahill, *prmnt, led aftr 3 out, edgd lft und pres and hdd after last, no extr.* ....(7 to 1 op 5 to 1 tchd 8 to 1) 2
3757^{5} HAND OF STRAW (Ire) 5-11-5 K Johnson, *mid-div, rdn aftr 5th, hdwy and ev ch bef 2 out, kpt on same pace frm last.* .... (11 to 2 op 4 to 1 tchd 6 to 1) 3
3757 LUMBACK LADY 7-11-0 B Storey, *hld up, hdwy hfwy, ch bef 2 out, rdn betw last two, sn btn*.......... (9 to 1 op 7 to 1) 4
3703 JAUNTY GENERAL 6-11-5 R Supple, *towards rear, styd on frm 3 out, nvr able to chal*..........(20 to 1 op 12 to 1) 5
2262^{8} LOST IN THE POST (Ire) 4-11-0 M Foster, *towards rear, styd on frm 2 out, nrst fnsh*.......... (20 to 1 op 12 to 1) 6
3663^{6} AMBER HOLLY 8-11-0 F Perratt, *sn tracking ldrs, ch 2 out, soon rdn, fdd*..........(25 to 1 op 20 to 1 tchd 33 to 1) 7
3663^{4} DONT FORGET CURTIS (Ire) 5-10-12 (7*) Miss S Lamb, *nvr dngrs*..........(33 to 1 op 25 to 1) 8
3657^{8} I'M TYSON (NZ) 9-11-0 (5*) R McGrath, *made most till hdd aftr 3 out, sn wknd*..........(12 to 1) 9
1280^{8} TEDDY EDWARD 7-10-12 (7*) Mr T J Barry, *trkd ldrs, rdn aftr 3 out, sn wknd*..........(50 to 1) 10
3583 TOPUP 4-10-9 (5*) S Taylor, *sn beh, tld off*........(100 to 1) 11
3003 RESPECTING 4-11-0 N Smith, *pld hrd early, sn beh, tld off.* ....(100 to 1) 12
3667^{7} DUNNELLIE 4-10-9 T Reed, *sn lost tch, wl tld off.* ....(66 to 1 op 50 to 1) 13
Dist: 3½l, 6l, 3½l, 8l, 6l, 2½l, 2½l, 3l, 14l, dist. 3m 45.50s. a 2.50s (13 Ran).
(Chris Deuters), J Berry

3867 Mason Organisation Centre Attraction Handicap Chase Class D for the Haddington Jubilee Cup (0-120 5-y-o and up) £3,986 3m 1f....... (6:50)

3758 NIJWAY [85] 7-10-0 B Storey, *trkd ldrs, led 14th, hrd pressed aftr last, styd on wl und pres*..........(6 to 1 op 5 to 1) 1
3601^{7} WHAAT FETTLE [100] 12-11-1 R Dunwoody, *nvr far away, rdn aftr last, sn ev ch, no extr fnl 100 yards.* ....(5 to 1 op 8 to 1) 2
3659^{3} WESTWELL BOY [100] 11-11-1 R Supple, *nvr far away, ev ch and rdn aftr 2 out, styd on same pace.* ....(9 to 2 fav op 6 to 1) 3
3678^{7} ROYAL VACATION [113] 8-12-0 J Callaghan, *beh and rdn hfwy, hdwy into midfield aftr 13th, kpt on same pace frm 3 out.* ....(6 to 1 tchd 13 to 2) 4
3601^{3} HURRICANE ANDREW (Ire) [86] 9-10-1 N Smith, *in tch, effrt aftr 16th, kpt on same pace.* .... (11 to 2 op 9 to 2 tchd 6 to 1) 5
3601^{4} FORWARD GLEN [87] (bl) 10-10-2^{2} Mr R Bevis, *mid-div, effrt aftr 14th, wknd bef 3 out*..........(20 to 1 op 16 to 1) 6
2536 SIDE OF HILL [91] 12-10-6 G Lee, *led till hdd 14th, wknd aftr 16th*.......... (50 to 1 tchd 66 to 1) 7
3353 LAST REFUGE (Ire) [91] 8-10-6^{4} T Reed, *beh most of way.* ....(20 to 1 op 16 to 1) 8
3659 JAUNTY GIG [85] (bl) 11-10-0 L O'Hara, *in tch till wknd aftr 15th*.......... (13 to 2 op 6 to 1 tchd 7 to 1) 9
3601^{5} GALE AHEAD (Ire) [95] (bl) 7-10-10 M Foster, *beh whn f 15th.* ....(8 to 1 op 11 to 2) f
3161^{2} WILLIE SPARKLE [85] 11-10-0 G Cahill, *towards rear, pld up lme aftr 16th*..........(33 to 1 tchd 50 to 1) pu
Dist: 2l, 10l, 1½l, 2½l, 8l, 2l, 3l, 15l. 6m 12.50s. a 15.50s (11 Ran).
(T A Barnes), M A Barnes

3868 Royal Bank Of Scotland Handicap Hurdle Class D (0-125 4-y-o and up) £4,788 2m 110yds............(7:25)

3759^{4} STASH THE CASH (Ire) [118] 6-12-0 R Garritty, *in tch, hdwy aftr 3 out, chalg whn blun last, sn rdn, ran on wl und pres to ld clsg stages*.......... (9 to 4 fav op 5 to 2) 1
3602^{2} KILLBALLY BOY (Ire) [90] 7-9-7 (7*) C McCormack, *led, rdn aftr last, hdd clsg stages, no extr.* ....(100 to 30 op 3 to 1 tchd 7 to 2) 2
3665* GLENUGIE [107] 6-11-3 N Bentley, *in tch, drvn alng aftr 3 out, no imprsn on ldrs, styd on frm last*.....(4 to 1 tchd 9 to 2) 3
3602* WELL APPOINTED (Ire) [96] 8-10-6 G Lee, *in tch, effrt aftr 3 out, no real hdwy*..........(3 to 1 tchd 7 to 2) 4
3002^{8} LIXOS [94] 6-10-4 M Moloney, *chsd ldr, ev ch 2 out, sn wknd, eased r-in whn no chance*..........(50 to 1 op 33 to 1) 5
1477^{3} RAGAMUFFIN ROMEO [90] 8-10-0 G Cahill, *sn beh, tld off.* ....(33 to 1 op 25 to 1) 6
3759 ASTRALEON (Ire) [103] 9-10-13 B Storey, *hld up in rear, lost tch frm 3 out, tld off and eased r-in.* .... (11 to 1 op 10 to 1 tchd 12 to 1) 7
Dist: 2l, 4l, ½l, 10l, dist, 12l. 3m 41.70s. b 1.30s (7 Ran).
SR: 39/9/22/10/ (G Shiel), M D Hammond

3869 Charlie Brown United Border Hunters' Chase Class H (5-y-o and up) £1,469 3m 1f........... (8:00)

WASHAKIE 12-11-12 Mr J Walton, *sn beh, some hdwy to chase ldrs aftr 13th, styd on wl frm 2 out, led last, all out.*
.........................(2 to 1 fav tchd 9 to 1) 1
3777⁷ ACROSS THE CARD 9-11-11 (7*) Mr M Bradburne, *beh, styd on frm 3 out, chsd wnr fnl 200 yards, no imprsn.*
.........................(11 to 4 op 5 tchd 3 to 1) 2
3777 RUSTY BLADE 8-11-7 (5*) Mr R Hale, *chsd ldr, blun 9th, rdn aftr 13th, ch last, kpt on same pace.*
.........................(12 to 1 op 14 to 1 tchd 16 to 1) 3
3713⁵ GREEN TIMES 12-11-7 (5*) Mr C Storey, *sn beh, nvr dngrs.*
.........................(14 to 1 tchd 16 to 1) 4
3539² SOVEREIGNS MATCH 9-11-7 (5*) Mr N Wilson, *led, clr 2 out, wknd quickly and hdd last, sn btn.....*(11 to 4 tchd 3 to 1) 5
SHINE A LIGHT 7-11-5 (7*) Captain A Ogden, *trkd ldrs, blun 8th, wknd quickly aftr 13th, tld off whn pld up bef last.*
.........................(9 to 1 op 8 to 1) pu
Dist: 1¼l, 3½l, 18l, 3½l. 6m 16.80s. a 19.80s (6 Ran).

(Mrs F T Walton), F T Walton

3870 Lothian Plumbing Handicap Hurdle Class D (0-125 4-y-o and up) £2,745 2¾m 110yds................ (8:30)

1827³ COLORFUL AMBITION [102] 7-10-12 J Supple, *hld up and beh, hdwy aftr 3 out, chsd wnr frm last, styd on und pres to ld last strds.*.........................(5 to 1 tchd 9 to 1) 1
2361³ SUPERTOP [111] 9-11-0 (7*) W Dowling, *led 5th, clr 3 out, rdn aftr last, ct last strds.*.........................(5 to 4 fav tchd 6 to 4) 2
3702 COQUI LANE [117] 10-11-13 D Parker, *hdwy to 5th, in tch, rdn and outpcd bef 3 out, no dngr aftr.*
.........................(13 to 2 op 7 to 1 tchd 8 to 1) 3
VERY EVIDENT (Ire) [90] 8-9-9 (5*) S Taylor, *in tch, rdn aftr 7th, sn outpcd, no dngr after.*.........................(6 to 1 op 8 to 1) 4
3657² STYLISH INTERVAL [92] 5-10-2 R Supple, *in tch, chsd ldr frm 7th, no imprsn, wknd aftr last.*..........(3 to 1 op 11 to 4) 5
3718 PARSONS BRIG [118] 11-12-0 Miss S Forster, *beh and rdn alng aftr 7th, sn lost tch, tld off.*
.........................(33 to 1 op 25 to 1 tchd 50 to 1) 6
Dist: Nk, 12l, 1l, 2½l, dist. 5m 14.10s. a 5.10s (6 Ran).

(F J Sainsbury), Mrs A Swinbank

PLUMPTON (good to firm)
Wednesday April 30th
Going Correction: MINUS 0.25 sec. per fur.

3871 April Claiming Hurdle Class F (4-y-o and up) £1,935 2½m........ (2:10)

2526⁷ CIRCUS COLOURS 7-11-2 S Fox, *hld up beh ldrs, led appr 3 out, drvn out.*.........................(8 to 1 op 6 to 1) 1
3558² PETER MONAMY (bl) 5-11-10 A P McCoy, *hld up, clr order appr 6th, rdn to chal fnl 2, unbl to quicken r-in.*
.........................(11 to 10 on op Evens tchd 5 to 4 on) 2
3771⁴ EWAR BOLD (bl) 4-10-1 (7*) D Slattery, *prmnt, led 7th, hdd appr 3 out, wknd bef nxt.*..........(20 to 1 tchd 25 to 1) 3
2977 FORTUNES ROSE (Ire) 5-10-7 T J Murphy, *prmnt, rdn aftr 4 out, wknd after nxt.....*(25 to 1 op 20 to 1 tchd 33 to 1) 4
669 JENZSOPH (Ire) 6-10-10 (5*) D J Kavanagh, *led, hit 4th, hdd 7th, wknd 3 out, fourth and btn whn blun and ran s out.*
.........................(13 to 8 op 6 to 4 tchd 7 to 4) ur
3621⁵ CASTLEBAY LAD (v) 14-11-4 Mr M Appleby, *hld up, not fluent and rdn alng 5th, tld off frm 4 out, pld up bef last.*
.........................(100 to 1 op 66 to 1) pu
SHEYL SEYMOUR 6-10-11 B Fenton, *slwly away, al beh, tld off frm 8th, pld up bef 2 out.*
.........................(40 to 1 op 33 to 1 tchd 50 to 1) pu
Dist: 1½l, 14l, 8l. 4m 50.10s. a 13.10s (7 Ran).

(S A Barningham), J R Jenkins

3872 Cooksbridge Novices' Handicap Hurdle Class E (0-100 4-y-o and up) £2,343 2½m.........(2:45)

3722 PERSIAN ELITE (Ire) [97] 6-12-0 J Osborne, *al hndy, pushed alng aftr 3 out, dived nxt, sn led, ran on wl.*
.........................(6 to 4 fav op 2 to 1 tchd 9 to 4 and 5 to 2) 1
3771³ NORDIC SPREE (Ire) [83] (v) 5-11-0 P Holley, *chsd ldr to 5th, led aftr 8th, hdd 3 out, styd on one pace r-in.*
.........................(8 to 1 op 9 to 2 tchd 9 to 1) 2
3489³ BEN BOWDEN [90] 4-10-11 (3*) L Aspell, *hld up, clr order 6th, led 3 out, hdd jst aftr nxt, one pace.....*(11 to 2 op 4 to 1) 3
2771 RED LIGHT [70] (v) 5-10-1 T J Murphy, *hld up beh ldrs, effrt appr 3 out, hit last, one pace.*
.........................(9 to 1 tchd 8 to 1) 4
3498⁶ CROWN IVORY (NZ) [71] 9-10-2 S Fox, *al beh.*
.........................(13 to 2 op 6 to 1 tchd 7 to 1) 5
3629² CLOCK WATCHERS [71] 9-10-2 D Morris, *led till aftr 8th, remained hndy till wknd appr 3 out.....*(9 to 2 tchd 5 to 1) 6
Dist: 4l, ½l, ½l, 16l, 6l. 4m 45.80s. a 8.80s (6 Ran).

(Elite Racing Club), C R Egerton

3873 Offham Novices' Chase Class E (5-y-o and up) £3,176 3m 1f 110yds
.........................(3:20)

3638 FRAZER ISLAND (Ire) 8-11-8 D O'Sullivan, *al gng easily, hld up, led 3 out, shaken up and came clr frm nxt.*
.........................(5 to 2 on op 9 to 4 on) 1
3444³ MALWOOD CASTLE (Ire) 7-11-8 P Holley, *led till appr second, rgned ld 4th, hdd 3 out, rdn and outpcd by wnr.*
.........................(7 to 2 op 3 to 1 tchd 4 to 1 and 9 to 2) 2
3739⁴ DREAM LEADER (Ire) 7-11-8 J Railton, *led appr second, hdd 4th, pressed ldr aftr to 15th, 3rd whn hit 16th, wkng when blun nxt, tld off.......*(9 to 2 op 4 to 1 tchd 5 to 1) 3
Dist: 8l, dist. 6m 33.40s. a 19.40s (3 Ran).

(Dr B Alexander), R Rowe

3874 Hove Four Years Old Fillies' Novices' Hurdle Class E £2,180 2m 1f.. (3:50)

3796* THEME ARENA (v) 11-7 A P McCoy, *made all, sn clr, blun 6th, drvn out......*(6 to 4 op 5 to 4 tchd 7 to 4 and 9 to 5) 1
3614⁸ PERSIAN DAWN 10-7 J Railton, *chsd wnr, rdn appr 2 out, 3 ls dwn but staying on whn blun last, no extr.*
.........................(50 to 1 op 20 to 1) 2
SALSIAN 10-7 T J Murphy, *hld up, rdn appr 3 out, sn btn, tld off.....*(33 to 1 op 12 to 1 tchd 40 to 1 and 50 to 1) 3
FORTUITIOUS (Ire) 10-7 S Fox, *not jump wl, al beh, tld off frm 3rd, pld up bef last.....*(25 to 1 op 12 to 1 tchd 33 to 1) 4
2775 THREESOCKS 10-7 I Lawrence, *not fluent, hld up, reminders appr 6th, sn beh, tld off whn pld up and dismounted bef 3 out, lme....* (7 to 4 on op 11 to 8 on tchd 5 to 4 on and 2 to 1 on) pu
Dist: 3l, dist. 4m 7.50s. a 10.50s (5 Ran).

(Antony Sofroniou), M C Pipe

3875 Wivelsfield Green Handicap Chase Class E (0-115 5-y-o and up) £2,946 2m 5f........................(4:20)

3613 LINDEN'S LOTTO (Ire) [98] 8-11-2 J R Kavanagh, *wtd wth, prog appr 4 out, led 2 out, rdn out.....* (4 to 1 tchd 7 to 2) 1
3685* COOLTEEN HERO (Ire) [94] 7-10-12 P Holley, *in tch, led 4 out, hdd 2 out, one pace.....* (11 to 4 op 5 to 2 tchd 3 to 1) 2
2005³ PAPER STAR [92] 10-10-10 B Powell, *led, hdd 4 out, sn wknd.*
.........................(7 to 2 op 4 to 1 tchd 9 to 2) 3
3502⁷ TURPIN'S GREEN [82] 14-10-0 T J Murphy, *prmnt, rdn alng aftr 8th, sn wknd.....*(25 to 1 op 20 to 1) 4
3412² BE SURPRISED [82] 11-9-7 (7*) M Batchelor, *trkd ldrs, rdn and wknd appr 3 out...* (14 to 1 op 10 to 1 tchd 16 to 1) 5
51 MERIVEL [110] 10-12-0 D O'Sullivan, *al beh.*
.........................(16 to 1 op 12 to 1) 6
3669² STORMHILL PILGRIM [82] 8-10-0 D Gallagher, *f second.*
.........................(9 to 4 fav op 2 to 1 tchd 5 to 2 and 11 to 4) f
Dict: 8l, 6l, 10l, 24l, 5l. 5m 7.60s. a 1.60s (7 Ran).
SR: 20/8/-/-/ (Crocketts Racing Club), J White

3876 Ladbroke Handicap Hurdle Class E (0-115 4-y-o and up) £2,241 2½m
.........................(4:50)

3635⁵ ALLTIME DANCER (Ire) [113] (bl) 5-12-0 J Osborne, *hld up, improved 3 out, led last, readily.....* (5 to 4 fav op 6 to 4) 1
3633³ NIGHT IN A MILLION [85] 6-10-0³ (3*) L Aspell, *led to last, no extr.....*.........................(9 to 4 op 6 to 4) 2
3078⁵ BIGWHEEL BILL (Ire) [85] 8-10-7 J Murphy, *prmnt till outpcd aftr 9th, rallied after nxt, one pace 2 out.*
.........................(10 to 1 op 7 to 1 tchd 15 to 2) 3
3773² ADILOV [85] 5-10-0 D Morris, *prmnt, blun 8th, wknd appr 2 out.*.........................(9 to 2 op 4 to 1 tchd 5 to 1) 4
Dist: 1¼l, 8l, 5l. 4m 43.40s. a 6.40s (4 Ran).

(H M Heyman), O Sherwood

CLONMEL (IRE) (good) Thursday May 1st

3877 Roscrea Beginners Chase (5-y-o and up) £2,226 3m............... (4:00)

88⁷ LITTLE-K (Ire) 7-11-6 (3*) K Whelan, ... (20 to 1) 1
3418⁵ AISEIRI 10-11-2 (7*) V T Keane, ... (16 to 1) 2
3447⁵ VIKING BUOY (Ire) 5-10-10 (3*) G Cotter, ... (7 to 1) 3
3418⁴ DEARBORN TEC (Ire) (bl) 8-12-0 T P Treacy, ...(6 to 1) 4
3420 HOTEL SALTEES (Ire) 9-11-4 K F Woods, ... (14 to 1) 5
3752⁷ PENNY BRIDE (Ire) 8-11-4 T P Rudd, ... (5 to 1) 6
2523³ WEJEMI (Ire) 8-11-2 (7*) Mr Paul Moloney, ... (7 to 1) 7
173⁶ HASTY HOURS (Ire) 7-11-4 C O'Dwyer, ... (7 to 2 fav) f
3693² LET BUNNY RUN (Ire) 7-11-9 D H O'Connor, ... (11 to 2) f
3752 MOON-FROG 10-11-9 J K Kinane, ... (25 to 1) pu
802 BALLY UPPER (Ire) 9-11-9 K F O'Brien, ... (16 to 1) pu
3088 BAILEYS BRIDGE (Ire) 6-11-2 (7*) M D Murphy, ... (16 to 1) pu
Dist: 8l, 11l, 20l, 6l. 6m 4.30s. (12 Ran).

(Miss D Keating), P R Lenihan

3878 Cahir Maiden Hurdle (4-y-o and up) £2,226 2½m................ (4:30)

802³ CRUCIAL MOVE (Ire) 6-11-1 T P Treacy, ...(13 to 8 fav) 1
3219⁶ BOCCACHERA (Ire) 5-11-0 A J O'Brien, ...(10 to 1) 2

541

36275 RAINBOW ERA (Ire) 4-10-13 C F Swan, ... (4 to 1) 3
2222 CORDAL DREAM (Ire) 5-11-10 M P Hourigan, ...(20 to 1) 4
1655 ROSE OF STRADBALLY (Ire) 6-10-12 (3*) K Whelan,
. . . .(12 to 1) 5
34327 MOSTA (Ire) 4-10-1 (7*) M J Collins, ... (12 to 1) 6
COOLE LADY (Ire) 6-10-8 (7*) V T Keane, ...(20 to 1) 7
2943 HARRY WELSH (Ire) (bl) 5-11-13 C O'Dwyer, ...(12 to 1) 8
3642 GRITRICK (Ire) 6-10-8 (7*) D A McLoughlin, ...(14 to 1) 9
KILBRANEY (Ire) 8-11-11 (3*) G Cotter, ... (10 to 1) 10
36255 GENOMIC (Ire) 5-11-5 K F O'Brien, ... (16 to 1) 11
RUSHING BYE (Ire) 6-11-6 F Woods, ...(20 to 1) 12
BABY BOP 6-11-6 T J Mitchell, ...(25 to 1) 13
HOMESTEAD NIECE (USA) 5-11-8 J Shortt, ...(12 to 1) 14
3547 KILLCHRIS DREAM (Ire) 6-11-1 D J Casey, ...(25 to 1) f
ORCHARD HOPE (Ire) 6-11-1 D O'Shea, ...(10 to 1) su
33439 SECRET PRINCE 6-11-3 (3*) D P Murphy, ... (10 to 1) pu
3183 INTERIM STATEMENT 4-10-8 T P Rudd, ... (20 to 1) pu
Dist: 3l, 13l, 1l, ¾l. 4m 51.50s. (18 Ran).

(John J M Murphy), S J Treacy

3879 Cashel Handicap Hurdle (0-123 4-y-o and up) £2,226 2m . . . . (5:00)

36074 BRONICA (Ire) [-] 5-11-1 C F Swan, ... (7 to 4 fav) 1
36262 CLASHBEG (Ire) [-] 6-10-7 (3*) K Whelan, ...(4 to 1) 2
32359 ILLBETHEREFORYOU (Ire) [-] 6-9-7 (5*) P G Hourigan,
. . . . (10 to 1) 3
9075 WESPERADA (Ire) [-] 5-11-2 (7*) B J Geraghty, ...(10 to 1) 4
828* BOB THE YANK (Ire) [-] 7-12-0 C O'Dwyer, ...(5 to 1) 5
36248 LEGITMAN (Ire) [-] 7-9-11 D J Casey, ... (12 to 1) 6
3337 BE MY FOLLY (Ire) [-] 5-9-13 (7*) M J Collins, ... (14 to 1) 7
3235 BEAU CYRANO (Ire) [-] 5-10-9 (7*) M D Murphy, ...(9 to 1) 8
36965 NORMINS HUSSAR (Ire) [-] 5-9-8[1] F Woods, ... (16 to 1) 9
3390 QUEEN OF ALL GALES (Ire) [-] 6-9-0 (7*) D A McLoughlin,
. . . . (25 to 1) 10
Dist: ¾l, hd, 2l, 1½l. 3m 51.60s. (10 Ran).

(Mrs Ranka Pollmeter), J E Kiely

3880 Carriganog I.N.H. Flat Race (5-y-o and up) £2,226 2½m. . . . . (5:30)

MUSIC AGAIN (Ire) 5-11-5 (3*) Mr R Walsh, ... (3 to 1 fav) 1
OZIER HILL (Ire) 9-12-0 Mr J A Berry, ... (9 to 2) 2
DEEJAYDEE (Ire) 5-11-6 (7*) Mr A FitzGerald, ...(10 to 1) 3
2838 SWIFT PICK (Ire) 5-11-13 Mr A J Martin, ... (14 to 1) 4
33422 CHOICE JENNY (Ire) 5-11-3 (5*) Mr A C Coyle, ...(6 to 1) 5
36079 MASTER CHUZZLEWIT (Ire) 6-11-7 (7*) Mr M J Daly,
. . . . (10 to 1) 6
FROSTBITTEN (Ire) 6-11-9 (5*) Mr G Elliott, ...(4 to 1) 7
34219 KILLALOONTY ROSE (Ire) 6-11-2 (7*) Mr D A Harney,
. . . . (16 to 1) 8
HAZEL HONEY (Ire) 6-11-2 (7*) Mr I Amond, ... (16 to 1) 9
AWALKINTHECLOUDS (Ire) 6-11-7 (7*) Mr P P Curran,
. . . . (12 to 1) 10
THUNDER PRINCESS (Ire) 5-11-1 (7*) Mr P Whelan,
. . . . (10 to 1) 11
CEANNABHALLA (Ire) 5-11-1 (7*) Mr P J Crowley, . .(10 to 1) 12
3697 MOLL'S CHOICE (Ire) 6-11-2 (7*) Mr J M Roche, . . . (16 to 1) 13
NOTTOBADOKAY (Ire) 6-12-0 Mr J P Dempsey, . . . (10 to 1) 14
COA GIRL (Ire) 7-11-9 Mr B M Cash, ...(8 to 1) 15
20807 GALLIC BEAUTY (Ire) 6-11-2 (7*) Mr R M Walsh, . . . (20 to 1) 16
LADY FONDA (Ire) 5-11-8 Mr P Fenton, ... (8 to 1) 17
Dist: 3½l, 1½l, 3½l, 2l. 4m 39.70s. (17 Ran).

(T Regan), W P Mullins

BANGOR (good)
Friday May 2nd
Going Correction: PLUS 0.15 sec. per fur.

3881 J. Scott Furnishers Novices' Hurdle Class E (4-y-o and up) £3,032 3m
. . . . (6:00)

3546 SHARP THYNE (Ire) 7-11-0 G Tormey, midfield, mstk 3rd, rdn
alng to improve 4 out, led 2 out, drvn clr r-in.
. . . . (40 to 1 op 25 to 1) 1
3735* SUPREME FLYER (Ire) 7-11-0 R Johnson, hld up, steady
hdwy 4th to track ldrs, not fluent 8th, styd on to take second
r-in, no imprsn on wnr. . . . .(7 to 4 jt-fav tchd 2 to 1) 2
37225 GOWER-SLAVE 5-11-0 B Fenton, al cl up, led 3 out to nxt, sn
one pace. . . . .(33 to 1 op 25 to 1) 3
37953 FOXIES LAD 6-10-11 (3*) Mr R Thornton, in tch, improved to
chase ldrs 7th, chlgd 2 out, sn no extr . . . .(7 to 4 jt-
fav tchd 15 to 8) 4
35063 RIVERBANK ROSE (v) 6-10-12 (3*) Guy Lewis, prmnt, blun
6th, led nxt to 3 out, wknd bef last. . . .(20 to 1 op 14 to 1) 5
37226 THE NAUGHTY VICAR (bl) 7-11-0 Richard Guest, midfield,
5th, wknd 3 out, sn eased. . . . .(33 to 1 op 25 to 1) 6
3833 TOMMY COOPER (Ire) 6-11-0 E Byrne, not fluent, towards
rear, nvr trbld ldrs. . . . .(25 to 1 op 20 to 1) 7
25175 DANZANTE (Ire) 5-11-0 D Gallagher, hld up, effrt 4 out, no
imprsn frm nxt. . . . .(33 to 1 op 25 to 1) 8
3019 PINXTON PENNY 5-10-6 (3*) E Husband, not fluent, in rear,
struggling frm hfwy, nvr a factor. . . . .(100 to 1 op 50 to 1) 9
30555 DOUBLE DASH (Ire) 4-10-13 D J Moffatt, midfield to 5th, sn
beh and rdn alng, nvr dngrs. . . . .(20 to 1 op 16 to 1) 10

1623 SEVEN POTATO MORE (Ire) 7-10-9 (5*) D J Kavanagh, keen
hold, in rear, struggling frm 8th, nvr a factor. . . . . . .(33 to 1) 11
3722 DUNSTON KNIGHT 4-10-7 Gary Lyons, hndy, lost pl 6th,
mstk nxt, sn struggling, no dngr whn mistake 4 out.
. . . .(100 to 1 op 50 to 1) 12
ITSGONNASHINE (Ire) 5-10-9 D Walsh, midfield, rdn alng aftr 6th,
wknd eighth. . . . .(100 to 1 op 50 to 1) 13
MOSEPHINE (Ire) 7-10-9 M Sharratt, hld up in tch, struggling
frm 7th, sn beh, tld off. . . . .(7 to 1 op 16 to 1) 14
37125 TILTY (USA) (v) 7-11-12 T Eley, led to 7th, cl up till wknd 4 out,
tld off whn pld up bef last, dismounted. . .(9 to 2 op 5 to 1) pu
2994 SCALE DOWN (Ire) 8-11-0 W Marston, strted slwly, pld hrd to
go prmnt 1st, wknd quickly and pulled up aftr 6th. . .(33 to 1) pu
31975 BIG STAN'S BOY 6-11-0 G Bradley, midfield, hdwy appr 5th
to go hndy, rdn and lost pl 7th, sn beh, tld off whn pld up bef 3
out. . . . .(20 to 1) pu
Dist: 4l, nk, 4l, sht-hd, 19l, ½l, 5l, 8l, 12l, 9l. 5m 46.70s. (17 Ran).

(Mrs R L Matson), P J Hobbs

3882 Jones Peckover Novices' Handicap Chase Class E (0-100 5-y-o and up) £3,468 2m 1f 110yds. . . . . (6:30)

36854 POND HOUSE (Ire) [97] 8-12-0 D Walsh, made all, rdn appr
last, kpt on whn pressed r-in.
. . . .(7 to 4 op 6 to 4 tchd 2 to 1) 1
37243 THE SECRET GREY [71] 6-10-2[2] T Jenks, chsd ldrs, chased
wnr appr 3 out, sn und pres, pckd 2 out, chlgd r-in, no extr cl
hme. . . . .(11 to 2 op 5 to 1) 2
36996 DESERT BRAVE (Ire) [77] 7-10-8 Richard Guest, in rear,
niggled along 8th, no imprsn frm 2 out.
. . . .(5 to 1 op 4 to 1 tchd 11 to 2) 3
35594 DANDIE IMP [73] 9-10-4 R Dunwoody, chsd wnr, hit 4th, lost
pl appr 3 out, sn drvn and wknd.
. . . .(11 to 8 fav op 6 to 4 tchd 7 to 4) 4
Dist: 1¼l, 8l, 1l. 4m 17.50s. 4 15.50s (4 Ran).

(C R Fleet), M C Pipe

3883 Crystal Ballgazers Selling Handicap Hurdle Class G (0-95 4-y-o and up) £2,130 2½m. . . . . (7:00)

38033 SKANE RIVER (Ire) [66] 6-10-9 R Dunwoody, trkd ldrs, chlgd
appr 2 out, led betw last two, drvn clr r-in.
. . . .(9 to 4 fav op 3 to 1) 1
35302 EDWARD SEYMOUR (USA) [84] 10-11-13 T Jenks, hld up,
hdwy aftr 6th to track ldrs, not quicken bef 2 out, kpt on r-in, no
imprsn on wnr. . . . .(7 to 2 op 5 to 2) 2
SQUEALING JEANIE [57] 8-10-0 B Fenton, strted slwly, sn
reco'red to track ldrs, led 4 out, hdd betw last 2, one pace.
. . . . (33 to 1) 3
2303 AAVASAKSA (Fr) [65] 4-9-13 (3*) Mr R Thornton, midfield,
chsd ldrs 6th, drvn whn mstk 3 out, sn outpcd.
. . . .(14 to 1 op 20 to 1 tchd 25 to 1) 4
105 SWEET NOBLE (Ire) [80] 8-11-9 M Sharratt, in tch, improved
to ld 7th, hdd 4 out, sn wknd. . . . .(25 to 1 op 14 to 1) 5
34765 GRANDMAN (Ire) [79] 6-11-8 D J Moffatt, hld up, mstk 5th,
effrt 7th, chasing ldrs whn mistake 3 out, sn outpcd.
. . . .(8 to 1 tchd 10 to 1) 6
35073 MARDOOD [64] 12-10-2 (5*) B Grattan, rear div, rdn alng frm
6th, nvr a factor. . . . .(16 to 1 op 12 to 1) 7
37035 GALLAGHENI (Ire) [77] 8-11-6 D Gallagher, chsd ldrs, wknd 4
out, sn no imprsn. . . . .(10 to 1 op 8 to 1) 8
36283 ITS GRAND [70] (v) 8-10-13 C Maude, prmnt till rdn and wknd
frm 7th. . . . .(10 to 1 op 8 to 1) 9
38103 AGAINST THE CLOCK [57] 5-9-7 (7*) L Cummins, led to 7th,
wkng whn mstk 4 out, tld off. . . . .(12 to 1 op 10 to 1) 10
33218 WHITEBONNET (Ire) [79] (bl) 7-11-8 J Osborne, hld up, struggling frm 4 out, eased from nxt, tld off. .(8 to 1 op 5 to 1) 11
56 LADY LOIS [57] 6-9-7 (7*) J Mogford, al beh, struggling frm
hfwy, tld off. . . . .(25 to 1 op 16 to 1) 12
37367 BUSTER [58] 9-10-1 E Byrne, al beh, lost tch frm 6th, tld off,
lme. . . . .(20 to 1 op 16 to 1) 13
Dist: 6l, 1¾l, 2l, 5l, ½l, 1¾l, 2½l, 14l, 23l, 7l. 4m 48.80s. a 18.80s (13 Ran).

(W J Peacock), G Richards

3884 Wynnstay Hunt Supporters Club Handicap Chase Class D (0-120 5-y-o and up) £4,182 2½m 110yds (7:30)

3067 JACOB'S WIFE [100] 7-10-8 J Osborne, cl up, pressed ldr
frm 4 out, narrowly led whn lft clr last. . . .(8 to 1 op 7 to 1) 1
33142 CHANGE THE ACT [109] 12-11-0 (3*) Mr R Thornton, prmnt,
lost pl 4th, struggling and beh 8th, drvn and kpt on stdly frm 3
out, lft second last. . . .(11 to 4 op 3 to 1 tchd 100 to 30) 2
37114 FRICKLEY [119] 11-11-13 R Dunwoody, hld up, took clr order
7th, blun 9th, sn lost pl and beh, no dngr afterwards.
. . . .(15 to 8 fav op 7 to 4 tchd 2 to 1) 3
3444* JAMES THE FIRST [120] 9-12-0 C Maude, hld up, hdwy to go
cl up 9th, wknd appr 3 out. . . . .(6 to 1 op 4 to 1) 4
7063 MAGGOTS GREEN [98] 10-10-6 B Fenton, led till mstk and
hdd 4 out, wknd quickly, tld off.
. . . .(9 to 1 op 8 to 1 tchd 10 to 1) 5
3730 OVER THE POLE [107] 7-10-10-12 (3*) Mr C Bonner, hld up in
rear, hdwy tenth, led 4 out, sn hrd pressed, narrowly ldd whn
f last. . . . . (7 to 1 op 6 to 1) f

3830 TOP BRASS (Ire) [99] (bl) 9-10-7 S McNeill, *hndy, wknd quickly tenth, tld off whn pld up bef 3 out.*
.... (20 to 1 op 14 to 1) pu
Dist: 12l, 19l, 5l, dist. 5m 5.50s. a 19.50s (7 Ran).

(The Black Sheep Flock), P R Webber

3885 Eastern Destiny Novices' Hunters' Chase Class H for the James Griffith Memorial Trophy (5-y-o and up) £1,548 3m 110yds............(8:00)

3567* BITOFAMIXUP (Ire) 6-12-4 (3*) Mr P Hacking, *nvr far away, led 14th, clr appr 2 out, easily.*
..............(4 to 1 on tchd 9 to 2 on and 7 to 2 on) 1
3671* MISTER HORATIO 7-11-11 (7*) Mr M Lewis, *prmnt, jmpd slwly 3rd, outpcd whn 14th, rdn to chase clr wnr appr 3 out. no ch when mstk last.*................. (9 to 2 op 7 to 2) 2
3723⁵ NADIAD 11-11-7 (7*) Mr A Wintle, *cl up, outpcd and beh 14th, no ch whn pckd 2 out.*.................(20 to 1 op 16 to 1) 3
DESMOND GOLD (Ire) 9-11-7 (7*) Mr D S Jones, *set slow pace, jmpd slwly 3rd, quickened appr 12th, hit and hdd 14th, wknd, tld off.*.................(16 to 1 op 12 to 1) 4
Dist: 25l, 4l, dist. 6m 26.10s. a 41.10s (4 Ran).

(Mike Roberts), M J Roberts

3886 Llandudno Handicap Hurdle Class F (0-105 4-y-o and up) £2,905 2m 1f ....(8:30)

2639⁵ WINSFORD HILL [84] 6-10-12 G Tormey, *hld up, hdwy on bit 3 out, led nxt, hit last, ran on wl.*
.................(12 to 1 tchd 14 to 1 and 16 to 1) 1
3278² MUIZENBERG [80] 10-10-8 D Gallagher, *al cl up, led 3rd, hdd 2 out, one pace.*.................(7 to 1 op 5 to 1) 2
3703⁹ NASHVILLE STAR (USA) [94] (v) 6-11-8 C Llewellyn, *led to 3rd, still cl up whn niggled alng 4 out, kpt on same pace und pres.*.................(10 to 1 op 7 to 1 tchd 12 to 1) 3
3674* DAILY SPORT GIRL [82] 8-10-10 Mr J L Llewellyn, *midfield, improved to go prmnt 4th, ev ch appr 2 out, wknd betw last two.*.................(8 to 1 op 6 to 1 tchd 9 to 1) 4
936* COINTOSSER (Ire) [105] 4-12-0 S Wynne, *hld up, hdwy to chase ldrs 3 out and effrt, wknd frm nxt.*
.........(15 to 8 fav op 5 to 2 tchd 3 to 1 and 7 to 4) 5
3558 CHRIS'S GLEN [83] (v) 8-10-11 B Fenton, *prmnt till lost pl 4th, effrt ag'n 3 out, wknd bef 2 out.*.......(20 to 1 op 12 to 1) 6
691⁶ NO LIGHT [99] 10-11-13 L Harvey, *pld hrd, hld up, no imprsn 3 out, eased bef nxt.*.................(9 to 1 op 6 to 1) 7
241³ LAWFUL LOVE (Ire) [78] 7-10-3 (3*) Mr R Thornton, *hld up, und pres 3 out, sn btn.*.................(11 to 2 op 5 to 1) 8
3819* EUROLINK THE REBEL (USA) [86] 5-10-9 (5*,6ex) B Grattan, *prmnt till wknd 4 out, tld off.*
.................(9 to 1 op 7 to 1 tchd 10 to 1) 9
3316⁸ MR LOWRY [80] 5-10-8 Derek Byrne, *hld up, hdwy 4th, hndy whn not fluent nxt, sn wknd, beh when pld up bef four out.*
.................(14 to 1 op 9 to 1) 10
Dist: 4l, 1½l, 10l, ½l, 2½l, 7l, 4l, 26l. 3m 59.70s. a 9.70s (10 Ran).
SR: 12/4/16/-/-/-/ (Six Horse Power), P J Hobbs

DUNDALK (IRE) (firm (races 1,2), good to firm (3,4,5)) Friday May 2nd

3887 Carlingford Handicap Chase (4-y-o and up) £2,551 3m............(5:15)

3609* LINDA'S BOY (Ire) [-] (bl) 7-10-13 (5*) P G Hourigan,
.................(7 to 4 on) 1
1538 TALK TO YOU LATER [-] 11-10-4 D H O'Connor, .. (33 to 1) 2
3230⁵ FANE'S TREASURE (Ire) [-] 8-9-13 (7*) B J Geraghty,
.................(10 to 1) f
3526³ PERSPEX GALE (Ire) [-] 9-10-11 C F Swan, ...(20 to 1) ur
Dist: 7l. 6m 10.30s. (4 Ran).

(Patrick Kearns), E Bolger

3888 Tallanstown Hunters Chase (5-y-o and up) £2,226 3m............(5:45)

3749⁵ TULLY BOY 10-11-7 (7*) Mr D McCartan, ...(8 to 1) 1
COOL IT (Ire) 7-11-7 (7*) Mr P Duggan, ...(25 to 1) 2
3646² HILTONSTOWN LASS (Ire) 7-11-2 (7*) Mr Richard J Walker,
.................(7 to 2) 3
HALF SCOTCH (Ire) 9-11-2 (7*) Mr A Stronge, ...(14 to 1) 4
170 ROYAL ARISTOCRAT (Ire) 8-11-6 (3*) Mr B R Hamilton,
.................(9 to 1) 5
FOREVER GOLD 12-11-7 (7*) Mr M Chesney, ...(25 to 1) 6
3748⁴ PERCUSIONIST 10-11-7 (7*) Mr J F Robinson, ...(12 to 1) 7
3770 KILLMURRAY BUCK (Ire) 9-11-2 (7*) Mr J P McNamara,
.................(16 to 1) 8
PRAYON PARSON (Ire) 9-11-7 (7*) Mr D P Daly, ...(12 to 1) 9
3391 PALMURA 10-11-7 (7*) Mr C P McGivern, ...(25 to 1) 10
VENERDI SANTO (Ire) 7-12-0 Mr B M Cash, ...(12 to 1) f
2844⁴ ONLY ONE (Ire) 7-11-7 (7*) Mr M O'Connor, ...(16 to 1) ur
3391³ CHRISTIMATT (Ire) 6-11-7 (7*) Mr L D McBratney, .(14 to 1) ur
2869 PAULS POINT 10-11-7 (7*) Mr A Tate, ...(16 to 1) ur
ONE WOMAN (Ire) 6-11-9 Mr M Phillips, ...(9 to 4 fav) ur

STATION MAN (Ire) 8-11-7 (7*) Mr R Kehoe, ...(25 to 1) pu
Dist: 3½l, 1½l, 6l, 10l. 6m 15.80s. (16 Ran).

(Philip McCartan), Philip McCartan

3889 Ardee Maiden Hurdle (4 & 5-y-o) £2,226 2m 135yds............(6:15)

3817³ BAILENAGUN (Ire) 4-10-8 (7*) B J Geraghty, ... (7 to 4 fav) 1
2942 HONEY TRADER 5-11-0 (5*) P G Hourigan, ...(8 to 1) 2
1143⁹ FOREST PRINCESS (Ire) 5-11-0 C F Swan, ...(9 to 2) 3
3547 SILVER RIVER (Ire) 5-11-0 C O'Dwyer, ...(16 to 1) 4
3376 JOHNS TOUGH LADY (Ire) 5-11-0 K F O'Brien, ... (25 to 1) 5
3625⁶ LOUGH SLANIA (Ire) 4-10-8 (7*) I Browne, ...(8 to 1) 6
3705 TINERANA GLOW (Ire) 5-11-0 D T Evans, ... (16 to 1) 7
1015 FLORAL EMBLEM (Ire) 5-10-1 (3*) B Bowens, ... (12 to 1) 8
2166 STORM COURSE (Ire) 5-10-7 (7*) D K Budds, ...(16 to 1) 9
PIER HOUSE (Ire) 5-11-10 (3*) U Smyth, ...(11 to 1) 10
3647⁷ MRS DOYLE (Ire) 5-11-0 F Woods, ...(20 to 1) 11
2270 PEYTO LAKE (Ire) 5-10-12 (7*) J A Robinson, ...(33 to 1) 12
3450 MAID TO MOVE (Ire) 4-10-8 (7*) Mr R P McNalley, (12 to 1) 13
3627⁹ BALLINTEMPLE TRAMP (Ire) 4-10-3 (7*) K A Kelly, (33 to 1) 14
3816 MEGA HUNTER (Ire) 5-11-5 M Moran, ...(33 to 1) 15
3183 TIMMYS CHOICE (Ire) 4-11-1 P Leech, ...(33 to 1) 16
2905 BALLERIN FLYER (Ire) 4-10-3 (7*) D M Bean, ...(50 to 1) 17
3389 ZAFFRIDGE (Ire) 5-11-0 (3*) D Bromley, ...(60 to 1) 18
SHABRA EXZOL (Ire) 5-11-5 P L Malone, ...(20 to 1) 19
1897⁸ KATSUKO (Ire) 5-11-0 H Rogers, ...(8 to 1) f
Dist: 2l, 3½l, 3½l, 13l. 3m 55.80s. (20 Ran).

(T M McDonnell), Noel Meade

3890 Carroll Trophy Handicap Hurdle (4-y-o and up) £5,780 2½m 153yds ....(6:45)

3750⁵ COLM'S ROCK [-] 6-11-1 C F Swan, ...(2 to 1 fav) 1
3768⁵ I REMEMBER IT WELL (Ire) [-] (bl) 5-9-9 (5*) P G Hourigan,
.................(6 to 1) 2
3754⁷ FIDDLERS BOW VI (Ire) [-] 9-10-1 (7*) B J Geraghty, (3 to 1) 3
3451⁹ METASTASIO [-] (bl) 5-11-4 H Rogers, ...(5 to 2) 4
3768² FANE PATH (Ire) [-] 5-9-12 (3*) G Cotter, ...(4 to 1) 5
Dist: 2l, 2l, 2½l, 7l, 4m 47.90s. (5 Ran).

(R Finnegan), A P O'Brien

3891 Greenore I.N.H. Flat Race (5-y-o and up) £2,226 2m 135yds............(8:15)

3456⁵ RING ALBERT 5-11-10 (3*) Mr R Walsh, ...(3 to 1) 1
3643 POLLTRIC (Ire) 6-12-0 Mrs C Barker, ...(10 to 1) 2
MASRIYNA 5-11-8 Mr J A Nash, ...(8 to 1) 3
3524⁷ MEN OF NINETYEIGHT (Ire) 5-11-13 Mr D Marnane,
.................(7 to 4 fav) 4
2235⁵ SCOUT AROUND (Ire) 5-11-13 Mr P Fenton, ...(5 to 1) 5
3551⁷ DANNKALIA (Ire) (bl) 5-11-8 J P Dempsey, ...(12 to 1) 6
RED EBREL (Ire) 6 11 1 (7*) Mr A J Dempsey, ...(10 to 1) 7
3642 NEW WEST (Ire) 7-11-7 (7*) Mr J D O'Connell, ...(20 to 1) 8
3390 JACKPOT JOHNNY (Ire) 6-11-12³ (5*) Mr G Farrell, (20 to 1) 9
3233 CRUISIN ON CREDIT (Ire) 6-11-7 (7*) Mr L J Temple,
.................(20 to 1) 10
3348⁹ STRONG IMAGE (Ire) 5-11-3 (5*) Mr G Elliott, ...(20 to 1) 11
2224 GRANNY BOWLY (Ire) 7-11-7⁵ (7*) Mr J P McCreesh,
.................(50 to 1) 12
3553⁷ JAPAMA 6-12-0 Mr A R Coonan, ...(14 to 1) 13
RAHANINE NATIVE (Ire) 5-11-1 (7*) Mr R F Coonan, (20 to 1) 14
THE BREAK (Ire) 8-11-2 (7*) Mr E G Durnin, ...(66 to 1) 15
3627⁸ PERFECT (Ire) 5-11-6 (7*) Mr M P Madden, ...(14 to 1) 16
LEGAL WHISPER (Ire) 6-11-7 (7*) Mr L Young, ...(66 to 1) 17
3697 SPENCER HOUSE (Ire) 5-11-6 (7*) Mr J J O'Sullivan,
.................(50 to 1) 18
ROBVILLE (Ire) 7-11-7 (7*) Mr J Keville, ...(33 to 1) 19
Dist: 11l, 3l, 1l, nk. 3m 44.70s. (19 Ran).

(Mrs J M Mullins), W P Mullins

NEWTON ABBOT (good to firm) Friday May 2nd
Going Correction: MINUS 0.15 sec. per fur.

3892 Theakstons Real Ale Stakes Maiden Hurdle Class E (4-y-o and up) £2,505 2m 1f.........................(1:50)

3296⁴ NORDANCE PRINCE (Ire) 6-11-0 A P McCoy, *hld up in tch, smooth hdwy to ld on bit sn aftr 3 out, hmpd by loose horse after nxt, soon reco'red, cmftbly.*.....(Evens fav op 6 to 4) 1
2828 ALLSTARS EXPRESS 4-10-2 (7*) Mr R Wakley, *al prmnt, led 4th till hdd sn aftr 3 out, ev ch nxt, one pace.*
.................(10 to 1 op 6 to 1) 2
2558⁶ HENRYS PORT 7-11-0 M Richards, *hld up in tch, cl 3rd but held whn blun badly last.*.... (10 to 1 op 6 to 1) 3
2810³ RACHEL LOUISE 5-10-9 S McNeill, *al prmnt, wknd appr 2 out.*.................(25 to 1 op 12 to 1) 4
3776² HE KNOWS THE RULES 5-11-0 B Powell, *prmnt till wknd appr 2 out.*.......(11 to 2 op 9 to 2 tchd 6 to 1) 5
3814² KETCHICAN 5-11-0 G Upton, *in rear, hdwy 4 out, one pace frm nxt.*.........(40 to 1 op 33 to 1 tchd 50 to 1) 6
IRENE'S PET 7-11-0 S Fox, *pld hrd, prmnt till wknd appr 3 out.*.................(25 to 1 op 16 to 1) 7

3106⁷ MAC'SMYUNCLE 6-11-0 J Frost, *al beh, tld off.*
.............................(100 to 1 op 33 to 1) 8
CALGARY GIRL 5-10-9 P Holley, *al beh, tld off.*
.............................(33 to 1 op 20 to 1) 9
THAT BIG BABY (Ire) 7-11-0 Miss L Blackford, *al beh, tld off*
hfwy..............................(200 to 1 op 66 to 1) 10
SUNRISE SPECIAL (Ire) 4-10-9 J F Titley, *al beh, tld off.*
.............................(100 to 1 op 33 to 1 tchd 200 to 1) 11
3542⁵ SPIRIT LEVEL 9-10-2 (7*) Mr S Durrack, *uns rdr 1st.*
.............................(100 to 1 op 33 to 1 tchd 200 to 1) ur
3623³ LUCKY ARCHER 4-10-9 M A Fitzgerald, *hmpd and uns rdr 1st.*.............................(5 to 1 op 7 to 2) ur
3736 NOQUITA (NZ) (bl) 10-10-9 (5*) X Aizpuru, *led to 4th, tld off whn pld up bef 2 out.*.....(200 to 1 op 50 to 1) pu
Dist: 4l, 5l, 6l, ¾l, 6l, 13l, 17l, 6l, 14l, 22l. 3m 59.50s. a 10.50s (14 Ran).
(Pinks Gym), Miss Venetia Williams

3893 Beamish Red Irish Ale Novices' Chase Class D (5-y-o and up) £3,436 2m 5f 110yds. ....(2:25)

3461³ CALL ME ALBI (Ire) (v) 6-11-0 M Richards, *hld up, rdn appr 6 out, led sn aftr 4 out, soon clr, drvn out.*
.............................(100 to 30 op 9 to 4) 1
3799² BLASKET HERO (bl) 9-11-6 A P McCoy, *in rear whn hit 8th, hdwy 4 out, rdn to chase wnr appr 2 out, no imprsn r-in.*
.............................(5 to 4 fav op 6 to 4 tchd 7 to 4) 2
2604 MEL (Ire) 7-11-0 B Powell, *al prmnt, wnt second 6 out, blun nxt, wknd appr 2 out...* (9 to 1 op 12 to 1 tchd 14 to 1) 3
3758⁵ JAC DEL PRINCE 7-11-0 P Hide, *led to second and 4th to 6th, ev ch four out, sn wknd....* (7 to 2 op 5 to 2 tchd 4 to 1) 4
3486² WALK IN THE WOODS 10-10-9 Mr A Holdsworth, *led second to 4th, led 6th till sn aftr four out, wknd quickly, virtually pld up r-in, tld off.*.........................(25 to 1 op 12 to 1) 5
TOMS CHOICE (Ire) 8-11-0 S McNeill, *in rear, some hdwy 4 out, btn whn wnt lme bef last, virtually pld up r-in, tld off.*
.............................(11 to 1 op 12 to 1 tchd 10 to 1) 6
Dist: 2l, 13l, 13l, dist, 2½l. 5m 20.20s. a 18.20s (6 Ran).
(Tony Rooth), Mrs L Richards

3894 Courage Best - Bristol Tradition Conditional Jockeys' Selling Handicap Hurdle Class G (0-95 4-y-o and up) £1,751 2m 1f. ....(2:55)

3859² MIRAMARE [60] 7-9-11 (3*) J Harris, *hld up, rdn and hdwy appr 3 out, led und pres bef nxt, ridden out.*
.............................(9 to 1 op 7 to 1 tchd 10 to 1) 1
3542¹ ON MY TOES [63] 6-9-12 (5*) B Moore, *led till hdd appr 2 out, rdn and one pace aftr..........*(6 to 1 tchd 13 to 2) 2
3487⁴ PRINCE OF SPADES [64] 5-10-4 O Burrows, *al prmnt, wknd aftr 3 out...*.............................(4 to 1 op 3 to 1 tchd 9 to 2) 3
3814 OCTOBER BREW (USA) [81] (bl) 7-11-7 G Supple, *hld up in rear, hdwy aftr 4th, rdn and wknd appr 2 out.*
.............................(9 to 4 fav op 11 to 4) 4
2436⁵ LANDSKER STAR [60] 7-10-0 D Salter, *in tch till wknd 3 out.*
.............................(20 to 1 op 16 to 1) 5
3814³ GABISH [60] 12-10-0 L Aspell, *prmnt early, beh frm 5th.*
.............................(25 to 1 op 20 to 1 tchd 33 to 1) 6
GALAXY HIGH [79] 10-11-5 Michael Brennan, *al beh, tld off hfwy.*.............................(10 to 1 tchd 8 to 1) 7
3673⁶ BODANTREE [88] 6-11-9 (5*) M Keighley, *trkd ldr to 4th, ev ch and gng wl whn f 3 out.*........(9 to 2 op 9 to 1) f
3810 MORE BILLS (Ire) [70] (v) 5-11-7 (3*) M Batchelor, *prmnt, trkd ldr 4th till appr 3 out, wl btn whn hit 2 out, sddl slpd, pld up bef last...................*(12 to 1 op 7 to 1 tchd 14 to 1) pu
Dist: 2½l, 15l, 2½l, 16l, 25l, 27l. 4m 1.00s. a 12.00s (9 Ran).
(Mrs Jonathan Bennett), R J Hodges

3895 Miller Time Classic Handicap Chase Class E (0-115 5-y-o and up) £2,900 2m 5f 110yds. ....(3:30)

3702⁵ RED BRANCH (Ire) [90] 8-11-1 T J Murphy, *jmpd wl and confidently rdn, led sn aftr 9th, in control frm 4 out.*
.....(Evens fav op 6 to 5 tchd 5 to 4 and 18 to 11 on) 1
3371³ BIT OF A TOUCH [83] 11-10-8 J Frost, *hld up, steady hdwy frm tenth, wnt second last, no imprsn.*
.............................(11 to 2 op 5 to 1 tchd 7 to 1) 2
3792³ SPRING TO GLORY [88] (v) 10-10-13 M A Fitzgerald, *trkd ldrs, chsd wnr 6 out to last, no extr r-in...*(7 to 1 op 6 to 1) 3
3371⁴ LAKE OF LOUGHREA (Ire) [99] 7-11-3 (7*) Mr R Wakley, *hld up in rear, hdwy 4 out, one pace aftr nxt.*(10 to 3 to 1) 4
3277³ SCOTONI [90] 11-11-1 S Curran, *led till sn aftr 9th, jmpd slwly nxt, soon wknd.*.............................(11 to 1 op 6 to 1) 5
1086⁴ DISTANT MEMORY [97] (bl) 8-11-8 A P McCoy, *wth ldr til hit 9th, wkng whn hit 6 out and nxt, tld off...*(6 to 1 op 4 to 1) 6
3404² GOLDEN OPAL [79] 12-10-4 B Powell, *al beh, tld off.*
.............................(20 to 1 op 14 to 1 tchd 25 to 1) 7
Dist: 1¼l, 1¼l, 8l, 30l, 10l, 18l. 5m 19.00s. a 17.00s (7 Ran).
(E J Mangan), J S King

3896 Holsten Pils - Get Real Classic Handicap Hurdle Class D (0-125 4-y-o and up) £2,735 2m 1f. ....(4:05)

3798⁷ YUBRALEE (USA) [118] 5-12-1 (5ex) A P McCoy, *made all, pushed clr 2 out, eased r-in, not extended.*
.............................(Evens fav op 11 to 10 tchd 11 to 10 on) 1
3633¹ OUT ON A PROMISE (Ire) [107] 5-11-4 M A Fitzgerald, *chsd wnr thrght, tried to cl 2 out, hld whn mstk last.*
.............................(15 to 8 op 6 to 4 tchd 2 to 1 and 9 to 4) 2
3275² HANDSON [90] 5-9-10 (5*) D Salter, *in tch till wknd appr 3 out, tld off...*.............................(11 to 2 op 4 to 1) 3
3062 INTERMAGIC [100] 7-10-11 S Fox, *al beh, lost tch hfwy, tld off...........................*(11 to 1 op 6 to 1 tchd 12 to 1) 4
Dist: 2l, dist, dist. 3m 53.10s. a 4.10s (4 Ran).
SR: 34/21/-/-/
(D A Johnson), M C Pipe

3897 Fosters Oval Handicap Chase Class D (0-125 5-y-o and up) £3,468 3¼m 110yds. ....(4:40)

3678² GOD SPEED YOU (Ire) [109] (bl) 8-11-4 J R Kavanagh, *led 1st, made rst, rdn out r-in.*
.............................(11 to 10 fav op 5 to 4 tchd 11 to 8) 1
3601⁶ BANNTOWN BILL (Ire) [97] (v) 8-10-6 A P McCoy, *led to 1st, cld on wnr 11th, rdn 3 out, no imprsn r-in.*
.............................(11 to 1 op 6 to 1) 2
3790⁶ DIAMOND FORT [97] 12-10-6 M A Fitzgerald, *hld up, hdwy to chase ldrs 6 out, one pace frm 2 out.*
.............................(6 to 1 op 4 to 1 tchd 7 to 1) 3
2895⁵ ACT OF PARLIAMENT (Ire) [117] (bl) 9-11-5 (7*) Mr R Wakley, *not fluent, beh till effrt 4 out, wknd nxt...*(3 to 1 op 9 to 4) 4
1859 RAINBOW CASTLE [105] 10-11-0 P Hide, *chsd ldrs till hit 14th, sn wknd, tld off..................*(10 to 1 op 7 to 2) 5
Dist: 1½l, 3l, 21l, dist. 6m 34.00s. a 14.00s (5 Ran).
(Wallop), C P Morlock

3898 Its Not All Over Yet Intermediate Open National Hunt Flat Class H (4,5,6-y-o) £1,264 2m 1f. ......(5:10)

EASTER ROSS 4-10-13 M A Fitzgerald, *hld up in tch, shaken up to ld o'r one furlong out, ran on.*
.............................(6 to 1 op 3 to 1 tchd 13 to 2) 1
VAGUE HOPE (Ire) 5-10-11 (7*) Mr O McPhail, *al in tch, led o'r 2 out, hdd over one out, kpt on one pace.*
.............................(7 to 1 op 10 to 1 tchd 14 to 1 and 8 to 1) 2
3135 BOZO (Ire) 6-11-4 G Upton, *al prmnt, ev ch 3 fs out, rdn and sn wknd..............*(7 to 4 fav op Evens tchd 2 to 1) 3
3302³ SALLY SCALLY 5-10-13 Mr L Jefford, *led till hdd 3 fs out, wknd................................*(4 to 1 op 5 to 1) 4
3408³ RUN FOR COVER (Ire) 5-10-13 A Procter, *mid-div, hdwy hfwy, one pace ins fnl 3 fs.............*(5 to 1 tchd 6 to 1) 5
3560 TWELVE CLUB 4-10-6 (7*) Mr R Wakley, *beh till hdwy o'r 4 fs out, no imprsn fnl 3 furlongs.........*(16 to 1 op 10 to 1) 6
KATY-BELLE 5-10-13 R Greene, *pld hrd, in rear till hdwy 5 fs out, nvr on terms.....................*(33 to 1 op 20 to 1) 7
3561 NATIONAL FIASCO 4-10-13 T Dascombe, *prmnt to hfwy, tld off...............................*(100 to 1 op 50 to 1) 8
ARCTIC VENTURE 5-10-13 M Richards, *mid-div to hfwy, tld off...........................*(100 to 1 op 25 to 1) 9
3408⁷ BABY LANCASTER 6-10-11 (7*) M Griffiths, *prmnt till wknd 5 fs out, tld off......................*(100 to 1 op 20 to 1) 10
ESKLEYBROOK 4-10-8 (5*) S Ryan, *slwly away, al beh, tld off........................*(100 to 1 op 20 to 1) 11
2179⁵ KING OF THE BLUES 5-11-4 T J Murphy, *prmnt till wknd o'r 3 fs out, eased, tld off..............*(10 to 1 tchd 14 to 1) 12
RUSTIC MISS 6-10-13 B Powell, *slwly away, al beh, tld off.*
.............................(20 to 1 op 12 to 1) 13
FABBL APPROVED 5-11-4 Mr A Holdsworth, *al beh, tld off hfwy..................................*(100 to 1 op 33 to 1) 14
Dist: 1¾l, 10l, hd, ¾l, 9l, 23l, 4l, 9l, 2½l. 3m 55.90s. (14 Ran).
(Queen Elizabeth), N J Henderson

SEDGEFIELD (good to firm)
Friday May 2nd
Going Correction: MINUS 0.10 sec. per fur.

3899 LCL Pils John Wade Haulage Selling Handicap Hurdle Class G (0-95 4-y-o and up) £1,992 2m 5f 110yds. (5:45)

1044³ FLINTLOCK (Ire) [68] 7-10-4 J Railton, *chsd ldrs, led 2 out, hrd pressed last, hld on wl und pres......*(12 to 1 op 10 to 1) 1
3507¹ BARTON HEIGHTS [85] 5-11-7 P Niven, *in tch, hdwy aftr 6th, rdn to chal last, ev ch till no extr towards finish.*
.............................(4 to 1 fav op 2 to 1) 2
3123 IJAB (Can) [72] 7-10-8 A Thornton, *trkd ldrs, ev ch whn hmpd appr 2 out, staying on whn hampered aftr last, not reco'r.*
.............................(4 to 1 fav op 5 to 1 tchd 12 to 1) 3
3819⁸ QUEEN'S COUNSEL (Ire) [71] 4-10-11 A S Smith, *hld up in tch, gd hdwy to ld 3 out, hmpd and hdd nxt, sn btn.*
.............................(10 to 1 op 7 to 1 tchd 11 to 1) 4
3803⁷ BARNSTORMER [70] (bl) 11-10-6 D Parker, *in tch, outpcd bef 3 out, no dngr aftr.................*(20 to 1 op 14 to 1) 5
3197³ SIMAND [71] 5-10-7 J Callaghan, *led 4th till hdd 3 out, wknd aftr three out.........*(10 to 1 op 7 to 1 tchd 11 to 1) 6
3399 DALUSMAN (Ire) [67] 9-10-3 B Storey, *prmnt till wknd appr 3 out.....................*(20 to 1 op 14 to 1) 7

KING OF THE HORSE (Ire) [80] 6-10-11 (5*) R McGrath, *hld up, some hdwy aftr 3 out, sn btn.*
.................................(13 to 2 op 6 to 1 tchd 7 to 1)   8
3582 ROSTINO (Ire) [64] 8-9-9 (5*) S Taylor, *nvr better than mid-div, lost tch bef 2 out.*...................(25 to 1 op 20 to 1)   9
1911⁸ FLY TO THE END (USA) [72] 7-10-8 L Wyer, *beh, lost tch bef 2 out, virtually pld up clsg stages.*.......(16 to 1 op 12 to 1) 10
FRIENDLY SOCIETY [65] 11-10-1 M Moloney, *beh whn f second*...........................(100 to 1 op 50 to 1)   f
SHARP TO OBLIGE [64] 10-10-0 O Pears, *beh whn brght dwn bend aftr 3rd*........(25 to 1 op 33 to 1 tchd 50 to 1) bd
3200⁵ COOL LUKE (Ire) [92] 8-11-7 (7*) N Horrocks, *strted slwly, towards rear whn slpd up bend aftr 3rd*..........(10 to 1) su
3658 FIERY SUN [73] 12-10-9 N Smith, *led hdd 4th, wknd bef 3 out, lost tch and pld up before nxt.*.......(9 to 1 op 5 to 1) pu
Dist: 1¼l, 6l, 6l, 1¾l, 7l, 2½l, 1¼l, 18l, 7l. 4m 56.50s. a 8.50s (14 Ran).
(Mrs J Watters), H Alexander

3900 Federation Special Conditional Jockeys' Novices' Hurdle Class E (4-y-o and up) £2,320 2m 1f......(6:15)

813² FATEHALKHAIR (Ire) 5-10-9 (5*) C McCormack, *made all, ran on srtly frm 2 out.*..........(11 to 4 op 3 to 1 tchd 7 to 2)   1
3127² COUNTRY ORCHID 6-10-9 G Lee, *badly hmpd 1st, sn in tch, hdwy and ch bef 2 out, soon rdn, no imprsn on wnr.*
.........................(11 to 10 fav op 11 to 8 tchd 7 to 4)   2
912⁸ SALKELD KING (Ire) 5-11-0 S Taylor, *chsd wnr, mstk 4th, outpcd bef 2 out, kpt on frm last.*.....(33 to 1 tchd 50 to 1)   3
3674⁵ JENDORCET (v) 7-10-9 R McGrath, *towards rear, hdwy aftr 5th, no imprsn on btm whn mstk last.*....(7 to 1 op 5 to 1)   4
3583² DIAMOND BEACH 4-11-2 E Callaghan, *badly hmpd 1st, beh, rdn bef 2 out, sn wknd*.................(3 to 1 op 2 to 1)   5
3356 BUDDLEIA 4-9-13 (5*) R Burns, *in tch till wknd aftr 5th, tld off.*
....(33 to 1)   6
3757 JUST WHISTLE 5-10-9 F Leahy, *f 1st.*
.....................(50 to 1 op 33 to 1 tchd 66 to 1)   f
3258 WEAPONS FREE 6-10-9 (5*) R McCarthy, *brght dwn 1st.*
.........................(20 to 1 op 14 to 1) bd
PATS CROSS (Ire) 8-11-0 M Newton, *in tch till wknd aftr 5th, tld off whn pld up bef 2 out*.........(20 to 1 op 12 to 1) pu
Dist: 12l, 4l, 1¼l, 18l, 21l. 3m 51.10s. a 5.10s (9 Ran).
SR: 18/1/2/-/-/-/   (Mrs Gwen Smith), B Ellison

3901 Kellys Lager Novices' Chase Class E (5-y-o and up) £3,059 3m 3f... (6:45)

3649* THE WHOLE HOG (Ire) 8-11-12 A Thornton, *nvr far away, mstk 16th, chsd ldr frm 2 out, styd on wl und pres to ld clsg stages.*...........(5 to 4 on op 11 to 8 on tchd 6 to 4 on)   1
3600⁵ MISS COLETTE 9-11-3 M Foster, *led, styd on wl frm 2 out, hdd clsg stages, no extr*............(100 to 30 op 7 to 2)   2
3660 GERMAN LEGEND 7-11-8 J Burke, *prmnt, mstk 11th, ev ch 3 out, rdn and wknd aftr nxt.*
........................(100 to 30 op 3 to 1 tchd 7 to 2)   3
3508⁴ EVENING RUSH 11-11-6 K Jones, *beh, lost tch frm 15th, tld off.*.............................(14 to 1 op 16 to 1)   4
Dist: Nk, 14l, dist. 6m 42.10s. a 9.10s (4 Ran).
(Mrs Sharon C Nelson), K C Bailey

3902 Federation Brewery Handicap Chase Class D (0-125 5-y-o and up) £3,821 2m 5f.............. (7:15)

3719³ WEAVER GEORGE (Ire) [108] 7-11-9 (5*) R McGrath, *hld up, steady hdwy to ld aftr 2 out, styd on wl.* (11 to 4 op 3 to 1)   1
3399 BLAZING DAWN [86] 10-10-6 T Reed, *trkd ldrs, outpcd aftr 2 out, styd on frm nxt.*.......(13 to 2 op 6 to 1 tchd 7 to 1)   2
3760⁶ REBEL KING [80] 7-9-9 (5*) S Taylor, *cl up, led 9th, hdd 3 out, kpt on same pace frm nxt.*
.......................(10 to 1 op 8 to 1 tchd 11 to 1)   3
3824⁷ CROSS CANNON [107] 11-11-13 B Storey, *trkd ldrs, led 3 out, hdd aftr nxt, 4th and btn whn f last.*
..................................(100 to 30 op 7 to 2)   f
3565⁴ ALY DALEY (Ire) [97] 9-11-3 A S Smith, *led till hdd 9th, rdn whn mstk nxt, 5th and btn when brght dwn last.*
.....................................(7 to 4 fav tchd 2 to 1) bd
WAIT YOU THERE (USA) [87] 12-10-7 Mr S Swiers, *beh, lost tch frm 9th, tld off whn pld up aftr 11th.* (14 to 1 op 12 to 1) pu
Dist: 1l, 2l. 5m 0.80s. a 4.80s (6 Ran).
SR: 31/8/-/   (Regent Decorators Ltd), W Storey

3903 Buchanan Novices' Hurdle Class E (4-y-o and up) £2,460 2m 5f 110yds .... (7:45)

3655² CATCH THE PIGEON 8-10-9 N Smith, *in tch, took clr order hfwy, led 2 out, sn quickened clr.*.......(11 to 4 op 7 to 2)   1
3727² NORTHERN SPLASH 4-11-7 (7*) Miss J Wormall, *cl up, led 6th, hdd 3 out, no rdn, outpcd aftr nxt, kpt on frm last.*
..............................(6 to 1 op 9 to 2)   2
2537² FLYAWAY BLUES 5-11-7 P Niven, *hld up, took clr order aftr 7th, rdn and outpcd aftr 3 out, styd on frm nxt, no extr r-in.*
.............(7 to 4 on op 2 to 1 on tchd 13 to 8 on)   3
3658² MOVIE MAN 5-10-7 (7*) R Burns, *prmnt, led 3 out, mstk and hdd nxt, sn btn.*...............(16 to 1 op 14 to 1)   4

1047 LADY SWIFT 6-10-9 M Foster, *trkd ldrs, dsptd ld hfwy, wknd appr 3 out, tld off.*..............(25 to 1 op 20 to 1)   5
3309 WOODHOUSE LANE 5-10-7 (7*) Miss C Metcalfe, *beh, lost tch aftr 7th, tld off.*..................(100 to 1 op 50 to 1)   6
3658 STRONG CHARACTER 11-11-0 J Burke, *made most to 6th, sn wknd, wl tld off.*...........(100 to 1 op 50 to 1)   7
Dist: 9l, ¾l, 3½l, dist, ½l, dist. 4m 57.70s. a 9.70s (7 Ran).
(Mrs R E Barr), R E Barr

3904 Keoghans Mares' Only Handicap Hurdle Class F (0-105 4-y-o and up) £2,092 2m 5f 110yds......... (8:15)

3803 WHITEGATESPRINCESS (Ire) [66] (v) 6-9-7 (7*) C McCormack, *trkd ldrs, led bef 2 out, styd on und pres.*
..................................(12 to 1 op 10 to 1)   1
3823⁵ RAISE A DOLLAR [75] 7-10-9 Mr S Swiers, *led 3rd to 5th, led 7th till hdd bef 2 out, styd on wl clsg stages, fnshd lme.*
....(5 to 2 op 7 to 2)   2
3761* PEGGY GORDON [77] 6-10-11 (7ex) Miss P Robson, *hld up, effrt aftr 3 out, kpt on same pace frm nxt.*
.............................(9 to 4 fav op 11 to 8)   3
3587⁹ AIDE MEMOIRE (Ire) [73] 8-10-7 K Johnson, *hld up, drvn alng bef 2 out, no hdwy.*.....(15 to 2 op 6 to 1 tchd 8 to 1)   4
3582² NITE SPRITE [66] 7-9-9 (5*) Scott Taylor, *prmnt, led 5th to 7th, wknd aftr 3 out.*......(15 to 2 op 7 to 1 tchd 8 to 1)   5
3331⁷ DAISY DAYS (Ire) [90] 7-11-10 A S Smith, *led to 3rd, pld up lme bef nxt.*.................(4 to 1 tchd 9 to 2) pu
Dist: 1¼l, 3½l, 1¼l, 1½l. 5m 6.20s. a 18.20s (6 Ran).
(Red Onion), B Ellison

HAYDOCK (good)
Saturday May 3rd
Going Correction: MINUS 0.05 sec. per fur.

3905 Crowther Homes Hell Nook Four Years Old Handicap Hurdle Class C £8,862 2m.................... (1:10)

3463² SEATTLE ALLEY (USA) [105] 11-3 J A McCarthy, *hld up, hdwy 4 out, slight ld last, all out.*............(7 to 1 op 8 to 1)   1
3641² FAIRLY SHARP (Ire) [103] 11-1 R Dunwoody, *chsd ldg pair, cld 3 out, led betw last 2, hdd last, ev ch r-in, jst hld.*
....(8 to 1 tchd 7 to 1)   2
3714* SHU GAA (Ire) [112] (bl) 11-10 J Osborne, *hld up in midfield, slightly outpcd 4 out, drvn and hdwy nxt, chsd ldrs and kpt on und pres frm 2 out.*............(5 to 1 op 7 to 1)   3
3610* KINNESCASH (Ire) [108] 11-6 M A Fitzgerald, *wth ldr, led 3 out, drvn and hdd betw last 2, not fluent last, one pace r-in.*
..................................(9 to 2 jt-fav op 4 to 1)   4
3802³ DOUBLE AGENT [102] 11-0 A S Smith, *hld up in tch, drvn and outpcd 3 out, not trble ldrs.*.........(20 to 1 op 14 to 1)   5
3483* MELT THE CLOUDS (Can) [113] (bl) 11-11 A P McCoy, *hld up in rear, hdwy to chase ldrs 3 out, mstk nxt, wknd bef last.*
....(8 to 1 op 5 to 1)   6
3714³ CLASH OF SWORDS [94] 10-6 L Wyer, *hld up in tch, effrt appr 3 out, wknd nxt.*..................(11 to 1 op 8 to 1)   7
3478⁵ GO WITH THE WIND [90] 10-2 D J Moffatt, *beh, niggled alng 3rd, nvr a factor.*.............(25 to 1 op 20 to 1)   8
3680 NOBLE COLOURS [95] 10-4 (3*) Mr R Thornton, *led till hdd 3 out, wknd quickly, tld off.*...........(9 to 2 jt-fav op 4 to 1)   9
3555 TIUTCHEV [93] 10-5 J Culloty, *in rear whn mstk and uns rdr 1st.*...............(14 to 1 op 10 to 1 tchd 16 to 1) ur
Dist: Sht-hd, 3½l, 2½l, 6l, 1½l, 4l, 1l, dist. 3m 44.80s. a 6.80s (10 Ran).
SR: 13/11/16/9/6/-/   (L & P Partnership), P R Webber

3906 Crowther Homes Long Distance Hurdle Class B (5-y-o and up) £8,524 2m 7f 110yds.................... (1:40)

3745² PRIDWELL 7-11-0 A P McCoy, *patiently rdn in rear, smooth hdwy 3 out, led narrowly nxt, very cheekily.*
...............................(5 to 4 fav tchd 6 to 4)   1
3579⁴ YAHMI (Ire) 7-11-0 J Osborne, *led till 2 out, sn und pres, no ch wth wnr.*...............(11 to 4 op 5 to 2 tchd 3 to 1)   2
3156 ROMANCER (Ire) 6-11-0 C Llewellyn, *chsd ldrs, pckd second, blun 4 out, sn und pres and lft beh.*....(9 to 1 op 10 to 1)   3
3151 CONQUERING LEADER (Ire) 8-10-9 M A Fitzgerald, *trkd ldr, chlgd 4 out, wknd 2 out, eased bef last, virtually pld up r-in.*
....(9 to 4 op 7 to 4)   4
Dist: 1¾l, 17l, dist. 5m 48.10s. a 17.10s (4 Ran).
(Jones, Berstock And Fleet Partnership), M C Pipe

3907 Crowther Homes Swinton Handicap Hurdle Class A Grade 3 (4-y-o and up) £23,197 2m................ (2:10)

3717⁵ DREAMS END [142] 9-11-11 (3*) L Aspell, *hld up, hdwy 3 out, sn chalg, led r-in, ran on wl.*........(14 to 1 op 12 to 1)   1
3562⁴ MISTER RM [114] 5-10-0 C Llewellyn, *hld up, hdwy und pres 3 out, sn chalg, lft in ld and hmpd last, hdd r-in, kpt on.*
....(16 to 1 op 14 to 1)   2
3766² SHANKAR (Ire) [137] 6-11-6 (3*) Mr R Thornton, *hld up, hdwy appr 3 out, ch approaching last, styd on same pace r-in.*
....(8 to 1 op 7 to 1)   3

3156* BARNA BOY (Ire) [135] 9-11-7 M A Fitzgerald, *mid-div, hmpd 1st, hdwy 4 out, ch and pres appr last, kpt on same pace r-in.*
.... (14 to 1 op 12 to 1) 4

3396* STAR SELECTION [122] 6-10-5 (3*) E Husband, *sn prmnt, und pres in 5th whn hmpd last, one pace run- in.*
.... (7 to 1 op 13 to 2 tchd 8 to 1) 5

3580⁷ TRAGIC HERO [134] (bl) 5-11-6 R Supple, *in tch, effrt 3 out, no imprsn on ldrs.*...........................(25 to 1) 6

3717⁴ INGLETONIAN [129] 8-11-1 B Storey, *in rear, swrvd to avoid faller second, hdwy und pres frm 3 out, nvr nrr.*
.... (12 to 1 op 10 to 1) 7

3717 EXPRESS GIFT [133] 8-11-5 P Niven, *hld up in rear, late hdwy, nvr nrr.*........................ (20 to 1 op 16 to 1) 8

3717³ EDELWEIS DU MOULIN (Fr) [135] 5-11-7 R Dunwoody, *midfield, hdwy appr 3 out, sn chasing ldrs, drvn and wknd bef last.*
.... (6 to 1 fav tchd 7 to 1) 9

3562⁶ GREEN GREEN DESERT (Fr) [125] 6-10-11 J Osborne, *hld up, hdwy 3 out, drvn and chasing ldrs aftr 4 out.*
.... (12 to 1 op 10 to 1) 10

3595 STOMPIN [139] (bl) 6-11-11 J Culloty, *trkd ldrs, rdn and wknd 3 out.*.................... (9 to 1 op 14 to 1) 11

3617⁶ KADASTROF (Fr) [135] 7-11-2 (5*) X Aizpuru, *cl up, pushed alng 4 out, wknd nxt.*................ (25 to 1 op 16 to 1) 12

3717⁹ MASTER BEVELED [138] 7-11-10 R Garritty, *in tch, blun 4th, sn lost pl and beh.*................. (20 to 1 op 16 to 1) 13

3156⁷ TOM BRODIE [127] 7-10-13 A S Smith, *midfield, swrvd to avoid faller second, hdwy aftr 4 out, drvn whn chasing ldrs nxt, wknd bef last.*.................. (20 to 1 op 16 to 1) 14

3595 KAITAK (Ire) [116] 6-10-2 L Wyer, *prmnt till f second.*
.... (25 to 1 op 20 to 1) f

3683* NORTHERN STARLIGHT [124] 6-10-10 A P McCoy, *led, pushed alng aftr 4 out, hrd pressed whn f last.*
.... (13 to 2 op 5 to 1 tchd 7 to 1) f

3562⁷ NORDIC BREEZE (Ire) [120] 5-10-6 C Maude, *f 1st.*
.... (10 to 1 op 14 to 1) f

3791⁴ MONNAIE FORTE (Ire) [114] 7-9-9 (5*) R McGrath, *hndy, lost pl aftr 4th, sn beh, tld off whn pld up bef last.*
.... (10 to 1 tchd 9 to 1) pu

3745⁴ ASHWELL BOY (Ire) [134] 6-11-6 B Powell, *al beh, struggling 4 out, tld off whn pld up bef last.*........ (10 to 1 op 7 to 2) pu

Dist: ¾l, 2½l, 3½l, nk, 5l, 3½l, nk, 1½l, ¾l, 15l. 3m 40.20s. a 2.20s (19 Ran).

SR: 70/41/61/55/42/49/40/44/44/ (T G Price), P Bowen

3908 Crowther Homes New Florida Handicap Hurdle Class B (0–140 4-y-o and up) £5,047 2½m........................ (2:45)

3478⁶ DIWALI DANCER [107] 7-10-1 B Powell, *made all, rdn appr last, edgd lft and kpt on cl hme.*........(9 to 1 op 11 to 2) 1

3715² SHERIFFMUIR [130] 8-11-10 J Osborne, *hndy, und pres frm 4 out and slightly outpcd, styd on run- in, crrd slightly lft cl hme.*............... (3 to 1 fav op 7 to 2 tchd 4 to 1) 2

3782² ELATION [108] (bl) 5-10-2 R Dunwoody, *trkd ldr, chlgd on bit 3 out, drvn appr last, not keen r-in, no extr.*
.... (11 to 2 op 5 to 1) 3

3717⁸ HOME COUNTIES (Ire) [132] 8-11-12 D J Moffatt, *hld up in rear, brief effrt 3 out, not trble ldrs....*(12 to 1 op 9 to 1) 4

3791 SUIVEZ [122] 7-11-2 M A Fitzgerald, *hld up, effrt 4 out, no imprsn.*....................(16 to 1 op 10 to 1) 5

3209⁴ MOVING OUT [112] 9-10-6 J Culloty, *in tch, rdn aftr 4 out, sn wknd.*.................... (12 to 1 op 10 to 1) 6

3759² DURANO [113] 6-10-7 R Garritty, *cl up, drvn appr 2 out, sn wknd and eased........*(14 to 1 op 7 to 1 tchd 6 to 1) 7

2217* STORM DUST [114] 8-10-5 (3*) Mr R Thornton, *in tch, lost pl 6th, drvn 4 out, no dngr aftrwards....*. (5 to 1 op 4 to 1) 8

3759⁸ RAINBOUR (Ire) [107] 5-10-1 A S Smith, *al beh, blun 5th, tld off...................*(14 to 1 tchd 16 to 1) 9

Dist: ¾l, ½l, 16l, ¾l, 21l, 1¼l, 1½l, dist. 4m 45.60s. a 9.60s (9 Ran).
(B E Case), M C Pipe

3909 Crowther Homes Edge Green Novices' Claiming Hurdle Class F (4-y-o and up) £2,015 2½m.........(3:15)

3805 JESSOLLE 5-10-10 R Dunwoody, *trkd ldrs, led 2 out, ran on wl.*.................... (9 to 4 op 7 to 4) 1

3714⁴ SOUSSE 4-10-5 G Lee, *led till aftr 1st, rgned ld appr 3rd, hdd 2 out, one pace.*.................. (4 to 1 op 3 to 1) 2

2807⁷ RECRUITMENT 4-10-8 R Supple, *led aftr 1st, hdd appr 3rd, no ch wth ldg pair frm 6th, blun whn no dngr 3 out.*
.... (25 to 1 op 14 to 1) 3

2749⁷ TUDOR TOWN 9-11-2 S Burrough, *in rear, mstk 3rd, nvr a factor........................*(25 to 1 op 16 to 1) 4

3846* COUNTRY LOVER (v) 6-12-0 A P McCoy, *hld up in rear, broke dwn and pld up bef second, destroyed.*
.... (11 to 10 fav op Evens tchd 5 to 4) pu

TEN MORE SINGHAS 7-10-12 T Eley, *al beh, lost tch 5th, tld off whn pld up bef last.*............ (33 to 1 op 25 to 1) pu

Dist: 3l, 23l, 9l. 4m 57.00s. a 21.00s (6 Ran).

(C R Fleet), G Richards

3910 Crowther Homes Dock Lane Novices' Hurdle Class D (4-y-o and up) £3,004 2m....................(3:50)

3111 SMOLENSK (Ire) 5-11-4 R Dunwoody, *hld up in 3rd pl, wnt second appr 3 out, led last, rdn out.*
.... (6 to 1 op 7 to 1 tchd 11 to 2) 1

3750 SHARPICAL 5-11-7 M A Fitzgerald, *rcd in last pl, cld 2 out, ev ch last, not quicken r-in.*
.... (11 to 4 on tchd 3 to 1 on and 5 to 2 on) 2

3555³ MOON DEVIL (Ire) 7-11-0 B Powell, *led till hdd last, kpt on same pace r-in.*............. (14 to 1 op 8 to 1) 3

3555* RIPARIUS (USA) 6-11-7 J Osborne, *trkd ldr, lost pl whn short of room on beng appr 3 out, ev ch 2 out, wknd bef last, sn eased, tld off....................*(4 to 10 op 7 to 2) 4

Dist: 2l, 2½l, dist. 3m 46.30s. a 8.30s (4 Ran).

(Mrs Chris Deuters), J Berry

HEREFORD (good)
Saturday May 3rd
Going Correction: PLUS 0.40 sec. per fur.

3911 Greig Middleton Selling Handicap Hurdle Class G (0–95 4-y-o and up) £1,725 2m 1f................ (2:25)

3819⁵ TURRILL HOUSE [65] 5-10-1 M Richards, *slwly away, hld up, gd hdwy appr 3 out, led bef nxt, sn clr, easily.*
.... (11 to 4 fav op 7 to 4 tchd 3 to 1) 1

2403 HONEYBED WOOD [64] 9-10-0 D Gallagher, *mstk second, wl in rear till hdwy frm 3 out, fnshd well to go second r-in.*
.... (11 to 2 op 10 to 1 tchd 12 to 1 and 5 to 1) 2

3457⁵ CUILLIN CAPER [70] (bl) 5-10-6 A Thornton, *led second, drvn clr 4 out, hdd appr 2 out, wknd bef last.* (11 to 2 op 3 to 1) 3

2983* CUILLIN CAPER [70] (bl) 5-10-6 A Thornton, *led second, drvn clr 4 out, hdd appr 2 out, wknd bef last.* (11 to 2 op 3 to 1) 4

786⁵ HARLEQUIN WALK (Ire) [81] 6-11-3 D O'Sullivan, *hld up, hdwy appr 5th, cl 3rd 2 out, wknd bef last.* (5 to 1 op 3 to 1) 5

3686³ COMMANCHE CREEK [75] 7-10-6 (3*) Sophie Mitchell, *in tch to 5th...................*(25 to 1 op 16 to 1) 6

3278 VISION OF FREEDOM (Ire) [92] 9-11-7 (7*) J Power, *trkd ldr till wknd 3 out................*(7 to 1 op 4 to 1 tchd 8 to 1) 7

3741⁹ JEWEL THIEF [68] (v) 7-10-4 B Fenton, *led to second, rdn aftr 4th, wknd four out......*(11 to 1 op 5 to 1 tchd 12 to 1) 8

3276 VITAL WONDER [64] 9-9-7 (7*) M Griffiths, *slwly away, blun 3rd, al beh.*...................... (11 to 2 op 4 to 1) 9

3542⁷ PATONG BEACH [64] 7-10-0 S Fox, *pld hrd, in tch till wknd 5th....................*(25 to 1 op 14 to 1) 10

Dist: 12l, 2l, 3l, 1½l, 8l, nk, 14l, 1¼l, 3l. 4m 0.10s. a 15.10s (10 Ran).

(J R Hawksley), W J Musson

3912 Mercury Asset Management Novices' Chase Class E (5-y-o and up) £2,690 2m 3f................ (2:55)

3486 DUBELLE 7-11-1 T J Murphy, *made all, in command frm 2 out, pushed out.*.............. (5 to 1 op 4 to 1) 1

44* EID (USA) 8-11-9 Richard Guest, *hld up, hdwy appr 3 out, wnt second nxt, no imprsn.*
.... (11 to 8 fav op 6 to 4 tchd 5 to 4 and 7 to 4) 2

3543 FIRST CLASS 7-11-0 R Greene, *not fluent, pld hrd, hdwy 3rd, chsd wnr to 2 out, sn btn.*
.... (7 to 2 op 5 to 2 tchd 4 to 1) 3

3573³ INDIAN TEMPLE 6-10-9 (5*) G Supple, *trkd wnr, reminders aftr 5th, hit 5 out, wknd after nxt....*(12 to 1 op 8 to 1) 4

3829² DIAMOND LIGHT 10-11-0 Mr S Lloyd, *al beh, hit 6th, sn tld off und ins rdr 3 out............*(14 to 1 op 8 to 1) ur

3502² ASTRAL INVASION (USA) 6-10-11 (3*) R Massey, *prmnt whn hit 5th, wknd 7th, tld off whn pld up bef 2 out.*
.... (7 to 1 op 6 to 1 tchd 8 to 1) pu

2561 DODGY DEALER (Ire) 7-11-0 Mr E James, *al beh, tld off 6th, pld up bef 2 out....*(20 to 1 op 12 to 1) pu

Dist: 8l, 5l, 17l. 4m 47.40s. a 22.40s (7 Ran).

(W J Lee), J S King

3913 Great Brampton House Antiques Novices' Hurdle Class E (4-y-o and up) £2,070 2m 3f 110yds......(3:25)

3793² EAU DE COLOGNE 5-11-6 M Richards, *hld up, hdwy 4 out, rdn to ld appr 2 out, clr last.*
.......(11 to 10 fav op Evens tchd 5 to 4 and 11 to 8) 1

2541⁶ SUPREME CHARM (Ire) 5-10-7 (7*) Mr R Wakley, *al prmnt, led 4 out, rdn and hdd appr 2 out, sn btn.* (8 to 1 tchd 10 to 1) 2

2871⁴ JUST JASMINE 5-10-9 R Greene, *al prmnt, wknd appr 2 out.*
.... (12 to 1 op 7 to 1) 3

3639³ HIGH SUMMER 7-11-0 G Upton, *prmnt, mstk 6th, lost pl appr 3 out, styd on aftr nxt...........*(10 to 1 tchd 12 to 1) 4

3097³ BROOK BEE 5-11-0 W Marston, *jmpd slwly 1st, led aftr second, hdd 8th, wknd appr 3 out....*. (33 to 1 op 20 to 1) 5

RUSHAWAY 6-11-0 D Gallagher, *led till aftr second, prmnt till wknd 3 out, eased......*(14 to 1 op 20 to 1 tchd 25 to 1) 6

1830⁵ BAY FAIR 5-10-9 I Lawrence, *reminderes and hdwy appr 7th, wknd nxt............*(14 to 1 op 8 to 1 tchd 16 to 1) 7

3534³ SICARIAN 5-11-0 Derek Byrne, *slwly away, beh till hdwy appr 7th, wknd nxt, tld off...............*(5 to 1 op 7 to 2) 8

2896² OPERETTO (Ire) 7-11-0 Mr E James, *prmnt till wknd 7th, tld off....................*(10 to 1 op 6 to 1 tchd 11 to 1) 9

3722⁶ WESTERN SUN 7-10-9 (5*) A Bates, *in tch, rdn aftr 5th, wknd 7th, tld off*..........................(100 to 1 op 66 to 1) 10

3735 FEARLESS HUSSAR 7-11-0 P Holley, *uns rdr nxt*.
..........................(100 to 1 op 66 to 1) ur
KING CURAN (USA) (bl) 6-11-0 Richard Guest, *mid-div, lost tch 6th, tld off whn pld up bef nxt*.........(10 to 1 op 6 to 1) pu
PEARLA DUBH (Ire) 8-11-0 V Slattery, *beh frm 5th, tld off whn blun 7th, pld up bef nxt*.................(33 to 1 op 25 to 1) pu

3513 SANDVILLE LAD 5-10-7 (7*) Mr A Wintle, *al beh, tld off frm 5th, pld up bef 3 out*........(66 to 1 op 50 to 1) pu

1592 ALI'S DELIGHT 6-11-0 A Thornton, *slwly away, al beh, tld off whn pld up bef 3 out*.........(100 to 1 op 66 to 1) pu

3729 MARLIES GOHR 5-10-9 T Dascombe, *al beh, tld off 6th, pld up bef 3 out*.....................(100 to 1 op 66 to 1) pu

Dist: 11l, ¾l, 3l, 23l, 1¾l, ½l, 18l, 4l, 4l. 4m 45.20s. a 27.20s (16 Ran).

(D And M Evans), Mrs L Richards

3914 Kidsons Impey Handicap Chase Class F (0-105 5-y-o and up) £2,560 3m 1f 110yds................(4:00)

NOVA CHAMP [81] 9-9-13 (5*) G F Ryan, *al gng wl beh ldrs, led on bit 3 out, clr nxt, easily*......(12 to 1 op 8 to 1) 1

2979* MR INVADER [93] 10-11-2 W Marston, *al prmnt, led 4 out, rdn and hdd nxt, no ch frm 2 out*..........(11 to 2 op 4 to 1) 2

3465* JUST ONE CANALETTO [77] (bl) 9-9-7 (7*) Mr J Goldstein, *hld up, hdwy 13th, ev ch 3 out, sn outpcd*.........(5 to 1 co-fav op 7 to 2) 3

3843⁶ BALLYDOUGAN (Ire) [77] (v) 9-10-0 T J Murphy, *wl beh till styd on frm 4 out, nvr nrr*...........(20 to 1 op 16 to 1) 4

757⁶ BOXING MATCH [77] 10-10-0 T Dascombe, *led second till hdd 4 out, wknd quickly, tld off*.........(20 to 1 op 14 to 1) 5

3739* SUPPOSIN [91] 9-11-0 Richard Guest, *beh whn hit tenth, hdwy 13th, wknd 4 out, tld off*.......(5 to 1 co-fav op 3 to 1) 6

3465⁴ MAXXUM EXPRESS (Ire) [80] 9-9-12 (5*) A Bates, *beh frm 6th, tld off*.........................(10 to 1 op 9 to 1) 7

3701 ROCKY PARK [95] 11-11-4 B Fenton, *beh frm 5th, tld off whn f 14th*.........(1 to 2 op 5 to 1 tchd 6 to 1 and 7 to 1) f

3461 BOTTLE BLACK [80] 10-10-3 P McLoughlin, *hld up in tch, rdn aftr tenth, beh whn f 14th*........(25 to 1 op 12 to 1) f

3688⁶ NORTHERN OPTIMIST [87] 9-10-10 Mr J L Llewellyn, *mid-div, lost tch 13th, tld off whn pld bef 4 out*.
..........................(20 to 1 op 12 to 1) pu

3790 DONT TELL THE WIFE [105] 11-12-0 A Thornton, *led to second, trkd ldrs, wkng whn hit 14th, tld off whn pld up bef 3 out*...................(12 to 1 op 10 to 1 tchd 14 to 1) pu

3739³ FURRY FOX (Ire) [78] 9-10-1 D Morris, *hld up, hdwy 7th, hit 11th, wknd and pld up bef nxt*.
..........................(6 to 1 op 7 to 1 tchd 8 to 1) pu

3640³ CAPO CASTANUM [92] 8-10-8 (7*) Mr A Wintle, *sn in tch, wknd appr 14th, tld off whn pld bef 3 out*......(5 to 1 co-fav op 7 to 2) pu

Dist: 13l, nk, ½l, 27l, 11l, 8l. 6m 20.20s. a 20.20s (13 Ran).

(Mrs C E Van Praagh), Mrs S J Smith

3915 Hereford Automatics Jackpot Novices' Handicap Hurdle Class E (0-100 4-y-o and up) £2,070 2m 1f ....(4:30)

3590² MAGICAL BLUES (Ire) [85] 5-11-4 K Gaule, *reluctant to strt, hdwy to ld 4 out, rdn out*..................(5 to 1 op 4 to 1) 1

3731³ NAHLA [80] 7-10-13 S Curran, *al prmnt, led 5th to nxt, ev ch 2 out, no extr appr last*......(9 to 2 op 4 to 1 tchd 5 to 1) 2

3728² THE BREWER [77] 5-10-10 R Bellamy, *hld up, hdwy appr 5th, rdn and no extr aftr 3 out*........(4 to 1 jt-fav op 7 to 2) 3

2898 ARIOSO [67] 9-9-9 (5*) A Bates, *hld up in rear, hdwy 3 out, nvr nrr*.............(13 to 2 op 4 to 1 tchd 7 to 1) 4

3731⁴ FENCER'S QUEST (Ire) [78] 4-10-6 S Wynne, *prmnt till wknd appr 3 out*.......................(9 to 2 op 3 to 1) 5

2874⁵ CREDO BOY [71] 8-10-4 R Greene, *mid-div, no hdwy frm 4 out*.......................(14 to 1 op 10 to 1) 6

3351 SOCCER BALL [67] 7-9-9 (5*) D J Kavanagh, *hld up hdwy 4 out, wknd nxt*...............(33 to 1 op 20 to 1) 7

1743⁶ KUMARI KING (Ire) [72] 7-10-5 D Morris, *in rear till hdwy 5th, wknd nxt*.............(16 to 1 tchd 20 to 1) 8

3148 ROYAL GLINT [67] 8-10-0 B Fenton, *mstk 1st, al beh*.
..........................(20 to 1 tchd 25 to 1) 9

3805² FAIRELAINE [79] (bl) 5-10-12 C O'Dwyer, *in tch to 5th, wl beh whn hit 3 out, tld off*.......(14 to 1 jt-fav op 7 to 2 tchd 8 to 1) 10

3729⁹ ASK ME (Ire) [87] 6-11-3 (3*) R Massey, *led to 5th, in wknd, f 3 out*................(20 to 1 op 12 to 1) f

3731 RITTO [93] 7-11-12 T Dascombe, *hld up in tch, hdwy appr 5th, mstk nxt, wknd quickly, tld off whn pld up aftr 2 out*.
..........................(8 to 1 op 7 to 1) pu

3731 AQUA AMBER [67] 5-9-11⁴ (7*) J Power, *prmnt, mstk second, wknd aftr 5th, tld off whn pld up bef 2 out*.
..........................(25 to 1 op 20 to 1) pu

Dist: 2½l, 3l, 3l, 7l, 1l, 2½l, 12l, 4l, 14l. 4m 1.90s. a 16.90s (13 Ran).

(Miss A Embiricos), Miss A E Embiricos

3916 Jail-Break Hunters' Chase Class H (5-y-o and up) £1,380 2m 3f..(5:05)

YQUEM 7-11-7 (7*) Mr R Wakley, *hld up, hdwy 6th, led 3 out, rdn whn lft clr last*...........(7 to 1 tchd 6 to 1) 1

3858⁴ FAMILIAR FRIEND (bl) 11-12-0 (7*) Mr J Lay, *hld up, hdwy 9th, wknd appr 3 out, lft poor second last*...(10 to 1 op 8 to 1) 2

LANDSKER MISSILE 8-11-9 (7*) Mr N Bradley, *al prmnt, rdn 4 out, wknd nxt, lft 3rd last*...........(7 to 4 fav op 6 to 4) 3

3733⁶ TELLAPOPKY [93] 8-11-7 (7*) Mr A Middleton, *slwly away, not jump wl, tld off frm 6th*.............(33 to 1 op 20 to 1) 4

3723 THORNHILL 7-11-2 (7*) Mr A Wood, *slwly away, in rear whn f 5th*............................(50 to 1 op 20 to 1) f

3851³ MY YOUNG MAN 12-12-0 (7*) Mr E James, *led second rdn and hdd 3 out, ev ch till hit and uns rdr last*.
..........................(4 to 1 op 7 to 2) ur

3733 TUFFNUT GEORGE 10-11-2 (7*) Mr A Phillips, *led to second, prmnt till wknd 9th, tld off whn pld up bef 2 out*.
..........................(8 to 1 op 5 to 1) pu
SUDANOR (Ire) 8-11-7 (7*) Mr M Munrowd, *in tch whn blun 8th, sn beh, tld off when pld up bef 4 out*.
..........................(20 to 1 op 12 to 1) pu
TWIST 'N' SCU 9-11-7 (7*) Mr R Lawther, *jmpd slwly 5th, tld off whn pld up bef tenth*.............(33 to 1 op 12 to 1) pu
ROO'S LEAP (Ire) 9-11-2 (7*) Mr O McPhail, *beh frm 7th, tld off whn pld up bef 9th*................(33 to 1 op 20 to 1) pu

3733* MANKIND 6-11-11 (7*) Mr L Baker, *in tch to 8th, sn beh, tld off whn pld up bef 3 out*........(7 to 2 op 5 to 2) pu

Dist: 15l, ¾l, dist. 4m 52.70s. a 27.70s (11 Ran).

(J J Boulter), A W Varey

3917 St. Michael's Hospice Mares' Only Standard National Hunt Flat Class H (4,5,6-y-o) £1,028 2m 1f......(5:35)

DAWN SPINNER 5-10-7 (7*) T Hagger, *pld hrd, al in tch, led appr fnl furlong, rallied to ld ag'n cl hme*. (8 to 1 op 5 to 1) 1

VICAR'S VASE 4-10-2 (7*) Mr R Wakley, *hld up in rear, gd hdwy 4 fs out, led ins last, hdd cl hme*..(10 to 1 op 6 to 1) 2

BE MY ROMANY (Ire) 5-10-9 (5*) A Bates, *led till hdd appr fnl furlong, kpt on one pace*...........(20 to 1 op 14 to 1) 3

FLORAL REEF 6-10-7 (7*) Mr M W Carroll, *hld up in tch, hdwy 4 fs out, ev ch 2 out, one pace aftr*....(20 to 1 op 14 to 1) 4

3807⁴ TARA GALE (Ire) 5-11-0 (7*) Mr A Wintle, *hld up, hdwy hfwy, ev ch o'r 2 fs out, one pace approaching last*.
..........................(5 to 2 fav op 3 to 1 tchd 7 to 2) 5

3197⁴ DUNSFOLD DOLLY 4-10-6 (3*) L Aspell, *al prmnt, ev ch 3 fs out till fdd o'r one out*............(10 to 1 op 3 to 1) 6

ABSOLUTE PROOF 4-10-2 (7*) J Power, *mid-div, hdwy o'r 3 fsn out, kpt on one pace fnl 2*......(12 to 1 op 7 to 1) 7

THE LADY SCORES (Ire) 5-10-7 (7*) S Scudder, *hld up, hdwy 6 fs out, wknd o'r 2 out*...........(8 to 1 op 5 to 1) 8

BOSSA NOVA 4-10-4 (5*) O Burrows, *pld hrd, in tchwknd o'r 3 fs out*.............(12 to 1 op 10 to 1 tchd 16 to 1) 9

3616³ SHIMMY DANCING 4-10-9 Miss A Embiricos, *prmnt till wknd 5 fs out*.............(10 to 1 op 7 to 1) 10

FLOSSIE HANDS (Ire) 5-11-3¹⁰ (7*) J T Nolan, *pld hrd, prmnt till wknd 5 fs out*.....................(12 to 1 op 10 to 1) 11

SEYMOURS SECRET 5-10-11 (3*) Sophie Mitchell, *al beh*.
..........................(20 to 1 op 12 to 1) 12

2784³ REDGRAVE WOLF 4-10-4 (5*) G Supple, *prmnt till wknd 6 fs out*...........(5 to 1 op 7 to 2 tchd 6 to 1) 13

AFTER TIME 5-10-7 (7*) P Maher, *al beh, tld off*.
..........................(8 to 1 op 6 to 1) 14

BRUNIDA 5-11-0 T Dascombe, *hld up hdwy hfwy, wknd 5 fs out, tld off*...........(8 to 1 op 6 to 1) 15

ALBERTINA 5-11-0 Mr E James, *slwly away, tld off aftr 6 fs*.
..........................(20 to 1 op 14 to 1) 16

PRINCESS HELEN (Ire) 4-10-2 (7*) M Lane, *al beh, tld off*.
..........................(10 to 1) 17

Dist: Hd, 3½l, 2l, nk, 1¼l, 3l, sht-hd, 15l, 9l, 4l. 3m 58.20s. (17 Ran).

(Sir Peter Miller), N J Henderson

HEXHAM (firm)
Saturday May 3rd
Going Correction: MINUS 0.30 sec. per fur.

3918 Chesters Stud Novices' Handicap Chase Class E (0-100 5-y-o and up) £3,440 2½m 110yds..........(6:00)

3758 TOUGH TEST (Ire) [86] 7-11-2 B Storey, *chsd ldrs, led 4 out, rdn clr 2 out, styd on strly*.
..........................(15 to 8 fav op 2 to 1 tchd 9 to 4 and 7 to 4) 1

3664² SHAWWELL [76] 10-10-6 T Reed, *led to 8th, lft in ld nxt, mstk and hdd 4 out, drvn and hit 2 out, sn one pace*.
..........................(10 to 1 op 5 to 1) 2

3655⁹ BANNER YEAR (Ire) [70] 6-10-0 G Cahill, *chsd ldrs, hmpd 9th, rdn alng and one pace frm 4 out*...(66 to 1 op 50 to 1) 3

3660⁶ MORE JOY [70] 9-9-7 (7*) C McCormack, *chsd ldrs, rdn alng and one pace frm 4 out*.........(7 to 1 op 6 to 1) 4

3663⁵ KINGS MINSTRAL (Ire) [74] 7-10-4³ J Burke, *in tch whn mstk 7th, sn outpcd and beh*...........(20 to 1) 5

3662⁵ QUIXALL CROSSETT [70] 12-9-9 (5*) Mr M H Naughton, *al beh, tld off frm hfwy*..................(66 to 1) 6

3660 MASTER FLASHMAN [73] (bl) 8-10-3 G Lee, *al rear, tld off frm hfwy*.............(11 to 2 op 5 to 1 tchd 6 to 1) 7

3821⁷ KARLOVAC [70] (bl) 11-10-0 F Perratt, *in tch, rdn alng and outpcd hfwy, sn tld off*.........(20 to 1 op 16 to 1) 8

547

3584^{6} TWIN FALLS (Ire) [94] (bl) 6-11-10 J Callaghan, *f 1st.* ....(6 to 1 op 5 to 1) f
3662^{3} JONAEM (Ire) [70] 7-10-0 K Johnson, *chsd ldrs, hdwy to ld 8th, f nxt.*....(8 to 1) f
2534 CLASSIC CREST (Ire) [70] (v) 6-10-0 M Foster, *al beh, tld off whn pld up aftr 2 out.*....(20 to 1 op 16 to 1) pu
Dist: 11l, 23l, 6l, 5l, 8l, 3l, 24l. 5m 2.50s. a 4.50s (11 Ran).
(J D Goodfellow), Mrs J D Goodfellow

3919 Dennis Waggott Builder Selling Handicap Hurdle Class G (0-95 4-y-o and up) £2,008 2m........(6:30)

3819^{3} TSANGA [69] 5-10-10 N Bentley, *al prmnt, led appr 2 out, clr last.*....(100 to 30 fav op 3 to 1 tchd 7 to 2) 1
3780* CHARLISTIONA [77] 6-10-11 (7*) S Melrose, *chsd ldrs, hdwy bef 3 out, rdn and one pace frm nxt.*....(4 to 1 op 3 to 1) 2
3703^{8} SKIDDAW SAMBA [83] 8-11-10 G Lee, *midfield, hdwy 4th, ev ch 3 out, sn rdn and one pace frm nxt.*....(7 to 2 tchd 4 to 1 and 3 to 1) 3
3780^{5} MONKEY WENCH (Ire) [82] 6-11-9 B Storey, *chsd ldrs till outpcd 4th, hdwy 3 out, sn rdn and one pace bef nxt.*....(8 to 1 tchd 9 to 1) 4
3469^{8} FRET (USA) [59] 7-10-0 M Foster, *cl up, led 5th till appr 2 out, grad wknd.*....(20 to 1) 5
3587^{8} STAGS FELL [64] 12-10-5 Carol Cuthbert, *chsd ldrs to 4th, sn lost pl and beh.*....(20 to 1 op 14 to 1) 6
3780 DARK MIDNIGHT (Ire) [64] 8-10-5^{5} J Burke, *al beh.*....(50 to 1 tchd 66 to 1) 7
3437^{7} IN A MOMENT (USA) [70] 6-10-11 R Garritty, *in tch till lost pl 3rd and sn beh.*....(6 to 1 tchd 7 to 1) 8
2983^{7} BLOOD BROTHER [59] 5-9-7 (7*) C McCormack, *led to 5th, grad wknd frm nxt.*.... (25 to 1 op 20 to 1 tchd 33 to 1) 9
3741^{6} BIRTHPLACE (Ire) [60] 7-10-1 K Johnson, *f 1st.*....(25 to 1 tchd 33 to 1) f
3803 SHUT UP [59] 8-10-0^{3} (3*) E Husband, *al beh, tld off whn sddl slpd and uns rdr aftr 2 out.*....(50 to 1) ur
3583^{9} OVER STATED (Ire) [67] 7-10-3 (5*) S Taylor, *brght dwn 1st.*....(16 to 1 tchd 20 to 1) bd
2855^{8} TIOTAO (Ire) [63] 7-10-4 D Parker, *brght dwn 1st.*....(10 to 1) bd
3762 SUPER GUY [60] 5-10-1^{1} G Cahill, *al beh, tld off whn pld up bef last.*....(50 to 1 tchd 66 to 1) pu
Dist: 2½l, 3l, 2½l, 13l, 4l, 2½l, 5l, 11l. (Time not taken) (14 Ran).
(J P Paternoster), G M Moore

3920 Gilesgate Subaru And Ssangyong Tant Pis Handicap Chase Class F (0-100 5-y-o and up) £2,887 2m 110yds........(7:00)

3662 SPEAKER'S HOUSE (USA) [86] 8-11-3 T Reed, *chsd ldr, led 4 out, clr 2 out, styd on.*.... (9 to 2 op 4 to 1 tchd 5 to 1) 1
3779^{6} CARDENDEN (Ire) [69] 9-10-0 B Storey, *led, rdn and hdd 4 out, kpt on und pres.*....(7 to 2 jt-fav tchd 4 to 1) 2
3664* BISHOPDALE [80] 16-10-11 F Perratt, *chsd ldrs, rdn alng 5 out and sn one pace.* (7 to 2 jt-fav op 3 to 1 tchd 4 to 1) 3
NORTH PRIDE (USA) [69] 12-10-0 G Cahill, *in tch, hit 6th, rdn alng 4 out, hit nxt and sn beh.*....(16 to 1 op 12 to 1) 4
MILS MIJ [97] 12-12-0 R Supple, *beh, some hdwy 4 out, rdn nxt and sn wknd.*....(4 to 1 op 7 to 2) 5
2412^{5} WILD BROOK (Ire) [72] 7-9-10 (7*) C McCormack, *blun 1st, al beh.*.... (7 to 1 op 10 to 1 tchd 12 to 1) 6
914 ANTHONY BELL [90] 11-11-7 N Smith, *al beh, tld off whn pld up 3 out.*....(8 to 1 tchd 9 to 1) pu
Dist: 4l, 6l, 18l, 2½l, 24l. 4m 1.00s. a 3.00s (7 Ran).
SR: 10/-/-/-/ (Mrs C G Greig), Miss Lucinda V Russell

3921 Gilesgate Subaru And Ssangyong 10th Anniversary Heart Of All England Maiden Hunters' Chase Class H (5-y-o and up) £2,388 3m 1f...(7:30)

CUMBERLAND BLUES (Ire) 8-11-7 (7*) Miss A Deniel, *made all, rdn 2 out, styd on wl frm last.*....(4 to 1 op 7 to 2) 1
COOLVAWN LADY (Ire) 8-11-2 (7*) Mr S Walker, *in tch, hdwy to chase ldrs 7th, effrt and dsptd ld 2 out, sn rdn and one pace last.*....(4 to 1 op 7 to 2 tchd 9 to 2) 2
WILL TRAVEL (Ire) 8-11-7 (7*) Mr A Robson, *chsd wnr, rdn 4 out, wknd aftr nxt.*....(5 to 2 fav op 3 to 1 tchd 9 to 4) 3
3666^{3} COOL YULE (Ire) 9-11-9 (5*) Miss P Robson, *beh till some hdwy frm 2 out, nvr a factor.*....(9 to 2 tchd 5 to 1) 4
EMU PARK 9-11-7 (7*) Mr J Thompson, *in tch till wknd frm tenth, tld off.*....(12 to 1 op 10 to 1 tchd 14 to 1) 5
TOD LAW 9-11-4 (5*) Mr C Storey, *al beh, tld off frm hfwy.*....(12 to 1 op 8 to 1) 6
DONSIDE 9-12-0 Mr J Walton, *chsd ldrs till slpd up aftr 4th.*....(16 to 1 op 14 to 1) su
FAST FUN 9-11-7 (7*) Mr R Morgan, *chsd ldrs to 7th, sn lost pl and beh, tld off whn pld up bef 3 out.*..(14 to 1 op 12 to 1) pu
Dist: 4l, 7l, 22l, dist, 20l. (Time not taken) (8 Ran).
(John L Holdroyd), Mrs A Lockwood

UTTOXETER (good)
Saturday May 3rd
Going Correction: NIL (races 1,2,5,7,8), PLUS 0.25 (3,4,6)

3922 Strebel Boilers & Radiators Juvenile Novices' Hurdle Class E for the Bill Love Trophy (4-y-o) £2,232 2m (2:10)

3566^{6} QUALITY (Ire) 11-5 N Williamson, *hld up in tch, chsd ldr 4 out, blun badly nxt, rdn appr last, styd on to ld nr finish.*....(11 to 8 fav op 5 to 4 tchd 6 to 4 and 13 to 8) 1
3332^{2} HISAR (Ire) 10-12 G Bradley, *led, mstk 1st, not fluent second, rdn appr last, hdd nr finish.*....(5 to 2 op 9 to 4 tchd 11 to 4) 2
3150 KINGS WITNESS (USA) 11-5 P Hide, *hld up, mstk second, hdwy 5th, rdn appr 3 out, wknd r-in.*....(9 to 4 op 7 to 4) 3
3150 SOCIETY GIRL 10-4 (3*) Michael Brennan, *chsd ldr 4 out, wknd nxt.*....(33 to 1 op 16 to 1) 4
AMBROSIA (Ire) 10-4 (3*) P Henley, *al towards rear, pckd 3rd, beh frm 4 out.*....(16 to 1 op 25 to 1 tchd 33 to 1) 5
3210 SHAWKEY (Ire) 10-12 D Walsh, *beh frm 5th, tld off and pld up bef 2 out.*....(50 to 1 op 33 to 1 tchd 66 to 1) pu
Dist: 1½l, 8l, 8l, dist. 3m 43.60s. a 6.60s (6 Ran).
SR: 25/16/15/ (D B O'Connor), P J Hobbs

3923 Stanton Plc Handicap Hurdle Class D (0-125 4-y-o and up) £2,913 2½m 110yds........(2:40)

3741^{2} STEVE FORD [92] 8-10-4 J R Kavanagh, *hld up, hdwy to chase ldr 4 out, mstk nxt, led 2 out, rdn out.*....(3 to 1 tchd 7 to 2) 1
3257* CLAIRESWAN (Ire) [102] (v) 5-11-0 J Railton, *chsd ldr, rdn 3 out, styd on same pace.*....(2 to 1 fav op 7 to 4 tchd 9 to 4) 2
DRUMMOND WARRIOR (Ire) [95] 8-10-7 N Williamson, *rcd keenly, led second, hdd 2 out, no extr r-in.*....(3 to 1 op 5 to 2) 3
3728 INNOCENT GEORGE [88] 8-9-7 (7*) T Siddall, *led to second, lost pl 5 out, rallied nxt, sn rdn and wknd.*....(12 to 1 op 9 to 1 tchd 14 to 1) 4
2028^{3} ROLFE (NZ) [112] (bl) 7-11-10 D Walsh, *trkd ldrs, rdn and wknd appr 3 out, pld up bef nxt.*....(4 to 1 op 7 to 2 tchd 9 to 2) pu
Dist: 3l, 1¼l, 18l. 4m 52.60s. a 13.60s (5 Ran).
(P J Morgan), C P Morlock

3924 Wateraid Handicap Chase Class B (5-y-o and up) £6,781 3¼m... (3:10)

3718^{5} COURT MELODY (Ire) [119] (bl) 9-11-4 P Hide, *al prmnt, led appr 5th, hdd nxt, led 4 out, styd on wl.*.. (4 to 1 op 5 to 2) 1
3678* LE MEILLE (Ire) [112] 8-10-11 N Williamson, *hld up, hdwy 13th, chsd wnr 3 out, sn rdn and no imprsn.*....(11 to 10 fav op 6 to 4 tchd Evens) 2
3114^{9} SIBTON ABBEY [125] 12-11-7 (3*) Michael Brennan, *led to appr 5th, rdn to ld 5 out, sn hdd, wknd 3 out.*....(20 to 1 op 10 to 1) 3
3153 LORD RELIC (NZ) [114] 11-10-13 D Walsh, *trkd ldrs, led 8th to tenth, wknd and eased 3 out.*....(7 to 1 op 9 to 2 tchd 8 to 1) 4
1382^{2} FACTOR TEN (Ire) [123] 9-11-8 J F Titley, *trkd ldr, led 6th till mstk and hdd 8th, led tenth, jmpd rght nxt, headed and wknd 5 out, pld up bef next.*....(7 to 2 op 4 to 1 tchd 9 to 2) pu
Dist: 4l, 10l, 26l. 6m 40.60s. a 28.60s (5 Ran).
(J W Aplin, P K Barber & Mick Coburn), P F Nicholls

3925 Peter J. Douglas Engineering Lord Gyllene Mares' Only Novices' Handicap Chase Class E (0-105 5-y-o and up) £3,468 2m 5f........ (3:45)

2863^{3} GEMMA'S WAGER (Ire) [79] 7-10-2^{2} W McFarland, *hld up, hit 4th, hdwy 5 out, led 2 out, styd on wl.*..(25 to 1 op 14 to 1) 1
3399 CULLANE LAKE (Ire) [78] 7-10-1 N Williamson, *chsd ldrs, mstk 9th, blun nxt (water), led 3 out to next, wkng whn hit last.*....(7 to 2 op 3 to 1) 2
3502^{8} LAMBRINI (Ire) [77] (bl) 7-10-0^{3} (3*) P Henley, *trkd ldrs, led 4 out, hdd and wknd nxt.* (66 to 1 op 33 to 1 tchd 100 to 1) 3
3440^{3} KADARI [91] (v) 8-10-11 (3*) Guy Lewis, *prmnt, rdn 8th, sn lost pl.*....(15 to 2 op 7 to 1 tchd 9 to 1) 4
2596^{5} WONDERFULL POLLY (Ire) [81] 9-10-4 P Hide, *in rear, mstk 8th, wknd tenth.*....(9 to 2 op 4 to 1 tchd 5 to 1) 5
3474^{2} QUICK QUOTE [86] 7-10-9 L Harvey, *wth ldr til led 8th, hdd and wknd 4 out.*....(7 to 2 op 3 to 1) 6
3799* JASILU [105] (v) 7-12-0 S McNeill, *chsd ldrs, rdn 9th wknd 5 out, pld up bef nxt.*....(3 to 1 fav tchd 7 to 1) pu
3434 MINDYEROWNBUSINESS (Ire) [82] 8-10-5^{5} J Railton, *made most to 8th, wknd quickly and pld up bef 5 out.*....(50 to 1 op 33 to 1 tchd 100 to 1) pu
3732^{4} JOY FOR LIFE (Ire) [77] 6-10-0 G Tormey, *in rear, hit 5th, lost tch hfwy, pld up bef 4 out.*....(20 to 1 tchd 33 to 1 and 50 to 1) pu
Dist: 13l, 7l, 24l, 19l, 1¾l. 5m 10.40s. a 12.40s (9 Ran).
SR: 2/-/-/-/-/ (Mr & Mrs Barry Noakes), Mark Campion

3926 Sedgwick UK Risk Services Handicap Hurdle Class D (0-125 4-y-o and

up) £2,927 3m 110yds....... (4:20)

3732 HI HEDLEY (Ire) [94] 7-9-13² (3*) P Henley, led 3rd, hrd rdn
r-in, all out........................(33 to 1 op 16 to 1) 1
3725² DERRING BRIDGE [94] 7-10-0 N Williamson, hld up, hdwy 5
out, chlgd 3 out, hrd rdn r-in, kpt on.... (7 to 1 tchd 8 to 1) 2
3568 SMITH TOO (Ire) [117] 9-11-2 (7*) R Garrard, al prmnt, rdn 2
out, styd on same pace... (9 to 2 op 7 to 2 tchd 11 to 2) 3
33216 NEEDWOOD POPPY [94] 9-10-0 B Clifford, hld up, styd on
frm 3 out, nvr plcd to chal.
..................(12 to 1 op 14 to 1 tchd 16 to 1) 4
3120 A MILLIONMEMORIES [94] 7-10-0 E Byrne, hld up, nvr plcd to
chal......................(33 to 1 op 25 to 1 tchd 40 to 1) 5
3774⁴ ULURU (Ire) [98] 9-10-4 J R Kavanagh, chsd ldrs, rdn 4 out,
wknd nxt.....................(9 to 1 op 8 to 1 tchd 10 to 1) 6
3712⁶ VICTOR BRAVO (NZ) [117] (bl) 10-11-9 C Llewellyn, prmnt,
jnd ldrs 4th, wknd appr 2 out, fnshd lme.
................(100 to 30 fav op 3 to 1 tchd 7 to 2) 7
3637⁵ OATIS ROSE [104] 7-10-5 (5*) X Aizpuru, sn drvn alng, tld off
frm hfwy............................(7 to 2 op 3 to 1) 8
3709 SHARE OPTIONS (Ire) [103] 6-10-9 G Bradley, led to 3rd, lost
pl nxt, sn rdn and tld off, pld up aftr 7th...(6 to 1 op 9 to 2) pu
Dist: ½l, 3½l, 10l, 14l, 4l, 12l, 27l. 5m 43.50s. a 6.50s (9 Ran).
SR: 7/6/25/-/-/-/   (G A Hubbard), G A Hubbard

3927 Biffa Waste Novices' Chase Class E (5-y-o and up) £2,866 2m..... (4:55)

3781⁴ TIDEBROOK 7-11-6 N Williamson, led till mstk and hdd second, led 5 out, lft wl clr nxt.
...................(6 to 4 on op 11 to 10 tchd 5 to 4) 1
2631⁴ SPECTRE BROWN 7-10-7 (7*) Mr T J Barry, pld hrd, blun 1st,
jnd ldr 6th, wknd aftr 5 out.
.........................(40 to 1 op 33 to 1 tchd 50 to 1) 2
3674⁴ ARCTIC BLOOM 11-10-9 Mr C Mulhall, in rear whn hmpd 7th,
nvr trbld ldrs................(9 to 1 op 8 to 1 tchd 10 to 1) 3
3360⁷ THE FENCE SHRINKER 6-10-11 (3*) P Henley, led 3rd, hdd 5
out, sn wknd..................(25 to 1 tchd 33 to 1) 4
3278⁴ ZINE LANE 6-10-5 (3*) Michael Brennan, led second, to nxt,
jnd wnr 5 out til f next.....(11 to 4 op 7 to 1 tchd 9 to 1) f
3528⁴ NIGHT BOAT 6-10-11 (3*) Guy Lewis, hld up, hit 3rd, blun and
clr rdr 7th..............(11 to 2 op 5 to 1 tchd 6 to 1) ur
Dist: 23l, 24l, 3l. 3m 57.70s. a 10.70s (6 Ran).
SR: 25/-/-/-/   (Richard Williams), K C Bailey

3928 Houghton Vaughan Maiden Open National Hunt Flat Class H (Div I) (4,5,6-y-o) £1,609 2m........ (5:25)

3721³ VALHALLA (Ire) 4-11-0 A P McCoy, hld up, hdwy 4 fs out, led
o'r one out, ran on wl. (11 to 8 fav op Evens tchd 6 to 4) 1
1675 OTAGO HEIGHTS (NZ) 5-11-5 D Leahy, hld up, hdwy hfwy,
led 4 fs out, hdd o'r one out, styd on same pace.
..................(12 to 1 op 14 to 1 tchd 16 to 1) 2
3482⁵ TOTEM FOLE 4-11-0 P Niven, hld up, styd on fnl 2 fs, nvr nrr.
.........................(6 to 1 tchd 13 to 2) 3
3720⁵ DONNYBROOK 4-10-9 (5*) B Grattan, hld up, hdwy hfwy,
rdn o'r 2 fs out, styd on same pace...........(20 to 1) 4
2899⁴ COUNT KARMUSKI 5-11-5 T Jenks, prmnt, rdn o'r 3 fs out,
styd on same pace................(14 to 1 tchd 16 to 1) 5
3282⁶ HOMME DE FER 5-11-5 S McNeill, hld up, nvr rchd chalg
pos.....................(10 to 1 tchd 12 to 1 and 14 to 1) 6
3721⁸ SKILLWISE 5-11-5 J Titley, hld up, rdn o'r 3 fs out, nvr able to
chal..........................(10 to 1 op 8 to 1 tchd 12 to 1) 7
3721⁹ CHOCOLATE DRUM (Ire) 6-11-5 L O'Hara, prmnt, rdn 4 fs out,
sn wknd..........................(16 to 1 op 14 to 1) 8
3475³ FRENCH COUNTY (Ire) 5-11-5 N Williamson, hld up, hdwy o'r
4 fs out, sn rdn and btn. (8 to 1 op 10 to 1 tchd 12 to 1) 9
3667⁴ BUCKLEY HOUSE 5-11-5 P Hide, pld hrd, led aftr one furlong, hdd 4 out, hng lft and sn btn.....(20 to 1 op 14 to 1) 10
3667⁶ GILSAN STAR 4-10-9 G Bradley, chsd ldrs til wknd o'r 4 fs out.
...........................(25 to 1 op 14 to 1) 11
3322 NIRVANA PRINCESS 5-10-7 (7*) J Mogford, mid-div, rdn 5 fs
out, sn beh..............(33 to 1 tchd 50 to 1 and 66 to 1) 12
2469 COQUETTISH 4-10-9 O Pears, prmnt to hfwy.
...........................(50 to 1 tchd 66 to 1) 13
3335⁸ ANOTHER RUMPUS 5-11-2 (3*) D Fortt, led for one furlong,
remained hndy til wknd o'r 4 out.....(20 to 1 op 14 to 1) 14
2723 TABBITTS HILL 5-11-0 Mr P Scott, mid-div, effrt 5 fs out,
virtually pld up o'r 3 out.............(33 to 1 op 20 to 1) 15
Dist: 4l, 3l, ½l, 1l, ½l, 12l, ½l, 5l, 3l. 3m 44.10s. (15 Ran).
(Great Head House Estates Limited), Martin Todhunter

3929 Houghton Vaughan Maiden Open National Hunt Flat Class H (Div II) (4,5,6-y-o) £1,598 2m........ (5:55)

3427² MURCHAN TYNE (Ire) 4-10-2 (7*) L Cummins, hld up, hdwy
hfwy, led o'r one furlong out, rdn out...........(7 to 2 jt-
fav op 3 to 1 tchd 4 to 1) 1
2402³ SQUADDIE 5-11-5 A P McCoy, rcd keenly, prmnt, rdn to ld 2
fs out, sn hdd, unbl to quicken ins last.
.........................(9 to 2 op 3 to 1 tchd 4 to 1) 2
3807⁵ TROUBLE AHEAD (Ire) 6-11-5 S McNeill, chsd ldrs, led 6 fs
out, hdd 2 furlongs, styd on same pace.
......................(8 to 1 op 7 to 1 tchd 9 to 1) 3

3439⁷ SALMON CELLAR (Ire) 4-11-0 D Leahy, hld up, hdwy 5 fs out,
rdn o'r 2 out, styd on same pace.
.........................(9 to 1 op 8 to 1 tchd 10 to 1) 4
3439 MAZZELMO 4-10-2 (7*) T Siddall, prmnt, drvn alng o'r 3 fs
out, sn btn..........................(16 to 1 op 9 to 1) 5
2723 GOOD TIME DANCER 5-11-0 Mr A Sansome, chsd ldrs, rdn
o'r 3 fs out, sn btn.........................(33 to 1) 6
WIN THE TOSS 5-11-5 N Williamson, hld up, hdwy 5 fs out,
rdn and wknd o'r 3 out...........(7 to 2 jt-fav op 6 to 1) 7
3282⁸ WHAT THE DEVIL 4-10-9 W Worthington, mid-div, effrt o'r 4 fs
out, not trble ldrs........(50 to 1 op 33 to 1 tchd 66 to 1) 8
3721 HACK ON 5-11-0 G Tormey, mid-div, rdn o'r 4 fs out, sn btn.
......................(10 to 1 op 9 to 1 tchd 12 to 1) 9
1809⁸ TRYMYPLY 5-11-2 (3*) D Fortt, prmnt till rdn and wknd o'r 4 fs
out......................(33 to 1 op 25 to 1) 10
3048 THE GNOME (Ire) 5-10-12 (7*) N Hannity, chsd ldrs, short of
room o'r 5 fs out, wknd over 3 out.
......................(16 to 1 op 10 to 1 tchd 20 to 1) 11
3661 NO TIME TO WAIT 6-11-5 O Pears, made most till 6 fs out,
wknd o'r 4 out...........................(33 to 1) 12
2764⁷ PAUSE FOR THOUGHT 4-11-0 P Niven, hld up, effrt 6 fs out,
wknd 4 out..............(8 to 1 op 10 to 1 tchd 12 to 1) 13
3322 OUTRAGEOUS AFFAIR 5-11-0 C Llewellyn, al in rear.
.........................(50 to 1 op 33 to 1) 14
3322 MICHIGAN BLUE 5-11-5 T Jenks, al in rear.
.........................(50 to 1 op 33 to 1) 15
3561 DESERT WAY 4-11-0 J F Titley, mid-div, hdwy o'r 5 fs out,
wknd and pld up over 2 out.
......................(11 to 1 op 7 to 1 tchd 12 to 1) pu
Dist: 4l, 1l, 4l, 12l, 2l, 3l, ½l, 1½l, 1¼l, 3l. 3m 41.00s. (16 Ran).
(Harrington-Worrall Racing), E J Alston

WARWICK (good to firm) Saturday May 3rd
Going Correction: MINUS 0.60 sec. per fur.

3930 Willoughby de Broke Challenge Trophy Novices' Hunters' Chase (5-y-o and up) £1,178 2½m 110yds.. (5:45)

LORD KILTON 9-11-7 (7*) Mr M Cowley, keen hold early, chsd
ldr, not fluent 3rd, lost tch tenth, rallied betw fnl 2, led r-in, ran
on.. 1
TOM FURZE 10-11-12 (7*) Mr M Batters, led clr frm tenth, in
command whn eased frm 2 out, hdd r-in, rdn and ran on wl,
jst flt... 2
Won by Nk. 5m 37.00s. a 42.00s (2 Ran).
SR: -/-/   (Mrs D Cowley), Mrs D Cowley

3931 Barford Selling Hurdle Class G (4,5,6-y-o) £1,642 2m........ (6:15)

3617⁹ FENIAN COURT (Ire) 6-10-9 M A Fitzgerald, al hndy, rdn to
chal frm 2 out, kpt on und pres to ld cl hme.
.........................(3 to 1 op 5 to 1) 1
3819² SUMMER VILLA (bl) 5-10-9 W Marston, in tch, led appr 2 out,
sn rdn, hdd cl hme.............(11 to 4 fav op 7 to 2) 2
NORTHERN GREY 5-11-0 N Mann, hld up, styd on frm 3 out,
4th whn blun nxt, one pace............(12 to 1 op 8 to 1) 3
3728⁶ NEVER SO BLUE (Ire) (bl) 6-11-0 R Dunwoody, led to 3rd,
rgned ld appr nxt, hdd approaching 2 out, sn btn.
.........................(100 to 30 op 9 to 4) 4
2804 RENO'S TREASURE (USA) 4-10-4 J Supple, hld up beh ldrs,
4th whn slpd on bend aftr 3rd, no dngr after.
......................(10 to 1 op 33 to 1 tchd 66 to 1) 5
FRANS LAD 5-11-0 Gary Lyons, beh frm 4th.
.........................(50 to 1 op 33 to 1) 6
3828 T'NIEL 6-10-6⁴ (7*) S Lycett, refused to race, took no part.
......................(66 to 1 op 33 to 1) ref
HIGHLAND SPIN 6-10-7 (7*) Mr S Durack, hld up in rear, slpd
up bend aftr 3rd..................(20 to 1 tchd 25 to 1) su
MINNISAM 4-10-9 R Greene, beh frm 4th, tld off whn pld up
bef 3 out..................(6 to 1 op 4 to 1) pu
3106⁹ NDABA 6-11-0 J R Kavanagh, took str hold, prmnt, led 3rd,
hdd appr nxt, sn wknd, tld off whn pld up bef 2 out.
......................(6 to 1 op 4 to 1) pu
3823⁸ TEEJAY'S FUTURE (Ire) 6-10-9 M Brennan, al beh, tld off whn
pld up bef 2 out..............(6 to 1 op 5 to 1 tchd 7 to 1) pu
Dist: Sht-hd, 8l, 8l, 28l, 2l. 3m 41.70s. a 2.70s (11 Ran).
(John Pugh), P D Evans

3932 Veterans Chase Class D £4,003 3 ¼m......................... (6:45)

3678³ COPPER MINE 11-11-2 J Osborne, made virtually all, clr frm
3 out, drvn out..............(Evens fav tchd 11 to 10) 1
3790³ HARRISTOWN LADY (bl) 10-10-7 B Clifford, in tch, chsd wnr
frm 7th, outpcd 3 out, rallied 2 out, styd on one pace.
..................(5 to 2 op 9 to 4 tchd 11 to 4) 2
3833 VICAR OF BRAY (v) 10-11-2 M Richards, jmpd slwly 3rd, lost
tch frm 5th, tld off from 14th........(33 to 1 tchd 40 to 1) 3
3678⁴ MUSTHAVEASWIG 11-11-7 (3*) Mr R Thornton, chsd wnr till
jmpd slwly 7th, pld up and dismounted bef nxt.
......................(5 to 2 op 3 to 1 tchd 11 to 4) pu
Dist: 1½l, dist. 6m 32.00s. a 18.00s (4 Ran).
(J Dougall), O Sherwood

3933 Mintex Handicap Hurdle Class C (0-135 4-y-o and up) £3,492 2m
.... (7:15)

3759* AMLAH (USA) [115] 5-11-3 B Powell, al hndy, led 4th, hdd last, hrd rdn and crrd lft r-in, kpt on to rgn ld cl hme.
...................................(11 to 8 fav op 5 to 4 tchd 6 to 4) 1
3734* BARFORD SOVEREIGN [116] 5-11-4 M A Fitzgerald, al prmnt, chsd wnr frm 3 out, led last, hrd drvn and edgd lft r-in, hdd cl hme...........(2 to 1 tchd 9 to 4 and 7 to 4) 2
3188⁴ JOSIFINA [110] 6-10-12 A Thornton, trkd ldrs, rdn alng appr 4th, lost tch 3 out.......................(14 to 1 op 8 to 1) 3
3831³ TEJANO GOLD (USA) [122] 7-11-10 R Dunwoody, led to 4th, rdn and wknd frm 3 out....(11 to 4 op 5 to 2 tchd 3 to 1) 4
Dist: ½l, 14l, 3½l. 3m 35.30s. b 3.70s (4 Ran).
SR: 30/30/10/18/   (In Touch Racing Club), P J Hobbs

3934 Alderminster Novices' Chase Class E (5-y-o and up) £2,900 2½m 110yds
.... (7:45)

3806³ WALLS COURT 10-11-2 L O'Hara, chsd ldr, led and hit 4 out, all out........(5 to 1 op 7 to 1 tchd 8 to 1) 1
3742* PLAN-A (Fr) 7-11-9 P Holley, in tch, not fluent 13th and nxt, chsd wnr aftr 3 out, jmpd slwly next, bad blund last, hrd rdn and rallied r-in, ran on wl.
...................................(11 to 10 on op 6 to 4 on tchd 6 to 5) 2
3792 RYTON RUN 12-11-6 B Fenton, led, reminders aftr 11th, hdd 4 out, wknd appr 2 out, tld off.
...................................(11 to 1 op 6 to 1 tchd 12 to 1) 3
3504 CHAPILLIERE (Fr) 7-11-2 G Upton, sn beh, tld off frm 11th.
...................................(7 to 2 op 3 to 1 tchd 4 to 1) 4
COTSWOLD CASTLE 11-10-13 (3*) Michael Brennan, sn beh, not fluent second and nxt, reminders aftr 7th, tld off frm tenth, pld up bef next..........(8 to 1 op 7 to 1 tchd 9 to 1) pu
Dist: Sht-hd, dist, dist. 5m 10.70s. a 15.70s (5 Ran).
(The Claret And Blue Partnership), J J Birkett

3935 Wasperton Hill Novices' Handicap Hurdle Class E (0-100 4-y-o and up) £2,731 2½m 110yds.........(8:15)

3331 LOCH NA KEAL [75] 5-11-1 C Llewellyn, hld up beh ldrs, led appr 2 out, clr whn hit last, readily.
...................................(5 to 2 fav op 3 to 1 tchd 7 to 2) 1
2678⁴ ARCTIC TRIUMPH [78] (bl) 6-11-4 P Holley, took str hold, led 3rd, clr nxt, hdd appr 2 out, one pace...(7 to 1 op 4 to 1) 2
3736* NAUTICAL JEWEL [82] 5-11-1 (7*) J Power, hld up, styd on frm 2 out, nvr nrr.......................(7 to 1 op 4 to 1) 3
3833 BROOKHAMPTON LANE (Ire) [70] (bl) 6-10-10 B Powell, took str hold, led to 3rd, wknd appr 2 out, no ch whn f last.
...................................(7 to 2 op 4 to 1 tchd 5 to 1) f
3310⁶ COOL HARRY (USA) [65] 6-9-12 (7*) Mr S Durack, beh frm 7th, tld off whn shied at fallen horse and uns rdr last.
...................................(4 to 1 op 8 to 1) ur
3528 DARK PHOENIX (Ire) [78] (v) 7-11-4 M Brennan, al beh, tld off 7th, pld up bef last.........(10 to 1 op 5 to 1) pu
Dist: 4l, 5l. 4m 55.10s. a 10.10s (6 Ran).
(S Kimber), C P Morlock

GOWRAN PARK (IRE) (good)
Sunday May 4th

3935a Tetratema Perpetual Cup (5-y-o and up) £3,425 3m.........(4:00)

3770 WHAT A HAND 9-12-7 Mr P Fenton,.........(5 to 4 on) 1
3749 TULLIBARDNICENEASY (Ire) 6-11-0 (5*) Mr A C Coyle,
...................................(16 to 1) 2
RADICAL-TIMES (Ire) 7-11-3 (7*) Mr P J Crowley, ..(25 to 1) 3
3153⁸ CRAZY DREAMS (Ire) 9-11-10 Mr P J Healy, ...(33 to 1) 4
CLONROSH SLAVE 10-11-3 (7*) Mr Paul Moloney, (33 to 1) f
3447³ SANDFAIR (Ire) 7-10-12 (7*) Mr C A Murphy, ...(16 to 1) f
3341 DROMOD POINT (Ire) 8-11-3 (7*) Mr D Whelan, ...(20 to 1) ur
3748 POULGILLIE (Ire) 7-11-5 (5*) Mr G Elliott, ...(14 to 1) ur
3770 DENFIELD (Ire) 6-11-6 (7*) Mr I Buchanan,.........(4 to 1) ur
3646* BEST INTEREST (Ire) 9-11-6 (7*) Mr John A Quinn, .(7 to 1) pu
3748* SALLY WILLOWS (Ire) 8-11-3 (7*) Mr J F Robinson, (14 to 1) pu
3748 THE EXECUTRIX (Ire) 5-10-8³ (7*) Mr J M O'Brien, (25 to 1) pu
Dist: 15l, 3½l, sht-hd. 6m 6.20s. (12 Ran).
(Frank A Bonsal Jr), E J O'Grady

3935b Great Oak Handicap Hurdle (0-123 4-y-o and up) £2,740 2½m
.... (4:30)

3835² STAGALIER (Ire) [-] 5-10-5 (7*) B J Geraghty, ...(4 to 1) 1
3764³ BORO BOW (Ire) [-] 6-11-12 T P Treacy, ...(9 to 4 fav) 2
3817* TOUREEN GALE (Ire) [-] 8-11-1 D J Casey, ...(3 to 1) 3
3837³ DOUBLE STRIKE (Ire) [-] (bl) 6-9-12¹ T P Rudd, ...(14 to 1) 4
3705³ NATIVE FLING (Ire) [-] 5-10-1 (7*) J Fleming, ...(16 to 1) 5
3431⁷ PRE ORDAINED (Ire) [-] 5-10-9 F J Flood, ...(9 to 1) 6
3150 EVRIZA (Ire) [-] 4-10-11 C F Swan, ...(7 to 1) 7
3416* CONAGHER BOY (Ire) [-] 7-10-11 A P McCoy, ...(10 to 1) 8
Dist: 3l, 2½l, nk, 25l. 5m 8.70s. (8 Ran).

(Gerard Callaghan), Noel Meade

3935c Avonmore Handicap Hurdle (0-140 4-y-o and up) £4,452 2m
.... (5:00)

3834* BAWNROCK (Ire) [-] 8-10-7 C F Swan, ...(100 to 30) 1
3377⁴ THE BOULD VIC (Ire) [-] 5-9-8 (7*) Mr J L Cullen, ..(6 to 1) 2
3752 ALWAYS IN TROUBLE [-] (bl) 10-9-12 T P Rudd, ... (5 to 1) 3
3214* CLIFDON FOG (Ire) [-] 6-12-0 A P McCoy,....(10 to 9 on) 4
2446³ IRISH PEACE (Ire) [-] 9-11-3 C O'Dwyer,.........(12 to 1) 5
Dist: 5l, 20l, 5l, 11l. 5m 49.60s. (5 Ran).
(New Road Syndicate), A P O'Brien

3935d Thomastown (Pro-Am) I.N.H. Flat Race (4-y-o and up) £2,740 2m
.... (5:30)

3553⁵ AS ROYAL (Ire) 6-12-1 (3*) Mr P English, ...(8 to 1) 1
3767² EDUARDO (Ire) 7-11-11 (7*) M D Murphy, ...(4 to 1) 2
CARJUNE (Ire) 5-11-3 (7*) Mr P Whelan, ...(25 to 1) 3
3553⁴ DRAMATIST (Ire) 6-11-11 (7*) J A Robinson, ...(10 to 1) 4
1005¹ BESSMOUNT LEADER (Ire) 5-12-3 Mr R Walsh, ...(9 to 2) 5
HAVE AT IT (Ire) 5-10-12 (7*) Mr P A Farrell, ...(14 to 1) 6
CLIFFS OF DOONEEN (Ire) 4-11-3 Mr G J Harford,
...................................(3 to 1 fav) 7
2649 FORTY SECRETS (Ire) 5-10-12 (7*) Mr J L Cullen, (33 to 1) 8
3627* KINGMAN (Ire) 5-11-10 (7*) Mr Paul Moloney, ...(10 to 1) 9
3769 SARAH SUPREME (Ire) 6-11-6 (7*) G T Hourigan, ...(7 to 1) 10
713⁹ LUNAR LADY (Ire) 5-10-12 (7*) Mr R F O'Gorman, (10 to 1) 11
600³ ATTACK AT DAWN (Ire) 6-11-6 (7*) Mr J P McNamara,
...................................(16 to 1) 12
LUCY CON (Ire) 5-10-12 (7*) L J Fleming, ...(14 to 1) 13
2073⁷ VARTRY BOY (Ire) 6-11-11 (7*) Mr D Breen, ...(14 to 1) 14
AHEAD OF THE POSSE (Ire) 5-11-3 (7*) Mr J P Hayden,
...................................(50 to 1) 15
3381⁷ OAKLAND BRIDGE (Ire) 6-11-6 (5*) Mr A C Coyle, (50 to 1) 16
1777 ROSIE FLYNN (Ire) 5-10-12 (7*) Mr Sean O O'Brien, (25 to 1) 17
2165 SALLY SUPREME (Ire) 6-10-13 (7*) Mr D Stack, ...(50 to 1) 18
122⁹ ANNFIELD HERITAGE (Ire) 6-10-13 (7*) Mr J J Fallon,
...................................(20 to 1) 19
POLLYPUTHEKETTLEON (Ire) 5-11-5 Mr P Fenton, (10 to 1) 20
Dist: 2l, 1l, 15l, ½l. 3m 52.60s. (20 Ran).
(Michael O'Dowd), Thomas Foley

EXETER (good (races 1,3,4,5,6), good to firm (2))
Monday May 5th
Going Correction: PLUS 0.35 sec. per fur.

3936 Steve Browning Good English Mares' Only Novices' Hurdle Class E (4-y-o and up) £2,218 2¼m... (2:00)

3382³ DISALLOWED (Ire) 4-11-3 A P McCoy, made all, not extended..................(12 to 1 on op 5 to 1 on) 1
3892⁴ RACHEL LOUISE 5-10-10 D Gallagher, jmpd slwly 1st and 3rd, hdwy frm 3 out, one pace frm nxt. (10 to 1 op 4 to 1) 2
3686⁶ UP THE TEMPO (Ire) 8-10-10 T Dascombe, dsptd second pl to 3rd, lost tch frm 3 out........(33 to 1 op 20 to 1) 3
ELLEN GAIL (Ire) 5-10-10 J Frost, al beh, lost tch 3 out.
...................................(10 to 1 op 5 to 1) 4
Dist: 10l, 5l, 7l. 4m 19.70s. a 20.70s (4 Ran).
(Million In Mind Partnership (6)), Miss H C Knight

3937 Gemini Radio Handicap Chase Class E (0-115 5-y-o and up) £2,881 2m 7f 110yds..................... (2:30)

3682³ TRUST DEED (USA) [82] (bl) 9-10-1 (5*) D Salter, wl beh till styd on frm 4 out, kpt on strly to ld r-in.
...................................(10 to 1 op 8 to 1 tchd 12 to 1) 1
3685³ MR PLAYFULL [91] 7-11-1 J Frost, mstks, hdwy to go second 4 out, led nxt, rdn and hdd r-in.
...................................(9 to 4 op 5 to 2 tchd 11 to 4) 2
3772* DECYBORG (Fr) [100] 6-11-10 A P McCoy, led, rdn appr 4 out, hdd nxt, ridden and wknd approaching last.
...................................(11 to 8 on op Evens tchd 11 to 10 and 6 to 4 on) 3
3862* HENLEY REGATTA [100] 9-11-10 (6ex) S Burrough, hld up, hdwy to chase ldr 9th, one pace frm 4 out.
...................................(6 to 1 op 4 to 1 tchd 13 to 2) 4
3138⁴ COASTING [76] 11-10-0 L Harvey, in tch to 7th, sn beh, tld off.........(33 to 1 op 16 to 1) 5
3405 BRAVO STAR (USA) [76] 12-10-0 T Dascombe, in tch till wknd 9th, tld off.
...................................(33 to 1 op 25 to 1 tchd 40 to 1 and 50 to 1) 6
Dist: 1¼l, 12l, 5l, dist, dist. 5m 49.30s. a 15.30s (6 Ran).
SR: 7/14/11/6/-/-/   (Malcolm Enticott), S G Knight

3938 Award Winning Gemini News Handicap Hurdle Class E (0-115 4-y-o and up) £2,361 2¼m... (3:00)

3809¹ ATH CHEANNAITHE (Fr) [86] (v) 5-10-0 T Dascombe, made all, sn clr, rdn 2 out, ran on r-in.........(6 to 4 op 2 to 1) 1

3745³ BLAIR CASTLE (Ire) [114] 6-12-0 A P McCoy, *trkd wnr frm second, hdwy to cl 2 out, rdn and not run on from last.* ....(5 to 4 fav op Evens tchd 6 to 4) 2
3894⁶ GABISH [86] 12-10-0 L Harvey, *chsd wnr to second, sn lost tch, tld off*..........................(50 to 1 op 25 to 1) 3
2760⁶ ROBERT'S TOY (Ire) [113] 6-11-6 (7*) B Moore, *hld up in rear, f second*..................................(3 to 1 op 5 to 2) f
Dist: 4l, dist. 4m 16.20s. a 17.20s (4 Ran).

(J Neville), J Neville

3939 Top Rating Gemini FM Novices' Handicap Chase Class E (0-100 5-y-o and up) £2,544 2m 3f 110yds (3:30)

3133 WIXOE WONDER (Ire) [77] (bl) 7-11-10 A P McCoy, *made all, clr 4th, mstks 8th and 3 out, unchlgd*..............(9 to 4 jt-fav tchd 5 to 2 and 2 to 1) 1
3682² JONJAS CHUDLEIGH [70] 10-11-3 J Frost, *hld up, hdwy appr 4 out, blun 2 out, reco'red to chase wnr r-in*.......(9 to 4 jt-fav op 5 to 2 tchd 2 to 1) 2
2498⁸ WOT NO GIN [65] 8-10-12 L Harvey, *chsd wnr 4th till hit tenth, wknd appr four out*.....................(3 to 1 op 2 to 1) 3
2388 ROLLED GOLD [64] 8-10-11 J F Titley, *hld up, hit 7th, hdwy to chase wnr tenth, wkng then jmpd lft 4 out and nxt.* ....(4 to 1 tchd 5 to 1) 4
3811⁵ MISTRESS ROSIE [71] 10-11-4 D Gallagher, *jmpd lft 5th, al beh, tld off whn pld up bef 4 out.* ....(7 to 1 op 5 to 1 tchd 8 to 1) pu
Dist: 16l, 13l, 7l. 4m 53.80s. a 20.80s (5 Ran).

(P J D Pottinger), M Bradstock

3940 West Of England Open Hunters' Chase Class H (6-y-o and up) £1,138 2m 7f 110yds.................(4:00)

CHILIPOUR 10-10-13 (7*) Mr L Baker, *hld up, hit 5th, hdwy 7th, led 11th, all out*............(6 to 4 on op 11 to 8 on) 1
MIGHTY FALCON 12-10-13 (7*) Miss E Tory, *sn in tch, led 9th to 11th, rallied to go second 3 out, chlgd nxt, kpt on und pres.* ....(7 to 1 tchd 8 to 1) 2
3578³ ABBOTSHAM 12-10-13 (7*) Mr E James, *hld up in rear, hit 6th, hdwy appr 9th, wnt second bef 4 out, wknd nxt.* ....(11 to 2 op 4 to 1 tchd 6 to 1) 3
ANJUBI 12-10-13 (7*) Mr R Widger, *trkd ldrs, outpcd tenth, styd on one pace frm 3 out.* ....(12 to 1 op 10 to 1 tchd 14 to 1) 4
SPITFIRE JUBILEE 11-10-13 (7*) Mr R Nuttall, *led to 9th, rdn and wknd 3 out*..........................(8 to 1 op 6 to 1) 5
INDIAN KNIGHT 12-10-13 (7*) Mr M G Miller, *trkd ldr to 9th, wkng whn hit 5 out, tld off*............(16 to 1 op 12 to 1) 6
KILLELAN LAD 15-10-13 (7*) Miss K Di Marte, *al in rear, hit tenth, tld off whn pld up bef 4 out*......(50 to 1 op 25 to 1) pu
TRY IT ALONE 15-10-13 (7*) Mr G Shenkin, *al beh, rdn appr 9th, tld off whn pld up bef 4 out*.......(33 to 1 op 16 to 1) pu
Dist: Nk, 8l, 2½l, 12l, dist. 6m 0.10s. a 26.10s (8 Ran).

(Nick Viney), Victor Dartnall

3941 Kevin Kane Maiden Open National Hunt Flat Class H (4,5,6-y-o) £1,413 2¼m.........................(4:30)

BRAMSHAW WOOD (Ire) 5-11-5 J Frost, *hld up in rear, hdwy 7 fs out, styd on und pres to ld cl hme.* (20 to 1 op 14 to 1) 1
STORM FORECAST (Ire) 5-11-5 J F Titley, *hld up, hdwy hfwy, led 4 fs out to 3 out, led appr last, rdn and hdd cl hme.* ....(11 to 8 fav op Evens tchd 5 to 4 on) 2
MY MICKY 6-11-5 L Harvey, *in tch, ev ch till wknd appr fnl furlong*.......................... (20 to 1 op 12 to 1) 3
3654³ BROTHER NERO (NZ) 5-11-5 R Greene, *led for 5 fs, kpt on one pace fnl 2*........................(20 to 1 op 12 to 1) 4
HILL'S ELECTRIC (Ire) 5-11-5 D Gallagher, *whippe round strt, sn in tch, led 3 out, hdd and wknd appr fnl furlong.* ....(20 to 1 op 12 to 1) 5
3408⁸ JIM'S QUEST 4-11-0 A P McCoy, *hld up in rear, hdwy 6 fs out, eery ch 2 out, wknd quickly ins last.* ....(5 to 1 op 6 to 1 tchd 7 to 1 and 8 to 1) 6
COOL NORMAN (NZ) 5-10-12 (7*) M Berry, *in tch, outpcd 7 fs out, nvr dngrs aftr*........(7 to 1 tchd 8 to 1 and 9 to 1) 7
ARDENT STEP (Ire) 4-10-4 (5*) O Burrows, *beh frm hfwy.* ....(11 to 2 op 4 to 1 tchd 6 to 1) 8
DUNGANNON LAD 6-10-12 (7*) N Willmington, *led aftr 5 fs, hdd 4 out, sn btn*..........................(20 to 1 op 12 to 1) 9
3654⁴ SEE PROSPERITY 5-10-12 (7*) L Cummins, *in tch till wknd hfwy*..................................(50 to 1 op 33 to 1) 10
BUDDY DIVER 4-11-0 T Dascombe, *in tch to hfwy, tld off.* ....(33 to 1 op 25 to 1) 11
IN HARMONY 5-10-9 (5*) D Salter, *al beh, tld off.* ....(14 to 1 op 12 to 1) 12
Dist: Nk, 7l, ¾l, 4l, 1¾l, 1l, 18l, 2½l, 23l, dist. 4m 16.20s. (12 Ran).

(Mrs U Wainwright), R H Alner

DOWN ROYAL (IRE) (yielding to soft)
Monday May 5th

3942 R.V.H. Bicentenary Handicap Hurdle (0-116 5-y-o and up) £1,712 2½m ....(2:35)

3837² FALLOW TRIX (Ire) [-] 5-10-8 (3*) D Bromley, ... (2 to 1 fav) 1
3070⁷ WADABLAST (Ire) [-] 7-9-4 (3*) B Bowens,........(10 to 1) 2
3643⁶ KILCAR (Ire) [-] 6-9-0 (7*) L J Fleming,............(12 to 1) 3
3696³ EIRE (Ire) [-] 8-9-0 (7*) R Burke,......................(7 to 1) 4
2647 IADA (Ire) [-] 6-10-1 D T Evans,......................(14 to 1) 5
3180⁸ THE PARSON'S FILLY (Ire) [-] 7-9-13 F J Flood, ... (14 to 1) 6
3068 BRACKENVALE (Ire) [-] 6-9-0 (7*) S P McCann, ... (20 to 1) 7
184* FRESH DEAL (Ire) [-] 5-12-0 L P Cusack, ... (6 to 1) 8
MASTER JOEY [-] 7-9-9⁴ (7*) C Rae, ...(14 to 1) 9
3389* COLLON DIAMONDS (Ire) [-] 9-9-6 (7*) Mr R P McNalley, ...(4 to 1) 10
3643⁸ JERMYN STREET (USA) [-] (bl) 6-9-9² P McWilliams, ...(16 to 1) pu
Dist: 8l, nk, 10l, 2½l. 4m 42.00s. (11 Ran).

(Laggallon Racing Syndicate), J R Cox

3943 Tyrone Crystal Q.R. Maiden Hurdle (4-y-o and up) £1,712 2¾m... (3:05)

3391 HAVEAFEWMANNERS (Ire) 7-10-10 (5*) Mr G Elliott, ... (7 to 2 jt-fav) 1
741 NOBODYWANTSME (Ire) 6-10-13 (7*) Mr R P McNalley, ...(16 to 1) 2
CASTLE DAWN (Ire) 7-10-13 (7*) Mr A J Dempsey, ..(6 to 1) 3
MARIES CALL (Ire) 7-10-8 (7*) Mr J Bright, ...(5 to 1) 4
JUST HOLD ON (Ire) 5-11-5 Mr R Walsh, ... (7 to 2 jt-fav) 5
884⁹ BANNAGH MOR (Ire) 6-11-1 (5*) Mr R J Patton, ... (11 to 2) 6
3380⁸ BORREEVA (Ire) 7-10-8 (7*) Mr K Ross, ...(12 to 1) 7
CHERISHTHELADY (Ire) 5-10-11 (3*) Mr P J Casey, (20 to 1) 8
NORTH CITY 6-10-13 (7*) Mr M O'Connor, ... (16 to 1) 9
WIND OF GLORY (Ire) 7-11-0¹ (7*) Mr P Jones, ... (20 to 1) pu
STRATA RIDGE (Ire) 7-10-13 (7*) Mr P Fahey, ... (8 to 1) pu
MAID O'TULLY (Ire) 6-10-12 (3*) Mr B R Hamilton, (12 to 1) pu
SPARTAN PARK 8-10-8 (7*) Mr W Ewing, ...(16 to 1) pu
Dist: 13l, 2l, ½l, dist. 5m 33.60s. (13 Ran).

(James Babes), A J Martin

3944 Isuzu Governor's Perpetual Cup EBF Handicap Chase (0-109 4-y-o and up) £3,425 2¾m...............(4:35)

3765 BALLYMACREVAN (Ire) [-] 7-11-7 (7*) Mr W Ewing, ...(100 to 30 fav) 1
3229⁴ LA-GREINE [-] 10-10-5 (7*) Mr K Ross, ...(7 to 1) 2
3839⁵ IF YOU BELIEVE (Ire) [-] 8-10-5 (3*) B Bowens, ...(5 to 1) 3
3645⁵ ROCHE MENTOR (Ire) [-] 7-9-7² (3*) D Bromley, ... (20 to 1) 4
3839⁷ GREEK MAGIC [-] 10-9-9² T J Mitchell, ... (12 to 1) 5
3753⁴ CABBERY ROSE (Ire) [-] 9-9-11 (7*) C Rae, ... (4 to 1) 6
3446⁴ HANNIES GIRL (Ire) [-] 8-10-5 (7*) L J Fleming, ... (7 to 1) 7
3393* MR FIVE WOOD (Ire) [-] 9-10-13 D T Evans, ...(7 to 2) ur
Dist: 4l, 4l, 4½l, 14l. 5m 38.50s. (8 Ran).

(Good Time Managers Syndicate), I A Duncan

3945 R.V.H. Bicentenary I.N.H. Flat Race (4-y-o and up) £1,712 2m.... (5:05)

3789 EASY FEELIN (Ire) 5-11-13 Mr P F Graffin, ...(10 to 1) 1
2115⁴ YOU MAKE ME LAUGH (Ire) 5-11-13 Mr A J Martin, ... (7 to 2 co-fav) 2
3767 HANDSOME ANTHONY (Ire) 6-11-11 (3*) Mr B R Hamilton, ...(12 to 1) 3
3840² CONAGHER LEADER (Ire) 6-12-0 Mr R Walsh, ... (6 to 1) 4
3647⁴ OTTER TRACK LADY (Ire) 4-10-8 (7*) Mr Philip Carberry, ...(7 to 1) 5
MACON EXPRESS (Ire) 4-10-13 (7*) Mr A J Dempsey, ...(8 to 1) 6
3349 THE TOLLAH (Ire) 5-11-8 (5*) Mr G Elliott, ... (7 to 1) 7
PRINCESS CATALDI (Ire) 7-11-4 (5*) Mr L Lennon, (33 to 1) 8
JOHNNY BRUSHASIDE (Ire) 4-11-6 Mr G J Harford, ... (7 to 2 co-fav) 9
VICTORIA'S BOY (Ire) 4-10-13 (7*) Mr W Ewing, ... (14 to 1) 10
3394⁵ KATOUCHE (Ire) 6-11-7 (7*) Mr A Parker, ... (14 to 1) 11
CUTE N'SHY (Ire) 4-10-10 (5*) Mr R J Patton, ... (16 to 1) 12
LIGHTNING JACK (Ire) 6-11-7 (7*) Mr Edgar Byrne, (14 to 1) 13
210 DUNMORE SUNSET (Ire) 5-11-6 (7*) Mr L J Gracey, (33 to 1) 14
3225 CAROLANNS CHOICE (Ire) 8-11-2 (7*) Mr R P McNalley, ...(33 to 1) 15
MY NATIVE GIRL (Ire) 4-11-1 Mr J P Dempsey, (7 to 2 co-fav) 16
BLUE TOO (Ire) 6-11-2 (7*) Mr P Fahey, ... (14 to 1) 17
MUST BE DONE (Ire) 5-11-6 (7*) Mr P Fisher, ... (33 to 1) 18
3394 JIMMYJOE (Ire) 4-10-13 (7*) Mr J J Canavan, ... (50 to 1) 19
Dist: 3l, 4l, ¾l, 3½l. 3m 53.30s. (19 Ran).

(S McAlister), P F Graffin

FONTWELL (good to firm)
Monday May 5th
Going Correction: MINUS 0.10 sec. per fur.

3946 Bracklesham Juvenile Novices' Hurdle Class E (4-y-o) £2,302 2¼m 110yds............................ (2:00)

3192* ELA AGAPI MOU (USA) 11-10 P Holley, *in tch, rdn 6th, led last, slyd on und pres.* (6 to 4 fav op 11 to 8 tchd 7 to 4) 1
3680² STERLING FELLOW 10-5 (7*) Mr S Durack, *led up near, outpcd 6th, hrd rdn and hdwy appr 2 out, not quicken r-in.*
.... (20 to 1 op 10 to 1) 2
3681² ANNA SOLEIL (Ire) 11-4 J Osborne, *chsd ldr, lft in ld 3 out, hdd and no extr last.....* (11 to 4 op 9 to 4 tchd 7 to 2) 3
3489⁴ BIGWIG (Ire) (v) 10-5 (7*) M Batchelor, *sn pushed alng in rear, lost tch 6th...........* (40 to 1 op 20 to 1 tchd 50 to 1) 4
2454 HEART 10-7 J Culloty, *keen hold, prmnt til appr 3 out, wknd.*
....(5 to 1 op 9 to 4) 5
3747² NAME OF OUR FATHER (USA) 11-4 R Johnson, *led till 13 out.*
............................(7 to 2 tchd 9 to 2 and 4 to 1) f
Dist: 2½l, 11l, 10l, 6l. 4m 26.20s. a 9.20s (6 Ran).

(Ballard (1834) Limited), G L Moore

3947 Beaumont Challenge Cup Novices' Chase Class E (6-y-o and up) £2,997 3¼m 110yds........................ (2:30)

3772² KEEP IT ZIPPED (Ire) (bl) 7-11-5 J Osborne, *made all, shaken up and wnt clr appr 2 out, eased r-in.*
................(11 to 8 on tchd 5 to 4 on and 6 to 4 on) 1
3858² MASTER CRUSADER 11-10-5 (7*) Mr S Durack, *in tch, wnt second 11th, no extr frm 3 out.*
....................(3 to 1 tchd 7 to 2 and 4 to 1) 2
674⁴ BAD BOY 10-12 (7*) A Dowling, *jmpd slwly, sn tld off, pld up bef 13th......................*(16 to 1 op 7 to 1) pu
PAGE ROYALE (Fr) 7-11-11 (3*) J Magee, *chsd wnr to 11th, tld off 16th, jmpd slwly and pld up 18th.*
....................................(7 to 2 op 3 to 1 tchd 4 to 1) pu
Dist: 10l. 6m 53.20s. a 23.20s (4 Ran).

(Mrs Luisa Stewart-Brown), O Sherwood

3948 Fittleworth Claiming Hurdle Class F (4-y-o and up) £2,057 2¼m 110yds
.... (3:00)

3871 JENZSOPH (Ire) (bl) 6-11-0 G Tormey, *set fst pace, jmpd wl, made all, sn clr, easily...*(9 to 4 op 7 to 4 tchd 5 to 2) 1
3871² PETER MONAMY (bl) 5-12-0 N Williamson, *chsd wnr, mstk 3 out, btn nxt....* (13 to 8 on op 7 to 4 on tchd 2 to 1) 2
3258⁹ THE GREY TEXAN 8-11-0 D O'Sullivan, *tld off till hdwy 3 out, styd on, not rch ldg pair.....*(33 to 1 op 20 to 1) 3
3409⁴ OLIVIPET 8-9-12 (7*) M Clinton, *sn outpcd, tld off frm 6th.*
....................(25 to 1 op 14 to 1 tchd 33 to 1) 4
3729⁷ GREEN KING 5-11-2 S McNeill, *some hdwy 4th, moderate 3rd whn ran very wide bend appr 6th, lost pl rpdly, sn tld off and virtually pld up.*
..............(9 to 1 op 14 to 1 tchd 20 to 1 and 25 to 1) 5
FRIAR'S OAK 5-11-2 J Culloty, *mstk 3rd, sn beh, tld off hfwy, pld up bef 2 out........*(25 to 1 op 20 to 1 tchd 33 to 1) pu
Dist: 19l, 3l, dist, dist. 4m 22.00s. a 5.00s (6 Ran).
SR: 20/15/-/

(A Stevens), P J Hobbs

3949 Madehurst Maiden Chase Class F (5-y-o and up) £2,444 2¼m...... (3:30)

3776⁷ FULL OF TRICKS 9-11-2 (3*) L Aspell, *led to second, led 7th, styd on frm 3 out.*
..........(10 to 1 op 6 to 1 tchd 12 to 1 and 14 to 1) 1
3792 EAU SO SLOE 6-11-2 (3*) J Magee, *hdwy 8th, jnd wnr 11th, hrd rdn and one pace frm 2 out.*
....................(20 to 1 op 14 to 1 tchd 33 to 1) 2
3738 SWIFT POKEY 7-10-12 (7*) Mr S Durack, *led second to 7th, lost tch tenth, remote 3rd whn refused and uns rdr 2 out, rmntd............................*(50 to 1 op 20 to 1) 3
3620² SNOWY PETREL (bl) 5-10-13 S McNeill, *cl 4th whn mstk and uns rdr 1st.............*(6 to 1 tchd 11 to 4 on) ur
Dist: 5l, dist. 4m 44.50s. a 24.50s (4 Ran).

(Brian J White), J J Bridger

3950 Diane Oughton Memorial Challenge Trophy Handicap Chase Class D (0-125 5-y-o and up) £3,827 2m 3f
.... (4:00)

3775* BLAZER MORINIERE (Fr) [90] 8-10-11 S Fox, *chsd ldrs, led tenth, ran on gmely whn chlgd r-in..................*(3 to 1) 1
3284* GROOVING (Ire) [103] 8-11-0 N Williamson, *hdwy tenth, wnt second 12th, str chal last, eased whn hld nr finish.*
....................(11 to 8 fav op 7 to 4 tchd 11 to 4 and 3 to 1) 2
3730⁴ POLDEN PRIDE [113] 9-11-10 B Clifford, *outpcd, some hdwy 11th, styd on frm 3 out, not rch ldrs.*
....................................(9 to 2 op 3 to 1 tchd 5 to 1) 3
3279⁷ RAMSTAR [100] 9-10-11 G Tormey, *made most to tenth, rdn nxt, wknd appr 3 out................*(14 to 1 op 10 to 1) 4
3630³ MASTER COMEDY [89] (bl) 13-10-0 J Culloty, *outpcd, sn tld off........*(25 to 1 op 20 to 1 tchd 33 to 1 and 50 to 1) 5
2437 BO KNOWS BEST (Ire) [110] (v) 8-11-7 P Holley, *rdn and lost tch hfwy, pld up bef 3 out........................*(10 to 1) pu

3951 Fontwell Handicap Hurdle Class E (0-110 5-y-o and up) £2,465 2¾m 110yds........................ (4:30)

3774⁴ ST VILLE [104] 11-11-5 (5*) G Supple, *prmnt, rdn to ld 8th, clr appr 2 out, hld on und pres r-in...........* (9 to 2 op 7 to 2) 1
3773* SCUD MISSILE (Ire) [95] 6-11-1 A Thornton, *rear, rdn and styd on wl frm 3 out, not rch wnr.*
.................(11 to 2 op 9 to 2 tchd 6 to 1) 2
2896² JACKSON FLINT [98] 9-11-4 J Culloty, *mid-div, 3 out, kpt on same pace.....................*(9 to 2 op 4 to 1) 3
3738³ ECU DE FRANCE (Ire) [80] 7-9-7 (7*) M Clinton, *rear, hdwy appr 2 out, styd on, nvr nr to chal.....* (50 to 1 op 33 to 1) 4
3494³ SMUGGLER'S POINT (USA) [103] 7-11-6 (3*) Sophie Mitchell, *led, pushed alng 4th, hdd 8th, wknd nxt.*
....................................(10 to 1 op 6 to 1) 5
3774³ GIVUS A CALL (Ire) [102] 7-11-5 (3*) L Aspell, *mid-div, rdn 7th, wknd 3 out..............* (9 to 1 op 5 to 1 tchd 6 to 1) 6
3614⁶ DERRYBELLE [80] 6-9-7 (7*) Mr S Durack, *prmnt till wknd 8th.*
....................................(33 to 1 op 20 to 1) 7
3725⁷ LAYHAM LOW (Ire) [84] 6-10-4 J Osborne, *prmnt till wknd 8th.*
....................(14 to 1 op 8 to 1 tchd 16 to 1) 8
3692³ PLINTH [82] 6-10-2 N Williamson, *mid-div, smooth hdwy whn hit 8th, chlgd 3 out, 4th and wkng whn mstk last, virtually pld up r-in................*(100 to 30 fav op 7 to 1 tchd 9 to 1) 9
3494⁵ KAREN'S TYPHOON (Ire) [80] 6-9-7 (7*) M Batchelor, *in tch whn slpd up bend aftr 1st..........*(25 to 1 tchd 33 to 1) su
Dist: 1½l, 1½l, 4l, 14l, 6l, dist, 6l, dist. 5m 32.90s. a 18.90s (10 Ran).

(Melplash Racing), R H Buckler

LIMERICK (IRE) (good)
Monday May 5th

3952 Pat Keogh Nissan Maiden Hurdle (4 & 5-y-o) £3,425 2m 1f........ (3:50)

3625³ LUNA FLEUR (Ire) 4-10-3 (7*) B J Geraghty, ...(3 to 1) 1
3816⁴ ASHJAR (USA) 4-11-1 (5*) P G Hourigan, ...(7 to 4 fav) 2
CONFECTIONER (Ire) 4-11-1 T P Treacy, ...(8 to 1) 3
3707⁷ DINGHY (Ire) 4-10-7 (3*) G Cotter, ...(10 to 1) 4
FIVE PALS (Ire) 5-11-5 M P Hourigan, ...(10 to 1) 5
3755 GOOD FOUNDATION (Ire) 4-10-3 (7*) Mr A Fleming,
.... 6
2336⁹ LITTLE MURRAY 4-10-8 (7*) Mr Paul Moloney, ...(16 to 1) 7
3818⁹ LOFTUS BELLE (Ire) 5-11-0 D J Casey, ...(9 to 1) 8
CALICO JACK (Ire) 5-10-12 (7*) M D Murphy, ...(16 to 1) 9
SISTER MARY (Ire) 5-11-0 A J O'Brien, ...(12 to 1) 10
GOOD TIMES AHEAD (Ire) 5-11-0 J R Barry, ...(20 to 1) 11
DROMALANE (Ire) 5-11-5 P A Roche, ...(14 to 1) 12
GRACES SUPREME (Ire) 5-10-11 (3*) K Whelan, ...(20 to 1) 13
487⁴ FRANCOSKID (Ire) 5-11-6 (7*) Mr J P McNamara, ...(10 to 1) 14
LARMELIA (Ire) 5-11-0 (5*) T Martin, ...(20 to 1) 15
3889 PEYTO LAKE (Ire) 5-10-12 (7*) J A Robinson, ...(14 to 1) 16
3232 MAGICAL MIST (Ire) 4-10-3 (7*) Mr P P O'Brien, ...(25 to 1) 17
3878 HOMESTEAD NIECE (USA) 5-11-1 (7*) M J Collins, ..(16 to 1) 18
PIPERS BOG (Ire) 5-10-12 (7*) Mr M Budds, ...(14 to 1) ur
1756 MYGLASS (Ire) 5-11-0 J Shortt, ...(12 to 1) ur
Dist: 14l, ¾l, 2½l, 4½l. 4m 9.90s. (20 Ran).

(Mrs M A Brennan), Noel Meade

3953 O'Reilly Associates Handicap Hurdle (0-109 4-y-o and up) £3,425 3m
.... (4:20)

3754 KASELECTRIC (Ire) [-] 6-11-7 (7*) Mr Paul Moloney, ..(14 to 1) 1
3837⁶ HEATHER VILLE (Ire) [-] 5-10-4 (7*) B J Geraghty, ...(7 to 1) 2
3234³ TULLOLOUGH [-] 14-9-13 W Slattery, ...(14 to 1) 3
3754 THE WISE KNIGHT (Ire) [-] 6-10-7 (7*) M D Murphy, ..(9 to 1) 4
3448⁵ CASEY JUNIOR (Ire) [-] (bl) 9-9-9 (7*) D W O'Sullivan,
....(12 to 1) 5
2016 MY BLUE (-) 5-9-4⁴ (7*) E F Cahalan, ...(14 to 1) 6
3428 BUCKMINSTER (-) 10-12-0 J Shortt, ...(12 to 1) 7
3072⁹ ANOTHER GROUSE (-) 10-11-1 T P Treacy, ...(9 to 1) 8
3223 RAINBOW TIMES (Ire) [-] 4-9-4 (3*) G Cotter, ...(25 to 1) 9
3695³ COOLREE LORD (Ire) [-] (bl) 6-9-8 (5*) P G Hourigan,
....(100 to 30 fav) 10
3695⁶ JOSHUA TREE [-] 12-10-4 J K Kinane, ...(14 to 1) 11
3878 SECRET PRINCE (Ire) [-] 6-9-7 C O'Brien, ...(12 to 1) 12
3837 EMPEROR GLEN (Ire) [-] 9-10-11 (3*) K Whelan, ...(14 to 1) 13
3645 JESSIE'S BOY (Ire) [-] 8-10-5 (5*) T Martin, ...(20 to 1) 14
563⁷ VERY LITTLE (Ire) [-] 9-10-6 M P Hourigan, ...(14 to 1) 15
3431⁹ TOURING-TURTLE (Ire) [-] 5-9-13 (5*) P Morris, ...(14 to 1) 16
3695⁷ DICK McCARTHY (Ire) [-] 5-10-5 D J Casey, ...(8 to 1) 17
3817⁹ CHELSEA BELLE (Ire) [-] 5-10-1 M Duffy, ...pu
Dist: 3½l, 11l, 6l, 6l. 4m 4.40s. (18 Ran).

(J J Canty), E McNamara

3954 Ballygeale Handicap Hurdle (0-102 4-y-o and up) £2,740 2m 1f... (4:50)

3817^{7} CLONMEL COMMERCIAL (Ire) [-] 6-9-11 (7*) D McCullagh, ...(6 to 1) 1
710^{5} FAIR SOCIETY (Ire) [-] 6-10-10 M P Hourigan, ...(12 to 1) 2
3346^{5} HILL OF HOPE (Ire) [-] 6-11-7 (3*) K Whelan, ...(12 to 1) 3
3817^{8} CHARLIE-O (Ire) [-] 5-11-9 J R Barry, ...(5 to 1 jt-fav) 4
3754 FRAU DANTE (Ire) [-] 7-11-6 P A Roche, ...(5 to 1 jt-fav) 5
3817 CNOCADRUM VI (Ire) [-] 6-10-0 W Slattery, ...(10 to 1) 6
3234 PERMIT ME (Ire) [-] 5-9-10 (7*) K A Kelly, ...(14 to 1) 7
DARCARI ROSE (Ire) [-] 8-10-8 (5*) T Martin, ...(14 to 1) 8
3337^{8} CLONEE PRIDE (Ire) [-] 6-9-5^{3} (5*) P D Carey, ...(20 to 1) 9
3817 RUN ROSE RUN (Ire) [-] (bl) 7-9-9 M Duffy, ...(12 to 1) 10
3446 MINSTREL FIRE (Ire) [-] 9-10-10 (7*) B J Geraghty, (10 to 1) 11
3216 NA HUIBHEACHU (Ire) [-] (bl) 6-10-1 (3*) G Cotter, (10 to 1) 12
2836 WACKO JACKO (Ire) [-] 8-11-5 T P Treacy, ...(14 to 1) 13
3878^{6} MOSTA (Ire) [-] 4-9-6 (7*) M J Collins, ...(10 to 1) 14
3419 SINGERS CORNER [-] (bl) 5-9-4 (7*) P J Dobbs, ...(14 to 1) 15
978 HIGH PARK LADY (Ire) [-] 6-9-3 (7*) S FitzGerald, ..(20 to 1) 16
3817 RIVER RUMPUS (Ire) [-] 5-9-12 (7*) M D Murphy, ..(12 to 1) 17
948^{4} MIDDLE MOGGS (Ire) [-] 5-10-9 (5*) P G Hourigan, (10 to 1) f
3608^{6} GALLIC HONEY (Ire) [-] 6-9-5 (7*) Mrs C Harrison, (14 to 1) pu
3345^{7} GIVEUPTHEFAGS (Ire) [-] 4-11-2 J Shortt, ...(10 to 1) pu

Dist: ½l, 4l, nk, nk. 4m 7.20s. (20 Ran).
(E P Hickey), Michael Donohoe

3955 Parteen I.N.H. Flat Race (6-y-o and up) £2,740 2½m.............. (5:20)

3416 STILLBYHERSELF (Ire) 7-11-2 (7*) Mr J P McNamara, ...(12 to 1) 1
3520^{2} SPLEODRACH (Ire) 7-11-9 Mr D Marnane, ...(5 to 1) 2
3608^{3} SARAH BLUE (Ire) 7-11-2 (7*) Mr K R O'Ryan, ...(8 to 1) 3
ORPHAN SPA (Ire) 6-12-0 Mr E Bolger, ...(7 to 1) 4
3836 THE RIGHT ATTITUDE (Ire) 7-11-7 (7*) Miss E Peck, (14 to 1) 5
MEENVANE (Ire) 7-11-7 (7*) Mr P J Crowley, ...(10 to 1) 6
3222^{5} DANGER FLYNN (Ire) 7-11-7 (7*) Mr K O'Sullivan, (14 to 1) 7
3818 BALLINREE (Ire) 6-11-4 (5*) Mr A C Coyle, ...(8 to 1) 8
720 GLEN GIRL (Ire) 7-11-2 (7*) Miss K Rudd, ...(20 to 1) 9
BUCKING LAURA (Ire) 6-11-2 (7*) Mr Paul Moloney, (5 to 1) 10
1776 GAIN CONTROL (Ire) 8-11-2 (7*) Miss O Hayes, ...(20 to 1) 11
3089 VALLEY OF KINGS (Ire) 7-11-7 (7*) Mr L J Temple, (14 to 1) 12
ASHLAR (Ire) 6-11-7 (7*) Mr R M Walsh, ...(9 to 2 fav) 13
BADALKA (Ire) 7-11-2 (7*) Mr T A J Corrigan, ...(14 to 1) 14
3233^{4} THE YELLOW BOG (Ire) 7-11-7 (7*) Mr B Moran, ..(14 to 1) 15
3421 GERRY O MALLEY (Ire) 7-11-9 (5*) Mr P A Deegan, (7 to 1) 16
CROHANE HILL (Ire) 6-11-7 (7*) Mr J P Hayden, ..(14 to 1) 17
140 JOSALADY (Ire) 8-11-2 (7*) Mr C T Kidd, ...(20 to 1) 18
NORTHERN HIGHWAY (Ire) 7-11-7 (7*) Mr D G McHale, ...(20 to 1) 19
WANDERING CHOICE (Ire) 7-11-2 (7*) Miss A Foley, ...(14 to 1) pu

Dist: Sht-hd, 5½l, 15l, 2l. 4m 54.40s. (20 Ran).
(Shannon Arches Syndicate), Thomas Foley

LUDLOW (good to firm) Monday May 5th

Going Correction: PLUS 0.40 sec. per fur.

3956 Tote Placepot Conditional Jockeys' Selling Hurdle Class G (4-y-o and up) £1,861 2m....................(2:30)

2973 BRIGHT ECLIPSE (USA) 4-10-4 (3*) M Griffiths, *chsd ldrs, rcd keenly, led 5th, hdd and btn whn lft clr last.* ....(11 to 2 op 5 to 1 tchd 6 to 1) 1
3731 SERIOUS OPTION (Ire) (v) 6-10-5 (7*) J Parkhouse, *chsd ldrs, ev ch appr 3 out, sn rdn and wknd, lft poor second last.* ....(25 to 1 op 20 to 1) 2
FLASH CHICK (Ire) 8-10-0 (7*) J Mogford, *al in rear, tld off frm 5th*...(66 to 1 op 50 to 1) 3
3554 RAKAPOSHI IMP (bl) 7-10-4 (3*) L Suthern, *chsd ldrs, mstk 1st, wknd 5th, tld off*.................(66 to 1 op 50 to 1) 4
3780^{4} ANLACE (v) 8-10-7 Chris Webb, *hld up, hdwy 5th, jnd ldr 3 out, led appr last, f*.......(3 to 1 op 11 to 4 tchd 7 to 2) f
ROYAL AG NAG 7-11-0 D J Kavanagh, *led till mstk and hdd 5th, rdn and wknd appr 3 out, sn pld up.* ....(11 to 8 on op Evens tchd 13 to 8 on) pu
3590 NORTHERN DIAMOND (Ire) 4-10-4 (3*) J Power, *hld up, effrt 5th wknd nxt, pld up bef 3 out.* ....(16 to 1 op 20 to 1 tchd 33 to 1) pu

Dist: 19l, 8l, dist. 3m 49.00s. a 17.00s (7 Ran).
(Allfor), J G M O'Shea

3957 Red Cross Novices' Hurdle Class E (4-y-o and up) £2,075 2m..... (3:05)

3296^{2} EMBANKMENT (Ire) 7-11-0 M A Fitzgerald, *trkd ldr, led appr 4th, cmftbly*.....(5 to 2 on op 2 to 1 on tchd 7 to 4 on) 1
2614^{6} FLOOSY 6-10-9 S Wynne, *al prmnt, rdn 2 out, ran on, no ch wth wnr*..............................(12 to 1 op 14 to 1) 2
3462^{2} MUSIC PLEASE 5-10-7 (7*) Mr R Wakley, *al prmnt, chsd wnr appr 3 out, no extr r-in*.....(4 to 1 op 5 to 2 tchd 9 to 2) 3
3500^{8} RED VIPER 5-11-0 Mr A Kinane, *mid-div, hdwy 4 out, wknd 2 out*..........................(16 to 1 op 25 to 1 tchd 33 to 1) 4
3825 NEW ROSS (Ire) 5-11-0 V Slattery, *led, hng lft and hdd bend aftr 3rd, wknd 3 out*.................(50 to 1 op 100 to 1) 5
3610 BACHE DINGLE 6-11-0 W Marston, *chsd ldrs, rdn 4 out, wknd nxt*...(100 to 1) 6
3825 PACKITIN PARKY 4-10-9 D Walsh, *patiently rdn, hdwy 4 out, ridden and wknd bef nxt*...........................(100 to 1) 7
SAPPHIRE SON (Ire) 5-11-0 B Fenton, *hld up, pld hrd, jmpd rght 3rd, wl beh frm nxt*..................(20 to 1 op 16 to 1) 8
873 JUST BECAUSE (Ire) 5-10-9 (5*) D J Kavanagh, *chsd ldrs, hmpd bend aftr 3rd, beh frm nxt*.....................(100 to 1) 9
2899 MISS MIGHTY 4-10-4 R Bellamy, *pld hrd, prmnt to 5th, tld off and pulled up bef 3 out*..............................(100 to 1) pu
3616 OGULLA 5-10-9 D Leahy, *prmnt, mstk 1st, lost pl nxt, beh frm 4th, tld off and pld up bef 3 out*.................(100 to 1) pu

Dist: 2l, 2½l, 10l, 4l, dist, 5l, 3l, 8l. 3m 49.70s. a 17.70s (11 Ran).
(Lady Tennant), N J Henderson

3958 Oldfield Novices' Handicap Chase Class E (0-100 5-y-o and up) £3,061 3m.............................. (3:35)

3742^{2} NORDIC VALLEY (Ire) [85] 6-11-10 D Walsh, *al prmnt, jnd ldrs appr 4 out, led last, rdn out*...........(11 to 4 op 2 to 1) 1
3914 FURRY FOX (Ire) [78] 9-11-3 D Morris, *hld up, hdwy 6 out, led 4 out, hdd last, unbl to quicken.* ....(4 to 1 op 7 to 2 tchd 9 to 2) 2
3822^{2} BOWLES PATROL (Ire) [80] 5-10-11 M A Fitzgerald, *hld up, mstk second, hdwy 6th, led briefly appr 4 out, rdn and hng lft approaching 2 out, sn btn.* ....(7 to 4 fav op 2 to 1 tchd 5 to 2) 3
3799^{4} PANDORA'S PRIZE [64] 11-10-3 S Wynne, *chsd ldr, led aftr 5 out, sn hdd, wknd after 4 out*.........(20 to 1 op 16 to 1) 4
3737 SIDE BAR [61] (v) 7-10-0 B Fenton, *led, blun 5 out, sn hdd, wknd appr 3 out*...... (20 to 1 op 25 to 1 tchd 33 to 1) 5
3470^{2} BARON'S HEIR [85] 10-11-10 W Marston, *chsd ldrs, blun 12th, sn lost tch*.............................. (4 to 1 op 3 to 1) 6
3620^{5} AEOLIAN [63] 6-9-9 (7*) Mr J Goldstein, *hld up, hdwy 6 out, wkng whn hit 3 out, blun and uns rdr nxt.* ....(40 to 1 op 33 to 1) ur
3611 FATTASH (USA) [69] (bl) 5-10-0^{7} (7*) F Quinlan, *jmpd lft 1st, al in rear, tld off 11th, pld up bef 5 out*....(50 to 1 op 25 to 1) pu
3141^{3} DEEP SONG [61] 7-10-0 R Bellamy, *rear, mstk 9th, sn pushed alng, lost tch 6 out, tld off and pld up bef 3 out.* ....(33 to 1 op 25 to 1) pu

Dist: 3l, 10l, 6l, dist, 13l. 6m 4.10s. a 17.10s (9 Ran).
SR: 21/11/-/-/-/-/ (Pond House Racing), M C Pipe

3959 Bet With The Tote Handicap Hurdle Class E (0-115 4-y-o and up) £3,061 2m.............................. (4:05)

3592 COURAGEOUS KNIGHT [82] 8-10-5 B Fenton, *chsd ldrs, led 3 out, edgd rght r-in, drvn out*..........(6 to 1 op 4 to 1) 1
3831 PERCY BRAITHWAITE (Ire) [105] 5-11-7 (7*) Mr J Goldstein, *chsd ldrs, led appr 3 out, sn hdd, ev ch last, crrd rght r-in, kpt on*..............(2 to 1 fav tchd 7 to 4 and 9 to 4) 2
2957 TANGO MAN (Ire) [77] 5-10-0 S Wynne, *hld up, hdwy 5th, ev ch frm 3 out, no extr r-in*..................(6 to 1 op 8 to 1) 3
803^{4} FRASER CAREY (Ire) [99] (bl) 5-11-8 M A Fitzgerald, *chsd ldrs, ev ch appr 3 out, wknd nxt*......... (7 to 1 op 9 to 2) 4
3673^{3} FOLLOW DE CALL [81] 7-10-4^{4} D Walsh, *hld up, mstk 3rd, hdwy 4 out, wknd nxt*................ (14 to 1 op 8 to 1) 5
3278 SWAHILI RUN [77] 9-9-7 (7*) M Griffiths, *led, clr 4th, hdd and wknd appr 3 out*..........................(33 to 1 op 20 to 1) 6
3831^{6} ROCA MURADA (Ire) [97] (v) 8-11-1 (5*) D J Kavanagh, *hld up, al beh*.................. (11 to 4 op 3 to 1 tchd 7 to 2) 7

Dist: ½l, 2l, 12l, 11l, 5l, 3l. 3m 47.60s. a 15.60s (7 Ran).
SR: -/7/-/-/ (L Kirkwood), P Hayward

3960 Ludlow Golf Club Novices' Chase Class E (5-y-o and up) £3,096 2m .... (4:35)

2938^{4} SIGMA RUN (Ire) 8-11-7 M A Fitzgerald, *led till hdd 5 out, btn whn lft clr last*.......(13 to 8 fav op 6 to 4 tchd 7 to 4) 1
3724^{4} EUROLINK SHADOW 5-10-8 D Walsh, *not jump wl, prmnt, mstk 5th (water), blun 7th, sn wknd, lft remote second last.* ....(5 to 1 tchd 9 to 2) 2
3740 HUGH DANIELS 9-10-7 (7*) Miss A Dudley, *chsd ldrs till wknd 6 out, lft poor 3rd last*...(33 to 1 op 25 to 1 tchd 50 to 1) 3
2186 PRIDEWOOD PICKER 10-11-0 B Fenton, *hld up, hdwy 6th, led 5 out, clr whn slpd on landing and f r-in.* ....(7 to 4 op 5 to 4) f
3620 QUARTER MARKER (Ire) 9-11-0 W Marston, *mstk 1st, prmnt, lost pl aftr 5th, sn wl beh, tld off and pld up bef 4 out.* .... (11 to 2 op 6 to 1) pu
3594 NUNS LUCY 6-10-9 D Leahy, *pckd 3rd, sn beh, tld off and pld up bef 4 out*.......................(50 to 1 op 20 to 1) pu

Dist: 25l, 6l. 4m 9.00s. a 19.00s (6 Ran).
(K W Bell & Son Ltd), J G M O'Shea

3961 St Johns' Novices' Handicap Hurdle Class E (0-100 4-y-o and up) £2,075 2m 5f 110yds................. (5:05)

3503 ONE MORE DIME (Ire) [62] 7-10-0 B Fenton, al prmnt, jnd ldr
6th, outpcd 3 out, rallied appr last, ran on wl to ld nr finish
.... (10 to 1 op 16 to 1)   1
3672⁴ THE EENS [67] 5-10-5 D Walsh, led 3rd, rdn appr 3 out, an clr,
wknd r-in, hdd nr finish....................(8 to 1 tchd 9 to 1)   2
3483³ GENEREUX [82] 4-10-9 (5*) Chris Webb, strted slwly, beh til
styd on frm 2 out, nrst finish........... (12 to 1 op 8 to 1)   3
3833⁷ VALLINGALE (Ire) [86] 6-11-3 (7*) Mr A Wintle, mid-div, effrt
5th, wknd 6 out...............................(7 to 1 op 4 to 1)   4
3190⁸ PROFESSOR PAGE (Ire) [74] (v) 7-10-12 M A Fitzgerald, hld
up in tch, mstk 1st, rdn 6th, sn lost touch. (9 to 1 op 8 to 1)   5
3422⁵ IMPERIAL HONORS (Ire) [62] 6-10-0 Mr A Kinane, sn pushed
alng, al in rear................................(50 to 1)   6
3611 EDEN STREAM [63] 10-10-1 D Leahy, prmnt, mstk 1st, wknd
6th..(33 to 1 op 25 to 1)   7
3771⁵ SOLDIER-B [62] 7-10-0 D Morris, led to 3rd, wknd 5th.
.... (25 to 1 op 20 to 1)   8
3796⁶ VITA NUOVA (Ire) [62] 6-10-0 V Slattery, prmnt, pld hrd, rdn
6th, sn beh.................................(33 to 1 op 16 to 1)   9
3820* HANCOCK [85] 5-11-9 W Marston, hld up, rdn aftr 5th, sn lost
tch, beh whn pld up bef 2 out.
.......................(15 to 8 fav op 2 to 1 tchd 7 to 4)   pu
3407¹ CONNAUGHT'S PRIDE [70] (bl) 6-10-3 (5*) D J Kavanagh,
prmnt, mstk 4th, wknd fve out, tld off and pld up bef 3 out.
.................................(4 to 1 op 7 to 2)   pu
Dist: ½l, 19l, 6l, dist, 8l, 21l, nk, sht-hd. 5m 17.80s. a 22.80s (11 Ran).
(J L Needham), J L Needham

NAVAN (IRE) (yielding to soft)
Monday May 5th

3962 Flower Hill Handicap Chase (5-y-o and up) £6,850 2½m......... (4:00)

3783⁴ BACK BAR (Ire) [-] 9-11-5 F Woods,...............(4 to 1)   1
3887 PERSPEX GALE (Ire) [-] 9-9-10³ C F Swan,........(13 to 2)   2
3763² ARCTIC WEATHER (Ire) [-] 8-11-11 T P Rudd, (9 to 4 jt-fav)   3
3752² HEADBANGER [-] 10-11-5 D H O'Connor, ... (9 to 4 jt-fav)   4
3431 FOURTH OF JULY [-] 13-10-8 C O'Dwyer,...........(10 to 1)   5
3839⁹ APPALACHEE BAY (Ire) [-] 7-9-7 (3*) J Butler, ...(13 to 2)   6
Dist: 1l, 3l, sht-hd, 10l. 5m 21.60s. (6 Ran).
(Patrick John McCarthy), A L T Moore

3963 Bective Maiden Hurdle (6-y-o and up) £3,082 2m 5f............. (4:30)

1536² WYATT (Ire) 7-11-6 K F O'Brien,..............(7 to 4 fav)   1
3083² DUISKE ABBEY (Ire) 7-11-9 C F Swan,.............(5 to 2)   2
2907³ KNOCKAULIN (Ire) 6-11-6 D H O'Connor, ...(14 to 1)   3
1649 JACKY FLYNN (Ire) 6-10-13 (7*) J E Casey, ...(14 to 1)   4
3227 KAVANAGHS DREAM (Ire) 8-12-0 H Rogers, ...(33 to 1)   5
3521³ GLOBAL LEGEND 7-11-6 C O'Dwyer, ...(3 to 1)   6
1715⁹ CHARMING DUKE (Ire) 7-10-13 (7*) B D Murtagh, (20 to 1)   7
1710 CORAL SEA (Ire) 7-11-7 (7*) Mr A Ross, ...(25 to 1)   8
3608 RODIRON PRIDE (Ire) 7-11-3 (3*) J Butler, ...(16 to 1)   9
DIPIE (Ire) 9-11-6 J P Byrne,...................(25 to 1)   10
3389⁶ KARA'S DREAM (Ire) 9-11-6 N Bowens, ...(20 to 1)   11
3213⁸ BITOFA DIVIL (Ire) 6-11-6 S C Lyons,..............(20 to 1)   12
2343 SOUNDSGOODTOME 6-11-1 P L Malone, ...(20 to 1)   13
3547 FANORE (Ire) 6-10-13 (7*) D A McLoughlin, ...(20 to 1)   14
PYRITE KING (Ire) 6-11-6 L P Cusack, ...(25 to 1)   15
1088⁶ SWISS THYNE (Ire) 7-10-11³ (7*) Mr R D Lee, ...(14 to 1)   16
2649 MAJESTIC LORD (Ire) 7-10-13 (7*) D K Budds, ...(33 to 1)   17
3224⁶ BODAWN BRADACH (Ire) 7-11-6 T P Rudd, ...(25 to 1)   18
1019 SAND EEL (Ire) 6-11-1 F Woods,...................(20 to 1)   19
YOU'RE SO FINE (Ire) 6-10-8 (7*) Mr M P Madden, (20 to 1)   pu
Dist: 3l, 7l, 20l, 3l. 5m 14.20s. (20 Ran).
(Seamus Ross), Noel Meade

3964 Navan Races Hurdle (4-y-o and up) £4,110 2m............. (5:00)

3754⁴ NATIVE-DARRIG (Ire) 6-12-0 C F Swan, ...(10 to 9 on)   1
3752 OWENDUFF (USA) 7-12-0 F Woods,................(3 to 1)   2
1908⁷ MARTYS STEP (Ire) 6-11-4 (3*) U Smyth, ...(7 to 1)   3
2222 HURRICANE DAVID (Ire) 8-11-7 L P Cusack, ...(25 to 1)   4
2048⁹ HIDDEN SPRINGS (Ire) 6-11-7 K F O'Brien, ...(33 to 1)   5
NEPI LAD (Ire) 9-11-0 (7*) D A McLoughlin, ...(16 to 1)   6
1204 LOUGHLINS PRIDE 8-11-2 Mr M Phillips, ...(20 to 1)   7
745⁷ SADALLAH (Ire) 6-11-6 C O'Dwyer, ...(14 to 1)   8
2225⁴ GLADIATORIAL (Ire) 5-11-13 P L Malone, ...(5 to 1)   f
2137 SWIFT GALE (Ire) 7-11-4 H Rogers, ...(20 to 1)   bd
Dist: 12l, 15l, 4l, 3½l. 4m 7.10s. (10 Ran).
(W P Kerwin), W P Mullins

3965 Kentstown I.N.H. Flat Race (5-y-o and up) £3,082 2m............. (5:30)

MAGIC CIRCLE (Fr) 5-11-13 Mr J A Berry, ...(7 to 4 fav)   1
3697⁷ THE TEXAS KID (Ire) 6-12-0 Mr P Fenton, ...(6 to 1)   2
LUCKY DANTE (Ire) 6-11-2 (7*) Mr D W Cullen, ...(8 to 1)   3
3456⁸ THE RED SIDE (Ire) 5-11-1 (7*) Mr P G Murphy, ..(8 to 1)   4
2383 RAGGLEPUSS (Ire) 7-11-2 (7*) Mr T Gibney, ...(25 to 1)   5
ONTHELIST (Ire) 5-11-6 (7*) Mr M O'Connor, ...(7 to 1)   6
3697 BYPHARTHEBEST (Ire) 5-11-1 (7*) Mr J Cash, ...(12 to 1)   7

3608⁸ BLACKWATER CISCO (Ire) 7-11-7 (7*) Mr P J Jennings,
.... (25 to 1)   8
PATS BOREEN (Ire) 6-11-7 (7*) Mr M P Madden, .. (12 to 1)   9
GLENMONT (Ire) 5-11-8 (5*) Mr D McGoona, ... (12 to 1)   10
3647 CANDY GALE (Ire) 5-11-1 (7*) Mr P J Prendergast, (25 to 1)   11
POLITICAL ANIMAL (Ire) 5-11-10 (3*) Mr D Valentine,
......................................(16 to 1)   12
CHECK THE DECK (Ire) 5-11-1 (3*) Mr P English, ..(8 to 1)   13
CRYPTIC MYTH (Ire) 5-11-1 (7*) Mr A K Wyse, ...(12 to 1)   14
782 SPARKEY SMITH (Ire) 5-11-8 Mr A R Coonan, ... (7 to 1)   15
DARI (Ire) 5-11-6 (7*) Mr P J Burke,..............(10 to 1)   16
3608⁸ ORANGE JUICE (Ire) 7-11-7 (7*) Mr A FitzGerald, ..(20 to 1)   17
2709⁷ LITTLE CANTER (Ire) 5-11-8 Mr J A Nash, ...(12 to 1)   18
3818 CAN'T BE STOPPED (Ire) (bl) 5-11-13 Mr M Phillips,
.... (25 to 1)   19
3789 TOWNLEYHALL (Ire) 5-11-6 (7*) Mr G A Kingston, (12 to 1)   20
3818 ESTHER'S CHOICE (Ire) 5-11-1 (7*) Mr C P McGivern,
......................................(14 to 1)   21
Dist: 3l, 13l, 4½l, 7l. 3m 55.10s. (21 Ran).
(Leo Schwyter), J A Berry

SOUTHWELL (good (races 1,2), good to soft (3,4,5), soft (6,7))
Monday May 5th
Going Correction: PLUS 1.10 sec. per fur.

3966 Clown Workshop & Bouncy Castle Novices' Handicap Chase Class F (0-95 5-y-o and up) £3,262 2m (2:30)

3474³ APPEARANCE MONEY (Ire) [72] 6-10-6 M Foster, hld up and
beh, steady hdwy 8th, effrt and chsd ldrs 3 out, 6 ls second
whn lft clr last.......................(6 to 1 tchd 7 to 1)   1
3781² COOL WEATHER (Ire) [70] (bl) 9-10-4 A S Smith, chsd clr ldr
till dsptd ld 7th, rdn and one pace frm 4 out.
.... (11 to 2 op 5 to 1)   2
3821² BALI TENDER (Ire) [66] 6-9-11 (3*) M R Thornton, chsd ldrs, hdwy
to dispute ld 4 out, rdn nxt and wknd 2 out.
.... (11 to 2 op 3 to 1)   3
3559 GIVRY (Ire) [80] 7-10-11 (3*) D Fortt, in tch to 5th, sn lost pl and
beh..........................(20 to 1 op 14 to 1)   4
3845³ BIT OF A DREAM (Ire) [66] 7-9-9 (5*) G F Ryan, chsd ldrs, rdn
alng bef 4 out and sn one pace.......(2 to 1 fav op 5 to 2)   5
2808⁷ STAGE PLAYER [82] 11-11-2 I Lawrence, al beh, tld off frm
hfwy.............................(10 to 1 op 7 to 1)   6
3668 CHORUS LINE (Ire) [90] 8-11-10 R Supple, led to aftr 1st, chsd
clr ldr till led 7th, rdn clear 3 out, 6 ls up whn blun and uns rdr
last...........................(5 to 1 op 7 to 1 tchd 9 to 2)   ur
PHARGOLD (Ire) [80] 8-11-0 J Supple, pld hrd, mstks, led aftr
1st and sn clr, wknd and hdd 7th, soon beh and tld off whn
pulled up bef last.......................(33 to 1 op 20 to 1)   pu
Dist: 5l, 5l, 10l, 3l, 19l. 4m 19.10s. a 25.10s (8 Ran).
SR: 3/-/-/-/-/   (Irish Festival Racing Club), F Murphy

3967 Southwell Racecourse Family Fun-day Novices' Chase Class E (5-y-o and up) £3,507 3m 110yds.... (3:00)

3327 PRINCE BUCK (Ire) 7-11-2 J Railton, cl up, led 3rd to 10th, led
ag'n 5 out, clr 3 out, hit last.
.... (13 to 2 op 5 to 1 tchd 7 to 1)   1
3726² ALASKAN HEIR (Ire) 6-11-2 T Eley, led to 3rd, cl up till led 10th,
hdd 5 out and sn drvn alng one pace frm 3 out.
......................(14 to 1 op 12 to 1 tchd 9 to 1)   2
3395 FERN LEADER (Ire) 7-11-2 J Supple, mstks and beh, hdwy
appr 4 out, sn approaching 2 out, nvr a factor.
......................................(8 to 1 op 6 to 1)   3
3395⁵ MAJORITY MAJOR (Ire) 8-11-8 A S Smith, chsd ldrs, drvn
alng 5 out, sn one pace.............(14 to 1 op 8 to 1)   4
GLENBRICKEN 11-11-2 Richard Guest, hld up in midfield,
hdwy 10th, rdn alng 4 out and sn wknd.
......................(9 to 1 op 8 to 1 tchd 10 to 1)   5
3716⁶ CROWN EQUERRY (Ire) 7-12-0 R Dunwoody, chsd ldrs, mstk
3rd, f 8th.........................(11 to 10 on op 6 to 1)   f
3724² EXEMPLAR (Ire) 9-10-11 (5*) G F Ryan, mstk 1st, blun and uns
rdr second..................................(6 to 1 op 4 to 1)   ur
2799 DAMCADA (Ire) 9-11-2 Mr O McPhail, chsd ldrs, rdn alng
and wknd 12th, tld off 5 out, pld up aftr nxt.
......................(33 to 1 op 25 to 1)   pu
3669 DOCTOR DUNKLIN (USA) 8-10-13 (3*) Michael Brennan, al
beh, tld off whn pld up bef 9th.........(50 to 1 op 33 to 1)   pu
Dist: 20l, 3l, 6l, hd. 6m 44.30s. a 50.30s (9 Ran).
(Mike Roberts), M J Roberts

3968 Malcolm Fisher 50th Birthday Hand-icap Chase Class E (0-115 5-y-o and up) £4,883 2½m 110yds...... (3:30)

3502⁶ ROYAL SQUARE (Can) [83] 11-9-11 (3*) Mr R Thornton, cl up,
led aftr 4 out, rdn clr after nxt, styd on wl.
......................................(16 to 1 op 12 to 1)   1
3670³ PERUVIAN GALE (Ire) [91] 8-10-8 Richard Guest, in tch,
pushed alng and outpcd 9th, hit 11th, hdwy frm 3 out, no ch
wth wnr.............................(5 to 2 op 3 to 1 tchd 7 to 2)   2

3760* ACAJOU III (Fr) [111] 9-12-0 R Dunwoody, *led, hit second, mstk 10th, rdn 4 out and sn hdd, drvn and wknd nxt, fnshd tired*........................(11 to 10 fav op 5 to 4 on) 3
3670* CHADWICK'S GINGER [100] 9-11-3 Derek Byrne, *hld up, hdwy to chase ldrs 6th, blun 10th, sn rdn and lost pl, tld off 4 out*.........................(11 to 4 tchd 3 to 1) 4
3797 APPLIANCEOFSCIENCE [84] 10-10-14 (3*) Michael Brennan, *beh, hit 4th, pld up aftr 6th*..........(25 to 1 tchd 33 to 1) pu
Dist: 10l, 20l, dist. 5m 27.60s. a 27.60s (5 Ran).
SR: 21/19/19/-/-/   (R A M Racecourses Ltd), N P Littmoden

3969 Double Decker Fun Bus Hunters' Chase Class H (6-y-o and up) £2,211 3m 110yds.................. (4:00)

35786 TRIFAST LAD 12-12-0 (3*) Mr P Hacking, *chsd clr ldr, hdwy 5 out, rdn to ld aftr 3 out, hld on w frm last*.
..........................(11 to 10 fav op 5 to 4 on tchd 5 to 4) 1
38514 KAMBALDA RAMBLER 13-11-7 (7*) Mr R Armson, *hld up and beh, gd hdwy bef 4 out, chlgd 2 out, ev ch last, kpt on*.
............................(4 to 1 tchd 5 to 1) 2
3777 FIFTH AMENDMENT (bl) 12-11-11 (3*) Mr R Thornton, *led and sn wl clr, rdn alng 5 out, hdd aftr 3 out, soon wknd*.
.........................(12 to 1) 3
37136 SOUTHERN MINSTREL 14-11-7 (7*) Miss C Metcalfe, *in tch, rdn alng 13th, beh frm 4 out*..............(4 to 1) 4
SHIP THE BUILDER 8-11-0 (7*) Mr T Whitaker, *prmnt, chsd ldr 4th till f 11th*..........................(20 to 1) f
ISHMA (Ire) 10-11-0 (7*) Mr D Page, *in rear, blun second, beh whn refused 9th*....................(8 to 1 op 12 to 1) ref
SHINING PENNY 10-11-0 (7*) Mr K Green, *beh and mstk 5th, blun 12th and pld up aftr*............(33 to 1 op 20 to 1) pu
Dist: ½l, 25l, 8l. 6m 56.50s. a 62.50s (7 Ran).
(Mike Roberts), M J Roberts

3970 Martin Orange 21st Birthday 'National Hunt' Novices' Hurdle Class E (4-y-o and up) £2,658 2¼m .... (4:30)

3709 JERVAULX (Ire) 6-11-6 R Dunwoody, *trkd ldrs gng wl, led 6th, rdn 2 out, styd on well appr last*.... (2 to 1 fav op 5 to 2) 1
2723 SILENT CRACKER 5-11-0 Derek Byrne, *hld up in tch, hdwy 4 out, chsd wnr 2 out, sn rdn and one pace last*.
.............................(12 to 1 tchd 14 to 1) 2
36723 GENERAL PARKER 6-11-0 A S Smith, *led to 6th, chsd wnr till den and wknd 2 out*................(11 to 2 op 4 to 1) 3
38234 POPPY'S DREAM 7-10-6 (3*) Mr R Thornton, *hedl up and beh, hdwy 3 out, kpt on frm nxt, nvr rch ldrs*.
.........................(3 to 1 op 7 to 2 tchd 5 to 2) 4
CHARIOT MAN (Ire) 5-11-0 Richard Guest, *hld up in midfield, hdwy 4 out, rdn alng aftr nxt and sn wknd*.
.........................(16 to 1 tchd 20 to 1) 5
2469 BLASTER WATSON 6-11-0 M Ranger, *jmpd slwly 1st, cl up till rdn and wknd 4 out, blun 2 out*...... (13 to 1 tchd 33 to 1) 6
3823 MOOR DANCE MAN 7-11-0 Gary Lyons, *midfield, effrt and rdn alng 4 out, no imprsn*......................(25 to 1) 7
3672 SUTTON BOY 8-11-0 N Bentley, *blun and uns rdr 1st*.
.........................(25 to 1) ur
DELUNE 5-11-0 M Foster, *mstks and sn beh, tld off whn refused 4th*......................(25 to 1 op 16 to 1) ref
DERRING WELL 7-10-9 I Lawrence, *al beh, tld off whn pld up bef last*...........................(25 to 1 op 20 to 1) pu
25678 LUDO'S ORCHESTRA (Ire) 6-11-0 P Niven, *al beh, tld off whn pld up bef 2 out*.........(20 to 1 op 16 to 1 tchd 25 to 1) pu
15036 CHIEF GALE (Ire) 5-10-11 (3*) Michael Brennan, *chsd ldrs till wknd aftr 4 out, beh whn pld up bef 2 out*.......... (8 to 1) pu
3805 THE STUFFED PUFFIN (Ire) 5-11-0 J Railton, *al beh, tld off whn pld up bef 2 out, broke blood vessel*.
.........................(10 to 1 op 8 to 1) pu
METHODIUS 5-11-0 R Supple, *in tch till rdn alng and wknd 4 out, beh whn pld up bef 2 out*. (20 to 1 tchd 25 to 1) pu
Dist: 2½l, 11l, 4l, 18l, 20l, 14l. 4m 51.40s. a 36.40s (14 Ran).
(Robert Ogden), G Richards

3971 Punch & Judy And Jazz Band Selling Hurdle Class G (4 - 7-y-o) £2,077 2m .... (5:00)

3782 FAIR AND FANCY (Fr) 6-11-0 A S Smith, *trkd ldrs, hdwy to ld 5th, rdn clr appr 2 out*..........(2 to 1 fav tchd 9 to 4) 1
3819 IRIE MON (Ire) 5-11-7 J Railton, *hld up and beh, hdwy 4 out, styd on betw last 2, no ch whn wnr*......(9 to 2 op 7 to 2) 2
1778 CRAIGARY 6-11-0 J Supple, *hld up and beh, hdwy to chase ldrs 4 out, rdn nxt and sn one pace*.....(9 to 2 op 5 to 1) 3
3844 HEVER GOLF DIAMOND 4-10-9 (7*) Mr P O'Keeffe, *al beh, tld off 4 out*......................(9 to 1 op 7 to 2) 4
LORDAN VELVET (Ire) 5-11-7 Richard Guest, *prmnt, led 4th to nxt, chsd wnr till rdn and wknd 2 out, fourth whn f last*.
.........................(5 to 1 tchd 9 to 2) f
2265 SULLAMELL 6-10-7 (7*) Mr O McPhail, *in tch to 4th, weakend quickly nxt and beh whn pld up aftr 3 out*.
.........................(25 to 1 op 33 to 1) pu
3823 CAN SHE CAN CAN 5-10-9 M Ranger, *chsd ldrs till lost pl 4th, sn beh and tld off whn pld up bef last*... (9 to 1 op 12 to 1) pu
Dist: 12l, 7l, dist. 4m 13.00s. a 27.00s (8 Ran).
(The F And F Partnership), Miss M K Milligan

3972 Bet With The Tote Handicap Hurdle Class E (0-115 4-y-o and up) £2,616 3m 110yds.................. (5:30)

36042 DOCKMASTER [87] 6-10-11 A S Smith, *prmnt, led 8th, clr aftr nxt, unchlgd*........................(7 to 2 op 3 to 1) 1
36589 SOLOMAN SPRINGS (USA) [76] 7-9-11 (3*) Mr R Thornton, *beh, hdwy 9th, rdn alng appr 3 out, styd on, no ch wth wnr*.
.........................(10 to 1 op 8 to 1) 2
37256 PHARARE (Ire) [92] 7-11-2 P Niven, *led to 8th, rdn alng nxt, sn drvn and wknd frm 9th*....................(4 to 1) 3
34073 LORD NITROGEN (USA) [80] 7-10-4 I Lawrence, *prmnt, chsd wnr frm 9th till rdn and wknd aftr 3 out*.(10 to 1 op 6 to 1) 4
34978 GI MOSS [76] (bl) 10-9-7 (7*) Mr O McPhail, *in tch, rdn alng 9th, sn lost pl and tld off bef 3 out*.... (20 to 1 op 12 to 1) 5
34618 TIM SOLDIER (Fr) [76] 10-10-0 R Supple, *al rear, beh whn pld up aftr 8th*.........................(7 to 2 op 9 to 2) pu
1739 ARRANGE A GAME [76] 10-10-0 T Eley, *in tch to 6th, beh whn pld up bef 9th*...........(33 to 1 op 25 to 1) pu
37612 GROSVENOR (Ire) [97] 6-11-7 R Dunwoody, *prmnt till lost pl 3rd, beh whn pld up aftr 6th*.
.........................(11 to 4 fav op 3 to 1 tchd 7 to 2) pu
Dist: 15l, dist, 1¾l, 20l. 6m 39.40s. a 57.40s (8 Ran).
(J D Gordon), Miss M K Milligan

TOWCESTER (good to firm)
Monday May 5th
Going Correction: PLUS 0.40 sec. per fur.

3973 Milton Keynes Jaipur Restaurant Novices' Selling Hurdle Class G (4-y-o and up) £1,950 2m....... (2:20)

35558 THE FLYING DOCTOR (Ire) 7-10-12 W McFarland, *steady hdwy appr 3 out, chlgd 2 out, sn led, drvn out*.
.........................(5 to 2 fav op 2 to 1) 1
38123 BAYERD (Ire) (bl) 6-11-5 J A McCarthy, *prmnt, chlgd 4th, led aftr 3 out, rdn and hdd sn after 2 out, one pace*.
.........................(7 to 2 op 3 to 1 tchd 9 to 2) 2
37362 OUR EDDIE (bl) 8-10-12 K Gaule, *hld up, hdwy 4th, chsd ldrs 3 out, one pace frm nxt*.................(3 to 1) 3
31635 CADDY'S FIRST (v) 5-10-12 T J Murphy, *chsd ldrs, rdn appr 2 out, sn wknd*.......(6 to 1 op 9 to 2 tchd 11 to 2) 4
MASTER SHOWMAN (bl) 6-10-12 T Jenks, *led till hdd aftr 3 out, sn wknd, tld off*.
.........................(16 to 1 op 25 to 1 tchd 33 to 1 and 50 to 1) 5
34625 STONE ISLAND 4-10-7 (7*) W Walsh, *sn beh, tld off*.
.........................(10 to 1 op 12 to 1) 6
3091 MEGA TID 5-10-9 (3*) P Henley, *prmnt to 4th, wknd quickly nxt, tld off*......................(33 to 1 op 20 to 1) 7
30665 COME ON IN 4-10-2 (5*) X Aizpuru, *in tch whn f 3rd*.
.........................(7 to 1 op 5 to 1 tchd 15 to 2) f
3828 A BADGE TOO FAR (Ire) (bl) 7-10-7 L O'Hara, *mstk 3rd, sn beh, tld off whn pld up bef last*..... (33 to 1 tchd 50 to 1) pu
Dist: 4l, ¾l, 15l, dist, 18l, ½l. 4m 0.80s. a 17.80s (9 Ran).
(The Rumble Racing Club), G B Balding

3974 Dove Naish Chartered Accountants Novices' Chase Class E (5-y-o and up) £3,013 2m 110yds....... (2:50)

25974 KHALIDI (Ire) 8-11-7 G Bradley, *led to 8th, led ag'n 3 out, hit 2 out, rdn last, drvn out*.
.........................(3 to 1 on tchd 5 to 2 on and 9 to 4 on) 1
37344 STAPLEFORD LADY 9-11-2 W McFarland, *rcd in 3rd till wnt second aftr 3 out, rdn to chal and not fluent last, sn btn*.
.........................(3 to 1 tchd 7 to 2) 2
38293 OLD REDWOOD 10-11-0 L O'Hara, *chsd wnr, hit 6th, chlgd 7th, led nxt, hdd 3 out, sn wknd, tld off*.
.........................(7 to 1 op 1 tchd 8 to 1) 3
Dist: 5l, dist. 4m 17.30s. a 20.30s (3 Ran).
(T J Whitley), D R Gandolfo

3975 Life Education Centre For Northampton Handicap Hurdle Class D (0-125 4-y-o and up) £2,819 2m 5f .... (3:20)

32723 EHTEFAAL (USA) [89] 6-11-7 T J Murphy, *made virtually all, came clr appr 2 out, eased r-in*.
.........................(15 to 8 fav op 6 to 4 tchd 9 to 4) 1
3852* ABLE PLAYER (USA) [92] 10-11-10 (6ex) M Sharratt, *lost tch 6th, styd on frm 3 out, took second appr last, hrd drvn and no ch wth wnr*...........(9 to 4 op 2 to 1 tchd 5 to 2) 2
3820 CAMBO (USA) [76] 11-10-1 (7*) R Studholme, *wth wnr to 3 out, outpcd frm 2 out*......(11 to 2 op 5 to 1 tchd 6 to 1) 3
3725 FED ON OATS [92] 9-11-10 J R Kavanagh, *trkd ldrs, chlgd 3 out, sn wknd, tld off whn f 2 out*.
.........................(5 to 2 op 3 to 1 tchd 7 to 2) f
Dist: 10l, dist. 5m 24.40s. a 25.40s (4 Ran).
(Mrs Marygold O'Kelly), J S King

3976 Tanswell Handicap Chase Class E (0-115 5-y-o and up) £3,000 2m

110yds...................... (3:50)

3740[2] CRACKLING FROST (Ire) [79] 9-10-3 (3*) P Henley, made
virtually all, hrd drvn aftr 2 out, all out.
.... (5 to 4 on op Evens tchd 11 to 10) 1
2356 MINE'S AN ACE (NZ) [95] 10-11-8 J R Kavanagh, wnt prmnt
4th, lft second 7th, stre chal frm 2 out till no extr nr finish.
.... (7 to 1 op 5 to 1) 2
3760[5] CHILL WIND [88] 8-11-1 G Bradley, wth wnr to 3rd, drpd rear
5th, hdwy and jmpd slwly 4 out, sn btn.
.... (7 to 2 op 3 to 1 tchd 4 to 1) 3
3740 YOUNG ALFIE [73] (bl) 12-10-0 T J Murphy, sn beh, rdn 6th,
tld off 4 out, fnshd lme................... (33 to 1 op 20 to 1) 4
3824[5] BALLY PARSON [97] 11-11-5 (5*) X Aizpuru, wth wnr to 3rd,
second whn blun and uns rdr 7th.
.... (4 to 1 op 3 to 1 tchd 9 to 2) ur
Dist: ½l, 25l, dist, 4m 13.50s. a 16.50s (5 Ran).
(The Unlucky For Some Partnership), Mrs D Haine

3977 Ironsides Solicitors Novices' Hunters' Chase Class H (5-y-o and up) £1,013 2¾m............. (4:20)

SEVERN INVADER 12-11-7 (7*) Miss H Gosling, plenty to do 4
out, steady hdwy frm nxt, styd on to ld aftr 2 out, readily.
.... (9 to 4 fav op 6 to 4 tchd 5 to 4 and 5 to 2) 1
3832[2] TEA CEE KAY 7-11-9 (5*) Mr A Sansome, led till aftr 4th, styd
wth ldr till led ag'n after 7th, rdn and hdd after 2 out, stayed on
same pace................... (4 to 1 op 5 to 1 tchd 7 to 2) 2
COPPER THISTLE (Ire) 9-12-0 (7*) Mr R Hunnisett, chsd ldrs
till drpd rear 7th, styd on frm 3 out, not rch ldrs.
.... (3 to 1 tchd 7 to 2) 3
3850[3] TAURA'S RASCAL 8-11-7 (7*) Mr F Brennan, chsd ldrs, hit 7th
and 11th, hit 3 out and sn wknd, no ch whn jmpd badly rght
last................... (100 to 30 op 7 to 2 tchd 4 to 1) 4
SHAREEF STAR (v) 9-11-7 (7*) Mr A Wood, jmpd badly till
tried to refuse and t 4th.
.... (50 to 1 op 25 to 1 tchd 100 to 1) f
BARICHSTE (bl) 9-11-7 (7*) Mr M Watson, tld off frm 5th, pld
up bef last................... (20 to 1 op 16 to 1 tchd 25 to 1) pu
ROAMING SHADOW 10-11-7 (7*) Mr J Barnes, led aftr 4th till
after 7th and wknd rpdly, tld off whn pld up bef 2 out.
.... (8 to 1 op 7 to 1 tchd 9 to 1) pu
Dist: 10l, 3l, 30l. 5m 52.20s. a 26.20s (7 Ran).
(Mrs Miles Gosling), Miss H Gosling

3978 Buttercup Conditional Jockeys' Mares' Only Novices' Handicap Hurdle Class F (0-100 4-y-o and up) £1,992 3m...................... (4:50)

3016[2] ARDENT LOVE (Ire) [73] 8-10-12 R Massey, led 5th to 6th, styd
prmnt, led 2 out, stayed on wl....... (6 to 4 fav op 7 to 4) 1
3828[5] MADAM'S WALK [85] 7-11-3 (7*) M Keighley, led second to
5th, led ag'n 7th, hdd 2 out, sn one pace and presssure.
.... (5 to 1 op 6 to 1) 2
3299[5] QUINAG [83] 6-11-1 (7*) W Walsh, beh, outpcd 4 out, rdn and
rallied appr 2 out, no imprsn on ldrs... (8 to 1 op 5 to 1) 3
2775 ANNIE RUTH (Ire) [65] 6-9-11 (7*) R Garrard, chsd ldrs, keen
hold, lost pos 4 out, styd on ag'n frm 2 out.
.... (25 to 1 op 16 to 1) 4
3473[4] CASTLE MEWS (Ire) [72] 6-10-11 S Ryan, in tch, chlgd 4 out
wknd aftr nxt................... (7 to 1 tchd 8 to 1 and 10 to 1) 5
3793[5] JAIME'S JOY [61] (v) 7-10-0 Martin Smith, prmnt, led 6th to
7th, lost pos 8th, sn reco'red, wknd aftr 3 out.
.... (50 to 1 op 33 to 1) 6
3845 FORTRIA ROSIE DAWN [68] 7-10-7 X Aizpuru, led to second,
pld hrd, wknd 8th, tld off whn pulled up bef 2 out.
.... (9 to 2 op 3 to 1 tchd 5 to 1) pu
3828[6] CARLINGFORD GALE (Ire) [77] 6-11-2 P Henley, al beh, lost
tch frm 8th, tld off whn pld up bef 3 out.
.... (5 to 1 op 1 op 10 to 1 tchd 12 to 1) pu
Dist: 7l, 14l, 8l, 21l, dist. 6m 13.10s. a 31.10s (8 Ran).
(Mrs Claire Smith), D Nicholson

WINCANTON (firm)
Tuesday May 6th
Going Correction: MINUS 0.45 sec. per fur. (races
1,3,4,5,6), MINUS 0.50 (2)

3979 Whitsbury 'National Hunt' Novices' Hurdle Class E (4-y-o and up) £1,952 2m........................ (5:45)

3743* MRS EM 5-11-7 (7*) L Cummins, al gng wl, led till aftr second,
chlgd 3 out, sn led ag'n, clr after 2 out, easily.
.... (10 to 3 on op 11 to 4 on tchd 4 to 1 on) 1
3812[2] RED TEL (Ire) 5-10-13 A P McCoy, rcd in 3rd, hdwy aftr 3 out,
chsd wnr and hit nxt, rdn and no imprsn r-in.
.... (3 to 1 op 9 to 4 tchd 100 to 30 and 7 to 2) 2
2893 ADMIRAL BRUNY (Ire) 6-10-13 C Llewellyn, pld hrd, led aftr
second, hdd aftr 3 out, wknd nxt.
.... (20 to 1 op 12 to 1 tchd 25 to 1) 3
Dist: 1¾l, 8l. 3m 34.40s. a 0.40s (3 Ran).
SR: 18/7/-/ (G Z Mizel), P F Nicholls

3980 Fonthill Novices' Handicap Chase Class E (0-100 5-y-o and up) £2,895 2m 5f........................(6:15)

3361[3] LITTLE ROWLEY [60] 8-10-4 M Richards, trkd ldr, chlgd 6th,
led nxt, hdd 9th, outpcd 11th, hit next, rallied 3 out, led next,
drvn out, fnshd lme................... (7 to 1 tchd 11 to 1) 1
787 MINERS REST [76] 9-10-13 (7*) Mr R Widger, led, jmpd slwly
second, hdd 7th, styd wth wnr till led 9th, clr 11th, jumped
slowly 4 out, mstk nxt, headed 2 out,on (2 to 1 tchd 9 to 4) 2
3726[5] FRONTIER FLIGHT (USA) [80] 7-11-7 (3*) E Husband, al
toiling in 3rd, blun second, jmpd slwly 4th and 5th, brief effrt
8th, no ch whn hit 3 out, tld off.
.... (6 to 1 op 5 to 4 on tchd 11 to 8 on) 3
Dist: ¾l, dist. 5m 23.30s. a 19.30s (3 Ran).
(J A Judd), Mrs L Richards

3981 Haynes Publishing 'National Hunt' Novices' Hurdle Class E (4-y-o and up) £2,442 2¾m............. (6:45)

3518[4] MR STRONG GALE (Ire) (bl) 6-11-7 R Johnson, led, clr second, steadied 6th, hit 7th and 8th, came clear appr 2 out, hit
last, easily... (10 to 3 on op 5 to 1 on tchd 3 to 1 on) 1
3735[4] WILLOWS ROULETTE 5-11-0 R Greene, chsd wnr, chlgd 6th,
rdn aftr 3 out, styd on but no ch wth winner.
.... (7 to 2 op 3 to 1 tchd 4 to 1) 2
3684[3] CARNIVAL CLOWN 5-10-9 (5*) G Supple, keen hold, rcd in
3rd, effrt to chase ldrs aftr 3 out, wknd appoaching 2 out.
.... (10 to 1 op 6 to 1) 3
Dist: 2l, 16l. 5m 11.10s. a 5.10s (3 Ran).
(T G A Chappell), P F Nicholls

3982 R. K. Harrison Insurance Brokers Novices' Hunters' Chase Class H (6-y-o and up) £1,713 2m 5f......(7:15)

3853[3] CLOBRACKEN LAD 9-11-7 (7*) Mr G Baines, made all, staying on wl whn hit 3 out, ran on r-in..........(15 to 8 jt-
fav op 6 to 4) 1
LINK COPPER 8-11-7 (7*) Miss L Blackford, al chasing wnr,
chlgd 9th and 4 out, rallied ag'n last, one pace.
.... (11 to 4 op 4 to 1) 2
CHISM (Ire) 6-11-7 (7*) Mr M G Miller, wnt 3rd aftr 8th, hdwy to
chase ldrs 11th, one pace frm 3 out.............(15 to 8 jt-
fav op 6 to 4) 3
BARROW STREET 7-11-7 (7*) Mr J Tizzard, rcd in 3rd till drpd
back to 4th at 8th, rdn 11th, wknd 13th....(9 to 1 op 6 to 1) 4
Dist: 2l, 15l, 27l. 5m 15.20s. a 11.20s (4 Ran).
(T J Swaffield), Mrs J Swaffield

3983 Chedington Handicap Chase Class D (0-120 5-y-o and up) £3,522 3m 1f 110yds........................ (7:45)

3651[3] DOUALAGO (Fr) [119] (bl) 7-12-0 A P McCoy, led 5th, hit
7th, styd pressing ldr till led 9th, rdn alng frm 4 out, stayed on
wl frm 3 out................... (5 to 1 op 4 to 1) 1
3678[5] JAMES PIGG [118] 10-11-13 R Johnson, trkd ldrs in 3rd, chsd
wnr frm 3 out, styd on r-in but no imprsn on winner.
.... (13 to 2 op 6 to 1 tchd 7 to 1) 2
3744[2] FROZEN DROP [100] 10-10-9 S Fox, al beh, lost tch frm 9th,
tld off................... (13 to 2 op 6 to 1) 3
3739 WOODLANDS GENHIRE [91] (bl) 12-10-0 C Llewellyn, al wl
beh, tld off frm 8th................... (50 to 1 op 25 to 1) 4
3813[4] FOXGROVE [91] 11-9-9 (5*) X Aizpuru, al beh, tld off frm 8th,
pld up bef 13th.......(16 to 1 op 12 to 1 tchd 20 to 1) pu
3813* SPINNING STEEL [96] 10-10-5 S Burrough, took keen hold,
wknd 9th, tld off whn pld up bef 11th.
.... (7 to 2 tchd 9 to 2 and 5 to 1) pu
3790[2] DRUMCULLEN (Ire) [100] 8-10-9 N Williamson, trkd wnr till
led 5th, hdd 9th, chlgd frm nxt, hit 16th hit 4 out, wknd next, 3rd
and no ch whn pld up 2 ou
.... (13 to 8 fav op 7 to 4 tchd 6 to 4) pu
Dist: 1¾l, dist, dist. 6m 10.00s. b 6.00s (7 Ran).
SR: 26/23/-/-/ (Martin Pipe Racing Club), M C Pipe

3984 Rockbourne Handicap Hurdle Class E (0-115 4-y-o and up) £2,095 2¾m........................ (8:15)

3771[5] GALATASORI JANE (Ire) [99] 7-11-3 (7*) L Cummins, not
fluent, chsd wnr, rdn 3 out, chlgd und pres and hit nxt, drvn to
ld r-in, all out. (11 to 8 on op 7 to 4 on tchd 5 to 4 on) 1
3683[3] SEVSO [87] 8-10-9 (3*) P Henley, led, hrd drvn frm 2 out, hdd
r-in, styd on................... (5 to 4 op 6 to 4) 2
1574[7] CHINA MAIL (Ire) [76] 5-10-1 T J Murphy, rcd in 3rd till lost
pos aftr 5th, effrt und pres 3 out, wknd appr nxt.
.... (11 to 1 op 5 to 1 tchd 25 to 1) 3
3686[7] STATION EXPRESS (Ire) [75] 9-9-7 (7*) M Griffiths, wnt 3rd aftr
5th, pressed ldr nxt, rdn 3 out, sn wknd.
.... (50 to 1 op 20 to 1 tchd 66 to 1) 4
Dist: Nk, 16l, 9l. 5m 6.40s. a 0.40s (4 Ran).
(B L Blinman), P F Nicholls

CHEPSTOW (good)
Wednesday May 7th
Going Correction: PLUS 0.05 sec. per fur. (races 1,2,4,6), PLUS 0.20 (3,5)

3985 Balmoral Juvenile Maiden Hurdle Class E (4-y-o) £2,248 2m 110yds
.... (2:25)

SONG OF THE SWORD 11-0 M A Fitzgerald, made all, set steady pace till quickened frm 4 out, blun last, pushed out, not extended.........(11 to 10 on op 6 to 4 on tchd Evens) 1

35413 TIMIDJAR (Ire) (bl) 11-0 R Dunwoody, hld up beh ldrs, hdwy to chase wnr frm 4 out, ev ch 2 out, no imprsn.
....................(11 to 2 op 4 to 1) 2

35554 SPRING CAMPAIGN (Ire) 11-0 A P McCoy, hld up beh, effrt aftr 4 out, styd on, lft 3rd 2 out, not pace to chal.
.....................(4 to 1 op 5 to 2) 3

36814 SPENCER STALLONE 11-0 W Marston, cl up, pushed along aftr 4th, wknd appr nxt, tld off.....(66 to 1 op 33 to 1) 4

35007 SASSY STREET (Ire) 11-0 D Gallagher, not fluent 1st, jmpd slwly nxt, hld up, pushed alng appr 4 out, sn btn, tld off.
.............(14 to 1 op 8 to 1 tchd 16 to 1) 5

SANTELLA CAPE 11-0 J Railton, cl up, outpcd aftr 4 out, btn 3rd whn f 2 out....................(25 to 1 op 16 to 1) f

ROMANTIC WARRIOR 10-11 (3") R Massey, hld up beh, outpcd 4 out, no ch whn hmpd and uns rdr 2 out.
....................(50 to 1 op 25 to 1) ur

36874 DUBAI DOLLY (Ire) 10-9 S Curran, hld up, hdwy appr 4 out, sn btn whn brght dwn 2 out........(7 to 1 op 20 to 1) bd

Dist: 3l, 24l, dist, 1½l. 3m 59.70s. a 12.70s (8 Ran).

(Lady Lloyd Webber), J A B Old

3986 Buckingham Novices' Handicap Hurdle Class E (0-100 5-y-o and up) £2,262 2m 110yds .... (2:55)

24323 ULTIMATE SMOOTHIE [95] 5-12-0 A P McCoy, hld up, smooth hdwy appr 4 out, led on bit approaching last, easily.
.............(11 to 2 op 3 to 1 tchd 6 to 1) 1

37315 ALPHA LEATHER [67] 6-9-7 (7") Mr O McPhail, chsd ldrs, hit 4 out and sn shaken up, kpt 2 out, no imprsn.
..........(7 to 1 op 6 to 1 tchd 8 to 1) 2

32873 MR POPPLETON [72] 8-10-5 L Harvey, led aftr 4th, rdn alng 3 out, hdd appr last, one pace.
....................(10 to 1 op 6 to 1 tchd 11 to 1) 3

3864* GEISWAY (Can) [84] 7-10-12 (5") X Aizpuru, hld up, pushed alng cl appr 4 out, drvn along and btn 2 out.
.................(Evens fav op 6 to 4) 4

34032 BLADE OF FORTUNE [86] 9-10-12 (7") Mr J Tizzard, led till aftr 4th, wknd 3 out............(7 to 1 op 9 to 2) 5

37962 DAYDREAM BELIEVER [68] 5-10-11 P Holley, hld up beh, effrt 4 out, no imprsn......(16 to 1 op 12 to 1 tchd 20 to 1) 6

582 MUTLEY [67] 7-10-0 R Greene, pld hrd, hld up, al beh.
....................(50 to 1 op 25 to 1 tchd 66 to 1) 7

35132 ROYAL RULER (Ire) [90] 6-11-9 R Dunwoody, chsd ldrs till wknd quickly appr 4 out, tld off.
....................(15 to 2 op 6 to 1 tchd 8 to 1) 8

Dist: 3l, 1¾l, 15l, 3½l, 9l, 2l, 21l. 3m 55.30s. a 8.30s (8 Ran).

SR: 26/-/-/10/-/ (Isca Bloodstock), M C Pipe

3987 Highgrove Handicap Chase Class C (0-130 5-y-o and up) £4,601 3m
.... (3:25)

34232 FUNCHEON GALE [98] 10-10-7 D Morris, hld up, cld appr 5 out, led aftr nxt, clr 2 out, easily.......(7 to 2 op 5 to 1) 1

38972 BANNTOWN BILL (Ire) [97] (v) 8-10-6 A P McCoy, led to 3rd, trkd ldr, rdn alng frm 13th, led nxt (5 out), hdd aftr 4 out, btn 2 out.................(7 to 2 op 5 to 2 tchd 4 to 1) 2

3613* BLACK CHURCH [110] 11-11-5 D O'Sullivan, hld up beh, mstk 13th, hrd drvn appr 4 out, btn quickly.
....................(7 to 4 fav op 11 to 10) 3

3605 DON'T LIGHT UP [115] (bl) 11-11-7 (3") Mr R Thornton, chsd ldrs to 7th, drpd rear 9th...........(10 to 1 tchd 12 to 1) 4

36884 PIMBERLEY PLACE (Ire) [110] 9-11-5 C Llewellyn, reminders to race, pld hrd, hdwy to ld 3rd, hdd 5 out, drpd out quickly.
....................(6 to 1 tchd 5 to 1) 5

38897 NICKLE JOE [95] 9-11-9-11 (7") Mr O McPhail, hit 3rd and uns rdr....................(16 to 1 tchd 20 to 1 and 14 to 1) ur

Dist: 10l, 20l, 5l, 2½l. 6m 1.00s. a 11.00s (6 Ran).

SR: 17/6/-/ (Kings Of The Road Partnership), R Curtis

3988 Sandringham Selling Handicap Hurdle Class G (0-95 4-y-o and up) £2,080 2½m 110yds........... (3:55)

38334 HELLO ME MAN (Ire) [78] 9-11-0 Mr J L Llewellyn, hld up, hdwy aftr 7th, led nxt (4 out), drvn alng and kpt on wl.
....................(9 to 2 tchd 5 to 1) 1

34052 STAR PERFORMER (Ire) [92] 6-11-7 (7") Mr G Shenkin, hld up beh ldg grp, cld 5th, chlgd wnr frm 3 out, ev ch whn hit last, no extr....................(10 to 1 op 7 to 1) 2

29772 KHAZARI (USA) [68] 9-10-4 L Harvey, hld up beh, hdwy 6th, rdn alng frm 4 out, kpt on.
....................(10 to 1 op 8 to 1 tchd 11 to 1) 3

3310 LOOK IN THE MIRROR [71] 6-10-7 C Llewellyn, al hndy, hrd rdn aftr 3 out, kpt on same pace.....(12 to 1 tchd 14 to 1) 4

34022 POWDER MONKEY [78] 7-11-0 G Tormey, hld up beh ldrs, took keen hold, cld 4th, shaken up four out, outpcd frm nxt, btn whn hit last....................(10 to 1 tchd 12 to 1) 5

3810* FLEET CADET [91] (v) 6-11-13 A P McCoy, hld up beh, hdwy 7th, hmpd by faller appr 4 out, not reco'r.
....................(5 to 2 fav tchd 11 to 4) 6

3859* KILLING TIME [80] 6-11-2 (7ex) D J Burchell, prmnt till wknd 7th....................(5 to 1 op 9 to 2 tchd 11 to 2) 7

30997 ROC AGE [67] 6-10-11 (3") Michael Brennan, led till wknd 4 out, sn hrd rdn and btn....................(25 to 1 tchd 33 to 1) 8

15676 PROVENCE [64] 10-9-7 (7") Mr J Goldstein, nvr far away, cld 5th, pushed alng aftr 7th, wknd 4 out..(14 to 1 op 16 to 1) 9

34957 CATWALKER (Ire) [64] 6-9-11 (3") Sophie Mitchell, al beh.
....................(50 to 1 op 33 to 1) 10

35543 STRIKE-A-POSE [68] 7-10-1 (3") Guy Lewis, chsd ldrs till wknd 7th, tld off....................(10 to 1 tchd 12 to 1) 11

35548 WESTCOAST [64] 6-9-7 (7") Mr O McPhail, pld hrd early, in tch till wknd aftr 7th, tld off.....(33 to 1 op 25 to 1) 12

33614 PRIZE MATCH [71] 8-10-7 S McNeill, mid-div till drpd beh 7th, tld off....................(14 to 1) 13

83 ASTROLABE [64] 5-10-0 B Fenton, chsd ldrs till rdn and wknd 6th, tld off.....(16 to 1 op 14 to 1 tchd 20 to 1) 14

3740 NAUTICAL GEORGE (Ire) [88] 7-11-5 (5") G Supple, al beh, tld off....................(20 to 1 op 16 to 1) 15

3668 MADAM ROSE (Ire) [64] (bl) 7-10-0 S Curran, chsd ldrs, mstk and drvn 5th, sn wknd, tld off......(33 to 1 op 20 to 1) 16

3617 SAAFI (Ire) [67] (bl) 6-10-3 V Slattery, mid-div, chasing ldrs whn slpd up appr 4 out............(25 to 1 op 16 to 1) su

Dist: ½l, 12l, ½l, 1l, 12l, sht-hd, 1¾l, nk, 6l, 15l. 4m 50.90s. a 12.90s (17 Ran).

(Lodge Cross Partnership), B J Llewellyn

3989 Jorrocks Novices' Hunters' Chase Class H (5-y-o and up) £1,067 3m
.... (4:30)

3832* PHAR TOO TOUCHY 10-11-7 (7") Mr N Harris, made all, shaken up r-in, ran on wl.
....................(11 to 8 on tchd 6 to 4 on and 5 to 4 on) 1

2918 SAVOY 10-11-7 (7") Captain A Ogden, hld up, hdwy to chase wnr frm 9th, reminders appr 2 out, no imprsn.
....................(6 to 4 op 6 to 5 tchd 13 to 8 and 7 to 4) 2

ARCHER (Ire) 10-11-7 (7") Mr M Harris, chsd wnr to 9th, wknd 11th, tld off....................(12 to 1 op 6 to 1 tchd 14 to 1) 3

3832 SULTAN'S SON 11-11-7 (7") Mr G Lewis, in cl tch till outpcd aftr 8th, tld off.
....................(16 to 1 op 10 to 1 tchd 20 to 1 and 25 to 1) 4

Dist: 4l, 19l, 17l. 6m 8.70s. a 18.70s (4 Ran).

(Miss R A Francis), Victor Dartnall

3990 South West Amateur Riders' Handicap Hurdle Class E (0-115 5-y-o and up) £2,360 3m................ (5:00)

18242 BALLINDOO [83] 8-11-0 (7") Mr R Armson, hld up beh, hdwy 4 out, led last, rdn out, ran on wl.......(11 to 2 op 4 to 1) 1

38416 APACHEE FLOWER [80] 7-10-11 (7") Mr R Widger, led briefly 1st, cl up, led ag'n 7th, hit 2 out, hdd last, kpt on, no extr nr finish....................(9 to 2 op 7 to 2 tchd 5 to 1) 2

3761 STAC-POLLAIDH [78] 7-10-9 (7") Mr R Wakley, hld up beh, hdwy 4 out, sn shaken up, outpcd appr last, kpt on wl r-in.
....................(11 to 2 op 9 to 2) 3

37983 ZINGIBAR [83] 5-11-0 (7") Mr O McPhail, trkd ldrs, hrd rdn aftr 4 out, one pace.............(11 to 2 op 4 to 1 tchd 6 to 1) 4

37613 COUNTRY STORE [96] 8-11-13 (7") Mr E James, led 3rd to 7th, drvn alng appr 4 out, sn outpcd.
....................(100 to 30 fav op 2 to 1) 5

3632 ICANTELYA (Ire) [81] 8-10-12 (7") Mr G Weatherley, hld up, took keen hold, outpcd appr 4 out....(33 to 1 op 20 to 1) 6

3725 BETTER BYTHE GLASS (Ire) [89] 8-11-10 (3") Mr M Rimell, chsd ldrs, pushed alng frm 7th, wknd appr 4 out.
....................(11 to 2 op 5 to 1 tchd 6 to 1) 7

3692 COLWALL [81] 6-10-12 (7") Mr J Goldstein, keen hold, sn led, hdd 3rd, cl up till rdn and wknd 4 out.
....................(8 to 1 tchd 9 to 1 and 10 to 1) 8

Dist: ¾l, 1l, 12l, 1¾l, 11l, 2l, 3l. 6m 0.50s. a 25.50s (8 Ran).

(R J Armson), R J Armson

UTTOXETER (good to soft)
Wednesday May 7th
Going Correction: PLUS 0.50 sec. per fur.

3991 Mobilefone Group Novices' Hunters' Chase Class H (5-y-o and up) £1,446 3¼m...................... (5:50)

FRONT COVER 7-11-2 (7") Miss S Vickery, trkd ldrs, shaken up aftr 16th, led nxt, sn clr, easily.(5 to 2 jt-fav tchd 9 to 4) 1

ROYAL SEGOS 10-11-7 (7") Mr C Stockton, led to 4 out, rdn and one pace frm nxt...(14 to 1 op 10 to 1 tchd 16 to 1) 2

557

GILLIE'S FOUNTAIN 6-11-7 (7*) Mr A Dalton, *settled rear, in tch till rdn and wknd 4 out, lft poor 3rd 2 out.*
.................................(16 to 1 op 12 to 1) 3
DOMINO NIGHT (Ire) 7-11-7 (7*) Mr G Hanmer, *keen hold, chsd ldr to appr 4 out, 3rd and wkng whn f 2 out. Dead.*
..................(10 to 1 op 12 to 1 tchd 14 to 1 and 16 to 1) f
3671 RYDERS WELLS 10-11-7 (7*) Mr S Walker, *jinked and uns rdr second.*.........................(12 to 1 op 7 to 1) ur
FISCAL POLICY 9-11-7 (7*) Mr R Trotter, *blun and uns rdr 1st.*
.................................(12 to 1 op 7 to 1) ur
3640⁴ BALASANI (Fr) 11-11-9 (5*) Mr A Sansome, *mstk 6th, last whn brght dwn 8th.*....................(5 to 1 tchd 11 to 2) bd
JUST MARMALADE 8-11-7 (7*) Mr R Burton, *chsd ldg pair till cannoned into by loose horse and brght dwn 8th.*
.................................(16 to 1 op 10 to 1 tchd 20 to 1) bd
3853⁶ VERY DARING 7-11-7 (7*) Miss S Sharratt, *in tch till brght dwn 8th.*........................(5 to 1 op 20 to 1) bd
ITA'S FELLOW (Ire) 9-11-7 (7*) Mrs C Ford, *keen hold, cl up, mstk 7th, brght dwn 8th.*..........(5 to 2 jt-fav op 2 to 1) bd
Dist: 13l, dist. 7m 1.50s. a 49.50s (10 Ran).

(Stewart Pike), S Pike

3992 Houghton Vaughan Selling Handicap Hurdle Class G (0-95 4-y-o and up) £1,878 2m....................(6:20)

3617⁴ BLOTOFT [73] 5-11-3 M A Fitzgerald, *hld up, prog to chase ldr 6th, led on bit aftr 3 out, sn clr, pushed out r-in.*
.................................(11 to 4 op 2 to 1) 1
MECADO [78] (v) 10-11-3 (5*) A Aizpuru, *mid-div, rdn and effrt 6th, styd on to chase wnr 2 out, no imprsn.*
.................................(12 to 1 op 8 to 1) 2
3803 PLAYFUL JULIET (Can) [76] (bl) 9-11-6 S Wynne, *led second to 4th, chsd ldr to 6th, kpt on und pres frm 2 out.*
.................................(4 to 1 op 3 to 1 tchd 9 to 2) 3
1472⁶ BRESIL (USA) [56] 8-9-7 (7*) Mark Brown, *hld up, rdn and prog 6th, one pace frm 3 out.*........(12 to 1 op 10 to 1) 4
3276⁶ KINGS VISION [60] 5-10-4 T Jenks, *chsd ldrs till rdn and struggling frm 6th.*.....................(14 to 1 op 12 to 1) 5
3617⁵ WORDSMITH (Ire) [70] 7-11-0 J Supple, *rear and rdn aftr 4th, no prog and pres frm 6th.*.........(9 to 4 fav op 3 to 1) 6
3722 ORINOCO VENTURE (Ire) [62] (bl) 6-10-6 Gary Lyons, *led to second and rem 4th, sn clr, wknd and hdd aftr 3 out.*
.................................(12 to 1 op 10 to 1) 7
2849⁸ ONLY A SIOUX [59] 5-10-3³ W Fry, *in tch till wknd aftr 6th.*
.................................(25 to 1 op 20 to 1) 8
3653⁷ DAYS OF THUNDER [74] 9-11-1 (3*) E Husband, *mstk 3rd, in tch in rear, wknd 6th.*...............(9 to 1 op 7 to 1) 9
Dist: 7l, hd, 13l, 3l, 1¾l, 3l, 10l, hd. 3m 58.10s. a 21.10s (9 Ran).

(R N Forman), S Gollings

3993 Bradshaw Bros. Open Hunters' Chase Class H for the Uttoxeter Premier Trophy (5-y-o and up) £1,840 4 ¼m........................(6:50)

3855² THE MALAKARMA (bl) 11-12-0 (5*) Mr B Pollock, *al prmnt and gng wl, led 19th, clr 3 out, rdn out run-in.*
.................................(11 to 2 op 4 to 1) 1
3856³ RYMING CUPLET 12-11-12 (7*) Mr L Jefford, *reminder 4th, prog tenth, chsd ldr 12th to 19th, chased wnr aftr nxt, styd on und pres.*.....................(12 to 1 op 10 to 1 tchd 14 to 1) 2
3855* RUSTY BRIDGE 10-12-2 (3*) Mr R Thornton, *led to 7th, lost pl 11th, rdn and lost tch 18th, kpt on und pres frm 4 out.*
.................................(9 to 2 op 7 to 2 tchd 5 to 1) 3
3713² ROYAL JESTER 13-12-2 (5*) Mr C Storey, *rear, struggling frm 16th, tld off from 5 out.*............(13 to 2 op 4 to 1) 4
3153 HOLLAND HOUSE 11-12-4 (3*) Mr C Bonner, *mstks, led 7th to 19th, wkng whn blun 3 out, 4th and wl btn whn f last.*
.......(11 to 10 fav op 5 to 4 tchd 11 to 8 and Evens) f
PEAJADE 13-11-7 (7*) Miss J Wormall, *mstks 7th and 8th, struggling aftr, tld off and pld up bef 19th.*
.................................(20 to 1 op 16 to 1) pu
3109² GRANVILLE GUEST 11-11-7 (7*) Mr J Tizzard, *trkd ldrs gng wl till rdn and no response 18th, tld off and pld up bef 4 out.*
.................................(11 to 1 op 8 to 1 tchd 12 to 1) pu
Dist: 7l, 17l, dist. 9m 1.50s. a 31.50s (7 Ran).

(Charles Dixey), Miss C Saunders

3994 Coutts & Co. Handicap Hurdle Class D (0-125 4-y-o and up) £2,717 2m....................(7:20)

3537⁴ FOURTH IN LINE (Ire) [110] 8-11-2 W Marston, *led 4th, quickened 6th, rdn 3 out, styd on wl.*....(7 to 2 op 3 to 1) 1
3077² WISE KING [106] 7-11-4 C Llewellyn, *led to 4th, chsd wnr aftr, pushed alng aftr 6th, rdn and no imprsn aftr 3 out.*
.................................(2 to 1 fav op 5 to 2 tchd 11 to 4) 2
3791² DARAKSHAN (Ire) [110] 5-11-8 J Culloty, *settled rear, pushed alng aftr 6th, rdn and effrt 3 out, no imprsn frm nxt.*
.................................(5 to 2 op 6 to 4 tchd 11 to 4) 3
3831 SAINT CIEL (USA) [102] 9-11-0 A P McCoy, *rcd wide, in tch, hrd rdn 3 out, wknd nxt.*...............(4 to 1 op 6 to 1) 4
3734² HANDY LASS [102] 8-11-0 M A Fitzgerald, *in tch till rdn and wknd appr 3 out, tld off.*...(5 to 1 op 4 to 1 tchd 11 to 2) 5
Dist: 4l, 6l, 12l, 7l. 29l. 3m 51.90s. a 14.90s (5 Ran).
SR: 31/17/15/-/-/ (John Nicholls (Banbury) Ltd), M J Wilkinson

3995 Lucia Farmer Handicap Chase Class D (0-125 5-y-o and up) £3,517 2½m....................(7:50)

3691* FORMAL INVITATION (Ire) [110] 8-11-7 (3*) Mr R Thornton, *trkd ldr, led aftr 4 out, shaken up after 2 out, drvn out run -in.*
.................................(7 to 4 jt-fav op 11 to 8 tchd 2 to 1) 1
3701⁹ ANDERMATT [108] 10-11-5 (3*) E Husband, *wtd wth, prog 11th, jnd wnr 3 out, rdn and unbl to quicken frm nxt.*
.................................(14 to 1 op 12 to 1 tchd 16 to 1) 2
3565⁸ SAILOR JIM [100] 10-11-0 A P McCoy, *led to aftr 4 out, wknd rpdly.*........................(7 to 4 jt-fav op 9 to 4) 3
3826 PLUNDER BAY (USA) [110] 6-11-10 M A Fitzgerald, *trkd ldg pair till wknd rpdly 4 out, fnshd tired.*
.................................(100 to 30 op 3 to 1 tchd 7 to 2) 4
3701⁸ WUDIMP [105] 8-11-5 Mr C Storey, *mstk 1st, nvr gng wl, mistake 7th, struggling frm nxt.*
.................................(7 to 1 tchd 8 to 1 and 6 to 1) 5
Dist: 3l, 25l, 15l, 2l. 5m 6.10s. a 22.10s (5 Ran).

(The Plough Partnership), D Nicholson

3996 A W Stokes Drums Novices' Hurdle Class E (4-y-o and up) £2,410 3m 110yds...........................(8:20)

3833² MR CHRISTIE 5-11-7 A Thornton, *wtd wth, rdn in mid-div aftr 9th, gd hdwy frm 3 out, led last, ran on strly.*
.................................(5 to 1 op 7 to 2 tchd 11 to 2) 1
3503² BEECHFIELD FLYER 6-11-0 G Tormey, *trkd ldr, rdn to ld 3 out, hdd and mstk last, unbl to quicken.*
.................................(4 to 1 op 7 to 2 tchd 9 to 2) 2
3778⁵ LOTTERY TICKET (Ire) 8-11-0 M A Fitzgerald, *al in tch, rdn 3 out, unbl to quicken appr last, styd on.*
.................................(4 to 1 op 6 to 1 tchd 7 to 1) 3
3503⁹ CYPRESS AVENUE (Ire) 5-10-11 (3*) Mr R Thornton, *rear, prog 8th, rdn and effrt appr 3 out, styd on one pace frm nxt.*
.................................(16 to 1 op 12 to 1 tchd 20 to 1) 4
2889² BANNY HILL LAD 7-11-0 J R Kavanagh, *trkd ldrs, led 9th, hrd rdn and hdd 3 out, wknd last.*
.................................(15 to 8 fav op 9 to 4 tchd 5 to 2 and 7 to 4) 5
3422⁴ KING'S RAINBOW (Ire) 8-10-9 J F Titley, *chsd ldrs, rdn and ev ch 3 out, not much room last, no extr r-in.*
.................................(16 to 1 op 10 to 1) 6
3729⁶ SIDNEY 8-11-0 S Wynne, *mid-div, hrd rdn and no prog aftr 8th, sn wknd, tld off.*................(66 to 1 op 33 to 1) 7
3435 PUSH ON POLLY (Ire) 7-10-9 J Supple, *sn rdn in mid-div, beh frm 9th, tld off.*..................(66 to 1 op 33 to 1) 8
2398 UPHAM SURPRISE 9-11-0 G Upton, *led to second, led 8th to 9th, sn wknd, tld off.*.....(8 to 1 op 7 to 1 tchd in mid-div, beh) 9
STEEL CHIMES (Ire) 8-11-0 Gary Lyons, *al beh, tld off and pld up bef 3 out.*...................(66 to 1 op 33 to 1) pu
3914 BOTTLE BLACK 10-11-0 P McLoughlin, *in tch till rdn and wknd 8th, tld off and pld up bef 2 out.*
.................................(66 to 1 op 50 to 1 tchd 100 to 1) pu
THREE JAYS 10-11-0 K Gaule, *al rear, tld off and pld up bef 8th.*..........................(33 to 1 op 25 to 1) pu
3881 SCALE DOWN (Ire) 8-11-0 W Marston, *led second till mstk and hdd 8th, wknd rpdly, pld up bef nxt.*.........(50 to 1) pu
MOOR HALL PRINCE 7-11-0 B Fenton, *prmnt to 4th, wknd rpdly, tld off and pld up bef 9th.*..............(50 to 1) pu
TRENTSIDE MAJOR 5-11-0 M Ranger, *al rear, hrd rdn 4th, tld off and pld up aftr 8th.*.................(33 to 1) pu
Dist: 6l, 1l, 1l, ½l, 1½l, dist, ½l, dist. 5m 2.80s. a 25.80s (15 Ran).

(David Mann Partnership), Miss L C Siddall

WETHERBY (good to soft)
Wednesday May 7th
Going Correction: PLUS 0.75 sec. per fur. (races 1,3,6), PLUS 0.55 (2,4,5)

3997 Washdale Conditional Jockeys' Juvenile Novices' Hurdle Class E (4-y-o) £2,232 2m....................(6:05)

3303⁵ OVERSMAN 10-12 F Leahy, *chsd ldrs, chalg whn lft in frnt 3 out, left clr nxt, drvn out.*
.................................(2 to 1 jt-fav op 9 to 4 tchd 5 to 2) 1
3802⁶ POLITICAL MANDATE 10-2 (5*) C McCormack, *cl up, chlgd 4 out, outpcd nxt, lft moderate second 2 out.*
.................................(20 to 1 op 16 to 1) 2
MR BRUNO 10-12 S Taylor, *hmpd 3rd, sn tld off.*
.................................(50 to 1 op 25 to 1) 3
3476 DOUBLE VINTAGE (Ire) 10-12 G Lee, *sn beh, tld off frm 4th.*
.................................(50 to 1 op 33 to 1) 4
3700⁷ REGAL EAGLE 10-12 L Aspell, *trkd ldrs, 4th whn f 3rd.*
.................................(9 to 4 op 6 to 4) f
IRISH OASIS (Ire) 10-12 B Grattan, *pld hrd, wth ldr, slightly hmpd 3 out, sn outpcd, 7 ls second whn f nxt.*
.................................(20 to 1 op 14 to 1) f
3820² AMAZING SAIL (Ire) 11-5 E Callaghan, *led, jnd aftr 4 out, slight ld whn f nxt.*.............(2 to 1 jt-fav op 9 to 4) f
Dist: 15l, dist, 1½l. 4m 1.70s. a 20.70s (7 Ran).

(Marquesa de Moratalla), J G FitzGerald

3998 Church Fenton Handicap Chase Class C (0-135 5-y-o and up) £4,532 2m.......................... (6:35)

3779³ POLITICAL TOWER [125] 10-11-4 B Storey, *in tch, pushed alng 5 out, reminders appr 2 out, ran on to ld last, kpt on gmely*......(4 to 1 op 5 to 1 tchd 11 to 2 and 7 to 2) 1
3842³ MISTER ODDY [127] 11-11-6 T J Murphy, *led, strly pressed 3 out, hdd last, kpt on same pace*....(2 to 1 fav tchd 9 to 4) 2
3711³ LEOTARD [135] 10-12-0 N Williamson, *pressed ldr, chlgd 3 out, pckd nxt, one pace und pres*
................................(9 to 4 op 7 to 4 tchd 5 to 2) 3
3842* CUMBRIAN CHALLENGE (Ire) [131] 8-11-10 (6ex) R Garritty, *hld up in tch, not fluent 6th (water) and nxt, drvn and outpcd aftr 3 out, sn no dngr*.... (5 to 2 op 9 to 1 tchd 11 to 4) 4
Dist: 3l, 1¼l, 16l. 4m 0.40s. a 13.40s (4 Ran).
SR: 44/43/49/29/   (G R S Nixon), R Nixon

3999 Racing Channel Novices' Hurdle Class D (4-y-o and up) £2,880 2½m 110yds....................... (7:05)

3160⁸ DIDDY RYMER 7-10-9 Richard Guest, *in tch, led appr 3 out, clr nxt, ran on strly*.....(10 to 1 op 8 to 1 tchd 12 to 1) 1
3704⁴ BOSTON MAN (bl) 6-11-6 R Dunwoody, *trkd ldrs, lost tch hfwy, styd on und pres to chase wnr betw last 2, nrst finish*.
....(7 to 1 op 6 to 1) 2
3401⁷ RIVEAUX (Ire) 7-11-0 P Carberry, *keen hold cl up, chalg whn blun 5th, drvn and outpcd aftr 3 out, pckd nxt, sn one pace*
....(7 to 1 op 6 to 1) 3
3729⁴ BECK AND CALL (Ire) 8-11-0 N Williamson, *chsd ldrs, not fluent 3rd, outpcd and hit 6th, styd on frm 2 out, unbl to chal*.
....(7 to 2 tchd 4 to 1) 4
3657³ SILENT GUEST (Ire) 4-11-0 R Garritty, *jnd ldrs 4th, hit 6th, outpcd appr 3 out, sn no dngr.*
....(13 to 2 op 5 to 1 tchd 7 to 1) 5
3535 PRAISE BE (Fr) (bl) 7-11-0 P Niven, *led till hdd appr 3 out, wknd quickly bef nxt*................(33 to 1 op 25 to 1) 6
3765⁵ LORD PAT (Ire) 6-11-0 A S Smith, *midfield, struggling 3 out, sn no dngr*.........................(33 to 1 op 25 to 1) 7
3808² CHINA KING (Ire) 8-11-0 B Storey, *hld up, chlgd 6th, not fluent 3 out, btn in 4th whn blun nxt, eased when beaten.*
..................................(3 to 1 fav op 5 to 1) 8
3583⁵ MILENBERG JOYS 5-11-0 D Parker, *hld up, some hdwy hfwy, struggling 3 out, sn lost tch*......(16 to 1 op 25 to 1) 9
3535⁷ TWEEDSWOOD (Ire) 7-11-0 R Supple, *beh, pushed alng 4th, blun and uns rdr 5th*................(5 to 1 tchd 6 to 1) ur
MOONLIGHT VENTURE 5-11-0 N Smith, *pushed alng in rear 4th, wl beh four out, tld off whn pld up bef 2 out.*
...............................(50 to 1 op 33 to 1) pu
1957⁷ JOLLY HEART (Ire) 7-11-0 M Brennan, *cl up, pld hrd, drpd rear 4th, wl tld off whn pulled up 3 out.*
.....................................(16 to 1 tchd 20 to 1) pu
Dist: 3½l, 10l, 1½l, 14l, hd, 7l, 3½l, 9l. 5m 8.10s. a 26.10s (12 Ran).
     (Brampton Royal Oak), Mrs S J Smith

4000 Headingley Handicap Chase Class C (0-130 5-y-o and up) £4,532 2½m 110yds....................... (7:35)

3760² NICHOLAS PLANT [99] 8-10-0 G Cahill, *led, blun 7th, hdd 5 out, rallied to ld ag'n 2 out, ran on gmely.* (3 to 1 op 5 to 2) 1
3711* DESTIN D'ESTRUVAL (Fr) [123] 6-11-10 R Johnson, *chsd ldrs, slight ld 5 out, not fluent 3 out, rdn and hdd nxt, kpt on same pace und pres.*
.................(9 to 4 op 2 to 1 tchd 5 to 2 and 11 to 4) 2
3508⁵ BRIGHTER SHADE (Ire) [105] 7-10-6 P Niven, *blun 1st, hld up, improved to chal 5 out, mstk nxt, drvn and outpcd appr 2 out.*
................................(2 to 1 fav tchd 9 to 4) 3
3760⁴ DEEP DECISION [99] 11-10-0 A S Smith, *chsd ldr, ev ch whn hit 4 out, struggling appr 2 out, sn btn.* (14 to 1 op 10 to 1) 4
3719⁴ GOLDEN HELLO [103] 6-10-4 N Williamson, *hld up, not fluent second, blun 9th (water), in tch whn f nxt.* (7 to 1 op 5 to 1) f
Dist: 4l, 12l, 4l. 5m 16.00s. a 23.00s (5 Ran).
     (Mrs M F Paterson), J S Goldie

4001 Cattal Novices' Chase Class D (5-y-o and up) £3,496 3m 1f........ (8:05)

3758* COLONEL IN CHIEF (Ire) 7-12-6 P Carberry, *led to 3rd, styd hndy, not fluent 7th, led on bit betw last 2, easily.*
................................(Evens fav tchd 11 to 10) 1
3726³ KILTULLA (Ire) 7-11-2 Richard Guest, *led 3rd, niggled alng 4 out, hdd betw last 2, no ch wth wnr.*
.............................(15 to 2 op 7 to 1 tchd 8 to 1) 2
DRAGONS BAY 8-11-2 P Niven, *hld up, chsd wnr 3rd, not fluent second and 3rd, midfield whn slight mstk 11th, sn lost tch.*
..................................(12 to 1 op 10 to 1) 3
3481² KARENASTINO 6-11-3 (5*) R Wilkinson, *str hold, chsd ldrs till outpcd 12th, no dngr aftr, tld off.*......(7 to 1 op 6 to 1) 4
3918⁶ QUIXALL CROSSETT 12-10-11 (5*) Mr M Naughton, *hld up, mstk and outpcd tenth, sn tld off.*.....(66 to 1 op 50 to 1) 5
3434⁴ TRUMP 8-11-2 D Parker, *hld up in rear, some hdwy whn hit tenth, lost tch aftr nxt, tld off when pld up after 4 out.*
....................................(4 to 1 op 7 to 2) pu

3250³ STRONGALONG (Ire) 7-11-2 A S Smith, *cl up, hit 6th, reminders and outpcd nxt, tld off whn pld up 4 out.*
.................................(12 to 1 op 10 to 1) pu
Dist: 5l, dist, 16l, dist. 6m 45.40s. a 37.40s (7 Ran).
     (Robert Ogden), G Richards

4002 Hunsingore Handicap Hurdle Class D (0-120 4-y-o and up) £2,705 2m
......................................(8:35)

3805* TEEJAY'N'AITCH (Ire) [85] 5-9-12 (5*) S Taylor, *led, quickened 3 out, clr appr last, drvn out.*
.....................................(11 to 4 jt-fav op 2 to 1 tchd 3 to 1) 1
3728³ KIERCHEM (Ire) [82] 6-10-0 N Williamson, *settled midfield, effrt aftr 4 out, chsd wnr frm 2 out, no imprsn....*(11 to 4 jt-fav op 5 to 2 tchd 3 to 1) 2
3665³ HIGHLAND WAY (Ire) [89] 9-10-0 (7*) C McCormack, *settled rear, clr order 4 out, outpcd whn slight mstk 2 out, sn no extr.*
..................................(3 to 1 op 9 to 4 tchd 10 to 1) 3
3540⁶ FOX SPARROW [90] (bl) 7-10-8 R Dunwoody, *trkd ldrs, niggled alng aftr 4 out, wknd appr 2 out.*
.............................(5 to 1 op 10 to 1 tchd 12 to 1) 4
3759⁶ SARMATIAN (USA) [110] 6-12-0 R Garritty, *hld up, clr order 4 out, niggled alng aftr nxt, sn btn........*(8 to 1 op 12 to 1) 5
3780 GOING PUBLIC [82] 10-10-0 A S Smith, *pressed ldr, hit 3rd, drpd rear appr 3 out, sn lost tch......*(20 to 1 op 16 to 1) 6
Dist: 5l, 9l, 1l, 20l, 30l. 3m 58.30s. a 17.30s (6 Ran).
SR: 22/14/12/13/12/-/   (Andrew Paterson), J S Goldie

TIPPERARY (IRE) (good to yielding) Thursday May 8th

4003 Greenvale 'Pulp 'n' Brew' Handicap Chase (0-102 4-y-o and up) £2,740 2 ¾m............................... (6:00)

3815⁵ TRIPTODICKS (Ire) [-] 7-10-10 C F Swan, ...(11 to 8 fav) 1
3838⁵ BROWNRATH KING [-] 8-10-3² K F O'Brien, .. (10 to 1) 2
3420⁷ WATERLOO KING [-] 10-10-6 (7*) J E Casey, ...(12 to 1) 3
2377 PHARALLEY (Ire) [-] 7-9-8 (7*) M D Murphy, ...(16 to 1) 4
3839 KILLERK LADY (Ire) [-] 6-9-2¹ (7*) B J Geraghty, ...(8 to 1) 5
3447² KILARA [-] 10-10-13 T P Rudd, ...(7 to 1) 6
3073⁷ CASEY'S TROUBLE [-] 12-10-7 (3*) Mr F J Casey, (14 to 1) 7
3815 MOUNTHENRY STAR (Ire) [-] 9-11-5 (7*) Mr Damien Murphy, ...(14 to 1) 8
3877¹ LITTLE-K (Ire) [-] 7-10-13 (3*) K Whelan, ...(7 to 1) f
1363⁸ WALKERS LADY (Ire) [-] 9-10-3 D T Evans, ...(10 to 1) pu
Dist: ½l, 13l, 20l, 15l. 5m 41.40s. (10 Ran).
     (M G O'Huallachain), David A Kiely

4004 Gowla 'Classic' Handicap Hurdle (0-102 4-y-o and up) £4,110 2m
......................................(7:00)

3754⁶ MARINERS REEF (Ire) [-] 6-10-7 (7*) D McCullagh, ...(11 to 4 fav) 1
3227³ NORDIC SENSATION (Ire) [-] 8-11-0 (7*) B J Geraghty, ...(5 to 1) 2
3954 RUN ROSE RUN (Ire) [-] 7-9-2 (7*) J M Maguire, ...(14 to 1) 3
2236 RUNABOUT (Ire) [-] 5-9-7 (7*) M D Murphy, ...(14 to 1) 4
3448⁴ JOHNNY HANDSOME (Ire) [-] 7-10-8 A J O'Brien, (10 to 1) 5
3696² LOUISES FANCY (Ire) [-] 7-10-11 (5*) P G Hourigan, (12 to 1) 6
2647 ADARAMANN (Ire) [-] 5-10-12 Mr R Walsh, ...(12 to 1) 7
3879⁷ BE MY FOLLY (Ire) [-] 5-10-12 C F Swan, ...(10 to 1) 8
3230³ JOHNNY'S DREAM (Ire) [-] 7-11-3 (3*) G Cotter, ...(10 to 1) 9
9439 MISSED CONNECTION (Ire) [-] 6-9-7 J K Kinane, ..(50 to 1) 10
2470 NASCIMENTO (USA) [-] 4-10-9 F J Flood, ...(14 to 1) 11
3817 ST CAROL (Ire) [-] (bl) 6-10-3 T P Treacy, ...(12 to 1) 12
3376⁴ SHE'LL BE GOOD (Ire) [-] 5-10-3 J R Barry, ...(10 to 1) 13
THE REGAL ROYAL (Ire) [-] 9-11-5 D J Casey, ...(14 to 1) 14
3767 BEHY BRIDGE (Ire) [-] 5-10-4 T J Mitchell, ...(20 to 1) 15
3520 CLASSPERFORMER (Ire) [-] 7-10-5 L P Cusack, ..(16 to 1) 16
2902 DUEONE (Ire) [-] 9-10-9 J Shortt, ...(14 to 1) 17
3073 NOBULL (Ire) [-] 7-11-9 K F O'Brien, ...(14 to 1) 18
3429 WINDTELIN (Ire) [-] 7-10-8 P A Roche, ...(25 to 1) 19
3231 POLITICAL TROUBLES (Ire) [-] 7-10-2 T P Rudd, ..(16 to 1) 20
Dist: 2½l, 8l, ½l, 2½l. 4m 0.90s. (20 Ran).
     (Mrs Sheila McCullagh), Michael McCullagh

4005 Gowla 'Breeder' Champion Mares Final (4-y-o and up) £4,110 2¼m
......................................(8:00)

GREENFLAG PRINCESS (Ire) 6-12-0 Mr F Fenton, (6 to 1) 1
SUPREME GOLD (Ire) 5-11-6 (7*) Mr P J Crowley, (10 to 1) 2
RURAL RUN (Ire) 6-11-7 (7*) Mr C A Murphy, ...(9 to 4 fav) 3
SHUIL NA MHUIRE (Ire) 7-11-7 Mr B Walsh, ...(14 to 1) 4
3222 UPSHEPOPS (Ire) 9-11-9 (5*) Mr Brian Moran, ...(20 to 1) 5
ORIENTAL BEAUTY (Ire) 6-11-7 (7*) Mr G Kearns, (12 to 1) 6
BEE-HIVE QUEEN (Ire) 5-11-6 (7*) Mr Paul Moloney, ...(12 to 1) 7
9834 MINELLA LASS 6-12-0 Mr D M O'Brien, ...(7 to 1) 8
CAP IT IF YOU CAN (Ire) 4-10-13 (7*) Mr J P McNamara, ...(10 to 1) 9
CUSH PRINCESS (Ire) 6-11-11 (3*) Mr T Lombard, (16 to 1) 10

3647[5] SOUNDS CONFIDENT (Ire) 5-11-6 (7*) Mr W Ewing,
.... (10 to 1)   11
   EVERLAUGHING (Ire) 6-12-0 Mr P J Healy, ... (16 to 1)   12
   CLASSIE CLAIRE (Ire) 6-11-7 (7*) Mr E Gallagher, (16 to 1)   13
1775 BUZZ ABOUT (Ire) 7-11-7 (7*) Mr J P Murphy, ...(20 to 1)   14
   AGLISH PRIDE (Ire) 5-11-13 Mr R Walsh, ...(7 to 2)   15
1040[7] FLYING IN THE GALE (Ire) 6-11-7 (7*) Mr T Cooper, (12 to 1)   16
   MISS ANNAGAUL (Ire) 6-11-7 (7*) Mr T J Beattie, (20 to 1)   17
   EASTER BARD 7-11-7 (7*) Mr D W Cullen, ...(20 to 1)   18
   MY NEW MERC (Ire) 5-11-6 (7*) Mr S P Hennessy, (20 to 1)   19
Dist: Dist, 5½l, 8l, 21l. 4m 38.50s. (19 Ran).

(Yawl Bay Seafoods Ltd), James Joseph Mangan

4006 Gowla 'Powerlytes' I.N.H. Flat Race (5-y-o and up) £4,110 2m..... (8:30)

2073[4] BE MY PLEASURE (Ire) 5-11-5 (7*) Mr Sean O O'Brien,
.... (9 to 1)   1
3836* HOW RAN ON (Ire) 6-12-4 Mr R Walsh, ...(9 to 1)   2
3789[3] STRONTIUM (Ire) 5-12-3 Mr P Fenton, ... (2 to 1 fav)   3
1019* NATIVE PLAYER (Ire) 5-11-10 (7*) Mr A Murphy, (12 to 1)   4
3789* RATHBAWN PRINCE (Ire) 5-11-10 (7*) Mr A J Dempsey,
.... (9 to 4)   5
2525[7] LADY RICHENDA (Ire) 9-10-13 (7*) Mr R Flavin, .. (25 to 1)   6
   DR CARTER (Ire) 7-11-4 (7*) Mr M A Cahill, ...(25 to 1)   7
   ARDBUTUS (Ire) 5-10-12 (7*) Mr J P McNamara, .. (25 to 1)   8
3840* INIS CARA (Ire) 5-11-10 (7*) Mr A FitzGerald, ... (10 to 1)   9
3697* KINNEGAD GIRL (Ire) 5-11-12 Mr A J Martin, ... (12 to 1)   10
3429[8] CEASERS REIGN (Ire) 5-11-3 (7*) Mr B Hassett, .. (33 to 1)   11
   PRINCE OF ROSSIAN (Ire) 5-11-10 Mr A J Nash, .. (20 to 1)   12
3456 WHAT A BARGAIN (Ire) 5-10-12 (7*) Mr A G Cash, (50 to 1)   13
3818 TURBINE (Ire) 5-11-10 Mr G J Harford, ...(33 to 1)   14
   PALM RIVER (Ire) 5-11-10 Mr J P Dempsey, ... (16 to 1)   15
3182 LA CIGALE (Ire) 6-11-0[1] (7*) Mr M Kavanagh, ...(50 to 1)   16
   THE DINGER (Ire) 5-11-3 (7*) Mr M T Hogg, ...(25 to 1)   17
   STAR VIEW (Ire) 5-10-12 (7*) Mr J A Smith, ...(50 to 1)   18
   TULIRA HILL (Ire) 6-11-4 (7*) Mr P Noonan, ...(25 to 1)   19
   SARATOGA SAL (Ire) 7-10-13 (7*) Mr R M Walsh, .. (33 to 1)   su
Dist: 15l, 6l, 3½l, 3½l. 3m 54.40s. (20 Ran).

(W O'Brien), Sean O O'Brien

SEDGEFIELD (good to firm)
Friday May 9th
Going Correction: PLUS 0.25 sec. per fur. (races 1,2,6), PLUS 0.20 (3,4,5)

4007 Alphameric Novices' Hurdle Class E (4-y-o and up) £2,355 2m 5f 110yds .... (2:00)

2952[8] TOSHIBA TALK 5-10-7 (7*) Mr C McCormack, hld up, gd
hdwy to ld aftr 3 out, sn clr, styd on wl. (16 to 1 op 14 to 1)   1
3903* CATCH THE PIGEON 8-11-2 N Smith, in tch, effrt aftr 3 out,
chasing wnr bef nxt, kpt on, no imprsn.
.............................(5 to 2 op 3 to 1 tchd 11 to 8)   2
3762* ROYAL YORK 5-11-2 P Carberry, hld up, effrt aftr 3 out, drvn
alng bef nxt, no imprsn on 1st 2.
.............................(11 to 10 fav op Evens tchd 11 to 8)   3
73[2] MUZRAK (Can) 6-11-7 R Garritty, trkd ldrs, outpcd aftr 3 out,
no dngr after.........................(8 to 1 op 7 to 2)   4
3262[3] ERNI (Fr) 5-10-7 (7*) R McCarthy, slight ld till hdd 7th, fdd frm
3 out.................................(12 to 1 op 10 to 1 tchd 14 to 1)   5
3820 RUBISLAW (v) 5-10-7 (7*) Miss S Lamb, in tch, gd hdwy to ld
7th, hdd aftr 3 out, wknd quickly bef nxt, tld off.
.... (100 to 1 op 66 to 1)   6
3903[7] STRONG CHARACTER 11-11-0 J Burke, beh, lost tch aftr 3
out, tld off.........................(200 to 1 op 100 to 1)   7
3435 ANOTHER GEORGE 7-11-0 A S Smith, prmnt till wknd
quickly bef 3 out, wl tld off............(12 to 1 op 20 to 1)   8
Dist: 5l, 5l, hd, 5l, 24l, 8l. 5m 5.40s. a 17.40s (8 Ran).

(Toshiba (UK) Ltd), B Ellison

4008 John Wade Group Of Companies Selling Handicap Hurdle Series Final Class G (4-y-o and up) £6,775 2m 5f 110yds...................... (2:30)

3820[6] SHELTON ABBEY [68] (bl) 11-10-3 P Carberry, hld up, sn aftr
6th, sn lost tch, hdwy und pres appr 2 out, str run frm last to ld
cl hme............................(12 to 1 op 10 to 1)   1
3899[2] BARTON HEIGHTS [85] 5-11-6 P Niven, ran in snatches, cl
up, led 3 out, ct close hme.
.............................(8 to 1 fav op 11 to 8 tchd 7 to 4)   2
3809[4] ROYAL HAND [72] (v) 7-10-7[7] Mr R Armson, in tch, took clr
order hfwy, ev ch 2 out, no extr whn mstk last.
.... (20 to 1 op 14 to 1)   3
3899* FLINTLOCK (Ire) [73] 7-10-3 (5*,5ex) R McGrath, hld up, hdwy
bef 3 out, ch nxt, kpt on same pace.....(9 to 2 op 5 to 2)   4
3904[5] NITE SPRITE [65] 7-9-9 (5*) S Taylor, in tch, drvn alng aftr 7th,
no hdwy..........................(12 to 1 op 10 to 1 tchd 14 to 1)   5
3405[6] SNOWY LANE (Ire) [71] (h,bl) 9-10-6[1] R Garritty, prmnt to
hfwy, sn outpcd, no dngr aftr.
.............................(10 to 1 op 10 to 1 tchd 12 to 1)   6
3587[1] RED JAM JAR [93] 12-12-0 K Johnson, made most till hdd 3
out, sn rdn and wknd......................(12 to 1 op 10 to 1)   7

3674[8] CATTON LADY [65] (bl) 7-9-9 (5*) B Grattan, al beh, tld off.
.............................(33 to 1 op 25 to 1)   8
3158 OBVIOUS RISK [65] 6-9-7 (7*) C McCormack, in tch, rdn bef 3
out, wknd quickly, pld up before nxt, lme.
.............................(14 to 1 op 12 to 1 tchd 16 to 1)   pu
Dist: Nk, 2l, 1l, 3½l, 2l, 3l, 17l. 5m 7.10s. a 19.10s (9 Ran).

(John Wade), J Wade

4009 Dudley Dukes Antique Fair Novices' Chase Class E (5-y-o and up) £3,127 2m 110yds.................. (3:00)

2576 LEPTON (Ire) (bl) 6-11-0 R Garritty, hld up, gd hdwy to chase
ldr aftr 3 out, rdn to ld after last, styd on.
.............................(33 to 1 op 20 to 1)   1
3584[5] HEE'S A DANCER (Ire) 5-10-8 A Thornton, prmnt, led aftr 9th, clr 2
out, rdn and hdd after last, no extr.
.............................(5 to 2 op 2 to 1 tchd 11 to 4)   2
   SUNKALA SHINE 9-10-7 (7*) Miss R Clark, towards rear, styd
on frm 2 out, nvr dngrs..........(50 to 1 op 33 to 1)   3
1161[2] MR REINER 9-11-0 P Carberry, chsd ldrs, some hdwy aftr
9th, kpt on same pace frm 3 out.
.............................(5 to 1 op 5 to 1 tchd 11 to 2)   4
3304[4] MOSS PAGEANT 7-11-0 B Storey, led, mstk 8th, hdd aftr nxt,
sn wknd, tld off.........(9 to 4 fav op 5 to 2 tchd 2 to 1)   5
3664[3] ARISTODEMUS (bl) 8-11-0 K Johnson, in tch, reminders aftr
4th, wknd bef 9th, tld off.........................(33 to 1)   6
3662 MESSONETTE 5-10-3 D Parker, al beh, lost tch frm 7th, wl tld
off.............................(100 to 1 op 50 to 1)   7
3865[4] NOBODYS FLAME (Ire) 9-11-4 A S Smith, beh frm hfwy, tld off
whn pld up bef 2 out.............(100 to 1 op 50 to 1)   pu
3244 CHILDSWAY 9-11-0 N Smith, sn lost tch, tld off whn pld up bef
6th.............................(66 to 1 op 50 to 1)   pu
3920[6] WILD BROOK (Ire) 7-10-7 (7*) C McCormack, towards rear
and rdn aftr 8th, wl beh whn pld up bef last.
.............................(20 to 1 op 33 to 1)   pu
3662* GONE ASHORE (Ire) 6-11-7 G Cahill, prmnt, wknd aftr tenth,
beh whn pld up bef last.....(5 to 1 op 5 to 1 tchd 6 to 1)   pu
Dist: 2½l, 9l, ¾l, 21l, 2½l, dist. 4m 5.40s. a 13.40s (11 Ran).

(J W P Curtis), J W Curtis

4010 George Carpenter Memorial Handicap Chase Class E (0-110 5-y-o and up) £3,574 3m 3f............. (3:30)

282[8] JIMMY O'DEA [90] (v) 10-10-5 (3*) E Husband, jmpd rght, cl
up, led 9th, quickened clr aftr 18th, cmftbly.
.............................(25 to 1 op 16 to 1)   1
3867[9] JAUNTY GIG [82] (bl) 11-10-0 L O'Hara, in tch, outpcd aftr
18th, styd on to chase wnr appr last, no imprsn.
.............................(14 to 1 op 14 to 1 tchd 16 to 1)   2
3352[5] JENDEE (Ire) [82] 9-9-7 (7*) C McCormack, towards rear, took
clr order 13th, outpcd aftr 18th, no dngr after.
.............................(12 to 1 op 14 to 1)   3
3804[3] TEMPLE GARTH [102] 8-11-6 R Supple, led till hdd 9th, prmnt
to 18th, grad wknd..................(6 to 1 op 5 to 1)   4
1739 SCRABO VIEW (Ire) [95] 9-10-8 (5*) B Grattan, beh till styd on
frm 2 out, nvr dngrs.....(12 to 1 op 12 to 1 tchd 14 to 1)   5
3708[6] BRIGHT DESTINY [82] (v) 8-9-7 (7*) Mr O McPhail, keen, trkd
ldrs, chsd wnr frm 18th, no imprsn, wknd betw last 2.
.............................(14 to 1 op 10 to 1 tchd 16 to 1)   6
3902[2] BLAZING DAWN [88] 10-10-6[2] T Reed, keen, hld up, effrt bef
17th, sn btn, wl beh whn pld up before last.
.............................(5 to 1 op 5 to 1 tchd 11 to 2)   pu
3659 OVER THE STREAM [96] 11-11-0 A S Smith, chsd ldrs, rdn
aftr 13th, tailing off whn blun 15th, sn pld up. ......(3 to 1 jt-
                         fav op 3 to 1 tchd 7 to 2)   pu
3739[6] MISCHIEVOUS GIRL [82] 9-10-0 Mrs F Needham, in tch,
mstks 13th and 15th, sn lost touch, tld off whn pld up bef 2 out.
.............................(50 to 1 op 33 to 1)   pu
3967 CROWN EQUERRY (Ire) [114] 7-12-4 P Carberry, early
reminders, towards rear, took clr order 6th, rdn and wknd aftr
15th, wl beh whn pld up bef 3 out. (3 to 1 jt-fav op 2 to 1)   pu
Dist: 5l, 7l, 3l, 3l, 5l. 6m 45.10s. a 12.10s (10 Ran).
SR: 13/-/-/10/-/-/

(J S Harlow), J Mackie

4011 Guy Cunard Hunters' Chase Class H (5-y-o and up) £1,842 2m 5f... (4:00)

3671[2] GREENMOUNT LAD (Ire) 9-12-3 (7*) Mr P Cornforth, nvr far
away, rdn aftr 13th, slight ld betw last 2, hdd and hit last, sn
led ag'n, styd on wl...................(5 to 2 op 2 to 1)   1
3164* WHAT CHANCE (Ire) 9-11-12 (7*) Mr A Charles-Jones, nvr far
away, led last, sn hdd, no extr.
.............................(9 to 4 op 9 to 4 tchd 5 to 2)   2
   KNOWE HEAD 13-12-9 (5*) Mr N Wilson, led till hdd betw last
2, no extr.............(13 to 8 fav op 13 to 8 tchd 9 to 4)   3
   BUCKANEER BAY 10-12-2 (5*) Mr R Hale, lost tch frm 7th, no
dngr aftr.............................(33 to 1 op 16 to 1)   4
3723 PRESS FOR ACTION 12-12-5 (5*) Miss P Robson, chsd ldr to
11th, wknd quickly aftr 13th.....(14 to 1 op 10 to 1)   5
3921 DONSIDE 9-12-7 Mr J Walton, sn wl beh, tld off.
.............................(12 to 1 op 10 to 1 tchd 14 to 1)   6
Dist: ¾l, 19l, 12l, 11l, dist. 5m 18.00s. a 22.00s (6 Ran).

(J Cornforth), J Cornforth

4012 Federation Brewery Handicap Hurdle Class F (0-100 5-y-o and up) £2,248 2m 1f................ (4:30)

3900* FATEHALKHAIR (Ire) [86] 5-10-8 (7*) C McCormack, *trkd ldr, led aftr 3 out and quickened, hit nxt, sn hrd pressed, hld on wl und pres frm last*......(5 to 4 fav op Evens tchd 11 to 8) 1
3780³ EDEN DANCER [95] 5-11-10 P Niven, *led till hdd aftr 3 out, rallied to chal after nxt, ev ch last, no extr und pres clsg stages*.............................(7 to 2 op 9 to 2) 2
3900⁴ JENDORCET [72] 7-10-1 F Perratt, *chsd ldrs, outpcd by 1st 2 aftr 3 out, kpt on same pace frm nxt*.....(7 to 1 op 8 to 1) 3
3762³ BEAU MATELOT [80] 5-10-9 A S Smith, *in tch, outpcd aftr 3 out, no dngr after*.........(8 to 1 op 6 to 1 tchd 9 to 1) 4
776³ SHARP SENSATION [99] 7-12-0 R Garritty, *in tch till wknd aftr 3 out, tld off*.....................(16 to 1 op 14 to 1) 5
IMPERIAL BID (Fr) [95] 9-11-10 M Foster, *beh, lost tch aftr 3 out, tld off*...................................... (20 to 1) 6
3798⁶ ERINY (USA) [86] 8-11-1 R Supple, *pld hrd, in tch till wknd aftr 3 out, beh whn pulled up and dismounted after nxt.*
......................................(7 to 1 op 6 to 1) pu
Dist: Nk, 13l, 7l, dist, nk. 3m 57.40s. a 11.40s (7 Ran).
SR: 15/24/-/-/ (Mrs Gwen Smith), B Ellison

STRATFORD (good)
Friday May 9th
Going Correction: PLUS 0.65 sec. per fur.

4013 Pragnell Trophy Class E Novices' Hurdle (Div I) (4-y-o and up) £2,010 2 ¾m 110yds..................(5:40)

3828² MAID FOR ADVENTURE (Ire) 6-11-1 J Culloty, *trkd ldrs, led 2 out, rdn appr last, drvn out.*
.... (11 to 10 on op 5 to 4 on tchd Evens) 1
3518³ REGAL GEM (Ire) 6-10-9 B Fenton, *beh till hdwy 8th, styd on to chase ldrs 2 out, chlgd last, stayed on same pace.*
.... (10 to 1 op 7 to 1 tchd 11 to 1) 2
3828⁹ LUCRATIVE PERK (Ire) 5-10-9 D Leahy, *hmpd second, styd tracking ldrs till led 4 out, hdd 2 out, one pace r-in.*
.... (100 to 1 op 33 to 1) 3
2822⁹ DOCS BOY 7-11-0 J Osborne, *hld up, hdwy 4 out, fdd aftr nxt.*
............................(8 to 1 op 3 to 1 tchd 9 to 1) 4
3729 FREELINE FONTAINE (Ire) 5-11-0 M A Fitzgerald, *hmpd second, styd tracking ldrs, chlgd 6th till led 8th, hdd 4 out, wknd aftr nxt*...... (7 to 2 op 3 to 1 tchd 4 to 1 and 9 to 2) 5
3388⁹ NICANJON 6-10-9 (5*) X Aizpuru, *led till hdd and f second.*
.... (50 to 1 op 20 to 1 tchd 66 to 1) f
3590 MUMMY'S MOLE 6-11-0 W Marston, *chsd ldrs, mstk 3rd, rdn 7th, blun and wknd 8th, tld off whn pld up bef 3 out.*
.............................(100 to 1 op 33 to 1) pu
SAFWAN 5-11-0 N Williamson, *hit 4th and beh, rdn and lost tch 8th, tld off whn pld up bef 2 out.*
........................(16 to 1 op 12 to 1 tchd 20 to 1) pu
3588 WOLDSMAN 7-11-0 C Llewellyn, *keen hold, prmnt and mstk 3rd, lost tch frm 7th, tld off whn pld up bef 2 out.*
.... (9 to 1 op 6 to 1 tchd 10 to 1) pu
2694 THUNDERBIRD 5-10-9 J A McCarthy, *led second, keen hold, hit 6th and 7th, hdd nxt, sn wknd, tld off whn pld up bef 2 out.*
.... (66 to 1 op 25 to 1) pu
Dist: ¾l, 4l, 8l, hd. 5m 46.00s. a 34.00s (10 Ran).
(Chris Brasher), Miss H C Knight

4014 Richardson Developments Novices' Chase Class D for The Sheldon Bosley Memorial Trophy (6-y-o and up) £3,652 2m 5f 110yds......... (6:10)

3822* MONKS SOHAM (Ire) 9-11-1 (3*) P Henley, *keen hold and rcd in 3rd till hdwy to chase ldr 12th, hit nxt, rdn alng to cl appr 2 out, led r-in, drvn out*..... (6 to 1 op 4 to 1 tchd 7 to 1) 1
3826² STATELY HOME (Ire) 6-11-8 R Johnson, *led aftr 1st, drvn clr 4 out, hrd rdn and hdd r-in, styd on gmely.*
..........................(6 to 4 on op 7 to 4 on tchd 11 to 8 on) 2
2862⁴ LITTLE GAINS 8-10-12 B Fenton, *led till aftr 1st, chsd ldr, hit tenth, wknd into 3rd 12th*............ (66 to 1 op 50 to 1) 3
3300 FINNIGAN FREE 7-10-8³ (7*) Mr M Frith, *al in 4th, in tch and effrt 9th, hit tenth, wknd 11th.*
..........................(50 to 1 op 33 to 1 tchd 66 to 1) 4
3691³ GREENBACK (Bel) 6-11-8 N Williamson, *al last, hit second, blun 5th, rdn alng 8th and sn lost tch.*
.............................(9 to 4 op 2 to 1 tchd 5 to 2) 5
Dist: 1¼l, 21l, 22l, 13l. 5m 20.60s. a 20.60s (5 Ran).
SR: 24/26/ (G A Hubbard), G A Hubbard

4015 Pragnell Trophy Class E Novices' Hurdle (Div II) (4-y-o and up) £1,996 2 ¾m 110yds..................(6:35)

3881³ GOWER-SLAVE 5-11-0 R Johnson, *chsd ldrs, rdn aftr 7th and lost pl, styd on to chase lder but no ch whn lft in lead 2 out, fnshd tired*..............(9 to 2 op 7 to 2 tchd 5 to 1) 1
3698 GENTLEMAN JIM 7-11-0 D Morris, *hld up, hdwy 7th, styd on to take 3rd aftr 3 out but no ch whn lft second 2 out, fnshd tired.*
.... (16 to 1 op 6 to 1) 2
3372² SIOUX TO SPEAK 5-11-0 J F Titley, *wth ldrs till rdn 7th, chsd lder 4 out till wknd aftr 3 out.*
............................(11 to 2 op 5 to 1 tchd 6 to 1) 3
2552⁹ SAUCY NUN (Ire) 5-10-9 B Powell, *beh till drvn and hdwy to chase ldrs 5th, wknd 8th.*
..........(11 to 1 op 10 to 1 tchd 9 to 1 and 12 to 1) 4
MARINERS MEMORY 9-10-11 (3*) R Massey, *hld up, rapid hdwy aftr 7th, ld after nxt, sn clr, f 2 out, unlucky.*
.... (66 to 1 op 50 to 1) f
3738* SHARP COMMAND 4-11-5 A P McCoy, *led till hdd aftr 8th, sn wknd, tld off whn pld up bef 3 out.*
............(6 to 4 on tchd 7 to 4 on and 11 to 8 on) pu
3283⁷ CURRA MINSTRAL (Ire) 7-10-9 Leesa Long, *tld off 5th, pld up bef 8th*.......................................(100 to 1) pu
2959 SUMMIT ELSE 6-10-9 C Llewellyn, *wth ldr till mstk and wknd 5th, sn wl beh, tld off whn pld up bef 2 out.*
......................(25 to 1 op 16 to 1 tchd 33 to 1) pu
2350⁹ MURRAY'S MILLION 5-11-0 W Marston, *hdwy 4th, hit 7th, sn rdn and beh, tld off whn pld up bef nxt*.......... (100 to 1) pu
Dist: 10l, ¾l, 15l. 5m 52.50s. a 40.50s (9 Ran).
(Bob Bevan), P Bowen

4016 Hartshorne Motor Services Ltd. Walsall Handicap Chase Class B for the Roddy Baker Gold Cup (0-140 5-y-o and up) £6,787 2m 5f 110yds (7:05)

3730* PHILIP'S WOODY [115] 9-10-4 M A Fitzgerald, *help up, outpcd 6th, hdwy frm 12th, quickened to chal last, led run in, ran on wl*..............................(10 to 1 op 6 to 1) 1
3208* DISCO DES MOTTES (Fr) [125] 6-11-0 P Carberry, *led, blun tenth, rdn 2 out, hdd r-in, one pace.*
.......(11 to 10 fav op Evens tchd 13 to 8 and 7 to 4) 2
3134³ AIR SHOT [135] 7-11-10 R Johnson, *rcd in 3rd, effrt and hit 4 out, chalg whn blun 2 out, styd on ag'n r-in.*
.... (7 to 4 op 2 to 1 tchd 9 to 4 and 6 to 4) 3
3711² DESTINY CALLS [122] 7-10-11 R Dunwoody, *chsd ldr, hit 8th, str chal frm 2 out till one pace r-in*......(7 to 1 op 5 to 1) 4
2220⁵ STRONG MEDICINE [131] 10-11-6 C O'Dwyer, *nvr gng wl, al beh, tld off frm tenth*....(16 to 1 op 10 to 1 tchd 20 to 1) 5
Dist: ½l, ½l, 1½l, dist. 5m 22.60s. a 22.60s (5 Ran).
(K G Knox), N J Henderson

4017 Needham & James Handicap Hurdle Class D (0-120 4-y-o and up) £2,861 2m 110yds.................. (7:35)

3595 MOST EQUAL [112] 7-11-13 A P McCoy, *hld up in rear, steady hdwy frm 3 out, chlgd 2 out till drvn to ld hear finish.*
....(7 to 2 op 3 to 1) 1
3896² OUT ON A PROMISE (Ire) [107] 5-11-8 N Williamson, *hld up, steady hdwy to track ldrs 3 out, led 2 out, rdn r-in, ct nr finish.*
....................(11 to 4 fav op 5 to 2 tchd 3 to 1) 2
2532 SEVERN GALE [102] 7-10-12 (5*) X Aizpuru, *led 4th, rdn 3 out, hdd nxt, sn outpcd*.....................(9 to 1 op 7 to 1) 3
3886³ NASHVILLE STAR (USA) [94] (v) 6-10-9 C Llewellyn, *chsd ldrs till outpcd 5th, hdwy to chase lders 4 out, wknd aftr 3 out.*
....(12 to 1 op 7 to 1) 4
GUNNER BE GOOD [85] 7-10-0 T Eley, *led to 4th, styd prmnt till wknd 3 out*......... (40 to 1 op 20 to 1 tchd 50 to 1) 5
1848⁶ PAIR OF JACKS (Ire) [91] 7-10-6 R Dunwoody, *in tch, hdwy 5th, wknd 3 out*..........(15 to 2 op 6 to 1 tchd 8 to 1) 6
3831⁸ KEEP ME IN MIND (Ire) [101] (bl) 8-11-2 J F Titley, *keen hold, in rear most of way, hmpd and lost tch 4 out*.......... (7 to 1) 7
3166⁵ ISAIAH [105] 8-11-6 T Kent, *chsd ldrs, cl 4th whn f four out.*
....(9 to 1 op 5 to 1) f
3831⁹ OUT RANKING (Fr) [112] 5-11-13 T Dascombe, *wl beh frm 4th, tld off from nxt, f 2 out*............(14 to 1 op 7 to 1) f
Dist: 1l, 13l, 11l, ½l, 3½l, 28l. 4m 3.00s. a 17.00s (9 Ran).
SR: 36/30/12/-/-/-/ (Heeru Kirpalani), M C Pipe

4018 John And Nigel Thorne Memorial Cup Class H Hunters' Chase (5-y-o and up) £2,108 3m...........(8:05)

3847⁴ KINO 10-11-7 (7*) Mr Andrew Martin, *outpcd 6th, hdwy to chase ldr 11th, wknd 3 out, lft poor second aftr 2 out, left in ld last, lucky*..........(10 to 1 op 7 to 1 tchd 11 to 1) 1
3857⁷ TARA BOY 12-11-7 (7*) Mr R Cambray, *rear and mstk 5th, nvr rchd ldrs, lft poor second whn hmpd 2 out, sn one pace.*
.... (20 to 1 op 10 to 1 tchd 25 to 1) 2
3578⁹ FARINGO 12-11-7 (7*) Miss C Grissell, *jmpd slwly second, al beh, lft poor 3rd at last*...........(50 to 1 op 20 to 1) 3
2790 THE MAJOR GENERAL 10-12-3 (7*) Captain A Ogden, *hld up in tch, lost pos 11th, hdwy to chase ldr 4 out, gng wl upsides whn lft clr 2 out, uns rdr last, rmntd.*
..............(5 to 2 op 7 to 4 tchd 11 to 4 and 3 to 1) 4
STILLTODO 10-11-2 (7*) Mr Chris Wilson, *led to 14th, sn wknd, tld of*.............(11 to 2 op 5 to 1 tchd 6 to 1) 5
3854³ HILL ISLAND 10-11-7 (7*) Mr Rupert Sweeting, *chsd ldr most of way till led 14th, rdn, still slight ld but hld whn f 2 out.*
..............(Evens fav tchd 11 to 8 and 11 to 10 on) f
Dist: 8l, 5l, 5l, dist. 6m 26.30s. a 41.30s (6 Ran).
(Andrew J Martin), Andrew J Martin

4019 A.H.P. Trailers Wombourne Novices' Handicap Hurdle Class E (0-100 4-y-o and up) £2,444 2m 110yds.. (8:35)

3852[2] SNOWSHILL SHAKER [91] 8-11-10 C Llewellyn, *trkd ldrs, gng wl whn hmpd bend aftr 3 out, slight ld nxt, readily.* ....(4 to 1 op 3 to 1 tchd 9 to 2) 1
3915[2] NAHLA [80] 7-10-13 S Curran, *prmnt, dsptd ld aftr 4 out, mstk 3 out, sn led, hdd 2 out, styd on.* ....(3 to 1 fav op 7 to 2 tchd 4 to 1) 2
3741[3] POSITIVO [70] 6-10-3 D Leahy, *al chasing ldrs, rdn frm 3 out, styd on*....................(14 to 1 op 12 to 1) 3
2973 ORCHARD KING [83] 7-11-2 M Brennan, *hld up, hdwy 4 out, styd on frm 2 out but not pace to trble ldrs.* ....(14 to 1 op 16 to 1 tchd 25 to 1) 4
1992* STONECUTTER [92] (v) 4-11-6 A Thornton, *trkd ldrs, led aftr 4 out, hdd after 3 out, wknd appr last.* ....(14 to 1 op 8 to 1 tchd 16 to 1) 5
2529[3] THE LANCER (Ire) [87] 8-11-6 R Dunwoody, *led till hdd aftr 4 out, wknd 2 out*....................(9 to 1 op 7 to 1 tchd 10 to 1) 6
936[5] ANDSOME BOY [84] 4-10-12 B Fenton, *hld up and keen hold, drvn and effrt 4 out, one pace appr 2 out.* ....(25 to 1 op 20 to 1 tchd 33 to 1) 7
3820[8] DOVETTO [77] 8-10-10 S Wynne, *hdwy 4th, rdn appr 3 out, wknd nxt*....................(12 to 1 op 8 to 1) 8
3915[8] KUMARI KING (Ire) [72] 7-10-5 D Morris, *beh frm 4th, tld off.* ....(33 to 1 op 20 to 1) 9
3734[3] SIBERIAN MYSTIC [90] 4-11-4 M A Fitzgerald, *mstk 4th, in tch whn badly hmpd four out, not reco'r, tld off.* ....(6 to 1 op 4 to 1) 10
3915 FAIRELAINE [79] 5-10-12 C O'Dwyer, *al beh, no ch whn badly hmpd 4 out, tld off*....................(20 to 1 op 10 to 1) 11
3042[7] WOODLANDS LAD TOO [67] 5-10-0 R Bellamy, *al beh, tld off.* ....(100 to 1 op 33 to 1) 12
3823[3] GIPSY GEOF (Ire) [95] 6-12-0 N Williamson, *hld up, steady hdwy and staying on whn f 4 out.* ....(13 to 2 op 7 to 2 tchd 7 to 1) f

Dist: 3l, hd, 3l, 1l, 2½l, 1l, ¾l, 25l, 7l, 16l. 4m 9.80s. a 23.80s (13 Ran).
(Austin P Knight), N A Twiston-Davies

HEXHAM (good to firm)
Saturday May 10th
Going Correction: MINUS 0.35 sec. per fur.

4020 Pensher Security Doors Ltd Conditional Jockeys' Novices' Hurdle Class E (4-y-o and up) £2,363 3m .... (2:20)

3663[2] PAPPA CHARLIE (USA) 6-11-0 F Leahy, *in tch, took clr order 9th, disputing ld whn lft clr 2 out, styd on und pres.* ....(4 to 1 tchd 3 to 1) 1
3538* MISTER TRICK (Ire) (bl) 7-10-9 (5*) W Dowling, *chsd ldr, outpcd aftr 3 out, styd on frm nxt*......(3 to 1 tchd 4 to 1) 2
3803[4] ETERNAL CITY 6-11-2 (5*) R Burns, *hld up, took clr order hfwy, outpcd aftr 3 out, styd on und pres frm nxt.* ....(15 to 2 op 6 to 1 tchd 8 to 1) 3
3655[4] CARNMONEY (Ire) 9-11-0 S Taylor, *chsd ldrs till wknd aftr 3 out*....................(20 to 1 op 16 to 1 tchd 25 to 1) 4
2359[4] THORNTOUN ESTATE (Ire) (v) 4-10-2 (5*) C McCormack, *chsd ldrs, ev ch 3 out, rdn and wknd appr nxt, fnshd lme.* ....(6 to 1 op 8 to 1 tchd 10 to 1) 5
3658[8] CHILL FACTOR 7-11-0 G Lee, *beh frm 8th, tld off.* ....(6 to 1 tchd 9 to 1) 6
3663* EASTCLIFFE (Ire) 5-11-4 (3*) D Thomas, *led, hrd pressed whn f 2 out, lme*.......... (5 to 2 fav op 2 to 1 tchd 11 to 4) f
3899 FRIENDLY SOCIETY 11-11-0 R McGrath, *lost tch frm 6th, tld off whn pld up aftr 8th*....................(50 to 1 op 33 to 1) pu
3803 MEADOWLECK 8-10-4 (5*) I Jardine, *lost tch frm 8th, sn tld off, pld up bef last*....................(100 to 1 op 66 to 1) pu
3258 RYE RUM (Ire) 6-10-11 (3*) B Grattan, *sn beh, tld off whn pld up aftr 8th*....................(100 to 1 op 66 to 1) pu
3655 TARTAN JOY (Ire) 6-10-11 (3*) R Wilkinson, *lost tch frm 8th, sn tld off, pld up bef last*....................(50 to 1 tchd 66 to 1) pu

Dist: 8l, 1½l, 21l, 6l, 20l. 5m 46.20s. b 1.80s (11 Ran).
SR: 20/12/17/-/-/-/ (Raymond Anderson Green), C Parker

4021 Pensher Security Doors Ltd 'National Hunt' Novices' Hurdle Class E (4-y-o and up) £2,607 2m .... (2:50)

3757[2] BOLD STATEMENT 5-11-6 N Bentley, *trkd ldr, led bef 2 out, sn clr*.........(11 to 10 on op 5 to 4 on tchd Evens) 1
3657 SILVER MINX 5-11-12 P Niven, *led till hdd bef 2 out, kpt on, no ch wth wnr*..............(15 to 8 op 7 to 4 tchd 9 to 4) 2
3866[7] AMBER HOLLY 8-10-9 B Storey, *towards rear, hdwy aftr 3 out, styd on same pace frm nxt*.....(20 to 1 tchd 25 to 1) 3
3928 BUCKLEY HOUSE 5-11-0 T Reed, *wl beh early, some late hdwy, nvr dngrs*...... (20 to 1 op 16 to 1 tchd 25 to 1) 4
3900 WEAPONS FREE 6-11-0 R Garritty, *rear div, gd hdwy aftr 3 out, no further prog frm nxt*..........(33 to 1 op 25 to 1) 5
2908[7] EDSTONE (Ire) 5-11-0 M Foster, *beh most of way.* ....(33 to 1 op 20 to 1) 6
3655[6] SALEM BEACH 5-10-2 (7*) C McCormack, *chsd ldrs till wknd aftr 3 out*.............(40 to 1 op 25 to 1 tchd 50 to 1) 7
3509[3] STARLIN SAM 8-11-0 P Carberry, *chsd ldrs till wknd aftr 5th.* ....(8 to 1 op 10 to 1) 8
3757 HUNTING SLANE 5-11-0 R Supple, *keen, in tch, rdn aftr 5th, wknd after 3 out*....................(100 to 1 op 33 to 1) 9
3970[5] CHARIOT MAN (Ire) 5-10-9 (5*) R Wilkinson, *towards rear whn f 3rd*............ (14 to 1 op 12 to 1 tchd 16 to 1) f
3439 ELLIOTT THE BUTLER 5-11-0 A S Smith, *blun and uns rdr 1st*....................(33 to 1) ur
WAVER LANE 4-9-13 (5*) S Taylor, *sn beh, tld off whn pld up bef 2 out*....................(50 to 1 op 33 to 1) pu

Dist: 20l, 9l, 2½l, sht-hd, 13l, 11l, 15l, 1½l. 3m 51.10s. a 2.10s (12 Ran).
SR: 15/1/-/-/-/-/ (R I Graham), G M Moore

4022 Bishops Skinner Ltd Novices' Chase Class E (5-y-o and up) £3,232 3m 1f .... (3:20)

3702[7] REAL TONIC 7-12-2 P Carberry, *settled midfield, steady hdwy to track ldr 3 out, rdn to ld fnl 100 yards.* ....(11 to 10 fav op 5 to 4 on tchd 5 to 4) 1
1819[6] PLUMBOB (Ire) 8-11-2 R Supple, *led till hdd fnl 100 yards, no extr*....................(7 to 1 op 5 to 1) 2
3967 EXEMPLAR (Ire) 9-10-11 (5*) R Wilkinson, *chsd ldrs, ev ch whn blun 3 out, sn rdn, kpt on same pace.* ....(4 to 1 op 7 to 2 tchd 9 to 2) 3
3582[7] BROOMHILL DUKER (Ire) 7-11-2 D Parker, *prmnt till grad wknd frm 16th*....................(33 to 1) 4
3660[3] TACTIX 7-10-11 A S Smith, *beh, some hdwy aftr 16th, no further prog frm 3 out*..............(20 to 1 tchd 25 to 1) 5
3438[7] JUST FOR ME (Ire) 8-10-11 (5*) Mr M H Naughton, *beh most of way*....................(33 to 1 op 25 to 1) 6
3761 FESTIVAL FANCY 10-10-11 G Lee, *beh most of way.* ....(25 to 1 op 20 to 1) 7
3470[3] PANTARA PRINCE (Ire) 8-11-2 B Storey, *in tch, hdwy to chase ldrs aftr 16th, wknd frm 3 out.* ....(9 to 2 op 6 to 1 tchd 7 to 2) 8
3778 PERSIAN GRANGE (Ire) 7-11-2 J Burke, *beh whn blun badly 12th, sn pld up*....................(50 to 1) pu
3660[4] ALICAT (Ire) 6-11-2 M Foster, *chsd ldrs, mstk 11th, tailing off whn blun 3 out, pld up bef last*....................(33 to 1) pu

Dist: Nk, 6l, 15l, 4l, 13l, ¾l, 13l. 6m 24.20s. a 19.20s (10 Ran).
(Robert Ogden), G Richards

4023 Lord's Taverners Selling Hurdle Class G (4 - 7-y-o) £1,800 2m (3:50)

3317[4] PALACE OF GOLD 7-11-0 R Supple, *led till hdd 4th, remained cl up, led bef 2 out, styd on wl und pres.* ....(11 to 8 fav op 2 to 1) 1
3819 NOIR ESPRIT 4-10-6 (3*) F Leahy, *in tch, hdwy to chase wnr betw last 2, sn rdn, no imprsn r-in*.................. (7 to 1) 2
3780[2] SUSELJA (Ire) 6-10-9 A S Smith, *hld up, hdwy bef 5th, kpt on same pace frm 2 out*....................(9 to 2 op 4 to 1) 3
3919 TIOTAO (Ire) 7-11-0 D Parker, *beh and rdn hfwy, hdwy aftr 3 out, no further prog frm nxt*..........(14 to 1 op 12 to 1) 4
3780 NONIOS (Ire) (bl) 6-10-7 (7*) T Hogg, *sn prmnt, led 4th, hdd bef 2 out, fdd*....................(7 to 2 op 5 to 2) 5
3919 OVER STATED (Ire) 7-10-9 (5*) S Taylor, *chsd ldrs till wknd aftr 3 out*....................(25 to 1 op 20 to 1) 6
3919[8] IN A MOMENT (USA) 6-11-7 P Niven, *early reminders, sn beh, lost tch frm 2 out, tld off*.........(12 to 1 op 16 to 1) 7
3709 KASIRAMA (Ire) 6-11-0 R Garritty, *towards rear, some hdwy aftr 3 out, wknd frm nxt, lost tch and pld up bef last.* ....(9 to 1 op 8 to 1 tchd 10 to 1) pu
3866 TEDDY EDWARD 7-10-7 (7*) Mr T J Barry, *al beh, lost tch and pld up bef 2 out*....................(33 to 1 op 25 to 1) pu

Dist: 4l, 7l, 10l, 3½l, 5l, dist. 3m 57.80s. a 8.80s (9 Ran).
(Mrs Barbara Lungo), L Lungo

4024 Ian Straker Memorial Trophy Class F Handicap Chase (0-105 5-y-o and up) £2,898 2m 110yds....... (4:20)

3821[3] TAPATCH (Ire) [86] 9-11-0 P Carberry, *beh and hrd rdn aftr mstk 5th, hdwy to track ldrs 8th, drvn alng after 2 out, styd on wl to ld fnl 100 yards*....................(5 to 2 jt-fav op 9 to 4 tchd 11 to 4) 1
3565[7] SUPER SANDY [72] 10-10-0 K Johnson, *made most till hdd 9th, drvn to ld appr last, headed fnl 100 yards, no extr.* ....(13 to 2 op 6 to 1 tchd 8 to 1) 2
3920[2] CARDENDEN (Ire) [72] 9-10-0 B Storey, *prmnt, led 9th, hdd appr last, sn btn*....................(3 to 1 op 4 to 1) 3
3867[2] WHAAT FETTLE [100] 12-12-0 P Niven, *outpcd and lost tch aftr 6th, no dngr after, tld off*....................(5 to 2 jt-fav op 9 to 4 tchd 11 to 4) 4
3865 SUPERMARINE [72] 11-10-0 G Lee, *chsd ldrs till wknd bef 3 out, tld off*....................(33 to 1 op 25 to 1) 5
3918 TWIN FALLS (Ire) [94] (bl) 6-11-8 N Bentley, *al beh, lost tch frm 6th, tld off*.................... (6 to 1 op 9 to 2) 6

Dist: 2l, 8l, 28l, 1¼l, 16l. 4m 6.70s. a 8.70s (6 Ran).
(Miss V Foster), M W Easterby

4025 Bishops Skinner Ltd Handicap Hurdle Class E (0-115 4-y-o and up)

£2,404 2½m 110yds. . . . . (4:50)

3820 KINDA GROOVY [86] (bl) 8-11-1 N Smith, *nvr far away, reminder aftr 5th, rdn to ld after 2 out, sn hrd pressed, styd on wl*. . . . .(9 to 1 op 12 to 1 tchd 5 to 1) 1
4002^{3} HIGHLAND WAY (Ire) [89] 9-10-11 (7*) C McCormack, *hld up, hdwy on bit to chal betw last 2, ev ch whn mstk last, sn rdn and no extr*. . . . .(9 to 2 op 7 to 2) 2
1038^{6} JUMBO STAR [80] 7-10-9 B Storey, *prmnt, led 3 out, hdd aftr nxt, sn rdn and wknd*. . . . . (12 to 1 op 10 to 1) 3
3866^{8} DONT FORGET CURTIS (Ire) [72] 5-9-8 (7*) Miss S Lamb, *prmnt early, drpd rear aftr 6th, no dngr after*. . . . . (10 to 1 op 8 to 1 tchd 12 to 1) 4
3604* RASCALLY [91] 7-11-6 M Foster, *led to second, in tch, ev ch 3 out, wknd bef nxt*. . .(11 to 8 on op 5 to 4 on tchd Evens) 5
3782 MOREOF A GUNNER [95] 7-11-10 R Garritty, *made most frm second till hdd 3 out, wknd bef nxt*. . . . .(8 to 1 op 12 to 1 tchd 14 to 1 and 16 to 1) 6

Dist: 1¼l, 18l, 1½l, 7l, 8l. 4m 59.80s. a 8.80s (6 Ran).

(Ian Park), I Park

KILLARNEY (IRE) (yielding to soft)
Saturday May 10th

4026 White Sands Hotel Maiden Hurdle (4-y-o) £3,425 2m 1f. . . . . (4:00)

BLUES PROJECT (Ire) 11-7 S H O'Donovan, ...(5 to 1) 1
3785^{2} SNOW FALCON 11-7 C F Swan, ...(9 to 4 on) 2
3705^{3} CELTIC PROJECT (Ire) (bl) 10-9 (7*) J M Maguire, . . .(6 to 1) 3
GLENSTAL FOREST (Ire) 10-6 (5*) P G Hourigan, . . .(16 to 1) 4
3087 DISPOSEN (Ire) 10-4 (7*) D Fisher, ...(25 to 1) 5
UNFORGOTTEN STAR (Ire) 11-2 F J Flood, ...(14 to 1) 6
3816 HENCARLAM (Ire) 11-2 K F O'Brien, ...(14 to 1) 7
3816 PATIENCE OF ANGELS (Ire) 10-11 D J Casey, ...(20 to 1) 8
3345 MARCHAWAY (Ire) 11-7 T J Mitchell, ...(12 to 1) 9
2337 KAYALIYNA (Ire) 10-11 M Moran, ...(12 to 1) 10
FANDANGO DE CHASSY (Fr) 11-2 F Woods, ...(10 to 1) 11
3415 GAELIC ROYALE (Ire) 10-8 (3*) R P O'Brien, ...(25 to 1) 12
LADY TIGER (Ire) 10-8 (3*) K Whelan, ...(16 to 1) 13

Dist: 4½l, 13l, 15l, 10l. 4m 12.30s. (13 Ran).

(Mrs J S Bolger), J S Bolger

4027 Killarney Racegoers Club Handicap Hurdle (0-102 4-y-o and up) £3,425 2½m. . . . . (4:30)

3954^{2} FAIR SOCIETY (Ire) [-] 6-10-0 M P Hourigan, ...(7 to 1) 1
3935* BAWNROCK (Ire) [-] 8-12-0 C F Swan, ...(6 to 1) 2
3835^{3} WELSH GRIT (Ire) [-] 8-11-6 D J Casey, ...(4 to 1 fav) 3
3626^{3} DOOK'S DELIGHT (Ire) [-] 6-10-2 L P Cusack, ... (11 to 1) 4
3431^{5} OWENBWEE (Ire) [-] (bl) 6-11-7 F Woods, ...(6 to 1) 5
3879* BRONICA (Ire) [-] 5-11-3 A J O'Brien, ...(7 to 1) 6
3953^{4} THE WISE KNIGHT (Ire) [-] 6-10-2 (7*) M D Murphy, (11 to 1) 7
3625* ONE MORE SPIN (Ire) [-] 4-10-13 (3*) K Whelan, ...(8 to 1) 8
2524 CRANNON BEAUTY (Ire) [-] 7-10-2 S H O'Donovan, ...(25 to 1) 9
3879^{6} LEGITMAN (Ire) [-] 7-9-5^{1} (5*) P G Hourigan, ... (12 to 1) 10
3377 CREATIVE BLAZE (Ire) [-] 8-11-11 K F O'Brien, ...(12 to 1) 11

Dist: Nk, 5l, 2½l, 4l. 5m 14.80s. (11 Ran).

(Fair Society Syndicate), Michael Hourigan

4028 Killarney Grand Hotel Handicap Chase (0-109 5-y-o and up) £3,425 2½m. . . . . (5:00)

3815^{8} YOUNG DUBLINER (Ire) [-] 8-11-2 (3*) K Whelan, . . .(6 to 1) 1
4003^{3} WATERLOO KING [-] 10-9-13 (7*) J E Casey, ...(7 to 1) 2
3839^{3} SILENTBROOK [-] 12-9-0 (7*) S FitzGerald, ...(10 to 1) 3
3706^{4} ROSSBEIGH CREEK [-] 10-11-2 F J Flood, ...(9 to 2) 4
2904* THE NOBLE ROUGE (Ire) [-] 8-11-7 (3*) G Cotter, (3 to 1 fav) 5
3765 STROLL HOME (Ire) [-] 7-12-0 C F Swan, ...(7 to 1) 6
3839^{4} YOUNG WOLF [-] 9-9-9 F Woods, ...(4 to 1) 7
3236^{8} CORRIBLOUGH (Ire) [-] 9-9-5 (7*) M D Murphy, ...(9 to 1) f

Dist: Nk, 15l, 2l, 15l. 5m 20.90s. (8 Ran).

(John A Cooper), E Bolger

4029 Killarney Racegoers Club INH Flat Race (5-y-o and up) £3,425 2m 1f . . . . (7:00)

MINELLA STORM (Ire) 5-11-13 Mr A J Martin, . .(5 to 2 fav) 1
2838^{8} OONAGH'S STAR (Ire) 5-11-8 (5*) Mr A C Coyle, . . (10 to 1) 2
2541 ONE FOR NAVIGATION (Ire) 5-11-13 Mr E Bolger, (10 to 1) 3
MAKING THE CUT (Ire) 5-11-1 (7*) Mr B J Crowley, (14 to 1) 4
3085^{9} GALE JOHNSTON (Ire) 6-11-2 (7*) Mr Paul Moloney, ...(20 to 1) 5
3769 CINQ FRANK (Ire) 7-12-0 Mr G J Harford, ... (12 to 1) 6
3840^{5} NOT CLEVER (Ire) 5-11-6 (7*) Mr A Ross, ...(10 to 1) 7
3840^{8} AUDACIOUS DANCER (Ire) 5-11-6 (7*) Mr A J Dempsey, ...(12 to 1) 8
3789^{9} EXECUTIVE HEIGHTS (Ire) 5-11-6 (7*) Mr P Cody, (10 to 1) 9
3524^{9} HOMEVILLE (Ire) 5-11-6 (7*) Mr J C Kelly, ... (10 to 1) 10
BARNEY THE MAN (Ire) 5-11-13 Mr R Walsh, ...(3 to 1) 11
3818^{4} INCHIQUIN CASTLE (Ire) 5-11-13 Mr P Fenton, ... (7 to 1) 12
253 DO THE BART (Ire) 5-11-6 (7*) Mr Sean O O'Brien, (12 to 1) 13
2754^{3} ACTIVE LADY (Ire) 5-11-1 (7*) Mr B Walsh, ... (20 to 1) 14
SIGNAL KNIGHT VI (Ire) 5-11-6 (7*) Mr J Boland, . . (20 to 1) 15
MOSSIE MCCARTHY (Ire) 5-11-13 Mr P J Healy, . . (20 to 1) 16
LORD OF THE GLEN (Ire) 5-11-6 (7*) Mr R Flavin, (10 to 1) pu
MAJOR BILL (Ire) 6-11-7 (7*) Mr M Budds, ...(20 to 1) pu

Dist: Nk, 20l, 1½l, 8l. 4m 7.30s. (18 Ran).

(John J Nallen), David Wachman

NEWTON ABBOT (good)
Saturday May 10th

Going Correction: PLUS 0.55 sec. per fur. (races 1,3,6), PLUS 0.10 (2,4,5)

4030 Newton Abbot Racecourse Corporate Club Novices' Hurdle Class D (4-y-o and up) £2,933 2m 1f. . . . . (6:05)

3957* EMBANKMENT (Ire) 7-11-6 M A Fitzgerald, *al cl up, led on bit 2 out, hrd hld*. . . . .(4 to 1 on op 3 to 1 on) 1
TARRAGON (Ire) 7-11-0 J A McCarthy, *pld hrd, led 1st to second, led 3rd to 2 out, sn btn*. . . . .(6 to 1 op 7 to 2) 2
3402 FINAL SCORE (Ire) 7-10-9 T Dascombe, *hld up, outpcd 4 out, lft poor 3rd last*. . . . . . . (40 to 1 op 33 to 1 tchd 50 to 1) 3
PRESS AGAIN 5-10-9 B Fenton, *led to 1st, wknd appr 5th, tld off 3 out*. . . . .(66 to 1 op 33 to 1) 4
2961 NEARLY A SCORE 5-10-9 J F Titley, *pld hrd, beh frm 3rd, tld off 4 out, hmpd 2 out*. . . . .(9 to 1 op 6 to 1 tchd 10 to 1) 5
1855 WESTERN PLAYBOY 5-11-0 V Slattery, *hld up, hdwy 5th, outpcd 3 out, poor 3rd whn f last*. . . . . (33 to 1 op 16 to 1) f

Dist: 8l, 25l, 24l, 6l. 4m 14.01s. a 25.01s (6 Ran).

(Lady Tennant), N J Henderson

4031 Horses Away Racing Club Handicap Chase Class E (0-115 5-y-o and up) £2,832 2m 110yds. . . . . (6:35)

3653* EVENING RAIN [86] 11-10-3 T Dascombe, *trkd ldr, led second to 5th, hrd rdn to ld last, all out*. . . . .(5 to 1 op 7 to 2) 1
2864^{3} THATS THE LIFE [83] 12-10-0 B Fenton, *led to second, led 5th, hrd rdn and hdd last, no extr r-in*. . .(4 to 1 tchd 5 to 1) 2
3828^{7} GLADYS EMMANUEL [83] 10-9-9 (5*) D J Kavanagh, *hld up, hdwy appr 4 out, one pace aftr nxt*. . . . .(7 to 2 op 4 to 1 tchd 3 to 1) 3
3685 TANGO'S DELIGHT [83] 9-10-0 V Slattery, *beh, some hdwy 5 out, nvr on terms*. . . . .(33 to 1 op 20 to 1) 4
3651^{4} BEAU BABILLARD [107] (bl) 10-11-10 M A Fitzgerald, *trkd ldrs, wknd 5 out*. . . . .(5 to 1 op 5 to 2) 5
3862^{2} BISHOPS CASTLE (Ire) [90] 9-10-7 J Frost, *hld up in rear, struggling frm 6th*. . . . (2 to 1 fav op 5 to 2 tchd 11 to 4) 6

Dist: 1¼l, 4l, 13l, 4l, 4l. 4m 4.90s. a 6.90s (6 Ran).

SR: 23/18/14/1/21/-/ (The Gardens Entertainments Ltd), R J Hodges

4032 Carl Nekola Memorial Handicap Hurdle Class C (0-130 4-y-o and up) £3,597 2¾m. . . . . (7:05)

3568 BRAVE TORNADO [130] 6-12-0 B Fenton, *hld up, rdn 4 out, led aftr nxt, pushed clr appr last*. . . . .(7 to 4 fav op 6 to 4 tchd 2 to 1) 1
3908^{6} MOVING OUT [109] 9-10-7 J F Titley, *led till hdd 4 out, rdn and ev ch whn mstk 2 out, no extr*. . . . . . (5 to 1 op 4 to 1) 2
3027* COUNTRY TARQUIN [102] 5-10-0 T Dascombe, *trkd ldrs, led 4 out, rdn and hdd aftr nxt, wknd*. . . . .(8 to 1 op 7 to 1 tchd 6 to 1) 3
923^{4} ECHO DE JANSER (Fr) [130] 5-12-0 R Greene, *f second, broke leg, dead*. . . . .(50 to 1 op 20 to 1) f
3677^{5} RHYTHM AND BLUES [102] 7-9-9 (5*) G Supple, *blun and uns rdr 4th*. . . . . (9 to 2 op 4 to 1 tchd 5 to 1) ur
3893^{2} BLASKET HERO [106] (bl) 9-10-4 G Tormey, *hld up, badly hmpd 4th, nvr gng wl aftr, beh whn mstk four out, broke leg, dead*. . . . .(3 to 1 op 4 to 1) pu
3881^{7} TOMMY COOPER [102] (bl) 6-10-0 E Byrne, *pld hrd, trkd ldr till wknd quickly appr 4 out, pulled up bef nxt*. . . . .(50 to 1 op 33 to 1) pu

Dist: 7l, 9l. 5m 19.00s. a 18.00s (7 Ran).

SR: 41/13/-/-/ (Miss B Swire), G B Balding

4033 Totnes And Bridgetown Novices' Hunters' Chase Class H (5-y-o and up) £1,030 2m 5f 110yds. . . . . (7:35)

KING TORUS (Ire) 7-11-9 (5*) Mr J Jukes, *al prmnt, led tenth, rdn 2 out, all out*. . . . .(11 to 8 fav op 6 to 4 tchd 7 to 4 and 2 to 1) 1
TICKET TO THE MOON 7-11-2 (7*) Mr J M Pritchard, *hld up in tch, hdwy to press wnr frm 4 out, no extr appr last*. . . . .(9 to 2 op 7 to 2) 2
FULL ALIRT 9-11-9 (7*) Miss S Young, *hld up in rear, hdwy 9th, one pace frm 3 out*. . . . . (14 to 1 op 10 to 1) 3
3885^{2} MISTER HORATIO 7-12-0 (7*) Mr M Lewis, *hld up, hdwy 9th, wknd appr 2 out*. . . . .(11 to 2 op 9 to 2) 4
3147* HERHORSE 10-11-9 (7*) Mr L Jefford, *hld up, hdwy whn hit 5 out, wkng when mstk 3 out*. . . . .(11 to 1 op 10 to 1 tchd 12 to 1) 5

MYHAMET 10-11-7 (7*) Mr N Harris, *hld up, hdwy 5 out, nvr nr to chal*................................(8 to 1 op 6 to 1) 6
NEWSKI EXPRESS 12-11-2 (7*) Mr G Shenkin, *f second*.
....(25 to 1 op 20 to 1) f
3857⁹ FLOWING RIVER (USA) (bl) 11-11-7 (7*) Mr N R Mitchell, *prmnt, led 4th to tenth, weakend quickly, tld off whn pld up bef 2 out*............................(33 to 1 op 20 to 1) pu
3832³ ANN'S AMBITION 6-11-7 (7*) Mr M Frith, *al beh, tld off whn pld up bef 2 out*.................(50 to 1 op 25 to 1) pu
3827 TOM'S GEMINI STAR 9-12-0 (7*) Mr T Dennis, *hld up, hdwy whn blun 4 out, pld up bef nxt*.......(10 to 1 tchd 11 to 1) pu
COMEDY GAYLE 10-11-7 (7*) Mr I Widdicombe, *al beh, tld off whn pld up aftr 9th*................(50 to 1 op 33 to 1) pu
FELLOW SIOUX 10-11-7 (7*) Mr I Dowrick, *pld hrd, prmnt till wknd tenth, tld off whn pulled up bef 2 out*.
....(14 to 1 op 10 to 1) pu
FRIENDLY VIKING 7-11-7 (7*) Mr R Darke, *al beh, tld off whn pld up aftr 9th*................(50 to 1 op 33 to 1) pu
3982⁴ BARROW STREET (v) 7-11-7 (7*) Mr J Tizzard, *led to 4th, weakend 9th, tld off whn pld up bef 2 out*.
....(50 to 1 op 33 to 1) pu
Dist: 1¾l, 9l, nk, 4l, nk. 5m 28.60s. a 26.60s (14 Ran).

(Nick Viney), Victor Dartnall

4034 Happy 50th Birthday Richard Brinsley Novices' Chase Class D (5-y-o and up) £3,403 2m 110yds (8:05)

3831 TIGHT FIST (Ire) 7-11-0 J F Titley, *trkd ldr, lft in ld 6th, hdd appr 4 out, led and pres 2 out, all out*.
....(13 to 8 op Evens tchd 7 to 4) 1
2991⁵ STRATTON FLYER 7-10-2 (7*) Mr R Widger, *lft cl second 6th, outpcd 3 out, rallied to go second r-in* (40 to 1 op 25 to 1) 2
3811⁴ RUN WITH JOY (Ire) 6-11-0 R Greene, *al prmnt, led appr 4 out, hdd 2 out, kpt on same pres*......(33 to 1 op 20 to 1) 3
3372⁷ STEER POINT 6-11-0 J Frost, *hld up, hdwy 5 out, ev ch till r-in and wknd appr last*........(9 to 1 op 8 to 1 tchd 10 to 1) 4
3829* LUCKY EDDIE 6-11-6 G Tormey, *in tch till hdwy appr 3 out*........................(4 to 1 fav op 7 to 4 tchd 2 to 1) 5
3861⁴ RUSTIC FLIGHT 10-10-7 (7*) M Griffiths, *beh whn jmpd slwly 7th, sn tld off*......................(20 to 1 op 16 to 1) 6
3826 TOM'S APACHE 8-11-0 Miss S Vickery, *pld hrd, sn clr, pulled up aftr 6th, lme*..........(4 to 1 op 7 to 2 tchd 9 to 2) pu
Dist: 1¼l, hd, 5l, 22l, dist. 4m 11.30s. a 13.30s (7 Ran).

(Mrs A M Davis), Miss H C Knight

4035 Blaze Of Glory Handicap Chase Class F (0-105 5-y-o and up) £1,944 3m 3f.........................(8:35)

3990² APACHEE FLOWER [80] 7-10-7 M A Fitzgerald, *al in cl tch and gng wl, wnt second 3 out, narrow ld nxt, kpt on und pres r-in*....................(9 to 4 fav op 5 to 2 tchd 11 to 4) 1
3926⁵ AMILLIONMEMORIES [82] 7-10-9 E Byrne, *hld up in rear, gd hdwy appr 4 out, chlgd 2 out, dsptd ld last, no extr nr finish*.
....(4 to 1 op 6 to 1) 2
3725 TIGER CLAW (Ire) [73] 11-10-2 R Greene, *hld up in mid-div, hdwy 3 out, one pace frm nxt*.........(10 to 1 op 5 to 1) 3
3833 LOUGHDOO (Ire) [73] 9-10-0 B Fenton, *al prmnt, led 3 out, hdd nxt, one pace*........(8 to 1 op 4 to 1 tchd 9 to 1) 4
3852³ PERSIAN VIEW (Ire) [97] 7-11-3 (7*) Mr R Wakley, *slwly away, in tch frm 4th, hdwy appr four out, weakend aftr nxt*.
....(6 to 1 op 7 to 2 tchd 8 to 1) 5
3407⁴ RISING'S LASS [73] 7-10-0 T Dascombe, *in tch to 8th, lost touch aftr*..........(9 to 1 op 8 to 1 tchd 10 to 1) 6
3883 WHITEBONNET [75] (bl) 7-9-13 (3*) Sophie Mitchell, *chsd ldr to 3 out, sn wknd*........(12 to 1 tchd 11 to 1) 7
3628² BAYLORD PRINCE (Ire) [73] 9-10-0 G Tormey, *rdn 6th, sn beh*.....................(20 to 1 op 16 to 1) 8
PURBECK POLLY [73] 7-9-7 (7*) M Griffiths, *in tch till wknd appr 4 out*..................(20 to 1 op 10 to 1) 9
3774⁵ NICK THE DREAMER [77] 12-9-11 (7*) N Willmington, *led till hdd 3 out, wknd quickly, tld off*......(16 to 1 op 10 to 1) 10
3909⁴ TUDOR TOWN [77] 9-10-4⁴ S Burrough, *pld hrd, in tch whn mstk 4th, wknd four out, tld off whn pulled up bef last*.
Dist: 1¼l, 2l, 1l, 8l, 8l, 7l, 5l, 9l, dist. 6m 42.40s. a 26.40s (11 Ran).

(John Tackley), H S Howe

WARWICK (good)
Saturday May 10th
Going Correction: PLUS 0.25 sec. per fur.

4036 Fusilier Handicap Hurdle Class E (0-115 4-y-o and up) £2,363 2m
.........................(5:20)

3886² MUIZENBERG [82] 10-10-4 A Thornton, *made all, sn clr, unchlgd*..................(7 to 2 op 3 to 1) 1
3844² ABOVE THE CUT (USA) [95] 5-11-3 C Llewellyn, *chsd wnr, rdn appr 2 out, styd on same pace*........(11 to 4 jt-fav op 2 to 1) 2
3731 SCHNOZZLE (Ire) [87] 6-10-9 G Bradley, *hld up, hdwy aftr 3 out, mstk nxt, sn rdn and no imprsn*...(8 to 1 op 12 to 1) 3

3894 BODANTREE [88] 6-10-10 J Culloty, *prmnt, outpcd 4 out, nvr dngrs aftrwards*...................(7 to 1 op 5 to 1) 4
3994⁴ SAINT CIEL (USA) [102] 9-11-10 Derek Byrne, *hld up, hdwy 4th, mstk nxt, wknd 2 out*...........(7 to 1 op 6 to 1) 5
3892 LUCKY ARCHER [92] 4-10-9 W Marston, *hld up, hdwy 4th, rdn 3 out, sn wknd*. (11 to 4 jt-fav op 9 to 4 tchd 3 to 1) 6
Dist: 9l, 1¼l, 2½l, 7l, nk. 3m 48.90s. a 9.90s (6 Ran).
SR: 17/21/11/9/16/1/

(Mrs Julia Owen), E H Owen Jun

4037 Flying Hackle Novices' Chase Class E (5-y-o and up) £2,770 2m....(5:50)

3528 ALPINE MIST (Ire) 5-10-5 (3*) Michael Brennan, *hld up, hdwy 6 out, chlgd 2 out, rdn to ld r-in, styd on wl*.
....(6 to 1 op 5 to 1 tchd 13 to 2) 1
3798⁵ VERDE LUNA 5-10-8 S McNeill, *chsd ldr til led 4th, hdd briefly aftr nxt, rdn and headed r-in, unbl to quicken*.
.......................(7 to 2 op 5 to 1 tchd 11 to 2 and 6 to 1) 2
3457² ALOSAILI 10-11-0 G Bradley, *al prmnt, rdn and mstk 2 out, styd on same pace*.............(14 to 1 op 33 to 1) 3
3949 SNOWY PETREL (Ire) (bl) 5-10-8 A Thornton, *chsd ldrs rdn 5 out, wknd 3 out*...(11 to 8 fav op 2 to 1 on tchd 6 to 4) 4
3974³ OLD REDWOOD 10-11-0 C Llewellyn, *led to 4th, led briefly aftr nxt, mstk four out sn wknd*......(6 to 1 op 10 to 1) 5
3903³ HUGH DANIELS 9-10-7 (7*) Miss A Dudley, *chsd ldrs, rcd keenly, wknd 6th*.............(20 to 1 tchd 25 to 1) 6
3620⁴ WHOD OF THOUGHT IT (Ire) 6-10-11 (3*) Mr C Bonner, *hld up in tch, blun and uns rdr 7th*.........(25 to 1 op 20 to 1) ur
3829⁴ LADY ROSEBURY 7-10-9 W Marston, *not jump wl, tld off whn refused 4th*.........(20 to 1 op 14 to 1 tchd 25 to 1) ref
2803 CUMBERLAND YOUTH 6-11-0 I Lawrence, *hld up, rdn and lost tch 6th, tld off and pld up bef 4 out*......(50 to 1) pu
Dist: 1½l, 5l, 15l, 9l, 23l. 4m 3.60s. a 11.60s (9 Ran).

(Catch-42), J G M O'Shea

4038 6th Of Foot Handicap Hurdle Class E (0-115 4-y-o and up) £2,352 2½m 110yds.........................(6:20)

3761 LORD MCMURROUGH (Ire) [110] 7-11-12 A P McCoy, *made all, sn wl clr, rdn and jmpd lft 2 out, all out*.....(9 to 4 jt-fav op 7 to 4) 1
3820 DESERT FORCE [88] (bl) 8-10-4¹ G Bradley, *chsd wnr 3rd, rdn appr 2 out, ran on wl, jst fld*...(12 to 1 op 6 to 1) 2
3641³ SUPER RAPIER (Ire) [84] 5-10-0 R Johnson, *chsd wnr to 3rd, remained hndy, outpcd 5 out, rallied 3 out, rdn nxt, styd on same pace*......................(5 to 1 op 9 to 1) 3
1477⁴ PRIME OF LIFE [89] 7-10-5 S McNeill, *hld up, rdn 5 out, sn lost tch*...............(9 to 1 op 7 to 1 tchd 10 to 1) 4
3844* CHIEF MOUSE [106] 4-11-2 J Osborne, *chsd ldrs till lost pl 6th, sn beh*...........(9 to 4 jt-fav tchd 11 to 4) 5
3871² CIRCUS COLOURS [98] 7-11-0 S Fox, *hld up, rdn appr 5 out, no imprsn*...................(7 to 1 op 4 to 1) 6
Dist: Sht-hd, 3l, 27l, 18l, 4l. 5m 6.60s. a 21.60s (6 Ran).

(J Neville), J Neville

4039 Blue Macaw 'National Hunt' Novices' Hurdle Class E (4-y-o and up) £2,761 2½m 110yds.........................(6:50)

ALBERMARLE (Ire) 6-11-0 J Osborne, *hld up, hdwy 6th, led aftr 3 out, sn clr, mstk nxt, eased r-in*.
.......................(6 to 1 op 7 to 1 tchd 9 to 1) 1
2951 GRATOMI (Ire) 7-11-0 S Fox, *strted slwly, hdwy 4 out, chsd wnr 2 out, kpt on*.....................(33 to 1) 2
3729⁴ ISIS DAWN 5-10-12 (3*) P Henley, *hld up, hdwy 5 out, wknd appr 3 out, lft 3rd last*.
.......................(11 to 4 fav op 5 to 2 tchd 3 to 1 and 7 to 2) 3
3097² SUPREME TROGLODYTE (Ire) 5-10-9 J R Kavanagh, *led to 4th, wknd four out*.........(14 to 1 op 10 to 1) 4
GAMAY 7-10-9 C Llewellyn, *prmnt to 5 out, sn no ch*.
....(20 to 1) 5
1735⁶ CROCKNAMOHILL (Ire) 6-11-0 W Marston, *chsd ldrs, drvn alng 5 out, sn wknd*.............(16 to 1 op 33 to 1) 6
3473⁵ DERRING FLOSS 7-10-2 (7*) Miss J Wormall, *in tch, chsd alng 5 out, sn wknd*................(33 to 1) 7
2123⁴ EDGE AHEAD (Ire) 7-11-0 R Dunwoody, *mid-div, rdn 5 out, sn lost tch*........................(10 to 1 op 5 to 1) 8
3639⁴ PEALINGS (Ire) 5-11-0 R Johnson, *chsd ldrs, rdn and wknd 4 out*.......................(14 to 1 op 8 to 1) 9
2277 TULLOW LADY (Ire) 6-10-9 M Brennan, *chsd ldrs, wknd 5 out*...............(20 to 1 op 16 to 1 tchd 25 to 1) 10
3534⁴ LABURNUM GOLD (Ire) 6-11-0 D Leahy, *led 4th, sn in tch, soon wknd, poor 3rd whn f last*.(5 to 1 op 9 to 2) f
HARINGTON HUNDREDS 7-11-0 A P McCoy, *al in rear, tld off and pld up bef 5 out*.......(20 to 1 tchd 25 to 1) pu
3312 BLAZING DOVE 6-11-0 A Thornton, *sn wl beh, tld off aftr 5th, broke blood vessel*..................(25 to 1) pu
3388⁵ MR BOJANGLES (Ire) 6-11-0 B Powell, *mid-div, rdn appr 5 out, sn beh, pld up bef 2 out*......(10 to 1 op 16 to 1) pu
3862³ BLOWING ROCK (Ire) 5-11-0 J Culloty, *prmnt to 5 out, tld off and pld up bef 2 out*.(7 to 1 op 5 to 1 tchd 8 to 1) pu
3405 ILEWINIT (Ire) 8-11-0 G Upton, *beh frm 6th, pld up bef 5 out*.......................(50 to 1) pu
3672⁶ BET WILTSHIRE 5-11-0 S Wynne, *sn wl beh, tld off and pld up bef 5 out*.............(20 to 1 tchd 25 to 1) pu
Dist: 7l, 28l, 2½l, 15l, ¾l, 20l, 11l, 6l, 30l. 5m 1.80s. a 16.80s (17 Ran).

564

(Robert Ogden), Capt T A Forster

4040 Willsford Handicap Chase Class C
(0-135 5-y-o and up) £4,597 3¼m
.... (7:20)

3753² MISS DISKIN (Ire) [100] 8-10-2 B Powell, wth ldr til led 7th, hit nxt, mstk tenth, hrd rdn r-in, all out.
..................(100 to 30 op 5 to 2 tchd 7 to 2) 1
2956 SOUNDS STRONG (Ire) [126] 8-12-0 R Johnson, hld up, hdwy 12th, jnd wnr 3 out, hrd rdn r-in, kpt on.
..................(11 to 2 op 5 to 2 tchd 5 to 1) 2
3932² HARRISTOWN LADY [103] (bl) 10-10-5 A P McCoy, prmnt, lost pl tenth, styd on frm 3 out.
..................(9 to 2 op 4 to 1 tchd 5 to 1) 3
3145⁴ ALLO GEORGE [110] 11-10-12 A Thornton, prmnt, jnd wnr 5 out, wknd aftr 3 out........................... (8 to 1) 4
3824³ MERRY PANTO (Ire) [98] 8-10-0 S McNeill, prmnt, rdn 6 out, sn wknd............. (11 to 1 op 8 to 1 tchd 12 to 1) 5
3790* GARRYLOUGH (Ire) [118] 8-11-6 R Dunwoody, made most to 7th, rdn appr 14th, sn wknd.
..................(5 to 2 fav op 9 to 4 tchd 11 to 4) 6
3790³ BIG BEN DUN [102] 11-10-4¹ G Bradley, chsd ldrs, mstk and lost pl 12th, drvn alng 14th, sn beh.
..................(10 to 1 op 8 to 1 tchd 11 to 1) 7
Dist: Sht-hd, dist, 2½l, 6l, 19l, 3l. 6m 37.20s. a 23.20s (7 Ran).
SR: 4/2/3/-/   (Martyn Forrester), R H Buckler

4041 Normandy Novices' Hunters' Chase
Class H (5-y-o and up) £991 3¼m
.... (7:50)

3967* PRINCE BUCK (Ire) 7-12-4 (3*) Mr P Hacking, made all, mstk second, styd on strly........... (6 to 4 on op 5 to 4 on) 1
TRUE FORTUNE 7-11-7 (7*) Mr D S Jones, al prmnt, chsd wnr 13th, rdn 3 out, sn btn.................(7 to 2 op 9 to 2) 2
DARTON RI 14-11-7 (7*) Mr J Maxse, prmnt, lost pl 6th, sn wl beh, no ch whn hmpd r-in, fnshd 4th, plcd 3rd.
..................(6 to 1 op 9 to 2) 3
3991 VERY DARING 7-11-7 (7*) Miss S Sharratt, chsd ldrs, rdn aftr 13th, sn wknd, fnshd 3rd, plcd 4th.... (20 to 1 op 16 to 1) 4
DAMERS TREASURE (bl) 11-11-7 (7*) Mr M Harris, chsd ldrs, mstk second, hit 11th, sn beh....... (16 to 1 op 10 to 1) 5
KELLYTINO 8-11-2 (7*) Mr P Scott, hld up, hdwy and in tch whn blun and uns rdr 12th...............(20 to 1 op 12 to 1) ur
POLYDEUCES 11-11-7 (7*) Capt R Inglesant, hld up in tch, jmpd rght 4th and 5th, chsd wnr nxt, wknd 12th, pld up bef 14th.........................(33 to 1 op 16 to 1) pu
BENTLEY MANOR 8-11-7 (7*) Mr G Hanmer, hld up, rdn and lost tenth, pld up bef 4 out.........(16 to 1 op 12 to 1) pu
Dist: 19l, dist, 3l, 20l. 6m 47.90s. a 33.90s (8 Ran).
                                                 (Mike Roberts), M J Roberts

4042 Arthur Hutt VC Memorial Standard
National Hunt Flat Class H (4,5,6-
y-o) £1,028 2m.................. (8:20)

ANDSUEPHI (Ire) 5-10-11 (7*) G Brace, chsd ldrs, shaken up o'r one furlong out, ran on to ld nr finish.
..................(16 to 1 op 12 to 1) 1
LUCY GLITTERS 5-10-8 (5*) A Bates, hld up, hdwy hfwy, led 3 fs out, rdn and hdd nr finish........... (10 to 1 op 8 to 1) 2
WINSTON RUN 5-10-11 (7*) F Bogle, hld up, hdwy o'r 4 fs out, rdn appr last, ran on.........................(16 to 1) 3
OI MOTHER (Ire) 5-10-10 (3*) R Massey, al prmnt, rdn and ev ch o'r one fs out, ran on one pace.
..................(11 to 10 fav op Evens tchd 6 to 4) 4
RUBY ROSA 5-10-6 (7*) J Mogford, hld up, hdwy hfwy, jnd ldrs 5 out, ran on one pace fnl 2 fs..... (20 to 1 op 16 to 1) 5
DARK HORSE 5-10-11 (7*) M Berry, hld up, hdwy o'r 3 fs out, hrd rdn over 2 out, nvr able to chal.
..................(14 to 1 op 10 to 1) 6
MELTON MADE (Ire) 4-10-10 (3*) Michael Brennan, chsd ldrs, led 5 fs out, hdd 3 out, sn rdn and btn.
..................(10 to 1 op 12 to 1 tchd 16 to 1) 7
TRUTHFULLY 4-10-3 (5*) X Aizpuru, nvr nr to chal.
..................(20 to 1 op 14 to 1) 8
SUMO 4-10-10 (3*) E Husband, mid-div, pushed alng o'r 6 fs out, nvr dngrs.........................(25 to 1 op 20 to 1) 9
BEACON LANE (Ire) 4-10-6 (7*) S O'Shea, hld up, hdwy o'r 5 fs out, wknd over 2 out...............(25 to 1 op 20 to 1) 10
HIGH IN THE SKY 4-10-6 (7*) D Yellowlees, hld up, hdwy hfwy, wknd 4 fs out.................(20 to 1 op 16 to 1) 11
DOUG ENG (Ire) 4-10-10 (3*) D Fortt, nvr trbld ldrs.
..................(5 to 1 op 4 to 1 tchd 6 to 1) 12
2831 WOODSTOCK WANDERER (Ire) 5-10-11 (7*) L Cummins, led to hfwy, wknd o'r 2 fs out. (8 to 1 op 10 to 1 tchd 6 to 1) 13
STORM HOME 5-11-4 Mr A Mitchell, prmnt, rdn o'r 4 fs out, sn wknd.........................(33 to 1 op 20 to 1) 14
CEDRIC TUDOR 4-10-13 Mr T McCarthy, prmnt, rdn 7 fs out, sn lost pl.........................(20 to 1 op 16 to 1) 15
STARDANTE (Ire) 5-11-1 (3*) P Henley, al beh.
..................(14 to 1 op 10 to 1 tchd 16 to 1) 16
MY FRIEND BILLY (Ire) 5-11-1 (3*) A Aspell, mid-div, drvn alng o'r 5 fs out, sn beh.........................(33 to 1) 17
DUNSTON SLICK 4-10-6 (7*) Miss L Boswell, chsd ldrs, led hfwy, hdd 6 fs out, wknd o'r 4 out............... (33 to 1) 18

POSTLIP ROYALE 4-10-1 (7*) Mr O McPhail, in tch to hfwy.
..................(50 to 1 op 33 to 1) 19
BRISTOL GOLD 4-10-6 (7*) L Suthern, prmnt, rdn hfwy, sn lost pl.........................(25 to 1 op 14 to 1) 20
2409 OLD MAN OF RAMAS 5-11-1 (3*) P Midgley, mid-div, rdn o'r 6 fs out, sn beh.........(20 to 1 op 12 to 1 tchd 25 to 1) 21
Dist: Nk, 2½l, 1¾l, 5l, 4l, 2l, 4l, ¾l, 3½l, 1½l. 3m 48.40s. (21 Ran).
                                      (Mrs J A Cohen), C P E Brooks

WORCESTER (good to soft)
Saturday May 10th
Going Correction: PLUS 1.25 sec. per fur.

4043 Holly Green Juvenile Novices' Hur-
dle Class E (4-y-o) £2,302 2m (2:10)

3905⁴ KINNESCASH (Ire) 11-12 M A Fitzgerald, made all, drw clr appr last, pushed out......(6 to 4 op Evens tchd 13 to 8) 1
3905 TIUTCHEV 10-12 J Culloty, hld up, prog 5th, rdn alng aftr 3 out, styd on to go second r-in, no imprsn on wnr.
..................(5 to 1 op 7 to 2 tchd 6 to 1) 2
3793³ INFLUENCE PEDLER 11-5 C Llewellyn, chsd wnr, chlgd 3 out, sn rdn, wknd appr last .... (11 to 10 on op 5 to 4) 3
3985 ROMANTIC WARRIOR 10-12 B Powell, wtd wth, rdn appr 3 out.........................(66 to 1 op 25 to 1) 4
3044 SUMMER PRINCESS 10-7 G Bradley, hld up, rdn appr 3 out, fdd, tld off.
..................(40 to 1 op 25 to 1 tchd 50 to 1 and 66 to 1) 5
Dist: 5l, 3l, 20l, dist. 4m 8.40s. a 28.40s (5 Ran).
SR: 14/-/   (D R James), P Bowen

4044 Great Malvern Novices' Chase Class
E (5-y-o and up) £2,977 2½m 110yds
.... (2:40)

1555⁵ WHO AM I (Ire) 7-11-0 A Thornton, hld up, clr order 6th, hit 8th, chalg whn pckd 3 out, led nxt, drvn out.
..................(16 to 1 op 10 to 1) 1
3716⁷ WITH IMPUNITY 8-11-7 R Johnson, in tch 5th, led 11th, blun 3 out, hdd nxt, rallied r-in, ran on.
..................(7 to 4 fav op 2 to 1 tchd 9 to 4) 2
3709⁷ THE BARGEMAN (NZ) 9-11-0 R Dunwoody, hld up, hdwy 7th, hit 4 out, sn rdn.........................(7 to 2 tchd 9 to 2) 3
3320⁴ CRANE HILL (bl) 7-11-0 W Marston, mstk second, nvr on terms.............(11 to 1 op 7 to 1 tchd 12 to 1) 4
3882³ DESERT BRAVE (Ire) 7-11-0 Richard Guest, hld up, took clr order 7th, wknd appr 4 out, no ch whn mstk last.
..................(16 to 1 op 10 to 1 tchd 50 to 1) 5
3912 ASTRAL INVASION (USA) 6-11-0 S Wynne, chsd ldr, led 4th, hit 8th, hdd 11th, 5th and wkng whn f 2 out.
..................(33 to 1 op 20 to 1 tchd 50 to 1) f
3191* HANGOVER 11-11-0 C Llewellyn, beh frm 8th, tld off whn pld up bef 2 out...........(10 to 1 op 8 to 1 tchd 12 to 1) pu
RICH LIFE (Ire) 7-11-7 M Richards, al beh, tld off whn pld up bef 11th.............(6 to 1 op 7 to 2 tchd 13 to 2) pu
3829 STEEL GOLD 7-10-10³ (7*) M R Burton, mstk second, al beh, tld off frm 6th, pld up bef 2 out.... (33 to 1 op 33 to 1) pu
3849⁸ NELL VALLEY 6-10-9 G Bradley, led to 4th, wknd quickly frm 6th, tld off whn pld up bef nxt....... (33 to 1 op 16 to 1) pu
Dist: 1½l, 12l, 9l, ¾l. 5m 28.80s. a 31.80s (10 Ran).
SR: 24/29/10/1/-/-/   (H Wellstead), R H Alner

4045 Horserace Betting Levy Board Hand-
icap Hurdle Class F (0-105 4-y-o and
up) £2,372 2m................. (3:10)

1705* STAY WITH ME (Fr) [98] 7-11-10 J Osborne, al prmnt, led 2 out, lft clr last, cmftbly.................(9 to 2 op 7 to 2) 1
3819 OUR ROBERT [92] (v) 5-11-4 T Eley, hld up, hdwy appr 3 out, badly hmpd last, ran on r-in........... (10 to 1 op 7 to 1) 2
3558 CLASSIC PAL (USA) [78] 6-10-4 D Skyrme, wtd wth, hdwy appr 3 out, sayed on r-in. (6 to 1 op 5 to 1 tchd 13 to 2) 3
3673² FONTANAYS (Ire) [94] (v) 9-10-13 (7*) R Hobson, prmnt, reminders and lost pl aftr 5th, styd on frm 2 out, lft second at last, one pace.......... (6 to 1 op 5 to 1 tchd 7 to 1) 4
3828⁸ MOLLIE SILVERS [76] 5-10-22 W McFarland, nvr nr to chal.
..................(50 to 1 op 20 to 1) 5
3459⁵ APACHE PARK (USA) [90] (bl) 4-10-11 D J Burchell, prmnt, led 3rd, hdd and mstk 3 out, wknd betw fnl 2.
..................(100 to 30 fav op 3 to 1) 6
3831⁵ EURO SINGER [102] 5-11-9 (5*) S Ryan, hld up beh ldrs, led 3 out to 2 out, sn rdn, second and held whn f last.
..................(13 to 2 op 7 to 2) 7
3886⁴ DAILY SPORT GIRL [82] 8-10-8 Mr J L Llewellyn, hld up, hdwy aftr 3 out, styd on frm 2 out, 3rd whn hmpd and uns rdr last.
..................(9 to 1 op 7 to 1) ur
3923⁴ INNOCENT GEORGE [82] 8-10-8 R Dunwoody, led to 3rd, wknd rpdly frm 5th, pld up and dismounted bef nxt.
..................(9 to 1 op 7 to 1 tchd 10 to 1) pu
3886 MR LOWRY [74] 5-10-0 S Wynne, hld up, brief effrt 3 out, sn btn, beh whn pld up bef nxt.
..................(20 to 1 op 16 to 1 tchd 25 to 1) pu
Dist: 4l, sht-hd, ½l, 1½l, 6l. 4m 8.80s. a 28.80s (10 Ran).
SR: 8/-/-/-/-/-/   (Mrs Sandra A Roe), C R Egerton

4046 Little Malvern Conditional Jockeys' Handicap Chase Class F (0–105 5-y-o and up) £2,827 2m 7f 110yds (3:40)

3739²	LAY IT OFF (Ire) [83] 8-10-6 L Aspell, *hld up, prog 9th, led and pckd tenth, hdd 12th, rgned ld nxt, lft clr last.* 1
	MARTELL BOY (NZ) [96] 10-11-5 P Henley, *prmnt, chalenging whn pckd 3 out, blun badly last, not reco'r.* .... (9 to 1 op 7 to 1 tchd 8 to 1) 2
3436	FARNEY GLEN [88] 10-10-4 (7*) D Jewett, *hld up, improved 11th, wknd appr 4 out.* ....(14 to 1 op 8 to 1) 3
3752⁴	COURT MASTER (Ire) [90] 9-10-13 R Massey, *prmnt, jmpd slwly second, led 12th to nxt, wknd appr 4 out.* ....(8 to 1 op 9 to 2) 4
3914⁴	NOVA CHAMP [87] 9-10-10 G F Ryan, *in tch, rdn appr 4 out, sn wknd...*(5 to 2 fav op 9 to 4 tchd 3 to 1 and 7 to 2) 5
3685	GOOD FOR A LAUGH [82] 13-10-5 O Burrows, *in tch till wknd 14th, tld off.* ....(20 to 1 op 16 to 1) 6
3914⁵	BOXING MATCH [77] 10-10-0 J Power, *chsd ldr, led 7th, hdd tenth, f nxt.* ....(40 to 1 op 33 to 1) f
3668³	NO FIDDLING (Ire) [82] 6-10-5 D Fortt, *beh till f 14th.* ....(4 to 1 op 11 to 2 tchd 7 to 1) f
2861	LITTLE-NIPPER [95] 12-11-4 J Magee, *not fluent, prmnt till blun 6th, wknd rpdly 9th, tld off whn pld up bef nxt.* ....(40 to 16 to 1 tchd 50 to 1) pu
3145²	JAILBREAKER [81] 10-10-4 D Salter, *hit 14th, al beh, tld off whn pld up bef 4 out...*(14 to 1 op 12 to 1 tchd 16 to 1) pu
3937⁷	TRUST DEED (USA) [88] (bl) 9-10-11 (6ex) X Aizpuru, *al beh, tld off whn pld up bef last.*..............(16 to 1 op 8 to 1) pu
3914	DONT TELL THE WIFE [105] (bl) 11-12-0 M Berry, *beh frm tenth, tld off whn pld up bef 2 out.* ....(25 to 1 op 20 to 1 tchd 33 to 1) pu
2745³	NEVADA GOLD [98] 11-11-7 Michael Brennan, *led to 7th, wknd rpdly 9th, tld off whn pld up bef nxt.* ....(20 to 1 op 14 to 1 tchd 25 to 1) pu
3895⁷	GOLDEN OPAL [77] 12-9-13⁶ (7*) J McDermott, *not fluent, hdwy 9th, wkng whn hit 13th, tld off whn hit 4 out, pld up bef nxt...* ....(33 to 1 op 20 to 1 tchd 40 to 1) pu
3193²	RIVER LEVEN [88] (bl) 8-10-11 Sophie Mitchell, *al beh, tld off whn pld up bef last.*..................(16 to 1 op 8 to 1) pu

Dist: 10, 13l, 13l, 4l, 4l, 21l. 6m 19.30s. (15 Ran).

(J G O'Neill), J G O'Neill

4047 INA Bearing Company Handicap Hurdle Class D (0–125 4-y-o and up) £2,903 3m ....(4:10)

3689²	THE TOISEACH (Ire) [117] (v) 6-12-0 J Osborne, *made all, given breather aftr 6th, styd on wl fnl 2.* ....(2 to 1 fav op 6 to 4 tchd 9 to 4) 1
3926²	DERRING BRIDGE [94] 7-10-5 R Johnson, *hld up, chsd wnr appr 8th, rdn approaching 2 out, no imprsn.* ....(11 to 4 op 4 to 1) 2
3557⁷	GENERAL MOUKTAR [107] 7-11-4 A P McCoy, *hld up and beh, prog 3 out, styd on r-in.* ....(3 to 1 op 5 to 2 tchd 7 to 2) 3
3926⁴	NEEDWOOD POPPY [89] 9-10-0 B Clifford, *nvr nr to chal.* ....(11 to 4 op 4 to 1) 4
	BULLENS BAY (Ire) [101] 8-10-12 B Powell, *beh frm 8th, tld off.* ....(16 to 1 op 12 to 1 tchd 20 to 1) 5
3689	SO PROUD [111] 12-11-8 R Dunwoody, *chsd wnr till appr 8th, sn wknd, tld off.*....................(20 to 1 op 12 to 1) 6

Dist: 6l, sht-hd, 6l, dist, 29l. 6m 21.90s. a 45.90s (6 Ran).

(T & J Vestey), J R Fanshawe

4048 Suckley Novices' Chase Class E (5-y-o and up) £3,455 2m 7f 110yds ....(4:40)

3716²	MACGEORGE (Ire) 7-12-0 R Dunwoody, *led second to 12th, rgned ld 4 out, all out.* (13 to 8 fav op 7 to 4 tchd 2 to 1) 1
3669¹	DREAM RIDE (Ire) 7-11-8 R Johnson, *hld up in tch, str chal und press frm 4 out, ran on.* (8 to 1 op 4 to 1 tchd 9 to 1) 2
3702⁹	LIEN DE FAMILLE (Ire) 7-11-8 A R Kavanagh, *prmnt, led 12th, pckd badly 14th, hdd 4 out, wknd nxt...*(33 to 1 op 12 to 1) 3
3718⁸	KAMIKAZE (bl) 7-11-8 J Osborne, *in tch, hit 7th, 4th whn hit four out, sn btn, tld off...*...(9 to 4 op 2 to 1 tchd 5 to 2) 4
3762⁶	CAREYSVILLE (Ire) 6-11-2 S Wynne, *mid-div, lost tch frm 13th, tld off.* ....(66 to 1 op 25 to 1) 5
2862⁶	BETTER FUTURE (Ire) (bl) 8-11-2 D Gallagher, *led to second, struggling frm 8th, tld off.* 6
2665⁵	STRAY HARMONY 7-10-11 D Walsh, *blun and uns rdr second.* ....(66 to 1 op 25 to 1 tchd 100 to 1) ur
3732³	MELNIK 6-11-8 G Upton, *al beh, tld off whn pld up bef 14th.* ....(16 to 1 op 10 to 1) pu
3669⁵	FIVE FLAGS (Ire) 9-11-2 Richard Guest, *not fluent, beh whn hit 7th, tld off whn pld up bef 4 out....*(33 to 1 op 16 to 1) pu
3612²	GLENGARRIF GIRL (Ire) (v) 7-10-11 A P McCoy, *not fluent, al beh, tld off whn pld up bef tenth.* ....(11 to 2 op 5 to 1 tchd 13 to 2 and 7 to 1) pu
2741	GERRY'S PRIDE (Ire) 6-11-2 S Curran, *blun tenth, al beh, tld off whn pld up bef 4 out.*............(66 to 1 op 25 to 1) pu

Dist: Nk, 19l, 24l, 3½l, dist. 6m 17.40s. (11 Ran).

(J H Watson), R Lee

4049 Longdon Intermediate National Hunt Flat Class H (Div I) (4,5,6-y-o) £1,413 2m ....(5:10)

	CONCHOBOR (Ire) 5-10-11 (7*) W Walsh, *gd prog o'r 4 fs out, led over 3 out, styd on strly.* (6 to 1 op 4 to 1 tchd 7 to 1) 1
	ROKER JOKER 6-10-13 (5*) Chris Webb, *trkd ldrs, chsd wnr frm 3 fs out, no imprsn.* (33 to 1 op 25 to 1 tchd 50 to 1) 2
	WHISTLING JAKE (Ire) 6-11-4 Mr R Bevis, *hld up, hdwy 4 fs out, styd on one pace fnl 2.* ....(10 to 1 op 7 to 1 tchd 12 to 1) 3
	SCALLY BLUE 6-11-5¹ Mr A H Crow, *led till o'r 3 fs out, sn btn.*..................(10 to 20 to 1 tchd 33 to 1) 4
	DEPUTY LEADER (Ire) 5-11-4 T C Murphy, *mid-div, prog 9 fs out, wknd o'r 4 out...*(4 to 1 fav tchd 5 to 1 and 11 to 2) 5
	DUNABRATTIN 4-10-8 (5*) S Ryan, *keen hold early, prmnt till hmpd and lost pl 7 fs out, rallied o'r 5 out, wknd over 4 out.* ....(8 to 1 op 6 to 1 tchd 9 to 1) 6
	ZENY THE NESTA 5-10-10 (3*) D Fortt, *nvr nr to chal.* ....(33 to 1 op 20 to 1) 7
	BARTON LIL 5-10-8 (5*) X Aizpuru, *nvr nr to chal.* ....(8 to 1 op 5 to 1 tchd 10 to 1) 8
	CASTLE OF LIGHT 6-11-4 Mr M Munrowd, *nvr better than mid-div...*........................(33 to 1 op 25 to 1) 9
	RARE GIFT (USA) 5-11-3¹ R Massey, *hld up in tch, wknd o'r 5 fs out.*..........(13 to 2 op 4 to 1 tchd 7 to 1) 10
3929	OUTRAGEOUS AFFAIR 5-10-10 (3*) J Magee, *nvr dngrs.* ....(50 to 1 op 33 to 1 tchd 66 to 1) 11
	RIGHT RON RUN 5-11-1 (3*) L Aspell, *beh fnl 6 fs.* ....(10 to 1 op 8 to 1 tchd 12 to 1) 12
	BERNERA 5-11-1 (3*) E Husband, *al beh.* ....(20 to 1 op 10 to 1) 13
	BABBLING BROOK (Ire) 5-10-11 (7*) Mr R Burton, *chsd ldrs till wknd 6 fs out.*......(16 to 1 op 12 to 1 tchd 20 to 1) 14
	CLOUDY BILL 5-10-11 (7*) Mr A Wintle, *nvr a dngr.* ....(6 to 1 op 4 to 1) 15
	BE BROADMINDED 5-10-11 (7*) Mr J Goldstein, *prmnt till wknd quickly hfwy, sn tld off, pld up 4 fs out.* ....(25 to 1 op 20 to 1 tchd 33 to 1) pu

Dist: 22l, 11l, 6l, ½l, 15l, ¾l, 14l, 3½l, 3½l, 8l. 4m 3.60s. (16 Ran).

(Scott Hardy Partnership), K C Bailey

4050 Longdon Intermediate National Hunt Flat Class H (Div II) (4,5,6-y-o) £1,402 2m ....(5:40)

	HOLLOA AWAY (Ire) 5-10-13 (5*) A Bates, *hld up, styd on frm o'r 2 fs out, led ins last, edgd lft last 50 yards.* ....(14 to 1 op 9 to 2) 1
3197²	COUNTRY HOUSE 6-10-10 (3*) Sophie Mitchell, *hld up, hdwy hfwy, outpcd 4 fs out, rallied 2 out, kpt on one pace.* 2
3661	GOING PRIMITIVE 6-11-1 (3*) D Fortt, *prmnt, led 3 fs out, hdd ins last, no extr.* ....(11 to 2 op 5 to 1 tchd 13 to 2) 3
3825	SWEET LITTLE BRIAR (Ire) 6-10-8 (5*) S Ryan, *hld up, hdwy o'r 4 fs out, ev ch over 3 out, btn appr last.* ....(25 to 1 op 10 to 1) 4
3561⁹	LIGHTENING STEEL 6-11-4 Mr A Phillips, *in tch till outpcd hfwy, styd on ag'n fnl 2 fs.*.........(33 to 1 op 16 to 1) 5
	PAMALYN 5-10-8 (5*) X Aizpuru, *prmnt till wknd o'r 3 fs out.* ....(10 to 1 op 12 to 1 tchd 7 to 1) 6
	LUCKY TOUCH 4-10-10 (3*) L Aspell, *prmnt, led o'r 4 fs out, hdd over 3 out, sn wknd.* ....(12 to 1 op 8 to 1) 7
	A VERSE TO ORDER 6-10-11 (7*) Mr J Goldstein, *nvr nrr.* 8
	THE KERRY LEDGEND (Ire) 4-10-6 (7*) C Scudder, *hld up, hdwy 5 fs out, ev ch 3 out, btn whn wndrd frm o'r 2 out.* ....(11 to 1 op 6 to 1 tchd 12 to 1 and 14 to 1) 9
	JO'S WEDDING 6-10-13 (5*) D Salter, *nvr on terms.* ....(33 to 1 op 14 to 1 tchd 40 to 1) 10
2810⁸	LADY BOCO 4-10-8 C Rae, *beh frm hfwy.* ....(50 to 1 op 20 to 1 tchd 66 to 1) 11
3197⁵	WHISKY WILMA 5-10-6 (7*) J Parkhouse, *al beh.* ....(33 to 1 op 16 to 1 tchd 50 to 1) 12
2642	PAPERPRINCE (NZ) 5-10-13 (5*) O Burrows, *in tch, effrt 4 fs out, sn wknd o'r 3 out.*......(33 to 1 op 12 to 1 tchd 50 to 1) 13
3197⁷	ABSOLUTE PROOF 4-10-1 (7*) J Power, *led till o'r 4 fs out, wknd quickly, tld off.* ....(16 to 1 op 10 to 1) 14
3616⁶	DANCING IN RIO 5-10-6 (7*) L Suthern, *prmnt, rdn 6 fs out, sn wknd, tld off...* (20 to 1 op 10 to 1 tchd 12 to 1) 15
	OBSIDIAN 15-11-1 (3*) R Massey, *beh frm hfwy, tld off.* ....(33 to 1 op 16 to 1) 16
	TURF SCORCHER 6-11-1 (3*) J Magee, *beh frm hfwy, tld off.* ....(25 to 1 op 16 to 1) 17

Dist: 1½l, ¾l, 6l, 2l, 2l, 1¾l, 10l, 2½l, 15l, 1¾l. 4m 10.50s. (17 Ran).

(W F Reid), Capt T A Forster

KILLARNEY (IRE) (yielding to soft) Sunday May 11th

4051 European Breeders Fund Mares Chase (5-y-o and up) £3,425 2¾m ....(2:40)

```
4005* GREENFLAG PRINCESS (Ire) 6-11-2 C F Swan, . (Evens fav)   1
3527⁸ MR K'S WINTERBLUES (Ire) (bl) 7-11-2 P Carberry, (8 to 1)  2
1242⁹ GRACEMARIE KATE (Ire) 8-10-9 (7*) M D Murphy, (12 to 1)   3
1462  KENTUCKY BABY (Ire) 7-11-8 C O'Dwyer, .........(9 to 2)   4
3392²  HERSILIA (Ire) 6-11-8 F J Flood, ..................(11 to 4)  f
3837  BOWES LADY (Ire) 6-10-13 (3*) G Cotter, .........(33 to 1)   f
Dist: Dist, 12l, 15l. 6m 5.70s. (6 Ran).
```
(Yawl Bay Seafoods Ltd), James Joseph Mangan

4052 Killarney Towers Hotel Maiden Hurdle (5-y-o and up) £3,425 2m 1f
.... (3:10)

```
3547⁴ CAVALIER D'OR (USA) 6-12-0 F Woods, .........(6 to 4 fav)   1
3769⁹ ABORIGINAL (Ire) 5-11-13 T P Treacy, ................(7 to 2)  2
      ARTY GREY (Ire) 7-11-6 J Shortt, ....................(20 to 1)  3
3889²  HONEY TRADER 5-11-5 P Carberry, .................(5 to 2)  4
3816  POWER CORE (Ire) 7-11-6 C F Swan, ...............(20 to 1)  5
3878⁵ ROSE OF STRADBALLY (Ire) 6-10-12 (3*) K Whelan,
      ................................................(10 to 1)  6
      THE WELL (Ire) 6-10-8 (7*) L A Hurley, ............(20 to 1)  7
3608  CAME AWAY (Ire) 6-11-1 J R Barry, ................(25 to 1)  8
4006  CEASERS REIGN (Ire) 5-11-5 T J Mitchell, .........(20 to 1)  9
3627  SCREEN LEADER (Ire) 5-11-5 F J Flood, ...........(20 to 1)  10
      SHANNON LIGHT (Ire) 5-11-5 P A Roche, ..........(20 to 1)  11
1193  AVALIN (Ire) 6-10-8 (7*) Mr A J O'Gorman, .......(25 to 1)  12
3816⁹ DAWN TO DUSK (Ire) 6-10-13 (7*) D McCullagh, . (20 to 1)  13
3336  RAY LORD (Ire) 6-11-6 K F O'Brien, ................(25 to 1)  14
3083  LADY DE HATTON (Ire) 5-10-9 (5*) P Morris, .......(20 to 1)  15
      MARINER'S TALE (Ire) 6-10-8 (7*) B J Geraghty, ..(14 to 1)  16
3878  RUSHING BYE (Ire) 6-11-6 C O'Dwyer, ..............(20 to 1)  17
      HANDS KNEES AND (Ire) 6-11-1 D H O'Connor, ..(20 to 1)  18
2754  ZACOPANI (Ire) 5-11-5 D J Casey, ...................(20 to 1)  19
434  CARNACREEVA GANE (Ire) 6-11-1 A J O'Brien, ..(12 to 1)  pu
Dist: 4l, 2½l, 3l, 7l. 4m 23.90s. (20 Ran).
```
(John P McManus), A L T Moore

4053 Randles/Nissan Beginners Chase (4-y-o and up) £3,425 2½m ...... (3:40)

```
3838²  CHATTERBUCK (Ire) 8-12-0 C O'Dwyer, ........ (5 to 4 on)   1
3835⁴ ECLIPTIC MOON (Ire) 7-12-0 T P Treacy, ...........(9 to 2)  2
1841  MAYASTA HOLME (Ire) 8-11-7 (7*) D A McLoughlin, ..(9 to 1)  3
      MUIR STATION (USA) 9-11-7 (7*) J E Casey, .......(7 to 1)  4
3344⁴ NIGHTMAN 8-12-0 T J Mitchell, ....................(8 to 1)  5
907  SHANRUE (Ire) 7-11-11 (3*) G Cotter, ...............(9 to 1)  6
3748²  GLENARD LAD (Ire) 9-11-7 (7*) Mr W Ewing, .....(12 to 1)  7
      CHATEAU ELAN (Ire) 6-12-0 D T Evans, ...........(20 to 1)  8
3818  HOLLOW FINGER (Ire) 6-12-0 D H O'Connor, .....(14 to 1)  pu
Dist: 15l, 15l, 4l, 25l. 5m 26.20s. (9 Ran).
```
(Mountrose Syndicate), J T R Dreaper

4054 Murphys Irish Stout Handicap Hurdle (Listed) (4-y-o and up) £16,250 2m 1f..............................(4:10)

```
3879⁵ BOB THE YANK (Ire) [-] 7-10-6 J Shortt, ..........(10 to 1)   1
3784⁴ SAVING BOND (Ire) [-] 5-10-7 B J Geraghty, .......(9 to 1)  2
3788⁵ SAMBARA (Ire) [-] 6-11-3 D J Casey, ................(6 to 1)  3
3086  MAYASTA (Ire) [-] 7-11-3 C O'Dwyer, ........ (11 to 4 fav)  4
3551⁶ REASILVIA (Ire) [-] 7-10-6 M D Murphy, .............(7 to 1)  5
3607³ TAITS CLOCK (Ire) [-] 8-10-0 K Whelan, ...........(12 to 1)  6
3766⁴ MYSTICAL CITY (Ire) [-] 7-12-0 P Morris, ...........(11 to 1)  7
3767⁷ JUST LITTLE [-] 5-11-7 P Carberry, ................(10 to 1)  8
3788  BLACK QUEEN (Ire) [-] 6-10-13 A J O'Brien, ........(4 to 1)  9
3890²  I REMEMBER IT WELL (Ire) [-] (bl) 5-10-0 M P Hourigan,
      ................................................(10 to 1)  10
3890*  COLM'S ROCK (Ire) [-] 6-11-2 (5ex) C F Swan, ......(6 to 1)  f
Dist: 7l, 5l, 5½l, ½l. 4m 17.60s. (11 Ran).
```
(R Phelan), P T Flavin

4055 Michael Lynch Plant Hire Handicap Chase (4-y-o and up) £3,425 2m 1f
.... (5:10)

```
3944⁷ HANNIES GIRL (Ire) [-] 8-10-10 (7*) L J Fleming, ..(6 to 1)   1
3645²  PERSIAN POWER (Ire) [-] 9-10-9 (7*) B J Geraghty,
      ................................................(7 to 2 fav)  2
3624  SANDY FOREST LADY (Ire) [-] 8-10-0 (3*) K Whelan,
      ................................................(10 to 1)  3
3838⁸ TIME AND CHARGES (Ire) [-] 7-11-0 C O'Dwyer, ..(11 to 2)  4
3420⁸ THE DASHER DOYLE (Ire) [-] 9-11-1 D J Casey, .....(4 to 1)  5
3340⁶ NORTHERN ACE [-] 11-9-7 W Slattery, ..............(7 to 1)  6
3954  MINSTREL FIRE (Ire) [-] 9-11-7 (7*) M D Murphy, ....(7 to 1)  7
3784  ANOTHER COURSE (Ire) [-] 9-10-7 D H O'Connor, ..(8 to 1)  8
3839⁶ RICH TRADITION (Ire) [-] 9-10-8 (3*) G Cotter, ......(6 to 1)  f
Dist: 1½l, 10l, 4l, 7l. 4m 25.00s. (9 Ran).
```
(Michael L Flynn), F Flood

4056 Kerry Petroleum I.N.H. Flat Race (4-y-o) £3,425 2m................ (5:40)

```
      AZINTER (Ire) 11-5 Mr J P Dempsey, ...........(10 to 1)   1
2905⁵ COULDN'T SAY (Ire) 11-5 (5*) Mr A C Coyle, .......(5 to 1)  2
      LORD OF THE CHASE (Ire) 11-10 Miss M Olivefalk, ..(8 to 1)  3
3755⁴ FIDALUS (Ire) 11-3 (7*) Mr M T Hartrey, ............(4 to 1)  4
3415⁸ MULTEEN JET (Ire) 11-3 (7*) Mr S P Hennessy, ....(20 to 1)  5
```

```
3345⁹ ARTIQUE FISH (Ire) 11-3 (7*) Mr K R O'Ryan, .....(12 to 1)   6
      10-12 (7*) Mr A J Dempsey, .....................(14 to 1)  7
3755  CONNIGAR BAY (Ire) 11-3 (7*) Mr P J Crowley, ...(12 to 1)  8
      SMOOTH MELODY (Ire) 11-10 Mr D Marnane, .....(12 to 1)  9
      TED DUGAL (Ire) 11-3 (7*) Mr G Kearns, ............(5 to 1)  10
      EURO PARADE (Ire) 11-3 (7*) Mr M J Walsh, .......(14 to 1)  pu
2518  THE KERRY REBEL (Ire) 11-3 (7*) Miss C Lambert, (20 to 1)  pu
Dist: 2l, 10l, 3½l, 8l. 4m 20.40s. (12 Ran).
```
(Dundalk Racing Club), John M Oxx

WOLVERHAMPTON (good)
Sunday May 11th
Going Correction: NIL

4057 Wolverhampton's Jumping Again Novices' Chase Class D (5-y-o and up) £4,902 2m............... (3:10)

```
3794²  SUBLIME FELLOW (Ire) 7-11-12 M A Fitzgerald, made all, sn
      clr, hit 5 out, lft wl clear 2 out, unchlgd.
      ...........(7 to 4 on op 6 to 4 on tchd 11 to 8 on)   1
3927⁴ THE FENCE SHRINKER 6-11-0 D Walsh, chsd wnr second till
      wknd 5 out, lft remote second 3 out................(20 to 1)  2
3821*  DARING PAST 7-11-8 R Garritty, mstks, chsd wnr till hit
      second, wnt second ag'n 6 out, clsg whn l 3 out.
      ...........................(15 to 8 op 5 to 4)  f
3970⁷ MOOR DANCE MAN 7-11-0 Gary Lyons, in tch whn blun and
      uns rdr 4th............................(25 to 1 op 33 to 1)  ur
Dist: Dist. 4m 16.50s. (4 Ran).
```
(Rory McGrath), N J Henderson

4058 New Chase Course Handicap Chase Class B (5-y-o and up) £17,348 3m 1f
.... (3:40)

```
3701³ CARIBOO GOLD (USA) [114] (bl) 8-10-3 J Osborne, hld up,
      hdwy 12th, led 3 out, clr appr last.
      ...................(100 to 30 op 2 to 1 tchd 7 to 2)   1
3826*  KENMORE-SPEED [113] 10-10-2† Richard Guest, chsd ldr,
      led 5 out, hdd 3 out, wknd appr last.
      ...................(9 to 4 fav op 9 to 4 tchd 5 to 2)  2
3924*  COURT MELODY (Ire) [121] (bl) 9-10-10 A P McCoy, prmnt,
      hmpd 3rd, mstk 6 out, wknd 4 out.......(3 to 1 op 4 to 1)  3
3830*  HAWAIIAN YOUTH (Ire) [111] 9-10-0 D Gallagher, led to sec-
      ond, blun and lost pl nxt, beh frm 6th... (7 to 1 op 8 to 1)  4
4014²  STATELY HOME (Ire) [135] 6-11-10 R Johnson, led second, sn
      clr, hdd 5 out, wkng whn l 3 out.
      ...................(13 to 2 op 4 to 1 tchd 7 to 1)  f
3711⁷ GLEMOT (Ire) [130] 9-11-5 G Bradley, hld up in tch, drvn alng
      5 out, wknd nxt, pld up bef 3 out......(12 to 1 op 10 to 1)  pu
Dist: 18l, 22l, 21l. 6m 41.70s. (6 Ran).
```
(Mrs Sharon C Nelson), K C Bailey

KILLARNEY (IRE) (yielding to soft)
Monday May 12th

4059 European Breeders Fund (Mares) Maiden Hurdle (5-y-o and up) £3,425 2½m....................... (5:30)

```
3834²  THE GREY MARE (Ire) 8-11-7 (7*) Mr P Fahey, ......(4 to 1)   1
3343²  LADY ARGYLE (Ire) 6-12-0 F J Flood, ...............(10 to 1)  2
3834  CORYROSE (Ire) 5-11-13 C F Swan, .........(11 to 8 fav)  3
4005⁴ SHUIL NA MHUIRE (Ire) 7-11-7 (7*) J E Casey, ....(10 to 1)  4
3705²  NEWBERRY ROSE (Ire) 5-11-10 (3*) Mr W M O'Sullivan,
      ................................................(7 to 1)  5
3835⁹ CONNA BRIDE LADY (Ire) 5-11-13 P Carberry, ....(16 to 1)  6
3955  GAIN CONTROL (Ire) 8-11-11 (3*) G Cotter, ........(25 to 1)  7
3952⁸ LOFTUS BELLE (Ire) 5-11-13 D J Casey, .............(10 to 1)  8
3834  BE THE ONE (Ire) 6-11-11 (3*) K Whelan, ..........(14 to 1)  9
3834⁶ NAN'S PET (bl) 7-12-0 F Woods, ...................(14 to 1)  10
3955⁸ BALLINREE (Ire) 6-12-0 T P Treacy, ................(10 to 1)  11
1777  JARSUN QUEEN (Ire) 5-11-6 (7*) L J Fleming, .....(20 to 1)  pu
3429⁷ BURREN VALLEY (Ire) 6-11-7 (7*) M D Murphy, ....(25 to 1)  pu
2525  ROMANCEINTHEDARK (Ire) (bl) 7-12-0 T J Mitchell,
      ................................................(20 to 1)  pu
Dist: 3½l, 5½l, 2½l, 3½l. 5m 2.50s. (14 Ran).
```
(Seamus Fahey), Seamus Fahey

4060 Hotel Dunloe Castle Handicap Hurdle (0-102 4-y-o and up) £3,425 2m 1f.................................... (6:00)

```
3180  MIRACLE ME (Ire) [-] 5-12-0 F Woods, .........(5 to 2 fav)   1
3817⁴ PHAREIGN (Ire) [-] 6-11-1 (7*) J M Maguire, ........(7 to 1)  2
3626  LADY OF GRANGE (Ire) [-] 5-10-8 F J Flood, ........(12 to 1)  3
2855⁵ ROBSERA (Ire) [-] 6-11-6 C F Swan, ................(5 to 1)  4
2640  FONTAINEROUGE (Ire) [-] 7-10-1 (7*) M D Murphy, (15 to 2)  5
2366  TEARDROP (Ire) [-] 5-11-2 J Shortt, ...............(14 to 1)  6
3223  BRIDGES DAUGHTER (Ire) [-] 6-11-1 P A Roche, ...(9 to 2)  7
3626  ASTRID (Ire) [-] 6-9-4 (3*) G Cotter, ................(20 to 1)  8
1617⁶ CARRICK GLEN (Ire) [-] 6-10-13 C O'Dwyer, .......(9 to 1)  9
3415⁹ KEEP RUNNING (Ire) [-] 4-10-6 (7*) D W O'Sullivan, (8 to 1)  10
Dist: 5l, hd, 4½l, 10l. 4m 8.40s. (10 Ran).
```

567

(Mrs D P Magnier), James Joseph Mangan

4061 Laurels Hunters Chase (5-y-o and up) £3,425 3m...............(7:00)

1016[4] LUCKY TOWN (Ire) 6-11-4 Mr R Walsh,..... (11 to 10 fav) 1
3888[9] PRAYON PARSON (Ire) 9-10-11 (7*) Mr D P Daly,.. (20 to 1) 2
741[9] ROSETOWN GIRL (Ire) 6-10-6 (7*) Mr L J Temple,.. (7 to 1) 3
TACK ROOM LADY (Ire) 6-10-6 (7*) Mr R Flavin,...(25 to 1) 4
4005[5] UPSHEPOPS (Ire) 9-10-8 (5*) Mr Brian Moran,.... (20 to 1) 5
3935 SANDFAIR (Ire) 7-10-6 (7*) Mr C A Murphy,....... (25 to 1) 6
GAELIC GLEN (Ire) 7-10-11 (7*) Mr E Gallagher,... (25 to 1) 7
GAYE BARD (Ire) 8-10-11 (7*) Mr P Cashman,.....(14 to 1) 8
BUILDERS LINE (Ire) 9-10-13 Mr M Phillips,...... (25 to 1) 9
2869* YES BOSS (Ire) 7-11-1 (5*) Mr G Elliott,..............(5 to 1) f
PHARWAYS (Ire) 7-10-11 (7*) Mr Damien Murphy, (25 to 1) f
3935[3] RADICAL-TIMES (Ire) (bl) 7-10-11 (7*) Mr Paul Moloney, ...(20 to 1) f
3447[7] TWO IN TUNE (Ire) 9-10-11 (7*) Mr K O'Sullivan,....(8 to 1) ur
2523[9] TEA BOX (Ire) 6-11-4 Mr P Fenton,.............. (16 to 1) ur
LOOKING AHEAD (Ire) 9-10-6 (7*) Mr P J Crowley, (25 to 1) pu

Dist: 12l, 4½l, 1l, 14l. 6m 4.60s. (15 Ran).

(Mrs Noreen McManus), E Bolger

4062 Killarney Racegoers Club INH Flat Race (6-y-o and up) £3,425 2m 1f ....(8:30)

3343[8] DON'T WASTE IT (Ire) 7-11-2 (7*) Mr A FitzGerald, (10 to 1) 1
3416[5] TENDER SITUATION 6-11-7 (7*) Mr Paul Moloney,..(5 to 2) 2
3818[5] AS AN SLI (Ire) 6-11-2 (7*) Mr D F Barry,..........(14 to 1) 3
CARBON WOOD (Ire) 7-11-7 (7*) Mr C A Murphy, (12 to 1) 4
3955[3] SARAH BLUE (Ire) 7-11-2 (7*) Mr K R O'Ryan,.... (10 to 1) 5
2675[5] PRIZE OF PEACE (Ire) 7-11-2 (7*) Mr M T Hartrey, (10 to 1) 6
2906[5] MR MAGNETIC (Ire) 6-12-0 Mr P Fenton,.........(10 to 1) 7
3818[3] MERRY CHIEFTAIN (Ire) 8-11-7 (7*) Mr B Hassett, (12 to 1) 8
SPRING BEAU (Ire) 6-12-0 Mr R Walsh,..........(10 to 1) 9
2276[3] GARRYHILL CHOICE (Ire) 6-11-11 (3*) Mr P English, ...(13 to 8 fav) 10
538[8] HIGH MOAT (Ire) 7-11-11 (3*) Mr W Cronin,....... (14 to 1) 11
3880[9] HAZEL HONEY (Ire) 6-11-2 (7*) Mr I Amond,...... (14 to 1) 12
3336 PAT BARRY (Ire) 6-11-2 (7*) Mr W Ewing,......... (33 to 1) 13
3965 ORANGE JUICE (Ire) 7-11-7 (7*) Mr K Kirwan,.....(20 to 1) 14
ROCK ON GIRL (Ire) 7-11-2 (7*) Miss L E A Doyle, (25 to 1) pu

Dist: ½l, 14l, nk, 3½l. 4m 5.50s. (15 Ran).

(T A O'Doherty), Michael Hourigan

TOWCESTER (soft (races 1,3,6), good to soft (2,4,5))
Monday May 12th
Going Correction: PLUS 1.00 sec. per fur. (races 1,3,6), PLUS 0.80 (2,4,5)

4063 Christie & Co Surveyors, Valuers And Agents Selling Hurdle Class G (4 - 7-y-o) £1,810 2m...........(5:45)

3973* THE FLYING DOCTOR (Ire) 7-11-6 W McFarland, *hld up in tch, clsg whn blun 3 out, rallied bef nxt, drw clr.* (15 to 8 jt-fav op 11 to 10 tchd 2 to 1) 1
3946[2] STERLING FELLOW 4-10-2 (7*) Mr S Durack, *hld up in rear, hdwy to challege appr 2 out, rdn and wknd bef last.* ....(15 to 8 jt-fav op 3 to 1) 2
3931[2] SUMMER VILLA (bl) 5-10-9 W Marston, *lft in ld 3rd, rdn and hdd appr 2 out, wknd......* (4 to 1 op 3 to 1 tchd 9 to 2) 3
ULTIMATE WARRIOR 7-11-0 M Richards, *in tch, jmpd rght 1st, wnt second 3 out, rdn and sn wknd.* ....(6 to 1 op 5 to 1 tchd 13 to 2 and 7 to 1) 4
3931[5] RENO'S TREASURE (USA) 4-10-4 J Supple, *led till hdd appr 3rd, wknd aftr nxt..*................. (66 to 1 op 25 to 1) 5
2625 ESPLA 6-10-11 (3*) J Magee, *wnt into ld bef ran out 3rd.* .... (20 to 1 op 10 to 1) ro
3948[5] GREEN KING (bl) 5-11-0 S McNeill, *whipped round strt, in tch frm second, wknd appr 5th, tld off whn pld up bef 2 out.* .... (16 to 1 op 14 to 1 tchd 25 to 1) pu

Dist: 11l, 15l, 1½l, 8l. 4m 8.30s. a 25.30s (7 Ran).

(The Rumble Racing Club), G B Balding

4064 Hartwell Land Rover Hunters' Chase Class H (5-y-o and up) £1,674 2m 110yds...................(6:15)

3851[5] NOT MY LINE (Ire) 8-11-11 (5*) Mr A Sansome, *led to 5th, led 7th, styd on wl.*........(14 to 1 op 10 to 1 tchd 16 to 1) 1
3916 MY YOUNG MAN 12-11-6 (7*) Mr E James, *hdwy 3rd, led 5th to 7th, hit 3 out, no headway aftr.* ....(11 to 4 op 5 to 2 tchd 100 to 30) 2
3858 NECTANEBO (Ire) 9-11-9 (7*) Mr M Frith, *mstks, hld up in rear, hdwy frm 4 out, one pace from 2 out.* ....(8 to 1 op 5 to 1 tchd 9 to 1) 3
FELTHAM MISTRESS 7-11-1 (7*) Mr E Babington, *hld up, hdwy 4 out, rdn appr 2 out, one pace.* (66 to 1 op 25 to 1) 4
3916* YQUEM (Ire) 7-11-9 (7*) Mr N R Mitchell, *in tch till wknd quickly appr 2 out..*.................(2 to 1 fav op 5 to 2) 5
AL HASHIMI 13-11-6 (7*) Mr N Ridout, *nvr on terms.* ....(25 to 1 op 16 to 1) 6
3733 EMERALD RULER 10-11-6 (7*) Mr P Cowley, *in tch, rdn 4 out, sn wknd.*............ (20 to 1 op 16 to 1 tchd 25 to 1) 7
3851[9] KILLIMOR LAD 10-11-6 (7*) Miss S Samworth, *al beh. y* .... (50 to 1 op 25 to 1) 8
SHUIL SAOR 10-11-6 (7*) Mr J Saville, *al beh, tld off.* .... (66 to 1 op 33 to 1) 9
NO WORD 10-11-6 (7*) Mr I Baker, *al beh, tld off.* .... (66 to 1 op 25 to 1) 10
DRIVING FORCE (bl) 11-11-6 (7*) Mr A Charles-Jones, *prmnt to 7th, tld off whn pld up bef last.* .... (9 to 1 op 7 to 1 tchd 10 to 1) pu
3499[3] HICKELTON LAD 13-11-6 (7*) Mr S Durack, *al beh, tld off whn pld up bef 2 out.*........ (12 to 1 op 9 to 1 tchd 14 to 1) pu
3723 KING OF SHADOWS 10-11-6 (7*) Mr S Prior, *prmnt to 5th, tld off whn pld up bef 3 out.*............. (33 to 1 op 20 to 1) pu
3916[2] FAMILIAR FRIEND (bl) 11-11-6 (7*) Mr L Lay, *prmnt till wknd quickly 3 out, pld up bef last.* .... (9 to 1 op 7 to 1 tchd 10 to 1) pu
3723[2] DALAMETRE 10-11-6 (7*) Mr M Munrowd, *beh frm 6th, tld off whn pld up bef last.*.............. (10 to 1 op 7 to 1) pu
LUCKY LANDING (Ire) 8-11-6 (7*) Mr Andrew Martin, *al towards rear, tld off whn pld up bef last.* .... (50 to 1 op 33 to 1) pu

Dist: 8l, 10l, ¾l, 2l, 4l, 1l, 7l, 12l, 15l. 4m 19.00s. a 22.00s (16 Ran).
SR: 14/3/-/-/-/-/ (P C Caudwell), Andy Morgan

4065 Shoosmiths Spring Handicap Hurdle Class F (0-105 4-y-o and up) £2,407 2m 5f.......................(6:45)

3872[2] NORDIC SPREE (Ire) [83] (v) 5-10-10 A P McCoy, *led to 3rd, led 5th, quickened 7th, rdn 2 out, drvn clr appr last.* ....(3 to 1 tchd 7 to 2) 1
3001[3] LUKE WARM [76] 7-10-0 (3*) Sophie Mitchell, *trkd ldrs wnt second 4 out, hrd rdn 2 out, no imprsn...* (7 to 1 op 4 to 1) 2
3975[3] CAMBO (USA) [82] 11-10-9 M Richards, *trkd ldr, led 3rd to 5th, rdn and wknd 2 out...*............. (7 to 2 op 5 to 2) 3
3554* A S JIM [74] 6-10-1 V Slattery, *hld up, hdwy appr 3 out, btn nxt.* ....(7 to 2 op 9 to 4) 4
3735[2] MOUNTAIN PATH [98] 7-11-11 M A Fitzgerald, *hld up, effrt 7th, wakened appr 3 out, tired whn jmpd lft nxt, tld off.* ....(9 to 4 fav op 2 to 1 tchd 11 to 4) 5

Dist: 6l, ¾l, sht-hd, 29l. 5m 42.50s. a 43.50s (5 Ran).

(Roger John Jones), G L Moore

4066 Land Rover Gentlemans Championship Hunters' Chase Class H (5-y-o and up) £4,162 3m 1f......... (7:15)

MAGNOLIA MAN 11-11-2 (7*) Mr N Harris, *hld up, steady hdwy frm 11th, led appr 2 out, styd on strly.* ....(9 to 4 op 6 to 4 tchd 5 to 2) 1
LUCKY CHRISTOPHER 12-11-9 (5*) Mr G Tarry, *al in tch, trkd ldr, short of room and swtchd lft on bend appr 2 out, rdn and kpt on one pace....*(7 to 4 fav tchd 15 to 8 and 13 to 8) 2
LUPY MINSTREL 12-11-11 (7*) Mr A Parker, *led to 4th, led 8th till hdd appr 2 out, rdn and kpt on one pace.* ....(8 to 1 op 4 to 1) 3
THE GENERAL'S DRUM 10-11-7 (7*) Mr K Heard, *hld up in rear, mstk 6th, wknd 4 out, tld off.* ....(9 to 4 op 2 to 1 tchd 5 to 2) 4
SYRUS P TURNTABLE 11-11-2 (7*) Mr J Saville, *prmnt, reminders aftr 9th, sn wknd, tld off whn pld up bef last.* .... (33 to 1 op 10 to 1) pu
SECRET TRUTH 8-10-11 (7*) Mr Andrew Martin, *mstk 1st, led 4th to 8th, wakened quickly, tld off whn pld up bef 11th.* ....(33 to 1 op 16 to 1 tchd 40 to 1) pu

Dist: 5l, 6l, 30l. 6m 47.70s. a 35.70s (6 Ran).

(Mrs D B Lunt), Ms D Cole

4067 Mulberry Insurance Novices' Chase Class E (5-y-o and up) £3,104 3m 1f ....(7:45)

3914[4] BALLYDOUGAN (Ire) (v) 9-11-1 D Walsh, *slwly away,and lost 20 ls strt, rdn and hdwy appr 8th, led last, swrvd badly lft r-in, jst hld on..*........................(14 to 1 op 12 to 1) 1
3167* BROGEEN LADY (Ire) 7-11-2 R Dunwoody, *led to tenth, led nxt till hdd last, swtchd rght whn short of room r-in, ev ch till cl hme..*................. (7 to 2 op 3 to 1 tchd 4 to 1) 2
3843 GRIZZLY BEAR (Ire) 7-11-7 J Culloty, *hld up in tch, ev ch 2 out, rdn and baulked r-in, kpt on..*........ (14 to 1 op 10 to 1) 3
3843[4] MR PICKPOCKET (Ire) 9-11-7 J F Titley, *trkd ldr led tenth to nxt, ev ch 2 out, wknd appr last.....*(7 to 4 fav op 2 to 1) 4
3732 MASTER TOBY 7-11-7 C Llewellyn, *mstk second, in tch whn pld up 3 out, lme..*........ (9 to 4 op 2 to 1 tchd 5 to 2) pu
3737[3] DERRYS PREROGATIVE 7-11-1 R Johnson, *trkd ldrs, blun 13th, sn lost tch, pld up appr 2 out.* .... (16 to 1 op 14 to 1 tchd 20 to 1) pu
3732 DEBONAIR DUDE (Ire) 7-11-1 M A Fitzgerald, *beind whn blun 13th, pld up bef nxt.....* (12 to 1 op 8 to 1 tchd 14 to 1) pu
3504 MUSICAL HIT (bl) 6-11-1 R Bellamy, *in tch to 8th, tld off whn pld up bef last.......* (66 to 1 op 50 to 1 tchd 100 to 1) pu

Dist: Nk, 1¾l, 8l. 6m 41.60s. a 29.60s (8 Ran).

(Mrs Robin Mathew), R Mathew

4068 Gibbs And Dandy 'National Hunt' Novices' Hurdle Class D (4-y-o and up) £2,966 2m............(8:15)

3692* STORMYFAIRWEATHER (Ire) 5-12-0 M A Fitzgerald, *hld up in tch, hdwy appr 4th, led on bit approaching last, cmftbly.*
..................(3 to 1 jt-fav op 6 to 4) 1
3233² RYTHM ROCK (Ire) 8-11-0 R Dunwoody, *al in tch, led 3 out, hrd rdn and hdd appr last, one pace.....*(5 to 1 op 7 to 2) 2
3846³ PHYSICAL FUN 6-10-11 (3*) P Henley, *al prmnt, led 4th to 5th, hrd rdn and one pace appr 2 out.........*(3 to 1 jt-
fav op 7 to 2 tchd 4 to 1 and 11 to 4) 3
2565⁵ CAPTAIN WALTER (Ire) 4-11-2 J Osborne, *hld up, outpcd appr 3 out, styd on frm nxt, nvr dngrs.*
..................(5 to 1 op 4 to 1 tchd 6 to 1) 4
BELARUS (Ire) 5-11-0 W McFarland, *beh till hdwy aftr 3 out, nvr dngrs...................*(33 to 1 op 16 to 1) 5
3795⁵ THE BIZZO 6-10-9 W Marston, *mid-div, lost tch 16th.*
..................(33 to 1 op 25 to 1 tchd 50 to 1) 6
UR ONLY YOUNG ONCE 7-10-9 J F Titley, *in tch till wknd 5th, tld off...................*(12 to 1 op 10 to 1) 7
HIGH PITCH 5-11-0 C Llewellyn, *al beh, tld off.*
..................(50 to 1 op 20 to 1) 9
OVER AND UNDER (Ire) 4-10-9 L Harvey, *tld off 3rd.*
..................(50 to 1 op 20 to 1) 9
1735 CAMP HEAD (Ire) 6-11-0 J A McCarthy, *prmnt, led 4 out, hdd and ran out nxt, hit slpd.*
..................(14 to 1 op 12 to 1 tchd 25 to 1) ro
3700 BOXGROVE MAN (Ire) 7-11-0 G Bradley, *al beh, tld off whn pld up bef last.........*(12 to 1 op 8 to 1 tchd 14 to 1) pu
2264 SINGLE SOURCING (Ire) 6-11-0 J Culloty, *led to 4th, hng lft bef nxt, sn wknd, tld off whn pld up before 2 out.*
..................(13 to 2 op 7 to 2) pu
3561 DANDE DOVE 6-11-0 S McNeill, *al beh, tld off whn pld up bef 2 out...................*(20 to 1 op 14 to 1) pu
Dist: 6l, 5l, 14l, 1½l, 14l, 30l, 18l. 4m 5.40s. a 22.40s (13 Ran).
SR: 36/16/11/-/-/-/ (Mrs Christopher Hanbury), N J Henderson

CHEPSTOW (good to soft (races 1,2,5,6,7), good (3,4)) Tuesday May 13th
Going Correction: PLUS 0.65 sec. per fur.

4069 Stirrup Cup Novices' Claiming Hurdle Class F (4-y-o and up) £2,108 2m 110yds........................(1:50)

3986⁵ BLADE OF FORTUNE 9-10-6 (7*) Mr J Tizzard, *made all, ran on gmely und pres frm 2 out...........*(9 to 2 op 4 to 1) 1
4045⁶ APACHE PARK (USA) 4-10-0 D J Burchell, *hld up, hdwy 3rd, chsd wnr aftr 4th till mstk 2 out, rallied to go second ag'n r-in.*
..................(7 to 2 fav op 5 to 2) 2
3796³ WITHERKAY 4-10-8 R Johnson, *lft second aftr 1st, 3rd appr 4 out, wnt second agaon 2 out, hng left and stumbled last, no extr r-in...........*(20 to 1 op 14 to 1 tchd 25 to 1) 3
3864⁵ CONTRACT BRIDGE (Ire) 4-10-6 W McFarland, *hld up, hdwy appr 4 out, wknd nxt.........*(9 to 2 op 4 to 1 tchd 5 to 1) 4
3812* LAURA LYE 7-11-0 G Upton, *hld up in rear, hdwy appr 4th, wkng whn mstk nxt.* (8 to 1 op 10 to 1 tchd 12 to 1) 5
3957⁴ RED VIPER 5-10-9 (7*) Mr L Baker, *hld up in tch, hdwy 4th, rdn four out, wkng whn mstk nxt.*
..................(25 to 1 op 20 to 1 tchd 33 to 1) 6
3809³ IRISH DOMINION 7-10-6 (7*) Mr G Shenkin, *beh whn blun badly second, nvr on terms aftr, tld off.*
..................(50 to 1 op 33 to 1 tchd 66 to 1) 7
3931 MINNISAM (bl) 4-10-5 R Greene, *prmnt till rdn and wknd appr 4 out, tld off.........*(16 to 1 tchd 20 to 1 and 25 to 1) 8
SWISS ACCOUNT 8-10-4 (7*) N Rossiter, *al beh, tld off.*
..................(66 to 1 op 50 to 1) 9
3334⁶ HONEYSHAN 5-11-9 S McNeill, *beh frm 4th, tld off.*
..................(20 to 1 op 14 to 1 tchd 25 to 1) 10
3402⁵ SCOTTISH PARK 8-10-5 D Walsh, *al beh, tld off whn pld up bef 4 out...........*(14 to 1 op 10 to 1) pu
3915 RITTO 7-11-8 A P McCoy, *hdwy 3rd, hit nxt, rdn and wknd 2 out, pld up bef last.........*(6 to 1 op 4 to 1) pu
3735 ABOVE THE CLOUDS 6-10-4¹ (7*) Mr P O'Keeffe, *pld hrd, jmpd lft 1st, sddl slpd, pulled up bef nxt...........*(100 to 1) pu
3684⁵ MORECEVA (Ire) 7-11-2 T Dascombe, *beh frm 3rd, tld off whn pld up bef last.........*(66 to 1 op 40 to 1) pu
Dist: 2l, nk, 14l, 1½l, 8l, 17l, 6l, 25l, 3l. 4m 4.30s. a 17.30s (14 Ran).
SR: 19/12/12/-/3/-/ (V G Greenway), V G Greenway

4070 Welsh Brewers Novices' Handicap Chase Class D (0-110 5-y-o and up) £3,715 3m........................(2:20)

3873² MALWOOD CASTLE (Ire) [88] 7-11-0 A Thornton, *hld up, hdwy 8th, wnt second 5 out, led and lft clr 2 out.*
..................(5 to 1 op 9 to 2) 1
3395³ THERMAL WARRIOR [81] 9-10-6 C Llewellyn, *al in tch, ev ch whn hit 5 out, btn when lft poor second 2 out.*
..................(2 to 1 fav op 9 to 4) 2
3958* NORDIC VALLEY [92] 6-11-3 (7ex) A P McCoy, *hld up, hdwy 13th, rdn appr 4 out, sn btn........*(7 to 1 op 5 to 1) 3

3841³ KARAR (Ire) [97] 7-11-8 D O'Sullivan, *hld up in rear, mstk tenth, nvr on terms aftr.................*(9 to 2 op 3 to 1) 4
3845* SEA PATROL [80] (bl) 10-10-5 M A Fitzgerald, *hld up, effrt 13th, sn tld off.............*(12 to 1 op 10 to 1) 5
3792 PREROGATIVE [99] (v) 7-11-7 (3*) Guy Lewis, *prmnt, chsd ldr aftr 7th, wknd 12th, tld off...........*(20 to 1 op 14 to 1) 6
3822⁵ CHIAPPUCCI (Ire) [80] 7-10-5 D Gallagher, *pld hrd, led to second, beh whn mstk 12th, tld off.........*(33 to 1) 7
3939* WIXOE WONDER (Ire) [84] (bl) 7-10-9 (7ex) G Bradley, *led second, rdn and hdd whn f 2 out.........*(33 to 1) f
3737⁶ SMART CASANOVA [75] 8-10-0 W Marston, *chsd ldr, hit 5th wknd and mstk 8th, pld up bef nxt.*
..................(66 to 1 op 50 to 1 tchd 100 to 1) pu
Dist: 26l, 10l, 1l, dist, 17l, 30l. 6m 12.20s. a 22.20s (9 Ran).
SR: 20/-/-/-/-/-/ (Mrs U Wainwright), R H Alner

4071 May Handicap Hurdle Class C (0-130 4-y-o and up) £3,488 2½m 110yds........................(2:55)

3908* DIWALI DANCER [113] 7-10-11 A P McCoy, *made all, mstk 5th, drw clr appr 2 out, eased r-in.*
..................(5 to 2 fav op 11 to 4 tchd 3 to 1) 1
3975⁴ EHTEFAAL (USA) [102] 6-10-0 (7ex) R Johnson, *not fluent, chsd wnr to 2 out, rallied to go second ag'n cl hme.*
..................(5 to 1 op 9 to 2 tchd 11 to 2) 2
4038* LORD MCMURROUGH (Ire) [117] 7-10-12 (3*,7ex) Mr R Thornton, *hld up, rdn and hdwy appr 4 out, chsd wnr 2 out till extr cl hme.........*(5 to 1 op 9 to 2 tchd 11 to 2) 3
3558 BALLET ROYAL (USA) [105] 8-9-10 (7*) A Dowling, *hld up, mstk 3rd, hdwy aftr 4 out, sn wknd appr 2 out..* (20 to 1) 4
3689³ EL DON [112] 5-10-10 J Ryan, *trkd ldrs till hit 7th, sn wknd, tld off...................*(4 to 1 op 3 to 1 tchd 9 to 2) 5
2701⁸ HEBRIDEAN [129] 10-11-13 M A Fitzgerald, *hld up in rear, effrt appr 4 out, tld off...........*(10 to 1 op 7 to 1) 6
3330⁴ MIM-LOU-AND [109] 5-10-7 J Culloty, *hld up in rear, lost tch appr 4 out, tld off...........*(10 to 1 op 7 to 1) 7
Dist: 4l, nk, 5l, dist, 8l, 8l. 5m 2.40s. a 24.40s (7 Ran).
(B E Case), M C Pipe

4072 Greig Middleton Ladies Championship Hunters' Chase Class H (5-y-o and up) £3,434 3m...........(3:25)

EARTHMOVER 6-11-2 (7*) Miss P Gundry, *hld up, hdwy to track ldr appr 7th, led aftr 13th, mstk 2 out, shaken up and quickened clr r-in...........*(2 to 1 on) 1
SAMS HERITAGE 13-11-9 (5*) Miss A Dare, *hld up, hdwy 9th, wnt second aftr 13th, ev ch last, outpcd r-in.*
..................(8 to 1 op 6 to 1) 2
CORNER BOY 10-11-11 (7*) Mrs J Dawson, *pld hrd, mstks, trkd ldr till appr 8th, wkng whn hit 5 out, btn when blun 3 out, tld off...........*(4 to 1 op 5 to 1) 3
LONESOME TRAVELLER (NZ) 8-11-2 (7*) Mrs A Hand, *in tch till wknd 13th, tld off...........*(66 to 1 op 33 to 1) 4
FALSE ECONOMY 12-11-11 (7*) Miss K Scorgie, *prmnt to 7th, tld off whn refused 4 out.........*(100 to 1 op 33 to 1) ref
MISTER GEBO 12-11-7 (7*) Miss C Dyson, *al beh, tld off whn pld up bef 2 out.........*(33 to 1 op 25 to 1) pu
3921* CUMBERLAND BLUES (Ire) 8-11-11 (7*) Miss A Deniel, *led, jmpd right, hdd aftr 13th, sn btn, tld off whn pld up bef 3 out.*
..................(14 to 1 op 8 to 1) pu
Dist: 9l, dist, 26l. 6m 22.70s. a 32.70s (7 Ran).
(R M Penny), R Barber

4073 Bargain-Buy Selling Handicap Hurdle Class G (0-90 4-y-o and up) £1,996 2m 110yds...........(3:55)

3911² HONEYBED WOOD [64] 9-10-2 R Johnson, *al prmnt, led appr 4 out to nxt, led ag'n bef mstk last, ran on wl.*
..................(7 to 2 op 3 to 1) 1
3911⁴ CUILLIN CAPER [70] 5-10-8 M A Fitzgerald, *al in tch, led on bit 3 out, hrd rdn and hdd appr last, no extr r-in.*
..................(10 to 1 op 7 to 1 tchd 11 to 1) 2
3892 SPIRIT LEVEL [63] 9-9-8 (7*) Mr S Durack, *al prmnt, outpcd appr 4 out, nvr dngrs aftr...........*(20 to 1 op 33 to 1) 3
3992⁴ BRESIL (USA) [62] 8-9-7 (7*) M Batchelor, *al prmnt, led 3rd till hdd appr 4 out, sn wknd...........*(25 to 1 tchd 33 to 1) 4
3988⁵ POWDER MONKEY [78] 7-11-2 G Tormey, *in tch till rdn and wknd appr 4 out...........*(11 to 2 op 5 to 1 tchd 6 to 1) 5
3992² MECADO [78] (v) 10-10-11 (5*) X Aizpuru, *in tch early, beh frm 3rd...........*(7 to 1 op 6 to 1 tchd 8 to 1) 6
2420 ILEWIN [88] 10-11-12 M Ahern, *al beh.*
..................(16 to 1 op 10 to 1 tchd 20 to 1) 7
SALLOW GLEN [62] 11-10-0 Dr P Pritchard, *prmnt till wknd 4th...................*(50 to 1) 8
3892⁹ CALGARY GIRL [62] 5-10-0 B Powell, *pld hrd, prmnt till wknd aftr 4th...................*(8 to 1) 9
3093² DO BE WARE [77] 7-11-1 B Fenton, *beh till effrt 4th, sn wknd, tld off...................*(7 to 1 op 6 to 1) 10
3894 MORE BILLS (Ire) [65] (v) 5-10-3 D J Burchell, *al beh, tld off...................*(33 to 1 op 20 to 1) 11
3979² RED TEL (Ire) [80] (bl) 5-11-4 A P McCoy, *led, reminders aftr second, hdd nxt, sn wknd, tld off whn pld up bef 4 out.*
..................(100 to 30 fav op 3 to 1 tchd 4 to 1) pu
Dist: 4l, 12l, 13l, 1¼l, 12l, 3l, 4l, 10l, 16l. 4m 6.60s. a 19.60s (12 Ran).

(R Herbert, T Doxsey And M Drake), M Sheppard

4074 Hue And Cry Handicap Chase Class D (0-120 5-y-o and up) £3,488 2m 3f 110yds................... (4:25)

3895*	RED BRANCH (Ire) [95] 8-10-3 J Culloty, jmpd wl, al in tch, led 4 out, clr last, ran on well. .... (11 to 10 fav op 5 to 4 tchd 11 to 8)	1
3740⁴	THE CARROT MAN [105] 9-10-10 (3") L Aspell, trkd ldrs, led 7th till hdd 4 out, btn wen blun badly last, reco'red wl. .... (11 to 2 op 5 to 1 tchd 6 to 1)	2
3688⁸	SEEK THE FAITH (USA) [110] 8-11-4 B Powell, hld up in rear, hdwy 7th, rdn 3 out, one pace aftr. .... (5 to 2 op 9 to 4 tchd 11 to 4)	3
3884⁴	JAMES THE FIRST [102] 9-12-0 M A Fitzgerald, hld up, hdwy aftr 11th, rdn and wknd appr 3 out....... (8 to 1 op 6 to 1)	4
3884⁵	MAGGOTS GREEN [98] 10-10-6 R Johnson, led to 4th, wknd tenth, tld off....... (16 to 1 op 14 to 1 tchd 20 to 1)	5
3730⁸	BORO VACATION (Ire) [120] 8-11-7 (7") Mr J Tizzard, bolted bef strt, pld hrd, led 4th to 7th, sn wknd, tld off whn pulled up four out.................(16 to 1 op 12 to 1)	pu

Dist: 12l, 4l, 20l, dist. 5m 7.30s. a 24.30s (6 Ran).

(E J Mangan), J S King

4075 End Of Season Intermediate Open National Hunt Flat Class H (4,5,6-y-o) £1,297 2m 110yds........ (4:55)

3721⁴	THE VILLAGE WAY (Ire) 6-11-4 R Johnson, rcd keenly, led o'r 4 fs out, ran green appr last, quickened wl ins. .... (7 to 4 on op 5 to 2 tchd 13 to 8 on and 6 to 4 on)	1
3560¹	RUPERT BLUES 5-11-4 (7") Mr O McPhail, trkd ldrs, rdn o'r 4 fs out, cased wnr fnl 2, no imprsn. .... (2 to 1 tchd 9 to 4 and 7 to 4)	2
	AMOTHEBAMBO (Ire) 4-10-6 (7") Mr G Shenkin, hld up, hdwy und pres 3 fs out, wknd appr last......(20 to 1 op 16 to 1)	3
	ODDA'S CHAPEL 4-10-13 B Powell, hld up in rear, hdwy aftr 6 fs, one pace ins fnl 3...............(16 to 1 op 14 to 1)	4
	MINIBELLE 5-10-13 M Clarke, prmnt till outpcd 5 fs out, nvr dngrs aftr..............(16 to 1 op 33 to 1)	5
2402⁶	JUST BAYARD 5-11-4 C Llewellyn, pld hrd, led 7 fs out, hdd o'r 4 out, rdn and sn wknd. .... (11 to 1 op 10 to 1 tchd 12 to 1 and 14 to 1)	6
3560	BALLINA 5-11-1 (3") Michael Brennan, led aftr one furlong, hdd 7 out, wknd 5 out................(20 to 1 op 33 to 1)	7
	IRISH MIST 5-11-4 V Slattery, hld up, effrt 6 fs out, sn wknd. .... (25 to 1 op 20 to 1)	8
3825	THE BOMBERS MOON 4-10-13 D Gallagher, led for one furlong, prmnt till wknd rpdly 6 fs out, tld off....(50 to 1)	9

Dist: 8l, 2½l, 3½l, 4l, 4l, 8l, 9l, 24l. 4m 10.80s. (9 Ran).

(St Mellion Estates Ltd), D Nicholson

KILLARNEY (IRE) (yielding to soft)
Tuesday May 13th

4076 Lake Hotel Hurdle (4-y-o and up) £3,425 2½m................(3:00)

4027²	BAWNROCK (Ire) 8-12-0 C F Swan,.............. (7 to 4)	1
3180⁹	TRUCKINABOUT (Ire) 7-10-8 (5") P G Hourigan, ..(25 to 1)	2
3963⁷	WYATT (Ire) 7-11-1 (7") B J Geraghty,.........(6 to 4 on)	3
3767⁷	COMKILRED (Ire) 5-11-2 T P Treacy,.............(8 to 1)	4
3834	CROHANE PRINCESS (Ire) 8-10-8 S H O'Donovan, (50 to 1)	5
2839	EXPERT ADVICE (Ire) 6-10-13 J R Barry, ...(33 to 1)	6
3450	KNOCKDOO (Ire) 4-10-4 F J Flood, ...(66 to 1)	7
	KISSANES PRIDE (Ire) 5-10-5 (7") S P McCann, ...(40 to 1)	8

Dist: 1l, 6l, 20l, 7l. 5m 9.90s. (8 Ran).

(New Road Syndicate), A P O'Brien

4077 Freefoam Handicap Hurdle (0-102 4-y-o and up) £3,425 2¾m.... (3:30)

3834⁴	WOODBORN LASS (Ire) [-] 7-9-11 (7") Miss A Sloane, ... (8 to 1)	1
4004⁴	RUNABOUT (Ire) [-] 5-10-2 C F Swan, ...(6 to 1)	2
3953³	TULLOLOUGH [-] 14-9-11 (7") M D Murphy, ...(10 to 1)	3
4059*	THE GREY MARE (Ire) [-] 8-11-6 (7",4ex) Mr P Fahey, (7 to 1)	4
4060⁷	BRIDGES DAUGHTER (Ire) [-] 6-10-10 P A Roche, (10 to 1)	5
3835	ANOTHER GALLOP (Ire) [-] 9-10-0 S H O'Donovan, (14 to 1)	6
3953²	HEATHER VILLE (Ire) [-] 5-10-11 (7") B J Geraghty, ..(5 to 1)	7
3834	OVER THE WALL (Ire) [-] 8-9-9 (7") J M Maguire, ..(14 to 1)	8
4060⁴	MIRACLE ME (Ire) [-] 5-11-13 (4ex) F Woods, ...(11 to 2)	9
3644	PADDY'S PET (Ire) [-] 8-11-3 C O'Dwyer, ...(8 to 1)	10
3626	GILLANA (Ire) [-] 7-10-3 (7") Mr Paul Moloney, (3 to 1 fav)	11
3953⁶	MY BLUE [-] 5-9-3 (7") E F Cahalan, ...(25 to 1)	12
	BILLIE'S MATE (Ire) [-] 6-10-4 J R Barry, ...(20 to 1)	13

Dist: Nk, 1l, 5½l, 6l. 5m 43.70s. (13 Ran).

(Miss F Fowley), Andrew Lee

4078 Menvier Handicap Chase (4-y-o and up) £6,850 2¾m................(4:30)

3347³	UNA'S CHOICE (Ire) [-] 9-11-0 F J Flood, ...(5 to 1)	1
3815⁶	SPRINGFORT LADY (Ire) [-] 8-9-10 (7") J E Casey, ..(8 to 1)	2
3815²	RYHANE (Ire) [-] 8-11-0 F Woods, ...(2 to 1 fav)	3

3446³	MACAUNTA (Ire) [-] 7-10-0 P Carberry, ...(7 to 1)	4
3754	MERRY PEOPLE (Ire) [-] 9-11-11 J Shortt, ...(12 to 1)	5
3765⁸	THE OUTBACK WAY (Ire) [-] (bl) 7-12-0 D H O'Connor, ... (10 to 1)	ur
3815	CASTALINO [-] 11-11-0 C O'Dwyer, ...(7 to 1)	pu
3763	DEEP HERITAGE (Ire) 11-11-13 C F Swan, ...(10 to 1)	pu
3753³	ALL IN THE GAME (Ire) [-] 9-9-7 (7") M D Murphy, ..(9 to 2)	pu

Dist: 1½l, ½l, 20l, sht-hd. 5m 51.30s. (9 Ran).

(Fish & Poultry Portions Ltd), F Flood

4079 Smurfit Corrugated Boxes INH Flat Race (4-y-o and up) £3,425 2m 1f .... (5:30)

3935⁵	BESSMOUNT LEADER (Ire) 5-12-3 Mr B M Cash, (6 to 4 jt-fav)	1
3789	STRONG CHOICE (Ire) 5-10-12 (7") Mr B J Crowley, ... (100 to 30)	2
1081*	BARHALE BOY (Ire) 5-11-10 (7") Mr C A Murphy, (6 to 4 jt-fav)	3
	DEEP ALTO (Ire) 5-10-12 (7") Mr B N Doyle, ...(14 to 1)	4
	JUMP FOR JOY (Ire) 4-10-5 (7") Miss A Sloane, ...(14 to 1)	su

Dist: 5½l, 7l, 8l. 4m 26.60s. (5 Ran).

(Miss J Butler), A P O'Brien

HEREFORD (good)
Wednesday May 14th
Going Correction: PLUS 0.55 sec. per fur. (races 1,2,4,5,7), PLUS 0.45 (3,6)

4080 Weobley Juvenile Novices' Hurdle Class E (4-y-o) £2,262 2m 1f.. (1:55)

3985*	SONG OF THE SWORD 11-5 M A Fitzgerald, hld up, pressed ldrs 4th, outpcd nxt, shaken up and chsd lder aftr four out, quickened on ins to lead appr last,easily. .... (7 to 4 on tchd 6 to 4 on and 11 to 8 on)	1
3905⁶	MELT THE CLOUDS (Can) (bl) 11-5 R Johnson, trkd ldr, led out, hdd aftr 2 out, hld and one pace whn hit last. .... (9 to 4 op 5 to 2 tchd 2 to 1)	2
3905⁹	NOBLE COLOURS 10-12 (7") Mr A Wintle, led to 4 out, sn rdn, wknd nxt................... (6 to 1 op 4 to 1)	3
3610⁶	STARTINGO 10-12 Mr A Charles-Jones, al wl beh, modest hdwy frm 3 out, nvr nrr.........(100 to 1 tchd 150 to 1)	4
1702	RED RUSTY (USA) 10-5 (7") M Clinton, al beh. .... (50 to 1 op 33 to 1)	5
	MORNING SIR 10-12 T Eley, not fluent, al beh. .... (50 to 1 op 33 to 1)	6

Dist: 4l, 14l, 14l, 16l, 3½l. 4m 0.90s. a 15.90s (6 Ran).
SR: 24/20/6/

(Lady Lloyd Webber), J A B Old

4081 Holmer Selling Hurdle Class G (4-7-y-o) £1,842 2m 3f 110yds... (2:25)

3988⁶	FLEET CADET (v) 6-11-7 (5") G Supple, hld up and confidently rdn, shaken up and hdwy 7th, led aftr 4 out, clr 2 out, easily. .... (9 to 4 op 2 to 1 tchd 4 to 1)	1
3988⁴	LOOK IN THE MIRROR 6-11-0 C Llewellyn, chsd leder to 6th, chlgd 4 out,led briefly sn aftr, rdn 2 out and styd on but no ch wth wnr........(7 to 2 op 3 to 1 tchd 4 to 1)	2
3810²	JUST FOR A REASON (bl) 5-11-0 J Railton, led, sn clr, mstk 4 out and soon hdd, wknd nxt............(8 to 1 op 5 to 1)	3
3973⁵	MASTER SHOWMAN (Ire) 6-10-7 (7") Mr A Wintle, keen hold, hdwy to chase ldr 6th, chlgd 4 out, sn rdn, wknd quickly 2 out. .... (40 to 1 op 33 to 1)	4
3978⁶	JAIME'S JOY (v) 7-10-2 (7") Martin Smith, al beh, tld off frm 4th.............(66 to 1 op 33 to 1 tchd 100 to 1)	5
3956⁴	RAKAPOSHI IMP 7-10-2 (7") L Suthern, prmnt, wknd 6th and sn tld off, pld up bef 3 out. .... (66 to 1 op 50 to 1 tchd 100 to 1)	pu
3672	HABERDASHER 6-11-0 W Marston, jmpd badly and sn tld off, pld up bef four out.. (66 to 1 op 50 to 1 tchd 100 to 1)	pu

Dist: 7l, 9l, 9l, dist. 4m 48.50s. a 30.50s (7 Ran).

(Sir John Swaine), M C Pipe

4082 Canon Pyon Handicap Chase Class E (0-115 5-y-o and up) £2,802 3m 1f 110yds....................... (3:00)

3830²	BALLY CLOVER [111] 10-12-0 N Williamson, trkd ldr, jmpd slwly 7th, hit tenth, led 14th, drvn clr frm 2 out, wknd nr finish and jst hld on.........(15 to 8 fav op 11 to 8 tchd 2 to 1)	1
3937⁵	COASTING [83] 11-9-7 (7") Mr S Durack, hdwy to track ldrs 11th, chsd wnr 4 out, rallied r-in, jst hld. (20 to 1 op 12 to 1)	2
3897³	DIAMOND FORT [95] 12-10-12 M A Fitzgerald, prmnt till drpd rear 8th, rdn and ran on frm 3 out, kpt on r-in. .... (9 to 4 op 2 to 1 tchd 5 to 2)	3
3895⁶	DISTANT MEMORY [97] (bl) 8-11-0 G Tormey, hld up, hdwy aftr and hit 9th, mstk 11th, rdn nxt, kpt on same pace frm 2 out. .... (7 to 1 op 7 to 2)	4
3875³	PAPER STAR [92] 10-10-9 B Powell, led to 14th, rallied to chal and hit 4 out, sn wknd, dismounted aftr line. .... (100 to 30 op 7 to 2 tchd 3 to 1)	5

Dist: Hd, 1¾l, 6l, 22l. 6m 29.20s. a 23.20s (5 Ran).

(James Williams), Miss Venetia Williams

4083 St Richards School Conditional Jockeys' Novices' Handicap Hurdle Class E (0-100 4-y-o and up) £2,332 2m 1f..............................(3:30)

2765³	TATHMIN [70] (v) 4-10-7 (3*) X Aizpuru, *hdwy to press ldrs 4 out, led aftr nxt, lft clr 2 out, readily.* ....(13 to 2 op 5 to 1 tchd 7 to 1)	1
3844⁶	FLOW BACK [70] 5-11-1 L Aspell, *beh till hdwy 4 out, chasing ldrs whn lft second 2 out, styd on same pace appr last.* ....(7 to 1 op 4 to 1 tchd 8 to 1)	2
3796⁴	TEE TEE TOO (Ire) [65] 5-10-5 (5*) R Studholme, *beh till styd on frm 2 out, not rch ldrs*............(14 to 1 op 12 to 1)	3
4019⁸	DOVETTO [77] 8-11-8 D J Kavanagh, *hdwy to chase ldrs 4th, chlgd four out, wknd aftr nxt*............(14 to 1 op 10 to 1)	4
3468⁵	ROYRACE [60] 5-10-5 R Massey, *prmnt early, drpd rear 3rd, moderate hdwy frm 2 out*............(14 to 1 op 10 to 1)	5
3988⁸	ROC AGE [67] 6-10-12 Michael Brennan, *led to 5th, chlgd ag'n 3 out, 3rd and wkng whn blun badly nxt.* ....(8 to 1 op 1 to 1 tchd 12 to 1)	6
3534⁸	FRENO (Ire) [70] 6-10-7 (8*) W Walsh, *in tch, chsd ldrs 4 out, wknd nxt*............(13 to 2 op 9 to 2 tchd 7 to 1)	7
3911⁹	VITAL WONDER [55] 9-9-11 (3*) O Burrows, *chsd ldrs to 5th, sn wknd*............(50 to 1 op 33 to 1)	8
2372	SOBER ISLAND [60] 8-10-5 Guy Lewis, *chsd ldrs to 5th, sn wknd*............(50 to 1 op 33 to 1)	9
3731²	REVERSE THRUST [79] 6-11-2 (8*) M Clinton, *hld up, keen hold, hdwy to chase ldrs 4th, led nxt, hdd aftr 3 out, second and held whn f next*............(6 to 4 fav tchd 7 to 4)	f

Dist: 4l, ¾l, 24l, 1½l, 1¼l, 4l, 6l, 2½l. 4m 0.80s. a 15.80s (10 Ran).
SR: 17/18/12/-/-/-/

(Miss J M Bodycote), M R Bosley

4084 Tillington Novices' Hurdle Class E (5-y-o and up) £2,332 2m 3f 110yds ....(4:00)

3722*	SPECIAL BEAT 5-11-2 (5*) Mr C Vigors, *al gng wl, chlgd 7th, sn ld, came clr frm 3 out, easily.* ....(13 to 8 on op 11 to 8 on)	1
3913⁶	RUSHAWAY 6-11-0 D Gallagher, *not fluent, led to 3rd, styd prmnt till outpcd 4 out, stayed to take poor second at last, tld off*............(12 to 1 op 8 to 1 tchd 14 to 1)	2
2723⁵	LORD FOLEY (NZ) 5-10-11 (3*) Michael Brennan, *rear and mstk 4th, hdwy 6th, wknd four out, tld off*............(20 to 1 op 16 to 1)	3
1815	FAIRIES FAREWELL 7-10-9 J A McCarthy, *led 3rd, hdd appr 7th, sn wknd, tld off*............(20 to 1 op 16 to 1)	4
3610³	AMI BLEU (Fr) 5-11-6 J F Titley, *chsd ldrs, led appr 7th, hdd sn aftr, chased wnr will wknd and lost second pl whn f last.* ....(100 to 30 op 5 to 1 tchd 7 to 2)	f
	HAYDOWN 5-10-7 (7*) Mr P Phillips, *beh frm 5th, sn tld off, pld up aftr 4 out*............(66 to 1 op 50 to 1)	pu
3913	SANDVILLE LAD 5-10-11 (3*) Guy Lewis, *beh and aftr 5th, tld off whn pld up bef 6th*............(66 to 1 op 50 to 1)	pu
3913⁵	BROOK BEE 5-11-0 W Marston, *beh frm 5th, tld off whn pld up bef 7th*............(20 to 1 op 14 to 1)	pu

Dist: Dist, 23l, 20l. 4m 41.20s. a 23.20s (8 Ran).

(C Marner), N J Henderson

4085 Brockhampton Hunters' Chase Class H (5-y-o and up) £1,194 3m 1f 110yds..............................(4:30)

3854*	MISS MILLBROOK 9-11-9 (7*) Mr E Williams, *hdwy tenth, led 14th, drvn out r-in.*............(2 to 1 fav op 7 to 4)	1
3969*	TRIFAST LAD 12-12-4 (3*) Mr P Hacking, *hdwy tenth, chsd wnr frm 3 out, styd on appr last but no imprsn on winner.* ....(5 to 1 op 9 to 1)	2
3993³	RUSTY BRIDGE 10-12-0 (7*) Mr O McPhail, *led till aftr 1st, rdn frm tenth, styd on ag'n from 2 out, took 3rd r-in.* ....(12 to 1 op 10 to 1 tchd 14 to 1)	3
	JACK SOUND 11-11-7 (7*) Mr D S Jones, *chsd ldr to 3 out, sn wknd*............(10 to 1 op 8 to 1)	4
3853*	VITAL SONG 11-12-0 (7*) Mr G Matthews, *led aftr 1st till mstk and hdd 14th, wknd 4 out.*............(9 to 2 op 4 to 1)	5
3854	J B LAD 11-11-7 (7*) Miss P Gundry, *hdwy 12th, wknd 4 out.* ....(50 to 1 op 33 to 1)	6
	LAYSTON D'OR 8-11-7 (7*) Mr A Charles-Jones, *al beh.* ....(50 to 1 op 33 to 1)	7
3857³	MY NOMINEE (bl) 9-12-0 (7*) Mr R Burton, *hdwy 11th, wknd 14th.*............(7 to 2 op 9 to 4)	8
	NO PANIC 13-11-7 (7*) Mr G Lewis, *hdwy 11th, sn wknd, tld off whn blun and uns rdr 4 out.*............(66 to 1 op 50 to 1)	ur
3940	KILLELAN LAD 15-11-7 (7*) Miss K Di Marte, *slwly away and jmpd poorly in rear, sn tld off, pld up bef 8th.* ....(66 to 1 op 50 to 1 tchd 100 to 1)	pu
	AL BILLAL 9-11-7 (7*) Miss P Cooper, *sn tld off, pld up bef 12th.*............(100 to 1)	pu

Dist: 3½l, 21l, 1¾l, 2l, ¾l, 18l, 22l. 6m 26.50s. a 20.50s (11 Ran).
SR: 11/11/-/-/-/-/

(D T Goldsworthy), D T Goldsworthy

4086 Marden Standard Open National Hunt Flat Class H (4,5,6-y-o) £1,030 2m 1f..............................(5:00)

	CASTLE OWEN (Ire) 5-11-1 (3*) Mr R Thornton, *hld up, steady hdwy 6 fs out, led o'r 2 out, sn clr, easily.* ....(5 to 4 on tchd 6 to 4 on)	1
2961⁵	CINNAMON CLUB 5-10-13 A Thornton, *trkd ldrs, led o'r 3 fs out, hdd over 2 out, sn outpcd*............(5 to 2 tchd 3 to 1)	2
3322⁷	BE IN SPACE 6-10-6 (7*) Mr O McPhail, *beh, rdn and hdwy frm 3, styd on fnl furlong*............(12 to 1 op 8 to 1)	3
2269	FRANKIE MUCK 5-10-11 (7*) Mr J Goldstein, *prmnt, drvn alng to stay chasing ldrs6 fs out, styd on same pace.* ....(12 to 1 op 8 to 1)	4
2309⁵	HURRICANE JANE (Ire) 5-10-13 J Railton, *beh, moderate hdwy fnl 2 fs*............(14 to 1 op 10 to 1)	5
	REGAL BLUFF 5-11-4 S Wynne, *set modest pace 4 fs, styd frnt rnk, dsptd ld frm 5 furlongs out till wknd 3 out.* ....(33 to 1 tchd 50 to 1)	6
3917⁹	BOSSA NOVA 4-10-3 (5*) O Burrows, *steady hdwy to track ldrs hfwy, led o'r 4 fs out till over 3 out, sn wknd*....(20 to 1)	7
	PRIDE OF PENNKER (Ire) 4-10-5 (3*) L Aspell, *chsd ldrs 11 fs.* ....(10 to 1 op 5 to 1 tchd 11 to 1)	8
3825⁶	MISS MOUSE 5-10-10 (3*) R Massey, *led aftr 4 fs, hdd o'r four furlongs out, sn wknd*............(14 to 1 op 10 to 1)	9
4049	BERNERA 5-11-4 T Eley, *chsd ldrs ten fs.* ....(33 to 1 op 25 to 1)	10

Dist: 12l, 9l, ½l, 3½l, 5l, 1¾l, 13l, 2l, 12l. 4m 6.10s. (10 Ran).

(Lord Vestey), D Nicholson

HUNTINGDON (good to firm)
Wednesday May 14th
Going Correction: MINUS 0.70 sec. per fur.

4087 Ladies Evening Selling Handicap Hurdle Class G (0-95 4-y-o and up) £1,891 2m 5f 110yds..........(6:05)

2177²	BRINDLEY HOUSE [92] 10-12-0 D Morris, *made all, lft clr 3 out, unchlgd*............(5 to 1 op 9 to 2 tchd 6 to 1)	1
3935³	NAUTICAL JEWEL [80] 5-10-9 (7*) Mr A Wintle, *in tch, styd on frm 3 out to go second last*............(7 to 2 tchd 4 to 1)	2
3852⁵	SCRIPT [66] 6-10-2 K Gaule, *al prmnt, lft second 3 out, no ch wth wnr whn mstk last*............(14 to 1 op 10 to 1)	3
3803	WEATHER ALERT (Ire) [67] (v) 6-10-3 R Johnson, *chsd ldrs till rdn and wknd appr 3 out*............(14 to 1 op 10 to 1)	4
3849⁶	CLERIC ON BROADWAY (Ire) [64] 9-10-0 J Culloty, *prmnt, hit 3rd, rdn 4 out, sn wknd*............(25 to 1 op 14 to 1 tchd 33 to 1)	5
3919⁵	FRET (USA) [64] 7-10-0 B Fenton, *al in rear.* ....(14 to 1 op 20 to 1)	6
3972⁵	GI MOSS [65] (bl) 10-10-1 S McNeill, *pld hrd, prmnt till wknd appr 7th, tld off, fnshd lme*............(25 to 1 op 12 to 1)	7
3951⁴	ECU DE FRANCE (Ire) [64] 7-9-7 (7*) N Willmington, *al in tch, gd headwway 6th, second whn stumbled and uns rdr 3 out.* ....(11 to 2 op 5 to 1 tchd 6 to 1)	ur
1020⁷	BEN CONNAN (Ire) [64] 7-9-11⁴ (7*) Mr R Wakley, *tld off 4th, f 6th*............(50 to 1 op 20 to 1)	ur
3990⁷	BETTER BYTHE GLASS (Ire) [89] 8-11-11 C Llewellyn, *sn beh, tld off 5th, pld up bef nxt.* ....(8 to 1 op 5 to 1 tchd 9 to 1)	pu
3190⁵	SPITFIRE BRIDGE (Ire) [68] 5-10-4 N Williamson, *hit second, prmnt frm 4th, hit 7th, wknd quickly appr 3 out, pld up bef nxt, fnshd lme*............(3 to 1 fav op 4 to 1)	pu

Dist: 9l, 7l, 2l, 3l, 2l, 19l. 4m 49.60s. a 0.60s (11 Ran).

(S B Glazer), R Curtis

4088 Health Spa Water Novices' Handicap Hurdle Class E (0-100 4-y-o and up) £2,407 3¼m.................(6:35)

3978*	ARDENT LOVE (Ire) [73] 8-10-9 R Johnson, *trkd ldrs, rdn to go second 8th, led und hrd pres to ld fnl 100 yards.* ....(7 to 4 fav op 6 to 4)	1
3833⁶	STORMY SESSION [78] 7-11-0 T Jenks, *led, rdn frm 2 out, hdd fnl 100 yards*.....(16 to 1 op 12 to 1 tchd 20 to 1)	2
3672*	FORBIDDEN WATERS (Ire) [73] 6-10-9 N Williamson, *hld up, hdwy 8th, ev ch 3 out till rdn and wknd appr last.* ....(100 to 30 op 3 to 1 tchd 7 to 2)	3
3903²	NORTHERN STAR [88] 6-11-3 (7*) Miss J Wormall, *prmnt till wknd appr 3 out*............(9 to 1 op 8 to 1 tchd 10 to 1)	4
3972	ARRANGE A GAME [64] 10-9-9 (5*) R Wilkinson, *not jump wl, lost tch 8th*............(9 to 1 op 5 to 1 tchd 40 to 1)	5
3872⁵	CROWN IVORY (NZ) [65] 9-10-1 S Fox, *al beh.* ....(10 to 1 op 12 to 1 tchd 16 to 1)	6
3961⁷	EDEN STREAM [64] 10-10-0 D Leahy, *in tch to 8th.* ....(14 to 1 op 20 to 1)	7
3951	KAREN'S TYPHOON (Ire) [72] 6-10-8 M A Fitzgerald, *beh till hdwy 7th, wknd appr 3 out, f last*.... (20 to 1 op 14 to 1)	f
3833⁵	SAMMORELLO (Ire) [80] 6-11-2 C Llewellyn, *prmnt, trkd ldr to 8th, sn wknd, tld off whn pld up bef 2 out.* ....(7 to 2 op 3 to 1 tchd 4 to 1)	pu

Dist: Nk, 10l, 1¾l, 16l, 2l, 6l. 5m 57.50s. a 5.50s (9 Ran).

(Mrs Claire Smith), D Nicholson

4089 Deloitte & Touche Chartered Accountants Novices' Chase Class E (5-y-o and up) £2,886 2m 110yds ....(7:05)

3370 GIMME (Ire) (v) 7-10-11 (3*) Michael Brennan, *hld up in rear and early mstks, gd hdwy to ld 4 out, drw clr frm 2 out.*
............(15 to 8 op 7 to 4 tchd 2 to 1 and 9 to 4) 1
2774 LOWAWATHA 9-11-7 D Gallagher, *led till hdd 4 out, rdn whn hit 2 out, wknd appr last...* (3 to 1 op 7 to 2 tchd 4 to 1) 2
787² TELMAR SYSTEMS 8-11-0 J R Kavanagh, *lft second 4th, hit four out, sn wknd......* (12 to 1 op 8 to 1 tchd 14 to 1) 3
4037 CUMBERLAND YOUTH 6-11-0 I Lawrence, *blun 5th, tld off nxt.....................* (40 to 1 op 33 to 1 tchd 50 to 1) 4
3923³ DRUMMOND WARRIOR (Ire) 8-11-0 M A Fitzgerald, *trkd ldr till f 4th.....................* (5 to 4 fav tchd Evens and 11 to 8) f
Dist: 14l, 21l, dist. 4m 0.10s. a 6.10s (5 Ran).

(Brian O'Kane), J G M O'Shea

4090 Hartley's Jam Quantum Leap Handicap Hurdle Class D (0-120 4-y-o and up) £2,756 2m 110yds........ (7:35)

3741* ANTIGUAN FLYER [90] (v) 8-10-1 (3*) Michael Brennan, *made all, clr 3rd, rdn 2 out, all out.*
............(11 to 4 op 5 to 2 tchd 9 to 4 and 9 to 4) 1
3595⁶ PRIZEFIGHTER [114] 6-12-0 D Gallagher, *trkd wnr, rdn and mstk 3 out, cld nxt, pressed winner to line.*
................(Evens fav op 5 to 4 on tchd 11 to 10) 2
3842⁴ TIME WON'T WAIT (Ire) [110] 8-11-10 N Williamson, *hld up dsptd second whn jmpd slwly 4th, wknd appr 3 out, tld off.*
.............(9 to 4 op 7 to 4 tchd 5 to 2) 3
Dist: 1l, dist. 3m 35.80s. b 5.20s (3 Ran).
SR: 12/35/-/

(George Prodromou), G Prodromou

4091 Q103 FM Novices' Handicap Chase Class E (0-100 5-y-o and up) £2,886 2½m 110yds................ (8:05)

3639 MISTER GOODGUY (Ire) [72] 8-10-0 D Morris, *hld up, trkd ldr 8th to nxt, chlgd appr 2 out, led bef last, ran on wl,*
.............(6 to 1 op 14 to 1 tchd 16 to 1) 1
3775² MILL O'THE RAGS (Ire) [100] 8-12-0 J F Titley, *led second till rdn and hdd appr last, kpt on one pace.*
.............(6 to 4 on tchd 7 to 4 on and 11 to 10 on) 2
3939³ WOT NO GIN [72] 8-10-0 L Harvey, *led to second, in rear 5th, one pace frm 3 out.*
.............(9 to 2 op 4 to 1 tchd 5 to 1 and 7 to 2) 3
2461⁶ GEORGE ASHFORD (Ire) [86] (bl) 7-11-0 M Sharratt, *trkd ldr 6th to 8th and nxt till wknd aftr 3 out....* (16 to 1 op 8 to 1) 4
3966⁸ STAGE PLAYER [82] 11-10-10 I Lawrence, *pld hrd, in tch till wknd appr 3 out.......*(10 to 1 op 6 to 1 tchd 12 to 1) 5
3821⁴ COPPER CABLE [72] 10-10-0 M Ranger, *in tch till wknd tenth.*
.............(12 to 1 op 7 to 1 tchd 14 to 1) 6
Dist: 4l, 10l, 1¾l, 12l, 1¼l. 4m 59.20s. a 12.20s (6 Ran).

(M O'Brien), R Curtis

4092 Yelling Novices' Hurdle Class E (4-y-o and up) £2,355 2m 110yds (8:35)

3892* NORDANCE PRINCE (Ire) 6-11-6 N Williamson, *al prmnt, led 5th, rdn clr appr last.*
.............(7 to 4 on op 6 to 4 on tchd 5 to 4 on) 1
3849⁷ REAL MADRID 6-11-6 R Johnson, *hld up in tch, hdwy to chase wnr 3 out, hrd rdn frm nxt, no imprsn r-in.*
.............(3 to 1 op 11 to 4 tchd 7 to 2) 2
3849³ UNDAWATERSCUBADIVA 5-11-0 M A Fitzgerald, *hld up, hdwy appr 3 out, wknd approaching nxt.* (8 to 1 op 7 to 1) 3
3957⁸ SAPPHIRE SON (Ire) 5-11-0 B Fenton, *hld up, hdwy to pass btn horses aftr 3 out....*(50 to 1 op 33 to 1 tchd 66 to 1) 4
3973³ OUR EDDIE (bl) 8-11-0 K Gaule, *pld hrd, led appr 4th, hdd nxt, wknd 3 out.....................* (20 to 1 op 16 to 1) 5
1423⁷ KAIFOON (USA) 8-11-0 S Fox, *led aftr 1st, hdd appr 4th, wknd nxt.....................* (50 to 1 op 14 to 1) 6
3928⁹ FRENCH COUNTY 5-11-0 G Bradley, *mid-div, lost tch 5th.....................* (10 to 1) 7
DUFFETOES 5-11-0 J Ryan, *led till aftr 1st, beh frm 5th.*
.............(25 to 1 op 10 to 1) 8
3957 OGULLA 5-10-9 D Leahy, *al beh, tld off.*
.............(66 to 1 op 33 to 1 tchd 100 to 1) 9
1800⁵ NASHAAT (USA) 9-11-0 A Larnach, *blun and uns rdr 3rd.*
.............(16 to 1 op 10 to 1 tchd 20 to 1) ur
Dist: 3½l, 7l, 6l, 2l, 8l, 3½l, 10l, 15l. 3m 42.70s. a 1.70s (10 Ran).

(Pinks Gym), Miss Venetia Williams

NAVAN (IRE) (yielding to soft)
Wednesday May 14th

4093 Garlow Cross Handicap Chase (0-116 4-y-o and up) £3,082 3m .... (7:00)

3962⁵ FOURTH OF JULY [-] 13-11-5 T P Treacy, ...(10 to 1) 1
3935⁵ IRISH PEACE (Ire) [-] (bl) 9-10-13 (3*) G Cotter, ...(7 to 1) 2
3783⁵ TEAL BRIDGE [-] 12-11-12 C O'Dwyer, ...(5 to 1) 3
3944³ IF YOU BELIEVE (Ire) [-] 8-10-2 (3*) B Bowens, ...(5 to 1) 4
3962² PERSPEX GALE (Ire) [-] 9-10-9 C F Swan, ...(9 to 4 fav) f
3236 J J JACKSON (Ire) [-] 9-8-8¹ F Woods, ...(11 to 2) f
3877² AISEIRI (Ire) [-] 10-9-10 S Curran, ...(14 to 1) ur
Dist: 1½l, dist, 9l. 6m 16.90s. (7 Ran).

(Joseph E Keeling), J T R Dreaper

4094 Oberstown Maiden Hurdle (4-y-o and up) £3,082 2¼m.........(7:30)

3963² DUISKE ABBEY (Ire) 7-11-9 C F Swan, ...(6 to 4 on) 1
3945⁴ CONAGHER LEADER (Ire) 6-12-0 A J O'Brien, ...(8 to 1) 2
3952³ CONFECTIONER (Ire) 4-11-6 T P Treacy, ...(6 to 1) 3
3547 ALVINE (Ire) 5-11-13 P Leech, ...(25 to 1) 4
3608⁷ MINSTRELS PRIDE (Ire) 6-11-11 (3*) U Smyth, ...(33 to 1) 5
1432 CHIEF DELANEY (Ire) 5-11-13 L P Cusack, ...(9 to 1) 6
3816² ASFREEASTHEWIND (Ire) 6-11-9 C O'Dwyer, ...(10 to 1) 7
393 WILLIE THE LION (Ire) 6-11-7 (7*) Mr K M Roche, (33 to 1) 8
3889⁵ JOHNS TOUGH LADY (Ire) 5-11-8 K F O'Brien, ...(14 to 1) 9
3965⁹ PATS BOREEN (Ire) 6-11-7 (7*) B J Geraghty, ...(14 to 1) 10
MELT DOWN (Ire) 6-11-9 F Flood, ...(14 to 1) 11
3380 APPLE RIVER (Ire) 4-10-8 (7*) M W Martin, ...(50 to 1) 12
3943⁹ NORTH CITY 6-11-7 (7*) D A McLoughlin, ...(66 to 1) 13
STYLISH LORD (Ire) 6-12-0 T P Rudd, ...(14 to 1) pu
HEAD TO TOE (Ire) 4-10-8 (7*) Mr M P Horan, ..(50 to 1) pu
Dist: 5½l, ¾l, 10l, 3l. 4m 26.20s. (15 Ran).

(Best of Ther Syndicate), S J Treacy

4095 Donoghmore Handicap Hurdle (0-116 5-y-o and up) £3,082 2½m .... (8:00)

3754² THAI ELECTRIC (Ire) [-] 6-10-12 T J Mitchell, ...(7 to 4 fav) 1
3890³ FIDDLERS BOW VI (Ire) [-] 9-11-3 (7*) B J Geraghty, (9 to 4) 2
3842⁴ EIRE (Ire) [-] 8-9-0 (7*) D A McLoughlin, ...(12 to 1) 3
3942⁷ FALLOW TRIX (Ire) [-] 5-10-13 (3*) D Bromley, ...(5 to 1) 4
3089 LAURA'S BEAU [-] 13-9-8 (7*) J P O'Gorman, ...(33 to 1) 5
3935⁴ DOUBLE STRIKE (Ire) [-] (bl) 6-10-3 T P Rudd, ...(10 to 1) 6
3942⁸ FRESH DEAL (Ire) [-] 5-12-0 L P Cusack, ...(12 to 1) 7
3754 SIBERIAN TALE (Ire) [-] 7-11-2 (3*) Mr P J Casey, ..(10 to 1) 8
Dist: 7l, 10l, 5½l, 7l. 4m 50.60s. (8 Ran).

(Mrs Brenda Byrne), Sean Byrne

4096 Rathfeigh I.N.H. Flat Race (5-y-o and up) £3,082 2m............ (8:30)

3965⁵ RAGGLEPUSS 7-11-2 (7*) Mr T Gibney, ...(20 to 1) 1
3880⁵ CHOICE JENNY (Ire) 5-11-3 (5*) Mr A C Coyle, (7 to 2 jt-fav) 2
DERRYMORE MIST (Ire) 5-11-6 (7*) Mr A Fleming, ..(9 to 2) 3
2735⁹ FOYLE WANDERER (Ire) 6-11-2 (7*) Miss S McDonogh,
.............(20 to 1) 4
3840⁷ BE MY TRUMP (Ire) 5-11-1 (7*) Mr P A Farrell, ...(12 to 1) 5
3647 FELICITY'S PRIDE (Ire) (bl) 6-11-2 (7*) D Kirwan, ..(20 to 1) 6
3945² YOU MAKE ME LAUGH (Ire) 5-11-13 Mr R Walsh, (7 to 2 jt-fav) 7
3945 BLUE TOO (Ire) 6-11-2 (7*) Mr P Fahey, ...(20 to 1) 8
3840 MODILE (Ire) 6-11-9 Mr G J Harford, ...(9 to 1) 9
3697⁵ CLANAWHILLAN (Ire) 7-12-0 Mr D Marnane, ...(5 to 1) 10
MEGAN'S RUN (Ire) 5-11-5 (3*) Mr D Valentine, ...(25 to 1) 11
3818 WOOLPACKER (Ire) 6-11-7 (7*) Mr E Sheehy, ...(20 to 1) 12
FOLLOW THE GUIDE (Ire) 5-11-1 (7*) Mr S Ryder, (12 to 1) 13
SCROUTHEA (Ire) 7-12-0 Mr P Fenton, ...(14 to 1) 14
ARCHDALL LADY (Ire) 5-11-1 (7*) Miss M McGuinness,
.............(20 to 1) 15
MASTER NATIVE (Ire) 5-11-13 Mr J A Nash, ...(14 to 1) 16
4006 THE DINGER (Ire) 5-11-6 (7*) Mr M T Hogan, ...(20 to 1) 17
3948 SERRANA BANK (Ire) 6-11-2 (7*) Mr A J Dempsey, (20 to 1) 18
3449 SMILING MINSTREL (Ire) 6-11-7 (7*) Mr G Finlay, ..(20 to 1) 19
MCAULEY JO (Ire) 5-11-3 (5*) Mr L Lennon, ...(25 to 1) 20
NEARLY A WOMAN VI (Ire) 5-11-5 (3*) Mr P M Kelly, (25 to 1) 21
Dist: 5½l, ¾l, 7l, 6l. 3m 47.10s. (21 Ran).

(Mrs E Keane), Gerard Keane

PERTH (soft)
Wednesday May 14th
Going Correction: PLUS 0.70 sec. per fur.

4097 Cameron Motors Maiden Hurdle Class E (4-y-o and up) £2,747 2½m 110yds........................ (6:20)

3305⁴ SUPREME SOVIET 7-11-5 B Storey, *pressed ldr, dsptd ld fnl circuit, lft clr appr 2 out, all out.*
.............(6 to 4 fav tchd 7 to 4 and 11 to 8) 1
3866³ HAND OF STRAW (Ire) 5-11-5 K Johnson, *midfield, improved hfwy, outpcd aftr 4 out, staying on whn blun last, rallied.*
.............(7 to 2 op 3 to 1) 2
3761 FRISKY THYNE (Ire) 8-11-5 R Garritty, *settled on ins, effrt 3 out, no imprsn frm nxt...* (10 to 1 op 8 to 1 tchd 11 to 1) 3
1789³ LORD OF THE LOCH 6-11-5 R Supple, *settled beh ldg grp, rdn alng aftr 3 out, struggling last 2.*
.............(3 to 1 tchd 7 to 2 and 4 to 1) 4
3757⁶ NORDISK LEGEND 5-11-5 T Reed, *hld up and beh, nvr on terms.....................*(20 to 1 op 14 to 1) 5
3698 SPRINGLEA TOWER 4-10-13 P Niven, *prmnt to hfwy, sn outpcd and beh.....................* (33 to 1) 6
5477 IHTIMAAM (Fr) 5-11-5 J Supple, *hld up in rear, pushed alng 4 out, nvr able to chal....* (16 to 1 op 10 to 1 tchd 20 to 1) 7
GOLD BITS (Ire) 6-11-5 R Dunwoody, *jmpd badly, chsd ldrs, 6th and wkng whn f 3 out.* (10 to 1 op 7 to 1 tchd 11 to 1) f
3808⁶ CALLING THE TUNE 6-11-5 D Bentley, *in tch, struggling fnl circuit, pld up bef 2 out.* ....(50 to 1) pu

3756 RAMBLING RAJAH 5-10-12 (7*) Mr M Bradburne, *led, jnd fnl circuit, slight ld whn pld up appr 2 out.*
.... (16 to 1 op 12 to 1 tchd 20 to 1) pu
Dist: 1l, 11l, 8l, 29l, 6l, dist. 5m 23.60s. a 43.60s (10 Ran).
(I Campbell), A C Whillans

4098 Break Through Breast Cancer Novices' Chase Class D (5-y-o and up) £3,517 3m .... (6:50)

3702 SLOTAMATIQUE (Ire) (bl) 8-11-7 R Dunwoody, *nvr far away, effrt and drvn 3 out, led last 100 yards, kpt on wl.*
.... (7 to 4 fav op 11 to 8) 1
3967³ FERN LEADER (Ire) (bl) 7-11-1 Mr Chris Wilson, *mstks, led and sn clr, blun 5 out, wknd and hdd last 100 yards.*
.... (6 to 1 op 4 to 1) 2
3925² CULLANE LAKE (Ire) 7-11-2 R Supple, *in tch, pushed alng 11th, rallied 4 out, no imprsn frm nxt.*
.... (4 to 1 op 7 to 2 tchd 9 to 2 and 5 to 1) 3
3781 ROYAL BANKER (Ire) (bl) 7-11-1 P Carberry, *chsd ldr till outpcd appr 4 out, sn btn.* .... (10 to 1 op 7 to 1) 4
4022⁷ FESTIVAL FANCY 10-10-10 G Lee, *hld up, struggling 11th, pld up bef 5 out.* .... (16 to 1) pu
      ANOTHER MEADOW 9-11-1 B Storey, *beh, mstk 3rd, tld off 11th, pld up bef 13th.* .... (33 to 1 op 25 to 1) pu
1930⁵ THE ENERGISER 11-11-1 J Burke, *beh, struggling 7th, pld up bef 12th.* .... (50 to 1 op 25 to 1) pu
4001³ DRAGONS BAY (Ire) 8-11-1 P Niven, *hld up in tch, effrt whn hit 5 out, struggling 3 out, pld up bef nxt.* (9 to 2 op 7 to 2) pu
Dist: 2½l, 30l, 28l. 6m 20.60s. a 25.60s (8 Ran).
SR: 5/-/-/-/-/ (Slotamatics (Bolton) Ltd), G Richards

4099 Macallan 10 Y.O. Single Malt Juvenile Novices' Hurdle Class E (4-y-o) £2,528 2m 110yds .... (7:20)

BREYDON 10-12 G Cahill, *keen hold, trkd ldrs, came wide strt and led 2 out, ran on und pres.*
.... (13 to 8 fav op 7 to 4 tchd 2 to 1 and 5 to 4) 1
      SHEEMORE (Ire) 10-12 R Garritty, *led, hng lft and hdd 2 out, flashed tail, rallied run in.* (5 to 2 op 7 to 4 tchd 11 to 4) 2
3303⁹ ANIKA'S GEM (Ire) 10-7 M Foster, *pressed ldr to 3 out, sn drvn alng, btn bef nxt.* .... (9 to 4 op 2 to 1 tchd 5 to 2) 3
3997³ MR BRUNO 10-7 (5*) S Taylor, *chsd ldrs, blun 4th, sn lost tch.*
.... (12 to 1 op 8 to 1) 4
Dist: Nk, 22l, 7l. 4m 11.60s. a 30.60s (4 Ran).
(The Dregs Of Humanity), P Monteith

4100 Famous Grouse Handicap Chase Class D (0-125 5-y-o and up) £3,436 2½m 110yds .... (7:50)

3902* WEAVER GEORGE (Ire) [109] 7-10-7 (5*) R McGrath, *hld up in last pl, improved aftr 9th, ev ch 3 out, sn outpcd, styd on strly frm last to ld last strd.* .... (5 to 2 co-fav tchd 11 to 4) 1
3918* TOUGH TEST (Ire) [97] 7-10-0 B Storey, *chsd ldrs, blun badly and rdr lost iron 6 out, reco'red and ev ch 3 out, led aftr last, hdd last strd.* .... (4 to 1 op 3 to 1) 2
4000* NICHOLAS PLANT [102] 8-10-5 (6ex) G Cahill, *blun 1st, led, hdd aftr last, kpt on same pace.* .... (5 to 2 co-fav op 9 to 4 tchd 11 to 4) 3
3968³ ACAJOU III (Fr) [111] 9-10-7 (7*) C McCormack, *mstks, pressed ldr, blun 5 out, fdd last 3.* .... (5 to 2 co-fav op 9 to 4 tchd 11 to 4) 4
889* WISE ADVICE (Ire) [98] 7-10-1 D Bentley, *chsd ldrs, struggling 6 out, sn lost tch.* .... (12 to 1 op 10 to 1) 5
Dist: Sht-hd, 7l, 13l, 20l. 5m 11.70s. a 19.70s (5 Ran).
SR: 30/18/16/12/-/ (Regent Decorators Ltd), W Storey

4101 Bunnahabhain 12 Y.O. Single Malt Selling Handicap Hurdle Class G (0-100 4-y-o and up) £2,775 3m 110yds .... (8:20)

3246³ KIRSTENBOSCH [80] 10-11-0 (7*) W Dowling, *hld up, improved 8th, led bef 2 out, sn clr, hng lft and nrly ran out last, ran on.* .... (9 to 2 op 4 to 1 tchd 5 to 1) 1
3883⁷ MARDOOD [60] 12-9-9* (7*) Miss R Clark, *chsd ldg grp, hit 3rd, outpcd 6th, rallied and ev ch 4 out, one pace fnl 2.*
.... (16 to 1 op 12 to 1 tchd 20 to 1 and 25 to 1) 2
3803 PRECIPICE RUN [83] 12-11-10 L O'Hara, *midfield, drvn alng and outpcd bef 3 out, no imprsn nxt...* (16 to 1 op 10 to 1) 3
3883* SKANE RIVER (Ire) [72] 6-10-13 R Dunwoody, *in tch, improved to ld 4 out, hdd bef 2 out, sn btn.*
.... (5 to 4 fav tchd 2 to 1) 4
3803 DON'T TELL JUDY (Ire) [59] 9-9-9 (5*) S Taylor, *prmnt, outpcd 8th, rallied to chase ldrs 4 out, outpaced aftr nxt.*
.... (16 to 1 tchd 20 to 1) 5
3919⁴ MONKEY WENCH (Ire) [80] 6-11-7 B Storey, *hld up, improved 8th, drvn and outpcd aftr 3 out...* (9 to 1 op 8 to 1) 6
3123⁹ RUBER [80] 10-11-7 D Parker, *cl up, led briefly aftr 8th, struggling fnl 3...* (9 to 2 op 4 to 1 tchd 5 to 1) 7
3904* WHITEGATESPRINCESS (Ire) [67] (v) 6-11-0 (7*) C McCormack, *beh, struggling bef 3 out, fdd...* (7 to 1 op 6 to 1) 8
3761 BUSY BOY [63] 10-10-4 J Burke, *not much room and ran out 1st...* .... (33 to 1 op 16 to 1) ro

3992³ PLAYFUL JULIET (Can) [76] (bl) 9-10-12 (5*) R McGrath, *led and sn clr, hdd aftr 8th, soon btn, pld up bef 2 out.*
.... (12 to 1 op 8 to 1) pu
4020 MEADOWLECK [59] 8-9-8¹ (7*) I Jardine, *cl up, struggling 8th, pld up bef 2 out...* .... (33 to 1 op 50 to 1) pu
Dist: 12l, 2l, ¾l, 12l, 1l, nk, dist. 6m 16.20s. a 34.20s (11 Ran).
(Mrs Barbara Lungo), L Lungo

4102 Highland Park 12 Y.O. Single Malt Conditional Jockeys' Handicap Hurdle Class E (0-115 4-y-o and up) £2,640 2m 110yds .... (8:50)

3759³ RACHAEL'S OWEN [90] 7-11-10 R McGrath, *sn pushed alng in rear, improved aftr 4 out, led 2 out, not much room, ran on gmely.* .... (7 to 4 fav op 13 to 8 tchd 15 to 8) 1
3761⁸ PARIAH (Ire) [93] 8-11-10 (3*) C McCormack, *trkd ldrs, chlgd and hng lft 2 out, kpt on und pres last.*
.... (3 to 1 op 7 to 2 tchd 4 to 1) 2
3919³ SKIDDAW SAMBA [82] 8-11-2 G Lee, *hld up, improved bef 3 out, rdn and no extr frm nxt...* (11 to 2 op 9 to 2) 3
2625⁵ HIGH LOW (USA) [91] 9-11-4 (7*) A Ede, *led and sn clr, hdd 2 out, soon btn...* .... (14 to 1 op 10 to 1) 4
      FRENCH PROJECT (Ire) [72] 5-10-6 G F Ryan, *prmnt, hit 4 out, outpcd frm nxt...* .... (33 to 1 op 20 to 1) 5
3013 MERRY MERMAID [92] 7-11-12 S Melrose, *cl up, outpcd bef 3 out, sn btn...* .... (6 to 1 op 9 to 2) 6
4002⁴ FOX SPARROW [90] (bl) 7-11-10 E Husband, *chsd ldg grp, struggling 5th, sn no dngr.* (9 to 1 op 8 to 1 tchd 10 to 1) 7
Dist: ¾l, 8l, 7l, 24l, 18l, 5l. 4m 3.30s. a 22.30s (7 Ran).
(Die-Hard Racing Club), J S Goldie

CLONMEL (IRE) (good)
Thursday May 15th

4103 John T.Purcell Memorial Handicap Chase (0-109 5-y-o and up) £2,226 2m 1f .... (7:00)

825⁶ SAVUTI (Ire) [-] 8-11-7 (7*) M D Murphy, ... (6 to 1) 1
3877³ VIKING BUOY (Ire) [-] 5-9-4 (3*) G Cotter, ... (6 to 1) 2
3887 FANE'S TREASURE (Ire) [-] 8-9-8 (7*) B J Geraghty, (8 to 1) 3
3446⁶ EVER SO BOLD [-] 10-10-8 T P Treacy, ... (10 to 1) 4
4055³ SANDY FOREST LADY (Ire) [-] 8-9-9² (3*) K Whelan, (5 to 1) 5
3839² CARAGH BRIDGE [-] 10-10-9 C F Swan, ... (13 to 8 fav) 6
3418³ LISHILLAUN (Ire) [-] 8-9-9 (5*) Susan A Finn, ... (14 to 1) 7
3838⁹ FLIP YOUR LID [-] 8-10-6 T J Mitchell, ... (10 to 1) 8
Dist: 2l, 11l, hd, 11l. 4m 13.40s. (8 Ran).
(Mrs David V Tipper), W J Burke

4104 Cahir Hurdle (4-y-o and up) £2,291 2½m .... (7:30)

1484* GLORIOUS GALE (Ire) 7-11-4 C F Swan, ... (5 to 4 on) 1
3878* CRUCIAL MOVE (Ire) 6-11-4 T P Treacy, ... (7 to 4) 2
3955* STILLBYHERSELF (Ire) 7-10-5 (3*) G Cotter, ... (5 to 1) 3
Dist: 7l, 7l. 4m 50.30s. (3 Ran).
(J G Leahy), A P O'Brien

4105 Avonmore Foods Handicap Hurdle (0-109 4-y-o and up) £3,596 2½m .... (8:00)

3419⁸ CLUB COUPE (Ire) [-] 5-10-6 (5*) P G Hourigan, (Evens fav) 1
3696* ANNAELAINE (Ire) [-] 6-9-12 (7*) B J Geraghty, ... (6 to 4) 2
4004 SHE'LL BE GOOD (Ire) [-] 5-9-12 J R Barry, ... (7 to 1) 3
4060⁶ TEARDROP (Ire) [-] 5-10-7 J Shortt, ... (12 to 1) 4
4004 NOBULL (Ire) [-] (bl) 7-11-4 K F O'Brien, ... (9 to 1) 5
3068 MAY BLOOM (Ire) [-] (bl) 6-9-7 D J Casey, ... (20 to 1) 6
Dist: 2l, 11l, 6l, 2½l. 4m 54.50s. (6 Ran).
(Martin Doran), P Hughes

4106 Tipperary I.N.H. Flat Race (4-y-o and up) £2,226 2m .... (8:30)

1241 BRASSIS HILL (Ire) 6-12-0 Mr P Fenton, ... (9 to 2) 1
3755 DOUBLE RESOLVE 4-11-1 Mr R Walsh, ... (10 to 1) 2
3836⁶ JOSH'S FANCY (Ire) 6-11-2 (7*) Mr A J Dempsey, .. (7 to 1) 3
3 NO GUARANTEE (Ire) 5-11-8 Mr B M Cash, ... (8 to 1) 4
      MONTY'S FANCY (Ire) 4-10-9¹ (7*) Mr C A Cronin, (14 to 1) 5
3068 CROMWELLS KEEP (Ire) 6-12-0 Mr J A Berry, .. (9 to 4 fav) 6
      PERFECT PEACE (Ire) 6-11-9 Mr M Phillips, ... (12 to 1) 7
3647⁹ MOUNT HALL (Ire) 5-11-8 Mr J A Nash, ... (14 to 1) 8
      LADY BELLAGHY (Ire) 6-11-2 (7*) Mr E Gallagher, (14 to 1) 9
1715 COMINOLE (Ire) 8-11-2 (7*) Miss D O'Neill, ... (14 to 1) 10
1907 AJKNAPP (Ire) 5-11-6 (7*) Mr M M A Flood, ... (20 to 1) 11
      TRIMMER LADY (Ire) 8-11-2 (7*) Miss N Scallan, .. (14 to 1) 12
      MT LEINSTER (Ire) 4-10-8 (7*) Mr J M O'Brien, ... (14 to 1) 13
3224 COOLTEEN LAD (Ire) 8-11-7 (7*) Mr M Kavanagh, (20 to 1) 14
      FAITCH'S LADY (Ire) 4-10-8 (7*) Mr A Daly, ... (14 to 1) 15
3965 LITTLE CANTER (Ire) 5-11-1 (7*) Mr G Finlay, ... (12 to 1) 16
      EXECUTIVE STRESS (Ire) 6-11-7 (7*) Mr J M Barcoe,
.... (10 to 1) su
Dist: 4l, 1½l, nk, 1½l. 3m 52.70s. (17 Ran).
(Mrs Margaret Mullins), Anthony Mullins

PERTH (good to soft)
Thursday May 15th
Going Correction: PLUS 0.55 sec. per fur.

4107 Pimms Charity Polo Tournament Novices' Chase Class E (5-y-o and up) £3,111 2m................ (1:55)

2631³ KNOW-NO-NO (Ire) 8-11-0 R Garritty, *nvr far away, smooth hdwy to ld aftr 3 out, drw clr frm nxt, easily.*
..................................(9 to 2 op 4 to 1) 1

3865 KINCARDINE BRIDGE (USA) 8-10-7 (7*) Mr M Bradburne, *led to second, cl up, led 6 out, blun 3 out, sn hdd, hit nxt, no extr.*
..................................(25 to 1 tchd 33 to 1) 2

3662² ALL CLEAR (Ire) 6-11-0 N Williamson, *cl up, chlgd 6 out, outpcd fnl 3.*
..................................(9 to 1 op 6 to 1) 3

3719⁵ RALLEGIO 8-11-12 G Cahill, *hld up, niggled to improve 6 out, mstk 4 out, sn outpcd.*....... (7 to 4 on tchd 13 to 8 on) 4

3927² SPECTRE BROWN 7-10-7 (7*) Mr T J Barry, *taken early to post, pld hrd, led second, jmpd rght, hdd 6 out, sn lost tch.*
..................................(16 to 1 tchd 20 to 1) 5

3781⁴ REGAL DOMAIN (Ire) 6-11-0 K Johnson, *jmpd badly in rear, nvr on terms.*..................(33 to 1 op 25 to 1) 6

4009³ SUNKALA SHINE 9-10-7 (7*) Miss R Clark, *chasing ldrs whn f 4th.*....................(12 to 1 op 8 to 1 tchd 14 to 1) f

3803 AKITO RACING (Ire) 6-10-2 (7*) C McCormack, *hld up, improved and in ld whn f 5 out.*......(50 to 1 op 25 to 1) f

Dist: 17l, 10l, 16l, 11l, 4l. 4m 6.10s. a 15.10s (8 Ran).
SR: 23/6/-/-/-/ (Mrs A Kane), M D Hammond

4108 Macdonalds Solicitors Quick Ransom Novices' Hurdle Class E (4-y-o and up) £2,276 3m 110yds.... (2:25)

3031⁶ MILITARY ACADEMY 8-11-12 P Carberry, *uns rdr and bolted one circuit bef strt, cl up, led before 8th, canter.* .(5 to 4 jt-fav op 6 to 4 on) 1

3756¹ PENTLANDS FLYER (Ire) 6-11-6 N Williamson, *hld up, improved to press wnr 4 out, mstk nxt, no ch wth winner fnl 2.*
..................................(5 to 4 jt-fav op 9 to 4) 2

3761 BLOOMING SPRING (Ire) 8-11-1 L O'Hara, *hld up, steady hdwy 7th, rdn and outpcd aftr 3 out, no dngr after.*
..................................(16 to 1 op 10 to 1) 3

3833 JIGGINSTOWN 10-10-7 (7*) L Cooper, *chsd ldrs till outpcd bef 2 out.*..........(10 to 1 op 8 to 1 tchd 12 to 1) 4

4001 STRONGADING (Ire) 7-11-0 A S Smith, *chsd ldrs, outpcd 3 out, sn btn.*..........(11 to 1 op 12 to 1 tchd 14 to 1) 5

3710⁶ SCALLY BEAU 6-11-0 R Supple, *hld up, lost tch frm 4 out.*
..................................(25 to 1 tchd 33 to 1) 6

3756 GUILE POINT 6-10-9 J Burke, *chsd ldrs till blun 8th, sn wknd and pld up bef nxt.*...............(40 to 1 op 50 to 1) pu

3663⁷ OTTADINI (Ire) 5-10-9 T Reed, *led till hdd bef 8th, sn wknd, tld off whn pld up before 2 out.*.....(33 to 1 op 25 to 1) pu

Dist: 3½l, 12l, 2½l, ½l, dist. 6m 17.30s. a 35.30s (8 Ran).
(Robert Ogden), G Richards

4109 Rhone-Poulenc Seed Protection Handicap Chase Class E (0-110 5-y-o and up) £3,590 3m......... (3:00)

1808¹ EAST HOUSTON [101] 8-11-5 (5*) R McGrath, *nvr far away, not much room aftr 4 out, led 2 out, rdn out.*
..................................(7 to 1 op 4 to 1 tchd 8 to 1) 1

3869³ RUSTY BLADE [80] 8-10-3 G Cahill, *chsd ldg grp, rdn and outpcd 4 out, styd on betw last 2, not rch wnr.*
..................................(10 to 1 op 8 to 1 tchd 12 to 1) 2

3867¹ NIJWAY [87] 7-10-10 B Storey, *cl up, dsptd ld frm 8th, hdd 2 out, not quicken.*.....(9 to 4 fav op 2 to 1 tchd 5 to 2) 3

4010⁶ BRIGHT DESTINY [77] 6-9-7 (7*) Mr O McPhail, *chsd ldrs, mstk and lost pl 6 out, styd on fnl 2, no imprsn.*
..................................(10 to 1 op 6 to 1 tchd 11 to 1) 4

3159³ GOLD PIGEON [77] 8-10-0 R Supple, *dsptd ld thrght till outpcd fnl 2.*............(11 to 2 op 5 to 1 tchd 6 to 1) 5

3758 KALAJO [95] 7-11-4 G Lee, *hld up, pushed alng to improve 9th, struggling bef 2 out, virtually pld up run in.*
..................................(9 to 2 op 3 to 1) 6

3967⁴ MAJORITY MAJOR (Ire) [80] 8-10-3 A S Smith, *dsptd ld till lost pl 5 out, sn btn.*.....(9 to 1 op 5 to 1 tchd 10 to 1) 7

3584 ITS A DEAL [77] 11-10-0 F Perratt, *jmpd badly, slight ld till 5th, lost pl nxt, tld off whn pld up bef 6 out.*
..................................(33 to 1 op 20 to 1) pu

Dist: 2l, 2½l, 1½l, 5l, dist, sht-hd. 6m 20.40s. a 25.40s (8 Ran).
(Highgreen Partnership), J J O'Neill

4110 Bell & Sime Handicap Hurdle Class D (0-120 4-y-o and up) £2,818 2½m 110yds........................ (3:30)

3782⁴ LINLATHEN [111] 7-12-0 P Niven, *made all, hng lft bef 2 out, drvn out frm last.*.. (5 to 4 fav op 11 to 10 tchd 11 to 8) 1

3976³ CHILL WIND [83] 8-10-0 R Supple, *nvr far away, rdn and ev ch 2 out, not quicken last.*..........(11 to 1 op 7 to 1) 2

3355² DUKE OF PERTH [95] 6-10-12 N Williamson, *pressed wnr, ev ch 3 out, sn rdn, one pace frm nxt.*......(11 to 4 op 5 to 2) 3

4102² PARIAH (Ire) [93] 8-10-10 R Dunwoody, *chsd ldrs, effrt bef 2 out, sn btn.*..........................(9 to 4 tchd 5 to 2) 4
Dist: 4l, 4l, 13l. 5m 10.80s. a 30.80s (4 Ran).
(Mrs J A Niven), Mrs M Reveley

4111 Reeves & Neylan Novices' Handicap Hurdle Class E (0-105 4-y-o and up) £2,710 2m 110yds............. (4:00)

4002¹ TEEJAY'N'AITCH (Ire) [92] 5-11-5 (5*,7ex) S Taylor, *made all, hit 4th, jnd aftr 3 out, ran on strly frm last.*
..................................(11 to 4 op 2 to 1) 1

3710⁵ HOPEFUL LORD (Ire) [78] 5-10-10 A S Smith, *hld up in rear, effrt 2 out, chsd wnr aftr last, kpt on.*
..................................(8 to 1 op 6 to 1 tchd 10 to 1) 2

3919² CHARLISTIONA [77] 6-10-2 (7*) S Melrose, *keen hold, settled in tch, improved 4 out, outpcd aftr nxt, styd on frm last.*
..................................(7 to 2 op 4 to 1 tchd 5 to 1) 3

3757¹ TAWAFIJ (USA) [92] 8-11-5 R Garritty, *hld up beh ldg grp, effrt bef 2 out, fdd run in.*..(3 to 1 op 11 to 4 tchd 7 to 2) 4

3805⁹ SIX CLERKS (Ire) [90] (bl) 4-11-3 P Carberry, *chsd ldrs gng wl, chlgd aftr 3 out, rdn and found nothing nxt.*
..................................(5 to 2 fav op 9 to 4 tchd 11 to 4) 5

3756 PRINCE BALTASAR [68] 8-10-0 R Supple, *pressed wnr, ev ch 3 out, struggling bef nxt.*..........(50 to 1 op 33 to 1) 6
Dist: 1¼l, hd, 6l, 15l, 14l. 4m 4.20s. a 23.20s (6 Ran).
(Andrew Paterson), J S Goldie

4112 Linlithgow & Stirlingshire Hunt Novices' Hunters' Chase Class H (5-y-o and up) £1,839 2½m 110yds.. (4:30)

3989² SAVOY 10-11-7 (7*) Captain A Ogden, *nvr far away, effrt bef 2 out, styd on wl to ld nr finish.*
..................................(11 to 8 fav op 5 to 4 tchd 6 to 4) 1

3777² HOWAYMAN 7-11-12 (7*) Mr A Parker, *cl up, dsptd ld frm 8th, led bef 3 out, hdd towards finish.*..(2 to 1 tchd 9 to 4) 2

3777⁸ MASTER KIT (Ire) 8-11-12 (7*) Mr J Billinge, *cl up on outsd till wknd bef 2 out.*..........(8 to 1 op 6 to 1) 3

3921³ WILL TRAVEL (Ire) 8-11-7 (7*) Mr A Robson, *led to 8th, struggling 5 out, tld off.*............(14 to 1 tchd 16 to 1) 4

REED 12-11-7 (7*) Mr O McPhail, *cl up, led 8th till hdd bef 3 out, btn whn blun badly 2 out.*
..................................(50 to 1 op 33 to 1 tchd 66 to 1) 5

HARDEN GLEN 6-11-7 (7*) Miss S Laidlaw, *mstks, chsd ldg bunch till blun and lost tch 6 out.*...(25 to 1 op 20 to 1) 6

KING SPRING 12-11-9 (5*) Mrs V Jackson, *al beh and detached, tld off whn pld up bef 4 out.* (33 to 1 op 25 to 1) pu

3777 DENIM BLUE 8-12-3 (5*) Miss P Robson, *nmpd strt, sddl slpd and sn pld up.*........(15 to 2 op 8 to 1 tchd 9 to 1) pu
Dist: Nk, 18l, 21l, 3l, dist. 5m 15.10s. a 23.10s (8 Ran).
(Robert Ogden), G Richards

4113 Perth Maiden National Hunt Flat Class H (4,5,6-y-o) £1,020 2m 110yds........................ (5:00)

QUEENSWAY (Ire) 5-11-7 (3*) F Leahy, *hld up, steady hdwy hfwy, rdn to ld o'r one furlong out, kpt on strly.*
..................................(7 to 1 tchd 8 to 1) 1

YOUNG TOMO (Ire) 5-11-3 (7*) Mr O McPhail, *cl up, led 3 fs out till o'r one out, kpt on same pace.* (20 to 1 op 12 to 1) 2

3661⁴ OLD BOMBAY (Ire) 5-11-3 (7*) C McCormack, *set steady pace, led hdd 3 fs out, sn outpcd.*...(4 to 1 tchd 6 to 1) 3

3048⁹ NOBLE TOM (Ire) 5-11-5 (5*) S Taylor, *sn prmnt, rdn and outpcd entering strt.*.................(14 to 1 op 10 to 1) 4

WOTSTHEPROBLEM 5-11-10 G Lee, *settled on outer, outpcd 5 fs out, no dngr after.*........(9 to 4 fav tchd 3 to 1) 5

3439⁶ BEN DOULA 5-11-3 (7*) M Herrington, *cl up, rdn o'r 5 fs out, sn outpcd.*..................(10 to 1 op 6 to 1) 6

INNOVATE (Ire) 5-11-2 (3*) P Midgley, *in tch, struggling appr strt, sn btn.*..........(25 to 1 op 20 to 1 tchd 33 to 1) 7

RISING DAWN 5-11-10 Mr Chris Wilson, *settled on ins, struggling entering strt, eased.*.........(14 to 1 op 10 to 1) 8

3808⁹ HANSEL'S STREAK 5-11-3 (7*) S Melrose, *beh, rdn hfwy, nvr on terms.*....................(50 to 1 op 33 to 1) 9

3015 CHAN MOVE (bl) 5-11-3 (7*) Mr T J Barry, *towards rear, struggling o'r 6 fs out, nvr on terms.*..(50 to 1 op 33 to 1) 10

693⁷ PAPERWORK PETE (Ire) 5-11-5 (5*) R McGrath, *midfield, struggling hfwy, sn btn..*(8 to 1 op 10 to 1 tchd 14 to 1) 11

SHE'S ALL HEART 4-11-0 Mr A Parker, *struggling hfwy, sn btn.*..........(14 to 1 op 12 to 1 tchd 16 to 1) 12

YEENOSO (Ire) 5-11-5 D Thomas, *pld hrd, in tch, btn o'r 4 fs out.*....................(33 to 1 op 20 to 1) 13

THE KEEK (Ire) 5-11-2 (3*) G F Ryan, *pld hrd, sn cl up, lost pl hfwy, tld off.*...............(14 to 1 op 8 to 1) 14
Dist: 6l, 9l, 10l, 1½l, 5l, nk, 8l, 12l, 1¾l, 20l. 3m 57.50s. (14 Ran).
(J G FitzGerald), J G FitzGerald

DOWNPATRICK (IRE) (good to firm)
Friday May 16th

4114 Heart Of Down Maiden Hurdle (4-y-o and up) £1,712 2m 1f 172yds (6:00)

3817 PILS INVADER (Ire) 9-11-1 D T Evans, ... (100 to 30) 1

3394[4] FRANKIE WILLOW (Ire) 4-11-6 C O'Dwyer, ... (Evens fav) 2
3963[5] KAVANAGHS DREAM (Ire) 8-12-0 H Rogers, ...(7 to 1) 3
3964[6] NEPI LAD (Ire) 9-11-7 (7*) D A McLoughlin, ...(7 to 1) 4
3840 SECRET TRIX (Ire) 5-11-2 (3*) D Bromley, ...(33 to 1) 5
3889 MAID TO MOVE (Ire) 4-10-8 (7*) Mr R P McNalley, .(10 to 1) 6
3755 MR BOSSMAN (Ire) 4-10-12 (3*) G Cotter, ...(14 to 1) 7
Dist: 11l, sht-hd, 20l, 8l. 4m 14.40s. (7 Ran).

(Poppies Punting Syndicate II), A D Evans

4115 Frank Fitzsimons Hunters Chase (5-y-o and up) £1,712 3m........ (7:30)

SIDEWAYS SALLY (Ire) 7-11-2 (7*) Mr R P McNalley,
....(12 to 1) 1
WILBAR (Ire) 8-11-7 (7*) Mr J G O'Connell, ... (6 to 1) 2
2869 CHENE ROSE (Ire) 9-11-2 (7*) Miss A McCartney, (33 to 1) 3
304[2] BABY JAKE (Ire) 7-11-7 (7*) Mr B Hassett, ...(6 to 4 on) 4
3646[4] FUNNY YE KNOW (Ire) 8-12-0 Mr P F Graffin, ...(20 to 1) 5
3935 DROMOD POINT (Ire) 8-11-7 (7*) Mr D Whelan, ...(25 to 1) 6
3888[4] HALF SCOTCH (Ire) 9-11-2 (7*) Mr A Stronge, ...(25 to 1) 7
CHARIOT DEL (Ire) 9-11-7 (7*) Mr W Ewing, ...(12 to 1) f
3888[2] COOL IT (Ire) 7-11-10[3] (7*) Mr P Duggan, ...(6 to 1) pu
3888[5] ROYAL ARISTOCRAT (Ire) 8-11-6 (3*) Mr B R Hamilton,
....(20 to 1) pu
3888 CHRISTIMATT (Ire) 6-11-9 (5*) Mr G Elliott, ...(25 to 1) pu
3888 PAULS POINT 10-11-8[1] (7*) Mr A Tate, ...(25 to 1) pu
3888[6] FOREVER GOLD 12-11-7 (7*) Mr K Ross, ...(25 to 1) pu
Dist: 2½l, ½l, 7l, 2l. 6m 5.00s. (13 Ran).

(J K Magee), A J Martin

4116 Toals Bookmakers Downpatrick Chase (5-y-o and up) £2,911 2¼m
....(8:00)

3699[3] POWER PACK (Ire) 9-11-11 (3*) Mr B R Hamilton, (2 to 1 on) 1
3838[6] SPECTACLE (Ire) 7-11-1[1] (7*) Mr C P McGivern, ...(10 to 1) 2
3838[3] COLLON (Ire) 8-11-2 (5*) Mr G Elliott, ...(3 to 1) 3
3891 GRANNY BOWLY (Ire) 7-10-13 (3*) D Bromley, ...(10 to 1) 4
3963 BITOFA DIVIL (Ire) 6-11-0 (7*) D A McLoughlin, ...(10 to 1) 5
3877 BALLY UPPER (Ire) 9-11-4 (3*) G Cotter, ...(33 to 1) f
2757 LADY MEARGAN (Ire) 6-10-11 (5*) T Martin, ...(25 to 1) f
3879[9] NORMINS HUSSAR (Ire) 5-11-0 T J Mitchell, ...(20 to 1) pu
Dist: 6l, 10l, 7l, 15l. 4m 32.50s. (8 Ran).

(P A D Scouller), J F C Maxwell

4117 Caithness I.N.H. Flat Race (4-y-o and up) £1,712 2m 1f 172yds..... (8:30)

3180 HEART 'N SOUL-ON (Ire) 6-11-9 (5*) Mr G Elliott, ...(8 to 1) 1
SUSHARI (Ire) 5-11-8 Mr B M Cash, ...(9 to 4) 2
3945[3] HANDSOME ANTHONY (Ire) 6-11-11 (3*) Mr B R Hamilton,
....(Evens fav) 3
3945 KATOUCHE (Ire) (bl) 6-12-0 Mr R Walsh, ...(6 to 1) 4
WEAVER'S STAR (Ire) 5-11-1 (7*) Mr P M Heaney, (12 to 1) 5
3945 DUNMORE SUNSET (Ire) 5-11-13 Mr A R Coonan, (33 to 1) 6
DEERFIELD (Ire) 7-11-7 (7*) Mr L J Gracey, ...(16 to 1) 7
A BIT OF A RASCAL (Ire) 8-11-7 (7*) Mr S Martin, ..(25 to 1) 8
MOIRAS DARLING 5-11-8 Mr A J Martin, ...(6 to 1) 9
3945 MUST BE DONE (Ire) 5-11-9 (7*) Mr C Cosgrave, ..(33 to 1) 10
REDS PARADISE (Ire) 5-11-8 (5*) Mr J T McNamara,
....(25 to 1) 11
Dist: ¾l, hd, ½l, 15l. 4m 8.20s. (11 Ran).

(Mrs Michael Cunningham), Michael Cunningham

FOLKESTONE (good)
Friday May 16th
Going Correction: MINUS 0.35 sec. per fur.

4118 Nigel Collison Fuels Novices' Hunters' Chase Class H for the Guy Peate Memorial Challenge Trophy (5-y-o and up) £1,990 3¼m... (5:50)

MISTER MAIN MAN (Ire) 9-12-0 (7*) Mr S Sporborg, led to 3
out, led ag'n nxt, rdn last, hld on und pres run-in.
..................................(13 to 8 fav op 6 to 4 tchd 2 to 1) 1
3832 NO JOKER (Ire) 9-12-0 (7*) Mr P Scott, trkd wnr till aftr 12th,
effrt to ld 3 out, hdd nxt, mstk last, rallied wl und pres.
....(7 to 1 op 4 to 1) 2
POLAR ANA (Ire) 8-11-9 (7*) Miss S Gladders, jmpd lft, in tch,
prog to chase wnr aftr 12th till 15th, ev ch aftr 3 out, sn wknd.
..................................(9 to 2 op 4 to 1 tchd 11 to 2 and 6 to 1) 3
KATES CASTLE 10-11-9 (7*) Mr J Van Praagh, prmnt till 4th
and wkng whn blun 3 out, no ch aftr... (13 to 1 op 10 to 1) 4
CENTRE STAGE 11-12-0 (7*) Mr A Warr, jmpd slwly 4th and
5th, al beh, tld off frm tenth..........(40 to 1 op 20 to 1) 5
BALLYALLIA CASTLE (Ire) 8-12-0 (7*) Mr N Bloom, trkd ldrs,
5th whn f 7th..................(9 to 2 op 7 to 2 tchd 5 to 1) f
SERIOUS MONEY (USA) 12-12-0 (7*) Miss C Savell, jmpd
very slwly, al tld off, refused 13th.....(100 to 1 op 50 to 1) ref
BRIGHT HOUR 12-12-0 (7*) Miss J Grant, nvr nr ldrs, beh frm
13th, tld off and pld up bef 3 out.
...................(66 to 1 op 33 to 1 tchd 100 to 1) pu

RUSTIC RAMBLE 11-12-4 (3*) Mr P Hacking, strted slwly, nvr
gng wl, tld off and pld up bef 13th.
.................................(9 to 1 op 8 to 1 tchd 10 to 1) pu
LINGER BALINDA (bl) 11-11-9 (7*) Mr P Bull, prmnt to tenth,
wkng in 5th whn blun 13th, tld off and pld up bef 3 out.
..........................(50 to 1 tchd 66 to 1 and 100 to 1) pu
Dist: ½l, 13l, 14l, dist. 6m 38.50s. a 23.50s (10 Ran).

(Sir Chippendale Keswick), C Sporborg

4119 Kent And Surrey Bloodhounds Challenge Cup Maiden Hunters' Chase Class H (5-y-o and up) £1,600 2m 5f
....(6:25)

STORMING LADY 7-11-13 (3*) Mr P Hacking, al gng wl, trkd
ldr tenth, led aftr nxt, drw well clr after 3 out, imprsv.
..................................(2 to 1 tchd 5 to 2) 1
WEDNESDAYS AUCTION (Ire) 9-12-2 (5*) Mr T McCarthy, last
whn pckd 1st, sn wl beh, tld off 7th, kpt on frm 11th, took poor
second aftr last.........(50 to 1 op 20 to 1 tchd 66 to 1) 2
BARN ELMS 10-12-0 (7*) Mr A Hickman, chsd ldr aftr 6th till
tenth, wknd 3 out, fnshd tired.
..................................(20 to 1 op 12 to 1 tchd 33 to 1) 3
SUPREME DEALER 12-12-0 (7*) Mr A Warr, chsd ldr till aftr
6th, wkng whn mstk 9th, sn wl beh.
..................................(20 to 1 op 14 to 1 tchd 25 to 1) 4
MR ORIENTAL 7-12-0 (7*) Mr G Gigantesco, mstks, rear frm
6th, tld off whn f 9th. (100 to 1 op 50 to 1 tchd 200 to 1) f
YOUR OPINION 11-12-0 (7*) Mr M Walters, prmnt, cl 4th whn
blun and uns rdr tenth. (50 to 1 op 33 to 1 tchd 66 to 1) ur
3848[2] COOL BANDIT (Ire) 7-12-0 (7*) Mr T Hills, led and sn clr, hdd
aftr 11th, second and wl btn whn blun and uns rdr 2 out.
..............(8 to 1 op 7 to 1 tchd 9 to 1 and 14 to 1) ur
KUMADA 10-12-0 (7*) Miss S Gritton, nvr gng wl, al beh, tld
off 8th, pld up bef 3 out..(25 to 1 op 8 to 1 tchd 33 to 1) pu
3850[2] MISTER SPECTATOR (Ire) 8-12-4 (3*) Mr Simon Andrews, not
gng wl and nvr gng well, lost pl 5th, well beh whn pld up bef
7th, lme.......(5 to 4 on op 6 to 4 on tchd 6 to 5 on) pu
ROSCOLVIN (Ire) 5-11-7 (7*) Mr P Bull, mstks, hld up, beh frm
7th, tld off and pld up bef 2 out.
..................................(12 to 1 op 7 to 1 tchd 14 to 1) pu
Dist: Dist, 7l, 14l. 5m 12.20s. a 1.20s (10 Ran).
SR: 16/-/-/-/-/-/

(Mike Roberts), M J Roberts

4120 IBS Appeal Open Hunters' Chase Class H for the Royal Judgement Challenge Trophy (5-y-o and up) £1,900 3¼m................(6:55)

VIRIDIAN 12-12-4 (3*) Mr M Rimell, chsd ldr 11th, chlgd frm 5
out, level and gng better whn lft wl clr 2 out, eased r-in.
..................................(6 to 4 fav op 7 to 4 tchd 2 to 1) 1
4018[3] FARINGO (bl) 12-12-0 (7*) Miss C Grissell, led to 5th, sn
pushed along, chsd ldr to 11th, wknd aftr nxt, lft poor second 2
out....................(40 to 1 op 25 to 1 tchd 50 to 1) 2
TEATRADER 11-11-8[1] (7*) Miss T Blazey, beh, hmpd 7th, no
prog frm 13th, sn tld off, lft poor 3rd 2 out.
..................................(14 to 1 op 10 to 1 tchd 16 to 1) 3
3850[6] GRASSINGTON (Ire) (v) 8-11-7 (7*) Mr Scott Quirk, trkd ldrs,
4th whn f 7th..........(50 to 1 op 25 to 1 tchd 66 to 1) f
FOXBOW (Ire) (bl) 7-11-9 (5*) Mr A Sansome, chsd ldr, led 5th,
rdn and pld whn f 2 out...................(11 to 1 op 6 to 1) f
3800[2] CAPE COTTAGE 13-12-7 (7*) Mr A Phillips, wtd wth, 5th and
in tch whn brght dwn 7th. (5 to 1 op 7 to 4 tchd 11 to 2) bd
CARDINAL RICHELIEU 10-11-7 (7*) Mr S Sporborg, strted
slwly, wl beh, some prog whn pld up bef 12th, lme.
..................................(7 to 4 tchd 15 to 8 and 11 to 8) pu
Dist: 19l, 7l. 6m 38.00s. a 23.00s (7 Ran).

(Denis Hine), D G Duggan

4121 Shepherd Neame United Hunts Open Champion Hunters' Chase Class H (6-y-o and up) £2,831 3m 7f... (7:30)

GLEN OAK 12-11-10 (7*) Mr J M Pritchard, wtd wth, prog to
chase ldr aftr 14th, pushed alng 3 out, led after nxt, styd on wl.
..................................(6 to 4 on op Evens tchd 13 to 8 on) 1
3274[2] SIRISAT 13-11-7 (7*) Miss T Blazey, led till aftr 2 out, not
quicken, wknd r-in.........(7 to 2 op 2 to 1 tchd 4 to 1) 2
3848[3] TAU 12-11-7 (7*) Mr A Warr, chsd ldr to 13th, sn wknd, no ch
frm 15th, took poor 3rd nr finish.......(50 to 1 op 25 to 1) 3
AMERICAN EYRE 12-11-7 (7*) Miss S Gladders, settled in
4th, outpcd aftr 14th, no imprsn ldrs nxt.
..................................(12 to 1 op 5 to 1 tchd 14 to 1) 4
EARLY MAN 10-11-11 (7*) Mr P Hacking, settled in 3rd, chsd
ldr 13th till mstk nxt, mistake and wknd 15th, pld up bef 3 out.
..................................(4 to 1 tchd 5 to 1) pu
Dist: 12l, 24l, 1½l. 7m 58.10s. a 28.10s (5 Ran).

(R J Mansell), D G Duggan

4122 Grant's Cherry Brandy South East Champion Novices' Hunters' Chase Final Class H (5-y-o and up) £1,800 2m 5f........................(8:00)

MUSKERRY MOYA (Ire) 8-11-9 (7*) Miss A Goschen, *made all, jnd 2 out, shaken up and ran on wl appr last.*
.........................(8 to 1 op 5 to 1 tchd 9 to 1) 1
REVEREND BROWN (Ire) 7-12-2 (5*) Mr A Sansome, *chsd wnr, mstk 9th, rdn 3 out, jnd winner nxt, wknd rpdly and jmpd last slwly, lme.*
.......(13 to 8 fav op 7 to 4 tchd 6 to 4 and 15 to 8) 2
MUTUAL MEMORIES 9-12-4 (3*) Mr Simon Andrews, *keen hold, chsd ldrs, mstk 9th, sn struggling, took poor 3rd und pres nr finish.*.....................(10 to 1 op 5 to 1) 3
RED CHANNEL (Ire) 7-12-0 (7*) Mr A Hickman, *strted slwly, pld hrd and hld up, prog to chase ldrs 7th, mstk 11th, wknd 3 out.*............................(5 to 2 op 3 to 1) 4
BISHOPS TALE 7-12-0 (7*) Mr R J Barrett, *strted very slwly, beh, rdn aftr 7th, no prog 9th, sn tld off...* (6 to 1 op 4 to 1) 5
SCARRA DARRAGH (Ire) 7-11-9 (7*) Mr A Charles-Jones, *several slow jumps, al beh, tld off frm 11th.*
....(33 to 1 tchd 50 to 1) 6
AND WHY NOT 9-12-0 (7*) Mr J Van Praagh, *f 1st.*
.......................(9 to 1 op 5 to 1 tchd 10 to 1) f
3969 ISHMA (Ire) 6-12-0 (7*) Mr D Page, *prmnt to 3rd, sn wknd, tld off and pld up bef 9th.*.................(50 to 1 op 25 to 1) pu
Dist: 29l, 18l, 1¼l, 23l, 11l. 5m 23.20s. a 12.20s (8 Ran).
(N W Rimington), J W Dufosee

4123 Pett Farm Equestrian Services United Hunts Open Challenge Cup Hunters' Chase Class H (5-y-o and up) £2,005 2m 5f............ (8:30)

3851* SLIEVENAMON MIST 11-12-9 (5*) Mr J Jukes, *hld up beh, prog to chase ldr aftr tenth, led appr 2 out, sn clr, eased r-in.*
.............(11 to 4 on op 5 to 2 on tchd 3 to 1 on) 1
3851² COUNTERBID (bl) 10-12-2 (5*) Mr A Sansome, *led, jmpd slwly 1st and sn hdd, led ag'n 4th, rdn and headed appr 2 out, no ch wth wnr.*
.............(15 to 2 op 5 to 1 tchd 9 to 1 and 10 to 1) 2
NO INHIBITIONS 10-12-0 (7*) Mr A Warr, *prmnt, chsd ldr briefly tenth, outpcd whn mstk nxt, no dngr aftr.*
..............................(50 to 1 op 20 to 1 tchd 66 to 1) 3
JUST JACK 11-12-4 (3*) Mr Simon Andrews, *mstk second, prmnt, chsd ldr aftr 8th till tenth, outpcd frm nxt.*
..........................(20 to 1 op 12 to 1 tchd 25 to 1) 4
EMERALD MOON 10-12-0 (7*) Mr T Hills, *in tch to tenth, sn outpcd and beh.*......(40 to 1 op 25 to 1 tchd 66 to 1) 5+
SURE PRIDE (USA) 9-12-0 (7*) Mr P G Hall, *al beh, tld off frm 9th.*.....................(50 to 1 op 33 to 1 tchd 66 to 1) 5+
3578* YOUNG NIMROD 10-12-0 (7*) Mr G Wragg, *wtd wth, 6th whn uns rdr 5th.*..........................(4 to 1 op 3 to 1) ur
BOLL WEEVIL 11-12-0 (7*) Miss J Grant, *led aftr 1st till 4th, chsd ldr till aftr 8th, wknd, tld off and pld up bef 2 out.*
...........................(25 to 1 op 33 to 1 tchd 33 to 1) pu
Dist: 6l, 22l, 13l, nk, dd-ht. 5m 17.40s. a 6.40s (8 Ran).
(Nick Viney), Victor Dartnall

AINTREE (good)
Friday May 16th
Going Correction: PLUS 0.40 sec. per fur.

4124 Aintree Novices' Hunters' Chase Class H (5-y-o and up) £1,738 3m 1f .... (5:45)

3991* FRONT COVER 7-11-7 (7*) Miss S Vickery, *nvr far away, reminder appr 5 out, sn led, clr 3 out, unchlgd.*
.................(9 to 4 on op 2 to 1 on tchd 7 to 4 on) 1
THE RUM MARINER 10-11-7 (7*) Mr D S Jones, *led, jmpd rght thrght, mstk 13th, hdd 5 out, wknd appr 3 out, sn no dngr.*
..........................(7 to 2 op 3 to 1 tchd 4 to 1) 2
4041* VERY DARING 7-11-7 (7*) Miss S Sharratt, *hld up, struggling frm hfwy, sn tld off..............*(33 to 1 op 25 to 1) 3
SAN REMO (bl) 10-11-7 (7*) Miss S Samworth, *cl up till outpcd 11th, sn wl beh, tld off..*(25 to 1 op 20 to 1) 4
3438 FROZEN STIFF (Ire) (bl) 9-11-7 (7*) Mr T J Barry, *almost uns rdr 1st, hld up, blun and unseated rider 4th.*
....(9 to 1 op 7 to 1) ur
3969 SHIP THE BUILDER 8-11-7 (7*) Mr T Whitaker, *beh, some hdwy and moderate 3rd whn blun and uns rdr 13th.*
.........................(20 to 1 op 16 to 1) ur
Dist: Dist, dist, 3l. 6m 33.30s. a 28.30s (6 Ran).
(Stewart Pike), S Pike

4125 Aughton Novices' Hurdle Class D (4-y-o and up) £2,788 2½m...... (6:15)

3562⁵ NIGEL'S LAD (Ire) 5-11-12 M Foster, *led, shaken up and drw clr appr 3 out, very easily.....*(15 to 8 on op 5 to 4 on) 1
3846² SAMANID (Ire) 5-11-12 R Dunwoody, *settled to track ldrs, chsd wnr frm 7th, outpcd 2 out, styd on..........(4 to 1)* 2
3680⁴ GIVE AND TAKE (bl) 4-11-0 A P McCoy, *pressed ldr, not fluent 3rd, blun nxt, mstk and outpcd 7th, sn struggling, tld off.*
.........................(9 to 1 op 7 to 2 tchd 5 to 1) 3
3999 TWEEDSWOOD (Ire) 7-11-0 R Supple, *jmpd slwly 1st, hld up, reminders 5th, wknd 4 out, tld off.....*(33 to 1 op 20 to 1) 4

3400 TREMENDISTO 7-11-6 T Jenks, *pld hrd in rear, not fluent 4th, outpcd 6th, tld off frm 5 out.....................(20 to 1)* 5
Dist: Dist, 14l, 13l, dist. 5m 1.60s. a 23.60s (5 Ran).
(N C Dunnington), P C Haslam

4126 Cedric Croston Handicap Chase Class D (0-125 5-y-o and up) £3,639 3m 1f......................... (6:45)

3983* DOUALAGO (Fr) [125] (bl) 7-12-0 (6ex) A P McCoy, *cl up, reminders frm hfwy, hrd drvn to chal 2 out, jmpd ahead last, kpt on gmely und pres...............(9 to 4 op 5 to 4)* 1
2393³ BAS DE LAINE (Fr) [124] (v) 11-11-13 R Garritty, *led, blun 6th, clr appr 4 out, strly pressed 2 out, mstk and hdd last, kpt on.*
..........................(3 to 1 tchd 11 to 4) 2
3968² PERUVIAN GALE (Ire) [97] 8-11-1 (3*) G F Ryan, *settled rear, mstk 7th, chsd ldrs 13th, reminders 4 out, fdd frm 2 out.*
.........................(7 to 1 op 6 to 1) 3
3760³ SEOD RIOGA (Ire) [115] 8-10-13 (5*) Chris Webb, *hld up, blun 8th, reminders 11th, struggling 5 out, sn tld off.*
.........................(11 to 4 op 9 to 4) 4
4010⁴ TEMPLE GARTH [102] 8-10-5 R Supple, *pressed ldrs till lost pl hfwy, jmpd slwly in rear 14th, tld off whn pld up bef 4 out.*
.........................(8 to 1 op 6 to 1) pu
Dist: 1¼l, 27l, 26l. 6m 26.00s. a 21.00s (5 Ran).
(Martin Pipe Racing Club), M C Pipe

4127 Weatherbys Insurance Services Handicap Hurdle Class C (0-135 4-y-o and up) £3,528 2m 110yds.. (7:20)

3896* YUBRALEE (USA) [122] 5-11-1 A P McCoy, *set gd pace, clr frm 3rd, mstk 2 out, eased considerably flt, unchlgd.*
.........................(13 to 8 on op 6 to 4 on tchd 11 to 8 on) 1
3791⁴ DANCING PADDY [135] 9-12-0 R Dunwoody, *chsd clr ldr, niggled alng 5th, outpcd appr 3 out, no ch wth wnr, eased whn btn.....................(100 to 30 op 3 to 1 tchd 7 to 2)* 2
3766 CHERYL'S LAD (Ire) [132] 7-11-8 (3*) Mr R Thornton, *hld up, not fluent, reminders and outpcd 4 out, sn beh.*
.........................(9 to 1 op 6 to 1 tchd 10 to 1) 3
3907⁶ TRAGIC HERO [132] (bl) 5-11-11 G Bradley, *hld up, effrt to chase clr ldr 4 out, moderate 3rd and btn whn l 3 out.*
.........................(11 to 2 op 5 to 1 tchd 6 to 1) f
Dist: 20l, 16l. 4m 5.50s. a 17.50s (4 Ran).
(D A Johnson), M C Pipe

4128 Liverpool Echo 'Woman Extra' Novices' Chase Class E (5-y-o and up) £2,951 2½m.................. (7:50)

2192³ MYTHICAL APPROACH (Ire) 7-10-11 (3*) Mr R Thornton, *trkd ldrs, al gng wl, jmpd ahead 2 out, clr last, cmftbly.*
.........................(6 to 4 fav op 5 to 4 tchd 7 to 4) 1
3912² EID (USA) 8-11-0 Richard Guest, *chsd ldr, led aftr 4th, strly pressed frm four out, slight mstk and hdd 2 out, one pace after.......................(9 to 4 op 2 to 1 tchd 5 to 2)* 2
3869⁵ SOVEREIGNS MATCH 9-11-0 B Storey, *led till aftr 4th, styd hndy, led briefly four out, drvn and outpcd after nxt.*
.........................(8 to 1 op 12 to 1) 3
4001⁵ QUIXALL CROSSETT 12-10-7 (7*) Mr T J Barry, *hld up, hit 3rd, niggled alng frm 11th, wknd appr 3 out.*
.........................(66 to 1 op 33 to 1) 4
3740⁶ NADJATI (USA) (bl) 8-11-6 R Dunwoody, *chsd ldrs, hit 7th, jnd lder and mstk 9th, drpd rear 11th, rallied briefly 3 out, btn whn jmpd slwly nxt.....................(4 to 1 op 7 to 2)* 5
3824⁴ CHEEKA 8-11-0 M Ranger, *chsd ldrs till lost pl 7th, hdwy 11th, struggling aftr 4 out, wl beh whn pld up bef 2 out.*
.........................(10 to 1 op 8 to 1) pu
Dist: 12l, 17l, 2½l, 3l. 5m 8.70s. a 20.70s (6 Ran).
(Lady Harris), D Nicholson

4129 Sunday Best Couture Handicap Chase Class D (0-125 5-y-o and up) £4,760 2m................... (8:20)

3882* POND HOUSE (Ire) [102] 8-10-12 A P McCoy, *set gd pace, jmpd wl, clr frm 6 out, mstk last, unchlgd.*
.........................(11 to 10 tchd Evens) 1
3779² STORM FALCON (USA) [114] 7-11-5 (5*) Chris Webb, *blun second, chsd ldr, struggling 6 out, wl beh whn hit 4 out and 2 out........................(5 to 4 on op 6 to 4 on)* 2
Won by Dist. 4m 2.80s. a 15.80s (2 Ran).
SR: -/-/
(C R Fleet), M C Pipe

4130 Carol Towner Spirit Of Merseyside 'National Hunt' Novices' Hurdle Class D (4-y-o and up) £2,814 2m 110yds......................... (8:50)

3721² GO NATIVE (Ire) 5-11-0 Richard Guest, *chsd ldr, not fluent early, chlgd gng wl 2 out, slight mstk last, sn led, pushed clr.*
.........................(11 to 10 op 7 to 4 tchd 6 to 5) 1
3979² MRS EM 5-11-6 (7*) L Cummins, *set steady pace, quickened appr 3 out, drvn and hdd flt, unbl to quicken.*
.........................(5 to 4 on op 5 to 2 on) 2

3970[6] BLASTER WATSON 6-11-0 M Ranger, *hld up and pld hrd, ran wide bend aftr 3rd, outpcd appr 3 out, sn no dngr.* ....(20 to 1 op 12 to 1) 3
Dist: 3l, 18l. 4m 9.60s. a 21.60s (3 Ran).
(Trevor Hemmings), Mrs S J Smith

STRATFORD (good (races 1,2,3,4,5), good to soft (6)) Friday May 16th

Going Correction: PLUS 0.40 sec. per fur.

4131 Richardsons Parkway Mares' Only Novices' Selling Hurdle Class G (4-y-o and up) £2,090 2m 110yds (6:00)

2515 PERSIAN BUTTERFLY 5-10-10 J Culloty, *al in tch, led appr last, rdn out*..........(14 to 1 op 12 to 1) 1
3296[9] CALLERMINE 8-10-3 (7*) Mr S Durack, *led till rdn and hdd appr 2 out, one pace*................(14 to 1 op 25 to 1) 2
3931* FENIAN COURT (Ire) (v) 6-11-3 M A Fitzgerald, *trkd ldr, led appr 2 out, hdd bef last, one pace.* ....(5 to 2 fav tchd 3 to 1 and 4 to 1) 3
3796[8] BOLD TIME MONKEY 6-10-10 C Llewellyn, *hld up in rear, hdwy 4 out, nvr on terms*.............(33 to 1 op 20 to 1) 4
3476[7] ANALOGICAL 4-10-5 V Slattery, *in tch, mstk 3rd, rdn and wknd appr 3 out*....................(10 to 1 op 7 to 1) 5
3874[2] PERSIAN DAWN 4-10-5 N Williamson, *hld up in rear, hdwy 4 out, nvr nr to chal*...................(11 to 2 op 5 to 1) 6
3265[7] HOW COULD-I (Ire) 4-10-5 A Thornton, *hld up, nvr nr to chal.* ....(8 to 1 op 6 to 1) 7
2457 WOODLANDS ENERGY 6-10-10 R Bellamy, *beh till efort 5th, nvr dngrs*..............................(66 to 1 op 50 to 1) 8
3170[3] PEDALTOTHEMETAL (Ire) 5-10-10 W Marston, *in tch till lost pl aftr 4th*................................(4 to 1 op 9 to 4) 9
3332 LIZIUM 5-10-10 S Fox, *prmnt till wknd 4 out.* ....(33 to 1 op 20 to 1) 10
880 GABRIELLE GERARD 5-10-10 D Bentley, *mstks, prmnt to 5th, sn wknd*..............................(10 to 1 op 8 to 1) 11
3561 ROSGLINN (Ire) 5-10-10 M Richards, *al beh, tld off.* ....(33 to 1 op 25 to 1) 12
3874[3] SALSIAN (bl) 4-10-5 T J Murphy, *mid-div, wknd appr 3 out, tld off*.......................................(50 to 1 op 33 to 1) 13
2503 GLENDRONACH 5-10-10 Gary Lyons, *beh 5th, sn tld off.* ....(66 to 1 op 50 to 1 tchd 100 to 1) 14
3828 HEATHYARDS JADE 4-10-5[3] (3*) L Aspell, *al beh, tld off whn pld up bef 3 out*.......................(33 to 1 op 25 to 1) pu
Dist: 4l, 2l, 10l, 2½l, 1¼l, hd, 1l, 2½l, 7l, 7l. 4m 6.40s. a 20.40s (15 Ran).
(David Hallums), R M Stronge

4132 Francis Graves Ltd Novices' Chase Class D for the Charles Lea Memorial Trophy (5-y-o and up) £3,548 2m 5f 110yds.....................(6:35)

3995* FORMAL INVITATION (Ire) 8-11-10 R Johnson, *hld up, mstks 3rd and 5th, trkd ldr hfwy, led sn aftr 3 out, clr frm nxt.* ....(11 to 8 on op Evens tchd 11 to 10) 1
2527[5] BAYLINE STAR (Ire) 7-11-0 J Culloty, *pld hrd,l hld up, hdwy appr 5 out, outpcd nxt, kpt on to go second last.* ....(5 to 1 op 11 to 4 tchd 11 to 2) 2
3822[3] IMPERIAL VINTAGE (Ire) 7-11-10 N Williamson, *led hit, 3 out, sn hdd, hld whn when stumbled badly on landing nxt,not reco'r*..................(2 to 1 op 6 to 4 tchd 9 to 4) 3
3732 LITTLE ELLIOT (Ire) 9-10-11 (3*) L Aspell, *trkd ldr to hfwy, wknd appr 5 out, tld off.* (33 to 1 op 20 to 1 tchd 50 to 1) 4
Dist: 4l, 11l, dist. 5m 24.10s. a 24.10s (4 Ran).
(The Plough Partnership), D Nicholson

4133 Birse Construction Handicap Hurdle Class E (0-115 4-y-o and up) £2,332 3m 3f.........................(7:05)

3557[9] JIMBALOU [80] 14-9-12 (3*) R Massey, *hld up in rear, hdwy tenth, chlgd 4 out, led appr 2 out, styd on strly.* ....(5 to 1 op 4 to 1) 1
3996[3] LOTTERY TICKET (Ire) [93] 8-11-0 M A Fitzgerald, *hld up, hdwy to lad appr 4 out, hdd bef 2 out, one pace*. . .(7 to 2 jt-fav op 4 to 1) 2
3951* ST VILLE [110] 11-12-3 (6ex) B Powell, *dsptd ld, ev ch till rdn and wknd appr 3 out*......(4 to 1 op 3 to 1 tchd 9 to 2) 3
3881* SHARP THYNE (Ire) [100] 7-11-7 G Tormey, *in cl tch till rdn appr 4 out, sn wknd.* (7 to 2 jt-fav op 3 to 1 tchd 4 to 1) 4
3803[8] FATHER O'BRIEN [83] 10-10-4 A Thornton, *sn led, hdd 6th, wknd appr 4 out, tld off*.............(16 to 1 op 14 to 1) 5
3871 CASTLEBAY LAD [79] 14-9-8[1] (7*) J Parkhouse, *in tch till wknd tenth, pld up aftr 4 out*........(100 to 1 op 50 to 1) pu
2770* MILLMOUNT (Ire) [92] (bl) 7-10-13 R Johnson, *hepd up in tch, rdn and wknd appr 4 out, tld off*......(5 to 1 tchd 4 to 1) pu
4035[7] WHITEBONNET (Ire) [79] (bl) 7-9-11 (3*) Sophie Mitchell, *prmnt, led 6th till hdd approahing 4 out, wknd quickly, pld up bef nxt*.................................(20 to 1 op 14 to 1) pu
3925 JOY FOR LIFE (Ire) [79] 6-10-0 J Culloty, *mstks in rear, al beh, pld up aftr 5th*...(33 to 1) pu
Dist: 6l, 3l, nk, dist. 6m 46.10s. a 28.10s (9 Ran).
(R G Brazington), R G Brazington

4134 Interlink Express Restricted Point-to-Point Final Novices' Hunters' Chase Class H For the Gay and Eve Sheppard Memorial Challenge Trophy (5-y-o and up) £2,976 3m (7:35)

ALLER MOOR (Ire) 6-11-7 (7*) Mr J Tizzard, *hld up, steady hdwy to go second 3 out, led nxt, tied up r-in, all out.* ....(9 to 4 op 5 to 2 tchd 3 to 1 and 2 to 1) 1
SWANSEA GOLD (Ire) 6-11-2 (7*) Mr D Alers-Hankey, *led to 4th, led 8th, clr four out, wknd and hdd 2 out, rallied gmely r-in*.......................................(12 to 1 op 10 to 1) 2
BARNEYS GOLD (Ire) 8-11-7 (7*) Mr A Bealby, *trkd ldrs till lost pl 8th, styd on frm 4 out, lft poor 3rd last.* ....(25 to 1 op 20 to 1 tchd 33 to 1) 3
BROWN BABY 11-11-3[1] (7*) Mr G Kerr, *pulle hrd, led 4th to 8th, wknd appr four out.* (25 to 1 op 20 to 1 tchd 33 to 1) 4
3599* GALLANTS DELIGHT 7-11-7 (7*) Mr A Robson, *hld up, hdwy whn mstk tenth, hit 12th, rallied 5 out, btn 3rd when blun and uns rdr last*........................(7 to 4 fav op 5 to 4) ur
BIT OF A CITIZEN (Ire) 6-11-2 (7*) Mr E Williams, *hld up, hdwy 11th, btn 3rd whn blun and uns rdr 3 out.* (11 to 1 op 8 to 1) ur
FIRST COMMAND (NZ) 10-11-7 (7*) Mr A Dalton, *chsd ldrs till wknd 12th, tld off whn pld up bef 3 out.* (33 to 1 op 20 to 1) pu
NEARLY AT SEA 8-11-2 (7*) Mr L Jefford, *mstks in rear, tld off whn pld up aftr 11th*.......(6 to 1 op 7 to 1 tchd 8 to 1) pu
MAMNOON (USA) 6-11-7 (7*) Mr R Armson, *beh, rdn aftr tenth, pld up after nxt*................(33 to 1 op 25 to 1) pu
MR BOBBIT (Ire) 7-11-7 (7*) Mr R Burton, *prmnt early, hit 6th, tld offwhn pld up aftr 3 out.* ....(16 to 1 op 14 to 1 tchd 20 to 1) pu
Dist: ½l, 18l, 21l. 6m 8.00s. a 23.00s (10 Ran).
(G Keirle), Mrs S Alner

4135 ROM Ltd. Handicap Chase Class C (0-135 5-y-o and up) £4,576 3m .... (8:10)

3830[3] BAVARD DIEU (Ire) [125] 9-11-10 C Llewellyn, *led to 3rd, outpcd 3 out, rallied appr last, hrd rdn to ld nr finish.* ....(11 to 2 op 6 to 1 tchd 5 to 1) 1
3924 FACTOR TEN (Ire) [123] 9-11-8 J F Titley, *sn trkd ldr, led 12th, hdd 4 out, rdn and badly hmpd bend bef 2 out, rallied to ld last, ct on line*...........................(4 to 1 op 11 to 4) 2
3730[2] SUPER COIN [114] 9-10-13 R Johnson, *hld up, not fluent, hit 5 out, led nxt, mstk 2 out, hdd last, wknd r-in.* ....(6 to 4 fav tchd 13 to 8) 3
3134 PASHTO [125] 10-11-10 M A Fitzgerald, *led 3rd to 12th, rdn and wknd appr 3 out, tld off*............(2 to 1 op 6 to 4) 4
Dist: Nk, 5l, dist. 6m 10.30s. a 25.30s (4 Ran).
(Saguaro Stables), N A Gaselee

4136 Hamer Ford 'National Hunt' Novices' Hurdle Class D (4-y-o and up) £3,090 2¾m 110yds.................. (8:40)

3546[4] MON AMIE 7-10-7 (7*) Mr G Shenkin, *pld hrd, hld up, mstk 8th, hdwy 4 out, led 2 out, all out.* ....(14 to 1 op 12 to 1 tchd 16 to 1)
CAMERA MAN 7-11-0 M A Fitzgerald, *al prmnt, led 8th, hdd 2 out, ran on one pace*..............................(12 to 1 op 8 to 1 tchd 14 to 1) 2
2638 LUCKY CALL (NZ) 6-11-0 R Greene, *hld up in rear, mstk 4 out, styd on strly r-in*...............................(33 to 1) 3
3935 COOL HARRY (USA) 6-10-7 (7*) Mr S Durack, *prmnt, hit 8th, ev ch appr 2 out, one pace*..........(33 to 1 op 16 to 1) 4
3709[2] MORPHEUS 8-11-0 R Johnson, *pld hrd, hld up, hdwy 7th, ev ch 2 out, wknd r-in.* ....(6 to 4 on tchd 11 to 8 on and 2 to 1 on) 5
4032 RHYTHM AND BLUES 7-11-6 B Powell, *hld up, hdwy appr 5th, outpcd approaching 2 out.* ....(100 to 30 op 7 to 2 tchd 5 to 1 and 11 to 2) 6
3729[5] IRISH DELIGHT 5-11-0 D Morris, *beh till hdwy 5 out, wknd quickly appr 2 out*.................(20 to 1 op 16 to 1) 7
4013 NICANJON 6-10-9 (5*) X Aizpuru, *mid-div, mstk second, lost tch 8th*..............................(100 to 1 op 50 to 1) 8
3892[7] IRENE'S PET 7-11-0 S Fox, *in tch, hdwy 6th, mstk nxt, wknd appr 3 out*..............................(33 to 1 op 20 to 1) 9
2605 FAITHLEGG (Ire) 6-10-9 J R Kavanagh, *mstk 3rd, beh frm hfwy*.....................................(20 to 1 op 14 to 1) 10
4015[4] SAUCY NUN (Ire) (bl) 5-10-9 N Williamson, *prmnt till wknd 7th, tld off*...(20 to 1) 11
3957[5] NEW ROSS (Ire) (bl) 5-11-0 V Slattery, *al beh, tld off.* ....(33 to 1 op 16 to 1) 12
1976 AMAZON HEIGHTS 5-10-9 Mr J Grassick, *prmnt, jmpd slwly 4th, wknd 8th, tld off*.................(100 to 1 op 66 to 1) 13
3692[6] GO FROLIC 9-10-9 A Thornton, *led to 8th, drpd out quickly, pld up bef 3 out*.........................(33 to 1 op 25 to 1) pu
Dist: Sht-hd, 2l, ½l, 3l, ¾l, 18l, 9l, 9l, 3½l, 22l. 5m 39.70s. a 27.70s (14 Ran).
(John Lister), A G Hobbs

BANGOR (good)
Saturday May 17th
Going Correction: PLUS 0.60 sec. per fur.

4137 Penycae Maiden Hurdle Class D (4-y-o and up) £2,970 2m 1f.... (11:50)

4045 MR LOWRY 5-11-5 S Wynne, *al in tch, improved to ld aftr 3 out, styd on gmely*..................(33 to 1 op 20 to 1) 1

3802[2] SADLER'S REALM 4-11-0 G Tormey, *in tch, improved 5th, sn chalg, ev ch last, not quicken r-in*..............(5 to 1 2 fav) 2

3757[4] WESTERN GENERAL 6-11-5 A P McCoy, *hld up 4 out, kpt on, no imprsn on ldrs*...........(4 to 1 tchd 9 to 2) 3

3823[6] DONNEGALE (Ire) 5-11-5 B Powell, *chsd ldrs, led appr 4 out, hdd aftr nxt, sn btn*.................(20 to 1 op 10 to 1) 4

2777[4] BIYA (Ire) 5-11-5 T Jenks, *in tch, improved to chal bef 3 out, sn drvn and wknd*........(25 to 1 op 16 to 1 tchd 33 to 1) 5

3970[2] SILENT CRACKER 5-11-5 J Culloty, *hld up to chase ldrs, wknd 4 out to chase ldrs, wknd nxt*................................ 6

3913 KING CURAN (USA) 6-11-5 N Williamson, *hld up, hdwy 5th, chsd ldrs nxt tld off*...........(16 to 1 op 12 to 1) 7

3720 THE OPERATOR (Ire) 6-11-5 J Osborne, *hld up, nvr plcd to chal*.........................(12 to 1 op 8 to 1) 8

4042 WOODSTOCK WANDERER (Ire) 5-11-5 R Johnson, *reluctant to race, wl beh, nvr dngrs*.........(20 to 1 op 14 to 1) 9

3957[9] JUST BECAUSE (Ire) 5-11-0 (5*) D J Kavanagh, *midfield, struggling 4 out, sn beh*.........(66 to 1 op 33 to 1) 10

3931[6] FRANS LAD 5-11-5 Gary Lyons, *al beh, nvr rchd chalg pos*...........................(66 to 1 op 33 to 1) 11

4037 LADY ROSEBURY 7-11-0 T J Murphy, *beh, blun 4th, sn no dngr*.........................(66 to 1 op 33 to 1) 12

3957[2] FLOOSY 6-11-0 M A Fitzgerald, *chsd ldrs, wknd quickly bef 3 out, sn eased, tld off*.....(11 to 1 op 5 to 1 tchd 6 to 1) 13

4042 STORM HOME 5-11-5 V Slattery, *not jump wl, al beh, lost tch 4th, tld off*...............(66 to 1 op 33 to 1) 14

3673 POLAR WIND 8-11-5 A Thornton, *keen hold, led till appr 4 out, wknd quickly, tld off whn pld up bef 2 out*.....................(100 to 1 op 33 to 1) pu

2145 HILTONS TRAVEL (Ire) 6-10-12 (7*) L Cummins, *unruly bef strt, wth ldr, mstk 4th, rdn alng and wknd quickly nxt, tld off whn pld up before 2 out*...............(50 to 1 op 25 to 1) pu

3780 NINE PIPES (Ire) 6-11-5 J R Kavanagh, *midfield to 4th, tld off whn pld up bef 2 out*................(50 to 1 op 33 to 1) pu

3957[6] BACHE DINGLE 6-11-5 W Marston, *al beh, tld off whn pld up bef 2 out*................................ pu

Dist: 1¼l, 2½l, 8l, 13l, 8l, 2l, 16l, 2½l, 1¼l, 3l. 4m 13.70s. a 23.70s (18 Ran).

(Doug Brereton), L J Barratt

4138 May Novices' Chase Class D (5-y-o and up) £3,355 2m 1f 110yds (12:20)

3787[3] FLYING INSTRUCTOR 7-11-7 N Williamson, *hld up, chsd ldr 5th (water), led 3 out, al on bit, canter*..................(11 to 2 on op 6 to 1 on tchd 5 to 1 on) 1

3882[4] DANDIE IMP 9-11-0 B Powell, *led to 3 out, sn und pres and no ch wth wnr*.....................(7 to 1 op 6 to 1) 2

3961[5] PROFESSOR PAGE (Ire) 7-11-0 M A Fitzgerald, *hld up in tch, improved 7th to track ldrs, outpcd frm nxt*..........(14 to 1) 3

3189[3] RELAXED LAD 8-11-0 R Bellamy, *chsd ldrs, hit 6th, pckd nxt, wknd 4 out*.........................(50 to 1) 4

3996 STEEL CHIMES (Ire) 8-11-0 Gary Lyons, *beh, lost tch 7th, tld off*.......(150 to 1 op 100 to 1 tchd 200 to 1) 5

4037[5] OLD REDWOOD (v) 10-11-0 C Llewellyn, *prmnt, drvn and wknd appr 8th, tld off*................(20 to 1 op 16 to 1) 6

Dist: 3l, 26l, 16l, dist, 4l. 4m 24.90s. a 22.90s (6 Ran).

(Lady Lyell), P R Webber

4139 Tote Credit Club Novices' Handicap Hurdle Class E (0-105 4-y-o and up) £2,738 2½m.............. (12:50)

3909* JESSOLE [95] 5-10-13 (2*) R Burns, *hld up, hdwy to track ldrs 4 out, led on bit 2 out, pushed out r-in*..................(5 to 1 op 4 to 1 tchd 11 to 2) 1

3946 NAME OF OUR FATHER (USA) [99] 4-11-4 R Johnson, *trkd ldrs, led 4 out, not fluent and hdd 2 out, sn one pace*..................(8 to 1 op 5 to 1) 2

3870[5] STYLISH INTERVAL [87] 5-10-12 P Carberry, *in tch, mstk 1st, pckd nxt and reminder, niggled alng appr 4 out, one pace and chasing ldrs frm next*.............(12 to 1 op 8 to 1) 3

4039[4] SUPREME TROGLODYTE (Ire) [80] 5-10-5 J R Kavanagh, *prmnt, und pres appr 2 out, sn btn*.....(20 to 1 op 12 to 1) 4

3280[4] MEG'S MEMORY (Ire) [93] 4-10-12 N Williamson, *keen hold, hld up in rear, improved 4 out, chlgd nxt, wknd 2 out*.........................(12 to 1 op 8 to 1) 5

3961[2] THE EENS [75] 5-10-0 S Wynne, *led to 4 out, sn wknd, eased bef 2 out*..............(10 to 1 op 8 to 1 tchd 12 to 1) 6

3986* ULTIMATE SMOOTHIE [103] 5-12-0 A P McCoy, *hld up in rear, hdwy on outsd 7th, rdn bef 3 out, wknd quickly*...................(6 to 5 fav op 7 to 4 tchd 11 to 10) 7

3988 WESTCOAST [75] 6-10-0 C Llewellyn, *wl beh frm 6th, tld off*.........................(66 to 1 op 33 to 1) 8

3559 BONNIFER (Ire) [76] (bl) 8-10-1 W Marston, *keen hold, prmnt, hld 5th, wknd quickly 7th, tld off*......(33 to 1 op 16 to 1) 9

3999* DIDDY RYMER [85] 7-10-10 Richard Guest, *in tch, effrt 4 out, wkng whn mstk nxt, sn pld up*.................(7 to 1 op 4 to 1 tchd 15 to 2) pu

Dist: 7l, ½l, 2l, 5l, 28l, 4l, 21l, 15l. 4m 59.00s. a 29.00s (10 Ran).

(C R Fleet), G Richards

4140 Marbury Handicap Chase Class E (0-115 5-y-o and up) £3,517 2½m 110yds.......................... (1:20)

3670[4] PEARL EPEE [90] 8-10-3 R Johnson, *led till blun badly 8th (water), sn beh, rnwd effrt appr 2 out, styd on strly to ld cl hme.*...............(9 to 2 op 7 to 2 tchd 5 to 1) 1

3995[4] ANDERMATT [108] 10-11-4 (3*) E Husband, *hld up in rear, hdwy tenth, led aftr 2 out, not fluent last, hdd and no extr cl hme*.................(2 to 1 fav op 11 to 4 tchd 3 to 1) 2

3968* ROYAL SQUARE (Can) [87] 11-9-11 (3*) Mr R Thornton, *hndy, on same pace*.............(7 to 1 op 5 to 1) 3

4024* TAPATCH [88] (bl) 9-10-1 P Carberry, *in tch, improved 7th, ch 3 out and drvn alng, btn frm nxt*......(7 to 1 op 6 to 1) 4

3884* JACOB'S WIFE [103] 7-11-2 J Osborne, *hld up appr 9th, ch 3 out, sn und pres and wknd.*...................(100 to 30 op 11 to 4 tchd 7 to 2) 5

1910[3] EARLYMORNING LIGHT (Ire) [115] 8-12-0 A P McCoy, *hndy, ld in ld 8th (water), mstk and hdd 3 out, wknd quickly, virtually pld up r-in*...........(7 to 1 op 4 to 1 tchd 15 to 2) 6

3987 NICKLE JOE [95] 11-10-8 W Marston, *cl up, reminders aftr 7th, sn lost pl, beh frm 11th, tld off*...........(25 to 1 op 20 to 1 tchd 33 to 1) 7

Dist: Nk, 1¾l, 8l, 5l, dist. 5m 13.80s. a 27.80s (7 Ran).

(Mrs A A Shutes), D Nicholson

4141 Win With The Tote Handicap Hurdle Class D (0-120 4-y-o and up) £3,485 2m 1f.............. (1:50)

3910[4] RIPARIUS (USA) [107] 6-11-2 J Osborne, *al cl up, pushed alng 3 out, styd on to ld last, drvn out.*.................(15 to 2 op 6 to 1 tchd 8 to 1) 1

4045[2] OUR ROBERT [93] (v) 5-10-2 N Williamson, *hld up, hdwy on bit whn mstk 4 out, rdn to ld 2 out, hdd last, no extr.*..............(13 to 2 op 7 to 1 tchd 15 to 2 and 6 to 1) 2

4043* KINNESCASH (Ire) [110] 4-11-0 M A Fitzgerald, *not fluent, led till hdd 2 out, no extr bef last*..............(11 to 10 fav) 3

3831* KINO'S CROSS [106] 8-11-1 L Harvey, *hld up, hdwy appr 5th, pushed alng whn chasing ldrs, 3 out, sn wknd.*................................ 4

2332[6] ALBERTITO (Fr) [92] 10-10-1 S Wynne, *prmnt till lost pl 4 out, no dngr aftrwards*................(33 to 1) 5

3933[4] TEJANO GOLD (USA) [119] 7-12-0 A P McCoy, *cl up, drvn appr 5th, wknd quickly nxt, tld off.*...........(9 to 2 op 4 to 1 tchd 5 to 1) 6

THIS IS MY LIFE (Ire) [100] 8-10-9 G Bradley, *slwly into strd, beh, sn in tch, not fluent 3rd, wknd 4 out, tld off*...............(14 to 1 op 8 to 1) 7

Dist: 2½l, 4l, 26l, 2l, 17l, 1½l. 4m 7.80s. a 17.80s (7 Ran).

SR: 12/-/3/-/ (Mrs David Blackburn), P R Webber

4142 North Western Area Point-to-Point Championship Final Hunters' Chase Class H for the Wynnstay Hunt Challenge Cup (5-y-o and up) £2,788 3m 110yds.......................... (2:20)

3727* NODFORM WONDER 10-12-0 (7*) Mr R Bevis, *led till appr 3rd, rgned ld 5th, pckd badly tenth, clr frm 12th, unchlgd.*.................(5 to 4 fav tchd 6 to 4 and 7 to 4) 1

NOTHING VENTURED 8-11-10 (7*) Mr A Beedles, *in tch, hdwy to chase wnr 9th, no ch wth clr winner frm 12th.*.................(100 to 30 op 3 to 1 tchd 7 to 2) 2

PAMELA'S LAD 11-11-10 (7*) Mr A Hanmer, *beh, hdwy to chase ldrs 13th, no imprsn and pace*....(25 to 1 op 20 to 1) 3

3991 ITA'S FELLOW (Ire) 9-11-10 (7*) Mrs C Ford, *midfield, effrt to chase ldrs 13th, sn no imprsn*.............(7 to 2 op 11 to 4) 4

3857[8] SIMPLY PERFECT 11-11-10 (7*) Miss S Swindells, *midfield, effrt 13th, nvr rchd chalg pos*...........(40 to 1 op 20 to 1) 5

4018[2] TARA BOY 12-11-10 (7*) Mr R Cambray, *al in rear, struggling 5 out, nvr a factor*......(25 to 1 op 20 to 1 tchd 33 to 1) 6

GLENROWAN (Ire) 9-11-12 (5*) Mr R Ford, *al wl beh, nvr a factor*...............(33 to 1 op 25 to 1) 7

SPY'S DELIGHT 11-11-10 (7*) Mr H Rayner, *in tch, mstk 5th, hmpd by faller tenth, lost touch frm 5 out, tld off*...................(33 to 1 op 14 to 1) 8

FIBREGUIDE TECH 14-11-10 (7*) Mr R Thomas, *midfield till f tenth*..................(33 to 1 op 20 to 1) f

NO MORE THE FOOL 11-11-10 (7*) Mr L Brennan, *slwly into strd, al beh, tld off 12th, pld up bef 5 out*.................(50 to 1 op 33 to 1) pu

ULTRASON IV (Fr) 11-11-10 (7*) Mr R Burton, *hndy till 9th, lost tch frm 12th, tld off whn pld up bef last*.(50 to 1 op 33 to 1) pu

NOBLE ANGEL (Ire) 9-11-10 (7*) Mr S Prior, *prmnt, led appr 3rd till hdd 5th, mstk and lost pl 9th, sn lost tch, tld off whn pld up bef 12th.*................(33 to 1 op 25 to 1) pu

Dist: 23l, 12l, 9l, 6l, 10l, 3l, 30l. 6m 26.10s. a 41.10s (12 Ran).

(D A Malam), R J Bevis

4143 Erddig Mares' Only Standard Open National Hunt Flat Class H (4,5,6-y-o) £1,287 2m 1f.............(2:50)

	SEA TARTH 6-11-1 N Williamson, *midfield, hdwy hfwy, led o'r 5 fs out, ran on ins last.* (33 to 1 op 20 to 1 tchd 40 to 1)	1
3929*	MURCHAN TYNE (Ire) 4-10-13 (7*) L Cummins, *midfield, hdwy hfwy, ev ch 3 fs out, chsd wnr fnl 2, kpt on und pres.*	
	.................(3 to 1 op 5 to 2 tchd 7 to 2)	2
	ORANGE IMP 4-10-10 W Dwan, *hld up, hdwy 7 fs out, ev ch o'r 2 out, sn one pace....*(8 to 1 op 5 to 1 tchd 10 to 1)	3
	DEEP C DIVA (Ire) 5-11-1 J Osborne, *hld up in rear, hdwy 5 fs out, sn chasing ldrs, one pace fnl 3.............*(9 to 4 jt-fav op 2 to 1 tchd 5 to 2)	4
	ACHILL RAMBLER 4-10-10 R Johnson, *hld up, hdwy hfwy, ev ch 3 fs out, btn o'r 2 out.........*(9 to 4 jt-fav op 2 to 1 tchd 5 to 2)	5
3825[8]	AILSAE 4-10-10 A Thornton, *midfield, improved to chase ldrs o'r 5 fs out, outpcd fnl 3..............*(20 to 1 op 14 to 1)	6
4042[8]	TRUTHFULLY 4-10-10 A P McCoy, *midfield, rdn alng hfwy, no imprsn on ldrs.......*(12 to 1 op 14 to 1 tchd 16 to 1)	7
	GREATEST FRIEND (Ire) 4-10-3 (7*) F Bogle, *prmnt till wknd o'r 3 fs out................*(33 to 1 tchd 40 to 1)	8
	DEE DEE 5-11-1 V Slattery, *hld up, nvr on terms wth ldrs.* ....(20 to 1 op 14 to 1)	9
4049[7]	ZENY THE NESTA 5-11-1 M A Fitzgerald, *cl up till wknd quickly o'r 3 fs out............*(33 to 1 op 25 to 1)	10
3825	CAHERMONE LADY (Ire) 6-11-1 Mr N Kent, *led till o'r 5 fs out, wknd quickly.......................*(50 to 1)	11
3374[8]	COMMUNITY SERVICE (Ire) 6-10-10 (5*) B Grattan, *chsd ldrs till wknd o'r 4 fs out.........*(33 to 1 tchd 50 to 1)	12
	SPLICETHEMAINBRACE 5-10-12 (3*) Michael Brennan, *trkd ldrs till lost pl hfwy, sn beh........*(25 to 1 op 14 to 1)	13
3928	NIRVANA PRINCESS 5-10-8 (7*) J Mogford, *cl up, reminders hfwy, sn wknd.............*(50 to 1 op 33 to 1)	14
2723	MISS FOLEY 4-10-10 R Bellamy, *in rear, pushed alng hfwy, tld off.............*(50 to 1 op 33 to 1 tchd 66 to 1)	15
	MISS MATCHMAKER 5-10-8 (7*) Mr T J Barry, *in tch, niggled alng o'r 6 fs out, wknd quickly, tld off.* (20 to 1 op 12 to 1)	16

Dist: 3½l, 6l, 4l, 2½l, 7l, 7l, 1¼l, 3½l, 7l, 9l. 4m 12.00s. (16 Ran).

(F P Luff), P Bowen

CORK (IRE) (good to firm)
Saturday May 17th

4144 Goggin & Buckley Maiden Hurdle (4-y-o and up) £4,110 2½m...... (2:00)

3450[4]	DOVALY 4-11-5 C F Swan, ...(5 to 1)	1
3935[2]	EDUARDO (Ire) 7-12-0 R Dunwoody, ...(5 to 2 jt-fav)	2
	ANCIENT ISLE (USA) 5-11-5 S H O'Donovan, ...(14 to 1)	3
3035	ATTACK AT DAWN (Ire) 5-11-5 T P Treacy, ...(20 to 1)	4
4005[8]	MINELLA LASS 6-11-1 J Shortt, ...(14 to 1)	5
4006[6]	LADY RICHENDA (Ire) 9-10-8 (7*) Mr R Flavin, ...(16 to 1)	6
4059[5]	NEWBERRY ROSE (Ire) 5-10-12[1] (3*) Mr W M O'Sullivan, ...(14 to 1)	7
4052	SHANNON LIGHT (Ire) 5-10-12 (7*) B J Geraghty, (33 to 1)	8
4052[6]	ROSE OF STRADBALLY (Ire) 6-10-12 (3*) K Whelan, ...(20 to 1)	9
3878[2]	BOCCACHERA (Ire) 5-11-0 C O'Dwyer, ...(14 to 1)	10
4094	SHUIL NA MHUIRE (Ire) 7-11-1 T P Rudd, ...(14 to 1)	11
3935[9]	KINGMAN (Ire) 5-11-13 P A Roche, ...(20 to 1)	12
4026	KAYALIYNA (Ire) 4-10-9 M Moran, ...(33 to 1)	13
3697	LORD PENNY (Ire) 5-11-5 D H O'Connor, ...(50 to 1)	14
	CHANGE THE SCRIPT (Ire) 7-10-13 (7*) M W Martin, ...(33 to 1)	15
	OLD TRAFFORD (Ire) 6-10-13 (7*) Mr Paul Moloney, ...(14 to 1)	16
4006*	MY PLEASURE (Ire) 5-11-8 K P Gaule, ...(5 to 2 jt-fav)	17
3964[7]	LOUGHLINS PRIDE 8-11-1 Mr M Phillips, ...(14 to 1)	18
3233	GROVE GALE (Ire) 6-11-1 C O'Brien, ...(33 to 1)	19
3878[7]	COOLE LADY (Ire) 6-10-8 (7*) V T Keane, ...(33 to 1)	20
2519	IN LINE FOR DALUS (Ire) 8-10-8 (7*) Miss C Gould, (33 to 1)	21
3642	WESTERN SEAS 4-11-5 F Woods, ...(33 to 1)	22
4052	CARNACREEVA GANE (Ire) 6-11-1 A J O'Brien, ..(33 to 1)	23
	THE APOSTLE (Ire) 7-11-1 (5*) M D Murphy, ...(33 to 1)	24
3816[5]	MIDNIGHT CYCLONE (Ire) 6-11-9 D J Casey, ...(10 to 1)	ur
611[9]	JUST A CHAT (Ire) 5-11-5 T J O'Sullivan, ...(50 to 1)	pu

Dist: 1l, 12l, hd, 1½l. 4m 51.20s. (26 Ran).

(D P Sharkey), M J P O'Brien

4145 Pierse New Stand Chase (5-y-o and up) £5,480 2m 5f............ (2:30)

4028[6]	STROLL HOME (Ire) 7-12-0 R Dunwoody, ...(100 to 30)	1
4003[6]	KILARA 10-10-11 (7*) Mr K O'Sullivan, ...(10 to 1)	2
2705	SAM VAUGHAN (Ire) 8-11-1 (3*) Mr W M O'Sullivan, (8 to 1)	3
3765[7]	LIVIN IT UP (Ire) 7-11-8 F Woods, ...(3 to 1 fav)	4
3935[3]	ALWAYS IN TROUBLE 10-11-8 T P Rudd, ...(11 to 2)	5
2367[3]	TAYLORS QUAY (Ire) 9-11-4 C O'Dwyer, ...(8 to 1)	6
3236	HAVE A BRANDY (Ire) 8-11-4 C O'Brien, ...(33 to 1)	ur
3753[6]	LOFTUS LAD (Ire) 9-11-6 (5*) M D Murphy, ...(12 to 1)	ur
3815[3]	VALERIE OWENS (Ire) 8-10-10 (7*) D K Budds, ..(7 to 1)	pu

Dist: 9l, 12l, hd, dist. 5m 18.50s. (9 Ran).

(Mrs M Mangan), James Joseph Mangan

4146 Paddy Power Bookmaker Handicap Hurdle (0-116 5-y-o and up) £6,850 2m 1f........................(3:00)

3964*	NATIVE-DARRIG (Ire) [-] 6-12-0 C F Swan, ...(5 to 2 fav)	1
3788[3]	RUPERT BELLE (Ire) [-] 6-11-4 (3*) P Henley, ...(6 to 1)	2
3879[2]	CLASHBEG (Ire) [-] 6-10-11 R Dunwoody, ...(7 to 1)	3
3768[4]	REGENCY RAKE (Ire) [-] 5-11-6 F Woods, ...(8 to 1)	4
3935[3]	TOUREEN GALE (Ire) [-] 8-11-9 D J Casey, ...(8 to 1)	5
2382[3]	DAWN ALERT (Ire) [-] 8-11-5 (7*) B J Geraghty, ..(14 to 1)	6
3705[4]	ANTICS (Ire) [-] 5-9-7 (7*) Mrs C Harrison, ...(16 to 1)	7
3954[3]	HILL OF HOPE (Ire) [-] 6-10-12 (3*) K Whelan, ..(14 to 1)	8
4004*	MARINERS REEF (Ire) [-] 6-10-1 (7*) D McCullagh, (13 to 2)	9
3419[4]	HEIGHT OF LUXURY (Ire) [-] 9-9-2 (5*) M D Murphy, (14 to 1)	10
3817[5]	LOCKBEG LASS (Ire) [-] 5-10-9 T P Treacy, ...(16 to 1)	11

Dist: 1½l, ¾l, 7l, 1l. 4m 6.80s. (11 Ran).

(W P Kerwin), W P Mullins

4147 Rathbarry Stud I.N.H. Flat Race (4-y-o and up) £4,110 2m 1f......(5:30)

4056[2]	COULDN'T SAY (Ire) 4-11-1 (5*) Mr A C Coyle, ...(9 to 4 fav)	1
	TO-DAY 4-10-13 (7*) Mr A FitzGerald, (14 to 1)	2
3707[3]	KEEP THE PEARL (Ire) 4-10-8 (7*) Mr A J Dempsey, (8 to 1)	3
3935[3]	CARJUNE (Ire) 5-11-13 Mr R Walsh, ...(14 to 1)	4
	MONEY MATTERS (Ire) 5-11-6 (7*) Mr P Cashman, (9 to 1)	5
	LESELTHY (Ire) 6-11-2 (7*) Mr B N Doyle, ...(33 to 1)	6
3955[6]	MEENVANE (Ire) 7-11-7 (7*) Mr P J Crowley, ...(14 to 1)	7
1409[2]	MR MONGOOSE (Ire) 5-11-6 (7*) Mr P J Prendergast,	
	...................................(10 to 1)	8
	BAWN BEAG (Ire) 5-11-1 (7*) Mr P Breen, ...(25 to 1)	9
3432[8]	LINEN HILL (Ire) 4-11-6 Mr P J Healy, ...(20 to 1)	10
	CARMEN FAIR (Ire) 5-11-1 (7*) Mr A K Wyse, ...(14 to 1)	11
	SMART MONTE (Ire) 4-10-8 (7*) Mr D A Harney, ..(20 to 1)	12
1090[5]	MAGICAL WAY (Ire) 7-12-0 Mr J A Nash, ...(16 to 1)	13
	NUOVO STYLE (Ire) 4-10-8 (7*) Mr Sean O O'Brien, (16 to 1)	14
	KILLASHEE PRINCESS (Ire) 4-10-12[4] (7*) Mr V Burke,	
	...................................(25 to 1)	15
4005[9]	CAP IT IF YOU CAN (Ire) 4-10-12 (3*) Mrs S McCarthy,	
	...................................(16 to 1)	16
	GLENBEVAN (Ire) 5-11-8 (5*) Mr J T McNamara, ..(16 to 1)	17
	WILD NOBLE (Ire) 6-11-6 (3*) Mr W M O'Sullivan, (14 to 1)	18
	BALLYCAR PRINCESS (Ire) 6-11-2 (7*) Mr D Ryan, (33 to 1)	19
1015	DEL MADERA (Ire) 5-11-6 (7*) Mr D O'Sullivan, ..(33 to 1)	pu
	HODDERS FOLLY (Ire) 5-11-13 Mr P Fenton, ...(14 to 1)	pu

Dist: 1l, 6l, 1½l, 2½l. 4m 1.10s. (21 Ran).

(Donal O'Brien), P Mullins

DOWNPATRICK (IRE) (good)
Saturday May 17th

4148 Killyleagh Maiden Hurdle (4-y-o and up) £1,712 2m 1f 172yds.....(2:30)

2964[8]	BIT O'SPEED (Ire) 6-11-11 (3*) G Cotter, ...(2 to 1)	1
3817	MR CAVALLO (Ire) 5-11-13 Mr A J Martin, ...(6 to 4 on)	2
3945[8]	PRINCESS CATALDI (Ire) 7-11-9 H Rogers, ...(14 to 1)	3
3642	CARA GAIL (Ire) 5-11-8 K F O'Brien, ...(12 to 1)	4
3218	KRIESLER (Ire) 5-11-8 (5*) P G Hourigan, ...(10 to 1)	5
3838	XANTHOS 7-12-0 L F Cusack, ...(16 to 1)	6
1096	COPPER SAND (Ire) 8-12-0 P L Malone, ...(33 to 1)	7
3392[4]	EASTERN FOX (Ire) 8-12-0 D T Evans, ...(16 to 1)	8
3889	TIMMYS CHOICE (Ire) 4-11-6 P Leech, ...(66 to 1)	9
3878	KILLCHRIS DREAM (Ire) 6-11-2 (7*) D Fisher, ...(33 to 1)	10
3644	BARORA GALE (Ire) 6-11-2 (7*) D A McLoughlin, ..(25 to 1)	11
3642[9]	STRATEGIC AFFAIR (Ire) 6-11-9 (5*) T Martin, ...(16 to 1)	f
3393	GOLDWREN (Ire) 8-11-2 (7*) Mr N W Toal, ...(33 to 1)	pu

Dist: 4l, 3l, 4l, 3½l. 4m 23.70s. (13 Ran).

(Peter S Thompson), T J Taaffe

4149 Irish Field Q.R. Maiden Hurdle (4-y-o and up) £1,712 2¾m.........(3:00)

3837[8]	STAR CLUB (Ire) 5-11-5 (3*) Mr B R Hamilton, ..(5 to 2 fav)	1
3942[3]	KILCAR (Ire) 6-10-13 (7*) Mr W Ewing, ...(3 to 1)	2
3606[5]	CHERGALE (Ire) 9-11-4 Mr G J Harford, ...(5 to 1)	3
	DRUMEE (Ire) 6-10-8 (7*) Mr N W Toal, ...(10 to 1)	4
3943[8]	CHERISHTHELADY (Ire) 6-11-6 (7*) Mr P J Casey, (25 to 1)	5
3889[6]	LOUGH SLANIA (Ire) 4-10-12 (3*) Mr P M Kelly, ..(7 to 1)	6
2670[8]	DUN CARRAIG (Ire) 9-12-0 Mr A R Coonan, ...(10 to 1)	7
	CLOGHRAN NATIVE (Ire) 5-10-7 (7*) Mr J O McGurgan,	
	...................................(25 to 1)	8
3891	THE BREAK (Ire) 8-10-8 (7*) Mr J Keville, ...(33 to 1)	9
3889[8]	STORM COURSE (Ire) 5-10-9 (5*) Mr G Elliott, ...(10 to 1)	10
4026[5]	DISPOSEN (Ire) 4-10-5[2] (7*) Mr D Groome, ...(10 to 1)	ur
	KAREN'S LEADER (Ire) 8-10-8 (7*) Mr K Ross, ...(33 to 1)	ur
	AMISTAR (Ire) 5-10-12 (7*) Mr J Young, ...(16 to 1)	pu

Dist: 1l, 25l, 7l, 10l. 5m 29.60s. (13 Ran).

(Range Syndicate), D G McArdle

4150 Willie Polly Memorial Handicap Hurdle (0-109 4-y-o and up) £2,055 2m 1f 172yds....................(3:30)

3643[9]	SLEWMORE (Ire) [-] 6-10-6 (7*) M P Cooney, ...(6 to 1)	1

3216 GO SASHA (Ire) [-] 4-11-9 (5*) T Martin, ... (5 to 2) 2
4004² NORDIC SENSATION (Ire) [-] 8-11-7 (3*) G Cotter,
. . . . (5 to 4 on) 3
2161⁵ DADDY'S HAT (Ire) [-] 4-11-2 P L Malone, ... (6 to 1) 4
Dist: 1½l, 1½l, dist. 4m 27.00s. (4 Ran).

(Mrs S Gilmore), Peter McCreery

4151 Downpatrick Handicap Chase (0-102 4-y-o and up) £1,712 2½m
. . . . (5:00)

3944² LA-GREINE [-] 10-11-2 (7*) Mr K Ross, ... (4 to 1) 1
4003² BROWNRATH KING (Ire) [-] 8-10-6 K F O'Brien, (7 to 4 fav) 2
3944 MR FIVE WOOD (Ire) [-] 9-11-9 D T Evans, ...(7 to 2) 3
3944 ROCHE MENTOR (Ire) [-] 7-10-0 (3*) D Bromley, . . (10 to 1) 4
3944⁵ GREEK MAGIC [-] 10-9-10 (3*) G Cotter, ... (12 to 1) 5
3944⁶ CABBERY ROSE (Ire) [-] 9-10-11 T J Mitchell, ...(10 to 1) 6
3953 JESSIE'S BOY (Ire) [-] (bl) 8-11-0 J K Kinane, ...(25 to 1) 7
3418 BLACKIE CONNORS (Ire) [-] 4-11-7 (7*) D M Bean, (14 to 1) 8
158⁹ WILLCHRIS [-] 10-10-10 (7*) Mr R P McNalley, ... (16 to 1) 9
Dist: ¾l, hd, 3½l, hd. 5m 20.30s. (9 Ran).

(T Bushe), I A Duncan

4152 Holestone Bloodhounds I.N.H. Flat Race (4-y-o and up) £1,712 2½m
. . . . (5:30)

AN TAIN SHIOC (Ire) 6-11-7 (7*) Mr A Ross, ... (7 to 1) 1
SERIOUS NOTE 9-11-9 Mr A J Martin, ... (9 to 4 fav) 2
DYSART O'DEA (Ire) 6-11-7 (7*) Mr B Hassett, ... (7 to 2) 3
3943² NOBODYWANTSME (Ire) 6-11-7 (7*) Mr R P McNalley,
. . . . (5 to 1) 4
3943 WIND OF GLORY (Ire) 7-11-7 (7*) Mr P Jones, ... (16 to 1) 5
FLORUCEVA (Ire) 7-11-4 (5*) Mr R J Patton, ... (14 to 1) 6
GLASTRYTURN (Ire) 6-11-7 (7*) Mr M O'Connor, . . (6 to 1) 7
LA MANCHA BOY 7-11-7 (7*) Mr D Boylan, ...(16 to 1) 8
BALLINAVARY VI (Ire) 6-11-9 (5*) Mr G Elliott, ... (12 to 1) 9
SAND DE VINCE 6-11-7 (7*) Mr B Potts, ... (16 to 1) 10
Dist: 9l, 6l, 3l, sht-hd. 5m 8.20s. (10 Ran).

(Mrs M B Casey), Patrick Martin

FAKENHAM (good)
Sunday May 18th
Going Correction: NIL

4153 Super Sunday Selling Handicap Hurdle Class G (0-95 4-y-o and up) £2,746 2m
. . . . (2:20)

3971⁴ HEVER GOLF DIAMOND [77] (bl) 4-10-11 (7*) Mr P O'Keeffe,
made all, rdn appr last, ran on wl.
. . . . (25 to 1 op 20 to 1 tchd 33 to 1) 1
3617² CAPTAIN TANDY (Ire) [70] 8-11-2 P McLoughlin, hld up, mstk
4th, hdwy appr 2 out, ran on . . . . (7 to 1 op 6 to 1) 2
3992* BLOTOFT [78] 5-11-10 M A Fitzgerald, hld up, hdwy 3 out,
chsd wnr nxt, rdn appr last, no imprsn . . . .(3 to 1 jt-
fav op 7 to 2 tchd 4 to 1) 3
2676³ CAPTAIN MARMALADE [75] 8-11-7 K Gaule, prmnt, lost pl
5th, rallied 2 out, ran on . . . .(7 to 1 op 6 to 1 tchd 8 to 1) 4
3820³ AJDAR [73] 6-11-5 M Brennan, mid-div, rdn appr 2 out, styd
on same pace . . . .(3 to 1 jt-fav op 7 to 2) 5
4073 DO BE WARE [77] (bl) 7-11-9 B Fenton, chsd ldrs, rdn 3 out,
btn nxt . . . . (14 to 1 op 12 to 1) 6
3736⁹ TUG YOUR FORELOCK [59] 6-10-5 J Culloty, prmnt till wknd
4 out . . . .(14 to 1 tchd 16 to 1) 7
3819⁴ LEBEDINSKI (Ire) [80] 4-11-7 V Smith, nvr nr to chal.
. . . . (16 to 1 op 14 to 1) 8
3673 EMERALD VENTURE [56] 10-10-2 C Rae, prmnt till wknd 3
out . . . . (33 to 1) 9
2801 WE'RE IN THE MONEY [60] 13-10-6 M Sharratt, beh frm 5th.
. . . . (33 to 1 op 20 to 1) 10
3469⁴ NAGOBELIA [78] 9-11-10 A P McCoy, hld up, hdwy 5th, wknd
nxt. . . . . (9 to 2 op 5 to 1) 11
Dist: 2l, sht-hd, hd, 2½l, 3l, 3½l, 1½l, ¾l, 12l, 2½l. 3m 53.00s. a 9.00s (11
Ran).
SR: -/-/4/-/-/-/

(H J Jarvis), J R Best

4154 Hood, Vores And Allwood Hunters' Chase Class H For Essandem Trophy (5-y-o and up) £2,594 3m 110yds
. . . . (2:55)

3847³ DROMIN LEADER 12-11-13 (5*) Mr A Sansome, made all, clr
aftr 3 out, all out. . . . .(7 to 4 tchd 2 to 1) 1
SANDYBRAES 12-11-5 (7*) Mr F Hutsby, chsd wnr thrght, hit
13th, blun 3 out, rdn appr last, no imprsn .(9 to 1 op 6 to 1) 2
CRACKING IDEA (Ire) 9-11-11 (7*) Mr C Ward Thomas, hld
up, hdwy 9th, outpcd 3 out, styd on und pres r-in.
. . . .(8 to 1 op 6 to 1 tchd 9 to 1) 3
3847 TAMMY'S FRIEND (Ire) 10-11-5 (7*) Mr R Wakley, prmnt, outpcd 3 out, styd on appr last . . . . (20 to 1 tchd 25 to 1) 4
ABBOTSHAM 12-11-5 (7*) Miss P Gundry, chsd ldrs, rdn 5
out, wknd 3 out . . . .(4 to 1 op 7 to 2) 5
3940* CHILIPOUR 10-12-3 (5*) Mr J Jukes, prmnt, blun 13th, rdn 3
out, no imprsn appr last, eased r-in. (5 to 4 on op 5 to 4) 6

LYME GOLD (Ire) (bl) 8-11-11 (7*) Mr D Keane, al in rear.
. . . . (50 to 1 op 33 to 1) 7
CARDINAL RED 10-11-11 (7*) Mr N King, sn beh, tried to
refuse tenth, pld up bef nxt.
. . . . (33 to 1 op 20 to 1 tchd 50 to 1) 8
SKERRY MEADOW 13-11-5 (7*) Miss V Roberts, hit 1st, sn wl
beh, blun 6th, pld up aftr tenth. . . . . . . (66 to 1 op 50 to 1) 9
Dist: 5l, ½l, 1¼l, 12l, 2l, dist. 6m 13.80s. a 16.80s (9 Ran).

(J M Turner), J M Turner

4155 Prince Of Wales Cup Handicap Chase Class E (0-110 5-y-o and up) £4,405 2m 5f 110yds. . . . . (3:30)

1706 MANOR MIEO [83] (v) 11-9-12 (3*) Michael Brennan, led 3rd
to 5th, led 7th, clr 4 out, wknd r-in, all out. (7 to 2 op 8 to 1) 1
3461² WHIPPERS DELIGHT (Ire) [90] 9-10-3 (5*) X Aizpuru, led
second to nxt, led 5th to 7th, outpcd 4 out, rallied appr last, ran
on wl. . . . . (9 to 2 op 5 to 1) 2
3976 BALLY PARSON [97] 11-11-1 J Culloty, prmnt, hit 5th, outpcd
4 out, styd on frm 2 out. . . .(15 to 2 op 7 to 1 tchd 8 to 1) 3
3972 TIM SOLDIER (Fr) [94] 10-10-12 R Supple, led to second,
remained hndy, hit 3 out, styd on same pace, fnshd lme.
. . . . (11 to 2 op 5 to 1) 4
3875* LINDEN'S LOTTO (Ire) [104] 8-11-8 J R Kavanagh, hld up,
hdwy und pres 5 out, wknd aftr 3 out.
. . . . (100 to 30 fav op 5 to 2 tchd 7 to 2) 5
3851 FISH QUAY [82] 14-9-7 (7*) Miss S Lamb, sn wl beh.
. . . . (100 to 1 op 50 to 1) 6
3980³ FRONTIER FLIGHT (USA) [82] 7-9-11 (3*) E Husband, prmnt,
to 6th, blun 8th, sn tld off, pld up bef 12th. (12 to 1 op 8 to 1) pu
4014* MONKS SOHAM (Ire) [119] 9-12-6 (3*) P Henley, hld up, hit
second, pld up bef 4 out. . . . . (7 to 2 op 9 to 4) pu
Dist: ½l, 3l, 5l, 17l, dist. 5m 18.70s. a 6.70s (8 Ran).
SR: 6/12/16/8/1/

(George Prodromou), G Prodromou

4156 King's Lynn Novices' Handicap Hurdle Class E (0-100 4-y-o and up) £3,022 2m 7f 110yds. . . . . . . (4:00)

3973⁶ STONE ISLAND [69] 4-10-12 (7*) Mr R Wakley, prmnt till lost
pl aftr 5th, remote second and virtually pld up after 5 out,
shaken up and lft wl clr bef nxt. . . . . (11 to 2 op 9 to 2) 1
3973 COME ON IN [74] 4-11-5 (5*) X Aizpuru, hld up, hdwy to chase
ldr 7th, rdn appr 5 out, virtually pld up afterwards, continued,
tld off . . . .(85 to 40 op 2 to 1 tchd 9 to 4) 2
3457 HOLKHAM BAY [61] 5-11-0 (3*) Michael Brennan, sn wl
clr, rdn appr 5 out, pld up bef nxt, continued but tld off.
. . . . (5 to 1 op 7 to 1) 3
4008³ ROYAL HAND [68] (v) 7-11-10 Mr R Armson, trkd ldr, 3rd whn
lft 7th. . . . .(11 to 10 fav op Evens tchd 11 to 8) f
Dist: Dist, dist. 5m 56.40s. a 29.40s (4 Ran).

(John Whyte), John Whyte

4157 West Norfolk Maiden Hunters' Chase Class H (5-y-o and up) £2,726 2m 5f 110yds. . . . . (4:35)

ROUGH EDGE 9-12-2 (5*) Mr W Wales, hld up, hdwy tenth, hit
nxt, chsd ldr 3 out, led last, styd on wl.
. . . .(5 to 2 fav op 9 to 4) 1
COOLVAWN LADY 8-11-9 (7*) Mr S Walker, al prmnt, led
9th, hdd and no extr last. . . . . (3 to 1 op 5 to 1) 2
3916⁴ TELLAPORKY 8-12-0 (7*) Mr A Middleton, hld up, hdwy 4 out,
not rch ldrs. . . . . (20 to 1 op 14 to 1 tchd 25 to 1) 3
BEECH BROOK 8-12-0 (7*) Mr T Lane, chsd ldrs, pckd tenth,
mstk 6 out, wknd 4 out. . . . .(9 to 2 op 7 to 2) 4
MENATURE (Ire) 8-12-2 (5*) Mr A Sansome, hld up, hdwy 12th
wknd nxt. . . . .(20 to 1 op 14 to 1) 5
RAKI CRAZY 6-12-0 (7*) Miss P Gundry, beh whn blun 3rd,
hdwy tenth, wknd 4 out. . . . .(16 to 1 op 12 to 1) 6
MCCARTNEY 11-12-0 (7*) Mr K Green, mid-divison, hdwy
and hit 11th, wknd appr 4 out. . . . . (25 to 1 op 20 to 1) 7
CHESTER BEN 8-12-4 (3*) Mr Simon Andrews, made most to
9th, wknd 4 out. . . . .(7 to 1 op 10 to 1) 8
ALAPA 10-12-0 (7*) Mr V Coogan, blun and uns rdr second.
. . . . (33 to 1 op 25 to 1 tchd 50 to 1) ur
AL JAWWAL 7-12-0 (7*) Mr R Wakley, in rear whn hit 4th, pld
up bef nxt. . . . .(10 to 1 op 8 to 1) pu
DARK RHYTHAM 8-12-0 (7*) Mr S Morris, prmnt to tenth, pld
up bef 4 out. . . . .(7 to 1 op 8 to 1) pu
Dist: bef 4 out, 7l, 12l, 22l, sht-hd, 28l, 2½l. 5m 28.40s. a 16.40s (11 Ran).

(David Wales), D A Wales

4158 Georgina And Paul's First Anniversary Novices' Hurdle Class D (4-y-o and up) £2,700 2½m. . . . . (5:10)

3872* PERSIAN ELITE (Ire) 6-12-0 J Osborne, made all, clr appr
last, unchlgd. . . . .(4 to 1 on tchd 13 to 8 on) 1
3872⁴ RED LIGHT (bl) 5-11-0 A P McCoy, prmnt, lost pl 3rd, hdwy 3
out, chsd wnr nxt, no imprsn. . . . . .(11 to 2 op 9 to 2) 2
4039⁹ PEALINGS (Ire) 5-10-11 (3*) Michael Brennan, mid-div, hdwy
5th, one pace frm 2 out. . . . . (7 to 1 op 6 to 1) 3
3971 CAN SHE CAN CAN 5-10-9 M Ranger, chsd wnr to appr 2 out,
sn btn. . . . .(25 to 1 op 20 to 1 tchd 33 to 1) 4

4025⁴ DONT FORGET CURTIS (Ire) 5-10-7 (7") Miss S Lamb, *hld up, styd on frm 3 out, nvr nr to chal.*
.... (12 to 1 op 10 to 1 tchd 14 to 1) 5
3931 TEEJAY'S FUTURE (Ire) 6-10-9 M Brennan, *hld up, hdwy 6th, wknd appr 2 out*................ (14 to 1 tchd 16 to 1) 6
3970 DERRING WELL 7-10-9 K Gaule, *in rear whn mstk 5th, nvr dngrs*.................................. (33 to 1 op 25 to 1) 7
HARVEST REAPER 5-11-0 R Supple, *prmnt, mstk 3rd, hit 7th, wknd appr 3 out*.................... (12 to 1 tchd 14 to 1) 8
3290⁸ PHILISITATE 8-10-9 B Fenton, *prmnt till lost pl 6th, sn wl beh.*
.... (33 to 1 op 20 to 1) 9
Dist: 4l, 8l, 2½l, 2½l, 3½l, 15l, 20l, 10l. 4m 48.90s. a 7.90s (9 Ran).
SR: 21/3/-/-/-/-/ (Elite Racing Club), C R Egerton

NAAS (IRE) (yielding)
Sunday May 18th

4159 Osberstown Handicap Hurdle (0-135 4-y-o and up) £3,082 2m 3f... (3:00)

4054 COLM'S ROCK (Ire) |-| 6-11-8 C F Swan, ... (2 to 1) 1
4027⁵ OWENBWEE (Ire) |-| 6-10-5 F Woods, ... (6 to 1) 2
2963 BUGGY (Ire) |-| 8-11-8 T J Mitchell, ... (8 to 1) 3
4054³ SAMBARA (Ire) |-| 6-11-8 D J Casey, ... (15 to 8 fav) 4
4095² FIDDLERS BOW VI (Ire) |-| 9-10-3 (7") B J Geraghty, (7 to 2) ur
Dist: 2l, hd, 2½l. 4m 42.90s. (5 Ran).
(R Finnegan), A P O'Brien

4160 Floods Horsefeeds Maiden Hurdle (4-y-o and up) £3,425 2m.... (3:30)

3450⁷ QUINZE 4-11-6 R Dunwoody, ... (9 to 4 fav) 1
3935⁴ DRAMATIST (Ire) 6-12-0 C F Swan, ... (11 to 2) 2
TRY FOR EVER (Ire) 5-11-1 (7") B J Geraghty, ... (3 to 1) 3
3767 TOTAL SUCCESS (Ire) 5-11-5 T P Treacy, ... (10 to 1) 4
2832³ DUNEMER (Ire) 4-11-1 Mr R Walsh, ... (10 to 1) 5
4094² CONAGHER LEADER (Ire) 6-11-6 A J O'Brien, ... (8 to 1) 6
2614⁴ FINLANA 4-10-3 (7") Miss E Doyle, ... (14 to 1) 7
2649 EQUIVOCATOR (Ire) 6-11-6 T P Rudd, ... (8 to 1) 8
720⁶ GOLD DEVON (Ire) 7-11-3 (3") K Whelan, ... (14 to 1) 9
4026⁸ PATIENCE OF ANGELS (Ire) 4-10-10 D J Casey, .. (20 to 1) 10
3964 SWIFT GALE (Ire) 6-11-6 H Rogers, ... (20 to 1) 11
3964³ MARTYS STEP (Ire) 6-11-3 (3") U Smyth, ... (8 to 1) 12
MULDALUS (Ire) 5-11-5 F Woods, ... (10 to 1) 13
3945¹⁷ THE TOLLAH (Ire) 5-11-5 D H O'Connor, ... (14 to 1) 14
3891⁷ RED EBREL (Ire) 5-10-11 (3") G Cotter, ... (14 to 1) 15
3178 MINNY DOZER (Ire) 5-10-13 (7") J P Deegan, ... (33 to 1) 16
3945 LIGHTNING JACK (Ire) 6-11-6 J Shortt, ... (20 to 1) 17
4026⁶ UNFORGOTTEN STAR (Ire) 4-11-1 F J Flood, ... (14 to 1) 18
3840 GOLDEN MICHELLE (Ire) 5-11-0 T J Mitchell, ... (20 to 1) 19
3697 SASSI LAD (Ire) 6-10-13 (7") D M Bean, ... (20 to 1) 20
3955 CROHANE HILL (Ire) 6-11-6 S H O'Donovan, ... (33 to 1) 21
3840 SOUNDWOMEN (Ire) 5-10-7 (7") L J Fleming, ... (33 to 1) 22
4006 PALM RIVER (Ire) 5-11-6 L P Cusack, ... (14 to 1) 23
3767 HELLO JOHN 4-10-8 (7") Mr D W Cullen, ... (33 to 1) 24
Dist: 6l, 2l, 2l, 2l. 3m 54.80s. (24 Ran).
(P C Byrne), P Hughes

4161 Blessington I.N.H. Flat Race (4-y-o and up) £3,082 2m 3f........ (5:30)

4029² OONAGH'S STAR (Ire) 5-11-8 (5") Mr A C Coyle, (9 to 4 fav) 1
3836⁴ FINCHOGUE (Ire) 5-11-8 Mr P Fenton, ... (7 to 1) 2
3935⁶ HAVE AT IT (Ire) 5-11-1 (7") Mr P A Farrell, ... (10 to 1) 3
3965² THE TEXAS KID (Ire) 6-11-7 (7") Mr A K Wyse, ... (8 to 1) 4
BUDALUS (Ire) 5-11-13 Mr J P Dempsey, ... (10 to 1) 5
LAKE SUPREME (Ire) 7-12-0 Mr D Marnane, ... (8 to 1) 6
REGAL KNIGHT (Ire) 5-11-13 Mr A R Coonan, ... (14 to 1) 7
SHERS HILL (Ire) 5-11-1 (7") Mr T J Doyle, ... (20 to 1) 8
3213⁴ SAIL AWAY SAILOR (Ire) 6-11-7 (7") Mrs B Haynes, (10 to 1) 9
3880² OZIER HILL (Ire) 9-12-0 Mr J A Berry, ... (3 to 1) 10
3524 GET EVEN (Ire) 5-11-13 Mr B M Cash, ... (10 to 1) 11
3524 DATEM (Ire) 5-11-13 Mr R Walsh, ... (12 to 1) 12
THE BALER BREAKER (Ire) 5-11-6 (7") Mr M G Whyte,
.... (14 to 1) 13
DAISY MUTLAR (Ire) 5-11-5 (3") Mr E Norris, ... (25 to 1) 14
3945⁶ MACON EXPRESS (Ire) 4-10-13 (7") Mr A J Dempsey,
.... (14 to 1) 15
3449 OLYMPIC LADY (Ire) 5-11-1 (7") Mr M A Cahill, .. (16 to 1) 16
3608 GARRYGLASS ROSE (Ire) 6-11-6 (3") D Valentine,
.... (20 to 1) 17
3836 HARRY'S SECRET (Ire) 7-12-1⁸ (7") Mr R Sheil, .. (33 to 1) 18
4029 BARNEY THE MAN (Ire) 5-11-6 (7") Mr I T Amond, (12 to 1) 19
CUSP OF CARABELLI (Ire) 5-11-1 (7") Mr C A Cronin,
.... (20 to 1) 20
PILARENE (Ire) 4-10-8 (7") Mr R Doran, ... (25 to 1) 21
3965 POLITICAL ANIMAL (Ire) 5-11-6 (7") Mr R J Barnwell,
.... (33 to 1) 22
722 KINGDOM GLORY (Ire) 6-12-0 Mr J A Nash, ... (33 to 1) pu
AUSSIE ROSE 7-11-2 (7") Mr J R Ryan, ... (25 to 1) pu
Dist: 4½l, 4l, ½l, nk. 4m 34.30s. (24 Ran).
(F P Taaffe), P Mullins

ROSCOMMON (IRE) (soft)
Monday May 19th

4162 Elphin Opportunity Handicap Hurdle (0-102 4-y-o and up) £2,740 2m
.... (2:30)

3954* CLONMEL COMMERCIAL (Ire) |-| 6-10-8 (4") D McCullagh,
.... (9 to 2 jt-fav) 1
3954⁸ DARCARI ROSE (Ire) |-| 8-10-13 (2") T Martin, ... (12 to 1) 2
3954⁶ CNOCADRUM VI (Ire) |-| 6-10-0 (2") M D Murphy, . (10 to 1) 3
3817² NOBLE TUNE (Ire) |-| 8-9-13 (4") K A Kelly, ... (11 to 2) 4
1017 MAJESTIC PADDY (Ire) |-| 7-12-0 U Smyth, ... (8 to 1) 5
4052⁵ POWER CORE (Ire) |-| 7-10-10 (4") J A Robinson, . (12 to 1) 6
3336² BORN TO WIN (Ire) |-| 7-11-9 (2") J M Donnelly, ... (4 to 1) 7
7013 SANDRA LOUISE (Ire) |-| 7-9-11 (4") L J Fleming, .. (10 to 1) 8
3837 ANOTHER BONNY |-| 11-9-3 (4") D A McLoughlin, (25 to 1) 9
3954 MIDDLE MOGGS (Ire) |-| 5-11-3 G Cotter, ... (9 to 2 jt-fav) 10
4096⁴ FOYLE WANDERER (Ire) |-| 6-10-7 (2") P G Hourigan,
.... (8 to 1) 11
4026³ CELTIC PROJECT (Ire) |-| (bl) 4-11-3 (4") J M Maguire,
.... (8 to 1) 12
4004 WINDTEKIN (Ire) |-| 4-11-1 (4") B J Geraghty, ... (20 to 1) 13
4060⁸ ASTRID (Ire) |-| 6-9-3 (4") P J Dobbs, ... (33 to 1) 14
3430 BUCK THE WEST (Ire) |-| 7-11-10 K Whelan, ... (20 to 1) 15
2585 FOREST STAR (USA) |-| 8-9-8 (4") D W O'Sullivan, (25 to 1) 16
Dist: 4½l, 1½l, 3½l, hd. 4m 4.40s. (16 Ran).
(E P Hickey), Michael Donohoe

4163 Villiger Hurdle (4-y-o and up) £3,253 2m........................ (3:00)

731 TAKLIF (Ire) 5-11-6 C F Swan, ... (5 to 4 fav) 1
1090⁹ OMAR (USA) 8-11-2 (5") P G Hourigan, ... (6 to 1) 2
3348⁴ FISHIN JOELLA (Ire) 5-11-5 (3") G Cotter, ... (2 to 1) 3
1778 THE SCEARDEEN (Ire) 8-11-2 J R Barry, ... (20 to 1) 4
3232³ COULTHARD (Ire) 4-10-6 (7") Miss S J Leahy, ... (12 to 1) 5
3963⁸ CORAL SEA (Ire) 7-11-2 (7") Mr A Ross, ... (16 to 1) 6
2751² NO AVAIL (Ire) 4-11-1 T P Treacy, ... (6 to 1) 7
3935 VARTRY BOY (Ire) 6-11-2 (5") M D Murphy, ... (20 to 1) 8
3416 EARL OF NAAS (Ire) 6-11-2 (5") T Martin, ... (50 to 1) 9
Dist: 5l, 4l, 13l, 13l. 4m 4.70s. (9 Ran).
(D P Sharkey), M J P O'Brien

4164 Frank Hannon Memorial Chase (5-y-o and up) £3,425 2m 5f..... (3:30)

2068⁶ PADASHPAN (USA) 8-11-10 C F Swan, ... (11 to 8 fav) 1
3962⁴ HEADBANGER 10-11-5 (5") Mr G Elliott, ... (7 to 2) 2
4053* CHATTERBUCK (Ire) 8-11-10 C O'Dwyer, ... (4 to 1) 3
3838 AMAZING ALL (Ire) 8-11-3 (3") D Bromley, ... (50 to 1) 4
3935⁸ CONAGHER BOY 7-11-3 (3") G Cotter, ... (16 to 1) 5
MUBADIR (USA) 9-11-3 B J Geraghty, ... (8 to 1) 6
3624 CASSFINN 11-10-10 (5") T Martin, ... (50 to 1) 7
WELCOME EXPRESS (Ire) 6-11-6 D T Evans, ... (25 to 1) 8
Dist: 4l, 3½l, ½l, 4½l. 5m 33.50s. (8 Ran).
(William Brennan), W P Mullins

4165 Flemings Super Valu Handicap Chase (0-123 4-y-o and up) £3,425 2m........................ (4:00)

4055² PERSIAN POWER (Ire) |-| 9-9-6 (7") B J Geraghty, ... (4 to 1) 1
4055* HANNIES GIRL (Ire) |-| 8-9-9 (7") L J Fleming, .. (7 to 2 fav) 2
4055⁴ TIME AND CHARGES (Ire) |-| 7-9-4 (3") G Cotter, .. (8 to 1) 3
2090 DRAMATIC VENTURE (Ire) |-| 8-11-2 C O'Dwyer, .. (10 to 1) 4
4103⁴ EVER SO BOLD |-| 10-9-11 T P Treacy, ... (16 to 1) 5
3962³ ARCTIC WEATHER (Ire) |-| 8-12-0 T P Rudd, ... (4 to 1) 6
CONGREGATION |-| 11-11-4 F Woods, ... (12 to 1) 7
214 HOLIWAY STAR (Ire) |-| 7-11-13 C F Swan, ... (4 to 1) 8
2840⁷ MIROSWAKI (USA) |-| 7-10-10 T J Mitchell, ... (10 to 1) 9
Dist: 6l, 2l, 3½l, 4l. 4m 11.60s. (9 Ran).
(P M Hunt), Noel Meade

4166 Kepak I.N.H. Flat Race (5-y-o and up) £3,425 2m.................... (5:00)

4005³ RURAL RUN (Ire) 6-11-2 (7") Mr C A Murphy, ... (5 to 1) 1
3527 BAVARD JET (Ire) 5-11-13 Mr R Walsh, ... (5 to 1) 2
3818² MONTEBA (Ire) 5-11-6 (7") Mr P Cashman, ... (4 to 1) 3
3456 BE MY MOT (Ire) 5-11-3 (5") Mr G Elliott, ... (8 to 1) 4
IONA FLYER (Ire) 5-11-3 (5") Mr J T McNamara, ... (10 to 1) 5
3834³ TULLY'S BALL (Ire) 7-12-0 Mr P Fenton, ... (5 to 2 fav) 6
1060³ MASK RIVER (Ire) 8-11-2 (7") Mr A Daly, ... (14 to 1) 7
3955 BADALKA (Ire) 7-11-2 (7") Mr T A J Corrigan, ... (25 to 1) 8
68 GLIDING AWAY (Ire) 7-11-2 (7") Mr P G Murphy, .. (33 to 1) 9
CLOONE STAR VI (Ire) 7-11-2 (7") Mr D A Harney, (16 to 1) 10
MISS BARNAMIRE (Ire) 7-11-2 (7") Mr D Breen, ... (33 to 1) 11
Dist: 5l, 13l, 2l, 15l. 4m 0.80s. (11 Ran).
(S Kennedy), A P O'Brien

FAIRYHOUSE (IRE) (yielding)
Tuesday May 20th
Going Correction: PLUS 0.20 sec. per fur.

4167 Porterstown Hurdle (4-y-o and up) £3,082 2m.................... (7:00)

2082* NOBLE THYNE (Ire) 7-12-4 T P Treacy, ... (Evens fav) 1
3767* STEP ON EYRE (Ire) 7-12-4 C F Swan, ... (11 to 10) 2
3450⁸ TAX REFORM (USA) 4-11-3 H Rogers, ... (25 to 1) 3
3891² POLLTRIC (Ire) 6-10-13 P L Malone, ... (20 to 1) 4
3889⁴ SILVER RIVER (Ire) 5-10-7 F Woods, ... (66 to 1) 5
3087 WELCOME PARADE 4-11-3 C O'Dwyer, ... (12 to 1) 6
2378 NOBLE SHOON (Ire) 6-11-1 (3*) G Cotter, ... (14 to 1) f
SR: 52/50/-/-/

(C Mayo), P Mullins

4168 Baltrasna Handicap Hurdle (0-109 4-y-o and up) £3,082 3m . . . . . (7:30)

3837⁴ HI KNIGHT (Ire) [-] 7-11-3 (7*) R Burke, ... (13 to 2) 1
4077³ TULLULOUGH [-] 14-9-3 (5*) M D Murphy, ... (10 to 1) 2
3837* MICK MAN (Ire) [-] 6-9-9 (7*) B J Geraghty, ... (8 to 1) 3
3768³ GENTLE MOSSY (Ire) [-] 5-11-1 D H O'Connor, (9 to 4 fav) 4
1904 STRONG RAIDER (Ire) [-] 7-9-8 (3*) G Cotter, ... (16 to 1) 5
828 ARCTIC KATE [-] 11-11-7 (7*) Mr J S O'Haire, . . . (14 to 1) 6
4149² KILCAR (Ire) [-] 6-9-10 P Carberry, ... (11 to 2) 7
4077⁶ ANOTHER GALLOP (Ire) [-] 9-9-0 (7*) J M Maguire, (25 to 1) 8
4149⁷ DUN CARRAIG (Ire) [-] (bl) 9-9-5 (3*) D Bromley, . . (20 to 1) 9
4109⁶ MAY BLOOM (Ire) [-] (bl) 6-9-7 D J Casey, ... (25 to 1) 10
4027⁹ CRANNON BEAUTY (Ire) [-] 7-10-2 C F Swan, ... (16 to 1) 11
4095³ EIRE (Ire) [-] 8-9-0 (7*) D A McLoughlin, ... (12 to 1) 12
3643³ DEIREADH AN SCEAL (Ire) [-] 7-9-13 T P Treacy, . . (16 to 1) pu
3817 DON'T LOOSE FAITH (Ire) [-] 5-10-5 J Shortt, ... (16 to 1) pu
3955 VALLEY OF KINGS (Ire) [-] 8-11-7 F Woods, ... (10 to 1) pu
3696⁶ GLEN CAMDEN (Ire) [-] (bl) 5-10-4 C O'Dwyer, . . . (16 to 1) pu
Dist: 2½l, 20l, 8l, 20l. 5m 51.70s. a 11.70s (16 Ran).
SR: 27/-/-/-/-/

(M D McGrath), J R H Fowler

4169 Macetown I.N.H. Flat Race (4-y-o and up) £3,082 2m . . . . (9:00)

SIBERIAN GALE 5-11-8 (5*) Mr A C Coyle, ... (11 to 10 fav) 1
KINGS BANQUET 4-11-6 Mr G J Harford, ... (10 to 1) 2
3697 BAY FALLOUGH (Ire) 8-11-7 (7*) Mr P J McCrickard, ... (16 to 1) 3
3707² KOHOUTEK 4-11-6 Mr R Walsh, ... (9 to 2) 4
3935 LUNAR LADY 5-11-1 (7*) Mr R F O'Gorman, ... (20 to 1) 5
4029⁶ CINQ FRANK (Ire) 7-12-0 Mr D Marnane, ... (14 to 1) 6
3816⁸ ANN'S DESIRE (Ire) 6-11-2 (7*) Mr J Keville, ... (12 to 1) 7
3075⁹ MISS HOT TAMALLI (Ire) 6-11-2 (7*) Miss S Collins, (20 to 1) 8
4062 GARRYHILL CHOICE (Ire) 6-11-11 (3*) Mr P English, ... (10 to 1) 9
GOODNIGHT MIKE (Ire) 5-11-6 (7*) Mr D Breen, . . . (16 to 1) 10
NEWTOWN STAR (Ire) 5-11-6 (7*) Mr W Ewing, . . . (16 to 1) 11
3891 JAPAMA (Ire) 6-12-0 Mr A R Coonan, ... (16 to 1) 12
3965 SNAP OUT OF IT (Ire) 5-11-7 (7*) Mr A J Dempsey, (16 to 1) 13
GLENMONT (Ire) 5-11-8 (5*) Mr D McGoona, ... (14 to 1) 14
BENGARI (Ire) 5-11-13 Mr P Fenton, ... (10 to 1) 15
ARD RI (Ire) 4-11-1 Mr B M Cash, ... (25 to 1) 16
945 KERRIA'S GIFT (Ire) 6-11-7 (7*) Mr S P Hennessy, (33 to 1) 17
HORGANS QUAY VI (Ire) 6-11-7 (7*) Mr P T Quinlan, ... (20 to 1) su
MY FUTURE (Ire) 5-11-1 (7*) Mr G A Kingston, ... (16 to 1) pu
Dist: 5l, ¾l, sht-hd, 4l. 3m 49.10s. (19 Ran).

(George Mullins), P Mullins

NEWTON ABBOT (good (races 1,2,3,4,5), good to soft (6))
Wednesday May 21st
Going Correction: NIL

4170 J C Milton Electricals Handicap Hurdle Class D (0-125 4-y-o and up) £2,669 2¾m . . . . (6:10)

3948* JENZSOPH (Ire) [103] (bl) 6-11-2 G Tormey, led, hrd rdn and hdd aftr 3 out, rallied to rgn ld last, all out. . . . . (9 to 4 op 2 to 1 tchd 5 to 2) 1
3948² PETER MONAMY [103] (v) 5-11-2 A P McCoy, chsd wnr, hit and shaken alng 5th, reminders aftr nxt, chlgd frm 7th, led after 3 out, hdd last, rallied r-in. . . . . (5 to 2 op 11 to 4 tchd 3 to 1 and 7 to 2) 2
3144² DEFENDTHEREALM [96] 6-10-9 J Frost, chsd ldg pair, lost tch appr 7th, tld off. . . (6 to 4 fav op 11 to 10 tchd Evens) 3
3635 HOLY WANDERER (USA) [112] 8-11-4 (7*) Mr R Morgan, hld in rear, rdn alng appr 7th, sn tld off, f last. . . . . (12 to 1 op 8 to 1 tchd 14 to 1) f
Dist: Nk, dist. 5m 14.00s. a 13.00s (4 Ran).

(A Stevens), P J Hobbs

4171 Mike Howard & Dick Spencer Memorial Hunters' Chase Class H (5-y-o and up) £1,152 3¼m 110yds. . . . . . (6:40)

BUZZ O'THE CROWD 10-11-0 (7*) Mr D Alers-Hankey, al hndy, led 16th, sn clr, unchlgd. . . . . (14 to 1 op 10 to 1 tchd 16 to 1) 1
3857⁵ FIGHT TO WIN (USA) 11-11-7 Mr J Grassick, wtd wth, improved 13th, lost pl 15th, styd on to take poor second 2 out, tld off. . . . . (50 to 1 op 25 to 1) 2

4033 TOM'S GEMINI STAR 9-11-7 (7*) Miss V Roberts, hld up, hit 13th, sn lost tch, moderate prog frm 3 out, tld off. . . . . (25 to 1 op 12 to 1) 3
3857² KNIFEBOARD 11-11-0 (7*) Mr E Williams, hld up, hdwy 8th, outpcd appr 15th, tld off. . . . . (6 to 1 op 4 to 1) 4
3989* PHAR TOO TOUCHY 10-11-5 (7*) Mr N Harris, hdwy to go prmnt 5th, led 7th, hit nxt, mstk and hdd 16th, sn wknd, tld off, fnshd distressed. . . . . (3 to 1 op 2 to 1 tchd 5 to 1) 5
JUST BEN 9-11-0 (7*) Miss J Cumings, chsd ldrs to 12th, sn wknd, tld off. (16 to 1 op 10 to 1) 6
EXPRESSMENT 13-11-7 (7*) Mr G Penfold, al beh, tld off. . . . . (33 to 1 op 20 to 1) 7
4085⁶ J B LAD 11-11-0 (7*) Mr S Shinton, prmnt, jmpd slwly 4th, beh frm 11th, tld off whn hit 16th, blun and uns rdr nxt. . . . . (50 to 1 op 33 to 1) ur
4018* KINO 10-11-10 (7*) Mr Andrew Martin, made most to 7th, wkng whn hit 15th, tld off when blun badly and almost uns rdr 3 out, pld up bef nxt. . . (25 to 1 op 16 to 1 tchd 33 to 1) pu
ALPHA ONE 12-11-0 (7*) Miss K Di Marte, al beh, tld off frm 8th, pld up bef 14th. . . . . (66 to 1 op 33 to 1 tchd 100 to 1) pu
3856⁴ SOME-TOY 11-11-10 (7*) Miss L Blackford, al beh, tld off 8th, pld up bef 4 out. . . . . (12 to 1 op 8 to 1 tchd 14 to 1) pu
Dist: Dist, 11l, 4l, 4l, 13l, 23l. 6m 39.00s. a 19.00s (11 Ran).

(B J Williams), Miss A V Handel

4172 Come Racing At Newton Abbot Novices' Hurdle Class D (4-y-o and up) £2,855 2m 1f. . . . . (7:10)

3907 NORDIC BREEZE (Ire) 5-11-7 A P McCoy, confidently rdn, not fluent 5th, improved to ld on bit aftr 3 out, not extended. . . . . (11 to 2 on op 7 to 1 on tchd 5 to 1 on) 1
2539² SPARKLING BUCK 5-10-6 (3*) Guy Lewis, hld up, hdwy 3 out, chlgd und pres appr nxt, sn held by wnr. (10 to 1 op 6 to 1) 2
3828 TECHNICAL MOVE (Ire) 6-10-9 S Burrough, chsd clr ldr to 3 out, fdd. . . . . (100 to 1 op 66 to 1) 3
3555 MORDROS 7-11-0 T Dascombe, keen hold, hld up, btn whn hit 3 out. . . . . (25 to 1 tchd 40 to 1 and 50 to 1) 4
WITH INTENT 5-11-0 Mr L Jefford, pld hrd, led, sn clr, tiring whn not fluent 3 out, soon hdd and fdd. . . . . (8 to 1 op 14 to 1 tchd 20 to 1 and 25 to 1) 5
4030³ FINAL SCORE (Ire) 7-11-0 (5*) O Burrows, hld up, rdn alng 5th, sn wknd, tld off. . . . . (25 to 1 op 12 to 1) 6
Dist: 1¼l, 21l, 1¼l, 1¼l, dist. 4m 16.40s. a 27.40s (6 Ran).

(Malcolm B Jones), M C Pipe

4173 Spa-Trans And Chagford Football Club Handicap Chase Class C (0-135 5-y-o and up) £4,287 2m 5f 110yds . . . . (7:40)

3950³ POLDEN PRIDE [113] 9-10-6 A P McCoy, wtd wth in rear, hit 7th, shaken alng 11th, rdn appr 2 out, led last, ran on wl. (2 to 1 op 7 to 4 tchd 9 to 4) 1
4040⁴ ALLO GEORGE [107] 11-10-0 A Thornton, jmpd rght, led to last, one pace. . . . . (100 to 30 op 9 to 2) 2
4016² PHILIP'S WOODY [116] 9-10-9 M A Fitzgerald, keen hold, chsd ldr, rdn alng frm 12th, wknd betw fnl 2, eased. (11 to 10 on op 5 to 4 on tchd 5 to 4) 3
Dist: 3l, 17l. 5m 26.90s. a 24.90s (3 Ran).

(D F Lockyer, C A Parry, G B Balding), G B Balding

4174 Florida Novices' Chase Class E (5-y-o and up) £2,836 2m 110yds (8:10)

3938 ROBERT'S TOY (Ire) (bl) 6-11-12 A P McCoy, made all, sn clr, not fluent 3 out, cheekily. (3 to 1 fav op 9 to 4 tchd 100 to 30) 1
4014⁴ FINNIGAN FREE 7-10-7 (7*) Mr M Frith, sn chasing wnr, hit 4 out, no imprsn frm nxt. . . (6 to 1 tchd 10 to 1 and 12 to 1) 2
ANOTHER HUBBLICK 6-11-0 V Slattery, hld up and beh, hit 4th, improved 8th, lft 3rd appr nxt, styd on one pace frm 3 out. . . . . (66 to 1 op 25 to 1 tchd 100 to 1) 3
3488⁴ HOLDIMCLOSE 7-11-0 J Frost, trkd ldrs to 7th, sn rdn and btn. . . . . (7 to 2 op 9 to 4) 4
4034² STRATTON FLYER 7-10-2 (7*) Mr R Widger, mid-div, beh frm 7th. . . . . (12 to 1 op 10 to 1 tchd 14 to 1) 5
3978 CARLINGFORD GALE (Ire) 6-10-9 L Harvey, hit 1st, hld up, improved 6th, lost pl nxt, no dngr aftr, tld off. . . . . (6 to 1 op 4 to 1) 6
4034³ RUN WITH JOY (Ire) 6-11-0 R Greene, in tch till wknd 8th, beh whn blun 4 out, tld off. . . . . (14 to 1 op 10 to 1) 7
3959⁷ ROCA MURADA (Ire) 8-11-0 N Williamson, hld up towards rear, gd hdwy on inner appr 7th, 3rd whn pld up bef 9th. . . . . (4 to 1 op 5 to 1 tchd 6 to 1) pu
3911 PATONG BEACH 7-10-9 M Ahern, al beh, tld off 8th, pld up bef 2 out. . . . . (66 to 1 op 25 to 1) pu
Dist: 1½l, 2½l, 26l, 1¾l, 9l, 11l. 4m 5.60s. a 7.60s (9 Ran).
SR: 22/8/5/-/-/-/

(Clive D Smith), M C Pipe

4175 Final Fling Handicap Hurdle Class F (0-105 4-y-o and up) £1,971 2m 1f . . . . (8:40)

4069* BLADE OF FORTUNE [90] 9-10-9 (7*,7ex) Mr J Tizzard, made all, quickened clr frm 3 out, mstk nxt, ran on wl. (15 to 8 op 6 to 4 tchd 2 to 1) 1

3831⁴ COOLEY'S VALVE (Ire) [98] 9-11-7 (3*) Mr R Thornton, *hld up, chsd wnr frm 5th, ev ch und pres last, one pace.*
....(7 to 2 op 3 to 1) 2
3863³ MISS SOUTER [74] 8-10-0 B Powell, *hld up, wth alng frm hfwy, lost tch aftr 3 out...*(10 to 1 op 8 to 1 tchd 12 to 1) 3
3863* MYSTIC HILL [91] 6-11-3 J Frost, *not fluent, chsd wnr to 5th, rdn alng frm 3 out, wknd bef nxt...*(11 to 8 fav op 7 to 4) 4
Dist: 1¼l, 17l, 7l. 4m 2.30s. a 13.30s (4 Ran).

(V G Greenway), V G Greenway

UTTOXETER (good to soft)
Wednesday May 21st
Going Correction: PLUS 0.40 sec. per fur.

4176 Carling Black Label Maiden Hurdle
Class E (4-y-o and up) £2,389 2m
..............................(6:25)

4068 SINGLE SOURCING (Ire) 6-11-5 J Culloty, *made all, hld narrow ld whn lft clr last, drvn out......*(6 to 1 op 3 to 1) 1
3743² ILEWIN JANINE (Ire) 6-11-0 C Maude, *hld up in rear, hdwy 4 out, ev ch whn mstk 2 out, one pace....*(6 to 1 op 5 to 1) 2
3985² TIMIDJAR (Ire) (bl) 4-11-0 R Dunwoody, *in tch, hdwy to chase ldrs appr 3 out, drvn and btn frm nxt.*
..................(6 to 4 on op 7 to 4 on tchd 11 to 8 on) 3
4092⁴ SAPPHIRE SON (Ire) 5-11-5 B Fenton, *pld hrd, hld up, hdwy to chase wnr aftr 4th, lost plf frm four out, wkng whn not fluent nxt, tld off...................*(7 to 1 op 5 to 1) 4
4019 WOODLANDS LAD TOO 5-11-5 R Bellamy, *al in rear, strug-gling 4 out, tld off..................*(66 to 1 op 33 to 1) 5
3996 TRENTSIDE MAJOR 5-11-5 M Ranger, *cl up, wkng whn mstk 4 out, tld off...................*(50 to 1 tchd 66 to 1) 6
CHINA LAL 5-11-0 O Pears, *beh, drvn and lost tch 5th, tld off.*
..................................(33 to 1 op 20 to 1) 7
3192⁵ TORAJA 5-11-5 D Leahy, *al prmnt, str chal frm 3 out, ev ch whn f last.......................*(10 to 1 op 8 to 1) f
DUNSTON QUEEN 4-10-9 Gary Lyons, *in tch, lost pl quickly 5th, sn drvn and beh, tld off whn pld up bef last.*
..................................(50 to 1 op 33 to 1) pu
Dist: 3½l, 7l, dist, 12l, nk, 5l. 3m 52.60s. a 15.60s (9 Ran).

(V J Adams), Miss H C Knight

4177 Draught Bass Novices' Handicap
Hurdle Class E (0-105 5-y-o and up)
£2,326 3m 110yds.............(6:55)

4023* PALACE OF GOLD [85] 7-11-3 R Supple, *chsd ldrs, led appr 4 out, hrd pressed whn jmpd rght nxt, drvn out r-in.*
..................................(9 to 1 op 8 to 1 tchd 12 to 1) 1
3996² MR CHRISTIE [96] 5-12-0 R Dunwoody, *chsd ldrs, rdn alng and slightly outpcd appr 3 out, styd on and swtchd lft to chal r-in, no extr cl hme..........*(2 to 1 fav op 5 to 2) 2
3797* QUITE A MAN [79] 9-10-11 C Maude, *hld up in tch, hdwy appr 4 out, sn chalg, ev ch whn blun last, tld.*
..................................(100 to 30 op 5 to 2) 3
4083⁵ ROYRACE [68] 5-9-11 (3*) R Massey, *hld up in rear, hdwy 7th, ev ch 3 out, sn und pres, wknd nxt....*(33 to 1 op 25 to 1) 4
4019² NAHLA [83] 7-11-1 S Curran, *hld up, hdwy to chase ldrs 4 out, wknd appr nxt......................*(4 to 1) 5
4020⁶ CHILL FACTOR [75] (bl) 7-10-7 P Niven, *prmnt, reminders bef 3rd, led appr 6th, hdd approaching 4 out, sn wknd, tld off.*
..................................(8 to 1 op 6 to 1) 6
935³ LITTLE TINCTURE (Ire) [70] 7-11-0 G Upton, *led till appr 6th, lost pl quickly nxt, sn beh, tld off.....*(12 to 1 op 10 to 1) 7
3470 KATBALLOU [68] 8-9-7 (7*) Mr S Durack, *hld up, took clr order 7th, wknd 4 out, tld off whn pld up bef nxt.*
..................................(14 to 1 op 12 to 1 tchd 10 to 1) pu
Dist: 1½l, 9l, 10l, 9l, dist, 3l. 5m 54.50s. a 17.50s (8 Ran).
SR: 21/12/-/-/-/ (Andrew W B Duncan), L Lungo

4178 Caffreys Irish Ale Handicap Chase
Class C for the Fred Dixon Memorial
Trophy (0-130 5-y-o and up) £4,260 3
¼m..............................(7:25)

4067² BROGEEN LADY (Ire) [100] 7-10-3 R Dunwoody, *made all, ran on wl frm 2 out, eased 2 out.*
..................................(15 to 8 fav op 13 to 8 tchd 2 to 1) 1
3770⁴ MR BOSTON [125] 12-12-0 P Niven, *hld up in last pl, hdwy to press wnr 14th (water), ev ch 2 out, no extr betw appr last.*
..................................(9 to 4 tchd 5 to 2) 2
4070² THERMAL WARRIOR [97] 9-10-0 C Llewellyn, *prmnt, rdn appr 4 out, one pace tld off.* (5 to 1 op 4 to 1 tchd 9 to 2) 3
3983² JAMES PIGG [118] 10-11-7 R Johnson, *prmnt, mstk 3rd, beh 15th, sn lost tch, tld off...............*(5 to 2 op 13 to 8) 4
Dist: 6l, 26l, 20l. 6m 52.20s. a 40.20s (4 Ran).

(Starlight Racing), D R Gandolfo

4179 Hooper's Hooch Conditional
Jockeys' Selling Handicap Hurdle
Class G (0-95 4-y-o and up) £1,868
2m..............................(7:55)

3988 STRIKE-A-POSE [65] 7-10-9 Michael Brennan, *hld up and beh, hdwy aftr 4 out, led appr 2 out, rdn clr r-in.*
..................................(6 to 1 op 12 to 1) 1
3476⁸ MUDLARK [76] 5-11-3 (3*) B Grattan, *hld up and beh, hdwy appr 3 out, kpt on und pres, no imprsn on wnr.*
..................................(12 to 1 op 10 to 1) 2
4069³ WITHERKAY [74] 4-10-10 (3*) L Cummins, *in tch, mstk 4th, effrt to chal aftr four out, one pace frm last.*
..................................(7 to 4 fav op 6 to 4) 3
3959⁵ FOLLOW DE CALL [72] 7-10-11 (5*) A Egan, *in tch, hdwy 4 out, led out till hng badly rght and hdd appr nxt, wknd last.*
..................................(12 to 1 op 10 to 1) 4
4092⁵ OUR EDDIE [77] (v) 8-11-7 S Ryan, *hld up, hdwy to chase ldrs appr 3 out, fdd frm nxt...........*(7 to 1 op 5 to 1) 5
3931⁴ NEVER SO BLUE (Ire) [78] 6-11-5 (3*) R Wilkinson, *midfield, reminder aftr 5th, no imprsn on ldrs frm 2 out.*
..................................(8 to 1 tchd 9 to 1) 6
3359⁴ BLATANT OUTBURST [74] (v) 7-11-4 Sophie Mitchell, *prmnt, led 4 out to nxt, sn wknd...*(11 to 2 op 9 to 2 tchd 6 to 1) 7
2999⁷ VERRO (USA) [56] 10-9-9 (5*) M Griffiths, *prmnt, drvn and wknd quickly appr 4 out...................*(50 to 1) 8
3915⁷ SOCCER BALL [60] 7-10-4 D J Kavanagh, *al in rear div, nvr a factor...........................*(16 to 1) 9
PREMIER STAR [56] 7-9-9 (5*) J Power, *al beh, stuggling and no dngr frm 4 out...................*(33 to 1) 10
3883 LADY LOIS [56] 6-9-9 (5*) J Mogford, *midfield, lost pl quickly 5th, sn beh, tld off..............*(33 to 1 op 50 to 1) 11
3992⁷ ORINOCO VENTURE (Ire) [57] (bl) 6-9-12 (3*) X Aizpuru, *hndy, lost pl hfwy, sn beh, tld off.......*(12 to 1 op 10 to 1) 12
3823 NEBAAL (USA) [56] (bl) 7-10-0 R Massey, *led to 4 out, wknd quickly, tld off whn pld up bef last....*(25 to 1 op 20 to 1) pu
Dist: 6l, 3½l, 5l, 1¾l, 3½l, 2l, hd, 2l, 14l, 18l. 3m 52.80s. a 15.80s (13 Ran).

(B J Llewellyn), B J Llewellyn

4180 Carling Premier Novices' Chase
Class D (5-y-o and up) £3,468 2m 5f
..............................(8:25)

4022² PLUMBOB (Ire) 8-11-0 R Supple, *nvr far away, mstk 11th, chsd ldr frm 4 out, styd on to ld cl hme.*
..................................(11 to 4 op 7 to 2 tchd 4 to 1 and 5 to 2) 1
4000³ BRIGHTER SHADE (Ire) 7-11-12 P Niven, *hld up, took clr order 6th, wth ldr 9th led 4 out, hrd pressed frm last, hdd and no extr close hme.........*(11 to 4 op 7 to 4 tchd 3 to 1) 2
4044² WITH IMPUNITY 8-11-6 R Johnson, *led to 4 out, sn drvn, wknd frm nxt....................*(7 to 4 fav op 7 to 4) 3
3947² MASTER CRUSADER 11-10-7 (7*) Mr S Durack, *hld up, reminder aftr 6th, struggling frm 9th sn no dngr.*
..................................(14 to 1 op 12 to 1 tchd 16 to 1) 4
4044 ASTRAL INVASION (USA) (bl) 6-11-0 S Wynne, *hndy, lost pl quickly 9th, sn beh.....*(25 to 1 op 20 to 1 tchd 33 to 1) 5
MIGHTY MERC 9-11-0 K Johnson, *keen hold, hld up, prmnt 4th, mstk 8th and lost pl, sn wl beh, tld off........*(33 to 1) 6
2184⁵ BRIDEPARK ROSE (Ire) 9-10-9 S Fox, *cl up, effrt 4 out, no response, eased frm nxt, fourth and no ch whn blun and uns rdr last..............*(5 to 1 op 9 to 2 tchd 11 to 2) ur
Dist: Hd, 15l, 12l, 15l, dist. 5m 22.40s. a 24.40s (7 Ran).

(Andrew W B Duncan), L Lungo

4181 Worthington Draught Bitter Novices'
Hurdle Class D (4-y-o and up) £2,899
2½m 110yds.................(8:55)

4136⁵ MORPHEUS 8-11-0 R Johnson, *hld up in tch, hdwy 4 out, chlgd und pres frm nxt, styd on to ld aftr last, drvn out.*
..................................(2 to 1 op 6 to 4) 1
4047⁵ BULLENS BAY (Ire) 8-11-0 Mr J L Llewellyn, *hld up, hdwy 4 out, slightly outpcd nxt, styd on ag'n r-in.*
..................................(14 to 1 op 10 to 1) 2
4068² RYTHM ROCK (Ire) 8-11-0 R Dunwoody, *in tch, clr order 4 out, led 2 out, mstk last, sn hdd, kpt on same pace.*
..................................(13 to 8 fav op 11 to 8 tchd 15 to 8) 3
4039⁵ GAMAY 7-11-0 C Llewellyn, *al cl up, effrt 3 out, kpt on one pace...............*(20 to 1 op 16 to 1) 4
4068 CAMP HEAD (Ire) 6-11-0 J A McCarthy, *in tch, improved to ld hdd 2 out, no extr bef last.....*(4 to 1 op 5 to 1) 5
4043⁴ ROMANTIC WARRIOR 4-10-5 (3*) R Massey, *cl up, mstk second, lost pl 6th, no dngr aftrwards.*
..................................(33 to 1 op 25 to 1 tchd 50 to 1) 6+
4050⁶ PAMALYN 5-10-9 C Maude, *trkd ldrs till lost pl 6th, rdn to renew effrt aftr 4 out, wknd bef 2 out....*(10 to 1 op 8 to 1) 6+
4039⁵ CROCKNAMOHILL (Ire) 6-11-0 W Marston, *led to 4 out, sn drvn and wknd...............*(20 to 1 op 25 to 1) 8
3996 MOOR HALL PRINCE 7-11-0 B Fenton, *strted slwly, al beh.*
..................................(50 to 1) 9
4013 SAFWAN 5-11-0 M Richards, *in rear, effrt appr 4 out, strug-gling bef nxt, tld off...................*(20 to 1 op 16 to 1) 10
3881 DUNSTON KNIGHT 4-10-8 Gary Lyons, *prmnt, niggled alng appr 4 out, sn wknd, tld off........*(100 to 1 op 50 to 1) 11
Dist: 1½l, 1¾l, 1¼l, 1¼l, 8l, 8l, 11l, 4l, dist, ¾l. 6m 10.50s. a 31.50s (11 Ran).

(Mrs M A Powis), D Nicholson

WORCESTER (soft)
Wednesday May 21st
Going Correction: PLUS 0.95 sec. per fur.

4182 Earls Croome Juvenile Novices' Hurdle Class E (4-y-o) £2,250 2m (2:20)

4080² MELT THE CLOUDS (Can) (bl) 11-5 A P McCoy, *led, rdn aftr 2 out, blun last, drvn out.*
.... (11 to 8 fav op 5 to 4 tchd 13 to 8 and 7 to 4) 1

3823² MAZAMET (USA) (v) 10-12 V Slattery, *chsd ldr, rdn and outpcd appr 3 out, rallied betw last 2, styd on r-in, unbl to quicken nr finish.....* (15 to 8 op 2 to 1 tchd 9 to 4 and 6 to 4) 2

3985 SANTELLA CAPE 10-12 J Railton, *hld up, rapid hdwy to chase ldr aftr 4 out, ev ch frm nxt, rdn and wknd after 2 out.*
.... (16 to 1 op 14 to 1 tchd 25 to 1) 3

3106* HAWANAFA 11-0 D Gallagher, *chsd ldr til pushed alng aftr 5th, lost tch after 4 out, jmpd badly rght last 3, tld off.*
.... (10 to 1 op 4 to 1 tchd 11 to 1) 4

3946² HEART 10-7 J Culloty, *chsd ldr til wknd aftr 4 out, beh whn pld up bef 2 out.............* (6 to 1 op 5 to 1 tchd 13 to 2) pu

Dist: 1¾l, 6l, dist. 4m 2.70s. a 22.70s (5 Ran).
SR: 16/7/1/-/-/ (Promo-Sherring Ltd), M C Pipe

4183 Ripple Novices' Handicap Hurdle Class E (0-100 4-y-o and up) £2,460 2½m......................... (2:50)

3988* HELLO ME MAN (Ire) [81] 9-11-4 Mr J L Llewellyn, *hld up, hdwy to track ldrs aftr 6th, led 3 out, jmpd rght last, hrd rdn and all out.........* (4 to 1 op 3 to 1 tchd 9 to 2) 1

3864³ LYPHARD'S FABLE (USA) [63] 6-10-0 R Johnson, *led til aftr 4th, led briefly four out, sn hdd, rdr lost whip aftr 2 out, ev ch last, unbl to quicken nr finish.*
.... (9 to 1 op 10 to 1 tchd 14 to 1 and 16 to 1) 2

4038⁴ PRIME OF LIFE [87] 7-11-10 S McNeill, *hld up, hdwy aftr 4th, chsd ldrs til wknd after 3 out........* (9 to 1 op 7 to 1) 3

3485³ JAY EM ESS (NZ) [78] 8-11-1 R Greene, *hld up, pushed alng aftr 4 out, no hdwy appr 3 out.*
.... (11 to 2 op 7 to 2 tchd 6 to 1) 4

4065⁴ A S JIM [74] 6-10-11 V Slattery, *hld up, chsd ldr frm 6th til wknd aftr 4 out............* (5 to 1 op 7 to 2 tchd 6 to 1) 5

4019³ POSITIVO [72] 6-10-9 D Leahy, *pushed alng aftr 5th, beh whn f 3 out.............* (11 to 2 op 7 to 2 tchd 6 to 1) f

3295⁴ MR LOVELY (Ire) [63] 6-10-0 T Dascombe, *chsd ldrs, rdn aftr 5 out, hmpd by broken top bar of hurdle and uns rdr after nxt.*
.... (12 to 1 op 20 to 1 tchd 14 to 1) ur

3986⁷ MUTLEY [64] 7-10-1¹ C Maude, *led aftr 4th, hit nxt, hdd after 5 out, sn wknd, tld off whn pld up r-in.* (20 to 1 op 14 to 1) pu

3992⁵ KINGS VISION [67] 5-10-4⁴ T Jenks, *hld up, drpd rear and pushed alng aftr 5th, sn lost tch, tld off whn pld up bef 3 out.*
.... (25 to 1 op 20 to 1 tchd 33 to 1) pu

3028 VIKING DREAM (Ire) [71] 5-10-8 S Fox, *chsd ldrs, mstk 4 out, sn wknd.* (7 to 2 fav op 6 to 1 tchd 13 to 2 and 7 to 1) pu

Dist: ¾l, 16l, 13l, 3½l. 5m 16.10s. a 40.10s (10 Ran).
(Lodge Cross Partnership), B J Llewellyn

4184 Brewery Traders Handicap Chase Class D (0-125 5-y-o and up) £3,614 2½m 110yds. (3:20)

4000² DESTIN D'ESTRUVAL (Fr) [122] 6-12-0 R Johnson, *hld up, mstk second, wnt second aftr 5 out, led on bit 2 out, clr last, easily........* (13 to 8 op 5 to 4 on tchd 11 to 8 on) 1

3974⁴ KHALIDI (Ire) [107] 8-10-13 R Dunwoody, *not fluent early, cld up 7th, led aftr 5 out to 2 out, sn no imprsn on wnr.*
.... (6 to 4 op 11 to 8 tchd 13 to 8 and 7 to 4) 2

4046 LITTLE-NIPPER [95] (bl) 12-10-1 C Maude, *led hdd aftr 5 out, sn wknd.........................* (20 to 1 op 12 to 1) 3

3950 BO KNOWS BEST (Ire) [110] (v) 8-11-2 P Holley, *chsd ldr til pushed alng aftr 8th, sn lost tch, tld off whn mstk 3 out.*
.... (20 to 1 op 14 to 1) 4

Dist: 11l, 20l, dist. 5m 33.00s. a 36.00s (4 Ran).
(Darren C Mercer), D Nicholson

4185 Brewery Traders 90th Anniversary Handicap Hurdle Class F (0-105 4-y-o and up) £2,040 2m......... (3:50)

4045¹ STAY WITH ME (Fr) [104] 7-12-0 J Osborne, *trkd ldrs, wnt second aftr 4th, led after four out, clr after 3 out, easily.*
.... (6 to 5 fav op 5 to 4 tchd Evens and 11 to 8) 1

4045³ CLASSIC PAL (USA) [79] 6-10-3¹ D Skyrme, *hld up, hdwy aftr 4 out, outpcd appr nxt, ran on ag'n after 2 out, no ch wth wnr.*
.... (5 to 1 op 3 to 1) 2

4045 DAILY SPORT GIRL [82] 8-10-6 Mr J L Llewellyn, *trkd ldr, cl up and ev ch aftr 4 out, rdn after 3 out, unbl to quicken betw last 2.......* (7 to 2 tchd 9 to 2 and 5 to 1) 3

3959⁷ COURAGEOUS KNIGHT [86] 8-10-10 B Fenton, *chsd ldrs til pushed alng aftr second, hit second after 4 out, styd on ag'n after 2 out, sn wknd, styd on one pace after 2 out.*
.... (8 to 1 tchd 10 to 1) 4

2730⁹ GREEN LANE (USA) [98] 9-11-8 C Llewellyn, *led til hdd aftr 4 out, sn wknd, styd on one pace after 2 out.*
.... (25 to 1 op 12 to 1) 5

Dist: 6l, ¾l, 3l, ¾l. 4m 2.50s. a 22.50s (5 Ran).
SR: 27/-/-/-/10/ (Mrs Sandra A Roe), C R Egerton

4186 Handley Castle Novices' Chase Class E (5-y-o and up) £3,114 2m 7f

---

110yds...................... (4:20)

4048 STRAY HARMONY 7-10-9 T J Murphy, *chsd ldr til wknd 6 out, distant 4th whn lft in ld and blun 2 out, fnshd alone.*
.... (66 to 1 op 50 to 1) 1

3737* WHO IS EQUINAME (Ire) (bl) 11-11-7 M A Fitzgerald, *led, rdn aftr 4 out, f 2 out.........* (4 to 1 tchd 13 to 8 and 7 to 4) f

4048⁵ CAREYSVILLE (Ire) 6-10-11 (3*) Mr R Thornton, *trkd ldr frm 9th, 3rd whn mstk 5 out, sn reco'red, cl second and hrd rdn when f 2 out.....* (50 to 1 op 25 to 1) f

4048² DREAM RIDE (Ire) 7-12-0 R Johnson, *trkd ldrs, blun 6 out, rdn whn mstk 3 out, 3rd and appeared hld when lft in ld and bright dwn 2 out......* (5 to 4 on op 7 to 4 on tchd 11 to 10) bd

3991 BALASANI (Fr) 11-10-11 (3*) L Aspell, *jmpd slwly 1st 2, pushed alng aftr 9th, lost tch 6 out, pld up bef 4 out, continued and refused four out.....* (14 to 1 op 16 to 1 tchd 25 to 1) ref

4041 KELLYTINO 8-10-9 R Bellamy, *hld up, hdwy aftr 11th, sn wknd, tld off whn pld up aftr 4 out, continued, refused 2 out.*
.... (33 to 1 op 16 to 1) ref

MR CAMPUS (Ire) 6-11-0 J R Kavanagh, *chase ldrs til wknd sn 9th, last whn jmpd slwly and pld up after tenth.*
.... (66 to 1 op 50 to 1) pu

4089⁴ CUMBERLAND YOUTH 6-11-0 I Lawrence, *hld up, reminders aftr 4th, blun badly 8th, beh whn pld up bef nxt.*
.... (100 to 1 op 50 to 1) pu

Dist: 6m 40.00s. (8 Ran).
(Winwood Connell Partnership), R J Smith

4187 Shrawley Standard Open National Hunt Flat Class H (Div I) (4,5,6-y-o) £1,255 2m....................(4:55)

LEWESDON MANOR 6-11-4 J Osborne, *hld up, hdwy 5 fs out, rdn to ld ins fnl furlong, drvn out.*
.... (9 to 1 op 10 to 1 tchd 12 to 1) 1

4075* THE VILLAGE WAY (Ire) 6-11-11 R Johnson, *hld up in middiv, trkd ldr 5 fs out, led o'r 2 furlongs out til hdd ins fnl furlong, ran on ag'n nr finish.*
..... (11 to 8 on op 5 to 4 on tchd 6 to 4 on and 11 to 10 on) 2

4075⁴ KERRY'S OATS 5-10-6 (7*) M Clinton, *hld up, hdwy 5 fs out, kpt on one pace ins fnl 2 furlongs..................* (20 to 1) 3

ROYAL TOAST (Ire) 5-11-4 J R Kavanagh, *hld up and beh, hdwy 5 fs out, no imprsn ins fnl 2 furlongs.*
.... (14 to 1 op 10 to 1 tchd 14 to 1) 4

3825² DOUBLE STAR 6-11-1 (3*) Mr R Thornton, *led til hdd o'r 2 fs out, kpt on one pace......* (7 to 1 op 4 to 1 tchd 8 to 1) 5

ESPERANZA IV (Fr) 5-10-13 J Railton, *trkd ldrs, ev ch o'r 5 fs out, styd on one pace......* (25 to 1 op 16 to 1) 6

3941⁵ HILL'S ELECTRIC (Ire) 5-11-4 D Gallagher, *hld up, hdwy aftr ten fs, styd on one pace.*
.... (14 to 1 op 10 to 1 tchd 16 to 1) 7

4086⁴ FRANKIE MUCK 5-11-4 C Llewellyn, *hld up, hdwy o'r 5 fs out, no imprsn......* (20 to 1 op 8 to 1) 8

3560² STAR ADVENTURE 5-11-4 Miss E James, *prid hrd, trkd ldrs til lost pl aftr ten fs.................* (8 to 1 op 5 to 1) 9

ARCTIC AFFAIR (Ire) 4-10-8 B Powell, *hld up, lost tch aftr ten fs......................* (20 to 1 op 10 to 1) 10

3941⁹ DUNGANNON LAD 6-10-11 (7*) L Cummins, *led for one furlong, trkd ldr til wknd quickly aftr ten fs, tld off.*
.... (50 to 1 op 20 to 1) 11

4050⁸ A VERSE TO ORDER 6-10-11 (7*) Mr O McPhail, *prmnt for one m, sn beh, tld off fnl 4 fs.*
.... (25 to 1 op 12 to 1 tchd 33 to 1) 12

4042 BRISTOL GOLD 4-10-6 (7*) L Suthern, *hld up, lost tch aftr ten fs, tld off fnl 4......* (50 to 1 op 25 to 1) 13

Dist: 1l, 5l, 2½l, 1½l, 7l, 5l, ¾l, sht-hd, 8l, dist. 4m 11.90s. (13 Ran).
(J G Phillips), P R Webber

4188 Shrawley Standard Open National Hunt Flat Class H (Div II) (4,5,6-y-o) £1,255 2m....................(5:25)

4042* ANDSUEPHI (Ire) 5-11-4 (7*) G Brace, *hld up, in tch whn not much room and lost pl o'r 6 fs out, quickened to ld over one furlong out, ran on wl.........................* (5 to 2 jt-fav op 5 to 4 on tchd 11 to 4) 1

STORMHILL STAG 5-10-11 (7*) L Cummins, *trkd ldg pair, 3rd strt, ev ch 2 fs out, unbl to quicken ins fnl furlong.*
.... (8 to 1 op 10 to 1 tchd 12 to 1 and 7 to 1) 2

1769⁹ NEVER IN DEBT 5-11-4 (7*) Mr G Shenkin, *hld up and beh, rapid hdwy o'r 3 fs out, ev ch 2 furlongs out, rdn and unbl to quicken.....* (11 to 2 op 6 to 1 tchd 8 to 1) 3

3929 TRYMYPLY 5-11-4 S McNeill, *hld up, rapid hdwy o'r 4 fs out, styd on ins fnl 2, unbl to quicken......* (33 to 1 op 20 to 1) 4

4042 BEACON LANE (Ire) 4-10-13 V Slattery, *chsd ldr, second strt, rdn and styd on one pace fnl 3 fs.*
.... (8 to 1 op 10 to 1 tchd 14 to 1) 5

4075⁵ MINIBELLE 5-10-13 M Clarke, *led til hdd o'r one furlong out, styd on one pace......* (12 to 1 op 10 to 1 tchd 16 to 1) 6

BLAZER 4-10-13 J R Kavanagh, *hld up, hdwy aftr ten fs, in tch o'r 4 furlongs out, wknd ins fnl 2.........* (5 to 2 jt-fav op 5 to 4 on tchd 11 to 4) 7

MOSSY BUCK (Ire) 5-11-4 J Railton, *reared strt and slwly away, hdwy to chase ldrs o'r 6 fs out, wknd over 3 out.*
.... (25 to 1 op 14 to 1) 8

HOW TO RUN 4-10-13 W Marston, *nvr rchd ldrs.*
.... (25 to 1 op 16 to 1) 9

4050 LADY BOCO 4-10-8 C Rae, *hld up and beh, hdwy aftr ten fs, chase ldrs til wknd o'r 4 out*..........(33 to 1) 10
3561[8] MISS BLUES SINGER 4-10-8 B Powell, *hld up and beh, hdwy aftr one m, wknd o'r 4 out*..........(33 to 1) 11
2567 COOLEST BY PHAR (Ire) 5-10-11 (7*) Mr O McPhail, *chsd ldrs til wknd aftr one m*..........(25 to 1 op 14 to 1) 12
4042 STARDANTE (Ire) 5-11-4 L Harvey, *mid-div til rdn and wknd quickly aftr one m, tld off.*
..........(25 to 1 op 20 to 1 tchd 33 to 1) 13
Dist: 3l, 1¾l. 4m 9.10s. (13 Ran).
(Mrs J A Cohen), C P E Brooks

EXETER (good)
Thursday May 22nd
Going Correction: PLUS 0.40 sec. per fur.

4189 Simpkins Edwards Branch Offices Selling Hurdle Class G (4 - 7-y-o) £1,818 2¼m..........(2:20)

3736[3] PAULTON (bl) 4-10-9 R Dunwoody, *al prmnt, reminders appr 2 out, led last, drvn out*....(7 to 1 op 6 to 1 tchd 15 to 2) 1
3894* MIRAMARE 7-10-7 (7*) Mr G Shenkin, *al prmnt, led 4th, briefly hdd 3 out, headed last, edgd lft r-in, no extr.*
..........(9 to 1 op 7 to 1 tchd 10 to 1) 2
3973[2] BAYERD (Ire) (bl) 6-11-6 N Williamson, *hld up, hdwy aftr 4th, one pace frm 2 out*..........(4 to 1 fav op 7 to 2) 3
4073[5] POWDER MONKEY 7-10-2 (7*) Mr J Tizzard, *hld up, rdn and hdwy 4th, one pace frm 2 out*..........(6 to 1 op 5 to 1) 4
3894[4] OCTOBER BREW (USA) (v) 7-10-9 (5*) G Supple, *hld up in tch, wnt second aftr 3 out, wknd frm nxt.* (10 to 1 op 7 to 1) 5
3911[8] JEWEL THIEF (v) 7-11-0 A P McCoy, *beh, rdn aftr 3 out, styd on one pace*..........(10 to 1 op 7 to 1) 6
3871[3] EWAR BOLD (bl) 4-10-9 M A Fitzgerald, *led to 4th, led ag'n briefly 3 out, sn wknd, mstk last*..........(11 to 1 op 8 to 1) 7
4073 RED TEL (Ire) 5-11-0 C Maude, *hld up in rear, rdn 3 out, nvr dngrs aftr*..........(8 to 1 op 5 to 1) 8
3810[4] GRIFFIN'S GIRL 5-10-6 (3*) Guy Lewis, *prmnt till wknd quickly appr 2 out*..........(14 to 1 op 10 to 1) 9
3402[4] LADY CALLERNISH 7-10-2 (7*) Mr S Durack, *beh whn rdn 4th, tld off when f four out.*
..........(10 to 1 op 25 to 1 tchd 33 to 1 and 50 to 1) f
4069[8] MINNISAM 4-10-9 R Greene, *prmnt till wknd 3 out, blun and uns rdr last*..........(25 to 1 op 20 to 1) ur
1354 MINNEOLA 5-10-9 L Harvey, *al towards rear, tld off whn pld up bef last*..........(66 to 1 op 33 to 1) pu
Dist: 2l, 1l, 4l, hd, 2l, 1l, ¾l, 8l. 4m 19.60s. a 20.60s (12 Ran).
(Business Forms Express), K Bishop

4190 Corporate Services Group Handicap Chase Class F (0-105 5-y-o and up) £3,249 2m 3f 110yds..........(2:50)

3937[2] MR PLAYFULL [91] 7-11-7 J Frost, *hld up in rear, steady hdwy frm 5 out, lft second last, str brst to ld last strds.*
..........(12 to 1 op 8 to 1 tchd 14 to 1) 1
3950* BLAZER MORINIERE (Fr) [93] 8-11-9 S Fox, *al in tch, led and lft clr last, hrd rdn and ct last strds.*
..........(4 to 1 op 7 to 2 tchd 9 to 2 and 5 to 1) 2
4046[4] COURT MASTER (Ire) [90] 9-11-6 B Powell, *hld up in mid-div, hdwy appr 4 out, nvr nr to chal*..........(14 to 1 op 8 to 1) 3
3792* BOOTS N ALL (Ire) [84] 7-11-0 B Fenton, *hld up, hdwy 8th, rdn appr 4 out, btn and 3rd whn hit 2 out*..........(7 to 4 fav) 4
4046 JAILBREAKER [81] 10-10-11 M A Fitzgerald, *mid-div, rdn appr 4 out, nvr dngrs aftr*..........(20 to 1 op 14 to 1) 5
1721[4] WILKINS [82] 8-10-12 N Williamson, *chsd ldrs, wknd 5 out.*
..........(14 to 1 op 8 to 1 tchd 16 to 1) 6
3950 BRIMPTON BERTIE [86] 8-11-2 G Upton, *al beh, lost tch 8th, tld off*..........(40 to 1 op 16 to 1) 7
DESERT RUN (Ire) [94] 9-11-10 S Burrough, *al beh, tld off 5th.*
..........(50 to 1 op 25 to 1) 8
3875[2] COOLTEEN HERO (Ire) [94] 7-11-10 P Holley, *led to 4th, blun 9th, sn reco'red, led appr four out, hdd and f last.*
..........(14 to 1 op 8 to 1) f
4031[3] GLADYS EMMANUEL [77] 10-10-2 (5*) D J Kavanagh, *in tch to 8th, tailing off whn refused 11th*.....(14 to 1 op 10 to 1) ref
4031[4] TANGO'S DELIGHT [70] 9-10-0 V Slattery, *al beh, tld off whn pld up bef last*..........(50 to 1 op 33 to 1) pu
4070 WIXOE WONDER (Ire) [83] (bl) 7-10-13 A P McCoy, *led 4th, clr 8th, hdd and wknd appr four out, pld up bef last.*
..........(5 to 1 op 6 to 1 tchd 13 to 2 and 9 to 2) pu
Dist: Nk, 8l, 6l, 15l, ¾l, 22l, dist. 4m 47.50s. a 14.50s (12 Ran).
SR: 26/28/17/5/-/-/ (P A Tylor), R G Frost

4191 Putting Your Business First Handicap Hurdle Class D (0-120 4-y-o and up) £2,676 2m 3f 110yds......(3:20)

3908[8] STORM DUST [113] 8-11-10 J Culloty, *hld up, making hdwy whn stumbled appr 2 out, chlgd last, led nr finish, all out.*
..........(9 to 2 op 5 to 1 tchd 11 to 2) 1
3650* BURLINGTON SAM (NZ) [91] 9-9-11 (5*) O Burrows, *chsd ldr, rdn and led appr 2 out, hdd und pres nr finish.*
..........(4 to 1 op 3 to 1) 2
3988[2] STAR PERFORMER (Ire) [97] 6-10-1 (7*) Mr G Shenkin, *hld up in rear, hdwy 4th, mstk 3 out, rallied and ran on r-in.*
..........(7 to 2 tchd 4 to 1 and 9 to 2) 3
3798[2] FAUSTINO [109] 5-11-6 N Williamson, *hld up, hdwy to second 2 out, wknd appr last.*
..........(11 to 4 fav op 5 to 2 tchd 9 to 4 and 3 to 1) 4
3938* ATH CHEANNAITHE (Fr) [91] (v) 5-10-2 T Dascombe, *led till hdd appr 2 out, sn btn, eased.*
..........(3 to 1 op 9 to 4 tchd 100 to 30) 5
Dist: Nk, 2½l, 2½l, 28l. 4m 42.20s. a 21.20s (5 Ran).
(R J Sunley Tice), Miss H C Knight

4192 ES Litigation Support Services Novices' Chase Class D (5-y-o and up) £3,550 2m 7f 110yds..........(3:50)

3689[4] SANTELLA BOY (USA) (bl) 5-10-7 R Dunwoody, *al gng wl, led on bit 2 out, sn clr, eased r-in.*
..........(11 to 4 op 5 to 2 tchd 3 to 1 and 100 to 30) 1
3718 STORMTRACKER (Ire) 8-12-0 M Richards, *made most to 11th, hrd rdn to ld 4 out, hdd 2 out, no ch aftr.*
..........(7 to 4 fav op 6 to 4 tchd 15 to 8 and 2 to 1) 2
3683[2] KIWI CRYSTAL (NZ) 8-10-9 R Greene, *blun second, sn prmnt, dsptd ld 6th, btn whn mstk 2 out.*
..........(12 to 1 op 10 to 1 tchd 14 to 1) 3
2480 WITHYCOMBE HILL 7-10-7 (7*) Mr R Widger, *hld up, hdwy to ld 11th, hdd and hit 4 out, wknd*..........(50 to 1 op 33 to 1) 4
3861 DUNLIR 7-11-0 M Sharratt, *al beh, tld off.*
..........(100 to 1 op 50 to 1) 5
3939[2] JONJAS CHUDLEIGH 10-11-0 J Frost, *al beh, tld off 5th.*
..........(20 to 1 op 16 to 1 tchd 25 to 1) 6
3556 HALKOPOUS 11-11-0 N Williamson, *beh whn hit 5th, tld off when pld up aftr 4 out*.....(5 to 2 op 2 to 1 tchd 11 to 4) pu
4048 GLENGARRIF GIRL (Ire) (v) 7-10-9 A P McCoy, *jmpd lft, mstk 6th, wknd 12th, tld off whn pld up 4 out.*
..........(11 to 1 op 8 to 1 tchd 12 to 1) pu
Dist: 8l, 1½l, 6l, 28l, 18l. 5m 57.00s. a 23.00s (8 Ran).
(The Link Leasing Partnership), C J Mann

4193 Business Development Group Novices' Handicap Hurdle Class E (0-100 4-y-o and up) £2,547 3¼m..........(4:20)

3894[2] ON MY TOES [65] 6-10-6[2] J Frost, *led appr 3rd, clr approaching 2 out, eased r-in*.....(11 to 1 op 8 to 1 tchd 12 to 1) 1
3864[3] PIPER'S ROCK (Ire) [87] 6-12-0 B Fenton, *led till appr 3rd, no ch wth wnr bef 2 out*..........(4 to 1 op 3 to 1 tchd 9 to 2) 2
4073[3] SPIRIT LEVEL [63] 9-9-11 (7*) Mr S Durack, *wl beh early, late hdwy to go 3rd r-in*.....(10 to 1 op 14 to 1 tchd 16 to 1) 3
3833 JOBSAGOODUN [81] 6-11-8 M A Fitzgerald, *mid-div, no ch 3 out*..........(8 to 1 op 5 to 1) 4
3978[4] ANNIE RUTH (Ire) [63] 6-9-11 (7*) R Garrard, *al beh.*
..........(11 to 1 op 8 to 1 tchd 12 to 1) 5
4087 ECU DE FRANCE (Ire) [65] 7-10-6 C Maude, *prmnt to hfwy.*
..........(7 to 2 fav op 5 to 1 tchd 6 to 1) 6
3984[3] CHINA MAIL (Ire) [70] 5-10-11 T J Murphy, *towards rear, hdwy 4 out, wknd appr 2 out*..........(25 to 1 op 10 to 1) 7
3594[2] KINGSWOOD MANOR [82] 5-11-9 N Williamson, *chsd ldrs early, tld off 3 out*..........(9 to 2 op 5 to 1 tchd 7 to 2) 8
145[6] HIDDEN FLOWER [59] 8-9-9[2] (7*) Mr R Widger, *al beh, tld off.*
..........(33 to 1 op 20 to 1) 9
3961[4] VALLINGALE (Ire) [84] 6-11-4 (7*) Mr A Wintle, *beh whn pld up bef last*..........(8 to 1 op 6 to 1 tchd 10 to 1) pu
3594 MUSIC CLASS (Ire) [71] 6-10-12 V Slattery, *al beh, tld off whn pld up bef 2 out*..........(33 to 1 op 16 to 1) pu
4069 MORECEVA (Ire) [59] (bl) 7-9-9 (5*) O Burrows, *beh whn pld up bef 2 out*..........(50 to 1 op 25 to 1) pu
Dist: 4l, 14l, sht-hd, 13l, 1l, 1¼l, dist, 9l. (Time not taken) (12 Ran).
(G Chambers), R G Frost

4194 Self Assessment Novices' Handicap Hurdle Class E (0-100 4-y-o and up) £2,295 2m 3f 110yds..........(4:55)

3972[4] LORD NITROGEN (USA) [76] 7-11-1 Mr J L Llewellyn, *prmnt, lft in ld 5th, clr 2 out, eased r-in.*
..........(6 to 1 op 8 to 1 tchd 10 to 1) 1
3936[3] UP THE TEMPO (Ire) [61] 8-10-0 T Dascombe, *wl beh till hdwy 2 out, took second cl hme.*
..........(8 to 1 op 10 to 1 tchd 12 to 1) 2
3961[3] GENEREUX [82] 4-10-11 (5*) Chris Webb, *chsd ldrs till outpcd 3 out, mstk nxt, kpt on r-in*..........(8 to 1 op 7 to 1) 3
3988 SAAFI (Ire) [67] (bl) 6-10-6 V Slattery, *beh, hdwy and kpt on one pace frm 2 out.*
..........(15 to 2 op 16 to 1 tchd 20 to 1 and 10 to 1) 4
3961 CONNAUGHT'S PRIDE [68] (bl) 6-10-7 N Williamson, *beh, rdn to go second appr 2 out, sn wknd.*
..........(5 to 1 op 6 to 1 tchd 7 to 1) 5
3864[2] SAFECRACKER [75] 4-10-9 D Gallagher, *led to 4th, wknd appr 2 out*..........(100 to 30 op 3 to 1 tchd 4 to 1) 6
4013[2] REGAL GEM (Ire) [82] 6-11-7 B Fenton, *prmnt, in ld 4th, blun badly and uns rdr nxt.* (5 to 2 fav op 3 to 1 tchd 7 to 2) ur
3981[3] CARNIVAL CLOWN [68] 5-10-7 R Greene, *beh whn pld up bef 3 out*..........(12 to 1 op 10 to 1 tchd 16 to 1) pu
Dist: 3½l, hd, 3l, 8½l, 1¼l. (Time not taken) (8 Ran).
(B J Llewellyn), B J Llewellyn

TIPPERARY (IRE) (yielding to soft)
Thursday May 22nd

4195 Fourstars Allstar Maiden Hurdle (4 & 5-y-o) £3,425 2m............. (7:30)

40064 NATIVE PLAYER (Ire) 5-11-13 C F Swan,........(Evens fav)	1
4052 LADY DE HATTON (Ire) 5-11-0 D J Casey,.........(14 to 1)	2
40095 BE MY TRUMP (Ire) 5-11-0 K F O'Brien,..........(12 to 1)	3
40524 HONEY TRADER 5-11-0 (5") P G Hourigan,.......(9 to 2)	4
39525 FIVE PALS (Ire) 5-11-5 C O'Dwyer,................(8 to 1)	5
HARDY CRACKER (Ire) 5-11-11 (3") G Cotter,....(25 to 1)	6
3450 SOVIET DREAMER 4-10-13 (7") J M Maguire,....(10 to 1)	7
3417 STONE HEAD (Ire) 4-10-12 (3") K Whelan,.......(16 to 1)	8
3818 MACCABAEUS (Ire) 5-11-5 G Bradley,.............(14 to 1)	9
ELFEET CASTLE 4-11-1 M P Hourigan,..............(20 to 1)	10
40946 CHIEF DELANEY (Ire) 5-11-5 L P Cusack,........(14 to 1)	11
3952 LARMELIA (Ire) 5-10-12 (7") C B Hynes,..........(50 to 1)	12
705 SEEKING DESTINY (Ire) 4-11-1 (5") T Martin,....(33 to 1)	13
36425 GOLD DEPOSITOR (Ire) 5-11-5 J Shortt,..........(10 to 1)	14
39529 CALICO JACK (Ire) 5-11-0 (5") M D Murphy,....(16 to 1)	15
LOC A LUA (Ire) 5-10-12 (7") M J Collins,........(25 to 1)	16
TOBAR NA CARRAIGE (Ire) 5-11-5 H Rogers,....(20 to 1)	17
FURRY ISLAND (Ire) 5-10-7 (7") K A Kelly,.......(25 to 1)	18
4094 APPLE RIVER (Ire) 4-10-3 (7") L J Fleming,......(25 to 1)	f
3818 THE SIDHE 5-11-0 J R Barry,......................(50 to 1)	pu

Dist: 7l, 2½l, 5l, 7l. 4m 10.40s. (20 Ran).

(Derek O'Keeffe), A P O'Brien

4196 Cashel Handicap Hurdle (0-116 4-y-o and up) £2,740 2½m........ (8:00)

40274 DOOK'S DELIGHT [-] 6-9-11 T J Mitchell,.........(10 to 1)	1
40273 WELSH GRIT [-] 8-11-5 D J Casey,...............(10 to 1)	2
38163 LEGATISSIMO (Ire) [-] 9-11-9 G Bradley,......(9 to 2 co-fav)	3
40272 FAIR SOCIETY (Ire) [-] 6-10-3 M P Hourigan, (9 to 2 co-fav)	4
4004 THE REGAL ROYAL (Ire) [-] 10-10-5 (7") P Morris, ..(14 to 1)	5
40272 THE WISE KNIGHT (Ire) [-] 6-10-5 T P Treacy,.....(14 to 1)	6
33377 UPPER MOUNT STREET (Ire) [-] 7-10-0 (3") G Cotter,	
....(10 to 1)	7
40775 BRIDGES DAUGHTER (Ire) [-] 6-9-9 J R Barry,......(12 to 1)	8
29659 WOODEN DANCE (Ire) [-] 4-9-3 (7") L J Fleming,...(14 to 1)	9
3235 TOMMY PAUD (Ire) [-] 8-11-3 (5") P G Hourigan, (9 to 2 co-fav)	10
40605 FONTAINEROUGE (Ire) [-] (bl) 7-9-2 (5") M D Murphy,	
....(12 to 1)	11
40957 FRESH DEAL (Ire) [-] 5-12-0 L P Cusack,........(10 to 1)	12
41626 POWER CORE (Ire) [-] 7-10-0 C F Swan,..........(12 to 1)	13
4162 BUCK THE WEST (Ire) [-] (bl) 7-10-7 (3") K Whelan, (25 to 1)	14
3390 FLOWERS OF MAY (Ire) [-] 5-9-7 P L Malone,....(33 to 1)	15

Dist: ½l, 2l, 4½l, 1½l. 5m 12.60s. (15 Ran).

(P T McNicholas), P D Osborne

4197 Nenagh I.N.H. Flat Race (4-y-o and up) £2,740 2½m............. (8:30)

40294 MAKING THE CUT (Ire) 5-11-1 (7") Mr B J Crowley, (6 to 1)	1
41448 SHANNON LIGHT (Ire) 5-11-6 (7") Mr R Flavin, ...(10 to 1)	2
16553 PARI PASSU (Ire) 5-11-3 (5") Mr A Coyle, ...(5 to 2 fav)	3
4052 ZACOPANI (Ire) 5-11-13 Mr R Walsh,.............(16 to 1)	4
41619 SAIL AWAY SAILOR (Ire) 6-11-7 (7") Mr Paul Moloney,	
....(8 to 1)	5
39539 RAINBOW TIMES (Ire) (bl) 4-10-9 (5") Mr G Elliott, (14 to 1)	6
41612 FINCHOGUE (Ire) 5-11-1 (7") Mr S P Hennessy, ...(9 to 2)	7
FUNCTION DREAM (Ire) 5-11-1 (7") Mr B Walsh, ...(12 to 1)	8
SUPER DOC (Ire) 7-12-0 Mr J A Berry,..........(14 to 1)	9
40052 SUPREME GOLD (Ire) 5-11-7 (7") Mr P J Crowley, ..(6 to 1)	10
27579 CLARA ROCK (Ire) 5-11-8 Mr P Fenton,...........(8 to 1)	11
4161 BARNEY THE MAN (Ire) 5-11-13 Mr J A Nash, ...(12 to 1)	12
4004 ST CAROL (Ire) 6-11-2 (7") Mr J M O'Brien, ...(14 to 1)	13
4096 MASTER NATIVE (Ire) 5-11-13 Mr D M O'Brien, ...(20 to 1)	14
41613 HAVE AT IT (Ire) 5-11-1 (7") Mr P A Farrell,.......(7 to 1)	15
MISS RYCUL (Ire) 5-11-1 (7") Mr P Fahey,........(20 to 1)	16
NIBALDA (Ire) 5-11-6 (7") Mr J E Finn,...........(20 to 1)	17
REGAL CHILD (Ire) 5-11-1 (7") Mr T J Nagle, ...(16 to 1)	18
ARDBUTUS (Ire) 5-11-1 (7") Mr J P McNamara, ..(14 to 1)	19
40068 BIGHEARTED ARTHUR (Ire) 5-11-6 (7") Mr A K Wyse,	
....(12 to 1)	20

Dist: 3½l, 9l, ½l, 2½l. 5m 6.40s. (20 Ran).

(Seamus O'Farrell), A P O'Brien

DUNDALK (IRE) (good)
Friday May 23rd

4198 Guinness Maiden Hurdle (4-y-o and up) £2,740 2m 135yds... (5:30)

39633 KNOCKAULIN (Ire) 6-11-6 F J Flood,.............(7 to 1)	1
ELEGANT KATE (Ire) 7-11-6 (3") G Cotter,.........(8 to 1)	2
41674 POLLTRIC (Ire) 6-11-6 P L Malone,...............(5 to 1)	3
20745 DUGGAN DUFF (Ire) 4-10-8 (7") D K Budds,......(20 to 1)	4
38893 FOREST PRINCESS (Ire) 5-11-0 C F Swan,.....(5 to 2 fav)	5
1696 NORDIC AIR (Ire) (bl) 6-11-6 D H O'Connor, ...(14 to 1)	6
3963 DIPIE (Ire) 9-11-6 J P Byrne,....................(7 to 1)	7

4199 Harp Lager Handicap Chase (0-102 4-y-o and up) £3,082 2m 3f... (7:30)

40289 SPRING BEAU (Ire) 6-10-13 (7") L J Fleming, ...(16 to 1)	8
39644 HURRICANE DAVID (Ire) 8-11-6 L P Cusack, ...(16 to 1)	9
41146 MAID TO MOVE (Ire) 4-11-1 H Rogers,...........(12 to 1)	10
3891 PERFECT (Ire) 5-10-12 (7") B J Geraghty, ...(16 to 1)	11
32168 US FOUR (Ire) (bl) 7-11-6 D J Casey,.............(10 to 1)	12
21058 ERNE PROJECT (Ire) 4-11-1 T J Mitchell,........(16 to 1)	13
EL CYRANO 4-10-12 (3") D Bromley,..........(25 to 1)	14
3834 MSADI MHULU (Ire) 6-11-1 T P Treacy,..........(16 to 1)	15
3840 ELECTRIC LAD (Ire) 6-11-6 J Shortt,.............(12 to 1)	16
39645 HIDDEN SPRINGS (Ire) 6-11-6 K F O'Brien,......(12 to 1)	17
928 SLIGO CHAMPION (Ire) 6-11-6 J K Kinane,......(50 to 1)	pu
4094 HEAD TO TOE (Ire) 4-10-3 (7") Mr D Broad,......(33 to 1)	pu

Dist: 4½l, 3l, 4½l, ½l. 3m 56.20s. (19 Ran).

(Mrs K L Urquhart), F Flood

(4199 continued — main section)

4028* YOUNG DUBLINER (Ire) [-] 8-11-11 (3") K Whelan, ..(7 to 2)	1
40284 ROSSBEIGH CREEK [-] 10-11-5 F J Flood,.......(5 to 1)	2
3954 WACKO JACKO (Ire) [-] 8-11-1 T P Treacy,.......(12 to 1)	3
37483 LINEKER (Ire) [-] 3-11-3 C O'Dwyer,.............(14 to 1)	4
4093 PERSPEX GALE (Ire) [-] 9-11-3 C F Swan, ...(5 to 2 fav)	5
41515 BLACKIE CONNORS (Ire) [-] 6-11-1 (7") D M Bean, (20 to 1)	6
3839* WALLYS RUN [-] 10-11-0 L P Cusack,..........(6 to 1)	7
3418 WHINNEY HILL [-] 7-9-4 (3") G Cotter,.........(33 to 1)	8
2039 THE BOURDA [-] 11-11-1 D J Casey,...........(20 to 1)	f
3888* TULLY BOY [-] 10-10-10† (7") M D McCartan, ...(8 to 1)	ur
4055 RICH TRADITION (Ire) [-] 9-10-12 T J Mitchell,...(12 to 1)	ur
40035 KILLERK LADY (Ire) [-] 6-9-2† (7") B J Geraghty, ..(10 to 1)	su
41517 JESSIE'S BOY (Ire) [-] (bl) 8-10-8 J K Kinane, ...(25 to 1)	pu
40534 KATIES HOLME (Ire) [-] 6-10-0 (7") D A McLoughlin, (16 to 1)	pu

Dist: Nk, 7l, 8l, hd. 4m 42.90s. (14 Ran).

(John A Cooper), E Bolger

4200 Louth Vintners Association (Pro/Am) Flat Race (4-y-o and up) £2,740 2m 135yds............. (8:30)

38916 DANNKALIA (Ire) (bl) 5-11-8 Mr J P Dempsey, ...(10 to 1)	1
35539 BELCAMP BELLE (Ire) 4-10-8 (7") Mr S P McCarthy,	2
40792 STRONG CHOICE (Ire) 5-11-1 (7") Mr B J Crowley,	
....(6 to 4 fav)	3
3965 CRYPTIC MYTH (Ire) 5-11-1 (7") A P Sweeney, ...(16 to 1)	4
20892 JANICE PRICE (Ire) 6-11-2 (7") Mr P Fahey,.......(10 to 1)	5
3755 AN BONNAN BUI (Ire) 4-10-8 (7") Mr T J Beattie, ..(12 to 1)	6
3935 LUCY CON (Ire) 5-11-1 (7") L J Fleming,..........(12 to 1)	7
41068 MOUNT HALL (Ire) 5-11-8 Mr J A Nash,..........(8 to 1)	8
WAKEUP LITTLESUSIE 10-11-2 (7") J P Deegan, ..(33 to 1)	9
34566 CHINA TEALEAF (Ire) 5-11-8 Mr P F Graffin, ...(5 to 2)	10
1490 MIGHTY TERM (Ire) 5-11-13 Mr B M Cash,........(7 to 1)	11
RIDGEWOOD WATER (Ire) 5-11-8 (5") Mr G Elliott, (14 to 1)	12
MR CHAIRMAN (Ire) 7-12-0 Mr G J Harford,........(14 to 1)	13
BAY-RATH (Ire) 6-11-2 (7") Mr K Ross,...........(20 to 1)	14
4006 STAR VIEW (Ire) 5-11-1 (7") D A McLoughlin, ...(20 to 1)	15
4106 MT LEINSTER (Ire) 4-10-8 (7") Mr J M O'Brien, ...(14 to 1)	16
GLITTERING JULY (Ire) 5-11-1 (7") Mr P M Heaney, (14 to 1)	pu

Dist: 2½l, ¾l, 4l, 1½l. 3m 51.90s. (17 Ran).

(Sandy Strand Syndicate), E D Delany

TOWCESTER (good)
Friday May 23rd
Going Correction: MINUS 0.05 sec. per fur.

4201 Yardley Graphics Novices' Hurdle Class E (4-y-o and up) £2,407 2m .... (6:20)

35002 JAMAICAN FLIGHT (USA) 4-10-9 J Railton, jmpd wl, made all, shaken up and ran on well whn chlgd 2 out.	
..................(6 to 1 tchd 13 to 2 and 7 to 1)	1
4092† NORDANCE PRINCE (Ire) 6-12-0 N Williamson, hld up in rear, hdwy frm 4th, wnt second aftr 3 out, chlgd nxt, rdn and sn btn..................(7 to 2 op 3 to 1 tchd 4 to 1)	2
39947 WISE KING 7-11-0 C Llewellyn, chsd wnr till rdn and wknd appr 2 out.	
...(11 to 8 on op 11 to 10 on tchd Evens and 6 to 4 on)	3
4183 POSITIVO 6-11-0 D Leahy, hld up in rear, styd on frm 3 out, nvr nrr.......................(20 to 1 op 16 to 1)	4
4019† ORCHARD KING 7-11-0 M Brennan, pld hrd, hdwy and 4th whn blun 5th, no ch aftr...............(8 to 1 op 7 to 1)	5
40687 UR ONLY YOUNG ONCE 7-10-9 A P McCoy, mstk 1st, chsd ldrs, ev ch 3 out, wknd quickly....(12 to 1 op 10 to 1)	6
40685 BELARUS 5-11-0 W McFarland, beh, effrt 4th, no ch frm nxt.......................................(16 to 1 op 14 to 1)	7
4049 RARE GIFT (USA) 6-11-0 R Johnson, beh frm second.	
...................(16 to 1 op 14 to 1 tchd 20 to 1)	8
40686 THE BIZZO 6-10-9 W Marston, prmnt early, beh frm 4th, tld off...............................(33 to 1 op 25 to 1)	9
4021 CHARIOT MAN 5-11-0 Richard Guest, al beh, tld off.	
...................(33 to 1 op 20 to 1)	10
3948 FRIAR'S OAK 5-10-7 (7") Mr O McPhail, prmnt early, sn beh, tld off...............................(66 to 1 op 33 to 1)	11

4068⁹ OVER AND UNDER (Ire) 4-10-9 L Harvey, *tld off 4th, pld up bef 3 out*..............................(33 to 1 op 20 to 1) pu

Dist: 4l, 11l, 9l, nk, 15l, 13l, ¾l, 14l, 1½l, 4l. 3m 48.80s. a 5.80s (12 Ran).

SR: 15/30/5/-/-/-/ (P Lamyman), Mrs S Lamyman

4202 National Letterbox Marketing Handicap Chase Class E (0-110 5-y-o and up) £3,137 3m 1f............ (6:45)

4046² MARTELL BOY (NZ) [96] 10-11-5 N Williamson, *led 5th, clr tenth, shaken up appr 2 out, unchlgd*....(3 to 1 op 9 to 4) 1
4040³ HARRISTOWN LADY [102] (bl) 10-11-11 A P McCoy, *hld up, hit 5th, hdwy to chase wnr appr 12th, no imprsn frm 3 out.* ....(4 to 1 op 9 to 2) 2
3406* FORTUNES COURSE (Ire) [97] 8-11-6 T J Murphy, *led to 5th, oupaced and wknd 4 out, blun nxt*......(4 to 1 op 3 to 1) 3
3987* FUNCHEON GALE [104] 10-11-13 D Morris, *hld up in rear, hdwy appr 12th, outpcd aftr nxt, tld off.* ....(11 to 4 fav op 5 to 2 tchd 3 to 1) 4
3996 BOTTLE BLACK [80] (bl) 10-10-3 C Llewellyn, *chsd ldrs till blun and uns rdr 11th*......................(66 to 1) ur
3739 JIM VALENTINE [99] 11-11-8 W Marston, *in rear whn blun 9th, tld off when pld up bef 2 out*......(4 to 1 op 5 to 1) pu
3932³ VICAR OF BRAY [87] (v) 10-10-10 M Richards, *in rear whn mstks tenth and 11th, tld off when pld up bef 14th.* ....(40 to 1 op 33 to 1) pu

Dist: 19l, 10l, 25l. 6m 24.70s. a 12.70s (7 Ran).

(David G Jones), Miss Venetia Williams

4203 Whitsun Novices' Hurdle Class D (4-y-o and up) £2,951 3m....... (7:15)

3579 SALMON BREEZE (Ire) 6-11-12 M A Fitzgerald, *hld up in tch, mstk 7th, led 4 out, clr frm 2 out.* ....(5 to 4 on op 7 to 4 on tchd 6 to 5 on and 11 to 10 on) 1
4007⁵ ERNI (Fr) 5-11-0 R Garritty, *nvr far away, ev ch 3 out, rdn and one pace aftr*......................(10 to 1 op 7 to 1) 2
2745 TIRLEY MISSILE 11-10-7 (7*) Mr O McPhail, *hld up, hdwy 8th, dsptd second 2 out, wknd appr last*....(25 to 1 op 16 to 1) 3
4039 TULLOW LADY (Ire) 6-10-9 M Brennan, *hld up, lost tch 7th, tld off.*....................(11 to 1 op 25 to 1) 4
3846⁴ LEAP FROG 6-11-0 W Marston, *not fluent, trkd ldr, led 8th, hdd 4 out, wknd bef nxt, tld off.* ....(11 to 4 op 5 to 2 tchd 3 to 1) 5
3736⁶ NISHMANN (Ire) 6-10-7 (7*) P Ryan, *al beh, tld off whn pld up bef 2 out.*.........................(50 to 1) pu
3312 ARCTIC CHARMER (USA) 5-10-7 (7*) Mr J Goldstein, *al beh, tld off whn pld up bef 2 out*............(50 to 1) pu
4065⁶ NORDIC SPREE (Ire) (v) 5-11-6 P Holley, *led till hit 8th, rdn and wknd, tld off whn pld up bef 2 out.* (9 to 2 tchd 5 to 1) pu

Dist: 5l, 3l, dist, dist. 6m 4.10s. a 22.10s (8 Ran).

(The Salmon Racing Partnership), N J Henderson

4204 Broadways Stampings Novices' Handicap Chase Class E (0-100 5-y-o and up) £3,182 2¾m....... (7:45)

3792² CARDINAL RULE (Ire) [90] 8-11-10 N Williamson, *al prmnt, led appr 2 out, rdn clr.* ....(9 to 2 op 4 to 1 tchd 5 to 1 and 11 to 2) 1
3708⁴ GEMS LAD [86] 10-11-6 Richard Guest, *al prmnt, led 6th to 7th, lft in ld nxt, rdn and appr 2 out, wknd approaching last.* ....(7 to 2 fav op 3 to 1 tchd 4 to 1) 2
3990⁵ COUNTRY STORE [88] 8-11-8 S McNeill, *chsd ldrs, lost tch 4 out.*......................(9 to 1 op 8 to 1 tchd 10 to 1) 3
4048 GERRY'S PRIDE (Ire) [66] 6-10-0 S Curran, *prmnt till rdn 11th, sn lost tch.*........................(50 to 1) 4
4067 MUSICAL HIT [66] (bl) 6-10-0 R Supple, *mstk in rear 7th, some hdwy 4 out, btn whn crrd wide by loose horse bef 2 out.* ....(50 to 1) 5
3996⁵ KING'S RAINBOW (Ire) [72] 8-10-3 (3*) P Henley, *prmnt till wknd appr 4 out*........(7 to 1 op 8 to 1 tchd 10 to 1) 6
3967⁵ GLENBRICKEN [71] 11-10-5 R Johnson, *mstk 5th, al in rear.*.........................(12 to 1 tchd 14 to 1) 7
4035⁵ PERSIAN VIEW (Ire) [90] 7-11-10 A Thornton, *whipped round and lost several ls strt, hit 6th, nvr on terms, tld off.* ....(14 to 1 op 10 to 1) 8
2892⁹ ROSIE-B [76] 7-10-10 V Slattery, *beh whn mstk 6th, tld off 11th.*........................(14 to 1 op 9 to 1) 9
3742³ GOLDEN DRUM (Ire) [69] (bl) 7-10-3 T J Murphy, *led to 6th, led ag'n 7th, blun badly and uns rdr nxt.* ....(14 to 1 op 12 to 1) ur
4091⁵ STAGE PLAYER [79] 11-10-13 L Lawrence, *not jump wl, al beh, tld off whn pld up bef 2 out.* ....(25 to 1 op 14 to 1 tchd 33 to 1) pu
4048⁶ BETTER FUTURE (Ire) [67] 8-10-1 D Gallagher, *mstk 3rd, sn tld off, pld up bef 9th*...(14 to 1 op 16 to 1 tchd 20 to 1) pu
3861* THUNDER ROAD (Ire) [75] 6-10-9 J Culloty, *mid-div whn blun 6th, sn beh, tld off whn pld up bef 3 out.* (4 to 1 op 5 to 1) pu

Dist: 11l, 25l, 1l, 1l, 4l, 2l, 10l, 8l. 5m 36.50s. a 10.50s (13 Ran).

(Peter J Burch), Miss Venetia Williams

4205 Towcester Handicap Chase Class D (0-125 5-y-o and up) £3,468 2m 110yds..................... (8:15)

3976² MINE'S AN ACE (NZ) [98] 10-10-3 R Greene, *hld up in tch, rdn 7th, led 3 out, drvn clr*.....................(9 to 2 op 5 to 1) 1
4091² MILL O'THE RAGS (Ire) [100] 8-10-2 (3*) P Henley, *trkd ldr, rdn and ev ch 3 out, one pace*......(13 to 8 fav op 7 to 4) 2
3618² RABA RIBA [123] 12-12-0 V Slattery, *led till hdd 3 out, rdn and outpcd, raillied r-in*......(4 to 1 op 3 to 1 tchd 9 to 2) 3
3842⁵ SOCIETY GUEST [120] 11-11-11 L Harvey, *jmpd lft and not al fluent, rdn and ev ch 3 out, sn wknd*...(3 to 1 tchd 7 to 2) 4

Dist: 6l, sht-hd, 6l. 4m 7.10s. a 10.10s (4 Ran).

(Michael A Knight), Miss Venetia Williams

4206 On Cue Design Handicap Hurdle Class D (0-125 4-y-o and up) £2,840 2m......................... (8:45)

4036² ABOVE THE CUT (USA) [95] 5-10-2 (7*) M Handley, *rcd keenly, made rst, rdn clr approaching last.* ....(6 to 1 op 5 to 1 tchd 13 to 2 and 7 to 1) 1
3823* TALATHATH (Fr) [114] 5-11-11 (3*) Mr R Thornton, *hld up, hdwy appr 3 out, wnt second nxt, not pace of wnr.* (11 to 4 jt-fav tchd 3 to 1 and 100 to 30) 2
4071⁴ BALLET ROYAL (USA) [105] 8-10-12 (7*) A Dowling, *hld up in rear, gd hdwy appr 3 out, outpcd frm nxt.* ....(12 to 1 op 7 to 1) 3
3791⁶ JOHN DRUMM [113] 6-11-13 J Osborne, *led to second, trkd wnr till wknd 2 out.* ....(11 to 4 jt-fav op 3 to 1 tchd 10 to 30) 4
4045⁴ FONTANAYS (Ire) [94] (v) 9-10-1 (7*) R Studholme, *prmnt, rdn appr 3 out, wkng whn mstk nxt*........(11 to 1 op 7 to 1) 5
3886⁷ NO LIGHT [97] 10-10-11 L Harvey, *pld hrd, hld up and hdwy 5th, wknd 3 out*......(10 to 1 op 8 to 1 tchd 11 to 1) 6
3946* ELA AGAPI MOU (USA) [117] 4-11-5 (7*) M Batchelor, *mid-div, beh frm 5th*.....................(14 to 1 op 12 to 1) 7
4070⁶ PREROGATIVE [104] 7-11-4 A P McCoy, *prmnt, reminders aftr 3rd, wknd 5th*...............(16 to 1 op 14 to 1) 8
3933³ JOSIFINA [108] 6-11-8 A Thornton, *in rear, nvr on terms.* ....(11 to 1 op 8 to 1 tchd 12 to 1) 9

Dist: 8l, hd, 6l, 3½l, 4l, 6l, 15l, ½l. 3m 48.80s. a 5.80s (9 Ran).

SR: 19/30/21/23/-/-/8/-/-/ (J P M & J W Cook), C P Morlock

CARTMEL (good)
Saturday May 24th
Going Correction: MINUS 0.50 sec. per fur.

4207 Moorgate Racing Handicap Hurdle Class E (0-115 4-y-o and up) £2,430 2m 1f 110yds................. (2:10)

3794* INDIAN JOCKEY [103] 5-11-9 A P McCoy, *made all, rdn appr last, kpt on gmely.*..................(11 to 8 fav op 7 to 4) 1
4002⁵ SARMATIAN (USA) [108] 6-11-11 (3*) Mr C Bonner, *chsd ldrs, effrt whn short of room on bend appr last, sn chasing wnr, no extr towards finish*....................(20 to 1 op 16 to 1) 2
4102⁴ HIGH LOW (USA) [87] 9-10-0 (7*) N Horrocks, *al prmnt, ev ch 2 out, sn und pres, one pace frm last*...(14 to 1 op 12 to 1) 3
4102* RACHAEL'S OWEN [95] 7-10-10 (5*) R McGrath, *in tch, cld 3 out, kpt on to chase ldrs frm nxt, no imprsn.* ....(8 to 1 op 6 to 1) 4
3866* CARLISLE BANDITO'S (Ire) [93] 5-10-13 D Parker, *in tch, und pressure 2 out, sn btn*..................(9 to 2 op 6 to 1) 5
4097* SUPREME SOVIET [94] 7-11-0 K Johnson, *hld up, drvn 3 out, nvr dngrs*........................(14 to 1 op 16 to 1) 6
3868³ GLENUGIE [107] 6-11-13 N Bentley, *in rear, reminders aftr second, sn drvn alng, hdwy 4 out, wknd nxt, soon eased.* ....(9 to 1 op 8 to 1 tchd 10 to 1) 7
3759⁷ BURES (Ire) [103] 6-11-4 (5*) B Grattan, *cl up, rdn 3 out, sn wknd*............................(20 to 1 op 14 to 1) 8
279² KARINSKA [96] 7-11-2 W Worthington, *hld up in tch, mstk 1st, beh frm 4 out.*..................(14 to 1) 9
4012* FATEHALKHAIR (Ire) [94] 5-11-0 R Dunwoody, *in tch, improved to chase ldrs aftr 4 out, wknd nxt.* ....(4 to 1 op 9 to 2) 10

Dist: ¾l, 4l, 2l, 1½l, 11l, ½l, 3l, sht-hd, 1¾l. 3m 57.90s. b 2.10s (10 Ran).

SR: 26/30/5/11/7/-/9/2/-/ (Stuart M Mercer), M C Pipe

4208 Marten Julian Novices' Handicap Chase Class E (0-100 5-y-o and up) £2,940 2m 1f 110yds......... (2:40)

4057 DARING PAST [95] (v) 7-11-12 R Dunwoody, *nvr far away, chlgd frm 2 out, ran on to ld bef strt, easily.* ....(11 to 8 on op 6 to 4 on tchd 5 to 4 on) 1
4107³ ALL CLEAR (Ire) [69] 6-9-9 (5*) R McGrath, *prmnt, mstk second, not fluent nxt (water), led 7th, hit 3 out, hdd bef strt, sn no ch wth wnr*.................(7 to 2 tchd 9 to 2) 2
3918⁸ KARLOVAC [79] 11-10-10 F Perratt, *beh, struggling 8th, kpt on clsg stages, nvr dngrs*......(25 to 1 op 20 to 1) 3
4057² THE FENCE SHRINKER [72] 6-10-3³ T Jenks, *led, mstk second, hdd 7th, wknd 4 out (water)*....(20 to 1 op 14 to 1) 4
3559 HIGH LEG [89] (bl) 9-10-0 W Marston, *cl up, lost pl 8th, no dngr aftrwards*..................(33 to 1 op 20 to 1) 5
4107⁶ REGAL DOMAIN (Ire) [69] 6-10-0 K Johnson, *strted slwly, wl beh, tld off.*......................(50 to 1 op 33 to 1) 6

3966* APPEARANCE MONEY (Ire) [72] 6-10-3 M Foster, hld up, hdwy to track ldrs 8th, still travelling wl whn f 3 out.
....(5 to 2 op 9 to 4) f
Dist: 3l, 25l, 5l, 2½l, dist. 4m 16.80s. a 5.80s (7 Ran).

(John A Petty), M D Hammond

4209 Dodson & Horrell Maiden Hunters' Chase Class H for the Fraser Cup (5-y-o and up) £1,852 3¼m...... (3:15)

3567⁴ SANDS OF GOLD (Ire) 9-11-7 (7*) Mr L Lay, al prmnt, hit 3 out, hrd drvn to ld entering strt, kpt on..... (5 to 1 tchd 6 to 1) 1
JAYANDOUBLEU (Ire) 8-11-7 (7*) Mr T Scott, led to 12th, cl up, outpcd last, kpt on one pace strt, no imprsn on wnr.
....(4 to 1 op 7 to 2) 2
WORLESTON FARRIER 9-11-7 (7*) Mr G Hanmer, wnt to post early, cl up, hit 9th, led 12th, clr aftr last till tired and hdd entering strt, no extr............(14 to 1 tchd 12 to 1) 3
3921⁴ COOL YULE (Ire) 9-11-9 (5*) Miss P Robson, in rear, hmpd by faller 11th, pushed alng appr 4 out (water), sn styd on, nrst finish...........................(10 to 1 op 7 to 1) 4
4022⁶ JUST FOR ME (Ire) 8-11-9 (5*) Mr M H Naughton, midfield, hit 7th, rdn appr 4 out, kpt on one pace, no imprsn on ldrs.
....(25 to 1 op 20 to 1) 5
WANG HOW 9-11-7 (7*) Mr A Robson, in tch early, beh and no ch whn mstk 3 out...............(33 to 1 op 25 to 1) 6
3921⁵ EMU PARK 9-11-7 (7*) Mr J Thompson, beh, hdwy 9th (water), in tch whn hit 12th, wknd 4 out (water).
....(33 to 1 op 16 to 1) 7
ORTON HOUSE 10-11-7 (7*) Mr R Burton, al beh, struggling frm 13th, nvr a factor...............(7 to 1 op 6 to 1) 8
RUSHING BURN 11-11-2 (7*) Miss N C Snowden, sn beh, tld off...(33 to 1) 9
CANISTER CASTLE 9-11-7 (7*) Mr D R McLeod, al beh, lost tch fnl circuit, tld off..............(20 to 1) 10
4041² TRUE FORTUNE 7-11-9 (5*) Mr J Jukes, in tch, hdwy to go cl up 7th, f 11th.................(5 to 4 fav op 2 to 1) f
ALL OR NOTHING 9-11-2 (7*) Mr J Ewart, beh, jmpd slwly second, hdwy frm 12th to chase ldrs, rdn alng whn blun and uns rdr 3 out.....................(20 to 1 op 16 to 1) ur
BUNNY HARE (Ire) 9-11-7 (7*) Mr R Forristal, midfield whn blun and uns rdr second..........(50 to 1 op 33 to 1) ur
4112 KING SPRING 12-11-9 (5*) Mrs V Jackson, al beh, tld off whn pld up bef 4 out (water)........(20 to 1 op 16 to 1) pu
Dist: 2½l, hd, 2½l, 1¾l, 19l, 9l, 4l, 20l, dist. 6m 30.40s. a 13.40s (14 Ran).

(Brett Badham), C N Nimmo

4210 Worthington Best Bitter Novices' Handicap Hurdle Class F (0-95 4-y-o and up) £2,542 2¾m......... (3:45)

4139³ STYLISH INTERVAL [87] 5-11-6 A P McCoy, al hndy, led 3 out, drvn aftr nxt, styd on...(4 to 1 op 9 to 2 tchd 5 to 1) 1
4007¹ TOSHIBA TALK (Ire) [95] 5-12-0 R Dunwoody, hld up, hdwy 4 out, chsd wnr aftr 2 out, kpt on und pres.
....(7 to 2 tchd 4 to 1) 2
3961* ONE MORE DIME (Ire) [67] 7-10-0 B Fenton, led to 3 out, sn one pace..............................(4 to 1 op 3 to 1) 3
3353⁴ MY MISSILE [67] 7-10-0 L O'Hara, prmnt till fdd frm 3 out.
....(9 to 1 op 7 to 1) 4
3918 JONAEM (Ire) [74] 7-10-7 K Johnson, cl up, und pres 3 out, sn wknd...................(10 to 1 op 8 to 1 tchd 11 to 1) 5
4020 TARTAN JOY [67] (v) 6-9-9 (5*) Mr M H Naughton, hld up in tch, hmpd by loose horse aftr 6th, struggling 4 out, btn whn blun nxt.........................(25 to 1 tchd 33 to 1) 6
3997 AMAZING SAIL (Ire) [90] 4-11-3 A S Smith, cl up whn f 3rd.
....(5 to 2 fav op 3 to 1) f
4139 DIDDY RHYTHM [82] 7-10-10 (5*) R Wilkinson, hld up whn brght dwn 3rd............(8 to 1 op 6 to 1) bd
3881 DOUBLE DASH (Ire) [78] (v) 4-10-5 D J Moffatt, hld up whn brght dwn 3rd...........(12 to 1 op 10 to 1) bd
4007⁷ STRONG CHARACTER [67] 11-10-0 J Burke, al beh, tld off whn pld up bef 3 out..........(33 to 1 op 25 to 1) pu
3997⁴ DOUBLE VINTAGE (Ire) [82] 4-10-9 W Worthington, nvr gng wl and al beh, tld off whn pld up bef 2 out.
....(33 to 1 op 20 to 1) pu
4101⁴ SKANE RIVER (Ire) [71] 6-9-13 (5*) R McGrath, in tch, short of room on bend aftr 6th, beh frm 3 out, tld off whn pld up r-in.
....(6 to 1 tchd 13 to 2) pu
Dist: 1¼l, 6l, 16l, 5l, 10l. 5m 16.00s. a 9.00s (12 Ran).

(Mrs J Waggott), N Waggott

4211 Laurent-Perrier Champagne Novices' Chase Class E for the McAlpine Cup (5-y-o and up) £2,841 3¼m
....(4:20)

4098¹ SLOTAMATIQUE (Ire) (v) 8-12-0 R Dunwoody, made all, lft clr 4 out (water), eased dwn to walk r-in.
....(6 to 5 on op 6 to 4 on tchd 13 to 8 on and 11 to 10 on) 1
4108⁵ STRONGALONG (Ire) 7-11-2 A P McCoy, wl beh, in tch 9th, sn drvn alng and well behind, lft poor second 2 out, tld off.
....(8 to 1 op 7 to 1) 2
4044 STEEL GOLD 7-10-10¹ (7*) Mr R Burton, cl up, lost pl 12th, sn und pres, lft poor second 4 out (water), blun 2 out and lost second, tld off......................(50 to 1) 3

4001² KILTULLA (Ire) 7-10-11 (5*) R Wilkinson, pressed wnr till f 4 out (water).....................(7 to 4 op 9 to 4) f
3925³ LAMBRINI (Ire) (bl) 7-10-8 (3*) P Henley, not jump wl, in rear, hdwy to go prmnt 8th, lost pl 12th, 4th and struggling whn f nxt.
....(10 to 1 op 7 to 1) f
3918⁵ KINGS MINSTRAL (Ire) 7-11-2 J Burke, refused to race, took no part............(25 to 1 op 16 to 1) l
Dist: Dist, dist. 6m 30.30s. a 13.30s (6 Ran).

(Slotamatique (Bolton) Ltd), G Richards

4212 Sticky Toffee Pudding Novices' Hurdle Class E (4-y-o and up) £3,072 2m 1f 110yds..................(4:50)

4021* BOLD STATEMENT 5-11-12 N Bentley, led 1st, made rst, drvn aftr last, styd on...............(9 to 4 op 2 to 1 tchd 5 to 2) 1
3198⁷ ADVANCE EAST 5-11-6 A P McCoy, hld up, hdwy whn mstk 4 out, chlgd aftr 2 out, chsd wnr r-in, no extr fnl finish.
....(4 to 1 tchd 7 to 2) 2
3910¹ SMOLENSK (Ire) 5-11-12 R Dunwoody, in tch, cld 4 out to track ldrs, ev ch on bit 2 out, no extr und pres r-in.
....(5 to 4 fav op 2 to 1) 3
3353 KINGFISHER BRAVE 4-10-9 B Fenton, prmnt, outpcd 4 out, no dngr aftrwards............(10 to 1 op 8 to 1) 4
1398⁷ ANOTHER QUARTER (Ire) 4-10-4 W Worthington, wnt to post early, led to 1st, remained cl up, ev ch 2 out, sn wknd.
....(25 to 1 op 16 to 1) 5
4097⁸ HAND OF STRAW (Ire) 5-11-0 K Johnson, midfield, jmpd slwly 1st, beh and no dngr frm 4 out.....(8 to 1 op 5 to 1) 6
3356 JOHNNEYS SPIRIT 5-11-0 L O'Hara, hld up in tch, struggling frm 4 out, sn beh, tld off............(33 to 1) 7
DRAMATIC PASS (Ire) 8-11-0 D J Moffatt, al beh, no ch whn f 4 out..........................(50 to 1) f
3971 SULLAMELL 6-11-0 W Marston, unruly strt, hld up in tch, struggling and beh 3 out, f nxt......(50 to 1 op 33 to 1) f
Dist: 2½l, 3½l, 5l, 2½l, nk, 23l. 4m 1.30s. a 1.30s (9 Ran).

(R I Graham), G M Moore

HEXHAM (good to firm)
Saturday May 24th
Going Correction: MINUS 0.20 sec. per fur.

4213 Co-operative Bank Novices' Hurdle Class E (4-y-o and up) £1,632 2½m 110yds..................(2:15)

4100⁴ ACAJOU III (Fr) 9-11-0 P Carberry, made virtually all, clr last, easily........................(5 to 2 op 2 to 1) 1
4007⁴ MUZRAK (Can) 6-11-8 R Garritty, nvr far away, chsd wnr 2 out, sn drvn alng, no imprsn last.
....(11 to 8 fav op 6 to 4 tchd 5 to 4) 2
3999² BOSTON MAN (bl) 6-11-8 M A Fitzgerald, al cl up, ev ch fnl circuit, outpcd 2 out, sn no dngr.....(3 to 1 tchd 7 to 2) 3
4007⁶ RUBISLAW 5-10-7 (7*) Miss S Lamb, sn wl beh, some hdwy bef 2 out, nvr on terms.........(100 to 1 op 50 to 1) 4
3999 MOONLIGHT VENTURE 5-11-0 P Niven, with ldr, struggling aftr 4 out, btn fnl 2.....(40 to 1 op 33 to 1 tchd 50 to 1) 5
3663 ALLERBY 9-11-0 J Supple, chsd main bunch, pushed alng aftr 3rd, tld off fnl circuit...........(16 to 1 op 14 to 1) 6
MINTULYAR 6-11-0 L Wyer, in tch, outpcd fnl circuit, btn last 3...(33 to 1) 7
SPLIT THE WIND 11-10-6 (3*) F Leahy, beh and sn detatched, struggling whn f 5th.................(66 to 1 op 50 to 1) f
4099⁴ MR BRUNO 4-10-8 B Storey, blun and uns rdr second.
....(50 to 1) ur
4113 CHAN MOVE 5-10-7 (7*) Mr T J Barry, jmpd badly in rear, blun 6th, sn pld up...........(100 to 1 op 50 to 1) pu
GARDENIA'S SONG 6-11-0 R Supple, chsd ldg bunch, outpcd aftr 6th, sn tld off, pld up after 2 out.(66 to 1 op 50 to 1) pu
Dist: 2½l, 7l, 28l, 2l, 17l, 4l. 4m 57.20s. a 6.20s (11 Ran).

(Robert Ogden), G Richards

4214 Thompsons Of Prudhoe Ltd Novices' Chase Class E (5-y-o and up) £2,193 2m 110yds........................(2:45)

4107¹ KNOW-NO-NO (Ire) 8-11-7 R Garritty, chsd ldg bunch, improved hfwy, led on bit bef last, easily.
....(Evens fav op 11 to 10 tchd 5 to 4) 1
3868⁷ ASTRALEON (Ire) 9-11-0 B Storey, settled in tch, improved to ld 3 out, hdd bef last, not quicken....(6 to 1 op 5 to 1) 2
4128³ SOVEREIGNS MATCH 9-11-0 P Carberry, led to second, cl up till outpcd frm 3 out...........(11 to 2 tchd 6 to 1) 3
4009⁵ MOSS PAGEANT 7-11-0 T Reed, led second, sn clr, hdd 3 out, tld...................(9 to 2 op 6 to 1 tchd 5 to 1) 4
HERBALIST 8-11-0 Richard Guest, sn beh, struggling whn mstk 6th, pld up 8th.........(20 to 1 tchd 25 to 1) pu
4107² KINCARDINE BRIDGE (USA) 8-10-7 (7*) Mr M Bradburne, in tch, effrt bef 7th, struggling whn hit 3 out, fdd, pld up before last.........................(10 to 1 tchd 12 to 1) pu
4107⁵ SPECTRE BROWN 7-10-7 (7*) Mr T J Barry, in tch to hfwy, sn lost touch, pld up bef 3 out......(33 to 1 op 25 to 1) pu
3353 WAR WHOOP 5-10-8 A Thornton, mstks, prmnt to hfwy, pld up 8th...........................(20 to 1) pu

4107 AKITO RACING (Ire) 6-10-9 P Niven, *sn tld off, pld up bef 4 out*..........................(25 to 1 tchd 33 to 1) pu
Dist: 9l, 9l, 16l. 4m 1.80s. a 3.80s (9 Ran).
SR: 22/6/-/-/-/-/ (Mrs A Kane), M D Hammond

4215 Claremont Garments Plc Handicap Chase Class E (0-115 5-y-o and up) £2,406 3m 1f................ (3:15)

4109³ NIJWAY [86] 7-10-1 A Thornton, *nvr far away, outpcd aftr 2 out, ran on wl frm last to ld post*.......(11 to 2 op 5 to 1) 1
3914⁶ SUPPOSIN [91] 9-10-6 Richard Guest, *held up in rear, steady hdwy 4 out, chlgd 2 out, led run in, hdd post.*
....(12 to 1 op 10 to 1) 2
4109² RUSTY BLADE [85] 8-10-0 R Johnson, *cl up, mstk 11th and sn pushed alng, led 2 out, hdd run in, rallied.* (6 to 1 op 5 to 1) 3
4024⁴ WHAAT FETTLE [100] 12-11-1 P Niven, *led till hdd 2 out, sn outpcd.*.................(5 to 1 tchd 6 to 1) 4
4010⁵ SCRABO VIEW (Ire) [94] 9-10-9 R Supple, *in tch, rdn alng 13th, outpcd last 3.*...............(14 to 1 tchd 16 to 1) 5
4109⁴ BRIGHT DESTINY [85] 6-9-7 (7*) Mr O McPhail, *cl up, strug-gling aftr 3 out, fdd.*...............(20 to 1 op 16 to 1) 6
3867⁴ ROYAL VACATION [113] 8-12-0 J Callaghan, *settled on ins, blun and lost pl 13th, sn struggling.*
....(7 to 1 op 6 to 1 tchd 15 to 2) 7
4010 MISCHIEVOUS GIRL [85] 9-10-0 Mrs F Needham, *prmnt on outsd, mstks 7th and nxt, sn lost pl, btn fnl circuit.*
....(50 to 1 tchd 66 to 1) 8
4009⁴ MR REINER (Ire) [85] 9-10-0 P Carberry, *chsd ldg grp, mstk 13th, struggling whn blun 3 out, tld off.* (12 to 1 op 10 to 1) 9
4102² TOUGH TEST (Ire) [96] 7-10-11 B Storey, *hld up in rear, blun, stumbled and uns rdr tenth.*
....(9 to 4 fav op 5 to 2 tchd 2 to 1) ur
Dist: Sht-hd, nk, 19l, 5l, 1½l, 5l, 30l, 22l. 6m 17.20s. a 12.20s (10 Ran).
(T A Barnes), M A Barnes

4216 S.C.S. Upholstery Specialists Mares' Only Handicap Hurdle Class E (0-115 4-y-o and up) £1,548 2m...... (3:45)

4007³ ROYAL YORK [90] 5-11-10 P Carberry, *nvr far away, chsd ldr hfwy, led on bit bef 2 out, clr last, very easily.* ....(5 to 2 jt-fav op 9 to 4 tchd 11 to 4) 1
3805⁴ PARSON'S LODGE (Ire) [80] 9-11-0 R Supple, *chsd ldr to hfwy, sn outpcd, rallied to chase wnr bef last, no imprsn.*
....(8 to 2 fav op 3 to 1) 2
3265* RADMORE BRANDY [90] 4-10-12 (7*) R Burns, *hld up, steady hdwy aftr 3 out, rdn nxt, sn one pace.* ....(4 to 1 op 7 to 2) 3
4102⁵ FRENCH PROJECT (Ire) [67] 5-9-12 (3*) G F Ryan, *chsd ldrs, rdn alng bef 2 out, outpcd before last.* (5 to 1 op 20 to 1) 4
4102³ SKIDDAW SAMBA [80] 8-11-0 G Lee, *prmnt on outsd, outpcd bef 2 out, sn btn.*...............(6 to 1 op 5 to 1) 5
2853⁶ BEST OF ALL (Ire) [94] 5-12-0 P Niven, *led till hdd bef 2 out, struggling before last.*.................(6 to 1) 6
4101⁸ WHITEGATESPRINCESS (Ire) [66] (v) 6-10-0 B Storey, *sn beh, rdn alng 3 out, nvr on terms.*.........(14 to 1 op 16 to 1) 7
4101 MEADOWLECK [66] 8-9-9 (5*) S Taylor, *beh, struggling 3 out, fdd.*.................................(50 to 1) 8
3246 NO TAKERS [66] 10-9-7 (7*) J O'Leary, *in tch, struggling 3 out, tld off.*.................(25 to 1 op 20 to 1) 9
Dist: 3l, 2l, 8l, 2½l, ½l, 10l, 3½l, dist. 3m 57.00s. a 8.00s (9 Ran).
(Robert Ogden), G Richards

4217 St. Oswalds Hospice Handicap Hurdle Class E (0-110 4-y-o and up) £2,075 2m 110yds....... (4:15)

3870* COLORFUL AMBITION [104] 7-11-13 J Supple, *hld up and beh, gd hdwy aftr 3 out, led bef last, ran on strly.*
....(15 to 8 fav op 5 to 2) 1
4025² HIGHLAND WAY (Ire) [89] 9-10-12 M A Fitzgerald, *keen hold, settled in tch, improved to ld 2 out, hdd bef last, not quicken run in.*...............(7 to 2 tchd 3 to 1 and 4 to 1) 2
4008* SHELTON ABBEY [77] 8-11-10-0 P Carberry, *settled in tch, drvn alng bef 2 out, styd on, no imprsn.* (7 to 1 op 11 to 2) 3
4012⁵ SHARP SENSATION [93] 7-11-2 P Niven, *hld up, effrt bef 2 out, drvn and kpt on last, nvr dngrs*.....(12 to 1 op 6 to 1) 4
4158⁵ DONT FORGET CURTIS (Ire) [77] 5-9-7 (7*) Miss S Lamb, *chsd ldrs till outpcd bef 2 out.*.........(25 to 1 op 16 to 1) 5
4025* KINDA GROOVY [89] 8-10-12 J Callaghan, *led till hdd 2 out, sn struggling.*...............(9 to 2 tchd 5 to 1) 6
3657² LONGCROFT [81] 5-10-4 R Johnson, *cl up till rdn and outpcd frm 2 out.*...............(9 to 1 op 7 to 1 tchd 10 to 1) 7
4025³ JUMBO STAR [78] 7-10-1 B Storey, *keen hold, pressed ldr, outpcd appr 2 out, sn btn.*...............(14 to 1 op 12 to 1) 8
RECLUSE [77] (bl) 6-10-0 L Wyer, *mstks, cl up, lost pl 3rd, tld off fnl circuit.*...............(33 to 1 op 16 to 1) 9
Dist: 4l, 4l, 2l, ¾l, ½l, 13l, 2l, 3½l. 4m 59.40s. a 8.40s (9 Ran).
(F J Sainsbury), Mrs A Swinbank

4218 Flying Ace Hunters' Chase Class H (5-y-o and up) £1,316 2½m 110yds .... (4:50)

4112² HOWAYMAN 7-12-2 (5*) Mr R Ford, *hld up, lft 3rd 3 out, led bef last, sn clr.*.... (11 to 10 on op Evens tchd 5 to 4 on) 1

4072 CUMBERLAND BLUES (Ire) 8-12-0 (7*) Miss A Deniel, *nvr far away, lft in ld and hmpd 3 out, hdd nxt, one pace frm last.*
....(10 to 1 op 7 to 1 tchd 12 to 1) 2
4112³ MASTER KIT (Ire) 8-12-0 (7*) Mr M Bradburne, *nvr far away, lft second 3 out, led nxt, hdd bef last, sn outpcd.*
....(9 to 1 op 6 to 1) 3
4112⁵ REED 12-11-7 (7*) Mr O McPhail, *beh, rdn hfwy, nvr on terms.*
....(33 to 1 op 14 to 1) 4
THANK U JIM 9-11-7 (7*) Miss T Jackson, *wth ldr, led 8th, f 3 out.*...............(15 to 2 op 12 to 1 tchd 7 to 1) f
4011³ KNOWE HEAD 13-12-0 (7*) Mr S Brisby, *cl up, mstk 7th, struggling fnl circuit, tld off whn pld up bef last.*
....(6 to 1 op 4 to 1 tchd 13 to 2) pu
4011⁴ BUCKANEER BAY 10-11-9 (5*) Mr R Hale, *beh, blun 8th, pld up bef nxt.*...............(33 to 1 op 14 to 1) pu
4124 FROZEN STIFF (Ire) 9-11-9 (5*) Mr N Wilson, *sn tld off, pld up bef 9th.*...............(20 to 1 op 14 to 1) pu
PERCY PIT 8-11-9 (5*) Mr R Johnson, *led to 8th, pld up bef tenth.*...............(50 to 1 op 33 to 1) pu
KINGS TOKEN 7-12-0 Mr J Walton, *sn tld off, pld up bef 9th.*
....(40 to 1 op 20 to 1) pu
Dist: 12l, 10l, 22l. 5m 7.10s. a 9.10s (10 Ran).
(Dennis Waggott), K Anderson

CARTMEL (good to firm)
Monday May 26th
Going Correction: MINUS 0.15 sec. per fur.

4219 Burlington Slate Selling Handicap Hurdle Class G (0-90 4-y-o and up) £2,402 2m 1f 110yds........ (2:00)

2030 HACKETTS CROSS (Ire) [83] 9-11-7 Richard Guest, *al prmnt, chlgd 2 out, led last, drvn clr r-in.*......(11 to 2 op 9 to 2) 1
3400⁶ BATTERY FIRED [72] 8-10-10 J Callaghan, *led, hit 3 out and hmpd by loose horse, mstk and hdd last, no extr.*
....(9 to 2 op 4 to 1) 2
3803⁶ FANADIYR (Ire) [64] 5-10-2 B Storey, *hld up, hdwy 4 out to chase ldrs, sn no imprsn.*..........(5 to 1 op 9 to 2) 3
3823 APACHE LEN (USA) [70] (v) 4-9-10 (7*) N Horrocks, *cl up to 3rd, sn beh, kpt on r-in.*...........(9 to 2 op 8 to 1) 4
4023⁷ IN A MOMENT (USA) [66] (bl) 6-11-0 R Supple, *slwly into strd, al niggled alng and beh, nvr dngrs....* (12 to 1 op 10 to 1) 5
3966 PHARGOLD (Ire) [63] 8-10-1 K Johnson, *in tch, not fluent 3rd and 4 out, wknd appr 2 out, tld off.*... (20 to 1 op 16 to 1) 6
3583 BELIEVE IT [65] 8-10-3 F Perratt, *prmnt to 3rd, struggling and wl beh 4 out, tld off.*...............(50 to 1) 7
3919 BIRTHPLACE (Ire) [62] 7-9-9 (5*) B Grattan, *in tch, mstk second, struggling and beh 4 out, tld off whn f last.* (33 to 1) f
4179⁶ NEVER SO BLUE (Ire) [78] (bl) 6-10-11 (5*) R Wilkinson, *midfield, hdwy to go prmnt 3rd, blun and uns rdr nxt.*
....(6 to 1 op 5 to 1 tchd 13 to 2) ur
SIMPLY GEORGE [90] 8-12-0 P Carberry, *hld up, effrt and hdwy appr 3 out, 5th whn pld up bef nxt, lme.*
....(2 to 1 op 5 to 2) pu
Dist: 5l, 14l, nk, 7l, 19l, 2½l. 4m 5.00s. a 5.00s (10 Ran).
SR: 18/2/-/-/-/-/ (G W Briscoe), P Eccles

4220 Victoria Trading Fruit Importers Ltd Novices' Chase Class E (5-y-o and up) £2,893 2m 5f 110yds......(2:35)

3966⁵ BIT OF A DREAM (Ire) 7-11-0 Richard Guest, *al hndy, half a l second whn lft wl clr and hmpd last.*
....(7 to 2 op 3 to 1 tchd 4 to 1) 1
4098⁴ ROYAL BANKER (Ire) 7-11-0 P Carberry, *prmnt, niggled alng and lost pl 6th, lost to 8th, wnt poor second in strt, no ch wth wnr.*..(12 to 1 op 5 to 1) 2
4022 PERSIAN GRANGE (Ire) 7-11-0 J Burke, *hld up in rear, hit 8th, hdwy and cl up whn blun nxt, sn wl beh, lft poor second last, second to strt.*...............(33 to 1 op 16 to 1) 3
3885³ NADIAD (v) 11-11-0 B Storey, *led till hdd 3 out, 3rd and und pres whn f nxt.*...........(11 to 2 op 5 to 1) f
4180* PLUMBOB (Ire) 8-11-6 R Supple, *al prmnt, wth ldr whn mstk 4 out (water), led nxt, rdn and half a l in frnt when blun and uns rdr last.*.......(2 to 1 on op 5 to 2 on tchd 15 to 8 on) ur
Dist: 23l, 2½l. 5m 17.90s. a 7.90s (5 Ran).
(The Cartmel Syndicate), Mrs S J Smith

4221 Burlington Slate Handicap Chase Class E Amateur Riders (0-125 5-y-o and up) £3,048 2m 5f 110yds (3:10)

3787⁷ FIVELEIGH BUILDS [122] 10-11-6 (7*) Mr M Bradburne, *not fluent, prmnt, lost grnd whn mstk 3rd, plenty to do tenth, cld 2 out, led aftr nxt, rdn clr, eased close hme.*
....(6 to 4 tchd 7 to 4 and 11 to 8) 1
3867⁵ HURRICANE ANDREW (Ire) [95] 9-9-9 (5*) Mr M H Naughton, *hmpd second, sn chasing ldr, drvn and mstk 2 out, kpt on one pace and no imprsn on wnr r-in......*(6 to 1 op 8 to 1) 2
4010 BLAZING DAWN [95] 10-9-9 S Lyons, *held second, clr 8th, mstk last, sn hdd and wknd.....*(6 to 1 tchd 6 to 1) 3
SARONA SMITH [119] 10-11-10⁴ Mr J Walton, *al beh, lost tch 8th, tld off.*...............(25 to 1 op 16 to 1) 4

BLACK SPUR [97] 15-10-2[9] (7*) Mr W Burnell, *led to second, cl up to 8th, 3rd and outpcd whn blun badly and uns rdr 9th.*
....(33 to 1 op 25 to 1)   ur
4126[2] BAS DE LAINE (Fr) [123] (v) 11-11-11 (3*) Mr C Bonner, *cl up whn blun and uns rdr second*......(11 to 10 fav op Evens)   ur
Dist: 3l, 6l, dist. 5m 16.20s. a 6.20s (6 Ran).

SR: 6/-/-/   (Miss Lucinda V Russell), Miss Lucinda V Russell

4222 Stanley Leisure Handicap Hurdle Class D (0-120 4-y-o and up) £2,710 3¼m................................(3:45)

4048 FIVE FLAGS (Ire) [86] 9-11-6 Richard Guest, *al prmnt, reminders 4th and 8th, led 3 out, hrd drvn and styd on wl r-in.*
....(9 to 4 op 5 to 2)   1
3852[6] PRIME DISPLAY (USA) [84] 11-11-4 R Supple, *nvr far away, pushed alng appr 3 out, str chal r-in, no extr nr finish.*
....(14 to 1 op 20 to 1)   2
3761[4] VALIANT DASH [81] 11-10-10 (5*) S Taylor, *led, not fluent 3rd, mstk and hdd 3 out, still ev ch nxt, styd on same pace und pres r-in.*
....(6 to 4 fav tchd 11 to 8)   3
4101[7] RUBER [78] 10-10-5 (7*) N Horrocks, *in rear, reminders bef 1st, mstk 6th, effrt 4 out, sn chasing ldrs, kpt on und pres r-in.*
....(4 to 1 op 3 to 1)   4
4210 DOUBLE VINTAGE (Ire) [73] 4-10-0 W Worthington, *al wl beh, reminders 7th, lost tch nxt, tld off.*..................(33 to 1)   5
1824[6] GYMCRAK CYRANO (Ire) [90] 8-11-3 (7*) Miss C Metcalfe, *strted slwly, hld up whn mstk and uns rdr 3rd.*
....(5 to 1 op 7 to 2)   ur
Dist: 1½l, nk, 1¼l, dist. 6m 12.20s. a 14.20s (6 Ran).

                                                    (Mrs S Smith), Mrs S J Smith

4223 Crowther Homes Juvenile Novices' Hurdle Class E (4-y-o) £2,654 2m 1f 110yds............................(4:20)

3905[8] GO WITH THE WIND 10-12 D J Moffatt, *chsd ldrs, hdwy whn not fluent 4 out, led nxt, rdn clr r-in.*
....(7 to 4 fav op 6 to 4 tchd 2 to 1)   1
3280[3] DOWN THE YARD 10-7 W Worthington, *in rear, mstk 4th, hdwy 3 out, chsd wnr aftr nxt, one pace r-in.*
....(6 to 1 op 5 to 1)   2
4212[5] ANOTHER QUARTER (Ire) 10-7 K Johnson, *in rear, hdwy to track ldrs 4 out, ev ch whn blun 2 out, wknd appr last.*
....(10 to 1 tchd 12 to 1)   3
4099[2] SHEEMORE (Ire) 10-5 (7*) N Horrocks, *chsd clr ldr, cld 4 out, und pres whn swshd tail and blun 2 out, sn wknd.*
....(9 to 4 op 2 to 1 tchd 7 to 4)   4
3819 PORT VALENSKA (Ire) 10-7 (5*) S Taylor, *in tch early, reminders 4th, beh and no ch frm four out.*
....(33 to 1 op 25 to 1)   5
819 ORANGE ORDER (Ire) 10-12 P Carberry, *rcd keenly, led and sn clr, mstk second, hrd pressed 4 out, hdd nxt, soon wknd and eased.*..........................(5 to 1 tchd 11 to 2)   6
3997[2] POLITICAL MANDATE 10-0 (7*) C McCormack, *chsd ldrs till wknd quickly 4 out, tld off.*..........(8 to 1 tchd 9 to 1)   7
Dist: 7l, 10l, 19l, 3l, 8l, 24l. 4m 6.60s. a 6.60s (7 Ran).

                                                    (Alf Chadwick), J S Goldie

4224 Swan Hotel At Newby Bridge Maiden Hurdle Class E (4-y-o and up) £2,447 2¾m................................(4:55)

2206[6] NOSAM 7-11-5 Richard Guest, *strted slwly, wl beh, in tch 6th, chsd ldr 3 out, led aftr last, sn clr.*......(7 to 1 op 5 to 1)   1
3972 GROSVENOR (Ire) (bl) 6-11-5 P Carberry, *chsd ldr, led appr 4 out, drvn aftr 2 out, hdd after last, eased whn no extr r-in.*
....(5 to 4 on op 5 to 2 on)   2
4212[6] HAND OF STRAW (Ire) 5-11-5 K Johnson, *in tch, jmpd slwly and reminder 4th, niggled alng to chase ldrs 3 out, sn no imprsn.*..................................(5 to 2 op 7 to 2)   3
1592 BARRIE STIR 5-11-5 J Callaghan, *not fluent, beh, rdn alng 4 out, nvr dngrs.*..........................(16 to 1 op 14 to 1)   4
3780 DE-VEERS CURRIE (Ire) 5-11-0 D J Moffatt, *led, mstk second, hdd appr 4 out and mistake, sn wknd, tld off.*
....(20 to 1 op 12 to 1)   5
NOBLE NORMAN 6-10-12 (7*) Mr J Davies, *in tch early, struggling 4 out, sn beh, tld off.*..........(16 to 1 op 14 to 1)   6
4212 DRAMATIC PASS (Ire) 8-11-5 W Worthington, *al beh, tld off whn pld up bef 2 out.*............(25 to 1 op 16 to 1)   pu
4063[6] RENO'S TREASURE (USA) 4-10-8 R Supple, *chsd ldrs early, beh 7th, tld off whn pld up bef 3 out...*(33 to 1 op 25 to 1)   pu
Dist: 9l, 8l, 9l, dist, 20l. 5m 22.00s. a 15.00s (8 Ran).

                                                    (N B Mason), N B Mason

FONTWELL (good to firm)
Monday May 26th
Going Correction: MINUS 0.50 sec. per fur.

4225 South Coast Radio Juvenile Novices' Hurdle Class E (4-y-o) £2,262 2¼m 110yds........................(2:00)

3681* MAJOR DUNDEE (Ire) (v) 11-10 C Maude, *made all, rdn 2 out, styd on und pres r-in.*
..........(11 to 10 fav op 5 to 4 tchd 11 to 8 and Evens)   1
3566[9] NOBLE LORD 12-2 B Powell, *chsd wnr to 3 out, rgned second appr last, not quicken r-in.*............(15 to 8 op 7 to 4)   2
3946[3] ANNA SOLEIL (Ire) 11-4 J A McCarthy, *cl up till hrd rdn and wknd appr last.*......................(7 to 2 tchd 4 to 1)   3
3985 DUBAI DOLLY (Ire) 10-7 S Curran, *sn outpcd in 4th, no ch whn mstk last.*..............(16 to 1 op 14 to 1 tchd 20 to 1)   4
P GRAYCO CHOICE 10-7 B Fenton, *sn rear, jmpd slwly second, lost tch nxt.*..............(100 to 1 op 66 to 1)   5
Dist: 4l, 16l, 10l, dist. 4m 15.20s. b 1.80s (5 Ran).

SR: 22/24/   (Michael R Jaye), M C Pipe

4226 Fontwell Selling Handicap Chase Class G (0-95 5-y-o and up) £2,366 2¼m................................(2:30)

3938[3] GABISH [67] 12-10-0 S Fox, *al prmnt, led 6th, hit 8th, hrd rdn and hld on gmely r-in.*..................(33 to 1 op 20 to 1)   1
1132[8] SHIKAREE (Ire) [87] (bl) 6-11-6 C Maude, *reminders 3rd, hdwy whn jmpd lft 7th, ev ch r-in, hrd rdn and kpt on.*
....(6 to 1 op 5 to 1 tchd 13 to 2)   2
4073[7] ILEWIN [82] 10-11-1 M Ahern, *prmnt, ev ch appr 3 out, one pace.*............................(16 to 1 op 10 to 1)   3
4033 FLOWING RIVER (USA) [67] (bl) 11-9-9 (5*) A Bates, *rear, hdwy tenth, 4th and hld whn mstk 2 out.*
....(20 to 1 op 12 to 1 tchd 25 to 1)   4
3862[5] RUSTIC GENT (Ire) [67] 9-10-0 D J Burchell, *beh, rdn and some hdwy 3 out, nvr nrr.*
....(8 to 1 op 7 to 1 tchd 10 to 1 and 11 to 1)   5
3958[5] SIDE BAR [67] (v) 7-10-0 S Curran, *mid-div whn hmpd bend aftr 1st, no dngr after...*(8 to 1 op 7 to 1 tchd 9 to 1)   6
4046 BOXING MATCH [71] 10-10-4 B Fenton, *in tch, effrt to press ldrs tenth, wknd 4 out...*(12 to 1 op 8 to 1 tchd 14 to 1)   7
3851 UPWARD SURGE (Ire) [67] 7-10-0 Mrs N Ledger, *prmnt early, beh frm hhwy.*..........(40 to 1 op 20 to 1 tchd 50 to 1)   8
4031* EVENING RAIN [86] 11-11-5 T Dascombe, *pressed ldrs till f tenth.*..........................(3 to 1 tchd 7 to 2)   f
4024[3] CARDENDEN (Ire) [69] 9-10-2 W McFarland, *led to 6th, prmnt whn blun and uns rdr 11th.* (7 to 2 op 4 to 1 tchd 5 to 1)   ur
3992[9] DAYS OF THUNDER [74] 9-10-7 T J Murphy, *wl beh frm hhwy, pld up bef 11th.*................(33 to 1 op 16 to 1)   pu
3371 PEACE OFFICER [95] 11-11-7 (7*) Mr O McPhail, *al rear, tld off whn pld up bef last.*..........(16 to 1 op 10 to 1)   pu
4046 GOLDEN OPAL [74] 12-10-7 B Powell, *al rear, beh whn pld up and dismounted aftr 8th.*
....(14 to 1 op 10 to 1 tchd 16 to 1)   pu
Dist: 1½l, 6l, 2½l, 13l, 7l, ¾l, dist. 4m 27.20s. a 7.20s (13 Ran).

                                                    (B Scriven), B Scriven

4227 Thornfield Handicap Chase Class E for the Lavington Challenge Cup (0-115 5-y-o and up) £2,943 3¼m 110yds............................(3:00)

4074* RED BRANCH (Ire) [102] 8-11-10 T J Murphy, *chsd ldrs, wnt second 5 out, rdn and led last, styd on wl.*
....(6 to 4 fav op 7 to 4 tchd 2 to 1)   1
3983 DRUMCULLEN (Ire) [100] 8-11-8 W McFarland, *led, hrd rdn and hdd last, no extr r-in.*(11 to 2 op 6 to 1 tchd 13 to 2)   2
3987[2] BANNTOWN BILL (Ire) [97] (v) 8-11-5 C Maude, *pressed ldr to 5 out, hrd rdn and wknd appr 3 out.*
....(4 to 1 op 3 to 1 tchd 5 to 1)   3
4074* KARAR (Ire) [95] 7-11-3 D O'Sullivan, *in tch, mstk second, outpcd 17th.* (11 to 2 op 6 to 1 tchd 7 to 1 and 5 to 1)   4
3950[5] MASTER COMEDY [78] (bl) 13-10-0 B Powell, *in tch till wknd 15th.*....................(11 to 2 op 7 to 1 tchd 16 to 1)   5
4046 TRUST DEED (USA) [84] (bl) 9-10-6 T Dascombe, *hdwy to chase ldrs 5th, cl second whn mstk and uns rdr 17th.*
....(11 to 1 op 7 to 1 tchd 12 to 1)   ur
230[6] FATHER DOWLING [81] (v) 10-10-3 B Fenton, *rear, lost tch 5th, tld off whn pld up bef tenth.*......(14 to 1 op 10 to 1)   pu
3983[3] FROZEN DROP [100] 10-11-8 S Fox, *nvr gng wl, chsd ldrs to 8th, lost tch 15th, pld up bef 4 out.*
....(10 to 1 op 6 to 1 tchd 11 to 1)   pu
Dist: 4l, 17l, 10l, 6l. 6m 33.60s. a 3.60s (8 Ran).

                                                    (E J Mangan), J S King

4228 Strebel Boilers And Radiators Handicap Hurdle Qualifier Class F (0-105 4-y-o and up) £2,048 2¾m 110yds..................................(3:30)

3990[4] ZINGIBAR [81] 5-10-9 B Fenton, *chsd ldrs, led 2 out, styd on wl.*......................(11 to 6 op 6 to 1 tchd 15 to 2)   1
4087[5] BRINDLEY HOUSE [100] 10-11-7 (7*) J Parkhouse, *set gd pace, hdd 2 out, kpt on gmely r-in.* (3 to 1 fav tchd 7 to 2)   2
3457[8] WICKLOW BOY (Ire) [72] 6-10-0 T J Murphy, *prmnt, kpt on same pace frm 3 out.*..............(50 to 1 op 33 to 1)   3
4191[3] STAR PERFORMER (Ire) [97] 6-11-4 (7*) Mr G Shenkin, *mid-div, rdn alng 7th, sn beh.*
....(7 to 2 op 5 to 1 tchd 11 to 2 and 6 to 1)   4
4063* THE FLYING DOCTOR (Ire) [97] 7-11-11 W McFarland, *hld up, in tch whn f 6th.*..................(7 to 2 tchd 4 to 1)   f

4069² APACHE PARK (USA) [88] 4-10-10 D J Burchell, *in tch till f 7th.*
.... (7 to 1 op 5 to 1 tchd 15 to 2) f
4065³ CAMBO (USA) [80] 11-10-8 D Skyrme, *chsd ldrs to 7th, 5th and no ch whn pld up and dismounted 2 out.*
............................(8 to 1 op 7 to 1 tchd 9 to 1) pu
3948³ THE GREY TEXAN [76] 8-10-4⁴ D O'Sullivan, *rear, lost tch 4th, pckd 5th, sn pld up and dismounted..........(10 to 1) pu
Dist: 3½l, 2½l, dist. 5m 17.90s. a 3.90s (8 Ran).

(D Holpin), J M Bradley

4229 Fontwell Park Hunters' Chase Class H (5-y-o and up) £1,203 3¼m 110yds .... (4:00)

MIGHTY FALCON 12-11-0 (7") Miss E Tory, *led 3rd till mstk and hdd tenth, lost pl 13th, rear 15th, plenty to do 4 out, gd hdwy to ld last, sn clr.*
............(9 to 2 op 4 to 1 tchd 11 to 2 and 6 to 1) 1
HEATHVIEW 10-11-7 (7") Mr M Portman, *hdwy 9th, led 12th to 15th, mstk nxt, led appr 3 out to last, sn outpcd.*
............(16 to 1 op 10 to 1 tchd 20 to 1) 2
3777⁴ FORDSTOWN (Ire) 8-11-7 (7") Mr Jamie Alexander, *led to 3rd, mstk and outpcd 16th, styd on frm 2 out.*
............(16 to 1 op 10 to 1 tchd 20 to 1) 3
4085² TRIFAST LAD 12-12-4 (3") Mr P Hacking, *settled towards rear, shaken up and hdwy 14th, effrt and chlgd appr last, wknd r-in.*............(6 to 4 fav tchd 7 to 4 and 2 to 1) 4
4154⁴ TAMMY'S FRIEND (bl) 10-11-0 (7") Mr A Wintle, *keen hold, prmnt, led tenth to 12th, wknd appr last.*
............(15 to 2 op 5 to 1 tchd 8 to 1) 5
4119 MR ORIENTAL 7-11-0 (7") Mr G Gigantesco, *mid-div, jmpd slwly second, rear whn bridle slpd and uns rdr aftr nxt.*
............(66 to 1 op 33 to 1 tchd 100 to 1) ur
4121⁴ AMERICAN EYRE 12-11-0 (7") Miss S Gladders, *al rear, lost tch 15th, pld up bef 4 out.*............(33 to 1 op 14 to 1) pu
4123³ NO INHIBITIONS 10-11-7 (7") Mr A Warr, *chsd ldrs till wknd quickly 4 out, beh whn pld up bef last.* (33 to 1 op 20 to 1) pu
HOWARYADOON 11-11-0 (7") Miss T Cave, *blun 3rd, rear aftr, beh whn pld up bef 3 out..........(14 to 1 op 8 to 1) pu
3327" COLONIAL KELLY 9-12-2 (5") Mr C Vigors, *hdwy to ld 15th, hdd appr 3 out, wknd 2 out, beh whn pld up lme r-in.*
............(5 to 2 tchd 11 to 4 and 9 to 1) pu
Dist: 13l, 3l, nk, 2½l. 6m 44.30s. a 14.30s (10 Ran).

(Miss Emma Tory), Miss Emma Tory

4230 Ted Triggs Memorial Handicap Hurdle Class E (0-110 4-y-o and up) £2,241 2¼m 110yds.......... (4:30)

2616⁴ CHIEFTAIN'S CROWN (USA) [87] 6-10-8 P McLoughlin, *cl up, led 2 out, hrd rdn appr last, styd on wl.*
............(6 to 1 op 9 to 2 tchd 6 to 1) 1
3776 LORD LOVE (Ire) [79] 5-10-0 T J Murphy, *keen hold, set steady pace, quickened 3 out, hdd nxt, kpt on r-in.*
............(9 to 1 op 7 to 1 tchd 10 to 1) 2
4185² CLASSIC PAL (USA) [86] 6-10-1¹ D Skyrme, *hld up rear, plenty to do 3 out, shaken up and ran on wl r-in.*
............(2 to 1 op 4 to 1 tchd 5 to 1 and 9 to 2) 3
3795² JOVIE KING (Ire) [95] 5-11-2 B Powell, *wth ldr, ev ch 3 out, sn outpcd, 3rd and btn whn mstk last.*
............(11 to 10 fav op 6 to 4 tchd 7 to 4) 4
4153⁶ DO BE WARE [79] (bl) 7-10-0 B Fenton, *chsd ldrs, rdn 6th, wknd nxt................(9 to 1 op 10 to 1 tchd 10 to 1) 5
Dist: 1¾l, 3l, nk, 16l. 4m 17.50s. a 0.50s (5 Ran).

(Miss J Rumford), T Hind

HEREFORD (good (races 1,3,4,5,6), good to firm (2))
Monday May 26th
Going Correction: PLUS 0.30 sec. per fur.

4231 Madley Novices' Hurdle Class E (4-y-o and up) £2,514 2m 1f.......(2:30)

4080" SONG OF THE SWORD 4-11-7 M A Fitzgerald, *chsd ldr, led 4th, quickend clr appr last, easily.*
......(11 to 2 on op 9 to 2 on tchd 6 to 1 on and 4 to 1 on) 1
4039 BLOWING ROCK (Ire) 5-11-0 J Culloty, *al prmnt, rdn 3 out, wnt second appr last, no ch whn wnr.*
............(15 to 2 op 8 to 1 tchd 10 to 1 and 7 to 1) 2
3959⁴ FRASER CAREY (Ire) (bl) 5-11-3 (3") Mr R Thornton, *led to 4th, ev ch 3 out, wknd appr last.*
............(6 to 1 op 4 to 1 tchd 13 to 2) 3
4073⁸ SALLOW GLEN 11-11-0 Dr P Pritchard, *beh, ran on appr last, nvr nrr..............(66 to 1 op 33 to 1 tchd 100 to 1) 4
3970 LUDO'S ORCHESTRA (Ire) 6-11-0 M Richards, *al in rear, tld off frm 5th.....................(50 to 1 op 33 to 1) 5
4137 JUST BECAUSE (Ire) 5-11-0 Mr D S Jones, *chsd ldrs, rdn and mstk 5th, f nxt........(100 to 1 op 50 to 1 tchd 150 to 1) f
2953 YONDER STAR 5-11-0 R Greene, *jmpd very slwly and uns rdr second......................(100 to 1 op 50 to 1) ur
ROGER DE MOWBRAY 7-11-0 L Harvey, *beh frm 5th, pld up and dismounted bef 2 out.......(50 to 1 op 33 to 1) pu
AMEER ALFAYAAFI (Ire) 4-10-6 (3") Sophie Mitchell, *hld up, ran out 3rd..............................(50 to 1 op 33 to 1) pu

---

Dist: 3l, 12l, nk, 17l. 3m 56.80s. a 11.80s (9 Ran).
SR: 26/16/10/4/-/-/

(Lady Lloyd Webber), J A B Old

4232 Orcop Selling Handicap Hurdle Class G (0-95 4-y-o and up) £2,038 3 ¼m........................... (3:00)

4101² MARDOOD [65] 12-9-8¹ (7") Miss R Clark, *al prmnt, led 2 out, rdn out........................(10 to 1 op 8 to 1) 1
3988⁹ PROVENCE [65] (v) 10-10-0 M Richards, *chsd ldrs, led 6 out, hdd 2 out, styd on........(12 to 1 op 7 to 1 tchd 14 to 1) 2
4035⁸ BAYLORD PRINCE (Ire) [65] 9-9-11 (3") Sophie Mitchell, *mid-div, hdwy 4 out, rdn 2 out, ran on r-in. (20 to 1 op 14 to 1) 3
2977⁹ KASHAN (Ire) [65] 9-10-0 I Lawrence, *chsd ldrs, outpcd 3 out, rallied appr last, ran on..............(10 to 1 op 8 to 1) 4
3801³ SONG FOR JESS (Ire) [72] 4-10-0³ (3") L Aspell, *hld up, hdwy 5 out, ev ch 3 out, one pace whn mstk last.*
............(10 to 1 op 8 to 1 tchd 12 to 1) 5
4053¹ TIGER CLAW (USA) [75] 11-10-10 R Greene, *sn beh and pushed alng, nvr nr ldrs................(5 to 1 op 4 to 1) 6
3801" AWESTRUCK [65] (bl) 7-9-7 (7") J Mogford, *nvr nr to chal.
....(6 to 1) 7
417 JENNYELLEN (Ire) [93] 8-12-0 M A Fitzgerald, *hld up, hdwy 5 out, mstk 2 out, sn wknd........(8 to 1 tchd 10 to 1) 8
3958⁴ PANDORA'S PRIZE [65] 11-10-0 J Culloty, *led to 3rd, led 7th to nxt, wknd 4 out.............(16 to 1 op 12 to 1) 9
4194² UP THE TEMPO (Ire) [65] 8-9-9 (5") O Burrows, *beh frm hfwy.
...................................(12 to 1 op 10 to 1) 10
3988³ KHAZARI (USA) [68] 9-10-3 L Harvey, *prmnt to 7th, pld up bef 4 out........................(7 to 1 op 5 to 1) pu
4088⁵ ARRANGE A GAME [65] 10-9-8¹ (7") M Handley, *beh frm 5th, tld off and pld up bef 5 out..........(16 to 1 op 12 to 1) pu
3725 KANO WARRIOR [67] (bl) 10-10-2 V Slattery, *chsd ldrs, led 5th to 7th, sn rdn and lost pl, pld up bef 5 out.*
...................................(20 to 1 op 14 to 1) pu
3951⁷ DERRYBELLE [73] 6-10-1 (7") Mr S Durack, *al in rear, pld up bef 4 out.......................(20 to 1 op 14 to 1) pu
3883³ SQUEALING JEANIE [65] 8-10-0 K Gaule, *mid-div, rdn 6 out, beh whn pld up bef 3 out.........(9 to 1 op 11 to 2) pu
4081² LOOK IN THE MIRROR [75] 6-10-5 C Llewellyn, *led 3rd to 5th, wknd 4 out, pld up bef nxt.........(3 to 1 fav op 5 to 1) pu
Dist: 1¾l, ½l, 2l, 2½l, 8l, sht-hd, 4l, 14l, 10l. 6m 19.30s. a 17.30s (16 Ran).

(S B Clark), S B Clark

4233 Craswell Novices' Chase Class E (5-y-o and up) £2,905 2m 3f......(3:30)

3591⁴ CHAN THE MAN 6-10-11 (3") Guy Lewis, *chsd ldr, led 9th, clr 2 out, cmftbly...........(11 to 2 op 8 to 1 tchd 5 to 1) 1
WESSHAUN 7-10-6 (3") L Aspell, *led, hdd and hit 9th, wknd 2 out, lft second appr last.*
............(12 to 1 op 10 to 1 tchd 14 to 1) 2
4174⁷ RUN WITH JOY (Ire) 6-11-0 R Greene, *chsd ldrs til wknd 3 out, lft 3rd appr last............(3 to 1 op 11 to 4 tchd 10 to 3) 3
3912 DIAMOND LIGHT 10-11-0 M Richards, *sn wl beh, tld off and pld up bef 7th..................................(6 to 1 op 7 to 1) pu
3737⁵ SORCIERE 6-11-1 B Clifford, *hld up, hdwy 4 out, chsd wnr but held whn broke leg and pld up bef last, dead.*
............(11 to 10 on op 5 to 4 on tchd Evens) pu
Dist: 22l, 1¾l. 4m 45.70s. a 20.70s (5 Ran).

(Mrs Sandra Worthington), D Burchell

4234 Michaelchurch Handicap Hurdle Class D (0-120 4-y-o and up) £2,864 2m 3f 110yds................(4:00)

4141³ KINNESCASH (Ire) [110] 4-11-6 M A Fitzgerald, *chsd ldr, mstk second, hit 5 out, cl up whn lft in clr ld 3 out.*
..(11 to 10 on op 5 to 4 on tchd 6 to 4 on Evens and 5 to 4 on) 1
3886⁹ EUROLINK THE REBEL (USA) [92] 5-10-0 (7") Miss R Clark, *chsd ldrs, rcd keenly, mstk 6th, wknd appr 3 out.*
......................................(10 to 1 op 7 to 1) 2
POLISH RIDER (USA) [86] 9-10-1 C Llewellyn, *hld up, rdn and wknd appr 3 out.........(11 to 2 op 5 to 1 tchd 7 to 1) 3
4017³ SEVERN GALE [100] 7-10-12 (3") Mr R Thornton, *led, mstk 6th, f 3 out...................(13 to 8 op 6 to 4 tchd 9 to 4) f
Dist: 12l, 7l. 4m 41.40s. a 23.40s (4 Ran).

(D R James), P Bowen

4235 Clive Maiden Hunters' Chase Class H (5-y-o and up) £1,160 3m 1f 110yds........................ (4:35)

4118² NO JOKER (Ire) 9-11-10 (7") Mr P Scott, *beh, hdwy 4 out, led last, styd on wl.......(7 to 2 fav tchd 4 to 1 and 9 to 4) 1
ANJUBI 12-11-10 (7") Mr S Mulcaire, *chsd ldrs, led 9th to 11th, led 6 out to 4 out, led appr last, sn hdd and no extr.
............(8 to 1 op 5 to 1 tchd 9 to 1) 2
4033 ANN'S AMBITION 10-11-10 (7") Mr M Frith, *al prmnt, led 4 out, hdd and no extr appr last........(25 to 1 op 14 to 1) 3
4124² THE RUM MARINER 10-11-10 (7") Mr D S Jones, *led 3rd to 9th, led 11th to 6 out, wknd 4 out......(13 to 2 op 5 to 1) 4
4120³ TEATRADER 11-11-10 (7") Mr S Durack, *led to 3rd, wknd 4 out................................(11 to 4 op 7 to 1) 5
3940⁶ INDIAN KNIGHT 12-11-10 (7") Mr E James, *in rear whn blun and uns rdr 6 out......(20 to 1 op 16 to 1 tchd 25 to 1) ur

ANDALUCIAN SUN (Ire) 9-11-10 (7*) Mr P G Moloney, *sn wl beh, sddl slpd, tried to refuse and uns rdr 5th.
.... (15 to 2 op 6 to 1 tchd 8 to 1) ur
MAJESTIC RIDE 13-11-10 (7*) Mr R Armson, *prmnt to 9th, beh whn pld up bef 3 out*..............(50 to 1 op 33 to 1) pu
3982² LINK COPPER 8-12-0 (3*) Mr R Treloggen, *hit 1st, beh frm 5th, pld up bef 6 out.*
.......(5 to 1 op 11 to 2 tchd 6 to 1 and 13 to 2) pu
CORN EXCHANGE 9-12-0 (3*) Mr M Rimell, *prmnt till wknd 5 out, blun badly 3 out, pld up bef nxt.*
.... (11 to 2 op 4 to 1 tchd 6 to 1) pu
PRIME COURSE (Ire) 8-11-10 (7*) Mr P Bull, *mstk 3rd, beh frm 9th, pld up bef 6 out*...............(33 to 1 tchd 40 to 1) pu
SALMON POUTCHER 8-11-7 (5*) Mr J Trice-Rolph, *beh frm 7th, pld up aftr tenth*................(33 to 1 op 16 to 1) pu
WATCHIT LAD 7-11-12 (7*) Mr M P Jones, *in rear whn hit 8th, tld off and pld up bef 2 out*......(50 to 1 op 33 to 1) pu
3855⁶ LURRIGA GLITTER (Ire) (bl) 9-11-12 (5*) Mr R Ford, *sn wl beh, pld up bef 4 out*............(7 to 1 op 6 to 1 tchd 8 to 1) pu
Dist: 3l, 4l, 22l, 26l. 6m 27.30s. a 21.30s (14 Ran).
(Brigadier R W S Hall), N A Gaselee

4236 **Carey Novices' Handicap Hurdle Class E (0-100 4-y-o and up) £2,472 2m 3f 110yds................. (5:05)**

3915* MAGICAL BLUES (Ire) [90] 5-11-10 K Gaule, *hld up, hdwy 4 out, led last, rdn out.*..........................(4 to 1 co-fav tchd 9 to 2 and 5 to 1) 1
3990⁸ COLWALL [77] 6-10-11 M A Fitzgerald, *hld up, hdwy 4 out, led 2 out, hdd last, unbl to quicken r-in*...(12 to 1 op 8 to 1) 2
4069⁷ IRISH DOMINION [66] 7-9-9 (5*) O Burrows, *hld up in tch, led appr 3 out, hdd nxt, sn btn.*
.............(14 to 1 op 16 to 1 tchd 20 to 1 and 25 to 1) 3
4015³ SIOUX TO SPEAK [85] 5-11-5 J Culloty, *prmnt, chsd ldr 5 out, wknd 3 out*.............(4 to 1 co-fav tchd 7 to 2 and 9 to 2) 4
4131² CALLERMINE [73] 8-10-4 (3*) Sophie Mitchell, *chsd ldr to 5 out, wknd appr 3 out*.......(5 to 1 op 9 to 2 tchd 11 to 2) 5
4063² STERLING FELLOW [85] (v) 4-10-7 (7*) Mr S Durack, *al beh.*
....................(5 to 1 op 9 to 2 tchd 11 to 2) 6
4183² LYPHARD'S FABLE (USA) [66] 6-10-0 M Richards, *mid-div whn f 5th.*...............(4 to 1 co-fav op 3 to 1) f
4083⁹ SOBER ISLAND [66] 8-9-13² (3*) Guy Lewis, *prmnt to 5 out, pld up bef 3 out*......(40 to 1 op 33 to 1 tchd 50 to 1) pu
3956³ FLASH CHICK (Ire) [66] 8-9-7 (7*) J Mogford, *al in rear, tld off whn pld up bef 3 out.*...........(25 to 1 op 16 to 1) pu
187⁴ LITTLE COURT [66] 6-10-0 V Slattery, *beh frm 5th, tld off and pld up bef 3 out.*............(14 to 1 op 7 to 1) pu
3979³ ADMIRAL BRUNY [75] 6-10-9 C Llewellyn, *led till hdd and wknd appr 3 out, pld up bef nxt.*
..............(7 to 1 op 6 to 1 tchd 8 to 1 and 9 to 1) pu
Dist: 2l, 10l, 14l, ½l, 6l. 4m 36.20s. a 13.20s (11 Ran).
(Miss A Embiricos), Miss A E Embiricos

HUNTINGDON (good to firm)
Monday May 26th
Going Correction: MINUS 0.55 sec. per fur.

4237 **Willmott Dixon Conditional Jockeys' Selling Handicap Hurdle Class G (0-95 4-y-o and up) £1,880 2m 110yds...................... (2:00)**

4153⁶ AJDAR [72] 6-10-5 R Massey, *chsd ldrs, chlgd 3 out, led appr nxt, hit last, drvn out.*...............(9 to 2 jt-fav op 3 to 1) 1
MAJOR'S LAW [84] 8-11-3 X Aizpuru, *hld up beh, hdwy 5th, led 3 out to appr nxt, hrd rdn and rallied r-in, jst held.*
.... (12 to 1 op 5 to 1 tchd 14 to 1) 2
4083⁸ TEE TEE TOO (Ire) [67] 5-9-9 (5*) R Studholme, *hld up in mid-div, cld aftr 5th, hrd rdn after 3 out, kpt on same pace und pres.*...............(11 to 1 op 7 to 1 tchd 12 to 1) 3
3780⁸ MAGGIES LAD [80] 9-10-13 P Henley, *cl up till rdn and outpcd aftr 3 out.* (12 to 1 op 7 to 1 tchd 12 to 1 and 14 to 1) 4
4063³ SUMMER VILLA [76] (bl) 5-10-6 (3*) J Power, *keen hold early, in tch, led 3 out to appr nxt, wknd.*
.....................(6 to 1 op 4 to 1 tchd 8 to 1) 5
2417⁹ ANGUS MCCOATUP (Ire) [85] 4-10-13 F Leahy, *hld up, cld aftr 5th, hrd rdn after 3 out, no imprsn.*
...........................(6 to 1 op 7 to 1 tchd 8 to 1) 6
3973⁴ CADDY'S FIRST [76] (v) 5-10-6 (3*) Chris Webb, *cl up, led briefly aftr 5th till 3 out, sn wknd*......(7 to 1 tchd 8 to 1) 7
4038⁵ CIRCUS COLOURS [95] 7-11-4 (10*) D Yellowlees, *beh, hrd rdn appr 3 out, no response.*..................(9 to 2 jt-fav op 4 to 1 tchd 5 to 1 and 11 to 2) 8
3798 KALZARI (USA) [79] 12-10-12 J Magee, *hld up in tch, pushed alng aftr 3 out, sn btn.*.....(7 to 1 tchd 8 to 1 and 9 to 1) 9
3959⁶ SWAHILI RUN [68] (v) 9-9-12 (3*) M Griffiths, *led, sn clr, hit 5th, rdn and hdd, pld up bef 2 out.*...(20 to 1 op 12 to 1) pu
Dist: Hd, 4l, 2l, 1¾l, 2½l, 5l, 4l, 16l. 3m 39.30s. b 1.70s (10 Ran).
SR: 4/16/-/6/-/-/ (Mrs Sue Catt), O Brennan

4238 **Swynford Paddocks Hotel Handicap Chase Class E (0-115 5-y-o and up) £3,137 2m 110yds........... (2:30)**

3976* CRACKLING FROST (Ire) [83] 9-10-9 R Dunwoody, *chsd ldg pair, chased wnr frm 4 out, sn niggled alng to cl, ev ch whn lft clr last.*.....................(5 to 4 fav op 9 to 4) 1
3668* DR ROCKET [82] (v) 12-10-3 (5*) X Aizpuru, *hld up in tch, outpcd 7th, styd on und pres frm last, no ch wth wnr.*
....................................(6 to 1 op 5 to 1) 2
3824⁶ ALLIMAC NOMIS [88] 8-11-0 R Garritty, *hld up in tch, outpcd 7th, no imprsn frm 2 out, fnshd lme, destroyed.*
.............(11 to 2 op 6 to 1 tchd 5 to 1 and 8 to 1) 3
COME ON DANCER (Ire) [83] 9-10-9 J R Kavanagh, *outpcd.*
...............................(25 to 1 op 12 to 1) 4
4064² MY YOUNG MAN [100] 12-11-12 G Bradley, *chsd ldr to 4 out, sn btn, tld off.*..................(6 to 1 op 4 to 1) 5
4129* POND HOUSE (Ire) [102] 8-12-0 J F Titley, *led, set gd pace, not fluent 4th, narrow advantage whn f last.*
....(3 to 1 op 9 to 4) f
4089² LOWAWATHA [93] 9-11-5 D Gallagher, *sn struggling in rear, tld off whn pld up bef 8th*...........(12 to 1 op 8 to 1) pu
Dist: 12l, 6l, 9l, 1¾l. 3m 59.10s. a 5.10s (7 Ran).
(The Unlucky For Some Partnership), Mrs D Haine

4239 **Qualitair Group Handicap Hurdle Class D (0-120 4-y-o and up) £2,924 2m 5f 110yds................. (3:05)**

4071* DIWALI DANCER [119] 7-11-13 R Dunwoody, *made all, shaken up aftr 3 out, rdn out.*
.............(11 to 10 on op 5 to 4 on tchd Evens) 1
3951² SCUD MISSILE (Ire) [97] 6-10-5 A Thornton, *hld up in tch, hdwy to chase wnr frm 3 out, hrd rdn and no extr r-in.*
.............(7 to 2 op 4 to 1 tchd 5 to 1 and 3 to 1) 2
1834 ROYAL CITIZEN (Ire) [92] 8-10-0 Derek Byrne, *hld up in last pl, steady hdwy appr 3 out, gng nicely, no imprsn frm nxt.*
.................(16 to 1 op 6 to 1 tchd 20 to 1) 3
4110* LINLATHEN [116] 7-11-10 P Niven, *chsd wnr till wknd 3 out, sn btn.*.....................(5 to 2 op 7 to 4) 4
3820 MOOBAKKR (USA) [92] 6-9-9 (5*) X Aizpuru, *chsd ldg pair till lost pl appr 6th, no dngr aftr.*
................(8 to 1 op 5 to 1 tchd 10 to 1) 5
Dist: 2l, 8l, 2l, 8l. 4m 51.50s. a 2.50s (5 Ran).
(B E Case), M C Pipe

4240 **Airfoyle Novices' Handicap Chase Class E (0-100 5-y-o and up) £3,068 3m....................... (3:35)**

4091* MISTER GOODGUY (Ire) [76] 8-10-8 D Morris, *trkd ldrs, mstk 13th, led 2 out, drvn out*...(5 to 2 op 2 to 1 tchd 3 to 1) 1
3118³ COLONEL COLT [68] 6-9-9 C Webb, *hld up, steady hdwy frm 14th, led 3 out to nxt, no extr r-in.*
................(16 to 1 op 12 to 1 tchd 20 to 1) 2
4138³ PROFESSOR PAGE (Ire) [68] 7-10-0 A Thornton, *trkd ldrs, chlgd 4 out, ev ch nxt, one pace appr 2 out.*
..............................(12 to 1 op 8 to 1) 3
3845⁵ MOZEMO [68] 10-9-11 (3*) R Massey, *hld up beh, steady hdwy frm 13th, cld aftr 3 out, sn one pace und pres.*
.............(10 to 1 op 6 to 1 tchd 12 to 1) 4
3855 SAINT BENE'T (Ire) [68] (bl) 9-9-9 (5*) X Aizpuru, *trkd ldrs, kpt on same pace frm 5 out.*
............(9 to 2 op 6 to 1 tchd 7 to 1 tchd 8 to 1) 5
4070* MALWOOD CASTLE (Ire) [96] 7-11-7 (7*) Mr J Tizzard, *hld up, not fluent 12th and sn drvn alng, no dngr aftr, tld off.*
...................(2 to 1 fav tchd 9 to 4) 6
3967 DAMCADA (Ire) [68] (bl) 9-10-0 D Gallagher, *led, hit 11th, not fluent and hdd 3 out, sn btn, tld off.*
..............(25 to 1 op 16 to 1 tchd 33 to 1) 7
3934 COTSWOLD CASTLE [68] (v) 11-9-7 (7*) M Griffiths, *not fluent, hld up, beh fnl circuit, pld up bef 3 out.*
...............................(33 to 1 op 20 to 1) pu
3914³ JUST ONE CANALETTO [75] (bl) 9-10-0 (7*) Mr J Goldstein, *hld up, cld 7th, lost pl 12th, tld off whn pld up bef 2 out, dismounted.*....................(8 to 1 op 4 to 1) pu
3918⁴ MORE JOY [68] 9-10-0 J R Kavanagh, *al beh, pld up bef 3 out.*
...............(25 to 1 op 20 to 1 tchd 33 to 1) pu
Dist: 3l, 2½l, 2l, 1½l, dist, 8l. 5m 58.20s. a 18.20s (10 Ran).
(M O'Brien), R Curtis

4241 **Edward Wootton Novices' Chase Class E (5-y-o and up) £2,977 2½m 110yds..................... (4:05)**

3822⁴ MISTER DRUM 8-12-7 R Dunwoody, *trkd ldr, led 8th, lft clr nxt, made rst, eased to walk r-in.*
.............(5 to 2 on op 7 to 2 on tchd 9 to 4 on) 1
3960* SIGMA RUN (Ire) 8-12-0 J R Kavanagh, *hld up, lft modest second at 9th, no ch wth wnr*........(3 to 1 op 7 to 2) 2
BUGSY MORAN (Ire) 7-11-0 G Bradley, *lft modest 3rd at 9th, blun badly 11th (water), tld off.*
.............(8 to 1 op 12 to 1 tchd 7 to 1) 3
4070⁷ CHIAPPUCCI (Ire) (bl) 7-11-0 D Gallagher, *led, hdd 8th, cl up whn f nxt.*...........(33 to 1 tchd 25 to 1) f
3970 METHODIUS (Ire) 5-10-7 D Morris, *al last, not fluent 1st 2, blun and uns rdr 8th*.............(33 to 1 tchd 25 to 1) ur
Dist: dist, dist. 5m 2.10s. a 15.10s (5 Ran).
(Malcolm Batchelor), M J Wilkinson

4242 Huntingdonshire Mencap Support Association Maiden Hurdle Class E (4-y-o and up) £2,687 2m 110yds
.... (4:35)

	FLIC ROYAL (Fr) 4-10-9 (5*) Chris Webb, hld up, hdwy 4 out, led 2 out, edgd lft r-in, kpt on wl..... (6 to 1 tchd 10 to 1)	1
3900²	COUNTRY ORCHID 6-11-0 P Niven, trkd ldrs, led briefly appr 2 out, ev ch last, no ex r-in...... (11 to 8 fav op 9 to 4)	2
3157⁵	QUALITAIR PRIDE 5-11-0 Derek Byrne, led till hdd appr 2 out, one pace.......................... (20 to 1 tchd 25 to 1)	3
4130³	BLASTER WATSON 6-11-5 M Ranger, trkd ldrs, one pace frm 3 out, btn whn not fluent last........ (12 to 1 op 10 to 1)	4
4092	NASHAAT (USA) 9-11-5 J F Titley, hld up, hdwy aftr 4 out, no imprsn appr 2 out.......(10 to 1 op 8 to 1 tchd 12 to 1)	5
	DUBLIN RIVER (USA) 4-11-0 J R Kavanagh, hld up, effrt 4 out, pushed alng whn nxt, sn btn, tld off. (5 to 1 tchd 9 to 1)	6
4158⁵	HARVEST REAPER 5-11-2 (3*) R Massey, trkd ldrs till wknd appr 5th, tld off........ (33 to 1 op 20 to 1 tchd 40 to 1)	7
3892	NOQUITA (NZ) (bl) 10-11-0 (5*) X Aizpuru, nvr on terms, tld off. ....(33 to 1 tchd 40 to 1)	8
9936⁴	ELLEN GAIL 5-11-0 A Thornton, ...(25 to 1 op 33 to 1)	9
	ALICIA LEA (Ire) 5-11-0 D Morris, al beh, tld off. ....(25 to 1 op 12 to 1)	10
2483⁷	TEDROSS 6-11-2 (3*) J Magee, hld up beh ldrs, wknd aftr 4th, tld off.................(33 to 1 tchd 40 to 1)	11
4030²	TARRAGON (Ire) 7-11-5 R Dunwoody, pld hrd beh ldrs, drpd out quickly 4th, tld off whn pulled up bef 3 out. ....(3 to 1 op 6 to 4 tchd 7 to 1)	pu

Dist: 1¼l, 11l, ½l, 7l, 20l, 4l, 8l, 2½l, 12l, 22l. 3m 38.40s. b 2.60s (12 Ran).
SR: 22/20/9/13/6/–/ (Ken Jaffa, John Lewis & David Shalson), S Mellor

KILBEGGAN (IRE) (good)
Monday May 26th

4243 Horse Leap Maiden Hurdle (5-y-o and up) £2,226 2m 3f........ (6:00)

3954⁷	PERMIT ME (Ire) 5-11-0 C F Swan, ...(9 to 2 jt-fav)	1
3963	FANORE (Ire) 6-10-13 (7*) D A McLoughlin, ...(20 to 1)	2
4076⁵	CROHANE PRINCESS (Ire) 8-11-1 S H O'Donovan, (14 to 1)	3
3953⁵	CASEY JUNIOR (Ire) (bl) 9-11-7 (7*) Mr Paul Moloney, ...(9 to 2 jt-fav)	4
3935	SALLY SUPREME (Ire) 6-10-8 (7*) S FitzGerald, ...(20 to 1)	5
4152²	SERIOUS NOTE (Ire) 9-10-8 (7*) Mr R P McNalley, ..(5 to 1)	6
4076⁶	EXPERT ADVICE (Ire) 6-11-6 J R Barry, ...(16 to 1)	7
	BOLD BREW (Ire) 9-11-6 J Short, ...(11 to 2)	8
4004	BEHY BRIDGE 5-11-0 T J Mitchell, ...(10 to 1)	9
4094⁸	WILLIE THE LION (Ire) 6-11-6 T P Treacy, ...(12 to 1)	10
4149	STORM COURSE 5-10-7 (7*) D K Budds, ...(14 to 1)	11
2378	HARRY HEANEY (Ire) 8-11-6 (7*) S Martin, ...(10 to 1)	12
4077	MY BLUE 5-10-7 (7*) E F Cahalan, ...(12 to 1)	f
4052	DAWN TO DUSK (Ire) 6-10-13 (7*) D McCullagh, ..(25 to 1)	su
	MOSS HEATH 12-11-1 D T Evans, ...(33 to 1)	pu
4059	JARSUN QUEEN (Ire) (bl) 5-10-7 (7*) L J Fleming, (16 to 1)	pu
	MARINO ROSE (Ire) 6-10-10 (5*) M D Murphy, ...(33 to 1)	pu
4148	BARORA GALE (Ire) 6-11-1 C O'Dwyer, ...(33 to 1)	pu

Dist: 4l, 9l, 20l, 2l. 4m 30.70s. (18 Ran).
(Patrick Lacey), Patrick Lacey

4244 Leinster/Petroleum Maiden Hurdle (5-y-o and up) £2,740 3m..... (6:30)

3880⁴	SWIFT PICK (Ire) 5-10-12 (7*) B J Geraghty, ...(8 to 1)	1
4144	CHANGE THE SCRIPT (Ire) 7-10-13 (7*) M W Martin, ...(20 to 1)	2
849	DREAM ETERNAL (Ire) 6-11-1 W Slattery, ...(16 to 1)	3
4160⁴	TOTAL SUCCESS (Ire) 5-11-5 T P Treacy, ...(10 to 9 on)	4
4144	LORD PENNY (Ire) 5-11-5 D H O'Connor, ...(25 to 1)	5
683	COLONIA SKY (Ire) 6-10-8 (7*) V T Keane, ...(25 to 1)	6
	DANTES WHISTLE (Ire) 6-11-1 D J Casey, ...(14 to 1)	7
3343	ROISIN BEAG (Ire) 6-10-10 (5*) M D Murphy, ...(33 to 1)	8
4104³	STILLYHERSELF (Ire) 7-11-6 (3*) G Cotter, ...(8 to 1)	9
720⁹	BLACK BOREEN (Ire) 7-12-0 P L Malone, ...(6 to 1)	10
4162	FOREST STAR (USA) 8-11-7 (7*) D W O'Sullivan, ...(25 to 1)	11
183⁵	GILLY'S HOPE (Ire) 6-11-3 (3*) K Whelan, ...(16 to 1)	12
3963⁷	CHARMING DUKE (Ire) 7-11-6 K F O'Brien, ...(20 to 1)	13
4144⁸	MINELLA LASS (Ire) 6-11-1 J Short, ...(12 to 1)	14
4148	KILLCHRIS DREAM (Ire) 6-10-8 (7*) D A McLoughlin, ...(33 to 1)	pu
4160	SOUNDWOMEN (Ire) 5-10-7 (7*) L J Fleming, ...(33 to 1)	pu
4149⁶	CLOGHRAN NATIVE (Ire) 5-11-0 C O'Dwyer, ...(20 to 1)	pu

Dist: Hd, 2l, hd, 8l. 5m 59.40s. (17 Ran).
(M J Halligan), Noel Meade

4245 Keenan Bros. Handicap Hurdle (0-116 4-y-o and up) £2,911 2m 3f
.... (7:00)

4027	LEGITMAN (Ire) [-] 7-9-10 D J Casey, ...(9 to 1)	1
3935²	THE BOULD VIC (Ire) [-] 5-10-13 (7*) B J Geraghty, ...(7 to 2 co-fav)	2
4054	I REMEMBER IT WELL (Ire) [-] (bl) 5-11-2 (5*) P G Hourigan, ...(7 to 2 co-fav)	3

3625	PERPETUAL PROSPECT (Ire) [-] 5-9-10 (7*) Mr Paul Moloney, ...(8 to 1)	4
4150²	GO SASHA (Ire) [-] 4-11-5 (7*) T Martin, ...(11 to 2)	5
4004⁸	BE MY FOLLY (Ire) [-] 5-10-3 T J O'Sullivan, ...(11 to 1)	6
4117*	HEART 'N SOUL-ON (Ire) [-] 6-10-3 C F Swan, ...(7 to 1)	7
4149	DISPOSEN (Ire) [-] 4-9-0 (7*) J M Maguire, ...(25 to 1)	8
	DUHARRA (Ire) [-] 9-11-13 P L Malone, ...(20 to 1)	9
3376*	JENSALEE (Ire) [-] 6-11-6 T P Treacy, ...(7 to 2 co-fav)	10

Dist: ½l, 1½l, 13l, nk. 4m 29.30s. (10 Ran).
(E Kavanagh), E Bolger

4246 Dawn Dairies Beginners Chase (4-y-o and up) £2,911 2m 5f.....(7:30)

354	TISRARA LADY (Ire) 7-11-9 S H O'Donovan, ...(10 to 1)	1
4146⁶	DAWN ALERT (Ire) 8-11-7 (7*) B J Geraghty, ...(7 to 4 fav)	2
4093²	IRISH PEACE (Ire) 9-11-11 (3*) G Cotter, ...(5 to 1)	3
4053²	ECLIPTIC MOON (Ire) 7-12-0 T P Treacy, ...(5 to 2)	4
4093	AISEIRI 10-11-7 (7*) V T Keane, ...(14 to 1)	5
3942⁶	THE PARSON'S FILLY (Ire) 7-11-6 (3*) G Kilfeather, (12 to 1)	6
3877	LET BUNNY RUN (Ire) 7-12-0 W Slattery, ...(10 to 1)	7
2673	CASTLELAKE LADY (Ire) 8-11-9 L P Cusack, ...(33 to 1)	8
3838	CORMAC LADY (Ire) 6-11-9 J K Kinane, ...(33 to 1)	9
4053⁶	SHANRUE (Ire) 7-12-0 M Moran, ...(12 to 1)	10
4152⁸	LA MANCHA BOY (Ire) 7-11-7 (7*) Mr J O McGurgan, ...(50 to 1)	11
4165⁹	MIROSWAKI (USA) 7-12-0 T J Mitchell, ...(12 to 1)	f
	OAKMONT (Ire) 4-10-4 (5*) M D Murphy, ...(12 to 1)	f
	CAPTAIN'S VIEW (Ire) (bl) 5-12-0 D J Casey, ...(50 to 1)	ur
4116	BALLY UPPER (Ire) 9-12-0 K F O'Brien, ...(33 to 1)	pu
3954	RIVER RUMPUS (Ire) 5-11-7 C O'Dwyer, ...(25 to 1)	pu

Dist: 2l, 7l, 9l, 11l. 5m 20.90s. (16 Ran).
(Thomas Kelly), Thomas Foley

4247 E.B.F. Usher Challenge Cup Handicap Chase (0-116 4-y-o and up) £2,911 3m 1f................. (8:00)

4003*	TRIPTODICKS (Ire) [-] 7-10-8 C F Swan, ...(6 to 4 fav)	1
4004⁴	PHARALLEY (Ire) [-] 7-9-7 D J Casey, ...(25 to 1)	2
4003	LITTLE-K (Ire) [-] 7-10-7 (3*) K Whelan, ...(20 to 1)	3
4093³	TEAL BRIDGE [-] 12-12-0 T J Mitchell, ...(11 to 4)	4
4151³	MR FIVE WOOD (Ire) [-] 9-11-0 D T Evans, ...(13 to 2)	5
4103⁶	CARAGH BRIDGE [-] 10-10-12 C O'Dwyer, ...(12 to 1)	6
4053	HERSILIA (Ire) [-] 6-11-3 F J Flood, ...(6 to 1)	7
4151²	BROWNRATH KING (Ire) [-] 8-9-11¹ T P Treacy, ...(7 to 2)	f
4115³	FUNNY YE KNOW (Ire) [-] 8-9-4 (3*) G Cotter, ...(25 to 1)	ur
	FURRY STAR [-] 11-11-6 Mr B M Cash, ...(20 to 1)	pu
1841	SWINGER (Ire) [-] 8-9-3 (7*) B J Geraghty, ...(16 to 1)	pu

Dist: 6l, 25l, nk, dist. 6m 21.50s. (11 Ran).
(M G O'Huallachain), David A Kiely

4248 Mullingar Hunters Chase (5-y-o and up) £2,226 3m 1f............. (8:30)

3770*	DIXON VARNER (Ire) 7-12-2 Mr R Walsh, ...(9 to 4 on)	1
4061²	PRAYON PARSON (Ire) 9-10-13 (7*) Mr D P Daly, ..(10 to 1)	2
	KNOW SOMETHING VI (Ire) 7-10-13 (7*) Mr Damien Murphy, ...(10 to 1)	3
3935	BEST INTEREST (Ire) 9-11-8 (3*) Mr B R Hamilton, (10 to 1)	4
	NO OTHER HILL (Ire) 5-10-13 Mr B M Cash, ...(20 to 1)	5
	MULLINELLO (Ire) 8-10-13 (7*) Mr A Fleming, ...(20 to 1)	6
3748	POLLS GALE 10-10-8 (7*) Mr P A Farrell, ...(12 to 1)	7
	SPARKLING ROSIE (Ire) 7-10-8 (7*) Mr M O'Connor, ...(10 to 1)	8
4061³	ROSETOWN GIRL (Ire) 6-10-8 (7*) Mr L J Temple, (10 to 1)	ur
3784³	FIND OUT MORE (Ire) 9-11-4 (7*) Mr B Potts, ...(12 to 1)	pu
3770	LOTTOVER (Ire) 8-10-8 (7*) Mr B Hassett, ...(10 to 1)	pu
4061	LOOKING AHEAD (Ire) 9-10-10 (5*) Mr J T McNamara, ...(25 to 1)	pu
4115*	SIDEWAYS SALLY (Ire) 7-10-13 (7*) Mr R P McNalley, ...(7 to 1)	pu
	MICRO VILLA (Ire) 5-10-1 (7*) Mr Paul Moloney, ..(16 to 1)	pu
	IRREGULAR PLANTING (Ire) 6-10-13 (7*) Mr G R Kenny, ...(20 to 1)	pu

Dist: 6l, 15l, 4½l. 6m 22.50s. (15 Ran).
(Mrs John Magnier), E Bolger

4249 Loughnagore I.N.H. Flat Race (5-y-o and up) £2,226 2½m.........(9:00)

4096²	CHOICE JENNY (Ire) 5-11-3 (5*) Mr A C Coyle, (6 to 4 fav)	1
4062	ROCK ON GIRL (Ire) 5-11-2 (7*) Mr A FitzGerald, ..(25 to 1)	2
4029⁸	AUDACIOUS DANCER (Ire) 5-11-13 Mr R Walsh, ...(14 to 1)	3
4029³	ONE FOR NAVIGATION (Ire) 5-11-13² Mr E Bolger, ..(7 to 2)	4
3880⁸	KILLALOONTY ROSE (Ire) 6-11-2 (7*) Mr D A Harney, ...(20 to 1)	5
4062⁶	PRIZE OF PEACE (Ire) 7-11-2 (7*) Mr M T Hartrey, (12 to 1)	6
4106³	JOSH'S FANCY (Ire) 6-11-2 (7*) Mr A J Dempsey, ..(5 to 1)	7
4006	WHAT A BARGAIN (Ire) 5-11-1 (7*) Mr A G Cash, ..(33 to 1)	8
	LARA'S BOY (Ire) 6-11-7 (7*) Mr D P Coakley, ...(16 to 1)	9
4200⁹	WAKEUP LITTLESUSIE 10-11-9 Mr M Phillips, ...(50 to 1)	10
	BLUE CASTLE (Ire) 5-11-8 (5*) Mr G Elliott, ...(25 to 1)	11
	BOSCO'S TOUCH (Ire) 6-11-7 Mr J A Collins, ...(12 to 1)	12
4062⁴	CARBON WOOD (Ire) 7-12-0 Mr B M Cash, ...(11 to 2)	13
4006	PRINCE OF ROSSIAN (Ire) 5-11-13 Mr J A Nash, ..(20 to 1)	14
	DICK AND DECLAN (Ire) 5-11-6 (7*) Mr N Nevin, ..(25 to 1)	15

4198 MSADI MHULU (Ire) (bl) 6-11-2 (7*) Mr P Fahey, . . . (25 to 1) 16
3231 ROSE'S PERK (Ire) 5-11-8 Mr P Fenton, ...(20 to 1) ref
Dist: ½l, 3l, 3l, 1½l. 4m 45.50s. (17 Ran).
(Mrs K Byrne), P Mullins

UTTOXETER (good to firm (races 1,2,3,4), good (5,6)) Monday May 26th

Going Correction: PLUS 0.05 sec. per fur.

4250 Mobilefone Group Maiden Chase Class E (5-y-o and up) £2,914 2m 7f . . . . (2:30)

3679 GLAMANGLITZ 7-11-2 A P McCoy, *made all, quickened clr fnl circuit, jmpd lft 4 out, unchlgd.* . . . .(2 to 1 fav op 5 to 2 tchd 7 to 4) 1
4014[3] LITTLE GAINS 8-11-2 J Railton, *settled wth chasing grp, styd on grimly frm 4 out, no imprsn on wnr.* (9 to 2 tchd 5 to 1) 2
2748 DARA'S COURSE (Ire) 8-10-11 S Burrough, *slwly into strd, given time to reco'r, wnt modest second 7 out, hrd at work last 4, no imprsn.* . . . .(25 to 1 op 20 to 1 tchd 33 to 1) 3
4138[5] STEEL CHIMES (Ire) 8-11-2 Gary Lyons, *struggling aftr one circuit, sn lost tch, tld off frm hfwy.* . . . . (33 to 1 op 25 to 1) 4
3893[3] MEL (Ire) 7-11-2 S McNeill, *chsd ldr, struggling and lost grnd quickly fnl circuit, tld off.* . . (15 to 2 op 5 to 1 tchd 8 to 1) 5
3958[6] BARON'S HEIR 10-11-2 W Marston, *jmpd sluggishly in rear, tld off whn pld up bef 8th.* . . . . (7 to 2 op 3 to 1) pu
FILL THE BOOT (Ire) 7-11-2 G Tormey, *struggling and reminders aftr one circuit, tailing off whn pld up bef tenth (water).* . . . .(4 to 1 op 9 to 2 tchd 5 to 1) pu
Dist: 9l, 12l, dist, 2l. 5m 39.40s. a 11.40s (7 Ran).
(Mrs Julie Martin), P T Dalton

4251 John Stubbs Memorial Selling Handicap Hurdle Class G (0-95 4-y-o and up) £1,899 2½m 110yds. . . . . . (3:00)

4179* STRIKE-A-POSE [65] 7-10-3 A P McCoy, *nvr far away, led aftr 6th, clr 4 out, rdn and styd on frm betw last 2.* . . . .(7 to 4 fav op 2 to 1 tchd 9 to 4) 1
4036[4] BODANTREE [86] 6-11-10 N Williamson, *wtd wth, improved to chase wnr frm 3 out, styd on und pres from betw last 2.* . . . .(4 to 1 op 9 to 2) 2
4153[9] EMERALD VENTURE [62] 10-10-0 C Rae, *settled to track ldrs, effrt and drvn alng appr 3 out, styd on same pace frm betw last 2.* . . . . (25 to 1 op 20 to 1) 3
3883[2] EDWARD SEYMOUR (USA) [84] 10-11-8 T Jenks, *patiently rdn, improved to go hndy hfwy, drvn alng 3 out, fdd nxt, tld off.* . . . . (9 to 4 op 5 to 2 tchd 11 to 4) 4
4073[9] CALGARY GIRL [62] 5-9-7 (7*) J McDermott, *settled in tch, took clr order hfwy, feeling pace aftr 4, wknd quickly nxt, tld off.* . . . .(20 to 1 op 12 to 1) 5
3984[4] STATION EXPRESS (Ire) [62] 9-9-9 (5*) D J Kavanagh, *al chasing ldrs, lost tch quickly passing hfwy, tld off bef 4 out.* . . . . (20 to 1 op 16 to 1) 6
4069[5] LAURA LYE (Ire) [78] 7-11-2 G Upton, *wtd wth, effrt hfwy, feeling pace appr 3 out, lost tch, tld off.* . . . . (13 to 2 op 6 to 1 tchd 7 to 1) 7
4073[6] MECADO [73] (v) 10-10-11 W Marston, *wth ldr, led briefly 6th, feeling pace 4 out, drpd out quickly and pld up bef nxt, lme.* . . . . (12 to 1 op 7 to 1) pu
153 ORCHESTRAL DESIGNS (Ire) [65] 6-10-3[3] T Kent, *led till hdd 6th, wknd rpdly, tld off whn pld up bef 2 out.* . . . . (50 to 1) pu
Dist: 3½l, 3½l, dist, 12l, 7l, 2½l. 4m 51.20s. a 12.20s (9 Ran).
(B J Llewellyn), B J Llewellyn

4252 Neville Lumb & Co. Handicap Chase Class D (0-125 5-y-o and up) £3,517 3¼m. . . . . (3:30)

4126* DOUALAGO (Fr) [125] (bl) 7-12-0 A P McCoy, *led or dsptd ld to 8th, styd second, reminders aftr twelfth, lft in lead after 3 out, stayed on, eased nring finish.* . . . .(2 to 1 jt-fav op 7 to 4 tchd 9 to 4) 1
4010* JIMMY O'DEA [97] (v) 10-9-11 (3*) E Husband, *led or dsptd ld, wnt clr tenth, 2 ls clear but wkng whn nrly uns rdr 3 out, one pace aftr.* . . . . (5 to 1 tchd 6 to 1) 2
3932* COPPER MINE [117] 11-11-6 J Osborne, *chsd ldrs for o'r a circuit, struggling and lost grnd quickly bef 8 out, plodded round.* . . . . (2 to 1 jt-fav op 3 to 1 tchd 7 to 2) 3
3972[2] SOLOMAN SPRINGS (USA) [97] 7-10-0 R Bellamy, *struggling thrght, tld off fnl circuit.* . . . .(25 to 1 op 16 to 1) 4
4046 NEVADA GOLD [98] 11-9-10 (5*) D J Kavanagh, *nvr gng particularly wl, lost tch fnl circuit, tld off whn pld up bef 5 out.* . . . .(16 to 1 op 12 to 1 tchd 20 to 1) pu
4132[3] IMPERIAL VINTAGE (Ire) [121] 7-11-10 N Williamson, *chsd ldrs, effrt to go 3rd fnl circuit, struggling bef 5 out, tld off whn pld up before 3 out.* . . . . (7 to 2 op 5 to 2 tchd 4 to 1) pu
Dist: 9l, 15l, 4l. 6m 34.80s. a 22.80s (6 Ran).
(Martin Pipe Racing Club), M C Pipe

4253 Back A Winner By Train Handicap Hurdle Class C for the Raisdorf Trophy (0-135 4-y-o and up) £3,436 2m . . . . (4:00)

3907 NORTHERN STARLIGHT [124] 6-11-10 A P McCoy, *made all, quickened clr frm 4 out, styd on wl from betw last 2.* . . . . (5 to 4 fav tchd 13 to 8) 1
3959[2] PERCY BRAITHWAITE (Ire) [107] 5-10-7 J Osborne, *trkd ldrs till lost pl hfwy, rallied frm 4 out, styd on to take second last 2, one pace r-in.* . . . . (5 to 1 tchd 11 to 2) 2
3933* AMLAH (USA) [118] 5-11-4 G Tormey, *chsd ldrs, feeling pace and lost grnd appr 4 out, styd on to take 3rd r-in, no imprsn.* . . . .(5 to 2 op 9 to 4 tchd 11 to 4) 3
3791[8] SERIOUS [113] 7-10-13 N Williamson, *wtd wth, improved to chase clr ldr 4 out, wknd and eased appr 2 out.* . . . . (13 to 2 op 5 to 1) 4
3791[7] ALBEMINE (USA) [117] (v) 8-11-3 T Kent, *pressed ldr, several reminders and lost pl quickly aftr 5th, sn lost tch, tld off.* . . . . (6 to 1 op 11 to 2) 5
Dist: 6l, 10l, 5l, dist. 3m 43.80s. a 6.80s (5 Ran).
SR: 36/13/14/4/-/ (Arthur Souch), M C Pipe

4254 Wellman Plc Novices' Handicap Chase Class E (0-100 5-y-o and up) £2,927 2m 5f. . . . . (4:30)

4091[3] WOT NO GIN [64] 8-10-6 N Williamson, *made most till hdd 10th (water), rallied to rgn ld appr 2 out, drw clr last.* . . . .(9 to 2 op 5 to 1) 1
4046 NO FIDDLING (Ire) [82] 6-11-7 (3*) D Fortt, *wtd wth, improved hfwy, drvn alng fnl circuit, styd on frm 3 out, no imprsn on wnr.* . . . .(7 to 2 op 3 to 1) 2
3980[2] MINERS REST [76] 9-10-11 (7*) Mr R Widger, *settled to track ldrs, drvn alng to chase clr ldg pair fnl circuit, styd on last 3, no imprsn.* . . . .(7 to 2 op 3 to 1) 3
4044 HANGOVER [68] 11-10-10 A P McCoy, *dsptd ld, definite advantage 10th (water), reminders frm nxt, rdn and hdd bef 2 out, stumbled last, fnshd tired.* . . . .(9 to 2 op 5 to 1 tchd 7 to 2) 4
3967[2] ALASKAN HEIR [72] (v) 6-11-0 T Eley, *wth ldrs, struggling to keep up sn aftr hfwy, lost tch, tld off frm 4 out.* . . . .(5 to 2 fav op 11 to 4 tchd 3 to 1) 5
4155 FRONTIER FLIGHT (USA) [80] (bl) 7-11-5 (3*) E Husband, *struggling and beh bef hfwy, sn tld off.* (16 to 1 op 10 to 1) 6
Dist: 27l, 3l, nk, 6l, 15l. 5m 18.90s. a 20.90s (6 Ran).
(The Up And Running Partnership), A J Wilson

4255 Twyfords Bathrooms Novices' Hurdle Class E (4-y-o and up) £2,389 2m . . . . (5:00)

4172* NORDIC BREEZE (Ire) 5-12-0 A P McCoy, *confidently rdn, smooth hdwy to ld appr 2 out, easily.* . . . .(5 to 2 on op 3 to 1 on tchd 9 to 4 on) 1
3823 BELLIDIUM 5-10-9 T Kent, *nvr far away, ev ch 4 out, hrd at work aftr nxt, kpt on, no chance wth wnr.* . . . . (100 to 1 op 50 to 1) 2
3722[4] KHALIKHOUM (Ire) 4-10-4 (5*) D J Kavanagh, *wth ldr, led frm 5th, clr appr 3 out, hdd aftr nxt, one pace from betw last 2.* . . . . (16 to 1 op 20 to 1) 3
4137* MR LOWRY 5-11-7 S Wynne, *al chasing ldrs, effrt aftr 4 out, hrd at work bef nxt, one pace.* . . . . (9 to 1 tchd 10 to 1) 4
FANCYTALKINTINKER (Ire) 7-11-0 T Jenks, *chsd ldrs, feeling pace and lost grnd 3 out, fdd.* . . . .(50 to 1 tchd 100 to 1) 5
4136 AMAZON HEIGHTS 5-10-9 Mr J Grassick, *pressed ldrs till wknd quickly aftr 4 out, tld off.* . . . .(100 to 1 op 50 to 1) 6
1852[4] SUPERMODEL 5-11-2 N Williamson, *led till hdd 5th, reminders bef nxt, lost tch before 3 out, pld up lme betw last 2.* . . . .(3 to 1 op 7 to 2 tchd 4 to 1) pu
Dist: 4l, 2l, 4l, 12l, dist. 3m 48.50s. a 11.50s (7 Ran).
(Malcolm B Jones), M C Pipe

WETHERBY (good to firm) Monday May 26th

Going Correction: MINUS 0.30 sec. per fur.

4256 Sandbeck Motors Claiming Hurdle Class F (4-y-o and up) £2,425 2½m 110yds. . . . . (2:15)

4101* KIRSTENBOSCH 10-10-5 (7*) W Dowling, *hld up, gd hdwy appr 3 out, led approaching last, ran on strly.* . . . .(5 to 1 op 6 to 1) 1
3909[2] SOUSSE 4-10-8 G Lee, *led, rdn appr 2 out, hdd approaching last, wknd flt.* . . . . (9 to 4 fav op 9 to 4 tchd 5 to 2) 2
3925[4] KADARI (v) 8-10-7 R Johnson, *al prmnt, chsd ldr hfwy till rdn 3 out and sn one pace.* . . . .(5 to 2 op 11 to 4 tchd 9 to 4 and 3 to 1) 3
3782[3] MASTER OF TROY 9-11-0 D Parker, *chsd ldrs, rdn alng 3 out and sn one pace.* . . . . (11 to 2 op 9 to 2) 4
3971* FAIR AND FANCY (Fr) 6-11-0 Mr S Swiers, *prmnt, rdn alng appr 3 out and sn one pace.* . . . . (13 to 2 op 11 to 2 tchd 8 to 1) 5
4087[6] FRET (USA) 7-10-10 Mr K Green, *midfield whn mstk 6th, sn lost pl and beh.* . . . .(25 to 1 op 16 to 1) 6

3899 FIERY SUN 12-10-10 N Smith, chsd ldrs, rdn alng and wknd
bef 3 out....................................(20 to 1 op 14 to 1)   7
2490⁶ COOL GAME 7-10-11 (3⁷) P Midgley, pld hrd, hld up, hdwy
hfwy, chsd ldrs and rdn 3 out, sn ridden and wknd, beh whn
hmpd and f last...(33 to 1)   f
3909³ RECRUITMENT 4-10-11 T Reed, hld up and beh, steady
hdwy 4 out, chsd ldrs nxt, rdn and btn whn f last.
....(33 to 1 op 20 to 1)   f
488³ MANOY 4-10-5 L Wyer, in tch, pushed alng and hdwy aftr 4
out, pld up lme bef nxt.....(8 to 1 op 7 to 1 tchd 9 to 1)   pu
Dist: 6l, 6l, 2½l, ¾l, 20l, 2½l. 4m 53.10s. a 11.10s (10 Ran).
(Mrs Barbara Lungo), L Lungo

4257 Moorside Landrover Centre Novices' Chase Class D (5-y-o and up) £3,415 3m 1f.........................(2:45)

4009⁴ LEPTON (Ire) (bl) 6-11-8 R Johnson, hld up and beh, steady
hdwy 12th, led on bit appr 2 out, rdn clr aftr last.
....(7 to 1 op 6 to 1 tchd 9 to 1)   1
3903⁴ MOVIE MAN 5-10-8 T Reed, hld up, hdwy to track ldrs hfwy,
effrt 4 out, rdn nxt, styd on appr last, no ch wh wnr. (16 to 1)   2
4044⁵ DESERT BRAVE (Ire) 7-10-13 (3⁷) G F Ryan, chsd ldrs, hdwy 4
out, rdn and hit nxt, drvn and one pace appr last.
....(8 to 1 op 6 to 1 tchd 9 to 1)   3
4211 KILTULLA (Ire) 7-11-2 L Wyer, cl up, led 5th, rdn 4 out, hdd bef
2 out and sn btn............(3 to 1 op 5 to 1 tchd 11 to 4)   4
3534 KNOCK STAR (Ire) 6-11-2 L O'Hara, cl up, chsd ldr frm hfwy
till rdn and mstk 4 out, sn wknd.....................(33 to 1)   5
3713⁴ NOW YOUNG MAN (Ire) 8-11-8 J Supple, hld up and not
fluent, effrt 11th and sn rdn alng, lost tch 5 out and soon beh.
....(5 to 2 op 2 to 1 tchd 11 to 4)   6
3901⁴ EVENING RUSH 11-11-6 D Parker, led to 5th, in tch till hit 10th
and sn lost pl, tld off 5 out....................................(33 to 1)   7
4128⁴ QUIXALL CROSSETT 12-10-9 (7⁷) Mr T J Barry, prmnt to 9th,
lost pl and pushed alng whn blun and uns rdr 11th
....(50 to 1 op 33 to 1)   ur
3806⁷ MALTA MAN (Ire) 7-11-3 (5⁷) R McGrath, hld up and not fluent,
hdwy to chase ldrs hfwy, rdn alng and outpcd 5 out, beh whn
pld up aftr nxt...........(2 to 1 fav op 2 to 1 tchd 5 to 2)   pu
Dist: 4l, 2l, 1½l, dist, ¾l, dist. 6m 16.30s. a 8.30s (9 Ran).
(J W P Curtis), M W Easterby

4258 'La Femme' Lady Riders' Handicap Hurdle Class D (0-120 4-y-o and up) £2,600 2m.........................(3:15)

4111⁴ TEEJAY'N'AITCH (Ire) [96] 5-10-10 Miss A Daniel, cl up, led
5th, rdn last and styd on wl........(7 to 4 fav op 13 to 8)   1
4002² KIERCHEM (Ire) [86] 6-10-0 Mrs S Grant, trkd ldrs, hdwy to
chase wnr 3 out, rdn and hit nxt, kpt on............(3 to 1)   2
2629⁵ MR MORIARTY (Ire) [96] 6-10-10 Mrs M Morris, led to 5th, cl
up till rdn 3 out and grad wknd frm nxt.
....(11 to 2 op 5 to 1 tchd 6 to 1)   3
1326² CONTRAFIRE (Ire) [108] 5-11-8 Mrs F Needham, prmnt, effrt
and rdn 3 out, sn wknd, blun last........(3 to 1 op 5 to 2)   4
249⁷ NORDIC SUN (Ire) [114] 9-11-7 (7⁷) Miss J Wormall, chsd ldrs,
rdn alng aftr 4 out wknd appr nxt.........(8 to 1 op 6 to 1)   5
3919⁶ STAGS FELL [87] 12-10-11 Carol Cuthbert, outpcd and beh
aftr 5th, sn tld off...........................(33 to 1 op 25 to 1)   6
SR: 21/9/14/18/18/-/ (Andrew Paterson), J S Goldie

4259 Godfrey Long Handicap Chase Class C (0-135 5-y-o and up) £4,730 3m 1f ....(3:45)

4058 GLEMOT (Ire) [130] 9-11-2 (7⁷) Mr R Wakley, made all, rdn 2
out, styd on wl flt...........(15 to 8 op 7 to 4 tchd 9 to 4)   1
4040² SOUNDS STRONG (Ire) [125] 8-11-4 R Johnson, trkd wnr,
effrt to chal and hit 3 out, sn rdn and kpt on wl flt.
....(9 to 4 on op 3 to 1 on)   2
Won by 1¾l. 6m 15.80s. a 7.80s (2 Ran).
SR: -/-/ (Dennis Yardy), K C Bailey

4260 Guy Cunard Hunters' Chase Class H (5-y-o and up) £1,308 2½m 110yds ....(4:15)

4085⁸ MY NOMINEE (bl) 9-12-0 (7⁷) Mr R Burton, prmnt, led aftr 7th,
hit 3 out, rdn nxt and styd on gmely........(4 to 1 op 5 to 2)   1
SHUIL SAOR 10-11-2 (7⁷) Mr C Mulhall, hld up, steady hdwy
....(9 to 1 op 6 to 1)   2
4142⁵ SIMPLY PERFECT 11-11-7 (7⁷) Miss K Swindells, al chasing
ldrs, effrt and ev ch 4 out, rdn nxt, one pace and hit last.
....(20 to 1 op 16 to 1)   3
4064⁴ NOT MY LINE (Ire) 8-12-2 (5⁷) Mr W Wales, led to 3rd, cl up,
effrt and ev ch 4 out, drvn nxt, hld whn blun last.
....(7 to 1 op 5 to 1 tchd 8 to 1)   4
CAMAN 7-11-2 (7⁷) Mrs S Grant, in tch till outpcd 5 out, styd
on frm 2 out, nrst finish............................(14 to 1)   5
INDIE ROCK 7-11-2 (7⁷) Mrs F Needham, mid-div, hdwy 4 out,
sn rdn and no imprsn frm nxt.
....(5 to 1 op 5 to 1 tchd 11 to 2)   6
3800⁷ GREAT GUSTO 11-11-11 (7⁷) Miss L Blackford, trkd ldrs,
hdwy 8th, cl up whn blun 10th, rdn alng appr 4 out, wknd bef
nxt...(2 to 1 fav op 5 to 2)   7

4171 ALPHA ONE 12-11-7 (7⁷) Miss K Di Marte, al beh. (33 to 1)   8
GOODHEAVENS MRTONY 10-11-2 (7⁷) Miss A Deniel,
reminders in rear hfwy, sn wl beh...................(33 to 1)   9
4066 SYRUS P TURNTABLE 11-11-2 (7⁷) Mr J Saville, beh frm
hfwy.............................(33 to 1 op 25 to 1)   10
EASTERN PLEASURE 10-11-2 (7⁷) Mr T J Barry, prmnt, rdn
alng 4 out, wkng whn f 2 out.........................(20 to 1)   f
4154² SANDYBRAES 12-11-7 (7⁷) Mr F Hutsby, beh and rdn alng
6th, pld up bef nxt........(13 to 2 op 6 to 1 tchd 7 to 1)   pu
4064 NO WORD 10-11-7 (7⁷) Mr I Baker, cl up, led aftr 7th,
wknd 10th, beh whn pld up lme bef 2 out............(33 to 1)   pu
JAPODENE 9-10-11 (7⁷) Mr M Haigh, al rear, wl beh whn pld
up bef 4 out...(33 to 1)   pu
GAELIC WARRIOR 10-11-9 Mr S Swiers, mid-divisn, hdwy to
chase ldrs 10th, rdn aftr nxt and wkng whn pld up after 4 out.
....(7 to 1 op 8 to 1 tchd 10 to 1)   pu
Dist: 1¼l, 2l, 1l, 1l, 11l, 1¼l, 7l, 33l, 10l. 5m 4.30s. a 11.30s (15 Ran).
(D E Nicholls), D E Nicholls

4261 Holiday Novices' Hurdle Class D (4-y-o and up) £2,757 2m.........(4:45)

1586⁶ LAGAN 4-11-2 R Johnson, made all and sn clr, jnd 4th, rdn
clear appr 2 out, easily..................(9 to 2 op 7 to 2)   1
4050³ GOING PRIMITIVE 6-11-0 D Parker, trkd ldrs, effrt and hdwy 3
out, chsd wnr nxt, sn rdn and no imprsn. (7 to 1 op 5 to 1)   2
SAILORMAITE 6-11-0 J Supple, hld up pulling hrd, rapid
hdwy to join ldr 4th, rdn 3 out, grad wknd.
....(14 to 1 op 10 to 1)   3
1656 IN GOOD FAITH 5-11-0 L Wyer, hld up in tch, hdwy 4 out, effrt
nxt and sn rdn, one pace 2 out.
....(15 to 8 fav op 7 to 4 tchd 2 to 1)   4
4111² HOPEFUL LORD (Ire) 5-10-9 (5⁷) R McGrath, hld up in tch,
hdwy to chase ldrs 4 out, rdn nxt and sn btn.
....(3 to 1 op 9 to 4)   5
4137³ WESTERN GENERAL 6-11-0 Mr S Swiers, hld up and beh,
hdwy to chase ldrs 3 out, sn rdn and btn. (9 to 2 op 5 to 1)   6
4113⁹ HANSEL'S STREAK 5-11-0 L O'Hara, in tch, rdn 4 out, sn
wknd and beh......(40 to 1 op 33 to 1 tchd 50 to 1)   7
3825 HONEYSUCKLE ROSE 4-10-4 Mr K Green, chsd ldres, blun
and lost pl, tld off whn pld up aftr four out....(33 to 1)   pu
Dist: 12l, 4l, nk, 1¼l, 1¼l, dist. 3m 44.40s. a 3.40s (8 Ran).
(Wild Racing), K A Morgan

HEXHAM (good to firm)
Tuesday May 27th
Going Correction: MINUS 0.40 sec. per fur.

4262 Buchanan High Level Brown Ale 'National Hunt' Novices' Hurdle Class E (5-y-o and up) £2,444 2½m 110yds.........................(6:35)

4020⁴ PAPPA CHARLIE (USA) 6-11-0 B Storey, al hndy, led betw
last 2, clr last, drvn out............(5 to 4 fav op 7 to 4)   1
EMPEROR'S MAGIC (Ire) 6-11-0 Richard Guest, midfield, clr
order hfwy, led and jmpd slwly 2 out, sn hdd and one pace.
....(6 to 1 op 5 to 1)   2
3970⁴ JERVAULX (Ire) 6-11-12 P Carberry, led, rdn and hdd 2 out, sn
wknd, wl btn whn hit last. (6 to 4 op 5 to 4 tchd 13 to 8)   3
4021⁵ WEAPONS FREE 6-11-0 R Garritty, settled rear, mstk 6th,
outpcd 3 out, sn wl beh............(25 to 1 op 12 to 1)   4
WITH RESPECT 6-11-0 K Johnson, str hold, cl up, hit 4th,
drpd rear 7th, sn tld off, pld up bef last.
....(100 to 1 op 33 to 1)   pu
BUCKLEY HOUSE 5-11-0 (7⁷) Mr L Mackey, pld hrd in rear, jmpd rght
5th, ran wide appr 7th, chlgd 3 out, wknd quickly nxt, pulled up
bef last...(8 to 1)   pu
Dist: 7l, dist, 13l. 4m 51.60s. a 0.60s (6 Ran).
(Raymond Anderson Green), C Parker

4263 Kellys Lager Maiden Chase Class F (5-y-o and up) £2,733 2½m 110yds ....(7:05)

3320 FORT ZEDDAAN (Ire) 7-11-3 Richard Guest, led to 7th, styd
hndy, hit 9th, rallied to ld ag'n 2 out, clr last, stayed on und
pres, jst hld on........(11 to 2 op 7 to 2 tchd 6 to 1)   1
3758 TWO FOR ONE (Ire) 8-11-3 A Thornton, chsd ldrs, drvn and
outpcd appr 2 out, rallied last, ran on strly, jst fld.
....(9 to 1 op 7 to 1 tchd 10 to 1)   2
3918³ BANNER YEAR (Ire) 6-11-3 P Niven, al hndy, reminders to
chase ldr appr 3 out, one pace aftr 2 out.
....(20 to 1 op 16 to 1 tchd 25 to 1)   3
3899⁹ ROSTINO (Ire) 8-11-3 P Carberry, beh, some hdwy 11th, nvr a
factor..(25 to 1 op 16 to 1)   4
40097 MEESONETTE 5-10-5 D Parker, sn beh, lost tch fnl circuit,
some hdwy frm 2 out, nvr dngrs.....(33 to 1 tchd 50 to 1)   5
4214³ SOVEREIGNS MATCH 9-11-3 B Storey, in tch, led 11th, hdd 2
out, sn wknd........(11 to 4 jt-fav op 5 to 2 tchd 3 to 1)   6
4009⁶ ARISTODEMUS (bl) 8-11-3 K Johnson, cl up, led 7th till mstk
and hdd 11th, not fluent 3 out, sn wknd. (25 to 1 op 20 to 1)   7
4022⁵ TACTIX 7-10-12 J Callaghan, sn drvn alng in rear, wl beh fnl
circuit, tld off.............................(13 to 2 op 5 to 1)   8

3672⁵ SINGH SONG 7-10-12 D Bentley, *pld hrd, cl up till blun and lost pl 8th, tld off frm 4 out*..........(12 to 1 op 10 to 1) 9

4024⁵ SUPERMARINE 11-11-3 G Lee, *midfield, blun and uns rdr 3rd*..........................(25 to 1 op 14 to 1) ur

3507⁶ CHARLVIC 7-10-10 (7⁵) L McGrath, *midfield, blun and uns rdr 7th*............................(33 to 1 tchd 50 to 1) ur

4098 THE ENERGISER (bl) 11-11-3 J Burke, *sn beh, tld off whn pld up aftr 8th*....................(33 to 1 op 20 to 1) pu

4009 CHILDSWAY 9-11-3 Mr C Mulhall, *al beh, tld off 5 out, pld up bef last*......................(33 to 1 op 25 to 1) pu

BILLY BUOYANT 8-11-3 T Reed, *al rear, wl beh hfwy, tld off whn pld up 4 out*....................(33 to 1 op 20 to 1) pu

2359 THE NEXT WALTZ (Ire) 6-11-3 R Supple, *hld up, gd hdwy 9th, chasing ldrs whn blun badly 11th, not reco'r, pld up 3 out*
......(11 to 4 jt-fav op 3 to 1 tchd 7 to 2 and 5 to 2) pu

Dist: Hd, 8l, 11l, 1¾l, 6l, 3½l, 24l, dist. 5m 8.20s. a 10.20s (15 Ran).
(Mrs S Smith), Mrs S J Smith

4264 Keoghans Novices' Hurdle Class E (4-y-o and up) £2,363 2m..... (7:35)

4216⁴ ROYAL YORK 5-11-11 (8ex) P Carberry, *made virtually all, shaken up to draw clr appr last, eased flt, cleverly*
..........(6 to 5 on op 5 to 4 on tchd 11 to 10 on) 1

3999⁸ CHINA KING (Ire) 6-11-0 B Storey, *hld up, not fluent second, hdwy to chase ldr betw last 2, styd on wl flt*
....(3 to 1 op 5 to 2) 2

3919⁷ TSANGA 5-11-8 N Bentley, *jnd ldr 3rd, ev ch till mstk 2 out, sn outpcd*....................(10 to 1 tchd 12 to 1) 3

3866² CAUGHT AT LAST (Ire) 6-11-0 P Niven, *pld hrd, chsd ldrs, drvn along appr 2 out, outpcd betw last two*
....(2 to 1 op 5 to 2) 4

Dist: ½l, 12l, 1¼l. 3m 49.70s. a 0.70s (4 Ran).
SR: 26/14/10/-/ (Robert Ogden), G Richards

4265 LCL Pils Handicap Chase Class F (0-105 5-y-o and up) £2,755 2½m 110yds..................... (8:05)

4022³ EXEMPLAR (Ire) [81] 9-10-11 R Guest, *in tch, hrd drvn to jump ahead last, styd on strly und pres, hld on wl*
.................................(3 to 1 fav op 11 to 4 tchd 100 to 30) 1

3902³ REBEL KING [77] 7-10-7 B Storey, *hld up, steady hdwy hfwy, led 12th till hdd last, rallied cl hme*....(6 to 1 op 4 to 1) 2

3585² THE TOASTER [96] 10-11-7 (5⁵) R McGrath, *al hndy, drvn alng frm 2 out, styd on same pace*
.....................................(7 to 2 op 4 to 1 tchd 5 to 2) 3

3867⁸ LAST REFUGE (Ire) [85] 8-11-1 T Reed, *hld up in rear, pushed alng and lost tch hfwy, styd on frm 3 out, nvr dngrs*.(16 to 1) 4

726³ BITACRACK [77] 10-10-4 L O'Hara, *led up, chlgd 8th, led tenth to 12th, cl up till mstk and wknd frm 2 out*....(14 to 1) 5

3918² SHAWWELL [76] 10-10-6 P Carberry, *led, blun 8th, hdd tenth, mstk and lost pl nxt, sn beh*.......(7 to 2 op 9 to 1) 6

3920⁵ MILS MIJ [95] 12-11-11 P Niven, *hld up, blun 7th, sn lost tch, tld off frm tenth*........................(5 to 1 op 4 to 1) 7

3821⁶ REVE DE VALSE (USA) [77] 10-10-7 K Johnson, *midfield, mstk and lost pl 7th, wl beh frm tenth, tld off*
....(14 to 1 op 12 to 1) 8

Dist: ½l, 8l, 2½l, 6l, 15l, 10l, 6l. 5m 3.80s. a 5.80s (8 Ran).
(Mrs S Smith), Mrs S J Smith

4266 Federation Brewery Handicap Hurdle Class F (0-105 4-y-o and up) £2,385 2m..................(8:35)

4008⁶ NITE SPRITE [66] 7-9-9 (5⁵) S Taylor, *chsd ldrs, pushed alng 7th, outpcd 3 out, rallied nxt, drvn to ld flt, styd on strly*
....(12 to 1 tchd 14 to 1) 1

3990⁴ BALLINDOO [90] 8-11-10 Mr R Armson, *nvr far away, slight ld 4 out, edgd rght betw last 2, mstk last, hdd and no extr flt*
.....................................(11 to 8 op 6 to 4) 2

4217⁵ DONT FORGET CURTIS (Ire) [69] 5-9-10 (7⁵) Miss S Lamb, *hld up, not fluent 4th, chlgd 3 out, drvn and one pace appr last*
...................................(6 to 1 op 5 to 1 tchd 7 to 1) 3

4008² BARTON HEIGHTS [86] 5-11-6 P Niven, *cl up till reminder and lost pl 7th, struggling appr 3 out, moderate hdwy aftr nxt, eased whn btn flt*...............(6 to 5 fav op 5 to 4 on) 4

3919 SHUT UP [66] (bl) 8-9-13² (3⁵) E Husband, *set modest pace, hdd 4 out, sn wknd and tld off*
...........................(40 to 1 op 33 to 1 tchd 50 to 1) 5

Dist: 2l, 5l, 20l, dist. 5m 50.30s. a 2.30s (5 Ran).
(R E Barr), R E Barr

4267 Jack Fawcus Memorial Challenge Cup Amateur Riders' Novices' Handicap Hurdle Class G (0-95 4-y-o and up) £2,042 2m.................(9:05)

1629⁶ COTTAGE PRINCE (Ire) [87] 4-11-3 (7⁵) Mr A Wintle, *hld up, clr order hfwy, pressed ldrs 2 out, quickened to ld flt, drvn out*
..........................(Evens fav tchd 11 to 8) 1

4012⁴ BEAU MATELOT [77] 5-11-0 (5⁵) Miss P Robson, *midfield, not fluent 3rd, effrt appr 2 out, chsd ldr betw last two, kpt on wl*
...................(7 to 2 op 4 to 1 tchd 3 to 1) 2

3868⁶ RAGAMUFFIN ROMEO [80] 8-11-3 (5⁵) Mr R Hale, *cl up, chlgd 3 out, sn led, hdd and no extr flt*
.................................(7 to 1 op 6 to 1 tchd 8 to 1) 3

4216⁷ WHITEGATESPRINCESS (Ire) [66] 6-10-3 (5⁵) Mr M H Naughton, *led till hdd aftr 3 out, drvn and no extr appr last*
.........................(11 to 2 op 5 to 1 tchd 6 to 1) 4

4213⁴ RUBISLAW [58] 5-9-7 (7⁵) Miss S Lamb, *chsd ldrs, ev ch whn slight mstk 2 out, sn rdn and one pace*.(25 to 1 op 20 to 1) 5

4087⁷ GI MOSS [68] (bl) 10-10-10¹⁷ (7⁵) Mr B Harriss, *beh, struggling frm hfwy, sn no chgr*
.................................(10 to 1 op 12 to 1 tchd 14 to 1) 6

3512⁷ SWANK GILBERT [58] 11-9-7 (7⁵) Miss H Cuthbert, *hld up, struggling appr 3 out, sn lost tch*...(33 to 1 op 20 to 1) 7

317⁵ NOTED STRAIN (Ire) [62] 9-9-11 (7⁵) Miss K Di Marte, *pld hrd, mstk second, cl up till wknd 3 out, tld off*
....(20 to 1 op 12 to 1) 8

DOC SPOT [67] 7-10-2 (7⁵) Mrs D Wilkinson, *hld up, struggling hfwy, tld off*.........(33 to 1 op 20 to 1) 9

Dist: 1l, sht-hd, 7l, ½l, 11l, 7l, 3½l, 12l. 3m 55.70s. a 6.70s (9 Ran).
(Mrs Kay Thomas), J J Quinn

CARTMEL (good to firm)
Wednesday May 28th
Going Correction: MINUS 0.15 sec. per fur.

4268 Jennings Bitter Mares' Only Novices' Selling Hurdle Class G (4-y-o and up) £2,276 2m 1f 110yds (2:00)

PALACE RIVER (Ire) 9-10-10 D J Moffatt, *hld up in tch, cld to chase ldrs 3 out, chalg whn hng lft r-in, styd on to ld towards finish*.........................(3 to 1 op 5 to 2) 1

4043⁵ SUMMER PRINCESS 4-10-5 Gary Lyons, *chsd ldr, led briefly 4 out, continued to press lder till led aftr last, hdd and no extr towards finish*..........(11 to 1 op 8 to 1 tchd 12 to 1) 2

3899⁴ QUEEN'S COUNSEL (Ire) 4-10-5 B Storey, *al cl up, led 3 out, drvn and hdd aftr last, kpt on und pres*
....(6 to 4 fav op 2 to 1) 3

3973 A BADGE TOO FAR (Ire) (bl) 7-10-10 L O'Hara, *hndy, lost pl 3rd, chsd ldrs but no imprsn frm 2 out*.(40 to 1 op 33 to 1) 4

4039⁷ DERRING FLOSS 7-10-3 (7⁵) Miss J Wormall, *cl up, drvn and wknd appr 2 out*.................(8 to 1 op 6 to 1) 5

4131 GABRIELLE GERARD 5-10-3 (7⁵) N Horrocks, *unruly bef strt, al beh, short of room on bend whn struggling aftr 4 out, mstk nxt, nvr dngrs*...................(14 to 1 op 8 to 1) 6

4216⁹ NO TAKERS 14-10-10 P Niven, *hld, hdd briefly 4 out, headed nxt, sn wknd*.........................(25 to 1 op 20 to 1) 7

TOLEPA (Ire) 4-10-0 (5⁵) R McGrath, *al beh, struggling 4 out, nvr on terms*.....................(14 to 1 op 12 to 1) 8

4216⁸ MEADOWLECK 8-10-5 (5⁵) S Taylor, *in rear, mstk second, niggled alng 4 out, nvr a factor*......(40 to 1 op 33 to 1) 9

4131⁵ ANALOGICAL 4-10-5 T Jenks, *in tch till l 3rd*
..............................(13 to 2 op 6 to 1 tchd 7 to 1) f

Dist: 2l, 1½l, 6l, 1¾l, 4l, 8l, 3l, 1¼l. 4m 10.15s. a 10.15s (10 Ran).
(G R Parrington), D Moffatt

4269 Stella Artois Handicap Chase Class D (0-125 5-y-o and up) £3,481 2m 1f 110yds.................... (2:30)

4207⁴ INDIAN JOCKEY [117] 5-12-0 A P McCoy, *made all, clr frm 6th, very easily*
...........................(6 to 4 on op 7 to 4 on tchd 11 to 8 on) 1

4221³ BLAZING DAWN [86] 10-10-3 B Storey, *rcd in 3rd pl, chsd clr wnr frm 7th, drvn alng last, no ch with winner*
....(7 to 2 op 4 to 1) 2

4226 CARDENDEN (Ire) [83] 9-10-0 P Carberry, *chsd clr wnr to 7th, rdn alng 4 out (water), sn no dngr*...(20 to 1 op 16 to 1) 3

3920⁴ SPEAKER'S HOUSE (USA) [92] 8-10-9 A Thornton, *al beh, lost tch 7th, tld off*........................(4 to 1) 4

Dist: 5l, 8l, dist. 4m 14.80s. a 3.80s (4 Ran).
SR: 37/7/-/-/ (Stuart M Mercer), M C Pipe

4270 Jennings Cumberland Ale Hunters' Chase Class H for the Horace D. Pain Memorial Trophy (5-y-o and up) £2,253 3¼m................(3:00)

HORNBLOWER (v) 10-11-7 (7⁵) Mrs C Ford, *led till aftr 6th, remained cl up, rgned ld 4 out (water), drw clr frm last, pushed out*............(11 to 8 fav op 6 to 4 tchd 5 to 4) 1

4229³ FORDSTOWN (Ire) 8-11-11 (7⁵) Mr Jamie Alexander, *prmnt, led aftr 6th, hdd 4 out (water), one pace*.......(14 to 1) 2

ACROSS THE CARD 9-11-11 (7⁵) Mr M Bradburne, *hld up and beh, late hdwy, nvr nrr*.......(4 to 1 tchd 9 to 2) 3

3969⁴ SOUTHERN MINSTREL 14-12-0 (7⁵) Miss C Metcalfe, *beh, some hdwy frl circuit, nvr dngrs*.....(10 to 1 op 8 to 1) 4

4066³ LUPY MINSTREL 12-12-2 (5⁵) Miss P Robson, *hld up, mstk tenth, effrt 13th, nvr trbld ldrs*...........(7 to 2 op 4 to 1) 5

PRIORY PIPER 8-11-7 (7⁵) Mr G Hanmer, *steadied strt, beh, mstk 3rd, nvr on terms*............(33 to 1 op 25 to 1) 6

4112⁴ WILL TRAVEL 8-11-7 (7⁵) Mr A Robson, *cl up till grad wknd frm 14th*......................(8 to 1 op 13 to 2) 7

4260⁸ ALPHA ONE 12-12-0 (7⁵) Miss K Di Marte, *in tch, mstk second, lost pl 7th, struggling and beh whn blun badly 13th, hot reco'r, pld up aftr nxt, dismounted*....(33 to 1 op 25 to 1) pu

RALLYING CRY (Ire) (bl) 9-11-7 (7*) Mr D R McLeod, *beh, mstk second and 4th, lost tch 6th, pld up aftr 8th, dismounted.*
.... (50 to 1 op 25 to 1) pu
DRUMCAIRN (Ire) (bl) 9-11-7 (7*) Mr M J Ruddy, *not jump wl, in tch, prmnt 7th, drvn alng and wknd 12th, blun nxt, pld up bef 14th.*
.... (33 to 1 op 25 to 1) pu
Dist: 6l, 3½l, 12l, 7l, 3½l, hd. 6m 35.80s. a 18.80s (10 Ran).

(N J Barrowclough), Richard Ford

4271 Dry Blackthorn Cider Maiden Hurdle Class E (5-y-o and up) £2,318 2m 1f 110yds...................... (3:35)

4261[4] IN GOOD FAITH 5-10-12 (7*) C McCormack, *nvr far away and al gng wl, led on bit last, sn clr, very easily.*
.... (7 to 4 fav op 5 to 4 tchd 15 to 8) 1
3900[3] SALKELD KING 5-11-5 B Storey, *in tch, blun 3rd, sn beh and lost touch, ran on und pres frm 2 out, wnt second r-in, no ch wth wnr.*.................... (7 to 1 tchd 8 to 1) 2
3820[4] DANTES AMOUR (Ire) 6-11-5 R Garritty, *hld up in tch, mstk 1st, reminders aftr 3rd, cld appr 3 out, one pace frm nxt.*
.... (9 to 4 op 3 to 1) 3
3999[6] PRAISE BE (Fr) (v) 7-11-5 P Niven, *led till hdd last, wknd quickly.*.................... (16 to 1 op 14 to 1) 4
493[6] STONE CROSS (Ire) 5-11-5 P Carberry, *hld up and beh, effrt aftr 4 out, und pres 2 out, no imprsn...* (14 to 1 op 10 to 1) 5
3919[7] DARK MIDNIGHT (Ire) (bl) 8-11-5 J Burke, *hndy, drvn and wknd quickly appr 2 out, tld off whn pld up bef last.*
.... (25 to 1 op 16 to 1) pu
4021[8] STARLIN SAM 8-11-5 Richard Guest, *chsd ldrs, reminders aftr 4th, wknd 3 out, tld off whn pld up bef last.*
.... (10 to 1 tchd 11 to 1) pu
4139[6] THE EENS 5-11-5 T Jenks, *prmnt, drvn appr 3 out, wknd nxt, wl beh whn pld up bef last.* (5 to 1 op 9 to 2 tchd 11 to 2) pu
Dist: 8l, 6l, 3l, 10l. 4m 7.40s. a 7.40s (8 Ran).

(Richard Dawson), J J Quinn

4272 Jennings Sneck Lifter Novices' Hurdle Class E (4-y-o and up) £2,350 3¼m...................... (4:05)

3657[6] GOOD HAND (USA) 11-11-12 P Niven, *prmnt, led appr 5th, hrd pressed and jnd 2 out, led ag'n aftr last, styd on wl towards finish...* (3 to 1 tchd 4 to 1 and 11 to 4) 1
4139* JESSOLLE 5-11-13 R Dunwoody, *hld up, hdwy appr 4 out, jnd issue on bit 2 out, drvn and hdd aftr last, no extr, fnshd sore.*
.... (2 to 1 on op 6 to 4 on) 2
4101[5] DON'T TELL JUDY (Ire) (bl) 9-10-7 (7*) C McCormack, *keen hold, chsd ldrs, outpcd frm 3 out...* (33 to 1 op 25 to 1) 3
4088[4] NORTHERN STAR 6-10-13 (7*) Miss J Wormall, *hndy till wknd appr 2 out.*.................... (13 to 2 op 5 to 1) 4
3903[6] WOODHOUSE LANE 5-10-7 (7*) Miss C Metcalfe, *beh, nvr on terms.*.................... (100 to 1 op 50 to 1) 5
3899[5] BARNSTORMER (bl) 11-11-0 D Parker, *prmnt, mstk second, wknd 2 out...*.................... (20 to 1 tchd 25 to 1) 6
4108[3] BLOOMING SPRING (Ire) 8-11-1 L O'Hara, *al beh, nvr a factor.*.................... (14 to 1) 7
4101 BUSY BOY 10-11-0 J Burke, *led till hdd appr 5th, wknd quickly, sn beh, tld off whn pld up aftr 8th.*
.... (100 to 1 op 50 to 1) pu
4177[4] ROYRACE 5-11-0 R Garritty, *hld up, effrt 4 out, sn no imprsn, wknd whn pld up bef 2 out...* (50 to 1 op 33 to 1) pu
Dist: 5l, 10l, 8l, 4l, ½l, 12l. 6m 11.30s. a 13.30s (9 Ran).

(Uncle Jacks Pub), S E Kettlewell

4273 Pioneer Foods Handicap Hurdle Class D (0-120 4-y-o and up) £2,815 2¾m...................... (4:35)

4217[2] HIGHLAND WAY (Ire) [91] 9-10-0 P Carberry, *rstrained in rear, cld on bit 2 out, led last, rdn out wth hands and heels.*
.... (4 to 1 tchd 7 to 2) 1
3778* LAGEN BRIDGE (Ire) [119] 8-12-0 D J Moffatt, *al prmnt, chlgd 2 out, ev ch r-in, styd on und pres.*
.... (6 to 5 fav op 11 to 10 tchd 4 to 1 and 11 to 8) 2
3870[2] SUPERTOP [111] 9-11-6 R Supple, *al hndy, effrt 2 out, kpt on und pres r-in...*.................... (2 to 1 tchd 7 to 2) 3
4222 GYMCRAK CYRANO (Ire) [91] 8-9-7 (7*) Miss C Metcalfe, *hld up in tch, effrt whn jmpd rght 2 out, one pace frm last.*
.... (16 to 1 op 14 to 1) 4
3904[3] PEGGY GORDON [91] 6-9-7 (7*) N Horrocks, *prmnt, led 3 out, hdd last, wknd quickly.*.................... (10 to 1) 5
4217[8] JUMBO STAR [91] 7-10-0 B Storey, *led to 3 out, sn und pres, wknd frm nxt.*.................... (33 to 1 op 25 to 1) 6
Dist: ½l, ½l, 4l, 5l, 5l. 5m 25.90s. a 18.90s (6 Ran).

(J D Gordon), Martin Todhunter

HEREFORD (good to firm)
Wednesday May 28th
Going Correction: PLUS 0.40 sec. per fur.

4274 Buttas Novices' Hurdle Class E (4-y-o and up) £2,472 2m 3f 110yds
.... (6:30)

4139[2] NAME OF OUR FATHER (USA) 4-11-1 R Johnson, *chsd ldr, led 5th, drvn out.*
.... (5 to 4 on op 7 to 4 on tchd 11 to 10 on) 1
4131[9] PEDALTOTHEMETAL (Ire) 5-10-9 Gary Lyons, *al prmnt, hrd rdn and wnt second appr 3 out, ran on wl frm last.*
.... (16 to 1 op 12 to 1) 2
4181[6] ROMANTIC WARRIOR 4-10-5 (3*) R Massey, *mstk 1st, prmnt till outpcd 8th, styd on frm 2 out...* (16 to 1 op 20 to 1) 3
4092[2] REAL MADRID 6-11-7 N Williamson, *steady hdwy 7th, rdn 3 out, 3rd and btn whn mstk 2 out.*
.... (15 to 8 op 2 to 1 tchd 7 to 4) 4
3915[4] ARIOSO 9-10-9 B Fenton, *gd hdwy to join wnr 7th, wknd 3 out.*.................... (9 to 1 op 14 to 1 tchd 16 to 1) 5
4139[8] WESTCOAST 6-11-0 C Llewellyn, *hdwy appr 3 out, wknd 2 out.*.................... (66 to 1 op 50 to 1) 6
4086[3] BE IN SPACE 6-10-2 (7*) Mr O McPhail, *wl beh frm 7th.*
.... (16 to 1 op 8 to 1) 7
3747[4] WESTFIELD 5-11-0 B Powell, *tld off frm 7th.*
.... (16 to 1 op 12 to 1) 8
1574[5] TROUBLE AT MILL 7-11-0 Mr D S Jones, *led to 5th, wknd quickly 7th, tld off...*.................... (66 to 1 op 50 to 1) 9
2804 TRIANNA 4-10-3 S Curran, *hrd rdn appr 7th, sn tld off.*
.... (66 to 1 op 33 to 1 tchd 100 to 1) pu
Dist: 1¼l, 16l, 9l, 4l, 4l, 14l, dist, dist. 4m 47.20s. a 29.20s (10 Ran).

(T M Morris), P Bowen

4275 Edwardian Selling Handicap Chase Class G (0-95 5-y-o and up) £2,780 3m 1f 110yds................. (7:00)

RAGLAN ROAD [86] 13-11-5 K Gaule, *hdwy tenth, led 2 out, al out.*.................... (8 to 1 op 6 to 1) 1
3861 SPRING TO IT [90] 11-11-9 A P McCoy, *led 6th, mstk and hdd 15th, led 3 out, mistake and headed 2 out, ran on...* (3 to 1 jt-fav op 5 to 2) 2
4232[9] PANDORA'S PRIZE [67] 11-10-0 S Wynne, *al prmnt, led on one pace frm 3 out...*.................... (25 to 1 tchd 33 to 1) 3
3875[4] TURPIN'S GREEN [71] 14-10-4 T J Murphy, *al prmnt, led 15th to 3 out, 3rd and btn whn blun 2 out...* (8 to 1 op 6 to 1) 4
4035[4] LOUGHDOO (Ire) [67] 9-10-0 B Fenton, *mstks, blun badly 7th, wl beh aftr...* (3 to 1 jt-fav op 7 to 1 tchd 5 to 1) 5
3899 COOL LUKE [72] 8-10-5 N Williamson, *hdwy 13th, rdn and wknd 4 out...*.................... (8 to 1 tchd 10 to 1) 6
4267[7] BOXING MATCH [71] 10-10-4 R Johnson, *prmnt till wknd 4 out.*.................... (14 to 1 op 12 to 1) 7
4190[8] DESERT RUN [94] 9-11-13 S Burrough, *f 1st.*
.... (33 to 1 op 25 to 1) f
3326[3] NAPOLEON'S GOLD [67] (v) 7-10-0 D Morris, *f 3rd.*
.... (25 to 1 op 16 to 1) f
3983[4] WOODLANDS GENHIRE [77] (bl) 12-10-10 C Llewellyn, *brght dwn 3rd.*.................... (20 to 1 op 16 to 1) bd
L'UOMO PIU [77] 13-10-3 (7*) Mr O McPhail, *led to 6th, wknd quickly tenth, tld off whn pld up bef 3 out.* (8 to 1 op 16 to 1) pu
RUSTINO [76] 11-10-2 (7*) Miss R Clark, *mstks, beh frm 11th, tld off whn pld up bef 2 out...* (14 to 1 op 12 to 1) pu
4226[5] RUSTIC GENT (Ire) [67] (bl) 9-10-0 J Burchell, *badly hmpd 1st, sn tld off, pld up bef 14th...* (12 to 1 op 10 to 1) pu
4132[4] LITTLE ELLIOT (Ire) [70] 9-10-3[3] C Maude, *tld off whn pld up bef 13th...*.................... (12 to 1 op 10 to 1 tchd 14 to 1) pu
3958 AEOLIAN [67] 6-10-0 J Culloty, *wl beh frm tenth, tld off whn pld up bef 3 out...*.................... (20 to 1 op 16 to 1) pu
Dist: 1½l, 3l, 17l, 17l, nk, 9l. 6m 26.70s. a 20.70s (15 Ran).

(Mark Johnson), Miss A E Embiricos

4276 Chairman's 80th Birthday Novices' Chase Class D (5-y-o and up) £3,452 2m...................... (7:30)

3792 SLEAZEY 6-11-6 S Curran, *made all, ran on wl.*
.... (9 to 4 op 4 to 1) 1
4019[9] KUMARI KING (Ire) 7-11-0 B Powell, *hdwy 4 out, 3rd whn mstk 3 out, ran on frm last, not rch wnr.* (20 to 1 op 12 to 1) 2
4034* TIGHT FIST (Ire) 7-11-6 J F Titley, *chsd wnr frm 5th till wknd last...*.................... (5 to 4 on op 2 to 1 on tchd 11 to 10 on) 3
4037[6] HUGH DANIELS 9-10-7 (7*) Miss A Dudley, *chsd ldrs till wknd 3 out...*.................... (40 to 1 op 33 to 1 tchd 50 to 1) 4
4107 SUNKALA SHINE 9-10-7 (7*) Miss R Clark, *mstks, in tch till wknd 4 out, tld off...*.................... (10 to 1 op 8 to 1) 5
3960 QUARTER MARKER 9-11-0 R Johnson, *chsd wnr to 6th, wknd 4 out...*.................... (12 to 1 op 9 to 1) 6
4034[4] STEER POINT 6-11-0 J Frost, *5th whn f 6th.*
.... (10 to 1 op 8 to 1) f
Dist: 4l, 1¾l, 7l, dist, 26l. 4m 3.50s. a 16.50s (7 Ran).

(J G O'Neill), J G O'Neill

4277 Richard Davis Memorial Conditional Jockeys' Handicap Hurdle Class F (0-105 4-y-o and up) £2,640 2m 1f
.... (8:00)

4081* FLEET CADET [91] (v) 6-11-7 (3*) G Supple, *hld up, led 5th, sn clr, easily.*.................... (5 to 4 fav tchd 13 to 8) 1
4228* ZINGIBAR [87] 5-11-6 (6ex) T Dascombe, *reminders 3rd, outpcd 5th, styd on frm 2 out, no ch wth wnr.*
.... (7 to 2 op 3 to 1) 2
3673[4] SALMAN (USA) [88] 11-11-7 P Henley, *chsd ldr, hrd rdn 3 out, wknd appr last.*.................... (7 to 1 op 6 to 1) 3

4083⁶ ROC AGE [67] 6-9-9 (5*) L Suthern, *led till wknd quickly 5th,
tld off*. . . . .(10 to 1 op 8 to 1 tchd 11 to 1) 4
4017⁶ PAIR OF JACKS (Ire) [89] 7-11-8 D J Kavanagh, *uns rdr 1st.*
. . . .(5 to 2 op 7 to 4) ur
Dist: 8l, 13l, dist. 4m 0.70s. a 15.70s (5 Ran).
SR: 7/-/ *(Sir John Swaine),* M C Pipe

4278 Garnstone Novices' Handicap Chase Class E (0-100 5-y-o and up) £2,983 2m 3f. . . . .(8:30)

3811² CASTLECONNER (Ire) [82] (bl) 6-11-1 J Frost, *al prmnt, led appr 3 out, ran on wl.* (3 to 1 jt-fav op 5 to 2 tchd 7 to 2) 1
3893¹ CALL ME ALBI (Ire) [84] (bl) 6-11-3 M Richards, *rdn and lost pl 8th, hdwy 2 out, ran on frm last.*
. . . .(4 to 1 op 7 to 2 tchd 9 to 2) 2
4204⁴ GERRY'S PRIDE (Ire) [67] 6-10-0 S Curran, *hdwy 9th, wth wnr and hrd rdn whn blun 2 out, wknd last.* (14 to 1 op 10 to 1) 3
3912⁵ DUBELLE [87] 7-11-6 T J Murphy, *chsd ldr, led 6th till appr 3 out, wknd 2 out, tld off*. . . . .(3 to 1 jt-fav op 5 to 2 tchd 100 to 30) 4
4254³ MINERS REST [76] 9-10-2 (7*) Mr R Widger, *in tch till mstk and wknd 4 out*. . . . . (12 to 1 op 5 to 1) 5
4193 VALLINGALE (Ire) [73] 6-10-6 J Culloty, *wl beh frm 6th, pld up bef 3 out*. . . . .(9 to 1 op 9 to 2 tchd 10 to 1) pu
3799³ INCH EMPEROR (Ire) [92] 7-11-11 B Powell, *led to 6th, wknd 8th, wl beh whn pld up bef 4 out.*
. . . .(7 to 2 op 3 to 1 tchd 4 to 1) pu
Dist: 8l, hd, 30l, 4l. 4m 46.40s. a 21.40s (7 Ran).
(Mrs G A Robarts), R G Frost

4279 Ledgemoor 'National Hunt' Novices' Hurdle Class E (5-y-o and up) £2,304 3¼m. . . . .(9:00)

3937³ DECYBORG (Fr) 6-11-0 A P McCoy, *made virtually all, all out.*
. . . . (7 to 4 on op 11 to 4 on tchd 13 to 8 on) 1
41816 PAMALYN 5-10-9 C Maude, *chsd wnr frm 8th, mstk 4 out, hng badly lft aftr 2 out, ran on wl from last.*.(5 to 1 op 10 to 1) 2
943 STEP IN LINE (Ire) 5-10-11 (3*) D Fortt, *hdwy 3 out, ran on frm last.*. . . . .(10 to 1 op 8 to 1) 3
2856 RELUCKINO (v) 7-11-0 M A Fitzgerald, *second whn blun and lost pl 7th, tld off frm 3 out.*. . (9 to 1 op 3 to 1 tchd 4 to 1) 4
TRUE FRED 8-11-0 Gary Lyons, *tld off frm 4 out.*
. . . .(14 to 1 op 12 to 1) 5
4137 LADY ROSEBURY 7-10-9 T J Murphy, *lost pl 7th, tld off frm 4 out.*. . . . .(33 to 1 tchd 66 to 1) 6
ANIMOSITY 7-10-9 T Dascombe, *tld off frm 8th, pld up bef 3 out*. . . . .(20 to 1 op 16 to 1) pu
Dist: 2l, 2½l, dist, 3½l, 8l. 6m 38.40s. a 36.40s (7 Ran).
(Terry Neill), M C Pipe

LEOPARDSTOWN (IRE) (good)
Wednesday May 28th

4280 James H.North & Co Q.R. Handicap Hurdle (0-116 4-y-o and up) £6,850 2m. . . . .(8:30)

3954⁵ FRAU DANTE (Ire) [-] 7-10-3 (7*) Mr J P McNamara, (10 to 1) 1
4196² WELSH GRIT (Ire) [-] 8-11-7 Mr R Walsh, ... (5 to 1) 2
4054⁶ TAITS CLOCK (Ire) [-] 8-10-13 (7*) Mr B Hassett, . .(10 to 1) 3
DUNFERNE CLASSIC (Ire) [-] 8-11-2 Mr F Fenton,
. . . .(5 to 2 fav) 4
3763⁵ OH SO GRUMPY [-] 9-11-11 (7*) Mr P Barrett, ...(20 to 1) 5
3889⁵ BAILENAGUN (Ire) [-] 4-9-13 (7*) Mr T Gibney, ...(14 to 1) 6
2128 FONTAINE LODGE (Ire) [-] 7-11-7 (5*) Mr G Elliott, . .(7 to 1) 7
3754 INNOVATIVE (Ire) [-] 6-9-11 (7*) Mr T J Beattie, . . .(25 to 1) 8
3345⁵ RED TONIC (USA) [-] 4-11-1 Mr G J Harford, ...(14 to 1) 9
4146⁴ REGENCY RAKE (Ire) [-] 5-10-13 (7*) Mr Paul Moloney,
. . . .(8 to 1) 10
3942² WADABLAST (Ire) [-] 7-9-11 (7*) Mr G T Morrow, . .(7 to 1) 11
1095⁷ KATIYMANN (Ire) [-] 5-11-8 Mr A J Martin, ...(9 to 1) 12
SIMPLY GLORIOUS (Ire) [-] 8-11-9 (7*) Mr B P Galvin,
. . . . (40 to 1) 13
Dist: 2l, 5l, hd, ½l. 3m 47.30s. a 3.30s (13 Ran).
SR: 25/34/28/24/39/-/ *(Mrs Austin Fenton),* Austin Fenton

4281 FIABCI (Pro/Am) I.N.H. Flat Race (4 & 5-y-o) £6,850 2m. . . . . (9:00)

4161¹ OONAGH'S STAR (Ire) 5-11-12 (5*) Mr A C Coyle, . .(5 to 1) 1
4029⁴ MINELLA STORM (Ire) 5-12-3 Mr A J Martin, ...(7 to 2) 2
2449² COLONEL HENDERSON (Ire) 5-11-10 Mr B M Cash,
. . . . (10 to 9 on) 3
3891⁴ RING ALBERT (Ire) 5-12-3 Mr R Walsh, ...(7 to 1) 4
4200² BELCAMP BELLE (Ire) 4-10-5 (7*) Mr S P McCarthy,
. . . .(14 to 1) 5
4147² TO-DAY TO-DAY (Ire) 4-10-10 (7*) Mr A FitzGerald, .(8 to 1) 6
1756 SUBLIME SPIRIT (Ire) 5-11-3 (7*) Mr D Buckley, . .(100 to 1) 7
Dist: 5l, 3½l, 12l, 2½l. 3m 40.80s. (7 Ran).
(F P Taaffe), P Mullins

BALLINROBE (IRE) (good)

Thursday May 29th

4282 Lough Carra Maiden Hurdle (4-y-o and up) £2,226 2m. . . . .(5:15)

4195⁴ HONEY TRADER 5-11-0 (5*) P G Hourigan, ...(6 to 4 fav) 1
1309 TALLY-HO MAJOR (Ire) 4-10-8 (7*) Mr A Ross, ...(12 to 1) 2
1709 PETASUS 4-10-13 (7*) N P Mulholland, ... (10 to 1) 3
4148³ PRINCESS CATALDI (Ire) 7-11-1 H Rogers, ...(5 to 1) 4
MISS TOFFEE NOSE (Ire) 5-10-7 (7*) Mr A J Dempsey,
. . . .(9 to 2) 5
RITA'S KILLALOE (Ire) 4-10-3 (7*) C B Hynes, ...(20 to 1) 6
2343⁸ TOCHAR BOY (Ire) 6-11-6 L P Cusack, ...(16 to 1) 7
4094 MELT DOWN (Ire) 6-11-1 F J Flood, ...(10 to 1) 8
HAGS HILL (Ire) (bl) 5-10-12 (7*) Mr S O'Callaghan, (20 to 1) 9
4144 CARNACREEVA GANE (Ire) 6-10-12 (3*) K Whelan, (16 to 1) 10
3952⁷ LITTLE MURRAY 4-11-1 S H O'Donovan, ...(14 to 1) 11
1275 HILL TOP LAD (Ire) 5-11-5 W Slattery, ...(20 to 1) 12
4052 MARINER'S TALE (Ire) 7-10-8 (7*) D McCullagh, . .(14 to 1) 13
LE PETIT GALLELOU (Ire) 7-11-6 C F Swan, ...(8 to 1) 14
4026 LADY TIGER (Ire) 4-10-10 T J Mitchell, ... (20 to 1) 15
Dist: 2½l, hd, 6l, 2½l. 4m 7.00s. (15 Ran).
(The Laune Syndicate), Michael Hourigan

4283 Harp Lager Handicap Chase (0-102 5-y-o and up) £3,425 2½m. . . .(8:00)

4103⁷ LISHILLAUN (Ire) [-] 7-9-2 (5*) Susan A Finn, ...(20 to 1) 1
4103⁵ SANDY FOREST LADY (Ire) [-] 8-10-0 (3*) K Whelan, (8 to 1) 2
3815 IRISH FOUNTAIN (Ire) [-] 9-11-7 (7*) Mr W Ewing, . . .(5 to 1) 3
4165³ TIME AND CHARGES (Ire) [-] 7-10-13 C O'Dwyer,
. . . . (3 to 1 fav) 4
4199 TULLY BOY [-] 10-10-11 (7*) Mr D McCartan, ...(6 to 1) 5
3706⁶ RATES RELIEF (Ire) [-] 7-11-11 C F Swan, ...(5 to 1) 6
4145 HAVE A BRANDY (Ire) [-] 8-9-10 W Slattery, ...(10 to 1) 7
4199 KILLERK LADY (Ire) [-] 6-9-2 (5*) B J Geraghty, ...(4 to 1) pu
Dist: 7l, ½l, 4½l, dist. 5m 22.10s. (8 Ran).
(Thomas Fitzsimons), Mrs Edwina Finn

4284 Flannerys Cornmarket I.N.H. Flat Race (4-y-o and up) £2,568 2m (8:30)

3755⁷ DARSARAK (Ire) 4-11-6 Mr A J Martin, ... (3 to 1) 1
4029⁷ NOT CLEVER (Ire) 5-11-6 (7*) Mr A J Dempsey, . . .(10 to 1) 2
3840⁴ DIGITAL SIGNAL (Ire) 4-11-6 Mr P Fenton, ...(5 to 1) 3
4147⁴ CARJUNE (Ire) 5-11-13 Mr R Walsh, ...(5 to 4 fav) 4
350⁴ A SLIDER (Ire) 5-11-1 (7*) Mr J P McNamara, ...(10 to 1) 5
2905⁹ DERRAVARAGH SECRET (Ire) 4-10-8 (7*) Mr A Ross,
. . . . (12 to 1) 6
4056⁵ MULTEEN JET (Ire) 4-10-13 (7*) Mr Paul Moloney, (12 to 1) 7
4197 ARDBUTUS (Ire) 5-11-1 (7*) Mr R J Cooper, ...(14 to 1) 8
RUN FOR A BUCK (Ire) 6-11-7 (7*) Mr D G McHale, (16 to 1) 9
4106 FAITCH'S LADY (Ire) 4-10-8 (7*) Mr A Daly, ...(25 to 1) 10
3880 THUNDER PRINCESS (Ire) 5-11-1 (7*) Mr P Whelan,
. . . . (25 to 1) ur
Dist: 5l, 2l, 2½l, 1l. 4m 4.80s. (11 Ran).
(P A McGuinness), A J Martin

UTTOXETER (good to firm)
Thursday May 29th
Going Correction: MINUS 0.05 sec. per fur.

4285 Britannia Unison Novices' Hurdle Class D (4-y-o and up) £2,927 2½m 110yds. . . . .(2:00)

4213⁷ ACAJOU III (Fr) 9-11-7 P Carberry, *made all, clr 2 out, unchlgd*. . . . .(5 to 4 fav tchd Evens) 1
4125³ GIVE AND TAKE (bl) 4-11-1 A P McCoy, *al prmnt, chsd wnr 3 out, no imprsn*. . . . .(1 op 6 to 1 tchd 9 to 1) 2
3881⁵ RIVERBANK ROSE (v) 6-11-2 G Tormey, *chsd wnr to appr 4 out, sn lost pl, styd on r-in.*
. . . .(9 to 1 op 14 to 1 tchd 25 to 1) 3
4125² SAMANID (Ire) 5-12-0 R Dunwoody, *hld up, hdwy hfwy, rdn and wknd appr 2 out.*. . . . .(9 to 2 op 7 to 2) 4
3682⁴ ELITE GOVERNOR (Ire) 8-10-11 (3*) Chris Webb, *prmnt till lost pl 4th, sn beh.*. . . . .(66 to 1 op 33 to 1) 5
3677⁴ SEABROOK LAD 6-11-7 W Marston, *hld up, hdwy 5th, chsd wnr and mstk 4 out, rdn nxt, sn wknd.*. . (5 to 1 op 4 to 1) 6
3970⁴ POPPY'S DREAM 7-10-9 N Williamson, *hld up, effrt appr 4 out, al in rear*. . . . .(10 to 1 op 7 to 1) 7
4045⁵ MOLLIE SILVERS 5-10-9 W McFarland, *hld up, effrt and mstk 4 out, al in rear*. . . . .(20 to 1 op 25 to 1 tchd 33 to 1) 8
4176⁶ TRENTSIDE MAJOR 5-11-0 M Ranger, *hld up, mstk 3rd, tld off and pld up bef 4 out*. . . . .(10 to 1 op 50 to 1) pu
Dist: 4l, 6l, 4l, 14l, 6l, 13l, dist. 4m 46.80s. a 7.80s (9 Ran).
SR: 5/-/-/-/-/-/ *(Robert Ogden),* G Richards

4286 Wellman Plc Novices' Chase Class D (5-y-o and up) £3,436 3¼m. . . . (2:30)

4180⁴ MASTER CRUSADER 11-10-9 (7*) Mr S Durack, *hld up in tch, chsd ldr 6th, led aftr six out, hrd rdn r-in, all out.*
. . . .(11 to 2 op 4 to 1) 1

NATIONAL HUNT RESULTS 1996-97

40673 GRIZZLY BEAR (Ire) 7-11-8 A P McCoy, chsd ldr, led tenth,
hdd aftr 6 out, ev ch frm 4 out, hrd rdn appr last, no extr r-in.
...(Evens fav op Evens tchd 11 to 10 and 11 to 10 on) 2
4257 QUIXALL CROSSETT 12-11-2 G Lyons, prmnt, lost pl tenth,
tld off 6 out, styd on strly frm 2 out....(33 to 1 op 25 to 1) 3
4204 THUNDER ROAD (Ire) (bl) 6-11-8 J Culloty, led to tenth, wknd
5 out.............................(11 to 2 op 9 to 2) 4
3967 DOCTOR DUNKLIN (USA) 8-11-2 J R Kavanagh, hld up,
hdwy 7th, rdn tenth, sn beh...........(33 to 1 op 16 to 1) 5
THEMOREYOUKNOW 8-11-2 Mr M Harris, hld up, hdwy 11th,
cl up whn f 13th.........(11 to 1 op 8 to 1 tchd 12 to 1) f
POPS ACADEMY (Ire) 6-11-2 M Richards, hld up, hit 1st, f
12th.........................(6 to 1 op 7 to 1 tchd 8 to 1) f
42045 MUSICAL HIT (bl) 6-11-2 R Supple, prmnt, mstk 6th, rdn 8th,
sn wknd, pld up bef six out.........(33 to 1 op 16 to 1) pu
Dist: 2l, 15l, 15l, dist. 6m 45.80s. a 33.80s (8 Ran).
(D L Williams), D L Williams

4287 Britannia Five Year Fixed Novices' Handicap Hurdle Class E (0-100 4-y-o and up) £2,400 2m......... (3:00)

40212 SILVER MINX [96] 5-11-10 P Niven, led second, clr 2 out,
jmpd lft last, eased nr finish...........(7 to 1 op 5 to 1) 1
40837 FRENO (Ire) [72] 6-10-0 N Williamson, hld up, hdwy 5th, chsd
wnr 4 out, one pace frm 2 out, lft second last.
.........................(25 to 1 op 16 to 1) 2
32683 APOLLONO [72] 5-10-0 R Johnson, prmnt, outpcd appr 3 out,
ran on r-in.........(5 to 1 op 6 to 1 tchd 13 to 2) 3
39997 OVERSMAN [90] 4-10-13 P Carberry, hld up, hdwy 4 out, rdn
whn pckd 2 out, styd on same pace......(11 to 2 op 4 to 1) 4
42163 RADMORE BRANDY [90] 4-10-13 R Dunwoody, mid-div, rdn
3 out, sn btn.........................(3 to 1 fav) 5
39862 ALPHA LEATHER [72] 6-10-0 Mr J Grassick, led to second, cl
up whn badly hmpd 4 out, not reco'r.
.........................(12 to 1 op 8 to 1 tchd 14 to 1) 6
41533 BLOTOFT [72] 5-10-7 M A Fitzgerald, hld up, rdn 3 out, no
response...............(7 to 1 op 6 to 1 tchd 8 to 1) 7
39224 SOCIETY GIRL [80] 4-10-3 R Supple, hld up in tch, effrt 4 out,
second and held whn f last.
.........................(11 to 1 op 8 to 1 tchd 14 to 1) f
40696 RED VIPER [76] 5-10-1 (3*) Chris Webb, hld up, hdwy 5 out, cl
up whn f nxt............(33 to 1 op 16 to 1 tchd 33 to 1) f
36862 TIME LEADER [72] 5-10-0 J Culloty, hld up, pld hrd, badly
hmpd 4 out, pulled up bef nxt.
.........................(11 to 1 op 8 to 1 tchd 12 to 1) pu
Dist: 6l, ½l, 2½l, 4l, 1¼l, 20l. 3m 45.40s. a 8.40s (10 Ran).
SR: 4/-/-/-/-/-/ (Mrs E A Kettlewell), Mrs M Reveley

4288 Britannia Simply Mortgages Handicap Chase Class E (0-115 5-y-o and up) £2,937 2m 5f............ (3:30)

41902 BLAZER MORINIERE (Fr) [93] 8-10-7 S Fox, al prmnt, jnd ldrs
4 out, led 2 out, styd on wl.
.........................(11 to 8 fav op 5 to 4 tchd 6 to 4) 1
40703 NORDIC VALLEY (Ire) [91] 6-10-5 A P McCoy, hld up, hdwy 6
out, led 4 out hdd 2 out, unbl to quicken r-in.
.........................(5 to 2 op 9 to 4 tchd 11 to 4) 2
39374 HENLEY REGATTA (Ire) [100] 9-11-0 M A Fitzgerald, hld up, hdwy
to join ldrs 4 out, rdn and wknd nxt.
.........................(9 to 2 op 4 to 1 tchd 5 to 1) 3
41406 EARLYMORNING LIGHT (Ire) [114] 8-12-0 R Dunwoody,
prmnt, chsd ldr 9th, ev ch 4 out, sn rdn and btn.
.........................(7 to 1 op 4 to 1) 4
41907 BRIMPTON BERTIE [86] 8-10-0 N Johnson, led second, hdd
and wknd 4 out.........(33 to 1 op 20 to 1 tchd 40 to 1) 5
3914 NORTHERN OPTIMIST [87] 9-10-1 N Williamson, led to second, wknd 5 out, pld up bef nxt.
.........................(14 to 1 op 12 to 1 tchd 16 to 1) pu
Dist: 1½l, 20l, 9l, 7l. 5m 6.00s. a 8.00s (6 Ran).
(John Pearl), P C Ritchens

4289 Britannia Members Loyalty Bonus Handicap Hurdle Class C for the Ken Boulton Cup (0-130 4-y-o and up) £3,485 3m 110yds........... (4:00)

39079 EDELWEIS DU MOULIN (Fr) [130] 5-12-0 P Carberry, hld up
and beh, hdwy 4 out, chsd ldr nxt, led on bit last, cmftbly.
.........................(3 to 1 op 5 to 2 tchd 100 to 30 and 7 to 2) 1
4047* THE TOISEACH (Ire) [121] (v) 6-11-5 J Osborne, trkd ldr, led
and lft wl clr 4th, hdd and mstk last, no ch wth wnr.
.........................(7 to 4 fav op 2 to 1 tchd 13 to 8) 2
4127 TRAGIC HERO [129] (bl) 5-11-13 A P McCoy, hld up and beh,
hdwy appr 3 out, sn rdn, and no imprsn.
.........................(10 to 1 op 14 to 1 tchd 11 to 2) 3
39962 BEECHFIELD FLYER [102] 6-10-0 G Tormey, in tch, hampered 4 out, chsd ldr four out to nxt, sn rdn and btn.
.........................(12 to 1 op 10 to 1 tchd 12 to 1) 4
1473* DON DU CADRAN (Fr) [104] 8-10-2² A Thornton, prmnt, chsd
ldr 5 out to nxt, sn wknd. (10 to 1 op 8 to 1 tchd 14 to 1) 5
40325 MOVING OUT [107] 9-10-5 J F Titley, led till hdd and f 4th.
.........................(33 to 1) f
3701 NORTHERN SQUIRE [110] 9-10-8 L Wyer, prmnt, lft second
4th, mstk 6th, wknd appr four out, tld off and pld up bef nxt.
.........................(33 to 1) pu

Dist: 2½l, 6l, 14l, dist. 5m 40.90s. a 3.90s (7 Ran).
SR: 49/37/39/-/ (Robert Ogden), G Richards

4290 Britannia Brighter Savers Novices' Hunters' Chase Class H for the Feilden Challenge Cup (5 - 8-y-o) £1,127 2m 5f............... (4:30)

KING TORUS (Ire) 7-12-1 (5*) Mr J Jukes, chsd ldrs, led appr 4
out, cmftbly...............(11 to 10 on op 11 to 10) 1
4209 TRUE FORTUNE 7-11-7 (7*) Mr D S Jones, al prmnt, chsd wnr
4 out, styd on.........................(8 to 1 op 6 to 1) 2
4122* MUSKERRY MOYA (Ire) 8-11-8 (7*) Miss A Goschen, led to
appr 4 out, wknd nxt, fnshd lme.
.........................(11 to 4 op 5 to 2 tchd 3 to 1) 3
41573 TELLAPORNEY 8-11-8¹ (7*) Mr A Middleton, wl beh til styd on
frm 2 out, nvr nrr...........(25 to 1 op 20 to 1) 4
EVERSO IRISH 8-11-7 (7*) Mr J Barnes, al beh.
.........................(33 to 1 op 25 to 1) 5
42343 VERY DARING 7-11-7 (7*) Miss S Sharratt, al beh.
.........................(50 to 1 op 33 to 1) 6
BEYOND THE STARS 6-11-11 (3*) Mr M Rimell, prmnt till f
7th.........................(14 to 1) f
THORNHILL 7-11-2 (7*) Mr R Widger, tld off frm 5th, pld up bef
6 out.........................(200 to 1 op 100 to 1) pu
4157 DARK RHYTHAM 8-11-7 (7*) Mr T Lane, led to second,
remained hndy til mstk and wknd 6 out, pld up bef 2 out.
.........................(25 to 1 tchd 33 to 1) pu
CHRISTMAS THYNE (Ire) 5-11-0 (7*) Mr A Phillips, mid-div,
rdn 8th, sn beh, tld off and pld up bef 4 out.
.........................(100 to 1 op 50 to 1) pu
4098 DRAGONS BAY 8-12-0 Mr S Swiers, strted slwly, hld up
and beh, steady hdwy 5 out, 5th whn pld up bef 3 out.
.........................(14 to 1 op 12 to 1) pu
Dist: 1½l, 28l, 11l, 14l, 25l. 5m 14.40s. a 16.40s (11 Ran).
(Nick Viney), Victor Dartnall

4291 Britannia Multiguard Maiden Open National Hunt Flat Class H (4,5,6-y-o) £1,287 2m............ (5:00)

41882 STORMHILL STAG 5-10-12 (7*) L Cummins, trkd ldrs, led o'r
2 fs out, rdn out.........(5 to 2 tchd 11 to 4 and 3 to 1) 1
40424 OI MOTHER (Ire) 5-10-11 (3*) R Massey, al prmnt, chsd wnr
o'r 2 fs out, rdn and hng lft over one out, unbl to quicken.
.........................(7 to 4 fav op 6 to 4 tchd 2 to 1) 2
30614 AMLWCH 4-11-0 D Parker, chsd ldrs, rdn 3 fs out, styd on
same pace.........(7 to 1 op 7 to 1 tchd 8 to 1) 3
41877 HILL'S ELECTRIC (Ire) 5-11-5 R Johnson, chsd ldrs, led o'r 5
fs out, hdd over 2 out, sn rdn and edgd lft, no extr.
.........................(16 to 1 op 10 to 1) 4
40426 DARK HORSE (Ire) 5-10-12 (7*) M Berry, hld up, hdwy hfwy,
rdn and hng lft o'r 3 fs out, sn btn...........(8 to 1) 5
41886 MINIBELLE 5-10-7 (7*) Mr S Durack, chsd ldrs, rdn o'r 4 fs
out, sn wknd.........(20 to 1 op 14 to 1) 6
40504 SWEET LITTLE BRIAR (Ire) 6-11-0 R Dunwoody, mid-div, effrt
o'r 5 fs out, wknd over 3 out.
.........................(7 to 1 op 8 to 1 tchd 10 to 1) 7
40429 SUMO 4-10-11 (3*) E Husband, chsd ldr, led 7 fs out, hdd o'r
5 out, wknd 3 out.........(33 to 1 op 50 to 1 tchd 100 to 1) 8
4143 CAHERMONE LADY (Ire) 6-11-0 O Pears, nvr nr to chal.
.........................(33 to 1 op 50 to 1 tchd 100 to 1) 9
3808 THE CHASE 6-11-5 L Wyer, hld up, hdwy o'r 4 fs out, sn rdn
and btn.........................(40 to 1 op 33 to 1) 10
38986 TWELVE CLUB 4-11-0 N Williamson, hld up, hdwy 5 fs out,
wknd o'r 3 out.........................(12 to 1 op 10 to 1) 11
4042 POSTLIP ROYALE 4-10-9 Mr J Grassick, hld up, pld hrd, al in
rear.........................(66 to 1) 12
38259 SPANISH SECRET (Ire) 5-11-5 M A Fitzgerald, led till hdd 7 fs
out, wknd 5 out.........(16 to 1 op 12 to 1 tchd 20 to 1) 13
4049 BE BROADMINDED 5-11-5 P Niven, hld up, beh frm hfwy.
.........................(66 to 1 op 50 to 1) 14
31429 DENSTAR (Ire) 4-10-7 (7*) F Quinlan, tld off frm hfwy.
.........................(50 to 1 tchd 66 to 1) 15
Dist: 2l, 7l, 5l, 11l, 2l, nk, 1½l, 7l, 3l, 10l. 3m 37.90s. (15 Ran).
(R Taylor), P Bowen

DOWN ROYAL (IRE) (good to firm) Friday May 30th

4292 Gain Horsefeeds Maiden Hurdle (4-y-o and up) £1,712 3m........ (5:55)

41687 KILCAR (Ire) 6-11-6 P Carberry,.............(7 to 4 fav) 1
37056 RACHEL'S SWALLOW (Ire) 5-11-5 (3*) B Bowens,.. (7 to 2) 2
41493 CHERGALE (Ire) 5-11-0 C O'Dwyer,.............(7 to 1) 3
41524 NOBODYWANTSME (Ire) 6-10-13 (7*) D A McLoughlin,
.........................(12 to 1) 4
36435 CORALDA (Ire) 6-10-8 (7*) D K Budds,.........(12 to 1) 5
4115 ROYAL ARISTOCRAT (Ire) 8-11-1 H Rogers,.....(16 to 1) pu
1580 ZUZUS PETALS (Ire) 7-10-8 (7*) J M Maguire,....(33 to 1) pu
3547 BITOFABUZZ (Ire) 6-10-13 (7*) M J Moore,.......(7 to 1) pu
41685 STRONG RAIDER (Ire) 7-11-6 K F O'Brien,........(4 to 1) pu
Dist: 12l, dist, 1l, 20l. 5m 44.00s. (9 Ran).
(John H Patton), Thomas Carberry

4293 Templepatrick Handicap Hurdle (0-102 4-y-o and up) £1,712 2m .... (6:25)

4162[8]	SANDRA LOUISE (Ire) [-] L J Fleming, ...(7 to 1)	1
3817	UNASSISTED (Ire) [-] 4-10-8 (3[*]) B Bowens,..........(5 to 1)	2
3606[3]	NOMINEE (Ire) [-] 5-10-9 L P Cusack, ...(5 to 1)	3
4280[6]	BAILENAGUN (Ire) [-] 4-11-1[*] P Carberry, ...(7 to 4 fav)	4
2132	BRADLEYS CORNER (Ire) [-] 6-11-6 K F O'Brien, ...(6 to 1)	5
4060	KEEP RUNNING (Ire) [-] 4-10-5 F J Flood, ...(16 to 1)	6
	NORA'S ERROR (Ire) [-] 8-11-6 D T Evans, ...(20 to 1)	7
4150[4]	DADDY'S HAT (Ire) [-] 4-10-13 P L Malone, ...(16 to 1)	8
907	SIR GANDOUGE (Ire) [-] 8-10-13 C O'Dwyer, ...(14 to 1)	9
3879	QUEEN OF ALL GALES (Ire) [-] (bl) 6-9-5 (7[*]) D A McLoughlin,	
	....(25 to 1)	10

Dist: 4l, 6l, 7l, 8l. 3m 43.00s. (10 Ran).

(M Foster), Cecil Ross

4294 Belfast Vintners Maiden Hurdle (4-y-o and up) £1,712 2m........ (6:55)

3231	LORD ESKER (Ire) 5-11-5 C N Bowers, ...(7 to 1)	1
4094[4]	ALVINE (Ire) 5-11-5 P Leech, ...(12 to 1)	2
	COPPER MOUNTAIN (Ire) 6-12-0 P Carberry, (Evens fav)	3
4168	EIRE (Ire) 8-11-7 (7[*]) D A McLoughlin, ...(10 to 1)	4
4117[6]	DUNMORE SUNSET (Ire) 5-11-5 K F O'Brien, ...(25 to 1)	5
4149[5]	CHERISHTHELADY (Ire) 5-10-9 (5[*]) T Martin, ...(25 to 1)	6
4114[2]	FRANKIE WILLOW (Ire) 4-11-6 F J Flood, ...(7 to 2)	7
137[*]	SINDABEZI (Ire) 5-11-8 C O'Dwyer, ...(3 to 1)	pu
	SEBRIMAR (Ire) 6-11-6 P McWilliams, ...(16 to 1)	pu

Dist: 4½l, 6l, 1½l, 15l. 3m 49.80s. (9 Ran).

(A P Brady), Victor Bowens

4295 Guinness I.N.H. Flat Race (4-y-o and up) £1,712 2m................ (8:25)

4096[*]	RAGGLEPUSS (Ire) 7-11-6 (7[*]) Mr T Gibney, ...(7 to 2)	1
4200[*]	DANNKALIA (Ire) (bl) 5-11-12 Mr J P Dempsey, ...(9 to 4 fav)	2
4161[4]	THE TEXAS KID (Ire) 6-11-4 (7[*]) Mr M O'Connor, ...(5 to 2)	3
	IT COULD BE YOU (Ire) 4-11-0 (3[*]) Mr B R Hamilton,	
	....(12 to 1)	4
4152[3]	WIND OF GLORY (Ire) 7-11-4 (7[*]) Mr P Jones, ...(16 to 1)	5
	WORLD O GOOD (Ire) 5-11-10 Mr P F Graffin, ...(8 to 1)	6
	EXECUTIVE SCORE (Ire) 6-11-11 Mr A J Martin, ...(11 to 2)	7

Dist: 1½l, 6l, 6l, 7l. 3m 46.20s. (7 Ran).

(Mrs E Keane), Gerard Keane

STRATFORD (good)
Friday May 30th
Going Correction: NIL

4296 Baileys Original Irish Cream Selling Handicap Hurdle Class G (0-95 4-y-o and up) £2,122 2m 110yds.... (6:35)

3810	NIGHT TIME [70] 5-10-3 (7[*]) Mr G Shenkin, wtd wth, improved 5th, chlgd 2 out, led appr last, drvn out. (16 to 1 op 33 to 1)	1
4153[*]	HEVER GOLF DIAMOND [83] (bl) 4-10-11 (7[*]) Mr P O'Keeffe, al hndy, led appr 6th, hdd approaching last, one pace.	
	....(11 to 2 op 5 to 2)	2
1110	MILZIG (USA) [64] 8-10-4 C Llewellyn, patiently rdn, prog appr 6th, ridden and one pace frm 2 out.	
	....(25 to 1 op 20 to 1)	3
4179[9]	OUR EDDIE [77] (v) 8-11-3 J Ryan, hld up, hdwy 6th, one pace 2 out,.......................(12 to 1 op 10 to 1 tchd 14 to 1)	4
4179[7]	BLATANT OUTBURST [74] (v) 7-11-0 A P McCoy, beh whn hit second, hdwy 6th, one pace appr nxt. (9 to 2 fav op 6 to 1)	5
3796	JUST ANDY [60] (bl) 6-9-7 (7[*]) J Mogford, nvr nr to chal.	
	....(66 to 1 op 50 to 1 tchd 100 to 1)	6
110[6]	STRIDING EDGE [62] 12-10-2[1] R Dunwoody, trkd ldrs till rdn and wknd 3 out,........................(10 to 1 op 8 to 1)	7
4277[3]	SALMAN (USA) [88] 14-11-11 (3[*]) Mr R Thornton, hld up beh ldrs, rdn appr 3 out, sn wknd,............(12 to 1 op 6 to 1)	8
1956	MY HARVINSKI [65] 7-10-5 D J Burchell, hld up beh ldrs, wknd appr 6th,.............(20 to 1 op 16 to 1 tchd 25 to 1)	9
4153[7]	TUG YOUR FORELOCK [60] 6-9-9 (5[*]) X Aizpuru, nvr on terms,..........................(20 to 1 op 25 to 1 tchd 33 to 1)	10
4179[8]	VERRO (USA) [60] (v) 10-9-7 (7[*]) M Griffiths, prmnt till wknd 6th,.......................................(50 to 1 op 33 to 1)	11
4189[8]	RED TEL (Ire) [78] (v) 5-10-13 (5[*]) G Supple, beh frm 5th.	
	....(12 to 1 op 6 to 1)	12
903	FAME AND FANTASY (Ire) [76] 6-11-2 R Johnson, in tch to 6th.	
	....(10 to 1 op 7 to 1 tchd 11 to 1)	13
4131	LIZIUM [61] 5-10-11 S Fox, hit 4th, nvr a factor.	
	....(33 to 1 tchd 40 to 1)	14
4153[9]	CAPTAIN TANDY (Ire) [72] 8-10-12 P McLoughlin, hld up, 5th and rdn alng whn f 2 out. (5 to 1 op 4 to 1 tchd 11 to 2)	f
4179[9]	SOCCER BALL [60] 7-10-0 W Marston, led till appr 6th, rdn whn f sixth,...............................(33 to 1)	f
4179	PREMIER STAR [60] 7-10-0 (7[*]) Mr S Durack, mstk and beh frm 5th, tld off whn pld up bef last,..........(50 to 1)	pu
4131[*]	PERSIAN BUTTERFLY [74] 5-11-0 J Culloty, in tch till pld up bef 5th,........................(9 to 1 op 5 to 1)	pu

Dist: 3½l, 2l, ¾l, 14l, 7l, 8l, 1½l, hd, 4l, ½l, hd. 3m 58.00s. (18 Ran).

(Mrs Maureen Shenkin), A G Hobbs

4297 Jean And Tony Hibbert 40th Wedding Anniversary Novices' Handicap Chase Class D (0-110 5-y-o and up) £3,548 2m 5f 110yds....... (7:05)

4138[2]	DANDIE IMP [73] 9-10-2 B Powell, made all, shaken up and drw clr frm 2 out, cmftbly...(9 to 4 op 2 to 1 tchd 5 to 2)	1
4082[4]	DISTANT MEMORY [95] (bl) 8-11-10 A P McCoy, hld up, chsd wnr frm 6th, rdn alng appr 12th, one pace 2 out.	
	....(5 to 2 tchd 11 to 4 and 9 to 4)	2
2295	LEGAL ARTIST (Ire) [79] 7-10-8 Richard Guest, hld up, not fluent 5th, drvn alng frm tenth, wknd 4 out.	
	....(8 to 1 op 5 to 1)	3
3895[3]	SPRING TO GLORY [84] (v) 10-10-13 M A Fitzgerald, chsd wnr till jmpd slwly 6th, reminders aftr 8th, hit 12th sn wknd.	
	....(13 to 8 fav op 6 to 4 tchd 2 to 1)	4

Dist: 15l, 20l, 6l. 5m 12.00s. + 12.00s. (4 Ran).

(Miss A Clift), A W Carroll

4298 Tarmac Construction Handicap Hurdle Class C (0-135 4-y-o and up) £3,626 2m 110yds............. (7:35)

4206[3]	BALLET ROYAL (USA) [104] 8-9-7 (7[*]) A Dowling, wtd wth, improved 6th, chalg whn llft in clr ld last.........(12 to 1)	1
4127[*]	YUBRALEE (USA) [132] 5-12-0 A P McCoy, led, sn clr, rdd fluent 4th, hdd appr 2 out, soon hld, llft in second pl last.	
	....(5 to 4 fav op 6 to 4)	2
3442[5]	CASTLE SECRET [120] 11-11-2 D J Burchell, hld up, drvn alng frm 6th, btn appr nxt...(4 to 1 op 3 to 1 tchd 9 to 2)	3
3907	KADASTROF (Fr) [132] 7-11-9 (5[*]) X Aizpuru, chsd ldr till appr 5th, wknd 3 out.........................(14 to 1 op 8 to 1)	4
4141[4]	KINO'S CROSS [105] 8-10-1 L Harvey, hld up, rdn and wknd appr 3 out.......................(25 to 1 op 14 to 1)	5
3652[*]	HAY DANCE [113] 6-10-9 N Williamson, hld up beh ldg pair, cld 4th, chsd ldr appr nxt, led approaching 2 out, f last.	
	....(2 to 1 op 9 to 4 tchd 5 to 2)	f

Dist: 12l, 6l, 3l, 5l. 3m 50.80s. + 4.80s (6 Ran).

SR: 24/40/22/26/-/-/

(H J Manners), H J Manners

4299 Horse And Hound Champion Novices' Hunters' Chase Class H for the John Corbet Cup (5-y-o and up) £4,272 3½m................... (8:05)

4072[*]	EARTHMOVER (Ire) 6-11-7 (7[*]) Miss P Gundry, hld up in midfield, hit 13th, steady prog frm 16th, led aftr 3 out, sn clr, ran on wl.......(7 to 4 fav op 6 to 4 tchd 15 to 8 and 2 to 1)	1
3850[*]	STRUGGLES GLORY (Ire) 11-11-13[6] (7[*]) Mr D C Robinson, led till aftr 3 out, styd on r-in.	
	....(2 to 1 op 9 to 4 tchd 5 to 2 and 15 to 8)	2
	SHUIL'S STAR (Ire) 6-11-7 (7[*]) Mr P Hamer, hld up and beh, hit 6th, gd hdwy 16th, cl 3rd whn hmpd 4 out, one pace frm nxt.	
	....(16 to 1 tchd 20 to 1)	3
4041[*]	PRINCE BUCK (Ire) 7-11-11 (3[*]) Mr P Hacking, in tch, chsd ldr frm 8th to 16th, wknd from 3 out, tiring whn mstk nxt.	
	....(9 to 2 tchd 5 to 1 and 11 to 2)	4
4011[*]	GREENMOUNT LAD (Ire) 9-11-7 (7[*]) Mr P Cornforth, hld up, mstks 7th and nxt, sn beh, tld off.....(33 to 1 op 14 to 1)	5
4171[3]	TOM'S GEMINI STAR 9-11-7 (7[*]) Miss V Roberts, blun second, al beh, tld off whn f 4 out...........(50 to 1 op 33 to 1)	f
4033[4]	MISTER HORATIO 7-11-7 (7[*]) Mr M Lewis, prmnt, chsd ldr frm 16th, chalg whn blun and uns rdr 4 out.	
	....(33 to 1 op 20 to 1)	ur
4171[5]	PHAR TOO TOUCHY 10-11-2 (7[*]) Mr N Harris, prmnt, mstk second, hit 13th, sn beh, pld up bef 16th. (11 to 2 op 4 to 1)	pu
3977[4]	TAURA'S RASCAL 8-11-7 (7[*]) Mr F Brennan, mid-div, hit tenth, blun badly 15th, beh whn pld up bef 17th.	
	....(50 to 1 op 25 to 1)	pu

Dist: 4l, 9l, 12l, dist. 7m 1.60s. + a 16.60s (9 Ran).

(R M Penny), R Barber

4300 Weatherbys Young Horse Awards Handicap Chase Class D (0-125 5-y-o and up) £3,418 2m 1f 110yds (8:35)

4269[*]	INDIAN JOCKEY [124] 5-11-9 (7ex) A P McCoy, led, sn clr, rdn alng appr 8th, hrd pressd 3 out, soon hdd, rallied approaching last, rgned ld r-in, ran on wl.	
	....(11 to 8 on op 9 to 4 on tchd 5 to 4 on)	1
2736	FIFTYSEVENCHANNELS (Ire) [108] 8-12-0 G Bradley, chsd wnr, chlgd 3 out, sn led, hdd r-in, no extr.	
	....(11 to 2 op 4 to 1 tchd 6 to 1)	2
4205[4]	SOCIETY GUEST [120] 11-11-11 L Harvey, hld up, drvn alng 9th, one pace.......................(9 to 1 op 8 to 1 tchd 12 to 1)	3
4129[2]	STORM FALCON (USA) [111] 7-11-2 R Dunwoody, hld up, mstk 4 out, sn btn.......................(5 to 2 op 3 to 1)	4

Dist: 4l, 10l, 8l. 4m 9.40s. + 7.40s (4 Ran).

SR: 21/22/9/-/

(Stuart M Mercer), M C Pipe

4301 Grandstand Consultants Novices' Hurdle Class D (4-y-o and up) £3,020 2m 110yds.................... (9:05)

3905² FAIRLY SHARP (Ire) 4-10-8 R Dunwoody, *al hndy, led 6th, clr*
frm nxt, eased r-in.
.... (11 to 10 on op Evens tchd 5 to 4 on) 1
4136⁹ IRENE'S PET 7-10-12 S Fox, *hld up, rdn alng 6th, styd on one*
pace frm 3 out, wnt second r-in, no imprsn on wnr.
.... (66 to 1 op 33 to 1) 2
4181⁵ CAMP HEAD (Ire) 6-10-12 J A McCarthy, *in tch frm 4th, effrt*
from 3 out, one pace nxt... (5 to 1 op 6 to 1 tchd 8 to 1) 3
ALAFLAK (Ire) 6-10-12 B Powell, *trkd ldrs, rdn 3 out, sn btn.*
.... (11 to 2 op 3 to 1 tchd 6 to 1) 4
3482⁷ NIGHT ESCAPADE (Ire) 5-10-7 M Richards, *beh, hit 4th, kpt*
on one pace fnl 2, nvr a dngr.
.... (33 to 1 op 25 to 1 tchd 50 to 1) 5
4201 FRIAR'S OAK 5-10-5 (7*) Mr O McPhail, *beh frm 5th.*
.... (100 to 1 op 66 to 1) 6
4030⁴ PRESS AGAIN 5-10-7 B Fenton, *blun 6th, nvr dngrs.*
.... (100 to 1 op 50 to 1) 7
EAU BENITE 6-10-12 R Johnson, *pld hrd early, nvr a factor.*
.... (100 to 1 op 50 to 1) 8
4182* MELT THE CLOUDS (Can) (bl) 4-11-5 A P McCoy, *led to 6th,*
wknd bef nxt... (100 to 30 op 5 to 2 tchd 7 to 2) 9
DAMARITA 6-10-11 (7*) Mr P O'Keeffe, *hld up, blun and uns*
rdr 3rd. ....(66 to 1 op 33 to 1) ur
3828 BLUE HAVANA 5-10-7 J Culloty, *hit second, prmnt to 4th,*
wknd quickly, tld off whn pld up bef 6th.
.... (100 to 1 op 50 to 1) pu
Dist: 13l, 2½l, 12l, 1¼l, 8l, 4l, 5l, 12l. 3m 58.60s. a 12.60s (11 Ran).

(Ms Caroline F Breay), Graeme Roe

WEXFORD (IRE) (good)
Friday May 30th

4302 Pinnacle Maiden Hurdle (4-y-o and up) £2,226 2¼m 100yds...... (5:30)

4144 KINGMAN (Ire) 5-11-13 P A Roche, ... (8 to 1) 1
BUCKLEUP (Ire) 8-11-7 (7*) Mr M Budds, ... (10 to 1) 2
2138² CROSSCHILD (Ire) 6-11-4 (5*) P G Hourigan, ...(9 to 4 fav) 3
TELESCOPE (Ire) 7-11-7 (7*) Mr A K Wyse, ... (13 to 2) 4
232⁵ BISHOP'S HILL (Ire) 8-12-0 T P Treacy, ...(7 to 2) 5
4195⁸ STONE HEAD (Ire) 4-11-3 (3*) K Whelan, ... (12 to 1) 6
4160 MINNY DOZER (Ire) 8-11-7 (7*) J P Deegan, ... (20 to 1) 7
4163⁸ VARTRY BOY (Ire) 6-11-9 (5*) B J Geraghty, ... (10 to 1) 8
4052⁸ CAME AWAY (Ire) 6-11-2 (7*) L A Hurley, ... (20 to 1) 9
3891⁸ NEW WEST (Ire) 7-11-7 (7*) S P McCann, ... (12 to 1) 10
4195 APPLE RIVER (Ire) 4-10-8 (7*) D Fisher, ...(20 to 1) 11
ISLAND OF DREAMS (Ire) 5-11-8 J Shortt, ... (14 to 1) 12
3840 KATIE DALY (Ire) 6-11-9 D J Casey, ... (10 to 1) 13
224⁵ ROLL OVER (Ire) 7-12-0 T J Mitchell, ...(7 to 1) f
Dist: 5l, nk, 5½l, 14l. 4m 23.50s. (14 Ran).

(T A Kent), T A Kent

4303 Mount Leinster Handicap Chase (0-130 4-y-o and up) £2,740 2½m
.... (6:00)

4164⁶ MUBADIR (USA) [-] 9-11-9 (5*) B J Geraghty, (9 to 4 jt-fav) 1
3752⁸ THE SUBBIE (Ire) [-] 8-11-1 T P Treacy, ...(5 to 2) 2
4165⁸ HOLIWAY STAR (Ire) [-] 7-11-7 C F Swan, ...(9 to 4 jt-fav) 3
63* HEARNS HILL (Ire) [-] 8-10-10 J Shortt, ... (5 to 1) f
Dist: 20l, 4½l. 4m 56.40s. (4 Ran).

(Liam Keating), Noel Meade

4304 Rosslare Handicap Hurdle (0-123 4-y-o and up) £2,740 2m...... (6:30)

4168⁴ GENTLE MOSSY (Ire) [-] 5-11-2 D H O'Connor, ...(9 to 2) 1
3235⁴ PAS POSSIBLE (Ire) [-] 5-11-11 T P Treacy, ...(9 to 2) 2
3952⁷ LUNA FLEUR (Ire) [-] 4-10-10 (5*) B J Geraghty, (9 to 4 fav) 3
4200⁵ JANICE PRICE (Ire) [-] 6-10-8 J Shortt, ... (8 to 1) 4
3952² ASHJAR (USA) [-] 4-10-6 (5*) P G Hourigan, ... (9 to 2) 5
3449 WINTER MELODY (Ire) [-] 5-9-11 (7*) W M Martin, (10 to 1) 6
4162⁵ MAJESTIC PADDY (Ire) [-] 7-11-4 T J Mitchell, ... (6 to 1) 7
3965⁸ BLACKWATER CISCO (Ire) [-] 7-10-3⁷ (7*) Mr J Quigley,
.... (33 to 1) 8
3816 BARNA GIRL (Ire) [-] 7-9-8¹ J R Barry, ... (33 to 1) 9
Dist: Hd, 8l, sht-hd, 20l. 3m 48.70s. (9 Ran).

(Purple and Gold Syndicate), James Joseph O'Connor

4305 Tusker Light I.N.H. Flat Race (4 & 5-y-o) £2,226 2m.............. (8:00)

3524 DOCKLINE (Ire) 5-11-6 (7*) Mr B J Crowley, ...(12 to 1) 1
RAISE THE GALE (Ire) 5-11-13 Mr J A Berry, ...(3 to 1 jt-fav) 2
ALONE TABANKULU (Ire) 5-11-5 (3*) Mr P English, (10 to 1) 3
3816² PARSEE (Ire) 5-11-1 (7*) Mr Paul Moloney, ...(5 to 1) 4
LEAPING LORD (Ire) 4-11-6 Mr P Fenton, ... (10 to 1) 5
4161⁵ BUDALUS (Ire) 5-11-13 Mr D Marnane, ... (5 to 1) 6
2172²⁹ BUTLER'S GROVE (Ire) 5-11-8 (5*) Mr A C Coyle, (3 to 1 jt-fav) 7
4096 MEGAN'S RUN (Ire) 5-11-5 (3*) Mr D Valentine, ... (20 to 1) 8
4106 AJKNAPP (Ire) 5-11-6 (7*) Mr M A Flood, ... (16 to 1) 9
4029⁸ MOSSIE MCCARTHY (Ire) 5-11-13 Mr P J Healy, .. (20 to 1) 10
BLACK IS BEAUTIFUL (Ire) 5-11-6 (7*) Mr J P McNamara,
.... (20 to 1) 11
2967⁸ DETROIT FLYER (Ire) 4-10-13 (7*) Mr A J Dempsey, (14 to 1) pu

Dist: Nk, 2l, 3½l, 1l. 3m 43.50s. (12 Ran).

(Seamus O'Farrell), A P O'Brien

4306 Three Rocks Mares I.N.H. Flat Race (Div I) (4-y-o and up) £2,226 2m
.... (8:30)

4169⁷ ANN'S DESIRE (Ire) 6-11-7 (7*) Mr J Keville, ... (8 to 1) 1
350² STRONG EDITION (Ire) 6-12-0 Mr J A Berry, ...(7 to 2) 2
3953 CHELSEA BELLE (Ire) 5-11-6 (7*) Mr T J Nagle, ... (12 to 1) 3
3965⁴ THE RED SIDE (Ire) 5-11-6 (7*) Mr P G Murphy, ...(9 to 2) 4
4005 AGLISH PRIDE (Ire) 5-11-13 Mr R Walsh, ... (3 to 1 fav) 5
4147⁹ BAWN BEAG (Ire) 5-11-10 (3*) Mr W M O'Sullivan, (12 to 1) 6
4197 ST CAROL (Ire) 6-11-9 (5*) Mr A C Coyle, ... (10 to 1) 7
4106 COMINOLE (Ire) 8-11-7 (7*) Miss C O'Neill, ... (16 to 1) 8
4059⁹ BE THE ONE (Ire) (bl) 6-12-0 Mr P Fenton, ... (10 to 1) 9
SANDY MISS (Ire) 7-11-11 (3*) Mr D Valentine, ... (14 to 1) 10
4096⁶ FELICITY'S PRIDE (Ire) (bl) 6-11-7 (7*) Mr D P Coakley,
.... (14 to 1) 11
DROIM ALTON GALE (Ire) 5-11-6 (7*) Mr Paul Moloney,
.... (14 to 1) 12
4106 TRIMMER LADY (Ire) 8-11-7 (7*) Mr O O'Connor, .. (12 to 1) 13
4106⁹ LADY BELLAGHY (Ire) 6-11-7 (7*) Mr E Gallagher, (14 to 1) 14
LACKEN STAR (Ire) 4-10-13 (7*) Mr W F Codd, ...(14 to 1) 15
Dist: ¾l, 1½l, ¾l, sht-hd. 3m 46.70s. (15 Ran).

(Mrs C Barker), Mrs C Barker

4307 Three Rocks Mares I.N.H. Flat Race (Div II) (4-y-o and up) £2,226 2m
.... (9:00)

4200³ STRONG CHOICE (Ire) 5-11-6 (7*) Mr B J Crowley, (9 to 4) 1
4029⁵ GALE JOHNSTON (Ire) 6-12-0 Mr P Fenton, ...(8 to 1) 2
4052⁷ THE WELL (Ire) 6-11-7 (7*) Mr K Culligan, ... (14 to 1) 3
4062⁵ SARAH BLUE (Ire) 7-11-7 (7*) Mr K R O'Ryan, ... (12 to 1) 4
4161⁸ SHERS HILL (Ire) 5-11-13 Mr B M Cash, ... (12 to 1) 5
4147³ KEEP THE PEARL 4-10-13 (7*) Mr A J Dempsey,
.... (5 to 4 fav) 6
1005 EASTERN CUSTOM (Ire) 6-11-7 (7*) Miss D O'Neill, (12 to 1) 7
4106⁵ MONTY'S FANCY (Ire) 4-10-13 (7*) Mr C A Cronin, (12 to 1) 8
MOVE ASIDE (Ire) 5-11-6 (7*) Mr Paul Moloney, ... (12 to 1) 9
LOST COIN 10-11-7 (7*) Mr J P Brennan, ...(14 to 1) 10
WOODVILLE PRINCESS (Ire) (bl) 6-11-11 (3*) Mr T Lombard,
.... (16 to 1) 11
CARRYONREGARDLESS (Ire) 6-11-7 (7*) Mr P J Jennings,
.... (25 to 1) 12
144 BIG STORM (Ire) 10-11-7 (3*) Mr P Walsh, ...(16 to 1) 13
4079⁴ DEEP ALTO (Ire) 5-11-6 (7*) Mr B N Doyle, ...(25 to 1) 14
4161 AUSSIE ROSE (Ire) 7-11-9 (5*) Mr A C Coyle, ... (25 to 1) 15
Dist: ½l, 1l, 7l, nk. 3m 48.70s. (15 Ran).

(Mrs Sandra McCarthy), P Mullins

GOWRAN PARK (IRE) (good)
Saturday May 31st

4308 Norevale Handicap Hurdle (0-135 4-y-o and up) £5,480 3m 1f... (2:30)

4247* TRIPTODICKS (Ire) [-] 7-10-1 T P Treacy, ...(9 to 2) 1
4059³ CORYROSE (Ire) [-] 5-9-10 (5*) P G Hourigan, ... (6 to 1) 2
4095* THE ELECTRIC (Ire) [-] 6-10-12 T J Mitchell, ...(7 to 4 fav) 3
4146⁵ TOUREEN GALE (Ire) [-] 8-10-13 D J Casey, ... (11 to 2) 4
3234 CLASHWILLIAM GIRL (Ire) [-] 9-10-11 J R Barry, ... (9 to 1) 5
4077⁷ HEATHER VILLE (Ire) [-] 5-9-7 (5*) B J Geraghty, ...(6 to 1) pu
ATHY SPIRIT [-] 12-11-11 J Shortt, ... (20 to 1) pu
4076* BAWNROCK (Ire) [-] 8-11-8 C F Swan, ... (9 to 2) pu
Dist: 7l, 20l, 5½l, 4½l. 5m 51.00s. (8 Ran).

(M G O'Huallachain), David A Kiely

4309 Barrowvale I.N.H. Flat Race (4-y-o) £2,226 2m.................... (5:30)

HURMUZAN (Ire) 11-2 (7*) Miss A Foley, ...(10 to 1) 1
BERKELEY FRONTIER (Ire) 11-9 Mr A J Martin, ... (8 to 1) 2
KARAKAM (Ire) 11-2 (7*) Mr Paul Moloney, ...(4 to 1 jt-fav) 3
SOVIET PRINCESS (Ire) 11-1 (3*) Mr P J Casey, ... (20 to 1) 4
MARBLE SOUND (Ire) 10-13 (5*) Mr A C Coyle, ... (7 to 1) 5
4056⁴ FIDALUS (Ire) 11-2 (7*) Mr M T Hartrey, ...(14 to 1) 6
LIME TREE ROAD (Ire) 11-9 Mr R Walsh, ...(4 to 1 jt-fav) 7
3952⁶ GOOD FOUNDATION (Ire) 11-4 Mr B M Cash, ... (10 to 1) 8
4056 THE KERRY REBEL (Ire) 11-2 (7*) Mr J P McNamara,
.... (16 to 1) 9
CARDIAC ARREST (Ire) 11-9 Mr J A Berry, ...(8 to 1) 10
3945⁵ OTTER TRACK LADY (Ire) 10-11 (7*) Mr Philip Carberry,
.... (12 to 1) 11
4056⁹ SMOOTH MELODY (Ire) 11-9 Mr D Marnane, ... (16 to 1) 12
STRONGDARA (Ire) 10-11 (7*) Mr J Cash, ... (12 to 1) 13
GOALDPOST (Ire) 11-2 (7*) Mr D A Harney, ...(14 to 1) 14
MONEY POT (Ire) 10-11 (7*) Mr P Fahey, ...(12 to 1) 15
Dist: 6l, 2½l, 11l, 6l. 3m 45.20s. (15 Ran).

(William Kelly), Thomas Foley

MARKET RASEN (good to firm)
Saturday May 31st

Going Correction: PLUS 0.05 sec. per fur.

4310 'End Of Season' Selling Handicap Hurdle Class G (0-90 4,5,6-y-o) £1,852 2m 1f 110yds......... (6:35)

3476⁵ LUCY TUFTY [71] 6-11-6 P Carberry, hld up in tch, smooth
hdwy to ld 2 out, pushed out run in
............................(7 to 2 op 3 to 1 tchd 4 to 1) 1
4081⁴ MASTER SHOWMAN (Ire) [58] 6-10-7 R Guest, chsd ldrs, rdn
to chal 2 out, kpt on run in.........(20 to 1 tchd 25 to 1) 2
4182⁴ HAWANAFA [71] (v) 4-11-1 R Dunwoody, led till hdd 2 out,
rallied and ev ch frm last, hld nr finish.
............................(3 to 1 op 7 to 2 tchd 11 to 4) 3
3971² IRIE MON (Ire) [78] 5-11-13 J Railton, hld up and beh, steady
hdwy aftr 3 out, rdn nxt, no imprsn......(7 to 1 op 6 to 1) 4
4237⁵ SUMMER VILLA [73] (bl) 5-11-8 J Ryan, hld up in rear, effrt
and drvn alng aftr 3 out, struggling nxt..(8 to 1 op 7 to 1) 5
4237* AJDAR [72] 6-11-4 (3*) R Massey, chsd ldrs, struggling aftr 3
out, sn btn............................(9 to 4 fav op 6 to 4) 6
3988 CATWALKER (Ire) [51] (bl) 6-10-0 M Richards, wth ldr to 3rd, cl
up, struggling aftr 3 out, fdd.............(20 to 1 tchd 25 to 1) 7
4176⁵ WOODLANDS LAD TOO [51] (bl) 5-10-0 T J Murphy, not
fluent in rear, struggling 5th, sn btn, tld off whn pld up bef 2
out..(33 to 1) pu
Dist: ½l, nk, 5l, 9l, 4l, 9l. 4m 14.30s. a 13.30s (8 Ran).

(G H Tufts), J Pearce

4311 Roger Johnstone & Partners Novices' Chase Class D (5-y-o and up) £3,803 2½m.....................(7:05)

4128² EID (USA) 8-11-0 Richard Guest, chsd ldr, led 5 out, drw clr
fnl 2.....................(7 to 4 on op 11 to 4 on) 1
OSGATHORPE 10-11-0 Mrs F Needham, chsd ldrs, chlgd 5
out, rdn and one pace fnl 2.
............................(11 to 4 op 3 to 1 tchd 100 to 30) 2
4286³ QUIXALL CROSSETT 12-11-0 Gary Lyons, led till hdd 5 out,
one pace last 3.........................(10 to 1 op 12 to 1) 3
3670 MORCAT 8-10-9 Mr C Mulhall, not fluent, in tch, outpcd tenth,
no dngr aftr..............................(12 to 1 op 10 to 1) 4
Dist: 12l, 1½l, 28l. 5m 4.60s. a 15.60s (4 Ran).

(N Wilby), Mrs S J Smith

4312 Lincolnshire Business Development Centre Handicap Chase Class E (0-110 5-y-o and up) £2,880 2m 1f 110yds.....................(7:35)

4140⁴ TAPATCH (Ire) [87] 9-11-10 P Carberry, sn chasing ldrs,
effrt 3 out, ev ch last, ran on wl und pres to ld post.
............................(6 to 4 fav tchd 2 to 1 and 11 to 8) 1
4031² THATS THE LIFE [78] 12-11-1 R Johnson, led till hdd 4 out,
rallied to rgn ld 2 out, ran on wl frm last, jst ct.
............................(9 to 4 op 7 to 4 tchd 5 to 2) 2
3821⁵ DASH TO THE PHONE (USA) [71] 5-10-2 R Supple, wth ldr,
led 4 out hdd 2 out, sn btn..............(10 to 1 op 7 to 1) 3
3775³ FICHU (USA) [82] 9-11-5 M Richards, sn beh, pushed alng
6th, struggling aftr 4 out, soon lost tch, fnshd tme.
............................(5 to 1 op 4 to 1 tchd 11 to 2) 4
895² THE YOKEL [70] 11-10-4 (3*) P Henley, in tch, struggling 4
out, pld up lme bef nxt................(6 to 1 op 7 to 1) pu
Dist: Sht-hd, 8l, dist. 4m 22.80s. a 8.80s (5 Ran).
SR: 17/8/

(Miss V Foster), M W Easterby

4313 H. & L. Garages Handicap Hurdle Class D (0-120 4-y-o and up) £2,951 2m 3f 110yds................(8:05)

4201* JAMAICAN FLIGHT (USA) [100] 4-10-8 J Railton, made virtually all, blun 3rd, clr whn blunded last, reco'red and ran on
strly.....................................(9 to 4 fav tchd 5 to 2) 1
4017² OUT ON A PROMISE (Ire) [110] 5-11-9 R Supple, keen hold in
rear, improved and ev ch 3 out, rdn nxt, one pace frm last.
............................(3 to 1 op 5 to 2 tchd 7 to 2) 2
4017⁴ NASHVILLE STAR (USA) [92] (v) 6-10-5 A Thornton, chsd ldrs,
drvn alng 3 out, outpcd bef nxt........(14 to 1 op 12 to 1) 3
4008⁷ RED JAM JAR [91] 12-10-4 K Johnson, wth ldr, struggling 3
out, sn btn..........................(14 to 1 op 10 to 1 tchd 16 to 1) 4
4071⁵ EL DON [112] 5-11-11 J Ryan, hld up, rdn alng 4 out, btn bef 2
out.....................................(5 to 1 op 4 to 1 tchd 11 to 2) 5
4213⁵ BOSTON MAN [88] 6-10-1 P Carberry, chsd ldrs, struggling
bef 3 out, fdd........................(9 to 2 op 4 to 1 tchd 7 to 2) 6
4071⁷ MIM-LOU-AND [106] 5-11-5 J Culloty, chsd ldrs, outpcd 4
out, btn whn blun 2 out, pld up bef last. (8 to 1 tchd 7 to 1) pu
Dist: 3½l, 8l, 1¾l, 8l, 22l. 4m 40.40s. a 10.40s (7 Ran).

(P Lamyman), Mrs S Lamyman

4314 Geostar Hunters' Chase Class H (5-y-o and up) £1,954 2¾m 110yds.....................(8:35)

4218² CUMBERLAND BLUES (Ire) 8-11-11 (7*) Miss A Deniel, led till
hdd 4 out, rallied to ld run in, gmely.
............................(11 to 8 fav op 6 to 4 tchd 7 to 4) 1

4260⁶ INDIE ROCK 7-11-3 (7*) Mrs F Needham, chsd ldrs, led 4 out,
hit last, sn hdd, kpt on wl............(9 to 2 tchd 4 to 1) 2
3969² KAMBALDA RAMBLER 13-12-3 (7*) Mr R Armson, nvr far
away, ev ch 4 out, outpcd aftr nxt.
............................(9 to 2 op 7 to 2 tchd 3 to 1) 3
4260² SHUIL SAOR 10-11-3 (7*) Mr C Mulhall, hld up, steady hdwy
9th, rdn 4 out, blun nxt, sn btn.
............................(4 to 1 op 7 to 2 tchd 9 to 2) 4
EARL GRAY (bl) 10-11-3 (7*) Miss J Eastwood, sn beh, nvr on
terms.....................................(33 to 1 op 25 to 1) 5
4270 ALPHA ONE 12-12-0 (7*) Miss K Di Marte, in tch, drpd rear
and struggling 8th, nvr dngrs aftr.....(33 to 1 op 25 to 1) 6
NEEDWOOD JOKER 6-11-3 (7*) Mr K Green, al wl beh.
............................(40 to 1 op 33 to 1) 7
AUNTIE CHRIS 7-10-12 (7*) Mr P Gee, whipped round and
uns rdr strt..........................(25 to 1 op 20 to 1) ur
4124 SHIP THE BUILDER 8-11-3 (7*) Mr S Brisby, jmpd badly in
rear, sn struggling, tld off whn pld up bef 2 out.
............................(16 to 1 op 8 to 1) pu
4066 SECRET TRUTH 8-10-12 (7*) Mr Andrew Martin, chsd wnr,
wkng whn hit tenth, tld off when pld up bef 3 out.
............................(20 to 1 op 25 to 1) pu
Dist: ½l, 10l, 5l, 16l, dist, 1¼l. 5m 39.50s. a 12.50s (10 Ran).

(John L Holdroyd), Mrs A Lockwood

4315 'Summer Festival Comes Next' Maiden Hurdle Class E (4-y-o and up) £2,547 2m 1f 110yds....... (9:05)

2463 RUSHEN RAIDER 5-11-5 R Garritty, hld up, improved 3 out,
led run in, ran on strly...................(5 to 1 op 9 to 2) 1
2397⁵ FRESH FRUIT DAILY 5-11-0 K Gaule, led, jmpd path and hdd
run in, not quicken. (11 to 8 on op 5 to 4 on tchd Evens) 2
370³ SILVERDALE LAD 6-11-5 M Foster, hld up, improved 5th, effrt
and rdn 2 out, styd on same pace frm last.
............................(11 to 2 op 9 to 2) 3
4201⁵ ORCHARD KING 7-11-2 (3*) R Massey, cl up, ev ch 3 out, sn
rdn, btn nxt.............................(5 to 1 op 7 to 2) 4
4158⁴ CAN SHE CAN CAN 5-11-0 M Ranger, chsd ldrs till outpcd
bef 3 out, fdd.........................(14 to 1 op 10 to 1) 5
4224 DRAMATIC PASS (Ire) 8-11-5 W Worthington, beh, struggling
hfwy, tld off.............................(66 to 1 op 33 to 1) 6
2852 GOOD VENTURE 6-11-0 N Smith, not jump wl, tld off fnl
circuit..................................(50 to 1 op 33 to 1) 7
4115⁴ ILKEHIM 10-11-5 Mr N Kent, cl up, outpcd bef 4th, sn lost tch,
tld off whn pld up before last.........(66 to 1 op 33 to 1) pu
Dist: 2½l, 8l, 8l, 3l, dist, dist. 4m 9.80s. a 8.80s (8 Ran).
SR: 12/4/1/-/-/

(Mrs Thelma White), K W Hogg

STRATFORD (good)
Saturday May 31st
Going Correction: MINUS 0.10 sec. per fur.

4316 J. P. Seafoods Novices' Hurdle Class D (4-y-o and up) £3,183 2¾m 110yds ....(2:25)

4181² BULLENS BAY (Ire) 8-10-13 Mr J L Llewellyn, patiently rdn,
improved fnl circuit, led 2 out, styd on wl to go clr r-in.
............................(4 to 1 op 5 to 2) 1
4182³ SANTELLA CAPE 4-10-7 J Railton, settled wth chasing grp.
chalg whn not fluent 3 out, rallied betw last 2, kpt on, no ch
with wnr...................(15 to 2 op 9 to 2 tchd 8 to 1) 2
4136 FAITHLEGG (Ire) 6-10-8 M A Fitzgerald, nvr far away, led aftr
7th to 4 out, led ag'n 3 out to nxt, one pace betw last 2.
............................(33 to 1 op 14 to 1) 3
187³ MOUNTAIN LEADER 7-10-13 B Powell, led till hdd 6th, lft in ld
nxt, headed 7th, led 4 out to next, fdd und pres betw last 2.
............................(33 to 1 op 25 to 1) 4
3810⁵ RAPID LINER 4-10-7 V Slattery, wtd wth, took clr order hfwy,
feeling pace appr 3 out, wknd quickly and lost tch.
............................(100 to 1 op 33 to 1) 5
4136⁴ COOL HARRY (USA) 6-10-6 (7*) Mr S Durack, chsd ldrs,
struggling bef 3 out, sn rdn and btn....(12 to 1 op 7 to 1) 6
4158⁷ DERRING WELL 7-10-8 K Gaule, last for a circuit, effrt hfwy,
drvn alng appr 3 out, sn lost tch, tld off.
............................(100 to 1 op 33 to 1) 7
3913* EAU DE COLOGNE 5-11-11 M Richards, wth ldr, led 6th, l
nxt.....................................(5 to 4 on op 11 to 10) f
ROYAL SILVER 6-10-6 (7*) J Mogford, wth ldrs whn l 4th.
............................(16 to 1 op 14 to 1) f
318 FIVE FROM HOME (Ire) 9-10-13 D Skyrme, lost tch aftr one
circuit, tld off whn pld up aftr 7th..........(33 to 1) pu
4209 BUNNY HARE (Ire) 9-10-13 L O'Hara, in tch for a circuit, tld off
whn pld up bef 4 out....................(100 to 1 op 66 to 1) pu
Dist: 3½l, 3l, 2l, 9l, 2½l, 24l. 5m 25.90s. a 13.90s (11 Ran).

(J Milton), B J Llewellyn

4317 Developer Of The Year 1997 Richardsons Handicap Chase Class C For the Gambling Prince Trophy (0-135 5-y-o and up) £4,532 2m 5f 110yds....................(2:55)

4058 STATELY HOME (Ire) [135] 6-12-0 N Williamson, jmpd boldly, wth ldr till led 5th, made rst, styd on srtly to go clr frm 2 out.
.................................(8 to 1 op 6 to 1) 1

4132* FORMAL INVITATION (Ire) [122] 8-11-1 R Johnson, ran in snatches, hit 5th, effrt and drvn alng fnl circuit, styd on frm 2 out, not rch wnr.
.......(13 to 8 fav op 7 to 4 tchd 15 to 8 and 6 to 4) 2

4126⁴ SEOD RIOGA (Ire) [114] 8-10-7 R Dunwoody, settled to track ldrs, ev ch 5 out, rdn and one pace frm 2 out.
.................................(9 to 1 op 7 to 1) 3

3744³ ALL FOR LUCK [119] 12-10-12 A P McCoy, last and niggled alng 1st circuit, took clr order appr 5 out, feeling pace and drvn along aftr 3 out, no extr.
.........................(15 to 2 op 5 to 1 tchd 8 to 1) 4

3884 OVER THE POLE [107] 10-10-0³ (3*) Mr C Bonner, settled in tch, ev ch 5 out, hrd at work aftr 3 out, fdd. (8 to 1 op 7 to 1) 5

4016⁵ STRONG MEDICINE [129] 10-11-8 A Thornton, pressed ldg pair for o'r a circuit, hrd at work whn pace quickened aftr 3 out, wknd quickly...............(20 to 1 op 14 to 1) 6

4259* GLEMOT (Ire) [136] 9-11-10 (5*,6ex) Mr R Wakley, led to 5th, styd upsides, disputing 3rd and drvn alng whn f 3 out.
.................................(8 to 1 op 5 to 1) f

4135² FACTOR TEN (Ire) [122] 9-11-1 J F Titley, chsd ldrs, feeling pace fnl circuit, wknd quickly and pld up aftr 3 out.
.........................(11 to 2 op 4 to 1) pu

Dist: 3½sl, 1½sl, 3½sl, 3½sl, 13l. 5m 4.80s. a 4.80s (8 Ran).
SR: 31/14/4/5/-/ (P Bowen), P Bowen

4318 A. C. Lloyd Handicap Hurdle Class E (0–115 5-y-o and up) £2,430 3m 3f
................................(3:25)

4252* DOUALAGO (Fr) [107] (bl) 7-11-11 (6ex) A P McCoy, made all, quickened pace fnl circuit, styd on srtly to go clr last 2, readily.
.........................(2 to 1 fav tchd 5 to 2) 1

3689⁵ HOLY JOE [98] 15-11-2 D J Burchell, settled wth chasing grp, drvn alng to improve fnl circuit, styd on frm 2 out, no imprsn on wnr...............(14 to 1 op 12 to 1 tchd 16 to 1) 2

4047² DERRING BRIDGE [93] 7-10-11 R Johnson, settled in tch, effrt and drvn alng fnl circuit, one pace frm 3 out.
.................................(8 to 1 op 9 to 1) 3

4133³ ST VILLE [109] 11-11-13 B Powell, bustled alng wth chasing grp, effrt fnl circuit, hrd at work aftr 3 out, no imprsn.
.................................(9 to 1 op 7 to 1) 4

4088² STORMY SESSION [84] 7-10-2 C Llewellyn, pressed wnr for more than one circuit, feeling pace and chsd alng frm 3 out, fdd.................................(7 to 1 op 4 to 1 tchd 11 to 2) 5

4133* JIMBALOU [90] 14-10-5 (3*) R Massey, struggling to keep in tch hfwy, lost touch fnl circuit, tld off whn pld up appr 2 out.
.........................(7 to 2 op 4 to 1 tchd 9 to 2) pu

4140⁷ NICKLE JOE [83] 11-9-10² (7*) Mr O McPhail, lost tch quickly hfwy, tld off whn pld up bef 4 out, lme. (50 to 1 op 25 to 1) pu

3926⁶ LIL URU (Ire) [94] 9-10-12 J A McCarthy, pressed ldg pair for one and a half circuits, struggling and lost grnd aftr 4 out, wknd quickly and pld up aftr nxt.....(16 to 1 op 12 to 1) pu

4141⁵ ALBERTITO (Fr) [87] 10-10-5 S Wynne, struggling to go pace hfwy, lost tch fnl circuit, pld up aftr 3 out...........(33 to 1) pu

4035* APACHEE FLOWER [87] 7-10-5² M A Fitzgerald, struggling pld up quickly 5th, tld off whn pld up 4 out.
.................................(7 to 1 op 6 to 1) pu

4177⁷ LITTLE TINCTURE (Ire) [84] 7-10-2² G Upton, struggling and lost tch quickly hfwy, tld off whn pld up appr 2 out..(50 to 1) pu

Dist: 4l, 6l, nk, sht-hd. 6m 26.10s. a 8.10s (11 Ran).
(Martin Pipe Racing Club), M C Pipe

4319 Spillers Horse Feeds Ladies' Hunters' Chase Class H (5-y-o and up) £2,136 3m................(3:55)

4218 THANK U JIM 9-10-7 (7*) Miss T Jackson, led to 3rd, styd upsides till rgned ld aftr 6 out, set str pace after, stayed on wl frm 2 out................(16 to 1 op 8 to 1 tchd 20 to 1) 1

FINAL PRIDE 11-10-9 (3*) Miss P Jones, wth ldr, led 3rd till hdd aftr 6 out, pressed wnr after, kpt on same pace frm 2 out.
.................................(6 to 5 on op 11 to 10 tchd 5 to 4 on) 2

WAKE UP LUV 12-10-7 (7*) Miss C Cooper, struggling to go pace and wl beh hfwy, str run frm 3 out, fnshd well.
.........................(33 to 1 op 20 to 1) 3

4072 MISTER GEBO 12-10-7 (7*) Miss C Dyson, struggling and drvn alng aftr one circuit, relentless prog to chase ldg pair fnl circuit, kpt on one pace frm 3 out........(50 to 1 op 25 to 1) 4

OLD MILL STREAM 11-10-7 (7*) Miss P Gundry, drvn alng wth chasing grp, effrt hfwy, struggling fnl circuit, nvr a threat.
.................................(5 to 1 op 4 to 1 tchd off fnl circuit. (16 to 1 op 8 to 1) 5

4011² WHAT CHANCE (Ire) 9-10-5² (7*) Mrs K Sunderland, struggling and drvn alng bef hfwy, tld off fnl circuit. (16 to 1 op 8 to 1) 6

4085 NO PANIC 13-10-7 (7*) Miss A Meakins, tld off bef hfwy, virtually pld up aftr last...............(66 to 1 op 33 to 1) 7

4072² SAMS HERITAGE 13-10-9 (5*) Miss A Dare, chsd clr ldg pair till pld up lme bef 12th.
.........................(11 to 4 op 2 to 1 tchd 100 to 30 and 7 to 2) pu

4064 HICKELTON LAD 13-10-10 (7*) Miss S Duckett, struggling and wl beh bef hfwy, tld off whn pld up before 2 out.
.........................(50 to 1 op 20 to 1) pu

Dist: 3½sl, 4l, ½sl, 20l, 24l, dist. 5m 52.20s. a 7.20s (9 Ran).
(Mrs G Sunter), Mrs G Sunter

4320 38th Year Of The Horse And Hound Cup Final Champion Hunters' Chase Class B (5-y-o and up) £12,575 3½m
................................(4:30)

3856¹ CELTIC ABBEY 9-12-0 Mr D S Jones, wth ldr, led 10th, quickened to go clr fnl circuit, styd on srtly frm 3 out, eased towards finish........(13 to 8 fav op 2 to 1 tchd 9 to 4) 1

3885* BITOFAMIXUP (Ire) 6-12-0 Mr P Hacking, patiently rdn, relentess prog fnl circuit, ch and drvn alng appr 3 out, no extr frm nxt.................................(9 to 4 tchd 2 to 1) 2

4178² MR BOSTON 12-12-0 Mr N Wilson, wtd wth, took clr order hfwy, drvn alng whn pace quickened fnl circuit, no imprsn frm 4 out.................................(8 to 1 op 6 to 1) 3

4121* GLEN OAK 12-12-0 Mr J M Pritchard, chsd ldrs, feeling pace and drvn alng fnl circuit, no imprsn on lders frm 4 out.
.........................(40 to 1 op 25 to 1) 4

3718 CAB ON TARGET 11-12-0 Mr S Swiers, patiently rdn, took clr order hfwy, feeling pace whn not fluent 6 out, no ch aftr.
.................................(7 to 2 op 3 to 1) 5

4120 CAPE COTTAGE 13-12-0 Mr A Phillips, al chasing ldrs, struggling to hold pl fnl circuit, sn lost tch..(40 to 1 op 33 to 1) 6

4085³ RUSTY BRIDGE 10-12-0 Mr R Burton, led till hdd 10th, lost pl quickly fnl circuit, tld off...........(33 to 1 tchd 50 to 1) 7

4121² SIRISAT 13-12-0 Miss T Blazey, wl plcd for a circuit, lost pl quickly appr 6 out, tld off......(66 to 1 op 50 to 1) 8

4154⁵ ABBOTSHAM 12-12-0 Mr R Thornton, reminders to keep up frm 5th, tld off whn pld up bef 5 out...(50 to 1 op 33 to 1) pu

4066² LUCKY CHRISTOPHER 12-12-0 Mr G Tarry, struggling to go pace whn nrly uns rdr 7th, hit nxt, tld off till pld up betw last 2.
.........................(25 to 1) pu

4066* MAGNOLIA MAN 11-12-0 Mr N Harris, sn struggling, tld off whn pld up bef 4 out...........(16 to 1 tchd 20 to 1) pu

Dist: 8l, 17l, 10l, 8l, 1¼l, 22l, 6l. 6m 49.20s. a 4.20s (11 Ran).
SR: 30/22/5/-/-/-/ (G J Powell), Miss Venetia Williams

4321 William Younger Handicap Chase Class D (0–125 5-y-o and up) £3,626 3½m........................(5:05)

4082³ DIAMOND FORT [95] 12-10-5 M A Fitzgerald, rcd in midfield, relentess prog fnl circuit, styd on grimly to ld r-in.
.................................(7 to 1 op 5 to 1) 1

3206⁶ SPECIAL ACCOUNT [94] 11-10-4 B Fenton, settled wth chasing grp, reminders fnl circuit, rallied to ld aftr 4 out, clr after nxt, hng lft and hld r-in, no extr.......(10 to 1 op 12 to 1) 2

3987⁴ DON'T LIGHT UP [110] 9-11-1-3 (3*) Mr R Thornton, reminders 4th, improved fnl circuit, led briefly aftr four out, rdn and one pace frm nxt...........(20 to 1 op 14 to 1) 3

4126³ PERUVIAN GALE (Ire) [90] 8-9-11 (3*) G F Ryan, nvr far away, led 7 out hld aftr 4 out, rdn and one pace frm nxt.
.................................(7 to 1 op 6 to 1) 4

3926³ SMITH TOO (Ire) [102] 9-10-12 D Leahy, wtd wth, took clr order hfwy, drvn alng whn pace quickened 3 out, fdd.
.........................(5 to 1 tchd 11 to 2 and 9 to 2) 5

4227³ BANNTOWN BILL (Ire) [97] (v) 8-10-7 A P McCoy, led to second, styd hndy, led 10th to 7 out, hrd at work 3 out, wknd and sn lost tch...............(6 to 1 op 5 to 1) 6

4275 WOODLANDS GENHIRE [90] (bl) 12-10-0 C Llewellyn, led second to 10th, lost tch fnl circuit, pld up bef 4 out.
.........................(33 to 1 op 50 to 1) pu

4202² HARRISTOWN LADY [101] (bl) 10-10-11 B Clifford, struggling and lost tch aftr one circuit, tld off whn pld up aftr 4 out.
.................................(7 to 1 tchd 8 to 1) pu

4186 BALASANI (Fr) [90] 11-10-0 S Curran, lost tch quickly and pld up bef 6 out.................................(33 to 1) pu

4171² FIGHT TO WIN (USA) [90] 9-9-10³ (7*) Mr O McPhail, struggling aftr one circuit, tld off whn pld up aftr 3 out.
.................................(33 to 1 tchd 50 to 1) pu

4082* BALLY CLOVER [114] 10-11-10 N Williamson, nvr gng wl, well beh whn pld up bef 7 out.....(4 to 1 fav op 9 to 2) pu

3875⁶ MERIVEL [110] 10-11-6 D O'Sullivan, struggling in rear whn hit 8 out, pld up bef 5 out...........(25 to 1 op 16 to 1) pu

Dist: ½l, 13l, 3l, nk, dist. 6m 52.60s. a 7.60s (12 Ran).
(Mrs R E Stocks), J C McConnochie

4322 Jones Spring's Darlaston Novices' Handicap Hurdle Class E (0–100 4-y-o and up) £2,556 2m 110yds.. (5:35)

4073² CUILLIN CAPER [72] 5-10-5² M A Fitzgerald, settled gng wl, nosed ahead appr 2 out, styd on well und pres.
.................................(6 to 1 op 5 to 1) 1

3163⁴ HAPPY BRAVE [77] 5-10-10 L Harvey, settled midfield, drvn alng to improve appr 2 out, rdn and kpt on wl frm betw last two................................(16 to 1 op 12 to 1) 2

4043² TIUTCHEV [93] 4-11-4 (3*) Mr R Thornton, nvr hndy hfwy nosed ahead aftr 3 out till appr nxt, one pace und pres r-in.
.................................(4 to 1 jt-fav op 5 to 1) 3

4255³ KHALIKHOUM (Ire) [83] 4-10-6 (5*) D J Kavanagh, wth ldr, hrd at work whn pace quickened aftr 3 out, one pace.
.........................(11 to 1 op 7 to 1 tchd 12 to 1) 4

4083 REVERSE THRUST [79] 6-10-5 (7*) M Clinton, patiently rdn, took clr order frm hfwy, ridden and not quicken from 3 out.
.........................(13 to 2 op 5 to 1 tchd 7 to 1) 5

3731[7] ANIF (USA) [68] 6-10-11 D Skyrme, *reminders to keep up hfwy, no imprsn on ldrs frm 3 out*....(25 to 1 op 20 to 1) 6

4156[3] HOLKHAM BAY [67] (bl) 5-9-9 (5*) A Aizpuru, *tried to make all, hdd aftr 3 out, wknd quickly*..........(25 to 1 op 20 to 1) 7

3913[7] BAY FAIR [85] 5-11-4 S McNeill, *chsd ldrs to hfwy, lost tch quickly bef 3 out*..................(16 to 1 op 14 to 1) 8

3911[3] SCALP 'EM (Ire) [67] 9-10-0 Dr P Pritchard, *pressed ldrs till wknd quickly appr 3 out, sn lost tch*.....(25 to 1 op 16 to 1) 9

3555[6] KEVASINGO [84] 5-11-3 V Slattery, *struggling frm hfwy, sn lost tch*....................................(16 to 1 op 14 to 1) 10

3959[3] TANGO MAN (Ire) [73] 5-10-6 A P McCoy, *wl plcd to hfwy, sn lost tch, tld off*................(4 to 1 jt-fav tchd 5 to 1) 11

4036[6] LUCKY ARCHER [90] 4-11-4 N Williamson, *beh, some hdwy whn hit 3 out, not reco'r, lost tch, tld off*.
....(13 to 2 op 5 to 1 tchd 7 to 1) 12

4131[4] BOLD TIME MONKEY [67] 6-10-0 C Llewellyn, *lost tch hfwy, tld off*..............(20 to 1 op 16 to 1 tchd 25 to 1) 13

4019[7] ANDSOME BOY [84] 4-10-12 B Fenton, *whipped round strt and lost many ls, al wl beh, tld off whn pld up bef 3 out*.
....(11 to 1 op 8 to 1) pu

4255[6] AMAZON HEIGHTS [67] 5-9-10[5] (7*) Mr O McPhail, *lost tch frm hfwy, tld off whn pld up bef 3 out*.(33 to 1 tchd 40 to 1) pu

Dist: 2l, 4l, hd, 6l, 14l, ½l, 8l, 2l, ¾l, 3½l. 3m 52.0s. 6.50s (15 Ran).
SR: -/-/6/-/-/-/ (Manor Farm Stud (Rutland)), T R Watson

BADEN-BADEN (GER) (good)
Sunday June 1st

4323 Iffezheimer Jagdrennen Chase £11,364 3m 1f 110yds........ (5:10)

REGISTANO (Ger) 10-11-0 D Fuhrmann, ... 1
GEORGE DE HAREB (Ire) 6-10-2 J Kousek, ... 2
3752[7] LINTON ROCKS 8-11-0 R Dunwoody, *prmnt to 2 out*...... 3
Dist: 2l, 1¾l, 10l, 3½l, 1½l, dist, dist. 6m 14.50s. (11 Ran).
(Gestut Sybille), U Stoltefuss

SLIGO (IRE) (good to firm)
Sunday June 1st

4324 Yeats Maiden Hurdle (4-y-o and up) £2,740 2m.................... (2:30)

1750[6] TOY'S AWAY (Ire) 4-10-8 (7*) Mr R P McNalley, (2 to 1 fav) 1
4162[7] BORN TO WIN (Ire) 7-11-1 T P Rudd, ...(4 to 1) 2
4198[7] DIPIE (Ire) 9-11-6 J P Byrne, ...(5 to 1) 3
4005 SOUNDS CONFIDENT (Ire) 5-11-3 (5*) G Kilfeather,
....(10 to 1) 4
4094 STYLISH LORD (Ire) 6-10-13 (7*) D A McLoughlin, .(4 to 1) 5
4160[5] DUNEMER (Ire) 4-11-1 Mr R Walsh, ...(7 to 2) 6
4198 MAID TO MOVE (Ire) 4-11-1 H Rogers, ...(9 to 1) 7
4094[5] MINSTRELS PRIDE (Ire) 6-11-6 J F Titley, ...(12 to 1) 8
4026 FANDANGO DE CHASSY (Fr) 4-10-8 (7*) D W O'Sullivan,
....(10 to 1) 9
3449 CASTLE-ETTA (Ire) 7-11-1 K F O'Brien, ...(40 to 1) 10
4160 PALM RIVER (Ire) 5-11-5 F J Flood, ...(25 to 1) 11
REGAL SECRET (Ire) 4-10-10 (5*) P G Hourigan, ..(8 to 1) 12
2907[9] CALLELLA PARSONS (Ire) 7-10-10 (5*) B J Geraghty,
....(40 to 1) 13
Dist: 2l, 13l, 5½l, hd. 3m 54.90s. (13 Ran).
(Mrs I M Murphy), A J Martin

4325 N.C.F. Meats Handicap Hurdle (0-109 4-y-o and up) £3,253 2m
.... (3:00)

4167[3] TAX REFORM (USA) [-] 4-11-6 H Rogers, ...(9 to 2) 1
4196[4] FAIR SOCIETY (Ire) [-] (bl) 6-10-11 M P Hourigan,
....(6 to 4 fav) 2
4150* SLEWMORE (Ire) [-] 6-10-5 (7*) M P Cooney, ...(3 to 1) 3
4148* BIT O'SPEED (Ire) [-] 6-10-12 P Carberry, ...(3 to 1) 4
4162[2] DARCARI ROSE (Ire) [-] 8-10-5 (5*) T Martin, ...(4 to 1) 5
SHIRWAN (Ire) [-] 8-10-13 (7*) D M Bean, ...(10 to 1) 6
4244 FOREST STAR (USA) [-] (bl) 8-9-6[8] (7*) D W O'Sullivan,
....(25 to 1) 7
Dist: 4l, ½l, 15l, 14l. 3m 49.40s. (7 Ran).
(D G McArdle), D G McArdle

4326 Covert Beginners Chase (5-y-o and up) £3,253 2½m............. (4:30)

3693[3] CORRIGEEN RAMBLER (Ire) 8-11-9 J F Titley, ...(7 to 1) 1
4159[2] OWENBWEE (Ire) 6-12-0 P Carberry, ...(6 to 4 fav) 2
4196 TOMMY PAUD (Ire) 8-12-0 J R Barry, ...(7 to 1) 3
4077[8] OVER THE WALL (Ire) 8-11-4 P A Roche, ...(16 to 1) 4
LONGMORE BOY 7-11-9 H Rogers, ...(25 to 1) 5
4053[7] GLENARD LAD (Ire) 9-11-6 (3*) Mr B R Hamilton, ..(20 to 1) ur
4116[2] SPECTACLE (Ire) 7-11-2 (7*) R Burke, ...(10 to 1) ur
4247 BROWNRATH KING (Ire) 8-12-0 K F O'Brien, ...(20 to 1) pu
4246[9] CORMAC LADY (Ire) 6-11-4 S H O'Donovan, ...(20 to 1) pu
3624 GONE ALL DAY (Ire) 7-11-9 T P Rudd, ...(25 to 1) pu
4164[7] CASSFINN 11-11-4 (5*) T Martin, ...(25 to 1) pu
Dist: 11l, 4½l, 4½l, dist. 5m 4.70s. (11 Ran).
(Edward O'Connor), Edward O'Connor

4327 Sportsmans I.N.H. Flat Race (4-y-o and up) £2,740 2m........... (5:00)

GRAN TURISMO (Ire) 4-10-13 (7*) Mr A J Dempsey, (6 to 1) 1
BRAVE MOVEMENT 5-11-10 (3*) Mr D Valentine, ...(4 to 1) 2
3840[6] EBONY PRINCE 5-11-13 Mr R Walsh, ...(7 to 2 fav) 3
WELL TED (Ire) 5-11-13 Mr P F Graffin, ...(4 to 1) 4
4166[4] BE MY MOT 5-11-3 (5*) Mr G Elliott, ...(7 to 1) 5
1013 TRY ONCE MORE (Ire) 6-11-2 Miss K Rudd, ...(7 to 1) 6
OWEN BART (Ire) 4-10-13 (7*) Mr J D Moore, ...(6 to 1) 7
3231 SWINFORD BOY (Ire) (bl) 9-11-7 (7*) Mr T Gibney, (20 to 1) 8
4249 ROSE'S PERK 5-11-1 (7*) Miss A Reilly, ...(14 to 1) 9
3343 HARBOUR BLAZE (Ire) 7-11-11 (3*) Mr B R Hamilton,
....(14 to 1) 10
Dist: Hd, 3l, 5l, 7l. 3m 45.90s. (10 Ran).
(D M O'Meara), Andrew Slattery

TRALEE (IRE) (firm)
Sunday June 1st

4328 Ballyheigue (C & G) Maiden Hurdle (4-y-o and up) £2,740 2½m... (2:35)

4243[8] BOLD BREW (Ire) 9-11-11 (3*) K Whelan, ...(7 to 2) 1
3834[8] COMAN'S JET (Ire) 7-12-0 C F Swan, ...(2 to 1 on) 2
FAIR REVIVAL 10-11-7 (7*) J D Pratt, ...(14 to 1) 3
4106[6] CROMWELLS KEEP (Ire) 6-12-0 T P Treacy, ...(7 to 2) 4
4195 TOBAR NA CARRAIGE (Ire) 5-11-13 N Williamson, (16 to 1) 5
Dist: 10l, 8l, 6l, nk. 5m 11.70s. (5 Ran).
(R Phelan), P T Flavin

4329 Stanley Racing Customer Comes First Handicap Hurdle (0-137 4-y-o and up) £4,110 2m............. (3:05)

4159* COLM'S ROCK (Ire) [-] 6-12-0 C F Swan, ...(6 to 4 fav) 1
4167[2] STEP ON EYRE (Ire) [-] 7-11-6 D J Casey, ...(13 to 8) 2
4054* BOB THE YANK (Ire) [-] 7-11-7 N Williamson, ...(9 to 4) f
Dist: 25l. 3m 52.70s. (3 Ran).
(R Finnegan), A P O'Brien

4330 Kingdom Beginners Chase (5-y-o and up) £2,740 2m............ (3:35)

9087 BENNY THE BISHOP (Ire) 7-11-7 (7*) Mr A Ross, ...(7 to 2) 1
4053[6] NIGHTMAN 8-12-0 T P Treacy, ...(10 to 1) 2
1362 BAY COTTAGE 8-11-9 D J Casey, ...(14 to 1) 3
4096 SMILING MINSTREL (Ire) 6-12-0 J K Kinane, ...(14 to 1) 4
4004[9] JOHNNY'S DREAM (Ire) 7-12-0 N Williamson, .. (Evens fav) f
3764[7] CLONAGAM (Ire) 8-12-0 T J Mitchell, ...(7 to 2) ur
Dist: Dist, 1½l, 9l. 4m 1.40s. (6 Ran).
(Mrs Salome Brennan), Cecil Ross

4331 Castlemaine I.N.H. Flat Race (6-y-o and up) £2,740 2½m......... (5:35)

1096 DARK MAGIC (Ire) 6-11-7 (7*) Miss C O'Neill, ...(12 to 1) 1
3525[3] HYELORD (Ire) 6-11-7 (7*) Mr B J Crowley, ...(15 to 8 fav) 2
4197[5] SAIL AWAY SAILOR (Ire) 6-11-7 (7*) Mr Paul Moloney,
....(10 to 1) 3
3238[8] ARDENTUM 6-11-9 (5*) Mr A C Coyle, ...(14 to 1) 4
3955[2] SPLEODRACH (Ire) 7-11-9 Mr P Fenton, ...(10 to 1) 5
4062[3] AS AN SLI (Ire) 6-11-2 (7*) Mr D F Barry, ...(10 to 1) 6
4062 HIGH MOAT (Ire) 7-11-11 (3*) Mr W Cronin, ...(10 to 1) 7
3840 GOLD CHARIOT (Ire) 6-11-2 (7*) Mr G A Kingston, (16 to 1) 8
BLACKBURN (Ire) 7-11-7 (7*) Mr E Sheehy, ...(12 to 1) 9
CLON CAW (Ire) (bl) 9-11-7 (7*) Mr D G O'Sullivan, (25 to 1) 10
NONREEN FANCY (Ire) 7-11-2 (7*) Mr M A Cahill, ...(25 to 1) 11
4062 HAZEL HONEY (Ire) 6-11-9 Mr J A Nash, ...(12 to 1) 12
3836[3] GAELTEACHT (Ire) 6-11-7 (7*) Mr M Scanlon, ...(5 to 2) pu
AT THE CROSSROADS (Ire) (bl) 6-11-2 (7*) Mr J P McNamara,
....(25 to 1) pu
Dist: Hd, 13l, 9l, nk. 4m 42.10s. (14 Ran).
(Paddy Fennelly), Paddy Fennelly

Index to National Hunt Results 1996-97

7 **A BADGE TOO FAR(IRE),** b m Heraldiste (USA) - Travel by Saritamer (USA) (Mrs L Williamson) 2565 2898 3184 3317 3554⁷ 3828 3973 4268⁴

8 **A BIT OF A RASCAL(IRE),** gr g Entre Nous - That's Amora (Raymund S Martin) 4117⁸

6 **A BOY CALLED ROSIE,** b g Derring Rose - Airy Fairy by Space King (J G M O'Shea) 2996

4 **A CHEF TOO FAR,** b g Be My Chief (USA) - Epithet by Mill Reef (USA) (R Rowe) 965² 1610 1790³

4 **A DAY ON THE DUB,** b g Presidium - Border Mouse by Border Chief (T P Tate) 3482

6 **A MILLION WATTS,** b g Belfort (FR) - Peters Pet Girl by Norwick (USA) (G M McCourt) 2387 2607

9 **A N C EXPRESS,** gr g Pragmatic - Lost In Silence by Silent Spring (J S King) 1687³ 2427² 2698⁶

6 **A S JIM,** b g Welsh Captain - Cawston's Arms by Cawston's Clown (O O'Neill) 873 1324² 1642⁸ 2999³ 3106² 3554¹ 4065⁴ 4183⁵

5 **A SLIDER(IRE),** gr m Millfontaine - No Breeze (John W Nicholson) 350⁴ 4284⁵

7 **A THOUSAND DREAMS(IRE),** b g Aristocracy - Ardellis Lady by Pollerton (P R Lenihan) 64⁴ 88⁴ 170⁶ 1715

6 **A VERSE TO ORDER,** b g Rymer - Born Bossy by Eborneezer (Miss P M Whittle) 4050⁸ 4187

8 **A WINDY CITIZEN(IRE),** ch m Phardante (FR) - Candolcis by Candy Cane (Mrs C Hicks) 2995¹ 3387

10 **AAL EL AAL,** b g High Top - Last Card (USA) by Full Out (USA) (P J Hobbs) 1918² 2282²

6 **AARDWOLF,** b g Dancing Brave (USA) - Pretoria by Habitat (C P E Brooks) 1287¹ 1757¹ 2043³ 2593 2794³ 3081³ 3453

4 **AAVASAKSA(FR),** b g Dancing Spree (USA) - Afkaza (FR) by Labus (FR) (A G Newcombe) 1412 2181¹⁸ 2303 3883⁴

5 **ABACO(USA),** ro g Theatrical - Jungle Dawn (AUS) (D K Weld) 624²

8 **ABALENE,** b g Forzando - Riva Renald by Try My Best (USA) (T W Donnelly) 247⁴

7 **ABBEY GALE(IRE),** b m Strong Gale - Monks Lass (Mrs John Harrington) 1119⁴ 1359 1432 2138

8 **ABBEY LAMP(IRE),** b g Miner's Lamp - Abbey Lodge by Master Owen (Miss Lucinda V Russell) 2347⁶ 2620⁵ 3250⁴

5 **ABBEY STREET(IRE),** b g Old Vic - Racquette by Ballymore (O Sherwood) 1612⁶ 2329 2695

6 **ABBEYDORAN,** b m Gildoran - Royal Lace by Royal Palace (Mrs J E Hawkins) 456⁹ 545⁶ 2668 2874 3299 3402 3614

9 **ABBEYLANDS(IRE),** gr g Cardinal Flower - Findabair by Sunny Way (J Howard Johnson) 1258¹ 2205

12 **ABBOTSHAM,** b g Ardross - Lucy Platter (FR) by Record Token (O J Carter) 57⁴ 154⁴ 188 3578³ 3940³ 4154⁵ 4320

7 **ABER GLEN,** ch m Oats - Springs To Mind by Miami Springs (N A Smith) 52 1648

5 **ABFAB,** b g Rabdan - Pas de Chat by Relko (K R Burke) 1809

5 **ABIGAIL ROSE(BEL),** gr m Abbey's Grey - Famille Rose (Mark McCausland) 1579⁴ 1839 2225⁷ 2379 2866 3070⁴ 3227⁷

5 **ABIGAILS STAR,** b g Arctic Lord - Bronze Age by Celtic Cone (P G Murphy) 3408²

11 **ABITMORFUN,** ch g Baron Blakeney - Mary Mile by Athenius (C F Coyne) 385⁴ 530⁵

6 **ABLE LADY(IRE),** ch f Glad Dancer - Egg Shells (J P Finn) 1908 2131

10 **ABLE PLAYER(USA),** b or br g Solford (USA) - Grecian Snow (CAN) by Snow Knight (K J Drewry) 58⁵ 125⁶ 725² 869² 1766³ 1848⁴ 3761⁹ 3852¹ 3975²

5 **ABORIGINAL(IRE),** b g Be My Native (USA) - Dundovail by Dunphy (P Mullins) 464¹ 611¹ 1533⁵ 1897⁵ 2049 3769⁹ 4052²

8 **ABOUT MIDNIGHT,** b m Jester - Princess Andromeda by Corvaro (USA) (F P Murtagh) 1521⁶ 1826 2117

6 **ABOVE SUSPICION(IRE),** b g Henbit (USA) - Cash Discount by Deep Run (C James) 1350 1809 2283

6 **ABOVE THE CLOUDS,** gr g Neltino - Goodnight Master by Gay Fandango (USA) (Miss A M Newton-Smith) 3735 4069

5 **ABOVE THE CUT(USA),** ch g Topsider (USA) - Placer Queen by Habitat (C P Morlock) 1215² 1410⁵ 1496⁶ 1958⁶ 2973² 3278¹ 3558⁵ 3844² 4036² 4206¹

6 **ABOVE THE GRASS(IRE),** b m Carlingford Castle - Mermaid by Furry Glen (D Robertson) 3061⁷

9 **ABSALOM'S LADY,** gr m Absalom - High Point Lady (CAN) by Knightly Dawn (USA) (Miss Gay Kelleway) 1210¹ 1394

7 **ABSALOM'S PILLAR,** ch g Absalom - Collapse by Busted (J Mackie) 1966⁵ 2389

11 **ABSENT MINDS,** br m Lir - Forgotten by Forlorn River (B R J Young) 3147

10 **ABSOLATUM,** b g Absalom - Omnia by Hill Clown (USA) (J Parfitt) 1140⁸ 1734⁶

5 **ABSOLUTE LIMIT,** gr g Absalom - Western Line by High Line (J T Gifford) 2405⁴ 2656⁴ 3064 3334 3634¹ 3795 3849²

4 **ABSOLUTE PROOF,** b f Interrex (CAN) - Kellyem by Absalom (W G M Turner) 3917⁷ 4050

9 **ABSOLUTELY JOHN(IRE),** ch g Goldhill - Rectory Lass by Even Money (Martin Todhunter) 2988 3158

6 **ABSOLUTLY EQUINAME(IRE),** gr g Roselier (FR) - Cotton Gale by Strong Gale (M J Heaton-Ellis) 1763³ 2298² 2822¹ 3310²

4 **ABSTRACT VIEW(USA),** b g Arctic Tern (USA) - Anya Ylina (USA) by Bold Reasoning (USA) (Mervyn Torrens) 1173 1430 1750

5 **ABYSS,** b g Charlotte's Dunce - Rebecca Sarah by Mansingh (USA) (N P Littmoden) 1181⁵ 2199⁸

4 **ACADEMY HOUSE(IRE),** b c Sadler's Wells (USA) - Shady Leaf by Glint Of Gold (R Akehurst) 1696²

9 **ACAJOU III(FR),** b g Cap Martin (FR) - Roxane II (FR) by Signani (FR) (G Richards) 2536 3014³ 3399⁴ 3760¹ 3968³ 4100⁴ 4213¹ 4285¹

4 **ACCOUNTANCY JEWEL(IRE),** b f Pennine Walk - Polyester Girl by Ridan (USA) (S J Treacy) 2161

244 606⁵ 727⁵ 912 1141⁵ 1386⁶ 1693⁴ 1911² 2487⁴ 3006⁵ 3587⁹ 3904⁴

8 **AIGUILLE(IRE),** b m Lancastrian - Cahernane Girl by Bargello (Andrew Heffernan) 2475² 2672⁸ 3179

4 **AILSAE,** b f Arctic Lord - Royal Snip by Royal Highway (Mrs J Brown) 3825⁸ 4143⁶

5 **AIMEES PRINCESS(IRE),** ch m Good Thyne (USA) - Sparkling Opera (F Flood) 2416

6 **AINSI SOIT IL(FR),** b or br g Amen (FR) - Crinolene (FR) by Rheffic (FR) (G M McCourt) 1298⁴ 1593 1747¹ 1938¹ 2246 2770² 2929 3267⁵

6 **AINTGOTWON,** b m Teenoso (USA) - Miss Deed by David Jack (A Hide) 1560 2309 2831⁹

5 **AIR BRIDGE,** b g Kind Of Hush - Spanish Beauty by Torus (R M Whitaker) 917⁸ 1390⁶ 1742² 2858⁸

7 **AIR COMMAND(BAR),** br g Concorde Hero (USA) - Hubbardair by Town And Country (M R Bosley) 398³ 479² 677⁴

6 **AIR COMMODORE(IRE),** b g Elegant Air - Belle Enfant by Beldale Flutter (USA) (D W P Arbuthnot) 3169³

5 **AIR FORCE ONE(IRE),** b g King's Ride - Solar Jet by Mandalus (W P Mullins) 2968³ 3238⁴ 3524⁶

7 **AIR SHOT,** b g Gunner B - Dans Le Vent by Pollerton (D Nicholson) 2696¹ 3134³ 4016³

4 **AIR WING,** ch c Risk Me (FR) - Greenstead Lass by Double-U-Jay (M H Tompkins) 1438

10 **AISEIRI,** ch g Crash Course - Catspaw by Laurence O (P R Lenihan) 1074 1358⁶ 1554⁹ 1904 3339⁹ 3418⁵ 3877² 4093 4246⁵

5 **AISLING ALAINN(IRE),** b g Pennine Walk - Chimela (Thomas Carberry) 2115⁵ 2383⁷ 3085⁷ 3642

6 **AJDAR,** b g Slip Anchor - Loucoum (FR) by Iron Duke (O Brennan) 1848⁹ 2407⁹ 2681² 2880 3166³ 3424⁹ 3728⁴ 3820³ 4153⁵ 4237¹ 4310⁶

5 **AJKNAPP(IRE),** b g Ajraas (USA) - Knapping (J A Berry) 1015 1907 4106 4305⁹

6 **AKITO RACING(IRE),** b m Royal Fountain - Belmont Lady by Quayside (Martin Todhunter) 1373⁷ 1521 1817⁸ 3803 4107 4214

7 **AKIYMANN(USA),** b g El Gran Senor (USA) - Akila (FR) by Top Ville (M C Pipe) 47 326⁶ 450¹ 582³ 650⁴ 1724⁷ 2741 3041 3466³

8 **AKTEON(IRE),** b g Actinium (FR) - Glitter On (M F Morris) 2900⁸ 3520

8 **AL BILLAL,** b h Enchantment - Liana Louise by Silly Season (R Williams) 4085

9 **AL CAPONE II(FR),** b g Italic (FR) - L'oranaise by Paris Jour (B Secly) 84² 682¹ 1301¹

8 **AL HAAL(USA),** b g Northern Baby (CAN) - Kit's Double (USA) by Spring Double (J Joseph) 1235⁵ 1811⁴ 2526 2768⁷

13 **AL HASHIMI,** b g Ile de Bourbon (USA) - Parmesh by Home Guard (USA) (N T Ridout) 2516 2974⁶ 3279 4064⁶

5 **AL HELAL,** b h In The Wings - Rosia Bay by High Top (J R Jenkins) 1155⁵ 1293 1438 1541⁵ 1805

7 **AL JAWWAL,** ch g Lead On Time (USA) - Littlefield by Bay Express (R Champion) 4157

6 **AL JINN,** ch g Hadeer - Mrs Musgrove by Jalmood (USA) (Martyn Wane) 2653 3262

11 **AL SKEET(USA),** b g L'emigrant (USA) - Processional (USA) by Reviewer (USA) (Ms M Collins) 372⁶ 479⁵

6 **ALABANG,** ch g Valiyar - Seleter by Hotfoot (M J Camacho) 1252¹ 1677¹

6 **ALAFLAK(IRE),** b h Caerleon (USA) - Safe Haven by Blakeney (Major W R Hern) 4301⁴

4 **ALAMBAR(IRE),** b c Fairy King (USA) - Lightino by Bustino (Noel Meade) 2337⁵ 2702⁴

8 **ALAMILLO(IRE),** ch m Lancastrian - Rossacurra by Deep Run (Peter McCreery) 1461 2077⁵ 2139⁴ 3380⁴

6 **ALAN'S PRIDE(IRE),** b m Supreme Leader - Mantilla Run by Deep Run (W McKeown) 1682 1989 2145⁹ 2489⁶ 2572 2853⁵ 3006 3433⁷

4 **ALANA'S BALLAD(IRE),** b f Be My Native (USA) - Radalgo by Ballad Rock (B P J Baugh) 2497

10 **ALAPA,** b h Alzao (USA) - Gay Folly by Wolver Hollow (A B Coogan) 3313 4157

4 **ALARICO(FR),** ch g Kadrou (FR) - Calabria (FR) by Vitiges (FR) (I P Williams) 1398⁹ 1854⁷

7 **ALASAD,** ch g Kris - Midway Lady (USA) by Alleged (USA) (Noel Meade) 303⁷ 730⁵ 897³ 1277⁴ 1433¹ 2018

6 **ALASKAN HEIR,** b g Northern State (USA) - Royal Meeting by Dara Monarch (A Streeter) 1835 1947 2407 2548⁵ 2762⁵ 3267⁶ 3481³ 3726² 3967² 4254⁵

4 **ALBAHA(USA),** br g Woodman (USA) - Linda's Magic (USA) by Far North (CAN) (J E Banks) 1922

7 **ALBEIT,** ch m Mandrake Major - Sioux Be It by Warpath (R Evans) 1351⁸

8 **ALBEMINE(USA),** b g Al Nasr (FR) - Lady Be Mine (USA) by Sir Ivor (Mrs J Cecil) 1572⁵ 1807² 2044¹ 2331⁹ 2501³ 2730⁶ 3635³ 3791⁷ 4253⁵

6 **ALBERMARLE(IRE),** ch g Phardante (FR) - Clarahill by Menelek (Capt T A Forster) 4039¹

10 **ALBERT BLAKE,** b g Roscoe Blake - Ablula by Abwah (T R Kinsey) 42³

5 **ALBERT THE LION(IRE),** gr g Celio Rufo - Esker Lady by Gala Performance (USA) (J Neville) 618

11 **ALBERT'S FANCY,** b g Furry Glen - Bride To Be by Prince Regent (FR) (P J P Doyle) 981 1079⁷

5 **ALBERTINA,** b m Phardante (FR) - Rambling Gold by Little Buskins (C James) 3917

10 **ALBERTITO(FR),** b g Esprit Du Nord (USA) - Aranita by Arctic Tern (USA) (R Hollinshead) 2004⁶ 2332⁶ 4141⁵ 4318

10 **ALBURY GREY,** gr m Petong - Infelice by Nishapour (FR) (T P McGovern) 1698⁴ 2482 2739

6 **ALCOVE,** ch g Faustus (USA) - Cubby Hole by Town And Country (G F Johnson Houghton) 689⁶

9 **ALDINGTON CHAPPLE,** b g Creetown - Aldington Miss by Legal Eagle (B Preece) 228⁴

10 **ALDWICK COLONNADE,** ch m Kind Of Hush - Money Supply by Brigadier Gerard (M D I Usher) 1811⁵ 2351 2663 2768⁹ 3148⁵ 3325⁶ 3628¹

9 **ALGAN(FR),** b g Le Pontet (FR) - Djaipour II by Gaur (F Doumen) 1310⁴

10 **ALI'S ALIBI,** br g Lucifer (USA) - Moppit-Up by Pitpan (Mrs M Reveley) 877² 1199⁴ 1632³ 1774² 2148² 2317³ 2935

6 **ALI'S DELIGHT,** br g Idiot's Delight - Almelikeh by Neltino (A J Wilson) 1217 1592 3913

6 **ALICAT(IRE),** b g Cataldi - Sweet Result by Owen Dudley (J W Curtis) 1330 2155³ 2650³ 2909³ 3660⁴ 4022

6 **ALICE BRENNAN(IRE),** ch f Good Thyne (USA) - Alice Starr (Patrick Joseph Flynn) 853⁷ 1902⁵ 2079 2131⁹ 2520 2752

7 **ALICE SHEER THORN(IRE),** ch m Sheer Grit - Rugged Thorn by Rugged Man (M J Gingell) 129

Keane) 8037 9474 10405 1361 18996 20381 21712 23811 2448 2646 32296 34554

4 AMOTHEBAMBO(IRE), b g Martin John - Twilight In Paris by Kampala (A G Hobbs) 40753

10 AMTRAK EXPRESS, ch g Black Minstrel - Four In A Row by Cracksman (Mrs J Pitman) 36363

4 AMYLOU, b f Dunbeath (USA) - La Chiquita by African Sky (R Allan) 664

4 AN BONNAN BUI(IRE), ch f Riverhead (USA) - Boggy Peak by Shirley Heights (Norman Cassidy) 3755 42006

8 AN MAINEACH(IRE), b g Lafontaine (USA) - Swanny Jane by Bargello (Capt D G Swan) 2001 252 293 4291 5531 3419 3550 37634

7 AN OON ISS AN OWL(IRE), ch g Lancastrian - Rev-Up by Menelek (William Flavin) 32221

5 AN SEABHAC(IRE), b g Lord Americo - October Lady by Lucifer (USA) (James O'Haire) 3973 7034 3789

8 AN SPAILPIN FANACH(IRE), b g Rymer - Sidhe Gaoth by Le Moss (D R Gandolfo) 3027 34944 3738

8 AN TAIN SHIOC(IRE), ch g Torus - Frost Bound (Patrick Martin) 41521

9 ANABATIC(IRE), b g Strong Gale - Loch Bracken by Royal Highway (M J P O'Brien) 2142 252 293 5636 6363 7192 7471 10042 11691 13941 18786

6 ANABRANCH, br m Kind Of Hush - An-Go-Look by Don't Look (J M Jefferson) 4232 6181 775 8793 12482 15881 18272 2149 25325 35402 37595

4 ANALOGICAL, br f Teenoso (USA) - The Howlet by New Brig (D McCain) 19431 25755 29999 32653 34767 41315 4268

5 ANALOGUE(IRE), b g Reference Point - Dancing Shadow by Dancer's Image (USA) (R J Eckley) 1733 1978

6 ANASTASIA WINDSOR, b m Leading Star - Causanna by Proverb (D Moffatt) 2811 29376

5 ANCHORENA, b m Slip Anchor - Canna by Caerleon (USA) (D W Barker) 5541 650 1775 1966 21225

4 ANCIENT CHINA(IRE), b c Old Vic - Shajan (Peter Casey) 38409

8 ANCIENT HISTORIAN(IRE), b g Niels - Valka (FR) by Val de Loir (W P Mullins) 10969 12786 14861 17133 20161

5 ANCIENT ISLE(USA), ch h Erins Isle - Sing A Message (USA) (J S Bolger) 41443

9 AND WHY NOT, ro g Baron Blakeney - Tamana Dancer by Gay Fandango (USA) (R Parker) 596 4122

9 ANDALUCIAN SUN(IRE), ch g Le Bavard (FR) - Sun Spray by Nice Guy (A Witcomb) 4235

6 ANDANITO(IRE), b g Darshaan - Newquay by Great Nephew (Lady Herries) 25944

8 ANDERMATT, b g Top Ville - Klarifi by Habitat (J Mackie) 33186 37019 39952 41402

8 ANDRE LAVAL(IRE), ch g Over The River (FR) - French Academy by Le Bavard (FR) (K C Bailey) 14991 17266

5 ANDREA COVA(IRE), b or br m Strong Gale - Blue Suede Shoes by Bargello (Victor Bowens) 16554 17569 20498 2343 26455 28701 33941 3769

10 ANDRELOT, b g Caerleon (USA) - Seminar by Don (ITY) (P Bowen) 1543 2022 2492 3274 5171 5864 7061 8093 11012 1204 16073 19262 21757

11 ANDRETTI'S HEIR, ch g Andretti - Mounemara by Ballymore (T S Sharpe) 3671

7 ANDROS DAWN(IRE), b m Buckskin (FR) - Aillwee Dawn by Deep Run (M F Morris) 1134 2165

12 ANDROS PRINCE, b g Blakeney - Ribamba by Ribocco (Miss A E Embiricos) 8092 11407 1529 25996

4 ANDSOME BOY, ch g Out Of Hand - My Home by Homing (C R Barwell) 4813 7673 9365 40197 4322

5 ANDSUEPHI(IRE), b g Montelimar (USA) - Butler's Daughter by Rhett Butler (C P E Brooks) 40421 41881

8 ANDY BURNETT(IRE), b g Orchestra - Trudy Belle (F Flood) 25192 2705 27555 2904

4 ANDY CLYDE, b g Rambo Dancer (CAN) - Leprechaun Lady by Royal Blend (A Bailey) 23325

6 ANDY COIN, ch m Andy Rew - Legal Coin by Official (W M Brisbourne) 8464

4 ANGAREB(IRE), b g Montekin - Falassa by Relko (Martin M Treacy) 872 8274

9 ANGELO'S DOUBLE(IRE), b g M Double M (USA) - Bebe Altesse (GER) by Alpenkonig (GER) (R H Buckler) 26382 2950 30922

8 ANGLESEY SEA VIEW, gr m Seymour Hicks (FR) - Lexham View by Abwah (A Bailey) 14643 15211 25507 31275

8 ANGRY NATIVE(IRE), b g Be My Native (USA) - An Grianan by Ballymore (J Wade) 3825

4 ANGUS MCCOATUP(IRE), ch c Mac's Imp (USA) - In For More by Don (M D Hammond) 19229 22567 24179 42376

6 ANIF(USA), b or br g Riverman (USA) - Marnie's Majik (USA) by Elocutionist (USA) (J Joseph) 2636 2725 31745 32924 34951 37317 43226

4 ANIKA'S GEM(IRE), b f Buckskin (FR) - Picton Lass by Rymer (Mrs S C Bradburne) 29152 33039 40993

7 ANIMOSITY, b m Latest Model - Perplexity by Pony Express (S G Knight) 4279

12 ANJUBI, b g Sunyboy - Dyna Bell by Double Jump (Miss M Bragg) 39404 42352

8 ANLACE, b m Sure Blade (USA) - Ascot Strike (USA) by Mr Prospector (USA) (S Mellor) 10517 1218 14166 15576 1857 32763 34248 3703 37804 3956

10 ANN'S AMBITION, b g Ovac (ITY) - Faultless Girl by Crash Course (Mrs C Hussey) 8043 950 35915 38323 4033 42353

6 ANN'S DESIRE(IRE), b m Dominion Royale - Winterlude by Wollow (Mrs C Barker) 4445 4973 6473 6863 10426 13598 16492 3547 36424 38168 41697 43061

5 ANNA BANNANNA, b m Prince Sabo - Top Berry by High Top (M C Pipe) 638

4 ANNA SOLEIL(IRE), b g Red Sunset - Flying Anna by Roan Rocket (O Sherwood) 23033 2628 28075 34891 36812 39463 42253

8 ANNABEL'S BABY(IRE), b m Alzao (USA) - Spyglass by Nigella (D J Wintle) 2403 31748

7 ANNADOT(IRE), gr m Roselier (FR) - Galliano by Royal Highway (F Flood) 9802 10891 14334 17529 20186 21344 2837 30869 34515

8 ANNAELAINE(IRE), gr m Wood Chanter - Hawaii's Princess (Noel Meade) 2582 2865 3089 36432 36961 41052

6 ANNFIELD HERITAGE(IRE), ch f Orchestra - Never A Whisper (Thomas Foley) 1154 1229 3935d

9 ANNFIELD LADY(IRE), b m Furry Glen - Never A Whisper by Crepello (Thomas Foley) 10785 1244

6 ANNIDA(IRE), ch f Torus - Subiacco (F Flood) 945

5 ANNIE OAKLEY(IRE), br m Buckskin (FR) - Helynsar (W Rock) 20409 2166

13 **BOREEN OWEN,** b g Boreen (FR) - Marble Owen by Master Owen (David Alan Harrison) 3586⁴

8 **BORING(USA),** ch g Foolish Pleasure (USA) - Arriya by Luthier (W Storey) 548⁵

6 **BORIS BROOK,** ch g Meadowbrook - Crella by Cagirama (R Allan) 1590⁸ 1829 2192⁶ 2346 2813⁶

6 **BORJITO(SPA),** b h Chayote (FR) - Tanaquil (FR) by Relkino (C R Barwell) 1956⁵ 3275

6 **BORLEAGH PILOT(IRE),** ch g Torus - Pilots Row (Mrs S A Bramall) 2137 2520 2865⁴ 3416

4 **BORN AT KINGS,** ch g Jupiter Island - My Coquette by Coquelin (USA) (J White) 3388 3616⁴

5 **BORN TO PLEASE(IRE),** ch g Waajib - Gratify by Grundy (P J Hobbs) 50² 262¹ 376³ 448² 554² 572¹ 772⁶ 869¹ 957¹ 3683⁵ 3773⁴

7 **BORN TO WIN(IRE),** b m Torus - Mugs Away by Mugatpura (M J P O'Brien) 2165 2413² 2582² 3235 3336⁷ 4162⁷ 4324²

6 **BORNACURRA KATIE(IRE),** b f Aristocracy - Bornacurra Ella (V T O'Brien) 1090

6 **BORO BOW(IRE),** b m Buckskin (FR) - Boro Quarter by Buckskin (FR) (P Mullins) 717¹ 984⁴ 1279 1554² 1622² 1901³ 2073³ 2166² 2275¹ 2582¹ 3551³ 3764³ 3935b²

4 **BORO SOVEREIGN(IRE),** b g King's Ride - Boro Penny (Anthony Mullins) 3707¹

4 **BORO VACATION(IRE),** b g Ovac (ITY) - Boro Quarter by Normandy (P F Nicholls) 252 293⁹ 1029 3730⁶ 4074

5 **BORODINO(IRE),** b g Strong Gale - Boro Quarter by Normandy (C P E Brooks) 1306 2510²

7 **BORREEVA(IRE),** ch f Boreen (FR) - Ardreeva (Seamus Fahey) 3380⁸ 3943⁷

9 **BORRISMORE FLASH(IRE),** ch g Le Moss - Deep Goddess by Deep Run (Lee Bowles) 604⁴ 680 3645 3693 3835

6 **BOSCO'S TOUCH(IRE),** b g Pimpernel's Tune - Last Touch (Mrs Edwina Finn) 4249

5 **BOSS DOYLE(IRE),** b g Lapierre - Prolific Scot by Northern Guest (USA) (M F Morris) 1143⁴ 1533² 2072² 2106¹ 2521² 3129 3417¹

4 **BOSSA NOVA,** b f Teenoso (USA) - Out Of Range by Faraway Times (USA) (L G Cottrell) 3917⁹ 4086⁷

8 **BOSSYMOSS(IRE),** b g Le Moss - Annes Wedding by Buckskin (FR) (A Streeter) 1413⁴ 1734 1994 2205 2896

6 **BOSTON BOMBER,** b g Wonderful Surprise - Miss Anax by Anax (R D E Woodhouse) 3008⁸

8 **BOSTON MAN,** b g True Song - Tempest Girl by Caliban (R D E Woodhouse) 735 1047 1679⁹ 1984³ 2120⁶ 2241 2762¹ 2885⁵ 3353⁷ 3704⁴ 3999² 4213³ 4313⁶

5 **BOSTON MELODY(IRE),** ch m Phardante (FR) - Brogeen View (John J Walsh) 68 943

9 **BOSWORTH FIELD(IRE),** br g Callernish - Another Lady VI by Anthony (Mrs Sarah Horner-Harker) 1253⁸ 1658 1820 1963¹ 2205

10 **BOTHA BOCHT,** b m Pauper - Tudor Saint by Tudor Music (Mrs Edwina Finn) 217

6 **BOTHAR GARBH(IRE),** b g Bar Dexter (USA) - Lady Bountiful (USA) (Sean O O'Brien) 253 407

10 **BOTTLE BLACK,** b g Kemal (FR) - Deep Sea Diver by Deep Diver (T Hind) 3149 3461 3914 3996 4202

5 **BOULABALLY(IRE),** ch g Dry Dock - Charming Whisper (T J Taaffe) 1120⁶ 1777 2645⁶ 2866

6 **BOULEVARD BAY(IRE),** b g Royal Fountain - Cairita by Pitcairn (O Sherwood) 3004⁸

6 **BOUND FOR GOLD,** b g Ovac (ITY) - Colly Cone by Celtic Cone (Miss H C Knight) 1053⁸

5 **BOUNDTOHONOUR(IRE),** b g Rashar (USA) - Densidal by Tanfirion (H Oliver) 52³ 2409 2899⁷ 3137⁶

4 **BOURBON DYNASTY(FR),** b g Rainbow Quest (USA) - Bourbon Girl by Ile de Bourbon (USA) (G Richards) 3303⁴ 3304 3396³

5 **BOURDONNER,** b g Pharly (FR) - Buzzbomb by Bustino (M D Hammond) 83⁴ 376¹ 414² 559¹ 725⁵ 3424² 3782¹

9 **BOURNEL,** ch m Sunley Builds - Golden Granite by Rugantino (C R Barwell) 1593⁹ 1916⁷ 2596⁹ 2741⁴ 3149³

BOUTRUS(IRE), (Michael Cosgrave) 3748

15 **BOW HANDY MAN,** ch g Nearly A Hand - Bellemarie by Beau Chapeau (Ms L C Plater) 3777⁶

6 **BOWCLIFFE,** b g Petoski - Gwiffina by Welsh Saint (E J Alston) 1371⁴ 1522³ 1823¹³ 1955² 2284⁵ 2617

5 **BOWCLIFFE COURT(IRE),** b g Slip Anchor - Res Nova (USA) by Blushing Groom (FR) (R Akehurst) 1641 1749¹ 1997³ 2594⁷

7 **BOWDEN SURPRISE,** ch g Morgans Choice - Bankers Surprise by Golden Surprise (R J Baker) 1915 3485¹ 3738⁵

6 **BOWES LADY(IRE),** b m Electric - Garraun (John Patrick Ryan) 1904 2518 3837 4051

11 **BOWL OF OATS,** ch g Oats - Bishop's Bow by Crozier (P G Warner) 3464³

6 **BOWLAND PARK,** b m Nicholas Bill - Macusla by Lighter (E J Alston) 262 473⁴ 609 660⁵

5 **BOWLES PATROL(IRE),** gr g Roselier (FR) - Another Dud by Le Bavard (FR) (John R Upson) 990⁷ 2407⁸ 2602⁹ 3477² 3822² 3958³

7 **BOXGROVE MAN(IRE),** br g Mandalus - Kittykelvin by Avocat (J A B Old) 3700 4068

10 **BOXING MATCH,** b g Royal Boxer - Mutchkin by Espresso (J M Bradley) 188⁷ 282⁵ 418⁵ 480 632³ 757⁶ 391⁴⁵ 4046 4226⁷ 4275⁷

7 **BOXIT AGAIN,** b g Kind Of Hush - Boxit by General Ironside (J Mackie) 874 1136

4 **BOY BLAKENEY,** b g Blakeney - Sarah Bear by Mansingh (USA) (Mrs S J Smith) 1249⁷ 1438⁴ 1629 1992² 2202 2804⁵ 3283³ 3736⁴

7 **BOYFRIEND,** b g Rolfe (USA) - Lady Sweetapples by Super Song (Mrs J Pitman) 2253 2982⁴

5 **BOYNE ROYALE(IRE),** ch g Boyne Valley - Moves Well (J J Lennon) 3097³

5 **BOYNE VIEW(IRE),** b m Buckskin (FR) - Dunacarney (Denis J Reddan) 705⁵ 802

6 **BOYO(IRE),** ch g Phardante (FR) - Bobs My Uncle by Deep Run (T D Easterby) 473 551⁵ 618

5 **BOYZONTOOWA(IRE),** b g Beau Sher - Lindabell by Over The River (FR) (R Collins) 1317 1817⁶ 2260⁸ 2538⁷ 3123

6 **BOZO(IRE),** b g Kefaah (USA) - Hossvend by Malinowski (USA) (B J M Ryall) 1735³ 3135 3898³

12 **BRABAZON(USA),** b g Cresta Rider (USA) - Brilliant Touch (USA) by Gleaming (USA) (Mrs E Scott) 3274⁵

11 **BRACKENFIELD,** ch g Le Moss - Stable Lass by Golden Love (R Barber) 3053¹ 3365

6 **BRACKENHEATH(IRE),** b g Le Moss - Stable Lass by Golden Love (D M Grissell) 1447⁷ 2738² 3119 3557

7 **BRACKENTHWAITE,** ch g Faustus (USA) - Cosset by Comedy Star (USA) (J L Eyre) 2485²

6 **BRACKENVALE(IRE),** b f Strong Gale - Matjup (J T R Dreaper) 1655⁵ 1901⁶ 2443 2704⁶ 2865⁷ 3068 3942⁷

4 **CHEERFUL ASPECT(IRE),** b g Cadeaux Genereux - Strike Home by Be My Guest (USA) (Capt T A Forster) 2423¹ 2954² 3192²

7 **CHEF COMEDIEN(IRE),** ch g Commanche Run - Clipper Queen by Balidar (M J Wilkinson) 1572³ 2949

5 **CHELSEA BELLE(IRE),** b m Supreme Leader - Chelsea Chick by London Bells (CAN) (T J Nagle) 2416 3224⁸ 3377³ 3817⁹ 3953 4306³

5 **CHELSEA KING(IRE),** b g Riot Helmet - Chelsea Chick (T J Nagle) 3222⁴ 3341⁴

5 **CHELWORTH WOLF,** ch g Little Wolf - Chelworth Countess by Noalto (J L Spearing) 445⁶ 506⁵

5 **CHEMIN-DE-FER,** b g Darshaan - Whitehaven by Top Ville (B A Pearce) 2015⁹

9 **CHENE ROSE(IRE),** ch m Denel (FR) - Jaybe's Gift by Dalesa (T Steele) 2869 4115³

5 **CHERGALE(IRE),** b f Strong Gale - Cherry Sorbet (Noel Meade) 3606⁵ 4149³ 4292³

5 **CHERISHTHELADY(IRE),** b f Legal Circles (USA) - Classy Chassis (E J Creighton) 3943⁸ 4149⁵ 4294⁶

6 **CHEROKEE CHIEF,** ch g Rakaposhi King - Coole Pilate by Celtic Cone (O Sherwood) 2288³ 2898² 3722²

12 **CHERRY CHAP,** b g Kabour - Mild Wind by Porto Bello (J Ibbott) 3460²

6 **CHERRY DEE,** ch m Ardross - Merry Cherry by Deep Run (P Beaumont) 1682² 2288⁹ 2619⁵ 2882³ 3057¹ 3400¹ 3704

9 **CHERRY ISLAND(IRE),** ch g King Persian - Tamar Di Bulgaria (ITY) by Duke Of Marmalade (USA) (H W Lavis) 2990²

10 **CHERRY ORCHID,** b g Callernish - Cherry Token by Prince Hansel (J L Needham) 1226 1475⁷

6 **CHERRYGARTH(IRE),** b g Lord Americo - Gallant Blade (M J P O'Brien) 211⁵

6 **CHERRYMORE(IRE),** br g Cataldi - Cherry Bow by Beau Chapeau (Mrs J Pitman) 2029¹ 2277⁷ 3700⁴

8 **CHERRYNUT,** b g Idiot's Delight - Merry Cherry by Deep Run (P F Nicholls) 1345¹ 2779 3115

7 **CHERYL'S LAD(IRE),** b g Mister Majestic - Two's Company by Sheshoon (D Nicholson) 1797² 1996³ 3156 3766 4127³

8 **CHESLOCK(IRE),** b g Orchestra - Swan Loch by Raise You Ten (John Monroe) 2090 2446 2587 2707³

8 **CHESTER BEN,** ro g Alias Smith (USA) - Saleander by Leander (Mrs P A Barthorpe) 4157⁸

5 **CHESTERS QUEST,** ch g Domynsky - Chess Mistress (USA) by Run The Gantlet (USA) (R Hollinshead) 533⁹

11 **CHESTNUT SHOON,** ch f Green Shoon - Aghavine (Philip Gould) 217⁷ 591

5 **CHIAPPELLI(IRE),** b m Buckskin (FR) - Lean Over by Over The River (FR) (T D Easterby) 1874

7 **CHIAPPUCCI(IRE),** b g Doulab (USA) - Jenny's Child by Crash Course (Mrs E H Heath) 1970⁹ 3364² 3669 3737⁴ 3822⁵ 4070⁷ 4241

9 **CHICKABIDDY,** b m Henbit (USA) - Shoshoni by Ballymoss (G F Edwards) 583³ 769³ 922² 1001² 1352¹

6 **CHICKAWICKA(IRE),** b h Dance Of Life (USA) - Shabby Doll by Northfields (USA) (B Palling) 1215¹ 1496³ 3385

5 **CHICODARI,** b g Shardari - Chicobin (USA) by J O Tobin (USA) (D Nicholson) 1346³ 1564³ 2329⁴ 2717³

4 **CHIEF CHIPPIE,** b g Mandalus - Little Katrina by Little Buskins (W T Kemp) 2363 2623 3303 3663⁸

5 **CHIEF DELANEY(IRE),** br g Caerleon (USA) - Stanerra's Song (USA) by Seattle Song (USA) (F Dunne) 1195 1432 4094⁶ 4195

5 **CHIEF GALE(IRE),** b g Strong Gale - Distant Lady by Buckskin (FR) (J G M O'Shea) 671⁴ 795² 952³ 1503⁶ 3970

10 **CHIEF JOSEPH,** b m General Ironside - Knollwood Court by Le Jean (N A Twiston-Davies) 2781

8 **CHIEF MINISTER(IRE),** br g Rainbow Quest (USA) - Riverlily (FR) by Green Dancer (USA) (M D Hammond) 2240² 2464² 2714¹ 3716⁴

4 **CHIEF MOUSE,** b g Be My Chief (USA) - Top Mouse by High Top (F Jordan) 481¹ 767² 1249¹ 1610 2430⁶ 2744 3276² 3680¹ 3844¹ 4038⁵

5 **CHIEF OF KHORASSAN(FR),** br g Nishapour (FR) - Amber's Image by Billion (USA) (S E Kettlewell) 74⁹ 2363⁸ 3661⁸

8 **CHIEF RAGER,** ch g Relkino - Metaxa by Khalkis (N A Twiston-Davies) 1767⁶ 2005 2268 2562 2719⁶

7 **CHIEF RANI(IRE),** ch g Salt Dome (USA) - Hada Rani by Jaazeiro (USA) (P Mullins) 67 396 929

5 **CHIEF'S LADY,** b m Reprimand - Pussy Foot by Red Sunset (J M Bradley) 423⁶ 641⁸

7 **CHIEF'S SONG,** b g Chief Singer - Tizzy by Formidable (USA) (S Dow) 966¹ 1393⁶ 2218⁵ 2451² 2591 3080⁹

6 **CHIEFTAIN'S CROWN(USA),** ch g Chief's Crown (USA) - Simple Taste (USA) by Sharpen Up (T Hind) 241⁵ 2532⁶ 2616⁴ 4230¹

9 **CHILDHAY CHOCOLATE,** b g Impecunious - Childhay by Roi Soleil (P F Nicholls) 809 1101³ 1426 1814 2434³ 2800³ 3121

6 **CHILDREN'S CHOICE(IRE),** b m Taufan (USA) - Alice Brackloon (USA) by Melyno (W J Musson) 1442⁶ 2973⁸

9 **CHILDSWAY,** b g Salmon Leap (USA) - Tharita by Thatch (USA) (S J Robinson) 608³ 2201⁸ 2576 2848⁵ 2985 3124 4009 4263

7 **CHILI HEIGHTS,** gr g Chilibang - Highest Tender by Prince Tenderfoot (USA) (K Bishop) 1729 1917⁵ 2185 3038 3614⁷ 3686⁴ 3859³

10 **CHILIPOUR,** gr g Nishapour (FR) - Con Carni by Blakeney (Victor Dartnall) 3578 3940¹ 4154⁶

7 **CHILL FACTOR,** br g Strong Gale - Icy Miss by Random Shot (Mrs M Reveley) 1039³ 1311⁴ 1631⁸ 2200³ 2653⁴ 3658⁸ 4020⁶ 4177⁶

8 **CHILL WIND,** gr g Siberian Express (USA) - Springwell by Miami Springs (N Bycroft) 2389 2629⁴ 2864² 3010¹ 3161 3355³ 3399 3760⁵ 3976³ 4110²

5 **CHILLED(IRE),** b g Mandalus - Phantom Thistle by Deep Run (Mrs J Pitman) 1447⁴

4 **CHILLINGTON,** gr g Chilibang - Saskia's Pride by Giacometti (W M Brisbourne) 848⁷ 1179 1943

6 **CHILLY LAD,** ch g High Kicker (USA) - Miss Poll Flinders by Swing Easy (USA) (R T Juckes) 2403

7 **CHILLY LORD(IRE),** ch g Good Thyne (USA) - Sleigh Lady (Thomas O'Neill) 88

4 **CHINA CASTLE,** b g Sayf El Arab (USA) - Honey Plum by Kind Of Hush (P C Haslam) 2879⁵

6 **CHINA GEM(IRE),** b g Idiot's Delight - Graeme's Gem by Pry (C P E Brooks) 1338 1545²

6 **CHINA KING(IRE),** b g King's Ride - China Jill by Strong Gale (J G FitzGerald) 3439⁵ 3808² 3999⁸ 4264²

5 **CHINA LAL,** b m Rakaposhi King - Doris Blake by Roscoe Blake (A Bailey) 4176[7]

5 **CHINA MAIL(IRE),** b g Slip Anchor - Fenney Mill by Levmoss (J A Bennett) 370[2] 451[1] 540[1] 585[3] 707[4] 830[4] 1343[6] 1574[7] 3984[3] 4193[7]

5 **CHINA TEALEAF(IRE),** b f Shardari - Reprint (Thomas O'Neill) 3456[6] 4200

7 **CHINESE GORDON(IRE),** b h Kahyasi - Abalvina (FR) by Abdos (J E Pease) 2109[3]

5 **CHINOOK'S DAUGHTER(IRE),** b m Strong Gale - Lulu's Daughter by Levanter (G Richards) 1390 1590 3757

11 **CHIP'N'RUN,** gr g Cruise Missile - Fairytale-Ending by Sweet Story (Ms M Teague) 3187[3]

4 **CHIPALATA,** b g Derrylin - Kirsheda by Busted (T W Donnelly) 893[1]

7 **CHIPPED OUT,** gr g Scallywag - City's Sister by Maystreak (Martin Todhunter) 1630[4] 1944[5] 3398[4] 3782

6 **CHISM(IRE),** br g Euphemism - Melody Gayle Vii by Damsire Unregistered (Mrs S Alner) 3982[3]

6 **CHOCOLATE DRUM(IRE),** br g Orchestra - Precious Petra by Bing II (J J Birkett) 3721[9] 3928[8]

6 **CHOCOLATE GIRL(IRE),** b f Le Bavard (FR) - Easter Beauty (James M O'Connor) 2087[7] 2165 2519

4 **CHOCOLATE ICE,** b c Shareef Dancer (USA) - Creake by Derring-Do (R J O'Sullivan) 2305[2]

8 **CHOICE COMPANY(IRE),** ch g Whistling Top - Audrey's Choice (David McBratney) 895[1] 135[8] 169 496

5 **CHOICE JENNY(IRE),** b m Saxco (FR) - Fern Glen by Furry Glen (P Mullins) 2228[5] 2649 2845[9] 3090[4] 3342[2] 3880[5] 4096[2] 4249[1]

7 **CHOISTY(IRE),** ch g Callernish - Rosemount Rose by Ashmore (FR) (Mrs A Swinbank) 1605 1820 2146[1] 2285[1] 2579

9 **CHOISYA(IRE),** b m Salmon Leap (USA) - Aingeal by Fordham (USA) (A P O'Brien) 345[2] 406

4 **CHOOSEY'S TREASURE(IRE),** gr f Treasure Kay - Catherine Linton (USA) by High Echelon (A P O'Brien) 882[4] 1173[1] 1309[1] 1403[3] 1616 2050[4] 2134[8] 2272[7] 2415[1] 2735[8]

7 **CHOPWELL CURTAINS,** ch g Town And Country - Liquer Candy by Laurence O (T D Easterby) 1152[2] 1585[1] 3319[1] 3577 3708[1] 3758

7 **CHOPWELL DRAPES(IRE),** b g Callernish - Sally Pond by Tarqogan (J Howard Johnson) 2463[4] 2972[3] 3308[4]

8 **CHORUS LINE(IRE),** b m Torus - Right Chimes by Even Money (P Beaumont) 1072[3] 1149[2] 2201[4] 2358 2576 2761[5] 3370[1] 3668 3966

8 **CHRIS'S GLEN,** ch g Librate - Misty Glen by Leander (J M Bradley) 707[3] 832[1] 957[3] 1055[6] 1262[5] 1857[4] 2184[4] 2604[3] 2748[3] 3104[3] 3252[3] 3558 3886[6]

7 **CHRISTCHURCH(FR),** b g Highlanders (FR) - Olchany (FR) by Labus (FR) (Simon Earle) 1942[7] 2976[3] 3310[8]

10 **CHRISTIAN SOLDIER,** b g Tickled Pink - Super Princess by Falcon (P Butler) 1061

8 **CHRISTIAN WARRIOR,** gr g Primo Dominie - Rashah by Blakeney (R E Peacock) 806

6 **CHRISTIMATT(IRE),** ch g Cidrax (FR) - Stonybridge by Avocat (C A McBratney) 3391[3] 3888 4115

5 **CHRISTINES GALE(IRE),** b m Strong Gale - Christines Frozen (M J P O'Brien) 713[4]

7 **CHRISTINES RUN(IRE),** ch m Tremblant - Christines Frozen by Deep Run (M J P O'Brien) 1278[2] 3182 3520[7]

11 **CHRISTMAS GORSE,** b g Celtic Cone - Spin Again by Royalty (N A Gaselee) 1645[1] 2005 2500 3115[9]

5 **CHRISTMAS THYNE(IRE),** b g Good Thyne (USA) - Shady Lady by Proverb (Mrs P Grainger) 4290

7 **CHUCK(IRE),** b g Kamehameha (USA) - Kill A Dawn by Kambalda (Michael McCullagh) 65 118 174[2] 195[6] 273[1] 302[6] 391[4] 432[5] 589[1] 684 849[4]

8 **CHUCK'S TREASURE(IRE),** b or br g Treasure Kay - Wisdom To Know by Bay Express (Seamus Fahey) 928

5 **CHUCKAWALLA(IRE),** b m Buckskin (FR) - Arctic Vista (J E Kiely) 66 176[8] 731[9]

14 **CHUCKLESTONE,** b g Chukaroo - Czar's Diamond by Queen's Hussar (J S King) 633[4]

4 **CHULPHOGA,** b f Warrshan (USA) - Lady Antoinette (J G Coogan) 1459 2161 2337

11 **CHUKKARIO,** b g Chukaroo - River Damsel by Forlorn River (J R Bosley) 769[9] 1001 1022

7 **CHUMMY'S SAGA,** ch g Caerleon (USA) - Sagar by Habitat (L Lungo) 1257[4] 1372[6] 1693[2] 2202[5] 2855[2] 3239[4]

10 **CHURCH LAW,** gr g Sexton Blake - Legal Argument by No Argument (Mrs L C Taylor) 1133[1] 1453 1645[2] 1853[2] 2310[9] 2599 3101[1] 3453

5 **CHURCH ROCK(IRE),** b g Lafontaine (USA) - Crupney Lass (J H Scott) 350[6] 898

7 **CHURCHTOWN PORT(IRE),** gr g Peacock (FR) - Portane Miss by Salluceva (P Butler) 2355[7] 2555 2729 2864

6 **CHURCHTOWN SPIRIT,** b m Town And Country - Kindled Spirit by Little Buskins (T P McGovern) 830 1447 1697[5]

6 **CHURCHWORTH,** b g Damister (USA) - Be Tuneful by Be Friendly (Miss H C Knight) 2893 3108 3239

6 **CIARA CANE(IRE),** b h Classic Secret (USA) - Rare Find by Rarity (Mrs B M Speirs) 579

6 **CIARA'S PRINCE(IRE),** b g Good Thyne (USA) - Sparkling Opera by Orchestra (F Flood) 1407[8] 1654 1752 2056[2] 2708[6] 2834[1] 2963[3] 3235[2] 3346[1]

4 **CICERO'S LAW(IRE),** ch g Glacial Storm (USA) - Royal Resemblance (Niall Madden) 3432

5 **CINDER'S SLIPPER(IRE),** b f Jareer (USA) - Farriers Slipper (John Turley) 3647

4 **CINDERELLA'S DREAM(IRE),** b f Un Desperado (FR) - Tattered Illusion (L W Doran) 2383

5 **CINNAMON CLUB,** b m Derrylin - Cinnamon Run by Deep Run (N A Gaselee) 2694[9] 2961[5] 4086[2]

4 **CINNIBAR,** b f Anshan - Kinkajoo (Mrs John Harrington) 3232[4] 3705[8]

7 **CINQ FRANK(IRE),** gr g Buckskin (FR) - Clever Milly (Donal Kinsella) 3769 4029[6] 4169[6]

5 **CINTARA(IRE),** b f Tidaro (USA) - Annynat (V T O'Brien) 3627

9 **CIPISEK(CZE),** b h Val II - Cecilka by Norbert (J Vana) 899[1]

7 **CIPRIANI QUEEN(IRE),** b m Seattle Dancer (USA) - Justsayno (USA) by Dr Blum (USA) (J T Gifford) 1155[1]

10 **CIRCLE BOY,** b g Carlingford Castle - Magic User by Deep Run (W Storey) 1257 1372 1911 1987[8]

4 **CIRCLED(USA),** gr f Cozzene (USA) - Hold The Hula (USA) by Hawaii (John A Harris) 2628

11 **CIRCULATION,** b g Town And Country - Veinarde by Derring-Do (D McCain) 240[4] 321[4] 505[2] 774[3] 914[1] 1176[2] 1327 1595[5] 1846

7 **CIRCUS COLOURS,** b g Rainbow Quest (USA) - Circus Plume by High Top (J R Jenkins) 44[6] 299[3] 382[4] 503[1] 675[2] 833[9] 2307[6] 2526[7] 3871[1] 4038[6] 4237[8]

6 **CIRCUS LINE,** ch g High Line - Mrs Mills by Ballad Rock (M W Easterby) 1465[2] 1635[1] 1835[1] 2257[1] 2389

5 **CONTRAFIRE(IRE)**, b g Contract Law (USA) - Fiery Song by Ballad Rock (Mrs A Swinbank) 879¹ 1033¹ 1326² 4258⁴

8 **CONVAMORE QUEEN(IRE)**, b m Carlingford Castle - Santa Ponsa by Wishing Star (N M Babbage) 2498 2726 2886

5 **COOKSGROVE ROSIE(IRE)**, b m Mandalus - Russell's Touch (S J Mahon) 898⁸ 1193 1432 1457⁷ 1901 2036⁸ 2380⁴ 3089 3180

6 **COOL AS A CUCUMBER(IRE)**, ch g Ballad Rock - Siberian Princess by Northfields (USA) (O Sherwood) 2409⁶ 2791⁸

7 **COOL BANDIT(IRE)**, b g Lancastrian - Madam Owen (Mrs D M Grissell) 3848² 4119

6 **COOL CAT(IRE)**, b g Cataldi - Arctic Sue by Arctic Slave (J C Tuck) 2871 3722

9 **COOL CHARACTER(IRE)**, b g Furry Glen - Raise The Standard by Distinctly (USA) (R H Buckler) 230 1420⁴ 1734⁶ 1859² 2293⁴ 2434⁴ 2741

9 **COOL DAWN(IRE)**, br g Over The River (FR) - Aran Tour by Arapaho (R H Alner) 1290⁴

7 **COOL GAME**, b g Scallywag - Word Game by Hasty Word (D W Barker) 2490⁵ 4256

7 **COOL GUNNER**, b g Gunner B - Coolek by Menelek (J S King) 1452⁶ 1958¹ 2267 2565⁴ 3039¹ 3275¹ 3709⁹

6 **COOL HARRY(USA)**, b or br g Sir Harry Lewis (USA) - No Chili by Glint Of Gold (H E Haynes) 1735 2744⁹ 2959⁴ 3144⁵ 3310⁶ 3935 4136⁴ 4316⁶

7 **COOL IT(IRE)**, b g Maculata - Cool As Ice by Prefairy (J R H Fowler) 3888² 4115

4 **COOL KEVIN**, b g Sharkskin Suit (USA) - Cool Snipe by Dynastic (Mrs M A Kendall) 2623⁶ 2858⁶ 3015⁴ 3439⁸

8 **COOL LUKE(IRE)**, b g Red Sunset - Watet Khet (FR) by Wittgenstein (USA) (F Murphy) 1225⁶ 1388⁶ 1635⁸ 2537⁵ 2854⁵ 3200⁵ 3899 4275⁶

6 **COOL MANDY**, b m Buzzards Bay - Petite Mandy by Mandamus (R J Price) 1261

5 **COOL N CALM**, br m Arctic Lord - Lovelyroseofclare (L Skehan) 1490⁷

9 **COOL NORMAN(NZ)**, b g First Norman (USA) - Ice Flake (NZ) by Icelandic (B de Haan) 3941⁷

7 **COOL RUNNER**, b g Sunyboy - Nosey's Daughter by Song (Mrs Susan Nock) 1347 2566⁷ 2772

4 **COOL SCOTCH(IRE)**, b f Glacial Storm (USA) - Not A Scotch (J R Cox) 2832 3450

9 **COOL SPOT(IRE)**, ch g Boyne Valley - Beagle Bay by Deep Run (G P Enright) 3192

5 **COOL STEEL(IRE)**, gr g Absalom - Formidable Task by Formidable (USA) (Mrs J Brown) 935⁵ 1631 1824 1953⁵ 2485⁸ 2577⁷ 2855⁶ 3042

6 **COOL VIRTUE(IRE)**, b m Zaffaran (USA) - Arctic Straight by Straight Lad (Capt T A Forster) 3028 3108⁹

9 **COOL WEATHER(IRE)**, b g Kemal (FR) - Arctic Tack by Arctic Slave (P Cheesbrough) 931⁵ 1183⁵ 1334⁵ 1739 2146⁶ 2258⁶ 2534⁵ 3259² 3511³ 3600⁴ 3781² 3966²

9 **COOL YULE(IRE)**, ch g Good Thyne (USA) - Sleigh Lady by Lord Gayle (USA) (R W Thomson) 3599⁴ 3666³ 3921⁴ 4209⁴

11 **COOLADERRA LADY**, b m Green Shoon - Road Scraper by Proverb (Philip Gould) 98⁴ 2197

8 **COOLAFINKA(IRE)**, b m Strong Statement (USA) - Petaluma Pet by Callernish (J A Berry) 1780⁵ 2021⁵ 2077² 2139² 2448² 2673³ 2842² 3133⁷ 3609³

7 **COOLE CHERRY**, b g Buckley - Cherry Opal by Saint Denys (C R Barwell) 1505⁶ 1995⁸ 2394⁴ 2601 3041⁴ 3190

6 **COOLE HILL(IRE)**, b or br m Strong Gale - Cool Girl by Menelek (D Nicholson) 1211⁵ 1419³ 1631⁴ 2025² 2298⁴ 2894²

6 **COOLE LADY(IRE)**, b or br f Architect (USA) - Rockfield Girl (P R Lenihan) 3878⁷ 4144

11 **COOLEGALE**, b g Strong Gale - Napoleone III by Bell Baraka (L Wells) 186⁶ 830³ 9897 1115⁹ 1343⁸ 3325⁸

5 **COOLEST BY PHAR(IRE)**, ch g Phardante (FR) - Gemma's Fridge by Frigid Aire (Miss P M Whittle) 2567 4188

9 **COOLEY'S VALVE(IRE)**, b g Pennine Walk - First Blush by Ela-Mana-Mou (Mrs S D Williams) 328⁶ 513⁴ 653¹ 754² 871³ 1141³ 3831⁴ 4175²

9 **COOLGREEN(IRE)**, ch g Andretti - Emanuela by Lorenzaccio (Mrs S L Bates) 65³ 212⁵ 2990

7 **COOLING CHIMES(IRE)**, b g Colmore Row - Charming Chimes by London Bells (CAN) (Denis FitzGerald) 91

9 **COOLMOREEN(IRE)**, ch g Carlingford Castle - Sirrahdis by Bally Joy (A J Wilson) 153 203⁵

9 **COOLREE(IRE)**, b h Gianchi - Positron by Free State (P F Nicholls) 1011¹ 1378² 1721³ 2175⁵ 2514¹ 2696 3314⁴

6 **COOLREE LORD(IRE)**, b g Mister Lord (USA) - Margeno's Love by Golden Love (Michael Hourigan) 781 977 1096⁷ 1359 1654 2366² 2585³ 2753⁵ 3234⁸ 3448¹ 3695³ 3953

8 **COOLRENY(IRE)**, ch g Bon Sang (FR) - Random Thatch by Random Shot (V Thompson) 1912 2576⁴ 2683

5 **COOLSHAMROCK(IRE)**, b m Buckskin (FR) - Arctic Conditions (Donal Hassett) 1121 1246⁹ 1533 1836 3234 3837

7 **COOLTEEN HERO(IRE)**, b g King Luthier - Running Stream by Paddy's Stream (R H Alner) 769⁶ 941¹ 1206² 1439 1557⁵ 2376 2612¹ 3173² 3360² 3685¹ 3875² 4190

8 **COOLTEEN LAD(IRE)**, ch g Roselier (FR) - River Farm (T Simmons) 3224 4106

8 **COOLVAWN LADY(IRE)**, b m Lancastrian - African Nelly by Pitpan (W R Halliday) 2891⁷ 3921² 4157²

8 **COOME HILL(IRE)**, b g Riot Helmet - Ballybrack by Golden Love (W W Dennis) 1101¹ 1304¹ 1639¹ 2452 2779¹ 3152⁷

11 **COONAWARA**, b g Corvaro (USA) - Why Don't Ye by Illa Laudo (Capt T A Forster) 3565

8 **COPPER BOY**, ch g Nearly A Hand - Learctic by Lepanto (GER) (R H Buckler) 1597¹ 2557¹ 3131

10 **COPPER CABLE**, ch g True Song - Princess Mey by Country Retreat (C Smith) 1216⁵ 1368⁴ 1707² 2261 3370⁴ 3496³ 3821⁴ 4091⁶

7 **COPPER COIL**, ch g Undulate (USA) - April Rose by Wollow (W G M Turner) 955² 1115³ 1234¹ 1355² 1663⁵ 1815¹ 2601⁵ 3190³ 3362³ 3594

4 **COPPER DIAMOND**, ch f So Careful - Lady Abbott by Grey Love (D Burchell) 481 614 893⁶

11 **COPPER MINE**, b g Kambalda - Devon Lark by Take A Reef (O Sherwood) 1177² 1395² 1563³ 2310 3678³ 3932¹ 4252³

6 **COPPER MOUNTAIN(IRE)**, b g Lomond (USA) - Flying Bid by Auction Ring (USA) (T J Taaffe) 4294³

8 **COPPER SAND(IRE)**, ch g Sandalay - Ballycahan Girl (James O'Haire) 1096 4148⁷

9 **COPPER THISTLE(IRE)**, b g Ovac (ITY) - Phantom Thistle by Deep Run (N J Pomfret) 2994¹ 3153⁹ 3977³

6 **COPPERHURST(IRE)**, ch m Royal Vulcan - Little Katrina by Little Buskins (W T Kemp) 550 890

9 **COQ HARDI AFFAIR(IRE),** b g The Parson - Deep Fern by Deep Run (Noel Meade) 2843³ 3453

6 **COQ HARDI VENTURE(IRE),** b g Roselier (FR) - Big Polly by Pollerton (Noel Meade) 2583¹ 2835⁷ 3071⁶ 3451⁷

6 **COQUET GOLD,** b m Rambling River - Carat Stick by Gold Rod (F T Walton) 1522⁸ 2147⁸ 2485 2847

4 **COQUETTISH,** b f Precocious - Cold Line by Exdirectory (J Hetherton) 2469 3928

10 **COQUI LANE,** ch g Le Coq D'Or - Gala Lane by Gala Performance (USA) (J M Dun) 1659³ 2319 2569³ 2683² 3058¹ 3306² 3600 3702 3870³

7 **CORAL SEA(IRE),** b g Corvaro (USA) - Seaville by Charlottesvilles Flyer (Cecil Ross) 929¹ 1042 1710 3963⁸ 4163⁶

6 **CORALCIOUS(IRE),** b g Precocious - Coral Heights by Shirley Heights (B Llewellyn) 297⁹

6 **CORALDA(IRE),** b f Kambalda - Wellknown Coraly (J Larkin) 946⁵ 1040⁴ 1244⁸ 1460⁹ 1581 3227⁹ 3643⁵ 4292⁵

7 **CORALETTE(IRE),** ch g Le Moss - Myralette by Deep Run (N J Henderson) 2873

7 **CORBLEU(IRE),** b g Corvaro (USA) - Another Daisy by Major Point (S B Bell) 1252 1775⁹ 1987³ 2856⁵ 3162¹ 3353⁶

5 **CORDAL DREAM(IRE),** b m Lancastrian - Emerson Supreme (Michael Hourigan) 1143 1246⁸ 2079 2222 3878⁴

6 **CORE BUSINESS,** b g Sizzling Melody - Abielle by Abwah (Lady Herries) 1115⁴

6 **CORKERS FLAME(IRE),** b g Corvaro - Preflame (T J O'Mara) 175⁵ 304 466⁶ 536

7 **CORKET(IRE),** b g Orchestra - Tor-Na-Grena by Torus (A P O'Brien) 2133¹ 2587¹ 2833¹ 3132⁵ 3765

10 **CORLY SPECIAL,** b g Lyphard's Special (USA) - Courreges by Manado (Miss S J K Scott) 2995³ 3256⁵

6 **CORMAC LADY(IRE),** b m Simply Great (FR) - Aiguiere (FR) by Native Guile (USA) (Michael McElhone) 134³ 175⁵ 197² 344 1581 3624⁷ 3838 4246⁹ 4326

4 **CORN ABBEY(IRE),** b c Runnett - Connaught Rose by Connaught (Miss S Collins) 1616⁶ 2050⁹ 2337² 2643³ 2832¹ 3345³

9 **CORN EXCHANGE,** b g Oats - Travellers Cheque by Kibenka (D G Duggan) 2502 2608 2997 4235

5 **CORNCAP(IRE),** b g Meneval (USA) - Laurabeg (S J Mahon) 2845 3090⁷ 3456

10 **CORNER BOY,** br g Callernish - Rescued by Sir Herbert (C D Dawson) 2993⁴ 4072³

11 **CORNET,** b g Coquelin (USA) - Corny Story by Oats (Denys Smith) 1785

9 **CORNS LITTLE FELLA,** ch g Royal Vulcan - Cornline by High Line (D P Geraghty) 2403

5 **COROMANDEL,** b m Prince Sabo - Jandell (NZ) by Shifnal (A H Harvey) 2302⁹ 2961 3475⁶

7 **CORPORAL KIRKWOOD(IRE),** br g Royal Fountain - The Black Bridge by Strong Gale (Martin Todhunter) 1681⁴ 1930 2534 3756

7 **CORPORATE IMAGE,** ch g Executive Man - Robis by Roan Rocket (T Hind) 3184⁸ 3554⁶ 3673

8 **CORPUS,** ch g Ballacashtal (CAN) - Millingdale by Tumble Wind (USA) (R J Hodges) 3185⁴ 3517¹ 3668

6 **CORRACHOILL(IRE),** b g Tremblant - Decent Slave (Peter McCreery) 2144¹ 2443⁴ 2964⁵ 3520⁸

13 **CORRARDER,** ch g True Song - Craig Maigy by Idiot's Delight (J G Smyth-Osbourne) 811 1323⁴ 2034²

8 **CORRIB SONG,** b g Pitpan - Platinum Blond by Warpath (Lady Herries) 2890⁴ 3171⁴

9 **CORRIBLOUGH(IRE),** b g Carlingford Castle - Good Oh by Pitpan (V T O'Brien) 576⁷ 729 982⁹ 1092 2648⁵ 2941³ 3074¹ 3236⁸ 4028

8 **CORRIGEEN RAMBLER(IRE),** gr g Step Together (USA) - Knocknahour Windy Vii (Edward O'Connor) 3341² 3693³ 4326¹

6 **CORRIMULZIE(IRE),** ch g Phardante (FR) - Scott's Hill by Dubassoff (USA) (K A Morgan) 2288 3289⁴

10 **CORRIN HILL,** b g Petorius - Pete's Money (USA) by Caucasus (USA) (R J Hodges) 666² 760³ 786³ 957²

9 **CORSTON DANCER(IRE),** b m Lafontaine (USA) - Corston Velvet by Bruni (J A Berry) 1169³ 1538 2169⁷ 2671⁴ 2756

7 **CORSTON JOKER,** b g Idiot's Delight - Corston Lass by Menelek (L Lungo) 1313 1823⁸ 2345⁷ 3030³ 3202¹ 3434³ 3702

6 **CORVARO FLYER(IRE),** b g Corvaro (USA) - Fiona's Blue (T Stack) 2757

8 **CORYMANDEL(IRE),** b g Mandalus - Curry Lunch by Pry (H de Bromhead) 714¹ 1003¹ 1408⁴ 2053⁵ 2273² 2734 2867 3453⁹

5 **CORYROSE(IRE),** gr m Roselier (FR) - Curry Lunch by Pry (H de Bromhead) 898³ 1409 1490⁵ 2079¹ 2129⁵ 2276⁷ 2445⁷ 2645 3430⁶ 3834 4059³ 4308²

7 **COSA FUAIR(IRE),** b g Roselier (FR) - Bold And True by Sir Herbert (K C Bailey) 975⁵ 1218²

5 **COSALT(IRE),** b m Eurobus - Eurosanta by Scorpio (FR) (J G Burns) 2040¹

6 **COSHEL LEADER(IRE),** b g Supreme Leader - Last Round by Lucky Guy (S J Treacy) 566²

9 **COSHLA EXPRESSO(IRE),** ch g Whitehall Bridge - Tanival by Carnival Night (A J Martin) 357² 496² 604¹ 714

13 **COSMIC FORCE(NZ),** b g Diagramatic (USA) - Cosmic Lass (NZ) by Roselander (M H Weston) 72³

7 **COSMIC STAR,** gr m Siberian Express (USA) - Miss Bunty by Song (P Winkworth) 1717⁶ 1843² 2174³ 3163

6 **COSTS SO MUCH(IRE),** ch f Roselier (FR) - Jaserdot (M A Gunn) 2675⁶

6 **COSY RIDE(IRE),** b g King's Ride - Fortysumthin (IRE) by Forties Field (FR) (N A Twiston-Davies) 1809⁵ 2213⁵

11 **COTSWOLD CASTLE,** ch g Carlingford Castle - Last Trip by Sun Prince (J G M O'Shea) 3934 4240

7 **COTTAGE JOKER,** b g Idiot's Delight - Pirate's Cottage by Pirate King (W A Bethell) 1763 1969

5 **COTTAGE LORD(IRE),** b f Mister Lord (USA) - Margeno's Love by Golden Love (Patrick Joseph Flynn) 2900 3090⁶ 3342³ 3697⁶

4 **COTTAGE PRINCE(IRE),** b g Classic Secret (USA) - Susan's Blues by Cure The Blues (USA) (J J Quinn) 664² 1024¹ 1249⁵ 1629⁸ 4267¹

6 **COTTEIR CHIEF(IRE),** b g Chief Singer - Hasty Key (USA) by Key To The Mint (USA) (J Neville) 2353² 2758⁵

6 **COTTESMORE,** b g Broadsword (USA) - Celestial Bride by Godswalk (USA) (Miss A E Embiricos) 2153

6 **COTTON EYED JIMMY(IRE),** b g Nordance (USA) - Sutica (M J Gilhooly) 3769

6 **COTTSTOWN BOY(IRE),** ch g King Luthier - Ballyanihan by Le Moss (Mrs S C Bradburne) 2322⁹ 2363 2817³ 3029⁷ 3710⁴ 3762⁵

4 **COULDN'T SAY(IRE),** b g Tirol - Sunlit Ride (P Mullins) 2370⁹ 2905⁵ 4056² 4147¹

10 **COULDNT BE BETTER,** br g Oats - Belle Bavard by Le Bavard (FR) (C P E Brooks) 1466² 1639⁸ 2273¹ 2821⁴

9 **COULTERS HILL(IRE),** b g Bustomi - Birdcage (Mrs D H Clyde) 1432 1580⁹

4 **COULTHARD(IRE),** ch g Glenstal (USA) - Royal Aunt by Martinmas (Augustine Leahy) 2270 2669³ 3232³ 4163⁵

10 **COULTON,** ch g Final Straw - Pontevecchio Due by Welsh Pageant (O Sherwood) 1084¹ 1210²

6 **COUNCILLOR(IRE),** b g Salt Dome (USA) - Virna (USA) by Coursing (G M Lyons) 1460 1654 1713 2022⁴ 2137 2172⁶ 2272 2383² 2675

8 **COUNT BALIOS(IRE),** b g Trojan Fen - Soyez Sage (FR) by Grundy (M H Wood) 2990⁵

9 **COUNT BARACHOIS(USA),** b g Barachois (CAN) - Seattle Queen (USA) by Seattle Slew (USA) (Mrs E H Heath) 1643⁷ 1808⁴ 1972⁴ 2194⁷ 2282³ 2408⁴ 2624⁷ 3367³ 3668⁴ 3740⁵

5 **COUNT KARMUSKI,** b g Ardross - Trimar Gold by Goldhill (W Jenks) 2899⁴ 3928⁵

7 **COUNT OF FLANDERS(IRE),** b g Green Desert (USA) - Marie de Flandre (FR) by Crystal Palace (FR) (K A Morgan) 263³ 416³ 704³ 1044¹ 1348⁷

10 **COUNT SURVEYOR,** ch g Corawice - Miss Magello by Bargello (T R Beadle) 3248

6 **COUNTER ATTACK(IRE),** b or br m Jolly Jake (NZ) - Night Invader by Brave Invader (USA) (Miss A E Embiricos) 1026⁸ 2889 3241⁶ 3473⁶ 3631⁵

10 **COUNTERBALANCE,** b m Orchestra - Lysanders Lady by Saulingo (J C McConnochie) 57³ 3371¹

10 **COUNTERBID,** gr g Celio Rufo - Biddy The Crow by Bargello (J M Turner) 3851² 4123²

5 **COUNTESS MILLIE,** ch m Rakaposhi King - Countess Carlotti by Hot Spark (L J Barratt) 1357⁸ 1642 2546

4 **COUNTESS OF CADIZ(USA),** b f Badger Land (USA) - Cokebutton by Be My Guest (USA) (Miss J F Craze) 930

6 **COUNTRY BEAU,** b g Town And Country - Chanelle by The Parson (J S King) 2248⁶ 2831¹ 3335¹

6 **COUNTRY BLUE,** b g Town And Country - Blue Breeze (USA) by Blue Times (USA) (P F Nicholls) 1271⁴

5 **COUNTRY COUSIN,** b g Town And Country - Archie's Niece by Sagaro (P F Nicholls) 2545⁴ 3859

6 **COUNTRY HOUSE,** b m Town And Country - Mearlin by Giolla Mear (J A B Old) 3197² 4050²

9 **COUNTRY KEEPER,** b g Town And Country - Mariban by Mummy's Pet (B J M Ryall) 1055 1236 1451³ 1687 1920² 2244⁴ 2638 2921 3484² 3771

5 **COUNTRY KRIS,** b g Town And Country - Mariban by Mummy's Pet (B J M Ryall) 1578 3408⁴ 3654²

6 **COUNTRY LOVER,** ch g Thatching - Fair Country by Town And Country (M C Pipe) 2242³ 2371³ 2758⁴ 3108⁴ 3546¹ 3684¹ 3747¹ 3846¹ 3909

6 **COUNTRY MINSTREL(IRE),** b g Black Minstrel - Madamme Highlights by Andretti (S A Douch) 654² 749 1474 1733⁴ 1947³ 2185 2323 2746 3268² 3528

6 **COUNTRY ORCHID,** b m Town And Country - Star Flower by Star Appeal (Mrs M Reveley) 1227² 1874⁶ 2363¹ 2810⁴ 3127² 3900² 4242²

6 **COUNTRY STAR(IRE),** b g Persian Bold - Sugar Plum Fairy by Sadler's Wells (USA) (C P E Brooks) 328¹ 465¹ 682² 1028¹ 1393⁴ 1886 1996⁵

8 **COUNTRY STORE,** ch m Sunyboy - Pollys Owen by Master Owen (A P Jones) 1207³ 1469³ 1916² 3017 3204 3761³ 3990⁵ 4204³

8 **COUNTRY STYLE,** ch m Town And Country - Win Green Hill by National Trust (R H Alner) 1961⁶ 2738 3514

8 **COUNTRY TARQUIN,** b h Town And Country - High Finesse by High Line (R J Hodges) 1456⁴ 1598⁹ 2215⁶ 2456⁹ 3027¹ 4032³

8 **COUNTRY TARROGEN,** b g Town And Country - Sweet Spice by Native Bazaar (T D Walford) 2790² 2993 3578

7 **COUNTRY TOWN,** b m Town And Country - Little Member by New Member (A P Jones) 1961 2726⁵ 2894⁴

6 **COUNTRYMAN(IRE),** ch g Henbit (USA) - Riancoir Alainn by Strong Gale (T R George) 1109² 2694⁴

8 **COUNTRYWIDE LAD,** ch g Lancastrian - Minor Furlong by Native Bazaar (M Madgwick) 152 251⁷

4 **COUNTY CAPTAIN(IRE),** b g Electric - Miss Daraheen (G M Lyons) 2130⁷

7 **COUP DE VENT,** ch g Viking (USA) - Callistro by Song (Mrs V C Ward) 2969⁸ 3820⁷

9 **COURAGE-MON-BRAVE,** gr g Bold Owl - Bri-Ette by Brittany (T R George) 2663

8 **COURAGEOUS KNIGHT,** gr g Midyan (USA) - Little Mercy by No Mercy (P Hayward) 152¹ 189⁷ 334⁴ 3328³ 3424 3592 3959¹ 4185⁴

5 **COURBARIL,** b g Warrshan (USA) - Free On Board by Free State (M C Pipe) 595¹ 689² 770¹ 859¹ 919¹ 1105¹ 1379 1561² 2215³ 2509¹ 3575² 3689¹

8 **COUREUR,** b g Ajdal (USA) - Nihad by Alleged (USA) (M D Hammond) 107¹ 279¹ 888⁷

9 **COURSING GLEN(IRE),** b g Crash Course - Glenartney by Furry Glen (Miss M E Rowland) 577³ 804 950²

6 **COURT AMBER(IRE),** b g Cataldi - Fine Cut (Michael Hourigan) 979 3179

8 **COURT CIRCULAR,** b g Miswaki (USA) - Round Tower by High Top (W Clay) 125⁸

6 **COURT JESTER,** gr g Petong - First Experience by Le Johnstan (M J Ryan) 322⁸ 376⁵ 484⁶ 506⁴

5 **COURT JOKER(IRE),** b g Fools Holme (USA) - Crimson Glen by Glenstal (USA) (H Alexander) 728 766³ 888⁵ 1313 1588³ 1823¹ 2122⁴ 2581 2880³ 3006 3350³

6 **COURT MASTER(IRE),** b or br g Bustinetto - Moycarkey by Raise You Ten (R H Buckler) 1341³ 1636¹ 1957² 2399⁵ 2928² 3067² 3143¹ 3559⁸ 3752⁴ 4046⁴ 4190³

9 **COURT MELODY(IRE),** b g Whistling Deer - Overwood Grove by Welsh Saint (P F Nicholls) 1133² 1767⁴ 2306¹ 2599³ 2986 3718⁵ 3924¹ 4058³

5 **COURT NAP(IRE),** ch g Waajib - Mirhar (FR) by Sharpen Up (S Mellor) 1888 2442 2658 3054⁶

4 **COURTING DANGER,** b g Tina's Pet - Court Town by Camden Town (D R Gandolfo) 2397 2628

7 **COVEN MOON,** ch m Crofthall - Mayspark by Stanford (C R Millington) 3168⁶

6 **COVER POINT(IRE),** b g Northiam (USA) - Angie by Prince Bee (J G FitzGerald) 1912² 2376⁴ 2650¹ 2808⁶

10 **COVERDALE LANE,** ch m Boreen (FR) - Princess Concorde by Great Heron (USA) (Mrs S J Smith) 1054³ 1312² 1734 1994¹ 2347³ 2912¹ 3204⁸ 3397¹

6 **CROMWELLS KEEP(IRE),** b g Castle Keep - Liffey Lady (J A Berry) 1782⁴ 2060⁴ 3068 4106⁶ 4328⁴

6 **CROOM ABU(IRE),** ch g The Noble Player (USA) - Anglesea Market (Lawrence Walshe) 66⁸ 131⁶ 408⁶ 619⁶

10 **CROPREDY LAD,** b g St Columbus - Lucky Story by Lucky Sovereign (P R Webber) 1177³ 1378⁴ 2386⁵ 2624⁵ 2800⁶ 3565

11 **CROSS CANNON,** b g Kambalda - Cushla by Zabeg (J Wade) 71⁷ 763³ 933⁴ 1165 1285³ 1932⁵ 2713⁴ 2911³ 3126¹ 3260² 3824⁷ 3902

5 **CROSS TALK(IRE),** b g Darshaan - Liaison (USA) by Blushing Groom (FR) (E A Wheeler) 1365³

6 **CROSSCHILD(IRE),** b m Buckskin (FR) - Mizuna by Ballymore (J A Berry) 185² 346¹ 773³ 1617⁸ 1776⁹ 2080⁴ 2138² 4302³

7 **CROSSEROADS(IRE),** b g Wylfa - Glenamara (T J Taaffe) 1486 2017 2649

8 **CROSSFARNOGUE(IRE),** br g Brewery Boy (AUS) - Rozmeen (FR) by Relko (A P O'Brien) 254¹ 303 1080⁸ 1276² 2052 2644⁶ 3073

10 **CROSSHOT,** b g Feelings (FR) - Gilzie Bank by New Brig (R McDonald) 1374⁹ 1912¹ 2345⁴ 2714⁴ 2884¹ 3199¹

11 **CROSSING THE STYX,** b g Lucifer (USA) - Glad Rain by Bahrain (K G Wingrove) 420

9 **CROSULA,** br g Sula Bula - Crosa by Crozier (M C Pipe) 149

4 **CROWN AND CUSHION,** b g High Adventure - Soulieana by Manado (T R Greathead) 1470¹ 1922 2550 2744

7 **CROWN EQUERRY(IRE),** b or br g Strong Gale - Ballybrowney Gold by Goldhill (G Richards) 1385 2237¹ 2319 2491¹ 2881² 3577 3716⁶ 3967 4010

4 **CROWN IVORY(NZ),** br g Ivory Hunter (USA) - Spotless (NZ) by Regalis (P C Ritchens) 60⁸ 401³ 519³ 667⁶ 919³ 1010¹ 1614⁶ 1801 3498⁶ 3872⁵ 4088⁶

6 **CROWNHILL CROSS,** ch g Dutch Treat - Royal Cross by Royal Smoke (F R Bown) 629⁶ 796 919⁸

6 **CRUCIAL MOVE(IRE),** b m Last Tycoon - Tough Battle by Captain James (S J Treacy) 66 685⁴ 802³ 3878¹ 4104²

11 **CRUISE CONTROL,** b g Cruise Missile - Kenda by Bargello (R Rowe) 1448 1941⁴ 2308 2726⁶ 2979 3254³ 3413³ 3632¹

8 **CRUISE FREE,** b g Cruise Missile - Lyons Charity by Impecunious (H J Manners) 519⁴

6 **CRUISIN ON CREDIT(IRE),** b g Dont Forget Me - Justine's Way (USA) (Michael Hourigan) 3233 3891

7 **CRUISINFORABRUISIN,** b g Cruise Missile - Bonsella by Gay Pilot (R J Price) 952⁴ 1263⁷

9 **CRUISING KATE,** b m Cruise Missile - Katebird by Birdbrook (S E Kettlewell) 862

7 **CRUSTYGUN,** b g Gunner B - Lady Crusty by Golden Dipper (O O'Neill) 1297 1716

4 **CRY BABY,** b g Bairn (USA) - Estonia by Kings Lake (USA) (A C Whillans) 1384⁸ 2188⁸ 2568¹ 2915³ 3400

5 **CRYPTIC MYTH(IRE),** b f Carlingford Castle - Cryptic Gold (Miss S Collins) 3965 4200⁴

5 **CRYSTAL GIFT,** b g Dominion - Grain Lady (USA) by Greinton (A C Whillans) 1388² 1631⁶

5 **CRYSTAL JEWEL,** b m Lir - Crystal Comet by Cosmo (P J Hobbs) 2552⁴ 2953⁴ 3807⁷

10 **CRYSTAL SPIRIT,** b g Kris - Crown Treasure (USA) by Graustark (I A Balding) 1871³

5 **CUBAN NIGHTS(USA),** b g Our Native (USA) - Havana Moon by Cox's Ridge (USA) (B J Llewellyn) 126² 2668⁶

10 **CUBAN QUESTION,** ch g Fidel - Straight Shot by Reformed Character (D T Hughes) 65⁶ 114² 158⁴ 209² 292⁹ 313² 471¹ 626¹ 721² 743

7 **CUBAN SKIES(IRE),** b g Strong Gale - Express Film (C C Trietline) 199 410 472⁹

9 **CUCHULLAINS GOLD(IRE),** ch g Denel (FR) - Rockford Lass by Walshford (T Casey) 164⁵ 201² 455¹ 605 699²

4 **CUE CALL(IRE),** br f In The Wings - Arousal by Rousillon (USA) (Mrs D Haine) 3176⁴ 3475²

5 **CUILLIN,** b m Emarati (USA) - Eyry by Falcon (R J Smith) 2371 3036 3332 3614

5 **CUILLIN CAPER,** b m Scottish Reel - That Space by Space King (T R Watson) 1251⁶ 1442⁹ 1951⁶ 2241 2983¹ 3911⁴ 4073² 4322¹

7 **CULLANE LAKE(IRE),** b m Strong Statement (USA) - Gusserane Lark by Napoleon Bonaparte (Miss M K Milligan) 1913⁵ 2187⁴ 2686⁴ 3161¹ 3399 3925² 4098³

6 **CULLENSTOWN LADY(IRE),** gr m Wood Chanter - Dawn Goddess by St Chad (P Hughes) 76⁴ 130² 179⁴ 254 302¹ 315⁴ 525² 625² 680¹

6 **CULPEPPERS DISH,** b g Lochnager - Faint Praise by Lepanto (GER) (Mrs L A Parker) 3746

6 **CULRAIN,** b g Hadeer - La Vie En Primrose by Henbit (USA) (T H Caldwell) 806³ 994¹ 1217³ 1330⁵ 2804

6 **CULRUA ROSIE(IRE),** b m Roselier (FR) - Coolyhennan (E Sheehy) 340 394⁷ 2144⁵ 2343 3380⁹

5 **CULTURAL ICON(USA),** b g Kris S (USA) - Sea Prospector (USA) by Mr Prospector (USA) (P Mitchell) 824⁹

7 **CUMBERLAND(FR),** 1310⁵

8 **CUMBERLAND BLUES(IRE),** b g Lancastrian - Tengello by Bargello (Mrs A Lockwood) 3921¹ 4072 4218² 4314¹

6 **CUMBERLAND YOUTH,** b g Town And Country - Key Biscayne by Deep Run (Miss C J E Caroe) 2458 2803 4037 4089⁴ 4186

8 **CUMBRIAN CHALLENGE(IRE),** ch g Be My Native (USA) - Sixpenny by English Prince (T D Easterby) 966⁵ 1184⁵ 1518⁷ 1773² 1871¹ 3318² 3711⁵ 3842¹ 3998⁴

4 **CUMBRIAN MAESTRO,** b g Puissance - Flicker Toa Flame (USA) by Empery (USA) (T D Easterby) 2145² 2852¹ 3003¹

9 **CUNNINGHAMS FORD(IRE),** b g Pollerton - Apicat by Buckskin (FR) (A H Harvey) 2562 2740 2892

5 **CUPRONICKEL(IRE),** b m Distant Relative - One Half Silver (CAN) by Plugged Nickle (USA) (D Burchell) 1669

7 **CURRA MINSTRAL(IRE),** ch m Black Minstrel - Owenacurra Lady by Pitpan (J E Long) 3283⁷ 4015

6 **CURRADUFF MOLL(IRE),** b m Good Thyne (USA) - Running Tide by Deep Run (N A Twiston-Davies) 1214¹ 2642² 3135

4 **CURRAGH COUNCIL(IRE),** b f Contract Law (USA) - Neshoma (J G Coogan) 1459 1709⁶ 2074⁶

10 **CURRAGH PETER,** b g Orchestra - Slaney Valley by Even Money (Mrs P Bickerton) 1010⁵ 1266 1510⁴ 1831³ 2201⁹ 2330³ 2457 3267 3371² 3726⁴

7 **CURRAGH RANGER(IRE),** b g Colmore Row - Derrinturn by Touch Paper (E J Creighton) 538⁶ 804⁵ 1041⁶

7 **CURRAVARING(IRE),** ch g Deep Society - Lady Harrier (Andrew Slattery) 2271

8 **CURRENCY BASKET(IRE),** b g Lafontaine (USA) - Trouville Lady by Tap On Wood (Patrick O'Leary) 1435⁶ 1618⁵ 2587² 2733

7 DANCING AT LAHARN(IRE), b g Euphemism - Beau Lady by Beau Chapeau (Miss S J Wilton) 55⁹ 111 1145⁴ 250² 1009²

5 DANCING CLODAGH(IRE), b m Dancing Dissident (USA) - An Tig Gaelige by Thatch (USA) (G M Lyons) 67⁵ 160² 222² 275² 428⁴ 579¹ 621⁸ 684 907 3768⁹

8 DANCING DANCER, b m Niniski (USA) - Verchinina by Star Appeal (D P Geraghty) 1068⁶ 2640

9 DANCING DOVE(IRE), ch m Denel (FR) - Curragh Breeze by Furry Glen (G Richards) 308²

10 DANCING HOLLY, br g Mufrij - Holly Doon by Doon (R S Wood) 3512

5 DANCING IN RIO(IRE), b m Lord Americo - Carnival Blossom by Carnival Night (T P Walshe) 3616⁶ 4050

9 DANCING PADDY, b g Nordance (USA) - Ninotchka by Niniski (USA) (K O Cunningham-Brown) 1507³ 1875¹ 2219 2590² 3154 3635⁴ 3791⁴ 4127²

5 DANCING POSER(IRE), b g Posen (USA) - Naughty Lass (Martin Brassil) 118⁵ 171⁴ 234⁷

6 DANCING RANGER, b g Broadsword (USA) - Elegant Nell by Free State (Miss S J Wilton) 1949

7 DANCING VISION(IRE), br g Vision (USA) - Dewan's Niece (USA) by Dewan (USA) (E McNamara) 944⁴ 980 1078³ 1274³ 1378¹ 1896³ 2071⁶ 2736⁵

6 DANDE DOVE, gr g Baron Blakeney - Ryans Dove by Rustingo (K C Bailey) 3561 4068

9 DANDIE IMP, b g Impecunious - Another Dandie by Communication (A W Carroll) 2498 2798 3098³ 3320 3559⁴ 3882⁴ 4138² 4297¹

6 DANDY DES PLAUTS(FR), b g Cap Martin (FR) - Pagode (FR) by Saumon (FR) (Mrs S J Smith) 2201 2486⁶ 2854⁴ 3434⁹

11 DANE ROSE, b m Full Of Hope - Roella by Gold Rod (P J Sheppard) 648⁷ 756⁶ 842⁴

5 DANEGOLD(IRE), b g Danehill (USA) - Cistus by Sun Prince (M R Channon) 1410² 1716¹ 2323³ 3080

5 DANGAN LAD(USA), b g Image Of Greatness - Cody Parker (T Costello) 347⁸ 468⁶

7 DANGER BABY, ch g Bairn (USA) - Swordlestown Miss by Apalachee (USA) (D L Williams) 1889³ 2393⁴ 2500 2742 2956⁶ 3115⁵ 3497³ 3613² 3790⁴

7 DANGER FLYNN(IRE), b g Boreen (FR) - Stramillian by Furry Glen (Michael Condon) 1118⁷ 3222⁵ 3955⁷

9 DANGEROUS REEF(IRE), b g Burslem - Tamara's Reef by Main Reef (B Lalor) 223⁸

5 DANJING(IRE), b g Danehill (USA) - Beijing (USA) by Northjet (M C Pipe) 1340 1381 3116³ 3568

6 DANNICUS, b g Derrylin - Kerris Melody by Furry Glen (N M Babbage) 1743³ 2298 2626 2877

5 DANNKALIA(IRE), b m Shernazar - Danakala by Mouktar (E D Delany) 1756 1901⁷ 2054 3389⁵ 3551⁷ 3891⁶ 4200¹ 4295²

6 DANNY GALE(IRE), b g Strong Gale - Mary The Rake by On Your Mark (G M McCourt) 654¹ 867 2765⁸ 2973 3099⁴ 3833⁸

9 DANOLI(IRE), b g The Parson - Blaze Gold by Arizona Duke (Thomas Foley) 1146¹ 1276¹ 1652 2052¹ 2231 2474¹ 3152

5 DANTE'S BATTLE(IRE), b or br g Phardante (FR) - No Battle (Mrs John Harrington) 2709 3217⁶ 3524

6 DANTE'S GOLD(IRE), ch g Phardante (FR) - Gold Bank by Over The River (FR) (C R Egerton) 2269⁹ 2402² 2858

5 DANTE'S MOON(IRE), b m Phardante (FR) - Shining Moon (Michael Cullen) 77⁶ 1143 1275

6 DANTE'S RUBICON(IRE), ch g Common Grounds - Dromorehill by Ballymore (N G Ayliffe) 900 2878

9 DANTE'S VIEW(USA), ch g Cox's Ridge (USA) - Only Star (USA) by Nureyev (USA) (P R Hedger) 1957³ 2176⁵ 2354³

5 DANTEAN, b g Warning - Danthonia (USA) by Northern Dancer (R J O'Sullivan) 419³ 652²

6 DANTES AMOUR(IRE), b g Phardante (FR) - Love Of Paris by Trojan Fen (M D Hammond) 1514 1968⁸ 2066⁴ 2490 3476³ 3598⁶ 3820⁴ 4271³

5 DANTES BANK(IRE), br g Phardante (FR) - Break The Bank (Miss A M McMahon) 3221⁵

7 DANTES CAVALIER(IRE), b g Phardante (FR) - Ring Road by Giolla Mear (D R Gandolfo) 1447² 1673² 1792¹ 2013⁴ 2691²

6 DANTES WHISTLE(IRE), ch f Phardante (FR) - Deep Whistle (David Wachman) 4244⁷

5 DANUCHA, ch m Derrylin - Connaught Queen by Connaught (J C Poulton) 3629 3780

5 DANZANTE(IRE), b g Ajraas (USA) - Baliana (CAN) by Riverman (USA) (R M Stronge) 1181¹ 1940⁶ 2394 2517⁵ 3881⁸

6 DANZIG ISLAND(IRE), b g Roi Danzig (USA) - Island Morn (USA) by Our Native (USA) (W Jenks) 1056 1321

8 DARA KNIGHT(IRE), br g Dara Monarch - Queen Of The Dance by Dancer's Image (USA) (R B Smyth) 950⁴ 1016 1373⁸ 1580 2383

8 DARA'S COURSE(IRE), b m Crash Course - Sliabh Dara by Prince Hansel (Miss P M Whittle) 2176⁷ 2461 2748 4250³

5 DARAKSHAN(IRE), b g Akarad (FR) - Dafayna by Habitat (Miss H C Knight) 1065³ 1322² 1594² 2260³ 2546¹ 2996¹ 3791² 3994³

5 DARAYDAN(IRE), b g Kahyasi - Delsy (FR) by Abdos (M C Pipe) 1437¹ 1573⁶ 1866¹ 2197³ 2323⁷ 3129³ 3442² 3639¹

8 DARCARI ROSE(IRE), b m Try My Best (USA) - Shikari Rose by Kala Shikari (Patrick Martin) 3954⁸ 4162² 4325⁵

7 DARDJINI(USA), b g Nijinsky (CAN) - Darara by Top Ville (N Meade) 1621¹ 1905² 2232³ 2706⁴ 3113

5 DARI(IRE), ch g Be My Native (USA) - Dedham Vale (J T R Dreaper) 3965

8 DARING DAY(IRE), b f Daring March - Somersday (Sean Aherne) 340⁶ 434⁶

7 DARING HEN(IRE), b m Henbit (USA) - Daring Glen by Furry Glen (R T Juckes) 153 1646 1747⁴ 2030 2403 2894

7 DARING KING, b g King Of Spain - Annacando by Derrylin (M J Bolton) 1207⁴ 1597 1700² 2740 3027⁴ 3459

5 DARING MAGIC, b m Daring March - Magic Chat by Le Bavard (FR) (J Hetherton) 2200

7 DARING PAST, b g Daring March - Better Buy Baileys by Sharpo (M D Hammond) 1828¹ 2201 2486⁴ 3479² 3699⁵ 3821¹ 4057 4208¹

6 DARING RYDE, b g Daring March - Mini Myra by Homing (J P Smith) 1295⁷ 1397 1731⁶ 2279⁶

8 DARINGLY, b h Daring March - Leylandia by Wolver Hollow (R Curtis) 82¹ 164² 265

4 DARK AGE(IRE), b c Darshaan - Sarela (USA) by Danzig (USA) (R Akehurst) 1790⁷

8 DARK BUOY, b g Idiot's Delight - Matilda Mile by Pardigras (B Mactaggart) 1587⁵ 1828⁴ 2237 2683

5 DARK CHALLENGER(IRE), b or br g Brush Aside (USA) - Great Aunt Emily by Traditionalist (USA) (Mrs J Pitman) 1306⁹ 1591³ 2156⁷

13 **DARK DAWN,** b g Pollerton - Cacodor's Pet by Chinatown (Mrs J M Newitt) 3603⁴ 3777⁵

12 **DARK HONEY,** b g Marechal (FR) - Caillou by Owen Anthony (S Dow) 1233⁶ 1637 1762⁵ 2389 2691⁶

5 **DARK HORSE(IRE),** br g Kambalda - Laurence Lady by Laurence O (C P E Brooks) 4042⁶ 4291⁵

6 **DARK MAGIC(IRE),** br g Over The River (FR) - Mwanamio (Paddy Fennelly) 1096 4331¹

8 **DARK MIDNIGHT(IRE),** br g Petorius - Gaelic Jewel by Scottish Rifle (D A Lamb) 610 660⁶ 792⁶ 912⁷ 1325 1693 1931⁷ 3780 3919⁷ 4271

7 **DARK NIGHTINGALE,** br m Strong Gale - First Things First by The Parson (O Sherwood) 1087¹ 1213² 1777⁵

11 **DARK OAK,** br g Kambalda - Dusky Jo by Dusky Boy (J W Curtis) 706⁴ 865² 1046¹ 1336³ 1774⁵ 2175³ 2579⁴ 3060 3505³

6 **DARK ORCHARD(IRE),** b g Black Minstrel - Ballyheda's Love by Golden Love (W R Muir) 1675² 2264⁴ 2688⁸

7 **DARK PHOENIX(IRE),** b m Camden Town - Hopeful Dawn by Prince Hansel (O Brennan) 1369⁶ 1540 1738⁴ 2296⁵ 2489² 2849³ 3137 3528 3935

8 **DARK RHYTHAM,** br g True Song - Crozanna by Crozier (G A Coombe) 2990⁶ 4157 4290

8 **DARK SILHOUETTE(IRE),** br g Good Thyne (USA) - Primrose Walk by Charlottown (O Brennan) 70

7 **DARK SWAN(IRE),** br g Soughaan (USA) - Last Stop by Charlottown (T J O'Mara) 944⁶ 1144⁶ 1407⁶ 1550 2068 2104¹ 2366 2708⁸

4 **DARK TRUFFLE,** br f Deploy - River Dove (USA) by Riverman (USA) (T R George) 1438³ 1599³ 2423⁹ 2746

8 **DARLEYFORDBAY,** b g Riberetto - Decorum by Quorum (S G Edwards) 82

9 **DARREN THE BRAVE,** ch g Sunyboy - Stey Brae by Malicious (C P E Brooks) 2268⁵ 2677³ 3329⁴ 3701⁴

4 **DARSARAK(IRE),** b g Shirley Heights - Darata (A J Martin) 2737 3755⁷ 4284¹

14 **DARTON RI,** b g Abednego - Boogie Woogie by No Argument (Mrs S Maxse) 4041³

4 **DARU(USA),** gr g Caro - Frau Daruma (ARG) by Frari (ARG) (R Hollinshead) 2973⁶

4 **DASH ON BY,** ch g Daster - Blue Condor by Condorcet (FR) (Miss A Stokell) 2858 3616

5 **DASH TO THE PHONE(USA),** b or br g Phone Trick (USA) - Dashing Partner (K A Morgan) 806⁵ 1070⁶ 1263⁹ 2576 3370 3821⁵ 4312³

6 **DASHANTI,** b g Rakaposhi King - Deep Line by Deep Run (D Nicholson) 1514⁶ 1805⁶

7 **DASHBOARD LIGHT,** b g Idiot's Delight - Good Lady by Deep Run (Mrs Charlotte Cooke) 2769 2990⁷

6 **DASHING DANCER(IRE),** ch g Conquering Hero (USA) - Santa Maria (GER) by Literat (D Shaw) 971⁸ 1293⁷ 1604

6 **DASHING DOLLAR(IRE),** b g Lord Americo - Cora Swan by Tarqogan (A P O'Brien) 928⁶ 1147¹ 1241³ 1549² 1621

9 **DASHING ROSE,** b m Mashhor Dancer (USA) - Speedy Rose by On Your Mark (Noel Meade) 1358⁵

10 **DASHMAR,** b g Rare One - Ballinattin Girl by Laurence O (Ms L C Plater) 1586² 1987⁵ 2241⁵ 3009 3246 3434 3803⁹

5 **DATEM(IRE),** b g Beau Sher - Comeragh Heather (T M Walsh) 3524 4161

6 **DATO STAR(IRE),** br g Accordion - Newgate Fairy by Flair Path (J M Jefferson) 1633³ 2208²

5 **DAUNT,** b g Darshaan - Minute Waltz by Sadler's Wells (USA) (F Jordan) 1977⁸ 2255⁷ 2451⁶ 2952⁷ 3110

6 **DAVENPORT BANQUET(IRE),** ch g Northiam (USA) - Crimson Kiss (USA) by Crimson Satan (W P Mullins) 1655¹ 2087²

10 **DAVY BLAKE,** b g Cool Guy (USA) - True Grit by Klairon (T N Dalgetty) 2536¹ 2850⁴

8 **DAWN ALERT(IRE),** br g Strong Gale - Gamonda by Gala Performance (USA) (Noel Meade) 1016² 1170² 2096 2143 2224⁴ 2382³ 4146⁶ 4246²

6 **DAWN CALLER(IRE),** b g Derrylin - Raise The Dawn (Mrs John Harrington) 304 393 685⁹

11 **DAWN CHANCE,** gr g Lighter - Main Chance by Midsummer Night II (R J Hodges) 771 895⁴ 1446¹ 1941⁶ 3490³ 3653

8 **DAWN FLIGHT,** b g Precocious - Sea Kestrel by Sea Hawk II (J R Jenkins) 206¹

7 **DAWN INFIDEL(IRE),** ch m Fidel - Clare Dawn by Prince Hansel (W P Mullins) 177 196³ 238¹

8 **DAWN LAD(IRE),** b g Lancastrian - Lek Dawn by Menelek (Mrs A Swinbank) 1035⁵ 1329 1585⁴ 1822¹ 2495⁷ 3261³

6 **DAWN LEADER(IRE),** b g Supreme Leader - Tudor Dawn by Deep Run (J A B Old) 2694¹ 3135

5 **DAWN MISSION,** b g Dunbeath (USA) - Bustellina by Busted (T D Easterby) 1148⁷ 1772⁷ 1883³ 3045⁸ 3398⁷

5 **DAWN SPINNER,** gr m Arctic Lord - Madame Russe by Bally Russe (N J Henderson) 3917¹

6 **DAWN TO DUSK(IRE),** br g Kambalda - Atlantic Breeze (Michael McCullagh) 2964 3816⁹ 4052 4243

5 **DAYDREAM BELIEVER,** b m Rakaposhi King - Petite Mirage by Hittite Glory (M Salaman) 1324⁴ 1675⁷ 2394⁸ 2539⁶ 3554⁴ 3731 3796² 3986⁶

4 **DAYDREAMER(USA),** b c Alleged (USA) - Stardusk (USA) by Stage Door Johnny (R H Buckler) 2303⁶ 2628⁷ 3091³

9 **DAYS OF THUNDER,** av Vaigly Great - Silent Prayer by Queen's Hussar (Mrs S M Odell) 360⁴ 505 2957 3410⁴ 3653⁷ 3992⁹ 4226

7 **DAYTONA BEACH(IRE),** ch g Bluebird (USA) - Water Spirit (USA) by Riverman (USA) (D J S ffrench Davis) 996

6 **DAYVILLE(IRE),** b g Homo Sapien - Golden Ingot (D G McArdle) 1539 1655 2443

5 **DAZZLE ME,** ch m Kalaglow - Defy Me by Bustino (A G Newcombe) 513

6 **DE CLARE DE MARE(IRE),** br f Royal Fountain - Rustic Star (J S Cullen) 3421

10 **DE JORDAAN,** br g Callernish - Gorge by Mount Hagen (FR) (W S Cunningham) 933³ 1108 3536⁴ 3670⁹

5 **DE-VEERS CURRIE(IRE),** b m Glenstal (USA) - Regent Star by Prince Regent (FR) (D Moffatt) 2572² 3127⁸ 3433 3780 4224⁵

7 **DEABHAILIN(IRE),** b g Broken Hearted - Devil's Drink (V T O'Brien) 62⁹ 90 135⁹ 3967 468³ 565⁹

5 **DEANO'S BEENO,** b g Far North (CAN) - Sans Dot by Busted (M C Pipe) 1919¹ 3111⁷ 3575⁵

6 **DEAR CHRIS(IRE),** f Supreme Leader - Our Chrisy (Patrick G Kelly) 3047 4727 622⁴

10 **DEAR DO,** b g Swinging Rebel - Earlsgift by Dusky Boy (N J Henderson) 1428² 1720² 2194⁴ 2478² 2864⁴

9 **DEAR EMILY,** b m Uncle Pokey - Malmar by Palm Track (J E Swiers) 79³ 164⁴ 239⁵ 885⁵ 2974

6 **DOUBLE STRIKE(IRE)**, b g Doubletour (USA) - Tamara's Reef by Main Reef (T G McCourt) 2016 2104⁴ 2366 2585 3180⁷ 3377⁵ 3837³ 3935b⁴ 4095⁶

9 **DOUBLE SYMPHONY(IRE)**, ch m Orchestra - Darling's Double by Menelek (C P E Brooks) 2451¹ 2590¹ 3155 3597

8 **DOUBLE THE STAKES(USA)**, b g Raise A Man (USA) - Je'da Qua (USA) by Fleet Nasrullah (Miss M Bragg) 3464

7 **DOUBLE THRILLER**, b g Dubassoff (USA) - Cape Thriller by Thriller (R C Wilkins) 3853⁴

6 **DOUBLE TROUBLE**, b g Little Wolf - Little Serenity by Little Buskins (D R Gandolfo) 1577 2766⁸

4 **DOUBLE VINTAGE(IRE)**, b g Double Schwartz - Great Alexandra by Runnett (M C Chapman) 3276⁸ 3476 3997⁴ 4210 4222⁵

4 **DOUBLEBACK(IRE)**, b f Simply Great (FR) - Wonder Woman (Michael Flynn) 1173 2965 3232⁵ 3415

6 **DOUBLING DICE**, b g Jalmood (USA) - Much Too Risky by Bustino (R Allan) 1657¹ 1823⁶ 2118⁷ 2359⁸ 2485⁶ 2630³

11 **DOUBTING DONNA**, gr m Tom Noddy - Dewy's Quince by Quorum (Mrs D Hughes) 3109 3746

4 **DOUG ENG(IRE)**, b g King's Ride - Euroville Lady by Light Brigade (Mrs J Pitman) 4042

6 **DOUGAL**, b g Mr Fluorocarbon - Natenka by Native Prince (B S Rothwell) 1738 1868 2463 2655 2972

4 **DOVALY**, b g Lycius (USA) - Sedova (USA) by Nijinsky (CAN) (M J P O'Brien) 3345² 3450⁴ 4144¹

8 **DOVETTO**, ch g Riberetto - Shadey Dove by Deadly Nightshade (A E Price) 3110³ 3820⁸ 4019⁸ 4083⁴

8 **DOWN THE FELL**, b g Say Primula - Sweet Dough by Reindeer (J Howard Johnson) 913⁴ 1049¹ 1281² 1527¹ 1758³ 2214⁴ 2466³ 3596¹

4 **DOWN THE YARD**, b f Batshoof - Sequin Lady by Star Appeal (M C Chapman) 488⁴ 614³ 3044⁶ 3280⁵ 4223²

6 **DOWSHI**, b m Baron Blakeney - Molinello by Balinger (L Lungo) 3308⁷ 3698

4 **DOYAWANAGIVEUP(IRE)**, ch f Be My Native (USA) - Knockananna (Bernard Jones) 3213

4 **DR BONES(IRE)**, b or br g Durgam (USA) - Rose Deer by Whistling Deer (M J P O'Brien) 1616 2230¹ 2731⁸ 3221¹

7 **DR CARTER(IRE)**, gr g Mister Lord (USA) - Caplight (M A Gunn) 4006⁷

4 **DR DAVE(IRE)**, b g Salluceva - Shule Doe by Royal Buck (P R Chamings) 243 3247 2265 2515³ 2676⁷ 3276⁴

6 **DR DOLITTLE(IRE)**, b g Orchestra - Lyngard (Miss Maura McGuinness) 2137 3226⁹ 3429

5 **DR EDGAR**, b g Most Welcome - African Dancer by Nijinsky (CAN) (M Dods) 728³ 1047 1657⁸ 1955⁸

5 **DR KING(IRE)**, b g Broken Hearted - Joanns Goddess by Godswalk (USA) (S Donohoe) 1195² 2041¹ 2235³ 3553¹ 3769

6 **DR LEUNT(IRE)**, ch g Kefaah (USA) - Not Mistaken (USA) by Mill Reef (USA) (P J Hobbs) 1268⁷ 2027⁵ 2329⁶ 2591 2695⁵ 3131⁶ 3568⁵ 3715⁷

12 **DR ROCKET**, b g Ragapan - Lady Hansel by Prince Hansel (R Dickin) 43³ 1764⁵ 1846² 1972³ 2261⁵ 2606² 2864⁷ 3104¹ 3185³ 3668¹ 4238²

6 **DRAGON FLY(IRE)**, ch g Phardante (FR) - Kix by King Emperor (C R Barwell) 157⁴ 336⁶

5 **DRAGON KING**, b g Rakaposhi King - Dunsilly Bell by London Bells (CAN) (C R Barwell) 3388²

7 **DRAGONMIST(IRE)**, b m Digamist (USA) - Etage by Ile de Bourbon (USA) (D Burchell) 667⁵ 756³ 924² 1261² 1355³ 1574¹ 2462⁴ 2665

8 **DRAGONS BAY(IRE)**, b g Radical - Logical View by Mandalus (Mrs M Reveley) 4001³ 4098 4290

6 **DRAKESTONE**, b g Motivate - Lyricist by Averof (R L Brown) 1006³ 1344⁹ 1573⁸ 1749³ 1976³

7 **DRAKEWRATH(IRE)**, b g Good Thyne (USA) - Velpol by Polyfoto (R A Bartlett) 1657⁵ 2619⁴ 2813

4 **DRAMATIC ACT**, gr f Tragic Role (USA) - Curious Feeling by Nishapour (FR) (C R Barwell) 1209

8 **DRAMATIC PASS(IRE)**, ch g Coquelin (USA) - Miss Flirt by Welsh Pageant (M C Chapman) 4212 4224 4315⁶

8 **DRAMATIC VENTURE(IRE)**, b g Phardante (FR) - Satelite Lady by General Ironside (W P Mullins) 1146⁷ 1242⁴ 1435² 1652 2020 2090 4165⁴

6 **DRAMATIST(IRE)**, b g Homo Sapien - Frostbite by Prince Tenderfoot (USA) (A P O'Brien) 121¹ 172² 2703 3068⁵ 3553⁴ 3935d⁴ 4160²

6 **DREAM ETERNAL(IRE)**, b m Strange Love (FR) - Blackwater Stream by Paddy's Stream (Andrew Slattery) 86⁴ 173 339² 424⁶ 561⁵ 685⁵ 781⁹ 849 4244³

9 **DREAM HERE**, b g Heres - Dream Buck by Pinturiscio (J C Fox) 103⁴ 326¹

7 **DREAM LEADER(IRE)**, b g Supreme Leader - Green Dream by Arapaho (M J Roberts) 1115² 1413¹ 1592⁵ 1938⁶ 2391 2776⁴ 3046⁵ 3492¹ 3739⁴ 3873³

5 **DREAM ON SONNY(IRE)**, b f Mazaad - Papette (Thomas O'Neill) 3349

7 **DREAM RIDE(IRE)**, b g King's Ride - Night Dreamer by Lochnager (D Nicholson) 1519² 1748² 2373¹ 2561⁴ 2955 3297³ 3669¹ 4048² 4186

6 **DREAM SOVEREIGN(IRE)**, b f Aristocracy - Bally Sovereign (Noel Meade) 829

7 **DREAMCATCHER(IRE)**, gr g Dromod Hill - Ulay by Charlaw (Thomas Foley) 139⁵ 853¹

7 **DREAMIN GEORGE(IRE)**, g Mandalus - Galway Grey (Michael Flynn) 64 122⁷ 183⁶

9 **DREAMS END**, ch h Rainbow Quest (USA) - Be Easy by Be Friendly (P Bowen) 303⁶ 1305¹ 1393⁸ 1761 2218⁸ 2442⁶ 2780¹ 3113 3595³ 3717⁵ 3907¹

7 **DRESS DANCE(IRE)**, b g Nordance - Pitaya by Princely Gift (N R Mitchell) 1349⁵ 1577⁴ 1698⁶ 2612⁴ 2873 3023 3559

5 **DRESSED IN STYLE(IRE)**, ch m Meneval (USA) - Inundated by Raise You Ten (M Bradstock) 2961⁶

6 **DREW'S BUCK(IRE)**, b g Buckskin (FR) - Twice Lucky (Raymund S Martin) 1042 1279⁹ 2037

10 **DREWITTS DANCER**, b g Balboa - Vermillon (FR) by Aureole (T P McGovern) 2767 2872

8 **DRINDOD(IRE)**, b g Welsh Term - Clearing Mist by Double Jump (J T R Dreaper) 261 429⁵ 646¹ 780 926² 1458 1896⁷ 2038⁶

10 **DRISHOGUE LAD**, b g The Parson - Elton's Lady (Noel Brett) 3068 3835¹

11 **DRIVING FORCE**, ch g Be My Native (USA) - Frederika (USA) by The Minstrel (CAN) (Mrs H Mobley) 2551⁴ 2974² 3368³ 4064

10 **DROICHEAD LAPEEN**, ch g Over The River (FR) - Merry Rambler by Wrekin Rambler (James O'Haire) 1618 1838⁹ 2100³ 2129⁷ 2339 2585 3089⁷

5 **DROIM ALTON GALE(IRE)**, b f Strong Gale - Mildred's Ball (M J Byrne) 4306

5 **DROMALANE(IRE)**, b g Vision (USA) - Clodianus by Bay Express (T A Kent) 3952

8 **ERNEST ARAGORN,** b g Laxton - Passage To Freedom by Pals Passage (Mrs S Lamyman) 1732 2201 2425 2625[7] 3184 3495

5 **ERNEST WILLIAM(IRE),** b or br g Phardante (FR) - Minerstown (IRE) by Miner's Lamp (G A Hubbard) 867 1155[4] 1367[5] 1738[8]

5 **ERNI(FR),** b g Un Numide (FR) - Quianoa (FR) by Beaugency (FR) (T P Tate) 1818[3] 2200[6] 3262[3] 4007[5] 4203[2]

5 **ERRAMORE(IRE),** b m Nordico (USA) - Naevog by Ela-Mana-Mou (A P O'Brien) 144[1] 255[3] 339[1] 732

9 **ERRIGAL ISLAND(IRE),** b g Buckskin (FR) - Crannon Girl by Polaroid (A P O'Brien) 1361

7 **ERZADJAN(IRE),** b g Kahyasi - Ezana by Ela-Mana-Mou (Mrs M Reveley) 1867[7] 2289[2] 2453[4] 3116 3568[7] 3712[3]

4 **ES GO,** ch g Dunbeath (USA) - Track Angel by Ardoon (R Bastiman) 2363[2] 2899[3]

8 **ESCADARO(USA),** b g Liloy (FR) - Mlle Chanteuse (USA) by The Minstrel (CAN) (Mrs V C Ward) 1971 2856

5 **ESCARTEFIGUE(FR),** b g Start Fast (FR) - Dona Clara by Crystal Palace (FR) (D Nicholson) 2232[5] 2563[2] 2830[3] 3151[5] 3568[1] 3786[2]

4 **ESKIMO KISS(IRE),** b f Distinctly North (USA) - Felicitas by Mr Fluorocarbon (G F Johnson Houghton) 2012 2292[3] 2607 3239[2] 3489

6 **ESKIMO NEL(IRE),** ch m Shy Groom (USA) - North Lady by Northfields (USA) (J L Spearing) 1305[5] 1761 2001[2] 2208[6] 2591

4 **ESKLEYBROOK,** b g Arzanni - Crystal Run Vii by Damsire Unregistered (T Keddy) 3898

5 **ESPERANZA IV(FR),** b m Quart de Vin (FR) - Relizane III (FR) by Diaghilev (M J Roberts) 4187[6]

5 **ESPLA,** b g Sure Blade (USA) - Morica by Moorestyle (J S Moore) 2390[9] 2625 4063

9 **ESTABLISH(IRE),** b m Salluceva - Royal Character by Reformed Character (J P Dodds) 1930 2062 2187 2491 2984[1] 3308

5 **ESTHER'S CHOICE(IRE),** b f King's Ride - Pil Eagle (FR) (John A White) 3818 3965

5 **ETAT MAJOR(FR),** b g Mont Basile - P'tite Poi (Mrs S A Bramall) 2054 2645

6 **ETERNAL CITY,** b g Kind Of Hush - Dark City by Sweet Monday (G Richards) 493[1] 654[5] 1962[9] 2635[2] 3013 3317[5] 3803[4] 4020[3]

6 **ETHBAAT(USA),** b or br g Chief's Crown (USA) - Alchaasibiyeh (USA) by Seattle Slew (USA) (M J Heaton-Ellis) 1646 1982[7] 2783

6 **ETHICAL NOTE(IRE),** ch g Orchestra - Ethel's Delight by Tiepolo II (Mrs S J Smith) 1162[6] 1377[6] 1587 1704[6] 2348

8 **ETON GALE(IRE),** b g Strong Gale - Lough Street by Milan (Thomas Foley) 1013[6] 1710[2] 2081 2445[3] 3131[8] 3520[6] 3607[2]

6 **ETTA DOVE,** b m Olympic Casino - Clifford's Dove by Rustingo (Miss Venetia Williams) 3408

5 **EUDIPE(FR),** b or br g Useful (FR) - Toskaninie (FR) by Kashnil (FR) (M C Pipe) 2457[1] 2554[2] 2788[1] 3132[2]

10 **EULOGY(FR),** br g Esprit Du Nord (USA) - Louange by Green Dancer (USA) (B C Morgan) 1803[4] 2033[2] 2604[6] 2859[9]

7 **EULOGY(IRE),** ch g Paean - Daly Preacher by Pry (R Rowe) 1427[3] 1852[3] 2253[9] 2438[7] 2690[2] 3050 3712

7 **EUPHONIC,** br g Elegant Air - Monalda (FR) by Claude (I A Balding) 1370[1]

4 **EURO EXPRESS,** ch g Domynsky - Teresa Deevey by Runnett (T D Easterby) 705 815[4]

4 **EURO PARADE(IRE),** b c Eurobus - Winter Parade (John J Walsh) 4056

5 **EURO SINGER,** br g Chief Singer - Crystal Gael by Sparkler (T Keddy) 1835[7] 1923[4] 2180[4] 3424[1] 3592[1] 3831[5] 4045

7 **EURO THYNE(IRE),** ch g Good Thyne (USA) - Cappagh Lady by Al Sirat (USA) (T D Easterby) 934[8]

4 **EUROBOX BOY,** ch g Savahra Sound - Princess Poquito by Hard Fought (A P Jarvis) 1024[5] 1398

6 **EUROCHIEF,** ch g Chief Singer - Tree Mallow by Malicious (R M Stronge) 1942 2283[8]

7 **EUROFAST PET(IRE),** b g Supreme Leader - Inagh's Image by Menelek (S A Brookshaw) 1350[7] 2315[7] 2791[5] 3210[5]

5 **EUROLINK SHADOW,** b g Be My Chief (USA) - Miss Top Ville (FR) by Top Ville (D McCain) 806[6] 1299[3] 1977[9] 3357[5] 3724[4] 3960[2]

10 **EUROLINK THE LAD,** b g Burslem - Shoshoni Princess by Prince Tenderfoot (USA) (D Burchell) 1803[6] 1990[7] 2526

5 **EUROLINK THE REBEL(USA),** ch g Timeless Native (USA) - Seeing Stars (USA) by Unconscious (USA) (S B Clark) 2238 2855 3042[4] 3512[4] 3741[7] 3819[1] 3886[9] 4234[2]

9 **EUROTHATCH(IRE),** gr g Thatching - Inch by English Prince (George Stewart) 1580[6] 1751[5] 1895 2735[7] 2865[1] 3072[3] 3390[5]

8 **EUROTWIST,** b g Viking (USA) - Orange Bowl by General Assembly (USA) (S E Kettlewell) 1465[5] 1625[2] 2257[9] 2526[3] 2880[7]

7 **EVANGELICA(USA),** b m Dahar (USA) - Rebut (USA) by Grallstark (USA) (M C Pipe) 188[1] 264[1] 375[5] 515[3] 797[2] 995[1] 1395[1] 1757[4] 2182[2] 3605

6 **EVE'S DAUGHTER(IRE),** b f Eve's Error - Crusheen Joy (Miss Ursula Ryan) 984 1195 1364 2906

9 **EVEN BLUE(IRE),** b g Gianchi - The Blue Pound by Even Money (Mrs C J Black) 1607[2] 1974[5] 2624[4]

11 **EVEN CALL,** br g Callernish - Even Doogles by Even Money (T Simmons) 98 406[5] 3378 3447[6]

4 **EVENING DANCER,** b g Nearly A Hand - Laval by Cheval (R J Hodges) 2510[7]

5 **EVENING DUSK(IRE),** b m Phardante (FR) - Red Dusk by Deep Run (J K M Oliver) 2533 2849 3198

11 **EVENING RAIN,** b g Hays - Fine Form (USA) by Fachendon (R J Hodges) 230[5] 3517 3653[1] 4031[1] 4226

11 **EVENING RUSH,** ch g Riot Helmet - Evening Bun by Baragoi (J Wade) 3508[4] 3901[4] 4257[7]

5 **EVENKEEL(IRE),** b g Horage - Corozal by Corvaro (USA) (D T Hughes) 2583[5] 2845[8] 3090[2] 3349[7] 3627[7]

8 **EVENTSINTERNASHNAL,** ch g Funny Man - Tamorina by Quayside (M Sheppard) 1054 1271 2498

5 **EVER BLESSED(IRE),** b g Lafontaine (USA) - Sanctify by Joshua (Mrs J Pitman) 1338[3]

10 **EVER SO BOLD,** ch h Never So Bold - Spinelle by Great Nephew (P Mullins) 409 851[4] 1004[8] 1245 2159[8] 3339[8] 3446[6] 4103[4] 4165[5]

6 **EVERLAUGHING(IRE),** b f Lancastrian - Lagerton (P J Healy) 4005

8 **EVERSO IRISH,** b g Hatim (USA) - Ever So by Mummy's Pet (J P Tulloch) 4290[5]

5 **EVEZIO RUFO,** b g Blakeney - Empress Corina by Free State (N P Littmoden) 934 1496[5] 1642[4] 1928[5] 2025[4] 2777 3016 3469[1] 3614[5] 3728[5] 3819

4 **EVRIZA(IRE),** b f Kahyasi - Evrana (USA) by Nureyev (USA) (A P O'Brien) 341[2] 522[2] 574[2] 620[1] 712[1] 1616[5] 2050 2230 2470[5] 3150 3935b[7]

4 **EWAR BOLD,** b c Bold Arrangement - Monaneigue Lady by Julio Mariner (K O

Cunningham-Brown) 1599 2265⁹ 2390⁶ 2640⁶ 2766⁵ 2977⁵ 3196 3771⁴ 3871³ 4189⁷

5 EWAR IMPERIAL, b g Legend Of France (USA) - Monaneigue Lady by Julio Mariner (K O Cunningham-Brown) 186⁵ 262²

5 EXALTED(IRE), b g High Estate - Heavenward (USA) by Conquistador Cielo (USA) (W Jenks) 2497² 2773⁴ 3150

8 EXCLUSION, ch g Ballad Rock - Great Exception by Grundy (J Hetherton) 156⁹ 228³ 412² 461 665⁸ 839⁴

8 EXCUSE ME(IRE), b g Toravich (USA) - Optimistic Baby by Konigssee (I R Ferguson) 135

5 EXECUTIVE(IRE), ch g Polish Precedent (USA) - Red Comes Up (USA) by Blushing Groom (FR) (D J S ffrench Davis) 2980

6 EXECUTIVE CHIEF(IRE), b g Executive Perk - Ceolbridge Baby (Francis Berry) 1898

5 EXECUTIVE DESIGN, b g Unfuwain (USA) - Seven Seas (FR) by Riverman (USA) (Mrs M Reveley) 1508¹ 2128⁷ 3131 3715⁵

5 EXECUTIVE HEIGHTS(IRE), br g Executive Perk - Monashuna (Redmond Cody) 566⁴ 686⁵ 3789⁹ 4029⁹

6 EXECUTIVE MERC(IRE), ch c Executive Perk - Barony Bush Vii (E P Hickey) 1539 2129 2228⁷

6 EXECUTIVE OPAL(IRE), ch f Executive Perk - Deep Captain (Michael Hourigan) 1060 1120⁸

8 EXECUTIVE OPTIONS(IRE), br g Strong Gale - Gala Noon by Gala Performance (USA) (J McCaghy) 1652³ 1898⁹ 2341⁴ 2446⁶ 2734 2842³

5 EXECUTIVE PEARL(IRE), b or br f Executive Perk - Kalamalka (C Roche) 3789

6 EXECUTIVE SCORE(IRE), b g Executive Perk - Fanny Dillon (A L T Moore) 4295⁷

7 EXECUTIVE STRESS(IRE), ch g Executive Perk - Mary Kate Finn (P Mullins) 4106

9 EXEMPLAR(IRE), b g Carlingford Castle - Mabbots Own by Royal Trip (Mrs S J Smith) 913⁵ 1036³ 1166¹ 1914⁵ 2238⁷ 2487⁹ 2762⁷ 3158² 3354³ 3724² 3967 4022³ 4265¹

7 EXPEDIENT EXPRESS(IRE), b g Torus - Paldamask by Native Prince (Joseph G Murphy) 2088⁹ 2104 2366 3180² 3448

7 EXPEDIENT OPTION(IRE), b g Sadler's Wells (USA) - Marwell by Habitat (A P O'Brien) 224² 302

6 EXPERT ADVICE(IRE), b or br g Torus - All Springs (Michael G Holden) 2339 2443 2518 2839 4076⁶ 4243⁷

5 EXPRESS AGAIN, b g Then Again - Before Long by Longleat (USA) (M J Haynes) 3082 3197⁷

8 EXPRESS GIFT, br g Bay Express - Annes Gift by Ballymoss (Mrs M Reveley) 2027³ 2128 2453 2693¹ 3080³ 3717 3907⁸

9 EXPRESS TRAVEL(IRE), b g New Express - Agher Glen by Apollo Eight (R Curtis) 1055¹ 1734 2401³

13 EXPRESSMENT, br g Battlement - Ruby Express by Pony Express (Miss A S Ross) 2875⁵ 3313⁵ 4171⁷

7 EXTERIOR PROFILES(IRE), b g Good Thyne (USA) - Best Of Kin by Pry (N A Twiston-Davies) 1647 2425⁴ 2597 2955³ 3383

4 EXTRA HOUR(IRE), b g Cyrano de Bergerac - Renzola by Dragonara Palace (USA) (W R Muir) 1922

5 EXTRA STOUT(IRE), ch g Buckskin (FR) - Bold Strike (FR) (Denis J Reddan) 171

5 EXTREMELY FRIENDLY, ch g Generous (IRE) - Water Woo (USA) by Tom Rolfe (Bob Jones) 1249 1737

6 EYE OF THE STORM(IRE), b g Strong Gale - Belon Brig by New Brig (J J Quinn) 671

4 EZANAK(IRE), b g Darshaan - Ezana by Ela-Mana-Mou (Miss H C Knight) 2628⁹ 2898³ 3501³

4 FAATEQ, b c Caerleon (USA) - Treble (USA) by Riverman (USA) (Anthony Mullins) 2669 3087 3345

5 FABBL APPROVED, br g Newski (USA) - What An Experiance by Chance Meeting (D C Turner) 3898

6 FABRIANO(USA), ch g El Gran Senor (USA) - Thorough by Thatch (USA) (M Halford) 3225³ 3642⁸

9 FABULOUS FRANCY(IRE), ch g Remainder Man - Francie's Treble by Quayside (Miss A E Embiricos) 868⁴ 1025³ 1448

7 FABULOUS MTOTO, b h Mtoto - El Fabulous (FR) by Fabulous Dancer (USA) (M S Saunders) 1860³

9 FACTOR TEN(IRE), b g Kemal (FR) - Kissowen by Pitpan (Miss H C Knight) 59¹ 821 877¹ 1382² 3924 4135² 4317

5 FAHEEN'S BOY(IRE), b g Don't Forget Me - Vibrant Hue (USA) (Ms E Cassidy) 1275 1897

5 FAHY'S FIELD(IRE), ch g Krayyan - Laurentino (Michael Hourigan) 2704 2942 3221

7 FAIR ALLY, gr g Scallywag - Fair Kitty by Saucy Kit (M E Sowersby) 1250⁵ 1587 1741⁵ 1963³ 2259 2971⁶ 3259⁴ 3481 3662

6 FAIR AND FANCY(FR), b g Always Fair (USA) - Fancy Star (FR) by Bellypha (Miss M K Milligan) 3782 3971¹ 4256⁵

5 FAIR ATTRACTION, ch g Charmer - Fairfields by Sharpen Up (J W Dufosee) 641

11 FAIR CROSSING, ch g Over The River (FR) - Golden Chestnut by Green Shoon (Mrs T J Hill) 3727

5 FAIR FONTAINE(IRE), b f Lafontaine (USA) - Fair Fantan (Daniel O'Connell) 3182⁷ 3430

11 FAIR GO, b g Torenaga - In Custody by Virginian Boy (Mrs C Harrison) 1003³ 1144⁸ 1538⁴ 1711⁵ 2059⁴ 2169⁴ 2448⁵ 2945⁵ 3420

6 FAIR HAUL, gr g Baron Blakeney - Cherry Meringue by Birdbrook (R G Frost) 1306 1598 1727 2479

10 FAIR REVIVAL, b g Tesoro Mio - Julia's Birthday by Bivouac (Denis Barry) 4328³

6 FAIR SET(IRE), b g Miner's Lamp - School Buck by Buckskin (FR) (F Flood) 1782⁸ 2041³ 2378⁸

6 FAIR SOCIETY(IRE), ch m Moscow Society (USA) - Fair Freda by Proverb (Michael Hourigan) 95² 135² 193⁴ 222 260⁴ 311³ 352¹ 408² 469 565⁷ 710⁵ 3954² 4027¹ 4196⁴ 4325²

5 FAIRELAINE, b m Zalazl (USA) - Blue And White by Busted (K C Bailey) 1669⁴ 1813² 2479³ 2607⁵ 3287⁸ 3805² 3915 4019

6 FAIRFIELD BRANDY(IRE), b f Mister Lord (USA) - Menek (Myles Coughlan) 2228

7 FAIRIES FAREWELL, ch m Broadsword (USA) - Fairies First by Nulli Secundus (O Sherwood) 1348⁵ 1815 4084⁴

4 FAIRLY SHARP(IRE), b f Glenstal (USA) - Bengala (FR) by Hard To Beat (Graeme Roe) 620² 712⁴ 882¹ 1309⁸ 2828⁶ 3044² 3315² 3641² 3905² 4301¹

5 FAIRY COURT(IRE), b h Fairy King (USA) - Gentle Freedom (D Thomas Sheridan) 1275 1488⁶

5 FAIRY KNIGHT, b h Fairy King (USA) - Vestal Flame by Habitat (R Hannon) 1641⁷ 1716³ 2782⁶

9 FAIRY MIST(IRE), gr g Roselier (FR) - Lochsollish by Raise You Ten (John Patrick Ryan) 1092⁴ 1538⁵ 1711⁷ 1837¹ 2059 2169⁵ 2867³ 3420¹

12 **FAIRY PARK,** ch g Don - Laricina by Tarboosh (USA) (H Oliver) 642 692² 809 1140 1799² 2031⁶ 2606 3139⁷ 3352 3404 3502³ 3670⁷

5 **FAIRY-LAND(IRE),** ch m Executive Perk - Season's Delight by Idiot's Delight (J Howard Johnson) 1783⁷ 2575

4 **FAITCH'S LADY(IRE),** b f Dock Leaf - Claregalway Lass (John Daly) 4106 4284

7 **FAITHFUL HAND,** ch g Nearly A Hand - Allende by Grand Roi (Mrs S J Smith) 749⁴ 1123⁴ 1280² 1695³ 1872² 3512³ 3673⁵

6 **FAITHLEGG(IRE),** b m Bold Owl - Combe Hill (N J Henderson) 2605 4136 4316³

4 **FALCARRAGH(IRE),** b g Common Grounds - Tatra by Niniski (USA) (A J Martin) 732⁵ 828⁹ 1040² 1273² 1581 1752 2051⁷ 2382⁶

4 **FALCON'S FIRE(IRE),** gr c Kalaglow - Regent's Folly by Touching Wood (USA) (J T Gorman) 2067⁶ 2337

4 **FALCON'S FLAME(USA),** b or br g Hawkster (USA) - Staunch Flame (USA) by Bold Forbes (USA) (V Thompson) 930² 2116³ 2357³ 2632⁴ 2849⁷ 3128⁸

10 **FALCONS DAWN,** b g Exhibitioner - African Bloom by African Sky (Mrs Stephanie J Castell) 446⁵ 511⁵

4 **FALLOW TRIX(IRE),** b g Peacock (FR) - Deer Trix by Buckskin (FR) (J R Cox) 928 1193⁵ 1579¹ 2016⁶ 2097³ 2208⁵ 2708⁴ 3837² 3942¹ 4095⁴

12 **FALSE ECONOMY,** ch g Torus - Vulvic by Vulgan (Mrs D D Scott) 4072

4 **FAMBO LAD(IRE),** b g Kemal (FR) - Knockatippaun by Bahrain (J A Berry) 780 1538

6 **FAME AND FANTASY(IRE),** b m Waajib - Birchwood by Fordham (USA) (Noel T Chance) 903 4296

4 **FAMILIAR ART,** b m Faustus (USA) - Mill D'Art by Artaius (USA) (D Moffatt) 1386⁸ 1693⁷ 1986 2202

11 **FAMILIAR FRIEND,** gr g John French - Bidula by Manacle (S J Gilmore) 3279 3387 3464² 3858⁴ 3916² 4064

4 **FAMILY PROJECT(IRE),** b f Project Manager - Favourite Niece by Busted (J S Bolger) 2230⁸ 2337 2702⁸ 3415⁵ 3767⁵

10 **FAMILY WAY,** b g Deep Run - Miss Miller by Lawrence O (A L T Moore) 1621² 2128⁴ 3131

12 **FAMOUS STOUT,** b g Strong Gale - Cinnamon Saint by Be Friendly (A J Martin) 3455² 3839

5 **FANADIYR(IRE),** b g Kahyasi - Fair Fight by Fine Blade (USA) (J S Goldie) 2485 3803⁶ 4219³

6 **FANCY NANCY(IRE),** b m Buckskin (FR) - Lils Melody by Grange Melody (Miss C Johnsey) 1260⁷ 2249⁷ 2749¹ 3016

7 **FANCYTALKINTINKER(IRE),** b g Bold Owl - Our Ena by Tower Walk (J N Dalton) 4255⁵

4 **FANDANGO DE CHASSY(FR),** b g Brezzo (FR) - Laita de Mercurey (FR) (A L T Moore) 4026 4324⁹

9 **FANE PARK(IRE),** br g Mummy's Treasure - Random Princess by Random Shot (C L Popham) 2295 2783 2977 3324

5 **FANE PATH(IRE),** br g Euphemism - Rowlandstown Lass by Rowlandson (Noel Meade) 180³ 210³ 329² 397² 472² 603¹ 802² 928² 2368⁴ 2583⁸ 2839² 2964⁴ 3226¹ 3419⁵ 3768² 3890⁵

8 **FANE'S TREASURE(IRE),** b g Mummy's Treasure - Fane Heights by First Consul (Noel Meade) 2735 2868⁹ 3073 3230⁵ 3887 4103³

4 **FANORE(IRE),** b g Homo Sapien - Dark Fluff (J A O'Connell) 238 1836 2443 3547 3963 4243²

5 **FANTASTIC FLEET(IRE),** b g Woodman (USA) - Gay Fantastic by Ela-Mana-Mou (Mrs J Webber) 515⁴ 669 3102 3858³

6 **FANTASY LINE,** b m Master Willie - Transcendence (USA) by Sham (USA) (P R Webber) 1556³ 1830⁶ 2153⁸ 2428⁴ 2882¹ 3331² 3506 3677

10 **FANTUS,** b g Green Shoon - Brave Dorney by Brave Invader (USA) (R Barber) 3153¹

5 **FAR AHEAD,** b g Soviet Star (USA) - Cut Ahead by Kalaglow (J L Eyre) 2711⁴ 2817¹ 3198¹ 3575⁴ 3709⁶

4 **FAR DAWN(USA),** b c Sunshine Forever (USA) - Dawn's Reality (USA) by In Reality (Mrs A J Perrett) 1412¹ 1854¹ 2195⁴ 2727² 3566²

8 **FAR EAST(NZ),** gr g Veloso (NZ) - East (USA) by Shecky Greene (USA) (B de Haan) 505¹

11 **FAR OUT,** b g Raga Navarro (ITY) - Spaced Out by Space King (O Brennan) 58

5 **FAR PASTURE,** br m Meadowbrook - Farm Consultation by Farm Walk (Mrs N Hope) 2363

11 **FAR SENIOR,** ch g Al Sirat (USA) - Ross Lady by Master Buck (P Wegmann) 1440³ 1645 2203 2389 2860 3321

6 **FAR SPRINGS(IRE),** b g Phardante (FR) - Ellasprings by Al Sirat (USA) (K C Bailey) 1479⁴

12 **FARINGO,** b g Rustingo - Royal Marie by Alba Rock (Mrs D M Grissell) 2641 2981² 3578⁹ 4018³ 4120²

8 **FARLEYER ROSE(IRE),** b m Phardante (FR) - Dane-Jor's by Take A Reef (Mrs L Richards) 2392 2661⁹ 2976⁵

6 **FARM LODGE(IRE),** b g Orchestra - Rossaleigh (I R Ferguson) 4977 644⁶

5 **FARM TALK,** ch g Palm Track - Kilkenny Gorge by Deep Run (M E Sowersby) 2262 2764 2984

5 **FARMER'S TERN(IRE),** ch m Sharrood (USA) - Winter Tern (USA) by Arctic Tern (USA) (P Butler) 990

5 **FARMERS SUBSIDY,** ch g Primitive Rising (USA) - Em-Kay-Em by Slim Jim (G M Moore) 795⁴ 1034 1703⁶ 1984⁷ 2241 2487

9 **FARNAN(IRE),** b g Mister Lord (USA) - Franzieflyer by Charlottesvilles Flyer (M V Manning) 1714⁶

10 **FARNEY GLEN,** b g Furry Glen - Windara by Double-U-Jay (J J O'Neill) 2151 2494⁶ 2759⁵ 2860¹ 3060³ 3436 4046³

5 **FARRIERS FANTASY,** ch m Alias Smith (USA) - Little Hut by Royal Palace (Mrs N Hope) 1128⁴

6 **FARVELLA(IRE),** b g Farhaan - Derryvella Lass (Miss Siobhan Reidy) 2757 3224

6 **FASHION LEADER(IRE),** br g Supreme Leader - Record Halmony by Record Token (C Weedon) 874 1115 2637 3628

7 **FASHION MAKER(IRE),** b g Creative Plan (USA) - Cailin Alainn by Sweet Revenge (Mrs I McKie) 1543³ 2951⁵ 3289³

4 **FASIL(IRE),** ch g Polish Patriot (USA) - Apple Peel by Pall Mall (N J H Walker) 2727⁸ 2893³ 3108¹ 3641⁴

5 **FASSAN(IRE),** br g Contract Law (USA) - Persian Susan (USA) by Herbager (M D Hammond) 1326⁵ 1772² 1983³ 2257⁸ 2879² 3396⁴

6 **FAST FORWARD FRED,** gr g Sharrood (USA) - Sun Street by Ile de Bourbon (USA) (L Montague Hall) 1208

9 **FAST FUN,** b g Germont - Fearful Fun by Harwell (K Robson) 3921

9 **FAST RUN(IRE),** ch g Commanche Run - Starlite Night (USA) by Star de Naskra (USA) (J W Mullins) 1567

12 **FAST STUDY,** b g Crash Course - Mary May by Little Buskins (S J Robinson) 3125⁵

7 **GLENFIELDS CASTLE(IRE),** ch g Carlingford Castle - Joy's Parade by Fidel (I A Duncan) 946³ 1041⁴ 1278⁸ 1581³ 1899⁸ 2037¹ 2229⁷ 2379 2585 3227⁵ 3390⁶ 3643¹ 3754⁵

9 **GLENFINN PRINCESS,** ch m Ginger Boy - Lady Amazon by Spartan General (P Bowen) 544 649³ 892¹ 1046⁵ 1674⁴ 1946² 3744¹ 3843

7 **GLENGARRIF GIRL(IRE),** b m Good Thyne (USA) - Mention Of Money by Le Bavard (FR) (M C Pipe) 302² 453¹ 643³ 1391² 1576 1867⁴ 2701³ 3612² 4048 4192

7 **GLENHAVEN ARTIST(IRE),** b f Supreme Leader - Loving Artist by Golden Love (F Flood) 2170 2272⁹ 2524⁹ 3072⁶

10 **GLENMAVIS,** b g King's Ride - Pink Quay by Quayside (Dr P Pritchard) 2028 2277 2603 3554⁵ 3617

5 **GLENMONT(IRE),** b g Montelimar (USA) - Glenamara (Frank Keogh) 3965 4169

5 **GLENMULLEN ROSE(IRE),** b f Roselier (FR) - Ballyeden Wish (W P Mullins) 3085

8 **GLENPATRICK PEACH(IRE),** b f Lafontaine (USA) - Seat Of Learning by Balliol (Mrs John Harrington) 2838 2907

8 **GLENREEF BOY(IRE),** b g Orange Reef - Lajnata by Nishipour (FR) (C P Donoghue) 245⁶ 304⁵ 722¹ 1013⁵ 1536⁷ 2081⁶ 2339 3754

9 **GLENROWAN(IRE),** b g Euphemism - Deity by Red God (Richard Ford) 4142⁷

4 **GLENSTAL FOREST(IRE),** b f Glenstal (USA) - Primrose Forest (Michael Hourigan) 4026⁴

9 **GLENTOWER(IRE),** b g Furry Glen - Helens Tower by Dual (C L Popham) 1229 1724⁴ 2434

6 **GLENUGIE,** b g Insan (USA) - Excavator Lady by Most Secret (G M Moore) 80⁶ 1914⁸ 2151⁶ 2238³ 2574⁸ 2815⁴ 3013⁵ 3263¹ 3587¹ 3665¹ 3868³ 4207⁷

6 **GLENVALLY,** gr m Belfort (FR) - Hivally by High Line (B W Murray) 387¹ 478⁴ 1044² 1736¹ 2257³

5 **GLEVUM,** gr m Town And Country - Peggy Wig by Counsel (N A Twiston-Davies) 3335⁹ 3721⁶

8 **GLIDE PATH(USA),** ch g Stalwart (USA) - Jolly Polka (USA) by Nice Dancer (CAN) (J R Jenkins) 2656² 2825⁷ 3382 3849⁹

7 **GLIDING AWAY(IRE),** ch f Tremblant - Ankar Maran Vii (William Hayes) 68 4166⁹

7 **GLINT OF AYR,** b m Glint Of Gold - Iyamski (USA) by Baldski (USA) (R H Goldie) 1657 2345

8 **GLINT OF EAGLES(IRE),** b g Treasure Hunter - Double Damask by Ardoon (W P Mullins) 1714² 2096² 2128

7 **GLISTENING DAWN,** ch m Beveled (USA) - Andrea Dawn by Run The Gantlet (USA) (T Keddy) 1002⁴ 1442¹ 1671⁵ 2158 2295 3692

7 **GLITTER ISLE(IRE),** gr g Roselier (FR) - Decent Dame by Decent Fellow (J T Gifford) 1573² 2425¹ 2638¹ 3132⁶

5 **GLITTERING JULY(IRE),** ch f Le Bavard (FR) - Perato (Patrick Martin) 4200

6 **GLOBAL DANCER,** b g Night Shift (USA) - Early Call by Kind Of Hush (L Wells) 3491 3610⁴ 3776³

7 **GLOBAL LEGEND,** b g Oats - Mirthful by Will Somers (J T R Dreaper) 3217⁷ 3521³ 3963⁶

4 **GLOBE RUNNER,** b c Adbass (USA) - Scenic Villa by Top Ville (J J O'Neill) 734² 930⁴ 1221² 1384 2602¹ 2818²

5 **GLORIANA,** b m Formidable (USA) - Tudor Pilgrim by Welsh Pageant (Lady Herries) 1423¹ 1669⁶

7 **GLORIOUS GALE(IRE),** br f Strong Gale - Bookmark by Shackleton (A P O'Brien) 1484¹ 4104¹

7 **GLOWING LINES(IRE),** br m Glow (USA) - Eye-liner (USA) by Raise A Native (Capt D G Swan) 87⁷ 730

4 **GLOWING MOON,** b f Kalaglow - Julia Flyte by Drone (Miss Gay Kelleway) 2961

7 **GLOWING PATH,** b g Kalaglow - Top Tina by High Top (R J Hodges) 891⁴ 998² 1175¹ 1235³ 1472¹ 1798² 1947² 2283¹ 2424⁵ 2663⁶ 3409³ 3652⁵

8 **GO BALLISTIC,** br g Celtic Cone - National Clover by National Trust (J G M O'Shea) 1056⁴ 1156¹ 1516² 1999¹ 2452 3152⁴ 3605

4 **GO CAHOOTS(USA),** gr g Sunshine Forever (USA) - Puss In Cahoots (USA) by The Axe II (Andrew Turnell) 3322¹

7 **GO FOR THE DOCTOR,** b g Doctor Wall - Mary Mile by Athenius (B A McMahon) 2029

9 **GO FROLIC,** ch m Rustingo - Go Perrys by High Hat (Miss C Phillips) 2513⁸ 3468⁴ 3692⁶ 4136

8 **GO GO GALLANT(IRE),** b g Over The River (FR) - Joyful Anna by Blurullah (Fergus Sutherland) 1194² 3181²

5 **GO GO HENRY(IRE),** br g Roselier (FR) - Glen-cairn Lass (Capt D G Swan) 2092

11 **GO MARY,** b m Raga Navarro (ITY) - Go Perrys by High Hat (Miss C Phillips) 3098⁶

5 **GO NATIVE(IRE),** br g Be My Native (USA) - Terrama Sioux by Relkino (Mrs S J Smith) 3251¹ 3721² 4130¹

7 **GO NOW(IRE),** b g Niniski (USA) - Aiguiere (FR) by Native Guile (USA) (Thomas Foley) 977⁵ 1076¹ 2837⁵ 3071⁵

5 **GO ROGER GO(IRE),** b g Phardante (FR) - Tonto's Girl by Strong Gale (E J O'Grady) 3087² 3456

4 **GO SASHA(IRE),** b g Magical Strike (USA) - Miss Flirt by Welsh Pageant (Patrick Martin) 574¹ 927² 1057³ 1750² 2050 2105² 2225³ 2669² 3216 4150² 4245⁵

11 **GO SILLY,** b g Silly Prices - Allez Stanwick by Goldhill (B Ellison) 662 865 1037⁵

9 **GO UNIVERSAL(IRE),** br g Teofane - Lady Dor-cet by Condorcet (FR) (C P E Brooks) 1613 1878² 2220 2325⁴

4 **GO WITH THE WIND,** b c Unfuwain (USA) - Cominna by Dominion (J S Goldie) 1854⁶ 2454⁴ 2656⁸ 3478⁵ 3905⁸ 4223¹

4 **GO-GO-POWER-RANGER,** ch g Golden Lahab (USA) - Nibelunga by Miami Springs (B Ellison) 482² 664¹

4 **GOALDPOST(IRE),** b g Tremblant - Snatchingly (W Harney) 4309

7 **GOATSFUT(IRE),** ch g Le Bavard (FR) - Kilbricken Glen by Furry Glen (B Preece) 1063 1882 2311 2954

5 **GOBALINO GIRL(IRE),** b m Over The River (FR) - Ogan Spa by Tarqogan (F Gray) 873⁹ 3299⁷

8 **GOD SPEED YOU(IRE),** gr g Roselier (FR) - Pitmark by Pitpan (C P Morlock) 1302¹ 1801¹ 2031² 2175⁶ 2301¹ 2600 3678² 3897¹

5 **GODS SQUAD,** ro g Gods Solution - My Always by Kalimnos (J Mackie) 2546² 2908¹ 3064

8 **GODSROCK VI(IRE),** b g Rptly By Rochebrun (FR) - Godsway (Thomas Foley) 1005⁹ 1147⁶

6 **GOING PRIMITIVE,** b g Primitive Rising (USA) - Good Going Girl by Import (J Hetherton) 3008² 3356⁴ 3661 4050³ 4261²

10 **GOING PUBLIC,** br g Strong Gale - Cairita by Pitcairn (P Cheesbrough) 2537 3780 4002⁶

6 **GOLD BITS(IRE),** b g Henbit (USA) - Ram-bling Gold by Little Buskins (G Richards) 4097

6 **GOLD CHARIOT(IRE),** ch f Noalto - Mum's Chariot (F Flood) 3840 4331⁸

5 **HARVEST REAPER,** gr g Bairn (USA) - Real Silver by Silly Season (J L Harris) 4158⁸ 4242⁷

5 **HARVEST STORM(IRE),** br m Strong Gale - New Talent (Miss N Hayes) 2525 3182

7 **HARVEST VIEW(IRE),** b m Good Thyne (USA) - In View Lass by Tepukei (C P E Brooks) 2596¹ 2781³ 3204⁴ 3726

14 **HARVEYSLAND,** b g Beau Charmeur (FR) - No Run by Deep Run (James O'Keeffe) 235⁶ 273⁶

8 **HARWELL LAD(IRE),** b g Over The River (FR) - Gayles Approach by Strong Gale (R H Alner) 1212 1767¹ 3441² 3827¹

7 **HASTY HOURS(IRE),** m Bulldozer - Hasty Years by Hul A Hul (Patrick Day) 64 173⁶ 3877

7 **HATCHAM BOY(IRE),** br g Roselier (FR) - Auling by Tarqogan (D Nicholson) 1611¹ 2043 2285² 2600 3311²

5 **HATTA BREEZE,** b m Night Shift (USA) - Jouvencelle by Rusticaro (FR) (D Nicholson) 1030² 2190 2591⁹

7 **HATTA RIVER(USA),** b g Irish River (FR) - Fallacieuse by Habitat (P T Dalton) 55 420³ 533⁶ 704⁸ 971 1399

8 **HAUGHTON LAD(IRE),** b g Drumalis - I'm The Latest by Polyfoto (J Parkes) 478⁵ 610⁹ 660² 862² 1313⁴ 1736⁶ 2241³ 2487 3123¹⁴

9 **HAUNTING MUSIC(IRE),** b g Cataldi - Theme Music by Tudor Music (Mrs A J Perrett) 1568⁴ 1793³ 2154⁵

4 **HAUTE CUISINE,** b g Petong - Nevis by Connaught (R J R Williams) 1844⁵ 2265

5 **HAVANA EXPRESS,** b g Cigar - On The Rocks by Julio Mariner (C A Dwyer) 693⁹ 1026

8 **HAVE A BRANDY(IRE),** gr g Roselier (FR) - Ardcress by Ardoon (Mrs F M O'Brien) 2410 2705⁵ 2904 3236 4145 4283

7 **HAVE A DROP(IRE),** b f Henbit (USA) - Clonsilla (John O'Callaghan) 212⁸ 257⁶ 406⁷

8 **HAVE A NIGHTCAP,** ch g Night Shift (USA) - Final Orders (USA) by Prince John (N P Littmoden) 49 476¹ 656⁶ 786

4 **HAVE AT IT(IRE),** b f Supreme Leader - Smokey River (P Hughes) 3935d⁶ 4161³ 4197

9 **HAVE TO THINK,** b g Impecunious - Dusty Run by Deep Run (P F Nicholls) 750² 1892³ 2182 2698 3744⁴

7 **HAVEAFEWMANNERS(IRE),** b m Celio Rufo - Ardagh Princess by Proverb (A J Martin) 3391 3943¹

10 **HAWAIIAN GODDESS(USA),** b m Hawaii - Destiny's Reward (USA) by Executioner (USA) (S W Campion) 42

7 **HAWAIIAN SAM(IRE),** b g Hawaiian Return (USA) - Thomastown Girl by Tekoah (Andrew Turnell) 1180² 1542³ 2391² 2657¹ 3132⁷ 3497⁶

9 **HAWAIIAN YOUTH(IRE),** ch g Hawaiian Return (USA) - Eternal Youth by Continuation (G M McCourt) 1686² 2395¹ 2729¹ 3024² 3165⁴ 3670⁵ 3830¹ 4058⁴

4 **HAWANAFA,** b f Tirol - Woodland View by Precipice Wood (Miss K M George) 1412⁸ 1610 1854 2267 2440⁴ 2611² 2804 3106¹ 4182⁴ 4310³

6 **HAWK HILL BOY,** b g Meadowbrook - Hawkes Hill Flyer by Nicholas Bill (F P Murtagh) 1677 2147 2346

6 **HAWKER HUNTER(USA),** b or br g Silver Hawk (USA) - Glorious Natalie (USA) by Reflected Glory (USA) (R Akehurst) 2259 2425 2561⁷

4 **HAWKERS DEAL,** b g K-Battery - Boreen Geal by Boreen (FR) (D A Nolan) 2206

9 **HAWTHORN'S WAY(IRE),** ch f Regular Guy - Daisy Spring by Straight Rule (J G Cosgrave) 171

10 **HAWTHORNE GLEN,** b g Furry Glen - Black Gnat by Typhoon (Mrs M E Long) 1888⁴ 2009⁴

11 **HAWWAM,** b g Glenstal (USA) - Hone by Sharpen Up (E J Alston) 1512⁴

6 **HAY DANCE,** b g Shareef Dancer (USA) - Hay Reef by Mill Reef (USA) (P J Hobbs) 140 192² 256¹ 291⁴ 1417³ 1601¹ 1759² 1982¹ 2290¹ 2323⁵ 2543³ 3652¹ 4298

4 **HAYAAIN,** b c Shirley Heights - Littlefield by Bay Express (K C Bailey) 2454¹ 2727⁴ 3150⁵ 3501¹

5 **HAYDOWN(IRE),** b or br g Petorius - Hay Knot by Main Reef (M R Bosley) 4084

4 **HAYLING-BILLY,** ch g Captain Webster - Mistress Royal by Royalty (P R Hedger) 1599⁴ 2526

8 **HAZAAF(USA),** ch h Woodman (USA) - Solo Disco (USA) by Solo Landing (USA) (A D Smith) 1415³ 1716

10 **HAZEL CREST,** b g Hays - Singing Wren by Julio Mariner (M E Sowersby) 885⁴ 1072² 1258⁵

6 **HAZEL HONEY(IRE),** b f Celio Rufo - Jim's Honey (W P Mullins) 3880⁹ 4062 4331

5 **HAZEL ROCK(IRE),** b f Over The River (FR) - Easter Beauty (Charles Reilly) 2737

10 **HAZLE WAND,** b g Le Moss - Pitcoke by Pitpan (T T Bill) 3556

5 **HAZY BUCK(IRE),** b g Buckskin (FR) - Queen Crab by Private Walk (John Murphy) 3349³

6 **HAZY WALK(IRE),** b m Henbit (USA) - Queen Crab by Private Walk (Martin M Treacy) 2271 2443 2519

5 **HE KNOWS THE RULES,** b g Tirol - Falls Of Lora by Scottish Rifle (R H Buckler) 2656⁵ 3296⁶ 3776² 3892⁵

7 **HE'S A KING(USA),** b g Key To The Kingdom (USA) - She's A Jay (USA) by Honey Jay (USA) (C L Popham) 755³ 904

7 **HE'S NO ANGEL(IRE),** b g Tremblant - Truly Deep by Deep Run (Capt D G Swan) 112³ 142⁸ 217⁶

6 **HEAD CHAPLAIN(IRE),** b g The Parson - Arctic Run (J R H Fowler) 1019 1463⁸ 1655⁸ 2081⁸ 2339 2839

4 **HEAD TO TOE(IRE),** b f Nashamaa - Tamar Di Bulgaria (ITY) (K O'Sullivan) 4094 4198

10 **HEADBANGER,** b g Wassl Merbayeh (USA) - High Fi by High Hat (Martin Michael Lynch) 1276⁴ 1534¹ 2052⁴ 2231⁵ 2587⁴ 3752² 3962⁴ 4164²

6 **HEADING NORTH,** ch g North Street - Penny Change by Money Business (O J Carter) 1917

6 **HEADS OR TAILS(IRE),** br m Spin Of A Coin - Moyadam Lady by Cherubino (B Mactaggart) 3396

6 **HEADWIND(IRE),** b g Strong Gale - Lady In Red by Royal Buck (J T Gifford) 1424²

6 **HEALING THOUGHT(IRE),** b g Soughaan (USA) - Fair Or Foul (Donal Hassett) 562

8 **HEARNS HILL(IRE),** b g Lancastrian - Bigwood by Precipice Wood (Mrs John Harrington) 63¹ 4303

4 **HEART,** ch f Cadeaux Genereux - Recipe by Bustino (Miss H C Knight) 2454 3946⁵ 4182

6 **HEART 'N SOUL-ON(IRE),** br g Roselier (FR) - Solinika by Dike (USA) (Michael Cunningham) 2443 2583⁹ 2865³ 3089 3180 4117¹ 4245⁷

4 **HEART OF AVONDALE(IRE),** b f Broken Hearted - Vita Veritas (Lindsay Woods) 3840³

5 **HEATHER VILLE(IRE),** b m Yashgan - Terracotta (GER) by Nebos (GER) (Noel Meade)

1655⁶ 2022³ 2368⁸ 3069² 3178³ 3343¹ 3837⁶ 3953²
4077⁷ 4308⁶

10 **HEATHVIEW,** b g Pitpan - Whosview by Fine
Blade (USA) (Mrs P Chamings) 4229²

7 **HEATHYARDS BOY,** b g Sayf El Arab (USA) -
French Cooking by Royal And Regal (USA)
(D McCain) 1138⁶ 1605 2026 2376⁵ 2747² 2823³
3079⁶ 3267² 3477⁴ 3726

4 **HEATHYARDS JADE,** b f Damister (USA) -
French Cooking by Royal And Regal (USA)
(A Streeter) 3828 4131

10 **HEATON(NZ),** b g Veloso (NZ) - Honey Queen
(NZ) by Better Honey (H G Rowsell) 585⁵ 667⁸

9 **HEAVENLY CITIZEN(IRE),** ch g Ovac (ITY) -
Miss Pushover by Push On (J L Gledson)
1967¹ 2203⁵ 2579² 2916⁷ 3159⁴ 3436⁶

5 **HEAVENS ABOVE,** br g Celestial Storm (USA)
- Regal Wonder by Stupendous (F Murphy)
911 1693⁶ 1953³ 2279³ 2359¹ 2635³

6 **HEAVY HUSTLER(IRE),** br g Strong Gale - Bal-
ingale by Balinger (A L T Moore) 1649 2081⁴
2583³ 3071⁹ 3520⁹

10 **HEDDON HAUGH(IRE),** b g Norwick (USA) - Pushkar
by Northfields (USA) (P R Webber) 1637⁹
2701⁸ 4071⁶

9 **HEDDON HAUGH(IRE),** br g Seclude (USA) -
Miss Kambalda by Kambalda (P
Cheesbrough) 723 935⁶ 1788² 1930¹ 2062

7 **HEDGEHOPPER(IRE),** b g Henbit (USA) -
Selham by Derring-Do (C Weedon) 1421³

8 **HEE'S A DANCER,** b g Rambo Dancer (CAN) -
Heemee by On Your Mark (Miss Lucinda V
Russell) 571⁶ 1786⁴ 2537⁸ 2631² 2985 3584⁵ 4009²

8 **HEIDIQUEENOFCLUBS(IRE),** b m Phardante
(FR) - Affordthe Queen by Pitpan (N A
Twiston-Davies) 2248⁷ 3720

9 **HEIGHT OF LUXURY(IRE),** ch m Orchestra -
Luxury by Ragapan (P N Walsh) 849⁸ 1273
1713⁴ 1839³ 2159⁴ 2674² 3337⁴ 3419⁴ 4146

6 **HEIGHTH OF FAME,** b g Shirley Heights -
Land Of Ivory (USA) by The Minstrel (CAN)
(J Hetherton) 1224⁷

8 **HEIST,** ch g Homeboy - Pilfer by Vaigly
Great (Noel Meade) 85² 553³ 925¹ 981 1434²
2071⁸ 3453⁷ 3783²

7 **HELENS BAY(IRE),** b f Montelimar (USA) -
Monkhouse by Monksfield (V Thompson)
1257⁶ 1331⁶ 1824⁹ 2064⁴ 3006 3123⁵

6 **HELL FOR LEATHER(IRE),** br g Decent Fellow -
Brideweir (John A White) 1487⁶ 1649

7 **HELLO EXCUSE ME(USA),** b g Storm Bird
(CAN) - Dream Play (USA) by Blushing
Groom (FR) (William J Fitzpatrick) 677¹ 158⁸

4 **HELLO JOHN,** b g Puissance - Real Party by
Realm (N Nelson) 3767 4160

9 **HELLO ME MAN(IRE),** b g Asir - Tide Gate by
Dike (USA) (B J Llewellyn) 1056 1452⁵ 1685²
1921 2428 2604 2977³ 3093⁴ 3833⁴ 3988¹ 4183¹

10 **HELLO MONKEY,** ch g Exhibitioner - Matjup
by Simbir (Thomas Foley) 87⁴ 2705⁶

5 **HELLO MR JOHNSON(IRE),** b g King Luthier -
Chat Her Up (T Cahill) 269⁶

8 **HELORHIWATER(IRE),** b m Aristocracy -
Smurfette by Baptism (E Sheehy) 86⁶ 277⁵
685⁶ 2943² 3337³ 3376³

5 **HELPERBY(IRE),** b or br g Brush Aside (USA) -
Kings de Lema (IRE) by King's Ride (J Howard Johnson) 2206 2651⁶ 2817⁵ 3351

5 **HEMERO(IRE),** br g Henbit (USA) - Garda
Spirit (R H Buckler) 731 782 850 1018

8 **HEMISPHERE(IRE),** ch g Dominion - Welsh
Fantasy by Welsh Pageant (D T Hughes)
1458¹ 1711¹ 1896² 2053³

6 **HEN HANSEL(IRE),** b g Henbit (USA) -
Another Cert by Prince Hansel (Sean O

O'Brien) 984⁶ 1075 1554⁴ 1649 2107⁵ 2276⁴ 2415⁴
2900⁴ 3233 3816

7 **HENBRIG,** b m Henbit (USA) - Malozza Brig
by New Brig (G R Oldroyd) 1968 2489 3127

4 **HENCARLAM(IRE),** b c Astronef - War Ballad
(FR) by Green Dancer (USA) (V T O'Brien)
442⁵ 574⁸ 3816 4026⁷

9 **HENLEY REGATTA,** b g Gorytus (USA) -
Straw Boater by Thatch (USA) (P R Rod-
ford) 48³ 102² 249³ 327² 447¹ 642⁴ 3685² 3862¹ 3937⁴
4288³

12 **HENLEY WOOD,** b g Leander - Allengrove by
Border Chief (P J Hobbs) 500¹ 674 831³ 938³
1356² 1491

8 **HENLEYDOWN(IRE),** b g Le Moss - Sunny Sunset (Daniel Lordan) 3378⁵

7 **HENNERWOOD OAK,** b m Lighter - Welsh Log
by King Log (Lady Susan Brooke) 2516² 3279

6 **HENPECKED(IRE),** b g Henbit (USA) - Desmond Lady by Maculata (M D Hammond)
700³ 1073⁹ 1695

7 **HENRIETTA HOWARD(IRE),** b m King's Ride -
Knockaville by Crozier (Mrs D Haine) 1402¹
1717⁴ 2253¹ 2530¹ 3116⁷ 3689

8 **HENRY CONE,** br g Celtic Cone - Misty Sunset by Le Bavard (FR) (Miss Venetia Williams) 3445⁶

7 **HENRY G'S(IRE),** b m The Parson - Break The
Bank by Gala Performance (USA) (F Flood)
158

8 **HENRY HOOLET,** b g Bold Owl - Genervera by
Spartan General (P Monteith) 2236 2344⁸
2485 2630⁴

7 **HENRYS PORT,** b g Royal Vulcan - Bright
Swan by Will Hays (USA) (Martyn Meade)
1594³ 1868 2277⁶ 2558⁶ 3892³

8 **HERBALIST,** b g Mandrake Major - Mohican
by Great Nephew (J Wade) 4214

5 **HERBALLISTIC,** ch m Rolfe (USA) - National
Clover by National Trust (J G M O'Shea)
1227⁷

7 **HERBERT BUCHANAN(IRE),** ch g Henbit (USA)
- Our Siveen by Deep Run (P F Nicholls) 642¹
759 857² 1114¹ 1301 1356⁴ 1602⁴ 3545³ 3571² 3797²

8 **HERBERT LODGE(IRE),** b g Montelimar (USA)
- Mindyourbusiness by Run The Gantlet
(USA) (K C Bailey) 1097¹ 1396² 1615³ 1868² 2119
2299⁵

7 **HERBIDACIOUS(IRE),** br m Lancastrian -
Lean Over by Over The River (FR) (M J
Roberts) 1113

5 **HERE COMES HERBIE,** ch g Golden Lahab
(USA) - Megan's Move by Move Off (W
Storey) 547³ 1986³ 2204 2359³ 2581⁵ 2815¹ 3203

8 **HERESTHEDEAL(IRE),** b g Martin John - Newgate Princess by Prince Regent (FR) (G M
McCourt) 325⁴ 594² 670² 762⁷ 904

7 **HERETICAL MISS,** br m Sayf El Arab (USA) -
Silent Prayer by Queen's Hussar (J Ffitch-
Heyes) 205⁸ 294³ 534⁵

10 **HERHORSE,** ch m Royal Vulcan - Ditchling
Beacon by High Line (Miss A Howard-
Chappell) 3147¹ 4033⁵

6 **HERSILIA(IRE),** br m Mandalus - Milan Pride
by Northern Guest (USA) (F Flood) 1118⁵
1273 1713⁶ 1778⁴ 2036⁴ 2103⁵ 2162⁹ 2868² 3230¹
3392² 4051 4247⁷

4 **HEVER GOLF DIAMOND,** b g Nomination -
Cadi Ha by Welsh Pageant (J R Best) 848¹
936⁴ 1188³ 1517⁵ 2730⁷ 3177¹ 3610⁵ 3844 3971⁴ 4153¹
4296²

4 **HEVER GOLF EAGLE,** b g Aragon - Elkie
Brooks by Relkino (T J Naughton) 3411⁶

4 **HEY SAM(IRE),** b g Samhoi (USA) - Beswick
Paper Lady by Giolla Mear (J Wade) 3356

4 **HEY ZOE**, ch f Hey Romeo - Whichford Lass by Indian Ruler (C H Jones) 3561

7 **HI HEDLEY(IRE)**, b g Henbit (USA) - Verbana by Boreen (FR) (G A Hubbard) 3732 3926[1]

5 **HI JAMIE(IRE)**, b g Parliament - Lilo Lil by Dunphy (A J Martin) 3525[7] 3770

7 **HI KNIGHT(IRE)**, b g King's Ride - Le Nuit by Le Bavard (FR) (J R H Fowler) 1407 2366[5] 2585[1] 2837 3072[4] 3837[4] 4168[1]

6 **HI MARBLE(IRE)**, ch m Wylfa - Red Marble by Le Bavard (FR) (Mrs Merrita Jones) 1641 1893 3172[5] 3594[3]

5 **HI-LO PICCOLO(IRE)**, b m Orchestra - Silent Twirl (Desmond McDonogh) 1756 2054[9] 2129[8] 2583

6 **HI-WAY TONIGHT(IRE)**, ch m Bold Arrangement - High Point Lady (CAN) (Anthony Mullins) 2900

7 **HIBBA(IRE)**, b m Doubletour (USA) - Country Niece (P R Lenihan) 3705

13 **HICKELTON LAD**, ch g Black Minstrel - Lupreno by Hugh Lupus (D L Williams) 2516[4] 3076[5] 3288[2] 3499[3] 4064 4319

7 **HIDDEN FLOWER**, b m Blakeney - Molucella by Connaught (H S Howe) 47 145[6] 4193[9]

6 **HIDDEN HOLLOW(IRE)**, b g Hollow Hand - Shady Ahan (John P Berry) 910[6] 1005[4] 1081[8]

9 **HIDDEN PLAY(IRE)**, b m Seclude (USA) - Play The Fool by Will Somers (James H Kelly) 2040 2137 2383[8]

11 **HIDDEN PLEASURE**, b g Furry Glen - Baloney by Balidar (T M Jones) 1698 1794 2304

6 **HIDDEN SPRINGS(IRE)**, ch g Carmelite House (USA) - Rosmarita (J A O'Connell) 1174[9] 1436 2048[9] 3964[5] 4198

5 **HIDDEN VALLEY**, b g St Columbus - Leven Valley by Ragstone (R G Frost) 942[9]

9 **HIGH ALLTITUDE(IRE)**, b g Coquelin (USA) - Donna Cressida by Don (ITY) (M J Heaton-Ellis) 1342 2555[2] 2922[2] 3314[3] 3730

10 **HIGH BURNSHOT**, br g Cardinal Flower - Andonian by Road House II (Mrs L C Jewell) 3119 3292[7]

6 **HIGH CELLESTE(IRE)**, b m Fat-Taak - Saulest by Saulingo (Martin Todhunter) 3061[8] 3356 3757

5 **HIGH FLOWN(USA)**, b g Lear Fan (USA) - Isticanna (USA) by Far North (CAN) (Ronald Thompson) 45[4] 205[5] 911[5]

5 **HIGH GALE(IRE)**, b g Strong Gale - High Board (A L T Moore) 3789

9 **HIGH GRADE**, b g High Top - Bright Sun by Mill Reef (USA) (Miss S J Wilton) 1265[2] 1481[2] 2797[2]

6 **HIGH HANDED(IRE)**, ch g Roselier (FR) - Slaney Pride by Busted (T H Caldwell) 1142 1329 1732 1881 2898[6]

6 **HIGH HOLME**, ch g Fools Holme (USA) - Corn Seed by Nicholas Bill (R H Buckler) 796

4 **HIGH HOPE HENRY(USA)**, b g Known Fact (USA) - Parquill (USA) by One For All (USA) (M D Hammond) 2357[4]

5 **HIGH IN THE CLOUDS(IRE)**, b g Scenic - Miracle Drug (USA) by Seattle Slew (USA) (Capt T A Forster) 2255[2] 2511[1] 2893[2] 3562[3]

4 **HIGH IN THE SKY**, b g Ilium - Sweet Canyon (NZ) by Headland II (J R Jenkins) 4042

7 **HIGH LEARIE**, b g Petoski - Lady Doubloon by Pieces Of Eight (A H Harvey) 2613[1] 2890[2] 3171[2] 3556[2]

9 **HIGH LOW(USA)**, b g Clever Trick (USA) - En Tiempo (USA) by Bold Hour (M D Hammond) 1349 2526[5] 2625[5] 4102[4] 4207[3]

8 **HIGH MIND(FR)**, br g Highest Honor (FR) - Gondolina (FR) by Vaguely Noble (Miss L C Siddall) 3703

7 **HIGH MOAT(IRE)**, ch g Pimpernels Tune - Run In Time by Deep Run (William Cronin) 62[2] 142[3] 286[3] 538[8] 4062 4331[7]

7 **HIGH MOOD**, b g Jalmood (USA) - Copt Hall Princess by Crowned Prince (USA) (T R George) 1540[7] 2637[8] 3007[4] 3781

11 **HIGH PADRE**, b g The Parson - High Energy by Dalesa (J G FitzGerald) 1199[5] 1626[3]

6 **HIGH PARK LADY(IRE)**, br f Phardante (FR) - Baranee (James Murphy) 277 339[6] 561[4] 716[7] 978 3954

5 **HIGH PATRIARCH(IRE)**, b g Alzao (USA) - Freesia by Shirley Heights (N J H Walker) 2725[3]

9 **HIGH PENHOWE**, ch m Ardross - Spritely by Charlottown (J J Quinn) 1951[5] 2422[3] 2761[7] 3045

6 **HIGH PILGRIM(IRE)**, b g Astronef - Inbisat (A J McNamara) 589[5]

5 **HIGH PITCH**, bl g Orchestra - Combe Hill by Crozier (N A Gaselee) 4068[8]

8 **HIGH POST**, b g Lidhame - Touch Of Class (FR) by Luthier (G A Ham) 47[2] 111[3] 2462[6] 2603 2746

9 **HIGH STAR(IRE)**, b g Leap High (USA) - Star Ali by Night Star (George Stewart) 3228[1] 3527

5 **HIGH STATESMAN**, b g High Kicker (USA) - Avenita Lady by Free State (T T Bill) 1350

7 **HIGH SUMMER**, b g Green Desert (USA) - Beacon Hill by Bustino (T Thomson Jones) 3312[5] 3639[3] 3913[4]

8 **HIGH TONE(IRE)**, ch g Orchestra - High Reign by Bahrain (J R Cox) 62[4] 181[4]

11 **HIGH-SPEC**, b g Strong Gale - Shine Your Light by Kemal (FR) (J E Kiely) 252[3] 338[2] 431[5] 553[6]

5 **HIGHBANK**, b g Puissance - Highland Daisy by He Loves Me (Mrs M Reveley) 1148[2] 1386[2]

6 **HIGHBEATH**, b g Dunbeath - Singing High by Julio Mariner (Mrs M Reveley) 934[3] 1067[1] 1775[8] 2348[5] 2763[4] 2971[1] 3824[1]

6 **HIGHEST CALL(IRE)**, b g Buckley - Call Me Anna by Giolla Mear (M Halford) 304[8] 365[2]

8 **HIGHLAND FLAME**, ch g Dunbeath (USA) - Blakesware Saint by Welsh Saint (A G Blackmore) 3139 3370 3496[4] 3668 3845

7 **HIGHLAND JACK**, ch g Nearly A Hand - Highland Path by Jock Scot (Andrew Turnell) 1498[1] 1718[5]

11 **HIGHLAND PARK**, ch g Simply Great (FR) - Perchance by Connaught (R Craggs) 1068[3] 1372[3] 2120[1] 2361[2] 3246

5 **HIGHLAND PRINCE**, ch g Le Moss - Rose Of The Glen by Respighi (J White) 3427

6 **HIGHLAND SPIN**, ch g Dunbeath (USA) - In A Spin by Windjammer (USA) (K G Wingrove) 3931

8 **HIGHLAND SUPREME(IRE)**, b g Supreme Leader - Right Love by Golden Love (Patrick G Kelly) 1360

9 **HIGHLAND WAY(IRE)**, b g Kemal (FR) - Peace Run by Deep Run (Martin Todhunter) 878 1049[2] 1587 1788 1986[5] 3013[7] 3350[2] 3587[3] 3665[3] 4002[3] 4025[2] 4217[2] 4273[1]

8 **HIGHLANDER(IRE)**, b g Shernazar - Bonny Brae by Cure The Blues (USA) (John Muldoon) 268[3] 730[4]

11 **HIGHLANDMAN**, b g Florida Son - Larne by Giolla Mear (J S Haldane) 2468[7] 2993[1] 3247[2] 3578[2] 3718

5 **HIGHLY CHARMING(IRE)**, b g Shirley Heights - Charmante Dame (FR) by Bellypha (Miss A Stokell) 652[9] 770[4] 992[2] 1215[4] 1733[7] 1955[3] 2256 2655[5] 3139[2]

9 **HUGH DANIELS,** b g Adonijah - Golden Realm by Red Regent (C J Hemsley) 100 266⁶ 1007⁶ 1138 2251 3740 3960³ 4037⁶ 4276⁴

6 **HUISH(IRE),** br g Orchestra - Lysanders Lady by Saulingo (G F H Charles-Jones) 2015⁷ 2199 2795⁸ 3077⁶ 3778

9 **HULA,** b g Broadsword (USA) - Blakes Lass by Blakeney (Miss Frances Wilson) 3599

5 **HULALEA(NZ),** ch g Hula Town (NZ) - Larilea (NZ) by Music Teacher (USA) (Miss S Edwards) 2483⁵ 2920 3296

8 **HULLO MARY DOLL,** br m Lidhame - Princess Story by Prince de Galles (A J Chamberlain) 903¹ 1139 1218³ 1417⁵ 1917⁴

5 **HUMBEL(USA),** b h Theatrical - Claxton's Slew by Seattle Slew (USA) (D K Weld) 2072³ 2443¹ 3111 3452²

6 **HUMMINBIRDPRINCESS,** b m Interrex (CAN) - Under The Wing by Aragon (J J Sheehan) 1115

7 **HUNCHEON CHANCE,** b or br g Tinoco - La Cazadora by Faraway Times (USA) (I R Ferguson) 315⁵

5 **HUNTERS ISLAND(IRE),** b m Celio Rufo - Caseys Cross (Basil King) 647

8 **HUNTERS ROCK(IRE),** ch g Treasure Hunter - Ring Twice by Prince Hansel (K C Bailey) 824⁷ 955¹ 1100¹ 1502⁵ 2559

6 **HUNTING LORE(IRE),** b or br g Lafontaine (USA) - Millies Luck by Al Sirat (USA) (N J Henderson) 1379¹

5 **HUNTING SLANE,** b g Move Off - Singing Slane by Cree Song (C Grant) 1968⁹ 2206 3003 3509 3757 4021⁹

5 **HUNYANI(IRE),** b g Hays - Aughaveans (Noel Meade) 3547

7 **HURDANTE(IRE),** ch g Phardante (FR) - Hurry by Deep Run (G B Balding) 1270² 1623⁷ 2249¹ 2438⁶ 3129 3575³

10 **HURDY,** ch g Arapahos (FR) - Demelza Carne by Woodville II (Mrs S A Bramall) 743³ 926

4 **HURMUZAN(IRE),** b g Shahrastani (USA) - Huraymila (Thomas Foley) 4309¹

9 **HURRICANE ANDREW(IRE),** ch g Hawaiian Return (USA) - Viable by Nagami (J A Moore) 1253 1589⁶ 2065¹ 2258 2633 3601³ 3867⁵ 4221²

8 **HURRICANE DAVID(IRE),** gr g Strong Gale - Sarsa (Gerard Stack) 2107 2222 3964⁴ 4198⁹

8 **HURRICANE GIRL(IRE),** b m Strong Gale - Baranee by My Swanee (John F Gleeson) 1484

5 **HURRICANE JANE(IRE),** br m Strong Gale - Jane Bond by Good Bond (M J Roberts) 1942⁵ 2309⁵ 4086⁵

6 **HURRICANE LAMP,** b g Derrylin - Lampstone by Ragstone (D Nicholson) 1496¹ 1849¹ 2292² 3077

10 **HURRYUP,** b g Duky - Delay by Tantivy (R Dickin) 57 154⁶ 230¹ 375⁸ 418 2252

5 **HURST FLYER,** gr m Neltino - True Missile by True Song (F P Murtagh) 1227³ 1874¹

9 **HUSO,** ch g Sharpo - Husnah (USA) by Caro (P C Haslam) 474¹ 550² 1375² 1819⁵

6 **HUTCEL BELL,** b m Belfort (FR) - Crammond Brig by New Brig (R D E Woodhouse) 322 370⁶ 1044

6 **HUTCEL LOCH,** b m Lochnager - Errema by Workboy (R D E Woodhouse) 880³ 1962 2117¹ 2419 2761²

5 **HUTCHIES LADY,** b m Efisio - Keep Mum by Mummy's Pet (R M McKellar) 1783⁵

7 **HYDEMILLA,** b m Idiot's Delight - Bellaloo by Privy Seal (Mrs T D Pilkington) 648⁸ 800 924³ 1132 1344³ 1614⁸

6 **HYDRO(IRE),** b g Electric - Loughanmore by Bargello (M D Hammond) 1532³ 2419⁵

10 **HYDROPIC,** b g Kabour - Hydrangea by Warpath (M A Barnes) 3762⁸

6 **HYELORD(IRE),** b or br g Mister Lord (USA) - Gradiska by Amoristic (USA) (A P O'Brien) 3525³ 4331²

6 **HYLTERS CHANCE(IRE),** ch g Zaffaran (USA) - Stickey Stream by Paddy's Stream (P J Hobbs) 650² 841¹ 906 1291² 1419⁵ 3692

6 **HYMOSS,** b m Idiot's Delight - Precipice Moss by Precipice Wood (W Jenks) 654⁷

5 **HYPERION LAD,** gr g Dawn Johnny (USA) - Hyperion Princess by Dragonara Palace (USA) (T T Bill) 2123

7 **'IGGINS(IRE),** br g Strong Gale - Gale Flash by News Item (J T Gifford) 2949⁹

6 **I DON'T THINK SO,** b m Mas Media - Misdevious (USA) by Alleged (USA) (T Hind) 103⁶ 145

10 **I HAVE HIM,** b g Orange Reef - Costerini by Soderini (Noel T Chance) 279³ 369

6 **I RECALL(IRE),** b g Don't Forget Me - Sable Lake by Thatching (P Hayward) 1429⁷ 1641⁹ 2558⁴ 2783⁷ 2952⁴ 3332⁵

5 **I REMEMBER IT WELL(IRE),** ch m Don't Forget Me - Star Cream by Star Appeal (Michael Hourigan) 67² 131 222 275⁴ 469¹ 598¹ 679¹ 742² 907² 1095² 3235⁸ 3768⁵ 3890² 4054 4245³

7 **I REMEMBER YOU(IRE),** ch g Don't Forget Me - Non Casual by Nonoalco (USA) (Mrs R G Henderson) 769⁵ 922³

4 **I SAY DANCER(IRE),** b f Distinctly North (USA) - Lady Marigot by Lord Gayle (USA) (L J Barratt) 991⁹

8 **I'LL FLY AWAY(IRE),** ch g Fairbairn - Princess Michico by Godswalk (USA) (Seamus P Murphy) 66⁷

6 **I'LL SAY NOTHING(IRE),** b g Tremblant - Lady Slavey (William Flavin) 3525⁵

7 **I'M A CHIPPY(IRE),** ch g Architect (USA) - Buckaway Rose (G B Balding) 1516⁶ 1876⁴

7 **I'M A DREAMER(IRE),** b g Mister Majestic - Lady Wise by Lord Gayle (USA) (Miss M E Rowland) 107⁴ 1719⁵ 1964³ 2296¹ 2973⁹ 3528⁸ 3635¹ 3791⁵

8 **I'M IN CLOVER(IRE),** ch g Good Thyne (USA) - Lady Cromer by Blakeney (J Norton) 2203 2763

5 **I'M SUPPOSIN(IRE),** b h Posen (USA) - Robinia (USA) by Roberto (USA) (R Rowe) 2049¹ 2342¹ 3113⁴ 3717⁷

6 **I'M THE MAN,** ro g Say Primula - Vinovia by Ribston (Mrs Dianne Sayer) 728⁵ 813⁴ 960⁷ 1162³

10 **I'M TOBY,** b g Celtic Cone - Easter Tinkle by Hot Brandy (Mrs R M Lampard) 3713

9 **I'M TYSON(NZ),** br g Tights (USA) - Rose Of Hawa (AUS) by Arch Sculptor (Mrs Dianne Sayer) 3002⁶ 3258⁵ 3587 3657⁸ 3869⁹

4 **IACCHUS(IRE),** br c Mac's Imp (USA) - Burkina by African Sky (A P O'Brien) 425¹ 927⁷ 1057⁸ 1309 1403⁴ 1616 2050 2105⁵

6 **IADA(IRE),** ch m Accordion - Riverhead by Quayside (F J Lacy) 1908⁵ 2131⁶ 2272⁵ 2647 3942⁵

8 **IADES BOY(NZ),** b g Iades (FR) - Phero's Bay (NZ) by Brazen Boy (AUS) (C J Mann) 1792

10 **IBN SINA(USA),** b g Dr Blum (USA) - Two On One (CAN) by Lord Durham (CAN) (W Clay) 659 878⁶

8 **ICANTELYA(IRE),** b g Meneval (USA) - Sky Road by Skyliner (J W Mullins) 65⁵ 171⁷ 212⁷ 868² 993⁴ 1684⁶ 2281 2482 3051 3365 3632 3990⁶

11 **ICARUS(USA),** b g Wind And Wuthering (USA) - Cedar Waxwing (USA) by Tom Fool (D H Brown) 2680

6 JEAN DE FLORETTE(USA), b g Our Native (USA) - The Branks (USA) by Hold Your Peace (USA) (R C Spicer) 648[6] 934

5 JEBI(USA), b g Phone Trick (USA) - Smokey Legend (USA) by Hawaii (C Murray) 377[3]

5 JED ABBEY, gr m Alias Smith (USA) - Lurdenlaw Rose by New Brig (R Shiels) 866 1039[8] 2117[8] 3663

7 JEFFELL, gr g Alias Smith (USA) - Saleander by Leander (A L T Moore) 1170 1405[1] 1779[1] 2052[6] 2733[1] 3522[2] 3787[1]

8 JEFFERIES, br g Sunyboy - Scotch Princess by Murrayfield (J A B Old) 1546[1] 1728[2] 2389[6] 2667[1] 3054[2]

4 JELALI(IRE), b g Last Tycoon - Lautreamont by Auction Ring (USA) (D J G Murray Smith) 1702[1] 2423 2803

6 JEMARO(IRE), b g Tidaro (USA) - Jeremique by Sunny Way (W Jenks) 1142 2723[3] 3722

6 JEMIMA PUDDLEDUCK, ch m Tate Gallery (USA) - Tittlemouse by Castle Keep (A Streeter) 1299 1807[2] 2204[3] 2581

6 JENBRO(IRE), b or br m Petorius - Golden Pheasant by Henbit (USA) (Patrick Martin) 424[7]

9 JENDEE(IRE), b g Dara Monarch - Bunch Of Blue by Martinmas (B Ellison) 663[4] 697 915[1] 1126[3] 1325 1988[4] 2203 2536[5] 3352[5] 4010[3]

7 JENDORCET, b m Grey Ghost - Jendor by Condorcet (FR) (C W Fairhurst) 3128[3] 3353 3674[5] 3900[4] 4012[3]

6 JENNIE'S PROSPECT, b g Rakaposhi King - Jennie Pat by Rymer (J J O'Neill) 1317 1887[8] 2858[3] 3011[9]

8 JENNYELLEN(IRE), b m Phardante (FR) - Kaltonia by Kala Shikari (P Bowen) 70[3] 225[1] 331 417 4232[8]

6 JENSALEE(IRE), b m Supreme Leader - Hopeful Chimes by Reformed Character (P Mullins) 2343[3] 2525[5] 2675[1] 2900[3] 3376[1] 4245

6 JENZSOPH(IRE), br m Glow (USA) - Taken By Force by Persian Bold (P J Hobbs) 299[1] 403[2] 543 669 3871 3948[1] 4170[1]

5 JER-MARIE(IRE), b g Torus - Esperia (J J Lennon) 782 898

6 JERMYN STREET(USA), b h Alleged (USA) - My Mother Mary (USA) by Boldnesian (Mark McCausland) 3069 3225[8] 3521[5] 3643[8] 3942

6 JERVAULX(IRE), b g Le Bavard (FR) - Saltee Star by Arapaho (G Richards) 1317 2344[1] 2572[2] 2785[7] 3034[2] 3321[7] 3709 3970[1] 4262[3]

6 JESSICA ONE(IRE), b m Supreme Leader - Lochadoo by Lochnager (Mrs M Reveley) 1317 2262[4] 2975[2]

8 JESSIE'S BOY(IRE), b g Flash Of Steel - Often by Ballymore (Luke Comer) 209 2376 495[1] 604[2] 744 748[7] 1080 1581 3344[5] 3645 3953 4151[7] 4199

5 JESSOLLE, gr m Scallywag - Dark City by Sweet Monday (G Richards) 1317 2496[5] 2711[9] 2791[9] 3316[3] 3598[1] 3805 3909[1] 4191[4] 4272[2]

7 JET BOYS(IRE), b g Le Bavard (FR) - Fast Adventure by Deep Run (Mrs J Pitman) 1271[2] 1545[5] 3373[3]

6 JET FILES(IRE), ro g Roselier (FR) - Deepdecending by Deep Run (Mrs J Pitman) 1769[5] 2311 2889

7 JET RULES(IRE), b g Roselier (FR) - Bell Walks Fancy by Entrechat (Mrs J Pitman) 1268[9] 2566[1] 2718[3]

4 JET SPECIALS(IRE), b g Be My Native (USA) - Glencuragh by Deep Run (Mrs J Pitman) 2831

5 JEWEL OF THE NIGHT(IRE), b g Prince Rupert (FR) - Tears Of A Prophet (IRE) by Mazaad (J P Kavanagh) 161[6] 275[8] 391[5]

7 JEWEL THIEF, b g Green Ruby (USA) - Miss Display by Touch Paper (G B Balding) 587[7] 1001[3] 1349[6] 1724[8] 3592[6] 3741[9] 3911[8] 4189[6]

5 JEWEL TRADER, b g Green Ruby (USA) - Maiden Bidder by Shack (USA) (Mrs L C Jewell) 1893

9 JHAL FREZI, b g Netherkelly - Warham Trout by Barolo (A Barrow) 975[4] 1237[6] 1724[5] 3611[1]

10 JIGGINSTOWN, b g Strong Gale - Galliano by Royal Highway (J J O'Neill) 1377[8] 1631 2025 2487[3] 2710[8] 3321[5] 3833 4108[4]

8 JIGTIME, b m Scottish Reel - Travel Again by Derrylin (J W Hughes) 3143[3] 3307[1] 3713[1]

7 JIHAAD(USA), b g Chief's Crown (USA) - Desirable by Lord Gayle (USA) (Michael A Kelly) 1839 2057[3] 2089[4] 2104[7] 2366 2735 2901[1] 2943[8] 3070[8] 3337 3419[7] 3837

9 JILLS JOY(IRE), b g Law Society (USA) - Cooliney Princess by Bruni (J Norton) 874[4] 1330[3] 1543[2] 1817 2200[8]

11 JIM VALENTINE, br g Furry Glen - Duessa by Linacre (D J Wintle) 188[5] 230[4] 327[5] 632[1] 840[1] 1253[3] 3739 4202

4 JIM'S QUEST, ch g Charmer - Salt Of The Earth by Sterling Bay (SWE) (P J Hobbs) 2179[3] 3335[7] 3408[8] 3941[6]

14 JIMBALOU, b g Jimsun - Midnight Pansy by Deadly Nightshade (R G Brazington) 3557[9] 4133[1] 4318

5 JIMMY JANE(IRE), ch m Cidrax (FR) - Banford's Choice (T J Canavan) 1579 2379 3227

6 JIMMY MAGEE(IRE), b g Strong Gale - Island Bridge (Francis Berry) 2964

10 JIMMY O'DEA, br g Funny Man - Premier Nell by Mandamus (J Mackie) 124[6] 188 282[8] 4010[4] 4252[2]

6 JIMMY SPRITE, b g Silly Prices - Little Mittens by Little Buskins (R E Barr) 2066[6]

10 JIMMY THE JACKDAW, b g Henbit (USA) - Organdy by Blakeney (P Butler) 362[5] 439[2]

9 JIMMY THE WEED(IRE), br g Sexton Blake - Miss Cheyne by Mansingh (USA) (Michael G Holden) 1433[9] 1899 2366 2585[2] 2837 3072[5] 3234[5]

7 JIMMY'S CROSS(IRE), ch g Phardante (FR) - Foredeline by Bonne Noel (G B Balding) 822

4 JIMMYJOE(IRE), ch g Cidrax (FR) - Banford's Choice (T J Canavan) 3394 3945

11 JIMMYS DOUBLE, b g Jimmy The Singer - Banford's Choice by Garland Knight (T J Canavan) 1582[7] 1896 2038

6 JIMSUE, gr g Afzal - Gentian by Roan Rocket (C H Jones) 2179

8 JO JO BOY(IRE), ch g Good Thyne (USA) - Sparkling Opera by Orchestra (F Flood) 526[7] 1058[5] 1190[3] 1535[5] 1621 1778 1899 2076[6]

4 JO LIGHTNING(IRE), b g Electric - Santa Jo by Pitpan (B Ellison) 2206 2687 3661 3808[9]

6 JO'S WEDDING, ch g Newski (USA) - Meant by Menelek (B R Millman) 4050

4 JOAN'S PRINCESS(IRE), b f Prince Rupert (FR) - Gay Krystyna (Leo McCreesh) 2383

5 JOBBER'S FIDDLE, b m Sizzling Melody - Island Mead by Pharly (FR) (D L Williams) 567 2265 2390[5] 2515 2977

7 JOBIE, b g Precocious - Lingering by Kind Of Hush (R T Phillips) 2662 3028

8 JOBSAGOODUN, b g Rakaposhi King - Donna Farina by Little Buskins (N J Henderson) 1615[4] 2152[8] 2601[8] 3833 4193[4]

4 JOCK, b g Scottish Reel - Northern Lady by The Brianstan (Miss S Williamson) 2145

6 JOCKS CROSS(IRE), ch g Riberetto - Shuil Le Dia by Kabale (G Richards) 1036[1] 1282[1] 2289[4] 2465[7] 2936[7]

4 **JUST NIP,** b g Lord Bud - Popping On by Sonnen Gold (J R Turner) 3661[1]

6 **JUST NORMAN,** b g Sunley Builds - Gameover Lady by Aragon (Miss H C Knight) 3335

9 **JUST ONE CANALETTO,** ch g Claude Monet (USA) - Mary Shelley by Ardross (N A Twiston-Davies) 1799[3] 2252[5] 2527 3465[1] 3914[3] 4240

7 **JUST ONE QUESTION(IRE),** b g Torus - Stormy Night by Deep Run (J J O'Neill) 1735[8] 2008 2546 3309[2]

5 **JUST POLLY,** b m Meadowbrook - Dajopede by Lighter (H Alexander) 2200 3308

4 **JUST RORY,** b g Skyliner - Judys Girl (IRE) by Simply Great (FR) (Miss Z A Green) 1629

6 **JUST SUPPOSEN(IRE),** b g Posen (USA) - Snipe Singer by Tyrnavos (B S Rothwell) 1048 2330 2464 2577 2762 2969[2] 3239[3]

6 **JUST SUPREME(IRE),** b g Supreme Leader - Just Ginger by The Parson (Michael Cunningham) 928 1013 2839 3075

5 **JUST WHISTLE,** gr m Absalom - Aunt Blue by Blue Refrain (Miss M K Milligan) 3401 3757 3900

5 **JUST-MANA-MOU(IRE),** b g Caerleon (USA) - Clarista (USA) by Riva Ridge (USA) (W G M Turner) 582[5] 2479[9]

7 **JUSTAWAY(IRE),** b g Millfontaine - Cruiseaway by Torus (A P O'Brien) 87[6] 174[5] 826[7] 980 1190[5] 1900[7] 2114[3] 2142[3] 2369[3] 2473[8]

5 **JUSTJIM,** b g Derring Rose - Crystal Run Vii by Damsire Unregistered (N A Twiston-Davies) 2029[8] 2283 3103[8]

6 **JUSTLIKEJIM,** ch g Say Primula - Trois Filles by French Marny (J L Harris) 1768[6] 2029[7]

5 **JUYUSH(USA),** b h Silver Hawk (USA) - Silken Doll (USA) by Chieftain II (J A B Old) 2242[1] 2405[1] 2656[1] 2820[1]

8 **JYMJAM JOHNNY(IRE),** b g Torus - Inventus by Pitpan (J J O'Neill) 1138 1376[4] 1806[3] 2150[5] 3304[6] 3399[2] 3782[8]

12 **K C'S DANCER,** ch g Buckskin (FR) - Lorna Lass by Laurence O (R Dickin) 727 840[3] 1101[5] 3578[4] 3855

4 **KABYLIE OUEST(FR),** ch f Franc Parler - Kadastra (FR) by Stradavinsky (R Dickin) 3082[7] 3335

8 **KADARI,** b m Commanche Run - Thoughtful by Northfields (USA) (W Clay) 1625[6] 1835[5] 1947[4] 2403[4] 2548[2] 2762[6] 2801[3] 3188[1] 3440[3] 3925[4] 4256[3]

7 **KADASTROF(FR),** ch h Port Etienne (FR) - Kadastra (FR) by Stradavinsky (R Dickin) 1888[2] 2329[9] 2442[1] 2695[7] 3080[6] 3330[1] 3523[6] 3717[6] 3907 4298[4]

8 **KADI(GER),** b g Shareef Dancer (USA) - Kaisertreue (GER) by Luciano (D Nicholson) 1571[3] 2235[5] 2466[2] 2779[5] 3114[8] 3565[3]

6 **KADIRI(IRE),** b g Darshaan - Kadissya (USA) by Blushing Groom (FR) (J R Bosley) 1574[9]

4 **KAI'S LADY(IRE),** b f Jareer (USA) - Rathnaleen by Scorpio (FR) (C L Popham) 705[7] 886[3] 1179 3569[2] 3648[5] 3810[6]

8 **KAIFOON(USA),** b g Woodman (USA) - Kitchen (USA) by Master Hand (USA) (P C Ritchens) 1423[7] 4092[6]

6 **KAILASH(USA),** b g Assert - Ambiente (USA) by Tentam (USA) (M C Pipe) 53[1] 191[1] 336[1] 900[1] 1103[1] 1396[1] 2042[4] 2795[2] 3111

6 **KAISER SOSA(IRE),** b g Welsh Term - Lucycello by Monksfield (T J Taaffe) 1457[6] 2583[6] 2902[1] 3451

6 **KAITAK(IRE),** ch g Broken Hearted - Klairelle by Klairon (J M Carr) 1184[3] 1508[4] 1772[3] 2128 2331[4] 2716[4] 2787[2] 3595 3907

6 **KAITHEY CHOICE(IRE),** b m Executive Perk - Reardans Fancy by Dramatic Bid (USA) (T Doyle) 945[5] 1364 1908[3] 2079[5] 2675[3] 3238 3421[5]

7 **KAJOSTAR,** ch m Country Classic - Rasimareem by Golden Mallard (S W Campion) 243 294[8] 704[7] 775 1044 1257[7]

6 **KALADROSS,** ch g Ardross - Calametta by Oats (W Jenks) 1344

7 **KALAJO,** b g Kala Shikari - Greenacres Joy by Tycoon II (B Mactaggart) 2362[4] 2686[7] 2914[1] 3056[1] 3250[1] 3758 4109[6]

12 **KALAKATE,** gr g Kalaglow - Old Kate by Busted (J J Bridger) 1444[7]

6 **KALAO TUA(IRE),** b f Shaadi (USA) - Lisa's Favourite by Gorytus (USA) (Mrs Merrita Jones) 819 991[2]

6 **KALASADI(USA),** b g Shahrastani (USA) - Kassiyda by Mill Reef (USA) (V Soane) 675[1] 1112[2] 1427 1597[2] 1834[5] 2217[5] 2559[8]

6 **KALDAN KHAN,** b g Topville - Kallista by Zeddaan (A P O'Brien) 291[2] 300[2] 1534[2] 2096[4] 2224[5] 2471[4]

7 **KALISKO(FR),** b g Cadoudal (FR) - Mista (FR) by Misti IV (R Allan) 2122[1]

10 **KALONA,** gr g Rough Lad - Bienfait by Le Tricolore (Michael Cunningham) 563[8]

6 **KALOORE,** ch g Ore - Cool Straight by Straight Lad (P Scholfield) 3147[2]

6 **KALORIEN,** b f Kalaglow - Orien (Patrick Joseph Flynn) 1539[7]

12 **KALZARI(USA),** b g Riverman (USA) - Kamisha (FR) by Lyphard (USA) (A W Carroll) 61[2] 143[3] 189[4] 996[2] 1098[3] 1417[6] 1596 2515[9] 3617[1] 3798 4237[9]

5 **KAMA SIMBA,** b g Lear Fan (USA) - Dance It (USA) by Believe It (USA) (J White) 55[8] 330 440

5 **KAMACTAY(IRE),** b g Kambalda - Miss Aglojo (D T Hughes) 3068[9]

13 **KAMBALDA RAMBLER,** b or br g Kambalda - Stroan Lass by Brave Invader (USA) (Mrs Helen Harvey) 2992[4] 3851[4] 3969[2] 4314[3]

6 **KAMBLETREE(IRE),** ch m Kambalda - Spindle Tree by Laurence O (M E Sowersby) 2200 2653 3127

7 **KAMIKAZE,** gr g Kris - Infamy by Shirley Heights (K C Bailey) 2259[1] 2566[4] 3207 3718[8] 4048[4]

6 **KANDYSON,** gr g Neltino - Kandy Belle by Hot Brandy (J R Jenkins) 3142[3]

10 **KANO WARRIOR,** b g Furry Glen - Last Princess by Le Prince (B Preece) 2957 3136[9] 3725 4232

6 **KANONA,** ch g Gunner B - Pugilistic by Hard Fought (Mrs A Swinbank) 610 761[3]

5 **KAPCO(IRE),** b g Be My Native (USA) - Shake Up by Paico (C P E Brooks) 3082[9] 3388[4]

9 **KARA'S DREAM(IRE),** b m Bulldozer - Rio's Glen by Rio Carmelo (USA) (Victor Bowens) 603[5] 647[4] 2839 3083 3389[6] 3963

8 **KARABAKH(IRE),** b g Bob Back (USA) - Such Moor by Santa Claus (W P Mullins) 2340 2708

4 **KARAKAM(IRE),** ch g Rainbow Quest (USA) - Karaferya (USA) (T A Kent) 4309[3]

7 **KARAR(IRE),** b g Shardari - Karaferya (USA) by Green Dancer (USA) (R Rowe) 833[5] 1112[4] 1576[2] 2254[4] 2600[5] 3116 3841[3] 4070[4] 4227[4]

6 **KARAWARA(IRE),** br m Doyoun - Karaferya (USA) by Green Dancer (USA) (Denis J Reddan) 347[4] 396[6]

8 **KAREN'S LEADER(IRE),** b f Supreme Leader - Ballinamona Karen (G Chesney) 4149

6 **KAREN'S TYPHOON(IRE),** b g Strong Gale - Pops Girl by Deep Run (T P McGovern) 667[7] 800[5] 1010[4] 1723[3] 2392[8] 2640 3016[4] 3494[5] 3951 4088

7 **KENDAL CAVALIER,** gr g Roselier (FR) - Kenda by Bargello (G B Balding) 1002² 1234¹ 1766⁵ 2014² 2245⁴ 2441⁷ 2921⁴ 3051 3272⁷

9 **KENILWORTH LAD,** br g Ring Bidder - Lucky Joker by Cawston's Clown (W S Cunningham) 3162 3355⁷

7 **KENMARE RIVER(IRE),** b g Over The River (FR) - Comeallye by Kambalda (R Collins) 1127³ 1605³ 1820 2203² 2534⁷

10 **KENMORE-SPEED,** gr g Scallywag - Quick Exit by David Jack (Mrs S J Smith) 1035⁷ 1250³ 1513² 1694¹ 1967² 2808² 3012¹ 3208² 3510¹ 3701¹ 3826¹ 4058²

8 **KENNETT SQUARE(IRE),** ro g Mansooj - Lumiere (USA) by Northjet (Lady Eliza Mays-Smith) 2428⁹ 3001

5 **KENNY'S PRINCESS(IRE),** b m Phardante (FR) - On The Blindside (Anthony Mullins) 898

6 **KENTAVRUS WAY(IRE),** b g Thatching - Phantom Row by Adonijah (G L Moore) 1111 1698 2010 2424³ 2610¹ 2765⁹ 3093

4 **KENTFORD CONQUISTA,** b f El Conquistador - Notinhand by Nearly A Hand (J W Mullins) 614⁷

6 **KENTFORD TINA,** b m Nearly A Hand - Notina by No Argument (J W Mullins) 1338⁹

7 **KENTUCKY BABY(IRE),** ch m Shy Groom (USA) - Ice Baby by Grundy (T J Taaffe) 162⁵ 311⁸ 471² 619² 626³ 711¹ 744 1462 4051⁴

8 **KENTUCKY GOLD(IRE),** b g Le Bavard (FR) - Darjoy by Darantus (Mrs L Williamson) 1609⁸ 1829 2288 2561 2799 3190 3395

8 **KENYATTA(USA),** b g Mogambo (USA) - Caranga (USA) by Caro (A Moore) 243⁴

8 **KEPHREN(USA),** ch g Kenmare (FR) - Marie de Russy (FR) by Sassafras (FR) (Patrick Joseph Flynn) 96¹ 292¹ 2735

4 **KEPPOLS PRINCESS(IRE),** br f Soviet Lad (USA) - Keppols (John Houghton) 3349 3755

5 **KERANI(USA),** b or br h Arctic Tern (USA) - Kerita (E J O'Grady) 288² 713³

4 **KERAWI,** b g Warning - Kerali by High Line (N A Twiston-Davies) 1027¹ 1188⁴ 1890 2553¹ 2828² 3150 3785

6 **KERCORLI(IRE),** br g Boreen (FR) - Ardreeva by Pauper (A J McNamara) 1273⁶ 1550³ 1778⁹ 2524⁵ 2753¹

4 **KERIALI(USA),** b g Irish River (FR) - Kerita by Formidable (USA) (M D Hammond) 3008⁴

7 **KERKY(IRE),** ch g Stalker - Blinky by Salvo (Martyn J McEnery) 3178⁹ 3375⁴

6 **KERNOF(IRE),** b g Rambo Dancer (CAN) - Empress Wu by High Line (M D Hammond) 320¹ 573² 815¹ 1188

6 **KERRIA'S GIFT(IRE),** b g Astronef - Kew Gift (John C Shearman) 581⁸ 945 4169

5 **KERRIER(IRE),** ch h Nashwan (USA) - Kerrera by Diesis (H J Manners) 401 3099 3443

4 **KERRY REEL(IRE),** b g Persian Heights - Spring Reel (Michael Hourigan) 1057 1173 1309 2074⁷

5 **KERRY'S OATS,** b m Derrylin - Kerry's Web by Oats (P R Hedger) 4187³

7 **KESANTA,** b m The Dissident - Nicaline by High Line (W G M Turner) 593 758² 854 924⁵ 1747 2477⁶

6 **KETABI(USA),** ch g Alydar (USA) - Ivory Fields (USA) by Sir Ivor (R Akehurst) 226

5 **KETCHICAN,** b g Joligeneration - Fair Melys (FR) by Welsh Pageant (S G Knight) 2877 3252⁵ 3573² 3731⁹ 3814² 3892⁶

10 **KETTLES,** b m Broadsword (USA) - Penny's Affair by Chingnu (M R Daniell) 2608 2875³ 3855⁷

5 **KEVASINGO,** b g Superpower - Katharina by Frankincense (R J Baker) 1743⁸ 1977³ 2242⁸ 3555⁶ 4322

8 **KEY PLAYER(IRE),** ch g Orchestra - Glenrula Queen by Royal Match (R Rowe) 2304¹ 2729³ 3094³ 3364 3461

7 **KEY TO MOYADE(IRE),** bl g Treasure Kay - Giorradana by Lord Ha Ha (M J Wilkinson) 1232 1368² 1670⁶ 1870² 2157³ 2808⁴ 3679³ 3843⁵

5 **KEYNOTE(IRE),** ch g Orchestra - St Moritz by Linacre (G B Balding) 3335

8 **KHALIDI(IRE),** b g Shernazar - Khaiyla by Mill Reef (USA) (D R Gandolfo) 1346⁴ 1762³ 1959⁴ 2282¹ 2597⁴ 3974¹ 4184²

4 **KHALIKHOUM(IRE),** b g Darshaan - Khalisiyn by Shakapour (Sir John Barlow Bt) 2284³ 2560 3044 3198 3722⁴ 4255³ 4322⁴

7 **KHARASAR(IRE),** b g Standaan (FR) - Khatima by Relko (Anthony Mullins) 1362⁶ 1552¹ 2052 2231⁴ 2733³ 3086⁸ 3787⁵

6 **KHATIR(CAN),** gr g Alwasmi (USA) - Perfect Poppy (USA) by Poppy Jay (M C Pipe) 1858⁷ 1956⁴ 2440⁷

5 **KHAYRAWANI(IRE),** br g Caerleon (USA) - Khaiyla by Mill Reef (USA) (C Roche) 220¹ 303⁴ 715¹ 2128⁶ 3523¹ 3766⁶

9 **KHAZARI(USA),** ch g Shahrastani (USA) - Kozana by Kris (R Brotherton) 155 225 2625⁸ 2977² 3988³ 4232

5 **KI CHI SAGA(USA),** ch g Miswaki (USA) - Cedilla (USA) by Caro (M Madgwick) 1719 1973

10 **KIBREET,** ch g Try My Best (USA) - Princess Pageant by Welsh Pageant (P J Hobbs) 1394 1875² 2219⁵ 2442⁴ 3154⁷

8 **KICKCASHTAL,** b g Ballacashtal (CAN) - Teenager by Never Say Die (Mrs C M Bowman) 2298 2653

6 **KIDSTUFF(IRE),** b g John French - Golden Vale Lady (Patrick G Kelly) 183 226⁶

6 **KIERCHEM(IRE),** b g Mazaad - Smashing Gale by Lord Gayle (USA) (C Grant) 1656 2202¹ 2485⁵ 2855⁹ 3002⁵ 3512¹ 3728³ 4002² 4258⁷

10 **KILARA,** b g Pollerton - Misty Boosh by Tarboosh (USA) (Michael O'Connor) 3447² 4003⁶ 4145²

4 **KILBAHA(IRE),** b f Petorius - Sable Royale (USA) by Real Value (USA) (Michael Hourigan) 522 620 1057⁶ 1430

6 **KILBOGGAN EXPRESS(IRE),** ch g Erin's Hope - Timeless Classic (Gerard Stack) 397

8 **KILBRANEY(IRE),** b g Amazing Bust - Royal Liatris by Ragapan (Thomas Foley) 3878

6 **KILBRICKEN GOLD(IRE),** b f Corvaro (USA) - Kilbricken Glen (Patrick Sinnott) 1147⁵

7 **KILBRICKEN MAID(IRE),** b m Meneval (USA) - Kilbricken Bay by Salluceva (Derek O'Keeffe) 1780³ 2021

5 **KILCALM KING(IRE),** b g King's Ride - Arctic Run by Deep Run (Noel Meade) 2845⁵ 3456² 3789²

6 **KILCAR(IRE),** ch g Phardante (FR) - Queen Of Swing by Kinghaven (Thomas Carberry) 1195⁹ 1460⁸ 2037 2583 2839 3068 3643⁶ 3942³ 4149² 4168⁷ 4292¹

6 **KILCARAMORE(IRE),** ch g Caerleon (USA) - Kasala (USA) by Blushing Groom (FR) (P J Healy) 91² 170¹ 272⁴ 355 746⁴ 1074³ 1361⁹ 2162 2366⁴ 3803³

7 **KILCARNE BAY(IRE),** b g Henbit (USA) - Thai Nang by Tap On Wood (O Sherwood) 1496⁴ 2250 2656⁶

5 **KILCOGY CROSS(IRE),** ch m Executive Perk - Dalus Dawn by Mandalus (A P O'Brien) 1019⁵ 1195⁵ 2079³ 2380⁵ 3342

10 **KING OF SHADOWS,** b or br g Connaught - Rhiannon by Welsh Pageant (Miss C M Carden) 2551 2897 3279[8] 3529[4] 3723 4064

4 **KING OF SPARTA,** b g Kefaah (USA) - Khaizaraan (CAN) by Sham (USA) (O Sherwood) 2284 3534[1] 3687[2]

11 **KING OF STEEL,** b g Kemal (FR) - Black Spangle by Black Tarquin (M D Hammond) 2912 3395

5 **KING OF SWING(IRE),** b g Lancastrian - Romantic Rhapsody by Ovac (ITY) (V Soane) 3176 3475

5 **KING OF THE BLUES,** b g Rakaposhi King - Colonial Princess by Roscoe Blake (J S King) 1357[3] 1802[2] 2179[5] 3898

6 **KING OF THE DAWN,** b g Rakaposhi King - Dawn Encounter by Rymer (P Mullins) 591[1] 733[4]

10 **KING OF THE GALES,** br g Strong Gale - Paulas Fancy by Lucky Guy (A L T Moore) 1243[6] 1537[6] 2085[2] 2127[3] 2474[5] 2734[2]

11 **KING OF THE GLEN,** b g King's Ride - Anabore by Darantus (A J McNamara) 780[1]

6 **KING OF THE HORSE(IRE),** ch g Hatim (USA) - Milly Whiteway by Great White Way (USA) (W Storey) 3899[8]

5 **KING OF THIEVES(IRE),** b g Executive Perk - Tom's Crofter (J L Hassett) 1247[4]

5 **KING PIN,** b g King's Ride - Bowling Fort by Bowling Pin (P Beaumont) 1280[4] 1656[3] 1962[1] 2318[1] 2721[3] 3709[5]

5 **KING PUCK(IRE),** b g Fairy King (USA) - Mrs Foodbroker by Home Guard (USA) (Patrick Martin) 928 1015

6 **KING RAT(IRE),** ch g King Of Clubs - Mrs Tittlemouse by Nonoalco (USA) (J G M O'Shea) 888[4] 1006[5] 1976[2] 2372 2852[5] 2999

12 **KING SPRING,** br g Royal Fountain - K-King by Fury Royal (Miss C E J Dawson) 4112 4209

7 **KING TORUS(IRE),** b g Torus - Kam A Dusk (Victor Dartnall) 4033[1] 4290[1]

8 **KING TYRANT(IRE),** ch g Mummy's Luck - Lady Thatch by Tyrant (USA) (M J Byrne) 65 114[7] 215[4] 237[2]

8 **KING UBAD(USA),** ch h Trempolino (USA) - Glitter (FR) by Reliance (K O Cunningham-Brown) 351[5]

8 **KING WAH GLORY(IRE),** b g Phardante (FR) - Rose's Best by Caribo (P Burke) 293[3] 719

12 **KING WILLIAM,** b g Dara Monarch - Norman Delight (USA) by Val de L'orne (FR) (N E Berry) 691[4]

7 **KING'S AFFAIR,** b g Rakaposhi King - Quelles Amours by Spartan General (P R Hedger) 2637 2980 3290

8 **KING'S COURTIER(IRE),** b g King's Ride - Glamorous Night by Sir Herbert (S Mellor) 1270[7] 1801 1937 2252 2392 2729 2888 3271

6 **KING'S FAYRE(IRE),** ch g King Luthier - Sizzle (J P N Parker) 3217[9]

5 **KING'S FLAGSHIP(IRE),** b g Contract Law (USA) - Cordon by Morston (FR) (Victor Bowens) 3816

7 **KING'S GOLD,** b g King Of Spain - Goldyke by Bustino (Mrs L Richards) 904 1111 1732[6] 2010 2267[5] 2932[5] 3295[3]

8 **KING'S MANDATE(IRE),** br g Mandalus - Shady Lucia (Thomas Kinane) 347[6] 424[3] 552[6] 1170 1779

8 **KING'S RAINBOW(IRE),** b m King's Ride - Royalement by Little Buskins (Mrs D Haine) 3019[5] 3422[4] 3996[6] 4204[6]

10 **KING'S SHILLING(USA),** b g Fit To Fight (USA) - Pride's Crossing (USA) by Riva Ridge (USA) (H Oliver) 189[6] 267[4] 308[4] 659[6] 755[5] 956[2] 1062[5] 1475[4] 1732 2512[2] 2604 3138[5] 3559 3852[4]

8 **KING'S TREASURE(USA),** b g King Of Clubs - Crown Treasure (USA) by Graustark (I A Balding) 3102[2] 3300

6 **KINGDOM GLORY(IRE),** gr g Wood Chanter - Ballybrennan (Capt D G Swan) 722 4161

7 **KINGDOM OF SHADES(USA),** ch g Risen Star (USA) - Dancers Countess (USA) by Northern Dancer (Andrew Turnell) 1441[2] 1744[6] 2557[2] 2787[3] 3062[2] 3568[9]

12 **KINGFISHER BAY,** b g Try My Best (USA) - Damiya (FR) by Direct Flight (O A Little) 2897[6] 3187 3746[7]

9 **KINGFISHER BLUES(IRE),** ch g Quayside - Night Spot by Midsummer Night II (Mrs P Grainger) 128[5]

4 **KINGFISHER BRAVE,** b g Rock City - Lambada Style (IRE) by Dancing Brave (USA) (M G Meagher) 1221[4] 1398[6] 1737[5] 3353 4212[4]

5 **KINGMAN(IRE),** b g King Luthier - Irish Lane by Boreen (FR) (T A Kent) 2092[2] 2588[7] 3178 3421 3627[1] 3935d[9] 4144 4302[1]

5 **KINGS ADVENTURE,** ch g Rakaposhi King - Mendick Adventure by Mandrake Major (B Mactaggart) 3598

4 **KINGS BANQUET,** b g Supreme Leader - Culinary by Tower Walk (Noel Meade) 4169[2]

6 **KINGS CAY(IRE),** b g Taufan (USA) - Provocation by Kings Lake (USA) (T H Caldwell) 1509

9 **KINGS CHERRY(IRE),** b g King's Ride - Another Cherry by Le Bavard (FR) (J A B Old) 1573[5] 1921[8] 2355[2] 2529[2] 2922[1] 3067[5] 3565

7 **KINGS HIGH(IRE),** br g King's Ride - Fatima Rose by The Parson (W T Kemp) 2116[8] 2192

8 **KINGS LANE,** b g Majestic Streak - Gala Lane by Gala Performance (USA) (J M Dun) 1824[8] 1984[5] 2241 2487[2] 2710 3057[3] 3162[4] 3400[7] 3658[1]

4 **KINGS MEASURE(IRE),** b g King's Ride - Snoqualmie (J M Jefferson) 3720[1]

7 **KINGS MINSTRAL(IRE),** ch g Andretti - Tara Minstral Vii (D A Lamb) 1257[2] 1586[1] 1787[3] 2122[9] 2349 3162 3262[6] 3663[5] 3918[5] 4211

4 **KINGS NIGHTCLUB,** b f Shareef Dancer (USA) - Troy Moon by Troy (J White) 363 501[4] 672[7] 936[6]

6 **KINGS RETURN(IRE),** b g King's Ride - Browne's Return by Deep Run (W P Mullins) 2110[1] 2140[1] 2445[5] 2670[1] 2835[4] 3071

5 **KINGS RUN(IRE),** b m King's Ride - Turbo Run (Roger Sweeney) 339 560

8 **KINGS SERMON(IRE),** b g King's Ride - Sunday Sermon by The Parson (P Beaumont) 1385[3] 1820[6] 2347[1] 2763 3005[2] 3511[1] 3702[3] 3758[4]

7 **KINGS TOKEN,** b g Rakaposhi King - Pro-Token by Proverb (F T Walton) 4218

5 **KINGS VISION,** gr g Absalom - Eye Sight by Roscoe Blake (W Jenks) 1348 2372 2999[8] 3276[6] 3992[5] 4183

4 **KINGS WITNESS(USA),** b g Lear Fan (USA) - Allison's Deeds by Sassafras (FR) (P F Nicholls) 2397[4] 2773[1] 3150 3922[3]

8 **KINGSFOLD PET,** b g Tina's Pet - Bella Lisa by River Chanter (M J Haynes) 1288 1612[7] 2820[6] 3020

6 **KINGSLAND TAVERNER,** ch g True Song - Princess Hecate by Autre Prince (O Sherwood) 3027[9]

8 **KINGSMILL QUAY,** b m Noble Imp - La Jolie Fille by Go Blue (Miss J Du Plessis) 1916

11 **KINGSTON WAY,** gr g Crash Course - Miragold by Grey Mirage (Mrs F M O'Brien) 314

11 **KINGSWELL BOY,** ch g Floriferous - Tide Gate by Dike (USA) (M C Pipe) 528 593[3]

4 **KINGSWOOD IMPERIAL,** ch g Absalom - Allied Newcastle by Crooner (R J O'Sullivan) 2483[3] 2831 3122

11 **LORD RELIC(NZ),** b g Zamazaan (FR) - Morning Order (NZ) by Bismark (S A Brookshaw) 2551[2] 2790[1] 2960[2] 3153 3924[4]

6 **LORD ROOBLE(IRE),** b g Jolly Jake (NZ) - Missing Note by Rarity (J T Gifford) 905[4] 1063[3] 1447[3] 1792[3] 2281[5] 2640[2] 2980[1] 3289[2] 3414[4]

9 **LORD SINGAPORE(IRE),** ch g Mister Lord (USA) - Demanoluma by Golden Love (John J Walsh) 553 719 981[2] 1434[1] 2071 3453[6]

5 **LORD TOMANICO(FR),** b g Tirol - Lady Beauvallon by Coquelin (USA) (C J Mann) 377[1] 451[3] 2397

8 **LORD VICK(IRE),** ch g Mister Lord (USA) - Vickies Gold by Golden Love (Miss A E Embiricos) 2301[5]

5 **LORDAN VELVET(IRE),** br g Lord Americo - Danny's Miracle by Superlative (Mrs W B Allen) 3971

11 **LORNA-GAIL,** b m Callernish - Gilt Course by Crash Course (R H Alner) 1776[5] 2742

5 **LOSLOMOS(IRE),** b g The Bart (USA) - Katebeaujolais (Donncha Duggan) 175[6] 233[8] 276[9]

4 **LOST ALPHABET(IRE),** b g Don't Forget Me - Zenga by Try My Best (Mrs John Harrington) 2449[9] 3183[2] 3349[2]

10 **LOST COIN,** b m Baragoi - Penny Levy by Levmoss (Michael Gleeson) 4307

4 **LOST IN THE POST(IRE),** ch g Don't Forget Me - Postie by Sharpo (Ronald Thompson) 2123[9] 2262[8] 3866[6]

6 **LOSTRIS(IRE),** b m Pennine Walk - Herila (FR) by Bold Lad (USA) (M Dods) 1679[7] 2147[2] 2346[8] 3203[4]

5 **LOTHIAN COMMANDER,** ch g Alias Smith (USA) - Lothian Lightning by Lighter (D McCain) 1540[8] 1623 2372[7] 2550[4] 3001[4] 3144[7] 3503[6]

7 **LOTHIAN COMMODORE,** ro g Alias Smith (USA) - Lothian Lightning by Lighter (G Richards) 3599[5]

8 **LOTHIAN JEM,** b m Skyliner - Lothian Countess by New Brig (J Wharton) 1439 1647 2158 2251

5 **LOTSCHBERG EXPRESS,** ch m Rymer - Chalet Waldegg by Monsanto (FR) (D R Gandolfo) 1214[8]

8 **LOTTERY TICKET(IRE),** b g The Parson - Beauty Run by Deep Run (T R George) 1339[2] 2799 2921 3778[5] 3996[3] 4133[2]

8 **LOTTOVER(IRE),** b m Over The River (FR) - Monaleigh by Sir Herbert (Donal Hassett) 943 3378[2] 3770 4248

10 **LOUGH ATALIA,** br g Over The River (FR) - Soft Drink by Gala Performance (USA) (V T O'Brien) 184[4] 348[1] 575[5] 679[6] 926 1059[6] 3446[1]

7 **LOUGH N UISCE(IRE),** ch m Boyne Valley - Moves Well by Green God (A P O'Brien) 142[5] 226[6]

4 **LOUGH SLANIA(IRE),** b c Pennine Walk - Sister Ursula by Ela-Mana-Mou (Kevin Prendergast) 1459[3] 1709 2067[3] 2230 2337 3625[8] 3889[6] 4149[6]

7 **LOUGH TULLY(IRE),** ch g Denel (FR) - Lough Hill Lady by Cantab (F Jordan) 796[6] 1134[4] 1543[5] 1815[2] 2158[3] 2661[1] 3001[1]

9 **LOUGHDOO(IRE),** ch g Avocat - Balmy Grove by Virginia Boy (R Lee) 1673[7] 2035[6] 2517[6] 3833 4035[4] 4275[5]

8 **LOUGHLINS PRIDE,** ch f Capricorn Line - Birdalova (M J Byrne) 120[4] 3964[7] 4144

6 **LOUGHLOONE(IRE),** b m Barbarolli (USA) - Tigora (A P O'Brien) 468[1] 732

7 **LOUIS THE LIP,** b g Strong Gale - Laurello by Bargello (J T R Dreaper) 1278

7 **LOUISES FANCY(IRE),** ch m Horage - Choclate Baby by Kashiwa (Mrs C Barker) 1246[4] 1654 2016[9] 2227[6] 3696[4] 4004[6]

5 **LOULISSARO(IRE),** b m Beau Sher - Rocket Cent Vii (P T Flavin) 434 590

6 **LOVE A CUDDLE(IRE),** ch m Orange Reef - Ger's Gift (Edward Power) 1782

9 **LOVE AND PORTER(IRE),** b m Sheer Grit - Divine Dibs by Raise You Ten (James Joseph O'Connor) 1194 1243[7] 1434 2071 2170 2584[9]

4 **LOVE HEART(IRE),** b c Kefaah (USA) - Cinnamon Fern by Sadler's Wells (USA) (T G McCourt) 620[7] 1750

5 **LOVE THE BLUES,** ch m Bluebird (USA) - Love Match (USA) by Affiliate (USA) (D Nicholson) 798[7] 2288[2] 2601[6] 2824[4]

7 **LOVE THE LORD(IRE),** b m Mister Lord (USA) - Margeno's Love by Golden Love (Daniel O'Connell) 981[7] 1079[3] 1243[3] 1434[5] 1551[5] 1753 2524[7] 2843[2] 3212[2]

8 **LOVELARK,** b m Crested Lark - Emily Love by Arctic Kanda (R Lee) 56 666[8] 768[3] 2030[2] 2403[6] 3016 3542[4] 3619[8]

5 **LOVELY LYNSEY(IRE),** b m Buckskin (FR) - Wessex Habit by Monksfield (D Carroll) 1279 2079 2137[6] 2343 2866[2]

9 **LOVELY OUTLOOK,** b g Teenoso (USA) - Black Penny by West Partisan (R M Carson) 3082

4 **LOVELY PROSPECT,** b f Lycius (USA) - Lovely Lagoon by Mill Reef (USA) (E Sheehy) 2161[9] 2337 2643

9 **LOVELY RASCAL,** gr m Scallywag - Owen Belle by Master Owen (J J O'Neill) 1227[5] 1476[2] 1809[7] 1989[7] 2492[6]

5 **LOVEYOUMILLIONS(IRE),** b g Law Society (USA) - Warning Sound by Red Alert (N Tinkler) 1371[7]

9 **LOVING AROUND(IRE),** b m Furry Glen - Shannon Ville by Deep Run (E J O'Grady) 1079[6]

9 **LOWAWATHA,** b g Dancing Brave (USA) - Shorthouse by Habitat (Mrs E H Heath) 79[4] 617[8] 870[2] 1104[4] 2774 4089[2] 4238

10 **LOWER BITHAM,** ch m Julio Mariner - Peggy by Port Corsair (R E Pocock) 1236

9 **LOYAL GAIT(NZ),** ch g Gaiter (NZ) - Lotsydamus (NZ) by Auk (USA) (A M Darlington) 3327 3640 3848

9 **LOYAL NOTE,** ch g Royal Vulcan - Maynote by Maystreak (S R Andrews) 2615[1] 2887[4] 3096[2] 3855[4]

6 **LUCAYAN CAY(IRE),** ch g Al Hareb (USA) - Flying Melody by Auction Ring (USA) (Mrs A J Bowlby) 2532[7] 2783[4] 3027

13 **LUCAYAN GOLD,** br g Ardross - Lucayan Lady by Swing Easy (USA) (K Bishop) 760[5]

6 **LUCIA FORTE,** b m Neltino - Celtic Well by Celtic Cone (K C Bailey) 1532[1] 1855[2] 2032 2315[4] 2541[3] 3331[1]

10 **LUCKER,** b g Anita's Prince - Musical Puss by Orchestra (Mrs E Moscrop) 3249[3] 3673

9 **LUCKNAM DREAMER,** b g Macmillion - River Damsel by Forlorn River (Mrs Barbara Waring) 1180

4 **LUCKY ARCHER,** b g North Briton - Preobrajenska by Double Form (P J Hobbs) 3334[4] 3623[3] 3892 4036[6] 4322

4 **LUCKY BEA,** b g Lochnager - Knocksharry by Palm Track (M W Easterby) 930[9] 1196 1629 2296[4] 2417 2577[1]

10 **LUCKY BLUE,** b g Blue Cashmere - Cooling by Tycoon II (Simon Earle) 2217 2530[8] 3580

7 **LUCKY BUST(IRE),** b g Amazing Bust - Perpetue by Proverb (W Harney) 741[3] 977[6] 1117[4] 1841[7] 2224 2446 2644[4] 2962[1] 3236[2] 3418 3753[5]

(USA) (Noel T Chance) 1097 1208 1893² 2499¹ 2697³ 3129⁸

12 **MARCHMAN,** b g Daring March - Saltation by Sallust (J S King) 587² 631⁴

10 **MARCHWOOD,** ch g Black Minstrel - Lisnagrough by Golden Love (N Chamberlain) 1375⁶ 1694 1967 2203⁸

7 **MARCO MAGNIFICO(USA),** b or br g Bering - Viscosity (USA) by Sir Ivor (Miss Lucinda V Russell) 727⁸ 912⁶ 1068⁵ 1122⁶ 1784

6 **MARDON(IRE),** br f Mandalus - Cherry Dancer (Ms M Flynn) 591 685

12 **MARDOOD,** b g Ela-Mana-Mou - Tigeen by Habitat (S B Clark) 1567⁵ 1824 2487 3123⁸ 3507³ 3883⁸ 4101² 4232¹

6 **MARELLO,** br m Supreme Leader - Clonmello by Le Bavard (FR) (Mrs M Reveley) 1227¹ 1464¹ 2711¹ 2917¹ 3710¹

9 **MAREMMA GALE(IRE),** b g Strong Gale - My Halo by Be Friendly (N R Mitchell) 855

5 **MARGALE(IRE),** b m Strong Gale - Tarmar (S Donohoe) 898 1019

7 **MARGIER,** br m Queen's Soldier (USA) - Princess Impala by Damsire Unregistered (D J Wintle) 3610⁷

6 **MARGOT'S BOY,** ch g Gypsy Castle - Rosinka by Raga Navarro (ITY) (D McCune) 3663

7 **MARGUERITA SONG,** b m Oats - Rhine Aria by Workboy (Edward P Mitchell) 99³ 223¹ 272⁶ 565⁴ 683⁹ 732 1552 1714 2077 2164 2274³ 2448 2646 3236⁹ 3706¹

7 **MARIA-NOELLE(IRE),** ch f King Luthier - Coshil Star (P Delaney) 2276⁹ 2675 2757

6 **MARIAN'S OWN(IRE),** br f Phardante (FR) - Own Acre (Ronald O'Leary) 527 983

6 **MARIE'S PRIDE(IRE),** b m Henbit (USA) - Cinderwood (Michael Hourigan) 92⁸ 135⁵ 238⁴ 274⁴ 304

7 **MARIES CALL(IRE),** b f Callernish - Chiminee Bee (J F Sleator) 3943⁴

7 **MARIES POLLY,** ch m Pollerton - Maries Party by The Parson (John A White) 1074⁶ 1242³ 1780⁴ 2021⁷ 2163 2411⁴ 2673 2868⁷ 2941 3340² 3446⁵

4 **MARIGLIANO(USA),** b g Riverman (USA) - Mount Holyoke by Golden Fleece (USA) (K A Morgan) 2758 3044⁸

7 **MARILLO(IRE),** br f Royal Fountain - Mameen's Gift by Boreen (FR) (Michael Hourigan) 983⁸ 1360⁹ 1550⁶ 1778

7 **MARINER'S TALE(IRE),** b m Mandalus - Knockbawn Lady by Push On (Michael McCullagh) 4052 4282

9 **MARINERS COVE,** br g Julio Mariner - Ionian Isle (FR) by Jim French (USA) (C D Broad) 41⁵ 1567

9 **MARINERS MEMORY,** b g Julio Mariner - Midnight Pansy by Deadly Nightshade (R G Brazington) 4015

10 **MARINERS MIRROR,** b m Julio Mariner - Sujono by Grey Mirage (N A Twiston-Davies) 1213³ 1312¹ 1732¹ 2014¹ 2437³ 2718²

6 **MARINERS REEF(IRE),** gr m Kambalda - Mariners Chain by Walshford (Michael McCullagh) 928 1013⁷ 1360⁴ 1550 2016² 2142² 2272³ 2447 2735² 2901³ 3216² 3377² 3754⁶ 4004¹ 4146⁹

6 **MARINO ROSE(IRE),** ch m Lord Chancellor (USA) - La Bellilotte (Gerard Stack) 4243

9 **MARIO'S DREAM(IRE),** ch g Boyne Valley - Its All A Dream by Le Moss (Mrs J G Retter) 279⁶ 330 629³ 918⁵ 998

7 **MARIUS(IRE),** b g Cyrano de Bergerac - Nesreen by The Parson (J T Gifford) 1572² 1807⁴ 2400¹ 2743² 3062⁴ 3328² 3791³

6 **MARJIMEL,** b m Backchat (USA) - Mary's Double by Majetta (Mrs A M Naughton) 2575⁹

7 **MARKET GOSSIP,** b g Rolfe (USA) - Buckbe by Ragstone (R H Alner) 1302 1734³

5 **MARKET LASS(IRE),** br f Orchestra - Tor-Na-Grena (Mrs John Harrington) 2166⁶

7 **MARKET MAYHEM,** b g Revlow - Miss Burgundy by Gambling Debt (J L Spearing) 1609² 1893 2546⁵ 2746 3143⁴

7 **MARKETING MAN,** b g Sizzling Melody - Best Offer by Crepello (J White) 128 251 416⁵

6 **MARKETPLACE(IRE),** b h Runnett - Ordinary Fare (USA) by What A Pleasure (USA) (Pavel Slozil) 1420⁶

13 **MARKS REFRAIN,** b g Blue Refrain - Markup by Appiani II (E M Caine) 1662

7 **MARKSMAN SPARKS,** b g Gunner B - Forty Watts by Sparkler (Dr D Chesney) 1478⁴ 2978

6 **MARLAST(IRE),** ch m Orchestra - Marla by Hul A Hul (J G Groome) 302⁷ 1435⁸ 1583³ 1714 2673

5 **MARLIES GOHR,** b m Arctic Bronze Vii - Miss Carvin by Carvin (T T Clement) 3729 3913

10 **MARLINGFORD,** ch g Be My Guest (USA) - Inchmarlo (USA) by Nashua (Mrs J Jordan) 1166⁶ 1386⁷ 1630⁷ 2205¹ 2286⁵ 2576³ 2826³ 2857⁴ 3399⁸

4 **MARLONETTE(IRE),** ch f Jareer (USA) - Marlova (FR) by Salvo (W P Mullins) 1430⁶ 1547³ 1709⁵ 2112¹ 2230⁵ 2470⁴ 2669¹ 2751¹ 3150⁶ 3566⁷ 3768⁷

5 **MARLOUSION(IRE),** ch m Montelimar (USA) - Ware Princess by Crash Course (C P E Brooks) 191² 545² 629 648⁴ 1369² 1570² 2725

6 **MARNIES WOLF,** ch g Little Wolf - Marnie's Girl by Crooner (R Tate) 1050⁶

5 **MARONETTA,** ch m Kristian - Suzannah's Song by Song (M J Ryan) 263

6 **MARROWFAT LADY(IRE),** b m Astronef - Lady Topknot by High Top (N E Berry) 2279 2390 2663

10 **MARSDEN ROCK,** b or br m Tina's Pet - Take My Hand by Precipice Wood (N B Mason) 912³ 1139⁶ 1331²

10 **MARSH'S LAW,** br g Kala Shikari - My Music by Sole Mio (USA) (G P Kelly) 617 1259⁶ 2969⁷ 3512⁸ 3820

10 **MARTELL BOY(NZ),** b g Princes Gate - Amorae (NZ) by Arragon (Miss Venetia Williams) 4046² 4202¹

5 **MARTELLO GIRL(IRE),** b m Buckskin (FR) - Moss Gale by Strong Gale (K S Bridgwater) 377

8 **MARTHA BUCKLE,** br m Lochnager - Bamdoro by Cavo Doro (J S Goldie) 2145 2349

8 **MARTHA'S DAUGHTER,** br m Majestic Maharaj - Lady Martha by Sidon (Capt T A Forster) 652 753⁴ 838² 956⁴

10 **MARTHA'S SON,** b g Idiot's Delight - Lady Martha by Sidon (Capt T A Forster) 2826 3130¹ 3576¹

10 **MARTOMICK,** br m Montelimar (USA) - Be My Joy by Be My Guest (USA) (K C Bailey) 1084³ 1395² 2327⁴

6 **MARTYS STEP(IRE),** gr g Step Together (USA) - Dozy Love by Bulldozer (Peter McCreery) 685² 850³ 977³ 1193 1359² 1649⁶ 1908⁷ 3964³ 4160

5 **MARY DONT BE LONG(IRE),** ch m The Bart (USA) - Righthand Lady (Henry Cleary) 1907⁹ 2144⁷ 2414

7 **MARY'S CASE(IRE),** b g Taufan (USA) - Second Service by Red Regent (Mrs J D Goodfellow) 1164⁸

INDEX TO NATIONAL HUNT RESULTS 1996-97

6 **MELDANTE VI(IRE),** b g Said To Be Phardante (FR) - By Skyliner (Michael Hourigan) 2374 2907 3134

4 **MELLOW MASTER,** b g Royal Academy (USA) - Upward Trend by Salmon Leap (USA) (N J H Walker) 2511 28861 34871 3648

6 **MELLOW YELLOW,** b g Derring Rose - Miss Nanna by Vayrann (J Mackie) 4154 5337 7755

6 **MELNIK,** ch g Nashwan (USA) - Melodist (USA) by The Minstrel (CAN) (Mrs A J Perrett) 19391 2280 2613 37323 4048

5 **MELODY MAID,** b m Strong Gale - Ribo Melody by Riboboy (USA) (N J Henderson) 25032 29611 35611 37696

6 **MELSTOCK MEGGIE,** ch m Cardinal Flower - Lake View Lady by Little Buskins (Mrs J Pitman) 14761 16691 18303 21583 27463

6 **MELT DOWN(IRE),** b f Tidaro (USA) - Sun Raker (F Flood) 4094 42828

4 **MELT THE CLOUDS(CAN),** ch g Diesis - Population by General Assembly (USA) (M C Pipe) 23032 24307 34831 39056 40802 41821 43019

4 **MELTEMISON,** b g Charmer - Salchow by Niniski (USA) (M D Hammond) 12218 16294 21885 26322 28188 37142

4 **MELTON MADE(IRE),** br g Strong Gale - Pamela's Princess by Black Minstrel (G A Hubbard) 40427

5 **MELVILLE ROSE(IRE),** br m Phardante (FR) - Melville (Michael A Kelly) 1364

6 **MELY MOSS(FR),** ch g Tip Moss (FR) - The Exception (FR) by Melyno (C R Egerton) 23141 25643 29472

5 **MEMORY'S MUSIC,** b h Dance Of Life (USA) - Sheer Luck by Shergar (M Madgwick) 14494 1697 2305 2610

6 **MEMSAHIB OFESTEEM,** gr m Neltino - Occatillo by Maris Piper (S Gollings) 28101 29753 3135

5 **MEN OF NINETYEIGHT(IRE),** b g King's Ride - Penny Holder by Strong Gale (P Hughes) 7825 32172 35247 38914

7 **MENALDI(IRE),** b g Meneval (USA) - Top Riggin by Jupiter Pluvius (P Cheesbrough) 12526 16319 2260 24893 26845 30345 33089 37562

8 **MENATURE(IRE),** ch g Meneval (USA) - Speedy Venture by Bargello (N J Pomfret) 1473 1883 41575

5 **MENDELUCI(IRE),** b g Nordico (USA) - Favourite Niece by Busted (J S Bolger) 3178 34294 36064 37059

7 **MENDIP PRINCE(IRE),** b g King's Ride - Atlantic Hope by Brave Invader (USA) (P J Hobbs) 12713 21566 2562 32714

7 **MENDIP SON,** b g Hallgate - Silver Surprise by Son Of Silver (Mrs H E Rees) 697

7 **MENELAVE(IRE),** b m Meneval (USA) - Harlave by Harwell (O Sherwood) 10661 14026 18073 26815 31864

7 **MENESONIC(IRE),** b g Meneval (USA) - Kandy Kate by Pry (R H Alner) 15024 16152 24383 27015 30411 33103

5 **MENSHAAR(USA),** b g Hawkster (USA) - Klassy Imp (USA) by Imp Society (USA) (L Lungo) 13135 17756 18291 20251 23203 31626

5 **MENTMORE TOWERS(IRE),** gr g Roselier (FR) - Decent Dame by Decent Fellow (Mrs J Pitman) 13972 22492 26011 35793

4 **MERAWANG(IRE),** b g Shahrastani (USA) - Modiyna by Nishapour (FR) (P F Nicholls) 24303 27443 3150

4 **MERCANTILE MAN(IRE),** b g Electric - Pride 'N' Poverty (J G Coogan) 3349

6 **MERCHANTS QUAY(IRE),** ch g Executive Perk - Foolish Lady by Signa Infesta (D T Hughes) 6281 17735 10132 13602 18362 21706 2647

10 **MERCHANTS ROAD,** ch g Kemal (FR) - Maggie's Turn by Garda's Revenge (USA) (V T O'Brien) 2902 32389 3834

6 **MERELY MORTAL,** b g Rolfe (USA) - Lagskona by Be Friendly (B Preece) 107 3104

7 **MERILENA(IRE),** b m Roselier (FR) - Scotsman Ice by Deep Run (G A Hubbard) 13707 17405 2679 27613 28928

10 **MERIVEL,** b g Buckskin (FR) - Island Varra by Deep Run (R Rowe) 51 38754 4321

8 **MERLINS DREAM(IRE),** ch g Callernish - Mystical Moonshine by Proverb (O Sherwood) 5412 7062 8722 10641 26271 31012 34971 37905

8 **MERLINS WISH(USA),** ch g Yukon (USA) - Dear Guinevere (USA) by Fearless Knight (M C Pipe) 266 2817 4175 5139 6387 9377

5 **MERRY CHANTER(IRE),** gr g Wood Chanter - Idle Taxi (Michael Cunningham) 288 3505 5779

8 **MERRY CHIEFTAIN(IRE),** g Supreme Leader - Merry Memories (Donal Hassett) 2907 38183 40628

9 **MERRY GALE(IRE),** br g Strong Gale - Merry Lesa by Dalesa (J T R Dreaper) 12434 15374 17532 20691 24744 26711 28363 35632

4 **MERRY MAJOR,** br g K-Battery - Merry Missus by Bargello (T D Barron) 32517

6 **MERRY MASQUERADE(IRE),** b g King's Ride - Merry Madness by Raise You Ten (Mrs M Reveley) 20083 22834 26231

13 **MERRY MASTER,** br g Le Coq D'Or - Merry Missus by Bargello (G M Moore) 1632 2334 2935

7 **MERRY MERMAID,** ch m Bairn (USA) - Manna Green by Bustino (P Monteith) 26182 2880 3013 41026

8 **MERRY PANTO(IRE),** ch g Lepanto (GER) - Merry Penny by St Chad (C P E Brooks) 9011 13422 1721 24595 37303 38243 40405

9 **MERRY PEOPLE(IRE),** b g Lafontaine (USA) - Merry Madness by Raise You Ten (John Queally) 1582 2162 3561 4706 6021 743 3754 40785

6 **MERRYHILL GOLD,** b g Glint Of Gold - Phlox by Floriana (J W Curtis) 7046 8623 1127 12506 21785 22854

8 **MERRYHILL MADAM,** b m Prince Sabo - Western Line by High Line (P Bradley) 756

6 **MESA VERDE(IRE),** b or br g Yashgan - Random Princess (J A Berry) 33811

6 **MESP(IRE),** br m Strong Gale - Queenie Kelly by The Parson (J G M O'Shea) 10536 12606 1570 18685 22987

5 **METASTASIO,** b h Petoski - Top Of The League by High Top (D G McArdle) 7152 10897 15353 16215 17523 20864 21285 23401 28415 3131 34519 38904

5 **METHODIUS(IRE),** b g Venetian Gate - Heaven Bound by Fine Blade (USA) (J R Jenkins) 3970 4241

6 **METRO FASHION(IRE),** ch g Carlingford Castle - Good Resemblance (M A Gunn) 3525

6 **MHEANMETOO,** ch g Roi Danzig (USA) - Spinster by Grundy (D L Williams) 2278 2498 29783 32933 37368

7 **MHEMEANLES,** br g Jalmood (USA) - Folle Idee (USA) by Foolish Pleasure (USA) (Frank Nicholls) 2792 3279

6 **MIA LADY(IRE),** b m Buckskin (FR) - Lady Helga (Thomas Foley) 1901 2079 2343

10 **MIAMI SPLASH,** ch g Miami Springs - Splash Of Red by Scallywag (Simon Earle) 1052

4 **MICHANDRA BOY,** b g Skyliner - Magdalene (IRE) by Runnett (Martyn Wane) 2687

6 **MICHELLES CRYSTAL,** b m Ovac (ITY) - Lochlairey by Lochnager (F L Matthews) 2995 3591

6 **MULLOVER,** ch g Ra Nova - True Divine by
True Song (Mrs John Harrington) 289⁹ 977⁴
1145¹ 1431⁴ 1620⁴ 2113² 2126² 2447

5 **MULTAN,** b g Indian Ridge - Patchinia by
Patch (G L Moore) 1641

4 **MULTEEN JET(IRE),** b g Homo Sapien - Ankar
Maran Vii (Daniel O'Connell) 2940⁶ 3415⁸
4056⁵ 4284⁷

7 **MULTI LINE,** ch m High Line - Waterford
Cream by Proverb (Mrs P Townsley) 2726⁹
2891⁸

5 **MULTIPIT(IRE),** b h Nashamaa - Opera Guest
by Be My Guest (USA) (E J Creighton) 221⁴
339⁵ 590

6 **MUMMY'S MOLE,** gr g Le Solaret (FR) - Tups
by Prince Regent (FR) (Graeme Roe) 3590
4013

6 **MUNTAFI,** b g Unfuwain (USA) - Princess
Sucree (USA) by Roberto (USA) (Mrs A J
Perrett) 1112⁹

7 **MURBERRY(IRE),** b or br m Strong Statement
(USA) - Lady Tarsel by Tarqogan (Mrs I
McKie) 153³ 262³ 295²

4 **MURCHAN TYNE(IRE),** ch f Good Thyne (USA)
- Ardnamurchan by Ardross (E J Alston)
3427² 3929¹ 4143²

5 **MURDER MOSS(IRE),** ch g Doulab (USA) -
Northern Wind by Northfields (USA) (S
Coltherd) 2634²

5 **MURGASTY(IRE),** b m Glacial Storm (USA) -
Shancarnan (AUS) (G T Hourigan) 603

6 **MURKELBUR(IRE),** b f Florida Son - Red For
Go (M O Cullinane) 1836 2131 2222

7 **MURLEYS CROSS(IRE),** ch g Over The River
(FR) - Private Dancer by Deep Run (J P
O'Keeffe) 1174¹

10 **MURPHAIDEEZ,** b g Le Moss - Toombeola by
Raise You Ten (R A Fahey) 2710 3123

6 **MURPHY'S GOLD(IRE),** ch g Salt Dome (USA)
- Winter Harvest by Grundy (R A Fahey)
1252⁵ 1397

8 **MURPHY'S LADY(IRE),** b m Over The River
(FR) - Rugged Lady by Rugged Man (Daniel
O'Connell) 63⁶ 93⁴ 212 236⁵ 338⁶ 406⁶

5 **MURPHY'S MALT(IRE),** ch g Mulhollande
(USA) - Rose Of The Sea (USA) by Diamonds Are Trump (USA) (A P O'Brien) 183²
407¹ 487¹ 731³ 850⁴ 1090² 1275¹ 1641⁶ 2965⁸

7 **MURPHY'S RUN(IRE),** b g Runnett - O'Hara
(GER) by Frontal (P Eccles) 735 1429 1716
2267 2977

9 **MURPHY'S TROUBLE(IRE),** ch f Orchestra -
Small Trouble by Deep Run (Peter Casey)
158³

5 **MURRAY'S MILLION,** b g Macmillion - Random Select by Random Shot (J S Smith)
1240 1735 2350⁹ 4015

10 **MUSE,** ch g High Line - Thoughtful by
Northfields (USA) (D R C Elsworth) 1268⁵
1506¹ 1877⁴ 2326⁴

6 **MUSEUM(IRE),** b g Tate Gallery (USA) - Go
Anywhere by Grundy (P Winkworth) 1410⁶
1646⁶ 2009² 2267⁸ 2765¹ 3049²

5 **MUSIC AGAIN(IRE),** ch f Orchestra - Kewanee
(W P Mullins) 3880¹

6 **MUSIC BLITZ,** b g Sizzling Melody - Sunny
Waters by High Top (Mrs D Thomson) 724
934⁷ 1374⁴ 1822⁴ 3304⁷ 3434⁷

7 **MUSIC CITY BEAT(IRE),** ch g Orchestra - Deep
Sunday (L J Fagan) 2737 2838

6 **MUSIC CLASS(IRE),** ch g Orchestra - Tacova
by Avocat (R J Baker) 2565⁹ 2771 3052⁶ 3333⁷
3594 4193

6 **MUSIC MAN(IRE),** ch g Mazaad - Star Music
(GER) (James Devereux) 394

7 **MUSIC MASTER(IRE),** ch g Orchestra - I Know
by Crespino (C R Egerton) 2152⁵ 2398⁴ 2889⁴
3167

5 **MUSIC PLEASE,** ch g Music Boy - Ask Mama
by Mummy's Pet (K C Bailey) 1716⁶ 2117⁵
2371⁵ 2511⁴ 3462² 3957³

11 **MUSIC SCORE,** ch g Orchestra - Hansel
Money by Prince Hansel (Mrs L C Taylor)
59⁴ 147 483 530² 649

8 **MUSICAL DUKE(IRE),** ch g Orchestra - What A
Duchess (Martin Michael Lynch) 345⁴ 576
982⁷ 1435⁷ 1714⁵ 2053 3074

6 **MUSICAL HIT,** ch g True Song - Rapagain by
Deep Run (P A Pritchard) 812 1129⁶ 1545 1763
2375³ 2566 2862⁷ 3504 4067 4204⁵ 4286

4 **MUSICAL MAYHEM(IRE),** b g Shernazar - Minstrels Folly (USA) by The Minstrel (CAN)
(D K Weld) 2449¹ 3135⁹

11 **MUSICAL MONARCH(NZ),** ch g Leader Of The
Band (USA) - Cheelbrite (NZ) by Head
Hunter (N J Hawke) 2253

6 **MUSICAL VOCATION(IRE),** ch m Orchestra -
Kentucky Calling by Pry (G L Edwards) 106

6 **MUSICAL WONDER(IRE),** b f Orchestra -
Wonder by Tekoah (Anthony Mullins) 2276²

7 **MUSKERRY EXPRESS(IRE),** b g Torenaga -
Home Rejoicing (John J Walsh) 1338 1241⁹
2164

6 **MUSKERRY KING(IRE),** ch g King Luthier -
Ware Princess by Crash Course (T J
O'Mara) 86² 133⁷ 211⁷ 337¹ 463⁴ 564 2674⁴ 2901⁷
3235³ 3419

8 **MUSKERRY MOYA(IRE),** ch m Rising - Muskerry Mary by Mon Capitaine (J W Dufosee)
4122¹ 4290³

6 **MUSKIN MORE(IRE),** ch g Electric - Clontinty
Queen by Laurence O (E J O'Grady) 1552⁵
1779⁷ 2096⁶ 2223³

8 **MUSKORA(IRE),** b g Muscatite - Singing
Wren by Julio Mariner (S H Shirley-
Beavan) 48⁵ 327³ 532 613

5 **MUST BE DONE(IRE),** ch g Furry Berg - Proan
(Mayne Kidd) 3945 4117

11 **MUSTHAVEASWIG,** gr g Croghan Hill - Gin An
Tonic by Osprey Hawk (D Nicholson) 1296³
1511 1884¹ 2310⁴ 2500¹ 2935⁴ 3206 3678⁴ 3932

4 **MUTANASSIB(IRE),** b g Mtoto - Lightning
Legacy (USA) by Super Concorde (USA) (M
C Pipe) 2426² 2636⁸ 2791³ 3150

7 **MUTAWALI(IRE),** ch g Exactly Sharp (USA) -
Ludovica by Bustino (R J Baker) 937¹ 1235⁶
1353³ 1800⁶

5 **MUTAZZ(USA),** b h Woodman (USA) -
Ghashtah (USA) by Nijinsky (CAN) (Major
W R Hern) 940³ 1265⁵ 3025⁴

7 **MUTLEY,** b g Rakaposhi King - Ferdee Free
by Netherkelly (N J Hawke) 103 186² 284³ 334³
446⁶ 582 3986⁷ 4183

10 **MUTUAL AGREEMENT,** ch m Quayside - Giolla's Bone by Pitpan (P F Nicholls) 455

6 **MUTUAL DECISION(IRE),** b m Supreme Leader
- Caddy Girl by Avocat (P F Graffin) 159 350³

9 **MUTUAL MEMORIES,** b g Relkino - Mind-
blowing by Pongee (S R Andrews) 376 4122³

13 **MUTUAL TRUST,** ch g Pollerton - Giolla's
Bone by Pitpan (P Bowen) 57 811⁴ 1086 1323

6 **MUZRAK(CAN),** ch g Forty Niner (USA) -
Linda North (USA) by Northern Dancer (M
D Hammond) 73² 4007⁴ 4132²

15 **MWEENISH,** b g Callernish - No Trix by No
Argument (P R Webber) 1974 2268

4 **MY BEAUTIFUL DREAM,** gr f Kalaglow - Cinderella Derek by Hittite Glory (A D Smith)
481⁵ 788

5 **MY BLACKBIRD(IRE),** br m Mandalus - Cherry
Park (D L Bolger) 199⁵ 2079⁷

8 **NADJATI(USA),** ch g Assert - Nayidiya by Riverman (USA) (D R Gandolfo) 48 106¹ 3740⁶ 4128⁵

5 **NAFERTITI(IRE),** b m Bob Back (USA) - Bold Lyndsey (J W Mullins) 1943

6 **NAGARA SOUND,** b f Lochnager - Safe 'N' Sound by Good Investment (USA) (B Preece) 976 2279 2432⁷ 2602⁶ 2973 3728

4 **NAGILLAH(IRE),** gr f Bob Back (USA) - Evil Edna (Michael Flynn) 1459

8 **NAGLE RICE(IRE),** b f Lancastrian - Raplist (William Cronin) 65 212 410

9 **NAGOBELIA,** b or br g Enchantment - Lost Valley by Perdu (J Pearce) 1402⁹ 1567 1848⁷ 2676² 2957³ 3163⁷ 3469⁴ 4153

7 **NAHLA,** b m Wassl - Bassita by Bustino (B de Haan) 3731³ 3915² 4019² 4177⁵

5 **NAHRANAH(IRE),** b m Brush Aside - Quaint Irene (T A Kent) 407 464

6 **NAHRAWALI(IRE),** b g Kahyasi - Nashkara by Shirley Heights (A Moore) 673¹ 1415¹

6 **NAHRI(USA),** ch g Riverman (USA) - Welden (USA) by Danzig (USA) (J Mackie) 1056² 1441¹

8 **NAHTHEN LAD(IRE),** b g Good Thyne (USA) - Current Call by Electrify (Mrs J Pitman) 1945⁶ 2209 2696² 3152 3605⁹

9 **NAIYSARI(IRE),** gr g Mouktar - Naiymat by Troy (P M Rich) 61⁴ 1138⁴ 1267³ 1627² 1889¹

5 **NAKED FEELINGS,** b g Feelings (FR) - Meg's Mantle by New Brig (Martin Todhunter) 879⁷ 1047

9 **NAKIR(FR),** b g Nikos - Nabita (FR) by Akarad (FR) (D Nicholson) 1210⁵ 1640²

8 **NAKURU(IRE),** b m Mandalus - Frivolity by Varano (P A Fahy) 258³ 288

4 **NAME OF OUR FATHER(USA),** b g Northern Baby (CAN) - Ten Hail Marys (USA) by Halo (USA) (P Bowen) 1922¹ 2454³ 2628⁶ 3623² 3747² 3946 4139² 4274¹

13 **NAMELOC,** ch g Deep Run - Kitty Cullen by Pollerton (J E Kiely) 944⁸

4 **NAMOODAJ,** b g Polish Precedent (USA) - Leipzig by Relkino (D Nicholson) 2230⁶ 2463⁸

7 **NAN'S PET(IRE),** b f Mister Lord (USA) - Flashing Gaze (Joseph Sheahan) 2519 3223⁹ 3834⁶ 4059

7 **NANCYS CHOICE,** b g Pitpan - Hope Of Oak by Leander (Mrs N Hope) 2357⁶ 2617⁴

6 **NANDURA,** b m Nordico (USA) - The Ranee by Royal Palace (Miss A E Embiricos) 69⁵ 146

6 **NANGEO BRAE(IRE),** br m Touch Boy - Xiara by Callernish (J L Eyre) 2975

5 **NANJIZAL,** b g Right Regent - Kaltezza Cross by Altezza (K S Bridgwater) 671 942 1181⁶ 1977⁷ 2744 3357⁷

7 **NANNAKA(USA),** b or br m Exceller (USA) - Najidiya (USA) by Riverman (USA) (P Mullins) 200² 235

4 **NANTGARW,** b f Teamster - Dikay (IRE) by Anita's Prince (D Burchell) 1599

7 **NAPOLEON'S GOLD(IRE),** ch g Over The River (FR) - Falcade by Falcon (A G Foster) 2391⁹ 3000 3326³ 4275

4 **NARROW FOCUS(USA),** b or br c Deputy Minister (CAN) - Starushka (USA) by Sham (USA) (Mervyn Torrens) 1173² 1430 1616⁷

7 **NASAYER(IRE),** b g Asir - Tourney's Girl by Yankee Gold (N B Mason) 2852⁶ 3011³ 3353⁸

4 **NASCIMENTO(USA),** b g Green Dancer (USA) - Miss Pele (USA) (Francis Berry) 2067 2230 2337 2470 4004

9 **NASHAAT(USA),** b g El Gran Senor (USA) - Absentia (USA) by Raise A Cup (USA) (K R Burke) 689³ 775² 1047³ 1248⁴ 1397⁷ 1800⁵ 4092 4242⁵

4 **NASHALONG(IRE),** ch g Nashamaa - Rousalong (J J Quinn) 882

6 **NASHVILLE STAR(USA),** ch g Star de Naskra (USA) - Mary Davies by Tyrnavos (R Mathew) 1465⁴ 1761 1982⁵ 2290⁴ 2329 2548¹ 2783⁹ 3424⁶ 3635⁶ 3703⁹ 3886³ 4017⁴ 4313³

6 **NASONE(IRE),** b g Nearly A Nose (USA) - Skateaway by Condorcet (FR) (J T Gifford) 1641⁴ 1849² 2277⁵ 3129 3709

11 **NATALIES FANCY,** b m The Parson - My Puttens by David Jack (James Joseph Mangan) 131³ 214¹ 433⁴

12 **NATHAN BLAKE,** gr g Sexton Blake - Nana by Forlorn River (W G M Turner) 844²

11 **NATIONAL CHOICE,** b g National Trust - Wrong Choice by Royal Smoke (K C Bailey) 568³

4 **NATIONAL FIASCO,** b g Pragmatic - Lady Barunbe by Deep Run (C L Popham) 3561 3898⁸

7 **NATIONAL FLAG(FR),** b g Sure Blade (USA) - On The Staff (USA) by Master Willie (K R Burke) 1425 1557³ 1846⁷ 2610

7 **NATIVE BABY(IRE),** b m Be My Native (USA) - Broadway Baby by Some Hand (W P Mullins) 68² 180² 253¹ 365³ 430³ 487² 637⁴ 733⁶

12 **NATIVE BLOOD VI,** b h Le Moss - Native Fashion by Zulu (W T Murphy) 1081

12 **NATIVE BORN,** b g Be My Native (USA) - Earth Mother by Baragoi (Liam McAteer) 92³ 195 234⁴

5 **NATIVE CAILIN(IRE),** ch m Be My Native (USA) - Chance Match (R B Smyth) 1579

8 **NATIVE CHAMPION(IRE),** ch g Be My Native (USA) - Dedham Vale by Dike (USA) (Lawrence Walshe) 1436 1554 1715 2089 2644

4 **NATIVE ECLIPSE(IRE),** br g Be My Native (USA) - Duessa by Linacre (A P O'Brien) 2067 2112² 2161² 2337 2702⁷ 2943⁶ 3216 3606²

5 **NATIVE ESTATES(IRE),** b g Be My Native (USA) - Sesetta by Lucky Brief (Noel Meade) 2137³ 3524²

7 **NATIVE FLECK(IRE),** b g Be My Native (USA) - Rare Find by Rarity (Michael Kiernan) 2271 2585 3547³ 3754

5 **NATIVE FLING(IRE),** b g Be My Native (USA) - Queens Romance by Imperial Fling (USA) (Peter McCreery) 951¹ 1275 2049⁹ 2168⁶ 2368³ 3705⁵ 3935b⁵

5 **NATIVE GALE(IRE),** br m Be My Native (USA) - Real Decent by Strong Gale (Patrick O'Leary) 732² 1407⁷ 1752⁸ 2753

10 **NATIVE MISSION,** ch g Be My Native (USA) - Sister Ida by Bustino (J G FitzGerald) 1993³ 2335² 2555³

5 **NATIVE PLAYER(IRE),** b g Be My Native (USA) - Kilbricken Bay by Salluceva (A P O'Brien) 782⁴ 1019¹ 4006⁴ 4195¹

7 **NATIVE RAMBLER(IRE),** ch g Le Bavard (FR) - Native Shot by Random Shot (Mrs A Price) 1009⁴ 2551

5 **NATIVE SHORE(IRE),** b m Be My Native (USA) - Castle Stream by Paddy's Stream (Martin Brassil) 884³ 1121³ 3090⁸ 3456⁷ 3647²

7 **NATIVE STATUS(IRE),** b g Be My Native (USA) - Run Wardasha by Run The Gantlet (USA) (Thomas Carberry) 1089⁴ 1461² 1895⁵ 2840² 3088

6 **NATIVE SUCCESS(IRE),** gr f Be My Native (USA) - Run Wardasha (Lawrence Walshe) 463 741

4 **NATIVE TANGO(IRE),** b f Be My Native (USA) - Rathshade (John Queally) 3707⁴

10 **NEW CHARGES,** b g Shernazar - Wise Blood by Kalamoun (P Beaumont) 2574⁶ 2710 3162⁸ 3761

9 **NEW CO(IRE),** ch g Deep Run - True Minstrel by Prince Hansel (M F Morris) 826³ 1172² 1653 1896¹ 2071¹ 2273² 2707³ 3134 3605

12 **NEW GHOST,** ch g New Member - St Mary Axe by Metropolis (G W Giddings) 3365 3790

6 **NEW INN,** b g Petoski - Pitroyal by Pitskelly (S Gollings) 1740⁶ 1885¹ 2004² 2149³ 2331² 2717⁴

5 **NEW LEAF(IRE),** b g Brush Aside (USA) - Page Of Gold by Goldhill (D R Gandolfo) 1350⁸ 2283² 2595⁶ 3401¹

7 **NEW LEGISLATION(IRE),** ch m Dominion Royale - Valary by Roman Warrior (M Halford) 159⁵ 169⁸ 424⁴ 494³ 601² 644¹ 948¹ 1040¹

4 **NEW REGIME(IRE),** b f Glenstal (USA) - Gay Refrain by Furry Glen (P T Dalton) 3099 3673

5 **NEW ROSS(IRE),** gr g Roselier (FR) - Miss Lucille by Fine Blade (USA) (O O'Neill) 3825 3957⁵ 4136

5 **NEW STOCK(IRE),** b f Bustomi - Worling-Pearl (T J Canavan) 3456

6 **NEW TRIBE(IRE),** b g Commanche Run - Red Partridge by Solinus (I R Ferguson) 947⁵ 1168⁶

7 **NEW WEST(IRE),** b g King Persian - Red Rust by Rusticaro (FR) (Eamon O'Connell) 142⁹ 192⁶ 276³ 805⁴ 951⁷ 3642 3891⁸ 4302

5 **NEWBERRY ROSE(IRE),** b or br m Black Minstrel - Bellusis by Belfalas (Eugene M O'Sullivan) 2414 2942⁸ 3233 3625² 3705² 4059⁵ 4147⁷

6 **NEWBOG LAD(IRE),** br g Phardante (FR) - Financial Burden (James M O'Connor) 444⁸ 686

4 **NEWGATE PIXIE(IRE),** b or br f Accordion - Newgate Fairy by Flair Path (B A McMahon) 2961

9 **NEWHALL PRINCE,** b g Prince Ragusa - Doyles Folly by Rheingold (A Streeter) 737³ 972 1175³ 1248³ 1525⁴ 1873² 2857³ 3479³ 3729⁹

11 **NEWLANDS-GENERAL,** ch g Oats - Spartiquick by Spartan General (P F Nicholls) 972⁴ 1052² 1267² 1428¹ 1672⁴ 2247 2294¹ 2947³ 3173 3517 3688²

7 **NEWPARK KATE(IRE),** b f Bustomi - New Park Girl (Michael Mellett) 1901⁸

5 **NEWS FLASH(IRE),** b g Strong Gale - Gale Flash by News Item (Andrew Turnell) 2920⁷

6 **NEWS FROM AFAR,** b g Ardross - My Purple Prose by Rymer (Mrs S D Williams) 1566⁴

12 **NEWSKI EXPRESS,** bl m Newski (USA) - Mint Express by Pony Express (John Lister) 4033

5 **NEWSKI LASS,** ch m Newski (USA) - Vitapep by Vital Season (P Wegmann) 2723

8 **NEWTON POINT,** b g Blakeney - Assertive (USA) by Assert (D Nicholson) 1032⁴

6 **NEWTOWN ROAD(IRE),** ch g Erin's Hope - Newtown Princess (S J Mahon) 3088⁶ 3454 3645

8 **NEWTOWN ROSIE(IRE),** gr m Roselier (FR) - Sicilian Princess by Sicilian Prince (Miss A E Embiricos) 807⁴ 1473⁴ 1611

5 **NEWTOWN STAR(IRE),** b f Denel (FR) - Pitsbox by Pitskelly (Thomas Carberry) 4169

4 **NEXSIS STAR,** ch g Absalom - The High Dancer by High Line (Mrs S J Smith) 1629 1909⁹ 2256³ 2417 2758⁸

5 **NIANTIC BAY(IRE),** b g Cataldi - Hansel's Queen (J G Groome) 2022 2737 3697⁹ 3818

5 **NIBALDA(IRE),** gr g Kambalda - Barrow Beg (Paul Nolan) 4197

6 **NICANJON,** ch g Nicholas Bill - Rosalina by Porto Bello (R Dickin) 1675 3388⁹ 4013 4136⁸

8 **NICHOLAS PLANT,** ch g Nicholas Bill - Bustilly by Busted (J S Goldie) 725⁵ 963¹ 1166³ 1388³ 1661⁵ 2151⁵ 2321 2573¹ 2622² 2846² 3056² 3702² 3760² 4000¹ 4100³

5 **NICHOLLS CROSS(IRE),** b g Mandalus - Milan Pride (Kevin O'Donnell) 3525⁴

5 **NICK DUNDEE(IRE),** b g Supreme Leader - Silent Run by Deep Run (E J O'Grady) 1247¹

5 **NICK OF TIME VI(IRE),** b g Reputedly By Eve's Err - Mags Daisy (Joseph Smith) 1756

6 **NICK ROSS,** b g Ardross - Nicolini by Nicholas Bill (R Brewis) 1280³ 1657³ 2917⁸ 3351 3598² 3704³

8 **NICK THE BEAK(IRE),** ch g Duky - Rainy Weather by Menelek (John R Upson) 1048⁶ 1558¹ 1744³ 2289¹ 2598⁹ 2801⁷ 3557

6 **NICK THE BILL,** b g Nicholas Bill - Another Treat by Derring-Do (J Wade) 1122⁹ 1257⁹

6 **NICK THE BISCUIT,** b g Nicholas Bill - Maryland Cookie (USA) by Bold Hour (J Rudge) 111 186

12 **NICK THE DREAMER,** ch g Nicholas Bill - Dream Of Fortune by Barbary Pirate (W G M Turner) 514⁷ 840⁵ 938 1086 1526⁴ 3405 3628⁴ 3774⁶ 4035

6 **NICKELLI(IRE),** b f Jolly Jake (NZ) - Reelin Surprise (J A Berry) 1195 1539 1617⁹

11 **NICKLE JOE,** ro g Plugged Nickle (USA) - Travois (USA) by Navajo (USA) (M Tate) 1624⁵ 1926⁷ 3689⁷ 3987 4140⁷ 4318

10 **NICKLUP,** ch m Netherkelly - Voolin by Jimmy Reppin (Capt T A Forster) 1366 1544²

7 **NICKY WILDE,** br g Strong Gale - Dark Trix by Peacock (FR) (C P E Brooks) 2371 2607³ 3736

5 **NICKYS PERIL,** ch m Nicholas Bill - Priceless Peril by Silly Prices (J S Haldane) 3356 3667⁸

8 **NICOLA MARIE(IRE),** ch f Cardinal Flower - China Dear (Ms M Flynn) 340⁸ 681¹ 773⁴ 1485⁹ 3177⁴ 3336⁶ 3575⁷ 3767⁶

5 **NIFAAF(USA),** b m Silver Hawk (USA) - Betty Money (USA) by Our Native (USA) (K A Morgan) 1050² 1968²

5 **NIGEL'S BOY,** b g Bold Fort - Furnace Lass Vii by Damsire Unregistered (D M Lloyd) 1306⁶

5 **NIGEL'S LAD(IRE),** b g Dominion Royale - Back To Earth (FR) by Vayrann (P C Haslam) 2711² 2849¹ 2937¹ 3562⁵ 4125¹

5 **NIGELS CHOICE,** gr g Teenoso (USA) - Warm Winter by Kalaglow (C J Hill) 1354

6 **NIGHT BOAT,** b g Night Shift (USA) - Billante (USA) by Graustark (W Clay) 45⁹ 806⁷ 1136² 1943⁹ 2515 3276² 3317¹ 3528⁴ 3927

6 **NIGHT CITY,** b g Kris - Night Secret by Nijinsky (CAN) (Lady Herries) 1716⁴ 1976⁵

5 **NIGHT DANCE,** ch h Weldnaas (USA) - Shift Over (USA) by Night Shift (USA) (K A Morgan) 1805⁴ 2256¹ 2580⁵

5 **NIGHT ESCAPADE(IRE),** b m Be My Native (USA) - Right Dark by Buckskin (FR) (C Weedon) 880⁴ 1514⁸ 2503 3482⁷ 4301⁵

9 **NIGHT FANCY,** ch g Night Shift (USA) - Smooth Siren (USA) by Sea Bird II (Mrs A M Woodrow) 1939⁷ 2604 2860⁴ 3138³ 3470⁴ 3611

5 **NIGHT FLARE(FR),** ch g Night Shift (USA) - Gold Flair by Tap On Wood (S Woodman) 1515 1716 2426⁶

6 **NIGHT IN A MILLION,** br g Night Shift (USA) - Ridalia by Ridan (USA) (S Woodman) 820⁴ 1111⁵ 1230⁵ 2479⁴ 2982⁷ 3119⁴ 3494¹ 3633³ 3876²

5 **NIGHT THYNE(IRE),** b g Good Thyne (USA) - Night Blade by Fine Blade (USA) (M J Roberts) 989 1703

5 **NOBLE GESTURE(IRE),** b g Welsh Term - Heirloom (Noel Meade) 2449 3349 3520

5 **NOBLE IRIS(IRE),** ch m The Noble Player (USA) - Sweet Glenbeigh (Michael Hourigan) 1060 1490

5 **NOBLE JEWEL(IRE),** b m Tremblant - Noble Flash (David J McGrath) 898 1246[6]

4 **NOBLE LORD,** ch g Lord Bud - Chasers' Bar by Oats (R H Buckler) 584[1] 634[1] 1422[1] 1530[2] 2324[2] 2553[3] 3442[4] 3566[9] 4225[2]

8 **NOBLE MONARCH(IRE),** br g Strong Gale - Perusia by Pirate King (J Howard Johnson) 1198[7] 1333[7] 1677[9]

6 **NOBLE NORMAN,** b g Grey Desire - Pokey's Pet by Uncle Pokey (Mrs A Swinbank) 4224[6]

6 **NOBLE SHOON(IRE),** b g Lord Americo - Dancing Shoon by Green Shoon (Michael Flynn) 685 883[2] 1018[4] 1145[2] 1649 2222[5] 2378 4167

9 **NOBLE SOCIETY,** b g Law Society (USA) - Be Noble by Vaguely Noble (K G Wingrove) 243 3592[7]

7 **NOBLE THYNE(IRE),** b g Good Thyne (USA) - Tina O'Flynn by Martinmas (P Mullins) 1404[1] 1651[3] 2082[1] 4167[1]

5 **NOBLE TOM(IRE),** b g The Noble Player (USA) - Hospitality by Homing (R Collins) 2262[2] 2469 3048[9] 4113[4]

8 **NOBLE TUNE(IRE),** b g Aristocracy - Melody All The Way (E Sheehy) 1715 2413 2520 3178 3608 3697 3817[2] 4162[4]

10 **NOBLY(USA),** b g Lyphard (USA) - Nonoalca (USA) by Nonoalco (USA) (R H Alner) 110[1] 167[3] 240[1] 296[2] 335[2] 386[2] 437[1] 500[2] 617[1] 651

4 **NOBLESSE OBLIGE,** b g Salse (USA) - Fair Rosamunda by Try My Best (USA) (K C Bailey) 2611 2893

9 **NOBODYS FLAME(IRE),** br g Dalsaan - Hamers Flame by Green Shoon (S I Pittendrigh) 1678 3124[8] 3584[9] 3865[4] 4009

11 **NOBODYS SON,** gr g Nobody Knows - Fine Performance by Gala Performance (USA) (Daniel O'Connell) 219[1] 252[2] 293 338 409[3] 429[4] 553

6 **NOBODYWANTSME(IRE),** b g Pennine Walk - Sachi by Kings Lake (USA) (E J Creighton) 112[6] 170 276 468[6] 741 3943[2] 4152[4] 4292[4]

7 **NOBULL(IRE),** b m Torus - Hansel's Queen by Prince Hansel (J G Groome) 2903 3073 4004 4105[5]

8 **NOCATCHIM,** b g Shardari - Solar by Hotfoot (K A Morgan) 45[1] 127[1] 202[1] 282[7] 386[3] 663[3]

7 **NODDADANTE(IRE),** b g Phardante (FR) - Loughcopple by Over The River (FR) (N R Mitchell) 1115[7] 1543 2479[8] 2977[1] 3190 3546[5]

10 **NODFORM WONDER,** b g Cut Above - Wonder by Tekoah (R J Bevis) 3727[1] 4142[1]

8 **NOELEENS DELIGHT(IRE),** ch m Le Bavard (FR) - Graham Dieu by Three Dons (Michael Cunningham) 395[2] 536[3] 622[1] 732

7 **NOELS DANCER(IRE),** ch g Nordance (USA) - Royal Desire by Royal Match (Michael Cunningham) 1435 2379[5] 2646 2868 3074[9] 3229

4 **NOIR ESPRIT,** br g Prince Daniel (USA) - Danse D'Esprit by Lidhame (J M Carr) 1524 1690[3] 2061[3] 2417[7] 2807[6] 3002[2] 3673[8] 3819 4023[2]

5 **NOISY MINER(IRE),** b g Kambalda - Furry Lady by Furry Glen (D Nicholson) 2784[1] 3302[1]

11 **NOISY WELCOME,** b g The Parson - Lady Pitpan by Pitpan (M P Jones) 2875

5 **NOMINEE(IRE),** br m Magical Strike (USA) - Royal Rumpus by Prince Tenderfoot (USA) (F Dunne) 3083 3547 3606[3] 4293[3]

6 **NON NON JOESEPHINE,** b m Dunbeath (USA) - Go Lightly by Galivanter (Miss Z A Green) 3807

6 **NON VINTAGE(IRE),** ch g Shy Groom (USA) - Great Alexandra by Runnett (M C Chapman) 80[4] 777[1] 1186[4] 1288[4] 1508 1633 1772[6] 1885[6] 2001[5] 2329 2530[7] 2760[1] 3131

7 **NONE STIRRED(IRE),** b g Supreme Leader - Double Wrapped by Double-U-Jay (J T Gifford) 1592[3] 2267[1]

6 **NONIOS(IRE),** b g Nashamaa - Bosquet by Queen's Hussar (G M Moore) 762[2] 864[2] 962[2] 1167[4] 1588[4] 1911[6] 3780 4023[5]

6 **NOORAN,** b g Risk Me (FR) - Susie Hall by Gold Rod (A C Whillans) 1167[6] 1337[9] 2345[2] 2714[3] 3030 3354[4] 3781[3]

7 **NOOSA SOUND(IRE),** br g Orchestra - Borecca by Boreen (FR) (L Lungo) 1825[5] 2347[2] 2620 2912

10 **NOQUITA(NZ),** ch g Nassipour (USA) - Memphis (AUS) by Boldest Melody (USA) (J C McConnochie) 1623 1940 1384[9] 3736 3892 4242[8]

8 **NORA'S ERROR(IRE),** ch g His Turn - Winning Nora by Northfields (USA) (Desmond McDonogh) 4293[7]

6 **NORD LYS(IRE),** b g Nordico (USA) - Beach Light by Bustino (B J Llewellyn) 398[1] 2424[7] 2663[9] 3317[2]

4 **NORD VENTE(IRE),** b f Distinctly North (USA) - Nelly Gail by Mount Hagen (FR) (A P O'Brien) 882 1173

6 **NORDANCE PRINCE(IRE),** b g Nordance (USA) - Shirleys Princess by Sandhurst Prince (Miss Venetia Williams) 1452[3] 1641[3] 2197[5] 2405[5] 3022[3] 3296[4] 3892[1] 4092[1] 4201[2]

8 **NORDANSK,** ch g Nordance (USA) - Free On Board by Free State (M Madgwick) 968[6] 1232

6 **NORDIC AIR(IRE),** b g Nordico (USA) - Phamond by Pharly (FR) (Thomas O'Neill) 169[6] 4198[6]

5 **NORDIC BREEZE(IRE),** b or br g Nordico (USA) - Baby Clair by Gulf Pearl (M C Pipe) 806[1] 1082[3] 1224[2] 2180 3111[3] 3562[7] 3907 4172[1] 4255[1]

6 **NORDIC CROWN(IRE),** b m Nordico (USA) - Fit The Halo by Dance In Time (CAN) (M C Pipe) 163[4] 225[5] 445[2] 903[2] 998[3]

9 **NORDIC FLIGHT,** b or br g Julio Mariner - Last Flight by Saucy Kit (R J Eckley) 1980[7] 2152 2403[7] 2862[8] 3000 3190

4 **NORDIC HERO(IRE),** b g Nordico (USA) - Postscript by Final Straw (A P Jarvis) 1024 1438 1992

6 **NORDIC PRINCE(IRE),** b g Nordance (USA) - Royal Desire by Royal Match (T P Tate) 2192[7] 2419[3]

7 **NORDIC QUEEN(IRE),** b m Nordico (USA) - Company Royale by King's Company (Donal Hassett) 66[4] 353

10 **NORDIC RACE,** b h Nordico (USA) - Lady Dulcinea (ARG) by General (FR) (John Roche) 87[5] 405

8 **NORDIC SENSATION(IRE),** b g Nordico (USA) - Royal Sensation by Prince Regent (FR) (Peadar Matthews) 2379 2841 3089[4] 3227[1] 4004[2] 4150[3]

5 **NORDIC SPREE(IRE),** b g Nordico (USA) - Moonsilk by Solinus (G L Moore) 1423[2] 2392[7] 2738 3196[5] 3414[3] 3771[3] 3872[2] 4065[1] 4203

9 **NORDIC SUN(IRE),** gr g Nordico (USA) - Cielsoleil (USA) by Conquistador Cielo (USA) (Mrs J Brown) 165[1] 249[7] 4258[5]

7 **NORDIC THORN(IRE),** b g Nordico (USA) - Rosemore by Ashmore (FR) (Martin Brassil) 65[1] 125[2] 312[4] 429[2] 730 1059[1] 1389[2]

6 **NORDIC VALLEY(IRE),** b g Nordico (USA) - Malia by Malacate (USA) (M C Pipe) 127[4] 190[3] 325[2] 366[2] 630[1] 771[1] 1352 1686[5] 1857 2154[2] 2431[3] 2877[8] 3118[4] 3742[2] 3958[1] 4070[3] 4288[2]

8 **NOT MY LINE(IRE)**, gr g Entre Nous - Uno Navarro by Raga Navarro (ITY) (Andy Morgan) 2531 2608[4] 3102[6] 3458[1] 3671[4] 3851[5] 4064[1] 4260[4]

5 **NOT SO PRIM**, b m Primitive Rising (USA) - Sobriquet by Roan Rocket (Mrs E Clark) 1128[6]

7 **NOT TO PANIC(IRE)**, ch m Torus - Quantas by Roan Rocket (K R Burke) 1205[5] 1716 1928[8] 2359[7] 3137[4]

8 **NOTABLE EXCEPTION**, b g Top Ville - Shorthouse by Habitat (Mrs M Reveley) 201[1] 764[1] 913[2] 1127[1] 1282[3]

11 **NOTARY-NOWELL**, b g Deep Run - Hamers Flame by Green Shoon (Mrs Richard Pilkington) 3848[4]

6 **NOTCOMPLAININGBUT(IRE)**, b m Supreme Leader - Dorcetta by Condorcet (FR) (P Mullins) 1172[3] 1900[6] 2128 2232[6] 2473[6] 2584[4]

9 **NOTED STRAIN(IRE)**, b g Gorytus (USA) - Almuadiyeh by Thatching (D F Bassett) 317[5] 4267[8]

8 **NOTHING DOING(IRE)**, b g Sarab - Spoons by Orchestra (W J Musson) 1477[7]

6 **NOTHING TO IT**, b g Lyphento (USA) - Corniche Rose by Punchinello (C P Morlock) 2939[8]

8 **NOTHING VENTURED**, b g Sonnen Gold - Dream Venture by Giolla Mear (Countess Goess-Saurau) 4142[2]

7 **NOTHINGTODOWITHME**, ch g Relkino - Lasses Nightshade by Deadly Nightshade (Capt T A Forster) 1272[3] 1546[5] 1798[5]

6 **NOTTOBADOKAY(IRE)**, b g Meneval (USA) - Plumelko (David Wachman) 3880

9 **NOVA CHAMP**, ch g Nearly A Hand - Laval by Cheval (Mrs S J Smith) 3914[1] 4046[5]

9 **NOVA RUN**, ch g Ra Nova - Sound Run by Deep Run (N J Henderson) 1351[1]

9 **NOVELLO ALLEGRO(USA)**, b g Sir Ivor - Tants by Vitiges (FR) (Noel Meade) 1538 1711

9 **NOW WE KNOW(IRE)**, ch g Denel (FR) - Struell Course by Green Shoon (M Sheppard) 1055[3]

8 **NOW YOUNG MAN(IRE)**, br g Callernish - Claddagh Pride by Bargello (Mrs A Swinbank) 3603[1] 3713[4] 4257[6]

9 **NOWHISKI**, b g Petoski - Be Faithful by Val de Loir (Tim Tarratt) 2995[2]

7 **NOYAN**, ch g Northern Baby (CAN) - Istiska (FR) by Irish River (FR) (R A Fahey) 1788[1] 2062 2201[1] 2597[2] 2808[1] 3134[4] 3765[1]

12 **NUAFFE**, b g Abednego - Miss Magello by Bargello (P A Fahy) 1079[8] 1243[8] 1434 2018[8] 2071 2273 2707[1] 2867 3605 3783

7 **NUAN(IRE)**, m Teofane - Rosenti (P M Lynch) 183 211

10 **NUCLEAR EXPRESS**, b g Martinmas - Halka by Daring March (J M Bradley) 2964 3603 4804

5 **NUKUD(USA)**, b g Topsider (USA) - Summer Silence (USA) by Stop The Music (USA) (G R Oldroyd) 806 1295[9] 1438

9 **NUNS CONE**, ch g Celtic Cone - Nunswalk by The Parson (R E Peacock) 1671 2789 3027

6 **NUNS LUCY**, ch m Toirdealbhach - Nuns Royal by Royal Boxer (F Jordan) 1474 1683 2371 3137 3594 3960

8 **NUNSON**, ch g Celtic Cone - Nunswalk by The Parson (R Dickin) 879 1591[4] 1729 2025 2176

4 **NUOVO STYLE(IRE)**, br f Be My Native (USA) - Santa Anita Jet (T J Nagle) 4147

7 **NUTTY SOLERA**, ch g Henbit (USA) - Friendly Cherry by Bargello (C Parker) 68[1] 1682[4] 1935[3] 2066[2] 2117[3] 2490[6] 2849[6] 3400

6 **NUZUM ROAD MAKERS(IRE)**, b g Lafontaine - Dark Gold (Michael Cunningham) 2131[8] 2443[8]

4 **NYMPH IN THE SKI(IRE)**, br f Scenic - Al Mansoura (USA) (William J Fitzpatrick) 620[6] 1750[9]

7 **O K KEALY**, gr g Absalom - Constanza by Sun Prince (M C Chapman) 2758

6 **O MY LOVE**, b m Idiot's Delight - Real Beauty by Kinglet (Miss H C Knight) 1594[7] 1961[5] 2267[6] 2603[4] 3528[6]

9 **O'SULLIVANS CHOISE(IRE)**, br g Sir Mordred - Kalypso (Michael J McDonagh) 464

5 **OAKBURY(IRE)**, ch g Common Grounds - Doon Belle by Ardoon (Miss L C Siddall) 73[6] 1261[4] 1604 1869[3] 2485[3] 2630[2] 2804[8] 3042[3] 3246 3530

7 **OAKDALE GIRL(IRE)**, ch f Lancastrian - Three Ladies (Augustine Leahy) 1241 1484[6]

6 **OAKLAND BRIDGE(IRE)**, ch g Digamist (USA) - Flo Kelly by Florescence (P Delaney) 2907[8] 3381[7] 3935d

8 **OAKLANDS BILLY**, b g Silly Prices - Fishermans Lass by Articulate (Mrs M Reveley) 3007 3259[6]

7 **OAKLER(IRE)**, b or br g Kings Lake (USA) - Melka by Relko (A P O'Brien) 828[6] 897[4]

8 **OAKLEY**, ch g Nicholas Bill - Scrub Oak by Burglar (Denys Smith) 2633

4 **OAKMONT(IRE)**, b c Pennine Walk - Heartland by Northfields (USA) (David A Kiely) 4246

6 **OAKS PRIDE(USA)**, ch g Afleet (CAN) - Field Point Road (USA) by Raja Baba (USA) (H de Bromhead) 1359 2160

9 **OAT COUTURE**, b g Oats - Marjoemin by Import (L Lungo) 1627[1] 2003 2348[4] 2574[1] 2789[8] 3059[2]

9 **OATIS REGRETS**, b g Oats - Joscilla by Joshua (Miss H C Knight) 1212[4] 1960[3]

7 **OATIS ROSE**, b m Oats - Constant Rose by Confusion (M Sheppard) 1454[3] 1576 1766[4] 1921[6] 2246[7] 2691[1] 2923[2] 3557[3] 3637[5] 3926[8]

8 **OATS N BARLEY**, b g Oats - Doon Silver by Doon (P R Rodford) 1994 2268 2441 3037

7 **OBAN**, ch g Scottish Reel - Sun Goddess (FR) by Deep Roots (Miss H C Knight) 1424[1] 1991[1] 2794[2]

15 **OBSIDIAN**, ch h Bustino - Quita II by Lavandin (Miss K M George) 4050

6 **OBVIOUS RISK**, b g Risk Me (FR) - Gymnopedie by Jaazeiro (USA) (E M Caine) 1656 2346[9] 2533[6] 2572[5] 2847[3] 2913[5] 2983[4] 3158 4008

6 **OCCOLD(IRE)**, b g Over The River (FR) - My Puttens by David Jack (G A Hubbard) 3729[3]

5 **OCEAN HAWK(USA)**, b g Hawkster (USA) - Society Sunrise by Imp Society (USA) (N A Twiston-Davies) 1233[1] 1520[2] 1998[1] 2210[1] 2830[8] 3151

10 **OCEAN LEADER**, b g Lord Ha Ha - Rough Tide by Moss Court (Mrs D Haine) 1706[1] 1994[5] 2258 3000 3481[1]

7 **OCTOBER BREW(USA)**, ch g Seattle Dancer (USA) - Princess Fager (USA) by Dr Fager (M C Pipe) 449[5] 1724[6] 2431[4] 2872 3485[4] 3814 3894[4] 4189[5]

6 **OCTOBER SEVENTH**, b g Derrylin - Cedar Shade (Charles O'Brien) 1096 1463[7] 1895[8] 2343 2443 3178

4 **ODDA'S CHAPEL**, b g Little Wolf - Pity's Pet by Stanford (M Sheppard) 4075[4]

7 **ODELL(IRE)**, br g Torus - Indian Isle by Warpath (K C Bailey) 1647[6] 3474[1]

4 **ODY MORODY(IRE)**, b f Kefaah (USA) - Arthur's Daughter (L Young) 882 1057

12 **ONE FOR THE POT,** ch g Nicholas Bill - Tea-Pot by Ragstone (Mrs A M Naughton) 1389[6] 1678[4] 1821[4] 2191[4] 2622[5]

4 **ONE IN THE EYE,** br c Arrasas (USA) - Mingalles by Prince de Galles (Jamie Poulton) 2265[2]

9 **ONE MAN(IRE),** gr g Remainder Man - Steal On by General Ironside (G Richards) 1187[1] 2045[1] 2327[1] 2507[2] 3152[6] 3563

7 **ONE MORE BILL,** b g Silly Prices - Another Treat by Derring-Do (J Wade) 1123[5] 1255[5]

7 **ONE MORE DIME(IRE),** b m Mandalus - Deep Dollar by Deep Run (J L Needham) 111[4] 1010[3] 1318[3] 2749[4] 3016 3359[3] 3503 3961[1] 4210[3]

6 **ONE MORE MAN(IRE),** b g Remainder Man - Pampered Sally by Paddy's Stream (J T Gifford) 1115 1503[5] 1791

6 **ONE MORE RUPEE,** b g Presidium - Little Token by Shack (USA) (C P Morlock) 1735 2298 2898

4 **ONE MORE SPIN(IRE),** b g Tirol - Manela Lady by Ela-Mana-Mou (E J O'Grady) 2270 3625[1] 4027[8]

4 **ONE STOP,** b f Silly Prices - Allerdale by Chebs Lad (M A Barnes) 2496[2] 2687 3029 3396

6 **ONE WOMAN(IRE),** b f Remainder Man - Violet Glade (M J Byrne) 3888

5 **ONE WORD(IRE),** b g Nordance (USA) - Purple Rain (FR) by Ahoonhora (Reginald Roberts) 2737[6] 3085[1] 3348[3] 3767[3]

7 **ONEDAYATATIME(IRE),** b g Buckskin (FR) - December Run by Deep Run (T Donohue) 562

7 **ONEOFTHECLAN(IRE),** b f Strong Statement (USA) - Telegram Mear (James Devereux) 68[4] 120[7]

5 **ONEOFTHEOLDONES,** b g Deploy - Waveguide by Double Form (J Norton) 1326 1642[9] 1823

8 **ONEOFUS,** b g Lochnager - Mountain Child by Mountain Call (Mrs L Richards) 2266 2657 2741 3195[4] 3845[4]

5 **ONLY A SIOUX,** b g Totem (USA) - Adder Howe by Amboise (J R Turner) 1590 2288 2419 2849[9] 3992[8]

8 **ONLY IF(IRE),** b f Strong Statement (USA) - Rosantus (Miss N Hayes) 88

7 **ONLY ONE(IRE),** ch g Salluceva - Sprightly's Last (J F Brennan) 1042 2844[4] 3888

8 **ONTHELIST(IRE),** br g Strong Gale - Maggies Turn (J F Brennan) 3965[6]

9 **ONTHEROADAGAIN(IRE),** b g Euphemism - Mugsaway by Mugatpura (M J P O'Brien) 732[7] 982 1170[1] 1461[6] 1779[3] 2020[2] 2078[2]

4 **ONYOUROWN(IRE),** b g Treasure Kay - Mursuma by Rarity (J Howard Johnson) 1530[3] 1629 1690[5] 3198 3353

5 **OONAGH'S STAR(IRE),** b g Brush Aside (USA) - Kimstar (P Mullins) 2838[8] 4029[2] 4161[1] 4281[1]

8 **OOZLEM(IRE),** b g Burslem - Fingers by Lord Gayle (USA) (L Montague Hall) 1130

10 **OPAL'S TENSPOT,** b g Royal Boxer - Opal Lady by Averof (J M Bradley) 986[5] 1140[6] 1471[5] 1799[1] 2252 2308[6] 2739[1] 2991 3191

4 **OPEN AFFAIR,** ch f Bold Arrangement - Key To Enchantment by Key To Content (USA) (H Akbary) 1438

4 **OPEN FAIRWAY,** ch g Opening Run (USA) - Golfe by Idiot's Delight (M Dods) 3356[7] 3721

8 **OPEN MARKET(USA),** b g Northern Baby (CAN) - Spiranthes (USA) by Vaguely Noble (D K Weld) 162[3] 252[1] 293

5 **OPERA FAN(IRE),** b g Taufan (USA) - Shannon Lady by Monsanto (K A Morgan) 1964[2] 2204[2] 2581[7]

9 **OPERA HAT(IRE),** b m Strong Gale - Tops O'Crush by Menelek (J R H Fowler) 719[4] 1094[3] 1537[1] 2085[3] 2233[6] 2836[1] 3086[3] 3751[5]

6 **OPERATIC DANCER,** b g Germont - Indian Dancer by Streak (R M McKellar) 2572

7 **OPERETTO(IRE),** b g Orchestra - Love From Judy by Quayside (Mrs Susan Nock) 1217 1379[4] 1592[6] 2603[2] 2896[2] 3913[9]

6 **OPTIMISM REIGNS(IRE),** b g Euphemism - Ellis Town by Camden Town (John J McLoughlin) 464 611[2] 1463[1] 2087[6]

6 **OPTIMISTIC AFFAIR,** b g Derring Rose - Bantel Belle by Lepanto (GER) (A Streeter) 1322[4] 1703[5]

6 **OR ROYAL(FR),** gr g Kendor (FR) - Pomme Royale (FR) by Shergar (M C Pipe) 1577[1] 1748[1] 1996[2] 3112[1] 3155[3]

4 **ORANGE IMP,** ch f Kind Of Hush - Sip Of Orange by Celtic Cone (J G FitzGerald) 4143[3]

7 **ORANGE JUICE(IRE),** b g Orange Reef - Vital Spirit (R V Shaw) 1170[7] 2107[6] 2132[4] 2271 2674 2941 3608[9] 3965 4062

5 **ORANGE LIL(IRE),** ch m Zaffaran (USA) - Espadrille (John A Quinn) 577 805[7] 951[6] 1042[7]

4 **ORANGE ORDER(IRE),** ch g Generous (IRE) - Fleur D'Oranger by Northfields (USA) (J White) 614[6] 819 4223[6]

11 **ORANGE RAGUSA,** ch g Orange Reef - Poncho by Ragusa (S H Shirley-Beavan) 3307[3] 3727[5]

6 **ORCHARD GENERATION,** b m Joligeneration - Miss Orchard by Latest Model (B R Millman) 545[9]

6 **ORCHARD HOPE(IRE),** b f Kambalda - Orchard Lass (Anthony Mullins) 3878

7 **ORCHARD KING,** ch g Rymer - Sprats Hill by Deep Run (O Brennan) 2565 2973 4019[4] 4201[5] 4315[4]

7 **ORCHARD SUNSET(IRE),** ch g Sandalay - Orchard Lass (Anthony Mullins) 4107 6786 826[5] 1193 1433 1842[7]

6 **ORCHESTRAL DESIGNS(IRE),** b g Fappiano (USA) - Elegance In Design by Habitat (R Harris) 100 153 4251

9 **ORCHESTRAL SUITE(IRE),** br g Orchestra - Sweetly Stung by Master Rocky (Miss Jennifer Pidgeon) 2531[1] 3102[1] 3567

6 **ORCHESTRAL WIND(IRE),** b f Orchestra - Angelas Gem (Peter Casey) 2845

5 **ORCHID HOUSE,** b m Town And Country - Tudor Orchid by Tudor Rhythm (N R Mitchell) 2614 2871 3022 3513[7]

8 **ORDOG MOR(IRE),** ch g Boreen (FR) - Minorette by Miralgo (M G Meagher) 46[2] 145[2] 203[1] 295[1] 519[1] 707[2] 779[3] 3001[7] 3244

13 **ORIENT ROVER,** b g Callernish - Oriental Infanta (John Daly) 93

6 **ORIENTAL BEAUTY(IRE),** b f Executive Perk - Sigginstown (John P Berry) 4005[6]

5 **ORIENTAL BOY(IRE),** b g Boreen (FR) - Arctic Sue by Arctic Slave (R Lee) 2409 2899

7 **ORIENTAL PEARL(IRE),** ch f Remainder Man - Gem Princess (Augustine Leahy) 978 1838

6 **ORINOCO VENTURE(IRE),** br g Doyoun - Push A Button by Bold Lad (IRE) (A Bailey) 539 638[8] 3722 3992[7] 4179

5 **ORMOND JENNY(IRE),** ch m Pennine Walk - Anner Princess by Prince Tenderfoot (USA) (A Seymour) 2270[5] 2645 2900 3705

6 **ORPHAN SPA(IRE),** ch g Phardante (FR) - Knockdrumagh (G M McCourt) 3955[4]

8 **ORSWELL LAD,** b g Pragmatic - Craftsmans Made by Jimsun (P J Hobbs) 1451[1] 1726[4] 2247[1] 2600 3145[1]

6 **PASJA(IRE),** b m Posen (USA) - Camogie by Celtic Ash (S Gollings) 70²

10 **PASSED PAWN,** b g Blakeney - Miss Millicent by Milesian (M C Pipe) 515⁵ 2435 2762

10 **PASSER-BY,** b g Lomond (USA) - Inisfree (USA) by Hoist The Flag (USA) (Peter McCreery) 235⁷ 344⁶ 426⁴ 471³ 623² 982 1092

9 **PAST MASTER(USA),** b g Chief's Crown (USA) - Passing Look (USA) by Buckpasser (S Gollings) 1047 1186 1872³ 1955⁵ 2296⁷ 2629⁶ 2855

13 **PASTORAL PRIDE(USA),** b g Exceller (USA) - Pastoral Miss by Northfields (USA) (Miss Polly Curling) 2516 3464

6 **PAT BARRY(IRE),** br f Delamain (USA) - Princess Heronia (John Roche) 3336 4062

6 **PAT BUCKLEY,** b g Buckley - Raheny by Sir Herbert (N A Twiston-Davies) 3735³ 3846⁸

7 **PAT HARTIGAN(IRE),** ch g Orchestra - Oriental Star by Falcon (A L T Moore) 2964¹ 3071²

7 **PAT THE HAT(IRE),** ch g Mr Fordette - Killonan Lass (John J Walsh) 65⁷ 300

4 **PATIENCE OF ANGELS(IRE),** b f Distinctly North (USA) - Cabin Brooke by Burslem (G T Hourigan) 3816 4026⁸ 4160

7 **PATONG BEACH,** ch m Infantry - Winter Resort by Miami Springs (P C Ritchens) 2765 2886⁸ 3542⁷ 3911 4174

6 **PATRAY LAD(IRE),** b g Executive Perk - Cathom (J M Wilson) 829 910 984 1060⁴

6 **PATS BOREEN(IRE),** ch g Boreen (FR) - Patrician Maid (Noel Meade) 3965⁹ 4094

8 **PATS CROSS(IRE),** b g Abednego - No Hunting by No Time (J Hetherton) 3900

6 **PATS FOLLY,** bl m Macmillion - Cavo Varka by Cavo Doro (F J Yardley) 101 186⁷ 454³ 1044

12 **PATS MINSTREL,** b g Black Minstrel - Lohunda Park by Malinowski (USA) (R Champion) 1223³ 1643⁶ 1845³ 1988⁵ 3165¹

6 **PATSCILLA,** b or br m Squill (USA) - Fortune Teller by Troy (R Dickin) 78⁸

5 **PATTERN ARMS,** b g Governor General - Early Doors by Ballad Rock (D Moffatt) 478⁶ 610 1033⁵

8 **PATTIE TIM(IRE),** ch g Orange Reef - Judy Cullen by Wrekin Rambler (Timothy O'Callaghan) 2585 2944³ 3086 3428 3835⁸

5 **PAUL(IRE),** b g Lapierre - Miss Philomena by Raise You Ten (Michael Hourigan) 213⁶ 346³ 410⁹ 472⁶ 898

4 **PAULA JANE(IRE),** b f Orchestra - Parsonetta (Michael Butler) 3524

7 **PAULA'S BOY(IRE),** br g Spin Of A Coin - Bunavoree by Rugged Man (D F Bassett) 2777⁷ 3283⁴ 3546⁶

10 **PAULS POINT,** b g Abednego - Corely Point (Bernard Jones) 2869 3888 4115

8 **PAULS RUN(IRE),** b g Cataldi - Annamoe by Ballymore (W J Lanigan) 1279¹ 1895⁶ 2094² 2271⁴ 3068⁴ 3430¹ 3767⁹

4 **PAULTON,** b g Lugana Beach - Runcina by Runnett (K Bishop) 1209 1470⁴ 1992⁶ 2181³ 2385⁸ 3106⁴ 3495² 3736³ 4189¹

7 **PAUSE FOR THOUGHT,** b g Bairn (USA) - Mill D'Art by Artaius (USA) (Mrs M Reveley) 2764¹ 3929

9 **PAVI'S BROTHER,** ch g Politico (USA) - May Moss by Sea Moss (P R Hedger) 2216² 2527⁶ 3556

7 **PAVLOVA(IRE),** ch m Montelimar (USA) - Light Foot by Little Buskins (R Rowe) 800⁹ 1700³ 2308⁵ 2480 2931¹ 3207⁴ 3630⁴

5 **PAY THE MAN(IRE),** ch g Remainder Man - Bail Out (E J O'Grady) 3090 3381

4 **PAYPNUTSGETMONKEYS(IRE),** b f Prince Rupert (FR) - Sweet Finale by Sallust (C A Smith) 2723 3439

5 **PEACE INITIATIVE,** b g Hadeer - Rostova by Blakeney (K Vincent) 2015⁵ 3197³

7 **PEACE LORD(IRE),** ch g Callernish - French Academy by Le Bavard (FR) (Mrs D Haine) 1065² 1397³ 2260² 2678¹ 2951³ 3372¹

11 **PEACE OFFICER,** br g Strong Gale - Peace Woman by Pitpan (A Barrow) 3371 4226

8 **PEACEFULL RIVER(IRE),** b m Over The River (FR) - No Battle by Khalkis (Norman Cassidy) 686 701¹ 828⁵ 1074

8 **PEAFIELD(IRE),** b g Torus - La'bavette by Le Bavard (FR) (James Murphy) 212² 338⁸ 406 729⁴

13 **PEAJADE,** b g Buckskin (FR) - Kaminaki by Deep Run (Miss Jill Wormall) 2468⁶ 2993² 3426³ 3993

9 **PEAK A BOO,** b m Le Coq D'Or - Peak Princess by Charlottown (D W Whillans) 3011 3396

4 **PEAK VIEW(IRE),** ch g Millfontaine - Canadian Native (Michael Hourigan) 1057 1430 1709

5 **PEALINGS(IRE),** gr g Wood Chanter - TenCents by Taste Of Honey (G A Hubbard) 1768⁷ 2656 3332⁶ 3480⁴ 3639⁴ 4039⁹ 4158³

8 **PEARL EPEE,** b m Broadsword (USA) - Pearly's Orphan by Precipice Wood (D Nicholson) 1568⁵ 1804 2026⁴ 2280 2799³ 3320¹ 3533² 3670⁴ 4140¹

5 **PEARL HART,** b m Puissance - Pearl Pet by Mummy's Pet (R T Phillips) 2668⁸ 3022 3491⁷

4 **PEARL SILK,** br f Cigar - Purrlea Atoll by Gulf Pearl (T T Bill) 2302 2552⁸

9 **PEARL'S CHOICE(IRE),** b m Deep Run - Vendevar by Pardigras (J C McConnochie) 1562⁴ 1916³ 2308³ 2596⁴ 2799²

4 **PEARLA DUBH(IRE),** b g Over The River (FR) - Canverb by Proverb (R J Baker) 3913

4 **PEARLS OF THOUGHT(IRE),** b f Persian Bold - Miss Loving by Northfields (USA) (A C Whillans) 2533 2811³ 3433³

5 **PEATSVILLE(IRE),** b g Ela-Mana-Mou - Windy Cheyenne (USA) by Tumble Wind (USA) (M R Channon) 1107² 1450

9 **PEATSWOOD,** ch g Rolfe (USA) - Cathy Jane by Lauso (M R Channon) 1105⁴ 2047² 2506⁵

7 **PEBBLE BEACH(IRE),** gr g Roselier (FR) - Indian Idol by Indian Ruler (USA) (G M Moore) 935¹ 1153³ 1311³ 2241² 2346 3160² 3787⁷

4 **PECAN PRINCESS(IRE),** b f Prince Rupert (FR) - Route Royale by Roi Soleil (C A Smith) 3282

4 **PEDALTOTHEMETAL(IRE),** b m Nordico (USA) - Full Choke by Shirley Heights (R T Juckes) 1717³ 1848² 2009⁵ 2462⁵ 2693³ 2982⁶ 3170³ 4131⁹ 4274²

9 **PEDE GALE(IRE),** b m Strong Gale - Deep Adventure by Deep Run (Capt D C Foster) 2868⁶ 3084⁵ 3229 3393⁴

5 **PEDLAR'S CROSS(IRE),** b g Lancastrian - Fine Debut by Fine Blade (USA) (G M McCourt) 2283 2939⁵

6 **PEEP O DAY,** b m Domynsky - Betrothed by Aglojo (J L Eyre) 2151

7 **PEERS FOLLY(IRE),** ch g Remainder Man - Bola Stream by Paddy's Stream (Miss H C Knight) 3332⁸ 3639

5 **PEETSIE(IRE),** b m Fairy King (USA) - Burning Ambition by Troy (N A Twiston-Davies) 2197⁶

6 **PEGASUS BAY,** b g Tina's Pet - Mossberry Fair by Mossberry (D E Cantillon) 46⁵ 150⁵ 242¹ 867⁵ 1006¹ 1175⁷ 1402⁷ 1568

6 **PEGGY GORDON,** b m Feelings (FR) - Megan's Way by Le Coq D'Or (Mrs D Thom-

son) 725[1] 1125[7] 1786[3] 2815[6] 3157[3] 3437[4] 3761[1] 3904[3] 4273[5]

14 PEGMARINE(USA), b g Text (USA) - Symbionese (USA) by Bold Reason (USA) (Mrs A M Woodrow) 1595[7] 1941[1] 2355[9] 2606[5] 2864[6]

4 PEGUS JUNIOR(IRE), b g Soviet Lad (USA) - La Maree by Tumble Wind (USA) (Patrick O'Leary) 1309[6] 1430 2074 2112[4] 2337[4] 2643[2] 2832[2] 2940[5] 3450[5] 3705[1]

5 PEJAYS DUCA(IRE), ch g Duca Di Busted - Whitechurch Gina (John F Gleeson) 713

6 PEMBRIDGE PLACE, b g Niniski (USA) - Rose D'Amour (USA) by Lines Of Power (USA) (G F Johnson Houghton) 60[2] 78[5] 284[6]

8 PENDIL'S DELIGHT, b m Scorpio (FR) - Pendella by Pendragon (M Stephenson) 201

11 PENIARTH, b m Oats - Rapenna by Straight Lad (R J Price) 379[2] 551[4] 612

10 PENLEA LADY, b m Leading Man - Pen Quill by Pendragon (Mrs S G Addinsell) 3187[1]

9 PENLET, b g Kinglet - Pensun by Jimsun (J I Pritchard) 2994[5]

9 PENNANT COTTAGE(IRE), b m Denel (FR) - The Hofsa by Varano (W Jenks) 841[4] 1234[6] 1847[5] 2254 2549 3190

7 PENNCALER(IRE), ch g Callernish - Pennyland by Le Bavard (FR) (P J Hobbs) 1793 2157[4] 2441[8] 2921[3] 3383

8 PENNDARA(IRE), gr g Pennine Walk - Adaraya (FR) by Zeddaan (A P O'Brien) 1018[2] 1120[1] 1841[2] 2052[7] 2231[3] 2367[1] 2733 3112[6] 3522

10 PENNINE PRIDE, b g Over The River (FR) - Pats'y Girl by Dadda Bert (M D Hammond) 1314[4] 1739[5] 1946[1] 2148 2715[7] 3159

10 PENNINE VIEW, ch g Slim Jim - Salvia by Salvo (J J Dixon) 3248[3] 3599[3]

7 PENNY A DAY(IRE), b g Supreme Leader - Mursuma by Rarity (Mrs M Reveley) 1772[1] 2128[3] 3156[3] 3580

8 PENNY BRIDE(IRE), ch m The Parson - Pennyland by Le Bavard (FR) (Timothy O'Callaghan) 983 1076 3624[3] 3752[7] 3877[6]

5 PENNY PEPPERMINT, b or br m Move Off - Cheeky Pigeon by Brave Invader (USA) (R E Barr) 2063[7] 2651[8] 3003[5] 3583

5 PENNY POET(IRE), b g Lafontaine - Penny Levy (A J McNamara) 1902 2055[9] 3429

5 PENNY POT, br m Lord Bud - Karmelanna by Silly Season (Mrs S A Bramall) 1077 2341 2410 2648 2868

5 PENNY'S WISHING, b m Clantime - Lady Pennington by Blue Cashmere (C Smith) 1642

6 PENNYAHEI, b m Malaspina - Pennyazena by Pamroy (S A Brookshaw) 2605

8 PENNYBRIDGE(IRE), ch g Orchestra - Little Snob by Aristocracy (I R Ferguson) 136[2] 2381[4] 2867[6] 3229[3] 3643[7]

4 PENNYBRYN, br f Teenoso (USA) - Be Bold by Bustino (J L Eyre) 3322[4]

8 PENNYMOOR PRINCE, b g Pragmatic - Warham Fantasy by Barolo (R G Frost) 1921 2442[7] 2701[6] 3039[6]

7 PENROSE LAD(NZ), b g Captain Jason (NZ) - Salimah (NZ) by Double Nearco (CAN) (D Nicholson) 1182[8] 1509[3] 1805[3] 2249[3] 2719[4] 3710[3]

6 PENTLAND SQUIRE, b g Belfort (FR) - Sparkler Superb by Grisaille (J M Jefferson) 806[9] 1033[3] 1677[2] 2006[3] 3351[5] 3598[5]

6 PENTLANDS FLYER(IRE), b g Phardante (FR) - Bunkilla by Arctic Slave (J Howard Johnson) 1053[5] 1224[8] 2490[4] 2712 3598[3] 3756[1] 4108[2]

4 PENZITA(IRE), ch f The Bart (USA) - Pendy (Gerard Stack) 620 882

4 PEPPANOORA(IRE), ch f Topanoora - Salt (J T Gorman) 2669[5]

5 PEPPER POT BOY(IRE), b g Lapierre - That's It by Adropejo (Mrs M Reveley) 3356[5]

7 PEPTIC LADY(IRE), b m Royal Fountain - In The Wood by Proverb (M C Pipe) 1494[4]

5 PERAMBIE(IRE), b m Executive Perk - Amber Ballad by Ballad Rock (A P O'Brien) 777 213[5] 269[3] 343[1] 430[5] 487[3] 560[9] 611[8] 731[6]

10 PERCUSIONIST, ch h Black Minstrel - Pleaseme by Javelot (P N Cummins) 3348[7] 3888[7]

5 PERCY BRAITHWAITE(IRE), b g Kahyasi - Nasseem (FR) by Zeddaan (Miss P M Whittle) 2023[4] 2173[1] 2509[7] 3064[7] 3623[1] 3831 3959[2] 4253[2]

5 PERCY PARROT, b g Lochnager - Soltago by Touching Wood (USA) (A C Whillans) 1371[6] 1657 1911

8 PERCY PIT, b g Pitpan - Technical Merit by Gala Performance (USA) (Mrs D McCormack) 4218

9 PERCY SMOLLETT, br g Oats - Misty Sunset by Le Bavard (FR) (D Nicholson) 2829[3] 3453

10 PERCY THROWER, gr g Oats - Arctic Advert by Birdbrook (N A Twiston-Davies) 1343[3] 1615[8]

5 PERCY'S JOY, b g Strong Gale - Knockeevan Girl by Tarqogan (T D Easterby) 3048 3661[9]

5 PERFECT(IRE), br g Castle Keep - Peaceful Rose (Noel Meade) 581 3627[8] 3891 4198

4 PERFECT ANSWER, ch f Keen - Hasty Key (USA) by Key To The Mint (USA) (J Neville) 3142

5 PERFECT BERTIE(IRE), b g Cyrano de Bergerac - Perfect Chance by Petorius (N M Babbage) 1856 2030[6]

6 PERFECT PAL(IRE), ch g Mulhollande (USA) - Gone by Whistling Wind (Miss Gay Kelleway) 1997 2350 2594

6 PERFECT PEACE(IRE), b f Lord Americo - Cailin Og (D Casey) 4106[7]

7 PERFECT TIMMER, b g Silly Prices - Hannah's Song by Saintly Song (A P O'Brien) 211[6] 276[2] 337[2] 352

7 PERIROYAL, ch g Royal Vulcan - Periplus by Galivanter (Mrs S J Smith) 1963

10 PERKNAPP, b g King Persian - Knapping by Busted (A Martin) 780[2] 1650[3] 2053[2] 2736 3154[3]

5 PERKY LAD(IRE), b g Executive Perk - Radalgo (T J Nagle) 3525

5 PERKY TOO(IRE), b g Executive Perk - Laud by Dual (J Howard Johnson) 2908 3351

5 PERMIT ME(IRE), br m Alzao (USA) - Kaweah Maid by General Assembly (USA) (Patrick Lacey) 560[4] 624[1] 731[4] 1275[9] 1777[6] 2089 2943 3234 3954[7] 4243[1]

4 PERPETUAL LIGHT, b f Petoski - Butosky by Busted (J J Quinn) 1690[8] 1909[6] 2188 2816[3]

5 PERPETUAL PROSPECT(IRE), gr g Shernazar - Manntika (C Roche) 343[9] 1015[9] 1193 1275 1533 3625 4245[4]

6 PERRYMAN(IRE), ch g Good Thyne (USA) - Poetic Lady by Rymer (K C Bailey) 3720

6 PERSIAN AMORE(IRE), gr f Celio Rufo - Persian Winter (Michael Cunningham) 1436

9 PERSIAN BUD(IRE), b or br g Persian Bold - Awakening Rose by Le Levanstell (M R Bosley) 1811[8]

5 PERSIAN BUTTERFLY, b m Dancing Dissident (USA) - Butterfly Kiss by Beldale Flutter (USA) (R M Stronge) 1496 1669[7] 1832 2279 2390[4] 2515 4131[1] 4296

5 PERSIAN DANSER(IRE), ch m Persian Bold - Ampersand (USA) by Stop The Music (USA) (Peter McCreery) 883[5] 1015[7] 1275 2114[7]

4 PERSIAN DAWN, br f Anshan - Visible Form by Formidable (USA) (R T Phillips) 1943 3614[8] 3874[2] 4131[6]

6 **PIXIE BLUE(IRE)**, f Henbit (USA) - Miss Spike (Thomas Carmody) 66 132⁹ 1013 1359 1899

7 **PIYALA(IRE)**, b f Paean - Diyala (FR) by Direct Flight (Anthony Mullins) 2675 2839 3178⁸ 3338³

5 **PLAID MAID(IRE)**, b m Executive Perk - Tipperary Tartan by Rarity (M Bradstock) 1560³

7 **PLAN-A(IRE)**, br g Creative Plan (USA) - Faravaun Rose by Good Thyne (USA) (R H Alner) 3742¹ 3934²

6 **PLANNING GAIN**, b g Blakeney - Romantiki (USA) by Giboulee (CAN) (Mrs J M Hollands) 3033

11 **PLAS-HENDY**, ch g Celtic Cone - Little Cindy II by Nine One (P M Rich) 3746⁸

8 **PLASSY BOY(IRE)**, ch g Over The River (FR) - Gillogue by Royal Orbit (USA) (K R Burke) 1815⁷ 2026² 2291⁵ 2741³ 2912 3000 3133 3679

14 **PLASTIC SPACEAGE**, b g The Parson - Chestnut Fire by Deep Run (J A B Old) 2427³ 2698⁶

5 **PLATIN GALE(IRE)**, b g Strong Gale - Dicklers Queen (S J Mahon) 2172 3069 3520

9 **PLAY GAMES(USA)**, ch g Nijinsky (CAN) - Playful Queen (USA) by Majestic Prince (Lady Eliza Mays-Smith) 2400 2982⁹

9 **PLAYFUL JULIET(CAN)**, b m Assert - Running Around (USA) by What A Pleasure (USA) (J C Haynes) 127³ 308⁶ 550¹ 3123 3803 3992³ 4101

9 **PLAYING TRUANT**, b g Teenoso (USA) - Elusive by Little Current (USA) (D R Gandolfo) 1001¹ 1605⁵ 1808 2308²

4 **PLAYPRINT**, ch c Persian Heights - Tawnais by Artaius (USA) (Michael Cunningham) 574 882 2643 2832⁸ 3089

5 **PLEASANT SURPRISE(FR)**, ch g Vaguely Pleasant (FR) - Surprise D'Hermite (FR) by Kashmir II (M C Pipe) 101⁴

8 **PLEASE CALL(IRE)**, b g Flair Path - Javana by Levanter (D P Geraghty) 659 1061²

10 **PLEASE NO TEARS**, b m Prince Rheingold - Mudinuri by Little Buskins (J E Mulhern) 217² 288³ 329⁴ 434⁴ 464² 527⁴ 622³ 1096⁸ 1174³ 1307⁴

7 **PLEASURE CRUISE**, b g Cruise Missile - Moment's Pleasure (USA) by What A Pleasure (USA) (J K Cresswell) 2626 3046

9 **PLEASURE SHARED(IRE)**, ch g Kemal (FR) - Love-In-A-Mist by Paddy's Stream (P J Hobbs) 1347¹ 1891 1998³ 2210² 2794 3037

4 **PLEASURELAND(IRE)**, ch g Don't Forget Me - Elminya (IRE) by Sure Blade (USA) (R Curtis) 1286² 1610⁶ 1861³ 2207 2423³ 2976¹ 3150 3422¹ 3637²

6 **PLINTH**, b g Dowsing (USA) - Pedestal by High Line (R H Alner) 83³ 371¹ 492² 659³ 1211 3692³ 3951⁹

7 **PLOUGH THE LEA(IRE)**, ch g Camden Town - Mo Mhuirnin by Miner's Lamp (D Carroll) 92 179⁵ 195² 234⁶ 495³ 2036⁷

8 **PLUMBOB(IRE)**, br g Bob Back (USA) - Naujella by Malinowski (USA) (L Lungo) 1315⁴ 1526² 1819⁶ 4022² 4180¹ 4220

9 **PLUMBRIDGE**, ch g Oats - Hayley by Indian Ruler (P R Chamings) 2638⁴ 2930 3195⁵

5 **PLUMPTON WOOD(IRE)**, br m Phardante (FR) - The Furnituremaker by Mandalus (J G Smyth-Osbourne) 3082 3482

6 **PLUNDER BAY(USA)**, b g Cutlass (USA) - La Ninouchka (USA) by Bombay Duck (USA) (N J Henderson) 1031¹ 1287 1518⁵ 2386⁴ 2728 2955⁶ 3531³ 3826 3995⁴

11 **POACHER'S DELIGHT**, ch g High Line - Moonlight Night (FR) by Levmoss (A G Newcombe) 249

7 **POCAIRE GAOITHE(IRE)**, gr g Roselier (FR) - Ervamoira by Energist (C L Popham) 1377⁴ 1631 1679 2241⁹ 2484⁶ 2620 3297⁴

7 **POCONO KNIGHT**, gr g Petong - Avahra by Sahib (C H Jones) 479⁶ 638⁴ 891 2676

4 **POETRY(IRE)**, gr f Treasure Kay - Silver Heart by Yankee Gold (M H Tompkins) 1844⁶ 2628

7 **POINT DUTY**, b g Reference Point - Vilikaia (USA) by Nureyev (USA) (F P Murtagh) 2533 2651 3258⁶ 3655

4 **POINT LUCK(IRE)**, b f Broken Hearted - Miss Flo Jo (T Stack) 2832 2940 3232⁹ 3415

5 **POINT REYES(IRE)**, b g Brush Aside (USA) - Lady's Wager by Girandole (C W Thornton) 1968¹

5 **POISON IVY(IRE)**, b m Kefaah (USA) - Darling Bud by Whistling Wind (Thomas G Walsh) 1143 1777 2413⁹ 2521⁷

9 **POKEY GRANGE**, gr g Uncle Pokey - Sudden Surrender by The Brianstan (S N Burt) 2990

8 **POKONO TRAIL(IRE)**, ch g Aristocracy - Frank's Choice by Whistling Deer (F Flood) 871¹

8 **POLAR ANA(IRE)**, b m Pollerton - O Ana by Laurence O (Mrs G M Gladders) 4118³

4 **POLAR KING(IRE)**, b g Glacial Storm (USA) - Our Little Lamb by Prince Regent (FR) (C W Thornton) 3251⁴ 3661⁵

11 **POLAR REGION**, br g Alzao (USA) - Bonny Hollow by Wolver Hollow (Mrs F Marner) 840 953⁵

8 **POLAR WIND**, ch g El Gran Senor (USA) - Tundra Goose by Habitat (N Waggott) 3534⁹ 3673 4137

9 **POLDEN PRIDE**, b g Vital Season - Bybrook by Border Chief (G B Balding) 48² 3273² 3545² 3651¹ 3730⁴ 3950³ 4173¹

8 **POLICEMANS PRIDE(FR)**, bl g Policeman (FR) - Proud Pet by Petingo (M Madgwick) 1082⁵ 1211 1722⁵ 2010³ 2304³ 2482³

6 **POLISH CONSUL**, ch g Polish Precedent (USA) - Consolation by Troy (Mark McCausland) 229³ 2443

9 **POLISH RIDER(USA)**, ch g Danzig Connection (USA) - Missy T (USA) by Lt Stevens (B J Llewellyn) 4234³

5 **POLITICAL ANIMAL(IRE)**, ch g Parliament - Orlita (Patrick Mooney) 3965 4161

6 **POLITICAL BILL**, ch g Politico (USA) - Trial Run by Deep Run (J I A Charlton) 1656 2200

13 **POLITICAL ISSUE**, b g Politico (USA) - Red Stockings by Red Pins (T L A Robson) 2634

4 **POLITICAL MANDATE**, br f Respect - Political Mill by Politico (USA) (R Nixon) 2687 2915⁶ 3598⁹ 3802⁶ 3997² 4237⁷

5 **POLITICAL MILLSTAR**, b g Leading Star - Political Mill by Politico (USA) (R Nixon) 1390 1682 2145⁵ 3308⁵

6 **POLITICAL PANTO(IRE)**, b g Phardante (FR) - Madam's Well by Pitpan (M C Pipe) 168³ 770² 1085²

6 **POLITICAL POWER**, b g Politico (USA) - Pauper Moon by Pauper (W Jenks) 2824⁶ 3439

8 **POLITICAL SAM**, ch g Politico (USA) - Samonia by Rolfe (USA) (David F Smith) 3004⁵

8 **POLITICAL SKIRMISH**, b m Politico (USA) - Bridgits' Girl by New Brig (I Park) 78

10 **POLITICAL TOWER**, b g Politico (USA) - Crosby Waves by Bing II (R Nixon) 863² 1151³ 1389¹ 1672³ 2335⁵ 2617³ 2911¹ 3154⁶ 3596 3719⁶ 3779³ 3998¹

7 **POLITICAL TROUBLES(IRE)**, b f Mandalus - Small Trouble (Peter Casey) 1901 2166⁹ 2380⁶ 2582 3231 4004

6 **PROFLUENT(USA)**, ch h Sunshine Forever (USA) - Proflare (USA) by Mr Prospective (J Bertran de Balanda) 351¹

10 **PROGRAMMED TO WIN**, b g Pollerton - Fair Corina by Menelek (W J Lanigan) 1711⁹ 2646

6 **PROLOGUE(IRE)**, b g Mandalus - Advance Notice (Mrs John Harrington) 802 910⁸ 1013 1712

5 **PROMALEE(IRE)**, b g Homo Sapien - Oralee by Prominer (A P O'Brien) 2054² 2115¹ 2235¹ 2737¹ 3769⁷

5 **PROMISE TO TRY(IRE)**, b m Orchestra - Haut Lafite by Tamerlane (M A Barnes) 1255⁶ 1464⁹ 2847 3128

9 **PROPAGANDA**, b g Nishapour (FR) - Mrs Moss by Reform (P R Webber) 3445⁷

4 **PROPER PRIMITIVE**, b f Primitive Rising (USA) - Nidd Bridges by Grey Ghost (C J Drewe) 2723⁹ 2961

8 **PROPHET'S THUMB(IRE)**, b g Arapahos (FR) - Smack On by Reformed Character (Patrick J McCarthy) 565⁸ 680⁶ 720⁸ 747⁵

6 **PROPHETS FIST(IRE)**, b g Lafontaine - Gorge (V T O'Brien) 185⁸ 343⁸ 686 850

4 **PROPOLIS POWER(IRE)**, ch g Simply Great (FR) - Now Then by Sandford Lad (M W Easterby) 930 1524⁵ 1737

6 **PROSPECT STAR(IRE)**, ch g Noalto - Alkouri (E Bolger) 827 982 1092 1754⁶

4 **PROSPERO**, b g Petong - Pennies To Pounds by Ile de Bourbon (USA) (Mrs A J Perrett) 2303

7 **PROTON**, b g Sure Blade (USA) - Banket by Glint Of Gold (R Akehurst) 1719¹ 2042³ 2509⁴

6 **PROTOTYPE**, b g Governor General - Sweet Enough by Caerleon (USA) (G F Johnson Houghton) 693¹ 1292³ 2302 2782 3028⁸ 3290³ 3414²

5 **PROUD IMAGE**, b g Zalazl (USA) - Fleur de Foret (USA) by Green Forest (USA) (G M McCourt) 1731³ 2390¹ 2663³ 2804² 3184² 3515¹ 3844⁵

7 **PROUD TOBY(IRE)**, b or br g Lancastrian - Lady Conkers by Domenico Fuoco (G B Balding) 1636 1765 3312

6 **PROUDANDAMBITIOUS(IRE)**, b g My Top - Kilvahine by Mandrake Major (Patrick Joseph Flynn) 1554⁶ 3083⁶ 3233⁸

6 **PROUDSTOWN LADY(IRE)**, br f Ashford (USA) - Baccata (Matthew McGoona) 159 210⁶ 1174

4 **PROVE THE POINT(IRE)**, b f Maelstrom Lake - In Review (Mrs P N Dutfield) 858¹ 1221 1438⁵ 1665 3027 3270⁴ 3542³

7 **PROVEN SCHEDULE(IRE)**, b g Buckskin (FR) - Moppet's Last (Miss A M McMahon) 562⁷

10 **PROVENCE**, ch g Rousillon (USA) - Premier Rose by Sharp Edge (A W Carroll) 1266⁹ 1400⁵ 1567⁶ 3989⁹ 4232²

4 **PROVINCE**, b g Dominion - Shih Ching (USA) by Secreto (USA) (C J Mann) 1702³ 1890⁵ 2828⁸ 3315³

6 **PRU'S PROFILES(IRE)**, b g Tale Quale - Hazy Hill by Goldhill (N A Twiston-Davies) 1260³ 1505

10 **PRUDENT PEGGY**, br m Kambalda - Arctic Raheen by Over The River (FR) (R G Frost) 335⁶ 514⁵ 639⁴ 756⁵ 1471² 1686⁴ 2606 2991⁷

5 **PRUSSIA**, b g Roi Danzig (USA) - Vagrant Maid (USA) by Honest Pleasure (USA) (W Clay) 150³ 229¹ 1263³ 2023³ 2311⁹ 2602⁷ 3129 3321² 3725⁸

5 **PRUSSIAN EAGLE(IRE)**, b m Strong Gale - Court Session by Seymour Hicks (FR) (R T Juckes) 1464⁷ 1663 3170

6 **PRUSSIAN STEEL(IRE)**, gr g Torus - Lady Barnaby by Young Barnaby (M Bradstock) 2567⁴ 2725

8 **PRUSSIAN STORM(IRE)**, b m Strong Gale - Let's Compromise by No Argument (Miss Venetia Williams) 1262

9 **PRYS PAUPER(IRE)**, b g Pauper - Prys Daughter by Pry (Patrick John Murphy) 463³

5 **PRYZON(IRE)**, b m Phardante (FR) - Pryoress (P T Flavin) 199 898

6 **PTARMIGAN LODGE**, br g Reference Point - Lomond Blossom by Lomond (USA) (Martin Michael Lynch) 908⁶ 1118³ 1358³ 1654⁸ 1899¹ 2134 2524⁶

7 **PUB TALK(IRE)**, br g Buckskin (FR) - Vixen's Red by Bargello (A P O'Brien) 344⁵

7 **PUBLIC WAY(IRE)**, b g Common Grounds - Kilpeacon by Florescence (N Chamberlain) 1371⁵

7 **PULKERRY(IRE)**, ch g King Luthier - Kylemore Abbey by Junius (USA) (P Winkworth) 929²

5 **PUNCH**, b g Reprimand - Cartooness (USA) by Achieved (N Tinkler) 652

12 **PUNCH'S HOTEL**, ch g Le Moss - Pops Girl by Deep Run (R Rowe) 833⁸ 2740 3120⁴

7 **PUNGAYNOR(IRE)**, b g Dock Leaf - Petite Paula (A Seymour) 91⁴ 233⁴ 468

10 **PUNTERS BAR**, ch g Le Moss - Miel Venture by Rockavon (Patrick Day) 63³ 85⁴ 2755⁴ 3454

7 **PUNTERS DREAM**, b g Teenoso (USA) - Princess Dina (Patrick Day) 1715 2081 2752

9 **PUNTERS OVERHEAD(IRE)**, b g Black Minstrel - Boyne Saint by Saint Crespin III (P F Nicholls) 1236¹ 1891

7 **PUNTING PETE(IRE)**, ch g Phardante (FR) - Silent Collection by Monksfield (W P Mullins) 1170 1276⁷ 1638³ 1905⁶ 2086⁸ 2133⁸ 2227⁹

8 **PURBECK CAVALIER**, ch g Sula Bula - Party Miss by West Partisan (R H Alner) 1236⁵ 1725⁶ 2352 2612² 2747 2928³

7 **PURBECK POLLY**, ch m Pollerton - Warwick Air by True Song (N R Mitchell) 4035⁹

6 **PURBECK RAMBLER**, b g Don't Forget Me - Sheer Nectar by Piaffer (USA) (G B Balding) 1498⁶ 1684⁵ 2354⁶ 2921 3023 3271⁶

4 **PURE SWING**, b g Shareef Dancer (USA) - Mrs Warren (USA) by Hail To Reason (J Pearce) 3176

6 **PUREVALUE(IRE)**, b or br g Kefaah (USA) - Blaze Of Light by Blakeney (M W Easterby) 1914³ 2332⁴ 2465¹ 2789⁶ 3200¹

8 **PURITAN(CAN)**, b g Alleged (USA) - Conform (CAN) by Blushing Groom (FR) (N Tinkler) 1401⁵ 1634⁵ 1785³ 1932² 2121² 2300² 2360

5 **PURPLE ACE(IRE)**, b g King's Ride - The Best I Can by Derring Rose (N A Gaselee) 2953⁸

7 **PURPLE SPLASH**, b g Ahonoora - Quay Line by High Line (P J Makin) 2797⁵ 3062

10 **PUSEY STREET BOY**, ch g Vaigly Great - Pusey Street by Native Bazaar (J R Bosley) 328⁴ 372 754⁹ 1020⁶

7 **PUSH ON POLLY(IRE)**, b m Salluceva - Brave Polly by Brave Invader (USA) (J Parkes) 1742⁴ 1968 2803 2889 3435 3996⁸

5 **PYLON(IRE)**, b g Electric - Hibiscus (Capt D G Swan) 637⁷

10 **PYR FOUR**, b g Strong Gale - Distant Castle by Deep Run (G M McCourt) 428⁶ 1095⁶ 1244 2069⁵ 3101³ 3329²

7 **PYRAMIS PRINCE(IRE)**, b g Fairy King (USA) - Midnight Patrol by Ashmore (FR) (John Whyte) 1370

6 **PYRITE KING(IRE)**, b or br g Tender King - Party Dancer (Gerard Stack) 3963

7 **PYRRHIC DANCE**, b g Sovereign Dancer (USA) - Cherubim (USA) by Stevward (M J Haynes) 1722 2044⁴ 3163

12 **RED MATCH,** ch g Royal Match - Hi Mary by High Line (R J Hodges) 895 1007 1203[7]

6 **RED OAK(IRE),** b g Supreme Leader - Please Oblige (J J Lennon) 1436[7] 1554[7] 3697

6 **RED OASSIS,** ch g Rymer - Heron's Mirage by Grey Mirage (H Oliver) 2199 2764[9] 3210[8] 3672

9 **RED PARADE(NZ),** b g Church Parade - Infra Ray (NZ) by Attalas (N J Hawke) 1726[3] 2245 2404[3] 2566

5 **RED PHANTOM(IRE),** ch g Kefaah (USA) - Highland Culture by Lomond (USA) (S Mellor) 1977 2255 2390 2872

7 **RED RADICAL(IRE),** ch g Radical - Galberstown by Signa Infesta (P E I Newell) 64[7] 245[4] 397[4] 581[1] 781[8] 908[8] 1189

4 **RED RAJA,** b g Persian Heights - Jenny Splendid by John Splendid (P Mitchell) 1610[8] 1790[1] 2012[2] 2423[5] 2727[1] 2828[5] 3315[1] 3785[9]

6 **RED RIVER(IRE),** ch m Over The River (FR) - Saroan Meed by Midsummer Night II (C J Drewe) 2560 3019[6]

4 **RED RUSTY(USA),** ch g The Carpenter (USA) - Super Sisters (AUS) by Call Report (USA) (P R Hedger) 1702 4080[5]

5 **RED SPECTACLE(IRE),** b g Red Sunset - Buz Kashi by Bold Lad (IRE) (P C Haslam) 473[1]

4 **RED SQUARE(IRE),** b f Soviet Lad (USA) - Mrs Dell (USA) (Victor Bowens) 882

6 **RED TEL(IRE),** b g Alzao (USA) - Arbour (USA) by Graustark (M C Pipe) 336[2] 456[1] 942[5] 1142[8] 1479 1703[3] 3812[2] 3979[2] 4073 4189[8] 4296

4 **RED TIE AFFAIR(USA),** b c Miswaki (USA) - Quiet Rendezvous (USA) by Nureyev (USA) (J M Bradley) 1922

4 **RED TIME,** br g Timeless Times (USA) - Crimson Dawn by Manado (M S Saunders) 936[8] 1599[8] 2292[8]

4 **RED TONIC(USA),** b g Cure The Blues (USA) - Glittering Heights (USA) by Golden Fleece (USA) (John Muldoon) 2161[3] 2337[9] 2702[3] 2940[1] 3345[5] 4280[9]

5 **RED TRIX,** ch m Primitive Rising (USA) - Daleena by Dalesa (W Raw) 546

6 **RED VALERIAN,** b g Robellino (USA) - Fleur Rouge by Pharly (FR) (G M Moore) 44[2] 606[1] 656[3] 765[1] 913

5 **RED VIPER,** b g Posen (USA) - Within A Whisper by Welsh Pageant (N M Lampard) 3500[8] 3957[4] 4069[6] 4287

8 **RED-STOAT(IRE),** ch m Oats - Rednael by Leander (Mrs J Storey) 2651

8 **REDEEMYOURSELF(IRE),** b g Royal Fountain - Reve Clair by Deep Run (J T Gifford) 1341[1]

4 **REDGRAVE WOLF,** ch f Little Wolf - Redgrave Rose by Tug Of War (K Bishop) 2784[3] 3917

5 **REDS PARADISE(IRE),** b or br g Treasure Hunter - Doalot Vii (Patrick J F Gillespie) 4117

7 **REDWOOD LAD,** b g Pitpan - Josephine Bruce by Supreme Red (J W Curtis) 2260

12 **REED,** b h Dara Monarch - Angelica (SWE) by Hornbeam (Mrs D Thomson) 4112[5] 4218[4]

5 **REEFA'S MILL(IRE),** b g Astronef - Pharly's Myth by Pharly (FR) (J Neville) 83[6] 513[5] 595[6] 891 937 1647[3] 1881

4 **REEM FEVER(IRE),** b f Fairy King (USA) - Jungle Jezebel by Thatching (D W P Arbuthnot) 1702[8] 1922

4 **REENIE(IRE),** b m Boreen (FR) - Slave Trade (John W Nicholson) 350 434[7] 561 802

8 **REESHLOCH,** b g Reesh - Abalone by Abwah (Andrew Turnell) 1349[2] 1557[2] 1957 2266[7] 2638[5] 3023[4]

5 **REEVES(IRE),** b g Caerleon (USA) - Kalkeen by Sheshoon (W P Mullins) 185[1] 316[1] 562[1] 715[7] 2170[9]

6 **REFLEX HAMMER,** b g Precious Metal - Khotso by Alcide (John R Upson) 1047[9] 1609[6] 1764[6]

7 **REGAL AURA(IRE),** ch g Glow (USA) - Dignified Air (FR) by Wolver Hollow (D C O'Brien) 2612[6] 3094[1] 3291[1] 3679[4]

6 **REGAL BLUFF,** ch g Regal Steel - Bangkok Boss by Balinger (J C McConnochie) 4086[6]

5 **REGAL CHILD(IRE),** b f King's Ride - Queen Kate (T J Nagle) 4197

6 **REGAL DOMAIN(IRE),** ro g Dominion Royale - Adaraya (FR) by Zeddaan (Mrs L Marshall) 1033[8] 1333 1657 3781[4] 4107[6] 4208[6]

4 **REGAL EAGLE,** b g Shirley Heights - On The Tiles by Thatch (USA) (M D Hammond) 3700[7] 3997

6 **REGAL GEM(IRE),** ch m Torus - Queen's Prize by Random Shot (C R Barwell) 52[1] 157[1] 231[6] 384[3] 446[4] 528[2] 800[8] 2541 3299[2] 3518[3] 4013[2] 4194

8 **REGAL GROVE(IRE),** b m King's Ride - Mayfield Grove by Khalkis (A P O'Brien) 272[1] 342[1]

7 **REGAL JEST,** gr m Jester - Royal Huntress by Royal Avenue (B W Murray) 2575 3317 3655

5 **REGAL KNIGHT(IRE),** b g King's Ride - Le Nuit (J R H Fowler) 4161[7]

6 **REGAL PURSUIT(IRE),** b m Roi Danzig (USA) - Pursue by Auction Ring (USA) (N J Henderson) 985[1] 1503[2] 3049[6] 3641[6] 3828[4]

9 **REGAL ROMPER(IRE),** b g Tender King - Fruit Of Passion by High Top (Mrs S J Smith) 875[3] 1151[1] 1316[1] 1389[3] 1678[3] 2191[2] 2493[2] 2774[2] 2911[2] 3126[4] 3536[3]

4 **REGAL SECRET(IRE),** b g Classic Secret (USA) - Majestic Nurse (T J Taaffe) 4324

4 **REGAL SPLENDOUR(CAN),** ch g Vice Regent (CAN) - Seattle Princess (USA) by Seattle Slew (USA) (R J O'Sullivan) 3022[6] 3332

5 **REGAL SPRING(IRE),** b g Royal Fountain - Ride The Rapids by Bulldozer (K C Bailey) 3561[5]

15 **REGARDLESS,** b g Quayside - Bel Arbre by Beau Chapeau (J P Leigh) 72[9] 124[4] 230 368

5 **REGENCY LEISURE,** ch g Mr Fluorocarbon - Pixie's Party by Celtic Cone (R J Eckley) 2567[7]

5 **REGENCY RAKE(IRE),** b g Ti King (FR) - Midnight Owl (FR) by Ardross (A L T Moore) 1195[8] 2055[1] 2142[4] 2674[6] 3216[3] 3768[4] 4146[4] 4280

5 **REGGIE'S HONOUR(IRE),** ch m Nashamaa - Silver Shoals (USA) by Mill Reef (USA) (Alan Clarke) 703[2] 782[5] 805 1195 3547

10 **REGISTANO(GER),** b g Tauchsport - Reklame by Immer (U Stoltefuss) 4323[1]

7 **REGIT(IRE),** b g Duky - Shenley Annabella by Thatching (Augustine Leahy) 2753 2901[5] 2943 3220 3339

7 **REIMEI,** b g Top Ville - Brilliant Reay by Ribero (R Akehurst) 1743[5] 2255[9]

5 **REINE DE LA CHASSE(FR),** ch m Ti King (FR) - Hunting Cottage by Pyjama Hunt (R J O'Sullivan) 783[4] 1271

4 **REKONDO(IRE),** b g Two Timing (USA) - Tuesday Morning (M J Grassick) 882 1403[6]

8 **RELATIVE CHANCE,** b g Relkino - Chance A Look by Don't Look (J S King) 1000[2] 1722[3]

8 **RELAXED LAD,** ro g Kalaglow - Relaxed by Homing (J H Peacock) 2747[3] 2998 3189[3] 4138[4]

7 **RELKANDER,** b g Relkino - Arctic Ander by Leander (Mrs J Pitman) 2920

8 **RELKEEL,** gr g Relkino - Secret Keel by Balinger (D Nicholson) 2563[2]

7 **RELKOWEN,** ch m Relkino - Pollys Owen by Master Owen (Andrew Turnell) 1667 2304 2877 3558

7 **RELUCKINO,** b g Buckley - Releta by Relkrino (J G M O'Shea) 1623 2392⁹ 2740² 2856 4279⁴

6 **REMAINDER STAR(IRE),** ch g Remainder Man - Temple Star by Irish Star (P A Fahy) 1117 1241⁶ 1584¹ 1838³ 2037

4 **REMEMBER STAR,** ch f Don't Forget Me - Star Girl Gay by Lord Gayle (USA) (A D Smith) 542⁶ 705 858⁶ 1353⁷ 2251⁴ 2477

4 **RENATA'S PRINCE(IRE),** b g Prince Rupert (FR) - Maria Renata by Jaazeiro (USA) (K R Burke) 442³ 522⁸

6 **RENNY(IRE),** b g Bold Arrangement - She Is The Boss by Skyliner (Augustine Leahy) 979

4 **RENO'S TREASURE(USA),** ch f Beau Genius (CAN) - Ligia M (USA) by Noholme Jr (USA) (John A Harris) 2804 3931⁵ 4065⁵ 4224

8 **RENT DAY,** b m Town And Country - Notinhand by Nearly A Hand (J W Mullins) 657³ 999 2388⁹ 2894⁶

5 **REPEAT OFFER,** b g Then Again - Bloffa by Derrylin (P D Cundell) 1578⁴ 2015³

4 **RESCUE TIME(IRE),** b c Mtoto - Tamassos by Dance In Time (CAN) (Kevin Prendergast) 1547¹ 1750⁷ 2050³ 2128 2369⁴ 2731⁵

6 **RESERVATION ROCK(IRE),** b g Ballad Rock - Crazyfoot by Luthier (T Hind) 3169⁶

7 **RESIST THE FORCE(USA),** br g Shadeed (USA) - Countess Tully by Hotfoot (C A Cyzer) 1515¹ 1759⁶ 2197

4 **RESPECTING,** b g Respect - Pricey by Silly Prices (J A Moore) 2061⁸ 3003 3866

5 **RESTANDBEJOYFUL,** ch m Takachiho - Restandbethankful by Random Shot (Mrs S Lamyman) 1874

6 **RESTATE(IRE),** b m Soviet Star (USA) - Busca (USA) by Mr Prospector (USA) (F Murphy) 1521⁸

4 **RET FREM(IRE),** b g Posen (USA) - New Light by Reform (C Parker) 567² 734⁶ 860²

12 **RETAIL RUNNER,** b g Trimmingham - Deep Rose by Deep Run (Miss S Edwards) 2308 2767³ 3138

10 **REVE DE VALSE(USA),** b g Conquistador Cielo (USA) - Dancing Vaguely (USA) by Vaguely Noble (R Johnson) 477¹ 555² 724³ 885³ 1072⁴ 1692¹ 1821³ 2261⁶ 3126³ 3585³ 3656⁴ 3821⁶ 4265⁸

7 **REVEREND BROWN(IRE),** b g The Parson - Let The Hare Sit by Politico (USA) (J M Turner) 3458⁴ 4122²

6 **REVERSE THRUST,** b g Ilium - Flying Straight by Straight Lad (P R Hedger) 1719⁷ 2277 2558⁵ 3022 3491¹ 3731² 4083 4322⁵

5 **REVOLT,** b g Primitive Rising (USA) - Fit For A King by Royalty (T D Easterby) 1682⁶ 1887⁵ 2192²

9 **REX TO THE RESCUE(IRE),** ch g Remainder Man - Cool Blue by Deep Run (R H Alner) 617³ 771² 894³ 1455³ 1721² 1926¹ 2386²

6 **RHOMAN FUN(IRE),** b g Rhoman Rule (USA) - Fun by Jukebox (R H Buckler) 1356 1471⁷ 1559² 2739⁵

5 **RHOMAN STAR(IRE),** b g Rhoman Rule (USA) - Star Of Dulargy (James Joseph Murphy) 713

9 **RHOSSILI BAY,** b g Idiot's Delight - Hitting Supreme by Supreme Sovereign (Mrs M Reveley) 167¹ 321

4 **RHUM DANCER(IRE),** b g Eurobus - Audata (FR) by Abdos (D K Weld) 341¹ 522¹ 712³

9 **RHYMING THOMAS,** ch g Rymer - Gokatiego by Huntercombe (J R Adam) 3246

7 **RHYTHM AND BLUES,** b g Myjinski (USA) - Pitskelly Blues by Pitskelly (R H Buckler) 1053⁴ 1208⁷ 2699⁵ 2927¹ 3253³ 3677⁵ 4032 4136⁶

9 **RHYTHMIC DANCER,** b g Music Boy - Stepping Gaily by Gay Fandango (USA) (D A Nolan) 661 728

6 **RI NA MARA(IRE),** b g King's Ride - Aqua Pura by Over The River (FR) (B A McMahon) 2959⁷

10 **RIAS RASCAL,** b g Lucifer (USA) - Bios Brrin by Pitpan (W Rock) 2869

8 **RICH DESIRE,** b m Grey Desire - Richesse (FR) by Faraway Son (USA) (F Murphy) 1312

7 **RICH LIFE(IRE),** b g Dance Of Life (USA) - Ringawoody by Auction Ring (USA) (C Weedon) 4044

9 **RICH TRADITION(IRE),** b g Torus - Dawn Of Spring Vii (Peter McCreery) 2411⁹ 2646 3229 3340⁵ 3706² 3839⁶ 4055 4199

8 **RICH TYCOON(IRE),** b g Buckskin (FR) - Stolen Gold by Tycoon II (P M Rich) 3144³ 3312

13 **RICHARD HUNT,** b g Celtic Cone - Member's Mistress by New Member (Mrs P Rowe) 2887

9 **RICHMOND(IRE),** ch g Hatim (USA) - On The Road by On Your Mark (Miss Z A Green) 558³ 608⁷ 695⁴ 818⁶

5 **RIDGEWOOD WATER(IRE),** b g Over The River (FR) - Galeshula by Strong Gale (Thomas O'Neill) 4200

7 **RIDING CROP(IRE),** b g King's Ride - Vintage Harvest by Deep Run (N J Henderson) 1155² 1615⁵ 2456³ 3569

6 **RIFAWAN(USA),** b g Cox's Ridge (USA) - Rifada by Ela-Mana-Mou (Mrs M Reveley) 2348

5 **RIGHT RON RUN,** b g Primitive Rising (USA) - Sheshells by Zino (F Murphy) 4049

7 **RIGHT WIN(IRE),** br h Law Society (USA) - Popular Win by Lorenzaccio (R Hannon) 1877⁶ 2208⁵ 2557⁵

5 **RILMOUNT(IRE),** ch f Roselier (FR) - Alice Starr (Miss I T Oakes) 3182

5 **RIMET(IRE),** ch m Montelimar (USA) - Rathcoffey Daisy (Eugene M O'Sullivan) 1247

9 **RIMOUSKI,** b h Sure Blade (USA) - Rimosa's Pet by Petingo (B R Cambidge) 2313² 2559 2801⁶ 3162⁵ 3498⁷

6 **RINEEN BREEZE(IRE),** b f Fresh Breeze (USA) - Poopee (Donal Hassett) 1060⁸

5 **RING ALBERT(IRE),** b or br g Miner's Lamp - Call-Me-Tara by Callernish (W P Mullins) 2108³ 2228² 2449⁷ 2946³ 3456⁵ 3891¹ 4281⁴

9 **RING CORBITTS,** b g Politico (USA) - Penny Pink by Spartan General (M J Roberts) 1706⁵ 1814² 2354 2566⁸

6 **RING FOR ROSIE,** br m Derrylin - Clear The Course by Crash Course (Capt T A Forster) 2775⁶ 3828¹

7 **RING HARRY(IRE),** b f Lancastrian - Hathaways Gazette by London Gazette (Andrew Slattery) 1484 1842⁶ 2079 2107 2519⁸ 2675⁹

6 **RING MAM(IRE),** b f King's Ride - Fubar (L Skehan) 829 3447

9 **RING O'ROSES(IRE),** b or br m Auction Ring (USA) - Coupe D'Hebe by Ile de Bourbon (USA) (W J Lanigan) 238⁶ 358⁷

5 **RING OF VISION(IRE),** br g Scenic - Circus Lady by High Top (C J Mann) 3028² 3296³ 3500¹ 3722³

8 **RINGRONE(IRE),** ch m Lancastrian - Naomi Night Vii by Damsire Unregistered (V Thompson) 1521⁷ 1826 2063⁸ 3124 3261

5 **RINUS MAJESTIC(IRE),** b g Gallic League - Deepwater Blues by Gulf Pearl (D McCain) 740 1026 1609

6 **RINUS MAJOR(IRE),** b g Don't Forget Me - Needy by High Top (D McCain) 2798 3316

INDEX TO NATIONAL HUNT RESULTS 1996-97

12 **RIO HAINA,** ch g St Columbus - Kruganko by Arctic Slave (G F Johnson Houghton) 2979 3461[4]

7 **RIOT LEADER(IRE),** b g Supreme Leader - Calamity Jane by Never Dwell (T R George) 2724[2]

6 **RIPARIUS(USA),** b g Riverman (USA) - Sweet Simone (FR) by Green Dancer (USA) (P R Webber) 3332[3] 3555[1] 3910[4] 4141[1]

5 **RIPOSTE(IRE),** br m Lord Americo - Fair Argument (A P O'Brien) 2100[6] 3705

11 **RISEUPWILLIEREILLY,** ch g Deep Run - Sinarga (D F Bassett) 3191 3490

8 **RISING BREEZE(IRE),** ch g Rising - On The Breeze by King's Equity (A P O'Brien) 158[6] 292[8] 355[4] 408[5] 523[5]

5 **RISING DAWN(IRE),** ch g Rising - Bawnard Lady by Ragapan (Mrs A Swinbank) 4113[8]

5 **RISING DOUGH(IRE),** br g Dowsing (USA) - Shortning Bread by Blakeney (G L Moore) 798[6] 2636[4] 2952[5] 3500[3]

6 **RISING MAN,** b g Primitive Rising (USA) - Dream Again by Blue Cashmere (J T Gifford) 1882[7] 3172[6]

6 **RISING MILL,** b g Primitive Rising (USA) - Milly L'attaque by Military (R Brewis) 3251

7 **RISING SAP,** ch g Brotherly (USA) - Miss Kewmill by Billion (USA) (J D Downes) 2531 2875 3102[8] 3529

9 **RISING WATERS(IRE),** b g Sure Blade (USA) - Over The Waves by Main Reef (Desmond McDonogh) 1752 1900[8] 2051 2126[6]

7 **RISING'S LASS(IRE),** ch m Rising - Gone by Whistling Wind (M J Weeden) 3407[4] 4035[6]

8 **RISK OF THUNDER(IRE),** b g Strong Gale - Park Delight by Saint Denys (E Bolger) 1754[1] 3784[1]

8 **RISKY DEE,** b g Risk Me (FR) - Linn O' Dee by King Of Spain (V Thompson) 1822[7] 1932[4] 2065[4] 2633[3] 2814[3] 3161[4]

5 **RISKY ROMEO,** b g Charmer - Chances Are by He Loves Me (G C Bravery) 423[4]

5 **RISKY ROSE,** b m Risk Me (FR) - Moharabuiee by Pas de Seul (R Hollinshead) 921[8]

6 **RISKY TU,** ch m Risk Me (FR) - Sarah Gillian (USA) by Zen (USA) (P A Kelleway) 2802 2980[6]

8 **RISZARD(USA),** ch g Danzig Connection (USA) - Tendresse (USA) by Secretariat (USA) (John J Walsh) 1242[7] 1362 1552[6] 2059[5] 2163[4]

4 **RITA'S KILLALOE(IRE),** gr f Magical Strike (USA) - She's Misty (P M Lynch) 4282[6]

5 **RITH DUBH(IRE),** b g Black Minstrel - Deep Bonnie by Deep Run (William Flavin) 3421[1]

7 **RITTO,** b g Arctic Tern (USA) - Melodrama by Busted (J Neville) 770[3] 905[1] 1082 1449[1] 3146 3731 3915 4069

7 **RIVA ROCK,** b g Roaring Riva - Kivulini by Hotfoot (T P McGovern) 227

6 **RIVA'S BOOK(USA),** b g Mari's Book (USA) - Riva's Revenge (USA) by Riva Ridge (USA) (Mrs L Williamson) 146[6] 206 417[3] 518[2]

7 **RIVEAUX(IRE),** b g Callernish - Bob's Hansel by Prince Hansel (G Richards) 2791[7] 2984[3] 3401[7] 3999[3]

6 **RIVER BAY(IRE),** b m Over The River (FR) - Derrynaflan by Karabas (Miss H C Knight) 1369[7] 1591[2] 1961[1] 2394[3] 3331 3698[3]

11 **RIVER BOUNTY,** ch g Over The River (FR) - Billie Gibb by Cavo Doro (C P E Brooks) 1613 2314[3] 2592[3] 2786

6 **RIVER CHALLENGE(IRE),** ch g Over The River (FR) - Floppy Disk by Patch (John R Upson) 371

5 **RIVER DAWN(IRE),** ch g Over The River (FR) - Morning Susan by Status Seeker (C P E Brooks) 2723[6] 2953

7 **RIVER GALA(IRE),** ch g Over The River (FR) - Silver Gala by Gala Performance (USA) (R J Hodges) 755[4] 787 3271 3493[2]

9 **RIVER ISLAND(USA),** b g Spend A Buck (USA) - Promising Risk (USA) by Exclusive Native (USA) (J A B Old) 1982[6] 2400[4] 2629

8 **RIVER LEVEN,** b g Nearly A Hand - Ana Mendoza by Don't Look (D R Gandolfo) 1806[1] 2010[2] 2304[4] 3193[3] 4046

8 **RIVER MAGNET(IRE),** ch g Over The River (FR) - Cacador's Magnet by Chinatown (C A McBratney) 3228

10 **RIVER MANDATE,** b or br g Mandalus - Liffey's Choice by Little Buskins (Capt T A Forster) 1607[1] 1974[2] 2404[2] 2589[2] 2948[3] 3114 3605

6 **RIVER MONARCH,** b h Just A Monarch - Costa Beck by Forlorn River (J T Gifford) 1515[8]

5 **RIVER MULLIGAN(IRE),** ch g Over The River (FR) - Miss Manhattan by Bally Joy (P J Hobbs) 3720

7 **RIVER OF DREAMS(IRE),** b g Over The River (FR) - Juverna Lass by Chinatown (Joseph Quinn) 3447[1]

11 **RIVER RED,** ch g Over The River (FR) - Monasootha by Paddy's Stream (K Frost) 1491[3] 2154[6] 3670

4 **RIVER ROCK(IRE),** ch g Classic Music (USA) - Borough Counsel (Victor Bowens) 1616

7 **RIVER ROOM,** ch g Gunner B - Final Melody by Final Straw (K C Bailey) 73[1] 168[1] 203[2] 1048[4] 1291[1] 1343[5] 1852[5]

5 **RIVER RUMPUS(IRE),** br g King's Ride - Sallybank (A J McNamara) 731 1015[8] 1143[8] 1488[5] 2057[8] 3817 3954 4246

7 **RIVER UNSHION(IRE),** ch g Aristocracy - Smurfette by Baptism (J Howard Johnson) 1771[3] 2686[2] 2909[1] 3261[1] 3758[3]

4 **RIVER VALLEY LADY(IRE),** b f Salt Dome (USA) - Princess Martina by English Prince (P Mullins) 620[8] 2337[7] 2643 2832[4]

5 **RIVER WYE(IRE),** b g Jareer (USA) - Sun Gift by Guillaume Tell (USA) (G H Yardley) 876[8] 2462[1] 2746

6 **RIVERBANK RED,** ch m Lighter - Gypsy Louise by Ascendant (W Clay) 1437 1604 2511[9] 2761 3281

6 **RIVERBANK ROSE,** b m Lighter - Queen Of Gypsy's by Knave To Play (W Clay) 812[4] 1266[4] 1442[3] 2025 2804[3] 3099[1] 3265[4] 3506[3] 3881[5] 4285[3]

4 **RIVERCARE(IRE),** b c Alzao (USA) - Still River by Kings Lake (USA) (M J Polglase) 1027[6]

6 **RIVERRUNSTHROUGHIT(IRE),** br f Jolly Jake (NZ) - River Of Wine (Henry Cleary) 173 278[9]

4 **RIVERS MAGIC,** b g Dominion - Rivers Maid by Rarity (J J Bridger) 1790[5] 2292

10 **RIVERSTOWN LAD,** b g Touching Wood (USA) - Malija (FR) by Malicious (Denis J Reddan) 565 947[3]

5 **RIZAL(USA),** ch g Zilzal (USA) - Sigy (FR) by Habitat (R J Eckley) 976 1097 1215

9 **ROAD BY THE RIVER(IRE),** b g Over The River (FR) - Ahadoon by Gulf Pearl (P Cheesbrough) 1632[2] 1988[3] 2150[4] 2488[5]

9 **ROAD TO AU BON(USA),** b g Strawberry Road (AUS) - Village Lady (USA) by Crimson Satan (R J Baker) 1603[1] 1959[5] 2295

7 **ROADRUNNER,** ch g Sunley Builds - Derraleena by Derrylin (Mrs L Richards) 2928[6] 3310

758

5 **ROUGH DIAMOND(IRE),** b g King's Ride -
Casaurina (IRE) by Le Moss (M Sheppard)
3555

9 **ROUGH EDGE,** b g Broadsword (USA) - Mini
Gazette by London Gazette (D A Wales)
4157[1]

11 **ROUGH QUEST,** b g Crash Course - Our Quest
by Private Walk (T Casey) 1940[1] 2045[2]

4 **ROUTE ONE(IRE),** br g Welsh Term - Skylin
by Skyliner (C P E Brooks) 3825[1]

9 **ROUTING,** b g Rousillon (USA) - Tura by
Northfields (USA) (N G Ayliffe) 189[1] 248[7]

11 **ROUYAN,** b g Akarad (FR) - Rosy Moon (FR)
by Sheshoon (Mrs J Pitman) 3563[3] 3711

6 **ROVESTAR,** b g Le Solaret (FR) - Gilberts
Choice by My Swanee (J S King) 1291[6] 1646[1]
2158 2428[7] 2877[3]

5 **ROWAN TREE(IRE),** b m Castle Keep - Three
Friars (Mrs John Harrington) 1077[7] 1275[5]

5 **ROWBET JACK,** b g Colmore Row - Bet Oliver
by Kala Shikari (K O Cunningham-Brown)
942

11 **ROWHEDGE,** ch g Tolomeo - Strident Note
by The Minstrel (CAN) (A P Jones) 510

5 **ROXY HICKS,** b m Seymour Hicks (FR) -
Damsong by Petong (R J Price) 3561 3796

4 **ROYAL ACTION,** b c Royal Academy (USA) -
Ivor's Honey by Sir Ivor (O Sherwood) 1844[3]
2336[2]

7 **ROYAL AG NAG,** b m Nicholas Bill - Murex by
Royalty (P J Hobbs) 3956

8 **ROYAL ALBERT(IRE),** b g Mandalus - Sparkling Stream by Paddy's Stream (Patrick
Joseph Flynn) 303

8 **ROYAL ARISTOCRAT(IRE),** b f Aristocracy -
Fosterstown by Royal Highway (I R Ferguson) 134[5] 170 3888[5] 4115 4292

7 **ROYAL BANKER(IRE),** b g Roselier (FR) - Dottie's Wasp by Tarqogan (Martin Todhunter) 3056 3395 3781 4098[4] 4220[2]

6 **ROYAL BELLE(IRE),** ch f Dominion Royale -
Dauricum (J F Bailey Jun) 1307

5 **ROYAL CHIP,** br g Rakaposhi King - Up Cooke
by Deep Run (Miss M K Milligan) 3008[5]

8 **ROYAL CIRCUS,** b g Kris - Circus Ring by
High Top (P R Webber) 414[1] 521[4] 606[6] 675 876[4]
963[5] 1218[6]

8 **ROYAL CITIZEN(IRE),** b g Caerleon (USA) -
Taking Steps by Gay Fandango (USA) (J F
Bottomley) 1388 1834 4239[3]

6 **ROYAL CRIMSON,** b g Danehill (USA) - Fine
Honey (USA) by Drone (M D Hammond)
2201[5] 2576[2] 2938

4 **ROYAL DIVERSION(IRE),** b f Marju (IRE) -
Royal Recreation (USA) by His Majesty
(USA) (M C Pipe) 1790[4] 2153

4 **ROYAL DIVIDE(IRE),** b g Lord Americo -
Divided Loyalties by Balidar (V Soane) 1769
2015

6 **ROYAL EVENT,** b g Rakaposhi King - Upham
Reunion by Paridel (D R Gandolfo) 1479[2]
1642[2] 1940[3] 2396[1] 2658[2] 3709

8 **ROYAL GLINT,** b m Glint Of Gold - Princess
Matilda by Habitat (H E Haynes) 109 152[7]
1733 2267 2432[6] 2957[9] 3148 3915[9]

7 **ROYAL HAND,** b g Nearly A Hand - Royal
Rushes by Royal Palace (R J Armson) 838
941[2] 1881 1963 2388[7] 2566 2653 3283[5] 3582[4] 3809[4]
4008[3] 4156

13 **ROYAL IRISH,** b g Le Bavard (FR) - Leuze by
Vimy (A C Ayres) 2660 3096

13 **ROYAL JESTER,** b g Royal Fountain - Tor-
mina by Tormento (C Storey) 2918[2] 3307[2]
3603[2] 3713[2] 3993[4]

5 **ROYAL MARINE(IRE),** b g King's Ride - Eurolink Sea Baby by Deep Run (A L T Moore)
2368[6] 2845[2]

4 **ROYAL MEMBER,** ch f Seven Hearts - Little
Member by New Member (Mrs Barbara
Waring) 3122 3402 3681[3] 3828

4 **ROYAL MIDYAN,** b c Midyan (USA) - Royal
Agreement (USA) by Vaguely Noble (J F
Bailey Jun) 1459 2067 3450[3] 3785

12 **ROYAL MILE,** b g Tyrnavos - Royal Rib by
Sovereign Path (F S Jackson) 42

4 **ROYAL MINT,** b g Bustino - Royal Seal by
Privy Seal (T Thomson Jones) 3825[5]

6 **ROYAL MIST(IRE),** b g Hays - Kings Perhaps
by King's Ride (Mrs J Pitman) 2377 3473

9 **ROYAL MOUNTBROWNE,** b g Royal Vulcan -
Star Shell by Queen's Hussar (A P O'Brien)
719[6] 981 1094[1] 1243[1] 1434[7] 1551[2] 1753[1] 1878[5] 2127[6]
2233[8] 2671[2] 2836[3]

6 **ROYAL OASIS(IRE),** b g Royal Fountain - Pro-
gello by Proverb (Patrick Heffernan) 2649
2840[5] 3336 3454[1] 3752

12 **ROYAL OATS,** b m Oats - Knights Queen by
Arctic Chevalier (Miss D Harries) 794

5 **ROYAL PALM,** b g Palm Track - Royal Export
by Import (V Thompson) 1255[8] 1656 1929[6]

9 **ROYAL PARIS(IRE),** b g Beau Charmeur (FR) -
Raised-In-Paris by Raise You Ten (Mrs S J
Smith) 1226[3] 1385 1820 2285[5] 2406[7] 2686 2861[4]

10 **ROYAL PIPER(NZ),** br g Piperhill - Blue Ice
(NZ) by Balkan Knight (A J Wilson) 1576[9]
1858[4] 2217[2] 2559[5] 2797[3] 3209[3] 3557[1]

6 **ROYAL POT BLACK(IRE),** b or br g Royal Fountain - Polly-Glide by Pollerton (P J Hobbs)
2248[3] 2409[2] 2642[4] 3388[3]

7 **ROYAL RANK(USA),** ch g Miswaki (USA) -
Westminster Palace by General Assembly
(USA) (D S Alder) 2538[9]

4 **ROYAL RAPPORT,** ch g Rich Charlie - Miss
Camellia by Sonnen Gold (J G M O'Shea)
481[2] 573[1]

6 **ROYAL RAVEN(IRE),** b g Castle Keep - Decent
Dame by Decent Fellow (J T Gifford) 1503[1]
1973[4] 2398[2] 2661

6 **ROYAL ROSY(IRE),** b m Dominion Royale -
Rosy Moon (FR) by Sheshoon (A P O'Brien)
944[2] 1074[8] 1550[2] 1780[2] 2021[3] 2077[1] 2171[3] 2274[1] 2648[2]
2842[4] 3765

6 **ROYAL RULER(IRE),** b m Strong Gale - Highland Party by Deep Run (J T Gifford) 1560[4]
1961 2426[7] 3513[2] 3986[6]

5 **ROYAL SALUTE,** ch g Royal Vulcan - Nuns
Royal by Royal Boxer (F Jordan) 336[7] 873

5 **ROYAL SANTAL(IRE),** br f Royal Fountain -
Santal Air (Michael Hourigan) 2414[9] 2645[7]
2965 3449[9]

11 **ROYAL SAXON,** b g Mandalus - La Campesina
by Arctic Slave (P Bowen) 1859 2482 2728[3]
2895[4] 3175[1] 3412[3] 3589[1] 3659[2] 3739

5 **ROYAL SCIMITAR(USA),** ch h Diesis - Princess
Of Man by Green God (Mrs A J Perrett) 2791[2]
3064[5]

10 **ROYAL SEGOS,** b g High Line - Segos by Runnymede (Miss S E Baxter) 3102[4] 3991[2]

6 **ROYAL SILVER,** gr g Kalaglow - Avon Royale
by Remainder (B Preece) 4316

6 **ROYAL SPRUCE(IRE),** b g Step Together
(USA) - Lacken Lady by Le Moss (G M
Moore) 2322[7] 2619 3435[8]

11 **ROYAL SQUARE(CAN),** ch g Gregorian (USA) -
Dance Crazy (USA) by Foolish Pleasure
(USA) (N P Littmoden) 2252 2459[7] 3138[6] 3502[6]
3968[1] 4140[3]

10 **ROYAL STANDARD,** b g Sadler's Wells (USA) -
Princess Tiara by Crowned Prince (USA) (P
M Rich) 1235[1] 1683[3] 1843[5]

5 **SHABO SHABO,** ch m Soldier Rose - Shaenas Girl Vii by Damsire Unregistered (Mrs S M Odell) 3506

5 **SHABRA EXZOL(IRE),** b or br g New Express - Shabra Girl (Desmond McDonogh) 3889

6 **SHADIRWAN(IRE),** b h Kahyasi - Shademah by Thatch (USA) (R Akehurst) 1866⁵ 2197

5 **SHADOW CHASER(IRE),** b m Krayyan - Great Kova (Thomas Bergin) 144⁸ 253⁹ 353

6 **SHADOW LEADER,** br g Tragic Role (USA) - Hush It Up by Tina's Pet (C R Egerton) 2397¹ 2594¹ 3111¹ 3717¹

9 **SHADOWS OF SILVER,** gr m Carwhite - Mimika by Lorenzaccio (Mrs M Reveley) 2463

5 **SHADY EMMA,** ch m Gunner B - Shady Legacy by Rymer (F Jordan) 654⁶ 1260 1976

9 **SHAHGRAM(IRE),** gr g Top Ville - Sharmada (FR) by Zeddaan (P Beaumont) 2204⁵ 2547

5 **SHAHRANI,** b g Lear Fan (USA) - Windmill Princess by Gorytus (USA) (M C Pipe) 150¹ 226¹ 370¹ 448¹ 696¹ 921¹ 1233 1443⁶ 2504⁸ 3049³ 3105⁴ 3544³ 3692⁴

4 **SHAHRUR(USA),** b or br c Riverman (USA) - Give Thanks by Relko (D K Weld) 2940² 3415

7 **SHALHOLME,** ch m Fools Holme (USA) - Shalati (FR) by High Line (J M Bradley) 830⁶ 937

7 **SHALIK(IRE),** ch g Pauper - Jasmine Girl by Jasmine Star (J R Jenkins) 359 387³ 440¹ 650 688² 776⁶ 971 1022² 1704⁴ 1941⁵ 1996

6 **SHALLOW RIVER(IRE),** b g Over The River (FR) - Rule The Waves by Deep Run (R Collins) 1315⁷ 1608³ 1825⁶ 2487

5 **SHALOM(IRE),** b or br g Brush Aside (USA) - Vixen's Red (Michael Hourigan) 577⁸ 718⁶ 850 1015 1121⁷ 2055⁶ 2368⁷ 2518⁵ 2942²

11 **SHAMARPHIL,** b m Sunyboy - Chaffcombe by Crozier (R H Alner) 1239³ 1420⁵ 1687⁶ 1946⁴ 2698⁹ 3020⁴ 3175²

8 **SHANAGARRY(IRE),** b g Mister Lord (USA) - Pachamama by Glen Quaich (Patrick Heffernan) 2273 2586³ 2843 3783³

7 **SHANAGORE HILL(IRE),** ch g Torus - Port La Joie by Charlottown (J C Poulton) 3493

6 **SHANAGORE WARRIOR(IRE),** b g Arapahos (FR) - Our Linda by Proverb (S Mellor) 1685⁴ 2013⁶ 2243³ 2640⁴ 3196³

10 **SHANAKEE,** b g Wassl - Sheeog by Reform (B J Llewellyn) 2663⁷ 2872⁴ 3136

6 **SHANAVOGH,** b g Idiot's Delight - Honeybuzzard (FR) by Sea Hawk II (G M Moore) 1034¹ 1198² 1623¹ 2318⁴ 2813¹ 3203³

7 **SHANES HERO(IRE),** ch g Phardante (FR) - Rent A Card by Raise You Ten (Peter McCreery) 1900 2128 2834

6 **SHANKAR(IRE),** gr g Shareef Dancer (USA) - Sibelle D'Oa (FR) by Kenmare (FR) (D Nicholson) 2778 3080 3330³ 3595¹ 3766² 3907³

10 **SHANKORAK,** b g Darshaan - Shanjarina (USA) by Blushing Groom (FR) (Francis Berry) 312⁸ 441⁵ 553 1089 2068

5 **SHANNON GALE(IRE),** b g Strong Gale - Shannon Spray by Le Bavard (FR) (C Roche) 1015 1404⁷ 1579² 2073¹

11 **SHANNON GLEN,** b g Furry Glen - Shannon Ville by Deep Run (P Baring) 57⁵

7 **SHANNON LAD(IRE),** ch g Montelimar (USA) - Dusty Busty by Bustino (A W Carroll) 1103² 1479 1796⁷ 3619⁴

5 **SHANNON LIGHT(IRE),** b or br g Electric - Shannon Lass (John Brassil) 4052 4144⁸ 4197²

5 **SHANNON OAK(IRE),** b g Montelimar (USA) - Mindyourbusiness by Run The Gantlet (USA) (J C Hayden) 884¹ 1409¹

5 **SHANNON SHOON(IRE),** b g Zaffaran (USA) - Carrick Shannon by Green Shoon (J Howard Johnson) 2469 2687 2858⁷

4 **SHANOORA(IRE),** gr f Don't Forget Me - Shalara by Dancer's Image (USA) (Mrs N Macauley) 1179⁸ 1438⁷ 1869⁸

7 **SHANRUE(IRE),** ch g Boyne Valley - Derrycastle Beauty by Hello Gorgeous (USA) (A P O'Brien) 142² 347¹ 463⁵ 710⁴ 907 4053⁶ 4246

5 **SHARATAN(IRE),** b g Kahyasi - Sharata (IRE) by Darshaan (Thomas Foley) 364¹ 715⁸ 943⁴ 1457⁴

6 **SHARE OPTIONS(IRE),** b or br g Executive Perk - Shannon Belle by Pollerton (T D Easterby) 934¹ 1770 1995⁵ 2200¹ 2465² 2910⁴ 3709 3926

5 **SHARED RISK,** ch g Risk Me (FR) - Late Idea by Tumble Wind (USA) (J Norton) 1047⁷ 1252² 2560⁴ 2712³

9 **SHAREEF STAR,** b g Shareef Dancer (USA) - Ultra Vires by High Line (F L Matthews) 3464 3977

7 **SHAREZA RIVER(IRE),** b g Over The River (FR) - Shahreza (Michael J McDonagh) 853

5 **SHARIAKANNDI(FR),** b g Lashkari - Shapaara by Rheingold (J S King) 1350⁹ 2015² 2243⁴ 2724⁵ 3698⁷

6 **SHARLENE(IRE),** b or br m Supreme Leader - Glissade by Furry Glen (Michael Cunningham) 288 348² 561⁶ 621⁴ 645⁵

5 **SHARLEY COP,** ch m Lord Bud - Buckby Folly by Netherkelly (M J Camacho) 3198

5 **SHARMOOR,** b m Shardari - Linpac North Moor by Moorestyle (Miss L C Siddall) 1442 1604⁴ 1969 2390⁸ 2577 2804 2847

7 **SHARONS PRIDE(IRE),** b f Buckskin (FR) - Perspex-Pride (Patrick Joseph Flynn) 1362 1780⁷ 2021⁶ 2756 2945 3237

4 **SHARP COMMAND,** ch g Sharpo - Bluish (USA) by Alleged (USA) (P Eccles) 2002 2893⁷ 3044⁴ 3655¹ 3725⁴ 3738¹ 4015

5 **SHARP ELVER(IRE),** ch m Sharp Victor (USA) - Blue Elver by Kings Lake (USA) (P R Hedger) 210² 269⁵ 346⁴ 1429 1598

5 **SHARP HOLLY(IRE),** b m Exactly Sharp (USA) - Children's Hour by Mummy's Pet (J A Bennett) 533⁸ 638

4 **SHARP OUTLOOK(IRE),** ch f Shernazar - Perfect Guest by What A Guest (M J P O'Brien) 2702⁶ 2940³ 3415³ 3606¹

7 **SHARP SAND,** ch g Broadsword (USA) - Sea Sand by Sousa (P Monteith) 2344 2570

7 **SHARP SENSATION,** ch g Crofthall - Pink Sensation by Sagaro (G A Harker) 698⁵ 776³ 4012⁵ 4217⁴

6 **SHARP THRILL,** ch g Squill (USA) - Brightelmstone by Prince Regent (FR) (B Smart) 641⁹ 937⁵ 1110² 1425³ 3184³ 3469²

7 **SHARP THYNE(IRE),** b g Good Thyne (USA) - Cornamucula (P J Hobbs) 3546 3881¹ 4133⁴

10 **SHARP TO OBLIGE,** ch g Dublin Taxi - Please Oblige by Le Levanstell (R M Whitaker) 3899

5 **SHARPICAL,** b g Sharpo - Magical Spirit by Top Ville (N J Henderson) 1805¹ 2197² 3172¹ 3562² 3750 3910²

10 **SHARROW BAY(NZ),** ch g Sovereign Parade (NZ) - Minella (NZ) by Causeur (A G Hobbs) 2679 3294

5 **SHAVANO,** ch g Indian Ridge - Out Of Range by Faraway Times (USA) (M Madgwick) 2221⁸

5 **SHAWAHIN,** b g Nashwan (USA) - Bempton by Blakeney (Noel Meade) 560⁷ 928 1015⁴ 1143⁶ 1899

INDEX TO NATIONAL HUNT RESULTS 1996-97

5 **SKYCAB(IRE),** b g Montelimar (USA) - Sams Money by Pry (J T Gifford) 2409⁴

4 **SKYLIGHT,** ch g Domynsky - Indian Flower by Mansingh (USA) (Miss M K Milligan) 567⁴

5 **SKYLITE BOY(IRE),** b g Jamesmead - Seraphic Wind (I A Duncan) 1579

6 **SLACK ALICE,** ro m Derring Rose - Fonmon by Blast (J L Spearing) 2248 2775

7 **SLANEY CHARM(IRE),** b g Strong Gale - Dark Gold by Raise You Ten (P J P Doyle) 603⁷ 984⁷ 1096³ 1622⁷ 1715⁵ 2088⁷

10 **SLANEY CHOICE,** b g Furry Glen - Berenice by King's Leap (P J P Doyle) 276

6 **SLANEY GLOW(IRE),** b m Glow (USA) - Santa Ana Wind by Busted (J S Cullen) 87³ 162 315⁶ 526⁶ 2051 2095⁴ 2170⁵ 2447² 2841⁸

4 **SLANEY NATIVE(IRE),** b g Be My Native (USA) - Mean To Me by Homing (Mrs John Harrington) 2234²

10 **SLANEY RASHER,** br g Strong Gale - Gala Noon by Gala Performance (USA) (B J Llewellyn) 140⁵ 3184

9 **SLANEY STANDARD(IRE),** b g Beau Charmeur (FR) - Dawn Even by Laurence O (P J P Doyle) 601⁴ 982⁵ 1362⁷ 1841⁵ 2091 2164 2413

9 **SLAUGHT SON(IRE),** br g Roselier (FR) - Stream Flyer by Paddy's Stream (Martin Todhunter) 125²

5 **SLAVE GALE(IRE),** b m Strong Gale - Apicat by Buckskin (FR) (A P O'Brien) 140⁷ 173² 224⁶ 392¹ 523² 575³ 679³ 803³

6 **SLAVICA,** gr m Roselier (FR) - Trimar Gold by Goldhill (Donal A Hayes) 2757² 2968⁴ 3380³

6 **SLEAZEY,** b g Executive Perk - Dane-Jor's by Take A Reef (J G O'Neill) 1928 2255 2546⁶ 2976³ 3284² 3496¹ 3668² 3792 4276¹

7 **SLEEPTITE(FR),** gr g Double Bed (FR) - Rajan Grey by Absalom (Miss H C Knight) 989¹ 1110⁴ 1178⁴ 1541⁷ 1856² 2030¹

4 **SLEEPY BOY,** br g Zero Watt (USA) - Furnace Lass Vii by Damsire Unregistered (W Storey) 664⁸

6 **SLEEPY RIVER(IRE),** ch g Over The River (FR) - Shreelane by Laurence O (A L T Moore) 1277⁷ 1752⁷ 2051⁵ 2340⁶ 3431¹ 3754

7 **SLEETMORE GALE(IRE),** b m Strong Gale - Lena's Reign by Quayside (T P McGovern) 233¹ 1939⁴ 2726⁸

6 **SLEW MAN(FR),** b h Baby Turk - Slew Of Fortune (USA) by Seattle Slew (USA) (M C Pipe) 1959⁶ 2442⁹ 2949⁴ 3156 3445⁹

6 **SLEWMORE(IRE),** br g Mister Majestic - Lola's Pet by Ahonoora (Peter McCreery) 1273 1580⁷ 2016 2159 2415⁵ 3227⁸ 3419¹ 3643⁹ 4150¹ 4325³

7 **SLIDE ON,** b g Seymour Hicks (FR) - Star Alliance by Big Morton (P D Evans) 2008¹ 2123⁵ 2199² 2758

8 **SLIDEOFHILL(IRE),** ch g Le Bavard (FR) - Queen Weasel by Gulf Pearl (J J O'Neill) 1804² 1970⁶ 2763² 3133 3708⁷

11 **SLIEVENAMON MIST,** ch g Thatching - La Generale by Brigadier Gerard (Victor Dartnall) 2556¹ 2974¹ 3851¹ 4123¹

6 **SLIEVROE(IRE),** b m Red Sunset - La Padma (J G Coogan) 134⁴ 169⁷ 275⁶ 391 619⁷ 644⁸

9 **SLIGHT PANIC,** b m Lighter - Midnight Panic by Panco (Miss J H Wickens) 955⁶

5 **SLIGHTLY SPECIAL(IRE),** ch g Digamist (USA) - Tunguska by Busted (D T Thom) 150 225 989⁶ 1061⁷ 1811² 1969⁶ 2251³ 2424² 2610⁷ 2982 3136⁸

4 **SLIGHTLY SPEEDY(IRE),** b g Prince Rupert (FR) - Moutalina by Ela-Mana-Mou (J T Gorman) 2050 2112⁶ 2643 2832

6 **SLIGO CHAMPION(IRE),** ch g Shy Groom (USA) - Miss Fandango (Michael McElhone) 122 716⁶ 928 4198

5 **SLIMLINE CAT(IRE),** b g Law Society (USA) - Fancy Dress (FR) (Edward Lynam) 2098⁶ 2172

7 **SLINGSBY(IRE),** b g Heraldiste (USA) - Tasmania Star by Captain James (N A Gaselee) 1216² 1568³ 1831¹ 2254¹ 2690

8 **SLIPMATIC,** b m Pragmatic - Slipalong by Slippered (Andrew Turnell) 1051⁵ 1413² 1663² 1991 2638

5 **SLIPPERY FIN,** b m Slip Anchor - Finyska (FR) by Niniski (USA) (W G M Turner) 1669³ 2893 3466⁴

13 **SLIPPERY MAX,** b g Nicholas Bill - Noammo by Realm (R T Juckes) 451² 518 666⁹ 785² 938⁴

7 **SLOE BRANDY,** b m Hotfoot - Emblazon by Wolver Hollow (Mrs H L Walton) 976 1464

8 **SLOTAMATIQUE(IRE),** b g Henbit (USA) - Press Luncheon by Be Friendly (G Richards) 1513³ 1825⁴ 2003¹ 2239³ 2483³ 3702 4098¹ 4211¹

9 **SLUSH PUPPY(IRE),** b g The Parson - Driven Snow by Deep Run (Mrs D J Coleman) 908² 1075¹ 1189³ 1751⁷

6 **SLYGUFF ROVER(IRE),** ch g Over The River (FR) - Serenade Run by Deep Run (S J Treacy) 945² 1096

6 **SMALL FLAME(IRE),** b m Camden Town - Hazel Gig by Captain's Gig (O Brennan) 1350 1541

7 **SMALL N SMART,** b g Germont - Sanjo by Kafu (D S Alder) 1256 1585

8 **SMART ACT,** br g Lighter - Miss Date by Mandamus (I R Brown) 1134 1261

7 **SMART APPROACH(IRE),** br m Buckskin (FR) - Smart Fashion by Carlburg (Mrs M Reveley) 723¹ 935² 1153⁴ 1331³ 1966² 2200² 2910² 2989¹

8 **SMART CASANOVA,** br g Oats - I'm Smart by Menelek (M J Wilkinson) 1437⁷ 2154 2304 2859⁷ 3737⁶ 4070

5 **SMART GUY,** ch g Gildoran - Talahache Bridge by New Brig (Mrs L C Jewell) 3176

7 **SMART IN SATIN,** ch g Scorpio (FR) - Smart In Amber by Sagaro (Miss Lucinda V Russell) 1377 1695 2344

8 **SMART IN SILK,** gr m Scorpio (FR) - Cool Down by Warpath (Miss Lucinda V Russell) 3699 3781

6 **SMART IN SOCKS,** ch g Jupiter Island - Cool Down by Warpath (Miss Lucinda V Russell) 740 1371⁹ 3700 3762⁹

7 **SMART IN VELVET,** gr m Scorpio (FR) - Cool Down by Warpath (P R Hedger) 900⁵ 1447

7 **SMART LORD,** br g Arctic Lord - Lady Catcher by Free Boy (M R Bosley) 618³ 976⁷ 1215³ 1646⁵ 1928⁴ 2972⁵ 3407

4 **SMART MONTE(IRE),** ch f Montelimar (USA) - Smart Cookie (W Harney) 4147

12 **SMART PAL,** b g Balinger - Smart Bird by Stephen George (B Knox) 3848⁵

9 **SMART REBAL(IRE),** b g Final Straw - Tomfoolery by Silly Season (J Akehurst) 1614

5 **SMART REMARK,** b g Broadsword (USA) - Miss Cervinia by Memling (T Hind) 157³ 231⁸ 2405⁹ 2795⁹ 3443⁵

7 **SMART ROOKIE(IRE),** b or br g King's Ride - Jim's Honey by Reformed Character (N J Henderson) 2792

6 **SMIDDY LAD,** ch g Crofthall - Carrapateira by Gunner B (R Shiels) 1682 2192 2346² 2538³ 2851⁵ 3031⁸

8 **SOLO GENT,** br g Le Bavard (FR) - Go-It-Alone by Linacre (A P Jones) 726² 1569¹ 1859⁴ 2252⁷ 2659 2772³ 3020⁶ 3465

8 **SOLO VOLUMES,** ch g Ballacashtal (CAN) - Miss Solo by Runnymede (H G Rowsell) 595 638 1082⁸ 1208

7 **SOLOMAN SPRINGS(USA),** ch g Wajima (USA) - Malilla (CHI) by Prologo (Mrs V C Ward) 1021 1708⁷ 2422² 2989² 3658⁹ 3972² 4252⁴

7 **SOLOMON'S DANCER(USA),** b or br g Al Nasr (FR) - Infinite Wisdom (USA) by Sassafras (FR) (G Richards) 1035¹ 1281¹ 1630² 2043² 3012² 3708² 3806²

6 **SOLSGIRTH,** br g Ardross - Lillies Brig by New Brig (J Barclay) 2192 2617¹ 3034³ 3400

5 **SOLVANG(IRE),** b g Carlingford Castle - Bramble Bird by Pitpan (David A Kiely) 3525¹ 3769

7 **SOLWAY KING,** b g Germont - Copper Tinsell by Crooner (M A Barnes) 2533 2849 3198

7 **SOLWAYSANDS,** b g Germont - Castle Point by Majestic Streak (K Little) 3438

12 **SOME DAY SOON,** b g Beau Charmeur (FR) - Our Day by Conte Grande (M Bradstock) 418² 953¹

5 **SOME ORCHESTRA(IRE),** b m Orchestra - Luxury (P N Walsh) 1247⁵ 1490⁹ 1907 3178 3765⁵

9 **SOME TOURIST(IRE),** b g Torus - Noellespir by Bargello (Nigel Benstead) 3850

11 **SOME-TOY,** ch g Arkan - Cedar Of Galaxy by Bauble (John Squire) 2608⁶ 3300⁴ 3615¹ 3690² 3856⁴ 4171

10 **SOMERSET DANCER(USA),** br g Green Dancer (USA) - Distant Song (FR) by Faraway Son (USA) (J J Bridger) 1596⁶ 1700

7 **SOMERSET PRIDE(IRE),** br m Supreme Leader - Susie Wuzie by Ardoon (W M Roper) 732

9 **SOMETHING CATCHY(IRE),** b m Toravich (USA) - Spring Flower II by Ozymandias (A Barrow) 3593³ 3861

5 **SOMETHING SPEEDY(IRE),** b m Sayf El Arab (USA) - Fabulous Pet by Somethingfabulous (USA) (M D Hammond) 1783³ 2063⁵ 2463 2853 3433⁸

8 **SOMMERSBY(IRE),** b g Vision (USA) - Echoing by Formidable (USA) (Mrs N Macauley) 262⁶

4 **SON OF ANSHAN,** b g Anshan - Anhaar by Ela-Mana-Mou (Mrs A Swinbank) 930 1221³ 1629² 1909¹ 2147 3055¹ 3303¹

9 **SON OF CAL(IRE),** g Callernish - Border Jewel (John Crowley) 2048

9 **SON OF IRIS,** br g Strong Gale - Sprats Hill by Deep Run (Mrs M Reveley) 1046 1253⁶ 1822⁵ 2239¹ 2495¹ 3306¹

8 **SON OF TEMPO(IRE),** b g Sandhurst Prince - Top Love (USA) by Topsider (USA) (Mrs K M Lamb) 3665⁴

10 **SON OF WAR,** gr g Pragmatic - Run Wardasha by Run The Gantlet (USA) (Peter McCreery) 1619² 1755¹ 2085⁵ 2734 2843

6 **SONG FOR AFRICA(IRE),** b m Orchestra - Live Aid by Little Buskins (M J Grassick) 1581² 1904 2104⁸ 2379²

4 **SONG FOR JESS(IRE),** b f Accordion - Ritual Girl by Ballad Rock (F Jordan) 305 411 542⁵ 614² 658⁴ 788 893⁷ 1869⁴ 2292⁶ 2886⁶ 3136⁴ 3466² 3801³ 4232⁵

5 **SONG OF KENDA,** b m Rolfe (USA) - Kenda by Bargello (B R Millman) 2668 3106⁵ 3402³

4 **SONG OF THE SWORD,** b g Kris - Melodist (USA) by The Minstrel (CAN) (J A B Old) 3985¹ 4080¹ 4231¹

8 **SONIC STAR(IRE),** b g Euphemism - Daraheen Blade by Fine Blade (USA) (D Nicholson) 298¹ 615¹ 655¹ 799²

13 **SONOFAGIPSY,** b g Sunyboy - Zingarella by Romany Air (J W Dufosee) 2544³ 2981⁵ 3365³ 3615⁶

5 **SONRISA(IRE),** b g Phardante (FR) - No Not by Ovac (ITY) (J White) 52 1763

6 **SOPHIE MAY,** b m Glint Of Gold - Rosana Park by Music Boy (L Montague Hall) 833² 1112⁸ 1557⁴ 1847⁴ 2266¹ 2729 2921

5 **SOPHIE VICTORIA(IRE),** b m Satco (FR) - Vein by Kalydon (Charles A Murphy) 77⁴ 1247³ 1756⁵ 1907⁷ 2525²

6 **SOPHIES DREAM,** ch g Librate - Misty Glen by Leander (J M Bradley) 1306 1609 1855⁹

6 **SORALENA(IRE),** b m Persian Bold - Entracte by Henbit (USA) (Francis Berry) 2097⁸ 2415⁶

10 **SORBIERE,** b g Deep Run - Irish Mint by Dusky Boy (N J Henderson) 1064⁴ 1231 1426² 1674 1937 2198⁵ 2559⁹ 3255³

6 **SORCERER'S DRUM(IRE),** b g Orchestra - Pearly Miss by Space King (A L T Moore) 1460⁷ 2131¹ 2447⁶ 3219

6 **SORCIERE,** ch m Hubbly Bubbly (USA) - Fernessa by Roman Warrior (G B Balding) 3543¹ 3737⁵ 4233

5 **SORISKY,** ch g Risk Me (FR) - Minabella by Dance In Time (CAN) (B Gubby) 226⁴ 297³ 971 1135⁷

10 **SORREL HILL,** b g Mandalus - Lamb's Head by Laser Light (P J Hobbs) 1453⁵ 1684⁴ 2245

11 **SORRY ABOUT THAT,** b g Cut Above - Mark Up by Appiani II (Thomas Carberry) 1650⁵ 1906³ 2226² 2444⁴ 2736² 3084⁴

6 **SOU SOU WESTERLY(IRE),** b g Strong Gale - Fair Fashion by Miner's Lamp (C Weedon) 1483

9 **SOUND CARRIER(USA),** br g Lord Gaylord (USA) - Bright Choice (USA) by Best Turn (USA) (C L Popham) 2700 3404⁵ 3742

9 **SOUND MAN(IRE),** b g Kemal (FR) - Frankford Run by Deep Run (E J O'Grady) 825¹ 1169² 1551¹ 1760¹ 2507³

6 **SOUND ORCHESTRA(IRE),** b g Orchestra - Northern Dandy (P Hughes) 745⁴ 951⁵

9 **SOUND REVEILLE,** b g Relkino - Loughanvalley by Candy Cane (C P E Brooks) 1640⁴ 1875³ 2212⁵ 2437

8 **SOUND STATEMENT(IRE),** ch g Strong Statement (USA) - Coolishall Again by Push On (Miss S Edwards) 2638 3699⁷

5 **SOUNDPOST,** b g Shareef Dancer (USA) - Cheerful Note by Cure The Blues (USA) (Mrs L Williamson) 1142⁷ 1390 1817⁷ 3722

5 **SOUNDS CONFIDENT(IRE),** b f Orchestra - Mrs Baggins (Derek Pugh) 3647⁵ 4005 4324¹

4 **SOUNDS DEVIOUS,** ch f Savahra Sound - Trust Ann by Capistrano (C Parker) 1384⁷ 1909 2344 2632

9 **SOUNDS GOLDEN,** br g Sonnen Gold - Tuneful Queen by Queen's Hussar (John Whyte) 1846⁵ 2254⁷

6 **SOUNDS LIKE FUN,** b g Neltino - Blakeney Sound by Blakeney (Miss H C Knight) 952¹ 2035⁴ 2323 3077¹ 3795¹

8 **SOUNDS STRONG(IRE),** br g Strong Gale - Jazz Bavard by Le Bavard (FR) (D Nicholson) 1069¹ 1495 1892¹ 2334⁶ 2956 4040² 4259²

6 **SOUNDSGOODTOME,** b f Supreme Leader - Laurello (J R H Fowler) 2343 3963

5 **SOUNDWOMEN(IRE),** ch f Buckskin (FR) - Clonaslee Baby (F Flood) 3840 4160 4244

5 **SOUPREME,** ch m Northern State (USA) - Soupcon by King Of Spain (Mrs M Reveley) 146

6 **SPRINGFIELD DANCER,** b m Rambo Dancer (CAN) - Nebiha by Nebbiolo (P J Hobbs) 331¹ 643

6 **SPRINGFIELD RHYME,** b m Idiot's Delight - Ledee by Le Bavard (FR) (S Gollings) 3823

8 **SPRINGFORT LADY(IRE),** b m Mister Lord (USA) - Ardglass Belle by Carnival Night (John J Walsh) 138⁵ 314⁶ 563² 588¹ 743 926³ 1194 1245⁶ 3706⁵ 3815⁶ 4078²

8 **SPRINGHILL QUAY(IRE),** br g Quayside - Home Rejoicing by Carlburg (G Richards) 1820⁴ 1963 2620

4 **SPRINGLEA TOWER,** b g Meadowbrook - Tringa (GER) by Kaiseradler (R Nixon) 3698 4097⁶

5 **SPRINGWELL MAY(IRE),** ch m Tremblant - Nello (USA) (W J Burke) 115⁶ 175 192⁵ 353⁹

9 **SPRINTFAYRE,** b g Magnolia Lad - Headliner by Pampered King (J E Long) 1425¹ 1541³ 1764¹ 1973² 3194⁵

5 **SPRITZER(IRE),** ch m Be My Native (USA) - Sipped by Ballyciptic (J G FitzGerald) 624⁶ 802 1193⁴ 1275⁷ 1775⁴ 2419¹ 2575² 2882⁵ 3535⁵

14 **SPROWSTON BOY,** ch g Dominion - Cavalier's Blush by King's Troop (M C Chapman) 1021¹ 1739⁶ 2258

4 **SPRUCE LODGE,** b g Full Extent (USA) - Miss Ticklemouse by Rhodomantade (J S King) 2784⁸

9 **SPUFFINGTON,** b g Sula Bula - Pita by Raffingora (J T Gifford) 1212⁵ 1544⁴ 1726⁵ 1974³ 2306³ 2439 2698³ 3063³ 3605 3718

5 **SPUMANTE,** ch g Executive Man - Midler by Comedy Star (USA) (M P Muggeridge) 689⁸ 919⁶ 1006⁸

4 **SPUNKIE,** ch g Jupiter Island - Super Sol by Rolfe (USA) (R F Johnson Houghton) 2377² 3122¹

9 **SPY DESSA,** br g Uncle Pokey - Jeanne Du Barry by Dubassoff (USA) (A G Newcombe) 104⁵ 2308 2638

11 **SPY'S DELIGHT,** b g Idiot's Delight - Ida Spider by Ben Novus (H N W Rayner) 2551 4142⁸

5 **SQUADDIE,** ch g Infantry - Mendelita by King's Company (J W Payne) 2402³ 3929²

8 **SQUEALING JEANIE,** b m Librate - Mutchkin by Espresso (J M Bradley) 3883³ 4232

8 **SQUIRE SILK,** b g Natroun (FR) - Rustle Of Silk by General Assembly (USA) (Andrew Turnell) 1725⁷ 2554¹ 2720² 3112² 3564¹

4 **SQUIRE'S OCCASION(CAN),** b g Black Tie Affair - Tayana by Wajima (USA) (R Curtis) 965³ 1154¹ 1286³ 1517⁴ 2333⁵ 2553 3680

10 **SQUIRRELLSDAUGHTER,** gr m Black Minstrel - Grey Squirell by Golden Gorden (J W Beddoes) 528⁵

5 **ST BARTS(IRE),** ch g Eve's Error - Eileens Fancy (Capt D G Swan) 2108⁹

6 **ST CAROL(IRE),** br f Orchestra - St Moritz by Linacre (P Mullins) 88 2137 2339 2520 2704 2900⁷ 3377 3626 3817 4004 4197 4306⁷

14 **ST COLEMAN'S WELL,** br g Callernish - Divided Loyalties by Balidar (John Crowley) 1549⁸

6 **ST KITTS,** b m Tragic Role (USA) - T Catty (USA) by Sensitive Prince (USA) (W G M Turner) 540

5 **ST MABYN INN BOY,** b g Lir - Weiss Rose (FR) by Pilgrim (USA) (P R Rodford) 2248 3108

7 **ST MELLION DRIVE,** b g Gunner B - Safeguard by Wolver Hollow (M C Pipe) 2243⁵ 2546³

8 **ST MELLION FAIRWAY(IRE),** b g Mandalus - Kilbricken Bay by Salluceva (D Nicholson) 1746³ 2189⁵ 2821³ 3453⁵

5 **ST MELLION LEISURE(IRE),** b g Lord Americo - Forthetimebeing by Prince Regent (FR) (M C Pipe) 1578⁷ 1942 2260 2766

4 **ST RITA,** gr f Bustino - Able Mabel by Absalom (M J P O'Brien) 2270

11 **ST VILLE,** b g Top Ville - Dame Julian by Blakeney (R H Buckler) 1576⁸ 1921⁷ 2246 2562⁷ 2740³ 2932² 3120¹ 3272² 3405² 3774¹ 3951¹ 4133³ 4318⁴

7 **STAC-POLLAIDH,** b m Tina's Pet - Erica Superba by Langton Heath (K C Bailey) 1213⁵ 1688 1971² 2295³ 2513⁵ 3140⁴ 3498² 3761 3990³

9 **STAFF(IRE),** b m Anita's Prince - Mashid by Fordham (USA) (A P O'Brien) 1310⁶

5 **STAGALIER(IRE),** gr m Roselier (FR) - Big Polly by Pollerton (Noel Meade) 2131² 2380¹ 3180¹ 3835² 3935b¹

6 **STAGE FRIGHT,** b g Sure Blade (USA) - First Act by Sadler's Wells (USA) (F Murphy) 229²

11 **STAGE PLAYER,** b g Ile de Bourbon (USA) - Popkins by Romulus (Miss C J E Caroe) 1571⁵ 1765⁶ 2010¹ 2457⁴ 2808⁷ 3966⁶ 4091⁵ 4204

12 **STAGS FELL,** gr g Step Together (USA) - Honey's Queen by Pals Passage (T A K Cuthbert) 698² 762⁵ 3587⁸ 3919⁶ 4258⁶

8 **STAIGUE FORT(IRE),** b f Standaan (FR) - Lady Beecham by Laurence O (C Storey) 548² 607² 662²

10 **STAMP DUTY,** b g Sunyboy - Royal Seal by Privy Seal (N J Henderson) 3559

5 **STAN'S PRIDE,** b g Lord Bud - Kilkilanne by Brave Invader (USA) (Mrs V A Aconley) 2469 2764

7 **STAN'S YOUR MAN,** b g Young Man (FR) - Charlotte's Festival by Gala Performance (USA) (Mrs J D Goodfellow) 1198¹ 1679⁴ 3203¹

8 **STAND ALONE(IRE),** br g Mandalus - Deep Slaney by Deep Run (John Brassil) 552⁷

6 **STANDARA(IRE),** b f Standaan (FR) - Tanndara (FR) (Basil King) 1902

8 **STANMORE(IRE),** b g Aristocracy - Lady Go Marching (USA) by Go Marching (USA) (C P E Brooks) 1483⁵ 2377⁸ 2694⁸

9 **STANSWAY(IRE),** b g Stansted - Rydal Way by Roscoe Blake (Michael O'Connor) 144² 177² 253² 410¹ 536 601⁵ 746⁶ 849

5 **STANWICK HALL,** b g Poetic Justice - Allez Stanwick by Goldhill (Miss S Williamson) 3008⁶

9 **STAPLEFORD LADY,** ch m Bairn (USA) - Marie Galante (FR) by King Of The Castle (USA) (J S Moore) 152⁴ 227³ 325¹ 369² 502³ 639⁸ 3633⁶ 3734⁴ 3974²

5 **STAR ADVENTURE,** b g Green Adventure (USA) - Lady Martha by Sidon (J T Evans) 3322⁶ 3560² 4187⁹

4 **STAR BLAKENEY,** b g Blakeney - Trikkala Star by Tachypous (G Barnett) 1221⁷ 2371⁷

5 **STAR CLUB(IRE),** b m Bluebird (USA) - Borough Counsel by Law Society (USA) (D G McArdle) 928 2583 2839⁷ 3085 3520⁵ 3837⁸ 4149¹

6 **STAR DEFECTOR(IRE),** ch g Soviet Star (USA) - Citissima by Simbir (John Muldoon) 183¹ 3416⁴

6 **STAR HAND(IRE),** b g Hollow Hand - Golden Moth (J A Berry) 686 853

4 **STAR ISLAND,** b g Jupiter Island - Gippeswyck Lady by Pas de Seul (J C Poulton) 2221⁶ 2402⁷

7 **STAR MARKET,** b g Celestial Storm (USA) - Think Ahead by Sharpen Up (J L Spearing) 248¹ 281³ 374³ 656¹ 808 871¹

6 **STAR MASTER,** b g Rainbow Quest (USA) - Chellita by Habitat (P Monteith) 1509⁶ 1770 1983⁸ 3700 3805⁶

4 **STRADBALLY KATE(IRE)**, b f Be My Native (USA) - Miss Mims (Thomas G Walsh) 3432

10 **STRAIGHT LACED(USA)**, b or br g Alleged (USA) - Swoonmist (USA) by Never Bend (P C Clarke) 596⁴

6 **STRAIGHT ON(IRE)**, b g Tremblant - Maybird by Royalty (J G Coogan) 89 171⁸ 604⁶ 645¹ 948²

10 **STRAIGHT TALK**, b g Ovac (ITY) - Golden Tipp by Golden Love (P F Nicholls) 821² 1156² 1304⁵ 1529 3605

8 **STRAIGHTFORWARD(IRE)**, b g Camden Town - Wild Lucy (Neil King) 464

9 **STRALDI(IRE)**, br g Ela-Mana-Mou - Cavurina by Cavo Doro (Mrs John Harrington) 2708 2841 3214⁴ 3451⁸

9 **STRANGE WAYS**, b g Reach - Burglar Tip by Burglar (H J Manners) 1216 1471 1541

7 **STRATA RIDGE(IRE)**, ch g Standaan (FR) - Andarta (Mrs John Harrington) 3943

6 **STRATEGIC AFFAIR(IRE)**, ch g Torus - Miss Inglewood (L T Reilly) 2022 3225 3642⁹ 4148

4 **STRATEGIC PLOY**, b f Deploy - Wryneck by Niniski (USA) (D P Kelly) 2074² 2337¹ 2470³ 2965⁴ 3087⁵ 3450² 3785

11 **STRATH ROYAL**, b g Furry Glen - Last Princess by Le Prince (O Brennan) 2850⁵ 3286⁴

6 **STRATHMINSTER**, gr g Minster Son - Strathdearn by Saritamer (USA) (K C Bailey) 1338⁸ 1973⁶ 3137

8 **STRATHMORE LODGE**, b m Skyliner - Coliemore by Coliseum (Miss Lucinda V Russell) 3056 3355 3803

6 **STRATHTORE DREAM(IRE)**, b or br m Jareer (USA) - Beyond Words by Ballad Rock (Miss L A Perratt) 724 1122⁸

7 **STRATTON FLYER**, b m Mas Media - Empress Valley by Gay Fandango (USA) (H S Howe) 2991⁵ 4034² 4174⁵

7 **STRAY HARMONY**, ch m Noalto - Kitty Come Home by Monsanto (FR) (R J Smith) 2665⁸ 4048 4186¹

7 **STREPHON(IRE)**, b g Fairy King (USA) - Madame Fair by Monseigneur (USA) (J P Leigh) 1736⁸

4 **STRETCHING(IRE)**, br g Contract Law (USA) - Mrs Mutton by Dancer's Image (USA) (A Bailey) 1530⁴

8 **STRICT TEMPO(IRE)**, b g Reasonable (FR) - Miss Disco (Patrick Heffernan) 224⁸ 2787 4077 1554⁵ 2416⁵ 2703

12 **STRIDING EDGE**, ch g Viking (USA) - Kospia by King Emperor (USA) (T Hind) 110⁶ 4296⁷

5 **STRIFFOLINO**, b g Robellino (USA) - Tizona by Pharly (FR) (Miss A E Embiricos) 3457

5 **STRIKE A LIGHT(IRE)**, b g Miner's Lamp - Rescued by Sir Herbert (Miss H C Knight) 1012⁴ 2871

7 **STRIKE-A-POSE**, ch m Blushing Scribe (USA) - My Bushbaby by Hul A Hul (B J Llewellyn) 1574⁸ 1731⁵ 1915³ 2440³ 2665⁹ 3317⁶ 3554³ 3988 4179¹ 4251¹

7 **STROKESAVER(IRE)**, ch g Orange Reef - Silver Love (USA) by The Axe II (C P E Brooks) 1597 1766⁶ 1970 2280 2480³ 2726² 2955⁵ 3252⁶ 3514¹

7 **STROLL HOME(IRE)**, ch g Tale Quale - Sales Centre by Deep Run (James Joseph Mangan) 97¹ 290¹ 300¹ 626 744³ 909³ 1059³ 3337 3522 3765 4028⁶ 4145¹

12 **STRONG APPROACH**, br g Strong Gale - Smart Fashion by Carlburg (J I A Charlton) 81

6 **STRONG AUCTION(IRE)**, b m Mazaad - Legal Puzzler (William J Fitzpatrick) 910 2094 3069

6 **STRONG BOOST(USA)**, b g Topsider (USA) - Final Figure (USA) by Super Concorde (USA) (Seamus O'Farrell) 604³ 680⁵ 711² 804⁴

9 **STRONG CASE(IRE)**, gr g Strong Gale - Sunshot by Candy Cane (M C Pipe) 201

11 **STRONG CHARACTER**, b g Strong Gale - Reinvite by Le Bavard (FR) (D A Lamb) 2578 3009⁸ 3658 3903⁷ 4007⁷ 4210

5 **STRONG CHOICE(IRE)**, br f Strong Gale - Innocent Choice (P Mullins) 3789 4079² 4200³ 4307¹

6 **STRONG DANCER(IRE)**, b g Strong Gale - Cailin Rialta (J Morrison) 394

9 **STRONG DEEL(IRE)**, b g Strong Gale - Gorryelm by Arctic Slave (F Murphy) 1199³ 1336 1632⁵ 1774

6 **STRONG EDITION(IRE)**, b f Strong Gale - My Maizey by Buckskin (FR) (J A Berry) 350² 4306²

9 **STRONG GLEN(IRE)**, br g Strong Gale - Merry And Bright by Beau Chapeau (P Wegmann) 2862

9 **STRONG HICKS(IRE)**, ch g Seymour Hicks (FR) - Deep Foliage by Deep Run (F Flood) 1014³ 1116⁵ 1408² 2020 2053⁶ 2274⁷ 2756⁴ 3236⁶ 3837⁹

7 **STRONG HOPE(IRE)**, br g Strong Gale - My Only Hope (James Buckle) 210

10 **STRONG HURRICANE**, b g Strong Gale - Gorryelm by Arctic Slave (P Hughes) 580³ 636⁵ 926⁶

5 **STRONG IMAGE(IRE)**, b f Strong Gale - Toi Figures (T G McCourt) 3348⁹ 3891

9 **STRONG JOHN(IRE)**, b g Strong Gale - Deep Khaletta by Deep Run (M E Sowersby) 125 206 241² 299² 606³ 665¹

5 **STRONG MAGIC(IRE)**, br g Strong Gale - Baybush by Boreen (FR) (Miss C Johnsey) 2469⁸ 2899

5 **STRONG MARTINA(IRE)**, b m Orchestra - Loreto Lady (Niall Madden) 1409⁶ 3069 3705

10 **STRONG MEDICINE**, b g Strong Gale - In The Forest by Crowded Room (K C Bailey) 1029¹ 1289¹ 1394⁷ 1613 1851² 1999⁵ 2220⁵ 4016⁵ 4317⁶

6 **STRONG MINT(IRE)**, br g Strong Gale - Derrygold by Derrylin (Mrs M Reveley) 1073⁵ 1390⁴ 1809¹ 2008 2908⁸

6 **STRONG PALADIN(IRE)**, b g Strong Gale - Kalanshoe by Random Shot (J T Gifford) 1479⁶ 1893⁷ 2871¹ 3253¹

6 **STRONG PROMISE(IRE)**, b or br g Strong Gale - Let's Compromise by No Argument (G A Hubbard) 688¹ 776² 1099¹ 1159¹ 1394² 1518¹ 2045⁴ 2507¹ 3130⁵ 3576² 3676¹

7 **STRONG RAIDER(IRE)**, br g Strong Gale - Sweet Tulip (M Phelan) 1013 1360 1486⁹ 1904 4168⁵ 4292

6 **STRONG SON(IRE)**, b g Strong Gale - Pryoress by Pry (Peter McCreery) 1539³ 2449

10 **STRONG SOUND**, b g Strong Gale - Jazz Music by Choral Society (P Cheesbrough) 71 165⁵ 3245³

7 **STRONG STUFF(IRE)**, b g Strong Gale - Must Rain by Raincheck (K C Bailey) 1399

7 **STRONG TARQUIN(IRE)**, br g Strong Gale - Trumpster by Tarqogan (P F Nicholls) 902¹ 1055⁴ 1451⁶ 2873

7 **STRONG TEL(IRE)**, b g Strong Gale - Arctic Snow Cat by Raise You Ten (M C Pipe) 1578³ 2920³ 3269

7 **STRONGALONG(IRE)**, b g Strong Gale - Cailin Cainnteach by Le Bavard (FR) (P Cheesbrough) 1334⁶ 1658 2484⁴ 2812² 3250³ 4001 4108⁵ 4211²

4 **STRONGDAKA(IRE)**, b f Strong Gale - Randaka (T J Taaffe) 4309

9 **SUNSET DAZZLE(IRE)**, ch g Kemal (FR) - Last Sunset (A P O'Brien) 196⁴

5 **SUNSET FLASH**, b g Good Times (ITY) - Political Prospect by Politico (USA) (Mrs J D Goodfellow) 2322

11 **SUNSET RUN**, b g Deep Run - Sunset Queen by Arctic Slave (Miss Catherine Tuke) 3458

6 **SUNSHINE BAY(IRE)**, b or br g Strong Gale - Mawbeg Holly by Golden Love (Fergus Sutherland) 2075⁶ 2519⁴ 2752² 3836²

5 **SUNSTRIKE**, ch g Super Sunrise - Gilzie's Touch by Feelings (FR) (R McDonald) 2206⁸ 2533⁸

6 **SUNSWORD**, b m Broadsword (USA) - Suntino by Rugantino (Miss A Stokell) 2503 3210

8 **SUNY BAY(IRE)**, gr g Roselier (FR) - Suny Salome by Sunyboy (C P E Brooks) 1480⁵ 2821¹ 3605²

6 **SUP A WHISKEY(IRE)**, b m Commanche Run - First In by Over The River (FR) (A P O'Brien) 410³ 472¹ 561⁸

5 **SUPER BRUSH(IRE)**, br m Brush Aside (USA) - Flying Silver by Master Buck (P R Johnson) 1129 1295

9 **SUPER COIN**, b g Scorpio (FR) - Penny Princess by Normandy (R Lee) 1236² 1577² 1748 2033¹ 2561² 3154 3730² 4135³

5 **SUPER DEALER(IRE)**, b g Supreme Leader - Death Or Glory by Hasdrubal (D T Hughes) 1907⁴ 2645¹ 3348²

7 **SUPER DOC(IRE)**, b g Lancastrian - Fairy Slip by Le Moss (Charles A Murphy) 4197⁹

10 **SUPER FLAME(CAN)**, b g Super Concorde (USA) - Flanders Flame by Busted (Joseph M Canty) 2142 2272 2735

5 **SUPER GUY**, b g Exodal (USA) - Custard Pie by Castle Keep (J Barclay) 740⁹ 960 1657 1929⁵ 3762 3919

5 **SUPER HIGH**, b g Superlative - Nell Of The North (USA) by Canadian Gil (CAN) (P Howling) 1997⁶

6 **SUPER NOVA**, b g Ra Nova - Windrush Song by True Song (C J Hemsley) 2377 3475⁹

5 **SUPER RAPIER(IRE)**, b g Strong Gale - Misty Venture by Foggy Bell (G A Hubbard) 1350⁴ 1556⁶ 2678³ 2980⁴ 3641³ 4038³

9 **SUPER RITCHART**, b g Starch Reduced - Karousa Girl by Rouser (B Palling) 1443⁵ 1727² 2254³ 2391³ 2748² 2859

7 **SUPER SAFFRON**, b m Pollerton - Sagora by Sagaro (B Smart) 2123⁸

10 **SUPER SANDY**, ch m Import - Super Satin by Lord Of Verona (F T Walton) 1316⁵ 1589 2150⁶ 2622³ 3010⁴ 3565⁷ 4024²

6 **SUPER SECRETARY(IRE)**, b f King's Ride - To-Us-All (S J Mahon) 159 210⁹ 343

9 **SUPER SHARP(NZ)**, ch g Brilliant Invader (AUS) - Aspen Annie (NZ) by Amalgam (USA) (H Oliver) 81⁴ 110³ 570¹ 639¹ 690² 895³ 1176¹ 3047⁴ 3360⁴

9 **SUPER TACTICS(IRE)**, b g Furry Glen - Hilarys Pet by Bonne Noel (R H Alner) 823² 964¹ 1342¹ 1480⁴ 1993¹ 2194¹ 2455 3544⁴ 3636²

7 **SUPERENSIS**, ch g Sayf El Arab (USA) - Superlife (USA) by Super Concorde (USA) (John Berry) 846² 1006⁶

5 **SUPEREXALT**, ch g Exorbitant - Super Sue by Lochnager (J G FitzGerald) 2496⁷ 3015⁹ 3509⁶

4 **SUPERGOLD(IRE)**, ch g Keen - Superflash by Superlative (F Kirby) 1922 2265

6 **SUPERHOO**, b g Superlative - Boo Hoo by Mummy's Pet (R Craggs) 70¹ 204² 765³

11 **SUPERIOR FINISH**, br g Oats - Emancipated by Mansingh (USA) (Mrs J Pitman) 2692³

8 **SUPERIOR RISK(IRE)**, b g Mandalus - Hal's Pauper by Official (N A Twiston-Davies) 1628

11 **SUPERMARINE**, b g Noalto - Lucky Love by Mummy's Pet (B Mactaggart) 3395 3662³ 3865 4024⁵ 4263

6 **SUPERMICK**, ch g Faustus (USA) - Lardana by Burglar (W R Muir) 1175² 1416¹ 1603⁷ 2396³ 2609⁴

4 **SUPERMISTER**, br g Damister (USA) - Superfina (USA) by Fluorescent Light (USA) (T D Easterby) 614

5 **SUPERMODEL**, gr m Unfuwain (USA) - Well Off by Welsh Pageant (Mrs N Macauley) 60⁴ 168⁴ 263² 1379² 1852⁴ 4255

7 **SUPERSONIA(IRE)**, b f Sheer Grit - Pitpan Lass (G Ducey) 68

9 **SUPERTOP**, b or br g High Top - Myth by Troy (L Lungo) 728² 792¹ 888¹ 1038² 1510¹ 1691⁵ 1933¹ 2120³ 2361³ 3870² 4273³

4 **SUPPORT ACT(IRE)**, b g Shernazar - Biserta (GER) (D K Weld) 2370⁵ 3755²

9 **SUPPOSIN**, b g Enchantment - Misty Rocket by Roan Rocket (Mrs S J Smith) 865³ 1037² 1253⁹ 1589 2239⁴ 2772 3161⁸ 3399⁷ 3739¹ 3914⁶ 4215²

7 **SUPREME ALLIANCE(IRE)**, b m Supreme Leader - Rambling Love by Golden Love (John C Shearman) 1536 2582⁷ 2839 3234

5 **SUPREME CHANTER(IRE)**, b g Supreme Leader - Blaithin by Le Bavard (FR) (T Donohue) 560 898³ 1247² 1307⁵ 1897³ 2054⁷ 3180

5 **SUPREME CHARM(IRE)**, b g Sovereign Water - Welsh Charmer by Welsh Captain (K C Bailey) 172¹ 1505⁴ 1997⁵ 2277 2541⁶ 3913²

5 **SUPREME COMFORT(IRE)**, b m Supreme Leader - Malozza Brig by New Brig (E M Caine) 74² 1073

6 **SUPREME CRUSADER(IRE)**, br g Supreme Leader - Seanaphobal Lady by Kambalda (W G McKenzie-Coles) 1675 3035 3192⁸

12 **SUPREME DEALER**, ch g The Parson - Vul's Money by Even Money (Mrs S Warr) 4119⁴

7 **SUPREME FLYER(IRE)**, b g Supreme Leader - Awbeg Lady by The Parson (K C Bailey) 1729² 2311³ 3241¹ 3735¹ 3881²

7 **SUPREME FUEL(IRE)**, b f Supreme Leader - Cheap Fuel (Thomas Foley) 2144⁹ 2416⁸

5 **SUPREME GAZETTE(IRE)**, b g Supreme Leader - Ladies Gazette (T Stack) 2060⁸ 2449 3381⁸

8 **SUPREME GENOTIN(IRE)**, b g Supreme Leader - Inagh's Image by Menelek (J A B Old) 1749² 1958² 2158⁹ 2952

5 **SUPREME GOLD(IRE)**, b f Supreme Leader - Palmers Well (Michael Cullen) 4005² 4197

4 **SUPREME ILLUSION(AUS)**, ch f Rory's Jester (AUS) - Counterfeit Coin (AUS) by Comeram (FR) (John Berry) 2611¹ 3042⁵ 3196 3519²

6 **SUPREME KELLYCARRA(IRE)**, b m Supreme Leader - Vamble by Vulgan (Miss H C Knight) 1270⁸

6 **SUPREME LADY(IRE)**, b m Supreme Leader - Tudor Lady by Green Shoon (Miss H C Knight) 1699¹ 2598¹ 3131 3715⁴

8 **SUPREME LINK(IRE)**, br g Supreme Leader - Broken Link (Michael Cullen) 1246⁷

6 **SUPREME MISS(IRE)**, b f Supreme Leader - Merry Miss (Michael Cunningham) 1901

8 **SUPREME RAMBLER(IRE)**, b g Supreme Leader - Panel Pin by Menelek (B Smart) 3310⁹

7 **SUPREME SOVIET**, ch g Presidium - Sylvan Song by Song (A C Whillans) 2316² 2538⁴ 2849² 3013⁹ 3305⁴ 4097¹ 4207⁶

INDEX TO NATIONAL HUNT RESULTS 1996-97

6 **THE FLYING PHANTOM,** gr g Sharrood (USA) - Miss Flossa (FR) by Big John (FR) (M H Tompkins) 2782[1] 3111 3382[7]

5 **THE FLYING YANK(IRE),** b m Architect (USA) - Time Please (Ronald Curran) 1756 2079

10 **THE FOOLISH ONE,** b m Idiot's Delight - The Ceiriog by Deep Diver (R H Alner) 106[7] 188

9 **THE FROG PRINCE(IRE),** b g Le Johnstan - Fine Lass by Royal Buck (N A Gaselee) 2947[4] 3565

5 **THE GADFLY,** br g Welsh Captain - Spartan Imp by Spartan General (R Dickin) 2409

7 **THE GALLOPIN'MAJOR(IRE),** ch g Orchestra - Pedalo by Legal Tender (Mrs M Reveley) 201 385 462[2] 551[2] 605[1] 662[1] 778[1] 915[2] 3481

10 **THE GENERAL'S DRUM,** b g Sergeant Drummer (USA) - Scottswood by Spartan General (R Fell) 4064[4]

4 **THE GENT(IRE),** b c Fairy King (USA) - Mosaique Bleue (M J Grassick) 574[6] 927[8]

9 **THE GLOW(IRE),** b g Glow (USA) - Full Choke by Shirley Heights (Mrs J Pitman) 2389[9] 2627[6]

5 **THE GNOME(IRE),** b g Polish Precedent (USA) - Argon Laser by Kris (G M Moore) 2858[4] 3048 3929

7 **THE GO AHEAD(IRE),** b g Le Bavard (FR) - Cantafleur by Cantab (Capt T A Forster) 1055 1339[4] 2527

8 **THE GOPHER(IRE),** ch g General View - Egg Shells by Miami Springs (T F Lacy) 525 729[1] 926[7] 1194[3] 1408 1903[3] 2020[4] 3526[1] 3765

6 **THE GOTHIC(IRE),** b g Supreme Leader - Cool Princess (John J Walsh) 552

4 **THE GREAT FLOOD,** ch g Risk Me (FR) - Yukosan by Absalom (C A Dwyer) 1024[4] 1524[1]

4 **THE GREY MARE(IRE),** gr m Roselier (FR) - Gem Princess by Little Buskins (Seamus Fahey) 1096[1] 2087[5] 2235[4] 2339 2838[2] 2902[2] 3213[3] 3520[4] 3834[2] 4059[1] 4077[4]

9 **THE GREY MONK(IRE),** gr g Roselier (FR) - Ballybeg Maid by Prince Hansel (G Richards) 1387[1] 1639[2] 2474 2819[1] 3453[3]

8 **THE GREY TEXAN,** gr g Nishapour (FR) - Houston Belle by Milford (R Rowe) 2847 3002 3258[9] 3948[3] 4228

4 **THE GREY WEAVER,** gr c Touch Of Grey - Foggy Dew by Smoggy (R M Flower) 991[8] 1179[9] 1412

7 **THE HEARTY LADY(IRE),** b m Hatim (USA) - Lady Leandra by Le Levanstell (E McNamara) 979[3] 1485[5] 1778

8 **THE HERBIVORE(IRE),** b g Lancastrian - Lean Over by Over The River (FR) (M J Roberts) 1411[3] 1718

5 **THE HOLY PARSON(IRE),** b g Satco - Holy Times by The Parson (Peter McCreery) 122[8] 1275 2160[4] 2416 2645[4] 3178[4]

12 **THE JOGGER,** b g Deep Run - Pollychant by Politico (USA) (C L Tizzard) 2793[1] 3153[7]

5 **THE KEEK(IRE),** b m Brush Aside (USA) - Fairgoi by Baragoi (J Howard Johnson) 4113

4 **THE KERRY LEDGEND(IRE),** b g Phardante (FR) - I'm Grannie by Perspex (Noel T Chance) 4050[9]

4 **THE KERRY REBEL(IRE),** b g Gallant Knight - Symphony Orchestra (Patrick Heffernan) 2518 4056 4309[9]

7 **THE KHOINOA(IRE),** b g Supreme Leader - Fine Drapes by Le Bavard (FR) (Mrs A Swinbank) 2199[1] 2346[5] 3011[8] 3396

5 **THE KNITTER,** ch g Derrylin - Meryett (BEL) by Le Grand Meaulnes (J J Birkett) 700[7] 866[6] 960 1097

8 **THE LAD,** b g Bold Owl - Solbella by Starch Reduced (L Montague Hall) 867[2] 1085[3]

5 **THE LADY CAPTAIN,** b m Neltino - Lady Seville by Orange Bay (D T Thom) 1742[1] 2409[5] 2678

5 **THE LADY SCORES(IRE),** br m Orchestra - Lysanders Lady by Saulingo (K C Bailey) 3917[8]

8 **THE LANCER(IRE),** b g Lancastrian - Bucktina by Buckskin (FR) (D R Gandolfo) 904[2] 1111[3] 1686[1] 1846[1] 2244[5] 2529[3] 4019[6]

6 **THE LAND AGENT,** b g Town And Country - Notinhand by Nearly A Hand (J W Mullins) 1727[2] 2384[8]

7 **THE LAST FLING(IRE),** ch g Avocat - Highway's Last by Royal Highway (Mrs S J Smith) 878[1] 1152[1] 1382 1773[1] 1891[3] 2466 2713[3] 3132 3577[2]

10 **THE LAST MISTRESS,** b m Mandalus - Slinky Persin by Jupiter Pluvius (A J Cook) 585[4] 920[7] 3746[5]

9 **THE LATVIAN LARK(IRE),** b g Buckskin (FR) - Dark Harbour by Deep Run (Noel Meade) 1018[1] 1242[2] 1461 1618[4] 2446[1] 3453

4 **THE LEGIONS PRIDE,** b c Rambo Dancer (CAN) - Immaculate Girl by Habat (J W Hills) 672[1]

4 **THE LIGHTMAKER(IRE),** b g Mac's Imp (USA) - Lady's Turn by Rymer (Simon Earle) 2831[4]

7 **THE LITTLE FERRET,** ch g Scottish Reel - Third Movement by Music Boy (A Moore) 242[3]

9 **THE LORRYMAN(IRE),** ch g Avocat - Perception by Star Moss (Nicky Mitchell) 102 188 327 418 3851[8]

10 **THE MAJOR GENERAL,** b g Pollerton - Cornamucla by Lucky Guy (G Richards) 2790 4018[4]

11 **THE MALAKARMA,** b g St Columbus - Impinge (USA) by Impressive (Miss C Saunders) 2502[1] 2960[1] 3274[3] 3690[6] 3855[2] 3993[1]

5 **THE MALL(IRE),** b g Be My Native (USA) - Swift Invader by Brave Invader (USA) (J F C Maxwell) 2866[9] 3226[5] 3520

8 **THE MARMALADE CAT,** ch g Escapism (USA) - Garrison Girl by Queen's Hussar (Mrs D Haine) 1804 1924

9 **THE MEXICANS GONE,** b g Royal Vulcan - Corncrop by Mycropolis (D P Geraghty) 2701 2923[8]

6 **THE MICKLETONIAN,** ch g K-Battery - Minature Miss by Move Off (J I A Charlton) 1818[8] 3583[4]

7 **THE MILL HEIGHT(IRE),** ch g Callernish - Cherry Gamble by Meadsville (K Tork) 3368

6 **THE MILLMAN(IRE),** ch g Noalto - Kitty Malone (S G Walsh) 2416 2907[6] 3381

6 **THE MILLMASTER(IRE),** b g Mister Lord (USA) - Rolling Mill by Hardboy (John R Upson) 1591[6] 1763 2388[5] 2527[9] 2741 3481

6 **THE MILLSTONE,** b g Welsh Captain - Blue Mint by Bilsborrow (C H Jones) 3427[9]

10 **THE MINDER(FR),** b or br h Miller's Mate - Clarandal by Young Generation (G F Edwards) 515[2]

10 **THE MINE CAPTAIN,** b g Shaab - Bal Casek by New Linacre (O Sherwood) 1666[3] 2184[2] 2328[1]

8 **THE MINISTER(IRE),** br g Black Minstrel - Miss Hi-Land by Tyrant (USA) (R Champion) 1349 1846[6]

11 **THE MOTCOMBE OAK,** ch g Brotherly (USA) - Yashama by Supreme Red (M Madgwick) 1445

6 **THE MUCKLE QUINE,** b m Hubbly Bubbly (USA) - Blessed Damsel by So Blessed (J J O'Neill) 2029 2206

9 **THUHOOL,** b g Formidable (USA) - Wurud (USA) by Green Dancer (USA) (R Rowe) 1051⁶

11 **THUMBS UP,** b g Fidel - Misclaire by Steeple Aston (G M McCourt) 1131³ 1157³ 1468¹ 1672² 2294² 2555⁴ 2689³ 2774¹ 3273¹ 3842²

5 **THUNDER PRINCESS(IRE),** b or br f Aristocracy - Chamonix Princess (P A Fahy) 3880 4284

6 **THUNDER ROAD(IRE),** b or br g Cardinal Flower - Ann Advancer by Even Money (Miss H C Knight) 1292 1981⁵ 2388⁶ 2480 3861¹ 4204 4286⁴

5 **THUNDERBIRD,** b m Funny Man - Carlton Valley by Barolo (A H Harvey) 2694 4013

5 **THUNDERPOINT(IRE),** b g Glacial Storm (USA) - Urdite (FR) by Concertino (FR) (T D Easterby) 2469⁷ 2687³ 2858⁵

11 **THUNDERSTRUCK,** b g Young Generation - Ringed Aureole by Aureole (J Howard Johnson) 914² 1201² 1327³ 1692 1822⁸

6 **THURSDAY NIGHT(IRE),** ch g Montelimar (USA) - Alsazia (FR) by Bolkonski (J G FitzGerald) 1225⁴ 1741 1991 2151³ 3045² 3205² 3537⁵ 3782⁶

11 **THURSDAY SWEEP,** br g Aristocracy - Regency Cherry by Master Duck (Edward P Mitchell) 2272

10 **TIBBI BLUES,** b m Cure The Blues (USA) - Tiberly (FR) by Lyphard (USA) (J S Goldie) 1198

8 **TIBBS INN,** ch g Adonijah - Historia by Northfields (USA) (A Barrow) 754⁸ 856 891 987³ 1261 1353⁴ 1670 1980

5 **TIBETAN,** b g Reference Point - Winter Queen by Welsh Pageant (Lady Herries) 2001⁴ 2465² 2787⁷

7 **TIBOULEN(IRE),** ch m General View - Kefflen's Lass by Flair Path (O Sherwood) 113⁶ 162⁶ 235⁴ 342³ 354² 564⁷ 579⁵ 732³

7 **TICKERTY'S GIFT,** b g Formidable (USA) - Handy Dancer by Green God (T E Powell) 1596⁵ 1699⁴ 1894⁴ 2009³ 2429¹ 2639³ 3194¹ 3328¹

7 **TICKET TO THE MOON,** b m Pollerton - Spring Rocket by Harwell (Mrs Janita Scott) 4033²

9 **TICO GOLD,** ch g Politico (USA) - Derigold by Hunter's Song (P Cheesbrough) 1183⁴ 1585³ 1681 1952² 2237³ 2418¹ 2652² 2909² 3005³ 3159⁵ 3511²

6 **TIDAL FORCE(IRE),** br g Strong Gale - Liffey Travel by Le Bavard (FR) (P J Hobbs) 1109¹ 2153 2277 3513⁶

6 **TIDAL PRINCESS(IRE),** b or br m Good Thyne (USA) - Gemini Gale by Strong Gale (W M Roper) 1836⁵ 2072⁶ 2845⁴ 3231¹

5 **TIDAL RACE(IRE),** b g Homo Sapien - Flowing Tide by Main Reef (J S Haldane) 1682 2206 3808

7 **TIDEBROOK,** ch h Callernish - Hayley by Indian Ruler (K C Bailey) 2499⁵ 3781¹ 3927¹

7 **TIDJANI(IRE),** b g Alleged (USA) - Tikarna (FR) (Francis Berry) 742¹ 1488⁴ 1621⁷ 1761³ 2473 2735 3156⁵

5 **TIED FOR TIME(IRE),** b g Montelimar (USA) - Cornamucla by Lucky Guy (Miss H C Knight) 3721

5 **TIFFANY VICTORIA(IRE),** b m Taufan - Victorian Pageant by Welsh Pageant (J C Harley) 161³ 208² 270⁵ 645²

5 **TIGANA,** b m Lugana Beach - Tina's Beauty by Tina's Pet (Mrs L C Jewell) 2886 3170 3292 3325

6 **TIGER BEE,** br m Town And Country - Ijazah by Touching Wood (USA) (N R Mitchell) 52

11 **TIGER CLAW(USA),** b g Diamond Shoal - Tiger Scout (USA) by Silent Screen (USA) (A G Hobbs) 1061¹ 1302 1567⁴ 1858⁶ 2177⁸ 2435³ 3140³ 3405³ 3725 4035³ 4232⁶

7 **TIGERALI(IRE),** b f Over The River (FR) - No Tigers (A P O'Brien) 117⁸ 192⁷ 233

9 **TIGH-NA-MARA,** b m Miramar Reef - Charlie's Sunshine by Jimsun (J M Jefferson) 419⁴ 609 761² 874² 1067 1331¹ 1442⁵

7 **TIGHT FIST(IRE),** b g Doulab (USA) - Fussy Budget by Wolver Hollow (Miss H C Knight) 1265⁴ 1647 3831 4034¹ 4276³

10 **TIGHTER BUDGET(USA),** b g Desert Wine (USA) - Silver Ice (USA) by Icecapade (USA) (Mrs Dianne Sayer) 739¹ 814¹ 959¹ 1165⁸ 1334² 1658³ 1785⁴ 3161⁶ 3306³ 3436

5 **TILAAL(USA),** ch h Gulch (USA) - Eye Drop (USA) by Irish River (FR) (M D Hammond) 2372⁴ 2817²

12 **TILT TECH FLYER,** b g Windjammer (USA) - Queen Kate by Queen's Hussar (I R Jones) 1917⁶ 2768 3148⁷ 3440

7 **TILTY(USA),** b g Linkage (USA) - En Tiempo (USA) by Bold Hour (A Streeter) 2025³ 2422¹ 2892³ 3140¹ 3712⁵ 3881

7 **TIM(IRE),** b g Sexton Blake - Wingau (FR) by Hard To Beat (J R Jenkins) 896⁵ 1402³ 1481¹ 1762² 2047¹ 2198⁴ 2453⁷ 2530³ 2797⁵ 3116

10 **TIM SOLDIER(FR),** ch g Tip Moss (FR) - Pali Dancer by Green Dancer (USA) (Miss A Stokell) 1569 1766 1954¹ 2203¹ 2421² 2772⁴ 3138² 3461¹ 3972 4155⁴

10 **TIMBUCKTOO,** b g Buckskin (FR) - Rugged Glen by Rugged Man (J K M Oliver) 747³ 1678² 2360⁵ 2493³ 3199⁵

7 **TIME AND CHARGES(IRE),** b g Good Thyne (USA) - Current Call by Electrify (Francis Berry) 909⁵ 1170⁶ 1276 1534⁷ 1618 2136 3838⁶ 4055⁴ 4165³ 4283⁴

8 **TIME ENOUGH(IRE),** ch g Callernish - Easter Gazette by London Gazette (C P E Brooks) 642² 995² 1177¹ 1418¹ 1745⁴

9 **TIME FOR A RUN,** b g Deep Run - Hourly Rate by Menelek (E J O'Grady) 1116⁴ 1537⁷ 1650⁶ 1753³ 2071³ 2127¹ 2836⁴ 3115²

6 **TIME FOR A WINNER(IRE),** b f Good Thyne - Ollies Return (G M Lyons) 928 1013 1189⁸ 1433

5 **TIME GOES ON,** b m Latest Model - Impromptu by My Swanee (R J Hodges) 2173 2430

5 **TIME LEADER,** ch g Lead On Time (USA) - Green Leaf (USA) by Alydar (USA) (R Dickin) 1263⁶ 1348⁵ 1614⁴ 1723² 1978⁵ 2158 2372⁵ 3686² 4287

5 **TIME TO GO(IRE),** b m Brush Aside (USA) - Vesper Time (Augustine Leahy) 253 365⁶

7 **TIME TO LEAD(IRE),** b g Supreme Leader - Hourly Rate by Menelek (E J O'Grady) 2098³ 2675² 3073 3344

6 **TIME TO PARLEZ,** b g Amboise - Image Of War by Warpath (C J Drewe) 2405⁷ 2792⁸

6 **TIME WARRIOR(IRE),** ch g Decent Fellow - Oonagh's Teddy by Quayside (G M Moore) 3356⁶ 3807²

8 **TIME WON'T WAIT(IRE),** b g Bulldozer - Time Will Wait by Milan (R T Phillips) 2212⁴ 2335³ 3154⁴ 3596 3842⁴ 4090³

6 **TIMEFORGOING(IRE),** br m Good Thyne (USA) - Kingstown Girl by Bright Will (M Halford) 238³

7 **TIMELY AFFAIR(IRE),** b m Don't Forget Me - In My Time by Levmoss (A L T Moore) 90⁹ 314 580² 729 1058⁶ 2038² 2223⁵

6 **TIMELY EXAMPLE(USA),** ch g Timeless Moment (USA) - Dearest Mongo (USA) by Mongo (B R Cambidge) 806⁸ 971⁷ 3495⁵ 3796⁷

5 **TIMELY MAGIC(IRE),** b g Good Thyne (USA) - Magic Quiz by Quisling (J Neville) 3082[3]

4 **TIMIDJAR(IRE),** b g Doyoun - Timissara (USA) by Shahrastani (USA) (D R Gandolfo) 2925[6] 3117[9] 3541[3] 3985[2] 4176[3]

4 **TIMMYS CHOICE(IRE),** br g Yashgan - Pampered Sneem (S J Mahon) 3183 3889 4148[9]

8 **TIMUR'S STAR,** b m Scorpio (FR) - Timur's Daughter by Tamerlane (J Parkes) 78

5 **TIN CUP,** b g Broadsword (USA) - Osmium (M F Morris) 3421

8 **TIN PAN ALLEY,** b g Pitpan - Also Kirsty by Twilight Alley (D M Grissell) 3355 3905 4043[2] 4322[3]

7 **TINAMONA(IRE),** b or br g Tanfirion - Evan's Love (Victor Bowens) 1432 1536

7 **TINERANA BOY(IRE),** gr g Razzo Forte - Regal Sound (Ronald O'Leary) 212[9]

5 **TINERANA GLOW(IRE),** ch m Glow (USA) - Hada Rani by Jaazeiro (USA) (T F Lacy) 3437 393[6] 444[2] 624[5] 681[5] 928 3625 3705 3889[7]

5 **TINGRITH LAD,** b g Reesh - Bracelet by Balidar (J A Bennett) 2377 3122[6]

6 **TINKER'S CUSS,** ch m Nearly A Hand - Little Member by New Member (A P Jones) 1476 1792 2183 2894

5 **TINKLERS FOLLY,** ch g Bairn (USA) - Lucky Straw by Tumble Wind (USA) (R M Whitaker) 610

6 **TINNOCK(IRE),** gr f Roselier (FR) - Adrian's Girl (R O'Connor) 394 611

7 **TINOTOPS,** br g Neltino - Topte by Copte (FR) (Mrs R A Vickery) 3274[1] 3857[1]

6 **TINVACOOSH(IRE),** b g Noalto - Lady Esmond (Eoin Griffin) 1539 1838 2343 3430

6 **TINY'S CARMEL(IRE),** b f Roselier (FR) - Boyne Mead (Peter McCreery) 2582 3338[6]

6 **TIOTAO(IRE),** b g Burslem - Linbel by Linacre (Mrs L C Jewell) 1259[3] 1872[4] 2118[2] 2485 2630[6] 2855[8] 3919 4023[4]

8 **TIP IT IN,** gr g Le Solaret (FR) - Alidante by Sahib (A Smith) 390[6] 932[8] 1248[1] 1588[2] 1691[1] 2581[8] 2760[2] 3006[7] 3820[9]

4 **TIP YOUR WAITRESS(IRE),** g Topanoora - Zazu (Augustine Leahy) 522[7] 1057 1547[9] 1709[4] 2105[6] 2415[8] 3219[5] 3835

14 **TIPP DOWN,** ch g Crash Course - Caramore Lady by Deep Run (Ms Helen Wallis) 2974

12 **TIPP MARINER,** ch g Sandalay - Knockbawn Lady by Push On (O Sherwood) 1133 1559

8 **TIPPING ALONG(IRE),** ch g Rising - Gone by Whistling Wind (D R Gandolfo) 544 667 906[3] 1061[4]

7 **TIPPING THE LINE,** b g Baron Blakeney - Lily Mab (FR) by Prince Mab (FR) (J R Best) 78[2] 155[1] 203 812[2] 1100[2] 1419[6]

6 **TIPSY QUEEN,** b m Rakaposhi King - Topsy Bee by Be Friendly (Miss H C Knight) 157 310[6]

5 **TIRADE(IRE),** b g Tirol - Sindos (Michael Hourigan) 3343

11 **TIRLEY MISSILE,** ch g Cruise Missile - Tic-On-Rose by Celtic Cone (J S Smith) 2745 4203[3]

6 **TIRMIZI(USA),** b g Shahrastani (USA) - Tikarna (FR) by Targowice (USA) (Mrs A Swinbank) 1604[7] 1953[1] 3006[9] 3398[9]

5 **TIRYAM(USA),** gr g Shahrastani (USA) - Tarkhana (Victor Bowens) 713[6] 3789

5 **TISNOTMYTURN(IRE),** bl m Roselier (FR) - Moreno (Ronald O'Neill) 1907 2525 2754 3380

7 **TISRARA LADY(IRE),** b m The Parson - My Deep Fort Vii (Thomas Foley) 118[8] 235[3] 354 4246[1]

8 **TISSISAT(USA),** ch g Green Forest (USA) - Expansive by Exbury (J Kirby) 2783[6] 2982[5]

8 **TITAN EMPRESS,** b m Oats - Stella Roma by Le Levanstell (S Mellor) 1207[2] 1445[5] 1674[6] 1814 1920[1] 2308

6 **TITANIUM HONDA(IRE),** gr g Doulab (USA) - Cumbrian Melody by Petong (D C O'Brien) 689

5 **TITATIUM(IRE),** ch g Lancastrian - Argu Ironside (John F Gleeson) 1077

10 **TITUS ANDRONICUS,** b g Oats - Lavilla by Tycoon II (N A Gaselee) 840[4]

4 **TIUTCHEV,** b g Soviet Star (USA) - Cut Ahead by Kalaglow (Miss H C Knight) 2497[4] 2925 3555 3905 4043[2] 4322[3]

10 **TO BE FAIR,** ch g Adonijah - Aquarula by Dominion (P J Hobbs) 612[7] 998[5] 1353[5]

7 **TO BE THE BEST,** ch g Superlative - Early Call by Kind Of Hush (D A Lamb) 695[1] 724[2]

7 **TO SAY THE LEAST,** ch g Sayyaf - Little Hut by Royal Palace (W T Kemp) 1034 1631

4 **TO-DAY TO-DAY(IRE),** b g Waajib - Balela (Miss A M McMahon) 4147[2] 4281[6]

5 **TOAST THE SPREECE(IRE),** b g Nordance (USA) - Pamphylia by Known Fact (USA) (A P O'Brien) 1777[1] 2017[1] 2132[1] 2473[1] 2732 3156 3750[4]

5 **TOAT CHIEFTAIN,** b g Puissance - Tribal Lady by Absalom (Miss A E Embiricos) 3265 3473[8]

5 **TOBAR NA CARRAIGE(IRE),** br g Mandalus - Swanny Jane (John J Walsh) 4195 4328[5]

7 **TOBARELLA(IRE),** ch m Henbit (USA) - Dreamello by Bargello (Martin Hurley) 144

4 **TOBERLONE,** b g K-Battery - Elisetta by Monsanto (FR) (J P Dodds) 3808

4 **TOBY,** b g Jendali (USA) - Au Revoir Sailor by Julio Mariner (G Richards) 3808[4]

8 **TOBY'S FRIEND(IRE),** ch f Fresh Breeze (USA) - Goggins Hill Plume (John Patrick Ryan) 1241 2079 2143[5] 2522[8]

7 **TOBYS PAL(IRE),** gr g Heraldiste (USA) - Excelling Miss (USA) by Exceller (USA) (Francis Ennis) 2228[6] 2383 2868

6 **TOCHAR BOY(IRE),** b g Tremblant - Gorabeth (J Fanning) 1195 2098[5] 2343[8] 4282[7]

9 **TOD LAW,** b m Le Moss - Owenburn by Menelek (Mrs R L Elliot) 3921[6]

6 **TODD(USA),** b g Theatrical - Boldara (USA) by Alydar (USA) (A H Harvey) 1006[2] 2153 2371 2771

10 **TODDLING INN,** b m Pragmatic - Arconist by Welsh Pageant (R J R Symonds) 3051 3365

5 **TODDYS LASS,** b m Rakaposhi King - Heaven And Earth by Midsummer Night II (J A Pickering) 1648 1809

4 **TOEJAM,** ch g Move Off - Cheeky Pigeon by Brave Invader (USA) (R E Barr) 3661

8 **TOLCARNE LADY,** b m Idiot's Delight - The Ceiriog by Deep Diver (K Bishop) 1237 2387

4 **TOLEPA(IRE),** b f Contract Law (USA) - Our Investment by Crofter (USA) (J J O'Neill) 4268[8]

8 **TOLL BOOTH,** b m Import - Little Hut by Royal Palace (Mrs N Hope) 457

7 **TOM BRODIE,** b g Ardross - Deep Line by Deep Run (J Howard Johnson) 962[1] 1200[1] 1528[1] 1885[4] 2218[4] 2467[2] 2716[3] 3156[7] 3907

5 **TOM DIAMOND,** ch g Right Regent - Shavegreen Holly Vii by Damsire Unregistered (L A Snook) 2784

10 **TOM FURZE,** b g Sula Bula - Bittleys Wood by Straight Lad (Mrs D Buckett) 3387[5] 3930[2]

INDEX TO NATIONAL HUNT RESULTS 1996-97

5 **TWO LORDS,** b g Arctic Lord - Doddycross by Deep Run (G A Ham) 2784 2899⁹

6 **TWO SHONAS(IRE),** b m Persian Heights - Olean by Sadler's Wells (USA) (J R Curran) 2094⁵ 2131 2222

13 **TWO STEP RHYTHM,** gr g Neltino - Niagara Rhythm by Military (J C McConnochie) 42⁷

4 **TYCOON PRINCE,** b g Last Tycoon - Princesse Vali (FR) by Val de L'orne (FR) (D Shaw) 2262

5 **TYLO STEAMER(IRE),** b g King's Ride - Chatty Actress by Le Bavard (FR) (A J McNamara) 1490²

6 **TYNDARIUS(IRE),** b g Mandalus - Lady Rerico (A L T Moore) 3348⁷

7 **TYPHOON(IRE),** br g Strong Gale - Bally Decent by Wrekin Rambler (Mark Campion) 1831 2373⁵ 2498 3103 3414

7 **TYPHOON EIGHT(IRE),** b h High Estate - Dance Date (IRE) by Sadler's Wells (USA) (R W Armstrong) 1919

4 **TYPHOON LAD,** ch g Risk Me (FR) - Muninga by St Alphage (S Dow) 965⁴

11 **UBU VAL(FR),** b g Kashneb (FR) - Lady Val (FR) by Credit Man (W A Bethell) 1314² 1767 2148⁴ 3014⁴

6 **UCKERBY LAD,** b g Tobin Lad (USA) - Chomolonga by High Top (Miss J Du Plessis) 2724

7 **UK HYGIENE(IRE),** br g Lepanto (GER) - Proceeding by Monsanto (FR) (M D Hammond) 1374⁸ 1587² 1741 2176⁴ 3656²

5 **ULTIMATE SMOOTHIE,** b g Highest Honor (FR) - Baino Charm (USA) by Diesis (M C Pipe) 129¹ 231¹ 693¹ 1240¹ 1609⁴ 2035¹ 2185⁵ 2432³ 3986¹ 4139⁷

7 **ULTIMATE WARRIOR,** b g Master Willie - Fighting Lady by Chebs Lad (Mrs L Richards) 4063⁴

10 **ULTRA FLUTTER,** b g Beldale Flutter (USA) - Ultra Vires by High Line (Michael Hourigan) 1172⁵ 1435⁵ 1618² 1898¹ 2058² 2125¹ 2341¹

10 **ULTRA MAGIC,** b m Magic Mirror - Cardane (FR) by Dan Cupid (T A Kent) 564⁴ 621⁵ 730

11 **ULTRASON IV(FR),** b g Quart de Vin (FR) - Jivati (FR) by Laniste (Mrs Amanda Bryan) 4142

9 **ULURU(IRE),** b g Kris - Mountain Lodge by Blakeney (C P Morlock) 1400³ 1867⁵ 2047⁵ 2559 3557⁶ 3774⁴ 3926⁶ 4318

4 **UMBERTON(IRE),** b g Nabeel Dancer (USA) - Pivotal Walk (IRE) by Pennine Walk (P R Hedger) 2594⁹

5 **UN POCO LOCO,** b g Lord Bud - Trailing Rose by Undulate (USA) (Mrs J Brown) 1280 2489 2852

9 **UNA'S CHOICE(IRE),** ch g Beau Charmeur (FR) - Laurabeg by Laurence O (F Flood) 2136⁷ 2226 2843⁵ 3181³ 3347³ 4078¹

4 **UNASSISTED(IRE),** b f Digamist (USA) - Velia by Welsh Saint (Victor Bowens) 1173 1403⁵ 1750⁸ 2067 2702 3415⁷ 3642¹ 3817 4293²

8 **UNCLE ALGY,** ch g Relkino - Great Aunt Emily by Traditionalist (USA) (Miss H C Knight) 1957 2254² 2527 2593 3845²

7 **UNCLE BERT(IRE),** b g Ovac (ITY) - Sweet Gum (USA) by Gummo (USA) (Miss Lucinda V Russell) 875⁵ 1206¹ 1692² 2191⁶

8 **UNCLE DOUG,** b g Common Grounds - Taqa by Blakeney (Mrs M Reveley) 1680⁵ 2190² 2467 2933⁶ 3305⁵

12 **UNCLE ERNIE,** b g Uncle Pokey - Ladyfold by Never Dwell (J G FitzGerald) 1157⁴ 1640³ 2819⁴ 3154¹

4 **UNCLE GEORGE,** ch g Anshan - Son Et Lumiere by Rainbow Quest (USA) (M H Tompkins) 614⁵ 705⁴

7 **UNCLE KEENY(IRE),** b g Phardante (FR) - Honeyburn by Straight Rule (J J O'Neill) 1045 1329

5 **UNCLE WAT,** b g Ardross - First Things First (Patrick Prendergast) 2054⁶

5 **UNDAWATERSCUBADIVA,** ch g Keen - Northern Scene by Habitat (M P Bielby) 3003³ 3258³ 3849³ 4092³

8 **UNDERSTANDING(IRE),** ch m Standaan (FR) - Sarania by Sassafras (FR) (Ms E Cassidy) 112⁷ 173 277

5 **UNFORGETABLE,** ch g Scottish Reel - Shercol by Monseigneur (USA) (K T Ivory) 2420⁹

4 **UNFORGOTTEN STAR(IRE),** b g Don't Forget Me - Murroe Star (F Flood) 4026⁶ 4160

9 **UNGUIDED MISSILE(IRE),** br g Deep Run - Legaun by Levanter (G Richards) 1466¹ 1999² 2209² 2779² 3152 3581¹ 3804¹

5 **UNITED FRONT,** br g Be My Chief (USA) - Julia Flyte by Drone (J Neville) 1141⁴ 1346⁷ 1606

6 **UNO NUMERO(IRE),** br g Mandalus - Kinneagh Queen (Mrs D J Coleman) 562 802⁷ 979

11 **UNOR(FR),** b g Pot D'Or (FR) - Fyrole II (FR) by Le Tyrol (P Monteith) 763

6 **UNPREJUDICE,** b g North Briton - Interviewme (USA) by Olden Times (M D Hammond) 2117⁶

8 **UNSINKABLE BOXER(IRE),** b g Sheer Grit - Softly Sarah by Hardboy (N J H Walker) 2398³ 2926³

7 **UNYOKE RAMBLER(IRE),** b f Castle Keep - Sparkling Stream (John P Berry) 1905⁸ 2166 2446

4 **UONI,** ch f Minster Son - Maid Of Essex by Bustino (P Butler) 3170⁵

8 **UP AND UNDER(IRE),** b g Garryowen - Merrywell (T K Geraghty) 2523⁶ 3391

8 **UP FOR RANSOME(IRE),** b g Boyne Valley - Fauvette (USA) by Youth (USA) (Mrs A M Naughton) 916⁵ 1127⁴ 2990³ 3248 3458² 3666²

5 **UP THE CREEK(IRE),** br m Supreme Leader - Jacob's Creek (IRE) by Buckskin (FR) (Miss M E Rowland) 975⁶

8 **UP THE TEMPO(IRE),** ch m Orchestra - Bailieboro by Bonne Noel (Paddy Farrell) 47 262⁵ 301⁵ 401² 540⁴ 1234 1501³ 1667 1724 3686⁶ 3936³ 4194² 4232

8 **UP TRUMPS(IRE),** ch g Torus - Lonely Wind by Tumble Wind (USA) (John J Walsh) 525³ 623¹

11 **UPHAM CLOSE,** ch m Oats - Real View by Royal Highway (Mrs Mandy Hand) 2544

6 **UPHAM RASCAL,** ch g Gunner B - Upham Kelly by Netherkelly (D R Gandolfo) 1202⁷ 1368 1568 1723 2372⁹ 3196

9 **UPHAM SURPRISE,** b g Sula Bula - Upham Lady by The Bo'sun (J A B Old) 2398 3996⁹

5 **UPPER CLUB(IRE),** b m Taufan (USA) - Sixpenny by English Prince (P R Webber) 1437⁶

7 **UPPER MOUNT STREET(IRE),** b m Strong Gale - Annick (FR) by Breton (J E Mulhern) 2369⁵ 2735⁴ 3337² 4196⁷

7 **UPRISING(IRE),** ch g Rising - Sea Skin by Buckskin (FR) (J A B Old) 2264⁷

9 **UPSHEPOPS(IRE),** b m The Parson - Avocan by Avocat (Miss Siobhan Reidy) 2844 3222 4005⁵ 4061⁵

7 **UPWARD SURGE(IRE),** ch g Kris - Sizes Vary by Be My Guest (USA) (R R Ledger) 3410⁵ 3775⁴ 3851 4226⁸

800

13 UPWELL, b g Tanfirion - Debnic by Counsel (R Johnson) 124³ 475⁵ 697³ 793² 816⁴ 915⁶ 3352⁴ 3586³ 3659⁶

7 UR ONLY YOUNG ONCE, b m Pitpan - H And K Hattrick by Green Shoon (Mrs D Haine) 4068⁷ 4201⁶

11 URANUS COLLONGES(FR), b g El Badr - Flika (FR) by Verdi (Mrs L Williamson) 1774 2005⁴ 2488 3264⁴ 3659

8 URBAN DANCING(USA), ch g Nureyev (USA) - Afifa (USA) by Dewan (USA) (B Ellison) 913 1167⁸ 1284² 1761⁸ 2201⁷ 2358¹

8 URBAN LILY, ch m Town And Country - Laval by Cheval (R J Hodges) 1450¹ 1723 1813¹ 1978⁴ 2295⁸ 2440⁵ 3148⁴

11 URON V(FR), b g Cap Martin (FR) - Jolivette (FR) by Laniste (C F Wall) 2530⁴ 2923⁷ 3116

9 URSHI-JADE, b m Pennine Walk - Treeline by High Top (J G M O'Shea) 2372 2853

7 URUBANDE(IRE), ch g Phardante (FR) - Truly Fair by Gulf Pearl (A P O'Brien) 1172¹ 1638² 2232⁴ 2584⁸ 3151 3597⁵

7 US FOUR(IRE), b g Mandalus - Rock Plant by Ovac (ITY) (S Donohoe) 64² 99⁶ 183⁹ 232⁹ 2172⁷ 2378³ 2735 3216⁸ 4198

7 V'SOSKE GALE(IRE), b m Strong Gale - Gentle Down (USA) by Naskra (USA) (James Joseph Mangan) 2410⁵ 2673 2705 2941¹ 3237⁵ 3340

7 VA UTU, b g Balliol - Flame by Firestreak (D M Lloyd) 2872 3186¹ 3403³ 3592² 3741⁴

6 VADLAWYS(FR), br h Always Fair (USA) - Vadlava (FR) by Bikala (S A Brookshaw) 2954³ 3316 3534²

6 VAGUE HOPE(IRE), b g Strong Gale - Misty's Wish by Furry Glen (J C McConnochie) 3898²

10 VAIN PRINCE, b g Sandhurst Prince - Vain Deb by Gay Fandango (USA) (N Tinkler) 281⁴ 390³ 508³ 571⁵ 737 818³ 962⁴

8 VAIN PRINCESS(IRE), ch m Lancastrian - Saint Cyde by Welsh Saint (Michael Hourigan) 91⁹ 140¹ 223³ 292³ 342 432⁴ 471⁴ 525¹ 3835

10 VAL D'ALENE(FR), b g Quart de Vin (FR) - Faribole (FR) by Or de Chine (F Doumen) 1310³

8 VAL DE RAMA(IRE), b g Lafontaine (USA) - Port Magee by Royal Highway (Denys Smith) 608¹ 764² 916³ 1127 1327² 1523³ 2121³

7 VALAMIR(IRE), ch g Valiyar - Alcinea (FR) by Sweet Revenge (P Delaney) 92⁵ 195⁸ 272⁷ 302 355⁵

6 VALE OF OAK, b m Meadowbrook - Farm Consultation by Farm Walk (Miss Scarlett J Crew) 700⁹

7 VALENTINE GALE(IRE), b m Strong Gale - Midnight Nurse by Ardoon (W P Mullins) 2582⁸ 2752⁷ 2964² 3223² 3375² 3551⁴

8 VALERIE OWENS(IRE), b or br m Lancastrian - Rugged Glen by Rugged Man (P Budds) 2673⁴ 2904⁴ 3236⁴ 3339¹ 3815⁵ 4145

4 VALES ALES, b g Dominion Royale - Keep Mum by Mummy's Pet (R M McKellar) 886

4 VALHALLA(IRE), b g Brush Aside (USA) - Eimers Pet by Paddy's Stream (Martin Todhunter) 3721³ 3928¹

7 VALIANT DASH, b g Valiyar - Dame Ashfield by Grundy (J S Goldie) 460³ 559² 738¹ 817 3507⁵ 3761⁴ 4223³

9 VALIANT WARRIOR, br g Valiyar - Jouvencelle by Rusticaro (FR) (M D Hammond) 2007² 2466⁵ 2713⁵ 3329³ 3605

9 VALIANTHE(USA), b h Antheus (USA) - Princess Vali by Val de L'orne (FR) (M C Pipe) 2768⁸ 3146

7 VALISKY, gr m Valiyar - Rocket Trip by Tyrnavos (R Lee) 47¹ 187

6 VALLEY ERNE(IRE), b g King's Ride - Erne Gold Vii (Michael Cunningham) 745² 910⁵ 1432⁹ 1580⁵ 1649⁷ 2022¹ 2129⁴ 2369¹ 2735¹ 3346⁴ 3523⁷ 3754¹

7 VALLEY GARDEN, b g Valiyar - April by Silly Season (J J O'Neill) 1944 2347 2569⁶

7 VALLEY OF KINGS(IRE), ch g King Luthier - Queenofthevalley by Deep Run (V T O'Brien) 929 1060² 1144² 1361 3089 3955 4168

5 VALLEY PLAYER(IRE), ch g The Noble Player (USA) - Queenofthevalley (V T O'Brien) 1279 2870 3625

6 VALLEY TINGO(IRE), ch g Martingo - Valley Range (M J Byrne) 121⁵

6 VALLINGALE(IRE), b m Strong Gale - Knockarctic by Quayside (Miss H C Knight) 749⁵ 874³ 2550² 3001 3833⁷ 3961⁴ 4193 4278

9 VALMAR(IRE), ch g Ovac (ITY) - Wine Lake by Guillaume Tell (USA) (D P Kelly) 565² 732¹ 828² 1273⁴ 1489² 2647² 2944

10 VALNAU(FR), b g Grandchant (FR) - Matale (FR) by Danoso (M C Pipe) 2268 3404⁶

8 VAN DER GRASS, ch g Van Der Linden (FR) - Fanny Keyser by Majority Blue (P Calver) 47

8 VANBOROUGH LAD, b g Precocious - Lustrous by Golden Act (USA) (M J Bolton) 2662⁹ 3028⁹ 3292³ 3457 3780⁶

8 VANCOUVER LAD(IRE), ch g Sheer Grit - Hi Style by Tarkhun (A G Sims) 2243 3051

6 VANSELL, b m Rambo Dancer (CAN) - Firmiter by Royal Palace (R H Buckler) 1578⁹ 1961⁹

10 VARECK II(FR), b g Brezzo (FR) - Kavala II (FR) by Danoso (M C Pipe) 902 999 1106 1302 1451⁷

6 VARTRY BOY(IRE), b g Tremblant - Millview Diamond by Diamonds Are Trump (USA) (J Fanning) 122¹ 1193 2073⁷ 3935d 4163⁸ 4302⁸

5 VASILIKI(IRE), ch g Le Bavard (FR) - Smiles Awake You by Floriferous (G T Hourigan) 716⁵ 850 1077² 1550⁵ 1756⁷ 2229² 2366¹ 2585 3234² 3451⁶ 3624

11 VAZON EXPRESS, b g Le Bavard (FR) - Grangecon Express by Bonne Noel (R Dalton) 124

10 VELEDA II(FR), ch g Olmeto - Herbe Fine (FR) by Francois Saubaber (Mrs S A Bramall) 1194 1408⁵ 1903⁴ 2169⁸ 2756⁹

7 VENDOON(IRE), b g Sanchi Steeple - Lovely Venture by He Loves Me (M J Heaton-Ellis) 1295⁵ 1614⁹

7 VENERDI SANTO(IRE), ch g Lord Chancellor (USA) - Deira (Miss I T Oakes) 3888

5 VENICE BEACH, b g Shirley Heights - Bold And Beautiful by Bold Lad (IRE) (C P E Brooks) 2662

5 VERDE LUNA, b g Green Desert (USA) - Mamaluna (USA) by Roberto (USA) (D W P Arbuthnot) 244² 333¹ 521³ 754³ 839 3403⁴ 3652⁴ 3798⁵ 4037²

4 VEREDARIUS(FR), b g Le Nain Jaune (FR) - Villa Verde (FR) by Top Ville (A L T Moore) 1118⁸ 1273 1899⁴ 2272⁴ 2585 2840 3215⁵ 3838¹

4 VERONICA FRANCO, b f Darshaan - Maiden Eileen by Stradavinsky (R Ingram) 1702⁴ 1854⁹ 2012 3139⁵ 3323³ 3489⁵ 3634³ 3776⁵

5 VERRAZANO BRIDGE(IRE), b or br g Be My Native (USA) - Shannon Ville by Deep Run (T J Taaffe) 3090¹

10 VERRO(USA), ch g Irish River (FR) - Royal Rafale (USA) by Reneged (K Bishop) 2999⁷ 4179⁸ 4296

4 VERULAM(IRE), b or br g Marju (IRE) - Hot Curry (USA) by Sharpen Up (J R Jenkins) 363² 436¹ 672 893⁸ 1024⁷

6 **WILD ROSE OF YORK,** gr m Unfuwain (USA) - Chepstow Vale (USA) by Key To The Mint (USA) (Thomas J Taaffe) 3964 4698

7 **WILD WEST WIND(IRE),** br g Strong Gale - Taggs Castle by Levmoss (Miss H C Knight) 13993 17253 23121 28631 31554

7 **WILDE MUSIC(IRE),** b g Orchestra - Run For Shelter by Strong Gale (C P E Brooks) 9684 10223 14782 33845

9 **WILDLIFE RANGER(IRE),** b h Orchestra - Midland Flight by Light Brigade (A P O'Brien) 2746 3585 3935 5524 6013 8028

8 **WILKINS,** b g Master Willie - Segos by Runnymede (R J O'Sullivan) 9023 11111 17214 41906

6 **WILL BROOK(IRE),** br g Royal Fountain - Clockonocra (Patrick J F Hassett) 853

6 **WILL I OR WONT I(IRE),** b f Black Minstrel - Four In A Row (John J Walsh) 2134 3405 394 1782 1908

11 **WILL IT LAST,** b m Roi Guillaume (FR) - Golden Annie by Le Tricolore (F L Matthews) 2790 2960

11 **WILL JAMES,** ch g Raga Navarro (ITY) - Sleekit by Blakeney (C J Drewe) 49 801 10518 12184 14167 1722

8 **WILL TRAVEL(IRE),** b g Mandalus - Kenga by Roman Warrior (Andrew Dickman) 39213 41124 42707

10 **WILLCHRIS,** b g Fidel - Culkeern by Master Buck (C A McBratney) 1368 1589 41519

5 **WILLIAM OF ORANGE,** ch g Nicholas Bill - Armonit by Town Crier (G Richards) 3721

5 **WILLIE BRENNAN(IRE),** b g Tremblant - Moss Ana by Le Moss (Sean O O'Brien) 4072 464

7 **WILLIE MAKEIT(IRE),** g Coquelin (USA) - Turbina by Tudor Melody (R T Phillips) 82 1562 2281 3831 5161 6396 10623 13193 16982 1941

11 **WILLIE SPARKLE,** b g Roi Guillaume (FR) - Adamay by Florescence (Mrs S C Bradburne) 726 8892 1254 15892 18228 20655 23216 25353 31612 3867

6 **WILLIE THE LION(IRE),** b g Hollow Hand - Serocco Wind (E Sheehy) 238 393 40948 4243

7 **WILLIE WANNABE(IRE),** gr g Roselier (FR) - Quincy Bay by Buckskin (FR) (Mrs D Thomson) 934 13777 1631 3009 3160

7 **WILLOW PARK(IRE),** ch g Ballad Rock - Seat Of Wisdom (W J Lanigan) 2093

4 **WILLOWMOUNT(IRE),** br g Neils - The Hofsa (E J O'Grady) 3232 3415

5 **WILLOWS ROULETTE,** b g High Season - Willows Casino by Olympic Casino (A G Hobbs) 11094 15788 19758 26374 37354 39812

14 **WILLSFORD,** b g Beau Charmeur (FR) - Wish Again by Three Wishes (Mrs J Pitman) 12905 1395

7 **WILLY STAR(BEL),** b g Minstrel Star - Landing Power by Hill's Forecast (Mrs S J Smith) 13651 15412 16041 18262 22966 25261 27776

6 **WILLY WEE(IRE),** b g Orchestra - Viacandella by Cantab (W Rock) 1042 32285 36463

5 **WILLYELKRA,** b g Welsh Term - Stonebroker (Lee Bowles) 28703 32319 3456

6 **WILMA'S CHOICE,** ch m Gildoran - Miss Colleen by Joshua (D P Geraghty) 25679

7 **WIN A HAND,** b m Nearly A Hand - Mariban by Mummy's Pet (B J M Ryall) 1100 2457 2664

11 **WIN I DID(IRE),** ch f Camden Town - Ask The Boss by Gulf Pearl (R H Alner) 2242 25393 31193 33625

5 **WIN THE TOSS,** b g Idiot's Delight - Mayfield (USA) by Alleged (USA) (C R Egerton) 39297

7 **WIND OF GLORY(IRE),** b g Henbit (USA) - Booly Bay (Bernard Jones) 3943 41525 42955

6 **WINDGAP HILL(IRE),** b g Supreme Leader - Deep Adventure by Deep Run (A L T Moore) 20607 21328 28386 32381 34299

5 **WINDLE BROOK,** b g Gildoran - Minigale by Strong Gale (K C Bailey) 35607

6 **WINDMILL STAR(IRE),** ch f Orchestra - Zaydeen (I R Ferguson) 2086

7 **WINDTEKIN(IRE),** ch g Montekin - Windy City by Windjammer (USA) (John Monroe) 3429 4004 4162

11 **WINDWARD ARIOM,** ch g Pas de Seul - Deja Vu (FR) by Be My Guest (USA) (P Mitchell) 616 656 22905 26127

6 **WINDY BEE(IRE),** ch m Aristocracy - Dozing Sinead by Bulldozer (Brian Nolan) 19081 20802 21661 25825 27324 2900 32231 35511 3786

4 **WINDYEDGE(USA),** ch g Woodman (USA) - Abeesh (USA) by Nijinsky (CAN) (Mrs A M Naughton) 2879 3044

7 **WINDYHOUSE WAY(IRE),** gr f Roselier (FR) - Wish You Wow (N P Doyle) 926

7 **WINGS COVE,** b g Elegant Air - Bel Esprit by Sagaro (Lady Herries) 23895 27978 30548

13 **WINGSPAN(USA),** b g Storm Bird (CAN) - Miss Renege (USA) by Riva Ridge (USA) (A G Newcombe) 5143 6175 7592 8317

4 **WINN CALEY,** ch f Beveled (USA) - Responder by Vitiges (FR) (C W Fairhurst) 1524

9 **WINN'S PRIDE(IRE),** b g Indian Ridge - Blue Bell Girl by Blakeney (R Hollinshead) 32091 33213

5 **WINNETKA GAL(IRE),** br m Phardante (FR) - Asigh Glen by Furry Glen (N A Twiston-Davies) 14766 1675

12 **WINNIE LORRAINE,** b m St Columbus - Win Green Hill by National Trust (Miss Tina Hammond) 73 375 586

7 **WINNOW,** ch m Oats - Anglophil by Philemon (Andrew Turnell) 12285 15436 19583 21843 23542 27484 32715 35592 37267

6 **WINSFORD HILL,** ch g Nearly A Hand - Gay Ticket by New Member (I P Williams) 14934 24075 26395 38861

7 **WINSPIT(IRE),** b g Desert Of Wind (USA) - Celestial Drive by Dublin Taxi (R H Alner) 1730 18463 23554 2606 29312 30942 34102

5 **WINSTON RUN,** ch g Derrylin - Craftsmans Made by Jimsun (I P Williams) 40423

9 **WINTER BELLE(USA),** b g Sportin' Life (USA) - Bella O'Reason (USA) by Belle O'Reason (USA) (J Howard Johnson) 215 373 16582 20622

8 **WINTER GEM,** b m Hasty Word - Masami by King Log (R J Price) 55

5 **WINTER MELODY(IRE),** ch g Dragon Palace (USA) - Winterlude (John Muldoon) 1897 2160 24439 29425 3449 43046

6 **WINTER PRINCESS,** b f Arctic Lord - Wayward Pam by Pamroy (I A Duncan) 9469 10423 1360 1584 33897 3644

6 **WINTER ROSE,** br g Derring Rose - Eleri by Rolfe (USA) (Miss P M Whittle) 47 7492 8766 10009 24582 27464 30161

13 **WINTER'S LANE,** ch g Leander - Roman Lilly by Romany Air (Ms Kay Rees) 3279

7 **WINTRY DAWN(IRE),** ch g Toca Madera - Julie Winters by Le Bavard (FR) (T J O'Mara) 2944 3234 3377

4 **WIRE MAN(IRE),** gr g Glenstal (USA) - Wire To Wire (Michael A Kelly) 1430

6 **WISE 'N' SHINE,** ch m Sunley Builds - More Wise by Ballymore (N M Lampard) 1082 12174 13448 19276 27667

7 **WISE ADVICE(IRE),** b g Duky - Down The Aisle by Godswalk (USA) (M D Hammond) 2496 2824 3693 4213 663 706 8891 41005

National Hunt Speed Ratings 1996-97

● THIS list derived from Sporting Life Average Times, represents the optimum time-rating of a horse after taking into account varying ground conditions, adjusted to 12st. To qualify for inclusion a horse must earn a speed rating of over 20. Supplementary information after the name and figure contains the distance, course, going based on times and date when the rating was achieved.

HURDLERS

Above The Cut (USA) 22² (2m ½f, Asco, G, Apr 29, *H*)

Added Dimension (IRE) 23¹ (2m 1f, Taun, S, Feb 26, *H*)

Aerion 28¹ (2m ½f, Newb, G, Nov 13)

Albemine (USA) 44² (2m ½f, Hunt, Y, Dec 10, *H*)

All On 29² (2m 4f, Edin, G, Feb 22, *H*)

Allegation 61² (2m 5f, Chel, G, Mar 12, *H*)

Alltime Dancer (IRE) 30⁵ (2m ½f, Chep, F, Oct 5, *H*)

Alzulu (IRE) 44¹ (2m, Newc, S, Feb 14)

Amaze 29³ (2m 2½f, Font, G, Aug 26, *H*)

Ambidextrous (IRE) 22⁵ (2m, Warw, G, Mar 1, *H*)

Ambleside (IRE) 41³ (2m 4f, Live, Y, Apr 4, *H*)

Amlah (USA) 31¹ (2m ½f, Pert, G, Apr 23, *H*)

Anabranch 33² (2m, Weth, G, Apr 1, *H*)

Ansuro Again 24¹ (3m ½f, Carl, S, Mar 6, *H*)

Anzum 67² (3m ½f, Chel, G, Mar 13, *G*)

Ardarroch Prince 26² (2m, Weth, G, Mar 31)

Ashwell Boy (IRE) 33¹ (2m ½f, Chep, F, Apr 22, *H*)

Ask The Butler (IRE) 26¹ (2m, Fair, G, Dec 1, *M*)

Avanti Express (IRE) 28² (2m 1f, Plum, S, Jan 27, *M*)

Ballet Royal (USA) 24¹ (2m ½f, Stra, G, May 30, *H*)

Ballyrihy Boy (IRE) 37 (2m 5f, Chel, G, Mar 12, *H*)

Bankhead (IRE) 36² (3m ½f, Utto, G, Mar 18, *H*)

Bardaros 24¹ (3m ½f, Carl, G, Jan 20, *H*)

Barford Sovereign 30² (2m, Warw, Hrd, May 3, *H*)

Barna Boy (IRE) 55⁴ (2m, Hayd, G, May 3, *G*)

Barton Scamp 23 (2m, Utto, G, Mar 18, *H*)

Bawnrock (IRE) 34² (2m, Punc, G, Jan 18, *M*)

Beaumont (IRE) 32³ (2m ½f, Donc, G, Mar 3, *H*)

Beggars Banquet (IRE) 27¹ (2m 4f, Newc, S, Dec 3)

Bells Bridge (IRE) 29¹ (2m 4f, Fair, Y, Feb 23, *M*)

Bietschhorn Bard 21¹ (2m 2f, Worc, G, Oct 26)

Big Strand (IRE) 41¹ (2m 5f, Chel, G, Mar 12, *H*)

Bimsey (IRE) 62¹ (2m 4f, Live, Y, Apr 5, *G*)

Black Queen (IRE) 51² (2m, Leop, G, Jan 11, *G*)

Blair Castle (IRE) 22³ (2m ½f, Chep, F, Apr 22, *H*)

Blast Freeze (IRE) 33³ (2m, Winc, Y, Feb 20, *G*)

Blaze Away (USA) 27³ (2m 5f, Chel, G, Oct 30, *H*)

Bless Me Sister (IRE) 37² (2m, Punc, G, Nov 3, *H*)

Blown Wind (IRE) 22¹ (2m, Worc, Hrd, Sep 13, *M*)

Blushing Sand (IRE) 30³ (2m 4f, Fair, Y, Feb 23, *M*)

Boardroom Shuffle (IRE) 52¹ (2m 1f, Chel, G, Jan 25, *H*)

Bold Statement 23¹ (2m, Hexh, S, Mar 24)

Bolino Star (IRE) 38⁵ (2m, Leop, S, Mar 2, *H*)

Bolivar (IRE) 27² (2m 1f, Chel, G, Jan 25, *H*)

Bonjour 22³ (2m, Utto, G, Jan 24)

Brackenheath (IRE) 20² (2m 6½f, Font, Hvy, Feb 17)

Brambles Way 24³ (2m 5½f, Sedg, G, Apr 12, *H*)

Brave Patriarch (IRE) 24² (2m ½f, Stra, G, Jun 20)

Brave Tornado 44¹ (2m 4½f, Chep, S, Feb 15, *H*)

Break The Rules 22¹ (2m, Hayd, Y, Feb 21)

Bukhari (IRE) 46² (2m, Punc, Hvy, Feb 16, *G*)

Bures (IRE) 26² (2m ½f, Kels, Hrd, Oct 6,

H)

Burnt Imp (USA) 33⁵ (2m 4f, Hayd, Y, Feb 21, *H)*

Cadougold (FR) 50¹ (2m 4f, Live, Y, Apr 4, *H)*

Caitriona's Choice (IRE) 37¹ (2m, Punc, G, Jan 13, *H)*

Callisoe Bay (IRE) 33 (2m ½f, Donc, G, Feb 22, *H)*

Cambo (USA) 20⁴ (2m, Warw, G, Mar 1, *H)*

Carlito Brigante 42¹ (2m ½f, Sand, G, Mar 8, *H)*

Castle Secret 34⁵ (2m ½f, Chep, F, Mar 31)

Castle Sweep (IRE) 69³ (2m 5f, Chel, G, Mar 12, *H)*

Cavalier D'Or (USA) 23⁴ (2m, Fair, F, Apr 2, *M)*

Celestial Choir 26⁴ (2m ½f, Stra, Y, Mar 10, *H)*

Centaur Express 30³ (2m, Catt, Y, Feb 8, *H)*

Charlie Foxtrot (IRE) 26⁴ (2m, Fair, G, Dec 1, *G)*

Charming Girl (USA) 32⁴ (2m ½f, Asco, G, Nov 2, *H)*

Cherrymore (IRE) 20 (2m ½f, Hunt, S, Jan 23)

Chickawicka (IRE) 26³ (2m, Warw, F, Nov 21)

Chicodari 39³ (2m ½f, Chel, G, Nov 26)

Chief Mouse 26¹ (2m ½f, Asco, G, Apr 29, *H)*

Chief's Song 53² (2m ½f, Sand, G, Feb 1)

Choosey's Treasure (IRE) 26¹ (2m, Leop, G, Nov 10)

Ciara's Prince (IRE) 33³ (2m, Leop, S, Mar 2, *H)*

Circus Line 34¹ (2m 1½f, Mark, G, Jan 21, *H)*

Circus Star 41³ (2m, Punc, Hrd, Apr 24, *G)*

Cittadino 23¹ (2m 4½f, Leic, Y, Jan 29, *H)*

Claireswan (IRE) 20¹ (2m 2½f, Font, G, Mar 18, *H)*

Clifdon Fog (IRE) 27³ (2m, Leop, Y, Dec 28, *H)*

Clifton Beat (USA) 52⁴ (2m ½f, Live, Y, Apr 5, *H)*

Clinton (IRE) 31² (2m ½f, Hunt, S, Jan 23)

Cockney Lad (IRE) 74¹ (2m, Punc, G, Nov 16, *G)*

Collier Bay 78¹ (2m, Towc, Y, Feb 7)

Colm's Rock (IRE) 53⁵ (2m, Punc, G, Apr 22, *G)*

Commanche Court (IRE) 41¹ (2m 1f,

Chel, G, Mar 13, *G)*

Common Sound (IRE) 25⁴ (2m, Ayr, Y, Jan 25, *H)*

Corrachoill (IRE) 25⁴ (2m 2f, Fair, G, Feb 1, *M)*

Country Lover 25³ (2m, Warw, G, Jan 28)

Country Orchid 20² (2m ½f, Hunt, Hrd, May 26, *M)*

Country Star (IRE) 40⁴ (2m ½f, Chel, G, Nov 16, *H)*

Courbaril 38¹ (2m 5½f, Chel, G, Apr 16, *H)*

Crack On 41¹ (2m ½f, Sand, G, Nov 9, *H)*

Cutthroat Kid (IRE) 26¹ (2m 3½f, Mark, G, Mar 17, *C)*

Dana Point (IRE) 35² (2m, Newc, S, Feb 14)

Dancing Dove (IRE) 23² (2m 4f, Bang, G, Aug 2, *H)*

Dancing Paddy 49⁴ (2m ½f, Asco, Y, Apr 25, *H)*

Danegold (IRE) 30³ (2m 1f, Chel, G, Jan 25, *H)*

Dantes Cavalier (IRE) 25² (2m 4f, Worc, S, Dec 2)

Darakshan (IRE) 26² (2m, Ludl, G, Nov 12)

Daraydan (IRE) 53² (2m ½f, Chep, F, Mar 31)

Dardjini (USA) 43³ (2m, Leop, G, Jan 19, *G)*

Dato Star (IRE) 67² (2m, Hayd, G, Jan 18, *G)*

Deano's Beeno 38 (2m ½f, Chel, F, Mar 11, *G)*

Decide Yourself (IRE) 23² (2m 2½f, Font, G, Mar 18, *H)*

Defendtherealm 23² (2m 6f, Newt, Hvy, Jan 20)

Delphi Lodge (IRE) 50³ (2m 2f, Leop, Y, Dec 27, *G)*

Denham Hill (IRE) 34¹ (2m 6½f, Font, Hvy, Feb 17)

Derannie (IRE) 20¹ (2m, Ayr, S, Mar 7, *M)*

Derisbay (IRE) 21¹ (2m 1f, Plum, G, Mar 29, *H)*

Desert Fighter 37¹ (2m, Weth, G, Apr 1, *H)*

Desert Mountain (IRE) 26¹ (2m 1½f, Folk, S, Jan 24, *M)*

Devon Peasant 25² (2m 3½f, Devo, Hvy, Mar 7, *H)*

Diamond Cut (FR) 25¹ (2m 4f, Bang, G, Aug 2, *H)*

Dictum (IRE) 21¹ (2m 4½f, Utto, G, Mar 18)

Difficult Times (IRE) 27 (2m 5f, Chel, G,

Mar 12, *G*)

Digin For Gold (IRE) 24[2] (2m 2f, Fair, G, Feb 1, *M*)

Direct Route (IRE) 60[3] (2m ½f, Newb, Y, Feb 8, *G*)

Disallowed (IRE) 24[2] (2m, Warw, G, Jan 28)

Diwali Dancer 34[2] (2m 4½f, Leic, G, Dec 11, *H*)

Doctoor (USA) 50[2] (2m ½f, Sand, G, Mar 8, *H*)

Doctor Green (FR) 25[5] (2m 1f, Taun, Y, Jan 31)

Done Well (USA) 21[3] (2m ½f, Kels, F, Apr 7, *H*)

Donnington (IRE) 30[1] (2m, Utto, G, Jan 24)

Dontleavethenest (IRE) 21[3] (2m 2f, Worc, G, Oct 26)

Double Symphony (IRE) 44[1] (2m ½f, Sand, G, Feb 1)

Dr Leunt (IRE) 41[6] (2m 5f, Chel, G, Mar 12, *H*)

Dreams End 70[1] (2m, Hayd, G, May 3, *G*)

Dromineer (IRE) 46[6] (2m, Punc, G, Apr 22, *G*)

Dual Image 20[4] (2m ½f, Kels, S, Feb 6, *H*)

Duky River 24[4] (2m 4f, Fair, G, Feb 1)

Dunferne Classic (IRE) 24[4] (2m, Leop, F, May 28, *H*)

Durano 29[2] (2m ½f, Pert, G, Apr 23, *H*)

Eagles Rest (IRE) 32[2] (2m ½f, Asco, G, Feb 5)

Eastcliffe (IRE) 24[1] (2m 4½f, Hexh, F, Apr 14)

Easy Listening (USA) 21[1] (2m 1f, Taun, Y, Jan 31)

Edelweis Du Moulin (FR) 49[1] (3m ½f, Utto, G, May 29, *H*)

Eden Dancer 24[2] (2m 1f, Sedg, G, May 9, *H*)

El Don 22[3] (2m 5½f, Chel, G, Apr 16, *H*)

Elpidos 30[4] (2m, Weth, S, Dec 7, *H*)

Embellished (IRE) 35 (2m ½f, Sand, G, Dec 7, *H*)

Endowment 28[1] (2m, Ayr, G, Nov 15, *M*)

Escartefigue (FR) 63[5] (3m ½f, Chel, G, Mar 13, *G*)

Eskimo Nel (IRE) 52[2] (2m ½f, Asco, G, Dec 21)

Eton Gale (IRE) 37 (2m 5f, Chel, G, Mar 12, *H*)

Euro Singer 20[1] (2m, Towc, G, Mar 29, *H*)

Ever Blessed (IRE) 24[3] (2m ½f, Newb, G, Nov 13)

Evriza (IRE) 23[5] (2m, Fair, G, Nov 30, *G*)

Exalted (IRE) 21[2] (2m, Warw, G, Feb 4)

Express Gift 57[3] (2m ½f, Sand, G, Mar 8, *H*)

Fairly Sharp (IRE) 22[2] (2m 1½f, Mark, G, Mar 7)

Falcon's Flame (USA) 21[2] (2m, Weth, F, Oct 16)

Fallow Trix (IRE) 24[5] (2m 6f, Leop, G, Jan 19, *H*)

Family Way 55[4] (2m, Leop, G, Jan 11, *G*)

Fane Path (IRE) 30[2] (2m 4f, Fair, Y, Feb 23, *M*)

Fantasy Line 32[2] (2m 5f, Newb, G, Mar 22, *H*)

Far Ahead 30[6] (2m 4f, Ayr, G, Apr 18, *H*)

Far Dawn (USA) 38[2] (2m ½f, Live, G, Apr 3, *G*)

Fasil (IRE) 20[3] (2m, Ludl, G, Feb 27)

Fassan (IRE) 20[2] (2m, Weth, S, Dec 7, *H*)

Fen Terrier 28[6] (2m, Ayr, G, Apr 17, *H*)

Fiddling The Facts (IRE) 25[3] (2m 5f, Newb, G, Mar 22, *H*)

Fieldridge 21[1] (2m 4f, Worc, F, Sep 14, *H*)

Fill The Bill (IRE) 32[3] (2m, Fair, G, Jan 15, *M*)

Fils de Cresson 21[3] (2m, Utto, G, Mar 15)

Finnegan's Hollow (IRE) 36[2] (2m 2f, Leop, G, Feb 2, *G*)

Fishin Joella (IRE) 40[1] (2m, Punc, G, Jan 18, *M*)

Fitzwilliam (USA) 27[1] (2m, Warw, G, Feb 4)

Flic Royal (FR) 22[1] (2m ½f, Hunt, Hrd, May 26, *M*)

Florid (USA) 41[1] (2m, Fake, F, Mar 14)

Flyaway Blues 21[1] (2m, Catt, G, Dec 4, *H*)

Flying Fiddler (IRE) 22[2] (2m, Winc, Y, Mar 6, *H*)

Flying Gunner 28[2] (3m, Leic, G, Jan 14)

Font Romeu (FR) 36[3] (2m, Hayd, G, Feb 22, *H*)

Fontaine Lodge (IRE) 24[3] (2m, Leop, G, Oct 28, *L*)

Fontanays (IRE) 20[2] (2m, Wind, G, Mar 3, *H*)

Forest Ivory (NZ) 44[4] (2m 5f, Chel, G, Mar 12, *G*)

Forestal 39[5] (2m ½f, Sand, G, Mar 8, *H*)

Fourth In Line (IRE) 31[1] (2m, Utto, Y, May 7, *H*)

Foxies Lad 26[2] (2m 3½f, Devo, Hvy, Mar 7)

Frau Dante (IRE) 25[1] (2m, Leop, F, May 28, *H*)

Freddie Muck 52[3] (2m 6½f, Utto, G, Feb

8, *H*)

Frickley 35 (2m ½f, Donc, G, Feb 22, *H*)

Frogmarch (USA) 33[5] (2m, Warw, G, Feb 15, *H*)

Frozen Sea (USA) 25[4] (2m 2½f, Font, G, Mar 18, *H*)

Furietto (IRE) 21[3] (2m 1½f, Folk, S, Jan 24, *S*)

Gales Cavalier (IRE) 51[2] (2m, Kemp, G, Jan 18, *H*)

Gazalani (IRE) 54[3] (2m, Punc, G, Apr 22, *G*)

General Tonic 20[2] (2m 4½f, Leic, G, Nov 18, *H*)

Gentle Mossy (IRE) 23[5] (2m, Fair, G, Jan 15, *M*)

Glanmerin (IRE) 35[2] (2m ½f, Hunt, G, Feb 6, *H*)

Glenugie 22[3] (2m ½f, Kels, F, Apr 30, *H*)

Glitter Isle (IRE) 24[2] (2m 4½f, Chep, S, Nov 27)

Globe Runner 27[2] (2m, Hayd, G, Feb 22, *H*)

Gods Squad 28[1] (2m, Weth, Hvy, Feb 27)

Goldingo 23[2] (2m, Winc, Y, Feb 6, *H*)

Good Glow 34[2] (2m, Punc, Y, Jan 28, *H*)

Good Vibes 35[1] (2m, Weth, G, Mar 31)

Grandinare (USA) 25[2] (2m, Ayr, G, Nov 15, *M*)

Graphic Equaliser (IRE) 42[5] (2m ½f, Chel, F, Mar 11, *G*)

Green Green Desert (FR) 40[1] (2m, Ludl, G, Feb 27)

Greenhue (IRE) 30[2] (2m, Leop, Y, Dec 26, *G*)

Grey Guy (IRE) 38[3] (2m, Fair, F, Mar 31, *G*)

Grimes 50[1] (2m, Punc, Hrd, Apr 24, *G*)

Ground Nut (IRE) 45[3] (2m ½f, Sand, G, Feb 1)

Guest Performance (IRE) 27[1] (2m 2f, Fair, G, Nov 30)

Haile Derring 27[1] (3m ½f, Carl, G, Nov 11, *H*)

Ham N'eggs 33[2] (2m, Weth, Hvy, Feb 26, *H*)

Hamilton Silk 54[2] (2m ½f, Newb, Y, Feb 8, *G*)

Hand Woven 29[4] (2m ½f, Chep, F, Oct 5, *H*)

Harbour Island 27[6] (2m 5f, Chel, G, Mar 12, *G*)

Hard News (USA) 32[2] (2m, Leop, G, Feb 2, *G*)

Hatta Breeze 36 (2m ½f, Newb, Y, Feb 8, *G*)

Hay Dance 34[1] (2m 1f, Newt, G, Apr 12, *H*)

Hayaain 32[5] (2m 1f, Chel, G, Mar 13, *G*)

Henrietta Howard (IRE) 25[1] (2m 4½f, Leic, G, Jan 21, *H*)

Henrys Port 23[6] (2m ½f, Hunt, S, Jan 23)

Hi Knight (IRE) 27[1] (3m, Fair, G, May 20, *H*)

High In The Clouds (IRE) 55[3] (2m ½f, Live, G, Apr 3, *G*)

Highbank 27[2] (2m, Ayr, Y, Nov 16, *H*)

Highly Motivated 23[2] (2m, Fair, G, Nov 30, *G*)

Hill Society (IRE) 70[5] (2m ½f, Chel, F, Mar 11, *G*)

Hisar (IRE) 20[2] (2m ½f, Newb, G, Mar 22)

Hoh Warrior (IRE) 36[1] (2m ½f, Newb, Y, Nov 30)

Holders Hill (IRE) 20[1] (2m ½f, Donc, G, Mar 1, *H*)

Home Counties (IRE) 51[3] (2m, Kemp, G, Oct 19)

House Captain 43[2] (2m 6½f, Utto, G, Feb 8, *H*)

Humbel (USA) 52[2] (2m, Fair, F, Mar 31, *G*)

Hurricane Lamp 36[2] (2m ½f, Donc, G, Jan 24, *G*)

I'm Supposin (IRE) 74[4] (2m ½f, Chel, F, Mar 11, *G*)

Indian Jockey 26[1] (2m 1½f, Cart, F, May 24, *H*)

Indrapura (IRE) 27[1] (2m, Worc, G, Nov 13, *H*)

Infamous (USA) 27[3] (2m, Wind, G, Feb 15)

Ingletonian 40 (2m, Hayd, G, May 3, *G*)

Inn At The Top 26[2] (2m 4f, Newc, S, Dec 3)

Ionio (USA) 26[1] (2m, Warw, G, Nov 30)

Iridal 29[2] (2m, Fair, F, Apr 2, *M*)

Iron N Gold 20[1] (2m ½f, Hunt, F, Mar 12, *H*)

Isaiah 26[2] (2m 1½f, Mark, G, Jan 21, *H*)

Istabraq (IRE) 57[1] (2m, Fair, G, Dec 1, *G*)

Ivy Edith 22[1] (2m, Utto, F, Jun 27, *H*)

Jack Yeats (IRE) 32[4] (2m, Fair, G, Jan 15, *M*)

Jakes Justice (IRE) 20[3] (2m ½f, Ling, S, Jan 22, *M*)

Jefferies 22[1] (2m 3½f, Taun, S, Feb 13, *H*)

Jenzsoph (IRE) 20[1] (2m 2½f, Font, G, May 5, *C*)

Jervaulx (IRE) 22[1] (2m, Ayr, S, Jan 27)

Jo Jo Boy (IRE) 25[3] (2m, Punc, G, Nov 3, *H*)

John Drumm 23[4] (2m, Towc, G, May 23, *H*)

Just Little 36[1] (2m ½f, Chel, G, Nov 15)

Justaway (IRE) 27[3] (2m, Punc, Y, Jan 28, H)
Juyush (USA) 60[1] (2m, Hayd, G, Feb 22)
Kadastrof (FR) 55[6] (2m ½f, Sand, G, Mar 8, H)
Kailash (USA) 32[2] (2m, Kemp, S, Feb 21)
Kaitak (IRE) 33[3] (2m, Weth, S, Dec 7, H)
Karshi 70[1] (3m ½f, Chel, G, Mar 13, G)
Kaselectric (IRE) 30[4] (2m 6f, Leop, G, Jan 19, H)
Kawa-Kawa 21[1] (2m, Punc, G, Nov 3, H)
Kerawi 33[2] (2m, Kemp, Y, Feb 22, G)
Khayrawani (IRE) 55[1] (2m, Fair, F, Apr 1, G)
Kibreet 31[4] (2m ½f, Chep, G, Feb 1, H)
Kind Cleric 21[3] (2m 4½f, Chep, S, Nov 27)
King Pin 31[5] (2m 4f, Ayr, G, Apr 18, H)
Kingdom Of Shades (USA) 41[2] (2m 4½f, Chep, S, Mar 8, H)
Kings Return (IRE) 29[5] (2m 4f, Fair, G, Feb 1)
Kinnescash (IRE) 20[2] (2m 1f, Bang, G, Mar 22)
Kissair (IRE) 43 (2m ½f, Newb, Y, Feb 8, G)
L'opera (FR) 36[4] (2m 1f, Chel, G, Mar 13, G)
Lady Arpel (IRE) 50[3] (2m, Punc, G, Nov 16, G)
Lady Daisy (IRE) 64[1] (2m, Punc, G, Apr 23, G)
Lady Peta (IRE) 26[1] (2m, Ludl, G, Nov 12)
Lagan 26[1] (2m, Weth, F, Oct 16)
Lagen Bridge (IRE) 31[1] (2m 4f, Ayr, S, Feb 8)
Lancastrian Pride (IRE) 20[4] (2m 4f, Fair, F, Apr 2, G)
Lansdowne 24[3] (3m ½f, Utto, G, Mar 18, H)
Large Action (IRE) 56[1] (2m 1f, Chel, Y, Dec 14, G)
Le Khoumf (FR) 25[1] (2m 1f, Taun, G, Jan 16, H)
Le Teteu (FR) 29[1] (2m ½f, Donc, G, Jan 24, G)
Leading Spirit (IRE) 20[3] (2m ½f, Asco, G, Feb 5)
Legible 31[1] (2m ½f, Hunt, S, Jan 23)
Lessons Lass (IRE) 27[1] (2m 2½f, Font, G, Feb 3, H)
Lightening Lad 40[2] (2m ½f, Sand, G, Nov 9, H)
Linton Rocks 28[6] (2m 6½f, Utto, G, Feb 8, H)
Liscahill Fort (IRE) 32[3] (2m 6f, Leop, G, Jan 19, H)

Little Shefford 21[2] (2m, Ludl, G, Mar 24)
Lively Encounter (IRE) 23[2] (2m ½f, Sand, S, Feb 14)
Liver Bird (IRE) 28[2] (2m 4f, Fair, F, Apr 2, G)
Lord McMurrough (IRE) 25[3] (2m 4½f, Leic, G, Dec 11, H)
Lord Rooble (IRE) 23[3] (2m 4f, Plum, S, Nov 18)
Lough Tully (IRE) 20[1] (2m 6f, Sand, S, Feb 13, H)
Lucia Forte 38[1] (2m 5f, Newb, G, Mar 22, H)
Lying Eyes 25[6] (2m 4½f, Chep, S, Feb 15, H)
Major Dundee (IRE) 22[1] (2m 2½f, Font, F, May 26)
Make A Stand 82[1] (2m ½f, Chel, F, Mar 11, G)
Mandys Mantino 56[1] (2m ½f, Chel, G, Nov 26)
Maple Bay (IRE) 20[2] (2m, Edin, G, Jan 10, M)
Marchant Ming (IRE) 41[4] (2m, Hayd, Y, Dec 21, H)
Marching Marquis (IRE) 28[3] (2m 4½f, Chep, S, Feb 15, G)
Marello 38[1] (2m, Newc, S, Feb 15)
Marius (IRE) 31[3] (2m ½f, Asco, Y, Apr 25, H)
Marlonette (IRE) 26[6] (2m 1f, Chel, G, Mar 13, G)
Master Beveled 54[2] (2m ½f, Sand, G, Dec 7, H)
Master Tribe (IRE) 56[1] (2m, Leop, G, Jan 11, G)
Mayasta (IRE) 30[4] (2m, Punc, G, Nov 16, G)
Meadow Hymn (IRE) 26[1] (2m 5½f, Sedg, G, Apr 12, H)
Melt The Clouds (CAN) 24[2] (2m 1½f, Folk, S, Jan 24, M)
Menesonic (IRE) 22[1] (3m 2f, Devo, Hvy, Mar 7)
Mentmore Towers (IRE) 26[2] (2m ½f, Hunt, G, Nov 16)
Metastasio 51[5] (2m, Leop, G, Jan 11, G)
Mid Day Chaser (IRE) 28[1] (2m 1f, Here, S, Dec 20, M)
Midnight Legend 63[1] (2m, Punc, G, Apr 22, G)
Mighty Moss (IRE) 48[2] (2m 5f, Chel, G, Mar 12, G)
Million Dancer 22[1] (2m, Worc, G, Jul 23)
Miltonfield 31[4] (2m, Leop, S, Mar 2, H)
Mim-Lou-And 31[2] (2m ½f, Chel, G, Nov 15)

Mister Morose (IRE) 51 (2m ½f, Newb, Y, Feb 8, *G*)

Mister Rm 45[4] (2m ½f, Live, G, Apr 3, *G*)

Mister Ross (IRE) 24[1] (2m ½f, Kels, Y, Dec 2)

Mistinguett (IRE) 66[1] (2m, Hayd, G, Jan 18, *G*)

Misty Moments (IRE) 32[2] (2m 4f, Fair, G, Feb 1)

Mithraic (IRE) 23[3] (2m, Weth, G, Nov 2)

Mizyan (IRE) 35[3] (2m, Leic, G, Nov 18, *H*)

Moment Of Glory (IRE) 37[2] (2m 4½f, Leic, Y, Jan 29, *H*)

Monica's Choice (IRE) 22[3] (2m, Ayr, S, Feb 11, *H*)

Monnaie Forte (IRE) 26[1] (2m ½f, Asco, Y, Apr 25, *H*)

Moorish 67 (2m ½f, Chel, F, Mar 11, *G*)

More Dash Thancash (IRE) 35 (2m ½f, Sand, G, Mar 8, *H*)

Morstock 37[6] (2m 1f, Chel, G, Mar 13, *G*)

Moscow Express (IRE) 32[1] (2m 4f, Fair, G, Feb 1)

Most Equal 36[1] (2m ½f, Stra, Y, May 9, *H*)

Motoqua 26[2] (2m 1f, Newt, Hvy, Jan 20, *M*)

Moving Out 21[5] (2m, Utto, S, Dec 20, *H*)

Mr Bureaucrat (NZ) 28[5] (2m, Weth, S, Dec 7, *H*)

Mr Knitwit 21[2] (2m 2f, Kels, Y, Dec 2, *H*)

Mr Percy (IRE) 44[3] (2m ½f, Asco, G, Dec 21)

Mr Wild (USA) 31[2] (2m, Kemp, G, Jan 17)

Murphy's Malt (IRE) 20[6] (2m ½f, Newb, Y, Nov 30)

Muse 39[5] (2m 4½f, Chep, S, Nov 9, *H*)

Music Please 23[5] (2m, Warw, G, Jan 28)

My Cheeky Man 34[1] (2m 1½f, Mark, Y, Feb 18)

Mystical City (IRE) 59[3] (2m, Fair, F, Apr 1, *G*)

Mytton's Choice (IRE) 43 (2m 1f, Chel, G, Mar 13, *G*)

Nagobelia 22[3] (2m, Warw, G, Mar 1, *H*)

Nahrawali (IRE) 23[1] (2m, Wind, F, Nov 16)

Nahri (USA) 31[1] (2m, Leic, G, Nov 18, *H*)

Naiysari (IRE) 28[4] (2m, Utto, F, Jun 9, *H*)

Nashville Star (USA) 21[1] (2m 1f, Bang, Y, Feb 7, *H*)

Nasone (IRE) 29[4] (2m ½f, Newb, Y, Nov 30)

Native Fleck (IRE) 24[3] (2m, Fair, F, Apr 2, *M*)

Native-Darrig (IRE) 23[4] (2m, Punc, G, Jan 18, *M*)

Near Gale (IRE) 42[4] (2m, Leop, G, Oct 28, *L*)

New Century (USA) 23[3] (2m, Weth, S, Feb 1)

New Inn 39[2] (2m ½f, Donc, G, Jan 25, *H*)

Nick The Beak (IRE) 24[3] (2m 4½f, Chep, S, Dec 7, *H*)

Nigel's Lad (IRE) 43[5] (2m ½f, Live, G, Apr 3, *G*)

Nine O Three (IRE) 25[2] (2m 3½f, Taun, S, Feb 13, *H*)

Nipper Reed 24[2] (2m 1f, Plum, S, Mar 10, *H*)

No More Hassle (IRE) 29[1] (2m, Hayd, G, Feb 22, *H*)

Noble Colours 23[1] (2m 1f, Here, G, Mar 31)

Noble Lord 30[4] (2m ½f, Chep, F, Mar 31)

Noble Shoon (IRE) 21[5] (2m, Punc, G, Jan 18, *M*)

Noble Thyne (IRE) 52[1] (2m, Fair, G, May 20)

Non Vintage (IRE) 39[6] (2m, Weth, S, Dec 7, *H*)

Nordance Prince (IRE) 33[3] (2m ½f, Newb, Y, Nov 30)

Nordic Breeze (IRE) 50[3] (2m ½f, Chel, F, Mar 11, *G*)

Northern Squire 22[1] (3m ½f, Carl, S, Feb 4, *H*)

Northern Starlight 41[1] (2m 1f, Newt, G, Mar 29, *H*)

Not For Turning (IRE) 23[1] (2m, Kemp, Y, Nov 20)

Nova Run 24[1] (2m 3½f, Taun, F, Nov 14, *H*)

Ocean Hawk (USA) 39[1] (3m ½f, Kemp, G, Nov 6, *H*)

Oh So Grumpy 39[5] (2m, Leop, F, May 28, *H*)

Oh So Risky 29[3] (2m ½f, Newb, F, Oct 25, *H*)

Olympian 24[4] (3m, Asco, F, Apr 12, *G*)

Once More For Luck (IRE) 22[5] (2m 1f, Carl, G, Jan 14, *H*)

Otto E Mezzo 23[5] (2m ½f, Sand, Y, Mar 7, *H*)

Our Kris 28[4] (2m, Kemp, G, Oct 19)

Out On A Promise (IRE) 30[2] (2m ½f, Stra, Y, May 9, *H*)

Out Ranking (FR) 30[3] (2m 1f, Newt, G, Apr 12, *H*)

Outset (IRE) 39[4] (2m 4f, Live, Y, Apr 4, *H*)

Padashpan (USA) 31[5] (2m, Punc, G, Nov 16, *G*)

Paddy's Return (IRE) 65[3] (3m ½f, Chel, G, Mar 13, *G*)

Palace Of Gold 21[1] (3m ½f, Utto, G, May

818

21, *H*)

Palette (IRE) 47[2] (2m, Fair, G, Dec 1, *G*)

Pappa Charlie (USA) 20[1] (3m, Hexh, F, May 10)

Peatswood 22[4] (2m 5f, Chel, G, Oct 30, *H*)

Pebble Beach (IRE) 24[2] (3m ½f, Carl, G, Jan 20, *H*)

Penndara (IRE) 21[2] (2m 2f, Punc, Y, Oct 24)

Penny A Day (IRE) 70[3] (2m, Leop, G, Jan 11, *G*)

Percy Braithwaite (IRE) 23[1] (2m, Ludl, G, Jan 16, *M*)

Percy Thrower 36[3] (3m ½f, Newb, G, Nov 13, *H*)

Persian Elite (IRE) 21[1] (2m 4f, Fake, G, May 18)

Phar From Funny 22[2] (2m, Winc, G, Nov 21, *H*)

Phardana (IRE) 20[3] (2m 2f, Fair, G, Feb 1, *M*)

Pharrambling (IRE) 20[3] (3m ½f, Carl, S, Mar 6, *H*)

Physical Fun 20[3] (2m 6f, Sand, S, Feb 13, *H*)

Polydamas 33 (2m ½f, Chel, F, Mar 11, *G*)

Pomme Secret (FR) 20[1] (2m 1f, Plum, S, Jan 27, *M*)

Potentate (USA) 57[1] (2m ½f, Chep, F, Mar 31)

Potter's Gale 28[2] (2m 1f, Chel, G, Jan 25, *H*)

Pridwell 69 (2m ½f, Chel, F, Mar 11, *G*)

Princeful (IRE) 51[2] (2m ½f, Chel, F, Mar 11, *G*)

Private Peace (IRE) 56[1] (2m, Punc, Hvy, Feb 16, *G*)

Prizefighter 35[2] (2m ½f, Hunt, Hrd, May 14, *H*)

Proton 28[3] (2m, Kemp, G, Dec 26)

Proud Image 20[1] (2m, Winc, Hrd, Mar 31)

Qattara (IRE) 20[1] (2m, Hexh, Y, Dec 20)

Quakers Field 43[1] (2m ½f, Live, G, Apr 3, *G*)

Quality (IRE) 27[3] (2m, Kemp, G, Jan 17)

Quango 20[5] (2m, Newc, S, Feb 15)

Queen Of Spades (IRE) 38[2] (2m ½f, Newb, Y, Nov 30)

Rangitikei (NZ) 33[2] (2m, Utto, G, Mar 15)

Rawy (USA) 29[2] (2m, Leop, Y, Dec 28, *H*)

Ready Money Creek (IRE) 31[2] (2m, Towc, Y, Feb 7)

Real Madrid 22[1] (2m ½f, Hunt, F, Apr 29)

Red Blazer 27[1] (2m, Towc, S, Dec 19)

Red Lighter 25[2] (2m 7f, Ling, S, Mar 15, *H*)

Red Raja 38[1] (2m ½f, Newb, G, Mar 21, *H*)

Red Valerian 23[1] (2m 5½f, Sedg, F, Sep 6, *H*)

Regency Rake (IRE) 26[3] (2m, Leop, G, Mar 16, *H*)

Relkeel 69[2] (2m, Towc, Y, Feb 7)

Rescue Time (IRE) 29[4] (2m, Punc, Y, Jan 28, *H*)

Right Win (IRE) 39[5] (2m, Hayd, G, Jan 18, *G*)

Ritto 25[1] (2m 1f, Newt, S, Oct 14, *M*)

Robert's Toy (IRE) 25[2] (2m ½f, Chel, Y, Nov 17, *H*)

Roll A Dollar 26 (2m 1f, Chel, G, Jan 25, *H*)

Romancer (IRE) 45[2] (2m, Winc, Y, Feb 20, *G*)

Ros Castle 31[5] (2m, Wind, G, Feb 15, *H*)

Roseberry Avenue (IRE) 21[1] (2m ½f, Ling, S, Dec 21)

Rosencrantz (IRE) 29[3] (2m 4½f, Leic, Y, Jan 29, *H*)

Rossel (USA) 26[1] (2m, Edin, F, Dec 27)

Royal Event 24[2] (2m, Warw, G, Nov 30)

Royal York 26[1] (2m, Hexh, F, May 27)

Russian Rascal (IRE) 22[1] (2m, Catt, Y, Jan 31)

Samanid (IRE) 25 (2m, Ayr, G, Apr 17, *H*)

Sanmartino (IRE) 70[6] (2m ½f, Chel, F, Mar 11, *G*)

Sarmatian (USA) 33[1] (2m, Ayr, Y, Nov 16, *H*)

Sassiver (USA) 24[3] (3m, Asco, F, Apr 12, *G*)

Saving Bond (IRE) 40[4] (2m, Fair, F, Apr 1, *G*)

Scotby (BEL) 33[1] (2m 6f, Newt, Hvy, Jan 20)

Sea Victor 30[3] (2m ½f, Donc, G, Mar 1, *H*)

Seasonal Splendour (IRE) 25[2] (2m, Wind, G, Dec 5, *H*)

Seattle Alley (USA) 28 (2m 1f, Chel, G, Mar 13, *G*)

Secret Spring (FR) 42[1] (2m, Kemp, G, Jan 17)

Sentosa Star (IRE) 45[2] (2m, Leop, S, Mar 2, *H*)

Serenity Prayer (USA) 58[2] (2m ½f, Chel, G, Nov 26)

Sesame Seed (IRE) 36[5] (2m ½f, Donc, G, Feb 22, *H*)

Severn Gale 22[1] (2m, Warw, G, Dec 16, *H*)

Shadow Leader 61[1] (2m ½f, Chel, F, Mar 11, *G*)

Shahrani 32[3] (2m ½f, Sand, Y, Mar 7, *H*)

Shanavogh 23[1] (2m 4f, Hayd, Y, Nov 30)
Shankar (IRE) 61[3] (2m, Hayd, G, May 3, G)
Sharpical 58[2] (2m ½f, Live, G, Apr 3, G)
Shekels (IRE) 36[1] (2m, Utto, G, Mar 15)
Shepherds Rest (IRE) 22[2] (2m, Wind, Feb 15, H)
Sheriffmuir 42[2] (2m 4f, Live, Y, Apr 4, H)
Shining Edge 47[1] (2m ½f, Donc, G, Feb 22, H)
Shoofk 22[2] (2m ½f, Asco, G, Nov 2, H)
Shooting Light (IRE) 38[3] (2m 1f, Chel, G, Mar 13, G)
Sierra Bay (IRE) 29[3] (2m ½f, Hunt, S, Jan 23)
Silly Money 29[1] (2m ½f, Donc, G, Mar 3, H)
Silver Groom (IRE) 61[5] (2m ½f, Newb, Y, Feb 8, G)
Silver Shred 36[3] (2m 4½f, Chep, S, Nov 9, H)
Silver Thyne (IRE) 28[2] (2m 4½f, Utto, G, Mar 18)
Silvian Bliss (USA) 38[1] (2m, Fair, F, Apr 2, M)
Sir Bob (IRE) 23[2] (2m 4f, Ayr, S, Feb 8)
Sir Dante (IRE) 26[1] (2m 4f, Chel, G, Apr 15, G)
Smith Too (IRE) 25[3] (3m ½f, Utto, G, May 3, H)
Smolensk (IRE) 20[2] (2m, Warw, F, Nov 21)
Snow Falcon 45[2] (2m, Punc, Hrd, Apr 24, G)
Sohrab (IRE) 63[4] (3m ½f, Chel, G, Mar 13, G)
Soldat (USA) 28[5] (2m 5f, Chel, G, Mar 12, G)
Son Of Anshan 30[1] (2m, Ayr, Hvy, Mar 8)
Song Of The Sword 26[1] (2m 1f, Here, G, May 26)
Southern Cross 21[2] (2m, Hexh, S, Mar 24)
Space Trucker (IRE) 76[3] (2m ½f, Chel, F, Mar 11, G)
Spaceage Gold 30[2] (3m ½f, Newb, G, Nov 13, H)
Sparkling Yasmin 41[2] (2m 4½f, Chep, S, Dec 7, H)
Spendid (IRE) 31[1] (2m, Towc, Y, Feb 7)
Spirit Dancer (IRE) 27[1] (2m, Fair, G, Nov 30, G)
Splendid Thyne 38[1] (2m ½f, Newb, S, Feb 28)
Sprintfayre 22[2] (2m, Towc, S, Dec 19)
Stan's Your Man 24[1] (2m 4f, Newc, G, Mar 15, H)

Star Market 29[1] (2m ½f, Hunt, F, Oct 11, H)
Star Rage (IRE) 54[2] (2m ½f, Donc, G, Feb 22, H)
Star Selection 42[5] (2m, Hayd, G, May 3, G)
Stash The Cash (IRE) 40[1] (2m, Ayr, Y, Jan 25, H)
Stay With Me (FR) 27[1] (2m, Worc, S, May 21, H)
Step On Eyre (IRE) 50[2] (2m, Fair, G, May 20)
Stormy Passage 20[1] (2m 1f, Newt, Hvy, Dec 3)
Stormyfairweather (IRE) 36[1] (2m, Towc, S, May 12)
Strategic Ploy 21[3] (2m, Leop, G, Feb 2, G)
Strong Tel (IRE) 20[3] (2m ½f, Newb, S, Feb 28)
Stylish Allure (USA) 34[4] (2m, Punc, Hrd, Apr 24, G)
Suas Leat (IRE) 23[1] (2m, Weth, G, Oct 27, H)
Suivez 33[2] (2m, Utto, F, Jun 27, H)
Summer Spell (USA) 34[1] (2m, Kemp, G, Jan 17)
Summerhill Special (IRE) 29[3] (2m ½f, Kels, S, Feb 6, H)
Sun Surfer (FR) 28[3] (3m, Bang, S, Dec 18, H)
Supertop 22[1] (2m, Hexh, F, Oct 12)
Supreme Lady (IRE) 46[1] (2m 6½f, Utto, G, Feb 8, H)
Supreme Soviet 20[2] (2m, Newc, S, Feb 24, M)
Sursum Corda 31[2] (2m ½f, Ling, S, Jan 22, M)
Swanbister (IRE) 22[2] (2m 4f, Hayd, Y, Nov 30)
Sylvester (IRE) 21[2] (2m, Warw, G, Mar 1, H)
Taits Clock (IRE) 28[3] (2m, Leop, F, May 28, H)
Talathath (FR) 30[2] (2m, Towc, G, May 23, H)
Tamarpour (USA) 39[5] (2m 5f, Chel, G, Mar 12, H)
Tarrs Bridge (IRE) 30 (3m ½f, Chel, G, Mar 13, G)
Teejay'N'aitch (IRE) 22[1] (2m, Weth, Y, May 7, H)
Teinein (FR) 48[1] (2m ½f, Hunt, Y, Nov 26, H)
Tejano Gold (USA) 36[3] (2m, Worc, S, Apr 26, H)
The Captain's Wish 34[4] (2m ½f, Newb,

The Latvian Lark (IRE) 33[1] (2m 2f, Punc, Y, Oct 24)

The Proms (IRE) 30[1] (2m, Hayd, Y, Feb 21, *H*)

The Toiseach (IRE) 37[2] (3m ½f, Utto, G, May 29, *H*)

Theatreworld (IRE) 77[2] (2m ½f, Chel, F, Mar 11, *G*)

Thornton Gate 37[3] (2m ½f, Kels, Y, Jan 17, *H*)

Three Farthings 26[1] (2m ½f, Ling, Y, Jan 31, *M*)

Three Rivers 23[2] (2m, Fair, G, Nov 20, *M*)

Three Scholars 43[3] (2m, Punc, Hvy, Feb 16, *G*)

Tibetan 38[4] (2m ½f, Asco, G, Dec 21)

Tickerty's Gift 30[1] (2m ½f, Ling, F, Mar 22, *H*)

Tidjani (IRE) 37[5] (2m 1f, Chel, G, Mar 13, *G*)

Toast The Spreece (IRE) 53[4] (2m, Punc, G, Apr 22, *G*)

Tom Brodie 47[4] (2m, Kemp, G, Jan 18, *H*)

Tompetoo (IRE) 24[5] (2m ½f, Newb, G, Nov 13)

Total Joy (IRE) 23[2] (2m 1f, Here, S, Dec 20, *M*)

Tower Street 24[2] (2m ½f, Newb, G, Nov 13)

Tragic Hero 49[6] (2m, Hayd, G, May 3, *G*)

Trainglot 51 (3m ½f, Chel, G, Mar 13, *G*)

Tree Creeper (IRE) 24[4] (2m, Warw, G, Jan 28)

Triennium (USA) 22[1] (2m, Edin, G, Jan 10, *H*)

Troodos 24[2] (3m 3½f, Sedg, G, Apr 12, *H*)

Tryfirion (IRE) 29[1] (2m 4f, Fair, Y, Feb 23, *H*)

Tullymurry Toff (IRE) 53[4] (2m 5f, Chel, G, Mar 12, *H*)

Ultimate Smoothie 26[1] (2m ½f, Chep, G, May 7, *H*)

Uncle Doug 40[2] (2m ½f, Kels, Y, Jan 17, *H*)

Urban Dancing (USA) 24[2] (2m, Newc, G, Nov 9, *H*)

Urubande (IRE) 34[4] (2m, Leop, G, Jan 19, *G*)

Valley Erne (IRE) 24[1] (2m, Punc, Y, Jan 28, *H*)

Vasiliki (IRE) 25[2] (2m 6f, Leop, G, Jan 19, *H*)

Victor Bravo (NZ) 24[6] (3m ½f, Live, G, Apr 3, *H*)

Vitus (USA) 25[1] (2m, Punc, G, Dec 7)

Wade Road (IRE) 46[4] (2m ½f, Chel, F, Mar 11, *G*)

Warm Spell 52[2] (2m, Kemp, G, Oct 19)

Wassl Street (IRE) 25[1] (2m, Towc, S, Mar 6, *H*)

Wayfarers Way (USA) 24[1] (2m 1f, Here, S, Dec 6, *H*)

Welsh Grit (IRE) 34[2] (2m, Leop, F, May 28, *H*)

West Leader (IRE) 20[3] (2m, Punc, G, Jan 18, *M*)

West On Bridge St (IRE) 20[4] (2m, Punc, G, Nov 3, *H*)

What A Question (IRE) 61[6] (3m ½f, Chel, G, Mar 13, *G*)

What's The Verdict (IRE) 59[2] (2m, Punc, G, Apr 22, *G*)

Whip Hand (IRE) 40[2] (2m 1½f, Mark, Y, Feb 18)

White Sea (IRE) 32[1] (2m ½f, Newb, G, Nov 29)

Windy Bee (IRE) 34[4] (2m, Punc, Hvy, Feb 16, *G*)

Wings Cove 33[5] (2m 4½f, Leic, Y, Jan 29, *H*)

Yet Again 20[1] (2m 1f, Taun, G, Dec 12)

Yubralee (USA) 40[2] (2m ½f, Stra, G, May 30, *H*)

Zabadi (IRE) 47[5] (2m ½f, Live, Y, Apr 5, *H*)

CHASERS

Aardwolf 34[1] (2m, Sand, G, Nov 9)

Abbeylands (IRE) 24[1] (2m ½f, Hexh, G, Nov 8, *H*)

Absalom's Lady 35[1] (2m 1½f, Devo, Y, Nov 5, *H*)

Act Of Faith 22[4] (3m, Newb, S, Nov 29)

Act Of Parliament (IRE) 27[1] (2m 5f, Wind, G, Dec 5, *H*)

Act The Wag (IRE) 35[1] (3m 4f, Sedg, G, Apr 12, *H*)

Addington Boy (IRE) 72[2] (2m 5f, Chel, G, Jan 25, *H*)

Air Shot 44[1] (2m 3½f, Chep, S, Feb 15)

Ali's Alibi 27[2] (3m 1f, Weth, Y, Dec 7, *H*)

Aljadeer (USA) 35[1] (2m 4f, Mark, S, Feb 18, *H*)

All For Luck 27[4] (3m 1f, Chel, G, Mar 11, *H*)

Aly Daley (IRE) 24[4] (2m 6f, Live, G, Apr 3, *H*)

Amancio (USA) 35[1] (2m, Plum, S, Jan 27)

Amber Spark (IRE) 23[3] (2m 5½f, Newt, Hvy, Nov 6)

Amble Speedy (IRE) 24[2] (3m 5f, Fair, G, Mar 31, *G*)

American Hero 53[1] (2m 1f, Kels, F, Apr 30)

Anabatic (IRE) 60[4] (2m 4½f, Chel, G, Nov 16, *G*)

Another Venture (IRE) 27[2] (3m 3f, Sedg, G, Apr 12)

Antonin (FR) 54[5] (3m, Leop, G, Dec 27, *G*)

Appearance Money (IRE) 21[2] (2m, Edin, G, Jan 28)

Applefort (IRE) 26[2] (2m 2f, Fair, G, Mar 31)

Arctic Kinsman 64[2] (2m, Kemp, Y, Feb 22)

Arctic Sandy (IRE) 24[3] (2m, Edin, G, Jan 28)

Arctic Weather (IRE) 43[2] (2m 3f, Leop, G, Jan 19, *L*)

Around The Horn 33[3] (2m, Asco, G, Dec 21, *H*)

Around The Gale (IRE) 29[1] (2m 1½f, Bang, S, Nov 1)

Art Prince (IRE) 36[1] (2m 5f, Utto, Y, Dec 21, *H*)

Artic Wings (IRE) 24[3] (2m 6f, Towc, G, Mar 29, *H*)

Ask Me Later (IRE) 25[1] (3m, Newc, Y, Feb 14)

Ask Tom (IRE) 83[2] (2m, Chel, F, Mar 12, *G*)

Avro Anson 69[3] (3m, Hayd, G, Jan 18, *G*)

Back Bar (IRE) 41[4] (3m, Leop, G, Dec 27, *G*)

Bally Parson 21[2] (2m, Warw, F, Nov 30, *H*)

Ballyea Boy (IRE) 25[1] (3m 1f, Towc, G, Nov 14, *H*)

Ballyline (IRE) 25[2] (2m ½f, Hexh, G, Nov 8, *H*)

Barnageera Boy (IRE) 34[1] (2m, Fair, Y, Dec 1, *H*)

Baronet (IRE) 29[1] (3m, Kemp, Y, Nov 6)

Barton Bank 68[5] (2m 4½f, Chel, G, Nov 16, *G*)

Bas de Laine (FR) 29[1] (2m 6½f, Kels, G, Nov 13, *H*)

Bavard Dieu (IRE) 23 (2m 4½f, Chel, G, Nov 16, *G*)

Beachy Head 30[1] (2m 4½f, Weth, Hvy, Feb 26, *H*)

Beakstown (IRE) 43 (2m, Chel, G, Mar 11, *G*)

Beatson (IRE) 25[1] (2m ½f, Towc, S, Dec 19, *H*)

Beau Babillard 21[5] (2m ½f, Newt, G, May 10, *H*)

Beldine 21[2] (2m, Pert, F, Aug 31, *H*)

Bell Staffboy (IRE) 37[1] (2m 3½f, Donc, G, Jan 24, *H*)

Bells Life (IRE) 52[1] (2m 6f, Live, G, Apr 3, *H*)

Belmont King (IRE) 53[1] (3m, Chep, Y, Dec 7, *G*)

Belvederian 52[4] (2m 3f, Leop, G, Jan 19, *L*)

Benjamin Lancaster 24[1] (2m ½f, Chep, G, Nov 9, *H*)

Bertone (IRE) 44[1] (2m 4f, Utto, F, Oct 5, *H*)

Berude Not To (IRE) 40[1] (3m, Kemp, S, Feb 21)

Betty's Boy (IRE) 38[5] (3m, Donc, G, Jan 25, *H*)

Big Matt (IRE) 66[3] (2m, Kemp, G, Jan 18, *G*)

Blair Castle (IRE) 20[4] (2m, Warw, F, Feb 15, *G*)

Blazer Moriniere (FR) 28[2] (2m 3½f, Devo, G, May 22, *H*)

Bobby Socks 21[1] (2m 4f, Mark, F, Jun 14, *H*)

Bobbyjo (IRE) 36[1] (3m 1f, Fair, S, Feb 23, *H*)

Bold Boss 30[2] (2m ½f, Newc, G, Feb 15)

Bradbury Star 52[3] (2m 4½f, Sand, Y, Dec 12, *H*)

Brave Fountain (IRE) 24[2] (2m 4f, Fair, Y, Feb 1)

Brazil Or Bust (IRE) 27[2] (2m, Warw, G, Jan 28, *H*)

Buckboard Bounce 37[4] (4m 4f, Live, G, Apr 7, *G*)

Cable Beach (IRE) 50[2] (2m, Fair, F, Apr 2, *L*)

Call It A Day (IRE) 52[3] (2m 3f, Leop, G, Jan 19, *L*)

Call Me River (IRE) 23[1] (3m, Wind, G, Nov 27, *H*)

Callisoe Bay (IRE) 53[2] (2m, Asco, G, Nov 22, *H*)

Camelot Knight 38[3] (4m 4f, Live, G, Apr 7, *G*)

Captain Khedive 34[1] (2m, Worc, F, Sep 13, *H*)

Cariboo Gold (USA) 28[1] (3m ½f, Bang, Hvy, Mar 5, *H*)

Castalino 23[4] (3m 1f, Fair, S, Feb 23, *H*)

Castle Chief (IRE) 22[2] (3m, Kemp, Y, Nov 6)

Castleroyal (IRE) 25[2] (2m 4½f, Carl, G, Oct 26)

Ceilidh Boy 20[2] (3m 4f, Kels, S, Feb 28, *H*)

Celibate (IRE) 66[3] (2m, Chel, G, Mar 11, *G*)

Celtic Abbey 30[1] (3m 4f, Stra, G, May 31)

Certainly Strong (IRE) 45[1] (2m, Sand, G, Feb 1, *H*)

Challenger Du Luc (FR) 65[1] (2m 4½f, Chel, G, Nov 16, *G*)

Change The Act 21[2] (2m 4f, Newb, G, Mar 21, *H*)

Charming Gale 21[1] (3m, Edin, F, Dec 9, *H*)

Chief Minister (IRE) 36[1] (2m ½f, Newc, G, Feb 15)

Clay County 66[2] (2m, Kemp, G, Jan 18, *G*)

Conquering Leader (IRE) 21[2] (2m 5f, Folk, S, Dec 17)

Conti D'Estruval (FR) 25[3] (2m 3½f, Donc, G, Mar 1, *H*)

Coolree (IRE) 26[3] (2m 5f, Wind, G, Dec 5, *H*)

Coome Hill (IRE) 50[1] (3m 1½f, Winc, Y, Feb 20)

Coq Hardi Affair (IRE) 42[3] (3m 1f, Fair, S, Feb 23, *H*)

Couldnt Be Better 45[2] (3m, Hayd, G, Nov 20, *H*)

Coulton 71[1] (2m 5f, Winc, G, Oct 27, *H*)

Court Master (IRE) 23[2] (2m 2f, Devo, S, Dec 18)

Court Melody (IRE) 29[3] (4m 2f, Utto, G, Feb 8, *H*)

Cover Point (IRE) 24[2] (2m ½f, Newc, G, Dec 16, *H*)

Crack On 23[3] (2m ½f, Hunt, S, Jan 23)

Cross Cannon 20[1] (2m ½f, Sedg, G, Mar 11, *H*)

Crystal Spirit 48[3] (2m 3½f, Donc, G, Dec 13, *H*)

Cumbrian Challenge (IRE) 46[1] (2m, Asco, G, Apr 29, *H*)

Cyborgo (FR) 29[1] (3m 1f, Live, Y, Apr 4, *G*)

Dakyns Boy 25[4] (3m 5½f, Chep, Y, Feb 1, *H*)

Dancing Paddy 59[3] (2m, Asco, G, Nov 22, *H*)

Danoli (IRE) 92[1] (3m, Leop, G, Feb 2, *G*)

Daring Past 22[1] (2m ½f, Hexh, G, Dec 11)

Dear Do 20[2] (2m, Wind, G, Dec 5, *H*)

Destin D'Estruval (FR) 38[5] (2m 5f, Chel, G, Mar 13)

Destiny Calls 36[2] (2m 3½f, Donc, G, Mar 1, *H*)

Diamond Fort 23[2] (3m 2½f, Newt, G, Mar 29, *H*)

Djeddah (FR) 22[3] (3m 1f, Chel, F, Mar 12, *G*)

Donjuan Collonges (FR) 23[1] (2m 3½f, Chep, Hvy, Mar 8, *H*)

Dorans Pride (IRE) 72[1] (2m 4f, Fair, G, Apr 1, *G*)

Doualago (FR) 32[1] (3m 1½f, Winc, F, May 6, *H*)

Double Symphony (IRE) 55[1] (2m 1f, Newb, Y, Feb 8, *G*)

Down The Fell 47[1] (2m, Live, Y, Apr 5, *G*)

Dream Ride (IRE) 31[2] (2m, Asco, G, Nov 23)

Dual Image 24[2] (2m 1½f, Mark, Y, Mar 7, *H*)

Dublin Flyer 84[1] (2m 5f, Chel, G, Jan 25, *H*)

Duke Of Aprolon 23[1] (2m 2f, Font, Y, Dec 4, *H*)

Easthorpe 52[2] (2m, Hayd, G, Jan 18, *H*)

Elzoba (FR) 28[1] (2m, Here, S, Feb 17)

Emerald Gale (IRE) 21[3] (2m 6f, Fair, G, Nov 30)

Eudipe (FR) 40[1] (2m 1½f, Stra, Y, Feb 1)

Even Blue (IRE) 23[2] (2m 4½f, Bang, Hvy, Nov 29, *H*)

Evening Rain 23[1] (2m ½f, Newt, G, May 10, *H*)

Exterior Profiles (IRE) 27[3] (2m 4½f, Warw, Y, Mar 1, *H*)

Father Sky 30[1] (3m 2f, Donc, G, Mar 1, *H*)

Feel The Power (IRE) 32[2] (2m 5f, Utto, G, Jan 24)

Fiftysevenchannels (IRE) 31[1] (2m 1f, Leop, G, Nov 10, *H*)

Finchpalm (IRE) 31[1] (2m 3f, Leop, G, Dec 30)

Fine Harvest 28[1] (2m, Warw, F, Nov 30, *H*)

Five To Seven (USA) 26[2] (2m 4½f, Ling, S, Dec 14, *H*)

Fiveleigh Builds 34[2] (2m 6½f, Kels, G, Nov 13, *H*)

Flight Lieutenant (USA) 29[1] (2m, Plum, G, Mar 20)

Flyer's Nap 46[1] (3m 5½f, Chep, Y, Feb 1, *H*)

Flying Instructor 64[4] (2m, Chel, G, Mar 11, *G*)

Fools Errand (IRE) 22[1] (2m 6f, Towc, G, Nov 23, *H*)

Fortunes Course (IRE) 22[1] (3m 2½f, Newt, G, Mar 29, *H*)

Frazer Island (IRE) 22[1] (2m 4½f, Hunt, S, Feb 20)

Frickley 26[1] (2m 3½f, Donc, G, Mar 1, *H*)

Full Of Oats 25[3] (3m 5½f, Chep, Y, Feb 1, *H*)

Funcheon Gale 20[1] (2m 6f, Towc, G, Mar 29, *H*)

Gales Cavalier (IRE) 62[3] (2m, Sand, G,

Feb 1, *H*)

Garnwin (IRE) 30[1] (2m 4½f, Warw, G, Feb 4)

Garolo (FR) 24[2] (2m, Ling, Y, Jan 31)

General Command (IRE) 57[1] (3m, Donc, G, Jan 25, *H*)

General Crack (IRE) 39[1] (3m, Chep, G, Oct 5, *H*)

General Wolfe 53[1] (3m, Hayd, G, Feb 21, *H*)

Gimme (IRE) 20[3] (2m ½f, Donc, G, Mar 1)

Giventime 26[1] (3m 2½f, Chep, Hvy, Mar 8, *H*)

Glemot (IRE) 45[2] (3m 1½f, Winc, G, Nov 9, *H*)

Glint Of Eagles (IRE) 29[2] (2m 3f, Leop, G, Dec 30)

Glitter Isle (IRE) 37[1] (2m 4½f, Ling, Hvy, Feb 12)

Go Ballistic 50[2] (3m ½f, Asco, G, Nov 23, *H*)

Go Universal (IRE) 44[2] (2m 5f, Chel, Y, Dec 14, *G*)

Golden Hello 28[3] (2m 1½f, Mark, S, Dec 6)

Golden Spinner 46[3] (3m, Donc, G, Jan 25, *H*)

Grange Brake 32[5] (3m, Chep, Y, Dec 7, *G*)

Greenback (BEL) 22[1] (2m, Folk, Y, Dec 9)

Grooving (IRE) 23[1] (2m 2f, Devo, S, Dec 18)

Guinda (IRE) 27[2] (2m ½f, Hunt, S, Jan 23)

Hanakham (IRE) 38[3] (3m 1½f, Winc, Y, Feb 20)

Harristown Lady 26[1] (3m 1f, Towc, G, Mar 19, *H*)

Harwell Lad (IRE) 30[1] (3m 1f, Towc, G, Dec 7, *H*)

Hatcham Boy (IRE) 27[1] (3m, Newb, S, Nov 29)

Haunting Music (IRE) 27[4] (2m 4½f, Hunt, S, Nov 26)

Hawaiian Sam (IRE) 26[2] (3m, Wind, G, Jan 29)

Headbanger 36[4] (2m 1f, Leop, G, Dec 26, *G*)

Headwind (IRE) 20[2] (2m 3f, Font, S, Nov 17)

Hee's A Dancer 24[2] (2m, Edin, G, Feb 12, *H*)

High Alltitude (IRE) 20[2] (2m 1f, Newb, S, Feb 28, *H*)

High Learie 28[2] (2m 4½f, Hunt, S, Feb 27)

Hill Of Tullow (IRE) 37[3] (2m 5f, Chel, G, Jan 25, *H*)

Him Of Praise (IRE) 25[1] (2m 6f, Towc, S, Mar 6)

Houghton 20[2] (2m, Worc, F, Sep 13, *H*)

Idiots Venture 64[3] (2m, Punc, G, Apr 22, *G*)

Iffeee 24[3] (3m, Chep, G, Oct 5, *H*)

Imperial Call (IRE) 70[3] (3m, Leop, G, Feb 2, *G*)

Imperial Vintage (IRE) 23[1] (2m 4f, Ludl, F, Apr 9, *H*)

Inchcailloch (IRE) 49[1] (3m ½f, Asco, G, Nov 23, *H*)

Indian Arrow (NZ) 30[1] (2m, Plum, S, Feb 28)

Indian Jockey 37[1] (2m 1½f, Cart, F, May 28, *H*)

Into The Red 31[4] (4m, Kels, G, Jan 17, *H*)

Island Chief (IRE) 28[1] (3m 1f, Weth, Y, Dec 7, *H*)

James Pigg 30[2] (3m 1½f, Winc, F, May 6, *H*)

James The First 25[1] (2m ½f, Newt, Hvy, Dec 16, *H*)

Jathib (CAN) 31[1] (2m ½f, Donc, G, Jan 24)

Jeffell 67[2] (2m 4f, Fair, G, Apr 1, *G*)

Jodami 90[2] (3m, Leop, G, Feb 2, *G*)

Johnny Setaside (IRE) 57[1] (3m, Leop, G, Dec 28, *G*)

Jultara (IRE) 36[1] (3m ½f, Asco, G, Mar 26)

Just Bruce 27[2] (2m ½f, Donc, G, Mar 1)

Jymjam Johnny (IRE) 20[3] (2m ½f, Hunt, S, Dec 10, *H*)

Kadi (GER) 49[3] (2m 6f, Live, G, Apr 3, *H*)

Kharasar (IRE) 22[4] (2m 1f, Leop, G, Jan 19, *G*)

Kibreet 47[5] (2m, Kemp, G, Jan 18, *G*)

Killeshin 29[4] (4m 2f, Utto, G, Mar 15, *G*)

King Lucifer (IRE) 56[2] (3m, Kemp, Y, Feb 22, *G*)

King Of The Gales 54[3] (3m, Leop, Y, Jan 11, *G*)

Kings Cherry (IRE) 22[1] (2m 1f, Newb, S, Feb 28, *H*)

Klairon Davis (FR) 89[1] (2m, Punc, G, Apr 22, *G*)

Know-No-No (IRE) 23[1] (2m, Pert, Y, May 15)

Konvekta King (IRE) 46[1] (2m 4½f, Weth, S, Feb 1, *H*)

Lackendara 20[3] (2m ½f, Towc, G, Mar 29, *H*)

Land Afar 42[1] (2m, Kemp, G, Jan 18)

Lansborough 21[2] (2m 4f, Ayr, Hvy, Feb 8)

Lasata 30[2] (2m, Wind, G, Nov 27, *H*)

Le Ginno (FR) 28[4] (2m 6f, Fair, Y, Nov 20)

Lemon's Mill (USA) 32[2] (2m 7f, Utto, F, Jun 9, *H*)
Leotard 49[3] (2m, Weth, Y, May 7, *H*)
Lightening Lad 62[5] (2m, Chel, G, Mar 11, *G*)
Linden's Lotto (IRE) 20[1] (2m 5f, Plum, F, Apr 30, *H*)
Little Martina (IRE) 29[1] (3m 3f, Sedg, G, Apr 12)
Lively Knight 29[1] (2m 5f, Plum, S, Mar 10)
Lo Stregone 52[3] (4m, Kels, G, Jan 17, *H*)
Lochnagrain (IRE) 30[2] (2m 4f, Mark, G, Mar 17, *H*)
Lord Dorcet (IRE) 68[6] (2m, Chel, F, Mar 12, *G*)
Lord Gyllene (NZ) 65[1] (4m 4f, Live, G, Apr 7, *G*)
Love The Lord (IRE) 44[2] (3m 1f, Fair, S, Feb 23, *H*)
Lucky Dollar 28[1] (3m, Ludl, G, Feb 5)
Maamur (USA) 33[4] (3m 1½f, Winc, Y, Feb 20)
Macgeorge (IRE) 35[1] (2m 4½f, Leic, G, Feb 11, *H*)
Major Bell 58[2] (2m 5f, Chel, G, Mar 13)
Major Nova 24[2] (2m 6f, Towc, S, Mar 6)
Malwood Castle (IRE) 20[1] (3m, Chep, Y, May 13, *H*)
Mammy's Choice (IRE) 26[3] (2m 4f, Newb, G, Mar 22, *H*)
Mandys Mantino 30[3] (2m, Kemp, G, Jan 18)
Manhattan Castle (IRE) 51[1] (2m 3f, Leop, G, Jan 19, *L*)
Mariners Mirror 29[1] (2m 4½f, Carl, G, Nov 11)
Martha's Son 88[1] (2m 4f, Live, Y, Apr 4, *G*)
Master Oats 58[5] (4m 4f, Live, G, Apr 7, *G*)
McGregor The Third 43[2] (3m, Hayd, G, Feb 21, *H*)
Melnik 28[1] (2m 5f, Folk, S, Dec 17)
Mely Moss (FR) 40[1] (2m 5f, Utto, G, Jan 24, *H*)
Merlins Dream (IRE) 29[1] (3m 1f, Towc, G, Mar 31, *H*)
Merry Gale (IRE) 45[4] (3m, Leop, G, Feb 2, *G*)
Mine's An Ace (NZ) 20[2] (2m 5f, Plum, G, Oct 22, *H*)
Mister Drum 38[1] (2m 1½f, Mark, S, Dec 6)
Mister Oddy 48[1] (2m, Sand, S, Feb 14, *H*)
Monicasman (IRE) 21[3] (2m 5f, Wind, G, Feb 15)

Monks Soham (IRE) 24[1] (2m 5½f, Stra, Y, May 9)
Mony-Skip (IRE) 38[2] (4m, Kels, G, Jan 17, *H*)
Monyman 32[1] (2m, Ayr, G, Apr 19, *H*)
Mr Knitwit 29[2] (2m 1f, Kels, G, Mar 21)
Mr Mulligan (IRE) 56[4] (3m, Chep, Y, Dec 7, *G*)
Mr Playfull 26[1] (2m 3½f, Devo, G, May 22, *H*)
Mudahim 51[1] (3m, Kemp, Y, Feb 22, *G*)
Mulligan 48[1] (2m 1f, Leop, G, Jan 19, *G*)
Nahthen Lad (IRE) 50[2] (2m 3½f, Chep, S, Feb 15)
Naiysari 26[1] (2m 4½f, Ling, S, Dec 14, *H*)
Nakir (FR) 48[2] (2m 1f, Newb, G, Nov 30, *H*)
Native Mission 39[3] (2m 1f, Newb, Y, Feb 7, *H*)
Native Status (IRE) 39[2] (2m 6f, Fair, Y, Nov 20)
Netherby Said 34[1] (2m 4f, Mark, G, Mar 17, *H*)
New Co (IRE) 51[1] (3m, Leop, G, Dec 27, *G*)
Newlands-General 38[2] (2m ½f, Chep, G, Nov 9, *H*)
No Pain No Gain (IRE) 24[5] (2m 6f, Live, G, Apr 3, *H*)
Noblely (USA) 21[1] (2m, Plum, Hrd, Aug 19, *H*)
Nordic Sun (IRE) 23[1] (2m 4f, Mark, G, Jul 3, *H*)
Nordic Thorn (IRE) 29[2] (2m, Ayr, Y, Nov 16, *H*)
Nordic Valley 21[1] (3m, Ludl, G, May 5, *H*)
Northern Hide 37[3] (2m 5f, Chel, Y, Dec 14, *G*)
Northern Squire 20[2] (3m, Newc, G, Mar 17, *H*)
Noyan 26[1] (2m 3½f, Donc, G, Feb 22, *H*)
Oat Couture 28[1] (2m, Hayd, G, Nov 30)
Oban 33[2] (3m, Kemp, S, Feb 21)
Oh So Grumpy 39[3] (2m, Fair, F, Apr 2, *L*)
Oh So Risky 38[1] (2m, Asco, G, Nov 23)
One Man (IRE) 85[1] (3m, Kemp, F, Dec 26, *G*)
Opera Hat (IRE) 52[5] (2m, Punc, G, Apr 22, *G*)
Or Royal (FR) 73[1] (2m, Chel, G, Mar 11, *G*)
Over The Pole 20[1] (2m 3½f, Donc, G, Feb 22, *H*)

Pagliaccio 22² (3m, Edin, F, Dec 9, *H*)

Palosanto (IRE) 36¹ (3m, Wind, G, Jan 29)

Papillon (IRE) 38¹ (2m 6f, Fair, Y, Nov 20)

Pariah (IRE) 23² (2m, Carl, S, Mar 6, *H*)

Pashto 32⁵ (2m 5f, Chel, G, Jan 25, *H*)

Penndara (IRE) 44⁶ (2m, Chel, G, Mar 11, G)

Perknapp 28³ (2m, Fair, Y, Dec 1, *H*)

Pharanear (IRE) 25¹ (2m 4½f, Worc, S, Dec 2)

Pimberley Place (IRE) 31 (2m 5f, Chel, G, Mar 13)

Plunder Bay (USA) 28⁴ (2m 4½f, Leic, G, Jan 29, *H*)

Political Tower 44¹ (2m, Weth, Y, May 7, *H*)

Postage Stamp 25⁶ (2m 4f, Mark, F, Jun 14, *H*)

Postman's Path 22² (2m 6f, Towc, G, Mar 29, *H*)

Potter's Bay (IRE) 30² (2m 5f, Chel, G, Jan 25, *H*)

Poucher (IRE) 21² (2m, Here, Y, Nov 20, *H*)

Power Pack (IRE) 26³ (2m, Ayr, G, Apr 17)

Prate Box (IRE) 39¹ (2m 4f, Fair, G, Mar 31, *H*)

Price's Hill 27¹ (3m 1f, Towc, S, Dec 19, *H*)

Punters Overhead (IRE) 29¹ (2m 5½f, Newt, Hvy, Nov 6)

Puritan (CAN) 29² (2m 3½f, Donc, G, Jan 24, *H*)

Quite A Man 24¹ (2m 4f, Ludl, G, Mar 24, *H*)

Raba Riba 20² (2m 4f, Ludl, F, Apr 9, *H*)

Rainbow Castle 20¹ (3m 2½f, Newt, G, Sep 29, *H*)

Rallegio 26¹ (2m ½f, Hexh, Y, Mar 13)

Ramallah 20² (2m 6f, Towc, S, Dec 19)

Real Tonic 27³ (2m 1f, Kels, G, Mar 21)

Rectory Garden (IRE) 31² (3m, Pert, G, Apr 25, *H*)

Red Bean 20⁴ (2m, Wind, G, Nov 27, *H*)

Red Branch (IRE) 30¹ (2m 4f, Newb, G, Mar 22, *H*)

Regal Romper (IRE) 27² (2m 1f, Kels, G, Jan 17, *H*)

Rex To The Rescue (IRE) 24² (2m 4½f, Leic, G, Jan 29, *H*)

River Bounty 25³ (2m 5f, Utto, G, Jan 24, *H*)

River Mandate 41² (3m 1f, Towc, S, Dec 19, *H*)

Robert's Toy (IRE) 22¹ (2m ½f, Newt, G, May 21)

Rockfield Native (IRE) 35¹ (2m 6f, Fair, G, Nov 30)

Romany Creek (IRE) 27² (3m, Ludl, G, Feb 27, *H*)

Rough Quest 73² (3m, Kemp, F, Dec 26, G)

Royal Mountbrowne 55⁵ (2m 5f, Chel, Y, Dec 14, G)

Royal Oasis (IRE) 28¹ (2m 2f, Fair, G, Mar 31)

Royal Square (CAN) 21¹ (2m 4½f, Sout, S, May 5, *H*)

Royal Vacation 20¹ (2m 6½f, Kels, G, Nov 2, *H*)

Run Up The Flag 28 (3m, Donc, G, Jan 25, *H*)

Rustic Air 24² (2m 4f, Mark, G, Apr 26, *H*)

Sail By The Stars 27¹ (2m 5f, Wind, G, Feb 15)

Saskia's Hero 26² (2m 1½f, Mark, F, Jun 15, *H*)

Scobie Boy (IRE) 27² (2m, Fair, Y, Dec 1, *H*)

Scoresheet (IRE) 21² (2m 4½f, Ling, S, Jan 22, *H*)

Scottish Bambi 27² (2m, Here, S, Dec 20, *H*)

Scotton Banks (IRE) 48⁴ (3m 1f, Weth, G, Nov 2, G)

See More Business (IRE) 37² (2m 4f, Fair, Y, Dec 1, G)

Senor El Betrutti (IRE) 37¹ (2m 5f, Winc, Y, Mar 6, *H*)

Seven Towers (IRE) 53¹ (4m 2f, Utto, G, Mar 15, G)

Shining Light (IRE) 31¹ (2m 4½f, Leic, G, Jan 29, *H*)

Shisoma (IRE) 30¹ (3m, Leop, G, Mar 16)

Silver Stick 37³ (3m 1f, Weth, G, Oct 27, *H*)

Simply Dashing (IRE) 27¹ (2m 4f, Mark, S, Nov 7)

Singing Sand 42² (2m, Ayr, G, Apr 17)

Sir Leonard (IRE) 21³ (2m 5f, Folk, S, Dec 17)

Sister Stephanie (IRE) 36³ (4m 2f, Utto, G, Mar 15, G)

Slingsby (IRE) 31³ (2m 4½f, Hunt, S, Nov 26)

Slotamatique (IRE) 21¹ (2m 4f, Hayd, Y, Dec 21)

Society Guest 35⁵ (2m, Asco, G, Apr 29, *H*)

Solomon's Dancer (USA) 22¹ (2m 4½f, Carl, G, Oct 26)

Son Of War 24⁵ (3m, Leop, G, Dec 28, G)

Sound Man (IRE) 59³ (2m 3½f, Asco, G, Feb 5, *G*)

Sound Reveille 45⁵ (2m, Hayd, G, Jan 18, *H*)

Sounds Strong (IRE) 36⁶ (3m, Donc, G, Jan 25, *H*)

Southampton 34² (2m, Chel, G, Nov 15, *H*)

Southerly Gale 22² (2m 6½f, Mark, F, Jun 15, *H*)

Spanish Light (IRE) 32² (2m 4f, Ludl, G, Feb 5, *H*)

Sparky Gayle 62¹ (2m 5f, Chel, G, Mar 13)

Spinnaker 20² (2m 4f, Hayd, Y, Dec 21)

Spring To Glory 22⁴ (2m 4f, Newb, G, Mar 22, *H*)

Spuffington 29³ (3m 1f, Towc, S, Dec 19, *H*)

Squire Silk 72² (2m, Chel, G, Mar 11, *G*)

St Mellion Fairway (IRE) 39³ (3m, Chep, Y, Dec 7, *G*)

Stately Home (IRE) 38¹ (2m 4½f, Sand, Y, Dec 12, *H*)

Stay Lucky (NZ) 26⁴ (2m 4½f, Worc, S, Dec 2)

Storm Alert 75¹ (2m, Asco, G, Dec 21, *H*)

Storm Falcon (USA) 27² (2m, Pert, G, Apr 24, *H*)

Straight Talk 37² (3m, Kemp, F, Oct 6, *H*)

Strokesaver (IRE) 25² (2m 5f, Wind, G, Feb 15)

Strong Medicine 40² (2m 4½f, Sand, Y, Dec 12, *H*)

Strong Promise (IRE) 83¹ (2m 5f, Chel, F, Apr 15, *G*)

Sublime Fellow (IRE) 37² (2m, Asco, G, Apr 25)

Sunley Bay 28² (3m 5½f, Chep, Y, Feb 1, *H*)

Suny Bay (IRE) 43² (4m 4f, Live, G, Apr 7, *G*)

Super Coin 29² (2m ½f, Chep, Y, Nov 27)

Super Tactics (IRE) 40¹ (2m, Utto, Y, Dec 20, *H*)

Sybillin 28⁵ (2m 1f, Kels, G, Jan 17, *H*)

Teaplanter 20² (3m 1f, Weth, S, Feb 1)

Teinein (FR) 24¹ (2m 4½f, Hunt, S, Feb 27)

Terao 41¹ (2m 4f, Newb, G, Mar 21, *H*)

The Carrig Rua (IRE) 33⁵ (2m 1f, Leop, G, Dec 26, *G*)

The Carrot Man 25⁴ (2m ½f, Towc, G, Apr 21, *H*)

The Crazy Bishop (IRE) 35⁴ (3m, Leop, Y, Jan 11, *G*)

The Gallopin'major (IRE) 21² (3m 3f,

The Grey Monk (IRE) 41³ (3m 5f, Fair, G, Mar 31, *G*)

The Last Fling (IRE) 28² (3m 1f, Live, Y, Apr 4, *G*)

The Latvian Lark (IRE) 39¹ (2m 4f, Fair, Y, Feb 1)

The Outback Way (IRE) 29³ (2m, Punc, S, Nov 16, *G*)

The Reverend Bert (IRE) 22¹ (2m 5f, Folk, G, Jan 30)

The Subbie (IRE) 29² (2m 4f, Punc, S, Nov 3, *G*)

Thumbs Up 45² (2m, Asco, G, Apr 29, *H*)

Tidebrook 25¹ (2m, Utto, G, May 3)

Timbucktoo 25² (2m ½f, Newc, Y, Dec 3, *H*)

Time For A Run 51² (3m 1f, Chel, G, Mar 11, *H*)

Time Won't Wait (IRE) 51⁴ (2m, Asco, G, Apr 29, *H*)

Toomuch Toosoon 22³ (2m ½f, Newt, F, Aug 15, *H*)

Travado 37⁴ (2m 1½f, Devo, Y, Nov 5, *H*)

Treasure Again (IRE) 24² (2m 4½f, Worc, S, Dec 2)

Trying Again 61² (3m, Chep, Y, Dec 7, *G*)

Turning Trix 44¹ (3m, Newc, Y, Nov 30, *H*)

Twin Falls (IRE) 23¹ (2m, Catt, G, Nov 23)

Ultra Flutter 33² (2m 6f, Fair, G, Nov 30)

Uncle Ernie 52³ (2m 1f, Newb, G, Nov 30, *H*)

Unguided Missile (IRE) 83² (3m, Hayd, G, Jan 18, *G*)

Urban Dancing (USA) 29¹ (2m, Edin, G, Jan 28)

Valiant Warrior 31⁵ (2m 4½f, Weth, S, Feb 1, *H*)

Viking Flagship 88⁴ (2m, Kemp, G, Jan 18, *G*)

Weaver George (IRE) 31¹ (2m 5f, Sedg, G, May 2, *H*)

Wee River (IRE) 42¹ (2m 1f, Kels, G, Jan 17, *H*)

Wee Windy (IRE) 31² (2m 4½f, Hunt, S, Nov 26)

Welcome Call (IRE) 25² (3m, Newb, Y, Nov 29)

Whaat Fettle 23³ (3m 4f, Kels, S, Feb 28, *H*)

Whale Of A Knight (IRE) 40² (3m, Leop, Y, Jan 11, *G*)

Whattabob (IRE) 23¹ (2m 6f, Towc, S, Dec 19)

Who Am I (IRE) 24¹ (2m 4½f, Worc, S, May 10)

Who Is Equiname (IRE) 35² (3m ½f,

Asco, G, Mar 26)

Wild West Wind (IRE) 39[4] (2m 5f, Chel, G, Mar 13)

Wise Approach 35[2] (2m 4f, Mark, F, Jun 14, *H*)

Wisley Wonder (IRE) 24[3] (3m, Newb, S, Nov 29)

With Impunity 29[2] (2m 4½f, Worc, S, May 10)

Wylde Hide 60[2] (3m, Leop, G, Dec 27, *G*)

Yeoman Warrior 34[2] (2m 6f, Live, G, Apr 3, *H*)

Yorkshire Gale 38[1] (3m 1f, Chel, G, Nov 26, *H*)

Young Hustler 54[3] (3m 1f, Weth, G, Nov 2, *G*)

Zambezi Spirit (IRE) 24[1] (2m 5f, Plum, G, Oct 22, *H*)

Zeredar (NZ) 31[1] (2m, Wind, G, Dec 5, *H*)

NOTES

NOTES

NOTES

NOTES